Profiles
of
Michigan

2015
Fourth Edition

Profiles
of
Michigan

A UNIVERSAL REFERENCE BOOK

Grey House
Publishing

PUBLISHER: Leslie Mackenzie
EDITORIAL DIRECTOR: Laura Mars
EDITOR: David Garoogian
MARKETING DIRECTOR: Jessica Moody

Grey House Publishing, Inc.
4919 Route 22
Amenia, NY 12501
518.789.8700
FAX 845.373.6390
www.greyhouse.com
e-mail: books @greyhouse.com

While every effort has been made to ensure the reliability of the information presented in this publication, Grey House Publishing neither guarantees the accuracy of the data contained herein nor assumes any responsibility for errors, omissions or discrepancies. Grey House accepts no payment for listing; inclusion in the publication of any organization, agency, institution, publication, service or individual does not imply endorsement of the editors or publisher.

Errors brought to the attention of the publisher and verified to the satisfaction of the publisher will be corrected in future editions.

First edition published 2006
Printed in the U.S.A.

ISBN: 978-1-61925-567-8

Table of Contents

Introduction

This is the fourth edition of *Profiles of Michigan—Facts, Figures & Statistics for 2,088 Populated Places in Michigan.* As with the other titles in our *State Profiles* series, it was built with content from Grey House Publishing's award-winning *Profiles of America*—a 4-volume compilation of data on more than 43,000 places in the United States. We have updated and included the Michigan chapter from *Profiles of America,* and added several new chapters of demographic information and ranking sections, so that *Profiles of Michigan* is the most comprehensive portrait of the state of Michigan ever published.

Profiles of Michigan provides data on all populated communities and counties in the state of Michigan for which the US Census provides individual statistics. This edition also includes profiles of 156 unincorporated places based on US Census data by zip code.

This premier reference work includes seven major sections that cover everything from **Education** to **Ethnic Backgrounds** to **Climate**. All sections include **Comparative Statistics** or **Rankings. About Michigan** at the front of the book, is comprised of detailed narrative and colorful photos and maps. Here is an overview of each section:

1. About Michigan
This 4-color section gives the researcher a real sense of the state and its history. It includes a Photo Gallery, and comprehensive sections on Michigan's History and Government, Land and Natural Resources, State Energy Profile, and Demographic Maps. With charts and maps, these 60 pages help to anchor the researcher to the state, both physically and politically.

2. Profiles
This section, organized by county, gives detailed profiles of 2,088 places plus 83 counties, based on Census 2010 and data from the American Community Survey. We have added current government statistics and original research, so that these profiles pull together statistical and descriptive information on every Census-recognized place in the state. Major fields of information include:

Geography	*Housing*	*Education*	*Religion*
Ancestry	*Transportation*	*Population*	*Climate*
Economy	*Industry*	*Health*	

NEW categories to this edition include public and private health insurance, language spoken at home, people with disabilities and veterans. In addition to place profiles, this section includes an **Place Name Index.**

3. Comparative Statistics
This section includes tables that compare Michigan's 100 largest communities by dozens of data points.

4. Community Rankings
This NEW section includes tables that rank the top 150 and bottom 150 communities with population over 10,000, in dozens of categories.

5. Education
This section begins with an **Educational State Profile,** summarizing number of schools, students, diplomas granted and educational dollars spent. Following the state profile are **School District Rankings** on 16 topics ranging from *Teacher/Student Ratios* to *High School Drop-Out Rates.* Following these rankings are statewide *National Assessment of Educational Progress (NAEP)* results and information about school and district performance from the Michigan Department of Education.

6. Ancestry and Ethnicity
This section provides a detailed look at the ancestral, Hispanic and racial makeup of Michigan's 200+ ethnic categories. Profiles are included for the state and for all counties and places with 50,000 or more residents. In the ranking section, data is displayed three ways: 1) by number, based on all places regardless of population;

2) by percent, based on all places regardless of population; 3) by percent, based on places with populations of 50,000 or more. You will discover, for example, that the city of Lansing has the greatest number of people reporting Somalian ancestry in the state (316), and that 19.1% of the population of Dearborn are of Lebanese ancestry.

7. Climate

This section includes a State Summary, three colorful maps and profiles of both National and Cooperative Weather Stations. In addition, you'll find Weather Station Rankings with hundreds of interesting details, such as Stambaugh 2 SSE and Stephenson 8 WNW reporting the lowest annual extreme minimum temperatures (-45° F).

These sections also include Significant Storm Event data from January 2000 through December 2009. Here you will learn that an ice storm caused $161 million in property damage in Southeast Lower Michigan in April 2003 and that a F2 tornado was responsible for two deaths in Ingham County in October 2007.

Note: The extensive **User Guide** that follows this introduction is segmented into four sections and examines, in some detail, each data field in the individual profiles and comparative sections for all chapters. It provides sources for all data points and statistical definitions as necessary.

User Guide

Places Covered

All 83 counties.

533 incorporated municipalities. Comprised of 277 cities and 256 villages.

1,240 Minor Civil Divisions (MCD). Comprise of 1,123 townships and 117 charter townships. These communities are included for states where the Census Bureau has determined that they serve as general-purpose governments. Those states are Connecticut, Maine, Massachusetts, Michigan, Minnesota, New Hampshire, New Jersey, New York, Pennsylvania, Rhode Island, Vermont, and Wisconsin. In some states incorporated municipalities are part of minor civil divisions and in some states they are independent of them.

159 Census Designated Places (CDP). The U.S. Bureau of the Census defines a CDP as "a statistical entity, defined for each decennial census according to Census Bureau guidelines, comprising a densely settled concentration of population that is not within an incorporated place, but is locally identified by a name. CDPs are delineated cooperatively by state and local officials and the Census Bureau, following Census Bureau guidelines.

156 unincorporated communities. The communities included have statistics for their ZIP Code Tabulation Area (ZCTA) available from the Census Bureau. They are referred to as "postal areas." "Postal areas" can span multiple ZCTAs. A ZCTA is a statistical entity developed by the Census Bureau to approximate the delivery area for a US Postal Service 5-digit or 3-digit ZIP Code in the US and Puerto Rico. A ZCTA is an aggregation of census blocks that have the same predominant ZIP Code associated with the mailing addresses in the Census Bureau's Master Address File. Thus, the Postal Service's delivery areas have been adjusted to encompass whole census blocks so that the Census Bureau can tabulate census data for the ZCTAs. ZCTAs do not include all ZIP Codes used for mail delivery and therefore do not precisely depict the area within which mail deliveries associated with that ZIP Code occur. Additionally, some areas that are known by a unique name, although they are part of a larger incorporated place, are also included as "postal areas."

For a more in-depth discussion of geographic areas, please refer to the Census Bureau's Geographic Areas Reference Manual at http://www.census.gov/geo/www/garm.html.

IMPORTANT NOTES

- Since the last decennial census, the U.S. Census replaced the long-form sample with the American Community Survey (ACS), which uses a series of monthly samples to produce annually updated estimates for the same areas. ACS estimates are based on data from a sample of housing units (3.54 million in 2013) and people in the population, not the full population. ACS sampling error (uncertainty of data) is greater for those areas with smaller populations. In an effort to provide the most accurate data, *Profiles of Michigan* reports ACS data for counties and communities with populations of 2,500 or more. The profiles for these places (2,500 or more population) also include data from Census 2010, including: population; population growth; population density; race; Hispanic origin; average household size; median age; age under 18; age 65 and over; males per 100 females; homeownership rate; homeowner vacancy rate; and rental vacancy rate. Profiles for counties and communities with 2,500 or less population show data from the Census 2010 only.

- *Profiles of Michigan* uses the term "community" to refer to all places except counties. The term "county" is used to refer to counties and county-equivalents. All places are defined as of the 2010 Census.

- If a community spans multiple counties, the community will be shown in the county that contains its largest population.

- Several states, including Michigan, have incorporated municipalities and minor civil divisions in the same county with the same name. Those communities are given separate entries (e.g. Harrisville, Michigan, in Alcona County will be listed under both the city and township of Adams).

- In each community profile, only school districts that have schools that are physically located within the community are shown. In addition, statistics for each school district cover the entire district, regardless of the physical location of the schools within the district.

- Special care should be taken when interpreting certain statistics for communities containing large colleges or universities. College students were counted as residents of the area in which they were living while attending college (as they have been since the 1950 census). One effect this may have is skewing the figures for population, income, housing, and educational attainment.

- Some information (e.g. income) is available for both counties and individual communities. Other information is available for just counties (e.g. election results), or just individual communities (e.g. local newspapers). Refer to the "Data Explanation and Sources" section for a complete listing.

- Some statistical information is available only for larger communities. In addition, the larger places are more apt to have services such as newspapers, airports, school districts, etc.

- For the most complete information on any community, users should also check the entry for the county in which the community is located. In addition, more information and services will be listed under the larger places in the county.

Data Explanation and Sources: County Profiles

PHYSICAL AND GEOGRAPHICAL CHARACTERISTICS

Physical Location: Describes the physical location of the county. *Source: Columbia University Press, The Columbia Gazetteer of North America and original research.*

Land and Water Area: Land and water area in square miles. *Source: U.S. Census Bureau, Census 2010*

Latitude and Longitude: Latitude and longitude in degrees. *Source: U.S. Census Bureau, Census 2010*

Time Zone: Lists the time zone. *Source: Original research*

Year Organized: Year the county government was organized. *Source: National Association of Counties*

County Seat: Lists the county seat. If a county has more than one seat, then both are listed. *Source: National Association of Counties*

Metropolitan Area: Indicates the metropolitan area the county is located in. Also lists all the component counties of that metropolitan area. The Office of Management and Budget (OMB) defines metropolitan and micropolitan statistical areas. The most current definitions are as of February 2013. *Source: U.S. Census Bureau*

Climate: Includes all weather stations located within the county. Indicates the station name and elevation as well as the monthly average high and low temperatures, average precipitation, and average snowfall. The period of record is generally 1980-2009, however, certain weather stations contain averages going back as far as 1900. *Source: Grey House Publishing, Weather America: A Thirty-Year Summary of Statistical Weather Data and Rankings, 2010*

POPULATION

Population: 2010 figures are a 100% count of population. *Source: U.S. Census Bureau, Census 2010*

Population Growth: The increase or decrease in population between 2000 and 2010. *Source: U.S. Census Bureau, Census 2000, Census 2010*

Population Density: Total 2010 population divided by the land area in square miles. *Source: U.S. Census Bureau, U.S. Census Bureau, Census 2010*

Race/Hispanic Origin: Figures include the U.S. Census Bureau categories of White alone; Black/African American alone; Asian alone; American Indian/Alaska Native alone; Native Hawaiian/Other Pacific Islander alone; two or more races; and Hispanic of any race. Alone refers to the fact that these figures are not in combination with any other race. *Source: U.S. Census Bureau, Census 2010*

The concept of race, as used by the Census Bureau, reflects self-identification by people according to the race or races with which they most closely identify. These categories are socio-political constructs and should not be interpreted as being scientific or anthropological in nature. Furthermore, the race categories include both racial and national-origin groups.

- **White.** A person having origins in any of the original peoples of Europe, the Middle East, or North Africa. It includes people who indicated their race(s) as "White" or reported entries such as Irish, German, Italian, Lebanese, Arab, Moroccan, or Caucasian.
- **Black/African American.** A person having origins in any of the Black racial groups of Africa. It includes people who indicated their race(s) as "Black, African Am., or Negro" or reported entries such as African American, Kenyan, Nigerian, or Haitian.
- **Asian.** A person having origins in any of the original peoples of the Far East, Southeast Asia, or the Indian subcontinent, including, for example, Cambodia, China, India, Japan, Korea, Malaysia, Pakistan, the Philippine Islands, Thailand, and Vietnam. It includes people who indicated their race(s) as "Asian" or reported entries such as "Asian Indian," "Chinese," "Filipino," "Korean," "Japanese," "Vietnamese," and "Other Asian" or provided other detailed Asian responses.
- **American Indian/Alaska Native.** A person having origins in any of the original peoples of North and South America (including Central America) and who maintains tribal affiliation or community attachment. This category includes people who indicated their race(s) as "American Indian or Alaska Native" or

reported their enrolled or principal tribe, such as Navajo, Blackfeet, Inupiat, Yup'ik, or Central American Indian groups or South American Indian groups.

- **Native Hawaiian/Other Pacific Islander.** A person having origins in any of the original peoples of Hawaii, Guam, Samoa, or other Pacific Islands. It includes people who indicated their race(s) as "Pacific Islander" or reported entries such as "Native Hawaiian," "Guamanian or Chamorro," "Samoan," and "Other Pacific Islander" or provided other detailed Pacific Islander responses..

- **Two or More Races.** People may choose to provide two or more races either by checking two or more race response check boxes, by providing multiple responses, or by some combination of check boxes and other responses. The race response categories shown on the questionnaire are collapsed into the five minimum race groups identified by OMB, and the Census Bureau's "Some Other Race" category.

- **Hispanic.** The data on the Hispanic or Latino population were derived from answers to a question that was asked of all people. The terms "Spanish," "Hispanic origin," and "Latino" are used interchangeably. Some respondents identify with all three terms while others may identify with only one of these three specific terms. Hispanics or Latinos who identify with the terms "Spanish," "Hispanic," or "Latino" are those who classify themselves in one of the specific Spanish, Hispanic, or Latino categories listed on the questionnaire ("Mexican," "Puerto Rican," or "Cuban") as well as those who indicate that they are "other Spanish/Hispanic/Latino." People who do not identify with one of the specific origins listed on the questionnaire but indicate that they are "other Spanish/Hispanic/Latino" are those whose origins are from Spain, the Spanish-speaking countries of Central or South America, the Dominican Republic, or people identifying themselves generally as Spanish, Spanish-American, Hispanic, Hispano, Latino, and so on. All write-in responses to the "other Spanish/Hispanic/Latino" category were coded. Origin can be viewed as the heritage, nationality group, lineage, or country of birth of the person or the person's parents or ancestors before their arrival in the United States. People who identify their origin as Spanish, Hispanic, or Latino may be of any race.

Average Household Size: Number of persons in the average household. *Source: U.S. Census Bureau, Census 2010*

Median Age: Median age of the population. *Source: U.S. Census Bureau, Census 2010*

Age Under 18: Percent of the total population under 18 years old. *Source: U.S. Census Bureau, Census 2010*

Age 65 and Over: Percent of the total population age 65 and over. *Source: U.S. Census Bureau, Census 2010*

Males per 100 Females: Number of males per 100 females. *Source: U.S. Census Bureau, Census 2010*

Marital Status: Percentage of population never married, now married, separated, widowed, or divorced. *Source: U.S. Census Bureau, American Community Survey, 2009-2013 Five-Year Estimates*

The marital status classification refers to the status at the time of enumeration. Data on marital status are tabulated only for the population 15 years old and over. Each person was asked whether they were "Now married," "Widowed," "Separated," "Divorced," or "Never married." Couples who live together (for example, people in common-law marriages) were able to report the marital status they considered to be the most appropriate.

- **Never married.** Never married includes all people who have never been married, including people whose only marriage(s) was annulled.

- **Now married.** All people whose current marriage has not ended by widowhood or divorce. This category includes people defined as "separated."

- **Separated.** Includes people legally separated or otherwise absent from their spouse because of marital discord. Those without a final divorce decree are classified as "separated." This category also includes people who have been deserted or who have parted because they no longer want to live together, but who have not obtained a divorce.

- **Widowed.** This category includes widows and widowers who have not remarried.

- **Divorced.** This category includes people who are legally divorced and who have not remarried.

Foreign Born: Percentage of population who were not U.S. citizens at birth. Foreign-born people are those who indicated they were either a U.S. citizen by naturalization or they were not a citizen of the United States. *Source: U.S. Census Bureau, American Community Survey, 2009-2013 Five-Year Estimates*

Speak English Only: Percent of population that reported speaking only English at home. *Source: U.S. Census Bureau, American Community Survey, 2009-2013 Five-Year Estimates*

With Disability: Percent of the civilian noninstitutionalized population that reported having a disability. Disability status is determined from from six types of difficulty: vision, hearing, cognitive, ambulatory, self-care, and independent living. For children under 5 years old, hearing and vision difficulty are used to determine disability status. For children between the ages of 5 and 14, disability status is determined from hearing, vision, cognitive, ambulatory, and self-care difficulties. For people aged 15 years and older, they are considered to have a disability if they have difficulty with any one of the six difficulty types. *Source: U.S. Census Bureau, American Community Survey, 2009-2013 Five-Year Estimates*

Veterans: Percent of the civilian population 18 years and over who have served (even for a short time), but are not currently serving, on active duty in the U.S. Army, Navy, Air Force, Marine Corps, or the Coast Guard, or who served in the U.S. Merchant Marine during World War II. People who served in the National Guard or Reserves are classified as veterans only if they were ever called or ordered to active duty, not counting the 4-6 months for initial training or yearly summer camps. All other civilians are classified as nonveterans. Note: While it is possible for 17 year olds to be veterans of the Armed Forces, ACS data products are restricted to the population 18 years and older. *Source: U.S. Census Bureau, American Community Survey, 2009-2013 Five-Year Estimates*

Ancestry: Largest ancestry groups reported (up to five). The data includes persons who report multiple ancestries. For example, if a person reported being Irish and Italian, they would be included in both categories. Thus, the sum of the percentages may be greater than 100%. *Source: U.S. Census Bureau, American Community Survey, 2009-2013 Five-Year Estimates*

The data represent self-classification by people according to the ancestry group or groups with which they most closely identify. Ancestry refers to a person's ethnic origin or descent, "roots," heritage, or the place of birth of the person, the person's parents, or their ancestors before their arrival in the United States. Some ethnic identities, such as Egyptian or Polish, can be traced to geographic areas outside the United States, while other ethnicities such as Pennsylvania German or Cajun evolved in the United States.

The ancestry question was intended to provide data for groups that were not included in the Hispanic origin and race questions. Therefore, although data on all groups are collected, the ancestry data shown in these tabulations are for non-Hispanic and non-race groups. *See* Race/Hispanic Origin for information on Hispanic and race groups.

RELIGION

Religion: Lists the largest religious groups (up to six) based on the number of adherents divided by the population of the county. Adherents are defined as "all members, including full members, their children and the estimated number of other regular participants who are not considered as communicant, confirmed or full members." *Source: American Religious Bodies, 2010 U.S. Religion Census: Religious Congregations & Membership Study*

ECONOMY

Unemployment Rate: Unemployment rate as of October 2014. Includes all civilians age 16 or over who were unemployed and looking for work. *Source: U.S. Department of Labor, Bureau of Labor Statistics, Local Area Unemployment Statistics*

Leading Industries: Lists the three largest industries (excluding government) based on the number of employees. *Source: U.S. Census Bureau, County Business Patterns 2012*

Farms: The total number of farms and the total acreage they occupy. *Source: U.S. Department of Agriculture, National Agricultural Statistics Service, 2012 Census of Agriculture*

Company Size: The numbers of companies at various employee headcounts. Includes private employers only. *Source: U.S. Census Bureau, County Business Patterns 2012*

- **Employ 1,000 or more persons.** The numbers of companies that employ 1,000 or more persons.
- **Employ 500-999 persons.** The numbers of companies that employ 500 to 999 persons.
- **Employ 100-499 persons.** The numbers of companies that employ 100 to 499 persons.
- **Employ 1-99 persons.** The numbers of companies that employ 1 to 99 persons.

Business Ownership: Number of businesses that are majority-owned by women or various minority groups. *Source: U.S. Census Bureau, 2007 Economic Census, Survey of Business Owners: Black-Owned Firms, 2007 (latest statistics available at time of publication)*

- **Women-Owned.** Number of businesses that are majority-owned by a woman. Majority ownership is defined as having 51 percent or more of the stock or equity in the business.
- **Black-Owned.** Number of businesses that are majority-owned by a Black or African-American person(s). Majority ownership is defined as having 51 percent or more of the stock or equity in the business. Black or African American is defined as a person having origins in any of the black racial groups of Africa, including those who consider themselves to be "Haitian."
- **Hispanic-Owned.** Number of businesses that are majority-owned by a person(s) of Hispanic or Latino origin. Majority ownership is defined as having 51 percent or more of the stock or equity in the business. Hispanic or Latino origin is defined as a person of Cuban, Mexican, Puerto Rican, South or Central American, or other Spanish culture or origin, regardless of race.
- **Asian-Owned.** Number of businesses that are majority-owned by an Asian person(s). Majority ownership is defined as having 51 percent or more of the stock or equity in the business.

EMPLOYMENT

Employment by Occupation: Percentage of the employed civilian population 16 years and over in management, professional, service, sales, farming, construction, and production occupations. *Source: U.S. Census Bureau, American Community Survey, 2009-2013 Five-Year Estimates*

- Management, business, and financial occupations include:
    Management occupations
    Business and financial operations occupations

- Computer, engineering, and science occupations include:
    Computer and mathematical occupations
    Architecture and engineering occupations
    Life, physical, and social science occupations

- Education, legal, community service, arts, and media occupations include:
    Community and social service occupations
    Legal occupations
    Education, training, and library occupations
    Arts, design, entertainment, sports, and media occupations

- Healthcare practitioners and technical occupations include:
    Health diagnosing and treating practitioners and other technical occupations
    Health technologists and technicians

- Service occupations include:
    Healthcare support occupations
    Protective service occupations:
        Fire fighting and prevention, and other protective service workers including supervisors
        Law enforcement workers including supervisors
    Food preparation and serving related occupations
    Building and grounds cleaning and maintenance occupations
    Personal care and service occupations

- Sales and office occupations include:
    Sales and related occupations
    Office and administrative support occupations

- Natural resources, construction, and maintenance occupations include:
    Farming, fishing, and forestry occupations
    Construction and extraction occupations
    Installation, maintenance, and repair occupations

- Production, transportation, and material moving occupations include:
    Production occupations
    Transportation occupations
    Material moving occupations

INCOME

Per Capita Income: Per capita income is the mean income computed for every man, woman, and child in a particular group. It is derived by dividing the total income of a particular group by the total population in that group. Per capita income is rounded to the nearest whole dollar. *Source: U.S. Census Bureau, American Community Survey, 2009-2013 Five-Year Estimates*

Median Household Income: Includes the income of the householder and all other individuals 15 years old and over in the household, whether they are related to the householder or not. The median divides the income distribution into two equal parts: one-half of the cases falling below the median income and one-half above the median. For households, the median income is based on the distribution of the total number of households including those with no income. Median income for households is computed on the basis of a standard distribution and is rounded to the nearest whole dollar. *Source: U.S. Census Bureau, American Community Survey, 2009-2013 Five-Year Estimates*

Average Household Income: Average household income is obtained by dividing total household income by the total number of households. *Source: U.S. Census Bureau, American Community Survey, 2009-2013 Five-Year Estimates*

Percent of Households with Income of $100,000 or more: Percent of households with income of $100,000 or more. *Source: U.S. Census Bureau, American Community Survey, 2009-2013 Five-Year Estimates*

Poverty Rate: Percentage of population with income below the poverty level. Based on individuals for whom poverty status is determined. Poverty status was determined for all people except institutionalized people, people in military group quarters, people in college dormitories, and unrelated individuals under 15 years old. *Source: U.S. Census Bureau, American Community Survey, 2009-2013 Five-Year Estimates*

EDUCATIONAL ATTAINMENT

Figures show the percent of population age 25 and over with the following levels of educational attainment. *Source: U.S. Census Bureau, American Community Survey, 2009-2013 Five-Year Estimates*

- **High school diploma or higher.** Includes people whose highest degree is a high school diploma or its equivalent (GED), people who attended college but did not receive a degree, and people who received a college, university, or professional degree.
- **Bachelor's degree or higher.** Includes people who received a bachelor's, master's, doctorate, or professional degree.
- **Graduate/professional degree or higher.** Includes people who received a master's, doctorate, or professional degree.

HOUSING

Homeownership Rate: Percentage of housing units that are owner-occupied. *Source: U.S. Census Bureau, Census 2010*

Median Home Value: Median value in dollars of all owner-occupied housing units as reported by the owner. *Source: U.S. Census Bureau, American Community Survey, 2009-2013 Five-Year Estimates*

Median Year Structure Built: Year structure built refers to when the building was first constructed, not when it was remodeled, added to, or converted. For mobile homes, houseboats, RVs, etc, the manufacturer's model year was assumed to be the year built. The data relate to the number of units built during the specified periods that were still in existence at the time of enumeration. *Source: U.S. Census Bureau, American Community Survey, 2009-2013 Five-Year Estimates*

Homeowner Vacancy Rate: Proportion of the homeowner inventory that is vacant "for sale." It is computed by dividing the number of vacant units "for sale only" by the sum of the owner-occupied units, vacant units that are "for sale only," and vacant units that have been sold but not yet occupied, and then multiplying by 100. This measure is rounded to the nearest tenth. *Source: U.S. Census Bureau, Census 2010*

Median Gross Rent: Median monthly gross rent in dollars on specified renter-occupied and specified vacant-for-rent units. Specified renter-occupied and specified vacant-for-rent units exclude 1-family houses on 10 acres or more. Gross rent is the contract rent plus the estimated average monthly cost of utilities (electricity, gas, and water and sewer) and fuels (oil, coal, kerosene, wood, etc.) if these are paid by the renter (or paid for the renter by someone else). Gross rent is intended to eliminate differentials that result from varying practices with respect to the inclusion of

xvi   Data Explanation and Sources: County Profiles

utilities and fuels as part of the rental payment. Contract rent is the monthly rent agreed to or contracted for, regardless of any furnishings, utilities, fees, meals, or services that may be included. For vacant units, it is the monthly rent asked for the rental unit at the time of enumeration. *Source: U.S. Census Bureau, American Community Survey, 2009-2013 Five-Year Estimates*

Rental Vacancy Rate: Proportion of the rental inventory that is vacant "for rent." It is computed by dividing the number of vacant units "for rent" by the sum of the renter-occupied units, vacant units that are "for rent," and vacant units that have been rented but not yet occupied, and then multiplying by 100. This measure is rounded to the nearest tenth. *Source: U.S. Census Bureau, Census 2010*

VITAL STATISTICS

Birth Rate: Estimated number of births per 10,000 population in 2013. *Source: U.S. Census Bureau, Annual Components of Population Change, July 1, 2010 - July 1, 2013*

Death Rate: Estimated number of deaths per 10,000 population in 2013. *Source: U.S. Census Bureau, Annual Components of Population Change, July 1, 2010 - July 1, 2013*

Age-adjusted Cancer Mortality Rate: Number of age-adjusted deaths from cancer per 100,000 population in 2011. Cancer is defined as International Classification of Disease (ICD) codes C00–D48.9 Neoplasms. *Source: Centers for Disease Control, CDC Wonder, 2011*

Age-adjusted death rates are weighted averages of the age-specific death rates, where the weights represent a fixed population by age. They are used because the rates of almost all causes of death vary by age. Age adjustment is a technique for "removing" the effects of age from crude rates, so as to allow meaningful comparisons across populations with different underlying age structures. For example, comparing the crude rate of heart disease in Virginia to that of California is misleading, because the relatively older population in Virginia will lead to a higher crude death rate, even if the age-specific rates of heart disease in Virginia and California are the same. For such a comparison, age-adjusted rates would be preferable. Age-adjusted rates should be viewed as relative indexes rather than as direct or actual measures of mortality risk.

Death rates based on counts of twenty or less (≤ 20) are flagged as "Unreliable". Death rates based on fewer than three years of data for counties with populations of less than 100,000 in the 2000 Census counts, are also flagged as "Unreliable" if the number of deaths is five or less (≤ 5).

HEALTH INSURANCE

Health insurance coverage in the ACS and other Census Bureau surveys define coverage to include plans and programs that provide comprehensive health coverage. Plans that provide insurance for specific conditions or situations such as cancer and long-term care policies are not considered coverage. Likewise, other types of insurance like dental, vision, life, and disability insurance are not considered health insurance coverage.

For reporting purposes, the Census Bureau broadly classifies health insurance coverage as private health insurance or public coverage. Private health insurance is a plan provided through an employer or union, a plan purchased by an individual from a private company, or TRICARE or other military health care. Public health coverage includes the federal programs Medicare, Medicaid, and VA Health Care (provided through the Department of Veterans Affairs); the Children's Health Insurance Program (CHIP); and individual state health plans. The types of health insurance are not mutually exclusive; people may be covered by more than one at the same time. People who had no reported health coverage, or those whose only health coverage was Indian Health Service, were considered uninsured. *Source: U.S. Census Bureau, American Community Survey, 2009-2013 Five-Year Estimates*

- **Have Insurance:** Percent of the civilian noninstitutionalized population with any type of comprehensive health insurance.
- **Have Private Insurance.** Percent of the civilian noninstitutionalized population with private health insurance. A person may report that they have both public and private health insurance, thus, the sum of the percentages may be greater than 100%.
- **Have Public Insurance.** Percent of the civilian noninstitutionalized population with public health insurance. A person may report that they have both public and private health insurance, thus, the sum of the percentages may be greater than 100%.
- **Do Not Have Insurance.** Percent of the civilian noninstitutionalized population with no health insurance.
- **Children Under 18 With No Insurance.** Percent of the civilian noninstitutionalized population under age 18 with no health insurance.

HEALTH CARE

Number of physicians, hospital beds and hospital admission per 10,000 population. *Source: Area Resource File (ARF) 2012-2013. U.S. Department of Health and Human Services, Health Resources and Services Administration, Bureau of Health Professions, Rockville, MD.*

- **Number of Physicians.** The number of active, non-federal physicians (MDs and DOs) per 10,000 population in 2011.
- **Number of Hospital Beds.** The number of hospital beds per 10,000 population in 2010.
- **Number of Hospital Admissions.** The number of hospital admissions per 10,000 population in 2010.

AIR QUALITY INDEX

The percentage of days in 2013 the AQI fell into the Good (0-50), Moderate (51-100), Unhealthy for Sensitive Groups (101-150), Unhealthy (151-200), Very Unhealthy (201-300), and Hazardous (300+) ranges. If a range does not appear, its value is zero. Data covers January 2013 through December 2013. *Source: AirData: Access to Air Pollution Data, U.S. Environmental Protection Agency, Office of Air and Radiation*

The AQI is an index for reporting daily air quality. It tells you how clean or polluted your air is, and what associated health concerns you should be aware of. The AQI focuses on health effects that can happen within a few hours or days after breathing polluted air. EPA uses the AQI for five major air pollutants regulated by the Clean Air Act: ground-level ozone, particulate matter, carbon monoxide, sulfur dioxide, and nitrogen dioxide. For each of these pollutants, EPA has established national air quality standards to protect against harmful health effects.

The AQI runs from 0 to 500. The higher the AQI value, the greater the level of air pollution and the greater the health danger. For example, an AQI value of 50 represents good air quality and little potential to affect public health, while an AQI value over 300 represents hazardous air quality. An AQI value of 100 generally corresponds to the national air quality standard for the pollutant, which is the level EPA has set to protect public health. So, AQI values below 100 are generally thought of as satisfactory. When AQI values are above 100, air quality is considered to be unhealthy—at first for certain sensitive groups of people, then for everyone as AQI values get higher. Each category corresponds to a different level of health concern. For example, when the AQI for a pollutant is between 51 and 100, the health concern is "Moderate." Here are the six levels of health concern and what they mean:

- "Good" The AQI value for your community is between 0 and 50. Air quality is considered satisfactory and air pollution poses little or no risk.
- "Moderate" The AQI for your community is between 51 and 100. Air quality is acceptable; however, for some pollutants there may be a moderate health concern for a very small number of individuals. For example, people who are unusually sensitive to ozone may experience respiratory symptoms.
- "Unhealthy for Sensitive Groups" Certain groups of people are particularly sensitive to the harmful effects of certain air pollutants. This means they are likely to be affected at lower levels than the general public. For example, children and adults who are active outdoors and people with respiratory disease are at greater risk from exposure to ozone, while people with heart disease are at greater risk from carbon monoxide. Some people may be sensitive to more than one pollutant. When AQI values are between 101 and 150, members of sensitive groups may experience health effects. The general public is not likely to be affected when the AQI is in this range.
- "Unhealthy" AQI values are between 151 and 200. Everyone may begin to experience health effects. Members of sensitive groups may experience more serious health effects.
- "Very Unhealthy" AQI values between 201 and 300 trigger a health alert, meaning everyone may experience more serious health effects.
- "Hazardous" AQI values over 300 trigger health warnings of emergency conditions. The entire population is more likely to be affected.

TRANSPORTATION

Commute to Work: Percentage of workers 16 years old and over that use the following means of transportation to commute to work: car; public transportation; walk; work from home. The means of transportation data for some areas may show workers using modes of public transportation that are not available in those areas (e.g. subway or elevated riders in a metropolitan area where there actually is no subway or elevated service). This result is largely due to people who worked during the reference week at a location that was different from their usual place of work (such as people away from home on business in an area where subway service was available) and people who used more than one

means of transportation each day but whose principal means was unavailable where they lived (e.g. residents of non-metropolitan areas who drove to the fringe of a metropolitan area and took the commuter railroad most of the distance to work). *Source: U.S. Census Bureau, American Community Survey, 2009-2013 Five-Year Estimates*

Median Travel Time to Work: Median travel time to work for workers 16 years old and over. Travel time to work refers to the total number of minutes that it usually took the person to get from home to work each day during the reference week. The elapsed time includes time spent waiting for public transportation, picking up passengers in carpools, and time spent in other activities related to getting to work. *Source: U.S. Census Bureau, American Community Survey, 2009-2013 Five-Year Estimates*

PRESIDENTIAL ELECTION

2012 Presidential election results. *Source: Dave Leip's Atlas of U.S. Presidential Elections*

NATIONAL AND STATE PARKS

Lists National/State parks located in the area. *Source: U.S. Geological Survey, Geographic Names Information System*

ADDITIONAL INFORMATION CONTACTS

General telephone number and website address (if available) of local government.

Data Explanation and Sources: Community Profiles

PHYSICAL AND GEOGRAPHICAL CHARACTERISTICS

Place Type: Lists the type of place (city, town, village, borough, Census-Designated Place (CDP), township, charter township, plantation, gore, district, grant, location, purchase, municipality, reservation, unorganized territory, or unincorporated postal area). *Source: U.S. Census Bureau, Census 2010 and U.S. Postal Service, City State File*

ZCTA: *This only appears within unincorporated postal areas.* The statistics that follow cover the corresponding ZIP Code Tabulation Area (ZCTA). A ZCTA is a statistical entity developed by the Census Bureau to approximate the delivery area for a US Postal Service 5-digit or 3-digit ZIP Code in the US and Puerto Rico. A ZCTA is an aggregation of census blocks that have the same predominant ZIP Code associated with the mailing addresses in the Census Bureau's Master Address File. Thus, the Postal Service's delivery areas have been adjusted to encompass whole census blocks so that the Census Bureau can tabulate census data for the ZCTAs. ZCTAs do not include all ZIP Codes used for mail delivery and therefore do not precisely depict the area within which mail deliveries associated with that ZIP Code occur. Additionally, some areas that are known by a unique name, although they are part of a larger incorporated place, are also included as "postal areas."

Land and Water Area: Land and water area in square miles. *Source: U.S. Census Bureau, Census 2010*

Latitude and Longitude: Latitude and longitude in degrees. *Source: U.S. Census Bureau, Census 2010.*

Elevation: Elevation in feet. *Source: U.S. Geological Survey, Geographic Names Information System (GNIS)*

HISTORY

Historical information. *Source: Columbia University Press, The Columbia Gazetteer of North America; Original research*

POPULATION

Population: 2010 figures are a 100% count of population. *Source: U.S. Census Bureau, Census 2010*

Population Growth: The increase or decrease in population between 2000 and 2010. *Source: U.S. Census Bureau, Census 2000, Census 2010*

Population Density: Total 2010 population divided by the land area in square miles. *Source: U.S. Census Bureau, U.S. Census Bureau, Census 2010*

Race/Hispanic Origin: Figures include the U.S. Census Bureau categories of White alone; Black/African American alone; Asian alone; American Indian/Alaska Native alone; Native Hawaiian/Other Pacific Islander alone; two or more races; and Hispanic of any race. Alone refers to the fact that these figures are not in combination with any other race. *Source: U.S. Census Bureau, Census 2010*

The concept of race, as used by the Census Bureau, reflects self-identification by people according to the race or races with which they most closely identify. These categories are socio-political constructs and should not be interpreted as being scientific or anthropological in nature. Furthermore, the race categories include both racial and national-origin groups.

- **White.** A person having origins in any of the original peoples of Europe, the Middle East, or North Africa. It includes people who indicated their race(s) as "White" or reported entries such as Irish, German, Italian, Lebanese, Arab, Moroccan, or Caucasian.
- **Black/African American.** A person having origins in any of the Black racial groups of Africa. It includes people who indicated their race(s) as "Black, African Am., or Negro" or reported entries such as African American, Kenyan, Nigerian, or Haitian.
- **Asian.** A person having origins in any of the original peoples of the Far East, Southeast Asia, or the Indian subcontinent, including, for example, Cambodia, China, India, Japan, Korea, Malaysia, Pakistan, the Philippine Islands, Thailand, and Vietnam. It includes people who indicated their race(s) as "Asian" or reported entries such as "Asian Indian," "Chinese," "Filipino," "Korean," "Japanese," "Vietnamese," and "Other Asian" or provided other detailed Asian responses.
- **American Indian/Alaska Native.** A person having origins in any of the original peoples of North and South America (including Central America) and who maintains tribal affiliation or community attachment.

This category includes people who indicated their race(s) as "American Indian or Alaska Native" or reported their enrolled or principal tribe, such as Navajo, Blackfeet, Inupiat, Yup'ik, or Central American Indian groups or South American Indian groups.

- **Native Hawaiian/Other Pacific Islander.** A person having origins in any of the original peoples of Hawaii, Guam, Samoa, or other Pacific Islands. It includes people who indicated their race(s) as "Pacific Islander" or reported entries such as "Native Hawaiian," "Guamanian or Chamorro," "Samoan," and "Other Pacific Islander" or provided other detailed Pacific Islander responses..

- **Two or More Races.** People may choose to provide two or more races either by checking two or more race response check boxes, by providing multiple responses, or by some combination of check boxes and other responses. The race response categories shown on the questionnaire are collapsed into the five minimum race groups identified by OMB, and the Census Bureau's "Some Other Race" category.

- **Hispanic.** The data on the Hispanic or Latino population were derived from answers to a question that was asked of all people. The terms "Spanish," "Hispanic origin," and "Latino" are used interchangeably. Some respondents identify with all three terms while others may identify with only one of these three specific terms. Hispanics or Latinos who identify with the terms "Spanish," "Hispanic," or "Latino" are those who classify themselves in one of the specific Spanish, Hispanic, or Latino categories listed on the questionnaire ("Mexican," "Puerto Rican," or "Cuban") as well as those who indicate that they are "other Spanish/Hispanic/Latino." People who do not identify with one of the specific origins listed on the questionnaire but indicate that they are "other Spanish/Hispanic/Latino" are those whose origins are from Spain, the Spanish-speaking countries of Central or South America, the Dominican Republic, or people identifying themselves generally as Spanish, Spanish-American, Hispanic, Hispano, Latino, and so on. All write-in responses to the "other Spanish/Hispanic/Latino" category were coded. Origin can be viewed as the heritage, nationality group, lineage, or country of birth of the person or the person's parents or ancestors before their arrival in the United States. People who identify their origin as Spanish, Hispanic, or Latino may be of any race.

Average Household Size: Number of persons in the average household. *Source: U.S. Census Bureau, Census 2010*

Median Age: Median age of the population. *Source: U.S. Census Bureau, Census 2010*

Age Under 18: Percent of the total population under 18 years old. *Source: U.S. Census Bureau, Census 2010*

Age 65 and Over: Percent of the total population age 65 and over. *Source: U.S. Census Bureau, Census 2010*

Males per 100 Females: Number of males per 100 females. *Source: U.S. Census Bureau, Census 2010*

Marital Status: Percentage of population never married, now married, separated, widowed, or divorced. *Source: U.S. Census Bureau, American Community Survey, 2009-2013 Five-Year Estimates*

The marital status classification refers to the status at the time of enumeration. Data on marital status are tabulated only for the population 15 years old and over. Each person was asked whether they were "Now married," "Widowed," "Separated," "Divorced," or "Never married." Couples who live together (for example, people in common-law marriages) were able to report the marital status they considered to be the most appropriate.

- **Never married.** Never married includes all people who have never been married, including people whose only marriage(s) was annulled.

- **Now married.** All people whose current marriage has not ended by widowhood or divorce. This category includes people defined as "separated."

- **Separated.** Includes people legally separated or otherwise absent from their spouse because of marital discord. Those without a final divorce decree are classified as "separated." This category also includes people who have been deserted or who have parted because they no longer want to live together, but who have not obtained a divorce.

- **Widowed.** This category includes widows and widowers who have not remarried.

- **Divorced.** This category includes people who are legally divorced and who have not remarried.

Foreign Born: Percentage of population who were not U.S. citizens at birth. Foreign-born people are those who indicated they were either a U.S. citizen by naturalization or they were not a citizen of the United States. *Source: U.S. Census Bureau, American Community Survey, 2009-2013 Five-Year Estimates*

Speak English Only: Percent of population that reported speaking only English at home. *Source: U.S. Census Bureau, American Community Survey, 2009-2013 Five-Year Estimates*

With Disability: Percent of the civilian noninstitutionalized population that reported having a disability. Disability status is determined from from six types of difficulty: vision, hearing, cognitive, ambulatory, self-care, and independent living. For children under 5 years old, hearing and vision difficulty are used to determine disability status. For children between the ages of 5 and 14, disability status is determined from hearing, vision, cognitive, ambulatory, and self-care difficulties. For people aged 15 years and older, they are considered to have a disability if they have difficulty with any one of the six difficulty types. *Source: U.S. Census Bureau, American Community Survey, 2009-2013 Five-Year Estimates*

Veterans: Percent of the civilian population 18 years and over who have served (even for a short time), but are not currently serving, on active duty in the U.S. Army, Navy, Air Force, Marine Corps, or the Coast Guard, or who served in the U.S. Merchant Marine during World War II. People who served in the National Guard or Reserves are classified as veterans only if they were ever called or ordered to active duty, not counting the 4-6 months for initial training or yearly summer camps. All other civilians are classified as nonveterans. Note: While it is possible for 17 year olds to be veterans of the Armed Forces, ACS data products are restricted to the population 18 years and older. *Source: U.S. Census Bureau, American Community Survey, 2009-2013 Five-Year Estimates*

Ancestry: Largest ancestry groups reported (up to five). The data includes persons who report multiple ancestries. For example, if a person reported being Irish and Italian, they would be included in both categories. Thus, the sum of the percentages may be greater than 100%. *Source: U.S. Census Bureau, American Community Survey, 2009-2013 Five-Year Estimates*

The data represent self-classification by people according to the ancestry group or groups with which they most closely identify. Ancestry refers to a person's ethnic origin or descent, "roots," heritage, or the place of birth of the person, the person's parents, or their ancestors before their arrival in the United States. Some ethnic identities, such as Egyptian or Polish, can be traced to geographic areas outside the United States, while other ethnicities such as Pennsylvania German or Cajun evolved in the United States.

The ancestry question was intended to provide data for groups that were not included in the Hispanic origin and race questions. Therefore, although data on all groups are collected, the ancestry data shown in these tabulations are for non-Hispanic and non-race groups. *See* Race/Hispanic Origin for information on Hispanic and race groups.

EMPLOYMENT

Employment by Occupation: Percentage of the employed civilian population 16 years and over in management, professional, service, sales, farming, construction, and production occupations. *Source: U.S. Census Bureau, American Community Survey, 2009-2013 Five-Year Estimates*

- Management, business, and financial occupations include:
    Management occupations
    Business and financial operations occupations

- Computer, engineering, and science occupations include:
    Computer and mathematical occupations
    Architecture and engineering occupations
    Life, physical, and social science occupations

- Education, legal, community service, arts, and media occupations include:
    Community and social service occupations
    Legal occupations
    Education, training, and library occupations
    Arts, design, entertainment, sports, and media occupations

- Healthcare practitioners and technical occupations include:
    Health diagnosing and treating practitioners and other technical occupations
    Health technologists and technicians

- Service occupations include:
    Healthcare support occupations
    Protective service occupations:
        Fire fighting and prevention, and other protective service workers including supervisors
        Law enforcement workers including supervisors
    Food preparation and serving related occupations
    Building and grounds cleaning and maintenance occupations
    Personal care and service occupations

- Sales and office occupations include:
    Sales and related occupations
    Office and administrative support occupations

- Natural resources, construction, and maintenance occupations include:
    Farming, fishing, and forestry occupations
    Construction and extraction occupations
    Installation, maintenance, and repair occupations

- Production, transportation, and material moving occupations include:
    Production occupations
    Transportation occupations
    Material moving occupations

INCOME

Per Capita Income: Per capita income is the mean income computed for every man, woman, and child in a particular group. It is derived by dividing the total income of a particular group by the total population in that group. Per capita income is rounded to the nearest whole dollar. *Source: U.S. Census Bureau, American Community Survey, 2009-2013 Five-Year Estimates*

Median Household Income: Includes the income of the householder and all other individuals 15 years old and over in the household, whether they are related to the householder or not. The median divides the income distribution into two equal parts: one-half of the cases falling below the median income and one-half above the median. For households, the median income is based on the distribution of the total number of households including those with no income. Median income for households is computed on the basis of a standard distribution and is rounded to the nearest whole dollar. *Source: U.S. Census Bureau, American Community Survey, 2009-2013 Five-Year Estimates*

Average Household Income: Average household income is obtained by dividing total household income by the total number of households. *Source: U.S. Census Bureau, American Community Survey, 2009-2013 Five-Year Estimates*

Percent of Households with Income of $100,000 or more: Percent of households with income of $100,000 or more. *Source: U.S. Census Bureau, American Community Survey, 2009-2013 Five-Year Estimates*

Poverty Rate: Percentage of population with income below the poverty level. Based on individuals for whom poverty status is determined. Poverty status was determined for all people except institutionalized people, people in military group quarters, people in college dormitories, and unrelated individuals under 15 years old. *Source: U.S. Census Bureau, American Community Survey, 2009-2013 Five-Year Estimates*

EDUCATIONAL ATTAINMENT

Figures show the percent of population age 25 and over with the following levels of educational attainment. *Source: U.S. Census Bureau, American Community Survey, 2009-2013 Five-Year Estimates*

- **High school diploma or higher.** Includes people whose highest degree is a high school diploma or its equivalent (GED), people who attended college but did not receive a degree, and people who received a college, university, or professional degree.
- **Bachelor's degree or higher.** Includes people who received a bachelor's, master's, doctorate, or professional degree.
- **Graduate/professional degree or higher.** Includes people who received a master's, doctorate, or professional degree.

SCHOOL DISTRICTS

Lists the name of each school district, the grade range (PK=pre-kindergarten; KG=kindergarten), the student enrollment, and the district headquarters' phone number. In each community profile, only school districts that have schools that are physically located within the community are shown. In addition, statistics for each school district cover the entire district, regardless of the physical location of the schools within the district. *Source: U.S. Department of Education, National Center for Educational Statistics, Directory of Public Elementary and Secondary Education Agencies, 2012-13*

COLLEGES

Four-year Colleges: Lists the name of each four-year college, the type of institution (private or public; for-profit or non-profit; religious affiliation; historically black), the total estimated student enrollment in 2013, the general telephone number, and the annual tuition and fees for full-time, first-time undergraduate students (in-state and out-of-state). *Source: U.S. Department of Education, National Center for Educational Statistics, IPEDS College Data, 2013-14*

Two-year Colleges: Lists the name of each two-year college, the type of institution (private or public; for-profit or non-profit; religious affiliation; historically black), the total estimated student enrollment in 2013, the general telephone number, and the annual tuition and fees for full-time, first-time undergraduate students (in-state and out-of-state). *Source: U.S. Department of Education, National Center for Educational Statistics, IPEDS College Data, 2013-14*

Vocational/Technical Schools: Lists the name of each vocational/technical school, the type of institution (private or public; for-profit or non-profit; religious affiliation; historically black), the total estimated student enrollment in 2013, the general telephone number, and the annual tuition and fees for full-time students. *Source: U.S. Department of Education, National Center for Educational Statistics, IPEDS College Data, 2013-14*

HOUSING

Homeownership Rate: Percentage of housing units that are owner-occupied. *Source: U.S. Census Bureau, Census 2010*

Median Home Value: Median value in dollars of all owner-occupied housing units as reported by the owner. *Source: U.S. Census Bureau, American Community Survey, 2009-2013 Five-Year Estimates*

Median Year Structure Built: Year structure built refers to when the building was first constructed, not when it was remodeled, added to, or converted. For mobile homes, houseboats, RVs, etc, the manufacturer's model year was assumed to be the year built. The data relate to the number of units built during the specified periods that were still in existence at the time of enumeration. *Source: U.S. Census Bureau, American Community Survey, 2009-2013 Five-Year Estimates*

Homeowner Vacancy Rate: Proportion of the homeowner inventory that is vacant "for sale." It is computed by dividing the number of vacant units "for sale only" by the sum of the owner-occupied units, vacant units that are "for sale only," and vacant units that have been sold but not yet occupied, and then multiplying by 100. This measure is rounded to the nearest tenth. *Source: U.S. Census Bureau, Census 2010*

Median Gross Rent: Median monthly gross rent in dollars on specified renter-occupied and specified vacant-for-rent units. Specified renter-occupied and specified vacant-for-rent units exclude 1-family houses on 10 acres or more. Gross rent is the contract rent plus the estimated average monthly cost of utilities (electricity, gas, and water and sewer) and fuels (oil, coal, kerosene, wood, etc.) if these are paid by the renter (or paid for the renter by someone else). Gross rent is intended to eliminate differentials that result from varying practices with respect to the inclusion of utilities and fuels as part of the rental payment. Contract rent is the monthly rent agreed to or contracted for, regardless of any furnishings, utilities, fees, meals, or services that may be included. For vacant units, it is the monthly rent asked for the rental unit at the time of enumeration. *Source: U.S. Census Bureau, American Community Survey, 2009-2013 Five-Year Estimates*

Rental Vacancy Rate: Proportion of the rental inventory that is vacant "for rent." It is computed by dividing the number of vacant units "for rent" by the sum of the renter-occupied units, vacant units that are "for rent," and vacant units that have been rented but not yet occupied, and then multiplying by 100. This measure is rounded to the nearest tenth. *Source: U.S. Census Bureau, Census 2010*

HEALTH INSURANCE

Health insurance coverage in the ACS and other Census Bureau surveys define coverage to include plans and programs that provide comprehensive health coverage. Plans that provide insurance for specific conditions or situations such as cancer and long-term care policies are not considered coverage. Likewise, other types of insurance like dental, vision, life, and disability insurance are not considered health insurance coverage.

For reporting purposes, the Census Bureau broadly classifies health insurance coverage as private health insurance or public coverage. Private health insurance is a plan provided through an employer or union, a plan purchased by an individual from a private company, or TRICARE or other military health care. Public health coverage includes the federal programs Medicare, Medicaid, and VA Health Care (provided through the Department of Veterans Affairs); the Children's Health Insurance Program (CHIP); and individual state health plans. The types of health insurance are not

mutually exclusive; people may be covered by more than one at the same time. People who had no reported health coverage, or those whose only health coverage was Indian Health Service, were considered uninsured. *Source: U.S. Census Bureau, American Community Survey, 2009-2013 Five-Year Estimates*

- **Have Insurance:** Percent of the civilian noninstitutionalized population with any type of comprehensive health insurance.
- **Have Private Insurance.** Percent of the civilian noninstitutionalized population with private health insurance. A person may report that they have both public and private health insurance, thus, the sum of the percentages may be greater than 100%.
- **Have Public Insurance.** Percent of the civilian noninstitutionalized population with public health insurance. A person may report that they have both public and private health insurance, thus, the sum of the percentages may be greater than 100%.
- **Do Not Have Insurance.** Percent of the civilian noninstitutionalized population with no health insurance.
- **Children Under 18 With No Insurance.** Percent of the civilian noninstitutionalized population under age 18 with no health insurance.

HOSPITALS

Lists the hospital name and the number of licensed beds. *Source: Grey House Publishing, The Comparative Guide to American Hospitals, 2014*

NEWSPAPERS

List of daily and weekly newspapers with circulation figures. *Source: Gebbie Press, 2015 All-In-One Media Directory*

SAFETY

Violent Crime Rate: Number of violent crimes reported per 10,000 population. Violent crimes include murder, forcible rape, robbery, and aggravated assault. *Source: Federal Bureau of Investigation, Uniform Crime Reports 2013*

Property Crime Rate: Number of property crimes reported per 10,000 population. Property crimes include burglary, larceny-theft, and motor vehicle theft. *Source: Federal Bureau of Investigation, Uniform Crime Reports 2013*

TRANSPORTATION

Commute to Work: Percentage of workers 16 years old and over that use the following means of transportation to commute to work: car; public transportation; walk; work from home. The means of transportation data for some areas may show workers using modes of public transportation that are not available in those areas (e.g. subway or elevated riders in a metropolitan area where there actually is no subway or elevated service). This result is largely due to people who worked during the reference week at a location that was different from their usual place of work (such as people away from home on business in an area where subway service was available) and people who used more than one means of transportation each day but whose principal means was unavailable where they lived (e.g. residents of non-metropolitan areas who drove to the fringe of a metropolitan area and took the commuter railroad most of the distance to work). *Source: U.S. Census Bureau, American Community Survey, 2009-2013 Five-Year Estimates*

Median Travel Time to Work: Median travel time to work for workers 16 years old and over. Travel time to work refers to the total number of minutes that it usually took the person to get from home to work each day during the reference week. The elapsed time includes time spent waiting for public transportation, picking up passengers in carpools, and time spent in other activities related to getting to work. *Source: U.S. Census Bureau, American Community Survey, 2009-2013 Five-Year Estimates*

Amtrak: Indicates if Amtrak rail or bus service is available. Please note that the cities being served continually change. *Source: National Railroad Passenger Corporation, Amtrak National Timetable, 2015*

AIRPORTS

Lists the local airport(s) along with type of service and hub size. *Source: U.S. Department of Transportation, Bureau of Transportation Statistics*

ADDITIONAL INFORMATION CONTACTS

General telephone number and website address (if available) of local government.

User Guide: Education Section

School District Rankings

Number of Schools: Total number of schools in the district. *Source: U.S. Department of Education, National Center for Education Statistics, Common Core of Data, Public Elementary/Secondary School Universe Survey: School Year 2011-2012.*

Number of Teachers: Teachers are defined as individuals who provide instruction to pre-kindergarten, kindergarten, grades 1 through 12, or ungraded classes, or individuals who teach in an environment other than a classroom setting, and who maintain daily student attendance records. Numbers reported are full-time equivalents (FTE). *Source: U.S. Department of Education, National Center for Education Statistics, Common Core of Data, Local Education Agency (School District) Universe Survey: School Year 2011-2012.*

Number of Students: A student is an individual for whom instruction is provided in an elementary or secondary education program that is not an adult education program and is under the jurisdiction of a school, school system, or other education institution. *Sources: U.S. Department of Education, National Center for Education Statistics, Common Core of Data, Local Education Agency (School District) Universe Survey: School Year 2011-2012 and Public Elementary/Secondary School Universe Survey: School Year 2011-2012*

Individual Education Program (IEP) Students: A written instructional plan for students with disabilities designated as special education students under IDEA-Part B. The written instructional plan includes a statement of present levels of educational performance of a child; statement of annual goals, including short-term instructional objectives; statement of specific educational services to be provided and the extent to which the child will be able to participate in regular educational programs; the projected date for initiation and anticipated duration of services; the appropriate objectives, criteria and evaluation procedures; and the schedules for determining, on at least an annual basis, whether instructional objectives are being achieved. *Source: U.S. Department of Education, National Center for Education Statistics, Common Core of Data, Local Education Agency (School District) Universe Survey: School Year 2011-2012*

English Language Learner (ELL) Students: Formerly referred to as Limited English Proficient (LEP). Students being served in appropriate programs of language assistance (e.g., English as a Second Language, High Intensity Language Training, bilingual education). Does not include pupils enrolled in a class to learn a language other than English. Also Limited-English-Proficient students are individuals who were not born in the United States or whose native language is a language other than English; or individuals who come from environments where a language other than English is dominant; or individuals who are American Indians and Alaskan Natives and who come from environments where a language other than English has had a significant impact on their level of English language proficiency; and who, by reason thereof, have sufficient difficulty speaking, reading, writing, or understanding the English language, to deny such individuals the opportunity to learn successfully in classrooms where the language of instruction is English or to participate fully in our society. *Source: U.S. Department of Education, National Center for Education Statistics, Common Core of Data, Local Education Agency (School District) Universe Survey: School Year 2011-2012*

Students Eligible for Free Lunch Program: The free lunch program is defined as a program under the National School Lunch Act that provides cash subsidies for free lunches to students based on family size and income criteria. *Source: U.S. Department of Education, National Center for Education Statistics, Common Core of Data, Public Elementary/Secondary School Universe Survey: School Year 2011-2012*

Students Eligible for Reduced-Price Lunch Program: A student who is eligible to participate in the Reduced-Price Lunch Program under the National School Lunch Act. *Source: U.S. Department of Education, National Center for Education Statistics, Common Core of Data, Public Elementary/Secondary School Universe Survey: School Year 2011-2012*

Student/Teacher Ratio: The number of students divided by the number of teachers (FTE). See Number of Students and Number of Teachers above for for information.

Student/Librarian Ratio: The number of students divided by the number of library and media support staff. Library and media support staff are defined as staff members who render other professional library and media services; also includes library aides and those involved in library/media support. Their duties include selecting, preparing, caring for, and making available to instructional staff, equipment, films, filmstrips, transparencies, tapes, TV programs, and similar materials maintained separately or as part of an instructional materials center. Also included are activities in the audio-visual center, TV studio, related-work-study areas, and services provided by audio-visual personnel.

Numbers are based on full-time equivalents. *Source: U.S. Department of Education, National Center for Education Statistics, Common Core of Data, Local Education Agency (School District) Universe Survey: School Year 2011-2012.*

Student/Counselor Ratio: The number of students divided by the number of guidance counselors. Guidance counselors are professional staff assigned specific duties and school time for any of the following activities in an elementary or secondary setting: counseling with students and parents; consulting with other staff members on learning problems; evaluating student abilities; assisting students in making educational and career choices; assisting students in personal and social development; providing referral assistance; and/or working with other staff members in planning and conducting guidance programs for students. The state applies its own standards in apportioning the aggregate of guidance counselors/directors into the elementary and secondary level components. Numbers reported are full-time equivalents. *Source: U.S. Department of Education, National Center for Education Statistics, Common Core of Data, Local Education Agency (School District) Universe Survey: School Year 2011-2012.*

Current Spending per Student: Expenditure for Instruction, Support Services, and Other Elementary/Secondary Programs. Includes salaries, employee benefits, purchased services, and supplies, as well as payments made by states on behalf of school districts. Also includes transfers made by school districts into their own retirement system. Excludes expenditure for Non-Elementary/Secondary Programs, debt service, capital outlay, and transfers to other governments or school districts. This item is formally called "Current Expenditures for Public Elementary/Secondary Education."

Instruction: Includes payments from all funds for salaries, employee benefits, supplies, materials, and contractual services for elementary/secondary instruction. It excludes capital outlay, debt service, and interfund transfers for elementary/secondary instruction. Instruction covers regular, special, and vocational programs offered in both the regular school year and summer school. It excludes instructional support activities as well as adult education and community services. Instruction salaries includes salaries for teachers and teacher aides and assistants.

Support Services: Relates to support services functions (series 2000) defined in Financial Accounting for Local and State School Systems (National Center for Education Statistics 2000). Includes payments from all funds for salaries, employee benefits, supplies, materials, and contractual services. It excludes capital outlay, debt service, and interfund transfers. It includes expenditure for the following functions:

- Business/Central/Other Support Services
- General Administration
- Instructional Staff Support
- Operation and Maintenance
- Pupil Support Services
- Pupil Transportation Services
- School Administration
- Nonspecified Support Services

Values shown are dollars per pupil per year. They were calculated by dividing the total dollar amounts by the fall membership. Fall membership is comprised of the total student enrollment on October 1 (or the closest school day to October 1) for all grade levels (including prekindergarten and kindergarten) and ungraded pupils. Membership includes students both present and absent on the measurement day. *Source: U.S. Department of Education, National Center for Education Statistics, Common Core of Data, School District Finance Survey (F-33), Fiscal Year 2011.*

Drop-out Rate: A dropout is a student who was enrolled in school at some time during the previous school year; was not enrolled at the beginning of the current school year; has not graduated from high school or completed a state or district approved educational program; and does not meet any of the following exclusionary conditions: has transferred to another public school district, private school, or state- or district-approved educational program; is temporarily absent due to suspension or school-approved illness; or has died. The values shown cover grades 9 through 12. *Note: Drop-out rates are no longer available to the general public disaggregated by grade, race/ethnicity, and gender at the school district level. Beginning with the 2005–06 school year the CCD is reporting dropout data aggregated from the local education agency (district) level to the state level. This allows data users to compare event dropout rates across states, regions, and other jurisdictions. Source: U.S. Department of Education, National Center for Education Statistics, Common Core of Data, Local Education Agency (School District) Universe Survey Dropout and Completion Data, 2008-2009; U.S. Department of Education, National Center for Education Statistics, Common Core of Data, State Dropout and Completion Data File, 2009-2010*

Average Freshman Graduation Rate (AFGR): The AFGR is the number of regular diploma recipients in a given year divided by the average of the membership in grades 8, 9, and 10, reported 5, 4, and 3 years earlier, respectively. For example, the denominator of the 2008–09 AFGR is the average of the 8th-grade membership in 2004–05, 9th-grade membership in 2005–06, and 10th-grade membership in 2006–07. Ungraded students are prorated into

these grades. Averaging these three grades provides an estimate of the number of first-time freshmen in the class of 2005–06 freshmen in order to estimate the on-time graduation rate for 2008–09.

Caution in interpreting the AFGR. Although the AFGR was selected as the best of the available alternatives, several factors make it fall short of a true on-time graduation rate. First, the AFGR does not take into account any imbalances in the number of students moving in and out of the nation or individual states over the high school years. As a result, the averaged freshman class is at best an approximation of the actual number of freshmen, where differences in the rates of transfers, retention, and dropping out in the three grades affect the average. Second, by including all graduates in a specific year, the graduates may include students who repeated a grade in high school or completed high school early and thus are not on-time graduates in that year. *Source: U.S. Department of Education, National Center for Education Statistics, Common Core of Data, Local Education Agency (School District) Universe Survey Dropout and Completion Data, 2008-2009; U.S. Department of Education, National Center for Education Statistics, Common Core of Data, State Dropout and Completion Data File, 2009-2010*

Number of Diploma Recipients: A student who has received a diploma during the previous school year or subsequent summer school. This category includes regular diploma recipients and other diploma recipients. A High School Diploma is a formal document certifying the successful completion of a secondary school program prescribed by the state education agency or other appropriate body. *Note: Diploma counts are no longer available to the general public disaggregated by grade, race/ethnicity, and gender at the school district level. Source: U.S. Department of Education, National Center for Education Statistics, Common Core of Data, Local Education Agency (School District) Universe Survey Dropout and Completion Data, 2008-2009; U.S. Department of Education, National Center for Education Statistics, Common Core of Data, State Dropout and Completion Data File, 2009-2010*

Note: n/a indicates data not available.

State Educational Profile

Please refer to the District Rankings section in the front of this User Guide for an explanation of data for all items except for the following:

Average Salary: The average salary for classroom teachers in 2013-2014. *Source: National Education Association, Rankings & Estimates: Rankings of the States 2013 and Estimates of School Statistics 2014*

College Entrance Exam Scores:

Scholastic Aptitude Test (SAT). *Note: Data covers all students during the 2013 school year. The College Board strongly discourages the comparison or ranking of states on the basis of SAT scores alone. Source: The College Board*

American College Testing Program (ACT). *Note: Data covers all students during the 2013 school year. Source: ACT, 2013 ACT National and State Scores*

National Assessment of Educational Progress (NAEP)

The National Assessment of Educational Progress (NAEP), also known as "the Nation's Report Card," is the only nationally representative and continuing assessment of what America's students know and can do in various subject areas. As a result of the "No Child Left Behind" legislation, all states are required to participate in NAEP.

For more information, visit the U.S. Department of Education, National Center for Education Statistics at http://nces.ed.gov/nationsreportcard.

User Guide: Ancestry and Ethnicity Section

Places Covered

The ancestry and ethnicity profile section of this book covers the state and all counties and places with populations of 50,000 or more. Places included fall into one of the following categories:

Incorporated Places. Depending on the state, places are incorporated as either cities, towns, villages, boroughs, municipalities, independent cities, or corporations. A few municipalities have a form of government combined with another entity (e.g. county) and are listed as special cities or consolidated, unified, or metropolitan governments.

Census Designated Places (CDP). The U.S. Census Bureau defines a CDP as "a statistical entity," defined for each decennial census according to Census Bureau guidelines, comprising a densely settled concentration of population that is not within an incorporated place, but is locally identified by a name. CDPs are delineated cooperatively by state and local officials and the Census Bureau, following Census Bureau guidelines.

Minor Civil Divisions (called charter townships, districts, gores, grants, locations, plantations, purchases, reservations, towns, townships, and unorganized territories) for the states where the Census Bureau has determined that they serve as general-purpose governments. Those states are Connecticut, Maine, Massachusetts, Michigan, Minnesota, New Hampshire, New Jersey, New York, Pennsylvania, Rhode Island, Vermont, and Wisconsin. In some states incorporated municipalities are part of minor civil divisions and in some states they are independent of them.

Note: Several states have incorporated municipalities and minor civil divisions in the same county with the same name. Those communities are given separate entries (e.g. Burlington, New Jersey, in Burlington County will be listed under both the city and township of Burlington). A few states have Census Designated Places and minor civil divisions in the same county with the same name. Those communities are given separate entries (e.g. Bridgewater, Massachusetts, in Plymouth County will be listed under both the CDP and town of Bridgewater).

Source of Data

The ethnicities shown in this book were compiled from two different sources. Data for Race and Hispanic Origin was taken from Census 2010 Summary File 1 (SF1) while Ancestry data was taken from the American Community Survey (ACS) 2006-2010 Five-Year Estimate. The distinction is important because SF1 contains 100-percent data, which is the information compiled from the questions asked of all people and about every housing unit. ACS estimates are compiled from a sampling of households. The 2006-2010 Five-Year Estimate is based on data collected from January 1, 2006 to December 31, 2010.

The American Community Survey (ACS) is a relatively new survey conducted by the U.S. Census Bureau. It uses a series of monthly samples to produce annually updated data for the same small areas (census tracts and block groups) formerly surveyed via the decennial census long-form sample. While some version of this survey has been in the field since 1999, it was not fully implemented in terms of coverage until 2006. In 2005 it was expanded to cover all counties in the country and the 1-in-40 households sampling rate was first applied. The full implementation of the (household) sampling strategy for ACS entails having the survey mailed to about 250,000 households nationwide every month of every year and was begun in January 2005. In January 2006 sampling of group quarters was added to complete the sample as planned. In any given year about 2.5% (1 in 40) of U.S. households will receive the survey. Over any 5-year period about 1 in 8 households should receive the survey (as compared to about 1 in 6 that received the census long form in the 2000 census). Since receiving the survey is not the same as responding to it, the Bureau has adopted a strategy of sampling for non-response, resulting in something closer to 1 in 11 households actually participating in the survey over any 5-year period. For more information about the American Community Survey visit http://www.census.gov/acs/www.

Ancestry

Ancestry refers to a person's ethnic origin, heritage, descent, or "roots," which may reflect their place of birth or that of previous generations of their family. Some ethnic identities, such as "Egyptian" or "Polish" can be traced to geographic areas outside the United States, while other ethnicities such as "Pennsylvania German" or "Cajun" evolved in the United States.

The intent of the ancestry question in the ACS was not to measure the degree of attachment the respondent had to a particular ethnicity, but simply to establish that the respondent had a connection to and self-identified with a particular

ethnic group. For example, a response of "Irish" might reflect total involvement in an Irish community or only a memory of ancestors several generations removed from the respondent.

The Census Bureau coded the responses into a numeric representation of over 1,000 categories. Responses initially were processed through an automated coding system; then, those that were not automatically assigned a code were coded by individuals trained in coding ancestry responses. The code list reflects the results of the Census Bureau's own research and consultations with many ethnic experts. Many decisions were made to determine the classification of responses. These decisions affected the grouping of the tabulated data. For example, the "Indonesian" category includes the responses of "Indonesian," "Celebesian," "Moluccan," and a number of other responses.

Ancestries Covered

Afghan	Palestinian	French, ex. Basque	Scottish
African, Sub-Saharan	Syrian	French Canadian	Serbian
African	Other Arab	German	Slavic
Cape Verdean	Armenian	German Russian	Slovak
Ethiopian	Assyrian/Chaldean/Syriac	Greek	Slovene
Ghanaian	Australian	Guyanese	Soviet Union
Kenyan	Austrian	Hungarian	Swedish
Liberian	Basque	Icelander	Swiss
Nigerian	Belgian	Iranian	Turkish
Senegalese	Brazilian	Irish	Ukrainian
Sierra Leonean	British	Israeli	Welsh
Somalian	Bulgarian	Italian	West Indian, ex.
South African	Cajun	Latvian	Hispanic
Sudanese	Canadian	Lithuanian	Bahamian
Ugandan	Carpatho Rusyn	Luxemburger	Barbadian
Zimbabwean	Celtic	Macedonian	Belizean
Other Sub-Saharan African	Croatian	Maltese	Bermudan
Albanian	Cypriot	New Zealander	British West Indian
Alsatian	Czech	Northern European	Dutch West Indian
American	Czechoslovakian	Norwegian	Haitian
Arab	Danish	Pennsylvania German	Jamaican
Arab	Dutch	Polish	Trinidadian/
Egyptian	Eastern European	Portuguese	Tobagonian
Iraqi	English	Romanian	U.S. Virgin Islander
Jordanian	Estonian	Russian	West Indian
Lebanese	European	Scandinavian	Other West Indian
Moroccan	Finnish	Scotch-Irish	Yugoslavian

The ancestry question allowed respondents to report one or more ancestry groups. Generally, only the first two responses reported were coded. If a response was in terms of a dual ancestry, for example, "Irish English," the person was assigned two codes, in this case one for Irish and another for English. However, in certain cases, multiple responses such as "French Canadian," "Scotch-Irish," "Greek Cypriot," and "Black Dutch" were assigned a single code reflecting their status as unique groups. If a person reported one of these unique groups in addition to another group, for example, "Scotch-Irish English," resulting in three terms, that person received one code for the unique group (Scotch-Irish) and another one for the remaining group (English). If a person reported "English Irish French," only English and Irish were coded. If there were more than two ancestries listed and one of the ancestries was a part of another, such as "German Bavarian Hawaiian," the responses were coded using the more detailed groups (Bavarian and Hawaiian).

The Census Bureau accepted "American" as a unique ethnicity if it was given alone or with one other ancestry. There were some groups such as "American Indian," "Mexican American," and "African American" that were coded and identified separately.

The ancestry question is asked for every person in the American Community Survey, regardless of age, place of birth, Hispanic origin, or race.

Although some people consider religious affiliation a component of ethnic identity, the ancestry question was not designed to collect any information concerning religion. Thus, if a religion was given as an answer to the ancestry question, it was listed in the "Other groups" category which is not shown in this book.

Ancestry should not be confused with a person's place of birth, although a person's place of birth and ancestry may be the same.

Hispanic Origin

The data on the Hispanic or Latino population were derived from answers to a Census 2010 question that was asked of all people. The terms "Spanish," "Hispanic origin," and "Latino" are used interchangeably. Some respondents identify with all three terms while others may identify with only one of these three specific terms. Hispanics or Latinos who identify with the terms "Spanish," "Hispanic," or "Latino" are those who classify themselves in one of the specific Spanish, Hispanic, or Latino categories listed on the questionnaire ("Mexican," "Puerto Rican," or "Cuban") as well as those who indicate that they are "other Spanish/Hispanic/Latino." People who do not identify with one of the specific origins listed on the questionnaire but indicate that they are "other Spanish/Hispanic/Latino" are those whose origins are from Spain, the Spanish-speaking countries of Central or South America, the Dominican Republic, or people identifying themselves generally as Spanish, Spanish-American, Hispanic, Hispano, Latino, and so on. All write-in responses to the "other Spanish/Hispanic/Latino" category were coded.

Hispanic Origins Covered

Hispanic or Latino	Salvadoran	Argentinean	Uruguayan
Central American, ex. Mexican	Other Central American	Bolivian	Venezuelan
Costa Rican	Cuban	Chilean	Other South American
Guatemalan	Dominican Republic	Colombian	Other Hispanic or Latino
Honduran	Mexican	Ecuadorian	
Nicaraguan	Puerto Rican	Paraguayan	
Panamanian	South American	Peruvian	

Origin can be viewed as the heritage, nationality group, lineage, or country of birth of the person or the person's parents or ancestors before their arrival in the United States. People who identify their origin as Hispanic, Latino, or Spanish may be of any race.

Ethnicities Based on Race

The data on race were derived from answers to the Census 2010 question on race that was asked of individuals in the United States. The Census Bureau collects racial data in accordance with guidelines provided by the U.S. Office of Management and Budget (OMB), and these data are based on self-identification.

The racial categories included in the census questionnaire generally reflect a social definition of race recognized in this country and not an attempt to define race biologically, anthropologically, or genetically. In addition, it is recognized that the categories of the race item include racial and national origin or sociocultural groups. People may choose to report more than one race to indicate their racial mixture, such as "American Indian" and "White." People who identify their origin as Hispanic, Latino, or Spanish may be of any race.

Racial Groups Covered

African-American/Black	Crow	Spanish American Indian	Korean
Not Hispanic	Delaware	Tlingit-Haida *(Alaska Native)*	Laotian
Hispanic	Hopi	Tohono O'Odham	Malaysian
American Indian/Alaska Native	Houma	Tsimshian *(Alaska Native)*	Nepalese
Not Hispanic	Inupiat *(Alaska Native)*	Ute	Pakistani
Hispanic	Iroquois	Yakama	Sri Lankan
Alaska Athabascan *(Ala. Nat.)*	Kiowa	Yaqui	Taiwanese
Aleut *(Alaska Native)*	Lumbee	Yuman	Thai
Apache	Menominee	Yup'ik *(Alaska Native)*	Vietnamese
Arapaho	Mexican American Indian	**Asian**	**Hawaii Native/Pacific Islander**
Blackfeet	Navajo	*Not Hispanic*	*Not Hispanic*
Canadian/French Am. Indian	Osage	*Hispanic*	*Hispanic*
Central American Indian	Ottawa	Bangladeshi	Fijian
Cherokee	Paiute	Bhutanese	Guamanian/Chamorro
Cheyenne	Pima	Burmese	Marshallese
Chickasaw	Potawatomi	Cambodian	Native Hawaiian
Chippewa	Pueblo	Chinese, ex. Taiwanese	Samoan
Choctaw	Puget Sound Salish	Filipino	Tongan
Colville	Seminole	Hmong	**White**
Comanche	Shoshone	Indian	*Not Hispanic*
Cree	Sioux	Indonesian	*Hispanic*
Creek	South American Indian	Japanese	

African American or Black: A person having origins in any of the Black racial groups of Africa. It includes people who indicated their race(s) as "Black, African Am., or Negro" or reported entries such as African American, Kenyan, Nigerian, or Haitian.

American Indian or Alaska Native: A person having origins in any of the original peoples of North and South America (including Central America) and who maintains tribal affiliation or community attachment. This category includes people who indicated their race(s) as "American Indian or Alaska Native" or reported their enrolled or principal tribe, such as Navajo, Blackfeet, Inupiat, Yup'ik, or Central American Indian groups or South American Indian groups.

Asian: A person having origins in any of the original peoples of the Far East, Southeast Asia, or the Indian subcontinent, including, for example, Cambodia, China, India, Japan, Korea, Malaysia, Pakistan, the Philippine Islands, Thailand, and Vietnam. It includes people who indicated their race(s) as "Asian" or reported entries such as "Asian Indian," "Chinese," "Filipino," "Korean," "Japanese," "Vietnamese," and "Other Asian" or provided other detailed Asian responses.

Native Hawaiian or Other Pacific Islander: A person having origins in any of the original peoples of Hawaii, Guam, Samoa, or other Pacific Islands. It includes people who indicated their race(s) as "Pacific Islander" or reported entries such as "Native Hawaiian," "Guamanian or Chamorro," "Samoan," and "Other Pacific Islander" or provided other detailed Pacific Islander responses.

White: A person having origins in any of the original peoples of Europe, the Middle East, or North Africa. It includes people who indicated their race(s) as "White" or reported entries such as Irish, German, Italian, Lebanese, Arab, Moroccan, or Caucasian.

Profiles

Each profile shows the name of the place, the county (if a place spans more than one county, the county that holds the majority of the population is shown), and the 2010 population (based on 100-percent data from Census 2010 Summary File 1). The rest of each profile is comprised of all 218 ethnicities grouped into three sections: ancestry; Hispanic origin; and race.

Column one displays the ancestry/Hispanic origin/race name, column two displays the number of people reporting each ancestry/Hispanic origin/race, and column three is the percent of the total population reporting each ancestry/Hispanic origin/race. The population figure shown is used to calculate the value in the "%" column for ethnicities based on race and Hispanic origin. The 2006-2010 estimated population figure from the American Community Survey (not shown) is used to calculate the value in the "%" column for all other ancestries.

For ethnicities in the ancestries group, the value in the "Number" column includes multiple ancestries reported. For example, if a person reported a multiple ancestry such as "French Danish," that response was counted twice in the tabulations, once in the French category and again in the Danish category. Thus, the sum of the counts is not the total population but the total of all responses. Numbers in parentheses indicate the number of people reporting a single ancestry. People reporting a single ancestry includes all people who reported only one ethnic group such as "German." Also included in this category are people with only a multiple-term response such as "Scotch-Irish" who are assigned a single code because they represent one distinct group. For example, the count for German would be interpreted as "The number of people who reported that German was their only ancestry."

For ethnicities based on Hispanic origin, the value in the "Number" column represents the number of people who reported being Mexican, Puerto Rican, Cuban or other Spanish/Hispanic/ Latino (all written-in responses were coded). All ethnicities based on Hispanic origin can be of any race.

For ethnicities based on race data the value in the "Number" column represents the total number of people who reported each category alone or in combination with one or more other race categories. This number represents the maximum number of people reporting and therefore the individual race categories may add up to more than the total population because people may be included in more than one category. The figures in parentheses show the number of people that reported that particular ethnicity alone, not in combination with any other race. For example, in Alabama, the entry for Korean shows 8,320 in parentheses and 10,624 in the "Number" column. This means that 8,320 people reported being Korean alone and 10,624 people reported being Korean alone or in combination with one or more other races.

Rankings

In the rankings section, each ethnicity has three tables. The first table shows the top 10 places sorted by ethnic population (based on all places, regardless of total population), the second table shows the top 10 places sorted by percent of the total population (based on all places, regardless of total population), the third table shows the top 10 places sorted by percent of the total population (based on places with total population of 50,000 or more).

Within each table, column one displays the place name, the state, and the county (if a place spans more than one county, the county that holds the majority of the population is shown). Column one in the first table displays the state only. Column two displays the number of people reporting each ancestry (includes people reporting multiple ancestries), Hispanic origin, or race (alone or in combination with any other race). Column three is the percent of the total population reporting each ancestry, Hispanic origin or race. For tables representing ethnicities based on race or Hispanic origin, the 100-percent population figure from SF1 is used to calculate the value in the "%" column. For all other ancestries, the 2006-2010 five-year estimated population figure from the American Community Survey is used to calculate the value in the "%" column.

Alphabetical Ethnicity Cross-Reference Guide

Afghan *see* Ancestry–Afghan
African *see* Ancestry–African, Sub-Saharan: African
African-American *see* Race–African-American/Black
African-American: Hispanic *see* Race–African-American/Black: Hispanic
African-American: Not Hispanic *see* Race–African-American/Black: Not Hispanic
Alaska Athabascan *see* Race–Alaska Native: Alaska Athabascan
Alaska Native *see* Race–American Indian/Alaska Native
Alaska Native: Hispanic *see* Race–American Indian/Alaska Native: Hispanic
Alaska Native: Not Hispanic *see* Race–American Indian/Alaska Native: Not Hispanic
Albanian *see* Ancestry–Albanian
Aleut *see* Race–Alaska Native: Aleut
Alsatian *see* Ancestry–Alsatian
American *see* Ancestry–American
American Indian *see* Race–American Indian/Alaska Native
American Indian: Hispanic *see* Race–American Indian/Alaska Native: Hispanic
American Indian: Not Hispanic *see* Race–American Indian/Alaska Native: Not Hispanic
Apache *see* Race–American Indian: Apache
Arab *see* Ancestry–Arab: Arab
Arab: Other *see* Ancestry–Arab: Other
Arapaho *see* Race–American Indian: Arapaho
Argentinean *see* Hispanic Origin–South American: Argentinean
Armenian *see* Ancestry–Armenian
Asian *see* Race–Asian
Asian Indian *see* Race–Asian: Indian
Asian: Hispanic *see* Race–Asian: Hispanic
Asian: Not Hispanic *see* Race–Asian: Not Hispanic
Assyrian *see* Ancestry–Assyrian/Chaldean/Syriac
Australian *see* Ancestry–Australian
Austrian *see* Ancestry–Austrian
Bahamian *see* Ancestry–West Indian: Bahamian, except Hispanic
Bangladeshi *see* Race–Asian: Bangladeshi
Barbadian *see* Ancestry–West Indian: Barbadian, except Hispanic
Basque *see* Ancestry–Basque
Belgian *see* Ancestry–Belgian
Belizean *see* Ancestry–West Indian: Belizean, except Hispanic
Bermudan *see* Ancestry–West Indian: Bermudan, except Hispanic
Bhutanese *see* Race–Asian: Bhutanese
Black *see* Race–African-American/Black
Black: Hispanic *see* Race–African-American/Black: Hispanic
Black: Not Hispanic *see* Race–African-American/Black: Not Hispanic
Blackfeet *see* Race–American Indian: Blackfeet
Bolivian *see* Hispanic Origin–South American: Bolivian
Brazilian *see* Ancestry–Brazilian
British *see* Ancestry–British

British West Indian *see* Ancestry–West Indian: British West Indian, except Hispanic
Bulgarian *see* Ancestry–Bulgarian
Burmese *see* Race–Asian: Burmese
Cajun *see* Ancestry–Cajun
Cambodian *see* Race–Asian: Cambodian
Canadian *see* Ancestry–Canadian
Canadian/French American Indian *see* Race–American Indian: Canadian/French American Indian
Cape Verdean *see* Ancestry–African, Sub-Saharan: Cape Verdean
Carpatho Rusyn *see* Ancestry–Carpatho Rusyn
Celtic *see* Ancestry–Celtic
Central American *see* Hispanic Origin–Central American, except Mexican
Central American Indian *see* Race–American Indian: Central American Indian
Central American: Other *see* Hispanic Origin–Central American: Other Central American
Chaldean *see* Ancestry–Assyrian/Chaldean/Syriac
Chamorro *see* Race–Hawaii Native/Pacific Islander: Guamanian or Chamorro
Cherokee *see* Race–American Indian: Cherokee
Cheyenne *see* Race–American Indian: Cheyenne
Chickasaw *see* Race–American Indian: Chickasaw
Chilean *see* Hispanic Origin–South American: Chilean
Chinese (except Taiwanese) *see* Race–Asian: Chinese, except Taiwanese
Chippewa *see* Race–American Indian: Chippewa
Choctaw *see* Race–American Indian: Choctaw
Colombian *see* Hispanic Origin–South American: Colombian
Colville *see* Race–American Indian: Colville
Comanche *see* Race–American Indian: Comanche
Costa Rican *see* Hispanic Origin–Central American: Costa Rican
Cree *see* Race–American Indian: Cree
Creek *see* Race–American Indian: Creek
Croatian *see* Ancestry–Croatian
Crow *see* Race–American Indian: Crow
Cuban *see* Hispanic Origin–Cuban
Cypriot *see* Ancestry–Cypriot
Czech *see* Ancestry–Czech
Czechoslovakian *see* Ancestry–Czechoslovakian
Danish *see* Ancestry–Danish
Delaware *see* Race–American Indian: Delaware
Dominican Republic *see* Hispanic Origin–Dominican Republic
Dutch *see* Ancestry–Dutch
Dutch West Indian *see* Ancestry–West Indian: Dutch West Indian, except Hispanic
Eastern European *see* Ancestry–Eastern European
Ecuadorian *see* Hispanic Origin–South American: Ecuadorian
Egyptian *see* Ancestry–Arab: Egyptian
English *see* Ancestry–English
Eskimo *see* Race–Alaska Native: Inupiat
Estonian *see* Ancestry–Estonian
Ethiopian *see* Ancestry–African, Sub-Saharan: Ethiopian
European *see* Ancestry–European
Fijian *see* Race–Hawaii Native/Pacific Islander: Fijian
Filipino *see* Race–Asian: Filipino
Finnish *see* Ancestry–Finnish
French (except Basque) *see* Ancestry–French, except Basque
French Canadian *see* Ancestry–French Canadian
German *see* Ancestry–German
German Russian *see* Ancestry–German Russian
Ghanaian *see* Ancestry–African, Sub-Saharan: Ghanaian
Greek *see* Ancestry–Greek
Guamanian *see* Race–Hawaii Native/Pacific Islander: Guamanian or Chamorro
Guatemalan *see* Hispanic Origin–Central American: Guatemalan
Guyanese *see* Ancestry–Guyanese
Haitian *see* Ancestry–West Indian: Haitian, except Hispanic
Hawaii Native *see* Race–Hawaii Native/Pacific Islander
Hawaii Native: Hispanic *see* Race–Hawaii Native/Pacific Islander: Hispanic

Hawaii Native: Not Hispanic *see* Race–Hawaii Native/Pacific Islander: Not Hispanic
Hispanic or Latino: *see* Hispanic Origin–Hispanic or Latino (of any race)
Hispanic or Latino: Other *see* Hispanic Origin–Other Hispanic or Latino
Hmong *see* Race–Asian: Hmong
Honduran *see* Hispanic Origin–Central American: Honduran
Hopi *see* Race–American Indian: Hopi
Houma *see* Race–American Indian: Houma
Hungarian *see* Ancestry–Hungarian
Icelander *see* Ancestry–Icelander
Indonesian *see* Race–Asian: Indonesian
Inupiat *see* Race–Alaska Native: Inupiat
Iranian *see* Ancestry–Iranian
Iraqi *see* Ancestry–Arab: Iraqi
Irish *see* Ancestry–Irish
Iroquois *see* Race–American Indian: Iroquois
Israeli *see* Ancestry–Israeli
Italian *see* Ancestry–Italian
Jamaican *see* Ancestry–West Indian: Jamaican, except Hispanic
Japanese *see* Race–Asian: Japanese
Jordanian *see* Ancestry–Arab: Jordanian
Kenyan *see* Ancestry–African, Sub-Saharan: Kenyan
Kiowa *see* Race–American Indian: Kiowa
Korean *see* Race–Asian: Korean
Laotian *see* Race–Asian: Laotian
Latvian *see* Ancestry–Latvian
Lebanese *see* Ancestry–Arab: Lebanese
Liberian *see* Ancestry–African, Sub-Saharan: Liberian
Lithuanian *see* Ancestry–Lithuanian
Lumbee *see* Race–American Indian: Lumbee
Luxemburger *see* Ancestry–Luxemburger
Macedonian *see* Ancestry–Macedonian
Malaysian *see* Race–Asian: Malaysian
Maltese *see* Ancestry–Maltese
Marshallese *see* Race–Hawaii Native/Pacific Islander: Marshallese
Menominee *see* Race–American Indian: Menominee
Mexican *see* Hispanic Origin–Mexican
Mexican American Indian *see* Race–American Indian: Mexican American Indian
Moroccan *see* Ancestry–Arab: Moroccan
Native Hawaiian *see* Race–Hawaii Native/Pacific Islander: Native Hawaiian
Navajo *see* Race–American Indian: Navajo
Nepalese *see* Race–Asian: Nepalese
New Zealander *see* Ancestry–New Zealander
Nicaraguan *see* Hispanic Origin–Central American: Nicaraguan
Nigerian *see* Ancestry–African, Sub-Saharan: Nigerian
Northern European *see* Ancestry–Northern European
Norwegian *see* Ancestry–Norwegian
Osage *see* Race–American Indian: Osage
Ottawa *see* Race–American Indian: Ottawa
Pacific Islander *see* Race–Hawaii Native/Pacific Islander
Pacific Islander: Hispanic *see* Race–Hawaii Native/Pacific Islander: Hispanic
Pacific Islander: Not Hispanic *see* Race–Hawaii Native/Pacific Islander: Not Hispanic
Paiute *see* Race–American Indian: Paiute
Pakistani *see* Race–Asian: Pakistani
Palestinian *see* Ancestry–Arab: Palestinian
Panamanian *see* Hispanic Origin–Central American: Panamanian
Paraguayan *see* Hispanic Origin–South American: Paraguayan
Pennsylvania German *see* Ancestry–Pennsylvania German
Peruvian *see* Hispanic Origin–South American: Peruvian
Pima *see* Race–American Indian: Pima
Polish *see* Ancestry–Polish
Portuguese *see* Ancestry–Portuguese
Potawatomi *see* Race–American Indian: Potawatomi

Pueblo *see* Race–American Indian: Pueblo
Puerto Rican *see* Hispanic Origin–Puerto Rican
Puget Sound Salish *see* Race–American Indian: Puget Sound Salish
Romanian *see* Ancestry–Romanian
Russian *see* Ancestry–Russian
Salvadoran *see* Hispanic Origin–Central American: Salvadoran
Samoan *see* Race–Hawaii Native/Pacific Islander: Samoan
Scandinavian *see* Ancestry–Scandinavian
Scotch-Irish *see* Ancestry–Scotch-Irish
Scottish *see* Ancestry–Scottish
Seminole *see* Race–American Indian: Seminole
Senegalese *see* Ancestry–African, Sub-Saharan: Senegalese
Serbian *see* Ancestry–Serbian
Shoshone *see* Race–American Indian: Shoshone
Sierra Leonean *see* Ancestry–African, Sub-Saharan: Sierra Leonean
Sioux *see* Race–American Indian: Sioux
Slavic *see* Ancestry–Slavic
Slovak *see* Ancestry–Slovak
Slovene *see* Ancestry–Slovene
Somalian *see* Ancestry–African, Sub-Saharan: Somalian
South African *see* Ancestry–African, Sub-Saharan: South African
South American *see* Hispanic Origin–South American
South American Indian *see* Race–American Indian: South American Indian
South American: Other *see* Hispanic Origin–South American: Other South American
Soviet Union *see* Ancestry–Soviet Union
Spanish American Indian *see* Race–American Indian: Spanish American Indian
Sri Lankan *see* Race–Asian: Sri Lankan
Sub-Saharan African *see* Ancestry–African, Sub-Saharan
Sub-Saharan African: Other *see* Ancestry–African, Sub-Saharan: Other
Sudanese *see* Ancestry–African, Sub-Saharan: Sudanese
Swedish *see* Ancestry–Swedish
Swiss *see* Ancestry–Swiss
Syriac *see* Ancestry–Assyrian/Chaldean/Syriac
Syrian *see* Ancestry–Arab: Syrian
Taiwanese *see* Race–Asian: Taiwanese
Thai *see* Race–Asian: Thai
Tlingit-Haida *see* Race–Alaska Native: Tlingit-Haida
Tohono O'Odham *see* Race–American Indian: Tohono O'Odham
Tongan *see* Race–Hawaii Native/Pacific Islander: Tongan
Trinidadian and Tobagonian *see* Ancestry–West Indian: Trinidadian and Tobagonian, except Hispanic
Tsimshian *see* Race–Alaska Native: Tsimshian
Turkish *see* Ancestry–Turkish
U.S. Virgin Islander *see* Ancestry–West Indian: U.S. Virgin Islander, except Hispanic
Ugandan *see* Ancestry–African, Sub-Saharan: Ugandan
Ukrainian *see* Ancestry–Ukrainian
Uruguayan *see* Hispanic Origin–South American: Uruguayan
Ute *see* Race–American Indian: Ute
Venezuelan *see* Hispanic Origin–South American: Venezuelan
Vietnamese *see* Race–Asian: Vietnamese
Welsh *see* Ancestry–Welsh
West Indian *see* Ancestry–West Indian: West Indian, except Hispanic
West Indian (except Hispanic) *see* Ancestry–West Indian, except Hispanic
West Indian: Other *see* Ancestry–West Indian: Other, except Hispanic
White *see* Race–White
White: Hispanic *see* Race–White: Hispanic
White: Not Hispanic *see* Race–White: Not Hispanic
Yakama *see* Race–American Indian: Yakama
Yaqui *see* Race–American Indian: Yaqui
Yugoslavian *see* Ancestry–Yugoslavian
Yuman *see* Race–American Indian: Yuman
Yup'ik *see* Race–Alaska Native: Yup'ik
Zimbabwean *see* Ancestry–African, Sub-Saharan: Zimbabwean

User Guide: Climate Section

SOURCES OF THE DATA

The National Climactic Data Center (NCDC) has two main classes or types of weather stations; first-order stations which are staffed by professional meteorologists and cooperative stations which are staffed by volunteers. All National Weather Service (NWS) stations included in this book are first-order stations.

The data in the climate section is compiled from several sources. The majority comes from the original NCDC computer tapes (DSI-3220 Summary of Month Cooperative). This data was used to create the entire table for each cooperative station and part of each National Weather Service station. The remainder of the data for each NWS station comes from the International Station Meteorological Climate Summary, Version 4.0, September 1996, which is also available from the NCDC.

Storm events come from the NCDC Storm Events Database which is accessible over the Internet at http://www4.ncdc.noaa.gov/ cgi-win/wwcgi.dll?wwevent~storms.

WEATHER STATION TABLES

The weather station tables are grouped by type (National Weather Service and Cooperative) and then arranged alphabetically. The station name is almost always a place name, and is shown here just as it appears in NCDC data. The station name is followed by the county in which the station is located (or by county equivalent name), the elevation of the station (at the time beginning of the thirty year period) and the latitude and longitude.

The National Weather Service Station tables contain 32 data elements which were compiled from two different sources, the International Station Meteorological Climate Summary (ISMCS) and NCDC DSI-3220 data tapes. The following 13 elements are from the ISMCS: maximum precipitation, minimum precipitation, maximum snowfall, maximum 24-hour snowfall, thunderstorm days, foggy days, predominant sky cover, relative humidity (morning and afternoon), dewpoint, wind speed and direction, and maximum wind gust. The remaining 19 elements come from the DSI-3220 data tapes. The period of record (POR) for data from the DSI-3220 data tapes is 1980-2009. The POR for ISMCS data varies from station to station and appears in a note below each station.

The Cooperative Station tables contain 19 data elements which were all compiled from the DSI-3220 data tapes with a POR of 1980-2009.

WEATHER ELEMENTS (NWS AND COOPERATIVE STATIONS)

The following elements were compiled by the editor from the NCDC DSI-3220 data tapes using a period of record of 1980-2009.

The average temperatures (maximum, minimum, and mean) are the average (see Methodology below) of those temperatures for all available values for a given month. For example, for a given station the average maximum temperature for July is the arithmetic average of all available maximum July temperatures for that station. (Maximum means the highest recorded temperature, minimum means the lowest recorded temperature, and mean means an arithmetic average temperature.)

The extreme maximum temperature is the highest temperature recorded in each month over the period 1980-2009. The extreme minimum temperature is the lowest temperature recorded in each month over the same time period. The extreme maximum daily precipitation is the largest amount of precipitation recorded over a 24-hour period in each month from 1980-2009. The maximum snow depth is the maximum snow depth recorded in each month over the period 1980-2009.

The days for maximum temperature and minimum temperature are the average number of days those criteria were met for all available instances. The symbol ≥ means greater than or equal to, the symbol ≤ means less than or equal to. For example, for a given station, the number of days the maximum temperature was greater than or equal to 90°F in July, is just an arithmetic average of the number of days in all the available Julys for that station.

Heating and cooling degree days are based on the median temperature for a given day and its variance from 65°F. For example, for a given station if the day's high temperature was 50°F and the day's low temperature was 30°F, the median (midpoint) temperature was 40°F. 40°F is 25 degrees below 65°F, hence on this day there would be 25 heating degree days. This also applies for cooling degree days. For example, for a given station if the day's high temperature was 80°F and the day's low temperature was 70°F, the median (midpoint) temperature was 75°F. 75°F is 10 degrees above 65°F, hence on this day there would be 10 cooling degree days. All heating and/or cooling degree

days in a month are summed for the month giving respective totals for each element for that month. These sums for a given month for a given station over the past thirty years are again summed and then arithmetically averaged. It should be noted that the heating and cooling degree days do not cancel each other out. It is possible to have both for a given station in the same month.

Precipitation data is computed the same as heating and cooling degree days. Mean precipitation and mean snowfall are arithmetic averages of cumulative totals for the month. All available values for the thirty year period for a given month for a given station are summed and then divided by the number of values. The same is true for days of greater than or equal to 0.1", 0.5",and 1.0" of precipitation, and days of greater than or equal to 1.0" of snow depth on the ground. The word trace appears for precipitation and snowfall amounts that are too small to measure.

Finally, remember that all values presented in the tables and the rankings are averages, maximums, or minimums of available data (see Methodology below) for that specific data element for the last thirty years (1980-2009).

WEATHER ELEMENTS (NWS STATIONS ONLY)

The following elements were taken directly from the International Station Meteorological Climate Summary. The periods of records vary per station and are noted at the bottom of each table.

Maximum precipitation, minimum precipitation, maximum snowfall, maximum snow depth, maximum 24-hour snowfall, thunderstorm days, foggy days, relative humidity (morning and afternoon), dewpoint, prevailing wind speed and direction, and maximum wind gust are all self-explanatory.

The word trace appears for precipitation and snowfall amounts that are too small to measure.

Predominant sky cover contains four possible entries: CLR (clear); SCT (scattered); BRK (broken); and OVR (overcast).

INCLUSION CRITERIA—HOW STATIONS WERE SELECTED

The basic criteria is that a station must have data for temperature, precipitation, heating and cooling degree days of sufficient quantity in order to create a meaningful average. More specifically, the definition of sufficiency here has two parts. First, there must be 22 values for a given data element, and second, ten of the nineteen elements included in the table must pass this sufficiency test. For example, in regard to mean maximum temperature (the first element on every data table), a given station needs to have a value for every month of at least 22 of the last thirty years in order to meet the criteria, and, in addition, every station included must have at least ten of the nineteen elements with at least this minimal level of completeness in order to fulfill the criteria. We then removed stations that were geographically close together, giving preference to stations with better data quality.

METHODOLOGY

The following discussion applies only to data compiled from the NCDC DSI-3220 data tapes and excludes weather elements that are extreme maximums or minimums.

The data is based on an arithmetic average of all available data for a specific data element at a given station. For example, the average maximum daily high temperature during July for any given station was abstracted from NCDC source tapes for the thirty Julys, starting in July, 1980 and ending in July, 2009. These thirty figures were then summed and divided by thirty to produce an arithmetic average. As might be expected, there were not thirty values for every data element on every table. For a variety of reasons, NCDC data is sometimes incomplete. Thus the following standards were established.

For those data elements where there were 26-30 values, the data was taken to be essentially complete and an average was computed. For data elements where there were 22-25 values, the data was taken as being partly complete but still valid enough to use to compute an average. Such averages are shown in **_bold italic_** type to indicate that there was less than 26 values. For the few data elements where there were not even 22 values, no average was computed and 'na' appears in the space. If any of the twelve months for a given data element reported a value of 'na', no annual average was computed and the annual average was reported as 'na' as well.

Thus the basic computational methodology used is designed to provide an arithmetic average. Because of this, such a pure arithmetic average is somewhat different from the special type of average (called a "normal") which NCDC procedures produces and appears in federal publications.

Perhaps the best outline of the contrasting normalization methodology is found in the following paragraph (which appears as part of an NCDC technical document titled, CLIM81 1961-1990 NORMALS TD-9641 prepared by Lewis France of NCDC in May, 1992):

Normals have been defined as the arithmetic mean of a climatological element computed over a long time period. International agreements eventually led to the decision that the appropriate time period would be three consecutive decades (Guttman, 1989). The data record should be consistent (have no changes in location, instruments, observation practices, etc.; these are identified here as "exposure changes") and have no missing values so a normal will reflect the actual average climatic conditions. If any significant exposure changes have occurred, the data record is said to be "inhomogeneous," and the normal may not reflect a true climatic average. Such data need to be adjusted to remove the nonclimatic inhomogeneities. The resulting (adjusted) record is then said to be "homogeneous." If no exposure changes have occurred at a station, the normal is calculated simply by averaging the appropriate 30 values from the 1961-1990 record.

In the main, there are two "inhomogeneities" that NCDC is correcting for with normalization: adjusting for variances in time of day of observation (at the so-called First Order stations data is based on midnight to midnight observation times and this practice is not necessarily followed at cooperative stations which are staffed by volunteers), and second, estimating data that is either missing or incongruent.

The editors had some concerns regarding the comparative results of the two methodologies. Would our methodology produce strikingly different results than NCDC's? To allay concerns, results of the two processes were compared for the time period normalized results are available (1971-2000). In short, what was found was that the answer to this question is no. Never the less, users should be aware that because of both the time period covered (1980-2009) and the methodology used, data is not compatible with data from other sources.

POTENTIAL CAUTIONS

First, as with any statistical reference work of this type, users need to be aware of the source of the data. The information here comes from NOAA, and it is the most comprehensive and reliable core data available. Although it is the best, it is not perfect. Most weather stations are staffed by volunteers, times of observation sometimes vary, stations occasionally are moved (especially over a thirty year period), equipment is changed or upgraded, and all of these factors affect the uniformity of the data. The editors do not attempt to correct for these factors, and this data is not intended for either climatologists or atmospheric scientists. Users with concerns about data collection and reporting protocols are both referred to NCDC technical documentation.

Second, users need to be aware of the methodology here which is described above. Although this methodology has produced fully satisfactory results, it is not directly compatible with other methodologies, hence variances in the results published here and those which appear in other publications will doubtlessly arise.

Third, is the trap of that informal logical fallacy known as "hasty generalization," and its corollaries. This may involve presuming the future will be like the past (specifically, next year will be an average year), or it may involve misunderstanding the limitations of an arithmetic average, but more interestingly, it may involve those mistakes made most innocently by generalizing informally on too broad a basis. As weather is highly localized, the data should be taken in that context. A weather station collects data about climatic conditions at that spot, and that spot may or may not be an effective paradigm for an entire town or area.

About Michigan

Governor	**Richard Dale "Rick" Snyder**
Lt Governor	**Brian Nelson Calley**
State Capital	Lansing
Date of Statehood	January 26, 1837 (26th state)
Before Statehood.	Michigan Territory
State Nicknames	Great Lake State; Wolverine State; Water Winter Wonderland
Largest City.	Detroit
Demonym	Michigander; Michiganian; Yooper (for residents of the Upper Peninsula)
Highest Point.	Mount Arvon (1,979 feet)
Lowest Point	Lake Erie (571 feet)
State Bird	American Robin *(Turdus migratorius)*
State Fish.	Brook Trout *(Salvelinus fontinalis)*
State Flower	Apple Blossom *(Pyrus coronaria)*
State Fossil	Mastodon
State Game Mammal.	White-Tailed Deer *(Odocoileus virginianus)*
State Gem	Isle Royal Greenstone *(Chlorastrolite)*
State Motto	"If you seek a pleasant peninsula, look about you" *("Si quaeris peninsulam amoenam circumspice")*
State Reptile	Painted Turtle *(Chrysemys picta)*
State Soil.	Kallkaska Soil Series *(Odocoileus virginianus)*
State Song	My Michigan
State Stone	Petoskey Stone *(Hexagonaria percarinata)*
State Tree	White Pine *(Pinus strobus)*
State Wildflower	Dwarf Lake Iris *(Iris lacustris)*

The state capitol building, top, was completed in 1878. It is located in Lansing, the capital of Michigan, and a National Historic Landmark. A statue of Austin Blair, the 13th governor of Michigan, stands in the foreground. The bottom photograph shows a typical Michigan farm. Farmers in the state grow more than 300 varieties of food, with corn, wheat and soybeans among the most popular crops. Agriculture contributes $101 billion to the state's economy, and the industry employs over 900,000 people.

The University of Michigan, originally founded in 1817 in Detroit, moved to Ann Arbor in 1837. It includes nearly 600 major buildings with satellite campuses located in Flint and Dearborn, and a student population of more than 43,000. The building pictured above houses the university's law school.

The city of Detroit, the most populous city in Michigan, is pictured top. It is a major port on the Detroit River, which connects the Great Lakes System to the Saint Lawrence Seaway, and is the largest city on the U.S./Canada border. The bottom photograph shows Point Iroquois Light, a lighthouse in Whitefish Bay, where Lake Superior connects with the other Great Lakes. It was the first lighthouse on the point and cost $5,000 to build. First lit in 1870, it was deactivated in 1963.

Pictured top is a historic building that once served as a hotel and opera house in the mining town of Fayette, Michigan. Fayette State Historical Park celebrates the once bustling town with Heritage Day and other annual events. The bottom photograph shows the city of Grand Rapids, the second largest city in Michigan. Home to five of the world's leading furniture manufacturers, it's nicknamed Furniture City. Another Grand Rapid nickname is River City, for the river for which it's named.

The Little Sable Point Light, pictured here, is a lighthouse south of the city of Pentwater on Lake Michigan. Public outcries following the loss of the Schooner Pride in 1866 led to Congressional approval for construction of the lighthouse, which was first lit in 1874. In 1955, the light was automated, and has a range of 15 nautical miles.

A Brief History of Michigan

Michigan Before the Europeans

When French explorers first visited Michigan in the early seventeenth century, there were approximately 100,000 Native Americans living in the Great Lakes region. Of these, the estimated population of what is now Michigan was approximately 15,000. Several tribes made the forests and river valleys here their home. The main groups, sometimes referred to as "The Three Fires," were the **Chippewa (Ojibway)**, who lived mainly in the Upper Peninsula and the eastern part of the Lower Peninsula; the **Ottawa**, who resided along the western part of the Lower Peninsula; and the **Potawatomi**, who occupied part of southwestern Michigan after migrating from what is now eastern Wisconsin. Other significant tribes in this region included the **Huron** (sometimes known as the Wyandot), who came to the southeastern area of Michigan from the Ontario side of Lake Huron; the **Sauk**, who resided in the Saginaw River valley; the **Miami**, who lived along the St. Joseph River before migrating to western Ohio; and the **Menominee**, who lived in northern Wisconsin and parts of the Upper Peninsula.

Most Native American settlements in the Great Lakes region were along river valleys or near the shoreline of the Great Lakes, and, much like today, most of the population located in the southern half of the Lower Peninsula. Tribal settlements were not permanent, with groups moving to new locations every few years. Although agriculture was limited by soil conditions and dense forest, the Native Americans of this region did cultivate crops. Corn, beans, and squash were grown and wild apples, berries, nuts, game, fish, honey, and wild rice provided other sources of food. Maple sugar was produced from the sap of maple trees and birch trees were used for housing materials and canoes.

The original inhabitants of this region were mobile people. They utilized the rivers and lakes for their transportation. Their trails, paths, and portages were later traversed by the coureurs de bois, English and French fur traders, and New England settlers. Several state and federal highways, including much of the interstate system, now follow pathways first traveled by these Native Americans.

The Native Americans of the pre-European era in Michigan left behind more than 1,000 **burial mounds** similar to those found in Ohio, Indiana, Illinois, and Missouri. Many mounds were discovered in the lower Grand River and Muskegon River valleys of west-central Michigan. The most puzzling prehistoric remnants, however, were the carefully designed and arranged ridges of earth described as "garden beds." These detailed geometric creations, long since destroyed by pioneers' plows, consisted of ridges of soil about eighteen inches high and covered many acres. Outside of a few found in Indiana and Wisconsin, the "garden beds" have been found only in Michigan. Their function remains a mystery.

Another question that has plagued historians and archaeologists for generations involves the copper fields of the western Upper Peninsula near Lake Superior. Prehistoric miners worked these fields along the Keweenaw Peninsula and on Isle Royale at least 4,000 years ago. Archaeological evidence indicates that **copper** was quarried from veins in open pits for hundreds of years by an unknown tribe or tribes. Nuggets of nearly pure native copper were hammered and annealed into the shape of tools, which were valued items of trade. Michigan copper was found among Native Americans as far south as the Gulf of Mexico and from the Rockies to the Alleghenies. Curiously, however, the use and mining of copper were unknown to the tribes in this region when the Europeans came to the Great Lakes in the seventeenth century.

The French Era

The first whites to see Michigan were French explorers. The earliest encounters between Europeans and Native Americans in this region were strongly influenced by a man who probably never visited Michigan, **Samuel de Champlain**. The founder of Quebec in 1608, Champlain is thought to have visited the eastern shores of Georgian Bay by 1612. He sent a young man named **Etienne Brulé** and a companion named Grenoble to travel west, seeking the fabled "northwest passage" to the Orient. It is believed that Brulé reached the Sault Ste. Marie area in 1618 and returned to Michigan in 1621, traveling as far west as the Keweenaw Peninsula, where he picked up samples of copper. Jean Nicolet, another Champlain protégé who was seeking access to the Orient, came through the Straits of Mackinac in 1634 before coming ashore along Green Bay dressed in garb designed to impress the Chinese he hoped to find.

Samuel de Champlain, in addition to advancing exploration of the Great Lakes, forged alliances and fostered conflict among various tribes that influenced Michigan's settlement for 200 years. In 1609, Champlain's use of his musket while assisting the Hurons in a battle with a small group of Mohawks, part of the Iroquois Nation, near Lake Champlain in New York made an enemy of what was probably the strongest group in the entire region. The incident also limited French access to the lower Great Lakes. As a result, the route taken by French explorers, traders, and missionaries followed the Ottawa River and Lake Nipissing instead of Lake Ontario, Lake Erie, and the Detroit River. Consequently, settlements in the Upper Peninsula of Michigan were established much earlier than in the southern portion of the state.

The earliest French explorers in the region were soon followed by **French missionaries**. These courageous and dedicated men endured unspeakable hardships in their attempt to convert the Native Americans to Christianity. They established missions and settlements throughout the lakes and the Mississippi River valley. Many Michigan landmarks memorialize their influence.

In 1641, Father Charles Raymbault and Father Isaac Jogues preached at Sault Ste. Marie. Father René Mesnard established the first regular mission at Keweenaw Bay in 1660. Beginning in 1665, Father Claude Allouez spent twenty-five years working among the people in the Keweenaw region, Green Bay, Sault Ste. Marie, Illinois, and southwestern Michigan, where he devoted most of his efforts. Father Jacques Marquette founded the first permanent settlement in Michigan at Sault Ste. Marie in 1668 and, in 1671, founded St. Ignace. That same year, a military post was established at St. Ignace and named Fort de Buade. This fort was later abandoned, and **Fort Michilimackinac** was built on the southern shore of the Straits. In 1679, René Robert Cavelier de La Salle established **Fort Miami** at the mouth of the St. Joseph River, and by 1690, Father Claude Aveneau established a mission at the site of present-day Niles, where Fort St. Joseph was soon built.

The Delisle Map. This 1703 map is thought to be the first to include Detroit.

French **coureurs de bois**, a loosely defined term for unlicensed traders, were a sharp contrast to the priests and nobility who established forts and missions. They were rugged individuals who lived among the Native Americans, respected their customs, and hunted and trapped the region's rich game.

Much of Michigan's early history was shaped by the long-standing conflicts between England and France. The military forts built in Michigan and elsewhere in the Great Lakes region were a response to a growing British interest in this area. In 1694, **Antoine de la Mothe Cadillac**, the commandant of the Michilimackinac post, saw the threat posed by the British, who were forming alliances with the Native Americans. Cadillac sought and received permission to establish a fortified settlement at "place du detroit." On July 24, 1701, Cadillac and a party of 100 established **Fort Pontchartrain**, which soon became a major trading post and a strategic location for the eventual settlement of the region. Within a short time, several thousand Native Americans settled near the area, and some French families moved in and established narrow "ribbon farms" along the Detroit River. Soon after the founding of Fort Pontchartrain, the area became the site of British-inspired raids by various Indians. At the same time, the fur trade was becoming more lucrative, and the intensity of British and French animosities resulted in the **French and Indian War**, the third Anglo-French war fought during the eighteenth century. Although no major battles of this war were fought in Michigan, the war ended the French era and began the British era following the British victory on the Plains of Abraham at Quebec in 1759. On November 19, 1760, the French formally surrendered Detroit to British Major Robert Rogers, thus ending almost a century and a half of French rule in Michigan.

The British Era

The British era of Michigan history was marked by great contentiousness, military activity, and armed hostilities. Michigan was both the site of many conflicts and the base from which attacks on other areas of the region were launched, such as the settlements in Ohio and Kentucky.

The arrival of the British in Michigan brought about great changes in the interactions between the Europeans and the Native Americans. The French treated the Native Americans with a certain measure of respect and a laissez-faire attitude. Many voyageurs took wives and lived among tribes. The French missionaries sought to "save" the Native American. French officials regularly gave gifts (including copious amounts of liquor) to the tribes. Traders were thought by Indians to be fair in their dealings.

The British, meanwhile, allied themselves with tribes that were traditional enemies of the tribes in Michigan in the 1600s. The English style of imposing law was in strong contrast to the more relaxed French approach. The British were intent upon developing the rich **fur trade**. They actively discouraged settlement of the interior region of Michigan in an effort to safeguard the fur empire. In spite of efforts to discourage development, settlers began making their way across the mountains and established settlements in Kentucky and along the Ohio River.

A combination of policy changes by the British and awareness of the threat presented by encroaching settlers led to **Pontiac's Rebellion**. Pontiac was a brilliant and forceful Ottawa leader. Encouraged by the French who remained in the region, Pontiac and leaders of other tribes across the interior devised a plan to oust the British. Pontiac was the architect of the plan in Michigan. Through a series of locally orchestrated attacks, all of the British forts, except for Detroit, Pitt, and Niagara, fell in 1763. In Detroit, Pontiac's plan was frustrated by an advance warning to Major Henry Gladwin, who learned of the plan and surprise attack. Instead, Pontiac laid siege to Detroit beginning in May, 1763, and continuing until November of that year, when the overall failure of the plan led to its abandonment and the siege of Detroit was lifted. Elsewhere, Fort Michilimackinac fell to the Chippewas on June 2, 1763, the British were defeated at Sault Ste. Marie, and Fort St. Joseph near Niles was abandoned.

The American Revolution, although it certainly changed Michigan's fortunes forever, had little immediate impact on this part of the country. Michigan was firmly controlled by the British. It was sparsely populated and remote from military engagements on the East Coast. In addition, its largely French and British residents did not feel a strong allegiance to the American cause.

Most of the military activity of the region consisted of British-supplied **tribal raids on American settlements** in Kentucky and southern Ohio. Governor Henry Hamilton paid for scalps brought to Detroit and earned himself the nickname "hair-buyer."

The famous 1778 capture of the British forts on the Wabash River in Indiana by **George Rogers Clark** prompted the British to build a new fort on Mackinac Island. The fort at Detroit was also rebuilt.

The 1783 **Treaty of Paris** signified the end of the American Revolution and stipulated an international boundary for the United States that included Michigan. However, it would be thirteen years before the British would relinquish their control of the area. The British ignored the treaty for several reasons. The British wished to keep peace and maintain their friendship with the Indians. They also felt the Americans failed to pay pre-war debts or compensate loyalists for losses during the war. The British coveted the lucrative fur trade of the Great Lakes and valued Michigan's strategic location. Finally, the British believed that another conflict between England and this upstart nation was imminent. Attempts made by George Washington to use diplomatic means to take Fort Detroit and Michigan into American possession were thwarted. Because of this situation, Michigan was included in Kent County of what was called the Province of Upper Canada. The **first elections held in Michigan** were to choose area representatives to the Upper Canadian Assembly in 1792.

After the American Revolution ended, the British in Detroit continued to orchestrate Indian raids on settlers in the Ohio River valley. The raids led to several major confrontations, including the loss in 1791 of hundreds of men under the command of **Arthur St. Clair**, the first governor of the Northwest Territory. President Washington then turned to Revolutionary War hero **"Mad Anthony" Wayne**, who defeated the British-backed Indians at the **Battle of Fallen Timbers** near Toledo in 1794. Shortly after this major victory and the signing of **Jay's Treaty** in 1794, British control of Michigan ended. On July 11, 1796, the American flag finally flew over Detroit.

Michigan as a Territory

Michigan's status changed many times even after it came under the control of the United States in 1796. Wayne County, part of the Northwest Territory under the **Ordinance of 1787**, included most of Wisconsin, all of Michigan, and the northern portions of Indiana and Ohio and sent delegates to the General Assembly of the Northwest Territory. In 1800, the western half of Michigan's Lower Peninsula and most of the Upper Peninsula became part of the **Indiana Territory**. Michigan's boundaries changed in response to the establishment of states from the Northwest Territory. For a brief period beginning in 1834, the Michigan Territory included Wisconsin, Minnesota, Iowa, and part of the Dakotas.

With the signature of President Thomas Jefferson on January 11, 1805, **Michigan became a separate territory**. Detroit, where most of the people lived, was designated the capital. The structure of government was determined by the Northwest Ordinance. This landmark document's basic provisions constituted a governmental blueprint that was followed by most of the states of our nation. According to the Northwest Ordinance, the first government that was uniquely Michigan's consisted of an assembly that, in effect, combined the executive, legislative, and judicial powers of government in one unit. The initial government was appointed entirely by President Jefferson and included William Hull from Massachusetts as the governor; Stanley Griswold from New Hampshire as the secretary; and Samuel Huntington from Ohio, Augustus Woodward from Washington, D.C., and Frederick Bates from Detroit as the judges. The governor and the judges constituted the lawmaking body, while the judges presided as the judicial equivalent of today's supreme court. Laws were to incorporate provisions already in effect in one or more of the states.

The first days of Michigan's new status as a territory were beset by hardship. On the very day the federal law was to take effect, July 1, 1805, Detroit was little more than ashes, the charred remains of a fire that had swept through the entire settlement. One of the first actions of the new government was to arrange for rebuilding the town.

At that time, Detroit was truly a frontier town, with pelts accepted as a medium of exchange. The English agents and fur traders who worked with Native Americans were headquartered at Fort Malden on the Canadian side of the Detroit River. In Detroit, French influence remained strong. French was probably spoken as much as English in most areas. **Father Gabriel Richard**, a French priest, brought one of the first printing presses to this side of the Alleghenies, published the first newspaper, and, together with the Reverend John Monteith and Judge Augustus Woodward, organized the **University of Michigan**. In 1823, Father Richard was Michigan's delegate to Congress, the only Catholic priest to sit in the United States House of Representatives until 1971.

Michigan's growth and development slowed at this time for a variety of reasons. Although a treaty was negotiated in 1807 with Native Americans involving the southeastern portion of the state, there were constant threats from British-incited Native Americans. Many of the same forces that inspired Pontiac in 1763 led Shawnee **Tecumseh** to attempt to unite western tribes to repel the region's settlers. Although Tecumseh's plan suffered a serious setback to future President William

Henry Harrison in 1811 at the Tippecanoe River in Indiana, the issue of British meddling in the west combined with concern over freedom of the seas on the East Coast to bring about the **War of 1812**.

Lewis Cass

Michigan soon found itself returned to British control. On the night of July 16, 1812, the British, who learned of the declaration of war before the Americans in Michigan, landed on the northern shore of Mackinac Island, forcing the surrender of the fort without a shot being fired. On August 16, 1812, after a few weeks of uncertain maneuvers in Canada, **Governor Hull**, fearing a massacre at the hands of Tecumseh's warriors and the British soldiers, turned Detroit over to the British. This surrender — the only time an American city has been surrendered to a foreign power — led to Governor Hull's court martial and sentence to be shot. Although spared from execution because of his heroism during the Revolution, Governor Hull was replaced by General **Lewis Cass**.

The War of 1812 resulted in many Michigan tragedies, most notably the defeat and slaughter of Americans at Frenchtown (Monroe) at the River Raisin in January 1813. However, with the dramatic victory of **Oliver Hazard Perry** over the British on Lake Erie and the triumph of William Henry Harrison over the British and Tecumseh at the Thames River in Canada, the British abandoned Detroit for the final time in September 1813. Britain, weary from war after fighting Napoleon and then the United States, ended the war with the **Treaty of Ghent** in 1814. In July 1815, the British returned Mackinac Island to the Americans and withdrew to Fort Collier on Drummond Island, which was then believed to be British territory.

After the war, federal surveyors commissioned to **survey the interior of Michigan** and secure lands to compensate those who had fought in the war effectively dismissed Michigan as uninhabitable because of swamplands. Much of the work of Governor Cass, including an expedition through the interior of the territory in 1820, aimed to promote **internal improvements** to disprove these claims and encourage the settlement needed for statehood.

As a result of the government surveyors' report that Michigan was unfit for cultivation, land in Illinois and Missouri instead was procured for veterans of the War of 1812. Although this decision delayed Michigan's inevitable growth, the most significant barrier to development was a lack of legally titled land. It was not until tribes relinquished their respective property rights that the pioneer era could begin. Governor Cass, who made many efforts to promote statehood, secured treaties with the Indians in 1819, 1820, and 1821 that provided the groundwork for a tremendous surge in population in Michigan in the 1820s and 1830s. Roads were soon built into the interior and, in 1818, the first public land sales were held along the southern tiers of counties. Settlement was aided by the **Territorial Road** and the Chicago Road, along which communities were

---

The Man With the Window to His Stomach

In 1822, an accident occurred on Mackinac Island that made possible important advances in medical science, specifically, the study of the process of digestion. The case involved a 19-year-old French-Canadian trapper and an Army surgeon.

On June 6, 1822, Alexis St. Martin suffered a severe gunshot wound at close range to his chest and abdomen. In spite of the seriousness of the wound, **Dr. William Beaumont**, an Army surgeon stationed at Fort Mackinac, was able to save the young man's life. The nature of the injury, however, was unique, for the damage of the blast and the subsequent healing left the stomach near the exterior of the abdomen, with an "opening" to the external wound. The result was a "window" to the stomach that remained after St. Martin returned to overall good health. In 1825, after Dr. Beaumont took St. Martin into his own family and supported him, the physician began a **series of physiological studies** using the French-Canadian's stomach. Dr. Beaumont carried out a variety of experiments with different foods to test his hypothesis that the process of digestion was essentially a chemical process. In addition to being able to observe the stomach, Dr. Beaumont could also extract some of its contents, thereby studying the stages of digestion. In 1833, Dr. Beaumont published *Experiments and Observations on the Gastric Juice and the Physiology of Digestion*. This work was an important contribution to medical knowledge.

Ironically, Alexis St. Martin outlived Dr. Beaumont by nearly thirty years. St. Martin died in 1880 after having lived a robust enough life to have fathered twenty children.

A twenty-six-star flag, reflecting Michigan's admission to the Union.

established. The onset of steam transportation to Michigan and the completion of the **Erie Canal** in New York in 1825 opened the floodgates as farmers and families from New England and New York joined the westward migration. By the 1830s, the rush to Michigan — **"Michigan Fever"** — was in full gear, and the territory grew faster than any other part of the country. In 1820, according to the census, Michigan had 8,896 people, excluding Indians. By 1830, the population had jumped to nearly 32,000, and in 1840, there were 212,267 inhabitants.

Statehood

By 1833, the Michigan Territory had more than the 60,000 inhabitants required by the Northwest Ordinance to form a state government and formally seek admission to the Union. By 1835, Michigan had **drafted a constitution** believed to be acceptable to the Congress. This constitution, which was to guide our state's development, was adopted by voters in October 1835 by a vote of 6,299 to 1,359. At this point, Michigan's admission into the Union may have proceeded smoothly but for one problem — a boundary dispute with the state of Ohio. While the dispute between Michigan and Ohio in 1835 has taken on a legendary quality over the years, it was never the full-fledged **"Toledo War"** as is sometimes claimed.

At stake was a 468-square-mile strip of land acknowledged to be Michigan's. People living in the area voted in Michigan elections and were governed by Michigan laws. The admission of Ohio as a state in 1803 enabled Ohio to exercise authority over the disputed territory and have a stronger voice through the Ohio congressional delegation. In 1835, a territorial militia was mobilized as volunteers organized to deal with the so-called "trespassers" from Ohio. In taking up arms, the "Boy Governor," Stevens T. Mason (1835-1840), enraged **President Andrew Jackson**, who removed him from office. Eventually, Congress proposed the compromise that gave the "Toledo Strip" to Ohio and the western four-fifths of the Upper Peninsula to Michigan. Michigan citizens did not accept this compromise immediately. At the first Convention of Assent in Ann Arbor in September 1836, delegates refused to accept this condition of statehood. However, in December, at the "Frostbitten Convention" in Ann Arbor, it was accepted. On January 26, 1837, Michigan became the twenty-sixth state.

With statehood achieved, an ambitious internal improvements program was begun. The new government embarked upon a plan to borrow five million dollars to finance a variety of projects. These included the construction of three railroads across the state, a network of roads, and a system of canals to facilitate river transportation. Although several elements of the plan were eventually completed, many of the projects, including the canal building, were never finished. Instead, because of the **Panic of 1837**, the internal improvements venture nearly crippled the state's finances.

The Panic of 1837 was a serious blow to the new state. It stemmed from lax banking practices due, in part, to President Jackson's attitude toward bankers, whom he considered to be "soulless monopolists." This attitude led to laws across the country, including Michigan, permitting virtually anyone to open a bank. As a result, a great amount of paper money was printed. This led to wild speculation, especially in places like Michigan where land sales were exploding. Rampant inflation followed, causing President Jackson to issue a directive (the Specie Circular) that government land could only be bought with gold or silver coin. Banks failed everywhere,

The Toledo War

One of the legendary events in Michigan history was the Toledo War. Although referred to as a "war," this conflict was more of a legal skirmish involving the Michigan Territory, the state of Ohio, and the U.S. Congress. This serious matter, which delayed Michigan's entry into the Union, also had its humorous side. The Toledo War made several contributions to Michigan folklore.

The Toledo War was the result of conflicting identification of the **boundaries separating Michigan and Ohio**. In 1787, as part of the establishment of the Northwest Territory, the state boundaries were to include a border running due east from the southernmost tip of Lake Michigan. This dividing line would have given Michigan a 468-square-mile strip of Ohio that includes Toledo. In 1803, Ohio was admitted to the Union with a boundary line that extended several miles to the north, enabling Ohio to include the mouth of the Maumee River, at Lake Erie. In 1805, Congress ignored the boundary set by Ohio and returned to the 1787 boundary line when it created the Michigan Territory, including the Toledo strip. People on this land considered themselves to be residents of Michigan. They voted in Michigan and were served by Michigan courts and county officials in Monroe.

As Michigan prepared for statehood, Acting Governor **Stevens T. Mason**, who was appointed to this post at the age of nineteen by President Andrew Jackson, led the effort to assert Michigan's dominion over this area. In April 1835, Governor Mason called for volunteers and mobilized troops to go to the Toledo strip to enforce laws passed by Michigan that imposed a fine or imprisonment on anyone who contested Michigan's authority on this land. Led by Mason, who was nicknamed "the Boy Governor," the Michigan militia arrested several surveyors who were representing Ohio's interests. The actions of Governor Mason incensed President Andrew Jackson, who removed Mason from office on August 29, 1835.

Stevens T. Mason

At the same time, the Buckeye State, under Governor Robert Lucas, had no interest in relinquishing land that was, according to its state constitution, clearly Ohio's. Ohio had a stronger voice in Congress because it was already a state, but Michigan had a strong legal case, based on several surveys. After nearly a two-year delay, Congress fashioned a **compromise** that was approved, on its second try, by the people of Michigan. The compromise granted Michigan more than 9,000 square miles of the Upper Peninsula.

In addition to Michigan's vast land acquisition, the Toledo War resulted in Michigan's nickname as the "**Wolverine State**." It is thought that this term originated as a derisive name given to the Michigan residents by the people of Ohio. The Ohioans were fond of comparing Michigan residents to an animal considered to be among the greediest, ugliest creatures.

especially in Michigan. This financial crisis, in addition to hampering the development of several visionary plans, left a lasting impression on the state's involvement in major projects.

Michigan's early development as a state included a strong **focus on education**. The Constitution of 1835 is notable in our nation's history for providing for the appointment of a permanent Superintendent of Public Instruction and for its promotion of "Intellectual, Scientifical, and Agricultural improvement." Following the leadership of Superintendent John D. Pierce and Isaac Crary, two prominent New England immigrants, a system of district libraries, township boards of school inspectors, and a primary school fund based upon money raised through the sale of lands was established. The University of Michigan, established in 1817, was now formally organized as a state institution at Ann Arbor.

John D. Pierce

In addition to establishing institutions throughout the state, including the State Prison at Jackson and the teachers' college at Ypsilanti in 1849, Michigan took steps to provide a **permanent seat of government** for the state. Although Detroit had been the center of most activity in the region and along the Great Lakes for many years, the founders of the state were aware of the need to locate the state capital in a more centralized place. As a state bordering a foreign country, one which the United States had engaged in war only a generation earlier, Michigan needed to establish a more secure location for its seat of government. There was also a strong sentiment that big cities, like Detroit, had a corrupting influence not appropriate for a state capital. Recognizing these concerns, the delegates who drafted the Constitution of 1835 provided that Detroit would serve as the state capital until 1847, when it was to be permanently located by the Legislature. In 1847, following intense debate over various locations, **Lansing Township** was selected. The area had few inhabitants and even fewer improvements. Nonetheless, the town, originally named "Michigan" and soon renamed Lansing, became the seat of government.

Reform Politics and the Civil War

Before the Civil War, Michigan's development, like much of the country's, was affected by the "second great awakening." This was an explosion of **religious fervor** that appears to have originated in New York State. Rooted in religious faith, this movement embraced the belief that each person had a duty to improve the world. In Michigan, this zeal led to sweeping social reforms in areas such as education, women's suffrage, slavery, prisons, and establishing institutions for the blind, deaf, and feebleminded.

The **state penitentiary** established at Jackson in 1838 replaced whipping posts and other severe forms of punishment with a system of prison discipline that was humane. This reflected what was, for the time, the enlightened idea that prisoners could be rehabilitated. In 1846, **capital punishment** was abolished in the wake of a highly publicized hanging in neighboring Ontario in which, it was later proved, an innocent man had been executed. Michigan became the first English-speaking jurisdiction to outlaw capital punishment.

Efforts on behalf of those with special needs included the establishment of the Kalamazoo Asylum for the Insane (1859), a state institution for the deaf and blind in 1854 in Flint, and the facility for the blind in Lansing in 1879.

In Battle Creek, Seventh Day Adventists built the **Western Health Reform Institute in 1866**. The first of a worldwide system of sanitaria, hospitals, and medical dispensaries, the institute became the Battle Creek Sanitarium in 1876. Work in the fields of health and nutrition aided the development of the cereal industry in the late nineteenth century.

During the antebellum period, several colleges with affiliations to various religious denominations were established. These included Kalamazoo College, Hillsdale College, Albion College, and Olivet College. Although it would be several generations before questions involving women's rights were addressed in earnest, Michigan was the scene of considerable activity related to women's suffrage. As early as 1846, people like Austin Blair, who later became Michigan's Civil War governor, and, a bit later, Kent County pioneer Rix Robinson promoted women's right to vote. In 1874, in a highly emotional campaign that attracted such leaders as Elizabeth Cady Stanton and **Susan B. Anthony**, the issue of **voting rights for women** was placed on the ballot in a statewide election. In 1867, limited voting rights were extended to women who owned property and wished to vote on school matters. Despite this early step, unabridged voting rights were not realized in Michigan until 1918 — only two years before the ratification of the Nineteenth Amendment to the Constitution of the United States.

Closely linked to women's rights was the issue of temperance. In pioneer America, the presence of hard liquor was a fact of life. Liquor — especially whiskey — exerted a tremendous impact on daily life, and it was a significant factor in many of the dealings between Native Americans and settlers. **Temperance groups** were established throughout Michigan following the 1833 establishment of the Michigan Temperance Society. Although abstinence from alcohol did not become part of American life (at least according to the law) until the Prohibition of the 1920s, there were efforts at the state and local levels to curb the making and selling of liquor in the 1850s.

Sojourner Truth

The most dramatic social reform in Michigan was the **antislavery movement**. The large number of small, proudly independent farmers that comprised the state's population contributed to the hatred of slavery. In 1850, according to the census, 35.4% of Michigan residents were born in Michigan; 33.6% were born in New York State; 7.8% were born in New England; and less than 1% were born in slave states. Antislavery societies flourished in Michigan. They were led by such prominent Quakers as Laura Haviland and Elizabeth Chandler. The popular sentiment of the people and Michigan's proximity to Canada made the state a hotbed of controversy concerning runaway slaves. The **Underground Railroad**, which included such remarkable individuals as **Sojourner Truth**, conducted a great deal of business in Michigan. Many courageous Michigan citizens were involved in this informal, loosely structured activity as "conductors" along the two main lines of the underground railway.

There were several notable confrontations between Michigan citizens and agents of slaveholders who journeyed north in an effort to recover slaves. One of the most famous incidents took place near Marshall, a major center of abolitionist strength. **Adam Crosswhite** and his family, fleeing Kentucky in 1844 by way of the Underground Railroad, lived in Marshall. In January of 1847, a group of Kentuckians came to Michigan to retrieve Crosswhite and his family. In a dramatic response, citizens of the town stood up to the Kentuckians and had them arrested and jailed while the Crosswhite family safely fled to Canada. The outcry from the southern states was deafening, with Henry Clay calling Michigan "a hotbed of radicals and renegades." The sentiment reflected in this incident and others like it elsewhere in the country led to the enactment by Congress of the controversial **Fugitive Slave Act of 1850**, which further divided the North and South.

An important outgrowth of the slavery question was the development of the **Republican Party**. This new element on the American political scene was founded in Michigan at the famed meeting "under the oaks" at Jackson in 1854. The new party, the dominant force in Michigan politics for many decades, resulted from the unification of former Whigs, some disenchanted Democrats, and several smaller parties and activist individuals rallying under the banner of antislavery and specific economic issues.

Michigan was loyal to the Union and to **Abraham Lincoln's** pledge to preserve it, and, when war broke out with the bombardment of Fort Sumter in South Carolina in April 1861, Michigan's citizens responded militarily and at home through agriculture and mining.

On May 16, 1861, the First Michigan Infantry arrived in Washington — the first regiment from the western states to heed President Lincoln's call for troops. A tearful Lincoln was reported to have exclaimed upon the arrival of the Michigan troops, "Thank God for Michigan." Michigan men fought in virtually all of the major campaigns and battles of the **Civil War**. In the face of war weariness, draft riots, which quickly became a race riot, occurred in Detroit in 1863. However, Michigan's response was overwhelmingly loyal. It is estimated that 23% of the male population of the state served in the Union armed forces. This percentage included some Indians and more than 1,600 black soldiers, an impressive total that included men who returned to Michigan from Canada to enlist. With the final victory in sight, the Union soldiers from Michigan were recognized by a grateful state ". . . for their unfaltering faith in the justice of our cause, their self-sacrificing patriotism, their patient endurance, their heroic fortitude, their unsurpassed valor, and their glorious victories."

Third Michigan Infantry. Between 1861 and 1865, 90,000 Michigan soldiers served in the Civil War.

Building Michigan's Economy

Known today as one of the world's greatest manufacturing centers and as a giant of the twentieth century industrial world, Michigan derived almost all of its economic strength in its earlier years from its natural resources, which propelled Michigan to the lead among the states in several key enterprises, including mining, lumbering, and agriculture.

Michigan's first enterprise was the **fur trade**. This activity was important to the development of the interior of the entire continent. Fur trading was a factor behind the hostilities that took place in the late eighteenth and nineteenth centuries. For many years, Mackinac Island was the regional center for the fur trade. Michigan furs helped German immigrant John Jacob Astor become America's first millionaire.

From the days when unknown Native American tribes mined it and when the first European explored the region, copper seemed a readily available resource awaiting development. Both the British and the French expressed interest in reports of copper. The British made some attempts to mine it, but, due to the remoteness of the region and greater interest in furs, never successfully pursued mining. **Dr. Douglass Houghton**, Michigan's first state geologist, noted the availability of this mineral in his 1841 report on the state's resources. Stories of the Ontonagon Boulder, a huge chunk of pure copper four feet long, three and one-half feet wide, and one and one-half feet thick, and the publicity created by reports of Henry Rowe Schoolcraft and others led to renewed interest in **copper mining**. By the mid-1840s, a copper boom was in the making, creating the country's first mineral rush. Many companies were established, and some mines yielded remarkable wealth. For forty years, until 1887, Michigan led the nation in the production of copper, and in many of those years produced more than one-half of the nation's supply.

About the same time, in 1844, rich **iron ore deposits** were discovered by surveyor William A. Burt in the Negaunee and Ishpeming area. From the 1850s until the turn of the century, Michigan was the nation's leader in iron ore production.

So important were the mineral riches of the Upper Peninsula that, in 1855, a remarkable engineering feat was completed, the construction of a **canal and locks along the St. Mary's River** at Sault Ste. Marie. The canal, operated by the state until it was turned over to the federal government in 1881, was financed by the sale of public land. The locks fostered growth in mining operations and facilitated the movement of essential minerals during the Civil War.

Michigan's most important economic activity was **agriculture**. The early dire warnings that Michigan soil could not support crops proved unfounded. Except for the farming activities of the Indians and the small "ribbon farms" of the French around the Detroit area, virtually the entire state remained uncultivated until the massive influx of New York and New England farmers in the 1820s and 1830s. As they penetrated the forest and cleared the land, the fertile quality of the southern Lower Peninsula became well known. Like most of the nation, Michigan's population was comprised of farmers.

The most important crop was wheat, and until the Great Plains gave way to the plow, Michigan was a national leader in this key crop. Michigan's unique combination of climate and soils was quickly noted by pioneer farmers, who began fruit production, especially apples and peaches, along Lake Michigan. Sugar beets and mint were also soon developed by the Michigan farmer.

Two areas of special interest in Michigan's agricultural development in the nineteenth century were the production of celery and the importance of cereals. In the Kalamazoo region, enterprising Dutch immigrants capitalized on the area's marshes and swamps to grow celery. Touting the healthful benefits of this crop put Kalamazoo celery on the nation's tables. In Battle Creek, noted health advocates **Dr. John Harvey Kellogg** and **C. W. Post** promoted the development of cereal products that eventually earned Battle Creek the nickname "Cereal City."

In 1855, the Legislature established the **Agricultural College of the State of Michigan,** the nation's pioneer land grant college. This college, now known as Michigan State University, required students to work on the school's farms as part of the curriculum and became an important contributor to farming and agricultural research.

One of the most famous and colorful activities of the nineteenth century was lumbering. The dense forests and ample river transportation provided a perfect combination for this enterprise. Lumbering became a large-scale industry after the Civil War and continued until approximately 1900. The harvest of Michigan's woodlands led the nation for many years and had a lasting influence on many communities, especially those affiliated with **furniture manufacturing** (Grand Rapids) or **papermaking** (Kalamazoo). Stories from the lumber camps constitute some of Michigan's richest folklore. Lumbering in Michigan had a strong national impact. For example, Michigan lumber largely rebuilt Chicago following its famous fire. Homes, barns, and fences throughout the Midwest were built with Michigan lumber. During peak years, Michigan produced one-fourth of the nation's lumber — almost equal to the production of the next three states combined. The total worth of Michigan's forests far exceeded the value derived from the famed gold rush of California.

During **Michigan's lumbering boom**, enormous capital was accumulated. Much of the capital later helped Michigan become a center for the automobile industry. However, the lumbering era also left its mark in less favorable ways. Fires occurred regularly, and in 1871 and 1881 Michigan was the site of some of the most severe and costly fires ever to ravage the country. The first disaster relief effort of the American Red Cross came in response to the 1881 fires.

A vital link in Michigan's economy was the availability of **reliable transportation**. During the nineteenth century, the stagecoach and canoe were supplanted by the railroad. Michigan embraced this new technology early. The first railroad chartered in the Northwest Territory was the Pontiac and Detroit Railway Company (1830). The first track laid in the old Northwest Territory (between Adrian and Toledo) was the Erie and Kalamazoo, the most successful early railroad. However, not everyone was thrilled with the arrival of the "iron horse." Farmers were greatly concerned for their livestock, which were often killed. This led to incidents in Jackson county that became known as the **"Great Railroad Conspiracy" of 1849-1851**. At that time, farmers stopped and derailed trains. One incident resulted in a highly publicized trial that brought **Senator William H. Seward** of New York as an attorney for the defense. (Seward later gained fame as U.S. Secretary of State by purchasing Alaska). Later in the nineteenth century, conflict between railroad interests and agriculture was the focus of fierce battles in the Legislature. Since railroads were the way farmers transported their goods to market, there was considerable interest in how rates were determined. The regulation and taxation of railroads were major programs of **Governor Hazen S. Pingree** (1897-1900).

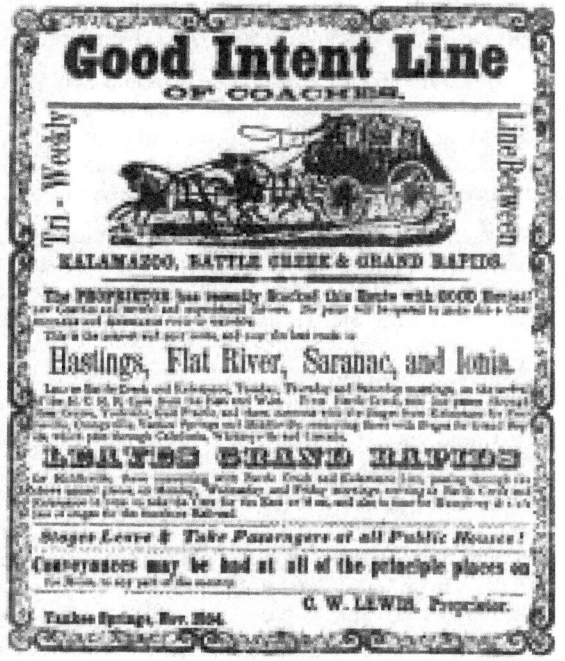

Good Intent Line opens stagecoach service to west Michigan.

Hermansville, Michigan, in the Upper Peninsula in 1892. This photo shows the aftermath of the clear-cut logging practices of the logging boom.

Conservation of Game and Resources

When first settled, Michigan was a pristine wilderness with abundant game, forests, and fish; however, it was not long before these resources were threatened by the onslaught of civilization. The saga of the passenger pigeon, a bird hunted to extinction in America during the nineteenth century, epitomized the potential consequences of uncontrolled hunting or fishing. It was reported that one million passenger pigeons were killed in a three-month period in 1878 near Petoskey. In addition, the effects of clear-cutting forestry practices demonstrated that even the most abundant resources were vulnerable. For many years, commercialized fishing and hunting operated freely. Deer were harvested in enormous quantities and fishing practices were so aggressive that they included using dynamite to take certain fish from streams.

Several efforts were made to deal with the rapidly disappearing game and fish. Hunting seasons were established, and other regulating measures attempted to protect certain animals, including swans, grayling, trout, and beaver. Enforcement of these restrictions, unfortunately, was difficult. In 1873, the **Board of Fish Commissioners** was established with an eye toward increasing the fish population through the use of hatcheries.

Michigan tried to cope with the problem of large-scale commercial hunting by prohibiting the taking of deer for consumption outside the state. In 1887, Michigan became a pioneer among the states in establishing the position of **Game Warden**. One of the early Game Wardens, Chase S. Osborn of Sault Ste. Marie, who served from 1895-1899, later served as governor (1911-1912).

Immigration and Human Resources

While much of Michigan's development and growth is associated with its natural resources, the key to this growth was the human resources that were needed to develop the mining, logging, agricultural, and industrial elements of the state's economy. Between 1860 and 1900, more than 700,000 immigrants came to Michigan, and nearly 400,000 of these new arrivals were born in foreign countries. In fact, the state began encouraging **immigrants** to settle in Michigan as early as 1845, when an Office of Foreign Emigration was established in New York. In early years, the Germans and Dutch were the most sought-after groups due to their strong religious beliefs, industriousness, and education. To increase immigration, the state's New York agent published a small pamphlet glorifying the virtues of the state. This type of promotion was to be repeated several times in Michigan and eventually in other states.

Following the success of this one-time venture, another agent was appointed to the post to continue the effort to attract Dutch and German settlers. He prepared a larger booklet which was also printed in German (*The Emigrants Guide to the State of Michigan* or *Des Auswanderers Wegweiser nach dem Staate Michigan*). This publication included more information about the state, including data on transportation, climate, agricultural and business opportunities, and matters of education, which were known to be important attractions for immigrants from Germany and the Netherlands. Thousands of these booklets were printed and the program proved to be a success.

The Civil War interrupted efforts to recruit new settlers, but in 1869, the governor appointed a commissioner of emigration to reside in Germany ". . . for the purpose of encouraging immigration to Michigan from German States and other countries of Europe." The agent, Max H. Allardt, lived in Germany from 1870-1875 where he published a periodical and a pamphlet extolling the wonders of Michigan. In 1881, successor commissioner Colonel Frederick Morley of Detroit distributed more than 40,000 copies of a lengthy publication in German, Dutch, French, and Swedish. The success of this program ultimately led to its own demise, for **Governor Josiah W. Begole** abolished the position of commissioner in 1885 as a result of the concern that immigrants were taking too many jobs. Programs to promote immigration to the state were abandoned until 1913, when another act was passed providing for a commissioner in an effort to attract people not only from Europe and Canada, but also from other states.

Poor harvests and the failed revolution of 1848 were responsible for the exodus of more than 3 million Germans from Europe to the United States. The thousands who came to Michigan played a significant role in the development of the state, particularly in education, agriculture, lumbering, and mining. Much of the state's Germanic heritage, which included a conscious effort to preserve the language and traditions of the homeland, was erased with the outbreak and outcome of World War I. In Michigan, German-Americans were urged to anglicize their names and forbidden to speak or teach the German language.

Other ethnic groups that contributed to Michigan's development were the Canadians, both English-speaking and French-speaking, who were quickly assimilated into American society; the Irish, who settled statewide and became an important political force in the city of Detroit; and the Dutch, who settled between the Grand and Kalamazoo rivers and were instrumental in establishing the furniture industry of Grand Rapids and the fruit and celery-growing industries of southwestern Michigan. In the Upper Peninsula, Cornish miners and a steady stream of Finns, Swedes, Norwegians, and Italians, who came after the Civil War, provided the human labor necessary to support the area's mining and lumbering enterprises.

By the turn of the century, a new wave of immigrants was pouring into the country and state. Unlike their predecessors, these immigrants were from southern and eastern Europe, particularly Poland, Austria-Hungary, Italy, and the Balkan States. These people were eager to reap the benefits of the American dream. The announcement by **Henry Ford** on January 5, 1914, that the Ford Motor Company would pay $5 for a day's work attracted many immigrants to Michigan and enticed residents of rural Michigan to migrate to urban areas to take advantage of job opportunities.

Between 1910 and 1930, Michigan was one of the fastest-growing states in the nation. This growth, which occurred mostly in southern Michigan, especially in the auto boom counties of Wayne, Oakland, and Genesee, expedited the state's transformation from rural-agrarian to urban-industrial. When the **influx of immigrants was restricted by Congress in 1924**, the state's industrial base began attracting workers from the South. While all major industrial centers continued to experience population growth, the city of Detroit was the chief destination for migrating southerners.

The Progressive Era

At the turn of the century, the forces of industrialization and dramatic population growth, together with urbanization and immigration, were forging a much different socioeconomic climate in Michigan. The lands of the northern Lower Peninsula and eastern Upper Peninsula had been stripped of pine and many lumber boomtowns had died out. The **state's economy underwent a transformation** from an extractive or resource-exploiting economy to a processing or industrial economy.

Between 1850 and 1900, the state population increased by over 600%, from 396,654 to 2,410,982. In addition, by 1900, nearly 40% of the state's population lived in urban areas. With increasing urbanization and industrialization came urban concerns, such as police and fire protection, water supply and sewage disposal, public health, and transportation.

This era gave rise to the **Progressive movement**, a national campaign for extensive economic, political, and social reforms manifested in different ways throughout the state and nation. Among the governmental reforms that characterized this movement were women's suffrage, primary elections, local home rule, the direct election of United States senators, and the initiative and referendum. Progressives also advocated measures, such as antitrust laws and railroad rate controls, that were designed to curb what they perceived to be big business's disregard for the public welfare. The agenda for social reform included labor safety and child labor laws, workers' disability compensation, and prohibition.

Virtually all of these reforms were considered and adopted in some form in Michigan. Hazen S. Pingree, a successful businessman who became mayor of Detroit and then governor of Michigan from 1897 to 1900, advocated many of these reforms, but was not successful in securing their adoption. Several of his gubernatorial successors, including Fred M. Warner (1905-1910), Chase S. Osborn (1911-1912), and Woodbridge N. Ferris (1913-1916), were responsible for achieving that success. During this period, Michigan revised its constitution. Though the **Constitution of 1908** was largely a reorganization of its 1850 predecessor, it did offer substantive changes that altered the relationship between state and local government. It had been the responsibility of the Legislature to both provide and amend the charters of local units with local legislation. The new constitution required the Legislature to enact statutes affording local units home rule powers and curbed the use of local legislation. Advocates of direct democracy, the initiative and the referendum, were initially disappointed by the limited form adopted in the new constitution. However, they were successful in expanding that power through an amendment adopted in 1913. Other reforms, such as the direct primary and workers' disability compensation, were also eventually adopted.

While the temperance movement in Michigan first surfaced in the mid-nineteenth century, support waned until the early twentieth century. In 1916, spurred by the efforts of such organizations as the Anti-Saloon League, the electorate approved a **prohibition amendment** to the state constitution by a substantial margin. Michigan thereby became officially "dry" more than a year before the controversial prohibition amendment to the U.S. Constitution was adopted. This prohibition experiment proved as unpopular in Michigan as it was elsewhere. With the escalating crime rates associated with the smuggling of liquor (Michigan's border with Canada was the entryway for much of the country's illicit spirits) and the financial crisis brought about by the Great Depression, support for legalizing liquor grew steadily. In 1932, Michigan voters repealed the state prohibition amendment, and on April 10, 1933, a state convention ratified the Twenty-First Amendment to the U.S. Constitution, ultimately ending prohibition on the national level.

Women's rights advocates had lobbied for women's suffrage in Michigan for many years. By 1867, taxpaying women were permitted to vote in school elections. The issue of women's suffrage was debated extensively during the Constitutional Convention of 1907-1908, and the Constitution of 1908 granted taxpaying women the right to vote on questions involving the expenditure of

public money. In 1912, a proposed constitutional amendment extending full voting rights to women was defeated by a narrow margin. The next year, another women's suffrage amendment was submitted to the voters, who once again rejected the proposal, this time by a substantial margin. The voters approved an amendment to the state constitution in 1918 **granting women voting rights in all Michigan elections**. When the Legislature ratified the Nineteenth Amendment to the U.S. Constitution on June 10, 1919, women were accorded full voting rights in all elections.

Women's suffrage movement in Michigan.

By the 1920s, Michigan's state governmental structure had evolved into a loose conglomeration of agencies, boards, and commissions, many of which were created to address the various problems associated with an emerging urban/industrial society and were independent of gubernatorial control. Elected in 1920 and returned to office for two additional terms, Governor Alex J. Groesbeck (1921-1926) successfully **streamlined and consolidated the executive branch of government**. At his urging, the Legislature enacted a statute creating the State Administrative Board to set administrative policy. Among the important administrative reforms implemented was the merging of thirty-three boards and agencies into five new departments — Agriculture, Conservation, Labor, Public Safety, and Welfare.

The Olds Motor Works in Lansing.

The Automobile

Although Michigan was not the birthplace of the automobile, no other state is more renowned for having put the nation, and indeed the world, on wheels. The automobile revolutionized American culture and society, affecting mobility, housing, clothing, morals, and leisure habits, and also had a **dramatic impact on the economic growth of the state** of Michigan. Automobile manufacturing in Michigan did not occur by accident. Between 1850 and 1900, the state's manufacturing capacity had grown considerably. The availability of raw materials and affordable transportation were also crucial factors. Enormous wealth had been generated by the lumber barons of the late nineteenth century and a host of enterprises related to timber resources sprang up, including a carriage and wagon industry. These factors, together with the presence of some of the most gifted and innovative technical minds in the world, combined to make Michigan the auto capital. By 1940, 60% of the world's automobiles were assembled in Michigan and nearly all passenger car manufacturers had plants within 250 miles of Detroit.

Ransom E. Olds of Lansing was one of the early automakers instrumental in popularizing this "newfangled machine." His success in the marketplace at the turn of the century inspired thousands of eager entrepreneurs to enter the auto industry. The most successful of these was undoubtedly **Henry Ford**. By concentrating on mass production techniques and reducing costs to produce an affordable, dependable, and durable auto, Ford became the industry's first true giant. In 1908, after years of experimenting with varying models, Ford introduced what would become America's most famous automobile — the **Model T** or "Tin Lizzie." The instant popularity of this vehicle and Ford's ability to mass produce it while passing on savings in production to the consumer through reduced prices helped propel the company to the top. By the 1920s, Ford had secured over half of the entire sales market.

Another of the great entrepreneurs of this era, **William Crapo Durant**, was the grandson of former Governor Henry Crapo (1865-1868), one of Michigan's most successful lumber dealers. A successful carriage maker, Durant assumed management of the struggling Buick Motor Company in 1904 and quickly transformed it into one of the nation's leading automakers. More importantly, he foresaw the potentially enormous public demand for automobiles and was determined to expand production capacity and introduce a wider variety of models. In 1908, he established the General Motors Company, a holding company that purchased and consolidated smaller auto firms and other auto-related businesses. Although General Motors experienced mixed fortunes in its early years and Durant was ultimately to lose control of the company not once, but twice, it was his vision and marketing ability that laid the foundation for the company's future success.

In 1922, a former General Motors executive, **Walter Chrysler**, took over the Maxwell-Briscoe Company. He reorganized the company as the Chrysler Corporation and, in addition to competing with Ford and General Motors in the mass market, targeted the luxury market, a move that would serve to insulate the company somewhat from the impact of the Great Depression.

Woodward Avenue, north of Detroit, not far from the site of the world's first mile of concrete rural highway.

Paving the Way

Michigan's first roads were constructed after the War of 1812 when Michigan was still a territory. Throughout the nineteenth century, **road construction** was a township responsibility. Due to the influence of railroads and interurban systems, the early roads were primarily "wagon roads" or "farm-to-market" routes. The growing popularity of the bicycle in the late nineteenth century generated enthusiasm for better roads, and groups such as the League of American Wheelmen began advocating road improvements. The approval by the electorate of a constitutional amendment permitting state spending on roads in 1905 marked the beginning of a new era with regard to "internal improvements."

In April 1909, the Wayne County Road Commission undertook the construction of the first mile of rural concrete highway in the country. Extending from the northerly line (Six Mile Road) of the village of Highland Park to Seven Mile Road, **Woodward Avenue** was paved with a strip of concrete eighteen feet wide and six and one-half inches thick at a cost of $13,537.59. Completed and opened for traffic in June 1909 amidst some skepticism, the Woodward Avenue project attracted road builders and engineers from across the country, who were greatly impressed with the results.

Good roads associations soon sprang up nationwide. The drive to promote better roads for auto travel was under way. By 1933, the United States boasted over 77,000 miles of rural concrete highway and nearly 25,000 miles of concrete city streets. The road-building boom reached its apex in 1956, when Congress authorized and initiated the most massive public works project in American history — the construction of the **federal interstate highway system**. The pioneering Wayne County Road Commission would go on to record a number of other "firsts," including the use of scrapers on trucks to remove snow (1915), the planting of trees to beautify highways (1918), and the painting of centerlines on highways (1920s).

The Working Class Hero

Among the reasons for the success of the Ford Motor Company was the favorable public image of founder **Henry Ford**. In today's world of hourly wages, benefit packages, and paid vacations, Ford's announcement on January 5, 1914, that he would pay his workers $5.00 for one day's work may not seem very significant, but it solidified his image as a true friend of the working class. A landmark in the history of industry, the five-dollar-day milestone represented more than a doubling of the customary autoworker wage of $2.30 per day. In less than a year, the other automakers were compelled to follow his lead.

While many have questioned Ford's true motives for making such a move, his statements that the people who assembled cars should be able to afford them elicited an enormously favorable public response. Despite the fact that many workers did not automatically qualify for the new wage and workers also had to adhere to Ford's strict moral code as enforced by the company's "sociological department," thousands flocked to the gates of the Ford plant to take advantage of the opportunity. Indeed, four days after the announcement, an angry throng of over 10,000 disappointed job seekers had to be dispersed with fire hoses when told that no more openings existed.

The **five-dollar-day rate** not only attracted more and more laborers, increasing the flow of immigrants to Michigan, it also afforded these workers with a small measure of wealth that, among other things, could be used to purchase a Ford automobile. Regardless of his motives, this historic wage helped earn Ford a reputation as an enlightened automaker.

Among other cars being manufactured in Michigan were the Columbia, Downing, Liberty, Ross, and Scripps-Booth of Detroit; the Dort and Paterson of Flint; the Briscoe, Hollier, and Handley of Jackson; and the Austin of Grand Rapids. The Michigan-based "Big Three" were supplying 75% of the nation's autos by the end of the 1920s, while a number of smaller Michigan firms continued to thrive.

The popularity of the motor car had a profound impact on virtually every aspect of the state's social and economic fabric. The meteoric **rise of the auto industry** led to the state's phenomenal population growth and accompanying social ills. Not only did Detroit swell from a population of 285,704 in 1910 to nearly 1.6 million in 1930, but other cities showed similar gains. Between 1900 and 1930, Flint's population jumped from 13,000 to more than 156,000. Dearborn's population grew from 1,000 to 50,000 during the same period, and small towns like Highland Park and Hamtramck became urban areas in less than a decade. Much of this growth resulted from the arrival of a new wave of immigrants, particularly from southern and eastern Europe.

Another offshoot of the burgeoning auto industry was the ultimate success of the "good roads movement," an initiative originally promoted by bicycle enthusiasts at the end of the nineteenth century. Under the leadership of such people as Horatio S. Earle, who became the state's first highway commissioner, the **"good roads movement"** gathered momentum. With the rapid acceptance of the automobile as the preferred mode of travel, the road-building boom began in earnest after World War I. Auto registrations in Michigan grew from 326,000 in 1919 to 1.4 million in 1929, and these motorists were able to take advantage of a growing network of roads and highways traversing the state.

The Great Depression and World War II

The unbridled optimism and progress of the 1920s died with the stock market crash of October 1929 and the ensuing Great Depression. The 1930s signaled the beginning of the **"age of isolationism,"** a period during which the mood of the nation reflected a general disdain for "internationalism" and a determination to resist involvement in the community of nations. The impact of the Great Depression was particularly acute in Michigan. The Lower Peninsula's industrial sector, the Upper Peninsula's mining industry, and agriculture were especially hard hit. Indeed, economic conditions in Michigan were such that the people suffered sooner and more severely than the rest of the nation. Unemployment figures alone provide a stark picture of the situation. By 1933, nearly 50% of the state's nonagricultural work force was unemployed, which was almost twice as high as the national rate.

Meanwhile, due in large part to the demands of an increasingly urban society, state and local expenditures grew considerably during the first part of the twentieth century. While public funds

were needed for health and sanitation, highway construction, conservation, and education, the Great Depression jeopardized progress in many of these areas. Local **relief programs** did not have the resources to respond to the crisis, and many private charitable organizations were bankrupt by 1932. Eventually, state and federal government resources were devoted to providing relief to those in need and to recovering from the economic malaise. By 1934, 800,000 of the state's 5 million residents were receiving some form of public relief. In 1932, the bonding limit of cities was raised so they could borrow money to provide more assistance. That same year, automobile weight tax funds were allocated directly to the counties. By 1933, Michigan had borrowed $21 million from the federal government through the Reconstruction Finance Corporation created under the Hoover Administration. These efforts, however, proved inadequate.

The burdens of the Depression were too much for a state tax system dependent on the property tax for revenue. Between 1914 and 1930, property taxes in Michigan had increased by 500%. Not surprisingly, by 1933, Michigan had the **highest property tax delinquency rate** in the nation. In November of 1932, voters approved an amendment to the Michigan constitution limiting property taxes to 1½% of assessed valuation, further straining available state revenues. Compelled to seek new sources of revenue, the Legislature enacted a 3% retail sales tax and forfeited the state's share of future property taxes. With the repeal of prohibition in 1933 and adoption of a state constitutional amendment authorizing the establishment of a Liquor Control Commission, a tax on the manufacture and sale of beer and wine was also enacted.

Among other measures adopted was a 1933 law providing old age assistance. And on February 14, 1933, Governor William A. Comstock (1933-1934) ordered most of the state's banks to close in an effort to save them from failure, thereby preceding the famed **"bank holiday"** declared by President Franklin Roosevelt at the national level on March 5, 1933. With many homeowners facing the possibility of losing their homes because of their failure to make mortgage payments or because of delinquent property taxes, **mortgage and land contract moratorium acts** were enacted. This legislation cancelled penalties and interest on delinquent property taxes, and provided for extensions on future property taxes. A state employment service was created to, among other things, administer the payment of unemployment insurance benefits under the Social Security Act passed by the U.S. Congress in 1935. By the end of the decade, direct relief financed by state and county funds was available. Yet, it would not be until World War II that the economy of the state and nation would recover enough to alleviate the effects of the Depression.

During this period, a sense of optimism and hope seemed to return, and by 1936 the auto industry appeared to be on the rebound. In addition, the misery and despair of the Depression were tempered somewhat by successes in the world of sports. The **Detroit Tigers** won the American League pennant in 1934 and 1935 and the World Series in 1935. Capping a truly banner year, the **Detroit Lions** won the National Football League title that same year and the **Detroit Red Wings** won their first of two consecutive Stanley Cups during the 1935-1936 season. In 1937, Detroit's own **Joe Louis** began his long reign as the heavyweight boxing champion of the world. Yet the problems of the Depression and the notion that the United States could "go it alone" in a hostile world were soon to be forgotten.

As the "Arsenal of Democracy," Michigan played an unparalleled role in fighting tyranny abroad during **World War II**. Even before the nation had been drawn into the global conflict, steps had been taken to prepare the vast industrial resources of the state for conversion to war production. The state's enormous industrial capacity, bolstered by mass production techniques, was ideally suited for the industrial and technological needs of modern warfare. The auto industry, which ceased civilian automotive production altogether in February 1942, quickly converted to the production of aircraft, tanks, guns, and other materials. By the end of the war, Michigan had contributed more than 4,000,000 engines, 25,000 tanks, and 8,500 B-24 Liberator bombers to the war effort. In terms of human resources for the armed forces, more than 600,000 Michigan men and women answered their nation's call to arms. As a result, thousands of people from other states, particularly the South, and from rural Michigan flocked to the cities to meet the demand for both skilled and nonskilled labor.

WPA projects employed thousands of displaced autoworkers.

The war effort at home. Many observers trace the origins of the modern women's movement and the growth of women in the work force to their heroic contributions as civilians during World War II.

Rosie the Riveter

Although the impact of World War II on the homefront was not nearly as traumatic for Americans as it was for people whose homelands became the world's battlefields, this global conflict had many profound influences on American society. The nature of the labor force was one of the areas that underwent dramatic change. In addition to bringing job seekers from other states to Michigan, **wartime labor shortages attracted increasing numbers of women to the war production effort**.

In 1940, there were 391,600 employed women in Michigan. By 1943, this number had more than doubled to 799,100, with women constituting nearly 35% of the nonagricultural work force. Many of those new to the labor force were older and married. What had been the domain of young, single, and relatively poor females was opened up to increasing numbers of middle-aged, middle-class mothers.

While women, particularly in the manufacturing sector, were not always welcomed with enthusiasm by their male co-workers, they became the subject of the country's publicity campaign to foster unity and patriotism for the war effort. The image of "Rosie the Riveter," the title of a popular patriotic song of the era, came to symbolize the contributions of women to the Arsenal of Democracy. Those women who had the added burden of being the head of a household were forced to endure other hardships such as meals lacking in nutrition, ration stamps for meats, sugar, butter, and coffee, and constant pleas from government to donate both certain important household commodities and time.

Organized Labor

Labor unions have existed in Michigan since statehood. The **Knights of Labor** proclaimed itself a union organized for all workers, skilled or unskilled, and succeeded in electing members to the Legislature during the 1880s. This led to the enactment of a variety of labor-oriented legislation, such as the establishment of a Michigan bureau of labor, a compulsory school education law, a ten-hour-day law, a child labor law, occupational safety laws, and a mine inspection law. But these successes were short-lived, and the Knights of Labor virtually disappeared by 1892. During the late nineteenth century and early twentieth century, the **American Federation of Labor** unsuccessfully attempted to unionize workers in the lumber, mining, and furniture industries. A bitter and sometimes violent strike of Upper Peninsula copper miners in 1913 ended with some concessions from management, but without union recognition.

A number of factors combined to encourage the growth of labor unions during the 1930s. Automation in the auto industry steadily reduced the proportion of skilled laborers needed to produce automobiles. In addition, the uncertainties of the Great Depression and the pro-labor New Deal environment revived the dormant labor movement. At this time, the **United Automobile Workers**, which had affiliated with the **Committee for Industrial Organization** and sought to organize the industry's growing unskilled labor force, began to assert itself. In 1936, the union targeted the General Motors Corporation, initiating a series of "sit-down" strikes throughout the country.

On December 30, 1936, the most famous of these confrontations, the **Flint sit-down strike**, began. As the strike dragged on, violence erupted between strikers and police. Governor Frank Murphy (1937-1938), who had just taken office, sent the National Guard to restore order, but refused to direct them to break the strike. Following intense negotiations between management and labor initiated by Governor Murphy, General Motors acquiesced and accepted the UAW as the sole bargaining agent for the workers. Before it ended, this strike and others throughout the country had idled 150,000 workers and closed more than sixty plants in fourteen states. While Chrysler and other smaller auto companies quickly recognized the UAW after brief work stoppages, the Ford Motor Company resisted the closed shop until 1941. The triumph of organized labor signaled a new era not only in American industry, but also in the politics of the Great Lake State.

Postwar Politics

One of the major developments of the post-World War II years in Michigan was the emergence of a competitive **two-party political arena**. Beginning with the Depression, the Democratic Party made inroads into what had been a Republican-dominated state since the 1850s. Democrats captured both houses of the Legislature in the 1932 election, lost both in the following election, and regained both in 1936, only to lose both once again in 1938. Labor union leadership, particularly the UAW, became much more active in politics in the postwar era, reflecting that union's interest in social issues beyond the workplace. After a disastrous 1946 election for the Democratic Party in Michigan, a new liberal-labor coalition emerged within the party and eventually wrested control. In 1948, **G. Mennen Williams** won the first of what would be six terms as Michigan's governor. That same year, a 95-5 Republican majority in the House was reduced to 61-39, while in the Senate, the Democrats gained an additional five seats, going from 28-4 to a 23-9 margin. The electoral support of blacks, whose population had more than doubled between 1940 and 1950, was another crucial factor in the resurgence of the Democratic Party. Beginning in the 1950s through the present day, Michigan politics reflect the characteristics of a highly competitive two-party state.

In national politics, Republican **U.S. Senator Arthur H. Vandenberg** emerged as one of the nation's foremost spokespersons in the area of foreign policy. During a distinguished career in the U.S. Senate, which began with his appointment in 1928 to fill a vacancy, Vandenberg made a significant and lasting contribution to the quickly evolving role of the United States in world affairs. Originally a staunch isolationist, he became the chief architect of the bipartisan postwar foreign policy that recognized the country's international responsibilities and resulted in such initiatives as the United Nations Charter, the Marshall Plan, and the North Atlantic Treaty Organization.

The 1950s

The 1950s marked an era of remarkable growth and prosperity in Michigan. Only Florida and California exceeded Michigan's population growth during the 1950s. The state's school-age population increased by over 50% between 1950 and 1958, straining the state's school system. Public demand led to a great **expansion of the state's educational system**, including more classrooms and teachers, the establishment of seven new community colleges, and important additions to a variety of higher education facilities.

As a state of both vast and unique dimensions, Michigan historically encountered problems of a geographic nature. Calls for the building of a bridge traversing the Straits of Mackinac and linking the two peninsulas began as early as 1884. The rapid growth of the automobile industry and the construction of Michigan's highway system generated further interest in such a project. In 1923, a state ferry service was established to facilitate traffic between the peninsulas. A report prepared by the State Highway Department in 1928 indicated that a bridge was feasible, but the onset of the Great Depression temporarily quelled enthusiasm for a bridge. Responding to the possible availability of federal public works funds, the Legislature created a Mackinac Straits Bridge Authority in 1934. However, its proposals were rejected by the federal government and the outbreak of World War II once again stalled bridge proponents.

The state's active promotion of overall economic development and the tourist industry also contributed to support for a bridge. An Economic Development Department was created in 1947 to coordinate efforts to strengthen and diversify the state's economy. The Michigan Tourist Council, established in 1945, promoted the state as a desirable destination for vacationers. Businesses related to the tourist industry prospered and efforts to capitalize on the growth continued. In 1950, the Mackinac Bridge Authority was reconstituted and, after the marketing of bonds to finance the project, work on the bridge began in 1954. The **Mackinac Bridge** officially opened on November 1, 1957, and Michigan's ultimate "internal improvement" was complete.

When the Mackinac Bridge opened in 1957, it represented an engineering marvel as well as the fulfillment of the dream of connecting Michigan's two great peninsulas.

Civil Rights

The struggle for social justice and equality epitomized by the **civil rights movement** characterized the decade of the 1960s. Racial tensions had erupted into violence on a number of occasions throughout Michigan's history. Indeed, the abolition movement of the antebellum and Civil War era flourished despite the widely held discriminatory attitudes toward blacks. In 1863, following the issuance of the Emancipation Proclamation and the initiation of a national draft, riots broke out in a number of cities in the North, including Detroit. As the city's black population increased dramatically in the twentieth century there were other incidents of racial unrest. Housing shortages, prejudice, and segregationist sentiments were instrumental in an outbreak of violence in 1925, when a black physician, Dr. Ossian Sweet, moved into a predominantly white neighborhood. Sweet's family was met by an angry mob of whites gathered outside their home. Shots were fired, resulting in the death of a bystander, and Dr. Sweet and his family were arrested and charged with murder. Although the persuasive arguments of the legendary **Clarence Darrow** led to the doctor's acquittal, racial tensions remained unchanged. In June 1943, a number of race riots broke out in several cities in the North and West, but the worst was in Detroit. After only one day of sustained violence, thirty-four people had died, hundreds were injured, and property loss was substantial.

There had been progress in Michigan over the years to preserve and protect civil rights. Throughout the state's history, laws were enacted to prohibit racial segregation in public education, to safeguard the demand of equal public accommodations, and to outlaw discrimination in the selection and qualification of jurors. In 1955, a Fair Employment Practices Commission was established to provide remedies for discrimination in employment opportunities. The 1963 Constitution contains strong provisions protecting civil rights, including the creation of a bipartisan **Civil Rights Commission** to investigate alleged discriminatory activities.

These initiatives, however, were not enough. On July 23, 1967, police raided an illegal drinking establishment in Detroit. Bystanders protested the arrests, and soon the nation's worst civil disturbance was under way as an astonished public followed the spectacle via national television newscasts. Before state and federal troops restored a semblance of order, forty-three people were killed, over 1,000 injured, more than 7,000 arrested, and property damage exceeding $50 million was incurred. This tragedy, one of several urban riots throughout the country, represented just one of a number of violent episodes that characterized the 1960s.

From the ashes of the riot emerged such positives as the **New Detroit Committee**, established to provide a forum for the city's community leaders to discuss the city's problems, and legislation designed to prohibit discrimination in the sale or rental of residential property.

Con-Con

The 1960s also marked a milestone in the development of state government. Michigan's evolution from rural-agrarian to urban-industrial was nearly complete as evidenced by the fact that over half of the state's population resided in southeastern Michigan. The politics of the 1950s had been marked by stalemate and, in part, represented the ongoing conflict between a dwindling rural minority that enjoyed certain political advantages and a growing and restless urban and suburban majority determined to gain a stronger voice. Moreover, a **general dissatisfaction with the governmental structure** of the state led to a consensus among a host of civic organizations that the 1908 constitution was outmoded and the root cause of the state's political immobilization.

A coalition of concerned citizens and reform groups sharing a desire to modernize Michigan's governmental structure succeeded in winning public approval for a revision of the state constitution. On April 3, 1961, voters approved a referendum to call a **constitutional convention**. The margin of victory in this referendum was achieved through majority votes in only Macomb, Oakland, Washtenaw, and Wayne Counties; the state's other seventy-nine counties opposed the proposal.

Legislative apportionment was one of the most intensely debated issues addressed by the delegates to the constitutional convention. However, decisions issued by the United States Supreme Court, both during and after the Constitutional Convention of 1961-1962, ultimately took precedence over Michigan's constitutional apportionment provisions. These decisions established the **"one person, one vote" principle** for state legislatures and had a dramatic impact in Michigan and across the country. Michigan voters adopted the new constitution on April 1, 1963. Among other things, the new constitution strengthened the governor's powers, particularly over the executive branch. In fiscal matters, the new document required balanced budgets and public approval of borrowing while prohibiting the adoption of a graduated income tax.

The decade of the 1960s began with promise, optimism, and great expectations. By its end, a host of social problems such as pollution, drug abuse, crime, poverty, and discrimination, many of which reflected the consequences of rapid growth and urbanization, posed major obstacles to continued progress and prosperity.

Environmental Concerns

If there is one recurring theme that has transcended all of Michigan's historical eras, it is the importance of natural resources to the growth and development of the state. Whether it was the early fur trade, the discovery of mineral deposits, the development of agriculture, the harvesting of the state's forests, or the growth of manufacturing, Michigan's resources have always played an integral role in the state's economy. Of course, the state's most visible and abundant resource is water. The Great Lakes are the largest single reservoir of fresh water in the world, and Michigan's geographic location within their watershed makes its stake in their protection and preservation especially high. In the wake of each wave of Michigan's economic development, there have been important lessons to be learned about the finite nature of the state's unique resources. While **environmental protection** and quality became major policy issues during the 1960s and 1970s, Michigan's involvement with environmental quality and the law can be traced back many years. With the creation of the Department of Conservation (forerunner to the Department of Natural Resources) in 1921, the Legislature recognized the state's responsibility to "protect and conserve the natural resources of the State of Michigan." Michigan's uniqueness has made it a focal point for the consideration of environmental issues. At the same time, the state's economy continues to depend on heavy manufacturing, farming, and tourism. The process of balancing the state's economic interests with this commitment to protect natural resources is an arduous one, but the people of Michigan have taken these lessons to heart.

The drafters of the Constitution of 1963 considered environmental protection important enough to include a mandate in the constitution directing the Legislature to protect the air, water, and other natural resources of the state from pollution, impairment, and destruction. Beginning in 1968 and repeatedly thereafter, the people of Michigan have demonstrated this commitment at the polls. That year, voters approved measures authorizing the issuance of $335 million in full faith and credit bonds for the prevention and abatement of water pollution and $100 million in full faith and credit bonds for funding public recreational facilities and programs. Concerns over litter led to the overwhelming approval of a citizen initiative in 1976 to enact a state law to prohibit the use of nonreturnable beverage containers. Michigan became one of the first states in the nation to require deposits for returnable containers. In 1984, the electorate approved an amendment to the state constitution establishing a **Natural Resources Trust Fund** to be used for, among other things, the acquisition of land for recreational uses or protection of the land because of its environmental importance or its scenic beauty. A $660 million environmental bond issue approved by voters in 1988 established a fund to clean up pollution sites and to provide money for solid waste management, wastewater treatment, and Great Lakes protection. An additional $140 million recreational bond issue was approved at the same time to finance state and local public recreation projects. In 1994, the public approved a state parks measure to provide a more permanent funding source for the maintenance and operation of Michigan's ninety-six state parks. Again in 1998, Michigan voters expressed their appreciation for our natural resources by authorizing a major bond program called the **Clean Michigan Initiative**.

Restructuring and Global Competition

As noted earlier, Michigan's economy has weathered many boom and bust cycles. Early fortunes were made and lost in fur trading, mining, and lumbering, but the state always rebounded. The 1970s presented another difficult challenge to the state when the **OPEC oil embargo** led to a sharp 23 percent drop in domestic auto sales in 1974 and sent the state into a deep recession. Intense competition from overseas automakers, who produced more fuel-efficient cars, cut further into Michigan's share of the market. These developments made clear to leaders in both the public and private sectors that it was necessary to further diversify Michigan's economy to reduce its dependency on the fortunes of the auto industry. Accordingly, the state has undergone a slow, but steady, economic restructuring since the mid-1970s. During the **1979-1982 recession**, the state lost over 300,000 of its manufacturing jobs. In contrast, service sector employment more than doubled between 1970 and 1990, generating over 530,000 new jobs. To establish and maintain a competitive position in a global economy, the state will likely continue this transition from a manufacturing to a service-oriented economy. With the changing nature of the technology and global strategies, even as the manufacturing sector recovers, there will likely be fewer of these types of jobs in the future. While many see this transition as necessary, it will not come without obstacles and challenges. Questions regarding life-styles, wages, and benefits will need to be addressed. However, Michigan's track record of adapting to change certainly bodes well for the future.

School Finance Reform and Education

Property taxes have served as a major source of revenue for governments since the colonial days. Michigan's first comprehensive property tax law was enacted by the Territorial Legislature in 1817 and a property tax was imposed in 1835 to finance the state's first constitutional convention. Over time, property taxes became the principal source for funding the public schools. As the property tax burden grew heavier, citizens expressed a desire to address the problem. In 1978, voters approved a **tax limitation amendment** to the state constitution that restricted the growth of tax revenues, but this measure did not address education finance.

For years, Michigan's heavy reliance on local property taxes to fund education and inequities in spending among school districts generated attempts to reform the education finance system. From 1970 to 1994, voters rejected a dozen ballot proposals concerning money for education and/or property taxes! Countless legislative plans and proposals of citizens and groups on this issue were thwarted even before reaching the ballot. The issue received national media attention when a small rural school district in the northern part of the state closed its schools in March 1993, three months before the end of the usual school year, because it had exhausted its revenues. In 1993, when the Legislature enacted legislation **eliminating local property taxes as a source of K-12 funding**, it became necessary to adopt a new system to fund schools. This time, the electorate was presented with two options — either approve a plan increasing the state sales tax to make up the lost funding or allow a statutory plan relying on an increased state income tax to take effect. The option chosen by voters in every previous ballot question — maintaining the status quo — was not available. On March 15, 1994, voters overwhelmingly approved the sales tax plan.

Coinciding with the call for education finance reform was a demand for **educational reform**. Such movements have sprung up periodically in history. The latter part of the 19th century witnessed a drive to improve curricula and instructional methods that were judged to be inferior to methods used in Europe. A strong "back-to-basics" movement arose in the early 1950s and the enactment of the National Defense Education Act of 1958, a direct response to the Soviet Union's launching of Sputnik, signaled a change to a new curriculum that emphasized science and mathematics. When the National Commission on Excellence in Education issued *A Nation at Risk: The Imperative for Education Reform* in 1983, another educational reform movement was initiated, and Michigan has responded accordingly.

School reform legislation enacted during the 1990s has defined more specific objectives for Michigan's education system. A model core curriculum, implementation of school improvement plans, addressing the problems of "at risk" children, experimentation with schools of choice and charter schools, and new strategies to address troubled districts are among the reforms that have been encouraged. With the enactment at the federal level of the Goals 2000: Educate America Act, the entire nation has become committed to better preparing our rising generations for the challenges of global competition.

The New Millennium

At the dawn of the Twenty-First Century and the start of the new millennium, Michigan is a far different state than the one that greeted 1900. At that time, the work of several visionary mechanics was touching off the age of the auto for our country and the world. Led by this revolutionary device, the state was transformed from a farming and natural resource economy into a giant of heavy industry. For the first two-thirds of the century, Michigan's population skyrocketed.

By the late 1970s and early 1980s, zooming fuel costs and other factors brought the painful realities of global competition and recession. Michigan lost population, as the number of manufacturing jobs both dropped dramatically and shifted to increased use of technology. Renewed efforts to diversify the economy and accentuate service sectors took root. By the year 2000, Michigan's solid recovery and low jobless rates reflect the resiliency that has marked the state's history. While the auto industry is still a key to our economic strength, aging plants are being replaced by a new generation of facilities. Workers are reaching new levels of training to use machines and materials Henry Ford could never have imagined.

Along with the reinvigoration of the Michigan economy, the population is rebounding. Major changes are taking place in how we work, what we do, and where the customers for our goods and services live. Our agriculture faces serious threats, and our ever-mobile society is making land use a key public policy concern for many. To deal with these challenges and to maintain the gains of recent years, the state is committed to strengthening our human resources. In the information age, just as in the ages of furs, mining, and manufacturing, it is these resources — nearly 10 million strong — that will shape Michigan's destiny.

Source: Michigan Legislature, http://www.legislature.mi.gov

An Introduction to Michigan State Government

Organization

Michigan state government contains three branches: legislative, judicial and executive.

The Legislative Branch

The legislative power of the State of Michigan is vested in a bicameral (2-chamber) body comprised of a Senate and a House of Representatives. The Senate consists of 38 members who are elected by the qualified electors of districts having approximately 212,400 to 263,500 residents. Senators are elected at the same time as the governor and serve 4-year terms concurrent with the governor's term of office. Terms for senators begin on January 1, following the November general election.

The House of Representatives consists of 110 members who are elected by the qualified electors of districts having approximately 77,000 to 91,000 residents. Representatives are elected in even-numbered years to 2-year terms. Legislative districts are drawn on the basis of population figures obtained through the federal decennial census.

The state legislature enacts the laws of Michigan; levies taxes and appropriates funds from money collected for the support of public institutions and the administration of the affairs of state government; proposes amendments to the state constitution, which must be approved by a majority vote of the electors; and considers legislation proposed by initiatory petitions. The legislature also provides oversight of the executive branch of government through the administrative rules and audit processes, committees, and the budget process; advises and consents, through the Senate, on gubernatorial appointments; and considers proposed amendments to the Constitution of the United States. The majority of the legislature's work, however, entails lawmaking. Through a process defined by the state constitution, statute, and legislative rules, the legislature considers thousands of bills (proposed laws) during each 2-year session.

The Judicial Branch

The Michigan Supreme Court

The Supreme Court is the highest court in the state, hearing cases appealed to it from the Court of Appeals. In addition to its judicial duties, the Supreme Court is responsible for the general administrative supervision of all courts in the state. The Supreme Court also establishes rules for practice and procedure in all courts. The Supreme Court consists of seven justices: the chief justice and six associate justices. The justices are elected to serve eight-year terms. Every two years one justice is selected by the court as chief justice. Although justices are nominated by political parties, they are elected on a nonpartisan ballot. A candidate for the Supreme Court must be a qualified elector, licensed to practice law in Michigan, and at the time of election must be less than 70 years of age.

The Supreme Court is Michigan's court of last resort. Each year, the Supreme Court receives over 2,000 applications for leave to appeal from litigants primarily seeking review of decisions by the Michigan Court of Appeals.

The Supreme Court's authority to hear cases is discretionary. The Court grants leave to those cases of greatest complexity and public import, where additional briefing and oral argument are essential to reaching a just outcome.

Each justice is responsible for reviewing each case to determine whether leave should be granted. Cases that are accepted for oral argument may be decided by an order, with or without an opinion. These orders may affirm or reverse the Michigan Court of Appeals, may remand a case to the trial court, or may adopt a correct Court of Appeals opinion.

Cases come before the Court during a term that starts August 1 and runs through July 31 of the following year. The Court hears oral arguments in Lansing beginning in October of each term. Decisions are released throughout the term, following oral arguments.

Michigan Court of Appeals

The Michigan Court of Appeals is one of the highest volume intermediate appellate courts in the country. It was created by the 1963 Michigan Constitution and heard its first cases in January 1965. Generally, decisions from final orders of a circuit court, as well as some probate court and agency orders, may be appealed to the court as a matter of right. Other lower court or tribunal decisions may be appealed only by application for leave to appeal, i.e., with permission of the court. The court also has jurisdiction to hear some original actions, such as complaints for mandamus or superintending control against government officers or actions alleging that state law has imposed an unfunded or inadequately funded mandate on local units of government.

The Court of Appeals started with only nine judges originally. The number of judgeships steadily increased through legislation over the years to accommodate the court's growing caseload-to 12 in 1969, to 18 in 1974, to 24 in 1988, and to 28 in 1993. Due to decreased filings in recent years, the size of the court was reduced in 2012 to 24 judges, which is to be achieved through attrition over time.

The judges of the Court of Appeals sit state-wide, although they are elected or appointed from one of four districts. The districts and their office locations are as follows: District I is based in Detroit, District II is based in Troy, District III is based in Grand Rapids, and District IV is based in Lansing. Hearings are held year-round before three-judge panels in Detroit, Lansing, and Grand Rapids. There is no courtroom at the Troy location. Hearings are also scheduled in Marquette and in a northern Lower Peninsula location in the spring and fall of each year for the convenience of the parties and their attorneys in those areas. Judges are randomly assigned to panels to sit in all courtroom locations so that a variety of judicial viewpoints are considered. At least two of the three judges on a panel must agree on the ruling in a case for it to be binding. Like most appellate courts, the Court of Appeals observes the principle of stare decisis so that the holding in an earlier decision serves as binding precedent in a later appeal. When a panel expresses its disagreement with a prior opinion, the court rules provide a mechanism by which a special seven-judge "conflict panel" may be convened to resolve the conflict between the earlier opinion and the later decision. MCR 7.215(J). Decisions of the court may generally be appealed by leave application to the Michigan Supreme Court.

Circuit Court

The circuit court is the trial court with the broadest powers in Michigan. In general, the circuit court handles all civil cases with claims of more than $25,000 and all felony criminal cases (cases where the accused, if found guilty, could be sent to prison). The family division of circuit court handles all cases regarding divorce, paternity, adoptions, personal protection actions, emancipation of minors, treatment and testing of infectious disease, safe delivery of newborns, name changes, juvenile offenses and delinquency, juvenile guardianship, and child abuse and neglect. In addition, the circuit court hears cases appealed from the other trial courts or from administrative agencies. The friend of the court office is part of the family division of the circuit court and handles domestic relations cases where minor children are involved.

In addition, there is a Court of Claims for filing cases against the State of Michigan in which a claim for money damages is made. As of November 12, 2013, the Court of Claims is part of the Michigan Court of Appeals. The Court of Claims is a specialized court that handles only claims over $1,000 filed against the State of Michigan or one of its departments.

There are 57 circuit courts in Michigan. Circuit court judges are elected for six-year terms.

District Court

The district court is often called the people's court. More people have contact with the district court than any other court. The district court handles most traffic violations, all civil cases with claims up to $25,000, landlord-tenant matters, most traffic tickets, and all misdemeanor criminal cases (generally, cases where the accused, if found guilty, cannot be sentenced to more than one year in jail). In addition, small claims cases are heard by a division of the district court. In Michigan, a few municipalities have chosen to retain a municipal

court rather than create a district court. The municipal courts have limited powers and are located in Grosse Pointe, Grosse Pointe Farms, Grosse Pointe Park, and Grosse Point Shores/Grosse Pointe Woods.

There are approximately 100 district courts in Michigan. District court judges are elected for six-year terms.

Probate Court

The probate court handles wills, administers estates and trusts, appoints guardians and conservators, and orders treatment for mentally ill and developmentally disabled persons.

There are 78 probate courts in Michigan; probate judges are elected for six-year terms.

Friend of the Court Bureau

The Friend of the Court Bureau (FOCB) was established to provide circuit courts across the state with management assistance in operating local friend of the court (FOC) offices, including development of local policies and procedures.

Executive Branch

In addition to the Governor and Lieutenant Governor, Michigan's voters elect two other executive branch officials statewide—the Secretary of State and the Attorney General. While candidates for the governor's office are chosen in the August primary election, candidates for the others are nominated at the regular year between presidential elections (voters cast one vote jointly for Governor and Lieutenant Governor). An amendment to the constitution adopted by the voters in 1992 limits these elected executives to two terms (eight years). This limitation applies to terms if office beginning on or after January 1, 1993. The 1963 Constitution requires that all permanent agencies or commissions, except universities, be assigned to one of a maximum of twenty principal departments. The principal departments are:

Agriculture and Rural Development

The mission of the Michigan Department of Agriculture & Rural Development is, "Assure the food safety, agricultural, environmental, and economic interests of the people of the State of Michigan are met through service, partnership and collaboration."

Attorney General

The attorney general is the lawyer for the State of Michigan. When public legal matters arise, he renders opinions on matters of law, and provides legal counsel for the legislature and for each officer, department, board, and commission of state government. He provides legal representation in court actions and assists in the conduct of official hearings held by state agencies.

Civil Rights

The Department of Civil Rights, in implementing the mission of the commission, secures the full enjoyment of civil rights guaranteed by law and the constitution through the elimination of discrimination. This is accomplished through the investigation and resolution of complaints of discrimination; outreach and education programs designed to promote voluntary compliance with civil rights laws; mediation; referral; crisis intervention; anti-hate crime programming; and the dissemination of information which explains citizen rights and responsibilities provided in a legal framework.

Civil Service Commission

The Civil Service Commission has overall responsibility for regulating conditions of employment for classified civil service workers in all of the departments of the executive branch of state government.

Corrections

The Department of Corrections administers Michigan's adult prison, probation, and parole systems. The department has jurisdiction over all adults convicted of felonies who are sentenced to prison. Convicted felons who are not sentenced to prison terms are either sentenced to a county jail term or are supervised in the community through a system called probation. Probation services for felons are provided by the department for the various felony courts in Michigan's counties.

Education

The Department of Education, under the direction of the Superintendent of Public Instruction, carries out the policies of the State Board of Education. The Department implements federal and state legislative mandates in education.

Environmental Quality

The department is dedicated to protecting human health and to preserving a healthy environment. The department will exemplify good environmental stewardship and affirm that a healthy environment is critical to our social, cultural, and economic well-being. The department will protect human health and the environment while fostering a healthy economy by effective and efficient administration of agency programs, and by providing for use of innovative strategies. This is being accomplished in a manner that is rebuilding the integrity of the department as an environmental protection agency that carries out this mission in a professional, just, and productive manner.

Health and Human Services

The Michigan Department of Health and Human Services strives to promote better health outcomes, reduce health risks, and support stable and safe families while encouraging self-sufficiency.

Insurance and Financial Services

The Department of Insurance and Financial Services (DIFS) is responsible for regulating Michigan's financial industries, including banks, credit unions, insurance, mortgage companies, and other consumer finance lenders.

Licensing and Regulatory Affairs

The Department of Licensing and Regulatory Affairs (LARA) supports business growth and job creation while safeguarding Michigan's citizens through a simple, fair, efficient and transparent regulatory structure.

Military and Veterans Affairs

The Department of Military and Veterans Affairs, also known as the state military establishment, has 3 primary missions: to execute the duties laid down by various statutes and the governor, administration of state-supported veterans programming, and military preparedness to assist both state and federal authorities. The Michigan Army and Air National Guard constitute the armed forces of the state and serve under the orders of the governor as commander-in-chief. The governor appoints an adjutant general to serve as commanding general of the Michigan National Guard and as director of the Department of Military and Veterans Affairs.

Natural Resources

The Michigan Department of Natural Resources is committed to the conservation, protection, management, use and enjoyment of the state's natural and cultural resources for current and future generations.

Secretary of State

The Department of State is the oldest department of Michigan state government and is administered by the secretary of state. Elected to a 4-year term, the secretary of state is a member of the executive branch of government and has constitutional as well as statutory duties.

State Police

The purpose of the department is to provide 24-hour statewide quality police service for the safety and protection of the people and their property in the state of Michigan. Its primary responsibilities are to reduce the opportunities for crime, to reduce traffic accidents through diligent and fair enforcement of the laws of this state, and to act as a first responder to any citizen's needs that can be addressed through the resources of the criminal justice system.

Talent and Economic Development

Joining job creation and economic development efforts under one umbrella, the Department of Talent and Economic Development consists of the Michigan Economic Development Corporation, the Michigan State Housing Development Authority, the Michigan Strategic Fund and the newly created Talent Investment Agency

(TIA). TED allows the state to leverage its ability to build talent with in-demand skills while helping state businesses grow and thrive.

Technology, Management and Budget

The Department of Technology, Management and Budget promotes a unified approach to information technology management and provides centralized administration of services including auditing, budgeting, employee resources, financial services, fleet management, mail, printing, property management, purchasing, records management, and retirement services for departments and agencies in the executive branch of state government.

Transportation

The primary functions of the Department of Transportation are the construction, improvement, and maintenance of the state highway system—the 9,620 miles of interstate, U.S.- and M-numbered highways, and the administration of other state transportation programs. Responsibilities include the development and implementation of comprehensive transportation plans for the entire state, including aeronautics and bus and rail transit, providing professional and technical assistance, and the administration of state and federal funds allocated for these programs. The director of the department is appointed by the governor, with the advice and consent of the senate.

Treasury

Treasury exists to provide quality financial, tax, and administrative services. The state treasurer acts as principal advisor to the governor on tax and fiscal policy issues. The state treasurer is the chairperson of the Michigan Debt Advisory Board, the Michigan Education Trust, the Michigan Higher Education Assistance Authority, the Michigan Higher Education Student Loan Authority, the Michigan Merit Award Board, the Michigan Municipal Bond Authority, and the Michigan School District Accountability Board.

Source: Michigan.gov, June 2015

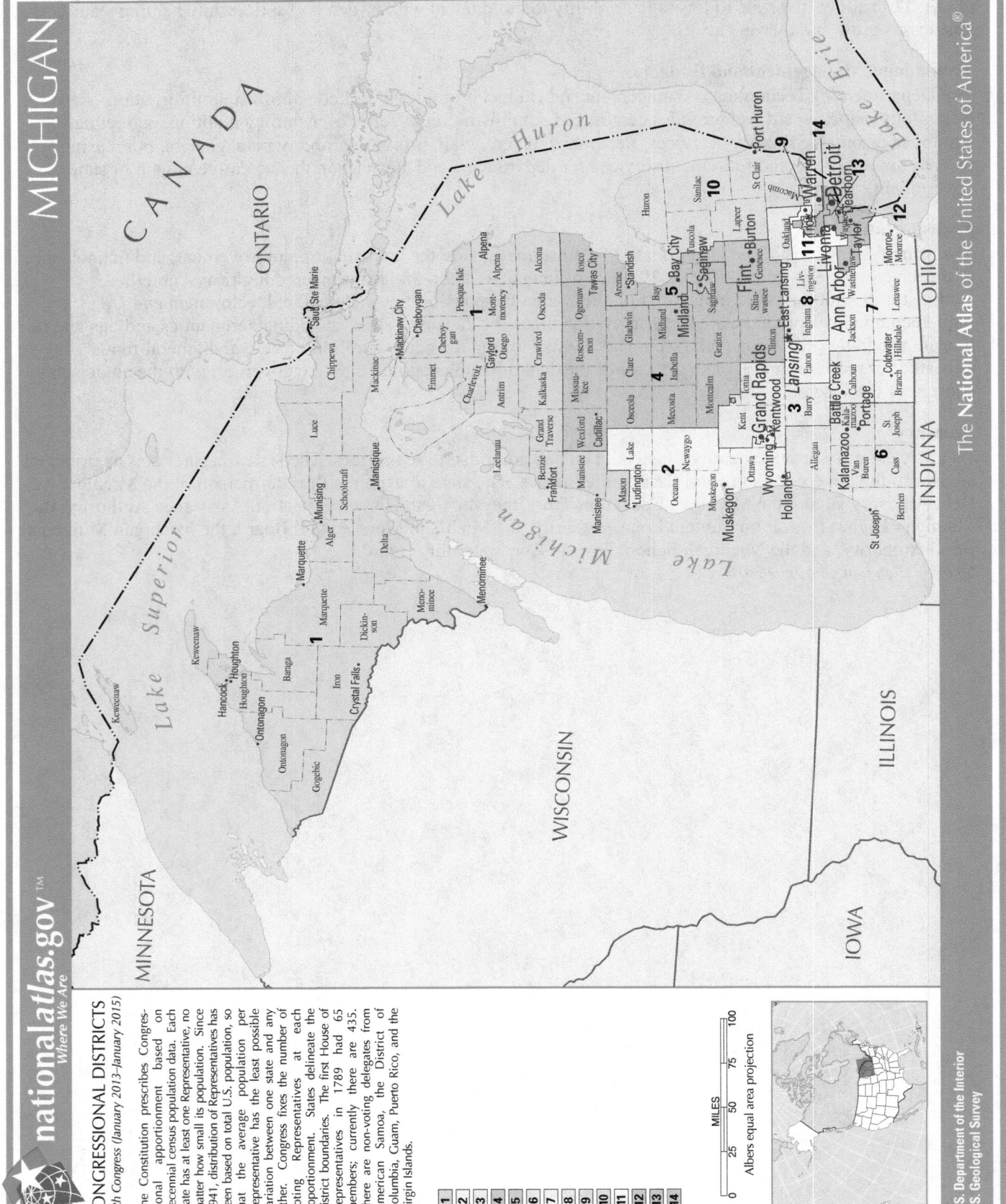

MICHIGAN

nationalatlas.gov ™
Where We Are

CONGRESSIONAL DISTRICTS
113th Congress (January 2013–January 2015)

The Constitution prescribes Congressional apportionment based on decennial census population data. Each state has at least one Representative, no matter how small its population. Since 1941, distribution of Representatives has been based on total U.S. population, so that the average population per Representative has the least possible variation between one state and any other. Congress fixes the number of voting Representatives at each apportionment. States delineate the district boundaries. The first House of Representatives in 1789 had 65 members; currently there are 435. There are non-voting delegates from American Samoa, the District of Columbia, Guam, Puerto Rico, and the Virgin Islands.

MILES

Albers equal area projection

U.S. Department of the Interior
U.S. Geological Survey

The **National Atlas** of the United States of America®

Percent of Population Who Voted for Barack Obama in 2012

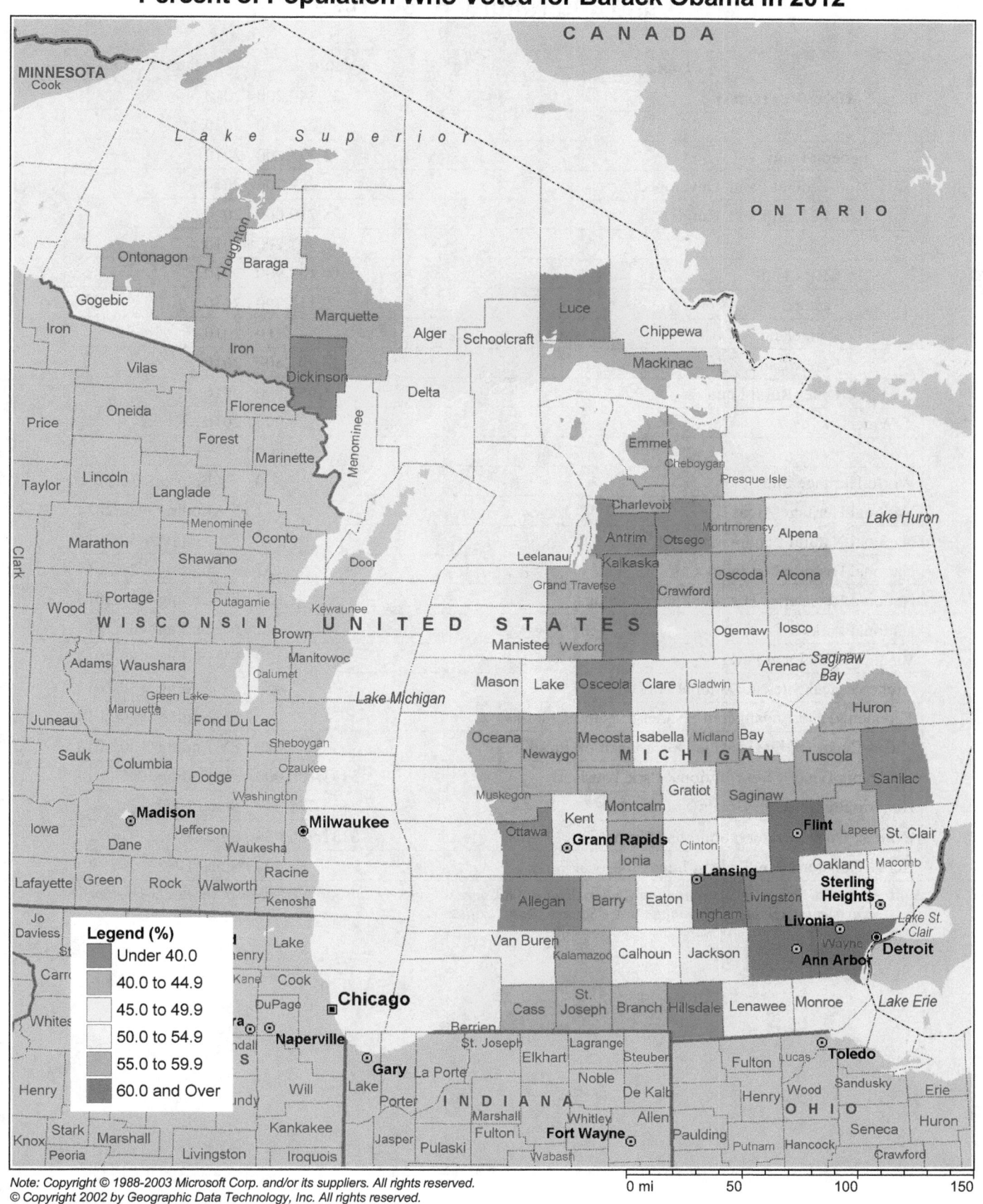

Land and Natural Resources

Topic	Value	Time Period
Total Surface Area (acres)	37,349,200	2010
Land	36,222,300	2010
Federal Land	3,273,600	2010
Non-Federal Land, Developed	4,229,700	2010
Non-Federal Land, Rural	28,719,000	2010
Cropland	7,907,200	2010
CRP Land	139,900	2010
Pastureland	2,115,700	2010
Rangeland	0.0	2010
Forest Land	16,597,400	2010
Other Rural Land	1,958,800	2010
Water	1,126,900	2010
World Heritage Sites	0	FY Ending 9/30/2014
National Heritage Areas	1	FY Ending 9/30/2014
National Natural Landmarks	12	FY Ending 9/30/2014
National Historic Landmarks	37	FY Ending 9/30/2014
National Register of Historic Places Listings	1,853	FY Ending 9/30/2014
National Parks	5	FY Ending 9/30/2014
Visitors to National Parks	1,993,139	FY Ending 9/30/2014
Archeological Sites in National Parks	458	FY Ending 9/30/2014
Threatened and Endangered Species in National Parks	3	FY Ending 9/30/2014
Places Recorded by Heritage Documentation Programs	626	FY Ending 9/30/2014
Economic Benefit from National Park Tourism	$173,100,000	FY Ending 9/30/2014
Historic Preservation Grants	$34,578,817	Since 1969
Land & Water Conservation Fund Grants	$131,985,684	Since 1965
Acres Transferred by Federal Lands to Local Parks	4,504	Since 1948

Sources: United States Department of Agriculture, Natural Resources Conservation Service, National Resources Inventory; U.S. Department of the Interior, National Park Service, State Profiles

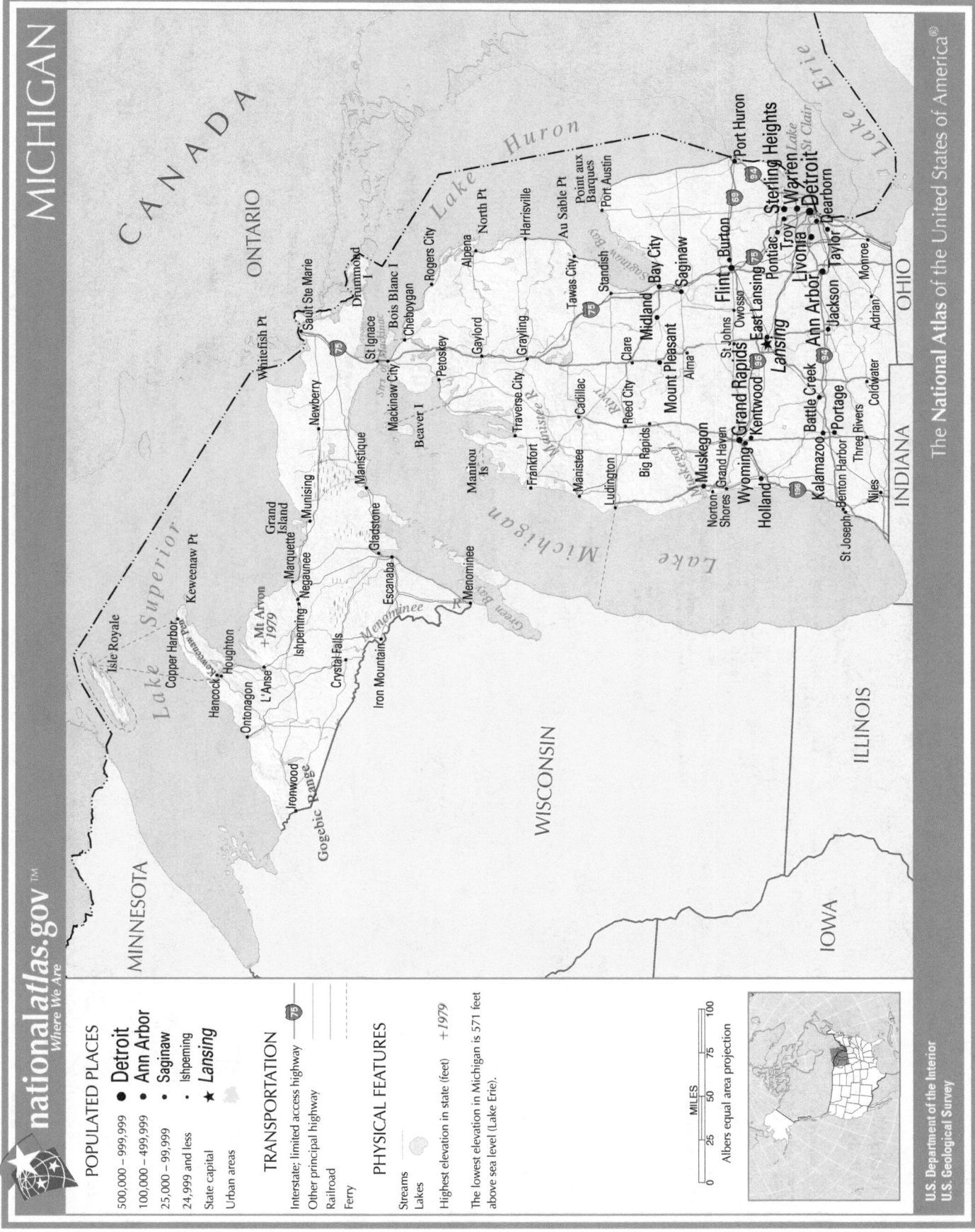

MICHIGAN

POPULATED PLACES

- **Detroit** 500,000 – 999,999
- **Ann Arbor** 100,000 – 499,999
- **Saginaw** 25,000 – 99,999
- Ishpeming 24,999 and less
- ★ *Lansing* State capital
- Urban areas

TRANSPORTATION

- 75 Interstate; limited access highway
- Other principal highway
- Railroad
- Ferry

PHYSICAL FEATURES

- Streams
- Lakes
- Highest elevation in state (feet)   + 1979

The lowest elevation in Michigan is 571 feet above sea level (Lake Erie).

MILES
0   25   50   75   100

Albers equal area projection

U.S. Department of the Interior
U.S. Geological Survey

The **National Atlas** of the United States of America®

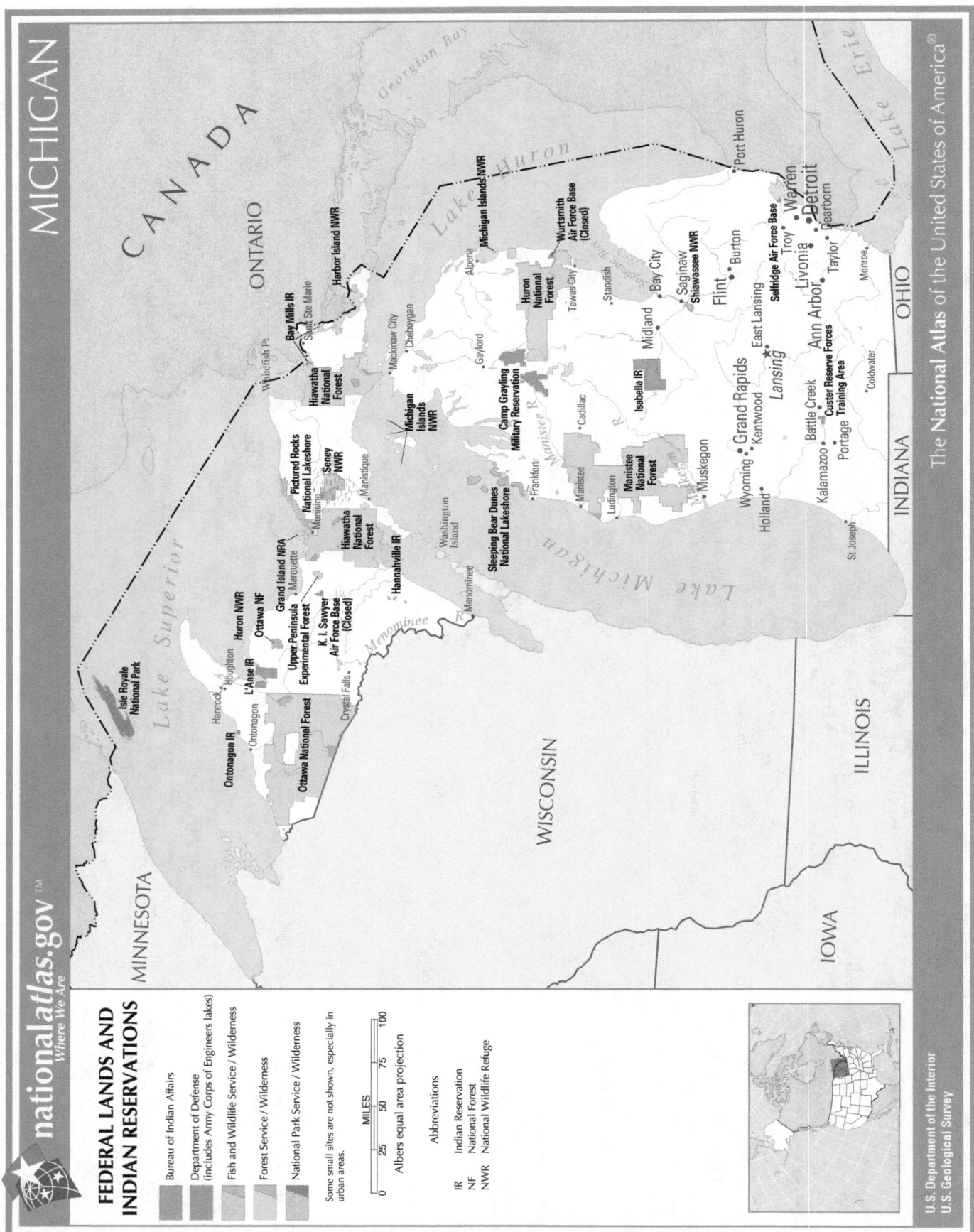

MICHIGAN

The National Atlas of the United States of America®

nationalatlas.gov™
Where We Are

FEDERAL LANDS AND
INDIAN RESERVATIONS

Bureau of Indian Affairs

Department of Defense
(includes Army Corps of Engineers lakes)

Fish and Wildlife Service / Wilderness

Forest Service / Wilderness

National Park Service / Wilderness

Some small sites are not shown, especially in
urban areas.

MILES
0   25   50   75   100
Albers equal area projection

Abbreviations

IR   Indian Reservation
NF   National Forest
NWR   National Wildlife Refuge

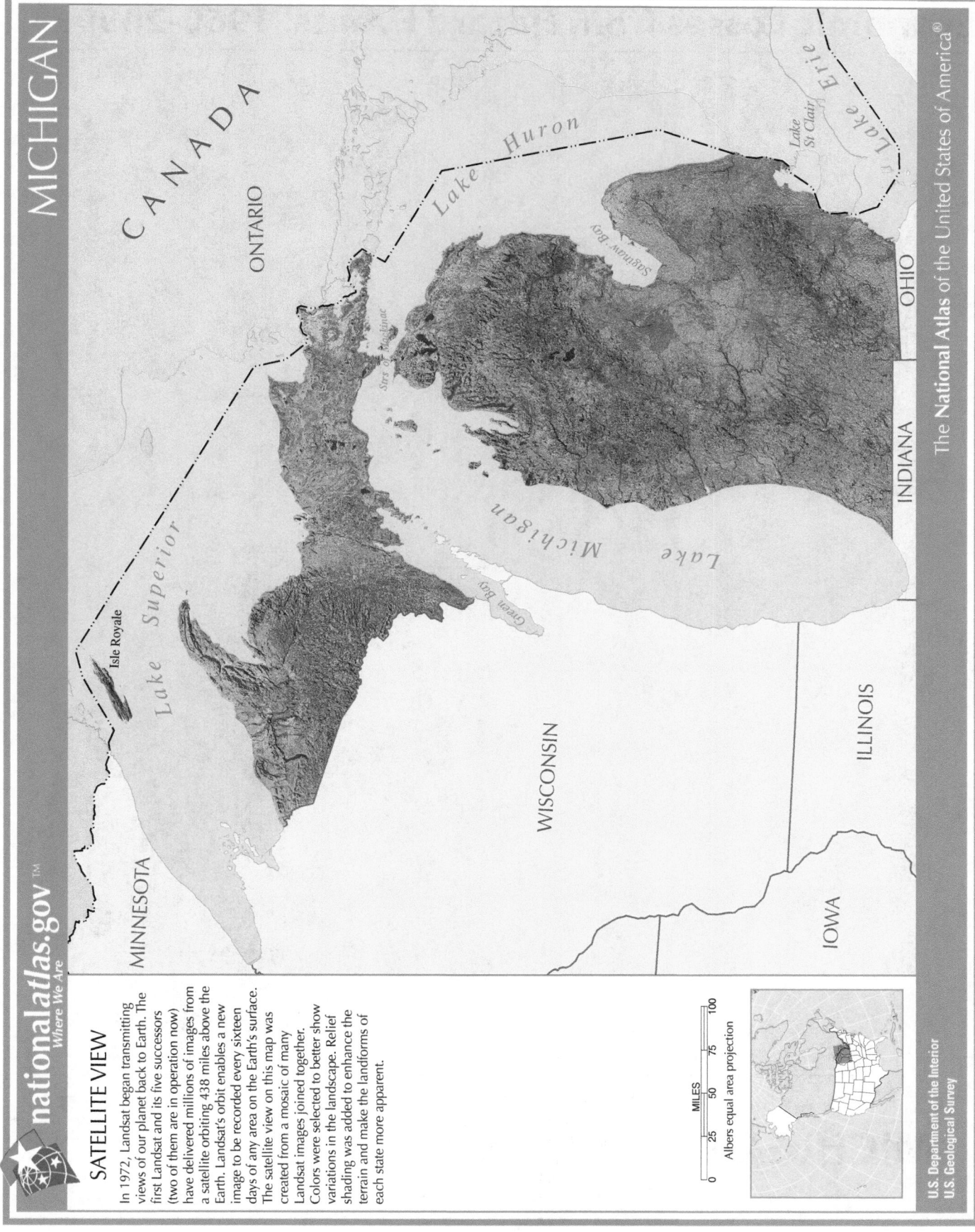

MICHIGAN

nationalatlas.gov™
Where We Are

SATELLITE VIEW

In 1972, Landsat began transmitting views of our planet back to Earth. The first Landsat and its five successors (two of them are in operation now) have delivered millions of images from a satellite orbiting 438 miles above the Earth. Landsat's orbit enables a new image to be recorded every sixteen days of any area on the Earth's surface. The satellite view on this map was created from a mosaic of many Landsat images joined together. Colors were selected to better show variations in the landscape. Relief shading was added to enhance the terrain and make the landforms of each state more apparent.

CANADA

ONTARIO

Lake Huron

Lake Superior

Isle Royale

Strs of Mackinac

Saginaw Bay

Lake Michigan

Green Bay

Lake St Clair

Lake Erie

MINNESOTA

WISCONSIN

IOWA

ILLINOIS

INDIANA

OHIO

The National Atlas of the United States of America®

MILES
0   25   50   75   100
Albers equal area projection

U.S. Department of the Interior
U.S. Geological Survey

Economic Losses from Hazard Events, 1960-2009

Minnesota

KEWEENAW

HOUGHTON

ONTONAGON

BARAGA

GOGEBIC

MARQUETTE   ALGER   LUCE   CHIPPEWA

IRON   SCHOOLCRAFT   MACKINAC

DICKINSON

DELTA

MENOMINEE

Wisconsin

EMMET   CHEBOYGAN   PRESQUE ISLE

CHARLEVOIX

ANTRIM   OTSEGO   MONTMORENCY   ALPENA

LEELANAU

BENZIE   GRAND TRAVERSE   KALKASKA   CRAWFORD   OSCODA   ALCONA

MANISTEE   WEXFORD   MISSAUKEE   ROSCOMMON   OGEMAW   IOSCO

MASON   LAKE   OSCEOLA   CLARE   GLADWIN   ARENAC

HURON

OCEANA   NEWAYGO   MECOSTA   ISABELLA   MIDLAND   BAY   TUSCOLA   SANILAC

MUSKEGON   MONTCALM   GRATIOT   SAGINAW   LAPEER

OTTAWA   KENT   IONIA   CLINTON SHIAWASSEE   GENESEE   ST. CLAIR

OAKLAND   MACOMB

ALLEGAN   BARRY   EATON   INGHAM LIVINGSTON

VAN BUREN   KALAMAZOO CALHOUN   JACKSON   WASHTENAW   WAYNE

Illinois

MONROE

BERRIEN   CASS   ST. JOSEPH   BRANCH   HILLSDALE   LENAWEE

Indiana   Ohio

MICHIGAN

Total Losses (Property and Crop)

- 3,288,641 – 7,001,016
- 7,001,017 – 15,025,876
- 15,025,877 – 58,535,790
- 58,535,791 – 117,073,748
- 117,073,749 – 960,885,454

Source: SHELDUS v. 8.0
Classification: Quantiles
Losses adjusted to 2009 Dollars
0   35   70 Miles

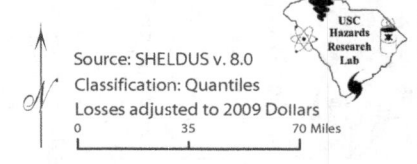

USC Hazards Research Lab

MICHIGAN
Hazard Losses ·
1960-2009

Distribution of Losses by Hazard Type
(in 2009 USD million)

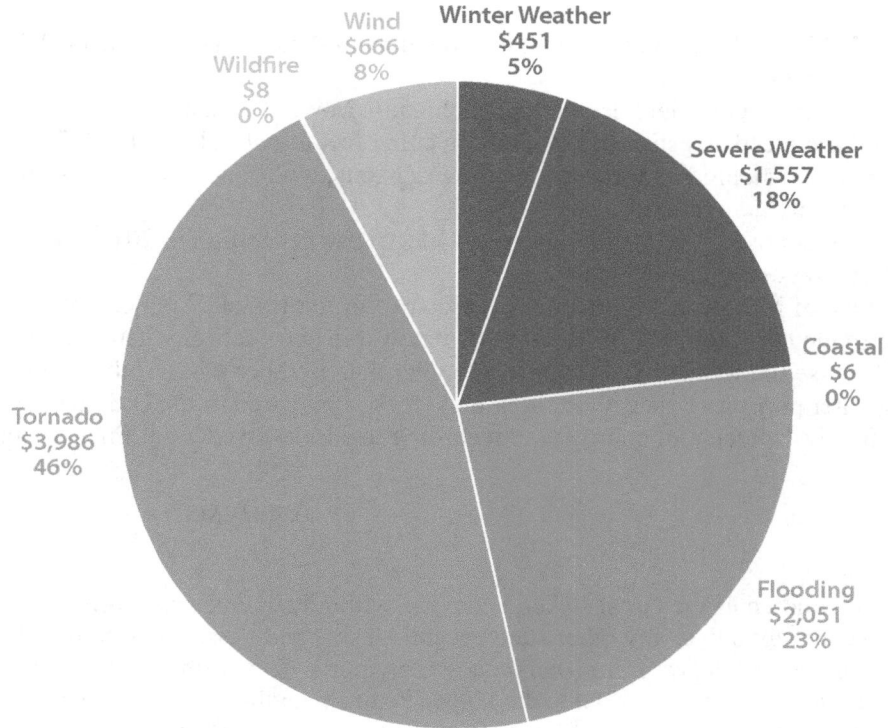

Wind
$666
8%

Winter Weather
$451
5%

Wildfire
$8
0%

Severe Weather
$1,557
18%

Coastal
$6
0%

Tornado
$3,986
46%

Flooding
$2,051
23%

Distribution of Hazard Events
(number of events)

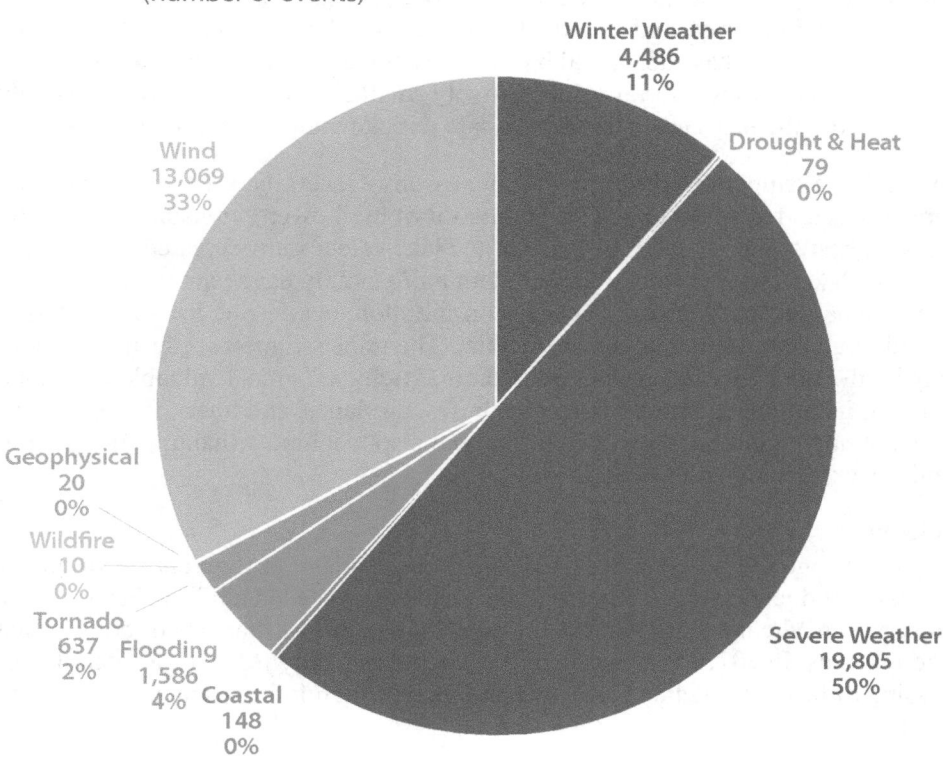

Winter Weather
4,486
11%

Drought & Heat
79
0%

Wind
13,069
33%

Geophysical
20
0%

Wildfire
10
0%

Tornado
637
2%

Flooding
1,586
4%

Coastal
148
0%

Severe Weather
19,805
50%

Michigan Energy Profile

Quick Facts

- In 2013, Michigan had more underground natural gas storage capacity–1.1 trillion cubic feet–than any other state in the nation.
- The Antrim Gas Field, located in Michigan's Lower Peninsula, is one of the nation's top 100 natural gas fields and produced an estimated 108 billion cubic feet of natural gas in 2012.
- In 2014, Michigan's three nuclear power plants, with four reactor units, provided 30% of the state's net electricity generation.
- Michigan used coal for 50% of its net electricity generation in 2014. Much of Michigan's coal is brought by rail from Wyoming and Montana.
- Much of Michigan's biomass energy comes from the state's almost 19 million acres of forest land. Biomass provided fuel for 35% of Michigan's renewable net electricity generation in 2014.
- Because the weather in Michigan is cooler than in other areas of the United States, space heating makes up a greater portion of energy use in homes (55%) compared to the U.S. average (41%), while air conditioning makes up only 1 percent of energy use, according to EIA's Residential Energy Consumption Survey.

Analysis

Overview

Michigan, known as the Great Lakes State, has within its boundaries portions of four of the five Great Lakes. The state has more shoreline than any other state except Alaska, and vessels that transit the Great Lakesâ€"Saint Lawrence Seaway arrive and depart from Michigan's many ports. The northern ends of Lake Michigan and Lake Huron divide the state into two distinct sections: the Upper Peninsula, which is lightly populated and heavily forested, and the Lower Peninsula, where most of the state's population lives and all of the major cities, manufacturing industries, and commercial agriculture are located. Michigan's largest and longest rivers are in the Lower Peninsula, but of the state's more than 150 waterfalls, all but one are located in the Upper Peninsula. With almost 40,000 square miles of the Great Lakes within its borders and thousands of smaller inland lakes and ponds, almost half of Michigan is water.

Michigan's energy resources include natural gas and crude oil, as well as renewable resources. With more than half of the state covered in forest, and abundant municipal solid waste and landfill gas provided by the state's large population, Michigan has substantial biomass resources. Dams on the state's many rivers provide hydroelectric power despite the generally level terrain and relatively small size of many of the rivers. Winds, occasionally of gale force, sweep in across the lakes and provide the state with an unobstructed wind resource.

Michigan has a temperate climate with four seasons. Generally, the Great Lakes moderate temperatures with the most extreme highs and lows occurring in the interior of the Lower Peninsula, away from the lakes. Snowfall, on the other hand, is highest along the lakes because of the lake-effect snows created by cold air blowing over the warmer lake waters. The lakes also provide Michigan with more cloudy days than most states. Michigan has a large population, ninth in the nation, and high total energy consumption, but despite its cold winters, Michigan is in the bottom one-third of all states in energy use per capita. The transportation sector is the leading energy consumer, followed closely by the industrial and residential sectors. Michigan's most valuable manufactured products are transportation equipment, including automobiles, trucks, buses, airplanes, and boats. Energy-intensive industrial activities in the state include not only automotive manufacturing, but also machinery manufacturing, fabricated metal products, chemicals, oil and gas extraction, and petroleum refining.

Petroleum

Michigan has one oil field that has produced more than 100 million barrels of oil since its discovery in 1957, and cumulative production from all fields in the state has exceeded a billion barrels. However, current crude oil production and reserves in Michigan are modest and account for far less than 1% of both the nation's total production and total proved reserves. In 2012, an upgrade of the Michigan's only refinery, located in Detroit, was completed, allowing the processing of heavy Canadian crude oils and increasing refinery capacity to 120,000 barrels per calendar day.

Several petroleum pipelines cross the state. Crude oil pipelines from western Canada enter Michigan from the northwest by way of Wisconsin and from the southwest by way of Wisconsin and Illinois. Other pipelines come up from the Gulf South. Petroleum product pipeline systems that supply Michigan markets enter the Lower Peninsula from the Chicago, Illinois, area to the southwest and also from the Toledo, Ohio, area to the southeast. There are no petroleum product pipelines in the Upper Peninsula. The majority of petroleum products consumed in Michigan are produced at refineries in Ohio, Indiana, and Illinois. The Lower Peninsula port cities of Detroit and Port Huron receive petroleum products from Canada. Port Huron also receives crude oil imports from Canada.

Petroleum is consumed in Michigan primarily as motor gasoline. Conventional motor gasoline can be sold in most of the state year-round. However, the vapor pressure of motor gasoline sold in all eight Detroit area counties during the summer ozone season is regulated to reduce emissions that contribute to ground-level ozone. Consumption of liquefied petroleum gas (LPG) is high in Michigan. The state has the largest residential LPG consumption in the nation and ranks among the top 10 in the use of LPG overall.

Natural Gas

Michigan has more than 10,000 producing natural gas wells. The Antrim Field in the northern portion of the Lower Peninsula is one of the top 100 natural gas fields in the nation as ranked by proved reserves. However, natural gas production in Michigan peaked in 1997 and is declining. The state's natural gas marketed production meets nearly one-sixth of the state's needs. Several natural gas pipelines cross Michigan on the way to markets in the northeastern United States and eastern Canada. Natural gas enters the state from Indiana, Ohio, and Wisconsin. Michigan also receives natural gas imports from Canada at St. Clair, Marysville, and Detroit. The bulk of the natural gas flowing out of Michigan flows into Canada at St. Clair, Detroit, Marysville, and Sault Ste. Marie.

Driven largely by the residential sector, Michigan's natural gas consumption is high. The state routinely ranks among the top five in residential use of natural gas and in the top 10 in total consumption. Nearly four-fifths of Michigan households use natural gas as their primary source for home heating. With more than one-tenth of U.S. capacity, Michigan has the most underground natural gas storage capacity of any state in the nation, and the second-largest number of natural gas storage fields after Pennsylvania. During the high-demand winter months, natural gas is withdrawn from storage to supply Michigan and neighboring states.

Coal

Although Michigan produced substantial amounts of coal between 1860 and 1949, there are no active coal mines in the state. However, Michigan's ports handle almost one-third of all Great Lakes coal shipments. The state relies heavily on coal for electricity generation, and some coal is used at Michigan's coke plants and by other industrial, commercial, and institutional users. The majority of the coal consumed in Michigan comes by rail from the West, primarily from Wyoming and Montana. A significant amount of coal also comes from nearby states, including some from the Appalachian coal fields of West Virginia and Kentucky.

Electricity

Because of Michigan's unique geography, the state is serviced by two major interstate electricity grids. One grid covers the Lower Peninsula and a small portion of the Upper Peninsula, and the other grid covers much of the Upper Peninsula. About half of the electricity generated in Michigan is produced by coal-fired power plants, the majority of which are in the southern half of the Lower Peninsula. Michigan's three nuclear power plants are also in the southern part of the state and typically supply more than one-fourth of the state's generation. Natural gas fuels much of the rest, with renewables, including hydroelectric power, contributing a small but rapidly increasing share of the electricity delivered to the grid.

Michigan's net electricity generation is greater than two-thirds of the states, but residential electricity sales per person in Michigan are below the national average, in part because less than one-tenth of Michigan households rely on electricity as their primary source of energy for home heating.

Renewable Energy

Michigan's renewable electricity generation comes predominantly from wind, which surpassed biomass as the state's primary renewable energy resource for electricity generation in 2014. Michigan's wind resource is ranked 18th in the nation. The state's wind capacity is among the fastest growing in the United States, and Michigan was among the top five states adding wind capacity in 2014. The state has more than 20 utility-scale wind farms with a combined total

capacity in excess of 1,500 megawatts. Substantial renewable electricity generation also comes from wood, wood waste, and other sources, including more than 100 hydroelectric power plants, several facilities that generate electricity using methane recovered from landfills, and anaerobic digesters on some of Michigan's many dairy farms. Overall, renewable resources contribute about 7% to the state's net electricity generation.

Michigan has six ethanol and four biodiesel production plants in operation. A major corn producer, Michigan uses corn as a feedstock for all but one of its ethanol plants, and those plants have the ability to produce more than 260 million gallons of ethanol each year from that feedstock. Michigan also has a small cellulosic ethanol plant that uses wood products waste as a feedstock. The state's biodiesel refineries can use a variety of feedstocks to produce more than 27 million gallons of biodiesel per year.

Michigan's Clean, Renewable, and Efficient Energy Act, enacted in 2008, requires that the state's electricity providers (investor-owned electric utilities, alternative retail suppliers, electric cooperatives, and municipal electric utilities) obtain at least 10% of the electricity they sell from renewable energy resources by 2015. The act defines renewable energy resources as biomass, solar and solar thermal energy, wind energy, kinetic energy of moving water, geothermal energy, municipal solid waste, and landfill gas. Electricity generation from hydroelectric facilities at newly constructed dams does not count toward the 10% requirement, but generation from modified facilities at existing dams does count. The standard also allows electric utilities to use energy efficiency and advanced cleaner energy technologies to fulfill part of the requirement. Michigan's two largest investor-owned electric utilities have additional requirements called renewable energy capacity standards. Those capacity standards are based on the number of customers each of the two utilities served at the beginning of 2008. The energy produced from new facilities that meet the capacity standards may be counted toward the 10% required from renewable energy resources for each of those electric utilities.

Michigan offers tax incentives in Renewable Energy Renaissance Zones (RERZs). These zones were created to promote the development of a renewable energy manufacturing industry in the state. RERZs must contain a renewable energy facility that creates energy, fuels, or chemicals from renewable resources or that does research, development, or manufacturing of those technologies. Facilities involved in the conversion of chemical energy for advanced battery technologies are also included. The zones can be located anywhere within the state.

Source: U.S. Energy Information Administration, State Profile and Energy Estimates, March 19, 2015

Household Energy Use in Michigan

A closer look at residential energy consumption

All data from EIA's 2009 Residential Energy Consumption Survey
www.eia.gov/consumption/residential/

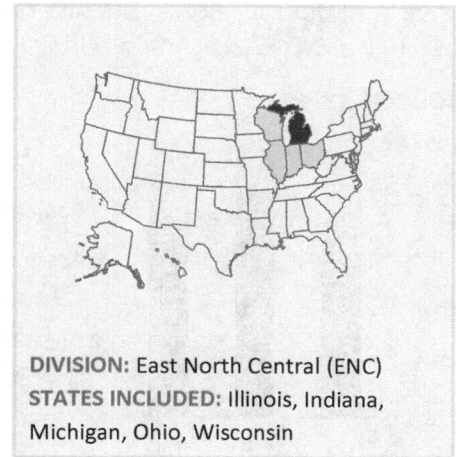

- Michigan households use 123 million Btu of energy per home, 38% more than the U.S. average.
- High consumption, combined with low costs for heating fuels compared to states with a similar climate, result in Michigan households spending 6% more for energy than the U.S. average.
- Less reliance on electricity for heating, as well as cool summers keeps average site electricity consumption in the state low relative to other parts of the U.S.
- Michigan homes are typically older than homes in other states.

DIVISION: East North Central (ENC)
STATES INCLUDED: Illinois, Indiana, Michigan, Ohio, Wisconsin

ALL ENERGY *average per household (excl. transportation)*

ELECTRICITY ONLY *average per household*

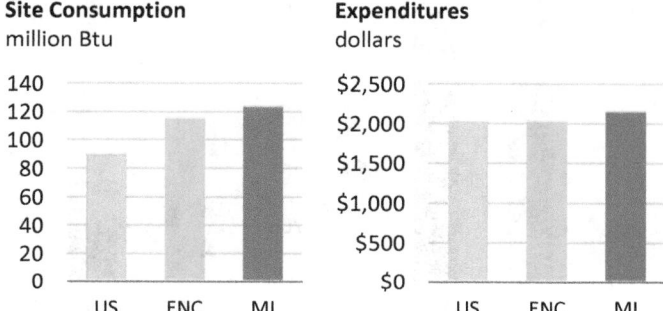
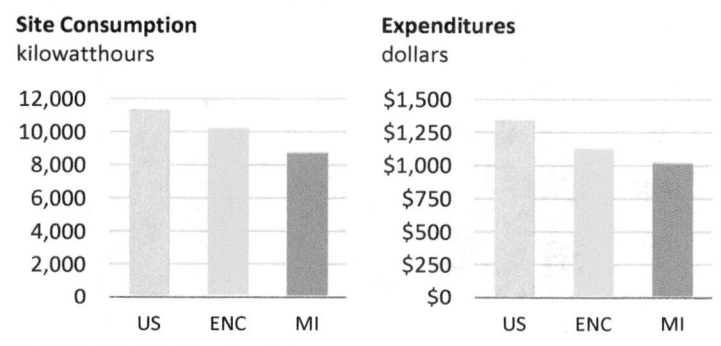

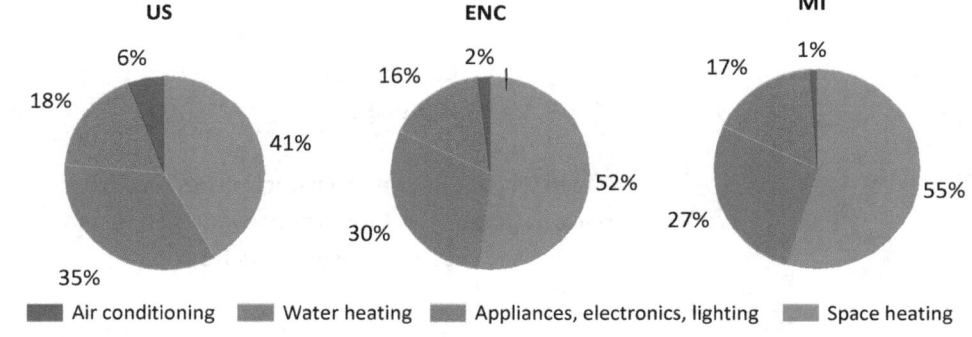

CONSUMPTION BY END USE

Since the weather in Michigan and the Midwest is cooler than other areas of the United States, space heating makes up a greater portion of energy use in homes compared to the U.S. average, and air conditioning makes up only 1% of energy use.

MAIN HEATING FUEL USED

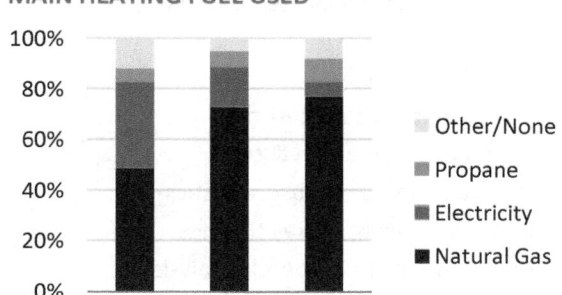

COOLING EQUIPMENT USED

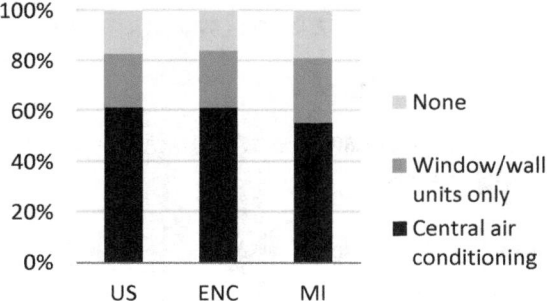

Compared to the U.S. average, a greater proportion (78%) of Michigan residents use natural gas for heating and a smaller proportion of residents (6%) use electricity for heating.

Nearly 20% of Michigan households do not use air conditioning, but those that do still predominantly rely on central air conditioning for cooling.

More highlights from RECS on housing characteristics and energy-related features per household...
US = United States | ENC = East North Central | MI = Michigan

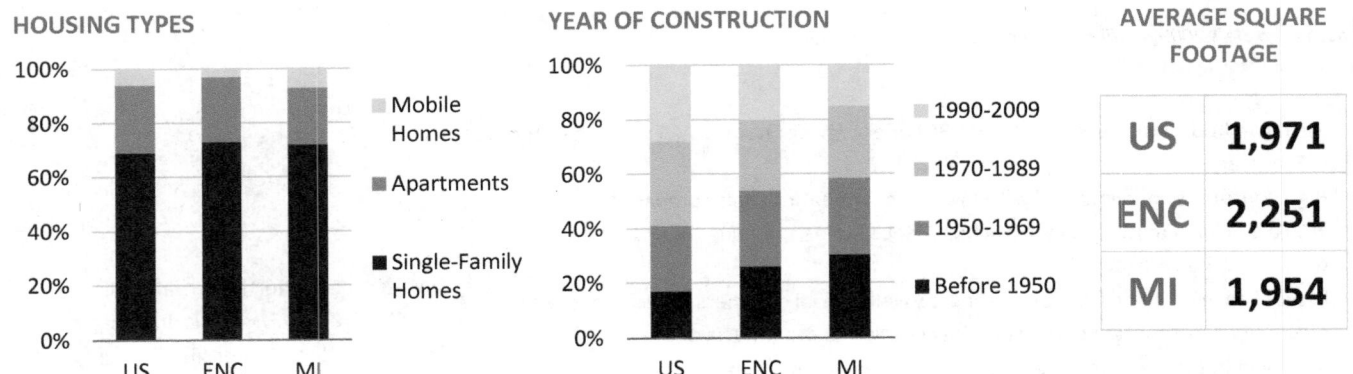

HOUSING TYPES

YEAR OF CONSTRUCTION

AVERAGE SQUARE FOOTAGE

US	1,971
ENC	2,251
MI	1,954

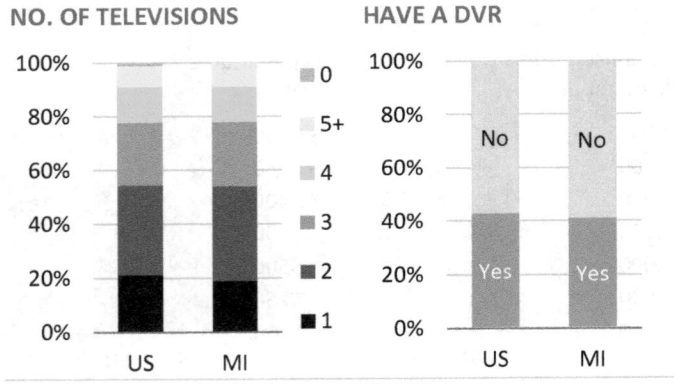

NO. OF TELEVISIONS   **HAVE A DVR**

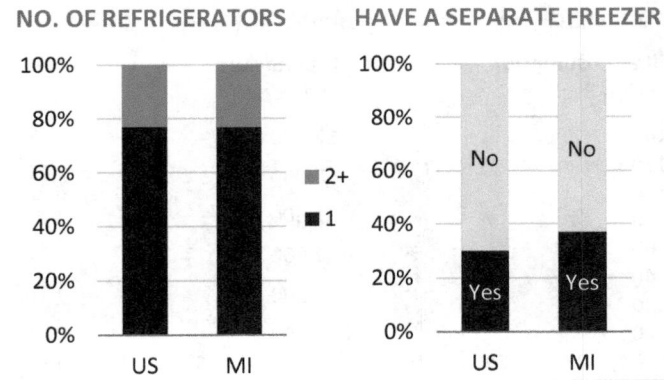

NO. OF REFRIGERATORS   **HAVE A SEPARATE FREEZER**

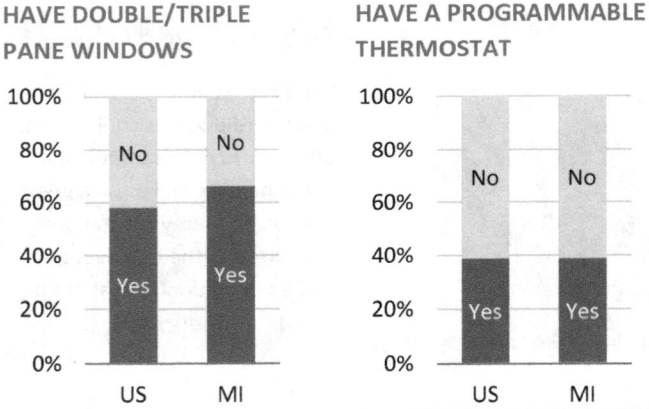

HAVE DOUBLE/TRIPLE PANE WINDOWS   **HAVE A PROGRAMMABLE THERMOSTAT**

About the Residential Energy Consumption Survey (RECS) Program

The RECS gathers energy characteristics through personal interviews from a nationwide sample of homes, and cost and consumption from energy suppliers.

The 2009 RECS is the thirteenth edition of the survey, which was first conducted in 1978.

Resulting products include:
- Home energy characteristics
- Average consumption & cost
- Detailed energy end-use statistics
- Reports highlighting key findings
- Microdata file for in-depth analysis

www.eia.gov/consumption/residential/

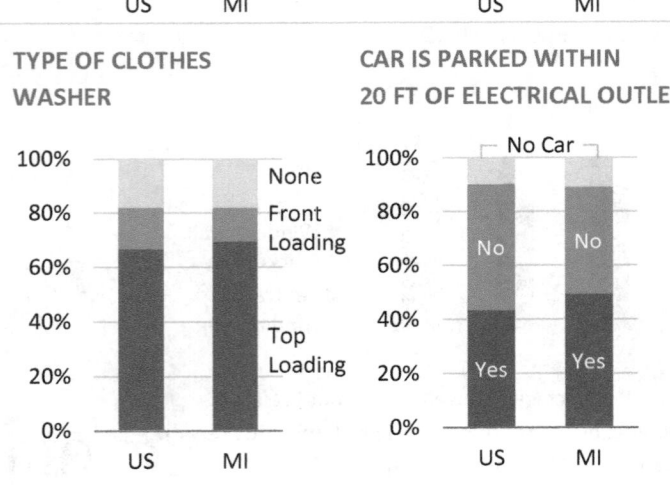

TYPE OF CLOTHES WASHER   **CAR IS PARKED WITHIN 20 FT OF ELECTRICAL OUTLET**

Population

Legend

- 100,000 and Over
- 75,000 to 99,999
- 50,000 to 74,999
- 25,000 to 49,999
- Under 25,000

0 mi   50   100   150

Percent White

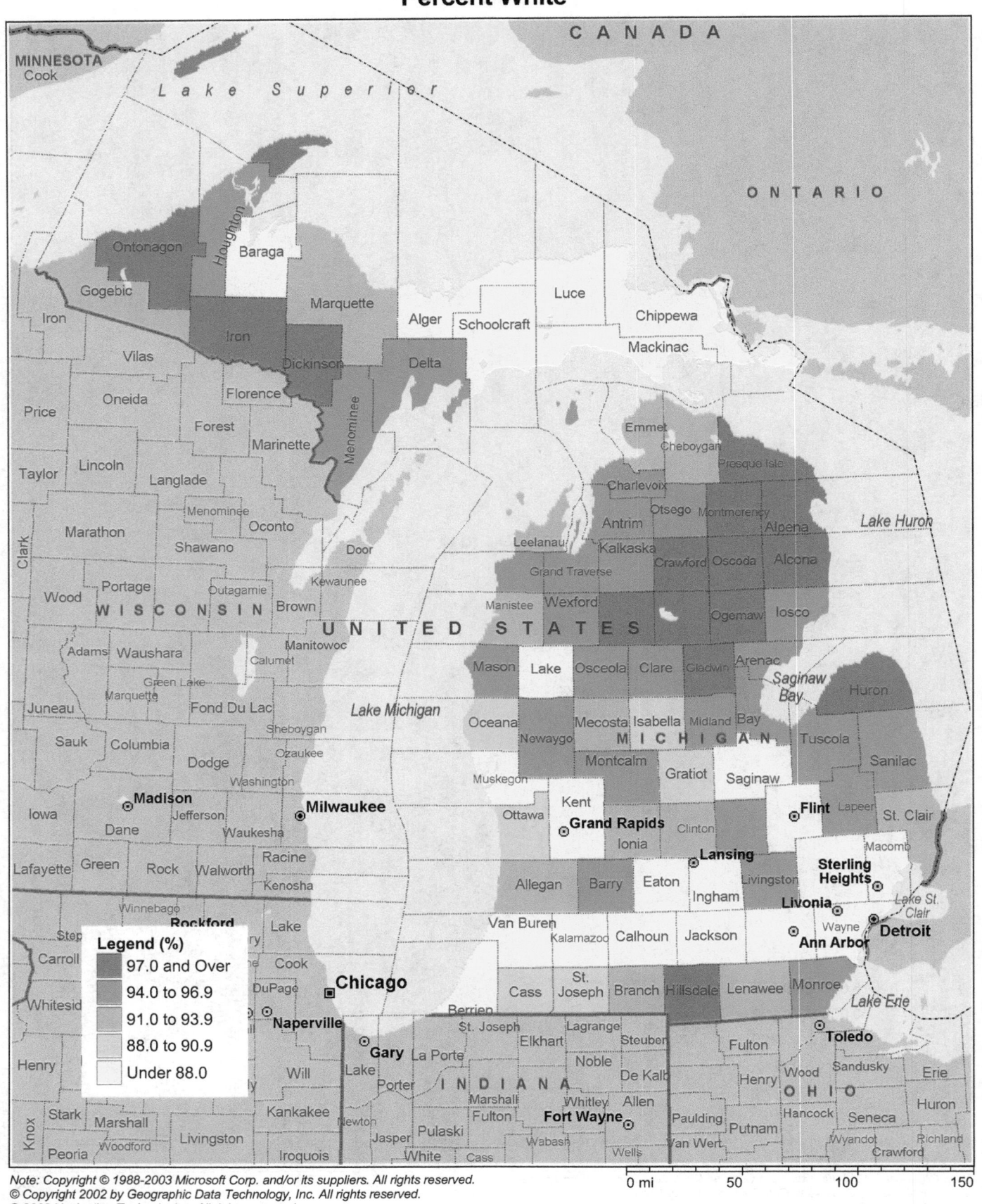

Legend (%)
- 97.0 and Over
- 94.0 to 96.9
- 91.0 to 93.9
- 88.0 to 90.9
- Under 88.0

0 mi   50   100   150

Percent Black

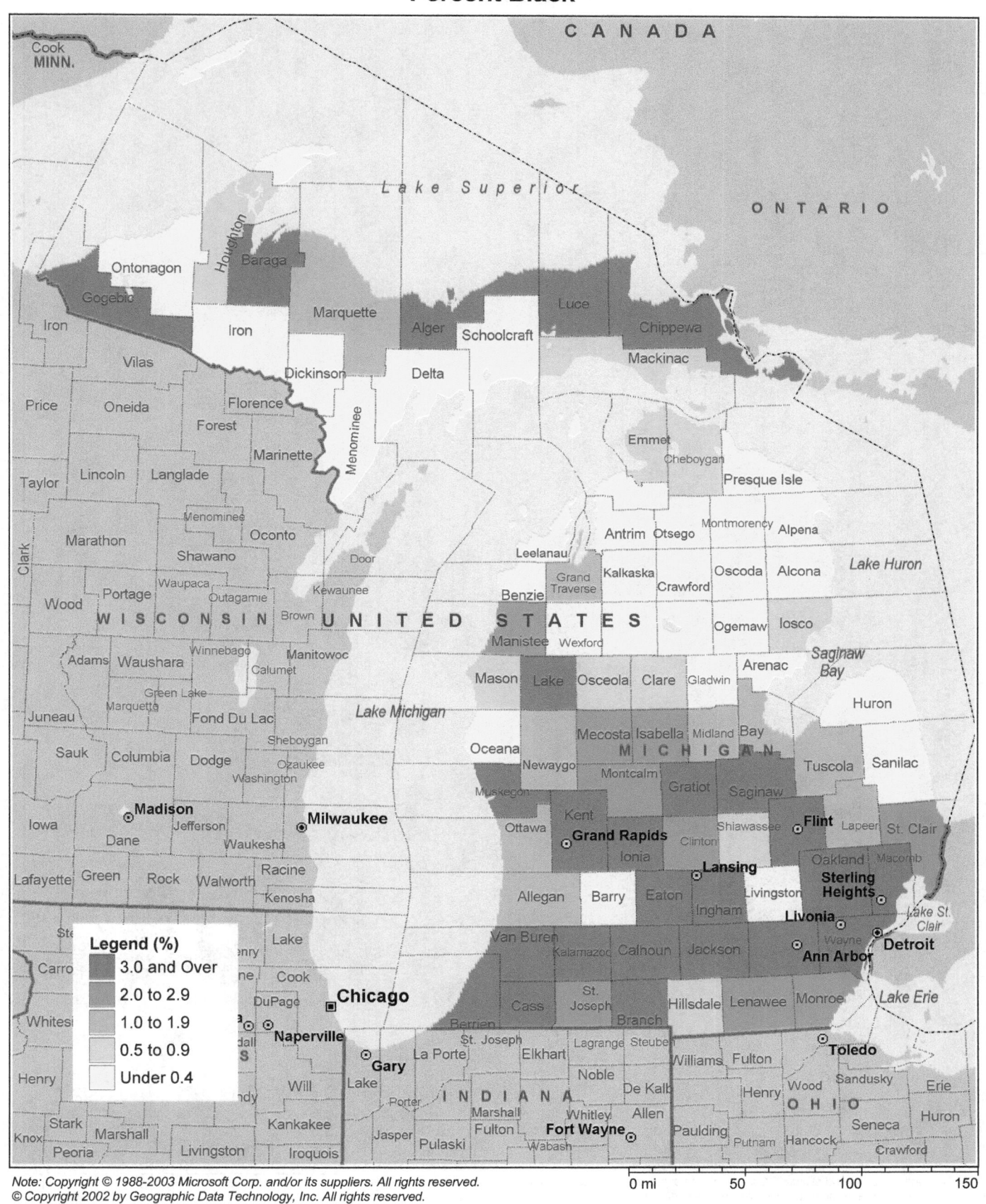

Legend (%)

- 3.0 and Over
- 2.0 to 2.9
- 1.0 to 1.9
- 0.5 to 0.9
- Under 0.4

0 mi   50   100   150

Percent Asian

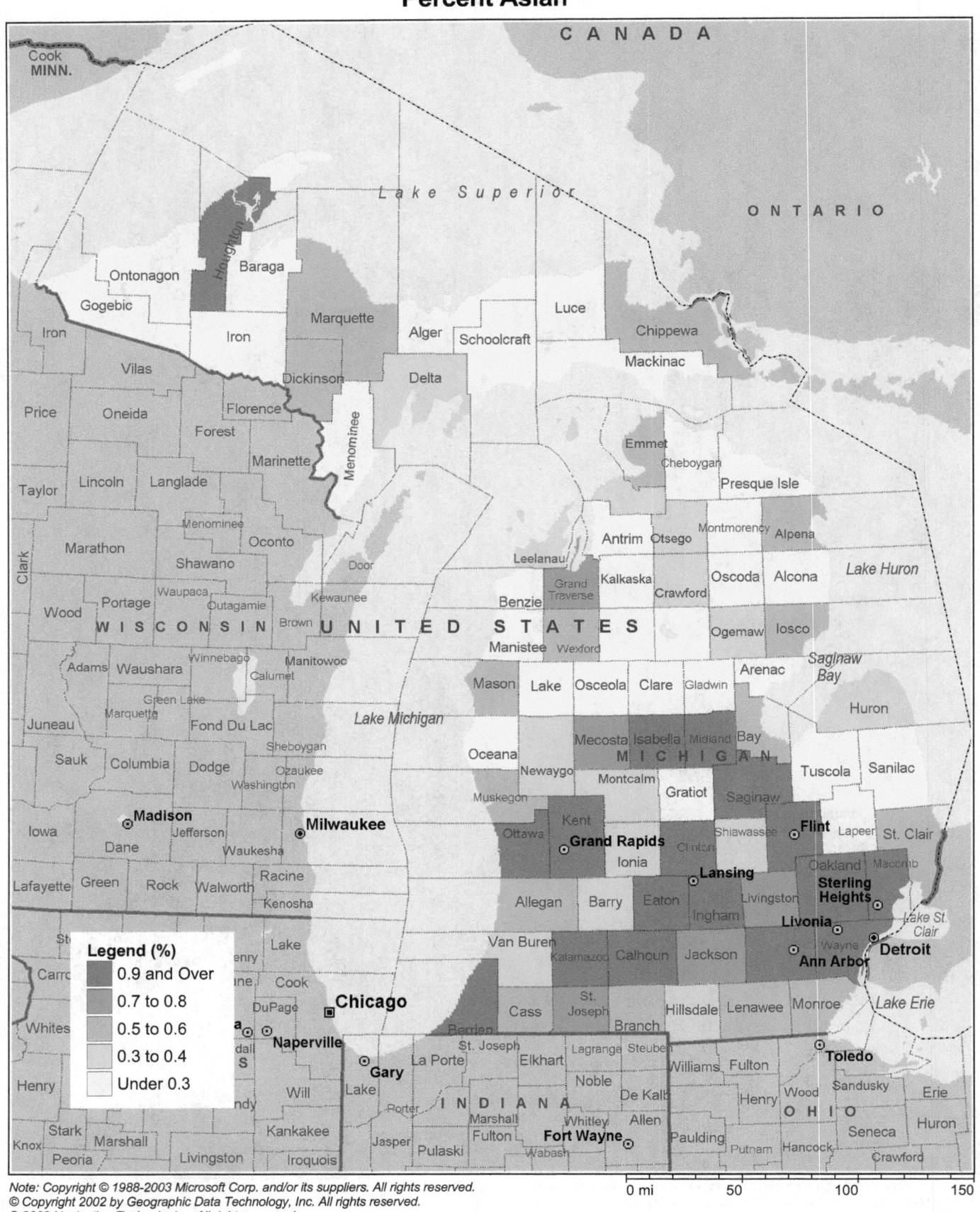

Legend (%)
- 0.9 and Over
- 0.7 to 0.8
- 0.5 to 0.6
- 0.3 to 0.4
- Under 0.3

0 mi   50   100   150

Percent Hispanic

Legend (%)
- 4.0 and Over
- 3.0 to 3.9
- 2.0 to 2.9
- 1.0 to 1.9
- Under 1.0

0 mi   50   100   150

Median Age

Legend (years)
- 43.0 and Over
- 41.0 to 42.9
- 39.0 to 40.9
- 37.0 to 38.9
- Under 37.0

0 mi   50   100   150

Median Household Income

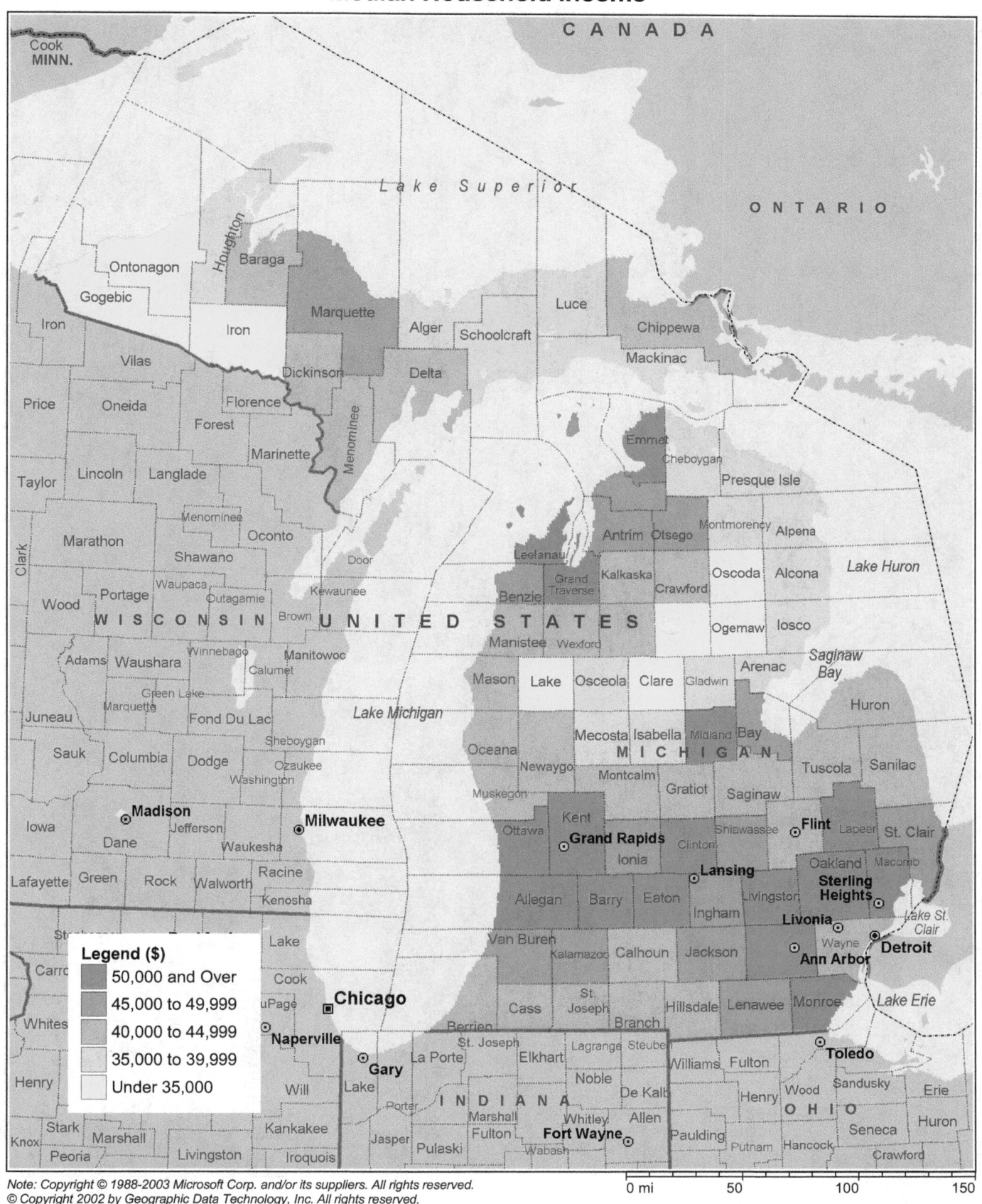

Legend ($)
- 50,000 and Over
- 45,000 to 49,999
- 40,000 to 44,999
- 35,000 to 39,999
- Under 35,000

0 mi   50   100   150

Median Home Value

Legend ($)
- 125,000 and Over
- 115,000 to 124,999
- 105,000 to 114,999
- 95,000 to 104,999
- Under 95,000

0 mi   50   100   150

High School Graduates*

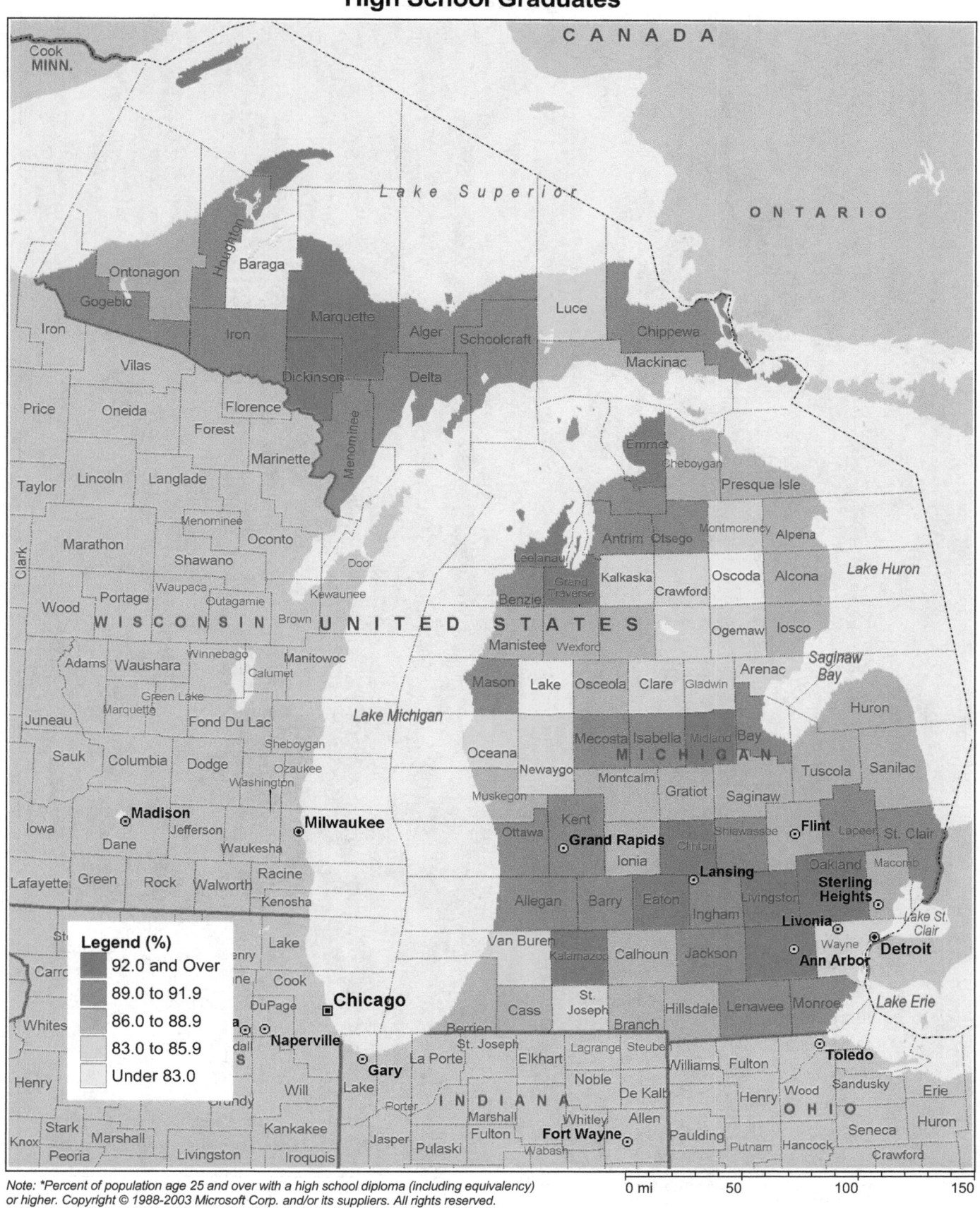

Legend (%)

- 92.0 and Over
- 89.0 to 91.9
- 86.0 to 88.9
- 83.0 to 85.9
- Under 83.0

Note: *Percent of population age 25 and over with a high school diploma (including equivalency)
or higher. Copyright © 1988-2003 Microsoft Corp. and/or its suppliers. All rights reserved.
© Copyright 2002 by Geographic Data Technology, Inc. All rights reserved.
© 2002 Navigation Technologies. All rights reserved.

0 mi   50   100   150

College Graduates*

Legend (%)
- 22.0 and Over
- 19.0 to 21.9
- 16.0 to 18.9
- 13.0 to 15.9
- Under 13.0

*Note: *Percent of population age 25 and over with a Bachelor's Degree or higher.*
Copyright © 1988-2003 Microsoft Corp. and/or its suppliers. All rights reserved.
© Copyright 2002 by Geographic Data Technology, Inc. All rights reserved.
© 2002 Navigation Technologies. All rights reserved.

0 mi   50   100   150

Profiles

Alcona County

Located in northeast Michigan; bounded on the east by Lake Huron; includes Hubbard Lake, and part of Huron National Forest. Covers a land area of 674.585 square miles, a water area of 1,115.997 square miles, and is located in the Eastern Time Zone at 44.68° N. Lat., 82.83° W. Long. The county was founded in 1840. County seat is Harrisville.

Population: 10,942; Growth (since 2000): -6.6%; Density: 16.2 persons per square mile; Race: 97.9% White, 0.1% Black/African American, 0.2% Asian, 0.6% American Indian/Alaska Native, 0.0% Native Hawaiian/Other Pacific Islander, 0.9% two or more races, 1.1% Hispanic of any race; Average household size: 2.13; Median age: 55.2; Age under 18: 14.6%; Age 65 and over: 31.4%; Males per 100 females: 103.1; Marriage status: 18.0% never married, 60.3% now married, 1.0% separated, 9.1% widowed, 12.6% divorced; Foreign born: 1.7%; Speak English only: 97.7%; With disability: 21.7%; Veterans: 18.4%; Ancestry: 29.0% German, 15.8% English, 13.1% Irish, 10.9% French, 9.7% Polish

Religion: Six largest groups: 7.3% Catholicism, 4.7% Lutheran, 3.5% Methodist/Pietist, 3.2% Pentecostal, 2.1% Non-denominational Protestant, 1.8% Baptist

Economy: Unemployment rate: 6.4%; Leading industries: 18.1% retail trade; 14.0% accommodation and food services; 13.0% construction; Farms: 235 totaling 38,309 acres; Company size: 0 employ 1,000 or more persons, 0 employ 500 to 999 persons, 0 employ 100 to 499 persons, 193 employ less than 100 persons; Business ownership: 191 women-owned, n/a Black-owned, n/a Hispanic-owned, n/a Asian-owned

Employment: 8.8% management, business, and financial, 2.4% computer, engineering, and science, 6.8% education, legal, community service, arts, and media, 6.5% healthcare practitioners, 23.7% service, 21.1% sales and office, 14.1% natural resources, construction, and maintenance, 16.6% production, transportation, and material moving

Income: Per capita: $22,719; Median household: $37,189; Average household: $48,679; Households with income of $100,000 or more: 8.5%; Poverty rate: 15.1%

Educational Attainment: High school diploma or higher: 86.9%; Bachelor's degree or higher: 13.0%; Graduate/professional degree or higher: 5.0%

Housing: Homeownership rate: 89.6%; Median home value: $102,800; Median year structure built: 1973; Homeowner vacancy rate: 5.1%; Median gross rent: $585 per month; Rental vacancy rate: 22.4%

Vital Statistics: Birth rate: 58.6 per 10,000 population; Death rate: 150.3 per 10,000 population; Age-adjusted cancer mortality rate: 179.5 deaths per 100,000 population

Health Insurance: 87.5% have insurance; 66.7% have private insurance; 53.0% have public insurance; 12.5% do not have insurance; 5.3% of children under 18 do not have insurance

Health Care: Physicians: 4.7 per 10,000 population; Hospital beds: 0.0 per 10,000 population; Hospital admissions: 0.0 per 10,000 population

Transportation: Commute: 88.1% car, 0.2% public transportation, 3.1% walk, 7.1% work from home; Median travel time to work: 21.7 minutes

Presidential Election: 40.6% Obama, 58.6% Romney (2012)

National and State Parks: Alpena State Forest; Harrisville State Park; Sturgeon Point State Park

Additional Information Contacts

Alcona Government. . . . . (989) 724-9400
   http://public.alconacountymi.com

Alcona County Communities

ALCONA (township). Covers a land area of 57.496 square miles and a water area of 8.867 square miles. Located at 44.81° N. Lat; 83.45° W. Long. Elevation is 591 feet.

Population: 968; Growth (since 2000): -11.1%; Density: 16.8 persons per square mile; Race: 98.7% White, 0.0% Black/African American, 0.3% Asian, 0.1% American Indian/Alaska Native, 0.0% Native Hawaiian/Other Pacific Islander, 0.2% Two or more races, 0.6% Hispanic of any race; Average household size: 1.95; Median age: 63.0; Age under 18: 9.6%; Age 65 and over: 45.8%; Males per 100 females: 107.3

Housing: Homeownership rate: 94.0%; Homeowner vacancy rate: 5.4%; Rental vacancy rate: 16.7%

BARTON CITY (unincorporated postal area)
ZCTA: 48705

Covers a land area of 88.389 square miles and a water area of 0.499 square miles. Located at 44.70° N. Lat; 83.66° W. Long. Elevation is 830 feet.

Population: 535; Growth (since 2000): -8.4%; Density: 6.1 persons per square mile; Race: 96.3% White, 0.0% Black/African American, 0.6% Asian, 0.9% American Indian/Alaska Native, 0.0% Native Hawaiian/Other Pacific Islander, 2.2% Two or more races, 0.2% Hispanic of any race; Average household size: 2.00; Median age: 58.7; Age under 18: 8.6%; Age 65 and over: 34.4%; Males per 100 females: 119.3

Housing: Homeownership rate: 92.8%; Homeowner vacancy rate: 6.1%; Rental vacancy rate: 22.2%

BLACK RIVER (unincorporated postal area)
ZCTA: 48721

Covers a land area of 27.462 square miles and a water area of 2.074 square miles. Located at 44.81° N. Lat; 83.34° W. Long. Elevation is 587 feet.

Population: 411; Growth (since 2000): -15.3%; Density: 15.0 persons per square mile; Race: 98.5% White, 0.0% Black/African American, 0.2% Asian, 0.0% American Indian/Alaska Native, 0.0% Native Hawaiian/Other Pacific Islander, 0.0% Two or more races, 1.5% Hispanic of any race; Average household size: 2.14; Median age: 55.1; Age under 18: 13.6%; Age 65 and over: 30.7%; Males per 100 females: 113.0

Housing: Homeownership rate: 91.7%; Homeowner vacancy rate: 4.3%; Rental vacancy rate: 23.8%

CALEDONIA (township). Covers a land area of 67.580 square miles and a water area of 5.148 square miles. Located at 44.83° N. Lat; 83.61° W. Long.

Population: 1,161; Growth (since 2000): -3.5%; Density: 17.2 persons per square mile; Race: 98.2% White, 0.0% Black/African American, 0.3% Asian, 0.3% American Indian/Alaska Native, 0.0% Native Hawaiian/Other Pacific Islander, 0.8% Two or more races, 1.8% Hispanic of any race; Average household size: 2.17; Median age: 56.7; Age under 18: 15.4%; Age 65 and over: 34.1%; Males per 100 females: 100.5

Housing: Homeownership rate: 92.3%; Homeowner vacancy rate: 3.7%; Rental vacancy rate: 14.6%

CURRAN (unincorporated postal area)
ZCTA: 48728

Covers a land area of 128.529 square miles and a water area of 1.235 square miles. Located at 44.73° N. Lat; 83.82° W. Long. Elevation is 922 feet.

Population: 290; Growth (since 2000): -5.5%; Density: 2.3 persons per square mile; Race: 99.0% White, 0.3% Black/African American, 0.0% Asian, 0.3% American Indian/Alaska Native, 0.0% Native Hawaiian/Other Pacific Islander, 0.0% Two or more races, 1.0% Hispanic of any race; Average household size: 1.96; Median age: 57.8; Age under 18: 10.0%; Age 65 and over: 27.9%; Males per 100 females: 100.0

Housing: Homeownership rate: 91.9%; Homeowner vacancy rate: 13.8%; Rental vacancy rate: 0.0%

CURTIS (township). Covers a land area of 68.391 square miles and a water area of 2.326 square miles. Located at 44.55° N. Lat; 83.78° W. Long.

Population: 1,236; Growth (since 2000): -10.3%; Density: 18.1 persons per square mile; Race: 97.8% White, 0.2% Black/African American, 0.1% Asian, 0.2% American Indian/Alaska Native, 0.0% Native Hawaiian/Other Pacific Islander, 1.5% Two or more races, 0.8% Hispanic of any race; Average household size: 2.08; Median age: 56.4; Age under 18: 13.3%; Age 65 and over: 33.6%; Males per 100 females: 109.1

School District(s)

Three Lakes Academy (KG-12)
   2012-13 Enrollment: 92. . . . . (906) 586-6631

Housing: Homeownership rate: 88.1%; Homeowner vacancy rate: 5.6%; Rental vacancy rate: 3.9%

GLENNIE (unincorporated postal area)
ZCTA: 48737
Covers a land area of 102.258 square miles and a water area of 3.658 square miles. Located at 44.55° N. Lat; 83.69° W. Long. Elevation is 1,017 feet.
Population: 1,245; Growth (since 2000): -7.4%; Density: 12.2 persons per square mile; Race: 98.0% White, 0.2% Black/African American, 0.0% Asian, 0.2% American Indian/Alaska Native, 0.0% Native Hawaiian/Other Pacific Islander, 1.5% Two or more races, 0.5% Hispanic of any race; Average household size: 2.06; Median age: 56.8; Age under 18: 12.6%; Age 65 and over: 34.5%; Males per 100 females: 108.2
Housing: Homeownership rate: 89.7%; Homeowner vacancy rate: 5.9%; Rental vacancy rate: 8.6%

GREENBUSH (township). Covers a land area of 24.923 square miles and a water area of 1.222 square miles. Located at 44.55° N. Lat; 83.38° W. Long. Elevation is 610 feet.
Population: 1,409; Growth (since 2000): -6.0%; Density: 56.5 persons per square mile; Race: 98.7% White, 0.1% Black/African American, 0.1% Asian, 0.6% American Indian/Alaska Native, 0.0% Native Hawaiian/Other Pacific Islander, 0.4% Two or more races, 0.7% Hispanic of any race; Average household size: 2.08; Median age: 57.9; Age under 18: 13.0%; Age 65 and over: 35.1%; Males per 100 females: 103.3
Housing: Homeownership rate: 91.8%; Homeowner vacancy rate: 6.6%; Rental vacancy rate: 46.2%

GUSTIN (township). Covers a land area of 35.686 square miles and a water area of 0.158 square miles. Located at 44.64° N. Lat; 83.47° W. Long. Elevation is 696 feet.
Population: 795; Growth (since 2000): -4.4%; Density: 22.3 persons per square mile; Race: 98.0% White, 0.0% Black/African American, 0.1% Asian, 0.6% American Indian/Alaska Native, 0.0% Native Hawaiian/Other Pacific Islander, 1.3% Two or more races, 1.4% Hispanic of any race; Average household size: 2.33; Median age: 45.3; Age under 18: 22.0%; Age 65 and over: 20.1%; Males per 100 females: 97.8
Housing: Homeownership rate: 81.1%; Homeowner vacancy rate: 1.8%; Rental vacancy rate: 30.4%

HARRISVILLE (city). County seat. Covers a land area of 0.612 square miles and a water area of 0 square miles. Located at 44.66° N. Lat; 83.29° W. Long. Elevation is 623 feet.
History: Harrisville, established in 1854 as Davison's Mills on the shores of Lake Huron, grew as a fishing village, particularly popular during the summer months.
Population: 493; Growth (since 2000): -4.1%; Density: 805.6 persons per square mile; Race: 96.6% White, 0.6% Black/African American, 0.2% Asian, 1.0% American Indian/Alaska Native, 0.0% Native Hawaiian/Other Pacific Islander, 1.0% Two or more races, 2.4% Hispanic of any race; Average household size: 1.96; Median age: 51.6; Age under 18: 16.4%; Age 65 and over: 29.6%; Males per 100 females: 81.9
Housing: Homeownership rate: 66.6%; Homeowner vacancy rate: 4.3%; Rental vacancy rate: 18.1%
Newspapers: Alcona County Review (weekly circulation 3400)

HARRISVILLE (township). Covers a land area of 30.332 square miles and a water area of 0.017 square miles. Located at 44.65° N. Lat; 83.35° W. Long. Elevation is 623 feet.
History: Harrisville Township was organized in 1860 and named for Benjamin Harris and his sons, Levi O. and Henry H. Harris, who had purchased the mill here from Crosier Davison.
Population: 1,348; Growth (since 2000): -4.5%; Density: 44.4 persons per square mile; Race: 96.9% White, 0.2% Black/African American, 0.4% Asian, 1.5% American Indian/Alaska Native, 0.1% Native Hawaiian/Other Pacific Islander, 0.8% Two or more races, 1.0% Hispanic of any race; Average household size: 2.19; Median age: 53.8; Age under 18: 15.3%; Age 65 and over: 29.8%; Males per 100 females: 98.2
Housing: Homeownership rate: 90.5%; Homeowner vacancy rate: 4.1%; Rental vacancy rate: 28.2%
Newspapers: Alcona County Review (weekly circulation 3400)

HAWES (township). Covers a land area of 69.961 square miles and a water area of 1.475 square miles. Located at 44.71° N. Lat; 83.51° W. Long.
Population: 1,107; Growth (since 2000): -5.1%; Density: 15.8 persons per square mile; Race: 98.6% White, 0.0% Black/African American, 0.0% Asian, 0.2% American Indian/Alaska Native, 0.0% Native Hawaiian/Other Pacific Islander, 1.2% Two or more races, 1.4% Hispanic of any race; Average household size: 2.22; Median age: 52.9; Age under 18: 15.5%; Age 65 and over: 28.3%; Males per 100 females: 110.1
Housing: Homeownership rate: 91.4%; Homeowner vacancy rate: 5.4%; Rental vacancy rate: 24.1%

HAYNES (township). Covers a land area of 34.928 square miles and a water area of 0.146 square miles. Located at 44.72° N. Lat; 83.35° W. Long.
Population: 722; Growth (since 2000): -0.3%; Density: 20.7 persons per square mile; Race: 97.9% White, 0.1% Black/African American, 0.4% Asian, 0.8% American Indian/Alaska Native, 0.0% Native Hawaiian/Other Pacific Islander, 0.6% Two or more races, 0.8% Hispanic of any race; Average household size: 2.11; Median age: 56.1; Age under 18: 13.7%; Age 65 and over: 30.6%; Males per 100 females: 99.4
Housing: Homeownership rate: 93.9%; Homeowner vacancy rate: 4.5%; Rental vacancy rate: 12.5%

HUBBARD LAKE (CDP). Covers a land area of 8.733 square miles and a water area of 13.815 square miles. Located at 44.82° N. Lat; 83.56° W. Long. Elevation is 748 feet.
Population: 1,002; Growth (since 2000): 0.9%; Density: 114.7 persons per square mile; Race: 98.6% White, 0.0% Black/African American, 0.4% Asian, 0.3% American Indian/Alaska Native, 0.0% Native Hawaiian/Other Pacific Islander, 0.1% Two or more races, 1.9% Hispanic of any race; Average household size: 1.98; Median age: 63.7; Age under 18: 9.8%; Age 65 and over: 47.2%; Males per 100 females: 102.8
Housing: Homeownership rate: 92.3%; Homeowner vacancy rate: 5.5%; Rental vacancy rate: 17.0%

LINCOLN (village). Covers a land area of 0.829 square miles and a water area of 0.229 square miles. Located at 44.68° N. Lat; 83.41° W. Long. Elevation is 814 feet.
History: Lincoln grew up around a lumber mill in 1885. It was incorporated as a village in 1907.
Population: 337; Growth (since 2000): -7.4%; Density: 406.4 persons per square mile; Race: 98.2% White, 0.0% Black/African American, 0.0% Asian, 0.0% American Indian/Alaska Native, 0.0% Native Hawaiian/Other Pacific Islander, 1.8% Two or more races, 2.7% Hispanic of any race; Average household size: 2.11; Median age: 43.2; Age under 18: 19.6%; Age 65 and over: 25.8%; Males per 100 females: 88.3
School District(s)
Alcona Community Schools (KG-12)
   2012-13 Enrollment: 773 . . . . (989) 736-6212
Housing: Homeownership rate: 69.4%; Homeowner vacancy rate: 3.4%; Rental vacancy rate: 19.7%

LOST LAKE WOODS (CDP). Covers a land area of 5.046 square miles and a water area of 0.139 square miles. Located at 44.80° N. Lat; 83.42° W. Long. Elevation is 860 feet.
Population: 312; Growth (since 2000): -8.0%; Density: 61.8 persons per square mile; Race: 98.7% White, 0.0% Black/African American, 0.3% Asian, 0.3% American Indian/Alaska Native, 0.0% Native Hawaiian/Other Pacific Islander, 0.3% Two or more races, 0.0% Hispanic of any race; Average household size: 1.80; Median age: 68.1; Age under 18: 6.4%; Age 65 and over: 62.2%; Males per 100 females: 100.0
Housing: Homeownership rate: 96.6%; Homeowner vacancy rate: 6.7%; Rental vacancy rate: 14.3%

MIKADO (township). Covers a land area of 71.359 square miles and a water area of 0.060 square miles. Located at 44.56° N. Lat; 83.51° W. Long. Elevation is 653 feet.
Population: 947; Growth (since 2000): -9.2%; Density: 13.3 persons per square mile; Race: 97.7% White, 0.1% Black/African American, 0.0% Asian, 0.8% American Indian/Alaska Native, 0.0% Native Hawaiian/Other Pacific Islander, 1.1% Two or more races, 1.3% Hispanic of any race; Average household size: 2.31; Median age: 49.4; Age under 18: 18.6%; Age 65 and over: 21.9%; Males per 100 females: 108.1

Housing: Homeownership rate: 89.7%; Homeowner vacancy rate: 5.4%; Rental vacancy rate: 8.5%

MILLEN (township).
Covers a land area of 70.780 square miles and a water area of 0.491 square miles. Located at 44.64° N. Lat; 83.64° W. Long.
Population: 404; Growth (since 2000): -12.7%; Density: 5.7 persons per square mile; Race: 95.8% White, 0.0% Black/African American, 1.0% Asian, 0.7% American Indian/Alaska Native, 0.0% Native Hawaiian/Other Pacific Islander, 2.2% Two or more races, 1.5% Hispanic of any race; Average household size: 2.00; Median age: 56.6; Age under 18: 9.2%; Age 65 and over: 32.7%; Males per 100 females: 112.6
Housing: Homeownership rate: 92.0%; Homeowner vacancy rate: 4.2%; Rental vacancy rate: 15.0%

MITCHELL (township).
Covers a land area of 142.538 square miles and a water area of 0.852 square miles. Located at 44.73° N. Lat; 83.80° W. Long.
Population: 352; Growth (since 2000): -11.1%; Density: 2.5 persons per square mile; Race: 98.3% White, 0.3% Black/African American, 0.0% Asian, 0.9% American Indian/Alaska Native, 0.0% Native Hawaiian/Other Pacific Islander, 0.6% Two or more races, 0.6% Hispanic of any race; Average household size: 1.91; Median age: 59.4; Age under 18: 7.7%; Age 65 and over: 31.8%; Males per 100 females: 107.1
Housing: Homeownership rate: 92.4%; Homeowner vacancy rate: 11.0%; Rental vacancy rate: 0.0%

SPRUCE (unincorporated postal area)
ZCTA: 48762
Covers a land area of 45.027 square miles and a water area of 0.140 square miles. Located at 44.82° N. Lat; 83.46° W. Long. Elevation is 778 feet.
Population: 1,139; Growth (since 2000): -14.3%; Density: 25.3 persons per square mile; Race: 98.8% White, 0.3% Black/African American, 0.0% Asian, 0.2% American Indian/Alaska Native, 0.0% Native Hawaiian/Other Pacific Islander, 0.7% Two or more races, 1.1% Hispanic of any race; Average household size: 2.18; Median age: 53.6; Age under 18: 17.2%; Age 65 and over: 30.6%; Males per 100 females: 104.9
Housing: Homeownership rate: 92.7%; Homeowner vacancy rate: 4.0%; Rental vacancy rate: 11.6%

Alger County

Located in northern Michigan, on the Upper Peninsula; bounded on the north by Lake Superior; includes part of Hiawatha National Forest. Covers a land area of 915.069 square miles, a water area of 4,132.666 square miles, and is located in the Eastern Time Zone at 47.08° N. Lat., 86.56° W. Long. The county was founded in 1885. County seat is Munising.

Weather Station: Grand Marais 2 E   Elevation: 624 feet

	Jan	Feb	Mar	Apr	May	Jun	Jul	Aug	Sep	Oct	Nov	Dec
High	26	29	38	50	62	71	76	76	69	55	41	31
Low	11	12	17	28	37	45	51	52	47	36	27	17
Precip	2.2	1.2	1.3	1.2	2.4	2.6	3.0	2.6	3.6	3.4	2.2	2.1
Snow	40.9	24.6	15.1	4.1	0.3	0.0	0.0	0.0	tr	0.6	11.7	35.7

High and Low temperatures in degrees Fahrenheit; Precipitation and Snow in inches

Weather Station: Munising   Elevation: 680 feet

	Jan	Feb	Mar	Apr	May	Jun	Jul	Aug	Sep	Oct	Nov	Dec
High	25	27	35	47	61	70	75	74	66	53	41	29
Low	11	11	20	30	40	48	55	55	49	38	28	17
Precip	3.3	2.1	2.2	2.2	2.8	2.8	3.2	3.0	3.9	4.2	3.1	3.6
Snow	42.5	28.2	19.3	7.2	0.4	0.0	0.0	0.0	tr	1.8	12.9	39.5

High and Low temperatures in degrees Fahrenheit; Precipitation and Snow in inches

Population: 9,601; Growth (since 2000): -2.6%; Density: 10.5 persons per square mile; Race: 86.3% White, 6.4% Black/African American, 0.3% Asian, 4.1% American Indian/Alaska Native, 0.0% Native Hawaiian/Other Pacific Islander, 2.7% two or more races, 1.2% Hispanic of any race; Average household size: 2.20; Median age: 47.3; Age under 18: 17.1%; Age 65 and over: 20.6%; Males per 100 females: 119.4; Marriage status: 30.7% never married, 48.3% now married, 0.6% separated, 7.3% widowed, 13.7% divorced; Foreign born: 1.4%; Speak English only: 96.8%; With disability: 19.8%; Veterans: 13.9%; Ancestry: 18.6% German, 13.0% Finnish, 12.5% Irish, 10.8% French, 10.3% English

Religion: Six largest groups: 25.9% Catholicism, 10.5% Lutheran, 2.7% Non-denominational Protestant, 2.0% Methodist/Pietist, 0.6% Adventist, 0.6% Holiness
Economy: Unemployment rate: 6.5%; Leading industries: 19.1% retail trade; 17.4% accommodation and food services; 14.4% construction; Farms: 93 totaling 17,781 acres; Company size: 0 employ 1,000 or more persons, 0 employ 500 to 999 persons, 3 employ 100 to 499 persons, 233 employ less than 100 persons; Business ownership: n/a women-owned, n/a Black-owned, n/a Hispanic-owned, n/a Asian-owned
Employment: 13.6% management, business, and financial, 2.5% computer, engineering, and science, 9.5% education, legal, community service, arts, and media, 3.6% healthcare practitioners, 25.4% service, 19.5% sales and office, 11.9% natural resources, construction, and maintenance, 14.2% production, transportation, and material moving
Income: Per capita: $19,717; Median household: $37,586; Average household: $48,564; Households with income of $100,000 or more: 8.7%; Poverty rate: 14.8%
Educational Attainment: High school diploma or higher: 89.4%; Bachelor's degree or higher: 17.1%; Graduate/professional degree or higher: 5.0%
Housing: Homeownership rate: 82.8%; Median home value: $117,100; Median year structure built: 1972; Homeowner vacancy rate: 3.2%; Median gross rent: $603 per month; Rental vacancy rate: 17.6%
Vital Statistics: Birth rate: 53.6 per 10,000 population; Death rate: 115.5 per 10,000 population; Age-adjusted cancer mortality rate: 160.3 deaths per 100,000 population
Health Insurance: 86.8% have insurance; 66.7% have private insurance; 43.0% have public insurance; 13.2% do not have insurance; 1.1% of children under 18 do not have insurance
Health Care: Physicians: 7.4 per 10,000 population; Hospital beds: 26.2 per 10,000 population; Hospital admissions: 202.0 per 10,000 population
Transportation: Commute: 82.3% car, 1.1% public transportation, 7.4% walk, 7.6% work from home; Median travel time to work: 21.1 minutes
Presidential Election: 48.0% Obama, 50.6% Romney (2012)
National and State Parks: Cusino State Wildlife Research Area; Escanaba River State Forest; Pictured Rocks National Lakeshore
Additional Information Contacts
Alger Government . . . . (906) 387-2076
    http://www.algercourthouse.com

Alger County Communities

AU TRAIN (township).
Covers a land area of 141.265 square miles and a water area of 16.777 square miles. Located at 46.34° N. Lat; 86.77° W. Long. Elevation is 610 feet.
Population: 1,138; Growth (since 2000): -2.9%; Density: 8.1 persons per square mile; Race: 90.8% White, 0.2% Black/African American, 0.0% Asian, 5.3% American Indian/Alaska Native, 0.0% Native Hawaiian/Other Pacific Islander, 3.7% Two or more races, 1.8% Hispanic of any race; Average household size: 2.18; Median age: 51.2; Age under 18: 16.1%; Age 65 and over: 21.2%; Males per 100 females: 102.5
Housing: Homeownership rate: 90.2%; Homeowner vacancy rate: 4.2%; Rental vacancy rate: 41.8%

BURT (township).
Covers a land area of 230.481 square miles and a water area of 27.545 square miles. Located at 46.57° N. Lat; 86.10° W. Long.
Population: 522; Growth (since 2000): 8.8%; Density: 2.3 persons per square mile; Race: 95.8% White, 0.4% Black/African American, 0.6% Asian, 0.8% American Indian/Alaska Native, 0.0% Native Hawaiian/Other Pacific Islander, 2.3% Two or more races, 1.3% Hispanic of any race; Average household size: 1.57; Median age: 62.6; Age under 18: 8.0%; Age 65 and over: 43.1%; Males per 100 females: 124.0
Housing: Homeownership rate: 80.7%; Homeowner vacancy rate: 2.5%; Rental vacancy rate: 20.0%

CHATHAM (village).
Covers a land area of 2.451 square miles and a water area of 0 square miles. Located at 46.34° N. Lat; 86.93° W. Long. Elevation is 876 feet.
History: Chatham was founded by James Finn in 1896 as a lumber camp. It was named for Chatham, Ontario. The Michigan Agricultural Experiment Station was established in Chatham in the late 1890's, as an extension of the Michigan State College of Agriculture.
Population: 220; Growth (since 2000): -4.8%; Density: 89.8 persons per square mile; Race: 88.6% White, 0.9% Black/African American, 0.0%

Asian, 7.3% American Indian/Alaska Native, 0.0% Native Hawaiian/Other Pacific Islander, 3.2% Two or more races, 0.0% Hispanic of any race; Average household size: 2.27; Median age: 44.3; Age under 18: 26.4%; Age 65 and over: 15.9%; Males per 100 females: 98.2
Housing: Homeownership rate: 75.2%; Homeowner vacancy rate: 2.6%; Rental vacancy rate: 17.2%

DEERTON (unincorporated postal area)
ZCTA: 49822
Covers a land area of 60.694 square miles and a water area of 8.014 square miles. Located at 46.43° N. Lat; 87.02° W. Long. Elevation is 728 feet.
Population: 220; Growth (since 2000): 34.1%; Density: 3.6 persons per square mile; Race: 95.9% White, 0.0% Black/African American, 0.5% Asian, 0.5% American Indian/Alaska Native, 0.0% Native Hawaiian/Other Pacific Islander, 2.7% Two or more races, 0.5% Hispanic of any race; Average household size: 2.04; Median age: 52.6; Age under 18: 13.2%; Age 65 and over: 22.7%; Males per 100 females: 96.4

School District(s)
Autrain-Onota Public Schools (PK-12)
    2012-13 Enrollment: 43 . . . . (906) 343-6632
Housing: Homeownership rate: 91.6%; Homeowner vacancy rate: 2.9%; Rental vacancy rate: 9.1%

EBEN JUNCTION (unincorporated postal area)
ZCTA: 49825
Covers a land area of 22.767 square miles and a water area of 0.087 square miles. Located at 46.35° N. Lat; 86.99° W. Long. Elevation is 965 feet.
Population: 299; Growth (since 2000): 39.7%; Density: 13.1 persons per square mile; Race: 96.0% White, 0.3% Black/African American, 0.0% Asian, 2.3% American Indian/Alaska Native, 0.0% Native Hawaiian/Other Pacific Islander, 1.3% Two or more races, 0.7% Hispanic of any race; Average household size: 2.32; Median age: 43.9; Age under 18: 24.7%; Age 65 and over: 17.1%; Males per 100 females: 95.4

School District(s)
Superior Central SD (KG-12)
    2012-13 Enrollment: 356 . . . . (906) 439-5531
Housing: Homeownership rate: 89.1%; Homeowner vacancy rate: 0.9%; Rental vacancy rate: 6.7%

GRAND ISLAND (township). Covers a land area of 22.479 square miles and a water area of 26.611 square miles. Located at 46.52° N. Lat; 86.66° W. Long.
History: Grand Island had a few settlers in the 1840's. Much of the land was owned by the Cleveland-Cliffs Iron Company, which conducted logging operations here. A lighthouse was built in 1856 on the northwest tip of the island, to help ships navigate on Lake Superior.
Population: 47; Growth (since 2000): 4.4%; Density: 2.1 persons per square mile; Race: 85.1% White, 0.0% Black/African American, 0.0% Asian, 8.5% American Indian/Alaska Native, 0.0% Native Hawaiian/Other Pacific Islander, 6.4% Two or more races, 0.0% Hispanic of any race; Average household size: 2.47; Median age: 50.5; Age under 18: 27.7%; Age 65 and over: 31.9%; Males per 100 females: 80.8
Housing: Homeownership rate: 94.7%; Homeowner vacancy rate: 0.0%; Rental vacancy rate: 50.0%

GRAND MARAIS (unincorporated postal area)
ZCTA: 49839
Covers a land area of 138.880 square miles and a water area of 22.873 square miles. Located at 46.62° N. Lat; 86.11° W. Long. Elevation is 627 feet.
Population: 479; Growth (since 2000): 10.6%; Density: 3.4 persons per square mile; Race: 95.4% White, 0.4% Black/African American, 0.6% Asian, 0.8% American Indian/Alaska Native, 0.0% Native Hawaiian/Other Pacific Islander, 2.5% Two or more races, 1.5% Hispanic of any race; Average household size: 1.55; Median age: 62.5; Age under 18: 7.5%; Age 65 and over: 43.6%; Males per 100 females: 124.9

School District(s)
Burt Township SD (KG-12)
    2012-13 Enrollment: 35 . . . . (906) 494-2543

Housing: Homeownership rate: 79.4%; Homeowner vacancy rate: 2.4%; Rental vacancy rate: 19.0%

LIMESTONE (township). Covers a land area of 74.225 square miles and a water area of 0.930 square miles. Located at 46.24° N. Lat; 87.02° W. Long. Elevation is 912 feet.
History: Limestone Township was first settled in 1889. It was named for the limestone bed of Johnson Creek, which runs through it.
Population: 438; Growth (since 2000): 7.6%; Density: 5.9 persons per square mile; Race: 95.9% White, 0.5% Black/African American, 0.0% Asian, 1.8% American Indian/Alaska Native, 0.0% Native Hawaiian/Other Pacific Islander, 1.6% Two or more races, 1.4% Hispanic of any race; Average household size: 2.38; Median age: 48.5; Age under 18: 21.0%; Age 65 and over: 21.0%; Males per 100 females: 93.0
Housing: Homeownership rate: 93.5%; Homeowner vacancy rate: 1.1%; Rental vacancy rate: 0.0%

MATHIAS (township). Covers a land area of 70.679 square miles and a water area of 1.345 square miles. Located at 46.21° N. Lat; 86.87° W. Long.
Population: 554; Growth (since 2000): -3.0%; Density: 7.8 persons per square mile; Race: 94.9% White, 0.0% Black/African American, 0.5% Asian, 1.1% American Indian/Alaska Native, 0.0% Native Hawaiian/Other Pacific Islander, 2.9% Two or more races, 1.3% Hispanic of any race; Average household size: 2.17; Median age: 48.7; Age under 18: 21.1%; Age 65 and over: 22.7%; Males per 100 females: 115.6
Housing: Homeownership rate: 87.4%; Homeowner vacancy rate: 2.2%; Rental vacancy rate: 11.1%

MUNISING (city). County seat. Covers a land area of 5.253 square miles and a water area of 3.781 square miles. Located at 46.43° N. Lat; 86.62° W. Long. Elevation is 614 feet.
History: Munising's name came from the Ojibway name for Grand Island, which was Gitchi-Menesing. A town was mapped out in the 1850's by a group of land speculators, but not until the 1870's did the town become a reality. Iron furnaces were the first industry, followed by a tannery and sawmills. Munising was incorporated as a village in 1897 and as a city in 1919.
Population: 2,355; Growth (since 2000): -7.2%; Density: 448.4 persons per square mile; Race: 91.2% White, 0.2% Black/African American, 0.7% Asian, 4.8% American Indian/Alaska Native, 0.0% Native Hawaiian/Other Pacific Islander, 3.0% Two or more races, 1.4% Hispanic of any race; Average household size: 2.13; Median age: 48.6; Age under 18: 18.7%; Age 65 and over: 26.3%; Males per 100 females: 90.2

School District(s)
Munising Public Schools (PK-12)
    2012-13 Enrollment: 647 . . . . (906) 387-2251
Housing: Homeownership rate: 64.3%; Homeowner vacancy rate: 4.2%; Rental vacancy rate: 11.2%
Hospitals: Munising Memorial Hospital
Safety: Violent crime rate: 8.6 per 10,000 population; Property crime rate: 180.6 per 10,000 population
Newspapers: Munising News (weekly circulation 2700)

MUNISING (township). Covers a land area of 202.211 square miles and a water area of 15.470 square miles. Located at 46.40° N. Lat; 86.51° W. Long. Elevation is 614 feet.
History: Incorporated as village 1897, as city 1916.
Population: 2,983; Growth (since 2000): -4.5%; Density: 14.8 persons per square mile; Race: 71.2% White, 19.9% Black/African American, 0.3% Asian, 5.7% American Indian/Alaska Native, 0.0% Native Hawaiian/Other Pacific Islander, 2.8% Two or more races, 1.0% Hispanic of any race; Average household size: 2.47; Median age: 40.4; Age under 18: 14.8%; Age 65 and over: 12.5%; Males per 100 females: 183.6; Marriage status: 48.1% never married, 38.8% now married, 0.0% separated, 3.1% widowed, 10.0% divorced; Foreign born: 1.9%; Speak English only: 95.8%; With disability: 18.1%; Veterans: 8.6%; Ancestry: 17.3% German, 9.0% Irish, 7.4% English, 7.4% American, 5.5% French
Employment: 5.8% management, business, and financial, 1.1% computer, engineering, and science, 11.2% education, legal, community service, arts, and media, 4.4% healthcare practitioners, 25.1% service, 23.4% sales and office, 13.2% natural resources, construction, and maintenance, 15.8% production, transportation, and material moving

Income: Per capita: $13,382; Median household: $43,000; Average household: $49,064; Households with income of $100,000 or more: 9.7%; Poverty rate: 18.2%

Educational Attainment: High school diploma or higher: 84.0%; Bachelor's degree or higher: 10.0%; Graduate/professional degree or higher: 3.2%

School District(s)
Munising Public Schools (PK-12)
    2012-13 Enrollment: 647 . . . . (906) 387-2251

Housing: Homeownership rate: 90.4%; Median home value: $120,400; Median year structure built: 1976; Homeowner vacancy rate: 3.5%; Median gross rent: $649 per month; Rental vacancy rate: 11.3%

Health Insurance: 88.3% have insurance; 67.9% have private insurance; 43.4% have public insurance; 11.7% do not have insurance; 0.0% of children under 18 do not have insurance

Hospitals: Munising Memorial Hospital

Newspapers: Munising News (weekly circulation 2700)

Transportation: Commute: 95.3% car, 0.3% public transportation, 0.0% walk, 2.7% work from home; Median travel time to work: 17.9 minutes

ONOTA (township).
Covers a land area of 87.732 square miles and a water area of 15.859 square miles. Located at 46.45° N. Lat; 87.00° W. Long. Elevation is 774 feet.

Population: 352; Growth (since 2000): 13.5%; Density: 4.0 persons per square mile; Race: 96.6% White, 0.0% Black/African American, 0.3% Asian, 0.9% American Indian/Alaska Native, 0.0% Native Hawaiian/Other Pacific Islander, 2.0% Two or more races, 0.9% Hispanic of any race; Average household size: 2.03; Median age: 56.6; Age under 18: 9.9%; Age 65 and over: 29.3%; Males per 100 females: 91.3

Housing: Homeownership rate: 94.2%; Homeowner vacancy rate: 2.4%; Rental vacancy rate: 64.5%

ROCK RIVER (township).
Covers a land area of 80.745 square miles and a water area of 0.252 square miles. Located at 46.35° N. Lat; 86.99° W. Long. Elevation is 614 feet.

Population: 1,212; Growth (since 2000): -0.1%; Density: 15.0 persons per square mile; Race: 95.2% White, 0.6% Black/African American, 0.1% Asian, 2.3% American Indian/Alaska Native, 0.0% Native Hawaiian/Other Pacific Islander, 1.8% Two or more races, 0.6% Hispanic of any race; Average household size: 2.32; Median age: 46.0; Age under 18: 23.3%; Age 65 and over: 14.9%; Males per 100 females: 102.7

Housing: Homeownership rate: 90.7%; Homeowner vacancy rate: 1.9%; Rental vacancy rate: 14.0%

RUMELY (unincorporated postal area)
ZCTA: 49826

Covers a land area of 14.283 square miles and a water area of 0.085 square miles. Located at 46.32° N. Lat; 87.05° W. Long. Elevation is 1,056 feet.

Population: 137; Growth (since 2000): 260.5%; Density: 9.6 persons per square mile; Race: 97.1% White, 0.0% Black/African American, 0.0% Asian, 0.7% American Indian/Alaska Native, 0.0% Native Hawaiian/Other Pacific Islander, 2.2% Two or more races, 0.0% Hispanic of any race; Average household size: 2.17; Median age: 49.9; Age under 18: 19.0%; Age 65 and over: 11.7%; Males per 100 females: 101.5

Housing: Homeownership rate: 95.3%; Homeowner vacancy rate: 1.6%; Rental vacancy rate: 0.0%

SHINGLETON (unincorporated postal area)
ZCTA: 49884

Covers a land area of 281.509 square miles and a water area of 11.075 square miles. Located at 46.41° N. Lat; 86.32° W. Long. Elevation is 827 feet.

Population: 552; Growth (since 2000): -41.4%; Density: 2.0 persons per square mile; Race: 84.4% White, 0.0% Black/African American, 0.0% Asian, 10.3% American Indian/Alaska Native, 0.0% Native Hawaiian/Other Pacific Islander, 5.3% Two or more races, 0.4% Hispanic of any race; Average household size: 2.45; Median age: 48.7; Age under 18: 18.8%; Age 65 and over: 19.9%; Males per 100 females: 103.7

Housing: Homeownership rate: 93.3%; Homeowner vacancy rate: 3.5%; Rental vacancy rate: 6.3%

TRENARY (unincorporated postal area)
ZCTA: 49891

Covers a land area of 85.212 square miles and a water area of 0.384 square miles. Located at 46.24° N. Lat; 87.02° W. Long. Elevation is 869 feet.

Population: 816; Growth (since 2000): -13.6%; Density: 9.6 persons per square mile; Race: 95.6% White, 0.2% Black/African American, 0.4% Asian, 1.5% American Indian/Alaska Native, 0.0% Native Hawaiian/Other Pacific Islander, 2.2% Two or more races, 0.6% Hispanic of any race; Average household size: 2.25; Median age: 47.8; Age under 18: 23.2%; Age 65 and over: 23.0%; Males per 100 females: 106.6

Housing: Homeownership rate: 88.9%; Homeowner vacancy rate: 1.5%; Rental vacancy rate: 9.1%

WETMORE (unincorporated postal area)
ZCTA: 49895

Covers a land area of 218.664 square miles and a water area of 7.816 square miles. Located at 46.17° N. Lat; 86.67° W. Long. Elevation is 876 feet.

Population: 765; Growth (since 2000): 15.4%; Density: 3.5 persons per square mile; Race: 89.7% White, 0.0% Black/African American, 0.5% Asian, 6.5% American Indian/Alaska Native, 0.0% Native Hawaiian/Other Pacific Islander, 3.1% Two or more races, 1.0% Hispanic of any race; Average household size: 2.20; Median age: 53.4; Age under 18: 16.6%; Age 65 and over: 21.2%; Males per 100 females: 97.7

Housing: Homeownership rate: 89.3%; Homeowner vacancy rate: 6.3%; Rental vacancy rate: 15.9%

Allegan County

Located in southwestern Michigan; bounded on the west by Lake Michigan. Covers a land area of 825.231 square miles, a water area of 1,008.057 square miles, and is located in the Eastern Time Zone at 42.60° N. Lat., 86.63° W. Long. The county was founded in 1831. County seat is Allegan.

Allegan County is part of the Holland, MI Micropolitan Statistical Area. The entire metro area includes: Allegan County, MI

Weather Station: Allegan 5 NE										Elevation: 750 feet		
	Jan	Feb	Mar	Apr	May	Jun	Jul	Aug	Sep	Oct	Nov	Dec
High	31	34	44	58	69	78	82	80	73	60	48	35
Low	16	17	24	35	45	54	58	57	50	39	31	21
Precip	3.0	2.1	2.5	3.4	4.6	3.6	3.9	3.9	4.0	3.3	3.8	3.2
Snow	25.6	17.3	8.5	2.6	tr	0.0	0.0	0.0	0.0	0.5	7.4	24.8

High and Low temperatures in degrees Fahrenheit; Precipitation and Snow in inches

Population: 111,408; Growth (since 2000): 5.4%; Density: 135.0 persons per square mile; Race: 92.9% White, 1.2% Black/African American, 0.6% Asian, 0.6% American Indian/Alaska Native, 0.0% Native Hawaiian/Other Pacific Islander, 1.9% two or more races, 6.7% Hispanic of any race; Average household size: 2.63; Median age: 39.2; Age under 18: 26.2%; Age 65 and over: 13.0%; Males per 100 females: 99.2; Marriage status: 23.7% never married, 60.0% now married, 1.2% separated, 5.3% widowed, 11.0% divorced; Foreign born: 3.2%; Speak English only: 94.3%; With disability: 11.4%; Veterans: 9.3%; Ancestry: 21.6% Dutch, 21.6% German, 9.8% English, 9.7% Irish, 6.4% American

Religion: Six largest groups: 9.0% Catholicism, 7.3% Presbyterian-Reformed, 3.5% Methodist/Pietist, 2.8% Non-denominational Protestant, 1.5% Lutheran, 1.0% Buddhism

Economy: Unemployment rate: 4.3%; Leading industries: 15.2% retail trade; 13.4% construction; 12.2% other services (except public administration); Farms: 1,396 totaling 270,282 acres; Company size: 3 employ 1,000 or more persons, 3 employ 500 to 999 persons, 44 employ 100 to 499 persons, 2,171 employs less than 100 persons; Business ownership: 2,639 women-owned, n/a Black-owned, 144 Hispanic-owned, 36 Asian-owned

Employment: 12.5% management, business, and financial, 4.0% computer, engineering, and science, 7.4% education, legal, community service, arts, and media, 4.3% healthcare practitioners, 15.7% service, 22.6% sales and office, 11.6% natural resources, construction, and maintenance, 21.7% production, transportation, and material moving

Income: Per capita: $24,140; Median household: $52,061; Average household: $63,833; Households with income of $100,000 or more: 16.1%; Poverty rate: 13.5%
Educational Attainment: High school diploma or higher: 90.0%; Bachelor's degree or higher: 20.2%; Graduate/professional degree or higher: 6.8%
Housing: Homeownership rate: 81.1%; Median home value: $140,200; Median year structure built: 1979; Homeowner vacancy rate: 2.8%; Median gross rent: $728 per month; Rental vacancy rate: 10.4%
Vital Statistics: Birth rate: 119.3 per 10,000 population; Death rate: 76.2 per 10,000 population; Age-adjusted cancer mortality rate: 174.4 deaths per 100,000 population
Health Insurance: 89.1% have insurance; 71.7% have private insurance; 30.5% have public insurance; 10.9% do not have insurance; 2.4% of children under 18 do not have insurance
Health Care: Physicians: 6.0 per 10,000 population; Hospital beds: 6.1 per 10,000 population; Hospital admissions: 210.9 per 10,000 population
Air Quality Index: 76.8% good, 21.2% moderate, 2.1% unhealthy for sensitive individuals, 0.0% unhealthy (percent of days)
Transportation: Commute: 92.9% car, 0.2% public transportation, 1.7% walk, 4.2% work from home; Median travel time to work: 24.4 minutes
Presidential Election: 39.8% Obama, 59.1% Romney (2012)
National and State Parks: Allegan State Forest; Saugatuck Dunes State Park
Additional Information Contacts
Allegan Government . . . . (269) 673-0205
  http://www.allegancounty.org

Allegan County Communities

ALLEGAN (city). County seat. Covers a land area of 3.847 square miles and a water area of 0.414 square miles. Located at 42.53° N. Lat; 85.85° W. Long. Elevation is 653 feet.
History: Allegan was settled in 1833. It was incorporated as a village in 1838 and as a city in 1907. The name was chosen by Henry Rowe Schoolcraft for the Alleghen tribe.
Population: 4,998; Growth (since 2000): 3.3%; Density: 1,299.1 persons per square mile; Race: 91.4% White, 4.3% Black/African American, 0.8% Asian, 0.6% American Indian/Alaska Native, 0.0% Native Hawaiian/Other Pacific Islander, 2.4% Two or more races, 3.8% Hispanic of any race; Average household size: 2.40; Median age: 34.6; Age under 18: 25.8%; Age 65 and over: 12.1%; Males per 100 females: 93.6; Marriage status: 26.1% never married, 47.6% now married, 1.9% separated, 9.5% widowed, 16.8% divorced; Foreign born: 0.5%; Speak English only: 97.8%; With disability: 18.0%; Veterans: 10.2%; Ancestry: 23.3% German, 17.4% English, 14.7% Irish, 12.5% Dutch, 4.8% American
Employment: 5.2% management, business, and financial, 3.1% computer, engineering, and science, 8.5% education, legal, community service, arts, and media, 1.1% healthcare practitioners, 12.7% service, 31.6% sales and office, 6.2% natural resources, construction, and maintenance, 31.7% production, transportation, and material moving
Income: Per capita: $20,203; Median household: $42,318; Average household: $47,015; Households with income of $100,000 or more: 8.9%; Poverty rate: 16.5%
Educational Attainment: High school diploma or higher: 89.7%; Bachelor's degree or higher: 14.0%; Graduate/professional degree or higher: 5.6%

School District(s)
Allegan Area Educational Service Agency (PK-12)
  2012-13 Enrollment: 349. . . . . (269) 673-2161
Allegan Public Schools (KG-12)
  2012-13 Enrollment: 2,657 . . . . (269) 673-5431
Outlook Academy (KG-12)
  2012-13 Enrollment: 35. . . . . (269) 561-7241
Housing: Homeownership rate: 55.0%; Median home value: $83,900; Median year structure built: 1954; Homeowner vacancy rate: 4.1%; Median gross rent: $751 per month; Rental vacancy rate: 11.3%
Health Insurance: 88.9% have insurance; 63.5% have private insurance; 41.2% have public insurance; 11.1% do not have insurance; 0.0% of children under 18 do not have insurance
Hospitals: Allegan General Hospital (63 beds)
Safety: Violent crime rate: 33.6 per 10,000 population; Property crime rate: 164.2 per 10,000 population
Newspapers: Allegan County News (weekly circulation 5500)

Transportation: Commute: 96.5% car, 0.0% public transportation, 1.9% walk, 1.6% work from home; Median travel time to work: 21.9 minutes
Airports: Padgham Field (general aviation)

ALLEGAN (township). Covers a land area of 30.404 square miles and a water area of 1.475 square miles. Located at 42.56° N. Lat; 85.83° W. Long. Elevation is 653 feet.
History: Settled 1834, incorporated as city 1907.
Population: 4,406; Growth (since 2000): 8.8%; Density: 144.9 persons per square mile; Race: 96.2% White, 1.1% Black/African American, 0.4% Asian, 0.4% American Indian/Alaska Native, 0.0% Native Hawaiian/Other Pacific Islander, 1.6% Two or more races, 2.0% Hispanic of any race; Average household size: 2.55; Median age: 43.6; Age under 18: 23.9%; Age 65 and over: 17.8%; Males per 100 females: 98.4; Marriage status: 24.4% never married, 55.7% now married, 0.7% separated, 8.2% widowed, 11.7% divorced; Foreign born: 0.7%; Speak English only: 97.9%; With disability: 18.5%; Veterans: 11.7%; Ancestry: 20.3% German, 10.7% Dutch, 10.4% Irish, 8.3% American, 7.1% English
Employment: 16.9% management, business, and financial, 5.5% computer, engineering, and science, 7.6% education, legal, community service, arts, and media, 5.2% healthcare practitioners, 11.7% service, 18.5% sales and office, 13.4% natural resources, construction, and maintenance, 21.1% production, transportation, and material moving
Income: Per capita: $23,977; Median household: $49,269; Average household: $63,189; Households with income of $100,000 or more: 21.5%; Poverty rate: 11.2%
Educational Attainment: High school diploma or higher: 90.8%; Bachelor's degree or higher: 19.3%; Graduate/professional degree or higher: 7.0%

School District(s)
Allegan Area Educational Service Agency (PK-12)
  2012-13 Enrollment: 349. . . . . (269) 673-2161
Allegan Public Schools (KG-12)
  2012-13 Enrollment: 2,657 . . . . (269) 673-5431
Outlook Academy (KG-12)
  2012-13 Enrollment: 35. . . . . (269) 561-7241
Housing: Homeownership rate: 87.1%; Median home value: $102,800; Median year structure built: 1978; Homeowner vacancy rate: 3.3%; Median gross rent: $794 per month; Rental vacancy rate: 10.2%
Health Insurance: 90.1% have insurance; 74.0% have private insurance; 35.6% have public insurance; 9.9% do not have insurance; 0.0% of children under 18 do not have insurance
Hospitals: Allegan General Hospital (63 beds)
Newspapers: Allegan County News (weekly circulation 5500)
Transportation: Commute: 94.1% car, 0.0% public transportation, 1.5% walk, 3.6% work from home; Median travel time to work: 18.1 minutes
Airports: Padgham Field (general aviation)

CASCO (township). Covers a land area of 38.871 square miles and a water area of 0.068 square miles. Located at 42.46° N. Lat; 86.20° W. Long. Elevation is 620 feet.
Population: 2,823; Growth (since 2000): -6.5%; Density: 72.6 persons per square mile; Race: 90.0% White, 3.1% Black/African American, 0.2% Asian, 1.1% American Indian/Alaska Native, 0.0% Native Hawaiian/Other Pacific Islander, 1.8% Two or more races, 9.1% Hispanic of any race; Average household size: 2.49; Median age: 45.8; Age under 18: 23.0%; Age 65 and over: 16.8%; Males per 100 females: 106.5; Marriage status: 25.6% never married, 58.9% now married, 1.3% separated, 6.6% widowed, 8.8% divorced; Foreign born: 10.0%; Speak English only: 89.0%; With disability: 17.4%; Veterans: 9.6%; Ancestry: 23.0% German, 14.9% English, 9.7% Dutch, 8.9% Irish, 4.6% Polish
Employment: 6.0% management, business, and financial, 1.3% computer, engineering, and science, 14.0% education, legal, community service, arts, and media, 3.9% healthcare practitioners, 19.3% service, 15.5% sales and office, 24.0% natural resources, construction, and maintenance, 15.9% production, transportation, and material moving
Income: Per capita: $29,272; Median household: $55,686; Average household: $79,594; Households with income of $100,000 or more: 17.7%; Poverty rate: 25.5%
Educational Attainment: High school diploma or higher: 87.4%; Bachelor's degree or higher: 21.7%; Graduate/professional degree or higher: 9.6%
Housing: Homeownership rate: 86.3%; Median home value: $181,300; Median year structure built: 1981; Homeowner vacancy rate: 4.1%; Median gross rent: $671 per month; Rental vacancy rate: 14.0%

Health Insurance: 82.1% have insurance; 55.1% have private insurance; 41.0% have public insurance; 17.9% do not have insurance; 4.7% of children under 18 do not have insurance
Transportation: Commute: 79.5% car, 1.0% public transportation, 8.4% walk, 11.1% work from home; Median travel time to work: 22.7 minutes

CHESHIRE (township). Covers a land area of 34.818 square miles and a water area of 1.097 square miles. Located at 42.47° N. Lat; 85.95° W. Long.
History: Cheshire Township was organized in 1851 around four sawmill villages.
Population: 2,199; Growth (since 2000): -5.8%; Density: 63.2 persons per square mile; Race: 92.9% White, 2.7% Black/African American, 0.2% Asian, 0.9% American Indian/Alaska Native, 0.0% Native Hawaiian/Other Pacific Islander, 1.7% Two or more races, 4.3% Hispanic of any race; Average household size: 2.63; Median age: 42.1; Age under 18: 23.6%; Age 65 and over: 13.5%; Males per 100 females: 103.6
Housing: Homeownership rate: 86.5%; Homeowner vacancy rate: 4.5%; Rental vacancy rate: 9.7%

CLYDE (township). Covers a land area of 34.802 square miles and a water area of 0.683 square miles. Located at 42.55° N. Lat; 86.06° W. Long.
History: Clyde Township was organized in 1859 and named for Clyde, New York, the former home of its first supervisor.
Population: 2,084; Growth (since 2000): -1.0%; Density: 59.9 persons per square mile; Race: 72.5% White, 1.6% Black/African American, 1.0% Asian, 0.8% American Indian/Alaska Native, 0.0% Native Hawaiian/Other Pacific Islander, 2.6% Two or more races, 34.5% Hispanic of any race; Average household size: 2.91; Median age: 38.5; Age under 18: 26.4%; Age 65 and over: 11.0%; Males per 100 females: 101.5
Housing: Homeownership rate: 89.4%; Homeowner vacancy rate: 2.6%; Rental vacancy rate: 7.2%

DORR (township). Covers a land area of 36.148 square miles and a water area of 0.025 square miles. Located at 42.72° N. Lat; 85.72° W. Long. Elevation is 699 feet.
Population: 7,439; Growth (since 2000): 13.1%; Density: 205.8 persons per square mile; Race: 97.0% White, 0.4% Black/African American, 0.3% Asian, 0.6% American Indian/Alaska Native, 0.0% Native Hawaiian/Other Pacific Islander, 1.1% Two or more races, 2.1% Hispanic of any race; Average household size: 3.03; Median age: 35.8; Age under 18: 29.7%; Age 65 and over: 8.2%; Males per 100 females: 97.4; Marriage status: 23.2% never married, 65.5% now married, 0.2% separated, 2.3% widowed, 9.0% divorced; Foreign born: 1.4%; Speak English only: 97.6%; With disability: 6.9%; Veterans: 6.5%; Ancestry: 28.9% Dutch, 24.5% German, 13.0% American, 10.1% Irish, 8.0% Polish
Employment: 15.0% management, business, and financial, 3.9% computer, engineering, and science, 8.3% education, legal, community service, arts, and media, 3.5% healthcare practitioners, 16.8% service, 20.2% sales and office, 15.1% natural resources, construction, and maintenance, 17.3% production, transportation, and material moving
Income: Per capita: $24,163; Median household: $70,069; Average household: $72,589; Households with income of $100,000 or more: 19.9%; Poverty rate: 7.5%
Educational Attainment: High school diploma or higher: 93.6%; Bachelor's degree or higher: 14.2%; Graduate/professional degree or higher: 4.3%
School District(s)
Hopkins Public Schools (KG-12)
    2012-13 Enrollment: 1,653 . . . . (269) 793-7261
Wayland Union Schools (PK-12)
    2012-13 Enrollment: 2,808 . . . . (269) 792-2181
Housing: Homeownership rate: 93.1%; Median home value: $154,900; Median year structure built: 1980; Homeowner vacancy rate: 1.3%; Median gross rent: $957 per month; Rental vacancy rate: 6.0%
Health Insurance: 94.7% have insurance; 81.8% have private insurance; 22.7% have public insurance; 5.3% do not have insurance; 0.0% of children under 18 do not have insurance
Transportation: Commute: 94.5% car, 0.5% public transportation, 0.8% walk, 3.2% work from home; Median travel time to work: 28.5 minutes

DOUGLAS (city). Covers a land area of 1.746 square miles and a water area of 0.225 square miles. Located at 42.64° N. Lat; 86.21° W. Long. Elevation is 610 feet.
History: Douglas grew around an art colony.
Population: 1,232; Growth (since 2000): 1.5%; Density: 705.6 persons per square mile; Race: 97.2% White, 0.6% Black/African American, 0.2% Asian, 0.2% American Indian/Alaska Native, 0.0% Native Hawaiian/Other Pacific Islander, 0.9% Two or more races, 3.7% Hispanic of any race; Average household size: 1.82; Median age: 54.3; Age under 18: 14.0%; Age 65 and over: 26.0%; Males per 100 females: 100.0
School District(s)
Saugatuck Public Schools (PK-12)
    2012-13 Enrollment: 858 . . . . (269) 857-1444
Housing: Homeownership rate: 74.6%; Homeowner vacancy rate: 4.4%; Rental vacancy rate: 19.9%

FENNVILLE (city). Covers a land area of 1.098 square miles and a water area of 0.010 square miles. Located at 42.59° N. Lat; 86.11° W. Long. Elevation is 663 feet.
Population: 1,398; Growth (since 2000): -4.2%; Density: 1,273.4 persons per square mile; Race: 72.6% White, 1.9% Black/African American, 0.1% Asian, 0.5% American Indian/Alaska Native, 0.0% Native Hawaiian/Other Pacific Islander, 4.2% Two or more races, 39.1% Hispanic of any race; Average household size: 2.77; Median age: 28.7; Age under 18: 34.9%; Age 65 and over: 7.7%; Males per 100 females: 101.2
School District(s)
Fennville Public Schools (PK-12)
    2012-13 Enrollment: 1,425 . . . . (269) 561-7331
Housing: Homeownership rate: 62.3%; Homeowner vacancy rate: 5.0%; Rental vacancy rate: 16.6%
Additional Information Contacts
City of Fennville . . . . (269) 561-8321
    http://www.fennville.com/cityoffennville.html

FILLMORE (township). Covers a land area of 28.352 square miles and a water area of 0.023 square miles. Located at 42.71° N. Lat; 86.07° W. Long. Elevation is 709 feet.
Population: 2,681; Growth (since 2000): -2.7%; Density: 94.6 persons per square mile; Race: 92.6% White, 0.5% Black/African American, 1.9% Asian, 0.4% American Indian/Alaska Native, 0.0% Native Hawaiian/Other Pacific Islander, 2.6% Two or more races, 6.5% Hispanic of any race; Average household size: 2.76; Median age: 39.2; Age under 18: 25.4%; Age 65 and over: 13.0%; Males per 100 females: 103.4; Marriage status: 22.5% never married, 62.3% now married, 1.1% separated, 5.3% widowed, 9.9% divorced; Foreign born: 1.6%; Speak English only: 96.4%; With disability: 10.6%; Veterans: 7.8%; Ancestry: 39.8% Dutch, 14.8% German, 5.6% English, 4.6% American, 4.1% Irish
Employment: 17.6% management, business, and financial, 5.3% computer, engineering, and science, 8.2% education, legal, community service, arts, and media, 3.2% healthcare practitioners, 9.4% service, 21.9% sales and office, 8.7% natural resources, construction, and maintenance, 25.7% production, transportation, and material moving
Income: Per capita: $25,219; Median household: $53,036; Average household: $70,049; Households with income of $100,000 or more: 17.8%; Poverty rate: 7.7%
Educational Attainment: High school diploma or higher: 89.6%; Bachelor's degree or higher: 17.8%; Graduate/professional degree or higher: 6.6%
Housing: Homeownership rate: 82.2%; Median home value: $150,700; Median year structure built: 1971; Homeowner vacancy rate: 2.8%; Median gross rent: $854 per month; Rental vacancy rate: 4.9%
Health Insurance: 94.8% have insurance; 81.6% have private insurance; 20.9% have public insurance; 5.2% do not have insurance; 0.9% of children under 18 do not have insurance
Transportation: Commute: 94.4% car, 0.0% public transportation, 0.0% walk, 4.9% work from home; Median travel time to work: 16.5 minutes

GANGES (township). Covers a land area of 32.049 square miles and a water area of 0.638 square miles. Located at 42.55° N. Lat; 86.19° W. Long. Elevation is 659 feet.
Population: 2,530; Growth (since 2000): 0.2%; Density: 78.9 persons per square mile; Race: 89.5% White, 0.2% Black/African American, 0.4% Asian, 0.2% American Indian/Alaska Native, 0.2% Native Hawaiian/Other Pacific Islander, 2.3% Two or more races, 16.8% Hispanic of any race; Average household size: 2.40; Median age: 45.9; Age under 18: 21.4%;

Age 65 and over: 16.8%; Males per 100 females: 101.6; Marriage status: 26.0% never married, 58.4% now married, 1.2% separated, 6.9% widowed, 8.6% divorced; Foreign born: 8.1%; Speak English only: 85.3%; With disability: 10.8%; Veterans: 11.0%; Ancestry: 15.7% German, 13.8% English, 11.9% Dutch, 9.6% Irish, 6.8% Polish
Employment: 14.4% management, business, and financial, 1.5% computer, engineering, and science, 7.3% education, legal, community service, arts, and media, 3.4% healthcare practitioners, 15.6% service, 20.2% sales and office, 14.1% natural resources, construction, and maintenance, 23.6% production, transportation, and material moving
Income: Per capita: $26,573; Median household: $48,452; Average household: $65,973; Households with income of $100,000 or more: 16.8%; Poverty rate: 16.4%
Educational Attainment: High school diploma or higher: 86.6%; Bachelor's degree or higher: 25.6%; Graduate/professional degree or higher: 10.0%
Housing: Homeownership rate: 85.2%; Median home value: $158,600; Median year structure built: 1982; Homeowner vacancy rate: 3.7%; Median gross rent: $744 per month; Rental vacancy rate: 13.4%
Health Insurance: 84.5% have insurance; 64.4% have private insurance; 36.4% have public insurance; 15.5% do not have insurance; 8.6% of children under 18 do not have insurance
Transportation: Commute: 83.7% car, 0.0% public transportation, 4.1% walk, 10.0% work from home; Median travel time to work: 29.2 minutes

GUN PLAIN (township). Covers a land area of 34.058 square miles and a water area of 0.315 square miles. Located at 42.46° N. Lat; 85.59° W. Long.
Population: 5,895; Growth (since 2000): 4.6%; Density: 173.1 persons per square mile; Race: 96.5% White, 0.9% Black/African American, 0.4% Asian, 0.5% American Indian/Alaska Native, 0.0% Native Hawaiian/Other Pacific Islander, 1.1% Two or more races, 2.2% Hispanic of any race; Average household size: 2.71; Median age: 41.0; Age under 18: 26.1%; Age 65 and over: 13.2%; Males per 100 females: 102.1; Marriage status: 22.0% never married, 66.6% now married, 0.4% separated, 1.6% widowed, 9.8% divorced; Foreign born: 1.7%; Speak English only: 97.3%; With disability: 10.9%; Veterans: 8.9%; Ancestry: 27.8% German, 15.8% English, 13.8% Dutch, 13.7% Irish, 5.3% American
Employment: 13.4% management, business, and financial, 6.3% computer, engineering, and science, 9.0% education, legal, community service, arts, and media, 7.8% healthcare practitioners, 10.9% service, 25.4% sales and office, 7.6% natural resources, construction, and maintenance, 19.6% production, transportation, and material moving
Income: Per capita: $27,544; Median household: $63,162; Average household: $72,471; Households with income of $100,000 or more: 21.9%; Poverty rate: 7.9%
Educational Attainment: High school diploma or higher: 93.4%; Bachelor's degree or higher: 26.3%; Graduate/professional degree or higher: 8.9%
Housing: Homeownership rate: 89.9%; Median home value: $158,700; Median year structure built: 1979; Homeowner vacancy rate: 2.1%; Median gross rent: $697 per month; Rental vacancy rate: 6.4%
Health Insurance: 93.0% have insurance; 78.8% have private insurance; 28.3% have public insurance; 7.0% do not have insurance; 0.0% of children under 18 do not have insurance
Transportation: Commute: 94.5% car, 0.0% public transportation, 0.0% walk, 4.3% work from home; Median travel time to work: 29.1 minutes

HEATH (township). Covers a land area of 35.372 square miles and a water area of 0.541 square miles. Located at 42.64° N. Lat; 85.95° W. Long.
Population: 3,317; Growth (since 2000): 7.0%; Density: 93.8 persons per square mile; Race: 97.3% White, 0.1% Black/African American, 0.7% Asian, 0.3% American Indian/Alaska Native, 0.0% Native Hawaiian/Other Pacific Islander, 0.6% Two or more races, 2.7% Hispanic of any race; Average household size: 2.84; Median age: 37.8; Age under 18: 28.5%; Age 65 and over: 7.8%; Males per 100 females: 106.8; Marriage status: 16.7% never married, 69.6% now married, 1.1% separated, 5.2% widowed, 8.6% divorced; Foreign born: 0.4%; Speak English only: 97.6%; With disability: 6.6%; Veterans: 6.6%; Ancestry: 41.1% Dutch, 21.0% German, 7.8% English, 4.8% Polish, 3.4% American
Employment: 12.3% management, business, and financial, 5.3% computer, engineering, and science, 6.4% education, legal, community service, arts, and media, 4.8% healthcare practitioners, 10.4% service,

19.7% sales and office, 15.0% natural resources, construction, and maintenance, 26.1% production, transportation, and material moving
Income: Per capita: $26,694; Median household: $58,611; Average household: $75,990; Households with income of $100,000 or more: 16.0%; Poverty rate: 5.0%
Educational Attainment: High school diploma or higher: 94.5%; Bachelor's degree or higher: 21.5%; Graduate/professional degree or higher: 7.8%
Housing: Homeownership rate: 90.3%; Median home value: $159,100; Median year structure built: 1985; Homeowner vacancy rate: 1.9%; Median gross rent: $844 per month; Rental vacancy rate: 18.6%
Health Insurance: 91.7% have insurance; 80.8% have private insurance; 18.4% have public insurance; 8.3% do not have insurance; 0.5% of children under 18 do not have insurance
Transportation: Commute: 97.8% car, 0.3% public transportation, 0.5% walk, 1.4% work from home; Median travel time to work: 22.2 minutes

HOPKINS (township). Covers a land area of 35.716 square miles and a water area of 0.309 square miles. Located at 42.63° N. Lat; 85.71° W. Long. Elevation is 712 feet.
Population: 2,601; Growth (since 2000): -2.6%; Density: 72.8 persons per square mile; Race: 96.7% White, 0.2% Black/African American, 0.2% Asian, 0.7% American Indian/Alaska Native, 0.0% Native Hawaiian/Other Pacific Islander, 1.8% Two or more races, 1.5% Hispanic of any race; Average household size: 2.77; Median age: 38.8; Age under 18: 26.1%; Age 65 and over: 11.3%; Males per 100 females: 107.7; Marriage status: 20.5% never married, 61.6% now married, 1.1% separated, 6.9% widowed, 11.0% divorced; Foreign born: 1.6%; Speak English only: 97.9%; With disability: 9.9%; Veterans: 14.3%; Ancestry: 27.0% German, 24.5% Dutch, 12.6% English, 10.4% Irish, 8.3% Polish
Employment: 10.6% management, business, and financial, 1.6% computer, engineering, and science, 7.3% education, legal, community service, arts, and media, 6.8% healthcare practitioners, 13.4% service, 21.1% sales and office, 15.9% natural resources, construction, and maintenance, 23.4% production, transportation, and material moving
Income: Per capita: $21,955; Median household: $51,000; Average household: $58,530; Households with income of $100,000 or more: 11.8%; Poverty rate: 8.7%
Educational Attainment: High school diploma or higher: 94.2%; Bachelor's degree or higher: 13.8%; Graduate/professional degree or higher: 3.9%
School District(s)
Hopkins Public Schools (KG-12)
    2012-13 Enrollment: 1,653 . . . . (269) 793-7261
Housing: Homeownership rate: 86.8%; Median home value: $138,800; Median year structure built: 1961; Homeowner vacancy rate: 1.6%; Median gross rent: $788 per month; Rental vacancy rate: 10.1%
Health Insurance: 89.9% have insurance; 78.7% have private insurance; 27.0% have public insurance; 10.1% do not have insurance; 0.3% of children under 18 do not have insurance
Transportation: Commute: 94.6% car, 0.0% public transportation, 1.2% walk, 3.4% work from home; Median travel time to work: 26.0 minutes

HOPKINS (village). Covers a land area of 0.479 square miles and a water area of 0 square miles. Located at 42.63° N. Lat; 85.76° W. Long. Elevation is 712 feet.
History: Hopkins grew up around the railroad station which was named Hopkins Station in 1874. The village was platted by John Hoffmaster.
Population: 610; Growth (since 2000): 3.0%; Density: 1,274.8 persons per square mile; Race: 93.8% White, 0.0% Black/African American, 0.2% Asian, 1.3% American Indian/Alaska Native, 0.0% Native Hawaiian/Other Pacific Islander, 3.1% Two or more races, 3.9% Hispanic of any race; Average household size: 2.69; Median age: 32.7; Age under 18: 30.2%; Age 65 and over: 9.2%; Males per 100 females: 102.0
School District(s)
Hopkins Public Schools (KG-12)
    2012-13 Enrollment: 1,653 . . . . (269) 793-7261
Housing: Homeownership rate: 75.3%; Homeowner vacancy rate: 2.8%; Rental vacancy rate: 15.2%
Safety: Violent crime rate: 0.0 per 10,000 population; Property crime rate: 65.9 per 10,000 population

LAKETOWN (township). Covers a land area of 21.549 square miles and a water area of 0.103 square miles. Located at 42.72° N. Lat; 86.17° W. Long.

Population: 5,505; Growth (since 2000): -1.0%; Density: 255.5 persons per square mile; Race: 95.2% White, 0.6% Black/African American, 0.7% Asian, 0.1% American Indian/Alaska Native, 0.0% Native Hawaiian/Other Pacific Islander, 1.8% Two or more races, 4.7% Hispanic of any race; Average household size: 2.45; Median age: 46.8; Age under 18: 22.1%; Age 65 and over: 17.7%; Males per 100 females: 98.1; Marriage status: 22.5% never married, 63.1% now married, 0.3% separated, 4.7% widowed, 9.7% divorced; Foreign born: 2.3%; Speak English only: 97.1%; With disability: 9.2%; Veterans: 13.5%; Ancestry: 38.7% Dutch, 22.6% German, 11.5% English, 8.4% Irish, 3.7% Polish
Employment: 16.8% management, business, and financial, 5.1% computer, engineering, and science, 11.9% education, legal, community service, arts, and media, 7.5% healthcare practitioners, 17.0% service, 23.6% sales and office, 7.4% natural resources, construction, and maintenance, 10.7% production, transportation, and material moving
Income: Per capita: $37,729; Median household: $67,333; Average household: $90,432; Households with income of $100,000 or more: 28.5%; Poverty rate: 6.3%
Educational Attainment: High school diploma or higher: 93.1%; Bachelor's degree or higher: 39.2%; Graduate/professional degree or higher: 15.2%
Housing: Homeownership rate: 85.8%; Median home value: $184,000; Median year structure built: 1986; Homeowner vacancy rate: 2.5%; Median gross rent: $759 per month; Rental vacancy rate: 6.1%
Health Insurance: 91.4% have insurance; 76.2% have private insurance; 32.8% have public insurance; 8.6% do not have insurance; 3.5% of children under 18 do not have insurance
Transportation: Commute: 92.0% car, 0.1% public transportation, 2.3% walk, 5.0% work from home; Median travel time to work: 18.3 minutes

LEE (township). Covers a land area of 35.178 square miles and a water area of 0.925 square miles. Located at 42.46° N. Lat; 86.08° W. Long. Elevation is 650 feet.

Population: 4,015; Growth (since 2000): -2.4%; Density: 114.1 persons per square mile; Race: 72.7% White, 4.8% Black/African American, 0.2% Asian, 1.3% American Indian/Alaska Native, 0.0% Native Hawaiian/Other Pacific Islander, 4.8% Two or more races, 27.9% Hispanic of any race; Average household size: 3.02; Median age: 31.8; Age under 18: 32.3%; Age 65 and over: 8.5%; Males per 100 females: 102.4; Marriage status: 33.1% never married, 50.1% now married, 2.7% separated, 5.6% widowed, 11.2% divorced; Foreign born: 11.2%; Speak English only: 77.9%; With disability: 13.8%; Veterans: 9.0%; Ancestry: 12.9% German, 10.7% Irish, 7.6% English, 3.2% French, 2.9% Dutch
Employment: 5.8% management, business, and financial, 2.4% computer, engineering, and science, 1.2% education, legal, community service, arts, and media, 2.7% healthcare practitioners, 23.5% service, 16.0% sales and office, 17.9% natural resources, construction, and maintenance, 30.5% production, transportation, and material moving
Income: Per capita: $13,970; Median household: $41,218; Average household: $44,846; Households with income of $100,000 or more: 4.3%; Poverty rate: 35.4%
Educational Attainment: High school diploma or higher: 75.7%; Bachelor's degree or higher: 7.0%; Graduate/professional degree or higher: 2.8%
Housing: Homeownership rate: 71.6%; Median home value: $87,900; Median year structure built: 1976; Homeowner vacancy rate: 3.1%; Median gross rent: $735 per month; Rental vacancy rate: 10.5%
Health Insurance: 77.1% have insurance; 48.0% have private insurance; 40.2% have public insurance; 22.9% do not have insurance; 1.8% of children under 18 do not have insurance
Transportation: Commute: 88.6% car, 0.0% public transportation, 1.3% walk, 10.2% work from home; Median travel time to work: 26.3 minutes

LEIGHTON (township). Covers a land area of 34.871 square miles and a water area of 0.724 square miles. Located at 42.73° N. Lat; 85.61° W. Long.

Population: 4,934; Growth (since 2000): 35.1%; Density: 141.5 persons per square mile; Race: 95.8% White, 0.5% Black/African American, 0.5% Asian, 0.7% American Indian/Alaska Native, 0.1% Native Hawaiian/Other Pacific Islander, 1.3% Two or more races, 3.0% Hispanic of any race; Average household size: 2.92; Median age: 35.0; Age under 18: 30.2%; Age 65 and over: 9.3%; Males per 100 females: 105.6; Marriage status: 20.0% never married, 69.4% now married, 1.2% separated, 1.8% widowed, 8.9% divorced; Foreign born: 2.7%; Speak English only: 97.8%; With disability: 7.2%; Veterans: 8.4%; Ancestry: 33.7% Dutch, 23.2% German, 8.8% Irish, 7.7% American, 6.9% English
Employment: 12.9% management, business, and financial, 5.1% computer, engineering, and science, 9.6% education, legal, community service, arts, and media, 4.3% healthcare practitioners, 16.9% service, 26.8% sales and office, 11.4% natural resources, construction, and maintenance, 12.9% production, transportation, and material moving
Income: Per capita: $26,011; Median household: $59,506; Average household: $70,800; Households with income of $100,000 or more: 17.3%; Poverty rate: 11.0
Educational Attainment: High school diploma or higher: 95.6%; Bachelor's degree or higher: 24.7%; Graduate/professional degree or higher: 8.1%
Housing: Homeownership rate: 87.6%; Median home value: $181,700; Median year structure built: 1998; Homeowner vacancy rate: 1.8%; Median gross rent: $926 per month; Rental vacancy rate: 4.1%
Health Insurance: 89.7% have insurance; 80.7% have private insurance; 22.0% have public insurance; 10.3% do not have insurance; 4.1% of children under 18 do not have insurance
Transportation: Commute: 93.6% car, 0.0% public transportation, 1.8% walk, 4.6% work from home; Median travel time to work: 28.2 minutes

MANLIUS (township). Covers a land area of 35.185 square miles and a water area of 0.770 square miles. Located at 42.64° N. Lat; 86.07° W. Long. Elevation is 587 feet.

Population: 3,017; Growth (since 2000): 14.5%; Density: 85.7 persons per square mile; Race: 92.1% White, 0.2% Black/African American, 0.6% Asian, 0.3% American Indian/Alaska Native, 0.0% Native Hawaiian/Other Pacific Islander, 1.8% Two or more races, 9.8% Hispanic of any race; Average household size: 2.82; Median age: 39.3; Age under 18: 29.7%; Age 65 and over: 10.2%; Males per 100 females: 104.4; Marriage status: 20.9% never married, 66.6% now married, 1.9% separated, 4.7% widowed, 7.8% divorced; Foreign born: 3.8%; Speak English only: 93.4%; With disability: 9.0%; Veterans: 10.3%; Ancestry: 30.0% Dutch, 19.7% German, 9.5% Irish, 7.1% English, 6.5% American
Employment: 10.2% management, business, and financial, 7.5% computer, engineering, and science, 7.8% education, legal, community service, arts, and media, 2.9% healthcare practitioners, 14.6% service, 19.7% sales and office, 12.3% natural resources, construction, and maintenance, 25.0% production, transportation, and material moving
Income: Per capita: $23,197; Median household: $52,019; Average household: $61,428; Households with income of $100,000 or more: 14.0%; Poverty rate: 12.0
Educational Attainment: High school diploma or higher: 86.8%; Bachelor's degree or higher: 22.0%; Graduate/professional degree or higher: 4.9%
Housing: Homeownership rate: 91.0%; Median home value: $170,200; Median year structure built: 1992; Homeowner vacancy rate: 2.3%; Median gross rent: $805 per month; Rental vacancy rate: 22.0%
Health Insurance: 94.7% have insurance; 80.3% have private insurance; 23.5% have public insurance; 5.3% do not have insurance; 2.7% of children under 18 do not have insurance
Transportation: Commute: 94.2% car, 0.1% public transportation, 0.4% walk, 5.1% work from home; Median travel time to work: 22.8 minutes

MARTIN (township). Covers a land area of 35.529 square miles and a water area of 0.440 square miles. Located at 42.55° N. Lat; 85.61° W. Long. Elevation is 830 feet.

Population: 2,629; Growth (since 2000): 4.6%; Density: 74.0 persons per square mile; Race: 94.6% White, 0.6% Black/African American, 0.4% Asian, 0.5% American Indian/Alaska Native, 0.0% Native Hawaiian/Other Pacific Islander, 1.9% Two or more races, 4.9% Hispanic of any race; Average household size: 2.76; Median age: 37.3; Age under 18: 28.5%; Age 65 and over: 12.8%; Males per 100 females: 101.0; Marriage status: 26.0% never married, 60.7% now married, 0.2% separated, 4.7% widowed, 8.5% divorced; Foreign born: 5.7%; Speak English only: 90.0%; With disability: 11.9%; Veterans: 8.2%; Ancestry: 24.9% Dutch, 19.4% German, 12.7% English, 7.9% Irish, 4.6% American
Employment: 12.2% management, business, and financial, 1.6% computer, engineering, and science, 7.1% education, legal, community service, arts, and media, 4.2% healthcare practitioners, 18.4% service, 15.3% sales and office, 14.9% natural resources, construction, and maintenance, 26.3% production, transportation, and material moving

Income: Per capita: $20,715; Median household: $50,282; Average household: $62,193; Households with income of $100,000 or more: 13.0%; Poverty rate: 18.8%

Educational Attainment: High school diploma or higher: 87.7%; Bachelor's degree or higher: 12.1%; Graduate/professional degree or higher: 3.6%

School District(s)

Martin Public Schools (PK-12)

    2012-13 Enrollment: 592 . . . . (269) 672-7194

Housing: Homeownership rate: 82.1%; Median home value: $121,200; Median year structure built: 1973; Homeowner vacancy rate: 3.0%; Median gross rent: $689 per month; Rental vacancy rate: 8.2%

Health Insurance: 87.6% have insurance; 68.9% have private insurance; 37.6% have public insurance; 12.4% do not have insurance; 5.5% of children under 18 do not have insurance

Transportation: Commute: 93.0% car, 0.0% public transportation, 2.8% walk, 3.3% work from home; Median travel time to work: 21.8 minutes

MARTIN (village). Covers a land area of 0.779 square miles and a water area of 0 square miles. Located at 42.54° N. Lat; 85.64° W. Long. Elevation is 830 feet.

Population: 410; Growth (since 2000): -5.7%; Density: 526.2 persons per square mile; Race: 92.9% White, 1.0% Black/African American, 0.0% Asian, 0.0% American Indian/Alaska Native, 0.0% Native Hawaiian/Other Pacific Islander, 3.2% Two or more races, 5.9% Hispanic of any race; Average household size: 2.53; Median age: 37.8; Age under 18: 24.9%; Age 65 and over: 13.4%; Males per 100 females: 103.0

School District(s)

Martin Public Schools (PK-12)

    2012-13 Enrollment: 592 . . . . (269) 672-7194

Housing: Homeownership rate: 69.8%; Homeowner vacancy rate: 2.5%; Rental vacancy rate: 9.3%

MOLINE (unincorporated postal area)

ZCTA: 49335

    Covers a land area of 0.948 square miles and a water area of 0 square miles. Located at 42.74° N. Lat; 85.67° W. Long. Elevation is 801 feet.

Population: 314; Growth (since 2000): 43.4%; Density: 331.1 persons per square mile; Race: 97.1% White, 0.3% Black/African American, 0.0% Asian, 0.6% American Indian/Alaska Native, 0.0% Native Hawaiian/Other Pacific Islander, 1.0% Two or more races, 2.5% Hispanic of any race; Average household size: 2.88; Median age: 34.2; Age under 18: 29.0%; Age 65 and over: 10.8%; Males per 100 females: 85.8

Housing: Homeownership rate: 86.2%; Homeowner vacancy rate: 4.1%; Rental vacancy rate: 0.0%

MONTEREY (township). Covers a land area of 35.705 square miles and a water area of 0.286 square miles. Located at 42.63° N. Lat; 85.83° W. Long.

Population: 2,356; Growth (since 2000): 14.1%; Density: 66.0 persons per square mile; Race: 93.7% White, 0.7% Black/African American, 0.1% Asian, 1.2% American Indian/Alaska Native, 0.0% Native Hawaiian/Other Pacific Islander, 2.6% Two or more races, 2.9% Hispanic of any race; Average household size: 2.89; Median age: 36.1; Age under 18: 27.8%; Age 65 and over: 8.2%; Males per 100 females: 101.7

Housing: Homeownership rate: 87.5%; Homeowner vacancy rate: 2.2%; Rental vacancy rate: 2.9%

OTSEGO (city). Covers a land area of 2.072 square miles and a water area of 0.063 square miles. Located at 42.46° N. Lat; 85.70° W. Long. Elevation is 709 feet.

History: Otsego grew up around its paper mills, with rapids on the Kalamazoo River generating power for the paper companies.

Population: 3,956; Growth (since 2000): 0.6%; Density: 1,908.8 persons per square mile; Race: 95.2% White, 0.6% Black/African American, 0.5% Asian, 0.3% American Indian/Alaska Native, 0.0% Native Hawaiian/Other Pacific Islander, 2.1% Two or more races, 3.3% Hispanic of any race; Average household size: 2.47; Median age: 36.1; Age under 18: 27.6%; Age 65 and over: 13.1%; Males per 100 females: 89.0; Marriage status: 21.5% never married, 51.7% now married, 2.0% separated, 8.1% widowed, 18.8% divorced; Foreign born: 1.1%; Speak English only: 98.5%; With disability: 18.2%; Veterans: 7.5%; Ancestry: 23.9% German, 16.9% Irish, 15.4% Dutch, 11.8% English, 9.0% American

Employment: 13.4% management, business, and financial, 3.7% computer, engineering, and science, 6.7% education, legal, community service, arts, and media, 4.2% healthcare practitioners, 19.6% service, 26.1% sales and office, 7.8% natural resources, construction, and maintenance, 18.4% production, transportation, and material moving

Income: Per capita: $19,605; Median household: $38,967; Average household: $48,090; Households with income of $100,000 or more: 8.3%; Poverty rate: 14.7%

Educational Attainment: High school diploma or higher: 91.5%; Bachelor's degree or higher: 13.7%; Graduate/professional degree or higher: 4.2%

School District(s)

Otsego Public Schools (PK-12)

    2012-13 Enrollment: 2,336 . . . . (269) 692-6066

Housing: Homeownership rate: 66.4%; Median home value: $104,300; Median year structure built: 1955; Homeowner vacancy rate: 2.3%; Median gross rent: $652 per month; Rental vacancy rate: 5.8%

Health Insurance: 88.8% have insurance; 68.4% have private insurance; 37.7% have public insurance; 11.2% do not have insurance; 3.8% of children under 18 do not have insurance

Safety: Violent crime rate: 20.2 per 10,000 population; Property crime rate: 167.0 per 10,000 population

Transportation: Commute: 93.7% car, 0.0% public transportation, 2.7% walk, 1.7% work from home; Median travel time to work: 23.9 minutes

Additional Information Contacts

City of Otsego . . . . (269) 692-3391

    http://www.cityofotsego.org

OTSEGO (township). Covers a land area of 33.228 square miles and a water area of 0.630 square miles. Located at 42.47° N. Lat; 85.73° W. Long. Elevation is 709 feet.

History: Settled 1832; incorporated as village 1865, as city 1918.

Population: 5,594; Growth (since 2000): 15.2%; Density: 168.3 persons per square mile; Race: 95.1% White, 0.7% Black/African American, 0.7% Asian, 0.4% American Indian/Alaska Native, 0.0% Native Hawaiian/Other Pacific Islander, 2.5% Two or more races, 2.9% Hispanic of any race; Average household size: 2.59; Median age: 40.5; Age under 18: 24.8%; Age 65 and over: 14.3%; Males per 100 females: 96.4; Marriage status: 24.6% never married, 59.3% now married, 0.7% separated, 6.2% widowed, 10.0% divorced; Foreign born: 0.9%; Speak English only: 98.5%; With disability: 13.5%; Veterans: 10.8%; Ancestry: 28.6% German, 16.1% Dutch, 12.3% English, 9.5% French, 8.5% Irish

Employment: 12.7% management, business, and financial, 3.3% computer, engineering, and science, 5.3% education, legal, community service, arts, and media, 3.6% healthcare practitioners, 15.8% service, 25.6% sales and office, 8.6% natural resources, construction, and maintenance, 25.1% production, transportation, and material moving

Income: Per capita: $26,415; Median household: $51,568; Average household: $67,318; Households with income of $100,000 or more: 16.9%; Poverty rate: 12.6%

Educational Attainment: High school diploma or higher: 91.1%; Bachelor's degree or higher: 16.3%; Graduate/professional degree or higher: 6.0%

School District(s)

Otsego Public Schools (PK-12)

    2012-13 Enrollment: 2,336 . . . . (269) 692-6066

Housing: Homeownership rate: 80.6%; Median home value: $126,600; Median year structure built: 1975; Homeowner vacancy rate: 1.6%; Median gross rent: $682 per month; Rental vacancy rate: 7.4%

Health Insurance: 90.9% have insurance; 79.9% have private insurance; 24.6% have public insurance; 9.1% do not have insurance; 2.6% of children under 18 do not have insurance

Transportation: Commute: 96.5% car, 0.2% public transportation, 0.4% walk, 1.7% work from home; Median travel time to work: 23.1 minutes

OVERISEL (township). Covers a land area of 35.645 square miles and a water area of 0.078 square miles. Located at 42.73° N. Lat; 85.95° W. Long. Elevation is 699 feet.

Population: 2,911; Growth (since 2000): 12.2%; Density: 81.7 persons per square mile; Race: 97.5% White, 0.4% Black/African American, 0.7% Asian, 0.0% American Indian/Alaska Native, 0.0% Native Hawaiian/Other Pacific Islander, 0.8% Two or more races, 2.8% Hispanic of any race; Average household size: 2.97; Median age: 33.9; Age under 18: 31.2%; Age 65 and over: 10.8%; Males per 100 females: 105.0; Marriage status: 20.9% never married, 72.1% now married, 0.9% separated, 2.5%

widowed, 4.5% divorced; Foreign born: 1.4%; Speak English only: 95.4%; With disability: 6.9%; Veterans: 8.1%; Ancestry: 60.0% Dutch, 12.1% German, 7.4% American, 3.8% Irish, 3.0% English

Employment: 12.0% management, business, and financial, 1.1% computer, engineering, and science, 3.8% education, legal, community service, arts, and media, 7.6% healthcare practitioners, 15.1% service, 23.6% sales and office, 14.6% natural resources, construction, and maintenance, 22.2% production, transportation, and material moving

Income: Per capita: $22,078; Median household: $63,631; Average household: $66,974; Households with income of $100,000 or more: 18.6%; Poverty rate: 8.1%

Educational Attainment: High school diploma or higher: 91.1%; Bachelor's degree or higher: 19.8%; Graduate/professional degree or higher: 6.0%

Housing: Homeownership rate: 91.0%; Median home value: $170,900; Median year structure built: 1971; Homeowner vacancy rate: 1.5%; Median gross rent: $800 per month; Rental vacancy rate: 7.3%

Health Insurance: 93.0% have insurance; 79.5% have private insurance; 23.8% have public insurance; 7.0% do not have insurance; 0.0% of children under 18 do not have insurance

Transportation: Commute: 92.3% car, 0.0% public transportation, 2.0% walk, 4.6% work from home; Median travel time to work: 21.5 minutes

PLAINWELL (city). Covers a land area of 1.975 square miles and a water area of 0.084 square miles. Located at 42.45° N. Lat; 85.65° W. Long. Elevation is 728 feet.

History: Plainwell, first settled in the early 1830's on the Kalamazoo River, developed around a paper mill, and later an office-equipment factory, and some canning plants.

Population: 3,804; Growth (since 2000): -3.3%; Density: 1,926.5 persons per square mile; Race: 96.0% White, 1.0% Black/African American, 0.4% Asian, 0.5% American Indian/Alaska Native, 0.1% Native Hawaiian/Other Pacific Islander, 1.5% Two or more races, 2.3% Hispanic of any race; Average household size: 2.33; Median age: 38.7; Age under 18: 23.8%; Age 65 and over: 15.9%; Males per 100 females: 87.8; Marriage status: 26.5% never married, 50.5% now married, 0.6% separated, 6.9% widowed, 16.1% divorced; Foreign born: 1.4%; Speak English only: 98.0%; With disability: 9.9%; Veterans: 12.8%; Ancestry: 22.0% German, 12.7% English, 11.5% Dutch, 10.2% American, 9.6% Irish

Employment: 10.9% management, business, and financial, 5.2% computer, engineering, and science, 6.6% education, legal, community service, arts, and media, 4.8% healthcare practitioners, 21.2% service, 25.6% sales and office, 8.0% natural resources, construction, and maintenance, 17.7% production, transportation, and material moving

Income: Per capita: $19,498; Median household: $41,863; Average household: $47,115; Households with income of $100,000 or more: 8.7%; Poverty rate: 13.0%

Educational Attainment: High school diploma or higher: 92.5%; Bachelor's degree or higher: 17.9%; Graduate/professional degree or higher: 5.1%

School District(s)
Plainwell Community Schools (KG-12)
    2012-13 Enrollment: 2,731 . . . . (269) 685-5823
Vocational/Technical School(s)
Michigan Career and Technical Institute (Public)
    Fall 2013 Enrollment: 200 . . . . (269) 664-4461
    2013-14 Tuition: In-state $17,496; Out-of-state $25,896

Housing: Homeownership rate: 63.9%; Median home value: $106,900; Median year structure built: 1954; Homeowner vacancy rate: 2.8%; Median gross rent: $697 per month; Rental vacancy rate: 7.8%

Health Insurance: 83.3% have insurance; 66.6% have private insurance; 27.0% have public insurance; 16.7% do not have insurance; 1.3% of children under 18 do not have insurance

Safety: Violent crime rate: 26.3 per 10,000 population; Property crime rate: 110.6 per 10,000 population

Newspapers: Union Enterprise (weekly circulation 600)

Transportation: Commute: 89.8% car, 0.0% public transportation, 4.9% walk, 5.1% work from home; Median travel time to work: 20.4 minutes

Additional Information Contacts
City of Plainwell. . . . . (269) 685-6821
  http://www.plainwell.org

PULLMAN (unincorporated postal area)
ZCTA: 49450
Covers a land area of 29.472 square miles and a water area of 0.462 square miles. Located at 42.48° N. Lat; 86.08° W. Long. Elevation is 650 feet.

Population: 3,302; Growth (since 2000): -1.4%; Density: 112.0 persons per square mile; Race: 71.7% White, 4.3% Black/African American, 0.3% Asian, 1.5% American Indian/Alaska Native, 0.0% Native Hawaiian/Other Pacific Islander, 5.0% Two or more races, 31.0% Hispanic of any race; Average household size: 3.08; Median age: 30.5; Age under 18: 34.4%; Age 65 and over: 7.7%; Males per 100 females: 101.6; Marriage status: 30.5% never married, 52.3% now married, 2.8% separated, 6.5% widowed, 10.7% divorced; Foreign born: 14.0%; Speak English only: 74.0%; With disability: 14.0%; Veterans: 9.3%; Ancestry: 14.8% German, 13.9% Irish, 5.4% English, 4.0% Dutch, 4.0% French

Employment: 2.3% management, business, and financial, 1.4% computer, engineering, and science, 3.2% education, legal, community service, arts, and media, 1.2% healthcare practitioners, 27.7% service, 15.7% sales and office, 20.9% natural resources, construction, and maintenance, 27.6% production, transportation, and material moving

Income: Per capita: $14,549; Median household: $42,179; Average household: $45,557; Households with income of $100,000 or more: 4.6%; Poverty rate: 34.1%

Educational Attainment: High school diploma or higher: 73.9%; Bachelor's degree or higher: 8.0%; Graduate/professional degree or higher: 2.4%

School District(s)
Bloomingdale Public SD (PK-12)
    2012-13 Enrollment: 1,180 . . . . (269) 521-3900

Housing: Homeownership rate: 72.3%; Median home value: $83,600; Median year structure built: 1976; Homeowner vacancy rate: 2.0%; Median gross rent: $673 per month; Rental vacancy rate: 10.6%

Health Insurance: 81.1% have insurance; 56.6% have private insurance; 39.4% have public insurance; 18.9% do not have insurance; 2.4% of children under 18 do not have insurance

Transportation: Commute: 92.4% car, 0.0% public transportation, 1.6% walk, 6.0% work from home; Median travel time to work: 23.1 minutes

SALEM (township). Covers a land area of 35.702 square miles and a water area of 0.332 square miles. Located at 42.72° N. Lat; 85.85° W. Long.

Population: 4,446; Growth (since 2000): 27.5%; Density: 124.5 persons per square mile; Race: 97.1% White, 0.2% Black/African American, 0.2% Asian, 0.6% American Indian/Alaska Native, 0.0% Native Hawaiian/Other Pacific Islander, 1.4% Two or more races, 2.2% Hispanic of any race; Average household size: 2.92; Median age: 34.8; Age under 18: 29.7%; Age 65 and over: 8.5%; Males per 100 females: 104.6; Marriage status: 21.4% never married, 65.8% now married, 0.0% separated, 4.9% widowed, 8.0% divorced; Foreign born: 1.3%; Speak English only: 97.6%; With disability: 8.8%; Veterans: 6.7%; Ancestry: 29.3% Dutch, 25.6% German, 11.0% English, 8.7% Irish, 7.1% American

Employment: 10.3% management, business, and financial, 3.4% computer, engineering, and science, 6.1% education, legal, community service, arts, and media, 2.6% healthcare practitioners, 16.3% service, 30.2% sales and office, 9.9% natural resources, construction, and maintenance, 21.3% production, transportation, and material moving

Income: Per capita: $23,207; Median household: $63,834; Average household: $68,221; Households with income of $100,000 or more: 16.1%; Poverty rate: 7.8%

Educational Attainment: High school diploma or higher: 91.7%; Bachelor's degree or higher: 13.0%; Graduate/professional degree or higher: 0.9%

Housing: Homeownership rate: 93.1%; Median home value: $161,800; Median year structure built: 1994; Homeowner vacancy rate: 0.9%; Median gross rent: $518 per month; Rental vacancy rate: 2.7%

Health Insurance: 90.9% have insurance; 80.4% have private insurance; 21.0% have public insurance; 9.1% do not have insurance; 2.3% of children under 18 do not have insurance

Transportation: Commute: 95.8% car, 0.0% public transportation, 0.6% walk, 3.6% work from home; Median travel time to work: 30.0 minutes

SAUGATUCK (city). Covers a land area of 1.177 square miles and a water area of 0.290 square miles. Located at 42.66° N. Lat; 86.20° W. Long. Elevation is 594 feet.

History: Saugatuck was first settled in the 1830's and developed as an art colony, attracting landscape painters to the Lake Michigan dunes region. James Fenimore Cooper spent time here. The name is the Pottawattomi term for the mouth of a river.

Population: 925; Growth (since 2000): -13.1%; Density: 785.7 persons per square mile; Race: 95.6% White, 0.6% Black/African American, 0.4% Asian, 0.6% American Indian/Alaska Native, 0.0% Native Hawaiian/Other Pacific Islander, 1.8% Two or more races, 3.8% Hispanic of any race; Average household size: 1.80; Median age: 53.3; Age under 18: 12.5%; Age 65 and over: 21.6%; Males per 100 females: 102.0

School District(s)

Saugatuck Public Schools (PK-12)

    2012-13 Enrollment: 858. . . . . (269) 857-1444

Housing: Homeownership rate: 66.7%; Homeowner vacancy rate: 6.8%; Rental vacancy rate: 24.3%

Newspapers: Commercial Record (weekly circulation 1700)

Additional Information Contacts

City of Saugatuck . . . . (269) 857-2603
    http://www.saugatuckcity.com

SAUGATUCK (township). Covers a land area of 23.373 square miles and a water area of 0.849 square miles. Located at 42.63° N. Lat; 86.18° W. Long. Elevation is 594 feet.

Population: 2,944; Growth (since 2000): -18.0%; Density: 126.0 persons per square mile; Race: 95.9% White, 0.3% Black/African American, 0.6% Asian, 0.5% American Indian/Alaska Native, 0.0% Native Hawaiian/Other Pacific Islander, 1.3% Two or more races, 4.6% Hispanic of any race; Average household size: 2.31; Median age: 46.8; Age under 18: 20.9%; Age 65 and over: 16.4%; Males per 100 females: 104.6; Marriage status: 20.2% never married, 64.2% now married, 0.8% separated, 7.7% widowed, 7.8% divorced; Foreign born: 2.6%; Speak English only: 92.2%; With disability: 8.7%; Veterans: 8.4%; Ancestry: 26.5% Dutch, 21.7% German, 10.6% Irish, 10.5% English, 8.6% Polish

Employment: 19.5% management, business, and financial, 9.9% computer, engineering, and science, 9.0% education, legal, community service, arts, and media, 1.4% healthcare practitioners, 15.0% service, 26.4% sales and office, 8.3% natural resources, construction, and maintenance, 10.4% production, transportation, and material moving

Income: Per capita: $28,944; Median household: $62,891; Average household: $73,540; Households with income of $100,000 or more: 26.9%; Poverty rate: 7.9%

Educational Attainment: High school diploma or higher: 95.5%; Bachelor's degree or higher: 43.5%; Graduate/professional degree or higher: 9.6%

School District(s)

Saugatuck Public Schools (PK-12)

    2012-13 Enrollment: 858. . . . . (269) 857-1444

Housing: Homeownership rate: 88.3%; Median home value: $244,900; Median year structure built: 1992; Homeowner vacancy rate: 5.2%; Median gross rent: $678 per month; Rental vacancy rate: 23.1%

Health Insurance: 89.1% have insurance; 78.6% have private insurance; 27.7% have public insurance; 10.9% do not have insurance; 2.2% of children under 18 do not have insurance

Newspapers: Commercial Record (weekly circulation 1700)

Transportation: Commute: 91.1% car, 1.8% public transportation, 0.0% walk, 7.1% work from home; Median travel time to work: 24.6 minutes

TROWBRIDGE (township). Covers a land area of 34.643 square miles and a water area of 1.152 square miles. Located at 42.46° N. Lat; 85.84° W. Long.

Population: 2,502; Growth (since 2000): -0.7%; Density: 72.2 persons per square mile; Race: 96.4% White, 0.8% Black/African American, 0.5% Asian, 0.5% American Indian/Alaska Native, 0.0% Native Hawaiian/Other Pacific Islander, 0.7% Two or more races, 1.9% Hispanic of any race; Average household size: 2.50; Median age: 43.2; Age under 18: 21.1%; Age 65 and over: 16.1%; Males per 100 females: 104.2; Marriage status: 17.2% never married, 62.4% now married, 2.0% separated, 6.9% widowed, 13.5% divorced; Foreign born: 1.1%; Speak English only: 99.6%; With disability: 11.6%; Veterans: 12.2%; Ancestry: 15.8% German, 15.4% English, 10.3% Dutch, 8.2% Irish, 6.7% American

Employment: 12.2% management, business, and financial, 3.3% computer, engineering, and science, 7.8% education, legal, community

service, arts, and media, 4.6% healthcare practitioners, 12.6% service, 21.8% sales and office, 11.9% natural resources, construction, and maintenance, 25.8% production, transportation, and material moving

Income: Per capita: $22,735; Median household: $53,854; Average household: $56,023; Households with income of $100,000 or more: 10.0%; Poverty rate: 12.0%

Educational Attainment: High school diploma or higher: 90.0%; Bachelor's degree or higher: 15.5%; Graduate/professional degree or higher: 4.6%

Housing: Homeownership rate: 83.3%; Median home value: $137,100; Median year structure built: 1973; Homeowner vacancy rate: 3.4%; Median gross rent: $639 per month; Rental vacancy rate: 12.5%

Health Insurance: 91.3% have insurance; 71.8% have private insurance; 29.7% have public insurance; 8.7% do not have insurance; 1.4% of children under 18 do not have insurance

Transportation: Commute: 94.1% car, 0.5% public transportation, 1.7% walk, 3.0% work from home; Median travel time to work: 27.2 minutes

VALLEY (township). Covers a land area of 32.921 square miles and a water area of 3.058 square miles. Located at 42.56° N. Lat; 85.96° W. Long.

Population: 2,018; Growth (since 2000): 10.2%; Density: 61.3 persons per square mile; Race: 95.3% White, 0.8% Black/African American, 0.4% Asian, 0.5% American Indian/Alaska Native, 0.0% Native Hawaiian/Other Pacific Islander, 2.4% Two or more races, 2.3% Hispanic of any race; Average household size: 2.63; Median age: 42.3; Age under 18: 24.7%; Age 65 and over: 12.4%; Males per 100 females: 102.4

Housing: Homeownership rate: 89.7%; Homeowner vacancy rate: 3.9%; Rental vacancy rate: 14.1%

WATSON (township). Covers a land area of 35.363 square miles and a water area of 0.735 square miles. Located at 42.55° N. Lat; 85.72° W. Long. Elevation is 810 feet.

Population: 2,063; Growth (since 2000): -1.1%; Density: 58.3 persons per square mile; Race: 97.1% White, 0.4% Black/African American, 0.2% Asian, 0.4% American Indian/Alaska Native, 0.0% Native Hawaiian/Other Pacific Islander, 1.6% Two or more races, 2.2% Hispanic of any race; Average household size: 2.77; Median age: 38.7; Age under 18: 25.4%; Age 65 and over: 11.0%; Males per 100 females: 112.2

Housing: Homeownership rate: 89.7%; Homeowner vacancy rate: 3.3%; Rental vacancy rate: 3.8%

WAYLAND (city). Covers a land area of 2.979 square miles and a water area of 0.045 square miles. Located at 42.67° N. Lat; 85.64° W. Long. Elevation is 771 feet.

History: Wayland developed as a center for a dairy area, with a Pet Milk Company processing plant located here.

Population: 4,079; Growth (since 2000): 3.6%; Density: 1,369.4 persons per square mile; Race: 95.0% White, 0.3% Black/African American, 0.3% Asian, 0.8% American Indian/Alaska Native, 0.0% Native Hawaiian/Other Pacific Islander, 2.6% Two or more races, 3.9% Hispanic of any race; Average household size: 2.56; Median age: 33.3; Age under 18: 28.7%; Age 65 and over: 11.7%; Males per 100 females: 88.8; Marriage status: 27.9% never married, 46.8% now married, 2.0% separated, 6.4% widowed, 18.9% divorced; Foreign born: 2.8%; Speak English only: 97.0%; With disability: 11.4%; Veterans: 9.0%; Ancestry: 25.8% German, 15.2% Dutch, 13.5% Irish, 11.8% American, 10.5% Polish

Employment: 7.6% management, business, and financial, 6.7% computer, engineering, and science, 8.5% education, legal, community service, arts, and media, 0.9% healthcare practitioners, 13.2% service, 33.1% sales and office, 8.5% natural resources, construction, and maintenance, 21.5% production, transportation, and material moving

Income: Per capita: $20,092; Median household: $50,134; Average household: $55,124; Households with income of $100,000 or more: 16.0%; Poverty rate: 13.4%

Educational Attainment: High school diploma or higher: 84.1%; Bachelor's degree or higher: 20.0%; Graduate/professional degree or higher: 8.7%

School District(s)

Wayland Union Schools (PK-12)

    2012-13 Enrollment: 2,808 . . . . (269) 792-2181

Housing: Homeownership rate: 63.8%; Median home value: $80,100; Median year structure built: 1985; Homeowner vacancy rate: 4.0%; Median gross rent: $711 per month; Rental vacancy rate: 11.5%

Health Insurance: 89.8% have insurance; 68.3% have private insurance; 30.6% have public insurance; 10.2% do not have insurance; 1.3% of children under 18 do not have insurance
Newspapers: Penasee Globe (weekly circulation 16000)
Transportation: Commute: 95.8% car, 0.0% public transportation, 2.1% walk, 0.0% work from home; Median travel time to work: 26.1 minutes
Additional Information Contacts
City of Wayland . . . . (269) 792-2265
  http://www.cityofwayland.org

WAYLAND (township). Covers a land area of 32.619 square miles and a water area of 0.814 square miles. Located at 42.64° N. Lat; 85.61° W. Long. Elevation is 771 feet.
History: Settled 1836, incorporated 1858.
Population: 3,088; Growth (since 2000): 2.5%; Density: 94.7 persons per square mile; Race: 95.9% White, 0.3% Black/African American, 0.5% Asian, 1.2% American Indian/Alaska Native, 0.0% Native Hawaiian/Other Pacific Islander, 1.7% Two or more races, 1.7% Hispanic of any race; Average household size: 2.71; Median age: 40.1; Age under 18: 24.6%; Age 65 and over: 9.6%; Males per 100 females: 103.4; Marriage status: 19.6% never married, 70.1% now married, 0.9% separated, 3.3% widowed, 6.9% divorced; Foreign born: 1.8%; Speak English only: 97.5%; With disability: 8.1%; Veterans: 9.1%; Ancestry: 26.5% German, 17.5% Dutch, 15.7% English, 7.5% Italian, 6.9% Irish
Employment: 15.7% management, business, and financial, 1.1% computer, engineering, and science, 3.8% education, legal, community service, arts, and media, 7.1% healthcare practitioners, 14.2% service, 16.0% sales and office, 13.0% natural resources, construction, and maintenance, 29.1% production, transportation, and material moving
Income: Per capita: $25,990; Median household: $57,632; Average household: $67,057; Households with income of $100,000 or more: 21.5%; Poverty rate: 9.5%
Educational Attainment: High school diploma or higher: 91.9%; Bachelor's degree or higher: 13.5%; Graduate/professional degree or higher: 3.5%
School District(s)
Wayland Union Schools (PK-12)
  2012-13 Enrollment: 2,808 . . . . (269) 792-2181
Housing: Homeownership rate: 89.1%; Median home value: $150,000; Median year structure built: 1982; Homeowner vacancy rate: 3.6%; Median gross rent: $1,043 per month; Rental vacancy rate: 11.3%
Health Insurance: 89.6% have insurance; 78.1% have private insurance; 25.6% have public insurance; 10.4% do not have insurance; 7.2% of children under 18 do not have insurance
Newspapers: Penasee Globe (weekly circulation 16000)
Transportation: Commute: 94.7% car, 0.0% public transportation, 0.9% walk, 4.4% work from home; Median travel time to work: 26.6 minutes

Alpena County

Located in northeastern Michigan; bounded on the east by Lake Huron. Covers a land area of 571.860 square miles, a water area of 1,123.062 square miles, and is located in the Eastern Time Zone at 44.89° N. Lat., 83.43° W. Long. The county was founded in 1840. County seat is Alpena.

Alpena County is part of the Alpena, MI Micropolitan Statistical Area. The entire metro area includes: Alpena County, MI

Weather Station: Alpena Phelps Collins Arpt   Elevation: 688 feet

	Jan	Feb	Mar	Apr	May	Jun	Jul	Aug	Sep	Oct	Nov	Dec
High	27	30	38	52	65	75	80	77	69	56	43	32
Low	11	11	19	31	40	50	55	54	46	36	28	18
Precip	1.7	1.3	1.9	2.5	2.6	2.6	3.0	3.3	2.9	2.6	2.1	1.8
Snow	21.4	18.0	11.0	na	na	na	na	na	tr	0.4	8.0	19.3

High and Low temperatures in degrees Fahrenheit; Precipitation and Snow in inches

Weather Station: Alpena Wastewater Pl   Elevation: 589 feet

	Jan	Feb	Mar	Apr	May	Jun	Jul	Aug	Sep	Oct	Nov	Dec
High	28	30	37	50	61	72	77	76	69	56	43	33
Low	13	14	22	33	44	54	59	58	51	40	30	21
Precip	1.8	1.5	1.7	2.5	2.9	2.6	3.1	3.5	3.3	2.7	2.2	1.9
Snow	15.3	11.8	6.3	2.4	tr	0.0	0.0	0.0	0.0	0.3	3.2	13.1

High and Low temperatures in degrees Fahrenheit; Precipitation and Snow in inches

Population: 29,598; Growth (since 2000): -5.5%; Density: 51.8 persons per square mile; Race: 97.5% White, 0.3% Black/African American, 0.5%

Asian, 0.5% American Indian/Alaska Native, 0.0% Native Hawaiian/Other Pacific Islander, 1.1% two or more races, 1.0% Hispanic of any race; Average household size: 2.27; Median age: 45.6; Age under 18: 20.9%; Age 65 and over: 19.5%; Males per 100 females: 96.4; Marriage status: 23.9% never married, 56.1% now married, 1.0% separated, 7.6% widowed, 12.4% divorced; Foreign born: 1.4%; Speak English only: 96.6%; With disability: 18.1%; Veterans: 12.0%; Ancestry: 33.2% German, 24.8% Polish, 13.5% French, 10.3% English, 9.8% Irish
Religion: Six largest groups: 22.8% Catholicism, 17.2% Lutheran, 2.1% Methodist/Pietist, 1.9% Presbyterian-Reformed, 1.7% Baptist, 1.7% Non-denominational Protestant
Economy: Unemployment rate: 6.0%; Leading industries: 18.7% retail trade; 13.2% other services (except public administration); 11.5% construction; Farms: 458 totaling 69,274 acres; Company size: 0 employ 1,000 or more persons, 2 employ 500 to 999 persons, 7 employ 100 to 499 persons, 784 employ less than 100 persons; Business ownership: 679 women-owned, n/a Black-owned, n/a Hispanic-owned, n/a Asian-owned
Employment: 10.1% management, business, and financial, 3.0% computer, engineering, and science, 9.1% education, legal, community service, arts, and media, 7.9% healthcare practitioners, 18.4% service, 26.8% sales and office, 10.3% natural resources, construction, and maintenance, 14.5% production, transportation, and material moving
Income: Per capita: $21,948; Median household: $38,016; Average household: $49,534; Households with income of $100,000 or more: 9.7%; Poverty rate: 17.3%
Educational Attainment: High school diploma or higher: 88.0%; Bachelor's degree or higher: 16.0%; Graduate/professional degree or higher: 7.2%
Housing: Homeownership rate: 78.8%; Median home value: $96,400; Median year structure built: 1967; Homeowner vacancy rate: 2.8%; Median gross rent: $545 per month; Rental vacancy rate: 9.6%
Vital Statistics: Birth rate: 92.8 per 10,000 population; Death rate: 113.4 per 10,000 population; Age-adjusted cancer mortality rate: 193.3 deaths per 100,000 population
Health Insurance: 87.2% have insurance; 65.9% have private insurance; 41.6% have public insurance; 12.8% do not have insurance; 4.9% of children under 18 do not have insurance
Health Care: Physicians: 27.4 per 10,000 population; Hospital beds: 42.6 per 10,000 population; Hospital admissions: 1,669.7 per 10,000 population
Transportation: Commute: 91.2% car, 0.5% public transportation, 1.1% walk, 5.3% work from home; Median travel time to work: 16.4 minutes
Presidential Election: 46.7% Obama, 52.1% Romney (2012)
National and State Parks: Alpena State Forest; Alpena State Park; Thunder Bay River State Forest
Additional Information Contacts
Alpena Government . . . . (989) 354-9500
  http://www.alpenacounty.org

Alpena County Communities

ALPENA (city). County seat. Covers a land area of 8.541 square miles and a water area of 0.689 square miles. Located at 45.07° N. Lat; 83.44° W. Long. Elevation is 591 feet.
History: The first settler came to Alpena in 1835, but the village was laid out in 1856 by several men from Detroit. They first called it Fremont, for General John C. Fremont, but the post office used the name of Alpena (Indian origin, meaning "partridge") when it was established in 1857. Daniel Carter was the first resident of the new town, followed by G.N. Fletcher who built a store and boarding house. Soon there were many lumber and shingle mills in Alpena. After 1900, limestone quarrying was begun.
Population: 10,483; Growth (since 2000): -7.3%; Density: 1,227.3 persons per square mile; Race: 96.8% White, 0.5% Black/African American, 0.7% Asian, 0.4% American Indian/Alaska Native, 0.1% Native Hawaiian/Other Pacific Islander, 1.4% Two or more races, 1.0% Hispanic of any race; Average household size: 2.13; Median age: 42.5; Age under 18: 20.7%; Age 65 and over: 19.4%; Males per 100 females: 91.1; Marriage status: 29.7% never married, 48.4% now married, 1.1% separated, 8.2% widowed, 13.7% divorced; Foreign born: 0.9%; Speak English only: 97.5%; With disability: 19.8%; Veterans: 10.8%; Ancestry: 32.3% German, 26.4% Polish, 13.2% French, 10.7% English, 10.6% Irish
Employment: 6.8% management, business, and financial, 3.1% computer, engineering, and science, 10.2% education, legal, community service, arts, and media, 5.9% healthcare practitioners, 22.2% service, 32.8% sales and

office, 4.8% natural resources, construction, and maintenance, 14.1% production, transportation, and material moving

Income: Per capita: $20,101; Median household: $33,311; Average household: $43,561; Households with income of $100,000 or more: 6.6%; Poverty rate: 22.4%

Educational Attainment: High school diploma or higher: 88.6%; Bachelor's degree or higher: 18.0%; Graduate/professional degree or higher: 8.1%

School District(s)
Alpena Public Schools (KG-12)
    2012-13 Enrollment: 3,965 . . . . (989) 358-5040
Alpena-Montmorency-Alcona ESD (PK-KG)
    2012-13 Enrollment: 177. . . . . (989) 354-3101
Bingham Arts Academy (PK-12)
    2012-13 Enrollment: 202. . . . . (989) 358-2500

Two-year College(s)
Alpena Community College (Public)
    Fall 2013 Enrollment: 1,712 . . . . (989) 356-9021
    2013-14 Tuition: In-state $5,790; Out-of-state $5,790

Housing: Homeownership rate: 66.4%; Median home value: $77,500; Median year structure built: 1952; Homeowner vacancy rate: 3.2%; Median gross rent: $519 per month; Rental vacancy rate: 8.8%

Health Insurance: 87.0% have insurance; 63.3% have private insurance; 42.7% have public insurance; 13.0% do not have insurance; 1.1% of children under 18 do not have insurance

Hospitals: Alpena Regional Medical Center (146 beds)

Safety: Violent crime rate: 44.7 per 10,000 population; Property crime rate: 252.5 per 10,000 population

Newspapers: Alpena News (daily circulation 10600)

Transportation: Commute: 90.5% car, 0.9% public transportation, 0.5% walk, 5.3% work from home; Median travel time to work: 12.8 minutes

Airports: Alpena County Regional (primary service/non-hub)

Additional Information Contacts
City of Alpena . . . . (989) 354-1700
    http://www.alpena.mi.us

ALPENA (township). Covers a land area of 104.451 square miles and a water area of 36.758 square miles. Located at 45.07° N. Lat; 83.36° W. Long. Elevation is 591 feet.

History: When Alpena Township was surveyed in 1839, land was offered to anyone in the survey party in lieu of wages, but there were no takers. The area was desolate cedar swamp.

Population: 9,060; Growth (since 2000): -7.4%; Density: 86.7 persons per square mile; Race: 97.4% White, 0.2% Black/African American, 0.6% Asian, 0.6% American Indian/Alaska Native, 0.0% Native Hawaiian/Other Pacific Islander, 1.1% Two or more races, 1.0% Hispanic of any race; Average household size: 2.25; Median age: 48.4; Age under 18: 19.5%; Age 65 and over: 22.1%; Males per 100 females: 95.0; Marriage status: 20.7% never married, 58.4% now married, 0.7% separated, 8.9% widowed, 12.0% divorced; Foreign born: 1.5%; Speak English only: 96.2%; With disability: 16.6%; Veterans: 10.9%; Ancestry: 31.9% German, 26.1% Polish, 14.7% French, 9.7% English, 7.2% Irish

Employment: 12.3% management, business, and financial, 4.2% computer, engineering, and science, 9.5% education, legal, community service, arts, and media, 10.5% healthcare practitioners, 15.5% service, 25.0% sales and office, 12.1% natural resources, construction, and maintenance, 10.8% production, transportation, and material moving

Income: Per capita: $25,247; Median household: $42,299; Average household: $55,557; Households with income of $100,000 or more: 13.0%; Poverty rate: 14.0%

Educational Attainment: High school diploma or higher: 89.7%; Bachelor's degree or higher: 17.6%; Graduate/professional degree or higher: 9.8%

School District(s)
Alpena Public Schools (KG-12)
    2012-13 Enrollment: 3,965 . . . . (989) 358-5040
Alpena-Montmorency-Alcona ESD (PK-KG)
    2012-13 Enrollment: 177. . . . . (989) 354-3101
Bingham Arts Academy (PK-12)
    2012-13 Enrollment: 202. . . . . (989) 358-2500

Two-year College(s)
Alpena Community College (Public)
    Fall 2013 Enrollment: 1,712 . . . . (989) 356-9021
    2013-14 Tuition: In-state $5,790; Out-of-state $5,790

Housing: Homeownership rate: 82.5%; Median home value: $117,000; Median year structure built: 1972; Homeowner vacancy rate: 2.5%; Median gross rent: $555 per month; Rental vacancy rate: 10.1%

Health Insurance: 89.4% have insurance; 70.6% have private insurance; 41.9% have public insurance; 10.6% do not have insurance; 1.0% of children under 18 do not have insurance

Hospitals: Alpena Regional Medical Center (146 beds)

Newspapers: Alpena News (daily circulation 10600)

Transportation: Commute: 92.7% car, 0.2% public transportation, 1.3% walk, 4.8% work from home; Median travel time to work: 14.3 minutes

Airports: Alpena County Regional (primary service/non-hub)

Additional Information Contacts
Alpena Township . . . . (989) 356-0297
    http://www.alpenatownship.com

GREEN (township). Covers a land area of 71.043 square miles and a water area of 9.013 square miles. Located at 45.01° N. Lat; 83.79° W. Long.

Population: 1,228; Growth (since 2000): 1.9%; Density: 17.3 persons per square mile; Race: 97.5% White, 0.1% Black/African American, 0.0% Asian, 1.3% American Indian/Alaska Native, 0.1% Native Hawaiian/Other Pacific Islander, 0.8% Two or more races, 1.1% Hispanic of any race; Average household size: 2.40; Median age: 48.9; Age under 18: 20.8%; Age 65 and over: 20.1%; Males per 100 females: 111.0

Housing: Homeownership rate: 92.3%; Homeowner vacancy rate: 3.1%; Rental vacancy rate: 9.1%

HERRON (unincorporated postal area)
ZCTA: 49744

    Covers a land area of 35.460 square miles and a water area of 0.043 square miles. Located at 44.99° N. Lat; 83.66° W. Long. Elevation is 741 feet.

    Population: 823; Growth (since 2000): 5.8%; Density: 23.2 persons per square mile; Race: 99.4% White, 0.1% Black/African American, 0.0% Asian, 0.1% American Indian/Alaska Native, 0.1% Native Hawaiian/Other Pacific Islander, 0.2% Two or more races, 0.4% Hispanic of any race; Average household size: 2.53; Median age: 44.2; Age under 18: 23.9%; Age 65 and over: 16.2%; Males per 100 females: 96.9

School District(s)
Alpena Public Schools (KG-12)
    2012-13 Enrollment: 3,965 . . . . (989) 358-5040
    Housing: Homeownership rate: 92.9%; Homeowner vacancy rate: 3.8%; Rental vacancy rate: 11.1%

LACHINE (unincorporated postal area)
ZCTA: 49753

    Covers a land area of 170.879 square miles and a water area of 4.835 square miles. Located at 45.02° N. Lat; 83.78° W. Long. Elevation is 735 feet.

    Population: 2,057; Growth (since 2000): -7.6%; Density: 12.0 persons per square mile; Race: 98.6% White, 0.0% Black/African American, 0.1% Asian, 0.4% American Indian/Alaska Native, 0.0% Native Hawaiian/Other Pacific Islander, 0.5% Two or more races, 1.1% Hispanic of any race; Average household size: 2.38; Median age: 47.8; Age under 18: 21.2%; Age 65 and over: 20.1%; Males per 100 females: 106.3

    Housing: Homeownership rate: 93.0%; Homeowner vacancy rate: 2.3%; Rental vacancy rate: 9.0%

LONG RAPIDS (township). Covers a land area of 54.193 square miles and a water area of 0.474 square miles. Located at 45.15° N. Lat; 83.68° W. Long. Elevation is 718 feet.

History: Long Rapids Township was organized in 1871 and named for the rapids on the Thunder Bay River, which traversed the township. A village grew up around a sawmill founded by Albert Merrill, and known for a time as Merrillsville.

Population: 1,010; Growth (since 2000): -0.9%; Density: 18.6 persons per square mile; Race: 98.6% White, 0.1% Black/African American, 0.1% Asian, 0.3% American Indian/Alaska Native, 0.0% Native Hawaiian/Other Pacific Islander, 0.6% Two or more races, 1.8% Hispanic of any race; Average household size: 2.42; Median age: 46.3; Age under 18: 22.0%; Age 65 and over: 17.4%; Males per 100 females: 105.3

Housing: Homeownership rate: 91.4%; Homeowner vacancy rate: 1.8%; Rental vacancy rate: 12.2%

MAPLE RIDGE (township). Covers a land area of 51.622 square miles and a water area of 2.197 square miles. Located at 45.13° N. Lat; 83.56° W. Long.
Population: 1,690; Growth (since 2000): -1.5%; Density: 32.7 persons per square mile; Race: 97.6% White, 0.2% Black/African American, 0.1% Asian, 1.2% American Indian/Alaska Native, 0.0% Native Hawaiian/Other Pacific Islander, 0.9% Two or more races, 0.4% Hispanic of any race; Average household size: 2.53; Median age: 42.3; Age under 18: 24.0%; Age 65 and over: 13.0%; Males per 100 females: 108.9
Housing: Homeownership rate: 90.1%; Homeowner vacancy rate: 2.0%; Rental vacancy rate: 4.2%

OSSINEKE (CDP). Covers a land area of 3.657 square miles and a water area of 0.011 square miles. Located at 44.91° N. Lat; 83.43° W. Long. Elevation is 659 feet.
Population: 938; Growth (since 2000): -11.4%; Density: 256.5 persons per square mile; Race: 97.5% White, 0.1% Black/African American, 0.7% Asian, 1.0% American Indian/Alaska Native, 0.1% Native Hawaiian/Other Pacific Islander, 0.5% Two or more races, 0.7% Hispanic of any race; Average household size: 2.37; Median age: 46.1; Age under 18: 21.5%; Age 65 and over: 18.7%; Males per 100 females: 100.0
School District(s)
Alpena Public Schools (KG-12)
   2012-13 Enrollment: 3,965 . . . . (989) 358-5040
Housing: Homeownership rate: 78.3%; Homeowner vacancy rate: 3.7%; Rental vacancy rate: 15.7%

OSSINEKE (township). Covers a land area of 105.740 square miles and a water area of 1.493 square miles. Located at 44.88° N. Lat; 83.65° W. Long. Elevation is 659 feet.
Population: 1,675; Growth (since 2000): -4.9%; Density: 15.8 persons per square mile; Race: 99.0% White, 0.1% Black/African American, 0.1% Asian, 0.4% American Indian/Alaska Native, 0.0% Native Hawaiian/Other Pacific Islander, 0.3% Two or more races, 1.4% Hispanic of any race; Average household size: 2.37; Median age: 47.1; Age under 18: 20.7%; Age 65 and over: 20.1%; Males per 100 females: 100.1
School District(s)
Alpena Public Schools (KG-12)
   2012-13 Enrollment: 3,965 . . . . (989) 358-5040
Housing: Homeownership rate: 92.0%; Homeowner vacancy rate: 3.0%; Rental vacancy rate: 12.3%

SANBORN (township). Covers a land area of 43.777 square miles and a water area of 5.948 square miles. Located at 44.89° N. Lat; 83.43° W. Long. Elevation is 673 feet.
Population: 2,116; Growth (since 2000): -1.7%; Density: 48.3 persons per square mile; Race: 97.4% White, 0.2% Black/African American, 0.9% Asian, 0.4% American Indian/Alaska Native, 0.0% Native Hawaiian/Other Pacific Islander, 0.5% Two or more races, 1.3% Hispanic of any race; Average household size: 2.50; Median age: 44.7; Age under 18: 24.0%; Age 65 and over: 17.2%; Males per 100 females: 100.0
Housing: Homeownership rate: 83.4%; Homeowner vacancy rate: 2.8%; Rental vacancy rate: 17.2%

WELLINGTON (township). Covers a land area of 53.224 square miles and a water area of 0.166 square miles. Located at 45.14° N. Lat; 83.81° W. Long.
Population: 307; Growth (since 2000): 3.7%; Density: 5.8 persons per square mile; Race: 98.0% White, 0.0% Black/African American, 0.7% Asian, 0.3% American Indian/Alaska Native, 0.0% Native Hawaiian/Other Pacific Islander, 1.0% Two or more races, 0.3% Hispanic of any race; Average household size: 2.42; Median age: 41.4; Age under 18: 22.5%; Age 65 and over: 19.2%; Males per 100 females: 106.0
Housing: Homeownership rate: 87.4%; Homeowner vacancy rate: 3.5%; Rental vacancy rate: 0.0%

WILSON (township). Covers a land area of 79.270 square miles and a water area of 0.534 square miles. Located at 45.01° N. Lat; 83.62° W. Long.
Population: 2,029; Growth (since 2000): -2.2%; Density: 25.6 persons per square mile; Race: 98.9% White, 0.1% Black/African American, 0.0% Asian, 0.3% American Indian/Alaska Native, 0.0% Native Hawaiian/Other Pacific Islander, 0.5% Two or more races, 0.6% Hispanic of any race; Average household size: 2.50; Median age: 45.3; Age under 18: 22.2%; Age 65 and over: 16.0%; Males per 100 females: 99.9

Housing: Homeownership rate: 90.7%; Homeowner vacancy rate: 2.5%; Rental vacancy rate: 7.2%

Antrim County

Located in northwestern Michigan; bounded on the west by Grand Traverse Bay; includes Torch Lake. Covers a land area of 475.703 square miles, a water area of 126.067 square miles, and is located in the Eastern Time Zone at 45.01° N. Lat., 85.18° W. Long. The county was founded in 1840. County seat is Bellaire.
Population: 23,580; Growth (since 2000): 2.0%; Density: 49.6 persons per square mile; Race: 96.8% White, 0.2% Black/African American, 0.2% Asian, 1.0% American Indian/Alaska Native, 0.0% Native Hawaiian/Other Pacific Islander, 1.4% two or more races, 1.7% Hispanic of any race; Average household size: 2.36; Median age: 47.4; Age under 18: 21.1%; Age 65 and over: 22.1%; Males per 100 females: 98.1; Marriage status: 20.9% never married, 62.1% now married, 0.9% separated, 6.2% widowed, 10.8% divorced; Foreign born: 2.0%; Speak English only: 97.1%; With disability: 14.8%; Veterans: 12.7%; Ancestry: 25.9% German, 15.4% English, 12.9% Irish, 7.9% Polish, 6.3% French
Religion: Six largest groups: 9.3% Catholicism, 6.1% Presbyterian-Reformed, 3.5% Methodist/Pietist, 2.3% Holiness, 1.7% Lutheran, 1.4% Baptist
Economy: Unemployment rate: 6.7%; Leading industries: 16.1% retail trade; 15.2% construction; 11.2% other services (except public administration); Farms: 415 totaling 64,167 acres; Company size: 0 employ 1,000 or more persons, 1 employs 500 to 999 persons, 2 employ 100 to 499 persons, 550 employ less than 100 persons; Business ownership: 731 women-owned, n/a Black-owned, n/a Hispanic-owned, n/a Asian-owned
Employment: 11.3% management, business, and financial, 1.7% computer, engineering, and science, 8.4% education, legal, community service, arts, and media, 4.4% healthcare practitioners, 24.1% service, 21.8% sales and office, 11.9% natural resources, construction, and maintenance, 16.4% production, transportation, and material moving
Income: Per capita: $24,370; Median household: $45,362; Average household: $57,580; Households with income of $100,000 or more: 11.9%; Poverty rate: 15.4%
Educational Attainment: High school diploma or higher: 90.7%; Bachelor's degree or higher: 23.8%; Graduate/professional degree or higher: 9.2%
Housing: Homeownership rate: 83.9%; Median home value: $141,300; Median year structure built: 1977; Homeowner vacancy rate: 4.2%; Median gross rent: $703 per month; Rental vacancy rate: 19.4%
Vital Statistics: Birth rate: 92.9 per 10,000 population; Death rate: 106.1 per 10,000 population; Age-adjusted cancer mortality rate: 185.7 deaths per 100,000 population
Health Insurance: 86.4% have insurance; 65.7% have private insurance; 41.9% have public insurance; 13.6% do not have insurance; 5.2% of children under 18 do not have insurance
Health Care: Physicians: 4.7 per 10,000 population; Hospital beds: 0.0 per 10,000 population; Hospital admissions: 0.0 per 10,000 population
Transportation: Commute: 89.1% car, 0.3% public transportation, 2.5% walk, 6.9% work from home; Median travel time to work: 24.5 minutes
Presidential Election: 38.7% Obama, 60.1% Romney (2012)
Additional Information Contacts
Antrim Government . . . . (231) 533-6353
   http://www.antrimcounty.org

Antrim County Communities

ALBA (CDP). Covers a land area of 2.723 square miles and a water area of 0 square miles. Located at 44.98° N. Lat; 84.97° W. Long. Elevation is 1,178 feet.
Population: 295; Growth (since 2000): n/a; Density: 108.4 persons per square mile; Race: 96.6% White, 0.7% Black/African American, 0.0% Asian, 0.7% American Indian/Alaska Native, 0.0% Native Hawaiian/Other Pacific Islander, 0.0% Two or more races, 6.1% Hispanic of any race; Average household size: 2.59; Median age: 41.3; Age under 18: 24.1%; Age 65 and over: 15.9%; Males per 100 females: 86.7
School District(s)
Alba Public Schools (PK-12)
   2012-13 Enrollment: 178 . . . . (231) 584-2000

Housing: Homeownership rate: 81.6%; Homeowner vacancy rate: 2.1%; Rental vacancy rate: 27.6%

ALDEN (CDP). Covers a land area of 0.400 square miles and a water area of 0 square miles. Located at 44.88° N. Lat; 85.27° W. Long. Elevation is 604 feet.
Population: 125; Growth (since 2000): n/a; Density: 312.4 persons per square mile; Race: 99.2% White, 0.0% Black/African American, 0.0% Asian, 0.0% American Indian/Alaska Native, 0.0% Native Hawaiian/Other Pacific Islander, 0.8% Two or more races, 1.6% Hispanic of any race; Average household size: 1.87; Median age: 59.2; Age under 18: 9.6%; Age 65 and over: 35.2%; Males per 100 females: 92.3
Housing: Homeownership rate: 79.1%; Homeowner vacancy rate: 0.0%; Rental vacancy rate: 17.6%

BANKS (township). Covers a land area of 44.943 square miles and a water area of 6.302 square miles. Located at 45.17° N. Lat; 85.31° W. Long.
Population: 1,609; Growth (since 2000): -11.3%; Density: 35.8 persons per square mile; Race: 95.9% White, 0.1% Black/African American, 0.3% Asian, 0.6% American Indian/Alaska Native, 0.0% Native Hawaiian/Other Pacific Islander, 1.4% Two or more races, 3.7% Hispanic of any race; Average household size: 2.48; Median age: 45.7; Age under 18: 22.7%; Age 65 and over: 17.4%; Males per 100 females: 106.0
Housing: Homeownership rate: 84.0%; Homeowner vacancy rate: 3.9%; Rental vacancy rate: 15.9%

BELLAIRE (village). County seat. Covers a land area of 1.840 square miles and a water area of 0.126 square miles. Located at 44.97° N. Lat; 85.21° W. Long. Elevation is 627 feet.
History: The site of Bellaire was chosen to be the seat of Elk Rapids County in 1879. The town was established on land belonging to Ambrose E. Palmer, who named it for the clear, pure air.
Population: 1,086; Growth (since 2000): -6.7%; Density: 590.2 persons per square mile; Race: 97.2% White, 0.1% Black/African American, 0.6% Asian, 0.7% American Indian/Alaska Native, 0.0% Native Hawaiian/Other Pacific Islander, 0.9% Two or more races, 2.4% Hispanic of any race; Average household size: 2.29; Median age: 42.2; Age under 18: 23.8%; Age 65 and over: 16.3%; Males per 100 females: 93.9
School District(s)
Bellaire Public Schools (KG-12)
    2012-13 Enrollment: 440. . . . . (231) 533-8141
Housing: Homeownership rate: 65.8%; Homeowner vacancy rate: 6.5%; Rental vacancy rate: 12.4%
Safety: Violent crime rate: 0.0 per 10,000 population; Property crime rate: 55.7 per 10,000 population
Newspapers: Antrim Review (weekly circulation 4400)
Airports: Antrim County (general aviation)

CENTRAL LAKE (township). Covers a land area of 27.503 square miles and a water area of 3.800 square miles. Located at 45.08° N. Lat; 85.28° W. Long. Elevation is 646 feet.
Population: 2,198; Growth (since 2000): -2.5%; Density: 79.9 persons per square mile; Race: 97.3% White, 0.1% Black/African American, 0.1% Asian, 0.5% American Indian/Alaska Native, 0.0% Native Hawaiian/Other Pacific Islander, 1.5% Two or more races, 1.2% Hispanic of any race; Average household size: 2.35; Median age: 48.2; Age under 18: 19.7%; Age 65 and over: 21.5%; Males per 100 females: 99.6
School District(s)
Central Lake Public Schools (KG-12)
    2012-13 Enrollment: 335. . . . . (231) 544-3141
Housing: Homeownership rate: 80.0%; Homeowner vacancy rate: 4.8%; Rental vacancy rate: 19.8%

CENTRAL LAKE (village). Covers a land area of 1.069 square miles and a water area of 0.176 square miles. Located at 45.07° N. Lat; 85.26° W. Long. Elevation is 646 feet.
History: The village of Central Lake was platted in 1883. The railroad came through in 1892, and in 1895 the village was incorporated.
Population: 952; Growth (since 2000): -3.8%; Density: 891.0 persons per square mile; Race: 96.0% White, 0.1% Black/African American, 0.3% Asian, 0.9% American Indian/Alaska Native, 0.0% Native Hawaiian/Other Pacific Islander, 2.3% Two or more races, 1.4% Hispanic of any race; Average household size: 2.44; Median age: 42.0; Age under 18: 23.4%; Age 65 and over: 15.1%; Males per 100 females: 93.9

School District(s)
Central Lake Public Schools (KG-12)
    2012-13 Enrollment: 335. . . . . (231) 544-3141
Housing: Homeownership rate: 68.5%; Homeowner vacancy rate: 4.6%; Rental vacancy rate: 18.7%
Safety: Violent crime rate: 0.0 per 10,000 population; Property crime rate: 116.4 per 10,000 population

CHESTONIA (township). Covers a land area of 35.274 square miles and a water area of 0.256 square miles. Located at 45.00° N. Lat; 85.03° W. Long. Elevation is 640 feet.
History: Chestonia Township was organized in 1874 with Thomas R. Van Wert as the first supervisor and postmster.
Population: 511; Growth (since 2000): -6.4%; Density: 14.5 persons per square mile; Race: 96.1% White, 0.4% Black/African American, 0.0% Asian, 0.6% American Indian/Alaska Native, 0.0% Native Hawaiian/Other Pacific Islander, 2.2% Two or more races, 0.4% Hispanic of any race; Average household size: 2.54; Median age: 46.2; Age under 18: 20.4%; Age 65 and over: 18.8%; Males per 100 females: 94.3
Housing: Homeownership rate: 88.0%; Homeowner vacancy rate: 5.3%; Rental vacancy rate: 25.0%

CUSTER (township). Covers a land area of 34.713 square miles and a water area of 0.492 square miles. Located at 44.90° N. Lat; 85.16° W. Long.
Population: 1,136; Growth (since 2000): 15.0%; Density: 32.7 persons per square mile; Race: 97.0% White, 0.3% Black/African American, 0.4% Asian, 0.4% American Indian/Alaska Native, 0.0% Native Hawaiian/Other Pacific Islander, 1.6% Two or more races, 2.1% Hispanic of any race; Average household size: 2.36; Median age: 47.3; Age under 18: 19.3%; Age 65 and over: 21.3%; Males per 100 females: 100.7
Housing: Homeownership rate: 87.1%; Homeowner vacancy rate: 5.6%; Rental vacancy rate: 54.6%

EASTPORT (CDP). Covers a land area of 1.996 square miles and a water area of 0.007 square miles. Located at 45.11° N. Lat; 85.35° W. Long. Elevation is 607 feet.
Population: 218; Growth (since 2000): n/a; Density: 109.2 persons per square mile; Race: 98.2% White, 0.0% Black/African American, 0.0% Asian, 1.4% American Indian/Alaska Native, 0.0% Native Hawaiian/Other Pacific Islander, 0.5% Two or more races, 0.9% Hispanic of any race; Average household size: 1.85; Median age: 62.0; Age under 18: 5.5%; Age 65 and over: 45.0%; Males per 100 females: 84.7
Housing: Homeownership rate: 90.8%; Homeowner vacancy rate: 6.6%; Rental vacancy rate: 33.3%

ECHO (township). Covers a land area of 34.847 square miles and a water area of 0.514 square miles. Located at 45.08° N. Lat; 85.16° W. Long.
Population: 877; Growth (since 2000): -5.5%; Density: 25.2 persons per square mile; Race: 96.0% White, 0.5% Black/African American, 0.0% Asian, 2.2% American Indian/Alaska Native, 0.0% Native Hawaiian/Other Pacific Islander, 1.1% Two or more races, 1.7% Hispanic of any race; Average household size: 2.50; Median age: 44.7; Age under 18: 22.7%; Age 65 and over: 17.7%; Males per 100 females: 107.3
Housing: Homeownership rate: 88.0%; Homeowner vacancy rate: 3.4%; Rental vacancy rate: 16.0%

ELK RAPIDS (township). Covers a land area of 7.080 square miles and a water area of 3.882 square miles. Located at 44.90° N. Lat; 85.40° W. Long. Elevation is 597 feet.
Population: 2,631; Growth (since 2000): -4.0%; Density: 371.6 persons per square mile; Race: 96.9% White, 0.5% Black/African American, 0.5% Asian, 0.8% American Indian/Alaska Native, 0.1% Native Hawaiian/Other Pacific Islander, 1.1% Two or more races, 1.7% Hispanic of any race; Average household size: 2.15; Median age: 53.0; Age under 18: 18.5%; Age 65 and over: 29.3%; Males per 100 females: 90.7; Marriage status: 21.7% never married, 58.0% now married, 0.4% separated, 10.2% widowed, 10.1% divorced; Foreign born: 1.7%; Speak English only: 96.0%; With disability: 12.9%; Veterans: 12.7%; Ancestry: 27.9% German, 18.3% English, 14.2% Irish, 8.2% Polish, 7.7% French
Employment: 15.9% management, business, and financial, 2.7% computer, engineering, and science, 6.7% education, legal, community service, arts, and media, 9.3% healthcare practitioners, 19.3% service,

29.7% sales and office, 4.8% natural resources, construction, and maintenance, 11.5% production, transportation, and material moving
Income: Per capita: $28,274; Median household: $49,145; Average household: $63,297; Households with income of $100,000 or more: 16.4%; Poverty rate: 14.8%
Educational Attainment: High school diploma or higher: 95.4%; Bachelor's degree or higher: 38.0%; Graduate/professional degree or higher: 16.5%

School District(s)
Elk Rapids Schools (PK-12)
    2012-13 Enrollment: 1,420 . . . . (231) 264-8692
Housing: Homeownership rate: 77.6%; Median home value: $229,600; Median year structure built: 1977; Homeowner vacancy rate: 3.4%; Median gross rent: $673 per month; Rental vacancy rate: 23.0%
Health Insurance: 88.8% have insurance; 72.0% have private insurance; 47.2% have public insurance; 11.2% do not have insurance; 1.2% of children under 18 do not have insurance
Transportation: Commute: 85.8% car, 0.0% public transportation, 2.9% walk, 7.8% work from home; Median travel time to work: 18.7 minutes
Additional Information Contacts
Elk Rapids Township. . . . . (231) 264-9333
    http://www.elkrapids.com/Township/index.htm

ELK RAPIDS (village). Covers a land area of 1.650 square miles and a water area of 0.359 square miles. Located at 44.90° N. Lat; 85.40° W. Long. Elevation is 597 feet.
History: Elk Rapids was settled in 1852 around a sawmill operated by power from the Elk River. A charcoal iron furnace and a chemical plant were also built here, but the area later became a summer resort village.
Population: 1,642; Growth (since 2000): -3.4%; Density: 995.3 persons per square mile; Race: 96.6% White, 0.7% Black/African American, 0.5% Asian, 1.2% American Indian/Alaska Native, 0.1% Native Hawaiian/Other Pacific Islander, 0.7% Two or more races, 1.3% Hispanic of any race; Average household size: 2.07; Median age: 52.4; Age under 18: 18.6%; Age 65 and over: 28.7%; Males per 100 females: 86.8

School District(s)
Elk Rapids Schools (PK-12)
    2012-13 Enrollment: 1,420 . . . . (231) 264-8692
Housing: Homeownership rate: 70.6%; Homeowner vacancy rate: 3.9%; Rental vacancy rate: 17.4%
Safety: Violent crime rate: 12.3 per 10,000 population; Property crime rate: 227.1 per 10,000 population

ELLSWORTH (village). Covers a land area of 0.718 square miles and a water area of 0.079 square miles. Located at 45.17° N. Lat; 85.24° W. Long. Elevation is 659 feet.
Population: 349; Growth (since 2000): -27.7%; Density: 485.9 persons per square mile; Race: 97.1% White, 0.6% Black/African American, 0.0% Asian, 0.0% American Indian/Alaska Native, 0.0% Native Hawaiian/Other Pacific Islander, 1.4% Two or more races, 0.6% Hispanic of any race; Average household size: 2.42; Median age: 42.9; Age under 18: 24.9%; Age 65 and over: 15.5%; Males per 100 females: 91.8

School District(s)
Ellsworth Community School (PK-12)
    2012-13 Enrollment: 224. . . . . (231) 588-2544
Housing: Homeownership rate: 72.5%; Homeowner vacancy rate: 2.8%; Rental vacancy rate: 8.7%

FOREST HOME (township). Covers a land area of 24.138 square miles and a water area of 9.392 square miles. Located at 44.98° N. Lat; 85.26° W. Long.
Population: 1,720; Growth (since 2000): -7.4%; Density: 71.3 persons per square mile; Race: 98.5% White, 0.0% Black/African American, 0.3% Asian, 0.5% American Indian/Alaska Native, 0.1% Native Hawaiian/Other Pacific Islander, 0.6% Two or more races, 1.3% Hispanic of any race; Average household size: 2.20; Median age: 53.4; Age under 18: 16.8%; Age 65 and over: 28.6%; Males per 100 females: 98.2
Housing: Homeownership rate: 88.0%; Homeowner vacancy rate: 3.5%; Rental vacancy rate: 5.7%

HELENA (township). Covers a land area of 16.203 square miles and a water area of 6.859 square miles. Located at 44.90° N. Lat; 85.27° W. Long.
Population: 1,001; Growth (since 2000): 14.0%; Density: 61.8 persons per square mile; Race: 98.4% White, 0.0% Black/African American, 0.2%

Asian, 0.5% American Indian/Alaska Native, 0.0% Native Hawaiian/Other Pacific Islander, 0.8% Two or more races, 0.9% Hispanic of any race; Average household size: 2.12; Median age: 55.6; Age under 18: 15.4%; Age 65 and over: 30.2%; Males per 100 females: 100.6
Housing: Homeownership rate: 90.0%; Homeowner vacancy rate: 2.3%; Rental vacancy rate: 14.5%

JORDAN (township). Covers a land area of 35.084 square miles and a water area of 0.146 square miles. Located at 45.07° N. Lat; 85.05° W. Long.
Population: 992; Growth (since 2000): 13.4%; Density: 28.3 persons per square mile; Race: 97.5% White, 0.1% Black/African American, 0.0% Asian, 0.8% American Indian/Alaska Native, 0.0% Native Hawaiian/Other Pacific Islander, 1.4% Two or more races, 1.6% Hispanic of any race; Average household size: 2.62; Median age: 41.0; Age under 18: 23.7%; Age 65 and over: 12.3%; Males per 100 females: 104.5
Housing: Homeownership rate: 88.9%; Homeowner vacancy rate: 1.7%; Rental vacancy rate: 10.4%

KEARNEY (township). Covers a land area of 34.239 square miles and a water area of 1.013 square miles. Located at 45.00° N. Lat; 85.14° W. Long.
Population: 1,765; Growth (since 2000): 0.1%; Density: 51.5 persons per square mile; Race: 96.9% White, 0.1% Black/African American, 0.3% Asian, 1.1% American Indian/Alaska Native, 0.0% Native Hawaiian/Other Pacific Islander, 1.2% Two or more races, 1.4% Hispanic of any race; Average household size: 2.33; Median age: 48.1; Age under 18: 20.8%; Age 65 and over: 26.4%; Males per 100 females: 89.4
Housing: Homeownership rate: 76.8%; Homeowner vacancy rate: 8.3%; Rental vacancy rate: 26.5%

KEWADIN (unincorporated postal area)
ZCTA: 49648
    Covers a land area of 26.607 square miles and a water area of 22.439 square miles. Located at 45.00° N. Lat; 85.34° W. Long. Elevation is 600 feet.
    Population: 2,098; Growth (since 2000): 3.6%; Density: 78.9 persons per square mile; Race: 95.5% White, 0.2% Black/African American, 0.1% Asian, 1.8% American Indian/Alaska Native, 0.1% Native Hawaiian/Other Pacific Islander, 1.2% Two or more races, 3.0% Hispanic of any race; Average household size: 2.20; Median age: 54.3; Age under 18: 16.8%; Age 65 and over: 29.8%; Males per 100 females: 97.7
    Housing: Homeownership rate: 91.1%; Homeowner vacancy rate: 3.3%; Rental vacancy rate: 14.4%

LAKES OF THE NORTH (CDP). Covers a land area of 16.582 square miles and a water area of 0.145 square miles. Located at 44.93° N. Lat; 84.89° W. Long.
Population: 925; Growth (since 2000): n/a; Density: 55.8 persons per square mile; Race: 97.9% White, 0.3% Black/African American, 0.2% Asian, 0.5% American Indian/Alaska Native, 0.0% Native Hawaiian/Other Pacific Islander, 0.9% Two or more races, 1.6% Hispanic of any race; Average household size: 2.26; Median age: 46.6; Age under 18: 19.9%; Age 65 and over: 21.4%; Males per 100 females: 100.2
Housing: Homeownership rate: 91.9%; Homeowner vacancy rate: 6.4%; Rental vacancy rate: 10.8%

MANCELONA (township). Covers a land area of 71.135 square miles and a water area of 0.249 square miles. Located at 44.89° N. Lat; 84.98° W. Long. Elevation is 1,125 feet.
History: Incorporated 1889.
Population: 4,400; Growth (since 2000): 7.3%; Density: 61.9 persons per square mile; Race: 96.2% White, 0.2% Black/African American, 0.0% Asian, 1.3% American Indian/Alaska Native, 0.0% Native Hawaiian/Other Pacific Islander, 2.3% Two or more races, 1.1% Hispanic of any race; Average household size: 2.63; Median age: 37.4; Age under 18: 27.6%; Age 65 and over: 13.6%; Males per 100 females: 99.0; Marriage status: 24.9% never married, 53.0% now married, 1.1% separated, 3.6% widowed, 18.5% divorced; Foreign born: 1.7%; Speak English only: 97.3%; With disability: 17.6%; Veterans: 13.5%; Ancestry: 26.7% German, 14.4% English, 9.3% Irish, 6.0% Polish, 5.8% French
Employment: 5.0% management, business, and financial, 1.1% computer, engineering, and science, 6.5% education, legal, community service, arts, and media, 0.4% healthcare practitioners, 33.8% service, 21.5% sales and

office, 12.1% natural resources, construction, and maintenance, 19.6% production, transportation, and material moving
Income: Per capita: $14,811; Median household: $35,612; Average household: $38,288; Households with income of $100,000 or more: 2.9%; Poverty rate: 32.5%
Educational Attainment: High school diploma or higher: 82.9%; Bachelor's degree or higher: 12.3%; Graduate/professional degree or higher: 1.7%

School District(s)
Mancelona Public Schools (PK-12)
    2012-13 Enrollment: 990 . . . . (231) 587-9764
Housing: Homeownership rate: 78.8%; Median home value: $81,800; Median year structure built: 1976; Homeowner vacancy rate: 4.5%; Median gross rent: $667 per month; Rental vacancy rate: 6.9%
Health Insurance: 85.1% have insurance; 54.8% have private insurance; 43.8% have public insurance; 14.9% do not have insurance; 2.3% of children under 18 do not have insurance
Transportation: Commute: 88.1% car, 0.5% public transportation, 5.4% walk, 4.8% work from home; Median travel time to work: 25.5 minutes; Amtrak: Bus service available.
Additional Information Contacts
Mancelona Township . . . . (231) 587-8651
    http://www.mancelonatownship.com

MANCELONA (village). Covers a land area of 1.003 square miles and a water area of 0 square miles. Located at 44.90° N. Lat; 85.06° W. Long. Elevation is 1,125 feet.
History: Mancelona grew up as a residential area for workers at the Antrim Iron Company furnace and sawmill, founded in 1882.
Population: 1,390; Growth (since 2000): -1.3%; Density: 1,385.8 persons per square mile; Race: 94.9% White, 0.1% Black/African American, 0.0% Asian, 1.2% American Indian/Alaska Native, 0.0% Native Hawaiian/Other Pacific Islander, 3.7% Two or more races, 0.9% Hispanic of any race; Average household size: 2.68; Median age: 34.1; Age under 18: 29.6%; Age 65 and over: 12.1%; Males per 100 females: 89.6

School District(s)
Mancelona Public Schools (PK-12)
    2012-13 Enrollment: 990 . . . . (231) 587-9764
Housing: Homeownership rate: 69.1%; Homeowner vacancy rate: 5.0%; Rental vacancy rate: 7.0%
Safety: Violent crime rate: 14.5 per 10,000 population; Property crime rate: 108.8 per 10,000 population

MILTON (township). Covers a land area of 25.563 square miles and a water area of 18.104 square miles. Located at 44.92° N. Lat; 85.34° W. Long.
Population: 2,204; Growth (since 2000): 6.4%; Density: 86.2 persons per square mile; Race: 95.2% White, 0.1% Black/African American, 0.3% Asian, 2.3% American Indian/Alaska Native, 0.0% Native Hawaiian/Other Pacific Islander, 1.2% Two or more races, 2.2% Hispanic of any race; Average household size: 2.31; Median age: 51.5; Age under 18: 19.7%; Age 65 and over: 26.3%; Males per 100 females: 97.3
Housing: Homeownership rate: 89.2%; Homeowner vacancy rate: 3.4%; Rental vacancy rate: 20.5%

STAR (township). Covers a land area of 34.389 square miles and a water area of 0.071 square miles. Located at 44.98° N. Lat; 84.92° W. Long.
Population: 926; Growth (since 2000): 24.3%; Density: 26.9 persons per square mile; Race: 96.5% White, 0.0% Black/African American, 0.1% Asian, 1.1% American Indian/Alaska Native, 0.0% Native Hawaiian/Other Pacific Islander, 1.6% Two or more races, 2.8% Hispanic of any race; Average household size: 2.41; Median age: 42.8; Age under 18: 22.2%; Age 65 and over: 15.6%; Males per 100 females: 101.7
Housing: Homeownership rate: 85.2%; Homeowner vacancy rate: 5.2%; Rental vacancy rate: 6.6%

TORCH LAKE (township). Covers a land area of 15.092 square miles and a water area of 6.011 square miles. Located at 45.04° N. Lat; 85.34° W. Long. Elevation is 617 feet.
History: Torch Lake got its name from the native custom of spearing fish at night by the light of torches.
Population: 1,194; Growth (since 2000): 3.0%; Density: 79.1 persons per square mile; Race: 97.1% White, 0.3% Black/African American, 0.1% Asian, 0.8% American Indian/Alaska Native, 0.3% Native Hawaiian/Other

Pacific Islander, 0.8% Two or more races, 2.8% Hispanic of any race; Average household size: 2.00; Median age: 59.8; Age under 18: 11.0%; Age 65 and over: 37.6%; Males per 100 females: 95.1
Housing: Homeownership rate: 94.2%; Homeowner vacancy rate: 4.1%; Rental vacancy rate: 25.5%

WARNER (township). Covers a land area of 35.498 square miles and a water area of 0.095 square miles. Located at 45.07° N. Lat; 84.93° W. Long.
Population: 416; Growth (since 2000): 6.9%; Density: 11.7 persons per square mile; Race: 97.8% White, 0.2% Black/African American, 0.0% Asian, 0.0% American Indian/Alaska Native, 0.5% Native Hawaiian/Other Pacific Islander, 1.2% Two or more races, 0.5% Hispanic of any race; Average household size: 2.83; Median age: 37.0; Age under 18: 30.0%; Age 65 and over: 11.8%; Males per 100 females: 99.0
Housing: Homeownership rate: 88.4%; Homeowner vacancy rate: 1.5%; Rental vacancy rate: 10.5%

Arenac County

Located in eastern Michigan; bounded on the southeast by Saginaw Bay. Covers a land area of 363.191 square miles, a water area of 317.499 square miles, and is located in the Eastern Time Zone at 44.04° N. Lat., 83.74° W. Long. The county was founded in 1883. County seat is Standish.

Weather Station: Standish 5 SW   Elevation: 645 feet

	Jan	Feb	Mar	Apr	May	Jun	Jul	Aug	Sep	Oct	Nov	Dec
High	29	32	41	55	67	76	81	79	72	59	45	34
Low	11	12	20	32	42	51	55	54	46	36	28	19
Precip	1.6	1.4	1.9	2.8	3.3	3.3	2.8	3.5	3.5	2.6	2.5	1.7
Snow	10.9	6.3	5.0	0.6	0.0	0.0	0.0	0.0	0.0	0.0	1.7	8.4

High and Low temperatures in degrees Fahrenheit; Precipitation and Snow in inches

Population: 15,899; Growth (since 2000): -7.9%; Density: 43.8 persons per square mile; Race: 96.8% White, 0.2% Black/African American, 0.2% Asian, 1.2% American Indian/Alaska Native, 0.1% Native Hawaiian/Other Pacific Islander, 1.3% two or more races, 1.4% Hispanic of any race; Average household size: 2.34; Median age: 46.7; Age under 18: 20.1%; Age 65 and over: 20.3%; Males per 100 females: 102.7; Marriage status: 23.3% never married, 57.3% now married, 1.1% separated, 8.2% widowed, 11.2% divorced; Foreign born: 0.7%; Speak English only: 97.8%; With disability: 19.1%; Veterans: 12.0%; Ancestry: 27.6% German, 13.8% Polish, 11.7% Irish, 10.9% English, 10.4% French
Religion: Six largest groups: 28.4% Catholicism, 7.0% Lutheran, 5.8% Methodist/Pietist, 1.2% Non-denominational Protestant, 1.1% Holiness, 1.1% Latter-day Saints
Economy: Unemployment rate: 7.2%; Leading industries: 21.4% retail trade; 14.5% accommodation and food services; 10.5% other services (except public administration); Farms: 421 totaling 81,677 acres; Company size: 0 employ 1,000 or more persons, 0 employ 500 to 999 persons, 4 employ 100 to 499 persons, 328 employ less than 100 persons; Business ownership: 356 women-owned, n/a Black-owned, n/a Hispanic-owned, n/a Asian-owned
Employment: 11.8% management, business, and financial, 2.5% computer, engineering, and science, 8.2% education, legal, community service, arts, and media, 5.2% healthcare practitioners, 19.1% service, 23.8% sales and office, 11.8% natural resources, construction, and maintenance, 17.5% production, transportation, and material moving
Income: Per capita: $20,039; Median household: $38,874; Average household: $48,650; Households with income of $100,000 or more: 8.0%; Poverty rate: 18.1%
Educational Attainment: High school diploma or higher: 84.3%; Bachelor's degree or higher: 11.4%; Graduate/professional degree or higher: 4.6%
Housing: Homeownership rate: 83.7%; Median home value: $90,200; Median year structure built: 1975; Homeowner vacancy rate: 3.3%; Median gross rent: $572 per month; Rental vacancy rate: 7.2%
Vital Statistics: Birth rate: 88.5 per 10,000 population; Death rate: 122.7 per 10,000 population; Age-adjusted cancer mortality rate: 213.0 deaths per 100,000 population
Health Insurance: 87.2% have insurance; 64.7% have private insurance; 43.0% have public insurance; 12.8% do not have insurance; 4.5% of children under 18 do not have insurance

Health Care: Physicians: 5.8 per 10,000 population; Hospital beds: 43.5 per 10,000 population; Hospital admissions: 618.9 per 10,000 population
Transportation: Commute: 90.5% car, 0.6% public transportation, 2.4% walk, 5.1% work from home; Median travel time to work: 27.1 minutes
Presidential Election: 46.9% Obama, 51.8% Romney (2012)
Additional Information Contacts
Arenac Government . . . . (989) 846-4626
   http://www.arenaccountygov.com

Arenac County Communities

ADAMS (township). Covers a land area of 35.638 square miles and a water area of 0.092 square miles. Located at 44.04° N. Lat; 84.10° W. Long.
Population: 563; Growth (since 2000): 2.4%; Density: 15.8 persons per square mile; Race: 97.3% White, 0.0% Black/African American, 0.0% Asian, 0.7% American Indian/Alaska Native, 0.7% Native Hawaiian/Other Pacific Islander, 1.1% Two or more races, 0.4% Hispanic of any race; Average household size: 2.66; Median age: 38.0; Age under 18: 26.5%; Age 65 and over: 12.3%; Males per 100 females: 112.5
Housing: Homeownership rate: 84.9%; Homeowner vacancy rate: 3.7%; Rental vacancy rate: 0.0%

ALGER (unincorporated postal area)
ZCTA: 48610
   Covers a land area of 117.476 square miles and a water area of 1.491 square miles. Located at 44.14° N. Lat; 84.19° W. Long. Elevation is 784 feet.
Population: 3,083; Growth (since 2000): -10.7%; Density: 26.2 persons per square mile; Race: 95.8% White, 0.3% Black/African American, 0.5% Asian, 1.6% American Indian/Alaska Native, 0.0% Native Hawaiian/Other Pacific Islander, 1.6% Two or more races, 1.5% Hispanic of any race; Average household size: 2.25; Median age: 51.4; Age under 18: 15.6%; Age 65 and over: 22.5%; Males per 100 females: 102.6; Marriage status: 23.2% never married, 57.1% now married, 2.0% separated, 7.9% widowed, 11.8% divorced; Foreign born: 1.2%; Speak English only: 98.4%; With disability: 25.0%; Veterans: 14.9%; Ancestry: 26.8% German, 13.3% Irish, 12.8% English, 7.9% American, 7.7% Polish
Employment: 9.3% management, business, and financial, 4.6% computer, engineering, and science, 4.8% education, legal, community service, arts, and media, 5.9% healthcare practitioners, 24.5% service, 29.4% sales and office, 5.4% natural resources, construction, and maintenance, 16.1% production, transportation, and material moving
Income: Per capita: $19,626; Median household: $37,015; Average household: $42,436; Households with income of $100,000 or more: 4.8%; Poverty rate: 20.2%
Educational Attainment: High school diploma or higher: 79.2%; Bachelor's degree or higher: 7.8%; Graduate/professional degree or higher: 2.9%
Housing: Homeownership rate: 89.0%; Median home value: $88,600; Median year structure built: 1978; Homeowner vacancy rate: 3.6%; Median gross rent: $679 per month; Rental vacancy rate: 6.6%
Health Insurance: 87.4% have insurance; 57.7% have private insurance; 55.3% have public insurance; 12.6% do not have insurance; 10.4% of children under 18 do not have insurance
Transportation: Commute: 93.7% car, 1.2% public transportation, 1.0% walk, 2.4% work from home; Median travel time to work: 31.3 minutes

ARENAC (township). Covers a land area of 35.775 square miles and a water area of 2.293 square miles. Located at 44.04° N. Lat; 83.86° W. Long. Elevation is 604 feet.
Population: 903; Growth (since 2000): -9.0%; Density: 25.2 persons per square mile; Race: 97.6% White, 0.2% Black/African American, 0.1% Asian, 1.0% American Indian/Alaska Native, 0.0% Native Hawaiian/Other Pacific Islander, 1.0% Two or more races, 1.1% Hispanic of any race; Average household size: 2.38; Median age: 46.5; Age under 18: 20.3%; Age 65 and over: 17.4%; Males per 100 females: 94.6
Housing: Homeownership rate: 88.4%; Homeowner vacancy rate: 2.6%; Rental vacancy rate: 10.0%

AU GRES (city). Covers a land area of 2.232 square miles and a water area of 0.101 square miles. Located at 44.04° N. Lat; 83.69° W. Long. Elevation is 591 feet.
History: Au Gres was settled by construction workers who came to work on the Saginaw-Au Sable State Road about 1862. The name of Au Gres refers to the "gritty stone" in the area, and was given to Point Au Gres by early French explorers. Au Gres was incorporated as a city in 1905.
Population: 889; Growth (since 2000): -13.5%; Density: 398.3 persons per square mile; Race: 97.5% White, 0.0% Black/African American, 0.0% Asian, 0.4% American Indian/Alaska Native, 0.0% Native Hawaiian/Other Pacific Islander, 1.9% Two or more races, 1.9% Hispanic of any race; Average household size: 2.00; Median age: 49.8; Age under 18: 17.9%; Age 65 and over: 25.5%; Males per 100 females: 108.7
School District(s)
Au Gres-Sims SD (KG-12)
   2012-13 Enrollment: 380 . . . . (989) 876-7150
Housing: Homeownership rate: 62.9%; Homeowner vacancy rate: 7.4%; Rental vacancy rate: 6.9%

AU GRES (township). Covers a land area of 33.349 square miles and a water area of 5.405 square miles. Located at 44.04° N. Lat; 83.74° W. Long. Elevation is 591 feet.
Population: 953; Growth (since 2000): -5.4%; Density: 28.6 persons per square mile; Race: 97.6% White, 0.2% Black/African American, 0.2% Asian, 0.4% American Indian/Alaska Native, 0.0% Native Hawaiian/Other Pacific Islander, 1.5% Two or more races, 0.2% Hispanic of any race; Average household size: 2.27; Median age: 50.7; Age under 18: 17.6%; Age 65 and over: 25.0%; Males per 100 females: 107.6
School District(s)
Au Gres-Sims SD (KG-12)
   2012-13 Enrollment: 380 . . . . (989) 876-7150
Housing: Homeownership rate: 94.0%; Homeowner vacancy rate: 5.0%; Rental vacancy rate: 3.7%

CLAYTON (township). Covers a land area of 32.065 square miles and a water area of 0.083 square miles. Located at 44.12° N. Lat; 84.00° W. Long.
Population: 1,097; Growth (since 2000): -0.4%; Density: 34.2 persons per square mile; Race: 97.5% White, 0.0% Black/African American, 0.1% Asian, 1.1% American Indian/Alaska Native, 0.0% Native Hawaiian/Other Pacific Islander, 1.3% Two or more races, 1.5% Hispanic of any race; Average household size: 2.62; Median age: 44.2; Age under 18: 21.1%; Age 65 and over: 15.0%; Males per 100 females: 107.8
Housing: Homeownership rate: 84.5%; Homeowner vacancy rate: 2.2%; Rental vacancy rate: 2.9%

DEEP RIVER (township). Covers a land area of 35.280 square miles and a water area of 0.247 square miles. Located at 44.04° N. Lat; 83.98° W. Long.
Population: 2,149; Growth (since 2000): -4.2%; Density: 60.9 persons per square mile; Race: 96.9% White, 0.3% Black/African American, 0.1% Asian, 1.0% American Indian/Alaska Native, 0.0% Native Hawaiian/Other Pacific Islander, 1.5% Two or more races, 1.5% Hispanic of any race; Average household size: 2.45; Median age: 44.5; Age under 18: 20.9%; Age 65 and over: 18.8%; Males per 100 females: 106.6
Housing: Homeownership rate: 87.1%; Homeowner vacancy rate: 2.6%; Rental vacancy rate: 7.6%

LINCOLN (township). Covers a land area of 20.996 square miles and a water area of 0.164 square miles. Located at 43.96° N. Lat; 84.01° W. Long.
Population: 942; Growth (since 2000): -38.1%; Density: 44.9 persons per square mile; Race: 95.9% White, 0.0% Black/African American, 0.0% Asian, 2.9% American Indian/Alaska Native, 0.0% Native Hawaiian/Other Pacific Islander, 1.0% Two or more races, 0.8% Hispanic of any race; Average household size: 2.43; Median age: 39.5; Age under 18: 24.3%; Age 65 and over: 17.1%; Males per 100 females: 106.6
Housing: Homeownership rate: 80.9%; Homeowner vacancy rate: 1.6%; Rental vacancy rate: 3.8%

MASON (township). Covers a land area of 32.045 square miles and a water area of 0.030 square miles. Located at 44.13° N. Lat; 83.86° W. Long.
Population: 851; Growth (since 2000): -14.4%; Density: 26.6 persons per square mile; Race: 97.5% White, 0.1% Black/African American, 0.1%

Asian, 1.3% American Indian/Alaska Native, 0.0% Native Hawaiian/Other Pacific Islander, 0.7% Two or more races, 1.9% Hispanic of any race; Average household size: 2.45; Median age: 45.0; Age under 18: 21.9%; Age 65 and over: 14.6%; Males per 100 females: 112.8
Housing: Homeownership rate: 86.5%; Homeowner vacancy rate: 2.6%; Rental vacancy rate: 4.1%

MOFFATT (township). Covers a land area of 31.507 square miles and a water area of 0.587 square miles. Located at 44.12° N. Lat; 84.11° W. Long.
Population: 1,184; Growth (since 2000): 5.6%; Density: 37.6 persons per square mile; Race: 97.5% White, 0.2% Black/African American, 0.3% Asian, 0.4% American Indian/Alaska Native, 0.0% Native Hawaiian/Other Pacific Islander, 1.5% Two or more races, 1.4% Hispanic of any race; Average household size: 2.28; Median age: 51.4; Age under 18: 16.3%; Age 65 and over: 23.7%; Males per 100 females: 95.4
Housing: Homeownership rate: 88.3%; Homeowner vacancy rate: 3.8%; Rental vacancy rate: 8.8%

OMER (city). Covers a land area of 1.133 square miles and a water area of 0.028 square miles. Located at 44.05° N. Lat; 83.86° W. Long. Elevation is 610 feet.
History: Omer was settled in 1873 and incorporated as a city in 1903. The Rifle River provided good fishing.
Population: 313; Growth (since 2000): -7.1%; Density: 276.2 persons per square mile; Race: 94.2% White, 0.3% Black/African American, 0.0% Asian, 4.2% American Indian/Alaska Native, 0.0% Native Hawaiian/Other Pacific Islander, 1.0% Two or more races, 0.0% Hispanic of any race; Average household size: 2.39; Median age: 40.8; Age under 18: 22.4%; Age 65 and over: 17.9%; Males per 100 females: 100.6
Housing: Homeownership rate: 84.0%; Homeowner vacancy rate: 1.7%; Rental vacancy rate: 21.4%

SIMS (township). Covers a land area of 11.505 square miles and a water area of 35.169 square miles. Located at 44.05° N. Lat; 83.58° W. Long.
Population: 1,095; Growth (since 2000): 0.4%; Density: 95.2 persons per square mile; Race: 95.8% White, 0.2% Black/African American, 0.6% Asian, 1.1% American Indian/Alaska Native, 0.0% Native Hawaiian/Other Pacific Islander, 2.3% Two or more races, 0.8% Hispanic of any race; Average household size: 2.08; Median age: 57.2; Age under 18: 13.1%; Age 65 and over: 31.7%; Males per 100 females: 97.7
Housing: Homeownership rate: 94.1%; Homeowner vacancy rate: 4.6%; Rental vacancy rate: 8.8%

STANDISH (city). County seat. Covers a land area of 2.155 square miles and a water area of <.001 square miles. Located at 43.98° N. Lat; 83.96° W. Long. Elevation is 623 feet.
History: Standish was named for John D. Standish of Detroit, who built a mill here in 1871. Standish developed as a shipping and trading center for a farming area that produced sugar beets and dairy products.
Population: 1,509; Growth (since 2000): -4.6%; Density: 700.4 persons per square mile; Race: 95.3% White, 0.5% Black/African American, 0.4% Asian, 1.5% American Indian/Alaska Native, 0.0% Native Hawaiian/Other Pacific Islander, 1.6% Two or more races, 2.6% Hispanic of any race; Average household size: 2.27; Median age: 40.0; Age under 18: 23.6%; Age 65 and over: 17.8%; Males per 100 females: 92.7
School District(s)
Bay-Arenac ISD (PK-12)
    2012-13 Enrollment: 614. . . . . (989) 686-4410
Standish-Sterling Community Schools (PK-12)
    2012-13 Enrollment: 1,628 . . . . (989) 846-3670
Housing: Homeownership rate: 57.0%; Homeowner vacancy rate: 3.5%; Rental vacancy rate: 4.3%
Hospitals: Saint Mary's Standish Community Hospital (68 beds)
Newspapers: Arenac County Independent (weekly circulation 6100)

STANDISH (township). Covers a land area of 27.632 square miles and a water area of 2.871 square miles. Located at 43.95° N. Lat; 83.91° W. Long. Elevation is 623 feet.
History: Incorporated as city 1903.
Population: 1,900; Growth (since 2000): -6.2%; Density: 68.8 persons per square mile; Race: 96.2% White, 0.2% Black/African American, 0.2% Asian, 1.8% American Indian/Alaska Native, 0.1% Native Hawaiian/Other Pacific Islander, 0.9% Two or more races, 2.1% Hispanic of any race;

Average household size: 2.48; Median age: 44.4; Age under 18: 22.4%; Age 65 and over: 16.4%; Males per 100 females: 101.1
School District(s)
Bay-Arenac ISD (PK-12)
    2012-13 Enrollment: 614. . . . . (989) 686-4410
Standish-Sterling Community Schools (PK-12)
    2012-13 Enrollment: 1,628 . . . . (989) 846-3670
Housing: Homeownership rate: 86.9%; Homeowner vacancy rate: 1.9%; Rental vacancy rate: 12.9%
Hospitals: Saint Mary's Standish Community Hospital (68 beds)
Newspapers: Arenac County Independent (weekly circulation 6100)

STERLING (village). Covers a land area of 0.977 square miles and a water area of 0.003 square miles. Located at 44.03° N. Lat; 84.02° W. Long. Elevation is 748 feet.
History: Sterling grew up around a sawmill built in 1871, and a railroad station established in 1872. It was named for lumberman William C. Sterling.
Population: 530; Growth (since 2000): -0.6%; Density: 542.3 persons per square mile; Race: 97.0% White, 0.0% Black/African American, 0.0% Asian, 0.9% American Indian/Alaska Native, 0.0% Native Hawaiian/Other Pacific Islander, 1.9% Two or more races, 1.7% Hispanic of any race; Average household size: 2.47; Median age: 42.7; Age under 18: 21.7%; Age 65 and over: 24.9%; Males per 100 females: 103.8
School District(s)
Standish-Sterling Community Schools (PK-12)
    2012-13 Enrollment: 1,628 . . . . (989) 846-3670
Housing: Homeownership rate: 78.9%; Homeowner vacancy rate: 1.3%; Rental vacancy rate: 7.1%

TURNER (township). Covers a land area of 31.145 square miles and a water area of 1.182 square miles. Located at 44.13° N. Lat; 83.75° W. Long. Elevation is 633 feet.
Population: 550; Growth (since 2000): -14.3%; Density: 17.7 persons per square mile; Race: 96.2% White, 0.4% Black/African American, 0.2% Asian, 1.3% American Indian/Alaska Native, 0.5% Native Hawaiian/Other Pacific Islander, 0.9% Two or more races, 0.2% Hispanic of any race; Average household size: 2.34; Median age: 49.3; Age under 18: 18.7%; Age 65 and over: 20.5%; Males per 100 females: 103.0
Housing: Homeownership rate: 91.5%; Homeowner vacancy rate: 1.8%; Rental vacancy rate: 20.0%

TURNER (village). Covers a land area of 1.024 square miles and a water area of <.001 square miles. Located at 44.14° N. Lat; 83.79° W. Long. Elevation is 633 feet.
Population: 114; Growth (since 2000): -18.0%; Density: 111.4 persons per square mile; Race: 95.6% White, 1.8% Black/African American, 0.0% Asian, 0.0% American Indian/Alaska Native, 0.0% Native Hawaiian/Other Pacific Islander, 2.6% Two or more races, 0.0% Hispanic of any race; Average household size: 2.65; Median age: 42.0; Age under 18: 25.4%; Age 65 and over: 14.9%; Males per 100 females: 83.9
Housing: Homeownership rate: 86.0%; Homeowner vacancy rate: 0.0%; Rental vacancy rate: 25.0%

TWINING (village). Covers a land area of 0.971 square miles and a water area of <.001 square miles. Located at 44.12° N. Lat; 83.81° W. Long. Elevation is 643 feet.
Population: 181; Growth (since 2000): -5.7%; Density: 186.4 persons per square mile; Race: 98.9% White, 0.0% Black/African American, 0.0% Asian, 0.6% American Indian/Alaska Native, 0.0% Native Hawaiian/Other Pacific Islander, 0.0% Two or more races, 1.7% Hispanic of any race; Average household size: 2.66; Median age: 34.5; Age under 18: 28.2%; Age 65 and over: 11.6%; Males per 100 females: 94.6
School District(s)
Arenac Eastern SD (PK-12)
    2012-13 Enrollment: 232. . . . . (989) 867-4234
Housing: Homeownership rate: 77.9%; Homeowner vacancy rate: 1.9%; Rental vacancy rate: 16.7%

WHITNEY (township). Covers a land area of 30.734 square miles and a water area of 13.888 square miles. Located at 44.11° N. Lat; 83.58° W. Long.
Population: 1,001; Growth (since 2000): -3.1%; Density: 32.6 persons per square mile; Race: 98.8% White, 0.1% Black/African American, 0.1% Asian, 0.4% American Indian/Alaska Native, 0.1% Native Hawaiian/Other

Pacific Islander, 0.5% Two or more races, 1.6% Hispanic of any race; Average household size: 2.16; Median age: 55.1; Age under 18: 15.1%; Age 65 and over: 30.4%; Males per 100 females: 104.3
Housing: Homeownership rate: 91.2%; Homeowner vacancy rate: 4.5%; Rental vacancy rate: 10.9%

Baraga County

Located in northwestern Michigan, on the Upper Peninsula; partly bounded on the north by Keweenaw and Huron Bays. Covers a land area of 898.257 square miles, a water area of 170.514 square miles, and is located in the Eastern Time Zone at 46.70° N. Lat., 88.36° W. Long. The county was founded in 1875. County seat is L'Anse.

Weather Station: Herman   Elevation: 1,740 feet

	Jan	Feb	Mar	Apr	May	Jun	Jul	Aug	Sep	Oct	Nov	Dec
High	21	26	36	50	64	72	76	74	66	52	37	25
Low	5	6	14	27	39	48	53	52	44	34	23	11
Precip	2.3	1.7	2.4	2.6	3.3	3.4	4.3	3.9	4.1	4.2	2.9	2.7
Snow	50.6	34.6	33.0	15.0	2.2	tr	0.0	0.0	0.2	9.3	28.8	47.8

High and Low temperatures in degrees Fahrenheit; Precipitation and Snow in inches

Population: 8,860; Growth (since 2000): 1.3%; Density: 9.9 persons per square mile; Race: 75.0% White, 7.2% Black/African American, 0.1% Asian, 13.1% American Indian/Alaska Native, 0.0% Native Hawaiian/Other Pacific Islander, 4.4% two or more races, 1.0% Hispanic of any race; Average household size: 2.28; Median age: 42.9; Age under 18: 20.2%; Age 65 and over: 17.3%; Males per 100 females: 121.7; Marriage status: 36.8% never married, 46.3% now married, 1.1% separated, 7.1% widowed, 9.9% divorced; Foreign born: 2.5%; Speak English only: 94.9%; With disability: 16.9%; Veterans: 11.3%; Ancestry: 19.0% Finnish, 13.0% German, 10.4% French, 7.9% Irish, 7.6% English
Religion: Six largest groups: 27.0% Catholicism, 22.1% Lutheran, 3.3% Methodist/Pietist, 0.6% Non-denominational Protestant, 0.2% Adventist, 0.0% Other Groups
Economy: Unemployment rate: 8.2%; Leading industries: 14.9% retail trade; 11.8% other services (except public administration); 10.8% manufacturing; Farms: 57 totaling 17,732 acres; Company size: 0 employ 1,000 or more persons, 0 employ 500 to 999 persons, 2 employ 100 to 499 persons, 193 employ less than 100 persons; Business ownership: n/a women-owned, n/a Black-owned, n/a Hispanic-owned, n/a Asian-owned
Employment: 12.2% management, business, and financial, 2.9% computer, engineering, and science, 6.2% education, legal, community service, arts, and media, 6.7% healthcare practitioners, 24.1% service, 21.9% sales and office, 7.9% natural resources, construction, and maintenance, 18.1% production, transportation, and material moving
Income: Per capita: $17,701; Median household: $41,189; Average household: $48,646; Households with income of $100,000 or more: 5.8%; Poverty rate: 13.2%
Educational Attainment: High school diploma or higher: 82.0%; Bachelor's degree or higher: 12.0%; Graduate/professional degree or higher: 3.4%
Housing: Homeownership rate: 77.2%; Median home value: $84,000; Median year structure built: 1967; Homeowner vacancy rate: 3.1%; Median gross rent: $509 per month; Rental vacancy rate: 9.2%
Vital Statistics: Birth rate: 87.4 per 10,000 population; Death rate: 117.3 per 10,000 population; Age-adjusted cancer mortality rate: 191.5 deaths per 100,000 population
Health Insurance: 88.7% have insurance; 68.2% have private insurance; 42.5% have public insurance; 11.3% do not have insurance; 4.3% of children under 18 do not have insurance
Health Care: Physicians: 11.5 per 10,000 population; Hospital beds: 17.0 per 10,000 population; Hospital admissions: 632.2 per 10,000 population
Transportation: Commute: 93.5% car, 0.1% public transportation, 1.9% walk, 3.4% work from home; Median travel time to work: 16.3 minutes
Presidential Election: 45.1% Obama, 53.5% Romney (2012)
National and State Parks: Baraga State Park
Additional Information Contacts
Baraga Government . . . . (906) 524-6183
    http://www.baragacounty.org

Baraga County Communities

ARVON (township). Covers a land area of 123.965 square miles and a water area of 7.380 square miles. Located at 46.85° N. Lat; 88.17° W. Long.
Population: 450; Growth (since 2000): -6.6%; Density: 3.6 persons per square mile; Race: 95.6% White, 0.0% Black/African American, 0.2% Asian, 1.8% American Indian/Alaska Native, 0.0% Native Hawaiian/Other Pacific Islander, 2.2% Two or more races, 0.0% Hispanic of any race; Average household size: 1.93; Median age: 58.0; Age under 18: 10.0%; Age 65 and over: 30.7%; Males per 100 females: 121.7
Housing: Homeownership rate: 93.1%; Homeowner vacancy rate: 5.2%; Rental vacancy rate: 22.7%

BARAGA (township). Covers a land area of 183.799 square miles and a water area of 3.399 square miles. Located at 46.75° N. Lat; 88.56° W. Long. Elevation is 630 feet.
History: Hanka Homestead, 1896 Finnish restored homestead. Native American relics found in vicinity.
Population: 3,815; Growth (since 2000): 7.7%; Density: 20.8 persons per square mile; Race: 62.1% White, 15.9% Black/African American, 0.1% Asian, 17.6% American Indian/Alaska Native, 0.0% Native Hawaiian/Other Pacific Islander, 4.2% Two or more races, 1.0% Hispanic of any race; Average household size: 2.36; Median age: 38.6; Age under 18: 19.2%; Age 65 and over: 12.3%; Males per 100 females: 157.2; Marriage status: 54.4% never married, 32.1% now married, 1.3% separated, 3.2% widowed, 10.4% divorced; Foreign born: 2.1%; Speak English only: 95.5%; With disability: 16.5%; Veterans: 9.0%; Ancestry: 14.5% Finnish, 8.3% German, 8.1% American, 7.5% French, 4.2% English
Employment: 11.7% management, business, and financial, 3.3% computer, engineering, and science, 4.4% education, legal, community service, arts, and media, 5.0% healthcare practitioners, 23.5% service, 21.8% sales and office, 7.3% natural resources, construction, and maintenance, 22.9% production, transportation, and material moving
Income: Per capita: $12,272; Median household: $37,014; Average household: $45,686; Households with income of $100,000 or more: 5.0%; Poverty rate: 19.4%
Educational Attainment: High school diploma or higher: 75.6%; Bachelor's degree or higher: 6.8%; Graduate/professional degree or higher: 1.9%
School District(s)
Baraga Area Schools (KG-12)
    2012-13 Enrollment: 493 . . . . (906) 353-6664
Two-year College(s)
Keweenaw Bay Ojibwa Community College (Public)
    Fall 2013 Enrollment: 106 . . . . (906) 353-4600
    2013-14 Tuition: In-state $2,660; Out-of-state $2,660
Housing: Homeownership rate: 74.0%; Median home value: $85,800; Median year structure built: 1969; Homeowner vacancy rate: 2.8%; Median gross rent: $417 per month; Rental vacancy rate: 7.4%
Health Insurance: 86.4% have insurance; 62.2% have private insurance; 39.1% have public insurance; 13.6% do not have insurance; 3.7% of children under 18 do not have insurance
Transportation: Commute: 92.5% car, 0.4% public transportation, 1.5% walk, 4.2% work from home; Median travel time to work: 15.5 minutes

BARAGA (village). Covers a land area of 2.117 square miles and a water area of 0.062 square miles. Located at 46.78° N. Lat; 88.50° W. Long. Elevation is 630 feet.
History: Baraga was named for Father Frederic Baraga, who founded a mission here in 1843. The village was incorporated in 1891, and became a summer resort area.
Population: 2,053; Growth (since 2000): 59.8%; Density: 969.9 persons per square mile; Race: 44.9% White, 29.4% Black/African American, 0.1% Asian, 22.0% American Indian/Alaska Native, 0.0% Native Hawaiian/Other Pacific Islander, 3.6% Two or more races, 1.0% Hispanic of any race; Average household size: 2.26; Median age: 35.7; Age under 18: 15.8%; Age 65 and over: 10.0%; Males per 100 females: 220.8
School District(s)
Baraga Area Schools (KG-12)
    2012-13 Enrollment: 493 . . . . (906) 353-6664

Keweenaw Bay Ojibwa Community College (Public)
    Fall 2013 Enrollment: 106 . . . . (906) 353-4600
    2013-14 Tuition: In-state $2,660; Out-of-state $2,660
    Housing: Homeownership rate: 54.0%; Homeowner vacancy rate: 1.7%;
Rental vacancy rate: 5.1%

COVINGTON (township).
Covers a land area of 192.258 square miles and a water area of 4.071 square miles. Located at 46.52° N. Lat; 88.50° W. Long. Elevation is 1,598 feet.
History: Covington was first settled by French Canadians. It was named by John Lyons, the first postmaster, after his former home in Covington, Kentucky.
Population: 476; Growth (since 2000): -16.3%; Density: 2.5 persons per square mile; Race: 95.8% White, 0.2% Black/African American, 0.0% Asian, 1.9% American Indian/Alaska Native, 0.0% Native Hawaiian/Other Pacific Islander, 2.1% Two or more races, 0.8% Hispanic of any race; Average household size: 2.09; Median age: 54.9; Age under 18: 14.9%; Age 65 and over: 29.2%; Males per 100 females: 113.5
Housing: Homeownership rate: 89.3%; Homeowner vacancy rate: 1.5%; Rental vacancy rate: 8.0%

L'ANSE (township).
Covers a land area of 247.405 square miles and a water area of 21.615 square miles. Located at 46.72° N. Lat; 88.31° W. Long. Elevation is 620 feet.
Population: 3,843; Growth (since 2000): -2.1%; Density: 15.5 persons per square mile; Race: 81.6% White, 0.7% Black/African American, 0.2% Asian, 12.2% American Indian/Alaska Native, 0.0% Native Hawaiian/Other Pacific Islander, 5.2% Two or more races, 1.0% Hispanic of any race; Average household size: 2.29; Median age: 43.0; Age under 18: 23.4%; Age 65 and over: 18.9%; Males per 100 females: 96.2; Marriage status: 22.1% never married, 57.2% now married, 1.1% separated, 11.7% widowed, 9.1% divorced; Foreign born: 3.3%; Speak English only: 95.1%; With disability: 15.4%; Veterans: 12.6%; Ancestry: 19.8% Finnish, 17.4% German, 13.6% French, 12.8% Irish, 10.2% English
Employment: 12.7% management, business, and financial, 2.8% computer, engineering, and science, 6.5% education, legal, community service, arts, and media, 7.1% healthcare practitioners, 24.5% service, 22.5% sales and office, 7.9% natural resources, construction, and maintenance, 15.9% production, transportation, and material moving
Income: Per capita: $21,846; Median household: $42,147; Average household: $49,521; Households with income of $100,000 or more: 6.1%; Poverty rate: 10.5%
Educational Attainment: High school diploma or higher: 87.3%; Bachelor's degree or higher: 16.0%; Graduate/professional degree or higher: 4.4%
Housing: Homeownership rate: 74.6%; Median home value: $77,700; Median year structure built: 1963; Homeowner vacancy rate: 3.0%; Median gross rent: $550 per month; Rental vacancy rate: 10.2%
Health Insurance: 89.3% have insurance; 70.7% have private insurance; 41.1% have public insurance; 10.7% do not have insurance; 4.9% of children under 18 do not have insurance
Hospitals: Baraga County Memorial Hospital (44 beds)
Transportation: Commute: 93.9% car, 0.0% public transportation, 2.3% walk, 2.8% work from home; Median travel time to work: 14.1 minutes; Amtrak: Bus service available.

L'ANSE (village).
County seat. Covers a land area of 2.528 square miles and a water area of 0.002 square miles. Located at 46.75° N. Lat; 88.45° W. Long. Elevation is 620 feet.
History: L'Anse grew up on a site that had been a campground for French explorers, trappers, and missionaries. The village was platted in 1871 when the Marquette, Houghton & Ontonagon Railroad arrived.
Population: 2,011; Growth (since 2000): -4.6%; Density: 795.4 persons per square mile; Race: 88.7% White, 1.4% Black/African American, 0.2% Asian, 5.0% American Indian/Alaska Native, 0.0% Native Hawaiian/Other Pacific Islander, 4.6% Two or more races, 0.9% Hispanic of any race; Average household size: 2.16; Median age: 41.7; Age under 18: 22.9%; Age 65 and over: 21.8%; Males per 100 females: 91.0
Housing: Homeownership rate: 66.3%; Homeowner vacancy rate: 4.6%; Rental vacancy rate: 7.8%
Hospitals: Baraga County Memorial Hospital (44 beds)

LANSE (unincorporated postal area)
ZCTA: 49946
Covers a land area of 271.666 square miles and a water area of 26.056 square miles. Located at 46.72° N. Lat; 88.32° W. Long..
Population: 4,040; Growth (since 2000): -2.6%; Density: 14.9 persons per square mile; Race: 82.1% White, 0.7% Black/African American, 0.2% Asian, 11.8% American Indian/Alaska Native, 0.0% Native Hawaiian/Other Pacific Islander, 5.0% Two or more races, 1.0% Hispanic of any race; Average household size: 2.28; Median age: 43.9; Age under 18: 22.8%; Age 65 and over: 19.2%; Males per 100 females: 97.1; Marriage status: 21.7% never married, 57.6% now married, 1.1% separated, 11.7% widowed, 9.1% divorced; Foreign born: 3.2%; Speak English only: 95.2%; With disability: 15.8%; Veterans: 12.6%; Ancestry: 20.1% Finnish, 17.5% German, 13.4% French, 13.0% Irish, 10.3% English
Employment: 12.9% management, business, and financial, 2.7% computer, engineering, and science, 6.8% education, legal, community service, arts, and media, 7.1% healthcare practitioners, 24.2% service, 22.5% sales and office, 7.8% natural resources, construction, and maintenance, 15.9% production, transportation, and material moving
Income: Per capita: $21,908; Median household: $42,165; Average household: $49,552; Households with income of $100,000 or more: 6.3%; Poverty rate: 10.5%
Educational Attainment: High school diploma or higher: 87.3%; Bachelor's degree or higher: 16.3%; Graduate/professional degree or higher: 4.4%

School District(s)
L'anse Area Schools (KG-12)
    2012-13 Enrollment: 683 . . . . (906) 524-6121
    Housing: Homeownership rate: 75.5%; Median home value: $78,500; Median year structure built: 1966; Homeowner vacancy rate: 3.3%; Median gross rent: $550 per month; Rental vacancy rate: 10.0%
    Health Insurance: 89.6% have insurance; 71.0% have private insurance; 41.3% have public insurance; 10.4% do not have insurance; 4.8% of children under 18 do not have insurance
Newspapers: L'Anse Sentinel (weekly circulation 3900)
    Transportation: Commute: 93.6% car, 0.0% public transportation, 2.3% walk, 3.1% work from home; Median travel time to work: 14.5 minutes

SKANEE (unincorporated postal area)
ZCTA: 49962
Covers a land area of 99.881 square miles and a water area of 6.452 square miles. Located at 46.84° N. Lat; 88.13° W. Long. Elevation is 745 feet.
Population: 260; Growth (since 2000): 4.8%; Density: 2.6 persons per square mile; Race: 96.9% White, 0.0% Black/African American, 0.0% Asian, 1.2% American Indian/Alaska Native, 0.0% Native Hawaiian/Other Pacific Islander, 1.9% Two or more races, 0.0% Hispanic of any race; Average household size: 1.90; Median age: 58.2; Age under 18: 8.5%; Age 65 and over: 33.8%; Males per 100 females: 124.1

School District(s)
Arvon Township SD (KG-12)
    2012-13 Enrollment: 8 . . . . (906) 524-7336
    Housing: Homeownership rate: 93.4%; Homeowner vacancy rate: 5.2%; Rental vacancy rate: 33.3%

SPURR (township).
Covers a land area of 150.830 square miles and a water area of 8.207 square miles. Located at 46.48° N. Lat; 88.24° W. Long.
Population: 276; Growth (since 2000): 21.6%; Density: 1.8 persons per square mile; Race: 90.9% White, 0.4% Black/African American, 0.7% Asian, 0.7% American Indian/Alaska Native, 0.0% Native Hawaiian/Other Pacific Islander, 6.2% Two or more races, 1.1% Hispanic of any race; Average household size: 2.28; Median age: 54.0; Age under 18: 16.7%; Age 65 and over: 21.0%; Males per 100 females: 114.0
Housing: Homeownership rate: 93.4%; Homeowner vacancy rate: 5.0%; Rental vacancy rate: 0.0%

WATTON (unincorporated postal area)
ZCTA: 49970
Covers a land area of 102.875 square miles and a water area of 1.100 square miles. Located at 46.55° N. Lat; 88.60° W. Long. Elevation is 1,463 feet.

Population: 243; Growth (since 2000): -32.5%; Density: 2.4 persons per square mile; Race: 95.5% White, 0.4% Black/African American, 0.0% Asian, 2.9% American Indian/Alaska Native, 0.0% Native Hawaiian/Other Pacific Islander, 1.2% Two or more races, 0.0% Hispanic of any race; Average household size: 2.04; Median age: 56.2; Age under 18: 15.2%; Age 65 and over: 25.5%; Males per 100 females: 115.0

Housing: Homeownership rate: 89.1%; Homeowner vacancy rate: 0.0%; Rental vacancy rate: 7.1%

ZEBA (CDP). Covers a land area of 3.609 square miles and a water area of 0.011 square miles. Located at 46.79° N. Lat; 88.41° W. Long. Elevation is 735 feet.

Population: 480; Growth (since 2000): n/a; Density: 133.0 persons per square mile; Race: 45.2% White, 0.0% Black/African American, 0.2% Asian, 46.9% American Indian/Alaska Native, 0.0% Native Hawaiian/Other Pacific Islander, 7.7% Two or more races, 1.3% Hispanic of any race; Average household size: 2.62; Median age: 34.0; Age under 18: 29.8%; Age 65 and over: 9.4%; Males per 100 females: 95.1

Housing: Homeownership rate: 71.1%; Homeowner vacancy rate: 0.0%; Rental vacancy rate: 17.2%

Barry County

Located in southwestern Michigan; drained by the Thornapple River. Covers a land area of 553.091 square miles, a water area of 23.950 square miles, and is located in the Eastern Time Zone at 42.58° N. Lat., 85.31° W. Long. The county was founded in 1829. County seat is Hastings.

Barry County is part of the Grand Rapids-Wyoming, MI Metropolitan Statistical Area. The entire metro area includes: Barry County, MI; Kent County, MI; Montcalm County, MI; Ottawa County, MI

Weather Station: Hastings										Elevation: 819 feet		
	Jan	Feb	Mar	Apr	May	Jun	Jul	Aug	Sep	Oct	Nov	Dec
High	32	35	45	58	70	79	83	81	74	61	48	35
Low	15	16	24	35	45	55	59	58	49	38	30	21
Precip	2.2	1.8	2.3	3.2	3.8	3.7	3.5	3.9	3.8	3.3	3.2	2.5
Snow	18.1	11.7	7.5	1.9	0.0	0.0	0.0	0.0	0.0	0.7	5.1	17.2

High and Low temperatures in degrees Fahrenheit; Precipitation and Snow in inches

Population: 59,173; Growth (since 2000): 4.3%; Density: 107.0 persons per square mile; Race: 96.9% White, 0.4% Black/African American, 0.4% Asian, 0.5% American Indian/Alaska Native, 0.0% Native Hawaiian/Other Pacific Islander, 1.3% two or more races, 2.3% Hispanic of any race; Average household size: 2.60; Median age: 41.2; Age under 18: 24.4%; Age 65 and over: 14.6%; Males per 100 females: 100.8; Marriage status: 22.4% never married, 60.8% now married, 0.9% separated, 6.1% widowed, 10.6% divorced; Foreign born: 1.3%; Speak English only: 97.6%; With disability: 14.0%; Veterans: 10.7%; Ancestry: 25.1% German, 16.6% English, 13.9% Dutch, 13.2% Irish, 10.2% American

Religion: Six largest groups: 6.8% Non-denominational Protestant, 4.5% Catholicism, 4.5% Methodist/Pietist, 2.0% Presbyterian-Reformed, 1.3% Holiness, 1.1% Lutheran

Economy: Unemployment rate: 4.2%; Leading industries: 15.3% other services (except public administration); 14.1% retail trade; 13.0% construction; Farms: 1,031 totaling 165,185 acres; Company size: 0 employ 1,000 or more persons, 2 employ 500 to 999 persons, 7 employ 100 to 499 persons, 871 employs less than 100 persons; Business ownership: 1,162 women-owned, n/a Black-owned, n/a Hispanic-owned, n/a Asian-owned

Employment: 11.9% management, business, and financial, 4.4% computer, engineering, and science, 6.6% education, legal, community service, arts, and media, 5.0% healthcare practitioners, 16.3% service, 22.6% sales and office, 13.0% natural resources, construction, and maintenance, 20.2% production, transportation, and material moving

Income: Per capita: $25,059; Median household: $52,186; Average household: $64,787; Households with income of $100,000 or more: 16.5%; Poverty rate: 11.7%

Educational Attainment: High school diploma or higher: 91.1%; Bachelor's degree or higher: 17.7%; Graduate/professional degree or higher: 6.4%

Housing: Homeownership rate: 83.8%; Median home value: $133,900; Median year structure built: 1972; Homeowner vacancy rate: 2.5%; Median gross rent: $717 per month; Rental vacancy rate: 11.2%

Vital Statistics: Birth rate: 99.3 per 10,000 population; Death rate: 87.0 per 10,000 population; Age-adjusted cancer mortality rate: 180.1 deaths per 100,000 population

Health Insurance: 89.8% have insurance; 72.8% have private insurance; 33.2% have public insurance; 10.2% do not have insurance; 3.7% of children under 18 do not have insurance

Health Care: Physicians: 8.6 per 10,000 population; Hospital beds: 9.8 per 10,000 population; Hospital admissions: 453.4 per 10,000 population

Transportation: Commute: 93.3% car, 0.1% public transportation, 1.9% walk, 3.9% work from home; Median travel time to work: 26.8 minutes

Presidential Election: 40.2% Obama, 58.7% Romney (2012)

National and State Parks: Barry State Game Area; Middleville State Game Area

Additional Information Contacts

Barry Government . . . . (269) 945-1285
http://www.barrycounty.org

Barry County Communities

ASSYRIA (township). Covers a land area of 35.870 square miles and a water area of 0.474 square miles. Located at 42.47° N. Lat; 85.12° W. Long. Elevation is 892 feet.

Population: 1,986; Growth (since 2000): 3.9%; Density: 55.4 persons per square mile; Race: 96.9% White, 0.4% Black/African American, 0.3% Asian, 0.5% American Indian/Alaska Native, 0.0% Native Hawaiian/Other Pacific Islander, 1.7% Two or more races, 1.3% Hispanic of any race; Average household size: 2.59; Median age: 43.4; Age under 18: 22.5%; Age 65 and over: 14.9%; Males per 100 females: 111.3

Housing: Homeownership rate: 91.0%; Homeowner vacancy rate: 2.5%; Rental vacancy rate: 4.2%

BALTIMORE (township). Covers a land area of 35.416 square miles and a water area of 0.788 square miles. Located at 42.56° N. Lat; 85.25° W. Long.

History: Baltimore Township was named for their former home by settlers who had come from Maryland.

Population: 1,861; Growth (since 2000): 0.9%; Density: 52.5 persons per square mile; Race: 97.9% White, 0.2% Black/African American, 0.2% Asian, 0.1% American Indian/Alaska Native, 0.0% Native Hawaiian/Other Pacific Islander, 1.1% Two or more races, 2.2% Hispanic of any race; Average household size: 2.54; Median age: 41.7; Age under 18: 23.5%; Age 65 and over: 15.5%; Males per 100 females: 102.5

Housing: Homeownership rate: 90.0%; Homeowner vacancy rate: 1.5%; Rental vacancy rate: 8.6%

BARRY (township). Covers a land area of 34.426 square miles and a water area of 2.077 square miles. Located at 42.47° N. Lat; 85.38° W. Long.

Population: 3,378; Growth (since 2000): -3.2%; Density: 98.1 persons per square mile; Race: 96.8% White, 0.4% Black/African American, 0.3% Asian, 0.3% American Indian/Alaska Native, 0.0% Native Hawaiian/Other Pacific Islander, 2.0% Two or more races, 1.5% Hispanic of any race; Average household size: 2.54; Median age: 44.5; Age under 18: 23.2%; Age 65 and over: 15.3%; Males per 100 females: 99.1; Marriage status: 26.8% never married, 53.4% now married, 4.5% separated, 9.3% widowed, 10.5% divorced; Foreign born: 2.9%; Speak English only: 98.2%; With disability: 16.3%; Veterans: 10.5%; Ancestry: 21.4% German, 15.3% French, 13.8% English, 12.5% Irish, 10.3% American

Employment: 18.3% management, business, and financial, 6.4% computer, engineering, and science, 7.5% education, legal, community service, arts, and media, 3.9% healthcare practitioners, 9.0% service, 19.6% sales and office, 17.9% natural resources, construction, and maintenance, 17.3% production, transportation, and material moving

Income: Per capita: $28,776; Median household: $55,625; Average household: $70,748; Households with income of $100,000 or more: 16.6%; Poverty rate: 11.3%

Educational Attainment: High school diploma or higher: 91.6%; Bachelor's degree or higher: 24.9%; Graduate/professional degree or higher: 9.9%

Housing: Homeownership rate: 85.2%; Median home value: $143,400; Median year structure built: 1972; Homeowner vacancy rate: 1.6%; Median gross rent: $1,063 per month; Rental vacancy rate: 7.5%

Health Insurance: 87.9% have insurance; 62.0% have private insurance; 41.4% have public insurance; 12.1% do not have insurance; 3.8% of children under 18 do not have insurance

Safety: Violent crime rate: 0.0 per 10,000 population; Property crime rate: 68.2 per 10,000 population
Transportation: Commute: 88.0% car, 0.0% public transportation, 2.5% walk, 9.5% work from home; Median travel time to work: 29.9 minutes

CARLTON (township). Covers a land area of 35.131 square miles and a water area of 0.555 square miles. Located at 42.72° N. Lat; 85.25° W. Long. Elevation is 830 feet.

Population: 2,391; Growth (since 2000): 2.6%; Density: 68.1 persons per square mile; Race: 96.4% White, 0.4% Black/African American, 0.2% Asian, 0.8% American Indian/Alaska Native, 0.0% Native Hawaiian/Other Pacific Islander, 1.5% Two or more races, 2.6% Hispanic of any race; Average household size: 2.71; Median age: 42.1; Age under 18: 23.5%; Age 65 and over: 14.3%; Males per 100 females: 100.1
Housing: Homeownership rate: 91.1%; Homeowner vacancy rate: 1.3%; Rental vacancy rate: 15.8%

CASTLETON (township). Covers a land area of 34.971 square miles and a water area of 0.798 square miles. Located at 42.64° N. Lat; 85.13° W. Long.

Population: 3,471; Growth (since 2000): -0.1%; Density: 99.3 persons per square mile; Race: 96.6% White, 0.3% Black/African American, 0.4% Asian, 0.5% American Indian/Alaska Native, 0.0% Native Hawaiian/Other Pacific Islander, 1.8% Two or more races, 2.1% Hispanic of any race; Average household size: 2.61; Median age: 38.7; Age under 18: 25.4%; Age 65 and over: 14.2%; Males per 100 females: 100.1; Marriage status: 24.3% never married, 53.2% now married, 0.8% separated, 5.9% widowed, 16.6% divorced; Foreign born: 1.3%; Speak English only: 96.8%; With disability: 20.1%; Veterans: 10.6%; Ancestry: 30.2% German, 22.0% English, 16.4% Irish, 10.5% American, 5.7% Dutch
Employment: 10.8% management, business, and financial, 1.0% computer, engineering, and science, 8.1% education, legal, community service, arts, and media, 2.7% healthcare practitioners, 18.8% service, 20.1% sales and office, 16.3% natural resources, construction, and maintenance, 22.3% production, transportation, and material moving
Income: Per capita: $18,513; Median household: $32,475; Average household: $45,730; Households with income of $100,000 or more: 11.4%; Poverty rate: 24.8%
Educational Attainment: High school diploma or higher: 87.6%; Bachelor's degree or higher: 10.9%; Graduate/professional degree or higher: 3.4%
Housing: Homeownership rate: 75.8%; Median home value: $68,400; Median year structure built: 1959; Homeowner vacancy rate: 5.3%; Median gross rent: $664 per month; Rental vacancy rate: 10.7%
Health Insurance: 90.7% have insurance; 56.6% have private insurance; 49.3% have public insurance; 9.3% do not have insurance; 1.4% of children under 18 do not have insurance
Transportation: Commute: 92.2% car, 0.0% public transportation, 4.9% walk, 2.5% work from home; Median travel time to work: 27.9 minutes

DELTON (CDP). Covers a land area of 2.160 square miles and a water area of 0.067 square miles. Located at 42.50° N. Lat; 85.41° W. Long. Elevation is 945 feet.

Population: 872; Growth (since 2000): n/a; Density: 403.7 persons per square mile; Race: 95.0% White, 1.0% Black/African American, 0.6% Asian, 0.6% American Indian/Alaska Native, 0.0% Native Hawaiian/Other Pacific Islander, 2.6% Two or more races, 1.6% Hispanic of any race; Average household size: 2.48; Median age: 43.6; Age under 18: 24.3%; Age 65 and over: 16.4%; Males per 100 females: 90.4
School District(s)
Delton Kellogg Schools (PK-12)
    2012-13 Enrollment: 1,484 . . . . (269) 623-9225
Housing: Homeownership rate: 73.6%; Homeowner vacancy rate: 3.4%; Rental vacancy rate: 8.8%

DOWLING (CDP). Covers a land area of 6.080 square miles and a water area of 0.202 square miles. Located at 42.53° N. Lat; 85.23° W. Long. Elevation is 955 feet.

Population: 374; Growth (since 2000): n/a; Density: 61.5 persons per square mile; Race: 98.4% White, 0.0% Black/African American, 0.8% Asian, 0.0% American Indian/Alaska Native, 0.0% Native Hawaiian/Other Pacific Islander, 0.8% Two or more races, 0.5% Hispanic of any race; Average household size: 2.49; Median age: 42.0; Age under 18: 22.7%; Age 65 and over: 16.3%; Males per 100 females: 98.9

Housing: Homeownership rate: 86.0%; Homeowner vacancy rate: 2.3%; Rental vacancy rate: 0.0%

FREEPORT (village). Covers a land area of 0.778 square miles and a water area of 0.005 square miles. Located at 42.76° N. Lat; 85.32° W. Long. Elevation is 787 feet.

Population: 483; Growth (since 2000): 8.8%; Density: 621.0 persons per square mile; Race: 97.1% White, 1.0% Black/African American, 0.2% Asian, 0.0% American Indian/Alaska Native, 0.0% Native Hawaiian/Other Pacific Islander, 1.2% Two or more races, 3.3% Hispanic of any race; Average household size: 2.73; Median age: 36.3; Age under 18: 27.1%; Age 65 and over: 9.1%; Males per 100 females: 99.6
Housing: Homeownership rate: 79.7%; Homeowner vacancy rate: 3.4%; Rental vacancy rate: 18.2%
Newspapers: Freeport News (weekly circulation 1000)

HASTINGS (charter township). Covers a land area of 30.017 square miles and a water area of 0.531 square miles. Located at 42.63° N. Lat; 85.24° W. Long. Elevation is 810 feet.

Population: 2,948; Growth (since 2000): 0.6%; Density: 98.2 persons per square mile; Race: 97.8% White, 0.0% Black/African American, 0.4% Asian, 0.2% American Indian/Alaska Native, 0.0% Native Hawaiian/Other Pacific Islander, 1.2% Two or more races, 1.3% Hispanic of any race; Average household size: 2.64; Median age: 44.7; Age under 18: 21.9%; Age 65 and over: 18.6%; Males per 100 females: 94.8; Marriage status: 18.3% never married, 63.5% now married, 0.7% separated, 7.6% widowed, 10.7% divorced; Foreign born: 1.3%; Speak English only: 98.2%; With disability: 15.3%; Veterans: 12.6%; Ancestry: 22.4% German, 13.9% English, 13.9% Irish, 11.0% Dutch, 9.2% American
Employment: 11.1% management, business, and financial, 6.0% computer, engineering, and science, 14.3% education, legal, community service, arts, and media, 6.2% healthcare practitioners, 13.0% service, 22.1% sales and office, 10.4% natural resources, construction, and maintenance, 16.9% production, transportation, and material moving
Income: Per capita: $24,341; Median household: $48,952; Average household: $62,853; Households with income of $100,000 or more: 18.5%; Poverty rate: 12.0%
Educational Attainment: High school diploma or higher: 88.9%; Bachelor's degree or higher: 19.4%; Graduate/professional degree or higher: 7.6%
School District(s)
Barry ISD (PK-12)
    2012-13 Enrollment: 131 . . . . (269) 945-9545
Hastings Area SD (PK-12)
    2012-13 Enrollment: 2,788 . . . . (269) 948-4400
Housing: Homeownership rate: 87.9%; Median home value: $126,900; Median year structure built: 1967; Homeowner vacancy rate: 1.9%; Median gross rent: $677 per month; Rental vacancy rate: 4.4%
Health Insurance: 87.9% have insurance; 72.0% have private insurance; 34.2% have public insurance; 12.1% do not have insurance; 13.3% of children under 18 do not have insurance
Hospitals: Pennock Hospital (88 beds)
Newspapers: J-Ad Graphics (weekly circulation 48000)
Transportation: Commute: 92.1% car, 0.5% public transportation, 0.3% walk, 4.2% work from home; Median travel time to work: 28.4 minutes

HASTINGS (city). County seat. Covers a land area of 5.195 square miles and a water area of 0.076 square miles. Located at 42.65° N. Lat; 85.29° W. Long. Elevation is 810 feet.

History: Hastings was settled in 1836 when a group of promoters purchased the land from Eurotas P. Hastings with the promise that the town would be the county seat, and it was so named in 1841. Hastings was incorporated as a village in 1855 and as a city in 1871. Native American mounds in vicinity.
Population: 7,350; Growth (since 2000): 3.6%; Density: 1,414.9 persons per square mile; Race: 96.9% White, 0.5% Black/African American, 0.3% Asian, 0.6% American Indian/Alaska Native, 0.0% Native Hawaiian/Other Pacific Islander, 1.2% Two or more races, 2.7% Hispanic of any race; Average household size: 2.47; Median age: 36.2; Age under 18: 26.6%; Age 65 and over: 15.4%; Males per 100 females: 88.2; Marriage status: 26.9% never married, 49.6% now married, 0.0% separated, 7.9% widowed, 15.6% divorced; Foreign born: 2.0%; Speak English only: 98.0%; With disability: 16.1%; Veterans: 8.8%; Ancestry: 28.4% German, 12.3% Irish, 12.3% American, 11.6% English, 6.7% Dutch

Employment: 8.3% management, business, and financial, 1.7% computer, engineering, and science, 8.8% education, legal, community service, arts, and media, 3.4% healthcare practitioners, 25.7% service, 23.0% sales and office, 7.9% natural resources, construction, and maintenance, 21.3% production, transportation, and material moving

Income: Per capita: $20,853; Median household: $42,747; Average household: $51,436; Households with income of $100,000 or more: 8.8%; Poverty rate: 18.5%

Educational Attainment: High school diploma or higher: 89.8%; Bachelor's degree or higher: 13.4%; Graduate/professional degree or higher: 7.9%

School District(s)

Barry ISD (PK-12)
    2012-13 Enrollment: 131 . . . . (269) 945-9545
Hastings Area SD (PK-12)
    2012-13 Enrollment: 2,788 . . . . (269) 948-4400

Housing: Homeownership rate: 64.4%; Median home value: $96,100; Median year structure built: 1962; Homeowner vacancy rate: 3.5%; Median gross rent: $708 per month; Rental vacancy rate: 7.9%

Health Insurance: 88.4% have insurance; 67.6% have private insurance; 36.4% have public insurance; 11.6% do not have insurance; 1.5% of children under 18 do not have insurance

Hospitals: Pennock Hospital (88 beds)

Safety: Violent crime rate: 19.2 per 10,000 population; Property crime rate: 196.2 per 10,000 population

Newspapers: J-Ad Graphics (weekly circulation 48000)

Transportation: Commute: 93.3% car, 0.0% public transportation, 2.5% walk, 3.1% work from home; Median travel time to work: 18.6 minutes

Additional Information Contacts

City of Hastings . . . . (269) 945-2468
    http://www.hastings.mi.us

HICKORY CORNERS (CDP).
Covers a land area of 2.070 square miles and a water area of 0.006 square miles. Located at 42.43° N. Lat; 85.39° W. Long. Elevation is 955 feet.

Population: 322; Growth (since 2000): n/a; Density: 155.5 persons per square mile; Race: 97.2% White, 0.3% Black/African American, 0.0% Asian, 0.0% American Indian/Alaska Native, 0.0% Native Hawaiian/Other Pacific Islander, 2.5% Two or more races, 1.2% Hispanic of any race; Average household size: 2.64; Median age: 39.0; Age under 18: 28.3%; Age 65 and over: 10.2%; Males per 100 females: 96.3

School District(s)

Gull Lake Community Schools (PK-12)
    2012-13 Enrollment: 2,930 . . . . (269) 488-5000

Housing: Homeownership rate: 84.5%; Homeowner vacancy rate: 4.6%; Rental vacancy rate: 13.6%

HOPE (township).
Covers a land area of 32.483 square miles and a water area of 3.611 square miles. Located at 42.55° N. Lat; 85.37° W. Long.

Population: 3,239; Growth (since 2000): -1.3%; Density: 99.7 persons per square mile; Race: 96.8% White, 0.4% Black/African American, 0.3% Asian, 0.5% American Indian/Alaska Native, 0.0% Native Hawaiian/Other Pacific Islander, 1.8% Two or more races, 1.5% Hispanic of any race; Average household size: 2.52; Median age: 44.7; Age under 18: 21.4%; Age 65 and over: 16.7%; Males per 100 females: 102.9; Marriage status: 26.2% never married, 49.6% now married, 3.3% separated, 12.4% widowed, 11.9% divorced; Foreign born: 0.0%; Speak English only: 98.6%; With disability: 15.9%; Veterans: 10.5%; Ancestry: 26.5% English, 20.7% German, 19.2% Dutch, 13.5% Irish, 13.0% American

Employment: 6.0% management, business, and financial, 1.9% computer, engineering, and science, 7.1% education, legal, community service, arts, and media, 1.7% healthcare practitioners, 30.0% service, 17.6% sales and office, 14.2% natural resources, construction, and maintenance, 21.4% production, transportation, and material moving

Income: Per capita: $19,980; Median household: $43,058; Average household: $44,673; Households with income of $100,000 or more: 3.6%; Poverty rate: 23.0%

Educational Attainment: High school diploma or higher: 91.5%; Bachelor's degree or higher: 10.5%; Graduate/professional degree or higher: 3.0%

Housing: Homeownership rate: 86.1%; Median home value: $135,500; Median year structure built: 1966; Homeowner vacancy rate: 2.9%; Median gross rent: $608 per month; Rental vacancy rate: 10.4%

Health Insurance: 80.5% have insurance; 65.6% have private insurance; 36.9% have public insurance; 19.5% do not have insurance; 18.8% of children under 18 do not have insurance

Transportation: Commute: 95.0% car, 0.0% public transportation, 0.0% walk, 5.0% work from home; Median travel time to work: 28.0 minutes

---

IRVING (township).
Covers a land area of 35.760 square miles and a water area of 0.331 square miles. Located at 42.72° N. Lat; 85.38° W. Long. Elevation is 751 feet.

History: Irving Township was settled about 1850 and developed around a dam and sawmill built by L.B. Hills. The township was named for American writer Washington Irving.

Population: 3,250; Growth (since 2000): 21.2%; Density: 90.9 persons per square mile; Race: 98.4% White, 0.3% Black/African American, 0.2% Asian, 0.3% American Indian/Alaska Native, 0.0% Native Hawaiian/Other Pacific Islander, 0.6% Two or more races, 1.9% Hispanic of any race; Average household size: 2.89; Median age: 38.5; Age under 18: 28.5%; Age 65 and over: 9.4%; Males per 100 females: 107.0; Marriage status: 20.4% never married, 68.0% now married, 0.8% separated, 3.7% widowed, 8.0% divorced; Foreign born: 1.1%; Speak English only: 98.7%; With disability: 11.6%; Veterans: 10.5%; Ancestry: 28.4% German, 19.4% Dutch, 14.1% Irish, 14.0% English, 10.6% Polish

Employment: 13.3% management, business, and financial, 5.3% computer, engineering, and science, 3.5% education, legal, community service, arts, and media, 4.9% healthcare practitioners, 11.1% service, 27.5% sales and office, 14.2% natural resources, construction, and maintenance, 20.1% production, transportation, and material moving

Income: Per capita: $26,219; Median household: $62,472; Average household: $72,332; Households with income of $100,000 or more: 20.9%; Poverty rate: 5.3%

Educational Attainment: High school diploma or higher: 94.0%; Bachelor's degree or higher: 18.2%; Graduate/professional degree or higher: 4.8%

Housing: Homeownership rate: 91.9%; Median home value: $152,500; Median year structure built: 1989; Homeowner vacancy rate: 1.6%; Median gross rent: $761 per month; Rental vacancy rate: 10.8%

Health Insurance: 91.6% have insurance; 80.9% have private insurance; 21.7% have public insurance; 8.4% do not have insurance; 3.5% of children under 18 do not have insurance

Transportation: Commute: 93.4% car, 0.4% public transportation, 2.7% walk, 3.3% work from home; Median travel time to work: 28.5 minutes

---

JOHNSTOWN (township).
Covers a land area of 34.950 square miles and a water area of 1.556 square miles. Located at 42.47° N. Lat; 85.25° W. Long.

History: Johnstown Township was organized in 1838 and named for John Mott, a Quaker preacher who planned to found a colony here. His plans changed, but the name remained.

Population: 3,008; Growth (since 2000): -1.9%; Density: 86.1 persons per square mile; Race: 97.4% White, 0.3% Black/African American, 0.3% Asian, 0.5% American Indian/Alaska Native, 0.0% Native Hawaiian/Other Pacific Islander, 1.1% Two or more races, 2.0% Hispanic of any race; Average household size: 2.48; Median age: 46.7; Age under 18: 21.1%; Age 65 and over: 17.3%; Males per 100 females: 102.7; Marriage status: 19.0% never married, 70.3% now married, 1.0% separated, 4.4% widowed, 6.3% divorced; Foreign born: 0.0%; Speak English only: 99.5%; With disability: 13.3%; Veterans: 15.4%; Ancestry: 18.3% German, 16.1% English, 15.8% Irish, 13.6% American, 5.6% Scottish

Employment: 23.1% management, business, and financial, 7.0% computer, engineering, and science, 4.0% education, legal, community service, arts, and media, 8.5% healthcare practitioners, 13.5% service, 18.5% sales and office, 6.9% natural resources, construction, and maintenance, 18.4% production, transportation, and material moving

Income: Per capita: $29,550; Median household: $63,835; Average household: $71,880; Households with income of $100,000 or more: 21.4%; Poverty rate: 7.4%

Educational Attainment: High school diploma or higher: 87.9%; Bachelor's degree or higher: 15.1%; Graduate/professional degree or higher: 5.3%

Housing: Homeownership rate: 87.6%; Median home value: $168,200; Median year structure built: 1966; Homeowner vacancy rate: 2.1%; Median gross rent: $825 per month; Rental vacancy rate: 6.2%

Health Insurance: 90.7% have insurance; 80.0% have private insurance; 35.7% have public insurance; 9.3% do not have insurance; 6.0% of children under 18 do not have insurance

Transportation: Commute: 92.5% car, 0.0% public transportation, 3.4% walk, 4.1% work from home; Median travel time to work: 25.8 minutes

MAPLE GROVE (township).
Covers a land area of 35.889 square miles and a water area of 0.128 square miles. Located at 42.55° N. Lat; 85.14° W. Long. Elevation is 971 feet.
Population: 1,593; Growth (since 2000): 8.3%; Density: 44.4 persons per square mile; Race: 98.1% White, 0.1% Black/African American, 0.2% Asian, 0.4% American Indian/Alaska Native, 0.0% Native Hawaiian/Other Pacific Islander, 1.1% Two or more races, 0.5% Hispanic of any race; Average household size: 2.74; Median age: 42.0; Age under 18: 23.1%; Age 65 and over: 14.4%; Males per 100 females: 101.1
Housing: Homeownership rate: 89.0%; Homeowner vacancy rate: 1.9%; Rental vacancy rate: 0.0%

MIDDLEVILLE (village).
Covers a land area of 2.282 square miles and a water area of 0.119 square miles. Located at 42.72° N. Lat; 85.47° W. Long. Elevation is 764 feet.
Population: 3,319; Growth (since 2000): 22.0%; Density: 1,454.4 persons per square mile; Race: 95.3% White, 0.2% Black/African American, 0.7% Asian, 0.7% American Indian/Alaska Native, 0.0% Native Hawaiian/Other Pacific Islander, 2.0% Two or more races, 4.4% Hispanic of any race; Average household size: 2.61; Median age: 32.4; Age under 18: 30.5%; Age 65 and over: 12.2%; Males per 100 females: 94.3; Marriage status: 14.7% never married, 62.8% now married, 1.5% separated, 6.9% widowed, 15.6% divorced; Foreign born: 0.8%; Speak English only: 98.3%; With disability: 13.3%; Veterans: 11.2%; Ancestry: 31.8% Dutch, 24.6% German, 18.9% English, 16.7% Irish, 9.9% American
Employment: 4.0% management, business, and financial, 8.1% computer, engineering, and science, 7.3% education, legal, community service, arts, and media, 1.4% healthcare practitioners, 17.0% service, 26.0% sales and office, 16.3% natural resources, construction, and maintenance, 20.0% production, transportation, and material moving
Income: Per capita: $19,481; Median household: $47,407; Average household: $51,676; Households with income of $100,000 or more: 5.7%; Poverty rate: 5.6%
Educational Attainment: High school diploma or higher: 90.3%; Bachelor's degree or higher: 15.0%; Graduate/professional degree or higher: 4.4%
School District(s)
Thornapple Kellogg SD (PK-12)
    2012-13 Enrollment: 3,055 . . . . (269) 795-5521
Housing: Homeownership rate: 71.8%; Median home value: $98,900; Median year structure built: 1982; Homeowner vacancy rate: 3.4%; Median gross rent: $752 per month; Rental vacancy rate: 23.8%
Health Insurance: 91.7% have insurance; 75.4% have private insurance; 33.6% have public insurance; 8.3% do not have insurance; 4.1% of children under 18 do not have insurance
Transportation: Commute: 98.2% car, 0.0% public transportation, 1.3% walk, 0.4% work from home; Median travel time to work: 28.0 minutes
Additional Information Contacts
Village of Middleville . . . . (269) 795-3385
    http://villageofmiddleville.org

NASHVILLE (village).
Covers a land area of 2.120 square miles and a water area of 0.107 square miles. Located at 42.60° N. Lat; 85.09° W. Long. Elevation is 820 feet.
History: Plotted 1865, incorporated 1869.
Population: 1,628; Growth (since 2000): -3.3%; Density: 767.8 persons per square mile; Race: 97.2% White, 0.2% Black/African American, 0.4% Asian, 0.6% American Indian/Alaska Native, 0.0% Native Hawaiian/Other Pacific Islander, 1.2% Two or more races, 2.1% Hispanic of any race; Average household size: 2.63; Median age: 35.9; Age under 18: 26.6%; Age 65 and over: 12.9%; Males per 100 females: 96.9
School District(s)
Maple Valley Schools (PK-12)
    2012-13 Enrollment: 1,197 . . . . (517) 852-9699
Housing: Homeownership rate: 61.6%; Homeowner vacancy rate: 3.5%; Rental vacancy rate: 13.1%
Safety: Violent crime rate: 12.3 per 10,000 population; Property crime rate: 160.3 per 10,000 population

ORANGEVILLE (township).
Covers a land area of 33.428 square miles and a water area of 2.231 square miles. Located at 42.55° N. Lat; 85.47° W. Long. Elevation is 774 feet.
Population: 3,311; Growth (since 2000): -0.3%; Density: 99.0 persons per square mile; Race: 95.5% White, 0.5% Black/African American, 0.2% Asian, 0.8% American Indian/Alaska Native, 0.0% Native Hawaiian/Other Pacific Islander, 1.4% Two or more races, 4.8% Hispanic of any race; Average household size: 2.57; Median age: 43.7; Age under 18: 23.3%; Age 65 and over: 15.3%; Males per 100 females: 105.9; Marriage status: 22.3% never married, 57.5% now married, 0.3% separated, 3.7% widowed, 16.5% divorced; Foreign born: 0.2%; Speak English only: 99.0%; With disability: 13.0%; Veterans: 13.3%; Ancestry: 20.5% German, 18.3% English, 15.1% Irish, 12.6% Dutch, 6.8% American
Employment: 9.2% management, business, and financial, 2.7% computer, engineering, and science, 8.2% education, legal, community service, arts, and media, 6.1% healthcare practitioners, 9.3% service, 18.9% sales and office, 16.8% natural resources, construction, and maintenance, 28.8% production, transportation, and material moving
Income: Per capita: $31,978; Median household: $47,261; Average household: $79,118; Households with income of $100,000 or more: 21.0%; Poverty rate: 19.6%
Educational Attainment: High school diploma or higher: 83.0%; Bachelor's degree or higher: 15.1%; Graduate/professional degree or higher: 7.0%
Housing: Homeownership rate: 84.4%; Median home value: $148,200; Median year structure built: 1969; Homeowner vacancy rate: 2.7%; Median gross rent: $527 per month; Rental vacancy rate: 6.8%
Health Insurance: 87.6% have insurance; 65.1% have private insurance; 36.1% have public insurance; 12.4% do not have insurance; 1.1% of children under 18 do not have insurance
Transportation: Commute: 95.0% car, 0.0% public transportation, 1.9% walk, 1.9% work from home; Median travel time to work: 30.6 minutes

PRAIRIEVILLE (township).
Covers a land area of 32.798 square miles and a water area of 3.687 square miles. Located at 42.47° N. Lat; 85.48° W. Long. Elevation is 981 feet.
History: Prairieville Township was organized in 1841. It was first called Spalding, for an early settler, but was renamed in 1843. The village of Prairieville formed around a tavern operated in 1837 by Hiram Lucas.
Population: 3,404; Growth (since 2000): 7.2%; Density: 103.8 persons per square mile; Race: 96.2% White, 1.1% Black/African American, 0.8% Asian, 0.3% American Indian/Alaska Native, 0.1% Native Hawaiian/Other Pacific Islander, 0.8% Two or more races, 2.5% Hispanic of any race; Average household size: 2.44; Median age: 44.8; Age under 18: 18.3%; Age 65 and over: 14.7%; Males per 100 females: 114.0; Marriage status: 23.0% never married, 63.6% now married, 0.6% separated, 4.5% widowed, 8.9% divorced; Foreign born: 3.6%; Speak English only: 93.4%; With disability: 14.1%; Veterans: 9.3%; Ancestry: 27.0% German, 19.9% English, 16.2% Irish, 12.4% Dutch, 8.2% American
Employment: 11.7% management, business, and financial, 4.6% computer, engineering, and science, 7.8% education, legal, community service, arts, and media, 5.2% healthcare practitioners, 19.7% service, 21.2% sales and office, 17.4% natural resources, construction, and maintenance, 12.4% production, transportation, and material moving
Income: Per capita: $32,098; Median household: $59,137; Average household: $83,174; Households with income of $100,000 or more: 22.8%; Poverty rate: 7.6%
Educational Attainment: High school diploma or higher: 94.0%; Bachelor's degree or higher: 30.2%; Graduate/professional degree or higher: 12.3%
Housing: Homeownership rate: 86.5%; Median home value: $174,900; Median year structure built: 1974; Homeowner vacancy rate: 3.1%; Median gross rent: $800 per month; Rental vacancy rate: 13.0%
Health Insurance: 87.6% have insurance; 73.8% have private insurance; 27.8% have public insurance; 12.4% do not have insurance; 3.9% of children under 18 do not have insurance
Transportation: Commute: 95.2% car, 0.0% public transportation, 0.9% walk, 3.1% work from home; Median travel time to work: 28.6 minutes

RUTLAND (charter township).
Covers a land area of 35.031 square miles and a water area of 1.105 square miles. Located at 42.64° N. Lat; 85.37° W. Long.
Population: 3,987; Growth (since 2000): 9.4%; Density: 113.8 persons per square mile; Race: 97.2% White, 0.0% Black/African American, 0.3% Asian, 0.3% American Indian/Alaska Native, 0.0% Native Hawaiian/Other

Pacific Islander, 1.4% Two or more races, 2.1% Hispanic of any race; Average household size: 2.67; Median age: 41.5; Age under 18: 25.2%; Age 65 and over: 13.9%; Males per 100 females: 104.7; Marriage status: 20.9% never married, 65.5% now married, 0.0% separated, 4.3% widowed, 9.4% divorced; Foreign born: 1.3%; Speak English only: 94.2%; With disability: 13.1%; Veterans: 11.1%; Ancestry: 21.0% German, 14.3% Dutch, 12.2% English, 11.1% Irish, 9.2% American

Employment: 11.7% management, business, and financial, 5.5% computer, engineering, and science, 2.2% education, legal, community service, arts, and media, 5.2% healthcare practitioners, 15.3% service, 26.2% sales and office, 12.2% natural resources, construction, and maintenance, 21.6% production, transportation, and material moving

Income: Per capita: $21,215; Median household: $53,056; Average household: $60,066; Households with income of $100,000 or more: 11.2%; Poverty rate: 9.9%

Educational Attainment: High school diploma or higher: 93.3%; Bachelor's degree or higher: 16.7%; Graduate/professional degree or higher: 7.2%

Housing: Homeownership rate: 90.5%; Median home value: $141,500; Median year structure built: 1978; Homeowner vacancy rate: 1.6%; Median gross rent: $944 per month; Rental vacancy rate: 9.0%

Health Insurance: 92.3% have insurance; 70.6% have private insurance; 39.3% have public insurance; 7.7% do not have insurance; 5.1% of children under 18 do not have insurance

Transportation: Commute: 94.5% car, 0.0% public transportation, 3.2% walk, 2.3% work from home; Median travel time to work: 29.9 minutes

SHELBYVILLE (unincorporated postal area)
ZCTA: 49344

Covers a land area of 32.286 square miles and a water area of 2.075 square miles. Located at 42.59° N. Lat; 85.59° W. Long..

Population: 3,410; Growth (since 2000): 2.9%; Density: 105.6 persons per square mile; Race: 95.1% White, 0.4% Black/African American, 0.3% Asian, 1.3% American Indian/Alaska Native, 0.0% Native Hawaiian/Other Pacific Islander, 1.6% Two or more races, 4.4% Hispanic of any race; Average household size: 2.51; Median age: 43.2; Age under 18: 22.9%; Age 65 and over: 13.4%; Males per 100 females: 105.3; Marriage status: 22.1% never married, 62.3% now married, 0.6% separated, 2.7% widowed, 12.9% divorced; Foreign born: 2.1%; Speak English only: 95.8%; With disability: 9.3%; Veterans: 8.0%; Ancestry: 18.7% German, 16.3% Dutch, 12.9% English, 8.2% American, 8.0% Irish

Employment: 11.6% management, business, and financial, 0.7% computer, engineering, and science, 6.4% education, legal, community service, arts, and media, 5.7% healthcare practitioners, 12.8% service, 18.5% sales and office, 14.1% natural resources, construction, and maintenance, 30.3% production, transportation, and material moving

Income: Per capita: $26,657; Median household: $52,389; Average household: $65,273; Households with income of $100,000 or more: 19.1%; Poverty rate: 11.9%

Educational Attainment: High school diploma or higher: 88.2%; Bachelor's degree or higher: 13.0%; Graduate/professional degree or higher: 4.2%

Housing: Homeownership rate: 84.6%; Median home value: $143,100; Median year structure built: 1969; Homeowner vacancy rate: 4.4%; Median gross rent: $828 per month; Rental vacancy rate: 10.5%

Health Insurance: 85.7% have insurance; 65.1% have private insurance; 33.2% have public insurance; 14.3% do not have insurance; 8.1% of children under 18 do not have insurance

Transportation: Commute: 95.7% car, 0.0% public transportation, 2.3% walk, 2.0% work from home; Median travel time to work: 29.1 minutes

THORNAPPLE (township). Covers a land area of 35.282 square miles and a water area of 0.645 square miles. Located at 42.72° N. Lat; 85.50° W. Long.

Population: 7,884; Growth (since 2000): 17.9%; Density: 223.5 persons per square mile; Race: 96.5% White, 0.4% Black/African American, 0.4% Asian, 0.5% American Indian/Alaska Native, 0.0% Native Hawaiian/Other Pacific Islander, 1.5% Two or more races, 2.8% Hispanic of any race; Average household size: 2.78; Median age: 36.2; Age under 18: 29.1%; Age 65 and over: 11.1%; Males per 100 females: 98.7; Marriage status: 16.4% never married, 69.1% now married, 0.6% separated, 5.5% widowed, 9.0% divorced; Foreign born: 0.7%; Speak English only: 98.7%; With disability: 10.1%; Veterans: 10.6%; Ancestry: 33.7% Dutch, 24.1% German, 16.6% English, 10.0% Irish, 7.0% American

Employment: 10.8% management, business, and financial, 7.0% computer, engineering, and science, 6.9% education, legal, community service, arts, and media, 6.3% healthcare practitioners, 13.1% service, 23.6% sales and office, 12.8% natural resources, construction, and maintenance, 19.5% production, transportation, and material moving

Income: Per capita: $24,055; Median household: $60,365; Average household: $66,566; Households with income of $100,000 or more: 18.2%; Poverty rate: 6.1%

Educational Attainment: High school diploma or higher: 94.4%; Bachelor's degree or higher: 21.5%; Graduate/professional degree or higher: 7.6%

Housing: Homeownership rate: 83.7%; Median home value: $138,600; Median year structure built: 1983; Homeowner vacancy rate: 2.3%; Median gross rent: $756 per month; Rental vacancy rate: 20.2%

Health Insurance: 95.6% have insurance; 85.2% have private insurance; 25.2% have public insurance; 4.4% do not have insurance; 1.8% of children under 18 do not have insurance

Transportation: Commute: 94.1% car, 0.0% public transportation, 0.7% walk, 5.2% work from home; Median travel time to work: 25.9 minutes

WOODLAND (township). Covers a land area of 35.384 square miles and a water area of 0.562 square miles. Located at 42.73° N. Lat; 85.13° W. Long. Elevation is 869 feet.

Population: 2,047; Growth (since 2000): -3.9%; Density: 57.9 persons per square mile; Race: 97.0% White, 0.6% Black/African American, 0.5% Asian, 0.4% American Indian/Alaska Native, 0.0% Native Hawaiian/Other Pacific Islander, 0.9% Two or more races, 3.2% Hispanic of any race; Average household size: 2.58; Median age: 42.8; Age under 18: 24.3%; Age 65 and over: 15.8%; Males per 100 females: 104.1

School District(s)
Lakewood Public Schools (PK-12)
  2012-13 Enrollment: 2,029 . . . . (616) 374-8043

Housing: Homeownership rate: 83.8%; Homeowner vacancy rate: 2.0%; Rental vacancy rate: 7.2%

WOODLAND (village). Covers a land area of 0.815 square miles and a water area of 0 square miles. Located at 42.73° N. Lat; 85.14° W. Long. Elevation is 869 feet.

Population: 425; Growth (since 2000): -14.1%; Density: 521.5 persons per square mile; Race: 96.9% White, 0.2% Black/African American, 0.2% Asian, 0.0% American Indian/Alaska Native, 0.0% Native Hawaiian/Other Pacific Islander, 0.7% Two or more races, 3.8% Hispanic of any race; Average household size: 2.62; Median age: 35.5; Age under 18: 27.1%; Age 65 and over: 12.7%; Males per 100 females: 104.3

School District(s)
Lakewood Public Schools (PK-12)
  2012-13 Enrollment: 2,029 . . . . (616) 374-8043

Housing: Homeownership rate: 67.9%; Homeowner vacancy rate: 3.4%; Rental vacancy rate: 8.8%

YANKEE SPRINGS (township). Covers a land area of 31.061 square miles and a water area of 4.794 square miles. Located at 42.65° N. Lat; 85.48° W. Long.

Population: 4,065; Growth (since 2000): -3.7%; Density: 130.9 persons per square mile; Race: 97.1% White, 0.1% Black/African American, 0.7% Asian, 0.6% American Indian/Alaska Native, 0.0% Native Hawaiian/Other Pacific Islander, 1.2% Two or more races, 1.4% Hispanic of any race; Average household size: 2.47; Median age: 44.1; Age under 18: 23.1%; Age 65 and over: 15.6%; Males per 100 females: 102.7; Marriage status: 19.3% never married, 68.4% now married, 0.4% separated, 6.1% widowed, 6.2% divorced; Foreign born: 1.1%; Speak English only: 99.1%; With disability: 15.2%; Veterans: 10.6%; Ancestry: 30.3% German, 17.7% English, 15.6% Irish, 14.0% Dutch, 11.2% American

Employment: 18.9% management, business, and financial, 5.5% computer, engineering, and science, 3.7% education, legal, community service, arts, and media, 5.1% healthcare practitioners, 12.0% service, 28.4% sales and office, 13.5% natural resources, construction, and maintenance, 12.8% production, transportation, and material moving

Income: Per capita: $29,645; Median household: $67,857; Average household: $74,436; Households with income of $100,000 or more: 22.0%; Poverty rate: 5.7%

Educational Attainment: High school diploma or higher: 95.2%; Bachelor's degree or higher: 23.4%; Graduate/professional degree or higher: 4.3%

Housing: Homeownership rate: 89.9%; Median home value: $170,500; Median year structure built: 1979; Homeowner vacancy rate: 2.5%; Median gross rent: $939 per month; Rental vacancy rate: 27.9%
Health Insurance: 91.4% have insurance; 76.8% have private insurance; 33.1% have public insurance; 8.6% do not have insurance; 0.0% of children under 18 do not have insurance
Transportation: Commute: 91.7% car, 0.3% public transportation, 1.1% walk, 3.4% work from home; Median travel time to work: 27.3 minutes
Additional Information Contacts
Yankee Springs Township. . . . . (269) 795-9091
http://www.yankeespringstwp.org

Bay County

Located in eastern Michigan; bounded on the east by Saginaw Bay and drained by the Saginaw River. Covers a land area of 442.302 square miles, a water area of 188.415 square miles, and is located in the Eastern Time Zone at 43.70° N. Lat., 83.98° W. Long. The county was founded in 1857. County seat is Bay City.

Bay County is part of the Bay City, MI Metropolitan Statistical Area. The entire metro area includes: Bay County, MI

Weather Station: Essexville   Elevation: 587 feet

	Jan	Feb	Mar	Apr	May	Jun	Jul	Aug	Sep	Oct	Nov	Dec
High	29	32	41	55	67	77	82	79	72	59	46	34
Low	16	17	25	37	48	57	62	60	52	41	32	22
Precip	1.7	1.5	1.8	3.1	3.3	3.2	2.6	3.4	4.2	2.9	2.7	1.8
Snow	12.6	8.4	5.3	0.9	0.0	0.0	0.0	0.0	0.0	tr	1.4	9.9

High and Low temperatures in degrees Fahrenheit; Precipitation and Snow in inches

Population: 107,771; Growth (since 2000): -2.2%; Density: 243.7 persons per square mile; Race: 94.1% White, 1.6% Black/African American, 0.5% Asian, 0.5% American Indian/Alaska Native, 0.0% Native Hawaiian/Other Pacific Islander, 2.2% two or more races, 4.7% Hispanic of any race; Average household size: 2.38; Median age: 41.7; Age under 18: 22.2%; Age 65 and over: 16.2%; Males per 100 females: 95.9; Marriage status: 28.2% never married, 52.5% now married, 1.3% separated, 7.5% widowed, 11.8% divorced; Foreign born: 1.4%; Speak English only: 96.6%; With disability: 15.6%; Veterans: 10.7%; Ancestry: 29.1% German, 19.7% Polish, 13.0% French, 11.8% Irish, 7.3% English
Religion: Six largest groups: 30.8% Catholicism, 13.7% Lutheran, 1.9% Methodist/Pietist, 1.9% Non-denominational Protestant, 1.3% Presbyterian-Reformed, 1.0% Holiness
Economy: Unemployment rate: 5.5%; Leading industries: 18.8% retail trade; 14.5% health care and social assistance; 11.9% other services (except public administration); Farms: 766 totaling 193,708 acres; Company size: 2 employ 1,000 or more persons, 1 employs 500 to 999 persons, 41 employs 100 to 499 persons, 2,218 employ less than 100 persons; Business ownership: 2,218 women-owned, n/a Black-owned, 139 Hispanic-owned, 42 Asian-owned
Employment: 10.1% management, business, and financial, 3.9% computer, engineering, and science, 8.0% education, legal, community service, arts, and media, 7.5% healthcare practitioners, 21.1% service, 25.6% sales and office, 8.8% natural resources, construction, and maintenance, 15.1% production, transportation, and material moving
Income: Per capita: $23,799; Median household: $45,376; Average household: $56,825; Households with income of $100,000 or more: 13.7%; Poverty rate: 14.7%
Educational Attainment: High school diploma or higher: 89.0%; Bachelor's degree or higher: 18.2%; Graduate/professional degree or higher: 5.5%
Housing: Homeownership rate: 77.8%; Median home value: $93,800; Median year structure built: 1961; Homeowner vacancy rate: 2.1%; Median gross rent: $630 per month; Rental vacancy rate: 8.9%
Vital Statistics: Birth rate: 105.2 per 10,000 population; Death rate: 104.9 per 10,000 population; Age-adjusted cancer mortality rate: 195.2 deaths per 100,000 population
Health Insurance: 89.2% have insurance; 69.7% have private insurance; 37.2% have public insurance; 10.8% do not have insurance; 2.7% of children under 18 do not have insurance
Health Care: Physicians: 15.1 per 10,000 population; Hospital beds: 33.9 per 10,000 population; Hospital admissions: 1,584.1 per 10,000 population
Air Quality Index: 82.5% good, 17.5% moderate, 0.0% unhealthy for sensitive individuals, 0.0% unhealthy (percent of days)

Transportation: Commute: 93.3% car, 0.7% public transportation, 2.1% walk, 2.9% work from home; Median travel time to work: 20.9 minutes
Presidential Election: 52.3% Obama, 46.7% Romney (2012)
National and State Parks: Bay City State Park; Tobico Marsh State Game Area
Additional Information Contacts
Bay Government . . . . (989) 895-4280
http://www.baycounty-mi.gov

Bay County Communities

AUBURN (city). Covers a land area of 1.045 square miles and a water area of 0.007 square miles. Located at 43.60° N. Lat; 84.08° W. Long. Elevation is 617 feet.
History: Auburn was settled by John Gaffney from Ireland in 1854. The village that grew up was first called Skinner, but was renamed Auburn in 1877, the name having been chosen from the first lines of Oliver Goldsmith's poem "The Deserted Village." Auburn was incorporated as a city in 1947.
Population: 2,087; Growth (since 2000): 3.8%; Density: 1,996.4 persons per square mile; Race: 97.5% White, 0.3% Black/African American, 0.5% Asian, 0.8% American Indian/Alaska Native, 0.1% Native Hawaiian/Other Pacific Islander, 0.5% Two or more races, 2.0% Hispanic of any race; Average household size: 2.24; Median age: 40.9; Age under 18: 22.0%; Age 65 and over: 17.6%; Males per 100 females: 90.8
School District(s)
Bay City SD (PK-12)
    2012-13 Enrollment: 8,200 . . . . (989) 686-9700
Housing: Homeownership rate: 69.2%; Homeowner vacancy rate: 1.8%; Rental vacancy rate: 3.7%

BANGOR (charter township). Covers a land area of 14.100 square miles and a water area of 8.000 square miles. Located at 43.65° N. Lat; 83.89° W. Long.
Population: 14,641; Growth (since 2000): -5.8%; Density: 1,038.4 persons per square mile; Race: 95.2% White, 0.9% Black/African American, 0.8% Asian, 0.6% American Indian/Alaska Native, 0.0% Native Hawaiian/Other Pacific Islander, 1.7% Two or more races, 3.9% Hispanic of any race; Average household size: 2.29; Median age: 45.6; Age under 18: 19.6%; Age 65 and over: 19.1%; Males per 100 females: 91.6; Marriage status: 23.2% never married, 55.1% now married, 1.5% separated, 9.1% widowed, 12.6% divorced; Foreign born: 2.1%; Speak English only: 96.7%; With disability: 16.7%; Veterans: 11.9%; Ancestry: 27.4% German, 15.8% Polish, 12.9% French, 12.6% Irish, 8.9% English
Employment: 10.2% management, business, and financial, 4.6% computer, engineering, and science, 7.2% education, legal, community service, arts, and media, 8.6% healthcare practitioners, 20.0% service, 26.2% sales and office, 8.9% natural resources, construction, and maintenance, 14.3% production, transportation, and material moving
Income: Per capita: $26,996; Median household: $44,947; Average household: $59,855; Households with income of $100,000 or more: 15.5%; Poverty rate: 13.5%
Educational Attainment: High school diploma or higher: 90.7%; Bachelor's degree or higher: 17.4%; Graduate/professional degree or higher: 4.5%
Housing: Homeownership rate: 76.8%; Median home value: $108,100; Median year structure built: 1968; Homeowner vacancy rate: 1.8%; Median gross rent: $711 per month; Rental vacancy rate: 9.2%
Health Insurance: 88.5% have insurance; 71.7% have private insurance; 37.5% have public insurance; 11.5% do not have insurance; 2.9% of children under 18 do not have insurance
Transportation: Commute: 92.3% car, 0.4% public transportation, 2.7% walk, 3.4% work from home; Median travel time to work: 19.8 minutes
Additional Information Contacts
Bangor Charter Township . . . . (989) 684-8931
http://www.bangortownship.org

BAY CITY (city). County seat. Covers a land area of 10.166 square miles and a water area of 1.039 square miles. Located at 43.59° N. Lat; 83.89° W. Long. Elevation is 594 feet.
History: Several small communities sprang up in the 1830's near the mouth of the Saginaw River on Lake Huron. The Tromble brothers, Joseph and Mader, built the first permanent frame house in 1836. The villages took the names of Lower Saginaw, Portsmouth, Wenona, Salzburg, and Banks. This was lumber country, and by 1872 there were 36 sawmills

operating in the area, regulating the life of the towns. In the 1860's, Lower Saginaw had annexed several of the nearby settlements and changed its name to Bay City, to distinguish it from the earlier established Saginaw upstream. The villages on the west bank merged as West Bay City. In 1903, Bay City and West Bay City were consolidated as Bay City. When the lumber industry declined in the early 1900's, Bay City turned to soft-coal mining, commercial fishing, and beet sugar.

Population: 34,932; Growth (since 2000): -5.1%; Density: 3,436.0 persons per square mile; Race: 89.7% White, 3.5% Black/African American, 0.5% Asian, 0.6% American Indian/Alaska Native, 0.0% Native Hawaiian/Other Pacific Islander, 3.9% Two or more races, 8.5% Hispanic of any race; Average household size: 2.38; Median age: 35.8; Age under 18: 24.9%; Age 65 and over: 12.3%; Males per 100 females: 95.0; Marriage status: 36.2% never married, 42.3% now married, 1.4% separated, 6.9% widowed, 14.6% divorced; Foreign born: 1.2%; Speak English only: 96.0%; With disability: 16.5%; Veterans: 9.9%; Ancestry: 26.7% German, 19.5% Polish, 12.3% French, 10.7% Irish, 6.7% English

Employment: 8.7% management, business, and financial, 2.4% computer, engineering, and science, 7.4% education, legal, community service, arts, and media, 5.5% healthcare practitioners, 25.7% service, 27.3% sales and office, 7.2% natural resources, construction, and maintenance, 15.7% production, transportation, and material moving

Income: Per capita: $18,922; Median household: $35,352; Average household: $44,981; Households with income of $100,000 or more: 7.7%; Poverty rate: 22.4%

Educational Attainment: High school diploma or higher: 86.1%; Bachelor's degree or higher: 15.9%; Graduate/professional degree or higher: 4.9%

School District(s)

Bangor Township Schools (PK-12)
    2012-13 Enrollment: 2,461 . . . . (989) 684-8121
Bay City Academy (KG-12)
    2012-13 Enrollment: 507 . . . . (989) 545-1555
Bay City SD (PK-12)
    2012-13 Enrollment: 8,200 . . . . (989) 686-9700
Bay County Psa (PK-12)
    2012-13 Enrollment: 197 . . . . (989) 684-6484
Bay-Arenac ISD (PK-12)
    2012-13 Enrollment: 614 . . . . (989) 686-4410

Vocational/Technical School(s)

Bayshire Academy of Beauty Craft Inc (Private, For-profit)
    Fall 2013 Enrollment: 41 . . . . (989) 894-4923
    2013-14 Tuition: $7,850

Housing: Homeownership rate: 68.1%; Median home value: $69,200; Median year structure built: 1942; Homeowner vacancy rate: 3.2%; Median gross rent: $563 per month; Rental vacancy rate: 8.6%

Health Insurance: 86.3% have insurance; 57.2% have private insurance; 43.0% have public insurance; 13.7% do not have insurance; 3.1% of children under 18 do not have insurance

Hospitals: Mclaren Bay Region (415 beds)

Safety: Violent crime rate: 63.1 per 10,000 population; Property crime rate: 272.7 per 10,000 population

Newspapers: Bay City Democrat (weekly circulation 800); Bay City Times (daily circulation 32700); Valley Farmer (weekly circulation 1200)

Transportation: Commute: 93.1% car, 0.7% public transportation, 2.3% walk, 2.3% work from home; Median travel time to work: 18.4 minutes; Amtrak: Train service available.

Additional Information Contacts

City of Bay City . . . . (989) 894-8200
    http://baycitymi.org

BEAVER (township). Covers a land area of 35.341 square miles and a water area of 0.020 square miles. Located at 43.69° N. Lat; 84.11° W. Long. Elevation is 630 feet.

Population: 2,885; Growth (since 2000): 2.8%; Density: 81.6 persons per square mile; Race: 98.3% White, 0.0% Black/African American, 0.2% Asian, 0.1% American Indian/Alaska Native, 0.0% Native Hawaiian/Other Pacific Islander, 0.8% Two or more races, 1.9% Hispanic of any race; Average household size: 2.68; Median age: 42.8; Age under 18: 23.8%; Age 65 and over: 14.4%; Males per 100 females: 105.9; Marriage status: 25.2% never married, 58.3% now married, 1.1% separated, 7.3% widowed, 9.2% divorced; Foreign born: 1.0%; Speak English only: 97.5%; With disability: 11.6%; Veterans: 10.1%; Ancestry: 30.7% German, 26.9% Polish, 9.4% French, 8.1% Irish, 5.6% American

Employment: 13.1% management, business, and financial, 4.1% computer, engineering, and science, 4.5% education, legal, community service, arts, and media, 8.3% healthcare practitioners, 15.0% service, 25.2% sales and office, 12.6% natural resources, construction, and maintenance, 17.2% production, transportation, and material moving

Income: Per capita: $24,462; Median household: $54,728; Average household: $70,430; Households with income of $100,000 or more: 19.2%; Poverty rate: 4.9%

Educational Attainment: High school diploma or higher: 90.3%; Bachelor's degree or higher: 17.0%; Graduate/professional degree or higher: 5.3%

Housing: Homeownership rate: 91.4%; Median home value: $122,600; Median year structure built: 1971; Homeowner vacancy rate: 0.9%; Median gross rent: $824 per month; Rental vacancy rate: 9.8%

Health Insurance: 90.9% have insurance; 75.5% have private insurance; 31.7% have public insurance; 9.1% do not have insurance; 3.3% of children under 18 do not have insurance

Transportation: Commute: 93.9% car, 0.4% public transportation, 0.3% walk, 3.7% work from home; Median travel time to work: 23.7 minutes

ESSEXVILLE (city). Covers a land area of 1.297 square miles and a water area of 0.110 square miles. Located at 43.61° N. Lat; 83.84° W. Long. Elevation is 587 feet.

History: Essexville developed around a beet-sugar refinery, one of the first in the state. In the early 1900's, the economy changed to commercial fishing, and cement manufacturing.

Population: 3,478; Growth (since 2000): -7.6%; Density: 2,681.1 persons per square mile; Race: 95.5% White, 0.9% Black/African American, 0.8% Asian, 0.6% American Indian/Alaska Native, 0.0% Native Hawaiian/Other Pacific Islander, 1.4% Two or more races, 3.0% Hispanic of any race; Average household size: 2.42; Median age: 42.3; Age under 18: 22.8%; Age 65 and over: 16.6%; Males per 100 females: 90.9; Marriage status: 29.2% never married, 47.6% now married, 3.0% separated, 10.6% widowed, 12.6% divorced; Foreign born: 0.0%; Speak English only: 98.9%; With disability: 16.8%; Veterans: 9.9%; Ancestry: 36.2% German, 17.2% Irish, 16.5% Polish, 16.4% French, 8.7% English

Employment: 6.5% management, business, and financial, 3.5% computer, engineering, and science, 4.8% education, legal, community service, arts, and media, 14.1% healthcare practitioners, 26.4% service, 30.1% sales and office, 4.3% natural resources, construction, and maintenance, 10.2% production, transportation, and material moving

Income: Per capita: $25,035; Median household: $48,563; Average household: $58,011; Households with income of $100,000 or more: 15.0%; Poverty rate: 5.8%

Educational Attainment: High school diploma or higher: 92.4%; Bachelor's degree or higher: 21.2%; Graduate/professional degree or higher: 6.2%

School District(s)

Bay-Arenac Community High School (KG-12)
    2012-13 Enrollment: 144 . . . . (989) 893-8811
Bay-Arenac ISD (PK-12)
    2012-13 Enrollment: 614 . . . . (989) 686-4410
Essexville-Hampton Public Schools (PK-12)
    2012-13 Enrollment: 1,773 . . . . (989) 894-9700

Housing: Homeownership rate: 89.4%; Median home value: $94,500; Median year structure built: 1954; Homeowner vacancy rate: 1.6%; Median gross rent: $854 per month; Rental vacancy rate: 6.7%

Health Insurance: 88.0% have insurance; 76.3% have private insurance; 31.7% have public insurance; 12.0% do not have insurance; 3.4% of children under 18 do not have insurance

Safety: Violent crime rate: 5.8 per 10,000 population; Property crime rate: 238.7 per 10,000 population

Transportation: Commute: 95.0% car, 0.0% public transportation, 2.4% walk, 1.8% work from home; Median travel time to work: 17.5 minutes

Additional Information Contacts

City of Essexville . . . . (989) 893-0772
    http://www.essexville.org

FRANKENLUST (township). Covers a land area of 21.053 square miles and a water area of 1.989 square miles. Located at 43.54° N. Lat; 83.97° W. Long.

Population: 3,562; Growth (since 2000): 40.8%; Density: 169.2 persons per square mile; Race: 93.8% White, 1.5% Black/African American, 2.1% Asian, 0.4% American Indian/Alaska Native, 0.0% Native Hawaiian/Other Pacific Islander, 1.1% Two or more races, 2.8% Hispanic of any race;

Average household size: 2.32; Median age: 44.7; Age under 18: 19.4%; Age 65 and over: 19.9%; Males per 100 females: 97.5; Marriage status: 22.2% never married, 65.1% now married, 0.9% separated, 6.4% widowed, 6.3% divorced; Foreign born: 2.9%; Speak English only: 96.2%; With disability: 9.6%; Veterans: 11.8%; Ancestry: 32.4% German, 15.8% Irish, 14.2% Polish, 9.8% English, 7.9% French

Employment: 14.9% management, business, and financial, 6.8% computer, engineering, and science, 9.4% education, legal, community service, arts, and media, 3.9% healthcare practitioners, 19.6% service, 25.7% sales and office, 9.8% natural resources, construction, and maintenance, 10.0% production, transportation, and material moving

Income: Per capita: $30,441; Median household: $63,681; Average household: $73,571; Households with income of $100,000 or more: 24.3%; Poverty rate: 8.5%

Educational Attainment: High school diploma or higher: 95.7%; Bachelor's degree or higher: 33.3%; Graduate/professional degree or higher: 14.0%

Housing: Homeownership rate: 77.3%; Median home value: $155,900; Median year structure built: 1978; Homeowner vacancy rate: 2.1%; Median gross rent: <$100 per month; Rental vacancy rate: 17.0%

Health Insurance: 97.1% have insurance; 88.7% have private insurance; 29.0% have public insurance; 2.9% do not have insurance; 0.0% of children under 18 do not have insurance

Transportation: Commute: 97.6% car, 0.4% public transportation, 0.0% walk, 0.5% work from home; Median travel time to work: 18.9 minutes

FRASER (township). Covers a land area of 32.434 square miles and a water area of 6.967 square miles. Located at 43.79° N. Lat; 83.98° W. Long.

Population: 3,192; Growth (since 2000): -5.4%; Density: 98.4 persons per square mile; Race: 98.2% White, 0.2% Black/African American, 0.2% Asian, 0.5% American Indian/Alaska Native, 0.0% Native Hawaiian/Other Pacific Islander, 0.8% Two or more races, 2.0% Hispanic of any race; Average household size: 2.39; Median age: 46.3; Age under 18: 19.0%; Age 65 and over: 17.6%; Males per 100 females: 102.4; Marriage status: 21.4% never married, 63.3% now married, 1.6% separated, 8.8% widowed, 6.5% divorced; Foreign born: 1.9%; Speak English only: 97.3%; With disability: 16.7%; Veterans: 11.0%; Ancestry: 29.2% German, 21.2% Polish, 18.5% French, 7.1% English, 6.6% Irish

Employment: 11.8% management, business, and financial, 4.9% computer, engineering, and science, 13.5% education, legal, community service, arts, and media, 8.4% healthcare practitioners, 14.3% service, 22.0% sales and office, 5.6% natural resources, construction, and maintenance, 19.6% production, transportation, and material moving

Income: Per capita: $25,515; Median household: $49,605; Average household: $58,082; Households with income of $100,000 or more: 13.8%; Poverty rate: 11.5%

Educational Attainment: High school diploma or higher: 91.9%; Bachelor's degree or higher: 16.3%; Graduate/professional degree or higher: 2.6%

Housing: Homeownership rate: 90.7%; Median home value: $93,800; Median year structure built: 1965; Homeowner vacancy rate: 1.9%; Median gross rent: $740 per month; Rental vacancy rate: 5.1%

Health Insurance: 92.8% have insurance; 78.9% have private insurance; 34.2% have public insurance; 7.2% do not have insurance; 0.0% of children under 18 do not have insurance

Transportation: Commute: 92.7% car, 0.0% public transportation, 2.2% walk, 4.4% work from home; Median travel time to work: 22.3 minutes

GARFIELD (township). Covers a land area of 35.670 square miles and a water area of 0.023 square miles. Located at 43.78° N. Lat; 84.10° W. Long.

History: Garfield Township was organized in 1887 and named for President James A. Garfield.

Population: 1,743; Growth (since 2000): -1.8%; Density: 48.9 persons per square mile; Race: 97.3% White, 0.2% Black/African American, 0.0% Asian, 1.0% American Indian/Alaska Native, 0.0% Native Hawaiian/Other Pacific Islander, 1.1% Two or more races, 2.6% Hispanic of any race; Average household size: 2.63; Median age: 42.9; Age under 18: 22.0%; Age 65 and over: 13.0%; Males per 100 females: 112.6

Housing: Homeownership rate: 94.2%; Homeowner vacancy rate: 1.7%; Rental vacancy rate: 9.5%

GIBSON (township). Covers a land area of 35.543 square miles and a water area of 0.046 square miles. Located at 43.95° N. Lat; 84.11° W. Long.

Population: 1,210; Growth (since 2000): -2.8%; Density: 34.0 persons per square mile; Race: 97.5% White, 0.1% Black/African American, 0.0% Asian, 0.7% American Indian/Alaska Native, 0.0% Native Hawaiian/Other Pacific Islander, 1.5% Two or more races, 1.1% Hispanic of any race; Average household size: 2.70; Median age: 38.7; Age under 18: 26.4%; Age 65 and over: 13.1%; Males per 100 females: 109.3

Housing: Homeownership rate: 87.5%; Homeowner vacancy rate: 0.8%; Rental vacancy rate: 5.1%

HAMPTON (charter township). Covers a land area of 27.328 square miles and a water area of 25.255 square miles. Located at 43.62° N. Lat; 83.77° W. Long.

Population: 9,652; Growth (since 2000): -2.5%; Density: 353.2 persons per square mile; Race: 94.8% White, 1.5% Black/African American, 0.6% Asian, 0.3% American Indian/Alaska Native, 0.0% Native Hawaiian/Other Pacific Islander, 2.2% Two or more races, 3.6% Hispanic of any race; Average household size: 2.22; Median age: 44.5; Age under 18: 20.9%; Age 65 and over: 19.6%; Males per 100 females: 92.7; Marriage status: 28.1% never married, 50.7% now married, 1.6% separated, 8.9% widowed, 12.3% divorced; Foreign born: 1.3%; Speak English only: 96.6%; With disability: 15.6%; Veterans: 9.4%; Ancestry: 21.3% German, 19.8% Polish, 14.4% Irish, 13.3% French, 5.4% American

Employment: 8.9% management, business, and financial, 3.0% computer, engineering, and science, 11.5% education, legal, community service, arts, and media, 10.6% healthcare practitioners, 14.8% service, 25.8% sales and office, 10.1% natural resources, construction, and maintenance, 15.3% production, transportation, and material moving

Income: Per capita: $23,016; Median household: $42,317; Average household: $53,837; Households with income of $100,000 or more: 14.8%; Poverty rate: 20.1%

Educational Attainment: High school diploma or higher: 86.9%; Bachelor's degree or higher: 18.5%; Graduate/professional degree or higher: 6.1%

Housing: Homeownership rate: 63.1%; Median home value: $130,600; Median year structure built: 1973; Homeowner vacancy rate: 1.3%; Median gross rent: $595 per month; Rental vacancy rate: 9.3%

Health Insurance: 89.2% have insurance; 68.0% have private insurance; 39.2% have public insurance; 10.8% do not have insurance; 3.3% of children under 18 do not have insurance

Safety: Violent crime rate: 13.6 per 10,000 population; Property crime rate: 286.8 per 10,000 population

Transportation: Commute: 94.6% car, 0.9% public transportation, 2.0% walk, 2.1% work from home; Median travel time to work: 21.2 minutes

Additional Information Contacts

Hampton Charter Township . . . . (989) 893-7541
   http://www.hamptontownship.org

KAWKAWLIN (township). Covers a land area of 32.407 square miles and a water area of 9.042 square miles. Located at 43.70° N. Lat; 83.98° W. Long. Elevation is 597 feet.

History: Kawkawlin developed around the water powered mill of James Fraser and the steam powered mill of Frederick A. Kaiser.

Population: 4,848; Growth (since 2000): -5.0%; Density: 149.6 persons per square mile; Race: 97.1% White, 0.2% Black/African American, 0.2% Asian, 0.6% American Indian/Alaska Native, 0.0% Native Hawaiian/Other Pacific Islander, 1.6% Two or more races, 1.9% Hispanic of any race; Average household size: 2.49; Median age: 45.3; Age under 18: 20.9%; Age 65 and over: 17.5%; Males per 100 females: 100.2; Marriage status: 21.9% never married, 64.2% now married, 1.3% separated, 4.1% widowed, 9.8% divorced; Foreign born: 1.1%; Speak English only: 98.5%; With disability: 16.4%; Veterans: 12.5%; Ancestry: 26.5% German, 17.3% Polish, 14.6% Irish, 14.0% French, 7.1% French Canadian

Employment: 11.5% management, business, and financial, 3.1% computer, engineering, and science, 6.7% education, legal, community service, arts, and media, 10.9% healthcare practitioners, 23.0% service, 20.0% sales and office, 12.0% natural resources, construction, and maintenance, 12.8% production, transportation, and material moving

Income: Per capita: $31,260; Median household: $58,824; Average household: $76,493; Households with income of $100,000 or more: 17.5%; Poverty rate: 8.5%

Educational Attainment: High school diploma or higher: 94.3%; Bachelor's degree or higher: 16.5%; Graduate/professional degree or higher: 5.0%

Housing: Homeownership rate: 87.3%; Median home value: $112,300; Median year structure built: 1973; Homeowner vacancy rate: 1.8%; Median gross rent: $608 per month; Rental vacancy rate: 14.1%

Health Insurance: 92.0% have insurance; 78.6% have private insurance; 30.6% have public insurance; 8.0% do not have insurance; 2.5% of children under 18 do not have insurance

Transportation: Commute: 92.4% car, 1.4% public transportation, 0.9% walk, 4.6% work from home; Median travel time to work: 23.9 minutes

LINWOOD (unincorporated postal area)
ZCTA: 48634

Covers a land area of 46.521 square miles and a water area of 2.436 square miles. Located at 43.75° N. Lat; 84.06° W. Long. Elevation is 584 feet.

Population: 4,371; Growth (since 2000): -6.7%; Density: 94.0 persons per square mile; Race: 97.9% White, 0.3% Black/African American, 0.2% Asian, 0.6% American Indian/Alaska Native, 0.0% Native Hawaiian/Other Pacific Islander, 0.7% Two or more races, 2.2% Hispanic of any race; Average household size: 2.45; Median age: 44.8; Age under 18: 20.4%; Age 65 and over: 16.8%; Males per 100 females: 103.4; Marriage status: 24.1% never married, 59.7% now married, 1.3% separated, 6.6% widowed, 9.6% divorced; Foreign born: 1.3%; Speak English only: 97.7%; With disability: 16.3%; Veterans: 8.6%; Ancestry: 32.8% German, 22.6% Polish, 15.5% French, 9.8% Irish, 7.5% English

Employment: 15.8% management, business, and financial, 5.6% computer, engineering, and science, 9.0% education, legal, community service, arts, and media, 9.9% healthcare practitioners, 15.1% service, 17.3% sales and office, 9.4% natural resources, construction, and maintenance, 18.0% production, transportation, and material moving

Income: Per capita: $28,803; Median household: $54,935; Average household: $69,530; Households with income of $100,000 or more: 18.5%; Poverty rate: 11.5%

Educational Attainment: High school diploma or higher: 89.6%; Bachelor's degree or higher: 18.0%; Graduate/professional degree or higher: 6.5%

School District(s)
Pinconning Area Schools (PK-12)
2012-13 Enrollment: 1,398 . . . . (989) 879-4556

Housing: Homeownership rate: 89.2%; Median home value: $106,200; Median year structure built: 1969; Homeowner vacancy rate: 2.0%; Median gross rent: $636 per month; Rental vacancy rate: 9.8%

Health Insurance: 91.6% have insurance; 73.8% have private insurance; 36.2% have public insurance; 8.4% do not have insurance; 2.5% of children under 18 do not have insurance

Transportation: Commute: 95.8% car, 0.0% public transportation, 1.7% walk, 0.8% work from home; Median travel time to work: 24.3 minutes

MERRITT (township). Covers a land area of 31.643 square miles and a water area of 0.029 square miles. Located at 43.52° N. Lat; 83.75° W. Long.

Population: 1,441; Growth (since 2000): -4.6%; Density: 45.5 persons per square mile; Race: 96.7% White, 0.1% Black/African American, 0.3% Asian, 0.6% American Indian/Alaska Native, 0.0% Native Hawaiian/Other Pacific Islander, 1.5% Two or more races, 2.8% Hispanic of any race; Average household size: 2.60; Median age: 41.7; Age under 18: 22.4%; Age 65 and over: 14.9%; Males per 100 females: 105.3

Housing: Homeownership rate: 91.7%; Homeowner vacancy rate: 0.8%; Rental vacancy rate: 2.1%

MONITOR (charter township). Covers a land area of 36.779 square miles and a water area of 0.197 square miles. Located at 43.61° N. Lat; 83.99° W. Long.

Population: 10,735; Growth (since 2000): 7.0%; Density: 291.9 persons per square mile; Race: 97.1% White, 0.4% Black/African American, 0.6% Asian, 0.3% American Indian/Alaska Native, 0.0% Native Hawaiian/Other Pacific Islander, 1.4% Two or more races, 2.4% Hispanic of any race; Average household size: 2.38; Median age: 46.9; Age under 18: 19.9%; Age 65 and over: 22.0%; Males per 100 females: 92.4; Marriage status: 23.1% never married, 59.7% now married, 1.1% separated, 8.8% widowed, 8.5% divorced; Foreign born: 1.0%; Speak English only: 97.0%; With disability: 15.8%; Veterans: 11.7%; Ancestry: 39.4% German, 25.5% Polish, 14.3% French, 12.2% Irish, 8.3% English

Employment: 12.3% management, business, and financial, 4.7% computer, engineering, and science, 9.0% education, legal, community service, arts, and media, 7.3% healthcare practitioners, 17.8% service, 26.2% sales and office, 7.9% natural resources, construction, and maintenance, 14.8% production, transportation, and material moving

Income: Per capita: $28,915; Median household: $55,470; Average household: $69,611; Households with income of $100,000 or more: 19.9%; Poverty rate: 7.1%

Educational Attainment: High school diploma or higher: 91.8%; Bachelor's degree or higher: 24.0%; Graduate/professional degree or higher: 7.8%

Housing: Homeownership rate: 92.3%; Median home value: $125,500; Median year structure built: 1972; Homeowner vacancy rate: 1.6%; Median gross rent: $579 per month; Rental vacancy rate: 6.3%

Health Insurance: 92.2% have insurance; 80.5% have private insurance; 33.1% have public insurance; 7.8% do not have insurance; 1.5% of children under 18 do not have insurance

Transportation: Commute: 94.0% car, 1.0% public transportation, 1.7% walk, 3.1% work from home; Median travel time to work: 20.6 minutes

Additional Information Contacts
Monitor Charter Township . . . . (989) 684-7203
http://www.monitortwp.org

MOUNT FOREST (township). Covers a land area of 35.910 square miles and a water area of 0.013 square miles. Located at 43.86° N. Lat; 84.12° W. Long. Elevation is 692 feet.

Population: 1,392; Growth (since 2000): -0.9%; Density: 38.8 persons per square mile; Race: 97.3% White, 0.2% Black/African American, 0.0% Asian, 0.9% American Indian/Alaska Native, 0.0% Native Hawaiian/Other Pacific Islander, 0.6% Two or more races, 3.1% Hispanic of any race; Average household size: 2.55; Median age: 44.7; Age under 18: 19.9%; Age 65 and over: 12.9%; Males per 100 females: 108.7

Housing: Homeownership rate: 92.3%; Homeowner vacancy rate: 1.9%; Rental vacancy rate: 2.3%

MUNGER (unincorporated postal area)
ZCTA: 48747

Covers a land area of 30.773 square miles and a water area of 0.017 square miles. Located at 43.52° N. Lat; 83.76° W. Long. Elevation is 594 feet.

Population: 1,494; Growth (since 2000): -3.1%; Density: 48.5 persons per square mile; Race: 96.9% White, 0.1% Black/African American, 0.3% Asian, 0.6% American Indian/Alaska Native, 0.0% Native Hawaiian/Other Pacific Islander, 1.4% Two or more races, 2.7% Hispanic of any race; Average household size: 2.58; Median age: 41.2; Age under 18: 22.6%; Age 65 and over: 14.6%; Males per 100 females: 103.5

Housing: Homeownership rate: 92.5%; Homeowner vacancy rate: 0.9%; Rental vacancy rate: 2.2%

PINCONNING (city). Covers a land area of 0.853 square miles and a water area of 0.001 square miles. Located at 43.86° N. Lat; 83.96° W. Long. Elevation is 600 feet.

History: The name of Pinconning is of Indian origin, meaning "place of the potato." The community was settled in 1866 and was an important rail center in logging days. Later it became a trading center in an area of sugar beets, chicory, and beans. Old maps show the Pinconning River as the Potato River.

Population: 1,307; Growth (since 2000): -5.7%; Density: 1,531.9 persons per square mile; Race: 96.5% White, 0.7% Black/African American, 0.3% Asian, 0.2% American Indian/Alaska Native, 0.0% Native Hawaiian/Other Pacific Islander, 2.1% Two or more races, 3.6% Hispanic of any race; Average household size: 2.24; Median age: 37.1; Age under 18: 25.4%; Age 65 and over: 16.1%; Males per 100 females: 89.7

School District(s)
Pinconning Area Schools (PK-12)
2012-13 Enrollment: 1,398 . . . . (989) 879-4556

Housing: Homeownership rate: 64.3%; Homeowner vacancy rate: 3.6%; Rental vacancy rate: 4.6%

Safety: Violent crime rate: 0.0 per 10,000 population; Property crime rate: 124.2 per 10,000 population

Newspapers: Pinconning Journal (weekly circulation 2000)

PINCONNING (township). Covers a land area of 36.682 square miles and a water area of 5.302 square miles. Located at 43.87° N. Lat; 83.97° W. Long. Elevation is 600 feet.
History: Settled c.1866; incorporated as village 1877, as city 1931.
Population: 2,431; Growth (since 2000): -6.8%; Density: 66.3 persons per square mile; Race: 97.1% White, 0.2% Black/African American, 0.2% Asian, 0.8% American Indian/Alaska Native, 0.0% Native Hawaiian/Other Pacific Islander, 1.5% Two or more races, 2.3% Hispanic of any race; Average household size: 2.49; Median age: 44.2; Age under 18: 22.2%; Age 65 and over: 16.2%; Males per 100 females: 103.4

School District(s)

Pinconning Area Schools (PK-12)
 . 2012-13 Enrollment: 1,398 . . . . (989) 879-4556
Housing: Homeownership rate: 88.2%; Homeowner vacancy rate: 1.3%; Rental vacancy rate: 8.0%
Newspapers: Pinconning Journal (weekly circulation 2000)

PORTSMOUTH (charter township). Covers a land area of 20.049 square miles and a water area of 0.166 square miles. Located at 43.56° N. Lat; 83.83° W. Long.
Population: 3,306; Growth (since 2000): -8.6%; Density: 164.9 persons per square mile; Race: 97.2% White, 0.6% Black/African American, 0.2% Asian, 0.4% American Indian/Alaska Native, 0.0% Native Hawaiian/Other Pacific Islander, 0.7% Two or more races, 3.9% Hispanic of any race; Average household size: 2.41; Median age: 47.0; Age under 18: 19.6%; Age 65 and over: 18.7%; Males per 100 females: 98.2; Marriage status: 27.5% never married, 54.7% now married, 2.4% separated, 9.4% widowed, 8.4% divorced; Foreign born: 1.5%; Speak English only: 92.0%; With disability: 11.9%; Veterans: 12.5%; Ancestry: 29.2% Polish, 27.0% German, 17.9% French, 8.2% Irish, 7.0% English
Employment: 8.9% management, business, and financial, 7.7% computer, engineering, and science, 11.9% education, legal, community service, arts, and media, 8.0% healthcare practitioners, 24.8% service, 16.2% sales and office, 10.8% natural resources, construction, and maintenance, 11.8% production, transportation, and material moving
Income: Per capita: $25,111; Median household: $49,333; Average household: $60,650; Households with income of $100,000 or more: 16.5%; Poverty rate: 8.8%
Educational Attainment: High school diploma or higher: 88.9%; Bachelor's degree or higher: 16.7%; Graduate/professional degree or higher: 4.8%
Housing: Homeownership rate: 92.7%; Median home value: $100,200; Median year structure built: 1962; Homeowner vacancy rate: 1.5%; Median gross rent: $1,036 per month; Rental vacancy rate: 23.7%
Health Insurance: 87.9% have insurance; 76.4% have private insurance; 35.2% have public insurance; 12.1% do not have insurance; 3.9% of children under 18 do not have insurance
Transportation: Commute: 91.0% car, 1.1% public transportation, 1.3% walk, 6.0% work from home; Median travel time to work: 20.5 minutes

WILLIAMS (charter township). Covers a land area of 33.552 square miles and a water area of 0.112 square miles. Located at 43.62° N. Lat; 84.10° W. Long.
Population: 4,772; Growth (since 2000): 6.2%; Density: 142.2 persons per square mile; Race: 97.3% White, 0.3% Black/African American, 0.5% Asian, 0.3% American Indian/Alaska Native, 0.0% Native Hawaiian/Other Pacific Islander, 1.1% Two or more races, 2.4% Hispanic of any race; Average household size: 2.62; Median age: 41.3; Age under 18: 24.0%; Age 65 and over: 13.9%; Males per 100 females: 102.0; Marriage status: 22.7% never married, 66.9% now married, 0.0% separated, 2.7% widowed, 7.6% divorced; Foreign born: 2.4%; Speak English only: 97.0%; With disability: 12.9%; Veterans: 9.3%; Ancestry: 30.9% German, 15.8% Polish, 8.9% Irish, 8.2% French, 7.9% American
Employment: 9.5% management, business, and financial, 6.8% computer, engineering, and science, 7.7% education, legal, community service, arts, and media, 7.7% healthcare practitioners, 23.1% service, 24.4% sales and office, 9.4% natural resources, construction, and maintenance, 11.4% production, transportation, and material moving
Income: Per capita: $23,999; Median household: $58,594; Average household: $66,985; Households with income of $100,000 or more: 16.5%; Poverty rate: 5.7%
Educational Attainment: High school diploma or higher: 89.7%; Bachelor's degree or higher: 20.8%; Graduate/professional degree or higher: 4.5%

Housing: Homeownership rate: 94.0%; Median home value: $115,400; Median year structure built: 1965; Homeowner vacancy rate: 1.6%; Median gross rent: $767 per month; Rental vacancy rate: 2.6%
Health Insurance: 91.7% have insurance; 81.5% have private insurance; 28.0% have public insurance; 8.3% do not have insurance; 2.8% of children under 18 do not have insurance
Transportation: Commute: 94.8% car, 0.0% public transportation, 0.0% walk, 4.5% work from home; Median travel time to work: 24.7 minutes
Additional Information Contacts
Williams Township . . . . (989) 662-4241
 http://williamstwp.com

Benzie County

Located in northwestern Michigan; bounded on the west by Lake Michigan; includes Crystal, Platte, and other lakes. Covers a land area of 319.704 square miles, a water area of 539.864 square miles, and is located in the Eastern Time Zone at 44.65° N. Lat., 86.49° W. Long. The county was founded in 1863. County seat is Beulah.

Benzie County is part of the Traverse City, MI Micropolitan Statistical Area. The entire metro area includes: Benzie County, MI; Grand Traverse County, MI; Kalkaska County, MI; Leelanau County, MI

Weather Station: Frankfort									Elevation: 720 feet		
	Jan	Feb	Mar	Apr	May	Jun	Jul	Aug	Sep	Oct	Nov	Dec
High	29	31	39	53	64	73	78	76	69	57	44	33
Low	18	19	25	35	44	53	59	60	53	42	33	23
Precip	2.5	1.8	2.0	2.7	3.0	3.1	3.0	3.3	4.0	3.5	3.0	2.7
Snow	30.6	20.3	13.9	4.0	0.1	0.0	0.0	0.0	tr	0.3	8.0	27.7

High and Low temperatures in degrees Fahrenheit; Precipitation and Snow in inches

Population: 17,525; Growth (since 2000): 9.5%; Density: 54.8 persons per square mile; Race: 96.1% White, 0.4% Black/African American, 0.3% Asian, 1.4% American Indian/Alaska Native, 0.0% Native Hawaiian/Other Pacific Islander, 1.3% two or more races, 1.7% Hispanic of any race; Average household size: 2.37; Median age: 46.2; Age under 18: 21.0%; Age 65 and over: 20.6%; Males per 100 females: 98.6; Marriage status: 21.6% never married, 58.5% now married, 0.9% separated, 6.5% widowed, 13.4% divorced; Foreign born: 1.6%; Speak English only: 95.6%; With disability: 17.7%; Veterans: 14.0%; Ancestry: 29.9% German, 16.1% English, 14.3% Irish, 6.7% Polish, 5.9% French
Religion: Six largest groups: 5.2% Lutheran, 5.0% Presbyterian-Reformed, 2.7% Catholicism, 2.6% Methodist/Pietist, 1.4% Baptist, 0.9% Holiness
Economy: Unemployment rate: 5.7%; Leading industries: 18.1% construction; 16.6% retail trade; 12.9% accommodation and food services; Farms: 181 totaling 20,646 acres; Company size: 0 employ 1,000 or more persons, 1 employs 500 to 999 persons, 2 employ 100 to 499 persons, 438 employ less than 100 persons; Business ownership: 472 women-owned, n/a Black-owned, n/a Hispanic-owned, n/a Asian-owned
Employment: 12.2% management, business, and financial, 2.7% computer, engineering, and science, 9.2% education, legal, community service, arts, and media, 7.1% healthcare practitioners, 21.8% service, 22.0% sales and office, 12.4% natural resources, construction, and maintenance, 12.6% production, transportation, and material moving
Income: Per capita: $24,831; Median household: $47,366; Average household: $57,171; Households with income of $100,000 or more: 11.5%; Poverty rate: 13.3%
Educational Attainment: High school diploma or higher: 90.3%; Bachelor's degree or higher: 24.9%; Graduate/professional degree or higher: 11.2%
Housing: Homeownership rate: 85.3%; Median home value: $149,700; Median year structure built: 1985; Homeowner vacancy rate: 3.8%; Median gross rent: $763 per month; Rental vacancy rate: 19.5%
Vital Statistics: Birth rate: 80.3 per 10,000 population; Death rate: 108.4 per 10,000 population; Age-adjusted cancer mortality rate: 247.2 deaths per 100,000 population
Health Insurance: 86.2% have insurance; 68.6% have private insurance; 38.8% have public insurance; 13.8% do not have insurance; 8.3% of children under 18 do not have insurance
Health Care: Physicians: 6.3 per 10,000 population; Hospital beds: 26.9 per 10,000 population; Hospital admissions: 44.1 per 10,000 population
Air Quality Index: 86.9% good, 12.6% moderate, 0.5% unhealthy for sensitive individuals, 0.0% unhealthy (percent of days)

Transportation: Commute: 89.0% car, 1.3% public transportation, 2.4% walk, 6.5% work from home; Median travel time to work: 25.2 minutes
Presidential Election: 47.6% Obama, 51.5% Romney (2012)
National and State Parks: Betsie River State Game Refuge; Pere Marquette State Forest
Additional Information Contacts
Benzie Government.............................. (231) 882-9671
  http://www.benzieco.net

Benzie County Communities

ALMIRA (township). Covers a land area of 33.748 square miles and a water area of 2.264 square miles. Located at 44.74° N. Lat; 85.89° W. Long.
History: Almira Township was named for Almira Burrell who had come here from New York in 1863.
Population: 3,645; Growth (since 2000): 29.7%; Density: 108.0 persons per square mile; Race: 97.5% White, 0.2% Black/African American, 0.2% Asian, 0.6% American Indian/Alaska Native, 0.0% Native Hawaiian/Other Pacific Islander, 1.1% Two or more races, 1.2% Hispanic of any race; Average household size: 2.63; Median age: 38.9; Age under 18: 26.5%; Age 65 and over: 10.9%; Males per 100 females: 99.4; Marriage status: 23.2% never married, 59.6% now married, 0.0% separated, 2.5% widowed, 14.7% divorced; Foreign born: 1.7%; Speak English only: 94.4%; With disability: 14.2%; Veterans: 9.7%; Ancestry: 35.2% German, 14.7% English, 9.9% Irish, 8.3% Dutch, 7.4% Polish
Employment: 14.9% management, business, and financial, 4.7% computer, engineering, and science, 14.5% education, legal, community service, arts, and media, 11.3% healthcare practitioners, 13.3% service, 21.2% sales and office, 12.1% natural resources, construction, and maintenance, 8.0% production, transportation, and material moving
Income: Per capita: $26,874; Median household: $62,545; Average household: $64,432; Households with income of $100,000 or more: 14.1%; Poverty rate: 5.8%
Educational Attainment: High school diploma or higher: 94.7%; Bachelor's degree or higher: 29.2%; Graduate/professional degree or higher: 13.0%
Housing: Homeownership rate: 90.9%; Median home value: $151,100; Median year structure built: 1997; Homeowner vacancy rate: 2.7%; Median gross rent: $726 per month; Rental vacancy rate: 15.1%
Health Insurance: 91.0% have insurance; 85.0% have private insurance; 20.6% have public insurance; 9.0% do not have insurance; 4.4% of children under 18 do not have insurance
Transportation: Commute: 94.7% car, 0.0% public transportation, 0.7% walk, 4.6% work from home; Median travel time to work: 26.8 minutes

BENDON (CDP). Covers a land area of 2.005 square miles and a water area of <.001 square miles. Located at 44.64° N. Lat; 85.85° W. Long. Elevation is 846 feet.
Population: 208; Growth (since 2000): n/a; Density: 103.8 persons per square mile; Race: 95.7% White, 0.5% Black/African American, 0.5% Asian, 3.4% American Indian/Alaska Native, 0.0% Native Hawaiian/Other Pacific Islander, 0.0% Two or more races, 0.5% Hispanic of any race; Average household size: 2.39; Median age: 38.5; Age under 18: 22.1%; Age 65 and over: 15.4%; Males per 100 females: 92.6
Housing: Homeownership rate: 79.3%; Homeowner vacancy rate: 4.2%; Rental vacancy rate: 0.0%

BENZONIA (township). Covers a land area of 27.806 square miles and a water area of 6.048 square miles. Located at 44.66° N. Lat; 86.12° W. Long. Elevation is 817 feet.
Population: 2,727; Growth (since 2000): -3.9%; Density: 98.1 persons per square mile; Race: 94.4% White, 0.5% Black/African American, 0.1% Asian, 2.5% American Indian/Alaska Native, 0.0% Native Hawaiian/Other Pacific Islander, 1.6% Two or more races, 2.7% Hispanic of any race; Average household size: 2.20; Median age: 50.6; Age under 18: 17.9%; Age 65 and over: 26.8%; Males per 100 females: 95.8; Marriage status: 25.6% never married, 51.7% now married, 1.1% separated, 8.9% widowed, 13.8% divorced; Foreign born: 0.8%; Speak English only: 96.5%; With disability: 22.0%; Veterans: 17.4%; Ancestry: 24.4% German, 14.8% English, 14.5% Irish, 9.8% Polish, 7.8% American
Employment: 9.6% management, business, and financial, 1.0% computer, engineering, and science, 9.8% education, legal, community service, arts, and media, 6.4% healthcare practitioners, 28.3% service, 18.1% sales and

office, 11.8% natural resources, construction, and maintenance, 15.0% production, transportation, and material moving
Income: Per capita: $23,179; Median household: $47,798; Average household: $53,103; Households with income of $100,000 or more: 11.7%; Poverty rate: 16.4%
Educational Attainment: High school diploma or higher: 88.9%; Bachelor's degree or higher: 28.9%; Graduate/professional degree or higher: 14.6%
School District(s)
Benzie County Central Schools (KG-12)
    2012-13 Enrollment: 1,616 .... (231) 882-9654
Housing: Homeownership rate: 82.4%; Median home value: $166,500; Median year structure built: 1977; Homeowner vacancy rate: 4.5%; Median gross rent: $900 per month; Rental vacancy rate: 23.6%
Health Insurance: 82.2% have insurance; 57.3% have private insurance; 47.5% have public insurance; 17.8% do not have insurance; 10.9% of children under 18 do not have insurance
Transportation: Commute: 87.9% car, 1.9% public transportation, 1.6% walk, 6.3% work from home; Median travel time to work: 21.3 minutes

BENZONIA (village). Covers a land area of 1.127 square miles and a water area of 0 square miles. Located at 44.62° N. Lat; 86.10° W. Long. Elevation is 817 feet.
History: Benzonia was platted in 1857 by a Congregational minister, Reverend Charles E. Bailey, who wanted to establish a Christian institution. The college closed in 1918.
Population: 497; Growth (since 2000): -4.2%; Density: 441.1 persons per square mile; Race: 93.2% White, 1.2% Black/African American, 0.0% Asian, 0.4% American Indian/Alaska Native, 0.0% Native Hawaiian/Other Pacific Islander, 2.8% Two or more races, 6.2% Hispanic of any race; Average household size: 2.38; Median age: 39.9; Age under 18: 25.6%; Age 65 and over: 18.5%; Males per 100 females: 82.1
School District(s)
Benzie County Central Schools (KG-12)
    2012-13 Enrollment: 1,616 .... (231) 882-9654
Housing: Homeownership rate: 77.5%; Homeowner vacancy rate: 6.1%; Rental vacancy rate: 7.8%

BEULAH (village). County seat. Covers a land area of 0.431 square miles and a water area of 0.001 square miles. Located at 44.63° N. Lat; 86.10° W. Long. Elevation is 607 feet.
History: Beulah, established on Crystal Lake about 1880, became the business center for the nearby tourist region. Smelt runs, the result of fish planted in Crystal Lake in 1912, attracted many sportsmen. The village was named by its founder, Reverend Charles E. Bailey, for the land of Beulah mentioned in Isaiah 62:4.
Population: 342; Growth (since 2000): -5.8%; Density: 793.2 persons per square mile; Race: 98.0% White, 0.3% Black/African American, 0.0% Asian, 0.3% American Indian/Alaska Native, 0.0% Native Hawaiian/Other Pacific Islander, 0.9% Two or more races, 2.3% Hispanic of any race; Average household size: 1.81; Median age: 52.7; Age under 18: 10.5%; Age 65 and over: 24.6%; Males per 100 females: 106.0
Housing: Homeownership rate: 59.7%; Homeowner vacancy rate: 8.5%; Rental vacancy rate: 27.0%

BLAINE (township). Covers a land area of 19.432 square miles and a water area of 1.621 square miles. Located at 44.57° N. Lat; 86.19° W. Long.
Population: 551; Growth (since 2000): 12.2%; Density: 28.4 persons per square mile; Race: 94.4% White, 0.4% Black/African American, 0.0% Asian, 0.4% American Indian/Alaska Native, 0.0% Native Hawaiian/Other Pacific Islander, 0.4% Two or more races, 7.1% Hispanic of any race; Average household size: 2.26; Median age: 53.3; Age under 18: 19.6%; Age 65 and over: 31.4%; Males per 100 females: 99.6
Housing: Homeownership rate: 88.5%; Homeowner vacancy rate: 2.8%; Rental vacancy rate: 38.6%

COLFAX (township). Covers a land area of 35.647 square miles and a water area of 0.260 square miles. Located at 44.56° N. Lat; 85.87° W. Long.
Population: 657; Growth (since 2000): 12.3%; Density: 18.4 persons per square mile; Race: 96.8% White, 0.2% Black/African American, 0.0% Asian, 2.1% American Indian/Alaska Native, 0.0% Native Hawaiian/Other Pacific Islander, 0.9% Two or more races, 1.1% Hispanic of any race;

Average household size: 2.47; Median age: 41.5; Age under 18: 20.9%; Age 65 and over: 11.9%; Males per 100 females: 113.3
Housing: Homeownership rate: 88.0%; Homeowner vacancy rate: 3.3%; Rental vacancy rate: 11.1%

CRYSTAL DOWNS COUNTRY CLUB (CDP). Covers a land area of 1.256 square miles and a water area of 0 square miles. Located at 44.70° N. Lat; 86.23° W. Long.
Population: 47; Growth (since 2000): n/a; Density: 37.4 persons per square mile; Race: 100.0% White, 0.0% Black/African American, 0.0% Asian, 0.0% American Indian/Alaska Native, 0.0% Native Hawaiian/Other Pacific Islander, 0.0% Two or more races, 0.0% Hispanic of any race; Average household size: 1.68; Median age: 65.5; Age under 18: 6.4%; Age 65 and over: 51.1%; Males per 100 females: 74.1
Housing: Homeownership rate: 92.9%; Homeowner vacancy rate: 10.3%; Rental vacancy rate: 0.0%

CRYSTAL LAKE (township). Covers a land area of 12.556 square miles and a water area of 4.522 square miles. Located at 44.64° N. Lat; 86.19° W. Long. Elevation is 863 feet.
Population: 957; Growth (since 2000): -0.3%; Density: 76.2 persons per square mile; Race: 97.6% White, 0.1% Black/African American, 0.3% Asian, 1.4% American Indian/Alaska Native, 0.0% Native Hawaiian/Other Pacific Islander, 0.6% Two or more races, 0.4% Hispanic of any race; Average household size: 2.16; Median age: 55.7; Age under 18: 14.4%; Age 65 and over: 31.2%; Males per 100 females: 101.1
Housing: Homeownership rate: 83.3%; Homeowner vacancy rate: 2.1%; Rental vacancy rate: 12.0%

CRYSTAL MOUNTAIN (CDP). Covers a land area of 1.645 square miles and a water area of 0.008 square miles. Located at 44.52° N. Lat; 86.00° W. Long.
Population: 54; Growth (since 2000): n/a; Density: 32.8 persons per square mile; Race: 98.1% White, 0.0% Black/African American, 0.0% Asian, 0.0% American Indian/Alaska Native, 0.0% Native Hawaiian/Other Pacific Islander, 1.9% Two or more races, 0.0% Hispanic of any race; Average household size: 2.00; Median age: 62.6; Age under 18: 5.6%; Age 65 and over: 33.3%; Males per 100 females: 100.0
Housing: Homeownership rate: 92.6%; Homeowner vacancy rate: 7.4%; Rental vacancy rate: 87.5%

ELBERTA (village). Covers a land area of 0.743 square miles and a water area of 0.252 square miles. Located at 44.62° N. Lat; 86.23° W. Long. Elevation is 591 feet.
History: Elberta grew around a charcoal-iron industry. When that closed, the town lagged until car-ferry service was begun from here to Manitowoc, Wisconsin, and to points in Upper Michigan.
Population: 372; Growth (since 2000): -18.6%; Density: 500.9 persons per square mile; Race: 95.2% White, 0.8% Black/African American, 0.3% Asian, 0.8% American Indian/Alaska Native, 0.0% Native Hawaiian/Other Pacific Islander, 2.2% Two or more races, 3.5% Hispanic of any race; Average household size: 2.15; Median age: 47.8; Age under 18: 18.5%; Age 65 and over: 21.5%; Males per 100 females: 107.8
Housing: Homeownership rate: 68.8%; Homeowner vacancy rate: 1.7%; Rental vacancy rate: 8.5%

FRANKFORT (city). Covers a land area of 1.385 square miles and a water area of 0.197 square miles. Located at 44.64° N. Lat; 86.23° W. Long. Elevation is 597 feet.
History: Frankfort was established on the hills overlooking Betsie Lake and the Betsie River, where docks accommodated the commercial fishing boats.
Population: 1,286; Growth (since 2000): -15.0%; Density: 928.2 persons per square mile; Race: 94.3% White, 1.1% Black/African American, 1.1% Asian, 2.0% American Indian/Alaska Native, 0.0% Native Hawaiian/Other Pacific Islander, 1.2% Two or more races, 2.0% Hispanic of any race; Average household size: 1.98; Median age: 54.6; Age under 18: 15.4%; Age 65 and over: 36.1%; Males per 100 females: 81.1
School District(s)
Frankfort-Elberta Area Schools (KG-12)
    2012-13 Enrollment: 529 . . . . (231) 352-4641
Housing: Homeownership rate: 68.9%; Homeowner vacancy rate: 7.8%; Rental vacancy rate: 21.6%
Hospitals: Paul Oliver Memorial Hospital (48 beds)

Safety: Violent crime rate: 15.6 per 10,000 population; Property crime rate: 281.0 per 10,000 population
Newspapers: Benzie Co Record Patriot (weekly circulation 4700)

GILMORE (township). Covers a land area of 7.132 square miles and a water area of 0.367 square miles. Located at 44.60° N. Lat; 86.19° W. Long.
Population: 821; Growth (since 2000): -3.4%; Density: 115.1 persons per square mile; Race: 95.9% White, 0.4% Black/African American, 0.1% Asian, 1.1% American Indian/Alaska Native, 0.0% Native Hawaiian/Other Pacific Islander, 2.2% Two or more races, 2.1% Hispanic of any race; Average household size: 2.28; Median age: 48.3; Age under 18: 18.6%; Age 65 and over: 22.9%; Males per 100 females: 105.8
Housing: Homeownership rate: 81.6%; Homeowner vacancy rate: 2.0%; Rental vacancy rate: 7.0%

HARDWOOD ACRES (CDP). Covers a land area of 0.523 square miles and a water area of 0.009 square miles. Located at 44.72° N. Lat; 85.82° W. Long.
Population: 432; Growth (since 2000): n/a; Density: 826.4 persons per square mile; Race: 97.5% White, 0.5% Black/African American, 0.5% Asian, 0.2% American Indian/Alaska Native, 0.0% Native Hawaiian/Other Pacific Islander, 1.4% Two or more races, 0.9% Hispanic of any race; Average household size: 2.94; Median age: 37.0; Age under 18: 30.1%; Age 65 and over: 4.9%; Males per 100 females: 99.1
Housing: Homeownership rate: 94.6%; Homeowner vacancy rate: 2.8%; Rental vacancy rate: 0.0%

HOMESTEAD (township). Covers a land area of 30.186 square miles and a water area of 0.101 square miles. Located at 44.65° N. Lat; 85.98° W. Long.
Population: 2,357; Growth (since 2000): 13.4%; Density: 78.1 persons per square mile; Race: 95.4% White, 0.8% Black/African American, 0.1% Asian, 1.4% American Indian/Alaska Native, 0.0% Native Hawaiian/Other Pacific Islander, 2.0% Two or more races, 1.4% Hispanic of any race; Average household size: 2.58; Median age: 42.5; Age under 18: 23.1%; Age 65 and over: 14.7%; Males per 100 females: 99.6
Housing: Homeownership rate: 84.9%; Homeowner vacancy rate: 5.7%; Rental vacancy rate: 9.1%

HONOR (village). Covers a land area of 0.538 square miles and a water area of 0.016 square miles. Located at 44.67° N. Lat; 86.02° W. Long. Elevation is 643 feet.
History: Honor was founded in 1895 on the Platte River when the Guelph Patent Cask Company was established here. It was named for the daughter of the company's general manager.
Population: 328; Growth (since 2000): 9.7%; Density: 610.2 persons per square mile; Race: 93.0% White, 0.3% Black/African American, 0.3% Asian, 2.4% American Indian/Alaska Native, 0.0% Native Hawaiian/Other Pacific Islander, 4.0% Two or more races, 2.4% Hispanic of any race; Average household size: 2.43; Median age: 38.0; Age under 18: 26.5%; Age 65 and over: 20.4%; Males per 100 females: 90.7
School District(s)
Benzie County Central Schools (KG-12)
    2012-13 Enrollment: 1,616 . . . . (231) 882-9654
Housing: Homeownership rate: 70.3%; Homeowner vacancy rate: 14.3%; Rental vacancy rate: 18.4%

INLAND (township). Covers a land area of 35.772 square miles and a water area of 0.411 square miles. Located at 44.64° N. Lat; 85.87° W. Long.
Population: 2,070; Growth (since 2000): 30.4%; Density: 57.9 persons per square mile; Race: 97.1% White, 0.3% Black/African American, 0.2% Asian, 1.4% American Indian/Alaska Native, 0.0% Native Hawaiian/Other Pacific Islander, 0.7% Two or more races, 1.7% Hispanic of any race; Average household size: 2.54; Median age: 39.7; Age under 18: 26.5%; Age 65 and over: 11.4%; Males per 100 females: 102.7
Housing: Homeownership rate: 87.1%; Homeowner vacancy rate: 2.2%; Rental vacancy rate: 10.1%

JOYFIELD (township). Covers a land area of 19.920 square miles and a water area of 0.060 square miles. Located at 44.54° N. Lat; 86.09° W. Long.
Population: 799; Growth (since 2000): 2.8%; Density: 40.1 persons per square mile; Race: 95.0% White, 0.6% Black/African American, 0.3%

Asian, 1.4% American Indian/Alaska Native, 0.0% Native Hawaiian/Other Pacific Islander, 2.4% Two or more races, 0.6% Hispanic of any race; Average household size: 2.55; Median age: 45.0; Age under 18: 22.7%; Age 65 and over: 18.4%; Males per 100 females: 100.8
Housing: Homeownership rate: 89.8%; Homeowner vacancy rate: 2.4%; Rental vacancy rate: 3.0%

LAKE (township). Covers a land area of 23.390 square miles and a water area of 11.733 square miles. Located at 44.71° N. Lat; 86.14° W. Long.
Population: 759; Growth (since 2000): 19.5%; Density: 32.4 persons per square mile; Race: 97.9% White, 0.0% Black/African American, 0.1% Asian, 1.3% American Indian/Alaska Native, 0.0% Native Hawaiian/Other Pacific Islander, 0.1% Two or more races, 1.1% Hispanic of any race; Average household size: 1.96; Median age: 64.3; Age under 18: 7.6%; Age 65 and over: 48.5%; Males per 100 females: 95.1
Housing: Homeownership rate: 93.8%; Homeowner vacancy rate: 3.9%; Rental vacancy rate: 57.6%

LAKE ANN (village). Covers a land area of 0.449 square miles and a water area of 0.031 square miles. Located at 44.73° N. Lat; 85.84° W. Long. Elevation is 827 feet.
History: Both the lake and the village of Lake Ann were named for the wife of A.P. Wheelock, the first settler here in 1862.
Population: 268; Growth (since 2000): -2.9%; Density: 596.8 persons per square mile; Race: 95.1% White, 0.4% Black/African American, 0.0% Asian, 1.5% American Indian/Alaska Native, 0.0% Native Hawaiian/Other Pacific Islander, 2.6% Two or more races, 0.4% Hispanic of any race; Average household size: 2.27; Median age: 48.2; Age under 18: 16.8%; Age 65 and over: 18.7%; Males per 100 females: 92.8
Housing: Homeownership rate: 75.4%; Homeowner vacancy rate: 0.0%; Rental vacancy rate: 16.7%

MAPLE GROVE (CDP). Covers a land area of 0.348 square miles and a water area of 0 square miles. Located at 44.71° N. Lat; 85.85° W. Long.
Population: 132; Growth (since 2000): n/a; Density: 379.2 persons per square mile; Race: 100.0% White, 0.0% Black/African American, 0.0% Asian, 0.0% American Indian/Alaska Native, 0.0% Native Hawaiian/Other Pacific Islander, 0.0% Two or more races, 2.3% Hispanic of any race; Average household size: 2.36; Median age: 42.4; Age under 18: 22.0%; Age 65 and over: 22.0%; Males per 100 females: 100.0
Housing: Homeownership rate: 87.5%; Homeowner vacancy rate: 3.9%; Rental vacancy rate: 12.5%

NESSEN CITY (CDP). Covers a land area of 1.214 square miles and a water area of <.001 square miles. Located at 44.52° N. Lat; 85.87° W. Long. Elevation is 856 feet.
Population: 97; Growth (since 2000): n/a; Density: 79.9 persons per square mile; Race: 94.8% White, 0.0% Black/African American, 0.0% Asian, 4.1% American Indian/Alaska Native, 0.0% Native Hawaiian/Other Pacific Islander, 1.0% Two or more races, 2.1% Hispanic of any race; Average household size: 2.62; Median age: 38.9; Age under 18: 20.6%; Age 65 and over: 16.5%; Males per 100 females: 110.9
Housing: Homeownership rate: 86.5%; Homeowner vacancy rate: 5.9%; Rental vacancy rate: 0.0%

PILGRIM (CDP). Covers a land area of 0.349 square miles and a water area of 0 square miles. Located at 44.66° N. Lat; 86.25° W. Long. Elevation is 617 feet.
Population: 11; Growth (since 2000): n/a; Density: 31.5 persons per square mile; Race: 100.0% White, 0.0% Black/African American, 0.0% Asian, 0.0% American Indian/Alaska Native, 0.0% Native Hawaiian/Other Pacific Islander, 0.0% Two or more races, 0.0% Hispanic of any race; Average household size: 1.57; Median age: 71.5; Age under 18: 0.0%; Age 65 and over: 54.5%; Males per 100 females: 175.0
Housing: Homeownership rate: 85.7%; Homeowner vacancy rate: 14.3%; Rental vacancy rate: 0.0%

PLATTE (township). Covers a land area of 36.300 square miles and a water area of 0.182 square miles. Located at 44.74° N. Lat; 85.99° W. Long.
Population: 354; Growth (since 2000): 3.5%; Density: 9.8 persons per square mile; Race: 96.9% White, 0.0% Black/African American, 0.6% Asian, 2.5% American Indian/Alaska Native, 0.0% Native Hawaiian/Other

Pacific Islander, 0.0% Two or more races, 0.0% Hispanic of any race; Average household size: 2.15; Median age: 51.4; Age under 18: 13.8%; Age 65 and over: 22.3%; Males per 100 females: 103.4
Housing: Homeownership rate: 89.1%; Homeowner vacancy rate: 1.3%; Rental vacancy rate: 14.3%

THOMPSONVILLE (village). Covers a land area of 0.996 square miles and a water area of <.001 square miles. Located at 44.52° N. Lat; 85.94° W. Long. Elevation is 794 feet.
Population: 441; Growth (since 2000): -3.5%; Density: 442.9 persons per square mile; Race: 94.8% White, 0.2% Black/African American, 0.2% Asian, 2.5% American Indian/Alaska Native, 0.0% Native Hawaiian/Other Pacific Islander, 2.0% Two or more races, 1.4% Hispanic of any race; Average household size: 2.41; Median age: 38.5; Age under 18: 23.1%; Age 65 and over: 15.6%; Males per 100 females: 99.5
School District(s)
Benzie County Central Schools (KG-12)
    2012-13 Enrollment: 1,616 . . . . (231) 882-9654
Housing: Homeownership rate: 78.7%; Homeowner vacancy rate: 8.0%; Rental vacancy rate: 15.2%

WELDON (township). Covers a land area of 36.430 square miles and a water area of 0.201 square miles. Located at 44.56° N. Lat; 86.00° W. Long. Elevation is 837 feet.
Population: 542; Growth (since 2000): 2.3%; Density: 14.9 persons per square mile; Race: 96.1% White, 0.2% Black/African American, 0.2% Asian, 0.9% American Indian/Alaska Native, 0.0% Native Hawaiian/Other Pacific Islander, 1.7% Two or more races, 1.8% Hispanic of any race; Average household size: 2.29; Median age: 46.6; Age under 18: 20.3%; Age 65 and over: 20.7%; Males per 100 females: 100.0
Housing: Homeownership rate: 84.4%; Homeowner vacancy rate: 7.7%; Rental vacancy rate: 38.3%

Berrien County

Located in southwestern Michigan; bounded on the south by Indiana, and on the west by Lake Michigan. Covers a land area of 567.747 square miles, a water area of 1,013.725 square miles, and is located in the Eastern Time Zone at 41.79° N. Lat., 86.74° W. Long. The county was founded in 1829. County seat is Saint Joseph.

Berrien County is part of the Niles-Benton Harbor, MI Metropolitan Statistical Area. The entire metro area includes: Berrien County, MI

Weather Station: Benton Harbor Ross Field   Elevation: 627 feet

	Jan	Feb	Mar	Apr	May	Jun	Jul	Aug	Sep	Oct	Nov	Dec
High	33	36	46	59	70	79	83	82	75	63	49	37
Low	19	21	27	37	46	56	61	59	52	42	33	23
Precip	2.0	1.6	2.1	3.3	3.5	3.2	3.2	4.1	4.1	3.5	3.3	2.3
Snow	29.6	20.0	7.6	0.8	tr	0.0	0.0	0.0	tr	0.4	3.5	23.8

High and Low temperatures in degrees Fahrenheit; Precipitation and Snow in inches

Weather Station: Eau Claire 4 NE   Elevation: 870 feet

	Jan	Feb	Mar	Apr	May	Jun	Jul	Aug	Sep	Oct	Nov	Dec
High	32	36	47	60	71	80	84	82	75	62	49	36
Low	19	21	29	39	49	59	64	62	55	44	34	23
Precip	2.2	1.8	2.3	3.2	3.4	3.3	3.7	4.4	3.6	3.7	3.3	2.6
Snow	26.2	16.5	8.5	1.7	tr	0.0	0.0	0.0	0.0	0.5	6.3	23.7

High and Low temperatures in degrees Fahrenheit; Precipitation and Snow in inches

Population: 156,813; Growth (since 2000): -3.5%; Density: 276.2 persons per square mile; Race: 78.3% White, 15.3% Black/African American, 1.6% Asian, 0.5% American Indian/Alaska Native, 0.1% Native Hawaiian/Other Pacific Islander, 2.4% two or more races, 4.5% Hispanic of any race; Average household size: 2.43; Median age: 41.0; Age under 18: 23.4%; Age 65 and over: 16.3%; Males per 100 females: 94.9; Marriage status: 29.4% never married, 51.5% now married, 1.5% separated, 7.4% widowed, 11.7% divorced; Foreign born: 5.6%; Speak English only: 92.2%; With disability: 14.4%; Veterans: 9.7%; Ancestry: 31.6% German, 11.9% Irish, 9.7% English, 5.5% American, 4.9% Polish
Religion: Six largest groups: 11.0% Catholicism, 7.3% Lutheran, 6.4% Adventist, 5.3% Baptist, 4.1% Methodist/Pietist, 2.7% Pentecostal
Economy: Unemployment rate: 5.4%; Leading industries: 16.2% retail trade; 11.2% other services (except public administration); 11.0% health care and social assistance; Farms: 1,063 totaling 156,418 acres; Company size: 3 employ 1,000 or more persons, 3 employ 500 to 999 persons, 62

employ 100 to 499 persons, 3,571 employs less than 100 persons; Business ownership: 3,973 women-owned, 1,235 Black-owned, 169 Hispanic-owned, 235 Asian-owned
Employment: 12.0% management, business, and financial, 4.7% computer, engineering, and science, 10.1% education, legal, community service, arts, and media, 5.7% healthcare practitioners, 20.1% service, 23.6% sales and office, 8.0% natural resources, construction, and maintenance, 15.7% production, transportation, and material moving
Income: Per capita: $24,013; Median household: $43,633; Average household: $59,724; Households with income of $100,000 or more: 15.0%; Poverty rate: 17.5%
Educational Attainment: High school diploma or higher: 87.4%; Bachelor's degree or higher: 24.2%; Graduate/professional degree or higher: 9.8%
Housing: Homeownership rate: 71.4%; Median home value: $129,300; Median year structure built: 1964; Homeowner vacancy rate: 3.0%; Median gross rent: $649 per month; Rental vacancy rate: 11.4%
Vital Statistics: Birth rate: 118.9 per 10,000 population; Death rate: 102.6 per 10,000 population; Age-adjusted cancer mortality rate: 183.0 deaths per 100,000 population
Health Insurance: 87.1% have insurance; 64.1% have private insurance; 37.4% have public insurance; 12.9% do not have insurance; 3.7% of children under 18 do not have insurance
Health Care: Physicians: 21.2 per 10,000 population; Hospital beds: 32.5 per 10,000 population; Hospital admissions: 1,157.6 per 10,000 population
Air Quality Index: 79.7% good, 19.5% moderate, 0.8% unhealthy for sensitive individuals, 0.0% unhealthy (percent of days)
Transportation: Commute: 91.8% car, 0.4% public transportation, 2.6% walk, 3.9% work from home; Median travel time to work: 19.8 minutes
Presidential Election: 46.4% Obama, 52.7% Romney (2012)
National and State Parks: Grand Mere State Park; Warren Dunes State Park; Warren Woods State Park
Additional Information Contacts
Berrien Government . . . . (269) 983-7111
http://www.berriencounty.org

Berrien County Communities

BAINBRIDGE (township). Covers a land area of 34.898 square miles and a water area of 0.450 square miles. Located at 42.11° N. Lat; 86.27° W. Long.
History: Bainbridge Township was surveyed in 1830 and named for the former home in New York of Jehiel Enos, who was responsible for the survey.
Population: 2,850; Growth (since 2000): -9.0%; Density: 81.7 persons per square mile; Race: 91.5% White, 0.7% Black/African American, 0.4% Asian, 0.6% American Indian/Alaska Native, 0.0% Native Hawaiian/Other Pacific Islander, 2.0% Two or more races, 8.2% Hispanic of any race; Average household size: 2.47; Median age: 45.0; Age under 18: 21.4%; Age 65 and over: 18.5%; Males per 100 females: 105.8; Marriage status: 24.1% never married, 62.7% now married, 0.9% separated, 3.9% widowed, 9.2% divorced; Foreign born: 6.9%; Speak English only: 85.9%; With disability: 13.8%; Veterans: 8.2%; Ancestry: 41.0% German, 11.5% English, 10.2% Irish, 9.6% American, 5.7% Dutch
Employment: 13.2% management, business, and financial, 5.2% computer, engineering, and science, 4.8% education, legal, community service, arts, and media, 7.7% healthcare practitioners, 11.3% service, 19.9% sales and office, 19.2% natural resources, construction, and maintenance, 18.6% production, transportation, and material moving
Income: Per capita: $23,778; Median household: $59,074; Average household: $71,303; Households with income of $100,000 or more: 16.1%; Poverty rate: 14.8%
Educational Attainment: High school diploma or higher: 85.5%; Bachelor's degree or higher: 15.7%; Graduate/professional degree or higher: 6.0%
Housing: Homeownership rate: 85.5%; Median home value: $140,600; Median year structure built: 1970; Homeowner vacancy rate: 1.1%; Median gross rent: $878 per month; Rental vacancy rate: 5.1%
Health Insurance: 86.2% have insurance; 59.2% have private insurance; 40.0% have public insurance; 13.8% do not have insurance; 2.3% of children under 18 do not have insurance
Transportation: Commute: 92.0% car, 0.0% public transportation, 2.1% walk, 5.9% work from home; Median travel time to work: 22.1 minutes

BARODA (township). Covers a land area of 17.766 square miles and a water area of 0.064 square miles. Located at 41.94° N. Lat; 86.48° W. Long. Elevation is 633 feet.
Population: 2,801; Growth (since 2000): -2.7%; Density: 157.7 persons per square mile; Race: 95.0% White, 0.9% Black/African American, 0.4% Asian, 0.4% American Indian/Alaska Native, 0.0% Native Hawaiian/Other Pacific Islander, 1.7% Two or more races, 4.5% Hispanic of any race; Average household size: 2.50; Median age: 41.8; Age under 18: 23.5%; Age 65 and over: 15.3%; Males per 100 females: 102.8; Marriage status: 25.6% never married, 53.9% now married, 1.1% separated, 7.4% widowed, 13.1% divorced; Foreign born: 4.3%; Speak English only: 93.7%; With disability: 11.5%; Veterans: 12.0%; Ancestry: 49.5% German, 11.8% English, 9.8% Irish, 8.0% American, 5.3% Italian
Employment: 13.9% management, business, and financial, 3.8% computer, engineering, and science, 7.7% education, legal, community service, arts, and media, 4.4% healthcare practitioners, 19.2% service, 27.4% sales and office, 14.1% natural resources, construction, and maintenance, 9.5% production, transportation, and material moving
Income: Per capita: $24,710; Median household: $49,904; Average household: $60,015; Households with income of $100,000 or more: 17.4%; Poverty rate: 9.9%
Educational Attainment: High school diploma or higher: 90.3%; Bachelor's degree or higher: 19.2%; Graduate/professional degree or higher: 4.8%
Housing: Homeownership rate: 82.3%; Median home value: $115,100; Median year structure built: 1973; Homeowner vacancy rate: 2.3%; Median gross rent: $703 per month; Rental vacancy rate: 9.4%
Health Insurance: 88.0% have insurance; 76.2% have private insurance; 29.5% have public insurance; 12.0% do not have insurance; 3.6% of children under 18 do not have insurance
Transportation: Commute: 95.8% car, 0.4% public transportation, 0.5% walk, 2.4% work from home; Median travel time to work: 24.6 minutes

BARODA (village). Covers a land area of 0.718 square miles and a water area of <.001 square miles. Located at 41.95° N. Lat; 86.49° W. Long. Elevation is 633 feet.
History: Baroda was named for a city in India. It was incorporated as a village in 1907.
Population: 873; Growth (since 2000): 1.7%; Density: 1,216.1 persons per square mile; Race: 95.6% White, 0.5% Black/African American, 0.1% Asian, 0.5% American Indian/Alaska Native, 0.1% Native Hawaiian/Other Pacific Islander, 2.1% Two or more races, 2.5% Hispanic of any race; Average household size: 2.29; Median age: 37.8; Age under 18: 24.1%; Age 65 and over: 14.0%; Males per 100 females: 95.3
Housing: Homeownership rate: 74.2%; Homeowner vacancy rate: 1.4%; Rental vacancy rate: 7.5%

BENTON (charter township). Covers a land area of 32.370 square miles and a water area of 0.446 square miles. Located at 42.11° N. Lat; 86.40° W. Long.
Population: 14,749; Growth (since 2000): -10.1%; Density: 455.6 persons per square mile; Race: 42.0% White, 51.7% Black/African American, 0.4% Asian, 0.5% American Indian/Alaska Native, 0.0% Native Hawaiian/Other Pacific Islander, 2.5% Two or more races, 6.0% Hispanic of any race; Average household size: 2.46; Median age: 37.2; Age under 18: 26.9%; Age 65 and over: 14.6%; Males per 100 females: 91.0; Marriage status: 35.3% never married, 40.0% now married, 2.7% separated, 9.5% widowed, 15.2% divorced; Foreign born: 4.0%; Speak English only: 93.6%; With disability: 17.8%; Veterans: 7.7%; Ancestry: 15.2% German, 7.0% Irish, 4.8% American, 4.0% English, 3.3% Italian
Employment: 6.9% management, business, and financial, 2.3% computer, engineering, and science, 6.5% education, legal, community service, arts, and media, 2.7% healthcare practitioners, 28.3% service, 25.2% sales and office, 8.9% natural resources, construction, and maintenance, 19.1% production, transportation, and material moving
Income: Per capita: $15,928; Median household: $25,083; Average household: $37,765; Households with income of $100,000 or more: 5.3%; Poverty rate: 34.2%
Educational Attainment: High school diploma or higher: 75.7%; Bachelor's degree or higher: 10.8%; Graduate/professional degree or higher: 4.2%
Housing: Homeownership rate: 56.2%; Median home value: $80,400; Median year structure built: 1962; Homeowner vacancy rate: 2.7%; Median gross rent: $557 per month; Rental vacancy rate: 10.8%

Health Insurance: 82.1% have insurance; 41.7% have private insurance; 52.3% have public insurance; 17.9% do not have insurance; 8.2% of children under 18 do not have insurance

Safety: Violent crime rate: 107.7 per 10,000 population; Property crime rate: 825.9 per 10,000 population

Transportation: Commute: 92.7% car, 1.2% public transportation, 0.4% walk, 3.6% work from home; Median travel time to work: 17.2 minutes

Additional Information Contacts
Benton Charter Township . . . . (269) 925-0616
  http://bentonchartertwp.org

BENTON HARBOR (city). Covers a land area of 4.427 square miles and a water area of 0.254 square miles. Located at 42.11° N. Lat; 86.45° W. Long. Elevation is 594 feet.

History: Benton Harbor was founded slightly after its neighboring city, St. Joseph, by settlers who preferred the less expensive, marshier land on the other side of the river. The fruit orchards that surrounded the early town were said to be started by Johnny Appleseed, but many pioneers brought young fruit trees with them from New York that contributed to southwestern Michigan's fruit industry. Benton Harbor grew larger than its earlier neighbor. In 1903 it attracted Benjamin Franklin Purnell, known as King Ben, who established a colony of the Israelite House of David here.

Population: 10,038; Growth (since 2000): -10.2%; Density: 2,267.5 persons per square mile; Race: 7.0% White, 89.2% Black/African American, 0.1% Asian, 0.3% American Indian/Alaska Native, 0.0% Native Hawaiian/Other Pacific Islander, 2.6% Two or more races, 2.2% Hispanic of any race; Average household size: 2.77; Median age: 28.3; Age under 18: 35.1%; Age 65 and over: 7.7%; Males per 100 females: 86.9; Marriage status: 57.6% never married, 21.6% now married, 3.9% separated, 6.9% widowed, 13.9% divorced; Foreign born: 0.6%; Speak English only: 97.7%; With disability: 21.3%; Veterans: 4.6%; Ancestry: 4.8% German, 2.0% American, 1.9% English, 0.9% Irish, 0.9% Dutch

Employment: 4.8% management, business, and financial, 1.5% computer, engineering, and science, 6.7% education, legal, community service, arts, and media, 4.2% healthcare practitioners, 33.7% service, 26.7% sales and office, 4.1% natural resources, construction, and maintenance, 18.3% production, transportation, and material moving

Income: Per capita: $10,083; Median household: $18,208; Average household: $25,566; Households with income of $100,000 or more: 1.4%; Poverty rate: 48.4%

Educational Attainment: High school diploma or higher: 71.8%; Bachelor's degree or higher: 4.8%; Graduate/professional degree or higher: 3.0%

School District(s)
Benton Harbor Area Schools (PK-12)
  2012-13 Enrollment: 2,770 . . . . (269) 605-1000
Benton Harbor Charter School (PK-12)
  2012-13 Enrollment: 388 . . . . (269) 925-3807
Coloma Community Schools (PK-12)
  2012-13 Enrollment: 1,739 . . . . (269) 468-2424
Countryside Academy (KG-12)
  2012-13 Enrollment: 568 . . . . (269) 944-3319
Dowagiac Union SD (PK-12)
  2012-13 Enrollment: 2,297 . . . . (269) 782-4402
Dream Academy (KG-12)
  2012-13 Enrollment: 253 . . . . (269) 926-1587
Hagar Township S/d #6 (KG-12)
  2012-13 Enrollment: 62 . . . . (269) 849-1343
Mildred C. Wells Preparatory Academy (KG-12)
  2012-13 Enrollment: 155 . . . . (269) 926-2885
Two-year College(s)
Lake Michigan College (Public)
  Fall 2013 Enrollment: 4,230 . . . . (269) 927-8100
  2013-14 Tuition: In-state $5,355; Out-of-state $6,705

Housing: Homeownership rate: 33.5%; Median home value: $49,800; Median year structure built: 1944; Homeowner vacancy rate: 3.1%; Median gross rent: $566 per month; Rental vacancy rate: 8.5%

Health Insurance: 83.6% have insurance; 26.3% have private insurance; 63.3% have public insurance; 16.4% do not have insurance; 1.9% of children under 18 do not have insurance

Safety: Violent crime rate: 224.1 per 10,000 population; Property crime rate: 703.3 per 10,000 population

Transportation: Commute: 92.1% car, 1.4% public transportation, 2.0% walk, 1.9% work from home; Median travel time to work: 13.6 minutes

Airports: Southwest Michigan Regional (general aviation)

Additional Information Contacts
City of Benton Harbor . . . . (269) 927-8400
  http://www.bentonharborcity.com

BENTON HEIGHTS (CDP). Covers a land area of 3.848 square miles and a water area of 0.002 square miles. Located at 42.12° N. Lat; 86.42° W. Long. Elevation is 633 feet.

History: Benton Heights was called Euclid Center until the name was changed by the residents in 1957.

Population: 4,084; Growth (since 2000): -25.2%; Density: 1,061.4 persons per square mile; Race: 29.2% White, 62.2% Black/African American, 0.2% Asian, 0.6% American Indian/Alaska Native, 0.0% Native Hawaiian/Other Pacific Islander, 2.8% Two or more races, 8.1% Hispanic of any race; Average household size: 2.79; Median age: 32.1; Age under 18: 31.4%; Age 65 and over: 12.3%; Males per 100 females: 92.6; Marriage status: 46.1% never married, 28.7% now married, 3.3% separated, 8.0% widowed, 17.2% divorced; Foreign born: 4.0%; Speak English only: 93.1%; With disability: 17.4%; Veterans: 3.2%; Ancestry: 11.5% German, 2.9% English, 2.1% Irish, 2.1% American, 2.0% Polish

Employment: 5.2% management, business, and financial, 0.0% computer, engineering, and science, 8.5% education, legal, community service, arts, and media, 1.9% healthcare practitioners, 42.3% service, 19.1% sales and office, 6.5% natural resources, construction, and maintenance, 16.4% production, transportation, and material moving

Income: Per capita: $8,739; Median household: $19,019; Average household: $25,829; Households with income of $100,000 or more: 0.7%; Poverty rate: 46.2%

Educational Attainment: High school diploma or higher: 67.8%; Bachelor's degree or higher: 4.8%; Graduate/professional degree or higher: 1.5%

Housing: Homeownership rate: 51.4%; Median home value: $59,800; Median year structure built: 1957; Homeowner vacancy rate: 2.0%; Median gross rent: $558 per month; Rental vacancy rate: 12.6%

Health Insurance: 80.2% have insurance; 25.6% have private insurance; 59.8% have public insurance; 19.8% do not have insurance; 3.0% of children under 18 do not have insurance

Transportation: Commute: 90.8% car, 5.1% public transportation, 1.1% walk, 0.9% work from home; Median travel time to work: 20.4 minutes

BERRIEN (township). Covers a land area of 35.066 square miles and a water area of 1.712 square miles. Located at 41.94° N. Lat; 86.29° W. Long.

History: Berrien Township was named for John M. Berrien, attorney general under President Andrew Jackson.

Population: 5,084; Growth (since 2000): 0.2%; Density: 145.0 persons per square mile; Race: 83.7% White, 6.4% Black/African American, 2.9% Asian, 0.4% American Indian/Alaska Native, 0.0% Native Hawaiian/Other Pacific Islander, 3.3% Two or more races, 8.6% Hispanic of any race; Average household size: 2.73; Median age: 43.0; Age under 18: 23.7%; Age 65 and over: 16.9%; Males per 100 females: 100.2; Marriage status: 26.2% never married, 55.7% now married, 0.5% separated, 6.0% widowed, 12.1% divorced; Foreign born: 8.6%; Speak English only: 85.0%; With disability: 15.1%; Veterans: 11.3%; Ancestry: 31.6% German, 8.1% Irish, 8.0% American, 6.6% English, 5.8% Italian

Employment: 8.7% management, business, and financial, 3.7% computer, engineering, and science, 20.4% education, legal, community service, arts, and media, 7.1% healthcare practitioners, 16.1% service, 19.6% sales and office, 13.5% natural resources, construction, and maintenance, 11.0% production, transportation, and material moving

Income: Per capita: $21,664; Median household: $57,730; Average household: $64,802; Households with income of $100,000 or more: 17.8%; Poverty rate: 16.0%

Educational Attainment: High school diploma or higher: 89.5%; Bachelor's degree or higher: 29.2%; Graduate/professional degree or higher: 15.9%

Housing: Homeownership rate: 82.7%; Median home value: $152,300; Median year structure built: 1970; Homeowner vacancy rate: 2.4%; Median gross rent: $855 per month; Rental vacancy rate: 10.7%

Health Insurance: 85.4% have insurance; 67.2% have private insurance; 31.8% have public insurance; 14.6% do not have insurance; 3.7% of children under 18 do not have insurance

Transportation: Commute: 95.0% car, 0.0% public transportation, 1.9% walk, 3.0% work from home; Median travel time to work: 24.0 minutes

BERRIEN CENTER (unincorporated postal area)
ZCTA: 49102

Covers a land area of 15.471 square miles and a water area of 0.648 square miles. Located at 41.95° N. Lat; 86.25° W. Long. Elevation is 771 feet.

Population: 1,563; Growth (since 2000): 4.7%; Density: 101.0 persons per square mile; Race: 85.4% White, 7.4% Black/African American, 2.2% Asian, 0.3% American Indian/Alaska Native, 0.0% Native Hawaiian/Other Pacific Islander, 2.6% Two or more races, 7.0% Hispanic of any race; Average household size: 2.71; Median age: 45.2; Age under 18: 23.1%; Age 65 and over: 22.5%; Males per 100 females: 103.8

School District(s)
Berrien Resa (PK-12)
    2012-13 Enrollment: 772 . . . . (269) 471-7725
Housing: Homeownership rate: 81.0%; Homeowner vacancy rate: 1.9%; Rental vacancy rate: 7.6%

BERRIEN SPRINGS (village). Covers a land area of 0.938 square miles and a water area of 0.081 square miles. Located at 41.95° N. Lat; 86.34° W. Long. Elevation is 666 feet.
History: Settlers came to Berrien Springs in 1829, to a site first called Wolf's Prairie. The village was platted in 1831, and named for John M. Berrien, attorney general under President Andrew Jackson, and for the many springs in the area.
Population: 1,800; Growth (since 2000): -3.3%; Density: 1,918.6 persons per square mile; Race: 72.7% White, 12.9% Black/African American, 5.1% Asian, 0.4% American Indian/Alaska Native, 0.4% Native Hawaiian/Other Pacific Islander, 4.7% Two or more races, 12.9% Hispanic of any race; Average household size: 2.35; Median age: 34.6; Age under 18: 22.8%; Age 65 and over: 13.7%; Males per 100 females: 92.1

School District(s)
Berrien Resa (PK-12)
    2012-13 Enrollment: 772 . . . . (269) 471-7725
Berrien Springs Public Schools (PK-12)
    2012-13 Enrollment: 2,224 . . . . (269) 471-2891

Four-year College(s)
Andrews University (Private, Not-for-profit, Seventh Day Adventists)
    Fall 2013 Enrollment: 3,516 . . . . (800) 253-2874
    2013-14 Tuition: In-state $25,470; Out-of-state $25,470
Housing: Homeownership rate: 57.0%; Homeowner vacancy rate: 2.0%; Rental vacancy rate: 10.5%
Newspapers: The Journal Era (weekly circulation 1800)

BERTRAND (township). Covers a land area of 34.435 square miles and a water area of 0.598 square miles. Located at 41.79° N. Lat; 86.37° W. Long. Elevation is 696 feet.
History: Bertrand Township was named for Joseph Bertrand, a French-Canadian who operated a trading post here in the early 1800's.
Population: 2,657; Growth (since 2000): 11.6%; Density: 77.2 persons per square mile; Race: 96.2% White, 1.0% Black/African American, 0.2% Asian, 1.2% American Indian/Alaska Native, 0.0% Native Hawaiian/Other Pacific Islander, 1.2% Two or more races, 1.4% Hispanic of any race; Average household size: 2.58; Median age: 45.9; Age under 18: 22.1%; Age 65 and over: 16.9%; Males per 100 females: 106.3; Marriage status: 20.5% never married, 65.4% now married, 0.6% separated, 4.6% widowed, 9.5% divorced; Foreign born: 0.8%; Speak English only: 97.3%; With disability: 11.2%; Veterans: 13.0%; Ancestry: 43.0% German, 14.1% Irish, 12.9% English, 8.5% Polish, 8.5% Dutch
Employment: 13.1% management, business, and financial, 3.2% computer, engineering, and science, 10.8% education, legal, community service, arts, and media, 8.3% healthcare practitioners, 13.1% service, 23.7% sales and office, 6.5% natural resources, construction, and maintenance, 21.2% production, transportation, and material moving
Income: Per capita: $30,269; Median household: $67,411; Average household: $79,680; Households with income of $100,000 or more: 29.3%; Poverty rate: 7.9%
Educational Attainment: High school diploma or higher: 94.3%; Bachelor's degree or higher: 27.3%; Graduate/professional degree or higher: 11.7%
Housing: Homeownership rate: 92.0%; Median home value: $166,800; Median year structure built: 1967; Homeowner vacancy rate: 2.2%; Median gross rent: $618 per month; Rental vacancy rate: 2.4%

Health Insurance: 89.7% have insurance; 78.9% have private insurance; 25.6% have public insurance; 10.3% do not have insurance; 5.4% of children under 18 do not have insurance
Transportation: Commute: 92.9% car, 0.0% public transportation, 2.1% walk, 2.8% work from home; Median travel time to work: 25.7 minutes

BRIDGMAN (city). Covers a land area of 2.897 square miles and a water area of 0.031 square miles. Located at 41.94° N. Lat; 86.57° W. Long. Elevation is 636 feet.
History: Bridgman grew as the location of plant nurseries, shipping plants to many locations in the United States and Canada. The village was named in 1870 for George C. Bridgman, owner of a lumber company. After uniting with nearby Charlotteville, Bridgman was incorporated as a village in 1927 and as a city in 1949.
Population: 2,291; Growth (since 2000): -5.6%; Density: 790.8 persons per square mile; Race: 95.3% White, 1.1% Black/African American, 1.0% Asian, 0.6% American Indian/Alaska Native, 0.0% Native Hawaiian/Other Pacific Islander, 1.2% Two or more races, 3.7% Hispanic of any race; Average household size: 2.30; Median age: 44.3; Age under 18: 22.1%; Age 65 and over: 20.5%; Males per 100 females: 90.4

School District(s)
Bridgman Public Schools (KG-12)
    2012-13 Enrollment: 980 . . . . (269) 466-0271
Housing: Homeownership rate: 70.4%; Homeowner vacancy rate: 3.4%; Rental vacancy rate: 12.7%
Additional Information Contacts
City of Bridgman . . . . (269) 465-5144
    http://www.bridgman.org

BUCHANAN (city). Covers a land area of 2.500 square miles and a water area of 0.073 square miles. Located at 41.83° N. Lat; 86.37° W. Long. Elevation is 692 feet.
History: Buchanan was once known as McCoy's Creek, settled by John Hatfield and Russell McCoy in 1834. It was later named for James Buchanan, who became the 15th U.S. president.
Population: 4,456; Growth (since 2000): -4.8%; Density: 1,782.1 persons per square mile; Race: 86.6% White, 7.5% Black/African American, 0.3% Asian, 1.2% American Indian/Alaska Native, 0.0% Native Hawaiian/Other Pacific Islander, 3.1% Two or more races, 3.3% Hispanic of any race; Average household size: 2.34; Median age: 37.6; Age under 18: 24.6%; Age 65 and over: 14.3%; Males per 100 females: 92.7; Marriage status: 27.0% never married, 49.0% now married, 3.7% separated, 10.5% widowed, 13.4% divorced; Foreign born: 4.1%; Speak English only: 91.4%; With disability: 17.3%; Veterans: 7.5%; Ancestry: 38.4% German, 22.5% English, 10.1% Irish, 6.4% American, 6.1% Polish
Employment: 5.0% management, business, and financial, 4.0% computer, engineering, and science, 10.3% education, legal, community service, arts, and media, 3.5% healthcare practitioners, 24.2% service, 27.6% sales and office, 5.8% natural resources, construction, and maintenance, 19.7% production, transportation, and material moving
Income: Per capita: $20,387; Median household: $36,051; Average household: $44,672; Households with income of $100,000 or more: 5.3%; Poverty rate: 16.8%
Educational Attainment: High school diploma or higher: 86.1%; Bachelor's degree or higher: 15.2%; Graduate/professional degree or higher: 6.5%

School District(s)
Buchanan Community Schools (PK-12)
    2012-13 Enrollment: 1,607 . . . . (269) 695-8401
Housing: Homeownership rate: 58.6%; Median home value: $97,800; Median year structure built: 1949; Homeowner vacancy rate: 2.8%; Median gross rent: $535 per month; Rental vacancy rate: 11.3%
Health Insurance: 87.3% have insurance; 64.5% have private insurance; 37.6% have public insurance; 12.7% do not have insurance; 3.8% of children under 18 do not have insurance
Newspapers: Berrien County Record (weekly circulation 2400)
Transportation: Commute: 97.1% car, 0.0% public transportation, 0.0% walk, 2.2% work from home; Median travel time to work: 22.8 minutes
Additional Information Contacts
City of Buchanan . . . . (269) 695-3844
    http://cityofbuchanan.com

BUCHANAN (township). Covers a land area of 32.136 square miles and a water area of 1.033 square miles. Located at 41.85° N. Lat; 86.39° W. Long. Elevation is 692 feet.

History: Buchanan Township was named for President James Buchanan.

Population: 3,523; Growth (since 2000): 0.4%; Density: 109.6 persons per square mile; Race: 94.9% White, 1.9% Black/African American, 0.3% Asian, 0.8% American Indian/Alaska Native, 0.0% Native Hawaiian/Other Pacific Islander, 1.8% Two or more races, 1.7% Hispanic of any race; Average household size: 2.63; Median age: 42.4; Age under 18: 24.4%; Age 65 and over: 16.0%; Males per 100 females: 100.4; Marriage status: 19.9% never married, 67.2% now married, 1.1% separated, 3.7% widowed, 9.2% divorced; Foreign born: 0.7%; Speak English only: 98.9%; With disability: 13.6%; Veterans: 10.2%; Ancestry: 40.2% German, 14.0% Irish, 12.2% English, 10.2% American, 6.6% Dutch

Employment: 8.9% management, business, and financial, 8.2% computer, engineering, and science, 12.5% education, legal, community service, arts, and media, 2.7% healthcare practitioners, 11.0% service, 27.4% sales and office, 12.0% natural resources, construction, and maintenance, 17.4% production, transportation, and material moving

Income: Per capita: $22,816; Median household: $62,125; Average household: $63,470; Households with income of $100,000 or more: 15.7%; Poverty rate: 13.1%

Educational Attainment: High school diploma or higher: 90.4%; Bachelor's degree or higher: 17.9%; Graduate/professional degree or higher: 3.9%

School District(s)
Buchanan Community Schools (PK-12)
    2012-13 Enrollment: 1,607 . . . . (269) 695-8401

Housing: Homeownership rate: 90.3%; Median home value: $118,200; Median year structure built: 1969; Homeowner vacancy rate: 2.7%; Median gross rent: $744 per month; Rental vacancy rate: 14.0%

Health Insurance: 82.7% have insurance; 65.2% have private insurance; 31.8% have public insurance; 17.3% do not have insurance; 3.8% of children under 18 do not have insurance

Newspapers: Berrien County Record (weekly circulation 2400)

Transportation: Commute: 95.2% car, 0.0% public transportation, 0.0% walk, 3.3% work from home; Median travel time to work: 23.5 minutes

CHIKAMING (township). Covers a land area of 21.937 square miles and a water area of 0.183 square miles. Located at 41.85° N. Lat; 86.62° W. Long.

History: Chickaming Township was organized in 1856. The name is of Indian origin meaning "lake."

Population: 3,100; Growth (since 2000): -15.7%; Density: 141.3 persons per square mile; Race: 95.1% White, 2.1% Black/African American, 0.7% Asian, 0.5% American Indian/Alaska Native, 0.0% Native Hawaiian/Other Pacific Islander, 1.4% Two or more races, 1.9% Hispanic of any race; Average household size: 2.11; Median age: 53.9; Age under 18: 14.0%; Age 65 and over: 27.8%; Males per 100 females: 96.6; Marriage status: 19.2% never married, 63.2% now married, 0.2% separated, 5.5% widowed, 12.1% divorced; Foreign born: 3.1%; Speak English only: 96.9%; With disability: 14.5%; Veterans: 11.8%; Ancestry: 42.1% German, 16.3% English, 14.6% Irish, 12.8% Swedish, 5.3% Polish

Employment: 11.6% management, business, and financial, 3.7% computer, engineering, and science, 7.6% education, legal, community service, arts, and media, 3.8% healthcare practitioners, 27.7% service, 30.4% sales and office, 7.2% natural resources, construction, and maintenance, 8.0% production, transportation, and material moving

Income: Per capita: $33,643; Median household: $47,398; Average household: $68,158; Households with income of $100,000 or more: 17.7%; Poverty rate: 4.9%

Educational Attainment: High school diploma or higher: 95.7%; Bachelor's degree or higher: 38.6%; Graduate/professional degree or higher: 18.2%

Housing: Homeownership rate: 87.9%; Median home value: $187,300; Median year structure built: 1963; Homeowner vacancy rate: 5.8%; Median gross rent: $960 per month; Rental vacancy rate: 21.2%

Health Insurance: 89.6% have insurance; 70.3% have private insurance; 48.9% have public insurance; 10.4% do not have insurance; 0.0% of children under 18 do not have insurance

Safety: Violent crime rate: 9.7 per 10,000 population; Property crime rate: 210.5 per 10,000 population

Transportation: Commute: 92.2% car, 1.2% public transportation, 0.0% walk, 6.7% work from home; Median travel time to work: 25.9 minutes

COLOMA (charter township). Covers a land area of 17.969 square miles and a water area of 1.111 square miles. Located at 42.21° N. Lat; 86.31° W. Long. Elevation is 663 feet.

Population: 5,020; Growth (since 2000): -3.8%; Density: 279.4 persons per square mile; Race: 93.6% White, 1.2% Black/African American, 0.5% Asian, 0.6% American Indian/Alaska Native, 0.1% Native Hawaiian/Other Pacific Islander, 1.8% Two or more races, 4.2% Hispanic of any race; Average household size: 2.43; Median age: 43.2; Age under 18: 22.2%; Age 65 and over: 16.9%; Males per 100 females: 97.6; Marriage status: 31.5% never married, 52.5% now married, 0.8% separated, 7.4% widowed, 8.5% divorced; Foreign born: 3.0%; Speak English only: 96.7%; With disability: 14.1%; Veterans: 16.7%; Ancestry: 37.5% German, 14.5% Irish, 10.0% English, 7.1% American, 6.7% Dutch

Employment: 13.2% management, business, and financial, 3.6% computer, engineering, and science, 5.7% education, legal, community service, arts, and media, 5.6% healthcare practitioners, 25.0% service, 21.3% sales and office, 6.0% natural resources, construction, and maintenance, 19.6% production, transportation, and material moving

Income: Per capita: $26,496; Median household: $46,397; Average household: $62,201; Households with income of $100,000 or more: 17.7%; Poverty rate: 11.0%

Educational Attainment: High school diploma or higher: 86.4%; Bachelor's degree or higher: 19.6%; Graduate/professional degree or higher: 4.8%

School District(s)
Coloma Community Schools (PK-12)
    2012-13 Enrollment: 1,739 . . . . (269) 468-2424

Housing: Homeownership rate: 81.6%; Median home value: $133,400; Median year structure built: 1968; Homeowner vacancy rate: 3.4%; Median gross rent: $627 per month; Rental vacancy rate: 13.7%

Health Insurance: 87.0% have insurance; 75.8% have private insurance; 28.7% have public insurance; 13.0% do not have insurance; 7.4% of children under 18 do not have insurance

Transportation: Commute: 97.8% car, 0.4% public transportation, 0.0% walk, 1.2% work from home; Median travel time to work: 23.8 minutes

COLOMA (city). Covers a land area of 0.887 square miles and a water area of 0.002 square miles. Located at 42.19° N. Lat; 86.31° W. Long. Elevation is 663 feet.

History: Coloma was settled by Stephen R. Gilson, who platted the village in 1855 and named it for the town in California where he had once lived. Coloma developed as a canning center. Incorporated as village 1893, as city 1942.

Population: 1,483; Growth (since 2000): -7.0%; Density: 1,672.8 persons per square mile; Race: 93.5% White, 1.2% Black/African American, 1.1% Asian, 0.5% American Indian/Alaska Native, 0.0% Native Hawaiian/Other Pacific Islander, 2.1% Two or more races, 3.9% Hispanic of any race; Average household size: 2.44; Median age: 38.6; Age under 18: 24.6%; Age 65 and over: 14.5%; Males per 100 females: 95.6

School District(s)
Coloma Community Schools (PK-12)
    2012-13 Enrollment: 1,739 . . . . (269) 468-2424

Housing: Homeownership rate: 72.7%; Homeowner vacancy rate: 1.6%; Rental vacancy rate: 8.8%

EAU CLAIRE (village). Covers a land area of 0.743 square miles and a water area of 0.002 square miles. Located at 41.98° N. Lat; 86.30° W. Long. Elevation is 712 feet.

Population: 625; Growth (since 2000): -4.7%; Density: 841.5 persons per square mile; Race: 82.6% White, 5.1% Black/African American, 0.0% Asian, 1.4% American Indian/Alaska Native, 0.0% Native Hawaiian/Other Pacific Islander, 3.7% Two or more races, 13.9% Hispanic of any race; Average household size: 2.92; Median age: 31.2; Age under 18: 30.7%; Age 65 and over: 9.0%; Males per 100 females: 93.5

School District(s)
Eau Claire Public Schools (PK-12)
    2012-13 Enrollment: 866 . . . . (269) 461-6947

Housing: Homeownership rate: 67.8%; Homeowner vacancy rate: 3.3%; Rental vacancy rate: 5.5%

Safety: Violent crime rate: 0.0 per 10,000 population; Property crime rate: 112.2 per 10,000 population

FAIR PLAIN (CDP).
Covers a land area of 4.210 square miles and a water area of 0.232 square miles. Located at 42.08° N. Lat; 86.45° W. Long. Elevation is 623 feet.

Population: 7,631; Growth (since 2000): -2.5%; Density: 1,812.8 persons per square mile; Race: 43.5% White, 51.7% Black/African American, 0.8% Asian, 0.4% American Indian/Alaska Native, 0.0% Native Hawaiian/Other Pacific Islander, 2.6% Two or more races, 3.3% Hispanic of any race; Average household size: 2.39; Median age: 40.0; Age under 18: 23.6%; Age 65 and over: 14.2%; Males per 100 females: 91.8; Marriage status: 29.1% never married, 51.2% now married, 2.4% separated, 6.5% widowed, 13.2% divorced; Foreign born: 1.4%; Speak English only: 98.4%; With disability: 13.8%; Veterans: 8.8%; Ancestry: 20.8% German, 10.9% Irish, 4.3% Italian, 4.2% English, 4.2% American

Employment: 6.9% management, business, and financial, 4.6% computer, engineering, and science, 11.1% education, legal, community service, arts, and media, 3.0% healthcare practitioners, 24.3% service, 24.9% sales and office, 3.3% natural resources, construction, and maintenance, 21.8% production, transportation, and material moving

Income: Per capita: $20,617; Median household: $34,329; Average household: $47,531; Households with income of $100,000 or more: 5.9%; Poverty rate: 22.2%

Educational Attainment: High school diploma or higher: 87.5%; Bachelor's degree or higher: 19.2%; Graduate/professional degree or higher: 7.0%

Housing: Homeownership rate: 66.6%; Median home value: $93,200; Median year structure built: 1957; Homeowner vacancy rate: 3.1%; Median gross rent: $617 per month; Rental vacancy rate: 10.3%

Health Insurance: 87.4% have insurance; 57.0% have private insurance; 43.4% have public insurance; 12.6% do not have insurance; 5.5% of children under 18 do not have insurance

Transportation: Commute: 91.4% car, 0.0% public transportation, 0.4% walk, 6.8% work from home; Median travel time to work: 15.6 minutes

GALIEN (township).
Covers a land area of 21.976 square miles and a water area of 0.078 square miles. Located at 41.79° N. Lat; 86.51° W. Long. Elevation is 676 feet.

Population: 1,452; Growth (since 2000): -9.9%; Density: 66.1 persons per square mile; Race: 97.1% White, 0.6% Black/African American, 0.2% Asian, 0.6% American Indian/Alaska Native, 0.0% Native Hawaiian/Other Pacific Islander, 1.4% Two or more races, 1.2% Hispanic of any race; Average household size: 2.41; Median age: 44.9; Age under 18: 20.4%; Age 65 and over: 18.2%; Males per 100 females: 103.4

School District(s)

Galien Township SD (PK-12)
    2012-13 Enrollment: n/a . . . . (269) 471-7725

Housing: Homeownership rate: 83.1%; Homeowner vacancy rate: 2.7%; Rental vacancy rate: 6.3%

GALIEN (village).
Covers a land area of 0.415 square miles and a water area of 0 square miles. Located at 41.80° N. Lat; 86.50° W. Long. Elevation is 676 feet.

History: Galien was settled in 1854 when George A. Blakeslee bought the mill here and built a store, which also served as the post office with Blakeslee as postmaster. The village was named for the nearby river, which had been named for Rene Brehant de Galinee, a priest who mapped the area in the 1670's.

Population: 549; Growth (since 2000): -7.4%; Density: 1,322.8 persons per square mile; Race: 96.4% White, 1.1% Black/African American, 0.2% Asian, 0.9% American Indian/Alaska Native, 0.0% Native Hawaiian/Other Pacific Islander, 1.3% Two or more races, 1.8% Hispanic of any race; Average household size: 2.42; Median age: 37.6; Age under 18: 24.0%; Age 65 and over: 15.7%; Males per 100 females: 101.1

School District(s)

Galien Township SD (PK-12)
    2012-13 Enrollment: n/a . . . . (269) 471-7725

Housing: Homeownership rate: 72.7%; Homeowner vacancy rate: 5.1%; Rental vacancy rate: 8.7%

GRAND BEACH (village).
Covers a land area of 0.908 square miles and a water area of 0 square miles. Located at 41.77° N. Lat; 86.79° W. Long. Elevation is 620 feet.

History: Grand Beach developed as a resort on Lake Michigan. It was incorporated as a village in 1934.

Population: 272; Growth (since 2000): 23.1%; Density: 299.7 persons per square mile; Race: 100.0% White, 0.0% Black/African American, 0.0%

Asian, 0.0% American Indian/Alaska Native, 0.0% Native Hawaiian/Other Pacific Islander, 0.0% Two or more races, 1.8% Hispanic of any race; Average household size: 2.05; Median age: 60.2; Age under 18: 15.8%; Age 65 and over: 35.7%; Males per 100 females: 92.9

Housing: Homeownership rate: 94.8%; Homeowner vacancy rate: 5.3%; Rental vacancy rate: 36.4%

Safety: Violent crime rate: 0.0 per 10,000 population; Property crime rate: 73.8 per 10,000 population

Additional Information Contacts

Village of Grand Beach . . . . (269) 469-3141
    http://www.grandbeach.org

HAGAR (township).
Covers a land area of 18.362 square miles and a water area of 0.328 square miles. Located at 42.19° N. Lat; 86.37° W. Long.

History: Hagar Township was named for William S. Hagar, whose son-in-law had been instrumental in the organizing of the township.

Population: 3,671; Growth (since 2000): -7.4%; Density: 199.9 persons per square mile; Race: 91.4% White, 3.7% Black/African American, 0.4% Asian, 0.7% American Indian/Alaska Native, 0.0% Native Hawaiian/Other Pacific Islander, 2.0% Two or more races, 3.5% Hispanic of any race; Average household size: 2.37; Median age: 44.4; Age under 18: 20.8%; Age 65 and over: 15.7%; Males per 100 females: 99.0; Marriage status: 26.4% never married, 55.8% now married, 1.5% separated, 6.5% widowed, 11.3% divorced; Foreign born: 1.6%; Speak English only: 94.5%; With disability: 20.3%; Veterans: 10.2%; Ancestry: 31.6% German, 16.2% Irish, 15.6% English, 6.6% Polish, 6.3% Italian

Employment: 12.7% management, business, and financial, 4.6% computer, engineering, and science, 6.4% education, legal, community service, arts, and media, 5.2% healthcare practitioners, 15.4% service, 27.3% sales and office, 12.7% natural resources, construction, and maintenance, 15.7% production, transportation, and material moving

Income: Per capita: $23,303; Median household: $43,705; Average household: $55,909; Households with income of $100,000 or more: 13.9%; Poverty rate: 15.5%

Educational Attainment: High school diploma or higher: 90.0%; Bachelor's degree or higher: 15.0%; Graduate/professional degree or higher: 6.1%

Housing: Homeownership rate: 73.8%; Median home value: $139,600; Median year structure built: 1964; Homeowner vacancy rate: 3.0%; Median gross rent: $714 per month; Rental vacancy rate: 18.1%

Health Insurance: 84.8% have insurance; 63.6% have private insurance; 36.6% have public insurance; 15.2% do not have insurance; 2.7% of children under 18 do not have insurance

Transportation: Commute: 95.7% car, 0.4% public transportation, 0.9% walk, 2.4% work from home; Median travel time to work: 21.6 minutes

LAKE (charter township).
Covers a land area of 18.625 square miles and a water area of 0.038 square miles. Located at 41.92° N. Lat; 86.54° W. Long.

Population: 2,972; Growth (since 2000): -5.6%; Density: 159.6 persons per square mile; Race: 96.4% White, 0.4% Black/African American, 0.9% Asian, 0.3% American Indian/Alaska Native, 0.0% Native Hawaiian/Other Pacific Islander, 1.3% Two or more races, 1.9% Hispanic of any race; Average household size: 2.42; Median age: 46.9; Age under 18: 20.0%; Age 65 and over: 19.1%; Males per 100 females: 102.7; Marriage status: 19.1% never married, 62.3% now married, 0.7% separated, 7.0% widowed, 11.6% divorced; Foreign born: 3.4%; Speak English only: 97.2%; With disability: 15.8%; Veterans: 16.9%; Ancestry: 46.9% German, 14.6% Irish, 6.5% American, 6.3% Polish, 5.8% Dutch

Employment: 19.5% management, business, and financial, 9.1% computer, engineering, and science, 10.1% education, legal, community service, arts, and media, 2.8% healthcare practitioners, 15.6% service, 22.5% sales and office, 7.9% natural resources, construction, and maintenance, 12.4% production, transportation, and material moving

Income: Per capita: $33,042; Median household: $57,406; Average household: $83,009; Households with income of $100,000 or more: 23.2%; Poverty rate: 7.6%

Educational Attainment: High school diploma or higher: 93.5%; Bachelor's degree or higher: 20.4%; Graduate/professional degree or higher: 5.3%

Housing: Homeownership rate: 86.1%; Median home value: $165,300; Median year structure built: 1975; Homeowner vacancy rate: 2.4%; Median gross rent: $618 per month; Rental vacancy rate: 9.2%

Health Insurance: 93.5% have insurance; 72.4% have private insurance; 32.8% have public insurance; 6.5% do not have insurance; 5.2% of children under 18 do not have insurance
Transportation: Commute: 93.9% car, 1.0% public transportation, 1.1% walk, 3.2% work from home; Median travel time to work: 18.1 minutes

LAKE MICHIGAN BEACH (CDP). Covers a land area of 3.835 square miles and a water area of 0.096 square miles. Located at 42.20° N. Lat; 86.38° W. Long. Elevation is 659 feet.
Population: 1,216; Growth (since 2000): -19.4%; Density: 317.1 persons per square mile; Race: 92.7% White, 1.4% Black/African American, 0.5% Asian, 0.7% American Indian/Alaska Native, 0.0% Native Hawaiian/Other Pacific Islander, 2.5% Two or more races, 4.3% Hispanic of any race; Average household size: 2.26; Median age: 46.8; Age under 18: 18.6%; Age 65 and over: 17.0%; Males per 100 females: 99.7
Housing: Homeownership rate: 73.5%; Homeowner vacancy rate: 4.1%; Rental vacancy rate: 29.7%

LAKESIDE (unincorporated postal area)
ZCTA: 49116
Covers a land area of 2.108 square miles and a water area of 0.961 square miles. Located at 41.85° N. Lat; 86.66° W. Long. Elevation is 643 feet.
Population: 394; Growth (since 2000): 57.6%; Density: 186.9 persons per square mile; Race: 94.9% White, 2.3% Black/African American, 0.0% Asian, 0.8% American Indian/Alaska Native, 0.0% Native Hawaiian/Other Pacific Islander, 1.8% Two or more races, 1.5% Hispanic of any race; Average household size: 2.00; Median age: 58.7; Age under 18: 9.6%; Age 65 and over: 35.0%; Males per 100 females: 92.2
Housing: Homeownership rate: 91.9%; Homeowner vacancy rate: 4.7%; Rental vacancy rate: 30.8%

LINCOLN (charter township). Covers a land area of 17.911 square miles and a water area of 0.305 square miles. Located at 42.02° N. Lat; 86.51° W. Long.
Population: 14,691; Growth (since 2000): 5.3%; Density: 820.2 persons per square mile; Race: 92.4% White, 2.2% Black/African American, 2.4% Asian, 0.3% American Indian/Alaska Native, 0.0% Native Hawaiian/Other Pacific Islander, 1.8% Two or more races, 2.8% Hispanic of any race; Average household size: 2.46; Median age: 42.3; Age under 18: 24.1%; Age 65 and over: 15.7%; Males per 100 females: 95.2; Marriage status: 20.5% never married, 64.4% now married, 1.1% separated, 6.0% widowed, 9.1% divorced; Foreign born: 7.4%; Speak English only: 91.8%; With disability: 9.4%; Veterans: 10.6%; Ancestry: 38.9% German, 13.6% Irish, 11.1% English, 8.5% Italian, 8.0% Polish
Employment: 20.0% management, business, and financial, 9.2% computer, engineering, and science, 11.1% education, legal, community service, arts, and media, 5.0% healthcare practitioners, 16.1% service, 22.5% sales and office, 5.6% natural resources, construction, and maintenance, 10.6% production, transportation, and material moving
Income: Per capita: $33,053; Median household: $65,023; Average household: $79,529; Households with income of $100,000 or more: 26.1%; Poverty rate: 5.4%
Educational Attainment: High school diploma or higher: 93.3%; Bachelor's degree or higher: 38.9%; Graduate/professional degree or higher: 14.2%
Housing: Homeownership rate: 80.0%; Median home value: $173,700; Median year structure built: 1976; Homeowner vacancy rate: 2.0%; Median gross rent: $799 per month; Rental vacancy rate: 9.8%
Health Insurance: 92.0% have insurance; 80.4% have private insurance; 26.6% have public insurance; 8.0% do not have insurance; 2.2% of children under 18 do not have insurance
Safety: Violent crime rate: 12.3 per 10,000 population; Property crime rate: 118.3 per 10,000 population
Transportation: Commute: 95.6% car, 0.1% public transportation, 0.1% walk, 3.7% work from home; Median travel time to work: 18.1 minutes
Additional Information Contacts
Lincoln Charter Township . . . . (269) 429-1589
http://www.lctberrien.org

MICHIANA (village). Covers a land area of 0.366 square miles and a water area of 0 square miles. Located at 41.76° N. Lat; 86.81° W. Long. Elevation is 607 feet.
Population: 182; Growth (since 2000): -9.0%; Density: 497.1 persons per square mile; Race: 98.4% White, 1.1% Black/African American, 0.5% Asian, 0.0% American Indian/Alaska Native, 0.0% Native Hawaiian/Other Pacific Islander, 0.0% Two or more races, 2.7% Hispanic of any race; Average household size: 1.73; Median age: 63.0; Age under 18: 4.9%; Age 65 and over: 42.3%; Males per 100 females: 97.8
Housing: Homeownership rate: 97.1%; Homeowner vacancy rate: 1.0%; Rental vacancy rate: 25.0%
Safety: Violent crime rate: 0.0 per 10,000 population; Property crime rate: 0.0 per 10,000 population

NEW BUFFALO (city). Covers a land area of 2.503 square miles and a water area of 0.025 square miles. Located at 41.79° N. Lat; 86.74° W. Long. Elevation is 623 feet.
History: New Buffalo was settled in 1835. A number of summer camps were established in the area.
Population: 1,883; Growth (since 2000): -14.4%; Density: 752.2 persons per square mile; Race: 93.4% White, 1.6% Black/African American, 0.3% Asian, 0.5% American Indian/Alaska Native, 0.2% Native Hawaiian/Other Pacific Islander, 1.3% Two or more races, 4.4% Hispanic of any race; Average household size: 2.14; Median age: 48.4; Age under 18: 17.3%; Age 65 and over: 21.3%; Males per 100 females: 97.4
School District(s)
New Buffalo Area Schools (PK-12)
2012-13 Enrollment: 652 . . . . (269) 469-6010
Housing: Homeownership rate: 71.6%; Homeowner vacancy rate: 10.7%; Rental vacancy rate: 14.9%
Newspapers: Harbor Country News (weekly circulation 19000); New Buffalo Times (weekly circulation 5500)

NEW BUFFALO (township). Covers a land area of 20.006 square miles and a water area of 0.246 square miles. Located at 41.79° N. Lat; 86.72° W. Long. Elevation is 623 feet.
History: Settled 1835, incorporated 1936.
Population: 2,386; Growth (since 2000): -3.3%; Density: 119.3 persons per square mile; Race: 94.7% White, 1.9% Black/African American, 0.8% Asian, 0.3% American Indian/Alaska Native, 0.1% Native Hawaiian/Other Pacific Islander, 1.0% Two or more races, 2.8% Hispanic of any race; Average household size: 2.20; Median age: 51.8; Age under 18: 17.5%; Age 65 and over: 25.7%; Males per 100 females: 96.7
School District(s)
New Buffalo Area Schools (PK-12)
2012-13 Enrollment: 652 . . . . (269) 469-6010
Housing: Homeownership rate: 84.1%; Homeowner vacancy rate: 4.8%; Rental vacancy rate: 14.9%
Newspapers: Harbor Country News (weekly circulation 19000); New Buffalo Times (weekly circulation 5500)
Additional Information Contacts
New Buffalo Township . . . . (269) 469-1011
http://www.newbuffalotownship.org

NEW TROY (CDP). Covers a land area of 1.325 square miles and a water area of 0.002 square miles. Located at 41.88° N. Lat; 86.54° W. Long. Elevation is 646 feet.
Population: 497; Growth (since 2000): n/a; Density: 375.2 persons per square mile; Race: 94.4% White, 2.0% Black/African American, 0.4% Asian, 0.6% American Indian/Alaska Native, 0.0% Native Hawaiian/Other Pacific Islander, 2.2% Two or more races, 1.0% Hispanic of any race; Average household size: 2.36; Median age: 43.1; Age under 18: 22.1%; Age 65 and over: 15.5%; Males per 100 females: 112.4
Housing: Homeownership rate: 79.7%; Homeowner vacancy rate: 3.4%; Rental vacancy rate: 6.4%

NILES (city). Covers a land area of 5.791 square miles and a water area of 0.158 square miles. Located at 41.83° N. Lat; 86.25° W. Long. Elevation is 692 feet.
History: Niles was an early stopping place on the stagecoach route between Detroit and Chicago. Prominent people who came from Niles are Montgomery Ward, who founded the department store and mail order chain, the Dodge brothers, who made automobiles, and writer Ring Lardner.

Population: 11,600; Growth (since 2000): -4.9%; Density: 2,003.0 persons per square mile; Race: 80.3% White, 12.4% Black/African American, 0.6% Asian, 0.6% American Indian/Alaska Native, 0.1% Native Hawaiian/Other Pacific Islander, 4.5% Two or more races, 5.7% Hispanic of any race; Average household size: 2.37; Median age: 36.1; Age under 18: 25.6%; Age 65 and over: 14.4%; Males per 100 females: 89.1; Marriage status: 34.1% never married, 44.1% now married, 2.5% separated, 7.0% widowed, 14.8% divorced; Foreign born: 3.7%; Speak English only: 90.4%; With disability: 18.3%; Veterans: 8.1%; Ancestry: 26.1% German, 14.3% Irish, 8.9% English, 6.7% Polish, 5.8% American

Employment: 6.3% management, business, and financial, 2.9% computer, engineering, and science, 6.0% education, legal, community service, arts, and media, 4.6% healthcare practitioners, 25.9% service, 25.9% sales and office, 5.7% natural resources, construction, and maintenance, 22.8% production, transportation, and material moving

Income: Per capita: $17,186; Median household: $31,841; Average household: $41,976; Households with income of $100,000 or more: 7.1%; Poverty rate: 27.6%

Educational Attainment: High school diploma or higher: 80.9%; Bachelor's degree or higher: 11.6%; Graduate/professional degree or higher: 3.7%

School District(s)
Brandywine Community Schools (PK-12)
    2012-13 Enrollment: 1,398 . . . . (269) 684-7150
Niles Community Schools (PK-12)
    2012-13 Enrollment: 3,809 . . . . (269) 683-0732
Housing: Homeownership rate: 57.2%; Median home value: $78,700; Median year structure built: 1953; Homeowner vacancy rate: 4.4%; Median gross rent: $588 per month; Rental vacancy rate: 10.9%
Health Insurance: 88.0% have insurance; 54.9% have private insurance; 46.8% have public insurance; 12.0% do not have insurance; 1.5% of children under 18 do not have insurance
Safety: Violent crime rate: 47.1 per 10,000 population; Property crime rate: 265.0 per 10,000 population
Newspapers: Cassopolis Vigilant (weekly circulation 600); Edwardsburg Argus (weekly circulation 900); Niles Daily Star (daily circulation 2400)
Transportation: Commute: 91.4% car, 0.7% public transportation, 3.5% walk, 2.5% work from home; Median travel time to work: 20.3 minutes; Amtrak: Train service available.
Airports: Jerry Tyler Memorial (general aviation)
Additional Information Contacts
City of Niles . . . . (269) 683-4700
    http://www.ci.niles.mi.us

NILES (township). Covers a land area of 37.316 square miles and a water area of 1.072 square miles. Located at 41.85° N. Lat; 86.28° W. Long. Elevation is 692 feet.
History: It was the site of a Jesuit Mission (1690) and of Fort St. Joseph, built by the French (1697). The fort fell to the British (1761), to the Native Americans (Pontiac's Rebellion, 1763), and to the Spanish and Native Americans (1780, 1781). Permanent settlement began in 1827, and as a station on the stagecoach route between Detroit and Chicago, Niles grew as a commercial and industrial center. Ring Lardner was born here. Incorporated 1829.
Population: 14,164; Growth (since 2000): 6.3%; Density: 379.6 persons per square mile; Race: 90.0% White, 3.7% Black/African American, 0.7% Asian, 0.7% American Indian/Alaska Native, 0.0% Native Hawaiian/Other Pacific Islander, 2.6% Two or more races, 4.5% Hispanic of any race; Average household size: 2.46; Median age: 41.9; Age under 18: 22.6%; Age 65 and over: 17.3%; Males per 100 females: 93.6; Marriage status: 30.5% never married, 48.6% now married, 1.6% separated, 8.6% widowed, 12.3% divorced; Foreign born: 3.7%; Speak English only: 94.0%; With disability: 16.1%; Veterans: 10.0%; Ancestry: 32.3% German, 13.7% Irish, 12.6% English, 5.6% Polish, 5.4% American
Employment: 10.8% management, business, and financial, 1.6% computer, engineering, and science, 7.9% education, legal, community service, arts, and media, 5.5% healthcare practitioners, 18.3% service, 22.4% sales and office, 9.5% natural resources, construction, and maintenance, 23.9% production, transportation, and material moving
Income: Per capita: $22,522; Median household: $42,672; Average household: $55,242; Households with income of $100,000 or more: 11.7%; Poverty rate: 16.4%
Educational Attainment: High school diploma or higher: 84.5%; Bachelor's degree or higher: 17.5%; Graduate/professional degree or higher: 6.3%

School District(s)
Brandywine Community Schools (PK-12)
    2012-13 Enrollment: 1,398 . . . . (269) 684-7150
Niles Community Schools (PK-12)
    2012-13 Enrollment: 3,809 . . . . (269) 683-0732
Housing: Homeownership rate: 80.3%; Median home value: $95,600; Median year structure built: 1968; Homeowner vacancy rate: 3.1%; Median gross rent: $677 per month; Rental vacancy rate: 14.6%
Health Insurance: 86.3% have insurance; 63.8% have private insurance; 38.4% have public insurance; 13.7% do not have insurance; 2.0% of children under 18 do not have insurance
Newspapers: Cassopolis Vigilant (weekly circulation 600); Edwardsburg Argus (weekly circulation 900); Niles Daily Star (daily circulation 2400)
Transportation: Commute: 93.7% car, 0.1% public transportation, 1.2% walk, 3.7% work from home; Median travel time to work: 23.2 minutes; Amtrak: Train service available.
Airports: Jerry Tyler Memorial (general aviation)
Additional Information Contacts
Niles Charter Township . . . . (269) 684-0870
    http://www.nilestownship.us

ORONOKO (charter township). Covers a land area of 32.330 square miles and a water area of 0.921 square miles. Located at 41.95° N. Lat; 86.41° W. Long.
Population: 9,193; Growth (since 2000): -6.6%; Density: 284.3 persons per square mile; Race: 63.4% White, 18.5% Black/African American, 8.0% Asian, 0.5% American Indian/Alaska Native, 0.8% Native Hawaiian/Other Pacific Islander, 4.4% Two or more races, 11.5% Hispanic of any race; Average household size: 2.49; Median age: 32.6; Age under 18: 18.9%; Age 65 and over: 13.7%; Males per 100 females: 95.5; Marriage status: 37.4% never married, 51.2% now married, 1.2% separated, 4.6% widowed, 6.8% divorced; Foreign born: 27.8%; Speak English only: 72.0%; With disability: 9.8%; Veterans: 6.8%; Ancestry: 19.4% German, 7.9% English, 7.3% Irish, 3.6% Jamaican, 3.2% American
Employment: 6.3% management, business, and financial, 3.6% computer, engineering, and science, 22.0% education, legal, community service, arts, and media, 7.8% healthcare practitioners, 24.9% service, 22.1% sales and office, 6.4% natural resources, construction, and maintenance, 6.7% production, transportation, and material moving
Income: Per capita: $17,519; Median household: $40,266; Average household: $52,594; Households with income of $100,000 or more: 12.1%; Poverty rate: 21.6%
Educational Attainment: High school diploma or higher: 93.8%; Bachelor's degree or higher: 51.0%; Graduate/professional degree or higher: 26.9%
Housing: Homeownership rate: 55.8%; Median home value: $149,900; Median year structure built: 1966; Homeowner vacancy rate: 2.4%; Median gross rent: $615 per month; Rental vacancy rate: 10.0%
Health Insurance: 84.3% have insurance; 69.2% have private insurance; 25.6% have public insurance; 15.7% do not have insurance; 10.0% of children under 18 do not have insurance
Transportation: Commute: 68.5% car, 0.3% public transportation, 20.3% walk, 7.7% work from home; Median travel time to work: 15.1 minutes
Additional Information Contacts
Oronoko Charter Township . . . . (269) 471-2824
    http://www.oronokotownship.org

PAW PAW LAKE (CDP). Covers a land area of 5.117 square miles and a water area of 1.657 square miles. Located at 42.21° N. Lat; 86.28° W. Long. Elevation is 636 feet.
History: The summer resort of Paw Paw Lake was opened in the 1850's. The operator of the hotel, William A. Baker, became the first postmaster in 1901.
Population: 3,511; Growth (since 2000): -11.0%; Density: 686.2 persons per square mile; Race: 93.7% White, 1.1% Black/African American, 0.7% Asian, 0.7% American Indian/Alaska Native, 0.1% Native Hawaiian/Other Pacific Islander, 2.1% Two or more races, 4.5% Hispanic of any race; Average household size: 2.28; Median age: 44.5; Age under 18: 20.4%; Age 65 and over: 19.7%; Males per 100 females: 101.4; Marriage status: 34.5% never married, 49.8% now married, 1.5% separated, 8.3% widowed, 7.5% divorced; Foreign born: 3.0%; Speak English only: 97.1%; With disability: 11.6%; Veterans: 14.8%; Ancestry: 44.7% German, 16.0% Irish, 9.5% English, 6.0% Dutch, 5.6% Italian
Employment: 13.0% management, business, and financial, 3.4% computer, engineering, and science, 5.0% education, legal, community

service, arts, and media, 3.7% healthcare practitioners, 19.7% service, 22.8% sales and office, 11.3% natural resources, construction, and maintenance, 21.1% production, transportation, and material moving
Income: Per capita: $25,721; Median household: $42,850; Average household: $59,440; Households with income of $100,000 or more: 13.2%; Poverty rate: 12.9%
Educational Attainment: High school diploma or higher: 85.6%; Bachelor's degree or higher: 19.3%; Graduate/professional degree or higher: 2.4%
Housing: Homeownership rate: 77.5%; Median home value: $127,800; Median year structure built: 1961; Homeowner vacancy rate: 3.7%; Median gross rent: $757 per month; Rental vacancy rate: 10.7%
Health Insurance: 86.2% have insurance; 77.3% have private insurance; 28.7% have public insurance; 13.8% do not have insurance; 0.0% of children under 18 do not have insurance
Transportation: Commute: 97.3% car, 0.0% public transportation, 0.0% walk, 1.9% work from home; Median travel time to work: 27.3 minutes

PIPESTONE (township). Covers a land area of 35.506 square miles and a water area of 0.418 square miles. Located at 42.02° N. Lat; 86.29° W. Long.
Population: 2,312; Growth (since 2000): -6.5%; Density: 65.1 persons per square mile; Race: 90.0% White, 3.2% Black/African American, 0.2% Asian, 0.9% American Indian/Alaska Native, 0.0% Native Hawaiian/Other Pacific Islander, 1.6% Two or more races, 7.9% Hispanic of any race; Average household size: 2.66; Median age: 44.5; Age under 18: 23.1%; Age 65 and over: 17.2%; Males per 100 females: 103.5
Housing: Homeownership rate: 84.0%; Homeowner vacancy rate: 1.8%; Rental vacancy rate: 8.7%

ROYALTON (township). Covers a land area of 18.121 square miles and a water area of 0.463 square miles. Located at 42.02° N. Lat; 86.43° W. Long.
History: Royalton was settled in the early 1830's by John Pike and his family from Fort Royal, South Carolina.
Population: 4,766; Growth (since 2000): 22.6%; Density: 263.0 persons per square mile; Race: 90.5% White, 2.7% Black/African American, 3.5% Asian, 0.4% American Indian/Alaska Native, 0.1% Native Hawaiian/Other Pacific Islander, 1.6% Two or more races, 4.2% Hispanic of any race; Average household size: 2.72; Median age: 42.6; Age under 18: 26.2%; Age 65 and over: 17.8%; Males per 100 females: 98.4; Marriage status: 18.2% never married, 62.1% now married, 2.0% separated, 9.1% widowed, 10.6% divorced; Foreign born: 7.1%; Speak English only: 94.4%; With disability: 13.8%; Veterans: 11.0%; Ancestry: 41.0% German, 8.3% English, 8.0% Irish, 4.9% Dutch, 4.1% Polish
Employment: 22.2% management, business, and financial, 5.8% computer, engineering, and science, 9.6% education, legal, community service, arts, and media, 7.7% healthcare practitioners, 15.0% service, 23.7% sales and office, 5.5% natural resources, construction, and maintenance, 10.4% production, transportation, and material moving
Income: Per capita: $33,561; Median household: $82,431; Average household: $97,909; Households with income of $100,000 or more: 37.3%; Poverty rate: 4.5%
Educational Attainment: High school diploma or higher: 94.0%; Bachelor's degree or higher: 39.9%; Graduate/professional degree or higher: 14.2%
Housing: Homeownership rate: 86.7%; Median home value: $243,000; Median year structure built: 1988; Homeowner vacancy rate: 2.2%; Median gross rent: $1,017 per month; Rental vacancy rate: 10.5%
Health Insurance: 96.4% have insurance; 87.1% have private insurance; 23.4% have public insurance; 3.6% do not have insurance; 1.1% of children under 18 do not have insurance
Transportation: Commute: 96.4% car, 0.3% public transportation, 0.0% walk, 2.8% work from home; Median travel time to work: 17.5 minutes
Additional Information Contacts
Royalton Township . . . . (269) 429-2501
  http://www.royaltontownship.org

SAINT JOSEPH (charter township). Covers a land area of 6.648 square miles and a water area of 0.318 square miles. Located at 42.07° N. Lat; 86.48° W. Long. Elevation is 633 feet.
Population: 10,028; Growth (since 2000): -0.1%; Density: 1,508.4 persons per square mile; Race: 81.6% White, 13.3% Black/African American, 2.6% Asian, 0.3% American Indian/Alaska Native, 0.0% Native Hawaiian/Other Pacific Islander, 1.6% Two or more races, 2.4% Hispanic of any race;

Average household size: 2.42; Median age: 46.2; Age under 18: 21.7%; Age 65 and over: 19.9%; Males per 100 females: 92.8; Marriage status: 17.9% never married, 65.8% now married, 0.5% separated, 6.9% widowed, 9.4% divorced; Foreign born: 4.4%; Speak English only: 96.1%; With disability: 11.5%; Veterans: 10.0%; Ancestry: 35.3% German, 17.6% Irish, 10.7% English, 7.3% Italian, 5.9% Polish
Employment: 16.1% management, business, and financial, 9.3% computer, engineering, and science, 14.0% education, legal, community service, arts, and media, 6.4% healthcare practitioners, 17.1% service, 21.4% sales and office, 3.0% natural resources, construction, and maintenance, 12.8% production, transportation, and material moving
Income: Per capita: $33,046; Median household: $62,088; Average household: $79,795; Households with income of $100,000 or more: 22.7%; Poverty rate: 4.6%
Educational Attainment: High school diploma or higher: 95.6%; Bachelor's degree or higher: 38.2%; Graduate/professional degree or higher: 15.9%

School District(s)
Berrien Resa (PK-12)
  2012-13 Enrollment: 772 . . . . (269) 471-7725
Saint Joseph Public Schools (PK-12)
  2012-13 Enrollment: 2,813 . . . . (269) 926-3100
Vocational/Technical School(s)
Twin City Beauty College (Private, For-profit)
  Fall 2013 Enrollment: 111 . . . . (616) 355-5010
  2013-14 Tuition: $15,300
Housing: Homeownership rate: 88.0%; Median home value: $147,400; Median year structure built: 1964; Homeowner vacancy rate: 1.9%; Median gross rent: $920 per month; Rental vacancy rate: 7.2%
Health Insurance: 93.9% have insurance; 83.1% have private insurance; 28.8% have public insurance; 6.1% do not have insurance; 1.4% of children under 18 do not have insurance
Hospitals: Lakeland Hospital - Saint Joseph (254 beds)
Safety: Violent crime rate: 19.1 per 10,000 population; Property crime rate: 143.7 per 10,000 population
Newspapers: Herald-Palladium (daily circulation 22200)
Transportation: Commute: 93.0% car, 0.0% public transportation, 0.6% walk, 5.7% work from home; Median travel time to work: 16.0 minutes; Amtrak: Train service available.
Additional Information Contacts
Saint Joseph Charter Township . . . . (269) 429-7703
  http://www.sjct.org

SAINT JOSEPH (city). County seat. Covers a land area of 3.215 square miles and a water area of 1.576 square miles. Located at 42.10° N. Lat; 86.49° W. Long. Elevation is 633 feet.
History: St. Joseph was preceded by the town of Newburyport, founded in 1831 at the mouth of the St. Joseph River. The constantly shifting sands won out over the residents, who abandoned the site in five years and moved farther up the hills onto the site of St. Joseph. St. Joseph was incorporated as a village in 1836. The town grew slowly, some of the settlers choosing to locate across the river where they established the town that became Benton Harbor. Rivalry between the two towns was bitter until around 1900. Later the two became so homogeneous that only residents knew exactly where the boundary lines were.
Population: 8,365; Growth (since 2000): -4.8%; Density: 2,601.9 persons per square mile; Race: 88.1% White, 5.3% Black/African American, 3.4% Asian, 0.3% American Indian/Alaska Native, 0.0% Native Hawaiian/Other Pacific Islander, 1.9% Two or more races, 2.8% Hispanic of any race; Average household size: 1.97; Median age: 41.6; Age under 18: 16.4%; Age 65 and over: 18.6%; Males per 100 females: 95.2; Marriage status: 33.8% never married, 42.0% now married, 0.7% separated, 9.0% widowed, 15.2% divorced; Foreign born: 5.7%; Speak English only: 93.5%; With disability: 10.9%; Veterans: 10.4%; Ancestry: 39.0% German, 13.7% Irish, 10.1% English, 8.9% Dutch, 5.6% Polish
Employment: 15.0% management, business, and financial, 6.6% computer, engineering, and science, 10.1% education, legal, community service, arts, and media, 13.0% healthcare practitioners, 16.6% service, 25.6% sales and office, 5.0% natural resources, construction, and maintenance, 8.0% production, transportation, and material moving
Income: Per capita: $36,084; Median household: $51,027; Average household: $75,619; Households with income of $100,000 or more: 21.5%; Poverty rate: 9.9%

Educational Attainment: High school diploma or higher: 94.6%; Bachelor's degree or higher: 37.5%; Graduate/professional degree or higher: 16.0%

School District(s)

Berrien Resa (PK-12)
    2012-13 Enrollment: 772......................(269) 471-7725
Saint Joseph Public Schools (PK-12)
    2012-13 Enrollment: 2,813...................(269) 926-3100

Vocational/Technical School(s)

Twin City Beauty College (Private, For-profit)
    Fall 2013 Enrollment: 111...................(616) 355-5010
    2013-14 Tuition: $15,300

Housing: Homeownership rate: 59.3%; Median home value: $152,500; Median year structure built: 1950; Homeowner vacancy rate: 3.1%; Median gross rent: $689 per month; Rental vacancy rate: 14.2%

Health Insurance: 86.1% have insurance; 73.5% have private insurance; 26.5% have public insurance; 13.9% do not have insurance; 1.4% of children under 18 do not have insurance

Hospitals: Lakeland Hospital - Saint Joseph (254 beds)

Newspapers: Herald-Palladium (daily circulation 22200)

Transportation: Commute: 91.6% car, 0.7% public transportation, 3.9% walk, 3.0% work from home; Median travel time to work: 17.5 minutes; Amtrak: Train service available.

Additional Information Contacts

City of Saint Joseph ....(269) 983-5541
    http://www.sjcity.com

SAWYER (unincorporated postal area)

ZCTA: 49125

Covers a land area of 13.495 square miles and a water area of 1.183 square miles. Located at 41.89° N. Lat; 86.58° W. Long. Elevation is 653 feet.

Population: 2,046; Growth (since 2000): -20.6%; Density: 151.6 persons per square mile; Race: 95.5% White, 1.0% Black/African American, 1.1% Asian, 0.4% American Indian/Alaska Native, 0.0% Native Hawaiian/Other Pacific Islander, 0.8% Two or more races, 2.6% Hispanic of any race; Average household size: 2.22; Median age: 50.3; Age under 18: 16.6%; Age 65 and over: 22.9%; Males per 100 females: 104.0

School District(s)

River Valley SD (PK-12)
    2012-13 Enrollment: 654......................(269) 756-9541
    Housing: Homeownership rate: 82.3%; Homeowner vacancy rate: 4.6%; Rental vacancy rate: 13.6%

SHOREHAM (village). Covers a land area of 0.582 square miles and a water area of 0 square miles. Located at 42.06° N. Lat; 86.51° W. Long. Elevation is 600 feet.

History: The village of Shoreham was founded by William Ducker, an early resident here who wanted to keep the area residential. He named the village for its location along the shore of Lake Michigan.

Population: 862; Growth (since 2000): 0.2%; Density: 1,480.6 persons per square mile; Race: 89.6% White, 3.5% Black/African American, 4.9% Asian, 0.1% American Indian/Alaska Native, 0.0% Native Hawaiian/Other Pacific Islander, 1.7% Two or more races, 3.0% Hispanic of any race; Average household size: 2.20; Median age: 48.1; Age under 18: 18.2%; Age 65 and over: 22.5%; Males per 100 females: 90.7

Housing: Homeownership rate: 73.5%; Homeowner vacancy rate: 1.7%; Rental vacancy rate: 5.3%

SHOREWOOD-TOWER HILLS-HARBERT (CDP). Covers a land area of 4.526 square miles and a water area of 0.032 square miles. Located at 41.88° N. Lat; 86.62° W. Long. Elevation is 640 feet.

Population: 1,344; Growth (since 2000): -17.0%; Density: 297.0 persons per square mile; Race: 96.1% White, 1.3% Black/African American, 1.3% Asian, 0.3% American Indian/Alaska Native, 0.0% Native Hawaiian/Other Pacific Islander, 0.6% Two or more races, 1.9% Hispanic of any race; Average household size: 2.13; Median age: 53.5; Age under 18: 15.1%; Age 65 and over: 28.0%; Males per 100 females: 94.2

Housing: Homeownership rate: 84.9%; Homeowner vacancy rate: 3.6%; Rental vacancy rate: 17.9%

SODUS (township). Covers a land area of 19.410 square miles and a water area of 0.581 square miles. Located at 42.04° N. Lat; 86.37° W. Long. Elevation is 669 feet.

History: The Sodus area was settled in the mid-1830's by William H. and David Rector. Sodus Township was separated out in 1859 and named by Rector for his home town of Sodus, New York.

Population: 1,932; Growth (since 2000): -9.7%; Density: 99.5 persons per square mile; Race: 83.4% White, 9.1% Black/African American, 0.6% Asian, 0.5% American Indian/Alaska Native, 0.0% Native Hawaiian/Other Pacific Islander, 1.4% Two or more races, 8.1% Hispanic of any race; Average household size: 2.38; Median age: 45.8; Age under 18: 21.9%; Age 65 and over: 20.4%; Males per 100 females: 95.0

School District(s)

Sodus Township S/d #5 (KG-12)
    2012-13 Enrollment: 75......................(269) 925-6757

Housing: Homeownership rate: 85.2%; Homeowner vacancy rate: 2.9%; Rental vacancy rate: 29.8%

STEVENSVILLE (village). Covers a land area of 1.042 square miles and a water area of 0.004 square miles. Located at 42.01° N. Lat; 86.53° W. Long. Elevation is 633 feet.

History: Stevensville was named for Thomas Stevens, who donated right-of-way land to the railroad and platted the village.

Population: 1,142; Growth (since 2000): -4.1%; Density: 1,096.2 persons per square mile; Race: 94.6% White, 2.1% Black/African American, 1.2% Asian, 1.0% American Indian/Alaska Native, 0.1% Native Hawaiian/Other Pacific Islander, 0.4% Two or more races, 2.4% Hispanic of any race; Average household size: 2.17; Median age: 44.2; Age under 18: 19.4%; Age 65 and over: 20.5%; Males per 100 females: 92.6

School District(s)

Lakeshore SD (Berrien) (PK-12)
    2012-13 Enrollment: 2,852...................(269) 428-1400

Housing: Homeownership rate: 69.2%; Homeowner vacancy rate: 2.4%; Rental vacancy rate: 14.7%

Additional Information Contacts

Village of Stevensville ....(269) 429-1802
    http://www.villageofstevensville.us

THREE OAKS (township). Covers a land area of 23.291 square miles and a water area of 0.187 square miles. Located at 41.79° N. Lat; 86.62° W. Long. Elevation is 679 feet.

History: Has museum containing Native American and historic relics. Settled 1850, incorporated 1867.

Population: 2,574; Growth (since 2000): -12.7%; Density: 110.5 persons per square mile; Race: 95.2% White, 1.0% Black/African American, 0.3% Asian, 0.9% American Indian/Alaska Native, 0.1% Native Hawaiian/Other Pacific Islander, 1.4% Two or more races, 3.0% Hispanic of any race; Average household size: 2.38; Median age: 43.0; Age under 18: 21.7%; Age 65 and over: 15.5%; Males per 100 females: 96.8; Marriage status: 26.8% never married, 54.7% now married, 1.8% separated, 7.7% widowed, 10.8% divorced; Foreign born: 2.9%; Speak English only: 95.0%; With disability: 13.3%; Veterans: 11.6%; Ancestry: 39.6% German, 14.0% Irish, 12.5% English, 8.1% Polish, 5.7% American

Employment: 11.3% management, business, and financial, 2.1% computer, engineering, and science, 8.5% education, legal, community service, arts, and media, 4.4% healthcare practitioners, 23.2% service, 24.0% sales and office, 9.0% natural resources, construction, and maintenance, 17.5% production, transportation, and material moving

Income: Per capita: $22,751; Median household: $38,542; Average household: $56,086; Households with income of $100,000 or more: 12.2%; Poverty rate: 13.7%

Educational Attainment: High school diploma or higher: 86.8%; Bachelor's degree or higher: 14.7%; Graduate/professional degree or higher: 5.6%

School District(s)

River Valley SD (PK-12)
    2012-13 Enrollment: 654......................(269) 756-9541

Housing: Homeownership rate: 78.8%; Median home value: $136,500; Median year structure built: 1955; Homeowner vacancy rate: 3.5%; Median gross rent: $695 per month; Rental vacancy rate: 11.9%

Health Insurance: 81.3% have insurance; 61.7% have private insurance; 35.8% have public insurance; 18.7% do not have insurance; 8.0% of children under 18 do not have insurance

Transportation: Commute: 91.7% car, 0.0% public transportation, 4.6% walk, 2.8% work from home; Median travel time to work: 21.6 minutes

THREE OAKS (village). Covers a land area of 0.987 square miles and a water area of 0 square miles. Located at 41.80° N. Lat; 86.61° W. Long. Elevation is 679 feet.
History: The village of Three Oaks was founded by Henry Chamberlain, who named it for the three trees that stood near the post office.
Population: 1,622; Growth (since 2000): -11.3%; Density: 1,642.7 persons per square mile; Race: 93.2% White, 1.1% Black/African American, 0.6% Asian, 1.4% American Indian/Alaska Native, 0.1% Native Hawaiian/Other Pacific Islander, 1.8% Two or more races, 4.4% Hispanic of any race; Average household size: 2.39; Median age: 39.3; Age under 18: 24.4%; Age 65 and over: 13.4%; Males per 100 females: 94.5
School District(s)
River Valley SD (PK-12)
　2012-13 Enrollment: 654 . . . . (269) 756-9541
Housing: Homeownership rate: 71.0%; Homeowner vacancy rate: 4.3%; Rental vacancy rate: 12.1%

UNION PIER (unincorporated postal area)
ZCTA: 49129
　Covers a land area of 5.014 square miles and a water area of 0.464 square miles. Located at 41.82° N. Lat; 86.69° W. Long. Elevation is 630 feet.
　Population: 609; Growth (since 2000): -16.2%; Density: 121.5 persons per square mile; Race: 88.5% White, 7.6% Black/African American, 1.3% Asian, 0.0% American Indian/Alaska Native, 0.0% Native Hawaiian/Other Pacific Islander, 1.6% Two or more races, 2.8% Hispanic of any race; Average household size: 2.00; Median age: 54.6; Age under 18: 14.1%; Age 65 and over: 26.6%; Males per 100 females: 93.3
　Housing: Homeownership rate: 84.9%; Homeowner vacancy rate: 12.1%; Rental vacancy rate: 36.1%

WATERVLIET (city). Covers a land area of 1.186 square miles and a water area of 0.038 square miles. Located at 42.19° N. Lat; 86.26° W. Long. Elevation is 650 feet.
History: Watervliet was settled in the early 1830's and named for the rapids that were once evident in the Paw Paw River.
Population: 1,735; Growth (since 2000): -5.9%; Density: 1,462.3 persons per square mile; Race: 94.3% White, 1.0% Black/African American, 0.2% Asian, 0.8% American Indian/Alaska Native, 0.0% Native Hawaiian/Other Pacific Islander, 2.7% Two or more races, 3.9% Hispanic of any race; Average household size: 2.55; Median age: 35.8; Age under 18: 27.9%; Age 65 and over: 11.6%; Males per 100 females: 91.9
School District(s)
Watervliet SD (PK-12)
　2012-13 Enrollment: 1,338 . . . . (269) 463-5566
Housing: Homeownership rate: 68.1%; Homeowner vacancy rate: 2.9%; Rental vacancy rate: 12.6%
Hospitals: Lakeland Community Hospital - Watervliet (70 beds)
Newspapers: Tri-City Record (weekly circulation 2700)

WATERVLIET (township). Covers a land area of 13.473 square miles and a water area of 1.012 square miles. Located at 42.20° N. Lat; 86.25° W. Long. Elevation is 650 feet.
History: Settled in 1830s; incorporated as village 1891, as city 1925.
Population: 3,102; Growth (since 2000): -8.5%; Density: 230.2 persons per square mile; Race: 90.7% White, 2.1% Black/African American, 0.7% Asian, 0.9% American Indian/Alaska Native, 0.0% Native Hawaiian/Other Pacific Islander, 2.8% Two or more races, 5.3% Hispanic of any race; Average household size: 2.38; Median age: 42.4; Age under 18: 22.6%; Age 65 and over: 17.2%; Males per 100 females: 97.6; Marriage status: 34.5% never married, 50.5% now married, 2.2% separated, 6.3% widowed, 8.7% divorced; Foreign born: 5.1%; Speak English only: 90.1%; With disability: 10.0%; Veterans: 9.1%; Ancestry: 41.0% German, 19.1% Irish, 8.2% American, 6.3% English, 5.5% Polish
Employment: 8.8% management, business, and financial, 5.9% computer, engineering, and science, 2.7% education, legal, community service, arts, and media, 4.1% healthcare practitioners, 8.2% service, 22.8% sales and office, 19.9% natural resources, construction, and maintenance, 27.6% production, transportation, and material moving
Income: Per capita: $17,413; Median household: $41,110; Average household: $46,500; Households with income of $100,000 or more: 5.4%; Poverty rate: 19.5%

Educational Attainment: High school diploma or higher: 80.0%; Bachelor's degree or higher: 14.4%; Graduate/professional degree or higher: 2.3%
School District(s)
Watervliet SD (PK-12)
　2012-13 Enrollment: 1,338 . . . . (269) 463-5566
Housing: Homeownership rate: 72.2%; Median home value: $101,800; Median year structure built: 1969; Homeowner vacancy rate: 2.6%; Median gross rent: $630 per month; Rental vacancy rate: 11.4%
Health Insurance: 82.1% have insurance; 54.8% have private insurance; 43.1% have public insurance; 17.9% do not have insurance; 2.5% of children under 18 do not have insurance
Hospitals: Lakeland Community Hospital - Watervliet (70 beds)
Newspapers: Tri-City Record (weekly circulation 2700)
Transportation: Commute: 97.8% car, 0.0% public transportation, 0.0% walk, 2.2% work from home; Median travel time to work: 24.7 minutes

WEESAW (township). Covers a land area of 35.437 square miles and a water area of 0.156 square miles. Located at 41.85° N. Lat; 86.50° W. Long.
Population: 1,936; Growth (since 2000): -6.2%; Density: 54.6 persons per square mile; Race: 95.3% White, 0.6% Black/African American, 0.3% Asian, 0.4% American Indian/Alaska Native, 0.0% Native Hawaiian/Other Pacific Islander, 1.8% Two or more races, 3.0% Hispanic of any race; Average household size: 2.43; Median age: 45.7; Age under 18: 20.5%; Age 65 and over: 16.9%; Males per 100 females: 106.2
Housing: Homeownership rate: 85.6%; Homeowner vacancy rate: 3.9%; Rental vacancy rate: 10.1%

Branch County

Located in southern Michigan; bounded on the south by Indiana. Covers a land area of 506.369 square miles, a water area of 13.307 square miles, and is located in the Eastern Time Zone at 41.92° N. Lat., 85.07° W. Long. The county was founded in 1829. County seat is Coldwater.

Branch County is part of the Coldwater, MI Micropolitan Statistical Area. The entire metro area includes: Branch County, MI

Weather Station: Coldwater State School　　　　　　　　Elevation: 983 feet

	Jan	Feb	Mar	Apr	May	Jun	Jul	Aug	Sep	Oct	Nov	Dec
High	31	34	44	58	69	78	82	80	73	60	47	34
Low	17	19	26	37	47	57	61	59	51	40	32	21
Precip	2.1	2.0	2.4	3.0	4.2	3.5	4.3	4.3	3.7	3.3	2.8	2.5
Snow	14.2	9.4	6.3	1.4	0.0	0.0	0.0	0.0	tr	0.5	3.6	12.1

High and Low temperatures in degrees Fahrenheit; Precipitation and Snow in inches

Population: 45,248; Growth (since 2000): -1.2%; Density: 89.4 persons per square mile; Race: 92.9% White, 3.1% Black/African American, 0.5% Asian, 0.4% American Indian/Alaska Native, 0.0% Native Hawaiian/Other Pacific Islander, 1.5% two or more races, 4.0% Hispanic of any race; Average household size: 2.56; Median age: 39.8; Age under 18: 23.9%; Age 65 and over: 14.7%; Males per 100 females: 111.4; Marriage status: 26.7% never married, 52.9% now married, 1.9% separated, 6.4% widowed, 14.1% divorced; Foreign born: 2.6%; Speak English only: 91.9%; With disability: 13.8%; Veterans: 9.3%; Ancestry: 31.8% German, 12.9% English, 10.7% Irish, 8.7% American, 7.4% Polish
Religion: Six largest groups: 13.2% Catholicism, 3.9% European Free-Church, 2.5% Methodist/Pietist, 2.4% Holiness, 2.2% Non-denominational Protestant, 2.1% Baptist
Economy: Unemployment rate: 5.4%; Leading industries: 16.5% retail trade; 12.7% other services (except public administration); 12.3% health care and social assistance; Farms: 1,054 totaling 244,208 acres; Company size: 0 employ 1,000 or more persons, 2 employ 500 to 999 persons, 17 employ 100 to 499 persons, 786 employ less than 100 persons; Business ownership: 623 women-owned, n/a Black-owned, n/a Hispanic-owned, n/a Asian-owned
Employment: 9.5% management, business, and financial, 2.2% computer, engineering, and science, 7.3% education, legal, community service, arts, and media, 5.4% healthcare practitioners, 17.8% service, 23.8% sales and office, 9.8% natural resources, construction, and maintenance, 24.1% production, transportation, and material moving
Income: Per capita: $19,947; Median household: $41,856; Average household: $53,518; Households with income of $100,000 or more: 10.4%; Poverty rate: 18.7%

Educational Attainment: High school diploma or higher: 86.4%; Bachelor's degree or higher: 13.4%; Graduate/professional degree or higher: 4.6%

Housing: Homeownership rate: 76.3%; Median home value: $98,000; Median year structure built: 1971; Homeowner vacancy rate: 3.0%; Median gross rent: $670 per month; Rental vacancy rate: 12.2%

Vital Statistics: Birth rate: 111.3 per 10,000 population; Death rate: 88.7 per 10,000 population; Age-adjusted cancer mortality rate: 193.4 deaths per 100,000 population

Health Insurance: 86.7% have insurance; 66.4% have private insurance; 35.2% have public insurance; 13.3% do not have insurance; 9.0% of children under 18 do not have insurance

Health Care: Physicians: 9.8 per 10,000 population; Hospital beds: 21.9 per 10,000 population; Hospital admissions: 798.5 per 10,000 population

Transportation: Commute: 89.9% car, 0.3% public transportation, 2.8% walk, 5.5% work from home; Median travel time to work: 24.8 minutes

Presidential Election: 40.1% Obama, 58.8% Romney (2012)

National and State Parks: Coldwater Lake State Park

Additional Information Contacts
Branch Government . . . . (517) 279-4300
   http://www.countyofbranch.com

Branch County Communities

ALGANSEE (township). Covers a land area of 35.528 square miles and a water area of 0.561 square miles. Located at 41.85° N. Lat; 84.88° W. Long. Elevation is 1,040 feet.

Population: 1,974; Growth (since 2000): -4.2%; Density: 55.6 persons per square mile; Race: 98.1% White, 0.5% Black/African American, 0.0% Asian, 0.1% American Indian/Alaska Native, 0.0% Native Hawaiian/Other Pacific Islander, 1.0% Two or more races, 1.0% Hispanic of any race; Average household size: 2.67; Median age: 42.2; Age under 18: 27.0%; Age 65 and over: 17.8%; Males per 100 females: 104.6

Housing: Homeownership rate: 88.2%; Homeowner vacancy rate: 2.5%; Rental vacancy rate: 11.2%

BATAVIA (township). Covers a land area of 35.725 square miles and a water area of 0.428 square miles. Located at 41.94° N. Lat; 85.12° W. Long. Elevation is 919 feet.

History: Batavia was named after Batavia, New York.

Population: 1,339; Growth (since 2000): -13.4%; Density: 37.5 persons per square mile; Race: 96.1% White, 0.3% Black/African American, 0.2% Asian, 0.4% American Indian/Alaska Native, 0.1% Native Hawaiian/Other Pacific Islander, 1.0% Two or more races, 3.4% Hispanic of any race; Average household size: 2.46; Median age: 42.6; Age under 18: 21.9%; Age 65 and over: 14.5%; Males per 100 females: 102.0

Housing: Homeownership rate: 78.6%; Homeowner vacancy rate: 1.2%; Rental vacancy rate: 14.2%

BETHEL (township). Covers a land area of 35.831 square miles and a water area of 0.240 square miles. Located at 41.85° N. Lat; 85.11° W. Long. Elevation is 997 feet.

History: The name of Bethel is Old Testament Hebrew meaning "House of the Lord." The area was settled in 1830.

Population: 1,434; Growth (since 2000): 0.9%; Density: 40.0 persons per square mile; Race: 90.3% White, 2.7% Black/African American, 0.4% Asian, 1.6% American Indian/Alaska Native, 0.0% Native Hawaiian/Other Pacific Islander, 0.6% Two or more races, 6.8% Hispanic of any race; Average household size: 2.80; Median age: 38.4; Age under 18: 26.1%; Age 65 and over: 13.2%; Males per 100 females: 101.7

Housing: Homeownership rate: 83.3%; Homeowner vacancy rate: 2.5%; Rental vacancy rate: 12.0%

BRONSON (city). Covers a land area of 1.367 square miles and a water area of 0.003 square miles. Located at 41.87° N. Lat; 85.19° W. Long. Elevation is 915 feet.

History: Jabez Bronson built a hunting lodge and tavern here in 1828. When the settlement was asked to serve as the first seat of Branch County, Bronson was the law and his tavern was the court. The village grew in the 1870's with the arrival of many Polish immigrants, attracted by the fertile land.

Population: 2,349; Growth (since 2000): -3.0%; Density: 1,718.0 persons per square mile; Race: 89.8% White, 0.8% Black/African American, 0.6% Asian, 0.6% American Indian/Alaska Native, 0.0% Native Hawaiian/Other Pacific Islander, 2.1% Two or more races, 15.4% Hispanic of any race;

Average household size: 2.80; Median age: 30.8; Age under 18: 31.1%; Age 65 and over: 10.3%; Males per 100 females: 97.4

School District(s)
Bronson Community SD (KG-12)
   2012-13 Enrollment: 1,050 . . . . (517) 369-3257

Housing: Homeownership rate: 63.6%; Homeowner vacancy rate: 2.9%; Rental vacancy rate: 11.9%

Safety: Violent crime rate: 17.1 per 10,000 population; Property crime rate: 277.8 per 10,000 population

BRONSON (township). Covers a land area of 34.618 square miles and a water area of 0.125 square miles. Located at 41.85° N. Lat; 85.24° W. Long. Elevation is 915 feet.

History: Bronson Township was first called Prairie River, but was renamed by the state legislature in 1837 for Jabez B. Bronson.

Population: 1,349; Growth (since 2000): -0.7%; Density: 39.0 persons per square mile; Race: 96.0% White, 0.6% Black/African American, 0.1% Asian, 0.5% American Indian/Alaska Native, 0.0% Native Hawaiian/Other Pacific Islander, 0.8% Two or more races, 7.6% Hispanic of any race; Average household size: 2.79; Median age: 38.9; Age under 18: 26.5%; Age 65 and over: 12.9%; Males per 100 females: 106.9

School District(s)
Bronson Community SD (KG-12)
   2012-13 Enrollment: 1,050 . . . . (517) 369-3257

Housing: Homeownership rate: 85.7%; Homeowner vacancy rate: 2.5%; Rental vacancy rate: 5.5%

BUTLER (township). Covers a land area of 35.625 square miles and a water area of 0.134 square miles. Located at 42.03° N. Lat; 84.88° W. Long. Elevation is 1,014 feet.

History: Butler Township was organized in 1838 and named for Butler, New York, the former home of many early residents.

Population: 1,467; Growth (since 2000): 7.7%; Density: 41.2 persons per square mile; Race: 99.2% White, 0.0% Black/African American, 0.1% Asian, 0.1% American Indian/Alaska Native, 0.0% Native Hawaiian/Other Pacific Islander, 0.5% Two or more races, 0.9% Hispanic of any race; Average household size: 3.02; Median age: 35.8; Age under 18: 29.6%; Age 65 and over: 12.8%; Males per 100 females: 101.2

Housing: Homeownership rate: 86.4%; Homeowner vacancy rate: 3.0%; Rental vacancy rate: 8.1%

CALIFORNIA (township). Covers a land area of 21.262 square miles and a water area of 0.042 square miles. Located at 41.79° N. Lat; 84.89° W. Long. Elevation is 1,060 feet.

History: California Township was settled in 1835 by Israel R. Hall and his family. The settlement that grew up around him was called Hall's Corners after Joseph Hall, who operated a general store here.

Population: 1,040; Growth (since 2000): 14.4%; Density: 48.9 persons per square mile; Race: 98.8% White, 0.0% Black/African American, 0.0% Asian, 0.2% American Indian/Alaska Native, 0.0% Native Hawaiian/Other Pacific Islander, 1.0% Two or more races, 1.6% Hispanic of any race; Average household size: 3.56; Median age: 24.2; Age under 18: 41.6%; Age 65 and over: 8.8%; Males per 100 females: 106.3

Housing: Homeownership rate: 82.3%; Homeowner vacancy rate: 0.4%; Rental vacancy rate: 1.9%

COLDWATER (city). County seat. Covers a land area of 8.033 square miles and a water area of 0.236 square miles. Located at 41.94° N. Lat; 85.00° W. Long. Elevation is 968 feet.

History: Coldwater grew up at the place where the Chicago Turnpike crossed the Coldwater River. A village was platted here in 1832, incorporated in 1837, and chartered as a city in 1861. Coldwater was an active and very successful station on the Underground Railroad, claiming that no slave was ever captured in the vicinity of Coldwater.

Population: 10,945; Growth (since 2000): -13.8%; Density: 1,362.5 persons per square mile; Race: 92.5% White, 0.6% Black/African American, 0.8% Asian, 0.2% American Indian/Alaska Native, 0.0% Native Hawaiian/Other Pacific Islander, 2.7% Two or more races, 6.6% Hispanic of any race; Average household size: 2.49; Median age: 35.2; Age under 18: 27.2%; Age 65 and over: 15.0%; Males per 100 females: 91.4; Marriage status: 31.5% never married, 44.7% now married, 3.0% separated, 8.6% widowed, 15.3% divorced; Foreign born: 5.1%; Speak English only: 88.3%; With disability: 15.1%; Veterans: 7.9%; Ancestry: 27.9% German, 12.3% English, 12.0% Irish, 10.2% American, 8.5% Polish

Employment: 8.0% management, business, and financial, 2.0% computer, engineering, and science, 7.3% education, legal, community service, arts, and media, 6.2% healthcare practitioners, 21.2% service, 24.6% sales and office, 7.2% natural resources, construction, and maintenance, 23.5% production, transportation, and material moving

Income: Per capita: $18,244; Median household: $36,014; Average household: $48,706; Households with income of $100,000 or more: 7.5%; Poverty rate: 20.1%

Educational Attainment: High school diploma or higher: 85.4%; Bachelor's degree or higher: 13.0%; Graduate/professional degree or higher: 5.2%

School District(s)

Branch ISD (PK-12)

    2012-13 Enrollment: 698 . . . . (517) 279-5730

Coldwater Community Schools (PK-12)

    2012-13 Enrollment: 2,860 . . . . (517) 279-5910

Pansophia Academy (KG-12)

    2012-13 Enrollment: 301 . . . . (517) 279-4686

Vocational/Technical School(s)

Salon Academy (Private, For-profit)

    Fall 2013 Enrollment: 48 . . . . (517) 279-2355

    2013-14 Tuition: $14,750

Housing: Homeownership rate: 60.6%; Median home value: $80,300; Median year structure built: 1962; Homeowner vacancy rate: 4.9%; Median gross rent: $675 per month; Rental vacancy rate: 11.4%

Health Insurance: 89.9% have insurance; 69.7% have private insurance; 35.6% have public insurance; 10.1% do not have insurance; 2.8% of children under 18 do not have insurance

Hospitals: Community Health Center of Branch County (96 beds)

Newspapers: Coldwater Daily Reporter (daily circulation 5300); Patriot Publications (weekly circulation 6000)

Transportation: Commute: 88.9% car, 0.6% public transportation, 3.3% walk, 4.7% work from home; Median travel time to work: 20.3 minutes

Airports: Branch County Memorial (general aviation)

Additional Information Contacts

City of Coldwater . . . . (517) 279-9501

    http://www.coldwater.org

COLDWATER (township). Covers a land area of 27.544 square miles and a water area of 1.175 square miles. Located at 41.96° N. Lat; 84.97° W. Long. Elevation is 968 feet.

History: Settled 1830; incorporated as village in 1837, as city in 1861.

Population: 6,102; Growth (since 2000): 65.9%; Density: 221.5 persons per square mile; Race: 78.4% White, 19.6% Black/African American, 0.5% Asian, 0.4% American Indian/Alaska Native, 0.0% Native Hawaiian/Other Pacific Islander, 0.6% Two or more races, 2.9% Hispanic of any race; Average household size: 2.44; Median age: 42.8; Age under 18: 11.8%; Age 65 and over: 12.0%; Males per 100 females: 255.0; Marriage status: 35.2% never married, 41.4% now married, 1.2% separated, 3.1% widowed, 20.4% divorced; Foreign born: 1.3%; Speak English only: 94.2%; With disability: 13.6%; Veterans: 11.8%; Ancestry: 26.8% German, 11.2% English, 9.5% Irish, 6.1% Dutch, 5.2% Polish

Employment: 7.1% management, business, and financial, 1.5% computer, engineering, and science, 14.8% education, legal, community service, arts, and media, 5.0% healthcare practitioners, 18.1% service, 28.3% sales and office, 8.9% natural resources, construction, and maintenance, 16.4% production, transportation, and material moving

Income: Per capita: $17,804; Median household: $45,037; Average household: $62,438; Households with income of $100,000 or more: 16.4%; Poverty rate: 9.8%

Educational Attainment: High school diploma or higher: 88.8%; Bachelor's degree or higher: 12.1%; Graduate/professional degree or higher: 3.9%

School District(s)

Branch ISD (PK-12)

    2012-13 Enrollment: 698 . . . . (517) 279-5730

Coldwater Community Schools (PK-12)

    2012-13 Enrollment: 2,860 . . . . (517) 279-5910

Pansophia Academy (KG-12)

    2012-13 Enrollment: 301 . . . . (517) 279-4686

Vocational/Technical School(s)

Salon Academy (Private, For-profit)

    Fall 2013 Enrollment: 48 . . . . (517) 279-2355

    2013-14 Tuition: $14,750

Housing: Homeownership rate: 83.9%; Median home value: $116,100; Median year structure built: 1972; Homeowner vacancy rate: 2.6%; Median gross rent: $659 per month; Rental vacancy rate: 13.2%

Health Insurance: 88.8% have insurance; 69.8% have private insurance; 35.5% have public insurance; 11.2% do not have insurance; 4.9% of children under 18 do not have insurance

Hospitals: Community Health Center of Branch County (96 beds)

Newspapers: Coldwater Daily Reporter (daily circulation 5300); Patriot Publications (weekly circulation 6000)

Transportation: Commute: 91.5% car, 0.9% public transportation, 1.4% walk, 5.5% work from home; Median travel time to work: 27.8 minutes

Airports: Branch County Memorial (general aviation)

GILEAD (township). Covers a land area of 21.059 square miles and a water area of 0.352 square miles. Located at 41.79° N. Lat; 85.12° W. Long. Elevation is 968 feet.

Population: 661; Growth (since 2000): -12.2%; Density: 31.4 persons per square mile; Race: 98.8% White, 0.3% Black/African American, 0.0% Asian, 0.5% American Indian/Alaska Native, 0.0% Native Hawaiian/Other Pacific Islander, 0.2% Two or more races, 1.5% Hispanic of any race; Average household size: 2.61; Median age: 42.6; Age under 18: 25.3%; Age 65 and over: 19.2%; Males per 100 females: 104.6

Housing: Homeownership rate: 88.2%; Homeowner vacancy rate: 1.3%; Rental vacancy rate: 3.2%

GIRARD (township). Covers a land area of 35.055 square miles and a water area of 1.104 square miles. Located at 42.03° N. Lat; 85.01° W. Long. Elevation is 955 feet.

Population: 1,780; Growth (since 2000): -7.1%; Density: 50.8 persons per square mile; Race: 96.9% White, 0.2% Black/African American, 0.3% Asian, 0.7% American Indian/Alaska Native, 0.0% Native Hawaiian/Other Pacific Islander, 1.4% Two or more races, 1.3% Hispanic of any race; Average household size: 2.39; Median age: 45.4; Age under 18: 20.7%; Age 65 and over: 18.8%; Males per 100 females: 100.5

Housing: Homeownership rate: 85.9%; Homeowner vacancy rate: 1.5%; Rental vacancy rate: 8.7%

KINDERHOOK (township). Covers a land area of 19.471 square miles and a water area of 1.884 square miles. Located at 41.78° N. Lat; 85.00° W. Long. Elevation is 1,001 feet.

History: Kinderhook Township was named to honor President Martin Van Buren, who had been born in Kinderhook, New York.

Population: 1,497; Growth (since 2000): -7.2%; Density: 76.9 persons per square mile; Race: 96.9% White, 0.2% Black/African American, 0.6% Asian, 0.5% American Indian/Alaska Native, 0.0% Native Hawaiian/Other Pacific Islander, 1.1% Two or more races, 1.7% Hispanic of any race; Average household size: 2.31; Median age: 50.6; Age under 18: 17.6%; Age 65 and over: 21.9%; Males per 100 females: 104.5

Housing: Homeownership rate: 86.6%; Homeowner vacancy rate: 2.1%; Rental vacancy rate: 17.0%

MATTESON (township). Covers a land area of 35.772 square miles and a water area of 0.538 square miles. Located at 41.94° N. Lat; 85.22° W. Long. Elevation is 902 feet.

Population: 1,218; Growth (since 2000): -5.2%; Density: 34.0 persons per square mile; Race: 96.4% White, 0.7% Black/African American, 0.0% Asian, 0.4% American Indian/Alaska Native, 0.0% Native Hawaiian/Other Pacific Islander, 2.0% Two or more races, 1.1% Hispanic of any race; Average household size: 2.53; Median age: 43.1; Age under 18: 22.8%; Age 65 and over: 16.3%; Males per 100 females: 104.4

Housing: Homeownership rate: 85.0%; Homeowner vacancy rate: 1.4%; Rental vacancy rate: 1.4%

NOBLE (township). Covers a land area of 20.965 square miles and a water area of 0.372 square miles. Located at 41.79° N. Lat; 85.23° W. Long.

Population: 520; Growth (since 2000): 0.4%; Density: 24.8 persons per square mile; Race: 95.2% White, 0.8% Black/African American, 0.6% Asian, 0.6% American Indian/Alaska Native, 0.0% Native Hawaiian/Other Pacific Islander, 2.5% Two or more races, 1.9% Hispanic of any race; Average household size: 2.77; Median age: 39.6; Age under 18: 26.9%; Age 65 and over: 14.0%; Males per 100 females: 107.2

Housing: Homeownership rate: 83.5%; Homeowner vacancy rate: 0.0%; Rental vacancy rate: 16.2%

OVID (township). Covers a land area of 33.179 square miles and a water area of 3.023 square miles. Located at 41.85° N. Lat; 85.00° W. Long.
Population: 2,326; Growth (since 2000): -4.4%; Density: 70.1 persons per square mile; Race: 98.5% White, 0.5% Black/African American, 0.2% Asian, 0.1% American Indian/Alaska Native, 0.0% Native Hawaiian/Other Pacific Islander, 0.4% Two or more races, 0.9% Hispanic of any race; Average household size: 2.24; Median age: 51.4; Age under 18: 16.8%; Age 65 and over: 23.7%; Males per 100 females: 100.9
Housing: Homeownership rate: 89.0%; Homeowner vacancy rate: 3.6%; Rental vacancy rate: 18.8%

QUINCY (township). Covers a land area of 35.229 square miles and a water area of 1.027 square miles. Located at 41.94° N. Lat; 84.88° W. Long. Elevation is 1,017 feet.
History: The first settler came to Quincy in 1830. Quincy Township was separated from Coldwater in 1836, and named for Quincy, Massachusetts, the former home of one of the settlers.
Population: 4,285; Growth (since 2000): -2.9%; Density: 121.6 persons per square mile; Race: 97.5% White, 0.2% Black/African American, 0.5% Asian, 0.2% American Indian/Alaska Native, 0.0% Native Hawaiian/Other Pacific Islander, 1.1% Two or more races, 1.9% Hispanic of any race; Average household size: 2.68; Median age: 37.7; Age under 18: 27.2%; Age 65 and over: 11.4%; Males per 100 females: 99.0; Marriage status: 26.8% never married, 55.0% now married, 0.9% separated, 5.4% widowed, 12.9% divorced; Foreign born: 1.3%; Speak English only: 91.7%; With disability: 11.3%; Veterans: 10.2%; Ancestry: 39.0% German, 13.4% English, 10.3% Irish, 6.9% American, 5.9% Polish
Employment: 6.7% management, business, and financial, 4.1% computer, engineering, and science, 8.2% education, legal, community service, arts, and media, 2.0% healthcare practitioners, 18.8% service, 26.7% sales and office, 6.9% natural resources, construction, and maintenance, 26.6% production, transportation, and material moving
Income: Per capita: $19,069; Median household: $42,287; Average household: $48,314; Households with income of $100,000 or more: 8.0%; Poverty rate: 16.7%
Educational Attainment: High school diploma or higher: 86.9%; Bachelor's degree or higher: 14.0%; Graduate/professional degree or higher: 4.1%

School District(s)
Quincy Community Schools (KG-12)
    2012-13 Enrollment: 1,180 . . . . (517) 639-7141
Housing: Homeownership rate: 78.2%; Median home value: $96,000; Median year structure built: 1972; Homeowner vacancy rate: 3.0%; Median gross rent: $702 per month; Rental vacancy rate: 18.4%
Health Insurance: 86.0% have insurance; 62.9% have private insurance; 35.5% have public insurance; 14.0% do not have insurance; 3.8% of children under 18 do not have insurance
Transportation: Commute: 89.5% car, 0.0% public transportation, 4.7% walk, 5.6% work from home; Median travel time to work: 27.6 minutes

QUINCY (village). Covers a land area of 1.220 square miles and a water area of <.001 square miles. Located at 41.94° N. Lat; 84.89° W. Long. Elevation is 1,017 feet.
History: A flour mill built in Quincy in 1863 became a cereal-foods and milling plant, the mainstay of the early economy, along with a Portland cement plant which used local clay.
Population: 1,652; Growth (since 2000): -2.9%; Density: 1,354.6 persons per square mile; Race: 96.9% White, 0.5% Black/African American, 0.4% Asian, 0.2% American Indian/Alaska Native, 0.0% Native Hawaiian/Other Pacific Islander, 1.3% Two or more races, 2.5% Hispanic of any race; Average household size: 2.61; Median age: 33.1; Age under 18: 29.6%; Age 65 and over: 8.2%; Males per 100 females: 97.6
School District(s)
Quincy Community Schools (KG-12)
    2012-13 Enrollment: 1,180 . . . . (517) 639-7141
Housing: Homeownership rate: 65.6%; Homeowner vacancy rate: 3.4%; Rental vacancy rate: 23.1%

SHERWOOD (township). Covers a land area of 34.644 square miles and a water area of 1.502 square miles. Located at 42.04° N. Lat; 85.22° W. Long. Elevation is 876 feet.
Population: 2,094; Growth (since 2000): -8.3%; Density: 60.4 persons per square mile; Race: 97.0% White, 0.3% Black/African American, 0.1% Asian, 1.0% American Indian/Alaska Native, 0.0% Native Hawaiian/Other Pacific Islander, 1.4% Two or more races, 1.0% Hispanic of any race;

Average household size: 2.54; Median age: 42.6; Age under 18: 23.4%; Age 65 and over: 14.6%; Males per 100 females: 102.7
Housing: Homeownership rate: 80.2%; Homeowner vacancy rate: 3.5%; Rental vacancy rate: 7.9%

SHERWOOD (village). Covers a land area of 0.983 square miles and a water area of 0 square miles. Located at 42.00° N. Lat; 85.24° W. Long. Elevation is 876 feet.
History: When Sherwood was founded on land belonging to E.F. Hazen in 1832, it was called Hazenville. The name was changed in 1839 to Sherwood for Sherwood Forest in England, the former home of early settler Alexander E. Tomlinson.
Population: 309; Growth (since 2000): -4.6%; Density: 314.4 persons per square mile; Race: 95.1% White, 0.6% Black/African American, 0.0% Asian, 3.6% American Indian/Alaska Native, 0.0% Native Hawaiian/Other Pacific Islander, 0.6% Two or more races, 0.3% Hispanic of any race; Average household size: 2.92; Median age: 39.2; Age under 18: 23.9%; Age 65 and over: 12.0%; Males per 100 females: 102.0
Housing: Homeownership rate: 79.2%; Homeowner vacancy rate: 1.2%; Rental vacancy rate: 20.7%

UNION (township). Covers a land area of 35.460 square miles and a water area of 0.559 square miles. Located at 42.03° N. Lat; 85.12° W. Long.
Population: 2,868; Growth (since 2000): -8.1%; Density: 80.9 persons per square mile; Race: 95.9% White, 0.3% Black/African American, 0.6% Asian, 0.6% American Indian/Alaska Native, 0.0% Native Hawaiian/Other Pacific Islander, 2.1% Two or more races, 1.4% Hispanic of any race; Average household size: 2.52; Median age: 39.2; Age under 18: 25.3%; Age 65 and over: 15.3%; Males per 100 females: 101.5; Marriage status: 24.1% never married, 55.1% now married, 2.7% separated, 6.4% widowed, 14.3% divorced; Foreign born: 0.6%; Speak English only: 98.7%; With disability: 15.2%; Veterans: 12.0%; Ancestry: 31.2% German, 15.1% English, 13.2% Irish, 12.8% American, 5.1% French
Employment: 13.1% management, business, and financial, 4.4% computer, engineering, and science, 7.1% education, legal, community service, arts, and media, 2.5% healthcare practitioners, 17.6% service, 24.3% sales and office, 9.2% natural resources, construction, and maintenance, 21.7% production, transportation, and material moving
Income: Per capita: $19,279; Median household: $43,148; Average household: $48,638; Households with income of $100,000 or more: 7.1%; Poverty rate: 14.7%
Educational Attainment: High school diploma or higher: 89.5%; Bachelor's degree or higher: 13.1%; Graduate/professional degree or higher: 2.5%
Housing: Homeownership rate: 77.2%; Median home value: $85,800; Median year structure built: 1961; Homeowner vacancy rate: 2.6%; Median gross rent: $581 per month; Rental vacancy rate: 13.7%
Health Insurance: 91.2% have insurance; 70.0% have private insurance; 34.1% have public insurance; 8.8% do not have insurance; 2.5% of children under 18 do not have insurance
Transportation: Commute: 91.4% car, 0.0% public transportation, 1.4% walk, 6.1% work from home; Median travel time to work: 25.6 minutes

UNION CITY (village). Covers a land area of 1.442 square miles and a water area of 0.049 square miles. Located at 42.07° N. Lat; 85.14° W. Long. Elevation is 906 feet.
History: Union City was named for the junction of the Coldwater and St. Joseph Rivers at this point. The village was a station on the Underground Railroad, helping slaves to freedom. Industries in the early 1900's included creamery products and dried milk processing.
Population: 1,599; Growth (since 2000): -11.4%; Density: 1,108.7 persons per square mile; Race: 95.2% White, 0.4% Black/African American, 0.8% Asian, 0.6% American Indian/Alaska Native, 0.0% Native Hawaiian/Other Pacific Islander, 2.8% Two or more races, 1.0% Hispanic of any race; Average household size: 2.53; Median age: 35.7; Age under 18: 27.6%; Age 65 and over: 13.8%; Males per 100 females: 94.3
School District(s)
Union City Community Schools (PK-12)
    2012-13 Enrollment: 1,084 . . . . (517) 741-8091
Housing: Homeownership rate: 70.9%; Homeowner vacancy rate: 3.2%; Rental vacancy rate: 17.1%
Safety: Violent crime rate: 12.6 per 10,000 population; Property crime rate: 326.8 per 10,000 population

Calhoun County

Located in southern Michigan; drained by the Kalamazoo and Saint Joseph Rivers. Covers a land area of 706.233 square miles, a water area of 12.120 square miles, and is located in the Eastern Time Zone at 42.24° N. Lat., 85.01° W. Long. The county was founded in 1829. County seat is Marshall.

Calhoun County is part of the Battle Creek, MI Metropolitan Statistical Area. The entire metro area includes: Calhoun County, MI

Weather Station: Battle Creek   Elevation: 955 feet

	Jan	Feb	Mar	Apr	May	Jun	Jul	Aug	Sep	Oct	Nov	Dec
High	32	36	46	60	71	79	83	81	73	61	47	36
Low	16	18	26	37	47	56	60	58	51	40	31	21
Precip	1.7	1.5	2.1	2.9	3.8	3.2	3.5	3.8	3.9	3.4	2.8	2.2
Snow	16.3	11.7	6.3	2.1	tr	0.0	0.0	0.0	tr	0.6	5.2	17.0

High and Low temperatures in degrees Fahrenheit; Precipitation and Snow in inches

Population: 136,146; Growth (since 2000): -1.3%; Density: 192.8 persons per square mile; Race: 82.2% White, 10.9% Black/African American, 1.6% Asian, 0.6% American Indian/Alaska Native, 0.0% Native Hawaiian/Other Pacific Islander, 3.1% two or more races, 4.5% Hispanic of any race; Average household size: 2.44; Median age: 39.2; Age under 18: 24.2%; Age 65 and over: 14.8%; Males per 100 females: 95.5; Marriage status: 29.1% never married, 49.6% now married, 2.0% separated, 6.7% widowed, 14.6% divorced; Foreign born: 3.6%; Speak English only: 93.9%; With disability: 15.2%; Veterans: 11.0%; Ancestry: 21.7% German, 12.8% English, 11.3% Irish, 7.7% American, 4.2% Polish
Religion: Six largest groups: 8.5% Catholicism, 4.0% Baptist, 3.8% Holiness, 3.2% Methodist/Pietist, 2.6% Non-denominational Protestant, 2.6% Lutheran
Economy: Unemployment rate: 5.1%; Leading industries: 18.7% retail trade; 12.3% health care and social assistance; 12.2% other services (except public administration); Farms: 1,023 totaling 224,877 acres; Company size: 5 employ 1,000 or more persons, 4 employ 500 to 999 persons, 60 employ 100 to 499 persons, 2,549 employ less than 100 persons; Business ownership: 2,933 women-owned, n/a Black-owned, n/a Hispanic-owned, 154 Asian-owned
Employment: 11.7% management, business, and financial, 3.3% computer, engineering, and science, 7.6% education, legal, community service, arts, and media, 5.2% healthcare practitioners, 19.5% service, 24.7% sales and office, 7.8% natural resources, construction, and maintenance, 20.1% production, transportation, and material moving
Income: Per capita: $22,978; Median household: $42,110; Average household: $56,836; Households with income of $100,000 or more: 13.5%; Poverty rate: 17.8%
Educational Attainment: High school diploma or higher: 88.8%; Bachelor's degree or higher: 19.5%; Graduate/professional degree or higher: 6.9%
Housing: Homeownership rate: 69.8%; Median home value: $98,300; Median year structure built: 1960; Homeowner vacancy rate: 2.9%; Median gross rent: $671 per month; Rental vacancy rate: 12.8%
Vital Statistics: Birth rate: 118.4 per 10,000 population; Death rate: 98.8 per 10,000 population; Age-adjusted cancer mortality rate: 193.9 deaths per 100,000 population
Health Insurance: 87.4% have insurance; 65.2% have private insurance; 37.8% have public insurance; 12.6% do not have insurance; 3.1% of children under 18 do not have insurance
Health Care: Physicians: 15.3 per 10,000 population; Hospital beds: 49.5 per 10,000 population; Hospital admissions: 1,297.4 per 10,000 population
Transportation: Commute: 91.4% car, 0.6% public transportation, 3.8% walk, 2.9% work from home; Median travel time to work: 20.0 minutes
Presidential Election: 50.3% Obama, 48.7% Romney (2012)
Additional Information Contacts
Calhoun Government . . . . (269) 781-0700
  http://www.calhouncountymi.org

Calhoun County Communities

ALBION (city). Covers a land area of 4.409 square miles and a water area of 0.103 square miles. Located at 42.25° N. Lat; 84.76° W. Long. Elevation is 951 feet.
History: Albion developed as an industrial city, taking its name from the Albion Company grist mill established in 1835 by Jesse Crowell, who had

formerly lived in Albion, New York. The village was platted by Crowell in 1836, incorporated as a village in 1855, and as a city in 1885.
Population: 8,616; Growth (since 2000): -5.8%; Density: 1,954.0 persons per square mile; Race: 63.6% White, 29.9% Black/African American, 1.1% Asian, 0.3% American Indian/Alaska Native, 0.2% Native Hawaiian/Other Pacific Islander, 3.9% Two or more races, 5.8% Hispanic of any race; Average household size: 2.39; Median age: 28.1; Age under 18: 21.7%; Age 65 and over: 13.0%; Males per 100 females: 87.2; Marriage status: 43.4% never married, 34.1% now married, 2.6% separated, 6.5% widowed, 16.0% divorced; Foreign born: 2.0%; Speak English only: 93.2%; With disability: 16.6%; Veterans: 6.8%; Ancestry: 17.1% German, 11.4% Irish, 8.5% English, 6.5% Polish, 3.4% American
Employment: 6.7% management, business, and financial, 0.9% computer, engineering, and science, 14.3% education, legal, community service, arts, and media, 1.6% healthcare practitioners, 26.9% service, 24.1% sales and office, 5.3% natural resources, construction, and maintenance, 20.2% production, transportation, and material moving
Income: Per capita: $14,455; Median household: $25,382; Average household: $36,057; Households with income of $100,000 or more: 6.0%; Poverty rate: 38.7%
Educational Attainment: High school diploma or higher: 84.0%; Bachelor's degree or higher: 18.3%; Graduate/professional degree or higher: 8.2%

School District(s)
Albion Public Schools (PK-12)
  2012-13 Enrollment: 723 . . . . (517) 629-9166
Calhoun ISD (PK-12)
  2012-13 Enrollment: 990 . . . . (269) 781-5141
Four-year College(s)
Albion College (Private, Not-for-profit, United Methodist)
  Fall 2013 Enrollment: 1,307 . . . . (517) 629-1000
  2013-14 Tuition: In-state $36,051; Out-of-state $36,051
Housing: Homeownership rate: 55.5%; Median home value: $63,700; Median year structure built: 1946; Homeowner vacancy rate: 4.7%; Median gross rent: $551 per month; Rental vacancy rate: 13.8%
Health Insurance: 86.3% have insurance; 51.5% have private insurance; 48.7% have public insurance; 13.7% do not have insurance; 7.1% of children under 18 do not have insurance
Safety: Violent crime rate: 68.0 per 10,000 population; Property crime rate: 281.6 per 10,000 population
Newspapers: Albion Recorder (weekly circulation 1100)
Transportation: Commute: 75.1% car, 0.0% public transportation, 20.0% walk, 2.7% work from home; Median travel time to work: 17.1 minutes; Amtrak: Train service available.
Additional Information Contacts
City of Albion . . . . (517) 629-5535
  http://www.ci.albion.mi.us

ALBION (township). Covers a land area of 32.631 square miles and a water area of 0.404 square miles. Located at 42.20° N. Lat; 84.76° W. Long. Elevation is 951 feet.
Population: 1,123; Growth (since 2000): -6.4%; Density: 34.4 persons per square mile; Race: 93.6% White, 2.5% Black/African American, 1.3% Asian, 0.6% American Indian/Alaska Native, 0.0% Native Hawaiian/Other Pacific Islander, 1.5% Two or more races, 1.8% Hispanic of any race; Average household size: 2.42; Median age: 47.2; Age under 18: 20.1%; Age 65 and over: 21.4%; Males per 100 females: 104.2
School District(s)
Albion Public Schools (PK-12)
  2012-13 Enrollment: 723 . . . . (517) 629-9166
Calhoun ISD (PK-12)
  2012-13 Enrollment: 990 . . . . (269) 781-5141
Four-year College(s)
Albion College (Private, Not-for-profit, United Methodist)
  Fall 2013 Enrollment: 1,307 . . . . (517) 629-1000
  2013-14 Tuition: In-state $36,051; Out-of-state $36,051
Housing: Homeownership rate: 83.8%; Homeowner vacancy rate: 2.8%; Rental vacancy rate: 6.2%
Newspapers: Albion Recorder (weekly circulation 1100)

ATHENS (township). Covers a land area of 35.936 square miles and a water area of 0.190 square miles. Located at 42.12° N. Lat; 85.24° W. Long. Elevation is 889 feet.
Population: 2,554; Growth (since 2000): -0.7%; Density: 71.1 persons per square mile; Race: 94.4% White, 0.4% Black/African American, 0.2%

Asian, 2.1% American Indian/Alaska Native, 0.1% Native Hawaiian/Other Pacific Islander, 2.4% Two or more races, 1.4% Hispanic of any race; Average household size: 2.56; Median age: 41.9; Age under 18: 22.5%; Age 65 and over: 17.6%; Males per 100 females: 102.2; Marriage status: 19.1% never married, 58.2% now married, 1.9% separated, 9.0% widowed, 13.8% divorced; Foreign born: 0.8%; Speak English only: 98.6%; With disability: 17.3%; Veterans: 13.1%; Ancestry: 25.4% German, 15.9% Irish, 13.5% English, 7.9% American, 5.8% Dutch

Employment: 9.0% management, business, and financial, 4.2% computer, engineering, and science, 4.2% education, legal, community service, arts, and media, 7.8% healthcare practitioners, 19.6% service, 20.5% sales and office, 11.4% natural resources, construction, and maintenance, 23.3% production, transportation, and material moving

Income: Per capita: $23,507; Median household: $54,890; Average household: $60,074; Households with income of $100,000 or more: 16.4%; Poverty rate: 9.1%

Educational Attainment: High school diploma or higher: 90.8%; Bachelor's degree or higher: 13.6%; Graduate/professional degree or higher: 3.7%

School District(s)
Athens Area Schools (PK-12)
    2012-13 Enrollment: 578 . . . . (269) 729-5427

Housing: Homeownership rate: 84.2%; Median home value: $95,000; Median year structure built: 1967; Homeowner vacancy rate: 1.7%; Median gross rent: $676 per month; Rental vacancy rate: 7.6%

Health Insurance: 88.9% have insurance; 76.8% have private insurance; 29.9% have public insurance; 11.1% do not have insurance; 4.7% of children under 18 do not have insurance

Transportation: Commute: 95.7% car, 0.0% public transportation, 2.6% walk, 1.5% work from home; Median travel time to work: 29.2 minutes

ATHENS (village).
Covers a land area of 1.007 square miles and a water area of 0.006 square miles. Located at 42.09° N. Lat; 85.24° W. Long. Elevation is 889 feet.

History: Athens was settled in 1831 along the Nottawaseepe River. In 1854, William Simons built a store here, and in 1860 the village was platted. Athens was named for Athens, New York, from which many of its early residents had come.

Population: 1,024; Growth (since 2000): -7.8%; Density: 1,016.8 persons per square mile; Race: 95.4% White, 0.5% Black/African American, 0.1% Asian, 0.9% American Indian/Alaska Native, 0.1% Native Hawaiian/Other Pacific Islander, 2.2% Two or more races, 1.4% Hispanic of any race; Average household size: 2.65; Median age: 38.9; Age under 18: 24.0%; Age 65 and over: 14.1%; Males per 100 females: 101.2

School District(s)
Athens Area Schools (PK-12)
    2012-13 Enrollment: 578 . . . . (269) 729-5427

Housing: Homeownership rate: 80.4%; Homeowner vacancy rate: 3.7%; Rental vacancy rate: 4.9%

BATTLE CREEK (city).
Covers a land area of 42.606 square miles and a water area of 1.117 square miles. Located at 42.30° N. Lat; 85.23° W. Long. Elevation is 840 feet.

History: Battle Creek was called Milton when it was first settled in 1831 by Samuel Guernsey of New York. When the post office was established in 1833, the community was renamed for the nearby creek, where a small battle between some individuals had taken place in 1825. Battle Creek's character was shaped in 1855 when Captain Joseph Bates moved the headquarters of the Seventh Day Adventist Church here. The church's emphasis on health reforms led to the founding of the Western Health Reform Institute, renamed the Battle Creek Sanitarium when Dr. John Harvey Kellogg took charge of it in 1876. Among other medical innovations, Kellogg perfected methods and machines for processing foods which resulted in new cereal and nut-food products. C.W. Post, who benefited from treatment at the sanitarium in 1891, established La Vita Inn in Battle Creek and began to serve a warm cereal drink, marketed as Postum. Later, the Kellogg and Post cereal factories were major employers in Battle Creek.

Population: 52,347; Growth (since 2000): -1.9%; Density: 1,228.6 persons per square mile; Race: 71.7% White, 18.2% Black/African American, 2.4% Asian, 0.7% American Indian/Alaska Native, 0.0% Native Hawaiian/Other Pacific Islander, 4.3% Two or more races, 6.7% Hispanic of any race; Average household size: 2.41; Median age: 36.3; Age under 18: 26.1%; Age 65 and over: 13.4%; Males per 100 females: 91.9; Marriage status: 32.2% never married, 45.6% now married, 2.5% separated, 7.1%

widowed, 15.1% divorced; Foreign born: 6.0%; Speak English only: 90.5%; With disability: 16.2%; Veterans: 11.1%; Ancestry: 19.2% German, 11.9% English, 10.9% Irish, 6.0% American, 3.8% Polish

Employment: 11.5% management, business, and financial, 3.6% computer, engineering, and science, 8.1% education, legal, community service, arts, and media, 5.1% healthcare practitioners, 20.4% service, 24.3% sales and office, 6.6% natural resources, construction, and maintenance, 20.4% production, transportation, and material moving

Income: Per capita: $22,154; Median household: $37,814; Average household: $55,091; Households with income of $100,000 or more: 12.1%; Poverty rate: 22.1%

Educational Attainment: High school diploma or higher: 88.3%; Bachelor's degree or higher: 21.9%; Graduate/professional degree or higher: 8.2%

School District(s)
Arbor Academy (KG-12)
    2012-13 Enrollment: 215 . . . . (269) 963-5851
Battle Creek Area Learning Center (KG-12)
    2012-13 Enrollment: 174 . . . . (269) 565-4782
Battle Creek Public Schools (PK-12)
    2012-13 Enrollment: 5,123 . . . . (269) 965-9465
Calhoun ISD (PK-12)
    2012-13 Enrollment: 990 . . . . (269) 781-5141
Endeavor Charter Academy (PK-12)
    2012-13 Enrollment: 672 . . . . (269) 962-9300
Harper Creek Community Schools (PK-12)
    2012-13 Enrollment: 2,599 . . . . (269) 441-6555
Lakeview SD (Calhoun) (PK-12)
    2012-13 Enrollment: 3,859 . . . . (269) 565-2411
Pennfield Schools (PK-12)
    2012-13 Enrollment: 2,094 . . . . (269) 961-9781

Four-year College(s)
The Robert B Miller College (Private, Not-for-profit)
    Fall 2013 Enrollment: 328 . . . . (269) 660-8021

Two-year College(s)
Kellogg Community College (Public)
    Fall 2013 Enrollment: 6,123 . . . . (269) 965-3931
    2013-14 Tuition: In-state $4,801; Out-of-state $6,762

Vocational/Technical School(s)
The Salon Spa Academy (Private, For-profit)
    Fall 2013 Enrollment: 61 . . . . (269) 962-4400
    2013-14 Tuition: $15,300
Wright Beauty Academy (Private, For-profit)
    Fall 2013 Enrollment: 45 . . . . (269) 964-4016
    2013-14 Tuition: $9,400

Housing: Homeownership rate: 60.6%; Median home value: $84,400; Median year structure built: 1955; Homeowner vacancy rate: 4.0%; Median gross rent: $689 per month; Rental vacancy rate: 12.8%

Health Insurance: 86.5% have insurance; 58.5% have private insurance; 43.0% have public insurance; 13.5% do not have insurance; 3.4% of children under 18 do not have insurance

Hospitals: Battle Creek VA Medical Center; Bronson Battle Creek Hospital (315 beds)

Newspapers: Battle Creek Enquirer (daily circulation 22600)

Transportation: Commute: 91.0% car, 1.4% public transportation, 3.5% walk, 2.7% work from home; Median travel time to work: 18.8 minutes; Amtrak: Train service available.

Airports: W K Kellogg (general aviation)

Additional Information Contacts
City of Battle Creek . . . . (269) 966-3378
    http://www.battlecreekmi.gov

BEDFORD (charter township).
Covers a land area of 29.100 square miles and a water area of 0.604 square miles. Located at 42.38° N. Lat; 85.24° W. Long. Elevation is 886 feet.

History: Bedford was named by Josiah Gilbert for his former home in Bedford, Westchester County, New York. Stagecoaches traveling between Grand Rapids and Battle Creek passed through Bedford.

Population: 9,357; Growth (since 2000): -1.7%; Density: 321.6 persons per square mile; Race: 83.9% White, 10.9% Black/African American, 0.4% Asian, 0.5% American Indian/Alaska Native, 0.1% Native Hawaiian/Other Pacific Islander, 3.1% Two or more races, 3.1% Hispanic of any race; Average household size: 2.47; Median age: 43.1; Age under 18: 21.8%; Age 65 and over: 15.8%; Males per 100 females: 101.4; Marriage status: 29.2% never married, 48.9% now married, 2.7% separated, 7.6%

widowed, 14.3% divorced; Foreign born: 1.6%; Speak English only: 97.8%; With disability: 16.7%; Veterans: 12.6%; Ancestry: 18.7% German, 11.6% English, 7.7% Irish, 7.3% American, 3.8% Italian

Employment: 10.7% management, business, and financial, 3.0% computer, engineering, and science, 5.4% education, legal, community service, arts, and media, 4.3% healthcare practitioners, 19.7% service, 26.2% sales and office, 7.2% natural resources, construction, and maintenance, 23.3% production, transportation, and material moving

Income: Per capita: $22,957; Median household: $45,702; Average household: $54,716; Households with income of $100,000 or more: 13.4%; Poverty rate: 11.5%

Educational Attainment: High school diploma or higher: 87.3%; Bachelor's degree or higher: 13.8%; Graduate/professional degree or higher: 4.7%

Housing: Homeownership rate: 86.5%; Median home value: $95,100; Median year structure built: 1960; Homeowner vacancy rate: 2.1%; Median gross rent: $791 per month; Rental vacancy rate: 10.3%

Health Insurance: 85.9% have insurance; 69.0% have private insurance; 33.4% have public insurance; 14.1% do not have insurance; 3.7% of children under 18 do not have insurance

Transportation: Commute: 91.1% car, 0.0% public transportation, 3.9% walk, 2.8% work from home; Median travel time to work: 18.5 minutes

Additional Information Contacts

Bedford Charter Township . . . . (269) 968-6917
    http://bedfordchartertownship.com

BROWNLEE PARK (CDP). Covers a land area of 2.006 square miles and a water area of 0.028 square miles. Located at 42.33° N. Lat; 85.13° W. Long. Elevation is 876 feet.

Population: 2,108; Growth (since 2000): -18.5%; Density: 1,050.9 persons per square mile; Race: 91.2% White, 2.1% Black/African American, 0.4% Asian, 0.6% American Indian/Alaska Native, 0.1% Native Hawaiian/Other Pacific Islander, 3.9% Two or more races, 5.5% Hispanic of any race; Average household size: 2.63; Median age: 36.2; Age under 18: 27.3%; Age 65 and over: 10.9%; Males per 100 females: 100.0

Housing: Homeownership rate: 75.8%; Homeowner vacancy rate: 3.3%; Rental vacancy rate: 39.9%

BURLINGTON (township). Covers a land area of 35.702 square miles and a water area of 0.428 square miles. Located at 42.11° N. Lat; 85.12° W. Long. Elevation is 932 feet.

History: Burlington Township was named for the gunboat "Burlington" which saw duty on the Great Lakes during the War of 1812.

Population: 1,941; Growth (since 2000): 0.6%; Density: 54.4 persons per square mile; Race: 97.4% White, 0.5% Black/African American, 0.2% Asian, 0.3% American Indian/Alaska Native, 0.0% Native Hawaiian/Other Pacific Islander, 1.4% Two or more races, 1.0% Hispanic of any race; Average household size: 2.56; Median age: 41.3; Age under 18: 24.8%; Age 65 and over: 14.6%; Males per 100 females: 103.9

Housing: Homeownership rate: 85.5%; Homeowner vacancy rate: 2.0%; Rental vacancy rate: 7.5%

BURLINGTON (village). Covers a land area of 0.651 square miles and a water area of 0.028 square miles. Located at 42.10° N. Lat; 85.08° W. Long. Elevation is 932 feet.

History: Burlington was founded in 1833 by William and Ansel Adams. The village as well as the township was named for a gunboat used in the War of 1812.

Population: 261; Growth (since 2000): -35.6%; Density: 400.7 persons per square mile; Race: 98.1% White, 0.0% Black/African American, 0.0% Asian, 0.0% American Indian/Alaska Native, 0.0% Native Hawaiian/Other Pacific Islander, 1.9% Two or more races, 0.0% Hispanic of any race; Average household size: 2.72; Median age: 37.3; Age under 18: 24.9%; Age 65 and over: 10.7%; Males per 100 females: 108.8

Housing: Homeownership rate: 81.3%; Homeowner vacancy rate: 10.1%; Rental vacancy rate: 10.0%

CERESCO (unincorporated postal area)
ZCTA: 49033

Covers a land area of 32.278 square miles and a water area of 0.386 square miles. Located at 42.23° N. Lat; 85.09° W. Long. Elevation is 896 feet.

Population: 1,760; Growth (since 2000): 7.4%; Density: 54.5 persons per square mile; Race: 97.7% White, 0.6% Black/African American, 0.4% Asian, 0.5% American Indian/Alaska Native, 0.0% Native

Hawaiian/Other Pacific Islander, 0.8% Two or more races, 1.4% Hispanic of any race; Average household size: 2.52; Median age: 46.2; Age under 18: 20.5%; Age 65 and over: 16.5%; Males per 100 females: 106.6

Housing: Homeownership rate: 91.0%; Homeowner vacancy rate: 0.8%; Rental vacancy rate: 6.0%

CLARENCE (township). Covers a land area of 32.545 square miles and a water area of 1.498 square miles. Located at 42.37° N. Lat; 84.78° W. Long. Elevation is 928 feet.

History: Clarence Township was first settled in 1836, and organized in 1838.

Population: 1,985; Growth (since 2000): -2.3%; Density: 61.0 persons per square mile; Race: 98.2% White, 0.3% Black/African American, 0.1% Asian, 0.4% American Indian/Alaska Native, 0.0% Native Hawaiian/Other Pacific Islander, 0.9% Two or more races, 1.1% Hispanic of any race; Average household size: 2.53; Median age: 44.7; Age under 18: 23.1%; Age 65 and over: 17.9%; Males per 100 females: 107.6

Housing: Homeownership rate: 82.7%; Homeowner vacancy rate: 2.1%; Rental vacancy rate: 9.9%

CLARENDON (township). Covers a land area of 35.537 square miles and a water area of 0.183 square miles. Located at 42.11° N. Lat; 84.88° W. Long. Elevation is 971 feet.

History: Many of the early residents in Clarendon Township had come from Clarendon, New York.

Population: 1,139; Growth (since 2000): 2.2%; Density: 32.1 persons per square mile; Race: 96.4% White, 0.5% Black/African American, 0.0% Asian, 0.6% American Indian/Alaska Native, 0.0% Native Hawaiian/Other Pacific Islander, 2.4% Two or more races, 1.4% Hispanic of any race; Average household size: 2.62; Median age: 40.9; Age under 18: 24.5%; Age 65 and over: 13.3%; Males per 100 females: 106.7

Housing: Homeownership rate: 87.1%; Homeowner vacancy rate: 2.0%; Rental vacancy rate: 3.4%

CONVIS (township). Covers a land area of 35.371 square miles and a water area of 1.111 square miles. Located at 42.38° N. Lat; 85.00° W. Long.

Population: 1,636; Growth (since 2000): -1.8%; Density: 46.3 persons per square mile; Race: 96.9% White, 0.2% Black/African American, 0.2% Asian, 0.5% American Indian/Alaska Native, 0.0% Native Hawaiian/Other Pacific Islander, 1.2% Two or more races, 2.7% Hispanic of any race; Average household size: 2.57; Median age: 44.3; Age under 18: 21.3%; Age 65 and over: 14.9%; Males per 100 females: 104.2

Housing: Homeownership rate: 91.6%; Homeowner vacancy rate: 1.9%; Rental vacancy rate: 1.9%

Additional Information Contacts

Convis Township . . . . (269) 789-0654
    http://www.convistownship.org

EAST LEROY (unincorporated postal area)
ZCTA: 49051

Covers a land area of 29.428 square miles and a water area of 0.213 square miles. Located at 42.18° N. Lat; 85.24° W. Long. Elevation is 919 feet.

Population: 2,436; Growth (since 2000): 6.1%; Density: 82.8 persons per square mile; Race: 97.3% White, 0.1% Black/African American, 0.6% Asian, 0.7% American Indian/Alaska Native, 0.1% Native Hawaiian/Other Pacific Islander, 1.0% Two or more races, 2.0% Hispanic of any race; Average household size: 2.61; Median age: 43.7; Age under 18: 22.6%; Age 65 and over: 15.8%; Males per 100 females: 98.9

School District(s)

Athens Area Schools (PK-12)
    2012-13 Enrollment: 578 . . . . (269) 729-5427
    Housing: Homeownership rate: 92.8%; Homeowner vacancy rate: 0.6%; Rental vacancy rate: 5.6%

ECKFORD (township). Covers a land area of 35.398 square miles and a water area of 0.259 square miles. Located at 42.19° N. Lat; 84.89° W. Long. Elevation is 951 feet.

Population: 1,303; Growth (since 2000): 1.6%; Density: 36.8 persons per square mile; Race: 97.4% White, 0.3% Black/African American, 0.8% Asian, 0.4% American Indian/Alaska Native, 0.0% Native Hawaiian/Other Pacific Islander, 1.0% Two or more races, 1.7% Hispanic of any race;

Average household size: 2.58; Median age: 43.6; Age under 18: 23.8%; Age 65 and over: 14.9%; Males per 100 females: 103.6
Housing: Homeownership rate: 86.3%; Homeowner vacancy rate: 2.0%; Rental vacancy rate: 12.7%

EMMETT (charter township). Covers a land area of 32.000 square miles and a water area of 0.501 square miles. Located at 42.28° N. Lat; 85.11° W. Long.
Population: 11,770; Growth (since 2000): -1.7%; Density: 367.8 persons per square mile; Race: 91.4% White, 3.1% Black/African American, 1.2% Asian, 0.6% American Indian/Alaska Native, 0.0% Native Hawaiian/Other Pacific Islander, 2.5% Two or more races, 3.9% Hispanic of any race; Average household size: 2.42; Median age: 40.6; Age under 18: 23.0%; Age 65 and over: 14.8%; Males per 100 females: 99.4; Marriage status: 27.6% never married, 54.2% now married, 1.0% separated, 5.2% widowed, 13.0% divorced; Foreign born: 2.7%; Speak English only: 96.2%; With disability: 12.1%; Veterans: 11.4%; Ancestry: 20.3% German, 14.1% English, 10.5% Irish, 9.0% American, 4.7% Dutch
Employment: 13.1% management, business, and financial, 1.8% computer, engineering, and science, 7.0% education, legal, community service, arts, and media, 5.6% healthcare practitioners, 16.5% service, 28.5% sales and office, 8.9% natural resources, construction, and maintenance, 18.6% production, transportation, and material moving
Income: Per capita: $26,056; Median household: $47,652; Average household: $65,806; Households with income of $100,000 or more: 16.9%; Poverty rate: 13.5%
Educational Attainment: High school diploma or higher: 90.4%; Bachelor's degree or higher: 18.8%; Graduate/professional degree or higher: 5.0%
Housing: Homeownership rate: 72.3%; Median home value: $117,900; Median year structure built: 1964; Homeowner vacancy rate: 2.3%; Median gross rent: $649 per month; Rental vacancy rate: 13.8%
Health Insurance: 88.9% have insurance; 74.6% have private insurance; 28.9% have public insurance; 11.1% do not have insurance; 0.5% of children under 18 do not have insurance
Safety: Violent crime rate: 46.4 per 10,000 population; Property crime rate: 552.9 per 10,000 population
Transportation: Commute: 94.4% car, 0.3% public transportation, 1.2% walk, 2.8% work from home; Median travel time to work: 17.7 minutes
Additional Information Contacts
Emmett Charter Township. . . . . (269) 968-0241
    http://www.emmett.org

FREDONIA (township). Covers a land area of 34.016 square miles and a water area of 0.829 square miles. Located at 42.20° N. Lat; 85.01° W. Long.
Population: 1,626; Growth (since 2000): -5.6%; Density: 47.8 persons per square mile; Race: 97.6% White, 0.0% Black/African American, 0.4% Asian, 0.6% American Indian/Alaska Native, 0.0% Native Hawaiian/Other Pacific Islander, 1.0% Two or more races, 1.5% Hispanic of any race; Average household size: 2.47; Median age: 45.6; Age under 18: 21.5%; Age 65 and over: 16.9%; Males per 100 females: 101.2
Housing: Homeownership rate: 85.3%; Homeowner vacancy rate: 2.8%; Rental vacancy rate: 1.0%

HOMER (township). Covers a land area of 35.657 square miles and a water area of 0.519 square miles. Located at 42.12° N. Lat; 84.78° W. Long. Elevation is 994 feet.
History: Homer Township was organized in 1834 and named for Homer, New York, at the request of residents who had come from New York.
Population: 3,015; Growth (since 2000): 0.2%; Density: 84.6 persons per square mile; Race: 97.6% White, 0.4% Black/African American, 0.2% Asian, 0.4% American Indian/Alaska Native, 0.0% Native Hawaiian/Other Pacific Islander, 1.0% Two or more races, 2.6% Hispanic of any race; Average household size: 2.83; Median age: 34.6; Age under 18: 30.1%; Age 65 and over: 12.6%; Males per 100 females: 94.9; Marriage status: 29.1% never married, 49.0% now married, 0.6% separated, 4.9% widowed, 16.9% divorced; Foreign born: 0.9%; Speak English only: 95.7%; With disability: 14.5%; Veterans: 9.6%; Ancestry: 25.7% German, 13.5% Irish, 11.2% American, 10.0% English, 4.4% Dutch
Employment: 11.3% management, business, and financial, 1.8% computer, engineering, and science, 5.2% education, legal, community service, arts, and media, 2.8% healthcare practitioners, 16.2% service, 17.1% sales and office, 8.7% natural resources, construction, and maintenance, 36.8% production, transportation, and material moving

Income: Per capita: $18,004; Median household: $36,853; Average household: $46,951; Households with income of $100,000 or more: 8.3%; Poverty rate: 20.4%
Educational Attainment: High school diploma or higher: 84.3%; Bachelor's degree or higher: 9.0%; Graduate/professional degree or higher: 3.2%
School District(s)
Homer Community SD (PK-12)
    2012-13 Enrollment: 1,053 . . . . (517) 568-4461
Housing: Homeownership rate: 72.7%; Median home value: $81,800; Median year structure built: 1970; Homeowner vacancy rate: 3.0%; Median gross rent: $505 per month; Rental vacancy rate: 19.1%
Health Insurance: 85.2% have insurance; 62.4% have private insurance; 37.2% have public insurance; 14.8% do not have insurance; 2.9% of children under 18 do not have insurance
Newspapers: Homer Index (weekly circulation 1800)
Transportation: Commute: 93.8% car, 0.0% public transportation, 3.1% walk, 2.5% work from home; Median travel time to work: 22.2 minutes

HOMER (village). Covers a land area of 1.395 square miles and a water area of 0.047 square miles. Located at 42.15° N. Lat; 84.81° W. Long. Elevation is 994 feet.
History: Homer was founded by Milton Barney, who built a sawmill and a grist mill here, and opened a store and an inn in the early 1830's. The village was first called Barneyville, but was later renamed for its township. Homer grew up on the burr oak plains, and became known for making products of wood and grains.
Population: 1,668; Growth (since 2000): -9.9%; Density: 1,195.4 persons per square mile; Race: 97.7% White, 0.3% Black/African American, 0.4% Asian, 0.4% American Indian/Alaska Native, 0.0% Native Hawaiian/Other Pacific Islander, 0.7% Two or more races, 2.8% Hispanic of any race; Average household size: 2.71; Median age: 33.5; Age under 18: 30.3%; Age 65 and over: 12.4%; Males per 100 females: 94.6
School District(s)
Homer Community SD (PK-12)
    2012-13 Enrollment: 1,053 . . . . (517) 568-4461
Housing: Homeownership rate: 65.7%; Homeowner vacancy rate: 3.3%; Rental vacancy rate: 20.8%
Newspapers: Homer Index (weekly circulation 1800)

LEE (township). Covers a land area of 36.218 square miles and a water area of 0.156 square miles. Located at 42.38° N. Lat; 84.89° W. Long.
Population: 1,213; Growth (since 2000): -3.5%; Density: 33.5 persons per square mile; Race: 95.7% White, 0.2% Black/African American, 0.0% Asian, 0.1% American Indian/Alaska Native, 0.0% Native Hawaiian/Other Pacific Islander, 3.3% Two or more races, 1.7% Hispanic of any race; Average household size: 2.70; Median age: 39.1; Age under 18: 25.1%; Age 65 and over: 12.7%; Males per 100 females: 111.3
Housing: Homeownership rate: 86.8%; Homeowner vacancy rate: 1.0%; Rental vacancy rate: 7.8%

LEROY (township). Covers a land area of 35.998 square miles and a water area of 0.449 square miles. Located at 42.20° N. Lat; 85.24° W. Long.
Population: 3,712; Growth (since 2000): 14.6%; Density: 103.1 persons per square mile; Race: 96.9% White, 0.8% Black/African American, 0.5% Asian, 0.7% American Indian/Alaska Native, 0.1% Native Hawaiian/Other Pacific Islander, 0.8% Two or more races, 2.4% Hispanic of any race; Average household size: 2.49; Median age: 46.0; Age under 18: 20.9%; Age 65 and over: 17.9%; Males per 100 females: 97.3; Marriage status: 12.0% never married, 63.8% now married, 0.0% separated, 7.7% widowed, 16.5% divorced; Foreign born: 3.3%; Speak English only: 94.9%; With disability: 15.0%; Veterans: 14.9%; Ancestry: 28.8% German, 17.4% English, 16.4% Irish, 12.1% American, 9.8% Dutch
Employment: 13.8% management, business, and financial, 3.5% computer, engineering, and science, 2.1% education, legal, community service, arts, and media, 12.0% healthcare practitioners, 16.0% service, 30.4% sales and office, 9.8% natural resources, construction, and maintenance, 12.5% production, transportation, and material moving
Income: Per capita: $34,349; Median household: $64,038; Average household: $81,895; Households with income of $100,000 or more: 30.7%; Poverty rate: 5.3%
Educational Attainment: High school diploma or higher: 96.4%; Bachelor's degree or higher: 20.1%; Graduate/professional degree or higher: 5.2%

Housing: Homeownership rate: 91.7%; Median home value: $130,700; Median year structure built: 1970; Homeowner vacancy rate: 1.4%; Median gross rent: $1,143 per month; Rental vacancy rate: 9.6%

Health Insurance: 89.8% have insurance; 82.6% have private insurance; 22.7% have public insurance; 10.2% do not have insurance; 0.0% of children under 18 do not have insurance

Transportation: Commute: 96.3% car, 0.0% public transportation, 0.0% walk, 3.0% work from home; Median travel time to work: 22.7 minutes

LEVEL PARK-OAK PARK (CDP).

Covers a land area of 5.183 square miles and a water area of 0.064 square miles. Located at 42.37° N. Lat; 85.27° W. Long. Elevation is 830 feet.

Population: 3,409; Growth (since 2000): -5.4%; Density: 657.7 persons per square mile; Race: 90.4% White, 4.3% Black/African American, 0.7% Asian, 0.4% American Indian/Alaska Native, 0.0% Native Hawaiian/Other Pacific Islander, 3.1% Two or more races, 2.7% Hispanic of any race; Average household size: 2.44; Median age: 42.9; Age under 18: 21.7%; Age 65 and over: 15.8%; Males per 100 females: 96.8; Marriage status: 29.0% never married, 49.0% now married, 2.7% separated, 8.3% widowed, 13.7% divorced; Foreign born: 2.1%; Speak English only: 97.7%; With disability: 16.7%; Veterans: 13.3%; Ancestry: 17.7% German, 12.1% English, 10.6% Irish, 8.9% American, 4.9% Italian

Employment: 13.9% management, business, and financial, 3.4% computer, engineering, and science, 5.1% education, legal, community service, arts, and media, 6.0% healthcare practitioners, 16.6% service, 31.4% sales and office, 5.3% natural resources, construction, and maintenance, 18.3% production, transportation, and material moving

Income: Per capita: $23,785; Median household: $44,805; Average household: $56,417; Households with income of $100,000 or more: 13.9%; Poverty rate: 13.5%

Educational Attainment: High school diploma or higher: 88.7%; Bachelor's degree or higher: 10.5%; Graduate/professional degree or higher: 4.3%

Housing: Homeownership rate: 87.8%; Median home value: $90,300; Median year structure built: 1957; Homeowner vacancy rate: 2.1%; Median gross rent: $791 per month; Rental vacancy rate: 8.5%

Health Insurance: 85.2% have insurance; 68.6% have private insurance; 30.5% have public insurance; 14.8% do not have insurance; 6.0% of children under 18 do not have insurance

Transportation: Commute: 90.5% car, 0.0% public transportation, 6.1% walk, 2.1% work from home; Median travel time to work: 16.9 minutes

MARENGO (township).

Covers a land area of 35.035 square miles and a water area of 0.679 square miles. Located at 42.29° N. Lat; 84.88° W. Long. Elevation is 928 feet.

Population: 2,213; Growth (since 2000): 3.8%; Density: 63.2 persons per square mile; Race: 96.5% White, 0.7% Black/African American, 0.2% Asian, 0.2% American Indian/Alaska Native, 0.0% Native Hawaiian/Other Pacific Islander, 1.6% Two or more races, 2.9% Hispanic of any race; Average household size: 2.57; Median age: 45.2; Age under 18: 22.8%; Age 65 and over: 18.9%; Males per 100 females: 93.6

Housing: Homeownership rate: 86.5%; Homeowner vacancy rate: 1.2%; Rental vacancy rate: 15.7%

MARSHALL (city).

County seat. Covers a land area of 6.278 square miles and a water area of 0.117 square miles. Located at 42.26° N. Lat; 84.96° W. Long. Elevation is 915 feet.

History: Marshall was settled in 1830 and named for U.S. Chief Justice John Marshall. An event that led to the passage of the New Fugitive Slave Bill of 1850 occurred in Marshall in 1846, when resident Adam Crosswhite, a slave who had escaped from Kentucky and had lived in Marshall for two years, was seized by slavehunters. The town not only freed Crosswhite and his family and sent them on to Canada on the Underground Railroad, but arrested those who had tried to take the Crosswhites. Marshall is also known as the place where John D. Pierce and Isaac E. Crary designed the Michigan State public school system.

Population: 7,088; Growth (since 2000): -5.0%; Density: 1,129.0 persons per square mile; Race: 95.1% White, 1.1% Black/African American, 0.7% Asian, 0.6% American Indian/Alaska Native, 0.0% Native Hawaiian/Other Pacific Islander, 1.8% Two or more races, 3.8% Hispanic of any race; Average household size: 2.25; Median age: 40.5; Age under 18: 24.0%; Age 65 and over: 18.2%; Males per 100 females: 90.6; Marriage status: 24.9% never married, 51.3% now married, 2.5% separated, 6.8% widowed, 17.0% divorced; Foreign born: 1.6%; Speak English only: 94.0%;

With disability: 13.1%; Veterans: 9.8%; Ancestry: 27.0% German, 16.1% Irish, 13.6% English, 7.4% Polish, 5.5% American

Employment: 13.7% management, business, and financial, 5.7% computer, engineering, and science, 10.4% education, legal, community service, arts, and media, 5.2% healthcare practitioners, 19.5% service, 21.5% sales and office, 7.5% natural resources, construction, and maintenance, 16.5% production, transportation, and material moving

Income: Per capita: $25,629; Median household: $46,886; Average household: $57,347; Households with income of $100,000 or more: 12.6%; Poverty rate: 10.6%

Educational Attainment: High school diploma or higher: 94.1%; Bachelor's degree or higher: 31.2%; Graduate/professional degree or higher: 11.7%

School District(s)

Calhoun ISD (PK-12)
    2012-13 Enrollment: 990 . . . . (269) 781-5141
Mar Lee SD (KG-12)
    2012-13 Enrollment: 320 . . . . (269) 781-5412
Marshall Academy (KG-12)
    2012-13 Enrollment: 240 . . . . (269) 781-6330
Marshall Public Schools (PK-12)
    2012-13 Enrollment: 2,238 . . . . (269) 781-1257

Housing: Homeownership rate: 64.3%; Median home value: $110,800; Median year structure built: 1959; Homeowner vacancy rate: 2.0%; Median gross rent: $687 per month; Rental vacancy rate: 9.3%

Health Insurance: 89.7% have insurance; 74.8% have private insurance; 33.1% have public insurance; 10.3% do not have insurance; 0.0% of children under 18 do not have insurance

Hospitals: Oaklawn Hospital (94 beds)

Safety: Violent crime rate: 22.7 per 10,000 population; Property crime rate: 219.9 per 10,000 population

Transportation: Commute: 83.4% car, 0.0% public transportation, 8.7% walk, 5.5% work from home; Median travel time to work: 19.3 minutes

Additional Information Contacts

City of Marshall . . . . (269) 781-5183
    http://www.cityofmarshall.com

MARSHALL (township).

Covers a land area of 31.135 square miles and a water area of 0.423 square miles. Located at 42.29° N. Lat; 85.01° W. Long. Elevation is 915 feet.

History: Historical homes. Settled 1831; incorporated as village 1836, as city 1859.

Population: 3,115; Growth (since 2000): 6.6%; Density: 100.0 persons per square mile; Race: 96.8% White, 0.2% Black/African American, 0.5% Asian, 0.6% American Indian/Alaska Native, 0.0% Native Hawaiian/Other Pacific Islander, 1.0% Two or more races, 3.0% Hispanic of any race; Average household size: 2.57; Median age: 44.8; Age under 18: 23.5%; Age 65 and over: 16.6%; Males per 100 females: 94.7; Marriage status: 17.9% never married, 70.6% now married, 0.0% separated, 3.7% widowed, 7.8% divorced; Foreign born: 1.8%; Speak English only: 96.6%; With disability: 7.6%; Veterans: 11.2%; Ancestry: 32.8% German, 17.9% English, 11.9% American, 10.6% Irish, 10.1% Polish

Employment: 19.0% management, business, and financial, 3.0% computer, engineering, and science, 9.7% education, legal, community service, arts, and media, 10.1% healthcare practitioners, 15.1% service, 24.4% sales and office, 6.6% natural resources, construction, and maintenance, 12.1% production, transportation, and material moving

Income: Per capita: $33,505; Median household: $73,125; Average household: $89,000; Households with income of $100,000 or more: 34.8%; Poverty rate: 0.9%

Educational Attainment: High school diploma or higher: 96.1%; Bachelor's degree or higher: 35.2%; Graduate/professional degree or higher: 15.6%

School District(s)

Calhoun ISD (PK-12)
    2012-13 Enrollment: 990 . . . . (269) 781-5141
Mar Lee SD (KG-12)
    2012-13 Enrollment: 320 . . . . (269) 781-5412
Marshall Academy (KG-12)
    2012-13 Enrollment: 240 . . . . (269) 781-6330
Marshall Public Schools (PK-12)
    2012-13 Enrollment: 2,238 . . . . (269) 781-1257

Housing: Homeownership rate: 87.9%; Median home value: $169,800; Median year structure built: 1975; Homeowner vacancy rate: 1.4%; Median gross rent: $812 per month; Rental vacancy rate: 6.4%

Health Insurance: 95.5% have insurance; 88.5% have private insurance; 20.2% have public insurance; 4.5% do not have insurance; 3.1% of children under 18 do not have insurance
Hospitals: Oaklawn Hospital (94 beds)
Transportation: Commute: 91.4% car, 0.0% public transportation, 3.5% walk, 4.8% work from home; Median travel time to work: 20.6 minutes

NEWTON (township). Covers a land area of 36.001 square miles and a water area of 0.377 square miles. Located at 42.21° N. Lat; 85.13° W. Long.
Population: 2,551; Growth (since 2000): 2.3%; Density: 70.9 persons per square mile; Race: 96.7% White, 0.9% Black/African American, 1.1% Asian, 0.4% American Indian/Alaska Native, 0.0% Native Hawaiian/Other Pacific Islander, 0.9% Two or more races, 1.1% Hispanic of any race; Average household size: 2.42; Median age: 48.5; Age under 18: 20.1%; Age 65 and over: 20.6%; Males per 100 females: 99.9; Marriage status: 19.6% never married, 66.1% now married, 0.8% separated, 4.9% widowed, 9.4% divorced; Foreign born: 0.7%; Speak English only: 99.5%; With disability: 14.5%; Veterans: 8.8%; Ancestry: 25.2% German, 18.9% English, 16.5% Irish, 9.3% American, 5.9% Dutch
Employment: 11.8% management, business, and financial, 6.5% computer, engineering, and science, 10.4% education, legal, community service, arts, and media, 7.0% healthcare practitioners, 8.0% service, 26.6% sales and office, 10.3% natural resources, construction, and maintenance, 19.5% production, transportation, and material moving
Income: Per capita: $30,375; Median household: $55,889; Average household: $75,626; Households with income of $100,000 or more: 25.0%; Poverty rate: 7.6%
Educational Attainment: High school diploma or higher: 91.8%; Bachelor's degree or higher: 22.3%; Graduate/professional degree or higher: 7.4%
Housing: Homeownership rate: 93.9%; Median home value: $171,500; Median year structure built: 1979; Homeowner vacancy rate: 2.9%; Median gross rent: $803 per month; Rental vacancy rate: 39.8%
Health Insurance: 93.8% have insurance; 83.1% have private insurance; 33.6% have public insurance; 6.2% do not have insurance; 2.8% of children under 18 do not have insurance
Transportation: Commute: 95.6% car, 0.0% public transportation, 0.8% walk, 3.0% work from home; Median travel time to work: 23.9 minutes

PENNFIELD (charter township). Covers a land area of 34.265 square miles and a water area of 0.835 square miles. Located at 42.38° N. Lat; 85.11° W. Long. Elevation is 843 feet.
Population: 9,001; Growth (since 2000): 1.0%; Density: 262.7 persons per square mile; Race: 90.0% White, 5.6% Black/African American, 0.6% Asian, 0.6% American Indian/Alaska Native, 0.1% Native Hawaiian/Other Pacific Islander, 2.5% Two or more races, 2.8% Hispanic of any race; Average household size: 2.45; Median age: 42.4; Age under 18: 22.6%; Age 65 and over: 15.1%; Males per 100 females: 97.1; Marriage status: 24.9% never married, 47.6% now married, 2.3% separated, 6.4% widowed, 21.2% divorced; Foreign born: 1.2%; Speak English only: 97.2%; With disability: 14.4%; Veterans: 12.3%; Ancestry: 25.2% German, 13.4% English, 11.3% Irish, 10.5% American, 6.3% Dutch
Employment: 10.9% management, business, and financial, 3.5% computer, engineering, and science, 5.4% education, legal, community service, arts, and media, 5.4% healthcare practitioners, 20.1% service, 25.7% sales and office, 8.9% natural resources, construction, and maintenance, 20.1% production, transportation, and material moving
Income: Per capita: $23,499; Median household: $44,769; Average household: $55,984; Households with income of $100,000 or more: 13.4%; Poverty rate: 13.1%
Educational Attainment: High school diploma or higher: 87.4%; Bachelor's degree or higher: 15.2%; Graduate/professional degree or higher: 6.1%
Housing: Homeownership rate: 75.7%; Median home value: $108,500; Median year structure built: 1966; Homeowner vacancy rate: 1.7%; Median gross rent: $651 per month; Rental vacancy rate: 12.9%
Health Insurance: 86.9% have insurance; 68.5% have private insurance; 35.7% have public insurance; 13.1% do not have insurance; 1.6% of children under 18 do not have insurance
Transportation: Commute: 96.4% car, 0.7% public transportation, 0.8% walk, 1.9% work from home; Median travel time to work: 20.7 minutes
Additional Information Contacts
Pennfield Charter Township . . . . (269) 968-8549
   http://www.pennfieldtwp.com

SHERIDAN (township). Covers a land area of 31.330 square miles and a water area of 0.437 square miles. Located at 42.30° N. Lat; 84.77° W. Long.
History: Sheridan was settled in the early 1830's, and the township was organized in 1836.
Population: 1,936; Growth (since 2000): -8.5%; Density: 61.8 persons per square mile; Race: 87.2% White, 8.5% Black/African American, 0.5% Asian, 0.5% American Indian/Alaska Native, 0.0% Native Hawaiian/Other Pacific Islander, 1.9% Two or more races, 4.1% Hispanic of any race; Average household size: 2.43; Median age: 42.3; Age under 18: 26.0%; Age 65 and over: 17.8%; Males per 100 females: 116.8
Housing: Homeownership rate: 82.4%; Homeowner vacancy rate: 1.9%; Rental vacancy rate: 9.6%

SPRINGFIELD (city). Covers a land area of 3.661 square miles and a water area of 0.037 square miles. Located at 42.32° N. Lat; 85.24° W. Long. Elevation is 883 feet.
History: First platted as Merrill Park, the name was changed to Springfield for Springfield, Illinois, former home of C.W. Post.
Population: 5,260; Growth (since 2000): 1.4%; Density: 1,436.7 persons per square mile; Race: 76.6% White, 9.6% Black/African American, 7.5% Asian, 0.5% American Indian/Alaska Native, 0.1% Native Hawaiian/Other Pacific Islander, 4.7% Two or more races, 4.1% Hispanic of any race; Average household size: 2.38; Median age: 33.8; Age under 18: 25.2%; Age 65 and over: 11.7%; Males per 100 females: 100.2; Marriage status: 38.9% never married, 38.0% now married, 2.5% separated, 8.5% widowed, 14.6% divorced; Foreign born: 7.6%; Speak English only: 88.6%; With disability: 14.3%; Veterans: 11.9%; Ancestry: 16.7% German, 11.8% English, 8.0% American, 6.7% Irish, 3.0% Dutch
Employment: 6.7% management, business, and financial, 2.7% computer, engineering, and science, 5.2% education, legal, community service, arts, and media, 2.6% healthcare practitioners, 19.6% service, 26.7% sales and office, 8.7% natural resources, construction, and maintenance, 27.8% production, transportation, and material moving
Income: Per capita: $17,605; Median household: $32,500; Average household: $39,776; Households with income of $100,000 or more: 2.3%; Poverty rate: 26.4%
Educational Attainment: High school diploma or higher: 81.1%; Bachelor's degree or higher: 10.1%; Graduate/professional degree or higher: 2.8%
School District(s)
Battle Creek Public Schools (PK-12)
   2012-13 Enrollment: 5,123 . . . . (269) 965-9465
Housing: Homeownership rate: 49.8%; Median home value: $65,400; Median year structure built: 1966; Homeowner vacancy rate: 3.6%; Median gross rent: $578 per month; Rental vacancy rate: 15.9%
Health Insurance: 80.2% have insurance; 51.9% have private insurance; 38.3% have public insurance; 19.8% do not have insurance; 8.1% of children under 18 do not have insurance
Safety: Violent crime rate: 25.0 per 10,000 population; Property crime rate: 261.0 per 10,000 population
Transportation: Commute: 96.3% car, 0.0% public transportation, 0.0% walk, 2.0% work from home; Median travel time to work: 16.0 minutes
Additional Information Contacts
City of Springfield . . . . (269) 965-2354
   http://www.springfieldmich.com

TEKONSHA (township). Covers a land area of 35.403 square miles and a water area of 0.866 square miles. Located at 42.11° N. Lat; 85.00° W. Long. Elevation is 942 feet.
Population: 1,645; Growth (since 2000): -5.1%; Density: 46.5 persons per square mile; Race: 96.8% White, 0.4% Black/African American, 0.4% Asian, 0.5% American Indian/Alaska Native, 0.0% Native Hawaiian/Other Pacific Islander, 1.7% Two or more races, 1.2% Hispanic of any race; Average household size: 2.55; Median age: 41.4; Age under 18: 24.7%; Age 65 and over: 17.6%; Males per 100 females: 92.8
School District(s)
Tekonsha Community Schools (PK-12)
   2012-13 Enrollment: 294 . . . . (517) 767-4121
Housing: Homeownership rate: 79.5%; Homeowner vacancy rate: 2.6%; Rental vacancy rate: 11.4%

TEKONSHA (village). Covers a land area of 0.708 square miles and a water area of 0.016 square miles. Located at 42.10° N. Lat; 84.99° W. Long. Elevation is 942 feet.

History: Tekonsha was settled in 1832 and named for a Potawatomi chief, Tekonquasha (1768-1825).

Population: 717; Growth (since 2000): 0.7%; Density: 1,013.3 persons per square mile; Race: 96.0% White, 0.0% Black/African American, 0.7% Asian, 0.4% American Indian/Alaska Native, 0.0% Native Hawaiian/Other Pacific Islander, 2.8% Two or more races, 0.8% Hispanic of any race; Average household size: 2.54; Median age: 40.0; Age under 18: 24.4%; Age 65 and over: 16.5%; Males per 100 females: 88.7

School District(s)

Tekonsha Community Schools (PK-12)

    2012-13 Enrollment: 294. . . . . (517) 767-4121

Housing: Homeownership rate: 75.9%; Homeowner vacancy rate: 1.8%; Rental vacancy rate: 5.6%

Cass County

Located in southwestern Michigan; bounded on the south by Indiana; drained by the Saint Joseph River and Short Dowagiac Creek. Covers a land area of 490.062 square miles, a water area of 18.255 square miles, and is located in the Eastern Time Zone at 41.92° N. Lat., 86.00° W. Long. The county was founded in 1829. County seat is Cassopolis.

Cass County is part of the South Bend-Mishawaka, IN-MI Metropolitan Statistical Area. The entire metro area includes: Saint Joseph County, IN; Cass County, MI

Weather Station: Dowagiac 1 W   Elevation: 740 feet

	Jan	Feb	Mar	Apr	May	Jun	Jul	Aug	Sep	Oct	Nov	Dec
High	32	36	46	58	70	79	83	81	74	61	49	36
Low	15	17	25	36	46	55	59	58	50	39	31	21
Precip	2.6	2.2	2.4	3.4	3.9	3.6	3.9	4.2	4.2	4.1	3.4	3.1
Snow	21.7	14.1	5.1	0.7	tr	0.0	0.0	0.0	0.0	0.1	4.3	19.4

High and Low temperatures in degrees Fahrenheit; Precipitation and Snow in inches

Population: 52,293; Growth (since 2000): 2.3%; Density: 106.7 persons per square mile; Race: 88.9% White, 5.4% Black/African American, 0.6% Asian, 1.0% American Indian/Alaska Native, 0.0% Native Hawaiian/Other Pacific Islander, 3.0% two or more races, 3.0% Hispanic of any race; Average household size: 2.51; Median age: 42.6; Age under 18: 23.4%; Age 65 and over: 16.0%; Males per 100 females: 99.6; Marriage status: 24.8% never married, 56.3% now married, 1.1% separated, 6.2% widowed, 12.7% divorced; Foreign born: 2.0%; Speak English only: 95.5%; With disability: 14.5%; Veterans: 11.6%; Ancestry: 30.7% German, 14.2% Irish, 12.4% English, 7.4% American, 6.9% Polish

Religion: Six largest groups: 5.0% Catholicism, 3.7% Methodist/Pietist, 1.7% Baptist, 1.1% Non-denominational Protestant, 1.0% Adventist, 1.0% Lutheran

Economy: Unemployment rate: 4.9%; Leading industries: 15.6% retail trade; 13.1% other services (except public administration); 10.8% construction; Farms: 798 totaling 188,690 acres; Company size: 0 employ 1,000 or more persons, 0 employ 500 to 999 persons, 12 employ 100 to 499 persons, 731 employs less than 100 persons; Business ownership: n/a women-owned, 138 Black-owned, 62 Hispanic-owned, n/a Asian-owned

Employment: 11.1% management, business, and financial, 3.5% computer, engineering, and science, 9.1% education, legal, community service, arts, and media, 5.3% healthcare practitioners, 16.6% service, 22.0% sales and office, 10.4% natural resources, construction, and maintenance, 22.1% production, transportation, and material moving

Income: Per capita: $22,743; Median household: $44,346; Average household: $58,045; Households with income of $100,000 or more: 14.0%; Poverty rate: 14.5%

Educational Attainment: High school diploma or higher: 87.2%; Bachelor's degree or higher: 16.2%; Graduate/professional degree or higher: 5.3%

Housing: Homeownership rate: 80.1%; Median home value: $124,800; Median year structure built: 1974; Homeowner vacancy rate: 3.0%; Median gross rent: $685 per month; Rental vacancy rate: 10.0%

Vital Statistics: Birth rate: 98.6 per 10,000 population; Death rate: 96.7 per 10,000 population; Age-adjusted cancer mortality rate: 179.1 deaths per 100,000 population

Health Insurance: 86.6% have insurance; 66.0% have private insurance; 35.0% have public insurance; 13.4% do not have insurance; 4.0% of children under 18 do not have insurance

Health Care: Physicians: 3.3 per 10,000 population; Hospital beds: 4.8 per 10,000 population; Hospital admissions: 158.2 per 10,000 population

Air Quality Index: 82.0% good, 17.5% moderate, 0.5% unhealthy for sensitive individuals, 0.0% unhealthy (percent of days)

Transportation: Commute: 94.1% car, 0.2% public transportation, 1.2% walk, 3.6% work from home; Median travel time to work: 25.6 minutes

Presidential Election: 42.7% Obama, 56.4% Romney (2012)

National and State Parks: Crane Pond State Game Area; Fred Russ State Forest

Additional Information Contacts

Cass Government . . . . (269) 445-4420
   http://www.casscountymi.org

Cass County Communities

CALVIN (township). Covers a land area of 34.338 square miles and a water area of 1.213 square miles. Located at 41.86° N. Lat; 85.92° W. Long.

History: Calvin Township was organized in 1835 and named for Calvin Britain, the territorial representative for the county at that time.

Population: 2,037; Growth (since 2000): -0.2%; Density: 59.3 persons per square mile; Race: 73.7% White, 18.7% Black/African American, 0.6% Asian, 0.6% American Indian/Alaska Native, 0.0% Native Hawaiian/Other Pacific Islander, 5.8% Two or more races, 1.4% Hispanic of any race; Average household size: 2.52; Median age: 44.3; Age under 18: 23.6%; Age 65 and over: 15.5%; Males per 100 females: 103.7

Housing: Homeownership rate: 80.3%; Homeowner vacancy rate: 4.0%; Rental vacancy rate: 11.6%

CASSOPOLIS (village). County seat. Covers a land area of 1.998 square miles and a water area of 0.245 square miles. Located at 41.91° N. Lat; 86.01° W. Long. Elevation is 889 feet.

History: Cassopolis was settled in 1829 and named for territorial governor Lewis Cass.

Population: 1,774; Growth (since 2000): 2.0%; Density: 888.1 persons per square mile; Race: 60.0% White, 29.3% Black/African American, 2.4% Asian, 1.1% American Indian/Alaska Native, 0.1% Native Hawaiian/Other Pacific Islander, 5.6% Two or more races, 4.5% Hispanic of any race; Average household size: 2.32; Median age: 35.4; Age under 18: 25.5%; Age 65 and over: 13.4%; Males per 100 females: 101.4

School District(s)

Cassopolis Public Schools (KG-12)

    2012-13 Enrollment: 1,048 . . . . (269) 445-0500

Lewis Cass ISD (PK-12)

    2012-13 Enrollment: 264. . . . . (269) 445-6204

Housing: Homeownership rate: 52.3%; Homeowner vacancy rate: 6.0%; Rental vacancy rate: 9.8%

Safety: Violent crime rate: 11.4 per 10,000 population; Property crime rate: 136.4 per 10,000 population

DOWAGIAC (city). Covers a land area of 4.464 square miles and a water area of 0.079 square miles. Located at 41.98° N. Lat; 86.11° W. Long. Elevation is 761 feet.

History: The city of Dowagiac grew up around the stove manufacturing industry, begun in the 1850's.

Population: 5,879; Growth (since 2000): -4.4%; Density: 1,317.0 persons per square mile; Race: 73.5% White, 14.3% Black/African American, 0.8% Asian, 3.0% American Indian/Alaska Native, 0.0% Native Hawaiian/Other Pacific Islander, 6.1% Two or more races, 5.4% Hispanic of any race; Average household size: 2.50; Median age: 32.0; Age under 18: 29.1%; Age 65 and over: 12.6%; Males per 100 females: 90.9; Marriage status: 28.0% never married, 50.5% now married, 1.8% separated, 7.7% widowed, 13.8% divorced; Foreign born: 1.5%; Speak English only: 95.8%; With disability: 16.5%; Veterans: 10.3%; Ancestry: 26.6% German, 13.6% Irish, 9.2% English, 6.3% American, 6.3% Polish

Employment: 3.7% management, business, and financial, 0.2% computer, engineering, and science, 9.6% education, legal, community service, arts, and media, 5.0% healthcare practitioners, 28.7% service, 26.6% sales and office, 7.3% natural resources, construction, and maintenance, 19.0% production, transportation, and material moving

Income: Per capita: $16,306; Median household: $31,685; Average household: $39,736; Households with income of $100,000 or more: 4.5%; Poverty rate: 20.4%

Educational Attainment: High school diploma or higher: 87.9%; Bachelor's degree or higher: 7.7%; Graduate/professional degree or higher: 1.6%

School District(s)

Dowagiac Union SD (PK-12)
   2012-13 Enrollment: 2,297 . . . . (269) 782-4402
Lewis Cass ISD (PK-12)
   2012-13 Enrollment: 264. . . . . (269) 445-6204

Two-year College(s)

Southwestern Michigan College (Public)
   Fall 2013 Enrollment: 2,802 . . . . (269) 782-1000
   2013-14 Tuition: In-state $5,681; Out-of-state $6,068

Housing: Homeownership rate: 53.8%; Median home value: $74,000; Median year structure built: 1954; Homeowner vacancy rate: 4.1%; Median gross rent: $590 per month; Rental vacancy rate: 9.3%

Health Insurance: 82.5% have insurance; 56.8% have private insurance; 38.5% have public insurance; 17.5% do not have insurance; 10.3% of children under 18 do not have insurance

Hospitals: Borgess - Lee Memorial Hospital (74 beds)

Newspapers: Dowagiac Daily News (daily circulation 1800)

Transportation: Commute: 96.1% car, 0.0% public transportation, 3.4% walk, 0.5% work from home; Median travel time to work: 19.0 minutes; Amtrak: Train service available.

Additional Information Contacts
City of Dowagiac . . . . (269) 782-2195
   http://www.cityofdowagiac.com

EDWARDSBURG (village).

Covers a land area of 0.914 square miles and a water area of 0.103 square miles. Located at 41.80° N. Lat; 86.08° W. Long. Elevation is 830 feet.

Population: 1,259; Growth (since 2000): 9.8%; Density: 1,377.2 persons per square mile; Race: 93.6% White, 1.5% Black/African American, 0.2% Asian, 0.8% American Indian/Alaska Native, 0.3% Native Hawaiian/Other Pacific Islander, 2.5% Two or more races, 3.2% Hispanic of any race; Average household size: 2.44; Median age: 36.1; Age under 18: 28.4%; Age 65 and over: 13.2%; Males per 100 females: 86.0

School District(s)

Edwardsburg Public Schools (PK-12)
   2012-13 Enrollment: 2,708 . . . . (269) 663-1053

Housing: Homeownership rate: 59.0%; Homeowner vacancy rate: 1.6%; Rental vacancy rate: 12.8%

HOWARD (township).

Covers a land area of 34.524 square miles and a water area of 0.766 square miles. Located at 41.86° N. Lat; 86.17° W. Long.

Population: 6,207; Growth (since 2000): -1.6%; Density: 179.8 persons per square mile; Race: 92.2% White, 3.8% Black/African American, 0.4% Asian, 0.5% American Indian/Alaska Native, 0.0% Native Hawaiian/Other Pacific Islander, 2.0% Two or more races, 2.5% Hispanic of any race; Average household size: 2.45; Median age: 44.9; Age under 18: 21.2%; Age 65 and over: 17.2%; Males per 100 females: 102.2; Marriage status: 21.7% never married, 59.8% now married, 1.2% separated, 8.4% widowed, 10.1% divorced; Foreign born: 1.6%; Speak English only: 96.0%; With disability: 12.2%; Veterans: 14.5%; Ancestry: 27.1% German, 12.2% English, 10.7% Irish, 7.4% Dutch, 7.3% American

Employment: 11.4% management, business, and financial, 3.6% computer, engineering, and science, 9.2% education, legal, community service, arts, and media, 5.5% healthcare practitioners, 14.3% service, 23.5% sales and office, 11.3% natural resources, construction, and maintenance, 21.3% production, transportation, and material moving

Income: Per capita: $23,679; Median household: $46,471; Average household: $57,928; Households with income of $100,000 or more: 14.4%; Poverty rate: 5.7%

Educational Attainment: High school diploma or higher: 88.0%; Bachelor's degree or higher: 16.0%; Graduate/professional degree or higher: 6.6%

Housing: Homeownership rate: 88.2%; Median home value: $117,400; Median year structure built: 1971; Homeowner vacancy rate: 1.7%; Median gross rent: $777 per month; Rental vacancy rate: 10.2%

Health Insurance: 87.8% have insurance; 70.2% have private insurance; 31.2% have public insurance; 12.2% do not have insurance; 0.0% of children under 18 do not have insurance

Transportation: Commute: 96.6% car, 0.2% public transportation, 0.6% walk, 1.7% work from home; Median travel time to work: 23.9 minutes

Additional Information Contacts
Howard Township . . . . (269) 684-0072
   http://www.howardtownship.net

JEFFERSON (township).

Covers a land area of 34.740 square miles and a water area of 1.267 square miles. Located at 41.85° N. Lat; 86.05° W. Long.

Population: 2,541; Growth (since 2000): 5.8%; Density: 73.1 persons per square mile; Race: 91.7% White, 4.7% Black/African American, 1.1% Asian, 0.3% American Indian/Alaska Native, 0.0% Native Hawaiian/Other Pacific Islander, 2.1% Two or more races, 1.1% Hispanic of any race; Average household size: 2.61; Median age: 44.6; Age under 18: 23.8%; Age 65 and over: 15.9%; Males per 100 females: 103.4; Marriage status: 24.2% never married, 57.3% now married, 1.0% separated, 6.0% widowed, 12.5% divorced; Foreign born: 0.4%; Speak English only: 97.8%; With disability: 14.0%; Veterans: 9.8%; Ancestry: 26.9% German, 16.2% English, 15.5% Irish, 10.5% American, 5.6% Polish

Employment: 14.1% management, business, and financial, 4.4% computer, engineering, and science, 7.8% education, legal, community service, arts, and media, 7.2% healthcare practitioners, 13.0% service, 18.4% sales and office, 11.9% natural resources, construction, and maintenance, 23.3% production, transportation, and material moving

Income: Per capita: $23,258; Median household: $49,018; Average household: $58,196; Households with income of $100,000 or more: 11.6%; Poverty rate: 9.4%

Educational Attainment: High school diploma or higher: 88.0%; Bachelor's degree or higher: 13.7%; Graduate/professional degree or higher: 4.7%

Housing: Homeownership rate: 89.2%; Median home value: $147,800; Median year structure built: 1976; Homeowner vacancy rate: 1.5%; Median gross rent: $716 per month; Rental vacancy rate: 6.4%

Health Insurance: 88.9% have insurance; 73.0% have private insurance; 32.9% have public insurance; 11.1% do not have insurance; 2.2% of children under 18 do not have insurance

Transportation: Commute: 98.9% car, 0.3% public transportation, 0.0% walk, 0.8% work from home; Median travel time to work: 27.5 minutes

---

JONES (unincorporated postal area)

ZCTA: 49061

Covers a land area of 37.464 square miles and a water area of 1.352 square miles. Located at 41.87° N. Lat; 85.82° W. Long. Elevation is 922 feet.

Population: 1,622; Growth (since 2000): -0.7%; Density: 43.3 persons per square mile; Race: 93.8% White, 2.5% Black/African American, 0.4% Asian, 0.5% American Indian/Alaska Native, 0.0% Native Hawaiian/Other Pacific Islander, 2.6% Two or more races, 1.7% Hispanic of any race; Average household size: 2.52; Median age: 42.1; Age under 18: 22.4%; Age 65 and over: 14.4%; Males per 100 females: 111.7

Housing: Homeownership rate: 79.9%; Homeowner vacancy rate: 5.1%; Rental vacancy rate: 1.5%

LAGRANGE (township).

Covers a land area of 33.181 square miles and a water area of 1.451 square miles. Located at 41.93° N. Lat; 86.04° W. Long.

History: La Grange Township was organized in 1829 and named for General LaFayette's home in France. Settlements were made around a sawmill built here in 1829, and a grist mill built in 1832.

Population: 3,500; Growth (since 2000): 4.8%; Density: 105.5 persons per square mile; Race: 72.5% White, 17.5% Black/African American, 1.6% Asian, 2.6% American Indian/Alaska Native, 0.0% Native Hawaiian/Other Pacific Islander, 4.7% Two or more races, 3.5% Hispanic of any race; Average household size: 2.39; Median age: 38.9; Age under 18: 22.7%; Age 65 and over: 14.9%; Males per 100 females: 96.0; Marriage status: 35.1% never married, 39.1% now married, 2.3% separated, 10.0% widowed, 15.8% divorced; Foreign born: 1.1%; Speak English only: 95.8%; With disability: 15.5%; Veterans: 11.5%; Ancestry: 23.1% German, 14.3% Irish, 9.3% English, 8.0% American, 4.6% Polish

Employment: 7.9% management, business, and financial, 3.2% computer, engineering, and science, 11.2% education, legal, community service, arts, and media, 0.3% healthcare practitioners, 26.2% service, 19.0% sales and office, 10.0% natural resources, construction, and maintenance, 22.3% production, transportation, and material moving

Income: Per capita: $19,923; Median household: $33,958; Average household: $46,621; Households with income of $100,000 or more: 9.5%; Poverty rate: 21.7%

Educational Attainment: High school diploma or higher: 82.7%; Bachelor's degree or higher: 12.1%; Graduate/professional degree or higher: 3.6%

Housing: Homeownership rate: 66.6%; Median home value: $112,500; Median year structure built: 1969; Homeowner vacancy rate: 3.8%; Median gross rent: $532 per month; Rental vacancy rate: 9.9%

Health Insurance: 86.4% have insurance; 56.6% have private insurance; 41.9% have public insurance; 13.6% do not have insurance; 1.3% of children under 18 do not have insurance

Transportation: Commute: 94.2% car, 0.2% public transportation, 3.8% walk, 1.1% work from home; Median travel time to work: 23.9 minutes

MARCELLUS (township). Covers a land area of 33.196 square miles and a water area of 1.681 square miles. Located at 42.03° N. Lat; 85.82° W. Long. Elevation is 896 feet.

History: Incorporated 1879.

Population: 2,539; Growth (since 2000): -6.4%; Density: 76.5 persons per square mile; Race: 96.4% White, 1.2% Black/African American, 0.3% Asian, 0.5% American Indian/Alaska Native, 0.0% Native Hawaiian/Other Pacific Islander, 1.5% Two or more races, 1.9% Hispanic of any race; Average household size: 2.59; Median age: 39.4; Age under 18: 24.9%; Age 65 and over: 15.7%; Males per 100 females: 105.4; Marriage status: 25.9% never married, 53.3% now married, 0.7% separated, 5.9% widowed, 14.9% divorced; Foreign born: 0.4%; Speak English only: 98.7%; With disability: 12.1%; Veterans: 9.9%; Ancestry: 37.7% German, 15.4% English, 15.1% Irish, 11.5% American, 5.1% Polish

Employment: 12.6% management, business, and financial, 6.2% computer, engineering, and science, 3.9% education, legal, community service, arts, and media, 3.1% healthcare practitioners, 20.7% service, 15.4% sales and office, 7.1% natural resources, construction, and maintenance, 31.0% production, transportation, and material moving

Income: Per capita: $20,679; Median household: $44,404; Average household: $55,061; Households with income of $100,000 or more: 15.8%; Poverty rate: 16.9%

Educational Attainment: High school diploma or higher: 88.1%; Bachelor's degree or higher: 14.7%; Graduate/professional degree or higher: 5.0%

School District(s)
Marcellus Community Schools (KG-12)
    2012-13 Enrollment: 723 . . . . (269) 646-7655

Housing: Homeownership rate: 80.2%; Median home value: $108,600; Median year structure built: 1968; Homeowner vacancy rate: 2.0%; Median gross rent: $643 per month; Rental vacancy rate: 12.9%

Health Insurance: 89.8% have insurance; 72.7% have private insurance; 29.7% have public insurance; 10.2% do not have insurance; 2.5% of children under 18 do not have insurance

Newspapers: Marcellus News (weekly circulation 1600)

Transportation: Commute: 93.3% car, 0.0% public transportation, 0.6% walk, 5.1% work from home; Median travel time to work: 29.1 minutes

MARCELLUS (village). Covers a land area of 0.583 square miles and a water area of 0.006 square miles. Located at 42.03° N. Lat; 85.81° W. Long. Elevation is 896 feet.

Population: 1,198; Growth (since 2000): 3.1%; Density: 2,055.6 persons per square mile; Race: 96.5% White, 1.6% Black/African American, 0.3% Asian, 0.3% American Indian/Alaska Native, 0.0% Native Hawaiian/Other Pacific Islander, 1.3% Two or more races, 1.5% Hispanic of any race; Average household size: 2.72; Median age: 34.9; Age under 18: 29.6%; Age 65 and over: 13.1%; Males per 100 females: 92.9

School District(s)
Marcellus Community Schools (KG-12)
    2012-13 Enrollment: 723 . . . . (269) 646-7655

Housing: Homeownership rate: 74.8%; Homeowner vacancy rate: 2.4%; Rental vacancy rate: 15.9%

Newspapers: Marcellus News (weekly circulation 1600)

MASON (township). Covers a land area of 20.224 square miles and a water area of 0.297 square miles. Located at 41.78° N. Lat; 85.93° W. Long.

Population: 2,945; Growth (since 2000): 17.1%; Density: 145.6 persons per square mile; Race: 95.6% White, 0.3% Black/African American, 0.8% Asian, 0.1% American Indian/Alaska Native, 0.0% Native Hawaiian/Other

Pacific Islander, 2.3% Two or more races, 2.3% Hispanic of any race; Average household size: 2.66; Median age: 40.1; Age under 18: 25.5%; Age 65 and over: 13.0%; Males per 100 females: 101.4; Marriage status: 29.2% never married, 53.3% now married, 2.4% separated, 4.2% widowed, 13.3% divorced; Foreign born: 1.1%; Speak English only: 98.1%; With disability: 11.1%; Veterans: 11.3%; Ancestry: 32.9% German, 19.4% Irish, 12.9% English, 8.2% American, 7.9% Polish

Employment: 10.5% management, business, and financial, 0.9% computer, engineering, and science, 5.7% education, legal, community service, arts, and media, 3.1% healthcare practitioners, 21.6% service, 22.9% sales and office, 12.6% natural resources, construction, and maintenance, 22.8% production, transportation, and material moving

Income: Per capita: $20,098; Median household: $47,378; Average household: $56,789; Households with income of $100,000 or more: 10.4%; Poverty rate: 16.4%

Educational Attainment: High school diploma or higher: 85.4%; Bachelor's degree or higher: 13.5%; Graduate/professional degree or higher: 3.3%

Housing: Homeownership rate: 78.7%; Median home value: $144,400; Median year structure built: 1984; Homeowner vacancy rate: 1.3%; Median gross rent: $690 per month; Rental vacancy rate: 13.5%

Health Insurance: 81.5% have insurance; 63.1% have private insurance; 26.7% have public insurance; 18.5% do not have insurance; 9.6% of children under 18 do not have insurance

Transportation: Commute: 94.0% car, 0.0% public transportation, 1.2% walk, 4.2% work from home; Median travel time to work: 22.7 minutes

MILTON (township). Covers a land area of 21.109 square miles and a water area of 0.213 square miles. Located at 41.79° N. Lat; 86.18° W. Long.

Population: 3,878; Growth (since 2000): 46.6%; Density: 183.7 persons per square mile; Race: 94.3% White, 1.8% Black/African American, 0.8% Asian, 0.2% American Indian/Alaska Native, 0.0% Native Hawaiian/Other Pacific Islander, 2.2% Two or more races, 1.9% Hispanic of any race; Average household size: 2.79; Median age: 43.9; Age under 18: 24.4%; Age 65 and over: 13.9%; Males per 100 females: 104.3; Marriage status: 22.7% never married, 64.7% now married, 2.3% separated, 5.9% widowed, 6.7% divorced; Foreign born: 2.4%; Speak English only: 96.5%; With disability: 12.3%; Veterans: 12.4%; Ancestry: 37.4% German, 15.6% Irish, 13.7% English, 6.5% American, 5.6% Polish

Employment: 14.8% management, business, and financial, 6.5% computer, engineering, and science, 7.5% education, legal, community service, arts, and media, 13.0% healthcare practitioners, 17.6% service, 19.0% sales and office, 7.2% natural resources, construction, and maintenance, 14.4% production, transportation, and material moving

Income: Per capita: $26,194; Median household: $54,419; Average household: $70,680; Households with income of $100,000 or more: 24.5%; Poverty rate: 9.7%

Educational Attainment: High school diploma or higher: 89.5%; Bachelor's degree or higher: 26.2%; Graduate/professional degree or higher: 8.1%

Housing: Homeownership rate: 93.1%; Median home value: $158,600; Median year structure built: 1978; Homeowner vacancy rate: 1.7%; Median gross rent: $777 per month; Rental vacancy rate: 17.8%

Health Insurance: 89.0% have insurance; 76.7% have private insurance; 27.0% have public insurance; 11.0% do not have insurance; 2.3% of children under 18 do not have insurance

Transportation: Commute: 96.9% car, 0.0% public transportation, 0.0% walk, 2.3% work from home; Median travel time to work: 22.4 minutes

Additional Information Contacts
Milton Township . . . . (269) 684-7262
    http://www.miltontwp.org

NEWBERG (township). Covers a land area of 34.545 square miles and a water area of 0.962 square miles. Located at 41.95° N. Lat; 85.81° W. Long.

Population: 1,632; Growth (since 2000): -4.2%; Density: 47.2 persons per square mile; Race: 93.9% White, 3.1% Black/African American, 0.4% Asian, 0.7% American Indian/Alaska Native, 0.0% Native Hawaiian/Other Pacific Islander, 1.9% Two or more races, 1.2% Hispanic of any race; Average household size: 2.47; Median age: 45.0; Age under 18: 20.8%; Age 65 and over: 15.5%; Males per 100 females: 107.9

Housing: Homeownership rate: 81.9%; Homeowner vacancy rate: 5.4%; Rental vacancy rate: 6.8%

Additional Information Contacts
Newberg Township . . . . (269) 244-8747
  http://newbergtwp.com

ONTWA (township). Covers a land area of 19.413 square miles and a water area of 1.578 square miles. Located at 41.79° N. Lat; 86.05° W. Long.
Population: 6,549; Growth (since 2000): 11.7%; Density: 337.3 persons per square mile; Race: 96.0% White, 0.9% Black/African American, 0.3% Asian, 0.3% American Indian/Alaska Native, 0.1% Native Hawaiian/Other Pacific Islander, 1.9% Two or more races, 1.8% Hispanic of any race; Average household size: 2.50; Median age: 41.6; Age under 18: 25.3%; Age 65 and over: 15.8%; Males per 100 females: 95.2; Marriage status: 21.5% never married, 58.4% now married, 0.2% separated, 5.5% widowed, 14.5% divorced; Foreign born: 4.5%; Speak English only: 92.6%; With disability: 13.3%; Veterans: 10.0%; Ancestry: 33.8% German, 15.7% Irish, 10.2% Polish, 9.2% English, 8.4% American
Employment: 10.3% management, business, and financial, 5.0% computer, engineering, and science, 12.1% education, legal, community service, arts, and media, 6.6% healthcare practitioners, 12.6% service, 22.2% sales and office, 10.3% natural resources, construction, and maintenance, 20.8% production, transportation, and material moving
Income: Per capita: $21,830; Median household: $49,067; Average household: $59,325; Households with income of $100,000 or more: 16.8%; Poverty rate: 10.8%
Educational Attainment: High school diploma or higher: 88.0%; Bachelor's degree or higher: 19.9%; Graduate/professional degree or higher: 6.3%
Housing: Homeownership rate: 81.4%; Median home value: $144,400; Median year structure built: 1977; Homeowner vacancy rate: 2.8%; Median gross rent: $735 per month; Rental vacancy rate: 8.9%
Health Insurance: 87.5% have insurance; 68.0% have private insurance; 34.1% have public insurance; 12.5% do not have insurance; 4.0% of children under 18 do not have insurance
Transportation: Commute: 95.9% car, 0.8% public transportation, 0.7% walk, 2.1% work from home; Median travel time to work: 29.4 minutes

PENN (township). Covers a land area of 33.557 square miles and a water area of 1.833 square miles. Located at 41.93° N. Lat; 85.93° W. Long. Elevation is 902 feet.
History: Penn Township was organized in 1829 and named for William Penn by its first settlers, who were Quakers from Pennsylvania.
Population: 1,774; Growth (since 2000): -6.7%; Density: 52.9 persons per square mile; Race: 83.0% White, 10.0% Black/African American, 2.3% Asian, 0.4% American Indian/Alaska Native, 0.0% Native Hawaiian/Other Pacific Islander, 4.0% Two or more races, 2.5% Hispanic of any race; Average household size: 2.46; Median age: 47.7; Age under 18: 20.4%; Age 65 and over: 20.7%; Males per 100 females: 104.1
Housing: Homeownership rate: 83.0%; Homeowner vacancy rate: 5.9%; Rental vacancy rate: 14.1%

POKAGON (township). Covers a land area of 34.000 square miles and a water area of 0.228 square miles. Located at 41.94° N. Lat; 86.17° W. Long. Elevation is 738 feet.
Population: 2,029; Growth (since 2000): -7.7%; Density: 59.7 persons per square mile; Race: 88.8% White, 5.6% Black/African American, 0.6% Asian, 0.8% American Indian/Alaska Native, 0.0% Native Hawaiian/Other Pacific Islander, 2.9% Two or more races, 2.8% Hispanic of any race; Average household size: 2.50; Median age: 45.0; Age under 18: 21.2%; Age 65 and over: 17.8%; Males per 100 females: 100.9
Housing: Homeownership rate: 87.6%; Homeowner vacancy rate: 2.4%; Rental vacancy rate: 13.7%

PORTER (township). Covers a land area of 51.522 square miles and a water area of 3.131 square miles. Located at 41.82° N. Lat; 85.83° W. Long.
History: Porter Township was organized in 1833 and named for George B. Porter, governor of Michigan.
Population: 3,798; Growth (since 2000): 0.1%; Density: 73.7 persons per square mile; Race: 96.8% White, 0.4% Black/African American, 0.2% Asian, 0.3% American Indian/Alaska Native, 0.0% Native Hawaiian/Other Pacific Islander, 1.9% Two or more races, 1.8% Hispanic of any race; Average household size: 2.37; Median age: 47.6; Age under 18: 19.2%; Age 65 and over: 17.1%; Males per 100 females: 102.6; Marriage status: 20.3% never married, 57.4% now married, 0.5% separated, 4.1%

widowed, 18.2% divorced; Foreign born: 1.3%; Speak English only: 97.5%; With disability: 17.3%; Veterans: 14.2%; Ancestry: 35.8% German, 15.1% English, 14.0% Irish, 9.1% French, 6.1% Polish
Employment: 16.6% management, business, and financial, 2.2% computer, engineering, and science, 7.8% education, legal, community service, arts, and media, 5.0% healthcare practitioners, 7.7% service, 25.2% sales and office, 7.8% natural resources, construction, and maintenance, 27.6% production, transportation, and material moving
Income: Per capita: $32,626; Median household: $46,731; Average household: $73,336; Households with income of $100,000 or more: 18.8%; Poverty rate: 17.4%
Educational Attainment: High school diploma or higher: 87.7%; Bachelor's degree or higher: 17.2%; Graduate/professional degree or higher: 3.6%
Housing: Homeownership rate: 84.7%; Median home value: $177,400; Median year structure built: 1973; Homeowner vacancy rate: 3.8%; Median gross rent: $724 per month; Rental vacancy rate: 5.0%
Health Insurance: 84.7% have insurance; 63.0% have private insurance; 37.2% have public insurance; 15.3% do not have insurance; 3.6% of children under 18 do not have insurance
Transportation: Commute: 90.4% car, 0.0% public transportation, 0.0% walk, 6.7% work from home; Median travel time to work: 29.6 minutes

SILVER CREEK (township). Covers a land area of 31.958 square miles and a water area of 2.264 square miles. Located at 42.03° N. Lat; 86.18° W. Long.
History: Silver Creek Township was organized in 1837. Silver Creek got its name from the silvery look to the marl bottom of the lake from which it runs.
Population: 3,218; Growth (since 2000): -7.8%; Density: 100.7 persons per square mile; Race: 90.0% White, 1.2% Black/African American, 0.1% Asian, 1.8% American Indian/Alaska Native, 0.0% Native Hawaiian/Other Pacific Islander, 2.2% Two or more races, 9.7% Hispanic of any race; Average household size: 2.47; Median age: 46.6; Age under 18: 21.3%; Age 65 and over: 22.2%; Males per 100 females: 97.3; Marriage status: 21.9% never married, 61.5% now married, 0.4% separated, 3.9% widowed, 12.7% divorced; Foreign born: 3.4%; Speak English only: 86.8%; With disability: 13.3%; Veterans: 9.7%; Ancestry: 26.8% German, 18.6% Irish, 14.7% English, 9.4% Polish, 5.7% American
Employment: 11.8% management, business, and financial, 0.7% computer, engineering, and science, 17.6% education, legal, community service, arts, and media, 3.6% healthcare practitioners, 14.4% service, 18.8% sales and office, 20.3% natural resources, construction, and maintenance, 12.8% production, transportation, and material moving
Income: Per capita: $22,131; Median household: $47,321; Average household: $58,672; Households with income of $100,000 or more: 12.0%; Poverty rate: 18.0%
Educational Attainment: High school diploma or higher: 83.7%; Bachelor's degree or higher: 22.4%; Graduate/professional degree or higher: 9.1%
Housing: Homeownership rate: 86.4%; Median home value: $154,700; Median year structure built: 1982; Homeowner vacancy rate: 5.0%; Median gross rent: $975 per month; Rental vacancy rate: 13.7%
Health Insurance: 87.9% have insurance; 61.2% have private insurance; 42.1% have public insurance; 12.1% do not have insurance; 0.0% of children under 18 do not have insurance
Transportation: Commute: 87.8% car, 0.0% public transportation, 0.0% walk, 10.4% work from home; Median travel time to work: 27.0 minutes

VANDALIA (village). Covers a land area of 0.988 square miles and a water area of <.001 square miles. Located at 41.92° N. Lat; 85.92° W. Long. Elevation is 879 feet.
Population: 301; Growth (since 2000): -29.8%; Density: 304.5 persons per square mile; Race: 41.5% White, 42.2% Black/African American, 7.6% Asian, 0.3% American Indian/Alaska Native, 0.0% Native Hawaiian/Other Pacific Islander, 6.6% Two or more races, 1.7% Hispanic of any race; Average household size: 2.81; Median age: 39.3; Age under 18: 25.6%; Age 65 and over: 16.9%; Males per 100 females: 113.5
Housing: Homeownership rate: 76.6%; Homeowner vacancy rate: 11.5%; Rental vacancy rate: 26.5%

VOLINIA (township). Covers a land area of 34.390 square miles and a water area of 0.726 square miles. Located at 42.03° N. Lat; 85.93° W. Long. Elevation is 863 feet.
Population: 1,112; Growth (since 2000): -5.3%; Density: 32.3 persons per square mile; Race: 95.8% White, 2.0% Black/African American, 0.7% Asian, 0.0% American Indian/Alaska Native, 0.0% Native Hawaiian/Other Pacific Islander, 1.3% Two or more races, 1.8% Hispanic of any race; Average household size: 2.60; Median age: 44.2; Age under 18: 24.3%; Age 65 and over: 15.6%; Males per 100 females: 102.6
Housing: Homeownership rate: 84.6%; Homeowner vacancy rate: 4.0%; Rental vacancy rate: 2.8%

WAYNE (township). Covers a land area of 34.251 square miles and a water area of 0.565 square miles. Located at 42.03° N. Lat; 86.05° W. Long. Elevation is 804 feet.
Population: 2,654; Growth (since 2000): -7.2%; Density: 77.5 persons per square mile; Race: 92.0% White, 1.7% Black/African American, 0.4% Asian, 1.5% American Indian/Alaska Native, 0.0% Native Hawaiian/Other Pacific Islander, 3.4% Two or more races, 3.1% Hispanic of any race; Average household size: 2.55; Median age: 45.5; Age under 18: 20.6%; Age 65 and over: 16.2%; Males per 100 females: 97.2; Marriage status: 27.5% never married, 53.1% now married, 0.2% separated, 4.5% widowed, 14.8% divorced; Foreign born: 1.3%; Speak English only: 98.6%; With disability: 20.9%; Veterans: 9.9%; Ancestry: 33.6% German, 18.3% English, 12.2% Irish, 9.8% Polish, 8.6% Dutch
Employment: 8.1% management, business, and financial, 4.3% computer, engineering, and science, 9.9% education, legal, community service, arts, and media, 3.1% healthcare practitioners, 23.3% service, 20.9% sales and office, 9.4% natural resources, construction, and maintenance, 20.8% production, transportation, and material moving
Income: Per capita: $21,502; Median household: $43,880; Average household: $56,514; Households with income of $100,000 or more: 14.6%; Poverty rate: 16.5%
Educational Attainment: High school diploma or higher: 87.7%; Bachelor's degree or higher: 11.8%; Graduate/professional degree or higher: 4.6%
Housing: Homeownership rate: 84.4%; Median home value: $109,300; Median year structure built: 1972; Homeowner vacancy rate: 1.2%; Median gross rent: $564 per month; Rental vacancy rate: 7.4%
Health Insurance: 87.4% have insurance; 59.7% have private insurance; 40.5% have public insurance; 12.6% do not have insurance; 1.0% of children under 18 do not have insurance
Transportation: Commute: 95.0% car, 0.0% public transportation, 2.5% walk, 2.1% work from home; Median travel time to work: 26.1 minutes

Charlevoix County

Located in northwestern Michigan; bounded on the northwest by Lake Michigan; drained by the Boyne and Jordan Rivers; includes the Beaver Islands, and Charlevoix and Walloon Lakes. Covers a land area of 416.339 square miles, a water area of 974.125 square miles, and is located in the Eastern Time Zone at 45.51° N. Lat., 85.45° W. Long. The county was founded in 1869. County seat is Charlevoix.

Weather Station: Boyne Falls   Elevation: 734 feet

	Jan	Feb	Mar	Apr	May	Jun	Jul	Aug	Sep	Oct	Nov	Dec
High	28	32	42	57	70	79	83	81	73	59	45	33
Low	13	13	20	32	42	52	56	55	49	39	30	20
Precip	2.4	1.6	1.8	2.5	2.9	2.8	2.6	3.6	3.8	3.9	3.0	2.7
Snow	31.1	21.4	11.0	4.5	0.3	0.0	0.0	0.0	tr	0.8	12.7	32.4

High and Low temperatures in degrees Fahrenheit; Precipitation and Snow in inches

Weather Station: East Jordan   Elevation: 589 feet

	Jan	Feb	Mar	Apr	May	Jun	Jul	Aug	Sep	Oct	Nov	Dec
High	30	33	42	56	69	78	82	80	73	59	46	34
Low	14	13	20	31	41	50	55	54	47	38	30	21
Precip	2.0	1.3	1.4	2.4	2.7	2.8	2.7	3.4	3.7	3.9	2.8	2.3
Snow	34.6	21.7	11.6	3.8	0.1	0.0	0.0	0.0	0.0	0.6	10.7	36.0

High and Low temperatures in degrees Fahrenheit; Precipitation and Snow in inches

Weather Station: St James 2 S Beaver Is   Elevation: 669 feet

	Jan	Feb	Mar	Apr	May	Jun	Jul	Aug	Sep	Oct	Nov	Dec
High	27	28	37	50	62	71	76	75	67	55	43	32
Low	15	14	21	32	42	51	57	58	52	41	32	22
Precip	2.5	1.4	2.0	2.7	2.8	2.4	2.5	2.8	3.6	3.7	2.7	2.6
Snow	26.4	15.9	11.3	4.5	0.2	0.0	0.0	0.0	tr	tr	5.9	22.5

High and Low temperatures in degrees Fahrenheit; Precipitation and Snow in inches

Population: 25,949; Growth (since 2000): -0.5%; Density: 62.3 persons per square mile; Race: 95.6% White, 0.3% Black/African American, 0.4% Asian, 1.5% American Indian/Alaska Native, 0.0% Native Hawaiian/Other Pacific Islander, 1.8% two or more races, 1.4% Hispanic of any race; Average household size: 2.36; Median age: 45.5; Age under 18: 22.0%; Age 65 and over: 18.6%; Males per 100 females: 97.0; Marriage status: 23.0% never married, 58.2% now married, 0.8% separated, 6.7% widowed, 12.2% divorced; Foreign born: 2.4%; Speak English only: 96.5%; With disability: 15.1%; Veterans: 11.6%; Ancestry: 26.2% German, 15.5% English, 15.3% Irish, 9.3% Polish, 7.1% American
Religion: Six largest groups: 12.8% Catholicism, 5.2% Presbyterian-Reformed, 4.0% Methodist/Pietist, 2.8% Lutheran, 2.4% Holiness, 1.4% Pentecostal
Economy: Unemployment rate: 5.9%; Leading industries: 15.5% construction; 14.4% retail trade; 11.1% other services (except public administration); Farms: 297 totaling 37,540 acres; Company size: 0 employ 1,000 or more persons, 1 employs 500 to 999 persons, 10 employ 100 to 499 persons, 789 employ less than 100 persons; Business ownership: 1,019 women-owned, n/a Black-owned, n/a Hispanic-owned, n/a Asian-owned
Employment: 11.3% management, business, and financial, 3.8% computer, engineering, and science, 8.4% education, legal, community service, arts, and media, 6.0% healthcare practitioners, 19.0% service, 24.7% sales and office, 10.3% natural resources, construction, and maintenance, 16.5% production, transportation, and material moving
Income: Per capita: $26,947; Median household: $45,949; Average household: $63,838; Households with income of $100,000 or more: 14.0%; Poverty rate: 13.3%
Educational Attainment: High school diploma or higher: 91.6%; Bachelor's degree or higher: 27.0%; Graduate/professional degree or higher: 11.1%
Housing: Homeownership rate: 79.4%; Median home value: $151,400; Median year structure built: 1975; Homeowner vacancy rate: 3.5%; Median gross rent: $635 per month; Rental vacancy rate: 13.1%
Vital Statistics: Birth rate: 96.1 per 10,000 population; Death rate: 99.9 per 10,000 population; Age-adjusted cancer mortality rate: 200.1 deaths per 100,000 population
Health Insurance: 88.7% have insurance; 70.6% have private insurance; 36.6% have public insurance; 11.3% do not have insurance; 5.8% of children under 18 do not have insurance
Health Care: Physicians: 18.4 per 10,000 population; Hospital beds: 9.6 per 10,000 population; Hospital admissions: 391.4 per 10,000 population
Transportation: Commute: 92.2% car, 0.6% public transportation, 2.1% walk, 4.1% work from home; Median travel time to work: 18.8 minutes
Presidential Election: 42.2% Obama, 56.9% Romney (2012)
National and State Parks: Beaver Islands State Wildlife Research Area; Fishermans Island State Park; Jordan River State Forest; Michigan Islands National Wildlife Refuge; Young State Park
Additional Information Contacts
Charlevoix Government. . . . . (231) 547-7200
   http://www.charlevoixcounty.org

Charlevoix County Communities

ADVANCE (CDP). Covers a land area of 2.720 square miles and a water area of 0.028 square miles. Located at 45.22° N. Lat; 85.08° W. Long. Elevation is 587 feet.
Population: 328; Growth (since 2000): n/a; Density: 120.6 persons per square mile; Race: 98.5% White, 0.0% Black/African American, 0.3% Asian, 0.9% American Indian/Alaska Native, 0.0% Native Hawaiian/Other Pacific Islander, 0.3% Two or more races, 0.0% Hispanic of any race; Average household size: 2.05; Median age: 57.6; Age under 18: 12.2%; Age 65 and over: 33.5%; Males per 100 females: 91.8
Housing: Homeownership rate: 86.9%; Homeowner vacancy rate: 2.8%; Rental vacancy rate: 22.2%

BAY (township). Covers a land area of 15.548 square miles and a water area of 3.344 square miles. Located at 45.30° N. Lat; 85.05° W. Long.
Population: 1,122; Growth (since 2000): 5.1%; Density: 72.2 persons per square mile; Race: 97.8% White, 0.0% Black/African American, 0.3% Asian, 0.3% American Indian/Alaska Native, 0.0% Native Hawaiian/Other Pacific Islander, 1.6% Two or more races, 0.4% Hispanic of any race;

Average household size: 2.52; Median age: 48.8; Age under 18: 20.9%; Age 65 and over: 21.3%; Males per 100 females: 101.4
Housing: Homeownership rate: 91.5%; Homeowner vacancy rate: 1.9%; Rental vacancy rate: 13.3%

BAY SHORE (CDP).
Note: Statistics that would complete this profile are not available because the CDP was created after the 2010 Census was released.

BEAVER ISLAND (unincorporated postal area)
ZCTA: 49782
Covers a land area of 72.692 square miles and a water area of 1.975 square miles. Located at 45.67° N. Lat; 85.54° W. Long..
Population: 657; Growth (since 2000): 19.2%; Density: 9.0 persons per square mile; Race: 97.3% White, 0.0% Black/African American, 0.0% Asian, 1.5% American Indian/Alaska Native, 0.0% Native Hawaiian/Other Pacific Islander, 1.1% Two or more races, 1.1% Hispanic of any race; Average household size: 1.96; Median age: 54.9; Age under 18: 13.7%; Age 65 and over: 26.3%; Males per 100 females: 107.3

School District(s)
Beaver Island Community School (KG-12)
    2012-13 Enrollment: 60 . . . . (231) 448-2744
Charlevoix Public Schools (KG-12)
    2012-13 Enrollment: 1,034 . . . . (231) 547-3200
Housing: Homeownership rate: 88.1%; Homeowner vacancy rate: 3.6%; Rental vacancy rate: 44.7%
Airports: Beaver Island (commercial service–non-primary); Welke (general aviation)

BOYNE CITY (city). Covers a land area of 4.058 square miles and a water area of 1.356 square miles. Located at 45.21° N. Lat; 85.01° W. Long. Elevation is 594 feet.
History: Boyne City developed along Lake Charlevoix as an area of summer homes and cottages. In the mid-1800's it was the site of a sawmill, and a charcoal foundry. In the 1900's, the tourist trade became the principal source of revenue, with the smelt run in the river in the spring attracting many visitors. The Boyne River, near which the city was established, was named for a river in Ireland.
Population: 3,735; Growth (since 2000): 6.6%; Density: 920.3 persons per square mile; Race: 94.9% White, 0.4% Black/African American, 0.5% Asian, 0.7% American Indian/Alaska Native, 0.1% Native Hawaiian/Other Pacific Islander, 3.2% Two or more races, 1.3% Hispanic of any race; Average household size: 2.27; Median age: 41.9; Age under 18: 23.9%; Age 65 and over: 16.9%; Males per 100 females: 94.0; Marriage status: 31.7% never married, 50.0% now married, 0.8% separated, 7.4% widowed, 10.9% divorced; Foreign born: 5.6%; Speak English only: 94.4%; With disability: 11.1%; Veterans: 8.7%; Ancestry: 25.0% German, 12.3% English, 11.5% Irish, 8.6% Polish, 5.7% American
Employment: 11.9% management, business, and financial, 4.8% computer, engineering, and science, 9.1% education, legal, community service, arts, and media, 3.6% healthcare practitioners, 22.6% service, 22.5% sales and office, 9.5% natural resources, construction, and maintenance, 15.9% production, transportation, and material moving
Income: Per capita: $20,720; Median household: $39,483; Average household: $49,011; Households with income of $100,000 or more: 6.0%; Poverty rate: 18.0%
Educational Attainment: High school diploma or higher: 93.6%; Bachelor's degree or higher: 20.1%; Graduate/professional degree or higher: 10.5%

School District(s)
Boyne City Public Schools (PK-12)
    2012-13 Enrollment: 1,335 . . . . (231) 439-8190
Charlevoix-Emmet ISD (PK-12)
    2012-13 Enrollment: 298 . . . . (231) 547-9947
Concord Academy Boyne (KG-12)
    2012-13 Enrollment: 215 . . . . (231) 582-0194
Housing: Homeownership rate: 67.2%; Median home value: $126,100; Median year structure built: 1972; Homeowner vacancy rate: 5.2%; Median gross rent: $631 per month; Rental vacancy rate: 7.8%
Health Insurance: 85.2% have insurance; 59.8% have private insurance; 35.2% have public insurance; 14.8% do not have insurance; 10.3% of children under 18 do not have insurance
Safety: Violent crime rate: 26.6 per 10,000 population; Property crime rate: 207.6 per 10,000 population

Transportation: Commute: 95.7% car, 0.6% public transportation, 0.4% walk, 3.0% work from home; Median travel time to work: 16.2 minutes
Additional Information Contacts
City of Boyne City . . . . (231) 582-6597
    http://gov.boynecity.com/government.phtml

BOYNE FALLS (village). Covers a land area of 0.553 square miles and a water area of 0.006 square miles. Located at 45.17° N. Lat; 84.91° W. Long. Elevation is 712 feet.
History: Boyne Falls was established when the Grand Rapids & Indiana Railroad arrived here in 1874. It was incorporated as a village in 1893, and named for the falls on the nearby Boyne River.
Population: 294; Growth (since 2000): -20.5%; Density: 531.7 persons per square mile; Race: 95.2% White, 0.7% Black/African American, 0.3% Asian, 1.0% American Indian/Alaska Native, 0.0% Native Hawaiian/Other Pacific Islander, 2.7% Two or more races, 0.7% Hispanic of any race; Average household size: 2.21; Median age: 41.7; Age under 18: 20.7%; Age 65 and over: 13.3%; Males per 100 females: 89.7

School District(s)
Boyne City Public Schools (PK-12)
    2012-13 Enrollment: 1,335 . . . . (231) 439-8190
Boyne Falls Public SD (KG-12)
    2012-13 Enrollment: 198 . . . . (231) 549-2211
Housing: Homeownership rate: 75.1%; Homeowner vacancy rate: 1.9%; Rental vacancy rate: 19.5%

BOYNE VALLEY (township). Covers a land area of 34.777 square miles and a water area of 0.677 square miles. Located at 45.15° N. Lat; 84.88° W. Long.
Population: 1,195; Growth (since 2000): -1.6%; Density: 34.4 persons per square mile; Race: 95.6% White, 0.3% Black/African American, 0.3% Asian, 1.8% American Indian/Alaska Native, 0.0% Native Hawaiian/Other Pacific Islander, 2.1% Two or more races, 1.4% Hispanic of any race; Average household size: 2.34; Median age: 45.9; Age under 18: 20.4%; Age 65 and over: 18.2%; Males per 100 females: 100.5
Housing: Homeownership rate: 83.5%; Homeowner vacancy rate: 2.3%; Rental vacancy rate: 12.5%

CHANDLER (township). Covers a land area of 35.603 square miles and a water area of 0.015 square miles. Located at 45.25° N. Lat; 84.78° W. Long.
Population: 248; Growth (since 2000): 7.8%; Density: 7.0 persons per square mile; Race: 94.4% White, 0.0% Black/African American, 0.4% Asian, 0.4% American Indian/Alaska Native, 0.0% Native Hawaiian/Other Pacific Islander, 2.0% Two or more races, 2.8% Hispanic of any race; Average household size: 2.64; Median age: 40.3; Age under 18: 23.0%; Age 65 and over: 10.9%; Males per 100 females: 108.4
Housing: Homeownership rate: 92.6%; Homeowner vacancy rate: 4.4%; Rental vacancy rate: 22.2%

CHARLEVOIX (city). County seat. Covers a land area of 2.048 square miles and a water area of 0.123 square miles. Located at 45.31° N. Lat; 85.25° W. Long. Elevation is 594 feet.
History: The first settlement here was called Pine River, and was the scene of a skirmish in 1853 between mainland settlers and those on Beaver Island. When the river was dredged between Round Lake and Lake Michigan, Charlevoix became a busy port of entry. Much lumber was shipped from here between 1876 and 1925. Charlevoix, which later became a popular resort, was named for the French explorer, Pierre Francois Xavier de Charlevoix.
Population: 2,513; Growth (since 2000): -16.1%; Density: 1,227.0 persons per square mile; Race: 94.2% White, 1.2% Black/African American, 0.5% Asian, 2.0% American Indian/Alaska Native, 0.0% Native Hawaiian/Other Pacific Islander, 1.8% Two or more races, 0.9% Hispanic of any race; Average household size: 1.94; Median age: 48.1; Age under 18: 17.5%; Age 65 and over: 23.6%; Males per 100 females: 89.4; Marriage status: 21.4% never married, 54.9% now married, 0.3% separated, 8.6% widowed, 15.1% divorced; Foreign born: 1.7%; Speak English only: 99.0%; With disability: 20.1%; Veterans: 13.9%; Ancestry: 27.1% German, 15.1% Irish, 14.3% English, 10.2% French, 8.6% Dutch
Employment: 7.0% management, business, and financial, 5.6% computer, engineering, and science, 10.3% education, legal, community service, arts, and media, 4.4% healthcare practitioners, 16.0% service, 31.9% sales and office, 9.6% natural resources, construction, and maintenance, 15.1% production, transportation, and material moving

Income: Per capita: $30,237; Median household: $34,792; Average household: $62,090; Households with income of $100,000 or more: 16.0%; Poverty rate: 23.0%

Educational Attainment: High school diploma or higher: 92.5%; Bachelor's degree or higher: 36.1%; Graduate/professional degree or higher: 14.6%

School District(s)
Charlevoix Public Schools (KG-12)
    2012-13 Enrollment: 1,034 . . . . (231) 547-3200
Charlevoix-Emmet ISD (PK-12)
    2012-13 Enrollment: 298 . . . . (231) 547-9947
Northwest Academy (KG-12)
    2012-13 Enrollment: 107 . . . . (231) 547-9000

Housing: Homeownership rate: 56.0%; Median home value: $167,200; Median year structure built: 1956; Homeowner vacancy rate: 3.7%; Median gross rent: $560 per month; Rental vacancy rate: 11.6%

Health Insurance: 94.0% have insurance; 70.7% have private insurance; 47.4% have public insurance; 6.0% do not have insurance; 0.0% of children under 18 do not have insurance

Hospitals: Charlevoix Area Hospital (50 beds)

Safety: Violent crime rate: 15.8 per 10,000 population; Property crime rate: 519.0 per 10,000 population

Newspapers: Charlevoix Courier (weekly circulation 3100)

Transportation: Commute: 82.1% car, 3.1% public transportation, 7.6% walk, 5.3% work from home; Median travel time to work: 12.5 minutes

Airports: Charlevoix Municipal (primary service/non-hub)

Additional Information Contacts
City of Charlevoix . . . . (231) 547-3270
    http://www.cityofcharlevoix.org

CHARLEVOIX (township). Covers a land area of 5.938 square miles and a water area of 6.138 square miles. Located at 45.31° N. Lat; 85.28° W. Long. Elevation is 594 feet.

History: Settled 1852; Incorporated as village 1879, as city 1905.

Population: 1,645; Growth (since 2000): -3.1%; Density: 277.0 persons per square mile; Race: 95.1% White, 0.1% Black/African American, 0.4% Asian, 1.9% American Indian/Alaska Native, 0.3% Native Hawaiian/Other Pacific Islander, 1.6% Two or more races, 1.0% Hispanic of any race; Average household size: 2.35; Median age: 47.5; Age under 18: 21.4%; Age 65 and over: 22.9%; Males per 100 females: 86.3

School District(s)
Charlevoix Public Schools (KG-12)
    2012-13 Enrollment: 1,034 . . . . (231) 547-3200
Charlevoix-Emmet ISD (PK-12)
    2012-13 Enrollment: 298 . . . . (231) 547-9947
Northwest Academy (KG-12)
    2012-13 Enrollment: 107 . . . . (231) 547-9000

Housing: Homeownership rate: 87.3%; Homeowner vacancy rate: 3.5%; Rental vacancy rate: 34.3%

Hospitals: Charlevoix Area Hospital (50 beds)

Newspapers: Charlevoix Courier (weekly circulation 3100)

Airports: Charlevoix Municipal (primary service/non-hub)

EAST JORDAN (city). Covers a land area of 3.047 square miles and a water area of 0.914 square miles. Located at 45.15° N. Lat; 85.13° W. Long. Elevation is 646 feet.

History: East Jordan was originally two settlements, East Jordan and South Arm, connected by a bridge across the Jordan River. The two were incorporated as one village in 1887 and as a city in 1911. First lumber and then canning and a creamery supported the East Jordan economy.

Population: 2,351; Growth (since 2000): -6.2%; Density: 771.7 persons per square mile; Race: 96.0% White, 0.2% Black/African American, 0.1% Asian, 1.6% American Indian/Alaska Native, 0.0% Native Hawaiian/Other Pacific Islander, 1.8% Two or more races, 2.3% Hispanic of any race; Average household size: 2.46; Median age: 37.1; Age under 18: 27.1%; Age 65 and over: 15.2%; Males per 100 females: 95.1

School District(s)
East Jordan Public Schools (PK-12)
    2012-13 Enrollment: 976 . . . . (231) 536-3131

Housing: Homeownership rate: 66.4%; Homeowner vacancy rate: 6.7%; Rental vacancy rate: 9.3%

Airports: East Jordan City (general aviation)

EVANGELINE (township). Covers a land area of 11.018 square miles and a water area of 3.716 square miles. Located at 45.25° N. Lat; 85.02° W. Long.

Population: 712; Growth (since 2000): -7.9%; Density: 64.6 persons per square mile; Race: 98.3% White, 0.0% Black/African American, 0.0% Asian, 0.6% American Indian/Alaska Native, 0.0% Native Hawaiian/Other Pacific Islander, 1.0% Two or more races, 0.3% Hispanic of any race; Average household size: 2.36; Median age: 49.7; Age under 18: 18.5%; Age 65 and over: 21.9%; Males per 100 females: 105.8

Housing: Homeownership rate: 84.8%; Homeowner vacancy rate: 2.3%; Rental vacancy rate: 15.8%

EVELINE (township). Covers a land area of 25.810 square miles and a water area of 10.936 square miles. Located at 45.25° N. Lat; 85.16° W. Long.

Population: 1,484; Growth (since 2000): -4.9%; Density: 57.5 persons per square mile; Race: 94.3% White, 0.1% Black/African American, 0.2% Asian, 2.6% American Indian/Alaska Native, 0.0% Native Hawaiian/Other Pacific Islander, 1.2% Two or more races, 2.3% Hispanic of any race; Average household size: 2.20; Median age: 52.9; Age under 18: 16.5%; Age 65 and over: 24.5%; Males per 100 females: 91.2

Housing: Homeownership rate: 86.8%; Homeowner vacancy rate: 3.8%; Rental vacancy rate: 16.0%

HAYES (township). Covers a land area of 30.090 square miles and a water area of 13.076 square miles. Located at 45.32° N. Lat; 85.15° W. Long.

Population: 1,919; Growth (since 2000): 1.4%; Density: 63.8 persons per square mile; Race: 94.1% White, 0.1% Black/African American, 0.4% Asian, 3.2% American Indian/Alaska Native, 0.1% Native Hawaiian/Other Pacific Islander, 1.9% Two or more races, 1.4% Hispanic of any race; Average household size: 2.37; Median age: 47.5; Age under 18: 18.9%; Age 65 and over: 19.1%; Males per 100 females: 99.1

Housing: Homeownership rate: 90.6%; Homeowner vacancy rate: 2.6%; Rental vacancy rate: 13.3%

HORTON BAY (CDP). Covers a land area of 4.820 square miles and a water area of <.001 square miles. Located at 45.29° N. Lat; 85.07° W. Long. Elevation is 673 feet.

Population: 512; Growth (since 2000): n/a; Density: 106.2 persons per square mile; Race: 98.4% White, 0.0% Black/African American, 0.0% Asian, 0.4% American Indian/Alaska Native, 0.0% Native Hawaiian/Other Pacific Islander, 1.2% Two or more races, 0.2% Hispanic of any race; Average household size: 2.46; Median age: 51.3; Age under 18: 19.9%; Age 65 and over: 23.6%; Males per 100 females: 105.6

Housing: Homeownership rate: 88.5%; Homeowner vacancy rate: 0.5%; Rental vacancy rate: 7.7%

HUDSON (township). Covers a land area of 34.308 square miles and a water area of 1.165 square miles. Located at 45.16° N. Lat; 84.80° W. Long.

Population: 691; Growth (since 2000): 8.1%; Density: 20.1 persons per square mile; Race: 95.7% White, 0.1% Black/African American, 0.7% Asian, 1.2% American Indian/Alaska Native, 0.0% Native Hawaiian/Other Pacific Islander, 2.3% Two or more races, 0.1% Hispanic of any race; Average household size: 2.51; Median age: 44.4; Age under 18: 22.7%; Age 65 and over: 14.9%; Males per 100 females: 110.7

Housing: Homeownership rate: 87.8%; Homeowner vacancy rate: 2.1%; Rental vacancy rate: 22.0%

IRONTON (CDP). Covers a land area of 0.987 square miles and a water area of 0 square miles. Located at 45.26° N. Lat; 85.19° W. Long. Elevation is 620 feet.

Population: 140; Growth (since 2000): n/a; Density: 141.8 persons per square mile; Race: 96.4% White, 1.4% Black/African American, 0.7% Asian, 0.7% American Indian/Alaska Native, 0.0% Native Hawaiian/Other Pacific Islander, 0.7% Two or more races, 0.0% Hispanic of any race; Average household size: 2.12; Median age: 48.2; Age under 18: 15.0%; Age 65 and over: 21.4%; Males per 100 females: 86.7

Housing: Homeownership rate: 81.8%; Homeowner vacancy rate: 1.8%; Rental vacancy rate: 20.0%

MARION (township). Covers a land area of 25.573 square miles and a water area of 0.949 square miles. Located at 45.25° N. Lat; 85.27° W. Long.

Population: 1,714; Growth (since 2000): 14.9%; Density: 67.0 persons per square mile; Race: 96.7% White, 0.4% Black/African American, 0.8% Asian, 0.8% American Indian/Alaska Native, 0.0% Native Hawaiian/Other Pacific Islander, 1.2% Two or more races, 1.1% Hispanic of any race; Average household size: 2.67; Median age: 41.2; Age under 18: 26.7%; Age 65 and over: 12.5%; Males per 100 females: 96.8

Housing: Homeownership rate: 87.8%; Homeowner vacancy rate: 1.9%; Rental vacancy rate: 8.0%

MELROSE (township). Covers a land area of 32.979 square miles and a water area of 2.019 square miles. Located at 45.24° N. Lat; 84.91° W. Long.

Population: 1,403; Growth (since 2000): 1.1%; Density: 42.5 persons per square mile; Race: 96.2% White, 0.3% Black/African American, 0.4% Asian, 0.8% American Indian/Alaska Native, 0.1% Native Hawaiian/Other Pacific Islander, 2.1% Two or more races, 1.9% Hispanic of any race; Average household size: 2.59; Median age: 42.6; Age under 18: 25.0%; Age 65 and over: 14.9%; Males per 100 females: 104.5

Housing: Homeownership rate: 85.3%; Homeowner vacancy rate: 4.3%; Rental vacancy rate: 20.0%

NORWOOD (CDP). Covers a land area of 2.032 square miles and a water area of <.001 square miles. Located at 45.23° N. Lat; 85.38° W. Long. Elevation is 656 feet.

Population: 142; Growth (since 2000): n/a; Density: 69.9 persons per square mile; Race: 97.2% White, 0.0% Black/African American, 1.4% Asian, 1.4% American Indian/Alaska Native, 0.0% Native Hawaiian/Other Pacific Islander, 0.0% Two or more races, 0.0% Hispanic of any race; Average household size: 2.54; Median age: 47.7; Age under 18: 19.7%; Age 65 and over: 24.6%; Males per 100 females: 102.9

Housing: Homeownership rate: 94.6%; Homeowner vacancy rate: 5.3%; Rental vacancy rate: 25.0%

NORWOOD (township). Covers a land area of 18.159 square miles and a water area of 6.246 square miles. Located at 45.26° N. Lat; 85.36° W. Long. Elevation is 656 feet.

Population: 723; Growth (since 2000): 1.3%; Density: 39.8 persons per square mile; Race: 97.0% White, 0.3% Black/African American, 0.3% Asian, 1.2% American Indian/Alaska Native, 0.0% Native Hawaiian/Other Pacific Islander, 1.2% Two or more races, 0.6% Hispanic of any race; Average household size: 2.47; Median age: 47.3; Age under 18: 21.9%; Age 65 and over: 20.1%; Males per 100 females: 95.9

Housing: Homeownership rate: 91.7%; Homeowner vacancy rate: 2.9%; Rental vacancy rate: 10.7%

PEAINE (township). Covers a land area of 52.346 square miles and a water area of 20.686 square miles. Located at 45.62° N. Lat; 85.54° W. Long.

Population: 292; Growth (since 2000): 19.7%; Density: 5.6 persons per square mile; Race: 99.0% White, 0.0% Black/African American, 0.0% Asian, 0.3% American Indian/Alaska Native, 0.0% Native Hawaiian/Other Pacific Islander, 0.7% Two or more races, 0.7% Hispanic of any race; Average household size: 1.85; Median age: 58.3; Age under 18: 8.6%; Age 65 and over: 28.8%; Males per 100 females: 117.9

Housing: Homeownership rate: 96.2%; Homeowner vacancy rate: 3.8%; Rental vacancy rate: 68.4%

SAINT JAMES (CDP). Covers a land area of 1.029 square miles and a water area of 0.003 square miles. Located at 45.74° N. Lat; 85.53° W. Long. Elevation is 604 feet.

Population: 205; Growth (since 2000): n/a; Density: 199.2 persons per square mile; Race: 95.1% White, 0.0% Black/African American, 0.0% Asian, 4.4% American Indian/Alaska Native, 0.0% Native Hawaiian/Other Pacific Islander, 0.5% Two or more races, 0.5% Hispanic of any race; Average household size: 1.93; Median age: 53.2; Age under 18: 17.1%; Age 65 and over: 27.3%; Males per 100 females: 101.0

Housing: Homeownership rate: 77.4%; Homeowner vacancy rate: 0.0%; Rental vacancy rate: 42.2%

SAINT JAMES (township). Covers a land area of 20.346 square miles and a water area of 295.558 square miles. Located at 45.81° N. Lat; 85.61° W. Long. Elevation is 604 feet.

History: St. James, on Beaver Island, was first inhabited by ancient mound builders. The island was called Isle du Castor by French adventurers in the 1600's and 1700's. A Mormon colony was established here in 1848, led by James Jesse Strang, known as King Strang. The colonists were forced to leave after Strang's death in 1856. Irish fishermen later rebuilt the town of St. James and reclaimed the farm lands, encouraging other Irish immigrants to settle here.

Population: 365; Growth (since 2000): 18.9%; Density: 17.9 persons per square mile; Race: 95.9% White, 0.0% Black/African American, 0.0% Asian, 2.5% American Indian/Alaska Native, 0.0% Native Hawaiian/Other Pacific Islander, 1.4% Two or more races, 1.4% Hispanic of any race; Average household size: 2.05; Median age: 51.5; Age under 18: 17.8%; Age 65 and over: 24.4%; Males per 100 females: 99.5

Housing: Homeownership rate: 80.9%; Homeowner vacancy rate: 3.4%; Rental vacancy rate: 36.8%

SOUTH ARM (township). Covers a land area of 30.639 square miles and a water area of 2.041 square miles. Located at 45.16° N. Lat; 85.17° W. Long.

History: South Arm was named for its location on the south arm of Pine Lake (later called Lake Charlevoix). A general store was opened here in the early 1870's.

Population: 1,873; Growth (since 2000): 1.6%; Density: 61.1 persons per square mile; Race: 95.9% White, 0.2% Black/African American, 0.2% Asian, 1.3% American Indian/Alaska Native, 0.0% Native Hawaiian/Other Pacific Islander, 1.8% Two or more races, 2.6% Hispanic of any race; Average household size: 2.49; Median age: 47.2; Age under 18: 21.5%; Age 65 and over: 22.4%; Males per 100 females: 92.7

Housing: Homeownership rate: 88.6%; Homeowner vacancy rate: 3.2%; Rental vacancy rate: 6.9%

WALLOON LAKE (CDP). Covers a land area of 1.355 square miles and a water area of 0 square miles. Located at 45.27° N. Lat; 84.94° W. Long. Elevation is 712 feet.

Population: 290; Growth (since 2000): n/a; Density: 214.1 persons per square mile; Race: 96.2% White, 0.0% Black/African American, 1.7% Asian, 0.0% American Indian/Alaska Native, 0.3% Native Hawaiian/Other Pacific Islander, 1.7% Two or more races, 1.4% Hispanic of any race; Average household size: 2.18; Median age: 51.8; Age under 18: 17.6%; Age 65 and over: 21.0%; Males per 100 females: 105.7

Housing: Homeownership rate: 82.3%; Homeowner vacancy rate: 4.5%; Rental vacancy rate: 39.5%

WILSON (township). Covers a land area of 34.053 square miles and a water area of 0.370 square miles. Located at 45.17° N. Lat; 85.03° W. Long.

Population: 1,964; Growth (since 2000): -2.9%; Density: 57.7 persons per square mile; Race: 96.2% White, 0.2% Black/African American, 0.9% Asian, 1.5% American Indian/Alaska Native, 0.0% Native Hawaiian/Other Pacific Islander, 1.0% Two or more races, 1.0% Hispanic of any race; Average household size: 2.67; Median age: 42.3; Age under 18: 25.5%; Age 65 and over: 12.5%; Males per 100 females: 111.2

Housing: Homeownership rate: 91.2%; Homeowner vacancy rate: 1.5%; Rental vacancy rate: 4.3%

Cheboygan County

Located in northern Michigan; bounded on the north by the Straits of Mackinac; drained by the Cheboygan, Black, and Sturgeon Rivers. Covers a land area of 715.264 square miles, a water area of 170.119 square miles, and is located in the Eastern Time Zone at 45.48° N. Lat., 84.50° W. Long. The county was founded in 1840. County seat is Cheboygan.

Weather Station: Cheboygan											Elevation: 589 feet	
	Jan	Feb	Mar	Apr	May	Jun	Jul	Aug	Sep	Oct	Nov	Dec
High	27	29	37	50	62	72	77	76	69	56	43	32
Low	10	10	17	31	41	51	58	57	49	38	29	18
Precip	1.7	1.3	1.8	2.6	2.8	2.6	3.1	3.4	3.4	3.5	2.5	2.0
Snow	25.4	19.3	12.1	4.0	0.1	0.0	0.0	0.0	0.0	0.6	7.0	24.3

High and Low temperatures in degrees Fahrenheit; Precipitation and Snow in inches

Population: 26,152; Growth (since 2000): -1.1%; Density: 36.6 persons per square mile; Race: 93.5% White, 0.5% Black/African American, 0.3% Asian, 3.0% American Indian/Alaska Native, 0.0% Native Hawaiian/Other Pacific Islander, 2.6% two or more races, 0.8% Hispanic of any race; Average household size: 2.31; Median age: 47.1; Age under 18: 20.4%; Age 65 and over: 21.5%; Males per 100 females: 99.1; Marriage status: 20.8% never married, 59.1% now married, 1.5% separated, 7.8% widowed, 12.3% divorced; Foreign born: 1.0%; Speak English only: 97.9%; With disability: 19.6%; Veterans: 13.0%; Ancestry: 24.4% German, 12.6% Irish, 12.4% English, 11.2% French, 10.8% Polish

Religion: Six largest groups: 14.2% Catholicism, 4.2% Methodist/Pietist, 3.8% Lutheran, 2.1% Pentecostal, 2.0% Non-denominational Protestant, 1.3% Latter-day Saints

Economy: Unemployment rate: 5.1%; Leading industries: 19.2% retail trade; 15.5% accommodation and food services; 14.8% construction; Farms: 313 totaling 45,567 acres; Company size: 0 employ 1,000 or more persons, 0 employ 500 to 999 persons, 4 employ 100 to 499 persons, 755 employ less than 100 persons; Business ownership: 849 women-owned, n/a Black-owned, n/a Hispanic-owned, n/a Asian-owned

Employment: 10.4% management, business, and financial, 1.5% computer, engineering, and science, 6.8% education, legal, community service, arts, and media, 6.0% healthcare practitioners, 22.2% service, 25.6% sales and office, 14.4% natural resources, construction, and maintenance, 13.1% production, transportation, and material moving

Income: Per capita: $23,412; Median household: $38,410; Average household: $52,189; Households with income of $100,000 or more: 9.7%; Poverty rate: 17.8%

Educational Attainment: High school diploma or higher: 87.8%; Bachelor's degree or higher: 16.3%; Graduate/professional degree or higher: 6.3%

Housing: Homeownership rate: 81.6%; Median home value: $112,500; Median year structure built: 1975; Homeowner vacancy rate: 4.5%; Median gross rent: $601 per month; Rental vacancy rate: 15.8%

Vital Statistics: Birth rate: 81.6 per 10,000 population; Death rate: 129.1 per 10,000 population; Age-adjusted cancer mortality rate: 227.3 deaths per 100,000 population

Health Insurance: 84.7% have insurance; 59.2% have private insurance; 46.3% have public insurance; 15.3% do not have insurance; 4.3% of children under 18 do not have insurance

Health Care: Physicians: 12.4 per 10,000 population; Hospital beds: 0.0 per 10,000 population; Hospital admissions: 0.0 per 10,000 population

Transportation: Commute: 90.4% car, 0.6% public transportation, 2.0% walk, 5.7% work from home; Median travel time to work: 26.4 minutes

Presidential Election: 43.9% Obama, 54.8% Romney (2012)

National and State Parks: Aloha State Park; Black Lake State Forest; Burt Lake State Park; Cheboygan State Park; Historic Mill Creek State Park; Michilimackinac State Park

Additional Information Contacts
Cheboygan Government . . . . (231) 627-8855
  http://www.cheboygancounty.net

Cheboygan County Communities

AFTON (unincorporated postal area)
ZCTA: 49705

Covers a land area of 75.873 square miles and a water area of 0.422 square miles. Located at 45.36° N. Lat; 84.46° W. Long. Elevation is 787 feet.

Population: 937; Growth (since 2000): 1.7%; Density: 12.3 persons per square mile; Race: 94.3% White, 0.1% Black/African American, 0.9% Asian, 1.9% American Indian/Alaska Native, 0.0% Native Hawaiian/Other Pacific Islander, 2.8% Two or more races, 0.4% Hispanic of any race; Average household size: 2.80; Median age: 38.5; Age under 18: 26.7%; Age 65 and over: 12.4%; Males per 100 females: 104.1

Housing: Homeownership rate: 85.5%; Homeowner vacancy rate: 3.1%; Rental vacancy rate: 19.7%

ALOHA (township). Covers a land area of 29.500 square miles and a water area of 2.884 square miles. Located at 45.49° N. Lat; 84.43° W. Long. Elevation is 604 feet.

Population: 949; Growth (since 2000): -8.8%; Density: 32.2 persons per square mile; Race: 92.0% White, 0.5% Black/African American, 1.3% Asian, 3.3% American Indian/Alaska Native, 0.0% Native Hawaiian/Other Pacific Islander, 3.0% Two or more races, 0.4% Hispanic of any race;

Average household size: 2.30; Median age: 51.3; Age under 18: 18.8%; Age 65 and over: 24.4%; Males per 100 females: 105.0

Housing: Homeownership rate: 89.1%; Homeowner vacancy rate: 4.4%; Rental vacancy rate: 10.0%

BEAUGRAND (township). Covers a land area of 23.829 square miles and a water area of 0.076 square miles. Located at 45.67° N. Lat; 84.56° W. Long.

History: Beaugrand Township was named for an early settler, Oliver Beaugrand. Settlement began here about 1852.

Population: 1,168; Growth (since 2000): 1.0%; Density: 49.0 persons per square mile; Race: 92.6% White, 0.1% Black/African American, 0.3% Asian, 3.0% American Indian/Alaska Native, 0.0% Native Hawaiian/Other Pacific Islander, 3.7% Two or more races, 0.7% Hispanic of any race; Average household size: 2.30; Median age: 50.5; Age under 18: 19.1%; Age 65 and over: 25.1%; Males per 100 females: 92.4

Housing: Homeownership rate: 86.8%; Homeowner vacancy rate: 3.1%; Rental vacancy rate: 2.9%

BENTON (township). Covers a land area of 58.661 square miles and a water area of 3.726 square miles. Located at 45.61° N. Lat; 84.37° W. Long.

Population: 3,206; Growth (since 2000): 4.1%; Density: 54.7 persons per square mile; Race: 92.7% White, 0.2% Black/African American, 0.4% Asian, 3.7% American Indian/Alaska Native, 0.0% Native Hawaiian/Other Pacific Islander, 3.0% Two or more races, 0.9% Hispanic of any race; Average household size: 2.37; Median age: 48.1; Age under 18: 19.9%; Age 65 and over: 20.4%; Males per 100 females: 98.4; Marriage status: 18.6% never married, 63.9% now married, 0.5% separated, 8.6% widowed, 8.9% divorced; Foreign born: 0.4%; Speak English only: 96.7%; With disability: 18.0%; Veterans: 17.7%; Ancestry: 22.0% German, 13.3% French, 11.6% Polish, 9.7% Swedish, 9.4% English

Employment: 13.1% management, business, and financial, 0.6% computer, engineering, and science, 8.7% education, legal, community service, arts, and media, 6.2% healthcare practitioners, 20.4% service, 29.2% sales and office, 17.3% natural resources, construction, and maintenance, 4.5% production, transportation, and material moving

Income: Per capita: $27,860; Median household: $40,357; Average household: $60,034; Households with income of $100,000 or more: 14.1%; Poverty rate: 11.5%

Educational Attainment: High school diploma or higher: 90.8%; Bachelor's degree or higher: 15.8%; Graduate/professional degree or higher: 6.9%

Housing: Homeownership rate: 89.9%; Median home value: $122,000; Median year structure built: 1981; Homeowner vacancy rate: 4.5%; Median gross rent: $613 per month; Rental vacancy rate: 12.3%

Health Insurance: 82.6% have insurance; 63.1% have private insurance; 42.2% have public insurance; 17.4% do not have insurance; 5.9% of children under 18 do not have insurance

Transportation: Commute: 96.5% car, 0.0% public transportation, 0.0% walk, 3.5% work from home; Median travel time to work: 28.9 minutes

BURT (township). Covers a land area of 19.732 square miles and a water area of 15.352 square miles. Located at 45.52° N. Lat; 84.65° W. Long. Elevation is 617 feet.

Population: 680; Growth (since 2000): 4.0%; Density: 34.5 persons per square mile; Race: 94.6% White, 0.1% Black/African American, 0.0% Asian, 3.4% American Indian/Alaska Native, 0.0% Native Hawaiian/Other Pacific Islander, 1.9% Two or more races, 1.2% Hispanic of any race; Average household size: 2.13; Median age: 58.2; Age under 18: 14.9%; Age 65 and over: 33.8%; Males per 100 females: 97.7

Housing: Homeownership rate: 94.7%; Homeowner vacancy rate: 1.9%; Rental vacancy rate: 9.1%

BURT LAKE (unincorporated postal area)
ZCTA: 49717

Covers a land area of 0.915 square miles and a water area of 0 square miles. Located at 45.43° N. Lat; 84.69° W. Long. Elevation is 705 feet.

Population: 72; Growth (since 2000): n/a; Density: 78.7 persons per square mile; Race: 98.6% White, 0.0% Black/African American, 0.0% Asian, 1.4% American Indian/Alaska Native, 0.0% Native Hawaiian/Other Pacific Islander, 0.0% Two or more races, 0.0% Hispanic of any race; Average household size: 1.80; Median age: 63.3; Age under 18: 11.1%; Age 65 and over: 47.2%; Males per 100 females: 94.6

Housing: Homeownership rate: 90.0%; Homeowner vacancy rate: 5.3%; Rental vacancy rate: 71.4%

CHEBOYGAN (city). County seat. Covers a land area of 6.797 square miles and a water area of 0.195 square miles. Located at 45.64° N. Lat; 84.47° W. Long. Elevation is 587 feet.

History: Cheboygan was established in 1844 on the Cheboygan River where it empties into Lake Huron. It developed as an important lumbering center in the late 1800's. When the timber was depleted, the land was used for fruit orchards.

Population: 4,867; Growth (since 2000): -8.1%; Density: 716.1 persons per square mile; Race: 90.8% White, 1.0% Black/African American, 0.2% Asian, 4.6% American Indian/Alaska Native, 0.0% Native Hawaiian/Other Pacific Islander, 3.2% Two or more races, 1.2% Hispanic of any race; Average household size: 2.23; Median age: 40.8; Age under 18: 22.1%; Age 65 and over: 19.0%; Males per 100 females: 91.9; Marriage status: 24.5% never married, 46.3% now married, 3.6% separated, 8.3% widowed, 20.9% divorced; Foreign born: 1.1%; Speak English only: 98.3%; With disability: 23.0%; Veterans: 9.4%; Ancestry: 18.2% German, 13.1% French, 11.1% English, 10.4% Irish, 8.6% Polish

Employment: 9.1% management, business, and financial, 1.4% computer, engineering, and science, 5.2% education, legal, community service, arts, and media, 4.3% healthcare practitioners, 24.7% service, 26.1% sales and office, 14.6% natural resources, construction, and maintenance, 14.5% production, transportation, and material moving

Income: Per capita: $15,080; Median household: $23,181; Average household: $32,771; Households with income of $100,000 or more: 4.0%; Poverty rate: 36.5%

Educational Attainment: High school diploma or higher: 79.7%; Bachelor's degree or higher: 10.4%; Graduate/professional degree or higher: 3.0%

School District(s)
Cheboygan Area Schools (PK-12)
    2012-13 Enrollment: 1,883 . . . . (231) 627-4436

Housing: Homeownership rate: 58.9%; Median home value: $75,600; Median year structure built: 1960; Homeowner vacancy rate: 4.5%; Median gross rent: $495 per month; Rental vacancy rate: 11.5%

Health Insurance: 84.0% have insurance; 41.6% have private insurance; 54.9% have public insurance; 16.0% do not have insurance; 1.9% of children under 18 do not have insurance

Safety: Violent crime rate: 41.8 per 10,000 population; Property crime rate: 400.9 per 10,000 population

Newspapers: Cheboygan Daily Tribune (daily circulation 4900); Mackinaw Journal (weekly circulation 1100)

Transportation: Commute: 87.3% car, 1.5% public transportation, 5.2% walk, 4.2% work from home; Median travel time to work: 22.0 minutes

Airports: Cheboygan County (general aviation)

ELLIS (township). Covers a land area of 35.575 square miles and a water area of 0.060 square miles. Located at 45.34° N. Lat; 84.55° W. Long.

Population: 596; Growth (since 2000): 14.8%; Density: 16.8 persons per square mile; Race: 96.0% White, 0.0% Black/African American, 0.2% Asian, 1.8% American Indian/Alaska Native, 0.0% Native Hawaiian/Other Pacific Islander, 2.0% Two or more races, 0.5% Hispanic of any race; Average household size: 2.51; Median age: 43.0; Age under 18: 23.0%; Age 65 and over: 18.0%; Males per 100 females: 103.4

Housing: Homeownership rate: 89.9%; Homeowner vacancy rate: 2.3%; Rental vacancy rate: 7.7%

FOREST (township). Covers a land area of 68.587 square miles and a water area of 0.933 square miles. Located at 45.29° N. Lat; 84.32° W. Long.

Population: 1,045; Growth (since 2000): -3.2%; Density: 15.2 persons per square mile; Race: 97.5% White, 0.1% Black/African American, 0.0% Asian, 0.6% American Indian/Alaska Native, 0.0% Native Hawaiian/Other Pacific Islander, 1.8% Two or more races, 1.1% Hispanic of any race; Average household size: 2.32; Median age: 48.7; Age under 18: 19.4%; Age 65 and over: 22.5%; Males per 100 females: 103.3

Housing: Homeownership rate: 87.8%; Homeowner vacancy rate: 2.5%; Rental vacancy rate: 14.9%

GRANT (township). Covers a land area of 48.802 square miles and a water area of 9.124 square miles. Located at 45.52° N. Lat; 84.30° W. Long.

Population: 846; Growth (since 2000): -10.7%; Density: 17.3 persons per square mile; Race: 95.9% White, 0.1% Black/African American, 0.0% Asian, 2.5% American Indian/Alaska Native, 0.0% Native Hawaiian/Other Pacific Islander, 1.2% Two or more races, 0.9% Hispanic of any race; Average household size: 2.10; Median age: 57.0; Age under 18: 13.4%; Age 65 and over: 33.9%; Males per 100 females: 108.9

Housing: Homeownership rate: 89.3%; Homeowner vacancy rate: 7.0%; Rental vacancy rate: 21.1%

HEBRON (township). Covers a land area of 34.053 square miles and a water area of 0.752 square miles. Located at 45.67° N. Lat; 84.66° W. Long.

Population: 269; Growth (since 2000): -11.2%; Density: 7.9 persons per square mile; Race: 94.4% White, 0.0% Black/African American, 0.0% Asian, 4.5% American Indian/Alaska Native, 0.0% Native Hawaiian/Other Pacific Islander, 1.1% Two or more races, 0.4% Hispanic of any race; Average household size: 2.40; Median age: 45.8; Age under 18: 19.0%; Age 65 and over: 16.4%; Males per 100 females: 120.5

Housing: Homeownership rate: 85.7%; Homeowner vacancy rate: 5.8%; Rental vacancy rate: 20.0%

INDIAN RIVER (CDP). Covers a land area of 12.870 square miles and a water area of 7.359 square miles. Located at 45.43° N. Lat; 84.62° W. Long. Elevation is 614 feet.

History: The village of Indian River was founded in 1878 by Floyd E. Martin, who named it for the river here. Indian River grew as a popular summer recreation center.

Population: 1,959; Growth (since 2000): -2.4%; Density: 152.2 persons per square mile; Race: 96.0% White, 0.1% Black/African American, 0.3% Asian, 1.9% American Indian/Alaska Native, 0.1% Native Hawaiian/Other Pacific Islander, 1.3% Two or more races, 0.9% Hispanic of any race; Average household size: 2.15; Median age: 51.6; Age under 18: 18.0%; Age 65 and over: 26.0%; Males per 100 females: 92.2

School District(s)
Cheb-Otsego-Presque Isle ESD (PK-PK)
    2012-13 Enrollment: 146 . . . . (231) 238-9394
Inland Lakes Schools (KG-12)
    2012-13 Enrollment: 799 . . . . (231) 238-6868

Housing: Homeownership rate: 78.9%; Homeowner vacancy rate: 5.1%; Rental vacancy rate: 15.1%

Newspapers: Community Voice (weekly circulation 1700); Straitsland Resorter (weekly circulation 2200)

INVERNESS (township). Covers a land area of 33.856 square miles and a water area of 3.344 square miles. Located at 45.59° N. Lat; 84.55° W. Long.

Population: 2,261; Growth (since 2000): -0.7%; Density: 66.8 persons per square mile; Race: 92.9% White, 0.1% Black/African American, 0.4% Asian, 3.7% American Indian/Alaska Native, 0.0% Native Hawaiian/Other Pacific Islander, 2.8% Two or more races, 0.5% Hispanic of any race; Average household size: 2.45; Median age: 45.3; Age under 18: 23.0%; Age 65 and over: 17.9%; Males per 100 females: 99.6

Housing: Homeownership rate: 86.9%; Homeowner vacancy rate: 5.3%; Rental vacancy rate: 9.7%

KOEHLER (township). Covers a land area of 43.556 square miles and a water area of 2.442 square miles. Located at 45.42° N. Lat; 84.52° W. Long.

Population: 1,283; Growth (since 2000): 9.8%; Density: 29.5 persons per square mile; Race: 96.3% White, 0.4% Black/African American, 0.3% Asian, 1.4% American Indian/Alaska Native, 0.2% Native Hawaiian/Other Pacific Islander, 1.4% Two or more races, 0.9% Hispanic of any race; Average household size: 2.56; Median age: 41.0; Age under 18: 25.6%; Age 65 and over: 16.3%; Males per 100 females: 109.0

Housing: Homeownership rate: 85.7%; Homeowner vacancy rate: 4.9%; Rental vacancy rate: 29.1%

MACKINAW (township). Covers a land area of 11.411 square miles and a water area of 1.037 square miles. Located at 45.74° N. Lat; 84.70° W. Long.

Population: 539; Growth (since 2000): -6.4%; Density: 47.2 persons per square mile; Race: 85.3% White, 8.0% Black/African American, 0.2%

Asian, 2.8% American Indian/Alaska Native, 0.0% Native Hawaiian/Other Pacific Islander, 3.5% Two or more races, 0.7% Hispanic of any race; Average household size: 1.95; Median age: 52.8; Age under 18: 14.1%; Age 65 and over: 27.3%; Males per 100 females: 81.5
Housing: Homeownership rate: 69.6%; Homeowner vacancy rate: 4.3%; Rental vacancy rate: 43.8%

MENTOR (township).
Covers a land area of 35.698 square miles and a water area of 0.159 square miles. Located at 45.33° N. Lat; 84.67° W. Long.
Population: 818; Growth (since 2000): 4.7%; Density: 22.9 persons per square mile; Race: 95.1% White, 0.2% Black/African American, 0.4% Asian, 1.8% American Indian/Alaska Native, 0.1% Native Hawaiian/Other Pacific Islander, 2.1% Two or more races, 0.5% Hispanic of any race; Average household size: 2.33; Median age: 46.9; Age under 18: 20.5%; Age 65 and over: 21.4%; Males per 100 females: 107.1
Housing: Homeownership rate: 84.9%; Homeowner vacancy rate: 2.3%; Rental vacancy rate: 13.1%

MULLETT (township).
Covers a land area of 18.995 square miles and a water area of 16.703 square miles. Located at 45.51° N. Lat; 84.56° W. Long. Elevation is 600 feet.
Population: 1,312; Growth (since 2000): 2.2%; Density: 69.1 persons per square mile; Race: 92.2% White, 0.5% Black/African American, 0.0% Asian, 4.8% American Indian/Alaska Native, 0.0% Native Hawaiian/Other Pacific Islander, 2.5% Two or more races, 0.7% Hispanic of any race; Average household size: 2.23; Median age: 52.1; Age under 18: 17.7%; Age 65 and over: 27.4%; Males per 100 females: 100.6
Housing: Homeownership rate: 89.5%; Homeowner vacancy rate: 8.2%; Rental vacancy rate: 30.0%

MUNRO (township).
Covers a land area of 28.400 square miles and a water area of 6.771 square miles. Located at 45.60° N. Lat; 84.66° W. Long.
Population: 571; Growth (since 2000): -15.9%; Density: 20.1 persons per square mile; Race: 96.1% White, 0.7% Black/African American, 0.0% Asian, 1.1% American Indian/Alaska Native, 0.0% Native Hawaiian/Other Pacific Islander, 2.1% Two or more races, 0.2% Hispanic of any race; Average household size: 2.15; Median age: 53.8; Age under 18: 13.7%; Age 65 and over: 29.6%; Males per 100 females: 99.0
Housing: Homeownership rate: 90.2%; Homeowner vacancy rate: 3.6%; Rental vacancy rate: 10.3%
Additional Information Contacts
Munro Township . . . . (231) 627-2603
  http://www.munrotownship.com

NUNDA (township).
Covers a land area of 70.263 square miles and a water area of 1.213 square miles. Located at 45.22° N. Lat; 84.49° W. Long.
Population: 1,042; Growth (since 2000): 12.6%; Density: 14.8 persons per square mile; Race: 92.9% White, 0.0% Black/African American, 0.4% Asian, 2.0% American Indian/Alaska Native, 0.0% Native Hawaiian/Other Pacific Islander, 4.2% Two or more races, 1.2% Hispanic of any race; Average household size: 2.47; Median age: 44.4; Age under 18: 21.3%; Age 65 and over: 15.5%; Males per 100 females: 109.7
Housing: Homeownership rate: 88.4%; Homeowner vacancy rate: 5.7%; Rental vacancy rate: 20.6%

TOPINABEE (unincorporated postal area)
ZCTA: 49791
  Covers a land area of 1.075 square miles and a water area of 0 square miles. Located at 45.49° N. Lat; 84.60° W. Long. Elevation is 640 feet.
  Population: 329; Growth (since 2000): 383.8%; Density: 306.1 persons per square mile; Race: 95.4% White, 0.0% Black/African American, 0.0% Asian, 4.0% American Indian/Alaska Native, 0.0% Native Hawaiian/Other Pacific Islander, 0.6% Two or more races, 0.3% Hispanic of any race; Average household size: 2.24; Median age: 51.8; Age under 18: 17.3%; Age 65 and over: 25.5%; Males per 100 females: 82.8
  Housing: Homeownership rate: 87.0%; Homeowner vacancy rate: 11.7%; Rental vacancy rate: 38.7%

TUSCARORA (township).
Covers a land area of 29.412 square miles and a water area of 12.539 square miles. Located at 45.43° N. Lat; 84.64° W. Long.
Population: 3,038; Growth (since 2000): -1.7%; Density: 103.3 persons per square mile; Race: 96.2% White, 0.1% Black/African American, 0.3% Asian, 1.7% American Indian/Alaska Native, 0.0% Native Hawaiian/Other Pacific Islander, 1.4% Two or more races, 0.7% Hispanic of any race; Average household size: 2.23; Median age: 49.5; Age under 18: 19.7%; Age 65 and over: 23.0%; Males per 100 females: 93.5; Marriage status: 24.2% never married, 57.8% now married, 1.8% separated, 8.0% widowed, 10.0% divorced; Foreign born: 1.0%; Speak English only: 97.1%; With disability: 17.7%; Veterans: 11.8%; Ancestry: 26.3% German, 13.2% Irish, 13.0% English, 9.6% European, 9.0% Polish
Employment: 10.3% management, business, and financial, 0.9% computer, engineering, and science, 4.8% education, legal, community service, arts, and media, 5.8% healthcare practitioners, 31.5% service, 24.2% sales and office, 12.8% natural resources, construction, and maintenance, 9.7% production, transportation, and material moving
Income: Per capita: $26,232; Median household: $41,990; Average household: $58,498; Households with income of $100,000 or more: 14.3%; Poverty rate: 13.2%
Educational Attainment: High school diploma or higher: 87.9%; Bachelor's degree or higher: 23.5%; Graduate/professional degree or higher: 5.8%
Housing: Homeownership rate: 80.8%; Median home value: $144,700; Median year structure built: 1972; Homeowner vacancy rate: 4.3%; Median gross rent: $613 per month; Rental vacancy rate: 17.4%
Health Insurance: 85.0% have insurance; 65.3% have private insurance; 44.0% have public insurance; 15.0% do not have insurance; 9.1% of children under 18 do not have insurance
Safety: Violent crime rate: 16.7 per 10,000 population; Property crime rate: 283.7 per 10,000 population
Transportation: Commute: 91.0% car, 0.0% public transportation, 1.0% walk, 6.9% work from home; Median travel time to work: 26.4 minutes
Additional Information Contacts
Tuscarora Township . . . . (231) 238-0970
  http://www.tuscaroratwp.com

WALKER (township).
Covers a land area of 34.191 square miles and a water area of 0.356 square miles. Located at 45.33° N. Lat; 84.41° W. Long.
Population: 327; Growth (since 2000): 12.0%; Density: 9.6 persons per square mile; Race: 93.3% White, 0.0% Black/African American, 1.2% Asian, 1.2% American Indian/Alaska Native, 0.0% Native Hawaiian/Other Pacific Islander, 4.3% Two or more races, 0.0% Hispanic of any race; Average household size: 2.76; Median age: 37.2; Age under 18: 26.0%; Age 65 and over: 14.7%; Males per 100 females: 109.6
Housing: Homeownership rate: 82.8%; Homeowner vacancy rate: 1.1%; Rental vacancy rate: 9.5%

WAVERLY (township).
Covers a land area of 48.186 square miles and a water area of 4.888 square miles. Located at 45.42° N. Lat; 84.34° W. Long.
Population: 457; Growth (since 2000): -3.2%; Density: 9.5 persons per square mile; Race: 97.4% White, 1.1% Black/African American, 0.2% Asian, 0.4% American Indian/Alaska Native, 0.4% Native Hawaiian/Other Pacific Islander, 0.4% Two or more races, 0.2% Hispanic of any race; Average household size: 2.34; Median age: 49.2; Age under 18: 19.3%; Age 65 and over: 21.9%; Males per 100 females: 105.9
Housing: Homeownership rate: 90.8%; Homeowner vacancy rate: 1.1%; Rental vacancy rate: 14.3%

WILMOT (township).
Covers a land area of 35.761 square miles and a water area of 0.245 square miles. Located at 45.25° N. Lat; 84.66° W. Long.
Population: 878; Growth (since 2000): 6.3%; Density: 24.6 persons per square mile; Race: 95.8% White, 0.1% Black/African American, 0.0% Asian, 1.9% American Indian/Alaska Native, 0.0% Native Hawaiian/Other Pacific Islander, 2.2% Two or more races, 0.5% Hispanic of any race; Average household size: 2.68; Median age: 40.3; Age under 18: 25.9%; Age 65 and over: 15.8%; Males per 100 females: 113.1
Housing: Homeownership rate: 84.5%; Homeowner vacancy rate: 4.1%; Rental vacancy rate: 5.6%

WOLVERINE (village). Covers a land area of 0.983 square miles and a water area of 0.007 square miles. Located at 45.27° N. Lat; 84.61° W. Long. Elevation is 817 feet.

History: Wolverine was settled as a sawmill center, and later grew as a resort area.

Population: 244; Growth (since 2000): -32.0%; Density: 248.3 persons per square mile; Race: 94.3% White, 0.0% Black/African American, 0.8% Asian, 0.0% American Indian/Alaska Native, 0.0% Native Hawaiian/Other Pacific Islander, 4.9% Two or more races, 1.2% Hispanic of any race; Average household size: 2.60; Median age: 40.3; Age under 18: 27.0%; Age 65 and over: 15.6%; Males per 100 females: 86.3

School District(s)

Wolverine Community SD (PK-12)
2012-13 Enrollment: 331. . . . . (231) 525-8201

Housing: Homeownership rate: 78.8%; Homeowner vacancy rate: 5.1%; Rental vacancy rate: 31.0%

Chippewa County

Located in northwestern Michigan on the Upper Peninsula; bounded on the east by Saint Marys River, on the north by Whitefish Bay, and on the south by Lake Huron; includes Sugar, Neebish, and Drummond Islands, and part of Marquette National Forest. Covers a land area of 1,558.420 square miles, a water area of 1,139.970 square miles, and is located in the Eastern Time Zone at 46.32° N. Lat., 84.52° W. Long. The county was founded in 1826. County seat is Sault Ste. Marie.

Chippewa County is part of the Sault Sainte Marie, MI Micropolitan Statistical Area. The entire metro area includes: Chippewa County, MI

Weather Station: Detour Village   Elevation: 595 feet

	Jan	Feb	Mar	Apr	May	Jun	Jul	Aug	Sep	Oct	Nov	Dec
High	25	27	34	47	60	70	76	75	66	53	41	31
Low	9	9	17	31	42	51	58	58	51	40	30	18
Precip	2.0	1.3	1.9	2.3	2.5	2.8	3.1	3.0	3.4	3.3	2.5	2.2
Snow	19.0	13.5	11.8	3.9	tr	0.0	0.0	0.0	0.0	0.3	5.3	17.8

High and Low temperatures in degrees Fahrenheit; Precipitation and Snow in inches

Weather Station: Rudyard 4 N   Elevation: 753 feet

	Jan	Feb	Mar	Apr	May	Jun	Jul	Aug	Sep	Oct	Nov	Dec
High	25	28	38	52	65	74	78	76	67	54	41	30
Low	7	8	16	29	38	47	52	52	45	34	26	15
Precip	1.8	1.3	1.6	2.3	2.4	3.1	3.1	3.1	3.9	3.7	2.9	2.5
Snow	22.9	14.6	12.4	5.4	tr	0.0	0.0	0.0	0.0	1.0	10.7	25.4

High and Low temperatures in degrees Fahrenheit; Precipitation and Snow in inches

Weather Station: Sault Ste Marie Sanderson Field   Elevation: 717 feet

	Jan	Feb	Mar	Apr	May	Jun	Jul	Aug	Sep	Oct	Nov	Dec
High	23	25	34	49	62	71	76	74	66	53	40	28
Low	6	8	16	30	40	47	53	53	47	37	27	15
Precip	2.3	1.4	1.9	2.5	2.6	2.7	2.9	3.1	3.6	3.8	3.3	2.9
Snow	32.5	18.2	13.2	na	na	na	na	tr	tr	2.1	16.5	37.8

High and Low temperatures in degrees Fahrenheit; Precipitation and Snow in inches

Weather Station: Tahquamenon Falls Stpk   Elevation: 745 feet

	Jan	Feb	Mar	Apr	May	Jun	Jul	Aug	Sep	Oct	Nov	Dec
High	23	27	35	48	63	72	77	75	67	53	39	28
Low	7	6	12	26	37	45	50	49	43	33	25	14
Precip	na	na	na	2.3	2.6	2.8	3.1	3.4	4.0	4.2	2.9	na
Snow	48.3	31.3	18.9	8.3	0.2	0.0	0.0	0.0	tr	1.3	18.6	50.3

High and Low temperatures in degrees Fahrenheit; Precipitation and Snow in inches

Weather Station: Trout Lake   Elevation: 839 feet

	Jan	Feb	Mar	Apr	May	Jun	Jul	Aug	Sep	Oct	Nov	Dec
High	25	28	37	51	64	73	77	75	67	54	41	30
Low	6	6	14	27	38	48	52	52	45	35	26	14
Precip	na	na	na	2.5	2.8	2.7	3.0	3.3	3.8	3.9	2.8	na
Snow	na	na	na	3.7	0.1	0.0	0.0	0.0	tr	0.5	na	21.1

High and Low temperatures in degrees Fahrenheit; Precipitation and Snow in inches

Weather Station: Whitefish Point   Elevation: 604 feet

	Jan	Feb	Mar	Apr	May	Jun	Jul	Aug	Sep	Oct	Nov	Dec
High	25	27	34	46	58	67	72	73	66	53	40	30
Low	12	11	17	29	38	46	52	55	49	39	29	19
Precip	2.3	1.5	1.8	2.2	2.5	2.7	3.2	3.1	3.5	3.7	2.8	2.8
Snow	36.1	21.7	12.7	4.7	0.1	0.0	0.0	0.0	tr	1.1	11.6	34.7

High and Low temperatures in degrees Fahrenheit; Precipitation and Snow in inches

Population: 38,520; Growth (since 2000): -0.1%; Density: 24.7 persons per square mile; Race: 72.3% White, 6.5% Black/African American, 0.6% Asian, 15.8% American Indian/Alaska Native, 0.1% Native Hawaiian/Other Pacific Islander, 4.6% two or more races, 1.2% Hispanic of any race; Average household size: 2.34; Median age: 39.5; Age under 18: 20.1%; Age 65 and over: 14.6%; Males per 100 females: 122.7; Marriage status: 33.9% never married, 48.0% now married, 1.4% separated, 5.7% widowed, 12.5% divorced; Foreign born: 2.8%; Speak English only: 94.9%; With disability: 18.0%; Veterans: 12.1%; Ancestry: 18.2% German, 11.6% Irish, 11.5% English, 7.4% French, 6.6% Polish

Religion: Six largest groups: 17.3% Catholicism, 2.6% Lutheran, 2.6% Presbyterian-Reformed, 2.4% Holiness, 2.2% Methodist/Pietist, 2.0% Baptist

Economy: Unemployment rate: 7.2%; Leading industries: 18.3% retail trade; 13.8% accommodation and food services; 12.4% construction; Farms: 409 totaling 93,032 acres; Company size: 1 employs 1,000 or more persons, 1 employs 500 to 999 persons, 7 employ 100 to 499 persons, 789 employ less than 100 persons; Business ownership: 679 women-owned, n/a Black-owned, n/a Hispanic-owned, n/a Asian-owned

Employment: 10.1% management, business, and financial, 2.1% computer, engineering, and science, 11.3% education, legal, community service, arts, and media, 5.8% healthcare practitioners, 27.1% service, 25.6% sales and office, 8.6% natural resources, construction, and maintenance, 9.5% production, transportation, and material moving

Income: Per capita: $20,589; Median household: $41,637; Average household: $52,648; Households with income of $100,000 or more: 10.3%; Poverty rate: 17.7%

Educational Attainment: High school diploma or higher: 89.8%; Bachelor's degree or higher: 18.5%; Graduate/professional degree or higher: 6.8%

Housing: Homeownership rate: 70.8%; Median home value: $101,600; Median year structure built: 1973; Homeowner vacancy rate: 2.8%; Median gross rent: $601 per month; Rental vacancy rate: 9.3%

Vital Statistics: Birth rate: 95.1 per 10,000 population; Death rate: 89.7 per 10,000 population; Age-adjusted cancer mortality rate: 204.9 deaths per 100,000 population

Health Insurance: 85.9% have insurance; 65.5% have private insurance; 37.2% have public insurance; 14.1% do not have insurance; 7.6% of children under 18 do not have insurance

Health Care: Physicians: 13.7 per 10,000 population; Hospital beds: 35.9 per 10,000 population; Hospital admissions: 856.6 per 10,000 population

Air Quality Index: 92.8% good, 7.2% moderate, 0.0% unhealthy for sensitive individuals, 0.0% unhealthy (percent of days)

Transportation: Commute: 87.5% car, 1.4% public transportation, 5.7% walk, 4.3% work from home; Median travel time to work: 16.2 minutes

Presidential Election: 45.6% Obama, 53.2% Romney (2012)

National and State Parks: Brimley State Park; De Tour State Park; Munuscong State Forest; Tahquamenon Falls State Park

Additional Information Contacts

Chippewa Government . . . . (906) 635-6300
http://www.chippewacountymi.gov

Chippewa County Communities

BARBEAU (unincorporated postal area)
ZCTA: 49710

Covers a land area of 36.401 square miles and a water area of 16.086 square miles. Located at 46.27° N. Lat; 84.17° W. Long. Elevation is 656 feet.

Population: 409; Growth (since 2000): -6.2%; Density: 11.2 persons per square mile; Race: 88.3% White, 0.0% Black/African American, 0.2% Asian, 7.6% American Indian/Alaska Native, 0.0% Native Hawaiian/Other Pacific Islander, 3.9% Two or more races, 2.2% Hispanic of any race; Average household size: 2.08; Median age: 57.4; Age under 18: 13.7%; Age 65 and over: 32.0%; Males per 100 females: 114.1

Housing: Homeownership rate: 90.3%; Homeowner vacancy rate: 3.2%; Rental vacancy rate: 20.8%

BAY MILLS (township). Covers a land area of 64.720 square miles and a water area of 33.216 square miles. Located at 46.42° N. Lat; 84.75° W. Long. Elevation is 604 feet.

Population: 1,477; Growth (since 2000): 21.7%; Density: 22.8 persons per square mile; Race: 42.2% White, 0.2% Black/African American, 0.2% Asian, 50.4% American Indian/Alaska Native, 0.4% Native Hawaiian/Other

Pacific Islander, 6.6% Two or more races, 0.3% Hispanic of any race; Average household size: 2.55; Median age: 37.9; Age under 18: 27.6%; Age 65 and over: 15.2%; Males per 100 females: 93.6
Housing: Homeownership rate: 76.7%; Homeowner vacancy rate: 0.7%; Rental vacancy rate: 5.6%

BRIMLEY (unincorporated postal area)
ZCTA: 49715

Covers a land area of 183.790 square miles and a water area of 30.080 square miles. Located at 46.40° N. Lat; 84.71° W. Long. Elevation is 656 feet.
Population: 3,130; Growth (since 2000): 12.1%; Density: 17.0 persons per square mile; Race: 57.7% White, 0.3% Black/African American, 0.2% Asian, 35.5% American Indian/Alaska Native, 0.2% Native Hawaiian/Other Pacific Islander, 6.0% Two or more races, 0.5% Hispanic of any race; Average household size: 2.54; Median age: 40.4; Age under 18: 25.8%; Age 65 and over: 15.3%; Males per 100 females: 94.7; Marriage status: 25.7% never married, 55.1% now married, 0.5% separated, 6.5% widowed, 12.7% divorced; Foreign born: 2.4%; Speak English only: 93.8%; With disability: 15.6%; Veterans: 17.6%; Ancestry: 12.3% German, 11.9% English, 11.2% Irish, 9.0% French, 3.7% Polish
Employment: 12.1% management, business, and financial, 2.6% computer, engineering, and science, 12.5% education, legal, community service, arts, and media, 5.0% healthcare practitioners, 30.0% service, 19.8% sales and office, 9.5% natural resources, construction, and maintenance, 8.4% production, transportation, and material moving
Income: Per capita: $23,604; Median household: $51,821; Average household: $57,931; Households with income of $100,000 or more: 9.7%; Poverty rate: 9.2%
Educational Attainment: High school diploma or higher: 89.7%; Bachelor's degree or higher: 23.1%; Graduate/professional degree or higher: 8.8%

School District(s)
Brimley Area Schools (KG-12)
    2012-13 Enrollment: 494. . . . . (906) 248-3219
Ojibwe Charter School (KG-12)
    2012-13 Enrollment: 85. . . . . (906) 248-2530
Four-year College(s)
Bay Mills Community College (Public)
    Fall 2013 Enrollment: 531 . . . . (906) 248-3354
    2013-14 Tuition: In-state $3,040; Out-of-state $3,040
Two-year College(s)
Bay Mills Community College (Public)
    Fall 2013 Enrollment: 531 . . . . (906) 248-3354
    2013-14 Tuition: In-state $3,040; Out-of-state $3,040
Vocational/Technical School(s)
Bay Mills Community College (Public)
    Fall 2013 Enrollment: 531 . . . . (906) 248-3354
    2013-14 Tuition: In-state $3,040; Out-of-state $3,040
Housing: Homeownership rate: 83.6%; Median home value: $116,100; Median year structure built: 1987; Homeowner vacancy rate: 1.6%; Median gross rent: $605 per month; Rental vacancy rate: 10.5%
Health Insurance: 90.7% have insurance; 77.1% have private insurance; 34.5% have public insurance; 9.3% do not have insurance; 6.3% of children under 18 do not have insurance
Transportation: Commute: 91.7% car, 1.2% public transportation, 1.9% walk, 3.9% work from home; Median travel time to work: 17.4 minutes

BRUCE (township). Covers a land area of 86.984 square miles and a water area of 3.666 square miles. Located at 46.31° N. Lat; 84.32° W. Long.
History: Bruce Township was named for Lord Bruce of the Shetland Islands, a friend of early settler Andrew J. Smith.
Population: 2,128; Growth (since 2000): 9.7%; Density: 24.5 persons per square mile; Race: 82.5% White, 0.1% Black/African American, 0.5% Asian, 12.0% American Indian/Alaska Native, 0.0% Native Hawaiian/Other Pacific Islander, 4.8% Two or more races, 0.8% Hispanic of any race; Average household size: 2.49; Median age: 43.5; Age under 18: 23.1%; Age 65 and over: 16.8%; Males per 100 females: 108.8
Housing: Homeownership rate: 92.7%; Homeowner vacancy rate: 1.2%; Rental vacancy rate: 11.0%

CHIPPEWA (township). Covers a land area of 94.841 square miles and a water area of 0.604 square miles. Located at 46.35° N. Lat; 85.00° W. Long.
Population: 213; Growth (since 2000): -10.5%; Density: 2.2 persons per square mile; Race: 89.7% White, 0.5% Black/African American, 0.0% Asian, 8.0% American Indian/Alaska Native, 0.0% Native Hawaiian/Other Pacific Islander, 1.9% Two or more races, 0.0% Hispanic of any race; Average household size: 2.37; Median age: 47.4; Age under 18: 23.5%; Age 65 and over: 15.0%; Males per 100 females: 108.8
Housing: Homeownership rate: 86.7%; Homeowner vacancy rate: 2.4%; Rental vacancy rate: 26.3%

DAFTER (township). Covers a land area of 47.800 square miles and a water area of 0.127 square miles. Located at 46.36° N. Lat; 84.44° W. Long. Elevation is 689 feet.
Population: 1,263; Growth (since 2000): -3.1%; Density: 26.4 persons per square mile; Race: 82.1% White, 0.2% Black/African American, 0.0% Asian, 13.1% American Indian/Alaska Native, 0.0% Native Hawaiian/Other Pacific Islander, 4.6% Two or more races, 0.1% Hispanic of any race; Average household size: 2.52; Median age: 42.3; Age under 18: 22.9%; Age 65 and over: 14.6%; Males per 100 females: 102.4
Housing: Homeownership rate: 89.6%; Homeowner vacancy rate: 2.0%; Rental vacancy rate: 11.9%

DE TOUR VILLAGE (village). Covers a land area of 3.545 square miles and a water area of 4.833 square miles. Located at 45.98° N. Lat; 83.91° W. Long. Elevation is 600 feet.
Population: 325; Growth (since 2000): -22.8%; Density: 91.7 persons per square mile; Race: 82.8% White, 0.0% Black/African American, 0.0% Asian, 12.9% American Indian/Alaska Native, 0.0% Native Hawaiian/Other Pacific Islander, 4.3% Two or more races, 0.6% Hispanic of any race; Average household size: 1.96; Median age: 57.6; Age under 18: 15.4%; Age 65 and over: 38.2%; Males per 100 females: 98.2
School District(s)
Detour Area Schools (KG-12)
    2012-13 Enrollment: 145. . . . . (906) 297-2011
Detour Arts and Technology Academy (KG-12)
    2012-13 Enrollment: 62. . . . . (906) 297-2011
Housing: Homeownership rate: 86.8%; Homeowner vacancy rate: 5.2%; Rental vacancy rate: 8.0%

DETOUR (township). Covers a land area of 48.771 square miles and a water area of 26.672 square miles. Located at 46.00° N. Lat; 84.01° W. Long.
History: The township was first called Warren, for Ebenezer Warren, the postmaster. The name change to Detour reflects the French Canadian heritage of the early settlers, and the sharp turns that ships had to make to enter St. Mary's River.
Population: 807; Growth (since 2000): -9.7%; Density: 16.5 persons per square mile; Race: 86.4% White, 0.0% Black/African American, 0.1% Asian, 10.5% American Indian/Alaska Native, 0.0% Native Hawaiian/Other Pacific Islander, 3.0% Two or more races, 0.4% Hispanic of any race; Average household size: 2.01; Median age: 57.8; Age under 18: 14.3%; Age 65 and over: 35.4%; Males per 100 females: 102.3
Housing: Homeownership rate: 89.5%; Homeowner vacancy rate: 5.7%; Rental vacancy rate: 14.0%

DRUMMOND (township). Covers a land area of 128.908 square miles and a water area of 120.079 square miles. Located at 46.00° N. Lat; 83.62° W. Long. Elevation is 620 feet.
History: Drummond Island, township, and village were named for Sir Gordon Drummond, a British commander who built a fort here after the War of 1812. Stone quarries were opened in Drummond in the late 1870's to furnish stone for the first lock at Sault Ste. Marie.
Population: 1,058; Growth (since 2000): 6.7%; Density: 8.2 persons per square mile; Race: 90.8% White, 0.0% Black/African American, 0.1% Asian, 4.3% American Indian/Alaska Native, 0.3% Native Hawaiian/Other Pacific Islander, 4.3% Two or more races, 0.8% Hispanic of any race; Average household size: 1.94; Median age: 57.1; Age under 18: 12.9%; Age 65 and over: 32.6%; Males per 100 females: 105.0
Housing: Homeownership rate: 85.7%; Homeowner vacancy rate: 6.4%; Rental vacancy rate: 34.4%

DRUMMOND ISLAND (unincorporated postal area)
ZCTA: 49726

Covers a land area of 128.721 square miles and a water area of 109.665 square miles. Located at 46.00° N. Lat; 83.62° W. Long..
Population: 1,058; Growth (since 2000): 6.7%; Density: 8.2 persons per square mile; Race: 90.8% White, 0.0% Black/African American, 0.1% Asian, 4.3% American Indian/Alaska Native, 0.3% Native Hawaiian/Other Pacific Islander, 4.3% Two or more races, 0.8% Hispanic of any race; Average household size: 1.94; Median age: 57.1; Age under 18: 12.9%; Age 65 and over: 32.6%; Males per 100 females: 105.0

School District(s)
Detour Area Schools (KG-12)
2012-13 Enrollment: 145 . . . . (906) 297-2011
Housing: Homeownership rate: 85.7%; Homeowner vacancy rate: 6.4%; Rental vacancy rate: 34.4%
Airports: Drummond Island (general aviation)

ECKERMAN (unincorporated postal area)
ZCTA: 49728

Covers a land area of 179.108 square miles and a water area of 26.699 square miles. Located at 46.41° N. Lat; 85.03° W. Long. Elevation is 774 feet.
Population: 334; Growth (since 2000): 0.9%; Density: 1.9 persons per square mile; Race: 90.4% White, 0.3% Black/African American, 0.0% Asian, 7.2% American Indian/Alaska Native, 0.0% Native Hawaiian/Other Pacific Islander, 2.1% Two or more races, 0.3% Hispanic of any race; Average household size: 2.20; Median age: 50.9; Age under 18: 18.0%; Age 65 and over: 23.7%; Males per 100 females: 112.7
Housing: Homeownership rate: 89.4%; Homeowner vacancy rate: 2.1%; Rental vacancy rate: 25.0%

GOETZVILLE (unincorporated postal area)
ZCTA: 49736

Covers a land area of 80.969 square miles and a water area of 43.979 square miles. Located at 46.07° N. Lat; 84.08° W. Long. Elevation is 745 feet.
Population: 578; Growth (since 2000): -3.5%; Density: 7.1 persons per square mile; Race: 89.3% White, 0.0% Black/African American, 0.0% Asian, 7.6% American Indian/Alaska Native, 0.0% Native Hawaiian/Other Pacific Islander, 3.1% Two or more races, 0.5% Hispanic of any race; Average household size: 2.14; Median age: 55.2; Age under 18: 15.9%; Age 65 and over: 31.1%; Males per 100 females: 94.0
Housing: Homeownership rate: 91.4%; Homeowner vacancy rate: 4.6%; Rental vacancy rate: 8.0%

HULBERT (township). Covers a land area of 70.851 square miles and a water area of 0.973 square miles. Located at 46.33° N. Lat; 85.19° W. Long. Elevation is 751 feet.
Population: 168; Growth (since 2000): -20.4%; Density: 2.4 persons per square mile; Race: 90.5% White, 0.0% Black/African American, 0.0% Asian, 3.0% American Indian/Alaska Native, 0.0% Native Hawaiian/Other Pacific Islander, 6.0% Two or more races, 1.2% Hispanic of any race; Average household size: 1.95; Median age: 54.8; Age under 18: 10.7%; Age 65 and over: 25.0%; Males per 100 females: 107.4
Housing: Homeownership rate: 81.4%; Homeowner vacancy rate: 2.8%; Rental vacancy rate: 40.7%

KINCHELOE (unincorporated postal area)
ZCTA: 49788

Covers a land area of 7.750 square miles and a water area of 0.036 square miles. Located at 46.27° N. Lat; 84.47° W. Long..
Population: 6,609; Growth (since 2000): 30.2%; Density: 852.8 persons per square mile; Race: 48.9% White, 35.8% Black/African American, 0.5% Asian, 11.1% American Indian/Alaska Native, 0.0% Native Hawaiian/Other Pacific Islander, 3.5% Two or more races, 1.9% Hispanic of any race; Average household size: 3.01; Median age: 35.3; Age under 18: 13.6%; Age 65 and over: 3.4%; Males per 100 females: 425.4; Marriage status: 59.9% never married, 22.8% now married, 2.0% separated, 2.3% widowed, 15.0% divorced; Foreign born: 2.6%; Speak English only: 90.0%; With disability: 17.6%; Veterans: 7.9%; Ancestry: 13.0% German, 10.2% Irish, 4.8% Polish, 4.8% English, 3.7% African

Employment: 10.7% management, business, and financial, 4.2% computer, engineering, and science, 9.4% education, legal, community service, arts, and media, 5.2% healthcare practitioners, 29.0% service, 22.1% sales and office, 6.4% natural resources, construction, and maintenance, 13.0% production, transportation, and material moving
Income: Per capita: $9,042; Median household: $39,625; Average household: $43,835; Households with income of $100,000 or more: 4.2%; Poverty rate: 31.3%
Educational Attainment: High school diploma or higher: 88.0%; Bachelor's degree or higher: 6.6%; Graduate/professional degree or higher: 2.3%
Housing: Homeownership rate: 42.5%; Median home value: $75,000; Median year structure built: 1959; Homeowner vacancy rate: 5.2%; Median gross rent: $671 per month; Rental vacancy rate: 14.8%
Health Insurance: 84.1% have insurance; 42.1% have private insurance; 49.6% have public insurance; 15.9% do not have insurance; 6.3% of children under 18 do not have insurance
Transportation: Commute: 91.0% car, 3.8% public transportation, 0.7% walk, 3.3% work from home; Median travel time to work: 24.3 minutes

KINROSS (charter township). Covers a land area of 119.717 square miles and a water area of 1.214 square miles. Located at 46.30° N. Lat; 84.68° W. Long. Elevation is 755 feet.
History: Kinross Township was named for Kinross, Scotland, by Scoth-Irish settlers.
Population: 7,561; Growth (since 2000): 27.7%; Density: 63.2 persons per square mile; Race: 53.2% White, 31.4% Black/African American, 0.5% Asian, 11.2% American Indian/Alaska Native, 0.0% Native Hawaiian/Other Pacific Islander, 3.6% Two or more races, 1.8% Hispanic of any race; Average household size: 2.89; Median age: 35.9; Age under 18: 14.8%; Age 65 and over: 4.6%; Males per 100 females: 340.4; Marriage status: 54.2% never married, 29.4% now married, 1.7% separated, 2.1% widowed, 14.3% divorced; Foreign born: 2.2%; Speak English only: 90.4%; With disability: 19.6%; Veterans: 8.6%; Ancestry: 14.7% German, 10.1% Irish, 8.4% English, 4.3% Dutch, 4.2% Polish
Employment: 12.5% management, business, and financial, 3.4% computer, engineering, and science, 10.7% education, legal, community service, arts, and media, 5.1% healthcare practitioners, 27.5% service, 22.8% sales and office, 6.9% natural resources, construction, and maintenance, 11.1% production, transportation, and material moving
Income: Per capita: $10,515; Median household: $40,625; Average household: $46,451; Households with income of $100,000 or more: 6.8%; Poverty rate: 29.8%
Educational Attainment: High school diploma or higher: 88.5%; Bachelor's degree or higher: 9.7%; Graduate/professional degree or higher: 2.9%
Housing: Homeownership rate: 56.0%; Median home value: $78,500; Median year structure built: 1965; Homeowner vacancy rate: 3.9%; Median gross rent: $666 per month; Rental vacancy rate: 14.2%
Health Insurance: 83.8% have insurance; 45.1% have private insurance; 48.5% have public insurance; 16.2% do not have insurance; 4.9% of children under 18 do not have insurance
Safety: Violent crime rate: 3.8 per 10,000 population; Property crime rate: 34.5 per 10,000 population
Transportation: Commute: 92.3% car, 2.8% public transportation, 1.0% walk, 3.1% work from home; Median travel time to work: 24.3 minutes
Additional Information Contacts
Kinross Charter Township . . . . (906) 495-5381
http://www.kinross.net

PICKFORD (township). Covers a land area of 108.262 square miles and a water area of 11.256 square miles. Located at 46.18° N. Lat; 84.34° W. Long. Elevation is 604 feet.
History: Pickford Township was named for Charles W. Pickford, the first settler here in 1877.
Population: 1,595; Growth (since 2000): 0.7%; Density: 14.7 persons per square mile; Race: 90.3% White, 0.0% Black/African American, 0.3% Asian, 6.2% American Indian/Alaska Native, 0.0% Native Hawaiian/Other Pacific Islander, 3.1% Two or more races, 0.6% Hispanic of any race; Average household size: 2.48; Median age: 43.1; Age under 18: 24.4%; Age 65 and over: 16.0%; Males per 100 females: 105.8

School District(s)
Pickford Public Schools (PK-12)
2012-13 Enrollment: 533 . . . . (906) 647-6285

Housing: Homeownership rate: 91.6%; Homeowner vacancy rate: 3.4%; Rental vacancy rate: 12.9%

RABER (township).
Covers a land area of 97.809 square miles and a water area of 45.279 square miles. Located at 46.11° N. Lat; 84.15° W. Long. Elevation is 597 feet.

History: Settlement began in the late 1870's in Raber, which was named for Mueller M. Raber, a lumberman who lived in that area.

Population: 647; Growth (since 2000): -3.4%; Density: 6.6 persons per square mile; Race: 90.0% White, 0.0% Black/African American, 0.3% Asian, 6.5% American Indian/Alaska Native, 0.0% Native Hawaiian/Other Pacific Islander, 3.2% Two or more races, 0.9% Hispanic of any race; Average household size: 2.14; Median age: 55.2; Age under 18: 16.2%; Age 65 and over: 30.8%; Males per 100 females: 97.9

Housing: Homeownership rate: 88.8%; Homeowner vacancy rate: 4.6%; Rental vacancy rate: 15.0%

RUDYARD (township).
Covers a land area of 89.637 square miles and a water area of 0.417 square miles. Located at 46.22° N. Lat; 84.62° W. Long. Elevation is 686 feet.

History: Rudyard was named in 1896 by Fred D. Underwood, general manager of the Baltimore & Ohio Railroad, for Rudyard Kipling, the English poet and author. In acknowledgment of the honor, Kipling sent a photograph with a poem on the back written about Michigan. Rudyard was established in dense forests and on swampy land, but became farming land.

Population: 1,370; Growth (since 2000): 4.2%; Density: 15.3 persons per square mile; Race: 87.7% White, 0.4% Black/African American, 0.7% Asian, 8.0% American Indian/Alaska Native, 0.0% Native Hawaiian/Other Pacific Islander, 3.2% Two or more races, 1.0% Hispanic of any race; Average household size: 2.66; Median age: 40.0; Age under 18: 28.7%; Age 65 and over: 14.9%; Males per 100 females: 98.8

School District(s)
Eastern Upper Peninsula ISD (PK-PK)
    2012-13 Enrollment: 185 . . . . (906) 632-3373
Rudyard Area Schools (PK-12)
    2012-13 Enrollment: 757 . . . . (906) 478-3771

Housing: Homeownership rate: 88.6%; Homeowner vacancy rate: 3.2%; Rental vacancy rate: 6.3%

SAULT SAINTE MARIE (city).
County seat. Covers a land area of 14.774 square miles and a water area of 5.388 square miles. Located at 46.48° N. Lat; 84.37° W. Long. Elevation is 617 feet.

History: Sault Ste. Marie, described by Henry Clay as the "remotest settlement in the United States, if not in the moon," was the first permanent settlement in Michigan. Etienne Brule, sent by Champlain to find a Northwest Passage, landed here in 1618. In 1668 the Jesuits built a mission at the Soo, as it was called. After more than two hundred years of French and British reign, the Soo came under American rule with the building of Fort Brady in 1823. The first canal and lock were built in 1855, and replaced by the improved Weitzel Lock in 1881. Poe Lock was added in 1896. Both the American Sault Ste. Marie and its Canadian counterpart of the same name, across the St. Marys River, attract many tourists.

Population: 14,144; Growth (since 2000): -14.5%; Density: 957.3 persons per square mile; Race: 74.8% White, 0.7% Black/African American, 0.9% Asian, 17.7% American Indian/Alaska Native, 0.1% Native Hawaiian/Other Pacific Islander, 5.5% Two or more races, 1.5% Hispanic of any race; Average household size: 2.22; Median age: 33.8; Age under 18: 21.3%; Age 65 and over: 13.9%; Males per 100 females: 94.1; Marriage status: 38.3% never married, 41.4% now married, 1.5% separated, 7.1% widowed, 13.2% divorced; Foreign born: 3.7%; Speak English only: 95.8%; With disability: 18.3%; Veterans: 10.4%; Ancestry: 19.7% German, 12.2% English, 11.3% Irish, 7.9% French, 7.4% Polish

Employment: 10.4% management, business, and financial, 1.3% computer, engineering, and science, 11.1% education, legal, community service, arts, and media, 5.8% healthcare practitioners, 28.1% service, 28.7% sales and office, 6.5% natural resources, construction, and maintenance, 8.0% production, transportation, and material moving

Income: Per capita: $21,265; Median household: $33,620; Average household: $49,086; Households with income of $100,000 or more: 9.2%; Poverty rate: 23.8%

Educational Attainment: High school diploma or higher: 89.2%; Bachelor's degree or higher: 20.9%; Graduate/professional degree or higher: 8.7%

School District(s)
Joseph K. Lumsden Bahweting Anishnabe Academy (KG-12)
    2012-13 Enrollment: 474 . . . . (906) 635-5055
Sault Sainte Marie Area Schools (PK-12)
    2012-13 Enrollment: 2,482 . . . . (906) 635-6609
Four-year College(s)
Lake Superior State University (Public)
    Fall 2013 Enrollment: 2,435 . . . . (906) 632-6841
    2013-14 Tuition: In-state $9,960; Out-of-state $14,880

Housing: Homeownership rate: 55.2%; Median home value: $81,400; Median year structure built: 1957; Homeowner vacancy rate: 2.1%; Median gross rent: $593 per month; Rental vacancy rate: 6.1%

Health Insurance: 83.5% have insurance; 62.4% have private insurance; 34.2% have public insurance; 16.5% do not have insurance; 9.8% of children under 18 do not have insurance

Hospitals: Chippewa County War Memorial Hospital

Safety: Violent crime rate: 25.3 per 10,000 population; Property crime rate: 279.5 per 10,000 population

Newspapers: Evening News (daily circulation 6800)

Transportation: Commute: 81.4% car, 1.6% public transportation, 11.1% walk, 4.1% work from home; Median travel time to work: 10.4 minutes; Amtrak: Bus service available.

Airports: Chippewa County International (primary service/non-hub)

Additional Information Contacts
City of Sault Sainte Marie . . . . (906) 632-5700
    http://www.sault-sainte-marie.mi.us

SOO (township).
Covers a land area of 50.130 square miles and a water area of 17.799 square miles. Located at 46.28° N. Lat; 84.20° W. Long.

Population: 3,141; Growth (since 2000): 18.4%; Density: 62.7 persons per square mile; Race: 73.9% White, 0.5% Black/African American, 0.8% Asian, 19.6% American Indian/Alaska Native, 0.0% Native Hawaiian/Other Pacific Islander, 5.1% Two or more races, 1.1% Hispanic of any race; Average household size: 2.44; Median age: 42.0; Age under 18: 22.6%; Age 65 and over: 15.7%; Males per 100 females: 101.9; Marriage status: 22.7% never married, 63.5% now married, 2.2% separated, 3.9% widowed, 9.9% divorced; Foreign born: 2.8%; Speak English only: 93.3%; With disability: 15.5%; Veterans: 12.7%; Ancestry: 17.0% German, 15.1% French, 14.0% Irish, 11.2% English, 10.7% Italian

Employment: 6.3% management, business, and financial, 3.9% computer, engineering, and science, 17.7% education, legal, community service, arts, and media, 6.4% healthcare practitioners, 28.5% service, 23.8% sales and office, 5.7% natural resources, construction, and maintenance, 7.7% production, transportation, and material moving

Income: Per capita: $28,146; Median household: $54,458; Average household: $66,694; Households with income of $100,000 or more: 17.0%; Poverty rate: 6.6%

Educational Attainment: High school diploma or higher: 92.9%; Bachelor's degree or higher: 27.3%; Graduate/professional degree or higher: 7.5%

Housing: Homeownership rate: 79.0%; Median home value: $154,600; Median year structure built: 1979; Homeowner vacancy rate: 1.7%; Median gross rent: $594 per month; Rental vacancy rate: 10.0%

Health Insurance: 90.1% have insurance; 79.0% have private insurance; 28.3% have public insurance; 9.9% do not have insurance; 4.1% of children under 18 do not have insurance

Transportation: Commute: 94.8% car, 1.0% public transportation, 1.1% walk, 2.1% work from home; Median travel time to work: 12.9 minutes

SUGAR ISLAND (township).
Covers a land area of 49.345 square miles and a water area of 27.116 square miles. Located at 46.44° N. Lat; 84.20° W. Long.

History: Boundary disputes between England and America kept the ownership of Sugar Island in question from 1783 to 1842, when it was placed in U.S. territory by the Webster Ashburton Treaty.

Population: 652; Growth (since 2000): -4.5%; Density: 13.2 persons per square mile; Race: 67.6% White, 0.0% Black/African American, 0.3% Asian, 27.1% American Indian/Alaska Native, 0.0% Native Hawaiian/Other Pacific Islander, 4.9% Two or more races, 0.9% Hispanic of any race; Average household size: 2.16; Median age: 54.1; Age under 18: 14.1%; Age 65 and over: 25.8%; Males per 100 females: 114.5

Housing: Homeownership rate: 88.7%; Homeowner vacancy rate: 3.6%; Rental vacancy rate: 10.5%

SUPERIOR (township). Covers a land area of 102.976 square miles and a water area of 1.698 square miles. Located at 46.38° N. Lat; 84.68° W. Long.
Population: 1,337; Growth (since 2000): 0.6%; Density: 13.0 persons per square mile; Race: 71.3% White, 0.4% Black/African American, 0.3% Asian, 22.7% American Indian/Alaska Native, 0.0% Native Hawaiian/Other Pacific Islander, 5.2% Two or more races, 0.8% Hispanic of any race; Average household size: 2.47; Median age: 44.3; Age under 18: 22.4%; Age 65 and over: 16.2%; Males per 100 females: 96.0
Housing: Homeownership rate: 88.5%; Homeowner vacancy rate: 2.6%; Rental vacancy rate: 19.5%

TROUT LAKE (township). Covers a land area of 141.392 square miles and a water area of 2.239 square miles. Located at 46.21° N. Lat; 84.95° W. Long. Elevation is 833 feet.
History: The Trout Lake area was settled in 1881 at a railway junction, and became a trading center for lumber camps.
Population: 384; Growth (since 2000): -17.4%; Density: 2.7 persons per square mile; Race: 89.3% White, 0.0% Black/African American, 0.5% Asian, 7.8% American Indian/Alaska Native, 0.0% Native Hawaiian/Other Pacific Islander, 1.8% Two or more races, 0.8% Hispanic of any race; Average household size: 2.03; Median age: 54.0; Age under 18: 13.0%; Age 65 and over: 30.2%; Males per 100 females: 113.3
Housing: Homeownership rate: 86.8%; Homeowner vacancy rate: 4.6%; Rental vacancy rate: 13.8%

WHITEFISH (township). Covers a land area of 241.501 square miles and a water area of 52.143 square miles. Located at 46.61° N. Lat; 85.11° W. Long.
Population: 575; Growth (since 2000): -2.2%; Density: 2.4 persons per square mile; Race: 94.1% White, 0.2% Black/African American, 0.0% Asian, 4.0% American Indian/Alaska Native, 0.0% Native Hawaiian/Other Pacific Islander, 1.6% Two or more races, 1.6% Hispanic of any race; Average household size: 1.96; Median age: 56.5; Age under 18: 13.0%; Age 65 and over: 31.8%; Males per 100 females: 105.4
Housing: Homeownership rate: 87.7%; Homeowner vacancy rate: 4.7%; Rental vacancy rate: 22.9%

Clare County

Located in central Michigan; drained by the Muskegon, Tobacco, and Small Cedar Rivers. Covers a land area of 564.315 square miles, a water area of 11.024 square miles, and is located in the Eastern Time Zone at 43.99° N. Lat., 84.84° W. Long. The county was founded in 1840. County seat is Harrison.
Population: 30,926; Growth (since 2000): -1.0%; Density: 54.8 persons per square mile; Race: 96.8% White, 0.5% Black/African American, 0.3% Asian, 0.7% American Indian/Alaska Native, 0.0% Native Hawaiian/Other Pacific Islander, 1.4% two or more races, 1.5% Hispanic of any race; Average household size: 2.36; Median age: 45.3; Age under 18: 20.9%; Age 65 and over: 19.9%; Males per 100 females: 99.7; Marriage status: 23.1% never married, 54.3% now married, 2.1% separated, 7.5% widowed, 15.1% divorced; Foreign born: 1.0%; Speak English only: 96.1%; With disability: 22.3%; Veterans: 13.1%; Ancestry: 28.2% German, 16.5% Irish, 16.1% English, 8.4% American, 6.2% French
Religion: Six largest groups: 16.2% Catholicism, 7.3% Holiness, 3.2% Methodist/Pietist, 2.1% European Free-Church, 2.1% Lutheran, 1.8% Latter-day Saints
Economy: Unemployment rate: 7.5%; Leading industries: 22.5% retail trade; 12.2% accommodation and food services; 11.3% health care and social assistance; Farms: 460 totaling 62,506 acres; Company size: 0 employ 1,000 or more persons, 0 employ 500 to 999 persons, 9 employ 100 to 499 persons, 515 employ less than 100 persons; Business ownership: 441 women-owned, n/a Black-owned, n/a Hispanic-owned, n/a Asian-owned
Employment: 10.3% management, business, and financial, 1.6% computer, engineering, and science, 7.9% education, legal, community service, arts, and media, 4.0% healthcare practitioners, 24.3% service, 24.7% sales and office, 12.3% natural resources, construction, and maintenance, 14.9% production, transportation, and material moving
Income: Per capita: $18,148; Median household: $32,668; Average household: $41,987; Households with income of $100,000 or more: 6.7%; Poverty rate: 26.5%

Educational Attainment: High school diploma or higher: 83.9%; Bachelor's degree or higher: 11.1%; Graduate/professional degree or higher: 3.8%
Housing: Homeownership rate: 79.0%; Median home value: $80,000; Median year structure built: 1974; Homeowner vacancy rate: 4.0%; Median gross rent: $581 per month; Rental vacancy rate: 9.8%
Vital Statistics: Birth rate: 108.9 per 10,000 population; Death rate: 116.5 per 10,000 population; Age-adjusted cancer mortality rate: 203.7 deaths per 100,000 population
Health Insurance: 84.3% have insurance; 55.2% have private insurance; 48.7% have public insurance; 15.7% do not have insurance; 7.7% of children under 18 do not have insurance
Health Care: Physicians: 4.6 per 10,000 population; Hospital beds: 15.8 per 10,000 population; Hospital admissions: 519.6 per 10,000 population
Transportation: Commute: 90.8% car, 0.9% public transportation, 2.4% walk, 4.4% work from home; Median travel time to work: 26.1 minutes
Presidential Election: 47.0% Obama, 51.8% Romney (2012)
National and State Parks: Wilson State Park
Additional Information Contacts
Clare Government . . . . (989) 539-4934
    http://www.clareco.net

Clare County Communities

ARTHUR (township). Covers a land area of 36.024 square miles and a water area of 0.185 square miles. Located at 43.95° N. Lat; 84.68° W. Long.
Population: 647; Growth (since 2000): -3.0%; Density: 18.0 persons per square mile; Race: 99.1% White, 0.5% Black/African American, 0.0% Asian, 0.0% American Indian/Alaska Native, 0.0% Native Hawaiian/Other Pacific Islander, 0.2% Two or more races, 0.3% Hispanic of any race; Average household size: 2.67; Median age: 44.8; Age under 18: 23.5%; Age 65 and over: 19.3%; Males per 100 females: 108.7
Housing: Homeownership rate: 89.6%; Homeowner vacancy rate: 1.8%; Rental vacancy rate: 3.8%

CLARE (city). Covers a land area of 3.391 square miles and a water area of 0.109 square miles. Located at 43.82° N. Lat; 84.77° W. Long. Elevation is 837 feet.
History: Clare was platted in 1870 when the Flint and Pere Marquette Railway was built, and named for County Clare in Ireland. It was incorporated as a village in 1879. Industries in the early 1900's included the manufacture of house trailers, highway equipment, and cheese. In 1930, oil and gas fields near the town added to the economic growth.
Population: 3,118; Growth (since 2000): -1.7%; Density: 919.5 persons per square mile; Race: 95.5% White, 0.7% Black/African American, 1.1% Asian, 0.6% American Indian/Alaska Native, 0.0% Native Hawaiian/Other Pacific Islander, 1.8% Two or more races, 1.5% Hispanic of any race; Average household size: 2.22; Median age: 36.1; Age under 18: 23.9%; Age 65 and over: 16.9%; Males per 100 females: 82.3; Marriage status: 34.6% never married, 41.5% now married, 3.2% separated, 8.7% widowed, 15.2% divorced; Foreign born: 1.0%; Speak English only: 97.8%; With disability: 17.5%; Veterans: 9.5%; Ancestry: 22.8% German, 19.0% Irish, 17.4% English, 8.3% American, 4.9% Dutch
Employment: 7.5% management, business, and financial, 2.5% computer, engineering, and science, 9.6% education, legal, community service, arts, and media, 2.0% healthcare practitioners, 36.4% service, 23.0% sales and office, 10.2% natural resources, construction, and maintenance, 8.9% production, transportation, and material moving
Income: Per capita: $17,541; Median household: $26,771; Average household: $37,871; Households with income of $100,000 or more: 7.1%; Poverty rate: 38.9%
Educational Attainment: High school diploma or higher: 83.4%; Bachelor's degree or higher: 20.6%; Graduate/professional degree or higher: 9.3%

School District(s)
Clare Public Schools (PK-12)
    2012-13 Enrollment: 1,524 . . . . (989) 386-9945
Clare-Gladwin Regional Education Service District (PK-PK)
    2012-13 Enrollment: 234 . . . . (989) 386-3851
Housing: Homeownership rate: 47.7%; Median home value: $90,600; Median year structure built: 1970; Homeowner vacancy rate: 3.8%; Median gross rent: $523 per month; Rental vacancy rate: 13.6%

Health Insurance: 81.0% have insurance; 43.2% have private insurance; 50.6% have public insurance; 19.0% do not have insurance; 7.6% of children under 18 do not have insurance
Hospitals: Midmichigan Medical Center - Clare (49 beds)
Safety: Violent crime rate: 58.2 per 10,000 population; Property crime rate: 313.4 per 10,000 population
Newspapers: Clare County Review (weekly circulation 10000); Clare Sentinel (weekly circulation 3300)
Transportation: Commute: 83.7% car, 1.3% public transportation, 3.3% walk, 7.6% work from home; Median travel time to work: 22.1 minutes
Airports: Clare Municipal (general aviation)
Additional Information Contacts
City of Clare. . . . . (989) 386-7541
   http://www.cityofclare.org

FARWELL (village). Covers a land area of 1.354 square miles and a water area of 0.045 square miles. Located at 43.84° N. Lat; 84.87° W. Long. Elevation is 928 feet.
History: Farwell came into existence when the Flint and Pere Marquette Railway was built through the area in 1870. For a time in the early 1900's, the Portland Cement Company had a plant here, using marl deposits from Littlefield Lake in the manufacture of cement.
Population: 871; Growth (since 2000): 1.9%; Density: 643.3 persons per square mile; Race: 97.8% White, 0.6% Black/African American, 0.1% Asian, 0.7% American Indian/Alaska Native, 0.1% Native Hawaiian/Other Pacific Islander, 0.6% Two or more races, 1.8% Hispanic of any race; Average household size: 2.30; Median age: 40.4; Age under 18: 22.0%; Age 65 and over: 18.4%; Males per 100 females: 93.1
School District(s)
Farwell Area Schools (PK-12)
   2012-13 Enrollment: 1,478 . . . . (989) 588-9917
Housing: Homeownership rate: 60.0%; Homeowner vacancy rate: 3.0%; Rental vacancy rate: 8.0%

FRANKLIN (township). Covers a land area of 35.326 square miles and a water area of 0.148 square miles. Located at 44.12° N. Lat; 84.66° W. Long.
Population: 825; Growth (since 2000): 2.0%; Density: 23.4 persons per square mile; Race: 98.5% White, 0.7% Black/African American, 0.1% Asian, 0.1% American Indian/Alaska Native, 0.0% Native Hawaiian/Other Pacific Islander, 0.5% Two or more races, 1.2% Hispanic of any race; Average household size: 2.33; Median age: 49.9; Age under 18: 20.0%; Age 65 and over: 24.2%; Males per 100 females: 108.3
Housing: Homeownership rate: 89.3%; Homeowner vacancy rate: 3.0%; Rental vacancy rate: 2.4%

FREEMAN (township). Covers a land area of 34.581 square miles and a water area of 1.217 square miles. Located at 43.96° N. Lat; 85.03° W. Long.
Population: 1,157; Growth (since 2000): 3.5%; Density: 33.5 persons per square mile; Race: 98.1% White, 0.5% Black/African American, 0.0% Asian, 0.3% American Indian/Alaska Native, 0.1% Native Hawaiian/Other Pacific Islander, 1.0% Two or more races, 0.9% Hispanic of any race; Average household size: 2.20; Median age: 55.3; Age under 18: 15.4%; Age 65 and over: 30.8%; Males per 100 females: 104.8
Housing: Homeownership rate: 89.3%; Homeowner vacancy rate: 2.3%; Rental vacancy rate: 4.9%

FROST (township). Covers a land area of 34.954 square miles and a water area of 0.562 square miles. Located at 44.11° N. Lat; 84.78° W. Long.
Population: 1,047; Growth (since 2000): -9.7%; Density: 30.0 persons per square mile; Race: 97.0% White, 0.0% Black/African American, 0.0% Asian, 0.2% American Indian/Alaska Native, 0.0% Native Hawaiian/Other Pacific Islander, 2.4% Two or more races, 1.1% Hispanic of any race; Average household size: 2.22; Median age: 50.5; Age under 18: 16.2%; Age 65 and over: 25.5%; Males per 100 females: 108.6
Housing: Homeownership rate: 87.7%; Homeowner vacancy rate: 2.6%; Rental vacancy rate: 11.9%
Safety: Violent crime rate: 0.0 per 10,000 population; Property crime rate: 202.5 per 10,000 population

GARFIELD (township). Covers a land area of 33.386 square miles and a water area of 2.381 square miles. Located at 43.86° N. Lat; 85.05° W. Long.
Population: 1,882; Growth (since 2000): -4.4%; Density: 56.4 persons per square mile; Race: 97.2% White, 0.2% Black/African American, 0.0% Asian, 1.3% American Indian/Alaska Native, 0.0% Native Hawaiian/Other Pacific Islander, 1.2% Two or more races, 1.6% Hispanic of any race; Average household size: 2.36; Median age: 47.7; Age under 18: 19.7%; Age 65 and over: 21.5%; Males per 100 females: 100.9
Housing: Homeownership rate: 83.9%; Homeowner vacancy rate: 3.4%; Rental vacancy rate: 5.9%

GRANT (township). Covers a land area of 32.762 square miles and a water area of 0.486 square miles. Located at 43.86° N. Lat; 84.79° W. Long.
Population: 3,259; Growth (since 2000): 7.4%; Density: 99.5 persons per square mile; Race: 97.4% White, 0.3% Black/African American, 0.3% Asian, 0.8% American Indian/Alaska Native, 0.0% Native Hawaiian/Other Pacific Islander, 0.9% Two or more races, 1.2% Hispanic of any race; Average household size: 2.59; Median age: 42.2; Age under 18: 24.7%; Age 65 and over: 16.0%; Males per 100 females: 101.7; Marriage status: 26.6% never married, 53.8% now married, 1.9% separated, 6.0% widowed, 13.6% divorced; Foreign born: 0.8%; Speak English only: 91.3%; With disability: 14.3%; Veterans: 11.5%; Ancestry: 34.9% German, 17.5% Irish, 15.7% English, 10.7% American, 5.9% French
Employment: 15.5% management, business, and financial, 2.6% computer, engineering, and science, 7.0% education, legal, community service, arts, and media, 2.8% healthcare practitioners, 20.6% service, 28.1% sales and office, 11.2% natural resources, construction, and maintenance, 12.2% production, transportation, and material moving
Income: Per capita: $20,037; Median household: $41,161; Average household: $51,362; Households with income of $100,000 or more: 12.3%; Poverty rate: 20.6%
Educational Attainment: High school diploma or higher: 80.9%; Bachelor's degree or higher: 12.7%; Graduate/professional degree or higher: 3.9%
Housing: Homeownership rate: 83.2%; Median home value: $104,100; Median year structure built: 1976; Homeowner vacancy rate: 2.8%; Median gross rent: $638 per month; Rental vacancy rate: 10.9%
Health Insurance: 84.9% have insurance; 60.7% have private insurance; 43.0% have public insurance; 15.1% do not have insurance; 6.1% of children under 18 do not have insurance
Transportation: Commute: 85.3% car, 0.0% public transportation, 4.9% walk, 7.7% work from home; Median travel time to work: 22.2 minutes

GREENWOOD (township). Covers a land area of 35.197 square miles and a water area of 0.304 square miles. Located at 44.02° N. Lat; 84.90° W. Long.
Population: 1,041; Growth (since 2000): -1.7%; Density: 29.6 persons per square mile; Race: 98.4% White, 0.3% Black/African American, 0.3% Asian, 0.1% American Indian/Alaska Native, 0.0% Native Hawaiian/Other Pacific Islander, 0.8% Two or more races, 1.2% Hispanic of any race; Average household size: 2.18; Median age: 51.5; Age under 18: 14.3%; Age 65 and over: 24.5%; Males per 100 females: 103.3
Housing: Homeownership rate: 89.6%; Homeowner vacancy rate: 3.8%; Rental vacancy rate: 3.8%

HAMILTON (township). Covers a land area of 35.868 square miles and a water area of 0.490 square miles. Located at 44.04° N. Lat; 84.69° W. Long.
History: Hamilton Township was subdivided from Hayes Township in 1885.
Population: 1,829; Growth (since 2000): -8.0%; Density: 51.0 persons per square mile; Race: 97.5% White, 0.3% Black/African American, 0.1% Asian, 0.7% American Indian/Alaska Native, 0.0% Native Hawaiian/Other Pacific Islander, 1.1% Two or more races, 1.9% Hispanic of any race; Average household size: 2.32; Median age: 48.5; Age under 18: 17.6%; Age 65 and over: 20.8%; Males per 100 females: 103.2
Housing: Homeownership rate: 87.6%; Homeowner vacancy rate: 4.0%; Rental vacancy rate: 6.7%

HARRISON (city). County seat. Covers a land area of 3.719 square miles and a water area of 0.312 square miles. Located at 44.01° N. Lat; 84.81° W. Long. Elevation is 1,165 feet.

History: Harrison was founded in 1879 as the seat of Clare County when the courthouse at Farwell was destroyed by fire. The new city was platted by the Pere Marquette Railway and named for President William Henry Harrison. Harrison became the center of a resort area offering hunting and fishing.

Population: 2,114; Growth (since 2000): 0.3%; Density: 568.4 persons per square mile; Race: 93.7% White, 1.7% Black/African American, 0.5% Asian, 0.8% American Indian/Alaska Native, 0.0% Native Hawaiian/Other Pacific Islander, 3.1% Two or more races, 2.5% Hispanic of any race; Average household size: 2.18; Median age: 42.1; Age under 18: 21.0%; Age 65 and over: 18.4%; Males per 100 females: 96.3

School District(s)

Harrison Community Schools (PK-12)
    2012-13 Enrollment: 1,481 . . . . (989) 539-7871

Two-year College(s)

Mid Michigan Community College (Public)
    Fall 2013 Enrollment: 4,552 . . . . (989) 386-6622
    2013-14 Tuition: In-state $4,988; Out-of-state $8,852

Housing: Homeownership rate: 57.8%; Homeowner vacancy rate: 3.8%; Rental vacancy rate: 12.3%

Newspapers: Clare County Cleaver (weekly circulation 5000)

HATTON (township). Covers a land area of 35.886 square miles and a water area of 0.252 square miles. Located at 43.94° N. Lat; 84.81° W. Long. Elevation is 997 feet.

Population: 933; Growth (since 2000): 1.1%; Density: 26.0 persons per square mile; Race: 96.5% White, 0.1% Black/African American, 0.2% Asian, 0.9% American Indian/Alaska Native, 0.0% Native Hawaiian/Other Pacific Islander, 2.4% Two or more races, 0.6% Hispanic of any race; Average household size: 2.56; Median age: 45.2; Age under 18: 22.0%; Age 65 and over: 17.4%; Males per 100 females: 112.0

Housing: Homeownership rate: 86.8%; Homeowner vacancy rate: 0.9%; Rental vacancy rate: 9.4%

HAYES (township). Covers a land area of 31.281 square miles and a water area of 0.885 square miles. Located at 44.04° N. Lat; 84.78° W. Long.

Population: 4,675; Growth (since 2000): -4.9%; Density: 149.5 persons per square mile; Race: 96.4% White, 0.4% Black/African American, 0.4% Asian, 0.8% American Indian/Alaska Native, 0.0% Native Hawaiian/Other Pacific Islander, 1.8% Two or more races, 1.5% Hispanic of any race; Average household size: 2.36; Median age: 43.4; Age under 18: 21.6%; Age 65 and over: 18.0%; Males per 100 females: 102.7; Marriage status: 22.0% never married, 51.0% now married, 1.1% separated, 7.7% widowed, 19.3% divorced; Foreign born: 0.0%; Speak English only: 97.0%; With disability: 24.8%; Veterans: 13.2%; Ancestry: 28.9% German, 16.2% English, 13.3% Irish, 8.7% Polish, 6.9% American

Employment: 10.2% management, business, and financial, 0.3% computer, engineering, and science, 7.7% education, legal, community service, arts, and media, 3.2% healthcare practitioners, 24.4% service, 25.8% sales and office, 10.3% natural resources, construction, and maintenance, 18.2% production, transportation, and material moving

Income: Per capita: $16,419; Median household: $28,606; Average household: $35,103; Households with income of $100,000 or more: 4.1%; Poverty rate: 33.3%

Educational Attainment: High school diploma or higher: 83.0%; Bachelor's degree or higher: 5.1%; Graduate/professional degree or higher: 1.2%

Housing: Homeownership rate: 81.8%; Median home value: $56,100; Median year structure built: 1972; Homeowner vacancy rate: 6.1%; Median gross rent: $618 per month; Rental vacancy rate: 7.6%

Health Insurance: 79.9% have insurance; 49.7% have private insurance; 49.7% have public insurance; 20.1% do not have insurance; 4.9% of children under 18 do not have insurance

Transportation: Commute: 94.9% car, 1.4% public transportation, 1.0% walk, 2.7% work from home; Median travel time to work: 23.9 minutes

LAKE GEORGE (unincorporated postal area)

ZCTA: 48633

    Covers a land area of 2.576 square miles and a water area of 0.296 square miles. Located at 43.94° N. Lat; 84.93° W. Long. Elevation is 1,112 feet.

Population: 210; Growth (since 2000): 223.1%; Density: 81.5 persons per square mile; Race: 96.2% White, 0.0% Black/African American, 0.0% Asian, 1.0% American Indian/Alaska Native, 0.0% Native Hawaiian/Other Pacific Islander, 2.4% Two or more races, 0.5% Hispanic of any race; Average household size: 1.84; Median age: 60.6; Age under 18: 5.2%; Age 65 and over: 35.7%; Males per 100 females: 96.3

Housing: Homeownership rate: 93.0%; Homeowner vacancy rate: 7.8%; Rental vacancy rate: 27.3%

LINCOLN (township). Covers a land area of 35.082 square miles and a water area of 0.845 square miles. Located at 43.94° N. Lat; 84.90° W. Long.

Population: 1,824; Growth (since 2000): 3.8%; Density: 52.0 persons per square mile; Race: 96.7% White, 0.3% Black/African American, 0.1% Asian, 0.8% American Indian/Alaska Native, 0.1% Native Hawaiian/Other Pacific Islander, 1.9% Two or more races, 2.0% Hispanic of any race; Average household size: 2.17; Median age: 52.6; Age under 18: 15.4%; Age 65 and over: 25.3%; Males per 100 females: 98.0

Housing: Homeownership rate: 90.4%; Homeowner vacancy rate: 6.7%; Rental vacancy rate: 9.8%

REDDING (township). Covers a land area of 34.903 square miles and a water area of 0.527 square miles. Located at 44.03° N. Lat; 85.02° W. Long. Elevation is 1,053 feet.

Population: 526; Growth (since 2000): 0.0%; Density: 15.1 persons per square mile; Race: 96.6% White, 0.0% Black/African American, 0.2% Asian, 0.6% American Indian/Alaska Native, 0.0% Native Hawaiian/Other Pacific Islander, 1.7% Two or more races, 3.2% Hispanic of any race; Average household size: 2.35; Median age: 49.0; Age under 18: 20.2%; Age 65 and over: 18.8%; Males per 100 females: 100.8

Housing: Homeownership rate: 83.4%; Homeowner vacancy rate: 6.5%; Rental vacancy rate: 9.8%

SHERIDAN (township). Covers a land area of 36.151 square miles and a water area of 0.347 square miles. Located at 43.85° N. Lat; 84.67° W. Long.

Population: 1,575; Growth (since 2000): -0.8%; Density: 43.6 persons per square mile; Race: 97.1% White, 1.1% Black/African American, 0.0% Asian, 0.3% American Indian/Alaska Native, 0.0% Native Hawaiian/Other Pacific Islander, 1.1% Two or more races, 2.0% Hispanic of any race; Average household size: 3.04; Median age: 33.6; Age under 18: 32.1%; Age 65 and over: 13.4%; Males per 100 females: 102.2

Housing: Homeownership rate: 85.6%; Homeowner vacancy rate: 1.6%; Rental vacancy rate: 14.0%

SUMMERFIELD (township). Covers a land area of 35.196 square miles and a water area of 0.704 square miles. Located at 44.11° N. Lat; 84.89° W. Long. Elevation is 1,096 feet.

Population: 456; Growth (since 2000): 0.7%; Density: 13.0 persons per square mile; Race: 98.9% White, 0.2% Black/African American, 0.2% Asian, 0.2% American Indian/Alaska Native, 0.0% Native Hawaiian/Other Pacific Islander, 0.4% Two or more races, 0.9% Hispanic of any race; Average household size: 2.06; Median age: 55.9; Age under 18: 8.8%; Age 65 and over: 29.6%; Males per 100 females: 113.1

Housing: Homeownership rate: 86.9%; Homeowner vacancy rate: 6.7%; Rental vacancy rate: 3.3%

SURREY (township). Covers a land area of 35.101 square miles and a water area of 0.711 square miles. Located at 43.86° N. Lat; 84.91° W. Long.

History: Surrey was settled in 1866 by the Wilkins family, and was named after Surrey in England.

Population: 3,606; Growth (since 2000): 1.4%; Density: 102.7 persons per square mile; Race: 97.4% White, 0.2% Black/African American, 0.2% Asian, 0.8% American Indian/Alaska Native, 0.1% Native Hawaiian/Other Pacific Islander, 0.9% Two or more races, 1.4% Hispanic of any race; Average household size: 2.36; Median age: 45.3; Age under 18: 20.7%; Age 65 and over: 20.7%; Males per 100 females: 96.6; Marriage status: 19.5% never married, 56.0% now married, 2.4% separated, 9.9% widowed, 14.6% divorced; Foreign born: 1.0%; Speak English only: 99.6%; With disability: 19.9%; Veterans: 12.8%; Ancestry: 24.8% German, 21.0% Irish, 14.3% English, 9.3% American, 5.1% Polish

Employment: 9.2% management, business, and financial, 1.8% computer, engineering, and science, 6.2% education, legal, community service, arts,

and media, 6.4% healthcare practitioners, 21.6% service, 24.4% sales and office, 11.3% natural resources, construction, and maintenance, 19.2% production, transportation, and material moving
Income: Per capita: $18,559; Median household: $34,832; Average household: $43,633; Households with income of $100,000 or more: 8.1%; Poverty rate: 17.7%
Educational Attainment: High school diploma or higher: 89.0%; Bachelor's degree or higher: 11.4%; Graduate/professional degree or higher: 3.6%
Housing: Homeownership rate: 78.8%; Median home value: $83,400; Median year structure built: 1972; Homeowner vacancy rate: 3.6%; Median gross rent: $636 per month; Rental vacancy rate: 4.8%
Health Insurance: 87.8% have insurance; 63.5% have private insurance; 43.0% have public insurance; 12.2% do not have insurance; 5.0% of children under 18 do not have insurance
Transportation: Commute: 95.0% car, 1.8% public transportation, 1.2% walk, 2.0% work from home; Median travel time to work: 27.3 minutes

WINTERFIELD (township). Covers a land area of 36.054 square miles and a water area of 0.559 square miles. Located at 44.13° N. Lat; 85.02° W. Long.
Population: 459; Growth (since 2000): -5.0%; Density: 12.7 persons per square mile; Race: 96.9% White, 0.0% Black/African American, 0.0% Asian, 0.9% American Indian/Alaska Native, 0.0% Native Hawaiian/Other Pacific Islander, 2.0% Two or more races, 0.4% Hispanic of any race; Average household size: 2.42; Median age: 47.4; Age under 18: 19.4%; Age 65 and over: 19.0%; Males per 100 females: 103.1
Housing: Homeownership rate: 84.2%; Homeowner vacancy rate: 3.6%; Rental vacancy rate: 0.0%

Clinton County

Located in south central Michigan; drained by the Maple, Lookingglass, and Grand Rivers. Covers a land area of 566.408 square miles, a water area of 8.149 square miles, and is located in the Eastern Time Zone at 42.95° N. Lat., 84.59° W. Long. The county was founded in 1831. County seat is Saint Johns.

Clinton County is part of the Lansing-East Lansing, MI Metropolitan Statistical Area. The entire metro area includes: Clinton County, MI; Eaton County, MI; Ingham County, MI

Weather Station: Lansing Capital City Arpt — Elevation: 840 feet

	Jan	Feb	Mar	Apr	May	Jun	Jul	Aug	Sep	Oct	Nov	Dec
High	30	33	44	57	69	78	82	80	73	60	47	34
Low	15	17	24	35	45	55	59	58	50	39	31	21
Precip	1.6	1.5	2.1	3.0	3.3	3.5	2.9	3.4	3.4	2.5	2.7	1.9
Snow	13.7	11.0	7.3	2.1	tr	tr	tr	0.0	tr	0.4	3.5	13.2

High and Low temperatures in degrees Fahrenheit; Precipitation and Snow in inches

Weather Station: St Johns — Elevation: 743 feet

	Jan	Feb	Mar	Apr	May	Jun	Jul	Aug	Sep	Oct	Nov	Dec
High	30	33	44	57	70	79	83	81	74	60	47	35
Low	15	17	24	35	46	56	60	58	50	40	31	21
Precip	1.8	1.5	2.1	3.3	3.6	3.2	3.2	3.4	3.7	3.0	2.7	1.7
Snow	13.5	9.5	5.8	1.3	tr	0.0	0.0	0.0	0.0	0.3	2.1	9.8

High and Low temperatures in degrees Fahrenheit; Precipitation and Snow in inches

Population: 75,382; Growth (since 2000): 16.4%; Density: 133.1 persons per square mile; Race: 92.9% White, 2.1% Black/African American, 1.5% Asian, 0.4% American Indian/Alaska Native, 0.0% Native Hawaiian/Other Pacific Islander, 2.0% two or more races, 3.9% Hispanic of any race; Average household size: 2.60; Median age: 38.4; Age under 18: 24.7%; Age 65 and over: 12.9%; Males per 100 females: 96.7; Marriage status: 28.2% never married, 57.0% now married, 1.0% separated, 5.1% widowed, 9.8% divorced; Foreign born: 2.9%; Speak English only: 95.4%; With disability: 10.3%; Veterans: 8.4%; Ancestry: 36.7% German, 14.8% Irish, 13.5% English, 8.6% American, 5.0% Polish
Religion: Six largest groups: 18.3% Catholicism, 5.1% Methodist/Pietist, 2.4% Non-denominational Protestant, 1.8% Lutheran, 1.2% Presbyterian-Reformed, 0.9% Holiness
Economy: Unemployment rate: 4.7%; Leading industries: 14.1% construction; 13.2% retail trade; 11.1% other services (except public administration); Farms: 1,128 totaling 243,815 acres; Company size: 1 employs 1,000 or more persons, 1 employs 500 to 999 persons, 17 employ 100 to 499 persons, 1,265 employ less than 100 persons; Business

ownership: 1,772 women-owned, n/a Black-owned, 65 Hispanic-owned, n/a Asian-owned
Employment: 15.0% management, business, and financial, 5.0% computer, engineering, and science, 11.0% education, legal, community service, arts, and media, 5.6% healthcare practitioners, 18.2% service, 25.0% sales and office, 8.1% natural resources, construction, and maintenance, 12.1% production, transportation, and material moving
Income: Per capita: $28,449; Median household: $60,466; Average household: $73,839; Households with income of $100,000 or more: 23.4%; Poverty rate: 11.1%
Educational Attainment: High school diploma or higher: 92.9%; Bachelor's degree or higher: 28.2%; Graduate/professional degree or higher: 10.3%
Housing: Homeownership rate: 78.6%; Median home value: $156,300; Median year structure built: 1977; Homeowner vacancy rate: 1.7%; Median gross rent: $764 per month; Rental vacancy rate: 9.5%
Vital Statistics: Birth rate: 92.0 per 10,000 population; Death rate: 66.6 per 10,000 population; Age-adjusted cancer mortality rate: 162.1 deaths per 100,000 population
Health Insurance: 91.7% have insurance; 80.7% have private insurance; 25.2% have public insurance; 8.3% do not have insurance; 3.8% of children under 18 do not have insurance
Health Care: Physicians: 9.9 per 10,000 population; Hospital beds: 3.3 per 10,000 population; Hospital admissions: 101.3 per 10,000 population
Air Quality Index: 90.7% good, 9.3% moderate, 0.0% unhealthy for sensitive individuals, 0.0% unhealthy (percent of days)
Transportation: Commute: 92.3% car, 1.0% public transportation, 1.4% walk, 4.3% work from home; Median travel time to work: 23.0 minutes
Presidential Election: 46.5% Obama, 52.7% Romney (2012)
National and State Parks: Maple River State Game Area; Rose Lake State Wildlife Research Area; Sleepy Hollow State Park
Additional Information Contacts
Clinton Government . . . . (989) 224-5100
    http://www.clinton-county.org

Clinton County Communities

BATH (CDP). Covers a land area of 5.739 square miles and a water area of 0.199 square miles. Located at 42.82° N. Lat; 84.45° W. Long. Elevation is 863 feet.
Population: 2,083; Growth (since 2000): n/a; Density: 362.9 persons per square mile; Race: 94.6% White, 1.4% Black/African American, 0.8% Asian, 0.9% American Indian/Alaska Native, 0.1% Native Hawaiian/Other Pacific Islander, 1.5% Two or more races, 4.1% Hispanic of any race; Average household size: 2.71; Median age: 37.6; Age under 18: 27.3%; Age 65 and over: 10.5%; Males per 100 females: 92.2
School District(s)
Bath Community Schools (PK-12)
    2012-13 Enrollment: 1,029 . . . . (517) 641-6721
Housing: Homeownership rate: 84.7%; Homeowner vacancy rate: 0.8%; Rental vacancy rate: 6.9%

BATH (charter township). Covers a land area of 31.835 square miles and a water area of 3.197 square miles. Located at 42.82° N. Lat; 84.42° W. Long. Elevation is 863 feet.
History: Bath Township was named in 1836 by Canadian Ira Cushman after Bath, England.
Population: 11,598; Growth (since 2000): 53.8%; Density: 364.3 persons per square mile; Race: 87.5% White, 5.2% Black/African American, 3.6% Asian, 0.4% American Indian/Alaska Native, 0.0% Native Hawaiian/Other Pacific Islander, 2.3% Two or more races, 3.4% Hispanic of any race; Average household size: 2.45; Median age: 30.1; Age under 18: 19.1%; Age 65 and over: 9.9%; Males per 100 females: 90.3; Marriage status: 40.8% never married, 47.1% now married, 1.0% separated, 2.7% widowed, 9.4% divorced; Foreign born: 5.6%; Speak English only: 91.6%; With disability: 9.7%; Veterans: 5.5%; Ancestry: 26.9% German, 16.2% Irish, 10.5% English, 5.1% American, 5.0% Italian
Employment: 17.8% management, business, and financial, 5.2% computer, engineering, and science, 14.4% education, legal, community service, arts, and media, 6.5% healthcare practitioners, 21.2% service, 22.7% sales and office, 4.6% natural resources, construction, and maintenance, 7.6% production, transportation, and material moving
Income: Per capita: $29,546; Median household: $56,844; Average household: $78,242; Households with income of $100,000 or more: 24.6%; Poverty rate: 23.2%

Educational Attainment: High school diploma or higher: 94.0%; Bachelor's degree or higher: 45.0%; Graduate/professional degree or higher: 18.1%

School District(s)
Bath Community Schools (PK-12)
  2012-13 Enrollment: 1,029 . . . . (517) 641-6721
Housing: Homeownership rate: 62.1%; Median home value: $167,800; Median year structure built: 1997; Homeowner vacancy rate: 2.4%; Median gross rent: $981 per month; Rental vacancy rate: 11.8%
Health Insurance: 89.8% have insurance; 79.5% have private insurance; 20.6% have public insurance; 10.2% do not have insurance; 7.7% of children under 18 do not have insurance
Safety: Violent crime rate: 16.2 per 10,000 population; Property crime rate: 123.3 per 10,000 population
Transportation: Commute: 88.9% car, 2.8% public transportation, 1.4% walk, 6.7% work from home; Median travel time to work: 20.2 minutes

BENGAL (township). Covers a land area of 36.529 square miles and a water area of 0.006 square miles. Located at 43.00° N. Lat; 84.67° W. Long.
Population: 1,188; Growth (since 2000): 1.2%; Density: 32.5 persons per square mile; Race: 95.5% White, 0.4% Black/African American, 0.5% Asian, 0.4% American Indian/Alaska Native, 0.0% Native Hawaiian/Other Pacific Islander, 0.6% Two or more races, 4.2% Hispanic of any race; Average household size: 2.96; Median age: 39.8; Age under 18: 27.3%; Age 65 and over: 10.6%; Males per 100 females: 102.7
Housing: Homeownership rate: 91.8%; Homeowner vacancy rate: 0.5%; Rental vacancy rate: 0.0%

BINGHAM (township). Covers a land area of 32.391 square miles and a water area of 0.019 square miles. Located at 42.98° N. Lat; 84.54° W. Long.
History: Bingham Township was named for Governor Kingsley S. Bingham.
Population: 2,859; Growth (since 2000): 3.0%; Density: 88.3 persons per square mile; Race: 95.8% White, 0.4% Black/African American, 0.4% Asian, 0.7% American Indian/Alaska Native, 0.0% Native Hawaiian/Other Pacific Islander, 1.5% Two or more races, 3.5% Hispanic of any race; Average household size: 2.78; Median age: 39.6; Age under 18: 26.8%; Age 65 and over: 12.1%; Males per 100 females: 103.5; Marriage status: 30.4% never married, 56.9% now married, 0.3% separated, 4.1% widowed, 8.6% divorced; Foreign born: 0.2%; Speak English only: 97.0%; With disability: 13.8%; Veterans: 9.3%; Ancestry: 43.7% German, 13.8% American, 12.4% English, 10.3% Irish, 5.3% Dutch
Employment: 12.4% management, business, and financial, 3.1% computer, engineering, and science, 6.2% education, legal, community service, arts, and media, 5.1% healthcare practitioners, 20.7% service, 27.6% sales and office, 8.4% natural resources, construction, and maintenance, 16.4% production, transportation, and material moving
Income: Per capita: $24,615; Median household: $61,859; Average household: $66,399; Households with income of $100,000 or more: 22.6%; Poverty rate: 16.6%
Educational Attainment: High school diploma or higher: 95.2%; Bachelor's degree or higher: 17.8%; Graduate/professional degree or higher: 4.9%
Housing: Homeownership rate: 89.3%; Median home value: $156,900; Median year structure built: 1980; Homeowner vacancy rate: 1.0%; Median gross rent: $713 per month; Rental vacancy rate: 11.3%
Health Insurance: 95.0% have insurance; 79.3% have private insurance; 26.8% have public insurance; 5.0% do not have insurance; 1.0% of children under 18 do not have insurance
Transportation: Commute: 89.8% car, 0.5% public transportation, 2.3% walk, 4.5% work from home; Median travel time to work: 20.6 minutes

DALLAS (township). Covers a land area of 36.390 square miles and a water area of 0.125 square miles. Located at 42.99° N. Lat; 84.77° W. Long.
Population: 2,369; Growth (since 2000): 2.0%; Density: 65.1 persons per square mile; Race: 98.0% White, 0.3% Black/African American, 0.4% Asian, 0.1% American Indian/Alaska Native, 0.0% Native Hawaiian/Other Pacific Islander, 0.8% Two or more races, 1.9% Hispanic of any race; Average household size: 2.86; Median age: 36.2; Age under 18: 30.8%; Age 65 and over: 15.1%; Males per 100 females: 102.3
Housing: Homeownership rate: 87.8%; Homeowner vacancy rate: 0.8%; Rental vacancy rate: 13.7%

DEWITT (charter township). Covers a land area of 31.030 square miles and a water area of 0.236 square miles. Located at 42.81° N. Lat; 84.54° W. Long. Elevation is 837 feet.
Population: 14,321; Growth (since 2000): 17.9%; Density: 461.5 persons per square mile; Race: 90.8% White, 2.6% Black/African American, 1.4% Asian, 0.6% American Indian/Alaska Native, 0.0% Native Hawaiian/Other Pacific Islander, 2.8% Two or more races, 6.1% Hispanic of any race; Average household size: 2.53; Median age: 40.4; Age under 18: 25.3%; Age 65 and over: 14.0%; Males per 100 females: 96.1; Marriage status: 26.0% never married, 56.7% now married, 0.8% separated, 5.6% widowed, 11.7% divorced; Foreign born: 2.6%; Speak English only: 95.6%; With disability: 11.9%; Veterans: 10.9%; Ancestry: 33.6% German, 15.8% Irish, 13.3% English, 6.9% American, 6.8% Polish
Employment: 16.4% management, business, and financial, 6.6% computer, engineering, and science, 10.4% education, legal, community service, arts, and media, 5.6% healthcare practitioners, 21.9% service, 23.4% sales and office, 5.1% natural resources, construction, and maintenance, 10.6% production, transportation, and material moving
Income: Per capita: $30,241; Median household: $60,815; Average household: $75,009; Households with income of $100,000 or more: 24.2%; Poverty rate: 7.8%
Educational Attainment: High school diploma or higher: 92.4%; Bachelor's degree or higher: 29.7%; Graduate/professional degree or higher: 9.3%

School District(s)
Dewitt Public Schools (PK-12)
  2012-13 Enrollment: 3,014 . . . . (517) 668-3000
Housing: Homeownership rate: 80.0%; Median home value: $146,200; Median year structure built: 1978; Homeowner vacancy rate: 2.4%; Median gross rent: $721 per month; Rental vacancy rate: 12.2%
Health Insurance: 89.9% have insurance; 78.4% have private insurance; 27.3% have public insurance; 10.1% do not have insurance; 4.7% of children under 18 do not have insurance
Transportation: Commute: 95.3% car, 0.5% public transportation, 0.0% walk, 3.0% work from home; Median travel time to work: 21.1 minutes
Additional Information Contacts
De Witt Charter Township . . . . (517) 668-0270
  http://www.dewitttownship.org

DEWITT (city). Covers a land area of 2.857 square miles and a water area of 0.125 square miles. Located at 42.84° N. Lat; 84.58° W. Long. Elevation is 837 feet.
History: DeWitt was named after DeWitt Clinton, Governor of New York during the 1830s. It was first settled by Captain David Scott, who moved here from Ann Arbor in 1833, and platted the land.
Population: 4,507; Growth (since 2000): -4.1%; Density: 1,577.4 persons per square mile; Race: 94.9% White, 1.4% Black/African American, 0.9% Asian, 0.4% American Indian/Alaska Native, 0.0% Native Hawaiian/Other Pacific Islander, 1.9% Two or more races, 3.5% Hispanic of any race; Average household size: 2.60; Median age: 39.8; Age under 18: 26.6%; Age 65 and over: 9.8%; Males per 100 females: 94.7; Marriage status: 21.0% never married, 62.3% now married, 1.2% separated, 5.3% widowed, 11.3% divorced; Foreign born: 1.7%; Speak English only: 95.6%; With disability: 5.6%; Veterans: 9.7%; Ancestry: 36.7% German, 17.0% English, 12.1% Irish, 8.3% American, 6.3% Dutch
Employment: 18.3% management, business, and financial, 4.2% computer, engineering, and science, 14.6% education, legal, community service, arts, and media, 8.6% healthcare practitioners, 16.6% service, 21.8% sales and office, 10.0% natural resources, construction, and maintenance, 5.9% production, transportation, and material moving
Income: Per capita: $35,891; Median household: $76,091; Average household: $93,500; Households with income of $100,000 or more: 28.7%; Poverty rate: 7.1%
Educational Attainment: High school diploma or higher: 97.8%; Bachelor's degree or higher: 45.4%; Graduate/professional degree or higher: 18.8%

School District(s)
Dewitt Public Schools (PK-12)
  2012-13 Enrollment: 3,014 . . . . (517) 668-3000
Housing: Homeownership rate: 76.1%; Median home value: $186,900; Median year structure built: 1978; Homeowner vacancy rate: 1.3%; Median gross rent: $1,016 per month; Rental vacancy rate: 5.2%
Health Insurance: 95.7% have insurance; 88.8% have private insurance; 18.5% have public insurance; 4.3% do not have insurance; 4.3% of children under 18 do not have insurance

Safety: Violent crime rate: 10.9 per 10,000 population; Property crime rate: 76.3 per 10,000 population

Transportation: Commute: 91.1% car, 0.0% public transportation, 0.0% walk, 8.9% work from home; Median travel time to work: 20.9 minutes

Additional Information Contacts

City of De Witt . . . . (517) 669-2441
http://www.dewittmi.org

DUPLAIN (township). Covers a land area of 35.121 square miles and a water area of 0.293 square miles. Located at 43.07° N. Lat; 84.42° W. Long. Elevation is 732 feet.

Population: 2,363; Growth (since 2000): 1.5%; Density: 67.3 persons per square mile; Race: 96.1% White, 0.5% Black/African American, 0.1% Asian, 0.3% American Indian/Alaska Native, 0.0% Native Hawaiian/Other Pacific Islander, 0.8% Two or more races, 5.4% Hispanic of any race; Average household size: 2.63; Median age: 40.4; Age under 18: 25.3%; Age 65 and over: 15.4%; Males per 100 females: 103.2

Housing: Homeownership rate: 80.6%; Homeowner vacancy rate: 1.6%; Rental vacancy rate: 4.3%

EAGLE (township). Covers a land area of 34.740 square miles and a water area of 0.643 square miles. Located at 42.82° N. Lat; 84.78° W. Long. Elevation is 837 feet.

Population: 2,671; Growth (since 2000): 14.5%; Density: 76.9 persons per square mile; Race: 97.0% White, 0.9% Black/African American, 0.3% Asian, 0.2% American Indian/Alaska Native, 0.0% Native Hawaiian/Other Pacific Islander, 1.0% Two or more races, 2.5% Hispanic of any race; Average household size: 2.64; Median age: 44.9; Age under 18: 22.7%; Age 65 and over: 14.6%; Males per 100 females: 102.5; Marriage status: 25.0% never married, 61.9% now married, 0.7% separated, 4.7% widowed, 8.5% divorced; Foreign born: 0.3%; Speak English only: 99.8%; With disability: 8.0%; Veterans: 11.1%; Ancestry: 44.1% German, 21.7% Irish, 17.6% English, 10.4% American, 5.2% Polish

Employment: 16.6% management, business, and financial, 5.7% computer, engineering, and science, 9.2% education, legal, community service, arts, and media, 8.4% healthcare practitioners, 11.2% service, 20.4% sales and office, 9.5% natural resources, construction, and maintenance, 19.0% production, transportation, and material moving

Income: Per capita: $32,326; Median household: $93,188; Average household: $84,924; Households with income of $100,000 or more: 44.9%; Poverty rate: 4.7%

Educational Attainment: High school diploma or higher: 95.8%; Bachelor's degree or higher: 31.2%; Graduate/professional degree or higher: 10.4%

School District(s)

Grand Ledge Public Schools (KG-12)
2012-13 Enrollment: 5,071 . . . . (517) 925-5400

Housing: Homeownership rate: 92.9%; Median home value: $160,900; Median year structure built: 1977; Homeowner vacancy rate: 0.9%; Median gross rent: $1,116 per month; Rental vacancy rate: 0.0%

Health Insurance: 93.0% have insurance; 88.4% have private insurance; 21.8% have public insurance; 7.0% do not have insurance; 1.2% of children under 18 do not have insurance

Transportation: Commute: 95.1% car, 0.0% public transportation, 0.6% walk, 4.0% work from home; Median travel time to work: 26.6 minutes

EAGLE (village). Covers a land area of 0.120 square miles and a water area of 0 square miles. Located at 42.81° N. Lat; 84.79° W. Long. Elevation is 837 feet.

Population: 123; Growth (since 2000): -5.4%; Density: 1,026.2 persons per square mile; Race: 99.2% White, 0.0% Black/African American, 0.0% Asian, 0.0% American Indian/Alaska Native, 0.0% Native Hawaiian/Other Pacific Islander, 0.0% Two or more races, 0.8% Hispanic of any race; Average household size: 2.56; Median age: 40.8; Age under 18: 23.6%; Age 65 and over: 13.8%; Males per 100 females: 89.2

School District(s)

Grand Ledge Public Schools (KG-12)
2012-13 Enrollment: 5,071 . . . . (517) 925-5400

Housing: Homeownership rate: 91.7%; Homeowner vacancy rate: 0.0%; Rental vacancy rate: 0.0%

ELSIE (village). Covers a land area of 1.161 square miles and a water area of 0.039 square miles. Located at 43.09° N. Lat; 84.39° W. Long. Elevation is 735 feet.

Population: 966; Growth (since 2000): -8.4%; Density: 832.3 persons per square mile; Race: 97.3% White, 0.4% Black/African American, 0.1% Asian, 0.6% American Indian/Alaska Native, 0.0% Native Hawaiian/Other Pacific Islander, 0.6% Two or more races, 2.4% Hispanic of any race; Average household size: 2.45; Median age: 39.7; Age under 18: 25.5%; Age 65 and over: 16.3%; Males per 100 females: 94.8

School District(s)

Ovid-Elsie Area Schools (PK-12)
2012-13 Enrollment: 1,712 . . . . (989) 834-2271

Housing: Homeownership rate: 73.7%; Homeowner vacancy rate: 1.7%; Rental vacancy rate: 2.8%

Safety: Violent crime rate: 0.0 per 10,000 population; Property crime rate: 82.6 per 10,000 population

ESSEX (township). Covers a land area of 35.356 square miles and a water area of 0.243 square miles. Located at 43.07° N. Lat; 84.66° W. Long.

Population: 1,910; Growth (since 2000): 5.4%; Density: 54.0 persons per square mile; Race: 97.6% White, 0.6% Black/African American, 0.3% Asian, 0.1% American Indian/Alaska Native, 0.0% Native Hawaiian/Other Pacific Islander, 0.7% Two or more races, 1.8% Hispanic of any race; Average household size: 2.73; Median age: 38.2; Age under 18: 28.2%; Age 65 and over: 12.7%; Males per 100 females: 104.7

Housing: Homeownership rate: 88.7%; Homeowner vacancy rate: 1.7%; Rental vacancy rate: 12.1%

FOWLER (village). Covers a land area of 1.320 square miles and a water area of 0.025 square miles. Located at 43.00° N. Lat; 84.74° W. Long. Elevation is 741 feet.

Population: 1,208; Growth (since 2000): 6.3%; Density: 915.3 persons per square mile; Race: 98.1% White, 0.4% Black/African American, 0.7% Asian, 0.0% American Indian/Alaska Native, 0.0% Native Hawaiian/Other Pacific Islander, 0.6% Two or more races, 2.5% Hispanic of any race; Average household size: 2.68; Median age: 36.1; Age under 18: 29.7%; Age 65 and over: 17.3%; Males per 100 females: 102.7

School District(s)

Fowler Public Schools (KG-12)
2012-13 Enrollment: 546 . . . . (989) 593-2250

Housing: Homeownership rate: 83.4%; Homeowner vacancy rate: 1.6%; Rental vacancy rate: 15.7%

GREENBUSH (township). Covers a land area of 35.176 square miles and a water area of 0.273 square miles. Located at 43.07° N. Lat; 84.53° W. Long.

Population: 2,199; Growth (since 2000): 4.0%; Density: 62.5 persons per square mile; Race: 97.2% White, 0.3% Black/African American, 0.2% Asian, 0.2% American Indian/Alaska Native, 0.0% Native Hawaiian/Other Pacific Islander, 1.5% Two or more races, 2.3% Hispanic of any race; Average household size: 2.69; Median age: 42.0; Age under 18: 25.5%; Age 65 and over: 13.9%; Males per 100 females: 100.8

Housing: Homeownership rate: 91.3%; Homeowner vacancy rate: 0.8%; Rental vacancy rate: 12.5%

LAKE VICTORIA (CDP). Covers a land area of 0.822 square miles and a water area of 0.229 square miles. Located at 42.92° N. Lat; 84.38° W. Long. Elevation is 810 feet.

Population: 930; Growth (since 2000): n/a; Density: 1,131.0 persons per square mile; Race: 96.3% White, 0.3% Black/African American, 0.9% Asian, 0.4% American Indian/Alaska Native, 0.0% Native Hawaiian/Other Pacific Islander, 1.6% Two or more races, 2.2% Hispanic of any race; Average household size: 2.67; Median age: 40.4; Age under 18: 24.7%; Age 65 and over: 12.7%; Males per 100 females: 97.0

Housing: Homeownership rate: 94.0%; Homeowner vacancy rate: 1.8%; Rental vacancy rate: 0.0%

LEBANON (township). Covers a land area of 35.099 square miles and a water area of 0.302 square miles. Located at 43.07° N. Lat; 84.77° W. Long.

Population: 605; Growth (since 2000): -14.2%; Density: 17.2 persons per square mile; Race: 98.0% White, 0.8% Black/African American, 0.2% Asian, 0.2% American Indian/Alaska Native, 0.0% Native Hawaiian/Other Pacific Islander, 0.7% Two or more races, 1.2% Hispanic of any race;

Average household size: 2.75; Median age: 42.2; Age under 18: 28.3%; Age 65 and over: 15.2%; Males per 100 females: 107.9
Housing: Homeownership rate: 89.0%; Homeowner vacancy rate: 0.5%; Rental vacancy rate: 14.3%

MAPLE RAPIDS (village). Covers a land area of 1.362 square miles and a water area of 0.056 square miles. Located at 43.11° N. Lat; 84.69° W. Long. Elevation is 686 feet.
Population: 672; Growth (since 2000): 4.5%; Density: 493.5 persons per square mile; Race: 97.5% White, 0.1% Black/African American, 0.6% Asian, 0.1% American Indian/Alaska Native, 0.0% Native Hawaiian/Other Pacific Islander, 1.6% Two or more races, 1.5% Hispanic of any race; Average household size: 2.68; Median age: 36.7; Age under 18: 27.8%; Age 65 and over: 12.2%; Males per 100 females: 104.3
Housing: Homeownership rate: 81.7%; Homeowner vacancy rate: 2.3%; Rental vacancy rate: 14.5%

OLIVE (township). Covers a land area of 35.631 square miles and a water area of 0.192 square miles. Located at 42.90° N. Lat; 84.55° W. Long.
Population: 2,476; Growth (since 2000): 6.6%; Density: 69.5 persons per square mile; Race: 95.8% White, 0.6% Black/African American, 0.8% Asian, 1.1% American Indian/Alaska Native, 0.0% Native Hawaiian/Other Pacific Islander, 1.1% Two or more races, 1.7% Hispanic of any race; Average household size: 2.69; Median age: 44.1; Age under 18: 24.7%; Age 65 and over: 15.8%; Males per 100 females: 109.5
Housing: Homeownership rate: 93.6%; Homeowner vacancy rate: 0.6%; Rental vacancy rate: 7.8%

OVID (township). Covers a land area of 35.838 square miles and a water area of 0.157 square miles. Located at 42.99° N. Lat; 84.41° W. Long. Elevation is 732 feet.
History: Plotted 1857; incorporated 1869.
Population: 3,795; Growth (since 2000): 8.7%; Density: 105.9 persons per square mile; Race: 95.9% White, 0.7% Black/African American, 0.2% Asian, 0.3% American Indian/Alaska Native, 0.1% Native Hawaiian/Other Pacific Islander, 1.7% Two or more races, 4.2% Hispanic of any race; Average household size: 2.74; Median age: 37.5; Age under 18: 28.4%; Age 65 and over: 13.5%; Males per 100 females: 91.2; Marriage status: 27.6% never married, 54.7% now married, 1.4% separated, 7.6% widowed, 10.0% divorced; Foreign born: 1.5%; Speak English only: 98.1%; With disability: 10.8%; Veterans: 6.4%; Ancestry: 29.3% German, 16.4% English, 15.7% American, 10.6% Irish, 5.7% French
Employment: 6.9% management, business, and financial, 2.1% computer, engineering, and science, 8.3% education, legal, community service, arts, and media, 4.3% healthcare practitioners, 22.7% service, 21.6% sales and office, 11.2% natural resources, construction, and maintenance, 22.8% production, transportation, and material moving
Income: Per capita: $20,748; Median household: $49,688; Average household: $56,634; Households with income of $100,000 or more: 10.3%; Poverty rate: 16.0%
Educational Attainment: High school diploma or higher: 87.5%; Bachelor's degree or higher: 13.1%; Graduate/professional degree or higher: 5.2%
School District(s)
Ovid-Elsie Area Schools (PK-12)
 2012-13 Enrollment: 1,712 . . . . (989) 834-2271
Housing: Homeownership rate: 82.9%; Median home value: $124,500; Median year structure built: 1966; Homeowner vacancy rate: 2.0%; Median gross rent: $566 per month; Rental vacancy rate: 4.5%
Health Insurance: 83.2% have insurance; 68.1% have private insurance; 30.0% have public insurance; 16.8% do not have insurance; 14.4% of children under 18 do not have insurance
Transportation: Commute: 94.9% car, 0.0% public transportation, 1.5% walk, 2.3% work from home; Median travel time to work: 22.9 minutes

OVID (village). Covers a land area of 0.924 square miles and a water area of 0.002 square miles. Located at 43.00° N. Lat; 84.38° W. Long. Elevation is 732 feet.
Population: 1,603; Growth (since 2000): 5.9%; Density: 1,735.4 persons per square mile; Race: 95.7% White, 0.4% Black/African American, 0.1% Asian, 0.3% American Indian/Alaska Native, 0.1% Native Hawaiian/Other Pacific Islander, 2.1% Two or more races, 5.7% Hispanic of any race; Average household size: 2.63; Median age: 35.0; Age under 18: 29.4%; Age 65 and over: 15.2%; Males per 100 females: 83.8

School District(s)
Ovid-Elsie Area Schools (PK-12)
 2012-13 Enrollment: 1,712 . . . . (989) 834-2271
Housing: Homeownership rate: 67.4%; Homeowner vacancy rate: 3.0%; Rental vacancy rate: 4.6%
Safety: Violent crime rate: 6.2 per 10,000 population; Property crime rate: 49.8 per 10,000 population

RILEY (township). Covers a land area of 35.714 square miles and a water area of 0.017 square miles. Located at 42.89° N. Lat; 84.65° W. Long. Elevation is 748 feet.
History: Riley Township was organized in 1841, after settlers had come to the area a few years earlier.
Population: 2,024; Growth (since 2000): 14.5%; Density: 56.7 persons per square mile; Race: 95.7% White, 0.6% Black/African American, 0.2% Asian, 0.4% American Indian/Alaska Native, 0.0% Native Hawaiian/Other Pacific Islander, 2.2% Two or more races, 3.8% Hispanic of any race; Average household size: 2.77; Median age: 41.4; Age under 18: 26.8%; Age 65 and over: 12.8%; Males per 100 females: 104.0
Housing: Homeownership rate: 93.4%; Homeowner vacancy rate: 0.1%; Rental vacancy rate: 2.0%

SAINT JOHNS (city). County seat. Covers a land area of 3.871 square miles and a water area of 0 square miles. Located at 43.00° N. Lat; 84.56° W. Long. Elevation is 794 feet.
History: St. Johns was laid out in 1853 by John Swegles, a surveyor for the Detroit & Milwaukee Railroad. The town was named for him, with the "Saint" added by Reverend C.A. Lamb, a Baptist minister. St. Johns was incorporated as a village in 1857 and as a city in 1904.
Population: 7,865; Growth (since 2000): 5.1%; Density: 2,031.8 persons per square mile; Race: 93.9% White, 1.4% Black/African American, 0.5% Asian, 0.6% American Indian/Alaska Native, 0.1% Native Hawaiian/Other Pacific Islander, 2.3% Two or more races, 4.6% Hispanic of any race; Average household size: 2.38; Median age: 37.2; Age under 18: 25.4%; Age 65 and over: 15.6%; Males per 100 females: 91.2; Marriage status: 29.0% never married, 48.4% now married, 2.1% separated, 9.7% widowed, 12.9% divorced; Foreign born: 1.2%; Speak English only: 97.3%; With disability: 14.0%; Veterans: 8.5%; Ancestry: 39.1% German, 14.1% Irish, 13.5% American, 12.4% English, 4.1% Italian
Employment: 10.0% management, business, and financial, 2.8% computer, engineering, and science, 7.9% education, legal, community service, arts, and media, 2.3% healthcare practitioners, 19.8% service, 37.8% sales and office, 4.5% natural resources, construction, and maintenance, 15.0% production, transportation, and material moving
Income: Per capita: $23,070; Median household: $39,824; Average household: $53,902; Households with income of $100,000 or more: 13.3%; Poverty rate: 15.1%
Educational Attainment: High school diploma or higher: 90.2%; Bachelor's degree or higher: 20.2%; Graduate/professional degree or higher: 8.9%
School District(s)
Clinton County Resa (PK-12)
 2012-13 Enrollment: 270 . . . . (989) 224-6831
Saint Johns Public Schools (PK-12)
 2012-13 Enrollment: 3,115 . . . . (989) 227-4050
Housing: Homeownership rate: 64.7%; Median home value: $119,200; Median year structure built: 1958; Homeowner vacancy rate: 2.8%; Median gross rent: $685 per month; Rental vacancy rate: 10.1%
Health Insurance: 92.0% have insurance; 70.9% have private insurance; 36.7% have public insurance; 8.0% do not have insurance; 0.0% of children under 18 do not have insurance
Hospitals: Sparrow Clinton Hospital (28 beds)
Safety: Violent crime rate: 10.1 per 10,000 population; Property crime rate: 141.7 per 10,000 population
Transportation: Commute: 90.8% car, 0.8% public transportation, 4.7% walk, 2.4% work from home; Median travel time to work: 23.3 minutes
Additional Information Contacts
City of Saint Johns . . . . (989) 224-8944
 http://www.cityofsaintjohnsmi.com

VICTOR (township). Covers a land area of 33.934 square miles and a water area of 2.029 square miles. Located at 42.90° N. Lat; 84.43° W. Long.
Population: 3,460; Growth (since 2000): 5.6%; Density: 102.0 persons per square mile; Race: 96.5% White, 0.2% Black/African American, 0.4%

Asian, 0.5% American Indian/Alaska Native, 0.0% Native Hawaiian/Other Pacific Islander, 1.6% Two or more races, 2.5% Hispanic of any race; Average household size: 2.70; Median age: 41.7; Age under 18: 24.8%; Age 65 and over: 12.3%; Males per 100 females: 100.8; Marriage status: 23.4% never married, 60.7% now married, 0.0% separated, 3.7% widowed, 12.2% divorced; Foreign born: 1.0%; Speak English only: 98.2%; With disability: 9.1%; Veterans: 11.4%; Ancestry: 28.8% German, 19.1% Irish, 16.9% English, 7.5% American, 5.9% Polish

Employment: 13.8% management, business, and financial, 4.4% computer, engineering, and science, 9.9% education, legal, community service, arts, and media, 9.3% healthcare practitioners, 13.1% service, 30.4% sales and office, 6.5% natural resources, construction, and maintenance, 12.6% production, transportation, and material moving

Income: Per capita: $29,047; Median household: $70,114; Average household: $76,018; Households with income of $100,000 or more: 24.6%; Poverty rate: 4.2%

Educational Attainment: High school diploma or higher: 94.0%; Bachelor's degree or higher: 22.6%; Graduate/professional degree or higher: 7.5%

Housing: Homeownership rate: 93.2%; Median home value: $152,300; Median year structure built: 1977; Homeowner vacancy rate: 1.0%; Median gross rent: $1,010 per month; Rental vacancy rate: 1.1%

Health Insurance: 92.3% have insurance; 85.1% have private insurance; 21.2% have public insurance; 7.7% do not have insurance; 2.8% of children under 18 do not have insurance

Transportation: Commute: 94.7% car, 1.1% public transportation, 1.2% walk, 2.5% work from home; Median travel time to work: 28.2 minutes

WACOUSTA (CDP). Covers a land area of 8.914 square miles and a water area of 0.078 square miles. Located at 42.82° N. Lat; 84.69° W. Long. Elevation is 797 feet.

Population: 1,440; Growth (since 2000): n/a; Density: 161.5 persons per square mile; Race: 94.5% White, 1.5% Black/African American, 0.8% Asian, 0.1% American Indian/Alaska Native, 0.1% Native Hawaiian/Other Pacific Islander, 2.2% Two or more races, 1.8% Hispanic of any race; Average household size: 2.52; Median age: 47.9; Age under 18: 19.9%; Age 65 and over: 15.1%; Males per 100 females: 102.8

Housing: Homeownership rate: 95.8%; Homeowner vacancy rate: 2.5%; Rental vacancy rate: 0.0%

WATERTOWN (charter township). Covers a land area of 35.505 square miles and a water area of 0.214 square miles. Located at 42.82° N. Lat; 84.65° W. Long.

Population: 4,836; Growth (since 2000): 16.2%; Density: 136.2 persons per square mile; Race: 93.6% White, 1.3% Black/African American, 1.3% Asian, 0.3% American Indian/Alaska Native, 0.0% Native Hawaiian/Other Pacific Islander, 2.2% Two or more races, 4.0% Hispanic of any race; Average household size: 2.70; Median age: 42.8; Age under 18: 25.2%; Age 65 and over: 12.5%; Males per 100 females: 101.8; Marriage status: 16.1% never married, 72.2% now married, 0.4% separated, 4.1% widowed, 7.6% divorced; Foreign born: 1.8%; Speak English only: 97.2%; With disability: 9.3%; Veterans: 5.9%; Ancestry: 36.1% German, 21.8% Irish, 17.6% English, 6.5% French, 6.5% Italian

Employment: 20.0% management, business, and financial, 7.1% computer, engineering, and science, 15.6% education, legal, community service, arts, and media, 5.0% healthcare practitioners, 15.4% service, 22.0% sales and office, 4.2% natural resources, construction, and maintenance, 10.6% production, transportation, and material moving

Income: Per capita: $40,240; Median household: $76,286; Average household: $99,262; Households with income of $100,000 or more: 37.7%; Poverty rate: 6.6%

Educational Attainment: High school diploma or higher: 95.2%; Bachelor's degree or higher: 36.6%; Graduate/professional degree or higher: 12.8%

Housing: Homeownership rate: 92.0%; Median home value: $194,000; Median year structure built: 1977; Homeowner vacancy rate: 2.0%; Median gross rent: $1,290 per month; Rental vacancy rate: 2.7%

Health Insurance: 94.8% have insurance; 90.2% have private insurance; 19.5% have public insurance; 5.2% do not have insurance; 1.6% of children under 18 do not have insurance

Transportation: Commute: 94.7% car, 0.4% public transportation, 0.0% walk, 4.5% work from home; Median travel time to work: 23.0 minutes

Additional Information Contacts
Watertown Charter Township . . . . (517) 626-6593
   http://www.twp.watertown.mi.us

WESTPHALIA (township). Covers a land area of 35.516 square miles and a water area of 0.072 square miles. Located at 42.90° N. Lat; 84.78° W. Long. Elevation is 761 feet.

Population: 2,365; Growth (since 2000): 4.8%; Density: 66.6 persons per square mile; Race: 97.8% White, 0.1% Black/African American, 0.2% Asian, 0.1% American Indian/Alaska Native, 0.0% Native Hawaiian/Other Pacific Islander, 1.1% Two or more races, 2.2% Hispanic of any race; Average household size: 2.84; Median age: 38.3; Age under 18: 29.7%; Age 65 and over: 16.6%; Males per 100 females: 101.6

School District(s)
Pewamo-Westphalia Community Schools (PK-12)
   2012-13 Enrollment: 636 . . . . (989) 587-5100
Housing: Homeownership rate: 90.2%; Homeowner vacancy rate: 0.7%; Rental vacancy rate: 0.0%

WESTPHALIA (village). Covers a land area of 1.114 square miles and a water area of 0.031 square miles. Located at 42.93° N. Lat; 84.80° W. Long. Elevation is 761 feet.

History: Westphalia was settled in 1836 by immigrants from Westphalia, Germany. The site was chosen by a priest, who established a parish for German-speaking Roman Catholics.

Population: 923; Growth (since 2000): 5.4%; Density: 828.6 persons per square mile; Race: 98.2% White, 0.1% Black/African American, 0.1% Asian, 0.1% American Indian/Alaska Native, 0.0% Native Hawaiian/Other Pacific Islander, 0.5% Two or more races, 3.0% Hispanic of any race; Average household size: 2.60; Median age: 39.4; Age under 18: 27.5%; Age 65 and over: 22.4%; Males per 100 females: 93.5

School District(s)
Pewamo-Westphalia Community Schools (PK-12)
   2012-13 Enrollment: 636 . . . . (989) 587-5100
Housing: Homeownership rate: 83.4%; Homeowner vacancy rate: 1.0%; Rental vacancy rate: 0.0%

Crawford County

Located in north central Michigan; drained by the North, Middle, and South Branches of the Au Sable River; includes part of Huron National Forest. Covers a land area of 556.280 square miles, a water area of 6.962 square miles, and is located in the Eastern Time Zone at 44.68° N. Lat., 84.61° W. Long. The county was founded in 1818. County seat is Grayling.

Weather Station: Grayling — Elevation: 1,140 feet

	Jan	Feb	Mar	Apr	May	Jun	Jul	Aug	Sep	Oct	Nov	Dec
High	26	29	38	53	66	76	80	78	70	56	42	30
Low	8	8	15	29	39	49	54	52	44	34	25	15
Precip	1.7	1.3	1.7	2.8	3.3	3.7	3.5	3.6	3.7	3.8	2.6	1.8
Snow	30.3	20.9	14.6	3.9	0.1	0.0	0.0	0.0	0.0	1.3	9.8	26.1

High and Low temperatures in degrees Fahrenheit; Precipitation and Snow in inches

Population: 14,074; Growth (since 2000): -1.4%; Density: 25.3 persons per square mile; Race: 97.5% White, 0.4% Black/African American, 0.4% Asian, 0.5% American Indian/Alaska Native, 0.0% Native Hawaiian/Other Pacific Islander, 1.1% two or more races, 1.3% Hispanic of any race; Average household size: 2.31; Median age: 47.7; Age under 18: 19.9%; Age 65 and over: 20.8%; Males per 100 females: 100.7; Marriage status: 22.8% never married, 56.2% now married, 1.7% separated, 7.6% widowed, 13.3% divorced; Foreign born: 1.7%; Speak English only: 98.4%; With disability: 20.8%; Veterans: 14.3%; Ancestry: 24.9% German, 15.4% English, 14.0% Irish, 7.5% French, 7.3% Polish

Religion: Six largest groups: 5.2% Catholicism, 5.1% Methodist/Pietist, 2.6% Lutheran, 1.4% Holiness, 1.2% Latter-day Saints, 0.9% Baptist

Economy: Unemployment rate: 6.4%; Leading industries: 20.0% retail trade; 14.3% accommodation and food services; 10.7% health care and social assistance; Farms: 49 totaling 2,755 acres; Company size: 0 employ 1,000 or more persons, 1 employs 500 to 999 persons, 1 employs 100 to 499 persons, 298 employ less than 100 persons; Business ownership: n/a women-owned, n/a Black-owned, n/a Hispanic-owned, n/a Asian-owned

Employment: 9.4% management, business, and financial, 2.2% computer, engineering, and science, 8.7% education, legal, community service, arts, and media, 6.3% healthcare practitioners, 25.7% service, 21.4% sales and office, 8.9% natural resources, construction, and maintenance, 17.4% production, transportation, and material moving

Income: Per capita: $21,492; Median household: $40,295; Average household: $49,624; Households with income of $100,000 or more: 8.3%; Poverty rate: 16.8%

Educational Attainment: High school diploma or higher: 85.4%; Bachelor's degree or higher: 15.2%; Graduate/professional degree or higher: 5.2%
Housing: Homeownership rate: 82.1%; Median home value: $96,400; Median year structure built: 1976; Homeowner vacancy rate: 3.4%; Median gross rent: $649 per month; Rental vacancy rate: 10.1%
Vital Statistics: Birth rate: 78.4 per 10,000 population; Death rate: 109.3 per 10,000 population; Age-adjusted cancer mortality rate: 219.6 deaths per 100,000 population
Health Insurance: 88.4% have insurance; 62.1% have private insurance; 46.6% have public insurance; 11.6% do not have insurance; 2.6% of children under 18 do not have insurance
Health Care: Physicians: 14.3 per 10,000 population; Hospital beds: 67.1 per 10,000 population; Hospital admissions: 2,684.9 per 10,000 population
Transportation: Commute: 90.8% car, 2.0% public transportation, 2.8% walk, 3.4% work from home; Median travel time to work: 21.2 minutes
Presidential Election: 43.9% Obama, 54.9% Romney (2012)
National and State Parks: Au Sable State Forest; Hanson State Game Refuge; Hartwick Pines State Park; Higgins Lake State Forest; North Higgins Lake State Park
Additional Information Contacts
Crawford Government . . . . (989) 348-2841
   http://www.crawfordco.org

Crawford County Communities

BEAVER CREEK (township). Covers a land area of 71.460 square miles and a water area of 0.097 square miles. Located at 44.56° N. Lat; 84.73° W. Long.
Population: 1,736; Growth (since 2000): 16.8%; Density: 24.3 persons per square mile; Race: 97.6% White, 0.5% Black/African American, 0.2% Asian, 0.6% American Indian/Alaska Native, 0.0% Native Hawaiian/Other Pacific Islander, 1.1% Two or more races, 1.1% Hispanic of any race; Average household size: 2.37; Median age: 47.8; Age under 18: 20.6%; Age 65 and over: 20.4%; Males per 100 females: 103.3
Housing: Homeownership rate: 89.7%; Homeowner vacancy rate: 3.9%; Rental vacancy rate: 5.0%

FREDERIC (township). Covers a land area of 71.396 square miles and a water area of 0.623 square miles. Located at 44.78° N. Lat; 84.79° W. Long. Elevation is 1,211 feet.
Population: 1,341; Growth (since 2000): -4.3%; Density: 18.8 persons per square mile; Race: 97.5% White, 0.1% Black/African American, 0.1% Asian, 1.0% American Indian/Alaska Native, 0.0% Native Hawaiian/Other Pacific Islander, 1.2% Two or more races, 1.0% Hispanic of any race; Average household size: 2.33; Median age: 47.5; Age under 18: 21.0%; Age 65 and over: 19.5%; Males per 100 females: 99.0
Housing: Homeownership rate: 86.0%; Homeowner vacancy rate: 2.7%; Rental vacancy rate: 13.3%

GRAYLING (charter township). Covers a land area of 170.736 square miles and a water area of 4.000 square miles. Located at 44.68° N. Lat; 84.64° W. Long. Elevation is 1,138 feet.
History: Incorporated as village 1903, as city 1934.
Population: 5,827; Growth (since 2000): -10.6%; Density: 34.1 persons per square mile; Race: 97.2% White, 0.3% Black/African American, 0.5% Asian, 0.5% American Indian/Alaska Native, 0.0% Native Hawaiian/Other Pacific Islander, 1.3% Two or more races, 1.2% Hispanic of any race; Average household size: 2.35; Median age: 47.5; Age under 18: 19.9%; Age 65 and over: 19.5%; Males per 100 females: 100.9; Marriage status: 22.2% never married, 54.8% now married, 1.7% separated, 7.9% widowed, 15.1% divorced; Foreign born: 1.2%; Speak English only: 99.4%; With disability: 20.8%; Veterans: 14.4%; Ancestry: 24.0% German, 15.4% English, 15.2% Irish, 8.8% French Canadian, 7.6% American
Employment: 10.1% management, business, and financial, 1.1% computer, engineering, and science, 9.3% education, legal, community service, arts, and media, 8.0% healthcare practitioners, 29.3% service, 20.2% sales and office, 7.3% natural resources, construction, and maintenance, 14.7% production, transportation, and material moving
Income: Per capita: $22,208; Median household: $45,332; Average household: $53,385; Households with income of $100,000 or more: 8.9%; Poverty rate: 13.5%
Educational Attainment: High school diploma or higher: 86.0%; Bachelor's degree or higher: 17.4%; Graduate/professional degree or higher: 4.8%

School District(s)
Crawford Ausable Schools (PK-12)
   2012-13 Enrollment: 1,625 . . . . (989) 344-3500
Michigan Department of Human Services (KG-12)
   2012-13 Enrollment: 46. . . . . (517) 373-2000
Housing: Homeownership rate: 85.2%; Median home value: $100,200; Median year structure built: 1975; Homeowner vacancy rate: 2.7%; Median gross rent: $703 per month; Rental vacancy rate: 11.7%
Health Insurance: 90.6% have insurance; 62.9% have private insurance; 44.8% have public insurance; 9.4% do not have insurance; 0.0% of children under 18 do not have insurance
Hospitals: Mercy Hospital - Grayling (130 beds)
Newspapers: Crawford County Avalanche (weekly circulation 5300)
Transportation: Commute: 88.9% car, 2.9% public transportation, 3.2% walk, 3.8% work from home; Median travel time to work: 18.9 minutes
Additional Information Contacts
Grayling Charter Township . . . . (989) 348-4361
   http://www.twp.grayling.mi.us

GRAYLING (city). County seat. Covers a land area of 2.006 square miles and a water area of 0.034 square miles. Located at 44.66° N. Lat; 84.71° W. Long. Elevation is 1,138 feet.
History: Grayling was named for the Michigan grayling fish, until 1884 a popular game fish in the Au Sable River. The grayling disappeared in the 1880's, and brook trout were planted in the Au Sable River.
Population: 1,884; Growth (since 2000): -3.5%; Density: 939.0 persons per square mile; Race: 97.2% White, 0.7% Black/African American, 0.5% Asian, 0.5% American Indian/Alaska Native, 0.1% Native Hawaiian/Other Pacific Islander, 0.9% Two or more races, 1.7% Hispanic of any race; Average household size: 2.27; Median age: 38.6; Age under 18: 23.8%; Age 65 and over: 20.7%; Males per 100 females: 87.5
School District(s)
Crawford Ausable Schools (PK-12)
   2012-13 Enrollment: 1,625 . . . . (989) 344-3500
Michigan Department of Human Services (KG-12)
   2012-13 Enrollment: 46. . . . . (517) 373-2000
Housing: Homeownership rate: 47.0%; Homeowner vacancy rate: 5.3%; Rental vacancy rate: 11.4%
Hospitals: Mercy Hospital - Grayling (130 beds)
Safety: Violent crime rate: 42.7 per 10,000 population; Property crime rate: 534.2 per 10,000 population
Newspapers: Crawford County Avalanche (weekly circulation 5300)
Additional Information Contacts
City of Grayling . . . . (989) 348-2131
   http://www.cityofgrayling.org

LOVELLS (township). Covers a land area of 100.551 square miles and a water area of 1.184 square miles. Located at 44.78° N. Lat; 84.46° W. Long. Elevation is 1,161 feet.
Population: 626; Growth (since 2000): 8.3%; Density: 6.2 persons per square mile; Race: 98.1% White, 0.8% Black/African American, 0.2% Asian, 0.3% American Indian/Alaska Native, 0.0% Native Hawaiian/Other Pacific Islander, 0.5% Two or more races, 2.4% Hispanic of any race; Average household size: 1.99; Median age: 57.5; Age under 18: 11.2%; Age 65 and over: 32.9%; Males per 100 females: 103.2
Housing: Homeownership rate: 91.4%; Homeowner vacancy rate: 5.9%; Rental vacancy rate: 0.0%

MAPLE FOREST (township). Covers a land area of 35.303 square miles and a water area of 0.289 square miles. Located at 44.81° N. Lat; 84.66° W. Long.
Population: 653; Growth (since 2000): 31.1%; Density: 18.5 persons per square mile; Race: 98.0% White, 0.3% Black/African American, 0.2% Asian, 0.9% American Indian/Alaska Native, 0.0% Native Hawaiian/Other Pacific Islander, 0.6% Two or more races, 0.5% Hispanic of any race; Average household size: 2.48; Median age: 46.8; Age under 18: 20.1%; Age 65 and over: 17.8%; Males per 100 females: 115.5
Housing: Homeownership rate: 89.4%; Homeowner vacancy rate: 5.2%; Rental vacancy rate: 3.3%

SOUTH BRANCH (township). Covers a land area of 104.828 square miles and a water area of 0.736 square miles. Located at 44.58° N. Lat; 84.45° W. Long.
Population: 2,007; Growth (since 2000): 9.0%; Density: 19.1 persons per square mile; Race: 98.2% White, 0.0% Black/African American, 0.4%

Asian, 0.2% American Indian/Alaska Native, 0.0% Native Hawaiian/Other Pacific Islander, 1.0% Two or more races, 1.4% Hispanic of any race; Average household size: 2.23; Median age: 50.8; Age under 18: 17.2%; Age 65 and over: 23.0%; Males per 100 females: 107.5
Housing: Homeownership rate: 89.3%; Homeowner vacancy rate: 2.9%; Rental vacancy rate: 3.9%

Delta County

Located in northwestern Michigan, on the Upper Peninsula; bounded on the south by Lake Michigan; drained by the Ford, Escanaba, Whitefish, and Days Rivers; includes part of Hiawatha National Forest. Covers a land area of 1,171.096 square miles, a water area of 820.228 square miles, and is located in the Eastern Time Zone at 45.81° N. Lat., 86.90° W. Long. The county was founded in 1843. County seat is Escanaba.

Delta County is part of the Escanaba, MI Micropolitan Statistical Area. The entire metro area includes: Delta County, MI

Population: 37,069; Growth (since 2000): -3.8%; Density: 31.7 persons per square mile; Race: 94.7% White, 0.2% Black/African American, 0.4% Asian, 2.4% American Indian/Alaska Native, 0.0% Native Hawaiian/Other Pacific Islander, 2.1% two or more races, 0.9% Hispanic of any race; Average household size: 2.28; Median age: 45.6; Age under 18: 20.9%; Age 65 and over: 19.1%; Males per 100 females: 98.2; Marriage status: 23.1% never married, 57.9% now married, 0.7% separated, 7.3% widowed, 11.7% divorced; Foreign born: 1.2%; Speak English only: 97.7%; With disability: 17.6%; Veterans: 14.9%; Ancestry: 20.1% German, 17.3% French, 12.8% Swedish, 12.0% Irish, 8.6% French Canadian
Religion: Six largest groups: 36.0% Catholicism, 10.9% Lutheran, 3.5% Baptist, 3.1% Methodist/Pietist, 1.6% Holiness, 1.4% Episcopalianism/Anglicanism
Economy: Unemployment rate: 5.9%; Leading industries: 16.8% retail trade; 11.7% other services (except public administration); 9.7% construction; Farms: 283 totaling 70,832 acres; Company size: 1 employs 1,000 or more persons, 1 employs 500 to 999 persons, 11 employs 100 to 499 persons, 1,065 employ less than 100 persons; Business ownership: n/a women-owned, n/a Black-owned, n/a Hispanic-owned, n/a Asian-owned
Employment: 8.6% management, business, and financial, 3.5% computer, engineering, and science, 7.9% education, legal, community service, arts, and media, 7.4% healthcare practitioners, 20.1% service, 23.0% sales and office, 10.2% natural resources, construction, and maintenance, 19.4% production, transportation, and material moving
Income: Per capita: $22,471; Median household: $42,676; Average household: $51,672; Households with income of $100,000 or more: 9.8%; Poverty rate: 16.4%
Educational Attainment: High school diploma or higher: 91.4%; Bachelor's degree or higher: 18.2%; Graduate/professional degree or higher: 4.7%
Housing: Homeownership rate: 79.0%; Median home value: $100,200; Median year structure built: 1965; Homeowner vacancy rate: 2.3%; Median gross rent: $554 per month; Rental vacancy rate: 7.5%
Vital Statistics: Birth rate: 103.8 per 10,000 population; Death rate: 107.8 per 10,000 population; Age-adjusted cancer mortality rate: 201.5 deaths per 100,000 population
Health Insurance: 88.0% have insurance; 67.8% have private insurance; 39.3% have public insurance; 12.0% do not have insurance; 5.1% of children under 18 do not have insurance
Health Care: Physicians: 14.1 per 10,000 population; Hospital beds: 13.0 per 10,000 population; Hospital admissions: 552.9 per 10,000 population
Transportation: Commute: 92.3% car, 0.5% public transportation, 2.7% walk, 3.1% work from home; Median travel time to work: 18.0 minutes
Presidential Election: 46.2% Obama, 52.8% Romney (2012)
National and State Parks: Fayette Historic State Park; Hiawatha National Forest; Manistique River State Forest; Portage Marsh State Wildlife Management Area
Additional Information Contacts
Delta Government . . . . (906) 789-5105
   http://www.deltacountymi.org

Delta County Communities

BALDWIN (township). Covers a land area of 83.859 square miles and a water area of 0.348 square miles. Located at 46.00° N. Lat; 87.10° W. Long.
History: Baldwin Township was named in 1873 for C.S. Baldwin, a railroad superintendent.
Population: 759; Growth (since 2000): 1.5%; Density: 9.1 persons per square mile; Race: 93.7% White, 0.0% Black/African American, 0.0% Asian, 3.7% American Indian/Alaska Native, 0.0% Native Hawaiian/Other Pacific Islander, 2.1% Two or more races, 0.8% Hispanic of any race; Average household size: 2.34; Median age: 48.6; Age under 18: 19.6%; Age 65 and over: 15.5%; Males per 100 females: 107.9
Housing: Homeownership rate: 90.8%; Homeowner vacancy rate: 2.3%; Rental vacancy rate: 6.3%

BARK RIVER (township). Covers a land area of 45.587 square miles and a water area of 0.057 square miles. Located at 45.71° N. Lat; 87.29° W. Long. Elevation is 741 feet.
History: Bark River was named by railway engineers for the quantities of birch bark floating in the river. The village of Bark River was established in 1871 as a station on the Chicago & Northwestern Railway.
Population: 1,578; Growth (since 2000): -4.4%; Density: 34.6 persons per square mile; Race: 94.1% White, 0.4% Black/African American, 0.4% Asian, 2.9% American Indian/Alaska Native, 0.0% Native Hawaiian/Other Pacific Islander, 2.0% Two or more races, 0.4% Hispanic of any race; Average household size: 2.54; Median age: 41.4; Age under 18: 24.7%; Age 65 and over: 14.8%; Males per 100 females: 105.2
Housing: Homeownership rate: 88.3%; Homeowner vacancy rate: 1.4%; Rental vacancy rate: 10.6%

BAY DE NOC (township). Covers a land area of 67.657 square miles and a water area of 23.392 square miles. Located at 45.77° N. Lat; 86.91° W. Long.
History: Bay de Noc Township was named for the Noquet Indians who once owned the land.
Population: 305; Growth (since 2000): -7.3%; Density: 4.5 persons per square mile; Race: 96.1% White, 0.0% Black/African American, 1.3% Asian, 0.7% American Indian/Alaska Native, 0.0% Native Hawaiian/Other Pacific Islander, 2.0% Two or more races, 0.0% Hispanic of any race; Average household size: 1.89; Median age: 58.7; Age under 18: 8.5%; Age 65 and over: 32.1%; Males per 100 females: 132.8
Housing: Homeownership rate: 95.0%; Homeowner vacancy rate: 7.7%; Rental vacancy rate: 0.0%

BRAMPTON (township). Covers a land area of 23.740 square miles and a water area of 1.806 square miles. Located at 45.92° N. Lat; 87.05° W. Long. Elevation is 738 feet.
History: Promoters for the Chicago & Northwestern Railroad, trying to interest investors in the area, named it Brampton after the city in England.
Population: 1,050; Growth (since 2000): -3.7%; Density: 44.2 persons per square mile; Race: 96.4% White, 0.0% Black/African American, 0.1% Asian, 2.2% American Indian/Alaska Native, 0.0% Native Hawaiian/Other Pacific Islander, 1.3% Two or more races, 0.7% Hispanic of any race; Average household size: 2.36; Median age: 50.5; Age under 18: 18.8%; Age 65 and over: 22.9%; Males per 100 females: 105.9
Housing: Homeownership rate: 92.7%; Homeowner vacancy rate: 1.2%; Rental vacancy rate: 8.3%

COOKS (unincorporated postal area)
ZCTA: 49817
   Covers a land area of 91.785 square miles and a water area of 0.473 square miles. Located at 45.96° N. Lat; 86.46° W. Long..
   Population: 615; Growth (since 2000): 7.5%; Density: 6.7 persons per square mile; Race: 88.0% White, 0.0% Black/African American, 0.5% Asian, 8.6% American Indian/Alaska Native, 0.0% Native Hawaiian/Other Pacific Islander, 2.9% Two or more races, 1.5% Hispanic of any race; Average household size: 2.33; Median age: 49.1; Age under 18: 19.0%; Age 65 and over: 22.0%; Males per 100 females: 112.1

School District(s)
Big Bay De Noc SD (PK-12)
   2012-13 Enrollment: 239 . . . . (906) 644-2773

Housing: Homeownership rate: 91.2%; Homeowner vacancy rate: 0.8%; Rental vacancy rate: 11.1%

CORNELL (township). Covers a land area of 59.727 square miles and a water area of 0.437 square miles. Located at 45.92° N. Lat; 87.30° W. Long. Elevation is 823 feet.

History: The township and village of Cornell were named for Cornell University, the alma mater of one of the town's founder, George H. Mashek.

Population: 593; Growth (since 2000): 6.5%; Density: 9.9 persons per square mile; Race: 97.3% White, 0.2% Black/African American, 0.2% Asian, 1.0% American Indian/Alaska Native, 0.0% Native Hawaiian/Other Pacific Islander, 1.2% Two or more races, 0.2% Hispanic of any race; Average household size: 2.43; Median age: 47.6; Age under 18: 21.4%; Age 65 and over: 20.4%; Males per 100 females: 110.3

Housing: Homeownership rate: 93.8%; Homeowner vacancy rate: 1.3%; Rental vacancy rate: 6.3%

ENSIGN (township). Covers a land area of 58.960 square miles and a water area of 6.839 square miles. Located at 45.87° N. Lat; 86.87° W. Long. Elevation is 709 feet.

Population: 748; Growth (since 2000): -4.1%; Density: 12.7 persons per square mile; Race: 96.0% White, 0.0% Black/African American, 0.0% Asian, 1.1% American Indian/Alaska Native, 0.0% Native Hawaiian/Other Pacific Islander, 2.9% Two or more races, 0.5% Hispanic of any race; Average household size: 2.15; Median age: 53.4; Age under 18: 14.4%; Age 65 and over: 27.1%; Males per 100 females: 114.9

Housing: Homeownership rate: 95.1%; Homeowner vacancy rate: 4.3%; Rental vacancy rate: 0.0%

ESCANABA (city). County seat. Covers a land area of 12.875 square miles and a water area of 3.622 square miles. Located at 45.75° N. Lat; 87.08° W. Long. Elevation is 607 feet.

History: Escanaba became an important iron-ore shipping port in 1863, when the first dock was constructed by the railroad. Commercial fishing was also a part of the early economy of Escanaba.

Population: 12,616; Growth (since 2000): -4.0%; Density: 979.9 persons per square mile; Race: 93.5% White, 0.4% Black/African American, 0.6% Asian, 2.6% American Indian/Alaska Native, 0.0% Native Hawaiian/Other Pacific Islander, 2.7% Two or more races, 1.2% Hispanic of any race; Average household size: 2.14; Median age: 41.4; Age under 18: 21.4%; Age 65 and over: 19.6%; Males per 100 females: 89.0; Marriage status: 28.1% never married, 47.1% now married, 0.6% separated, 10.3% widowed, 14.5% divorced; Foreign born: 0.9%; Speak English only: 97.1%; With disability: 21.2%; Veterans: 11.8%; Ancestry: 20.7% French, 18.5% German, 11.5% Swedish, 11.1% Irish, 7.9% French Canadian

Employment: 7.2% management, business, and financial, 2.7% computer, engineering, and science, 7.8% education, legal, community service, arts, and media, 7.3% healthcare practitioners, 25.3% service, 24.2% sales and office, 7.8% natural resources, construction, and maintenance, 17.8% production, transportation, and material moving

Income: Per capita: $19,556; Median household: $27,328; Average household: $41,797; Households with income of $100,000 or more: 7.1%; Poverty rate: 26.8%

Educational Attainment: High school diploma or higher: 89.7%; Bachelor's degree or higher: 16.0%; Graduate/professional degree or higher: 3.2%

School District(s)

Delta-Schoolcraft ISD (PK-12)
    2012-13 Enrollment: 116 . . . . (906) 786-9300
Escanaba Area Public Schools (KG-12)
    2012-13 Enrollment: 2,479 . . . . (906) 786-5411
Michigan Department of Human Services (KG-12)
    2012-13 Enrollment: 46 . . . . (517) 373-2000

Two-year College(s)

Bay de Noc Community College (Public)
    Fall 2013 Enrollment: 2,305 . . . . (906) 786-5802
    2013-14 Tuition: In-state $7,126; Out-of-state $11,218

Vocational/Technical School(s)

Paul Mitchell the School-Escanaba (Private, For-profit)
    Fall 2013 Enrollment: 41 . . . . (906) 239-3222
    2013-14 Tuition: $12,000

Housing: Homeownership rate: 61.3%; Median home value: $82,500; Median year structure built: 1947; Homeowner vacancy rate: 2.3%; Median gross rent: $521 per month; Rental vacancy rate: 6.3%

Health Insurance: 83.5% have insurance; 56.8% have private insurance; 44.9% have public insurance; 16.5% do not have insurance; 8.5% of children under 18 do not have insurance

Hospitals: Saint Francis Hospital

Safety: Violent crime rate: 20.7 per 10,000 population; Property crime rate: 501.2 per 10,000 population

Newspapers: Daily Press (daily circulation 9000)

Transportation: Commute: 89.3% car, 0.5% public transportation, 5.1% walk, 3.1% work from home; Median travel time to work: 13.4 minutes; Amtrak: Bus service available.

Airports: Delta County (primary service/non-hub)

Additional Information Contacts

City of Escanaba . . . . (906) 786-9402
    http://www.escanaba.org

ESCANABA (township). Covers a land area of 59.650 square miles and a water area of 0.641 square miles. Located at 45.85° N. Lat; 87.17° W. Long. Elevation is 607 feet.

History: Settled 1852; Incorporated 1883.

Population: 3,482; Growth (since 2000): -2.9%; Density: 58.4 persons per square mile; Race: 96.0% White, 0.0% Black/African American, 0.5% Asian, 2.3% American Indian/Alaska Native, 0.0% Native Hawaiian/Other Pacific Islander, 1.1% Two or more races, 0.5% Hispanic of any race; Average household size: 2.54; Median age: 45.7; Age under 18: 21.6%; Age 65 and over: 13.9%; Males per 100 females: 105.8; Marriage status: 22.0% never married, 62.8% now married, 0.0% separated, 2.9% widowed, 12.3% divorced; Foreign born: 1.0%; Speak English only: 98.7%; With disability: 11.6%; Veterans: 15.6%; Ancestry: 18.3% German, 15.3% Swedish, 15.1% French Canadian, 13.8% French, 11.4% Irish

Employment: 9.3% management, business, and financial, 4.6% computer, engineering, and science, 11.3% education, legal, community service, arts, and media, 7.2% healthcare practitioners, 11.8% service, 19.5% sales and office, 13.0% natural resources, construction, and maintenance, 23.2% production, transportation, and material moving

Income: Per capita: $29,260; Median household: $63,015; Average household: $69,052; Households with income of $100,000 or more: 13.7%; Poverty rate: 9.2%

Educational Attainment: High school diploma or higher: 94.6%; Bachelor's degree or higher: 19.0%; Graduate/professional degree or higher: 8.2%

School District(s)

Delta-Schoolcraft ISD (PK-12)
    2012-13 Enrollment: 116 . . . . (906) 786-9300
Escanaba Area Public Schools (KG-12)
    2012-13 Enrollment: 2,479 . . . . (906) 786-5411
Michigan Department of Human Services (KG-12)
    2012-13 Enrollment: 46 . . . . (517) 373-2000

Two-year College(s)

Bay de Noc Community College (Public)
    Fall 2013 Enrollment: 2,305 . . . . (906) 786-5802
    2013-14 Tuition: In-state $7,126; Out-of-state $11,218

Vocational/Technical School(s)

Paul Mitchell the School-Escanaba (Private, For-profit)
    Fall 2013 Enrollment: 41 . . . . (906) 239-3222
    2013-14 Tuition: $12,000

Housing: Homeownership rate: 95.5%; Median home value: $156,200; Median year structure built: 1978; Homeowner vacancy rate: 1.8%; Median gross rent: $646 per month; Rental vacancy rate: 12.9%

Health Insurance: 92.9% have insurance; 83.8% have private insurance; 21.7% have public insurance; 7.1% do not have insurance; 0.0% of children under 18 do not have insurance

Hospitals: Saint Francis Hospital

Newspapers: Daily Press (daily circulation 9000)

Transportation: Commute: 96.0% car, 0.0% public transportation, 0.0% walk, 2.2% work from home; Median travel time to work: 15.7 minutes; Amtrak: Bus service available.

Airports: Delta County (primary service/non-hub)

FAIRBANKS (township). Covers a land area of 47.337 square miles and a water area of 251.876 square miles. Located at 45.61° N. Lat; 86.69° W. Long.

Population: 281; Growth (since 2000): -12.5%; Density: 5.9 persons per square mile; Race: 86.8% White, 0.0% Black/African American, 0.0% Asian, 6.0% American Indian/Alaska Native, 1.4% Native Hawaiian/Other Pacific Islander, 5.0% Two or more races, 1.1% Hispanic of any race;

Average household size: 2.10; Median age: 55.2; Age under 18: 17.4%; Age 65 and over: 25.6%; Males per 100 females: 99.3
Housing: Homeownership rate: 91.1%; Homeowner vacancy rate: 2.4%; Rental vacancy rate: 23.5%

FORD RIVER (township).
Covers a land area of 64.884 square miles and a water area of 0.357 square miles. Located at 45.67° N. Lat; 87.21° W. Long. Elevation is 584 feet.
History: Ford River Township was named for Thomas Ford, a governor of Illinois and an explorer of the Upper Peninsula in the 1840's. Ford wrote a history of Michigan in which he described the river.
Population: 2,054; Growth (since 2000): -8.3%; Density: 31.7 persons per square mile; Race: 97.0% White, 0.0% Black/African American, 0.1% Asian, 1.8% American Indian/Alaska Native, 0.0% Native Hawaiian/Other Pacific Islander, 1.1% Two or more races, 0.6% Hispanic of any race; Average household size: 2.29; Median age: 49.9; Age under 18: 17.5%; Age 65 and over: 19.0%; Males per 100 females: 109.8
Housing: Homeownership rate: 90.5%; Homeowner vacancy rate: 2.6%; Rental vacancy rate: 9.5%

GARDEN (township).
Covers a land area of 159.837 square miles and a water area of 24.345 square miles. Located at 45.94° N. Lat; 86.53° W. Long. Elevation is 591 feet.
History: Garden Township was named for the good soil that made it a garden spot on the Upper Peninsula.
Population: 750; Growth (since 2000): -8.2%; Density: 4.7 persons per square mile; Race: 90.4% White, 0.0% Black/African American, 0.3% Asian, 4.5% American Indian/Alaska Native, 0.0% Native Hawaiian/Other Pacific Islander, 4.8% Two or more races, 1.3% Hispanic of any race; Average household size: 2.08; Median age: 53.8; Age under 18: 15.5%; Age 65 and over: 27.3%; Males per 100 females: 116.1
Housing: Homeownership rate: 91.4%; Homeowner vacancy rate: 2.1%; Rental vacancy rate: 5.9%

GARDEN (village).
Covers a land area of 0.810 square miles and a water area of 0.209 square miles. Located at 45.77° N. Lat; 86.56° W. Long. Elevation is 591 feet.
History: Garden was established on the peninsula that creates Big Bay de Noc from a corner of Lake Michigan. Philomen Thompson built a cabin here in 1850, and was joined by other settlers of French ancestry. The village was incorporated in 1886.
Population: 221; Growth (since 2000): -7.9%; Density: 272.7 persons per square mile; Race: 87.3% White, 0.0% Black/African American, 0.0% Asian, 5.0% American Indian/Alaska Native, 0.0% Native Hawaiian/Other Pacific Islander, 7.7% Two or more races, 0.5% Hispanic of any race; Average household size: 2.21; Median age: 49.4; Age under 18: 21.3%; Age 65 and over: 22.2%; Males per 100 females: 108.5
Housing: Homeownership rate: 82.9%; Homeowner vacancy rate: 4.7%; Rental vacancy rate: 5.3%

GLADSTONE (city).
Covers a land area of 5.003 square miles and a water area of 2.924 square miles. Located at 45.85° N. Lat; 87.03° W. Long. Elevation is 604 feet.
History: Gladstone was founded in 1887 as a railroad shipping center for grain shipments. The city was incorporated in 1889. A cooperage company was founded here in 1892 and expanded into the making of hardwood flooring. Gladstone was named for William E. Gladstone, British prime minister.
Population: 4,973; Growth (since 2000): -1.2%; Density: 993.9 persons per square mile; Race: 95.4% White, 0.2% Black/African American, 0.3% Asian, 1.9% American Indian/Alaska Native, 0.0% Native Hawaiian/Other Pacific Islander, 1.8% Two or more races, 1.0% Hispanic of any race; Average household size: 2.27; Median age: 43.6; Age under 18: 22.7%; Age 65 and over: 21.1%; Males per 100 females: 91.1; Marriage status: 20.7% never married, 56.0% now married, 1.3% separated, 8.8% widowed, 14.5% divorced; Foreign born: 3.3%; Speak English only: 96.6%; With disability: 19.4%; Veterans: 16.3%; Ancestry: 21.6% German, 19.8% Irish, 14.3% French, 12.0% Swedish, 10.0% English
Employment: 8.2% management, business, and financial, 5.0% computer, engineering, and science, 7.5% education, legal, community service, arts, and media, 9.6% healthcare practitioners, 19.6% service, 25.1% sales and office, 9.5% natural resources, construction, and maintenance, 15.5% production, transportation, and material moving

Income: Per capita: $22,347; Median household: $42,936; Average household: $52,680; Households with income of $100,000 or more: 9.6%; Poverty rate: 10.7%
Educational Attainment: High school diploma or higher: 92.4%; Bachelor's degree or higher: 23.9%; Graduate/professional degree or higher: 5.9%
School District(s)
Gladstone Area Schools (KG-12)
    2012-13 Enrollment: 1,497 . . . . (906) 428-2417
Housing: Homeownership rate: 76.8%; Median home value: $79,800; Median year structure built: 1958; Homeowner vacancy rate: 2.5%; Median gross rent: $516 per month; Rental vacancy rate: 9.0%
Health Insurance: 87.7% have insurance; 68.5% have private insurance; 40.2% have public insurance; 12.3% do not have insurance; 4.8% of children under 18 do not have insurance
Safety: Violent crime rate: 10.2 per 10,000 population; Property crime rate: 158.7 per 10,000 population
Transportation: Commute: 88.9% car, 0.4% public transportation, 5.2% walk, 4.4% work from home; Median travel time to work: 16.1 minutes
Additional Information Contacts
City of Gladstone. . . . . (906) 428-2311
    http://www.gladstonemi.org

MAPLE RIDGE (township).
Covers a land area of 108.257 square miles and a water area of 0 square miles. Located at 46.09° N. Lat; 87.14° W. Long.
Population: 766; Growth (since 2000): -5.2%; Density: 7.1 persons per square mile; Race: 97.7% White, 0.0% Black/African American, 0.3% Asian, 1.0% American Indian/Alaska Native, 0.0% Native Hawaiian/Other Pacific Islander, 0.9% Two or more races, 1.0% Hispanic of any race; Average household size: 2.27; Median age: 47.9; Age under 18: 20.1%; Age 65 and over: 19.3%; Males per 100 females: 108.2
Housing: Homeownership rate: 92.9%; Homeowner vacancy rate: 4.3%; Rental vacancy rate: 7.7%

MASONVILLE (township).
Covers a land area of 167.797 square miles and a water area of 2.654 square miles. Located at 46.04° N. Lat; 86.89° W. Long. Elevation is 600 feet.
History: Masonville was the site of the first sawmill in Delta County, built in 1847 by Darius Clark.
Population: 1,734; Growth (since 2000): -7.6%; Density: 10.3 persons per square mile; Race: 92.7% White, 0.1% Black/African American, 0.2% Asian, 3.2% American Indian/Alaska Native, 0.0% Native Hawaiian/Other Pacific Islander, 3.9% Two or more races, 0.8% Hispanic of any race; Average household size: 2.27; Median age: 49.1; Age under 18: 20.2%; Age 65 and over: 19.4%; Males per 100 females: 105.5
Housing: Homeownership rate: 85.1%; Homeowner vacancy rate: 3.0%; Rental vacancy rate: 16.2%

NAHMA (township).
Covers a land area of 166.370 square miles and a water area of 22.480 square miles. Located at 45.97° N. Lat; 86.72° W. Long. Elevation is 587 feet.
History: The name of Nahma is of Indian origin meaning "sturgeon." The town, located at the mouth of the Sturgeon River, developed as a sawmill village.
Population: 495; Growth (since 2000): -0.8%; Density: 3.0 persons per square mile; Race: 95.8% White, 0.2% Black/African American, 0.0% Asian, 3.4% American Indian/Alaska Native, 0.0% Native Hawaiian/Other Pacific Islander, 0.2% Two or more races, 0.2% Hispanic of any race; Average household size: 2.13; Median age: 53.9; Age under 18: 15.6%; Age 65 and over: 29.1%; Males per 100 females: 102.0
Housing: Homeownership rate: 90.9%; Homeowner vacancy rate: 5.7%; Rental vacancy rate: 19.2%

PERKINS (unincorporated postal area)
ZCTA: 49872
    Covers a land area of 18.959 square miles and a water area of 0 square miles. Located at 46.02° N. Lat; 87.08° W. Long. Elevation is 784 feet.
    Population: 206; Growth (since 2000): 249.2%; Density: 10.9 persons per square mile; Race: 91.7% White, 0.0% Black/African American, 0.0% Asian, 6.3% American Indian/Alaska Native, 0.0% Native Hawaiian/Other Pacific Islander, 1.0% Two or more races, 1.5% Hispanic of any race; Average household size: 2.29; Median age: 46.2; Age under 18: 20.9%; Age 65 and over: 17.5%; Males per 100 females: 108.1

Housing: Homeownership rate: 86.7%; Homeowner vacancy rate: 2.5%; Rental vacancy rate: 14.3%

ROCK (unincorporated postal area)
ZCTA: 49880

Covers a land area of 216.344 square miles and a water area of 0.851 square miles. Located at 46.11° N. Lat; 87.22° W. Long. Elevation is 968 feet.

Population: 1,142; Growth (since 2000): -5.9%; Density: 5.3 persons per square mile; Race: 96.8% White, 0.0% Black/African American, 0.4% Asian, 1.5% American Indian/Alaska Native, 0.0% Native Hawaiian/Other Pacific Islander, 1.1% Two or more races, 0.9% Hispanic of any race; Average household size: 2.27; Median age: 49.3; Age under 18: 18.7%; Age 65 and over: 19.2%; Males per 100 females: 106.9

School District(s)
Mid Peninsula SD (PK-12)
2012-13 Enrollment: 230. . . . . (906) 359-4387
Housing: Homeownership rate: 93.0%; Homeowner vacancy rate: 3.5%; Rental vacancy rate: 5.4%

WELLS (township). Covers a land area of 39.555 square miles and a water area of 0.351 square miles. Located at 45.78° N. Lat; 87.17° W. Long. Elevation is 630 feet.

Population: 4,885; Growth (since 2000): -3.2%; Density: 123.5 persons per square mile; Race: 96.3% White, 0.0% Black/African American, 0.3% Asian, 1.8% American Indian/Alaska Native, 0.0% Native Hawaiian/Other Pacific Islander, 1.5% Two or more races, 0.5% Hispanic of any race; Average household size: 2.49; Median age: 45.7; Age under 18: 21.5%; Age 65 and over: 16.0%; Males per 100 females: 103.1; Marriage status: 18.6% never married, 70.5% now married, 0.7% separated, 4.8% widowed, 6.1% divorced; Foreign born: 0.2%; Speak English only: 99.2%; With disability: 15.2%; Veterans: 20.1%; Ancestry: 21.3% German, 16.7% French, 13.1% Swedish, 10.7% French Canadian, 7.7% Irish
Employment: 6.4% management, business, and financial, 2.3% computer, engineering, and science, 8.1% education, legal, community service, arts, and media, 7.5% healthcare practitioners, 18.0% service, 24.9% sales and office, 7.9% natural resources, construction, and maintenance, 25.0% production, transportation, and material moving
Income: Per capita: $23,425; Median household: $54,288; Average household: $60,237; Households with income of $100,000 or more: 11.5%; Poverty rate: 11.6%
Educational Attainment: High school diploma or higher: 90.5%; Bachelor's degree or higher: 16.3%; Graduate/professional degree or higher: 3.2%
Housing: Homeownership rate: 92.2%; Median home value: $118,400; Median year structure built: 1974; Homeowner vacancy rate: 1.3%; Median gross rent: $679 per month; Rental vacancy rate: 6.1%
Health Insurance: 94.3% have insurance; 75.7% have private insurance; 38.9% have public insurance; 5.7% do not have insurance; 3.4% of children under 18 do not have insurance
Transportation: Commute: 96.3% car, 1.1% public transportation, 0.0% walk, 1.6% work from home; Median travel time to work: 15.7 minutes

Dickinson County

Located in northwestern Michigan on the Upper Peninsula; bounded on the southwest by Wisconsin; drained by the Menominee, Ford, and Escanaba Rivers. Covers a land area of 761.400 square miles, a water area of 15.650 square miles, and is located in the Central Time Zone at 46.01° N. Lat., 87.87° W. Long. The county was founded in 1891. County seat is Iron Mountain.

Dickinson County is part of the Iron Mountain, MI-WI Micropolitan Statistical Area. The entire metro area includes: Dickinson County, MI; Florence County, WI

Weather Station: Iron Mtn-Kingsford WWTP   Elevation: 1,060 feet

	Jan	Feb	Mar	Apr	May	Jun	Jul	Aug	Sep	Oct	Nov	Dec
High	24	29	39	54	67	76	80	78	70	56	41	28
Low	3	6	17	30	41	51	56	54	46	34	24	11
Precip	1.3	1.0	1.6	2.3	3.0	3.3	3.4	3.5	3.5	3.1	1.9	1.5
Snow	14.2	9.4	10.6	4.6	0.6	0.0	0.0	0.0	tr	0.7	5.8	13.8

High and Low temperatures in degrees Fahrenheit; Precipitation and Snow in inches

Population: 26,168; Growth (since 2000): -4.7%; Density: 34.4 persons per square mile; Race: 97.2% White, 0.3% Black/African American, 0.5% Asian, 0.6% American Indian/Alaska Native, 0.0% Native Hawaiian/Other Pacific Islander, 1.2% two or more races, 1.0% Hispanic of any race; Average household size: 2.26; Median age: 45.4; Age under 18: 21.4%; Age 65 and over: 19.0%; Males per 100 females: 96.9; Marriage status: 22.6% never married, 58.8% now married, 0.9% separated, 7.9% widowed, 10.8% divorced; Foreign born: 1.4%; Speak English only: 97.4%; With disability: 15.3%; Veterans: 13.6%; Ancestry: 23.0% German, 15.9% Italian, 13.2% Swedish, 11.4% French, 11.2% Irish
Religion: Six largest groups: 35.7% Catholicism, 15.0% Lutheran, 6.8% Methodist/Pietist, 2.8% Baptist, 2.3% Presbyterian-Reformed, 1.5% Pentecostal
Economy: Unemployment rate: 5.0%; Leading industries: 17.2% retail trade; 13.1% health care and social assistance; 11.1% other services (except public administration); Farms: 162 totaling 28,614 acres; Company size: 1 employs 1,000 or more persons, 3 employ 500 to 999 persons, 11 employs 100 to 499 persons, 880 employ less than 100 persons; Business ownership: n/a women-owned, n/a Black-owned, n/a Hispanic-owned, n/a Asian-owned
Employment: 9.4% management, business, and financial, 2.6% computer, engineering, and science, 9.9% education, legal, community service, arts, and media, 6.3% healthcare practitioners, 17.6% service, 27.1% sales and office, 10.3% natural resources, construction, and maintenance, 16.7% production, transportation, and material moving
Income: Per capita: $24,611; Median household: $44,136; Average household: $55,951; Households with income of $100,000 or more: 12.2%; Poverty rate: 12.7%
Educational Attainment: High school diploma or higher: 93.8%; Bachelor's degree or higher: 20.0%; Graduate/professional degree or higher: 6.1%
Housing: Homeownership rate: 80.2%; Median home value: $85,500; Median year structure built: 1961; Homeowner vacancy rate: 2.6%; Median gross rent: $586 per month; Rental vacancy rate: 9.1%
Vital Statistics: Birth rate: 95.0 per 10,000 population; Death rate: 115.7 per 10,000 population; Age-adjusted cancer mortality rate: 163.7 deaths per 100,000 population
Health Insurance: 88.9% have insurance; 70.3% have private insurance; 38.8% have public insurance; 11.1% do not have insurance; 5.6% of children under 18 do not have insurance
Health Care: Physicians 24.7 per 10,000 population; Hospital beds: 43.3 per 10,000 population; Hospital admissions: 1,520.8 per 10,000 population
Transportation: Commute: 92.0% car, 0.1% public transportation, 3.2% walk, 3.3% work from home; Median travel time to work: 15.2 minutes
Presidential Election: 38.7% Obama, 60.1% Romney (2012)
National and State Parks: Sturgeon River State Forest
Additional Information Contacts
Dickinson Government . . . . (906) 774-0988
  http://www.dickinsoncountymi.gov

Dickinson County Communities

BREEN (township). Covers a land area of 86.688 square miles and a water area of 1.690 square miles. Located at 45.98° N. Lat; 87.70° W. Long.

Population: 499; Growth (since 2000): 4.2%; Density: 5.8 persons per square mile; Race: 96.2% White, 0.0% Black/African American, 0.0% Asian, 2.4% American Indian/Alaska Native, 0.0% Native Hawaiian/Other Pacific Islander, 1.4% Two or more races, 0.0% Hispanic of any race; Average household size: 2.41; Median age: 45.1; Age under 18: 25.1%; Age 65 and over: 18.6%; Males per 100 females: 105.3
Housing: Homeownership rate: 87.5%; Homeowner vacancy rate: 4.7%; Rental vacancy rate: 3.4%

BREITUNG (charter township). Covers a land area of 64.266 square miles and a water area of 3.621 square miles. Located at 45.87° N. Lat; 88.00° W. Long.

Population: 5,853; Growth (since 2000): -1.3%; Density: 91.1 persons per square mile; Race: 97.6% White, 0.4% Black/African American, 0.4% Asian, 0.4% American Indian/Alaska Native, 0.1% Native Hawaiian/Other Pacific Islander, 0.9% Two or more races, 0.7% Hispanic of any race; Average household size: 2.35; Median age: 48.7; Age under 18: 20.0%; Age 65 and over: 19.4%; Males per 100 females: 101.1; Marriage status: 23.0% never married, 63.1% now married, 0.3% separated, 6.3% widowed, 7.6% divorced; Foreign born: 1.1%; Speak English only: 97.9%;

With disability: 15.7%; Veterans: 12.8%; Ancestry: 23.6% German, 15.8% Swedish, 14.9% Italian, 12.8% French, 10.3% English

Employment: 9.3% management, business, and financial, 2.5% computer, engineering, and science, 12.7% education, legal, community service, arts, and media, 7.5% healthcare practitioners, 18.0% service, 28.8% sales and office, 9.9% natural resources, construction, and maintenance, 11.3% production, transportation, and material moving

Income: Per capita: $29,382; Median household: $50,296; Average household: $72,353; Households with income of $100,000 or more: 19.3%; Poverty rate: 8.3%

Educational Attainment: High school diploma or higher: 94.0%; Bachelor's degree or higher: 24.5%; Graduate/professional degree or higher: 9.2%

Housing: Homeownership rate: 93.2%; Median home value: $114,100; Median year structure built: 1975; Homeowner vacancy rate: 1.5%; Median gross rent: $677 per month; Rental vacancy rate: 9.1%

Health Insurance: 91.8% have insurance; 75.1% have private insurance; 38.1% have public insurance; 8.2% do not have insurance; 2.7% of children under 18 do not have insurance

Transportation: Commute: 94.0% car, 0.0% public transportation, 0.4% walk, 3.6% work from home; Median travel time to work: 13.6 minutes

CHANNING (unincorporated postal area)

ZCTA: 49815

Covers a land area of 117.398 square miles and a water area of 2.023 square miles. Located at 46.19° N. Lat; 87.96° W. Long. Elevation is 1,401 feet.

Population: 488; Growth (since 2000): -10.3%; Density: 4.2 persons per square mile; Race: 99.4% White, 0.0% Black/African American, 0.2% Asian, 0.2% American Indian/Alaska Native, 0.0% Native Hawaiian/Other Pacific Islander, 0.2% Two or more races, 0.4% Hispanic of any race; Average household size: 2.21; Median age: 51.0; Age under 18: 19.1%; Age 65 and over: 22.5%; Males per 100 females: 107.7

Housing: Homeownership rate: 90.0%; Homeowner vacancy rate: 0.5%; Rental vacancy rate: 4.3%

FELCH (township).
Covers a land area of 141.842 square miles and a water area of 1.971 square miles. Located at 46.08° N. Lat; 87.87° W. Long. Elevation is 1,204 feet.

Population: 752; Growth (since 2000): 3.6%; Density: 5.3 persons per square mile; Race: 98.4% White, 0.0% Black/African American, 0.4% Asian, 0.1% American Indian/Alaska Native, 0.0% Native Hawaiian/Other Pacific Islander, 0.9% Two or more races, 0.1% Hispanic of any race; Average household size: 2.37; Median age: 45.8; Age under 18: 21.4%; Age 65 and over: 18.9%; Males per 100 females: 109.5

School District(s)

North Dickinson County Schools (KG-12)

    2012-13 Enrollment: 300 . . . . (906) 542-9281

Housing: Homeownership rate: 89.6%; Homeowner vacancy rate: 5.0%; Rental vacancy rate: 13.2%

FOSTER CITY (unincorporated postal area)

ZCTA: 49834

Covers a land area of 36.062 square miles and a water area of 0.660 square miles. Located at 45.95° N. Lat; 87.77° W. Long. Elevation is 1,033 feet.

Population: 284; Growth (since 2000): 1.8%; Density: 7.9 persons per square mile; Race: 95.8% White, 0.0% Black/African American, 0.0% Asian, 3.2% American Indian/Alaska Native, 0.0% Native Hawaiian/Other Pacific Islander, 1.1% Two or more races, 0.0% Hispanic of any race; Average household size: 2.51; Median age: 44.7; Age under 18: 27.1%; Age 65 and over: 19.7%; Males per 100 females: 113.5

Housing: Homeownership rate: 87.6%; Homeowner vacancy rate: 2.0%; Rental vacancy rate: 5.9%

IRON MOUNTAIN (city).
County seat. Covers a land area of 7.368 square miles and a water area of 0.671 square miles. Located at 45.83° N. Lat; 88.06° W. Long. Elevation is 1,138 feet.

History: Iron Mountain was named for the nearby bluff that was stratified with iron ore. The city developed as a manufacturing and distribution point for the Menominee Range district, which produced hematite. Mining declined here in the 1930's.

Population: 7,624; Growth (since 2000): -6.5%; Density: 1,034.7 persons per square mile; Race: 96.3% White, 0.5% Black/African American, 0.7% Asian, 0.6% American Indian/Alaska Native, 0.0% Native Hawaiian/Other Pacific Islander, 1.7% Two or more races, 1.6% Hispanic of any race; Average household size: 2.21; Median age: 42.4; Age under 18: 22.6%; Age 65 and over: 17.2%; Males per 100 females: 96.7; Marriage status: 22.8% never married, 56.6% now married, 1.0% separated, 7.8% widowed, 12.9% divorced; Foreign born: 1.3%; Speak English only: 97.4%; With disability: 15.5%; Veterans: 11.8%; Ancestry: 24.0% German, 17.3% Italian, 13.4% Irish, 11.8% Swedish, 10.9% Polish

Employment: 11.7% management, business, and financial, 2.5% computer, engineering, and science, 9.3% education, legal, community service, arts, and media, 5.2% healthcare practitioners, 16.9% service, 27.9% sales and office, 9.3% natural resources, construction, and maintenance, 17.1% production, transportation, and material moving

Income: Per capita: $22,855; Median household: $38,351; Average household: $50,864; Households with income of $100,000 or more: 10.4%; Poverty rate: 12.2%

Educational Attainment: High school diploma or higher: 93.6%; Bachelor's degree or higher: 23.1%; Graduate/professional degree or higher: 5.7%

School District(s)

Iron Mountain Public Schools (PK-12)

    2012-13 Enrollment: 1,106 . . . . (906) 779-2600

Housing: Homeownership rate: 70.4%; Median home value: $76,000; Median year structure built: 1948; Homeowner vacancy rate: 3.5%; Median gross rent: $534 per month; Rental vacancy rate: 9.0%

Health Insurance: 89.4% have insurance; 69.7% have private insurance; 38.8% have public insurance; 10.6% do not have insurance; 2.1% of children under 18 do not have insurance

Hospitals: Dickinson County Memorial Hospital (96 beds); Iron Mountain MI VA Medical Center (61 beds)

Newspapers: Daily News (daily circulation 9100)

Transportation: Commute: 90.9% car, 0.1% public transportation, 3.6% walk, 3.9% work from home; Median travel time to work: 12.5 minutes

Airports: Ford (primary service/non-hub)

Additional Information Contacts

City of Iron Mountain . . . . (906) 774-8530

    http://cityofironmountain.com

KINGSFORD (city).
Covers a land area of 4.322 square miles and a water area of 0.257 square miles. Located at 45.81° N. Lat; 88.10° W. Long. Elevation is 1,099 feet.

History: Kingsford was planned around the Ford Motor Company plant, and was named for a Ford Company official, Edward G. Kingsford. Kingsford was incorporated as a village in 1924 and as a city in 1947. Ford's holdings here included a sawmill, a chemical plant, a hydroelectric plant on the Menominee River, and several plants that made wood parts for the cars.

Population: 5,133; Growth (since 2000): -7.5%; Density: 1,187.6 persons per square mile; Race: 97.2% White, 0.4% Black/African American, 0.5% Asian, 0.4% American Indian/Alaska Native, 0.0% Native Hawaiian/Other Pacific Islander, 1.2% Two or more races, 1.1% Hispanic of any race; Average household size: 2.22; Median age: 44.0; Age under 18: 21.7%; Age 65 and over: 20.7%; Males per 100 females: 87.2; Marriage status: 19.8% never married, 55.0% now married, 1.4% separated, 10.7% widowed, 14.5% divorced; Foreign born: 2.1%; Speak English only: 96.8%; With disability: 14.3%; Veterans: 15.8%; Ancestry: 20.3% German, 12.5% Italian, 12.1% Irish, 11.7% Swedish, 10.0% Polish

Employment: 9.6% management, business, and financial, 2.8% computer, engineering, and science, 14.3% education, legal, community service, arts, and media, 5.6% healthcare practitioners, 16.8% service, 26.9% sales and office, 10.3% natural resources, construction, and maintenance, 13.5% production, transportation, and material moving

Income: Per capita: $24,736; Median household: $37,188; Average household: $53,037; Households with income of $100,000 or more: 9.7%; Poverty rate: 17.3%

Educational Attainment: High school diploma or higher: 94.8%; Bachelor's degree or higher: 18.1%; Graduate/professional degree or higher: 5.0%

School District(s)

Breitung Township SD (PK-12)

    2012-13 Enrollment: 1,658 . . . . (906) 779-2650

Dickinson-Iron ISD (PK-12)

    2012-13 Enrollment: 161 . . . . (906) 779-2690

Housing: Homeownership rate: 74.0%; Median home value: $70,900; Median year structure built: 1954; Homeowner vacancy rate: 2.3%; Median gross rent: $627 per month; Rental vacancy rate: 6.4%
Health Insurance: 88.7% have insurance; 67.1% have private insurance; 40.5% have public insurance; 11.3% do not have insurance; 2.4% of children under 18 do not have insurance
Transportation: Commute: 87.3% car, 0.4% public transportation, 8.6% walk, 2.4% work from home; Median travel time to work: 12.2 minutes

LORETTO (unincorporated postal area)
ZCTA: 49852
Covers a land area of 0.237 square miles and a water area of 0.030 square miles. Located at 45.79° N. Lat; 87.82° W. Long. Elevation is 899 feet.
Population: 120; Growth (since 2000): 4.3%; Density: 506.0 persons per square mile; Race: 95.8% White, 0.0% Black/African American, 0.0% Asian, 1.7% American Indian/Alaska Native, 0.0% Native Hawaiian/Other Pacific Islander, 2.5% Two or more races, 0.0% Hispanic of any race; Average household size: 2.18; Median age: 45.0; Age under 18: 20.8%; Age 65 and over: 27.5%; Males per 100 females: 93.5
Housing: Homeownership rate: 87.2%; Homeowner vacancy rate: 3.9%; Rental vacancy rate: 0.0%

NORWAY (city). Covers a land area of 8.724 square miles and a water area of 0.083 square miles. Located at 45.81° N. Lat; 87.92° W. Long. Elevation is 955 feet.
History: Norway came into existence because of the Vulcan hematite vein, where mining began in 1877.
Population: 2,845; Growth (since 2000): -3.9%; Density: 326.1 persons per square mile; Race: 97.4% White, 0.0% Black/African American, 0.2% Asian, 0.8% American Indian/Alaska Native, 0.0% Native Hawaiian/Other Pacific Islander, 1.4% Two or more races, 1.4% Hispanic of any race; Average household size: 2.25; Median age: 41.9; Age under 18: 23.5%; Age 65 and over: 18.5%; Males per 100 females: 93.5; Marriage status: 33.6% never married, 49.1% now married, 1.4% separated, 7.7% widowed, 9.6% divorced; Foreign born: 1.6%; Speak English only: 95.1%; With disability: 17.1%; Veterans: 12.7%; Ancestry: 24.9% Italian, 23.8% German, 21.1% French, 12.2% Irish, 10.9% Swedish
Employment: 1.9% management, business, and financial, 0.0% computer, engineering, and science, 5.5% education, legal, community service, arts, and media, 2.8% healthcare practitioners, 19.2% service, 32.3% sales and office, 8.6% natural resources, construction, and maintenance, 29.6% production, transportation, and material moving
Income: Per capita: $18,420; Median household: $37,443; Average household: $41,296; Households with income of $100,000 or more: 5.7%; Poverty rate: 17.2%
Educational Attainment: High school diploma or higher: 91.0%; Bachelor's degree or higher: 12.8%; Graduate/professional degree or higher: 5.1%
School District(s)
Norway-Vulcan Area Schools (PK-12)
    2012-13 Enrollment: 724 . . . . (906) 563-9552
Housing: Homeownership rate: 76.0%; Median home value: $62,500; Median year structure built: 1949; Homeowner vacancy rate: 2.9%; Median gross rent: $568 per month; Rental vacancy rate: 9.8%
Health Insurance: 77.9% have insurance; 57.0% have private insurance; 40.2% have public insurance; 22.1% do not have insurance; 28.0% of children under 18 do not have insurance
Newspapers: The Current (weekly circulation 1500)
Transportation: Commute: 97.0% car, 0.0% public transportation, 2.0% walk, 1.1% work from home; Median travel time to work: 15.2 minutes
Additional Information Contacts
City of Norway . . . . (906) 563-9961
    http://www.norwaymi.com

NORWAY (township). Covers a land area of 88.523 square miles and a water area of 2.190 square miles. Located at 45.87° N. Lat; 87.88° W. Long. Elevation is 955 feet.
History: Norway Spring, artesian spring created in 1903 by 1,904 foot drill-hole made in search of iron deposits. Settled c.1879, incorporated 1891.
Population: 1,489; Growth (since 2000): -9.2%; Density: 16.8 persons per square mile; Race: 98.6% White, 0.1% Black/African American, 0.3% Asian, 0.0% American Indian/Alaska Native, 0.0% Native Hawaiian/Other

Pacific Islander, 0.9% Two or more races, 0.4% Hispanic of any race; Average household size: 2.36; Median age: 47.8; Age under 18: 19.1%; Age 65 and over: 19.3%; Males per 100 females: 104.0
School District(s)
Norway-Vulcan Area Schools (PK-12)
    2012-13 Enrollment: 724 . . . . (906) 563-9552
Housing: Homeownership rate: 90.7%; Homeowner vacancy rate: 2.1%; Rental vacancy rate: 32.6%
Newspapers: The Current (weekly circulation 1500)

QUINNESEC (CDP). Covers a land area of 1.094 square miles and a water area of 0.084 square miles. Located at 45.80° N. Lat; 87.99° W. Long. Elevation is 1,040 feet.
History: Quinnesec developed as a mining town in the Menominee Range, with ore being extracted here as early as 1873.
Population: 1,191; Growth (since 2000): 0.3%; Density: 1,088.7 persons per square mile; Race: 97.2% White, 1.0% Black/African American, 0.3% Asian, 0.5% American Indian/Alaska Native, 0.0% Native Hawaiian/Other Pacific Islander, 0.7% Two or more races, 0.7% Hispanic of any race; Average household size: 2.52; Median age: 45.5; Age under 18: 21.5%; Age 65 and over: 15.1%; Males per 100 females: 101.5
Housing: Homeownership rate: 94.9%; Homeowner vacancy rate: 0.9%; Rental vacancy rate: 22.6%

RALPH (unincorporated postal area)
ZCTA: 49877
Covers a land area of 121.783 square miles and a water area of 0.431 square miles. Located at 46.15° N. Lat; 87.71° W. Long. Elevation is 1,138 feet.
Population: 67; Growth (since 2000): 31.4%; Density: 0.6 persons per square mile; Race: 98.5% White, 0.0% Black/African American, 0.0% Asian, 1.5% American Indian/Alaska Native, 0.0% Native Hawaiian/Other Pacific Islander, 0.0% Two or more races, 1.5% Hispanic of any race; Average household size: 2.03; Median age: 57.5; Age under 18: 16.4%; Age 65 and over: 28.4%; Males per 100 females: 116.1
Housing: Homeownership rate: 97.0%; Homeowner vacancy rate: 5.9%; Rental vacancy rate: 0.0%

SAGOLA (township). Covers a land area of 159.709 square miles and a water area of 3.037 square miles. Located at 46.11° N. Lat; 88.04° W. Long. Elevation is 1,434 feet.
History: Sagola grew around the Sagola Lumber Company operation, begun in the 1880's. The name comes from the Indian word for welcome.
Population: 1,106; Growth (since 2000): -5.4%; Density: 6.9 persons per square mile; Race: 98.3% White, 0.4% Black/African American, 0.3% Asian, 0.7% American Indian/Alaska Native, 0.0% Native Hawaiian/Other Pacific Islander, 0.4% Two or more races, 0.3% Hispanic of any race; Average household size: 2.24; Median age: 49.4; Age under 18: 19.4%; Age 65 and over: 20.2%; Males per 100 females: 106.0
Housing: Homeownership rate: 90.1%; Homeowner vacancy rate: 1.8%; Rental vacancy rate: 3.9%

VULCAN (unincorporated postal area)
ZCTA: 49892
Covers a land area of 162.873 square miles and a water area of 3.459 square miles. Located at 45.82° N. Lat; 87.79° W. Long. Elevation is 955 feet.
Population: 1,948; Growth (since 2000): -4.8%; Density: 12.0 persons per square mile; Race: 98.6% White, 0.1% Black/African American, 0.2% Asian, 0.2% American Indian/Alaska Native, 0.0% Native Hawaiian/Other Pacific Islander, 0.9% Two or more races, 0.3% Hispanic of any race; Average household size: 2.27; Median age: 49.2; Age under 18: 18.1%; Age 65 and over: 18.7%; Males per 100 females: 106.4
Housing: Homeownership rate: 91.0%; Homeowner vacancy rate: 1.9%; Rental vacancy rate: 16.1%

WAUCEDAH (township). Covers a land area of 88.502 square miles and a water area of 1.739 square miles. Located at 45.83° N. Lat; 87.76° W. Long. Elevation is 899 feet.
Population: 804; Growth (since 2000): 0.5%; Density: 9.1 persons per square mile; Race: 98.1% White, 0.0% Black/African American, 0.2% Asian, 0.5% American Indian/Alaska Native, 0.0% Native Hawaiian/Other Pacific Islander, 1.1% Two or more races, 0.1% Hispanic of any race;

Average household size: 2.20; Median age: 50.5; Age under 18: 16.5%; Age 65 and over: 21.0%; Males per 100 females: 103.0
Housing: Homeownership rate: 90.9%; Homeowner vacancy rate: 2.3%; Rental vacancy rate: 2.9%

WEST BRANCH (township). Covers a land area of 111.457 square miles and a water area of 0.392 square miles. Located at 46.16° N. Lat; 87.71° W. Long.
Population: 63; Growth (since 2000): -6.0%; Density: 0.6 persons per square mile; Race: 98.4% White, 0.0% Black/African American, 0.0% Asian, 1.6% American Indian/Alaska Native, 0.0% Native Hawaiian/Other Pacific Islander, 0.0% Two or more races, 1.6% Hispanic of any race; Average household size: 2.03; Median age: 57.1; Age under 18: 17.5%; Age 65 and over: 28.6%; Males per 100 females: 117.2
Housing: Homeownership rate: 96.7%; Homeowner vacancy rate: 6.3%; Rental vacancy rate: 0.0%

Eaton County

Located in south central Michigan; drained by the Grand and Thornapple Rivers. Covers a land area of 575.175 square miles, a water area of 4.258 square miles, and is located in the Eastern Time Zone at 42.59° N. Lat., 84.85° W. Long. The county was founded in 1837. County seat is Charlotte.

Eaton County is part of the Lansing-East Lansing, MI Metropolitan Statistical Area. The entire metro area includes: Clinton County, MI; Eaton County, MI; Ingham County, MI

Weather Station: Charlotte										Elevation: 901 feet	
	Jan	Feb	Mar	Apr	May	Jun	Jul	Aug	Sep	Oct	Nov	Dec
High	30	33	43	57	68	78	81	79	72	60	46	34
Low	15	16	24	35	45	55	59	57	49	38	30	20
Precip	1.8	1.5	2.1	3.1	3.7	3.3	3.0	3.6	3.7	3.2	2.9	2.2
Snow	13.3	8.7	6.4	1.2	0.0	0.0	0.0	0.0	0.0	0.5	1.9	10.9

High and Low temperatures in degrees Fahrenheit; Precipitation and Snow in inches

Population: 107,759; Growth (since 2000): 4.0%; Density: 187.4 persons per square mile; Race: 87.8% White, 6.3% Black/African American, 1.7% Asian, 0.4% American Indian/Alaska Native, 0.0% Native Hawaiian/Other Pacific Islander, 2.6% two or more races, 4.7% Hispanic of any race; Average household size: 2.44; Median age: 40.3; Age under 18: 23.3%; Age 65 and over: 14.0%; Males per 100 females: 95.3; Marriage status: 28.0% never married, 54.4% now married, 1.3% separated, 5.8% widowed, 11.7% divorced; Foreign born: 3.5%; Speak English only: 93.9%; With disability: 13.3%; Veterans: 9.8%; Ancestry: 27.7% German, 15.1% English, 13.5% Irish, 6.3% American, 4.8% Dutch
Religion: Six largest groups: 14.2% Pentecostal, 6.0% Catholicism, 4.2% Methodist/Pietist, 3.3% Lutheran, 1.6% Presbyterian-Reformed, 1.5% Baptist
Economy: Unemployment rate: 5.4%; Leading industries: 16.3% retail trade; 11.7% other services (except public administration); 11.5% health care and social assistance; Farms: 1,163 totaling 223,239 acres; Company size: 4 employ 1,000 or more persons, 3 employ 500 to 999 persons, 52 employ 100 to 499 persons, 1,989 employ less than 100 persons; Business ownership: 2,495 women-owned, 273 Black-owned, n/a Hispanic-owned, 113 Asian-owned
Employment: 13.7% management, business, and financial, 6.3% computer, engineering, and science, 9.1% education, legal, community service, arts, and media, 5.0% healthcare practitioners, 17.3% service, 26.7% sales and office, 7.3% natural resources, construction, and maintenance, 14.6% production, transportation, and material moving
Income: Per capita: $26,582; Median household: $54,115; Average household: $64,824; Households with income of $100,000 or more: 18.1%; Poverty rate: 10.8%
Educational Attainment: High school diploma or higher: 93.4%; Bachelor's degree or higher: 24.6%; Graduate/professional degree or higher: 8.8%
Housing: Homeownership rate: 72.6%; Median home value: $138,300; Median year structure built: 1976; Homeowner vacancy rate: 2.3%; Median gross rent: $759 per month; Rental vacancy rate: 9.3%
Vital Statistics: Birth rate: 106.3 per 10,000 population; Death rate: 84.1 per 10,000 population; Age-adjusted cancer mortality rate: 176.0 deaths per 100,000 population

Health Insurance: 90.9% have insurance; 77.1% have private insurance; 29.9% have public insurance; 9.1% do not have insurance; 2.6% of children under 18 do not have insurance
Health Care: Physicians: 8.2 per 10,000 population; Hospital beds: 4.2 per 10,000 population; Hospital admissions: 94.7 per 10,000 population
Transportation: Commute: 93.9% car, 0.7% public transportation, 1.2% walk, 3.3% work from home; Median travel time to work: 22.6 minutes
Presidential Election: 51.0% Obama, 47.9% Romney (2012)
Additional Information Contacts
Eaton Government . . . . (517) 543-7500
  http://www.eatoncounty.org

Eaton County Communities

BELLEVUE (township). Covers a land area of 36.380 square miles and a water area of 0.247 square miles. Located at 42.47° N. Lat; 85.02° W. Long. Elevation is 866 feet.
History: Settled 1830; incorporated 1867.
Population: 3,150; Growth (since 2000): 0.2%; Density: 86.6 persons per square mile; Race: 96.8% White, 0.7% Black/African American, 0.2% Asian, 0.2% American Indian/Alaska Native, 0.0% Native Hawaiian/Other Pacific Islander, 1.7% Two or more races, 2.0% Hispanic of any race; Average household size: 2.56; Median age: 40.5; Age under 18: 24.2%; Age 65 and over: 13.2%; Males per 100 females: 92.4; Marriage status: 26.7% never married, 55.7% now married, 1.7% separated, 6.5% widowed, 11.1% divorced; Foreign born: 0.2%; Speak English only: 98.9%; With disability: 17.4%; Veterans: 11.4%; Ancestry: 25.9% German, 13.8% English, 8.6% Irish, 7.8% American, 6.1% Polish
Employment: 10.5% management, business, and financial, 5.2% computer, engineering, and science, 5.2% education, legal, community service, arts, and media, 7.6% healthcare practitioners, 11.3% service, 27.1% sales and office, 15.3% natural resources, construction, and maintenance, 17.7% production, transportation, and material moving
Income: Per capita: $23,208; Median household: $47,898; Average household: $58,502; Households with income of $100,000 or more: 16.0%; Poverty rate: 5.8%
Educational Attainment: High school diploma or higher: 85.0%; Bachelor's degree or higher: 14.2%; Graduate/professional degree or higher: 4.4%
School District(s)
Bellevue Community Schools (PK-12)
  2012-13 Enrollment: 589. . . . . (269) 763-9432
Housing: Homeownership rate: 84.7%; Median home value: $98,600; Median year structure built: 1959; Homeowner vacancy rate: 1.8%; Median gross rent: $649 per month; Rental vacancy rate: 12.4%
Health Insurance: 88.0% have insurance; 65.0% have private insurance; 39.3% have public insurance; 12.0% do not have insurance; 9.1% of children under 18 do not have insurance
Transportation: Commute: 92.4% car, 0.0% public transportation, 1.2% walk, 3.7% work from home; Median travel time to work: 29.2 minutes

BELLEVUE (village). Covers a land area of 1.016 square miles and a water area of 0.076 square miles. Located at 42.44° N. Lat; 85.02° W. Long. Elevation is 866 feet.
History: Bellevue, laid out in 1835, served as the seat of Eaton County from 1838 to 1840. The name was first spelled Bellvue; the extra "e" was added in 1841.
Population: 1,282; Growth (since 2000): -6.1%; Density: 1,261.7 persons per square mile; Race: 96.2% White, 0.6% Black/African American, 0.2% Asian, 0.2% American Indian/Alaska Native, 0.0% Native Hawaiian/Other Pacific Islander, 2.2% Two or more races, 1.7% Hispanic of any race; Average household size: 2.48; Median age: 35.4; Age under 18: 26.1%; Age 65 and over: 13.9%; Males per 100 females: 85.8
School District(s)
Bellevue Community Schools (PK-12)
  2012-13 Enrollment: 589. . . . . (269) 763-9432
Housing: Homeownership rate: 73.5%; Homeowner vacancy rate: 0.8%; Rental vacancy rate: 13.8%

BENTON (township). Covers a land area of 33.542 square miles and a water area of 0.090 square miles. Located at 42.65° N. Lat; 84.79° W. Long.
Population: 2,796; Growth (since 2000): 3.1%; Density: 83.4 persons per square mile; Race: 96.2% White, 0.9% Black/African American, 0.3% Asian, 0.4% American Indian/Alaska Native, 0.1% Native Hawaiian/Other

Pacific Islander, 1.3% Two or more races, 3.8% Hispanic of any race; Average household size: 2.61; Median age: 43.6; Age under 18: 22.2%; Age 65 and over: 14.0%; Males per 100 females: 102.0; Marriage status: 21.3% never married, 62.0% now married, 0.3% separated, 6.1% widowed, 10.6% divorced; Foreign born: 0.7%; Speak English only: 97.3%; With disability: 13.6%; Veterans: 13.0%; Ancestry: 27.1% German, 19.2% English, 13.3% Irish, 10.0% American, 5.8% Dutch

Employment: 12.3% management, business, and financial, 7.1% computer, engineering, and science, 5.0% education, legal, community service, arts, and media, 4.7% healthcare practitioners, 12.6% service, 27.1% sales and office, 14.1% natural resources, construction, and maintenance, 17.2% production, transportation, and material moving

Income: Per capita: $27,568; Median household: $65,172; Average household: $72,837; Households with income of $100,000 or more: 21.1%; Poverty rate: 4.3%

Educational Attainment: High school diploma or higher: 94.8%; Bachelor's degree or higher: 17.2%; Graduate/professional degree or higher: 4.6%

Housing: Homeownership rate: 90.2%; Median home value: $152,700; Median year structure built: 1974; Homeowner vacancy rate: 1.6%; Median gross rent: $944 per month; Rental vacancy rate: 5.4%

Health Insurance: 92.0% have insurance; 84.7% have private insurance; 22.5% have public insurance; 8.0% do not have insurance; 0.9% of children under 18 do not have insurance

Transportation: Commute: 95.1% car, 0.0% public transportation, 0.8% walk, 3.6% work from home; Median travel time to work: 25.2 minutes

BROOKFIELD (township). Covers a land area of 36.068 square miles and a water area of 0.306 square miles. Located at 42.47° N. Lat; 84.79° W. Long. Elevation is 922 feet.

History: Brookfield Township was organized in 1841.

Population: 1,537; Growth (since 2000): 7.6%; Density: 42.6 persons per square mile; Race: 96.4% White, 0.7% Black/African American, 0.3% Asian, 0.6% American Indian/Alaska Native, 0.0% Native Hawaiian/Other Pacific Islander, 0.8% Two or more races, 2.8% Hispanic of any race; Average household size: 2.63; Median age: 42.4; Age under 18: 23.7%; Age 65 and over: 15.0%; Males per 100 females: 104.1

Housing: Homeownership rate: 88.3%; Homeowner vacancy rate: 0.8%; Rental vacancy rate: 0.0%

CARMEL (township). Covers a land area of 34.017 square miles and a water area of 0.054 square miles. Located at 42.55° N. Lat; 84.90° W. Long.

Population: 2,855; Growth (since 2000): 8.7%; Density: 83.9 persons per square mile; Race: 97.3% White, 0.4% Black/African American, 0.2% Asian, 0.2% American Indian/Alaska Native, 0.0% Native Hawaiian/Other Pacific Islander, 1.2% Two or more races, 3.9% Hispanic of any race; Average household size: 2.68; Median age: 41.6; Age under 18: 25.1%; Age 65 and over: 13.9%; Males per 100 females: 102.6; Marriage status: 18.9% never married, 65.8% now married, 0.0% separated, 5.0% widowed, 10.4% divorced; Foreign born: 0.4%; Speak English only: 96.3%; With disability: 11.2%; Veterans: 8.5%; Ancestry: 28.6% German, 16.3% English, 11.7% Irish, 7.2% Dutch, 5.4% Polish

Employment: 18.4% management, business, and financial, 5.4% computer, engineering, and science, 9.2% education, legal, community service, arts, and media, 4.1% healthcare practitioners, 16.0% service, 23.5% sales and office, 9.1% natural resources, construction, and maintenance, 14.2% production, transportation, and material moving

Income: Per capita: $27,030; Median household: $64,886; Average household: $72,516; Households with income of $100,000 or more: 23.3%; Poverty rate: 9.0%

Educational Attainment: High school diploma or higher: 95.1%; Bachelor's degree or higher: 20.5%; Graduate/professional degree or higher: 6.7%

Housing: Homeownership rate: 92.4%; Median home value: $162,200; Median year structure built: 1977; Homeowner vacancy rate: 1.3%; Median gross rent: $1,058 per month; Rental vacancy rate: 9.0%

Health Insurance: 95.8% have insurance; 86.4% have private insurance; 26.5% have public insurance; 4.2% do not have insurance; 0.0% of children under 18 do not have insurance

Transportation: Commute: 93.7% car, 0.0% public transportation, 0.0% walk, 6.3% work from home; Median travel time to work: 25.0 minutes

CHARLOTTE (city). County seat. Covers a land area of 6.448 square miles and a water area of 0.048 square miles. Located at 42.57° N. Lat; 84.83° W. Long. Elevation is 909 feet.

History: Charlotte was founded in the 1830's and named for the wife of one of the founders. Incorporated as a village in 1863 and as a city in 1871, Charlotte developed as a distribution center for maple sugar products.

Population: 9,074; Growth (since 2000): 8.2%; Density: 1,407.3 persons per square mile; Race: 95.1% White, 1.2% Black/African American, 0.5% Asian, 0.4% American Indian/Alaska Native, 0.0% Native Hawaiian/Other Pacific Islander, 2.0% Two or more races, 4.6% Hispanic of any race; Average household size: 2.38; Median age: 35.8; Age under 18: 26.0%; Age 65 and over: 14.0%; Males per 100 females: 93.3; Marriage status: 28.7% never married, 52.1% now married, 2.5% separated, 6.9% widowed, 12.2% divorced; Foreign born: 1.6%; Speak English only: 97.5%; With disability: 16.0%; Veterans: 8.6%; Ancestry: 27.3% German, 18.5% English, 14.4% Irish, 7.2% American, 5.3% Dutch

Employment: 6.5% management, business, and financial, 3.5% computer, engineering, and science, 9.4% education, legal, community service, arts, and media, 4.0% healthcare practitioners, 22.8% service, 22.6% sales and office, 10.0% natural resources, construction, and maintenance, 21.2% production, transportation, and material moving

Income: Per capita: $20,942; Median household: $40,536; Average household: $50,173; Households with income of $100,000 or more: 8.9%; Poverty rate: 18.0%

Educational Attainment: High school diploma or higher: 91.8%; Bachelor's degree or higher: 16.0%; Graduate/professional degree or higher: 5.4%

School District(s)

Charlotte Public Schools (PK-12)
    2012-13 Enrollment: 2,670 . . . . (517) 541-5100
Eaton ISD (PK-12)
    2012-13 Enrollment: 187 . . . . (517) 541-8720
Relevant Academy of Eaton County (KG-12)
    2012-13 Enrollment: 143 . . . . (517) 541-8934

Housing: Homeownership rate: 62.1%; Median home value: $111,000; Median year structure built: 1969; Homeowner vacancy rate: 3.1%; Median gross rent: $678 per month; Rental vacancy rate: 7.8%

Health Insurance: 87.9% have insurance; 66.2% have private insurance; 41.1% have public insurance; 12.1% do not have insurance; 2.0% of children under 18 do not have insurance

Hospitals: Hayes Green Beach Memorial Hospital (45 beds)

Safety: Violent crime rate: 31.0 per 10,000 population; Property crime rate: 277.5 per 10,000 population

Newspapers: Lansing Community Newspapers (weekly circulation 30000)

Transportation: Commute: 90.9% car, 1.2% public transportation, 1.0% walk, 4.0% work from home; Median travel time to work: 24.0 minutes

Additional Information Contacts
City of Charlotte . . . . (517) 543-2750
    http://www.charlottemi.org

CHESTER (township). Covers a land area of 36.026 square miles and a water area of 0.040 square miles. Located at 42.64° N. Lat; 84.90° W. Long. Elevation is 909 feet.

Population: 1,747; Growth (since 2000): -1.7%; Density: 48.5 persons per square mile; Race: 98.3% White, 0.5% Black/African American, 0.1% Asian, 0.1% American Indian/Alaska Native, 0.0% Native Hawaiian/Other Pacific Islander, 0.8% Two or more races, 1.3% Hispanic of any race; Average household size: 2.64; Median age: 45.3; Age under 18: 23.1%; Age 65 and over: 14.3%; Males per 100 females: 101.0

Housing: Homeownership rate: 90.5%; Homeowner vacancy rate: 1.5%; Rental vacancy rate: 1.5%

DELTA (charter township). Covers a land area of 32.464 square miles and a water area of 0.749 square miles. Located at 42.73° N. Lat; 84.66° W. Long. Elevation is 866 feet.

Population: 32,408; Growth (since 2000): 9.2%; Density: 998.3 persons per square mile; Race: 78.6% White, 11.6% Black/African American, 3.8% Asian, 0.5% American Indian/Alaska Native, 0.0% Native Hawaiian/Other Pacific Islander, 3.6% Two or more races, 6.2% Hispanic of any race; Average household size: 2.26; Median age: 41.4; Age under 18: 20.9%; Age 65 and over: 15.9%; Males per 100 females: 91.5; Marriage status: 29.2% never married, 52.0% now married, 1.2% separated, 6.3% widowed, 12.5% divorced; Foreign born: 6.5%; Speak English only: 89.3%;

With disability: 12.4%; Veterans: 9.9%; Ancestry: 25.6% German, 13.3% English, 12.1% Irish, 5.8% Polish, 4.7% American

Employment: 17.2% management, business, and financial, 9.2% computer, engineering, and science, 10.3% education, legal, community service, arts, and media, 5.4% healthcare practitioners, 15.8% service, 27.4% sales and office, 3.8% natural resources, construction, and maintenance, 10.8% production, transportation, and material moving

Income: Per capita: $32,290; Median household: $60,902; Average household: $70,139; Households with income of $100,000 or more: 22.1%; Poverty rate: 7.9%

Educational Attainment: High school diploma or higher: 95.2%; Bachelor's degree or higher: 36.6%; Graduate/professional degree or higher: 14.0%

Housing: Homeownership rate: 64.0%; Median home value: $150,500; Median year structure built: 1978; Homeowner vacancy rate: 2.0%; Median gross rent: $783 per month; Rental vacancy rate: 8.3%

Health Insurance: 92.3% have insurance; 82.8% have private insurance; 26.2% have public insurance; 7.7% do not have insurance; 1.7% of children under 18 do not have insurance

Transportation: Commute: 95.6% car, 0.3% public transportation, 1.0% walk, 2.6% work from home; Median travel time to work: 19.0 minutes

Additional Information Contacts
Delta Charter Township. . . . . (517) 323-8500
   http://www.deltami.gov

DIMONDALE (village).
Covers a land area of 0.895 square miles and a water area of 0.044 square miles. Located at 42.65° N. Lat; 84.65° W. Long. Elevation is 860 feet.

Population: 1,234; Growth (since 2000): -8.0%; Density: 1,378.6 persons per square mile; Race: 92.7% White, 0.7% Black/African American, 0.8% Asian, 0.9% American Indian/Alaska Native, 0.0% Native Hawaiian/Other Pacific Islander, 3.2% Two or more races, 4.1% Hispanic of any race; Average household size: 2.43; Median age: 47.0; Age under 18: 21.1%; Age 65 and over: 16.3%; Males per 100 females: 89.3

School District(s)
Holt Public Schools (KG-12)
   2012-13 Enrollment: 5,792 . . . . (517) 694-5715

Housing: Homeownership rate: 80.9%; Homeowner vacancy rate: 1.9%; Rental vacancy rate: 4.9%

Additional Information Contacts
Village of Dimondale. . . . . (517) 646-0230
   http://dcdcmi.web.officelive.com

EATON (township).
Covers a land area of 32.023 square miles and a water area of 0.105 square miles. Located at 42.54° N. Lat; 84.77° W. Long.

Population: 4,073; Growth (since 2000): -4.8%; Density: 127.2 persons per square mile; Race: 96.6% White, 0.9% Black/African American, 0.8% Asian, 0.2% American Indian/Alaska Native, 0.0% Native Hawaiian/Other Pacific Islander, 1.1% Two or more races, 3.2% Hispanic of any race; Average household size: 2.63; Median age: 44.5; Age under 18: 22.3%; Age 65 and over: 14.7%; Males per 100 females: 98.4; Marriage status: 21.6% never married, 61.9% now married, 1.8% separated, 4.3% widowed, 12.3% divorced; Foreign born: 1.1%; Speak English only: 97.1%; With disability: 14.5%; Veterans: 11.7%; Ancestry: 32.2% German, 14.0% English, 11.7% Irish, 9.4% Dutch, 9.2% American

Employment: 16.7% management, business, and financial, 8.8% computer, engineering, and science, 9.6% education, legal, community service, arts, and media, 3.2% healthcare practitioners, 8.9% service, 26.3% sales and office, 11.4% natural resources, construction, and maintenance, 15.2% production, transportation, and material moving

Income: Per capita: $26,323; Median household: $61,488; Average household: $69,177; Households with income of $100,000 or more: 21.8%; Poverty rate: 10.3%

Educational Attainment: High school diploma or higher: 94.6%; Bachelor's degree or higher: 21.3%; Graduate/professional degree or higher: 8.3%

Housing: Homeownership rate: 91.4%; Median home value: $147,600; Median year structure built: 1978; Homeowner vacancy rate: 1.2%; Median gross rent: $1,025 per month; Rental vacancy rate: 3.6%

Health Insurance: 90.3% have insurance; 80.0% have private insurance; 30.1% have public insurance; 9.7% do not have insurance; 1.2% of children under 18 do not have insurance

Transportation: Commute: 91.4% car, 0.0% public transportation, 0.0% walk, 6.1% work from home; Median travel time to work: 25.5 minutes

Additional Information Contacts
Eaton Township. . . . . (517) 543-3308
   http://www.eatontownship.com

EATON RAPIDS (city).
Covers a land area of 3.389 square miles and a water area of 0.116 square miles. Located at 42.51° N. Lat; 84.65° W. Long. Elevation is 873 feet.

History: Eaton Rapids grew up around woolen mills, powered by water from the Grand River. The city was established as the center for a large sheep raising area.

Population: 5,214; Growth (since 2000): -2.2%; Density: 1,538.6 persons per square mile; Race: 95.1% White, 0.7% Black/African American, 0.5% Asian, 0.4% American Indian/Alaska Native, 0.0% Native Hawaiian/Other Pacific Islander, 2.6% Two or more races, 4.4% Hispanic of any race; Average household size: 2.49; Median age: 34.8; Age under 18: 27.7%; Age 65 and over: 11.1%; Males per 100 females: 93.4; Marriage status: 31.5% never married, 46.8% now married, 0.5% separated, 9.4% widowed, 12.3% divorced; Foreign born: 2.1%; Speak English only: 97.9%; With disability: 13.8%; Veterans: 8.1%; Ancestry: 29.0% German, 21.7% English, 14.1% Irish, 7.4% American, 6.2% French

Employment: 4.9% management, business, and financial, 3.7% computer, engineering, and science, 11.6% education, legal, community service, arts, and media, 7.4% healthcare practitioners, 24.8% service, 18.8% sales and office, 10.0% natural resources, construction, and maintenance, 18.8% production, transportation, and material moving

Income: Per capita: $17,638; Median household: $43,088; Average household: $46,156; Households with income of $100,000 or more: 5.9%; Poverty rate: 24.7%

Educational Attainment: High school diploma or higher: 92.1%; Bachelor's degree or higher: 15.4%; Graduate/professional degree or higher: 6.2%

School District(s)
Eaton Rapids Public Schools (PK-12)
   2012-13 Enrollment: 2,609 . . . . (517) 663-8155
Island City Academy (KG-12)
   2012-13 Enrollment: 213. . . . . (517) 663-0111

Housing: Homeownership rate: 60.0%; Median home value: $96,400; Median year structure built: 1957; Homeowner vacancy rate: 4.5%; Median gross rent: $837 per month; Rental vacancy rate: 10.9%

Health Insurance: 84.2% have insurance; 60.6% have private insurance; 43.1% have public insurance; 15.8% do not have insurance; 2.3% of children under 18 do not have insurance

Hospitals: Eaton Rapids Medical Center (20 beds)

Safety: Violent crime rate: 15.4 per 10,000 population; Property crime rate: 153.9 per 10,000 population

Transportation: Commute: 95.5% car, 1.1% public transportation, 0.4% walk, 3.0% work from home; Median travel time to work: 22.9 minutes

Additional Information Contacts
City of Eaton Rapids . . . . (517) 663-8118
   http://www.cityofeatonrapids.com

EATON RAPIDS (township).
Covers a land area of 34.150 square miles and a water area of 0.236 square miles. Located at 42.56° N. Lat; 84.67° W. Long. Elevation is 873 feet.

History: Settled 1837; incorporated as village 1871, as city 1881.

Population: 4,113; Growth (since 2000): 7.6%; Density: 120.4 persons per square mile; Race: 96.0% White, 0.9% Black/African American, 0.7% Asian, 0.3% American Indian/Alaska Native, 0.0% Native Hawaiian/Other Pacific Islander, 1.7% Two or more races, 4.1% Hispanic of any race; Average household size: 2.71; Median age: 43.4; Age under 18: 23.5%; Age 65 and over: 12.5%; Males per 100 females: 100.3; Marriage status: 19.8% never married, 70.7% now married, 0.0% separated, 1.2% widowed, 8.3% divorced; Foreign born: 0.5%; Speak English only: 96.1%; With disability: 8.5%; Veterans: 8.9%; Ancestry: 27.7% German, 15.7% Irish, 14.7% English, 6.1% American, 4.0% French

Employment: 17.5% management, business, and financial, 7.6% computer, engineering, and science, 4.2% education, legal, community service, arts, and media, 6.2% healthcare practitioners, 14.4% service, 25.6% sales and office, 9.1% natural resources, construction, and maintenance, 15.4% production, transportation, and material moving

Income: Per capita: $32,083; Median household: $81,008; Average household: $93,023; Households with income of $100,000 or more: 33.5%; Poverty rate: 4.1%

Educational Attainment: High school diploma or higher: 98.4%; Bachelor's degree or higher: 23.7%; Graduate/professional degree or higher: 9.6%

School District(s)
Eaton Rapids Public Schools (PK-12)
   2012-13 Enrollment: 2,609 . . . . (517) 663-8155
Island City Academy (KG-12)
   2012-13 Enrollment: 213 . . . . (517) 663-0111
Housing: Homeownership rate: 91.4%; Median home value: $166,700; Median year structure built: 1983; Homeowner vacancy rate: 1.7%; Median gross rent: <$100 per month; Rental vacancy rate: 6.4%
Health Insurance: 92.8% have insurance; 83.0% have private insurance; 25.2% have public insurance; 7.2% do not have insurance; 2.9% of children under 18 do not have insurance
Hospitals: Eaton Rapids Medical Center (20 beds)
Transportation: Commute: 97.5% car, 0.5% public transportation, 0.4% walk, 1.6% work from home; Median travel time to work: 27.8 minutes
Additional Information Contacts
Eaton Rapids Township . . . . (517) 663-7407

GRAND LEDGE (city). Covers a land area of 3.574 square miles and a water area of 0.082 square miles. Located at 42.75° N. Lat; 84.74° W. Long. Elevation is 837 feet.
History: Grand Ledge was named for the sandstone ledges that overhang the river in this area. The sandstone furnished material for the tile and clay product factories of the city.
Population: 7,786; Growth (since 2000): -0.3%; Density: 2,178.5 persons per square mile; Race: 94.4% White, 0.9% Black/African American, 0.8% Asian, 0.5% American Indian/Alaska Native, 0.1% Native Hawaiian/Other Pacific Islander, 2.5% Two or more races, 4.6% Hispanic of any race; Average household size: 2.31; Median age: 38.8; Age under 18: 24.3%; Age 65 and over: 14.1%; Males per 100 females: 91.3; Marriage status: 28.0% never married, 50.6% now married, 1.8% separated, 7.3% widowed, 14.1% divorced; Foreign born: 1.1%; Speak English only: 94.9%; With disability: 15.8%; Veterans: 9.4%; Ancestry: 33.5% German, 18.1% Irish, 15.6% English, 7.1% French, 6.1% Dutch
Employment: 11.4% management, business, and financial, 2.5% computer, engineering, and science, 13.1% education, legal, community service, arts, and media, 2.9% healthcare practitioners, 22.6% service, 29.4% sales and office, 5.9% natural resources, construction, and maintenance, 12.2% production, transportation, and material moving
Income: Per capita: $26,156; Median household: $50,104; Average household: $60,739; Households with income of $100,000 or more: 12.6%; Poverty rate: 9.1%
Educational Attainment: High school diploma or higher: 96.8%; Bachelor's degree or higher: 27.5%; Graduate/professional degree or higher: 10.7%

School District(s)
Grand Ledge Public Schools (KG-12)
   2012-13 Enrollment: 5,071 . . . . (517) 925-5400
Oneida Township S/d #3 (KG-12)
   2012-13 Enrollment: 14 . . . . (517) 749-9832
Housing: Homeownership rate: 64.6%; Median home value: $119,300; Median year structure built: 1971; Homeowner vacancy rate: 2.8%; Median gross rent: $713 per month; Rental vacancy rate: 8.5%
Health Insurance: 90.8% have insurance; 74.5% have private insurance; 30.8% have public insurance; 9.2% do not have insurance; 1.4% of children under 18 do not have insurance
Safety: Violent crime rate: 7.7 per 10,000 population; Property crime rate: 133.8 per 10,000 population
Transportation: Commute: 94.9% car, 0.4% public transportation, 2.4% walk, 1.4% work from home; Median travel time to work: 18.4 minutes
Airports: Abrams Municipal (general aviation)
Additional Information Contacts
City of Grand Ledge . . . . (517) 627-2149
   http://www.grand-ledge.com

HAMLIN (township). Covers a land area of 34.358 square miles and a water area of 0.213 square miles. Located at 42.46° N. Lat; 84.66° W. Long.
History: Hamlin Township was set off from Eaton Rapids Township in 1869 by the legislature. It was named for Samuel Hamlin who had built a road through the northwestern part of the county.
Population: 3,343; Growth (since 2000): 13.2%; Density: 97.3 persons per square mile; Race: 95.8% White, 1.4% Black/African American, 0.1%

Asian, 0.8% American Indian/Alaska Native, 0.0% Native Hawaiian/Other Pacific Islander, 1.6% Two or more races, 2.1% Hispanic of any race; Average household size: 2.75; Median age: 41.4; Age under 18: 25.5%; Age 65 and over: 12.4%; Males per 100 females: 98.5; Marriage status: 20.1% never married, 62.7% now married, 0.7% separated, 5.5% widowed, 11.6% divorced; Foreign born: 11.0%; Speak English only: 91.5%; With disability: 7.8%; Veterans: 11.2%; Ancestry: 23.7% German, 19.9% Irish, 18.0% English, 9.1% American, 8.9% Assyrian/Chaldean/Syriac
Employment: 7.7% management, business, and financial, 5.0% computer, engineering, and science, 7.2% education, legal, community service, arts, and media, 10.2% healthcare practitioners, 16.0% service, 25.2% sales and office, 7.8% natural resources, construction, and maintenance, 20.8% production, transportation, and material moving
Income: Per capita: $21,791; Median household: $55,521; Average household: $63,539; Households with income of $100,000 or more: 16.9%; Poverty rate: 15.9%
Educational Attainment: High school diploma or higher: 87.8%; Bachelor's degree or higher: 21.7%; Graduate/professional degree or higher: 6.0%
Housing: Homeownership rate: 90.8%; Median home value: $132,700; Median year structure built: 1983; Homeowner vacancy rate: 2.0%; Median gross rent: $1,097 per month; Rental vacancy rate: 3.5%
Health Insurance: 94.6% have insurance; 75.5% have private insurance; 33.2% have public insurance; 5.4% do not have insurance; 1.2% of children under 18 do not have insurance
Transportation: Commute: 93.2% car, 0.0% public transportation, 0.9% walk, 3.8% work from home; Median travel time to work: 23.7 minutes

KALAMO (township). Covers a land area of 36.595 square miles and a water area of 0.142 square miles. Located at 42.56° N. Lat; 85.02° W. Long. Elevation is 942 feet.
Population: 1,842; Growth (since 2000): 5.7%; Density: 50.3 persons per square mile; Race: 96.6% White, 0.1% Black/African American, 0.1% Asian, 0.5% American Indian/Alaska Native, 0.0% Native Hawaiian/Other Pacific Islander, 2.0% Two or more races, 2.0% Hispanic of any race; Average household size: 2.65; Median age: 41.6; Age under 18: 24.5%; Age 65 and over: 14.4%; Males per 100 females: 106.3
Housing: Homeownership rate: 90.9%; Homeowner vacancy rate: 0.3%; Rental vacancy rate: 0.0%

MULLIKEN (village). Covers a land area of 1.044 square miles and a water area of 0 square miles. Located at 42.76° N. Lat; 84.90° W. Long. Elevation is 866 feet.
Population: 553; Growth (since 2000): -0.7%; Density: 529.9 persons per square mile; Race: 96.6% White, 0.0% Black/African American, 0.0% Asian, 0.2% American Indian/Alaska Native, 0.0% Native Hawaiian/Other Pacific Islander, 2.4% Two or more races, 3.1% Hispanic of any race; Average household size: 2.71; Median age: 35.3; Age under 18: 24.8%; Age 65 and over: 8.5%; Males per 100 females: 110.3
Housing: Homeownership rate: 88.6%; Homeowner vacancy rate: 6.3%; Rental vacancy rate: 0.0%

OLIVET (city). Covers a land area of 1.020 square miles and a water area of 0.001 square miles. Located at 42.44° N. Lat; 84.93° W. Long. Elevation is 938 feet.
History: Olivet College was founded in Olivet in 1844 by the Congregational Church. The site was chosen by Reverend John Shiperd, the founder of Oberlin College in Ohio, who got lost in the woods here and decided this must be the place to locate a new college.
Population: 1,605; Growth (since 2000): -8.7%; Density: 1,573.4 persons per square mile; Race: 89.8% White, 6.8% Black/African American, 0.6% Asian, 0.2% American Indian/Alaska Native, 0.0% Native Hawaiian/Other Pacific Islander, 1.9% Two or more races, 3.1% Hispanic of any race; Average household size: 2.52; Median age: 21.7; Age under 18: 15.4%; Age 65 and over: 6.0%; Males per 100 females: 110.1

School District(s)
Olivet Community Schools (PK-12)
   2012-13 Enrollment: 1,566 . . . . (269) 749-4572
Four-year College(s)
Olivet College (Private, Not-for-profit, United Church of Christ)
   Fall 2013 Enrollment: 1,133 . . . . (800) 456-7189
   2013-14 Tuition: In-state $23,021; Out-of-state $23,021
Housing: Homeownership rate: 47.8%; Homeowner vacancy rate: 3.3%; Rental vacancy rate: 13.8%

Safety: Violent crime rate: 6.2 per 10,000 population; Property crime rate: 62.1 per 10,000 population

ONEIDA (charter township).
Covers a land area of 32.559 square miles and a water area of 0.103 square miles. Located at 42.72° N. Lat; 84.80° W. Long.
Population: 3,865; Growth (since 2000): 4.4%; Density: 118.7 persons per square mile; Race: 95.8% White, 0.9% Black/African American, 0.5% Asian, 0.4% American Indian/Alaska Native, 0.0% Native Hawaiian/Other Pacific Islander, 1.6% Two or more races, 3.0% Hispanic of any race; Average household size: 2.64; Median age: 46.1; Age under 18: 22.3%; Age 65 and over: 15.8%; Males per 100 females: 98.4; Marriage status: 24.0% never married, 60.0% now married, 0.8% separated, 6.1% widowed, 9.9% divorced; Foreign born: 1.3%; Speak English only: 98.7%; With disability: 8.3%; Veterans: 10.6%; Ancestry: 30.1% German, 16.7% English, 13.8% Irish, 5.5% Italian, 4.9% Dutch
Employment: 14.5% management, business, and financial, 5.4% computer, engineering, and science, 9.1% education, legal, community service, arts, and media, 4.7% healthcare practitioners, 14.9% service, 38.0% sales and office, 5.8% natural resources, construction, and maintenance, 7.6% production, transportation, and material moving
Income: Per capita: $32,548; Median household: $75,750; Average household: $84,522; Households with income of $100,000 or more: 29.9%; Poverty rate: 5.9%
Educational Attainment: High school diploma or higher: 95.1%; Bachelor's degree or higher: 24.3%; Graduate/professional degree or higher: 5.9%
Housing: Homeownership rate: 91.1%; Median home value: $175,000; Median year structure built: 1977; Homeowner vacancy rate: 1.4%; Median gross rent: $575 per month; Rental vacancy rate: 7.8%
Health Insurance: 97.0% have insurance; 89.0% have private insurance; 20.3% have public insurance; 3.0% do not have insurance; 0.0% of children under 18 do not have insurance
Transportation: Commute: 90.9% car, 3.1% public transportation, 0.0% walk, 6.0% work from home; Median travel time to work: 22.1 minutes
Additional Information Contacts
Oneida Charter Township .... (517) 622-8078
  http://www.oneidatownship.org

POTTERVILLE (city).
Covers a land area of 1.682 square miles and a water area of 0.139 square miles. Located at 42.63° N. Lat; 84.75° W. Long. Elevation is 899 feet.
History: Linus Potter and his family settled here in 1844. The eldest son, George, built a sawmill and a boarding house that later became a hotel. Potterville developed as the center of an area known for its purebred sheep, cattle, and Percheron horses.
Population: 2,617; Growth (since 2000): 20.7%; Density: 1,556.0 persons per square mile; Race: 94.2% White, 1.3% Black/African American, 0.5% Asian, 0.6% American Indian/Alaska Native, 0.0% Native Hawaiian/Other Pacific Islander, 2.6% Two or more races, 5.7% Hispanic of any race; Average household size: 2.75; Median age: 32.4; Age under 18: 31.2%; Age 65 and over: 7.1%; Males per 100 females: 94.7; Marriage status: 28.0% never married, 51.4% now married, 1.8% separated, 3.1% widowed, 17.5% divorced; Foreign born: 1.5%; Speak English only: 95.8%; With disability: 16.1%; Veterans: 9.0%; Ancestry: 30.4% German, 18.8% Irish, 11.8% English, 6.7% Dutch, 5.8% American
Employment: 9.1% management, business, and financial, 5.4% computer, engineering, and science, 8.7% education, legal, community service, arts, and media, 4.5% healthcare practitioners, 19.4% service, 29.3% sales and office, 10.3% natural resources, construction, and maintenance, 13.3% production, transportation, and material moving
Income: Per capita: $24,040; Median household: $51,750; Average household: $61,078; Households with income of $100,000 or more: 13.5%; Poverty rate: 14.2%
Educational Attainment: High school diploma or higher: 90.9%; Bachelor's degree or higher: 16.5%; Graduate/professional degree or higher: 3.4%
School District(s)
Potterville Public Schools (PK-12)
  2012-13 Enrollment: 928......................... (517) 645-2662
Housing: Homeownership rate: 75.0%; Median home value: $95,500; Median year structure built: 1978; Homeowner vacancy rate: 5.7%; Median gross rent: $606 per month; Rental vacancy rate: 24.7%

Health Insurance: 89.0% have insurance; 70.7% have private insurance; 28.0% have public insurance; 11.0% do not have insurance; 2.4% of children under 18 do not have insurance
Safety: Violent crime rate: 0.0 per 10,000 population; Property crime rate: 283.2 per 10,000 population
Transportation: Commute: 93.2% car, 1.2% public transportation, 1.7% walk, 1.4% work from home; Median travel time to work: 22.8 minutes

ROXAND (township).
Covers a land area of 36.425 square miles and a water area of 0.050 square miles. Located at 42.73° N. Lat; 84.90° W. Long. Elevation is 873 feet.
History: Roxand was settled in the 1830's. It was named for a woman, Roxana, an early settler here. The "a" became a "d" through a clerk's error.
Population: 1,848; Growth (since 2000): -2.9%; Density: 50.7 persons per square mile; Race: 97.8% White, 0.1% Black/African American, 0.0% Asian, 0.2% American Indian/Alaska Native, 0.0% Native Hawaiian/Other Pacific Islander, 1.4% Two or more races, 2.8% Hispanic of any race; Average household size: 2.66; Median age: 39.6; Age under 18: 23.4%; Age 65 and over: 11.8%; Males per 100 females: 104.0
Housing: Homeownership rate: 88.9%; Homeowner vacancy rate: 2.8%; Rental vacancy rate: 2.5%

SUNFIELD (township).
Covers a land area of 36.090 square miles and a water area of 0.399 square miles. Located at 42.72° N. Lat; 85.02° W. Long. Elevation is 866 feet.
Population: 1,997; Growth (since 2000): -8.3%; Density: 55.3 persons per square mile; Race: 97.2% White, 0.4% Black/African American, 0.3% Asian, 0.0% American Indian/Alaska Native, 0.0% Native Hawaiian/Other Pacific Islander, 1.4% Two or more races, 3.0% Hispanic of any race; Average household size: 2.57; Median age: 42.1; Age under 18: 23.5%; Age 65 and over: 14.0%; Males per 100 females: 95.0
School District(s)
Lakewood Public Schools (PK-12)
  2012-13 Enrollment: 2,029 .... (616) 374-8043
Housing: Homeownership rate: 85.0%; Homeowner vacancy rate: 3.2%; Rental vacancy rate: 10.1%
Newspapers: Sunfield Sentinel (weekly circulation 500)

SUNFIELD (village).
Covers a land area of 0.798 square miles and a water area of 0 square miles. Located at 42.76° N. Lat; 85.00° W. Long. Elevation is 866 feet.
History: The village of Sunfield was laid out by land speculators and was named for the township.
Population: 578; Growth (since 2000): -2.2%; Density: 724.0 persons per square mile; Race: 96.7% White, 0.0% Black/African American, 0.2% Asian, 0.0% American Indian/Alaska Native, 0.0% Native Hawaiian/Other Pacific Islander, 1.7% Two or more races, 3.6% Hispanic of any race; Average household size: 2.65; Median age: 32.4; Age under 18: 31.3%; Age 65 and over: 10.2%; Males per 100 females: 78.4
School District(s)
Lakewood Public Schools (PK-12)
  2012-13 Enrollment: 2,029 .... (616) 374-8043
Housing: Homeownership rate: 69.7%; Homeowner vacancy rate: 6.1%; Rental vacancy rate: 5.8%
Newspapers: Sunfield Sentinel (weekly circulation 500)

VERMONTVILLE (township).
Covers a land area of 36.105 square miles and a water area of 0.256 square miles. Located at 42.64° N. Lat; 85.02° W. Long. Elevation is 932 feet.
Population: 2,053; Growth (since 2000): -2.2%; Density: 56.9 persons per square mile; Race: 97.7% White, 0.0% Black/African American, 0.2% Asian, 0.4% American Indian/Alaska Native, 0.0% Native Hawaiian/Other Pacific Islander, 1.4% Two or more races, 1.8% Hispanic of any race; Average household size: 2.74; Median age: 39.6; Age under 18: 26.1%; Age 65 and over: 13.3%; Males per 100 females: 110.1
School District(s)
Maple Valley Schools (PK-12)
  2012-13 Enrollment: 1,197 .... (517) 852-9699
Housing: Homeownership rate: 84.3%; Homeowner vacancy rate: 1.6%; Rental vacancy rate: 7.6%

VERMONTVILLE (village). Covers a land area of 1.264 square miles and a water area of 0.012 square miles. Located at 42.63° N. Lat; 85.03° W. Long. Elevation is 932 feet.

History: Vermontville was settled in 1836 by a group from Vermont, who brought the maple sugar industry with them.

Population: 759; Growth (since 2000): -3.8%; Density: 600.5 persons per square mile; Race: 97.1% White, 0.0% Black/African American, 0.3% Asian, 0.8% American Indian/Alaska Native, 0.0% Native Hawaiian/Other Pacific Islander, 1.8% Two or more races, 2.4% Hispanic of any race; Average household size: 2.61; Median age: 36.3; Age under 18: 26.2%; Age 65 and over: 14.1%; Males per 100 females: 109.1

School District(s)

Maple Valley Schools (PK-12)

    2012-13 Enrollment: 1,197 . . . . (517) 852-9699

Housing: Homeownership rate: 76.0%; Homeowner vacancy rate: 3.9%; Rental vacancy rate: 9.8%

WALTON (township). Covers a land area of 35.210 square miles and a water area of 0.284 square miles. Located at 42.47° N. Lat; 84.89° W. Long.

Population: 2,266; Growth (since 2000): 12.7%; Density: 64.4 persons per square mile; Race: 96.6% White, 0.5% Black/African American, 0.5% Asian, 0.3% American Indian/Alaska Native, 0.0% Native Hawaiian/Other Pacific Islander, 1.0% Two or more races, 3.4% Hispanic of any race; Average household size: 2.84; Median age: 38.8; Age under 18: 27.4%; Age 65 and over: 10.4%; Males per 100 females: 104.5

Housing: Homeownership rate: 88.4%; Homeowner vacancy rate: 1.0%; Rental vacancy rate: 8.0%

WAVERLY (CDP). Covers a land area of 9.068 square miles and a water area of 0.055 square miles. Located at 42.74° N. Lat; 84.63° W. Long. Elevation is 860 feet.

Population: 23,925; Growth (since 2000): 47.7%; Density: 2,638.5 persons per square mile; Race: 75.2% White, 13.8% Black/African American, 4.2% Asian, 0.5% American Indian/Alaska Native, 0.0% Native Hawaiian/Other Pacific Islander, 4.0% Two or more races, 6.9% Hispanic of any race; Average household size: 2.15; Median age: 40.7; Age under 18: 19.7%; Age 65 and over: 16.4%; Males per 100 females: 89.6; Marriage status: 30.4% never married, 49.7% now married, 1.5% separated, 6.5% widowed, 13.4% divorced; Foreign born: 6.5%; Speak English only: 88.9%; With disability: 13.7%; Veterans: 10.3%; Ancestry: 23.5% German, 12.5% English, 11.8% Irish, 5.1% Polish, 4.6% Dutch

Employment: 17.4% management, business, and financial, 8.9% computer, engineering, and science, 8.8% education, legal, community service, arts, and media, 4.9% healthcare practitioners, 16.1% service, 28.3% sales and office, 3.9% natural resources, construction, and maintenance, 11.8% production, transportation, and material moving

Income: Per capita: $31,100; Median household: $53,520; Average household: $64,392; Households with income of $100,000 or more: 17.6%; Poverty rate: 9.1%

Educational Attainment: High school diploma or higher: 95.2%; Bachelor's degree or higher: 35.2%; Graduate/professional degree or higher: 12.1%

Housing: Homeownership rate: 56.0%; Median home value: $142,700; Median year structure built: 1978; Homeowner vacancy rate: 1.8%; Median gross rent: $779 per month; Rental vacancy rate: 8.2%

Health Insurance: 91.5% have insurance; 80.8% have private insurance; 28.2% have public insurance; 8.5% do not have insurance; 1.4% of children under 18 do not have insurance

Transportation: Commute: 95.2% car, 0.2% public transportation, 1.0% walk, 2.9% work from home; Median travel time to work: 18.4 minutes

WINDSOR (charter township). Covers a land area of 34.491 square miles and a water area of 0.579 square miles. Located at 42.64° N. Lat; 84.66° W. Long.

Population: 6,838; Growth (since 2000): -6.8%; Density: 198.3 persons per square mile; Race: 92.2% White, 2.7% Black/African American, 1.5% Asian, 0.5% American Indian/Alaska Native, 0.0% Native Hawaiian/Other Pacific Islander, 1.8% Two or more races, 4.0% Hispanic of any race; Average household size: 2.37; Median age: 49.6; Age under 18: 18.2%; Age 65 and over: 19.1%; Males per 100 females: 95.1; Marriage status: 22.8% never married, 57.1% now married, 0.4% separated, 7.8% widowed, 12.3% divorced; Foreign born: 2.9%; Speak English only: 96.1%; With disability: 14.7%; Veterans: 13.2%; Ancestry: 32.0% German, 17.9% English, 14.4% Irish, 8.1% American, 5.6% Dutch

Employment: 17.4% management, business, and financial, 6.4% computer, engineering, and science, 5.9% education, legal, community service, arts, and media, 8.4% healthcare practitioners, 11.1% service, 31.2% sales and office, 9.4% natural resources, construction, and maintenance, 10.2% production, transportation, and material moving

Income: Per capita: $27,264; Median household: $58,625; Average household: $67,315; Households with income of $100,000 or more: 17.6%; Poverty rate: 5.2%

Educational Attainment: High school diploma or higher: 94.2%; Bachelor's degree or higher: 22.4%; Graduate/professional degree or higher: 7.8%

Housing: Homeownership rate: 91.3%; Median home value: $156,900; Median year structure built: 1979; Homeowner vacancy rate: 2.9%; Median gross rent: $866 per month; Rental vacancy rate: 8.8%

Health Insurance: 95.2% have insurance; 86.8% have private insurance; 26.9% have public insurance; 4.8% do not have insurance; 1.2% of children under 18 do not have insurance

Transportation: Commute: 96.5% car, 0.8% public transportation, 1.3% walk, 1.2% work from home; Median travel time to work: 20.5 minutes

Additional Information Contacts

Windsor Charter Township . . . . (517) 646-0772
   http://www.twp.windsor.mi.us

Emmet County

Located in northwestern Michigan; bounded on the west by Little Traverse Bay and Lake Michigan, and on the north by the Straits of Mackinac; drained by the Maple River. Covers a land area of 467.494 square miles, a water area of 414.503 square miles, and is located in the Eastern Time Zone at 45.59° N. Lat., 84.99° W. Long. The county was founded in 1853. County seat is Petoskey.

Weather Station: Cross Village   Elevation: 743 feet

	Jan	Feb	Mar	Apr	May	Jun	Jul	Aug	Sep	Oct	Nov	Dec
High	27	30	38	52	64	71	76	75	68	55	43	32
Low	13	12	19	31	41	51	57	57	51	40	31	21
Precip	1.8	1.2	1.8	2.6	2.7	2.6	2.1	3.2	3.4	3.6	2.6	2.1
Snow	21.4	16.3	10.5	4.9	0.1	0.0	0.0	0.0	tr	0.3	5.8	20.5

High and Low temperatures in degrees Fahrenheit; Precipitation and Snow in inches

Weather Station: Pellston Emmet County Arpt   Elevation: 714 feet

	Jan	Feb	Mar	Apr	May	Jun	Jul	Aug	Sep	Oct	Nov	Dec
High	27	29	38	52	66	75	79	77	69	56	43	31
Low	9	9	17	30	40	49	54	53	46	36	28	18
Precip	2.0	1.4	1.9	2.4	2.7	2.3	2.5	3.1	3.5	3.6	2.7	2.1
Snow	na	na	10.3	4.3	0.1	0.0	na	na	na	na	na	na

High and Low temperatures in degrees Fahrenheit; Precipitation and Snow in inches

Weather Station: Petoskey   Elevation: 609 feet

	Jan	Feb	Mar	Apr	May	Jun	Jul	Aug	Sep	Oct	Nov	Dec
High	28	29	37	50	61	70	75	75	68	56	44	33
Low	15	14	21	33	42	53	59	59	52	41	32	22
Precip	2.1	1.4	1.9	2.6	2.9	2.8	2.8	3.4	3.4	3.8	2.6	2.6
Snow	35.6	23.8	12.0	4.2	0.2	0.0	0.0	0.0	tr	0.5	9.6	37.5

High and Low temperatures in degrees Fahrenheit; Precipitation and Snow in inches

Population: 32,694; Growth (since 2000): 4.0%; Density: 69.9 persons per square mile; Race: 92.9% White, 0.5% Black/African American, 0.5% Asian, 3.7% American Indian/Alaska Native, 0.0% Native Hawaiian/Other Pacific Islander, 2.2% two or more races, 1.3% Hispanic of any race; Average household size: 2.37; Median age: 43.1; Age under 18: 22.6%; Age 65 and over: 16.6%; Males per 100 females: 97.0; Marriage status: 23.5% never married, 58.5% now married, 0.8% separated, 5.8% widowed, 12.2% divorced; Foreign born: 2.2%; Speak English only: 96.8%; With disability: 12.3%; Veterans: 11.2%; Ancestry: 28.3% German, 16.9% Irish, 15.9% English, 10.7% Polish, 6.6% French

Religion: Six largest groups: 17.3% Catholicism, 4.2% Methodist/Pietist, 3.0% Non-denominational Protestant, 2.6% Lutheran, 2.4% Holiness, 2.3% Presbyterian-Reformed

Economy: Unemployment rate: 5.8%; Leading industries: 19.6% retail trade; 14.6% construction; 12.4% health care and social assistance; Farms: 287 totaling 39,805 acres; Company size: 1 employs 1,000 or more persons, 1 employs 500 to 999 persons, 12 employ 100 to 499 persons, 1,486 employ less than 100 persons; Business ownership: 1,142 women-owned, n/a Black-owned, n/a Hispanic-owned, n/a Asian-owned

Employment: 13.5% management, business, and financial, 3.3% computer, engineering, and science, 9.6% education, legal, community service, arts, and media, 7.4% healthcare practitioners, 21.4% service, 25.7% sales and office, 10.5% natural resources, construction, and maintenance, 8.5% production, transportation, and material moving

Income: Per capita: $29,718; Median household: $50,929; Average household: $71,028; Households with income of $100,000 or more: 17.3%; Poverty rate: 10.9%

Educational Attainment: High school diploma or higher: 93.8%; Bachelor's degree or higher: 31.8%; Graduate/professional degree or higher: 12.4%

Housing: Homeownership rate: 74.3%; Median home value: $167,700; Median year structure built: 1980; Homeowner vacancy rate: 4.0%; Median gross rent: $744 per month; Rental vacancy rate: 17.5%

Vital Statistics: Birth rate: 97.8 per 10,000 population; Death rate: 86.6 per 10,000 population; Age-adjusted cancer mortality rate: 191.0 deaths per 100,000 population

Health Insurance: 86.5% have insurance; 70.6% have private insurance; 32.3% have public insurance; 13.5% do not have insurance; 4.8% of children under 18 do not have insurance

Health Care: Physicians: 52.2 per 10,000 population; Hospital beds: 54.3 per 10,000 population; Hospital admissions: 2,684.0 per 10,000 population

Transportation: Commute: 88.5% car, 0.3% public transportation, 4.1% walk, 5.3% work from home; Median travel time to work: 19.3 minutes

Presidential Election: 40.7% Obama, 57.7% Romney (2012)

National and State Parks: Craig Lake State Park; Fort Michilimackinac State Park; Hardwood State Forest; Petoskey State Park; Wilderness State Park

Additional Information Contacts

Emmet Government . . . . (231) 348-1702
http://www.co.emmet.mi.us

Emmet County Communities

ALANSON (village). Covers a land area of 0.988 square miles and a water area of 0.031 square miles. Located at 45.44° N. Lat; 84.79° W. Long. Elevation is 617 feet.

History: Alanson was settled in 1875. First called Hinman, it was later named for Alanson Cook, a railroad official with the Grand Rapids & Indiana. The village was incorporated in 1905.

Population: 738; Growth (since 2000): -6.0%; Density: 747.2 persons per square mile; Race: 92.4% White, 0.0% Black/African American, 0.3% Asian, 5.0% American Indian/Alaska Native, 0.0% Native Hawaiian/Other Pacific Islander, 2.3% Two or more races, 1.4% Hispanic of any race; Average household size: 2.40; Median age: 36.3; Age under 18: 25.1%; Age 65 and over: 11.7%; Males per 100 females: 101.6

School District(s)

Alanson Public Schools (PK-12)
    2012-13 Enrollment: 287. . . . . (231) 548-2261

Housing: Homeownership rate: 72.7%; Homeowner vacancy rate: 8.2%; Rental vacancy rate: 27.4%

BAY VIEW (CDP). Covers a land area of 0.374 square miles and a water area of 0 square miles. Located at 45.39° N. Lat; 84.93° W. Long. Elevation is 617 feet.

Population: 133; Growth (since 2000): n/a; Density: 355.3 persons per square mile; Race: 98.5% White, 0.0% Black/African American, 0.0% Asian, 0.8% American Indian/Alaska Native, 0.0% Native Hawaiian/Other Pacific Islander, 0.8% Two or more races, 0.0% Hispanic of any race; Average household size: 2.25; Median age: 48.2; Age under 18: 21.1%; Age 65 and over: 21.8%; Males per 100 females: 92.8

Housing: Homeownership rate: 62.7%; Homeowner vacancy rate: 0.0%; Rental vacancy rate: 12.0%

BEAR CREEK (township). Covers a land area of 39.574 square miles and a water area of 6.112 square miles. Located at 45.35° N. Lat; 84.90° W. Long.

Population: 6,201; Growth (since 2000): 17.7%; Density: 156.7 persons per square mile; Race: 93.3% White, 0.7% Black/African American, 0.9% Asian, 3.1% American Indian/Alaska Native, 0.0% Native Hawaiian/Other Pacific Islander, 1.8% Two or more races, 1.5% Hispanic of any race; Average household size: 2.41; Median age: 40.8; Age under 18: 25.4%; Age 65 and over: 15.7%; Males per 100 females: 94.6; Marriage status: 28.2% never married, 56.8% now married, 1.2% separated, 4.1% widowed, 11.0% divorced; Foreign born: 2.3%; Speak English only: 97.0%;

With disability: 9.8%; Veterans: 10.1%; Ancestry: 25.9% German, 24.7% Irish, 15.7% English, 9.8% Polish, 5.5% European

Employment: 8.1% management, business, and financial, 7.8% computer, engineering, and science, 10.5% education, legal, community service, arts, and media, 6.8% healthcare practitioners, 22.6% service, 25.8% sales and office, 8.2% natural resources, construction, and maintenance, 10.2% production, transportation, and material moving

Income: Per capita: $24,670; Median household: $51,391; Average household: $62,078; Households with income of $100,000 or more: 15.6%; Poverty rate: 11.5%

Educational Attainment: High school diploma or higher: 96.9%; Bachelor's degree or higher: 34.1%; Graduate/professional degree or higher: 11.2%

Housing: Homeownership rate: 64.6%; Median home value: $163,900; Median year structure built: 1982; Homeowner vacancy rate: 2.6%; Median gross rent: $836 per month; Rental vacancy rate: 16.8%

Health Insurance: 87.7% have insurance; 69.8% have private insurance; 32.7% have public insurance; 12.3% do not have insurance; 1.8% of children under 18 do not have insurance

Transportation: Commute: 91.7% car, 0.3% public transportation, 2.0% walk, 5.3% work from home; Median travel time to work: 16.9 minutes

BLISS (township). Covers a land area of 43.658 square miles and a water area of 2.368 square miles. Located at 45.70° N. Lat; 84.92° W. Long. Elevation is 764 feet.

History: Bliss Township was named for Aaron T. Bliss, a lumberman who became a governor of Michigan.

Population: 620; Growth (since 2000): 8.4%; Density: 14.2 persons per square mile; Race: 87.7% White, 0.5% Black/African American, 0.0% Asian, 6.6% American Indian/Alaska Native, 0.0% Native Hawaiian/Other Pacific Islander, 5.0% Two or more races, 1.1% Hispanic of any race; Average household size: 2.41; Median age: 44.7; Age under 18: 23.2%; Age 65 and over: 19.4%; Males per 100 females: 103.9

Housing: Homeownership rate: 90.2%; Homeowner vacancy rate: 1.3%; Rental vacancy rate: 13.8%

BRUTUS (CDP). Covers a land area of 2.812 square miles and a water area of 0.002 square miles. Located at 45.49° N. Lat; 84.78° W. Long. Elevation is 686 feet.

Population: 218; Growth (since 2000): n/a; Density: 77.5 persons per square mile; Race: 95.4% White, 0.0% Black/African American, 0.5% Asian, 2.3% American Indian/Alaska Native, 0.0% Native Hawaiian/Other Pacific Islander, 1.8% Two or more races, 0.0% Hispanic of any race; Average household size: 2.56; Median age: 45.0; Age under 18: 22.0%; Age 65 and over: 17.9%; Males per 100 females: 94.6

Housing: Homeownership rate: 80.0%; Homeowner vacancy rate: 1.4%; Rental vacancy rate: 22.7%

CARP LAKE (CDP). Covers a land area of 2.059 square miles and a water area of 2.718 square miles. Located at 45.70° N. Lat; 84.75° W. Long. Elevation is 732 feet.

Population: 357; Growth (since 2000): n/a; Density: 173.4 persons per square mile; Race: 91.9% White, 0.6% Black/African American, 0.0% Asian, 3.4% American Indian/Alaska Native, 0.0% Native Hawaiian/Other Pacific Islander, 3.9% Two or more races, 0.6% Hispanic of any race; Average household size: 2.18; Median age: 51.7; Age under 18: 16.2%; Age 65 and over: 28.9%; Males per 100 females: 94.0

Housing: Homeownership rate: 81.7%; Homeowner vacancy rate: 8.8%; Rental vacancy rate: 71.7%

CARP LAKE (township). Covers a land area of 32.347 square miles and a water area of 2.806 square miles. Located at 45.69° N. Lat; 84.80° W. Long. Elevation is 732 feet.

Population: 759; Growth (since 2000): -5.9%; Density: 23.5 persons per square mile; Race: 91.2% White, 1.2% Black/African American, 0.0% Asian, 2.9% American Indian/Alaska Native, 0.0% Native Hawaiian/Other Pacific Islander, 4.6% Two or more races, 0.5% Hispanic of any race; Average household size: 2.30; Median age: 48.0; Age under 18: 19.5%; Age 65 and over: 22.0%; Males per 100 females: 100.8

Housing: Homeownership rate: 85.5%; Homeowner vacancy rate: 6.0%; Rental vacancy rate: 62.8%

CENTER (township). Covers a land area of 34.297 square miles and a water area of 0.963 square miles. Located at 45.60° N. Lat; 84.92° W. Long.
Population: 568; Growth (since 2000): 13.8%; Density: 16.6 persons per square mile; Race: 89.4% White, 0.4% Black/African American, 0.5% Asian, 6.3% American Indian/Alaska Native, 0.0% Native Hawaiian/Other Pacific Islander, 3.3% Two or more races, 1.4% Hispanic of any race; Average household size: 2.52; Median age: 41.3; Age under 18: 23.8%; Age 65 and over: 13.0%; Males per 100 females: 112.7
Housing: Homeownership rate: 87.5%; Homeowner vacancy rate: 2.9%; Rental vacancy rate: 12.5%

CONWAY (CDP). Covers a land area of 0.421 square miles and a water area of 0.002 square miles. Located at 45.41° N. Lat; 84.87° W. Long. Elevation is 607 feet.
Population: 204; Growth (since 2000): n/a; Density: 484.4 persons per square mile; Race: 92.6% White, 2.0% Black/African American, 0.0% Asian, 5.4% American Indian/Alaska Native, 0.0% Native Hawaiian/Other Pacific Islander, 0.0% Two or more races, 2.5% Hispanic of any race; Average household size: 1.94; Median age: 45.3; Age under 18: 13.2%; Age 65 and over: 23.5%; Males per 100 females: 92.5
Housing: Homeownership rate: 76.2%; Homeowner vacancy rate: 15.6%; Rental vacancy rate: 16.1%

CROSS VILLAGE (CDP). Covers a land area of 0.734 square miles and a water area of 0 square miles. Located at 45.64° N. Lat; 85.03° W. Long. Elevation is 666 feet.
Population: 93; Growth (since 2000): n/a; Density: 126.7 persons per square mile; Race: 87.1% White, 1.1% Black/African American, 0.0% Asian, 11.8% American Indian/Alaska Native, 0.0% Native Hawaiian/Other Pacific Islander, 0.0% Two or more races, 0.0% Hispanic of any race; Average household size: 1.86; Median age: 53.9; Age under 18: 16.1%; Age 65 and over: 21.5%; Males per 100 females: 126.8
Housing: Homeownership rate: 82.0%; Homeowner vacancy rate: 2.4%; Rental vacancy rate: 25.0%

CROSS VILLAGE (township). Covers a land area of 10.102 square miles and a water area of 0.227 square miles. Located at 45.64° N. Lat; 85.01° W. Long. Elevation is 666 feet.
History: The cross for which Cross Village was named may have been placed here by Father Marquette. The area was known as La Croix (French, the cross) in the early 1800's, and was given its present name in 1875.
Population: 281; Growth (since 2000): -4.4%; Density: 27.8 persons per square mile; Race: 81.9% White, 0.4% Black/African American, 0.0% Asian, 13.2% American Indian/Alaska Native, 0.0% Native Hawaiian/Other Pacific Islander, 4.6% Two or more races, 1.1% Hispanic of any race; Average household size: 1.99; Median age: 53.6; Age under 18: 14.9%; Age 65 and over: 21.7%; Males per 100 females: 128.5
Housing: Homeownership rate: 86.6%; Homeowner vacancy rate: 4.7%; Rental vacancy rate: 13.6%

FRIENDSHIP (township). Covers a land area of 31.447 square miles and a water area of 0.007 square miles. Located at 45.51° N. Lat; 85.04° W. Long.
Population: 889; Growth (since 2000): 5.3%; Density: 28.3 persons per square mile; Race: 94.6% White, 0.3% Black/African American, 0.0% Asian, 2.7% American Indian/Alaska Native, 0.0% Native Hawaiian/Other Pacific Islander, 2.4% Two or more races, 0.7% Hispanic of any race; Average household size: 2.51; Median age: 44.9; Age under 18: 22.9%; Age 65 and over: 15.5%; Males per 100 females: 104.8
Housing: Homeownership rate: 91.5%; Homeowner vacancy rate: 4.8%; Rental vacancy rate: 11.4%

HARBOR SPRINGS (city). Covers a land area of 1.295 square miles and a water area of 0 square miles. Located at 45.43° N. Lat; 84.99° W. Long. Elevation is 669 feet.
History: The Mission of the Holy Childhood of Jesus was founded here in 1827 by Father Peter de Jean. The town of Harbor Springs was settled in the 1870's as a lumber and fishing center, but later became dependent on the summer vacationers for its revenue.
Population: 1,194; Growth (since 2000): -23.8%; Density: 922.2 persons per square mile; Race: 92.0% White, 0.3% Black/African American, 0.8% Asian, 4.8% American Indian/Alaska Native, 0.1% Native Hawaiian/Other Pacific Islander, 2.0% Two or more races, 0.7% Hispanic of any race;

Average household size: 1.93; Median age: 55.8; Age under 18: 15.7%; Age 65 and over: 32.2%; Males per 100 females: 77.9

School District(s)
Harbor Springs SD (PK-12)
   2012-13 Enrollment: 867 . . . . (231) 526-4545
Housing: Homeownership rate: 71.8%; Homeowner vacancy rate: 6.6%; Rental vacancy rate: 14.4%
Safety: Violent crime rate: 8.3 per 10,000 population; Property crime rate: 232.6 per 10,000 population
Newspapers: Harbor Light (weekly circulation 2200)
Airports: Harbor Springs (general aviation)

LEVERING (CDP). Covers a land area of 0.436 square miles and a water area of 0 square miles. Located at 45.63° N. Lat; 84.78° W. Long. Elevation is 764 feet.
Population: 215; Growth (since 2000): n/a; Density: 492.9 persons per square mile; Race: 91.2% White, 0.0% Black/African American, 0.9% Asian, 4.2% American Indian/Alaska Native, 0.0% Native Hawaiian/Other Pacific Islander, 3.7% Two or more races, 0.9% Hispanic of any race; Average household size: 2.42; Median age: 39.4; Age under 18: 24.2%; Age 65 and over: 9.3%; Males per 100 females: 106.7
Housing: Homeownership rate: 69.8%; Homeowner vacancy rate: 7.7%; Rental vacancy rate: 16.1%

LITTLE TRAVERSE (township). Covers a land area of 17.964 square miles and a water area of 2.394 square miles. Located at 45.44° N. Lat; 84.91° W. Long.
Population: 2,380; Growth (since 2000): -1.9%; Density: 132.5 persons per square mile; Race: 96.5% White, 0.6% Black/African American, 0.1% Asian, 1.7% American Indian/Alaska Native, 0.0% Native Hawaiian/Other Pacific Islander, 0.9% Two or more races, 1.0% Hispanic of any race; Average household size: 2.34; Median age: 44.6; Age under 18: 21.8%; Age 65 and over: 15.9%; Males per 100 females: 98.2
Housing: Homeownership rate: 80.9%; Homeowner vacancy rate: 4.3%; Rental vacancy rate: 17.0%

LITTLEFIELD (township). Covers a land area of 21.723 square miles and a water area of 2.836 square miles. Located at 45.43° N. Lat; 84.78° W. Long.
Population: 2,978; Growth (since 2000): 7.0%; Density: 137.1 persons per square mile; Race: 92.7% White, 0.3% Black/African American, 0.2% Asian, 4.4% American Indian/Alaska Native, 0.0% Native Hawaiian/Other Pacific Islander, 2.4% Two or more races, 0.9% Hispanic of any race; Average household size: 2.48; Median age: 41.2; Age under 18: 22.7%; Age 65 and over: 13.9%; Males per 100 females: 102.7; Marriage status: 25.1% never married, 60.0% now married, 1.2% separated, 7.1% widowed, 7.8% divorced; Foreign born: 1.0%; Speak English only: 99.2%; With disability: 21.0%; Veterans: 11.5%; Ancestry: 33.5% German, 18.7% English, 17.4% Irish, 10.8% Polish, 6.5% American
Employment: 12.6% management, business, and financial, 0.6% computer, engineering, and science, 9.6% education, legal, community service, arts, and media, 5.8% healthcare practitioners, 20.1% service, 19.9% sales and office, 17.2% natural resources, construction, and maintenance, 14.2% production, transportation, and material moving
Income: Per capita: $20,086; Median household: $44,286; Average household: $50,451; Households with income of $100,000 or more: 5.9%; Poverty rate: 9.1%
Educational Attainment: High school diploma or higher: 88.4%; Bachelor's degree or higher: 16.7%; Graduate/professional degree or higher: 8.8%
Housing: Homeownership rate: 80.0%; Median home value: $97,800; Median year structure built: 1983; Homeowner vacancy rate: 4.0%; Median gross rent: $736 per month; Rental vacancy rate: 25.9%
Health Insurance: 76.3% have insurance; 59.6% have private insurance; 31.7% have public insurance; 23.7% do not have insurance; 17.0% of children under 18 do not have insurance
Transportation: Commute: 97.0% car, 0.0% public transportation, 0.5% walk, 1.9% work from home; Median travel time to work: 19.9 minutes

MACKINAW CITY (village). Covers a land area of 3.383 square miles and a water area of 4.217 square miles. Located at 45.78° N. Lat; 84.76° W. Long.
History: Mackinaw City grew as a gateway to the Upper Peninsula for tourists and vacationers. There was a fort here in the mid-1700's, called Fort Michilimackinac, as were several forts in the area. Built by the French,

the fort was taken over by the British in 1761, who moved it to Mackinac Island in 1780.

Population: 806; Growth (since 2000): -6.2%; Density: 238.2 persons per square mile; Race: 87.8% White, 5.3% Black/African American, 0.0% Asian, 4.3% American Indian/Alaska Native, 0.0% Native Hawaiian/Other Pacific Islander, 2.4% Two or more races, 2.4% Hispanic of any race; Average household size: 1.95; Median age: 49.5; Age under 18: 16.5%; Age 65 and over: 24.8%; Males per 100 females: 82.4

School District(s)
Mackinaw City Public Schools (PK-12)
    2012-13 Enrollment: 192. . . . . (231) 436-8211
Housing: Homeownership rate: 59.0%; Homeowner vacancy rate: 5.0%; Rental vacancy rate: 38.0%
Safety: Violent crime rate: 37.1 per 10,000 population; Property crime rate: 457.9 per 10,000 population
Additional Information Contacts
Village of Mackinaw City . . . . (231) 436-5351
    http://www.mackinawcity.org

MAPLE RIVER (township). Covers a land area of 35.324 square miles and a water area of 0.146 square miles. Located at 45.50° N. Lat; 84.80° W. Long.

Population: 1,348; Growth (since 2000): 9.4%; Density: 38.2 persons per square mile; Race: 92.7% White, 0.2% Black/African American, 0.1% Asian, 3.9% American Indian/Alaska Native, 0.0% Native Hawaiian/Other Pacific Islander, 2.7% Two or more races, 1.0% Hispanic of any race; Average household size: 2.73; Median age: 40.7; Age under 18: 26.9%; Age 65 and over: 12.8%; Males per 100 females: 108.0
Housing: Homeownership rate: 86.4%; Homeowner vacancy rate: 2.9%; Rental vacancy rate: 15.2%

MCKINLEY (township). Covers a land area of 35.109 square miles and a water area of 0.067 square miles. Located at 45.59° N. Lat; 84.79° W. Long.

Population: 1,297; Growth (since 2000): 2.2%; Density: 36.9 persons per square mile; Race: 88.0% White, 0.2% Black/African American, 1.3% Asian, 6.2% American Indian/Alaska Native, 0.0% Native Hawaiian/Other Pacific Islander, 4.2% Two or more races, 1.8% Hispanic of any race; Average household size: 2.54; Median age: 38.5; Age under 18: 28.1%; Age 65 and over: 12.3%; Males per 100 females: 95.0
Housing: Homeownership rate: 76.4%; Homeowner vacancy rate: 3.7%; Rental vacancy rate: 17.8%

ODEN (CDP). Covers a land area of 0.614 square miles and a water area of 0 square miles. Located at 45.43° N. Lat; 84.83° W. Long. Elevation is 620 feet.

Population: 363; Growth (since 2000): n/a; Density: 591.6 persons per square mile; Race: 91.5% White, 0.3% Black/African American, 0.3% Asian, 4.4% American Indian/Alaska Native, 0.0% Native Hawaiian/Other Pacific Islander, 3.3% Two or more races, 1.9% Hispanic of any race; Average household size: 2.36; Median age: 41.7; Age under 18: 21.2%; Age 65 and over: 12.1%; Males per 100 females: 107.4
Housing: Homeownership rate: 65.6%; Homeowner vacancy rate: 7.3%; Rental vacancy rate: 19.7%

PELLSTON (village). Covers a land area of 1.911 square miles and a water area of <.001 square miles. Located at 45.55° N. Lat; 84.78° W. Long. Elevation is 699 feet.

History: Pellston was platted in 1882 by William H. Pells, who named the town for himself. Pellston grew up around a large lumber mill and a station on the Grand Rapids & Indiana Railroad. It was incorporated as a village in 1907.
Population: 822; Growth (since 2000): 6.6%; Density: 430.2 persons per square mile; Race: 86.5% White, 0.2% Black/African American, 0.1% Asian, 8.0% American Indian/Alaska Native, 0.0% Native Hawaiian/Other Pacific Islander, 4.9% Two or more races, 1.9% Hispanic of any race; Average household size: 2.67; Median age: 34.1; Age under 18: 30.8%; Age 65 and over: 9.2%; Males per 100 females: 95.2
School District(s)
Pellston Public Schools (KG-12)
    2012-13 Enrollment: 628. . . . . (231) 539-8682
Housing: Homeownership rate: 73.3%; Homeowner vacancy rate: 4.2%; Rental vacancy rate: 10.9%
Airports: Pellston Regional Airport of Emmet County (primary service/non-hub)

PETOSKEY (city). County seat. Covers a land area of 5.089 square miles and a water area of 0.200 square miles. Located at 45.36° N. Lat; 85.01° W. Long. Elevation is 666 feet.

History: Petoskey was established on Little Traverse Bay, and named for Chief Bidasiga (Rising Sun), who owned this land when the Presbyterians founded a mission in 1852.
Population: 5,670; Growth (since 2000): -6.7%; Density: 1,114.1 persons per square mile; Race: 91.7% White, 0.7% Black/African American, 0.4% Asian, 4.7% American Indian/Alaska Native, 0.0% Native Hawaiian/Other Pacific Islander, 2.1% Two or more races, 1.9% Hispanic of any race; Average household size: 2.10; Median age: 39.8; Age under 18: 19.4%; Age 65 and over: 16.1%; Males per 100 females: 89.8; Marriage status: 31.7% never married, 45.5% now married, 0.5% separated, 7.6% widowed, 15.2% divorced; Foreign born: 3.3%; Speak English only: 95.8%; With disability: 11.3%; Veterans: 8.5%; Ancestry: 25.8% German, 16.7% English, 16.0% Irish, 13.0% Polish, 5.8% French
Employment: 18.6% management, business, and financial, 1.1% computer, engineering, and science, 11.9% education, legal, community service, arts, and media, 7.5% healthcare practitioners, 22.0% service, 29.1% sales and office, 6.5% natural resources, construction, and maintenance, 3.3% production, transportation, and material moving
Income: Per capita: $36,862; Median household: $41,827; Average household: $78,457; Households with income of $100,000 or more: 15.8%; Poverty rate: 13.5%
Educational Attainment: High school diploma or higher: 94.4%; Bachelor's degree or higher: 39.5%; Graduate/professional degree or higher: 15.6%
School District(s)
Concord Academy - Petoskey (KG-12)
    2012-13 Enrollment: 245. . . . . (231) 439-6800
Public Schools of Petoskey (PK-12)
    2012-13 Enrollment: 2,891. . . . . (231) 348-2100
Two-year College(s)
North Central Michigan College (Public)
    Fall 2013 Enrollment: 2,790 . . . . (231) 348-6600
    2013-14 Tuition: In-state $4,786; Out-of-state $6,038
Housing: Homeownership rate: 52.9%; Median home value: $190,100; Median year structure built: 1966; Homeowner vacancy rate: 6.8%; Median gross rent: $650 per month; Rental vacancy rate: 8.6%
Health Insurance: 88.9% have insurance; 74.2% have private insurance; 32.3% have public insurance; 11.1% do not have insurance; 1.2% of children under 18 do not have insurance
Hospitals: Mclaren - Northern Michigan (243 beds)
Safety: Violent crime rate: 1.7 per 10,000 population; Property crime rate: 134.6 per 10,000 population
Newspapers: Petoskey News-Review (daily circulation 10600); The Graphic (weekly circulation 14000)
Transportation: Commute: 73.2% car, 0.4% public transportation, 14.8% walk, 7.2% work from home; Median travel time to work: 14.4 minutes; Amtrak: Bus service available.
Additional Information Contacts
City of Petoskey . . . . (231) 347-2500
    http://www.petoskey.us

PLEASANTVIEW (township). Covers a land area of 35.604 square miles and a water area of 0.086 square miles. Located at 45.50° N. Lat; 84.90° W. Long.

History: Pleasant View Township was organized in 1876.
Population: 823; Growth (since 2000): -12.7%; Density: 23.1 persons per square mile; Race: 95.4% White, 0.9% Black/African American, 0.4% Asian, 1.2% American Indian/Alaska Native, 0.0% Native Hawaiian/Other Pacific Islander, 1.9% Two or more races, 1.3% Hispanic of any race; Average household size: 2.35; Median age: 45.2; Age under 18: 21.5%; Age 65 and over: 15.4%; Males per 100 females: 105.2
Housing: Homeownership rate: 82.3%; Homeowner vacancy rate: 2.4%; Rental vacancy rate: 42.2%

PONSHEWAING (CDP). Covers a land area of 0.088 square miles and a water area of 0 square miles. Located at 45.42° N. Lat; 84.81° W. Long. Elevation is 610 feet.

Population: 69; Growth (since 2000): n/a; Density: 784.3 persons per square mile; Race: 98.6% White, 0.0% Black/African American, 1.4% Asian, 0.0% American Indian/Alaska Native, 0.0% Native Hawaiian/Other Pacific Islander, 0.0% Two or more races, 1.4% Hispanic of any race;

Average household size: 2.09; Median age: 52.3; Age under 18: 14.5%; Age 65 and over: 23.2%; Males per 100 females: 122.6
Housing: Homeownership rate: 66.7%; Homeowner vacancy rate: 0.0%; Rental vacancy rate: 8.3%

READMOND (township). Covers a land area of 31.028 square miles and a water area of <.001 square miles. Located at 45.57° N. Lat; 85.04° W. Long.
Population: 581; Growth (since 2000): 17.8%; Density: 18.7 persons per square mile; Race: 93.5% White, 0.0% Black/African American, 0.0% Asian, 3.3% American Indian/Alaska Native, 0.0% Native Hawaiian/Other Pacific Islander, 2.9% Two or more races, 2.4% Hispanic of any race; Average household size: 2.30; Median age: 49.2; Age under 18: 19.6%; Age 65 and over: 21.9%; Males per 100 females: 107.5
Housing: Homeownership rate: 92.9%; Homeowner vacancy rate: 4.8%; Rental vacancy rate: 33.3%

RESORT (township). Covers a land area of 19.132 square miles and a water area of 2.463 square miles. Located at 45.33° N. Lat; 85.02° W. Long.
Population: 2,697; Growth (since 2000): 8.8%; Density: 141.0 persons per square mile; Race: 94.0% White, 0.4% Black/African American, 1.6% Asian, 2.1% American Indian/Alaska Native, 0.0% Native Hawaiian/Other Pacific Islander, 1.8% Two or more races, 1.0% Hispanic of any race; Average household size: 2.63; Median age: 42.9; Age under 18: 24.5%; Age 65 and over: 14.5%; Males per 100 females: 100.4; Marriage status: 11.7% never married, 74.1% now married, 0.0% separated, 5.0% widowed, 9.2% divorced; Foreign born: 3.9%; Speak English only: 96.3%; With disability: 11.2%; Veterans: 11.8%; Ancestry: 31.3% German, 19.2% Irish, 13.2% English, 8.9% Polish, 8.4% French
Employment: 12.6% management, business, and financial, 1.2% computer, engineering, and science, 6.1% education, legal, community service, arts, and media, 15.6% healthcare practitioners, 19.5% service, 28.4% sales and office, 12.4% natural resources, construction, and maintenance, 4.2% production, transportation, and material moving
Income: Per capita: $37,905; Median household: $71,026; Average household: $97,059; Households with income of $100,000 or more: 31.7%; Poverty rate: 4.5%
Educational Attainment: High school diploma or higher: 95.1%; Bachelor's degree or higher: 35.2%; Graduate/professional degree or higher: 18.2%
Housing: Homeownership rate: 88.7%; Median home value: $193,100; Median year structure built: 1985; Homeowner vacancy rate: 2.8%; Median gross rent: $655 per month; Rental vacancy rate: 22.4%
Health Insurance: 92.9% have insurance; 82.1% have private insurance; 28.0% have public insurance; 7.1% do not have insurance; 4.2% of children under 18 do not have insurance
Transportation: Commute: 92.9% car, 0.0% public transportation, 0.8% walk, 2.7% work from home; Median travel time to work: 16.7 minutes

SPRINGVALE (township). Covers a land area of 44.708 square miles and a water area of 2.349 square miles. Located at 45.34° N. Lat; 84.80° W. Long.
Population: 2,141; Growth (since 2000): 24.0%; Density: 47.9 persons per square mile; Race: 95.0% White, 0.3% Black/African American, 0.2% Asian, 1.7% American Indian/Alaska Native, 0.1% Native Hawaiian/Other Pacific Islander, 2.7% Two or more races, 1.0% Hispanic of any race; Average household size: 2.81; Median age: 38.6; Age under 18: 27.0%; Age 65 and over: 11.2%; Males per 100 females: 105.7
Housing: Homeownership rate: 88.8%; Homeowner vacancy rate: 1.7%; Rental vacancy rate: 11.5%

WAWATAM (township). Covers a land area of 15.727 square miles and a water area of 4.651 square miles. Located at 45.73° N. Lat; 84.78° W. Long.
Population: 661; Growth (since 2000): -6.2%; Density: 42.0 persons per square mile; Race: 92.6% White, 0.3% Black/African American, 0.0% Asian, 5.3% American Indian/Alaska Native, 0.0% Native Hawaiian/Other Pacific Islander, 1.7% Two or more races, 2.3% Hispanic of any race; Average household size: 2.09; Median age: 49.3; Age under 18: 19.1%; Age 65 and over: 24.8%; Males per 100 females: 84.1
Housing: Homeownership rate: 67.1%; Homeowner vacancy rate: 4.9%; Rental vacancy rate: 32.3%

WEST TRAVERSE (township). Covers a land area of 13.366 square miles and a water area of 0.028 square miles. Located at 45.45° N. Lat; 85.04° W. Long.
Population: 1,606; Growth (since 2000): 10.9%; Density: 120.2 persons per square mile; Race: 94.6% White, 0.0% Black/African American, 0.4% Asian, 3.8% American Indian/Alaska Native, 0.0% Native Hawaiian/Other Pacific Islander, 1.2% Two or more races, 1.2% Hispanic of any race; Average household size: 2.22; Median age: 54.4; Age under 18: 17.3%; Age 65 and over: 27.1%; Males per 100 females: 93.3
Housing: Homeownership rate: 87.7%; Homeowner vacancy rate: 3.7%; Rental vacancy rate: 14.2%

Genesee County

Located in southeast central Michigan; drained by the Flint and Shiawassee Rivers. Covers a land area of 636.977 square miles, a water area of 12.610 square miles, and is located in the Eastern Time Zone at 43.02° N. Lat., 83.71° W. Long. The county was founded in 1835. County seat is Flint.

Genesee County is part of the Flint, MI Metropolitan Statistical Area. The entire metro area includes: Genesee County, MI

Weather Station: Flint Bishop Arpt   Elevation: 766 feet

	Jan	Feb	Mar	Apr	May	Jun	Jul	Aug	Sep	Oct	Nov	Dec
High	30	33	44	57	69	78	82	80	73	60	47	35
Low	16	17	25	36	46	55	60	58	50	40	32	21
Precip	1.6	1.5	2.0	2.9	3.0	3.0	3.4	3.3	3.8	2.5	2.6	2.0
Snow	13.0	10.3	6.8	2.6	tr	tr	tr	tr	0.0	0.4	2.5	11.8

High and Low temperatures in degrees Fahrenheit; Precipitation and Snow in inches

Population: 425,790; Growth (since 2000): -2.4%; Density: 668.5 persons per square mile; Race: 74.5% White, 20.7% Black/African American, 0.9% Asian, 0.5% American Indian/Alaska Native, 0.0% Native Hawaiian/Other Pacific Islander, 2.6% two or more races, 3.0% Hispanic of any race; Average household size: 2.48; Median age: 38.5; Age under 18: 25.0%; Age 65 and over: 13.7%; Males per 100 females: 93.1; Marriage status: 33.0% never married, 47.1% now married, 1.9% separated, 6.7% widowed, 13.3% divorced; Foreign born: 2.3%; Speak English only: 96.6%; With disability: 16.0%; Veterans: 9.3%; Ancestry: 17.0% German, 10.5% Irish, 9.8% English, 5.9% American, 5.6% Polish
Religion: Six largest groups: 10.7% Catholicism, 7.0% Baptist, 3.4% Non-denominational Protestant, 3.2% Lutheran, 3.0% Methodist/Pietist, 3.0% Pentecostal
Economy: Unemployment rate: 6.2%; Leading industries: 18.7% retail trade; 16.6% health care and social assistance; 11.1% other services (except public administration); Farms: 835 totaling 123,276 acres; Company size: 5 employ 1,000 or more persons, 9 employ 500 to 999 persons, 149 employ 100 to 499 persons, 7,650 employ less than 100 persons; Business ownership: 12,004 women-owned, 4,442 Black-owned, 314 Hispanic-owned, 547 Asian-owned
Employment: 10.3% management, business, and financial, 3.7% computer, engineering, and science, 9.5% education, legal, community service, arts, and media, 7.0% healthcare practitioners, 20.3% service, 25.4% sales and office, 7.9% natural resources, construction, and maintenance, 16.1% production, transportation, and material moving
Income: Per capita: $22,380; Median household: $42,089; Average household: $55,534; Households with income of $100,000 or more: 13.9%; Poverty rate: 21.0%
Educational Attainment: High school diploma or higher: 88.7%; Bachelor's degree or higher: 18.9%; Graduate/professional degree or higher: 7.0%
Housing: Homeownership rate: 70.3%; Median home value: $91,700; Median year structure built: 1967; Homeowner vacancy rate: 3.1%; Median gross rent: $711 per month; Rental vacancy rate: 13.5%
Vital Statistics: Birth rate: 117.2 per 10,000 population; Death rate: 101.5 per 10,000 population; Age-adjusted cancer mortality rate: 185.4 deaths per 100,000 population
Health Insurance: 89.9% have insurance; 63.7% have private insurance; 41.8% have public insurance; 10.1% do not have insurance; 3.3% of children under 18 do not have insurance
Health Care: Physicians: 26.6 per 10,000 population; Hospital beds: 28.2 per 10,000 population; Hospital admissions: 1,467.7 per 10,000 population
Air Quality Index: 85.3% good, 14.7% moderate, 0.0% unhealthy for sensitive individuals, 0.0% unhealthy (percent of days)

Transportation: Commute: 93.8% car, 1.1% public transportation, 1.2% walk, 3.1% work from home; Median travel time to work: 25.5 minutes
Presidential Election: 63.3% Obama, 35.2% Romney (2012)
Additional Information Contacts
Genesee Government. . . . . (810) 257-3163
  http://www.gc4me.com

Genesee County Communities

ARGENTINE (CDP). Covers a land area of 2.368 square miles and a water area of 0.908 square miles. Located at 42.79° N. Lat; 83.84° W. Long. Elevation is 873 feet.
Population: 2,525; Growth (since 2000): 10.5%; Density: 1,066.4 persons per square mile; Race: 97.1% White, 0.4% Black/African American, 0.1% Asian, 0.4% American Indian/Alaska Native, 0.1% Native Hawaiian/Other Pacific Islander, 1.5% Two or more races, 2.1% Hispanic of any race; Average household size: 2.53; Median age: 41.6; Age under 18: 24.2%; Age 65 and over: 12.1%; Males per 100 females: 104.5; Marriage status: 15.0% never married, 62.4% now married, 1.9% separated, 4.7% widowed, 17.9% divorced; Foreign born: 5.0%; Speak English only: 98.4%; With disability: 15.1%; Veterans: 9.1%; Ancestry: 26.6% German, 14.1% Polish, 8.6% English, 7.2% Irish, 5.0% French
Employment: 16.8% management, business, and financial, 3.5% computer, engineering, and science, 14.9% education, legal, community service, arts, and media, 6.1% healthcare practitioners, 10.2% service, 15.1% sales and office, 8.8% natural resources, construction, and maintenance, 24.5% production, transportation, and material moving
Income: Per capita: $30,701; Median household: $67,500; Average household: $75,885; Households with income of $100,000 or more: 28.4%; Poverty rate: 10.1%
Educational Attainment: High school diploma or higher: 89.9%; Bachelor's degree or higher: 22.8%; Graduate/professional degree or higher: 11.6%
Housing: Homeownership rate: 85.5%; Median home value: $169,500; Median year structure built: 1979; Homeowner vacancy rate: 2.8%; Median gross rent: $633 per month; Rental vacancy rate: 7.2%
Health Insurance: 94.2% have insurance; 81.7% have private insurance; 27.1% have public insurance; 5.8% do not have insurance; 0.0% of children under 18 do not have insurance
Transportation: Commute: 95.1% car, 0.0% public transportation, 0.8% walk, 2.5% work from home; Median travel time to work: 28.7 minutes

ARGENTINE (township). Covers a land area of 34.652 square miles and a water area of 1.655 square miles. Located at 42.83° N. Lat; 83.86° W. Long. Elevation is 873 feet.
Population: 6,913; Growth (since 2000): 6.0%; Density: 199.5 persons per square mile; Race: 97.7% White, 0.3% Black/African American, 0.1% Asian, 0.3% American Indian/Alaska Native, 0.0% Native Hawaiian/Other Pacific Islander, 1.2% Two or more races, 1.4% Hispanic of any race; Average household size: 2.67; Median age: 40.3; Age under 18: 25.5%; Age 65 and over: 10.6%; Males per 100 females: 104.3; Marriage status: 23.0% never married, 61.4% now married, 2.1% separated, 4.9% widowed, 10.8% divorced; Foreign born: 3.3%; Speak English only: 97.5%; With disability: 11.6%; Veterans: 8.0%; Ancestry: 25.1% German, 11.6% English, 11.0% Irish, 7.7% Polish, 7.1% American
Employment: 11.7% management, business, and financial, 3.1% computer, engineering, and science, 10.5% education, legal, community service, arts, and media, 5.8% healthcare practitioners, 13.9% service, 20.9% sales and office, 12.9% natural resources, construction, and maintenance, 21.1% production, transportation, and material moving
Income: Per capita: $26,367; Median household: $64,135; Average household: $72,627; Households with income of $100,000 or more: 24.7%; Poverty rate: 12.2%
Educational Attainment: High school diploma or higher: 91.7%; Bachelor's degree or higher: 21.6%; Graduate/professional degree or higher: 7.9%
Housing: Homeownership rate: 89.8%; Median home value: $156,800; Median year structure built: 1983; Homeowner vacancy rate: 2.0%; Median gross rent: $864 per month; Rental vacancy rate: 5.4%
Health Insurance: 92.8% have insurance; 78.3% have private insurance; 25.7% have public insurance; 7.2% do not have insurance; 1.1% of children under 18 do not have insurance
Transportation: Commute: 95.3% car, 0.0% public transportation, 0.5% walk, 3.7% work from home; Median travel time to work: 31.9 minutes

ATLAS (township). Covers a land area of 35.215 square miles and a water area of 0.717 square miles. Located at 42.92° N. Lat; 83.52° W. Long. Elevation is 860 feet.
Population: 7,993; Growth (since 2000): 10.1%; Density: 227.0 persons per square mile; Race: 97.1% White, 0.7% Black/African American, 0.7% Asian, 0.2% American Indian/Alaska Native, 0.0% Native Hawaiian/Other Pacific Islander, 0.9% Two or more races, 2.1% Hispanic of any race; Average household size: 2.88; Median age: 41.5; Age under 18: 27.5%; Age 65 and over: 10.5%; Males per 100 females: 102.7; Marriage status: 23.1% never married, 65.1% now married, 0.8% separated, 4.7% widowed, 7.0% divorced; Foreign born: 2.9%; Speak English only: 97.1%; With disability: 8.0%; Veterans: 5.9%; Ancestry: 20.8% German, 15.6% Irish, 15.4% English, 10.3% Polish, 5.9% Italian
Employment: 12.8% management, business, and financial, 6.2% computer, engineering, and science, 13.7% education, legal, community service, arts, and media, 9.3% healthcare practitioners, 15.8% service, 18.4% sales and office, 11.5% natural resources, construction, and maintenance, 12.3% production, transportation, and material moving
Income: Per capita: $35,486; Median household: $83,575; Average household: $100,489; Households with income of $100,000 or more: 39.5%; Poverty rate: 5.1%
Educational Attainment: High school diploma or higher: 94.8%; Bachelor's degree or higher: 31.4%; Graduate/professional degree or higher: 14.6%
Housing: Homeownership rate: 92.8%; Median home value: $187,200; Median year structure built: 1988; Homeowner vacancy rate: 1.6%; Median gross rent: $932 per month; Rental vacancy rate: 4.3%
Health Insurance: 95.5% have insurance; 86.2% have private insurance; 21.1% have public insurance; 4.5% do not have insurance; 2.8% of children under 18 do not have insurance
Transportation: Commute: 96.2% car, 0.0% public transportation, 0.2% walk, 2.7% work from home; Median travel time to work: 31.1 minutes
Additional Information Contacts
Atlas Township . . . . (810) 636-2548
  http://www.atlastownship.org

BEECHER (CDP). Covers a land area of 5.882 square miles and a water area of 0.019 square miles. Located at 43.09° N. Lat; 83.70° W. Long. Elevation is 801 feet.
Population: 10,232; Growth (since 2000): -20.0%; Density: 1,739.5 persons per square mile; Race: 25.3% White, 69.1% Black/African American, 0.1% Asian, 0.8% American Indian/Alaska Native, 0.0% Native Hawaiian/Other Pacific Islander, 3.4% Two or more races, 3.5% Hispanic of any race; Average household size: 2.74; Median age: 32.9; Age under 18: 30.5%; Age 65 and over: 12.4%; Males per 100 females: 91.8; Marriage status: 50.2% never married, 29.0% now married, 2.4% separated, 6.8% widowed, 14.0% divorced; Foreign born: 0.5%; Speak English only: 98.7%; With disability: 23.6%; Veterans: 7.9%; Ancestry: 4.6% German, 3.8% Irish, 2.6% African, 2.4% American, 1.8% English
Employment: 3.4% management, business, and financial, 0.2% computer, engineering, and science, 7.0% education, legal, community service, arts, and media, 3.9% healthcare practitioners, 33.9% service, 26.0% sales and office, 6.2% natural resources, construction, and maintenance, 19.4% production, transportation, and material moving
Income: Per capita: $13,813; Median household: $25,568; Average household: $38,175; Households with income of $100,000 or more: 2.5%; Poverty rate: 42.2%
Educational Attainment: High school diploma or higher: 79.0%; Bachelor's degree or higher: 6.0%; Graduate/professional degree or higher: 1.3%
Housing: Homeownership rate: 62.6%; Median home value: $45,600; Median year structure built: 1960; Homeowner vacancy rate: 3.6%; Median gross rent: $777 per month; Rental vacancy rate: 20.8%
Health Insurance: 89.0% have insurance; 33.8% have private insurance; 70.0% have public insurance; 11.0% do not have insurance; 2.5% of children under 18 do not have insurance
Transportation: Commute: 85.9% car, 4.2% public transportation, 0.8% walk, 4.8% work from home; Median travel time to work: 24.0 minutes

BURTON (city). Covers a land area of 23.355 square miles and a water area of 0.068 square miles. Located at 43.00° N. Lat; 83.62° W. Long. Elevation is 774 feet.
Population: 29,999; Growth (since 2000): -1.0%; Density: 1,284.5 persons per square mile; Race: 88.1% White, 7.3% Black/African American, 0.6% Asian, 0.6% American Indian/Alaska Native, 0.0% Native Hawaiian/Other

Pacific Islander, 2.5% Two or more races, 3.1% Hispanic of any race; Average household size: 2.50; Median age: 38.6; Age under 18: 24.0%; Age 65 and over: 13.2%; Males per 100 females: 95.3; Marriage status: 30.9% never married, 47.9% now married, 1.5% separated, 7.5% widowed, 13.7% divorced; Foreign born: 1.2%; Speak English only: 97.9%; With disability: 17.4%; Veterans: 9.6%; Ancestry: 19.6% German, 12.6% Irish, 10.1% English, 7.2% American, 5.9% French

Employment: 8.5% management, business, and financial, 2.8% computer, engineering, and science, 8.8% education, legal, community service, arts, and media, 5.9% healthcare practitioners, 20.3% service, 26.3% sales and office, 7.6% natural resources, construction, and maintenance, 19.7% production, transportation, and material moving

Income: Per capita: $21,804; Median household: $43,983; Average household: $54,482; Households with income of $100,000 or more: 11.5%; Poverty rate: 19.7%

Educational Attainment: High school diploma or higher: 88.8%; Bachelor's degree or higher: 14.2%; Graduate/professional degree or higher: 4.3%

School District(s)

Atherton Community Schools (KG-12)
   2012-13 Enrollment: 799. . . . . (810) 591-9182
Bendle Public Schools (PK-12)
   2012-13 Enrollment: 2,295 . . . . (810) 591-2501
Bentley Community SD in the County of Genesee (PK-12)
   2012-13 Enrollment: 793. . . . . (810) 591-9100
Burton Glen Charter Academy (KG-12)
   2012-13 Enrollment: 665. . . . . (810) 744-2300
Carman-Ainsworth Community Schools (PK-12)
   2012-13 Enrollment: 4,594 . . . . (810) 591-3205
Kearsley Community SD (PK-12)
   2012-13 Enrollment: 3,266 . . . . (810) 591-8000
Madison Academy (KG-12)
   2012-13 Enrollment: 576. . . . . (810) 655-2949

Housing: Homeownership rate: 74.7%; Median home value: $74,600; Median year structure built: 1962; Homeowner vacancy rate: 3.5%; Median gross rent: $766 per month; Rental vacancy rate: 8.1%

Health Insurance: 89.0% have insurance; 65.4% have private insurance; 38.6% have public insurance; 11.0% do not have insurance; 6.7% of children under 18 do not have insurance

Safety: Violent crime rate: 40.7 per 10,000 population; Property crime rate: 423.4 per 10,000 population

Transportation: Commute: 96.1% car, 0.2% public transportation, 0.4% walk, 2.4% work from home; Median travel time to work: 23.2 minutes

Additional Information Contacts
City of Burton. . . . . (810) 743-1500
   http://www.burtonmi.com

CLAYTON (charter township). Covers a land area of 34.159 square miles and a water area of 0.054 square miles. Located at 43.01° N. Lat; 83.87° W. Long.

Population: 7,581; Growth (since 2000): 0.5%; Density: 221.9 persons per square mile; Race: 93.2% White, 3.2% Black/African American, 0.7% Asian, 0.5% American Indian/Alaska Native, 0.1% Native Hawaiian/Other Pacific Islander, 1.5% Two or more races, 2.8% Hispanic of any race; Average household size: 2.61; Median age: 43.5; Age under 18: 23.0%; Age 65 and over: 16.0%; Males per 100 females: 94.9; Marriage status: 27.0% never married, 56.2% now married, 0.3% separated, 5.2% widowed, 11.5% divorced; Foreign born: 1.8%; Speak English only: 95.1%; With disability: 17.5%; Veterans: 10.4%; Ancestry: 24.0% German, 15.9% Irish, 13.9% English, 8.1% American, 6.5% Polish

Employment: 9.6% management, business, and financial, 1.9% computer, engineering, and science, 9.7% education, legal, community service, arts, and media, 7.4% healthcare practitioners, 21.7% service, 27.5% sales and office, 9.9% natural resources, construction, and maintenance, 12.3% production, transportation, and material moving

Income: Per capita: $26,808; Median household: $57,688; Average household: $69,348; Households with income of $100,000 or more: 19.5%; Poverty rate: 10.1%

Educational Attainment: High school diploma or higher: 92.4%; Bachelor's degree or higher: 17.6%; Graduate/professional degree or higher: 5.8%

Housing: Homeownership rate: 89.1%; Median home value: $111,700; Median year structure built: 1973; Homeowner vacancy rate: 2.4%; Median gross rent: $741 per month; Rental vacancy rate: 11.3%

Health Insurance: 91.6% have insurance; 75.3% have private insurance; 35.9% have public insurance; 8.4% do not have insurance; 1.2% of children under 18 do not have insurance

Safety: Violent crime rate: 16.4 per 10,000 population; Property crime rate: 103.8 per 10,000 population

Transportation: Commute: 96.1% car, 0.1% public transportation, 0.0% walk, 3.4% work from home; Median travel time to work: 26.2 minutes

CLIO (city). Covers a land area of 1.112 square miles and a water area of 0.011 square miles. Located at 43.18° N. Lat; 83.74° W. Long. Elevation is 722 feet.

History: A sawmill was built here in 1837, and the village grew with the arrival of the Pere Marquette Railroad in 1861. Clio was incorporated as a village in 1873 and as a city in 1928.

Population: 2,646; Growth (since 2000): 6.6%; Density: 2,380.2 persons per square mile; Race: 95.2% White, 1.1% Black/African American, 0.2% Asian, 0.6% American Indian/Alaska Native, 0.0% Native Hawaiian/Other Pacific Islander, 2.1% Two or more races, 3.2% Hispanic of any race; Average household size: 2.21; Median age: 35.7; Age under 18: 24.3%; Age 65 and over: 15.5%; Males per 100 females: 89.3; Marriage status: 30.4% never married, 47.7% now married, 6.7% separated, 7.7% widowed, 14.1% divorced; Foreign born: 1.6%; Speak English only: 98.2%; With disability: 16.4%; Veterans: 10.9%; Ancestry: 18.2% Irish, 15.0% German, 14.3% English, 9.2% American, 7.7% Polish

Employment: 8.9% management, business, and financial, 3.2% computer, engineering, and science, 10.2% education, legal, community service, arts, and media, 9.9% healthcare practitioners, 19.8% service, 22.4% sales and office, 10.1% natural resources, construction, and maintenance, 15.4% production, transportation, and material moving

Income: Per capita: $18,049; Median household: $32,500; Average household: $38,157; Households with income of $100,000 or more: 4.1%; Poverty rate: 16.9%

Educational Attainment: High school diploma or higher: 87.5%; Bachelor's degree or higher: 14.0%; Graduate/professional degree or higher: 4.1%

School District(s)

Clio Area SD (PK-12)
   2012-13 Enrollment: 3,473 . . . . (810) 591-7490

Housing: Homeownership rate: 51.4%; Median home value: $78,500; Median year structure built: 1972; Homeowner vacancy rate: 3.4%; Median gross rent: $613 per month; Rental vacancy rate: 10.7%

Health Insurance: 89.6% have insurance; 65.0% have private insurance; 43.2% have public insurance; 10.4% do not have insurance; 0.0% of children under 18 do not have insurance

Safety: Violent crime rate: 15.5 per 10,000 population; Property crime rate: 395.3 per 10,000 population

Transportation: Commute: 93.3% car, 0.0% public transportation, 3.0% walk, 1.7% work from home; Median travel time to work: 29.5 minutes

Additional Information Contacts
City of Clio. . . . . (810) 686-5850
   http://www.clio.govoffice.com

DAVISON (city). Covers a land area of 1.976 square miles and a water area of 0 square miles. Located at 43.03° N. Lat; 83.52° W. Long. Elevation is 794 feet.

History: Davison developed as a service center for the surrounding farming area, and a residential center for workers employed in Flint factories.

Population: 5,173; Growth (since 2000): -6.6%; Density: 2,617.9 persons per square mile; Race: 94.9% White, 1.8% Black/African American, 0.3% Asian, 0.3% American Indian/Alaska Native, 0.0% Native Hawaiian/Other Pacific Islander, 2.0% Two or more races, 2.9% Hispanic of any race; Average household size: 2.18; Median age: 39.5; Age under 18: 23.5%; Age 65 and over: 16.9%; Males per 100 females: 82.5; Marriage status: 32.8% never married, 43.2% now married, 2.6% separated, 5.9% widowed, 18.2% divorced; Foreign born: 0.9%; Speak English only: 99.4%; With disability: 14.3%; Veterans: 9.1%; Ancestry: 24.7% German, 20.2% English, 15.4% Irish, 7.8% French, 7.6% Polish

Employment: 14.2% management, business, and financial, 4.8% computer, engineering, and science, 7.7% education, legal, community service, arts, and media, 4.7% healthcare practitioners, 18.3% service, 33.7% sales and office, 3.1% natural resources, construction, and maintenance, 13.4% production, transportation, and material moving

Income: Per capita: $22,140; Median household: $35,861; Average household: $48,435; Households with income of $100,000 or more: 11.8%; Poverty rate: 15.1%

Educational Attainment: High school diploma or higher: 92.4%; Bachelor's degree or higher: 22.8%; Graduate/professional degree or higher: 9.0%

School District(s)
Davison Community Schools (PK-12)
    2012-13 Enrollment: 5,565 . . . . (810) 591-0801

Vocational/Technical School(s)
Ross Medical Education Center-Davison (Private, For-profit)
    Fall 2013 Enrollment: 181 . . . . (810) 658-1424
    2013-14 Tuition: $15,680

Housing: Homeownership rate: 54.8%; Median home value: $94,500; Median year structure built: 1967; Homeowner vacancy rate: 2.2%; Median gross rent: $598 per month; Rental vacancy rate: 12.0%

Health Insurance: 84.3% have insurance; 64.1% have private insurance; 37.9% have public insurance; 15.7% do not have insurance; 3.5% of children under 18 do not have insurance

Newspapers: Davison Index (weekly circulation 11000)

Transportation: Commute: 95.8% car, 0.4% public transportation, 2.0% walk, 0.9% work from home; Median travel time to work: 23.3 minutes

Additional Information Contacts
City of Davison . . . . (810) 653-2191
    http://www.cityofdavison.org

DAVISON (township). Covers a land area of 33.318 square miles and a water area of 0.315 square miles. Located at 43.00° N. Lat; 83.52° W. Long. Elevation is 794 feet.

History: Settled 1836; incorporated as village 1889, as city 1939.

Population: 19,575; Growth (since 2000): 10.5%; Density: 587.5 persons per square mile; Race: 93.3% White, 2.9% Black/African American, 0.8% Asian, 0.6% American Indian/Alaska Native, 0.0% Native Hawaiian/Other Pacific Islander, 1.9% Two or more races, 3.2% Hispanic of any race; Average household size: 2.38; Median age: 38.4; Age under 18: 23.7%; Age 65 and over: 13.9%; Males per 100 females: 91.2; Marriage status: 30.9% never married, 48.6% now married, 0.8% separated, 6.0% widowed, 14.5% divorced; Foreign born: 1.5%; Speak English only: 96.3%; With disability: 12.5%; Veterans: 9.7%; Ancestry: 20.5% German, 14.9% English, 14.3% Irish, 9.0% Polish, 6.2% American

Employment: 12.2% management, business, and financial, 4.3% computer, engineering, and science, 10.1% education, legal, community service, arts, and media, 6.4% healthcare practitioners, 16.0% service, 27.9% sales and office, 6.1% natural resources, construction, and maintenance, 17.0% production, transportation, and material moving

Income: Per capita: $25,953; Median household: $50,739; Average household: $62,579; Households with income of $100,000 or more: 18.1%; Poverty rate: 9.2%

Educational Attainment: High school diploma or higher: 94.7%; Bachelor's degree or higher: 21.7%; Graduate/professional degree or higher: 7.9%

School District(s)
Davison Community Schools (PK-12)
    2012-13 Enrollment: 5,565 . . . . (810) 591-0801

Vocational/Technical School(s)
Ross Medical Education Center-Davison (Private, For-profit)
    Fall 2013 Enrollment: 181 . . . . (810) 658-1424
    2013-14 Tuition: $15,680

Housing: Homeownership rate: 65.7%; Median home value: $120,200; Median year structure built: 1979; Homeowner vacancy rate: 2.5%; Median gross rent: $632 per month; Rental vacancy rate: 8.5%

Health Insurance: 91.2% have insurance; 76.0% have private insurance; 33.0% have public insurance; 8.8% do not have insurance; 2.4% of children under 18 do not have insurance

Safety: Violent crime rate: 14.1 per 10,000 population; Property crime rate: 204.0 per 10,000 population

Newspapers: Davison Index (weekly circulation 11000)

Transportation: Commute: 95.7% car, 0.2% public transportation, 1.2% walk, 2.6% work from home; Median travel time to work: 26.3 minutes

Additional Information Contacts
Davison Township . . . . (810) 653-4156
    http://davisontwp-mi.org

FENTON (charter township). Covers a land area of 23.803 square miles and a water area of 3.728 square miles. Located at 42.84° N. Lat; 83.75° W. Long. Elevation is 906 feet.

History: Settled 1834, incorporated 1863.

Population: 15,552; Growth (since 2000): 19.9%; Density: 653.4 persons per square mile; Race: 96.5% White, 0.4% Black/African American, 1.0% Asian, 0.4% American Indian/Alaska Native, 0.0% Native Hawaiian/Other Pacific Islander, 1.4% Two or more races, 1.8% Hispanic of any race; Average household size: 2.59; Median age: 42.7; Age under 18: 24.3%; Age 65 and over: 13.7%; Males per 100 females: 99.0; Marriage status: 20.7% never married, 62.4% now married, 0.5% separated, 5.2% widowed, 11.6% divorced; Foreign born: 2.3%; Speak English only: 96.7%; With disability: 9.0%; Veterans: 9.7%; Ancestry: 26.3% German, 14.6% Irish, 12.3% English, 9.4% Polish, 6.2% American

Employment: 15.1% management, business, and financial, 7.5% computer, engineering, and science, 11.7% education, legal, community service, arts, and media, 7.9% healthcare practitioners, 15.0% service, 23.5% sales and office, 6.5% natural resources, construction, and maintenance, 12.9% production, transportation, and material moving

Income: Per capita: $31,948; Median household: $71,667; Average household: $83,193; Households with income of $100,000 or more: 31.0%; Poverty rate: 8.9%

Educational Attainment: High school diploma or higher: 94.4%; Bachelor's degree or higher: 33.0%; Graduate/professional degree or higher: 12.2%

School District(s)
Fenton Area Public Schools (PK-12)
    2012-13 Enrollment: 3,466 . . . . (810) 591-4700
Lake Fenton Community Schools (PK-12)
    2012-13 Enrollment: 1,987 . . . . (810) 591-2532

Housing: Homeownership rate: 89.7%; Median home value: $173,500; Median year structure built: 1987; Homeowner vacancy rate: 2.4%; Median gross rent: $891 per month; Rental vacancy rate: 11.5%

Health Insurance: 92.7% have insurance; 84.8% have private insurance; 22.6% have public insurance; 7.3% do not have insurance; 3.6% of children under 18 do not have insurance

Newspapers: Tri-County Times (weekly circulation 24000)

Transportation: Commute: 95.4% car, 0.3% public transportation, 0.6% walk, 2.9% work from home; Median travel time to work: 28.5 minutes

Additional Information Contacts
Fenton Township . . . . (810) 629-1537
    http://www.fentontownship.org

FENTON (city). Covers a land area of 6.678 square miles and a water area of 0.324 square miles. Located at 42.80° N. Lat; 83.71° W. Long. Elevation is 906 feet.

History: Fenton developed around a cement plant, utilizing marl taken from the many nearby lakes.

Population: 11,756; Growth (since 2000): 11.1%; Density: 1,760.5 persons per square mile; Race: 95.1% White, 1.3% Black/African American, 0.7% Asian, 0.3% American Indian/Alaska Native, 0.0% Native Hawaiian/Other Pacific Islander, 2.0% Two or more races, 2.5% Hispanic of any race; Average household size: 2.27; Median age: 36.0; Age under 18: 24.1%; Age 65 and over: 14.4%; Males per 100 females: 88.1; Marriage status: 29.5% never married, 48.3% now married, 2.0% separated, 9.0% widowed, 13.2% divorced; Foreign born: 3.4%; Speak English only: 96.7%; With disability: 10.3%; Veterans: 9.3%; Ancestry: 26.4% German, 14.6% Irish, 10.3% English, 9.8% Polish, 6.5% American

Employment: 12.6% management, business, and financial, 5.7% computer, engineering, and science, 8.3% education, legal, community service, arts, and media, 4.6% healthcare practitioners, 20.3% service, 23.3% sales and office, 8.4% natural resources, construction, and maintenance, 16.8% production, transportation, and material moving

Income: Per capita: $23,841; Median household: $43,852; Average household: $56,285; Households with income of $100,000 or more: 14.7%; Poverty rate: 15.6%

Educational Attainment: High school diploma or higher: 90.4%; Bachelor's degree or higher: 27.3%; Graduate/professional degree or higher: 9.8%

School District(s)
Fenton Area Public Schools (PK-12)
    2012-13 Enrollment: 3,466 . . . . (810) 591-4700
Lake Fenton Community Schools (PK-12)
    2012-13 Enrollment: 1,987 . . . . (810) 591-2532

Housing: Homeownership rate: 58.9%; Median home value: $105,800; Median year structure built: 1983; Homeowner vacancy rate: 3.9%; Median gross rent: $781 per month; Rental vacancy rate: 8.5%
Health Insurance: 86.5% have insurance; 69.3% have private insurance; 30.2% have public insurance; 13.5% do not have insurance; 5.2% of children under 18 do not have insurance
Safety: Violent crime rate: 14.8 per 10,000 population; Property crime rate: 287.1 per 10,000 population
Newspapers: Tri-County Times (weekly circulation 24000)
Transportation: Commute: 93.8% car, 0.5% public transportation, 1.1% walk, 4.5% work from home; Median travel time to work: 27.0 minutes
Additional Information Contacts
City of Fenton . . . . (810) 629-2261
  http://www.cityoffenton.org

FLINT (charter township). Covers a land area of 23.281 square miles and a water area of 0.217 square miles. Located at 43.00° N. Lat; 83.77° W. Long. Elevation is 751 feet.
Population: 31,929; Growth (since 2000): -5.2%; Density: 1,371.4 persons per square mile; Race: 68.0% White, 25.7% Black/African American, 1.9% Asian, 0.5% American Indian/Alaska Native, 0.0% Native Hawaiian/Other Pacific Islander, 3.1% Two or more races, 2.9% Hispanic of any race; Average household size: 2.34; Median age: 40.6; Age under 18: 23.0%; Age 65 and over: 17.2%; Males per 100 females: 86.8; Marriage status: 32.9% never married, 44.4% now married, 3.0% separated, 8.7% widowed, 14.1% divorced; Foreign born: 4.2%; Speak English only: 94.2%; With disability: 17.0%; Veterans: 8.9%; Ancestry: 13.6% German, 8.8% English, 8.4% Irish, 4.7% American, 4.0% Polish
Employment: 7.6% management, business, and financial, 3.2% computer, engineering, and science, 9.8% education, legal, community service, arts, and media, 6.5% healthcare practitioners, 25.0% service, 23.8% sales and office, 6.6% natural resources, construction, and maintenance, 17.4% production, transportation, and material moving
Income: Per capita: $22,347; Median household: $40,888; Average household: $53,009; Households with income of $100,000 or more: 11.1%; Poverty rate: 19.2%
Educational Attainment: High school diploma or higher: 87.2%; Bachelor's degree or higher: 19.1%; Graduate/professional degree or higher: 7.1%
School District(s)
Academy of Flint (KG-12)
  2012-13 Enrollment: 425. . . . . (810) 789-9484
Beecher Community SD (PK-12)
  2012-13 Enrollment: 1,360 . . . . (810) 591-9201
Bendle Public Schools (PK-12)
  2012-13 Enrollment: 2,295 . . . . (810) 591-2501
Carman-Ainsworth Community Schools (PK-12)
  2012-13 Enrollment: 4,594 . . . . (810) 591-3205
Flint SD (PK-12)
  2012-13 Enrollment: 8,485 . . . . (810) 760-1249
Genesee ISD (PK-12)
  2012-13 Enrollment: 1,776 . . . . (810) 591-4402
International Academy of Flint (KG-12)
  2012-13 Enrollment: 1,098 . . . . (810) 600-5000
Kearsley Community SD (PK-12)
  2012-13 Enrollment: 3,266 . . . . (810) 591-8000
Linden Charter Academy (KG-12)
  2012-13 Enrollment: 745. . . . . (810) 720-0515
Mich School F/t Deaf/mich School F/t Blind-Lio (PK-12)
  2012-13 Enrollment: 110. . . . . (810) 257-1467
Mt. Morris Consolidated Schools (PK-12)
  2012-13 Enrollment: 2,457 . . . . (810) 591-8760
Northridge Academy (KG-12)
  2012-13 Enrollment: 261. . . . . (810) 785-8811
Richfield Public Schools Academy (PK-12)
  2012-13 Enrollment: 633. . . . . (810) 736-1281
Westwood Heights Schools (PK-12)
  2012-13 Enrollment: 842. . . . . (810) 591-0870
Four-year College(s)
Baker College Center for Graduate Studies (Private, Not-for-profit)
  Fall 2013 Enrollment: 5,270 . . . . (810) 766-4021
  2013-14 Tuition: In-state $10,800; Out-of-state $10,800
Baker College of Flint (Private, Not-for-profit)
  Fall 2013 Enrollment: 4,977 . . . . (810) 766-4000
  2013-14 Tuition: In-state $8,100; Out-of-state $8,100

Kettering University (Private, Not-for-profit)
  Fall 2013 Enrollment: 1,985 . . . . (800) 955-4464
  2013-14 Tuition: In-state $35,600; Out-of-state $35,600
University of Michigan-Flint (Public)
  Fall 2013 Enrollment: 8,555 . . . . (810) 762-3000
  2013-14 Tuition: In-state $9,356; Out-of-state $18,238
Two-year College(s)
Flint Institute of Barbering Inc (Private, For-profit)
  Fall 2013 Enrollment: 56. . . . . (810) 232-4711
Mott Community College (Public)
  Fall 2013 Enrollment: 9,683 . . . . (810) 762-0200
  2013-14 Tuition: In-state $4,498; Out-of-state $6,228
Vocational/Technical School(s)
Regency Beauty Institute-Flint (Private, For-profit)
  Fall 2013 Enrollment: 130. . . . . (800) 787-6456
  2013-14 Tuition: $17,300
Ross Medical Education Center-Flint (Private, For-profit)
  Fall 2013 Enrollment: 307. . . . . (810) 733-7488
  2013-14 Tuition: $15,680
Housing: Homeownership rate: 65.1%; Median home value: $85,300; Median year structure built: 1969; Homeowner vacancy rate: 2.7%; Median gross rent: $716 per month; Rental vacancy rate: 14.5%
Health Insurance: 89.9% have insurance; 63.7% have private insurance; 44.0% have public insurance; 10.1% do not have insurance; 3.4% of children under 18 do not have insurance
Hospitals: Hurley Medical Center (443 beds); Mclaren Flint (452 beds)
Safety: Violent crime rate: 107.8 per 10,000 population; Property crime rate: 629.9 per 10,000 population
Newspapers: Flint Journal (daily circulation 83500); Suburban Newspaper Group (weekly circulation 93000)
Transportation: Commute: 93.8% car, 0.9% public transportation, 1.6% walk, 2.9% work from home; Median travel time to work: 22.0 minutes; Amtrak: Train service available.
Airports: Bishop International (primary service/small hub)
Additional Information Contacts
Flint Charter Township . . . . (810) 732-1350
  http://www.flinttownship.com

FLINT (city). County seat. Covers a land area of 33.416 square miles and a water area of 0.636 square miles. Located at 43.02° N. Lat; 83.69° W. Long. Elevation is 751 feet.
History: Jacob Smith settled on the site of Flint after negotiating a treaty with the local tribes in 1819. Others joined him, including John Todd in 1830, who operated a tavern and a ferry across the Flint River. When Michigan became a state in 1837, Flint was a village of 300 and the seat of Genesee County. The early lumbering industry led to the manufacture of two-wheeled carts, which later gave way to carriage shops. Flint was ready in 1904 for the founding of the Buick Motor Company, which added engines to Flint's carriages. Pioneers in Flint's automobile industry were C.W. Nash, Walter P. Chrysler, and William C. Durant.
Population: 102,434; Growth (since 2000): -18.0%; Density: 3,065.4 persons per square mile; Race: 37.4% White, 56.6% Black/African American, 0.5% Asian, 0.5% American Indian/Alaska Native, 0.0% Native Hawaiian/Other Pacific Islander, 3.9% Two or more races, 3.9% Hispanic of any race; Average household size: 2.45; Median age: 33.6; Age under 18: 27.3%; Age 65 and over: 10.7%; Males per 100 females: 92.2; Marriage status: 48.0% never married, 30.1% now married, 3.2% separated, 6.3% widowed, 15.7% divorced; Foreign born: 1.2%; Speak English only: 97.4%; With disability: 20.6%; Veterans: 7.9%; Ancestry: 6.3% German, 5.4% Irish, 4.1% English, 3.7% American, 1.8% French
Employment: 6.1% management, business, and financial, 2.2% computer, engineering, and science, 9.0% education, legal, community service, arts, and media, 4.4% healthcare practitioners, 28.3% service, 24.4% sales and office, 7.0% natural resources, construction, and maintenance, 18.7% production, transportation, and material moving
Income: Per capita: $14,360; Median household: $24,834; Average household: $34,085; Households with income of $100,000 or more: 4.4%; Poverty rate: 41.5%
Educational Attainment: High school diploma or higher: 81.7%; Bachelor's degree or higher: 11.0%; Graduate/professional degree or higher: 4.0%
School District(s)
Academy of Flint (KG-12)
  2012-13 Enrollment: 425. . . . . (810) 789-9484

Beecher Community SD (PK-12)
    2012-13 Enrollment: 1,360 . . . . (810) 591-9201
Bendle Public Schools (PK-12)
    2012-13 Enrollment: 2,295 . . . . (810) 591-2501
Carman-Ainsworth Community Schools (PK-12)
    2012-13 Enrollment: 4,594 . . . . (810) 591-3205
Flint SD (PK-12)
    2012-13 Enrollment: 8,485 . . . . (810) 760-1249
Genesee ISD (PK-12)
    2012-13 Enrollment: 1,776 . . . . (810) 591-4402
International Academy of Flint (KG-12)
    2012-13 Enrollment: 1,098 . . . . (810) 600-5000
Kearsley Community SD (PK-12)
    2012-13 Enrollment: 3,266 . . . . (810) 591-8000
Linden Charter Academy (KG-12)
    2012-13 Enrollment: 745 . . . . (810) 720-0515
Mich School F/t Deaf/mich School F/t Blind-Lio (PK-12)
    2012-13 Enrollment: 110 . . . . (810) 257-1467
Mt. Morris Consolidated Schools (PK-12)
    2012-13 Enrollment: 2,457 . . . . (810) 591-8760
Northridge Academy (KG-12)
    2012-13 Enrollment: 261 . . . . (810) 785-8811
Richfield Public Schools Academy (PK-12)
    2012-13 Enrollment: 633 . . . . (810) 736-1281
Westwood Heights Schools (PK-12)
    2012-13 Enrollment: 842 . . . . (810) 591-0870

Four-year College(s)

Baker College Center for Graduate Studies (Private, Not-for-profit)
    Fall 2013 Enrollment: 5,270 . . . . (810) 766-4021
    2013-14 Tuition: In-state $10,800; Out-of-state $10,800
Baker College of Flint (Private, Not-for-profit)
    Fall 2013 Enrollment: 4,977 . . . . (810) 766-4000
    2013-14 Tuition: In-state $8,100; Out-of-state $8,100
Kettering University (Private, Not-for-profit)
    Fall 2013 Enrollment: 1,985 . . . . (800) 955-4464
    2013-14 Tuition: In-state $35,600; Out-of-state $35,600
University of Michigan-Flint (Public)
    Fall 2013 Enrollment: 8,555 . . . . (810) 762-3000
    2013-14 Tuition: In-state $9,356; Out-of-state $18,238

Two-year College(s)

Flint Institute of Barbering Inc (Private, For-profit)
    Fall 2013 Enrollment: 56 . . . . (810) 232-4711
Mott Community College (Public)
    Fall 2013 Enrollment: 9,683 . . . . (810) 762-0200
    2013-14 Tuition: In-state $4,498; Out-of-state $6,228

Vocational/Technical School(s)

Regency Beauty Institute-Flint (Private, For-profit)
    Fall 2013 Enrollment: 130 . . . . (800) 787-6456
    2013-14 Tuition: $17,300
Ross Medical Education Center-Flint (Private, For-profit)
    Fall 2013 Enrollment: 307 . . . . (810) 733-7488
    2013-14 Tuition: $15,680

Housing: Homeownership rate: 55.2%; Median home value: $41,700; Median year structure built: 1954; Homeowner vacancy rate: 3.9%; Median gross rent: $668 per month; Rental vacancy rate: 16.5%
Health Insurance: 86.7% have insurance; 39.3% have private insurance; 60.2% have public insurance; 13.3% do not have insurance; 3.0% of children under 18 do not have insurance
Hospitals: Hurley Medical Center (443 beds); Mclaren Flint (452 beds)
Safety: Violent crime rate: 190.8 per 10,000 population; Property crime rate: 426.4 per 10,000 population
Newspapers: Flint Journal (daily circulation 83500); Suburban Newspaper Group (weekly circulation 93000)
Transportation: Commute: 88.0% car, 4.4% public transportation, 3.0% walk, 3.5% work from home; Median travel time to work: 21.7 minutes; Amtrak: Train service available.
Airports: Bishop International (primary service/small hub)
Additional Information Contacts
City of Flint . . . . (810) 766-7015
    http://www.cityofflint.com

FLUSHING (charter township). Covers a land area of 31.366 square miles and a water area of 0.306 square miles. Located at 43.10° N. Lat; 83.87° W. Long. Elevation is 699 feet.
History: Indian mounds nearby. Settled 1833, incorporated 1877.

Population: 10,640; Growth (since 2000): 4.0%; Density: 339.2 persons per square mile; Race: 94.4% White, 2.1% Black/African American, 0.8% Asian, 0.6% American Indian/Alaska Native, 0.0% Native Hawaiian/Other Pacific Islander, 1.6% Two or more races, 2.4% Hispanic of any race; Average household size: 2.64; Median age: 42.9; Age under 18: 23.9%; Age 65 and over: 15.2%; Males per 100 females: 97.0; Marriage status: 22.6% never married, 58.8% now married, 0.8% separated, 7.0% widowed, 11.6% divorced; Foreign born: 2.1%; Speak English only: 96.7%; With disability: 14.3%; Veterans: 10.6%; Ancestry: 28.3% German, 15.1% English, 12.1% Irish, 8.4% Polish, 7.7% French
Employment: 13.8% management, business, and financial, 4.5% computer, engineering, and science, 12.9% education, legal, community service, arts, and media, 8.0% healthcare practitioners, 13.9% service, 26.6% sales and office, 7.9% natural resources, construction, and maintenance, 12.4% production, transportation, and material moving
Income: Per capita: $27,243; Median household: $61,224; Average household: $71,192; Households with income of $100,000 or more: 18.9%; Poverty rate: 9.1%
Educational Attainment: High school diploma or higher: 95.7%; Bachelor's degree or higher: 30.3%; Graduate/professional degree or higher: 9.1%

School District(s)

Flushing Community Schools (PK-12)
    2012-13 Enrollment: 4,090 . . . . (810) 591-1180
Genesee ISD (PK-12)
    2012-13 Enrollment: 1,776 . . . . (810) 591-4402

Housing: Homeownership rate: 93.5%; Median home value: $113,700; Median year structure built: 1976; Homeowner vacancy rate: 1.7%; Median gross rent: $1,178 per month; Rental vacancy rate: 22.0%
Health Insurance: 94.1% have insurance; 78.2% have private insurance; 34.0% have public insurance; 5.9% do not have insurance; 4.1% of children under 18 do not have insurance
Transportation: Commute: 94.3% car, 0.0% public transportation, 0.0% walk, 5.7% work from home; Median travel time to work: 29.3 minutes
Additional Information Contacts
Flushing Township . . . . (810) 659-0800
    http://www.flushingtownship.com

FLUSHING (city). Covers a land area of 3.623 square miles and a water area of 0.170 square miles. Located at 43.06° N. Lat; 83.84° W. Long. Elevation is 699 feet.
Population: 8,389; Growth (since 2000): 0.5%; Density: 2,315.4 persons per square mile; Race: 94.8% White, 2.4% Black/African American, 0.4% Asian, 0.4% American Indian/Alaska Native, 0.0% Native Hawaiian/Other Pacific Islander, 1.6% Two or more races, 2.2% Hispanic of any race; Average household size: 2.30; Median age: 45.1; Age under 18: 21.7%; Age 65 and over: 21.7%; Males per 100 females: 85.4; Marriage status: 27.0% never married, 52.2% now married, 1.2% separated, 7.0% widowed, 13.9% divorced; Foreign born: 2.8%; Speak English only: 96.7%; With disability: 14.7%; Veterans: 10.3%; Ancestry: 24.2% German, 15.1% English, 14.2% Irish, 10.3% Polish, 7.0% French
Employment: 12.0% management, business, and financial, 3.9% computer, engineering, and science, 9.5% education, legal, community service, arts, and media, 10.6% healthcare practitioners, 17.0% service, 30.3% sales and office, 7.5% natural resources, construction, and maintenance, 9.2% production, transportation, and material moving
Income: Per capita: $28,121; Median household: $55,082; Average household: $66,269; Households with income of $100,000 or more: 20.0%; Poverty rate: 10.3%
Educational Attainment: High school diploma or higher: 95.4%; Bachelor's degree or higher: 27.7%; Graduate/professional degree or higher: 11.6%

School District(s)

Flushing Community Schools (PK-12)
    2012-13 Enrollment: 4,090 . . . . (810) 591-1180
Genesee ISD (PK-12)
    2012-13 Enrollment: 1,776 . . . . (810) 591-4402

Housing: Homeownership rate: 74.1%; Median home value: $112,200; Median year structure built: 1972; Homeowner vacancy rate: 1.8%; Median gross rent: $568 per month; Rental vacancy rate: 11.0%
Health Insurance: 94.9% have insurance; 83.1% have private insurance; 31.8% have public insurance; 5.1% do not have insurance; 2.3% of children under 18 do not have insurance
Safety: Violent crime rate: 6.1 per 10,000 population; Property crime rate: 124.3 per 10,000 population

Transportation: Commute: 96.8% car, 0.0% public transportation, 1.0% walk, 2.2% work from home; Median travel time to work: 26.1 minutes
Additional Information Contacts
City of Flushing . . . . (810) 659-5665
  http://www.flushingcity.com

FOREST (township). Covers a land area of 35.700 square miles and a water area of 0.455 square miles. Located at 43.18° N. Lat; 83.53° W. Long. Elevation is 814 feet.
Population: 4,702; Growth (since 2000): -0.8%; Density: 131.7 persons per square mile; Race: 97.7% White, 0.4% Black/African American, 0.1% Asian, 0.5% American Indian/Alaska Native, 0.0% Native Hawaiian/Other Pacific Islander, 0.9% Two or more races, 1.6% Hispanic of any race; Average household size: 2.58; Median age: 44.4; Age under 18: 22.2%; Age 65 and over: 14.6%; Males per 100 females: 102.0; Marriage status: 19.5% never married, 62.8% now married, 2.6% separated, 6.3% widowed, 11.4% divorced; Foreign born: 1.1%; Speak English only: 97.9%; With disability: 17.7%; Veterans: 8.6%; Ancestry: 22.8% German, 14.8% English, 13.5% American, 11.6% Irish, 5.9% Dutch
Employment: 8.7% management, business, and financial, 0.8% computer, engineering, and science, 8.9% education, legal, community service, arts, and media, 7.9% healthcare practitioners, 20.8% service, 23.1% sales and office, 10.9% natural resources, construction, and maintenance, 18.9% production, transportation, and material moving
Income: Per capita: $21,897; Median household: $49,142; Average household: $55,809; Households with income of $100,000 or more: 9.4%; Poverty rate: 9.0%
Educational Attainment: High school diploma or higher: 92.5%; Bachelor's degree or higher: 12.9%; Graduate/professional degree or higher: 4.0%
Housing: Homeownership rate: 89.6%; Median home value: $112,800; Median year structure built: 1974; Homeowner vacancy rate: 1.6%; Median gross rent: $722 per month; Rental vacancy rate: 9.9%
Health Insurance: 87.3% have insurance; 74.3% have private insurance; 34.8% have public insurance; 12.7% do not have insurance; 13.2% of children under 18 do not have insurance
Transportation: Commute: 90.4% car, 0.3% public transportation, 3.0% walk, 5.9% work from home; Median travel time to work: 33.3 minutes

GAINES (township). Covers a land area of 35.097 square miles and a water area of 0.136 square miles. Located at 42.91° N. Lat; 83.88° W. Long. Elevation is 856 feet.
History: Gaines Township was organized in 1842 and named for General E.P. Gaines, a friend of an early settler.
Population: 6,820; Growth (since 2000): 5.1%; Density: 194.3 persons per square mile; Race: 96.9% White, 0.9% Black/African American, 0.2% Asian, 0.6% American Indian/Alaska Native, 0.0% Native Hawaiian/Other Pacific Islander, 1.2% Two or more races, 2.4% Hispanic of any race; Average household size: 2.72; Median age: 42.2; Age under 18: 24.3%; Age 65 and over: 13.2%; Males per 100 females: 99.9; Marriage status: 24.3% never married, 60.8% now married, 1.0% separated, 5.5% widowed, 9.4% divorced; Foreign born: 0.4%; Speak English only: 98.9%; With disability: 13.3%; Veterans: 10.5%; Ancestry: 29.1% German, 13.1% Irish, 11.0% English, 9.3% Polish, 6.5% American
Employment: 14.3% management, business, and financial, 4.8% computer, engineering, and science, 8.3% education, legal, community service, arts, and media, 5.5% healthcare practitioners, 15.4% service, 25.4% sales and office, 10.1% natural resources, construction, and maintenance, 16.1% production, transportation, and material moving
Income: Per capita: $25,398; Median household: $59,816; Average household: $70,331; Households with income of $100,000 or more: 21.0%; Poverty rate: 8.5%
Educational Attainment: High school diploma or higher: 91.7%; Bachelor's degree or higher: 15.8%; Graduate/professional degree or higher: 4.6%
School District(s)
Swartz Creek Community Schools (PK-12)
  2012-13 Enrollment: 3,980 . . . . (810) 591-2300
Housing: Homeownership rate: 92.7%; Median home value: $122,500; Median year structure built: 1976; Homeowner vacancy rate: 1.5%; Median gross rent: $816 per month; Rental vacancy rate: 6.5%
Health Insurance: 93.6% have insurance; 80.7% have private insurance; 31.5% have public insurance; 6.4% do not have insurance; 0.1% of children under 18 do not have insurance

Transportation: Commute: 95.9% car, 0.1% public transportation, 0.5% walk, 3.0% work from home; Median travel time to work: 29.4 minutes

GAINES (village). Covers a land area of 0.372 square miles and a water area of 0 square miles. Located at 42.87° N. Lat; 83.91° W. Long. Elevation is 856 feet.
History: The area was settled in the 1830's, but the village of Gaines began when the railroad depot was built in 1856.
Population: 380; Growth (since 2000): 3.8%; Density: 1,021.7 persons per square mile; Race: 97.9% White, 0.3% Black/African American, 0.0% Asian, 0.5% American Indian/Alaska Native, 0.0% Native Hawaiian/Other Pacific Islander, 1.1% Two or more races, 1.8% Hispanic of any race; Average household size: 2.47; Median age: 38.5; Age under 18: 26.6%; Age 65 and over: 12.1%; Males per 100 females: 101.1
School District(s)
Swartz Creek Community Schools (PK-12)
  2012-13 Enrollment: 3,980 . . . . (810) 591-2300
Housing: Homeownership rate: 72.1%; Homeowner vacancy rate: 3.4%; Rental vacancy rate: 4.2%

GENESEE (charter township). Covers a land area of 29.061 square miles and a water area of 1.207 square miles. Located at 43.10° N. Lat; 83.63° W. Long. Elevation is 755 feet.
Population: 21,581; Growth (since 2000): -10.5%; Density: 742.6 persons per square mile; Race: 87.2% White, 8.6% Black/African American, 0.2% Asian, 0.8% American Indian/Alaska Native, 0.0% Native Hawaiian/Other Pacific Islander, 2.5% Two or more races, 3.8% Hispanic of any race; Average household size: 2.55; Median age: 40.8; Age under 18: 24.0%; Age 65 and over: 15.0%; Males per 100 females: 94.9; Marriage status: 29.8% never married, 50.3% now married, 2.0% separated, 6.8% widowed, 13.2% divorced; Foreign born: 1.5%; Speak English only: 97.5%; With disability: 19.4%; Veterans: 12.0%; Ancestry: 19.0% German, 13.2% Irish, 10.1% English, 7.6% American, 6.2% French
Employment: 6.8% management, business, and financial, 2.6% computer, engineering, and science, 4.8% education, legal, community service, arts, and media, 5.6% healthcare practitioners, 20.5% service, 28.1% sales and office, 12.5% natural resources, construction, and maintenance, 19.2% production, transportation, and material moving
Income: Per capita: $20,455; Median household: $39,429; Average household: $49,467; Households with income of $100,000 or more: 10.6%; Poverty rate: 19.2%
Educational Attainment: High school diploma or higher: 85.2%; Bachelor's degree or higher: 11.6%; Graduate/professional degree or higher: 3.2%
School District(s)
Genesee SD (PK-12)
  2012-13 Enrollment: 805 . . . . (810) 591-1650
Housing: Homeownership rate: 79.6%; Median home value: $72,300; Median year structure built: 1968; Homeowner vacancy rate: 4.1%; Median gross rent: $798 per month; Rental vacancy rate: 19.6%
Health Insurance: 89.9% have insurance; 62.8% have private insurance; 45.2% have public insurance; 10.1% do not have insurance; 4.9% of children under 18 do not have insurance
Safety: Violent crime rate: 56.3 per 10,000 population; Property crime rate: 187.3 per 10,000 population
Transportation: Commute: 93.8% car, 1.2% public transportation, 0.8% walk, 2.8% work from home; Median travel time to work: 29.6 minutes
Additional Information Contacts
Genesee Charter Township . . . . (810) 640-2000
  http://www.geneseetwp.com

GOODRICH (village). Covers a land area of 2.195 square miles and a water area of 0.072 square miles. Located at 42.91° N. Lat; 83.52° W. Long. Elevation is 879 feet.
History: Goodrich was settled in 1835 by the Goodrich brothers (Enos, Moses, and Levi) and their families. The village was first called Atlas, but renamed Goodrich when Reuben Goodrich became the postmaster in 1849.
Population: 1,860; Growth (since 2000): 37.5%; Density: 847.3 persons per square mile; Race: 98.1% White, 0.9% Black/African American, 0.2% Asian, 0.2% American Indian/Alaska Native, 0.0% Native Hawaiian/Other Pacific Islander, 0.5% Two or more races, 2.2% Hispanic of any race; Average household size: 2.83; Median age: 36.9; Age under 18: 32.6%; Age 65 and over: 10.3%; Males per 100 females: 98.9

School District(s)

Goodrich Area Schools (PK-12)

2012-13 Enrollment: 2,086 . . . . (810) 591-2201

Housing: Homeownership rate: 85.6%; Homeowner vacancy rate: 2.8%; Rental vacancy rate: 3.1%

GRAND BLANC (charter township). Covers a land area of 32.700 square miles and a water area of 0.339 square miles. Located at 42.91° N. Lat; 83.63° W. Long. Elevation is 840 feet.

History: Settled 1823, incorporated 1930.

Population: 37,508; Growth (since 2000): 25.8%; Density: 1,147.0 persons per square mile; Race: 82.6% White, 10.7% Black/African American, 3.4% Asian, 0.4% American Indian/Alaska Native, 0.0% Native Hawaiian/Other Pacific Islander, 2.3% Two or more races, 3.1% Hispanic of any race; Average household size: 2.52; Median age: 36.8; Age under 18: 26.5%; Age 65 and over: 12.3%; Males per 100 females: 93.3; Marriage status: 26.9% never married, 56.6% now married, 1.6% separated, 5.5% widowed, 11.1% divorced; Foreign born: 6.3%; Speak English only: 92.5%; With disability: 9.9%; Veterans: 9.6%; Ancestry: 19.5% German, 10.5% English, 10.0% Irish, 8.0% Polish, 6.0% American

Employment: 15.4% management, business, and financial, 6.5% computer, engineering, and science, 11.2% education, legal, community service, arts, and media, 12.3% healthcare practitioners, 15.1% service, 23.8% sales and office, 5.0% natural resources, construction, and maintenance, 10.6% production, transportation, and material moving

Income: Per capita: $30,084; Median household: $58,521; Average household: $76,603; Households with income of $100,000 or more: 24.5%; Poverty rate: 9.8%

Educational Attainment: High school diploma or higher: 94.8%; Bachelor's degree or higher: 34.5%; Graduate/professional degree or higher: 13.7%

School District(s)

Grand Blanc Academy (KG-12)

2012-13 Enrollment: 437. . . . . (810) 953-3140

Grand Blanc Community Schools (PK-12)

2012-13 Enrollment: 8,684 . . . . (810) 591-6014

Woodland Park Academy (KG-12)

2012-13 Enrollment: 405. . . . . (810) 695-4710

Vocational/Technical School(s)

Sharps Academy of Hair Styling (Private, For-profit)

Fall 2013 Enrollment: 73 . . . . (810) 695-6742

2013-14 Tuition: $10,905

Housing: Homeownership rate: 68.6%; Median home value: $130,800; Median year structure built: 1981; Homeowner vacancy rate: 3.3%; Median gross rent: $744 per month; Rental vacancy rate: 10.9%

Health Insurance: 92.4% have insurance; 79.8% have private insurance; 26.5% have public insurance; 7.6% do not have insurance; 1.7% of children under 18 do not have insurance

Hospitals: Genesys Regional Medical Center - Health Park (410 beds)

Safety: Violent crime rate: 17.1 per 10,000 population; Property crime rate: 165.5 per 10,000 population

Transportation: Commute: 96.1% car, 0.1% public transportation, 0.3% walk, 3.3% work from home; Median travel time to work: 25.2 minutes

Additional Information Contacts

Grand Blanc Township . . . . (810) 424-2600

http://www.twp.grand-blanc.mi.us

GRAND BLANC (city). Covers a land area of 3.610 square miles and a water area of 0.015 square miles. Located at 42.93° N. Lat; 83.62° W. Long. Elevation is 840 feet.

History: Grand Blanc took its name from the nickname given to a fur trader named Fisher, who with Antoine Campau established a post here. Fisher was a large man, known as Le Grand Blanc (French, "the big white"). Settlement began here in the 1820's; Rufus Stevens opened a trading post in 1826.

Population: 8,276; Growth (since 2000): 0.4%; Density: 2,292.3 persons per square mile; Race: 82.5% White, 11.1% Black/African American, 2.8% Asian, 0.4% American Indian/Alaska Native, 0.0% Native Hawaiian/Other Pacific Islander, 2.9% Two or more races, 2.6% Hispanic of any race; Average household size: 2.28; Median age: 39.1; Age under 18: 24.3%; Age 65 and over: 16.3%; Males per 100 females: 86.1; Marriage status: 32.2% never married, 47.9% now married, 2.5% separated, 8.9% widowed, 11.1% divorced; Foreign born: 4.1%; Speak English only: 94.9%; With disability: 14.8%; Veterans: 7.3%; Ancestry: 15.4% German, 12.8% Irish, 10.3% English, 5.5% Polish, 4.4% French

Employment: 15.8% management, business, and financial, 3.2% computer, engineering, and science, 12.7% education, legal, community service, arts, and media, 9.3% healthcare practitioners, 14.1% service, 29.9% sales and office, 3.0% natural resources, construction, and maintenance, 12.2% production, transportation, and material moving

Income: Per capita: $32,011; Median household: $50,742; Average household: $74,299; Households with income of $100,000 or more: 27.3%; Poverty rate: 14.5%

Educational Attainment: High school diploma or higher: 95.0%; Bachelor's degree or higher: 40.3%; Graduate/professional degree or higher: 17.8%

School District(s)

Grand Blanc Academy (KG-12)

2012-13 Enrollment: 437. . . . . (810) 953-3140

Grand Blanc Community Schools (PK-12)

2012-13 Enrollment: 8,684 . . . . (810) 591-6014

Woodland Park Academy (KG-12)

2012-13 Enrollment: 405. . . . . (810) 695-4710

Vocational/Technical School(s)

Sharps Academy of Hair Styling (Private, For-profit)

Fall 2013 Enrollment: 73 . . . . (810) 695-6742

2013-14 Tuition: $10,905

Housing: Homeownership rate: 56.8%; Median home value: $136,500; Median year structure built: 1974; Homeowner vacancy rate: 2.2%; Median gross rent: $717 per month; Rental vacancy rate: 5.1%

Health Insurance: 91.6% have insurance; 74.9% have private insurance; 32.0% have public insurance; 8.4% do not have insurance; 1.3% of children under 18 do not have insurance

Hospitals: Genesys Regional Medical Center - Health Park (410 beds)

Safety: Violent crime rate: 14.8 per 10,000 population; Property crime rate: 171.5 per 10,000 population

Transportation: Commute: 95.9% car, 0.0% public transportation, 2.3% walk, 1.1% work from home; Median travel time to work: 25.8 minutes

Additional Information Contacts

City of Grand Blanc . . . . (810) 694-1118

http://www.cityofgrandblanc.com

LAKE FENTON (CDP). Covers a land area of 5.507 square miles and a water area of 1.692 square miles. Located at 42.85° N. Lat; 83.71° W. Long. Elevation is 879 feet.

History: A community was platted as "Mount Pleasant" by John Cook in 1840. The name was changed to Long Lake in 1850. The lake was subsequently renamed Lake Fenton and the platted settlement became extinct. In 1932, the United States Board on Geographic Names decided on "Lake Fenton" as the official name of the lake.

Population: 5,559; Growth (since 2000): 14.0%; Density: 1,009.4 persons per square mile; Race: 96.6% White, 0.6% Black/African American, 1.0% Asian, 0.3% American Indian/Alaska Native, 0.0% Native Hawaiian/Other Pacific Islander, 1.2% Two or more races, 2.2% Hispanic of any race; Average household size: 2.47; Median age: 43.8; Age under 18: 22.3%; Age 65 and over: 15.8%; Males per 100 females: 95.4; Marriage status: 16.6% never married, 69.3% now married, 0.5% separated, 4.5% widowed, 9.6% divorced; Foreign born: 3.1%; Speak English only: 96.4%; With disability: 8.4%; Veterans: 8.4%; Ancestry: 25.3% German, 11.7% Irish, 9.7% English, 7.6% French, 7.2% American

Employment: 13.6% management, business, and financial, 5.8% computer, engineering, and science, 12.9% education, legal, community service, arts, and media, 8.0% healthcare practitioners, 16.3% service, 23.1% sales and office, 6.0% natural resources, construction, and maintenance, 14.2% production, transportation, and material moving

Income: Per capita: $32,936; Median household: $73,470; Average household: $80,170; Households with income of $100,000 or more: 32.2%; Poverty rate: 8.0%

Educational Attainment: High school diploma or higher: 94.1%; Bachelor's degree or higher: 34.3%; Graduate/professional degree or higher: 9.8%

Housing: Homeownership rate: 85.3%; Median home value: $172,600; Median year structure built: 1985; Homeowner vacancy rate: 2.4%; Median gross rent: $749 per month; Rental vacancy rate: 12.4%

Health Insurance: 91.0% have insurance; 86.3% have private insurance; 21.2% have public insurance; 9.0% do not have insurance; 7.7% of children under 18 do not have insurance

Transportation: Commute: 98.5% car, 0.0% public transportation, 0.7% walk, 0.8% work from home; Median travel time to work: 24.0 minutes

LINDEN (city). Covers a land area of 2.357 square miles and a water area of 0.067 square miles. Located at 42.82° N. Lat; 83.78° W. Long. Elevation is 876 feet.

History: Linden was settled in 1835 by Richard and Perry Lamb. It was incorporated as a village in 1871.

Population: 3,991; Growth (since 2000): 39.5%; Density: 1,692.9 persons per square mile; Race: 96.8% White, 0.5% Black/African American, 0.4% Asian, 0.5% American Indian/Alaska Native, 0.0% Native Hawaiian/Other Pacific Islander, 1.3% Two or more races, 2.0% Hispanic of any race; Average household size: 2.51; Median age: 39.5; Age under 18: 25.6%; Age 65 and over: 19.9%; Males per 100 females: 88.7; Marriage status: 12.8% never married, 69.8% now married, 0.0% separated, 8.4% widowed, 9.0% divorced; Foreign born: 2.3%; Speak English only: 98.0%; With disability: 11.2%; Veterans: 10.9%; Ancestry: 26.3% German, 16.5% Irish, 12.8% English, 12.0% Polish, 8.8% American

Employment: 10.9% management, business, and financial, 5.2% computer, engineering, and science, 12.9% education, legal, community service, arts, and media, 8.1% healthcare practitioners, 20.9% service, 20.9% sales and office, 7.4% natural resources, construction, and maintenance, 13.5% production, transportation, and material moving

Income: Per capita: $27,447; Median household: $62,065; Average household: $71,038; Households with income of $100,000 or more: 19.4%; Poverty rate: 5.1%

Educational Attainment: High school diploma or higher: 97.1%; Bachelor's degree or higher: 28.3%; Graduate/professional degree or higher: 13.1%

School District(s)
Lake Fenton Community Schools (PK-12)
    2012-13 Enrollment: 1,987 . . . . (810) 591-2532
Linden Community Schools (PK-12)
    2012-13 Enrollment: 2,958 . . . . (810) 591-0980

Housing: Homeownership rate: 83.0%; Median home value: $136,000; Median year structure built: 1990; Homeowner vacancy rate: 3.4%; Median gross rent: $673 per month; Rental vacancy rate: 12.5%

Health Insurance: 94.3% have insurance; 84.5% have private insurance; 31.5% have public insurance; 5.7% do not have insurance; 0.0% of children under 18 do not have insurance

Safety: Violent crime rate: 20.5 per 10,000 population; Property crime rate: 69.3 per 10,000 population

Transportation: Commute: 95.9% car, 0.1% public transportation, 0.5% walk, 3.5% work from home; Median travel time to work: 31.5 minutes

MONTROSE (charter township). Covers a land area of 34.249 square miles and a water area of 0.395 square miles. Located at 43.18° N. Lat; 83.87° W. Long. Elevation is 673 feet.

Population: 6,224; Growth (since 2000): -1.8%; Density: 181.7 persons per square mile; Race: 95.4% White, 1.7% Black/African American, 0.1% Asian, 0.6% American Indian/Alaska Native, 0.0% Native Hawaiian/Other Pacific Islander, 1.7% Two or more races, 2.5% Hispanic of any race; Average household size: 2.79; Median age: 40.7; Age under 18: 24.5%; Age 65 and over: 13.7%; Males per 100 females: 99.4; Marriage status: 28.5% never married, 51.6% now married, 1.4% separated, 6.8% widowed, 13.1% divorced; Foreign born: 1.0%; Speak English only: 97.6%; With disability: 19.1%; Veterans: 13.0%; Ancestry: 20.5% German, 12.3% English, 8.0% Irish, 5.9% American, 5.8% French

Employment: 8.9% management, business, and financial, 1.8% computer, engineering, and science, 6.4% education, legal, community service, arts, and media, 6.6% healthcare practitioners, 18.9% service, 26.9% sales and office, 17.1% natural resources, construction, and maintenance, 13.3% production, transportation, and material moving

Income: Per capita: $21,862; Median household: $48,036; Average household: $63,527; Households with income of $100,000 or more: 15.5%; Poverty rate: 16.4%

Educational Attainment: High school diploma or higher: 88.1%; Bachelor's degree or higher: 9.6%; Graduate/professional degree or higher: 2.8%

School District(s)
Montrose Community Schools (PK-12)
    2012-13 Enrollment: 1,376 . . . . (810) 591-7267

Housing: Homeownership rate: 86.3%; Median home value: $105,100; Median year structure built: 1973; Homeowner vacancy rate: 3.2%; Median gross rent: $787 per month; Rental vacancy rate: 18.7%

Health Insurance: 89.8% have insurance; 66.7% have private insurance; 39.9% have public insurance; 10.2% do not have insurance; 1.1% of children under 18 do not have insurance

Safety: Violent crime rate: 14.3 per 10,000 population; Property crime rate: 250.5 per 10,000 population

Transportation: Commute: 93.2% car, 0.9% public transportation, 1.5% walk, 3.3% work from home; Median travel time to work: 30.9 minutes

MONTROSE (city). Covers a land area of 0.977 square miles and a water area of 0 square miles. Located at 43.18° N. Lat; 83.89° W. Long. Elevation is 673 feet.

Population: 1,657; Growth (since 2000): 2.3%; Density: 1,696.6 persons per square mile; Race: 96.8% White, 0.7% Black/African American, 0.2% Asian, 0.7% American Indian/Alaska Native, 0.0% Native Hawaiian/Other Pacific Islander, 0.7% Two or more races, 2.4% Hispanic of any race; Average household size: 2.46; Median age: 36.4; Age under 18: 27.2%; Age 65 and over: 12.9%; Males per 100 females: 88.3

School District(s)
Montrose Community Schools (PK-12)
    2012-13 Enrollment: 1,376 . . . . (810) 591-7267

Housing: Homeownership rate: 64.6%; Homeowner vacancy rate: 4.8%; Rental vacancy rate: 7.8%

MOUNT MORRIS (city). Covers a land area of 1.197 square miles and a water area of 0 square miles. Located at 43.12° N. Lat; 83.70° W. Long. Elevation is 771 feet.

History: Mount Morris developed as a residential center for workers employed in Flint's industrial plants.

Population: 3,086; Growth (since 2000): -3.4%; Density: 2,578.1 persons per square mile; Race: 80.1% White, 13.4% Black/African American, 0.5% Asian, 0.6% American Indian/Alaska Native, 0.0% Native Hawaiian/Other Pacific Islander, 4.3% Two or more races, 4.4% Hispanic of any race; Average household size: 2.34; Median age: 34.0; Age under 18: 27.1%; Age 65 and over: 9.4%; Males per 100 females: 86.0; Marriage status: 41.2% never married, 37.4% now married, 0.9% separated, 8.5% widowed, 12.9% divorced; Foreign born: 0.8%; Speak English only: 98.3%; With disability: 22.7%; Veterans: 6.5%; Ancestry: 14.1% German, 11.8% Irish, 9.5% English, 5.6% French, 5.3% Italian

Employment: 3.3% management, business, and financial, 1.1% computer, engineering, and science, 3.1% education, legal, community service, arts, and media, 5.0% healthcare practitioners, 26.5% service, 35.1% sales and office, 7.8% natural resources, construction, and maintenance, 18.2% production, transportation, and material moving

Income: Per capita: $13,340; Median household: $21,778; Average household: $33,706; Households with income of $100,000 or more: 4.3%; Poverty rate: 38.4%

Educational Attainment: High school diploma or higher: 77.8%; Bachelor's degree or higher: 2.6%; Graduate/professional degree or higher: 0.6%

School District(s)
Beecher Community SD (PK-12)
    2012-13 Enrollment: 1,360 . . . . (810) 591-9201
Mt. Morris Consolidated Schools (PK-12)
    2012-13 Enrollment: 2,457 . . . . (810) 591-8760

Housing: Homeownership rate: 54.3%; Median home value: $62,200; Median year structure built: 1956; Homeowner vacancy rate: 6.0%; Median gross rent: $648 per month; Rental vacancy rate: 12.6%

Health Insurance: 94.8% have insurance; 48.0% have private insurance; 63.0% have public insurance; 5.2% do not have insurance; 0.9% of children under 18 do not have insurance

Safety: Violent crime rate: 83.0 per 10,000 population; Property crime rate: 292.2 per 10,000 population

Newspapers: Genesee County Herald (weekly circulation 3800)

Transportation: Commute: 99.9% car, 0.0% public transportation, 0.0% walk, 0.0% work from home; Median travel time to work: 27.5 minutes

MOUNT MORRIS (township). Covers a land area of 31.506 square miles and a water area of 0.113 square miles. Located at 43.09° N. Lat; 83.76° W. Long. Elevation is 771 feet.

History: Settled 1842; incorporated as village 1867, as city 1930.

Population: 21,501; Growth (since 2000): -9.4%; Density: 682.4 persons per square mile; Race: 51.7% White, 42.8% Black/African American, 0.3% Asian, 0.7% American Indian/Alaska Native, 0.0% Native Hawaiian/Other Pacific Islander, 3.5% Two or more races, 3.3% Hispanic of any race; Average household size: 2.61; Median age: 37.0; Age under 18: 27.4%; Age 65 and over: 14.3%; Males per 100 females: 92.2; Marriage status: 37.1% never married, 40.4% now married, 1.7% separated, 7.6% widowed, 14.9% divorced; Foreign born: 1.8%; Speak English only: 97.6%;

With disability: 19.6%; Veterans: 9.7%; Ancestry: 11.5% German, 7.2% Irish, 6.7% English, 4.4% American, 4.1% Polish

Employment: 9.6% management, business, and financial, 1.4% computer, engineering, and science, 7.3% education, legal, community service, arts, and media, 4.6% healthcare practitioners, 26.1% service, 26.9% sales and office, 6.8% natural resources, construction, and maintenance, 17.4% production, transportation, and material moving

Income: Per capita: $18,211; Median household: $34,697; Average household: $47,275; Households with income of $100,000 or more: 8.0%; Poverty rate: 30.8%

Educational Attainment: High school diploma or higher: 84.1%; Bachelor's degree or higher: 11.5%; Graduate/professional degree or higher: 2.8%

School District(s)

Beecher Community SD (PK-12)
    2012-13 Enrollment: 1,360 . . . . (810) 591-9201
Mt. Morris Consolidated Schools (PK-12)
    2012-13 Enrollment: 2,457 . . . . (810) 591-8760

Housing: Homeownership rate: 72.1%; Median home value: $65,500; Median year structure built: 1964; Homeowner vacancy rate: 3.4%; Median gross rent: $796 per month; Rental vacancy rate: 17.0%

Health Insurance: 88.0% have insurance; 49.8% have private insurance; 54.9% have public insurance; 12.0% do not have insurance; 2.9% of children under 18 do not have insurance

Safety: Violent crime rate: 71.0 per 10,000 population; Property crime rate: 426.9 per 10,000 population

Newspapers: Genesee County Herald (weekly circulation 3800)

Transportation: Commute: 93.1% car, 2.2% public transportation, 0.6% walk, 3.1% work from home; Median travel time to work: 24.0 minutes

Additional Information Contacts
Mount Morris Township . . . . (810) 785-0817
    http://www.mtmorristwp.org

MUNDY (township). Covers a land area of 36.033 square miles and a water area of 0.147 square miles. Located at 42.91° N. Lat; 83.76° W. Long.

Population: 15,082; Growth (since 2000): 23.7%; Density: 418.6 persons per square mile; Race: 92.1% White, 4.3% Black/African American, 1.0% Asian, 0.3% American Indian/Alaska Native, 0.1% Native Hawaiian/Other Pacific Islander, 1.8% Two or more races, 2.4% Hispanic of any race; Average household size: 2.45; Median age: 41.5; Age under 18: 22.9%; Age 65 and over: 15.0%; Males per 100 females: 95.4; Marriage status: 24.8% never married, 58.1% now married, 0.9% separated, 5.9% widowed, 11.2% divorced; Foreign born: 2.2%; Speak English only: 96.4%; With disability: 15.2%; Veterans: 10.1%; Ancestry: 18.3% German, 11.6% English, 9.7% Irish, 8.3% American, 7.0% Polish

Employment: 12.5% management, business, and financial, 4.6% computer, engineering, and science, 11.4% education, legal, community service, arts, and media, 9.4% healthcare practitioners, 14.3% service, 24.0% sales and office, 7.7% natural resources, construction, and maintenance, 16.2% production, transportation, and material moving

Income: Per capita: $26,014; Median household: $55,041; Average household: $65,414; Households with income of $100,000 or more: 17.3%; Poverty rate: 7.7%

Educational Attainment: High school diploma or higher: 94.0%; Bachelor's degree or higher: 21.5%; Graduate/professional degree or higher: 9.5%

Housing: Homeownership rate: 82.8%; Median home value: $116,200; Median year structure built: 1979; Homeowner vacancy rate: 2.5%; Median gross rent: $808 per month; Rental vacancy rate: 9.0%

Health Insurance: 92.9% have insurance; 78.0% have private insurance; 32.7% have public insurance; 7.1% do not have insurance; 3.0% of children under 18 do not have insurance

Safety: Violent crime rate: 15.6 per 10,000 population; Property crime rate: 236.1 per 10,000 population

Transportation: Commute: 95.6% car, 0.2% public transportation, 0.6% walk, 3.2% work from home; Median travel time to work: 26.1 minutes

Additional Information Contacts
Mundy Township . . . . (810) 655-4631
    http://mundytwp-mi.gov

OTISVILLE (village). Covers a land area of 0.881 square miles and a water area of 0.094 square miles. Located at 43.17° N. Lat; 83.53° W. Long. Elevation is 814 feet.

Population: 864; Growth (since 2000): -2.0%; Density: 980.8 persons per square mile; Race: 97.8% White, 0.5% Black/African American, 0.1% Asian, 0.5% American Indian/Alaska Native, 0.0% Native Hawaiian/Other Pacific Islander, 1.0% Two or more races, 1.2% Hispanic of any race; Average household size: 2.53; Median age: 36.9; Age under 18: 27.3%; Age 65 and over: 13.2%; Males per 100 females: 98.6

School District(s)

Lakeville Community SD (PK-12)
    2012-13 Enrollment: 1,467 . . . . (810) 591-3980

Housing: Homeownership rate: 76.9%; Homeowner vacancy rate: 3.3%; Rental vacancy rate: 14.1%

Safety: Violent crime rate: 0.0 per 10,000 population; Property crime rate: 95.2 per 10,000 population

RICHFIELD (township). Covers a land area of 35.057 square miles and a water area of 1.309 square miles. Located at 43.10° N. Lat; 83.52° W. Long.

Population: 8,730; Growth (since 2000): 6.9%; Density: 249.0 persons per square mile; Race: 94.6% White, 2.1% Black/African American, 0.5% Asian, 0.5% American Indian/Alaska Native, 0.0% Native Hawaiian/Other Pacific Islander, 1.8% Two or more races, 2.6% Hispanic of any race; Average household size: 2.69; Median age: 40.9; Age under 18: 24.8%; Age 65 and over: 13.6%; Males per 100 females: 97.5; Marriage status: 21.9% never married, 62.0% now married, 0.4% separated, 5.8% widowed, 10.3% divorced; Foreign born: 0.5%; Speak English only: 98.1%; With disability: 12.0%; Veterans: 10.3%; Ancestry: 23.2% German, 16.6% English, 16.3% Irish, 9.9% American, 5.8% Polish

Employment: 9.4% management, business, and financial, 1.9% computer, engineering, and science, 10.1% education, legal, community service, arts, and media, 8.5% healthcare practitioners, 16.1% service, 24.2% sales and office, 9.8% natural resources, construction, and maintenance, 20.1% production, transportation, and material moving

Income: Per capita: $26,020; Median household: $57,901; Average household: $69,010; Households with income of $100,000 or more: 20.6%; Poverty rate: 9.2%

Educational Attainment: High school diploma or higher: 90.0%; Bachelor's degree or higher: 16.8%; Graduate/professional degree or higher: 6.6%

Housing: Homeownership rate: 90.5%; Median home value: $116,400; Median year structure built: 1977; Homeowner vacancy rate: 2.3%; Median gross rent: $1,070 per month; Rental vacancy rate: 6.3%

Health Insurance: 93.2% have insurance; 77.1% have private insurance; 34.4% have public insurance; 6.8% do not have insurance; 1.5% of children under 18 do not have insurance

Safety: Violent crime rate: 11.7 per 10,000 population; Property crime rate: 110.3 per 10,000 population

Transportation: Commute: 95.0% car, 0.0% public transportation, 0.0% walk, 5.0% work from home; Median travel time to work: 27.9 minutes

Additional Information Contacts
Richfield Township . . . . (810) 653-3564
    http://richfieldtwp.org

SWARTZ CREEK (city). Covers a land area of 4.044 square miles and a water area of 0.002 square miles. Located at 42.96° N. Lat; 83.83° W. Long. Elevation is 787 feet.

History: First called Miller Settlement for Adam Miller, who came here in 1836, the town was named Swartz Creek in 1843. The earliest residents were German immigrants.

Population: 5,758; Growth (since 2000): 12.9%; Density: 1,423.7 persons per square mile; Race: 91.6% White, 5.1% Black/African American, 0.8% Asian, 0.2% American Indian/Alaska Native, 0.0% Native Hawaiian/Other Pacific Islander, 1.8% Two or more races, 2.3% Hispanic of any race; Average household size: 2.25; Median age: 41.0; Age under 18: 22.6%; Age 65 and over: 20.1%; Males per 100 females: 81.1; Marriage status: 26.6% never married, 50.2% now married, 0.6% separated, 8.8% widowed, 14.4% divorced; Foreign born: 1.9%; Speak English only: 98.5%; With disability: 16.5%; Veterans: 13.8%; Ancestry: 24.0% German, 17.9% English, 12.8% Irish, 9.8% American, 6.8% Polish

Employment: 9.5% management, business, and financial, 2.9% computer, engineering, and science, 12.8% education, legal, community service, arts, and media, 12.0% healthcare practitioners, 16.4% service, 21.2% sales

and office, 8.3% natural resources, construction, and maintenance, 16.9% production, transportation, and material moving
Income: Per capita: $22,556; Median household: $43,105; Average household: $52,679; Households with income of $100,000 or more: 10.6%; Poverty rate: 21.8%
Educational Attainment: High school diploma or higher: 89.8%; Bachelor's degree or higher: 18.5%; Graduate/professional degree or higher: 6.1%

School District(s)
Carman-Ainsworth Community Schools (PK-12)
    2012-13 Enrollment: 4,594 . . . . (810) 591-3205
Swartz Creek Community Schools (PK-12)
    2012-13 Enrollment: 3,980 . . . . (810) 591-2300

Four-year College(s)
ITT Technical Institute-Swartz Creek (Private, For-profit)
    Fall 2013 Enrollment: 402 . . . . (810) 628-2500
    2013-14 Tuition: In-state $18,048; Out-of-state $18,048

Housing: Homeownership rate: 70.9%; Median home value: $106,300; Median year structure built: 1973; Homeowner vacancy rate: 3.2%; Median gross rent: $774 per month; Rental vacancy rate: 8.3%
Health Insurance: 93.3% have insurance; 67.4% have private insurance; 46.5% have public insurance; 6.7% do not have insurance; 0.0% of children under 18 do not have insurance
Safety: Violent crime rate: 17.7 per 10,000 population; Property crime rate: 193.1 per 10,000 population
Transportation: Commute: 91.6% car, 0.7% public transportation, 0.7% walk, 6.1% work from home; Median travel time to work: 22.3 minutes

---

THETFORD (township). Covers a land area of 34.549 square miles and a water area of 0.112 square miles. Located at 43.17° N. Lat; 83.63° W. Long.
Population: 7,049; Growth (since 2000): -14.8%; Density: 204.0 persons per square mile; Race: 94.7% White, 2.1% Black/African American, 0.3% Asian, 0.7% American Indian/Alaska Native, 0.0% Native Hawaiian/Other Pacific Islander, 1.7% Two or more races, 2.6% Hispanic of any race; Average household size: 2.63; Median age: 41.8; Age under 18: 21.2%; Age 65 and over: 12.0%; Males per 100 females: 105.8; Marriage status: 26.6% never married, 55.4% now married, 1.7% separated, 5.1% widowed, 12.9% divorced; Foreign born: 1.4%; Speak English only: 97.8%; With disability: 15.4%; Veterans: 10.5%; Ancestry: 28.2% German, 15.0% Irish, 14.3% English, 7.2% American, 6.6% Polish
Employment: 10.7% management, business, and financial, 3.9% computer, engineering, and science, 5.7% education, legal, community service, arts, and media, 5.5% healthcare practitioners, 15.1% service, 25.5% sales and office, 14.4% natural resources, construction, and maintenance, 19.3% production, transportation, and material moving
Income: Per capita: $25,081; Median household: $51,797; Average household: $66,144; Households with income of $100,000 or more: 19.3%; Poverty rate: 13.9%
Educational Attainment: High school diploma or higher: 88.3%; Bachelor's degree or higher: 10.4%; Graduate/professional degree or higher: 4.1%
Housing: Homeownership rate: 87.5%; Median home value: $98,900; Median year structure built: 1973; Homeowner vacancy rate: 3.5%; Median gross rent: $809 per month; Rental vacancy rate: 30.1%
Health Insurance: 86.4% have insurance; 67.5% have private insurance; 35.6% have public insurance; 13.6% do not have insurance; 7.5% of children under 18 do not have insurance
Safety: Violent crime rate: 4.4 per 10,000 population; Property crime rate: 27.6 per 10,000 population
Transportation: Commute: 96.0% car, 0.1% public transportation, 1.8% walk, 1.8% work from home; Median travel time to work: 28.4 minutes

---

VIENNA (charter township). Covers a land area of 35.006 square miles and a water area of 0.110 square miles. Located at 43.18° N. Lat; 83.76° W. Long.
Population: 13,255; Growth (since 2000): 1.1%; Density: 378.7 persons per square mile; Race: 94.7% White, 1.8% Black/African American, 0.4% Asian, 0.6% American Indian/Alaska Native, 0.0% Native Hawaiian/Other Pacific Islander, 1.9% Two or more races, 2.6% Hispanic of any race; Average household size: 2.52; Median age: 42.5; Age under 18: 22.3%; Age 65 and over: 16.7%; Males per 100 females: 96.9; Marriage status: 27.5% never married, 53.7% now married, 1.3% separated, 7.2% widowed, 11.6% divorced; Foreign born: 2.2%; Speak English only: 97.3%;

With disability: 13.1%; Veterans: 10.2%; Ancestry: 21.9% German, 13.6% Irish, 10.6% English, 8.5% American, 8.1% Polish
Employment: 9.3% management, business, and financial, 2.2% computer, engineering, and science, 7.2% education, legal, community service, arts, and media, 5.7% healthcare practitioners, 21.0% service, 31.1% sales and office, 9.9% natural resources, construction, and maintenance, 13.6% production, transportation, and material moving
Income: Per capita: $23,386; Median household: $52,684; Average household: $60,558; Households with income of $100,000 or more: 14.2%; Poverty rate: 10.6%
Educational Attainment: High school diploma or higher: 88.4%; Bachelor's degree or higher: 16.2%; Graduate/professional degree or higher: 6.2%
Housing: Homeownership rate: 82.0%; Median home value: $113,200; Median year structure built: 1973; Homeowner vacancy rate: 2.6%; Median gross rent: $691 per month; Rental vacancy rate: 10.2%
Health Insurance: 89.0% have insurance; 75.0% have private insurance; 31.9% have public insurance; 11.0% do not have insurance; 7.8% of children under 18 do not have insurance
Transportation: Commute: 95.7% car, 0.2% public transportation, 1.1% walk, 1.3% work from home; Median travel time to work: 25.1 minutes
Additional Information Contacts
Vienna Charter Township . . . . (810) 686-7580
    http://viennatwp.com

Gladwin County

Located in east central Michigan; drained by the Tittabawassee and Tobacco Rivers; includes many small lakes. Covers a land area of 501.779 square miles, a water area of 14.151 square miles, and is located in the Eastern Time Zone at 43.99° N. Lat., 84.39° W. Long. The county was founded in 1855. County seat is Gladwin.

Weather Station: Gladwin — Elevation: 774 feet

	Jan	Feb	Mar	Apr	May	Jun	Jul	Aug	Sep	Oct	Nov	Dec
High	29	32	42	56	69	78	82	80	72	59	45	33
Low	12	13	21	32	42	52	57	55	47	36	28	19
Precip	2.0	1.6	2.1	2.9	3.4	3.1	3.0	3.5	3.6	2.9	2.8	2.1
Snow	14.0	9.1	7.8	1.9	tr	0.0	0.0	0.0	0.0	0.3	3.3	11.3

High and Low temperatures in degrees Fahrenheit; Precipitation and Snow in inches

Population: 25,692; Growth (since 2000): -1.3%; Density: 51.2 persons per square mile; Race: 97.7% White, 0.2% Black/African American, 0.3% Asian, 0.5% American Indian/Alaska Native, 0.0% Native Hawaiian/Other Pacific Islander, 1.0% two or more races, 1.2% Hispanic of any race; Average household size: 2.36; Median age: 47.7; Age under 18: 20.1%; Age 65 and over: 22.8%; Males per 100 females: 99.9; Marriage status: 20.3% never married, 60.4% now married, 1.4% separated, 7.5% widowed, 11.7% divorced; Foreign born: 1.6%; Speak English only: 95.1%; With disability: 19.6%; Veterans: 12.8%; Ancestry: 28.1% German, 11.0% Irish, 10.8% English, 7.8% Polish, 7.4% American
Religion: Six largest groups: 11.1% Catholicism, 7.3% Lutheran, 2.7% European Free-Church, 2.2% Non-denominational Protestant, 2.1% Methodist/Pietist, 1.7% Holiness
Economy: Unemployment rate: 7.4%; Leading industries: 20.4% retail trade; 14.7% construction; 10.7% accommodation and food services; Farms: 533 totaling 67,150 acres; Company size: 0 employ 1,000 or more persons, 0 employ 500 to 999 persons, 5 employ 100 to 499 persons, 397 employ less than 100 persons; Business ownership: n/a women-owned, n/a Black-owned, n/a Hispanic-owned, n/a Asian-owned
Employment: 10.7% management, business, and financial, 2.0% computer, engineering, and science, 6.7% education, legal, community service, arts, and media, 5.4% healthcare practitioners, 18.5% service, 24.8% sales and office, 14.4% natural resources, construction, and maintenance, 17.5% production, transportation, and material moving
Income: Per capita: $20,368; Median household: $37,626; Average household: $47,560; Households with income of $100,000 or more: 8.4%; Poverty rate: 21.4%
Educational Attainment: High school diploma or higher: 83.9%; Bachelor's degree or higher: 11.8%; Graduate/professional degree or higher: 4.7%
Housing: Homeownership rate: 84.7%; Median home value: $103,300; Median year structure built: 1978; Homeowner vacancy rate: 3.6%; Median gross rent: $572 per month; Rental vacancy rate: 8.3%

Vital Statistics: Birth rate: 83.6 per 10,000 population; Death rate: 137.7 per 10,000 population; Age-adjusted cancer mortality rate: 171.9 deaths per 100,000 population
Health Insurance: 84.9% have insurance; 62.7% have private insurance; 46.0% have public insurance; 15.1% do not have insurance; 16.4% of children under 18 do not have insurance
Health Care: Physicians: 5.9 per 10,000 population; Hospital beds: 9.7 per 10,000 population; Hospital admissions: 229.0 per 10,000 population
Transportation: Commute: 91.4% car, 0.7% public transportation, 3.2% walk, 4.0% work from home; Median travel time to work: 29.2 minutes
Presidential Election: 45.9% Obama, 53.1% Romney (2012)
National and State Parks: Gladwin State Park
Additional Information Contacts
Gladwin Government. . . . . (989) 426-4821
　http://www.gladwinco.com

Gladwin County Communities

BEAVERTON (city). Covers a land area of 1.028 square miles and a water area of 0.284 square miles. Located at 43.88° N. Lat; 84.49° W. Long. Elevation is 722 feet.
History: Beaverton was settled by lumbermen about 1863. It later developed as a farming center, and was incorporated as a village in 1901 and as a city in 1903. First known as Grand Forks for its location at the forks of the Tobacco and Cedar Rivers, it was later named for Beaverton, Ontario, the former home of settler Donald Gunn Ross.
Population: 1,071; Growth (since 2000): -3.2%; Density: 1,041.5 persons per square mile; Race: 97.7% White, 0.4% Black/African American, 0.0% Asian, 0.7% American Indian/Alaska Native, 0.0% Native Hawaiian/Other Pacific Islander, 1.2% Two or more races, 0.7% Hispanic of any race; Average household size: 2.32; Median age: 36.2; Age under 18: 27.1%; Age 65 and over: 17.5%; Males per 100 females: 90.2
School District(s)
Beaverton Rural Schools (PK-12)
　2012-13 Enrollment: 1,313 . . . . (989) 246-3000
Housing: Homeownership rate: 55.6%; Homeowner vacancy rate: 5.5%; Rental vacancy rate: 16.3%

BEAVERTON (township). Covers a land area of 35.031 square miles and a water area of 0.302 square miles. Located at 43.85° N. Lat; 84.57° W. Long. Elevation is 722 feet.
Population: 1,964; Growth (since 2000): 8.2%; Density: 56.1 persons per square mile; Race: 98.0% White, 0.3% Black/African American, 0.0% Asian, 0.2% American Indian/Alaska Native, 0.0% Native Hawaiian/Other Pacific Islander, 0.9% Two or more races, 2.3% Hispanic of any race; Average household size: 2.68; Median age: 40.3; Age under 18: 24.6%; Age 65 and over: 15.6%; Males per 100 females: 104.8
School District(s)
Beaverton Rural Schools (PK-12)
　2012-13 Enrollment: 1,313 . . . . (989) 246-3000
Housing: Homeownership rate: 83.1%; Homeowner vacancy rate: 2.2%; Rental vacancy rate: 6.7%

BENTLEY (township). Covers a land area of 34.696 square miles and a water area of 1.100 square miles. Located at 43.86° N. Lat; 84.23° W. Long.
History: Bentley Township was named for Murray Bentley, a storekeeper and first supervisor of the township.
Population: 844; Growth (since 2000): -1.7%; Density: 24.3 persons per square mile; Race: 98.6% White, 0.0% Black/African American, 0.0% Asian, 0.4% American Indian/Alaska Native, 0.0% Native Hawaiian/Other Pacific Islander, 0.6% Two or more races, 1.1% Hispanic of any race; Average household size: 2.48; Median age: 43.8; Age under 18: 20.5%; Age 65 and over: 14.5%; Males per 100 females: 100.0
Housing: Homeownership rate: 93.5%; Homeowner vacancy rate: 2.2%; Rental vacancy rate: 8.3%

BILLINGS (township). Covers a land area of 21.557 square miles and a water area of 1.638 square miles. Located at 43.87° N. Lat; 84.33° W. Long. Elevation is 705 feet.
Population: 2,416; Growth (since 2000): -11.0%; Density: 112.1 persons per square mile; Race: 97.1% White, 0.5% Black/African American, 0.3% Asian, 0.7% American Indian/Alaska Native, 0.0% Native Hawaiian/Other Pacific Islander, 1.0% Two or more races, 1.3% Hispanic of any race;

Average household size: 2.20; Median age: 51.6; Age under 18: 15.8%; Age 65 and over: 23.5%; Males per 100 females: 106.8
Housing: Homeownership rate: 89.3%; Homeowner vacancy rate: 4.8%; Rental vacancy rate: 9.8%

BOURRET (township). Covers a land area of 32.337 square miles and a water area of 0.388 square miles. Located at 44.10° N. Lat; 84.25° W. Long.
Population: 461; Growth (since 2000): -2.1%; Density: 14.3 persons per square mile; Race: 93.3% White, 1.3% Black/African American, 0.0% Asian, 2.8% American Indian/Alaska Native, 0.0% Native Hawaiian/Other Pacific Islander, 1.7% Two or more races, 1.5% Hispanic of any race; Average household size: 2.12; Median age: 54.4; Age under 18: 14.3%; Age 65 and over: 29.1%; Males per 100 females: 118.5
Housing: Homeownership rate: 92.1%; Homeowner vacancy rate: 4.3%; Rental vacancy rate: 4.8%

BUCKEYE (township). Covers a land area of 34.172 square miles and a water area of 0.392 square miles. Located at 43.94° N. Lat; 84.42° W. Long.
Population: 1,308; Growth (since 2000): -1.9%; Density: 38.3 persons per square mile; Race: 98.0% White, 0.2% Black/African American, 0.5% Asian, 0.2% American Indian/Alaska Native, 0.1% Native Hawaiian/Other Pacific Islander, 0.8% Two or more races, 1.0% Hispanic of any race; Average household size: 2.55; Median age: 42.8; Age under 18: 22.5%; Age 65 and over: 13.7%; Males per 100 females: 111.3
Housing: Homeownership rate: 85.6%; Homeowner vacancy rate: 3.9%; Rental vacancy rate: 1.3%

BUTMAN (township). Covers a land area of 33.995 square miles and a water area of 1.647 square miles. Located at 44.12° N. Lat; 84.43° W. Long. Elevation is 961 feet.
History: Butman Township was organized in 1883 and named for Myron Butman, a businessman from Saginaw. The Lovell P. Sherman family of Rhode Island had settled here in 1878.
Population: 1,999; Growth (since 2000): 2.7%; Density: 58.8 persons per square mile; Race: 98.6% White, 0.2% Black/African American, 0.1% Asian, 0.4% American Indian/Alaska Native, 0.0% Native Hawaiian/Other Pacific Islander, 0.7% Two or more races, 0.7% Hispanic of any race; Average household size: 2.14; Median age: 60.6; Age under 18: 11.9%; Age 65 and over: 39.7%; Males per 100 females: 107.4
Housing: Homeownership rate: 92.7%; Homeowner vacancy rate: 4.5%; Rental vacancy rate: 2.8%
Additional Information Contacts
Butman Township . . . . (989) 426-4351
　http://www.butmantownship.com

CLEMENT (township). Covers a land area of 20.043 square miles and a water area of 0.805 square miles. Located at 44.12° N. Lat; 84.33° W. Long.
Population: 901; Growth (since 2000): -9.4%; Density: 45.0 persons per square mile; Race: 97.6% White, 0.1% Black/African American, 0.1% Asian, 0.6% American Indian/Alaska Native, 0.0% Native Hawaiian/Other Pacific Islander, 1.2% Two or more races, 1.6% Hispanic of any race; Average household size: 2.14; Median age: 55.0; Age under 18: 15.1%; Age 65 and over: 29.5%; Males per 100 females: 100.7
Housing: Homeownership rate: 91.4%; Homeowner vacancy rate: 4.2%; Rental vacancy rate: 5.3%

GLADWIN (city). County seat. Covers a land area of 2.891 square miles and a water area of 0.024 square miles. Located at 43.98° N. Lat; 84.49° W. Long. Elevation is 784 feet.
History: The community of Gladwin was established in the early 1870's by lumbermen. First called Cedar, it soon took the name of the county, which had been named for Major Henry Gladwin, British commander at Detroit.
Population: 2,933; Growth (since 2000): -2.3%; Density: 1,014.5 persons per square mile; Race: 96.8% White, 0.1% Black/African American, 0.7% Asian, 0.4% American Indian/Alaska Native, 0.0% Native Hawaiian/Other Pacific Islander, 1.4% Two or more races, 1.1% Hispanic of any race; Average household size: 2.19; Median age: 40.4; Age under 18: 23.5%; Age 65 and over: 22.3%; Males per 100 females: 81.4; Marriage status: 24.7% never married, 45.5% now married, 3.7% separated, 13.6% widowed, 16.2% divorced; Foreign born: 1.8%; Speak English only: 97.6%; With disability: 22.9%; Veterans: 12.0%; Ancestry: 28.9% German, 14.7% Irish, 12.1% English, 8.3% Polish, 5.1% Italian

Employment: 7.3% management, business, and financial, 0.7% computer, engineering, and science, 14.4% education, legal, community service, arts, and media, 6.2% healthcare practitioners, 22.5% service, 25.9% sales and office, 6.4% natural resources, construction, and maintenance, 16.6% production, transportation, and material moving
Income: Per capita: $16,394; Median household: $25,174; Average household: $34,635; Households with income of $100,000 or more: 3.9%; Poverty rate: 30.7%
Educational Attainment: High school diploma or higher: 87.6%; Bachelor's degree or higher: 21.0%; Graduate/professional degree or higher: 11.4%

School District(s)
Gladwin Community Schools (PK-12)
    2012-13 Enrollment: 1,796 . . . . (989) 426-9255
Housing: Homeownership rate: 58.1%; Median home value: $83,200; Median year structure built: 1976; Homeowner vacancy rate: 4.0%; Median gross rent: $511 per month; Rental vacancy rate: 9.0%
Health Insurance: 89.4% have insurance; 61.3% have private insurance; 47.7% have public insurance; 10.6% do not have insurance; 3.2% of children under 18 do not have insurance
Hospitals: Midmichigan Medical Center - Gladwin (25 beds)
Safety: Violent crime rate: 51.6 per 10,000 population; Property crime rate: 364.6 per 10,000 population
Newspapers: Gladwin County Record (weekly circulation 7200)
Transportation: Commute: 93.5% car, 1.2% public transportation, 2.8% walk, 2.5% work from home; Median travel time to work: 19.8 minutes
Additional Information Contacts
City of Gladwin . . . . (989) 426-9231
    http://www.gladwin.org

GLADWIN (township). Covers a land area of 35.216 square miles and a water area of 0.077 square miles. Located at 44.03° N. Lat; 84.42° W. Long. Elevation is 784 feet.
History: Settled 1865; incorporated as village 1885, as city 1893.
Population: 1,116; Growth (since 2000): 6.9%; Density: 31.7 persons per square mile; Race: 98.1% White, 0.2% Black/African American, 0.4% Asian, 0.2% American Indian/Alaska Native, 0.0% Native Hawaiian/Other Pacific Islander, 0.8% Two or more races, 0.4% Hispanic of any race; Average household size: 2.94; Median age: 40.0; Age under 18: 28.3%; Age 65 and over: 17.7%; Males per 100 females: 100.4

School District(s)
Gladwin Community Schools (PK-12)
    2012-13 Enrollment: 1,796 . . . . (989) 426-9255
Housing: Homeownership rate: 90.5%; Homeowner vacancy rate: 1.4%; Rental vacancy rate: 11.6%
Hospitals: Midmichigan Medical Center - Gladwin (25 beds)
Newspapers: Gladwin County Record (weekly circulation 7200)

GRIM (township). Covers a land area of 70.297 square miles and a water area of 1.025 square miles. Located at 43.99° N. Lat; 84.23° W. Long.
Population: 136; Growth (since 2000): 5.4%; Density: 1.9 persons per square mile; Race: 98.5% White, 0.0% Black/African American, 0.0% Asian, 0.7% American Indian/Alaska Native, 0.0% Native Hawaiian/Other Pacific Islander, 0.7% Two or more races, 0.0% Hispanic of any race; Average household size: 2.43; Median age: 41.5; Age under 18: 24.3%; Age 65 and over: 9.6%; Males per 100 females: 112.5
Housing: Homeownership rate: 89.3%; Homeowner vacancy rate: 2.0%; Rental vacancy rate: 0.0%

GROUT (township). Covers a land area of 34.181 square miles and a water area of 0.611 square miles. Located at 43.95° N. Lat; 84.56° W. Long.
History: Grout Township was settled in 1863 by Benjamin Teeple, but Willard Grout had filed the first homestead claim here, and the township was named for him. Grout became the postmaster in 1874.
Population: 1,964; Growth (since 2000): 5.1%; Density: 57.5 persons per square mile; Race: 98.4% White, 0.1% Black/African American, 0.3% Asian, 0.4% American Indian/Alaska Native, 0.0% Native Hawaiian/Other Pacific Islander, 0.7% Two or more races, 1.6% Hispanic of any race; Average household size: 2.72; Median age: 41.9; Age under 18: 25.5%; Age 65 and over: 18.7%; Males per 100 females: 96.8
Housing: Homeownership rate: 88.4%; Homeowner vacancy rate: 1.3%; Rental vacancy rate: 3.4%

HAY (township). Covers a land area of 21.454 square miles and a water area of 1.239 square miles. Located at 43.95° N. Lat; 84.34° W. Long.
Population: 1,362; Growth (since 2000): -2.9%; Density: 63.5 persons per square mile; Race: 97.3% White, 0.2% Black/African American, 0.1% Asian, 0.5% American Indian/Alaska Native, 0.0% Native Hawaiian/Other Pacific Islander, 1.3% Two or more races, 1.9% Hispanic of any race; Average household size: 2.24; Median age: 50.8; Age under 18: 16.0%; Age 65 and over: 23.6%; Males per 100 females: 108.3
Housing: Homeownership rate: 87.9%; Homeowner vacancy rate: 3.2%; Rental vacancy rate: 2.6%

RHODES (unincorporated postal area)
ZCTA: 48652
    Covers a land area of 53.507 square miles and a water area of 1.188 square miles. Located at 43.86° N. Lat; 84.20° W. Long. Elevation is 732 feet.
    Population: 1,548; Growth (since 2000): 1.8%; Density: 28.9 persons per square mile; Race: 98.3% White, 0.0% Black/African American, 0.1% Asian, 0.6% American Indian/Alaska Native, 0.0% Native Hawaiian/Other Pacific Islander, 0.4% Two or more races, 1.6% Hispanic of any race; Average household size: 2.50; Median age: 44.0; Age under 18: 21.2%; Age 65 and over: 14.9%; Males per 100 females: 104.5
    Housing: Homeownership rate: 93.5%; Homeowner vacancy rate: 1.7%; Rental vacancy rate: 7.0%

SAGE (township). Covers a land area of 34.229 square miles and a water area of 1.199 square miles. Located at 44.03° N. Lat; 84.55° W. Long.
Population: 2,457; Growth (since 2000): -6.1%; Density: 71.8 persons per square mile; Race: 98.0% White, 0.0% Black/African American, 0.7% Asian, 0.4% American Indian/Alaska Native, 0.0% Native Hawaiian/Other Pacific Islander, 0.9% Two or more races, 0.9% Hispanic of any race; Average household size: 2.48; Median age: 47.0; Age under 18: 21.7%; Age 65 and over: 21.9%; Males per 100 females: 93.3
Housing: Homeownership rate: 91.4%; Homeowner vacancy rate: 4.0%; Rental vacancy rate: 8.6%

SECORD (township). Covers a land area of 22.027 square miles and a water area of 1.481 square miles. Located at 44.05° N. Lat; 84.33° W. Long. Elevation is 735 feet.
History: Marcel Secord settled here in the early 1860's, where he operated a boarding house for lumbermen.
Population: 1,151; Growth (since 2000): 1.0%; Density: 52.3 persons per square mile; Race: 97.7% White, 0.4% Black/African American, 0.2% Asian, 0.6% American Indian/Alaska Native, 0.0% Native Hawaiian/Other Pacific Islander, 0.9% Two or more races, 0.8% Hispanic of any race; Average household size: 1.95; Median age: 61.3; Age under 18: 7.3%; Age 65 and over: 38.8%; Males per 100 females: 97.4
Housing: Homeownership rate: 94.6%; Homeowner vacancy rate: 5.2%; Rental vacancy rate: 13.5%

SHERMAN (township). Covers a land area of 34.870 square miles and a water area of 0.469 square miles. Located at 44.12° N. Lat; 84.54° W. Long.
Population: 1,043; Growth (since 2000): 1.4%; Density: 29.9 persons per square mile; Race: 96.1% White, 0.5% Black/African American, 0.4% Asian, 1.1% American Indian/Alaska Native, 0.0% Native Hawaiian/Other Pacific Islander, 2.0% Two or more races, 0.8% Hispanic of any race; Average household size: 2.44; Median age: 47.7; Age under 18: 21.0%; Age 65 and over: 21.4%; Males per 100 females: 112.4
Housing: Homeownership rate: 89.2%; Homeowner vacancy rate: 3.3%; Rental vacancy rate: 0.0%

TOBACCO (township). Covers a land area of 33.752 square miles and a water area of 1.472 square miles. Located at 43.85° N. Lat; 84.41° W. Long.
Population: 2,566; Growth (since 2000): 0.5%; Density: 76.0 persons per square mile; Race: 99.0% White, 0.1% Black/African American, 0.2% Asian, 0.2% American Indian/Alaska Native, 0.0% Native Hawaiian/Other Pacific Islander, 0.4% Two or more races, 1.4% Hispanic of any race; Average household size: 2.45; Median age: 47.7; Age under 18: 19.6%; Age 65 and over: 20.9%; Males per 100 females: 103.2; Marriage status: 18.7% never married, 65.2% now married, 0.9% separated, 6.2% widowed, 10.0% divorced; Foreign born: 1.0%; Speak English only: 98.0%;

With disability: 14.9%; Veterans: 12.9%; Ancestry: 26.2% German, 12.3% Irish, 10.8% American, 10.6% French, 9.8% English

Employment: 15.4% management, business, and financial, 2.9% computer, engineering, and science, 3.8% education, legal, community service, arts, and media, 5.2% healthcare practitioners, 11.3% service, 27.2% sales and office, 13.0% natural resources, construction, and maintenance, 21.4% production, transportation, and material moving

Income: Per capita: $25,734; Median household: $48,311; Average household: $62,235; Households with income of $100,000 or more: 16.8%; Poverty rate: 9.5%

Educational Attainment: High school diploma or higher: 87.9%; Bachelor's degree or higher: 12.1%; Graduate/professional degree or higher: 4.2%

Housing: Homeownership rate: 90.9%; Median home value: $119,700; Median year structure built: 1982; Homeowner vacancy rate: 2.4%; Median gross rent: $1,028 per month; Rental vacancy rate: 4.0%

Health Insurance: 90.9% have insurance; 73.9% have private insurance; 43.9% have public insurance; 9.1% do not have insurance; 9.1% of children under 18 do not have insurance

Transportation: Commute: 84.6% car, 0.0% public transportation, 4.9% walk, 9.3% work from home; Median travel time to work: 29.5 minutes

Gogebic County

Located in northwestern Michigan on the Upper Peninsula; bounded on the northwest by Lake Superior, and on the south and southwest by Wisconsin; drained by the Montreal, Presque Isle, and Ontonagon Rivers; includes part of Ottawa National Forest, and many small lakes and waterfalls. Covers a land area of 1,101.849 square miles, a water area of 374.495 square miles, and is located in the Central Time Zone at 46.49° N. Lat., 89.79° W. Long. The county was founded in 1881. County seat is Bessemer.

Weather Station: Ironwood										Elevation: 1,430 feet		
	Jan	Feb	Mar	Apr	May	Jun	Jul	Aug	Sep	Oct	Nov	Dec
High	21	25	35	50	63	72	77	75	66	52	37	24
Low	2	4	14	28	40	50	55	53	45	34	22	9
Precip	2.0	1.3	2.0	2.6	3.1	3.5	4.1	3.4	4.0	3.9	2.7	2.1
Snow	45.2	26.7	24.6	11.4	1.8	0.0	0.0	0.0	0.3	6.8	24.9	45.5

High and Low temperatures in degrees Fahrenheit; Precipitation and Snow in inches

Population: 16,427; Growth (since 2000): -5.4%; Density: 14.9 persons per square mile; Race: 91.7% White, 4.1% Black/African American, 0.2% Asian, 2.4% American Indian/Alaska Native, 0.0% Native Hawaiian/Other Pacific Islander, 1.4% two or more races, 0.9% Hispanic of any race; Average household size: 2.11; Median age: 46.8; Age under 18: 16.9%; Age 65 and over: 21.4%; Males per 100 females: 114.3; Marriage status: 28.2% never married, 48.1% now married, 1.4% separated, 9.6% widowed, 14.1% divorced; Foreign born: 1.0%; Speak English only: 96.0%; With disability: 16.7%; Veterans: 14.4%; Ancestry: 19.9% Finnish, 17.2% German, 11.6% Italian, 9.8% American, 9.5% Polish

Religion: Six largest groups: 29.1% Catholicism, 20.0% Lutheran, 5.9% Baptist, 2.2% Non-denominational Protestant, 1.3% Methodist/Pietist, 0.3% Episcopalianism/Anglicanism

Economy: Unemployment rate: 6.7%; Leading industries: 19.0% retail trade; 14.4% accommodation and food services; 14.4% other services (except public administration); Farms: 62 totaling 6,078 acres; Company size: 0 employ 1,000 or more persons, 0 employ 500 to 999 persons, 7 employ 100 to 499 persons, 403 employ less than 100 persons; Business ownership: 491 women-owned, n/a Black-owned, n/a Hispanic-owned, n/a Asian-owned

Employment: 8.8% management, business, and financial, 4.1% computer, engineering, and science, 7.6% education, legal, community service, arts, and media, 6.6% healthcare practitioners, 22.8% service, 20.1% sales and office, 13.4% natural resources, construction, and maintenance, 16.6% production, transportation, and material moving

Income: Per capita: $20,330; Median household: $34,252; Average household: $45,318; Households with income of $100,000 or more: 7.8%; Poverty rate: 20.3%

Educational Attainment: High school diploma or higher: 91.7%; Bachelor's degree or higher: 18.3%; Graduate/professional degree or higher: 5.7%

Housing: Homeownership rate: 78.7%; Median home value: $66,800; Median year structure built: 1954; Homeowner vacancy rate: 4.1%; Median gross rent: $594 per month; Rental vacancy rate: 23.5%

Vital Statistics: Birth rate: 77.3 per 10,000 population; Death rate: 135.7 per 10,000 population; Age-adjusted cancer mortality rate: 234.6 deaths per 100,000 population

Health Insurance: 82.8% have insurance; 58.4% have private insurance; 44.7% have public insurance; 17.2% do not have insurance; 6.5% of children under 18 do not have insurance

Health Care: Physicians: 19.3 per 10,000 population; Hospital beds: 15.5 per 10,000 population; Hospital admissions: 307.4 per 10,000 population

Transportation: Commute: 90.2% car, 0.6% public transportation, 5.1% walk, 2.8% work from home; Median travel time to work: 19.2 minutes

Presidential Election: 53.6% Obama, 45.5% Romney (2012)

National and State Parks: Gogebic Lake State Park

Additional Information Contacts

Gogebic Government . . . . (906) 663-4518
  http://www.gogebic.org

Gogebic County Communities

BESSEMER (city). County seat. Covers a land area of 5.465 square miles and a water area of 0 square miles. Located at 46.48° N. Lat; 90.05° W. Long. Elevation is 1,427 feet.

History: Bessemer was established at a point where a copper lode to the north and an iron lode to the south met. Bessemer experienced rapid growth in the 1890's, when the expansion of the railroads created a wide market for Bessemer steel rails. The city was named for Sir Henry Bessemer (1813-1898), who devised the smelting process that made his name well-known.

Population: 1,905; Growth (since 2000): -11.3%; Density: 348.6 persons per square mile; Race: 96.4% White, 0.5% Black/African American, 0.3% Asian, 0.9% American Indian/Alaska Native, 0.0% Native Hawaiian/Other Pacific Islander, 1.6% Two or more races, 0.7% Hispanic of any race; Average household size: 2.11; Median age: 45.4; Age under 18: 20.3%; Age 65 and over: 21.0%; Males per 100 females: 96.6

School District(s)

Bessemer Area SD (PK-12)
  2012-13 Enrollment: 435. . . . . (906) 667-0802
Ironwood Area Schools of Gogebic County (PK-12)
  2012-13 Enrollment: 887. . . . . (906) 932-0200

Housing: Homeownership rate: 72.1%; Homeowner vacancy rate: 3.0%; Rental vacancy rate: 14.4%

BESSEMER (township). Covers a land area of 113.733 square miles and a water area of 1.561 square miles. Located at 46.39° N. Lat; 89.92° W. Long. Elevation is 1,427 feet.

History: Bessemer Township was named for Sir Henry Bessemer (1813-1898), a British metallurgist whose name became associated with the Bessemer process for making steel by blasting compressed air through molten iron.

Population: 1,176; Growth (since 2000): -7.4%; Density: 10.3 persons per square mile; Race: 99.1% White, 0.2% Black/African American, 0.1% Asian, 0.1% American Indian/Alaska Native, 0.0% Native Hawaiian/Other Pacific Islander, 0.6% Two or more races, 0.3% Hispanic of any race; Average household size: 2.15; Median age: 49.7; Age under 18: 18.5%; Age 65 and over: 22.1%; Males per 100 females: 113.4

School District(s)

Bessemer Area SD (PK-12)
  2012-13 Enrollment: 435. . . . . (906) 667-0802
Ironwood Area Schools of Gogebic County (PK-12)
  2012-13 Enrollment: 887. . . . . (906) 932-0200

Housing: Homeownership rate: 90.0%; Homeowner vacancy rate: 3.7%; Rental vacancy rate: 39.1%

ERWIN (township). Covers a land area of 47.453 square miles and a water area of 0.902 square miles. Located at 46.38° N. Lat; 90.09° W. Long.

Population: 326; Growth (since 2000): -8.7%; Density: 6.9 persons per square mile; Race: 97.2% White, 0.0% Black/African American, 0.0% Asian, 0.6% American Indian/Alaska Native, 0.0% Native Hawaiian/Other Pacific Islander, 2.1% Two or more races, 0.0% Hispanic of any race; Average household size: 2.26; Median age: 49.6; Age under 18: 18.4%; Age 65 and over: 15.3%; Males per 100 females: 109.0

Housing: Homeownership rate: 94.4%; Homeowner vacancy rate: 1.4%; Rental vacancy rate: 0.0%

IRONWOOD (charter township). Covers a land area of 175.402 square miles and a water area of 13.526 square miles. Located at 46.58° N. Lat; 90.16° W. Long. Elevation is 1,506 feet.

History: Founded 1885, Incorporated 1889.

Population: 2,333; Growth (since 2000): 0.1%; Density: 13.3 persons per square mile; Race: 97.6% White, 0.2% Black/African American, 0.2% Asian, 0.6% American Indian/Alaska Native, 0.0% Native Hawaiian/Other Pacific Islander, 1.3% Two or more races, 0.9% Hispanic of any race; Average household size: 2.17; Median age: 47.8; Age under 18: 17.0%; Age 65 and over: 21.8%; Males per 100 females: 103.8

School District(s)
Ironwood Area Schools of Gogebic County (PK-12)
    2012-13 Enrollment: 887 . . . . (906) 932-0200
Two-year College(s)
Gogebic Community College (Public)
    Fall 2013 Enrollment: 1,099 . . . . (906) 932-4231
    2013-14 Tuition: In-state $5,292; Out-of-state $6,253

Housing: Homeownership rate: 83.0%; Homeowner vacancy rate: 5.5%; Rental vacancy rate: 46.2%

Hospitals: Aspirus Grand View Hospital (25 beds)

Newspapers: Daily Globe (daily circulation 6500)

Airports: Gogebic-Iron County (commercial service–non-primary)

IRONWOOD (city). Covers a land area of 6.420 square miles and a water area of 0 square miles. Located at 46.45° N. Lat; 90.15° W. Long. Elevation is 1,506 feet.

History: Lumbering and mining both contributed to the development of Ironwood, the central city of the mining area that included Bessemer, Ramsay, and Wakefield. Iron ore was discovered in 1884 in this area, and the railroad line was extended in 1885 to tap the new resources. Ironwood was platted by the railroad in 1885, incorporated as a village in 1887, and chartered as a city in 1889. Ironwood was named for James R. Wood, known as "Iron" Wood.

Population: 5,387; Growth (since 2000): -14.4%; Density: 839.0 persons per square mile; Race: 96.0% White, 0.5% Black/African American, 0.2% Asian, 1.1% American Indian/Alaska Native, 0.0% Native Hawaiian/Other Pacific Islander, 1.8% Two or more races, 1.2% Hispanic of any race; Average household size: 2.09; Median age: 45.5; Age under 18: 19.3%; Age 65 and over: 21.7%; Males per 100 females: 92.7; Marriage status: 27.3% never married, 42.8% now married, 1.8% separated, 12.8% widowed, 17.1% divorced; Foreign born: 1.2%; Speak English only: 97.0%; With disability: 18.7%; Veterans: 14.8%; Ancestry: 22.8% Finnish, 15.9% German, 11.8% Italian, 10.5% Polish, 10.1% Irish

Employment: 8.2% management, business, and financial, 4.7% computer, engineering, and science, 5.6% education, legal, community service, arts, and media, 6.1% healthcare practitioners, 20.7% service, 20.4% sales and office, 13.0% natural resources, construction, and maintenance, 21.4% production, transportation, and material moving

Income: Per capita: $18,902; Median household: $27,349; Average household: $38,839; Households with income of $100,000 or more: 6.2%; Poverty rate: 27.2%

Educational Attainment: High school diploma or higher: 89.7%; Bachelor's degree or higher: 15.7%; Graduate/professional degree or higher: 4.1%

School District(s)
Ironwood Area Schools of Gogebic County (PK-12)
    2012-13 Enrollment: 887 . . . . (906) 932-0200
Two-year College(s)
Gogebic Community College (Public)
    Fall 2013 Enrollment: 1,099 . . . . (906) 932-4231
    2013-14 Tuition: In-state $5,292; Out-of-state $6,253

Housing: Homeownership rate: 70.4%; Median home value: $52,300; Median year structure built: Before 1940; Homeowner vacancy rate: 4.1%; Median gross rent: $618 per month; Rental vacancy rate: 11.7%

Health Insurance: 80.3% have insurance; 51.4% have private insurance; 46.7% have public insurance; 19.7% do not have insurance; 3.4% of children under 18 do not have insurance

Hospitals: Aspirus Grand View Hospital (25 beds)

Safety: Violent crime rate: 25.0 per 10,000 population; Property crime rate: 174.9 per 10,000 population

Newspapers: Daily Globe (daily circulation 6500)

Transportation: Commute: 89.6% car, 0.6% public transportation, 5.6% walk, 1.8% work from home; Median travel time to work: 17.3 minutes

Airports: Gogebic-Iron County (commercial service–non-primary)

MARENISCO (CDP). Covers a land area of 3.446 square miles and a water area of 0 square miles. Located at 46.37° N. Lat; 89.71° W. Long. Elevation is 1,519 feet.

Population: 254; Growth (since 2000): n/a; Density: 73.7 persons per square mile; Race: 92.5% White, 0.0% Black/African American, 0.0% Asian, 5.9% American Indian/Alaska Native, 0.0% Native Hawaiian/Other Pacific Islander, 1.2% Two or more races, 0.4% Hispanic of any race; Average household size: 2.25; Median age: 45.7; Age under 18: 16.5%; Age 65 and over: 19.7%; Males per 100 females: 120.9

Housing: Homeownership rate: 89.3%; Homeowner vacancy rate: 7.3%; Rental vacancy rate: 7.7%

MARENISCO (township). Covers a land area of 310.892 square miles and a water area of 15.010 square miles. Located at 46.38° N. Lat; 89.58° W. Long. Elevation is 1,519 feet.

Population: 1,727; Growth (since 2000): 64.3%; Density: 5.6 persons per square mile; Race: 61.7% White, 36.5% Black/African American, 0.2% Asian, 1.2% American Indian/Alaska Native, 0.0% Native Hawaiian/Other Pacific Islander, 0.3% Two or more races, 0.3% Hispanic of any race; Average household size: 2.07; Median age: 39.3; Age under 18: 4.3%; Age 65 and over: 9.4%; Males per 100 females: 554.2

Housing: Homeownership rate: 92.7%; Homeowner vacancy rate: 6.9%; Rental vacancy rate: 39.4%

RAMSAY (unincorporated postal area)
ZCTA: 49959
    Covers a land area of 0.706 square miles and a water area of 0 square miles. Located at 46.47° N. Lat; 90.00° W. Long. Elevation is 1,467 feet.
    Population: 344; Growth (since 2000): -10.4%; Density: 487.4 persons per square mile; Race: 98.3% White, 0.0% Black/African American, 0.0% Asian, 0.0% American Indian/Alaska Native, 0.0% Native Hawaiian/Other Pacific Islander, 1.7% Two or more races, 0.6% Hispanic of any race; Average household size: 2.05; Median age: 47.2; Age under 18: 18.3%; Age 65 and over: 24.4%; Males per 100 females: 106.0
    Housing: Homeownership rate: 87.5%; Homeowner vacancy rate: 3.3%; Rental vacancy rate: 4.3%

WAKEFIELD (city). Covers a land area of 8.016 square miles and a water area of 0.566 square miles. Located at 46.48° N. Lat; 89.93° W. Long. Elevation is 1,539 feet.

History: Wakefield grew up, literally, around several mines which were located within the boundaries of the city. The village was named for George M. Wakefield, a mine owner, who platted it in 1886. Wakefield was incorporated as a city in 1919.

Population: 1,851; Growth (since 2000): -11.2%; Density: 230.9 persons per square mile; Race: 96.8% White, 0.1% Black/African American, 0.4% Asian, 1.1% American Indian/Alaska Native, 0.0% Native Hawaiian/Other Pacific Islander, 1.1% Two or more races, 1.0% Hispanic of any race; Average household size: 2.11; Median age: 50.1; Age under 18: 17.1%; Age 65 and over: 26.7%; Males per 100 females: 93.6

School District(s)
Wakefield-Marenisco SD (PK-12)
    2012-13 Enrollment: 288 . . . . (906) 224-9421

Housing: Homeownership rate: 82.9%; Homeowner vacancy rate: 1.9%; Rental vacancy rate: 11.4%

Newspapers: Wakefield News (weekly circulation 1400)

WAKEFIELD (township). Covers a land area of 179.697 square miles and a water area of 0.790 square miles. Located at 46.55° N. Lat; 89.87° W. Long. Elevation is 1,539 feet.

History: Settled 1866; incorporated as village 1887, as city 1919.

Population: 305; Growth (since 2000): -16.2%; Density: 1.7 persons per square mile; Race: 99.7% White, 0.0% Black/African American, 0.0% Asian, 0.0% American Indian/Alaska Native, 0.0% Native Hawaiian/Other Pacific Islander, 0.3% Two or more races, 0.3% Hispanic of any race; Average household size: 2.07; Median age: 51.1; Age under 18: 16.4%; Age 65 and over: 22.3%; Males per 100 females: 108.9

School District(s)
Wakefield-Marenisco SD (PK-12)
    2012-13 Enrollment: 288 . . . . (906) 224-9421

Housing: Homeownership rate: 92.5%; Homeowner vacancy rate: 9.9%; Rental vacancy rate: 87.4%

Newspapers: Wakefield News (weekly circulation 1400)

WATERSMEET (CDP). Covers a land area of 9.200 square miles and a water area of 0.005 square miles. Located at 46.30° N. Lat; 89.21° W. Long. Elevation is 1,604 feet.

Population: 428; Growth (since 2000): n/a; Density: 46.5 persons per square mile; Race: 67.5% White, 0.2% Black/African American, 0.0% Asian, 29.4% American Indian/Alaska Native, 0.0% Native Hawaiian/Other Pacific Islander, 2.8% Two or more races, 1.4% Hispanic of any race; Average household size: 2.40; Median age: 42.0; Age under 18: 26.2%; Age 65 and over: 20.6%; Males per 100 females: 104.8

School District(s)
Watersmeet Township SD (KG-12)
    2012-13 Enrollment: 176. . . . . (906) 358-4555
Housing: Homeownership rate: 82.0%; Homeowner vacancy rate: 6.9%; Rental vacancy rate: 17.5%

WATERSMEET (township). Covers a land area of 254.770 square miles and a water area of 23.002 square miles. Located at 46.25° N. Lat; 89.21° W. Long. Elevation is 1,604 feet.

History: Watersmeet was named for the junction of the middle branch of the Ontonagon River and Duck Creek, which was the apex of three watersheds, water draining to Lake Superior on the north, to Lake Michigan on the east, and to the Mississippi Valley on the south.

Population: 1,417; Growth (since 2000): -3.7%; Density: 5.6 persons per square mile; Race: 79.6% White, 0.1% Black/African American, 0.1% Asian, 18.5% American Indian/Alaska Native, 0.0% Native Hawaiian/Other Pacific Islander, 1.8% Two or more races, 1.1% Hispanic of any race; Average household size: 2.11; Median age: 55.2; Age under 18: 16.6%; Age 65 and over: 28.4%; Males per 100 females: 106.9

School District(s)
Watersmeet Township SD (KG-12)
    2012-13 Enrollment: 176. . . . . (906) 358-4555
Housing: Homeownership rate: 85.5%; Homeowner vacancy rate: 4.3%; Rental vacancy rate: 22.7%

Grand Traverse County

Located in northwestern Michigan; drained by the Boardman and Betsie Rivers; includes Traverse Bay in the north, and Green, Duck, and Long Lakes. Covers a land area of 464.331 square miles, a water area of 136.984 square miles, and is located in the Eastern Time Zone at 44.72° N. Lat., 85.55° W. Long. The county was founded in 1851. County seat is Traverse City.

Grand Traverse County is part of the Traverse City, MI Micropolitan Statistical Area. The entire metro area includes: Benzie County, MI; Grand Traverse County, MI; Kalkaska County, MI; Leelanau County, MI

Weather Station: Old Mission 3 SSW   Elevation: 649 feet

	Jan	Feb	Mar	Apr	May	Jun	Jul	Aug	Sep	Oct	Nov	Dec
High	29	31	39	52	65	74	79	77	70	56	44	33
Low	16	16	21	32	41	51	57	57	50	39	30	22
Precip	1.3	0.9	1.2	2.2	2.6	3.0	2.5	3.5	3.4	3.2	2.0	1.6
Snow	na	na	na	na	tr	0.0	0.0	0.0	0.0	0.0	na	na

High and Low temperatures in degrees Fahrenheit; Precipitation and Snow in inches

Population: 86,986; Growth (since 2000): 12.0%; Density: 187.3 persons per square mile; Race: 94.7% White, 1.2% Black/African American, 0.7% Asian, 1.2% American Indian/Alaska Native, 0.0% Native Hawaiian/Other Pacific Islander, 1.7% two or more races, 2.2% Hispanic of any race; Average household size: 2.39; Median age: 41.3; Age under 18: 22.1%; Age 65 and over: 15.0%; Males per 100 females: 97.5; Marriage status: 27.5% never married, 53.7% now married, 0.9% separated, 5.8% widowed, 12.9% divorced; Foreign born: 2.0%; Speak English only: 96.6%; With disability: 12.0%; Veterans: 10.4%; Ancestry: 28.1% German, 13.3% Irish, 12.8% English, 11.6% American, 8.6% Polish

Religion: Six largest groups: 16.1% Catholicism, 5.9% Non-denominational Protestant, 4.4% Lutheran, 4.0% Presbyterian-Reformed, 3.2% Methodist/Pietist, 1.5% Holiness

Economy: Unemployment rate: 4.6%; Leading industries: 17.1% retail trade; 12.0% health care and social assistance; 11.2% professional, scientific, and technical services; Farms: 504 totaling 54,558 acres; Company size: 1 employs 1,000 or more persons, 2 employ 500 to 999 persons, 44 employ 100 to 499 persons, 3,260 employ less than 100 persons; Business ownership: 2,569 women-owned, 34 Black-owned, n/a Hispanic-owned, n/a Asian-owned

Employment: 13.5% management, business, and financial, 3.0% computer, engineering, and science, 8.9% education, legal, community service, arts, and media, 7.2% healthcare practitioners, 21.0% service, 26.5% sales and office, 9.0% natural resources, construction, and maintenance, 10.9% production, transportation, and material moving

Income: Per capita: $27,660; Median household: $51,766; Average household: $68,384; Households with income of $100,000 or more: 17.8%; Poverty rate: 11.7%

Educational Attainment: High school diploma or higher: 93.3%; Bachelor's degree or higher: 30.4%; Graduate/professional degree or higher: 12.0%

Housing: Homeownership rate: 75.0%; Median home value: $168,300; Median year structure built: 1982; Homeowner vacancy rate: 2.7%; Median gross rent: $847 per month; Rental vacancy rate: 9.9%

Vital Statistics: Birth rate: 101.0 per 10,000 population; Death rate: 83.6 per 10,000 population; Age-adjusted cancer mortality rate: 147.7 deaths per 100,000 population

Health Insurance: 87.5% have insurance; 71.7% have private insurance; 31.4% have public insurance; 12.5% do not have insurance; 5.5% of children under 18 do not have insurance

Health Care: Physicians: 46.5 per 10,000 population; Hospital beds: 44.3 per 10,000 population; Hospital admissions: 2,652.4 per 10,000 population

Transportation: Commute: 91.6% car, 0.4% public transportation, 1.8% walk, 4.1% work from home; Median travel time to work: 20.3 minutes

Presidential Election: 43.6% Obama, 55.4% Romney (2012)

National and State Parks: Interlochen State Park; Petobego State Game Area; Traverse City State Park

Additional Information Contacts
Grand Traverse Government . . . . (231) 922-4700
    http://www.co.grand-traverse.mi.us

Grand Traverse County Communities

ACME (township). Covers a land area of 25.007 square miles and a water area of 0.275 square miles. Located at 44.79° N. Lat; 85.46° W. Long. Elevation is 594 feet.

Population: 4,375; Growth (since 2000): 1.0%; Density: 175.0 persons per square mile; Race: 96.3% White, 0.3% Black/African American, 0.5% Asian, 0.8% American Indian/Alaska Native, 0.0% Native Hawaiian/Other Pacific Islander, 1.7% Two or more races, 1.5% Hispanic of any race; Average household size: 2.42; Median age: 46.6; Age under 18: 21.8%; Age 65 and over: 18.7%; Males per 100 females: 93.9; Marriage status: 28.5% never married, 56.7% now married, 0.6% separated, 3.4% widowed, 11.4% divorced; Foreign born: 3.1%; Speak English only: 97.5%; With disability: 6.9%; Veterans: 11.3%; Ancestry: 26.1% German, 14.3% American, 14.1% Polish, 12.8% English, 11.2% Irish

Employment: 13.0% management, business, and financial, 5.0% computer, engineering, and science, 12.5% education, legal, community service, arts, and media, 10.3% healthcare practitioners, 13.0% service, 30.0% sales and office, 8.0% natural resources, construction, and maintenance, 8.3% production, transportation, and material moving

Income: Per capita: $39,085; Median household: $75,500; Average household: $104,763; Households with income of $100,000 or more: 30.3%; Poverty rate: 7.6%

Educational Attainment: High school diploma or higher: 97.8%; Bachelor's degree or higher: 42.6%; Graduate/professional degree or higher: 18.7%

Housing: Homeownership rate: 81.7%; Median home value: $196,800; Median year structure built: 1982; Homeowner vacancy rate: 2.3%; Median gross rent: $797 per month; Rental vacancy rate: 23.2%

Health Insurance: 92.1% have insurance; 83.0% have private insurance; 23.2% have public insurance; 7.9% do not have insurance; 1.6% of children under 18 do not have insurance

Transportation: Commute: 91.1% car, 0.0% public transportation, 0.9% walk, 6.9% work from home; Median travel time to work: 17.4 minutes

BLAIR (township). Covers a land area of 35.610 square miles and a water area of 0.367 square miles. Located at 44.63° N. Lat; 85.61° W. Long.

Population: 8,209; Growth (since 2000): 27.3%; Density: 230.5 persons per square mile; Race: 93.1% White, 0.4% Black/African American, 1.0% Asian, 1.9% American Indian/Alaska Native, 0.1% Native Hawaiian/Other Pacific Islander, 2.4% Two or more races, 3.5% Hispanic of any race; Average household size: 2.79; Median age: 34.2; Age under 18: 27.8%; Age 65 and over: 8.3%; Males per 100 females: 102.6; Marriage status:

26.7% never married, 50.0% now married, 0.9% separated, 3.5% widowed, 19.8% divorced; Foreign born: 1.4%; Speak English only: 95.7%; With disability: 15.9%; Veterans: 9.4%; Ancestry: 28.2% German, 11.1% American, 9.8% English, 8.8% Irish, 7.3% Dutch

Employment: 10.4% management, business, and financial, 2.1% computer, engineering, and science, 5.1% education, legal, community service, arts, and media, 3.7% healthcare practitioners, 22.6% service, 33.3% sales and office, 8.0% natural resources, construction, and maintenance, 14.8% production, transportation, and material moving

Income: Per capita: $19,254; Median household: $46,971; Average household: $54,318; Households with income of $100,000 or more: 10.2%; Poverty rate: 10.8%

Educational Attainment: High school diploma or higher: 88.4%; Bachelor's degree or higher: 13.6%; Graduate/professional degree or higher: 4.6%

Housing: Homeownership rate: 83.8%; Median home value: $117,700; Median year structure built: 1989; Homeowner vacancy rate: 2.7%; Median gross rent: $897 per month; Rental vacancy rate: 6.9%

Health Insurance: 79.6% have insurance; 64.0% have private insurance; 30.1% have public insurance; 20.4% do not have insurance; 15.4% of children under 18 do not have insurance

Transportation: Commute: 96.0% car, 0.0% public transportation, 1.0% walk, 0.9% work from home; Median travel time to work: 19.9 minutes

CHUMS CORNER (CDP). Covers a land area of 2.660 square miles and a water area of 0.004 square miles. Located at 44.67° N. Lat; 85.65° W. Long. Elevation is 889 feet.

Population: 946; Growth (since 2000): n/a; Density: 355.7 persons per square mile; Race: 95.2% White, 0.3% Black/African American, 1.8% Asian, 1.3% American Indian/Alaska Native, 0.0% Native Hawaiian/Other Pacific Islander, 1.1% Two or more races, 1.4% Hispanic of any race; Average household size: 2.76; Median age: 38.4; Age under 18: 24.9%; Age 65 and over: 13.4%; Males per 100 females: 96.7

Housing: Homeownership rate: 86.9%; Homeowner vacancy rate: 2.0%; Rental vacancy rate: 6.3%

EAST BAY (township). Covers a land area of 39.928 square miles and a water area of 2.466 square miles. Located at 44.69° N. Lat; 85.51° W. Long.

Population: 10,663; Growth (since 2000): 7.5%; Density: 267.1 persons per square mile; Race: 96.1% White, 0.3% Black/African American, 0.7% Asian, 1.0% American Indian/Alaska Native, 0.0% Native Hawaiian/Other Pacific Islander, 1.5% Two or more races, 1.6% Hispanic of any race; Average household size: 2.48; Median age: 41.1; Age under 18: 23.1%; Age 65 and over: 11.9%; Males per 100 females: 98.6; Marriage status: 28.4% never married, 56.3% now married, 0.2% separated, 3.0% widowed, 12.4% divorced; Foreign born: 1.4%; Speak English only: 97.9%; With disability: 8.9%; Veterans: 9.7%; Ancestry: 28.7% German, 12.7% Irish, 12.4% English, 9.4% American, 9.4% Polish

Employment: 13.4% management, business, and financial, 2.8% computer, engineering, and science, 7.3% education, legal, community service, arts, and media, 8.7% healthcare practitioners, 19.8% service, 29.8% sales and office, 9.5% natural resources, construction, and maintenance, 8.8% production, transportation, and material moving

Income: Per capita: $26,704; Median household: $56,621; Average household: $67,255; Households with income of $100,000 or more: 14.6%; Poverty rate: 8.1%

Educational Attainment: High school diploma or higher: 93.2%; Bachelor's degree or higher: 29.8%; Graduate/professional degree or higher: 12.3%

Housing: Homeownership rate: 81.8%; Median home value: $163,900; Median year structure built: 1982; Homeowner vacancy rate: 2.4%; Median gross rent: $824 per month; Rental vacancy rate: 13.3%

Health Insurance: 89.1% have insurance; 76.2% have private insurance; 26.9% have public insurance; 10.9% do not have insurance; 1.0% of children under 18 do not have insurance

Transportation: Commute: 93.7% car, 0.0% public transportation, 1.1% walk, 4.1% work from home; Median travel time to work: 20.0 minutes

Additional Information Contacts
East Bay Charter Township . . . . (231) 947-8647
   http://www.eastbaytwp.org

FIFE LAKE (township). Covers a land area of 34.601 square miles and a water area of 1.372 square miles. Located at 44.56° N. Lat; 85.39° W. Long. Elevation is 1,060 feet.

Population: 2,791; Growth (since 2000): 84.0%; Density: 80.7 persons per square mile; Race: 74.2% White, 23.0% Black/African American, 0.4% Asian, 1.2% American Indian/Alaska Native, 0.0% Native Hawaiian/Other Pacific Islander, 1.1% Two or more races, 3.4% Hispanic of any race; Average household size: 2.42; Median age: 38.4; Age under 18: 12.3%; Age 65 and over: 9.2%; Males per 100 females: 279.2; Marriage status: 40.3% never married, 37.5% now married, 2.2% separated, 2.7% widowed, 19.5% divorced; Foreign born: 1.0%; Speak English only: 95.1%; With disability: 18.6%; Veterans: 13.0%; Ancestry: 21.0% German, 10.5% American, 9.7% Irish, 9.1% English, 5.1% French

Employment: 7.2% management, business, and financial, 5.2% computer, engineering, and science, 6.2% education, legal, community service, arts, and media, 5.6% healthcare practitioners, 20.5% service, 24.0% sales and office, 13.0% natural resources, construction, and maintenance, 18.3% production, transportation, and material moving

Income: Per capita: $16,776; Median household: $48,214; Average household: $59,580; Households with income of $100,000 or more: 15.0%; Poverty rate: 9.2%

Educational Attainment: High school diploma or higher: 86.7%; Bachelor's degree or higher: 9.0%; Graduate/professional degree or higher: 3.6%

School District(s)
Forest Area Community Schools (PK-12)
   2012-13 Enrollment: 614 . . . . (231) 369-4191
Housing: Homeownership rate: 77.7%; Median home value: $118,600; Median year structure built: 1977; Homeowner vacancy rate: 2.3%; Median gross rent: $650 per month; Rental vacancy rate: 8.1%

Health Insurance: 80.9% have insurance; 65.7% have private insurance; 33.9% have public insurance; 19.1% do not have insurance; 8.7% of children under 18 do not have insurance

Transportation: Commute: 94.4% car, 2.2% public transportation, 1.3% walk, 2.1% work from home; Median travel time to work: 36.7 minutes

FIFE LAKE (village). Covers a land area of 0.750 square miles and a water area of 0.453 square miles. Located at 44.58° N. Lat; 85.35° W. Long. Elevation is 1,060 feet.

Population: 443; Growth (since 2000): -4.9%; Density: 590.6 persons per square mile; Race: 95.7% White, 0.7% Black/African American, 0.0% Asian, 1.6% American Indian/Alaska Native, 0.0% Native Hawaiian/Other Pacific Islander, 2.0% Two or more races, 1.8% Hispanic of any race; Average household size: 2.34; Median age: 41.1; Age under 18: 22.8%; Age 65 and over: 15.6%; Males per 100 females: 96.0

School District(s)
Forest Area Community Schools (PK-12)
   2012-13 Enrollment: 614 . . . . (231) 369-4191
Housing: Homeownership rate: 65.6%; Homeowner vacancy rate: 6.8%; Rental vacancy rate: 13.2%

GARFIELD (charter township). Covers a land area of 26.592 square miles and a water area of 1.101 square miles. Located at 44.72° N. Lat; 85.64° W. Long.

History: Garfield Township was organized in 1882 and named for President James A. Garfield, who had just been assassinated.

Population: 16,256; Growth (since 2000): 17.5%; Density: 611.3 persons per square mile; Race: 93.9% White, 0.8% Black/African American, 1.1% Asian, 1.2% American Indian/Alaska Native, 0.0% Native Hawaiian/Other Pacific Islander, 2.4% Two or more races, 2.4% Hispanic of any race; Average household size: 2.16; Median age: 43.0; Age under 18: 20.1%; Age 65 and over: 20.4%; Males per 100 females: 84.4; Marriage status: 28.9% never married, 47.9% now married, 1.2% separated, 9.9% widowed, 13.3% divorced; Foreign born: 1.8%; Speak English only: 97.1%; With disability: 15.6%; Veterans: 11.9%; Ancestry: 26.5% German, 14.9% Irish, 12.7% English, 12.7% American, 9.3% Polish

Employment: 14.5% management, business, and financial, 2.7% computer, engineering, and science, 7.3% education, legal, community service, arts, and media, 5.8% healthcare practitioners, 22.4% service, 30.7% sales and office, 5.3% natural resources, construction, and maintenance, 11.3% production, transportation, and material moving

Income: Per capita: $26,217; Median household: $44,152; Average household: $57,602; Households with income of $100,000 or more: 14.0%; Poverty rate: 14.3%

Educational Attainment: High school diploma or higher: 92.8%; Bachelor's degree or higher: 28.8%; Graduate/professional degree or higher: 10.1%

Housing: Homeownership rate: 60.7%; Median home value: $159,600; Median year structure built: 1990; Homeowner vacancy rate: 3.4%; Median gross rent: $856 per month; Rental vacancy rate: 11.0%

Health Insurance: 88.5% have insurance; 65.8% have private insurance; 41.2% have public insurance; 11.5% do not have insurance; 3.2% of children under 18 do not have insurance

Transportation: Commute: 94.3% car, 0.2% public transportation, 0.6% walk, 3.1% work from home; Median travel time to work: 17.1 minutes

Additional Information Contacts

Garfield Charter Township . . . . (231) 941-1620
  http://www.garfield-twp.com

GRANT (township). Covers a land area of 35.201 square miles and a water area of 0.817 square miles. Located at 44.56° N. Lat; 85.77° W. Long.

History: Grant Township was organized in 1866 and named for General Ulysses S. Grant.

Population: 1,066; Growth (since 2000): 12.6%; Density: 30.3 persons per square mile; Race: 98.1% White, 0.1% Black/African American, 0.1% Asian, 0.4% American Indian/Alaska Native, 0.0% Native Hawaiian/Other Pacific Islander, 1.1% Two or more races, 1.1% Hispanic of any race; Average household size: 2.46; Median age: 44.9; Age under 18: 22.7%; Age 65 and over: 14.5%; Males per 100 females: 106.2

Housing: Homeownership rate: 87.1%; Homeowner vacancy rate: 3.3%; Rental vacancy rate: 5.1%

GRAWN (CDP). Covers a land area of 0.634 square miles and a water area of 0 square miles. Located at 44.66° N. Lat; 85.69° W. Long. Elevation is 876 feet.

Population: 772; Growth (since 2000): n/a; Density: 1,217.9 persons per square mile; Race: 90.5% White, 0.5% Black/African American, 0.4% Asian, 2.7% American Indian/Alaska Native, 0.0% Native Hawaiian/Other Pacific Islander, 3.5% Two or more races, 5.7% Hispanic of any race; Average household size: 2.65; Median age: 37.0; Age under 18: 23.6%; Age 65 and over: 8.3%; Males per 100 females: 111.5

Housing: Homeownership rate: 81.4%; Homeowner vacancy rate: 0.8%; Rental vacancy rate: 10.0%

GREEN LAKE (township). Covers a land area of 29.179 square miles and a water area of 7.224 square miles. Located at 44.64° N. Lat; 85.76° W. Long. Elevation is 843 feet.

Population: 5,784; Growth (since 2000): 15.5%; Density: 198.2 persons per square mile; Race: 96.4% White, 0.3% Black/African American, 0.6% Asian, 1.2% American Indian/Alaska Native, 0.1% Native Hawaiian/Other Pacific Islander, 1.4% Two or more races, 1.8% Hispanic of any race; Average household size: 2.52; Median age: 39.5; Age under 18: 24.2%; Age 65 and over: 11.9%; Males per 100 females: 99.2; Marriage status: 27.3% never married, 55.9% now married, 0.6% separated, 3.4% widowed, 13.3% divorced; Foreign born: 4.1%; Speak English only: 92.9%; With disability: 10.4%; Veterans: 7.7%; Ancestry: 26.8% German, 17.5% American, 11.6% English, 8.8% Irish, 7.9% Polish

Employment: 7.4% management, business, and financial, 1.6% computer, engineering, and science, 6.7% education, legal, community service, arts, and media, 5.2% healthcare practitioners, 21.6% service, 26.1% sales and office, 18.4% natural resources, construction, and maintenance, 13.1% production, transportation, and material moving

Income: Per capita: $19,866; Median household: $52,866; Average household: $57,400; Households with income of $100,000 or more: 11.4%; Poverty rate: 11.2%

Educational Attainment: High school diploma or higher: 91.9%; Bachelor's degree or higher: 20.1%; Graduate/professional degree or higher: 8.1%

Housing: Homeownership rate: 88.2%; Median home value: $132,600; Median year structure built: 1991; Homeowner vacancy rate: 3.2%; Median gross rent: $995 per month; Rental vacancy rate: 10.9%

Health Insurance: 80.0% have insurance; 60.0% have private insurance; 30.9% have public insurance; 20.0% do not have insurance; 7.8% of children under 18 do not have insurance

Transportation: Commute: 90.2% car, 1.1% public transportation, 2.0% walk, 6.1% work from home; Median travel time to work: 24.6 minutes

INTERLOCHEN (CDP). Covers a land area of 1.241 square miles and a water area of 0.032 square miles. Located at 44.65° N. Lat; 85.77° W. Long. Elevation is 843 feet.

Population: 583; Growth (since 2000): n/a; Density: 470.0 persons per square mile; Race: 95.2% White, 0.5% Black/African American, 0.0% Asian, 2.2% American Indian/Alaska Native, 0.2% Native Hawaiian/Other Pacific Islander, 1.7% Two or more races, 1.9% Hispanic of any race; Average household size: 2.38; Median age: 32.3; Age under 18: 25.4%; Age 65 and over: 8.4%; Males per 100 females: 104.6

School District(s)

Benzie County Central Schools (KG-12)
  2012-13 Enrollment: 1,616 . . . . (231) 882-9654
Traverse City Area Public Schools (PK-12)
  2012-13 Enrollment: 9,786 . . . . (231) 933-1725

Housing: Homeownership rate: 77.5%; Homeowner vacancy rate: 6.0%; Rental vacancy rate: 8.5%

KINGSLEY (village). Covers a land area of 1.416 square miles and a water area of 0.023 square miles. Located at 44.59° N. Lat; 85.53° W. Long. Elevation is 968 feet.

History: The village of Kingsley was laid out on land belonging to Judson W. Kingsley, and called Kingsley Station when the Grand Rapids & Indiana Railroad built a depot here in 1874.

Population: 1,480; Growth (since 2000): 0.7%; Density: 1,045.5 persons per square mile; Race: 95.6% White, 0.7% Black/African American, 0.1% Asian, 1.1% American Indian/Alaska Native, 0.2% Native Hawaiian/Other Pacific Islander, 2.2% Two or more races, 2.4% Hispanic of any race; Average household size: 2.83; Median age: 32.6; Age under 18: 31.4%; Age 65 and over: 9.5%; Males per 100 females: 92.7

School District(s)

Kingsley Area Schools (PK-12)
  2012-13 Enrollment: 1,412 . . . . (231) 263-5261

Housing: Homeownership rate: 73.6%; Homeowner vacancy rate: 2.3%; Rental vacancy rate: 8.4%

LONG LAKE (township). Covers a land area of 29.897 square miles and a water area of 5.769 square miles. Located at 44.71° N. Lat; 85.75° W. Long.

History: Long Lake Township was organized in 1867. The Hannah, Lay & Company built a sawmill here in 1871.

Population: 8,662; Growth (since 2000): 13.3%; Density: 289.7 persons per square mile; Race: 96.7% White, 0.2% Black/African American, 0.5% Asian, 0.9% American Indian/Alaska Native, 0.0% Native Hawaiian/Other Pacific Islander, 1.3% Two or more races, 2.0% Hispanic of any race; Average household size: 2.60; Median age: 41.4; Age under 18: 25.1%; Age 65 and over: 11.0%; Males per 100 females: 98.7; Marriage status: 18.8% never married, 69.4% now married, 0.4% separated, 3.9% widowed, 7.9% divorced; Foreign born: 0.7%; Speak English only: 98.3%; With disability: 8.8%; Veterans: 10.0%; Ancestry: 29.6% German, 13.5% English, 11.9% Irish, 8.7% French, 8.4% Polish

Employment: 12.6% management, business, and financial, 3.2% computer, engineering, and science, 9.2% education, legal, community service, arts, and media, 11.3% healthcare practitioners, 21.6% service, 19.6% sales and office, 11.5% natural resources, construction, and maintenance, 11.0% production, transportation, and material moving

Income: Per capita: $29,113; Median household: $63,292; Average household: $72,977; Households with income of $100,000 or more: 24.7%; Poverty rate: 10.9%

Educational Attainment: High school diploma or higher: 93.1%; Bachelor's degree or higher: 28.6%; Graduate/professional degree or higher: 11.3%

Housing: Homeownership rate: 86.6%; Median home value: $185,700; Median year structure built: 1990; Homeowner vacancy rate: 2.6%; Median gross rent: $1,090 per month; Rental vacancy rate: 12.1%

Health Insurance: 90.3% have insurance; 80.6% have private insurance; 25.5% have public insurance; 9.7% do not have insurance; 5.2% of children under 18 do not have insurance

Transportation: Commute: 97.3% car, 0.0% public transportation, 0.2% walk, 2.5% work from home; Median travel time to work: 21.3 minutes

Additional Information Contacts

Long Lake Township . . . . (231) 946-2249
  http://www.longlaketownship.com

MAYFIELD (township). Covers a land area of 35.924 square miles and a water area of 0.122 square miles. Located at 44.56° N. Lat; 85.63° W. Long. Elevation is 837 feet.
Population: 1,550; Growth (since 2000): 22.0%; Density: 43.1 persons per square mile; Race: 97.9% White, 0.3% Black/African American, 0.3% Asian, 0.3% American Indian/Alaska Native, 0.2% Native Hawaiian/Other Pacific Islander, 1.0% Two or more races, 0.4% Hispanic of any race; Average household size: 2.77; Median age: 37.7; Age under 18: 27.1%; Age 65 and over: 11.4%; Males per 100 females: 97.2
Housing: Homeownership rate: 85.5%; Homeowner vacancy rate: 2.7%; Rental vacancy rate: 4.8%

PARADISE (township). Covers a land area of 52.871 square miles and a water area of 0.113 square miles. Located at 44.58° N. Lat; 85.50° W. Long.
Population: 4,713; Growth (since 2000): 12.5%; Density: 89.1 persons per square mile; Race: 96.8% White, 0.7% Black/African American, 0.1% Asian, 0.7% American Indian/Alaska Native, 0.1% Native Hawaiian/Other Pacific Islander, 1.4% Two or more races, 2.3% Hispanic of any race; Average household size: 2.86; Median age: 35.5; Age under 18: 28.9%; Age 65 and over: 9.2%; Males per 100 females: 100.9; Marriage status: 33.4% never married, 51.8% now married, 1.4% separated, 2.1% widowed, 12.8% divorced; Foreign born: 0.1%; Speak English only: 97.5%; With disability: 8.5%; Veterans: 8.3%; Ancestry: 35.8% German, 16.3% Irish, 15.8% English, 8.5% American, 6.8% Polish
Employment: 7.5% management, business, and financial, 2.4% computer, engineering, and science, 9.9% education, legal, community service, arts, and media, 5.0% healthcare practitioners, 24.9% service, 20.5% sales and office, 15.1% natural resources, construction, and maintenance, 14.7% production, transportation, and material moving
Income: Per capita: $20,740; Median household: $48,918; Average household: $60,933; Households with income of $100,000 or more: 18.5%; Poverty rate: 15.9%
Educational Attainment: High school diploma or higher: 93.5%; Bachelor's degree or higher: 17.5%; Graduate/professional degree or higher: 4.2%
School District(s)
Whitefish Township Schools (PK-12)
    2012-13 Enrollment: 45 . . . . (906) 492-3353
Housing: Homeownership rate: 84.7%; Median home value: $131,900; Median year structure built: 1991; Homeowner vacancy rate: 2.6%; Median gross rent: $772 per month; Rental vacancy rate: 8.0%
Health Insurance: 88.9% have insurance; 71.0% have private insurance; 25.9% have public insurance; 11.1% do not have insurance; 2.2% of children under 18 do not have insurance
Transportation: Commute: 94.2% car, 0.5% public transportation, 1.7% walk, 3.0% work from home; Median travel time to work: 28.8 minutes

PENINSULA (township). Covers a land area of 27.892 square miles and a water area of 4.018 square miles. Located at 44.89° N. Lat; 85.52° W. Long.
History: The township is coterminous with the Old Mission Peninsula, which projects into the Grand Traverse Bay of Lake Michigan. The Old Mission Point Lighthouse is located at the northern end of the peninsula. The peninsula is included in the Old Mission Peninsula AVA, an American Viticultural Area known for its fine Michigan wine.
Population: 5,433; Growth (since 2000): 3.2%; Density: 194.8 persons per square mile; Race: 96.7% White, 0.1% Black/African American, 0.9% Asian, 0.4% American Indian/Alaska Native, 0.0% Native Hawaiian/Other Pacific Islander, 0.7% Two or more races, 2.3% Hispanic of any race; Average household size: 2.31; Median age: 53.4; Age under 18: 18.8%; Age 65 and over: 25.9%; Males per 100 females: 94.3; Marriage status: 14.3% never married, 67.8% now married, 0.0% separated, 9.2% widowed, 8.6% divorced; Foreign born: 4.7%; Speak English only: 95.6%; With disability: 11.9%; Veterans: 13.0%; Ancestry: 29.8% German, 18.3% English, 17.7% Irish, 13.0% American, 6.8% Polish
Employment: 23.5% management, business, and financial, 5.0% computer, engineering, and science, 14.6% education, legal, community service, arts, and media, 12.1% healthcare practitioners, 15.2% service, 19.9% sales and office, 2.1% natural resources, construction, and maintenance, 7.6% production, transportation, and material moving
Income: Per capita: $49,920; Median household: $71,139; Average household: $105,695; Households with income of $100,000 or more: 29.8%; Poverty rate: 5.4%

Educational Attainment: High school diploma or higher: 97.6%; Bachelor's degree or higher: 60.6%; Graduate/professional degree or higher: 30.3%
Housing: Homeownership rate: 89.5%; Median home value: $327,300; Median year structure built: 1979; Homeowner vacancy rate: 2.4%; Median gross rent: $896 per month; Rental vacancy rate: 7.8%
Health Insurance: 96.9% have insurance; 88.2% have private insurance; 35.5% have public insurance; 3.1% do not have insurance; 0.0% of children under 18 do not have insurance
Transportation: Commute: 85.4% car, 0.0% public transportation, 0.7% walk, 10.5% work from home; Median travel time to work: 20.3 minutes
Additional Information Contacts
Peninsula Township . . . . (231) 223-7322
    http://www.peninsulatownship.com

TRAVERSE CITY (city). County seat. Covers a land area of 8.326 square miles and a water area of 0.332 square miles. Located at 44.75° N. Lat; 85.60° W. Long. Elevation is 597 feet.
History: Traverse City began in 1847 when the Boardmans, father and son, purchased land and built a mill near the mouth of Mill Creek. Other mills soon followed, and Traverse City was incorporated in 1895. Apples were the first commercial crop in Traverse City after the lumber mills closed, but it soon became known as the cherry capital of the state. The Traverse City Canning Company was established in 1907 to can cherries.
Population: 14,674; Growth (since 2000): 1.0%; Density: 1,762.5 persons per square mile; Race: 94.4% White, 0.7% Black/African American, 0.7% Asian, 1.8% American Indian/Alaska Native, 0.0% Native Hawaiian/Other Pacific Islander, 1.9% Two or more races, 1.9% Hispanic of any race; Average household size: 2.08; Median age: 40.8; Age under 18: 18.2%; Age 65 and over: 16.7%; Males per 100 females: 90.0; Marriage status: 33.6% never married, 44.1% now married, 1.1% separated, 7.5% widowed, 14.7% divorced; Foreign born: 2.0%; Speak English only: 96.1%; With disability: 12.6%; Veterans: 9.2%; Ancestry: 28.1% German, 16.4% Irish, 13.3% English, 11.2% Polish, 10.1% American
Employment: 17.1% management, business, and financial, 3.1% computer, engineering, and science, 11.2% education, legal, community service, arts, and media, 7.2% healthcare practitioners, 23.9% service, 24.4% sales and office, 5.3% natural resources, construction, and maintenance, 7.7% production, transportation, and material moving
Income: Per capita: $29,593; Median household: $45,497; Average household: $66,223; Households with income of $100,000 or more: 18.3%; Poverty rate: 15.7%
Educational Attainment: High school diploma or higher: 95.1%; Bachelor's degree or higher: 40.3%; Graduate/professional degree or higher: 14.6%
School District(s)
Grand Traverse Academy (KG-12)
    2012-13 Enrollment: 1,176 . . . . (231) 995-0665
The Greenspire School (KG-12)
    2012-13 Enrollment: 60 . . . . (231) 946-4400
Traverse Bay Area ISD (PK-12)
    2012-13 Enrollment: 833 . . . . (231) 922-6200
Traverse City Area Public Schools (PK-12)
    2012-13 Enrollment: 9,786 . . . . (231) 933-1725
Traverse City College Preparatory Academy (KG-12)
    2012-13 Enrollment: 58 . . . . (231) 929-4539
Woodland School (KG-12)
    2012-13 Enrollment: 200 . . . . (231) 947-7474
Four-year College(s)
Northwestern Michigan College (Public)
    Fall 2013 Enrollment: 4,724 . . . . (231) 995-1000
    2013-14 Tuition: In-state $5,093; Out-of-state $6,436
Housing: Homeownership rate: 58.2%; Median home value: $168,900; Median year structure built: 1958; Homeowner vacancy rate: 2.8%; Median gross rent: $808 per month; Rental vacancy rate: 6.3%
Health Insurance: 86.6% have insurance; 70.7% have private insurance; 29.9% have public insurance; 13.4% do not have insurance; 4.1% of children under 18 do not have insurance
Hospitals: Munson Medical Center (391 beds)
Newspapers: Grand Traverse Insider (weekly circulation 1100); Northern Express (weekly circulation 30000); Traverse City Record-Eagle (daily circulation 27700)
Transportation: Commute: 82.3% car, 1.2% public transportation, 5.5% walk, 4.8% work from home; Median travel time to work: 15.0 minutes; Amtrak: Bus service available.

Airports: Cherry Capital (primary service/non-hub)
Additional Information Contacts
City of Traverse City . . . . (231) 922-4480
  http://www.ci.traverse-city.mi.us

UNION (township). Covers a land area of 35.813 square miles and a water area of 0.194 square miles. Located at 44.64° N. Lat; 85.41° W. Long.
Population: 405; Growth (since 2000): -2.9%; Density: 11.3 persons per square mile; Race: 97.5% White, 0.0% Black/African American, 0.5% Asian, 1.0% American Indian/Alaska Native, 0.2% Native Hawaiian/Other Pacific Islander, 0.7% Two or more races, 1.7% Hispanic of any race; Average household size: 2.55; Median age: 45.9; Age under 18: 23.5%; Age 65 and over: 11.9%; Males per 100 females: 97.6
Housing: Homeownership rate: 90.5%; Homeowner vacancy rate: 3.3%; Rental vacancy rate: 11.8%

WHITEWATER (township). Covers a land area of 47.841 square miles and a water area of 5.722 square miles. Located at 44.76° N. Lat; 85.39° W. Long.
Population: 2,597; Growth (since 2000): 5.3%; Density: 54.3 persons per square mile; Race: 96.5% White, 0.2% Black/African American, 0.5% Asian, 0.9% American Indian/Alaska Native, 0.0% Native Hawaiian/Other Pacific Islander, 1.2% Two or more races, 1.6% Hispanic of any race; Average household size: 2.57; Median age: 46.1; Age under 18: 21.8%; Age 65 and over: 14.6%; Males per 100 females: 103.2; Marriage status: 20.9% never married, 64.3% now married, 1.0% separated, 7.7% widowed, 7.1% divorced; Foreign born: 1.8%; Speak English only: 96.9%; With disability: 11.5%; Veterans: 11.7%; Ancestry: 29.3% German, 18.9% Irish, 13.1% American, 13.0% Polish, 11.0% English
Employment: 10.3% management, business, and financial, 3.3% computer, engineering, and science, 9.3% education, legal, community service, arts, and media, 4.5% healthcare practitioners, 14.7% service, 28.1% sales and office, 16.8% natural resources, construction, and maintenance, 12.9% production, transportation, and material moving
Income: Per capita: $35,387; Median household: $67,587; Average household: $86,719; Households with income of $100,000 or more: 25.9%; Poverty rate: 3.2%
Educational Attainment: High school diploma or higher: 95.3%; Bachelor's degree or higher: 28.8%; Graduate/professional degree or higher: 12.6%
Housing: Homeownership rate: 89.8%; Median home value: $188,200; Median year structure built: 1985; Homeowner vacancy rate: 2.0%; Median gross rent: $1,230 per month; Rental vacancy rate: 9.5%
Health Insurance: 90.0% have insurance; 78.1% have private insurance; 29.3% have public insurance; 10.0% do not have insurance; 7.0% of children under 18 do not have insurance
Transportation: Commute: 92.1% car, 0.5% public transportation, 0.7% walk, 4.2% work from home; Median travel time to work: 29.5 minutes

WILLIAMSBURG (unincorporated postal area)
ZCTA: 49690
  Covers a land area of 76.805 square miles and a water area of 13.666 square miles. Located at 44.79° N. Lat; 85.40° W. Long. Elevation is 738 feet.
  Population: 6,182; Growth (since 2000): -7.5%; Density: 80.5 persons per square mile; Race: 96.9% White, 0.2% Black/African American, 0.5% Asian, 0.6% American Indian/Alaska Native, 0.0% Native Hawaiian/Other Pacific Islander, 1.1% Two or more races, 1.5% Hispanic of any race; Average household size: 2.44; Median age: 47.6; Age under 18: 20.6%; Age 65 and over: 19.0%; Males per 100 females: 97.4; Marriage status: 27.1% never married, 57.4% now married, 0.4% separated, 5.7% widowed, 9.9% divorced; Foreign born: 2.4%; Speak English only: 97.5%; With disability: 9.5%; Veterans: 10.3%; Ancestry: 27.6% German, 14.4% Polish, 14.1% English, 13.5% Irish, 13.1% American
  Employment: 13.0% management, business, and financial, 2.8% computer, engineering, and science, 9.6% education, legal, community service, arts, and media, 8.2% healthcare practitioners, 12.6% service, 29.3% sales and office, 13.5% natural resources, construction, and maintenance, 11.0% production, transportation, and material moving
  Income: Per capita: $37,762; Median household: $73,201; Average household: $98,446; Households with income of $100,000 or more: 28.3%; Poverty rate: 5.0%

Educational Attainment: High school diploma or higher: 96.8%; Bachelor's degree or higher: 37.7%; Graduate/professional degree or higher: 17.3%
School District(s)
Elk Rapids Schools (PK-12)
  2012-13 Enrollment: 1,420 . . . . (231) 264-8692
Traverse City Area Public Schools (PK-12)
  2012-13 Enrollment: 9,786 . . . . (231) 933-1725
  Housing: Homeownership rate: 85.0%; Median home value: $203,500; Median year structure built: 1983; Homeowner vacancy rate: 2.4%; Median gross rent: $1,084 per month; Rental vacancy rate: 22.1%
  Health Insurance: 91.3% have insurance; 81.8% have private insurance; 25.0% have public insurance; 8.7% do not have insurance; 3.5% of children under 18 do not have insurance
  Transportation: Commute: 91.2% car, 0.2% public transportation, 0.9% walk, 6.3% work from home; Median travel time to work: 22.3 minutes

Gratiot County

Located in central Michigan; drained by the Maple, Pine, and Bad Rivers. Covers a land area of 568.464 square miles, a water area of 3.147 square miles, and is located in the Eastern Time Zone at 43.29° N. Lat., 84.60° W. Long. The county was founded in 1855. County seat is Ithaca.

Gratiot County is part of the Alma, MI Micropolitan Statistical Area. The entire metro area includes: Gratiot County, MI

Weather Station: Alma — Elevation: 759 feet

	Jan	Feb	Mar	Apr	May	Jun	Jul	Aug	Sep	Oct	Nov	Dec
High	30	33	43	57	69	79	83	81	73	60	46	34
Low	14	15	23	34	45	54	58	57	49	38	29	20
Precip	1.9	1.6	2.1	3.1	3.5	3.3	2.8	3.4	3.5	3.0	2.8	2.1
Snow	11.0	8.3	6.0	1.8	tr	0.0	0.0	0.0	0.0	0.3	2.8	9.8

High and Low temperatures in degrees Fahrenheit; Precipitation and Snow in inches

Population: 42,476; Growth (since 2000): 0.5%; Density: 74.7 persons per square mile; Race: 90.6% White, 5.5% Black/African American, 0.3% Asian, 0.5% American Indian/Alaska Native, 0.0% Native Hawaiian/Other Pacific Islander, 1.4% two or more races, 5.4% Hispanic of any race; Average household size: 2.49; Median age: 38.7; Age under 18: 21.5%; Age 65 and over: 14.8%; Males per 100 females: 113.7; Marriage status: 32.6% never married, 49.5% now married, 1.3% separated, 6.3% widowed, 11.6% divorced; Foreign born: 1.4%; Speak English only: 95.9%; With disability: 15.4%; Veterans: 9.2%; Ancestry: 27.3% German, 13.1% English, 12.3% Irish, 6.9% American, 5.0% French
Religion: Six largest groups: 11.0% Catholicism, 4.0% Methodist/Pietist, 3.8% Holiness, 3.1% Baptist, 2.4% Lutheran, 1.7% Presbyterian-Reformed
Economy: Unemployment rate: 6.0%; Leading industries: 18.5% retail trade; 14.1% health care and social assistance; 11.4% other services (except public administration); Farms: 878 totaling 289,376 acres; Company size: 0 employ 1,000 or more persons, 2 employ 500 to 999 persons, 16 employ 100 to 499 persons, 718 employ less than 100 persons; Business ownership: 784 women-owned, n/a Black-owned, n/a Hispanic-owned, n/a Asian-owned
Employment: 10.5% management, business, and financial, 2.6% computer, engineering, and science, 8.5% education, legal, community service, arts, and media, 5.8% healthcare practitioners, 22.8% service, 21.9% sales and office, 9.8% natural resources, construction, and maintenance, 18.1% production, transportation, and material moving
Income: Per capita: $18,836; Median household: $40,359; Average household: $51,756; Households with income of $100,000 or more: 10.7%; Poverty rate: 19.1%
Educational Attainment: High school diploma or higher: 87.7%; Bachelor's degree or higher: 14.0%; Graduate/professional degree or higher: 4.8%
Housing: Homeownership rate: 74.8%; Median home value: $86,600; Median year structure built: 1961; Homeowner vacancy rate: 2.2%; Median gross rent: $593 per month; Rental vacancy rate: 7.7%
Vital Statistics: Birth rate: 103.4 per 10,000 population; Death rate: 100.1 per 10,000 population; Age-adjusted cancer mortality rate: 174.4 deaths per 100,000 population
Health Insurance: 87.6% have insurance; 66.3% have private insurance; 37.0% have public insurance; 12.4% do not have insurance; 6.2% of children under 18 do not have insurance
Health Care: Physicians: 14.5 per 10,000 population; Hospital beds: 32.3 per 10,000 population; Hospital admissions: 1,362.2 per 10,000 population

Transportation: Commute: 89.5% car, 0.1% public transportation, 3.6% walk, 5.6% work from home; Median travel time to work: 22.3 minutes
Presidential Election: 47.5% Obama, 51.4% Romney (2012)
Additional Information Contacts
Gratiot Government. . . . . (989) 875-5215
  http://www.co.gratiot.mi.us

Gratiot County Communities

ALMA (city). Covers a land area of 5.926 square miles and a water area of 0.161 square miles. Located at 43.38° N. Lat; 84.66° W. Long. Elevation is 735 feet.
History: Alma was settled in 1853 by General Ralph Ely, who built a sawmill here and platted the village in 1856. First called Elyton, the name was changed to Alma by a Mr. Gargett when he platted an addition to the town. Alma was incorporated as a village in 1872 and as a city in 1905.
Population: 9,383; Growth (since 2000): 1.2%; Density: 1,583.3 persons per square mile; Race: 92.8% White, 0.9% Black/African American, 0.8% Asian, 0.6% American Indian/Alaska Native, 0.0% Native Hawaiian/Other Pacific Islander, 2.2% Two or more races, 8.1% Hispanic of any race; Average household size: 2.30; Median age: 30.8; Age under 18: 21.4%; Age 65 and over: 15.6%; Males per 100 females: 88.3; Marriage status: 44.0% never married, 36.0% now married, 1.1% separated, 6.3% widowed, 13.6% divorced; Foreign born: 2.4%; Speak English only: 95.3%; With disability: 13.6%; Veterans: 6.9%; Ancestry: 27.1% German, 11.7% Irish, 10.1% English, 6.9% Dutch, 5.4% Polish
Employment: 8.4% management, business, and financial, 1.5% computer, engineering, and science, 14.2% education, legal, community service, arts, and media, 4.3% healthcare practitioners, 27.5% service, 24.9% sales and office, 5.7% natural resources, construction, and maintenance, 13.5% production, transportation, and material moving
Income: Per capita: $15,171; Median household: $32,550; Average household: $39,942; Households with income of $100,000 or more: 4.8%; Poverty rate: 31.6%
Educational Attainment: High school diploma or higher: 88.0%; Bachelor's degree or higher: 20.9%; Graduate/professional degree or higher: 9.0%
School District(s)
Alma Public Schools (PK-12)
  2012-13 Enrollment: 2,199 . . . . (989) 463-3111
Four-year College(s)
Alma College (Private, Not-for-profit, Presbyterian Church (USA))
  Fall 2013 Enrollment: 1,419 . . . . (989) 463-7111
  2013-14 Tuition: In-state $32,660; Out-of-state $32,660
Housing: Homeownership rate: 55.8%; Median home value: $76,500; Median year structure built: 1957; Homeowner vacancy rate: 2.5%; Median gross rent: $543 per month; Rental vacancy rate: 8.1%
Health Insurance: 86.5% have insurance; 62.6% have private insurance; 36.8% have public insurance; 13.5% do not have insurance; 9.5% of children under 18 do not have insurance
Hospitals: Midmichigan Medical Center - Gratiot (142 beds)
Safety: Violent crime rate: 23.8 per 10,000 population; Property crime rate: 224.7 per 10,000 population
Transportation: Commute: 80.8% car, 0.0% public transportation, 8.6% walk, 9.1% work from home; Median travel time to work: 12.8 minutes
Additional Information Contacts
City of Alma. . . . . (989) 463-8336
  http://www.ci.alma.mi.us

ARCADA (township). Covers a land area of 32.168 square miles and a water area of 0.289 square miles. Located at 43.33° N. Lat; 84.68° W. Long.
Population: 1,681; Growth (since 2000): -1.6%; Density: 52.3 persons per square mile; Race: 96.3% White, 0.1% Black/African American, 0.7% Asian, 0.3% American Indian/Alaska Native, 0.0% Native Hawaiian/Other Pacific Islander, 1.2% Two or more races, 6.1% Hispanic of any race; Average household size: 2.52; Median age: 44.7; Age under 18: 23.4%; Age 65 and over: 18.3%; Males per 100 females: 99.9
Housing: Homeownership rate: 86.6%; Homeowner vacancy rate: 1.4%; Rental vacancy rate: 6.3%

ASHLEY (village). Covers a land area of 0.641 square miles and a water area of 0 square miles. Located at 43.19° N. Lat; 84.48° W. Long. Elevation is 669 feet.
History: Ashley was laid out in 1883, and incorporated as a village in 1887. It was named for John M. Ashley, who was responsible for the railroad branch being built to the town.
Population: 563; Growth (since 2000): 7.0%; Density: 877.9 persons per square mile; Race: 97.9% White, 1.1% Black/African American, 0.2% Asian, 0.0% American Indian/Alaska Native, 0.0% Native Hawaiian/Other Pacific Islander, 0.2% Two or more races, 3.2% Hispanic of any race; Average household size: 2.51; Median age: 41.3; Age under 18: 24.9%; Age 65 and over: 21.3%; Males per 100 females: 84.6
School District(s)
Ashley Community Schools (PK-12)
  2012-13 Enrollment: 287 . . . . (989) 847-4000
Housing: Homeownership rate: 77.0%; Homeowner vacancy rate: 3.8%; Rental vacancy rate: 17.9%

BANNISTER (unincorporated postal area)
ZCTA: 48807
  Covers a land area of 27.939 square miles and a water area of 0.024 square miles. Located at 43.15° N. Lat; 84.40° W. Long. Elevation is 673 feet.
  Population: 916; Growth (since 2000): -0.4%; Density: 32.8 persons per square mile; Race: 97.5% White, 0.1% Black/African American, 0.1% Asian, 0.2% American Indian/Alaska Native, 0.0% Native Hawaiian/Other Pacific Islander, 1.6% Two or more races, 2.3% Hispanic of any race; Average household size: 2.57; Median age: 41.7; Age under 18: 22.8%; Age 65 and over: 14.8%; Males per 100 females: 105.8
  Housing: Homeownership rate: 85.5%; Homeowner vacancy rate: 1.9%; Rental vacancy rate: 3.7%

BETHANY (township). Covers a land area of 34.573 square miles and a water area of 0.131 square miles. Located at 43.43° N. Lat; 84.54° W. Long.
History: Bethany Township was organized in 1858, and named for a Lutheran mission, called Bethanien, that had been founded here in 1847.
Population: 1,407; Growth (since 2000): -59.7%; Density: 40.7 persons per square mile; Race: 95.5% White, 0.7% Black/African American, 0.1% Asian, 0.6% American Indian/Alaska Native, 0.0% Native Hawaiian/Other Pacific Islander, 1.6% Two or more races, 4.7% Hispanic of any race; Average household size: 2.67; Median age: 42.6; Age under 18: 24.2%; Age 65 and over: 16.3%; Males per 100 females: 103.9
Housing: Homeownership rate: 86.0%; Homeowner vacancy rate: 1.1%; Rental vacancy rate: 7.6%

BRECKENRIDGE (village). Covers a land area of 1.074 square miles and a water area of 0.003 square miles. Located at 43.41° N. Lat; 84.48° W. Long. Elevation is 735 feet.
History: Breckenridge grew up in 1872 around a station of the Pere Marquette Railroad. The village was named for Daniel W. and Justin A. Breckenridge, who owned a mill here.
Population: 1,328; Growth (since 2000): -0.8%; Density: 1,236.5 persons per square mile; Race: 96.8% White, 0.5% Black/African American, 0.0% Asian, 0.8% American Indian/Alaska Native, 0.0% Native Hawaiian/Other Pacific Islander, 1.2% Two or more races, 4.4% Hispanic of any race; Average household size: 2.48; Median age: 35.8; Age under 18: 27.6%; Age 65 and over: 13.5%; Males per 100 females: 93.3
School District(s)
Breckenridge Community Schools (PK-12)
  2012-13 Enrollment: 829 . . . . (989) 842-3182
Housing: Homeownership rate: 65.4%; Homeowner vacancy rate: 1.9%; Rental vacancy rate: 7.0%
Safety: Violent crime rate: 7.6 per 10,000 population; Property crime rate: 160.6 per 10,000 population

ELBA (township). Covers a land area of 34.990 square miles and a water area of 0.094 square miles. Located at 43.16° N. Lat; 84.43° W. Long.
Population: 1,396; Growth (since 2000): 0.1%; Density: 39.9 persons per square mile; Race: 97.3% White, 0.5% Black/African American, 0.4% Asian, 0.1% American Indian/Alaska Native, 0.3% Native Hawaiian/Other Pacific Islander, 1.1% Two or more races, 2.7% Hispanic of any race;

Average household size: 2.58; Median age: 40.8; Age under 18: 25.3%; Age 65 and over: 17.8%; Males per 100 females: 97.7
Housing: Homeownership rate: 83.0%; Homeowner vacancy rate: 2.5%; Rental vacancy rate: 13.7%

ELWELL (unincorporated postal area)
ZCTA: 48832
Covers a land area of 25.923 square miles and a water area of 0.165 square miles. Located at 43.41° N. Lat; 84.78° W. Long. Elevation is 771 feet.
Population: 1,393; Growth (since 2000): -2.9%; Density: 53.7 persons per square mile; Race: 98.1% White, 0.1% Black/African American, 0.0% Asian, 0.4% American Indian/Alaska Native, 0.0% Native Hawaiian/Other Pacific Islander, 1.4% Two or more races, 2.7% Hispanic of any race; Average household size: 2.51; Median age: 43.7; Age under 18: 21.6%; Age 65 and over: 17.3%; Males per 100 females: 98.2
Housing: Homeownership rate: 85.7%; Homeowner vacancy rate: 1.0%; Rental vacancy rate: 4.8%

EMERSON (township). Covers a land area of 34.287 square miles and a water area of 0.013 square miles. Located at 43.34° N. Lat; 84.54° W. Long.
Population: 952; Growth (since 2000): -1.4%; Density: 27.8 persons per square mile; Race: 97.3% White, 0.2% Black/African American, 0.2% Asian, 0.4% American Indian/Alaska Native, 0.0% Native Hawaiian/Other Pacific Islander, 0.7% Two or more races, 3.5% Hispanic of any race; Average household size: 2.67; Median age: 41.3; Age under 18: 25.2%; Age 65 and over: 15.5%; Males per 100 females: 94.7
Housing: Homeownership rate: 84.0%; Homeowner vacancy rate: 1.3%; Rental vacancy rate: 6.6%

FULTON (township). Covers a land area of 34.989 square miles and a water area of 0.824 square miles. Located at 43.16° N. Lat; 84.66° W. Long.
Population: 2,521; Growth (since 2000): 4.5%; Density: 72.1 persons per square mile; Race: 95.4% White, 0.6% Black/African American, 0.2% Asian, 0.4% American Indian/Alaska Native, 0.0% Native Hawaiian/Other Pacific Islander, 1.4% Two or more races, 4.1% Hispanic of any race; Average household size: 2.56; Median age: 42.1; Age under 18: 23.2%; Age 65 and over: 15.2%; Males per 100 females: 98.2; Marriage status: 19.7% never married, 64.0% now married, 0.5% separated, 6.8% widowed, 9.5% divorced; Foreign born: 0.8%; Speak English only: 96.1%; With disability: 16.1%; Veterans: 8.9%; Ancestry: 31.7% German, 17.9% Irish, 13.6% English, 8.0% American, 4.8% French
Employment: 6.9% management, business, and financial, 2.0% computer, engineering, and science, 4.7% education, legal, community service, arts, and media, 7.2% healthcare practitioners, 18.0% service, 28.6% sales and office, 12.7% natural resources, construction, and maintenance, 19.9% production, transportation, and material moving
Income: Per capita: $23,865; Median household: $49,708; Average household: $62,268; Households with income of $100,000 or more: 15.1%; Poverty rate: 15.8%
Educational Attainment: High school diploma or higher: 88.3%; Bachelor's degree or higher: 10.7%; Graduate/professional degree or higher: 2.7%
Housing: Homeownership rate: 81.2%; Median home value: $120,800; Median year structure built: 1969; Homeowner vacancy rate: 2.5%; Median gross rent: $670 per month; Rental vacancy rate: 4.7%
Health Insurance: 89.1% have insurance; 74.8% have private insurance; 33.5% have public insurance; 10.9% do not have insurance; 7.0% of children under 18 do not have insurance
Transportation: Commute: 93.4% car, 0.5% public transportation, 0.6% walk, 5.4% work from home; Median travel time to work: 39.1 minutes

HAMILTON (township). Covers a land area of 34.663 square miles and a water area of 0.202 square miles. Located at 43.25° N. Lat; 84.42° W. Long.
Population: 465; Growth (since 2000): -5.3%; Density: 13.4 persons per square mile; Race: 98.7% White, 0.4% Black/African American, 0.2% Asian, 0.6% American Indian/Alaska Native, 0.0% Native Hawaiian/Other Pacific Islander, 0.0% Two or more races, 2.6% Hispanic of any race; Average household size: 2.46; Median age: 43.1; Age under 18: 21.7%; Age 65 and over: 16.1%; Males per 100 females: 104.8

Housing: Homeownership rate: 84.1%; Homeowner vacancy rate: 0.6%; Rental vacancy rate: 9.1%

ITHACA (city). County seat. Covers a land area of 5.230 square miles and a water area of 0.052 square miles. Located at 43.29° N. Lat; 84.60° W. Long. Elevation is 794 feet.
History: Ithaca was settled in the 1850's and developed as the center of a farming community. First called Gratiot Center, it was renamed in 1857 for Ithaca, New York. The economy was boosted in the 1920's by the discovery of oil in the county.
Population: 2,910; Growth (since 2000): -6.1%; Density: 556.4 persons per square mile; Race: 94.7% White, 0.5% Black/African American, 0.6% Asian, 0.9% American Indian/Alaska Native, 0.0% Native Hawaiian/Other Pacific Islander, 1.8% Two or more races, 6.2% Hispanic of any race; Average household size: 2.36; Median age: 39.2; Age under 18: 23.9%; Age 65 and over: 15.2%; Males per 100 females: 90.6; Marriage status: 33.2% never married, 52.4% now married, 1.5% separated, 5.5% widowed, 8.9% divorced; Foreign born: 0.9%; Speak English only: 97.9%; With disability: 16.0%; Veterans: 10.1%; Ancestry: 33.8% German, 22.8% English, 9.0% American, 8.2% Irish, 7.1% Dutch
Employment: 10.8% management, business, and financial, 5.3% computer, engineering, and science, 5.0% education, legal, community service, arts, and media, 6.1% healthcare practitioners, 26.1% service, 19.0% sales and office, 8.7% natural resources, construction, and maintenance, 19.0% production, transportation, and material moving
Income: Per capita: $22,843; Median household: $42,297; Average household: $52,203; Households with income of $100,000 or more: 12.2%; Poverty rate: 12.0%
Educational Attainment: High school diploma or higher: 92.9%; Bachelor's degree or higher: 16.7%; Graduate/professional degree or higher: 4.9%
School District(s)
Ithaca Public Schools (KG-12)
2012-13 Enrollment: 1,272 . . . . (989) 875-3700
Housing: Homeownership rate: 71.9%; Median home value: $82,400; Median year structure built: 1956; Homeowner vacancy rate: 3.3%; Median gross rent: $560 per month; Rental vacancy rate: 9.9%
Health Insurance: 90.9% have insurance; 78.0% have private insurance; 32.9% have public insurance; 9.1% do not have insurance; 0.0% of children under 18 do not have insurance
Newspapers: Gratiot County Herald (weekly circulation 8000)
Transportation: Commute: 87.2% car, 0.0% public transportation, 4.1% walk, 5.3% work from home; Median travel time to work: 23.3 minutes

LAFAYETTE (township). Covers a land area of 36.001 square miles and a water area of 0.005 square miles. Located at 43.34° N. Lat; 84.43° W. Long. Elevation is 705 feet.
Population: 591; Growth (since 2000): -9.9%; Density: 16.4 persons per square mile; Race: 97.0% White, 0.0% Black/African American, 0.0% Asian, 0.2% American Indian/Alaska Native, 0.0% Native Hawaiian/Other Pacific Islander, 1.2% Two or more races, 4.7% Hispanic of any race; Average household size: 2.69; Median age: 42.4; Age under 18: 23.7%; Age 65 and over: 17.4%; Males per 100 females: 101.0
Housing: Homeownership rate: 88.7%; Homeowner vacancy rate: 1.5%; Rental vacancy rate: 16.7%

MIDDLETON (unincorporated postal area)
ZCTA: 48856
Covers a land area of 27.505 square miles and a water area of 0.006 square miles. Located at 43.20° N. Lat; 84.73° W. Long. Elevation is 741 feet.
Population: 966; Growth (since 2000): 3.1%; Density: 35.1 persons per square mile; Race: 91.6% White, 0.3% Black/African American, 0.0% Asian, 0.3% American Indian/Alaska Native, 0.0% Native Hawaiian/Other Pacific Islander, 2.3% Two or more races, 10.2% Hispanic of any race; Average household size: 2.78; Median age: 35.6; Age under 18: 26.4%; Age 65 and over: 12.8%; Males per 100 females: 100.4
School District(s)
Fulton Schools (PK-12)
2012-13 Enrollment: 1,049 . . . . (989) 236-7300
Housing: Homeownership rate: 72.3%; Homeowner vacancy rate: 3.4%; Rental vacancy rate: 5.9%

NEW HAVEN (township). Covers a land area of 35.573 square miles and a water area of 0.082 square miles. Located at 43.25° N. Lat; 84.78° W. Long. Elevation is 778 feet.
Population: 1,004; Growth (since 2000): -1.2%; Density: 28.2 persons per square mile; Race: 98.8% White, 0.4% Black/African American, 0.0% Asian, 0.3% American Indian/Alaska Native, 0.0% Native Hawaiian/Other Pacific Islander, 0.3% Two or more races, 3.2% Hispanic of any race; Average household size: 2.59; Median age: 41.2; Age under 18: 24.7%; Age 65 and over: 15.5%; Males per 100 females: 107.4
Housing: Homeownership rate: 84.3%; Homeowner vacancy rate: 2.1%; Rental vacancy rate: 3.2%

NEWARK (township). Covers a land area of 34.377 square miles and a water area of 0.036 square miles. Located at 43.24° N. Lat; 84.66° W. Long. Elevation is 751 feet.
Population: 1,093; Growth (since 2000): -4.9%; Density: 31.8 persons per square mile; Race: 94.1% White, 0.8% Black/African American, 0.1% Asian, 0.3% American Indian/Alaska Native, 0.1% Native Hawaiian/Other Pacific Islander, 1.1% Two or more races, 6.6% Hispanic of any race; Average household size: 2.57; Median age: 42.6; Age under 18: 22.5%; Age 65 and over: 17.0%; Males per 100 females: 106.2
Housing: Homeownership rate: 80.1%; Homeowner vacancy rate: 2.5%; Rental vacancy rate: 5.7%

NORTH SHADE (township). Covers a land area of 35.606 square miles and a water area of 0.010 square miles. Located at 43.16° N. Lat; 84.78° W. Long.
Population: 665; Growth (since 2000): -5.8%; Density: 18.7 persons per square mile; Race: 94.1% White, 0.5% Black/African American, 0.2% Asian, 0.0% American Indian/Alaska Native, 0.0% Native Hawaiian/Other Pacific Islander, 1.1% Two or more races, 6.3% Hispanic of any race; Average household size: 2.92; Median age: 37.1; Age under 18: 28.4%; Age 65 and over: 14.1%; Males per 100 females: 92.8
Housing: Homeownership rate: 86.8%; Homeowner vacancy rate: 2.0%; Rental vacancy rate: 6.1%

NORTH STAR (township). Covers a land area of 34.102 square miles and a water area of 0.054 square miles. Located at 43.24° N. Lat; 84.54° W. Long. Elevation is 718 feet.
Population: 888; Growth (since 2000): -10.8%; Density: 26.0 persons per square mile; Race: 96.8% White, 0.9% Black/African American, 0.0% Asian, 0.0% American Indian/Alaska Native, 0.2% Native Hawaiian/Other Pacific Islander, 1.5% Two or more races, 4.1% Hispanic of any race; Average household size: 2.53; Median age: 42.5; Age under 18: 22.3%; Age 65 and over: 17.9%; Males per 100 females: 109.4
Housing: Homeownership rate: 89.4%; Homeowner vacancy rate: 2.2%; Rental vacancy rate: 19.6%

PERRINTON (village). Covers a land area of 0.632 square miles and a water area of 0.008 square miles. Located at 43.18° N. Lat; 84.68° W. Long. Elevation is 735 feet.
History: Perrinton was established when the Toledo, Saginaw & Muskegon Railroad was built through here in 1886. The Perrin for whom it was named was the head of a law firm that had interests in the land here.
Population: 406; Growth (since 2000): -7.5%; Density: 642.0 persons per square mile; Race: 95.6% White, 0.2% Black/African American, 0.2% Asian, 0.0% American Indian/Alaska Native, 0.0% Native Hawaiian/Other Pacific Islander, 1.5% Two or more races, 3.2% Hispanic of any race; Average household size: 2.52; Median age: 38.4; Age under 18: 24.6%; Age 65 and over: 13.8%; Males per 100 females: 97.1
Housing: Homeownership rate: 65.2%; Homeowner vacancy rate: 1.9%; Rental vacancy rate: 8.2%

PINE RIVER (township). Covers a land area of 30.314 square miles and a water area of 0.164 square miles. Located at 43.43° N. Lat; 84.67° W. Long.
Population: 2,279; Growth (since 2000): -7.0%; Density: 75.2 persons per square mile; Race: 96.0% White, 0.2% Black/African American, 0.5% Asian, 0.5% American Indian/Alaska Native, 0.0% Native Hawaiian/Other Pacific Islander, 1.4% Two or more races, 4.7% Hispanic of any race; Average household size: 2.48; Median age: 45.7; Age under 18: 21.0%; Age 65 and over: 18.8%; Males per 100 females: 95.8
Housing: Homeownership rate: 90.1%; Homeowner vacancy rate: 2.8%; Rental vacancy rate: 3.1%

POMPEII (unincorporated postal area)
ZCTA: 48874
Covers a land area of 0.576 square miles and a water area of 0 square miles. Located at 43.19° N. Lat; 84.59° W. Long. Elevation is 715 feet.
Population: 180; Growth (since 2000): 3.4%; Density: 312.6 persons per square mile; Race: 98.3% White, 0.0% Black/African American, 0.0% Asian, 0.0% American Indian/Alaska Native, 0.0% Native Hawaiian/Other Pacific Islander, 0.6% Two or more races, 5.6% Hispanic of any race; Average household size: 3.00; Median age: 29.4; Age under 18: 37.2%; Age 65 and over: 3.3%; Males per 100 females: 85.6
Housing: Homeownership rate: 81.7%; Homeowner vacancy rate: 2.0%; Rental vacancy rate: 0.0%

RIVERDALE (unincorporated postal area)
ZCTA: 48877
Covers a land area of 33.694 square miles and a water area of 0.409 square miles. Located at 43.40° N. Lat; 84.84° W. Long. Elevation is 794 feet.
Population: 2,392; Growth (since 2000): -3.4%; Density: 71.0 persons per square mile; Race: 98.0% White, 0.2% Black/African American, 0.0% Asian, 0.2% American Indian/Alaska Native, 0.0% Native Hawaiian/Other Pacific Islander, 0.7% Two or more races, 2.9% Hispanic of any race; Average household size: 2.65; Median age: 40.5; Age under 18: 24.4%; Age 65 and over: 13.0%; Males per 100 females: 102.0
Housing: Homeownership rate: 81.9%; Homeowner vacancy rate: 2.3%; Rental vacancy rate: 1.8%

SAINT LOUIS (city). Covers a land area of 3.343 square miles and a water area of 0.189 square miles. Located at 43.41° N. Lat; 84.61° W. Long. Elevation is 732 feet.
History: St. Louis was settled in 1853 around a sawmill. First called Pine River, it was consolidated with a nearby settlement called St. Louis in 1865. St. Louis later grew as a spa and health resort when the therapeutic value of its water was discovered. The mineral baths were especially sought by those suffering from rheumatism.
Population: 7,482; Growth (since 2000): 66.5%; Density: 2,238.4 persons per square mile; Race: 67.7% White, 29.1% Black/African American, 0.2% Asian, 0.6% American Indian/Alaska Native, 0.0% Native Hawaiian/Other Pacific Islander, 1.0% Two or more races, 5.7% Hispanic of any race; Average household size: 2.45; Median age: 36.1; Age under 18: 13.5%; Age 65 and over: 8.9%; Males per 100 females: 265.7; Marriage status: 47.7% never married, 29.0% now married, 1.8% separated, 6.6% widowed, 16.7% divorced; Foreign born: 1.2%; Speak English only: 94.1%; With disability: 20.0%; Veterans: 9.6%; Ancestry: 17.3% German, 10.4% English, 9.9% Irish, 5.5% French, 4.0% Scottish
Employment: 10.3% management, business, and financial, 2.4% computer, engineering, and science, 4.5% education, legal, community service, arts, and media, 4.5% healthcare practitioners, 23.9% service, 23.9% sales and office, 9.8% natural resources, construction, and maintenance, 20.6% production, transportation, and material moving
Income: Per capita: $10,344; Median household: $28,063; Average household: $42,832; Households with income of $100,000 or more: 10.0%; Poverty rate: 27.7%
Educational Attainment: High school diploma or higher: 80.5%; Bachelor's degree or higher: 8.5%; Graduate/professional degree or higher: 2.7%

School District(s)
Saint Louis Public Schools (PK-12)
    2012-13 Enrollment: 1,130 . . . . (989) 681-2545
Housing: Homeownership rate: 66.7%; Median home value: $62,400; Median year structure built: 1961; Homeowner vacancy rate: 3.0%; Median gross rent: $558 per month; Rental vacancy rate: 8.0%
Health Insurance: 86.3% have insurance; 49.5% have private insurance; 48.0% have public insurance; 13.7% do not have insurance; 2.3% of children under 18 do not have insurance
Safety: Violent crime rate: 10.8 per 10,000 population; Property crime rate: 83.6 per 10,000 population
Transportation: Commute: 98.1% car, 0.0% public transportation, 0.4% walk, 0.6% work from home; Median travel time to work: 20.0 minutes

SEVILLE (township). Covers a land area of 35.538 square miles and a water area of 0.377 square miles. Located at 43.42° N. Lat; 84.78° W. Long.

History: Seville Township was organized in 1856, the first settler in the area having arrived the previous year.

Population: 2,173; Growth (since 2000): -8.5%; Density: 61.1 persons per square mile; Race: 98.0% White, 0.0% Black/African American, 0.0% Asian, 0.2% American Indian/Alaska Native, 0.0% Native Hawaiian/Other Pacific Islander, 1.2% Two or more races, 3.0% Hispanic of any race; Average household size: 2.52; Median age: 43.6; Age under 18: 21.5%; Age 65 and over: 16.8%; Males per 100 females: 99.4

Housing: Homeownership rate: 85.1%; Homeowner vacancy rate: 1.6%; Rental vacancy rate: 3.7%

SUMNER (township). Covers a land area of 35.648 square miles and a water area of 0.276 square miles. Located at 43.34° N. Lat; 84.79° W. Long. Elevation is 761 feet.

History: Sumner Township was organized in 1855 and named for pioneer settler Charles Sumner. For a time the village here was called Belltown, for its principal landowner, and later Stover, for its first storekeeper.

Population: 1,930; Growth (since 2000): 1.0%; Density: 54.1 persons per square mile; Race: 98.5% White, 0.1% Black/African American, 0.1% Asian, 0.2% American Indian/Alaska Native, 0.0% Native Hawaiian/Other Pacific Islander, 0.7% Two or more races, 1.8% Hispanic of any race; Average household size: 2.66; Median age: 41.1; Age under 18: 25.7%; Age 65 and over: 14.0%; Males per 100 females: 104.0

Housing: Homeownership rate: 82.4%; Homeowner vacancy rate: 1.2%; Rental vacancy rate: 3.7%

WASHINGTON (township). Covers a land area of 35.255 square miles and a water area of 0.181 square miles. Located at 43.16° N. Lat; 84.54° W. Long.

Population: 870; Growth (since 2000): -4.3%; Density: 24.7 persons per square mile; Race: 96.8% White, 0.1% Black/African American, 0.1% Asian, 0.3% American Indian/Alaska Native, 0.0% Native Hawaiian/Other Pacific Islander, 0.9% Two or more races, 3.2% Hispanic of any race; Average household size: 2.66; Median age: 41.0; Age under 18: 23.8%; Age 65 and over: 15.2%; Males per 100 females: 106.2

Housing: Homeownership rate: 84.4%; Homeowner vacancy rate: 1.4%; Rental vacancy rate: 8.9%

WHEELER (township). Covers a land area of 35.882 square miles and a water area of 0.010 square miles. Located at 43.42° N. Lat; 84.42° W. Long. Elevation is 718 feet.

Population: 2,786; Growth (since 2000): 0.0%; Density: 77.6 persons per square mile; Race: 97.0% White, 0.3% Black/African American, 0.0% Asian, 0.4% American Indian/Alaska Native, 0.0% Native Hawaiian/Other Pacific Islander, 0.8% Two or more races, 4.8% Hispanic of any race; Average household size: 2.59; Median age: 40.1; Age under 18: 25.9%; Age 65 and over: 15.1%; Males per 100 females: 99.3; Marriage status: 20.1% never married, 63.7% now married, 1.5% separated, 6.3% widowed, 9.9% divorced; Foreign born: 0.3%; Speak English only: 98.0%; With disability: 16.4%; Veterans: 11.3%; Ancestry: 31.0% German, 15.0% Irish, 11.4% English, 8.4% American, 7.1% Polish

Employment: 10.9% management, business, and financial, 0.7% computer, engineering, and science, 7.3% education, legal, community service, arts, and media, 5.2% healthcare practitioners, 21.1% service, 19.2% sales and office, 11.2% natural resources, construction, and maintenance, 24.4% production, transportation, and material moving

Income: Per capita: $22,291; Median household: $38,258; Average household: $53,838; Households with income of $100,000 or more: 14.7%; Poverty rate: 16.2%

Educational Attainment: High school diploma or higher: 93.0%; Bachelor's degree or higher: 10.4%; Graduate/professional degree or higher: 4.9%

Housing: Homeownership rate: 77.5%; Median home value: $82,900; Median year structure built: 1963; Homeowner vacancy rate: 1.4%; Median gross rent: $600 per month; Rental vacancy rate: 6.2%

Health Insurance: 90.6% have insurance; 69.8% have private insurance; 39.0% have public insurance; 9.4% do not have insurance; 0.5% of children under 18 do not have insurance

Transportation: Commute: 92.2% car, 0.0% public transportation, 3.7% walk, 3.1% work from home; Median travel time to work: 25.8 minutes

Hillsdale County

Located in southern Michigan; bounded on the south by Ohio; drained by headstreams of the Kalamazoo and Saint Joseph Rivers; includes many small lakes. Covers a land area of 598.133 square miles, a water area of 8.873 square miles, and is located in the Eastern Time Zone at 41.86° N. Lat., 84.64° W. Long. The county was founded in 1835. County seat is Hillsdale.

Hillsdale County is part of the Hillsdale, MI Micropolitan Statistical Area. The entire metro area includes: Hillsdale County, MI

Weather Station: Hillsdale   Elevation: 1,080 feet

	Jan	Feb	Mar	Apr	May	Jun	Jul	Aug	Sep	Oct	Nov	Dec
High	31	34	44	57	69	79	82	80	73	61	47	35
Low	15	16	24	35	45	56	59	57	49	39	30	20
Precip	2.2	1.9	2.4	3.3	3.9	3.9	3.6	3.8	3.8	3.2	2.9	2.5
Snow	13.7	9.6	6.3	1.8	tr	0.0	0.0	0.0	0.0	0.3	3.0	11.0

High and Low temperatures in degrees Fahrenheit; Precipitation and Snow in inches

Population: 46,688; Growth (since 2000): 0.3%; Density: 78.1 persons per square mile; Race: 97.0% White, 0.5% Black/African American, 0.4% Asian, 0.4% American Indian/Alaska Native, 0.0% Native Hawaiian/Other Pacific Islander, 1.3% two or more races, 1.8% Hispanic of any race; Average household size: 2.53; Median age: 40.5; Age under 18: 23.8%; Age 65 and over: 15.7%; Males per 100 females: 98.5; Marriage status: 24.8% never married, 57.3% now married, 1.7% separated, 6.2% widowed, 11.7% divorced; Foreign born: 0.7%; Speak English only: 95.1%; With disability: 14.6%; Veterans: 10.4%; Ancestry: 34.7% German, 14.4% Irish, 13.5% English, 9.3% American, 5.1% French

Religion: Six largest groups: 4.7% Catholicism, 4.2% Methodist/Pietist, 3.0% Non-denominational Protestant, 2.4% Holiness, 2.2% Baptist, 1.7% European Free-Church

Economy: Unemployment rate: 6.0%; Leading industries: 17.5% retail trade; 13.1% health care and social assistance; 11.1% other services (except public administration); Farms: 1,530 totaling 262,363 acres; Company size: 0 employ 1,000 or more persons, 2 employ 500 to 999 persons, 14 employ 100 to 499 persons, 768 employ less than 100 persons; Business ownership: 881 women-owned, n/a Black-owned, n/a Hispanic-owned, n/a Asian-owned

Employment: 10.0% management, business, and financial, 2.6% computer, engineering, and science, 8.7% education, legal, community service, arts, and media, 5.6% healthcare practitioners, 17.7% service, 20.8% sales and office, 9.7% natural resources, construction, and maintenance, 24.9% production, transportation, and material moving

Income: Per capita: $20,379; Median household: $41,759; Average household: $52,346; Households with income of $100,000 or more: 10.9%; Poverty rate: 19.7%

Educational Attainment: High school diploma or higher: 87.0%; Bachelor's degree or higher: 15.3%; Graduate/professional degree or higher: 6.4%

Housing: Homeownership rate: 78.4%; Median home value: $103,700; Median year structure built: 1970; Homeowner vacancy rate: 2.9%; Median gross rent: $639 per month; Rental vacancy rate: 9.2%

Vital Statistics: Birth rate: 109.5 per 10,000 population; Death rate: 93.9 per 10,000 population; Age-adjusted cancer mortality rate: 181.8 deaths per 100,000 population

Health Insurance: 85.4% have insurance; 63.8% have private insurance; 37.1% have public insurance; 14.6% do not have insurance; 11.9% of children under 18 do not have insurance

Health Care: Physicians: 7.1 per 10,000 population; Hospital beds: 18.0 per 10,000 population; Hospital admissions: 764.9 per 10,000 population

Transportation: Commute: 89.3% car, 0.3% public transportation, 4.1% walk, 5.0% work from home; Median travel time to work: 24.1 minutes

Presidential Election: 37.2% Obama, 61.5% Romney (2012)

National and State Parks: Pittsford State Game Area

Additional Information Contacts

Hillsdale Government . . . . (517) 437-3391
   http://www.co.hillsdale.mi.us

Hillsdale County Communities

ADAMS (township). Covers a land area of 35.636 square miles and a water area of 0.380 square miles. Located at 41.94° N. Lat; 84.54° W. Long.

History: Adams became a township in 1836, being separated out from Moscow Township. It was named for Henry P. Adams, an early settler.

Population: 2,493; Growth (since 2000): -0.2%; Density: 70.0 persons per square mile; Race: 97.4% White, 0.4% Black/African American, 0.4% Asian, 0.4% American Indian/Alaska Native, 0.0% Native Hawaiian/Other Pacific Islander, 1.2% Two or more races, 0.6% Hispanic of any race; Average household size: 2.53; Median age: 43.9; Age under 18: 23.2%; Age 65 and over: 18.7%; Males per 100 females: 99.1

Housing: Homeownership rate: 81.3%; Homeowner vacancy rate: 2.2%; Rental vacancy rate: 6.0%

ALLEN (township). Covers a land area of 36.006 square miles and a water area of 0.224 square miles. Located at 41.94° N. Lat; 84.76° W. Long. Elevation is 1,076 feet.

Population: 1,657; Growth (since 2000): 1.6%; Density: 46.0 persons per square mile; Race: 97.9% White, 0.4% Black/African American, 0.2% Asian, 0.2% American Indian/Alaska Native, 0.0% Native Hawaiian/Other Pacific Islander, 1.1% Two or more races, 1.6% Hispanic of any race; Average household size: 2.61; Median age: 40.7; Age under 18: 25.2%; Age 65 and over: 13.5%; Males per 100 females: 104.6

Housing: Homeownership rate: 82.5%; Homeowner vacancy rate: 2.0%; Rental vacancy rate: 10.4%

ALLEN (village). Covers a land area of 0.155 square miles and a water area of 0 square miles. Located at 41.96° N. Lat; 84.77° W. Long. Elevation is 1,076 feet.

History: Allen was settled by Captain Moses Allen and his family in 1827.

Population: 191; Growth (since 2000): -15.1%; Density: 1,231.7 persons per square mile; Race: 97.9% White, 0.0% Black/African American, 1.0% Asian, 0.0% American Indian/Alaska Native, 0.0% Native Hawaiian/Other Pacific Islander, 1.0% Two or more races, 0.0% Hispanic of any race; Average household size: 2.39; Median age: 45.8; Age under 18: 19.4%; Age 65 and over: 24.1%; Males per 100 females: 99.0

Housing: Homeownership rate: 81.3%; Homeowner vacancy rate: 1.5%; Rental vacancy rate: 11.8%

AMBOY (township). Covers a land area of 29.962 square miles and a water area of 0.677 square miles. Located at 41.72° N. Lat; 84.60° W. Long.

History: Amboy Township was separated from Rowland in 1850.

Population: 1,173; Growth (since 2000): -4.2%; Density: 39.1 persons per square mile; Race: 97.7% White, 0.1% Black/African American, 0.9% Asian, 0.0% American Indian/Alaska Native, 0.0% Native Hawaiian/Other Pacific Islander, 0.5% Two or more races, 2.1% Hispanic of any race; Average household size: 2.55; Median age: 46.9; Age under 18: 21.4%; Age 65 and over: 15.6%; Males per 100 females: 105.1

Housing: Homeownership rate: 92.0%; Homeowner vacancy rate: 3.4%; Rental vacancy rate: 7.5%

CAMBRIA (township). Covers a land area of 34.809 square miles and a water area of 1.335 square miles. Located at 41.86° N. Lat; 84.64° W. Long. Elevation is 1,079 feet.

History: Cambria Township was established in 1841 by the Willits brothers (Moses, Barron, and Jonathan) and named for their former home of Cambria, New York.

Population: 2,533; Growth (since 2000): -0.5%; Density: 72.8 persons per square mile; Race: 97.2% White, 0.6% Black/African American, 0.4% Asian, 0.4% American Indian/Alaska Native, 0.0% Native Hawaiian/Other Pacific Islander, 1.1% Two or more races, 1.5% Hispanic of any race; Average household size: 2.53; Median age: 43.7; Age under 18: 23.6%; Age 65 and over: 15.8%; Males per 100 females: 100.1; Marriage status: 18.9% never married, 65.5% now married, 2.6% separated, 4.1% widowed, 11.6% divorced; Foreign born: 0.4%; Speak English only: 98.3%; With disability: 12.8%; Veterans: 13.6%; Ancestry: 32.1% German, 15.6% English, 14.3% American, 8.5% Irish, 3.4% Scottish

Employment: 10.1% management, business, and financial, 0.4% computer, engineering, and science, 10.6% education, legal, community service, arts, and media, 5.0% healthcare practitioners, 15.6% service,

18.4% sales and office, 13.2% natural resources, construction, and maintenance, 26.6% production, transportation, and material moving

Income: Per capita: $24,321; Median household: $46,550; Average household: $56,566; Households with income of $100,000 or more: 13.2%; Poverty rate: 15.5%

Educational Attainment: High school diploma or higher: 89.8%; Bachelor's degree or higher: 12.7%; Graduate/professional degree or higher: 6.2%

Housing: Homeownership rate: 82.4%; Median home value: $112,100; Median year structure built: 1972; Homeowner vacancy rate: 2.9%; Median gross rent: $663 per month; Rental vacancy rate: 10.1%

Health Insurance: 84.6% have insurance; 69.4% have private insurance; 32.0% have public insurance; 15.4% do not have insurance; 7.1% of children under 18 do not have insurance

Transportation: Commute: 98.3% car, 0.0% public transportation, 1.7% walk, 0.0% work from home; Median travel time to work: 18.6 minutes

CAMDEN (township). Covers a land area of 42.362 square miles and a water area of 0.240 square miles. Located at 41.76° N. Lat; 84.78° W. Long. Elevation is 1,020 feet.

History: Camden Township was named for Camden, New York, the name being suggested by Easton T. Chester who had lived there previously.

Population: 2,047; Growth (since 2000): -2.0%; Density: 48.3 persons per square mile; Race: 99.1% White, 0.1% Black/African American, 0.1% Asian, 0.1% American Indian/Alaska Native, 0.0% Native Hawaiian/Other Pacific Islander, 0.5% Two or more races, 0.7% Hispanic of any race; Average household size: 2.82; Median age: 36.7; Age under 18: 30.0%; Age 65 and over: 13.6%; Males per 100 females: 102.3

School District(s)

Camden-Frontier School (KG-12)
    2012-13 Enrollment: 562. . . . . (517) 368-5991

Housing: Homeownership rate: 80.6%; Homeowner vacancy rate: 4.6%; Rental vacancy rate: 9.0%

CAMDEN (village). Covers a land area of 0.842 square miles and a water area of 0 square miles. Located at 41.76° N. Lat; 84.76° W. Long. Elevation is 1,020 feet.

History: Camden grew up around the sawmills built in the late 1830's. It was incorporated as a village in 1899, and named for Camden, New York.

Population: 512; Growth (since 2000): -6.9%; Density: 607.7 persons per square mile; Race: 99.4% White, 0.0% Black/African American, 0.0% Asian, 0.2% American Indian/Alaska Native, 0.0% Native Hawaiian/Other Pacific Islander, 0.4% Two or more races, 0.2% Hispanic of any race; Average household size: 2.89; Median age: 32.6; Age under 18: 31.2%; Age 65 and over: 9.4%; Males per 100 females: 97.7

School District(s)

Camden-Frontier School (KG-12)
    2012-13 Enrollment: 562. . . . . (517) 368-5991

Housing: Homeownership rate: 67.6%; Homeowner vacancy rate: 11.0%; Rental vacancy rate: 10.8%

FAYETTE (township). Covers a land area of 22.831 square miles and a water area of 0.277 square miles. Located at 41.97° N. Lat; 84.65° W. Long. Elevation is 1,076 feet.

Population: 3,326; Growth (since 2000): -0.7%; Density: 145.7 persons per square mile; Race: 95.8% White, 1.4% Black/African American, 0.8% Asian, 0.5% American Indian/Alaska Native, 0.0% Native Hawaiian/Other Pacific Islander, 1.2% Two or more races, 1.8% Hispanic of any race; Average household size: 2.46; Median age: 40.2; Age under 18: 25.6%; Age 65 and over: 17.6%; Males per 100 females: 93.4; Marriage status: 24.4% never married, 53.5% now married, 1.1% separated, 8.7% widowed, 13.4% divorced; Foreign born: 0.5%; Speak English only: 97.9%; With disability: 21.5%; Veterans: 11.1%; Ancestry: 27.1% German, 17.4% English, 15.9% Irish, 8.6% American, 7.1% French

Employment: 10.0% management, business, and financial, 3.4% computer, engineering, and science, 12.4% education, legal, community service, arts, and media, 4.4% healthcare practitioners, 21.5% service, 20.5% sales and office, 9.1% natural resources, construction, and maintenance, 18.7% production, transportation, and material moving

Income: Per capita: $20,284; Median household: $40,234; Average household: $50,658; Households with income of $100,000 or more: 10.8%; Poverty rate: 17.3%

Educational Attainment: High school diploma or higher: 93.0%; Bachelor's degree or higher: 17.3%; Graduate/professional degree or higher: 7.9%

Housing: Homeownership rate: 79.2%; Median home value: $108,800; Median year structure built: 1961; Homeowner vacancy rate: 3.7%; Median gross rent: $634 per month; Rental vacancy rate: 9.3%
Health Insurance: 88.4% have insurance; 68.6% have private insurance; 39.7% have public insurance; 11.6% do not have insurance; 0.4% of children under 18 do not have insurance
Transportation: Commute: 93.0% car, 0.0% public transportation, 0.7% walk, 5.0% work from home; Median travel time to work: 21.6 minutes

HILLSDALE (city). County seat. Covers a land area of 5.916 square miles and a water area of 0.270 square miles. Located at 41.93° N. Lat; 84.64° W. Long. Elevation is 1,119 feet.

History: Hillsdale was settled in 1834 by Jeremiah Arnold. In the 1840's, the railroad built a station here, the Free Will Baptist organization founded a college, and Hillsdale was made the seat of Hillsdale County.
Population: 8,305; Growth (since 2000): 0.9%; Density: 1,403.7 persons per square mile; Race: 95.8% White, 0.7% Black/African American, 0.7% Asian, 0.4% American Indian/Alaska Native, 0.0% Native Hawaiian/Other Pacific Islander, 2.0% Two or more races, 2.3% Hispanic of any race; Average household size: 2.35; Median age: 30.2; Age under 18: 22.1%; Age 65 and over: 13.6%; Males per 100 females: 88.6; Marriage status: 43.5% never married, 36.9% now married, 2.4% separated, 6.8% widowed, 12.8% divorced; Foreign born: 0.8%; Speak English only: 97.8%; With disability: 14.9%; Veterans: 7.4%; Ancestry: 41.3% German, 16.6% Irish, 11.5% English, 7.0% French, 6.7% American
Employment: 6.5% management, business, and financial, 1.0% computer, engineering, and science, 11.4% education, legal, community service, arts, and media, 4.7% healthcare practitioners, 27.8% service, 22.0% sales and office, 4.6% natural resources, construction, and maintenance, 22.1% production, transportation, and material moving
Income: Per capita: $15,818; Median household: $30,741; Average household: $41,792; Households with income of $100,000 or more: 6.9%; Poverty rate: 31.6%
Educational Attainment: High school diploma or higher: 86.9%; Bachelor's degree or higher: 15.6%; Graduate/professional degree or higher: 7.2%

School District(s)
Hillsdale Community Schools (KG-12)
    2012-13 Enrollment: 1,431 . . . . (517) 437-4401
Hillsdale ISD (PK-12)
    2012-13 Enrollment: 318. . . . . (517) 437-0990
Hillsdale Preparatory School (PK-12)
    2012-13 Enrollment: 109. . . . . (517) 437-4625
Will Carleton Charter School Academy (KG-12)
    2012-13 Enrollment: 361. . . . . (517) 437-2000

Vocational/Technical School(s)
Hillsdale Beauty College (Private, For-profit)
    Fall 2013 Enrollment: 35 . . . . (517) 437-4670
    2013-14 Tuition: $11,200
Housing: Homeownership rate: 51.9%; Median home value: $81,200; Median year structure built: 1947; Homeowner vacancy rate: 4.0%; Median gross rent: $563 per month; Rental vacancy rate: 11.4%
Health Insurance: 90.1% have insurance; 59.2% have private insurance; 44.1% have public insurance; 9.9% do not have insurance; 1.0% of children under 18 do not have insurance
Hospitals: Hillsdale Community Health Center (65 beds)
Safety: Violent crime rate: 39.1 per 10,000 population; Property crime rate: 205.2 per 10,000 population
Newspapers: County Sampler (weekly circulation 5000); Hillsdale Daily News (daily circulation 7300)
Transportation: Commute: 77.1% car, 0.5% public transportation, 15.5% walk, 5.8% work from home; Median travel time to work: 14.9 minutes
Airports: Hillsdale Municipal (general aviation)
Additional Information Contacts
City of Hillsdale . . . . (517) 437-6441
    http://www.cityofhillsdale.org

HILLSDALE (township). Covers a land area of 12.321 square miles and a water area of 0.573 square miles. Located at 41.92° N. Lat; 84.66° W. Long. Elevation is 1,119 feet.

History: Seat of Hillsdale College, with 60-acre Slayton Arboretum. Native American mounds nearby. Settled 1834; incorporated as village 1847, as city 1869.
Population: 2,033; Growth (since 2000): 3.5%; Density: 165.0 persons per square mile; Race: 97.0% White, 0.5% Black/African American, 0.8%

Asian, 0.3% American Indian/Alaska Native, 0.0% Native Hawaiian/Other Pacific Islander, 0.7% Two or more races, 2.0% Hispanic of any race; Average household size: 2.55; Median age: 46.1; Age under 18: 22.3%; Age 65 and over: 18.8%; Males per 100 females: 95.7

School District(s)
Hillsdale Community Schools (KG-12)
    2012-13 Enrollment: 1,431 . . . . (517) 437-4401
Hillsdale ISD (PK-12)
    2012-13 Enrollment: 318. . . . . (517) 437-0990
Hillsdale Preparatory School (PK-12)
    2012-13 Enrollment: 109. . . . . (517) 437-4625
Will Carleton Charter School Academy (KG-12)
    2012-13 Enrollment: 361. . . . . (517) 437-2000

Vocational/Technical School(s)
Hillsdale Beauty College (Private, For-profit)
    Fall 2013 Enrollment: 35 . . . . (517) 437-4670
    2013-14 Tuition: $11,200
Housing: Homeownership rate: 88.8%; Homeowner vacancy rate: 1.0%; Rental vacancy rate: 7.6%
Hospitals: Hillsdale Community Health Center (65 beds)
Newspapers: County Sampler (weekly circulation 5000); Hillsdale Daily News (daily circulation 7300)
Airports: Hillsdale Municipal (general aviation)

JEFFERSON (township). Covers a land area of 35.494 square miles and a water area of 0.607 square miles. Located at 41.85° N. Lat; 84.54° W. Long.

History: Jefferson Township was set off from Moscow Township in 1837, when it was named Florida. In 1849 the name was changed to Jefferson.
Population: 3,063; Growth (since 2000): -2.5%; Density: 86.3 persons per square mile; Race: 97.2% White, 0.4% Black/African American, 0.5% Asian, 0.3% American Indian/Alaska Native, 0.0% Native Hawaiian/Other Pacific Islander, 1.5% Two or more races, 0.8% Hispanic of any race; Average household size: 2.51; Median age: 42.7; Age under 18: 22.3%; Age 65 and over: 16.1%; Males per 100 females: 101.6; Marriage status: 15.0% never married, 68.2% now married, 2.1% separated, 4.7% widowed, 12.1% divorced; Foreign born: 0.2%; Speak English only: 98.2%; With disability: 15.3%; Veterans: 15.0%; Ancestry: 26.6% German, 13.2% American, 12.4% Irish, 8.1% English, 6.6% Italian
Employment: 5.0% management, business, and financial, 0.0% computer, engineering, and science, 11.4% education, legal, community service, arts, and media, 3.0% healthcare practitioners, 15.2% service, 24.3% sales and office, 7.8% natural resources, construction, and maintenance, 33.3% production, transportation, and material moving
Income: Per capita: $20,801; Median household: $47,242; Average household: $50,985; Households with income of $100,000 or more: 7.0%; Poverty rate: 11.6%
Educational Attainment: High school diploma or higher: 85.1%; Bachelor's degree or higher: 15.3%; Graduate/professional degree or higher: 4.8%
Housing: Homeownership rate: 82.0%; Median home value: $106,200; Median year structure built: 1970; Homeowner vacancy rate: 2.9%; Median gross rent: $640 per month; Rental vacancy rate: 8.3%
Health Insurance: 90.6% have insurance; 71.6% have private insurance; 34.9% have public insurance; 9.4% do not have insurance; 0.0% of children under 18 do not have insurance
Transportation: Commute: 96.4% car, 0.0% public transportation, 1.7% walk, 1.1% work from home; Median travel time to work: 27.9 minutes

JONESVILLE (village). Covers a land area of 2.888 square miles and a water area of 0.032 square miles. Located at 41.98° N. Lat; 84.67° W. Long. Elevation is 1,073 feet.

History: Jonesville was settled in 1829 at a place where the St. Joseph River could be forded. The village was platted by Benaiah Jones in 1831 and named for him.
Population: 2,258; Growth (since 2000): -3.4%; Density: 781.8 persons per square mile; Race: 95.3% White, 2.1% Black/African American, 0.9% Asian, 0.3% American Indian/Alaska Native, 0.0% Native Hawaiian/Other Pacific Islander, 1.1% Two or more races, 2.1% Hispanic of any race; Average household size: 2.41; Median age: 37.6; Age under 18: 26.3%; Age 65 and over: 17.4%; Males per 100 females: 90.2

School District(s)
Hillsdale ISD (PK-12)
    2012-13 Enrollment: 318. . . . . (517) 437-0990

Jonesville Community Schools (KG-12)
2012-13 Enrollment: 1,466 . . . . (517) 849-9075
Housing: Homeownership rate: 73.3%; Homeowner vacancy rate: 4.3%;
Rental vacancy rate: 9.8%
Safety: Violent crime rate: 9.0 per 10,000 population; Property crime rate:
318.2 per 10,000 population

LITCHFIELD (city). Covers a land area of 2.497 square miles and a
water area of 0.037 square miles. Located at 42.04° N. Lat; 84.75° W.
Long. Elevation is 1,024 feet.
History: Litchfield was settled in 1834 and platted as Smithville in 1836. It
was later named Litchfield for the town of that name in Connecticut, the
former home of some of the early residents.
Population: 1,369; Growth (since 2000): -6.1%; Density: 548.3 persons
per square mile; Race: 96.9% White, 0.3% Black/African American, 0.1%
Asian, 0.7% American Indian/Alaska Native, 0.0% Native Hawaiian/Other
Pacific Islander, 0.9% Two or more races, 2.9% Hispanic of any race;
Average household size: 2.44; Median age: 38.4; Age under 18: 25.6%;
Age 65 and over: 15.0%; Males per 100 females: 99.3
School District(s)
Litchfield Community Schools (PK-12)
2012-13 Enrollment: 312. . . . . (517) 542-2388
Housing: Homeownership rate: 63.2%; Homeowner vacancy rate: 3.5%;
Rental vacancy rate: 4.6%
Safety: Violent crime rate: 14.8 per 10,000 population; Property crime rate:
221.4 per 10,000 population
Additional Information Contacts
City of Litchfield. . . . . (517) 542-2921
http://www.ci.litchfield.mi.us

LITCHFIELD (township). Covers a land area of 32.974 square miles
and a water area of 0.075 square miles. Located at 42.02° N. Lat; 84.77°
W. Long. Elevation is 1,024 feet.
Population: 1,003; Growth (since 2000): 3.5%; Density: 30.4 persons per
square mile; Race: 97.0% White, 0.6% Black/African American, 0.2%
Asian, 0.4% American Indian/Alaska Native, 0.0% Native Hawaiian/Other
Pacific Islander, 1.7% Two or more races, 1.2% Hispanic of any race;
Average household size: 2.54; Median age: 46.1; Age under 18: 21.5%;
Age 65 and over: 17.7%; Males per 100 females: 107.2
School District(s)
Litchfield Community Schools (PK-12)
2012-13 Enrollment: 312. . . . . (517) 542-2388
Housing: Homeownership rate: 91.6%; Homeowner vacancy rate: 1.6%;
Rental vacancy rate: 13.2%

MONTGOMERY (village). Covers a land area of 1.000 square miles
and a water area of 0.004 square miles. Located at 41.78° N. Lat; 84.81°
W. Long. Elevation is 1,050 feet.
Population: 342; Growth (since 2000): -11.4%; Density: 342.1 persons
per square mile; Race: 98.0% White, 0.0% Black/African American, 0.6%
Asian, 0.3% American Indian/Alaska Native, 0.0% Native Hawaiian/Other
Pacific Islander, 1.2% Two or more races, 2.0% Hispanic of any race;
Average household size: 2.61; Median age: 35.7; Age under 18: 30.1%;
Age 65 and over: 17.3%; Males per 100 females: 111.1
Housing: Homeownership rate: 79.3%; Homeowner vacancy rate: 3.8%;
Rental vacancy rate: 16.1%

MOSCOW (township). Covers a land area of 35.154 square miles and
a water area of 0.279 square miles. Located at 42.02° N. Lat; 84.52° W.
Long. Elevation is 1,096 feet.
History: In the Moscow area, stagecoach drivers forded the Kalamazoo
River, then a river of some size. A log tavern erected at the ford in 1831
was replaced about 1850 by the Moscow Tavern.
Population: 1,470; Growth (since 2000): 1.7%; Density: 41.8 persons per
square mile; Race: 97.0% White, 0.3% Black/African American, 0.1%
Asian, 0.2% American Indian/Alaska Native, 0.0% Native Hawaiian/Other
Pacific Islander, 1.2% Two or more races, 1.5% Hispanic of any race;
Average household size: 2.66; Median age: 42.7; Age under 18: 23.1%;
Age 65 and over: 14.4%; Males per 100 females: 103.9
Housing: Homeownership rate: 85.5%; Homeowner vacancy rate: 1.2%;
Rental vacancy rate: 10.0%

NORTH ADAMS (village). Covers a land area of 0.518 square miles
and a water area of 0 square miles. Located at 41.97° N. Lat; 84.53° W.
Long. Elevation is 1,194 feet.
Population: 477; Growth (since 2000): -7.2%; Density: 921.5 persons per
square mile; Race: 98.1% White, 0.0% Black/African American, 0.4%
Asian, 0.4% American Indian/Alaska Native, 0.0% Native Hawaiian/Other
Pacific Islander, 0.8% Two or more races, 0.2% Hispanic of any race;
Average household size: 2.52; Median age: 40.2; Age under 18: 24.5%;
Age 65 and over: 17.6%; Males per 100 females: 92.3
School District(s)
North Adams-Jerome Public Schools (PK-12)
2012-13 Enrollment: 393. . . . . (517) 287-4263
Housing: Homeownership rate: 75.7%; Homeowner vacancy rate: 4.6%;
Rental vacancy rate: 14.8%

OSSEO (unincorporated postal area)
ZCTA: 49266
Covers a land area of 44.205 square miles and a water area of 0.604
square miles. Located at 41.84° N. Lat; 84.55° W. Long. Elevation is
1,109 feet.
Population: 2,942; Growth (since 2000): -1.0%; Density: 66.6 persons
per square mile; Race: 97.5% White, 0.4% Black/African American,
0.3% Asian, 0.2% American Indian/Alaska Native, 0.0% Native
Hawaiian/Other Pacific Islander, 1.4% Two or more races, 0.8%
Hispanic of any race; Average household size: 2.57; Median age: 42.5;
Age under 18: 22.8%; Age 65 and over: 16.0%; Males per 100 females:
106.5; Marriage status: 16.3% never married, 67.2% now married, 1.8%
separated, 5.7% widowed, 10.8% divorced; Foreign born: 0.3%; Speak
English only: 98.2%; With disability: 16.7%; Veterans: 14.8%; Ancestry:
28.6% German, 11.6% Irish, 11.4% American, 9.2% English, 5.0%
Italian
Employment: 3.5% management, business, and financial, 1.1%
computer, engineering, and science, 6.3% education, legal, community
service, arts, and media, 3.4% healthcare practitioners, 14.1% service,
29.0% sales and office, 6.7% natural resources, construction, and
maintenance, 35.9% production, transportation, and material moving
Income: Per capita: $21,058; Median household: $47,303; Average
household: $50,810; Households with income of $100,000 or more:
6.4%; Poverty rate: 11.2%
Educational Attainment: High school diploma or higher: 86.0%;
Bachelor's degree or higher: 11.2%; Graduate/professional degree or
higher: 4.5%
Housing: Homeownership rate: 83.2%; Median home value: $109,400;
Median year structure built: 1969; Homeowner vacancy rate: 3.1%;
Median gross rent: $645 per month; Rental vacancy rate: 7.6%
Health Insurance: 91.7% have insurance; 72.4% have private
insurance; 34.2% have public insurance; 8.3% do not have insurance;
4.1% of children under 18 do not have insurance
Transportation: Commute: 96.2% car, 0.0% public transportation, 1.0%
walk, 2.0% work from home; Median travel time to work: 27.7 minutes

PITTSFORD (township). Covers a land area of 35.423 square miles
and a water area of 0.164 square miles. Located at 41.86° N. Lat; 84.42°
W. Long. Elevation is 1,089 feet.
Population: 1,603; Growth (since 2000): 0.2%; Density: 45.3 persons per
square mile; Race: 96.3% White, 0.3% Black/African American, 0.4%
Asian, 0.6% American Indian/Alaska Native, 0.0% Native Hawaiian/Other
Pacific Islander, 1.2% Two or more races, 2.1% Hispanic of any race;
Average household size: 2.58; Median age: 43.2; Age under 18: 23.4%;
Age 65 and over: 16.7%; Males per 100 females: 95.0
School District(s)
Pittsford Area Schools (KG-12)
2012-13 Enrollment: 683. . . . . (517) 523-3481
Housing: Homeownership rate: 87.7%; Homeowner vacancy rate: 0.7%;
Rental vacancy rate: 6.1%

RANSOM (township). Covers a land area of 30.082 square miles and a
water area of 0.094 square miles. Located at 41.78° N. Lat; 84.53° W.
Long. Elevation is 1,007 feet.
Population: 932; Growth (since 2000): -5.1%; Density: 31.0 persons per
square mile; Race: 99.0% White, 0.0% Black/African American, 0.1%
Asian, 0.1% American Indian/Alaska Native, 0.0% Native Hawaiian/Other
Pacific Islander, 0.6% Two or more races, 2.3% Hispanic of any race;
Average household size: 2.90; Median age: 40.8; Age under 18: 25.5%;
Age 65 and over: 14.7%; Males per 100 females: 112.3

Housing: Homeownership rate: 89.4%; Homeowner vacancy rate: 2.0%; Rental vacancy rate: 2.8%

READING (city). Covers a land area of 1.012 square miles and a water area of 0 square miles. Located at 41.84° N. Lat; 84.75° W. Long. Elevation is 1,194 feet.

History: Reading was first called Basswood Corners for a group of seven basswood trees near the four corners of the village, as it was laid out. It became Reading in 1840, named after its township. Reading grew around a sawmill built in 1852, and a railroad station established in 1869. It was incorporated as a village in 1873, and as a city in 1934.

Population: 1,078; Growth (since 2000): -4.9%; Density: 1,065.0 persons per square mile; Race: 98.9% White, 0.1% Black/African American, 0.1% Asian, 0.2% American Indian/Alaska Native, 0.0% Native Hawaiian/Other Pacific Islander, 0.6% Two or more races, 0.8% Hispanic of any race; Average household size: 2.72; Median age: 33.3; Age under 18: 32.2%; Age 65 and over: 11.2%; Males per 100 females: 99.6

School District(s)
Reading Community Schools (KG-12)
    2012-13 Enrollment: 828 . . . . (517) 283-2166
Housing: Homeownership rate: 67.9%; Homeowner vacancy rate: 3.6%; Rental vacancy rate: 5.9%
Safety: Violent crime rate: 0.0 per 10,000 population; Property crime rate: 94.1 per 10,000 population

READING (township). Covers a land area of 33.976 square miles and a water area of 1.034 square miles. Located at 41.86° N. Lat; 84.77° W. Long. Elevation is 1,194 feet.

History: Settled 1840; incorporated as village 1873; as city 1934.

Population: 1,765; Growth (since 2000): -0.9%; Density: 51.9 persons per square mile; Race: 98.3% White, 0.1% Black/African American, 0.1% Asian, 0.1% American Indian/Alaska Native, 0.0% Native Hawaiian/Other Pacific Islander, 0.9% Two or more races, 1.1% Hispanic of any race; Average household size: 2.40; Median age: 48.7; Age under 18: 20.2%; Age 65 and over: 21.7%; Males per 100 females: 109.4

School District(s)
Reading Community Schools (KG-12)
    2012-13 Enrollment: 828 . . . . (517) 283-2166
Housing: Homeownership rate: 90.3%; Homeowner vacancy rate: 2.8%; Rental vacancy rate: 10.1%

SCIPIO (township). Covers a land area of 29.211 square miles and a water area of 0.234 square miles. Located at 42.04° N. Lat; 84.64° W. Long.

History: Scipio Township was organized in 1836.

Population: 1,884; Growth (since 2000): 3.4%; Density: 64.5 persons per square mile; Race: 97.0% White, 0.2% Black/African American, 0.2% Asian, 0.6% American Indian/Alaska Native, 0.0% Native Hawaiian/Other Pacific Islander, 1.1% Two or more races, 1.8% Hispanic of any race; Average household size: 2.71; Median age: 38.8; Age under 18: 27.1%; Age 65 and over: 12.7%; Males per 100 females: 104.3
Housing: Homeownership rate: 80.0%; Homeowner vacancy rate: 1.8%; Rental vacancy rate: 4.1%

SOMERSET (township). Covers a land area of 33.415 square miles and a water area of 2.142 square miles. Located at 42.03° N. Lat; 84.42° W. Long. Elevation is 1,066 feet.

History: Somerset was settled in the early 1830's, when it was known as Wheatland. Somerset Township was organized later and named for Somerset in New York.

Population: 4,623; Growth (since 2000): 8.1%; Density: 138.4 persons per square mile; Race: 97.2% White, 0.5% Black/African American, 0.2% Asian, 0.4% American Indian/Alaska Native, 0.0% Native Hawaiian/Other Pacific Islander, 1.0% Two or more races, 2.4% Hispanic of any race; Average household size: 2.40; Median age: 47.3; Age under 18: 19.6%; Age 65 and over: 18.8%; Males per 100 females: 98.9; Marriage status: 16.9% never married, 65.3% now married, 0.7% separated, 6.4% widowed, 11.4% divorced; Foreign born: 1.1%; Speak English only: 99.0%; With disability: 12.2%; Veterans: 11.4%; Ancestry: 29.4% German, 25.0% English, 20.2% Irish, 9.5% American, 8.7% Polish
Employment: 12.8% management, business, and financial, 7.6% computer, engineering, and science, 9.9% education, legal, community service, arts, and media, 8.3% healthcare practitioners, 9.9% service, 26.2% sales and office, 9.5% natural resources, construction, and maintenance, 15.8% production, transportation, and material moving

Income: Per capita: $28,488; Median household: $57,561; Average household: $63,752; Households with income of $100,000 or more: 16.5%; Poverty rate: 8.7%
Educational Attainment: High school diploma or higher: 90.5%; Bachelor's degree or higher: 26.1%; Graduate/professional degree or higher: 12.6%
Housing: Homeownership rate: 90.2%; Median home value: $142,500; Median year structure built: 1986; Homeowner vacancy rate: 4.2%; Median gross rent: $955 per month; Rental vacancy rate: 7.8%
Health Insurance: 91.3% have insurance; 80.1% have private insurance; 31.8% have public insurance; 8.7% do not have insurance; 3.3% of children under 18 do not have insurance
Safety: Violent crime rate: 2.2 per 10,000 population; Property crime rate: 61.1 per 10,000 population
Transportation: Commute: 93.9% car, 1.9% public transportation, 0.0% walk, 4.2% work from home; Median travel time to work: 29.4 minutes

SOMERSET CENTER (unincorporated postal area)
ZCTA: 49282
    Covers a land area of 2.929 square miles and a water area of 0.640 square miles. Located at 42.03° N. Lat; 84.40° W. Long. Elevation is 1,060 feet.

Population: 372; Growth (since 2000): -52.6%; Density: 127.0 persons per square mile; Race: 94.9% White, 3.5% Black/African American, 0.5% Asian, 0.3% American Indian/Alaska Native, 0.0% Native Hawaiian/Other Pacific Islander, 0.8% Two or more races, 5.1% Hispanic of any race; Average household size: 2.10; Median age: 49.1; Age under 18: 14.8%; Age 65 and over: 23.1%; Males per 100 females: 101.1
Housing: Homeownership rate: 85.9%; Homeowner vacancy rate: 16.9%; Rental vacancy rate: 21.9%

WALDRON (village). Covers a land area of 1.000 square miles and a water area of 0 square miles. Located at 41.72° N. Lat; 84.42° W. Long. Elevation is 902 feet.

Population: 538; Growth (since 2000): -8.8%; Density: 538.2 persons per square mile; Race: 97.6% White, 0.6% Black/African American, 0.0% Asian, 0.9% American Indian/Alaska Native, 0.0% Native Hawaiian/Other Pacific Islander, 0.9% Two or more races, 0.7% Hispanic of any race; Average household size: 2.55; Median age: 34.1; Age under 18: 30.1%; Age 65 and over: 11.9%; Males per 100 females: 90.1

School District(s)
Waldron Area Schools (KG-12)
    2012-13 Enrollment: 294 . . . . (517) 286-6251
Housing: Homeownership rate: 71.6%; Homeowner vacancy rate: 4.8%; Rental vacancy rate: 6.3%

WHEATLAND (township). Covers a land area of 35.651 square miles and a water area of 0.029 square miles. Located at 41.94° N. Lat; 84.41° W. Long. Elevation is 1,099 feet.

Population: 1,351; Growth (since 2000): 7.4%; Density: 37.9 persons per square mile; Race: 97.1% White, 0.1% Black/African American, 0.1% Asian, 0.3% American Indian/Alaska Native, 0.0% Native Hawaiian/Other Pacific Islander, 1.8% Two or more races, 3.4% Hispanic of any race; Average household size: 2.66; Median age: 42.5; Age under 18: 23.2%; Age 65 and over: 15.0%; Males per 100 females: 108.2
Housing: Homeownership rate: 85.8%; Homeowner vacancy rate: 1.1%; Rental vacancy rate: 5.3%

WOODBRIDGE (township). Covers a land area of 30.052 square miles and a water area of 0.031 square miles. Located at 41.77° N. Lat; 84.64° W. Long.

Population: 1,325; Growth (since 2000): -0.9%; Density: 44.1 persons per square mile; Race: 97.3% White, 0.0% Black/African American, 0.2% Asian, 0.3% American Indian/Alaska Native, 0.0% Native Hawaiian/Other Pacific Islander, 1.7% Two or more races, 1.1% Hispanic of any race; Average household size: 3.12; Median age: 34.4; Age under 18: 32.2%; Age 65 and over: 11.4%; Males per 100 females: 99.8
Housing: Homeownership rate: 85.2%; Homeowner vacancy rate: 1.6%; Rental vacancy rate: 16.0%

WRIGHT (township). Covers a land area of 43.349 square miles and a water area of 0.171 square miles. Located at 41.76° N. Lat; 84.41° W. Long.
Population: 1,655; Growth (since 2000): -7.4%; Density: 38.2 persons per square mile; Race: 97.2% White, 0.2% Black/African American, 0.1% Asian, 1.1% American Indian/Alaska Native, 0.0% Native Hawaiian/Other Pacific Islander, 1.0% Two or more races, 1.6% Hispanic of any race; Average household size: 2.62; Median age: 40.1; Age under 18: 26.1%; Age 65 and over: 14.3%; Males per 100 females: 99.4
Housing: Homeownership rate: 81.3%; Homeowner vacancy rate: 2.9%; Rental vacancy rate: 5.6%

Houghton County

Located in northwestern Michigan, on the Upper Peninsula; includes part of the Keweenaw Peninsula, extending into Lake Superior; partly bounded on the southeast by Keweenaw Bay; drained by the Ontonagon and Sturgeon Rivers. Covers a land area of 1,009.099 square miles, a water area of 492.402 square miles, and is located in the Eastern Time Zone at 47.00° N. Lat., 88.65° W. Long. The county was founded in 1845. County seat is Houghton.

Houghton County is part of the Houghton, MI Micropolitan Statistical Area. The entire metro area includes: Houghton County, MI; Keweenaw County, MI

Weather Station: Hancock Houghton Co Arpt   Elevation: 1,074 feet

	Jan	Feb	Mar	Apr	May	Jun	Jul	Aug	Sep	Oct	Nov	Dec
High	22	25	33	47	61	70	75	74	64	51	37	26
Low	10	10	18	30	41	50	56	55	48	37	26	15
Precip	2.8	1.5	1.8	1.9	2.5	2.6	2.8	2.4	3.3	3.1	2.3	2.6
Snow	na	na	na	na	na	na	na	na	na	na	na	na

High and Low temperatures in degrees Fahrenheit; Precipitation and Snow in inches

Population: 36,628; Growth (since 2000): 1.7%; Density: 36.3 persons per square mile; Race: 94.5% White, 0.5% Black/African American, 2.9% Asian, 0.6% American Indian/Alaska Native, 0.0% Native Hawaiian/Other Pacific Islander, 1.3% two or more races, 1.1% Hispanic of any race; Average household size: 2.38; Median age: 33.1; Age under 18: 20.6%; Age 65 and over: 15.0%; Males per 100 females: 118.0; Marriage status: 38.9% never married, 45.3% now married, 0.7% separated, 6.8% widowed, 9.0% divorced; Foreign born: 4.7%; Speak English only: 93.0%; With disability: 12.1%; Veterans: 10.3%; Ancestry: 31.8% Finnish, 19.5% German, 10.1% English, 9.7% French, 8.2% Irish
Religion: Six largest groups: 22.9% Catholicism, 10.0% Lutheran, 3.4% Methodist/Pietist, 2.2% Non-denominational Protestant, 1.4% Baptist, 0.7% Pentecostal
Economy: Unemployment rate: 5.6%; Leading industries: 16.8% retail trade; 12.4% accommodation and food services; 11.4% construction; Farms: 177 totaling 27,194 acres; Company size: 0 employ 1,000 or more persons, 1 employs 500 to 999 persons, 4 employ 100 to 499 persons, 888 employ less than 100 persons; Business ownership: 617 women-owned, n/a Black-owned, n/a Hispanic-owned, n/a Asian-owned
Employment: 10.3% management, business, and financial, 6.7% computer, engineering, and science, 14.3% education, legal, community service, arts, and media, 5.4% healthcare practitioners, 25.4% service, 20.6% sales and office, 8.7% natural resources, construction, and maintenance, 8.5% production, transportation, and material moving
Income: Per capita: $19,783; Median household: $35,430; Average household: $49,967; Households with income of $100,000 or more: 11.4%; Poverty rate: 23.0%
Educational Attainment: High school diploma or higher: 91.0%; Bachelor's degree or higher: 28.9%; Graduate/professional degree or higher: 11.2%
Housing: Homeownership rate: 69.1%; Median home value: $88,400; Median year structure built: 1947; Homeowner vacancy rate: 2.7%; Median gross rent: $595 per month; Rental vacancy rate: 5.4%
Vital Statistics: Birth rate: 98.3 per 10,000 population; Death rate: 93.9 per 10,000 population; Age-adjusted cancer mortality rate: 166.5 deaths per 100,000 population
Health Insurance: 89.3% have insurance; 72.3% have private insurance; 31.9% have public insurance; 10.7% do not have insurance; 2.6% of children under 18 do not have insurance
Health Care: Physicians: 16.7 per 10,000 population; Hospital beds: 33.0 per 10,000 population; Hospital admissions: 770.3 per 10,000 population

Transportation: Commute: 83.4% car, 0.5% public transportation, 9.6% walk, 4.4% work from home; Median travel time to work: 14.7 minutes
Presidential Election: 44.1% Obama, 54.3% Romney (2012)
National and State Parks: Baraga State Forest; Keweenaw National Historical Park; McLain State Park
Additional Information Contacts
Houghton Government . . . . (906) 482-1150
  http://www.houghtoncounty.net

Houghton County Communities

ADAMS (township). Covers a land area of 47.050 square miles and a water area of 0.508 square miles. Located at 47.06° N. Lat; 88.68° W. Long. Elevation is 1,299 feet.
Population: 2,573; Growth (since 2000): -6.3%; Density: 54.7 persons per square mile; Race: 97.1% White, 0.2% Black/African American, 0.6% Asian, 0.6% American Indian/Alaska Native, 0.0% Native Hawaiian/Other Pacific Islander, 1.5% Two or more races, 0.7% Hispanic of any race; Average household size: 2.49; Median age: 35.3; Age under 18: 26.8%; Age 65 and over: 14.7%; Males per 100 females: 108.7; Marriage status: 32.2% never married, 55.2% now married, 1.8% separated, 4.4% widowed, 8.2% divorced; Foreign born: 1.6%; Speak English only: 95.9%; With disability: 16.7%; Veterans: 14.2%; Ancestry: 49.9% Finnish, 10.6% German, 9.3% American, 7.9% English, 6.9% Italian
Employment: 7.6% management, business, and financial, 2.4% computer, engineering, and science, 6.4% education, legal, community service, arts, and media, 5.2% healthcare practitioners, 27.6% service, 28.3% sales and office, 10.0% natural resources, construction, and maintenance, 12.5% production, transportation, and material moving
Income: Per capita: $17,980; Median household: $39,508; Average household: $47,909; Households with income of $100,000 or more: 7.1%; Poverty rate: 13.3%
Educational Attainment: High school diploma or higher: 86.0%; Bachelor's degree or higher: 15.0%; Graduate/professional degree or higher: 3.9%
Housing: Homeownership rate: 81.0%; Median home value: $72,500; Median year structure built: Before 1940; Homeowner vacancy rate: 2.0%; Median gross rent: $465 per month; Rental vacancy rate: 5.6%
Health Insurance: 91.5% have insurance; 68.0% have private insurance; 40.4% have public insurance; 8.5% do not have insurance; 1.4% of children under 18 do not have insurance
Transportation: Commute: 99.3% car, 0.0% public transportation, 0.0% walk, 0.7% work from home; Median travel time to work: 13.8 minutes

ATLANTIC MINE (unincorporated postal area)
ZCTA: 49905
  Covers a land area of 59.342 square miles and a water area of 12.040 square miles. Located at 47.12° N. Lat; 88.72° W. Long. Elevation is 1,050 feet.
  Population: 2,005; Growth (since 2000): 24.3%; Density: 33.8 persons per square mile; Race: 98.0% White, 0.3% Black/African American, 0.3% Asian, 0.8% American Indian/Alaska Native, 0.0% Native Hawaiian/Other Pacific Islander, 0.5% Two or more races, 0.7% Hispanic of any race; Average household size: 2.91; Median age: 30.4; Age under 18: 33.7%; Age 65 and over: 8.5%; Males per 100 females: 108.4
                    School District(s)
Stanton Township Public Schools (KG-12)
  2012-13 Enrollment: 152. . . . . (906) 482-2797
  Housing: Homeownership rate: 87.1%; Homeowner vacancy rate: 1.6%; Rental vacancy rate: 1.1%

CALUMET (charter township). Covers a land area of 33.160 square miles and a water area of 0.125 square miles. Located at 47.26° N. Lat; 88.44° W. Long. Elevation is 1,214 feet.
History: Village grew after development of Calumet and Hecla copper mine here in 1860s. Incorporated 1875 as Red Jacket, renamed 1929.
Population: 6,489; Growth (since 2000): -7.3%; Density: 195.7 persons per square mile; Race: 97.0% White, 0.3% Black/African American, 0.2% Asian, 0.7% American Indian/Alaska Native, 0.0% Native Hawaiian/Other Pacific Islander, 1.5% Two or more races, 1.2% Hispanic of any race; Average household size: 2.38; Median age: 39.5; Age under 18: 26.1%; Age 65 and over: 16.6%; Males per 100 females: 100.6; Marriage status: 32.8% never married, 47.5% now married, 0.6% separated, 8.6% widowed, 11.1% divorced; Foreign born: 1.4%; Speak English only: 94.3%;

With disability: 15.7%; Veterans: 13.5%; Ancestry: 36.8% Finnish, 17.1% German, 11.5% English, 9.9% French, 7.5% Irish
Employment: 6.4% management, business, and financial, 4.3% computer, engineering, and science, 9.8% education, legal, community service, arts, and media, 5.5% healthcare practitioners, 32.4% service, 18.6% sales and office, 10.4% natural resources, construction, and maintenance, 12.5% production, transportation, and material moving
Income: Per capita: $17,149; Median household: $32,073; Average household: $40,956; Households with income of $100,000 or more: 5.0%; Poverty rate: 21.4%
Educational Attainment: High school diploma or higher: 85.8%; Bachelor's degree or higher: 19.1%; Graduate/professional degree or higher: 5.6%
School District(s)
Public Schools of Calumet (KG-12)
    2012-13 Enrollment: 1,459 . . . . (906) 337-0311
Housing: Homeownership rate: 74.2%; Median home value: $60,800; Median year structure built: Before 1940; Homeowner vacancy rate: 4.4%; Median gross rent: $548 per month; Rental vacancy rate: 8.7%
Health Insurance: 84.9% have insurance; 56.8% have private insurance; 46.5% have public insurance; 15.1% do not have insurance; 3.4% of children under 18 do not have insurance
Transportation: Commute: 87.4% car, 0.2% public transportation, 8.8% walk, 2.7% work from home; Median travel time to work: 16.9 minutes

CALUMET (village). Covers a land area of 0.197 square miles and a water area of 0 square miles. Located at 47.25° N. Lat; 88.45° W. Long. Elevation is 1,214 feet.
History: Calumet developed as a company town for the Calumet and Hecla Consolidated Copper Company, formed in 1871 from the consolidation of two smaller companies. The name of Calumet refers to the clay stone bowl of a peace pipe.
Population: 726; Growth (since 2000): -17.4%; Density: 3,691.6 persons per square mile; Race: 96.8% White, 0.4% Black/African American, 0.3% Asian, 0.4% American Indian/Alaska Native, 0.0% Native Hawaiian/Other Pacific Islander, 1.8% Two or more races, 2.5% Hispanic of any race; Average household size: 1.93; Median age: 40.4; Age under 18: 20.4%; Age 65 and over: 18.2%; Males per 100 females: 97.3
School District(s)
Public Schools of Calumet (KG-12)
    2012-13 Enrollment: 1,459 . . . . (906) 337-0311
Housing: Homeownership rate: 28.2%; Homeowner vacancy rate: 11.7%; Rental vacancy rate: 10.2%
Safety: Violent crime rate: 55.9 per 10,000 population; Property crime rate: 153.6 per 10,000 population

CHASSELL (township). Covers a land area of 48.328 square miles and a water area of 3.443 square miles. Located at 46.99° N. Lat; 88.53° W. Long. Elevation is 620 feet.
History: Chassell was named for its founder, a French farmer named John Chassell.
Population: 1,812; Growth (since 2000): -0.5%; Density: 37.5 persons per square mile; Race: 97.9% White, 0.2% Black/African American, 0.4% Asian, 0.4% American Indian/Alaska Native, 0.0% Native Hawaiian/Other Pacific Islander, 1.0% Two or more races, 0.6% Hispanic of any race; Average household size: 2.39; Median age: 43.4; Age under 18: 24.2%; Age 65 and over: 18.7%; Males per 100 females: 100.2
School District(s)
Chassell Township SD (KG-12)
    2012-13 Enrollment: 268. . . . . (906) 523-4691
Housing: Homeownership rate: 84.3%; Homeowner vacancy rate: 1.1%; Rental vacancy rate: 9.1%

COPPER CITY (village). Covers a land area of 0.084 square miles and a water area of 0 square miles. Located at 47.28° N. Lat; 88.39° W. Long. Elevation is 876 feet.
History: Copper City was established as a station on the rail line, in a copper mining region. It was incorporated in 1917.
Population: 190; Growth (since 2000): -7.3%; Density: 2,254.8 persons per square mile; Race: 97.4% White, 0.0% Black/African American, 0.0% Asian, 0.0% American Indian/Alaska Native, 0.0% Native Hawaiian/Other Pacific Islander, 2.6% Two or more races, 0.5% Hispanic of any race; Average household size: 2.38; Median age: 43.0; Age under 18: 26.8%; Age 65 and over: 17.9%; Males per 100 females: 100.0

Housing: Homeownership rate: 83.8%; Homeowner vacancy rate: 5.6%; Rental vacancy rate: 7.1%

DODGEVILLE (unincorporated postal area)
ZCTA: 49921
    Covers a land area of 0.406 square miles and a water area of 0.002 square miles. Located at 47.09° N. Lat; 88.58° W. Long. Elevation is 984 feet.
    Population: 360; Growth (since 2000): -12.8%; Density: 887.7 persons per square mile; Race: 95.8% White, 0.6% Black/African American, 0.6% Asian, 0.0% American Indian/Alaska Native, 0.0% Native Hawaiian/Other Pacific Islander, 2.2% Two or more races, 2.2% Hispanic of any race; Average household size: 2.42; Median age: 30.8; Age under 18: 18.1%; Age 65 and over: 10.3%; Males per 100 females: 157.1
    Housing: Homeownership rate: 74.5%; Homeowner vacancy rate: 0.0%; Rental vacancy rate: 11.6%

DOLLAR BAY (CDP). Covers a land area of 4.073 square miles and a water area of 0.558 square miles. Located at 47.13° N. Lat; 88.51° W. Long. Elevation is 627 feet.
Population: 1,082; Growth (since 2000): n/a; Density: 265.7 persons per square mile; Race: 97.5% White, 0.2% Black/African American, 0.8% Asian, 0.6% American Indian/Alaska Native, 0.0% Native Hawaiian/Other Pacific Islander, 0.9% Two or more races, 0.4% Hispanic of any race; Average household size: 2.54; Median age: 37.7; Age under 18: 28.3%; Age 65 and over: 15.3%; Males per 100 females: 101.9
School District(s)
Dollar Bay-Tamarack City Area Schools (KG-12)
    2012-13 Enrollment: 306. . . . . (906) 482-5800
Housing: Homeownership rate: 79.1%; Homeowner vacancy rate: 1.7%; Rental vacancy rate: 6.3%

DUNCAN (township). Covers a land area of 176.112 square miles and a water area of 1.551 square miles. Located at 46.52° N. Lat; 88.81° W. Long.
Population: 236; Growth (since 2000): -15.7%; Density: 1.3 persons per square mile; Race: 98.3% White, 0.0% Black/African American, 0.4% Asian, 1.3% American Indian/Alaska Native, 0.0% Native Hawaiian/Other Pacific Islander, 0.0% Two or more races, 0.0% Hispanic of any race; Average household size: 1.89; Median age: 56.0; Age under 18: 9.7%; Age 65 and over: 35.2%; Males per 100 females: 101.7
Housing: Homeownership rate: 92.8%; Homeowner vacancy rate: 5.7%; Rental vacancy rate: 9.1%

ELM RIVER (township). Covers a land area of 91.263 square miles and a water area of 1.991 square miles. Located at 46.89° N. Lat; 88.84° W. Long.
Population: 177; Growth (since 2000): 4.7%; Density: 1.9 persons per square mile; Race: 98.9% White, 0.0% Black/African American, 0.0% Asian, 0.6% American Indian/Alaska Native, 0.0% Native Hawaiian/Other Pacific Islander, 0.6% Two or more races, 0.0% Hispanic of any race; Average household size: 2.21; Median age: 54.8; Age under 18: 11.9%; Age 65 and over: 24.9%; Males per 100 females: 118.5
Housing: Homeownership rate: 95.0%; Homeowner vacancy rate: 3.8%; Rental vacancy rate: 44.4%

FRANKLIN (township). Covers a land area of 19.859 square miles and a water area of 0.740 square miles. Located at 47.16° N. Lat; 88.53° W. Long. Elevation is 1,135 feet.
Population: 1,466; Growth (since 2000): 11.1%; Density: 73.8 persons per square mile; Race: 97.7% White, 0.1% Black/African American, 0.3% Asian, 0.3% American Indian/Alaska Native, 0.0% Native Hawaiian/Other Pacific Islander, 1.6% Two or more races, 0.8% Hispanic of any race; Average household size: 2.68; Median age: 31.7; Age under 18: 30.5%; Age 65 and over: 10.4%; Males per 100 females: 108.8
Housing: Homeownership rate: 80.6%; Homeowner vacancy rate: 2.0%; Rental vacancy rate: 3.6%

HANCOCK (city). Covers a land area of 2.598 square miles and a water area of 0.373 square miles. Located at 47.13° N. Lat; 88.60° W. Long. Elevation is 692 feet.
History: Hancock was named for the patriot John Hancock, a signer of the Declaration of Independence. It developed as a copper mining center, with

the Quincy Copper Mine opening in 1848. Suomi College was founded here in 1899 by the Finnish Evangelical Lutheran Church.
Population: 4,634; Growth (since 2000): 7.2%; Density: 1,783.8 persons per square mile; Race: 94.7% White, 1.2% Black/African American, 1.7% Asian, 1.0% American Indian/Alaska Native, 0.1% Native Hawaiian/Other Pacific Islander, 1.3% Two or more races, 1.4% Hispanic of any race; Average household size: 2.20; Median age: 34.1; Age under 18: 16.7%; Age 65 and over: 19.3%; Males per 100 females: 98.0; Marriage status: 38.8% never married, 36.5% now married, 1.1% separated, 12.5% widowed, 12.1% divorced; Foreign born: 3.4%; Speak English only: 94.0%; With disability: 11.5%; Veterans: 13.8%; Ancestry: 29.6% Finnish, 24.1% German, 11.7% English, 11.6% French, 8.0% Irish
Employment: 12.3% management, business, and financial, 7.5% computer, engineering, and science, 16.4% education, legal, community service, arts, and media, 5.6% healthcare practitioners, 25.6% service, 23.3% sales and office, 2.3% natural resources, construction, and maintenance, 7.0% production, transportation, and material moving
Income: Per capita: $22,528; Median household: $27,873; Average household: $45,753; Households with income of $100,000 or more: 13.6%; Poverty rate: 25.6%
Educational Attainment: High school diploma or higher: 90.3%; Bachelor's degree or higher: 36.9%; Graduate/professional degree or higher: 12.8%

School District(s)
Copper Country ISD (PK-12)
    2012-13 Enrollment: 283 . . . . (906) 482-4250
Dollar Bay-Tamarack City Area Schools (KG-12)
    2012-13 Enrollment: 306 . . . . (906) 482-5800
Hancock Public Schools (KG-12)
    2012-13 Enrollment: 818 . . . . (906) 487-5925
Four-year College(s)
Finlandia University (Private, Not-for-profit, Evangelical Lutheran Church)
    Fall 2013 Enrollment: 525 . . . . (906) 482-5300
    2013-14 Tuition: In-state $20,480; Out-of-state $20,480
Housing: Homeownership rate: 53.9%; Median home value: $100,000; Median year structure built: 1941; Homeowner vacancy rate: 4.0%; Median gross rent: $554 per month; Rental vacancy rate: 5.3%
Health Insurance: 89.0% have insurance; 74.4% have private insurance; 29.9% have public insurance; 11.0% do not have insurance; 1.5% of children under 18 do not have insurance
Hospitals: Portage Health (74 beds)
Safety: Violent crime rate: 8.7 per 10,000 population; Property crime rate: 95.4 per 10,000 population
Transportation: Commute: 82.7% car, 0.4% public transportation, 7.0% walk, 7.2% work from home; Median travel time to work: 10.5 minutes; Amtrak: Bus service available.
Airports: Houghton County Memorial (primary service/non-hub)

HANCOCK (township). Covers a land area of 15.889 square miles and a water area of 1.005 square miles. Located at 47.20° N. Lat; 88.59° W. Long. Elevation is 692 feet.
History: Seat of Suomi College. Historic Arcadian Copper Mines (tours). Plotted 1859; incorporated as village 1875, as city 1903.
Population: 461; Growth (since 2000): 13.0%; Density: 29.0 persons per square mile; Race: 99.3% White, 0.0% Black/African American, 0.2% Asian, 0.0% American Indian/Alaska Native, 0.0% Native Hawaiian/Other Pacific Islander, 0.2% Two or more races, 0.4% Hispanic of any race; Average household size: 2.79; Median age: 40.3; Age under 18: 32.3%; Age 65 and over: 15.4%; Males per 100 females: 96.2
School District(s)
Copper Country ISD (PK-12)
    2012-13 Enrollment: 283 . . . . (906) 482-4250
Dollar Bay-Tamarack City Area Schools (KG-12)
    2012-13 Enrollment: 306 . . . . (906) 482-5800
Hancock Public Schools (KG-12)
    2012-13 Enrollment: 818 . . . . (906) 487-5925
Four-year College(s)
Finlandia University (Private, Not-for-profit, Evangelical Lutheran Church)
    Fall 2013 Enrollment: 525 . . . . (906) 482-5300
    2013-14 Tuition: In-state $20,480; Out-of-state $20,480
Housing: Homeownership rate: 94.0%; Homeowner vacancy rate: 1.3%; Rental vacancy rate: 0.0%
Hospitals: Portage Health (74 beds)
Airports: Houghton County Memorial (primary service/non-hub)

HOUGHTON (city). County seat. Covers a land area of 4.445 square miles and a water area of 0.236 square miles. Located at 47.11° N. Lat; 88.57° W. Long. Elevation is 643 feet.
History: Houghton was founded in 1852 and named for Douglass Houghton, a geologist. The town became a copper center, and later a governmental and business center. The Michigan College of Mining and Technology was founded here.
Population: 7,708; Growth (since 2000): 10.0%; Density: 1,734.1 persons per square mile; Race: 85.2% White, 1.0% Black/African American, 11.2% Asian, 0.4% American Indian/Alaska Native, 0.1% Native Hawaiian/Other Pacific Islander, 1.8% Two or more races, 1.8% Hispanic of any race; Average household size: 2.37; Median age: 22.1; Age under 18: 10.1%; Age 65 and over: 7.0%; Males per 100 females: 179.9; Marriage status: 67.2% never married, 24.7% now married, 0.3% separated, 2.9% widowed, 5.2% divorced; Foreign born: 13.7%; Speak English only: 85.5%; With disability: 7.9%; Veterans: 3.8%; Ancestry: 24.4% German, 13.0% Irish, 11.1% Finnish, 9.1% English, 6.6% French
Employment: 10.3% management, business, and financial, 11.6% computer, engineering, and science, 25.5% education, legal, community service, arts, and media, 3.4% healthcare practitioners, 21.9% service, 17.3% sales and office, 5.9% natural resources, construction, and maintenance, 4.1% production, transportation, and material moving
Income: Per capita: $16,810; Median household: $27,661; Average household: $50,431; Households with income of $100,000 or more: 14.5%; Poverty rate: 42.1%
Educational Attainment: High school diploma or higher: 93.5%; Bachelor's degree or higher: 50.8%; Graduate/professional degree or higher: 28.5%

School District(s)
Houghton-Portage Township SD (KG-12)
    2012-13 Enrollment: 1,373 . . . . (906) 482-0451
Four-year College(s)
Michigan Technological University (Public)
    Fall 2013 Enrollment: 6,975 . . . . (906) 487-1885
    2013-14 Tuition: In-state $13,728; Out-of-state $28,608
Housing: Homeownership rate: 34.3%; Median home value: $127,900; Median year structure built: 1972; Homeowner vacancy rate: 2.9%; Median gross rent: $647 per month; Rental vacancy rate: 2.1%
Health Insurance: 90.7% have insurance; 82.4% have private insurance; 18.1% have public insurance; 9.3% do not have insurance; 3.6% of children under 18 do not have insurance
Safety: Violent crime rate: 10.4 per 10,000 population; Property crime rate: 144.2 per 10,000 population
Newspapers: Daily Mining Gazette (daily circulation 9500)
Transportation: Commute: 61.9% car, 1.3% public transportation, 29.3% walk, 3.1% work from home; Median travel time to work: 10.3 minutes; Amtrak: Bus service available.
Additional Information Contacts
City of Houghton . . . . (906) 482-1700
    http://www.cityofhoughton.com

HUBBELL (CDP). Covers a land area of 1.867 square miles and a water area of 0.011 square miles. Located at 47.18° N. Lat; 88.44° W. Long. Elevation is 627 feet.
History: The community of Hubbell, which began with a sawmill, developed around the Calumet and Hecla Smelting Works.
Population: 946; Growth (since 2000): -14.4%; Density: 506.6 persons per square mile; Race: 98.2% White, 0.0% Black/African American, 1.1% Asian, 0.2% American Indian/Alaska Native, 0.0% Native Hawaiian/Other Pacific Islander, 0.5% Two or more races, 0.6% Hispanic of any race; Average household size: 2.26; Median age: 46.9; Age under 18: 18.6%; Age 65 and over: 20.4%; Males per 100 females: 93.5
Housing: Homeownership rate: 87.3%; Homeowner vacancy rate: 4.0%; Rental vacancy rate: 2.0%

KEARSARGE (unincorporated postal area)
ZCTA: 49942
    Covers a land area of 1.020 square miles and a water area of 0.007 square miles. Located at 47.27° N. Lat; 88.41° W. Long. Elevation is 1,122 feet.
    Population: 156; Growth (since 2000): -37.6%; Density: 153.0 persons per square mile; Race: 98.7% White, 0.0% Black/African American, 0.6% Asian, 0.0% American Indian/Alaska Native, 0.0% Native Hawaiian/Other Pacific Islander, 0.6% Two or more races, 1.3% Hispanic of any race; Average household size: 2.29; Median age: 40.5;

Age under 18: 25.6%; Age 65 and over: 20.5%; Males per 100 females: 88.0

Housing: Homeownership rate: 91.2%; Homeowner vacancy rate: 3.1%; Rental vacancy rate: 0.0%

LAIRD (township). Covers a land area of 187.297 square miles and a water area of 2.079 square miles. Located at 46.70° N. Lat; 88.79° W. Long.

Population: 555; Growth (since 2000): -12.5%; Density: 3.0 persons per square mile; Race: 97.5% White, 0.0% Black/African American, 0.4% Asian, 0.9% American Indian/Alaska Native, 0.0% Native Hawaiian/Other Pacific Islander, 1.3% Two or more races, 0.4% Hispanic of any race; Average household size: 2.27; Median age: 44.4; Age under 18: 21.1%; Age 65 and over: 15.7%; Males per 100 females: 120.2

Housing: Homeownership rate: 87.7%; Homeowner vacancy rate: 0.9%; Rental vacancy rate: 0.0%

LAKE LINDEN (village). Covers a land area of 0.771 square miles and a water area of 0.117 square miles. Located at 47.20° N. Lat; 88.41° W. Long. Elevation is 617 feet.

History: First settled in 1851, the community of Lake Linden grew up around the Calumet and Hecla Stamping Mills located here in 1867. The town was named for the linden trees that lined the lake shore.

Population: 1,007; Growth (since 2000): -6.8%; Density: 1,306.0 persons per square mile; Race: 97.4% White, 0.0% Black/African American, 0.2% Asian, 0.7% American Indian/Alaska Native, 0.0% Native Hawaiian/Other Pacific Islander, 1.5% Two or more races, 0.8% Hispanic of any race; Average household size: 2.07; Median age: 44.1; Age under 18: 21.4%; Age 65 and over: 23.4%; Males per 100 females: 104.3

School District(s)

Lake Linden-Hubbell SD (PK-12)
    2012-13 Enrollment: 508 . . . . (906) 296-6211

Housing: Homeownership rate: 66.3%; Homeowner vacancy rate: 3.6%; Rental vacancy rate: 6.8%

Safety: Violent crime rate: 10.0 per 10,000 population; Property crime rate: 129.9 per 10,000 population

Additional Information Contacts

Village of Lake Linden . . . . (906) 296-9911
    http://www.lakelinden.net

LAURIUM (village). Covers a land area of 0.651 square miles and a water area of 0 square miles. Located at 47.24° N. Lat; 88.44° W. Long. Elevation is 1,237 feet.

History: Laurium was platted by the Laurium Mining Company and developed as a residential area for workers in Calumet. Notre Dame University football player George Gipp was a native of Laurium.

Population: 1,977; Growth (since 2000): -7.0%; Density: 3,036.5 persons per square mile; Race: 96.6% White, 0.7% Black/African American, 0.1% Asian, 0.7% American Indian/Alaska Native, 0.0% Native Hawaiian/Other Pacific Islander, 1.5% Two or more races, 1.2% Hispanic of any race; Average household size: 2.43; Median age: 38.1; Age under 18: 27.3%; Age 65 and over: 15.4%; Males per 100 females: 98.7

Housing: Homeownership rate: 73.3%; Homeowner vacancy rate: 5.5%; Rental vacancy rate: 7.6%

Hospitals: Aspirus Keweenaw Hospital

Safety: Violent crime rate: 5.1 per 10,000 population; Property crime rate: 122.3 per 10,000 population

NISULA (unincorporated postal area)
ZCTA: 49952

Covers a land area of 65.777 square miles and a water area of 1.361 square miles. Located at 46.70° N. Lat; 88.79° W. Long. Elevation is 1,043 feet.

Population: 143; Growth (since 2000): 95.9%; Density: 2.2 persons per square mile; Race: 95.1% White, 0.0% Black/African American, 0.0% Asian, 3.5% American Indian/Alaska Native, 0.0% Native Hawaiian/Other Pacific Islander, 1.4% Two or more races, 1.4% Hispanic of any race; Average household size: 2.17; Median age: 45.6; Age under 18: 18.9%; Age 65 and over: 18.2%; Males per 100 females: 134.4

Housing: Homeownership rate: 90.9%; Homeowner vacancy rate: 0.0%; Rental vacancy rate: 0.0%

OSCEOLA (township). Covers a land area of 24.819 square miles and a water area of 1.164 square miles. Located at 47.19° N. Lat; 88.48° W. Long. Elevation is 1,224 feet.

History: Osceola grew up around the Osceola Mine, a unit of the Calumet and Hecla Consolidated Copper Company.

Population: 1,888; Growth (since 2000): -1.0%; Density: 76.1 persons per square mile; Race: 96.9% White, 1.0% Black/African American, 0.7% Asian, 0.3% American Indian/Alaska Native, 0.0% Native Hawaiian/Other Pacific Islander, 1.1% Two or more races, 0.7% Hispanic of any race; Average household size: 2.47; Median age: 40.8; Age under 18: 26.7%; Age 65 and over: 15.3%; Males per 100 females: 105.9

Housing: Homeownership rate: 83.9%; Homeowner vacancy rate: 1.9%; Rental vacancy rate: 5.3%

PAINESDALE (unincorporated postal area)
ZCTA: 49955

Covers a land area of 11.331 square miles and a water area of 0.091 square miles. Located at 47.01° N. Lat; 88.69° W. Long. Elevation is 1,299 feet.

Population: 371; Growth (since 2000): -45.8%; Density: 32.7 persons per square mile; Race: 98.1% White, 0.0% Black/African American, 0.3% Asian, 0.3% American Indian/Alaska Native, 0.0% Native Hawaiian/Other Pacific Islander, 1.3% Two or more races, 0.0% Hispanic of any race; Average household size: 2.49; Median age: 38.1; Age under 18: 25.9%; Age 65 and over: 18.1%; Males per 100 females: 115.7

School District(s)

Adams Township SD (KG-12)
    2012-13 Enrollment: 447 . . . . (906) 482-0599

Housing: Homeownership rate: 90.0%; Homeowner vacancy rate: 6.3%; Rental vacancy rate: 11.8%

PELKIE (unincorporated postal area)
ZCTA: 49958

Covers a land area of 121.192 square miles and a water area of 5.101 square miles. Located at 46.83° N. Lat; 88.67° W. Long..

Population: 1,270; Growth (since 2000): -1.2%; Density: 10.5 persons per square mile; Race: 96.3% White, 0.1% Black/African American, 0.2% Asian, 1.8% American Indian/Alaska Native, 0.1% Native Hawaiian/Other Pacific Islander, 1.3% Two or more races, 0.2% Hispanic of any race; Average household size: 2.29; Median age: 47.0; Age under 18: 19.8%; Age 65 and over: 17.1%; Males per 100 females: 119.3

School District(s)

Baraga Area Schools (KG-12)
    2012-13 Enrollment: 493 . . . . (906) 353-6664

Housing: Homeownership rate: 87.8%; Homeowner vacancy rate: 2.8%; Rental vacancy rate: 8.1%

PORTAGE (charter township). Covers a land area of 112.087 square miles and a water area of 4.486 square miles. Located at 46.97° N. Lat; 88.64° W. Long.

Population: 3,221; Growth (since 2000): 2.1%; Density: 28.7 persons per square mile; Race: 96.1% White, 0.4% Black/African American, 1.1% Asian, 0.7% American Indian/Alaska Native, 0.2% Native Hawaiian/Other Pacific Islander, 1.2% Two or more races, 1.1% Hispanic of any race; Average household size: 2.43; Median age: 37.7; Age under 18: 20.5%; Age 65 and over: 14.1%; Males per 100 females: 129.9; Marriage status: 36.2% never married, 50.8% now married, 0.3% separated, 5.3% widowed, 7.7% divorced; Foreign born: 5.7%; Speak English only: 93.4%; With disability: 11.7%; Veterans: 6.6%; Ancestry: 25.7% Finnish, 22.3% German, 10.7% English, 9.6% Irish, 9.3% French

Employment: 15.7% management, business, and financial, 8.7% computer, engineering, and science, 16.8% education, legal, community service, arts, and media, 6.9% healthcare practitioners, 28.2% service, 15.0% sales and office, 4.2% natural resources, construction, and maintenance, 4.6% production, transportation, and material moving

Income: Per capita: $23,448; Median household: $50,156; Average household: $65,207; Households with income of $100,000 or more: 23.4%; Poverty rate: 24.8%

Educational Attainment: High school diploma or higher: 97.3%; Bachelor's degree or higher: 41.3%; Graduate/professional degree or higher: 12.9%

Housing: Homeownership rate: 75.3%; Median home value: $134,300; Median year structure built: 1967; Homeowner vacancy rate: 1.6%; Median gross rent: $779 per month; Rental vacancy rate: 11.2%
Health Insurance: 91.1% have insurance; 77.1% have private insurance; 26.2% have public insurance; 8.9% do not have insurance; 0.0% of children under 18 do not have insurance
Transportation: Commute: 87.4% car, 0.4% public transportation, 2.0% walk, 7.3% work from home; Median travel time to work: 14.3 minutes

QUINCY (township). Covers a land area of 3.823 square miles and a water area of 0 square miles. Located at 47.16° N. Lat; 88.59° W. Long.
Population: 270; Growth (since 2000): 7.6%; Density: 70.6 persons per square mile; Race: 99.3% White, 0.4% Black/African American, 0.0% Asian, 0.0% American Indian/Alaska Native, 0.4% Native Hawaiian/Other Pacific Islander, 0.0% Two or more races, 0.7% Hispanic of any race; Average household size: 2.33; Median age: 40.0; Age under 18: 16.3%; Age 65 and over: 14.4%; Males per 100 females: 116.0
Housing: Homeownership rate: 76.8%; Homeowner vacancy rate: 1.1%; Rental vacancy rate: 7.1%

SCHOOLCRAFT (township). Covers a land area of 40.121 square miles and a water area of 0.727 square miles. Located at 47.20° N. Lat; 88.29° W. Long.
Population: 1,839; Growth (since 2000): -1.3%; Density: 45.8 persons per square mile; Race: 97.6% White, 0.1% Black/African American, 0.3% Asian, 0.5% American Indian/Alaska Native, 0.1% Native Hawaiian/Other Pacific Islander, 1.3% Two or more races, 0.8% Hispanic of any race; Average household size: 2.27; Median age: 43.7; Age under 18: 23.4%; Age 65 and over: 20.7%; Males per 100 females: 105.5
Housing: Homeownership rate: 77.2%; Homeowner vacancy rate: 2.3%; Rental vacancy rate: 6.5%

SIDNAW (unincorporated postal area)
ZCTA: 49961
Covers a land area of 59.989 square miles and a water area of 0.680 square miles. Located at 46.52° N. Lat; 88.73° W. Long. Elevation is 1,368 feet.
Population: 107; Growth (since 2000): -24.1%; Density: 1.8 persons per square mile; Race: 100.0% White, 0.0% Black/African American, 0.0% Asian, 0.0% American Indian/Alaska Native, 0.0% Native Hawaiian/Other Pacific Islander, 0.0% Two or more races, 0.0% Hispanic of any race; Average household size: 1.91; Median age: 60.2; Age under 18: 13.1%; Age 65 and over: 41.1%; Males per 100 females: 94.5
Housing: Homeownership rate: 92.8%; Homeowner vacancy rate: 1.9%; Rental vacancy rate: 0.0%

SOUTH RANGE (village). Covers a land area of 0.363 square miles and a water area of 0 square miles. Located at 47.07° N. Lat; 88.64° W. Long. Elevation is 1,138 feet.
History: South Range was founded by the Whealkate Mining Company in 1902, and grew as an ore-shipping point on the Copper Range Railroad. Many of the early residents of South Range were of Italian heritage.
Population: 758; Growth (since 2000): 4.3%; Density: 2,088.1 persons per square mile; Race: 95.9% White, 0.0% Black/African American, 1.2% Asian, 0.4% American Indian/Alaska Native, 0.0% Native Hawaiian/Other Pacific Islander, 2.4% Two or more races, 1.1% Hispanic of any race; Average household size: 2.19; Median age: 40.2; Age under 18: 23.4%; Age 65 and over: 19.7%; Males per 100 females: 108.2
School District(s)
Adams Township SD (KG-12)
    2012-13 Enrollment: 447 . . . . (906) 482-0599
Housing: Homeownership rate: 69.3%; Homeowner vacancy rate: 0.8%; Rental vacancy rate: 7.5%

STANTON (township). Covers a land area of 122.382 square miles and a water area of 1.325 square miles. Located at 47.09° N. Lat; 88.78° W. Long.
Population: 1,419; Growth (since 2000): 11.9%; Density: 11.6 persons per square mile; Race: 98.5% White, 0.1% Black/African American, 0.3% Asian, 0.3% American Indian/Alaska Native, 0.0% Native Hawaiian/Other Pacific Islander, 0.8% Two or more races, 0.4% Hispanic of any race; Average household size: 2.73; Median age: 38.1; Age under 18: 30.9%; Age 65 and over: 13.3%; Males per 100 females: 105.4

Housing: Homeownership rate: 91.9%; Homeowner vacancy rate: 2.1%; Rental vacancy rate: 4.5%

TOIVOLA (unincorporated postal area)
ZCTA: 49965
Covers a land area of 207.027 square miles and a water area of 2.380 square miles. Located at 46.95° N. Lat; 88.86° W. Long. Elevation is 1,273 feet.
Population: 440; Growth (since 2000): 0.7%; Density: 2.1 persons per square mile; Race: 97.3% White, 0.2% Black/African American, 0.5% Asian, 0.2% American Indian/Alaska Native, 0.0% Native Hawaiian/Other Pacific Islander, 1.6% Two or more races, 0.9% Hispanic of any race; Average household size: 2.09; Median age: 54.3; Age under 18: 11.6%; Age 65 and over: 24.8%; Males per 100 females: 121.1
School District(s)
Elm River Township SD (KG-12)
    2012-13 Enrollment: 5 . . . . (906) 288-3751
Housing: Homeownership rate: 93.3%; Homeowner vacancy rate: 2.0%; Rental vacancy rate: 28.6%

TORCH LAKE (township). Covers a land area of 79.868 square miles and a water area of 13.056 square miles. Located at 47.10° N. Lat; 88.38° W. Long.
Population: 1,880; Growth (since 2000): 1.1%; Density: 23.5 persons per square mile; Race: 98.5% White, 0.1% Black/African American, 0.5% Asian, 0.4% American Indian/Alaska Native, 0.0% Native Hawaiian/Other Pacific Islander, 0.5% Two or more races, 0.5% Hispanic of any race; Average household size: 2.29; Median age: 50.3; Age under 18: 19.0%; Age 65 and over: 24.3%; Males per 100 females: 103.9
Housing: Homeownership rate: 89.0%; Homeowner vacancy rate: 2.4%; Rental vacancy rate: 2.1%

Huron County

Located in eastern Michigan, at the tip of the Thumb; bounded on the east and north by Lake Huron, and on the west by Saginaw Bay; drained by headwaters of the Cass and by Pigeon and Willow Rivers. Covers a land area of 835.706 square miles, a water area of 1,301.096 square miles, and is located in the Eastern Time Zone at 43.91° N. Lat., 82.86° W. Long. The county was founded in 1840. County seat is Bad Axe.

Weather Station: Bad Axe										Elevation: 714 feet		
	Jan	Feb	Mar	Apr	May	Jun	Jul	Aug	Sep	Oct	Nov	Dec
High	28	31	40	53	66	76	80	78	71	58	45	33
Low	15	15	23	33	43	53	58	57	50	40	31	21
Precip	1.8	1.8	2.0	2.9	3.2	2.9	3.2	3.6	4.0	2.7	2.8	2.1
Snow	12.3	9.7	7.2	2.2	0.1	0.0	0.0	0.0	0.0	0.4	3.4	10.8

High and Low temperatures in degrees Fahrenheit; Precipitation and Snow in inches

Weather Station: Harbor Beach 1 SSE										Elevation: 600 feet		
	Jan	Feb	Mar	Apr	May	Jun	Jul	Aug	Sep	Oct	Nov	Dec
High	29	31	39	50	61	71	77	76	70	57	45	34
Low	15	16	23	33	43	53	59	58	51	40	31	21
Precip	2.5	2.0	2.1	3.0	3.2	2.8	2.8	3.5	4.0	2.9	2.9	2.5
Snow	na	10.4	7.0	2.0	0.1	0.0	0.0	0.0	0.0	0.1	1.7	11.5

High and Low temperatures in degrees Fahrenheit; Precipitation and Snow in inches

Population: 33,118; Growth (since 2000): -8.2%; Density: 39.6 persons per square mile; Race: 97.5% White, 0.4% Black/African American, 0.4% Asian, 0.3% American Indian/Alaska Native, 0.0% Native Hawaiian/Other Pacific Islander, 0.9% two or more races, 2.0% Hispanic of any race; Average household size: 2.27; Median age: 46.8; Age under 18: 20.7%; Age 65 and over: 21.7%; Males per 100 females: 98.5; Marriage status: 23.3% never married, 57.8% now married, 1.1% separated, 8.7% widowed, 10.3% divorced; Foreign born: 1.7%; Speak English only: 96.7%; With disability: 17.1%; Veterans: 10.2%; Ancestry: 44.6% German, 20.0% Polish, 10.0% Irish, 9.0% English, 5.7% French
Religion: Six largest groups: 20.4% Catholicism, 15.8% Lutheran, 7.8% Methodist/Pietist, 1.9% European Free-Church, 1.7% Latter-day Saints, 1.7% Holiness
Economy: Unemployment rate: 5.1%; Leading industries: 16.7% retail trade; 14.1% construction; 11.3% other services (except public administration); Farms: 1,205 totaling 452,370 acres; Company size: 0 employ 1,000 or more persons, 0 employ 500 to 999 persons, 20 employ 100 to 499 persons, 943 employ less than 100 persons; Business

ownership: n/a women-owned, n/a Black-owned, n/a Hispanic-owned, n/a Asian-owned

Employment: 13.2% management, business, and financial, 2.7% computer, engineering, and science, 5.7% education, legal, community service, arts, and media, 6.3% healthcare practitioners, 18.6% service, 20.4% sales and office, 13.6% natural resources, construction, and maintenance, 19.4% production, transportation, and material moving

Income: Per capita: $22,120; Median household: $40,204; Average household: $50,996; Households with income of $100,000 or more: 9.5%; Poverty rate: 15.8%

Educational Attainment: High school diploma or higher: 86.9%; Bachelor's degree or higher: 13.7%; Graduate/professional degree or higher: 4.4%

Housing: Homeownership rate: 81.8%; Median home value: $96,100; Median year structure built: 1965; Homeowner vacancy rate: 3.0%; Median gross rent: $589 per month; Rental vacancy rate: 12.8%

Vital Statistics: Birth rate: 81.9 per 10,000 population; Death rate: 141.8 per 10,000 population; Age-adjusted cancer mortality rate: 181.8 deaths per 100,000 population

Health Insurance: 89.2% have insurance; 69.1% have private insurance; 41.4% have public insurance; 10.8% do not have insurance; 3.8% of children under 18 do not have insurance

Health Care: Physicians: 12.0 per 10,000 population; Hospital beds: 41.3 per 10,000 population; Hospital admissions: 698.0 per 10,000 population

Air Quality Index: 92.9% good, 6.6% moderate, 0.5% unhealthy for sensitive individuals, 0.0% unhealthy (percent of days)

Transportation: Commute: 90.0% car, 0.5% public transportation, 4.1% walk, 4.4% work from home; Median travel time to work: 20.7 minutes

Presidential Election: 42.1% Obama, 56.9% Romney (2012)

National and State Parks: Albert E Sleeper State Park; Port Crescent State Park; Wild Fowl Bay State Park

Additional Information Contacts

Huron Government . . . . (989) 269-9942
http://www.co.huron.mi.us

Huron County Communities

BAD AXE (city). County seat. Covers a land area of 2.262 square miles and a water area of <.001 square miles. Located at 43.80° N. Lat; 83.00° W. Long. Elevation is 758 feet.

History: Local legend says that Bad Axe received its unusual name from a broken axe found on the site when it was surveyed. For a time, mail was delivered to Bad Axe if it had the sketch of a broken axe on the envelope. The village was planned in 1873, incorporated as a village in 1885 and as a city in 1905. For a time in the early 1900's it was known as Huron, but the residents voted back in the name of Bad Axe.

Population: 3,129; Growth (since 2000): -9.6%; Density: 1,383.2 persons per square mile; Race: 95.1% White, 0.8% Black/African American, 1.5% Asian, 0.9% American Indian/Alaska Native, 0.0% Native Hawaiian/Other Pacific Islander, 1.2% Two or more races, 2.4% Hispanic of any race; Average household size: 2.16; Median age: 42.9; Age under 18: 21.3%; Age 65 and over: 20.5%; Males per 100 females: 86.9; Marriage status: 33.7% never married, 40.4% now married, 4.1% separated, 10.9% widowed, 15.1% divorced; Foreign born: 1.7%; Speak English only: 97.0%; With disability: 23.2%; Veterans: 8.2%; Ancestry: 42.7% German, 21.4% Polish, 10.6% English, 9.3% Irish, 6.0% French

Employment: 9.9% management, business, and financial, 3.2% computer, engineering, and science, 4.8% education, legal, community service, arts, and media, 5.7% healthcare practitioners, 21.4% service, 30.2% sales and office, 10.3% natural resources, construction, and maintenance, 14.5% production, transportation, and material moving

Income: Per capita: $18,987; Median household: $29,255; Average household: $41,544; Households with income of $100,000 or more: 8.9%; Poverty rate: 30.1%

Educational Attainment: High school diploma or higher: 84.0%; Bachelor's degree or higher: 14.1%; Graduate/professional degree or higher: 7.0%

School District(s)
Bad Axe Public Schools (KG-12)
    2012-13 Enrollment: 1,118 . . . . (989) 269-9938
Church SD (KG-12)
    2012-13 Enrollment: 24 . . . . (989) 269-7772
Colfax Township S/d #1f (KG-12)
    2012-13 Enrollment: 25 . . . . (989) 269-8853

Huron ISD (PK-12)
    2012-13 Enrollment: 141 . . . . (989) 269-6406
Sigel Township S/d #3f (KG-12)
    2012-13 Enrollment: 7 . . . . (989) 269-8944
Verona Township S/d #1f (KG-12)
    2012-13 Enrollment: 26 . . . . (989) 269-7054

Housing: Homeownership rate: 60.8%; Median home value: $87,900; Median year structure built: 1958; Homeowner vacancy rate: 6.0%; Median gross rent: $579 per month; Rental vacancy rate: 7.7%

Health Insurance: 91.2% have insurance; 56.9% have private insurance; 52.4% have public insurance; 8.8% do not have insurance; 2.4% of children under 18 do not have insurance

Hospitals: Huron Medical Center (64 beds)

Safety: Violent crime rate: 45.9 per 10,000 population; Property crime rate: 196.6 per 10,000 population

Newspapers: Huron Daily Tribune (daily circulation 7000); Newsweekly (weekly circulation 5000)

Transportation: Commute: 89.7% car, 0.5% public transportation, 6.2% walk, 2.6% work from home; Median travel time to work: 13.9 minutes

Airports: Huron County Memorial (general aviation)

BAY PORT (CDP). Covers a land area of 3.347 square miles and a water area of 0.032 square miles. Located at 43.84° N. Lat; 83.37° W. Long. Elevation is 600 feet.

Population: 477; Growth (since 2000): n/a; Density: 142.5 persons per square mile; Race: 98.7% White, 0.4% Black/African American, 0.4% Asian, 0.2% American Indian/Alaska Native, 0.0% Native Hawaiian/Other Pacific Islander, 0.0% Two or more races, 1.9% Hispanic of any race; Average household size: 2.14; Median age: 46.9; Age under 18: 17.0%; Age 65 and over: 19.9%; Males per 100 females: 105.6

Housing: Homeownership rate: 84.3%; Homeowner vacancy rate: 3.6%; Rental vacancy rate: 11.9%

BINGHAM (township). Covers a land area of 35.756 square miles and a water area of 0.109 square miles. Located at 43.72° N. Lat; 82.94° W. Long.

History: Bingham Township was organized in 1863 and named for Governor Kingsley S. Bingham.

Population: 1,709; Growth (since 2000): -2.4%; Density: 47.8 persons per square mile; Race: 98.6% White, 0.3% Black/African American, 0.1% Asian, 0.1% American Indian/Alaska Native, 0.0% Native Hawaiian/Other Pacific Islander, 0.8% Two or more races, 0.7% Hispanic of any race; Average household size: 2.44; Median age: 40.9; Age under 18: 24.9%; Age 65 and over: 16.0%; Males per 100 females: 95.5

Housing: Homeownership rate: 81.6%; Homeowner vacancy rate: 1.2%; Rental vacancy rate: 11.0%

BLOOMFIELD (township). Covers a land area of 35.737 square miles and a water area of 0.231 square miles. Located at 43.90° N. Lat; 82.83° W. Long.

Population: 455; Growth (since 2000): -15.0%; Density: 12.7 persons per square mile; Race: 98.7% White, 0.4% Black/African American, 0.0% Asian, 0.0% American Indian/Alaska Native, 0.0% Native Hawaiian/Other Pacific Islander, 0.9% Two or more races, 3.1% Hispanic of any race; Average household size: 2.43; Median age: 45.4; Age under 18: 22.2%; Age 65 and over: 19.8%; Males per 100 females: 115.6

Housing: Homeownership rate: 86.7%; Homeowner vacancy rate: 0.0%; Rental vacancy rate: 0.0%

BROOKFIELD (township). Covers a land area of 35.492 square miles and a water area of 0 square miles. Located at 43.71° N. Lat; 83.30° W. Long.

History: Brookfield Township was first settled by A.H. Burton, whose home was the location of the first township election in 1868. He named the township for his former home in New York.

Population: 760; Growth (since 2000): -16.8%; Density: 21.4 persons per square mile; Race: 98.2% White, 0.0% Black/African American, 0.1% Asian, 0.1% American Indian/Alaska Native, 0.0% Native Hawaiian/Other Pacific Islander, 1.1% Two or more races, 3.2% Hispanic of any race; Average household size: 2.35; Median age: 44.3; Age under 18: 21.3%; Age 65 and over: 18.3%; Males per 100 females: 99.5

Housing: Homeownership rate: 82.5%; Homeowner vacancy rate: 1.1%; Rental vacancy rate: 14.1%

CASEVILLE (township).
Covers a land area of 13.717 square miles and a water area of 130.631 square miles. Located at 43.91° N. Lat; 83.39° W. Long. Elevation is 600 feet.

History: Caseville Township was named for Leonard Case, who owned land in the area.

Population: 2,570; Growth (since 2000): -5.6%; Density: 187.4 persons per square mile; Race: 98.1% White, 0.1% Black/African American, 0.2% Asian, 0.2% American Indian/Alaska Native, 0.0% Native Hawaiian/Other Pacific Islander, 1.2% Two or more races, 1.7% Hispanic of any race; Average household size: 1.98; Median age: 57.2; Age under 18: 14.2%; Age 65 and over: 33.7%; Males per 100 females: 99.4; Marriage status: 16.6% never married, 68.1% now married, 0.2% separated, 7.5% widowed, 7.9% divorced; Foreign born: 1.1%; Speak English only: 98.1%; With disability: 18.0%; Veterans: 18.6%; Ancestry: 36.7% German, 12.7% Polish, 12.6% English, 10.5% Irish, 7.6% French

Employment: 14.4% management, business, and financial, 2.8% computer, engineering, and science, 6.3% education, legal, community service, arts, and media, 8.2% healthcare practitioners, 22.5% service, 20.2% sales and office, 17.1% natural resources, construction, and maintenance, 8.4% production, transportation, and material moving

Income: Per capita: $26,735; Median household: $45,192; Average household: $58,066; Households with income of $100,000 or more: 12.0%; Poverty rate: 13.7%

Educational Attainment: High school diploma or higher: 94.1%; Bachelor's degree or higher: 19.7%; Graduate/professional degree or higher: 7.5%

School District(s)
Caseville Public Schools (KG-12)
    2012-13 Enrollment: 258 . . . . (989) 856-2940

Housing: Homeownership rate: 83.0%; Median home value: $161,600; Median year structure built: 1976; Homeowner vacancy rate: 5.1%; Median gross rent: $624 per month; Rental vacancy rate: 21.1%

Health Insurance: 91.0% have insurance; 71.5% have private insurance; 55.0% have public insurance; 9.0% do not have insurance; 0.0% of children under 18 do not have insurance

Transportation: Commute: 94.8% car, 0.0% public transportation, 1.6% walk, 3.6% work from home; Median travel time to work: 25.1 minutes

CASEVILLE (city).
Covers a land area of 1.104 square miles and a water area of 0.030 square miles. Located at 43.94° N. Lat; 83.28° W. Long. Elevation is 600 feet.

History: Caseville was first settled in 1836, when it was known as Pigeon River Settlement. Once an industrial center with lake and rail shipping facilities for its salt and iron works, Caseville later became a tourist village, drawing vacationers to the shores of Saginaw Bay.

Population: 777; Growth (since 2000): -12.5%; Density: 703.8 persons per square mile; Race: 97.8% White, 0.4% Black/African American, 0.1% Asian, 0.1% American Indian/Alaska Native, 0.0% Native Hawaiian/Other Pacific Islander, 1.4% Two or more races, 0.9% Hispanic of any race; Average household size: 1.84; Median age: 55.1; Age under 18: 11.3%; Age 65 and over: 28.4%; Males per 100 females: 98.7

School District(s)
Caseville Public Schools (KG-12)
    2012-13 Enrollment: 258 . . . . (989) 856-2940

Housing: Homeownership rate: 66.8%; Homeowner vacancy rate: 4.4%; Rental vacancy rate: 11.3%

Safety: Violent crime rate: 0.0 per 10,000 population; Property crime rate: 317.5 per 10,000 population

CHANDLER (township).
Covers a land area of 35.295 square miles and a water area of 0.104 square miles. Located at 43.90° N. Lat; 83.17° W. Long.

History: Chandler Township was organized in 1880 and named for Zachariah Chandler, a U.S. senator from Michigan.

Population: 472; Growth (since 2000): -5.8%; Density: 13.4 persons per square mile; Race: 97.5% White, 0.8% Black/African American, 0.0% Asian, 0.6% American Indian/Alaska Native, 0.0% Native Hawaiian/Other Pacific Islander, 0.0% Two or more races, 2.1% Hispanic of any race; Average household size: 2.61; Median age: 42.1; Age under 18: 23.7%; Age 65 and over: 13.3%; Males per 100 females: 107.0

Housing: Homeownership rate: 91.1%; Homeowner vacancy rate: 1.2%; Rental vacancy rate: 20.0%

COLFAX (township).
Covers a land area of 34.554 square miles and a water area of 0.294 square miles. Located at 43.81° N. Lat; 83.07° W. Long.

Population: 1,884; Growth (since 2000): -3.6%; Density: 54.5 persons per square mile; Race: 96.7% White, 0.3% Black/African American, 0.9% Asian, 0.3% American Indian/Alaska Native, 0.0% Native Hawaiian/Other Pacific Islander, 1.4% Two or more races, 1.6% Hispanic of any race; Average household size: 2.43; Median age: 45.0; Age under 18: 22.9%; Age 65 and over: 20.8%; Males per 100 females: 86.2

Housing: Homeownership rate: 86.9%; Homeowner vacancy rate: 2.1%; Rental vacancy rate: 8.7%

DWIGHT (township).
Covers a land area of 35.726 square miles and a water area of 0.250 square miles. Located at 43.99° N. Lat; 82.96° W. Long.

Population: 758; Growth (since 2000): -18.5%; Density: 21.2 persons per square mile; Race: 98.0% White, 0.0% Black/African American, 0.3% Asian, 0.0% American Indian/Alaska Native, 0.0% Native Hawaiian/Other Pacific Islander, 0.8% Two or more races, 1.3% Hispanic of any race; Average household size: 2.29; Median age: 44.9; Age under 18: 21.6%; Age 65 and over: 16.2%; Males per 100 females: 108.2

Housing: Homeownership rate: 83.3%; Homeowner vacancy rate: 1.8%; Rental vacancy rate: 8.2%

ELKTON (village).
Covers a land area of 1.001 square miles and a water area of 0 square miles. Located at 43.82° N. Lat; 83.18° W. Long. Elevation is 640 feet.

Population: 808; Growth (since 2000): -6.4%; Density: 807.0 persons per square mile; Race: 96.4% White, 0.1% Black/African American, 0.0% Asian, 0.4% American Indian/Alaska Native, 0.0% Native Hawaiian/Other Pacific Islander, 2.5% Two or more races, 2.5% Hispanic of any race; Average household size: 2.32; Median age: 36.3; Age under 18: 26.1%; Age 65 and over: 15.5%; Males per 100 females: 91.9

Housing: Homeownership rate: 68.2%; Homeowner vacancy rate: 3.6%; Rental vacancy rate: 8.3%

Safety: Violent crime rate: 0.0 per 10,000 population; Property crime rate: 63.3 per 10,000 population

FAIRHAVEN (township).
Covers a land area of 21.498 square miles and a water area of 119.238 square miles. Located at 43.80° N. Lat; 83.47° W. Long. Elevation is 584 feet.

Population: 1,107; Growth (since 2000): -12.1%; Density: 51.5 persons per square mile; Race: 98.2% White, 0.4% Black/African American, 0.2% Asian, 0.8% American Indian/Alaska Native, 0.0% Native Hawaiian/Other Pacific Islander, 0.3% Two or more races, 2.0% Hispanic of any race; Average household size: 2.20; Median age: 46.2; Age under 18: 18.1%; Age 65 and over: 18.9%; Males per 100 females: 110.1

Housing: Homeownership rate: 83.5%; Homeowner vacancy rate: 3.7%; Rental vacancy rate: 11.5%

FILION (unincorporated postal area)
ZCTA: 48432

Covers a land area of 33.387 square miles and a water area of 0.304 square miles. Located at 43.90° N. Lat; 82.97° W. Long. Elevation is 715 feet.

Population: 636; Growth (since 2000): -19.9%; Density: 19.0 persons per square mile; Race: 96.7% White, 0.3% Black/African American, 0.3% Asian, 0.8% American Indian/Alaska Native, 0.0% Native Hawaiian/Other Pacific Islander, 1.3% Two or more races, 3.0% Hispanic of any race; Average household size: 2.36; Median age: 45.8; Age under 18: 22.3%; Age 65 and over: 17.9%; Males per 100 females: 115.6

Housing: Homeownership rate: 93.6%; Homeowner vacancy rate: 1.6%; Rental vacancy rate: 15.0%

GORE (township).
Covers a land area of 6.804 square miles and a water area of 43.113 square miles. Located at 43.95° N. Lat; 82.71° W. Long.

History: Gore Township was organized in 1862 and named for the triangular shape formed by its boundaries.

Population: 144; Growth (since 2000): 3.6%; Density: 21.2 persons per square mile; Race: 97.9% White, 0.0% Black/African American, 0.0% Asian, 2.1% American Indian/Alaska Native, 0.0% Native Hawaiian/Other Pacific Islander, 0.0% Two or more races, 0.7% Hispanic of any race; Average household size: 2.01; Median age: 61.4; Age under 18: 9.0%; Age 65 and over: 35.4%; Males per 100 females: 102.8

Housing: Homeownership rate: 87.1%; Homeowner vacancy rate: 1.6%; Rental vacancy rate: 0.0%

GRANT (township). Covers a land area of 35.352 square miles and a water area of 0.076 square miles. Located at 43.72° N. Lat; 83.17° W. Long.
History: Grant Township was first settled by Levin Williamson in 1863. The township was organized in 1867 and named for General Ulysses S. Grant.
Population: 913; Growth (since 2000): 9.6%; Density: 25.8 persons per square mile; Race: 98.9% White, 0.3% Black/African American, 0.2% Asian, 0.0% American Indian/Alaska Native, 0.0% Native Hawaiian/Other Pacific Islander, 0.1% Two or more races, 2.3% Hispanic of any race; Average household size: 2.74; Median age: 39.9; Age under 18: 28.5%; Age 65 and over: 12.9%; Males per 100 females: 103.8
Housing: Homeownership rate: 90.0%; Homeowner vacancy rate: 1.3%; Rental vacancy rate: 8.3%

HARBOR BEACH (city). Covers a land area of 1.748 square miles and a water area of 0.337 square miles. Located at 43.84° N. Lat; 82.65° W. Long. Elevation is 607 feet.
History: Harbor Beach was founded in 1837. Earlier names of Barnettsville and Sand Beach were replaced in 1889 with Harbor Beach. Harbor Beach had an unusual early industry in the making of counterfeit money, both U.S. currency and Mexican dollars being made here and distributed in large quantities. Later, the town became a resort and commercial fishing center.
Population: 1,703; Growth (since 2000): -7.3%; Density: 974.0 persons per square mile; Race: 96.4% White, 0.2% Black/African American, 1.1% Asian, 0.4% American Indian/Alaska Native, 0.0% Native Hawaiian/Other Pacific Islander, 1.8% Two or more races, 0.6% Hispanic of any race; Average household size: 2.14; Median age: 47.7; Age under 18: 20.4%; Age 65 and over: 22.7%; Males per 100 females: 90.5
School District(s)
Harbor Beach Community Schools (KG-12)
    2012-13 Enrollment: 508........................ (989) 479-3261
Sigel Township S/d #4f (KG-12)
    2012-13 Enrollment: 20......................... (989) 479-9266
Sigel Township S/d #6 (KG-12)
    2012-13 Enrollment: 7.......................... (989) 269-7863
Housing: Homeownership rate: 71.4%; Homeowner vacancy rate: 2.9%; Rental vacancy rate: 15.8%
Hospitals: Harbor Beach Community Hospital (61 beds)
Safety: Violent crime rate: 36.2 per 10,000 population; Property crime rate: 271.2 per 10,000 population

HUME (township). Covers a land area of 29.799 square miles and a water area of 5.445 square miles. Located at 43.98° N. Lat; 83.06° W. Long.
History: Hume Township was organized in 1860 and named for Walter Hume, who had come from Canada to settle here in 1844.
Population: 749; Growth (since 2000): -6.5%; Density: 25.1 persons per square mile; Race: 99.5% White, 0.4% Black/African American, 0.0% Asian, 0.1% American Indian/Alaska Native, 0.0% Native Hawaiian/Other Pacific Islander, 0.0% Two or more races, 1.5% Hispanic of any race; Average household size: 2.07; Median age: 52.3; Age under 18: 15.2%; Age 65 and over: 23.4%; Males per 100 females: 108.1
Housing: Homeownership rate: 90.8%; Homeowner vacancy rate: 4.1%; Rental vacancy rate: 39.3%

HURON (township). Covers a land area of 33.533 square miles and a water area of 2.155 square miles. Located at 43.98° N. Lat; 82.83° W. Long.
Population: 437; Growth (since 2000): 3.3%; Density: 13.0 persons per square mile; Race: 96.3% White, 0.0% Black/African American, 0.0% Asian, 0.5% American Indian/Alaska Native, 0.0% Native Hawaiian/Other Pacific Islander, 0.0% Two or more races, 7.3% Hispanic of any race; Average household size: 2.24; Median age: 54.3; Age under 18: 18.3%; Age 65 and over: 31.4%; Males per 100 females: 109.1
Housing: Homeownership rate: 88.7%; Homeowner vacancy rate: 1.7%; Rental vacancy rate: 0.0%

KINDE (village). Covers a land area of 1.178 square miles and a water area of 0.009 square miles. Located at 43.94° N. Lat; 83.00° W. Long. Elevation is 699 feet.
History: Kinde was established as a station on the Port Huron & Northwestern Railroad in 1884, and was named for storekeeper John Kinde. Many of the early residents of Kinde were of Polish ancestry. The village grew as the center of a farming area.
Population: 448; Growth (since 2000): -16.1%; Density: 380.3 persons per square mile; Race: 96.4% White, 0.0% Black/African American, 0.9% Asian, 1.8% American Indian/Alaska Native, 0.0% Native Hawaiian/Other Pacific Islander, 0.7% Two or more races, 0.9% Hispanic of any race; Average household size: 2.30; Median age: 40.0; Age under 18: 25.2%; Age 65 and over: 18.1%; Males per 100 females: 101.8
School District(s)
North Huron SD (KG-12)
    2012-13 Enrollment: 459........................ (989) 874-4100
Housing: Homeownership rate: 81.6%; Homeowner vacancy rate: 3.6%; Rental vacancy rate: 11.9%
Safety: Violent crime rate: 0.0 per 10,000 population; Property crime rate: 0.0 per 10,000 population

LAKE (township). Covers a land area of 20.506 square miles and a water area of 69.533 square miles. Located at 43.99° N. Lat; 83.17° W. Long.
Population: 855; Growth (since 2000): -14.2%; Density: 41.7 persons per square mile; Race: 98.2% White, 0.0% Black/African American, 0.7% Asian, 0.0% American Indian/Alaska Native, 0.0% Native Hawaiian/Other Pacific Islander, 1.1% Two or more races, 0.2% Hispanic of any race; Average household size: 1.95; Median age: 60.3; Age under 18: 10.3%; Age 65 and over: 39.9%; Males per 100 females: 92.1
Housing: Homeownership rate: 93.4%; Homeowner vacancy rate: 4.0%; Rental vacancy rate: 41.2%

LINCOLN (township). Covers a land area of 35.476 square miles and a water area of 0.319 square miles. Located at 43.91° N. Lat; 82.94° W. Long.
History: Lincoln Township was organized in 1877 and named for Abraham Lincoln.
Population: 807; Growth (since 2000): -7.6%; Density: 22.7 persons per square mile; Race: 97.4% White, 0.1% Black/African American, 0.5% Asian, 1.0% American Indian/Alaska Native, 0.0% Native Hawaiian/Other Pacific Islander, 0.7% Two or more races, 0.6% Hispanic of any race; Average household size: 2.46; Median age: 42.9; Age under 18: 25.4%; Age 65 and over: 18.1%; Males per 100 females: 113.5
Housing: Homeownership rate: 91.1%; Homeowner vacancy rate: 2.0%; Rental vacancy rate: 9.4%

MCKINLEY (township). Covers a land area of 20.178 square miles and a water area of 3.440 square miles. Located at 43.87° N. Lat; 83.29° W. Long.
Population: 445; Growth (since 2000): -11.5%; Density: 22.1 persons per square mile; Race: 98.0% White, 0.0% Black/African American, 0.4% Asian, 0.0% American Indian/Alaska Native, 0.0% Native Hawaiian/Other Pacific Islander, 0.9% Two or more races, 2.9% Hispanic of any race; Average household size: 2.24; Median age: 50.1; Age under 18: 17.5%; Age 65 and over: 24.0%; Males per 100 females: 115.0
Housing: Homeownership rate: 89.9%; Homeowner vacancy rate: 1.6%; Rental vacancy rate: 16.7%

MEADE (township). Covers a land area of 35.639 square miles and a water area of 0.007 square miles. Located at 43.89° N. Lat; 83.07° W. Long.
Population: 720; Growth (since 2000): -9.9%; Density: 20.2 persons per square mile; Race: 97.9% White, 0.1% Black/African American, 0.3% Asian, 0.7% American Indian/Alaska Native, 0.0% Native Hawaiian/Other Pacific Islander, 0.6% Two or more races, 1.8% Hispanic of any race; Average household size: 2.35; Median age: 45.5; Age under 18: 21.7%; Age 65 and over: 16.4%; Males per 100 females: 101.7
Housing: Homeownership rate: 91.2%; Homeowner vacancy rate: 0.7%; Rental vacancy rate: 12.9%

OLIVER (township). Covers a land area of 35.307 square miles and a water area of 0.046 square miles. Located at 43.80° N. Lat; 83.17° W. Long. Elevation is 640 feet.
Population: 1,483; Growth (since 2000): -8.8%; Density: 42.0 persons per square mile; Race: 97.1% White, 0.4% Black/African American, 0.1% Asian, 0.2% American Indian/Alaska Native, 0.0% Native Hawaiian/Other Pacific Islander, 1.7% Two or more races, 2.7% Hispanic of any race; Average household size: 2.39; Median age: 39.5; Age under 18: 24.4%; Age 65 and over: 15.2%; Males per 100 females: 98.5
Housing: Homeownership rate: 75.3%; Homeowner vacancy rate: 2.9%; Rental vacancy rate: 8.4%

OWENDALE (village). Covers a land area of 0.743 square miles and a water area of 0 square miles. Located at 43.73° N. Lat; 83.27° W. Long. Elevation is 640 feet.
Population: 241; Growth (since 2000): -18.6%; Density: 324.2 persons per square mile; Race: 96.3% White, 0.0% Black/African American, 0.0% Asian, 0.4% American Indian/Alaska Native, 0.0% Native Hawaiian/Other Pacific Islander, 2.9% Two or more races, 2.9% Hispanic of any race; Average household size: 2.43; Median age: 35.5; Age under 18: 25.7%; Age 65 and over: 14.9%; Males per 100 females: 100.8
School District(s)
Owendale-Gagetown Area SD (PK-12)
    2012-13 Enrollment: 191. . . . . (989) 678-4261
Housing: Homeownership rate: 82.8%; Homeowner vacancy rate: 3.5%; Rental vacancy rate: 32.0%

PARIS (township). Covers a land area of 36.014 square miles and a water area of 0.013 square miles. Located at 43.74° N. Lat; 82.83° W. Long.
Population: 481; Growth (since 2000): -13.6%; Density: 13.4 persons per square mile; Race: 97.3% White, 2.5% Black/African American, 0.2% Asian, 0.0% American Indian/Alaska Native, 0.0% Native Hawaiian/Other Pacific Islander, 0.0% Two or more races, 0.6% Hispanic of any race; Average household size: 2.56; Median age: 41.3; Age under 18: 26.6%; Age 65 and over: 19.1%; Males per 100 females: 113.8
School District(s)
Big Jackson SD (KG-12)
    2012-13 Enrollment: 33. . . . . (231) 796-8947
Housing: Homeownership rate: 84.6%; Homeowner vacancy rate: 2.4%; Rental vacancy rate: 3.3%

PIGEON (village). Covers a land area of 0.859 square miles and a water area of 0 square miles. Located at 43.83° N. Lat; 83.27° W. Long. Elevation is 623 feet.
History: Pigeon was founded in 1888, and named for the nearby Pigeon River, where many wild pigeons were seen.
Population: 1,208; Growth (since 2000): 0.1%; Density: 1,406.0 persons per square mile; Race: 98.6% White, 0.3% Black/African American, 0.2% Asian, 0.2% American Indian/Alaska Native, 0.0% Native Hawaiian/Other Pacific Islander, 0.5% Two or more races, 2.8% Hispanic of any race; Average household size: 2.13; Median age: 47.2; Age under 18: 19.5%; Age 65 and over: 28.2%; Males per 100 females: 85.0
School District(s)
Elkton-Pigeon-Bay Port Laker Schools (KG-12)
    2012-13 Enrollment: 882. . . . . (989) 453-4600
Housing: Homeownership rate: 67.9%; Homeowner vacancy rate: 2.1%; Rental vacancy rate: 13.9%
Hospitals: Scheurer Hospital

POINTE AUX BARQUES (township). Covers a land area of 1.310 square miles and a water area of 2.550 square miles. Located at 44.06° N. Lat; 82.95° W. Long. Elevation is 591 feet.
History: At the tip of Michigan's "thumb," Pointe Aux Barques is believed to be named for the large rocks off shore, which resemble the prows of ships. The area became a resort center, and the location of estates owned by wealthy Detroit families.
Population: 10; Growth (since 2000): 0.0%; Density: 7.6 persons per square mile; Race: 100.0% White, 0.0% Black/African American, 0.0% Asian, 0.0% American Indian/Alaska Native, 0.0% Native Hawaiian/Other Pacific Islander, 0.0% Two or more races, 0.0% Hispanic of any race; Average household size: 1.67; Median age: 69.5; Age under 18: 0.0%; Age 65 and over: 60.0%; Males per 100 females: 100.0

Housing: Homeownership rate: 83.3%; Homeowner vacancy rate: 0.0%; Rental vacancy rate: 0.0%

PORT AUSTIN (township). Covers a land area of 16.304 square miles and a water area of 153.970 square miles. Located at 44.07° N. Lat; 82.91° W. Long. Elevation is 597 feet.
History: Grindstone City to East, with 6-ft-diameter grindstones on beach produced at nearby quarries in pioneer days. Port Crescent State Park to West has petroglyphs in sandstone outcrops.
Population: 1,424; Growth (since 2000): -10.5%; Density: 87.3 persons per square mile; Race: 97.5% White, 0.1% Black/African American, 0.5% Asian, 0.1% American Indian/Alaska Native, 0.3% Native Hawaiian/Other Pacific Islander, 0.9% Two or more races, 2.0% Hispanic of any race; Average household size: 1.96; Median age: 55.5; Age under 18: 13.1%; Age 65 and over: 30.8%; Males per 100 females: 99.4
Housing: Homeownership rate: 83.2%; Homeowner vacancy rate: 5.7%; Rental vacancy rate: 20.4%

PORT AUSTIN (village). Covers a land area of 1.029 square miles and a water area of 0.013 square miles. Located at 44.04° N. Lat; 83.00° W. Long. Elevation is 597 feet.
History: The first "settler" in Port Austin was reportedly a fugitive from Canada, who hid in a cove on the shore here in 1837. Others found the hideaway a good place to live, and the village of Port Austin grew up. It became a resort center.
Population: 664; Growth (since 2000): -9.9%; Density: 645.4 persons per square mile; Race: 96.1% White, 0.2% Black/African American, 1.1% Asian, 0.2% American Indian/Alaska Native, 0.6% Native Hawaiian/Other Pacific Islander, 1.5% Two or more races, 1.7% Hispanic of any race; Average household size: 1.91; Median age: 55.4; Age under 18: 14.6%; Age 65 and over: 30.3%; Males per 100 females: 98.8
Housing: Homeownership rate: 75.7%; Homeowner vacancy rate: 8.9%; Rental vacancy rate: 21.7%

PORT HOPE (village). Covers a land area of 1.011 square miles and a water area of 0 square miles. Located at 43.94° N. Lat; 82.71° W. Long. Elevation is 610 feet.
History: Port Hope was supposedly named in 1855 by sailors whose ship had been wrecked on the rocks off shore. The village grew up around a lumber mill built in 1858. Port Hope later became a summer home location for vacationers.
Population: 267; Growth (since 2000): -13.9%; Density: 264.0 persons per square mile; Race: 93.3% White, 0.0% Black/African American, 0.0% Asian, 1.9% American Indian/Alaska Native, 0.0% Native Hawaiian/Other Pacific Islander, 4.9% Two or more races, 2.2% Hispanic of any race; Average household size: 2.01; Median age: 54.9; Age under 18: 15.7%; Age 65 and over: 34.5%; Males per 100 females: 99.3
School District(s)
Port Hope Community Schools (PK-12)
    2012-13 Enrollment: 74. . . . . (989) 428-4151
Housing: Homeownership rate: 85.7%; Homeowner vacancy rate: 5.0%; Rental vacancy rate: 5.0%

RUBICON (township). Covers a land area of 23.685 square miles and a water area of 27.004 square miles. Located at 43.92° N. Lat; 82.69° W. Long.
Population: 732; Growth (since 2000): -5.9%; Density: 30.9 persons per square mile; Race: 96.4% White, 0.0% Black/African American, 0.1% Asian, 1.1% American Indian/Alaska Native, 0.0% Native Hawaiian/Other Pacific Islander, 1.9% Two or more races, 2.2% Hispanic of any race; Average household size: 2.22; Median age: 50.7; Age under 18: 17.8%; Age 65 and over: 27.0%; Males per 100 females: 111.0
Housing: Homeownership rate: 89.4%; Homeowner vacancy rate: 3.0%; Rental vacancy rate: 5.4%

RUTH (unincorporated postal area)
ZCTA: 48470
    Covers a land area of 40.007 square miles and a water area of 0.016 square miles. Located at 43.74° N. Lat; 82.75° W. Long. Elevation is 758 feet.
    Population: 784; Growth (since 2000): -14.9%; Density: 19.6 persons per square mile; Race: 96.8% White, 2.2% Black/African American, 0.0% Asian, 0.0% American Indian/Alaska Native, 0.0% Native Hawaiian/Other Pacific Islander, 1.0% Two or more races, 1.1% Hispanic of any race; Average household size: 2.53; Median age: 40.4;

Age under 18: 24.9%; Age 65 and over: 18.6%; Males per 100 females: 102.6

Housing: Homeownership rate: 87.4%; Homeowner vacancy rate: 2.2%; Rental vacancy rate: 0.0%

SAND BEACH (township).
Covers a land area of 36.359 square miles and a water area of 11.781 square miles. Located at 43.82° N. Lat; 82.68° W. Long.

Population: 1,221; Growth (since 2000): -16.9%; Density: 33.6 persons per square mile; Race: 97.0% White, 0.2% Black/African American, 0.4% Asian, 0.7% American Indian/Alaska Native, 0.0% Native Hawaiian/Other Pacific Islander, 0.8% Two or more races, 1.1% Hispanic of any race; Average household size: 2.43; Median age: 46.7; Age under 18: 23.4%; Age 65 and over: 21.3%; Males per 100 females: 108.4

Housing: Homeownership rate: 91.0%; Homeowner vacancy rate: 1.9%; Rental vacancy rate: 6.3%

SEBEWAING (township).
Covers a land area of 32.511 square miles and a water area of 2.831 square miles. Located at 43.72° N. Lat; 83.40° W. Long. Elevation is 587 feet.

History: Sebewaing was settled by a group led by Reverend John F.J. Auch, a Luthern minister from Ann Arbor, who came in 1845. The name is of Indian origin, meaning "crooked creek."

Population: 2,724; Growth (since 2000): -7.5%; Density: 83.8 persons per square mile; Race: 97.5% White, 0.2% Black/African American, 0.3% Asian, 0.1% American Indian/Alaska Native, 0.0% Native Hawaiian/Other Pacific Islander, 0.8% Two or more races, 3.7% Hispanic of any race; Average household size: 2.30; Median age: 44.7; Age under 18: 21.8%; Age 65 and over: 19.3%; Males per 100 females: 95.5; Marriage status: 26.2% never married, 58.7% now married, 1.5% separated, 4.7% widowed, 10.5% divorced; Foreign born: 1.0%; Speak English only: 98.4%; With disability: 14.0%; Veterans: 8.7%; Ancestry: 57.7% German, 9.7% English, 7.1% Irish, 6.1% American, 4.5% French

Employment: 10.6% management, business, and financial, 2.7% computer, engineering, and science, 8.9% education, legal, community service, arts, and media, 8.2% healthcare practitioners, 17.6% service, 16.5% sales and office, 15.3% natural resources, construction, and maintenance, 20.3% production, transportation, and material moving

Income: Per capita: $22,085; Median household: $44,096; Average household: $51,621; Households with income of $100,000 or more: 7.6%; Poverty rate: 10.7%

Educational Attainment: High school diploma or higher: 90.5%; Bachelor's degree or higher: 11.8%; Graduate/professional degree or higher: 3.1%

School District(s)
Unionville-Sebewaing Area S.d. (PK-12)
    2012-13 Enrollment: 778 . . . . (989) 883-2360

Housing: Homeownership rate: 78.3%; Median home value: $80,600; Median year structure built: 1950; Homeowner vacancy rate: 3.6%; Median gross rent: $441 per month; Rental vacancy rate: 14.0%

Health Insurance: 86.7% have insurance; 75.4% have private insurance; 28.9% have public insurance; 13.3% do not have insurance; 5.0% of children under 18 do not have insurance

Transportation: Commute: 86.7% car, 0.6% public transportation, 6.8% walk, 3.1% work from home; Median travel time to work: 22.5 minutes

SEBEWAING (village).
Covers a land area of 1.579 square miles and a water area of 0.126 square miles. Located at 43.73° N. Lat; 83.45° W. Long. Elevation is 587 feet.

History: Commercial fishing has been important to Sebewaing, situated at the mouth of the Sebewaing River on Saginaw Bay. Early industries also included a beet sugar refinery, a brewery, and a plant that manufactured fish-net anchors.

Population: 1,759; Growth (since 2000): -10.9%; Density: 1,114.1 persons per square mile; Race: 97.5% White, 0.0% Black/African American, 0.2% Asian, 0.2% American Indian/Alaska Native, 0.0% Native Hawaiian/Other Pacific Islander, 0.9% Two or more races, 4.3% Hispanic of any race; Average household size: 2.19; Median age: 44.9; Age under 18: 20.8%; Age 65 and over: 20.8%; Males per 100 females: 97.0

School District(s)
Unionville-Sebewaing Area S.d. (PK-12)
    2012-13 Enrollment: 778 . . . . (989) 883-2360

Housing: Homeownership rate: 72.8%; Homeowner vacancy rate: 4.2%; Rental vacancy rate: 15.8%

Safety: Violent crime rate: 11.7 per 10,000 population; Property crime rate: 128.3 per 10,000 population

SHERIDAN (township).
Covers a land area of 36.145 square miles and a water area of 0.007 square miles. Located at 43.73° N. Lat; 83.07° W. Long.

History: John McIntosh settled in Sheridan in 1859 and became its first supervisor when the township was organized in 1866. Sheridan was named for General Philip H. Sheridan.

Population: 712; Growth (since 2000): -3.3%; Density: 19.7 persons per square mile; Race: 98.6% White, 0.0% Black/African American, 0.4% Asian, 0.0% American Indian/Alaska Native, 0.0% Native Hawaiian/Other Pacific Islander, 0.6% Two or more races, 2.5% Hispanic of any race; Average household size: 2.62; Median age: 42.3; Age under 18: 24.9%; Age 65 and over: 17.3%; Males per 100 females: 99.4

Housing: Homeownership rate: 87.6%; Homeowner vacancy rate: 0.8%; Rental vacancy rate: 2.9%

SHERMAN (township).
Covers a land area of 43.994 square miles and a water area of 6.237 square miles. Located at 43.73° N. Lat; 82.67° W. Long.

Population: 1,083; Growth (since 2000): -7.0%; Density: 24.6 persons per square mile; Race: 97.9% White, 0.5% Black/African American, 0.5% Asian, 0.0% American Indian/Alaska Native, 0.0% Native Hawaiian/Other Pacific Islander, 1.0% Two or more races, 1.8% Hispanic of any race; Average household size: 2.44; Median age: 44.3; Age under 18: 22.8%; Age 65 and over: 19.8%; Males per 100 females: 104.7

Housing: Homeownership rate: 90.1%; Homeowner vacancy rate: 2.7%; Rental vacancy rate: 4.3%

SIGEL (township).
Covers a land area of 35.637 square miles and a water area of 0.062 square miles. Located at 43.82° N. Lat; 82.83° W. Long.

History: Sigel Township was organized in 1863 and named (though spelled differently) for General Franz Seigel who served during the Civil War.

Population: 465; Growth (since 2000): -19.3%; Density: 13.0 persons per square mile; Race: 99.4% White, 0.2% Black/African American, 0.2% Asian, 0.0% American Indian/Alaska Native, 0.0% Native Hawaiian/Other Pacific Islander, 0.2% Two or more races, 0.4% Hispanic of any race; Average household size: 2.64; Median age: 41.4; Age under 18: 23.2%; Age 65 and over: 17.6%; Males per 100 females: 103.1

Housing: Homeownership rate: 89.7%; Homeowner vacancy rate: 1.3%; Rental vacancy rate: 5.3%

UBLY (village).
Covers a land area of 1.335 square miles and a water area of <.001 square miles. Located at 43.71° N. Lat; 82.93° W. Long. Elevation is 784 feet.

Population: 858; Growth (since 2000): -1.7%; Density: 642.5 persons per square mile; Race: 98.1% White, 0.6% Black/African American, 0.2% Asian, 0.2% American Indian/Alaska Native, 0.0% Native Hawaiian/Other Pacific Islander, 0.7% Two or more races, 1.0% Hispanic of any race; Average household size: 2.22; Median age: 40.8; Age under 18: 23.0%; Age 65 and over: 19.2%; Males per 100 females: 85.7

School District(s)
Ubly Community Schools (KG-12)
    2012-13 Enrollment: 782 . . . . (989) 658-8202

Housing: Homeownership rate: 73.3%; Homeowner vacancy rate: 2.1%; Rental vacancy rate: 12.8%

VERONA (township).
Covers a land area of 34.133 square miles and a water area of 0.071 square miles. Located at 43.82° N. Lat; 82.94° W. Long. Elevation is 804 feet.

Population: 1,259; Growth (since 2000): -6.7%; Density: 36.9 persons per square mile; Race: 96.9% White, 1.7% Black/African American, 0.4% Asian, 0.2% American Indian/Alaska Native, 0.0% Native Hawaiian/Other Pacific Islander, 0.8% Two or more races, 1.1% Hispanic of any race; Average household size: 2.48; Median age: 45.5; Age under 18: 22.2%; Age 65 and over: 16.1%; Males per 100 females: 96.4

Housing: Homeownership rate: 92.3%; Homeowner vacancy rate: 2.1%; Rental vacancy rate: 4.9%

WINSOR (township). Covers a land area of 35.233 square miles and a water area of 0.144 square miles. Located at 43.81° N. Lat; 83.29° W. Long.

Population: 1,907; Growth (since 2000): -6.7%; Density: 54.1 persons per square mile; Race: 98.7% White, 0.3% Black/African American, 0.1% Asian, 0.1% American Indian/Alaska Native, 0.0% Native Hawaiian/Other Pacific Islander, 0.5% Two or more races, 2.6% Hispanic of any race; Average household size: 2.24; Median age: 47.6; Age under 18: 19.6%; Age 65 and over: 23.9%; Males per 100 females: 95.0

Housing: Homeownership rate: 75.3%; Homeowner vacancy rate: 1.7%; Rental vacancy rate: 13.3%

Ingham County

Located in south central Michigan; drained by the Grand and Red Cedar Rivers. Covers a land area of 556.120 square miles, a water area of 4.592 square miles, and is located in the Eastern Time Zone at 42.60° N. Lat., 84.37° W. Long. The county was founded in 1838. County seat is Mason.

Ingham County is part of the Lansing-East Lansing, MI Metropolitan Statistical Area. The entire metro area includes: Clinton County, MI; Eaton County, MI; Ingham County, MI

Weather Station: East Lansing 4 S									Elevation: 879 feet		
	Jan	Feb	Mar	Apr	May	Jun	Jul	Aug	Sep	Oct	Nov	Dec
High	30	33	43	57	69	78	82	81	74	60	47	35
Low	15	16	24	35	46	55	59	58	49	38	31	20
Precip	1.6	1.4	1.7	2.8	3.3	3.4	3.1	3.3	3.6	2.6	2.6	1.6
Snow	12.0	8.7	4.9	1.0	0.0	0.0	0.0	0.0	0.0	0.3	1.7	9.7

High and Low temperatures in degrees Fahrenheit; Precipitation and Snow in inches

Population: 280,895; Growth (since 2000): 0.6%; Density: 505.1 persons per square mile; Race: 76.2% White, 11.8% Black/African American, 5.2% Asian, 0.6% American Indian/Alaska Native, 0.0% Native Hawaiian/Other Pacific Islander, 4.0% two or more races, 7.3% Hispanic of any race; Average household size: 2.36; Median age: 31.4; Age under 18: 20.9%; Age 65 and over: 10.5%; Males per 100 females: 94.7; Marriage status: 43.3% never married, 41.7% now married, 1.2% separated, 4.3% widowed, 10.6% divorced; Foreign born: 8.5%; Speak English only: 88.2%; With disability: 11.9%; Veterans: 7.3%; Ancestry: 22.9% German, 12.9% Irish, 11.8% English, 5.9% Polish, 5.0% American

Religion: Six largest groups: 15.9% Catholicism, 5.2% Non-denominational Protestant, 3.0% Methodist/Pietist, 2.8% Presbyterian-Reformed, 2.8% Lutheran, 2.6% Baptist

Economy: Unemployment rate: 5.1%; Leading industries: 15.0% retail trade; 13.2% health care and social assistance; 13.1% other services (except public administration); Farms: 944 totaling 200,578 acres; Company size: 5 employ 1,000 or more persons, 7 employ 500 to 999 persons, 142 employ 100 to 499 persons, 5,988 employ less than 100 persons; Business ownership: 7,116 women-owned, n/a Black-owned, 493 Hispanic-owned, 998 Asian-owned

Employment: 13.3% management, business, and financial, 6.6% computer, engineering, and science, 14.0% education, legal, community service, arts, and media, 5.0% healthcare practitioners, 20.2% service, 24.5% sales and office, 5.4% natural resources, construction, and maintenance, 11.1% production, transportation, and material moving

Income: Per capita: $24,754; Median household: $45,321; Average household: $62,161; Households with income of $100,000 or more: 17.5%; Poverty rate: 21.9%

Educational Attainment: High school diploma or higher: 91.1%; Bachelor's degree or higher: 36.5%; Graduate/professional degree or higher: 16.2%

Housing: Homeownership rate: 59.3%; Median home value: $120,500; Median year structure built: 1967; Homeowner vacancy rate: 2.9%; Median gross rent: $775 per month; Rental vacancy rate: 8.8%

Vital Statistics: Birth rate: 117.2 per 10,000 population; Death rate: 71.6 per 10,000 population; Age-adjusted cancer mortality rate: 169.7 deaths per 100,000 population

Health Insurance: 90.4% have insurance; 72.2% have private insurance; 30.1% have public insurance; 9.6% do not have insurance; 3.3% of children under 18 do not have insurance

Health Care: Physicians: 39.7 per 10,000 population; Hospital beds: 35.2 per 10,000 population; Hospital admissions: 1,733.9 per 10,000 population

Air Quality Index: 89.8% good, 10.2% moderate, 0.0% unhealthy for sensitive individuals, 0.0% unhealthy (percent of days)

Transportation: Commute: 85.0% car, 3.0% public transportation, 5.6% walk, 3.9% work from home; Median travel time to work: 19.8 minutes

Presidential Election: 63.0% Obama, 35.3% Romney (2012)

Additional Information Contacts

Ingham Government . . . . (517) 676-7204
   http://www.ingham.org

Ingham County Communities

ALAIEDON (township). Covers a land area of 35.596 square miles and a water area of 0.172 square miles. Located at 42.63° N. Lat; 84.43° W. Long.

History: Many of the early residents of Alaiedon were German immigrants, and the community was first called German Settlement. The township was formed in 1842.

Population: 2,894; Growth (since 2000): -17.3%; Density: 81.3 persons per square mile; Race: 94.7% White, 1.2% Black/African American, 1.4% Asian, 0.6% American Indian/Alaska Native, 0.0% Native Hawaiian/Other Pacific Islander, 1.3% Two or more races, 2.7% Hispanic of any race; Average household size: 2.56; Median age: 47.4; Age under 18: 20.0%; Age 65 and over: 17.7%; Males per 100 females: 98.6; Marriage status: 21.0% never married, 67.0% now married, 0.9% separated, 5.4% widowed, 6.6% divorced; Foreign born: 5.8%; Speak English only: 93.9%; With disability: 11.8%; Veterans: 12.7%; Ancestry: 28.2% German, 22.8% English, 12.9% Irish, 10.4% American, 4.3% Polish

Employment: 23.8% management, business, and financial, 3.7% computer, engineering, and science, 12.6% education, legal, community service, arts, and media, 6.4% healthcare practitioners, 11.1% service, 24.4% sales and office, 3.7% natural resources, construction, and maintenance, 14.3% production, transportation, and material moving

Income: Per capita: $43,564; Median household: $77,989; Average household: $113,270; Households with income of $100,000 or more: 38.3%; Poverty rate: 5.7%

Educational Attainment: High school diploma or higher: 92.8%; Bachelor's degree or higher: 39.4%; Graduate/professional degree or higher: 17.9%

Housing: Homeownership rate: 89.3%; Median home value: $176,100; Median year structure built: 1970; Homeowner vacancy rate: 1.3%; Median gross rent: $1,017 per month; Rental vacancy rate: 9.8%

Health Insurance: 94.5% have insurance; 82.5% have private insurance; 29.4% have public insurance; 5.5% do not have insurance; 3.5% of children under 18 do not have insurance

Transportation: Commute: 93.6% car, 1.0% public transportation, 0.4% walk, 3.5% work from home; Median travel time to work: 19.8 minutes

AURELIUS (township). Covers a land area of 36.410 square miles and a water area of 0.062 square miles. Located at 42.56° N. Lat; 84.55° W. Long. Elevation is 974 feet.

History: Aurelius Township was named by early settler Elijah Woodworth for his former home in Cayuga County, New York.

Population: 3,525; Growth (since 2000): 6.2%; Density: 96.8 persons per square mile; Race: 96.7% White, 1.0% Black/African American, 0.3% Asian, 0.3% American Indian/Alaska Native, 0.0% Native Hawaiian/Other Pacific Islander, 0.9% Two or more races, 3.1% Hispanic of any race; Average household size: 2.73; Median age: 42.6; Age under 18: 24.5%; Age 65 and over: 12.9%; Males per 100 females: 101.3; Marriage status: 24.3% never married, 62.8% now married, 0.2% separated, 3.7% widowed, 9.2% divorced; Foreign born: 4.4%; Speak English only: 93.9%; With disability: 10.5%; Veterans: 7.9%; Ancestry: 30.7% German, 19.1% Irish, 16.7% English, 13.5% American, 6.6% French

Employment: 11.7% management, business, and financial, 4.7% computer, engineering, and science, 12.1% education, legal, community service, arts, and media, 8.8% healthcare practitioners, 15.2% service, 26.6% sales and office, 8.2% natural resources, construction, and maintenance, 12.7% production, transportation, and material moving

Income: Per capita: $28,397; Median household: $75,409; Average household: $83,123; Households with income of $100,000 or more: 34.2%; Poverty rate: 1.9%

Educational Attainment: High school diploma or higher: 94.7%; Bachelor's degree or higher: 26.0%; Graduate/professional degree or higher: 9.8%

Housing: Homeownership rate: 92.0%; Median home value: $168,800; Median year structure built: 1973; Homeowner vacancy rate: 1.2%; Median gross rent: $1,201 per month; Rental vacancy rate: 1.0%

Health Insurance: 97.3% have insurance; 91.4% have private insurance; 18.3% have public insurance; 2.7% do not have insurance; 0.0% of children under 18 do not have insurance
Transportation: Commute: 94.8% car, 0.0% public transportation, 0.4% walk, 3.2% work from home; Median travel time to work: 23.2 minutes

BUNKER HILL (township). Covers a land area of 32.881 square miles and a water area of 0.047 square miles. Located at 42.47° N. Lat; 84.31° W. Long. Elevation is 945 feet.
History: Bunker Hill Township was organized in 1839, and was probably named for Adam Bunker, an early settler here.
Population: 2,119; Growth (since 2000): 7.1%; Density: 64.4 persons per square mile; Race: 97.3% White, 0.2% Black/African American, 0.1% Asian, 0.2% American Indian/Alaska Native, 0.0% Native Hawaiian/Other Pacific Islander, 1.5% Two or more races, 3.2% Hispanic of any race; Average household size: 2.80; Median age: 39.4; Age under 18: 27.2%; Age 65 and over: 11.3%; Males per 100 females: 104.1
Housing: Homeownership rate: 87.0%; Homeowner vacancy rate: 1.1%; Rental vacancy rate: 2.9%

DANSVILLE (village). Covers a land area of 1.005 square miles and a water area of <.001 square miles. Located at 42.56° N. Lat; 84.30° W. Long. Elevation is 968 feet.
Population: 563; Growth (since 2000): 31.2%; Density: 559.9 persons per square mile; Race: 95.6% White, 0.7% Black/African American, 0.7% Asian, 1.1% American Indian/Alaska Native, 0.0% Native Hawaiian/Other Pacific Islander, 1.6% Two or more races, 1.6% Hispanic of any race; Average household size: 2.92; Median age: 33.4; Age under 18: 31.8%; Age 65 and over: 8.2%; Males per 100 females: 96.9

School District(s)
Dansville Schools (KG-12)
    2012-13 Enrollment: 864 . . . . (517) 623-6120
Housing: Homeownership rate: 87.1%; Homeowner vacancy rate: 3.4%; Rental vacancy rate: 3.8%

DELHI (charter township). Covers a land area of 28.610 square miles and a water area of 0.417 square miles. Located at 42.63° N. Lat; 84.54° W. Long. Elevation is 883 feet.
Population: 25,877; Growth (since 2000): 14.7%; Density: 904.5 persons per square mile; Race: 86.8% White, 5.2% Black/African American, 2.9% Asian, 0.5% American Indian/Alaska Native, 0.0% Native Hawaiian/Other Pacific Islander, 3.1% Two or more races, 5.3% Hispanic of any race; Average household size: 2.52; Median age: 37.7; Age under 18: 25.5%; Age 65 and over: 10.9%; Males per 100 females: 93.2; Marriage status: 23.9% never married, 59.0% now married, 1.0% separated, 4.8% widowed, 12.3% divorced; Foreign born: 5.2%; Speak English only: 92.2%; With disability: 11.4%; Veterans: 10.3%; Ancestry: 26.1% German, 12.6% English, 11.7% Irish, 7.4% American, 5.7% Polish
Employment: 17.4% management, business, and financial, 6.5% computer, engineering, and science, 8.6% education, legal, community service, arts, and media, 7.4% healthcare practitioners, 17.2% service, 27.7% sales and office, 4.5% natural resources, construction, and maintenance, 10.6% production, transportation, and material moving
Income: Per capita: $29,064; Median household: $61,273; Average household: $73,493; Households with income of $100,000 or more: 26.1%; Poverty rate: 10.0%
Educational Attainment: High school diploma or higher: 93.5%; Bachelor's degree or higher: 32.2%; Graduate/professional degree or higher: 10.7%
Housing: Homeownership rate: 74.0%; Median home value: $151,200; Median year structure built: 1983; Homeowner vacancy rate: 2.1%; Median gross rent: $914 per month; Rental vacancy rate: 6.6%
Health Insurance: 91.6% have insurance; 80.7% have private insurance; 24.7% have public insurance; 8.4% do not have insurance; 2.3% of children under 18 do not have insurance
Transportation: Commute: 92.2% car, 1.5% public transportation, 0.7% walk, 4.0% work from home; Median travel time to work: 20.6 minutes
Additional Information Contacts
Delhi Charter Township. . . . . (517) 694-2135
    http://www.delhitownship.com

EAST LANSING (city). Covers a land area of 13.594 square miles and a water area of 0.080 square miles. Located at 42.75° N. Lat; 84.48° W. Long. Elevation is 856 feet.
History: In 1849, D. Robert Burcham bought land and settled on the site that became East Lansing. This was the location of the first agricultural college in the United States, authorized by the state in 1855 and opened in 1857 as the Michigan Agricultural College (later Michigan State College of Agriculture and Applied Science). When East Lansing was granted a city charter in 1907, the residents favored College Park as a name, but the post office insisted on East Lansing.
Population: 48,579; Growth (since 2000): 4.4%; Density: 3,573.5 persons per square mile; Race: 78.4% White, 6.8% Black/African American, 10.6% Asian, 0.3% American Indian/Alaska Native, 0.0% Native Hawaiian/Other Pacific Islander, 2.9% Two or more races, 3.4% Hispanic of any race; Average household size: 2.23; Median age: 21.6; Age under 18: 7.5%; Age 65 and over: 6.4%; Males per 100 females: 94.3; Marriage status: 76.7% never married, 17.6% now married, 0.5% separated, 2.2% widowed, 3.5% divorced; Foreign born: 14.9%; Speak English only: 82.8%; With disability: 5.1%; Veterans: 2.4%; Ancestry: 22.4% German, 15.1% Irish, 10.6% English, 9.6% Polish, 8.3% Italian
Employment: 11.0% management, business, and financial, 8.1% computer, engineering, and science, 20.7% education, legal, community service, arts, and media, 3.7% healthcare practitioners, 27.4% service, 22.7% sales and office, 2.7% natural resources, construction, and maintenance, 3.7% production, transportation, and material moving
Income: Per capita: $18,650; Median household: $32,953; Average household: $62,193; Households with income of $100,000 or more: 18.7%; Poverty rate: 41.1%
Educational Attainment: High school diploma or higher: 97.2%; Bachelor's degree or higher: 68.5%; Graduate/professional degree or higher: 38.3%

School District(s)
East Lansing SD (PK-12)
    2012-13 Enrollment: 3,489 . . . . (517) 333-7424
Four-year College(s)
Michigan State University (Public)
    Fall 2013 Enrollment: 49,317 . . . . (517) 355-1855
    2013-14 Tuition: In-state $12,862; Out-of-state $33,750
Michigan State University-College of Law (Private, Not-for-profit)
    Fall 2013 Enrollment: 998 . . . . (517) 432-6800
Vocational/Technical School(s)
Douglas J Aveda Institute (Private, For-profit)
    Fall 2013 Enrollment: 977 . . . . (517) 333-9656
    2013-14 Tuition: $20,600
Protege Academy (Private, For-profit)
    Fall 2013 Enrollment: 74 . . . . (517) 324-3388
    2013-14 Tuition: $13,900
Housing: Homeownership rate: 33.6%; Median home value: $177,000; Median year structure built: 1970; Homeowner vacancy rate: 2.8%; Median gross rent: $856 per month; Rental vacancy rate: 6.0%
Health Insurance: 93.8% have insurance; 88.0% have private insurance; 12.9% have public insurance; 6.2% do not have insurance; 2.2% of children under 18 do not have insurance
Safety: Violent crime rate: 22.5 per 10,000 population; Property crime rate: 164.7 per 10,000 population
Transportation: Commute: 58.5% car, 5.5% public transportation, 22.2% walk, 5.6% work from home; Median travel time to work: 15.3 minutes; Amtrak: Train service available.
Additional Information Contacts
City of East Lansing . . . . (517) 337-1731
    http://www.cityofeastlansing.com

EDGEMONT PARK (CDP). Covers a land area of 0.830 square miles and a water area of 0 square miles. Located at 42.75° N. Lat; 84.59° W. Long. Elevation is 876 feet.
Population: 2,358; Growth (since 2000): -3.4%; Density: 2,840.7 persons per square mile; Race: 74.4% White, 15.6% Black/African American, 1.7% Asian, 0.1% American Indian/Alaska Native, 0.0% Native Hawaiian/Other Pacific Islander, 5.4% Two or more races, 9.3% Hispanic of any race; Average household size: 2.19; Median age: 37.7; Age under 18: 22.6%; Age 65 and over: 15.1%; Males per 100 females: 84.9
Housing: Homeownership rate: 69.2%; Homeowner vacancy rate: 2.5%; Rental vacancy rate: 7.9%

HASLETT (CDP). Covers a land area of 15.370 square miles and a water area of 0.895 square miles. Located at 42.75° N. Lat; 84.40° W. Long. Elevation is 876 feet.

Population: 19,220; Growth (since 2000): 70.3%; Density: 1,250.5 persons per square mile; Race: 84.7% White, 4.4% Black/African American, 6.5% Asian, 0.4% American Indian/Alaska Native, 0.0% Native Hawaiian/Other Pacific Islander, 3.0% Two or more races, 4.3% Hispanic of any race; Average household size: 2.15; Median age: 39.4; Age under 18: 20.1%; Age 65 and over: 14.5%; Males per 100 females: 89.0; Marriage status: 31.8% never married, 50.4% now married, 1.1% separated, 7.7% widowed, 10.1% divorced; Foreign born: 9.9%; Speak English only: 88.8%; With disability: 9.6%; Veterans: 8.6%; Ancestry: 24.7% German, 16.4% Irish, 14.5% English, 5.4% Polish, 4.3% French

Employment: 19.8% management, business, and financial, 9.2% computer, engineering, and science, 18.3% education, legal, community service, arts, and media, 7.2% healthcare practitioners, 12.9% service, 26.0% sales and office, 1.5% natural resources, construction, and maintenance, 5.1% production, transportation, and material moving

Income: Per capita: $35,195; Median household: $55,785; Average household: $76,467; Households with income of $100,000 or more: 26.4%; Poverty rate: 13.9%

Educational Attainment: High school diploma or higher: 96.4%; Bachelor's degree or higher: 58.1%; Graduate/professional degree or higher: 28.8%

School District(s)
Haslett Public Schools (PK-12)
    2012-13 Enrollment: 2,709 . . . . (517) 339-8242

Housing: Homeownership rate: 59.3%; Median home value: $169,900; Median year structure built: 1980; Homeowner vacancy rate: 2.2%; Median gross rent: $777 per month; Rental vacancy rate: 7.4%

Health Insurance: 90.5% have insurance; 82.3% have private insurance; 22.5% have public insurance; 9.5% do not have insurance; 3.4% of children under 18 do not have insurance

Transportation: Commute: 92.1% car, 1.5% public transportation, 1.1% walk, 4.5% work from home; Median travel time to work: 20.2 minutes

HOLT (CDP). Covers a land area of 15.674 square miles and a water area of 0.198 square miles. Located at 42.64° N. Lat; 84.53° W. Long. Elevation is 889 feet.

History: The first settlement was made here in 1837, and was known as Delhi or Delhi Center, for the township. It was renamed Holt by the post office in 1860 for John Holt, postmaster general.

Population: 23,973; Growth (since 2000): 111.9%; Density: 1,529.5 persons per square mile; Race: 86.3% White, 5.6% Black/African American, 3.1% Asian, 0.5% American Indian/Alaska Native, 0.0% Native Hawaiian/Other Pacific Islander, 3.2% Two or more races, 5.4% Hispanic of any race; Average household size: 2.52; Median age: 37.0; Age under 18: 25.7%; Age 65 and over: 10.6%; Males per 100 females: 92.6; Marriage status: 24.0% never married, 58.7% now married, 1.0% separated, 4.6% widowed, 12.7% divorced; Foreign born: 4.8%; Speak English only: 92.7%; With disability: 11.3%; Veterans: 10.3%; Ancestry: 26.1% German, 12.7% English, 12.0% Irish, 7.0% American, 6.0% Polish

Employment: 18.3% management, business, and financial, 6.7% computer, engineering, and science, 8.7% education, legal, community service, arts, and media, 7.7% healthcare practitioners, 16.2% service, 27.1% sales and office, 4.4% natural resources, construction, and maintenance, 10.8% production, transportation, and material moving

Income: Per capita: $28,740; Median household: $60,237; Average household: $73,150; Households with income of $100,000 or more: 26.1%; Poverty rate: 9.7%

Educational Attainment: High school diploma or higher: 93.6%; Bachelor's degree or higher: 32.5%; Graduate/professional degree or higher: 10.8%

School District(s)
Holt Public Schools (KG-12)
    2012-13 Enrollment: 5,792 . . . . (517) 694-5715

Housing: Homeownership rate: 72.8%; Median home value: $148,700; Median year structure built: 1985; Homeowner vacancy rate: 2.2%; Median gross rent: $910 per month; Rental vacancy rate: 6.7%

Health Insurance: 92.0% have insurance; 80.9% have private insurance; 24.3% have public insurance; 8.0% do not have insurance; 2.4% of children under 18 do not have insurance

Transportation: Commute: 92.2% car, 1.6% public transportation, 0.7% walk, 4.0% work from home; Median travel time to work: 20.2 minutes

INGHAM (township). Covers a land area of 32.671 square miles and a water area of 0.050 square miles. Located at 42.56° N. Lat; 84.31° W. Long.

History: Ingham Township was named for Samuel D. Ingham, who served as secretary of the treasury under President Andrew Jackson.

Population: 2,452; Growth (since 2000): 19.0%; Density: 75.1 persons per square mile; Race: 97.5% White, 0.5% Black/African American, 0.3% Asian, 0.3% American Indian/Alaska Native, 0.0% Native Hawaiian/Other Pacific Islander, 1.1% Two or more races, 1.8% Hispanic of any race; Average household size: 2.86; Median age: 40.7; Age under 18: 27.3%; Age 65 and over: 11.9%; Males per 100 females: 101.8

Housing: Homeownership rate: 92.9%; Homeowner vacancy rate: 2.1%; Rental vacancy rate: 4.7%

LANSING (charter township). Covers a land area of 4.934 square miles and a water area of 0.126 square miles. Located at 42.74° N. Lat; 84.59° W. Long. Elevation is 853 feet.

History: Lansing Township was organized in 1841 and named for Lansing, New York, the former home of an early resident. The New York town had been named for John Lansing, a Revolutionary War hero.

Population: 8,126; Growth (since 2000): -3.9%; Density: 1,647.0 persons per square mile; Race: 76.3% White, 12.5% Black/African American, 2.6% Asian, 0.5% American Indian/Alaska Native, 0.0% Native Hawaiian/Other Pacific Islander, 4.7% Two or more races, 10.9% Hispanic of any race; Average household size: 2.06; Median age: 35.0; Age under 18: 18.8%; Age 65 and over: 12.9%; Males per 100 females: 92.5; Marriage status: 41.8% never married, 40.2% now married, 0.7% separated, 4.3% widowed, 13.7% divorced; Foreign born: 7.0%; Speak English only: 87.6%; With disability: 11.0%; Veterans: 9.0%; Ancestry: 22.4% German, 11.3% Irish, 8.7% English, 5.0% Italian, 3.7% American

Employment: 12.1% management, business, and financial, 4.2% computer, engineering, and science, 11.8% education, legal, community service, arts, and media, 3.4% healthcare practitioners, 16.4% service, 30.2% sales and office, 8.6% natural resources, construction, and maintenance, 13.4% production, transportation, and material moving

Income: Per capita: $23,120; Median household: $42,488; Average household: $50,150; Households with income of $100,000 or more: 8.9%; Poverty rate: 17.0%

Educational Attainment: High school diploma or higher: 91.7%; Bachelor's degree or higher: 32.2%; Graduate/professional degree or higher: 10.1%

School District(s)
Cole Academy (KG-12)
    2012-13 Enrollment: 193. . . . . (517) 708-3512
El-Hajj Malik El-Shabazz Academy (PK-12)
    2012-13 Enrollment: 343. . . . . (517) 267-8474
Grand Ledge Public Schools (KG-12)
    2012-13 Enrollment: 5,071 . . . . (517) 925-5400
Ingham ISD (PK-12)
    2012-13 Enrollment: 1,144 . . . . (517) 244-1214
Lansing Charter Academy (PK-12)
    2012-13 Enrollment: 657. . . . . (517) 882-9585
Lansing Public SD (PK-12)
    2012-13 Enrollment: 12,249 . . . . (517) 755-1010
Mid-Michigan Leadership Academy (PK-12)
    2012-13 Enrollment: 223. . . . . (517) 485-5379
Waverly Community Schools (PK-12)
    2012-13 Enrollment: 2,778 . . . . (517) 321-7265
Windemere Park Charter Academy (KG-12)
    2012-13 Enrollment: 714. . . . . (517) 327-0700

Four-year College(s)
Great Lakes Christian College (Private, Not-for-profit, Christian Churches and Churches of Christ)
    Fall 2013 Enrollment: 194. . . . . (517) 321-0242
    2013-14 Tuition: In-state $14,500; Out-of-state $14,500
Thomas M Cooley Law Schoo (Private, Not-for-profit)
    Fall 2013 Enrollment: 2,477 . . . . (517) 371-5140

Two-year College(s)
Career Quest Learning Centers-Lansing (Private, For-profit)
    Fall 2013 Enrollment: 422. . . . . (517) 318-3330
Lansing Community College (Public)
    Fall 2013 Enrollment: 17,562 . . . . (517) 483-1957
    2013-14 Tuition: In-state $5,210; Out-of-state $7,700

Vocational/Technical School(s)

Dorsey Business Schools-Lansing (Private, For-profit)
  Fall 2013 Enrollment: 156 . . . . (517) 272-4018
  2013-14 Tuition: In-state $17,568; Out-of-state $17,568
Regency Beauty Institute-Lansing (Private, For-profit)
  Fall 2013 Enrollment: 80 . . . . (800) 787-6456
  2013-14 Tuition: $17,300
Ross Medical Education Center-Lansing (Private, For-profit)
  Fall 2013 Enrollment: 151 . . . . (517) 703-9044
  2013-14 Tuition: $15,680

Housing: Homeownership rate: 51.6%; Median home value: $103,200; Median year structure built: 1962; Homeowner vacancy rate: 2.5%; Median gross rent: $669 per month; Rental vacancy rate: 10.4%

Health Insurance: 89.4% have insurance; 67.5% have private insurance; 32.6% have public insurance; 10.6% do not have insurance; 5.8% of children under 18 do not have insurance

Hospitals: Edward W Sparrow Hospital (535 beds); Mclaren - Greater Lansing

Newspapers: City Pulse (weekly circulation 20000); Lansing State Journal (daily circulation 63000)

Transportation: Commute: 91.3% car, 1.9% public transportation, 2.3% walk, 2.7% work from home; Median travel time to work: 16.4 minutes

Airports: Capital Region International (primary service/non-hub)

Additional Information Contacts
Lansing Charter Township . . . . (517) 485-4063
  http://www.lansingtownship.org

LANSING (city). State capital. Covers a land area of 36.049 square miles and a water area of 0.626 square miles. Located at 42.71° N. Lat; 84.56° W. Long. Elevation is 853 feet.

History: When Lansing was chosen as the state capital in 1847, it had only one log house and a sawmill. The few families here had come from Lansing, New York, and named their settlement after their former home, which had been named for Chancellor John Lansing of New York. Though its choice as capital seemed a joke, the community arose to the honor and erected a capitol building the same year. Lansing was incorporated as a city in 1859. Industrial development came after 1871, when the railroads connected the city with the rest of the state. Ransom E. Olds, automobile pioneer, brought Lansing into the auto manufacturing scene in the early 1900's.

Population: 114,297; Growth (since 2000): -4.1%; Density: 3,170.6 persons per square mile; Race: 61.2% White, 23.7% Black/African American, 3.7% Asian, 0.8% American Indian/Alaska Native, 0.0% Native Hawaiian/Other Pacific Islander, 6.2% Two or more races, 12.5% Hispanic of any race; Average household size: 2.33; Median age: 32.2; Age under 18: 24.2%; Age 65 and over: 9.7%; Males per 100 females: 93.8; Marriage status: 43.3% never married, 38.3% now married, 2.1% separated, 4.4% widowed, 13.9% divorced; Foreign born: 8.1%; Speak English only: 87.0%; With disability: 16.5%; Veterans: 7.5%; Ancestry: 18.7% German, 10.0% Irish, 8.3% English, 4.4% Polish, 4.2% American

Employment: 10.4% management, business, and financial, 5.1% computer, engineering, and science, 11.1% education, legal, community service, arts, and media, 3.8% healthcare practitioners, 23.4% service, 25.2% sales and office, 6.1% natural resources, construction, and maintenance, 14.9% production, transportation, and material moving

Income: Per capita: $19,440; Median household: $36,054; Average household: $44,652; Households with income of $100,000 or more: 7.1%; Poverty rate: 28.7%

Educational Attainment: High school diploma or higher: 86.2%; Bachelor's degree or higher: 24.7%; Graduate/professional degree or higher: 9.0%

School District(s)

Cole Academy (KG-12)
  2012-13 Enrollment: 193 . . . . (517) 708-3512
El-Hajj Malik El-Shabazz Academy (PK-12)
  2012-13 Enrollment: 343 . . . . (517) 267-8474
Grand Ledge Public Schools (KG-12)
  2012-13 Enrollment: 5,071 . . . . (517) 925-5400
Ingham ISD (PK-12)
  2012-13 Enrollment: 1,144 . . . . (517) 244-1214
Lansing Charter Academy (PK-12)
  2012-13 Enrollment: 657 . . . . (517) 882-9585
Lansing Public SD (PK-12)
  2012-13 Enrollment: 12,249 . . . . (517) 755-1010

Mid-Michigan Leadership Academy (PK-12)
  2012-13 Enrollment: 223 . . . . (517) 485-5379
Waverly Community Schools (PK-12)
  2012-13 Enrollment: 2,778 . . . . (517) 321-7265
Windemere Park Charter Academy (KG-12)
  2012-13 Enrollment: 714 . . . . (517) 327-0700

Four-year College(s)

Great Lakes Christian College (Private, Not-for-profit, Christian Churches and Churches of Christ)
  Fall 2013 Enrollment: 194 . . . . (517) 321-0242
  2013-14 Tuition: In-state $14,500; Out-of-state $14,500
Thomas M Cooley Law Schoo (Private, Not-for-profit)
  Fall 2013 Enrollment: 2,477 . . . . (517) 371-5140

Two-year College(s)

Career Quest Learning Centers-Lansing (Private, For-profit)
  Fall 2013 Enrollment: 422 . . . . (517) 318-3330
Lansing Community College (Public)
  Fall 2013 Enrollment: 17,562 . . . . (517) 483-1957
  2013-14 Tuition: In-state $5,210; Out-of-state $7,700

Vocational/Technical School(s)

Dorsey Business Schools-Lansing (Private, For-profit)
  Fall 2013 Enrollment: 156 . . . . (517) 272-4018
  2013-14 Tuition: In-state $17,568; Out-of-state $17,568
Regency Beauty Institute-Lansing (Private, For-profit)
  Fall 2013 Enrollment: 80 . . . . (800) 787-6456
  2013-14 Tuition: $17,300
Ross Medical Education Center-Lansing (Private, For-profit)
  Fall 2013 Enrollment: 151 . . . . (517) 703-9044
  2013-14 Tuition: $15,680

Housing: Homeownership rate: 53.7%; Median home value: $85,000; Median year structure built: 1959; Homeowner vacancy rate: 3.9%; Median gross rent: $729 per month; Rental vacancy rate: 10.3%

Health Insurance: 87.1% have insurance; 55.8% have private insurance; 42.7% have public insurance; 12.9% do not have insurance; 3.6% of children under 18 do not have insurance

Hospitals: Edward W Sparrow Hospital (535 beds); Mclaren - Greater Lansing

Safety: Violent crime rate: 105.7 per 10,000 population; Property crime rate: 347.7 per 10,000 population

Newspapers: City Pulse (weekly circulation 20000); Lansing State Journal (daily circulation 63000)

Transportation: Commute: 88.5% car, 4.4% public transportation, 2.7% walk, 2.7% work from home; Median travel time to work: 19.1 minutes

Airports: Capital Region International (primary service/non-hub)

Additional Information Contacts
City of Lansing . . . . (517) 483-4131
  http://www.cityoflansingmi.com

LEROY (township). Covers a land area of 34.127 square miles and a water area of 0.080 square miles. Located at 42.64° N. Lat; 84.21° W. Long.

Population: 3,530; Growth (since 2000): -3.4%; Density: 103.4 persons per square mile; Race: 96.3% White, 0.5% Black/African American, 0.7% Asian, 0.5% American Indian/Alaska Native, 0.0% Native Hawaiian/Other Pacific Islander, 1.3% Two or more races, 2.0% Hispanic of any race; Average household size: 2.66; Median age: 38.5; Age under 18: 25.6%; Age 65 and over: 10.9%; Males per 100 females: 103.3; Marriage status: 29.4% never married, 49.1% now married, 1.5% separated, 5.3% widowed, 16.3% divorced; Foreign born: 0.5%; Speak English only: 96.1%; With disability: 9.9%; Veterans: 14.5%; Ancestry: 31.0% German, 20.1% Irish, 18.3% English, 5.6% Italian, 5.1% French

Employment: 5.6% management, business, and financial, 2.4% computer, engineering, and science, 4.5% education, legal, community service, arts, and media, 4.9% healthcare practitioners, 16.9% service, 29.9% sales and office, 9.7% natural resources, construction, and maintenance, 26.0% production, transportation, and material moving

Income: Per capita: $23,073; Median household: $51,161; Average household: $60,859; Households with income of $100,000 or more: 15.6%; Poverty rate: 18.0%

Educational Attainment: High school diploma or higher: 89.3%; Bachelor's degree or higher: 14.9%; Graduate/professional degree or higher: 6.3%

Housing: Homeownership rate: 82.1%; Median home value: $115,300; Median year structure built: 1977; Homeowner vacancy rate: 2.4%; Median gross rent: $873 per month; Rental vacancy rate: 7.6%

Health Insurance: 88.5% have insurance; 76.5% have private insurance; 27.8% have public insurance; 11.5% do not have insurance; 13.9% of children under 18 do not have insurance

Transportation: Commute: 95.0% car, 0.0% public transportation, 1.4% walk, 2.9% work from home; Median travel time to work: 25.8 minutes

LESLIE (city).
Covers a land area of 1.287 square miles and a water area of 0.001 square miles. Located at 42.45° N. Lat; 84.43° W. Long. Elevation is 935 feet.

History: Leslie was settled in 1836 as the center of a farming area. In North Leslie, an ancient burial mound revealed a human skull and thigh bone of very large dimensions.

Population: 1,851; Growth (since 2000): -9.4%; Density: 1,438.0 persons per square mile; Race: 96.5% White, 0.9% Black/African American, 0.5% Asian, 0.3% American Indian/Alaska Native, 0.0% Native Hawaiian/Other Pacific Islander, 1.5% Two or more races, 2.6% Hispanic of any race; Average household size: 2.64; Median age: 35.7; Age under 18: 28.5%; Age 65 and over: 9.7%; Males per 100 females: 97.3

School District(s)
Leslie Public Schools (PK-12)
    2012-13 Enrollment: 1,374 . . . . (517) 589-8200
White Pine Academy (KG-12)
    2012-13 Enrollment: 117 . . . . (517) 589-8961
Housing: Homeownership rate: 76.6%; Homeowner vacancy rate: 6.2%; Rental vacancy rate: 16.6%

LESLIE (township).
Covers a land area of 34.896 square miles and a water area of 0.159 square miles. Located at 42.47° N. Lat; 84.42° W. Long. Elevation is 935 feet.

History: Settled 1836, incorporated 1869.

Population: 2,389; Growth (since 2000): 2.7%; Density: 68.5 persons per square mile; Race: 97.8% White, 0.2% Black/African American, 0.1% Asian, 0.2% American Indian/Alaska Native, 0.0% Native Hawaiian/Other Pacific Islander, 0.6% Two or more races, 3.1% Hispanic of any race; Average household size: 2.67; Median age: 42.9; Age under 18: 23.6%; Age 65 and over: 13.6%; Males per 100 females: 105.9

School District(s)
Leslie Public Schools (PK-12)
    2012-13 Enrollment: 1,374 . . . . (517) 589-8200
White Pine Academy (KG-12)
    2012-13 Enrollment: 117 . . . . (517) 589-8961
Housing: Homeownership rate: 91.3%; Homeowner vacancy rate: 1.2%; Rental vacancy rate: 11.4%

Additional Information Contacts
Leslie Township . . . . (517) 589-8201
    http://www.leslietownship.org

LOCKE (township).
Covers a land area of 35.837 square miles and a water area of 0.225 square miles. Located at 42.73° N. Lat; 84.21° W. Long.

Population: 1,791; Growth (since 2000): 7.2%; Density: 50.0 persons per square mile; Race: 97.0% White, 0.3% Black/African American, 0.5% Asian, 0.3% American Indian/Alaska Native, 0.3% Native Hawaiian/Other Pacific Islander, 1.2% Two or more races, 2.3% Hispanic of any race; Average household size: 2.84; Median age: 42.6; Age under 18: 25.7%; Age 65 and over: 12.2%; Males per 100 females: 99.7

Housing: Homeownership rate: 91.1%; Homeowner vacancy rate: 2.2%; Rental vacancy rate: 8.2%

MASON (city).
County seat. Covers a land area of 5.100 square miles and a water area of 0.028 square miles. Located at 42.58° N. Lat; 84.44° W. Long. Elevation is 915 feet.

History: Mason was settled in 1836 at the junction of two trails. It became the seat of Ingham County in 1840.

Population: 8,252; Growth (since 2000): 22.9%; Density: 1,618.1 persons per square mile; Race: 90.2% White, 5.9% Black/African American, 0.9% Asian, 0.4% American Indian/Alaska Native, 0.0% Native Hawaiian/Other Pacific Islander, 1.7% Two or more races, 3.7% Hispanic of any race; Average household size: 2.29; Median age: 37.8; Age under 18: 21.8%; Age 65 and over: 13.5%; Males per 100 females: 103.2; Marriage status: 34.7% never married, 45.3% now married, 2.3% separated, 5.5% widowed, 14.4% divorced; Foreign born: 1.2%; Speak English only: 98.1%; With disability: 12.9%; Veterans: 10.0%; Ancestry: 26.0% German, 19.2% Irish, 16.1% English, 5.9% American, 5.7% French

Employment: 10.9% management, business, and financial, 7.1% computer, engineering, and science, 12.5% education, legal, community service, arts, and media, 5.6% healthcare practitioners, 14.7% service, 29.1% sales and office, 5.8% natural resources, construction, and maintenance, 14.3% production, transportation, and material moving

Income: Per capita: $24,132; Median household: $53,396; Average household: $61,228; Households with income of $100,000 or more: 17.7%; Poverty rate: 10.5%

Educational Attainment: High school diploma or higher: 91.7%; Bachelor's degree or higher: 26.7%; Graduate/professional degree or higher: 11.1%

School District(s)
Ingham ISD (PK-12)
    2012-13 Enrollment: 1,144 . . . . (517) 244-1214
Mason Public Schools (Ingham) (PK-12)
    2012-13 Enrollment: 3,051 . . . . (517) 676-2484
Housing: Homeownership rate: 66.6%; Median home value: $113,900; Median year structure built: 1981; Homeowner vacancy rate: 2.0%; Median gross rent: $818 per month; Rental vacancy rate: 10.4%

Health Insurance: 94.5% have insurance; 76.0% have private insurance; 34.1% have public insurance; 5.5% do not have insurance; 2.5% of children under 18 do not have insurance

Safety: Violent crime rate: 8.5 per 10,000 population; Property crime rate: 202.5 per 10,000 population

Transportation: Commute: 93.3% car, 0.2% public transportation, 3.7% walk, 1.5% work from home; Median travel time to work: 20.2 minutes

Additional Information Contacts
City of Mason . . . . (517) 676-9155
    http://www.mason.mi.us

MERIDIAN (charter township).
Covers a land area of 30.485 square miles and a water area of 1.084 square miles. Located at 42.73° N. Lat; 84.42° W. Long. Elevation is 896 feet.

Population: 39,688; Growth (since 2000): 1.5%; Density: 1,301.9 persons per square mile; Race: 80.0% White, 4.9% Black/African American, 10.9% Asian, 0.4% American Indian/Alaska Native, 0.0% Native Hawaiian/Other Pacific Islander, 2.8% Two or more races, 3.8% Hispanic of any race; Average household size: 2.26; Median age: 38.2; Age under 18: 20.8%; Age 65 and over: 13.3%; Males per 100 females: 90.7; Marriage status: 32.5% never married, 52.1% now married, 0.8% separated, 6.1% widowed, 9.3% divorced; Foreign born: 12.8%; Speak English only: 84.9%; With disability: 8.5%; Veterans: 8.1%; Ancestry: 25.0% German, 14.0% Irish, 13.6% English, 6.1% Polish, 4.2% American

Employment: 19.1% management, business, and financial, 11.1% computer, engineering, and science, 21.2% education, legal, community service, arts, and media, 6.8% healthcare practitioners, 13.5% service, 21.7% sales and office, 2.3% natural resources, construction, and maintenance, 4.2% production, transportation, and material moving

Income: Per capita: $37,732; Median household: $62,145; Average household: $85,330; Households with income of $100,000 or more: 30.6%; Poverty rate: 13.1%

Educational Attainment: High school diploma or higher: 97.1%; Bachelor's degree or higher: 64.8%; Graduate/professional degree or higher: 33.6%

Housing: Homeownership rate: 60.9%; Median home value: $184,400; Median year structure built: 1979; Homeowner vacancy rate: 2.0%; Median gross rent: $794 per month; Rental vacancy rate: 7.6%

Health Insurance: 92.4% have insurance; 84.3% have private insurance; 21.5% have public insurance; 7.6% do not have insurance; 2.5% of children under 18 do not have insurance

Safety: Violent crime rate: 28.6 per 10,000 population; Property crime rate: 229.3 per 10,000 population

Transportation: Commute: 89.7% car, 1.7% public transportation, 2.1% walk, 4.9% work from home; Median travel time to work: 19.8 minutes

Additional Information Contacts
Meridian Charter Township . . . . (517) 853-4000
    http://www.meridian.mi.us

OKEMOS (CDP).
Covers a land area of 16.763 square miles and a water area of 0.148 square miles. Located at 42.71° N. Lat; 84.41° W. Long. Elevation is 840 feet.

History: The settlement of Hamilton was founded in 1839 by Freeman Bray as a trading point with the surrounding Ojibwa people and as a farming community. In 1859, one year following the death of Chief John

Okemos (on whose treaty lands the city was built), the city was renamed Okemos to honor the Native American chief.

Population: 21,369; Growth (since 2000): -6.3%; Density: 1,274.8 persons per square mile; Race: 76.5% White, 5.1% Black/African American, 14.4% Asian, 0.3% American Indian/Alaska Native, 0.1% Native Hawaiian/Other Pacific Islander, 2.6% Two or more races, 3.3% Hispanic of any race; Average household size: 2.38; Median age: 37.9; Age under 18: 21.3%; Age 65 and over: 12.3%; Males per 100 females: 92.8; Marriage status: 32.8% never married, 54.4% now married, 0.6% separated, 4.4% widowed, 8.4% divorced; Foreign born: 14.6%; Speak English only: 82.3%; With disability: 7.4%; Veterans: 7.8%; Ancestry: 25.4% German, 13.4% English, 12.9% Irish, 7.5% Polish, 4.5% American

Employment: 18.3% management, business, and financial, 12.8% computer, engineering, and science, 23.4% education, legal, community service, arts, and media, 6.1% healthcare practitioners, 14.6% service, 17.7% sales and office, 3.6% natural resources, construction, and maintenance, 3.6% production, transportation, and material moving

Income: Per capita: $39,889; Median household: $70,781; Average household: $94,266; Households with income of $100,000 or more: 35.8%; Poverty rate: 11.6%

Educational Attainment: High school diploma or higher: 97.9%; Bachelor's degree or higher: 70.0%; Graduate/professional degree or higher: 37.2%

School District(s)
Michigan Connections Academy (KG-12)
    2012-13 Enrollment: 813. . . . . (517) 507-5390
Okemos Public Schools (PK-12)
    2012-13 Enrollment: 3,910 . . . . (517) 706-5010

Housing: Homeownership rate: 63.8%; Median home value: $193,300; Median year structure built: 1977; Homeowner vacancy rate: 1.7%; Median gross rent: $822 per month; Rental vacancy rate: 7.8%

Health Insurance: 94.2% have insurance; 86.5% have private insurance; 20.7% have public insurance; 5.8% do not have insurance; 1.6% of children under 18 do not have insurance

Transportation: Commute: 88.1% car, 1.9% public transportation, 3.0% walk, 5.0% work from home; Median travel time to work: 20.1 minutes

ONONDAGA (township).
Covers a land area of 36.114 square miles and a water area of 0.372 square miles. Located at 42.47° N. Lat; 84.55° W. Long. Elevation is 902 feet.

Population: 3,158; Growth (since 2000): 6.8%; Density: 87.4 persons per square mile; Race: 95.4% White, 0.7% Black/African American, 0.4% Asian, 0.6% American Indian/Alaska Native, 0.0% Native Hawaiian/Other Pacific Islander, 1.8% Two or more races, 3.7% Hispanic of any race; Average household size: 2.77; Median age: 39.8; Age under 18: 27.3%; Age 65 and over: 9.5%; Males per 100 females: 100.1; Marriage status: 26.0% never married, 56.7% now married, 0.5% separated, 4.5% widowed, 12.8% divorced; Foreign born: 0.7%; Speak English only: 96.4%; With disability: 15.4%; Veterans: 11.5%; Ancestry: 27.8% German, 16.1% American, 15.2% English, 9.0% Irish, 6.6% French

Employment: 13.4% management, business, and financial, 4.8% computer, engineering, and science, 8.0% education, legal, community service, arts, and media, 4.5% healthcare practitioners, 20.4% service, 16.3% sales and office, 6.4% natural resources, construction, and maintenance, 26.2% production, transportation, and material moving

Income: Per capita: $25,304; Median household: $61,636; Average household: $70,112; Households with income of $100,000 or more: 18.6%; Poverty rate: 11.3%

Educational Attainment: High school diploma or higher: 92.9%; Bachelor's degree or higher: 17.9%; Graduate/professional degree or higher: 7.1%

School District(s)
Ingham ISD (PK-12)
    2012-13 Enrollment: 1,144 . . . . (517) 244-1214

Housing: Homeownership rate: 88.4%; Median home value: $139,700; Median year structure built: 1980; Homeowner vacancy rate: 2.7%; Median gross rent: $775 per month; Rental vacancy rate: 3.8%

Health Insurance: 88.7% have insurance; 76.0% have private insurance; 26.0% have public insurance; 11.3% do not have insurance; 4.5% of children under 18 do not have insurance

Transportation: Commute: 94.4% car, 0.3% public transportation, 0.2% walk, 4.2% work from home; Median travel time to work: 27.8 minutes

STOCKBRIDGE (township).
Covers a land area of 35.457 square miles and a water area of 0.461 square miles. Located at 42.46° N. Lat; 84.20° W. Long. Elevation is 942 feet.

Population: 3,896; Growth (since 2000): 13.4%; Density: 109.9 persons per square mile; Race: 96.5% White, 0.6% Black/African American, 0.3% Asian, 0.7% American Indian/Alaska Native, 0.0% Native Hawaiian/Other Pacific Islander, 1.6% Two or more races, 2.6% Hispanic of any race; Average household size: 2.75; Median age: 39.2; Age under 18: 26.7%; Age 65 and over: 12.0%; Males per 100 females: 100.0; Marriage status: 25.5% never married, 59.9% now married, 1.0% separated, 5.3% widowed, 9.4% divorced; Foreign born: 1.5%; Speak English only: 95.9%; With disability: 13.8%; Veterans: 8.5%; Ancestry: 24.1% German, 17.2% English, 16.6% Irish, 11.7% American, 5.7% French

Employment: 11.1% management, business, and financial, 4.3% computer, engineering, and science, 11.6% education, legal, community service, arts, and media, 7.1% healthcare practitioners, 13.8% service, 22.1% sales and office, 6.3% natural resources, construction, and maintenance, 23.7% production, transportation, and material moving

Income: Per capita: $25,583; Median household: $54,107; Average household: $69,615; Households with income of $100,000 or more: 20.2%; Poverty rate: 13.2%

Educational Attainment: High school diploma or higher: 89.0%; Bachelor's degree or higher: 19.4%; Graduate/professional degree or higher: 6.5%

School District(s)
Stockbridge Community Schools (PK-12)
    2012-13 Enrollment: 1,541 . . . . (517) 851-7188

Housing: Homeownership rate: 79.7%; Median home value: $132,400; Median year structure built: 1973; Homeowner vacancy rate: 2.4%; Median gross rent: $728 per month; Rental vacancy rate: 8.4%

Health Insurance: 88.2% have insurance; 71.1% have private insurance; 32.0% have public insurance; 11.8% do not have insurance; 9.1% of children under 18 do not have insurance

Newspapers: Stockbridge Town Crier (weekly circulation 10000)

Transportation: Commute: 93.2% car, 0.1% public transportation, 4.2% walk, 2.5% work from home; Median travel time to work: 33.3 minutes

STOCKBRIDGE (village).
Covers a land area of 1.508 square miles and a water area of 0.016 square miles. Located at 42.45° N. Lat; 84.18° W. Long. Elevation is 942 feet.

History: Stockbridge was settled in 1835 by Herman Lowe. The village was first called Pekin by Elijah Smith, who platted it and named it for his former home in New York. The name was later changed to that of the township.

Population: 1,218; Growth (since 2000): -3.3%; Density: 807.8 persons per square mile; Race: 96.7% White, 0.2% Black/African American, 0.2% Asian, 0.9% American Indian/Alaska Native, 0.0% Native Hawaiian/Other Pacific Islander, 1.8% Two or more races, 3.1% Hispanic of any race; Average household size: 2.53; Median age: 36.8; Age under 18: 29.4%; Age 65 and over: 12.3%; Males per 100 females: 88.0

School District(s)
Stockbridge Community Schools (PK-12)
    2012-13 Enrollment: 1,541 . . . . (517) 851-7188

Housing: Homeownership rate: 59.6%; Homeowner vacancy rate: 3.4%; Rental vacancy rate: 8.9%

Safety: Violent crime rate: 40.9 per 10,000 population; Property crime rate: 286.4 per 10,000 population

Newspapers: Stockbridge Town Crier (weekly circulation 10000)

VEVAY (township).
Covers a land area of 31.562 square miles and a water area of 0.082 square miles. Located at 42.54° N. Lat; 84.42° W. Long.

Population: 3,537; Growth (since 2000): -2.1%; Density: 112.1 persons per square mile; Race: 96.4% White, 0.5% Black/African American, 0.3% Asian, 0.6% American Indian/Alaska Native, 0.0% Native Hawaiian/Other Pacific Islander, 1.3% Two or more races, 2.6% Hispanic of any race; Average household size: 2.67; Median age: 43.3; Age under 18: 22.7%; Age 65 and over: 12.9%; Males per 100 females: 99.6; Marriage status: 23.8% never married, 66.2% now married, 0.6% separated, 3.2% widowed, 6.8% divorced; Foreign born: 2.7%; Speak English only: 94.8%; With disability: 7.4%; Veterans: 10.2%; Ancestry: 30.2% German, 23.5% English, 14.4% Irish, 7.9% American, 5.6% French

Employment: 21.9% management, business, and financial, 0.0% computer, engineering, and science, 7.1% education, legal, community service, arts, and media, 5.2% healthcare practitioners, 11.9% service,

23.5% sales and office, 18.1% natural resources, construction, and maintenance, 12.4% production, transportation, and material moving
Income: Per capita: $29,800; Median household: $72,026; Average household: $82,564; Households with income of $100,000 or more: 28.8%; Poverty rate: 3.8%
Educational Attainment: High school diploma or higher: 94.7%; Bachelor's degree or higher: 23.8%; Graduate/professional degree or higher: 10.1%
Housing: Homeownership rate: 93.2%; Median home value: $165,200; Median year structure built: 1977; Homeowner vacancy rate: 2.0%; Median gross rent: $496 per month; Rental vacancy rate: 27.4%
Health Insurance: 95.1% have insurance; 82.1% have private insurance; 28.4% have public insurance; 4.9% do not have insurance; 3.8% of children under 18 do not have insurance
Transportation: Commute: 86.1% car, 0.0% public transportation, 5.2% walk, 8.0% work from home; Median travel time to work: 23.6 minutes

WEBBERVILLE (village). Covers a land area of 1.832 square miles and a water area of 0.012 square miles. Located at 42.66° N. Lat; 84.18° W. Long. Elevation is 896 feet.
Population: 1,272; Growth (since 2000): -15.4%; Density: 694.2 persons per square mile; Race: 97.5% White, 0.6% Black/African American, 0.1% Asian, 0.2% American Indian/Alaska Native, 0.0% Native Hawaiian/Other Pacific Islander, 0.9% Two or more races, 2.7% Hispanic of any race; Average household size: 2.50; Median age: 35.6; Age under 18: 26.4%; Age 65 and over: 9.2%; Males per 100 females: 98.4
School District(s)
Webberville Community Schools (KG-12)
    2012-13 Enrollment: 611 . . . . (517) 521-3422
Housing: Homeownership rate: 77.9%; Homeowner vacancy rate: 2.9%; Rental vacancy rate: 13.7%

WHEATFIELD (township). Covers a land area of 29.139 square miles and a water area of 0.063 square miles. Located at 42.64° N. Lat; 84.32° W. Long.
Population: 1,632; Growth (since 2000): -0.5%; Density: 56.0 persons per square mile; Race: 94.4% White, 0.4% Black/African American, 1.3% Asian, 0.4% American Indian/Alaska Native, 0.0% Native Hawaiian/Other Pacific Islander, 2.8% Two or more races, 1.9% Hispanic of any race; Average household size: 2.61; Median age: 46.3; Age under 18: 22.3%; Age 65 and over: 16.5%; Males per 100 females: 93.8
Housing: Homeownership rate: 88.7%; Homeowner vacancy rate: 1.1%; Rental vacancy rate: 5.4%

WHITE OAK (township). Covers a land area of 36.283 square miles and a water area of 0.197 square miles. Located at 42.56° N. Lat; 84.20° W. Long. Elevation is 968 feet.
Population: 1,173; Growth (since 2000): -0.3%; Density: 32.3 persons per square mile; Race: 95.7% White, 0.6% Black/African American, 0.3% Asian, 1.2% American Indian/Alaska Native, 0.0% Native Hawaiian/Other Pacific Islander, 1.7% Two or more races, 1.6% Hispanic of any race; Average household size: 2.67; Median age: 44.9; Age under 18: 22.9%; Age 65 and over: 12.9%; Males per 100 females: 114.1
Housing: Homeownership rate: 89.6%; Homeowner vacancy rate: 3.0%; Rental vacancy rate: 4.3%

WILLIAMSTON (city). Covers a land area of 2.435 square miles and a water area of 0.116 square miles. Located at 42.68° N. Lat; 84.28° W. Long. Elevation is 869 feet.
History: Williamston developed in an area where large clay pits contained layers of soft coal. Both clay and coal have been mined commercially.
Population: 3,854; Growth (since 2000): 12.0%; Density: 1,582.5 persons per square mile; Race: 94.4% White, 0.9% Black/African American, 1.1% Asian, 0.5% American Indian/Alaska Native, 0.1% Native Hawaiian/Other Pacific Islander, 2.3% Two or more races, 3.1% Hispanic of any race; Average household size: 2.40; Median age: 35.9; Age under 18: 28.0%; Age 65 and over: 11.7%; Males per 100 females: 91.1; Marriage status: 24.0% never married, 56.5% now married, 0.0% separated, 6.5% widowed, 13.1% divorced; Foreign born: 3.8%; Speak English only: 92.8%; With disability: 10.6%; Veterans: 5.6%; Ancestry: 29.8% German, 14.5% English, 13.7% Irish, 12.1% Polish, 6.9% American
Employment: 26.1% management, business, and financial, 3.9% computer, engineering, and science, 17.9% education, legal, community service, arts, and media, 3.8% healthcare practitioners, 17.0% service,

18.0% sales and office, 5.6% natural resources, construction, and maintenance, 7.6% production, transportation, and material moving
Income: Per capita: $29,436; Median household: $50,956; Average household: $71,827; Households with income of $100,000 or more: 24.0%; Poverty rate: 16.0%
Educational Attainment: High school diploma or higher: 92.9%; Bachelor's degree or higher: 43.2%; Graduate/professional degree or higher: 19.2%
School District(s)
Williamston Community Schools (PK-12)
    2012-13 Enrollment: 1,837 . . . . (517) 655-4361
Housing: Homeownership rate: 66.2%; Median home value: $125,900; Median year structure built: 1983; Homeowner vacancy rate: 4.6%; Median gross rent: $643 per month; Rental vacancy rate: 11.5%
Health Insurance: 92.1% have insurance; 71.6% have private insurance; 34.1% have public insurance; 7.9% do not have insurance; 1.2% of children under 18 do not have insurance
Safety: Violent crime rate: 5.2 per 10,000 population; Property crime rate: 54.7 per 10,000 population
Transportation: Commute: 90.1% car, 1.5% public transportation, 2.6% walk, 5.9% work from home; Median travel time to work: 24.5 minutes

WILLIAMSTOWN (township). Covers a land area of 29.088 square miles and a water area of 0.171 square miles. Located at 42.74° N. Lat; 84.31° W. Long.
History: Originally Called Phelpstown Township The name of the township was changed from Phelpstown to Williamstown, by act of the Legislature, Feb. 17, 1857.
Population: 4,978; Growth (since 2000): 3.0%; Density: 171.1 persons per square mile; Race: 96.1% White, 0.8% Black/African American, 1.2% Asian, 0.3% American Indian/Alaska Native, 0.0% Native Hawaiian/Other Pacific Islander, 1.3% Two or more races, 2.0% Hispanic of any race; Average household size: 2.66; Median age: 47.2; Age under 18: 23.0%; Age 65 and over: 15.0%; Males per 100 females: 99.1; Marriage status: 27.6% never married, 63.9% now married, 0.9% separated, 3.8% widowed, 4.7% divorced; Foreign born: 2.0%; Speak English only: 96.5%; With disability: 13.4%; Veterans: 8.6%; Ancestry: 26.6% German, 20.8% English, 19.8% Irish, 11.1% Polish, 5.6% Scottish
Employment: 17.8% management, business, and financial, 5.7% computer, engineering, and science, 17.6% education, legal, community service, arts, and media, 7.4% healthcare practitioners, 19.6% service, 20.5% sales and office, 5.7% natural resources, construction, and maintenance, 5.7% production, transportation, and material moving
Income: Per capita: $47,273; Median household: $100,484; Average household: $122,657; Households with income of $100,000 or more: 51.0%; Poverty rate: 4.8%
Educational Attainment: High school diploma or higher: 96.8%; Bachelor's degree or higher: 49.0%; Graduate/professional degree or higher: 25.2%
Housing: Homeownership rate: 92.4%; Median home value: $222,900; Median year structure built: 1974; Homeowner vacancy rate: 1.0%; Median gross rent: $1,324 per month; Rental vacancy rate: 12.9%
Health Insurance: 97.4% have insurance; 89.8% have private insurance; 25.0% have public insurance; 2.6% do not have insurance; 0.0% of children under 18 do not have insurance
Transportation: Commute: 95.8% car, 0.6% public transportation, 0.9% walk, 2.7% work from home; Median travel time to work: 25.1 minutes

Ionia County

Located in south central Michigan; crossed by the Grand River; drained by the Flat, Lookingglass, and Maple Rivers. Covers a land area of 571.304 square miles, a water area of 8.742 square miles, and is located in the Eastern Time Zone at 42.94° N. Lat., 85.07° W. Long. The county was founded in 1837. County seat is Ionia.

Ionia County is part of the Ionia, MI Micropolitan Statistical Area. The entire metro area includes: Ionia County, MI

Weather Station: Ionia 2 SSW   Elevation: 805 feet

	Jan	Feb	Mar	Apr	May	Jun	Jul	Aug	Sep	Oct	Nov	Dec
High	30	33	43	57	69	78	82	80	73	59	46	34
Low	15	16	23	34	45	55	59	57	49	38	30	20
Precip	2.1	1.9	2.5	2.9	3.7	3.1	3.4	3.9	3.8	3.3	3.0	2.2
Snow	14.5	10.3	7.3	1.3	tr	0.0	0.0	0.0	0.0	0.5	3.8	14.0

High and Low temperatures in degrees Fahrenheit; Precipitation and Snow in inches

Population: 63,905; Growth (since 2000): 3.9%; Density: 111.9 persons per square mile; Race: 91.6% White, 4.7% Black/African American, 0.4% Asian, 0.5% American Indian/Alaska Native, 0.0% Native Hawaiian/Other Pacific Islander, 1.4% two or more races, 4.4% Hispanic of any race; Average household size: 2.64; Median age: 37.0; Age under 18: 24.5%; Age 65 and over: 11.3%; Males per 100 females: 116.0; Marriage status: 29.4% never married, 52.4% now married, 1.3% separated, 5.6% widowed, 12.6% divorced; Foreign born: 1.4%; Speak English only: 96.3%; With disability: 15.4%; Veterans: 9.9%; Ancestry: 29.8% German, 13.1% Irish, 12.0% English, 6.9% American, 6.8% Dutch
Religion: Six largest groups: 19.4% Catholicism, 4.1% Non-denominational Protestant, 4.1% Methodist/Pietist, 1.9% Holiness, 1.7% Presbyterian-Reformed, 1.0% Lutheran
Economy: Unemployment rate: 5.0%; Leading industries: 16.7% retail trade; 12.3% other services (except public administration); 12.1% health care and social assistance; Farms: 1,109 totaling 248,418 acres; Company size: 0 employ 1,000 or more persons, 2 employ 500 to 999 persons, 17 employ 100 to 499 persons, 844 employ less than 100 persons; Business ownership: 1,191 women-owned, n/a Black-owned, n/a Hispanic-owned, n/a Asian-owned
Employment: 11.8% management, business, and financial, 3.4% computer, engineering, and science, 7.8% education, legal, community service, arts, and media, 3.9% healthcare practitioners, 17.4% service, 24.3% sales and office, 12.6% natural resources, construction, and maintenance, 18.7% production, transportation, and material moving
Income: Per capita: $20,206; Median household: $47,892; Average household: $56,197; Households with income of $100,000 or more: 12.9%; Poverty rate: 15.8%
Educational Attainment: High school diploma or higher: 87.9%; Bachelor's degree or higher: 14.0%; Graduate/professional degree or higher: 4.1%
Housing: Homeownership rate: 77.7%; Median home value: $111,000; Median year structure built: 1970; Homeowner vacancy rate: 2.6%; Median gross rent: $664 per month; Rental vacancy rate: 13.4%
Vital Statistics: Birth rate: 113.9 per 10,000 population; Death rate: 74.9 per 10,000 population; Age-adjusted cancer mortality rate: 163.6 deaths per 100,000 population
Health Insurance: 89.5% have insurance; 69.7% have private insurance; 33.8% have public insurance; 10.5% do not have insurance; 2.8% of children under 18 do not have insurance
Health Care: Physicians: 4.5 per 10,000 population; Hospital beds: 3.9 per 10,000 population; Hospital admissions: 78.5 per 10,000 population
Transportation: Commute: 93.6% car, 0.1% public transportation, 1.7% walk, 3.8% work from home; Median travel time to work: 27.6 minutes
Presidential Election: 42.8% Obama, 55.7% Romney (2012)
National and State Parks: Ionia State Recreation Area; Lowell State Game Area; Portland State Game Area
Additional Information Contacts
Ionia Government . . . . (616) 527-5322
    http://www.ioniacounty.org

Ionia County Communities

BELDING (city). Covers a land area of 4.721 square miles and a water area of 0.181 square miles. Located at 43.10° N. Lat; 85.23° W. Long. Elevation is 778 feet.
History: Belding was first known as Broas Rapids for Charles Broas, who settled on the site in 1839. Later it was named Patterson's Mills, when Lucius Patterson bought an interest in the Broas mill property. In 1864, the Belding brothers founded a silk mill here. The mill was purchased in 1928 by a group of New York bankers, who abandoned the enterprise when the economic depression hit the country. The citizens of Belding later reopened the mill.
Population: 5,757; Growth (since 2000): -2.0%; Density: 1,219.4 persons per square mile; Race: 95.2% White, 0.3% Black/African American, 0.5% Asian, 0.5% American Indian/Alaska Native, 0.1% Native Hawaiian/Other Pacific Islander, 1.8% Two or more races, 5.0% Hispanic of any race; Average household size: 2.61; Median age: 33.7; Age under 18: 28.7%; Age 65 and over: 12.7%; Males per 100 females: 90.8; Marriage status: 29.2% never married, 47.5% now married, 1.9% separated, 5.4% widowed, 17.9% divorced; Foreign born: 1.6%; Speak English only: 96.9%; With disability: 21.5%; Veterans: 9.1%; Ancestry: 23.2% German, 13.3% Irish, 9.0% English, 6.9% American, 5.8% Dutch

Employment: 6.9% management, business, and financial, 3.0% computer, engineering, and science, 4.5% education, legal, community service, arts, and media, 2.9% healthcare practitioners, 23.4% service, 24.9% sales and office, 13.6% natural resources, construction, and maintenance, 20.6% production, transportation, and material moving
Income: Per capita: $17,238; Median household: $36,509; Average household: $44,786; Households with income of $100,000 or more: 7.0%; Poverty rate: 24.2%
Educational Attainment: High school diploma or higher: 80.7%; Bachelor's degree or higher: 10.1%; Graduate/professional degree or higher: 2.0%
School District(s)
Belding Area SD (PK-12)
    2012-13 Enrollment: 1,997 . . . . (616) 794-4700
Grattan Academy (KG-12)
    2012-13 Enrollment: 271 . . . . (616) 754-9360
Housing: Homeownership rate: 65.0%; Median home value: $82,200; Median year structure built: 1955; Homeowner vacancy rate: 3.3%; Median gross rent: $546 per month; Rental vacancy rate: 12.4%
Health Insurance: 86.0% have insurance; 55.5% have private insurance; 46.6% have public insurance; 14.0% do not have insurance; 0.7% of children under 18 do not have insurance
Safety: Violent crime rate: 12.2 per 10,000 population; Property crime rate: 262.6 per 10,000 population
Transportation: Commute: 95.3% car, 0.0% public transportation, 1.3% walk, 2.6% work from home; Median travel time to work: 32.0 minutes
Additional Information Contacts
City of Belding . . . . (616) 794-1900
    http://www.ci.belding.mi.us

BERLIN (township). Covers a land area of 41.546 square miles and a water area of 0.227 square miles. Located at 42.91° N. Lat; 85.13° W. Long.
History: Berlin Township was organized in 1839.
Population: 2,116; Growth (since 2000): -24.1%; Density: 50.9 persons per square mile; Race: 96.9% White, 0.3% Black/African American, 0.3% Asian, 0.5% American Indian/Alaska Native, 0.0% Native Hawaiian/Other Pacific Islander, 1.3% Two or more races, 2.0% Hispanic of any race; Average household size: 2.63; Median age: 40.8; Age under 18: 25.2%; Age 65 and over: 17.0%; Males per 100 females: 98.7
Housing: Homeownership rate: 83.2%; Homeowner vacancy rate: 2.5%; Rental vacancy rate: 4.2%

BOSTON (township). Covers a land area of 35.076 square miles and a water area of 0.890 square miles. Located at 42.89° N. Lat; 85.26° W. Long.
History: Boston Township was named by its early settlers who had come from New England.
Population: 5,709; Growth (since 2000): 15.1%; Density: 162.8 persons per square mile; Race: 96.6% White, 0.5% Black/African American, 0.4% Asian, 0.5% American Indian/Alaska Native, 0.0% Native Hawaiian/Other Pacific Islander, 1.1% Two or more races, 2.5% Hispanic of any race; Average household size: 2.62; Median age: 38.5; Age under 18: 26.2%; Age 65 and over: 11.6%; Males per 100 females: 100.3; Marriage status: 22.3% never married, 58.1% now married, 0.7% separated, 6.5% widowed, 13.1% divorced; Foreign born: 0.7%; Speak English only: 98.3%; With disability: 15.3%; Veterans: 10.3%; Ancestry: 30.3% German, 13.7% Irish, 11.7% English, 11.5% Dutch, 9.6% American
Employment: 13.7% management, business, and financial, 6.9% computer, engineering, and science, 8.4% education, legal, community service, arts, and media, 2.2% healthcare practitioners, 16.7% service, 24.0% sales and office, 12.6% natural resources, construction, and maintenance, 15.6% production, transportation, and material moving
Income: Per capita: $24,337; Median household: $58,300; Average household: $65,441; Households with income of $100,000 or more: 16.3%; Poverty rate: 15.3%
Educational Attainment: High school diploma or higher: 92.0%; Bachelor's degree or higher: 22.7%; Graduate/professional degree or higher: 5.6%
Housing: Homeownership rate: 81.0%; Median home value: $147,300; Median year structure built: 1981; Homeowner vacancy rate: 2.1%; Median gross rent: $503 per month; Rental vacancy rate: 5.2%
Health Insurance: 90.3% have insurance; 69.3% have private insurance; 33.3% have public insurance; 9.7% do not have insurance; 4.6% of children under 18 do not have insurance

Transportation: Commute: 94.4% car, 0.5% public transportation, 0.8% walk, 4.3% work from home; Median travel time to work: 31.5 minutes

CAMPBELL (township). Covers a land area of 35.734 square miles and a water area of 0.185 square miles. Located at 42.82° N. Lat; 85.25° W. Long.

History: Campbell Township was named for Jeremiah and Martin Campbell, Irish immigrants who settled here in 1840. The township was organized in 1849.

Population: 2,388; Growth (since 2000): 6.5%; Density: 66.8 persons per square mile; Race: 96.6% White, 0.2% Black/African American, 0.5% Asian, 0.5% American Indian/Alaska Native, 0.0% Native Hawaiian/Other Pacific Islander, 1.7% Two or more races, 2.3% Hispanic of any race; Average household size: 2.68; Median age: 38.2; Age under 18: 26.4%; Age 65 and over: 12.2%; Males per 100 females: 104.3

Housing: Homeownership rate: 87.4%; Homeowner vacancy rate: 1.9%; Rental vacancy rate: 7.4%

CLARKSVILLE (village). Covers a land area of 0.504 square miles and a water area of 0 square miles. Located at 42.84° N. Lat; 85.24° W. Long. Elevation is 823 feet.

History: Clarksville was settled in 1840 by two brothers who had immigrated from Ireland. First called Skipperville, the village was renamed in 1875 for Clark L. Howard, who opened a store here and secured a post office.

Population: 394; Growth (since 2000): 24.3%; Density: 781.5 persons per square mile; Race: 94.7% White, 0.5% Black/African American, 2.0% Asian, 0.3% American Indian/Alaska Native, 0.0% Native Hawaiian/Other Pacific Islander, 2.3% Two or more races, 2.8% Hispanic of any race; Average household size: 2.40; Median age: 32.4; Age under 18: 25.4%; Age 65 and over: 15.5%; Males per 100 females: 115.3

School District(s)

Lakewood Public Schools (PK-12)
  2012-13 Enrollment: 2,029 . . . . (616) 374-8043

Housing: Homeownership rate: 74.4%; Homeowner vacancy rate: 2.4%; Rental vacancy rate: 10.6%

DANBY (township). Covers a land area of 35.106 square miles and a water area of 0.864 square miles. Located at 42.81° N. Lat; 84.90° W. Long.

Population: 2,988; Growth (since 2000): 10.8%; Density: 85.1 persons per square mile; Race: 97.9% White, 0.1% Black/African American, 0.4% Asian, 0.2% American Indian/Alaska Native, 0.0% Native Hawaiian/Other Pacific Islander, 1.0% Two or more races, 1.1% Hispanic of any race; Average household size: 2.83; Median age: 39.1; Age under 18: 27.4%; Age 65 and over: 10.9%; Males per 100 females: 102.0; Marriage status: 19.7% never married, 64.9% now married, 0.5% separated, 4.2% widowed, 11.2% divorced; Foreign born: 0.8%; Speak English only: 97.8%; With disability: 10.4%; Veterans: 10.4%; Ancestry: 36.4% German, 12.2% English, 12.2% Irish, 7.4% Dutch, 7.1% Polish

Employment: 18.7% management, business, and financial, 4.6% computer, engineering, and science, 5.4% education, legal, community service, arts, and media, 3.7% healthcare practitioners, 15.8% service, 24.5% sales and office, 11.2% natural resources, construction, and maintenance, 16.1% production, transportation, and material moving

Income: Per capita: $28,031; Median household: $69,297; Average household: $78,724; Households with income of $100,000 or more: 31.1%; Poverty rate: 7.9%

Educational Attainment: High school diploma or higher: 95.5%; Bachelor's degree or higher: 25.1%; Graduate/professional degree or higher: 5.4%

Housing: Homeownership rate: 92.0%; Median home value: $165,800; Median year structure built: 1979; Homeowner vacancy rate: 0.7%; Median gross rent: $682 per month; Rental vacancy rate: 3.4%

Health Insurance: 93.7% have insurance; 85.3% have private insurance; 22.1% have public insurance; 6.3% do not have insurance; 1.1% of children under 18 do not have insurance

Transportation: Commute: 95.0% car, 0.2% public transportation, 1.2% walk, 3.3% work from home; Median travel time to work: 32.3 minutes

EASTON (township). Covers a land area of 28.424 square miles and a water area of 0.167 square miles. Located at 42.99° N. Lat; 85.14° W. Long.

Population: 3,082; Growth (since 2000): 8.7%; Density: 108.4 persons per square mile; Race: 95.5% White, 0.4% Black/African American, 0.3%

Asian, 0.2% American Indian/Alaska Native, 0.0% Native Hawaiian/Other Pacific Islander, 1.3% Two or more races, 5.4% Hispanic of any race; Average household size: 2.57; Median age: 40.6; Age under 18: 25.4%; Age 65 and over: 14.1%; Males per 100 females: 97.9; Marriage status: 20.3% never married, 66.3% now married, 0.4% separated, 5.8% widowed, 7.6% divorced; Foreign born: 0.9%; Speak English only: 98.3%; With disability: 15.0%; Veterans: 8.5%; Ancestry: 32.8% German, 14.3% English, 13.9% Irish, 7.2% American, 6.1% Dutch

Employment: 10.2% management, business, and financial, 5.3% computer, engineering, and science, 10.6% education, legal, community service, arts, and media, 3.6% healthcare practitioners, 13.0% service, 26.7% sales and office, 13.5% natural resources, construction, and maintenance, 17.2% production, transportation, and material moving

Income: Per capita: $23,342; Median household: $54,896; Average household: $59,271; Households with income of $100,000 or more: 14.8%; Poverty rate: 11.8%

Educational Attainment: High school diploma or higher: 88.6%; Bachelor's degree or higher: 12.2%; Graduate/professional degree or higher: 4.7%

Housing: Homeownership rate: 83.7%; Median home value: $119,400; Median year structure built: 1978; Homeowner vacancy rate: 2.3%; Median gross rent: $599 per month; Rental vacancy rate: 23.5%

Health Insurance: 94.0% have insurance; 78.9% have private insurance; 27.5% have public insurance; 6.0% do not have insurance; 0.0% of children under 18 do not have insurance

Transportation: Commute: 96.6% car, 0.0% public transportation, 0.7% walk, 2.8% work from home; Median travel time to work: 26.9 minutes

HUBBARDSTON (village). Covers a land area of 1.542 square miles and a water area of 0.075 square miles. Located at 43.09° N. Lat; 84.84° W. Long. Elevation is 682 feet.

History: Hubbardston began in 1865 when a town was laid out around a dam and sawmill built in the early 1850's by Joseph Brown. The town was named for Thomas Hubbard, one of the men who platted it.

Population: 395; Growth (since 2000): 0.3%; Density: 256.2 persons per square mile; Race: 97.2% White, 0.3% Black/African American, 0.3% Asian, 0.0% American Indian/Alaska Native, 0.0% Native Hawaiian/Other Pacific Islander, 0.8% Two or more races, 4.3% Hispanic of any race; Average household size: 2.69; Median age: 41.8; Age under 18: 23.0%; Age 65 and over: 14.9%; Males per 100 females: 103.6

Housing: Homeownership rate: 81.6%; Homeowner vacancy rate: 0.9%; Rental vacancy rate: 7.4%

IONIA (city). County seat. Covers a land area of 5.346 square miles and a water area of 0.130 square miles. Located at 42.98° N. Lat; 85.07° W. Long. Elevation is 718 feet.

History: Ionia was established in 1833 by settlers who purchased wigwams and fields of corn, melons, and squash from the native inhabitants. Named for the county, which had been named for the ancient Greek province, the town became a shipping point for beans, as well as a producer of furniture, pottery, and flour.

Population: 11,394; Growth (since 2000): 7.8%; Density: 2,131.3 persons per square mile; Race: 70.9% White, 25.0% Black/African American, 0.4% Asian, 0.7% American Indian/Alaska Native, 0.0% Native Hawaiian/Other Pacific Islander, 1.4% Two or more races, 7.7% Hispanic of any race; Average household size: 2.53; Median age: 32.3; Age under 18: 15.7%; Age 65 and over: 6.4%; Males per 100 females: 246.1; Marriage status: 49.9% never married, 28.3% now married, 2.0% separated, 4.8% widowed, 17.0% divorced; Foreign born: 1.1%; Speak English only: 94.3%; With disability: 17.9%; Veterans: 8.8%; Ancestry: 16.2% German, 9.3% Irish, 9.2% English, 6.5% Polish, 6.1% American

Employment: 7.6% management, business, and financial, 1.5% computer, engineering, and science, 6.3% education, legal, community service, arts, and media, 7.0% healthcare practitioners, 19.9% service, 25.0% sales and office, 9.6% natural resources, construction, and maintenance, 23.2% production, transportation, and material moving

Income: Per capita: $12,270; Median household: $36,419; Average household: $40,949; Households with income of $100,000 or more: 4.9%; Poverty rate: 24.4%

Educational Attainment: High school diploma or higher: 83.7%; Bachelor's degree or higher: 9.0%; Graduate/professional degree or higher: 2.5%

School District(s)

Berlin Township S/d #3 (KG-12)
  2012-13 Enrollment: 16 . . . . (616) 527-4900

Easton Township S/d #6 (KG-12)
  2012-13 Enrollment: 34 . . . . (616) 527-4900
Ionia ISD (PK-12)
  2012-13 Enrollment: 403 . . . . (616) 527-4900
Ionia Public Schools (PK-12)
  2012-13 Enrollment: 3,046 . . . . (616) 527-9280
Ionia Township S/d #2 (KG-12)
  2012-13 Enrollment: 18 . . . . (616) 527-4900
Michigan Department of Corrections (09-12)
  2012-13 Enrollment: 56 . . . . (517) 373-0720

Two-year College(s)

School of Missionary Aviation Technology (Private, Not-for-profit)
  Fall 2013 Enrollment: 66 . . . . (616) 527-4160
Housing: Homeownership rate: 53.8%; Median home value: $82,600; Median year structure built: Before 1940; Homeowner vacancy rate: 5.7%; Median gross rent: $642 per month; Rental vacancy rate: 11.6%
Health Insurance: 86.2% have insurance; 57.1% have private insurance; 40.2% have public insurance; 13.8% do not have insurance; 2.6% of children under 18 do not have insurance
Hospitals: Sparrow Ionia Hospital (25 beds)
Safety: Violent crime rate: 18.4 per 10,000 population; Property crime rate: 181.9 per 10,000 population
Newspapers: Sentinel-Standard (daily circulation 2900)
Transportation: Commute: 94.5% car, 0.3% public transportation, 1.6% walk, 1.8% work from home; Median travel time to work: 24.4 minutes
Additional Information Contacts
City of Ionia . . . . (616) 527-4170
  http://www.ci.ionia.mi.us

IONIA (township). Covers a land area of 33.504 square miles and a water area of 0.445 square miles. Located at 42.99° N. Lat; 85.01° W. Long. Elevation is 718 feet.
History: Settled 1833; incorporated as village 1865, as city 1873.
Population: 3,779; Growth (since 2000): 3.0%; Density: 112.8 persons per square mile; Race: 94.0% White, 0.5% Black/African American, 0.4% Asian, 0.3% American Indian/Alaska Native, 0.0% Native Hawaiian/Other Pacific Islander, 2.4% Two or more races, 5.9% Hispanic of any race; Average household size: 2.71; Median age: 38.3; Age under 18: 26.7%; Age 65 and over: 11.9%; Males per 100 females: 98.5; Marriage status: 25.8% never married, 52.3% now married, 3.1% separated, 9.7% widowed, 12.3% divorced; Foreign born: 1.6%; Speak English only: 98.5%; With disability: 17.8%; Veterans: 14.6%; Ancestry: 31.2% German, 12.9% Irish, 11.7% American, 9.9% English, 3.9% French
Employment: 12.6% management, business, and financial, 0.1% computer, engineering, and science, 9.1% education, legal, community service, arts, and media, 0.9% healthcare practitioners, 17.6% service, 21.7% sales and office, 17.3% natural resources, construction, and maintenance, 20.6% production, transportation, and material moving
Income: Per capita: $19,532; Median household: $38,051; Average household: $49,046; Households with income of $100,000 or more: 9.0%; Poverty rate: 11.8%
Educational Attainment: High school diploma or higher: 83.9%; Bachelor's degree or higher: 7.4%; Graduate/professional degree or higher: 3.7%

School District(s)

Berlin Township S/d #3 (KG-12)
  2012-13 Enrollment: 16 . . . . (616) 527-4900
Easton Township S/d #6 (KG-12)
  2012-13 Enrollment: 34 . . . . (616) 527-4900
Ionia ISD (PK-12)
  2012-13 Enrollment: 403 . . . . (616) 527-4900
Ionia Public Schools (PK-12)
  2012-13 Enrollment: 3,046 . . . . (616) 527-9280
Ionia Township S/d #2 (KG-12)
  2012-13 Enrollment: 18 . . . . (616) 527-4900
Michigan Department of Corrections (09-12)
  2012-13 Enrollment: 56 . . . . (517) 373-0720

Two-year College(s)

School of Missionary Aviation Technology (Private, Not-for-profit)
  Fall 2013 Enrollment: 66 . . . . (616) 527-4160
Housing: Homeownership rate: 82.9%; Median home value: $93,100; Median year structure built: 1976; Homeowner vacancy rate: 2.5%; Median gross rent: $713 per month; Rental vacancy rate: 42.9%

Health Insurance: 90.6% have insurance; 62.8% have private insurance; 41.4% have public insurance; 9.4% do not have insurance; 3.1% of children under 18 do not have insurance
Hospitals: Sparrow Ionia Hospital (25 beds)
Newspapers: Sentinel-Standard (daily circulation 2900)
Transportation: Commute: 97.2% car, 0.0% public transportation, 0.8% walk, 0.7% work from home; Median travel time to work: 21.3 minutes

KEENE (township). Covers a land area of 35.580 square miles and a water area of 0.293 square miles. Located at 42.99° N. Lat; 85.25° W. Long.
History: Keene Township was organized in 1842 and named for Keene, New Hampshire, the former home of early settler Edward Butterfield.
Population: 1,831; Growth (since 2000): 10.3%; Density: 51.5 persons per square mile; Race: 94.9% White, 0.2% Black/African American, 0.1% Asian, 1.1% American Indian/Alaska Native, 0.0% Native Hawaiian/Other Pacific Islander, 1.4% Two or more races, 4.9% Hispanic of any race; Average household size: 2.94; Median age: 39.3; Age under 18: 26.9%; Age 65 and over: 10.3%; Males per 100 females: 103.2
Housing: Homeownership rate: 90.6%; Homeowner vacancy rate: 1.4%; Rental vacancy rate: 3.3%

LAKE ODESSA (village). Covers a land area of 0.893 square miles and a water area of <.001 square miles. Located at 42.78° N. Lat; 85.14° W. Long. Elevation is 863 feet.
History: Lake Odessa was founded on the shores of both Jordan and Tupper Lakes in 1887, and named for the Russian city.
Population: 2,018; Growth (since 2000): -11.2%; Density: 2,260.9 persons per square mile; Race: 91.4% White, 0.1% Black/African American, 0.8% Asian, 0.4% American Indian/Alaska Native, 0.0% Native Hawaiian/Other Pacific Islander, 3.1% Two or more races, 10.3% Hispanic of any race; Average household size: 2.41; Median age: 34.6; Age under 18: 27.0%; Age 65 and over: 13.5%; Males per 100 females: 93.3

School District(s)

Lakewood Public Schools (PK-12)
  2012-13 Enrollment: 2,029 . . . . (616) 374-8043
Housing: Homeownership rate: 70.7%; Homeowner vacancy rate: 2.8%; Rental vacancy rate: 11.5%
Safety: Violent crime rate: 24.8 per 10,000 population; Property crime rate: 94.2 per 10,000 population
Additional Information Contacts
Village of Lake Odessa . . . . (616) 374-7110
  http://www.lakeodessa.org

LYONS (township). Covers a land area of 35.923 square miles and a water area of 0.969 square miles. Located at 42.99° N. Lat; 84.90° W. Long. Elevation is 653 feet.
History: Lyons Township was organized in 1837 when it was called Maple. It was renamed Lyons in 1840.
Population: 3,465; Growth (since 2000): 0.6%; Density: 96.5 persons per square mile; Race: 96.2% White, 0.2% Black/African American, 0.4% Asian, 0.5% American Indian/Alaska Native, 0.0% Native Hawaiian/Other Pacific Islander, 2.3% Two or more races, 3.0% Hispanic of any race; Average household size: 2.71; Median age: 38.2; Age under 18: 26.5%; Age 65 and over: 11.7%; Males per 100 females: 107.0; Marriage status: 25.7% never married, 59.7% now married, 0.9% separated, 4.7% widowed, 9.8% divorced; Foreign born: 0.0%; Speak English only: 98.0%; With disability: 13.1%; Veterans: 8.2%; Ancestry: 42.8% German, 15.0% English, 12.3% Irish, 5.7% American, 5.3% Polish
Employment: 15.2% management, business, and financial, 4.5% computer, engineering, and science, 4.9% education, legal, community service, arts, and media, 2.6% healthcare practitioners, 17.9% service, 23.5% sales and office, 17.3% natural resources, construction, and maintenance, 14.2% production, transportation, and material moving
Income: Per capita: $21,876; Median household: $54,481; Average household: $58,137; Households with income of $100,000 or more: 9.8%; Poverty rate: 10.7%
Educational Attainment: High school diploma or higher: 92.8%; Bachelor's degree or higher: 9.5%; Graduate/professional degree or higher: 2.4%
Housing: Homeownership rate: 83.8%; Median home value: $88,100; Median year structure built: 1971; Homeowner vacancy rate: 3.4%; Median gross rent: $595 per month; Rental vacancy rate: 11.4%

Health Insurance: 90.8% have insurance; 76.3% have private insurance; 31.3% have public insurance; 9.2% do not have insurance; 5.5% of children under 18 do not have insurance
Transportation: Commute: 92.1% car, 0.0% public transportation, 2.7% walk, 4.9% work from home; Median travel time to work: 32.1 minutes

LYONS (village). Covers a land area of 1.217 square miles and a water area of 0.130 square miles. Located at 42.99° N. Lat; 84.94° W. Long. Elevation is 653 feet.
History: This site was owned by Lucius Lyon, who platted it in 1836 with the thought that it would become an important town. Lyons was incorporated as a village in 1859.
Population: 789; Growth (since 2000): 8.7%; Density: 648.1 persons per square mile; Race: 95.4% White, 0.4% Black/African American, 0.3% Asian, 0.0% American Indian/Alaska Native, 0.0% Native Hawaiian/Other Pacific Islander, 2.8% Two or more races, 4.1% Hispanic of any race; Average household size: 2.66; Median age: 37.8; Age under 18: 25.7%; Age 65 and over: 11.3%; Males per 100 females: 109.8
Housing: Homeownership rate: 83.2%; Homeowner vacancy rate: 3.5%; Rental vacancy rate: 3.8%

MUIR (village). Covers a land area of 0.713 square miles and a water area of 0.045 square miles. Located at 43.00° N. Lat; 84.94° W. Long. Elevation is 653 feet.
Population: 604; Growth (since 2000): -4.7%; Density: 847.6 persons per square mile; Race: 94.7% White, 0.2% Black/African American, 1.5% Asian, 1.0% American Indian/Alaska Native, 0.0% Native Hawaiian/Other Pacific Islander, 1.8% Two or more races, 3.0% Hispanic of any race; Average household size: 2.66; Median age: 35.6; Age under 18: 27.2%; Age 65 and over: 10.4%; Males per 100 females: 98.7

School District(s)
Ionia Public Schools (PK-12)
    2012-13 Enrollment: 3,046 . . . . (616) 527-9280
Housing: Homeownership rate: 68.7%; Homeowner vacancy rate: 6.5%; Rental vacancy rate: 12.3%

NORTH PLAINS (township). Covers a land area of 35.753 square miles and a water area of 0.213 square miles. Located at 43.07° N. Lat; 84.91° W. Long.
Population: 1,279; Growth (since 2000): -6.4%; Density: 35.8 persons per square mile; Race: 98.3% White, 0.2% Black/African American, 0.1% Asian, 0.2% American Indian/Alaska Native, 0.0% Native Hawaiian/Other Pacific Islander, 0.5% Two or more races, 2.1% Hispanic of any race; Average household size: 2.57; Median age: 42.5; Age under 18: 20.8%; Age 65 and over: 14.3%; Males per 100 females: 112.1
Housing: Homeownership rate: 84.9%; Homeowner vacancy rate: 4.9%; Rental vacancy rate: 11.0%

ODESSA (township). Covers a land area of 35.578 square miles and a water area of 0.539 square miles. Located at 42.81° N. Lat; 85.14° W. Long.
Population: 3,778; Growth (since 2000): -6.4%; Density: 106.2 persons per square mile; Race: 93.7% White, 0.3% Black/African American, 0.6% Asian, 0.3% American Indian/Alaska Native, 0.0% Native Hawaiian/Other Pacific Islander, 2.4% Two or more races, 6.6% Hispanic of any race; Average household size: 2.57; Median age: 37.8; Age under 18: 26.5%; Age 65 and over: 13.5%; Males per 100 females: 95.9; Marriage status: 24.4% never married, 57.4% now married, 1.5% separated, 7.8% widowed, 10.4% divorced; Foreign born: 1.0%; Speak English only: 96.4%; With disability: 14.5%; Veterans: 9.5%; Ancestry: 34.4% German, 15.6% Irish, 14.8% English, 8.4% Dutch, 7.2% Italian
Employment: 6.9% management, business, and financial, 3.6% computer, engineering, and science, 6.5% education, legal, community service, arts, and media, 4.4% healthcare practitioners, 23.3% service, 29.3% sales and office, 7.2% natural resources, construction, and maintenance, 18.9% production, transportation, and material moving
Income: Per capita: $20,905; Median household: $42,772; Average household: $55,533; Households with income of $100,000 or more: 14.7%; Poverty rate: 20.0%
Educational Attainment: High school diploma or higher: 89.9%; Bachelor's degree or higher: 15.5%; Graduate/professional degree or higher: 3.1%
Housing: Homeownership rate: 79.0%; Median home value: $101,000; Median year structure built: 1957; Homeowner vacancy rate: 2.6%; Median gross rent: $689 per month; Rental vacancy rate: 9.9%

Health Insurance: 91.2% have insurance; 72.1% have private insurance; 32.8% have public insurance; 8.8% do not have insurance; 2.9% of children under 18 do not have insurance
Transportation: Commute: 91.9% car, 0.0% public transportation, 5.4% walk, 1.9% work from home; Median travel time to work: 24.7 minutes

ORANGE (township). Covers a land area of 35.930 square miles and a water area of 0.043 square miles. Located at 42.90° N. Lat; 85.03° W. Long.
Population: 987; Growth (since 2000): -5.1%; Density: 27.5 persons per square mile; Race: 97.6% White, 0.1% Black/African American, 0.1% Asian, 0.6% American Indian/Alaska Native, 0.0% Native Hawaiian/Other Pacific Islander, 0.1% Two or more races, 2.5% Hispanic of any race; Average household size: 2.58; Median age: 41.7; Age under 18: 23.7%; Age 65 and over: 13.4%; Males per 100 females: 97.4
Housing: Homeownership rate: 85.6%; Homeowner vacancy rate: 1.5%; Rental vacancy rate: 5.1%

ORLEANS (township). Covers a land area of 35.170 square miles and a water area of 1.086 square miles. Located at 43.08° N. Lat; 85.13° W. Long. Elevation is 860 feet.
Population: 2,743; Growth (since 2000): 0.3%; Density: 78.0 persons per square mile; Race: 95.6% White, 0.1% Black/African American, 0.2% Asian, 0.6% American Indian/Alaska Native, 0.0% Native Hawaiian/Other Pacific Islander, 1.4% Two or more races, 5.0% Hispanic of any race; Average household size: 2.71; Median age: 39.0; Age under 18: 26.6%; Age 65 and over: 11.8%; Males per 100 females: 103.6; Marriage status: 27.1% never married, 55.8% now married, 0.4% separated, 3.8% widowed, 13.3% divorced; Foreign born: 3.0%; Speak English only: 95.2%; With disability: 23.4%; Veterans: 11.5%; Ancestry: 22.8% German, 13.6% Irish, 12.5% English, 10.5% American, 6.1% Dutch
Employment: 9.8% management, business, and financial, 1.1% computer, engineering, and science, 6.0% education, legal, community service, arts, and media, 2.4% healthcare practitioners, 18.0% service, 21.2% sales and office, 18.3% natural resources, construction, and maintenance, 23.1% production, transportation, and material moving
Income: Per capita: $17,254; Median household: $36,116; Average household: $46,472; Households with income of $100,000 or more: 5.8%; Poverty rate: 24.8%
Educational Attainment: High school diploma or higher: 81.8%; Bachelor's degree or higher: 6.9%; Graduate/professional degree or higher: 1.7%

School District(s)
Threshold Academy (KG-12)
    2012-13 Enrollment: 163 . . . . (616) 754-9315
Housing: Homeownership rate: 81.1%; Median home value: $91,800; Median year structure built: 1977; Homeowner vacancy rate: 2.1%; Median gross rent: $823 per month; Rental vacancy rate: 9.9%
Health Insurance: 87.0% have insurance; 56.7% have private insurance; 49.1% have public insurance; 13.0% do not have insurance; 2.5% of children under 18 do not have insurance
Transportation: Commute: 91.0% car, 0.0% public transportation, 1.3% walk, 6.8% work from home; Median travel time to work: 30.2 minutes

OTISCO (township). Covers a land area of 30.973 square miles and a water area of 0.959 square miles. Located at 43.08° N. Lat; 85.26° W. Long.
Population: 2,282; Growth (since 2000): 1.7%; Density: 73.7 persons per square mile; Race: 98.2% White, 0.1% Black/African American, 0.7% Asian, 0.2% American Indian/Alaska Native, 0.0% Native Hawaiian/Other Pacific Islander, 0.6% Two or more races, 1.5% Hispanic of any race; Average household size: 2.69; Median age: 41.1; Age under 18: 24.8%; Age 65 and over: 10.9%; Males per 100 females: 103.6
Housing: Homeownership rate: 86.4%; Homeowner vacancy rate: 1.2%; Rental vacancy rate: 9.4%

PALO (unincorporated postal area)
ZCTA: 48870
    Covers a land area of 0.059 square miles and a water area of 0 square miles. Located at 43.11° N. Lat; 84.98° W. Long. Elevation is 791 feet.
    Population: 148; Growth (since 2000): n/a; Density: 2,501.9 persons per square mile; Race: 98.6% White, 0.0% Black/African American, 0.0% Asian, 0.0% American Indian/Alaska Native, 0.0% Native Hawaiian/Other Pacific Islander, 0.7% Two or more races, 2.7% Hispanic of any race; Average household size: 3.16; Median age: 34.7;

Age under 18: 29.1%; Age 65 and over: 9.5%; Males per 100 females: 102.7

Housing: Homeownership rate: 84.4%; Homeowner vacancy rate: 2.6%; Rental vacancy rate: 22.2%

PEWAMO (village). Covers a land area of 0.998 square miles and a water area of 0 square miles. Located at 43.00° N. Lat; 84.85° W. Long. Elevation is 738 feet.

History: Pewamo began in 1857 as a station on the Detroit & Milwaukee Railroad, and was founded as a village in 1859.

Population: 469; Growth (since 2000): -16.3%; Density: 469.8 persons per square mile; Race: 95.1% White, 0.2% Black/African American, 0.4% Asian, 1.1% American Indian/Alaska Native, 0.0% Native Hawaiian/Other Pacific Islander, 3.2% Two or more races, 1.3% Hispanic of any race; Average household size: 2.52; Median age: 39.9; Age under 18: 24.3%; Age 65 and over: 16.8%; Males per 100 females: 97.9

School District(s)

Pewamo-Westphalia Community Schools (PK-12)
   2012-13 Enrollment: 636. . . . . (989) 587-5100

Housing: Homeownership rate: 81.7%; Homeowner vacancy rate: 5.5%; Rental vacancy rate: 10.5%

PORTLAND (city). Covers a land area of 2.639 square miles and a water area of 0.145 square miles. Located at 42.87° N. Lat; 84.90° W. Long. Elevation is 725 feet.

History: Portland was established in the 1830's at the junction of the Looking Glass and Grand Rivers, and became an industrial center and a shipping point for farm produce.

Population: 3,883; Growth (since 2000): 2.5%; Density: 1,471.5 persons per square mile; Race: 96.7% White, 0.7% Black/African American, 0.2% Asian, 0.4% American Indian/Alaska Native, 0.0% Native Hawaiian/Other Pacific Islander, 1.4% Two or more races, 3.1% Hispanic of any race; Average household size: 2.37; Median age: 35.6; Age under 18: 25.4%; Age 65 and over: 13.0%; Males per 100 females: 96.0; Marriage status: 29.0% never married, 50.6% now married, 0.7% separated, 7.4% widowed, 13.1% divorced; Foreign born: 2.0%; Speak English only: 95.8%; With disability: 11.7%; Veterans: 7.7%; Ancestry: 42.4% German, 16.9% Irish, 13.3% English, 6.4% French, 5.8% Dutch

Employment: 9.0% management, business, and financial, 4.4% computer, engineering, and science, 14.8% education, legal, community service, arts, and media, 4.5% healthcare practitioners, 18.1% service, 35.0% sales and office, 5.5% natural resources, construction, and maintenance, 8.8% production, transportation, and material moving

Income: Per capita: $24,830; Median household: $50,972; Average household: $59,707; Households with income of $100,000 or more: 18.7%; Poverty rate: 6.7%

Educational Attainment: High school diploma or higher: 93.2%; Bachelor's degree or higher: 23.2%; Graduate/professional degree or higher: 9.8%

School District(s)

Portland Public Schools (PK-12)
   2012-13 Enrollment: 1,984 . . . . (517) 647-4161

Housing: Homeownership rate: 65.4%; Median home value: $119,200; Median year structure built: 1968; Homeowner vacancy rate: 1.7%; Median gross rent: $760 per month; Rental vacancy rate: 12.3%

Health Insurance: 92.9% have insurance; 83.0% have private insurance; 23.3% have public insurance; 7.1% do not have insurance; 0.0% of children under 18 do not have insurance

Transportation: Commute: 91.9% car, 0.0% public transportation, 2.3% walk, 4.3% work from home; Median travel time to work: 26.1 minutes

Additional Information Contacts

City of Portland . . . . (517) 647-7531
   http://www.portland-michigan.org

PORTLAND (township). Covers a land area of 32.175 square miles and a water area of 1.147 square miles. Located at 42.91° N. Lat; 84.90° W. Long. Elevation is 725 feet.

Population: 3,404; Growth (since 2000): 38.4%; Density: 105.8 persons per square mile; Race: 97.2% White, 0.3% Black/African American, 0.3% Asian, 0.3% American Indian/Alaska Native, 0.0% Native Hawaiian/Other Pacific Islander, 1.1% Two or more races, 2.2% Hispanic of any race; Average household size: 2.83; Median age: 38.3; Age under 18: 29.4%; Age 65 and over: 11.0%; Males per 100 females: 98.7; Marriage status: 22.5% never married, 58.9% now married, 2.3% separated, 6.2% widowed, 12.4% divorced; Foreign born: 2.2%; Speak English only: 97.3%;

With disability: 14.6%; Veterans: 15.9%; Ancestry: 41.8% German, 15.1% English, 8.1% Irish, 7.2% Dutch, 6.4% Polish

Employment: 16.5% management, business, and financial, 2.8% computer, engineering, and science, 9.9% education, legal, community service, arts, and media, 4.3% healthcare practitioners, 9.2% service, 25.4% sales and office, 14.2% natural resources, construction, and maintenance, 17.6% production, transportation, and material moving

Income: Per capita: $25,720; Median household: $61,076; Average household: $71,410; Households with income of $100,000 or more: 19.7%; Poverty rate: 10.0%

Educational Attainment: High school diploma or higher: 96.4%; Bachelor's degree or higher: 19.9%; Graduate/professional degree or higher: 8.0%

School District(s)

Portland Public Schools (PK-12)
   2012-13 Enrollment: 1,984 . . . . (517) 647-4161

Housing: Homeownership rate: 86.2%; Median home value: $144,500; Median year structure built: 1979; Homeowner vacancy rate: 2.7%; Median gross rent: $751 per month; Rental vacancy rate: 13.5%

Health Insurance: 91.2% have insurance; 78.9% have private insurance; 26.6% have public insurance; 8.8% do not have insurance; 2.6% of children under 18 do not have insurance

Transportation: Commute: 93.3% car, 0.5% public transportation, 2.8% walk, 3.3% work from home; Median travel time to work: 25.3 minutes

---

RONALD (township). Covers a land area of 36.185 square miles and a water area of 0.221 square miles. Located at 43.08° N. Lat; 85.02° W. Long.

Population: 1,869; Growth (since 2000): -1.8%; Density: 51.7 persons per square mile; Race: 96.6% White, 0.4% Black/African American, 0.2% Asian, 0.2% American Indian/Alaska Native, 0.0% Native Hawaiian/Other Pacific Islander, 0.9% Two or more races, 4.1% Hispanic of any race; Average household size: 2.68; Median age: 39.3; Age under 18: 25.0%; Age 65 and over: 13.4%; Males per 100 females: 104.3

Housing: Homeownership rate: 88.0%; Homeowner vacancy rate: 3.9%; Rental vacancy rate: 15.3%

SARANAC (village). Covers a land area of 1.151 square miles and a water area of 0.051 square miles. Located at 42.93° N. Lat; 85.21° W. Long. Elevation is 646 feet.

History: The village of Saranac was laid out in the 1830's and named for the resort town in New York, hoping to attract more settlers from New York.

Population: 1,325; Growth (since 2000): -0.1%; Density: 1,151.2 persons per square mile; Race: 97.4% White, 0.2% Black/African American, 0.4% Asian, 0.2% American Indian/Alaska Native, 0.0% Native Hawaiian/Other Pacific Islander, 1.1% Two or more races, 2.7% Hispanic of any race; Average household size: 2.31; Median age: 37.2; Age under 18: 28.0%; Age 65 and over: 15.1%; Males per 100 females: 90.9

School District(s)

Saranac Community Schools (PK-12)
   2012-13 Enrollment: 1,125 . . . . (616) 642-1400

Housing: Homeownership rate: 57.4%; Homeowner vacancy rate: 3.2%; Rental vacancy rate: 6.5%

SEBEWA (township). Covers a land area of 35.941 square miles and a water area of 0.038 square miles. Located at 42.81° N. Lat; 85.02° W. Long.

History: Sebewa Township was organized in 1845 and named for Sebewa ("little river") Creek. The first permanent settlements in the area were made in the 1830's.

Population: 1,171; Growth (since 2000): -2.6%; Density: 32.6 persons per square mile; Race: 98.3% White, 0.3% Black/African American, 0.3% Asian, 0.1% American Indian/Alaska Native, 0.0% Native Hawaiian/Other Pacific Islander, 0.4% Two or more races, 2.3% Hispanic of any race; Average household size: 2.72; Median age: 39.0; Age under 18: 25.7%; Age 65 and over: 13.2%; Males per 100 females: 104.4

Housing: Homeownership rate: 86.9%; Homeowner vacancy rate: 1.0%; Rental vacancy rate: 5.1%

Iosco County

Located in northeastern Michigan; bounded on the east by Lake Huron; drained by the Au Sable, Au Gres, and Tawas Rivers; includes part of

Huron National Forest, and Tawas and Van Ettan Lakes. Covers a land area of 549.096 square miles, a water area of 1,340.961 square miles, and is located in the Eastern Time Zone at 44.33° N. Lat., 82.85° W. Long. The county was founded in 1840. County seat is Tawas City.

Weather Station: East Tawas   Elevation: 585 feet

	Jan	Feb	Mar	Apr	May	Jun	Jul	Aug	Sep	Oct	Nov	Dec
High	30	32	41	53	65	75	80	78	71	58	46	34
Low	13	14	21	33	43	53	58	57	49	38	30	20
Precip	2.0	1.7	2.1	2.8	3.0	3.0	2.7	3.4	3.5	2.8	2.6	2.1
Snow	16.8	12.7	8.1	1.9	0.1	0.0	0.0	0.0	tr	0.1	2.7	11.2

High and Low temperatures in degrees Fahrenheit; Precipitation and Snow in inches

Weather Station: Hale Loud Dam   Elevation: 814 feet

	Jan	Feb	Mar	Apr	May	Jun	Jul	Aug	Sep	Oct	Nov	Dec
High	29	32	41	55	67	76	81	79	71	58	45	33
Low	11	11	19	31	42	52	57	55	48	37	28	18
Precip	1.7	1.2	1.5	2.5	2.9	3.2	3.0	3.4	3.3	2.7	2.4	1.7
Snow	12.5	7.9	5.4	1.3	0.2	0.0	0.0	0.0	tr	tr	2.5	8.7

High and Low temperatures in degrees Fahrenheit; Precipitation and Snow in inches

Population: 25,887; Growth (since 2000): -5.3%; Density: 47.1 persons per square mile; Race: 96.4% White, 0.5% Black/African American, 0.5% Asian, 0.7% American Indian/Alaska Native, 0.1% Native Hawaiian/Other Pacific Islander, 1.5% two or more races, 1.6% Hispanic of any race; Average household size: 2.17; Median age: 51.0; Age under 18: 17.6%; Age 65 and over: 26.1%; Males per 100 females: 97.3; Marriage status: 21.0% never married, 53.7% now married, 1.5% separated, 10.3% widowed, 15.0% divorced; Foreign born: 2.4%; Speak English only: 97.3%; With disability: 21.7%; Veterans: 16.4%; Ancestry: 29.5% German, 14.1% Irish, 12.8% English, 9.1% Polish, 8.7% French
Religion: Six largest groups: 11.9% Catholicism, 8.5% Lutheran, 7.0% Methodist/Pietist, 3.8% Non-denominational Protestant, 3.0% Baptist, 1.5% Latter-day Saints
Economy: Unemployment rate: 7.4%; Leading industries: 19.1% retail trade; 13.4% accommodation and food services; 12.7% construction; Farms: 283 totaling 37,996 acres; Company size: 0 employ 1,000 or more persons, 1 employs 500 to 999 persons, 8 employ 100 to 499 persons, 597 employ less than 100 persons; Business ownership: 793 women-owned, n/a Black-owned, n/a Hispanic-owned, n/a Asian-owned
Employment: 9.6% management, business, and financial, 1.7% computer, engineering, and science, 6.7% education, legal, community service, arts, and media, 6.4% healthcare practitioners, 23.8% service, 24.8% sales and office, 11.6% natural resources, construction, and maintenance, 15.4% production, transportation, and material moving
Income: Per capita: $22,047; Median household: $36,236; Average household: $48,282; Households with income of $100,000 or more: 7.8%; Poverty rate: 19.0%
Educational Attainment: High school diploma or higher: 87.4%; Bachelor's degree or higher: 14.0%; Graduate/professional degree or higher: 5.4%
Housing: Homeownership rate: 81.7%; Median home value: $90,300; Median year structure built: 1970; Homeowner vacancy rate: 4.8%; Median gross rent: $588 per month; Rental vacancy rate: 12.5%
Vital Statistics: Birth rate: 94.4 per 10,000 population; Death rate: 143.9 per 10,000 population; Age-adjusted cancer mortality rate: 205.9 deaths per 100,000 population
Health Insurance: 87.3% have insurance; 60.8% have private insurance; 51.6% have public insurance; 12.7% do not have insurance; 3.3% of children under 18 do not have insurance
Health Care: Physicians: 11.8 per 10,000 population; Hospital beds: 7.8 per 10,000 population; Hospital admissions: 436.1 per 10,000 population
Transportation: Commute: 91.9% car, 0.2% public transportation, 2.0% walk, 4.7% work from home; Median travel time to work: 21.1 minutes
Presidential Election: 46.8% Obama, 51.8% Romney (2012)
National and State Parks: Tawas Point State Park; Tuttle Marsh National Wildlife Area
Additional Information Contacts
Iosco Government. . . . . (517) 362-3497
    http://iosco.m33access.com

Iosco County Communities

ALABASTER (township). Covers a land area of 22.224 square miles and a water area of 0 square miles. Located at 44.20° N. Lat; 83.60° W. Long. Elevation is 591 feet.
History: Alabaster rock had been quarried here for some 25 years before the township was formed in 1866. The U.S. Gypsum Company used the docks here to ship gypsum from its mine.
Population: 487; Growth (since 2000): -3.2%; Density: 21.9 persons per square mile; Race: 97.5% White, 0.0% Black/African American, 1.6% Asian, 0.2% American Indian/Alaska Native, 0.0% Native Hawaiian/Other Pacific Islander, 0.4% Two or more races, 0.4% Hispanic of any race; Average household size: 2.02; Median age: 60.2; Age under 18: 11.1%; Age 65 and over: 37.0%; Males per 100 females: 105.5
Housing: Homeownership rate: 92.9%; Homeowner vacancy rate: 3.5%; Rental vacancy rate: 10.5%

AU SABLE (CDP). Covers a land area of 2.097 square miles and a water area of 0.033 square miles. Located at 44.41° N. Lat; 83.34° W. Long. Elevation is 597 feet.
Population: 1,404; Growth (since 2000): -8.4%; Density: 669.5 persons per square mile; Race: 95.7% White, 0.6% Black/African American, 0.9% Asian, 0.9% American Indian/Alaska Native, 0.0% Native Hawaiian/Other Pacific Islander, 1.6% Two or more races, 3.6% Hispanic of any race; Average household size: 2.26; Median age: 47.0; Age under 18: 20.2%; Age 65 and over: 21.6%; Males per 100 females: 97.7
Housing: Homeownership rate: 81.9%; Homeowner vacancy rate: 5.4%; Rental vacancy rate: 14.5%

AU SABLE (charter township). Covers a land area of 20.626 square miles and a water area of 0.494 square miles. Located at 44.39° N. Lat; 83.38° W. Long. Elevation is 597 feet.
History: A village was platted here in 1849 by Curtis Emerson and James Eldridge. Incorporated as a village in 1872 and as a city in 1889, Au Sable relinquished its city charter in 1931 and became a township. The name is French for "sandy."
Population: 2,047; Growth (since 2000): -8.2%; Density: 99.2 persons per square mile; Race: 95.8% White, 0.7% Black/African American, 0.7% Asian, 0.7% American Indian/Alaska Native, 0.0% Native Hawaiian/Other Pacific Islander, 1.4% Two or more races, 3.0% Hispanic of any race; Average household size: 2.16; Median age: 49.5; Age under 18: 18.4%; Age 65 and over: 23.9%; Males per 100 females: 98.7
Housing: Homeownership rate: 81.0%; Homeowner vacancy rate: 5.6%; Rental vacancy rate: 21.0%
Additional Information Contacts
Au Sable Charter Township . . . . (989) 739-9169
    http://www.ausabletownship.net

BALDWIN (township). Covers a land area of 28.417 square miles and a water area of 2.891 square miles. Located at 44.32° N. Lat; 83.47° W. Long.
Population: 1,694; Growth (since 2000): -1.9%; Density: 59.6 persons per square mile; Race: 96.9% White, 0.5% Black/African American, 0.4% Asian, 1.0% American Indian/Alaska Native, 0.0% Native Hawaiian/Other Pacific Islander, 0.9% Two or more races, 1.0% Hispanic of any race; Average household size: 2.14; Median age: 53.5; Age under 18: 16.4%; Age 65 and over: 28.3%; Males per 100 females: 99.8
Housing: Homeownership rate: 87.2%; Homeowner vacancy rate: 4.7%; Rental vacancy rate: 18.3%

BURLEIGH (township). Covers a land area of 34.644 square miles and a water area of 0.013 square miles. Located at 44.20° N. Lat; 83.82° W. Long.
Population: 787; Growth (since 2000): 1.5%; Density: 22.7 persons per square mile; Race: 95.6% White, 0.0% Black/African American, 0.1% Asian, 1.5% American Indian/Alaska Native, 0.0% Native Hawaiian/Other Pacific Islander, 2.7% Two or more races, 2.2% Hispanic of any race; Average household size: 2.56; Median age: 45.5; Age under 18: 21.6%; Age 65 and over: 20.8%; Males per 100 females: 102.8
Housing: Homeownership rate: 84.7%; Homeowner vacancy rate: 2.3%; Rental vacancy rate: 13.0%

EAST TAWAS (city). Covers a land area of 2.841 square miles and a water area of 0.447 square miles. Located at 44.29° N. Lat; 83.48° W. Long. Elevation is 587 feet.

History: East Tawas developed at the mouth of the Tawas River, where it emptied into Tawas Bay on Lake Huron. A twin with the city of Tawas, East Tawas grew with the lumber industry. Later, tourism provided a source of revenue, with the shops of the Detroit & Mackinac Railroad located here.

Population: 2,808; Growth (since 2000): -4.8%; Density: 988.3 persons per square mile; Race: 95.7% White, 0.2% Black/African American, 1.1% Asian, 0.3% American Indian/Alaska Native, 0.1% Native Hawaiian/Other Pacific Islander, 1.9% Two or more races, 2.0% Hispanic of any race; Average household size: 2.06; Median age: 50.9; Age under 18: 18.6%; Age 65 and over: 27.5%; Males per 100 females: 82.5; Marriage status: 23.8% never married, 52.1% now married, 0.0% separated, 11.1% widowed, 12.9% divorced; Foreign born: 2.3%; Speak English only: 98.0%; With disability: 23.0%; Veterans: 13.5%; Ancestry: 33.9% German, 16.6% French, 15.6% Irish, 12.6% Polish, 10.4% English

Employment: 12.8% management, business, and financial, 0.7% computer, engineering, and science, 7.5% education, legal, community service, arts, and media, 7.1% healthcare practitioners, 18.7% service, 33.6% sales and office, 11.1% natural resources, construction, and maintenance, 8.6% production, transportation, and material moving

Income: Per capita: $27,391; Median household: $39,857; Average household: $57,912; Households with income of $100,000 or more: 10.0%; Poverty rate: 18.9%

Educational Attainment: High school diploma or higher: 86.5%; Bachelor's degree or higher: 22.9%; Graduate/professional degree or higher: 6.0%

Housing: Homeownership rate: 70.5%; Median home value: $93,100; Median year structure built: 1970; Homeowner vacancy rate: 3.3%; Median gross rent: $563 per month; Rental vacancy rate: 5.9%

Health Insurance: 91.7% have insurance; 65.5% have private insurance; 53.8% have public insurance; 8.3% do not have insurance; 0.0% of children under 18 do not have insurance

Newspapers: Iosco County News-Herald (weekly circulation 6500)

Transportation: Commute: 81.2% car, 0.0% public transportation, 7.2% walk, 8.2% work from home; Median travel time to work: 11.6 minutes

Additional Information Contacts

City of East Tawas . . . . (989) 362-6161
   http://www.easttawas.com

GRANT (township). Covers a land area of 34.880 square miles and a water area of 0.571 square miles. Located at 44.30° N. Lat; 83.71° W. Long.

Population: 1,546; Growth (since 2000): -0.9%; Density: 44.3 persons per square mile; Race: 97.3% White, 0.2% Black/African American, 0.4% Asian, 0.3% American Indian/Alaska Native, 0.0% Native Hawaiian/Other Pacific Islander, 1.4% Two or more races, 1.2% Hispanic of any race; Average household size: 2.17; Median age: 52.1; Age under 18: 17.8%; Age 65 and over: 25.4%; Males per 100 females: 103.4

Housing: Homeownership rate: 89.2%; Homeowner vacancy rate: 4.5%; Rental vacancy rate: 9.4%

HALE (unincorporated postal area)
ZCTA: 48739

Covers a land area of 93.172 square miles and a water area of 5.096 square miles. Located at 44.37° N. Lat; 83.84° W. Long. Elevation is 856 feet.

Population: 4,043; Growth (since 2000): -12.4%; Density: 43.4 persons per square mile; Race: 97.4% White, 0.6% Black/African American, 0.1% Asian, 0.7% American Indian/Alaska Native, 0.0% Native Hawaiian/Other Pacific Islander, 1.1% Two or more races, 0.9% Hispanic of any race; Average household size: 2.15; Median age: 53.5; Age under 18: 15.9%; Age 65 and over: 29.8%; Males per 100 females: 104.7; Marriage status: 18.8% never married, 59.4% now married, 2.5% separated, 9.1% widowed, 12.7% divorced; Foreign born: 1.2%; Speak English only: 98.6%; With disability: 25.5%; Veterans: 18.6%; Ancestry: 33.7% German, 17.3% English, 14.4% Irish, 8.7% American, 7.9% Polish

Employment: 9.9% management, business, and financial, 2.3% computer, engineering, and science, 4.8% education, legal, community service, arts, and media, 4.4% healthcare practitioners, 29.7% service, 21.8% sales and office, 13.0% natural resources, construction, and maintenance, 14.2% production, transportation, and material moving

Income: Per capita: $19,456; Median household: $34,536; Average household: $43,042; Households with income of $100,000 or more: 6.6%; Poverty rate: 22.3%

Educational Attainment: High school diploma or higher: 85.9%; Bachelor's degree or higher: 9.6%; Graduate/professional degree or higher: 3.9%

School District(s)

Hale Area Schools (PK-12)
   2012-13 Enrollment: 464 . . . . (989) 728-7661
   Housing: Homeownership rate: 88.6%; Median home value: $97,800; Median year structure built: 1971; Homeowner vacancy rate: 4.2%; Median gross rent: $697 per month; Rental vacancy rate: 11.1%
   Health Insurance: 84.5% have insurance; 55.6% have private insurance; 56.4% have public insurance; 15.5% do not have insurance; 2.5% of children under 18 do not have insurance
   Transportation: Commute: 90.6% car, 0.1% public transportation, 3.2% walk, 3.6% work from home; Median travel time to work: 29.7 minutes

NATIONAL CITY (unincorporated postal area)
ZCTA: 48748

Covers a land area of 46.322 square miles and a water area of 1.274 square miles. Located at 44.35° N. Lat; 83.61° W. Long. Elevation is 673 feet.

Population: 1,693; Growth (since 2000): -4.7%; Density: 36.5 persons per square mile; Race: 97.1% White, 0.2% Black/African American, 0.5% Asian, 0.4% American Indian/Alaska Native, 0.0% Native Hawaiian/Other Pacific Islander, 1.6% Two or more races, 0.8% Hispanic of any race; Average household size: 2.11; Median age: 54.8; Age under 18: 14.9%; Age 65 and over: 28.6%; Males per 100 females: 103.7

Housing: Homeownership rate: 90.5%; Homeowner vacancy rate: 3.6%; Rental vacancy rate: 8.2%

OSCODA (CDP). Covers a land area of 0.870 square miles and a water area of 0.078 square miles. Located at 44.42° N. Lat; 83.33° W. Long. Elevation is 587 feet.

Population: 903; Growth (since 2000): -9.0%; Density: 1,037.4 persons per square mile; Race: 93.0% White, 1.8% Black/African American, 1.3% Asian, 0.6% American Indian/Alaska Native, 0.7% Native Hawaiian/Other Pacific Islander, 2.3% Two or more races, 2.8% Hispanic of any race; Average household size: 2.13; Median age: 46.7; Age under 18: 20.7%; Age 65 and over: 23.4%; Males per 100 females: 90.1

School District(s)

Oscoda Area Schools (PK-12)
   2012-13 Enrollment: 1,275 . . . . (989) 739-2033
Housing: Homeownership rate: 69.8%; Homeowner vacancy rate: 5.8%; Rental vacancy rate: 15.9%

Newspapers: Oscoda Press (weekly circulation 6000)

Airports: Oscoda-Wurtsmith (general aviation)

OSCODA (charter township). Covers a land area of 121.992 square miles and a water area of 9.289 square miles. Located at 44.47° N. Lat; 83.54° W. Long. Elevation is 587 feet.

Population: 6,997; Growth (since 2000): -3.5%; Density: 57.4 persons per square mile; Race: 95.2% White, 0.7% Black/African American, 0.5% Asian, 1.0% American Indian/Alaska Native, 0.1% Native Hawaiian/Other Pacific Islander, 2.0% Two or more races, 2.0% Hispanic of any race; Average household size: 2.14; Median age: 50.9; Age under 18: 17.5%; Age 65 and over: 26.4%; Males per 100 females: 98.1; Marriage status: 20.9% never married, 47.1% now married, 0.6% separated, 11.3% widowed, 20.6% divorced; Foreign born: 4.6%; Speak English only: 97.0%; With disability: 21.1%; Veterans: 16.5%; Ancestry: 24.8% German, 12.6% English, 11.2% Irish, 10.1% French, 8.5% American

Employment: 8.8% management, business, and financial, 1.2% computer, engineering, and science, 6.1% education, legal, community service, arts, and media, 6.1% healthcare practitioners, 27.4% service, 21.0% sales and office, 11.9% natural resources, construction, and maintenance, 17.4% production, transportation, and material moving

Income: Per capita: $22,775; Median household: $33,869; Average household: $48,548; Households with income of $100,000 or more: 6.9%; Poverty rate: 22.3%

Educational Attainment: High school diploma or higher: 87.5%; Bachelor's degree or higher: 16.4%; Graduate/professional degree or higher: 7.4%

School District(s)

Oscoda Area Schools (PK-12)
  2012-13 Enrollment: 1,275 . . . . (989) 739-2033
Housing: Homeownership rate: 77.1%; Median home value: $79,600; Median year structure built: 1970; Homeowner vacancy rate: 7.2%; Median gross rent: $560 per month; Rental vacancy rate: 15.5%
Health Insurance: 87.0% have insurance; 53.5% have private insurance; 56.4% have public insurance; 13.0% do not have insurance; 3.6% of children under 18 do not have insurance
Safety: Violent crime rate: 29.3 per 10,000 population; Property crime rate: 347.6 per 10,000 population
Newspapers: Oscoda Press (weekly circulation 6000)
Transportation: Commute: 95.0% car, 0.0% public transportation, 0.2% walk, 4.8% work from home; Median travel time to work: 19.9 minutes
Airports: Oscoda-Wurtsmith (general aviation)
Additional Information Contacts
Oscoda Township . . . . (989) 739-3211
  http://www.oscodatwp.com

PLAINFIELD (township). Covers a land area of 103.732 square miles and a water area of 3.774 square miles. Located at 44.42° N. Lat; 83.77° W. Long.
Population: 3,799; Growth (since 2000): -11.5%; Density: 36.6 persons per square mile; Race: 97.4% White, 0.6% Black/African American, 0.1% Asian, 0.6% American Indian/Alaska Native, 0.0% Native Hawaiian/Other Pacific Islander, 1.2% Two or more races, 0.8% Hispanic of any race; Average household size: 2.11; Median age: 53.8; Age under 18: 15.8%; Age 65 and over: 29.7%; Males per 100 females: 104.2; Marriage status: 17.5% never married, 55.9% now married, 3.3% separated, 12.6% widowed, 14.0% divorced; Foreign born: 1.5%; Speak English only: 98.7%; With disability: 31.3%; Veterans: 18.8%; Ancestry: 31.6% German, 15.3% Irish, 12.5% English, 9.1% Polish, 8.1% French
Employment: 9.5% management, business, and financial, 0.3% computer, engineering, and science, 6.2% education, legal, community service, arts, and media, 4.9% healthcare practitioners, 25.1% service, 25.8% sales and office, 13.3% natural resources, construction, and maintenance, 14.9% production, transportation, and material moving
Income: Per capita: $18,968; Median household: $31,320; Average household: $39,558; Households with income of $100,000 or more: 5.3%; Poverty rate: 24.1%
Educational Attainment: High school diploma or higher: 85.5%; Bachelor's degree or higher: 7.2%; Graduate/professional degree or higher: 2.6%
Housing: Homeownership rate: 87.6%; Median home value: $90,900; Median year structure built: 1970; Homeowner vacancy rate: 4.2%; Median gross rent: $725 per month; Rental vacancy rate: 11.1%
Health Insurance: 85.7% have insurance; 56.1% have private insurance; 59.9% have public insurance; 14.3% do not have insurance; 1.6% of children under 18 do not have insurance
Transportation: Commute: 93.6% car, 0.1% public transportation, 1.1% walk, 2.0% work from home; Median travel time to work: 27.9 minutes

RENO (township). Covers a land area of 35.274 square miles and a water area of 0.056 square miles. Located at 44.28° N. Lat; 83.82° W. Long.
Population: 590; Growth (since 2000): -10.1%; Density: 16.7 persons per square mile; Race: 98.5% White, 0.0% Black/African American, 0.2% Asian, 0.3% American Indian/Alaska Native, 0.0% Native Hawaiian/Other Pacific Islander, 0.8% Two or more races, 0.8% Hispanic of any race; Average household size: 2.44; Median age: 47.5; Age under 18: 20.8%; Age 65 and over: 19.3%; Males per 100 females: 111.5
Housing: Homeownership rate: 92.1%; Homeowner vacancy rate: 3.0%; Rental vacancy rate: 17.4%

SAND LAKE (CDP). Covers a land area of 14.949 square miles and a water area of 1.270 square miles. Located at 44.33° N. Lat; 83.67° W. Long. Elevation is 787 feet.
Population: 1,412; Growth (since 2000): n/a; Density: 94.5 persons per square mile; Race: 97.0% White, 0.2% Black/African American, 0.5% Asian, 0.4% American Indian/Alaska Native, 0.0% Native Hawaiian/Other Pacific Islander, 1.6% Two or more races, 1.1% Hispanic of any race; Average household size: 2.09; Median age: 55.3; Age under 18: 15.4%; Age 65 and over: 29.7%; Males per 100 females: 99.4
Housing: Homeownership rate: 90.5%; Homeowner vacancy rate: 4.1%; Rental vacancy rate: 9.6%

SHERMAN (township). Covers a land area of 35.933 square miles and a water area of 0.005 square miles. Located at 44.21° N. Lat; 83.70° W. Long.
Population: 448; Growth (since 2000): -9.1%; Density: 12.5 persons per square mile; Race: 98.0% White, 0.2% Black/African American, 0.2% Asian, 0.4% American Indian/Alaska Native, 0.0% Native Hawaiian/Other Pacific Islander, 0.9% Two or more races, 0.7% Hispanic of any race; Average household size: 2.30; Median age: 49.4; Age under 18: 15.8%; Age 65 and over: 23.2%; Males per 100 females: 105.5
Housing: Homeownership rate: 88.0%; Homeowner vacancy rate: 0.0%; Rental vacancy rate: 4.2%

TAWAS (township). Covers a land area of 33.394 square miles and a water area of 0.004 square miles. Located at 44.29° N. Lat; 83.59° W. Long.
Population: 1,744; Growth (since 2000): 3.6%; Density: 52.2 persons per square mile; Race: 97.8% White, 0.1% Black/African American, 0.1% Asian, 0.6% American Indian/Alaska Native, 0.0% Native Hawaiian/Other Pacific Islander, 1.3% Two or more races, 0.6% Hispanic of any race; Average household size: 2.38; Median age: 48.9; Age under 18: 20.4%; Age 65 and over: 22.1%; Males per 100 females: 96.4
Housing: Homeownership rate: 91.0%; Homeowner vacancy rate: 2.1%; Rental vacancy rate: 4.4%
Safety: Violent crime rate: 22.1 per 10,000 population; Property crime rate: 201.1 per 10,000 population

TAWAS CITY (city). County seat. Covers a land area of 1.719 square miles and a water area of 0.423 square miles. Located at 44.27° N. Lat; 83.52° W. Long. Elevation is 591 feet.
History: Tawas City, a twin with East Tawas, both located on Tawas Bay of Lake Huron, developed an early dependence on tourism for its source of revenue. The Tawas City Perch Festival was originated in 1936 to exploit the popularity of perch fishing in Tawas Bay.
Population: 1,827; Growth (since 2000): -8.9%; Density: 1,063.1 persons per square mile; Race: 96.9% White, 0.7% Black/African American, 0.9% Asian, 0.2% American Indian/Alaska Native, 0.0% Native Hawaiian/Other Pacific Islander, 0.8% Two or more races, 1.4% Hispanic of any race; Average household size: 2.22; Median age: 47.4; Age under 18: 17.9%; Age 65 and over: 24.6%; Males per 100 females: 89.1

School District(s)

Iosco Resa (PK-12)
  2012-13 Enrollment: 151. . . . . (989) 362-3006
Tawas Area Schools (PK-12)
  2012-13 Enrollment: 1,264 . . . . (989) 984-2250
Housing: Homeownership rate: 75.8%; Homeowner vacancy rate: 5.3%; Rental vacancy rate: 6.0%
Hospitals: Tawas Saint Joseph Hospital (49 beds)

WHITTEMORE (city). Covers a land area of 0.985 square miles and a water area of 0 square miles. Located at 44.23° N. Lat; 83.80° W. Long. Elevation is 778 feet.
Population: 384; Growth (since 2000): -19.3%; Density: 390.0 persons per square mile; Race: 94.8% White, 1.3% Black/African American, 0.0% Asian, 0.5% American Indian/Alaska Native, 0.0% Native Hawaiian/Other Pacific Islander, 2.1% Two or more races, 3.1% Hispanic of any race; Average household size: 2.10; Median age: 47.0; Age under 18: 19.0%; Age 65 and over: 19.0%; Males per 100 females: 82.9

School District(s)

Whittemore-Prescott Area Schools (PK-12)
  2012-13 Enrollment: 962. . . . . (989) 756-2500
Housing: Homeownership rate: 67.7%; Homeowner vacancy rate: 6.8%; Rental vacancy rate: 13.2%

WILBER (township). Covers a land area of 72.436 square miles and a water area of 0.192 square miles. Located at 44.38° N. Lat; 83.52° W. Long. Elevation is 656 feet.
Population: 729; Growth (since 2000): -1.5%; Density: 10.1 persons per square mile; Race: 98.8% White, 0.0% Black/African American, 0.5% Asian, 0.1% American Indian/Alaska Native, 0.0% Native Hawaiian/Other Pacific Islander, 0.5% Two or more races, 0.5% Hispanic of any race; Average household size: 2.24; Median age: 52.0; Age under 18: 14.1%; Age 65 and over: 23.7%; Males per 100 females: 99.7
Housing: Homeownership rate: 92.0%; Homeowner vacancy rate: 2.3%; Rental vacancy rate: 6.9%

Iron County

Located in northwestern Michigan, on the Upper Peninsula; bounded on the south by Wisconsin; drained by the Brule, Michigamme, Paint, and Iron Rivers; includes part of Ottawa National Forest, the Menominee range, and many small lakes. Covers a land area of 1,166.149 square miles, a water area of 45.061 square miles, and is located in the Central Time Zone at 46.17° N. Lat., 88.54° W. Long. The county was founded in 1885. County seat is Crystal Falls.

Weather Station: Stambaugh 2 SSE   Elevation: 1,560 feet

	Jan	Feb	Mar	Apr	May	Jun	Jul	Aug	Sep	Oct	Nov	Dec
High	22	27	37	51	65	73	77	75	66	53	38	26
Low	0	1	11	26	37	46	50	49	41	30	20	7
Precip	1.0	0.8	1.4	2.2	3.0	3.6	4.1	3.1	3.5	3.1	1.9	1.3
Snow	14.9	10.6	11.5	5.8	0.4	0.0	0.0	tr	tr	2.0	8.7	15.2

High and Low temperatures in degrees Fahrenheit; Precipitation and Snow in inches

Population: 11,817; Growth (since 2000): -10.1%; Density: 10.1 persons per square mile; Race: 97.1% White, 0.1% Black/African American, 0.3% Asian, 0.9% American Indian/Alaska Native, 0.0% Native Hawaiian/Other Pacific Islander, 1.4% two or more races, 1.4% Hispanic of any race; Average household size: 2.06; Median age: 51.9; Age under 18: 17.1%; Age 65 and over: 26.3%; Males per 100 females: 97.1; Marriage status: 23.0% never married, 53.8% now married, 1.2% separated, 11.3% widowed, 11.9% divorced; Foreign born: 1.8%; Speak English only: 96.4%; With disability: 21.2%; Veterans: 15.1%; Ancestry: 20.9% German, 13.8% Italian, 13.3% Finnish, 12.1% Polish, 11.7% Swedish
Religion: Six largest groups: 29.2% Catholicism, 13.7% Lutheran, 4.7% Methodist/Pietist, 0.9% Presbyterian-Reformed, 0.8% Baptist, 0.7% Pentecostal
Economy: Unemployment rate: 6.0%; Leading industries: 16.9% retail trade; 12.7% construction; 11.1% other services (except public administration); Farms: 117 totaling 22,939 acres; Company size: 0 employ 1,000 or more persons, 0 employ 500 to 999 persons, 3 employ 100 to 499 persons, 358 employ less than 100 persons; Business ownership: n/a women-owned, n/a Black-owned, n/a Hispanic-owned, n/a Asian-owned
Employment: 9.4% management, business, and financial, 2.7% computer, engineering, and science, 6.9% education, legal, community service, arts, and media, 6.7% healthcare practitioners, 23.7% service, 23.9% sales and office, 10.8% natural resources, construction, and maintenance, 15.9% production, transportation, and material moving
Income: Per capita: $21,499; Median household: $34,685; Average household: $45,656; Households with income of $100,000 or more: 7.1%; Poverty rate: 14.2%
Educational Attainment: High school diploma or higher: 89.2%; Bachelor's degree or higher: 18.4%; Graduate/professional degree or higher: 6.0%
Housing: Homeownership rate: 81.8%; Median home value: $75,100; Median year structure built: 1955; Homeowner vacancy rate: 4.0%; Median gross rent: $490 per month; Rental vacancy rate: 12.4%
Vital Statistics: Birth rate: 79.9 per 10,000 population; Death rate: 162.4 per 10,000 population; Age-adjusted cancer mortality rate: 188.8 deaths per 100,000 population
Health Insurance: 88.4% have insurance; 64.7% have private insurance; 47.9% have public insurance; 11.6% do not have insurance; 4.2% of children under 18 do not have insurance
Health Care: Physicians: 8.6 per 10,000 population; Hospital beds: 21.3 per 10,000 population; Hospital admissions: 770.5 per 10,000 population
Transportation: Commute: 91.5% car, 0.1% public transportation, 4.4% walk, 3.1% work from home; Median travel time to work: 19.5 minutes
Presidential Election: 44.9% Obama, 53.9% Romney (2012)
National and State Parks: Iron Range State Forest
Additional Information Contacts
Iron Government . . . . (906) 875-3221
  http://www.ironmi.org

Iron County Communities

ALPHA (village). Covers a land area of 0.942 square miles and a water area of 0.052 square miles. Located at 46.04° N. Lat; 88.38° W. Long. Elevation is 1,424 feet.
History: The settlement at Alpha grew up around the Mastodon Mine, opened in 1881. First called Mastodon, the village was incorporated as Alpha in 1914.

Population: 145; Growth (since 2000): -26.8%; Density: 153.9 persons per square mile; Race: 100.0% White, 0.0% Black/African American, 0.0% Asian, 0.0% American Indian/Alaska Native, 0.0% Native Hawaiian/Other Pacific Islander, 0.0% Two or more races, 0.0% Hispanic of any race; Average household size: 1.71; Median age: 56.5; Age under 18: 13.1%; Age 65 and over: 28.3%; Males per 100 females: 101.4
Housing: Homeownership rate: 80.0%; Homeowner vacancy rate: 4.2%; Rental vacancy rate: 5.6%

AMASA (CDP). Covers a land area of 4.036 square miles and a water area of 0.006 square miles. Located at 46.23° N. Lat; 88.46° W. Long. Elevation is 1,440 feet.
Population: 283; Growth (since 2000): n/a; Density: 70.1 persons per square mile; Race: 97.5% White, 0.0% Black/African American, 0.0% Asian, 2.5% American Indian/Alaska Native, 0.0% Native Hawaiian/Other Pacific Islander, 0.0% Two or more races, 1.1% Hispanic of any race; Average household size: 1.99; Median age: 47.4; Age under 18: 18.4%; Age 65 and over: 18.7%; Males per 100 females: 109.6
Housing: Homeownership rate: 78.8%; Homeowner vacancy rate: 2.6%; Rental vacancy rate: 0.0%

BATES (township). Covers a land area of 125.691 square miles and a water area of 5.768 square miles. Located at 46.25° N. Lat; 88.62° W. Long.
Population: 921; Growth (since 2000): -9.8%; Density: 7.3 persons per square mile; Race: 97.2% White, 0.0% Black/African American, 0.4% Asian, 0.4% American Indian/Alaska Native, 0.0% Native Hawaiian/Other Pacific Islander, 1.4% Two or more races, 1.6% Hispanic of any race; Average household size: 2.12; Median age: 52.3; Age under 18: 17.8%; Age 65 and over: 26.1%; Males per 100 females: 98.9
Housing: Homeownership rate: 91.5%; Homeowner vacancy rate: 4.8%; Rental vacancy rate: 15.9%

CASPIAN (city). Covers a land area of 1.425 square miles and a water area of 0 square miles. Located at 46.07° N. Lat; 88.63° W. Long. Elevation is 1,496 feet.
History: The Chicago & Northwestern Railroad built a branch line station here in 1884. The village was platted in 1908 by the Veroner Mining Company to provide housing for employees in the Caspian, Baltic, and Fogarty mines.
Population: 906; Growth (since 2000): -9.1%; Density: 635.8 persons per square mile; Race: 95.0% White, 0.0% Black/African American, 0.7% Asian, 1.4% American Indian/Alaska Native, 0.0% Native Hawaiian/Other Pacific Islander, 2.9% Two or more races, 1.2% Hispanic of any race; Average household size: 2.11; Median age: 46.4; Age under 18: 21.4%; Age 65 and over: 23.6%; Males per 100 females: 95.3
Housing: Homeownership rate: 73.0%; Homeowner vacancy rate: 6.8%; Rental vacancy rate: 9.3%

CRYSTAL FALLS (city). County seat. Covers a land area of 3.473 square miles and a water area of 0.145 square miles. Located at 46.09° N. Lat; 88.32° W. Long. Elevation is 1,473 feet.
History: Crystal Falls, named for a cascade on the Paint River, was first a lumber village but grew with the development of the Bristol Mine which opened in 1882.
Population: 1,469; Growth (since 2000): -18.0%; Density: 422.9 persons per square mile; Race: 96.9% White, 0.2% Black/African American, 0.2% Asian, 0.7% American Indian/Alaska Native, 0.0% Native Hawaiian/Other Pacific Islander, 1.8% Two or more races, 1.0% Hispanic of any race; Average household size: 2.06; Median age: 48.3; Age under 18: 19.7%; Age 65 and over: 22.5%; Males per 100 females: 97.4
School District(s)
Forest Park SD (PK-12)
    2012-13 Enrollment: 468 . . . . (906) 875-6761
Housing: Homeownership rate: 78.0%; Homeowner vacancy rate: 4.4%; Rental vacancy rate: 7.2%
Safety: Violent crime rate: 7.0 per 10,000 population; Property crime rate: 125.8 per 10,000 population
Additional Information Contacts
City of Crystal Falls . . . . (906) 875-3212
  http://www.crystalfalls.org

CRYSTAL FALLS (township). Covers a land area of 228.412 square miles and a water area of 6.977 square miles. Located at 46.25° N. Lat; 88.31° W. Long. Elevation is 1,473 feet.
History: Incorporated as village 1889, as city 1899.
Population: 1,743; Growth (since 2000): 1.2%; Density: 7.6 persons per square mile; Race: 97.9% White, 0.0% Black/African American, 0.3% Asian, 0.6% American Indian/Alaska Native, 0.0% Native Hawaiian/Other Pacific Islander, 0.8% Two or more races, 1.4% Hispanic of any race; Average household size: 2.02; Median age: 55.5; Age under 18: 14.5%; Age 65 and over: 32.6%; Males per 100 females: 95.8
School District(s)
Forest Park SD (PK-12)
    2012-13 Enrollment: 468. . . . . (906) 875-6761
Housing: Homeownership rate: 87.9%; Homeowner vacancy rate: 1.7%; Rental vacancy rate: 5.1%

GAASTRA (city). Covers a land area of 1.640 square miles and a water area of 0 square miles. Located at 46.06° N. Lat; 88.61° W. Long. Elevation is 1,621 feet.
History: Gaastra was laid out in 1908 and named for Douwe Gaastra, a real estate speculator who owned the land. Gaastra was incorporated as a village in 1919 and as a city in 1949.
Population: 347; Growth (since 2000): 2.4%; Density: 211.6 persons per square mile; Race: 98.3% White, 0.0% Black/African American, 0.0% Asian, 0.6% American Indian/Alaska Native, 0.0% Native Hawaiian/Other Pacific Islander, 1.2% Two or more races, 1.2% Hispanic of any race; Average household size: 2.30; Median age: 46.7; Age under 18: 23.3%; Age 65 and over: 25.9%; Males per 100 females: 79.8
Housing: Homeownership rate: 86.7%; Homeowner vacancy rate: 2.2%; Rental vacancy rate: 4.8%

HEMATITE (township). Covers a land area of 153.450 square miles and a water area of 2.198 square miles. Located at 46.34° N. Lat; 88.48° W. Long.
Population: 338; Growth (since 2000): -4.0%; Density: 2.2 persons per square mile; Race: 96.2% White, 0.0% Black/African American, 0.3% Asian, 2.1% American Indian/Alaska Native, 0.0% Native Hawaiian/Other Pacific Islander, 0.6% Two or more races, 1.8% Hispanic of any race; Average household size: 1.99; Median age: 47.9; Age under 18: 18.0%; Age 65 and over: 20.4%; Males per 100 females: 108.6
Housing: Homeownership rate: 80.0%; Homeowner vacancy rate: 3.5%; Rental vacancy rate: 0.0%

IRON RIVER (city). Covers a land area of 6.736 square miles and a water area of 0.021 square miles. Located at 46.10° N. Lat; 88.64° W. Long. Elevation is 1,512 feet.
History: Iron River was settled in 1881 when the Nanaina Mine was producing, and was known for a time as Nanaina. Iron River was incorporated as a village in 1885 and as a city in 1926.
Population: 3,029; Growth (since 2000): 57.0%; Density: 449.7 persons per square mile; Race: 96.3% White, 0.2% Black/African American, 0.3% Asian, 1.2% American Indian/Alaska Native, 0.1% Native Hawaiian/Other Pacific Islander, 1.7% Two or more races, 1.9% Hispanic of any race; Average household size: 2.02; Median age: 47.6; Age under 18: 19.6%; Age 65 and over: 24.7%; Males per 100 females: 88.8; Marriage status: 25.7% never married, 45.9% now married, 1.5% separated, 14.5% widowed, 13.9% divorced; Foreign born: 4.0%; Speak English only: 94.2%; With disability: 27.7%; Veterans: 14.9%; Ancestry: 21.5% German, 14.2% Finnish, 13.4% Swedish, 12.4% English, 10.8% Italian
Employment: 8.7% management, business, and financial, 1.3% computer, engineering, and science, 5.8% education, legal, community service, arts, and media, 3.8% healthcare practitioners, 31.2% service, 20.5% sales and office, 12.9% natural resources, construction, and maintenance, 15.7% production, transportation, and material moving
Income: Per capita: $18,244; Median household: $26,168; Average household: $34,305; Households with income of $100,000 or more: 3.0%; Poverty rate: 25.2%
Educational Attainment: High school diploma or higher: 86.9%; Bachelor's degree or higher: 16.0%; Graduate/professional degree or higher: 2.4%
School District(s)
West Iron County Public Schools (PK-12)
    2012-13 Enrollment: 887. . . . . (906) 265-9218

Housing: Homeownership rate: 69.1%; Median home value: $51,700; Median year structure built: 1943; Homeowner vacancy rate: 5.4%; Median gross rent: $476 per month; Rental vacancy rate: 13.0%
Health Insurance: 85.3% have insurance; 52.4% have private insurance; 57.3% have public insurance; 14.7% do not have insurance; 0.9% of children under 18 do not have insurance
Hospitals: Northstar Health System (67 beds)
Safety: Violent crime rate: 16.9 per 10,000 population; Property crime rate: 423.6 per 10,000 population
Newspapers: Iron Co Reporter (weekly circulation 6000)
Transportation: Commute: 84.4% car, 0.0% public transportation, 9.7% walk, 4.3% work from home; Median travel time to work: 16.1 minutes

IRON RIVER (township). Covers a land area of 238.253 square miles and a water area of 4.273 square miles. Located at 46.24° N. Lat; 88.79° W. Long. Elevation is 1,512 feet.
History: Settled by iron-ore prospectors c.1881; incorporated as village 1885, as city 1926.
Population: 1,027; Growth (since 2000): -35.2%; Density: 4.3 persons per square mile; Race: 97.2% White, 0.0% Black/African American, 0.2% Asian, 1.5% American Indian/Alaska Native, 0.0% Native Hawaiian/Other Pacific Islander, 1.2% Two or more races, 1.0% Hispanic of any race; Average household size: 2.11; Median age: 53.0; Age under 18: 15.6%; Age 65 and over: 23.4%; Males per 100 females: 105.0
School District(s)
West Iron County Public Schools (PK-12)
    2012-13 Enrollment: 887. . . . . (906) 265-9218
Housing: Homeownership rate: 88.7%; Homeowner vacancy rate: 2.9%; Rental vacancy rate: 8.3%
Hospitals: Northstar Health System (67 beds)
Newspapers: Iron Co Reporter (weekly circulation 6000)

MANSFIELD (township). Covers a land area of 99.076 square miles and a water area of 8.384 square miles. Located at 46.21° N. Lat; 88.15° W. Long. Elevation is 1,381 feet.
Population: 241; Growth (since 2000): -0.8%; Density: 2.4 persons per square mile; Race: 100.0% White, 0.0% Black/African American, 0.0% Asian, 0.0% American Indian/Alaska Native, 0.0% Native Hawaiian/Other Pacific Islander, 0.0% Two or more races, 0.4% Hispanic of any race; Average household size: 1.96; Median age: 56.9; Age under 18: 9.5%; Age 65 and over: 29.5%; Males per 100 females: 115.2
Housing: Homeownership rate: 95.9%; Homeowner vacancy rate: 1.7%; Rental vacancy rate: 0.0%

MASTODON (township). Covers a land area of 126.504 square miles and a water area of 8.930 square miles. Located at 46.02° N. Lat; 88.28° W. Long. Elevation is 1,394 feet.
Population: 656; Growth (since 2000): -1.8%; Density: 5.2 persons per square mile; Race: 98.9% White, 0.0% Black/African American, 0.2% Asian, 0.3% American Indian/Alaska Native, 0.0% Native Hawaiian/Other Pacific Islander, 0.5% Two or more races, 0.9% Hispanic of any race; Average household size: 1.95; Median age: 58.7; Age under 18: 11.7%; Age 65 and over: 33.1%; Males per 100 females: 106.3
Housing: Homeownership rate: 92.0%; Homeowner vacancy rate: 2.2%; Rental vacancy rate: 6.9%

STAMBAUGH (township). Covers a land area of 181.489 square miles and a water area of 8.365 square miles. Located at 46.25° N. Lat; 88.87° W. Long. Elevation is 1,634 feet.
History: Settled c.1878; incorporated as village 1895, as city 1923.
Population: 1,140; Growth (since 2000): -8.7%; Density: 6.3 persons per square mile; Race: 97.6% White, 0.4% Black/African American, 0.1% Asian, 0.9% American Indian/Alaska Native, 0.0% Native Hawaiian/Other Pacific Islander, 1.1% Two or more races, 1.1% Hispanic of any race; Average household size: 2.08; Median age: 55.4; Age under 18: 11.0%; Age 65 and over: 28.1%; Males per 100 females: 109.2
Housing: Homeownership rate: 94.2%; Homeowner vacancy rate: 4.8%; Rental vacancy rate: 52.3%

Isabella County

Located in central Michigan; drained by the Chippewa and Pine Rivers. Covers a land area of 572.677 square miles, a water area of 5.004 square

miles, and is located in the Eastern Time Zone at 43.65° N. Lat., 84.84° W. Long. The county was founded in 1831. County seat is Mount Pleasant.

Isabella County is part of the Mount Pleasant, MI Micropolitan Statistical Area. The entire metro area includes: Isabella County, MI

Population: 70,311; Growth (since 2000): 11.0%; Density: 122.8 persons per square mile; Race: 89.2% White, 2.4% Black/African American, 1.6% Asian, 3.4% American Indian/Alaska Native, 0.0% Native Hawaiian/Other Pacific Islander, 2.8% two or more races, 3.1% Hispanic of any race; Average household size: 2.49; Median age: 25.1; Age under 18: 18.0%; Age 65 and over: 9.7%; Males per 100 females: 94.8; Marriage status: 50.6% never married, 36.1% now married, 0.7% separated, 3.9% widowed, 9.5% divorced; Foreign born: 3.0%; Speak English only: 94.5%; With disability: 12.4%; Veterans: 6.2%; Ancestry: 30.6% German, 16.4% Irish, 12.9% English, 8.2% Polish, 5.6% French
Religion: Six largest groups: 14.5% Catholicism, 2.8% Non-denominational Protestant, 2.4% Methodist/Pietist, 2.2% Muslim Estimate, 2.0% Lutheran, 1.6% Presbyterian-Reformed
Economy: Unemployment rate: 4.5%; Leading industries: 15.6% retail trade; 14.7% health care and social assistance; 11.1% other services (except public administration); Farms: 928 totaling 188,465 acres; Company size: 1 employs 1,000 or more persons, 2 employ 500 to 999 persons, 27 employ 100 to 499 persons, 1,349 employ less than 100 persons; Business ownership: 1,401 women-owned, n/a Black-owned, n/a Hispanic-owned, 92 Asian-owned
Employment: 10.0% management, business, and financial, 2.6% computer, engineering, and science, 11.6% education, legal, community service, arts, and media, 3.6% healthcare practitioners, 27.9% service, 27.1% sales and office, 7.7% natural resources, construction, and maintenance, 9.5% production, transportation, and material moving
Income: Per capita: $19,061; Median household: $36,372; Average household: $51,284; Households with income of $100,000 or more: 11.4%; Poverty rate: 31.5%
Educational Attainment: High school diploma or higher: 90.1%; Bachelor's degree or higher: 25.3%; Graduate/professional degree or higher: 11.4%
Housing: Homeownership rate: 58.1%; Median home value: $119,800; Median year structure built: 1980; Homeowner vacancy rate: 2.0%; Median gross rent: $698 per month; Rental vacancy rate: 6.1%
Vital Statistics: Birth rate: 91.9 per 10,000 population; Death rate: 59.2 per 10,000 population; Age-adjusted cancer mortality rate: 164.4 deaths per 100,000 population
Health Insurance: 86.8% have insurance; 71.3% have private insurance; 26.8% have public insurance; 13.2% do not have insurance; 4.7% of children under 18 do not have insurance
Health Care: Physicians: 13.2 per 10,000 population; Hospital beds: 11.0 per 10,000 population; Hospital admissions: 539.9 per 10,000 population
Transportation: Commute: 85.7% car, 1.3% public transportation, 7.4% walk, 3.6% work from home; Median travel time to work: 17.7 minutes
Presidential Election: 53.7% Obama, 44.5% Romney (2012)
Additional Information Contacts
Isabella Government . . . . (989) 772-0911
    http://www.isabellacounty.org

Isabella County Communities

BEAL CITY (CDP). Covers a land area of 4.013 square miles and a water area of 0.001 square miles. Located at 43.66° N. Lat; 84.90° W. Long. Elevation is 863 feet.
History: Beal City was founded by a Mr. Beal who operated a grocery store here in the 1880's.
Population: 357; Growth (since 2000): 3.5%; Density: 89.0 persons per square mile; Race: 95.5% White, 0.0% Black/African American, 0.3% Asian, 1.1% American Indian/Alaska Native, 0.0% Native Hawaiian/Other Pacific Islander, 3.1% Two or more races, 1.1% Hispanic of any race; Average household size: 2.75; Median age: 37.6; Age under 18: 33.3%; Age 65 and over: 15.4%; Males per 100 females: 88.9
School District(s)
Beal City Public Schools (PK-12)
    2012-13 Enrollment: 701 . . . . (989) 644-3901
Housing: Homeownership rate: 89.3%; Homeowner vacancy rate: 0.9%; Rental vacancy rate: 17.6%

BLANCHARD (unincorporated postal area)
ZCTA: 49310
    Covers a land area of 89.225 square miles and a water area of 0.227 square miles. Located at 43.51° N. Lat; 85.05° W. Long. Elevation is 971 feet.
Population: 3,016; Growth (since 2000): 9.4%; Density: 33.8 persons per square mile; Race: 94.6% White, 0.9% Black/African American, 0.2% Asian, 0.9% American Indian/Alaska Native, 0.0% Native Hawaiian/Other Pacific Islander, 3.3% Two or more races, 1.8% Hispanic of any race; Average household size: 2.69; Median age: 38.9; Age under 18: 27.8%; Age 65 and over: 12.2%; Males per 100 females: 105.3; Marriage status: 34.6% never married, 51.9% now married, 0.8% separated, 3.7% widowed, 9.7% divorced; Foreign born: 1.6%; Speak English only: 83.3%; With disability: 12.5%; Veterans: 8.6%; Ancestry: 38.8% German, 11.0% English, 10.1% Irish, 6.8% American, 6.0% Dutch
Employment: 12.4% management, business, and financial, 1.5% computer, engineering, and science, 6.5% education, legal, community service, arts, and media, 1.6% healthcare practitioners, 19.1% service, 19.9% sales and office, 20.2% natural resources, construction, and maintenance, 18.8% production, transportation, and material moving
Income: Per capita: $17,270; Median household: $40,550; Average household: $50,293; Households with income of $100,000 or more: 8.1%; Poverty rate: 12.2%
Educational Attainment: High school diploma or higher: 87.6%; Bachelor's degree or higher: 12.3%; Graduate/professional degree or higher: 4.6%
School District(s)
Montabella Community Schools (PK-12)
    2012-13 Enrollment: 822 . . . . (989) 427-5148
Housing: Homeownership rate: 87.8%; Median home value: $104,900; Median year structure built: 1976; Homeowner vacancy rate: 3.4%; Median gross rent: $736 per month; Rental vacancy rate: 6.8%
Health Insurance: 88.1% have insurance; 69.7% have private insurance; 34.0% have public insurance; 11.9% do not have insurance; 2.0% of children under 18 do not have insurance
Transportation: Commute: 74.8% car, 0.4% public transportation, 2.5% walk, 21.8% work from home; Median travel time to work: 26.1 minutes

BROOMFIELD (township). Covers a land area of 34.918 square miles and a water area of 0.860 square miles. Located at 43.60° N. Lat; 85.04° W. Long.
History: Broomfield Township was organized in 1866 and named for William Broomfield, an early settler.
Population: 1,849; Growth (since 2000): 14.1%; Density: 53.0 persons per square mile; Race: 95.2% White, 0.6% Black/African American, 0.3% Asian, 1.6% American Indian/Alaska Native, 0.0% Native Hawaiian/Other Pacific Islander, 1.9% Two or more races, 2.4% Hispanic of any race; Average household size: 2.54; Median age: 40.5; Age under 18: 23.1%; Age 65 and over: 16.3%; Males per 100 females: 97.1
Housing: Homeownership rate: 86.4%; Homeowner vacancy rate: 2.9%; Rental vacancy rate: 13.2%

CHIPPEWA (township). Covers a land area of 35.854 square miles and a water area of 0.312 square miles. Located at 43.59° N. Lat; 84.66° W. Long.
Population: 4,654; Growth (since 2000): 0.8%; Density: 129.8 persons per square mile; Race: 74.8% White, 0.6% Black/African American, 0.4% Asian, 18.0% American Indian/Alaska Native, 0.1% Native Hawaiian/Other Pacific Islander, 5.3% Two or more races, 5.6% Hispanic of any race; Average household size: 2.71; Median age: 34.9; Age under 18: 27.3%; Age 65 and over: 9.9%; Males per 100 females: 100.9; Marriage status: 34.8% never married, 43.3% now married, 2.4% separated, 4.8% widowed, 17.1% divorced; Foreign born: 1.3%; Speak English only: 95.9%; With disability: 16.5%; Veterans: 8.0%; Ancestry: 24.2% German, 16.0% Irish, 13.0% English, 5.1% Scottish, 4.7% Polish
Employment: 9.3% management, business, and financial, 1.7% computer, engineering, and science, 5.1% education, legal, community service, arts, and media, 3.7% healthcare practitioners, 29.9% service, 26.4% sales and office, 12.0% natural resources, construction, and maintenance, 11.8% production, transportation, and material moving
Income: Per capita: $23,236; Median household: $43,293; Average household: $62,183; Households with income of $100,000 or more: 15.4%; Poverty rate: 23.6%

Educational Attainment: High school diploma or higher: 84.1%; Bachelor's degree or higher: 15.5%; Graduate/professional degree or higher: 4.1%
Housing: Homeownership rate: 78.4%; Median home value: $118,400; Median year structure built: 1983; Homeowner vacancy rate: 2.1%; Median gross rent: $703 per month; Rental vacancy rate: 6.0%
Health Insurance: 84.2% have insurance; 63.6% have private insurance; 33.1% have public insurance; 15.8% do not have insurance; 6.3% of children under 18 do not have insurance
Transportation: Commute: 89.4% car, 2.0% public transportation, 3.4% walk, 4.3% work from home; Median travel time to work: 15.4 minutes

COE (township). Covers a land area of 36.165 square miles and a water area of 0.061 square miles. Located at 43.52° N. Lat; 84.66° W. Long. Elevation is 761 feet.
History: Coe Township was organized in 1855 and named for Lt. Governor George A. Coe.
Population: 3,079; Growth (since 2000): 2.9%; Density: 85.1 persons per square mile; Race: 95.2% White, 0.4% Black/African American, 0.3% Asian, 1.3% American Indian/Alaska Native, 0.0% Native Hawaiian/Other Pacific Islander, 1.8% Two or more races, 3.1% Hispanic of any race; Average household size: 2.49; Median age: 39.3; Age under 18: 24.8%; Age 65 and over: 14.0%; Males per 100 females: 92.3; Marriage status: 30.6% never married, 54.1% now married, 0.7% separated, 5.0% widowed, 10.3% divorced; Foreign born: 0.4%; Speak English only: 99.5%; With disability: 14.5%; Veterans: 9.2%; Ancestry: 40.4% German, 15.7% English, 15.1% Irish, 10.7% American, 6.6% Dutch
Employment: 14.7% management, business, and financial, 1.7% computer, engineering, and science, 8.7% education, legal, community service, arts, and media, 6.2% healthcare practitioners, 23.8% service, 23.2% sales and office, 4.1% natural resources, construction, and maintenance, 17.6% production, transportation, and material moving
Income: Per capita: $21,753; Median household: $47,482; Average household: $53,512; Households with income of $100,000 or more: 9.7%; Poverty rate: 10.4%
Educational Attainment: High school diploma or higher: 90.4%; Bachelor's degree or higher: 18.2%; Graduate/professional degree or higher: 8.5%
Housing: Homeownership rate: 76.6%; Median home value: $108,600; Median year structure built: 1970; Homeowner vacancy rate: 1.5%; Median gross rent: $614 per month; Rental vacancy rate: 17.0%
Health Insurance: 84.5% have insurance; 72.6% have private insurance; 29.1% have public insurance; 15.5% do not have insurance; 7.0% of children under 18 do not have insurance
Transportation: Commute: 96.8% car, 0.0% public transportation, 0.9% walk, 1.8% work from home; Median travel time to work: 18.3 minutes
Additional Information Contacts
Coe Township . . . . (989) 828-5960
 http://www.coetownship.com

COLDWATER (township). Covers a land area of 35.916 square miles and a water area of 0.120 square miles. Located at 43.77° N. Lat; 85.02° W. Long.
Population: 777; Growth (since 2000): 5.4%; Density: 21.6 persons per square mile; Race: 94.7% White, 0.4% Black/African American, 0.0% Asian, 1.9% American Indian/Alaska Native, 0.0% Native Hawaiian/Other Pacific Islander, 2.8% Two or more races, 1.5% Hispanic of any race; Average household size: 2.45; Median age: 45.1; Age under 18: 20.8%; Age 65 and over: 18.0%; Males per 100 females: 103.4
School District(s)
Coldwater Community Schools (PK-12)
 2012-13 Enrollment: 2,860 . . . . (517) 279-5910
Housing: Homeownership rate: 83.6%; Homeowner vacancy rate: 2.5%; Rental vacancy rate: 0.0%

DEERFIELD (township). Covers a land area of 35.452 square miles and a water area of 0.387 square miles. Located at 43.60° N. Lat; 84.90° W. Long.
History: The first white settler of Deerfield came to reside here in 1834, and his. family was for a year or more the only family in town. This man's name was John How. He was born near Carlisle, England, in the village of Dalston, April 19, 1814.
Population: 3,188; Growth (since 2000): 3.5%; Density: 89.9 persons per square mile; Race: 93.1% White, 0.4% Black/African American, 0.9% Asian, 3.5% American Indian/Alaska Native, 0.0% Native Hawaiian/Other

Pacific Islander, 1.7% Two or more races, 2.6% Hispanic of any race; Average household size: 2.65; Median age: 43.7; Age under 18: 23.5%; Age 65 and over: 12.7%; Males per 100 females: 103.8; Marriage status: 20.2% never married, 66.0% now married, 0.3% separated, 4.2% widowed, 9.5% divorced; Foreign born: 1.6%; Speak English only: 96.7%; With disability: 10.5%; Veterans: 9.8%; Ancestry: 37.4% German, 18.9% Irish, 16.1% English, 6.6% American, 4.9% Polish
Employment: 16.1% management, business, and financial, 3.3% computer, engineering, and science, 12.4% education, legal, community service, arts, and media, 5.9% healthcare practitioners, 18.6% service, 22.1% sales and office, 10.4% natural resources, construction, and maintenance, 11.0% production, transportation, and material moving
Income: Per capita: $33,669; Median household: $67,358; Average household: $86,639; Households with income of $100,000 or more: 25.8%; Poverty rate: 5.2%
Educational Attainment: High school diploma or higher: 93.3%; Bachelor's degree or higher: 36.0%; Graduate/professional degree or higher: 16.1%
School District(s)
Britton Deerfield Schools (PK-12)
 2012-13 Enrollment: 756 . . . . (517) 451-4581
Housing: Homeownership rate: 90.9%; Median home value: $157,700; Median year structure built: 1983; Homeowner vacancy rate: 1.5%; Median gross rent: $667 per month; Rental vacancy rate: 8.3%
Health Insurance: 90.5% have insurance; 83.6% have private insurance; 21.6% have public insurance; 9.5% do not have insurance; 2.2% of children under 18 do not have insurance
Transportation: Commute: 96.9% car, 0.4% public transportation, 0.3% walk, 2.1% work from home; Median travel time to work: 23.3 minutes

DENVER (township). Covers a land area of 36.408 square miles and a water area of 0.034 square miles. Located at 43.69° N. Lat; 84.66° W. Long.
Population: 1,148; Growth (since 2000): 0.1%; Density: 31.5 persons per square mile; Race: 86.2% White, 0.7% Black/African American, 0.4% Asian, 9.0% American Indian/Alaska Native, 0.0% Native Hawaiian/Other Pacific Islander, 3.2% Two or more races, 2.5% Hispanic of any race; Average household size: 2.58; Median age: 39.5; Age under 18: 25.1%; Age 65 and over: 11.1%; Males per 100 females: 95.2
Housing: Homeownership rate: 88.1%; Homeowner vacancy rate: 2.0%; Rental vacancy rate: 7.0%

FREMONT (township). Covers a land area of 35.852 square miles and a water area of 0.045 square miles. Located at 43.50° N. Lat; 84.91° W. Long.
Population: 1,455; Growth (since 2000): 7.1%; Density: 40.6 persons per square mile; Race: 95.7% White, 1.2% Black/African American, 0.1% Asian, 0.7% American Indian/Alaska Native, 0.0% Native Hawaiian/Other Pacific Islander, 2.1% Two or more races, 3.0% Hispanic of any race; Average household size: 2.73; Median age: 38.2; Age under 18: 27.1%; Age 65 and over: 10.9%; Males per 100 females: 100.1
Housing: Homeownership rate: 90.3%; Homeowner vacancy rate: 3.2%; Rental vacancy rate: 11.9%

GILMORE (township). Covers a land area of 35.593 square miles and a water area of 0.422 square miles. Located at 43.77° N. Lat; 84.92° W. Long.
History: Gilmore Township was organized in 1870 and named for General Gilmore.
Population: 1,459; Growth (since 2000): 6.0%; Density: 41.0 persons per square mile; Race: 96.4% White, 0.1% Black/African American, 0.2% Asian, 1.3% American Indian/Alaska Native, 0.0% Native Hawaiian/Other Pacific Islander, 1.6% Two or more races, 2.1% Hispanic of any race; Average household size: 2.59; Median age: 44.3; Age under 18: 24.2%; Age 65 and over: 15.1%; Males per 100 females: 97.7
Housing: Homeownership rate: 88.3%; Homeowner vacancy rate: 0.4%; Rental vacancy rate: 4.3%

ISABELLA (township). Covers a land area of 36.321 square miles and a water area of 0.061 square miles. Located at 43.68° N. Lat; 84.79° W. Long.
Population: 2,253; Growth (since 2000): 5.0%; Density: 62.0 persons per square mile; Race: 90.6% White, 0.9% Black/African American, 0.2% Asian, 4.4% American Indian/Alaska Native, 0.0% Native Hawaiian/Other Pacific Islander, 3.4% Two or more races, 2.7% Hispanic of any race;

Average household size: 2.58; Median age: 38.6; Age under 18: 25.9%; Age 65 and over: 13.1%; Males per 100 females: 92.9
Housing: Homeownership rate: 81.8%; Homeowner vacancy rate: 0.4%; Rental vacancy rate: 3.7%

LAKE ISABELLA (village). Covers a land area of 3.513 square miles and a water area of 1.136 square miles. Located at 43.64° N. Lat; 85.00° W. Long. Elevation is 892 feet.
Population: 1,681; Growth (since 2000): n/a; Density: 478.5 persons per square mile; Race: 95.1% White, 0.4% Black/African American, 0.5% Asian, 1.1% American Indian/Alaska Native, 0.1% Native Hawaiian/Other Pacific Islander, 2.0% Two or more races, 3.6% Hispanic of any race; Average household size: 2.41; Median age: 41.1; Age under 18: 22.4%; Age 65 and over: 17.8%; Males per 100 females: 95.9
Housing: Homeownership rate: 92.1%; Homeowner vacancy rate: 4.3%; Rental vacancy rate: 8.2%

LINCOLN (township). Covers a land area of 36.124 square miles and a water area of 0.101 square miles. Located at 43.51° N. Lat; 84.79° W. Long.
Population: 2,115; Growth (since 2000): 9.2%; Density: 58.5 persons per square mile; Race: 94.5% White, 0.4% Black/African American, 0.5% Asian, 1.0% American Indian/Alaska Native, 0.0% Native Hawaiian/Other Pacific Islander, 2.1% Two or more races, 3.5% Hispanic of any race; Average household size: 2.76; Median age: 36.0; Age under 18: 26.4%; Age 65 and over: 12.1%; Males per 100 females: 106.5
Housing: Homeownership rate: 86.2%; Homeowner vacancy rate: 1.3%; Rental vacancy rate: 8.6%

LOOMIS (CDP). Covers a land area of 2.801 square miles and a water area of 0.018 square miles. Located at 43.78° N. Lat; 84.66° W. Long. Elevation is 810 feet.
Population: 213; Growth (since 2000): n/a; Density: 76.1 persons per square mile; Race: 98.1% White, 0.0% Black/African American, 0.5% Asian, 1.4% American Indian/Alaska Native, 0.0% Native Hawaiian/Other Pacific Islander, 0.0% Two or more races, 2.3% Hispanic of any race; Average household size: 2.49; Median age: 36.4; Age under 18: 24.4%; Age 65 and over: 10.3%; Males per 100 females: 99.1
Housing: Homeownership rate: 74.7%; Homeowner vacancy rate: 3.1%; Rental vacancy rate: 0.0%

MOUNT PLEASANT (city). County seat. Covers a land area of 7.741 square miles and a water area of 0.090 square miles. Located at 43.60° N. Lat; 84.78° W. Long. Elevation is 771 feet.
History: Mount Pleasant, which began as a trading post, developed as a residential and college city. The Central State Teachers College was founded here in 1895.
Population: 26,016; Growth (since 2000): 0.3%; Density: 3,360.8 persons per square mile; Race: 87.6% White, 3.9% Black/African American, 3.0% Asian, 2.0% American Indian/Alaska Native, 0.0% Native Hawaiian/Other Pacific Islander, 2.8% Two or more races, 3.3% Hispanic of any race; Average household size: 2.35; Median age: 22.0; Age under 18: 11.0%; Age 65 and over: 7.2%; Males per 100 females: 90.0; Marriage status: 67.9% never married, 21.5% now married, 0.5% separated, 3.2% widowed, 7.4% divorced; Foreign born: 5.6%; Speak English only: 92.2%; With disability: 10.1%; Veterans: 4.0%; Ancestry: 27.4% German, 15.4% Irish, 10.8% Polish, 10.0% English, 6.4% Italian
Employment: 9.1% management, business, and financial, 3.0% computer, engineering, and science, 15.9% education, legal, community service, arts, and media, 2.7% healthcare practitioners, 32.5% service, 27.6% sales and office, 3.2% natural resources, construction, and maintenance, 6.1% production, transportation, and material moving
Income: Per capita: $15,945; Median household: $28,336; Average household: $45,515; Households with income of $100,000 or more: 10.6%; Poverty rate: 45.3%
Educational Attainment: High school diploma or higher: 92.7%; Bachelor's degree or higher: 39.1%; Graduate/professional degree or higher: 20.5%

School District(s)
Beal City Public Schools (PK-12)
    2012-13 Enrollment: 701. . . . . (989) 644-3901
Gratiot-Isabella Resd (PK-12)
    2012-13 Enrollment: 184 . . . . (989) 875-5101
Mt. Pleasant City SD (PK-12)
    2012-13 Enrollment: 3,454 . . . . (989) 775-2301

Renaissance Public Schools Academy (PK-12)
    2012-13 Enrollment: 341. . . . . (989) 773-9889
Shepherd Public Schools (PK-12)
    2012-13 Enrollment: 1,765 . . . . (989) 828-5520
Four-year College(s)
Central Michigan University (Public)
    Fall 2013 Enrollment: 26,841 . . . . (989) 774-4000
    2013-14 Tuition: In-state $11,220; Out-of-state $23,670
Two-year College(s)
Saginaw Chippewa Tribal College (Public)
    Fall 2013 Enrollment: 117 . . . . (989) 775-4123
    2013-14 Tuition: In-state $2,040; Out-of-state $2,040
Vocational/Technical School(s)
M J Murphy Beauty College of Mount Pleasant (Private, For-profit)
    Fall 2013 Enrollment: 82 . . . . (989) 773-8629
    2013-14 Tuition: $8,600
Housing: Homeownership rate: 34.7%; Median home value: $123,400; Median year structure built: 1974; Homeowner vacancy rate: 2.1%; Median gross rent: $687 per month; Rental vacancy rate: 6.6%
Health Insurance: 87.8% have insurance; 74.4% have private insurance; 21.3% have public insurance; 12.2% do not have insurance; 3.1% of children under 18 do not have insurance
Hospitals: Mclaren Central Michigan (137 beds)
Safety: Violent crime rate: 22.1 per 10,000 population; Property crime rate: 187.1 per 10,000 population
Newspapers: Morning Sun (daily circulation 10200)
Transportation: Commute: 76.3% car, 1.1% public transportation, 16.2% walk, 2.9% work from home; Median travel time to work: 14.4 minutes
Airports: Mount Pleasant Municipal (general aviation)
Additional Information Contacts
City of Mount Pleasant . . . . (989) 779-5361
    http://www.mt-pleasant.org

NOTTAWA (township). Covers a land area of 35.307 square miles and a water area of 0.622 square miles. Located at 43.68° N. Lat; 84.91° W. Long.
Population: 2,282; Growth (since 2000): 0.2%; Density: 64.6 persons per square mile; Race: 93.0% White, 0.2% Black/African American, 0.3% Asian, 3.5% American Indian/Alaska Native, 0.0% Native Hawaiian/Other Pacific Islander, 3.0% Two or more races, 1.8% Hispanic of any race; Average household size: 2.65; Median age: 39.2; Age under 18: 27.9%; Age 65 and over: 12.5%; Males per 100 females: 104.7
Housing: Homeownership rate: 87.8%; Homeowner vacancy rate: 1.2%; Rental vacancy rate: 7.8%

ROLLAND (township). Covers a land area of 35.764 square miles and a water area of 0.133 square miles. Located at 43.50° N. Lat; 85.02° W. Long.
Population: 1,305; Growth (since 2000): 7.9%; Density: 36.5 persons per square mile; Race: 94.9% White, 0.8% Black/African American, 0.3% Asian, 0.7% American Indian/Alaska Native, 0.0% Native Hawaiian/Other Pacific Islander, 3.1% Two or more races, 1.7% Hispanic of any race; Average household size: 2.59; Median age: 39.0; Age under 18: 27.1%; Age 65 and over: 11.4%; Males per 100 females: 107.8
Housing: Homeownership rate: 86.7%; Homeowner vacancy rate: 3.5%; Rental vacancy rate: 9.5%

ROSEBUSH (village). Covers a land area of 0.889 square miles and a water area of 0.002 square miles. Located at 43.70° N. Lat; 84.76° W. Long. Elevation is 781 feet.
History: Rosebush was settled in the 1840's. In 1868, James L. Bush platted the village, donating land to the Ann Arbor Railroad for a station. He named the village for his wife, Rose Bush.
Population: 368; Growth (since 2000): -2.9%; Density: 414.0 persons per square mile; Race: 88.6% White, 1.1% Black/African American, 0.0% Asian, 3.8% American Indian/Alaska Native, 0.0% Native Hawaiian/Other Pacific Islander, 5.2% Two or more races, 6.3% Hispanic of any race; Average household size: 2.13; Median age: 39.0; Age under 18: 19.8%; Age 65 and over: 17.1%; Males per 100 females: 80.4
Housing: Homeownership rate: 57.0%; Homeowner vacancy rate: 2.0%; Rental vacancy rate: 5.2%

SHEPHERD (village). Covers a land area of 0.968 square miles and a water area of 0 square miles. Located at 43.52° N. Lat; 84.69° W. Long. Elevation is 774 feet.

History: Shepherd was founded by lumberman Isaac N. Shepherd.

Population: 1,515; Growth (since 2000): -1.4%; Density: 1,565.7 persons per square mile; Race: 94.2% White, 0.5% Black/African American, 0.3% Asian, 1.3% American Indian/Alaska Native, 0.0% Native Hawaiian/Other Pacific Islander, 2.8% Two or more races, 3.2% Hispanic of any race; Average household size: 2.36; Median age: 37.5; Age under 18: 24.5%; Age 65 and over: 13.0%; Males per 100 females: 87.7

School District(s)

Morey Public Schools Academy (PK-12)
    2012-13 Enrollment: 138. . . . . (989) 866-6739
Shepherd Public Schools (PK-12)
    2012-13 Enrollment: 1,765 . . . . (989) 828-5520

Housing: Homeownership rate: 66.4%; Homeowner vacancy rate: 1.6%; Rental vacancy rate: 15.7%

Safety: Violent crime rate: 26.2 per 10,000 population; Property crime rate: 137.7 per 10,000 population

Newspapers: Shepherd Argus (weekly circulation 1800)

SHERMAN (township). Covers a land area of 34.714 square miles and a water area of 0.997 square miles. Located at 43.68° N. Lat; 85.03° W. Long.

Population: 2,991; Growth (since 2000): 14.3%; Density: 86.2 persons per square mile; Race: 94.1% White, 0.6% Black/African American, 0.4% Asian, 1.6% American Indian/Alaska Native, 0.1% Native Hawaiian/Other Pacific Islander, 2.7% Two or more races, 2.7% Hispanic of any race; Average household size: 2.49; Median age: 40.2; Age under 18: 23.3%; Age 65 and over: 16.7%; Males per 100 females: 97.3; Marriage status: 23.0% never married, 56.6% now married, 1.4% separated, 6.1% widowed, 14.3% divorced; Foreign born: 0.9%; Speak English only: 99.6%; With disability: 14.6%; Veterans: 9.7%; Ancestry: 36.4% German, 21.3% Irish, 19.6% English, 8.0% French, 6.0% Canadian

Employment: 9.3% management, business, and financial, 0.2% computer, engineering, and science, 12.1% education, legal, community service, arts, and media, 4.2% healthcare practitioners, 17.4% service, 29.6% sales and office, 11.2% natural resources, construction, and maintenance, 16.1% production, transportation, and material moving

Income: Per capita: $18,303; Median household: $38,421; Average household: $45,583; Households with income of $100,000 or more: 7.8%; Poverty rate: 25.8%

Educational Attainment: High school diploma or higher: 87.8%; Bachelor's degree or higher: 14.3%; Graduate/professional degree or higher: 4.5%

Housing: Homeownership rate: 87.3%; Median home value: $83,600; Median year structure built: 1978; Homeowner vacancy rate: 3.8%; Median gross rent: $793 per month; Rental vacancy rate: 7.6%

Health Insurance: 89.8% have insurance; 62.5% have private insurance; 47.4% have public insurance; 10.2% do not have insurance; 0.0% of children under 18 do not have insurance

Transportation: Commute: 98.6% car, 0.8% public transportation, 0.3% walk, 0.0% work from home; Median travel time to work: 29.3 minutes

UNION (charter township). Covers a land area of 28.157 square miles and a water area of 0.330 square miles. Located at 43.58° N. Lat; 84.82° W. Long.

Population: 12,927; Growth (since 2000): 69.8%; Density: 459.1 persons per square mile; Race: 87.6% White, 3.8% Black/African American, 1.9% Asian, 3.2% American Indian/Alaska Native, 0.0% Native Hawaiian/Other Pacific Islander, 2.9% Two or more races, 3.2% Hispanic of any race; Average household size: 2.46; Median age: 22.8; Age under 18: 14.3%; Age 65 and over: 6.3%; Males per 100 females: 92.1; Marriage status: 66.2% never married, 24.5% now married, 0.6% separated, 2.1% widowed, 7.2% divorced; Foreign born: 2.5%; Speak English only: 95.5%; With disability: 10.1%; Veterans: 3.8%; Ancestry: 27.2% German, 19.2% Irish, 12.8% English, 11.6% Polish, 6.3% French

Employment: 7.8% management, business, and financial, 3.0% computer, engineering, and science, 9.7% education, legal, community service, arts, and media, 2.8% healthcare practitioners, 33.5% service, 32.6% sales and office, 4.6% natural resources, construction, and maintenance, 6.0% production, transportation, and material moving

Income: Per capita: $16,976; Median household: $25,590; Average household: $42,880; Households with income of $100,000 or more: 8.8%; Poverty rate: 46.5%

Educational Attainment: High school diploma or higher: 92.3%; Bachelor's degree or higher: 29.7%; Graduate/professional degree or higher: 12.5%

Housing: Homeownership rate: 34.7%; Median home value: $129,700; Median year structure built: 1994; Homeowner vacancy rate: 1.6%; Median gross rent: $702 per month; Rental vacancy rate: 3.8%

Health Insurance: 81.6% have insurance; 69.7% have private insurance; 18.5% have public insurance; 18.4% do not have insurance; 12.1% of children under 18 do not have insurance

Transportation: Commute: 91.8% car, 2.0% public transportation, 4.2% walk, 0.8% work from home; Median travel time to work: 13.7 minutes

VERNON (township). Covers a land area of 35.344 square miles and a water area of 0.334 square miles. Located at 43.76° N. Lat; 84.80° W. Long.

Population: 1,369; Growth (since 2000): 2.0%; Density: 38.7 persons per square mile; Race: 96.3% White, 0.9% Black/African American, 0.4% Asian, 1.2% American Indian/Alaska Native, 0.0% Native Hawaiian/Other Pacific Islander, 1.0% Two or more races, 1.3% Hispanic of any race; Average household size: 2.57; Median age: 41.5; Age under 18: 23.4%; Age 65 and over: 15.7%; Males per 100 females: 98.7

Housing: Homeownership rate: 85.6%; Homeowner vacancy rate: 1.3%; Rental vacancy rate: 2.5%

WEIDMAN (CDP). Covers a land area of 5.653 square miles and a water area of 0.296 square miles. Located at 43.70° N. Lat; 84.98° W. Long. Elevation is 889 feet.

Population: 959; Growth (since 2000): 9.1%; Density: 169.6 persons per square mile; Race: 92.6% White, 0.9% Black/African American, 0.3% Asian, 4.4% American Indian/Alaska Native, 0.0% Native Hawaiian/Other Pacific Islander, 1.8% Two or more races, 1.6% Hispanic of any race; Average household size: 2.45; Median age: 39.7; Age under 18: 24.9%; Age 65 and over: 17.2%; Males per 100 females: 102.7

School District(s)

Chippewa Hills SD (PK-12)
    2012-13 Enrollment: 2,180 . . . . (989) 967-2000

Housing: Homeownership rate: 80.7%; Homeowner vacancy rate: 2.5%; Rental vacancy rate: 7.2%

WINN (unincorporated postal area)
ZCTA: 48896
    Covers a land area of 0.273 square miles and a water area of 0 square miles. Located at 43.52° N. Lat; 84.90° W. Long. Elevation is 869 feet.
    Population: 154; Growth (since 2000): 31.6%; Density: 565.1 persons per square mile; Race: 98.7% White, 1.3% Black/African American, 0.0% Asian, 0.0% American Indian/Alaska Native, 0.0% Native Hawaiian/Other Pacific Islander, 0.0% Two or more races, 0.6% Hispanic of any race; Average household size: 2.52; Median age: 33.0; Age under 18: 29.2%; Age 65 and over: 6.5%; Males per 100 females: 65.6

School District(s)

Shepherd Public Schools (PK-12)
    2012-13 Enrollment: 1,765 . . . . (989) 828-5520
    Housing: Homeownership rate: 83.6%; Homeowner vacancy rate: 8.9%; Rental vacancy rate: 16.7%

WISE (township). Covers a land area of 36.500 square miles and a water area of 0.094 square miles. Located at 43.78° N. Lat; 84.67° W. Long. Elevation is 751 feet.

Population: 1,397; Growth (since 2000): 7.4%; Density: 38.3 persons per square mile; Race: 96.2% White, 0.1% Black/African American, 0.3% Asian, 1.8% American Indian/Alaska Native, 0.0% Native Hawaiian/Other Pacific Islander, 1.4% Two or more races, 1.9% Hispanic of any race; Average household size: 2.64; Median age: 38.7; Age under 18: 25.6%; Age 65 and over: 13.9%; Males per 100 females: 112.0

Housing: Homeownership rate: 85.8%; Homeowner vacancy rate: 1.1%; Rental vacancy rate: 3.8%

Jackson County

Located in southern Michigan; drained by the Grand and Raisin Rivers; includes many small lakes. Covers a land area of 701.666 square miles, a water area of 21.830 square miles, and is located in the Eastern Time

Zone at 42.25° N. Lat., 84.42° W. Long. The county was founded in 1832. County seat is Jackson.

Jackson County is part of the Jackson, MI Metropolitan Statistical Area. The entire metro area includes: Jackson County, MI

Weather Station: Jackson Reynolds Field   Elevation: 998 feet

	Jan	Feb	Mar	Apr	May	Jun	Jul	Aug	Sep	Oct	Nov	Dec
High	31	34	45	58	69	79	82	80	73	60	47	35
Low	17	18	26	37	47	56	60	59	51	40	32	22
Precip	1.5	1.3	1.8	2.7	3.2	3.2	3.5	3.6	3.5	2.7	2.5	2.0
Snow	na	na	na	na	na	na	na	na	na	na	na	na

High and Low temperatures in degrees Fahrenheit; Precipitation and Snow in inches

Population: 160,248; Growth (since 2000): 1.2%; Density: 228.4 persons per square mile; Race: 87.7% White, 7.9% Black/African American, 0.7% Asian, 0.4% American Indian/Alaska Native, 0.0% Native Hawaiian/Other Pacific Islander, 2.5% two or more races, 3.0% Hispanic of any race; Average household size: 2.48; Median age: 39.7; Age under 18: 23.2%; Age 65 and over: 14.2%; Males per 100 females: 104.0; Marriage status: 30.0% never married, 50.1% now married, 1.5% separated, 6.2% widowed, 13.7% divorced; Foreign born: 1.7%; Speak English only: 96.5%; With disability: 15.0%; Veterans: 10.1%; Ancestry: 24.2% German, 16.9% English, 15.5% Irish, 8.5% American, 7.7% Polish
Religion: Six largest groups: 12.3% Catholicism, 3.4% Holiness, 3.1% Baptist, 2.5% Lutheran, 2.4% Methodist/Pietist, 2.2% Non-denominational Protestant
Economy: Unemployment rate: 5.8%; Leading industries: 17.9% retail trade; 11.9% health care and social assistance; 10.4% other services (except public administration); Farms: 1,073 totaling 183,111 acres; Company size: 2 employ 1,000 or more persons, 6 employ 500 to 999 persons, 59 employ 100 to 499 persons, 2,896 employ less than 100 persons; Business ownership: 3,473 women-owned, 337 Black-owned, 135 Hispanic-owned, n/a Asian-owned
Employment: 11.5% management, business, and financial, 4.4% computer, engineering, and science, 8.1% education, legal, community service, arts, and media, 5.2% healthcare practitioners, 20.1% service, 24.7% sales and office, 8.0% natural resources, construction, and maintenance, 17.8% production, transportation, and material moving
Income: Per capita: $22,613; Median household: $46,615; Average household: $58,365; Households with income of $100,000 or more: 14.8%; Poverty rate: 17.0%
Educational Attainment: High school diploma or higher: 89.1%; Bachelor's degree or higher: 18.8%; Graduate/professional degree or higher: 6.1%
Housing: Homeownership rate: 73.4%; Median home value: $112,800; Median year structure built: 1966; Homeowner vacancy rate: 3.0%; Median gross rent: $722 per month; Rental vacancy rate: 14.0%
Vital Statistics: Birth rate: 113.2 per 10,000 population; Death rate: 95.5 per 10,000 population; Age-adjusted cancer mortality rate: 194.4 deaths per 100,000 population
Health Insurance: 88.3% have insurance; 67.1% have private insurance; 35.9% have public insurance; 11.7% do not have insurance; 4.0% of children under 18 do not have insurance
Health Care: Physicians: 11.9 per 10,000 population; Hospital beds: 31.2 per 10,000 population; Hospital admissions: 1,375.9 per 10,000 population
Transportation: Commute: 93.2% car, 0.4% public transportation, 2.0% walk, 3.0% work from home; Median travel time to work: 23.3 minutes
Presidential Election: 46.6% Obama, 52.4% Romney (2012)
National and State Parks: Sharonville State Wildlife Management Area; Waterloo State Recreation Area
Additional Information Contacts
Jackson Government . . . . (517) 788-4268
  http://www.co.jackson.mi.us

Jackson County Communities

BLACKMAN (charter township). Covers a land area of 31.709 square miles and a water area of 0.195 square miles. Located at 42.30° N. Lat; 84.42° W. Long.
History: Blackman Township was organized in 1857 and named for Horace Blackman who had settled here in 1829.
Population: 24,051; Growth (since 2000): 5.5%; Density: 758.5 persons per square mile; Race: 79.1% White, 16.6% Black/African American, 1.0% Asian, 0.5% American Indian/Alaska Native, 0.0% Native Hawaiian/Other Pacific Islander, 1.9% Two or more races, 3.6% Hispanic of any race;

Average household size: 2.23; Median age: 39.2; Age under 18: 16.2%; Age 65 and over: 13.7%; Males per 100 females: 164.4; Marriage status: 34.3% never married, 38.4% now married, 2.0% separated, 7.6% widowed, 19.7% divorced; Foreign born: 0.9%; Speak English only: 95.7%; With disability: 19.0%; Veterans: 10.7%; Ancestry: 23.2% German, 14.7% Irish, 12.5% English, 8.5% Polish, 7.6% American
Employment: 11.3% management, business, and financial, 3.3% computer, engineering, and science, 8.6% education, legal, community service, arts, and media, 2.8% healthcare practitioners, 23.4% service, 26.1% sales and office, 6.5% natural resources, construction, and maintenance, 18.1% production, transportation, and material moving
Income: Per capita: $18,389; Median household: $36,324; Average household: $49,380; Households with income of $100,000 or more: 10.5%; Poverty rate: 16.4%
Educational Attainment: High school diploma or higher: 86.4%; Bachelor's degree or higher: 13.0%; Graduate/professional degree or higher: 3.8%
Housing: Homeownership rate: 55.5%; Median home value: $100,500; Median year structure built: 1975; Homeowner vacancy rate: 2.5%; Median gross rent: $728 per month; Rental vacancy rate: 17.5%
Health Insurance: 87.4% have insurance; 67.5% have private insurance; 37.0% have public insurance; 12.6% do not have insurance; 2.3% of children under 18 do not have insurance
Transportation: Commute: 92.8% car, 0.6% public transportation, 1.8% walk, 1.6% work from home; Median travel time to work: 20.2 minutes
Additional Information Contacts
Blackman Charter Township . . . . (517) 788-4345
  http://www.blackmantwp.com

BROOKLYN (village). Covers a land area of 1.007 square miles and a water area of 0.011 square miles. Located at 42.11° N. Lat; 84.25° W. Long. Elevation is 994 feet.
History: Brooklyn was first called Swainesville for early settler Calvin H. Swaine, who built a sawmill in 1833. The name was changed in 1836 after Brooklyn, New York.
Population: 1,206; Growth (since 2000): 2.6%; Density: 1,197.1 persons per square mile; Race: 96.9% White, 0.2% Black/African American, 1.3% Asian, 0.7% American Indian/Alaska Native, 0.0% Native Hawaiian/Other Pacific Islander, 0.8% Two or more races, 2.9% Hispanic of any race; Average household size: 2.09; Median age: 43.6; Age under 18: 22.7%; Age 65 and over: 23.0%; Males per 100 females: 76.6
School District(s)
Columbia SD (PK-12)
  2012-13 Enrollment: 1,452 . . . . (517) 592-6641
Housing: Homeownership rate: 53.7%; Homeowner vacancy rate: 5.4%; Rental vacancy rate: 11.5%
Newspapers: The Brooklyn Exponent (weekly circulation 6000)
Additional Information Contacts
Village of Brooklyn . . . . (517) 592-2591
  http://www.villageofbrooklyn.com

CLARKLAKE (unincorporated postal area)
ZCTA: 49234
  Covers a land area of 21.914 square miles and a water area of 1.317 square miles. Located at 42.13° N. Lat; 84.37° W. Long. Elevation is 974 feet.
Population: 2,579; Growth (since 2000): -4.6%; Density: 117.7 persons per square mile; Race: 97.8% White, 0.1% Black/African American, 0.3% Asian, 0.5% American Indian/Alaska Native, 0.0% Native Hawaiian/Other Pacific Islander, 0.9% Two or more races, 2.5% Hispanic of any race; Average household size: 2.38; Median age: 48.5; Age under 18: 18.8%; Age 65 and over: 17.5%; Males per 100 females: 100.7; Marriage status: 22.8% never married, 52.2% now married, 0.3% separated, 7.3% widowed, 17.6% divorced; Foreign born: 0.3%; Speak English only: 98.5%; With disability: 15.7%; Veterans: 13.1%; Ancestry: 29.3% German, 22.9% English, 18.0% Irish, 10.2% Italian, 7.4% Polish
Employment: 4.3% management, business, and financial, 4.0% computer, engineering, and science, 7.4% education, legal, community service, arts, and media, 6.1% healthcare practitioners, 24.6% service, 27.8% sales and office, 9.9% natural resources, construction, and maintenance, 16.0% production, transportation, and material moving
Income: Per capita: $30,245; Median household: $58,250; Average household: $79,692; Households with income of $100,000 or more: 26.0%; Poverty rate: 16.7%

Educational Attainment: High school diploma or higher: 95.0%; Bachelor's degree or higher: 25.2%; Graduate/professional degree or higher: 7.6%

School District(s)

Columbia SD (PK-12)
    2012-13 Enrollment: 1,452 . . . . (517) 592-6641
Housing: Homeownership rate: 86.6%; Median home value: $185,800; Median year structure built: 1970; Homeowner vacancy rate: 2.0%; Median gross rent: $954 per month; Rental vacancy rate: 5.8%
Health Insurance: 89.3% have insurance; 70.6% have private insurance; 32.6% have public insurance; 10.7% do not have insurance; 9.8% of children under 18 do not have insurance
Transportation: Commute: 97.2% car, 0.0% public transportation, 0.0% walk, 2.2% work from home; Median travel time to work: 32.0 minutes

COLUMBIA (township). Covers a land area of 36.638 square miles and a water area of 2.961 square miles. Located at 42.10° N. Lat; 84.27° W. Long.
Population: 7,420; Growth (since 2000): 2.6%; Density: 202.5 persons per square mile; Race: 97.5% White, 0.2% Black/African American, 0.7% Asian, 0.4% American Indian/Alaska Native, 0.0% Native Hawaiian/Other Pacific Islander, 1.0% Two or more races, 1.9% Hispanic of any race; Average household size: 2.37; Median age: 46.7; Age under 18: 20.5%; Age 65 and over: 19.0%; Males per 100 females: 99.0; Marriage status: 20.7% never married, 61.2% now married, 0.3% separated, 6.4% widowed, 11.7% divorced; Foreign born: 1.9%; Speak English only: 97.5%; With disability: 14.9%; Veterans: 11.1%; Ancestry: 29.5% German, 21.7% English, 15.5% Irish, 7.6% Polish, 5.6% French
Employment: 12.0% management, business, and financial, 5.0% computer, engineering, and science, 9.0% education, legal, community service, arts, and media, 7.3% healthcare practitioners, 17.0% service, 23.8% sales and office, 8.0% natural resources, construction, and maintenance, 18.0% production, transportation, and material moving
Income: Per capita: $28,798; Median household: $60,686; Average household: $72,116; Households with income of $100,000 or more: 23.3%; Poverty rate: 11.4%
Educational Attainment: High school diploma or higher: 94.0%; Bachelor's degree or higher: 24.1%; Graduate/professional degree or higher: 7.8%
Housing: Homeownership rate: 82.0%; Median home value: $172,700; Median year structure built: 1975; Homeowner vacancy rate: 3.2%; Median gross rent: $777 per month; Rental vacancy rate: 10.0%
Health Insurance: 91.6% have insurance; 72.8% have private insurance; 35.8% have public insurance; 8.4% do not have insurance; 4.0% of children under 18 do not have insurance
Safety: Violent crime rate: 24.3 per 10,000 population; Property crime rate: 43.2 per 10,000 population
Transportation: Commute: 95.0% car, 0.0% public transportation, 1.1% walk, 3.4% work from home; Median travel time to work: 32.2 minutes

CONCORD (township). Covers a land area of 35.725 square miles and a water area of 0.473 square miles. Located at 42.21° N. Lat; 84.65° W. Long. Elevation is 1,024 feet.
Population: 2,723; Growth (since 2000): 1.2%; Density: 76.2 persons per square mile; Race: 98.2% White, 0.3% Black/African American, 0.1% Asian, 0.3% American Indian/Alaska Native, 0.0% Native Hawaiian/Other Pacific Islander, 0.9% Two or more races, 1.6% Hispanic of any race; Average household size: 2.63; Median age: 40.8; Age under 18: 26.1%; Age 65 and over: 13.5%; Males per 100 females: 99.0; Marriage status: 24.8% never married, 64.7% now married, 0.6% separated, 4.0% widowed, 6.5% divorced; Foreign born: 0.5%; Speak English only: 98.7%; With disability: 10.3%; Veterans: 13.0%; Ancestry: 26.8% German, 26.6% English, 14.3% Irish, 7.6% American, 6.8% Polish
Employment: 15.3% management, business, and financial, 1.8% computer, engineering, and science, 10.2% education, legal, community service, arts, and media, 7.3% healthcare practitioners, 10.7% service, 21.0% sales and office, 16.8% natural resources, construction, and maintenance, 16.9% production, transportation, and material moving
Income: Per capita: $24,165; Median household: $55,813; Average household: $64,951; Households with income of $100,000 or more: 15.3%; Poverty rate: 10.8%
Educational Attainment: High school diploma or higher: 95.2%; Bachelor's degree or higher: 19.0%; Graduate/professional degree or higher: 7.8%

School District(s)

Concord Community Schools (KG-12)
    2012-13 Enrollment: 788 . . . . (517) 524-8850
Housing: Homeownership rate: 85.4%; Median home value: $140,100; Median year structure built: 1971; Homeowner vacancy rate: 1.6%; Median gross rent: $710 per month; Rental vacancy rate: 24.3%
Health Insurance: 90.8% have insurance; 81.5% have private insurance; 23.1% have public insurance; 9.2% do not have insurance; 0.0% of children under 18 do not have insurance
Transportation: Commute: 94.4% car, 0.0% public transportation, 1.8% walk, 2.9% work from home; Median travel time to work: 23.7 minutes

CONCORD (village). Covers a land area of 1.499 square miles and a water area of 0.124 square miles. Located at 42.18° N. Lat; 84.65° W. Long. Elevation is 1,024 feet.
History: The name of Concord reflects the good relationship among the residents when they applied for a post office. The community was first called Van Fossenville for William Van Fossen, the first settler here in 1832.
Population: 1,050; Growth (since 2000): -4.6%; Density: 700.6 persons per square mile; Race: 99.0% White, 0.3% Black/African American, 0.1% Asian, 0.1% American Indian/Alaska Native, 0.0% Native Hawaiian/Other Pacific Islander, 0.4% Two or more races, 1.8% Hispanic of any race; Average household size: 2.55; Median age: 40.9; Age under 18: 26.0%; Age 65 and over: 15.6%; Males per 100 females: 95.5

School District(s)

Concord Community Schools (KG-12)
    2012-13 Enrollment: 788 . . . . (517) 524-8850
Housing: Homeownership rate: 79.3%; Homeowner vacancy rate: 2.1%; Rental vacancy rate: 34.4%
Safety: Violent crime rate: 9.5 per 10,000 population; Property crime rate: 85.8 per 10,000 population

GRASS LAKE (charter township). Covers a land area of 46.431 square miles and a water area of 1.576 square miles. Located at 42.25° N. Lat; 84.19° W. Long. Elevation is 997 feet.
Population: 5,684; Growth (since 2000): 23.9%; Density: 122.4 persons per square mile; Race: 96.4% White, 1.1% Black/African American, 0.2% Asian, 0.5% American Indian/Alaska Native, 0.1% Native Hawaiian/Other Pacific Islander, 1.4% Two or more races, 1.9% Hispanic of any race; Average household size: 2.65; Median age: 40.2; Age under 18: 24.9%; Age 65 and over: 12.2%; Males per 100 females: 100.3; Marriage status: 20.8% never married, 65.9% now married, 0.3% separated, 4.7% widowed, 8.5% divorced; Foreign born: 1.1%; Speak English only: 97.9%; With disability: 9.0%; Veterans: 12.5%; Ancestry: 30.4% German, 18.9% Irish, 18.6% English, 8.0% American, 7.3% Polish
Employment: 12.1% management, business, and financial, 8.6% computer, engineering, and science, 5.8% education, legal, community service, arts, and media, 7.1% healthcare practitioners, 12.3% service, 23.8% sales and office, 13.9% natural resources, construction, and maintenance, 16.5% production, transportation, and material moving
Income: Per capita: $28,816; Median household: $61,332; Average household: $73,950; Households with income of $100,000 or more: 21.7%; Poverty rate: 5.6%
Educational Attainment: High school diploma or higher: 95.8%; Bachelor's degree or higher: 25.6%; Graduate/professional degree or higher: 9.9%

School District(s)

Grass Lake Community Schools (KG-12)
    2012-13 Enrollment: 1,233 . . . . (517) 522-5540
Housing: Homeownership rate: 87.0%; Median home value: $177,400; Median year structure built: 1980; Homeowner vacancy rate: 3.3%; Median gross rent: $714 per month; Rental vacancy rate: 8.4%
Health Insurance: 93.9% have insurance; 84.9% have private insurance; 20.6% have public insurance; 6.1% do not have insurance; 3.7% of children under 18 do not have insurance
Transportation: Commute: 95.3% car, 0.0% public transportation, 2.2% walk, 2.1% work from home; Median travel time to work: 30.5 minutes

GRASS LAKE (village). Covers a land area of 0.940 square miles and a water area of 0.001 square miles. Located at 42.25° N. Lat; 84.21° W. Long. Elevation is 997 feet.
History: The village of Grass Lake was established in the 1840's on the south shore of the lake for which it was named. For a time, Grass Lake's

economy was supported by a furniture factory. Later it depended on dairying and agriculture.
Population: 1,173; Growth (since 2000): 8.4%; Density: 1,248.5 persons per square mile; Race: 94.7% White, 1.1% Black/African American, 0.1% Asian, 1.2% American Indian/Alaska Native, 0.0% Native Hawaiian/Other Pacific Islander, 2.0% Two or more races, 1.5% Hispanic of any race; Average household size: 2.54; Median age: 36.9; Age under 18: 26.4%; Age 65 and over: 10.8%; Males per 100 females: 96.5
School District(s)
Grass Lake Community Schools (KG-12)
    2012-13 Enrollment: 1,233 . . . . (517) 522-5540
Housing: Homeownership rate: 69.7%; Homeowner vacancy rate: 3.0%; Rental vacancy rate: 6.5%

HANOVER (township). Covers a land area of 34.841 square miles and a water area of 0.935 square miles. Located at 42.12° N. Lat; 84.53° W. Long. Elevation is 1,115 feet.
Population: 3,695; Growth (since 2000): -2.6%; Density: 106.1 persons per square mile; Race: 97.6% White, 0.3% Black/African American, 0.4% Asian, 0.1% American Indian/Alaska Native, 0.1% Native Hawaiian/Other Pacific Islander, 1.2% Two or more races, 1.5% Hispanic of any race; Average household size: 2.61; Median age: 43.1; Age under 18: 24.4%; Age 65 and over: 15.4%; Males per 100 females: 103.2; Marriage status: 27.1% never married, 59.2% now married, 0.3% separated, 3.2% widowed, 10.4% divorced; Foreign born: 1.3%; Speak English only: 96.9%; With disability: 11.8%; Veterans: 12.8%; Ancestry: 32.1% German, 25.7% English, 14.2% Irish, 6.7% French, 5.9% Polish
Employment: 9.7% management, business, and financial, 5.7% computer, engineering, and science, 6.0% education, legal, community service, arts, and media, 5.5% healthcare practitioners, 13.2% service, 21.8% sales and office, 11.9% natural resources, construction, and maintenance, 26.1% production, transportation, and material moving
Income: Per capita: $27,916; Median household: $67,839; Average household: $81,012; Households with income of $100,000 or more: 22.6%; Poverty rate: 7.7%
Educational Attainment: High school diploma or higher: 94.6%; Bachelor's degree or higher: 18.9%; Graduate/professional degree or higher: 6.1%
School District(s)
Hanover-Horton SD (PK-12)
    2012-13 Enrollment: 1,222 . . . . (517) 563-0100
Housing: Homeownership rate: 89.4%; Median home value: $134,800; Median year structure built: 1973; Homeowner vacancy rate: 1.9%; Median gross rent: $600 per month; Rental vacancy rate: 28.3%
Health Insurance: 92.1% have insurance; 77.7% have private insurance; 28.9% have public insurance; 7.9% do not have insurance; 3.2% of children under 18 do not have insurance
Transportation: Commute: 92.5% car, 0.0% public transportation, 2.0% walk, 5.3% work from home; Median travel time to work: 29.2 minutes

HANOVER (village). Covers a land area of 0.419 square miles and a water area of 0.017 square miles. Located at 42.10° N. Lat; 84.55° W. Long. Elevation is 1,115 feet.
History: Hanover was named for Hanover, Germany, the former home of Henry Wickman who came here in 1836. The village was platted when the railroad came in 1870.
Population: 441; Growth (since 2000): 4.0%; Density: 1,052.5 persons per square mile; Race: 95.7% White, 0.9% Black/African American, 0.0% Asian, 0.5% American Indian/Alaska Native, 0.0% Native Hawaiian/Other Pacific Islander, 2.3% Two or more races, 4.3% Hispanic of any race; Average household size: 2.69; Median age: 32.1; Age under 18: 32.0%; Age 65 and over: 10.0%; Males per 100 females: 90.9
School District(s)
Hanover-Horton SD (PK-12)
    2012-13 Enrollment: 1,222 . . . . (517) 563-0100
Housing: Homeownership rate: 69.5%; Homeowner vacancy rate: 1.7%; Rental vacancy rate: 15.0%

HENRIETTA (township). Covers a land area of 35.981 square miles and a water area of 1.065 square miles. Located at 42.37° N. Lat; 84.31° W. Long.
History: Henrietta Township was organized in 1837 and named West Portage until 1839, when it was renamed for Henrietta, New York, former home of settler Henry Hurd.

Population: 4,705; Growth (since 2000): 5.0%; Density: 130.8 persons per square mile; Race: 96.8% White, 0.5% Black/African American, 0.2% Asian, 0.4% American Indian/Alaska Native, 0.0% Native Hawaiian/Other Pacific Islander, 1.4% Two or more races, 2.3% Hispanic of any race; Average household size: 2.53; Median age: 43.2; Age under 18: 22.1%; Age 65 and over: 13.5%; Males per 100 females: 104.7; Marriage status: 22.2% never married, 60.3% now married, 2.9% separated, 4.1% widowed, 13.4% divorced; Foreign born: 1.9%; Speak English only: 97.1%; With disability: 13.0%; Veterans: 9.7%; Ancestry: 28.0% German, 24.6% Irish, 14.1% English, 10.6% Polish, 7.8% American
Employment: 10.3% management, business, and financial, 9.7% computer, engineering, and science, 7.6% education, legal, community service, arts, and media, 4.0% healthcare practitioners, 22.4% service, 21.2% sales and office, 6.5% natural resources, construction, and maintenance, 18.3% production, transportation, and material moving
Income: Per capita: $22,631; Median household: $60,278; Average household: $62,476; Households with income of $100,000 or more: 16.6%; Poverty rate: 18.6%
Educational Attainment: High school diploma or higher: 86.1%; Bachelor's degree or higher: 16.4%; Graduate/professional degree or higher: 4.9%
Housing: Homeownership rate: 89.7%; Median home value: $145,900; Median year structure built: 1976; Homeowner vacancy rate: 1.4%; Median gross rent: $722 per month; Rental vacancy rate: 7.2%
Health Insurance: 91.8% have insurance; 68.1% have private insurance; 35.9% have public insurance; 8.2% do not have insurance; 1.5% of children under 18 do not have insurance
Transportation: Commute: 95.6% car, 0.3% public transportation, 0.0% walk, 4.1% work from home; Median travel time to work: 28.7 minutes

JACKSON (city). County seat. Covers a land area of 10.865 square miles and a water area of 0.118 square miles. Located at 42.24° N. Lat; 84.40° W. Long. Elevation is 932 feet.
History: The site chosen for Jackson was at the intersection of the Grand River and an old trail. Lumbering was the first industry, followed by a gristmill. Jackson achieved fame in 1854 when the Republican Pary was formed and named at a convention held here. The convention meetings were held outdoors under the oak trees. The party's first platform included repeal of the fugitive slave law. Jackson's industrial importance grew when the Michigan Central Railroad established its shops here in 1871. The manufacture of carriages was an early industry, replaced in the early 1900's by industries related to auto manufacturing.
Population: 33,534; Growth (since 2000): -7.7%; Density: 3,086.6 persons per square mile; Race: 71.4% White, 20.4% Black/African American, 0.7% Asian, 0.4% American Indian/Alaska Native, 0.0% Native Hawaiian/Other Pacific Islander, 5.5% Two or more races, 5.3% Hispanic of any race; Average household size: 2.46; Median age: 32.2; Age under 18: 28.5%; Age 65 and over: 10.3%; Males per 100 females: 91.2; Marriage status: 40.1% never married, 38.1% now married, 2.6% separated, 6.4% widowed, 15.4% divorced; Foreign born: 1.9%; Speak English only: 96.0%; With disability: 17.8%; Veterans: 7.5%; Ancestry: 18.6% German, 13.2% Irish, 13.1% English, 7.9% Polish, 7.9% African
Employment: 7.6% management, business, and financial, 2.3% computer, engineering, and science, 6.8% education, legal, community service, arts, and media, 4.1% healthcare practitioners, 26.0% service, 27.5% sales and office, 6.7% natural resources, construction, and maintenance, 19.0% production, transportation, and material moving
Income: Per capita: $15,336; Median household: $28,309; Average household: $38,176; Households with income of $100,000 or more: 5.8%; Poverty rate: 34.7%
Educational Attainment: High school diploma or higher: 82.9%; Bachelor's degree or higher: 13.5%; Graduate/professional degree or higher: 4.0%
School District(s)
Da Vinci Institute (KG-12)
    2012-13 Enrollment: 263 . . . . (517) 796-0031
East Jackson Community Schools (KG-12)
    2012-13 Enrollment: 1,225 . . . . (517) 764-2090
Jackson ISD (PK-12)
    2012-13 Enrollment: 987 . . . . (517) 768-5200
Jackson Public Schools (PK-12)
    2012-13 Enrollment: 5,899 . . . . (517) 841-2202
Napoleon Community Schools (PK-12)
    2012-13 Enrollment: 1,431 . . . . (517) 536-8667

Northwest Community Schools (PK-12)
    2012-13 Enrollment: 2,788 . . . . (517) 817-4710
Paragon Charter Academy (KG-12)
    2012-13 Enrollment: 685 . . . . (517) 750-9500
Vandercook Lake Public Schools (PK-12)
    2012-13 Enrollment: 1,259 . . . . (517) 782-9044
Western SD (PK-12)
    2012-13 Enrollment: 2,927 . . . . (517) 841-8100
                        Four-year College(s)
Baker College of Jackson (Private, Not-for-profit)
    Fall 2013 Enrollment: 2,257 . . . . (517) 789-6123
    2013-14 Tuition: In-state $8,100; Out-of-state $8,100
                        Two-year College(s)
Career Quest Learning Centers-Jackson (Private, For-profit)
    Fall 2013 Enrollment: 329 . . . . (517) 990-9595
Jackson College (Public)
    Fall 2013 Enrollment: 5,665 . . . . (517) 787-0800
    2013-14 Tuition: In-state $4,704; Out-of-state $6,024
Housing: Homeownership rate: 52.7%; Median home value: $66,900; Median year structure built: Before 1940; Homeowner vacancy rate: 4.6%; Median gross rent: $636 per month; Rental vacancy rate: 12.4%
Health Insurance: 81.4% have insurance; 44.1% have private insurance; 47.3% have public insurance; 18.6% do not have insurance; 5.9% of children under 18 do not have insurance
Hospitals: Allegiance Health (411 beds)
Safety: Violent crime rate: 110.9 per 10,000 population; Property crime rate: 518.9 per 10,000 population
Newspapers: Jackson Citizen Patriot (daily circulation 33000)
Transportation: Commute: 90.1% car, 1.4% public transportation, 3.2% walk, 2.9% work from home; Median travel time to work: 18.3 minutes; Amtrak: Train service available.
Airports: Jackson County-Reynolds Field (general aviation)
Additional Information Contacts
City of Jackson . . . . (517) 788-4025
    http://www.cityofjackson.org

LEONI (township). Covers a land area of 48.544 square miles and a water area of 2.678 square miles. Located at 42.27° N. Lat; 84.30° W. Long. Elevation is 984 feet.
Population: 13,807; Growth (since 2000): 2.6%; Density: 284.4 persons per square mile; Race: 95.3% White, 1.2% Black/African American, 0.5% Asian, 0.4% American Indian/Alaska Native, 0.0% Native Hawaiian/Other Pacific Islander, 2.1% Two or more races, 2.4% Hispanic of any race; Average household size: 2.52; Median age: 41.2; Age under 18: 23.5%; Age 65 and over: 14.4%; Males per 100 females: 99.8; Marriage status: 29.0% never married, 46.9% now married, 0.9% separated, 6.7% widowed, 17.4% divorced; Foreign born: 1.6%; Speak English only: 95.8%; With disability: 16.9%; Veterans: 11.1%; Ancestry: 29.2% German, 17.4% Irish, 14.8% English, 10.7% Polish, 10.2% American
Employment: 12.3% management, business, and financial, 5.0% computer, engineering, and science, 4.0% education, legal, community service, arts, and media, 5.3% healthcare practitioners, 18.8% service, 24.6% sales and office, 8.2% natural resources, construction, and maintenance, 22.0% production, transportation, and material moving
Income: Per capita: $22,018; Median household: $43,245; Average household: $53,207; Households with income of $100,000 or more: 11.5%; Poverty rate: 16.2%
Educational Attainment: High school diploma or higher: 85.9%; Bachelor's degree or higher: 16.0%; Graduate/professional degree or higher: 4.8%
Housing: Homeownership rate: 82.9%; Median home value: $109,100; Median year structure built: 1964; Homeowner vacancy rate: 2.4%; Median gross rent: $837 per month; Rental vacancy rate: 14.3%
Health Insurance: 88.0% have insurance; 68.6% have private insurance; 37.6% have public insurance; 12.0% do not have insurance; 6.2% of children under 18 do not have insurance
Transportation: Commute: 96.7% car, 0.0% public transportation, 1.0% walk, 1.6% work from home; Median travel time to work: 22.7 minutes
Additional Information Contacts
Leoni Township . . . . (517) 764-4694
    http://www.leonitownship.com

LIBERTY (township). Covers a land area of 34.272 square miles and a water area of 1.345 square miles. Located at 42.11° N. Lat; 84.42° W. Long. Elevation is 1,004 feet.
History: Liberty Township was organized in 1837. The patriotic name was inspired by Patrick Henry's words, "Give me liberty or give me death."
Population: 2,961; Growth (since 2000): 2.0%; Density: 86.4 persons per square mile; Race: 97.8% White, 0.2% Black/African American, 0.4% Asian, 0.4% American Indian/Alaska Native, 0.0% Native Hawaiian/Other Pacific Islander, 0.9% Two or more races, 2.0% Hispanic of any race; Average household size: 2.53; Median age: 45.8; Age under 18: 21.7%; Age 65 and over: 16.5%; Males per 100 females: 100.6; Marriage status: 22.0% never married, 56.0% now married, 1.2% separated, 6.9% widowed, 15.1% divorced; Foreign born: 0.5%; Speak English only: 98.0%; With disability: 12.6%; Veterans: 14.7%; Ancestry: 27.9% German, 18.5% English, 18.1% Irish, 9.7% Polish, 7.5% American
Employment: 9.5% management, business, and financial, 3.3% computer, engineering, and science, 8.0% education, legal, community service, arts, and media, 9.6% healthcare practitioners, 12.1% service, 28.6% sales and office, 13.2% natural resources, construction, and maintenance, 15.7% production, transportation, and material moving
Income: Per capita: $30,894; Median household: $62,014; Average household: $76,853; Households with income of $100,000 or more: 24.3%; Poverty rate: 6.9%
Educational Attainment: High school diploma or higher: 93.0%; Bachelor's degree or higher: 23.7%; Graduate/professional degree or higher: 6.4%
Housing: Homeownership rate: 90.4%; Median home value: $160,600; Median year structure built: 1972; Homeowner vacancy rate: 2.1%; Median gross rent: $950 per month; Rental vacancy rate: 5.1%
Health Insurance: 92.9% have insurance; 83.3% have private insurance; 28.7% have public insurance; 7.1% do not have insurance; 2.1% of children under 18 do not have insurance
Transportation: Commute: 94.4% car, 0.0% public transportation, 1.2% walk, 2.6% work from home; Median travel time to work: 26.9 minutes

MICHIGAN CENTER (CDP). Covers a land area of 5.040 square miles and a water area of 0.659 square miles. Located at 42.23° N. Lat; 84.32° W. Long. Elevation is 945 feet.
Population: 4,672; Growth (since 2000): 0.7%; Density: 927.0 persons per square mile; Race: 96.6% White, 0.4% Black/African American, 0.3% Asian, 0.5% American Indian/Alaska Native, 0.0% Native Hawaiian/Other Pacific Islander, 1.8% Two or more races, 1.9% Hispanic of any race; Average household size: 2.44; Median age: 41.8; Age under 18: 22.2%; Age 65 and over: 15.2%; Males per 100 females: 101.7; Marriage status: 29.6% never married, 46.8% now married, 0.6% separated, 5.8% widowed, 17.8% divorced; Foreign born: 1.8%; Speak English only: 97.4%; With disability: 17.0%; Veterans: 11.9%; Ancestry: 27.7% German, 17.4% Irish, 16.8% English, 13.0% American, 11.4% Polish
Employment: 15.5% management, business, and financial, 2.9% computer, engineering, and science, 4.5% education, legal, community service, arts, and media, 7.6% healthcare practitioners, 19.5% service, 22.5% sales and office, 11.7% natural resources, construction, and maintenance, 15.8% production, transportation, and material moving
Income: Per capita: $20,120; Median household: $44,897; Average household: $48,222; Households with income of $100,000 or more: 8.1%; Poverty rate: 16.6%
Educational Attainment: High school diploma or higher: 83.9%; Bachelor's degree or higher: 18.5%; Graduate/professional degree or higher: 4.3%
                        School District(s)
Michigan Center SD (PK-12)
    2012-13 Enrollment: 1,385 . . . . (517) 764-5778
Housing: Homeownership rate: 81.8%; Median home value: $114,300; Median year structure built: 1956; Homeowner vacancy rate: 2.9%; Median gross rent: $780 per month; Rental vacancy rate: 8.1%
Health Insurance: 80.5% have insurance; 65.1% have private insurance; 33.2% have public insurance; 19.5% do not have insurance; 14.0% of children under 18 do not have insurance
Transportation: Commute: 95.9% car, 0.0% public transportation, 2.2% walk, 2.0% work from home; Median travel time to work: 18.8 minutes

MUNITH (unincorporated postal area)
ZCTA: 49259

Covers a land area of 27.986 square miles and a water area of 0.971 square miles. Located at 42.37° N. Lat; 84.26° W. Long. Elevation is 945 feet.

Population: 2,523; Growth (since 2000): -9.5%; Density: 90.2 persons per square mile; Race: 97.3% White, 0.1% Black/African American, 0.2% Asian, 0.3% American Indian/Alaska Native, 0.0% Native Hawaiian/Other Pacific Islander, 1.6% Two or more races, 2.0% Hispanic of any race; Average household size: 2.65; Median age: 41.2; Age under 18: 23.8%; Age 65 and over: 13.0%; Males per 100 females: 103.3; Marriage status: 29.6% never married, 54.0% now married, 0.0% separated, 5.6% widowed, 10.8% divorced; Foreign born: 0.4%; Speak English only: 99.0%; With disability: 19.2%; Veterans: 9.5%; Ancestry: 33.6% German, 20.7% Irish, 13.7% American, 12.8% English, 5.5% Polish

Employment: 9.4% management, business, and financial, 4.1% computer, engineering, and science, 7.4% education, legal, community service, arts, and media, 7.1% healthcare practitioners, 13.3% service, 28.0% sales and office, 4.7% natural resources, construction, and maintenance, 26.0% production, transportation, and material moving

Income: Per capita: $26,139; Median household: $56,993; Average household: $67,934; Households with income of $100,000 or more: 13.1%; Poverty rate: 12.2%

Educational Attainment: High school diploma or higher: 88.6%; Bachelor's degree or higher: 13.9%; Graduate/professional degree or higher: 5.5%

Housing: Homeownership rate: 89.2%; Median home value: $118,500; Median year structure built: 1979; Homeowner vacancy rate: 5.5%; Median gross rent: $724 per month; Rental vacancy rate: 11.0%

Health Insurance: 92.6% have insurance; 69.3% have private insurance; 39.0% have public insurance; 7.4% do not have insurance; 1.5% of children under 18 do not have insurance

Transportation: Commute: 99.7% car, 0.3% public transportation, 0.0% walk, 0.0% work from home; Median travel time to work: 31.8 minutes

NAPOLEON (CDP). Covers a land area of 2.621 square miles and a water area of 0.024 square miles. Located at 42.16° N. Lat; 84.24° W. Long. Elevation is 965 feet.

Population: 1,258; Growth (since 2000): 0.3%; Density: 480.0 persons per square mile; Race: 96.2% White, 0.3% Black/African American, 0.1% Asian, 0.4% American Indian/Alaska Native, 0.2% Native Hawaiian/Other Pacific Islander, 2.6% Two or more races, 1.7% Hispanic of any race; Average household size: 2.65; Median age: 37.3; Age under 18: 27.2%; Age 65 and over: 12.5%; Males per 100 females: 99.1

School District(s)
Napoleon Community Schools (PK-12)
   2012-13 Enrollment: 1,431 . . . . (517) 536-8667
Housing: Homeownership rate: 77.1%; Homeowner vacancy rate: 3.9%; Rental vacancy rate: 14.0%

NAPOLEON (township). Covers a land area of 28.938 square miles and a water area of 2.471 square miles. Located at 42.18° N. Lat; 84.30° W. Long. Elevation is 965 feet.

Population: 6,776; Growth (since 2000): -2.7%; Density: 234.2 persons per square mile; Race: 97.0% White, 0.6% Black/African American, 0.3% Asian, 0.3% American Indian/Alaska Native, 0.0% Native Hawaiian/Other Pacific Islander, 1.4% Two or more races, 2.2% Hispanic of any race; Average household size: 2.54; Median age: 42.3; Age under 18: 23.1%; Age 65 and over: 13.4%; Males per 100 females: 99.1; Marriage status: 25.1% never married, 52.7% now married, 0.7% separated, 6.1% widowed, 16.1% divorced; Foreign born: 0.2%; Speak English only: 99.5%; With disability: 11.7%; Veterans: 10.0%; Ancestry: 20.8% German, 17.4% English, 12.8% Irish, 12.7% American, 7.9% Polish

Employment: 11.2% management, business, and financial, 2.2% computer, engineering, and science, 6.5% education, legal, community service, arts, and media, 4.3% healthcare practitioners, 21.0% service, 27.8% sales and office, 7.9% natural resources, construction, and maintenance, 19.1% production, transportation, and material moving

Income: Per capita: $28,302; Median household: $57,687; Average household: $70,103; Households with income of $100,000 or more: 21.9%; Poverty rate: 7.2%

Educational Attainment: High school diploma or higher: 92.7%; Bachelor's degree or higher: 17.1%; Graduate/professional degree or higher: 3.5%

School District(s)
Napoleon Community Schools (PK-12)
   2012-13 Enrollment: 1,431 . . . . (517) 536-8667
Housing: Homeownership rate: 83.4%; Median home value: $134,400; Median year structure built: 1973; Homeowner vacancy rate: 2.7%; Median gross rent: $725 per month; Rental vacancy rate: 17.2%
Health Insurance: 90.9% have insurance; 80.3% have private insurance; 27.3% have public insurance; 9.1% do not have insurance; 1.1% of children under 18 do not have insurance
Safety: Violent crime rate: 3.0 per 10,000 population; Property crime rate: 84.2 per 10,000 population
Transportation: Commute: 98.0% car, 0.0% public transportation, 0.6% walk, 1.4% work from home; Median travel time to work: 25.7 minutes

NORVELL (township). Covers a land area of 29.532 square miles and a water area of 2.633 square miles. Located at 42.13° N. Lat; 84.16° W. Long. Elevation is 948 feet.

Population: 2,963; Growth (since 2000): 1.4%; Density: 100.3 persons per square mile; Race: 97.1% White, 0.5% Black/African American, 0.2% Asian, 0.3% American Indian/Alaska Native, 0.0% Native Hawaiian/Other Pacific Islander, 1.1% Two or more races, 2.0% Hispanic of any race; Average household size: 2.45; Median age: 47.7; Age under 18: 19.8%; Age 65 and over: 18.2%; Males per 100 females: 102.5; Marriage status: 26.3% never married, 53.3% now married, 2.2% separated, 5.6% widowed, 14.8% divorced; Foreign born: 0.9%; Speak English only: 98.3%; With disability: 15.8%; Veterans: 13.0%; Ancestry: 30.1% German, 15.9% Irish, 15.7% English, 8.6% American, 7.7% French

Employment: 17.1% management, business, and financial, 5.9% computer, engineering, and science, 3.4% education, legal, community service, arts, and media, 0.6% healthcare practitioners, 24.4% service, 22.7% sales and office, 13.2% natural resources, construction, and maintenance, 12.7% production, transportation, and material moving

Income: Per capita: $23,987; Median household: $44,135; Average household: $56,609; Households with income of $100,000 or more: 13.4%; Poverty rate: 13.0%

Educational Attainment: High school diploma or higher: 91.8%; Bachelor's degree or higher: 16.1%; Graduate/professional degree or higher: 4.0%

Housing: Homeownership rate: 90.5%; Median home value: $140,500; Median year structure built: 1971; Homeowner vacancy rate: 2.7%; Median gross rent: $672 per month; Rental vacancy rate: 9.4%
Health Insurance: 86.2% have insurance; 64.3% have private insurance; 36.8% have public insurance; 13.8% do not have insurance; 8.7% of children under 18 do not have insurance
Transportation: Commute: 97.1% car, 0.0% public transportation, 0.0% walk, 2.9% work from home; Median travel time to work: 28.7 minutes

PARMA (township). Covers a land area of 36.295 square miles and a water area of 0.103 square miles. Located at 42.29° N. Lat; 84.66° W. Long. Elevation is 1,001 feet.

Population: 2,726; Growth (since 2000): 1.1%; Density: 75.1 persons per square mile; Race: 93.5% White, 3.3% Black/African American, 0.3% Asian, 0.6% American Indian/Alaska Native, 0.0% Native Hawaiian/Other Pacific Islander, 1.7% Two or more races, 2.8% Hispanic of any race; Average household size: 2.71; Median age: 40.8; Age under 18: 24.0%; Age 65 and over: 13.8%; Males per 100 females: 97.7; Marriage status: 22.8% never married, 60.9% now married, 0.5% separated, 6.1% widowed, 10.2% divorced; Foreign born: 1.8%; Speak English only: 98.4%; With disability: 13.0%; Veterans: 11.2%; Ancestry: 19.0% Irish, 18.5% German, 14.0% English, 8.7% American, 4.8% Polish

Employment: 5.2% management, business, and financial, 1.5% computer, engineering, and science, 4.3% education, legal, community service, arts, and media, 1.1% healthcare practitioners, 23.9% service, 28.7% sales and office, 9.8% natural resources, construction, and maintenance, 25.4% production, transportation, and material moving

Income: Per capita: $19,565; Median household: $48,333; Average household: $54,993; Households with income of $100,000 or more: 13.6%; Poverty rate: 7.9%

Educational Attainment: High school diploma or higher: 86.2%; Bachelor's degree or higher: 10.6%; Graduate/professional degree or higher: 1.8%

School District(s)
Western SD (PK-12)
   2012-13 Enrollment: 2,927 . . . . (517) 841-8100

Housing: Homeownership rate: 85.5%; Median home value: $101,300; Median year structure built: 1972; Homeowner vacancy rate: 1.9%; Median gross rent: $669 per month; Rental vacancy rate: 10.3%
Health Insurance: 89.1% have insurance; 74.3% have private insurance; 32.1% have public insurance; 10.9% do not have insurance; 1.3% of children under 18 do not have insurance
Newspapers: County Press (weekly circulation 1500)
Transportation: Commute: 95.4% car, 0.8% public transportation, 2.7% walk, 0.0% work from home; Median travel time to work: 25.4 minutes

PARMA (village). Covers a land area of 1.057 square miles and a water area of 0 square miles. Located at 42.27° N. Lat; 84.55° W. Long. Elevation is 1,001 feet.

History: Parma was settled in the 1830's, at a place known as Cracker Hill. Many of the early residents were Quakers, and for a time there was a Quaker meeting house in Parma.
Population: 769; Growth (since 2000): -15.2%; Density: 727.4 persons per square mile; Race: 95.8% White, 0.4% Black/African American, 0.9% Asian, 0.4% American Indian/Alaska Native, 0.0% Native Hawaiian/Other Pacific Islander, 1.8% Two or more races, 2.5% Hispanic of any race; Average household size: 2.62; Median age: 36.5; Age under 18: 29.0%; Age 65 and over: 12.6%; Males per 100 females: 106.2

School District(s)
Western SD (PK-12)
    2012-13 Enrollment: 2,927 . . . . (517) 841-8100
Housing: Homeownership rate: 75.6%; Homeowner vacancy rate: 1.8%; Rental vacancy rate: 19.5%
Newspapers: County Press (weekly circulation 1500)

PLEASANT LAKE (unincorporated postal area)
ZCTA: 49272
    Covers a land area of 11.340 square miles and a water area of 0.821 square miles. Located at 42.39° N. Lat; 84.35° W. Long. Elevation is 958 feet.
    Population: 2,417; Growth (since 2000): 0.2%; Density: 213.1 persons per square mile; Race: 96.5% White, 0.8% Black/African American, 0.2% Asian, 0.4% American Indian/Alaska Native, 0.0% Native Hawaiian/Other Pacific Islander, 1.3% Two or more races, 2.9% Hispanic of any race; Average household size: 2.43; Median age: 44.0; Age under 18: 21.3%; Age 65 and over: 13.0%; Males per 100 females: 102.4
    Housing: Homeownership rate: 89.8%; Homeowner vacancy rate: 1.2%; Rental vacancy rate: 8.9%

PULASKI (township). Covers a land area of 36.185 square miles and a water area of 0.493 square miles. Located at 42.12° N. Lat; 84.66° W. Long. Elevation is 1,089 feet.

History: Pulaski Township was organized in 1838 and named for Count Casimir Pulaski, Polish hero in the American Revolution.
Population: 2,075; Growth (since 2000): 7.5%; Density: 57.3 persons per square mile; Race: 96.1% White, 1.3% Black/African American, 0.1% Asian, 0.1% American Indian/Alaska Native, 0.0% Native Hawaiian/Other Pacific Islander, 1.4% Two or more races, 1.9% Hispanic of any race; Average household size: 2.72; Median age: 41.2; Age under 18: 25.0%; Age 65 and over: 13.8%; Males per 100 females: 105.2
Housing: Homeownership rate: 85.1%; Homeowner vacancy rate: 0.9%; Rental vacancy rate: 10.9%

RIVES (township). Covers a land area of 35.790 square miles and a water area of 0.493 square miles. Located at 42.37° N. Lat; 84.42° W. Long.

Population: 4,683; Growth (since 2000): -0.9%; Density: 130.8 persons per square mile; Race: 97.2% White, 0.9% Black/African American, 0.2% Asian, 0.4% American Indian/Alaska Native, 0.0% Native Hawaiian/Other Pacific Islander, 1.1% Two or more races, 1.8% Hispanic of any race; Average household size: 2.69; Median age: 40.6; Age under 18: 24.9%; Age 65 and over: 12.8%; Males per 100 females: 102.5; Marriage status: 32.4% never married, 47.8% now married, 0.0% separated, 7.4% widowed, 12.4% divorced; Foreign born: 0.2%; Speak English only: 98.4%; With disability: 10.0%; Veterans: 8.3%; Ancestry: 23.7% German, 15.6% English, 15.5% Irish, 11.8% American, 7.5% Polish
Employment: 7.9% management, business, and financial, 5.3% computer, engineering, and science, 7.0% education, legal, community service, arts, and media, 4.3% healthcare practitioners, 24.6% service, 29.8% sales and

office, 6.9% natural resources, construction, and maintenance, 14.1% production, transportation, and material moving
Income: Per capita: $22,167; Median household: $56,964; Average household: $63,746; Households with income of $100,000 or more: 19.1%; Poverty rate: 11.5%
Educational Attainment: High school diploma or higher: 92.0%; Bachelor's degree or higher: 15.7%; Graduate/professional degree or higher: 6.8%
Housing: Homeownership rate: 88.7%; Median home value: $116,500; Median year structure built: 1979; Homeowner vacancy rate: 1.8%; Median gross rent: $1,194 per month; Rental vacancy rate: 28.9%
Health Insurance: 92.7% have insurance; 79.9% have private insurance; 24.7% have public insurance; 7.3% do not have insurance; 1.7% of children under 18 do not have insurance
Transportation: Commute: 97.7% car, 0.3% public transportation, 1.1% walk, 0.5% work from home; Median travel time to work: 28.7 minutes

RIVES JUNCTION (unincorporated postal area)
ZCTA: 49277
    Covers a land area of 35.520 square miles and a water area of 0.546 square miles. Located at 42.39° N. Lat; 84.47° W. Long. Elevation is 925 feet.
    Population: 3,668; Growth (since 2000): -1.9%; Density: 103.3 persons per square mile; Race: 97.9% White, 0.6% Black/African American, 0.2% Asian, 0.1% American Indian/Alaska Native, 0.0% Native Hawaiian/Other Pacific Islander, 0.8% Two or more races, 2.7% Hispanic of any race; Average household size: 2.71; Median age: 42.2; Age under 18: 24.1%; Age 65 and over: 13.8%; Males per 100 females: 105.5; Marriage status: 24.4% never married, 56.3% now married, 0.1% separated, 7.2% widowed, 12.1% divorced; Foreign born: 0.7%; Speak English only: 99.0%; With disability: 13.0%; Veterans: 7.6%; Ancestry: 33.5% German, 18.0% Irish, 16.2% English, 7.6% American, 5.1% Dutch
    Employment: 10.1% management, business, and financial, 4.1% computer, engineering, and science, 6.8% education, legal, community service, arts, and media, 6.5% healthcare practitioners, 22.4% service, 26.0% sales and office, 9.0% natural resources, construction, and maintenance, 15.0% production, transportation, and material moving
    Income: Per capita: $25,175; Median household: $57,143; Average household: $64,909; Households with income of $100,000 or more: 18.9%; Poverty rate: 7.4%
    Educational Attainment: High school diploma or higher: 95.2%; Bachelor's degree or higher: 16.3%; Graduate/professional degree or higher: 7.3%
    Housing: Homeownership rate: 89.9%; Median home value: $133,000; Median year structure built: 1977; Homeowner vacancy rate: 1.7%; Median gross rent: $661 per month; Rental vacancy rate: 6.7%
    Health Insurance: 93.4% have insurance; 84.0% have private insurance; 22.8% have public insurance; 6.6% do not have insurance; 5.2% of children under 18 do not have insurance
    Transportation: Commute: 96.9% car, 0.0% public transportation, 1.8% walk, 0.0% work from home; Median travel time to work: 28.0 minutes

SANDSTONE (township). Covers a land area of 36.004 square miles and a water area of 0.180 square miles. Located at 42.29° N. Lat; 84.55° W. Long. Elevation is 971 feet.

History: Sandstone was settled in the 1830's and named for the large deposit of sandstone along Sandstone Creek.
Population: 3,984; Growth (since 2000): 4.8%; Density: 110.7 persons per square mile; Race: 95.8% White, 1.0% Black/African American, 0.5% Asian, 0.5% American Indian/Alaska Native, 0.0% Native Hawaiian/Other Pacific Islander, 2.0% Two or more races, 1.6% Hispanic of any race; Average household size: 2.66; Median age: 43.4; Age under 18: 24.6%; Age 65 and over: 15.1%; Males per 100 females: 100.9; Marriage status: 21.5% never married, 65.0% now married, 1.4% separated, 3.9% widowed, 9.6% divorced; Foreign born: 1.7%; Speak English only: 97.3%; With disability: 12.5%; Veterans: 14.0%; Ancestry: 28.9% German, 23.6% English, 16.2% Irish, 9.9% American, 7.0% Polish
Employment: 15.3% management, business, and financial, 3.6% computer, engineering, and science, 5.7% education, legal, community service, arts, and media, 9.8% healthcare practitioners, 20.6% service, 20.8% sales and office, 7.7% natural resources, construction, and maintenance, 16.7% production, transportation, and material moving

Income: Per capita: $28,437; Median household: $60,417; Average household: $72,600; Households with income of $100,000 or more: 20.8%; Poverty rate: 4.8%

Educational Attainment: High school diploma or higher: 91.7%; Bachelor's degree or higher: 19.6%; Graduate/professional degree or higher: 7.3%

Housing: Homeownership rate: 88.3%; Median home value: $126,200; Median year structure built: 1982; Homeowner vacancy rate: 2.6%; Median gross rent: $875 per month; Rental vacancy rate: 17.4%

Health Insurance: 91.6% have insurance; 82.6% have private insurance; 25.3% have public insurance; 8.4% do not have insurance; 0.6% of children under 18 do not have insurance

Transportation: Commute: 97.3% car, 0.0% public transportation, 0.4% walk, 2.3% work from home; Median travel time to work: 19.5 minutes

SPRING ARBOR (CDP). Covers a land area of 2.776 square miles and a water area of 0.034 square miles. Located at 42.21° N. Lat; 84.56° W. Long. Elevation is 1,004 feet.

Population: 2,881; Growth (since 2000): 31.7%; Density: 1,037.6 persons per square mile; Race: 94.4% White, 2.9% Black/African American, 0.9% Asian, 0.2% American Indian/Alaska Native, 0.0% Native Hawaiian/Other Pacific Islander, 1.4% Two or more races, 2.4% Hispanic of any race; Average household size: 2.24; Median age: 22.4; Age under 18: 12.7%; Age 65 and over: 18.6%; Males per 100 females: 71.7; Marriage status: 54.4% never married, 31.1% now married, 0.7% separated, 9.7% widowed, 4.8% divorced; Foreign born: 2.2%; Speak English only: 96.8%; With disability: 9.6%; Veterans: 5.1%; Ancestry: 25.5% English, 21.2% German, 15.8% Irish, 8.0% Finnish, 7.0% Dutch

Employment: 5.5% management, business, and financial, 8.2% computer, engineering, and science, 20.0% education, legal, community service, arts, and media, 0.0% healthcare practitioners, 30.6% service, 24.5% sales and office, 1.9% natural resources, construction, and maintenance, 9.3% production, transportation, and material moving

Income: Per capita: $18,730; Median household: $53,482; Average household: $69,861; Households with income of $100,000 or more: 22.7%; Poverty rate: 1.5%

Educational Attainment: High school diploma or higher: 90.9%; Bachelor's degree or higher: 34.6%; Graduate/professional degree or higher: 13.3%

School District(s)
Western SD (PK-12)
    2012-13 Enrollment: 2,927 . . . . (517) 841-8100
Four-year College(s)
Spring Arbor University (Private, Not-for-profit, Free Methodist)
    Fall 2013 Enrollment: 3,962 . . . . (517) 750-1200
    2013-14 Tuition: In-state $23,400; Out-of-state $23,400

Housing: Homeownership rate: 53.1%; Median home value: $140,700; Median year structure built: 1978; Homeowner vacancy rate: 2.9%; Median gross rent: $646 per month; Rental vacancy rate: 9.8%

Health Insurance: 94.2% have insurance; 83.5% have private insurance; 21.8% have public insurance; 5.8% do not have insurance; 0.0% of children under 18 do not have insurance

Transportation: Commute: 67.7% car, 0.3% public transportation, 19.8% walk, 8.0% work from home; Median travel time to work: 16.7 minutes

SPRING ARBOR (township). Covers a land area of 35.095 square miles and a water area of 0.656 square miles. Located at 42.21° N. Lat; 84.54° W. Long. Elevation is 1,004 feet.

History: Spring Arbor was settled in the 1830's, and named for a spring in the area. Isaac N. Swain founded the village of Spring Arbor in 1839.

Population: 8,267; Growth (since 2000): 9.1%; Density: 235.6 persons per square mile; Race: 95.5% White, 1.5% Black/African American, 0.9% Asian, 0.3% American Indian/Alaska Native, 0.0% Native Hawaiian/Other Pacific Islander, 1.5% Two or more races, 1.7% Hispanic of any race; Average household size: 2.58; Median age: 36.3; Age under 18: 21.7%; Age 65 and over: 15.6%; Males per 100 females: 89.0; Marriage status: 36.1% never married, 51.3% now married, 0.8% separated, 5.5% widowed, 7.1% divorced; Foreign born: 2.0%; Speak English only: 97.7%; With disability: 9.7%; Veterans: 7.0%; Ancestry: 31.6% English, 23.2% German, 16.2% Irish, 4.7% Dutch, 4.6% French

Employment: 9.4% management, business, and financial, 6.0% computer, engineering, and science, 17.3% education, legal, community service, arts, and media, 3.8% healthcare practitioners, 22.5% service, 25.7% sales and office, 6.1% natural resources, construction, and maintenance, 9.2% production, transportation, and material moving

Income: Per capita: $23,240; Median household: $56,745; Average household: $71,418; Households with income of $100,000 or more: 21.9%; Poverty rate: 13.9%

Educational Attainment: High school diploma or higher: 92.0%; Bachelor's degree or higher: 34.0%; Graduate/professional degree or higher: 11.0%

School District(s)
Western SD (PK-12)
    2012-13 Enrollment: 2,927 . . . . (517) 841-8100
Four-year College(s)
Spring Arbor University (Private, Not-for-profit, Free Methodist)
    Fall 2013 Enrollment: 3,962 . . . . (517) 750-1200
    2013-14 Tuition: In-state $23,400; Out-of-state $23,400

Housing: Homeownership rate: 78.9%; Median home value: $135,200; Median year structure built: 1976; Homeowner vacancy rate: 3.8%; Median gross rent: $726 per month; Rental vacancy rate: 15.3%

Health Insurance: 92.9% have insurance; 74.9% have private insurance; 31.4% have public insurance; 7.1% do not have insurance; 3.5% of children under 18 do not have insurance

Safety: Violent crime rate: 1.2 per 10,000 population; Property crime rate: 68.9 per 10,000 population

Transportation: Commute: 81.9% car, 0.1% public transportation, 7.2% walk, 7.9% work from home; Median travel time to work: 20.0 minutes

SPRINGPORT (township). Covers a land area of 36.100 square miles and a water area of 0.269 square miles. Located at 42.39° N. Lat; 84.65° W. Long. Elevation is 1,004 feet.

Population: 2,159; Growth (since 2000): -1.1%; Density: 59.8 persons per square mile; Race: 97.0% White, 0.5% Black/African American, 0.1% Asian, 0.5% American Indian/Alaska Native, 0.0% Native Hawaiian/Other Pacific Islander, 1.6% Two or more races, 1.5% Hispanic of any race; Average household size: 2.68; Median age: 40.0; Age under 18: 25.0%; Age 65 and over: 12.3%; Males per 100 females: 99.7

School District(s)
Springport Public Schools (PK-12)
    2012-13 Enrollment: 1,032 . . . .! (517) 857-3495

Housing: Homeownership rate: 77.2%; Homeowner vacancy rate: 1.9%; Rental vacancy rate: 8.5%

Newspapers: Springport Signal (weekly circulation 1400)

SPRINGPORT (village). Covers a land area of 1.260 square miles and a water area of 0 square miles. Located at 42.38° N. Lat; 84.70° W. Long. Elevation is 1,004 feet.

History: Springport was founded in 1836 by John Oyer, when it was called Oyer's Corners. It developed around a station of the Lake Shore & Michigan Southern Railroad which arrived here in 1876.

Population: 800; Growth (since 2000): 13.6%; Density: 635.1 persons per square mile; Race: 96.1% White, 0.1% Black/African American, 0.4% Asian, 0.5% American Indian/Alaska Native, 0.0% Native Hawaiian/Other Pacific Islander, 2.3% Two or more races, 1.9% Hispanic of any race; Average household size: 2.73; Median age: 33.6; Age under 18: 29.0%; Age 65 and over: 10.4%; Males per 100 females: 89.6

School District(s)
Springport Public Schools (PK-12)
    2012-13 Enrollment: 1,032 . . . . (517) 857-3495

Housing: Homeownership rate: 59.4%; Homeowner vacancy rate: 0.6%; Rental vacancy rate: 7.8%

Newspapers: Springport Signal (weekly circulation 1400)

SUMMIT (township). Covers a land area of 29.090 square miles and a water area of 0.919 square miles. Located at 42.20° N. Lat; 84.43° W. Long.

History: Summit Township was set off in 1857 from the old township of Jackson, and named for having the highest elevation in the county.

Population: 22,508; Growth (since 2000): 4.5%; Density: 773.7 persons per square mile; Race: 89.6% White, 5.3% Black/African American, 1.5% Asian, 0.3% American Indian/Alaska Native, 0.1% Native Hawaiian/Other Pacific Islander, 2.5% Two or more races, 2.7% Hispanic of any race; Average household size: 2.42; Median age: 42.8; Age under 18: 23.1%; Age 65 and over: 18.5%; Males per 100 females: 91.9; Marriage status: 24.9% never married, 58.8% now married, 1.4% separated, 6.5% widowed, 9.7% divorced; Foreign born: 3.8%; Speak English only: 94.8%; With disability: 13.8%; Veterans: 10.8%; Ancestry: 23.9% German, 17.1% English, 16.1% Irish, 10.5% American, 7.6% Polish

Employment: 16.2% management, business, and financial, 6.4% computer, engineering, and science, 11.9% education, legal, community service, arts, and media, 7.2% healthcare practitioners, 15.4% service, 22.7% sales and office, 6.3% natural resources, construction, and maintenance, 14.0% production, transportation, and material moving
Income: Per capita: $28,578; Median household: $56,103; Average household: $70,595; Households with income of $100,000 or more: 20.2%; Poverty rate: 11.7%
Educational Attainment: High school diploma or higher: 93.9%; Bachelor's degree or higher: 30.5%; Graduate/professional degree or higher: 10.5%
Housing: Homeownership rate: 79.3%; Median home value: $118,400; Median year structure built: 1964; Homeowner vacancy rate: 3.0%; Median gross rent: $889 per month; Rental vacancy rate: 11.5%
Health Insurance: 91.3% have insurance; 73.3% have private insurance; 35.3% have public insurance; 8.7% do not have insurance; 2.4% of children under 18 do not have insurance
Transportation: Commute: 93.6% car, 0.1% public transportation, 1.1% walk, 4.3% work from home; Median travel time to work: 21.1 minutes
Additional Information Contacts
Summit Township . . . . (517) 788-4113
    http://www.summittwp.com

TOMPKINS (township). Covers a land area of 36.012 square miles and a water area of 0.344 square miles. Located at 42.38° N. Lat; 84.54° W. Long. Elevation is 912 feet.
Population: 2,671; Growth (since 2000): -3.2%; Density: 74.2 persons per square mile; Race: 97.7% White, 0.6% Black/African American, 0.2% Asian, 0.3% American Indian/Alaska Native, 0.0% Native Hawaiian/Other Pacific Islander, 0.9% Two or more races, 2.4% Hispanic of any race; Average household size: 2.61; Median age: 43.2; Age under 18: 22.2%; Age 65 and over: 14.0%; Males per 100 females: 102.8; Marriage status: 18.5% never married, 62.3% now married, 0.2% separated, 7.6% widowed, 11.6% divorced; Foreign born: 1.1%; Speak English only: 97.9%; With disability: 15.7%; Veterans: 9.0%; Ancestry: 23.4% German, 20.4% English, 13.4% American, 10.8% Irish, 4.4% French
Employment: 16.1% management, business, and financial, 3.4% computer, engineering, and science, 8.7% education, legal, community service, arts, and media, 4.4% healthcare practitioners, 18.0% service, 15.8% sales and office, 13.3% natural resources, construction, and maintenance, 20.2% production, transportation, and material moving
Income: Per capita: $26,753; Median household: $56,226; Average household: $65,400; Households with income of $100,000 or more: 18.1%; Poverty rate: 7.5%
Educational Attainment: High school diploma or higher: 91.6%; Bachelor's degree or higher: 11.1%; Graduate/professional degree or higher: 5.8%
Housing: Homeownership rate: 88.1%; Median home value: $135,600; Median year structure built: 1977; Homeowner vacancy rate: 1.6%; Median gross rent: $690 per month; Rental vacancy rate: 6.2%
Health Insurance: 90.8% have insurance; 75.1% have private insurance; 27.6% have public insurance; 9.2% do not have insurance; 7.9% of children under 18 do not have insurance
Transportation: Commute: 94.6% car, 0.0% public transportation, 3.1% walk, 0.5% work from home; Median travel time to work: 29.2 minutes

VANDERCOOK LAKE (CDP). Covers a land area of 4.573 square miles and a water area of 0.258 square miles. Located at 42.19° N. Lat; 84.39° W. Long. Elevation is 968 feet.
Population: 4,721; Growth (since 2000): -1.8%; Density: 1,032.3 persons per square mile; Race: 95.3% White, 1.3% Black/African American, 0.2% Asian, 0.2% American Indian/Alaska Native, 0.0% Native Hawaiian/Other Pacific Islander, 2.3% Two or more races, 2.3% Hispanic of any race; Average household size: 2.56; Median age: 40.1; Age under 18: 24.8%; Age 65 and over: 14.5%; Males per 100 females: 92.9; Marriage status: 31.1% never married, 53.3% now married, 2.6% separated, 6.7% widowed, 8.8% divorced; Foreign born: 1.0%; Speak English only: 98.7%; With disability: 15.4%; Veterans: 9.4%; Ancestry: 24.0% German, 17.7% Irish, 16.8% English, 12.3% American, 8.4% Polish
Employment: 10.0% management, business, and financial, 1.4% computer, engineering, and science, 7.6% education, legal, community service, arts, and media, 6.2% healthcare practitioners, 20.3% service, 20.2% sales and office, 11.5% natural resources, construction, and maintenance, 22.8% production, transportation, and material moving

Income: Per capita: $22,023; Median household: $47,031; Average household: $56,930; Households with income of $100,000 or more: 14.0%; Poverty rate: 19.1%
Educational Attainment: High school diploma or higher: 87.8%; Bachelor's degree or higher: 12.6%; Graduate/professional degree or higher: 5.6%
Housing: Homeownership rate: 84.4%; Median home value: $84,600; Median year structure built: 1960; Homeowner vacancy rate: 2.3%; Median gross rent: $803 per month; Rental vacancy rate: 8.6%
Health Insurance: 91.9% have insurance; 70.9% have private insurance; 36.6% have public insurance; 8.1% do not have insurance; 1.3% of children under 18 do not have insurance
Transportation: Commute: 94.1% car, 0.0% public transportation, 3.0% walk, 1.7% work from home; Median travel time to work: 23.1 minutes

VINEYARD LAKE (CDP). Covers a land area of 2.563 square miles and a water area of 0.868 square miles. Located at 42.09° N. Lat; 84.22° W. Long.
Population: 980; Growth (since 2000): n/a; Density: 382.4 persons per square mile; Race: 97.9% White, 0.4% Black/African American, 0.0% Asian, 0.4% American Indian/Alaska Native, 0.0% Native Hawaiian/Other Pacific Islander, 1.2% Two or more races, 1.1% Hispanic of any race; Average household size: 2.12; Median age: 50.3; Age under 18: 15.4%; Age 65 and over: 23.0%; Males per 100 females: 104.6
Housing: Homeownership rate: 90.0%; Homeowner vacancy rate: 4.4%; Rental vacancy rate: 4.2%

WATERLOO (township). Covers a land area of 47.619 square miles and a water area of 1.923 square miles. Located at 42.37° N. Lat; 84.19° W. Long. Elevation is 958 feet.
Population: 2,856; Growth (since 2000): -6.9%; Density: 60.0 persons per square mile; Race: 97.5% White, 0.3% Black/African American, 0.1% Asian, 0.1% American Indian/Alaska Native, 0.0% Native Hawaiian/Other Pacific Islander, 1.6% Two or more races, 1.6% Hispanic of any race; Average household size: 2.60; Median age: 43.0; Age under 18: 22.6%; Age 65 and over: 13.1%; Males per 100 females: 102.6; Marriage status: 28.5% never married, 59.4% now married, 0.2% separated, 4.0% widowed, 8.1% divorced; Foreign born: 0.6%; Speak English only: 97.5%; With disability: 14.5%; Veterans: 11.6%; Ancestry: 31.6% German, 16.2% Irish, 14.8% English, 11.5% American, 8.1% Polish
Employment: 11.5% management, business, and financial, 4.1% computer, engineering, and science, 7.1% education, legal, community service, arts, and media, 10.8% healthcare practitioners, 13.5% service, 25.3% sales and office, 12.0% natural resources, construction, and maintenance, 15.6% production, transportation, and material moving
Income: Per capita: $31,087; Median household: $70,217; Average household: $81,036; Households with income of $100,000 or more: 24.8%; Poverty rate: 6.3%
Educational Attainment: High school diploma or higher: 95.0%; Bachelor's degree or higher: 21.2%; Graduate/professional degree or higher: 9.2%
Housing: Homeownership rate: 89.8%; Median home value: $152,100; Median year structure built: 1983; Homeowner vacancy rate: 5.7%; Median gross rent: $647 per month; Rental vacancy rate: 11.6%
Health Insurance: 93.5% have insurance; 78.5% have private insurance; 28.1% have public insurance; 6.5% do not have insurance; 1.7% of children under 18 do not have insurance
Transportation: Commute: 91.0% car, 1.9% public transportation, 1.2% walk, 5.3% work from home; Median travel time to work: 32.2 minutes

Kalamazoo County

Located in southwestern Michigan; drained by the Kalamazoo and Portage Rivers; includes many small lakes. Covers a land area of 561.658 square miles, a water area of 18.639 square miles, and is located in the Eastern Time Zone at 42.25° N. Lat., 85.53° W. Long. The county was founded in 1829. County seat is Kalamazoo.

Kalamazoo County is part of the Kalamazoo-Portage, MI Metropolitan Statistical Area. The entire metro area includes: Kalamazoo County, MI; Van Buren County, MI

Weather Station: Gull Lake Biol Sta   Elevation: 910 feet

	Jan	Feb	Mar	Apr	May	Jun	Jul	Aug	Sep	Oct	Nov	Dec
High	32	36	47	61	73	82	85	83	75	63	49	36
Low	17	19	27	37	48	57	61	60	52	42	33	22
Precip	2.2	1.9	2.6	3.6	3.9	3.7	3.7	4.2	4.7	3.4	3.3	2.8
Snow	17.1	10.9	5.5	0.9	tr	0.0	0.0	0.0	0.0	0.4	3.9	16.9

High and Low temperatures in degrees Fahrenheit; Precipitation and Snow in inches

Population: 250,331; Growth (since 2000): 4.9%; Density: 445.7 persons per square mile; Race: 81.7% White, 10.9% Black/African American, 2.1% Asian, 0.4% American Indian/Alaska Native, 0.0% Native Hawaiian/Other Pacific Islander, 3.3% two or more races, 4.0% Hispanic of any race; Average household size: 2.40; Median age: 34.1; Age under 18: 22.7%; Age 65 and over: 12.3%; Males per 100 females: 95.9; Marriage status: 37.1% never married, 46.5% now married, 1.4% separated, 5.2% widowed, 11.2% divorced; Foreign born: 4.8%; Speak English only: 93.0%; With disability: 12.5%; Veterans: 7.9%; Ancestry: 23.2% German, 13.5% Irish, 12.9% English, 12.1% Dutch, 5.5% Polish

Religion: Six largest groups: 9.5% Catholicism, 8.6% Non-denominational Protestant, 6.6% Presbyterian-Reformed, 3.0% Methodist/Pietist, 2.9% Baptist, 1.9% Lutheran

Economy: Unemployment rate: 4.7%; Leading industries: 15.7% retail trade; 11.9% health care and social assistance; 11.4% other services (except public administration); Farms: 734 totaling 143,540 acres; Company size: 7 employ 1,000 or more persons, 13 employ 500 to 999 persons, 126 employ 100 to 499 persons, 5,386 employ less than 100 persons; Business ownership: 6,690 women-owned, 1,260 Black-owned, 144 Hispanic-owned, 433 Asian-owned

Employment: 14.4% management, business, and financial, 6.1% computer, engineering, and science, 10.9% education, legal, community service, arts, and media, 6.7% healthcare practitioners, 19.5% service, 23.8% sales and office, 6.5% natural resources, construction, and maintenance, 12.1% production, transportation, and material moving

Income: Per capita: $25,757; Median household: $45,775; Average household: $63,610; Households with income of $100,000 or more: 17.8%; Poverty rate: 19.1%

Educational Attainment: High school diploma or higher: 92.6%; Bachelor's degree or higher: 34.0%; Graduate/professional degree or higher: 13.3%

Housing: Homeownership rate: 63.9%; Median home value: $136,700; Median year structure built: 1972; Homeowner vacancy rate: 2.4%; Median gross rent: $717 per month; Rental vacancy rate: 10.2%

Vital Statistics: Birth rate: 119.1 per 10,000 population; Death rate: 79.3 per 10,000 population; Age-adjusted cancer mortality rate: 181.4 deaths per 100,000 population

Health Insurance: 89.2% have insurance; 72.2% have private insurance; 30.0% have public insurance; 10.8% do not have insurance; 3.5% of children under 18 do not have insurance

Health Care: Physicians: 36.3 per 10,000 population; Hospital beds: 39.0 per 10,000 population; Hospital admissions: 1,706.7 per 10,000 population

Air Quality Index: 81.8% good, 18.2% moderate, 0.0% unhealthy for sensitive individuals, 0.0% unhealthy (percent of days)

Transportation: Commute: 91.1% car, 1.3% public transportation, 3.0% walk, 3.5% work from home; Median travel time to work: 20.0 minutes

Presidential Election: 56.2% Obama, 42.9% Romney (2012)

National and State Parks: Fort Custer State Park; Fulton State Game Area; Gourdneck State Game Area

Additional Information Contacts
Kalamazoo Government . . . . (269) 383-8840
   http://www.kalcounty.com

Kalamazoo County Communities

ALAMO (township). Covers a land area of 36.202 square miles and a water area of 0.191 square miles. Located at 42.38° N. Lat; 85.69° W. Long. Elevation is 781 feet.

History: Alamo Township was formed in 1838 and named for the Alamo in Texas.

Population: 3,762; Growth (since 2000): -1.5%; Density: 103.9 persons per square mile; Race: 95.9% White, 1.4% Black/African American, 0.5% Asian, 0.4% American Indian/Alaska Native, 0.0% Native Hawaiian/Other Pacific Islander, 1.2% Two or more races, 1.7% Hispanic of any race; Average household size: 2.53; Median age: 46.5; Age under 18: 21.6%; Age 65 and over: 17.9%; Males per 100 females: 97.8; Marriage status: 19.1% never married, 61.1% now married, 1.9% separated, 7.3%

widowed, 12.5% divorced; Foreign born: 1.4%; Speak English only: 97.4%; With disability: 9.7%; Veterans: 9.5%; Ancestry: 28.0% Dutch, 20.6% German, 11.8% Irish, 10.3% English, 9.2% American

Employment: 13.8% management, business, and financial, 4.2% computer, engineering, and science, 11.3% education, legal, community service, arts, and media, 4.5% healthcare practitioners, 12.2% service, 25.6% sales and office, 17.9% natural resources, construction, and maintenance, 10.4% production, transportation, and material moving

Income: Per capita: $25,529; Median household: $58,087; Average household: $66,546; Households with income of $100,000 or more: 20.7%; Poverty rate: 10.6%

Educational Attainment: High school diploma or higher: 92.2%; Bachelor's degree or higher: 26.4%; Graduate/professional degree or higher: 9.5%

Housing: Homeownership rate: 91.9%; Median home value: $138,200; Median year structure built: 1975; Homeowner vacancy rate: 2.3%; Median gross rent: $932 per month; Rental vacancy rate: 8.6%

Health Insurance: 89.3% have insurance; 81.5% have private insurance; 25.1% have public insurance; 10.7% do not have insurance; 4.9% of children under 18 do not have insurance

Transportation: Commute: 93.2% car, 0.0% public transportation, 0.9% walk, 5.9% work from home; Median travel time to work: 20.5 minutes

Additional Information Contacts
Alamo Township . . . . (269) 382-3366
   http://www.alamotownship.org

AUGUSTA (village). Covers a land area of 1.015 square miles and a water area of 0.014 square miles. Located at 42.34° N. Lat; 85.35° W. Long. Elevation is 807 feet.

History: Augusta was the home of scientist Dr. William T. Bovie. The village was platted in 1836, and incorporated in 1869.

Population: 885; Growth (since 2000): -1.6%; Density: 872.3 persons per square mile; Race: 94.0% White, 1.5% Black/African American, 0.1% Asian, 1.4% American Indian/Alaska Native, 0.0% Native Hawaiian/Other Pacific Islander, 2.0% Two or more races, 2.4% Hispanic of any race; Average household size: 2.44; Median age: 39.2; Age under 18: 24.2%; Age 65 and over: 11.0%; Males per 100 females: 99.3

School District(s)
Galesburg-Augusta Community Schools (PK-12)
   2012-13 Enrollment: 1,128 . . . . (269) 484-2000

Housing: Homeownership rate: 71.3%; Homeowner vacancy rate: 0.4%; Rental vacancy rate: 12.5%

BRADY (township). Covers a land area of 34.831 square miles and a water area of 1.428 square miles. Located at 42.11° N. Lat; 85.47° W. Long.

Population: 4,248; Growth (since 2000): -0.4%; Density: 122.0 persons per square mile; Race: 97.6% White, 0.5% Black/African American, 0.3% Asian, 0.2% American Indian/Alaska Native, 0.0% Native Hawaiian/Other Pacific Islander, 1.1% Two or more races, 1.5% Hispanic of any race; Average household size: 2.66; Median age: 43.2; Age under 18: 23.4%; Age 65 and over: 16.1%; Males per 100 females: 102.6; Marriage status: 22.4% never married, 59.9% now married, 0.4% separated, 6.0% widowed, 11.8% divorced; Foreign born: 0.6%; Speak English only: 99.8%; With disability: 13.9%; Veterans: 8.6%; Ancestry: 32.8% German, 18.2% Irish, 17.2% Dutch, 13.2% English, 5.4% Polish

Employment: 17.2% management, business, and financial, 5.6% computer, engineering, and science, 2.6% education, legal, community service, arts, and media, 5.7% healthcare practitioners, 9.6% service, 28.6% sales and office, 13.6% natural resources, construction, and maintenance, 17.2% production, transportation, and material moving

Income: Per capita: $26,156; Median household: $52,263; Average household: $69,034; Households with income of $100,000 or more: 18.9%; Poverty rate: 12.6%

Educational Attainment: High school diploma or higher: 93.7%; Bachelor's degree or higher: 19.4%; Graduate/professional degree or higher: 6.5%

Housing: Homeownership rate: 91.3%; Median home value: $147,900; Median year structure built: 1965; Homeowner vacancy rate: 1.9%; Median gross rent: $906 per month; Rental vacancy rate: 14.7%

Health Insurance: 86.7% have insurance; 72.3% have private insurance; 27.9% have public insurance; 13.3% do not have insurance; 11.2% of children under 18 do not have insurance

Transportation: Commute: 93.7% car, 0.0% public transportation, 1.7% walk, 4.6% work from home; Median travel time to work: 23.9 minutes

Additional Information Contacts
Brady Township. . . . . (269) 649-1813
http://www.bradytwp.org

CHARLESTON (township).
Covers a land area of 34.777 square miles and a water area of 0.790 square miles. Located at 42.29° N. Lat; 85.35° W. Long.

Population: 1,975; Growth (since 2000): 8.9%; Density: 56.8 persons per square mile; Race: 96.2% White, 1.0% Black/African American, 0.4% Asian, 0.3% American Indian/Alaska Native, 0.0% Native Hawaiian/Other Pacific Islander, 1.4% Two or more races, 1.6% Hispanic of any race; Average household size: 2.61; Median age: 43.0; Age under 18: 22.6%; Age 65 and over: 14.7%; Males per 100 females: 102.4

Housing: Homeownership rate: 90.0%; Homeowner vacancy rate: 0.9%; Rental vacancy rate: 20.2%

CLIMAX (township).
Covers a land area of 36.142 square miles and a water area of 0.166 square miles. Located at 42.20° N. Lat; 85.36° W. Long. Elevation is 965 feet.

History: Climax was named Climax Prairie by its early settlers because it climaxed the end of their search for a place to live.

Population: 2,463; Growth (since 2000): 2.1%; Density: 68.1 persons per square mile; Race: 98.0% White, 0.4% Black/African American, 0.1% Asian, 0.3% American Indian/Alaska Native, 0.0% Native Hawaiian/Other Pacific Islander, 0.9% Two or more races, 1.5% Hispanic of any race; Average household size: 2.69; Median age: 41.9; Age under 18: 24.4%; Age 65 and over: 14.7%; Males per 100 females: 102.7

School District(s)
Climax-Scotts Community Schools (KG-12)
2012-13 Enrollment: 537 . . . . (269) 746-2400

Housing: Homeownership rate: 89.3%; Homeowner vacancy rate: 1.0%; Rental vacancy rate: 4.8%

Newspapers: Climax Crescent (weekly circulation 1000)

CLIMAX (village).
Covers a land area of 1.055 square miles and a water area of 0 square miles. Located at 42.24° N. Lat; 85.34° W. Long. Elevation is 965 feet.

History: The village of Climax was settled in 1838 and took the name of the township, referring to the settlers end of a search for a place to live.

Population: 767; Growth (since 2000): -3.0%; Density: 726.9 persons per square mile; Race: 98.3% White, 0.5% Black/African American, 0.1% Asian, 0.0% American Indian/Alaska Native, 0.0% Native Hawaiian/Other Pacific Islander, 0.8% Two or more races, 2.0% Hispanic of any race; Average household size: 2.74; Median age: 37.9; Age under 18: 26.5%; Age 65 and over: 9.4%; Males per 100 females: 101.3

School District(s)
Climax-Scotts Community Schools (KG-12)
2012-13 Enrollment: 537 . . . . (269) 746-2400

Housing: Homeownership rate: 82.8%; Homeowner vacancy rate: 1.3%; Rental vacancy rate: 9.4%

Newspapers: Climax Crescent (weekly circulation 1000)

COMSTOCK (charter township).
Covers a land area of 33.314 square miles and a water area of 1.937 square miles. Located at 42.29° N. Lat; 85.47° W. Long. Elevation is 778 feet.

History: Comstock was named for General Horace Comstock, who supported the development of the settlement in 1831 and became the first postmaster. His efforts to have Comstock named as the seat of Kalamazoo County were unsuccessful, and he returned to New York.

Population: 14,854; Growth (since 2000): 7.2%; Density: 445.9 persons per square mile; Race: 88.1% White, 5.6% Black/African American, 1.9% Asian, 0.5% American Indian/Alaska Native, 0.1% Native Hawaiian/Other Pacific Islander, 2.9% Two or more races, 3.0% Hispanic of any race; Average household size: 2.45; Median age: 38.9; Age under 18: 23.6%; Age 65 and over: 13.3%; Males per 100 females: 96.8; Marriage status: 29.0% never married, 54.2% now married, 1.6% separated, 5.4% widowed, 11.4% divorced; Foreign born: 5.5%; Speak English only: 93.7%; With disability: 15.4%; Veterans: 10.3%; Ancestry: 22.1% German, 16.2% Dutch, 13.1% English, 12.5% Irish, 7.0% American

Employment: 13.6% management, business, and financial, 8.3% computer, engineering, and science, 6.9% education, legal, community service, arts, and media, 7.0% healthcare practitioners, 17.4% service, 22.8% sales and office, 9.2% natural resources, construction, and maintenance, 14.7% production, transportation, and material moving

Income: Per capita: $26,261; Median household: $50,041; Average household: $62,901; Households with income of $100,000 or more: 15.5%; Poverty rate: 14.7%

Educational Attainment: High school diploma or higher: 89.8%; Bachelor's degree or higher: 26.1%; Graduate/professional degree or higher: 9.9%

Housing: Homeownership rate: 70.7%; Median home value: $130,500; Median year structure built: 1975; Homeowner vacancy rate: 1.8%; Median gross rent: $693 per month; Rental vacancy rate: 15.7%

Health Insurance: 90.9% have insurance; 72.0% have private insurance; 34.5% have public insurance; 9.1% do not have insurance; 3.8% of children under 18 do not have insurance

Transportation: Commute: 93.5% car, 0.6% public transportation, 0.7% walk, 4.1% work from home; Median travel time to work: 19.1 minutes

Additional Information Contacts
Comstock Charter Township . . . . (269) 381-2360
http://www.comstockmi.com

COMSTOCK NORTHWEST (CDP).
Covers a land area of 3.166 square miles and a water area of 0.017 square miles. Located at 42.32° N. Lat; 85.52° W. Long.

Population: 5,455; Growth (since 2000): 22.0%; Density: 1,723.1 persons per square mile; Race: 81.0% White, 10.6% Black/African American, 3.3% Asian, 0.3% American Indian/Alaska Native, 0.0% Native Hawaiian/Other Pacific Islander, 3.6% Two or more races, 3.2% Hispanic of any race; Average household size: 2.20; Median age: 34.7; Age under 18: 22.3%; Age 65 and over: 13.3%; Males per 100 females: 94.9; Marriage status: 40.9% never married, 41.4% now married, 0.5% separated, 5.1% widowed, 12.6% divorced; Foreign born: 10.3%; Speak English only: 89.3%; With disability: 14.4%; Veterans: 11.4%; Ancestry: 18.1% German, 14.4% Dutch, 13.6% English, 8.2% Irish, 6.1% American

Employment: 14.8% management, business, and financial, 11.8% computer, engineering, and science, 8.5% education, legal, community service, arts, and media, 8.7% healthcare practitioners, 17.7% service, 18.4% sales and office, 5.2% natural resources, construction, and maintenance, 14.8% production, transportation, and material moving

Income: Per capita: $24,182; Median household: $48,098; Average household: $54,812; Households with income of $100,000 or more: 12.8%; Poverty rate: 18.1%

Educational Attainment: High school diploma or higher: 95.3%; Bachelor's degree or higher: 32.9%; Graduate/professional degree or higher: 10.9%

Housing: Homeownership rate: 51.4%; Median home value: $132,200; Median year structure built: 1987; Homeowner vacancy rate: 1.5%; Median gross rent: $685 per month; Rental vacancy rate: 17.5%

Health Insurance: 94.4% have insurance; 74.8% have private insurance; 29.9% have public insurance; 5.6% do not have insurance; 2.4% of children under 18 do not have insurance

Transportation: Commute: 94.3% car, 0.9% public transportation, 0.0% walk, 4.2% work from home; Median travel time to work: 19.3 minutes

COOPER (charter township).
Covers a land area of 36.335 square miles and a water area of 0.309 square miles. Located at 42.38° N. Lat; 85.59° W. Long. Elevation is 873 feet.

History: Cooper Township was organized in 1836 by General Horace Comstock, who named it for his wife, a niece of James Fenimore Cooper.

Population: 10,111; Growth (since 2000): 15.5%; Density: 278.3 persons per square mile; Race: 93.2% White, 3.0% Black/African American, 1.0% Asian, 0.4% American Indian/Alaska Native, 0.0% Native Hawaiian/Other Pacific Islander, 2.1% Two or more races, 1.6% Hispanic of any race; Average household size: 2.53; Median age: 40.5; Age under 18: 22.6%; Age 65 and over: 13.6%; Males per 100 females: 96.3; Marriage status: 28.7% never married, 55.5% now married, 0.5% separated, 5.2% widowed, 10.6% divorced; Foreign born: 2.1%; Speak English only: 97.3%; With disability: 12.8%; Veterans: 9.6%; Ancestry: 24.3% German, 18.9% English, 15.2% Dutch, 12.6% Irish, 7.6% Polish

Employment: 12.6% management, business, and financial, 6.3% computer, engineering, and science, 8.9% education, legal, community service, arts, and media, 8.4% healthcare practitioners, 16.4% service, 21.1% sales and office, 10.9% natural resources, construction, and maintenance, 15.4% production, transportation, and material moving

Income: Per capita: $26,597; Median household: $56,424; Average household: $66,781; Households with income of $100,000 or more: 18.3%; Poverty rate: 9.8%

Educational Attainment: High school diploma or higher: 91.2%; Bachelor's degree or higher: 28.0%; Graduate/professional degree or higher: 10.1%

Housing: Homeownership rate: 79.8%; Median home value: $140,800; Median year structure built: 1973; Homeowner vacancy rate: 1.3%; Median gross rent: $889 per month; Rental vacancy rate: 6.2%

Health Insurance: 93.2% have insurance; 80.2% have private insurance; 28.3% have public insurance; 6.8% do not have insurance; 2.3% of children under 18 do not have insurance

Transportation: Commute: 94.8% car, 1.5% public transportation, 1.2% walk, 1.6% work from home; Median travel time to work: 21.6 minutes

Additional Information Contacts

Cooper Charter Township . . . . (269) 382-0223
  http://coopertwp.org

EASTWOOD (CDP). Covers a land area of 1.956 square miles and a water area of 0.013 square miles. Located at 42.30° N. Lat; 85.54° W. Long. Elevation is 860 feet.

Population: 6,340; Growth (since 2000): 1.2%; Density: 3,241.5 persons per square mile; Race: 62.5% White, 28.3% Black/African American, 0.7% Asian, 0.4% American Indian/Alaska Native, 0.0% Native Hawaiian/Other Pacific Islander, 5.7% Two or more races, 6.0% Hispanic of any race; Average household size: 2.45; Median age: 32.2; Age under 18: 26.6%; Age 65 and over: 8.8%; Males per 100 females: 94.7; Marriage status: 36.7% never married, 42.1% now married, 2.3% separated, 4.2% widowed, 16.9% divorced; Foreign born: 3.3%; Speak English only: 93.6%; With disability: 15.0%; Veterans: 10.6%; Ancestry: 17.6% German, 15.3% Irish, 12.7% Dutch, 8.3% English, 3.8% American

Employment: 7.0% management, business, and financial, 5.0% computer, engineering, and science, 7.0% education, legal, community service, arts, and media, 4.0% healthcare practitioners, 29.6% service, 24.6% sales and office, 7.2% natural resources, construction, and maintenance, 15.5% production, transportation, and material moving

Income: Per capita: $18,599; Median household: $40,318; Average household: $45,338; Households with income of $100,000 or more: 7.3%; Poverty rate: 25.2%

Educational Attainment: High school diploma or higher: 88.3%; Bachelor's degree or higher: 18.2%; Graduate/professional degree or higher: 7.4%

Housing: Homeownership rate: 61.0%; Median home value: $78,500; Median year structure built: 1953; Homeowner vacancy rate: 3.3%; Median gross rent: $733 per month; Rental vacancy rate: 14.0%

Health Insurance: 83.9% have insurance; 54.0% have private insurance; 39.8% have public insurance; 16.1% do not have insurance; 9.9% of children under 18 do not have insurance

Transportation: Commute: 86.8% car, 5.1% public transportation, 1.3% walk, 4.3% work from home; Median travel time to work: 19.4 minutes

---

GALESBURG (city). Covers a land area of 1.405 square miles and a water area of 0.041 square miles. Located at 42.29° N. Lat; 85.42° W. Long. Elevation is 791 feet.

History: Galesburg, established at the intersection of several trails, was a stopping place for travelers going between St. Joseph and Fort Dearborn. The town was first called Morton when it was founded in 1835 by George L. Gale, but in 1838 the residents changed the name to Galesburg, in honor of the founder.

Population: 2,009; Growth (since 2000): 1.1%; Density: 1,429.4 persons per square mile; Race: 93.5% White, 2.4% Black/African American, 0.3% Asian, 0.5% American Indian/Alaska Native, 0.0% Native Hawaiian/Other Pacific Islander, 2.6% Two or more races, 2.4% Hispanic of any race; Average household size: 2.47; Median age: 35.6; Age under 18: 25.8%; Age 65 and over: 12.4%; Males per 100 females: 89.7

School District(s)

Galesburg-Augusta Community Schools (PK-12)
  2012-13 Enrollment: 1,128 . . . . (269) 484-2000

Housing: Homeownership rate: 63.9%; Homeowner vacancy rate: 2.6%; Rental vacancy rate: 10.3%

KALAMAZOO (charter township). Covers a land area of 11.680 square miles and a water area of 0.112 square miles. Located at 42.31° N. Lat; 85.62° W. Long. Elevation is 787 feet.

History: The seat of Western Michigan University, Kalamazoo College and Nazareth College. Incorporated 1883.

Population: 21,918; Growth (since 2000): 1.1%; Density: 1,876.6 persons per square mile; Race: 75.7% White, 16.4% Black/African American, 1.3%

Asian, 0.4% American Indian/Alaska Native, 0.0% Native Hawaiian/Other Pacific Islander, 4.1% Two or more races, 4.6% Hispanic of any race; Average household size: 2.32; Median age: 33.3; Age under 18: 22.3%; Age 65 and over: 12.9%; Males per 100 females: 96.0; Marriage status: 32.7% never married, 45.4% now married, 1.4% separated, 5.9% widowed, 15.9% divorced; Foreign born: 3.4%; Speak English only: 94.2%; With disability: 13.9%; Veterans: 9.0%; Ancestry: 21.6% German, 13.6% Irish, 13.1% Dutch, 11.0% English, 4.9% Polish

Employment: 11.4% management, business, and financial, 6.0% computer, engineering, and science, 11.0% education, legal, community service, arts, and media, 4.9% healthcare practitioners, 24.3% service, 22.4% sales and office, 7.0% natural resources, construction, and maintenance, 12.8% production, transportation, and material moving

Income: Per capita: $22,097; Median household: $38,685; Average household: $48,208; Households with income of $100,000 or more: 9.3%; Poverty rate: 18.9%

Educational Attainment: High school diploma or higher: 90.2%; Bachelor's degree or higher: 29.8%; Graduate/professional degree or higher: 10.8%

School District(s)

Comstock Public Schools (PK-12)
  2012-13 Enrollment: 1,952 . . . . (269) 250-8900
Forest Academy (KG-12)
  2012-13 Enrollment: 133 . . . . (269) 488-2315
Kalamazoo Public Schools (PK-12)
  2012-13 Enrollment: 12,455 . . . . (269) 337-0123
Kalamazoo Resa (PK-12)
  2012-13 Enrollment: 1,223 . . . . (269) 250-9205
Otsego Public Schools (PK-12)
  2012-13 Enrollment: 2,336 . . . . (269) 692-6066
Paramount Charter Academy (KG-12)
  2012-13 Enrollment: 621 . . . . (269) 553-6400
Parchment SD (PK-12)
  2012-13 Enrollment: 1,805 . . . . (269) 488-1050
Plainwell Community Schools (KG-12)
  2012-13 Enrollment: 2,731 . . . . (269) 685-5823
Youth Advancement Academy (KG-12)
  2012-13 Enrollment: 42 . . . . (269) 488-2804

Four-year College(s)

Kalamazoo College (Private, Not-for-profit)
  Fall 2013 Enrollment: 1,458 . . . . (269) 337-7000
  2013-14 Tuition: In-state $39,450; Out-of-state $39,450
Western Michigan University (Public)
  Fall 2013 Enrollment: 24,294 . . . . (269) 387-1000
  2013-14 Tuition: In-state $10,355; Out-of-state $24,109

Two-year College(s)

Career Quest Learning Center-Kalamazoo (Private, For-profit)
  Fall 2013 Enrollment: 99 . . . . (269) 364-2300
Kalamazoo Valley Community College (Public)
  Fall 2013 Enrollment: 10,192 . . . . (269) 488-4100
  2013-14 Tuition: In-state $4,711; Out-of-state $6,354
West Michigan College of Barbering and Beauty (Private, For-profit)
  Fall 2013 Enrollment: 87 . . . . (269) 381-4424

Vocational/Technical School(s)

Everest Institute-Kalamazoo (Private, For-profit)
  Fall 2013 Enrollment: 356 . . . . (269) 381-9616
  2013-14 Tuition: $18,556

Housing: Homeownership rate: 65.6%; Median home value: $97,600; Median year structure built: 1961; Homeowner vacancy rate: 2.4%; Median gross rent: $737 per month; Rental vacancy rate: 11.9%

Health Insurance: 86.1% have insurance; 66.4% have private insurance; 34.0% have public insurance; 13.9% do not have insurance; 5.0% of children under 18 do not have insurance

Hospitals: Borgess Medical Center (424 beds); Bronson Methodist Hospital (343 beds)

Newspapers: Kalamazoo Gazette (daily circulation 52400); The Commercial-Express (weekly circulation 2000)

Transportation: Commute: 90.6% car, 3.2% public transportation, 1.6% walk, 2.5% work from home; Median travel time to work: 18.9 minutes; Amtrak: Train service available.

Airports: Kalamazoo/Battle Creek International (primary service/non-hub)

Additional Information Contacts

Kalamazoo Charter Township . . . . (269) 381-8080
  http://www.kalamazootownship.org

KALAMAZOO (city). County seat. Covers a land area of 24.684 square miles and a water area of 0.432 square miles. Located at 42.28° N. Lat; 85.59° W. Long. Elevation is 787 feet.

History: The name first applied to the river was Kee-Kalamazoo, meaning "where the water boils in the pot," in reference to the bubbling springs in the river. A trading post was established here in 1823, followed in 1847 by a group of Hollanders seeking religious freedom. Kalamazoo was the birthplace of celery, whose seeds were introduced about 1850 by Scotsman James Taylor. Cultivation was begun by Marinus DeBruin, and by 1870 much swampland had been converted into celery farms. Other industries that began before the turn of the century were the Kalamazoo Paper Company, forerunner of a group that made the city a paper-mill center, and Dr. William E. Upjohn's pill company, which developed into the pharmaceutical industry.

Population: 74,262; Growth (since 2000): -3.7%; Density: 3,008.5 persons per square mile; Race: 68.1% White, 22.2% Black/African American, 1.7% Asian, 0.5% American Indian/Alaska Native, 0.0% Native Hawaiian/Other Pacific Islander, 4.6% Two or more races, 6.4% Hispanic of any race; Average household size: 2.29; Median age: 26.2; Age under 18: 20.5%; Age 65 and over: 9.4%; Males per 100 females: 97.4; Marriage status: 55.5% never married, 27.9% now married, 1.7% separated, 4.6% widowed, 12.1% divorced; Foreign born: 6.3%; Speak English only: 89.3%; With disability: 13.1%; Veterans: 5.4%; Ancestry: 18.9% German, 10.9% Irish, 9.6% English, 8.4% Dutch, 5.7% Polish

Employment: 11.1% management, business, and financial, 4.2% computer, engineering, and science, 12.3% education, legal, community service, arts, and media, 4.7% healthcare practitioners, 26.1% service, 25.2% sales and office, 4.8% natural resources, construction, and maintenance, 11.6% production, transportation, and material moving

Income: Per capita: $18,468; Median household: $31,893; Average household: $46,381; Households with income of $100,000 or more: 10.1%; Poverty rate: 34.3%

Educational Attainment: High school diploma or higher: 89.4%; Bachelor's degree or higher: 31.9%; Graduate/professional degree or higher: 13.4%

School District(s)

Comstock Public Schools (PK-12)
    2012-13 Enrollment: 1,952 . . . . (269) 250-8900
Forest Academy (KG-12)
    2012-13 Enrollment: 133. . . . . (269) 488-2315
Kalamazoo Public Schools (PK-12)
    2012-13 Enrollment: 12,455 . . . . (269) 337-0123
Kalamazoo Resa (PK-12)
    2012-13 Enrollment: 1,223 . . . . (269) 250-9205
Otsego Public Schools (PK-12)
    2012-13 Enrollment: 2,336 . . . . (269) 692-6066
Paramount Charter Academy (KG-12)
    2012-13 Enrollment: 621. . . . . (269) 553-6400
Parchment SD (PK-12)
    2012-13 Enrollment: 1,805 . . . . (269) 488-1050
Plainwell Community Schools (KG-12)
    2012-13 Enrollment: 2,731 . . . . (269) 685-5823
Youth Advancement Academy (KG-12)
    2012-13 Enrollment: 42 . . . . (269) 488-2804

Four-year College(s)

Kalamazoo College (Private, Not-for-profit)
    Fall 2013 Enrollment: 1,458 . . . . (269) 337-7000
    2013-14 Tuition: In-state $39,450; Out-of-state $39,450
Western Michigan University (Public)
    Fall 2013 Enrollment: 24,294 . . . . (269) 387-1000
    2013-14 Tuition: In-state $10,355; Out-of-state $24,109

Two-year College(s)

Career Quest Learning Center-Kalamazoo (Private, For-profit)
    Fall 2013 Enrollment: 99. . . . . (269) 364-2300
Kalamazoo Valley Community College (Public)
    Fall 2013 Enrollment: 10,192 . . . . (269) 488-4100
    2013-14 Tuition: In-state $4,711; Out-of-state $6,354
West Michigan College of Barbering and Beauty (Private, For-profit)
    Fall 2013 Enrollment: 87. . . . . (269) 381-4424

Vocational/Technical School(s)

Everest Institute-Kalamazoo (Private, For-profit)
    Fall 2013 Enrollment: 356. (269) 381-9616
    2013-14 Tuition: $18,556

Housing: Homeownership rate: 43.6%; Median home value: $97,600; Median year structure built: 1957; Homeowner vacancy rate: 3.9%; Median gross rent: $707 per month; Rental vacancy rate: 9.0%

Health Insurance: 85.8% have insurance; 62.7% have private insurance; 33.4% have public insurance; 14.2% do not have insurance; 5.2% of children under 18 do not have insurance

Hospitals: Borgess Medical Center (424 beds); Bronson Methodist Hospital (343 beds)

Newspapers: Kalamazoo Gazette (daily circulation 52400); The Commercial-Express (weekly circulation 2000)

Transportation: Commute: 85.6% car, 2.4% public transportation, 7.6% walk, 3.3% work from home; Median travel time to work: 18.0 minutes; Amtrak: Train service available.

Airports: Kalamazoo/Battle Creek International (primary service/non-hub)

Additional Information Contacts
City of Kalamazoo . . . . (269) 337-8792
    http://www.kalamazoocity.org

NAZARETH (unincorporated postal area)
ZCTA: 49074

Covers a land area of 0.071 square miles and a water area of 0 square miles. Located at 42.32° N. Lat; 85.54° W. Long..

Population: 149; Growth (since 2000): n/a; Density: 2,099.2 persons per square mile; Race: 90.6% White, 8.1% Black/African American, 0.7% Asian, 0.0% American Indian/Alaska Native, 0.0% Native Hawaiian/Other Pacific Islander, 0.7% Two or more races, 0.7% Hispanic of any race; Average household size: 1.04; Median age: 80.2; Age under 18: 0.0%; Age 65 and over: 86.6%; Males per 100 females: 14.6

Housing: Homeownership rate: n/a; Homeowner vacancy rate: 0.0%; Rental vacancy rate: 2.8%

OSHTEMO (charter township). Covers a land area of 35.869 square miles and a water area of 0.135 square miles. Located at 42.29° N. Lat; 85.71° W. Long. Elevation is 968 feet.

History: Oshtemo developed as a trading center for grape and apple growers. The township was established in 1838, and the post office was founded in 1857.

Population: 21,705; Growth (since 2000): 27.7%; Density: 605.1 persons per square mile; Race: 80.0% White, 12.2% Black/African American, 2.8% Asian, 0.3% American Indian/Alaska Native, 0.0% Native Hawaiian/Other Pacific Islander, 3.3% Two or more races, 4.0% Hispanic of any race; Average household size: 2.21; Median age: 32.0; Age under 18: 18.4%; Age 65 and over: 15.2%; Males per 100 females: 90.9; Marriage status: 41.0% never married, 43.8% now married, 1.7% separated, 6.4% widowed, 8.8% divorced; Foreign born: 6.5%; Speak English only: 91.9%; With disability: 12.7%; Veterans: 7.9%; Ancestry: 24.4% German, 14.3% English, 12.3% Irish, 12.2% Dutch, 4.9% Polish

Employment: 11.5% management, business, and financial, 5.4% computer, engineering, and science, 13.9% education, legal, community service, arts, and media, 6.8% healthcare practitioners, 24.9% service, 23.0% sales and office, 4.4% natural resources, construction, and maintenance, 10.1% production, transportation, and material moving

Income: Per capita: $27,918; Median household: $41,675; Average household: $61,155; Households with income of $100,000 or more: 18.8%; Poverty rate: 23.5%

Educational Attainment: High school diploma or higher: 95.7%; Bachelor's degree or higher: 44.1%; Graduate/professional degree or higher: 18.3%

Housing: Homeownership rate: 50.5%; Median home value: $167,200; Median year structure built: 1986; Homeowner vacancy rate: 2.5%; Median gross rent: $695 per month; Rental vacancy rate: 11.9%

Health Insurance: 90.5% have insurance; 74.6% have private insurance; 30.3% have public insurance; 9.5% do not have insurance; 4.5% of children under 18 do not have insurance

Transportation: Commute: 92.9% car, 0.9% public transportation, 1.3% walk, 3.3% work from home; Median travel time to work: 20.9 minutes

Additional Information Contacts
Oshtemo Charter Township . . . . (269) 375-4260
    http://www.oshtemo.org

PARCHMENT (city). Covers a land area of 0.921 square miles and a water area of 0.014 square miles. Located at 42.33° N. Lat; 85.57° W. Long. Elevation is 774 feet.

History: Parchment was established as a model village around the Kalamazoo Vegetable Parchment Paper factory. Jacob Kindleberger built the town for the factory workers in 1909, when he opened the paper mill.

Population: 1,804; Growth (since 2000): -6.8%; Density: 1,959.2 persons per square mile; Race: 84.6% White, 8.5% Black/African American, 1.3% Asian, 0.2% American Indian/Alaska Native, 0.0% Native Hawaiian/Other Pacific Islander, 4.0% Two or more races, 3.4% Hispanic of any race; Average household size: 2.30; Median age: 38.5; Age under 18: 24.2%; Age 65 and over: 12.0%; Males per 100 females: 86.0

Housing: Homeownership rate: 62.6%; Homeowner vacancy rate: 3.3%; Rental vacancy rate: 12.9%

PAVILION (township). Covers a land area of 35.007 square miles and a water area of 1.359 square miles. Located at 42.21° N. Lat; 85.48° W. Long. Elevation is 866 feet.

Population: 6,222; Growth (since 2000): 6.7%; Density: 177.7 persons per square mile; Race: 94.2% White, 1.4% Black/African American, 0.5% Asian, 0.3% American Indian/Alaska Native, 0.0% Native Hawaiian/Other Pacific Islander, 2.7% Two or more races, 2.7% Hispanic of any race; Average household size: 2.69; Median age: 38.9; Age under 18: 26.1%; Age 65 and over: 11.6%; Males per 100 females: 100.8; Marriage status: 25.8% never married, 57.7% now married, 0.7% separated, 3.3% widowed, 13.3% divorced; Foreign born: 0.5%; Speak English only: 98.7%; With disability: 12.6%; Veterans: 10.3%; Ancestry: 29.5% German, 16.3% Dutch, 15.5% English, 13.9% Irish, 11.3% American

Employment: 13.7% management, business, and financial, 9.1% computer, engineering, and science, 5.8% education, legal, community service, arts, and media, 8.1% healthcare practitioners, 13.5% service, 20.1% sales and office, 9.6% natural resources, construction, and maintenance, 20.1% production, transportation, and material moving

Income: Per capita: $27,071; Median household: $57,045; Average household: $74,357; Households with income of $100,000 or more: 21.8%; Poverty rate: 13.9%

Educational Attainment: High school diploma or higher: 90.9%; Bachelor's degree or higher: 18.8%; Graduate/professional degree or higher: 5.8%

Housing: Homeownership rate: 90.4%; Median home value: $153,400; Median year structure built: 1977; Homeowner vacancy rate: 1.6%; Median gross rent: $1,026 per month; Rental vacancy rate: 10.9%

Health Insurance: 90.9% have insurance; 72.7% have private insurance; 31.0% have public insurance; 9.1% do not have insurance; 1.9% of children under 18 do not have insurance

Transportation: Commute: 92.7% car, 0.0% public transportation, 0.6% walk, 5.1% work from home; Median travel time to work: 20.9 minutes

PORTAGE (city). Covers a land area of 32.225 square miles and a water area of 2.941 square miles. Located at 42.20° N. Lat; 85.59° W. Long. Elevation is 879 feet.

History: Portage was settled in 1830, and given a post office in 1836, when it was called Sweetland. In 1839 it was renamed Portage, like the township.

Population: 46,292; Growth (since 2000): 3.1%; Density: 1,436.5 persons per square mile; Race: 86.9% White, 4.9% Black/African American, 3.8% Asian, 0.4% American Indian/Alaska Native, 0.0% Native Hawaiian/Other Pacific Islander, 3.0% Two or more races, 3.1% Hispanic of any race; Average household size: 2.40; Median age: 38.1; Age under 18: 24.8%; Age 65 and over: 13.6%; Males per 100 females: 92.1; Marriage status: 28.7% never married, 55.8% now married, 1.6% separated, 5.2% widowed, 10.2% divorced; Foreign born: 5.0%; Speak English only: 93.8%; With disability: 11.3%; Veterans: 8.4%; Ancestry: 25.4% German, 15.9% Irish, 13.8% English, 12.1% Dutch, 6.1% Polish

Employment: 18.7% management, business, and financial, 7.5% computer, engineering, and science, 11.1% education, legal, community service, arts, and media, 8.3% healthcare practitioners, 12.7% service, 25.2% sales and office, 5.9% natural resources, construction, and maintenance, 10.6% production, transportation, and material moving

Income: Per capita: $29,738; Median household: $55,036; Average household: $71,816; Households with income of $100,000 or more: 21.8%; Poverty rate: 11.7%

Educational Attainment: High school diploma or higher: 95.7%; Bachelor's degree or higher: 39.8%; Graduate/professional degree or higher: 14.7%

Kalamazoo Resa (PK-12)
    2012-13 Enrollment: 1,223 . . . . (269) 250-9205
Oakland Academy (KG-12)
    2012-13 Enrollment: 232 . . . . (269) 324-8951
Portage Public Schools (PK-12)
    2012-13 Enrollment: 8,707 . . . . (269) 323-5000

Vocational/Technical School(s)

Ross Medical Education Center-Portage (Private, For-profit)
    Fall 2013 Enrollment: 136 . . . . (269) 324-0431
    2013-14 Tuition: $15,680
Wright Beauty Academy (Private, For-profit)
    Fall 2013 Enrollment: 84 . . . . (269) 321-8708
    2013-14 Tuition: $11,300

Housing: Homeownership rate: 68.9%; Median home value: $148,100; Median year structure built: 1975; Homeowner vacancy rate: 2.1%; Median gross rent: $712 per month; Rental vacancy rate: 10.4%

Health Insurance: 90.7% have insurance; 77.7% have private insurance; 26.8% have public insurance; 9.3% do not have insurance; 2.5% of children under 18 do not have insurance

Safety: Violent crime rate: 18.6 per 10,000 population; Property crime rate: 338.9 per 10,000 population

Transportation: Commute: 94.1% car, 0.5% public transportation, 1.2% walk, 3.2% work from home; Median travel time to work: 20.0 minutes

Additional Information Contacts

City of Portage . . . . (269) 329-4400
   http://www.portagemi.gov

PRAIRIE RONDE (township). Covers a land area of 35.828 square miles and a water area of 0.632 square miles. Located at 42.12° N. Lat; 85.70° W. Long.

Population: 2,250; Growth (since 2000): 7.9%; Density: 62.8 persons per square mile; Race: 97.0% White, 0.4% Black/African American, 0.1% Asian, 0.6% American Indian/Alaska Native, 0.0% Native Hawaiian/Other Pacific Islander, 1.2% Two or more races, 2.1% Hispanic of any race; Average household size: 2.82; Median age: 42.6; Age under 18: 26.6%; Age 65 and over: 10.4%; Males per 100 females: 101.8

Housing: Homeownership rate: 93.9%; Homeowner vacancy rate: 1.3%; Rental vacancy rate: 3.9%

RICHLAND (township). Covers a land area of 34.428 square miles and a water area of 1.751 square miles. Located at 42.38° N. Lat; 85.47° W. Long. Elevation is 932 feet.

History: Richland Township was organized in 1832 and named by Simeon Mills.

Population: 7,580; Growth (since 2000): 16.8%; Density: 220.2 persons per square mile; Race: 91.6% White, 3.9% Black/African American, 1.3% Asian, 0.3% American Indian/Alaska Native, 0.1% Native Hawaiian/Other Pacific Islander, 1.9% Two or more races, 3.0% Hispanic of any race; Average household size: 2.56; Median age: 41.0; Age under 18: 26.4%; Age 65 and over: 13.5%; Males per 100 females: 94.4; Marriage status: 25.0% never married, 59.7% now married, 1.5% separated, 4.9% widowed, 10.4% divorced; Foreign born: 5.1%; Speak English only: 94.9%; With disability: 11.2%; Veterans: 9.5%; Ancestry: 29.1% German, 18.3% English, 16.7% Irish, 13.9% Dutch, 6.9% Italian

Employment: 21.0% management, business, and financial, 5.1% computer, engineering, and science, 10.1% education, legal, community service, arts, and media, 12.3% healthcare practitioners, 16.2% service, 21.1% sales and office, 4.6% natural resources, construction, and maintenance, 9.6% production, transportation, and material moving

Income: Per capita: $37,618; Median household: $64,638; Average household: $97,766; Households with income of $100,000 or more: 32.0%; Poverty rate: 5.9%

Educational Attainment: High school diploma or higher: 94.9%; Bachelor's degree or higher: 42.4%; Graduate/professional degree or higher: 17.6%

School District(s)

Gull Lake Community Schools (PK-12)
    2012-13 Enrollment: 2,930 . . . . (269) 488-5000

Housing: Homeownership rate: 80.4%; Median home value: $196,700; Median year structure built: 1982; Homeowner vacancy rate: 1.8%; Median gross rent: $686 per month; Rental vacancy rate: 9.4%

Health Insurance: 93.3% have insurance; 82.9% have private insurance; 25.0% have public insurance; 6.7% do not have insurance; 0.3% of children under 18 do not have insurance

Transportation: Commute: 94.1% car, 0.0% public transportation, 0.3% walk, 4.4% work from home; Median travel time to work: 22.4 minutes

RICHLAND (village).
Covers a land area of 1.015 square miles and a water area of <.001 square miles. Located at 42.37° N. Lat; 85.46° W. Long. Elevation is 932 feet.

History: The village of Richland was platted in 1833 and called Gull Corners, for nearby Gull Lake. It was renamed for the township in 1840, and incorporated as a village in 1871.

Population: 751; Growth (since 2000): 26.6%; Density: 740.0 persons per square mile; Race: 94.7% White, 0.4% Black/African American, 1.2% Asian, 0.0% American Indian/Alaska Native, 0.0% Native Hawaiian/Other Pacific Islander, 3.5% Two or more races, 1.5% Hispanic of any race; Average household size: 2.16; Median age: 46.8; Age under 18: 21.6%; Age 65 and over: 22.1%; Males per 100 females: 78.4

School District(s)
Gull Lake Community Schools (PK-12)
   2012-13 Enrollment: 2,930 . . . . (269) 488-5000

Housing: Homeownership rate: 81.6%; Homeowner vacancy rate: 2.7%; Rental vacancy rate: 8.6%

Safety: Violent crime rate: 0.0 per 10,000 population; Property crime rate: 13.0 per 10,000 population

ROSS (township).
Covers a land area of 33.337 square miles and a water area of 2.687 square miles. Located at 42.38° N. Lat; 85.35° W. Long.

History: Ross Township was organized in 1839 and named by the legislature. John Van Vleck built a tavern here in 1843.

Population: 4,664; Growth (since 2000): -7.6%; Density: 139.9 persons per square mile; Race: 95.7% White, 0.8% Black/African American, 0.9% Asian, 0.5% American Indian/Alaska Native, 0.0% Native Hawaiian/Other Pacific Islander, 1.9% Two or more races, 1.6% Hispanic of any race; Average household size: 2.39; Median age: 47.7; Age under 18: 20.5%; Age 65 and over: 16.6%; Males per 100 females: 100.3; Marriage status: 23.1% never married, 61.0% now married, 0.5% separated, 7.5% widowed, 8.4% divorced; Foreign born: 3.1%; Speak English only: 95.5%; With disability: 15.4%; Veterans: 12.5%; Ancestry: 26.5% German, 17.6% English, 14.6% Irish, 10.1% Dutch, 6.5% American

Employment: 17.0% management, business, and financial, 7.0% computer, engineering, and science, 14.1% education, legal, community service, arts, and media, 7.6% healthcare practitioners, 13.9% service, 19.9% sales and office, 5.8% natural resources, construction, and maintenance, 14.7% production, transportation, and material moving

Income: Per capita: $33,559; Median household: $64,956; Average household: $84,273; Households with income of $100,000 or more: 30.2%; Poverty rate: 4.6%

Educational Attainment: High school diploma or higher: 95.8%; Bachelor's degree or higher: 43.5%; Graduate/professional degree or higher: 13.7%

Housing: Homeownership rate: 85.5%; Median home value: $192,400; Median year structure built: 1964; Homeowner vacancy rate: 2.2%; Median gross rent: $892 per month; Rental vacancy rate: 12.2%

Health Insurance: 90.1% have insurance; 80.9% have private insurance; 24.8% have public insurance; 9.9% do not have insurance; 0.6% of children under 18 do not have insurance

Transportation: Commute: 94.2% car, 0.7% public transportation, 1.8% walk, 3.0% work from home; Median travel time to work: 21.4 minutes

SCHOOLCRAFT (township).
Covers a land area of 34.272 square miles and a water area of 1.800 square miles. Located at 42.11° N. Lat; 85.59° W. Long. Elevation is 879 feet.

Population: 8,214; Growth (since 2000): 13.1%; Density: 239.7 persons per square mile; Race: 95.8% White, 0.7% Black/African American, 0.5% Asian, 0.5% American Indian/Alaska Native, 0.0% Native Hawaiian/Other Pacific Islander, 1.9% Two or more races, 2.2% Hispanic of any race; Average household size: 2.58; Median age: 39.5; Age under 18: 25.2%; Age 65 and over: 13.2%; Males per 100 females: 99.5; Marriage status: 25.7% never married, 57.3% now married, 1.2% separated, 4.5% widowed, 12.6% divorced; Foreign born: 1.4%; Speak English only: 97.2%; With disability: 12.1%; Veterans: 9.3%; Ancestry: 26.7% German, 17.0% English, 16.0% Irish, 14.0% Dutch, 6.6% American

Employment: 13.9% management, business, and financial, 8.6% computer, engineering, and science, 7.9% education, legal, community service, arts, and media, 9.0% healthcare practitioners, 17.3% service,

22.4% sales and office, 7.7% natural resources, construction, and maintenance, 13.3% production, transportation, and material moving

Income: Per capita: $29,382; Median household: $57,623; Average household: $74,411; Households with income of $100,000 or more: 19.7%; Poverty rate: 13.4%

Educational Attainment: High school diploma or higher: 93.5%; Bachelor's degree or higher: 24.0%; Graduate/professional degree or higher: 7.3%

School District(s)
Schoolcraft Community Schools (KG-12)
   2012-13 Enrollment: 1,102 . . . . (269) 488-7390

Housing: Homeownership rate: 78.6%; Median home value: $140,700; Median year structure built: 1973; Homeowner vacancy rate: 1.8%; Median gross rent: $654 per month; Rental vacancy rate: 8.9%

Health Insurance: 90.3% have insurance; 79.1% have private insurance; 26.0% have public insurance; 9.7% do not have insurance; 4.6% of children under 18 do not have insurance

Transportation: Commute: 93.3% car, 0.0% public transportation, 1.9% walk, 3.7% work from home; Median travel time to work: 23.7 minutes

SCHOOLCRAFT (village).
Covers a land area of 0.978 square miles and a water area of 0 square miles. Located at 42.12° N. Lat; 85.63° W. Long. Elevation is 879 feet.

History: It was in Schoolcraft that James Fenimore Cooper stayed while collecting material for his book "Oak Openings." Schoolcraft was a station on the Underground Railroad to freedom for slaves from the south. The town was named for Henry Rowe Schoolcraft when it was founded in 1831 by Lucius Lyon, a surveyor.

Population: 1,525; Growth (since 2000): -3.9%; Density: 1,559.1 persons per square mile; Race: 95.6% White, 1.0% Black/African American, 0.6% Asian, 1.0% American Indian/Alaska Native, 0.0% Native Hawaiian/Other Pacific Islander, 1.4% Two or more races, 2.0% Hispanic of any race; Average household size: 2.48; Median age: 38.1; Age under 18: 26.4%; Age 65 and over: 12.9%; Males per 100 females: 97.5

School District(s)
Schoolcraft Community Schools (KG-12)
   2012-13 Enrollment: 1,102 . . . . (269) 488-7390

Housing: Homeownership rate: 69.9%; Homeowner vacancy rate: 2.9%; Rental vacancy rate: 7.0%

SCOTTS (unincorporated postal area)
ZCTA: 49088
   Covers a land area of 32.111 square miles and a water area of 0.844 square miles. Located at 42.18° N. Lat; 85.42° W. Long. Elevation is 915 feet.

Population: 3,648; Growth (since 2000): 20.8%; Density: 113.6 persons per square mile; Race: 97.7% White, 0.5% Black/African American, 0.3% Asian, 0.2% American Indian/Alaska Native, 0.0% Native Hawaiian/Other Pacific Islander, 1.0% Two or more races, 1.2% Hispanic of any race; Average household size: 2.66; Median age: 41.7; Age under 18: 24.7%; Age 65 and over: 13.5%; Males per 100 females: 104.5; Marriage status: 25.0% never married, 62.0% now married, 0.8% separated, 3.0% widowed, 10.0% divorced; Foreign born: 0.1%; Speak English only: 99.4%; With disability: 9.8%; Veterans: 12.4%; Ancestry: 29.5% German, 16.0% Dutch, 15.7% Irish, 14.5% English, 11.8% American

Employment: 17.3% management, business, and financial, 10.3% computer, engineering, and science, 4.6% education, legal, community service, arts, and media, 6.2% healthcare practitioners, 9.4% service, 21.5% sales and office, 9.3% natural resources, construction, and maintenance, 21.5% production, transportation, and material moving

Income: Per capita: $26,370; Median household: $62,966; Average household: $72,080; Households with income of $100,000 or more: 25.0%; Poverty rate: 7.3%

Educational Attainment: High school diploma or higher: 93.2%; Bachelor's degree or higher: 23.0%; Graduate/professional degree or higher: 5.3%

School District(s)
Climax-Scotts Community Schools (KG-12)
   2012-13 Enrollment: 537 . . . . (269) 746-2400
Vicksburg Community Schools (PK-12)
   2012-13 Enrollment: 2,636 . . . . (269) 321-1000

Housing: Homeownership rate: 92.4%; Median home value: $165,500; Median year structure built: 1973; Homeowner vacancy rate: 1.6%; Median gross rent: $982 per month; Rental vacancy rate: 4.5%

Health Insurance: 93.9% have insurance; 82.4% have private insurance; 24.6% have public insurance; 6.1% do not have insurance; 0.7% of children under 18 do not have insurance
Transportation: Commute: 94.9% car, 0.0% public transportation, 0.0% walk, 3.7% work from home; Median travel time to work: 22.8 minutes

SOUTH GULL LAKE (CDP).
Covers a land area of 1.351 square miles and a water area of 1.797 square miles. Located at 42.39° N. Lat; 85.41° W. Long. Elevation is 879 feet.
Population: 1,182; Growth (since 2000): -22.5%; Density: 875.2 persons per square mile; Race: 97.2% White, 0.4% Black/African American, 1.4% Asian, 0.2% American Indian/Alaska Native, 0.0% Native Hawaiian/Other Pacific Islander, 0.8% Two or more races, 0.9% Hispanic of any race; Average household size: 2.30; Median age: 51.6; Age under 18: 18.7%; Age 65 and over: 20.9%; Males per 100 females: 97.0
Housing: Homeownership rate: 86.9%; Homeowner vacancy rate: 4.3%; Rental vacancy rate: 11.7%

TEXAS (charter township).
Covers a land area of 34.383 square miles and a water area of 1.915 square miles. Located at 42.20° N. Lat; 85.71° W. Long.
History: Texas Township was formed from Brady township in 1838, and derives its name, doubtless, from the Lone Star State, which even then began to appear as an important factor in the history of the American Republic.
Population: 14,697; Growth (since 2000): 34.6%; Density: 427.4 persons per square mile; Race: 90.6% White, 2.5% Black/African American, 4.1% Asian, 0.3% American Indian/Alaska Native, 0.0% Native Hawaiian/Other Pacific Islander, 2.0% Two or more races, 2.1% Hispanic of any race; Average household size: 2.81; Median age: 39.5; Age under 18: 28.8%; Age 65 and over: 10.5%; Males per 100 females: 99.0; Marriage status: 21.1% never married, 68.3% now married, 0.1% separated, 4.1% widowed, 6.5% divorced; Foreign born: 5.9%; Speak English only: 92.7%; With disability: 7.0%; Veterans: 7.7%; Ancestry: 26.0% German, 16.5% Irish, 15.4% English, 13.4% Dutch, 7.4% Polish
Employment: 23.8% management, business, and financial, 8.7% computer, engineering, and science, 12.4% education, legal, community service, arts, and media, 8.7% healthcare practitioners, 11.8% service, 21.4% sales and office, 5.0% natural resources, construction, and maintenance, 8.2% production, transportation, and material moving
Income: Per capita: $40,837; Median household: $90,882; Average household: $120,156; Households with income of $100,000 or more: 45.2%; Poverty rate: 5.1%
Educational Attainment: High school diploma or higher: 97.1%; Bachelor's degree or higher: 52.9%; Graduate/professional degree or higher: 24.2%
Housing: Homeownership rate: 90.8%; Median home value: $242,200; Median year structure built: 1991; Homeowner vacancy rate: 2.1%; Median gross rent: $869 per month; Rental vacancy rate: 5.5%
Health Insurance: 95.8% have insurance; 87.0% have private insurance; 19.4% have public insurance; 4.2% do not have insurance; 0.0% of children under 18 do not have insurance
Transportation: Commute: 92.2% car, 0.0% public transportation, 0.2% walk, 6.8% work from home; Median travel time to work: 21.0 minutes
Additional Information Contacts
Texas Charter Township . . . . (269) 375-1591
http://www.texastownship.org

VICKSBURG (village).
Covers a land area of 3.014 square miles and a water area of 0.141 square miles. Located at 42.12° N. Lat; 85.54° W. Long. Elevation is 856 feet.
History: Known for Egyptian lotuses grown nearby. Annual Vicksburg Old Car Festival. Incorporated 1871.
Population: 2,906; Growth (since 2000): 25.3%; Density: 964.3 persons per square mile; Race: 95.9% White, 0.6% Black/African American, 0.6% Asian, 0.3% American Indian/Alaska Native, 0.0% Native Hawaiian/Other Pacific Islander, 2.1% Two or more races, 3.2% Hispanic of any race; Average household size: 2.59; Median age: 33.0; Age under 18: 28.4%; Age 65 and over: 11.3%; Males per 100 females: 97.3; Marriage status: 29.3% never married, 46.9% now married, 0.5% separated, 5.3% widowed, 18.4% divorced; Foreign born: 1.9%; Speak English only: 97.3%; With disability: 14.9%; Veterans: 7.5%; Ancestry: 25.9% German, 19.4% Irish, 13.3% English, 9.9% Dutch, 6.3% French
Employment: 10.8% management, business, and financial, 5.7% computer, engineering, and science, 6.1% education, legal, community

service, arts, and media, 7.5% healthcare practitioners, 13.3% service, 26.6% sales and office, 12.6% natural resources, construction, and maintenance, 17.3% production, transportation, and material moving
Income: Per capita: $34,198; Median household: $56,583; Average household: $87,875; Households with income of $100,000 or more: 18.3%; Poverty rate: 15.1%
Educational Attainment: High school diploma or higher: 92.3%; Bachelor's degree or higher: 22.3%; Graduate/professional degree or higher: 7.6%
School District(s)
Vicksburg Community Schools (PK-12)
   2012-13 Enrollment: 2,636 . . . . (269) 321-1000
Housing: Homeownership rate: 73.5%; Median home value: $119,300; Median year structure built: 1960; Homeowner vacancy rate: 2.5%; Median gross rent: $683 per month; Rental vacancy rate: 13.8%
Health Insurance: 90.1% have insurance; 69.2% have private insurance; 33.7% have public insurance; 9.9% do not have insurance; 2.2% of children under 18 do not have insurance
Safety: Violent crime rate: 23.4 per 10,000 population; Property crime rate: 200.5 per 10,000 population
Transportation: Commute: 94.7% car, 0.0% public transportation, 1.3% walk, 4.0% work from home; Median travel time to work: 25.4 minutes

WAKESHMA (township).
Covers a land area of 36.018 square miles and a water area of 0 square miles. Located at 42.11° N. Lat; 85.35° W. Long. Elevation is 919 feet.
Population: 1,301; Growth (since 2000): -8.0%; Density: 36.1 persons per square mile; Race: 97.0% White, 0.2% Black/African American, 0.7% Asian, 0.2% American Indian/Alaska Native, 0.0% Native Hawaiian/Other Pacific Islander, 0.6% Two or more races, 1.8% Hispanic of any race; Average household size: 2.60; Median age: 41.0; Age under 18: 22.8%; Age 65 and over: 12.7%; Males per 100 females: 104.9
Housing: Homeownership rate: 87.4%; Homeowner vacancy rate: 0.7%; Rental vacancy rate: 3.1%

WESTWOOD (CDP).
Covers a land area of 2.855 square miles and a water area of 0 square miles. Located at 42.30° N. Lat; 85.63° W. Long. Elevation is 942 feet.
Population: 8,653; Growth (since 2000): -5.1%; Density: 3,030.7 persons per square mile; Race: 82.1% White, 11.5% Black/African American, 1.8% Asian, 0.3% American Indian/Alaska Native, 0.0% Native Hawaiian/Other Pacific Islander, 3.1% Two or more races, 2.7% Hispanic of any race; Average household size: 2.07; Median age: 32.1; Age under 18: 16.0%; Age 65 and over: 15.7%; Males per 100 females: 94.5; Marriage status: 34.0% never married, 44.5% now married, 1.2% separated, 7.3% widowed, 14.2% divorced; Foreign born: 3.0%; Speak English only: 96.0%; With disability: 12.2%; Veterans: 8.2%; Ancestry: 26.3% German, 13.7% Dutch, 13.7% English, 12.0% Irish, 7.0% Polish
Employment: 15.8% management, business, and financial, 6.3% computer, engineering, and science, 17.4% education, legal, community service, arts, and media, 5.2% healthcare practitioners, 24.2% service, 19.1% sales and office, 5.1% natural resources, construction, and maintenance, 7.0% production, transportation, and material moving
Income: Per capita: $26,404; Median household: $38,578; Average household: $50,651; Households with income of $100,000 or more: 12.0%; Poverty rate: 16.2%
Educational Attainment: High school diploma or higher: 95.1%; Bachelor's degree or higher: 45.7%; Graduate/professional degree or higher: 17.7%
Housing: Homeownership rate: 58.8%; Median home value: $114,300; Median year structure built: 1964; Homeowner vacancy rate: 1.8%; Median gross rent: $736 per month; Rental vacancy rate: 11.9%
Health Insurance: 86.4% have insurance; 76.4% have private insurance; 26.3% have public insurance; 13.6% do not have insurance; 0.0% of children under 18 do not have insurance
Transportation: Commute: 92.2% car, 3.4% public transportation, 1.6% walk, 1.3% work from home; Median travel time to work: 18.5 minutes

Kalkaska County

Located in northwest central Michigan; drained by the Manistee and Boardman Rivers; includes many lakes. Covers a land area of 559.865 square miles, a water area of 10.841 square miles, and is located in the Eastern Time Zone at 44.68° N. Lat., 85.09° W. Long. The county was founded in 1870. County seat is Kalkaska.

Kalkaska County is part of the Traverse City, MI Micropolitan Statistical Area. The entire metro area includes: Benzie County, MI; Grand Traverse County, MI; Kalkaska County, MI; Leelanau County, MI

Population: 17,153; Growth (since 2000): 3.5%; Density: 30.6 persons per square mile; Race: 96.8% White, 0.3% Black/African American, 0.2% Asian, 0.9% American Indian/Alaska Native, 0.0% Native Hawaiian/Other Pacific Islander, 1.6% two or more races, 1.2% Hispanic of any race; Average household size: 2.44; Median age: 43.0; Age under 18: 22.7%; Age 65 and over: 16.5%; Males per 100 females: 103.3; Marriage status: 22.6% never married, 55.6% now married, 1.4% separated, 6.3% widowed, 15.6% divorced; Foreign born: 1.0%; Speak English only: 98.3%; With disability: 17.0%; Veterans: 12.1%; Ancestry: 26.6% German, 15.5% English, 14.0% Irish, 7.0% Polish, 6.2% French
Religion: Six largest groups: 4.5% Catholicism, 4.2% Baptist, 2.0% Lutheran, 1.9% Methodist/Pietist, 1.7% Non-denominational Protestant, 1.2% Pentecostal
Economy: Unemployment rate: 6.6%; Leading industries: 15.9% retail trade; 12.3% construction; 11.7% other services (except public administration); Farms: 224 totaling 25,819 acres; Company size: 0 employ 1,000 or more persons, 0 employ 500 to 999 persons, 4 employ 100 to 499 persons, 330 employ less than 100 persons; Business ownership: 588 women-owned, n/a Black-owned, n/a Hispanic-owned, n/a Asian-owned
Employment: 7.7% management, business, and financial, 1.6% computer, engineering, and science, 6.7% education, legal, community service, arts, and media, 4.0% healthcare practitioners, 23.2% service, 24.6% sales and office, 13.6% natural resources, construction, and maintenance, 18.5% production, transportation, and material moving
Income: Per capita: $20,258; Median household: $40,140; Average household: $48,457; Households with income of $100,000 or more: 8.6%; Poverty rate: 16.3%
Educational Attainment: High school diploma or higher: 85.9%; Bachelor's degree or higher: 12.1%; Graduate/professional degree or higher: 4.6%
Housing: Homeownership rate: 82.6%; Median home value: $98,800; Median year structure built: 1980; Homeowner vacancy rate: 4.8%; Median gross rent: $692 per month; Rental vacancy rate: 11.5%
Vital Statistics: Birth rate: 86.1 per 10,000 population; Death rate: 91.9 per 10,000 population; Age-adjusted cancer mortality rate: 196.9 deaths per 100,000 population
Health Insurance: 84.4% have insurance; 60.0% have private insurance; 41.8% have public insurance; 15.6% do not have insurance; 6.5% of children under 18 do not have insurance
Health Care: Physicians: 4.7 per 10,000 population; Hospital beds: 56.1 per 10,000 population; Hospital admissions: 106.9 per 10,000 population
Transportation: Commute: 95.1% car, 0.1% public transportation, 1.3% walk, 2.5% work from home; Median travel time to work: 27.5 minutes
Presidential Election: 39.5% Obama, 59.1% Romney (2012)
National and State Parks: Kalkaska State Forest
Additional Information Contacts
Kalkaska Government . . . . (231) 258-3300
  http://www.kalkaskacounty.net

Kalkaska County Communities

BEAR LAKE (CDP). Covers a land area of 5.761 square miles and a water area of 0.660 square miles. Located at 44.72° N. Lat; 84.96° W. Long.
Population: 327; Growth (since 2000): n/a; Density: 56.8 persons per square mile; Race: 97.2% White, 0.0% Black/African American, 0.0% Asian, 0.9% American Indian/Alaska Native, 0.0% Native Hawaiian/Other Pacific Islander, 1.8% Two or more races, 1.5% Hispanic of any race; Average household size: 1.85; Median age: 60.7; Age under 18: 7.3%; Age 65 and over: 38.8%; Males per 100 females: 104.4
School District(s)
Bear Lake Schools (PK-12)
  2012-13 Enrollment: 355 . . . . (231) 864-3133
Housing: Homeownership rate: 93.8%; Homeowner vacancy rate: 5.1%; Rental vacancy rate: 38.1%

BEAR LAKE (township). Covers a land area of 71.086 square miles and a water area of 1.238 square miles. Located at 44.68° N. Lat; 84.90° W. Long.
Population: 667; Growth (since 2000): -10.6%; Density: 9.4 persons per square mile; Race: 97.8% White, 0.0% Black/African American, 0.0% Asian, 0.4% American Indian/Alaska Native, 0.0% Native Hawaiian/Other Pacific Islander, 1.8% Two or more races, 0.9% Hispanic of any race; Average household size: 1.93; Median age: 57.1; Age under 18: 10.5%; Age 65 and over: 32.7%; Males per 100 females: 107.1
Housing: Homeownership rate: 91.1%; Homeowner vacancy rate: 5.7%; Rental vacancy rate: 21.4%

BLUE LAKE (township). Covers a land area of 34.958 square miles and a water area of 1.271 square miles. Located at 44.81° N. Lat; 84.91° W. Long.
Population: 387; Growth (since 2000): -9.6%; Density: 11.1 persons per square mile; Race: 97.2% White, 0.5% Black/African American, 0.0% Asian, 0.0% American Indian/Alaska Native, 0.0% Native Hawaiian/Other Pacific Islander, 2.3% Two or more races, 0.5% Hispanic of any race; Average household size: 1.94; Median age: 59.4; Age under 18: 9.0%; Age 65 and over: 37.5%; Males per 100 females: 95.5
Housing: Homeownership rate: 92.9%; Homeowner vacancy rate: 3.1%; Rental vacancy rate: 36.4%

BOARDMAN (township). Covers a land area of 36.052 square miles and a water area of 0.180 square miles. Located at 44.65° N. Lat; 85.26° W. Long.
Population: 1,530; Growth (since 2000): 11.4%; Density: 42.4 persons per square mile; Race: 97.3% White, 0.5% Black/African American, 0.1% Asian, 1.2% American Indian/Alaska Native, 0.0% Native Hawaiian/Other Pacific Islander, 0.9% Two or more races, 0.6% Hispanic of any race; Average household size: 2.71; Median age: 37.8; Age under 18: 28.0%; Age 65 and over: 12.0%; Males per 100 females: 106.2
Housing: Homeownership rate: 82.8%; Homeowner vacancy rate: 4.1%; Rental vacancy rate: 11.8%

CLEARWATER (township). Covers a land area of 31.168 square miles and a water area of 2.623 square miles. Located at 44.81° N. Lat; 85.27° W. Long.
Population: 2,444; Growth (since 2000): 2.6%; Density: 78.4 persons per square mile; Race: 96.6% White, 0.2% Black/African American, 0.1% Asian, 0.5% American Indian/Alaska Native, 0.0% Native Hawaiian/Other Pacific Islander, 2.5% Two or more races, 0.9% Hispanic of any race; Average household size: 2.41; Median age: 45.1; Age under 18: 21.8%; Age 65 and over: 17.5%; Males per 100 females: 105.7
Housing: Homeownership rate: 84.7%; Homeowner vacancy rate: 3.8%; Rental vacancy rate: 14.8%

COLDSPRINGS (township). Covers a land area of 34.508 square miles and a water area of 1.761 square miles. Located at 44.81° N. Lat; 85.03° W. Long.
Population: 1,464; Growth (since 2000): 1.0%; Density: 42.4 persons per square mile; Race: 97.5% White, 0.4% Black/African American, 0.2% Asian, 0.7% American Indian/Alaska Native, 0.0% Native Hawaiian/Other Pacific Islander, 1.0% Two or more races, 0.8% Hispanic of any race; Average household size: 2.37; Median age: 48.7; Age under 18: 18.4%; Age 65 and over: 20.3%; Males per 100 females: 106.2
Housing: Homeownership rate: 92.2%; Homeowner vacancy rate: 3.6%; Rental vacancy rate: 22.6%

EXCELSIOR (township). Covers a land area of 35.325 square miles and a water area of 0.898 square miles. Located at 44.72° N. Lat; 85.04° W. Long.
Population: 953; Growth (since 2000): 11.5%; Density: 27.0 persons per square mile; Race: 97.7% White, 0.6% Black/African American, 0.1% Asian, 0.8% American Indian/Alaska Native, 0.0% Native Hawaiian/Other Pacific Islander, 0.7% Two or more races, 0.5% Hispanic of any race; Average household size: 2.44; Median age: 44.5; Age under 18: 21.6%; Age 65 and over: 17.1%; Males per 100 females: 104.5
Housing: Homeownership rate: 83.8%; Homeowner vacancy rate: 5.2%; Rental vacancy rate: 8.6%

GARFIELD (township). Covers a land area of 106.160 square miles and a water area of 0.572 square miles. Located at 44.56° N. Lat; 85.03° W. Long.

Population: 804; Growth (since 2000): 1.3%; Density: 7.6 persons per square mile; Race: 98.4% White, 0.0% Black/African American, 0.0% Asian, 0.7% American Indian/Alaska Native, 0.0% Native Hawaiian/Other Pacific Islander, 0.7% Two or more races, 0.7% Hispanic of any race; Average household size: 2.26; Median age: 48.3; Age under 18: 19.4%; Age 65 and over: 21.0%; Males per 100 females: 108.8

Housing: Homeownership rate: 89.9%; Homeowner vacancy rate: 4.5%; Rental vacancy rate: 7.7%

KALKASKA (township). Covers a land area of 70.439 square miles and a water area of 0.786 square miles. Located at 44.73° N. Lat; 85.21° W. Long. Elevation is 1,033 feet.

History: Incorporated 1887.

Population: 4,722; Growth (since 2000): -2.2%; Density: 67.0 persons per square mile; Race: 96.3% White, 0.3% Black/African American, 0.5% Asian, 1.0% American Indian/Alaska Native, 0.0% Native Hawaiian/Other Pacific Islander, 1.7% Two or more races, 1.7% Hispanic of any race; Average household size: 2.44; Median age: 38.9; Age under 18: 24.6%; Age 65 and over: 15.4%; Males per 100 females: 96.5; Marriage status: 23.6% never married, 49.7% now married, 2.6% separated, 9.1% widowed, 17.6% divorced; Foreign born: 0.8%; Speak English only: 98.7%; With disability: 16.9%; Veterans: 10.0%; Ancestry: 27.3% German, 18.6% Irish, 15.3% English, 7.3% Polish, 5.6% French

Employment: 7.9% management, business, and financial, 1.2% computer, engineering, and science, 6.6% education, legal, community service, arts, and media, 3.9% healthcare practitioners, 26.9% service, 25.9% sales and office, 12.0% natural resources, construction, and maintenance, 15.6% production, transportation, and material moving

Income: Per capita: $19,545; Median household: $40,246; Average household: $47,568; Households with income of $100,000 or more: 9.7%; Poverty rate: 11.9%

Educational Attainment: High school diploma or higher: 87.1%; Bachelor's degree or higher: 12.6%; Graduate/professional degree or higher: 4.2%

School District(s)
Excelsior Township S/d #1 (KG-12)
    2012-13 Enrollment: 45 . . . . (231) 258-8438
Kalkaska Public Schools (KG-12)
    2012-13 Enrollment: 1,597 . . . . (231) 258-9109

Housing: Homeownership rate: 70.1%; Median home value: $93,100; Median year structure built: 1978; Homeowner vacancy rate: 5.5%; Median gross rent: $639 per month; Rental vacancy rate: 9.1%

Health Insurance: 83.1% have insurance; 58.1% have private insurance; 37.7% have public insurance; 16.9% do not have insurance; 10.2% of children under 18 do not have insurance

Hospitals: Kalkaska Memorial Health Center

Newspapers: Leader & Kalkaskian (weekly circulation 3000)

Transportation: Commute: 94.8% car, 0.0% public transportation, 1.9% walk, 1.7% work from home; Median travel time to work: 23.6 minutes; Amtrak: Bus service available.

KALKASKA (village). County seat. Covers a land area of 3.116 square miles and a water area of 0.051 square miles. Located at 44.73° N. Lat; 85.18° W. Long. Elevation is 1,033 feet.

History: Kalkaska was first settled as a logging and railroad grading camp. In 1873, a tannery and sawmill were established, and the village became a supply center for the nearby farms. Later, Kalkaska developed as a resort area for fishermen and vacationers.

Population: 2,020; Growth (since 2000): -9.3%; Density: 648.3 persons per square mile; Race: 95.6% White, 0.6% Black/African American, 0.6% Asian, 1.3% American Indian/Alaska Native, 0.0% Native Hawaiian/Other Pacific Islander, 1.7% Two or more races, 1.8% Hispanic of any race; Average household size: 2.22; Median age: 37.9; Age under 18: 23.4%; Age 65 and over: 17.1%; Males per 100 females: 88.4

School District(s)
Excelsior Township S/d #1 (KG-12)
    2012-13 Enrollment: 45 . . . . (231) 258-8438
Kalkaska Public Schools (KG-12)
    2012-13 Enrollment: 1,597 . . . . (231) 258-9109

Housing: Homeownership rate: 50.0%; Homeowner vacancy rate: 9.3%; Rental vacancy rate: 7.6%

Hospitals: Kalkaska Memorial Health Center

Safety: Violent crime rate: 0.0 per 10,000 population; Property crime rate: 123.9 per 10,000 population

Newspapers: Leader & Kalkaskian (weekly circulation 3000)

MANISTEE LAKE (CDP). Covers a land area of 3.557 square miles and a water area of 1.378 square miles. Located at 44.78° N. Lat; 85.01° W. Long.

Population: 456; Growth (since 2000): n/a; Density: 128.2 persons per square mile; Race: 98.2% White, 0.4% Black/African American, 0.0% Asian, 0.2% American Indian/Alaska Native, 0.0% Native Hawaiian/Other Pacific Islander, 0.9% Two or more races, 1.1% Hispanic of any race; Average household size: 2.22; Median age: 50.5; Age under 18: 14.9%; Age 65 and over: 25.0%; Males per 100 females: 100.9

Housing: Homeownership rate: 87.8%; Homeowner vacancy rate: 3.7%; Rental vacancy rate: 33.3%

OLIVER (township). Covers a land area of 35.728 square miles and a water area of 0.313 square miles. Located at 44.64° N. Lat; 85.04° W. Long.

Population: 281; Growth (since 2000): 6.8%; Density: 7.9 persons per square mile; Race: 97.5% White, 0.0% Black/African American, 0.0% Asian, 1.8% American Indian/Alaska Native, 0.4% Native Hawaiian/Other Pacific Islander, 0.4% Two or more races, 0.4% Hispanic of any race; Average household size: 2.32; Median age: 43.9; Age under 18: 19.2%; Age 65 and over: 19.9%; Males per 100 females: 108.1

Housing: Homeownership rate: 88.4%; Homeowner vacancy rate: 7.8%; Rental vacancy rate: 0.0%

ORANGE (township). Covers a land area of 34.226 square miles and a water area of 0.584 square miles. Located at 44.65° N. Lat; 85.14° W. Long.

Population: 1,233; Growth (since 2000): 4.8%; Density: 36.0 persons per square mile; Race: 97.5% White, 0.1% Black/African American, 0.1% Asian, 0.6% American Indian/Alaska Native, 0.0% Native Hawaiian/Other Pacific Islander, 1.6% Two or more races, 1.8% Hispanic of any race; Average household size: 2.70; Median age: 39.5; Age under 18: 25.5%; Age 65 and over: 12.0%; Males per 100 females: 106.2

Housing: Homeownership rate: 86.8%; Homeowner vacancy rate: 3.2%; Rental vacancy rate: 7.6%

RAPID CITY (CDP). Covers a land area of 5.408 square miles and a water area of 0.090 square miles. Located at 44.84° N. Lat; 85.29° W. Long. Elevation is 630 feet.

Population: 1,352; Growth (since 2000): n/a; Density: 250.0 persons per square mile; Race: 95.0% White, 0.4% Black/African American, 0.1% Asian, 0.6% American Indian/Alaska Native, 0.0% Native Hawaiian/Other Pacific Islander, 3.8% Two or more races, 0.8% Hispanic of any race; Average household size: 2.38; Median age: 43.1; Age under 18: 23.1%; Age 65 and over: 17.1%; Males per 100 females: 103.0

School District(s)
Kalkaska Public Schools (KG-12)
    2012-13 Enrollment: 1,597 . . . . (231) 258-9109

Housing: Homeownership rate: 81.0%; Homeowner vacancy rate: 5.5%; Rental vacancy rate: 15.6%

RAPID RIVER (township). Covers a land area of 35.130 square miles and a water area of 0.124 square miles. Located at 44.82° N. Lat; 85.15° W. Long.

Population: 1,145; Growth (since 2000): 13.9%; Density: 32.6 persons per square mile; Race: 94.4% White, 0.1% Black/African American, 0.3% Asian, 2.4% American Indian/Alaska Native, 0.0% Native Hawaiian/Other Pacific Islander, 2.4% Two or more races, 1.9% Hispanic of any race; Average household size: 2.56; Median age: 38.4; Age under 18: 25.3%; Age 65 and over: 9.9%; Males per 100 females: 100.5

School District(s)
Rapid River Public Schools (KG-12)
    2012-13 Enrollment: 374 . . . . (906) 474-6411

Housing: Homeownership rate: 88.1%; Homeowner vacancy rate: 7.3%; Rental vacancy rate: 14.5%

SOUTH BOARDMAN (CDP). Covers a land area of 3.294 square miles and a water area of 0.041 square miles. Located at 44.64° N. Lat; 85.29° W. Long. Elevation is 1,007 feet.

Population: 536; Growth (since 2000): n/a; Density: 162.7 persons per square mile; Race: 96.6% White, 0.9% Black/African American, 0.0%

Asian, 1.7% American Indian/Alaska Native, 0.0% Native Hawaiian/Other Pacific Islander, 0.7% Two or more races, 0.6% Hispanic of any race; Average household size: 2.68; Median age: 37.7; Age under 18: 27.8%; Age 65 and over: 13.8%; Males per 100 females: 117.0

School District(s)

Forest Area Community Schools (PK-12)

2012-13 Enrollment: 614 . . . . (231) 369-4191

Housing: Homeownership rate: 71.5%; Homeowner vacancy rate: 3.4%; Rental vacancy rate: 14.9%

SPRINGFIELD (township). Covers a land area of 35.086 square miles and a water area of 0.494 square miles. Located at 44.55° N. Lat; 85.29° W. Long.

Population: 1,523; Growth (since 2000): 19.9%; Density: 43.4 persons per square mile; Race: 96.7% White, 0.5% Black/African American, 0.3% Asian, 0.3% American Indian/Alaska Native, 0.0% Native Hawaiian/Other Pacific Islander, 1.6% Two or more races, 1.8% Hispanic of any race; Average household size: 2.66; Median age: 40.5; Age under 18: 24.6%; Age 65 and over: 12.6%; Males per 100 females: 112.1

Housing: Homeownership rate: 86.9%; Homeowner vacancy rate: 4.8%; Rental vacancy rate: 8.6%

Kent County

Located in southwestern Michigan; crossed by the Grand River; drained by the Flat, Rogue, and Thornapple Rivers. Covers a land area of 846.948 square miles, a water area of 24.996 square miles, and is located in the Eastern Time Zone at 43.03° N. Lat., 85.55° W. Long. The county was founded in 1836. County seat is Grand Rapids.

Kent County is part of the Grand Rapids-Wyoming, MI Metropolitan Statistical Area. The entire metro area includes: Barry County, MI; Kent County, MI; Montcalm County, MI; Ottawa County, MI

Weather Station: Grand Rapids Kent County Intl   Elevation: 784 feet

	Jan	Feb	Mar	Apr	May	Jun	Jul	Aug	Sep	Oct	Nov	Dec
High	30	33	44	58	69	79	82	80	73	60	47	34
Low	17	19	26	37	47	57	61	60	52	41	32	22
Precip	2.1	1.8	2.4	3.3	3.9	3.6	3.8	3.6	4.3	3.2	3.4	2.5
Snow	20.9	14.2	8.3	2.0	tr	tr	tr	tr	tr	0.6	6.8	21.9

High and Low temperatures in degrees Fahrenheit; Precipitation and Snow in inches

Population: 602,622; Growth (since 2000): 4.9%; Density: 711.5 persons per square mile; Race: 79.9% White, 9.7% Black/African American, 2.3% Asian, 0.5% American Indian/Alaska Native, 0.0% Native Hawaiian/Other Pacific Islander, 3.0% two or more races, 9.7% Hispanic of any race; Average household size: 2.60; Median age: 34.4; Age under 18: 26.2%; Age 65 and over: 11.1%; Males per 100 females: 96.0; Marriage status: 32.9% never married, 52.0% now married, 1.5% separated, 4.8% widowed, 10.3% divorced; Foreign born: 7.3%; Speak English only: 88.7%; With disability: 10.7%; Veterans: 7.6%; Ancestry: 20.8% German, 18.9% Dutch, 11.5% Irish, 9.7% English, 8.1% Polish

Religion: Six largest groups: 19.0% Catholicism, 11.9% Presbyterian-Reformed, 9.3% Non-denominational Protestant, 2.8% Methodist/Pietist, 2.5% Lutheran, 2.2% Holiness

Economy: Unemployment rate: 4.0%; Leading industries: 13.7% retail trade; 10.6% professional, scientific, and technical services; 10.4% other services (except public administration); Farms: 1,159 totaling 157,493 acres; Company size: 21 employs 1,000 or more persons, 37 employ 500 to 999 persons, 494 employ 100 to 499 persons, 14,996 employ less than 100 persons; Business ownership: 15,469 women-owned, 3,127 Black-owned, 1,034 Hispanic-owned, 1,439 Asian-owned

Employment: 14.1% management, business, and financial, 4.9% computer, engineering, and science, 10.5% education, legal, community service, arts, and media, 5.7% healthcare practitioners, 16.4% service, 25.4% sales and office, 7.0% natural resources, construction, and maintenance, 16.1% production, transportation, and material moving

Income: Per capita: $25,889; Median household: $51,667; Average household: $67,629; Households with income of $100,000 or more: 18.7%; Poverty rate: 15.5%

Educational Attainment: High school diploma or higher: 89.4%; Bachelor's degree or higher: 31.7%; Graduate/professional degree or higher: 10.7%

Housing: Homeownership rate: 69.6%; Median home value: $137,500; Median year structure built: 1972; Homeowner vacancy rate: 2.2%; Median gross rent: $745 per month; Rental vacancy rate: 10.3%

Vital Statistics: Birth rate: 143.3 per 10,000 population; Death rate: 69.8 per 10,000 population; Age-adjusted cancer mortality rate: 167.9 deaths per 100,000 population

Health Insurance: 89.4% have insurance; 72.2% have private insurance; 28.7% have public insurance; 10.6% do not have insurance; 3.4% of children under 18 do not have insurance

Health Care: Physicians: 33.4 per 10,000 population; Hospital beds: 37.3 per 10,000 population; Hospital admissions: 1,581.3 per 10,000 population

Air Quality Index: 73.2% good, 26.3% moderate, 0.5% unhealthy for sensitive individuals, 0.0% unhealthy (percent of days)

Transportation: Commute: 91.2% car, 1.7% public transportation, 1.7% walk, 4.2% work from home; Median travel time to work: 21.1 minutes

Presidential Election: 45.5% Obama, 53.4% Romney (2012)

National and State Parks: Cannonsburg State Game Area; Rogue River State Game Area

Additional Information Contacts

Kent Government . . . . (616) 632-7590
http://www.co.kent.mi.us

Kent County Communities

ADA (township). Covers a land area of 36.036 square miles and a water area of 1.077 square miles. Located at 42.98° N. Lat; 85.49° W. Long. Elevation is 640 feet.

History: Ada was founded in 1821 as a trading post and sawmill site. It later became a trading center for a farming area. Both the township and the town of Ada were named for Ada Smith, the daughter of the first postmaster in 1837.

Population: 13,142; Growth (since 2000): 33.0%; Density: 364.7 persons per square mile; Race: 93.3% White, 1.0% Black/African American, 3.6% Asian, 0.2% American Indian/Alaska Native, 0.0% Native Hawaiian/Other Pacific Islander, 1.6% Two or more races, 1.7% Hispanic of any race; Average household size: 2.95; Median age: 39.8; Age under 18: 31.3%; Age 65 and over: 9.2%; Males per 100 females: 97.8; Marriage status: 19.6% never married, 72.7% now married, 0.0% separated, 2.8% widowed, 5.0% divorced; Foreign born: 5.5%; Speak English only: 93.4%; With disability: 5.0%; Veterans: 6.2%; Ancestry: 26.8% German, 24.0% Dutch, 14.9% Irish, 13.0% English, 6.4% Polish

Employment: 28.2% management, business, and financial, 5.5% computer, engineering, and science, 11.2% education, legal, community service, arts, and media, 10.6% healthcare practitioners, 11.0% service, 26.8% sales and office, 3.1% natural resources, construction, and maintenance, 3.6% production, transportation, and material moving

Income: Per capita: $47,925; Median household: $112,466; Average household: $144,485; Households with income of $100,000 or more: 56.8%; Poverty rate: 2.7%

Educational Attainment: High school diploma or higher: 99.0%; Bachelor's degree or higher: 59.1%; Graduate/professional degree or higher: 24.5%

School District(s)

Forest Hills Public Schools (PK-12)

2012-13 Enrollment: 10,101 . . . . (616) 493-8800

Housing: Homeownership rate: 92.0%; Median home value: $260,000; Median year structure built: 1988; Homeowner vacancy rate: 1.2%; Median gross rent: $1,474 per month; Rental vacancy rate: 9.1%

Health Insurance: 97.4% have insurance; 93.1% have private insurance; 13.5% have public insurance; 2.6% do not have insurance; 2.0% of children under 18 do not have insurance

Transportation: Commute: 93.2% car, 0.7% public transportation, 0.6% walk, 4.7% work from home; Median travel time to work: 20.4 minutes

Additional Information Contacts

Ada Township . . . . (616) 676-9191
http://www.ada.mi.us

ALGOMA (township). Covers a land area of 34.129 square miles and a water area of 0.796 square miles. Located at 43.16° N. Lat; 85.62° W. Long.

History: Algoma Township was organized in 1849 and named for a steamer, the "Algoma," which operated on the Grand River between Grand Rapids and Grand Haven.

Population: 9,932; Growth (since 2000): 30.8%; Density: 291.0 persons per square mile; Race: 96.8% White, 0.4% Black/African American, 0.7% Asian, 0.2% American Indian/Alaska Native, 0.0% Native Hawaiian/Other Pacific Islander, 1.3% Two or more races, 2.0% Hispanic of any race; Average household size: 2.89; Median age: 38.6; Age under 18: 28.5%;

Age 65 and over: 9.8%; Males per 100 females: 98.8; Marriage status: 18.2% never married, 71.6% now married, 1.1% separated, 3.4% widowed, 6.8% divorced; Foreign born: 1.1%; Speak English only: 97.9%; With disability: 10.9%; Veterans: 11.0%; Ancestry: 26.8% German, 18.1% Dutch, 16.8% Irish, 12.4% English, 8.4% Polish

Employment: 18.6% management, business, and financial, 3.7% computer, engineering, and science, 13.4% education, legal, community service, arts, and media, 6.6% healthcare practitioners, 6.8% service, 30.0% sales and office, 6.2% natural resources, construction, and maintenance, 14.7% production, transportation, and material moving

Income: Per capita: $29,507; Median household: $77,534; Average household: $85,345; Households with income of $100,000 or more: 30.4%; Poverty rate: 8.3%

Educational Attainment: High school diploma or higher: 96.7%; Bachelor's degree or higher: 35.2%; Graduate/professional degree or higher: 10.7%

Housing: Homeownership rate: 94.7%; Median home value: $173,400; Median year structure built: 1992; Homeowner vacancy rate: 1.1%; Median gross rent: $811 per month; Rental vacancy rate: 10.8%

Health Insurance: 93.5% have insurance; 84.2% have private insurance; 24.1% have public insurance; 6.5% do not have insurance; 4.4% of children under 18 do not have insurance

Transportation: Commute: 93.0% car, 0.3% public transportation, 1.0% walk, 5.4% work from home; Median travel time to work: 25.2 minutes

Additional Information Contacts

Algoma Township . . . . (616) 866-1583
  http://www.algomatwp.org

ALPINE (township). Covers a land area of 35.903 square miles and a water area of 0.310 square miles. Located at 43.07° N. Lat; 85.73° W. Long. Elevation is 758 feet.

History: Alpine Township was organized in 1847 and named for the pine trees that grew in the area.

Population: 13,336; Growth (since 2000): -4.6%; Density: 371.4 persons per square mile; Race: 81.9% White, 6.2% Black/African American, 1.0% Asian, 0.6% American Indian/Alaska Native, 0.0% Native Hawaiian/Other Pacific Islander, 3.6% Two or more races, 13.0% Hispanic of any race; Average household size: 2.52; Median age: 32.6; Age under 18: 25.8%; Age 65 and over: 10.7%; Males per 100 females: 95.6; Marriage status: 38.3% never married, 45.2% now married, 0.7% separated, 5.3% widowed, 11.2% divorced; Foreign born: 7.7%; Speak English only: 85.9%; With disability: 10.9%; Veterans: 7.5%; Ancestry: 21.4% German, 13.1% Dutch, 12.3% Polish, 8.6% Irish, 6.4% English

Employment: 8.3% management, business, and financial, 3.3% computer, engineering, and science, 5.3% education, legal, community service, arts, and media, 2.7% healthcare practitioners, 21.1% service, 31.0% sales and office, 9.0% natural resources, construction, and maintenance, 19.2% production, transportation, and material moving

Income: Per capita: $22,538; Median household: $43,252; Average household: $56,977; Households with income of $100,000 or more: 14.8%; Poverty rate: 19.9%

Educational Attainment: High school diploma or higher: 85.2%; Bachelor's degree or higher: 18.3%; Graduate/professional degree or higher: 5.4%

Housing: Homeownership rate: 58.3%; Median home value: $127,200; Median year structure built: 1979; Homeowner vacancy rate: 1.9%; Median gross rent: $682 per month; Rental vacancy rate: 14.7%

Health Insurance: 83.8% have insurance; 61.4% have private insurance; 33.7% have public insurance; 16.2% do not have insurance; 3.7% of children under 18 do not have insurance

Transportation: Commute: 90.6% car, 0.9% public transportation, 1.6% walk, 5.4% work from home; Median travel time to work: 19.6 minutes

Additional Information Contacts

Alpine Township . . . . (616) 784-1262
  http://www.alpinetwp.org

ALTO (unincorporated postal area)
ZCTA: 49302

Covers a land area of 48.760 square miles and a water area of 0.903 square miles. Located at 42.82° N. Lat; 85.40° W. Long. Elevation is 814 feet.

Population: 7,585; Growth (since 2000): 17.3%; Density: 155.6 persons per square mile; Race: 96.2% White, 0.6% Black/African American, 1.0% Asian, 0.3% American Indian/Alaska Native, 0.0% Native Hawaiian/Other Pacific Islander, 1.1% Two or more races, 2.2%

Hispanic of any race; Average household size: 2.94; Median age: 39.7; Age under 18: 28.1%; Age 65 and over: 9.2%; Males per 100 females: 105.7; Marriage status: 20.0% never married, 68.6% now married, 0.2% separated, 3.5% widowed, 7.9% divorced; Foreign born: 2.9%; Speak English only: 96.2%; With disability: 8.3%; Veterans: 9.8%; Ancestry: 29.2% German, 21.0% Dutch, 12.4% English, 12.2% Irish, 8.4% Polish

Employment: 16.2% management, business, and financial, 4.4% computer, engineering, and science, 11.1% education, legal, community service, arts, and media, 6.5% healthcare practitioners, 11.8% service, 27.4% sales and office, 9.9% natural resources, construction, and maintenance, 12.7% production, transportation, and material moving

Income: Per capita: $28,436; Median household: $75,616; Average household: $85,666; Households with income of $100,000 or more: 30.7%; Poverty rate: 7.1%

Educational Attainment: High school diploma or higher: 95.0%; Bachelor's degree or higher: 35.2%; Graduate/professional degree or higher: 11.4%

School District(s)

Caledonia Community Schools (KG-12)
  2012-13 Enrollment: 4,368 . . . . (616) 891-8185
Lowell Area Schools (PK-12)
  2012-13 Enrollment: 3,799 . . . . (616) 987-2500

Housing: Homeownership rate: 93.1%; Median home value: $208,900; Median year structure built: 1982; Homeowner vacancy rate: 1.3%; Median gross rent: $1,019 per month; Rental vacancy rate: 5.9%

Health Insurance: 92.9% have insurance; 84.6% have private insurance; 17.9% have public insurance; 7.1% do not have insurance; 0.5% of children under 18 do not have insurance

Transportation: Commute: 94.7% car, 0.0% public transportation, 0.2% walk, 4.7% work from home; Median travel time to work: 25.7 minutes

---

BELMONT (unincorporated postal area)
ZCTA: 49306

Covers a land area of 19.812 square miles and a water area of 0.495 square miles. Located at 43.08° N. Lat; 85.57° W. Long. Elevation is 663 feet.

Population: 9,244; Growth (since 2000): 15.4%; Density: 466.6 persons per square mile; Race: 96.0% White, 0.5% Black/African American, 1.1% Asian, 0.3% American Indian/Alaska Native, 0.0% Native Hawaiian/Other Pacific Islander, 1.4% Two or more races, 2.2% Hispanic of any race; Average household size: 2.72; Median age: 41.6; Age under 18: 25.9%; Age 65 and over: 12.4%; Males per 100 females: 99.8; Marriage status: 23.0% never married, 64.5% now married, 0.1% separated, 3.3% widowed, 9.2% divorced; Foreign born: 2.6%; Speak English only: 96.4%; With disability: 7.7%; Veterans: 8.2%; Ancestry: 24.9% Dutch, 22.7% German, 17.3% Irish, 16.0% English, 8.7% Polish

Employment: 18.9% management, business, and financial, 3.7% computer, engineering, and science, 11.5% education, legal, community service, arts, and media, 8.5% healthcare practitioners, 13.9% service, 25.4% sales and office, 4.8% natural resources, construction, and maintenance, 13.4% production, transportation, and material moving

Income: Per capita: $32,425; Median household: $76,550; Average household: $93,050; Households with income of $100,000 or more: 31.8%; Poverty rate: 5.5%

Educational Attainment: High school diploma or higher: 95.1%; Bachelor's degree or higher: 35.9%; Graduate/professional degree or higher: 13.5%

School District(s)

Chandler Woods Charter Academy (KG-12)
  2012-13 Enrollment: 693 . . . . (616) 866-6000
Rockford Public Schools (PK-12)
  2012-13 Enrollment: 7,921 . . . . (616) 863-6557

Housing: Homeownership rate: 94.9%; Median home value: $172,200; Median year structure built: 1990; Homeowner vacancy rate: 1.4%; Median gross rent: $668 per month; Rental vacancy rate: 8.1%

Health Insurance: 94.2% have insurance; 87.9% have private insurance; 17.8% have public insurance; 5.8% do not have insurance; 1.0% of children under 18 do not have insurance

Transportation: Commute: 90.6% car, 0.0% public transportation, 1.1% walk, 7.4% work from home; Median travel time to work: 22.5 minutes

BOWNE (township). Covers a land area of 35.530 square miles and a water area of 0.496 square miles. Located at 42.82° N. Lat; 85.38° W. Long.

Population: 3,084; Growth (since 2000): 12.4%; Density: 86.8 persons per square mile; Race: 95.9% White, 0.6% Black/African American, 0.8% Asian, 0.3% American Indian/Alaska Native, 0.0% Native Hawaiian/Other Pacific Islander, 1.1% Two or more races, 3.2% Hispanic of any race; Average household size: 3.04; Median age: 38.5; Age under 18: 28.6%; Age 65 and over: 9.1%; Males per 100 females: 102.9; Marriage status: 25.7% never married, 68.2% now married, 1.0% separated, 2.1% widowed, 3.9% divorced; Foreign born: 3.8%; Speak English only: 94.8%; With disability: 5.7%; Veterans: 7.8%; Ancestry: 25.2% German, 22.0% Dutch, 10.3% English, 6.3% American

Employment: 14.8% management, business, and financial, 4.4% computer, engineering, and science, 11.5% education, legal, community service, arts, and media, 3.8% healthcare practitioners, 13.0% service, 21.8% sales and office, 12.9% natural resources, construction, and maintenance, 18.0% production, transportation, and material moving

Income: Per capita: $26,447; Median household: $75,852; Average household: $80,011; Households with income of $100,000 or more: 26.4%; Poverty rate: 9.4%

Educational Attainment: High school diploma or higher: 95.1%; Bachelor's degree or higher: 30.1%; Graduate/professional degree or higher: 9.4%

Housing: Homeownership rate: 91.7%; Median home value: $198,800; Median year structure built: 1977; Homeowner vacancy rate: 1.2%; Median gross rent: $728 per month; Rental vacancy rate: 5.7%

Health Insurance: 91.3% have insurance; 85.1% have private insurance; 15.5% have public insurance; 8.7% do not have insurance; 0.3% of children under 18 do not have insurance

Transportation: Commute: 94.2% car, 0.0% public transportation, 0.6% walk, 4.2% work from home; Median travel time to work: 27.3 minutes

BYRON (township). Covers a land area of 36.098 square miles and a water area of 0.074 square miles. Located at 42.81° N. Lat; 85.72° W. Long. Elevation is 748 feet.

History: Byron Township was organized in 1836.

Population: 20,317; Growth (since 2000): 15.7%; Density: 562.8 persons per square mile; Race: 92.8% White, 1.6% Black/African American, 1.6% Asian, 0.5% American Indian/Alaska Native, 0.0% Native Hawaiian/Other Pacific Islander, 1.9% Two or more races, 4.2% Hispanic of any race; Average household size: 2.68; Median age: 38.8; Age under 18: 26.3%; Age 65 and over: 14.1%; Males per 100 females: 98.4; Marriage status: 23.7% never married, 62.7% now married, 1.2% separated, 4.8% widowed, 8.7% divorced; Foreign born: 4.2%; Speak English only: 93.4%; With disability: 10.0%; Veterans: 9.6%; Ancestry: 37.3% Dutch, 23.4% German, 11.7% Irish, 8.5% English, 5.1% Polish

Employment: 15.4% management, business, and financial, 5.6% computer, engineering, and science, 8.3% education, legal, community service, arts, and media, 4.3% healthcare practitioners, 13.5% service, 26.1% sales and office, 10.8% natural resources, construction, and maintenance, 16.0% production, transportation, and material moving

Income: Per capita: $26,917; Median household: $57,310; Average household: $74,324; Households with income of $100,000 or more: 22.4%; Poverty rate: 9.9%

Educational Attainment: High school diploma or higher: 90.7%; Bachelor's degree or higher: 28.4%; Graduate/professional degree or higher: 8.0%

Housing: Homeownership rate: 83.1%; Median home value: $160,800; Median year structure built: 1991; Homeowner vacancy rate: 1.7%; Median gross rent: $804 per month; Rental vacancy rate: 12.0%

Health Insurance: 93.3% have insurance; 79.2% have private insurance; 27.4% have public insurance; 6.7% do not have insurance; 2.9% of children under 18 do not have insurance

Transportation: Commute: 94.5% car, 0.2% public transportation, 0.9% walk, 2.9% work from home; Median travel time to work: 21.6 minutes

Additional Information Contacts
Byron Township. . . . . (616) 878-9066
http://www.byrontownship.org

BYRON CENTER (CDP). Covers a land area of 5.083 square miles and a water area of 0.018 square miles. Located at 42.81° N. Lat; 85.73° W. Long. Elevation is 748 feet.

Population: 5,822; Growth (since 2000): 54.1%; Density: 1,145.3 persons per square mile; Race: 95.6% White, 0.9% Black/African American, 1.0%

Asian, 0.4% American Indian/Alaska Native, 0.0% Native Hawaiian/Other Pacific Islander, 1.4% Two or more races, 2.7% Hispanic of any race; Average household size: 2.84; Median age: 37.9; Age under 18: 30.7%; Age 65 and over: 13.9%; Males per 100 females: 94.4; Marriage status: 21.3% never married, 67.6% now married, 0.7% separated, 6.3% widowed, 4.8% divorced; Foreign born: 4.6%; Speak English only: 94.9%; With disability: 7.6%; Veterans: 9.4%; Ancestry: 40.8% Dutch, 22.9% German, 12.8% English, 9.7% Irish, 8.8% Polish

Employment: 17.4% management, business, and financial, 7.3% computer, engineering, and science, 10.2% education, legal, community service, arts, and media, 3.5% healthcare practitioners, 15.6% service, 29.0% sales and office, 5.3% natural resources, construction, and maintenance, 11.7% production, transportation, and material moving

Income: Per capita: $29,140; Median household: $66,915; Average household: $83,140; Households with income of $100,000 or more: 23.7%; Poverty rate: 9.0%

Educational Attainment: High school diploma or higher: 92.3%; Bachelor's degree or higher: 37.1%; Graduate/professional degree or higher: 11.3%

School District(s)
Byron Center Charter School (KG-12)
    2012-13 Enrollment: 258. . . . . (616) 878-4852
Byron Center Public Schools (PK-12)
    2012-13 Enrollment: 3,571. (616) 878-6100
Cross Creek Charter Academy (KG-12)
    2012-13 Enrollment: 758. . . . . (616) 656-4000

Housing: Homeownership rate: 87.8%; Median home value: $185,200; Median year structure built: 1999; Homeowner vacancy rate: 1.0%; Median gross rent: $1,156 per month; Rental vacancy rate: 10.6%

Health Insurance: 92.2% have insurance; 81.3% have private insurance; 24.4% have public insurance; 7.8% do not have insurance; 7.3% of children under 18 do not have insurance

Transportation: Commute: 92.2% car, 0.0% public transportation, 1.2% walk, 4.3% work from home; Median travel time to work: 20.0 minutes

CALEDONIA (township). Covers a land area of 34.913 square miles and a water area of 0.784 square miles. Located at 42.80° N. Lat; 85.50° W. Long. Elevation is 814 feet.

Population: 12,332; Growth (since 2000): 37.6%; Density: 353.2 persons per square mile; Race: 95.2% White, 1.2% Black/African American, 1.2% Asian, 0.3% American Indian/Alaska Native, 0.0% Native Hawaiian/Other Pacific Islander, 1.6% Two or more races, 2.3% Hispanic of any race; Average household size: 2.80; Median age: 37.8; Age under 18: 28.0%; Age 65 and over: 10.1%; Males per 100 females: 102.4; Marriage status: 22.4% never married, 65.8% now married, 0.5% separated, 3.6% widowed, 8.2% divorced; Foreign born: 3.6%; Speak English only: 94.8%; With disability: 8.1%; Veterans: 8.6%; Ancestry: 29.3% German, 20.6% Dutch, 13.5% Irish, 13.3% English, 7.9% Polish

Employment: 18.0% management, business, and financial, 5.9% computer, engineering, and science, 9.5% education, legal, community service, arts, and media, 10.0% healthcare practitioners, 11.5% service, 24.6% sales and office, 6.9% natural resources, construction, and maintenance, 13.5% production, transportation, and material moving

Income: Per capita: $29,959; Median household: $78,690; Average household: $85,635; Households with income of $100,000 or more: 30.7%; Poverty rate: 4.1%

Educational Attainment: High school diploma or higher: 94.7%; Bachelor's degree or higher: 37.4%; Graduate/professional degree or higher: 12.0%

School District(s)
Caledonia Community Schools (KG-12)
    2012-13 Enrollment: 4,368 . . . . (616) 891-8185
Kentwood Public Schools (PK-12)
    2012-13 Enrollment: 8,718 . . . . (616) 455-4400

Housing: Homeownership rate: 89.1%; Median home value: $198,000; Median year structure built: 1992; Homeowner vacancy rate: 1.8%; Median gross rent: $798 per month; Rental vacancy rate: 6.2%

Health Insurance: 95.2% have insurance; 88.8% have private insurance; 16.5% have public insurance; 4.8% do not have insurance; 1.7% of children under 18 do not have insurance

Transportation: Commute: 92.3% car, 0.0% public transportation, 2.8% walk, 4.5% work from home; Median travel time to work: 22.9 minutes

Additional Information Contacts
Caledonia Charter Township. . . . . (616) 891-0070
http://www.caledoniatownship.org

CALEDONIA (village). Covers a land area of 1.327 square miles and a water area of 0.080 square miles. Located at 42.79° N. Lat; 85.52° W. Long. Elevation is 814 feet.

History: Caledonia was settled in 1838 and named for Caledonia, New York. The village was incorporated in 1888.

Population: 1,511; Growth (since 2000): 37.1%; Density: 1,138.4 persons per square mile; Race: 96.8% White, 0.7% Black/African American, 0.7% Asian, 0.1% American Indian/Alaska Native, 0.0% Native Hawaiian/Other Pacific Islander, 1.0% Two or more races, 2.7% Hispanic of any race; Average household size: 2.86; Median age: 30.7; Age under 18: 34.9%; Age 65 and over: 5.8%; Males per 100 females: 98.0

School District(s)

Caledonia Community Schools (KG-12)

    2012-13 Enrollment: 4,368 . . . . (616) 891-8185

Kentwood Public Schools (PK-12)

    2012-13 Enrollment: 8,718 . . . . (616) 455-4400

Housing: Homeownership rate: 74.7%; Homeowner vacancy rate: 1.0%; Rental vacancy rate: 5.6%

CANNON (township). Covers a land area of 35.260 square miles and a water area of 1.712 square miles. Located at 43.08° N. Lat; 85.49° W. Long.

History: The township took its name from the small settlement of Cannonsburgh, which had been founded in 1842 at the direction of LeGrand Cannon, described as an eastern capitalist.

Population: 13,336; Growth (since 2000): 10.4%; Density: 378.2 persons per square mile; Race: 96.3% White, 0.7% Black/African American, 0.8% Asian, 0.2% American Indian/Alaska Native, 0.1% Native Hawaiian/Other Pacific Islander, 1.5% Two or more races, 1.8% Hispanic of any race; Average household size: 2.91; Median age: 40.5; Age under 18: 30.1%; Age 65 and over: 8.8%; Males per 100 females: 99.6; Marriage status: 22.6% never married, 66.7% now married, 0.4% separated, 2.4% widowed, 8.4% divorced; Foreign born: 3.1%; Speak English only: 94.7%; With disability: 5.6%; Veterans: 6.8%; Ancestry: 28.5% German, 20.6% Dutch, 19.9% English, 17.4% Irish, 8.0% Polish

Employment: 23.1% management, business, and financial, 5.8% computer, engineering, and science, 11.8% education, legal, community service, arts, and media, 7.7% healthcare practitioners, 12.8% service, 25.9% sales and office, 5.6% natural resources, construction, and maintenance, 7.3% production, transportation, and material moving

Income: Per capita: $34,959; Median household: $89,452; Average household: $106,137; Households with income of $100,000 or more: 45.0%; Poverty rate: 4.9%

Educational Attainment: High school diploma or higher: 96.9%; Bachelor's degree or higher: 48.6%; Graduate/professional degree or higher: 18.9%

Housing: Homeownership rate: 93.0%; Median home value: $223,300; Median year structure built: 1991; Homeowner vacancy rate: 1.2%; Median gross rent: $1,137 per month; Rental vacancy rate: 5.8%

Health Insurance: 95.8% have insurance; 91.4% have private insurance; 15.1% have public insurance; 4.2% do not have insurance; 1.2% of children under 18 do not have insurance

Transportation: Commute: 93.4% car, 0.2% public transportation, 0.9% walk, 5.1% work from home; Median travel time to work: 25.7 minutes

Additional Information Contacts

Cannon Township . . . . (616) 874-6966

    http://www.cannontwp.org

CASCADE (charter township). Covers a land area of 33.884 square miles and a water area of 0.972 square miles. Located at 42.90° N. Lat; 85.49° W. Long. Elevation is 666 feet.

History: Mineral springs in the Cascade area attracted health seekers when they were first discovered, but soon the springs undermined the hotel and it collapsed. The area developed as a residential suburb of Grand Rapids.

Population: 17,134; Growth (since 2000): 13.4%; Density: 505.7 persons per square mile; Race: 93.5% White, 1.5% Black/African American, 3.1% Asian, 0.2% American Indian/Alaska Native, 0.0% Native Hawaiian/Other Pacific Islander, 1.3% Two or more races, 1.9% Hispanic of any race; Average household size: 2.72; Median age: 43.3; Age under 18: 28.0%; Age 65 and over: 14.5%; Males per 100 females: 97.3; Marriage status: 17.8% never married, 71.4% now married, 0.4% separated, 4.6% widowed, 6.2% divorced; Foreign born: 6.1%; Speak English only: 93.2%; With disability: 6.7%; Veterans: 8.1%; Ancestry: 28.4% German, 15.9% Dutch, 15.8% Irish, 15.7% English, 6.8% Polish

Employment: 26.6% management, business, and financial, 6.2% computer, engineering, and science, 14.1% education, legal, community service, arts, and media, 11.1% healthcare practitioners, 8.2% service, 23.6% sales and office, 2.1% natural resources, construction, and maintenance, 8.1% production, transportation, and material moving

Income: Per capita: $50,936; Median household: $101,273; Average household: $139,009; Households with income of $100,000 or more: 51.3%; Poverty rate: 2.4%

Educational Attainment: High school diploma or higher: 97.8%; Bachelor's degree or higher: 63.8%; Graduate/professional degree or higher: 28.5%

Housing: Homeownership rate: 92.2%; Median home value: $258,500; Median year structure built: 1983; Homeowner vacancy rate: 1.4%; Median gross rent: $1,281 per month; Rental vacancy rate: 11.8%

Health Insurance: 95.3% have insurance; 89.1% have private insurance; 18.7% have public insurance; 4.7% do not have insurance; 1.9% of children under 18 do not have insurance

Transportation: Commute: 92.0% car, 0.1% public transportation, 0.5% walk, 6.6% work from home; Median travel time to work: 20.0 minutes

Additional Information Contacts

Cascade Township . . . . (616) 949-1500

    http://www.cascadetwp.com

CASNOVIA (village). Covers a land area of 1.078 square miles and a water area of 0.009 square miles. Located at 43.23° N. Lat; 85.79° W. Long. Elevation is 899 feet.

Population: 319; Growth (since 2000): 1.3%; Density: 296.1 persons per square mile; Race: 88.4% White, 0.3% Black/African American, 0.0% Asian, 1.9% American Indian/Alaska Native, 0.0% Native Hawaiian/Other Pacific Islander, 5.0% Two or more races, 11.6% Hispanic of any race; Average household size: 2.64; Median age: 41.9; Age under 18: 22.3%; Age 65 and over: 12.9%; Males per 100 females: 103.2

Housing: Homeownership rate: 82.6%; Homeowner vacancy rate: 3.8%; Rental vacancy rate: 8.7%

CEDAR SPRINGS (city). Covers a land area of 2.029 square miles and a water area of 0.066 square miles. Located at 43.22° N. Lat; 85.55° W. Long. Elevation is 856 feet.

History: Cedar Springs was settled in 1855 and platted in 1859. On the Grand Rapids & Indiana Railroad after 1868, Cedar Springs developed as a summer resort.

Population: 3,509; Growth (since 2000): 12.8%; Density: 1,729.3 persons per square mile; Race: 94.3% White, 0.8% Black/African American, 0.4% Asian, 0.6% American Indian/Alaska Native, 0.0% Native Hawaiian/Other Pacific Islander, 3.0% Two or more races, 4.2% Hispanic of any race; Average household size: 2.81; Median age: 29.6; Age under 18: 32.9%; Age 65 and over: 9.9%; Males per 100 females: 89.1; Marriage status: 28.7% never married, 48.8% now married, 2.9% separated, 4.9% widowed, 17.6% divorced; Foreign born: 0.8%; Speak English only: 97.7%; With disability: 16.7%; Veterans: 10.2%; Ancestry: 25.3% German, 14.7% Dutch, 13.2% Irish, 11.0% English, 8.2% Polish

Employment: 8.0% management, business, and financial, 2.5% computer, engineering, and science, 4.1% education, legal, community service, arts, and media, 3.7% healthcare practitioners, 19.2% service, 24.5% sales and office, 12.4% natural resources, construction, and maintenance, 25.7% production, transportation, and material moving

Income: Per capita: $16,449; Median household: $37,025; Average household: $42,074; Households with income of $100,000 or more: 5.0%; Poverty rate: 20.2%

Educational Attainment: High school diploma or higher: 84.6%; Bachelor's degree or higher: 11.5%; Graduate/professional degree or higher: 2.3%

School District(s)

Cedar Springs Public Schools (PK-12)

    2012-13 Enrollment: 3,374 . . . . (616) 696-1204

Creative Technologies Academy (KG-12)

    2012-13 Enrollment: 300. . . . . (616) 696-4905

Housing: Homeownership rate: 62.5%; Median home value: $87,800; Median year structure built: 1974; Homeowner vacancy rate: 1.5%; Median gross rent: $732 per month; Rental vacancy rate: 6.3%

Health Insurance: 79.8% have insurance; 55.0% have private insurance; 40.6% have public insurance; 20.2% do not have insurance; 12.9% of children under 18 do not have insurance

Safety: Violent crime rate: 36.5 per 10,000 population; Property crime rate: 252.5 per 10,000 population

Newspapers: Cedar Springs Post (weekly circulation 5000)
Transportation: Commute: 97.3% car, 0.0% public transportation, 0.4% walk, 2.3% work from home; Median travel time to work: 26.0 minutes
Additional Information Contacts
City of Cedar Springs . . . . (616) 696-1330
  http://www.cityofcedarsprings.org

COMSTOCK PARK (CDP). Covers a land area of 3.880 square miles and a water area of 0.009 square miles. Located at 43.04° N. Lat; 85.68° W. Long. Elevation is 659 feet.

History: Previously known as North Park and Mill Creek, Comstock Park was renamed in 1906 for Charles C. Comstock, a congressional representative from the district.
Population: 10,088; Growth (since 2000): -5.5%; Density: 2,600.2 persons per square mile; Race: 78.7% White, 8.0% Black/African American, 1.2% Asian, 0.7% American Indian/Alaska Native, 0.0% Native Hawaiian/Other Pacific Islander, 4.0% Two or more races, 14.3% Hispanic of any race; Average household size: 2.42; Median age: 30.8; Age under 18: 25.8%; Age 65 and over: 9.5%; Males per 100 females: 93.4; Marriage status: 39.0% never married, 43.3% now married, 0.9% separated, 5.1% widowed, 12.6% divorced; Foreign born: 9.1%; Speak English only: 82.8%; With disability: 11.1%; Veterans: 7.4%; Ancestry: 17.8% German, 12.3% Dutch, 10.9% Polish, 9.3% Irish, 5.7% American
Employment: 7.5% management, business, and financial, 3.9% computer, engineering, and science, 4.8% education, legal, community service, arts, and media, 1.7% healthcare practitioners, 24.7% service, 31.1% sales and office, 7.0% natural resources, construction, and maintenance, 19.2% production, transportation, and material moving
Income: Per capita: $21,095; Median household: $39,177; Average household: $51,460; Households with income of $100,000 or more: 12.6%; Poverty rate: 22.3%
Educational Attainment: High school diploma or higher: 84.7%; Bachelor's degree or higher: 18.6%; Graduate/professional degree or higher: 5.1%

School District(s)
Comstock Park Public Schools (PK-12)
    2012-13 Enrollment: 2,243 . . . . (616) 254-5002
Kenowa Hills Public Schools (PK-12)
    2012-13 Enrollment: 3,296 . . . . (616) 784-2511
Housing: Homeownership rate: 47.5%; Median home value: $122,600; Median year structure built: 1978; Homeowner vacancy rate: 2.4%; Median gross rent: $679 per month; Rental vacancy rate: 14.5%
Health Insurance: 82.0% have insurance; 58.1% have private insurance; 32.5% have public insurance; 18.0% do not have insurance; 3.2% of children under 18 do not have insurance
Transportation: Commute: 92.3% car, 1.1% public transportation, 2.0% walk, 3.4% work from home; Median travel time to work: 19.2 minutes

COURTLAND (township). Covers a land area of 34.699 square miles and a water area of 1.273 square miles. Located at 43.17° N. Lat; 85.49° W. Long.

Population: 7,678; Growth (since 2000): 32.0%; Density: 221.3 persons per square mile; Race: 96.7% White, 0.3% Black/African American, 1.1% Asian, 0.3% American Indian/Alaska Native, 0.0% Native Hawaiian/Other Pacific Islander, 1.1% Two or more races, 1.6% Hispanic of any race; Average household size: 2.97; Median age: 37.2; Age under 18: 30.0%; Age 65 and over: 8.6%; Males per 100 females: 104.0; Marriage status: 23.1% never married, 64.4% now married, 0.3% separated, 2.4% widowed, 10.1% divorced; Foreign born: 1.7%; Speak English only: 95.7%; With disability: 9.8%; Veterans: 8.4%; Ancestry: 28.1% German, 18.7% Dutch, 13.1% Irish, 12.5% Polish, 11.3% English
Employment: 20.6% management, business, and financial, 4.6% computer, engineering, and science, 13.2% education, legal, community service, arts, and media, 4.2% healthcare practitioners, 14.0% service, 23.2% sales and office, 7.1% natural resources, construction, and maintenance, 13.1% production, transportation, and material moving
Income: Per capita: $28,680; Median household: $72,864; Average household: $84,092; Households with income of $100,000 or more: 32.0%; Poverty rate: 3.5%
Educational Attainment: High school diploma or higher: 95.4%; Bachelor's degree or higher: 34.1%; Graduate/professional degree or higher: 11.5%
Housing: Homeownership rate: 95.1%; Median home value: $201,100; Median year structure built: 1991; Homeowner vacancy rate: 1.2%; Median gross rent: $940 per month; Rental vacancy rate: 3.7%

Health Insurance: 94.9% have insurance; 85.0% have private insurance; 21.5% have public insurance; 5.1% do not have insurance; 1.9% of children under 18 do not have insurance
Transportation: Commute: 90.7% car, 0.0% public transportation, 0.4% walk, 6.9% work from home; Median travel time to work: 29.0 minutes

CUTLERVILLE (CDP). Covers a land area of 5.869 square miles and a water area of 0.015 square miles. Located at 42.84° N. Lat; 85.67° W. Long. Elevation is 676 feet.

History: Cutlerville was settled in 1853 by John Cutler and his family of ten children. One of his sons, John, built the Cutler mansion in 1891, which became the Pine Rest Christian Hospital in 1910.
Population: 14,370; Growth (since 2000): -4.9%; Density: 2,448.3 persons per square mile; Race: 82.2% White, 7.2% Black/African American, 3.0% Asian, 0.8% American Indian/Alaska Native, 0.0% Native Hawaiian/Other Pacific Islander, 3.1% Two or more races, 8.2% Hispanic of any race; Average household size: 2.45; Median age: 35.8; Age under 18: 24.1%; Age 65 and over: 12.9%; Males per 100 females: 95.7; Marriage status: 32.1% never married, 49.1% now married, 1.9% separated, 5.3% widowed, 13.5% divorced; Foreign born: 4.9%; Speak English only: 91.7%; With disability: 14.2%; Veterans: 10.2%; Ancestry: 25.6% Dutch, 23.5% German, 11.3% Irish, 6.9% English, 4.9% American
Employment: 9.9% management, business, and financial, 5.3% computer, engineering, and science, 5.6% education, legal, community service, arts, and media, 3.5% healthcare practitioners, 17.8% service, 25.7% sales and office, 9.4% natural resources, construction, and maintenance, 22.8% production, transportation, and material moving
Income: Per capita: $20,851; Median household: $42,453; Average household: $52,696; Households with income of $100,000 or more: 12.0%; Poverty rate: 19.2%
Educational Attainment: High school diploma or higher: 87.0%; Bachelor's degree or higher: 18.4%; Graduate/professional degree or higher: 4.9%
Housing: Homeownership rate: 69.4%; Median home value: $115,600; Median year structure built: 1985; Homeowner vacancy rate: 2.5%; Median gross rent: $763 per month; Rental vacancy rate: 11.4%
Health Insurance: 90.6% have insurance; 66.7% have private insurance; 37.6% have public insurance; 9.4% do not have insurance; 2.5% of children under 18 do not have insurance
Transportation: Commute: 92.9% car, 2.5% public transportation, 1.1% walk, 2.5% work from home; Median travel time to work: 21.1 minutes

EAST GRAND RAPIDS (city). Covers a land area of 2.934 square miles and a water area of 0.468 square miles. Located at 42.95° N. Lat; 85.61° W. Long. Elevation is 751 feet.

History: East Grand Rapids was first settled in the early 1830s by the Reed Family from New York, New York. Originally part of Paris Township, residents voted to establish the Village of East Grand Rapids in 1891. The Village was incorporated into a Home Rule City in 1926 when the population was approximately 1,300.
Population: 10,694; Growth (since 2000): -0.7%; Density: 3,645.3 persons per square mile; Race: 95.4% White, 1.1% Black/African American, 1.5% Asian, 0.1% American Indian/Alaska Native, 0.0% Native Hawaiian/Other Pacific Islander, 1.6% Two or more races, 1.5% Hispanic of any race; Average household size: 2.80; Median age: 39.8; Age under 18: 31.6%; Age 65 and over: 9.7%; Males per 100 females: 93.6; Marriage status: 19.4% never married, 67.3% now married, 0.1% separated, 3.0% widowed, 10.3% divorced; Foreign born: 4.7%; Speak English only: 94.0%; With disability: 5.2%; Veterans: 6.6%; Ancestry: 23.8% German, 19.3% Dutch, 18.1% Irish, 17.1% English, 8.1% Polish
Employment: 22.7% management, business, and financial, 7.9% computer, engineering, and science, 24.8% education, legal, community service, arts, and media, 10.8% healthcare practitioners, 6.2% service, 23.0% sales and office, 1.3% natural resources, construction, and maintenance, 3.2% production, transportation, and material moving
Income: Per capita: $54,452; Median household: $101,875; Average household: $147,979; Households with income of $100,000 or more: 50.7%; Poverty rate: 3.2%
Educational Attainment: High school diploma or higher: 99.2%; Bachelor's degree or higher: 77.9%; Graduate/professional degree or higher: 34.2%
Housing: Homeownership rate: 91.5%; Median home value: $246,100; Median year structure built: 1953; Homeowner vacancy rate: 1.3%; Median gross rent: $1,135 per month; Rental vacancy rate: 7.4%

Health Insurance: 97.3% have insurance; 91.6% have private insurance; 14.1% have public insurance; 2.7% do not have insurance; 2.2% of children under 18 do not have insurance
Safety: Violent crime rate: 2.7 per 10,000 population; Property crime rate: 124.3 per 10,000 population
Transportation: Commute: 86.0% car, 2.7% public transportation, 2.5% walk, 7.4% work from home; Median travel time to work: 17.7 minutes
Additional Information Contacts
City of East Grand Rapids . . . . (616) 949-2110
  http://www.eastgr.org

FOREST HILLS (CDP). Covers a land area of 49.270 square miles and a water area of 1.531 square miles. Located at 42.96° N. Lat; 85.49° W. Long. Elevation is 630 feet.
History: The Forest Hills community comprises parts of Ada Township, Cascade Township, Michigan, Grand Rapids Township, and Paris Township (now the city of Kentwood), The Forest Hills area has experienced significant growth since the 1950s when various small rural school districts were cobbled together to form a unified district, which now ranks as one of the best public school districts in the state of Michigan.
Population: 25,867; Growth (since 2000): 23.5%; Density: 525.0 persons per square mile; Race: 93.4% White, 1.2% Black/African American, 3.4% Asian, 0.2% American Indian/Alaska Native, 0.0% Native Hawaiian/Other Pacific Islander, 1.3% Two or more races, 1.7% Hispanic of any race; Average household size: 2.87; Median age: 41.2; Age under 18: 30.1%; Age 65 and over: 11.2%; Males per 100 females: 98.0; Marriage status: 18.9% never married, 72.3% now married, 0.2% separated, 3.3% widowed, 5.5% divorced; Foreign born: 5.5%; Speak English only: 93.8%; With disability: 5.2%; Veterans: 6.7%; Ancestry: 27.5% German, 20.7% Dutch, 16.1% Irish, 15.0% English, 6.3% Polish
Employment: 28.2% management, business, and financial, 6.1% computer, engineering, and science, 12.8% education, legal, community service, arts, and media, 11.5% healthcare practitioners, 9.3% service, 23.6% sales and office, 2.4% natural resources, construction, and maintenance, 6.0% production, transportation, and material moving
Income: Per capita: $50,807; Median household: $112,454; Average household: $148,079; Households with income of $100,000 or more: 56.1%; Poverty rate: 2.3%
Educational Attainment: High school diploma or higher: 98.2%; Bachelor's degree or higher: 63.8%; Graduate/professional degree or higher: 27.9%
Housing: Homeownership rate: 93.3%; Median home value: $262,700; Median year structure built: 1985; Homeowner vacancy rate: 1.2%; Median gross rent: $1,336 per month; Rental vacancy rate: 7.4%
Health Insurance: 96.6% have insurance; 91.7% have private insurance; 15.4% have public insurance; 3.4% do not have insurance; 1.7% of children under 18 do not have insurance
Transportation: Commute: 92.7% car, 0.5% public transportation, 0.6% walk, 5.5% work from home; Median travel time to work: 20.2 minutes

GAINES (charter township). Covers a land area of 35.703 square miles and a water area of 0.057 square miles. Located at 42.80° N. Lat; 85.60° W. Long.
Population: 25,146; Growth (since 2000): 25.0%; Density: 704.3 persons per square mile; Race: 80.5% White, 9.3% Black/African American, 4.6% Asian, 0.5% American Indian/Alaska Native, 0.0% Native Hawaiian/Other Pacific Islander, 2.7% Two or more races, 6.1% Hispanic of any race; Average household size: 2.69; Median age: 34.8; Age under 18: 27.5%; Age 65 and over: 10.5%; Males per 100 females: 96.4; Marriage status: 28.2% never married, 57.6% now married, 1.6% separated, 3.9% widowed, 10.3% divorced; Foreign born: 4.9%; Speak English only: 91.8%; With disability: 12.0%; Veterans: 8.7%; Ancestry: 28.0% Dutch, 20.4% German, 9.8% Irish, 9.0% English, 7.0% Polish
Employment: 13.0% management, business, and financial, 5.3% computer, engineering, and science, 8.7% education, legal, community service, arts, and media, 5.7% healthcare practitioners, 17.4% service, 26.8% sales and office, 5.1% natural resources, construction, and maintenance, 17.9% production, transportation, and material moving
Income: Per capita: $26,485; Median household: $55,929; Average household: $68,186; Households with income of $100,000 or more: 20.6%; Poverty rate: 11.5%
Educational Attainment: High school diploma or higher: 90.6%; Bachelor's degree or higher: 29.9%; Graduate/professional degree or higher: 10.2%

Housing: Homeownership rate: 71.6%; Median home value: $153,400; Median year structure built: 1990; Homeowner vacancy rate: 1.8%; Median gross rent: $743 per month; Rental vacancy rate: 11.6%
Health Insurance: 91.6% have insurance; 75.9% have private insurance; 26.1% have public insurance; 8.4% do not have insurance; 2.5% of children under 18 do not have insurance
Transportation: Commute: 94.6% car, 1.7% public transportation, 0.9% walk, 2.3% work from home; Median travel time to work: 20.3 minutes
Additional Information Contacts
Gaines Charter Township . . . . (616) 698-6640
  http://www.gainestownship.org

GOWEN (unincorporated postal area)
ZCTA: 49326
  Covers a land area of 23.428 square miles and a water area of 2.206 square miles. Located at 43.25° N. Lat; 85.32° W. Long..
Population: 3,752; Growth (since 2000): 8.9%; Density: 160.1 persons per square mile; Race: 96.2% White, 0.8% Black/African American, 0.2% Asian, 0.3% American Indian/Alaska Native, 0.0% Native Hawaiian/Other Pacific Islander, 1.8% Two or more races, 2.9% Hispanic of any race; Average household size: 2.60; Median age: 41.4; Age under 18: 23.9%; Age 65 and over: 13.8%; Males per 100 females: 109.0; Marriage status: 24.3% never married, 57.5% now married, 0.9% separated, 4.5% widowed, 13.8% divorced; Foreign born: 1.1%; Speak English only: 95.8%; With disability: 16.0%; Veterans: 10.5%; Ancestry: 27.4% German, 14.3% Irish, 9.5% Dutch, 8.8% English, 6.9% Polish
Employment: 11.1% management, business, and financial, 3.0% computer, engineering, and science, 6.4% education, legal, community service, arts, and media, 5.3% healthcare practitioners, 17.7% service, 23.0% sales and office, 14.6% natural resources, construction, and maintenance, 18.7% production, transportation, and material moving
Income: Per capita: $23,281; Median household: $52,792; Average household: $63,361; Households with income of $100,000 or more: 19.7%; Poverty rate: 18.3%
Educational Attainment: High school diploma or higher: 87.7%; Bachelor's degree or higher: 14.2%; Graduate/professional degree or higher: 6.2%
Housing: Homeownership rate: 89.5%; Median home value: $126,500; Median year structure built: 1977; Homeowner vacancy rate: 2.5%; Median gross rent: $733 per month; Rental vacancy rate: 11.3%
Health Insurance: 90.1% have insurance; 63.1% have private insurance; 40.8% have public insurance; 9.9% do not have insurance; 0.0% of children under 18 do not have insurance
Transportation: Commute: 95.5% car, 0.0% public transportation, 1.2% walk, 2.4% work from home; Median travel time to work: 34.6 minutes

GRAND RAPIDS (charter township). Covers a land area of 15.342 square miles and a water area of 0.221 square miles. Located at 42.99° N. Lat; 85.58° W. Long. Elevation is 640 feet.
History: The Township was first organized as the Town of Kent in 1834 with Rix Robinson as the moderator. The State of Michigan designated Grand Rapids Township in 1842. Grand Rapids Township became a "Charter" Township in 1979 under the Charter Township Act of the State of Michigan.
Population: 16,661; Growth (since 2000): 18.5%; Density: 1,086.0 persons per square mile; Race: 91.5% White, 1.8% Black/African American, 4.4% Asian, 0.2% American Indian/Alaska Native, 0.0% Native Hawaiian/Other Pacific Islander, 1.7% Two or more races, 2.0% Hispanic of any race; Average household size: 2.72; Median age: 41.3; Age under 18: 27.3%; Age 65 and over: 15.3%; Males per 100 females: 93.8; Marriage status: 23.0% never married, 61.2% now married, 0.3% separated, 7.7% widowed, 8.2% divorced; Foreign born: 6.8%; Speak English only: 93.2%; With disability: 8.1%; Veterans: 8.7%; Ancestry: 24.1% German, 18.3% Dutch, 16.1% English, 15.0% Irish, 9.2% Polish
Employment: 20.6% management, business, and financial, 7.1% computer, engineering, and science, 13.7% education, legal, community service, arts, and media, 10.4% healthcare practitioners, 11.9% service, 23.7% sales and office, 4.8% natural resources, construction, and maintenance, 7.8% production, transportation, and material moving
Income: Per capita: $39,086; Median household: $78,071; Average household: $108,890; Households with income of $100,000 or more: 36.8%; Poverty rate: 2.8%
Educational Attainment: High school diploma or higher: 96.8%; Bachelor's degree or higher: 54.2%; Graduate/professional degree or higher: 20.8%

School District(s)

East Grand Rapids Public Schools (PK-12)
  2012-13 Enrollment: 2,990 . . . . (616) 235-3535
Excel Charter Academy (KG-12)
  2012-13 Enrollment: 1,347 . . . . (616) 281-9339
Forest Hills Public Schools (PK-12)
  2012-13 Enrollment: 10,101 . . . . (616) 493-8800
Godwin Heights Public Schools (PK-12)
  2012-13 Enrollment: 2,224 . . . . (616) 252-2090
Grand Rapids Child Discovery Center (KG-12)
  2012-13 Enrollment: 209 . . . . (616) 459-0330
Grand Rapids Public Schools (PK-12)
  2012-13 Enrollment: 17,038 . . . . (616) 819-2000
Grandville Public Schools (PK-12)
  2012-13 Enrollment: 5,625 . . . . (616) 254-6570
Hope Academy of West Michigan (KG-12)
  2012-13 Enrollment: 428 . . . . (616) 977-4917
Kelloggsville Public Schools (PK-12)
  2012-13 Enrollment: 2,211 . . . . (616) 538-7460
Kenowa Hills Public Schools (PK-12)
  2012-13 Enrollment: 3,296 . . . . (616) 784-2511
Kentwood Public Schools (PK-12)
  2012-13 Enrollment: 8,718 . . . . (616) 455-4400
Knapp Charter Academy (KG-12)
  2012-13 Enrollment: 742 . . . . (616) 364-1100
Lighthouse Academy (KG-12)
  2012-13 Enrollment: 302 . . . . (616) 949-2287
Michigan Virtual Charter Academy (KG-12)
  2012-13 Enrollment: 948 . . . . (616) 309-1600
New Branches School (KG-12)
  2012-13 Enrollment: 352 . . . . (616) 243-6221
Northview Public Schools (PK-12)
  2012-13 Enrollment: 3,444 . . . . (616) 363-6861
Ridge Park Charter Academy (KG-12)
  2012-13 Enrollment: 669 . . . . (616) 222-0093
Vista Charter Academy (KG-12)
  2012-13 Enrollment: 718 . . . . (616) 246-6920
Walker Charter Academy (KG-12)
  2012-13 Enrollment: 743 . . . . (616) 785-2700
Wellspring Preparatory High School (KG-12)
  2012-13 Enrollment: 303 . . . . (616) 235-9500
West Mi Academy of Environmental Science (KG-12)
  2012-13 Enrollment: 591 . . . . (616) 791-7454
West Michigan Aviation Academy (KG-12)
  2012-13 Enrollment: 245 . . . . (616) 446-8886
William C. Abney Academy (KG-12)
  2012-13 Enrollment: 556 . . . . (616) 454-5541

Four-year College(s)

Aquinas College (Private, Not-for-profit, Roman Catholic)
  Fall 2013 Enrollment: 2,001 . . . . (616) 632-8900
  2013-14 Tuition: In-state $26,460; Out-of-state $26,460
Calvin College (Private, Not-for-profit, Christian Reformed Church)
  Fall 2013 Enrollment: 4,034 . . . . (616) 526-6000
  2013-14 Tuition: In-state $28,250; Out-of-state $28,250
Calvin Theological Seminary (Private, Not-for-profit, Christian Reformed Church)
  Fall 2013 Enrollment: 306 . . . . (616) 957-6036
Compass College of Cinematic Arts (Private, Not-for-profit)
  Fall 2013 Enrollment: 81 . . . . (616) 988-1000
  2013-14 Tuition: In-state $13,915; Out-of-state $13,915
Cornerstone University (Private, Not-for-profit, Interdenominational)
  Fall 2013 Enrollment: 2,809 . . . . (616) 949-5300
  2013-14 Tuition: In-state $24,168; Out-of-state $24,168
Davenport University (Private, Not-for-profit)
  Fall 2013 Enrollment: 9,591 . . . . (616) 698-7111
  2013-14 Tuition: In-state $14,096; Out-of-state $14,096
Kuyper College (Private, Not-for-profit, Other Protestant)
  Fall 2013 Enrollment: 291 . . . . (616) 222-3000
  2013-14 Tuition: In-state $18,454; Out-of-state $18,454

Two-year College(s)

Grand Rapids Community College (Public)
  Fall 2013 Enrollment: 16,590 . . . . (616) 234-4000
  2013-14 Tuition: In-state $5,742; Out-of-state $8,310
Sanford-Brown College-Grand Rapids (Private, For-profit)
  Fall 2013 Enrollment: 57 . . . . (616) 977-8400

Vocational/Technical School(s)

Empire Beauty School-Michigan (Private, For-profit)
  Fall 2013 Enrollment: 365 . . . . (800) 920-4593
  2013-14 Tuition: $15,180
Everest Institute-Grand Rapids (Private, For-profit)
  Fall 2013 Enrollment: 576 . . . . (616) 364-8464
  2013-14 Tuition: $18,556
International Cosmetology Academy (Private, For-profit)
  Fall 2013 Enrollment: 47 . . . . (616) 248-3335
  2013-14 Tuition: $13,015

Housing: Homeownership rate: 88.5%; Median home value: $211,000; Median year structure built: 1983; Homeowner vacancy rate: 1.5%; Median gross rent: $1,187 per month; Rental vacancy rate: 12.0%

Health Insurance: 94.9% have insurance; 88.9% have private insurance; 20.8% have public insurance; 5.1% do not have insurance; 2.2% of children under 18 do not have insurance

Hospitals: Saint Mary's Health Care (324 beds); Spectrum Health - Butterworth Campus (986 beds)

Newspapers: Grand Rapids Press (daily circulation 132000); Grand Rapids Times (weekly circulation 5000); Kalamazoo Times (weekly circulation 5000)

Transportation: Commute: 90.9% car, 0.1% public transportation, 0.5% walk, 7.5% work from home; Median travel time to work: 17.6 minutes; Amtrak: Train service available.

Airports: Gerald R. Ford International (primary service/small hub)

Additional Information Contacts
Grand Rapids Charter Township . . . . (616) 361-7391
  http://www.grandrapidstwp.org

GRAND RAPIDS (city). County seat. Covers a land area of 44.395 square miles and a water area of 0.870 square miles. Located at 42.96° N. Lat; 85.66° W. Long. Elevation is 640 feet.

History: A Baptist mission in 1826 and a fur trading post in 1827 were the beginnings of Grand Rapids, named for the rapids on the Grand River. Louis Campau, who had built the trading post, laid out the town in 1831, besting Lucius Lyon's attempts in a similar endeavor. For a time Lyon's town name of Kent was the official post office name, but in 1842 the town again became Grand Rapids. Logging, the first industry of importance, led to furniture making as early as 1838. By 1876 the Grand Rapids furniture trade was established. Incorporated as a city 1926.

Population: 188,040; Growth (since 2000): -4.9%; Density: 4,235.6 persons per square mile; Race: 64.6% White, 20.9% Black/African American, 1.9% Asian, 0.7% American Indian/Alaska Native, 0.1% Native Hawaiian/Other Pacific Islander, 4.2% Two or more races, 15.6% Hispanic of any race; Average household size: 2.49; Median age: 30.8; Age under 18: 24.7%; Age 65 and over: 11.1%; Males per 100 females: 94.9; Marriage status: 43.7% never married, 40.0% now married, 2.4% separated, 5.4% widowed, 10.9% divorced; Foreign born: 10.1%; Speak English only: 84.5%; With disability: 11.9%; Veterans: 6.7%; Ancestry: 15.6% German, 14.7% Dutch, 8.8% Irish, 7.5% Polish, 6.8% English

Employment: 11.7% management, business, and financial, 4.1% computer, engineering, and science, 12.6% education, legal, community service, arts, and media, 4.5% healthcare practitioners, 19.6% service, 23.4% sales and office, 7.1% natural resources, construction, and maintenance, 17.1% production, transportation, and material moving

Income: Per capita: $20,214; Median household: $39,227; Average household: $50,908; Households with income of $100,000 or more: 10.6%; Poverty rate: 26.8%

Educational Attainment: High school diploma or higher: 83.9%; Bachelor's degree or higher: 29.4%; Graduate/professional degree or higher: 10.1%

School District(s)

East Grand Rapids Public Schools (PK-12)
  2012-13 Enrollment: 2,990 . . . . (616) 235-3535
Excel Charter Academy (KG-12)
  2012-13 Enrollment: 1,347 . . . . (616) 281-9339
Forest Hills Public Schools (PK-12)
  2012-13 Enrollment: 10,101 . . . . (616) 493-8800
Godwin Heights Public Schools (PK-12)
  2012-13 Enrollment: 2,224 . . . . (616) 252-2090
Grand Rapids Child Discovery Center (KG-12)
  2012-13 Enrollment: 209 . . . . (616) 459-0330
Grand Rapids Public Schools (PK-12)
  2012-13 Enrollment: 17,038 . . . . (616) 819-2000

Grandville Public Schools (PK-12)
   2012-13 Enrollment: 5,625 . . . . (616) 254-6570
Hope Academy of West Michigan (KG-12)
   2012-13 Enrollment: 428. . . . . (616) 977-4917
Kelloggsville Public Schools (PK-12)
   2012-13 Enrollment: 2,211 . . . . (616) 538-7460
Kenowa Hills Public Schools (PK-12)
   2012-13 Enrollment: 3,296 . . . . (616) 784-2511
Kentwood Public Schools (PK-12)
   2012-13 Enrollment: 8,718 . . . . (616) 455-4400
Knapp Charter Academy (KG-12)
   2012-13 Enrollment: 742. . . . . (616) 364-1100
Lighthouse Academy (KG-12)
   2012-13 Enrollment: 302. . . . . (616) 949-2287
Michigan Virtual Charter Academy (KG-12)
   2012-13 Enrollment: 948. . . . . (616) 309-1600
New Branches School (KG-12)
   2012-13 Enrollment: 352. . . . . (616) 243-6221
Northview Public Schools (PK-12)
   2012-13 Enrollment: 3,444 . . . . (616) 363-6861
Ridge Park Charter Academy (KG-12)
   2012-13 Enrollment: 669. . . . . (616) 222-0093
Vista Charter Academy (KG-12)
   2012-13 Enrollment: 718. . . . . (616) 246-6920
Walker Charter Academy (KG-12)
   2012-13 Enrollment: 743. . . . . (616) 785-2700
Wellspring Preparatory High School (KG-12)
   2012-13 Enrollment: 303. . . . . (616) 235-9500
West Mi Academy of Environmental Science (KG-12)
   2012-13 Enrollment: 591. . . . . (616) 791-7454
West Michigan Aviation Academy (KG-12)
   2012-13 Enrollment: 245. . . . . (616) 446-8886
William C. Abney Academy (KG-12)
   2012-13 Enrollment: 556. . . . . (616) 454-5541

Four-year College(s)

Aquinas College (Private, Not-for-profit, Roman Catholic)
   Fall 2013 Enrollment: 2,001 . . . . (616) 632-8900
   2013-14 Tuition: In-state $26,460; Out-of-state $26,460
Calvin College (Private, Not-for-profit, Christian Reformed Church)
   Fall 2013 Enrollment: 4,034 . . . . (616) 526-6000
   2013-14 Tuition: In-state $28,250; Out-of-state $28,250
Calvin Theological Seminary (Private, Not-for-profit, Christian Reformed Church)
   Fall 2013 Enrollment: 306 . . . . (616) 957-6036
Compass College of Cinematic Arts (Private, Not-for-profit)
   Fall 2013 Enrollment: 81 . . . . (616) 988-1000
   2013-14 Tuition: In-state $13,915; Out-of-state $13,915
Cornerstone University (Private, Not-for-profit, Interdenominational)
   Fall 2013 Enrollment: 2,809 . . . . (616) 949-5300
   2013-14 Tuition: In-state $24,168; Out-of-state $24,168
Davenport University (Private, Not-for-profit)
   Fall 2013 Enrollment: 9,591 . . . . (616) 698-7111
   2013-14 Tuition: In-state $14,096; Out-of-state $14,096
Kuyper College (Private, Not-for-profit, Other Protestant)
   Fall 2013 Enrollment: 291. . . . . (616) 222-3000
   2013-14 Tuition: In-state $18,454; Out-of-state $18,454

Two-year College(s)

Grand Rapids Community College (Public)
   Fall 2013 Enrollment: 16,590 . . . . (616) 234-4000
   2013-14 Tuition: In-state $5,742; Out-of-state $8,310
Sanford-Brown College-Grand Rapids (Private, For-profit)
   Fall 2013 Enrollment: 57 . . . . (616) 977-8400

Vocational/Technical School(s)

Empire Beauty School-Michigan (Private, For-profit)
   Fall 2013 Enrollment: 365. . . . . (800) 920-4593
   2013-14 Tuition: $15,180
Everest Institute-Grand Rapids (Private, For-profit)
   Fall 2013 Enrollment: 576. . . . . (616) 364-8464
   2013-14 Tuition: $18,556
International Cosmetology Academy (Private, For-profit)
   Fall 2013 Enrollment: 47 . . . . (616) 248-3335
   2013-14 Tuition: $13,015

Housing: Homeownership rate: 56.0%; Median home value: $109,400; Median year structure built: 1952; Homeowner vacancy rate: 3.3%; Median gross rent: $758 per month; Rental vacancy rate: 10.2%

Health Insurance: 86.4% have insurance; 60.1% have private insurance; 37.6% have public insurance; 13.6% do not have insurance; 3.0% of children under 18 do not have insurance

Hospitals: Saint Mary's Health Care (324 beds); Spectrum Health - Butterworth Campus (986 beds)

Safety: Violent crime rate: 69.3 per 10,000 population; Property crime rate: 323.6 per 10,000 population

Newspapers: Grand Rapids Press (daily circulation 132000); Grand Rapids Times (weekly circulation 5000); Kalamazoo Times (weekly circulation 5000)

Transportation: Commute: 86.7% car, 3.5% public transportation, 3.3% walk, 4.9% work from home; Median travel time to work: 19.5 minutes; Amtrak: Train service available.

Airports: Gerald R. Ford International (primary service/small hub)

Additional Information Contacts

City of Grand Rapids. . . . . (616) 456-3000
   http://www.ci.grand-rapids.mi.us

GRANDVILLE (city).

Covers a land area of 7.273 square miles and a water area of 0.398 square miles. Located at 42.90° N. Lat; 85.75° W. Long. Elevation is 604 feet.

History: Grandville was established in the 1830's by a company of land operators from an eastern state. Grandville was incorporated as a village in 1887 and as a city in 1933.

Population: 15,378; Growth (since 2000): -5.4%; Density: 2,114.4 persons per square mile; Race: 92.0% White, 2.2% Black/African American, 1.5% Asian, 0.2% American Indian/Alaska Native, 0.0% Native Hawaiian/Other Pacific Islander, 2.4% Two or more races, 6.2% Hispanic of any race; Average household size: 2.54; Median age: 36.3; Age under 18: 24.8%; Age 65 and over: 14.6%; Males per 100 females: 93.6; Marriage status: 29.0% never married, 55.0% now married, 0.4% separated, 5.3% widowed, 10.6% divorced; Foreign born: 3.6%; Speak English only: 95.4%; With disability: 11.6%; Veterans: 7.7%; Ancestry: 30.6% Dutch, 26.3% German, 11.8% Irish, 10.2% Polish, 8.9% English

Employment: 13.2% management, business, and financial, 4.4% computer, engineering, and science, 11.1% education, legal, community service, arts, and media, 6.3% healthcare practitioners, 15.4% service, 26.5% sales and office, 6.6% natural resources, construction, and maintenance, 16.5% production, transportation, and material moving

Income: Per capita: $24,141; Median household: $53,701; Average household: $62,653; Households with income of $100,000 or more: 14.1%; Poverty rate: 9.9%

Educational Attainment: High school diploma or higher: 93.5%; Bachelor's degree or higher: 32.7%; Graduate/professional degree or higher: 9.6%

School District(s)

Grandville Public Schools (PK-12)
   2012-13 Enrollment: 5,625 . . . . (616) 254-6570

Housing: Homeownership rate: 71.9%; Median home value: $135,000; Median year structure built: 1975; Homeowner vacancy rate: 1.6%; Median gross rent: $674 per month; Rental vacancy rate: 8.0%

Health Insurance: 90.2% have insurance; 75.4% have private insurance; 29.7% have public insurance; 9.8% do not have insurance; 5.4% of children under 18 do not have insurance

Safety: Violent crime rate: 16.6 per 10,000 population; Property crime rate: 458.2 per 10,000 population

Transportation: Commute: 91.7% car, 2.1% public transportation, 1.9% walk, 3.8% work from home; Median travel time to work: 22.1 minutes

Additional Information Contacts

City of Grandville. . . . . (616) 531-3030
   http://www.cityofgrandville.com

GRATTAN (township).

Covers a land area of 33.858 square miles and a water area of 3.089 square miles. Located at 43.08° N. Lat; 85.36° W. Long. Elevation is 830 feet.

History: Grattan Township was named for Henry Grattan, an Irish statesman and orator. The first settlers here in the mid-1840's were Irish. Edward S. Bellamy and Nathan Holmes built a grist mill in 1850.

Population: 3,621; Growth (since 2000): 2.0%; Density: 106.9 persons per square mile; Race: 96.5% White, 0.7% Black/African American, 0.5% Asian, 0.4% American Indian/Alaska Native, 0.0% Native Hawaiian/Other Pacific Islander, 1.1% Two or more races, 2.1% Hispanic of any race; Average household size: 2.61; Median age: 44.7; Age under 18: 22.5%; Age 65 and over: 12.0%; Males per 100 females: 101.5; Marriage status: 24.4% never married, 62.5% now married, 0.4% separated, 4.9%

widowed, 8.2% divorced; Foreign born: 1.9%; Speak English only: 98.1%; With disability: 10.2%; Veterans: 9.8%; Ancestry: 29.2% German, 20.9% Dutch, 17.1% Irish, 15.5% English, 10.2% Polish

Employment: 12.4% management, business, and financial, 2.1% computer, engineering, and science, 10.5% education, legal, community service, arts, and media, 4.3% healthcare practitioners, 15.7% service, 32.6% sales and office, 9.0% natural resources, construction, and maintenance, 13.4% production, transportation, and material moving

Income: Per capita: $34,375; Median household: $63,931; Average household: $84,814; Households with income of $100,000 or more: 26.3%; Poverty rate: 5.6%

Educational Attainment: High school diploma or higher: 96.1%; Bachelor's degree or higher: 28.7%; Graduate/professional degree or higher: 6.9%

Housing: Homeownership rate: 91.0%; Median home value: $223,900; Median year structure built: 1977; Homeowner vacancy rate: 2.8%; Median gross rent: $938 per month; Rental vacancy rate: 5.3%

Health Insurance: 92.3% have insurance; 81.4% have private insurance; 23.1% have public insurance; 7.7% do not have insurance; 0.0% of children under 18 do not have insurance

Transportation: Commute: 92.0% car, 0.0% public transportation, 2.1% walk, 4.5% work from home; Median travel time to work: 31.9 minutes

KENT CITY (village). Covers a land area of 1.322 square miles and a water area of <.001 square miles. Located at 43.22° N. Lat; 85.76° W. Long. Elevation is 810 feet.

History: Kent City was platted in 1870 for John W. Thompson. It was named after its township, which had been named for New York jurist James Kent (1763-1847).

Population: 1,057; Growth (since 2000): -0.4%; Density: 799.4 persons per square mile; Race: 88.8% White, 0.9% Black/African American, 0.2% Asian, 0.3% American Indian/Alaska Native, 0.0% Native Hawaiian/Other Pacific Islander, 2.1% Two or more races, 17.8% Hispanic of any race; Average household size: 2.83; Median age: 30.6; Age under 18: 30.7%; Age 65 and over: 7.7%; Males per 100 females: 93.2

School District(s)

Kent City Community Schools (PK-12)
    2012-13 Enrollment: 1,278 . . . . (616) 678-7714

Housing: Homeownership rate: 72.7%; Homeowner vacancy rate: 2.2%; Rental vacancy rate: 11.9%

KENTWOOD (city). Covers a land area of 20.904 square miles and a water area of 0.050 square miles. Located at 42.88° N. Lat; 85.59° W. Long. Elevation is 689 feet.

Population: 48,707; Growth (since 2000): 7.6%; Density: 2,330.1 persons per square mile; Race: 70.1% White, 15.4% Black/African American, 6.6% Asian, 0.4% American Indian/Alaska Native, 0.1% Native Hawaiian/Other Pacific Islander, 3.9% Two or more races, 8.5% Hispanic of any race; Average household size: 2.45; Median age: 34.3; Age under 18: 25.4%; Age 65 and over: 11.5%; Males per 100 females: 92.2; Marriage status: 34.9% never married, 49.6% now married, 1.3% separated, 4.8% widowed, 10.7% divorced; Foreign born: 13.5%; Speak English only: 81.4%; With disability: 11.7%; Veterans: 7.4%; Ancestry: 17.0% German, 15.0% Dutch, 10.0% Irish, 7.6% English, 5.0% Polish

Employment: 12.8% management, business, and financial, 6.3% computer, engineering, and science, 8.6% education, legal, community service, arts, and media, 5.3% healthcare practitioners, 16.1% service, 27.7% sales and office, 4.5% natural resources, construction, and maintenance, 18.7% production, transportation, and material moving

Income: Per capita: $24,851; Median household: $48,368; Average household: $60,855; Households with income of $100,000 or more: 15.6%; Poverty rate: 13.5%

Educational Attainment: High school diploma or higher: 90.9%; Bachelor's degree or higher: 33.1%; Graduate/professional degree or higher: 10.3%

Vocational/Technical School(s)

Ross Medical Education Center-Kentwood (Private, For-profit)
    Fall 2013 Enrollment: 176 . . . . (616) 698-3075
    2013-14 Tuition: $15,680

Housing: Homeownership rate: 61.1%; Median home value: $129,200; Median year structure built: 1980; Homeowner vacancy rate: 2.5%; Median gross rent: $762 per month; Rental vacancy rate: 13.1%

Health Insurance: 89.0% have insurance; 72.1% have private insurance; 27.7% have public insurance; 11.0% do not have insurance; 5.0% of children under 18 do not have insurance

Safety: Violent crime rate: 28.2 per 10,000 population; Property crime rate: 242.5 per 10,000 population

Transportation: Commute: 93.3% car, 1.3% public transportation, 1.1% walk, 2.9% work from home; Median travel time to work: 18.8 minutes

Additional Information Contacts

City of Kentwood . . . . (616) 698-9610
    http://www.ci.kentwood.mi.us

LOWELL (charter township). Covers a land area of 32.571 square miles and a water area of 0.747 square miles. Located at 42.90° N. Lat; 85.37° W. Long. Elevation is 633 feet.

History: Resort. Settled 1821, incorporated 1859.

Population: 5,949; Growth (since 2000): 14.0%; Density: 182.6 persons per square mile; Race: 96.2% White, 0.5% Black/African American, 0.5% Asian, 0.5% American Indian/Alaska Native, 0.0% Native Hawaiian/Other Pacific Islander, 1.5% Two or more races, 2.5% Hispanic of any race; Average household size: 2.72; Median age: 38.4; Age under 18: 26.3%; Age 65 and over: 9.8%; Males per 100 females: 97.2; Marriage status: 25.2% never married, 60.4% now married, 0.5% separated, 2.8% widowed, 11.6% divorced; Foreign born: 1.0%; Speak English only: 98.3%; With disability: 10.6%; Veterans: 9.6%; Ancestry: 23.7% German, 20.4% Dutch, 18.3% English, 12.0% Irish, 9.9% Polish

Employment: 11.4% management, business, and financial, 4.5% computer, engineering, and science, 6.5% education, legal, community service, arts, and media, 5.5% healthcare practitioners, 16.1% service, 32.6% sales and office, 7.8% natural resources, construction, and maintenance, 15.5% production, transportation, and material moving

Income: Per capita: $24,105; Median household: $63,954; Average household: $70,511; Households with income of $100,000 or more: 18.7%; Poverty rate: 10.7%

Educational Attainment: High school diploma or higher: 93.9%; Bachelor's degree or higher: 26.1%; Graduate/professional degree or higher: 5.6%

School District(s)

Lowell Area Schools (PK-12)
    2012-13 Enrollment: 3,799 . . . . (616) 987-2500

Housing: Homeownership rate: 84.4%; Median home value: $157,200; Median year structure built: 1978; Homeowner vacancy rate: 1.0%; Median gross rent: $854 per month; Rental vacancy rate: 5.8%

Health Insurance: 90.9% have insurance; 78.3% have private insurance; 25.2% have public insurance; 9.1% do not have insurance; 0.9% of children under 18 do not have insurance

Newspapers: Lowell Ledger (weekly circulation 3000)

Transportation: Commute: 94.0% car, 0.0% public transportation, 1.7% walk, 3.1% work from home; Median travel time to work: 23.4 minutes

Additional Information Contacts

Lowell Charter Township . . . . (616) 897-7600
    http://www.twp.lowell.mi.us

LOWELL (city). Covers a land area of 2.875 square miles and a water area of 0.221 square miles. Located at 42.93° N. Lat; 85.35° W. Long. Elevation is 633 feet.

History: Lowell was settled in 1821 at the mouth of the Flat River, and incorporated as a village in 1861. Industries in the early 1900's included a milling plant, chick hatchery, and a button factory that used mussel shells gathered by clam-diggers on the Grand, Flat, and Thornapple Rivers.

Population: 3,783; Growth (since 2000): -5.7%; Density: 1,315.8 persons per square mile; Race: 94.1% White, 1.3% Black/African American, 0.6% Asian, 0.6% American Indian/Alaska Native, 0.0% Native Hawaiian/Other Pacific Islander, 2.3% Two or more races, 3.0% Hispanic of any race; Average household size: 2.50; Median age: 37.1; Age under 18: 25.7%; Age 65 and over: 15.0%; Males per 100 females: 86.1; Marriage status: 24.5% never married, 45.8% now married, 1.6% separated, 9.8% widowed, 19.9% divorced; Foreign born: 1.0%; Speak English only: 98.9%; With disability: 19.5%; Veterans: 11.6%; Ancestry: 20.1% German, 17.0% English, 11.4% Dutch, 11.1% Irish, 7.0% American

Employment: 12.8% management, business, and financial, 5.7% computer, engineering, and science, 6.4% education, legal, community service, arts, and media, 4.2% healthcare practitioners, 17.3% service, 28.6% sales and office, 6.1% natural resources, construction, and maintenance, 18.9% production, transportation, and material moving

Income: Per capita: $21,365; Median household: $44,364; Average household: $50,991; Households with income of $100,000 or more: 7.9%; Poverty rate: 13.8%

Educational Attainment: High school diploma or higher: 86.5%; Bachelor's degree or higher: 19.3%; Graduate/professional degree or higher: 4.1%

School District(s)

Lowell Area Schools (PK-12)
   2012-13 Enrollment: 3,799 . . . . (616) 987-2500
Housing: Homeownership rate: 62.5%; Median home value: $99,800; Median year structure built: 1966; Homeowner vacancy rate: 2.6%; Median gross rent: $631 per month; Rental vacancy rate: 11.3%
Health Insurance: 92.7% have insurance; 76.1% have private insurance; 36.3% have public insurance; 7.3% do not have insurance; 0.0% of children under 18 do not have insurance
Safety: Violent crime rate: 67.4 per 10,000 population; Property crime rate: 329.2 per 10,000 population
Newspapers: Lowell Ledger (weekly circulation 3000)
Transportation: Commute: 92.8% car, 0.1% public transportation, 3.3% walk, 1.9% work from home; Median travel time to work: 22.8 minutes

NELSON (township). Covers a land area of 35.209 square miles and a water area of 0.750 square miles. Located at 43.26° N. Lat; 85.49° W. Long.

Population: 4,764; Growth (since 2000): 13.6%; Density: 135.3 persons per square mile; Race: 96.9% White, 0.8% Black/African American, 0.3% Asian, 0.3% American Indian/Alaska Native, 0.0% Native Hawaiian/Other Pacific Islander, 1.1% Two or more races, 2.4% Hispanic of any race; Average household size: 2.83; Median age: 36.5; Age under 18: 27.7%; Age 65 and over: 8.7%; Males per 100 females: 102.7; Marriage status: 26.8% never married, 61.4% now married, 1.0% separated, 3.2% widowed, 8.6% divorced; Foreign born: 0.1%; Speak English only: 99.6%; With disability: 11.2%; Veterans: 8.4%; Ancestry: 25.4% German, 14.9% English, 14.4% Dutch, 12.3% Irish, 11.1% American
Employment: 12.5% management, business, and financial, 6.3% computer, engineering, and science, 7.6% education, legal, community service, arts, and media, 4.3% healthcare practitioners, 12.8% service, 24.1% sales and office, 13.2% natural resources, construction, and maintenance, 19.2% production, transportation, and material moving
Income: Per capita: $22,967; Median household: $67,953; Average household: $65,440; Households with income of $100,000 or more: 20.8%; Poverty rate: 11.9%
Educational Attainment: High school diploma or higher: 87.5%; Bachelor's degree or higher: 19.0%; Graduate/professional degree or higher: 5.0%
Housing: Homeownership rate: 88.8%; Median home value: $131,900; Median year structure built: 1985; Homeowner vacancy rate: 1.6%; Median gross rent: $445 per month; Rental vacancy rate: 1.6%
Health Insurance: 93.7% have insurance; 73.7% have private insurance; 34.2% have public insurance; 6.3% do not have insurance; 1.5% of children under 18 do not have insurance
Transportation: Commute: 94.0% car, 0.2% public transportation, 1.8% walk, 3.2% work from home; Median travel time to work: 34.5 minutes
Additional Information Contacts
Nelson Township. . . . . (616) 636-5332
   http://www.nelsontownship.org

NORTHVIEW (CDP). Covers a land area of 10.336 square miles and a water area of 0.699 square miles. Located at 43.04° N. Lat; 85.60° W. Long. Elevation is 745 feet.

Population: 14,541; Growth (since 2000): -1.3%; Density: 1,406.8 persons per square mile; Race: 91.5% White, 3.6% Black/African American, 1.3% Asian, 0.3% American Indian/Alaska Native, 0.1% Native Hawaiian/Other Pacific Islander, 2.6% Two or more races, 2.9% Hispanic of any race; Average household size: 2.44; Median age: 39.8; Age under 18: 23.5%; Age 65 and over: 13.7%; Males per 100 females: 91.1; Marriage status: 28.9% never married, 53.3% now married, 1.5% separated, 5.8% widowed, 11.9% divorced; Foreign born: 2.3%; Speak English only: 95.2%; With disability: 11.4%; Veterans: 8.6%; Ancestry: 28.2% German, 19.8% Dutch, 13.6% Irish, 11.7% Polish, 11.3% English
Employment: 19.5% management, business, and financial, 3.9% computer, engineering, and science, 9.2% education, legal, community service, arts, and media, 6.9% healthcare practitioners, 16.3% service, 25.1% sales and office, 4.9% natural resources, construction, and maintenance, 14.1% production, transportation, and material moving
Income: Per capita: $29,038; Median household: $53,090; Average household: $70,622; Households with income of $100,000 or more: 18.3%; Poverty rate: 11.2%

Educational Attainment: High school diploma or higher: 95.4%; Bachelor's degree or higher: 30.4%; Graduate/professional degree or higher: 10.0%
Housing: Homeownership rate: 74.7%; Median home value: $140,900; Median year structure built: 1975; Homeowner vacancy rate: 1.7%; Median gross rent: $689 per month; Rental vacancy rate: 10.1%
Health Insurance: 89.9% have insurance; 76.0% have private insurance; 27.7% have public insurance; 10.1% do not have insurance; 0.2% of children under 18 do not have insurance
Transportation: Commute: 92.3% car, 0.7% public transportation, 0.6% walk, 5.1% work from home; Median travel time to work: 18.4 minutes

OAKFIELD (township). Covers a land area of 33.813 square miles and a water area of 2.600 square miles. Located at 43.17° N. Lat; 85.37° W. Long.

Population: 5,782; Growth (since 2000): 14.3%; Density: 171.0 persons per square mile; Race: 96.9% White, 0.4% Black/African American, 0.5% Asian, 0.3% American Indian/Alaska Native, 0.0% Native Hawaiian/Other Pacific Islander, 1.4% Two or more races, 2.6% Hispanic of any race; Average household size: 2.73; Median age: 40.4; Age under 18: 25.8%; Age 65 and over: 10.0%; Males per 100 females: 104.3; Marriage status: 19.0% never married, 69.6% now married, 2.4% separated, 2.7% widowed, 8.7% divorced; Foreign born: 1.8%; Speak English only: 96.7%; With disability: 9.8%; Veterans: 7.5%; Ancestry: 33.3% German, 11.9% Dutch, 10.2% Irish, 9.4% English, 7.5% Polish
Employment: 8.3% management, business, and financial, 3.9% computer, engineering, and science, 3.9% education, legal, community service, arts, and media, 7.7% healthcare practitioners, 13.1% service, 27.6% sales and office, 13.9% natural resources, construction, and maintenance, 21.4% production, transportation, and material moving
Income: Per capita: $23,280; Median household: $61,333; Average household: $66,573; Households with income of $100,000 or more: 16.3%; Poverty rate: 10.3%
Educational Attainment: High school diploma or higher: 90.7%; Bachelor's degree or higher: 16.8%; Graduate/professional degree or higher: 5.4%
Housing: Homeownership rate: 92.1%; Median home value: $142,600; Median year structure built: 1984; Homeowner vacancy rate: 2.6%; Median gross rent: $827 per month; Rental vacancy rate: 13.5%
Health Insurance: 94.9% have insurance; 82.4% have private insurance; 26.7% have public insurance; 5.1% do not have insurance; 1.0% of children under 18 do not have insurance
Transportation: Commute: 94.7% car, 0.0% public transportation, 0.0% walk, 3.1% work from home; Median travel time to work: 31.7 minutes

PLAINFIELD (charter township). Covers a land area of 35.045 square miles and a water area of 1.687 square miles. Located at 43.07° N. Lat; 85.61° W. Long.

History: Plainfield Township was organized in 1838 and named for the level of much of the land within its boundaries.
Population: 30,952; Growth (since 2000): 2.5%; Density: 883.2 persons per square mile; Race: 93.7% White, 2.1% Black/African American, 1.2% Asian, 0.3% American Indian/Alaska Native, 0.0% Native Hawaiian/Other Pacific Islander, 2.1% Two or more races, 2.6% Hispanic of any race; Average household size: 2.59; Median age: 39.7; Age under 18: 25.1%; Age 65 and over: 12.3%; Males per 100 females: 94.6; Marriage status: 26.8% never married, 58.8% now married, 0.8% separated, 4.7% widowed, 9.7% divorced; Foreign born: 2.3%; Speak English only: 95.9%; With disability: 10.1%; Veterans: 9.0%; Ancestry: 26.8% German, 21.4% Dutch, 15.5% Irish, 12.4% English, 11.1% Polish
Employment: 18.1% management, business, and financial, 4.7% computer, engineering, and science, 10.8% education, legal, community service, arts, and media, 6.7% healthcare practitioners, 16.3% service, 25.7% sales and office, 5.3% natural resources, construction, and maintenance, 12.4% production, transportation, and material moving
Income: Per capita: $29,375; Median household: $60,218; Average household: $75,963; Households with income of $100,000 or more: 22.7%; Poverty rate: 7.4%
Educational Attainment: High school diploma or higher: 95.0%; Bachelor's degree or higher: 33.2%; Graduate/professional degree or higher: 10.5%
Housing: Homeownership rate: 83.0%; Median home value: $155,000; Median year structure built: 1981; Homeowner vacancy rate: 1.6%; Median gross rent: $696 per month; Rental vacancy rate: 9.5%

Health Insurance: 92.1% have insurance; 81.4% have private insurance; 23.6% have public insurance; 7.9% do not have insurance; 1.4% of children under 18 do not have insurance
Transportation: Commute: 92.0% car, 0.4% public transportation, 0.9% walk, 5.7% work from home; Median travel time to work: 20.0 minutes
Additional Information Contacts
Plainfield Charter Township . . . . (616) 364-8466
    http://www.plainfieldchartertwp.org

ROCKFORD (city).
Covers a land area of 3.242 square miles and a water area of 0.067 square miles. Located at 43.14° N. Lat; 85.55° W. Long. Elevation is 702 feet.
History: Rockford was settled in the 1840's, and was known for a time as Laphamsville for its first settler, Smith Lapham. Renamed Rockford in 1866, the town grew up around a tanning, shoe, and glove factory. Its location on the Rogue River and Rum Creek also made it a resort area.
Population: 5,719; Growth (since 2000): 23.6%; Density: 1,763.8 persons per square mile; Race: 95.0% White, 0.7% Black/African American, 1.2% Asian, 0.5% American Indian/Alaska Native, 0.1% Native Hawaiian/Other Pacific Islander, 2.0% Two or more races, 3.7% Hispanic of any race; Average household size: 2.58; Median age: 33.7; Age under 18: 30.9%; Age 65 and over: 10.7%; Males per 100 females: 90.2; Marriage status: 23.5% never married, 58.2% now married, 1.5% separated, 6.1% widowed, 12.2% divorced; Foreign born: 3.0%; Speak English only: 92.4%; With disability: 8.9%; Veterans: 10.3%; Ancestry: 21.3% German, 17.9% Dutch, 17.2% English, 12.7% Irish, 12.1% Polish
Employment: 18.3% management, business, and financial, 8.4% computer, engineering, and science, 9.5% education, legal, community service, arts, and media, 8.5% healthcare practitioners, 16.5% service, 18.3% sales and office, 7.0% natural resources, construction, and maintenance, 13.5% production, transportation, and material moving
Income: Per capita: $24,692; Median household: $47,093; Average household: $65,232; Households with income of $100,000 or more: 19.7%; Poverty rate: 15.6%
Educational Attainment: High school diploma or higher: 96.2%; Bachelor's degree or higher: 38.0%; Graduate/professional degree or higher: 13.8%
School District(s)
Rockford Public Schools (PK-12)
    2012-13 Enrollment: 7,921 . . . . (616) 863-6557
Housing: Homeownership rate: 70.0%; Median home value: $145,200; Median year structure built: 1984; Homeowner vacancy rate: 1.7%; Median gross rent: $595 per month; Rental vacancy rate: 4.6%
Health Insurance: 91.7% have insurance; 80.5% have private insurance; 24.6% have public insurance; 8.3% do not have insurance; 9.0% of children under 18 do not have insurance
Safety: Violent crime rate: 11.9 per 10,000 population; Property crime rate: 149.3 per 10,000 population
Newspapers: Rockford Squire (weekly circulation 12000)
Transportation: Commute: 95.7% car, 0.0% public transportation, 1.5% walk, 2.6% work from home; Median travel time to work: 22.8 minutes; Amtrak: Bus service available.
Additional Information Contacts
City of Rockford. . . . . (616) 866-1537
    http://www.rockford.mi.us

SAND LAKE (village).
Covers a land area of 0.709 square miles and a water area of 0.032 square miles. Located at 43.29° N. Lat; 85.52° W. Long. Elevation is 915 feet.
History: Lumber operations began in the Sand Lake area in the late 1860's. The village was platted and named in 1871. Sand Lake grew as a resort area.
Population: 500; Growth (since 2000): 1.6%; Density: 704.8 persons per square mile; Race: 94.6% White, 0.8% Black/African American, 1.0% Asian, 0.2% American Indian/Alaska Native, 0.0% Native Hawaiian/Other Pacific Islander, 2.0% Two or more races, 5.2% Hispanic of any race; Average household size: 2.66; Median age: 33.2; Age under 18: 28.6%; Age 65 and over: 11.8%; Males per 100 females: 90.1
School District(s)
Tri County Area Schools (PK-12)
    2012-13 Enrollment: 2,181 . . . . (616) 636-5454
Housing: Homeownership rate: 62.3%; Homeowner vacancy rate: 1.7%; Rental vacancy rate: 0.0%
Safety: Violent crime rate: 0.0 per 10,000 population; Property crime rate: 214.8 per 10,000 population

SOLON (township).
Covers a land area of 34.718 square miles and a water area of 1.558 square miles. Located at 43.26° N. Lat; 85.62° W. Long.
History: Solon Township was organized in 1857, a few years after the area was settled by J.M. Rounds and a Mr. Beals.
Population: 5,974; Growth (since 2000): 28.1%; Density: 172.1 persons per square mile; Race: 95.8% White, 0.4% Black/African American, 0.6% Asian, 0.4% American Indian/Alaska Native, 0.0% Native Hawaiian/Other Pacific Islander, 1.7% Two or more races, 2.7% Hispanic of any race; Average household size: 2.75; Median age: 37.5; Age under 18: 26.0%; Age 65 and over: 11.5%; Males per 100 females: 99.5; Marriage status: 17.9% never married, 65.1% now married, 1.5% separated, 4.1% widowed, 12.9% divorced; Foreign born: 2.0%; Speak English only: 96.3%; With disability: 11.0%; Veterans: 10.4%; Ancestry: 27.5% German, 14.2% Dutch, 13.4% English, 13.1% Irish, 6.9% American
Employment: 7.5% management, business, and financial, 4.8% computer, engineering, and science, 7.7% education, legal, community service, arts, and media, 9.5% healthcare practitioners, 15.3% service, 26.1% sales and office, 9.1% natural resources, construction, and maintenance, 20.0% production, transportation, and material moving
Income: Per capita: $23,952; Median household: $60,306; Average household: $68,020; Households with income of $100,000 or more: 19.1%; Poverty rate: 8.2%
Educational Attainment: High school diploma or higher: 83.4%; Bachelor's degree or higher: 16.2%; Graduate/professional degree or higher: 4.1%
Housing: Homeownership rate: 92.4%; Median home value: $127,500; Median year structure built: 1986; Homeowner vacancy rate: 2.4%; Median gross rent: $882 per month; Rental vacancy rate: 4.6%
Health Insurance: 92.2% have insurance; 81.4% have private insurance; 26.8% have public insurance; 7.8% do not have insurance; 0.0% of children under 18 do not have insurance
Transportation: Commute: 97.0% car, 0.0% public transportation, 0.0% walk, 2.6% work from home; Median travel time to work: 31.6 minutes

SPARTA (township).
Covers a land area of 36.427 square miles and a water area of 0.052 square miles. Located at 43.16° N. Lat; 85.73° W. Long. Elevation is 758 feet.
History: Plotted 1869, incorporated 1883.
Population: 9,110; Growth (since 2000): 1.9%; Density: 250.1 persons per square mile; Race: 94.5% White, 0.7% Black/African American, 0.4% Asian, 0.3% American Indian/Alaska Native, 0.0% Native Hawaiian/Other Pacific Islander, 1.7% Two or more races, 5.3% Hispanic of any race; Average household size: 2.65; Median age: 35.6; Age under 18: 28.0%; Age 65 and over: 12.4%; Males per 100 females: 94.4; Marriage status: 29.3% never married, 49.3% now married, 1.8% separated, 6.1% widowed, 15.3% divorced; Foreign born: 1.8%; Speak English only: 96.6%; With disability: 13.6%; Veterans: 8.7%; Ancestry: 31.4% German, 14.9% Dutch, 13.6% Irish, 13.0% English, 8.3% Polish
Employment: 11.3% management, business, and financial, 3.7% computer, engineering, and science, 6.9% education, legal, community service, arts, and media, 5.5% healthcare practitioners, 17.8% service, 20.5% sales and office, 12.2% natural resources, construction, and maintenance, 22.1% production, transportation, and material moving
Income: Per capita: $23,903; Median household: $48,226; Average household: $60,702; Households with income of $100,000 or more: 12.5%; Poverty rate: 13.4%
Educational Attainment: High school diploma or higher: 91.6%; Bachelor's degree or higher: 17.0%; Graduate/professional degree or higher: 4.9%
School District(s)
Sparta Area Schools (PK-12)
    2012-13 Enrollment: 2,702 . . . . (616) 887-8253
Housing: Homeownership rate: 76.5%; Median home value: $114,700; Median year structure built: 1974; Homeowner vacancy rate: 2.3%; Median gross rent: $635 per month; Rental vacancy rate: 7.1%
Health Insurance: 88.9% have insurance; 70.3% have private insurance; 32.5% have public insurance; 11.1% do not have insurance; 1.4% of children under 18 do not have insurance
Transportation: Commute: 94.2% car, 0.5% public transportation, 1.7% walk, 3.3% work from home; Median travel time to work: 27.0 minutes
Airports: Paul C. Miller-Sparta (general aviation)
Additional Information Contacts
Sparta Township . . . . (616) 887-8863
    http://www.sparta-township.com

SPARTA (village). Covers a land area of 2.461 square miles and a water area of 0.007 square miles. Located at 43.16° N. Lat; 85.71° W. Long. Elevation is 758 feet.

History: Sparta was founded by Jonathan P. Nash, and first called Nashville. In 1850, Sparta took the name of its township.

Population: 4,140; Growth (since 2000): -0.5%; Density: 1,682.4 persons per square mile; Race: 94.5% White, 1.3% Black/African American, 0.5% Asian, 0.4% American Indian/Alaska Native, 0.0% Native Hawaiian/Other Pacific Islander, 1.7% Two or more races, 4.2% Hispanic of any race; Average household size: 2.51; Median age: 34.0; Age under 18: 28.5%; Age 65 and over: 13.8%; Males per 100 females: 88.9; Marriage status: 28.9% never married, 46.2% now married, 2.8% separated, 8.9% widowed, 16.1% divorced; Foreign born: 1.1%; Speak English only: 96.3%; With disability: 13.2%; Veterans: 8.3%; Ancestry: 27.6% German, 17.8% Irish, 16.6% Dutch, 14.2% English, 7.4% American

Employment: 8.6% management, business, and financial, 3.9% computer, engineering, and science, 7.2% education, legal, community service, arts, and media, 6.0% healthcare practitioners, 21.9% service, 20.9% sales and office, 8.9% natural resources, construction, and maintenance, 22.6% production, transportation, and material moving

Income: Per capita: $20,658; Median household: $41,274; Average household: $48,274; Households with income of $100,000 or more: 6.3%; Poverty rate: 10.4%

Educational Attainment: High school diploma or higher: 92.5%; Bachelor's degree or higher: 18.6%; Graduate/professional degree or higher: 5.1%

School District(s)

Sparta Area Schools (PK-12)
    2012-13 Enrollment: 2,702 . . . . (616) 887-8253

Housing: Homeownership rate: 61.4%; Median home value: $102,300; Median year structure built: 1969; Homeowner vacancy rate: 3.5%; Median gross rent: $620 per month; Rental vacancy rate: 7.8%

Health Insurance: 89.9% have insurance; 71.0% have private insurance; 31.5% have public insurance; 10.1% do not have insurance; 0.0% of children under 18 do not have insurance

Safety: Violent crime rate: 33.1 per 10,000 population; Property crime rate: 196.5 per 10,000 population

Transportation: Commute: 96.6% car, 0.0% public transportation, 2.0% walk, 0.9% work from home; Median travel time to work: 25.5 minutes

Airports: Paul C. Miller-Sparta (general aviation)

Additional Information Contacts
Village of Sparta . . . . (616) 887-8251
    http://www.spartami.org

SPENCER (township). Covers a land area of 33.970 square miles and a water area of 2.687 square miles. Located at 43.25° N. Lat; 85.37° W. Long.

Population: 3,960; Growth (since 2000): 7.6%; Density: 116.6 persons per square mile; Race: 96.8% White, 0.7% Black/African American, 0.2% Asian, 0.4% American Indian/Alaska Native, 0.0% Native Hawaiian/Other Pacific Islander, 1.3% Two or more races, 2.4% Hispanic of any race; Average household size: 2.60; Median age: 40.6; Age under 18: 25.1%; Age 65 and over: 13.7%; Males per 100 females: 107.3; Marriage status: 25.4% never married, 62.8% now married, 1.2% separated, 3.2% widowed, 8.6% divorced; Foreign born: 1.6%; Speak English only: 93.0%; With disability: 15.7%; Veterans: 11.6%; Ancestry: 26.5% German, 14.3% Irish, 14.2% English, 12.1% Dutch, 7.3% Polish

Employment: 11.9% management, business, and financial, 3.3% computer, engineering, and science, 7.5% education, legal, community service, arts, and media, 5.8% healthcare practitioners, 15.7% service, 19.4% sales and office, 18.7% natural resources, construction, and maintenance, 17.6% production, transportation, and material moving

Income: Per capita: $24,291; Median household: $56,074; Average household: $64,166; Households with income of $100,000 or more: 16.2%; Poverty rate: 14.1%

Educational Attainment: High school diploma or higher: 88.9%; Bachelor's degree or higher: 19.0%; Graduate/professional degree or higher: 5.9%

Housing: Homeownership rate: 88.6%; Median home value: $136,600; Median year structure built: 1984; Homeowner vacancy rate: 3.1%; Median gross rent: $925 per month; Rental vacancy rate: 10.5%

Health Insurance: 91.7% have insurance; 73.3% have private insurance; 34.6% have public insurance; 8.3% do not have insurance; 1.2% of children under 18 do not have insurance

Transportation: Commute: 95.5% car, 0.4% public transportation, 1.2% walk, 2.1% work from home; Median travel time to work: 37.8 minutes

TYRONE (township). Covers a land area of 36.123 square miles and a water area of 0.235 square miles. Located at 43.25° N. Lat; 85.73° W. Long.

Population: 4,731; Growth (since 2000): 9.9%; Density: 131.0 persons per square mile; Race: 93.6% White, 0.6% Black/African American, 0.2% Asian, 0.7% American Indian/Alaska Native, 0.0% Native Hawaiian/Other Pacific Islander, 1.5% Two or more races, 8.7% Hispanic of any race; Average household size: 2.93; Median age: 34.9; Age under 18: 28.9%; Age 65 and over: 9.5%; Males per 100 females: 102.5; Marriage status: 26.6% never married, 56.7% now married, 1.2% separated, 4.9% widowed, 11.9% divorced; Foreign born: 6.1%; Speak English only: 90.2%; With disability: 10.9%; Veterans: 10.3%; Ancestry: 18.6% German, 15.7% Dutch, 11.5% Irish, 9.7% English, 9.4% Polish

Employment: 13.4% management, business, and financial, 4.0% computer, engineering, and science, 8.4% education, legal, community service, arts, and media, 5.2% healthcare practitioners, 10.2% service, 27.1% sales and office, 14.5% natural resources, construction, and maintenance, 17.3% production, transportation, and material moving

Income: Per capita: $19,214; Median household: $47,635; Average household: $55,403; Households with income of $100,000 or more: 8.6%; Poverty rate: 10.5%

Educational Attainment: High school diploma or higher: 86.0%; Bachelor's degree or higher: 11.5%; Graduate/professional degree or higher: 1.8%

Housing: Homeownership rate: 87.7%; Median home value: $114,400; Median year structure built: 1983; Homeowner vacancy rate: 1.6%; Median gross rent: $846 per month; Rental vacancy rate: 8.2%

Health Insurance: 85.1% have insurance; 69.1% have private insurance; 30.6% have public insurance; 14.9% do not have insurance; 6.9% of children under 18 do not have insurance

Transportation: Commute: 94.9% car, 0.3% public transportation, 1.0% walk, 3.9% work from home; Median travel time to work: 35.8 minutes

Additional Information Contacts
Tyrone Township . . . . (616) 678-4779
    http://www.tyronetownship.org

VERGENNES (township). Covers a land area of 34.485 square miles and a water area of 0.903 square miles. Located at 42.98° N. Lat; 85.38° W. Long.

Population: 4,189; Growth (since 2000): 16.0%; Density: 121.5 persons per square mile; Race: 96.3% White, 0.9% Black/African American, 0.6% Asian, 0.1% American Indian/Alaska Native, 0.1% Native Hawaiian/Other Pacific Islander, 1.5% Two or more races, 1.8% Hispanic of any race; Average household size: 2.97; Median age: 39.2; Age under 18: 29.1%; Age 65 and over: 8.9%; Males per 100 females: 104.2; Marriage status: 25.5% never married, 66.0% now married, 1.1% separated, 1.9% widowed, 6.6% divorced; Foreign born: 1.9%; Speak English only: 97.3%; With disability: 7.4%; Veterans: 3.6%; Ancestry: 28.6% German, 17.2% Dutch, 15.7% English, 14.5% Irish, 13.3% Polish

Employment: 18.2% management, business, and financial, 5.4% computer, engineering, and science, 12.3% education, legal, community service, arts, and media, 4.7% healthcare practitioners, 15.4% service, 22.3% sales and office, 10.3% natural resources, construction, and maintenance, 11.3% production, transportation, and material moving

Income: Per capita: $27,663; Median household: $79,415; Average household: $81,313; Households with income of $100,000 or more: 25.4%; Poverty rate: 4.6%

Educational Attainment: High school diploma or higher: 95.7%; Bachelor's degree or higher: 36.6%; Graduate/professional degree or higher: 10.9%

Housing: Homeownership rate: 93.8%; Median home value: $184,200; Median year structure built: 1984; Homeowner vacancy rate: 0.7%; Median gross rent: $979 per month; Rental vacancy rate: 3.3%

Health Insurance: 92.5% have insurance; 85.4% have private insurance; 15.5% have public insurance; 7.5% do not have insurance; 3.7% of children under 18 do not have insurance

Transportation: Commute: 90.4% car, 0.0% public transportation, 1.8% walk, 6.3% work from home; Median travel time to work: 25.5 minutes

Additional Information Contacts
Vergennes Township . . . . (616) 897-5671
    http://www.vergennestwp.org

WALKER (city). Covers a land area of 24.942 square miles and a water area of 0.544 square miles. Located at 43.00° N. Lat; 85.76° W. Long. Elevation is 748 feet.
Population: 23,537; Growth (since 2000): 7.8%; Density: 943.7 persons per square mile; Race: 91.3% White, 2.8% Black/African American, 1.9% Asian, 0.5% American Indian/Alaska Native, 0.0% Native Hawaiian/Other Pacific Islander, 2.1% Two or more races, 4.1% Hispanic of any race; Average household size: 2.40; Median age: 34.6; Age under 18: 22.9%; Age 65 and over: 12.1%; Males per 100 females: 95.0; Marriage status: 32.6% never married, 50.1% now married, 0.8% separated, 5.8% widowed, 11.4% divorced; Foreign born: 3.8%; Speak English only: 93.9%; With disability: 11.1%; Veterans: 7.6%; Ancestry: 25.9% Dutch, 23.4% German, 16.1% Polish, 14.4% Irish, 9.8% English
Employment: 14.3% management, business, and financial, 7.0% computer, engineering, and science, 10.9% education, legal, community service, arts, and media, 6.9% healthcare practitioners, 14.7% service, 24.9% sales and office, 7.6% natural resources, construction, and maintenance, 13.6% production, transportation, and material moving
Income: Per capita: $26,694; Median household: $50,828; Average household: $61,898; Households with income of $100,000 or more: 17.3%; Poverty rate: 11.7%
Educational Attainment: High school diploma or higher: 92.8%; Bachelor's degree or higher: 28.5%; Graduate/professional degree or higher: 7.7%

Four-year College(s)
University of Phoenix-West Michigan Campus (Private, For-profit)
    Fall 2013 Enrollment: 306 . . . . (866) 766-0766
    2013-14 Tuition: In-state $11,320; Out-of-state $11,320
Vocational/Technical School(s)
Regency Beauty Institute-Grand Rapids (Private, For-profit)
    Fall 2013 Enrollment: 87 . . . . (800) 787-6456
    2013-14 Tuition: $17,300
Housing: Homeownership rate: 62.8%; Median home value: $145,900; Median year structure built: 1982; Homeowner vacancy rate: 1.3%; Median gross rent: $694 per month; Rental vacancy rate: 12.3%
Health Insurance: 91.0% have insurance; 80.5% have private insurance; 21.6% have public insurance; 9.0% do not have insurance; 4.5% of children under 18 do not have insurance
Safety: Violent crime rate: 16.6 per 10,000 population; Property crime rate: 280.7 per 10,000 population
Transportation: Commute: 95.0% car, 1.2% public transportation, 0.9% walk, 2.2% work from home; Median travel time to work: 19.2 minutes
Additional Information Contacts
City of Walker . . . . (616) 453-6311
    http://www.ci.walker.mi.us

WYOMING (city). Covers a land area of 24.639 square miles and a water area of 0.234 square miles. Located at 42.89° N. Lat; 85.71° W. Long. Elevation is 643 feet.
History: Native American mounds in adjacent Grandville. Settled 1832, incorporated 1959.
Population: 72,125; Growth (since 2000): 4.0%; Density: 2,927.3 persons per square mile; Race: 75.8% White, 7.2% Black/African American, 2.8% Asian, 0.6% American Indian/Alaska Native, 0.0% Native Hawaiian/Other Pacific Islander, 3.8% Two or more races, 19.4% Hispanic of any race; Average household size: 2.66; Median age: 32.1; Age under 18: 27.1%; Age 65 and over: 9.0%; Males per 100 females: 97.3; Marriage status: 33.5% never married, 51.1% now married, 1.9% separated, 4.3% widowed, 11.1% divorced; Foreign born: 10.8%; Speak English only: 81.5%; With disability: 10.9%; Veterans: 6.8%; Ancestry: 21.1% Dutch, 18.0% German, 10.8% Irish, 7.7% English, 7.1% Polish
Employment: 9.8% management, business, and financial, 3.8% computer, engineering, and science, 6.6% education, legal, community service, arts, and media, 3.8% healthcare practitioners, 18.5% service, 27.8% sales and office, 8.2% natural resources, construction, and maintenance, 21.5% production, transportation, and material moving
Income: Per capita: $21,246; Median household: $45,477; Average household: $55,718; Households with income of $100,000 or more: 11.7%; Poverty rate: 16.7%
Educational Attainment: High school diploma or higher: 85.2%; Bachelor's degree or higher: 19.4%; Graduate/professional degree or higher: 5.1%

School District(s)
Godfrey-Lee Public Schools (PK-12)
    2012-13 Enrollment: 1,778 . . . . (616) 241-4722

Godwin Heights Public Schools (PK-12)
    2012-13 Enrollment: 2,224 . . . . (616) 252-2090
Grandville Public Schools (PK-12)
    2012-13 Enrollment: 5,625 . . . . (616) 254-6570
Vanguard Charter Academy (KG-12)
    2012-13 Enrollment: 755 . . . . (616) 538-3630
Wyoming Public Schools (PK-12)
    2012-13 Enrollment: 4,568 . . . . (616) 530-7555
Four-year College(s)
Grace Bible College (Private, Not-for-profit, Other Protestant)
    Fall 2013 Enrollment: 579 . . . . (616) 538-2330
    2013-14 Tuition: In-state $12,235; Out-of-state $12,235
ITT Technical Institute-Grand Rapids (Private, For-profit)
    Fall 2013 Enrollment: 51 . . . . (616) 406-1200
    2013-14 Tuition: In-state $18,048; Out-of-state $18,048
ITT Technical Institute-Wyoming (Private, For-profit)
    Fall 2013 Enrollment: 343 . . . . (616) 406-1200
    2013-14 Tuition: In-state $18,048; Out-of-state $18,048
Housing: Homeownership rate: 66.0%; Median home value: $103,500; Median year structure built: 1966; Homeowner vacancy rate: 2.9%; Median gross rent: $714 per month; Rental vacancy rate: 7.7%
Health Insurance: 84.6% have insurance; 67.4% have private insurance; 26.9% have public insurance; 15.4% do not have insurance; 6.0% of children under 18 do not have insurance
Hospitals: Metro Health Hospital (208 beds)
Safety: Violent crime rate: 41.9 per 10,000 population; Property crime rate: 223.2 per 10,000 population
Transportation: Commute: 93.4% car, 1.6% public transportation, 0.8% walk, 3.0% work from home; Median travel time to work: 20.3 minutes
Additional Information Contacts
City of Wyoming . . . . (616) 530-7226
    http://www.ci.wyoming.mi.us

Keweenaw County

Located in northwestern Michigan, on the Upper Peninsula; on the Keweenaw Peninsula in Lake Superior; includes Isle Royale. Covers a land area of 540.112 square miles, a water area of 5,426.077 square miles, and is located in the Eastern Time Zone at 47.68° N. Lat., 88.15° W. Long. The county was founded in 1861. County seat is Eagle River.

Keweenaw County is part of the Houghton, MI Micropolitan Statistical Area. The entire metro area includes: Houghton County, MI; Keweenaw County, MI

Population: 2,156; Growth (since 2000): -6.3%; Density: 4.0 persons per square mile; Race: 98.5% White, 0.1% Black/African American, 0.0% Asian, 0.1% American Indian/Alaska Native, 0.0% Native Hawaiian/Other Pacific Islander, 1.2% two or more races, 0.7% Hispanic of any race; Average household size: 2.12; Median age: 51.6; Age under 18: 17.9%; Age 65 and over: 24.0%; Males per 100 females: 105.5
Religion: Five largest groups: 15.1% Lutheran, 11.9% Catholicism, 1.8% Methodist/Pietist, 0.3% Episcopalianism/Anglicanism, 0.1% Other Groups
Housing: Homeownership rate: 89.8%; Homeowner vacancy rate: 4.6%; Rental vacancy rate: 23.4%
Health Care: Physicians: 4.5 per 10,000 population; Hospital beds: 0.0 per 10,000 population; Hospital admissions: 0.0 per 10,000 population
Air Quality Index: 100.0% good, 0.0% moderate, 0.0% unhealthy for sensitive individuals, 0.0% unhealthy (percent of days)
Presidential Election: 41.9% Obama, 55.8% Romney (2012)
National and State Parks: Fort Wilkins State Park; Isle Royale National Park
Additional Information Contacts
Keweenaw Government . . . . (906) 337-2229
    http://www.keweenawcountyonline.org

Keweenaw County Communities

AHMEEK (village). Covers a land area of 0.069 square miles and a water area of 0 square miles. Located at 47.30° N. Lat; 88.40° W. Long. Elevation is 873 feet.
History: Ahmeek grew up around the Ahmeek Copper Mine. The village was founded in 1904 by John Bosch, and incorporated as a village in 1909. The name is Chippewa for "beaver."

Population: 146; Growth (since 2000): -7.0%; Density: 2,131.2 persons per square mile; Race: 99.3% White, 0.0% Black/African American, 0.0% Asian, 0.7% American Indian/Alaska Native, 0.0% Native Hawaiian/Other Pacific Islander, 0.0% Two or more races, 0.0% Hispanic of any race; Average household size: 2.00; Median age: 45.7; Age under 18: 18.5%; Age 65 and over: 18.5%; Males per 100 females: 94.7
Housing: Homeownership rate: 84.9%; Homeowner vacancy rate: 4.5%; Rental vacancy rate: 15.4%

ALLOUEZ (township). Covers a land area of 54.619 square miles and a water area of 0.071 square miles. Located at 47.37° N. Lat; 88.35° W. Long. Elevation is 1,007 feet.
History: Allouez took its name from the Allouez Mining Company, which had been named for Claude Jean Allouez, a French Jesuit missionary. The Allouez Mining Company opened a copper mine here in 1859.
Population: 1,571; Growth (since 2000): -0.8%; Density: 28.8 persons per square mile; Race: 98.8% White, 0.1% Black/African American, 0.0% Asian, 0.1% American Indian/Alaska Native, 0.0% Native Hawaiian/Other Pacific Islander, 1.0% Two or more races, 0.6% Hispanic of any race; Average household size: 2.28; Median age: 46.6; Age under 18: 22.7%; Age 65 and over: 19.3%; Males per 100 females: 101.7
Housing: Homeownership rate: 88.6%; Homeowner vacancy rate: 2.5%; Rental vacancy rate: 12.9%

COPPER HARBOR (CDP). Covers a land area of 1.513 square miles and a water area of 0.914 square miles. Located at 47.47° N. Lat; 87.87° W. Long. Elevation is 620 feet.
Population: 108; Growth (since 2000): n/a; Density: 71.4 persons per square mile; Race: 97.2% White, 0.0% Black/African American, 0.0% Asian, 0.0% American Indian/Alaska Native, 0.0% Native Hawaiian/Other Pacific Islander, 2.8% Two or more races, 0.0% Hispanic of any race; Average household size: 1.86; Median age: 53.0; Age under 18: 9.3%; Age 65 and over: 22.2%; Males per 100 females: 120.4
School District(s)
Grant Township S/d #2 (PK-12)
    2012-13 Enrollment: 4 . . . . (906) 289-4447
Housing: Homeownership rate: 77.6%; Homeowner vacancy rate: 10.0%; Rental vacancy rate: 38.1%

EAGLE HARBOR (CDP). Covers a land area of 1.803 square miles and a water area of 0.256 square miles. Located at 47.45° N. Lat; 88.15° W. Long. Elevation is 620 feet.
Population: 76; Growth (since 2000): n/a; Density: 42.2 persons per square mile; Race: 98.7% White, 0.0% Black/African American, 0.0% Asian, 0.0% American Indian/Alaska Native, 0.0% Native Hawaiian/Other Pacific Islander, 1.3% Two or more races, 3.9% Hispanic of any race; Average household size: 1.69; Median age: 66.3; Age under 18: 5.3%; Age 65 and over: 53.9%; Males per 100 females: 81.0
Housing: Homeownership rate: 97.7%; Homeowner vacancy rate: 4.3%; Rental vacancy rate: 87.5%

EAGLE HARBOR (township). Covers a land area of 180.408 square miles and a water area of 362.599 square miles. Located at 47.96° N. Lat; 88.93° W. Long. Elevation is 620 feet.
History: The Eagle Harbor area developed as a resort center, after the days when copper was shipped from here to the markets of the world. It was in Eagle Harbor that Justus H. Rathbone, a school teacher, wrote the rituals for the Order of Knights of Pythias, later founded in Washington, D.C.
Population: 217; Growth (since 2000): -22.8%; Density: 1.2 persons per square mile; Race: 98.2% White, 0.5% Black/African American, 0.0% Asian, 0.5% American Indian/Alaska Native, 0.0% Native Hawaiian/Other Pacific Islander, 0.9% Two or more races, 1.8% Hispanic of any race; Average household size: 1.70; Median age: 63.9; Age under 18: 2.3%; Age 65 and over: 46.1%; Males per 100 females: 106.7
Housing: Homeownership rate: 94.3%; Homeowner vacancy rate: 7.8%; Rental vacancy rate: 50.0%

EAGLE RIVER (CDP). County seat. Covers a land area of 5.945 square miles and a water area of 0.019 square miles. Located at 47.40° N. Lat; 88.26° W. Long. Elevation is 650 feet.
Population: 71; Growth (since 2000): n/a; Density: 11.9 persons per square mile; Race: 100.0% White, 0.0% Black/African American, 0.0% Asian, 0.0% American Indian/Alaska Native, 0.0% Native Hawaiian/Other Pacific Islander, 0.0% Two or more races, 0.0% Hispanic of any race;

Average household size: 1.72; Median age: 61.3; Age under 18: 4.2%; Age 65 and over: 31.0%; Males per 100 females: 136.7
Housing: Homeownership rate: 100.0%; Homeowner vacancy rate: 4.9%; Rental vacancy rate: 100.0%

GRANT (township). Covers a land area of 119.204 square miles and a water area of 83.528 square miles. Located at 47.40° N. Lat; 87.90° W. Long.
Population: 219; Growth (since 2000): 27.3%; Density: 1.8 persons per square mile; Race: 97.7% White, 0.0% Black/African American, 0.5% Asian, 0.0% American Indian/Alaska Native, 0.0% Native Hawaiian/Other Pacific Islander, 1.8% Two or more races, 0.0% Hispanic of any race; Average household size: 1.87; Median age: 57.9; Age under 18: 7.3%; Age 65 and over: 31.5%; Males per 100 females: 121.2
Housing: Homeownership rate: 88.9%; Homeowner vacancy rate: 8.8%; Rental vacancy rate: 48.0%

HOUGHTON (township). Covers a land area of 120.724 square miles and a water area of 396.694 square miles. Located at 48.10° N. Lat; 88.57° W. Long.
Population: 82; Growth (since 2000): -59.8%; Density: 0.7 persons per square mile; Race: 100.0% White, 0.0% Black/African American, 0.0% Asian, 0.0% American Indian/Alaska Native, 0.0% Native Hawaiian/Other Pacific Islander, 0.0% Two or more races, 0.0% Hispanic of any race; Average household size: 1.70; Median age: 62.0; Age under 18: 3.7%; Age 65 and over: 35.4%; Males per 100 females: 134.3
Housing: Homeownership rate: 95.6%; Homeowner vacancy rate: 6.4%; Rental vacancy rate: 33.3%

MOHAWK (unincorporated postal area)
ZCTA: 49950
    Covers a land area of 178.668 square miles and a water area of 11.428 square miles. Located at 47.39° N. Lat; 88.13° W. Long. Elevation is 1,033 feet.
    Population: 1,121; Growth (since 2000): -21.0%; Density: 6.3 persons per square mile; Race: 99.3% White, 0.2% Black/African American, 0.0% Asian, 0.1% American Indian/Alaska Native, 0.0% Native Hawaiian/Other Pacific Islander, 0.4% Two or more races, 0.4% Hispanic of any race; Average household size: 2.08; Median age: 52.5; Age under 18: 16.5%; Age 65 and over: 26.3%; Males per 100 females: 109.9
School District(s)
Public Schools of Calumet (KG-12)
    2012-13 Enrollment: 1,459 . . . . (906) 337-0311
    Housing: Homeownership rate: 89.2%; Homeowner vacancy rate: 4.8%; Rental vacancy rate: 25.0%

SHERMAN (township). Covers a land area of 65.157 square miles and a water area of 4.088 square miles. Located at 47.27° N. Lat; 88.21° W. Long.
Population: 67; Growth (since 2000): 11.7%; Density: 1.0 persons per square mile; Race: 92.5% White, 0.0% Black/African American, 0.0% Asian, 0.0% American Indian/Alaska Native, 0.0% Native Hawaiian/Other Pacific Islander, 6.0% Two or more races, 3.0% Hispanic of any race; Average household size: 1.81; Median age: 58.2; Age under 18: 7.5%; Age 65 and over: 25.4%; Males per 100 females: 116.1
Housing: Homeownership rate: 94.6%; Homeowner vacancy rate: 12.5%; Rental vacancy rate: 0.0%

Lake County

Located in west central Michigan; drained by Pere Marquette and Little Manistee Rivers; includes part of Manistee National Forest. Covers a land area of 567.370 square miles, a water area of 6.910 square miles, and is located in the Eastern Time Zone at 44.00° N. Lat., 85.81° W. Long. The county was founded in 1870. County seat is Baldwin.
Population: 11,539; Growth (since 2000): 1.8%; Density: 20.3 persons per square mile; Race: 87.0% White, 9.2% Black/African American, 0.1% Asian, 0.8% American Indian/Alaska Native, 0.0% Native Hawaiian/Other Pacific Islander, 2.6% two or more races, 2.1% Hispanic of any race; Average household size: 2.16; Median age: 50.1; Age under 18: 17.9%; Age 65 and over: 23.7%; Males per 100 females: 104.6; Marriage status: 24.8% never married, 44.7% now married, 1.4% separated, 12.0% widowed, 18.6% divorced; Foreign born: 0.9%; Speak English only: 97.9%;

With disability: 26.2%; Veterans: 13.5%; Ancestry: 22.5% German, 11.7% Irish, 11.0% English, 5.5% American, 5.3% Dutch

Religion: Six largest groups: 7.1% Catholicism, 3.0% Non-denominational Protestant, 2.5% Methodist/Pietist, 1.3% Presbyterian-Reformed, 1.2% Adventist, 1.1% Holiness

Economy: Unemployment rate: 8.2%; Leading industries: 18.5% retail trade; 18.5% accommodation and food services; 12.3% other services (except public administration); Farms: 200 totaling 26,025 acres; Company size: 0 employ 1,000 or more persons, 0 employ 500 to 999 persons, 1 employs 100 to 499 persons, 161 employs less than 100 persons; Business ownership: 128 women-owned, n/a Black-owned, n/a Hispanic-owned, n/a Asian-owned

Employment: 7.3% management, business, and financial, 2.1% computer, engineering, and science, 6.1% education, legal, community service, arts, and media, 3.0% healthcare practitioners, 25.9% service, 22.8% sales and office, 11.3% natural resources, construction, and maintenance, 21.5% production, transportation, and material moving

Income: Per capita: $16,202; Median household: $29,379; Average household: $38,197; Households with income of $100,000 or more: 5.7%; Poverty rate: 27.9%

Educational Attainment: High school diploma or higher: 80.3%; Bachelor's degree or higher: 8.4%; Graduate/professional degree or higher: 3.2%

Housing: Homeownership rate: 81.6%; Median home value: $79,700; Median year structure built: 1978; Homeowner vacancy rate: 4.8%; Median gross rent: $544 per month; Rental vacancy rate: 8.1%

Vital Statistics: Birth rate: 82.6 per 10,000 population; Death rate: 123.0 per 10,000 population; Age-adjusted cancer mortality rate: 236.1 deaths per 100,000 population

Health Insurance: 83.8% have insurance; 48.9% have private insurance; 56.3% have public insurance; 16.2% do not have insurance; 7.1% of children under 18 do not have insurance

Health Care: Physicians: 3.5 per 10,000 population; Hospital beds: 0.0 per 10,000 population; Hospital admissions: 0.0 per 10,000 population

Transportation: Commute: 92.3% car, 0.6% public transportation, 3.1% walk, 2.7% work from home; Median travel time to work: 25.2 minutes

Presidential Election: 52.1% Obama, 47.0% Romney (2012)

National and State Parks: Manistee National Forest; Pere Marquette State Forest; North Country National Scenic Trail

Additional Information Contacts

Lake Government . . . . (231) 745-2725
   http://www.lakecounty-michigan.com

Lake County Communities

BALDWIN (village). County seat. Covers a land area of 1.263 square miles and a water area of 0.002 square miles. Located at 43.90° N. Lat; 85.85° W. Long. Elevation is 840 feet.

History: Baldwin grew up at the junction of two rail lines, in an area of many lakes and streams that attracted vacationers. After being called Hannibal for an early settler, the name was changed to Baldwin in 1872 to honor Henry P. Baldwin, a governor of Michigan.

Population: 1,208; Growth (since 2000): 9.1%; Density: 956.1 persons per square mile; Race: 62.8% White, 29.0% Black/African American, 0.1% Asian, 0.9% American Indian/Alaska Native, 0.0% Native Hawaiian/Other Pacific Islander, 6.5% Two or more races, 4.1% Hispanic of any race; Average household size: 2.07; Median age: 36.8; Age under 18: 20.3%; Age 65 and over: 15.2%; Males per 100 females: 114.2

School District(s)

Baldwin Community Schools (PK-12)
   2012-13 Enrollment: 542 . . . . (231) 745-4791

Housing: Homeownership rate: 35.2%; Homeowner vacancy rate: 7.2%; Rental vacancy rate: 6.0%

CHASE (township). Covers a land area of 35.395 square miles and a water area of 0.147 square miles. Located at 43.85° N. Lat; 85.64° W. Long. Elevation is 1,096 feet.

History: Chase Township was named for Salmon Portland Chase, a governor of Ohio.

Population: 1,137; Growth (since 2000): -4.8%; Density: 32.1 persons per square mile; Race: 93.6% White, 3.8% Black/African American, 0.1% Asian, 0.4% American Indian/Alaska Native, 0.0% Native Hawaiian/Other Pacific Islander, 1.9% Two or more races, 1.1% Hispanic of any race; Average household size: 2.53; Median age: 40.7; Age under 18: 23.8%; Age 65 and over: 14.3%; Males per 100 females: 104.5

Housing: Homeownership rate: 89.1%; Homeowner vacancy rate: 2.2%; Rental vacancy rate: 9.3%

CHERRY VALLEY (township). Covers a land area of 35.612 square miles and a water area of 0 square miles. Located at 43.94° N. Lat; 85.74° W. Long.

Population: 396; Growth (since 2000): 7.6%; Density: 11.1 persons per square mile; Race: 90.4% White, 6.6% Black/African American, 0.0% Asian, 0.3% American Indian/Alaska Native, 0.0% Native Hawaiian/Other Pacific Islander, 2.8% Two or more races, 0.5% Hispanic of any race; Average household size: 2.22; Median age: 53.4; Age under 18: 18.9%; Age 65 and over: 28.3%; Males per 100 females: 98.0

Housing: Homeownership rate: 89.9%; Homeowner vacancy rate: 4.8%; Rental vacancy rate: 19.2%

DOVER (township). Covers a land area of 36.860 square miles and a water area of 0.073 square miles. Located at 44.12° N. Lat; 85.63° W. Long.

Population: 395; Growth (since 2000): 19.0%; Density: 10.7 persons per square mile; Race: 95.4% White, 0.0% Black/African American, 0.3% Asian, 0.8% American Indian/Alaska Native, 0.0% Native Hawaiian/Other Pacific Islander, 3.0% Two or more races, 2.5% Hispanic of any race; Average household size: 2.34; Median age: 48.9; Age under 18: 20.8%; Age 65 and over: 20.0%; Males per 100 females: 100.5

Housing: Homeownership rate: 84.0%; Homeowner vacancy rate: 0.7%; Rental vacancy rate: 12.9%

EDEN (township). Covers a land area of 36.442 square miles and a water area of 0.057 square miles. Located at 44.12° N. Lat; 85.86° W. Long.

Population: 487; Growth (since 2000): 29.2%; Density: 13.4 persons per square mile; Race: 98.4% White, 0.6% Black/African American, 0.2% Asian, 0.6% American Indian/Alaska Native, 0.0% Native Hawaiian/Other Pacific Islander, 0.2% Two or more races, 1.8% Hispanic of any race; Average household size: 2.14; Median age: 53.1; Age under 18: 15.8%; Age 65 and over: 21.8%; Males per 100 females: 114.5

Housing: Homeownership rate: 83.3%; Homeowner vacancy rate: 5.5%; Rental vacancy rate: 2.6%

ELK (township). Covers a land area of 35.508 square miles and a water area of 1.247 square miles. Located at 44.12° N. Lat; 85.98° W. Long.

Population: 985; Growth (since 2000): 9.4%; Density: 27.7 persons per square mile; Race: 97.2% White, 0.7% Black/African American, 0.1% Asian, 0.4% American Indian/Alaska Native, 0.0% Native Hawaiian/Other Pacific Islander, 1.4% Two or more races, 2.2% Hispanic of any race; Average household size: 1.99; Median age: 57.2; Age under 18: 12.3%; Age 65 and over: 34.2%; Males per 100 females: 116.5

Housing: Homeownership rate: 89.8%; Homeowner vacancy rate: 3.7%; Rental vacancy rate: 5.6%

ELLSWORTH (township). Covers a land area of 35.162 square miles and a water area of 0.200 square miles. Located at 44.03° N. Lat; 85.62° W. Long.

Population: 817; Growth (since 2000): -0.5%; Density: 23.2 persons per square mile; Race: 96.5% White, 0.6% Black/African American, 0.1% Asian, 0.6% American Indian/Alaska Native, 0.0% Native Hawaiian/Other Pacific Islander, 2.1% Two or more races, 1.6% Hispanic of any race; Average household size: 2.40; Median age: 46.0; Age under 18: 21.5%; Age 65 and over: 19.2%; Males per 100 females: 100.7

Housing: Homeownership rate: 90.0%; Homeowner vacancy rate: 4.9%; Rental vacancy rate: 5.4%

IDLEWILD (unincorporated postal area)
ZCTA: 49642

Covers a land area of 18.130 square miles and a water area of 0.295 square miles. Located at 43.87° N. Lat; 85.76° W. Long. Elevation is 853 feet.

Population: 842; Growth (since 2000): 22.9%; Density: 46.4 persons per square mile; Race: 54.2% White, 41.0% Black/African American, 0.0% Asian, 0.8% American Indian/Alaska Native, 0.1% Native Hawaiian/Other Pacific Islander, 3.8% Two or more races, 1.0% Hispanic of any race; Average household size: 2.11; Median age: 50.2; Age under 18: 20.8%; Age 65 and over: 23.9%; Males per 100 females: 96.3

Housing: Homeownership rate: 70.0%; Homeowner vacancy rate: 7.7%; Rental vacancy rate: 12.8%

IRONS (unincorporated postal area)
ZCTA: 49644

Covers a land area of 115.075 square miles and a water area of 1.862 square miles. Located at 44.11° N. Lat; 85.92° W. Long. Elevation is 856 feet.

Population: 2,033; Growth (since 2000): 15.1%; Density: 17.7 persons per square mile; Race: 97.5% White, 0.5% Black/African American, 0.1% Asian, 0.6% American Indian/Alaska Native, 0.0% Native Hawaiian/Other Pacific Islander, 1.2% Two or more races, 1.8% Hispanic of any race; Average household size: 2.05; Median age: 55.8; Age under 18: 13.9%; Age 65 and over: 29.9%; Males per 100 females: 113.6

Housing: Homeownership rate: 87.2%; Homeowner vacancy rate: 3.9%; Rental vacancy rate: 5.2%

LAKE (township).
Covers a land area of 33.887 square miles and a water area of 2.039 square miles. Located at 43.86° N. Lat; 85.98° W. Long.

Population: 862; Growth (since 2000): 1.5%; Density: 25.4 persons per square mile; Race: 95.0% White, 2.6% Black/African American, 0.2% Asian, 0.5% American Indian/Alaska Native, 0.0% Native Hawaiian/Other Pacific Islander, 1.3% Two or more races, 1.0% Hispanic of any race; Average household size: 1.97; Median age: 57.7; Age under 18: 11.4%; Age 65 and over: 32.8%; Males per 100 females: 102.3

Housing: Homeownership rate: 93.8%; Homeowner vacancy rate: 6.3%; Rental vacancy rate: 3.6%

LUTHER (village).
Covers a land area of 0.919 square miles and a water area of 0.010 square miles. Located at 44.04° N. Lat; 85.68° W. Long. Elevation is 1,033 feet.

History: When Luther was settled in 1880, it was called Wilson, for the owner of the sawmill. The next year it was platted and renamed for B.T. Luther, the other owner of the sawmill. Luther was incorporated as a village in 1893.

Population: 318; Growth (since 2000): -6.2%; Density: 346.1 persons per square mile; Race: 95.9% White, 0.3% Black/African American, 0.0% Asian, 1.9% American Indian/Alaska Native, 0.0% Native Hawaiian/Other Pacific Islander, 1.9% Two or more races, 2.8% Hispanic of any race; Average household size: 2.32; Median age: 40.8; Age under 18: 24.5%; Age 65 and over: 18.2%; Males per 100 females: 93.9

School District(s)
Pine River Area Schools (PK-12)
2012-13 Enrollment: 1,120 . . . . (231) 829-3141

Housing: Homeownership rate: 80.2%; Homeowner vacancy rate: 5.2%; Rental vacancy rate: 20.6%

NEWKIRK (township).
Covers a land area of 72.797 square miles and a water area of 0.042 square miles. Located at 44.09° N. Lat; 85.75° W. Long.

Population: 632; Growth (since 2000): -12.1%; Density: 8.7 persons per square mile; Race: 94.6% White, 0.8% Black/African American, 0.0% Asian, 2.5% American Indian/Alaska Native, 0.0% Native Hawaiian/Other Pacific Islander, 1.9% Two or more races, 1.6% Hispanic of any race; Average household size: 2.16; Median age: 49.5; Age under 18: 18.2%; Age 65 and over: 25.9%; Males per 100 females: 115.0

Housing: Homeownership rate: 80.8%; Homeowner vacancy rate: 5.8%; Rental vacancy rate: 20.0%

PEACOCK (township).
Covers a land area of 34.920 square miles and a water area of 0.850 square miles. Located at 44.02° N. Lat; 85.86° W. Long. Elevation is 866 feet.

Population: 492; Growth (since 2000): 10.6%; Density: 14.1 persons per square mile; Race: 96.5% White, 1.2% Black/African American, 0.4% Asian, 0.2% American Indian/Alaska Native, 0.0% Native Hawaiian/Other Pacific Islander, 0.8% Two or more races, 3.7% Hispanic of any race; Average household size: 2.01; Median age: 56.6; Age under 18: 12.4%; Age 65 and over: 31.3%; Males per 100 females: 100.8

Housing: Homeownership rate: 87.4%; Homeowner vacancy rate: 2.7%; Rental vacancy rate: 3.1%

PINORA (township).
Covers a land area of 35.472 square miles and a water area of 0.041 square miles. Located at 43.94° N. Lat; 85.61° W. Long.

Population: 717; Growth (since 2000): 11.5%; Density: 20.2 persons per square mile; Race: 97.1% White, 0.7% Black/African American, 0.0% Asian, 0.4% American Indian/Alaska Native, 0.0% Native Hawaiian/Other Pacific Islander, 1.8% Two or more races, 0.3% Hispanic of any race; Average household size: 2.49; Median age: 46.1; Age under 18: 20.9%; Age 65 and over: 18.5%; Males per 100 females: 102.5

Housing: Homeownership rate: 85.7%; Homeowner vacancy rate: 2.4%; Rental vacancy rate: 6.8%

PLEASANT PLAINS (township).
Covers a land area of 34.734 square miles and a water area of 0.557 square miles. Located at 43.86° N. Lat; 85.86° W. Long.

Population: 1,581; Growth (since 2000): 3.0%; Density: 45.5 persons per square mile; Race: 78.1% White, 16.2% Black/African American, 0.0% Asian, 0.9% American Indian/Alaska Native, 0.0% Native Hawaiian/Other Pacific Islander, 4.4% Two or more races, 4.0% Hispanic of any race; Average household size: 2.20; Median age: 45.0; Age under 18: 22.6%; Age 65 and over: 18.3%; Males per 100 females: 102.7

Housing: Homeownership rate: 70.8%; Homeowner vacancy rate: 7.4%; Rental vacancy rate: 8.7%

SAUBLE (township).
Covers a land area of 34.630 square miles and a water area of 0.715 square miles. Located at 44.03° N. Lat; 85.99° W. Long. Elevation is 735 feet.

Population: 333; Growth (since 2000): 3.1%; Density: 9.6 persons per square mile; Race: 95.2% White, 0.0% Black/African American, 0.3% Asian, 1.5% American Indian/Alaska Native, 0.0% Native Hawaiian/Other Pacific Islander, 1.5% Two or more races, 1.8% Hispanic of any race; Average household size: 1.86; Median age: 59.6; Age under 18: 9.6%; Age 65 and over: 36.3%; Males per 100 females: 97.0

Housing: Homeownership rate: 91.6%; Homeowner vacancy rate: 3.5%; Rental vacancy rate: 11.8%

SWEETWATER (township).
Covers a land area of 35.691 square miles and a water area of 0.065 square miles. Located at 43.94° N. Lat; 85.98° W. Long.

Population: 245; Growth (since 2000): 2.9%; Density: 6.9 persons per square mile; Race: 89.0% White, 7.3% Black/African American, 0.0% Asian, 0.4% American Indian/Alaska Native, 0.0% Native Hawaiian/Other Pacific Islander, 2.9% Two or more races, 1.6% Hispanic of any race; Average household size: 2.03; Median age: 53.5; Age under 18: 12.7%; Age 65 and over: 29.4%; Males per 100 females: 111.2

Housing: Homeownership rate: 90.5%; Homeowner vacancy rate: 2.8%; Rental vacancy rate: 0.0%

WEBBER (township).
Covers a land area of 34.969 square miles and a water area of 0.561 square miles. Located at 43.95° N. Lat; 85.86° W. Long.

Population: 1,699; Growth (since 2000): -9.4%; Density: 48.6 persons per square mile; Race: 72.5% White, 21.1% Black/African American, 0.4% Asian, 1.1% American Indian/Alaska Native, 0.0% Native Hawaiian/Other Pacific Islander, 4.5% Two or more races, 3.1% Hispanic of any race; Average household size: 2.04; Median age: 45.8; Age under 18: 16.5%; Age 65 and over: 21.5%; Males per 100 females: 104.7

Housing: Homeownership rate: 64.0%; Homeowner vacancy rate: 6.2%; Rental vacancy rate: 4.7%

YATES (township).
Covers a land area of 35.289 square miles and a water area of 0.317 square miles. Located at 43.85° N. Lat; 85.73° W. Long.

Population: 761; Growth (since 2000): 6.6%; Density: 21.6 persons per square mile; Race: 55.6% White, 39.9% Black/African American, 0.0% Asian, 0.9% American Indian/Alaska Native, 0.1% Native Hawaiian/Other Pacific Islander, 3.4% Two or more races, 1.4% Hispanic of any race; Average household size: 2.01; Median age: 52.0; Age under 18: 18.0%; Age 65 and over: 26.3%; Males per 100 females: 97.7

Housing: Homeownership rate: 71.5%; Homeowner vacancy rate: 6.1%; Rental vacancy rate: 10.0%

Lapeer County

Located in eastern Michigan; drained by the Flint and Belle Rivers; includes many small lakes. Covers a land area of 643.013 square miles, a water area of 19.831 square miles, and is located in the Eastern Time Zone at 43.09° N. Lat., 83.22° W. Long. The county was founded in 1837. County seat is Lapeer.

Lapeer County is part of the Detroit-Warren-Dearborn, MI Metropolitan Statistical Area. The entire metro area includes: Detroit-Dearborn-Livonia, MI Metropolitan Division (Wayne County, MI); Warren-Troy-Farmington Hills, MI Metropolitan Division (Lapeer County, MI; Livingston County, MI; Macomb County, MI; Oakland County, MI; Saint Clair County, MI)

Weather Station: Lapeer WWTP										Elevation: 819 feet		
	Jan	Feb	Mar	Apr	May	Jun	Jul	Aug	Sep	Oct	Nov	Dec
High	30	33	43	57	69	78	82	80	73	60	47	34
Low	15	16	24	35	45	54	59	57	50	39	31	21
Precip	1.6	1.5	1.8	2.7	3.1	3.0	3.7	3.3	3.9	2.9	2.6	1.8
Snow	10.0	7.9	4.7	1.3	0.0	0.0	0.0	0.0	0.0	0.1	1.4	8.1

High and Low temperatures in degrees Fahrenheit; Precipitation and Snow in inches

Population: 88,319; Growth (since 2000): 0.5%; Density: 137.4 persons per square mile; Race: 95.5% White, 1.0% Black/African American, 0.3% Asian, 0.5% American Indian/Alaska Native, 0.0% Native Hawaiian/Other Pacific Islander, 1.4% two or more races, 4.1% Hispanic of any race; Average household size: 2.64; Median age: 41.6; Age under 18: 24.2%; Age 65 and over: 13.3%; Males per 100 females: 101.7; Marriage status: 24.9% never married, 59.9% now married, 1.2% separated, 5.2% widowed, 9.9% divorced; Foreign born: 2.7%; Speak English only: 95.9%; With disability: 12.7%; Veterans: 9.7%; Ancestry: 27.2% German, 13.8% Irish, 12.8% English, 9.8% Polish, 7.3% American
Religion: Six largest groups: 15.3% Catholicism, 3.5% Lutheran, 2.6% Methodist/Pietist, 2.3% Non-denominational Protestant, 1.7% Baptist, 1.6% Pentecostal
Economy: Unemployment rate: 7.7%; Leading industries: 15.2% retail trade; 12.8% health care and social assistance; 12.2% construction; Farms: 1,133 totaling 175,598 acres; Company size: 0 employ 1,000 or more persons, 1 employs 500 to 999 persons, 27 employ 100 to 499 persons, 1,540 employ less than 100 persons; Business ownership: n/a women-owned, n/a Black-owned, 88 Hispanic-owned, n/a Asian-owned
Employment: 10.8% management, business, and financial, 5.2% computer, engineering, and science, 8.3% education, legal, community service, arts, and media, 6.1% healthcare practitioners, 16.6% service, 22.2% sales and office, 10.4% natural resources, construction, and maintenance, 20.4% production, transportation, and material moving
Income: Per capita: $23,907; Median household: $52,939; Average household: $64,003; Households with income of $100,000 or more: 17.5%; Poverty rate: 11.0%
Educational Attainment: High school diploma or higher: 90.2%; Bachelor's degree or higher: 17.0%; Graduate/professional degree or higher: 5.9%
Housing: Homeownership rate: 83.6%; Median home value: $137,600; Median year structure built: 1977; Homeowner vacancy rate: 2.9%; Median gross rent: $757 per month; Rental vacancy rate: 11.1%
Vital Statistics: Birth rate: 95.4 per 10,000 population; Death rate: 86.9 per 10,000 population; Age-adjusted cancer mortality rate: 182.4 deaths per 100,000 population
Health Insurance: 88.5% have insurance; 73.3% have private insurance; 31.3% have public insurance; 11.5% do not have insurance; 3.3% of children under 18 do not have insurance
Health Care: Physicians: 9.3 per 10,000 population; Hospital beds: 17.8 per 10,000 population; Hospital admissions: 785.2 per 10,000 population
Transportation: Commute: 92.6% car, 0.7% public transportation, 1.2% walk, 4.4% work from home; Median travel time to work: 32.8 minutes
Presidential Election: 43.7% Obama, 55.1% Romney (2012)
National and State Parks: Lapeer State Game Area; Metamora-Hadley State Recreation Area; Ortonville State Recreation Area
Additional Information Contacts
Lapeer Government . . . . (810) 667-0366
    http://www.lapeercountyweb.org

Lapeer County Communities

ALMONT (township). Covers a land area of 36.660 square miles and a water area of 0.313 square miles. Located at 42.93° N. Lat; 83.05° W. Long. Elevation is 853 feet.
History: Incorporated 1885.
Population: 6,583; Growth (since 2000): 9.0%; Density: 179.6 persons per square mile; Race: 95.8% White, 0.2% Black/African American, 0.2% Asian, 0.2% American Indian/Alaska Native, 0.0% Native Hawaiian/Other Pacific Islander, 0.9% Two or more races, 4.4% Hispanic of any race; Average household size: 2.72; Median age: 40.7; Age under 18: 25.5%; Age 65 and over: 11.7%; Males per 100 females: 102.5; Marriage status: 24.3% never married, 60.4% now married, 0.2% separated, 5.9% widowed, 9.3% divorced; Foreign born: 2.7%; Speak English only: 95.0%; With disability: 10.0%; Veterans: 9.1%; Ancestry: 30.2% German, 18.2% Polish, 13.0% English, 11.8% Irish, 7.4% American
Employment: 13.9% management, business, and financial, 9.1% computer, engineering, and science, 8.2% education, legal, community service, arts, and media, 4.1% healthcare practitioners, 12.8% service, 21.3% sales and office, 11.2% natural resources, construction, and maintenance, 19.4% production, transportation, and material moving
Income: Per capita: $26,473; Median household: $57,952; Average household: $70,882; Households with income of $100,000 or more: 25.8%; Poverty rate: 5.6%
Educational Attainment: High school diploma or higher: 93.0%; Bachelor's degree or higher: 20.4%; Graduate/professional degree or higher: 8.8%

School District(s)
Almont Community Schools (PK-12)
    2012-13 Enrollment: 1,530 . . . . (810) 798-8561
Housing: Homeownership rate: 89.5%; Median home value: $160,400; Median year structure built: 1980; Homeowner vacancy rate: 2.2%; Median gross rent: $640 per month; Rental vacancy rate: 9.6%
Health Insurance: 92.3% have insurance; 80.8% have private insurance; 27.2% have public insurance; 7.7% do not have insurance; 0.2% of children under 18 do not have insurance
Transportation: Commute: 94.8% car, 0.1% public transportation, 1.0% walk, 3.7% work from home; Median travel time to work: 36.6 minutes

ALMONT (village). Covers a land area of 1.424 square miles and a water area of <.001 square miles. Located at 42.92° N. Lat; 83.04° W. Long. Elevation is 853 feet.
History: Almont was first settled by James Deneen in 1828. First called Newburg, the name was changed in 1846 to honor the Mexican general Juan N. Almonte.
Population: 2,674; Growth (since 2000): -4.6%; Density: 1,877.9 persons per square mile; Race: 93.1% White, 0.3% Black/African American, 0.2% Asian, 0.3% American Indian/Alaska Native, 0.0% Native Hawaiian/Other Pacific Islander, 1.1% Two or more races, 7.4% Hispanic of any race; Average household size: 2.60; Median age: 37.2; Age under 18: 26.9%; Age 65 and over: 11.4%; Males per 100 females: 100.8; Marriage status: 26.3% never married, 54.1% now married, 0.6% separated, 7.5% widowed, 12.0% divorced; Foreign born: 2.0%; Speak English only: 95.2%; With disability: 9.1%; Veterans: 10.6%; Ancestry: 32.8% German, 22.2% Polish, 14.3% Irish, 14.2% English, 8.0% French
Employment: 8.8% management, business, and financial, 9.2% computer, engineering, and science, 9.1% education, legal, community service, arts, and media, 2.4% healthcare practitioners, 13.3% service, 24.0% sales and office, 10.8% natural resources, construction, and maintenance, 22.5% production, transportation, and material moving
Income: Per capita: $23,017; Median household: $42,692; Average household: $58,980; Households with income of $100,000 or more: 19.0%; Poverty rate: 7.7%
Educational Attainment: High school diploma or higher: 90.7%; Bachelor's degree or higher: 15.3%; Graduate/professional degree or higher: 6.2%

School District(s)
Almont Community Schools (PK-12)
    2012-13 Enrollment: 1,530 . . . . (810) 798-8561
Housing: Homeownership rate: 82.1%; Median home value: $106,000; Median year structure built: 1976; Homeowner vacancy rate: 3.6%; Median gross rent: $599 per month; Rental vacancy rate: 10.6%

Health Insurance: 92.7% have insurance; 78.9% have private insurance; 27.3% have public insurance; 7.3% do not have insurance; 0.6% of children under 18 do not have insurance
Safety: Violent crime rate: 29.9 per 10,000 population; Property crime rate: 190.4 per 10,000 population
Transportation: Commute: 95.4% car, 0.0% public transportation, 0.6% walk, 3.1% work from home; Median travel time to work: 36.2 minutes

ARCADIA (township).
Covers a land area of 35.049 square miles and a water area of 1.121 square miles. Located at 43.10° N. Lat; 83.17° W. Long.
Population: 3,113; Growth (since 2000): -2.6%; Density: 88.8 persons per square mile; Race: 97.1% White, 0.4% Black/African American, 0.3% Asian, 0.4% American Indian/Alaska Native, 0.0% Native Hawaiian/Other Pacific Islander, 1.4% Two or more races, 1.9% Hispanic of any race; Average household size: 2.65; Median age: 44.0; Age under 18: 22.8%; Age 65 and over: 14.6%; Males per 100 females: 105.3; Marriage status: 19.7% never married, 69.0% now married, 1.5% separated, 5.1% widowed, 6.3% divorced; Foreign born: 0.9%; Speak English only: 97.9%; With disability: 13.3%; Veterans: 13.3%; Ancestry: 27.2% German, 15.7% Polish, 11.8% English, 11.1% Irish, 11.1% American
Employment: 9.8% management, business, and financial, 4.1% computer, engineering, and science, 12.0% education, legal, community service, arts, and media, 8.2% healthcare practitioners, 17.4% service, 17.0% sales and office, 9.9% natural resources, construction, and maintenance, 21.6% production, transportation, and material moving
Income: Per capita: $23,913; Median household: $52,813; Average household: $62,563; Households with income of $100,000 or more: 16.5%; Poverty rate: 10.5%
Educational Attainment: High school diploma or higher: 85.0%; Bachelor's degree or higher: 14.0%; Graduate/professional degree or higher: 4.4%
Housing: Homeownership rate: 92.5%; Median home value: $149,700; Median year structure built: 1978; Homeowner vacancy rate: 1.4%; Median gross rent: $1,071 per month; Rental vacancy rate: 4.4%
Health Insurance: 86.9% have insurance; 71.6% have private insurance; 32.7% have public insurance, 13.1% do not have insurance; 5.9% of children under 18 do not have insurance
Transportation: Commute: 95.3% car, 0.3% public transportation, 0.0% walk, 3.5% work from home; Median travel time to work: 32.8 minutes

ATTICA (CDP).
Covers a land area of 4.775 square miles and a water area of 0.193 square miles. Located at 43.02° N. Lat; 83.16° W. Long. Elevation is 896 feet.
Population: 994; Growth (since 2000): n/a; Density: 208.2 persons per square mile; Race: 97.2% White, 0.1% Black/African American, 0.0% Asian, 0.3% American Indian/Alaska Native, 0.0% Native Hawaiian/Other Pacific Islander, 1.1% Two or more races, 4.8% Hispanic of any race; Average household size: 2.63; Median age: 41.3; Age under 18: 22.8%; Age 65 and over: 14.9%; Males per 100 females: 101.6
School District(s)
Lapeer ISD (PK-12)
   2012-13 Enrollment: 186 . . . . (810) 664-5917
Housing: Homeownership rate: 89.1%; Homeowner vacancy rate: 1.2%; Rental vacancy rate: 4.7%

ATTICA (township).
Covers a land area of 35.091 square miles and a water area of 1.132 square miles. Located at 43.02° N. Lat; 83.16° W. Long. Elevation is 896 feet.
Population: 4,755; Growth (since 2000): 1.6%; Density: 135.5 persons per square mile; Race: 96.6% White, 0.2% Black/African American, 0.1% Asian, 0.3% American Indian/Alaska Native, 0.0% Native Hawaiian/Other Pacific Islander, 1.3% Two or more races, 4.8% Hispanic of any race; Average household size: 2.69; Median age: 41.9; Age under 18: 23.6%; Age 65 and over: 13.6%; Males per 100 females: 103.6; Marriage status: 28.9% never married, 59.8% now married, 1.4% separated, 2.3% widowed, 9.0% divorced; Foreign born: 1.2%; Speak English only: 96.6%; With disability: 13.5%; Veterans: 7.1%; Ancestry: 29.6% German, 14.8% Irish, 14.4% English, 9.3% Polish, 7.0% American
Employment: 5.3% management, business, and financial, 7.7% computer, engineering, and science, 6.5% education, legal, community service, arts, and media, 3.4% healthcare practitioners, 16.5% service, 23.5% sales and office, 12.0% natural resources, construction, and maintenance, 25.0% production, transportation, and material moving

Income: Per capita: $23,075; Median household: $53,343; Average household: $62,851; Households with income of $100,000 or more: 13.6%; Poverty rate: 11.7%
Educational Attainment: High school diploma or higher: 94.6%; Bachelor's degree or higher: 8.9%; Graduate/professional degree or higher: 2.3%
School District(s)
Lapeer ISD (PK-12)
   2012-13 Enrollment: 186 . . . . (810) 664-5917
Housing: Homeownership rate: 88.8%; Median home value: $139,500; Median year structure built: 1977; Homeowner vacancy rate: 2.1%; Median gross rent: $710 per month; Rental vacancy rate: 3.4%
Health Insurance: 89.0% have insurance; 79.3% have private insurance; 27.1% have public insurance; 11.0% do not have insurance; 0.0% of children under 18 do not have insurance
Transportation: Commute: 94.6% car, 0.3% public transportation, 0.5% walk, 3.6% work from home; Median travel time to work: 30.2 minutes
Additional Information Contacts
Attica Township . . . . (810) 724-8128
   http://atticatownship.org

BARNES LAKE-MILLERS LAKE (CDP).
Covers a land area of 3.057 square miles and a water area of 0.400 square miles. Located at 43.18° N. Lat; 83.31° W. Long.
Population: 1,093; Growth (since 2000): -7.9%; Density: 357.5 persons per square mile; Race: 97.9% White, 0.1% Black/African American, 0.3% Asian, 0.5% American Indian/Alaska Native, 0.0% Native Hawaiian/Other Pacific Islander, 1.1% Two or more races, 2.6% Hispanic of any race; Average household size: 2.39; Median age: 45.2; Age under 18: 20.4%; Age 65 and over: 15.8%; Males per 100 females: 106.2
Housing: Homeownership rate: 83.7%; Homeowner vacancy rate: 2.8%; Rental vacancy rate: 9.5%

BURLINGTON (township).
Covers a land area of 34.989 square miles and a water area of 0.626 square miles. Located at 43.28° N. Lat; 83.17° W. Long.
Population: 1,478; Growth (since 2000): 5.4%; Density: 42.2 persons per square mile; Race: 97.2% White, 0.6% Black/African American, 0.1% Asian, 0.2% American Indian/Alaska Native, 0.1% Native Hawaiian/Other Pacific Islander, 1.4% Two or more races, 1.8% Hispanic of any race; Average household size: 2.74; Median age: 40.3; Age under 18: 25.1%; Age 65 and over: 14.1%; Males per 100 females: 107.6
Housing: Homeownership rate: 82.0%; Homeowner vacancy rate: 3.6%; Rental vacancy rate: 10.0%

BURNSIDE (township).
Covers a land area of 53.369 square miles and a water area of 0.707 square miles. Located at 43.22° N. Lat; 83.06° W. Long. Elevation is 850 feet.
History: Burnside Township began as Allison Township, organized in 1855. The name was changed in 1866 to honor Union General Ambrose E. Burnside.
Population: 1,864; Growth (since 2000): -2.9%; Density: 34.9 persons per square mile; Race: 96.3% White, 0.4% Black/African American, 0.2% Asian, 0.6% American Indian/Alaska Native, 0.0% Native Hawaiian/Other Pacific Islander, 1.7% Two or more races, 4.0% Hispanic of any race; Average household size: 2.66; Median age: 42.1; Age under 18: 24.1%; Age 65 and over: 11.5%; Males per 100 females: 107.3
Housing: Homeownership rate: 86.6%; Homeowner vacancy rate: 2.1%; Rental vacancy rate: 5.0%

CLIFFORD (village).
Covers a land area of 1.508 square miles and a water area of 0.001 square miles. Located at 43.32° N. Lat; 83.18° W. Long. Elevation is 830 feet.
History: Clifford was founded in the early 1860's by Arden W. Lyman, who operated a store and post office from his home. Lyman named the village for his son, Clifford Lyman.
Population: 324; Growth (since 2000): 0.0%; Density: 214.8 persons per square mile; Race: 96.9% White, 0.3% Black/African American, 0.0% Asian, 0.3% American Indian/Alaska Native, 0.0% Native Hawaiian/Other Pacific Islander, 2.2% Two or more races, 1.9% Hispanic of any race; Average household size: 2.77; Median age: 39.3; Age under 18: 26.5%; Age 65 and over: 13.0%; Males per 100 females: 107.7
Housing: Homeownership rate: 73.6%; Homeowner vacancy rate: 5.3%; Rental vacancy rate: 3.0%

COLUMBIAVILLE (village). Covers a land area of 0.845 square miles and a water area of 0.296 square miles. Located at 43.16° N. Lat; 83.40° W. Long. Elevation is 771 feet.

History: Columbiaville was settled in 1847 and developed around a sawmill. It was first known as Niverville, and later renamed for Columbia County, New York.

Population: 787; Growth (since 2000): -3.4%; Density: 931.1 persons per square mile; Race: 95.2% White, 0.0% Black/African American, 0.1% Asian, 0.4% American Indian/Alaska Native, 0.0% Native Hawaiian/Other Pacific Islander, 1.8% Two or more races, 4.6% Hispanic of any race; Average household size: 2.63; Median age: 36.4; Age under 18: 27.1%; Age 65 and over: 11.9%; Males per 100 females: 91.5

School District(s)

Lakeville Community SD (PK-12)

    2012-13 Enrollment: 1,467 . . . . (810) 591-3980

Housing: Homeownership rate: 71.9%; Homeowner vacancy rate: 2.2%; Rental vacancy rate: 12.5%

DEERFIELD (township). Covers a land area of 35.409 square miles and a water area of 0.911 square miles. Located at 43.19° N. Lat; 83.29° W. Long.

Population: 5,695; Growth (since 2000): -0.7%; Density: 160.8 persons per square mile; Race: 97.7% White, 0.3% Black/African American, 0.1% Asian, 0.4% American Indian/Alaska Native, 0.0% Native Hawaiian/Other Pacific Islander, 1.2% Two or more races, 2.7% Hispanic of any race; Average household size: 2.79; Median age: 39.7; Age under 18: 26.0%; Age 65 and over: 10.9%; Males per 100 females: 102.3; Marriage status: 23.5% never married, 58.2% now married, 1.0% separated, 5.3% widowed, 13.0% divorced; Foreign born: 1.9%; Speak English only: 97.3%; With disability: 11.9%; Veterans: 7.9%; Ancestry: 21.6% German, 14.5% English, 13.9% Irish, 12.0% American, 6.0% Polish

Employment: 11.8% management, business, and financial, 3.6% computer, engineering, and science, 8.6% education, legal, community service, arts, and media, 5.9% healthcare practitioners, 14.7% service, 22.2% sales and office, 15.5% natural resources, construction, and maintenance, 17.7% production, transportation, and material moving

Income: Per capita: $20,793; Median household: $50,278; Average household: $60,038; Households with income of $100,000 or more: 15.2%; Poverty rate: 10.1%

Educational Attainment: High school diploma or higher: 91.7%; Bachelor's degree or higher: 11.8%; Graduate/professional degree or higher: 4.5%

Housing: Homeownership rate: 88.5%; Median home value: $104,500; Median year structure built: 1979; Homeowner vacancy rate: 3.5%; Median gross rent: $891 per month; Rental vacancy rate: 7.5%

Health Insurance: 81.9% have insurance; 65.0% have private insurance; 32.6% have public insurance; 18.1% do not have insurance; 5.3% of children under 18 do not have insurance

Transportation: Commute: 95.7% car, 0.0% public transportation, 0.9% walk, 2.4% work from home; Median travel time to work: 31.6 minutes

DRYDEN (township). Covers a land area of 34.937 square miles and a water area of 1.267 square miles. Located at 42.94° N. Lat; 83.17° W. Long. Elevation is 938 feet.

Population: 4,768; Growth (since 2000): 3.1%; Density: 136.5 persons per square mile; Race: 97.7% White, 0.1% Black/African American, 0.4% Asian, 0.3% American Indian/Alaska Native, 0.0% Native Hawaiian/Other Pacific Islander, 1.1% Two or more races, 1.4% Hispanic of any race; Average household size: 2.69; Median age: 44.6; Age under 18: 23.5%; Age 65 and over: 13.3%; Males per 100 females: 105.3; Marriage status: 24.6% never married, 65.4% now married, 1.0% separated, 2.5% widowed, 7.5% divorced; Foreign born: 4.1%; Speak English only: 96.3%; With disability: 8.9%; Veterans: 8.3%; Ancestry: 28.8% German, 14.0% Irish, 12.3% Polish, 11.2% Italian, 6.4% French

Employment: 12.0% management, business, and financial, 8.0% computer, engineering, and science, 7.2% education, legal, community service, arts, and media, 8.1% healthcare practitioners, 10.7% service, 25.2% sales and office, 10.8% natural resources, construction, and maintenance, 17.8% production, transportation, and material moving

Income: Per capita: $30,676; Median household: $68,889; Average household: $83,029; Households with income of $100,000 or more: 29.7%; Poverty rate: 8.4%

Educational Attainment: High school diploma or higher: 96.3%; Bachelor's degree or higher: 23.9%; Graduate/professional degree or higher: 9.5%

School District(s)

Dryden Community Schools (PK-12)

    2012-13 Enrollment: 642 . . . . (810) 796-9534

Housing: Homeownership rate: 89.4%; Median home value: $211,000; Median year structure built: 1987; Homeowner vacancy rate: 2.2%; Median gross rent: $778 per month; Rental vacancy rate: 4.6%

Health Insurance: 92.0% have insurance; 83.2% have private insurance; 22.2% have public insurance; 8.0% do not have insurance; 4.4% of children under 18 do not have insurance

Safety: Violent crime rate: 4.2 per 10,000 population; Property crime rate: 81.7 per 10,000 population

Transportation: Commute: 92.2% car, 0.3% public transportation, 0.6% walk, 6.1% work from home; Median travel time to work: 36.5 minutes

Additional Information Contacts

Dryden Township . . . . (810) 796-2248

DRYDEN (village). Covers a land area of 1.100 square miles and a water area of 0 square miles. Located at 42.95° N. Lat; 83.12° W. Long. Elevation is 938 feet.

History: Dryden was first called Lamb's Corners, but was renamed for the English poet, John Dryden. The village developed as the center of a farming and horse-breeding region.

Population: 951; Growth (since 2000): 16.7%; Density: 864.9 persons per square mile; Race: 98.0% White, 0.0% Black/African American, 0.2% Asian, 0.4% American Indian/Alaska Native, 0.0% Native Hawaiian/Other Pacific Islander, 1.1% Two or more races, 1.1% Hispanic of any race; Average household size: 2.57; Median age: 38.6; Age under 18: 27.1%; Age 65 and over: 12.2%; Males per 100 females: 99.4

School District(s)

Dryden Community Schools (PK-12)

    2012-13 Enrollment: 642 . . . . (810) 796-9534

Housing: Homeownership rate: 78.3%; Homeowner vacancy rate: 2.4%; Rental vacancy rate: 2.4%

ELBA (township). Covers a land area of 31.611 square miles and a water area of 2.149 square miles. Located at 43.02° N. Lat; 83.39° W. Long. Elevation is 850 feet.

Population: 5,250; Growth (since 2000): -3.9%; Density: 166.1 persons per square mile; Race: 97.1% White, 0.4% Black/African American, 0.3% Asian, 0.6% American Indian/Alaska Native, 0.0% Native Hawaiian/Other Pacific Islander, 1.2% Two or more races, 2.0% Hispanic of any race; Average household size: 2.59; Median age: 45.0; Age under 18: 21.5%; Age 65 and over: 14.4%; Males per 100 females: 101.1; Marriage status: 19.0% never married, 68.4% now married, 1.2% separated, 2.4% widowed, 10.2% divorced; Foreign born: 2.2%; Speak English only: 98.1%; With disability: 12.6%; Veterans: 12.7%; Ancestry: 26.9% German, 14.4% Irish, 13.8% English, 10.6% American, 8.4% Polish

Employment: 12.5% management, business, and financial, 6.7% computer, engineering, and science, 8.9% education, legal, community service, arts, and media, 11.7% healthcare practitioners, 11.9% service, 24.7% sales and office, 9.3% natural resources, construction, and maintenance, 14.2% production, transportation, and material moving

Income: Per capita: $30,459; Median household: $65,599; Average household: $73,915; Households with income of $100,000 or more: 21.0%; Poverty rate: 7.2%

Educational Attainment: High school diploma or higher: 97.7%; Bachelor's degree or higher: 24.7%; Graduate/professional degree or higher: 8.9%

Housing: Homeownership rate: 89.3%; Median home value: $154,900; Median year structure built: 1979; Homeowner vacancy rate: 2.3%; Median gross rent: $1,044 per month; Rental vacancy rate: 4.3%

Health Insurance: 90.2% have insurance; 82.1% have private insurance; 31.4% have public insurance; 9.8% do not have insurance; 0.0% of children under 18 do not have insurance

Transportation: Commute: 94.5% car, 3.1% public transportation, 1.0% walk, 0.9% work from home; Median travel time to work: 33.3 minutes

GOODLAND (township). Covers a land area of 35.583 square miles and a water area of 0.180 square miles. Located at 43.11° N. Lat; 83.05° W. Long. Elevation is 837 feet.

History: Goodland Township was organized in 1855. The name was suggested by James Hill, who had settled here in 1851.

Population: 1,828; Growth (since 2000): 5.4%; Density: 51.4 persons per square mile; Race: 97.0% White, 0.4% Black/African American, 0.1% Asian, 0.2% American Indian/Alaska Native, 0.0% Native Hawaiian/Other

Pacific Islander, 1.9% Two or more races, 3.0% Hispanic of any race; Average household size: 2.77; Median age: 41.8; Age under 18: 23.9%; Age 65 and over: 13.2%; Males per 100 females: 104.7
Housing: Homeownership rate: 87.8%; Homeowner vacancy rate: 2.5%; Rental vacancy rate: 4.8%

HADLEY (township). Covers a land area of 33.443 square miles and a water area of 2.574 square miles. Located at 42.93° N. Lat; 83.39° W. Long. Elevation is 902 feet.
Population: 4,528; Growth (since 2000): -2.7%; Density: 135.4 persons per square mile; Race: 97.7% White, 0.2% Black/African American, 0.4% Asian, 0.2% American Indian/Alaska Native, 0.0% Native Hawaiian/Other Pacific Islander, 1.1% Two or more races, 1.2% Hispanic of any race; Average household size: 2.72; Median age: 46.4; Age under 18: 21.8%; Age 65 and over: 13.8%; Males per 100 females: 104.1; Marriage status: 22.9% never married, 66.3% now married, 1.1% separated, 3.5% widowed, 7.3% divorced; Foreign born: 1.4%; Speak English only: 96.2%; With disability: 10.0%; Veterans: 9.0%; Ancestry: 25.5% German, 18.5% Irish, 12.1% English, 11.4% Polish, 6.3% American
Employment: 11.5% management, business, and financial, 9.0% computer, engineering, and science, 9.8% education, legal, community service, arts, and media, 7.5% healthcare practitioners, 14.9% service, 18.0% sales and office, 11.7% natural resources, construction, and maintenance, 17.7% production, transportation, and material moving
Income: Per capita: $26,348; Median household: $64,886; Average household: $73,154; Households with income of $100,000 or more: 21.7%; Poverty rate: 9.5%
Educational Attainment: High school diploma or higher: 86.8%; Bachelor's degree or higher: 21.0%; Graduate/professional degree or higher: 6.7%
Housing: Homeownership rate: 94.2%; Median home value: $163,700; Median year structure built: 1981; Homeowner vacancy rate: 1.4%; Median gross rent: $1,236 per month; Rental vacancy rate: 3.9%
Health Insurance: 91.8% have insurance; 76.7% have private insurance; 28.4% have public insurance; 8.2% do not have insurance; 3.1% of children under 18 do not have insurance
Transportation: Commute: 93.2% car, 0.1% public transportation, 1.8% walk, 4.9% work from home; Median travel time to work: 36.3 minutes

IMLAY (township). Covers a land area of 33.552 square miles and a water area of 0.176 square miles. Located at 43.02° N. Lat; 83.05° W. Long.
History: Imlay Township was organized in 1850 and named for William H. Imlay, a Connecticut capitalist who owned land here.
Population: 3,128; Growth (since 2000): 15.3%; Density: 93.2 persons per square mile; Race: 94.3% White, 0.3% Black/African American, 0.5% Asian, 0.4% American Indian/Alaska Native, 0.0% Native Hawaiian/Other Pacific Islander, 1.7% Two or more races, 9.0% Hispanic of any race; Average household size: 2.90; Median age: 39.7; Age under 18: 26.4%; Age 65 and over: 11.9%; Males per 100 females: 99.9; Marriage status: 26.0% never married, 60.9% now married, 0.2% separated, 4.8% widowed, 8.4% divorced; Foreign born: 6.2%; Speak English only: 87.9%; With disability: 9.1%; Veterans: 8.0%; Ancestry: 30.6% German, 14.4% Polish, 7.9% Irish, 6.9% English, 6.7% Italian
Employment: 9.7% management, business, and financial, 1.7% computer, engineering, and science, 8.4% education, legal, community service, arts, and media, 1.7% healthcare practitioners, 16.6% service, 19.3% sales and office, 11.7% natural resources, construction, and maintenance, 30.9% production, transportation, and material moving
Income: Per capita: $21,066; Median household: $53,851; Average household: $64,274; Households with income of $100,000 or more: 16.7%; Poverty rate: 10.8%
Educational Attainment: High school diploma or higher: 82.8%; Bachelor's degree or higher: 10.7%; Graduate/professional degree or higher: 1.8%
Housing: Homeownership rate: 89.4%; Median home value: $153,400; Median year structure built: 1972; Homeowner vacancy rate: 3.8%; Median gross rent: $830 per month; Rental vacancy rate: 4.2%
Health Insurance: 80.5% have insurance; 70.8% have private insurance; 23.7% have public insurance; 19.5% do not have insurance; 15.9% of children under 18 do not have insurance
Transportation: Commute: 92.7% car, 3.6% public transportation, 0.8% walk, 2.6% work from home; Median travel time to work: 27.1 minutes

IMLAY CITY (city). Covers a land area of 2.367 square miles and a water area of 0 square miles. Located at 43.02° N. Lat; 83.08° W. Long. Elevation is 827 feet.
History: Imlay City, named for landowner William H. Imlay, began in 1870 when the Port Huron & Lake Michigan Railroad arrived. The town grew as a market center for an agricultural area. Celery was a leading crop in the early 1900's.
Population: 3,597; Growth (since 2000): -7.0%; Density: 1,519.7 persons per square mile; Race: 82.9% White, 0.9% Black/African American, 0.6% Asian, 0.3% American Indian/Alaska Native, 0.0% Native Hawaiian/Other Pacific Islander, 3.2% Two or more races, 29.0% Hispanic of any race; Average household size: 2.64; Median age: 33.0; Age under 18: 30.2%; Age 65 and over: 12.8%; Males per 100 females: 90.2; Marriage status: 33.3% never married, 47.1% now married, 2.1% separated, 9.4% widowed, 10.3% divorced; Foreign born: 17.3%; Speak English only: 75.0%; With disability: 14.7%; Veterans: 7.9%; Ancestry: 20.7% German, 8.2% English, 7.4% American, 7.4% Irish, 4.7% French Canadian
Employment: 7.3% management, business, and financial, 4.0% computer, engineering, and science, 4.5% education, legal, community service, arts, and media, 3.1% healthcare practitioners, 24.8% service, 18.3% sales and office, 7.4% natural resources, construction, and maintenance, 30.7% production, transportation, and material moving
Income: Per capita: $16,816; Median household: $34,287; Average household: $43,177; Households with income of $100,000 or more: 6.4%; Poverty rate: 20.5%
Educational Attainment: High school diploma or higher: 74.6%; Bachelor's degree or higher: 15.9%; Graduate/professional degree or higher: 4.2%

School District(s)
Imlay City Community Schools (PK-12)
    2012-13 Enrollment: 2,143 . . . . (810) 724-9861
Housing: Homeownership rate: 57.0%; Median home value: $90,700; Median year structure built: 1964; Homeowner vacancy rate: 3.7%; Median gross rent: $598 per month; Rental vacancy rate: 22.3%
Health Insurance: 79.7% have insurance; 56.3% have private insurance; 38.0% have public insurance; 20.3% do not have insurance; 6.2% of children under 18 do not have insurance
Safety: Violent crime rate: 39.0 per 10,000 population; Property crime rate: 225.9 per 10,000 population
Newspapers: Tri-City Times (weekly circulation 6300)
Transportation: Commute: 87.7% car, 0.0% public transportation, 2.2% walk, 6.4% work from home; Median travel time to work: 22.0 minutes

LAPEER (city). County seat. Covers a land area of 7.134 square miles and a water area of 0.254 square miles. Located at 43.05° N. Lat; 83.33° W. Long. Elevation is 856 feet.
History: Lapeer was founded in 1831, when the Pontiac Mill Company built a sawmill here. Its name comes from the French word for stone, perhaps referring to the flints found along the Flint River. First a lumber town, Lapeer became a furniture manufacturing center.
Population: 8,841; Growth (since 2000): -2.5%; Density: 1,239.2 persons per square mile; Race: 88.6% White, 7.6% Black/African American, 0.8% Asian, 0.6% American Indian/Alaska Native, 0.0% Native Hawaiian/Other Pacific Islander, 1.8% Two or more races, 3.9% Hispanic of any race; Average household size: 2.22; Median age: 36.0; Age under 18: 24.1%; Age 65 and over: 13.5%; Males per 100 females: 106.3; Marriage status: 38.0% never married, 38.3% now married, 3.0% separated, 6.9% widowed, 16.8% divorced; Foreign born: 2.1%; Speak English only: 95.8%; With disability: 19.0%; Veterans: 9.7%; Ancestry: 20.9% German, 15.9% Irish, 10.7% English, 7.8% American, 6.8% Polish
Employment: 6.7% management, business, and financial, 4.0% computer, engineering, and science, 10.1% education, legal, community service, arts, and media, 4.5% healthcare practitioners, 20.8% service, 20.4% sales and office, 11.5% natural resources, construction, and maintenance, 21.9% production, transportation, and material moving
Income: Per capita: $17,583; Median household: $35,266; Average household: $44,552; Households with income of $100,000 or more: 8.4%; Poverty rate: 24.7%
Educational Attainment: High school diploma or higher: 85.5%; Bachelor's degree or higher: 14.5%; Graduate/professional degree or higher: 4.0%

School District(s)
Chatfield School (KG-12)
    2012-13 Enrollment: 463 . . . . (810) 667-8970

Lapeer Community Schools (PK-12)
  2012-13 Enrollment: 5,828 . . . . (810) 667-2401
Housing: Homeownership rate: 51.0%; Median home value: $86,900; Median year structure built: 1976; Homeowner vacancy rate: 6.0%; Median gross rent: $715 per month; Rental vacancy rate: 14.9%
Health Insurance: 86.5% have insurance; 58.4% have private insurance; 43.9% have public insurance; 13.5% do not have insurance; 2.5% of children under 18 do not have insurance
Hospitals: Mclaren Lapeer Region (185 beds)
Safety: Violent crime rate: 47.6 per 10,000 population; Property crime rate: 425.2 per 10,000 population
Newspapers: County Line Reminder (weekly circulation 8300); LA View (weekly circulation 35000); The County Press (weekly circulation 16500)
Transportation: Commute: 90.1% car, 0.6% public transportation, 3.2% walk, 2.1% work from home; Median travel time to work: 27.0 minutes; Amtrak: Train service available.
Additional Information Contacts
City of Lapeer . . . . (810) 664-2902
  http://www.ci.lapeer.mi.us

LAPEER (township). Covers a land area of 29.986 square miles and a water area of 0.927 square miles. Located at 43.01° N. Lat; 83.27° W. Long. Elevation is 856 feet.
History: Settled 1831, incorporated as city 1869.
Population: 5,056; Growth (since 2000): -0.4%; Density: 168.6 persons per square mile; Race: 96.6% White, 0.2% Black/African American, 0.6% Asian, 0.6% American Indian/Alaska Native, 0.0% Native Hawaiian/Other Pacific Islander, 1.3% Two or more races, 2.7% Hispanic of any race; Average household size: 2.69; Median age: 44.3; Age under 18: 22.4%; Age 65 and over: 14.7%; Males per 100 females: 103.0; Marriage status: 17.0% never married, 67.6% now married, 1.2% separated, 6.5% widowed, 8.8% divorced; Foreign born: 2.1%; Speak English only: 97.3%; With disability: 15.7%; Veterans: 11.3%; Ancestry: 22.9% German, 16.3% Irish, 15.3% English, 9.2% Polish, 7.4% American
Employment: 10.9% management, business, and financial, 5.4% computer, engineering, and science, 10.2% education, legal, community service, arts, and media, 9.4% healthcare practitioners, 15.8% service, 20.8% sales and office, 4.5% natural resources, construction, and maintenance, 22.9% production, transportation, and material moving
Income: Per capita: $30,233; Median household: $61,005; Average household: $75,778; Households with income of $100,000 or more: 22.8%; Poverty rate: 6.8%
Educational Attainment: High school diploma or higher: 89.1%; Bachelor's degree or higher: 20.4%; Graduate/professional degree or higher: 8.5%
School District(s)
Chatfield School (KG-12)
  2012-13 Enrollment: 463 . . . . (810) 667-8970
Lapeer Community Schools (PK-12)
  2012-13 Enrollment: 5,828 . . . . (810) 667-2401
Housing: Homeownership rate: 89.0%; Median home value: $155,900; Median year structure built: 1978; Homeowner vacancy rate: 2.2%; Median gross rent: $896 per month; Rental vacancy rate: 6.8%
Health Insurance: 91.5% have insurance; 77.6% have private insurance; 32.4% have public insurance; 8.5% do not have insurance; 1.6% of children under 18 do not have insurance
Hospitals: Mclaren Lapeer Region (185 beds)
Safety: Violent crime rate: 2.0 per 10,000 population; Property crime rate: 51.5 per 10,000 population
Newspapers: County Line Reminder (weekly circulation 8300); LA View (weekly circulation 35000); The County Press (weekly circulation 16500)
Transportation: Commute: 92.7% car, 0.6% public transportation, 1.8% walk, 3.4% work from home; Median travel time to work: 31.3 minutes; Amtrak: Train service available.

MARATHON (township). Covers a land area of 32.853 square miles and a water area of 1.591 square miles. Located at 43.19° N. Lat; 83.40° W. Long.
Population: 4,568; Growth (since 2000): -2.8%; Density: 139.0 persons per square mile; Race: 96.4% White, 0.3% Black/African American, 0.1% Asian, 0.8% American Indian/Alaska Native, 0.0% Native Hawaiian/Other Pacific Islander, 1.5% Two or more races, 3.0% Hispanic of any race; Average household size: 2.71; Median age: 40.4; Age under 18: 24.3%; Age 65 and over: 12.2%; Males per 100 females: 102.8; Marriage status: 23.1% never married, 61.5% now married, 2.2% separated, 5.3%

widowed, 10.0% divorced; Foreign born: 0.8%; Speak English only: 97.9%; With disability: 13.0%; Veterans: 10.5%; Ancestry: 29.1% German, 20.1% Irish, 15.4% English, 10.4% Polish, 6.5% French
Employment: 8.1% management, business, and financial, 5.2% computer, engineering, and science, 7.8% education, legal, community service, arts, and media, 6.3% healthcare practitioners, 13.5% service, 20.5% sales and office, 14.7% natural resources, construction, and maintenance, 24.0% production, transportation, and material moving
Income: Per capita: $21,479; Median household: $54,728; Average household: $59,234; Households with income of $100,000 or more: 14.4%; Poverty rate: 12.3%
Educational Attainment: High school diploma or higher: 88.1%; Bachelor's degree or higher: 13.0%; Graduate/professional degree or higher: 3.3%
Housing: Homeownership rate: 86.9%; Median home value: $103,700; Median year structure built: 1972; Homeowner vacancy rate: 3.0%; Median gross rent: $707 per month; Rental vacancy rate: 9.0%
Health Insurance: 89.0% have insurance; 72.5% have private insurance; 31.2% have public insurance; 11.0% do not have insurance; 2.5% of children under 18 do not have insurance
Transportation: Commute: 94.5% car, 0.8% public transportation, 1.7% walk, 2.7% work from home; Median travel time to work: 43.8 minutes

MAYFIELD (township). Covers a land area of 33.118 square miles and a water area of 1.626 square miles. Located at 43.10° N. Lat; 83.29° W. Long.
Population: 7,955; Growth (since 2000): 3.9%; Density: 240.2 persons per square mile; Race: 97.4% White, 0.3% Black/African American, 0.2% Asian, 0.6% American Indian/Alaska Native, 0.0% Native Hawaiian/Other Pacific Islander, 1.2% Two or more races, 2.7% Hispanic of any race; Average household size: 2.58; Median age: 43.3; Age under 18: 23.1%; Age 65 and over: 16.6%; Males per 100 females: 95.5; Marriage status: 23.4% never married, 58.0% now married, 1.0% separated, 8.9% widowed, 9.6% divorced; Foreign born: 1.2%; Speak English only: 98.8%; With disability: 11.7%; Veterans: 12.3%; Ancestry: 31.5% German, 15.3% English, 10.5% Irish, 8.9% Italian, 7.6% Polish
Employment: 10.8% management, business, and financial, 3.4% computer, engineering, and science, 7.0% education, legal, community service, arts, and media, 6.1% healthcare practitioners, 23.8% service, 23.5% sales and office, 7.7% natural resources, construction, and maintenance, 17.6% production, transportation, and material moving
Income: Per capita: $23,765; Median household: $47,500; Average household: $61,942; Households with income of $100,000 or more: 20.7%; Poverty rate: 10.7%
Educational Attainment: High school diploma or higher: 92.7%; Bachelor's degree or higher: 17.0%; Graduate/professional degree or higher: 6.8%
Housing: Homeownership rate: 88.0%; Median home value: $127,200; Median year structure built: 1976; Homeowner vacancy rate: 3.7%; Median gross rent: $635 per month; Rental vacancy rate: 4.3%
Health Insurance: 90.5% have insurance; 72.5% have private insurance; 36.2% have public insurance; 9.5% do not have insurance; 1.2% of children under 18 do not have insurance
Transportation: Commute: 92.2% car, 0.8% public transportation, 0.7% walk, 6.4% work from home; Median travel time to work: 30.2 minutes
Additional Information Contacts
Mayfield Township. . . . . (810) 664-0821
  http://www.mayfieldtownship.com

METAMORA (township). Covers a land area of 34.213 square miles and a water area of 1.072 square miles. Located at 42.93° N. Lat; 83.27° W. Long. Elevation is 1,043 feet.
Population: 4,249; Growth (since 2000): 1.6%; Density: 124.2 persons per square mile; Race: 97.5% White, 0.5% Black/African American, 0.4% Asian, 0.4% American Indian/Alaska Native, 0.0% Native Hawaiian/Other Pacific Islander, 0.7% Two or more races, 2.1% Hispanic of any race; Average household size: 2.63; Median age: 44.7; Age under 18: 23.4%; Age 65 and over: 14.6%; Males per 100 females: 101.6; Marriage status: 19.7% never married, 68.3% now married, 1.3% separated, 5.1% widowed, 6.8% divorced; Foreign born: 2.8%; Speak English only: 98.6%; With disability: 8.9%; Veterans: 9.5%; Ancestry: 29.1% German, 16.5% Irish, 13.1% English, 8.7% Polish, 6.2% French
Employment: 18.5% management, business, and financial, 4.3% computer, engineering, and science, 8.8% education, legal, community service, arts, and media, 7.1% healthcare practitioners, 15.3% service,

26.9% sales and office, 5.8% natural resources, construction, and maintenance, 13.2% production, transportation, and material moving

Income: Per capita: $26,842; Median household: $68,194; Average household: $75,524; Households with income of $100,000 or more: 19.3%; Poverty rate: 8.0%

Educational Attainment: High school diploma or higher: 91.7%; Bachelor's degree or higher: 28.3%; Graduate/professional degree or higher: 9.1%

School District(s)
Lapeer Community Schools (PK-12)
    2012-13 Enrollment: 5,828 . . . . (810) 667-2401

Housing: Homeownership rate: 87.6%; Median home value: $185,900; Median year structure built: 1983; Homeowner vacancy rate: 3.7%; Median gross rent: $930 per month; Rental vacancy rate: 10.7%

Health Insurance: 91.2% have insurance; 82.3% have private insurance; 24.4% have public insurance; 8.8% do not have insurance; 2.1% of children under 18 do not have insurance

Safety: Violent crime rate: 4.7 per 10,000 population; Property crime rate: 99.1 per 10,000 population

Transportation: Commute: 92.6% car, 0.6% public transportation, 0.2% walk, 6.1% work from home; Median travel time to work: 34.3 minutes

---

METAMORA (village). Covers a land area of 0.834 square miles and a water area of 0.002 square miles. Located at 42.95° N. Lat; 83.29° W. Long. Elevation is 1,043 feet.

Population: 565; Growth (since 2000): 11.4%; Density: 677.7 persons per square mile; Race: 98.1% White, 0.4% Black/African American, 0.2% Asian, 0.5% American Indian/Alaska Native, 0.0% Native Hawaiian/Other Pacific Islander, 0.7% Two or more races, 1.4% Hispanic of any race; Average household size: 2.62; Median age: 39.4; Age under 18: 27.8%; Age 65 and over: 11.7%; Males per 100 females: 94.2

School District(s)
Lapeer Community Schools (PK-12)
    2012-13 Enrollment: 5,828 . . . . (810) 667-2401

Housing: Homeownership rate: 81.1%; Homeowner vacancy rate: 1.7%; Rental vacancy rate: 10.9%

NORTH BRANCH (township). Covers a land area of 36.081 square miles and a water area of 0.300 square miles. Located at 43.20° N. Lat; 83.18° W. Long. Elevation is 810 feet.

Population: 3,645; Growth (since 2000): 1.4%; Density: 101.0 persons per square mile; Race: 96.9% White, 0.4% Black/African American, 0.1% Asian, 0.4% American Indian/Alaska Native, 0.1% Native Hawaiian/Other Pacific Islander, 1.6% Two or more races, 3.0% Hispanic of any race; Average household size: 2.74; Median age: 38.6; Age under 18: 26.9%; Age 65 and over: 11.9%; Males per 100 females: 99.8; Marriage status: 28.1% never married, 55.3% now married, 0.3% separated, 3.9% widowed, 12.8% divorced; Foreign born: 0.8%; Speak English only: 98.3%; With disability: 17.2%; Veterans: 8.8%; Ancestry: 35.2% German, 16.9% Irish, 14.9% English, 8.6% Polish, 6.3% French

Employment: 10.3% management, business, and financial, 2.1% computer, engineering, and science, 9.0% education, legal, community service, arts, and media, 5.5% healthcare practitioners, 14.7% service, 23.9% sales and office, 9.1% natural resources, construction, and maintenance, 25.3% production, transportation, and material moving

Income: Per capita: $20,792; Median household: $47,982; Average household: $54,009; Households with income of $100,000 or more: 13.4%; Poverty rate: 13.4%

Educational Attainment: High school diploma or higher: 90.3%; Bachelor's degree or higher: 15.1%; Graduate/professional degree or higher: 5.0%

School District(s)
North Branch Area Schools (PK-12)
    2012-13 Enrollment: 2,425 . . . . (810) 688-3570

Housing: Homeownership rate: 79.7%; Median home value: $117,000; Median year structure built: 1973; Homeowner vacancy rate: 3.6%; Median gross rent: $622 per month; Rental vacancy rate: 6.2%

Health Insurance: 89.4% have insurance; 65.2% have private insurance; 39.2% have public insurance; 10.6% do not have insurance; 1.6% of children under 18 do not have insurance

Transportation: Commute: 88.4% car, 1.3% public transportation, 0.8% walk, 9.2% work from home; Median travel time to work: 37.3 minutes

---

NORTH BRANCH (village). Covers a land area of 1.331 square miles and a water area of 0 square miles. Located at 43.23° N. Lat; 83.19° W. Long. Elevation is 810 feet.

Population: 1,033; Growth (since 2000): 0.6%; Density: 776.1 persons per square mile; Race: 96.5% White, 0.2% Black/African American, 0.2% Asian, 0.2% American Indian/Alaska Native, 0.2% Native Hawaiian/Other Pacific Islander, 1.5% Two or more races, 3.9% Hispanic of any race; Average household size: 2.45; Median age: 34.0; Age under 18: 27.7%; Age 65 and over: 13.8%; Males per 100 females: 85.1

School District(s)
North Branch Area Schools (PK-12)
    2012-13 Enrollment: 2,425 . . . . (810) 688-3570

Housing: Homeownership rate: 57.1%; Homeowner vacancy rate: 9.2%; Rental vacancy rate: 8.7%

OREGON (township). Covers a land area of 32.553 square miles and a water area of 2.643 square miles. Located at 43.09° N. Lat; 83.40° W. Long.

Population: 5,786; Growth (since 2000): -6.2%; Density: 177.7 persons per square mile; Race: 97.1% White, 0.1% Black/African American, 0.4% Asian, 0.5% American Indian/Alaska Native, 0.0% Native Hawaiian/Other Pacific Islander, 1.5% Two or more races, 2.2% Hispanic of any race; Average household size: 2.67; Median age: 43.9; Age under 18: 22.1%; Age 65 and over: 12.0%; Males per 100 females: 99.0; Marriage status: 21.1% never married, 67.9% now married, 0.3% separated, 3.8% widowed, 7.2% divorced; Foreign born: 3.1%; Speak English only: 96.7%; With disability: 12.0%; Veterans: 9.4%; Ancestry: 26.2% German, 14.6% English, 14.0% Irish, 7.9% American, 7.8% Polish

Employment: 11.2% management, business, and financial, 5.1% computer, engineering, and science, 10.3% education, legal, community service, arts, and media, 6.9% healthcare practitioners, 15.5% service, 26.3% sales and office, 10.6% natural resources, construction, and maintenance, 14.0% production, transportation, and material moving

Income: Per capita: $27,262; Median household: $62,750; Average household: $74,473; Households with income of $100,000 or more: 19.3%; Poverty rate: 4.1%

Educational Attainment: High school diploma or higher: 94.1%; Bachelor's degree or higher: 18.3%; Graduate/professional degree or higher: 6.5%

Housing: Homeownership rate: 93.4%; Median home value: $144,600; Median year structure built: 1975; Homeowner vacancy rate: 2.1%; Median gross rent: $1,028 per month; Rental vacancy rate: 9.5%

Health Insurance: 89.1% have insurance; 80.1% have private insurance; 24.2% have public insurance; 10.9% do not have insurance; 3.5% of children under 18 do not have insurance

Transportation: Commute: 94.5% car, 0.9% public transportation, 0.6% walk, 3.6% work from home; Median travel time to work: 31.4 minutes

---

OTTER LAKE (village). Covers a land area of 0.761 square miles and a water area of 0.081 square miles. Located at 43.21° N. Lat; 83.46° W. Long. Elevation is 869 feet.

Population: 389; Growth (since 2000): -11.0%; Density: 511.3 persons per square mile; Race: 94.3% White, 0.3% Black/African American, 0.3% Asian, 1.3% American Indian/Alaska Native, 0.3% Native Hawaiian/Other Pacific Islander, 3.3% Two or more races, 1.8% Hispanic of any race; Average household size: 2.70; Median age: 38.4; Age under 18: 25.7%; Age 65 and over: 11.6%; Males per 100 females: 121.0

School District(s)
Lakeville Community SD (PK-12)
    2012-13 Enrollment: 1,467 . . . . (810) 591-3980

Housing: Homeownership rate: 78.5%; Homeowner vacancy rate: 7.9%; Rental vacancy rate: 8.8%

RICH (township). Covers a land area of 34.980 square miles and a water area of 0.261 square miles. Located at 43.28° N. Lat; 83.29° W. Long.

History: Rich was settled in the mid-1850's and grew around a grist mill. Rich Township, organized in 1858, was named for Charles Rich.

Population: 1,623; Growth (since 2000): 14.9%; Density: 46.4 persons per square mile; Race: 96.9% White, 0.6% Black/African American, 0.2% Asian, 0.4% American Indian/Alaska Native, 0.0% Native Hawaiian/Other Pacific Islander, 1.7% Two or more races, 2.3% Hispanic of any race; Average household size: 2.88; Median age: 37.2; Age under 18: 29.5%; Age 65 and over: 13.3%; Males per 100 females: 99.6

Housing: Homeownership rate: 86.8%; Homeowner vacancy rate: 3.9%; Rental vacancy rate: 1.3%

Leelanau County

Located in northwestern Michigan; a peninsula, bounded on the west by Lake Michigan, and on the east by Grand Traverse Bay; includes Leelanau and Glen Lakes. Covers a land area of 347.171 square miles, a water area of 2,185.021 square miles, and is located in the Eastern Time Zone at 45.15° N. Lat., 86.05° W. Long. The county was founded in 1863. County seat is Leland.

Leelanau County is part of the Traverse City, MI Micropolitan Statistical Area. The entire metro area includes: Benzie County, MI; Grand Traverse County, MI; Kalkaska County, MI; Leelanau County, MI

Weather Station: Maple City   Elevation: 729 feet

	Jan	Feb	Mar	Apr	May	Jun	Jul	Aug	Sep	Oct	Nov	Dec
High	29	32	41	55	67	77	81	79	71	58	45	34
Low	17	17	22	33	42	52	57	57	50	40	31	22
Precip	2.6	1.8	1.8	2.7	2.8	2.9	2.6	3.3	4.2	3.7	3.2	3.0
Snow	44.6	27.6	14.3	4.4	tr	0.0	0.0	0.0	0.0	0.4	11.3	41.2

High and Low temperatures in degrees Fahrenheit; Precipitation and Snow in inches

Population: 21,708; Growth (since 2000): 2.8%; Density: 62.5 persons per square mile; Race: 93.1% White, 0.3% Black/African American, 0.4% Asian, 3.5% American Indian/Alaska Native, 0.0% Native Hawaiian/Other Pacific Islander, 1.7% two or more races, 3.7% Hispanic of any race; Average household size: 2.31; Median age: 50.3; Age under 18: 19.5%; Age 65 and over: 23.4%; Males per 100 females: 97.3; Marriage status: 20.2% never married, 63.2% now married, 0.6% separated, 6.4% widowed, 10.2% divorced; Foreign born: 3.1%; Speak English only: 94.7%; With disability: 12.4%; Veterans: 12.6%; Ancestry: 28.7% German, 15.1% English, 12.7% Irish, 11.2% Polish, 9.8% American
Religion: Six largest groups: 27.0% Catholicism, 5.5% Lutheran, 5.4% Methodist/Pietist, 3.2% Presbyterian-Reformed, 0.5% Baptist, 0.2% Episcopalianism/Anglicanism
Economy: Unemployment rate: 4.4%; Leading industries: 17.0% retail trade; 16.3% construction; 9.9% professional, scientific, and technical services; Farms: 494 totaling 59,481 acres; Company size: 0 employ 1,000 or more persons, 0 employ 500 to 999 persons, 2 employ 100 to 499 persons, 732 employ less than 100 persons; Business ownership: 931 women-owned, n/a Black-owned, n/a Hispanic-owned, n/a Asian-owned
Employment: 16.4% management, business, and financial, 2.6% computer, engineering, and science, 12.1% education, legal, community service, arts, and media, 6.8% healthcare practitioners, 19.6% service, 21.5% sales and office, 12.0% natural resources, construction, and maintenance, 9.0% production, transportation, and material moving
Income: Per capita: $31,462; Median household: $55,018; Average household: $74,759; Households with income of $100,000 or more: 21.5%; Poverty rate: 11.2%
Educational Attainment: High school diploma or higher: 94.2%; Bachelor's degree or higher: 39.2%; Graduate/professional degree or higher: 16.5%
Housing: Homeownership rate: 84.8%; Median home value: $235,600; Median year structure built: 1981; Homeowner vacancy rate: 3.4%; Median gross rent: $822 per month; Rental vacancy rate: 16.8%
Vital Statistics: Birth rate: 83.7 per 10,000 population; Death rate: 97.0 per 10,000 population; Age-adjusted cancer mortality rate: 126.7 deaths per 100,000 population
Health Insurance: 88.2% have insurance; 75.6% have private insurance; 34.5% have public insurance; 11.8% do not have insurance; 7.6% of children under 18 do not have insurance
Health Care: Physicians: 11.6 per 10,000 population; Hospital beds: 0.0 per 10,000 population; Hospital admissions: 0.0 per 10,000 population
Transportation: Commute: 85.8% car, 0.6% public transportation, 3.4% walk, 9.0% work from home; Median travel time to work: 22.2 minutes
Presidential Election: 46.4% Obama, 52.8% Romney (2012)
National and State Parks: D H Day State Park; Fife Lake State Forest; Leelanau State Park; Sleeping Bear Dunes National Lakeshore
Additional Information Contacts
Leelanau Government . . . . (231) 256-9824
    http://www.leelanau.cc

Leelanau County Communities

BINGHAM (township). Covers a land area of 23.573 square miles and a water area of 15.766 square miles. Located at 44.91° N. Lat; 85.64° W. Long. Elevation is 722 feet.
History: Bingham Township was named for former Michigan Governor Kingsley Bingham in 1861.
Population: 2,497; Growth (since 2000): 3.0%; Density: 105.9 persons per square mile; Race: 94.2% White, 0.2% Black/African American, 0.1% Asian, 2.5% American Indian/Alaska Native, 0.0% Native Hawaiian/Other Pacific Islander, 2.0% Two or more races, 3.4% Hispanic of any race; Average household size: 2.40; Median age: 49.2; Age under 18: 21.3%; Age 65 and over: 20.1%; Males per 100 females: 99.8
Housing: Homeownership rate: 89.6%; Homeowner vacancy rate: 1.8%; Rental vacancy rate: 14.2%

CEDAR (CDP). Covers a land area of 0.180 square miles and a water area of 0 square miles. Located at 44.85° N. Lat; 85.79° W. Long. Elevation is 597 feet.
Population: 93; Growth (since 2000): n/a; Density: 517.4 persons per square mile; Race: 94.6% White, 2.2% Black/African American, 1.1% Asian, 1.1% American Indian/Alaska Native, 0.0% Native Hawaiian/Other Pacific Islander, 1.1% Two or more races, 0.0% Hispanic of any race; Average household size: 2.11; Median age: 39.8; Age under 18: 23.7%; Age 65 and over: 16.1%; Males per 100 females: 89.8
Housing: Homeownership rate: 68.2%; Homeowner vacancy rate: 0.0%; Rental vacancy rate: 0.0%

CENTERVILLE (township). Covers a land area of 27.700 square miles and a water area of 2.724 square miles. Located at 44.91° N. Lat; 85.76° W. Long.
Population: 1,274; Growth (since 2000): 16.3%; Density: 46.0 persons per square mile; Race: 96.9% White, 0.2% Black/African American, 0.4% Asian, 0.8% American Indian/Alaska Native, 0.0% Native Hawaiian/Other Pacific Islander, 1.3% Two or more races, 2.5% Hispanic of any race; Average household size: 2.48; Median age: 46.7; Age under 18: 22.2%; Age 65 and over: 19.8%; Males per 100 females: 102.5
Housing: Homeownership rate: 86.8%; Homeowner vacancy rate: 3.1%; Rental vacancy rate: 13.6%

CLEVELAND (township). Covers a land area of 30.687 square miles and a water area of 39.952 square miles. Located at 44.95° N. Lat; 85.91° W. Long.
Population: 1,031; Growth (since 2000): -0.9%; Density: 33.6 persons per square mile; Race: 96.5% White, 0.1% Black/African American, 0.3% Asian, 1.2% American Indian/Alaska Native, 0.1% Native Hawaiian/Other Pacific Islander, 1.2% Two or more races, 1.1% Hispanic of any race; Average household size: 2.14; Median age: 52.1; Age under 18: 16.2%; Age 65 and over: 24.9%; Males per 100 females: 100.6
Housing: Homeownership rate: 89.0%; Homeowner vacancy rate: 7.2%; Rental vacancy rate: 41.8%

ELMWOOD (charter township). Covers a land area of 19.935 square miles and a water area of 10.963 square miles. Located at 44.82° N. Lat; 85.66° W. Long.
Population: 4,503; Growth (since 2000): 5.6%; Density: 225.9 persons per square mile; Race: 96.2% White, 0.3% Black/African American, 0.7% Asian, 0.8% American Indian/Alaska Native, 0.0% Native Hawaiian/Other Pacific Islander, 1.0% Two or more races, 2.5% Hispanic of any race; Average household size: 2.34; Median age: 48.7; Age under 18: 20.6%; Age 65 and over: 22.3%; Males per 100 females: 95.7; Marriage status: 21.6% never married, 62.1% now married, 0.4% separated, 6.7% widowed, 9.6% divorced; Foreign born: 4.9%; Speak English only: 94.5%; With disability: 10.4%; Veterans: 13.0%; Ancestry: 29.2% German, 15.9% English, 9.9% Irish, 7.8% French, 7.7% American
Employment: 18.2% management, business, and financial, 1.7% computer, engineering, and science, 13.2% education, legal, community service, arts, and media, 7.1% healthcare practitioners, 17.0% service, 23.8% sales and office, 11.9% natural resources, construction, and maintenance, 7.1% production, transportation, and material moving
Income: Per capita: $36,771; Median household: $63,328; Average household: $87,028; Households with income of $100,000 or more: 27.2%; Poverty rate: 7.3%

Educational Attainment: High school diploma or higher: 94.7%; Bachelor's degree or higher: 41.5%; Graduate/professional degree or higher: 21.2%

Housing: Homeownership rate: 83.7%; Median home value: $221,400; Median year structure built: 1985; Homeowner vacancy rate: 4.0%; Median gross rent: $899 per month; Rental vacancy rate: 9.3%

Health Insurance: 91.3% have insurance; 84.3% have private insurance; 32.3% have public insurance; 8.7% do not have insurance; 2.5% of children under 18 do not have insurance

Transportation: Commute: 89.3% car, 0.0% public transportation, 0.7% walk, 7.9% work from home; Median travel time to work: 17.6 minutes

EMPIRE (township). Covers a land area of 35.241 square miles and a water area of 7.552 square miles. Located at 44.82° N. Lat; 86.01° W. Long. Elevation is 610 feet.

Population: 1,182; Growth (since 2000): 8.9%; Density: 33.5 persons per square mile; Race: 98.5% White, 0.0% Black/African American, 0.2% Asian, 0.7% American Indian/Alaska Native, 0.0% Native Hawaiian/Other Pacific Islander, 0.4% Two or more races, 1.4% Hispanic of any race; Average household size: 2.02; Median age: 56.2; Age under 18: 13.9%; Age 65 and over: 28.7%; Males per 100 females: 95.0

Housing: Homeownership rate: 84.3%; Homeowner vacancy rate: 2.8%; Rental vacancy rate: 22.0%

EMPIRE (village). Covers a land area of 1.148 square miles and a water area of 0.092 square miles. Located at 44.81° N. Lat; 86.06° W. Long. Elevation is 610 feet.

History: Empire began as a lumber town, boasting the largest sawmill in Leelanau County at one time. Later, cherry orchards became the source of revenue.

Population: 375; Growth (since 2000): -0.8%; Density: 326.6 persons per square mile; Race: 99.2% White, 0.0% Black/African American, 0.0% Asian, 0.8% American Indian/Alaska Native, 0.0% Native Hawaiian/Other Pacific Islander, 0.0% Two or more races, 0.8% Hispanic of any race; Average household size: 1.78; Median age: 56.8; Age under 18: 13.3%; Age 65 and over: 29.6%; Males per 100 females: 83.8

Housing: Homeownership rate: 70.1%; Homeowner vacancy rate: 3.2%; Rental vacancy rate: 16.0%

GLEN ARBOR (CDP). Covers a land area of 1.028 square miles and a water area of 0.016 square miles. Located at 44.90° N. Lat; 85.99° W. Long. Elevation is 591 feet.

Population: 229; Growth (since 2000): n/a; Density: 222.9 persons per square mile; Race: 98.7% White, 0.4% Black/African American, 0.4% Asian, 0.0% American Indian/Alaska Native, 0.0% Native Hawaiian/Other Pacific Islander, 0.4% Two or more races, 1.3% Hispanic of any race; Average household size: 1.96; Median age: 62.8; Age under 18: 11.8%; Age 65 and over: 42.4%; Males per 100 females: 86.2

Housing: Homeownership rate: 86.3%; Homeowner vacancy rate: 12.9%; Rental vacancy rate: 28.0%

GLEN ARBOR (township). Covers a land area of 28.333 square miles and a water area of 59.252 square miles. Located at 44.91° N. Lat; 86.03° W. Long. Elevation is 591 feet.

Population: 859; Growth (since 2000): 9.0%; Density: 30.3 persons per square mile; Race: 97.8% White, 0.5% Black/African American, 0.9% Asian, 0.1% American Indian/Alaska Native, 0.0% Native Hawaiian/Other Pacific Islander, 0.6% Two or more races, 1.0% Hispanic of any race; Average household size: 1.98; Median age: 60.9; Age under 18: 14.8%; Age 65 and over: 40.5%; Males per 100 females: 94.8

Housing: Homeownership rate: 91.2%; Homeowner vacancy rate: 6.3%; Rental vacancy rate: 65.8%

GREILICKVILLE (CDP). Covers a land area of 4.517 square miles and a water area of 2.593 square miles. Located at 44.80° N. Lat; 85.66° W. Long. Elevation is 584 feet.

History: Greilickville was first called Norristown in honor of two brothers who founded the village and built a gristmill, tannery and brickyard. The name of Greilickville came from Godfrey Greilick and his sons (John, Anthony, and Edward) who came from Austria in 1848. One of the seven sawmills operated by the Greilicks was at Morristown. The Greilickville name came into use when the Manistee & Northwestern Railroad called its station that in 1893.

Population: 1,530; Growth (since 2000): 8.1%; Density: 338.7 persons per square mile; Race: 98.7% White, 0.1% Black/African American, 0.4%

Asian, 0.1% American Indian/Alaska Native, 0.0% Native Hawaiian/Other Pacific Islander, 0.5% Two or more races, 1.7% Hispanic of any race; Average household size: 2.03; Median age: 55.9; Age under 18: 14.3%; Age 65 and over: 35.7%; Males per 100 females: 86.8

Housing: Homeownership rate: 76.7%; Homeowner vacancy rate: 4.5%; Rental vacancy rate: 6.9%

KASSON (township). Covers a land area of 35.911 square miles and a water area of 0.391 square miles. Located at 44.83° N. Lat; 85.88° W. Long.

History: Kasson Township was organized in 1865 and named for Kasson Freeman, county surveyor.

Population: 1,609; Growth (since 2000): 2.0%; Density: 44.8 persons per square mile; Race: 98.1% White, 0.2% Black/African American, 0.4% Asian, 0.5% American Indian/Alaska Native, 0.0% Native Hawaiian/Other Pacific Islander, 0.5% Two or more races, 1.1% Hispanic of any race; Average household size: 2.51; Median age: 45.6; Age under 18: 22.4%; Age 65 and over: 15.8%; Males per 100 females: 101.4

Housing: Homeownership rate: 85.2%; Homeowner vacancy rate: 2.0%; Rental vacancy rate: 2.1%

LAKE LEELANAU (CDP). Covers a land area of 0.255 square miles and a water area of 0.004 square miles. Located at 44.98° N. Lat; 85.72° W. Long. Elevation is 617 feet.

Population: 253; Growth (since 2000): n/a; Density: 992.6 persons per square mile; Race: 83.0% White, 0.4% Black/African American, 3.2% Asian, 10.7% American Indian/Alaska Native, 0.0% Native Hawaiian/Other Pacific Islander, 1.6% Two or more races, 10.7% Hispanic of any race; Average household size: 2.56; Median age: 36.5; Age under 18: 25.3%; Age 65 and over: 12.6%; Males per 100 females: 82.0

Housing: Homeownership rate: 63.7%; Homeowner vacancy rate: 3.1%; Rental vacancy rate: 9.8%

Newspapers: Leelanau Enterprise (weekly circulation 7700)

LEELANAU (township). Covers a land area of 49.153 square miles and a water area of 178.319 square miles. Located at 45.16° N. Lat; 85.61° W. Long.

History: The name of Leelanau is of Indian origin and means "delight of life."

Population: 2,027; Growth (since 2000): -5.2%; Density: 41.2 persons per square mile; Race: 93.0% White, 0.5% Black/African American, 0.0% Asian, 3.8% American Indian/Alaska Native, 0.0% Native Hawaiian/Other Pacific Islander, 1.6% Two or more races, 4.4% Hispanic of any race; Average household size: 2.16; Median age: 58.0; Age under 18: 13.3%; Age 65 and over: 33.6%; Males per 100 females: 97.0

Housing: Homeownership rate: 89.2%; Homeowner vacancy rate: 2.4%; Rental vacancy rate: 21.6%

LELAND (CDP). County seat. Covers a land area of 0.976 square miles and a water area of 0.022 square miles. Located at 45.02° N. Lat; 85.76° W. Long. Elevation is 594 feet.

Population: 377; Growth (since 2000): n/a; Density: 386.4 persons per square mile; Race: 97.9% White, 0.0% Black/African American, 1.3% Asian, 0.0% American Indian/Alaska Native, 0.0% Native Hawaiian/Other Pacific Islander, 0.3% Two or more races, 2.7% Hispanic of any race; Average household size: 1.89; Median age: 59.1; Age under 18: 13.8%; Age 65 and over: 37.9%; Males per 100 females: 91.4

School District(s)

Leland Public SD (PK-12)

    2012-13 Enrollment: 409 . . . . (231) 256-9857

Housing: Homeownership rate: 83.6%; Homeowner vacancy rate: 1.2%; Rental vacancy rate: 5.7%

LELAND (township). Covers a land area of 45.370 square miles and a water area of 101.207 square miles. Located at 45.12° N. Lat; 85.98° W. Long. Elevation is 594 feet.

History: Leland developed as a summer resort and a community of commercial fishermen. A sawmill was erected here in 1853, and docks supplied cordwood to steamers.

Population: 2,043; Growth (since 2000): 0.5%; Density: 45.0 persons per square mile; Race: 93.7% White, 0.1% Black/African American, 0.7% Asian, 1.6% American Indian/Alaska Native, 0.0% Native Hawaiian/Other Pacific Islander, 1.4% Two or more races, 6.9% Hispanic of any race; Average household size: 2.27; Median age: 52.7; Age under 18: 18.1%; Age 65 and over: 27.7%; Males per 100 females: 99.3

School District(s)

Leland Public SD (PK-12)
    2012-13 Enrollment: 409 . . . . (231) 256-9857
Housing: Homeownership rate: 83.3%; Homeowner vacancy rate: 2.1%;
Rental vacancy rate: 6.2%

MAPLE CITY (CDP).
Covers a land area of 0.433 square miles and a water area of 0 square miles. Located at 44.86° N. Lat; 85.86° W. Long. Elevation is 705 feet.
Population: 207; Growth (since 2000): n/a; Density: 477.8 persons per square mile; Race: 97.6% White, 0.5% Black/African American, 0.0% Asian, 0.5% American Indian/Alaska Native, 0.0% Native Hawaiian/Other Pacific Islander, 1.4% Two or more races, 0.0% Hispanic of any race; Average household size: 2.23; Median age: 39.7; Age under 18: 25.6%; Age 65 and over: 11.1%; Males per 100 females: 102.9

School District(s)
Glen Lake Community Schools (PK-12)
    2012-13 Enrollment: 775 . . . . (231) 334-3061
Housing: Homeownership rate: 58.1%; Homeowner vacancy rate: 5.3%;
Rental vacancy rate: 0.0%

NORTHPORT (village).
Covers a land area of 1.650 square miles and a water area of 0.004 square miles. Located at 45.13° N. Lat; 85.62° W. Long. Elevation is 607 feet.
History: Northport was an important shipping center during the last half of the 19th century.
Population: 526; Growth (since 2000): -18.8%; Density: 318.8 persons per square mile; Race: 93.2% White, 0.6% Black/African American, 0.2% Asian, 2.5% American Indian/Alaska Native, 0.0% Native Hawaiian/Other Pacific Islander, 3.2% Two or more races, 6.1% Hispanic of any race; Average household size: 2.10; Median age: 57.5; Age under 18: 14.4%; Age 65 and over: 36.1%; Males per 100 females: 86.5

School District(s)
Northport Public SD (PK-12)
    2012-13 Enrollment: 163 . . . . (231) 386-5153
Housing: Homeownership rate: 85.2%; Homeowner vacancy rate: 4.4%;
Rental vacancy rate: 30.9%

OMENA (CDP).
Covers a land area of 4.519 square miles and a water area of 0.050 square miles. Located at 45.06° N. Lat; 85.60° W. Long. Elevation is 604 feet.
Population: 267; Growth (since 2000): n/a; Density: 59.1 persons per square mile; Race: 91.0% White, 0.4% Black/African American, 0.0% Asian, 7.9% American Indian/Alaska Native, 0.0% Native Hawaiian/Other Pacific Islander, 0.0% Two or more races, 4.5% Hispanic of any race; Average household size: 2.15; Median age: 60.1; Age under 18: 12.4%; Age 65 and over: 38.2%; Males per 100 females: 102.3
Housing: Homeownership rate: 88.7%; Homeowner vacancy rate: 1.8%;
Rental vacancy rate: 0.0%

SOLON (township).
Covers a land area of 26.394 square miles and a water area of 3.253 square miles. Located at 44.82° N. Lat; 85.77° W. Long. Elevation is 627 feet.
History: Solon Township was settled in the 1860's and named for Solon, Ohio, the former home of some of the early residents.
Population: 1,509; Growth (since 2000): -2.1%; Density: 57.2 persons per square mile; Race: 96.8% White, 0.3% Black/African American, 0.5% Asian, 1.2% American Indian/Alaska Native, 0.0% Native Hawaiian/Other Pacific Islander, 1.1% Two or more races, 0.5% Hispanic of any race; Average household size: 2.42; Median age: 46.8; Age under 18: 21.3%; Age 65 and over: 14.6%; Males per 100 females: 99.6
Housing: Homeownership rate: 87.0%; Homeowner vacancy rate: 1.8%;
Rental vacancy rate: 8.8%

SUTTONS BAY (township).
Covers a land area of 24.522 square miles and a water area of 17.364 square miles. Located at 45.00° N. Lat; 85.64° W. Long. Elevation is 597 feet.
Population: 2,982; Growth (since 2000): 0.0%; Density: 121.6 persons per square mile; Race: 76.3% White, 0.7% Black/African American, 0.4% Asian, 16.6% American Indian/Alaska Native, 0.0% Native Hawaiian/Other Pacific Islander, 4.5% Two or more races, 8.9% Hispanic of any race; Average household size: 2.45; Median age: 48.1; Age under 18: 22.0%; Age 65 and over: 21.4%; Males per 100 females: 92.8; Marriage status: 24.2% never married, 60.6% now married, 1.3% separated, 4.4% widowed, 10.8% divorced; Foreign born: 2.3%; Speak English only: 93.3%;

With disability: 15.1%; Veterans: 14.6%; Ancestry: 28.1% German, 11.0% Irish, 9.8% American, 9.7% English, 7.7% Polish
Employment: 16.0% management, business, and financial, 3.3% computer, engineering, and science, 12.7% education, legal, community service, arts, and media, 6.4% healthcare practitioners, 28.3% service, 17.6% sales and office, 7.6% natural resources, construction, and maintenance, 8.0% production, transportation, and material moving
Income: Per capita: $26,833; Median household: $44,123; Average household: $67,559; Households with income of $100,000 or more: 17.1%; Poverty rate: 23.7%
Educational Attainment: High school diploma or higher: 90.4%; Bachelor's degree or higher: 31.3%; Graduate/professional degree or higher: 9.1%

School District(s)
Leelanau Montessori Public Schools Academy (PK-12)
    2012-13 Enrollment: 74 . . . . (231) 271-8609
Suttons Bay Public Schools (PK-12)
    2012-13 Enrollment: 731 . . . . (231) 271-8604
Housing: Homeownership rate: 76.0%; Median home value: $234,100; Median year structure built: 1985; Homeowner vacancy rate: 4.3%; Median gross rent: $671 per month; Rental vacancy rate: 12.3%
Health Insurance: 82.1% have insurance; 58.9% have private insurance; 39.1% have public insurance; 17.9% do not have insurance; 9.1% of children under 18 do not have insurance
Transportation: Commute: 87.4% car, 0.9% public transportation, 5.2% walk, 5.9% work from home; Median travel time to work: 24.7 minutes

SUTTONS BAY (village).
Covers a land area of 1.251 square miles and a water area of <.001 square miles. Located at 44.98° N. Lat; 85.65° W. Long. Elevation is 597 feet.
History: Suttons Bay was founded in 1854 on land owned by Harry C. Sutton. The town developed around sawmills and docks, where lumber was shipped. The location on Suttons Bay later became a resort area.
Population: 618; Growth (since 2000): 4.9%; Density: 493.9 persons per square mile; Race: 93.7% White, 0.2% Black/African American, 1.1% Asian, 2.8% American Indian/Alaska Native, 0.0% Native Hawaiian/Other Pacific Islander, 2.3% Two or more races, 0.3% Hispanic of any race; Average household size: 2.02; Median age: 58.8; Age under 18: 12.8%; Age 65 and over: 39.3%; Males per 100 females: 80.7

School District(s)
Leelanau Montessori Public Schools Academy (PK-12)
    2012-13 Enrollment: 74 . . . . (231) 271-8609
Suttons Bay Public Schools (PK-12)
    2012-13 Enrollment: 731 . . . . (231) 271-8604
Housing: Homeownership rate: 71.5%; Homeowner vacancy rate: 12.6%;
Rental vacancy rate: 14.1%

Lenawee County

Located in southeastern Michigan; bounded on the south by Ohio; drained by the Raisin and Tiffin Rivers. Covers a land area of 749.555 square miles, a water area of 11.854 square miles, and is located in the Eastern Time Zone at 41.90° N. Lat., 84.07° W. Long. The county was founded in 1822. County seat is Adrian.

Lenawee County is part of the Adrian, MI Micropolitan Statistical Area. The entire metro area includes: Lenawee County, MI

Weather Station: Adrian 2 NNE   Elevation: 759 feet

	Jan	Feb	Mar	Apr	May	Jun	Jul	Aug	Sep	Oct	Nov	Dec
High	33	35	46	59	71	80	84	81	75	62	49	36
Low	16	18	26	36	46	55	59	58	50	39	30	21
Precip	2.1	2.0	2.5	3.2	3.7	3.9	3.2	3.9	3.6	2.8	2.9	2.6
Snow	8.9	6.8	4.6	0.7	0.0	0.0	0.0	0.0	0.0	0.1	1.6	7.0

High and Low temperatures in degrees Fahrenheit; Precipitation and Snow in inches

Population: 99,892; Growth (since 2000): 1.0%; Density: 133.3 persons per square mile; Race: 92.3% White, 2.5% Black/African American, 0.5% Asian, 0.5% American Indian/Alaska Native, 0.0% Native Hawaiian/Other Pacific Islander, 2.2% two or more races, 7.6% Hispanic of any race; Average household size: 2.52; Median age: 40.0; Age under 18: 23.2%; Age 65 and over: 14.6%; Males per 100 females: 102.1; Marriage status: 28.8% never married, 53.6% now married, 1.7% separated, 6.0% widowed, 11.7% divorced; Foreign born: 2.0%; Speak English only: 95.2%; With disability: 14.7%; Veterans: 9.9%; Ancestry: 30.9% German, 15.2% Irish, 12.9% English, 6.1% American, 5.9% Polish

Religion: Six largest groups: 13.6% Catholicism, 5.1% Methodist/Pietist, 4.8% Lutheran, 3.9% Non-denominational Protestant, 2.7% Baptist, 2.5% Pentecostal

Economy: Unemployment rate: 5.6%; Leading industries: 16.5% retail trade; 13.0% other services (except public administration); 12.7% health care and social assistance; Farms: 1,618 totaling 344,347 acres; Company size: 1 employs 1,000 or more persons, 4 employ 500 to 999 persons, 25 employ 100 to 499 persons, 1,803 employ less than 100 persons; Business ownership: 2,112 women-owned, n/a Black-owned, n/a Hispanic-owned, n/a Asian-owned

Employment: 11.3% management, business, and financial, 3.4% computer, engineering, and science, 9.0% education, legal, community service, arts, and media, 5.2% healthcare practitioners, 20.2% service, 23.9% sales and office, 9.7% natural resources, construction, and maintenance, 17.3% production, transportation, and material moving

Income: Per capita: $22,395; Median household: $47,766; Average household: $57,679; Households with income of $100,000 or more: 13.9%; Poverty rate: 14.1%

Educational Attainment: High school diploma or higher: 89.1%; Bachelor's degree or higher: 19.3%; Graduate/professional degree or higher: 6.6%

Housing: Homeownership rate: 77.5%; Median home value: $116,900; Median year structure built: 1967; Homeowner vacancy rate: 2.7%; Median gross rent: $710 per month; Rental vacancy rate: 11.9%

Vital Statistics: Birth rate: 108.8 per 10,000 population; Death rate: 93.7 per 10,000 population; Age-adjusted cancer mortality rate: 185.9 deaths per 100,000 population

Health Insurance: 88.7% have insurance; 71.6% have private insurance; 33.3% have public insurance; 11.3% do not have insurance; 4.8% of children under 18 do not have insurance

Health Care: Physicians: 9.0 per 10,000 population; Hospital beds: 12.7 per 10,000 population; Hospital admissions: 589.5 per 10,000 population

Air Quality Index: 85.3% good, 14.7% moderate, 0.0% unhealthy for sensitive individuals, 0.0% unhealthy (percent of days)

Transportation: Commute: 92.2% car, 0.3% public transportation, 3.4% walk, 3.0% work from home; Median travel time to work: 26.6 minutes

Presidential Election: 48.8% Obama, 50.1% Romney (2012)

National and State Parks: Cambridge State Historic Park; Hayes State Park; Lake Hudson State Park; Lake Hudson State Recreation Area; Onsted State Wildlife Management Area

Additional Information Contacts
Lenawee Government . . . . (517) 264-4599
  http://www.lenawee.mi.us

Lenawee County Communities

ADDISON (village). Covers a land area of 0.956 square miles and a water area of 0.044 square miles. Located at 41.99° N. Lat; 84.35° W. Long. Elevation is 1,050 feet.

History: Addison was named for Addison J. Comstock, a banker who owned land here and had the town platted in 1851. Before that, the settlement had been called Manetau, Peru, Brownell's Mills, Jackson's Mills, and Harrison. Addison was incorporated in 1893.

Population: 605; Growth (since 2000): -3.5%; Density: 633.0 persons per square mile; Race: 97.0% White, 0.5% Black/African American, 0.0% Asian, 0.0% American Indian/Alaska Native, 0.0% Native Hawaiian/Other Pacific Islander, 2.1% Two or more races, 1.0% Hispanic of any race; Average household size: 2.47; Median age: 35.1; Age under 18: 26.8%; Age 65 and over: 10.7%; Males per 100 females: 87.9

School District(s)
Addison Community Schools (KG-12)
  2012-13 Enrollment: 873 . . . . (517) 547-6123

Housing: Homeownership rate: 60.4%; Homeowner vacancy rate: 4.5%; Rental vacancy rate: 8.5%

ADRIAN (city). County seat. Covers a land area of 7.953 square miles and a water area of 0.149 square miles. Located at 41.90° N. Lat; 84.04° W. Long. Elevation is 774 feet.

History: Adrian was founded as Logan in 1828 by Addison J. Comstock. His wife wanted the town named for her hero, the Roman emperor Hadrian, and it became Adrian. Adrian was incorporated as a village in 1836 and as a city in 1853. This was the home of Elmer D. Smith, who originated 586 varieties of chrysanthemums.

Population: 21,133; Growth (since 2000): -2.0%; Density: 2,657.1 persons per square mile; Race: 84.1% White, 4.4% Black/African American, 0.9%

Asian, 0.6% American Indian/Alaska Native, 0.0% Native Hawaiian/Other Pacific Islander, 4.0% Two or more races, 18.8% Hispanic of any race; Average household size: 2.37; Median age: 32.5; Age under 18: 23.0%; Age 65 and over: 14.2%; Males per 100 females: 91.4; Marriage status: 43.7% never married, 37.6% now married, 3.5% separated, 6.2% widowed, 12.4% divorced; Foreign born: 2.8%; Speak English only: 90.7%; With disability: 18.4%; Veterans: 8.9%; Ancestry: 23.6% German, 12.6% Irish, 9.0% English, 5.0% Polish, 4.6% American

Employment: 8.7% management, business, and financial, 2.9% computer, engineering, and science, 10.0% education, legal, community service, arts, and media, 3.9% healthcare practitioners, 27.1% service, 24.3% sales and office, 5.4% natural resources, construction, and maintenance, 17.8% production, transportation, and material moving

Income: Per capita: $16,604; Median household: $30,094; Average household: $42,195; Households with income of $100,000 or more: 8.5%; Poverty rate: 30.9%

Educational Attainment: High school diploma or higher: 81.2%; Bachelor's degree or higher: 19.9%; Graduate/professional degree or higher: 8.1%

School District(s)
Adrian SD (PK-12)
  2012-13 Enrollment: 3,098 . . . . (517) 264-6640
Lenawee ISD (PK-12)
  2012-13 Enrollment: 438 . . . . (517) 265-1627
Madison SD (Lenawee) (PK-12)
  2012-13 Enrollment: 1,559 . . . . (517) 263-0741
Tecumseh Public Schools (PK-12)
  2012-13 Enrollment: 2,944 . . . . (517) 424-7318

Four-year College(s)
Adrian College (Private, Not-for-profit, United Methodist)
  Fall 2013 Enrollment: 1,658 . . . . (517) 265-5161
  2013-14 Tuition: In-state $30,758; Out-of-state $30,758
Siena Heights University (Private, Not-for-profit, Roman Catholic)
  Fall 2013 Enrollment: 2,684 . . . . (517) 263-0731
  2013-14 Tuition: In-state $21,890; Out-of-state $21,890

Housing: Homeownership rate: 55.1%; Median home value: $74,200; Median year structure built: 1955; Homeowner vacancy rate: 4.1%; Median gross rent: $679 per month; Rental vacancy rate: 14.2%

Health Insurance: 84.7% have insurance; 55.3% have private insurance; 44.2% have public insurance; 15.3% do not have insurance; 4.8% of children under 18 do not have insurance

Hospitals: Emma L Bixby Medical Center (88 beds)

Newspapers: Daily Telegram (daily circulation 14500)

Transportation: Commute: 84.0% car, 0.2% public transportation, 11.7% walk, 2.1% work from home; Median travel time to work: 16.5 minutes

Airports: Lenawee County (general aviation)

Additional Information Contacts
City of Adrian . . . . (517) 263-2161
  http://www.ci.adrian.mi.us

ADRIAN (township). Covers a land area of 33.991 square miles and a water area of 0.017 square miles. Located at 41.95° N. Lat; 84.07° W. Long. Elevation is 774 feet.

History: The township was named Logan until 1838, when the name was changed to Adrian by the legislature.

Population: 6,035; Growth (since 2000): 5.0%; Density: 177.5 persons per square mile; Race: 95.2% White, 1.2% Black/African American, 0.6% Asian, 0.3% American Indian/Alaska Native, 0.0% Native Hawaiian/Other Pacific Islander, 1.6% Two or more races, 7.4% Hispanic of any race; Average household size: 2.51; Median age: 45.3; Age under 18: 21.8%; Age 65 and over: 18.2%; Males per 100 females: 93.3; Marriage status: 20.7% never married, 58.7% now married, 0.9% separated, 9.9% widowed, 10.7% divorced; Foreign born: 2.2%; Speak English only: 95.1%; With disability: 13.4%; Veterans: 10.9%; Ancestry: 32.1% German, 15.4% English, 13.3% Irish, 8.2% Polish, 7.9% French

Employment: 15.0% management, business, and financial, 1.7% computer, engineering, and science, 8.9% education, legal, community service, arts, and media, 3.7% healthcare practitioners, 19.1% service, 26.6% sales and office, 11.6% natural resources, construction, and maintenance, 13.4% production, transportation, and material moving

Income: Per capita: $26,024; Median household: $48,547; Average household: $63,209; Households with income of $100,000 or more: 14.7%; Poverty rate: 7.2%

Educational Attainment: High school diploma or higher: 92.2%; Bachelor's degree or higher: 26.2%; Graduate/professional degree or higher: 9.6%

School District(s)

Adrian SD (PK-12)
    2012-13 Enrollment: 3,098 . . . . (517) 264-6640
Lenawee ISD (PK-12)
    2012-13 Enrollment: 438. . . . . (517) 265-1627
Madison SD (Lenawee) (PK-12)
    2012-13 Enrollment: 1,559 . . . . (517) 263-0741
Tecumseh Public Schools (PK-12)
    2012-13 Enrollment: 2,944 . . . . (517) 424-7318

Four-year College(s)

Adrian College (Private, Not-for-profit, United Methodist)
    Fall 2013 Enrollment: 1,658 . . . . (517) 265-5161
    2013-14 Tuition: In-state $30,758; Out-of-state $30,758
Siena Heights University (Private, Not-for-profit, Roman Catholic)
    Fall 2013 Enrollment: 2,684 . . . . (517) 263-0731
    2013-14 Tuition: In-state $21,890; Out-of-state $21,890

Housing: Homeownership rate: 86.3%; Median home value: $144,000; Median year structure built: 1977; Homeowner vacancy rate: 2.7%; Median gross rent: $825 per month; Rental vacancy rate: 9.8%

Health Insurance: 95.1% have insurance; 81.5% have private insurance; 31.8% have public insurance; 4.9% do not have insurance; 3.0% of children under 18 do not have insurance

Hospitals: Emma L Bixby Medical Center (88 beds)

Newspapers: Daily Telegram (daily circulation 14500)

Transportation: Commute: 95.2% car, 0.7% public transportation, 0.0% walk, 4.0% work from home; Median travel time to work: 20.3 minutes

Airports: Lenawee County (general aviation)

BLISSFIELD (township). Covers a land area of 20.881 square miles and a water area of 0.173 square miles. Located at 41.86° N. Lat; 83.86° W. Long. Elevation is 689 feet.

History: Blissfield Township was organized in 1827 and named for Hervey Bliss, who settled here in 1824.

Population: 3,973; Growth (since 2000): 1.5%; Density: 190.3 persons per square mile; Race: 96.7% White, 0.3% Black/African American, 0.2% Asian, 0.4% American Indian/Alaska Native, 0.0% Native Hawaiian/Other Pacific Islander, 1.6% Two or more races, 4.8% Hispanic of any race; Average household size: 2.51; Median age: 39.2; Age under 18: 25.5%; Age 65 and over: 15.7%; Males per 100 females: 94.3; Marriage status: 24.3% never married, 55.9% now married, 1.5% separated, 6.7% widowed, 13.1% divorced; Foreign born: 1.5%; Speak English only: 96.6%; With disability: 15.6%; Veterans: 10.1%; Ancestry: 40.6% German, 11.8% Irish, 9.2% English, 8.0% American, 5.0% Italian

Employment: 11.6% management, business, and financial, 3.4% computer, engineering, and science, 6.9% education, legal, community service, arts, and media, 5.9% healthcare practitioners, 17.3% service, 29.3% sales and office, 8.2% natural resources, construction, and maintenance, 17.3% production, transportation, and material moving

Income: Per capita: $24,328; Median household: $48,107; Average household: $57,029; Households with income of $100,000 or more: 14.4%; Poverty rate: 13.5%

Educational Attainment: High school diploma or higher: 94.2%; Bachelor's degree or higher: 21.3%; Graduate/professional degree or higher: 4.8%

School District(s)

Blissfield Community Schools (KG-12)
    2012-13 Enrollment: 1,257 . . . . (517) 486-2205

Housing: Homeownership rate: 78.9%; Median home value: $104,000; Median year structure built: 1957; Homeowner vacancy rate: 2.8%; Median gross rent: $814 per month; Rental vacancy rate: 8.5%

Health Insurance: 89.8% have insurance; 72.2% have private insurance; 36.4% have public insurance; 10.2% do not have insurance; 2.5% of children under 18 do not have insurance

Newspapers: Blissfield Advance (weekly circulation 2700)

Transportation: Commute: 92.8% car, 0.0% public transportation, 2.1% walk, 4.0% work from home; Median travel time to work: 29.4 minutes

---

BLISSFIELD (village). Covers a land area of 2.237 square miles and a water area of 0.055 square miles. Located at 41.83° N. Lat; 83.86° W. Long. Elevation is 689 feet.

History: Blissfield was incorporated as a village in 1875.

Population: 3,340; Growth (since 2000): 3.6%; Density: 1,492.8 persons per square mile; Race: 96.6% White, 0.3% Black/African American, 0.2% Asian, 0.5% American Indian/Alaska Native, 0.0% Native Hawaiian/Other Pacific Islander, 1.6% Two or more races, 5.1% Hispanic of any race; Average household size: 2.48; Median age: 38.8; Age under 18: 25.6%; Age 65 and over: 15.5%; Males per 100 females: 93.4; Marriage status: 24.8% never married, 55.5% now married, 1.3% separated, 5.2% widowed, 14.5% divorced; Foreign born: 1.7%; Speak English only: 96.1%; With disability: 16.1%; Veterans: 11.2%; Ancestry: 38.5% German, 12.1% Irish, 9.8% English, 9.3% American, 5.8% Italian

Employment: 11.6% management, business, and financial, 3.9% computer, engineering, and science, 7.1% education, legal, community service, arts, and media, 6.0% healthcare practitioners, 16.0% service, 32.6% sales and office, 6.3% natural resources, construction, and maintenance, 16.4% production, transportation, and material moving

Income: Per capita: $24,753; Median household: $47,695; Average household: $56,779; Households with income of $100,000 or more: 13.4%; Poverty rate: 15.3%

Educational Attainment: High school diploma or higher: 94.3%; Bachelor's degree or higher: 22.0%; Graduate/professional degree or higher: 4.6%

School District(s)

Blissfield Community Schools (KG-12)
    2012-13 Enrollment: 1,257 . . . . (517) 486-2205

Housing: Homeownership rate: 77.9%; Median home value: $101,100; Median year structure built: 1957; Homeowner vacancy rate: 3.1%; Median gross rent: $808 per month; Rental vacancy rate: 8.9%

Health Insurance: 88.2% have insurance; 69.4% have private insurance; 38.7% have public insurance; 11.8% do not have insurance; 2.9% of children under 18 do not have insurance

Newspapers: Blissfield Advance (weekly circulation 2700)

Transportation: Commute: 92.5% car, 0.0% public transportation, 1.7% walk, 4.5% work from home; Median travel time to work: 29.7 minutes

---

BRITTON (village). Covers a land area of 0.788 square miles and a water area of 0 square miles. Located at 41.99° N. Lat; 83.83° W. Long. Elevation is 699 feet.

History: Britton was named for John Britton, who operated a store here and became the first postmaster in 1881.

Population: 586; Growth (since 2000): -16.2%; Density: 743.5 persons per square mile; Race: 98.6% White, 0.2% Black/African American, 0.3% Asian, 0.2% American Indian/Alaska Native, 0.0% Native Hawaiian/Other Pacific Islander, 0.3% Two or more races, 1.9% Hispanic of any race; Average household size: 2.47; Median age: 38.8; Age under 18: 22.2%; Age 65 and over: 11.8%; Males per 100 females: 102.1

School District(s)

Britton Deerfield Schools (PK-12)
    2012-13 Enrollment: 756. . . . . (517) 451-4581

Housing: Homeownership rate: 75.5%; Homeowner vacancy rate: 1.1%; Rental vacancy rate: 18.1%

CAMBRIDGE (township). Covers a land area of 31.849 square miles and a water area of 3.585 square miles. Located at 42.02° N. Lat; 84.18° W. Long.

History: Cambridge Junction was originally the intersection of the Chicago Turnpike and the Monroe Turnpike from Lake Erie. The Walker Tavern was a stopover spot on the stagecoach journey between Chicago and Detroit. As such, it entertained such guests as Daniel Webster and James Fenimore Cooper.

Population: 5,733; Growth (since 2000): 8.2%; Density: 180.0 persons per square mile; Race: 96.9% White, 0.4% Black/African American, 0.4% Asian, 0.5% American Indian/Alaska Native, 0.1% Native Hawaiian/Other Pacific Islander, 1.2% Two or more races, 2.6% Hispanic of any race; Average household size: 2.51; Median age: 45.6; Age under 18: 22.4%; Age 65 and over: 16.1%; Males per 100 females: 100.5; Marriage status: 23.7% never married, 57.7% now married, 0.9% separated, 6.1% widowed, 12.5% divorced; Foreign born: 1.2%; Speak English only: 98.6%; With disability: 12.4%; Veterans: 9.7%; Ancestry: 27.2% German, 21.5% Irish, 13.3% English, 10.2% Polish, 5.6% Italian

Employment: 10.5% management, business, and financial, 2.6% computer, engineering, and science, 7.7% education, legal, community service, arts, and media, 6.0% healthcare practitioners, 21.2% service, 25.0% sales and office, 8.4% natural resources, construction, and maintenance, 18.7% production, transportation, and material moving

Income: Per capita: $26,817; Median household: $53,893; Average household: $64,175; Households with income of $100,000 or more: 18.0%; Poverty rate: 12.5%

Educational Attainment: High school diploma or higher: 94.6%; Bachelor's degree or higher: 20.2%; Graduate/professional degree or higher: 8.9%

Housing: Homeownership rate: 88.1%; Median home value: $159,400; Median year structure built: 1979; Homeowner vacancy rate: 2.2%; Median gross rent: $636 per month; Rental vacancy rate: 6.8%

Health Insurance: 87.7% have insurance; 76.4% have private insurance; 30.0% have public insurance; 12.3% do not have insurance; 7.1% of children under 18 do not have insurance

Safety: Violent crime rate: 1.8 per 10,000 population; Property crime rate: 31.8 per 10,000 population

Transportation: Commute: 92.5% car, 0.0% public transportation, 2.8% walk, 4.5% work from home; Median travel time to work: 31.5 minutes

CEMENT CITY (village). Covers a land area of 0.905 square miles and a water area of 0.035 square miles. Located at 42.07° N. Lat; 84.33° W. Long. Elevation is 1,060 feet.

History: Cement City began as Woodstock. It was renamed in 1900 when a cement company built a plant here. The village was incorporated in 1953.

Population: 438; Growth (since 2000): -3.1%; Density: 484.1 persons per square mile; Race: 95.7% White, 0.0% Black/African American, 0.7% Asian, 0.0% American Indian/Alaska Native, 0.0% Native Hawaiian/Other Pacific Islander, 2.5% Two or more races, 2.5% Hispanic of any race; Average household size: 2.52; Median age: 40.4; Age under 18: 24.7%; Age 65 and over: 13.9%; Males per 100 females: 103.7

Housing: Homeownership rate: 78.7%; Homeowner vacancy rate: 2.1%; Rental vacancy rate: 2.6%

CLAYTON (village). Covers a land area of 0.713 square miles and a water area of 0 square miles. Located at 41.86° N. Lat; 84.23° W. Long. Elevation is 892 feet.

History: Clayton was settled in 1836 and platted in 1843. It was named for a Presbyterian minister in New York, a friend of Reuben E. Bird who platted the village.

Population: 344; Growth (since 2000): 5.5%; Density: 482.4 persons per square mile; Race: 93.6% White, 1.7% Black/African American, 0.3% Asian, 0.3% American Indian/Alaska Native, 0.0% Native Hawaiian/Other Pacific Islander, 2.3% Two or more races, 5.5% Hispanic of any race; Average household size: 2.92; Median age: 31.5; Age under 18: 30.5%; Age 65 and over: 11.9%; Males per 100 females: 108.5

Housing: Homeownership rate: 68.7%; Homeowner vacancy rate: 2.4%; Rental vacancy rate: 2.6%

CLINTON (township). Covers a land area of 18.131 square miles and a water area of 0.075 square miles. Located at 42.06° N. Lat; 83.95° W. Long. Elevation is 837 feet.

Population: 3,604; Growth (since 2000): -0.6%; Density: 198.8 persons per square mile; Race: 96.3% White, 0.3% Black/African American, 0.5% Asian, 0.4% American Indian/Alaska Native, 0.0% Native Hawaiian/Other Pacific Islander, 2.1% Two or more races, 2.2% Hispanic of any race; Average household size: 2.55; Median age: 40.3; Age under 18: 25.1%; Age 65 and over: 13.4%; Males per 100 females: 93.9; Marriage status: 23.9% never married, 58.6% now married, 1.8% separated, 6.1% widowed, 11.4% divorced; Foreign born: 2.9%; Speak English only: 96.4%; With disability: 13.2%; Veterans: 12.5%; Ancestry: 26.6% German, 12.2% Irish, 10.3% English, 8.9% American, 7.1% Italian

Employment: 10.6% management, business, and financial, 3.8% computer, engineering, and science, 9.0% education, legal, community service, arts, and media, 8.1% healthcare practitioners, 18.0% service, 19.1% sales and office, 10.4% natural resources, construction, and maintenance, 20.9% production, transportation, and material moving

Income: Per capita: $21,204; Median household: $52,799; Average household: $55,327; Households with income of $100,000 or more: 11.1%; Poverty rate: 6.2%

Educational Attainment: High school diploma or higher: 92.7%; Bachelor's degree or higher: 20.3%; Graduate/professional degree or higher: 3.5%

School District(s)
Clinton Community Schools (PK-12)
    2012-13 Enrollment: 1,112 . . . . (517) 456-6501

Lenawee ISD (PK-12)
    2012-13 Enrollment: 438 . . . . (517) 265-1627

Housing: Homeownership rate: 84.1%; Median home value: $126,600; Median year structure built: 1973; Homeowner vacancy rate: 3.7%; Median gross rent: $730 per month; Rental vacancy rate: 16.2%

Health Insurance: 82.4% have insurance; 69.6% have private insurance; 28.0% have public insurance; 17.6% do not have insurance; 15.1% of children under 18 do not have insurance

Newspapers: Clinton Local (weekly circulation 2100)

Transportation: Commute: 92.4% car, 0.9% public transportation, 4.2% walk, 2.0% work from home; Median travel time to work: 31.6 minutes

CLINTON (village). Covers a land area of 1.843 square miles and a water area of 0.035 square miles. Located at 42.07° N. Lat; 83.97° W. Long. Elevation is 837 feet.

History: Clinton was called Oak Plains when it was incorporated in 1838. An early industry in Clinton was the woolen mill. The town was named for DeWitt Clinton of New York.

Population: 2,336; Growth (since 2000): 1.9%; Density: 1,267.3 persons per square mile; Race: 96.6% White, 0.2% Black/African American, 0.7% Asian, 0.5% American Indian/Alaska Native, 0.0% Native Hawaiian/Other Pacific Islander, 1.6% Two or more races, 2.4% Hispanic of any race; Average household size: 2.49; Median age: 37.2; Age under 18: 27.0%; Age 65 and over: 12.6%; Males per 100 females: 89.0

School District(s)
Clinton Community Schools (PK-12)
    2012-13 Enrollment: 1,112 . . . . (517) 456-6501
Lenawee ISD (PK-12)
    2012-13 Enrollment: 438 . . . . (517) 265-1627

Housing: Homeownership rate: 81.7%; Homeowner vacancy rate: 4.6%; Rental vacancy rate: 17.3%

Newspapers: Clinton Local (weekly circulation 2100)

Additional Information Contacts
Village of Clinton . . . . (517) 456-7494
    http://www.villageofclinton.org

DEERFIELD (township). Covers a land area of 25.010 square miles and a water area of 0.144 square miles. Located at 41.89° N. Lat; 83.80° W. Long. Elevation is 679 feet.

Population: 1,568; Growth (since 2000): -11.4%; Density: 62.7 persons per square mile; Race: 96.1% White, 0.3% Black/African American, 0.1% Asian, 0.9% American Indian/Alaska Native, 0.0% Native Hawaiian/Other Pacific Islander, 2.0% Two or more races, 5.7% Hispanic of any race; Average household size: 2.67; Median age: 39.6; Age under 18: 25.9%; Age 65 and over: 13.6%; Males per 100 females: 101.8

Housing: Homeownership rate: 85.2%; Homeowner vacancy rate: 2.4%; Rental vacancy rate: 12.1%

DEERFIELD (village). Covers a land area of 0.958 square miles and a water area of 0 square miles. Located at 41.89° N. Lat; 83.78° W. Long. Elevation is 679 feet.

Population: 898; Growth (since 2000): -10.6%; Density: 937.2 persons per square mile; Race: 95.0% White, 0.4% Black/African American, 0.1% Asian, 0.9% American Indian/Alaska Native, 0.0% Native Hawaiian/Other Pacific Islander, 3.1% Two or more races, 4.1% Hispanic of any race; Average household size: 2.62; Median age: 38.4; Age under 18: 26.3%; Age 65 and over: 12.9%; Males per 100 females: 95.6

Housing: Homeownership rate: 82.5%; Homeowner vacancy rate: 3.1%; Rental vacancy rate: 14.1%

DOVER (township). Covers a land area of 35.081 square miles and a water area of 0.106 square miles. Located at 41.86° N. Lat; 84.18° W. Long.

Population: 1,834; Growth (since 2000): 2.6%; Density: 52.3 persons per square mile; Race: 93.8% White, 0.7% Black/African American, 0.3% Asian, 0.6% American Indian/Alaska Native, 0.0% Native Hawaiian/Other Pacific Islander, 2.5% Two or more races, 7.7% Hispanic of any race; Average household size: 2.70; Median age: 39.9; Age under 18: 26.0%; Age 65 and over: 14.4%; Males per 100 females: 105.4

Housing: Homeownership rate: 80.4%; Homeowner vacancy rate: 2.9%; Rental vacancy rate: 6.3%

FAIRFIELD (township). Covers a land area of 42.029 square miles and a water area of 0 square miles. Located at 41.77° N. Lat; 84.06° W. Long. Elevation is 768 feet.
Population: 1,764; Growth (since 2000): 0.5%; Density: 42.0 persons per square mile; Race: 96.0% White, 0.6% Black/African American, 0.2% Asian, 0.3% American Indian/Alaska Native, 0.0% Native Hawaiian/Other Pacific Islander, 1.9% Two or more races, 2.9% Hispanic of any race; Average household size: 2.66; Median age: 41.4; Age under 18: 23.4%; Age 65 and over: 13.4%; Males per 100 females: 111.5
Housing: Homeownership rate: 86.1%; Homeowner vacancy rate: 2.2%; Rental vacancy rate: 11.5%

FRANKLIN (township). Covers a land area of 38.333 square miles and a water area of 0.864 square miles. Located at 42.03° N. Lat; 84.07° W. Long.
Population: 3,174; Growth (since 2000): 8.0%; Density: 82.8 persons per square mile; Race: 96.6% White, 0.3% Black/African American, 0.4% Asian, 0.6% American Indian/Alaska Native, 0.0% Native Hawaiian/Other Pacific Islander, 1.6% Two or more races, 2.5% Hispanic of any race; Average household size: 2.68; Median age: 43.1; Age under 18: 23.9%; Age 65 and over: 13.6%; Males per 100 females: 107.3; Marriage status: 24.0% never married, 60.3% now married, 1.7% separated, 5.0% widowed, 10.7% divorced; Foreign born: 1.1%; Speak English only: 98.4%; With disability: 10.1%; Veterans: 6.5%; Ancestry: 31.8% German, 16.3% Irish, 14.3% English, 9.3% Polish, 8.5% American
Employment: 13.0% management, business, and financial, 7.5% computer, engineering, and science, 7.4% education, legal, community service, arts, and media, 4.0% healthcare practitioners, 15.0% service, 23.8% sales and office, 13.3% natural resources, construction, and maintenance, 16.1% production, transportation, and material moving
Income: Per capita: $26,278; Median household: $61,715; Average household: $71,792; Households with income of $100,000 or more: 20.8%; Poverty rate: 3.6%
Educational Attainment: High school diploma or higher: 95.4%; Bachelor's degree or higher: 22.8%; Graduate/professional degree or higher: 8.8%
Housing: Homeownership rate: 88.7%; Median home value: $168,800; Median year structure built: 1976; Homeowner vacancy rate: 1.7%; Median gross rent: $913 per month; Rental vacancy rate: 6.3%
Health Insurance: 92.9% have insurance; 80.0% have private insurance; 29.7% have public insurance; 7.1% do not have insurance; 0.0% of children under 18 do not have insurance
Transportation: Commute: 94.4% car, 0.6% public transportation, 3.2% walk, 1.4% work from home; Median travel time to work: 36.7 minutes

HUDSON (city). Covers a land area of 2.190 square miles and a water area of 0.006 square miles. Located at 41.86° N. Lat; 84.35° W. Long. Elevation is 915 feet.
History: Hudson was settled in the 1830's and first known as Bean Creek, then Lanesville. Renamed Hudson in 1840, it developed as a shipping point for a farming area, and the home of industries producing harnesses and pumps. Hudson was incorporated as a city in 1893.
Population: 2,307; Growth (since 2000): -7.7%; Density: 1,053.4 persons per square mile; Race: 96.2% White, 0.7% Black/African American, 0.3% Asian, 0.5% American Indian/Alaska Native, 0.0% Native Hawaiian/Other Pacific Islander, 1.9% Two or more races, 4.2% Hispanic of any race; Average household size: 2.63; Median age: 33.4; Age under 18: 29.5%; Age 65 and over: 10.7%; Males per 100 females: 96.2
School District(s)
Hudson Area Schools (PK-12)
    2012-13 Enrollment: 940. . . . . (517) 448-8912
Housing: Homeownership rate: 66.8%; Homeowner vacancy rate: 2.5%; Rental vacancy rate: 9.8%
Newspapers: Hudson Post-Gazette (weekly circulation 1600)

HUDSON (township). Covers a land area of 35.388 square miles and a water area of 1.074 square miles. Located at 41.85° N. Lat; 84.30° W. Long. Elevation is 915 feet.
History: Hudson Township was named for Dr. Daniel Hudson, one of the first landowners, who had come from New York.
Population: 1,497; Growth (since 2000): -5.0%; Density: 42.3 persons per square mile; Race: 98.3% White, 0.3% Black/African American, 0.1% Asian, 0.0% American Indian/Alaska Native, 0.0% Native Hawaiian/Other Pacific Islander, 1.0% Two or more races, 1.7% Hispanic of any race;

Average household size: 2.36; Median age: 48.1; Age under 18: 18.0%; Age 65 and over: 22.6%; Males per 100 females: 95.7
School District(s)
Hudson Area Schools (PK-12)
    2012-13 Enrollment: 940 . . . . (517) 448-8912
Housing: Homeownership rate: 90.0%; Homeowner vacancy rate: 2.1%; Rental vacancy rate: 6.0%
Newspapers: Hudson Post-Gazette (weekly circulation 1600)

JASPER (CDP). Covers a land area of 4.032 square miles and a water area of 0 square miles. Located at 41.79° N. Lat; 84.04° W. Long. Elevation is 735 feet.
Population: 412; Growth (since 2000): n/a; Density: 102.2 persons per square mile; Race: 94.4% White, 0.5% Black/African American, 0.0% Asian, 0.2% American Indian/Alaska Native, 0.0% Native Hawaiian/Other Pacific Islander, 2.4% Two or more races, 5.6% Hispanic of any race; Average household size: 2.73; Median age: 33.7; Age under 18: 26.7%; Age 65 and over: 12.9%; Males per 100 females: 105.0
Housing: Homeownership rate: 82.1%; Homeowner vacancy rate: 3.1%; Rental vacancy rate: 0.0%

MACON (township). Covers a land area of 32.685 square miles and a water area of 0.003 square miles. Located at 42.04° N. Lat; 83.83° W. Long. Elevation is 830 feet.
History: The Macon area was owned by Henry Ford, and devoted largely to soy-bean production.
Population: 1,486; Growth (since 2000): 2.6%; Density: 45.5 persons per square mile; Race: 92.0% White, 5.7% Black/African American, 0.1% Asian, 0.6% American Indian/Alaska Native, 0.3% Native Hawaiian/Other Pacific Islander, 0.9% Two or more races, 2.4% Hispanic of any race; Average household size: 2.69; Median age: 41.1; Age under 18: 27.7%; Age 65 and over: 13.4%; Males per 100 females: 130.7
Housing: Homeownership rate: 91.4%; Homeowner vacancy rate: 1.7%; Rental vacancy rate: 4.3%

MADISON (charter township). Covers a land area of 30.391 square miles and a water area of 0.260 square miles. Located at 41.85° N. Lat; 84.07° W. Long.
Population: 8,621; Growth (since 2000): 5.1%; Density: 283.7 persons per square mile; Race: 81.2% White, 13.6% Black/African American, 0.4% Asian, 0.6% American Indian/Alaska Native, 0.0% Native Hawaiian/Other Pacific Islander, 2.0% Two or more races, 8.5% Hispanic of any race; Average household size: 2.63; Median age: 39.6; Age under 18: 18.6%; Age 65 and over: 12.0%; Males per 100 females: 166.6; Marriage status: 36.1% never married, 47.7% now married, 1.5% separated, 4.9% widowed, 11.3% divorced; Foreign born: 1.7%; Speak English only: 95.4%; With disability: 15.1%; Veterans: 7.1%; Ancestry: 30.4% German, 12.2% Irish, 10.6% English, 5.2% American, 3.8% Polish
Employment: 12.2% management, business, and financial, 0.5% computer, engineering, and science, 9.2% education, legal, community service, arts, and media, 2.1% healthcare practitioners, 25.8% service, 27.6% sales and office, 8.9% natural resources, construction, and maintenance, 13.7% production, transportation, and material moving
Income: Per capita: $17,966; Median household: $53,487; Average household: $58,866; Households with income of $100,000 or more: 11.8%; Poverty rate: 7.6%
Educational Attainment: High school diploma or higher: 86.7%; Bachelor's degree or higher: 13.2%; Graduate/professional degree or higher: 4.6%
Housing: Homeownership rate: 83.4%; Median home value: $109,700; Median year structure built: 1974; Homeowner vacancy rate: 1.9%; Median gross rent: $743 per month; Rental vacancy rate: 7.1%
Health Insurance: 90.7% have insurance; 77.2% have private insurance; 31.4% have public insurance; 9.3% do not have insurance; 5.6% of children under 18 do not have insurance
Safety: Violent crime rate: 8.2 per 10,000 population; Property crime rate: 91.0 per 10,000 population
Transportation: Commute: 98.8% car, 0.0% public transportation, 0.0% walk, 0.8% work from home; Median travel time to work: 20.1 minutes
Additional Information Contacts
Madison Charter Township . . . . (517) 263-9313
    http://www.madisontwp.com

MANITOU BEACH-DEVILS LAKE (CDP). Covers a land area of 6.831 square miles and a water area of 2.858 square miles. Located at 41.97° N. Lat; 84.30° W. Long.
Population: 2,019; Growth (since 2000): -2.9%; Density: 295.6 persons per square mile; Race: 97.3% White, 0.2% Black/African American, 0.4% Asian, 0.3% American Indian/Alaska Native, 0.0% Native Hawaiian/Other Pacific Islander, 1.2% Two or more races, 2.0% Hispanic of any race; Average household size: 2.18; Median age: 50.3; Age under 18: 17.4%; Age 65 and over: 19.6%; Males per 100 females: 104.4
Housing: Homeownership rate: 84.1%; Homeowner vacancy rate: 2.4%; Rental vacancy rate: 29.0%

MEDINA (township). Covers a land area of 47.536 square miles and a water area of 0.090 square miles. Located at 41.76° N. Lat; 84.30° W. Long. Elevation is 837 feet.
Population: 1,090; Growth (since 2000): -11.2%; Density: 22.9 persons per square mile; Race: 96.9% White, 0.3% Black/African American, 0.2% Asian, 0.1% American Indian/Alaska Native, 0.2% Native Hawaiian/Other Pacific Islander, 1.5% Two or more races, 3.2% Hispanic of any race; Average household size: 2.59; Median age: 43.9; Age under 18: 22.8%; Age 65 and over: 15.5%; Males per 100 females: 109.2
Housing: Homeownership rate: 86.1%; Homeowner vacancy rate: 3.7%; Rental vacancy rate: 9.1%

MORENCI (city). Covers a land area of 2.120 square miles and a water area of 0 square miles. Located at 41.72° N. Lat; 84.22° W. Long. Elevation is 764 feet.
History: Incorporated as city 1934.
Population: 2,220; Growth (since 2000): -7.4%; Density: 1,047.4 persons per square mile; Race: 96.2% White, 1.0% Black/African American, 0.3% Asian, 0.3% American Indian/Alaska Native, 0.1% Native Hawaiian/Other Pacific Islander, 1.4% Two or more races, 4.5% Hispanic of any race; Average household size: 2.68; Median age: 34.1; Age under 18: 28.7%; Age 65 and over: 13.4%; Males per 100 females: 92.5
School District(s)
Morenci Area Schools (PK-12)
    2012-13 Enrollment: 709 . . . . (517) 458-7501
Housing: Homeownership rate: 70.2%; Homeowner vacancy rate: 3.3%; Rental vacancy rate: 19.3%
Safety: Violent crime rate: 22.8 per 10,000 population; Property crime rate: 127.9 per 10,000 population
Newspapers: State Line Observer (weekly circulation 2400)

OGDEN (township). Covers a land area of 42.105 square miles and a water area of 0 square miles. Located at 41.77° N. Lat; 83.94° W. Long. Elevation is 709 feet.
Population: 973; Growth (since 2000): -8.5%; Density: 23.1 persons per square mile; Race: 97.2% White, 0.2% Black/African American, 0.2% Asian, 0.2% American Indian/Alaska Native, 0.0% Native Hawaiian/Other Pacific Islander, 1.6% Two or more races, 3.8% Hispanic of any race; Average household size: 2.59; Median age: 45.9; Age under 18: 20.3%; Age 65 and over: 13.7%; Males per 100 females: 116.2
Housing: Homeownership rate: 85.9%; Homeowner vacancy rate: 1.2%; Rental vacancy rate: 5.3%

ONSTED (village). Covers a land area of 0.965 square miles and a water area of 0 square miles. Located at 42.01° N. Lat; 84.19° W. Long. Elevation is 988 feet.
Population: 917; Growth (since 2000): 12.8%; Density: 950.4 persons per square mile; Race: 96.2% White, 0.2% Black/African American, 0.4% Asian, 1.6% American Indian/Alaska Native, 0.0% Native Hawaiian/Other Pacific Islander, 1.3% Two or more races, 1.6% Hispanic of any race; Average household size: 2.48; Median age: 39.3; Age under 18: 26.9%; Age 65 and over: 15.8%; Males per 100 females: 95.5
School District(s)
Onsted Community Schools (KG-12)
    2012-13 Enrollment: 1,517 . . . . (517) 467-2174
Housing: Homeownership rate: 71.9%; Homeowner vacancy rate: 1.8%; Rental vacancy rate: 4.5%

PALMYRA (township). Covers a land area of 36.503 square miles and a water area of 0.285 square miles. Located at 41.87° N. Lat; 83.95° W. Long. Elevation is 709 feet.
History: Palmyra was settled in 1827 and named for Palmyra, New York, the former home of an early settler.
Population: 2,084; Growth (since 2000): -11.9%; Density: 57.1 persons per square mile; Race: 96.4% White, 0.5% Black/African American, 0.2% Asian, 0.3% American Indian/Alaska Native, 0.0% Native Hawaiian/Other Pacific Islander, 2.0% Two or more races, 7.0% Hispanic of any race; Average household size: 2.61; Median age: 42.3; Age under 18: 21.7%; Age 65 and over: 15.2%; Males per 100 females: 107.6
Housing: Homeownership rate: 84.4%; Homeowner vacancy rate: 2.0%; Rental vacancy rate: 6.2%

RAISIN (township). Covers a land area of 36.129 square miles and a water area of 0.391 square miles. Located at 41.95° N. Lat; 83.94° W. Long.
Population: 7,559; Growth (since 2000): 16.2%; Density: 209.2 persons per square mile; Race: 95.0% White, 0.7% Black/African American, 0.6% Asian, 0.4% American Indian/Alaska Native, 0.0% Native Hawaiian/Other Pacific Islander, 1.8% Two or more races, 5.3% Hispanic of any race; Average household size: 2.75; Median age: 40.1; Age under 18: 25.2%; Age 65 and over: 12.5%; Males per 100 females: 102.3; Marriage status: 23.9% never married, 63.0% now married, 0.2% separated, 3.4% widowed, 9.6% divorced; Foreign born: 2.0%; Speak English only: 97.6%; With disability: 9.6%; Veterans: 10.4%; Ancestry: 32.8% German, 17.5% Irish, 14.6% English, 7.8% French, 6.5% Dutch
Employment: 11.4% management, business, and financial, 5.9% computer, engineering, and science, 8.8% education, legal, community service, arts, and media, 7.8% healthcare practitioners, 18.1% service, 25.4% sales and office, 8.9% natural resources, construction, and maintenance, 13.8% production, transportation, and material moving
Income: Per capita: $25,591; Median household: $64,951; Average household: $73,501; Households with income of $100,000 or more: 23.6%; Poverty rate: 8.4%
Educational Attainment: High school diploma or higher: 91.8%; Bachelor's degree or higher: 19.5%; Graduate/professional degree or higher: 5.0%
Housing: Homeownership rate: 92.9%; Median home value: $141,600; Median year structure built: 1985; Homeowner vacancy rate: 1.5%; Median gross rent: $977 per month; Rental vacancy rate: 10.9%
Health Insurance: 93.5% have insurance; 82.5% have private insurance; 23.8% have public insurance; 6.5% do not have insurance; 0.6% of children under 18 do not have insurance
Safety: Violent crime rate: 0.0 per 10,000 population; Property crime rate: 13.4 per 10,000 population
Transportation: Commute: 94.4% car, 0.4% public transportation, 0.7% walk, 3.6% work from home; Median travel time to work: 32.2 minutes

RIDGEWAY (township). Covers a land area of 28.649 square miles and a water area of 0.025 square miles. Located at 41.97° N. Lat; 83.83° W. Long. Elevation is 738 feet.
History: Ridgeway was settled in the late 1820's. It was named for an old path over a ridge, called the ridge way.
Population: 1,542; Growth (since 2000): -2.4%; Density: 53.8 persons per square mile; Race: 96.4% White, 0.3% Black/African American, 1.2% Asian, 0.4% American Indian/Alaska Native, 0.1% Native Hawaiian/Other Pacific Islander, 1.2% Two or more races, 2.6% Hispanic of any race; Average household size: 2.66; Median age: 39.5; Age under 18: 22.7%; Age 65 and over: 12.8%; Males per 100 females: 97.4
Housing: Homeownership rate: 82.0%; Homeowner vacancy rate: 2.6%; Rental vacancy rate: 14.6%

RIGA (township). Covers a land area of 40.860 square miles and a water area of <.001 square miles. Located at 41.77° N. Lat; 83.83° W. Long. Elevation is 696 feet.
Population: 1,406; Growth (since 2000): -2.3%; Density: 34.4 persons per square mile; Race: 97.2% White, 0.0% Black/African American, 0.2% Asian, 0.3% American Indian/Alaska Native, 0.0% Native Hawaiian/Other Pacific Islander, 1.3% Two or more races, 3.6% Hispanic of any race; Average household size: 2.71; Median age: 42.5; Age under 18: 22.8%; Age 65 and over: 14.7%; Males per 100 females: 102.6
Housing: Homeownership rate: 86.5%; Homeowner vacancy rate: 0.7%; Rental vacancy rate: 1.4%

ROLLIN (township). Covers a land area of 33.679 square miles and a water area of 2.413 square miles. Located at 41.94° N. Lat; 84.30° W. Long. Elevation is 981 feet.

History: Rollin Township was named for Reverend David Rollin. It was settled in the mid-1830's and grew up around a sawmill.

Population: 3,270; Growth (since 2000): 3.0%; Density: 97.1 persons per square mile; Race: 97.1% White, 0.2% Black/African American, 0.3% Asian, 0.4% American Indian/Alaska Native, 0.0% Native Hawaiian/Other Pacific Islander, 1.3% Two or more races, 2.6% Hispanic of any race; Average household size: 2.37; Median age: 46.5; Age under 18: 20.5%; Age 65 and over: 18.1%; Males per 100 females: 101.6; Marriage status: 20.4% never married, 59.5% now married, 2.5% separated, 4.2% widowed, 16.0% divorced; Foreign born: 1.8%; Speak English only: 95.0%; With disability: 18.6%; Veterans: 11.4%; Ancestry: 37.4% German, 19.3% Irish, 17.7% English, 8.8% Polish, 6.8% French

Employment: 9.8% management, business, and financial, 1.0% computer, engineering, and science, 19.6% education, legal, community service, arts, and media, 9.1% healthcare practitioners, 13.8% service, 24.1% sales and office, 9.6% natural resources, construction, and maintenance, 13.0% production, transportation, and material moving

Income: Per capita: $25,948; Median household: $46,118; Average household: $58,936; Households with income of $100,000 or more: 8.7%; Poverty rate: 15.3%

Educational Attainment: High school diploma or higher: 89.9%; Bachelor's degree or higher: 27.9%; Graduate/professional degree or higher: 9.6%

Housing: Homeownership rate: 82.6%; Median home value: $125,600; Median year structure built: 1964; Homeowner vacancy rate: 2.1%; Median gross rent: $709 per month; Rental vacancy rate: 21.2%

Health Insurance: 86.7% have insurance; 66.3% have private insurance; 39.2% have public insurance; 13.3% do not have insurance; 7.3% of children under 18 do not have insurance

Transportation: Commute: 97.0% car, 0.0% public transportation, 1.3% walk, 1.7% work from home; Median travel time to work: 36.9 minutes

ROME (township). Covers a land area of 35.864 square miles and a water area of 0.028 square miles. Located at 41.94° N. Lat; 84.19° W. Long. Elevation is 906 feet.

Population: 1,791; Growth (since 2000): 1.1%; Density: 49.9 persons per square mile; Race: 96.9% White, 0.3% Black/African American, 0.0% Asian, 0.3% American Indian/Alaska Native, 0.1% Native Hawaiian/Other Pacific Islander, 2.0% Two or more races, 3.2% Hispanic of any race; Average household size: 2.72; Median age: 43.6; Age under 18: 23.6%; Age 65 and over: 13.7%; Males per 100 females: 104.2

Housing: Homeownership rate: 90.7%; Homeowner vacancy rate: 2.0%; Rental vacancy rate: 0.0%

SAND CREEK (unincorporated postal area)
ZCTA: 49279

Covers a land area of 26.346 square miles and a water area of 0 square miles. Located at 41.78° N. Lat; 84.10° W. Long. Elevation is 778 feet.

Population: 797; Growth (since 2000): -14.3%; Density: 30.3 persons per square mile; Race: 97.6% White, 0.5% Black/African American, 0.0% Asian, 0.5% American Indian/Alaska Native, 0.0% Native Hawaiian/Other Pacific Islander, 1.1% Two or more races, 1.9% Hispanic of any race; Average household size: 2.68; Median age: 42.9; Age under 18: 24.5%; Age 65 and over: 14.7%; Males per 100 females: 104.9

School District(s)
Sand Creek Community Schools (PK-12)
    2012-13 Enrollment: 937 . . . . (517) 436-3108
Housing: Homeownership rate: 89.2%; Homeowner vacancy rate: 0.7%; Rental vacancy rate: 15.8%

SENECA (township). Covers a land area of 40.054 square miles and a water area of 0.059 square miles. Located at 41.76° N. Lat; 84.17° W. Long. Elevation is 797 feet.

History: Seneca Township was organized in 1836 and named for Seneca County, New York, the former home of many of its first residents.

Population: 1,230; Growth (since 2000): -5.6%; Density: 30.7 persons per square mile; Race: 97.6% White, 0.2% Black/African American, 0.2% Asian, 0.5% American Indian/Alaska Native, 0.0% Native Hawaiian/Other Pacific Islander, 1.2% Two or more races, 3.4% Hispanic of any race; Average household size: 2.64; Median age: 43.1; Age under 18: 22.8%; Age 65 and over: 14.3%; Males per 100 females: 106.0

Housing: Homeownership rate: 86.5%; Homeowner vacancy rate: 1.2%; Rental vacancy rate: 4.5%

TECUMSEH (city). Covers a land area of 5.702 square miles and a water area of 0.241 square miles. Located at 42.01° N. Lat; 83.94° W. Long. Elevation is 804 feet.

History: Tecumseh was incorporated as a village in 1837, and was named for the great Shawnee chief Tecumseh. The first house built in Lenawee County was erected by Musgrove and Abi Evans in 1824 in Tecumseh. The village grew as a trading center for a farm area that raised celery.

Population: 8,521; Growth (since 2000): -0.6%; Density: 1,494.4 persons per square mile; Race: 96.0% White, 0.4% Black/African American, 0.7% Asian, 0.4% American Indian/Alaska Native, 0.0% Native Hawaiian/Other Pacific Islander, 1.6% Two or more races, 4.4% Hispanic of any race; Average household size: 2.35; Median age: 39.8; Age under 18: 24.7%; Age 65 and over: 15.5%; Males per 100 females: 87.9; Marriage status: 21.1% never married, 56.5% now married, 2.2% separated, 7.9% widowed, 14.4% divorced; Foreign born: 1.9%; Speak English only: 96.1%; With disability: 14.7%; Veterans: 13.9%; Ancestry: 34.0% German, 23.3% Irish, 16.8% English, 8.8% Polish, 5.9% American

Employment: 13.1% management, business, and financial, 6.8% computer, engineering, and science, 11.3% education, legal, community service, arts, and media, 5.7% healthcare practitioners, 21.2% service, 20.9% sales and office, 7.9% natural resources, construction, and maintenance, 13.0% production, transportation, and material moving

Income: Per capita: $26,746; Median household: $49,856; Average household: $60,634; Households with income of $100,000 or more: 16.1%; Poverty rate: 9.3%

Educational Attainment: High school diploma or higher: 93.0%; Bachelor's degree or higher: 23.1%; Graduate/professional degree or higher: 7.6%

School District(s)
Tecumseh Public Schools (PK-12)
    2012-13 Enrollment: 2,944 . . . . (517) 424-7318
Housing: Homeownership rate: 70.7%; Median home value: $114,200; Median year structure built: 1968; Homeowner vacancy rate: 3.9%; Median gross rent: $681 per month; Rental vacancy rate: 8.2%

Health Insurance: 91.5% have insurance; 80.8% have private insurance; 28.8% have public insurance; 8.5% do not have insurance; 2.3% of children under 18 do not have insurance

Hospitals: Promedica Herrick Hospital (100 beds)
Newspapers: Tecumseh Herald (weekly circulation 6000)
Transportation: Commute: 94.2% car, 0.2% public transportation, 0.9% walk, 3.3% work from home; Median travel time to work: 30.5 minutes
Additional Information Contacts
City of Tecumseh . . . . (517) 423-2107
    http://www.mytecumseh.org

TECUMSEH (township). Covers a land area of 12.567 square miles and a water area of 0.069 square miles. Located at 42.03° N. Lat; 83.92° W. Long. Elevation is 804 feet.

History: Has Native-American village sites and earthworks. Settled 1824, incorporated 1837.

Population: 1,972; Growth (since 2000): 4.8%; Density: 156.9 persons per square mile; Race: 95.0% White, 0.9% Black/African American, 0.3% Asian, 0.8% American Indian/Alaska Native, 0.0% Native Hawaiian/Other Pacific Islander, 2.6% Two or more races, 4.5% Hispanic of any race; Average household size: 2.70; Median age: 43.9; Age under 18: 22.6%; Age 65 and over: 14.9%; Males per 100 females: 105.0

School District(s)
Tecumseh Public Schools (PK-12)
    2012-13 Enrollment: 2,944 . . . . (517) 424-7318
Housing: Homeownership rate: 93.7%; Homeowner vacancy rate: 1.1%; Rental vacancy rate: 9.8%

Hospitals: Promedica Herrick Hospital (100 beds)
Newspapers: Tecumseh Herald (weekly circulation 6000)

TIPTON (unincorporated postal area)
ZCTA: 49287

Covers a land area of 28.137 square miles and a water area of 0.575 square miles. Located at 42.02° N. Lat; 84.07° W. Long. Elevation is 899 feet.

Population: 2,099; Growth (since 2000): 9.0%; Density: 74.6 persons per square mile; Race: 97.0% White, 0.5% Black/African American, 0.6% Asian, 0.2% American Indian/Alaska Native, 0.0% Native

Hawaiian/Other Pacific Islander, 1.1% Two or more races, 2.8% Hispanic of any race; Average household size: 2.70; Median age: 42.7; Age under 18: 24.0%; Age 65 and over: 13.3%; Males per 100 females: 106.6

Housing: Homeownership rate: 88.2%; Homeowner vacancy rate: 1.6%; Rental vacancy rate: 5.1%

WESTON (unincorporated postal area)

ZCTA: 49289

Covers a land area of 0.719 square miles and a water area of 0 square miles. Located at 41.77° N. Lat; 84.11° W. Long. Elevation is 755 feet.

Population: 167; Growth (since 2000): 67.0%; Density: 232.3 persons per square mile; Race: 92.8% White, 0.6% Black/African American, 1.8% Asian, 2.4% American Indian/Alaska Native, 0.0% Native Hawaiian/Other Pacific Islander, 2.4% Two or more races, 2.4% Hispanic of any race; Average household size: 2.69; Median age: 40.3; Age under 18: 19.8%; Age 65 and over: 6.6%; Males per 100 females: 135.2

Housing: Homeownership rate: 82.2%; Homeowner vacancy rate: 7.3%; Rental vacancy rate: 38.9%

WOODSTOCK (township). Covers a land area of 33.876 square miles and a water area of 1.799 square miles. Located at 42.03° N. Lat; 84.31° W. Long.

Population: 3,505; Growth (since 2000): 1.1%; Density: 103.5 persons per square mile; Race: 96.7% White, 0.5% Black/African American, 0.2% Asian, 0.3% American Indian/Alaska Native, 0.0% Native Hawaiian/Other Pacific Islander, 1.9% Two or more races, 1.3% Hispanic of any race; Average household size: 2.39; Median age: 46.5; Age under 18: 19.9%; Age 65 and over: 16.9%; Males per 100 females: 103.4; Marriage status: 23.8% never married, 57.5% now married, 0.5% separated, 7.8% widowed, 10.9% divorced; Foreign born: 1.1%; Speak English only: 94.7%; With disability: 15.0%; Veterans: 13.2%; Ancestry: 38.8% German, 15.5% English, 13.8% Irish, 6.6% Polish, 4.4% American

Employment: 7.7% management, business, and financial, 2.2% computer, engineering, and science, 13.0% education, legal, community service, arts, and media, 3.4% healthcare practitioners, 14.8% service, 27.3% sales and office, 8.3% natural resources, construction, and maintenance, 23.3% production, transportation, and material moving

Income: Per capita: $23,018; Median household: $44,360; Average household: $55,146; Households with income of $100,000 or more: 13.7%; Poverty rate: 12.3%

Educational Attainment: High school diploma or higher: 92.4%; Bachelor's degree or higher: 18.4%; Graduate/professional degree or higher: 4.6%

Housing: Homeownership rate: 84.7%; Median home value: $130,700; Median year structure built: 1973; Homeowner vacancy rate: 2.5%; Median gross rent: $754 per month; Rental vacancy rate: 13.3%

Health Insurance: 87.2% have insurance; 72.0% have private insurance; 32.1% have public insurance; 12.8% do not have insurance; 18.7% of children under 18 do not have insurance

Transportation: Commute: 89.9% car, 0.0% public transportation, 2.3% walk, 4.5% work from home; Median travel time to work: 29.2 minutes

Livingston County

Located in southeastern Michigan; drained by the Red Cedar, Huron, and Shiawassee Rivers; includes many lakes. Covers a land area of 565.254 square miles, a water area of 20.150 square miles, and is located in the Eastern Time Zone at 42.60° N. Lat., 83.91° W. Long. The county was founded in 1836. County seat is Howell.

Livingston County is part of the Detroit-Warren-Dearborn, MI Metropolitan Statistical Area. The entire metro area includes: Detroit-Dearborn-Livonia, MI Metropolitan Division (Wayne County, MI); Warren-Troy-Farmington Hills, MI Metropolitan Division (Lapeer County, MI; Livingston County, MI; Macomb County, MI; Oakland County, MI; Saint Clair County, MI)

Weather Station: Milford Gm Proving Ground   Elevation: 990 feet

	Jan	Feb	Mar	Apr	May	Jun	Jul	Aug	Sep	Oct	Nov	Dec
High	30	33	43	56	68	77	81	79	71	59	46	34
Low	15	16	24	35	46	56	60	59	51	40	31	20
Precip	1.6	1.9	1.8	2.5	3.2	3.3	2.8	3.0	3.0	2.4	2.5	2.0
Snow	11.0	7.6	3.5	1.2	tr	0.0	0.0	0.0	0.0	0.1	1.6	8.4

High and Low temperatures in degrees Fahrenheit; Precipitation and Snow in inches

Population: 180,967; Growth (since 2000): 15.3%; Density: 320.2 persons per square mile; Race: 96.7% White, 0.4% Black/African American, 0.8% Asian, 0.4% American Indian/Alaska Native, 0.0% Native Hawaiian/Other Pacific Islander, 1.3% two or more races, 1.9% Hispanic of any race; Average household size: 2.67; Median age: 40.9; Age under 18: 25.5%; Age 65 and over: 12.0%; Males per 100 females: 100.1; Marriage status: 24.0% never married, 60.5% now married, 0.7% separated, 4.8% widowed, 10.7% divorced; Foreign born: 3.0%; Speak English only: 96.2%; With disability: 9.3%; Veterans: 8.9%; Ancestry: 28.1% German, 17.2% Irish, 14.3% English, 12.3% Polish, 7.0% Italian

Religion: Six largest groups: 20.4% Catholicism, 4.7% Lutheran, 3.2% Non-denominational Protestant, 2.5% Presbyterian-Reformed, 2.3% Methodist/Pietist, 1.9% Holiness

Economy: Unemployment rate: 6.9%; Leading industries: 14.6% retail trade; 13.3% construction; 12.5% professional, scientific, and technical services; Farms: 734 totaling 86,141 acres; Company size: 1 employs 1,000 or more persons, 3 employ 500 to 999 persons, 63 employ 100 to 499 persons, 4,026 employ less than 100 persons; Business ownership: 5,193 women-owned, 45 Black-owned, n/a Hispanic-owned, 262 Asian-owned

Employment: 16.5% management, business, and financial, 7.2% computer, engineering, and science, 8.5% education, legal, community service, arts, and media, 6.4% healthcare practitioners, 15.1% service, 25.2% sales and office, 9.0% natural resources, construction, and maintenance, 12.0% production, transportation, and material moving

Income: Per capita: $32,129; Median household: $72,359; Average household: $85,656; Households with income of $100,000 or more: 31.6%; Poverty rate: 6.2%

Educational Attainment: High school diploma or higher: 94.4%; Bachelor's degree or higher: 32.9%; Graduate/professional degree or higher: 11.2%

Housing: Homeownership rate: 85.3%; Median home value: $183,100; Median year structure built: 1986; Homeowner vacancy rate: 2.0%; Median gross rent: $917 per month; Rental vacancy rate: 9.4%

Vital Statistics: Birth rate: 92.3 per 10,000 population; Death rate: 71.0 per 10,000 population; Age-adjusted cancer mortality rate: 165.6 deaths per 100,000 population

Health Insurance: 92.1% have insurance; 83.2% have private insurance; 22.0% have public insurance; 7.9% do not have insurance; 2.4% of children under 18 do not have insurance

Health Care: Physicians: 11.2 per 10,000 population; Hospital beds: 8.4 per 10,000 population; Hospital admissions: 364.2 per 10,000 population

Transportation: Commute: 93.2% car, 0.3% public transportation, 0.9% walk, 4.7% work from home; Median travel time to work: 31.4 minutes

Presidential Election: 38.0% Obama, 61.3% Romney (2012)

National and State Parks: Brighton State Recreation Area; Gregory State Game Area; Island Lake State Recreation Area; Oak Grove State Game Area; Southern Michigan State Forest Nursery; Unadilla State Wildlife Area

Additional Information Contacts

Livingston Government . . . . (517) 546-3669
   http://www.co.livingston.mi.us

Livingston County Communities

BRIGHTON (city). Covers a land area of 3.557 square miles and a water area of 0.129 square miles. Located at 42.53° N. Lat; 83.78° W. Long. Elevation is 925 feet.

History: Brighton was first settled in 1832 by Maynard Maltby, who called it Ore Creek. The community, renamed by residents from New York for the town of Brighton there, developed around a grist mill.

Population: 7,444; Growth (since 2000): 11.1%; Density: 2,092.8 persons per square mile; Race: 96.0% White, 0.7% Black/African American, 1.1% Asian, 0.4% American Indian/Alaska Native, 0.0% Native Hawaiian/Other Pacific Islander, 1.2% Two or more races, 2.3% Hispanic of any race; Average household size: 2.02; Median age: 43.4; Age under 18: 19.0%; Age 65 and over: 21.7%; Males per 100 females: 86.0; Marriage status: 27.7% never married, 43.3% now married, 0.9% separated, 12.0% widowed, 17.0% divorced; Foreign born: 2.9%; Speak English only: 97.8%; With disability: 12.0%; Veterans: 11.1%; Ancestry: 28.2% German, 16.7% Irish, 14.2% English, 12.1% Polish, 8.8% Italian

Employment: 17.4% management, business, and financial, 4.9% computer, engineering, and science, 7.5% education, legal, community service, arts, and media, 8.2% healthcare practitioners, 19.2% service, 27.2% sales and office, 6.0% natural resources, construction, and maintenance, 9.6% production, transportation, and material moving

Income: Per capita: $32,350; Median household: $53,259; Average household: $63,593; Households with income of $100,000 or more: 19.0%; Poverty rate: 8.4%
Educational Attainment: High school diploma or higher: 93.4%; Bachelor's degree or higher: 37.7%; Graduate/professional degree or higher: 12.6%

School District(s)
Brighton Area Schools (KG-12)
  2012-13 Enrollment: 5,980 . . . . (810) 299-4040
Charyl Stockwell Academy (KG-12)
  2012-13 Enrollment: 1,082 . . . . (810) 632-2200
Flextech High School (KG-12)
  2012-13 Enrollment: 256 . . . . (810) 844-3366
Hartland Consolidated Schools (PK-12)
  2012-13 Enrollment: 5,490 . . . . (810) 626-2100

Vocational/Technical School(s)
Brighton Institute of Cosmetology (Private, For-profit)
  Fall 2013 Enrollment: 55 . . . . (810) 229-5066
  2013-14 Tuition: $13,915
Ross Medical Education Center-Brighton (Private, For-profit)
  Fall 2013 Enrollment: 127 . . . . (810) 227-0160
  2013-14 Tuition: $15,680
Housing: Homeownership rate: 59.0%; Median home value: $163,500; Median year structure built: 1982; Homeowner vacancy rate: 1.9%; Median gross rent: $806 per month; Rental vacancy rate: 10.7%
Health Insurance: 91.7% have insurance; 81.9% have private insurance; 27.9% have public insurance; 8.3% do not have insurance; 3.1% of children under 18 do not have insurance
Hospitals: Brighton Hospital (63 beds)
Safety: Violent crime rate: 2.6 per 10,000 population; Property crime rate: 193.8 per 10,000 population
Transportation: Commute: 91.4% car, 0.0% public transportation, 4.0% walk, 2.6% work from home; Median travel time to work: 26.7 minutes
Additional Information Contacts
City of Brighton . . . . (810) 227-1911
  http://www.brightoncity.org

BRIGHTON (township). Covers a land area of 32.958 square miles and a water area of 1.641 square miles. Located at 42.56° N. Lat; 83.73° W. Long. Elevation is 925 feet.
History: Settled 1832; incorporated 1867 as village and 1928 as city.
Population: 17,791; Growth (since 2000): 0.7%; Density: 539.8 persons per square mile; Race: 97.0% White, 0.6% Black/African American, 0.9% Asian, 0.3% American Indian/Alaska Native, 0.0% Native Hawaiian/Other Pacific Islander, 1.0% Two or more races, 1.7% Hispanic of any race; Average household size: 2.76; Median age: 43.8; Age under 18: 24.6%; Age 65 and over: 11.7%; Males per 100 females: 103.8; Marriage status: 25.8% never married, 62.4% now married, 0.1% separated, 4.0% widowed, 7.8% divorced; Foreign born: 4.0%; Speak English only: 96.5%; With disability: 7.4%; Veterans: 8.9%; Ancestry: 24.7% German, 15.7% Irish, 14.6% English, 14.2% Polish, 8.5% Italian
Employment: 18.0% management, business, and financial, 8.6% computer, engineering, and science, 11.3% education, legal, community service, arts, and media, 7.7% healthcare practitioners, 12.7% service, 25.0% sales and office, 6.1% natural resources, construction, and maintenance, 10.6% production, transportation, and material moving
Income: Per capita: $37,350; Median household: $89,919; Average household: $104,412; Households with income of $100,000 or more: 43.7%; Poverty rate: 4.2%
Educational Attainment: High school diploma or higher: 96.8%; Bachelor's degree or higher: 43.1%; Graduate/professional degree or higher: 15.3%

School District(s)
Brighton Area Schools (KG-12)
  2012-13 Enrollment: 5,980 . . . . (810) 299-4040
Charyl Stockwell Academy (KG-12)
  2012-13 Enrollment: 1,082 . . . . (810) 632-2200
Flextech High School (KG-12)
  2012-13 Enrollment: 256 . . . . (810) 844-3366
Hartland Consolidated Schools (PK-12)
  2012-13 Enrollment: 5,490 . . . . (810) 626-2100

Vocational/Technical School(s)
Brighton Institute of Cosmetology (Private, For-profit)
  Fall 2013 Enrollment: 55 . . . . (810) 229-5066
  2013-14 Tuition: $13,915

Ross Medical Education Center-Brighton (Private, For-profit)
  Fall 2013 Enrollment: 127 . . . . (810) 227-0160
  2013-14 Tuition: $15,680
Housing: Homeownership rate: 92.7%; Median home value: $224,100; Median year structure built: 1981; Homeowner vacancy rate: 1.7%; Median gross rent: $1,174 per month; Rental vacancy rate: 6.0%
Health Insurance: 93.1% have insurance; 87.0% have private insurance; 18.6% have public insurance; 6.9% do not have insurance; 3.0% of children under 18 do not have insurance
Hospitals: Brighton Hospital (63 beds)
Transportation: Commute: 93.3% car, 0.0% public transportation, 0.7% walk, 5.5% work from home; Median travel time to work: 29.7 minutes
Additional Information Contacts
Brighton Charter Township . . . . (810) 229-0550
  http://www.brightontwp.com

COHOCTAH (township). Covers a land area of 37.922 square miles and a water area of 0.454 square miles. Located at 42.73° N. Lat; 83.98° W. Long. Elevation is 886 feet.
Population: 3,317; Growth (since 2000): -2.3%; Density: 87.5 persons per square mile; Race: 97.4% White, 0.1% Black/African American, 0.5% Asian, 0.4% American Indian/Alaska Native, 0.1% Native Hawaiian/Other Pacific Islander, 1.2% Two or more races, 1.4% Hispanic of any race; Average household size: 2.82; Median age: 41.9; Age under 18: 24.6%; Age 65 and over: 11.2%; Males per 100 females: 104.5; Marriage status: 33.9% never married, 48.9% now married, 1.1% separated, 5.0% widowed, 12.3% divorced; Foreign born: 1.8%; Speak English only: 98.2%; With disability: 10.0%; Veterans: 10.0%; Ancestry: 35.5% German, 19.1% English, 16.7% Irish, 8.8% French, 8.6% American
Employment: 7.8% management, business, and financial, 11.2% computer, engineering, and science, 6.4% education, legal, community service, arts, and media, 3.3% healthcare practitioners, 21.0% service, 21.8% sales and office, 10.4% natural resources, construction, and maintenance, 18.1% production, transportation, and material moving
Income: Per capita: $23,544; Median household: $62,148; Average household: $66,020; Households with income of $100,000 or more: 23.1%; Poverty rate: 9.2%
Educational Attainment: High school diploma or higher: 89.8%; Bachelor's degree or higher: 17.5%; Graduate/professional degree or higher: 7.3%
Housing: Homeownership rate: 92.0%; Median home value: $148,400; Median year structure built: 1978; Homeowner vacancy rate: 1.4%; Median gross rent: $1,039 per month; Rental vacancy rate: 10.5%
Health Insurance: 84.2% have insurance; 69.9% have private insurance; 27.3% have public insurance; 15.8% do not have insurance; 6.5% of children under 18 do not have insurance
Transportation: Commute: 92.1% car, 0.3% public transportation, 0.3% walk, 4.0% work from home; Median travel time to work: 35.3 minutes

CONWAY (township). Covers a land area of 37.726 square miles and a water area of 0.065 square miles. Located at 42.74° N. Lat; 84.09° W. Long.
Population: 3,546; Growth (since 2000): 29.8%; Density: 94.0 persons per square mile; Race: 96.4% White, 0.3% Black/African American, 0.8% Asian, 0.8% American Indian/Alaska Native, 0.0% Native Hawaiian/Other Pacific Islander, 1.6% Two or more races, 1.7% Hispanic of any race; Average household size: 2.95; Median age: 37.0; Age under 18: 28.9%; Age 65 and over: 8.5%; Males per 100 females: 108.7; Marriage status: 28.8% never married, 55.8% now married, 0.6% separated, 5.4% widowed, 10.0% divorced; Foreign born: 1.5%; Speak English only: 98.2%; With disability: 11.5%; Veterans: 7.4%; Ancestry: 23.9% German, 20.6% Irish, 20.0% English, 7.6% American, 5.7% Italian
Employment: 13.0% management, business, and financial, 3.3% computer, engineering, and science, 7.2% education, legal, community service, arts, and media, 5.2% healthcare practitioners, 11.5% service, 24.5% sales and office, 18.1% natural resources, construction, and maintenance, 17.2% production, transportation, and material moving
Income: Per capita: $24,671; Median household: $63,919; Average household: $74,690; Households with income of $100,000 or more: 20.8%; Poverty rate: 11.0%
Educational Attainment: High school diploma or higher: 92.4%; Bachelor's degree or higher: 14.7%; Graduate/professional degree or higher: 5.0%

Housing: Homeownership rate: 93.5%; Median home value: $168,100; Median year structure built: 1992; Homeowner vacancy rate: 1.5%; Median gross rent: $983 per month; Rental vacancy rate: 7.1%
Health Insurance: 88.7% have insurance; 72.1% have private insurance; 27.4% have public insurance; 11.3% do not have insurance; 7.2% of children under 18 do not have insurance
Transportation: Commute: 95.6% car, 0.0% public transportation, 0.0% walk, 2.8% work from home; Median travel time to work: 34.8 minutes

DEERFIELD (township). Covers a land area of 36.171 square miles and a water area of 1.469 square miles. Located at 42.75° N. Lat; 83.87° W. Long.
Population: 4,170; Growth (since 2000): 2.0%; Density: 115.3 persons per square mile; Race: 97.1% White, 0.3% Black/African American, 0.6% Asian, 0.6% American Indian/Alaska Native, 0.1% Native Hawaiian/Other Pacific Islander, 1.3% Two or more races, 1.3% Hispanic of any race; Average household size: 2.81; Median age: 43.1; Age under 18: 25.6%; Age 65 and over: 10.7%; Males per 100 females: 102.9; Marriage status: 24.9% never married, 59.2% now married, 1.1% separated, 2.9% widowed, 13.0% divorced; Foreign born: 2.2%; Speak English only: 97.8%; With disability: 11.1%; Veterans: 10.6%; Ancestry: 24.7% German, 19.6% Irish, 13.8% English, 12.3% Polish, 7.9% Italian
Employment: 15.0% management, business, and financial, 5.4% computer, engineering, and science, 6.4% education, legal, community service, arts, and media, 6.8% healthcare practitioners, 13.9% service, 29.7% sales and office, 12.2% natural resources, construction, and maintenance, 10.6% production, transportation, and material moving
Income: Per capita: $28,589; Median household: $72,148; Average household: $79,015; Households with income of $100,000 or more: 27.6%; Poverty rate: 8.0%
Educational Attainment: High school diploma or higher: 95.6%; Bachelor's degree or higher: 28.3%; Graduate/professional degree or higher: 6.3%
Housing: Homeownership rate: 92.9%; Median home value: $205,400; Median year structure built: 1981; Homeowner vacancy rate: 2.1%; Median gross rent: $928 per month; Rental vacancy rate: 3.7%
Health Insurance: 94.4% have insurance; 84.2% have private insurance; 24.3% have public insurance; 5.6% do not have insurance; 2.5% of children under 18 do not have insurance
Transportation: Commute: 92.3% car, 1.8% public transportation, 1.3% walk, 4.1% work from home; Median travel time to work: 36.1 minutes

FOWLERVILLE (village). Covers a land area of 2.344 square miles and a water area of 0.037 square miles. Located at 42.66° N. Lat; 84.07° W. Long. Elevation is 906 feet.
History: Fowlerville was established in 1835.
Population: 2,886; Growth (since 2000): -2.9%; Density: 1,231.3 persons per square mile; Race: 96.8% White, 0.2% Black/African American, 0.3% Asian, 0.6% American Indian/Alaska Native, 0.0% Native Hawaiian/Other Pacific Islander, 1.7% Two or more races, 2.3% Hispanic of any race; Average household size: 2.40; Median age: 35.2; Age under 18: 26.9%; Age 65 and over: 13.4%; Males per 100 females: 92.9; Marriage status: 31.6% never married, 42.0% now married, 0.6% separated, 5.5% widowed, 20.8% divorced; Foreign born: 3.7%; Speak English only: 90.2%; With disability: 14.6%; Veterans: 7.7%; Ancestry: 30.2% German, 21.3% Irish, 9.4% English, 6.3% Polish, 5.3% Scottish
Employment: 22.3% management, business, and financial, 3.0% computer, engineering, and science, 2.5% education, legal, community service, arts, and media, 7.3% healthcare practitioners, 17.5% service, 22.6% sales and office, 12.2% natural resources, construction, and maintenance, 12.7% production, transportation, and material moving
Income: Per capita: $19,672; Median household: $45,000; Average household: $47,931; Households with income of $100,000 or more: 6.8%; Poverty rate: 13.7%
Educational Attainment: High school diploma or higher: 90.2%; Bachelor's degree or higher: 13.8%; Graduate/professional degree or higher: 6.1%
School District(s)
Fowlerville Community Schools (PK-12)
    2012-13 Enrollment: 2,894 . . . . (517) 223-6001
Housing: Homeownership rate: 62.7%; Median home value: $101,100; Median year structure built: 1974; Homeowner vacancy rate: 4.7%; Median gross rent: $791 per month; Rental vacancy rate: 7.2%

Health Insurance: 82.5% have insurance; 59.7% have private insurance; 34.8% have public insurance; 17.5% do not have insurance; 8.1% of children under 18 do not have insurance
Safety: Violent crime rate: 34.4 per 10,000 population; Property crime rate: 360.8 per 10,000 population
Transportation: Commute: 90.3% car, 0.3% public transportation, 5.7% walk, 0.0% work from home; Median travel time to work: 21.2 minutes

GENOA (township). Covers a land area of 34.048 square miles and a water area of 2.341 square miles. Located at 42.56° N. Lat; 83.86° W. Long.
History: Before there was the new Township Hall, the land belonged to the Herbst family. 45 acres were sold to the township. The township hall sits on property that originally belonged to the Carl Christian Conrad family. It was first purchased from the United States Government in 1830. After the Civil War, there was no one left to farm the land, and it was purchased by John Schoenhals.
Population: 19,821; Growth (since 2000): 24.7%; Density: 582.1 persons per square mile; Race: 96.1% White, 0.6% Black/African American, 1.0% Asian, 0.4% American Indian/Alaska Native, 0.0% Native Hawaiian/Other Pacific Islander, 1.4% Two or more races, 2.1% Hispanic of any race; Average household size: 2.54; Median age: 42.7; Age under 18: 24.2%; Age 65 and over: 14.4%; Males per 100 females: 96.1; Marriage status: 22.3% never married, 62.0% now married, 0.2% separated, 4.5% widowed, 11.2% divorced; Foreign born: 3.9%; Speak English only: 95.7%; With disability: 10.3%; Veterans: 9.2%; Ancestry: 28.0% German, 16.8% Irish, 15.4% English, 11.7% Polish, 6.4% Italian
Employment: 16.7% management, business, and financial, 7.2% computer, engineering, and science, 10.3% education, legal, community service, arts, and media, 5.5% healthcare practitioners, 18.0% service, 25.0% sales and office, 6.6% natural resources, construction, and maintenance, 10.7% production, transportation, and material moving
Income: Per capita: $36,579; Median household: $73,574; Average household: $92,616; Households with income of $100,000 or more: 33.1%; Poverty rate: 4.4%
Educational Attainment: High school diploma or higher: 95.8%; Bachelor's degree or higher: 38.4%; Graduate/professional degree or higher: 14.4%
Housing: Homeownership rate: 82.5%; Median home value: $200,100; Median year structure built: 1992; Homeowner vacancy rate: 2.0%; Median gross rent: $971 per month; Rental vacancy rate: 8.3%
Health Insurance: 91.2% have insurance; 83.7% have private insurance; 23.4% have public insurance; 8.8% do not have insurance; 2.8% of children under 18 do not have insurance
Transportation: Commute: 93.5% car, 0.2% public transportation, 0.4% walk, 5.2% work from home; Median travel time to work: 29.4 minutes
Additional Information Contacts
Genoa Township . . . . (810) 227-5225
    http://www.genoa.org

GREEN OAK (township). Covers a land area of 34.300 square miles and a water area of 2.668 square miles. Located at 42.48° N. Lat; 83.72° W. Long. Elevation is 928 feet.
History: In September 2005, the township board voted to incorporate as a charter township, becoming the second charter township in Livingston County.
Population: 17,476; Growth (since 2000): 11.9%; Density: 509.5 persons per square mile; Race: 96.6% White, 0.7% Black/African American, 0.9% Asian, 0.5% American Indian/Alaska Native, 0.0% Native Hawaiian/Other Pacific Islander, 1.1% Two or more races, 1.9% Hispanic of any race; Average household size: 2.69; Median age: 42.3; Age under 18: 25.1%; Age 65 and over: 11.7%; Males per 100 females: 101.1; Marriage status: 24.6% never married, 59.4% now married, 0.3% separated, 6.0% widowed, 10.0% divorced; Foreign born: 3.0%; Speak English only: 96.4%; With disability: 8.9%; Veterans: 7.3%; Ancestry: 26.9% German, 16.0% Irish, 13.0% English, 12.4% Polish, 9.0% Italian
Employment: 16.7% management, business, and financial, 7.3% computer, engineering, and science, 10.7% education, legal, community service, arts, and media, 5.5% healthcare practitioners, 13.6% service, 26.8% sales and office, 8.5% natural resources, construction, and maintenance, 11.1% production, transportation, and material moving
Income: Per capita: $33,258; Median household: $74,510; Average household: $87,048; Households with income of $100,000 or more: 35.2%; Poverty rate: 5.8%

Educational Attainment: High school diploma or higher: 94.8%; Bachelor's degree or higher: 35.1%; Graduate/professional degree or higher: 13.6%
Housing: Homeownership rate: 89.0%; Median home value: $194,000; Median year structure built: 1984; Homeowner vacancy rate: 2.2%; Median gross rent: $972 per month; Rental vacancy rate: 9.5%
Health Insurance: 92.0% have insurance; 83.9% have private insurance; 19.7% have public insurance; 8.0% do not have insurance; 1.7% of children under 18 do not have insurance
Safety: Violent crime rate: 12.2 per 10,000 population; Property crime rate: 128.5 per 10,000 population
Transportation: Commute: 94.5% car, 0.0% public transportation, 0.2% walk, 4.8% work from home; Median travel time to work: 29.9 minutes
Additional Information Contacts
Green Oak Charter Township . . . . (810) 231-1333
    http://www.greenoaktwp.com

GREGORY (unincorporated postal area)
ZCTA: 48137
Covers a land area of 42.436 square miles and a water area of 2.437 square miles. Located at 42.46° N. Lat; 84.08° W. Long. Elevation is 935 feet.
Population: 4,796; Growth (since 2000): 6.3%; Density: 113.0 persons per square mile; Race: 97.4% White, 0.4% Black/African American, 0.2% Asian, 0.6% American Indian/Alaska Native, 0.0% Native Hawaiian/Other Pacific Islander, 1.3% Two or more races, 1.4% Hispanic of any race; Average household size: 2.63; Median age: 42.7; Age under 18: 23.8%; Age 65 and over: 12.3%; Males per 100 females: 103.8; Marriage status: 18.0% never married, 67.4% now married, 0.2% separated, 3.8% widowed, 10.9% divorced; Foreign born: 3.0%; Speak English only: 96.0%; With disability: 12.9%; Veterans: 12.6%; Ancestry: 34.7% German, 15.6% Irish, 11.3% Polish, 11.1% English, 6.4% Italian
Employment: 14.8% management, business, and financial, 8.2% computer, engineering, and science, 11.3% education, legal, community service, arts, and media, 8.0% healthcare practitioners, 14.4% service, 20.0% sales and office, 9.4% natural resources, construction, and maintenance, 13.9% production, transportation, and material moving
Income: Per capita: $31,624; Median household: $74,022; Average household: $84,190; Households with income of $100,000 or more: 33.4%; Poverty rate: 6.1%
Educational Attainment: High school diploma or higher: 93.8%; Bachelor's degree or higher: 32.0%; Graduate/professional degree or higher: 9.6%
Housing: Homeownership rate: 92.6%; Median home value: $170,300; Median year structure built: 1975; Homeowner vacancy rate: 2.7%; Median gross rent: $914 per month; Rental vacancy rate: 10.3%
Health Insurance: 93.7% have insurance; 84.6% have private insurance; 25.1% have public insurance; 6.3% do not have insurance; 0.8% of children under 18 do not have insurance
Transportation: Commute: 91.0% car, 0.0% public transportation, 1.8% walk, 6.3% work from home; Median travel time to work: 35.1 minutes

HAMBURG (township). Covers a land area of 32.241 square miles and a water area of 3.779 square miles. Located at 42.47° N. Lat; 83.85° W. Long. Elevation is 899 feet.
History: A plat was recorded in 1837. Nineteen men met to choose a name for the town. The three Germans were not allowed to vote and the others deadlocked 8-8, split between naming it "Steuben" or "Knox". The others finally agreed to allow the Messrs. Grisson to decide, and they choose the name of their hometown, Hamburg, Germany.
Population: 21,165; Growth (since 2000): 2.6%; Density: 656.5 persons per square mile; Race: 97.2% White, 0.3% Black/African American, 0.6% Asian, 0.3% American Indian/Alaska Native, 0.0% Native Hawaiian/Other Pacific Islander, 1.3% Two or more races, 1.3% Hispanic of any race; Average household size: 2.69; Median age: 42.6; Age under 18: 25.3%; Age 65 and over: 11.0%; Males per 100 females: 101.8; Marriage status: 21.4% never married, 65.6% now married, 0.7% separated, 4.1% widowed, 8.8% divorced; Foreign born: 2.6%; Speak English only: 96.0%; With disability: 9.7%; Veterans: 8.3%; Ancestry: 28.2% German, 18.5% Irish, 17.1% English, 13.0% Polish, 7.1% Italian
Employment: 17.9% management, business, and financial, 7.7% computer, engineering, and science, 8.8% education, legal, community service, arts, and media, 7.9% healthcare practitioners, 13.8% service, 24.0% sales and office, 8.8% natural resources, construction, and maintenance, 11.2% production, transportation, and material moving

Income: Per capita: $35,101; Median household: $78,191; Average household: $93,123; Households with income of $100,000 or more: 34.0%; Poverty rate: 3.8%
Educational Attainment: High school diploma or higher: 95.1%; Bachelor's degree or higher: 36.8%; Graduate/professional degree or higher: 13.2%
Housing: Homeownership rate: 91.9%; Median home value: $193,800; Median year structure built: 1984; Homeowner vacancy rate: 1.9%; Median gross rent: $938 per month; Rental vacancy rate: 6.3%
Health Insurance: 94.8% have insurance; 87.7% have private insurance; 18.7% have public insurance; 5.2% do not have insurance; 1.6% of children under 18 do not have insurance
Safety: Violent crime rate: 2.3 per 10,000 population; Property crime rate: 75.5 per 10,000 population
Transportation: Commute: 91.9% car, 0.1% public transportation, 0.7% walk, 6.9% work from home; Median travel time to work: 32.7 minutes
Additional Information Contacts
Hamburg Township . . . . (810) 231-1000
    http://www.hamburg.mi.us

HANDY (township). Covers a land area of 34.343 square miles and a water area of 0.165 square miles. Located at 42.63° N. Lat; 84.09° W. Long.
Population: 8,006; Growth (since 2000): 14.3%; Density: 233.1 persons per square mile; Race: 96.9% White, 0.4% Black/African American, 0.4% Asian, 0.5% American Indian/Alaska Native, 0.0% Native Hawaiian/Other Pacific Islander, 1.4% Two or more races, 2.2% Hispanic of any race; Average household size: 2.67; Median age: 35.1; Age under 18: 27.6%; Age 65 and over: 10.1%; Males per 100 females: 99.5; Marriage status: 27.7% never married, 53.9% now married, 1.2% separated, 5.0% widowed, 13.4% divorced; Foreign born: 2.5%; Speak English only: 94.2%; With disability: 10.1%; Veterans: 7.8%; Ancestry: 29.2% German, 20.3% Irish, 15.1% English, 9.7% Polish, 4.9% American
Employment: 14.9% management, business, and financial, 5.0% computer, engineering, and science, 3.4% education, legal, community service, arts, and media, 6.8% healthcare practitioners, 15.9% service, 21.8% sales and office, 18.4% natural resources, construction, and maintenance, 13.7% production, transportation, and material moving
Income: Per capita: $23,010; Median household: $58,466; Average household: $62,835; Households with income of $100,000 or more: 19.4%; Poverty rate: 12.6
Educational Attainment: High school diploma or higher: 93.2%; Bachelor's degree or higher: 16.8%; Graduate/professional degree or higher: 4.8%
Housing: Homeownership rate: 78.7%; Median home value: $130,100; Median year structure built: 1987; Homeowner vacancy rate: 3.0%; Median gross rent: $833 per month; Rental vacancy rate: 9.9%
Health Insurance: 85.1% have insurance; 70.0% have private insurance; 25.4% have public insurance; 14.9% do not have insurance; 5.8% of children under 18 do not have insurance
Transportation: Commute: 92.8% car, 0.1% public transportation, 1.9% walk, 3.3% work from home; Median travel time to work: 30.6 minutes

HARTLAND (township). Covers a land area of 35.857 square miles and a water area of 1.438 square miles. Located at 42.65° N. Lat; 83.74° W. Long. Elevation is 948 feet.
History: Hartland is one of the communities of Hartland Township, an unincorporated community situated near the center of the township, just north of the junction of US 23 and M-59; the other is Parshallville, an unincorporated community partially located in the northwest corner of the township.
Population: 14,663; Growth (since 2000): 33.3%; Density: 408.9 persons per square mile; Race: 96.6% White, 0.5% Black/African American, 1.0% Asian, 0.3% American Indian/Alaska Native, 0.0% Native Hawaiian/Other Pacific Islander, 1.3% Two or more races, 2.3% Hispanic of any race; Average household size: 2.84; Median age: 39.3; Age under 18: 28.6%; Age 65 and over: 10.6%; Males per 100 females: 101.6; Marriage status: 24.0% never married, 64.4% now married, 0.9% separated, 3.8% widowed, 7.8% divorced; Foreign born: 2.3%; Speak English only: 97.2%; With disability: 5.9%; Veterans: 8.5%; Ancestry: 27.8% German, 20.1% Irish, 12.8% English, 12.8% Polish, 8.5% Italian
Employment: 17.6% management, business, and financial, 8.1% computer, engineering, and science, 8.4% education, legal, community service, arts, and media, 8.1% healthcare practitioners, 14.8% service,

24.1% sales and office, 8.7% natural resources, construction, and maintenance, 10.2% production, transportation, and material moving
Income: Per capita: $31,775; Median household: $81,706; Average household: $95,800; Households with income of $100,000 or more: 38.1%; Poverty rate: 3.6%
Educational Attainment: High school diploma or higher: 94.9%; Bachelor's degree or higher: 37.9%; Graduate/professional degree or higher: 11.4%

School District(s)
Hartland Consolidated Schools (PK-12)
    2012-13 Enrollment: 5,490 . . . . (810) 626-2100
Housing: Homeownership rate: 87.4%; Median home value: $199,000; Median year structure built: 1992; Homeowner vacancy rate: 1.8%; Median gross rent: $1,059 per month; Rental vacancy rate: 6.4%
Health Insurance: 94.1% have insurance; 89.5% have private insurance; 15.9% have public insurance; 5.9% do not have insurance; 1.2% of children under 18 do not have insurance
Transportation: Commute: 94.4% car, 0.2% public transportation, 1.1% walk, 2.9% work from home; Median travel time to work: 32.3 minutes
Additional Information Contacts
Hartland Township . . . . (810) 632-7498
    http://www.hartlandtwp.com

HOWELL (city). County seat. Covers a land area of 4.752 square miles and a water area of 0.198 square miles. Located at 42.61° N. Lat; 83.93° W. Long. Elevation is 935 feet.
History: Howell began as a lumber town, but later turned to dairying, becoming a center for Holstein cattle. The Know-Nothing movement, organized to influence changes in the immigration laws, was strong in Howell in the 1850's.
Population: 9,489; Growth (since 2000): 2.8%; Density: 1,996.8 persons per square mile; Race: 94.8% White, 0.4% Black/African American, 1.1% Asian, 0.7% American Indian/Alaska Native, 0.3% Native Hawaiian/Other Pacific Islander, 1.3% Two or more races, 3.5% Hispanic of any race; Average household size: 2.25; Median age: 35.2; Age under 18: 23.2%; Age 65 and over: 13.5%; Males per 100 females: 93.2; Marriage status: 30.2% never married, 43.7% now married, 2.0% separated, 7.3% widowed, 18.7% divorced; Foreign born: 5.2%; Speak English only: 92.6%; With disability: 12.0%; Veterans: 7.1%; Ancestry: 29.3% German, 14.7% English, 13.0% Polish, 12.6% Irish, 7.3% Italian
Employment: 10.6% management, business, and financial, 7.8% computer, engineering, and science, 5.5% education, legal, community service, arts, and media, 3.5% healthcare practitioners, 21.4% service, 28.7% sales and office, 5.8% natural resources, construction, and maintenance, 16.6% production, transportation, and material moving
Income: Per capita: $23,158; Median household: $43,206; Average household: $53,893; Households with income of $100,000 or more: 12.0%; Poverty rate: 16.4%
Educational Attainment: High school diploma or higher: 90.1%; Bachelor's degree or higher: 23.2%; Graduate/professional degree or higher: 5.2%

School District(s)
Charyl Stockwell Academy (KG-12)
    2012-13 Enrollment: 1,082 . . . . (810) 632-2200
Hartland Consolidated Schools (PK-12)
    2012-13 Enrollment: 5,490 . . . . (810) 626-2100
Howell Public Schools (PK-12)
    2012-13 Enrollment: 7,802 . . . . (517) 548-6234
Kensington Woods High School (KG-12)
    2012-13 Enrollment: 130 . . . . (517) 545-0828
Livingston Esa (01-12)
    2012-13 Enrollment: 548 . . . . (517) 546-5550
Housing: Homeownership rate: 53.4%; Median home value: $119,800; Median year structure built: 1978; Homeowner vacancy rate: 2.4%; Median gross rent: $776 per month; Rental vacancy rate: 13.4%
Health Insurance: 88.0% have insurance; 68.9% have private insurance; 31.9% have public insurance; 12.0% do not have insurance; 2.1% of children under 18 do not have insurance
Hospitals: Saint Joseph Mercy Livingston Hospital (136 beds)
Safety: Violent crime rate: 29.4 per 10,000 population; Property crime rate: 193.4 per 10,000 population
Newspapers: Daily Press & Argus (daily circulation 13700)
Transportation: Commute: 92.2% car, 1.4% public transportation, 2.1% walk, 2.2% work from home; Median travel time to work: 26.7 minutes
Airports: Livingston County Spencer J. Hardy (general aviation)

Additional Information Contacts
City of Howell . . . . (517) 546-3500
    http://www.cityofhowell.org

HOWELL (township). Covers a land area of 31.817 square miles and a water area of 0.226 square miles. Located at 42.64° N. Lat; 83.97° W. Long. Elevation is 935 feet.
History: Settled 1834; Incorporated as village 1863, as city 1915.
Population: 6,702; Growth (since 2000): 18.0%; Density: 210.6 persons per square mile; Race: 97.0% White, 0.3% Black/African American, 0.6% Asian, 0.4% American Indian/Alaska Native, 0.0% Native Hawaiian/Other Pacific Islander, 1.0% Two or more races, 1.9% Hispanic of any race; Average household size: 2.59; Median age: 40.9; Age under 18: 23.3%; Age 65 and over: 13.6%; Males per 100 females: 96.7; Marriage status: 22.5% never married, 58.4% now married, 0.5% separated, 5.7% widowed, 13.4% divorced; Foreign born: 1.6%; Speak English only: 97.7%; With disability: 9.8%; Veterans: 10.2%; Ancestry: 29.9% German, 19.6% Irish, 15.7% English, 10.4% Polish, 7.7% French
Employment: 14.7% management, business, and financial, 5.4% computer, engineering, and science, 7.6% education, legal, community service, arts, and media, 6.7% healthcare practitioners, 19.6% service, 20.2% sales and office, 10.5% natural resources, construction, and maintenance, 15.2% production, transportation, and material moving
Income: Per capita: $27,816; Median household: $64,803; Average household: $70,183; Households with income of $100,000 or more: 23.6%; Poverty rate: 6.6%
Educational Attainment: High school diploma or higher: 91.8%; Bachelor's degree or higher: 22.4%; Graduate/professional degree or higher: 7.6%

School District(s)
Charyl Stockwell Academy (KG-12)
    2012-13 Enrollment: 1,082 . . . . (810) 632-2200
Hartland Consolidated Schools (PK-12)
    2012-13 Enrollment: 5,490 . . . . (810) 626-2100
Howell Public Schools (PK-12)
    2012-13 Enrollment: 7,802 . . . . (517) 548-6234
Kensington Woods High School (KG-12)
    2012-13 Enrollment: 130 . . . . (517) 545-0828
Livingston Esa (01-12)
    2012-13 Enrollment: 548 . . . . (517) 546-5550
Housing: Homeownership rate: 89.9%; Median home value: $151,600; Median year structure built: 1991; Homeowner vacancy rate: 3.1%; Median gross rent: $1,202 per month; Rental vacancy rate: 6.5%
Health Insurance: 89.5% have insurance; 77.6% have private insurance; 26.0% have public insurance; 10.5% do not have insurance; 4.8% of children under 18 do not have insurance
Hospitals: Saint Joseph Mercy Livingston Hospital (136 beds)
Newspapers: Daily Press & Argus (daily circulation 13700)
Transportation: Commute: 95.3% car, 0.0% public transportation, 0.0% walk, 3.7% work from home; Median travel time to work: 35.1 minutes
Airports: Livingston County Spencer J. Hardy (general aviation)

IOSCO (township). Covers a land area of 35.193 square miles and a water area of 0.251 square miles. Located at 42.55° N. Lat; 84.08° W. Long.
Population: 3,801; Growth (since 2000): 25.1%; Density: 108.0 persons per square mile; Race: 97.4% White, 0.1% Black/African American, 0.2% Asian, 0.5% American Indian/Alaska Native, 0.0% Native Hawaiian/Other Pacific Islander, 1.6% Two or more races, 1.3% Hispanic of any race; Average household size: 2.97; Median age: 38.9; Age under 18: 28.1%; Age 65 and over: 8.4%; Males per 100 females: 109.0; Marriage status: 16.9% never married, 70.2% now married, 0.0% separated, 2.5% widowed, 10.4% divorced; Foreign born: 2.0%; Speak English only: 96.6%; With disability: 11.7%; Veterans: 9.2%; Ancestry: 34.6% German, 12.8% English, 12.6% Polish, 11.7% Irish, 8.7% American
Employment: 8.4% management, business, and financial, 8.2% computer, engineering, and science, 8.9% education, legal, community service, arts, and media, 2.8% healthcare practitioners, 14.5% service, 25.8% sales and office, 12.6% natural resources, construction, and maintenance, 18.9% production, transportation, and material moving
Income: Per capita: $29,782; Median household: $75,117; Average household: $79,256; Households with income of $100,000 or more: 29.6%; Poverty rate: 3.8%

Educational Attainment: High school diploma or higher: 91.5%; Bachelor's degree or higher: 23.0%; Graduate/professional degree or higher: 7.5%

Housing: Homeownership rate: 94.5%; Median home value: $169,300; Median year structure built: 1988; Homeowner vacancy rate: 1.5%; Median gross rent: $975 per month; Rental vacancy rate: 6.6%

Health Insurance: 91.8% have insurance; 82.8% have private insurance; 24.9% have public insurance; 8.2% do not have insurance; 4.2% of children under 18 do not have insurance

Transportation: Commute: 93.8% car, 0.0% public transportation, 1.0% walk, 5.3% work from home; Median travel time to work: 33.9 minutes

MARION (township). Covers a land area of 34.895 square miles and a water area of 0.935 square miles. Located at 42.55° N. Lat; 83.97° W. Long.

Population: 9,996; Growth (since 2000): 47.9%; Density: 286.5 persons per square mile; Race: 97.3% White, 0.1% Black/African American, 0.8% Asian, 0.4% American Indian/Alaska Native, 0.0% Native Hawaiian/Other Pacific Islander, 1.2% Two or more races, 1.6% Hispanic of any race; Average household size: 2.85; Median age: 40.9; Age under 18: 27.0%; Age 65 and over: 11.2%; Males per 100 females: 101.5; Marriage status: 19.0% never married, 68.7% now married, 0.6% separated, 3.9% widowed, 8.5% divorced; Foreign born: 2.3%; Speak English only: 96.0%; With disability: 7.3%; Veterans: 7.5%; Ancestry: 28.5% German, 21.2% Irish, 14.8% Polish, 13.2% English, 7.5% Italian

Employment: 19.3% management, business, and financial, 7.6% computer, engineering, and science, 7.1% education, legal, community service, arts, and media, 4.6% healthcare practitioners, 11.4% service, 29.6% sales and office, 8.0% natural resources, construction, and maintenance, 12.4% production, transportation, and material moving

Income: Per capita: $33,933; Median household: $85,387; Average household: $99,276; Households with income of $100,000 or more: 41.9%; Poverty rate: 4.9%

Educational Attainment: High school diploma or higher: 94.9%; Bachelor's degree or higher: 28.7%; Graduate/professional degree or higher: 8.9%

Housing: Homeownership rate: 94.6%; Median home value: $189,200; Median year structure built: 1992; Homeowner vacancy rate: 1.6%; Median gross rent: $1,548 per month; Rental vacancy rate: 6.9%

Health Insurance: 95.4% have insurance; 89.0% have private insurance; 18.5% have public insurance; 4.6% do not have insurance; 0.9% of children under 18 do not have insurance

Transportation: Commute: 93.0% car, 0.5% public transportation, 0.0% walk, 6.5% work from home; Median travel time to work: 33.4 minutes

Additional Information Contacts
Marion Township . . . . (517) 546-1588
    http://www.mariontownship.com

OCEOLA (township). Covers a land area of 36.119 square miles and a water area of 0.636 square miles. Located at 42.65° N. Lat; 83.86° W. Long.

Population: 11,936; Growth (since 2000): 42.7%; Density: 330.5 persons per square mile; Race: 96.7% White, 0.4% Black/African American, 0.9% Asian, 0.4% American Indian/Alaska Native, 0.1% Native Hawaiian/Other Pacific Islander, 1.4% Two or more races, 1.9% Hispanic of any race; Average household size: 2.93; Median age: 37.5; Age under 18: 29.9%; Age 65 and over: 9.1%; Males per 100 females: 100.6; Marriage status: 23.0% never married, 64.3% now married, 0.7% separated, 4.0% widowed, 8.7% divorced; Foreign born: 3.0%; Speak English only: 94.8%; With disability: 7.7%; Veterans: 9.7%; Ancestry: 29.1% German, 17.3% Irish, 13.2% English, 12.8% Polish, 6.1% American

Employment: 21.9% management, business, and financial, 6.7% computer, engineering, and science, 7.8% education, legal, community service, arts, and media, 8.9% healthcare practitioners, 11.6% service, 25.2% sales and office, 10.2% natural resources, construction, and maintenance, 7.7% production, transportation, and material moving

Income: Per capita: $31,547; Median household: $80,731; Average household: $90,321; Households with income of $100,000 or more: 34.7%; Poverty rate: 3.2%

Educational Attainment: High school diploma or higher: 96.4%; Bachelor's degree or higher: 35.8%; Graduate/professional degree or higher: 12.1%

Housing: Homeownership rate: 91.0%; Median home value: $187,000; Median year structure built: 1995; Homeowner vacancy rate: 1.4%; Median gross rent: $988 per month; Rental vacancy rate: 6.6%

Health Insurance: 94.1% have insurance; 88.2% have private insurance; 17.8% have public insurance; 5.9% do not have insurance; 1.9% of children under 18 do not have insurance

Transportation: Commute: 92.1% car, 0.6% public transportation, 1.4% walk, 4.9% work from home; Median travel time to work: 33.0 minutes

Additional Information Contacts
Oceola Township . . . . (517) 546-3259
    http://oceolatwp.org

PINCKNEY (village). Covers a land area of 1.597 square miles and a water area of 0.057 square miles. Located at 42.45° N. Lat; 83.95° W. Long. Elevation is 906 feet.

History: Pinckney was founded by William Kirkland, who named the village for his brother, Charles Pinckney Kirkland, a New York lawyer. The village was first settled in 1836.

Population: 2,427; Growth (since 2000): 13.4%; Density: 1,520.0 persons per square mile; Race: 97.9% White, 0.1% Black/African American, 0.3% Asian, 0.2% American Indian/Alaska Native, 0.0% Native Hawaiian/Other Pacific Islander, 1.2% Two or more races, 1.8% Hispanic of any race; Average household size: 2.78; Median age: 34.1; Age under 18: 31.2%; Age 65 and over: 7.4%; Males per 100 females: 96.0

School District(s)
Pinckney Community Schools (PK-12)
    2012-13 Enrollment: 4,012 . . . . (810) 225-3900

Housing: Homeownership rate: 79.4%; Homeowner vacancy rate: 2.4%; Rental vacancy rate: 8.2%

Safety: Violent crime rate: 0.0 per 10,000 population; Property crime rate: 158.5 per 10,000 population

PUTNAM (township). Covers a land area of 34.086 square miles and a water area of 1.501 square miles. Located at 42.47° N. Lat; 83.97° W. Long.

Population: 8,248; Growth (since 2000): 10.0%; Density: 242.0 persons per square mile; Race: 97.7% White, 0.3% Black/African American, 0.4% Asian, 0.1% American Indian/Alaska Native, 0.0% Native Hawaiian/Other Pacific Islander, 1.2% Two or more races, 1.4% Hispanic of any race; Average household size: 2.71; Median age: 41.1; Age under 18: 25.1%; Age 65 and over: 10.9%; Males per 100 females: 101.8; Marriage status: 24.0% never married, 58.8% now married, 0.6% separated, 5.3% widowed, 11.9% divorced; Foreign born: 3.8%; Speak English only: 96.4%; With disability: 12.5%; Veterans: 11.6%; Ancestry: 30.4% German, 15.0% Irish, 10.1% Polish, 8.2% English, 5.4% European

Employment: 14.2% management, business, and financial, 7.2% computer, engineering, and science, 7.2% education, legal, community service, arts, and media, 3.9% healthcare practitioners, 16.9% service, 23.4% sales and office, 10.8% natural resources, construction, and maintenance, 16.4% production, transportation, and material moving

Income: Per capita: $32,911; Median household: $63,646; Average household: $84,923; Households with income of $100,000 or more: 29.0%; Poverty rate: 7.3%

Educational Attainment: High school diploma or higher: 90.2%; Bachelor's degree or higher: 24.5%; Graduate/professional degree or higher: 9.0%

Housing: Homeownership rate: 85.4%; Median home value: $174,200; Median year structure built: 1978; Homeowner vacancy rate: 1.9%; Median gross rent: $848 per month; Rental vacancy rate: 8.6%

Health Insurance: 90.2% have insurance; 79.0% have private insurance; 25.5% have public insurance; 9.8% do not have insurance; 1.5% of children under 18 do not have insurance

Transportation: Commute: 93.4% car, 0.4% public transportation, 1.1% walk, 4.8% work from home; Median travel time to work: 33.4 minutes

TYRONE (township). Covers a land area of 35.405 square miles and a water area of 1.282 square miles. Located at 42.74° N. Lat; 83.74° W. Long.

History: It was named after County Tyrone in Northern Ireland.

Population: 10,020; Growth (since 2000): 18.5%; Density: 283.0 persons per square mile; Race: 96.4% White, 0.5% Black/African American, 0.7% Asian, 0.4% American Indian/Alaska Native, 0.0% Native Hawaiian/Other Pacific Islander, 1.6% Two or more races, 2.2% Hispanic of any race; Average household size: 2.84; Median age: 42.4; Age under 18: 26.5%; Age 65 and over: 12.0%; Males per 100 females: 102.1; Marriage status: 23.1% never married, 66.2% now married, 0.7% separated, 2.4% widowed, 8.2% divorced; Foreign born: 3.0%; Speak English only: 96.9%;

With disability: 8.7%; Veterans: 9.2%; Ancestry: 25.9% German, 15.4% English, 15.1% Polish, 13.3% Irish, 8.7% American

Employment: 17.5% management, business, and financial, 7.7% computer, engineering, and science, 9.1% education, legal, community service, arts, and media, 5.3% healthcare practitioners, 14.8% service, 24.5% sales and office, 9.0% natural resources, construction, and maintenance, 12.1% production, transportation, and material moving

Income: Per capita: $32,730; Median household: $81,351; Average household: $95,257; Households with income of $100,000 or more: 35.6%; Poverty rate: 5.7%

Educational Attainment: High school diploma or higher: 95.7%; Bachelor's degree or higher: 35.2%; Graduate/professional degree or higher: 10.9%

Housing: Homeownership rate: 90.8%; Median home value: $195,400; Median year structure built: 1984; Homeowner vacancy rate: 1.7%; Median gross rent: $993 per month; Rental vacancy rate: 9.4%

Health Insurance: 93.7% have insurance; 84.7% have private insurance; 22.7% have public insurance; 6.3% do not have insurance; 0.9% of children under 18 do not have insurance

Transportation: Commute: 93.9% car, 0.1% public transportation, 0.3% walk, 5.8% work from home; Median travel time to work: 31.1 minutes

Additional Information Contacts
Tyrone Township. . . . . (810) 629-8631
  http://www.tyronetownship.us

UNADILLA (township). Covers a land area of 33.754 square miles and a water area of 0.974 square miles. Located at 42.47° N. Lat; 84.07° W. Long. Elevation is 902 feet.

Population: 3,366; Growth (since 2000): 5.5%; Density: 99.7 persons per square mile; Race: 97.7% White, 0.4% Black/African American, 0.3% Asian, 0.6% American Indian/Alaska Native, 0.0% Native Hawaiian/Other Pacific Islander, 1.0% Two or more races, 1.3% Hispanic of any race; Average household size: 2.60; Median age: 42.0; Age under 18: 22.5%; Age 65 and over: 12.7%; Males per 100 females: 102.9; Marriage status: 17.4% never married, 63.8% now married, 2.4% separated, 4.5% widowed, 14.2% divorced; Foreign born: 1.6%; Speak English only: 98.4%; With disability: 11.7%; Veterans: 9.4%; Ancestry: 34.9% German, 18.3% Irish, 12.7% Polish, 7.7% English, 7.5% Italian

Employment: 12.3% management, business, and financial, 5.2% computer, engineering, and science, 10.6% education, legal, community service, arts, and media, 8.2% healthcare practitioners, 13.5% service, 23.5% sales and office, 9.2% natural resources, construction, and maintenance, 17.6% production, transportation, and material moving

Income: Per capita: $26,825; Median household: $61,045; Average household: $71,685; Households with income of $100,000 or more: 23.8%; Poverty rate: 10.4%

Educational Attainment: High school diploma or higher: 93.8%; Bachelor's degree or higher: 23.4%; Graduate/professional degree or higher: 8.9%

Housing: Homeownership rate: 89.9%; Median home value: $153,800; Median year structure built: 1974; Homeowner vacancy rate: 3.1%; Median gross rent: $880 per month; Rental vacancy rate: 5.7%

Health Insurance: 93.3% have insurance; 81.1% have private insurance; 32.0% have public insurance; 6.7% do not have insurance; 2.2% of children under 18 do not have insurance

Safety: Violent crime rate: 17.6 per 10,000 population; Property crime rate: 85.2 per 10,000 population

Transportation: Commute: 92.8% car, 0.0% public transportation, 3.6% walk, 1.5% work from home; Median travel time to work: 36.6 minutes

Luce County

Located in northwestern Michigan, on the Upper Peninsula; bounded on the north by Lake Superior; drained by the Tahquamenon and Two Hearted Rivers; includes part of Manistique and North Manistique Lakes, and Tahquamenon Falls. Covers a land area of 899.078 square miles, a water area of 1,013.409 square miles, and is located in the Eastern Time Zone at 46.94° N. Lat., 85.58° W. Long. The county was founded in 1887. County seat is Newberry.

Weather Station: Newberry 3 S   Elevation: 850 feet

	Jan	Feb	Mar	Apr	May	Jun	Jul	Aug	Sep	Oct	Nov	Dec
High	23	27	36	50	64	72	77	75	67	54	40	29
Low	8	10	17	29	40	48	54	54	47	36	27	15
Precip	na	na	na	1.7	2.5	2.8	2.9	3.3	3.6	3.2	na	na
Snow	na	17.6	15.1	4.9	0.1	0.0	0.0	0.0	tr	0.6	9.5	25.0

High and Low temperatures in degrees Fahrenheit; Precipitation and Snow in inches

Population: 6,631; Growth (since 2000): -5.6%; Density: 7.4 persons per square mile; Race: 80.4% White, 11.1% Black/African American, 0.3% Asian, 5.0% American Indian/Alaska Native, 0.0% Native Hawaiian/Other Pacific Islander, 3.1% two or more races, 1.2% Hispanic of any race; Average household size: 2.25; Median age: 43.0; Age under 18: 17.9%; Age 65 and over: 17.9%; Males per 100 females: 136.5; Marriage status: 30.0% never married, 48.0% now married, 2.7% separated, 7.6% widowed, 14.4% divorced; Foreign born: 2.0%; Speak English only: 96.3%; With disability: 22.3%; Veterans: 11.1%; Ancestry: 18.8% German, 11.1% Irish, 8.6% English, 7.0% French, 5.6% American

Religion: Six largest groups: 8.9% Catholicism, 7.8% Lutheran, 3.4% Non-denominational Protestant, 3.2% Pentecostal, 2.8% Methodist/Pietist, 1.3% Baptist

Economy: Unemployment rate: 6.6%; Leading industries: 15.5% retail trade; 13.1% accommodation and food services; 10.1% other services (except public administration); Farms: 43 totaling 11,599 acres; Company size: 0 employ 1,000 or more persons, 0 employ 500 to 999 persons, 2 employ 100 to 499 persons, 166 employ less than 100 persons; Business ownership: 49 women-owned, n/a Black-owned, n/a Hispanic-owned, n/a Asian-owned

Employment: 9.7% management, business, and financial, 4.2% computer, engineering, and science, 6.9% education, legal, community service, arts, and media, 5.9% healthcare practitioners, 26.9% service, 22.4% sales and office, 8.7% natural resources, construction, and maintenance, 15.2% production, transportation, and material moving

Income: Per capita: $18,768; Median household: $39,469; Average household: $49,130; Households with income of $100,000 or more: 8.2%; Poverty rate: 18.6%

Educational Attainment: High school diploma or higher: 85.8%; Bachelor's degree or higher: 12.7%; Graduate/professional degree or higher: 3.3%

Housing: Homeownership rate: 79.9%; Median home value: $79,400; Median year structure built: 1973; Homeowner vacancy rate: 4.2%; Median gross rent: $599 per month; Rental vacancy rate: 9.6%

Vital Statistics: Birth rate: 84.6 per 10,000 population; Death rate: 124.6 per 10,000 population; Age-adjusted cancer mortality rate: 223.2 deaths per 100,000 population

Health Insurance: 88.1% have insurance; 59.1% have private insurance; 46.8% have public insurance; 11.9% do not have insurance; 4.6% of children under 18 do not have insurance

Health Care: Physicians: 15.4 per 10,000 population; Hospital beds: 111.9 per 10,000 population; Hospital admissions: 772.8 per 10,000 population

Transportation: Commute: 91.0% car, 0.0% public transportation, 4.6% walk, 3.7% work from home; Median travel time to work: 14.2 minutes

Presidential Election: 38.2% Obama, 60.9% Romney (2012)

National and State Parks: Lake Superior State Forest; Muskallonge Lake State Park; Tahquamenon River State Forest

Additional Information Contacts
Luce Government . . . . (906) 293-5521
  http://www.lucecountymi.org

Luce County Communities

COLUMBUS (township). Covers a land area of 140.338 square miles and a water area of 2.821 square miles. Located at 46.42° N. Lat; 85.74° W. Long.

Population: 204; Growth (since 2000): -5.1%; Density: 1.5 persons per square mile; Race: 97.5% White, 0.0% Black/African American, 0.0% Asian, 2.0% American Indian/Alaska Native, 0.0% Native Hawaiian/Other Pacific Islander, 0.5% Two or more races, 0.0% Hispanic of any race; Average household size: 2.19; Median age: 50.5; Age under 18: 16.2%; Age 65 and over: 24.0%; Males per 100 females: 117.0

Housing: Homeownership rate: 88.2%; Homeowner vacancy rate: 7.9%; Rental vacancy rate: 15.4%

LAKEFIELD (township). Covers a land area of 63.178 square miles and a water area of 8.776 square miles. Located at 46.28° N. Lat; 85.74° W. Long.
Population: 1,061; Growth (since 2000): -1.2%; Density: 16.8 persons per square mile; Race: 96.1% White, 0.4% Black/African American, 0.4% Asian, 1.6% American Indian/Alaska Native, 0.0% Native Hawaiian/Other Pacific Islander, 1.4% Two or more races, 0.6% Hispanic of any race; Average household size: 2.23; Median age: 52.5; Age under 18: 17.5%; Age 65 and over: 25.7%; Males per 100 females: 102.9
Housing: Homeownership rate: 93.1%; Homeowner vacancy rate: 6.8%; Rental vacancy rate: 13.5%

MCMILLAN (township). Covers a land area of 588.776 square miles and a water area of 15.570 square miles. Located at 46.51° N. Lat; 85.52° W. Long. Elevation is 781 feet.
History: McMillan developed as a supply base for lumber and charcoal camps. It was named in 1881 for James Stoughton McMillan, a railroad executive and U.S. senator.
Population: 2,692; Growth (since 2000): -31.8%; Density: 4.6 persons per square mile; Race: 89.2% White, 0.3% Black/African American, 0.2% Asian, 6.2% American Indian/Alaska Native, 0.1% Native Hawaiian/Other Pacific Islander, 4.1% Two or more races, 1.6% Hispanic of any race; Average household size: 2.20; Median age: 44.6; Age under 18: 22.8%; Age 65 and over: 20.7%; Males per 100 females: 92.8; Marriage status: 24.1% never married, 48.8% now married, 2.6% separated, 10.6% widowed, 16.5% divorced; Foreign born: 1.6%; Speak English only: 97.1%; With disability: 24.2%; Veterans: 9.5%; Ancestry: 16.2% German, 13.7% Irish, 9.4% French, 8.8% English, 5.9% American
Employment: 11.3% management, business, and financial, 0.4% computer, engineering, and science, 8.3% education, legal, community service, arts, and media, 5.0% healthcare practitioners, 30.1% service, 24.2% sales and office, 6.4% natural resources, construction, and maintenance, 14.3% production, transportation, and material moving
Income: Per capita: $19,598; Median household: $30,260; Average household: $42,197; Households with income of $100,000 or more: 4.6%; Poverty rate: 24.0%
Educational Attainment: High school diploma or higher: 86.3%; Bachelor's degree or higher: 10.0%; Graduate/professional degree or higher: 2.8%
Housing: Homeownership rate: 72.6%; Median home value: $62,800; Median year structure built: 1964; Homeowner vacancy rate: 3.2%; Median gross rent: $545 per month; Rental vacancy rate: 9.0%
Health Insurance: 85.7% have insurance; 50.7% have private insurance; 53.0% have public insurance; 14.3% do not have insurance; 5.8% of children under 18 do not have insurance
Transportation: Commute: 91.4% car, 0.0% public transportation, 6.7% walk, 1.9% work from home; Median travel time to work: 13.9 minutes

NEWBERRY (village). County seat. Covers a land area of 0.981 square miles and a water area of 0 square miles. Located at 46.35° N. Lat; 85.51° W. Long. Elevation is 771 feet.
History: Newberry developed as a lumber town, changing gradually to woodworking and trading for the Tahquamenon Valley. The Newberry Lumber and Chemical Company was founded here in 1882 as a charcoal kiln and iron-furnace operation, converting hardwood into charcoal for use in smelting iron ore.
Population: 1,519; Growth (since 2000): -43.4%; Density: 1,547.6 persons per square mile; Race: 89.3% White, 0.4% Black/African American, 0.3% Asian, 6.3% American Indian/Alaska Native, 0.1% Native Hawaiian/Other Pacific Islander, 3.6% Two or more races, 2.8% Hispanic of any race; Average household size: 2.26; Median age: 41.1; Age under 18: 25.9%; Age 65 and over: 19.8%; Males per 100 females: 91.8
School District(s)
Tahquamenon Area Schools (KG-12)
    2012-13 Enrollment: 738 . . . . (906) 293-3226
Housing: Homeownership rate: 68.7%; Homeowner vacancy rate: 4.4%; Rental vacancy rate: 10.1%
Hospitals: Helen Newberry Joy Hospital
Newspapers: Newberry News (weekly circulation 3600)
Airports: Luce County (general aviation)

PENTLAND (township). Covers a land area of 106.786 square miles and a water area of 0.559 square miles. Located at 46.29° N. Lat; 85.42° W. Long. Elevation is 869 feet.
Population: 2,674; Growth (since 2000): 49.6%; Density: 25.0 persons per square mile; Race: 64.0% White, 27.2% Black/African American, 0.3% Asian, 5.5% American Indian/Alaska Native, 0.0% Native Hawaiian/Other Pacific Islander, 3.0% Two or more races, 1.2% Hispanic of any race; Average household size: 2.35; Median age: 39.4; Age under 18: 13.2%; Age 65 and over: 11.4%; Males per 100 females: 238.1; Marriage status: 41.1% never married, 37.5% now married, 4.2% separated, 4.9% widowed, 16.5% divorced; Foreign born: 3.6%; Speak English only: 94.3%; With disability: 17.3%; Veterans: 7.8%; Ancestry: 17.0% German, 8.7% English, 7.2% Irish, 5.8% American, 4.4% Italian
Employment: 6.2% management, business, and financial, 10.6% computer, engineering, and science, 4.5% education, legal, community service, arts, and media, 8.0% healthcare practitioners, 18.5% service, 24.9% sales and office, 10.3% natural resources, construction, and maintenance, 17.1% production, transportation, and material moving
Income: Per capita: $15,192; Median household: $47,036; Average household: $57,237; Households with income of $100,000 or more: 15.8%; Poverty rate: 20.7%
Educational Attainment: High school diploma or higher: 84.2%; Bachelor's degree or higher: 10.9%; Graduate/professional degree or higher: 3.6%
Housing: Homeownership rate: 82.7%; Median home value: $91,300; Median year structure built: 1975; Homeowner vacancy rate: 3.2%; Median gross rent: $738 per month; Rental vacancy rate: 9.4%
Health Insurance: 90.7% have insurance; 64.7% have private insurance; 40.2% have public insurance; 9.3% do not have insurance; 4.7% of children under 18 do not have insurance
Transportation: Commute: 91.8% car, 0.0% public transportation, 1.6% walk, 4.4% work from home; Median travel time to work: 10.6 minutes

Mackinac County

Located in northwestern Michigan on the Upper Peninsula; bounded on the south by Lakes Michigan and Huron and the Straits of Mackinac; drained by the Carp and Pine Rivers; includes Mackinac and Bois Blanc Islands, several lakes, and part of Marquette National Forest. Covers a land area of 1,021.569 square miles, a water area of 1,079.075 square miles, and is located in the Eastern Time Zone at 46.17° N. Lat., 85.30° W. Long. The county was founded in 1818. County seat is Saint Ignace.

Weather Station: St Ignace Mackinac Br — Elevation: 600 feet

	Jan	Feb	Mar	Apr	May	Jun	Jul	Aug	Sep	Oct	Nov	Dec
High	26	28	35	48	60	70	75	74	67	54	42	31
Low	13	12	19	32	41	52	58	59	52	41	31	21
Precip	1.3	0.9	1.2	2.0	2.5	2.6	2.5	2.7	3.0	3.5	2.3	1.6
Snow	na	na	7.1	2.9	tr	0.0	0.0	0.0	0.0	tr	3.6	na

High and Low temperatures in degrees Fahrenheit; Precipitation and Snow in inches

Population: 11,113; Growth (since 2000): -6.9%; Density: 10.9 persons per square mile; Race: 76.5% White, 0.5% Black/African American, 0.2% Asian, 17.3% American Indian/Alaska Native, 0.0% Native Hawaiian/Other Pacific Islander, 5.3% two or more races, 1.1% Hispanic of any race; Average household size: 2.19; Median age: 49.0; Age under 18: 18.7%; Age 65 and over: 22.4%; Males per 100 females: 102.0; Marriage status: 21.4% never married, 57.5% now married, 1.3% separated, 7.9% widowed, 13.3% divorced; Foreign born: 2.0%; Speak English only: 95.6%; With disability: 19.0%; Veterans: 14.0%; Ancestry: 25.3% German, 12.7% Irish, 12.0% English, 8.9% French, 6.7% Polish
Religion: Six largest groups: 36.4% Catholicism, 6.7% Non-denominational Protestant, 5.6% Lutheran, 4.0% Methodist/Pietist, 1.8% European Free-Church, 1.5% Presbyterian-Reformed
Economy: Unemployment rate: 4.1%; Leading industries: 25.7% accommodation and food services; 20.1% retail trade; 13.7% construction; Farms: 103 totaling 22,420 acres; Company size: 0 employ 1,000 or more persons, 0 employ 500 to 999 persons, 1 employs 100 to 499 persons, 451 employs less than 100 persons; Business ownership: 253 women-owned, n/a Black-owned, n/a Hispanic-owned, n/a Asian-owned
Employment: 11.4% management, business, and financial, 1.4% computer, engineering, and science, 7.5% education, legal, community service, arts, and media, 5.4% healthcare practitioners, 25.8% service, 25.4% sales and office, 13.9% natural resources, construction, and maintenance, 9.2% production, transportation, and material moving

Income: Per capita: $22,622; Median household: $38,704; Average household: $50,112; Households with income of $100,000 or more: 8.4%; Poverty rate: 15.3%

Educational Attainment: High school diploma or higher: 88.3%; Bachelor's degree or higher: 18.5%; Graduate/professional degree or higher: 6.9%

Housing: Homeownership rate: 78.4%; Median home value: $119,300; Median year structure built: 1975; Homeowner vacancy rate: 3.5%; Median gross rent: $593 per month; Rental vacancy rate: 11.1%

Vital Statistics: Birth rate: 65.1 per 10,000 population; Death rate: 111.2 per 10,000 population; Age-adjusted cancer mortality rate: 161.3 deaths per 100,000 population

Health Insurance: 82.8% have insurance; 62.9% have private insurance; 41.1% have public insurance; 17.2% do not have insurance; 13.1% of children under 18 do not have insurance

Health Care: Physicians: 10.8 per 10,000 population; Hospital beds: 56.9 per 10,000 population; Hospital admissions: 289.2 per 10,000 population

Transportation: Commute: 83.1% car, 2.3% public transportation, 4.3% walk, 4.2% work from home; Median travel time to work: 19.6 minutes

Presidential Election: 43.5% Obama, 55.7% Romney (2012)

National and State Parks: Brown's Brook State Roadside Park; Mackinac Island State Park; Mackinac State Forest; Straits State Park

Additional Information Contacts

Mackinac Government . . . . (906) 643-7300
    http://www.mackinaccounty.net

Mackinac County Communities

BOIS BLANC (township). Covers a land area of 35.115 square miles and a water area of 13.603 square miles. Located at 45.78° N. Lat; 84.48° W. Long.

History: The name of Bois Blanc is French for "white wood," referring to the many birch trees here.

Population: 95; Growth (since 2000): 33.8%; Density: 2.7 persons per square mile; Race: 88.4% White, 0.0% Black/African American, 0.0% Asian, 5.3% American Indian/Alaska Native, 0.0% Native Hawaiian/Other Pacific Islander, 6.3% Two or more races, 0.0% Hispanic of any race; Average household size: 1.86; Median age: 63.5; Age under 18: 8.4%; Age 65 and over: 41.1%; Males per 100 females: 102.1

Housing: Homeownership rate: 94.1%; Homeowner vacancy rate: 0.0%; Rental vacancy rate: 25.0%

BREVORT (township). Covers a land area of 92.482 square miles and a water area of 6.353 square miles. Located at 46.05° N. Lat; 84.84° W. Long. Elevation is 597 feet.

History: The township, lake, river, and village were named for Henry Brevort, a surveyor who subdivided the area in 1845. Many people of Swedish ancestry settled in Brevort in the 1860's. The post office was established in 1890.

Population: 594; Growth (since 2000): -8.5%; Density: 6.4 persons per square mile; Race: 81.1% White, 0.7% Black/African American, 0.0% Asian, 12.1% American Indian/Alaska Native, 0.2% Native Hawaiian/Other Pacific Islander, 5.9% Two or more races, 1.2% Hispanic of any race; Average household size: 2.27; Median age: 51.0; Age under 18: 17.3%; Age 65 and over: 23.6%; Males per 100 females: 92.9

Housing: Homeownership rate: 95.4%; Homeowner vacancy rate: 3.5%; Rental vacancy rate: 0.0%

CLARK (township). Covers a land area of 78.974 square miles and a water area of 22.631 square miles. Located at 46.01° N. Lat; 84.35° W. Long.

Population: 2,056; Growth (since 2000): -6.5%; Density: 26.0 persons per square mile; Race: 84.4% White, 0.2% Black/African American, 0.0% Asian, 11.6% American Indian/Alaska Native, 0.0% Native Hawaiian/Other Pacific Islander, 3.7% Two or more races, 1.5% Hispanic of any race; Average household size: 2.16; Median age: 50.5; Age under 18: 17.9%; Age 65 and over: 25.5%; Males per 100 females: 100.8

Housing: Homeownership rate: 79.6%; Homeowner vacancy rate: 3.5%; Rental vacancy rate: 7.6%

ENGADINE (unincorporated postal area)
ZCTA: 49827

Covers a land area of 102.809 square miles and a water area of 1.951 square miles. Located at 46.18° N. Lat; 85.56° W. Long. Elevation is 673 feet.

Population: 897; Growth (since 2000): -5.1%; Density: 8.7 persons per square mile; Race: 84.7% White, 0.0% Black/African American, 0.1% Asian, 8.1% American Indian/Alaska Native, 0.0% Native Hawaiian/Other Pacific Islander, 5.9% Two or more races, 1.2% Hispanic of any race; Average household size: 2.28; Median age: 45.7; Age under 18: 23.9%; Age 65 and over: 24.1%; Males per 100 females: 112.1

School District(s)

Engadine Consolidated Schools (KG-12)

2012-13 Enrollment: 271 . . . . (906) 477-6313

Housing: Homeownership rate: 81.9%; Homeowner vacancy rate: 4.4%; Rental vacancy rate: 15.5%

GARFIELD (township). Covers a land area of 134.515 square miles and a water area of 3.048 square miles. Located at 46.16° N. Lat; 85.50° W. Long. Elevation is 623 feet.

Population: 1,146; Growth (since 2000): -8.4%; Density: 8.5 persons per square mile; Race: 82.4% White, 0.0% Black/African American, 0.1% Asian, 11.6% American Indian/Alaska Native, 0.0% Native Hawaiian/Other Pacific Islander, 5.1% Two or more races, 1.0% Hispanic of any race; Average household size: 2.20; Median age: 50.2; Age under 18: 20.6%; Age 65 and over: 26.5%; Males per 100 females: 109.1

Housing: Homeownership rate: 85.2%; Homeowner vacancy rate: 3.7%; Rental vacancy rate: 18.8%

GOULD CITY (unincorporated postal area)
ZCTA: 49838

Covers a land area of 139.458 square miles and a water area of 5.382 square miles. Located at 46.03° N. Lat; 85.74° W. Long. Elevation is 741 feet.

Population: 504; Growth (since 2000): 47.8%; Density: 3.6 persons per square mile; Race: 88.9% White, 1.0% Black/African American, 0.4% Asian, 7.5% American Indian/Alaska Native, 0.0% Native Hawaiian/Other Pacific Islander, 2.2% Two or more races, 0.8% Hispanic of any race; Average household size: 2.12; Median age: 55.0; Age under 18: 15.9%; Age 65 and over: 25.2%; Males per 100 females: 111.8

Housing: Homeownership rate: 88.6%; Homeowner vacancy rate: 3.2%; Rental vacancy rate: 25.0%

HENDRICKS (township). Covers a land area of 78.966 square miles and a water area of 2.137 square miles. Located at 46.13° N. Lat; 85.15° W. Long.

Population: 153; Growth (since 2000): -16.4%; Density: 1.9 persons per square mile; Race: 75.2% White, 0.0% Black/African American, 0.0% Asian, 15.7% American Indian/Alaska Native, 0.0% Native Hawaiian/Other Pacific Islander, 8.5% Two or more races, 1.3% Hispanic of any race; Average household size: 2.10; Median age: 54.8; Age under 18: 17.0%; Age 65 and over: 32.7%; Males per 100 females: 118.6

Housing: Homeownership rate: 89.1%; Homeowner vacancy rate: 1.5%; Rental vacancy rate: 11.1%

HESSEL (unincorporated postal area)
ZCTA: 49745

Covers a land area of 78.711 square miles and a water area of 10.328 square miles. Located at 46.04° N. Lat; 84.52° W. Long. Elevation is 594 feet.

Population: 1,089; Growth (since 2000): 433.8%; Density: 13.8 persons per square mile; Race: 74.7% White, 0.2% Black/African American, 0.3% Asian, 19.4% American Indian/Alaska Native, 0.0% Native Hawaiian/Other Pacific Islander, 5.5% Two or more races, 0.5% Hispanic of any race; Average household size: 2.23; Median age: 50.1; Age under 18: 18.2%; Age 65 and over: 21.5%; Males per 100 females: 104.3

Housing: Homeownership rate: 86.9%; Homeowner vacancy rate: 3.6%; Rental vacancy rate: 3.0%

HUDSON (township). Covers a land area of 68.768 square miles and a water area of 0.650 square miles. Located at 46.17° N. Lat; 85.30° W. Long.

Population: 181; Growth (since 2000): -15.4%; Density: 2.6 persons per square mile; Race: 65.7% White, 0.0% Black/African American, 0.6% Asian, 27.1% American Indian/Alaska Native, 0.0% Native Hawaiian/Other Pacific Islander, 6.6% Two or more races, 1.1% Hispanic of any race;

Average household size: 1.93; Median age: 54.8; Age under 18: 11.0%; Age 65 and over: 27.6%; Males per 100 females: 94.6
Housing: Homeownership rate: 89.3%; Homeowner vacancy rate: 4.5%; Rental vacancy rate: 16.7%

MACKINAC ISLAND (city). Covers a land area of 4.352 square miles and a water area of 14.491 square miles. Located at 45.86° N. Lat; 84.62° W. Long. Elevation is 594 feet.

History: The island, first called Michilimackinac ("the great turtle"), stands in the Straits of Mackinac between Lake Huron and Lake Michigan, and attracts many tourists. The British transferred their garrison from the mainland to Mackinac Island in 1781, and refused to evacuate the post when the island was ceded to America by the Treaty of Paris in 1783. The island changed hands several times until coming under permanent American rule in 1814, and John Jacob Astor soon centered the activities of the American Fur Company at Mackinac Island. When fur trading declined after 1830, Mackinac Island was promoted as a resort center and a place for summer estates, especially after ferry service was begun in 1881.

Population: 492; Growth (since 2000): -5.9%; Density: 113.1 persons per square mile; Race: 73.8% White, 1.2% Black/African American, 0.6% Asian, 18.1% American Indian/Alaska Native, 0.2% Native Hawaiian/Other Pacific Islander, 5.9% Two or more races, 2.2% Hispanic of any race; Average household size: 2.05; Median age: 42.5; Age under 18: 17.7%; Age 65 and over: 13.4%; Males per 100 females: 112.1

School District(s)
Mackinac Island Public Schools (KG-12)
    2012-13 Enrollment: 86........................ (906) 847-3377
Housing: Homeownership rate: 56.7%; Homeowner vacancy rate: 4.8%; Rental vacancy rate: 14.3%
Safety: Violent crime rate: 40.5 per 10,000 population; Property crime rate: 4,210.5 per 10,000 population
Airports: Mackinac Island (general aviation)

MARQUETTE (township). Covers a land area of 97.054 square miles and a water area of 39.115 square miles. Located at 46.08° N. Lat; 84.57° W. Long.

Population: 603; Growth (since 2000): -8.5%; Density: 6.2 persons per square mile; Race: 83.3% White, 0.0% Black/African American, 0.3% Asian, 12.1% American Indian/Alaska Native, 0.0% Native Hawaiian/Other Pacific Islander, 4.3% Two or more races, 2.3% Hispanic of any race; Average household size: 2.35; Median age: 48.5; Age under 18: 20.2%; Age 65 and over: 20.7%; Males per 100 females: 112.3
Housing: Homeownership rate: 91.9%; Homeowner vacancy rate: 4.1%; Rental vacancy rate: 4.5%

MORAN (township). Covers a land area of 127.525 square miles and a water area of 6.836 square miles. Located at 46.04° N. Lat; 84.94° W. Long. Elevation is 705 feet.

Population: 994; Growth (since 2000): -8.0%; Density: 7.8 persons per square mile; Race: 72.0% White, 0.4% Black/African American, 0.2% Asian, 20.7% American Indian/Alaska Native, 0.0% Native Hawaiian/Other Pacific Islander, 6.6% Two or more races, 1.0% Hispanic of any race; Average household size: 2.31; Median age: 48.9; Age under 18: 18.2%; Age 65 and over: 19.1%; Males per 100 females: 106.7
Housing: Homeownership rate: 85.8%; Homeowner vacancy rate: 3.2%; Rental vacancy rate: 19.5%

NAUBINWAY (unincorporated postal area)
ZCTA: 49762
    Covers a land area of 218.757 square miles and a water area of 89.186 square miles. Located at 46.10° N. Lat; 85.34° W. Long. Elevation is 597 feet.
    Population: 639; Growth (since 2000): -12.6%; Density: 2.9 persons per square mile; Race: 72.8% White, 0.0% Black/African American, 0.2% Asian, 21.3% American Indian/Alaska Native, 0.0% Native Hawaiian/Other Pacific Islander, 5.6% Two or more races, 0.6% Hispanic of any race; Average household size: 2.00; Median age: 56.6; Age under 18: 13.3%; Age 65 and over: 31.0%; Males per 100 females: 106.8
    Housing: Homeownership rate: 91.9%; Homeowner vacancy rate: 3.0%; Rental vacancy rate: 22.9%

NEWTON (township). Covers a land area of 148.596 square miles and a water area of 6.317 square miles. Located at 46.03° N. Lat; 85.74° W. Long.

Population: 427; Growth (since 2000): 19.9%; Density: 2.9 persons per square mile; Race: 88.3% White, 1.2% Black/African American, 0.2% Asian, 7.7% American Indian/Alaska Native, 0.0% Native Hawaiian/Other Pacific Islander, 2.6% Two or more races, 0.9% Hispanic of any race; Average household size: 2.10; Median age: 54.6; Age under 18: 15.9%; Age 65 and over: 23.9%; Males per 100 females: 106.3
Housing: Homeownership rate: 88.6%; Homeowner vacancy rate: 2.2%; Rental vacancy rate: 20.7%

POINTE AUX PINS (unincorporated postal area)
ZCTA: 49775
    Covers a land area of 35.115 square miles and a water area of 13.293 square miles. Located at 45.78° N. Lat; 84.48° W. Long. Elevation is 587 feet.
    Population: 95; Growth (since 2000): 33.8%; Density: 2.7 persons per square mile; Race: 88.4% White, 0.0% Black/African American, 0.0% Asian, 5.3% American Indian/Alaska Native, 0.0% Native Hawaiian/Other Pacific Islander, 6.3% Two or more races, 0.0% Hispanic of any race; Average household size: 1.86; Median age: 63.5; Age under 18: 8.4%; Age 65 and over: 41.1%; Males per 100 females: 102.1

School District(s)
Bois Blanc Pines SD (KG-12)
    2012-13 Enrollment: 3........................ (231) 634-7225
    Housing: Homeownership rate: 94.1%; Homeowner vacancy rate: 0.0%; Rental vacancy rate: 25.0%

PORTAGE (township). Covers a land area of 55.435 square miles and a water area of 16.829 square miles. Located at 46.18° N. Lat; 85.77° W. Long.

Population: 981; Growth (since 2000): -7.0%; Density: 17.7 persons per square mile; Race: 95.1% White, 0.2% Black/African American, 0.2% Asian, 2.8% American Indian/Alaska Native, 0.0% Native Hawaiian/Other Pacific Islander, 1.7% Two or more races, 0.1% Hispanic of any race; Average household size: 2.06; Median age: 54.5; Age under 18: 14.6%; Age 65 and over: 28.7%; Males per 100 females: 106.1
Housing: Homeownership rate: 83.8%; Homeowner vacancy rate: 3.2%; Rental vacancy rate: 19.8%

SAINT IGNACE (city). County seat. Covers a land area of 2.680 square miles and a water area of 0.008 square miles. Located at 45.89° N. Lat; 84.73° W. Long. Elevation is 587 feet.

History: The town of St. Ignace had its beginning when Father Jacques Marquette built a mission here in 1671. In 1706, seeing that he had few parishioners, the last priest burned the chapel as he left. When the Jesuits came again in 1834, they found that fishermen had settled here. It was the establishment of railroad ferry service across the Mackinac Straits that brought about the founding of an iron smelting furnace, the rise of the lumber industry, and the settlement of a town. St. Ignace was incorporated as a village in 1882, and as a city in 1883. The iron smelter and the lumber industry soon declined, but St. Ignace developed as an entry to the Upper Peninsula and as a commercial fishing center.

Population: 2,452; Growth (since 2000): -8.4%; Density: 914.9 persons per square mile; Race: 63.4% White, 1.0% Black/African American, 0.3% Asian, 27.8% American Indian/Alaska Native, 0.0% Native Hawaiian/Other Pacific Islander, 7.3% Two or more races, 1.1% Hispanic of any race; Average household size: 2.24; Median age: 44.5; Age under 18: 21.3%; Age 65 and over: 17.7%; Males per 100 females: 93.2

School District(s)
Moran Township SD (KG-12)
    2012-13 Enrollment: 81........................ (906) 643-7970
Saint Ignace Area Schools (PK-12)
    2012-13 Enrollment: 626........................ (906) 643-8145
Housing: Homeownership rate: 62.0%; Homeowner vacancy rate: 5.0%; Rental vacancy rate: 8.5%
Hospitals: Mackinac Straits Hospital & Health Center
Safety: Violent crime rate: 20.4 per 10,000 population; Property crime rate: 342.3 per 10,000 population
Newspapers: St. Ignace News (weekly circulation 6600)
Airports: Mackinac County (general aviation)

SAINT IGNACE (township). Covers a land area of 97.108 square miles and a water area of 44.988 square miles. Located at 46.04° N. Lat; 84.69° W. Long. Elevation is 587 feet.

Population: 939; Growth (since 2000): -8.3%; Density: 9.7 persons per square mile; Race: 61.2% White, 0.7% Black/African American, 0.2% Asian, 31.1% American Indian/Alaska Native, 0.0% Native Hawaiian/Other Pacific Islander, 6.7% Two or more races, 0.6% Hispanic of any race; Average household size: 2.29; Median age: 46.0; Age under 18: 20.3%; Age 65 and over: 19.1%; Males per 100 females: 103.2

School District(s)

Moran Township SD (KG-12)

    2012-13 Enrollment: 81 . . . . (906) 643-7970

Saint Ignace Area Schools (PK-12)

    2012-13 Enrollment: 626 . . . . (906) 643-8145

Housing: Homeownership rate: 77.0%; Homeowner vacancy rate: 0.6%; Rental vacancy rate: 2.1%

Hospitals: Mackinac Straits Hospital & Health Center

Newspapers: St. Ignace News (weekly circulation 6600)

Airports: Mackinac County (general aviation)

Macomb County

Located in southeastern Michigan; bounded on the southeast by Lake Saint Clair and Anchor Bay; drained by the Clinton River. Covers a land area of 479.223 square miles, a water area of 91.627 square miles, and is located in the Eastern Time Zone at 42.67° N. Lat., 82.91° W. Long. The county was founded in 1818. County seat is Mount Clemens.

Macomb County is part of the Detroit-Warren-Dearborn, MI Metropolitan Statistical Area. The entire metro area includes: Detroit-Dearborn-Livonia, MI Metropolitan Division (Wayne County, MI); Warren-Troy-Farmington Hills, MI Metropolitan Division (Lapeer County, MI; Livingston County, MI; Macomb County, MI; Oakland County, MI; Saint Clair County, MI)

Weather Station: Mount Clemens Selfridge Fld										Elevation: 580 feet		
	Jan	Feb	Mar	Apr	May	Jun	Jul	Aug	Sep	Oct	Nov	Dec
High	32	34	44	57	68	78	82	80	73	60	48	36
Low	18	19	26	37	47	57	62	61	53	42	33	23
Precip	1.8	1.7	2.2	na	na	2.9	3.1	3.0	3.3	na	2.8	na
Snow	10.6	7.7	5.0	0.8	tr	0.0	0.0	0.0	tr	0.1	0.8	na

High and Low temperatures in degrees Fahrenheit; Precipitation and Snow in inches

Population: 840,978; Growth (since 2000): 6.7%; Density: 1,754.9 persons per square mile; Race: 85.4% White, 8.6% Black/African American, 3.0% Asian, 0.3% American Indian/Alaska Native, 0.0% Native Hawaiian/Other Pacific Islander, 2.1% two or more races, 2.3% Hispanic of any race; Average household size: 2.51; Median age: 39.9; Age under 18: 23.0%; Age 65 and over: 14.3%; Males per 100 females: 94.6; Marriage status: 30.3% never married, 51.7% now married, 1.2% separated, 7.1% widowed, 10.9% divorced; Foreign born: 10.3%; Speak English only: 86.4%; With disability: 13.4%; Veterans: 8.5%; Ancestry: 20.9% German, 16.8% Polish, 12.5% Italian, 10.7% Irish, 6.9% English

Religion: Six largest groups: 29.7% Catholicism, 4.8% Lutheran, 2.0% Non-denominational Protestant, 1.4% Baptist, 1.1% Eastern Liturgical (Orthodox), 1.1% Orthodox

Economy: Unemployment rate: 7.8%; Leading industries: 15.5% retail trade; 12.9% health care and social assistance; 9.7% construction; Farms: 502 totaling 67,960 acres; Company size: 13 employ 1,000 or more persons, 26 employ 500 to 999 persons, 379 employ 100 to 499 persons, 17,635 employ less than 100 persons; Business ownership: 18,006 women-owned, 3,146 Black-owned, 786 Hispanic-owned, 2,193 Asian-owned

Employment: 13.4% management, business, and financial, 5.9% computer, engineering, and science, 8.1% education, legal, community service, arts, and media, 5.6% healthcare practitioners, 18.0% service, 27.0% sales and office, 7.4% natural resources, construction, and maintenance, 14.6% production, transportation, and material moving

Income: Per capita: $26,748; Median household: $53,451; Average household: $66,735; Households with income of $100,000 or more: 20.3%; Poverty rate: 12.5%

Educational Attainment: High school diploma or higher: 88.2%; Bachelor's degree or higher: 22.5%; Graduate/professional degree or higher: 7.7%

Housing: Homeownership rate: 76.4%; Median home value: $123,100; Median year structure built: 1973; Homeowner vacancy rate: 2.2%; Median gross rent: $824 per month; Rental vacancy rate: 10.2%

Vital Statistics: Birth rate: 105.5 per 10,000 population; Death rate: 92.9 per 10,000 population; Age-adjusted cancer mortality rate: 185.4 deaths per 100,000 population

Health Insurance: 88.6% have insurance; 72.8% have private insurance; 30.2% have public insurance; 11.4% do not have insurance; 3.6% of children under 18 do not have insurance

Health Care: Physicians: 16.2 per 10,000 population; Hospital beds: 15.5 per 10,000 population; Hospital admissions: 796.6 per 10,000 population

Air Quality Index: 84.4% good, 14.3% moderate, 1.2% unhealthy for sensitive individuals, 0.0% unhealthy (percent of days)

Transportation: Commute: 95.2% car, 0.8% public transportation, 0.8% walk, 2.5% work from home; Median travel time to work: 26.8 minutes

Presidential Election: 51.6% Obama, 47.6% Romney (2012)

National and State Parks: Dodge Brothers State Park Number 8; Rochester-Utica State Recreation Area

Additional Information Contacts

Macomb Government . . . . (586) 469-5120

    http://www.macombcountymi.gov

Macomb County Communities

ARMADA (township). Covers a land area of 36.476 square miles and a water area of 0.061 square miles. Located at 42.85° N. Lat; 82.92° W. Long. Elevation is 751 feet.

Population: 5,379; Growth (since 2000): 2.5%; Density: 147.5 persons per square mile; Race: 98.0% White, 0.3% Black/African American, 0.4% Asian, 0.2% American Indian/Alaska Native, 0.0% Native Hawaiian/Other Pacific Islander, 0.6% Two or more races, 1.8% Hispanic of any race; Average household size: 2.79; Median age: 42.6; Age under 18: 24.7%; Age 65 and over: 13.7%; Males per 100 females: 100.6; Marriage status: 24.8% never married, 60.5% now married, 0.9% separated, 7.3% widowed, 7.4% divorced; Foreign born: 2.5%; Speak English only: 95.8%; With disability: 9.6%; Veterans: 10.2%; Ancestry: 38.6% German, 25.2% Polish, 11.7% Irish, 11.1% Italian, 8.5% English

Employment: 15.1% management, business, and financial, 8.2% computer, engineering, and science, 8.0% education, legal, community service, arts, and media, 7.3% healthcare practitioners, 16.2% service, 22.3% sales and office, 8.2% natural resources, construction, and maintenance, 14.6% production, transportation, and material moving

Income: Per capita: $31,117; Median household: $75,388; Average household: $85,234; Households with income of $100,000 or more: 33.1%; Poverty rate: 4.6%

Educational Attainment: High school diploma or higher: 91.5%; Bachelor's degree or higher: 21.1%; Graduate/professional degree or higher: 6.2%

School District(s)

Armada Area Schools (PK-12)

    2012-13 Enrollment: 2,007 . . . . (586) 784-2112

Housing: Homeownership rate: 88.9%; Median home value: $174,500; Median year structure built: 1979; Homeowner vacancy rate: 1.3%; Median gross rent: $750 per month; Rental vacancy rate: 4.9%

Health Insurance: 91.1% have insurance; 85.5% have private insurance; 20.3% have public insurance; 8.9% do not have insurance; 4.6% of children under 18 do not have insurance

Transportation: Commute: 96.1% car, 0.0% public transportation, 1.4% walk, 2.1% work from home; Median travel time to work: 32.5 minutes

ARMADA (village). Covers a land area of 0.761 square miles and a water area of 0.002 square miles. Located at 42.84° N. Lat; 82.88° W. Long. Elevation is 751 feet.

History: Armada was established in 1834 when Henry B. Ten Eyck hosted the first town meeting in his home. Armada was incorporated as a village in 1867.

Population: 1,730; Growth (since 2000): 10.0%; Density: 2,273.8 persons per square mile; Race: 98.0% White, 0.3% Black/African American, 0.1% Asian, 0.1% American Indian/Alaska Native, 0.1% Native Hawaiian/Other Pacific Islander, 0.9% Two or more races, 2.6% Hispanic of any race; Average household size: 2.73; Median age: 38.6; Age under 18: 27.9%; Age 65 and over: 15.1%; Males per 100 females: 89.9

School District(s)

Armada Area Schools (PK-12)

    2012-13 Enrollment: 2,007 . . . . (586) 784-2112

Housing: Homeownership rate: 77.9%; Homeowner vacancy rate: 2.7%; Rental vacancy rate: 6.9%
Safety: Violent crime rate: 5.8 per 10,000 population; Property crime rate: 46.3 per 10,000 population

BRUCE (township). Covers a land area of 36.750 square miles and a water area of 0.425 square miles. Located at 42.85° N. Lat; 83.04° W. Long.
Population: 8,700; Growth (since 2000): 6.6%; Density: 236.7 persons per square mile; Race: 95.1% White, 1.6% Black/African American, 0.5% Asian, 0.2% American Indian/Alaska Native, 0.0% Native Hawaiian/Other Pacific Islander, 1.4% Two or more races, 4.8% Hispanic of any race; Average household size: 2.81; Median age: 42.5; Age under 18: 24.7%; Age 65 and over: 13.1%; Males per 100 females: 101.6; Marriage status: 27.0% never married, 60.7% now married, 1.1% separated, 5.3% widowed, 7.0% divorced; Foreign born: 4.4%; Speak English only: 90.9%; With disability: 11.3%; Veterans: 9.5%; Ancestry: 35.1% German, 14.2% Polish, 13.1% Irish, 12.7% Italian, 11.7% English
Employment: 17.4% management, business, and financial, 7.0% computer, engineering, and science, 9.1% education, legal, community service, arts, and media, 5.1% healthcare practitioners, 11.3% service, 24.3% sales and office, 8.1% natural resources, construction, and maintenance, 17.7% production, transportation, and material moving
Income: Per capita: $31,213; Median household: $74,261; Average household: $88,762; Households with income of $100,000 or more: 34.8%; Poverty rate: 7.3%
Educational Attainment: High school diploma or higher: 90.5%; Bachelor's degree or higher: 25.8%; Graduate/professional degree or higher: 11.0%
Housing: Homeownership rate: 92.2%; Median home value: $189,600; Median year structure built: 1983; Homeowner vacancy rate: 2.4%; Median gross rent: $784 per month; Rental vacancy rate: 15.5%
Health Insurance: 90.3% have insurance; 81.7% have private insurance; 24.6% have public insurance; 9.7% do not have insurance; 4.0% of children under 18 do not have insurance
Transportation: Commute: 92.7% car, 0.0% public transportation, 2.3% walk, 4.3% work from home; Median travel time to work: 28.8 minutes
Additional Information Contacts
Bruce Township . . . . (586) 752-4585
  http://www.brucetwp.org

CENTER LINE (city). Covers a land area of 1.741 square miles and a water area of 0 square miles. Located at 42.48° N. Lat; 83.03° W. Long. Elevation is 623 feet.
History: Center Line was named by the French because it was on the middle of three trails from Detroit to the northern trading posts. The first general store was opened here in 1863.
Population: 8,257; Growth (since 2000): -3.2%; Density: 4,743.2 persons per square mile; Race: 82.5% White, 12.0% Black/African American, 2.5% Asian, 0.4% American Indian/Alaska Native, 0.0% Native Hawaiian/Other Pacific Islander, 2.5% Two or more races, 1.7% Hispanic of any race; Average household size: 2.22; Median age: 41.2; Age under 18: 21.4%; Age 65 and over: 17.7%; Males per 100 females: 85.7; Marriage status: 33.6% never married, 39.3% now married, 2.0% separated, 8.4% widowed, 18.7% divorced; Foreign born: 6.4%; Speak English only: 92.8%; With disability: 20.1%; Veterans: 8.9%; Ancestry: 23.5% German, 16.8% Polish, 14.2% Irish, 8.6% Italian, 8.3% English
Employment: 12.1% management, business, and financial, 3.4% computer, engineering, and science, 4.8% education, legal, community service, arts, and media, 3.9% healthcare practitioners, 20.5% service, 32.5% sales and office, 5.0% natural resources, construction, and maintenance, 17.9% production, transportation, and material moving
Income: Per capita: $19,543; Median household: $30,752; Average household: $42,514; Households with income of $100,000 or more: 8.2%; Poverty rate: 21.3%
Educational Attainment: High school diploma or higher: 85.9%; Bachelor's degree or higher: 14.0%; Graduate/professional degree or higher: 3.1%
School District(s)
Center Line Public Schools (PK-12)
  2012-13 Enrollment: 2,705 . . . . (586) 510-2000
Housing: Homeownership rate: 54.4%; Median home value: $65,700; Median year structure built: 1957; Homeowner vacancy rate: 2.2%; Median gross rent: $474 per month; Rental vacancy rate: 5.3%

Health Insurance: 88.0% have insurance; 56.8% have private insurance; 45.1% have public insurance; 12.0% do not have insurance; 6.3% of children under 18 do not have insurance
Safety: Violent crime rate: 44.8 per 10,000 population; Property crime rate: 283.6 per 10,000 population
Transportation: Commute: 95.7% car, 0.9% public transportation, 1.4% walk, 1.0% work from home; Median travel time to work: 21.4 minutes
Additional Information Contacts
City of Center Line . . . . (586) 757-6800
  http://www.centerline.gov

CHESTERFIELD (township). Covers a land area of 27.577 square miles and a water area of 3.026 square miles. Located at 42.68° N. Lat; 82.81° W. Long. Elevation is 607 feet.
Population: 43,381; Growth (since 2000): 16.0%; Density: 1,573.1 persons per square mile; Race: 90.8% White, 5.3% Black/African American, 1.0% Asian, 0.4% American Indian/Alaska Native, 0.0% Native Hawaiian/Other Pacific Islander, 1.8% Two or more races, 2.4% Hispanic of any race; Average household size: 2.66; Median age: 38.2; Age under 18: 26.1%; Age 65 and over: 9.4%; Males per 100 females: 96.1; Marriage status: 26.3% never married, 57.2% now married, 1.2% separated, 5.3% widowed, 11.2% divorced; Foreign born: 4.4%; Speak English only: 93.8%; With disability: 10.2%; Veterans: 8.6%; Ancestry: 26.6% German, 20.4% Polish, 14.4% Italian, 12.4% Irish, 7.7% American
Employment: 13.8% management, business, and financial, 6.5% computer, engineering, and science, 7.7% education, legal, community service, arts, and media, 5.5% healthcare practitioners, 16.7% service, 26.3% sales and office, 7.4% natural resources, construction, and maintenance, 16.0% production, transportation, and material moving
Income: Per capita: $29,221; Median household: $65,392; Average household: $76,805; Households with income of $100,000 or more: 27.3%; Poverty rate: 8.8%
Educational Attainment: High school diploma or higher: 90.1%; Bachelor's degree or higher: 21.8%; Graduate/professional degree or higher: 6.1%
School District(s)
Anchor Bay SD (PK-12)
  2012-13 Enrollment: 6,214 . . . . (586) 725-2861
L'anse Creuse Public Schools (PK-12)
  2012-13 Enrollment: 11,518 . . . . (586) 783-6300
Housing: Homeownership rate: 83.3%; Median home value: $150,600; Median year structure built: 1991; Homeowner vacancy rate: 2.7%; Median gross rent: $936 per month; Rental vacancy rate: 13.1%
Health Insurance: 91.2% have insurance; 78.4% have private insurance; 23.9% have public insurance; 8.8% do not have insurance; 1.5% of children under 18 do not have insurance
Safety: Violent crime rate: 27.2 per 10,000 population; Property crime rate: 165.8 per 10,000 population
Transportation: Commute: 95.7% car, 0.5% public transportation, 0.3% walk, 2.9% work from home; Median travel time to work: 29.5 minutes
Additional Information Contacts
Chesterfield Township . . . . (586) 949-0400
  http://chesterfieldtwp.org

CLINTON (charter township). Covers a land area of 28.097 square miles and a water area of 0.272 square miles. Located at 42.59° N. Lat; 82.92° W. Long. Elevation is 607 feet.
Population: 96,796; Growth (since 2000): 1.2%; Density: 3,445.0 persons per square mile; Race: 82.1% White, 13.0% Black/African American, 1.8% Asian, 0.3% American Indian/Alaska Native, 0.0% Native Hawaiian/Other Pacific Islander, 2.2% Two or more races, 2.4% Hispanic of any race; Average household size: 2.29; Median age: 40.7; Age under 18: 20.9%; Age 65 and over: 16.2%; Males per 100 females: 88.6; Marriage status: 32.0% never married, 47.0% now married, 1.5% separated, 8.1% widowed, 13.0% divorced; Foreign born: 7.3%; Speak English only: 90.2%; With disability: 15.1%; Veterans: 9.2%; Ancestry: 20.4% German, 16.7% Polish, 14.1% Italian, 10.3% Irish, 6.5% English
Employment: 12.1% management, business, and financial, 4.6% computer, engineering, and science, 8.4% education, legal, community service, arts, and media, 5.7% healthcare practitioners, 20.6% service, 27.2% sales and office, 6.8% natural resources, construction, and maintenance, 14.8% production, transportation, and material moving
Income: Per capita: $26,168; Median household: $47,609; Average household: $60,107; Households with income of $100,000 or more: 15.4%; Poverty rate: 11.8%

Educational Attainment: High school diploma or higher: 89.3%; Bachelor's degree or higher: 20.5%; Graduate/professional degree or higher: 7.2%

School District(s)
Chippewa Valley Schools (PK-12)
 2012-13 Enrollment: 16,422 . . . . (586) 723-2782
Clintondale Community Schools (PK-12)
 2012-13 Enrollment: 3,407 . . . . (586) 791-6300
Fraser Public Schools (PK-12)
 2012-13 Enrollment: 5,291 . . . . (586) 439-7000
L'anse Creuse Public Schools (PK-12)
 2012-13 Enrollment: 11,518 . . . . (586) 783-6300
Macomb Academy (12-12)
 2012-13 Enrollment: 72 . . . . (586) 228-2201
Macomb ISD (PK-12)
 2012-13 Enrollment: 2,316 . . . . (586) 228-3300

Four-year College(s)
Baker College of Clinton Township (Private, Not-for-profit)
 Fall 2013 Enrollment: 4,383 . . . . (586) 791-6610
 2013-14 Tuition: In-state $8,100; Out-of-state $8,100

Vocational/Technical School(s)
Gallery College of Beauty (Private, For-profit)
 Fall 2013 Enrollment: 193 . . . . (586) 783-7358
 2013-14 Tuition: $16,500

Housing: Homeownership rate: 67.1%; Median home value: $119,100; Median year structure built: 1979; Homeowner vacancy rate: 2.2%; Median gross rent: $784 per month; Rental vacancy rate: 10.5%

Health Insurance: 87.4% have insurance; 71.0% have private insurance; 33.5% have public insurance; 12.6% do not have insurance; 5.3% of children under 18 do not have insurance

Hospitals: Henry Ford Macomb Hospital (435 beds)

Safety: Violent crime rate: 29.1 per 10,000 population; Property crime rate: 217.6 per 10,000 population

Newspapers: Advisor & Source Newspapers (weekly circulation 125000)

Transportation: Commute: 95.2% car, 1.4% public transportation, 0.5% walk, 2.3% work from home; Median travel time to work: 26.9 minutes

Additional Information Contacts
Clinton Charter Township . . . . (586) 286-8000
 http://www.clintontownship-mi.gov

EASTPOINTE (city).
Covers a land area of 5.143 square miles and a water area of 0.002 square miles. Located at 42.47° N. Lat; 82.95° W. Long. Elevation is 614 feet.

Population: 32,442; Growth (since 2000): -4.8%; Density: 6,307.4 persons per square mile; Race: 65.6% White, 29.5% Black/African American, 1.1% Asian, 0.4% American Indian/Alaska Native, 0.0% Native Hawaiian/Other Pacific Islander, 2.9% Two or more races, 2.1% Hispanic of any race; Average household size: 2.58; Median age: 36.3; Age under 18: 25.7%; Age 65 and over: 11.3%; Males per 100 females: 93.8; Marriage status: 38.7% never married, 39.6% now married, 2.1% separated, 7.3% widowed, 14.4% divorced; Foreign born: 3.2%; Speak English only: 94.1%; With disability: 16.2%; Veterans: 7.4%; Ancestry: 16.7% German, 11.0% Polish, 10.3% Irish, 10.2% Italian, 4.5% English

Employment: 6.4% management, business, and financial, 3.2% computer, engineering, and science, 6.4% education, legal, community service, arts, and media, 4.0% healthcare practitioners, 21.9% service, 32.2% sales and office, 6.6% natural resources, construction, and maintenance, 19.4% production, transportation, and material moving

Income: Per capita: $18,940; Median household: $43,207; Average household: $48,863; Households with income of $100,000 or more: 8.4%; Poverty rate: 22.6%

Educational Attainment: High school diploma or higher: 84.8%; Bachelor's degree or higher: 13.0%; Graduate/professional degree or higher: 4.9%

School District(s)
East Detroit Public Schools (KG-12)
 2012-13 Enrollment: 3,833 . . . . (586) 533-3024
Eaton Academy (KG-12)
 2012-13 Enrollment: 477 . . . . (586) 777-1519
South Lake Schools (KG-12)
 2012-13 Enrollment: 2,052 . . . . (586) 435-1600

Housing: Homeownership rate: 78.0%; Median home value: $62,500; Median year structure built: 1954; Homeowner vacancy rate: 3.5%; Median gross rent: $1,025 per month; Rental vacancy rate: 7.6%

Health Insurance: 87.3% have insurance; 59.8% have private insurance; 39.6% have public insurance; 12.7% do not have insurance; 1.9% of children under 18 do not have insurance

Safety: Violent crime rate: 91.0 per 10,000 population; Property crime rate: 359.9 per 10,000 population

Transportation: Commute: 94.1% car, 0.9% public transportation, 2.2% walk, 1.4% work from home; Median travel time to work: 23.6 minutes

Additional Information Contacts
City of Eastpointe . . . . (586) 445-5026
 http://www.cityofeastpointe.net

FRASER (city).
Covers a land area of 4.141 square miles and a water area of 0.016 square miles. Located at 42.54° N. Lat; 82.95° W. Long. Elevation is 614 feet.

History: Named for Alex Fraser (or Frazer) who founded the village in 1857. Incorporated as a village 1894, as a city 1957.

Population: 14,480; Growth (since 2000): -5.3%; Density: 3,496.6 persons per square mile; Race: 92.0% White, 3.9% Black/African American, 1.5% Asian, 0.5% American Indian/Alaska Native, 0.0% Native Hawaiian/Other Pacific Islander, 1.8% Two or more races, 2.1% Hispanic of any race; Average household size: 2.36; Median age: 42.9; Age under 18: 21.4%; Age 65 and over: 16.2%; Males per 100 females: 86.6; Marriage status: 28.3% never married, 51.3% now married, 1.4% separated, 8.3% widowed, 12.1% divorced; Foreign born: 4.7%; Speak English only: 94.8%; With disability: 12.9%; Veterans: 8.7%; Ancestry: 29.7% German, 18.9% Polish, 14.8% Italian, 13.4% Irish, 7.7% English

Employment: 12.9% management, business, and financial, 6.1% computer, engineering, and science, 9.1% education, legal, community service, arts, and media, 4.5% healthcare practitioners, 16.9% service, 29.1% sales and office, 8.1% natural resources, construction, and maintenance, 13.3% production, transportation, and material moving

Income: Per capita: $28,474; Median household: $51,585; Average household: $67,343; Households with income of $100,000 or more: 20.0%; Poverty rate: 9.7%

Educational Attainment: High school diploma or higher: 90.0%; Bachelor's degree or higher: 18.9%; Graduate/professional degree or higher: 5.9%

School District(s)
Arts Academy in the Woods (KG-12)
 2012-13 Enrollment: 314 . . . . (586) 294-0391
Fraser Public Schools (PK-12)
 2012-13 Enrollment: 5,291 . . . . (586) 439-7000

Housing: Homeownership rate: 70.5%; Median home value: $113,900; Median year structure built: 1971; Homeowner vacancy rate: 2.2%; Median gross rent: $689 per month; Rental vacancy rate: 6.1%

Health Insurance: 90.6% have insurance; 77.2% have private insurance; 30.4% have public insurance; 9.4% do not have insurance; 5.8% of children under 18 do not have insurance

Safety: Violent crime rate: 20.0 per 10,000 population; Property crime rate: 270.5 per 10,000 population

Transportation: Commute: 95.4% car, 0.6% public transportation, 1.4% walk, 1.8% work from home; Median travel time to work: 25.6 minutes

Additional Information Contacts
City of Fraser . . . . (586) 293-3100
 http://www.fraser.govoffice.com

HARRISON (charter township).
Covers a land area of 14.456 square miles and a water area of 9.311 square miles. Located at 42.59° N. Lat; 82.82° W. Long.

Population: 24,587; Growth (since 2000): 0.5%; Density: 1,700.9 persons per square mile; Race: 89.0% White, 7.4% Black/African American, 0.7% Asian, 0.3% American Indian/Alaska Native, 0.0% Native Hawaiian/Other Pacific Islander, 1.8% Two or more races, 2.6% Hispanic of any race; Average household size: 2.21; Median age: 43.5; Age under 18: 19.2%; Age 65 and over: 13.7%; Males per 100 females: 97.1; Marriage status: 29.4% never married, 50.7% now married, 1.7% separated, 6.4% widowed, 13.5% divorced; Foreign born: 4.2%; Speak English only: 94.1%; With disability: 13.7%; Veterans: 11.4%; Ancestry: 23.6% German, 17.4% Polish, 12.7% Italian, 11.0% Irish, 10.6% American

Employment: 13.1% management, business, and financial, 5.5% computer, engineering, and science, 9.5% education, legal, community service, arts, and media, 6.5% healthcare practitioners, 17.3% service, 25.5% sales and office, 10.0% natural resources, construction, and maintenance, 12.7% production, transportation, and material moving

Income: Per capita: $31,259; Median household: $52,125; Average household: $68,293; Households with income of $100,000 or more: 23.1%; Poverty rate: 12.1%
Educational Attainment: High school diploma or higher: 92.0%; Bachelor's degree or higher: 24.8%; Graduate/professional degree or higher: 10.0%
Housing: Homeownership rate: 69.3%; Median home value: $150,200; Median year structure built: 1977; Homeowner vacancy rate: 3.0%; Median gross rent: $798 per month; Rental vacancy rate: 14.3%
Health Insurance: 88.7% have insurance; 74.3% have private insurance; 29.7% have public insurance; 11.3% do not have insurance; 3.9% of children under 18 do not have insurance
Transportation: Commute: 94.3% car, 0.5% public transportation, 1.1% walk, 2.6% work from home; Median travel time to work: 28.8 minutes
Additional Information Contacts
Harrison Charter Township . . . . (586) 466-1400
  http://www.harrison-township.org

HARRISON TOWNSHIP (unincorporated postal area)
ZCTA: 48045
  Covers a land area of 14.615 square miles and a water area of 9.225 square miles. Located at 42.59° N. Lat; 82.82° W. Long..
  Population: 24,604; Growth (since 2000): 3.0%; Density: 1,683.5 persons per square mile; Race: 89.0% White, 7.4% Black/African American, 0.7% Asian, 0.3% American Indian/Alaska Native, 0.0% Native Hawaiian/Other Pacific Islander, 1.8% Two or more races, 2.6% Hispanic of any race; Average household size: 2.21; Median age: 43.5; Age under 18: 19.2%; Age 65 and over: 13.7%; Males per 100 females: 97.1; Marriage status: 29.4% never married, 50.7% now married, 1.7% separated, 6.4% widowed, 13.6% divorced; Foreign born: 4.2%; Speak English only: 94.1%; With disability: 13.6%; Veterans: 11.4%; Ancestry: 23.6% German, 17.4% Polish, 12.6% Italian, 11.0% Irish, 10.6% American
  Employment: 13.1% management, business, and financial, 5.5% computer, engineering, and science, 9.5% education, legal, community service, arts, and media, 6.5% healthcare practitioners, 17.3% service, 25.4% sales and office, 10.0% natural resources, construction, and maintenance, 12.7% production, transportation, and material moving
  Income: Per capita: $31,327; Median household: $52,214; Average household: $68,438; Households with income of $100,000 or more: 23.2%; Poverty rate: 12.1%
  Educational Attainment: High school diploma or higher: 92.0%; Bachelor's degree or higher: 24.8%; Graduate/professional degree or higher: 10.0%

School District(s)
L'anse Creuse Public Schools (PK-12)
  2012-13 Enrollment: 11,518 . . . . (586) 783-6300
  Housing: Homeownership rate: 69.2%; Median home value: $150,400; Median year structure built: 1977; Homeowner vacancy rate: 3.0%; Median gross rent: $798 per month; Rental vacancy rate: 14.3%
  Health Insurance: 88.6% have insurance; 74.3% have private insurance; 29.6% have public insurance; 11.4% do not have insurance; 3.9% of children under 18 do not have insurance
  Transportation: Commute: 94.3% car, 0.5% public transportation, 1.1% walk, 2.6% work from home; Median travel time to work: 29.0 minutes

LENOX (township). Covers a land area of 38.706 square miles and a water area of 0.222 square miles. Located at 42.76° N. Lat; 82.80° W. Long.
  Population: 10,470; Growth (since 2000): 24.2%; Density: 270.5 persons per square mile; Race: 81.0% White, 14.5% Black/African American, 0.5% Asian, 0.5% American Indian/Alaska Native, 0.0% Native Hawaiian/Other Pacific Islander, 2.6% Two or more races, 3.8% Hispanic of any race; Average household size: 2.83; Median age: 36.8; Age under 18: 24.7%; Age 65 and over: 8.8%; Males per 100 females: 123.5; Marriage status: 35.1% never married, 50.5% now married, 1.2% separated, 5.5% widowed, 8.9% divorced; Foreign born: 2.4%; Speak English only: 95.1%; With disability: 13.8%; Veterans: 9.7%; Ancestry: 20.5% German, 17.7% Polish, 12.5% Irish, 11.8% English, 11.3% Italian
  Employment: 13.5% management, business, and financial, 4.1% computer, engineering, and science, 4.7% education, legal, community service, arts, and media, 2.3% healthcare practitioners, 14.7% service, 29.1% sales and office, 12.3% natural resources, construction, and maintenance, 19.2% production, transportation, and material moving

Income: Per capita: $21,847; Median household: $56,319; Average household: $66,696; Households with income of $100,000 or more: 18.5%; Poverty rate: 10.3%
Educational Attainment: High school diploma or higher: 88.6%; Bachelor's degree or higher: 12.5%; Graduate/professional degree or higher: 4.2%
Housing: Homeownership rate: 84.9%; Median home value: $132,000; Median year structure built: 1987; Homeowner vacancy rate: 4.3%; Median gross rent: $911 per month; Rental vacancy rate: 11.5%
Health Insurance: 89.1% have insurance; 72.4% have private insurance; 29.3% have public insurance; 10.9% do not have insurance; 4.2% of children under 18 do not have insurance
Transportation: Commute: 94.8% car, 0.4% public transportation, 1.9% walk, 2.6% work from home; Median travel time to work: 32.5 minutes
Additional Information Contacts
Lenox Township . . . . (586) 727-2085
  http://lenoxtwp.org

MACOMB (township). Covers a land area of 36.225 square miles and a water area of 0.119 square miles. Located at 42.67° N. Lat; 82.91° W. Long. Elevation is 627 feet.
Population: 79,580; Growth (since 2000): 57.7%; Density: 2,196.8 persons per square mile; Race: 90.5% White, 3.9% Black/African American, 3.1% Asian, 0.2% American Indian/Alaska Native, 0.0% Native Hawaiian/Other Pacific Islander, 1.6% Two or more races, 2.3% Hispanic of any race; Average household size: 2.99; Median age: 37.4; Age under 18: 29.1%; Age 65 and over: 9.3%; Males per 100 females: 98.1; Marriage status: 25.4% never married, 64.2% now married, 0.8% separated, 4.2% widowed, 6.3% divorced; Foreign born: 10.4%; Speak English only: 85.3%; With disability: 7.8%; Veterans: 6.9%; Ancestry: 20.7% German, 20.7% Italian, 19.0% Polish, 9.2% Irish, 7.0% American
Employment: 17.8% management, business, and financial, 8.6% computer, engineering, and science, 9.6% education, legal, community service, arts, and media, 6.8% healthcare practitioners, 13.7% service, 26.7% sales and office, 5.9% natural resources, construction, and maintenance, 11.0% production, transportation, and material moving
Income: Per capita: $31,715; Median household: $82,957; Average household: $93,655; Households with income of $100,000 or more: 39.6%; Poverty rate: 5.1%
Educational Attainment: High school diploma or higher: 92.2%; Bachelor's degree or higher: 33.8%; Graduate/professional degree or higher: 11.7%

School District(s)
Chippewa Valley Schools (PK-12)
  2012-13 Enrollment: 16,422 . . . . (586) 723-2782
L'anse Creuse Public Schools (PK-12)
  2012-13 Enrollment: 11,518 . . . . (586) 783-6300
Macomb ISD (PK-12)
  2012-13 Enrollment: 2,316 . . . . (586) 228-3300
Utica Community Schools (PK-12)
  2012-13 Enrollment: 28,415 . . . . (586) 797-1000
Housing: Homeownership rate: 93.5%; Median home value: $204,000; Median year structure built: 1998; Homeowner vacancy rate: 1.9%; Median gross rent: $1,142 per month; Rental vacancy rate: 8.1%
Health Insurance: 94.3% have insurance; 86.5% have private insurance; 18.2% have public insurance; 5.7% do not have insurance; 1.5% of children under 18 do not have insurance
Transportation: Commute: 95.9% car, 0.2% public transportation, 0.2% walk, 3.3% work from home; Median travel time to work: 31.0 minutes
Additional Information Contacts
Macomb Township . . . . (586) 992-0710
  http://www.macomb-mi.gov

MEMPHIS (city). Covers a land area of 1.120 square miles and a water area of 0.029 square miles. Located at 42.90° N. Lat; 82.77° W. Long. Elevation is 758 feet.
Population: 1,183; Growth (since 2000): 4.8%; Density: 1,056.2 persons per square mile; Race: 97.6% White, 0.8% Black/African American, 0.0% Asian, 0.3% American Indian/Alaska Native, 0.0% Native Hawaiian/Other Pacific Islander, 0.8% Two or more races, 2.1% Hispanic of any race; Average household size: 2.47; Median age: 39.4; Age under 18: 24.3%; Age 65 and over: 13.8%; Males per 100 females: 91.7

School District(s)
Memphis Community Schools (PK-12)
  2012-13 Enrollment: 961 . . . . (810) 392-2151

Housing: Homeownership rate: 66.3%; Homeowner vacancy rate: 1.3%; Rental vacancy rate: 13.5%
Safety: Violent crime rate: 34.0 per 10,000 population; Property crime rate: 101.9 per 10,000 population

MOUNT CLEMENS (city). County seat. Covers a land area of 4.069 square miles and a water area of 0.131 square miles. Located at 42.60° N. Lat; 82.88° W. Long. Elevation is 610 feet.

History: Named for Christian Clemens, an early settler who operated a distillery. Mount Clemens developed around sulphur springs as a spa with bathhouses and hotels. The water, which contained about 30 different chemical elements, was also marketed in containers for medicinal purposes. In Mount Clemens, at the Grand Trunk Station, Thomas Edison learned telegraphy.
Population: 16,314; Growth (since 2000): -5.8%; Density: 4,009.1 persons per square mile; Race: 70.0% White, 24.8% Black/African American, 0.5% Asian, 0.3% American Indian/Alaska Native, 0.0% Native Hawaiian/Other Pacific Islander, 3.6% Two or more races, 2.9% Hispanic of any race; Average household size: 2.19; Median age: 38.3; Age under 18: 20.6%; Age 65 and over: 13.0%; Males per 100 females: 106.2; Marriage status: 41.7% never married, 34.4% now married, 2.9% separated, 7.6% widowed, 16.3% divorced; Foreign born: 2.7%; Speak English only: 96.0%; With disability: 21.3%; Veterans: 7.0%; Ancestry: 21.2% German, 10.0% Irish, 8.2% American, 7.9% Polish, 6.3% French
Employment: 12.5% management, business, and financial, 4.6% computer, engineering, and science, 10.2% education, legal, community service, arts, and media, 4.6% healthcare practitioners, 22.9% service, 23.5% sales and office, 6.6% natural resources, construction, and maintenance, 15.0% production, transportation, and material moving
Income: Per capita: $21,725; Median household: $33,208; Average household: $46,917; Households with income of $100,000 or more: 9.2%; Poverty rate: 21.8%
Educational Attainment: High school diploma or higher: 83.2%; Bachelor's degree or higher: 18.2%; Graduate/professional degree or higher: 6.8%

School District(s)
Chippewa Valley Schools (PK-12)
    2012-13 Enrollment: 16,422 . . . . (586) 723-2782
L'anse Creuse Public Schools (PK-12)
    2012-13 Enrollment: 11,518 . . . . (586) 783-6300
Mount Clemens Community SD (PK-12)
    2012-13 Enrollment: 1,539 . . . . (586) 461-3766
Mt. Clemens Montessori Academy (KG-12)
    2012-13 Enrollment: 320 . . . . (586) 465-5545
Prevail Academy (KG-12)
    2012-13 Enrollment: 501 . . . . (586) 783-0173
Housing: Homeownership rate: 57.9%; Median home value: $76,800; Median year structure built: 1956; Homeowner vacancy rate: 3.5%; Median gross rent: $591 per month; Rental vacancy rate: 11.9%
Health Insurance: 83.9% have insurance; 57.4% have private insurance; 40.6% have public insurance; 16.1% do not have insurance; 3.6% of children under 18 do not have insurance
Hospitals: Mclaren Macomb (288 beds)
Transportation: Commute: 89.9% car, 2.9% public transportation, 3.6% walk, 2.4% work from home; Median travel time to work: 23.5 minutes
Airports: Selfridge Angb (general aviation)
Additional Information Contacts
City of Mount Clemens . . . . (586) 469-6818
    http://www.cityofmountclemens.com

NEW BALTIMORE (city). Covers a land area of 4.608 square miles and a water area of 2.124 square miles. Located at 42.69° N. Lat; 82.74° W. Long. Elevation is 587 feet.

History: First a lumbering center with a sawmill and dock, New Baltimore became a year-round resort with fishing, duck hunting, and ice fishing on Lake St. Clair.
Population: 12,084; Growth (since 2000): 63.2%; Density: 2,622.2 persons per square mile; Race: 94.4% White, 2.7% Black/African American, 0.9% Asian, 0.4% American Indian/Alaska Native, 0.0% Native Hawaiian/Other Pacific Islander, 1.4% Two or more races, 1.8% Hispanic of any race; Average household size: 2.72; Median age: 37.1; Age under 18: 28.8%; Age 65 and over: 9.8%; Males per 100 females: 95.9; Marriage status: 19.4% never married, 63.6% now married, 0.9% separated, 5.8% widowed, 11.2% divorced; Foreign born: 2.1%; Speak English only: 95.5%;

With disability: 9.0%; Veterans: 10.1%; Ancestry: 27.7% German, 16.1% Polish, 13.5% Irish, 12.2% Italian, 7.7% English
Employment: 16.8% management, business, and financial, 3.3% computer, engineering, and science, 8.5% education, legal, community service, arts, and media, 6.3% healthcare practitioners, 15.6% service, 28.9% sales and office, 9.6% natural resources, construction, and maintenance, 11.1% production, transportation, and material moving
Income: Per capita: $30,972; Median household: $79,267; Average household: $84,543; Households with income of $100,000 or more: 35.1%; Poverty rate: 6.6%
Educational Attainment: High school diploma or higher: 93.6%; Bachelor's degree or higher: 26.6%; Graduate/professional degree or higher: 11.5%

School District(s)
Anchor Bay SD (PK-12)
    2012-13 Enrollment: 6,214 . . . . (586) 725-2861
Vocational/Technical School(s)
Ross Medical Education Center-New Baltimore (Private, For-profit)
    Fall 2013 Enrollment: 116 . . . . (586) 716-3837
    2013-14 Tuition: $15,680
Housing: Homeownership rate: 79.0%; Median home value: $168,700; Median year structure built: 1993; Homeowner vacancy rate: 1.6%; Median gross rent: $647 per month; Rental vacancy rate: 12.0%
Health Insurance: 93.9% have insurance; 87.3% have private insurance; 20.2% have public insurance; 6.1% do not have insurance; 2.4% of children under 18 do not have insurance
Safety: Violent crime rate: 7.4 per 10,000 population; Property crime rate: 56.0 per 10,000 population
Newspapers: Voice Newspapers (weekly circulation 80000)
Transportation: Commute: 97.2% car, 0.1% public transportation, 0.7% walk, 2.0% work from home; Median travel time to work: 31.5 minutes

NEW HAVEN (village). Covers a land area of 2.534 square miles and a water area of 0.001 square miles. Located at 42.73° N. Lat; 82.80° W. Long. Elevation is 627 feet.

History: Incorporated 1869.
Population: 4,642; Growth (since 2000): 51.2%; Density: 1,831.8 persons per square mile; Race: 76.3% White, 16.9% Black/African American, 0.5% Asian, 0.5% American Indian/Alaska Native, 0.1% Native Hawaiian/Other Pacific Islander, 4.5% Two or more races, 4.8% Hispanic of any race; Average household size: 2.96; Median age: 31.1; Age under 18: 33.0%; Age 65 and over: 6.0%; Males per 100 females: 94.1; Marriage status: 36.0% never married, 47.0% now married, 2.0% separated, 4.7% widowed, 12.3% divorced; Foreign born: 0.3%; Speak English only: 97.0%; With disability: 15.8%; Veterans: 8.2%; Ancestry: 20.8% German, 15.1% Irish, 11.3% American, 10.6% Polish, 10.2% English
Employment: 12.2% management, business, and financial, 4.6% computer, engineering, and science, 3.6% education, legal, community service, arts, and media, 3.3% healthcare practitioners, 12.6% service, 33.4% sales and office, 10.6% natural resources, construction, and maintenance, 19.7% production, transportation, and material moving
Income: Per capita: $20,858; Median household: $58,558; Average household: $65,170; Households with income of $100,000 or more: 19.7%; Poverty rate: 13.4%
Educational Attainment: High school diploma or higher: 85.3%; Bachelor's degree or higher: 14.3%; Graduate/professional degree or higher: 4.8%

School District(s)
L'anse Creuse Public Schools (PK-12)
    2012-13 Enrollment: 11,518 . . . . (586) 783-6300
Merritt Academy (PK-12)
    2012-13 Enrollment: 515 . . . . (586) 749-6000
New Haven Community Schools (PK-12)
    2012-13 Enrollment: 1,348 . . . . (586) 749-5123
Housing: Homeownership rate: 79.4%; Median home value: $101,900; Median year structure built: 1993; Homeowner vacancy rate: 4.5%; Median gross rent: $875 per month; Rental vacancy rate: 13.0%
Health Insurance: 87.6% have insurance; 66.5% have private insurance; 31.3% have public insurance; 12.4% do not have insurance; 1.2% of children under 18 do not have insurance
Transportation: Commute: 94.3% car, 0.0% public transportation, 2.7% walk, 2.2% work from home; Median travel time to work: 33.3 minutes

RAY (township). Covers a land area of 36.580 square miles and a water area of 0.114 square miles. Located at 42.76° N. Lat; 82.92° W. Long.
Population: 3,739; Growth (since 2000): 0.0%; Density: 102.2 persons per square mile; Race: 97.6% White, 0.4% Black/African American, 0.7% Asian, 0.3% American Indian/Alaska Native, 0.0% Native Hawaiian/Other Pacific Islander, 0.5% Two or more races, 1.7% Hispanic of any race; Average household size: 2.66; Median age: 45.2; Age under 18: 21.6%; Age 65 and over: 14.9%; Males per 100 females: 106.8; Marriage status: 20.7% never married, 65.8% now married, 0.0% separated, 4.5% widowed, 9.0% divorced; Foreign born: 8.3%; Speak English only: 89.6%; With disability: 14.2%; Veterans: 7.5%; Ancestry: 29.4% German, 18.9% Polish, 12.8% Italian, 10.4% Irish, 7.1% English
Employment: 10.7% management, business, and financial, 10.3% computer, engineering, and science, 12.4% education, legal, community service, arts, and media, 1.9% healthcare practitioners, 14.7% service, 24.4% sales and office, 8.5% natural resources, construction, and maintenance, 16.9% production, transportation, and material moving
Income: Per capita: $32,021; Median household: $76,102; Average household: $79,109; Households with income of $100,000 or more: 29.9%; Poverty rate: 4.4%
Educational Attainment: High school diploma or higher: 89.0%; Bachelor's degree or higher: 22.2%; Graduate/professional degree or higher: 10.2%

School District(s)
New Haven Community Schools (PK-12)
    2012-13 Enrollment: 1,348 . . . . (586) 749-5123
Housing: Homeownership rate: 88.5%; Median home value: $177,600; Median year structure built: 1973; Homeowner vacancy rate: 1.6%; Median gross rent: $1,269 per month; Rental vacancy rate: 2.4%
Health Insurance: 89.7% have insurance; 78.7% have private insurance; 24.9% have public insurance; 10.3% do not have insurance; 0.0% of children under 18 do not have insurance
Transportation: Commute: 94.3% car, 0.0% public transportation, 0.9% walk, 2.6% work from home; Median travel time to work: 30.8 minutes

RICHMOND (city). Covers a land area of 2.850 square miles and a water area of 0.039 square miles. Located at 42.81° N. Lat; 82.75° W. Long. Elevation is 732 feet.
History: Richmond was first known as Beebe's Corners. A settlement about a mile east was called Ridgeway, and later Lenox. A business district developed between the two settlements, and in 1879 the whole was merged and incorporated as Richmond. Harness racing was popular at the Sportsman's Park in Richmond beginning in the 1880's.
Population: 5,735; Growth (since 2000): 17.1%; Density: 2,012.1 persons per square mile; Race: 94.2% White, 1.0% Black/African American, 0.2% Asian, 0.3% American Indian/Alaska Native, 0.2% Native Hawaiian/Other Pacific Islander, 1.5% Two or more races, 4.6% Hispanic of any race; Average household size: 2.49; Median age: 39.9; Age under 18: 23.8%; Age 65 and over: 15.5%; Males per 100 females: 93.0; Marriage status: 23.9% never married, 57.7% now married, 0.5% separated, 6.5% widowed, 11.8% divorced; Foreign born: 6.7%; Speak English only: 90.5%; With disability: 15.2%; Veterans: 13.9%; Ancestry: 33.1% German, 17.1% Polish, 11.8% Irish, 8.9% English, 8.4% Italian
Employment: 12.8% management, business, and financial, 6.0% computer, engineering, and science, 4.2% education, legal, community service, arts, and media, 8.5% healthcare practitioners, 23.4% service, 17.5% sales and office, 11.5% natural resources, construction, and maintenance, 16.1% production, transportation, and material moving
Income: Per capita: $26,893; Median household: $48,465; Average household: $61,469; Households with income of $100,000 or more: 16.5%; Poverty rate: 17.3%
Educational Attainment: High school diploma or higher: 86.1%; Bachelor's degree or higher: 14.0%; Graduate/professional degree or higher: 6.2%

School District(s)
Richmond Community Schools (PK-12)
    2012-13 Enrollment: 1,646 . . . . (586) 727-3565
Housing: Homeownership rate: 74.9%; Median home value: $113,900; Median year structure built: 1981; Homeowner vacancy rate: 2.4%; Median gross rent: $683 per month; Rental vacancy rate: 17.4%
Health Insurance: 89.2% have insurance; 71.3% have private insurance; 35.5% have public insurance; 10.8% do not have insurance; 3.1% of children under 18 do not have insurance
Safety: Violent crime rate: 29.6 per 10,000 population; Property crime rate: 210.8 per 10,000 population

Transportation: Commute: 93.8% car, 0.0% public transportation, 1.8% walk, 4.4% work from home; Median travel time to work: 26.8 minutes
Additional Information Contacts
City of Richmond . . . . (586) 727-7571
    http://www.cityofrichmond.net

RICHMOND (township). Covers a land area of 37.491 square miles and a water area of 0.057 square miles. Located at 42.85° N. Lat; 82.81° W. Long. Elevation is 732 feet.
History: Richmond Township was named in 1840 for Richmond, New York, by its first postmaster, who had formerly lived in New York.
Population: 3,665; Growth (since 2000): 7.3%; Density: 97.8 persons per square mile; Race: 96.5% White, 0.9% Black/African American, 0.1% Asian, 0.4% American Indian/Alaska Native, 0.0% Native Hawaiian/Other Pacific Islander, 1.2% Two or more races, 1.8% Hispanic of any race; Average household size: 2.94; Median age: 42.0; Age under 18: 24.5%; Age 65 and over: 11.6%; Males per 100 females: 110.5; Marriage status: 22.6% never married, 67.7% now married, 0.3% separated, 4.6% widowed, 5.1% divorced; Foreign born: 1.6%; Speak English only: 98.2%; With disability: 10.8%; Veterans: 9.5%; Ancestry: 36.9% German, 19.3% Polish, 9.9% English, 9.5% Italian, 7.6% Irish
Employment: 14.1% management, business, and financial, 2.0% computer, engineering, and science, 8.5% education, legal, community service, arts, and media, 5.3% healthcare practitioners, 19.0% service, 21.2% sales and office, 14.6% natural resources, construction, and maintenance, 15.4% production, transportation, and material moving
Income: Per capita: $28,494; Median household: $68,015; Average household: $84,001; Households with income of $100,000 or more: 27.2%; Poverty rate: 8.3%
Educational Attainment: High school diploma or higher: 90.0%; Bachelor's degree or higher: 18.4%; Graduate/professional degree or higher: 5.3%

School District(s)
Richmond Community Schools (PK-12)
    2012-13 Enrollment: 1,646 . . . . (586) 727-3565
Housing: Homeownership rate: 92.6%; Median home value: $182,200; Median year structure built: 1979; Homeowner vacancy rate: 1.0%; Median gross rent: $979 per month; Rental vacancy rate: 7.1%
Health Insurance: 95.2% have insurance; 88.4% have private insurance; 22.0% have public insurance; 4.8% do not have insurance; 0.0% of children under 18 do not have insurance
Transportation: Commute: 94.5% car, 0.0% public transportation, 0.0% walk, 4.3% work from home; Median travel time to work: 31.5 minutes

ROMEO (village). Covers a land area of 2.017 square miles and a water area of <.001 square miles. Located at 42.80° N. Lat; 83.00° W. Long. Elevation is 810 feet.
History: Romeo was settled by a group of New Englanders in the 1820's. Their interest in culture and education led to the literary name for the town, as well as to a number of academies that flourished in the 1800's.
Population: 3,596; Growth (since 2000): -3.4%; Density: 1,783.0 persons per square mile; Race: 91.9% White, 3.8% Black/African American, 0.5% Asian, 0.2% American Indian/Alaska Native, 0.0% Native Hawaiian/Other Pacific Islander, 2.6% Two or more races, 5.7% Hispanic of any race; Average household size: 2.36; Median age: 40.9; Age under 18: 23.5%; Age 65 and over: 15.3%; Males per 100 females: 86.4; Marriage status: 27.8% never married, 48.5% now married, 1.4% separated, 8.4% widowed, 15.4% divorced; Foreign born: 2.3%; Speak English only: 94.3%; With disability: 15.7%; Veterans: 9.6%; Ancestry: 35.3% German, 14.9% Polish, 14.8% English, 13.7% Irish, 12.7% Italian
Employment: 8.5% management, business, and financial, 5.6% computer, engineering, and science, 11.0% education, legal, community service, arts, and media, 4.1% healthcare practitioners, 19.7% service, 21.0% sales and office, 9.2% natural resources, construction, and maintenance, 20.9% production, transportation, and material moving
Income: Per capita: $25,733; Median household: $43,786; Average household: $57,610; Households with income of $100,000 or more: 15.5%; Poverty rate: 11.2%
Educational Attainment: High school diploma or higher: 86.8%; Bachelor's degree or higher: 23.1%; Graduate/professional degree or higher: 10.1%

School District(s)
Romeo Community Schools (PK-12)
    2012-13 Enrollment: 5,287 . . . . (586) 752-0225

Housing: Homeownership rate: 72.2%; Median home value: $141,300; Median year structure built: 1956; Homeowner vacancy rate: 3.4%; Median gross rent: $753 per month; Rental vacancy rate: 13.9%
Health Insurance: 85.8% have insurance; 63.9% have private insurance; 37.7% have public insurance; 14.2% do not have insurance; 3.2% of children under 18 do not have insurance
Safety: Violent crime rate: 13.9 per 10,000 population; Property crime rate: 97.3 per 10,000 population
Newspapers: Romeo Observer (weekly circulation 6700)
Transportation: Commute: 87.1% car, 0.0% public transportation, 4.7% walk, 7.5% work from home; Median travel time to work: 27.2 minutes

ROSEVILLE (city). Covers a land area of 9.826 square miles and a water area of 0.029 square miles. Located at 42.51° N. Lat; 82.94° W. Long. Elevation is 617 feet.
History: Named for William C. Rose, a local tavern-keeper who became the first postmaster in 1836. Roseville began in the 1840's, but grew with the industrial expansion of Detroit in the 1900's, when many residences were built here for people employed in the larger city.
Population: 47,299; Growth (since 2000): -1.7%; Density: 4,813.9 persons per square mile; Race: 83.1% White, 11.8% Black/African American, 1.6% Asian, 0.4% American Indian/Alaska Native, 0.0% Native Hawaiian/Other Pacific Islander, 2.6% Two or more races, 2.0% Hispanic of any race; Average household size: 2.41; Median age: 37.9; Age under 18: 23.0%; Age 65 and over: 13.1%; Males per 100 females: 93.8; Marriage status: 36.1% never married, 41.7% now married, 1.2% separated, 7.6% widowed, 14.6% divorced; Foreign born: 3.6%; Speak English only: 93.7%; With disability: 17.1%; Veterans: 7.9%; Ancestry: 23.9% German, 17.2% Polish, 11.8% Italian, 11.7% Irish, 6.5% English
Employment: 8.3% management, business, and financial, 4.2% computer, engineering, and science, 5.9% education, legal, community service, arts, and media, 3.1% healthcare practitioners, 22.8% service, 27.0% sales and office, 9.1% natural resources, construction, and maintenance, 19.5% production, transportation, and material moving
Income: Per capita: $20,578; Median household: $40,337; Average household: $48,564; Households with income of $100,000 or more: 8.2%; Poverty rate: 16.3%
Educational Attainment: High school diploma or higher: 85.3%; Bachelor's degree or higher: 9.8%; Graduate/professional degree or higher: 2.4%

School District(s)
Conner Creek Academy East (KG-12)
    2012-13 Enrollment: 1,115 . . . . (586) 779-8055
Fraser Public Schools (PK-12)
    2012-13 Enrollment: 5,291 . . . . (586) 439-7000
Global Preparatory Academy (PK-12)
    2012-13 Enrollment: 163 . . . . (586) 575-9500
Reach Charter Academy (KG-12)
    2012-13 Enrollment: 686 . . . . (586) 498-9171
Roseville Community Schools (PK-12)
    2012-13 Enrollment: 5,129 . . . . (586) 445-5505
Vocational/Technical School(s)
Dorsey Business Schools-Roseville (Private, For-profit)
    Fall 2013 Enrollment: 515 . . . . (586) 296-3225
    2013-14 Tuition: In-state $19,728; Out-of-state $19,728
Dorsey Business Schools-Roseville Culinary Academy (Private, For-profit)
    Fall 2013 Enrollment: 165 . . . . (586) 296-3225
    2013-14 Tuition: In-state $20,736; Out-of-state $20,736
Housing: Homeownership rate: 70.3%; Median home value: $66,100; Median year structure built: 1959; Homeowner vacancy rate: 2.8%; Median gross rent: $846 per month; Rental vacancy rate: 8.8%
Health Insurance: 85.7% have insurance; 64.3% have private insurance; 35.8% have public insurance; 14.3% do not have insurance; 3.4% of children under 18 do not have insurance
Safety: Violent crime rate: 46.1 per 10,000 population; Property crime rate: 416.7 per 10,000 population
Transportation: Commute: 93.7% car, 1.7% public transportation, 1.4% walk, 2.3% work from home; Median travel time to work: 24.7 minutes
Additional Information Contacts
City of Roseville. . . . . (586) 445-5443
    http://www.roseville-mi.gov

SAINT CLAIR SHORES (city). Covers a land area of 11.619 square miles and a water area of 2.659 square miles. Located at 42.49° N. Lat; 82.89° W. Long. Elevation is 581 feet.
History: The area of St. Clair Shores was settled in the 1770's by French families from Detroit. The village was named and incorporated in 1925, after having been called L'Anse Cruise (deep bay) by the residents. St. Clair Shores was incorporated as a city in 1950.
Population: 59,715; Growth (since 2000): -5.4%; Density: 5,139.5 persons per square mile; Race: 92.7% White, 3.9% Black/African American, 1.0% Asian, 0.3% American Indian/Alaska Native, 0.0% Native Hawaiian/Other Pacific Islander, 1.7% Two or more races, 1.7% Hispanic of any race; Average household size: 2.24; Median age: 44.2; Age under 18: 19.0%; Age 65 and over: 19.2%; Males per 100 females: 91.5; Marriage status: 29.1% never married, 49.1% now married, 0.8% separated, 9.0% widowed, 12.8% divorced; Foreign born: 4.9%; Speak English only: 93.4%; With disability: 15.1%; Veterans: 10.6%; Ancestry: 24.0% German, 18.2% Polish, 15.2% Irish, 14.3% Italian, 8.4% English
Employment: 13.7% management, business, and financial, 4.4% computer, engineering, and science, 8.9% education, legal, community service, arts, and media, 7.3% healthcare practitioners, 17.5% service, 26.6% sales and office, 8.8% natural resources, construction, and maintenance, 12.8% production, transportation, and material moving
Income: Per capita: $29,479; Median household: $53,069; Average household: $64,420; Households with income of $100,000 or more: 17.8%; Poverty rate: 10.3%
Educational Attainment: High school diploma or higher: 91.8%; Bachelor's degree or higher: 24.1%; Graduate/professional degree or higher: 7.4%

School District(s)
Lake Shore Public Schools (Macomb) (KG-12)
    2012-13 Enrollment: 3,667 . . . . (586) 285-8480
Lakeview Public Schools (Macomb) (PK-12)
    2012-13 Enrollment: 3,864 . . . . (586) 445-4000
South Lake Schools (KG-12)
    2012-13 Enrollment: 2,052 . . . . (586) 435-1600
Housing: Homeownership rate: 81.9%; Median home value: $94,600; Median year structure built: 1957; Homeowner vacancy rate: 2.1%; Median gross rent: $865 per month; Rental vacancy rate: 10.2%
Health Insurance: 89.0% have insurance; 77.4% have private insurance; 29.6% have public insurance; 11.0% do not have insurance; 3.4% of children under 18 do not have insurance
Transportation: Commute: 94.9% car, 1.5% public transportation, 0.6% walk, 2.4% work from home; Median travel time to work: 26.6 minutes
Additional Information Contacts
City of Saint Clair Shores . . . . (586) 447-3311
    http://www.stclairshores.net

SHELBY (charter township). Covers a land area of 34.257 square miles and a water area of 0.887 square miles. Located at 42.67° N. Lat; 83.04° W. Long. Elevation is 682 feet.
Population: 73,804; Growth (since 2000): 13.3%; Density: 2,154.4 persons per square mile; Race: 90.9% White, 3.2% Black/African American, 3.3% Asian, 0.3% American Indian/Alaska Native, 0.0% Native Hawaiian/Other Pacific Islander, 1.7% Two or more races, 2.4% Hispanic of any race; Average household size: 2.60; Median age: 41.0; Age under 18: 22.7%; Age 65 and over: 14.5%; Males per 100 females: 96.5; Marriage status: 26.8% never married, 57.8% now married, 0.7% separated, 6.5% widowed, 8.9% divorced; Foreign born: 13.2%; Speak English only: 83.9%; With disability: 10.6%; Veterans: 8.4%; Ancestry: 19.0% German, 14.9% Polish, 13.7% Italian, 10.2% Irish, 9.2% American
Employment: 17.0% management, business, and financial, 7.5% computer, engineering, and science, 9.3% education, legal, community service, arts, and media, 5.9% healthcare practitioners, 15.3% service, 26.6% sales and office, 6.3% natural resources, construction, and maintenance, 11.9% production, transportation, and material moving
Income: Per capita: $30,947; Median household: $63,212; Average household: $79,646; Households with income of $100,000 or more: 27.9%; Poverty rate: 9.6%
Educational Attainment: High school diploma or higher: 90.6%; Bachelor's degree or higher: 30.2%; Graduate/professional degree or higher: 11.5%

School District(s)
Utica Community Schools (PK-12)
    2012-13 Enrollment: 28,415 . . . . (586) 797-1000

Vocational/Technical School(s)

Regency Beauty Institute-Detroit Lakeside (Private, For-profit)
Fall 2013 Enrollment: 102 . . . . (800) 787-6456
2013-14 Tuition: $17,300

Housing: Homeownership rate: 78.3%; Median home value: $182,300; Median year structure built: 1986; Homeowner vacancy rate: 1.8%; Median gross rent: $909 per month; Rental vacancy rate: 14.0%

Health Insurance: 90.4% have insurance; 79.8% have private insurance; 25.6% have public insurance; 9.6% do not have insurance; 4.4% of children under 18 do not have insurance

Transportation: Commute: 96.3% car, 0.3% public transportation, 0.5% walk, 2.6% work from home; Median travel time to work: 27.6 minutes

Additional Information Contacts

Shelby Charter Township . . . . (586) 731-5102
http://www.shelbytwp.org

STERLING HEIGHTS (city). Covers a land area of 36.505 square miles and a water area of 0.294 square miles. Located at 42.58° N. Lat; 83.03° W. Long. Elevation is 614 feet.

History: Sterling Heights began as the township of Jefferson, but was renamed to honor early settler Azariah W. Sterling. In 1966 the township was incorporated as a city.

Population: 129,699; Growth (since 2000): 4.2%; Density: 3,552.9 persons per square mile; Race: 85.1% White, 5.2% Black/African American, 6.7% Asian, 0.2% American Indian/Alaska Native, 0.0% Native Hawaiian/Other Pacific Islander, 2.2% Two or more races, 1.9% Hispanic of any race; Average household size: 2.61; Median age: 40.4; Age under 18: 21.7%; Age 65 and over: 15.2%; Males per 100 females: 94.1; Marriage status: 29.3% never married, 54.8% now married, 1.0% separated, 7.3% widowed, 8.5% divorced; Foreign born: 24.2%; Speak English only: 69.6%; With disability: 12.8%; Veterans: 7.4%; Ancestry: 16.3% German, 15.6% Polish, 9.8% Italian, 8.6% Irish, 8.0% Assyrian/Chaldean/Syriac

Employment: 13.3% management, business, and financial, 7.4% computer, engineering, and science, 8.6% education, legal, community service, arts, and media, 5.9% healthcare practitioners, 18.0% service, 26.4% sales and office, 6.5% natural resources, construction, and maintenance, 13.9% production, transportation, and material moving

Income: Per capita: $26,691; Median household: $57,075; Average household: $68,810; Households with income of $100,000 or more: 22.1%; Poverty rate: 13.0%

Educational Attainment: High school diploma or higher: 85.8%; Bachelor's degree or higher: 25.8%; Graduate/professional degree or higher: 9.2%

School District(s)

Huron Academy (KG-12)
2012-13 Enrollment: 520 . . . . (586) 446-9170
Macomb ISD (PK-12)
2012-13 Enrollment: 2,316 . . . . (586) 228-3300
Noor International Academy (KG-12)
2012-13 Enrollment: 107 . . . . (313) 565-0507
Utica Community Schools (PK-12)
2012-13 Enrollment: 28,415 . . . . (586) 797-1000
Warren Consolidated Schools (KG-12)
2012-13 Enrollment: 15,193 . . . . (586) 825-2400

Vocational/Technical School(s)

Paul Mitchell the School-Michigan (Private, For-profit)
Fall 2013 Enrollment: 237 . . . . (586) 939-8600
2013-14 Tuition: $15,550

Housing: Homeownership rate: 76.2%; Median home value: $144,200; Median year structure built: 1976; Homeowner vacancy rate: 1.7%; Median gross rent: $856 per month; Rental vacancy rate: 8.7%

Health Insurance: 87.7% have insurance; 71.2% have private insurance; 30.1% have public insurance; 12.3% do not have insurance; 4.3% of children under 18 do not have insurance

Safety: Violent crime rate: 18.7 per 10,000 population; Property crime rate: 190.3 per 10,000 population

Transportation: Commute: 96.3% car, 0.4% public transportation, 0.6% walk, 2.2% work from home; Median travel time to work: 25.7 minutes

Additional Information Contacts

City of Sterling Heights . . . . (586) 446-2489
http://www.ci.sterling-heights.mi.us

UTICA (city). Covers a land area of 1.710 square miles and a water area of 0.032 square miles. Located at 42.63° N. Lat; 83.02° W. Long. Elevation is 656 feet.

History: Utica was first called Hog's Hollow. It was settled by a group of German immigrants in 1817.

Population: 4,757; Growth (since 2000): 3.9%; Density: 2,782.6 persons per square mile; Race: 90.4% White, 1.9% Black/African American, 3.5% Asian, 0.5% American Indian/Alaska Native, 0.0% Native Hawaiian/Other Pacific Islander, 1.8% Two or more races, 3.8% Hispanic of any race; Average household size: 2.13; Median age: 41.7; Age under 18: 17.9%; Age 65 and over: 17.4%; Males per 100 females: 90.1; Marriage status: 31.3% never married, 43.1% now married, 1.4% separated, 10.5% widowed, 15.0% divorced; Foreign born: 12.6%; Speak English only: 87.9%; With disability: 17.3%; Veterans: 9.4%; Ancestry: 26.3% German, 12.3% Polish, 10.9% Italian, 10.8% Irish, 9.6% American

Employment: 11.6% management, business, and financial, 5.0% computer, engineering, and science, 7.2% education, legal, community service, arts, and media, 4.1% healthcare practitioners, 19.2% service, 33.5% sales and office, 7.2% natural resources, construction, and maintenance, 12.2% production, transportation, and material moving

Income: Per capita: $24,689; Median household: $45,500; Average household: $56,311; Households with income of $100,000 or more: 13.7%; Poverty rate: 10.7%

Educational Attainment: High school diploma or higher: 90.4%; Bachelor's degree or higher: 15.0%; Graduate/professional degree or higher: 4.5%

School District(s)

Utica Community Schools (PK-12)
2012-13 Enrollment: 28,415 . . . . (586) 797-1000

Housing: Homeownership rate: 58.1%; Median home value: $114,000; Median year structure built: 1972; Homeowner vacancy rate: 4.7%; Median gross rent: $706 per month; Rental vacancy rate: 10.7%

Health Insurance: 83.2% have insurance; 69.8% have private insurance; 29.8% have public insurance; 16.8% do not have insurance; 3.6% of children under 18 do not have insurance

Safety: Violent crime rate: 52.5 per 10,000 population; Property crime rate: 379.9 per 10,000 population

Transportation: Commute: 93.9% car, 1.7% public transportation, 1.4% walk, 3.1% work from home; Median travel time to work: 24.3 minutes

Additional Information Contacts

City of Utica . . . . (586) 739-1600
http://www.cityofutica.org

WARREN (city). Covers a land area of 34.381 square miles and a water area of 0.077 square miles. Located at 42.49° N. Lat; 83.03° W. Long. Elevation is 623 feet.

History: Named for General Joseph Warren, Revolutionary War leader who fell at the Battle of Bunker Hill. Established 1837. Incorporated as a city 1957.

Population: 134,056; Growth (since 2000): -3.0%; Density: 3,899.2 persons per square mile; Race: 78.4% White, 13.5% Black/African American, 4.6% Asian, 0.4% American Indian/Alaska Native, 0.0% Native Hawaiian/Other Pacific Islander, 2.6% Two or more races, 2.1% Hispanic of any race; Average household size: 2.49; Median age: 39.4; Age under 18: 22.7%; Age 65 and over: 16.1%; Males per 100 females: 93.8; Marriage status: 34.4% never married, 46.0% now married, 1.4% separated, 8.6% widowed, 11.0% divorced; Foreign born: 11.4%; Speak English only: 85.0%; With disability: 15.9%; Veterans: 8.7%; Ancestry: 17.8% Polish, 17.8% German, 10.5% Irish, 8.9% Italian, 6.3% English

Employment: 10.9% management, business, and financial, 4.4% computer, engineering, and science, 6.2% education, legal, community service, arts, and media, 4.9% healthcare practitioners, 20.4% service, 28.4% sales and office, 8.0% natural resources, construction, and maintenance, 16.9% production, transportation, and material moving

Income: Per capita: $21,744; Median household: $43,962; Average household: $53,776; Households with income of $100,000 or more: 11.8%; Poverty rate: 18.2%

Educational Attainment: High school diploma or higher: 83.8%; Bachelor's degree or higher: 16.3%; Graduate/professional degree or higher: 4.9%

School District(s)

Academy of Warren (KG-12)
2012-13 Enrollment: 657 . . . . (586) 552-8010
Center Line Public Schools (PK-12)
2012-13 Enrollment: 2,705 . . . . (586) 510-2000

Clintondale Community Schools (PK-12)
   2012-13 Enrollment: 3,407 . . . . (586) 791-6300
Conner Creek Academy East (KG-12)
   2012-13 Enrollment: 1,115 . . . . (586) 779-8055
Fitzgerald Public Schools (PK-12)
   2012-13 Enrollment: 2,878 . . . . (586) 757-1750
Great Oaks Academy (KG-12)
   2012-13 Enrollment: 718 . . . . (586) 427-4540
Macomb ISD (PK-12)
   2012-13 Enrollment: 2,316 . . . . (586) 228-3300
Van Dyke Public Schools (PK-12)
   2012-13 Enrollment: 2,892 . . . . (586) 758-8334
Warren Consolidated Schools (KG-12)
   2012-13 Enrollment: 15,193 . . . . (586) 825-2400
Warren Woods Public Schools (PK-12)
   2012-13 Enrollment: 3,341 . . . . (586) 439-4469

Two-year College(s)
Macomb Community College (Public)
   Fall 2013 Enrollment: 23,446 . . . . (586) 445-7999
   2013-14 Tuition: In-state $4,316; Out-of-state $5,556

Vocational/Technical School(s)
Mr Bela's School of Cosmetology Inc (Private, For-profit)
   Fall 2013 Enrollment: 117 . . . . (586) 751-4000
   2013-14 Tuition: $14,325

Housing: Homeownership rate: 74.4%; Median home value: $89,500; Median year structure built: 1964; Homeowner vacancy rate: 2.2%; Median gross rent: $804 per month; Rental vacancy rate: 9.0%

Health Insurance: 85.7% have insurance; 63.7% have private insurance; 36.5% have public insurance; 14.3% do not have insurance; 4.3% of children under 18 do not have insurance

Hospitals: Saint John Macomb - Oakland Hospital - Macomb Center (535 beds); Southeast Michigan Surgical Hospital (20 beds)

Safety: Violent crime rate: 50.6 per 10,000 population; Property crime rate: 261.5 per 10,000 population

Newspapers: C & G Newspapers (weekly circulation 545000)

Transportation: Commute: 94.8% car, 1.0% public transportation, 0.9% walk, 1.9% work from home; Median travel time to work: 23.8 minutes

Additional Information Contacts
City of Warren . . . . (586) 574-4500
   http://www.cityofwarren.org

WASHINGTON (township).
Covers a land area of 35.476 square miles and a water area of 1.276 square miles. Located at 42.77° N. Lat; 83.05° W. Long. Elevation is 702 feet.

Population: 25,139; Growth (since 2000): 31.8%; Density: 708.6 persons per square mile; Race: 94.8% White, 1.6% Black/African American, 1.0% Asian, 0.2% American Indian/Alaska Native, 0.0% Native Hawaiian/Other Pacific Islander, 1.3% Two or more races, 3.9% Hispanic of any race; Average household size: 2.70; Median age: 41.3; Age under 18: 25.0%; Age 65 and over: 14.1%; Males per 100 females: 95.9; Marriage status: 23.9% never married, 62.3% now married, 0.5% separated, 3.7% widowed, 10.2% divorced; Foreign born: 10.5%; Speak English only: 87.1%; With disability: 9.3%; Veterans: 8.1%; Ancestry: 23.7% German, 17.2% Polish, 14.6% Italian, 10.7% Irish, 8.7% English

Employment: 18.7% management, business, and financial, 7.3% computer, engineering, and science, 9.3% education, legal, community service, arts, and media, 6.9% healthcare practitioners, 12.0% service, 24.7% sales and office, 8.2% natural resources, construction, and maintenance, 12.8% production, transportation, and material moving

Income: Per capita: $35,562; Median household: $75,449; Average household: $94,759; Households with income of $100,000 or more: 33.5%; Poverty rate: 6.6%

Educational Attainment: High school diploma or higher: 93.1%; Bachelor's degree or higher: 30.7%; Graduate/professional degree or higher: 10.8%

School District(s)
Romeo Community Schools (PK-12)
   2012-13 Enrollment: 5,287 . . . . (586) 752-0225

Housing: Homeownership rate: 84.0%; Median home value: $216,100; Median year structure built: 1992; Homeowner vacancy rate: 2.1%; Median gross rent: $941 per month; Rental vacancy rate: 13.0%

Health Insurance: 90.4% have insurance; 78.8% have private insurance; 25.6% have public insurance; 9.6% do not have insurance; 3.1% of children under 18 do not have insurance

Transportation: Commute: 93.2% car, 0.0% public transportation, 1.0% walk, 4.5% work from home; Median travel time to work: 28.4 minutes

Additional Information Contacts
Washington Charter Township . . . . (586) 786-0010
   http://www.washingtontownship.org

Manistee County

Located in northwestern Michigan; bounded on the west by Lake Michigan; drained by the Manistee and Little Manistee Rivers; includes part of Manistee National Forest, and several lakes. Covers a land area of 542.149 square miles, a water area of 738.415 square miles, and is located in the Eastern Time Zone at 44.35° N. Lat., 86.60° W. Long. The county was founded in 1855. County seat is Manistee.

Weather Station: Manistee 3 SE										Elevation: 669 feet	
	Jan	Feb	Mar	Apr	May	Jun	Jul	Aug	Sep	Oct	Nov	Dec
High	30	33	42	56	66	76	80	78	71	58	45	34
Low	18	19	24	35	44	53	58	58	51	41	32	23
Precip	2.1	1.5	1.9	3.1	3.2	3.6	3.2	3.6	3.6	3.5	3.2	2.4
Snow	na	na	na	na	tr	0.0	0.0	0.0	0.0	tr	na	na

High and Low temperatures in degrees Fahrenheit; Precipitation and Snow in inches

Population: 24,733; Growth (since 2000): 0.8%; Density: 45.6 persons per square mile; Race: 92.2% White, 2.9% Black/African American, 0.3% Asian, 2.1% American Indian/Alaska Native, 0.1% Native Hawaiian/Other Pacific Islander, 1.9% two or more races, 2.6% Hispanic of any race; Average household size: 2.27; Median age: 47.1; Age under 18: 19.1%; Age 65 and over: 20.7%; Males per 100 females: 107.4; Marriage status: 25.0% never married, 54.7% now married, 1.4% separated, 7.9% widowed, 12.3% divorced; Foreign born: 1.4%; Speak English only: 95.9%; With disability: 18.6%; Veterans: 14.1%; Ancestry: 27.2% German, 15.4% Polish, 12.7% Irish, 11.1% English, 5.6% French

Religion: Six largest groups: 20.6% Catholicism, 8.9% Lutheran, 5.1% Methodist/Pietist, 1.7% Baptist, 1.2% Presbyterian-Reformed, 0.9% European Free-Church

Economy: Unemployment rate: 5.9%; Leading industries: 18.8% retail trade; 11.8% other services (except public administration); 11.4% health care and social assistance; Farms: 324 totaling 44,298 acres; Company size: 0 employ 1,000 or more persons, 1 employs 500 to 999 persons, 5 employ 100 to 499 persons, 563 employ less than 100 persons; Business ownership: 616 women-owned, n/a Black-owned, n/a Hispanic-owned, n/a Asian-owned

Employment: 10.6% management, business, and financial, 2.3% computer, engineering, and science, 8.3% education, legal, community service, arts, and media, 5.6% healthcare practitioners, 24.6% service, 23.4% sales and office, 11.1% natural resources, construction, and maintenance, 14.1% production, transportation, and material moving

Income: Per capita: $22,702; Median household: $41,551; Average household: $53,044; Households with income of $100,000 or more: 9.9%; Poverty rate: 16.9%

Educational Attainment: High school diploma or higher: 88.8%; Bachelor's degree or higher: 19.1%; Graduate/professional degree or higher: 7.5%

Housing: Homeownership rate: 78.9%; Median home value: $109,900; Median year structure built: 1971; Homeowner vacancy rate: 4.0%; Median gross rent: $669 per month; Rental vacancy rate: 13.9%

Vital Statistics: Birth rate: 68.7 per 10,000 population; Death rate: 116.6 per 10,000 population; Age-adjusted cancer mortality rate: 202.1 deaths per 100,000 population

Health Insurance: 87.2% have insurance; 65.1% have private insurance; 43.1% have public insurance; 12.8% do not have insurance; 5.0% of children under 18 do not have insurance

Health Care: Physicians: 14.6 per 10,000 population; Hospital beds: 13.8 per 10,000 population; Hospital admissions: 674.5 per 10,000 population

Air Quality Index: 86.5% good, 12.7% moderate, 0.8% unhealthy for sensitive individuals, 0.0% unhealthy (percent of days)

Transportation: Commute: 90.4% car, 0.4% public transportation, 2.6% walk, 5.4% work from home; Median travel time to work: 19.5 minutes

Presidential Election: 52.2% Obama, 46.3% Romney (2012)

National and State Parks: Manistee River State Game Area; Orchard Beach State Park

Additional Information Contacts
Manistee Government . . . . (231) 398-3500
   http://www.manisteecountymi.gov

Manistee County Communities

ARCADIA (CDP). Covers a land area of 0.522 square miles and a water area of <.001 square miles. Located at 44.49° N. Lat; 86.24° W. Long. Elevation is 594 feet.
Population: 291; Growth (since 2000): n/a; Density: 557.7 persons per square mile; Race: 99.3% White, 0.0% Black/African American, 0.3% Asian, 0.0% American Indian/Alaska Native, 0.0% Native Hawaiian/Other Pacific Islander, 0.3% Two or more races, 1.7% Hispanic of any race; Average household size: 2.03; Median age: 61.8; Age under 18: 12.7%; Age 65 and over: 42.6%; Males per 100 females: 98.0
Housing: Homeownership rate: 87.4%; Homeowner vacancy rate: 4.5%; Rental vacancy rate: 20.8%

ARCADIA (township). Covers a land area of 18.594 square miles and a water area of 0.387 square miles. Located at 44.47° N. Lat; 86.20° W. Long. Elevation is 594 feet.
History: Arcadia Township was organized in 1870. The village of Arcadia was settled by a German immigrant.
Population: 639; Growth (since 2000): 2.9%; Density: 34.4 persons per square mile; Race: 94.8% White, 0.0% Black/African American, 0.2% Asian, 0.6% American Indian/Alaska Native, 0.0% Native Hawaiian/Other Pacific Islander, 2.0% Two or more races, 4.7% Hispanic of any race; Average household size: 2.16; Median age: 56.1; Age under 18: 17.7%; Age 65 and over: 31.9%; Males per 100 females: 101.6
Housing: Homeownership rate: 89.9%; Homeowner vacancy rate: 2.9%; Rental vacancy rate: 20.5%

BEAR LAKE (township). Covers a land area of 34.689 square miles and a water area of 1.394 square miles. Located at 44.38° N. Lat; 86.13° W. Long. Elevation is 791 feet.
Population: 1,751; Growth (since 2000): 10.3%; Density: 50.5 persons per square mile; Race: 97.0% White, 0.3% Black/African American, 0.0% Asian, 1.1% American Indian/Alaska Native, 0.1% Native Hawaiian/Other Pacific Islander, 1.1% Two or more races, 2.1% Hispanic of any race; Average household size: 2.49; Median age: 44.5; Age under 18: 23.6%; Age 65 and over: 20.2%; Males per 100 females: 100.8
School District(s)
Bear Lake Schools (PK-12)
   2012-13 Enrollment: 355 . . . . (231) 864-3133
Housing: Homeownership rate: 85.5%; Homeowner vacancy rate: 4.2%; Rental vacancy rate: 17.3%

BEAR LAKE (village). Covers a land area of 0.308 square miles and a water area of 0.026 square miles. Located at 44.42° N. Lat; 86.15° W. Long. Elevation is 791 feet.
History: Bear Lake Village, on the shores of Bear Lake, was first a lumber center, but became a tourist trading center and a shipping point for fruit from the surrounding farms and orchards. The village was settled in 1863 by Russell F. Smith, and incorporated in 1893.
Population: 286; Growth (since 2000): -10.1%; Density: 927.4 persons per square mile; Race: 94.1% White, 0.0% Black/African American, 0.0% Asian, 3.1% American Indian/Alaska Native, 0.3% Native Hawaiian/Other Pacific Islander, 1.4% Two or more races, 1.4% Hispanic of any race; Average household size: 2.42; Median age: 40.6; Age under 18: 23.8%; Age 65 and over: 18.5%; Males per 100 females: 95.9
Housing: Homeownership rate: 72.0%; Homeowner vacancy rate: 10.5%; Rental vacancy rate: 10.8%
Additional Information Contacts
Village of Bear Lake . . . . (231) 864-4300
   http://www.bearlakemichigan.org

BRETHREN (CDP). Covers a land area of 3.117 square miles and a water area of 0.035 square miles. Located at 44.29° N. Lat; 86.01° W. Long. Elevation is 722 feet.
Population: 410; Growth (since 2000): n/a; Density: 131.5 persons per square mile; Race: 97.6% White, 0.0% Black/African American, 0.2% Asian, 1.0% American Indian/Alaska Native, 0.0% Native Hawaiian/Other Pacific Islander, 1.0% Two or more races, 0.7% Hispanic of any race; Average household size: 2.41; Median age: 43.6; Age under 18: 25.6%; Age 65 and over: 15.4%; Males per 100 females: 108.1
School District(s)
Kaleva Norman Dickson SD (KG-12)
   2012-13 Enrollment: 576 . . . . (231) 477-5353

Housing: Homeownership rate: 82.4%; Homeowner vacancy rate: 3.4%; Rental vacancy rate: 6.3%

BROWN (township). Covers a land area of 35.644 square miles and a water area of 0.503 square miles. Located at 44.31° N. Lat; 86.11° W. Long.
History: Brown Township was organized in 1855 and named for Henry L. Brown, who settled here in 1853.
Population: 747; Growth (since 2000): 4.9%; Density: 21.0 persons per square mile; Race: 97.6% White, 0.1% Black/African American, 0.3% Asian, 0.9% American Indian/Alaska Native, 0.0% Native Hawaiian/Other Pacific Islander, 0.9% Two or more races, 1.3% Hispanic of any race; Average household size: 2.43; Median age: 47.8; Age under 18: 21.3%; Age 65 and over: 20.1%; Males per 100 females: 99.2
Housing: Homeownership rate: 85.4%; Homeowner vacancy rate: 3.4%; Rental vacancy rate: 2.2%

CLEON (township). Covers a land area of 36.065 square miles and a water area of 0.082 square miles. Located at 44.47° N. Lat; 85.89° W. Long.
Population: 957; Growth (since 2000): 2.7%; Density: 26.5 persons per square mile; Race: 95.9% White, 0.0% Black/African American, 0.0% Asian, 0.9% American Indian/Alaska Native, 0.0% Native Hawaiian/Other Pacific Islander, 1.7% Two or more races, 5.2% Hispanic of any race; Average household size: 2.45; Median age: 43.7; Age under 18: 21.8%; Age 65 and over: 13.5%; Males per 100 females: 113.6
Housing: Homeownership rate: 84.6%; Homeowner vacancy rate: 3.8%; Rental vacancy rate: 3.2%

COPEMISH (village). Covers a land area of 0.934 square miles and a water area of 0.044 square miles. Located at 44.48° N. Lat; 85.93° W. Long. Elevation is 817 feet.
History: The Buckley Douglass Lumber Company began operations here about 1883. The town of Copemish was established when the railroad came in 1889. The name means "big beech" referring to a legendary beech tree in the community.
Population: 194; Growth (since 2000): -16.4%; Density: 207.8 persons per square mile; Race: 93.3% White, 0.0% Black/African American, 0.0% Asian, 1.5% American Indian/Alaska Native, 0.0% Native Hawaiian/Other Pacific Islander, 0.0% Two or more races, 13.4% Hispanic of any race; Average household size: 2.49; Median age: 42.8; Age under 18: 21.6%; Age 65 and over: 14.4%; Males per 100 females: 110.9
Housing: Homeownership rate: 76.9%; Homeowner vacancy rate: 7.7%; Rental vacancy rate: 0.0%

DICKSON (township). Covers a land area of 69.531 square miles and a water area of 2.009 square miles. Located at 44.30° N. Lat; 85.95° W. Long.
Population: 993; Growth (since 2000): 6.9%; Density: 14.3 persons per square mile; Race: 97.9% White, 0.0% Black/African American, 0.2% Asian, 1.0% American Indian/Alaska Native, 0.0% Native Hawaiian/Other Pacific Islander, 0.8% Two or more races, 1.8% Hispanic of any race; Average household size: 2.29; Median age: 49.2; Age under 18: 19.5%; Age 65 and over: 22.5%; Males per 100 females: 106.9
Housing: Homeownership rate: 86.9%; Homeowner vacancy rate: 3.1%; Rental vacancy rate: 3.4%

EASTLAKE (village). Covers a land area of 1.165 square miles and a water area of 0.335 square miles. Located at 44.25° N. Lat; 86.29° W. Long.
Population: 512; Growth (since 2000): 16.1%; Density: 439.6 persons per square mile; Race: 89.8% White, 0.6% Black/African American, 0.2% Asian, 3.1% American Indian/Alaska Native, 0.0% Native Hawaiian/Other Pacific Islander, 5.7% Two or more races, 2.9% Hispanic of any race; Average household size: 2.22; Median age: 46.8; Age under 18: 19.1%; Age 65 and over: 22.1%; Males per 100 females: 91.8
Housing: Homeownership rate: 86.1%; Homeowner vacancy rate: 2.4%; Rental vacancy rate: 33.3%

FILER (charter township). Covers a land area of 15.745 square miles and a water area of 0.386 square miles. Located at 44.20° N. Lat; 86.32° W. Long.
Population: 2,325; Growth (since 2000): 5.3%; Density: 147.7 persons per square mile; Race: 96.3% White, 0.2% Black/African American, 0.5% Asian, 1.2% American Indian/Alaska Native, 0.0% Native Hawaiian/Other

Pacific Islander, 1.3% Two or more races, 2.1% Hispanic of any race; Average household size: 2.33; Median age: 50.3; Age under 18: 19.2%; Age 65 and over: 23.8%; Males per 100 females: 92.9

Housing: Homeownership rate: 83.9%; Homeowner vacancy rate: 2.4%; Rental vacancy rate: 2.4%

FILER CITY (CDP). Covers a land area of 0.259 square miles and a water area of 0 square miles. Located at 44.21° N. Lat; 86.29° W. Long. Elevation is 607 feet.

Population: 116; Growth (since 2000): n/a; Density: 447.1 persons per square mile; Race: 92.2% White, 0.0% Black/African American, 0.0% Asian, 0.9% American Indian/Alaska Native, 0.0% Native Hawaiian/Other Pacific Islander, 6.9% Two or more races, 1.7% Hispanic of any race; Average household size: 2.64; Median age: 37.5; Age under 18: 26.7%; Age 65 and over: 13.8%; Males per 100 females: 107.1

Housing: Homeownership rate: 79.6%; Homeowner vacancy rate: 0.0%; Rental vacancy rate: 0.0%

KALEVA (village). Covers a land area of 1.103 square miles and a water area of 0 square miles. Located at 44.37° N. Lat; 86.01° W. Long. Elevation is 748 feet.

History: The name of Kaleva came from the Finnish national epic, the Kalevala. Kaleva was founded as a Finnish settlement by the Michigan Land Society in the 1890's, at a railroad junction. The village was platted in 1894.

Population: 470; Growth (since 2000): -7.7%; Density: 426.3 persons per square mile; Race: 94.7% White, 0.2% Black/African American, 0.4% Asian, 0.6% American Indian/Alaska Native, 0.0% Native Hawaiian/Other Pacific Islander, 2.1% Two or more races, 6.0% Hispanic of any race; Average household size: 2.28; Median age: 39.6; Age under 18: 23.0%; Age 65 and over: 11.7%; Males per 100 females: 91.8

Housing: Homeownership rate: 67.5%; Homeowner vacancy rate: 5.4%; Rental vacancy rate: 5.6%

MANISTEE (city). County seat. Covers a land area of 3.285 square miles and a water area of 1.177 square miles. Located at 44.25° N. Lat; 86.33° W. Long. Elevation is 656 feet.

History: Many of the early residents of Manistee were of Swedish and Norwegian descent. The name is of Chippewa origin meaning "spirit of the woods."

Population: 6,226; Growth (since 2000): -5.5%; Density: 1,895.0 persons per square mile; Race: 91.5% White, 0.5% Black/African American, 0.4% Asian, 3.8% American Indian/Alaska Native, 0.0% Native Hawaiian/Other Pacific Islander, 3.0% Two or more races, 3.4% Hispanic of any race; Average household size: 2.18; Median age: 43.6; Age under 18: 21.9%; Age 65 and over: 18.0%; Males per 100 females: 94.0; Marriage status: 26.6% never married, 48.8% now married, 1.2% separated, 8.9% widowed, 15.7% divorced; Foreign born: 1.4%; Speak English only: 96.7%; With disability: 18.2%; Veterans: 12.4%; Ancestry: 23.5% German, 21.2% Polish, 11.2% Irish, 9.8% English, 5.9% American

Employment: 10.8% management, business, and financial, 2.0% computer, engineering, and science, 14.5% education, legal, community service, arts, and media, 4.9% healthcare practitioners, 22.7% service, 25.2% sales and office, 8.5% natural resources, construction, and maintenance, 11.4% production, transportation, and material moving

Income: Per capita: $22,374; Median household: $41,015; Average household: $49,769; Households with income of $100,000 or more: 8.4%; Poverty rate: 17.9%

Educational Attainment: High school diploma or higher: 92.6%; Bachelor's degree or higher: 24.5%; Graduate/professional degree or higher: 9.3%

School District(s)

Casman Alternative Academy (KG-12)
   2012-13 Enrollment: 83 . . . . (231) 723-4981
Manistee Area Public Schools (PK-12)
   2012-13 Enrollment: 1,661 . . . . (231) 723-3521
Manistee ISD (PK-PK)
   2012-13 Enrollment: 35 . . . . (231) 723-4264

Housing: Homeownership rate: 60.9%; Median home value: $91,500; Median year structure built: 1951; Homeowner vacancy rate: 5.5%; Median gross rent: $629 per month; Rental vacancy rate: 15.3%

Health Insurance: 87.7% have insurance; 60.9% have private insurance; 45.9% have public insurance; 12.3% do not have insurance; 0.6% of children under 18 do not have insurance

Hospitals: West Shore Medical Center

Safety: Violent crime rate: 17.9 per 10,000 population; Property crime rate: 256.6 per 10,000 population

Newspapers: Manistee News-Advocate (daily circulation 5000)

Transportation: Commute: 90.6% car, 0.2% public transportation, 2.9% walk, 4.6% work from home; Median travel time to work: 14.5 minutes

Airports: Manistee County-Blacker (general aviation)

Additional Information Contacts
City of Manistee. . . . . (231) 398-2803
   http://www.ci.manistee.mi.us

MANISTEE (township). Covers a land area of 44.379 square miles and a water area of 3.889 square miles. Located at 44.29° N. Lat; 86.25° W. Long. Elevation is 656 feet.

History: Incorporated as city 1869.

Population: 4,084; Growth (since 2000): 8.5%; Density: 92.0 persons per square mile; Race: 78.2% White, 16.3% Black/African American, 0.1% Asian, 2.7% American Indian/Alaska Native, 0.3% Native Hawaiian/Other Pacific Islander, 2.0% Two or more races, 2.4% Hispanic of any race; Average household size: 2.26; Median age: 44.1; Age under 18: 12.4%; Age 65 and over: 19.4%; Males per 100 females: 165.5; Marriage status: 35.6% never married, 44.7% now married, 1.2% separated, 7.4% widowed, 12.3% divorced; Foreign born: 1.2%; Speak English only: 93.4%; With disability: 15.3%; Veterans: 14.9%; Ancestry: 21.6% German, 14.5% Polish, 11.0% Irish, 7.1% English, 7.0% African

Employment: 9.1% management, business, and financial, 4.0% computer, engineering, and science, 6.4% education, legal, community service, arts, and media, 9.5% healthcare practitioners, 24.7% service, 21.6% sales and office, 11.7% natural resources, construction, and maintenance, 12.9% production, transportation, and material moving

Income: Per capita: $19,218; Median household: $44,694; Average household: $54,410; Households with income of $100,000 or more: 12.7%; Poverty rate: 15.4%

Educational Attainment: High school diploma or higher: 87.5%; Bachelor's degree or higher: 14.8%; Graduate/professional degree or higher: 6.0%

School District(s)

Casman Alternative Academy (KG-12)
   2012-13 Enrollment: 83 . . . . (231) 723-4981
Manistee Area Public Schools (PK-12)
   2012-13 Enrollment: 1,661 . . . . (231) 723-3521
Manistee ISD (PK-PK)
   2012-13 Enrollment: 35 . . . . (231) 723-4264

Housing: Homeownership rate: 87.3%; Median home value: $108,700; Median year structure built: 1968; Homeowner vacancy rate: 1.8%; Median gross rent: $625 per month; Rental vacancy rate: 16.1%

Health Insurance: 89.7% have insurance; 72.3% have private insurance; 41.5% have public insurance; 10.3% do not have insurance; 3.3% of children under 18 do not have insurance

Hospitals: West Shore Medical Center

Newspapers: Manistee News-Advocate (daily circulation 5000)

Transportation: Commute: 89.7% car, 0.4% public transportation, 1.9% walk, 6.2% work from home; Median travel time to work: 15.4 minutes

Airports: Manistee County-Blacker (general aviation)

Additional Information Contacts
Manistee Township . . . . (231) 723-6507
   http://manisteetownship.com

MAPLE GROVE (township). Covers a land area of 35.565 square miles and a water area of 0.215 square miles. Located at 44.39° N. Lat; 86.00° W. Long.

Population: 1,316; Growth (since 2000): 2.4%; Density: 37.0 persons per square mile; Race: 95.1% White, 0.1% Black/African American, 0.2% Asian, 1.6% American Indian/Alaska Native, 0.0% Native Hawaiian/Other Pacific Islander, 2.0% Two or more races, 3.5% Hispanic of any race; Average household size: 2.43; Median age: 43.5; Age under 18: 23.0%; Age 65 and over: 13.4%; Males per 100 females: 97.6

Housing: Homeownership rate: 80.2%; Homeowner vacancy rate: 3.6%; Rental vacancy rate: 8.5%

MARILLA (township). Covers a land area of 35.465 square miles and a water area of 0.154 square miles. Located at 44.39° N. Lat; 85.90° W. Long. Elevation is 945 feet.

Population: 393; Growth (since 2000): 8.6%; Density: 11.1 persons per square mile; Race: 96.7% White, 0.0% Black/African American, 0.3% Asian, 0.8% American Indian/Alaska Native, 0.0% Native Hawaiian/Other

Pacific Islander, 0.8% Two or more races, 3.6% Hispanic of any race; Average household size: 2.54; Median age: 49.9; Age under 18: 20.6%; Age 65 and over: 20.4%; Males per 100 females: 88.9

Housing: Homeownership rate: 90.3%; Homeowner vacancy rate: 4.8%; Rental vacancy rate: 0.0%

NORMAN (township). Covers a land area of 70.812 square miles and a water area of 1.504 square miles. Located at 44.20° N. Lat; 85.94° W. Long.

Population: 1,553; Growth (since 2000): -7.3%; Density: 21.9 persons per square mile; Race: 95.6% White, 0.6% Black/African American, 0.3% Asian, 1.7% American Indian/Alaska Native, 0.0% Native Hawaiian/Other Pacific Islander, 1.5% Two or more races, 1.5% Hispanic of any race; Average household size: 2.18; Median age: 51.3; Age under 18: 16.5%; Age 65 and over: 24.0%; Males per 100 females: 110.4

Housing: Homeownership rate: 85.8%; Homeowner vacancy rate: 5.2%; Rental vacancy rate: 10.5%

OAK HILL (CDP). Covers a land area of 0.503 square miles and a water area of 0 square miles. Located at 44.22° N. Lat; 86.30° W. Long. Elevation is 656 feet.

Population: 569; Growth (since 2000): n/a; Density: 1,131.8 persons per square mile; Race: 96.0% White, 0.7% Black/African American, 0.2% Asian, 1.2% American Indian/Alaska Native, 0.0% Native Hawaiian/Other Pacific Islander, 1.2% Two or more races, 4.0% Hispanic of any race; Average household size: 2.30; Median age: 42.1; Age under 18: 21.3%; Age 65 and over: 22.0%; Males per 100 females: 94.2

Housing: Homeownership rate: 76.2%; Homeowner vacancy rate: 1.5%; Rental vacancy rate: 3.3%

ONEKAMA (township). Covers a land area of 18.424 square miles and a water area of 5.021 square miles. Located at 44.38° N. Lat; 86.22° W. Long. Elevation is 594 feet.

Population: 1,329; Growth (since 2000): -12.2%; Density: 72.1 persons per square mile; Race: 96.9% White, 0.1% Black/African American, 0.5% Asian, 1.0% American Indian/Alaska Native, 0.0% Native Hawaiian/Other Pacific Islander, 1.3% Two or more races, 1.1% Hispanic of any race; Average household size: 2.09; Median age: 55.2; Age under 18: 15.3%; Age 65 and over: 29.9%; Males per 100 females: 92.9

School District(s)
Onekama Consolidated Schools (KG-12)
    2012-13 Enrollment: 388 . . . . (231) 889-4251
Housing: Homeownership rate: 83.3%; Homeowner vacancy rate: 5.0%; Rental vacancy rate: 13.5%

ONEKAMA (village). Covers a land area of 0.583 square miles and a water area of 0 square miles. Located at 44.37° N. Lat; 86.20° W. Long. Elevation is 594 feet.

History: Onekama developed around the cucumber fields of the nearby farms, and as a supply center for the resorts in Manistee County. A channel dredged between Portage Lake and Lake Michigan made Onekama a harbor town.

Population: 411; Growth (since 2000): -36.5%; Density: 704.8 persons per square mile; Race: 96.6% White, 0.2% Black/African American, 0.2% Asian, 1.2% American Indian/Alaska Native, 0.0% Native Hawaiian/Other Pacific Islander, 1.7% Two or more races, 1.9% Hispanic of any race; Average household size: 1.98; Median age: 54.4; Age under 18: 15.1%; Age 65 and over: 28.5%; Males per 100 females: 82.7

School District(s)
Onekama Consolidated Schools (KG-12)
    2012-13 Enrollment: 388 . . . . (231) 889-4251
Housing: Homeownership rate: 73.2%; Homeowner vacancy rate: 8.5%; Rental vacancy rate: 9.4%

PARKDALE (CDP). Covers a land area of 1.548 square miles and a water area of 0 square miles. Located at 44.27° N. Lat; 86.28° W. Long. Elevation is 600 feet.

Population: 704; Growth (since 2000): n/a; Density: 454.9 persons per square mile; Race: 92.6% White, 0.7% Black/African American, 0.1% Asian, 3.7% American Indian/Alaska Native, 0.9% Native Hawaiian/Other Pacific Islander, 1.6% Two or more races, 2.1% Hispanic of any race; Average household size: 2.10; Median age: 55.5; Age under 18: 11.2%; Age 65 and over: 36.8%; Males per 100 females: 91.8

Housing: Homeownership rate: 85.5%; Homeowner vacancy rate: 2.2%; Rental vacancy rate: 5.1%

PLEASANTON (township). Covers a land area of 33.548 square miles and a water area of 1.899 square miles. Located at 44.47° N. Lat; 86.13° W. Long. Elevation is 886 feet.

Population: 818; Growth (since 2000): 0.1%; Density: 24.4 persons per square mile; Race: 98.4% White, 0.0% Black/African American, 0.1% Asian, 0.4% American Indian/Alaska Native, 0.0% Native Hawaiian/Other Pacific Islander, 1.0% Two or more races, 1.1% Hispanic of any race; Average household size: 2.24; Median age: 50.0; Age under 18: 18.1%; Age 65 and over: 27.9%; Males per 100 females: 102.5

Housing: Homeownership rate: 88.7%; Homeowner vacancy rate: 5.0%; Rental vacancy rate: 37.9%

SPRINGDALE (township). Covers a land area of 35.424 square miles and a water area of 0.200 square miles. Located at 44.48° N. Lat; 85.99° W. Long.

History: Springdale Township was organized in 1870 and named for the many perennial springs in the area.

Population: 781; Growth (since 2000): 7.0%; Density: 22.0 persons per square mile; Race: 98.1% White, 0.0% Black/African American, 0.1% Asian, 0.3% American Indian/Alaska Native, 0.0% Native Hawaiian/Other Pacific Islander, 1.0% Two or more races, 1.8% Hispanic of any race; Average household size: 2.24; Median age: 47.5; Age under 18: 22.2%; Age 65 and over: 21.8%; Males per 100 females: 106.6

Housing: Homeownership rate: 83.1%; Homeowner vacancy rate: 6.1%; Rental vacancy rate: 15.7%

STRONACH (CDP). Covers a land area of 0.348 square miles and a water area of 0 square miles. Located at 44.21° N. Lat; 86.27° W. Long. Elevation is 604 feet.

Population: 162; Growth (since 2000): n/a; Density: 465.2 persons per square mile; Race: 98.8% White, 0.0% Black/African American, 0.0% Asian, 0.0% American Indian/Alaska Native, 0.0% Native Hawaiian/Other Pacific Islander, 1.2% Two or more races, 1.9% Hispanic of any race; Average household size: 2.49; Median age: 39.0; Age under 18: 26.5%; Age 65 and over: 14.8%; Males per 100 females: 90.6

Housing: Homeownership rate: 89.3%; Homeowner vacancy rate: 1.7%; Rental vacancy rate: 12.5%

STRONACH (township). Covers a land area of 54.978 square miles and a water area of 0.537 square miles. Located at 44.21° N. Lat; 86.15° W. Long. Elevation is 604 feet.

Population: 821; Growth (since 2000): 2.1%; Density: 14.9 persons per square mile; Race: 95.4% White, 0.4% Black/African American, 0.2% Asian, 2.4% American Indian/Alaska Native, 0.0% Native Hawaiian/Other Pacific Islander, 1.3% Two or more races, 1.3% Hispanic of any race; Average household size: 2.32; Median age: 50.4; Age under 18: 17.3%; Age 65 and over: 19.2%; Males per 100 females: 105.3

Housing: Homeownership rate: 90.1%; Homeowner vacancy rate: 3.0%; Rental vacancy rate: 20.5%

WELLSTON (CDP). Covers a land area of 0.974 square miles and a water area of 0.041 square miles. Located at 44.22° N. Lat; 85.96° W. Long. Elevation is 774 feet.

Population: 311; Growth (since 2000): n/a; Density: 319.1 persons per square mile; Race: 95.2% White, 0.3% Black/African American, 0.3% Asian, 3.2% American Indian/Alaska Native, 0.0% Native Hawaiian/Other Pacific Islander, 0.6% Two or more races, 1.6% Hispanic of any race; Average household size: 2.29; Median age: 46.8; Age under 18: 20.3%; Age 65 and over: 16.7%; Males per 100 females: 99.4

Housing: Homeownership rate: 74.2%; Homeowner vacancy rate: 6.4%; Rental vacancy rate: 7.9%

Marquette County

Located in northwestern Michigan on the Upper Peninsula; bounded on the north by Lake Superior; drained by the Dead and Michigamme Rivers; includes the Marquette Iron Range and Huron Mountains, and several lakes. Covers a land area of 1,808.401 square miles, a water area of 1,616.139 square miles, and is located in the Eastern Time Zone at 46.66° N. Lat., 87.58° W. Long. The county was founded in 1843. County seat is Marquette.

Marquette County is part of the Marquette, MI Micropolitan Statistical Area. The entire metro area includes: Marquette County, MI

Weather Station: Champion Van Riper Prk   Elevation: 1,564 feet

	Jan	Feb	Mar	Apr	May	Jun	Jul	Aug	Sep	Oct	Nov	Dec
High	23	27	38	52	66	74	79	76	67	54	38	26
Low	2	2	11	24	35	45	50	49	42	31	21	8
Precip	1.8	1.2	2.1	2.4	3.0	3.3	3.8	3.3	3.5	3.5	2.2	1.9
Snow	25.9	16.1	19.3	6.8	0.5	0.0	0.0	0.0	0.1	4.3	15.6	26.1

High and Low temperatures in degrees Fahrenheit; Precipitation and Snow in inches

Weather Station: Marquette County Arpt   Elevation: 1,415 feet

	Jan	Feb	Mar	Apr	May	Jun	Jul	Aug	Sep	Oct	Nov	Dec
High	22	26	35	48	62	72	76	74	66	52	37	26
Low	6	7	14	28	39	49	54	53	45	34	24	12
Precip	2.4	2.1	3.0	3.1	3.1	2.7	2.8	3.1	3.7	3.9	3.2	2.5
Snow	43.4	35.8	34.8	14.5	1.3	tr	tr	tr	0.1	6.4	24.5	42.2

High and Low temperatures in degrees Fahrenheit; Precipitation and Snow in inches

Weather Station: Marquette Wbo   Elevation: 676 feet

	Jan	Feb	Mar	Apr	May	Jun	Jul	Aug	Sep	Oct	Nov	Dec
High	26	29	37	48	60	69	75	75	67	54	41	30
Low	13	14	21	32	41	50	57	58	51	40	29	18
Precip	1.9	1.3	2.0	2.4	2.6	2.5	2.6	2.6	3.3	3.2	2.6	1.9
Snow	28.3	21.2	20.7	7.6	0.6	0.0	0.0	0.0	0.1	1.0	10.8	25.1

High and Low temperatures in degrees Fahrenheit; Precipitation and Snow in inches

Population: 67,077; Growth (since 2000): 3.8%; Density: 37.1 persons per square mile; Race: 93.8% White, 1.7% Black/African American, 0.6% Asian, 1.7% American Indian/Alaska Native, 0.0% Native Hawaiian/Other Pacific Islander, 2.0% two or more races, 1.1% Hispanic of any race; Average household size: 2.26; Median age: 39.4; Age under 18: 18.7%; Age 65 and over: 14.7%; Males per 100 females: 102.1; Marriage status: 34.8% never married, 48.6% now married, 0.7% separated, 5.9% widowed, 10.7% divorced; Foreign born: 1.3%; Speak English only: 96.4%; With disability: 12.3%; Veterans: 11.9%; Ancestry: 18.7% Finnish, 17.8% German, 13.7% English, 10.9% French, 10.2% Irish

Religion: Six largest groups: 23.3% Catholicism, 13.3% Lutheran, 4.0% Methodist/Pietist, 1.8% Baptist, 1.0% Non-denominational Protestant, 0.8% Holiness

Economy: Unemployment rate: 5.1%; Leading industries: 16.7% retail trade; 14.4% health care and social assistance; 12.5% other services (except public administration); Farms: 168 totaling 30,693 acres; Company size: 1 employs 1,000 or more persons, 2 employ 500 to 999 persons, 18 employ 100 to 499 persons, 1,640 employ less than 100 persons; Business ownership: n/a women-owned, n/a Black-owned, n/a Hispanic-owned, n/a Asian-owned

Employment: 10.3% management, business, and financial, 3.6% computer, engineering, and science, 9.3% education, legal, community service, arts, and media, 8.7% healthcare practitioners, 22.8% service, 23.0% sales and office, 12.2% natural resources, construction, and maintenance, 10.2% production, transportation, and material moving

Income: Per capita: $23,789; Median household: $45,622; Average household: $58,015; Households with income of $100,000 or more: 15.0%; Poverty rate: 15.7%

Educational Attainment: High school diploma or higher: 93.5%; Bachelor's degree or higher: 29.1%; Graduate/professional degree or higher: 9.1%

Housing: Homeownership rate: 68.9%; Median home value: $126,600; Median year structure built: 1967; Homeowner vacancy rate: 1.8%; Median gross rent: $607 per month; Rental vacancy rate: 9.9%

Vital Statistics: Birth rate: 93.8 per 10,000 population; Death rate: 92.9 per 10,000 population; Age-adjusted cancer mortality rate: 191.4 deaths per 100,000 population

Health Insurance: 88.1% have insurance; 74.3% have private insurance; 29.5% have public insurance; 11.9% do not have insurance; 3.4% of children under 18 do not have insurance

Health Care: Physicians: 37.3 per 10,000 population; Hospital beds: 44.6 per 10,000 population; Hospital admissions: 1,768.3 per 10,000 population

Transportation: Commute: 89.6% car, 0.4% public transportation, 5.3% walk, 2.9% work from home; Median travel time to work: 18.0 minutes

Presidential Election: 56.4% Obama, 42.3% Romney (2012)

National and State Parks: Escanaba River State Forest; Huron National Wildlife Refuge; Michigamme State Forest

Additional Information Contacts
Marquette Government . . . . (906) 225-8151
    http://www.co.marquette.mi.us

Marquette County Communities

ARNOLD (unincorporated postal area)
ZCTA: 49819
    Covers a land area of 13.005 square miles and a water area of 0.079 square miles. Located at 46.11° N. Lat; 87.46° W. Long. Elevation is 1,030 feet.
    Population: 36; Growth (since 2000): n/a; Density: 2.8 persons per square mile; Race: 100.0% White, 0.0% Black/African American, 0.0% Asian, 0.0% American Indian/Alaska Native, 0.0% Native Hawaiian/Other Pacific Islander, 0.0% Two or more races, 0.0% Hispanic of any race; Average household size: 2.12; Median age: 49.5; Age under 18: 19.4%; Age 65 and over: 19.4%; Males per 100 females: 125.0

School District(s)
Wells Township SD (KG-12)
    2012-13 Enrollment: 11 . . . . (906) 238-4200
    Housing: Homeownership rate: 88.2%; Homeowner vacancy rate: 0.0%; Rental vacancy rate: 0.0%

BIG BAY (CDP). Covers a land area of 3.780 square miles and a water area of 2.155 square miles. Located at 46.82° N. Lat; 87.71° W. Long. Elevation is 682 feet.
    Population: 319; Growth (since 2000): 20.4%; Density: 84.4 persons per square mile; Race: 94.7% White, 0.3% Black/African American, 1.3% Asian, 1.9% American Indian/Alaska Native, 0.0% Native Hawaiian/Other Pacific Islander, 1.9% Two or more races, 0.6% Hispanic of any race; Average household size: 1.87; Median age: 57.9; Age under 18: 10.0%; Age 65 and over: 29.2%; Males per 100 females: 107.1

School District(s)
Powell Township Schools (PK-12)
    2012-13 Enrollment: 43 . . . . (906) 345-9355
    Housing: Homeownership rate: 88.3%; Homeowner vacancy rate: 3.2%; Rental vacancy rate: 13.0%

CHAMPION (township). Covers a land area of 120.892 square miles and a water area of 3.972 square miles. Located at 46.64° N. Lat; 87.84° W. Long. Elevation is 1,591 feet.
    Population: 297; Growth (since 2000): 0.0%; Density: 2.5 persons per square mile; Race: 97.0% White, 0.0% Black/African American, 0.0% Asian, 1.7% American Indian/Alaska Native, 0.0% Native Hawaiian/Other Pacific Islander, 1.0% Two or more races, 0.0% Hispanic of any race; Average household size: 2.27; Median age: 45.4; Age under 18: 24.9%; Age 65 and over: 17.5%; Males per 100 females: 94.1
    Housing: Homeownership rate: 88.6%; Homeowner vacancy rate: 1.6%; Rental vacancy rate: 6.3%

CHOCOLAY (charter township). Covers a land area of 58.985 square miles and a water area of 1.817 square miles. Located at 46.46° N. Lat; 87.25° W. Long.
    History: The name of Chocolay Township came from that of a French fur trader, M. Choquette.
    Population: 5,903; Growth (since 2000): -17.4%; Density: 100.1 persons per square mile; Race: 94.3% White, 0.3% Black/African American, 0.3% Asian, 3.0% American Indian/Alaska Native, 0.0% Native Hawaiian/Other Pacific Islander, 2.0% Two or more races, 0.6% Hispanic of any race; Average household size: 2.40; Median age: 44.7; Age under 18: 20.8%; Age 65 and over: 14.2%; Males per 100 females: 102.5; Marriage status: 26.0% never married, 63.4% now married, 0.2% separated, 5.4% widowed, 5.3% divorced; Foreign born: 1.1%; Speak English only: 98.8%; With disability: 12.2%; Veterans: 13.3%; Ancestry: 23.7% German, 15.2% English, 13.8% Finnish, 13.5% Irish, 8.7% French
    Employment: 13.4% management, business, and financial, 2.1% computer, engineering, and science, 12.4% education, legal, community service, arts, and media, 9.4% healthcare practitioners, 16.8% service, 26.0% sales and office, 10.3% natural resources, construction, and maintenance, 9.6% production, transportation, and material moving
    Income: Per capita: $28,400; Median household: $59,894; Average household: $70,761; Households with income of $100,000 or more: 19.5%; Poverty rate: 5.9%
    Educational Attainment: High school diploma or higher: 94.4%; Bachelor's degree or higher: 39.7%; Graduate/professional degree or higher: 14.3%

Housing: Homeownership rate: 84.6%; Median home value: $168,100; Median year structure built: 1972; Homeowner vacancy rate: 0.9%; Median gross rent: $617 per month; Rental vacancy rate: 7.6%
Health Insurance: 93.4% have insurance; 84.4% have private insurance; 26.7% have public insurance; 6.6% do not have insurance; 0.7% of children under 18 do not have insurance
Safety: Violent crime rate: 0.0 per 10,000 population; Property crime rate: 64.7 per 10,000 population
Transportation: Commute: 95.9% car, 0.0% public transportation, 1.1% walk, 1.8% work from home; Median travel time to work: 20.0 minutes
Additional Information Contacts
Chocolay Township . . . . (906) 249-1448
  http://www.chocolaytownship.org

ELY (township). Covers a land area of 137.273 square miles and a water area of 3.254 square miles. Located at 46.42° N. Lat; 87.81° W. Long.
Population: 1,952; Growth (since 2000): -2.9%; Density: 14.2 persons per square mile; Race: 97.1% White, 0.1% Black/African American, 0.1% Asian, 1.2% American Indian/Alaska Native, 0.1% Native Hawaiian/Other Pacific Islander, 1.4% Two or more races, 0.6% Hispanic of any race; Average household size: 2.57; Median age: 43.3; Age under 18: 23.8%; Age 65 and over: 13.5%; Males per 100 females: 111.0
Housing: Homeownership rate: 93.9%; Homeowner vacancy rate: 1.1%; Rental vacancy rate: 2.1%

EWING (township). Covers a land area of 48.292 square miles and a water area of 0.565 square miles. Located at 46.10° N. Lat; 87.29° W. Long.
Population: 160; Growth (since 2000): 0.6%; Density: 3.3 persons per square mile; Race: 96.9% White, 0.0% Black/African American, 1.3% Asian, 1.3% American Indian/Alaska Native, 0.0% Native Hawaiian/Other Pacific Islander, 0.6% Two or more races, 0.0% Hispanic of any race; Average household size: 2.03; Median age: 55.6; Age under 18: 7.5%; Age 65 and over: 20.0%; Males per 100 females: 116.2
Housing: Homeownership rate: 97.4%; Homeowner vacancy rate: 2.5%; Rental vacancy rate: 0.0%

FORSYTH (township). Covers a land area of 177.672 square miles and a water area of 5.102 square miles. Located at 46.25° N. Lat; 87.45° W. Long.
Population: 6,164; Growth (since 2000): 27.8%; Density: 34.7 persons per square mile; Race: 92.0% White, 1.1% Black/African American, 0.7% Asian, 2.1% American Indian/Alaska Native, 0.0% Native Hawaiian/Other Pacific Islander, 3.9% Two or more races, 2.3% Hispanic of any race; Average household size: 2.40; Median age: 41.7; Age under 18: 23.6%; Age 65 and over: 15.6%; Males per 100 females: 98.3; Marriage status: 28.4% never married, 53.7% now married, 1.1% separated, 5.5% widowed, 12.4% divorced; Foreign born: 1.5%; Speak English only: 94.8%; With disability: 16.7%; Veterans: 19.4%; Ancestry: 21.1% German, 12.2% English, 11.9% Finnish, 11.3% French, 10.5% Irish
Employment: 17.8% management, business, and financial, 6.6% computer, engineering, and science, 9.3% education, legal, community service, arts, and media, 4.7% healthcare practitioners, 17.1% service, 21.1% sales and office, 11.4% natural resources, construction, and maintenance, 12.0% production, transportation, and material moving
Income: Per capita: $23,007; Median household: $45,836; Average household: $54,894; Households with income of $100,000 or more: 12.1%; Poverty rate: 15.8%
Educational Attainment: High school diploma or higher: 94.6%; Bachelor's degree or higher: 18.9%; Graduate/professional degree or higher: 5.8%
Housing: Homeownership rate: 69.8%; Median home value: $108,800; Median year structure built: 1969; Homeowner vacancy rate: 3.2%; Median gross rent: $599 per month; Rental vacancy rate: 32.0%
Health Insurance: 85.4% have insurance; 61.3% have private insurance; 43.5% have public insurance; 14.6% do not have insurance; 13.9% of children under 18 do not have insurance
Safety: Violent crime rate: 19.1 per 10,000 population; Property crime rate: 132.2 per 10,000 population
Transportation: Commute: 95.3% car, 0.0% public transportation, 1.1% walk, 2.6% work from home; Median travel time to work: 25.7 minutes

GWINN (CDP). Covers a land area of 4.920 square miles and a water area of 0.152 square miles. Located at 46.30° N. Lat; 87.43° W. Long. Elevation is 1,099 feet.
History: Gwinn was built in 1907 by the Cleveland Cliffs Iron Company as a model community for its employees. It was named by William Gwinn Mather, the company president, for his mother whose maiden name was Gwinn.
Population: 1,917; Growth (since 2000): -2.4%; Density: 389.7 persons per square mile; Race: 93.7% White, 1.0% Black/African American, 0.9% Asian, 1.8% American Indian/Alaska Native, 0.0% Native Hawaiian/Other Pacific Islander, 2.3% Two or more races, 1.7% Hispanic of any race; Average household size: 2.29; Median age: 46.2; Age under 18: 20.8%; Age 65 and over: 20.0%; Males per 100 females: 97.8
School District(s)
Gwinn Area Community Schools (KG-12)
    2012-13 Enrollment: 1,200 . . . . (906) 346-9283
Housing: Homeownership rate: 80.2%; Homeowner vacancy rate: 2.6%; Rental vacancy rate: 20.9%
Airports: Sawyer International (primary service/non-hub)

HARVEY (CDP). Covers a land area of 1.993 square miles and a water area of 0.558 square miles. Located at 46.49° N. Lat; 87.35° W. Long. Elevation is 653 feet.
History: Harvey grew up in 1860 around the blast furnace of the Northern Iron Company. Established on the Chocolay River near the shore of Lake Superior, Harvey was named for Charles T. Harvey. The town developed as an agricultural center, and later as a summer resort.
Population: 1,393; Growth (since 2000): 5.5%; Density: 698.8 persons per square mile; Race: 94.5% White, 0.5% Black/African American, 0.3% Asian, 2.3% American Indian/Alaska Native, 0.0% Native Hawaiian/Other Pacific Islander, 2.4% Two or more races, 0.5% Hispanic of any race; Average household size: 2.21; Median age: 41.9; Age under 18: 19.7%; Age 65 and over: 13.1%; Males per 100 females: 105.5
Housing: Homeownership rate: 68.1%; Homeowner vacancy rate: 1.4%; Rental vacancy rate: 13.0%

HUMBOLDT (township). Covers a land area of 92.671 square miles and a water area of 2.997 square miles. Located at 46.36° N. Lat; 87.92° W. Long. Elevation is 1,542 feet.
Population: 464; Growth (since 2000): -1.1%; Density: 5.0 persons per square mile; Race: 97.8% White, 0.0% Black/African American, 0.0% Asian, 0.2% American Indian/Alaska Native, 0.2% Native Hawaiian/Other Pacific Islander, 1.7% Two or more races, 0.2% Hispanic of any race; Average household size: 2.20; Median age: 50.9; Age under 18: 17.0%; Age 65 and over: 22.4%; Males per 100 females: 122.0
Housing: Homeownership rate: 88.6%; Homeowner vacancy rate: 2.6%; Rental vacancy rate: 0.0%

ISHPEMING (city). Covers a land area of 8.743 square miles and a water area of 0.609 square miles. Located at 46.47° N. Lat; 87.67° W. Long. Elevation is 1,407 feet.
History: The name of Ishpeming is of Indian origin meaning "high grounds" or "heaven." The city developed around the mining of ore from the Marquette Range, with the Cleveland Cliffs Iron Company, the Oliver Mining Company, and a mine opened by Henry Ford. The Norden Ski Club was formed in 1888 in Ishpeming and instituted jumping contests, which became the Ishpeming Ski Tournament.
Population: 6,470; Growth (since 2000): -3.2%; Density: 740.0 persons per square mile; Race: 96.0% White, 0.2% Black/African American, 0.3% Asian, 1.1% American Indian/Alaska Native, 0.0% Native Hawaiian/Other Pacific Islander, 2.2% Two or more races, 1.0% Hispanic of any race; Average household size: 2.23; Median age: 40.3; Age under 18: 21.7%; Age 65 and over: 17.0%; Males per 100 females: 93.1; Marriage status: 26.2% never married, 48.3% now married, 0.2% separated, 9.3% widowed, 16.2% divorced; Foreign born: 0.9%; Speak English only: 97.7%; With disability: 14.2%; Veterans: 13.7%; Ancestry: 24.9% Finnish, 19.5% English, 15.1% Italian, 11.6% French, 11.6% German
Employment: 5.5% management, business, and financial, 0.5% computer, engineering, and science, 6.0% education, legal, community service, arts, and media, 8.7% healthcare practitioners, 24.6% service, 25.5% sales and office, 16.8% natural resources, construction, and maintenance, 12.5% production, transportation, and material moving
Income: Per capita: $19,215; Median household: $36,536; Average household: $43,711; Households with income of $100,000 or more: 8.2%; Poverty rate: 17.3%

Educational Attainment: High school diploma or higher: 93.7%; Bachelor's degree or higher: 19.1%; Graduate/professional degree or higher: 5.0%

School District(s)
Ishpeming Public SD No. 1 (KG-12)
    2012-13 Enrollment: 831 . . . . (906) 485-5501
Nice Community SD (PK-12)
    2012-13 Enrollment: 1,175 . . . . (906) 485-1021
Housing: Homeownership rate: 65.4%; Median home value: $73,500; Median year structure built: Before 1940; Homeowner vacancy rate: 2.7%; Median gross rent: $486 per month; Rental vacancy rate: 7.2%
Health Insurance: 85.1% have insurance; 67.9% have private insurance; 34.5% have public insurance; 14.9% do not have insurance; 4.1% of children under 18 do not have insurance
Hospitals: Bell Hospital (69 beds)
Safety: Violent crime rate: 12.2 per 10,000 population; Property crime rate: 151.9 per 10,000 population
Transportation: Commute: 94.5% car, 0.3% public transportation, 3.0% walk, 1.8% work from home; Median travel time to work: 17.4 minutes

ISHPEMING (township). Covers a land area of 86.291 square miles and a water area of 5.193 square miles. Located at 46.63° N. Lat; 87.69° W. Long. Elevation is 1,407 feet.

History: U.S. National Ski Hall of Fame; birthplace of skiing in America; ski tournaments held here since 1888. Incorporated as village 1871, as city 1873.
Population: 3,513; Growth (since 2000): -0.3%; Density: 40.7 persons per square mile; Race: 97.0% White, 0.2% Black/African American, 0.4% Asian, 0.8% American Indian/Alaska Native, 0.0% Native Hawaiian/Other Pacific Islander, 1.5% Two or more races, 0.3% Hispanic of any race; Average household size: 2.43; Median age: 45.1; Age under 18: 21.7%; Age 65 and over: 18.0%; Males per 100 females: 97.2; Marriage status: 26.2% never married, 58.6% now married, 0.9% separated, 6.4% widowed, 8.8% divorced; Foreign born: 1.9%; Speak English only: 96.1%; With disability: 9.6%; Veterans: 10.9%; Ancestry: 27.2% Finnish, 18.1% English, 14.0% French, 12.1% Italian, 12.1% German
Employment: 10.8% management, business, and financial, 2.7% computer, engineering, and science, 9.2% education, legal, community service, arts, and media, 10.6% healthcare practitioners, 19.6% service, 19.4% sales and office, 19.6% natural resources, construction, and maintenance, 8.2% production, transportation, and material moving
Income: Per capita: $27,976; Median household: $50,377; Average household: $68,577; Households with income of $100,000 or more: 22.2%; Poverty rate: 10.7%
Educational Attainment: High school diploma or higher: 95.1%; Bachelor's degree or higher: 25.9%; Graduate/professional degree or higher: 4.8%

School District(s)
Ishpeming Public SD No. 1 (KG-12)
    2012-13 Enrollment: 831 . . . . (906) 485-5501
Nice Community SD (PK-12)
    2012-13 Enrollment: 1,175 . . . . (906) 485-1021
Housing: Homeownership rate: 91.6%; Median home value: $111,200; Median year structure built: 1964; Homeowner vacancy rate: 0.6%; Median gross rent: n/a per month; Rental vacancy rate: 8.6%
Health Insurance: 91.8% have insurance; 80.8% have private insurance; 27.9% have public insurance; 8.2% do not have insurance; 0.0% of children under 18 do not have insurance
Hospitals: Bell Hospital (69 beds)
Safety: Violent crime rate: 0.0 per 10,000 population; Property crime rate: 30.7 per 10,000 population
Transportation: Commute: 97.6% car, 0.1% public transportation, 0.9% walk, 0.6% work from home; Median travel time to work: 18.1 minutes

K. I. SAWYER (CDP). Covers a land area of 1.712 square miles and a water area of 0.021 square miles. Located at 46.33° N. Lat; 87.37° W. Long.

Population: 2,624; Growth (since 2000): n/a; Density: 1,533.2 persons per square mile; Race: 85.1% White, 2.8% Black/African American, 0.5% Asian, 3.8% American Indian/Alaska Native, 0.0% Native Hawaiian/Other Pacific Islander, 7.5% Two or more races, 3.9% Hispanic of any race; Average household size: 2.72; Median age: 27.6; Age under 18: 34.0%; Age 65 and over: 5.3%; Males per 100 females: 94.9; Marriage status: 35.2% never married, 45.1% now married, 3.2% separated, 4.9% widowed, 14.9% divorced; Foreign born: 0.9%; Speak English only: 96.2%;

With disability: 17.4%; Veterans: 17.5%; Ancestry: 23.4% German, 12.1% Irish, 8.8% French, 8.3% American, 6.3% English
Employment: 18.0% management, business, and financial, 4.2% computer, engineering, and science, 7.2% education, legal, community service, arts, and media, 5.6% healthcare practitioners, 18.8% service, 21.0% sales and office, 8.6% natural resources, construction, and maintenance, 16.5% production, transportation, and material moving
Income: Per capita: $13,912; Median household: $30,186; Average household: $36,929; Households with income of $100,000 or more: 3.1%; Poverty rate: 30.5%
Educational Attainment: High school diploma or higher: 93.9%; Bachelor's degree or higher: 12.9%; Graduate/professional degree or higher: 3.7%
Housing: Homeownership rate: 20.8%; Median home value: $50,500; Median year structure built: 1965; Homeowner vacancy rate: 5.1%; Median gross rent: $617 per month; Rental vacancy rate: 38.3%
Health Insurance: 80.7% have insurance; 42.9% have private insurance; 51.0% have public insurance; 19.3% do not have insurance; 3.7% of children under 18 do not have insurance
Transportation: Commute: 91.5% car, 0.5% public transportation, 2.7% walk, 1.7% work from home; Median travel time to work: 28.2 minutes

LITTLE LAKE (unincorporated postal area)
ZCTA: 49833
    Covers a land area of 8.095 square miles and a water area of 0.653 square miles. Located at 46.29° N. Lat; 87.33° W. Long. Elevation is 1,132 feet.
    Population: 266; Growth (since 2000): 6.8%; Density: 32.9 persons per square mile; Race: 94.7% White, 0.0% Black/African American, 1.1% Asian, 3.0% American Indian/Alaska Native, 0.4% Native Hawaiian/Other Pacific Islander, 0.0% Two or more races, 1.9% Hispanic of any race; Average household size: 2.27; Median age: 48.3; Age under 18: 18.4%; Age 65 and over: 20.7%; Males per 100 females: 100.0
    Housing: Homeownership rate: 85.5%; Homeowner vacancy rate: 4.7%; Rental vacancy rate: 15.0%

MARQUETTE (charter township). Covers a land area of 55.297 square miles and a water area of 5.500 square miles. Located at 46.60° N. Lat; 87.51° W. Long. Elevation is 666 feet.

History: Once an iron ore shipping port. Seat of Northern Michigan University\(has Olympic Training Center). Maritime Museum. Settled 1849, Incorporated as a city 1871.
Population: 3,905; Growth (since 2000): 18.8%; Density: 70.6 persons per square mile; Race: 94.6% White, 0.5% Black/African American, 1.0% Asian, 1.9% American Indian/Alaska Native, 0.0% Native Hawaiian/Other Pacific Islander, 1.9% Two or more races, 0.7% Hispanic of any race; Average household size: 2.24; Median age: 43.9; Age under 18: 18.1%; Age 65 and over: 15.9%; Males per 100 females: 96.6; Marriage status: 29.1% never married, 51.1% now married, 0.8% separated, 7.9% widowed, 11.9% divorced; Foreign born: 3.1%; Speak English only: 94.3%; With disability: 11.0%; Veterans: 13.6%; Ancestry: 19.2% Finnish, 14.8% German, 11.7% Irish, 10.8% English, 10.6% French
Employment: 12.7% management, business, and financial, 0.8% computer, engineering, and science, 14.2% education, legal, community service, arts, and media, 15.3% healthcare practitioners, 19.9% service, 14.5% sales and office, 10.7% natural resources, construction, and maintenance, 11.9% production, transportation, and material moving
Income: Per capita: $30,592; Median household: $54,929; Average household: $68,397; Households with income of $100,000 or more: 17.0%; Poverty rate: 7.7%
Educational Attainment: High school diploma or higher: 93.2%; Bachelor's degree or higher: 36.5%; Graduate/professional degree or higher: 15.8%

School District(s)
Marquette Area Public Schools (PK-12)
    2012-13 Enrollment: 3,100 . . . . (906) 225-5326
Marquette-Alger Resa (PK-12)
    2012-13 Enrollment: 89 . . . . (906) 226-5101
North Star Academy (KG-12)
    2012-13 Enrollment: 269 . . . . (906) 226-0156
Four-year College(s)
Northern Michigan University (Public)
    Fall 2013 Enrollment: 8,918 . . . . (906) 227-2650
    2013-14 Tuition: In-state $9,037; Out-of-state $14,113

Housing: Homeownership rate: 67.0%; Median home value: $167,500; Median year structure built: 1982; Homeowner vacancy rate: 1.4%; Median gross rent: $814 per month; Rental vacancy rate: 1.5%
Health Insurance: 88.5% have insurance; 80.9% have private insurance; 23.9% have public insurance; 11.5% do not have insurance; 2.6% of children under 18 do not have insurance
Hospitals: Marquette General Hospital (352 beds)
Newspapers: Mining Journal (daily circulation 14600)
Transportation: Commute: 91.2% car, 0.5% public transportation, 1.0% walk, 3.7% work from home; Median travel time to work: 15.4 minutes; Amtrak: Bus service available.

MARQUETTE (city). County seat. Covers a land area of 11.393 square miles and a water area of 8.063 square miles. Located at 46.55° N. Lat; 87.40° W. Long. Elevation is 666 feet.

History: In 1830 iron ore was discovered on the south shore of Lake Superior, and in 1846 the Jackson mine was opened about 14 miles inland from the site of Marquette. A shipping point was needed for the ore, and the site selected was the natural harbor at the mouth of the Carp River. The community that grew up here was first called Worcester, for the Massachusetts home of an early resident. In 1850 the town was renamed for the Jesuit missionary Marquette, whose explorations had helped to open the Northwest Territory. Marquette was incorporated as a village in 1859, and as a city in 1871.
Population: 21,355; Growth (since 2000): 8.6%; Density: 1,874.4 persons per square mile; Race: 91.1% White, 4.4% Black/African American, 0.9% Asian, 1.5% American Indian/Alaska Native, 0.0% Native Hawaiian/Other Pacific Islander, 1.8% Two or more races, 1.4% Hispanic of any race; Average household size: 2.05; Median age: 29.1; Age under 18: 12.2%; Age 65 and over: 13.0%; Males per 100 females: 107.7; Marriage status: 51.1% never married, 34.6% now married, 0.8% separated, 4.6% widowed, 9.7% divorced; Foreign born: 1.5%; Speak English only: 95.4%; With disability: 10.0%; Veterans: 8.8%; Ancestry: 20.1% German, 11.2% Irish, 10.7% English, 10.7% Finnish, 8.5% French
Employment: 9.6% management, business, and financial, 4.5% computer, engineering, and science, 9.7% education, legal, community service, arts, and media, 8.5% healthcare practitioners, 29.7% service, 23.8% sales and office, 7.6% natural resources, construction, and maintenance, 6.7% production, transportation, and material moving
Income: Per capita: $21,764; Median household: $37,770; Average household: $55,470; Households with income of $100,000 or more: 14.6%; Poverty rate: 25.5%
Educational Attainment: High school diploma or higher: 93.2%; Bachelor's degree or higher: 37.0%; Graduate/professional degree or higher: 12.2%

School District(s)
Marquette Area Public Schools (PK-12)
    2012-13 Enrollment: 3,100 . . . . (906) 225-5326
Marquette-Alger Resa (PK-12)
    2012-13 Enrollment: 89. . . . . (906) 226-5101
North Star Academy (KG-12)
    2012-13 Enrollment: 269. . . . . (906) 226-0156

Four-year College(s)
Northern Michigan University (Public)
    Fall 2013 Enrollment: 8,918 . . . . (906) 227-2650
    2013-14 Tuition: In-state $9,037; Out-of-state $14,113
Housing: Homeownership rate: 48.0%; Median home value: $159,600; Median year structure built: 1963; Homeowner vacancy rate: 1.9%; Median gross rent: $648 per month; Rental vacancy rate: 3.8%
Health Insurance: 85.6% have insurance; 73.4% have private insurance; 25.1% have public insurance; 14.4% do not have insurance; 1.4% of children under 18 do not have insurance
Hospitals: Marquette General Hospital (352 beds)
Safety: Violent crime rate: 8.8 per 10,000 population; Property crime rate: 148.7 per 10,000 population
Newspapers: Mining Journal (daily circulation 14600)
Transportation: Commute: 78.2% car, 0.8% public transportation, 13.5% walk, 4.4% work from home; Median travel time to work: 11.7 minutes; Amtrak: Bus service available.
Additional Information Contacts
City of Marquette. . . . . (906) 228-0435
    http://www.mqtcty.org

MICHIGAMME (CDP). Covers a land area of 2.379 square miles and a water area of 2.275 square miles. Located at 46.53° N. Lat; 88.06° W. Long. Elevation is 1,631 feet.

Population: 271; Growth (since 2000): -5.6%; Density: 113.9 persons per square mile; Race: 97.0% White, 0.0% Black/African American, 0.0% Asian, 0.4% American Indian/Alaska Native, 0.0% Native Hawaiian/Other Pacific Islander, 2.6% Two or more races, 0.0% Hispanic of any race; Average household size: 2.17; Median age: 52.7; Age under 18: 15.9%; Age 65 and over: 19.9%; Males per 100 females: 105.3
Housing: Homeownership rate: 93.6%; Homeowner vacancy rate: 3.3%; Rental vacancy rate: 0.0%

MICHIGAMME (township). Covers a land area of 133.192 square miles and a water area of 8.839 square miles. Located at 46.65° N. Lat; 87.98° W. Long. Elevation is 1,631 feet.

Population: 349; Growth (since 2000): -7.4%; Density: 2.6 persons per square mile; Race: 97.1% White, 0.0% Black/African American, 0.0% Asian, 0.6% American Indian/Alaska Native, 0.0% Native Hawaiian/Other Pacific Islander, 2.3% Two or more races, 0.0% Hispanic of any race; Average household size: 2.14; Median age: 54.7; Age under 18: 13.5%; Age 65 and over: 24.4%; Males per 100 females: 102.9
Housing: Homeownership rate: 95.1%; Homeowner vacancy rate: 2.5%; Rental vacancy rate: 38.5%

NEGAUNEE (city). Covers a land area of 13.557 square miles and a water area of 0.894 square miles. Located at 46.50° N. Lat; 87.59° W. Long. Elevation is 1,371 feet.

History: Iron ore was discovered in 1844 in the Marquette Range by a surveying party. Development of the community of Negaunee was slow, because of the difficulty of transporting the ore via forest trails to the dock at Marquette, and then unloading it to be carried around the rapids at Sault Ste. Marie. By 1855 a plank road had been completed, and the first locks at Sault Ste. Marie made shipping easier. The railroad connection between Negaunee and Marquette in 1857 brought more growth, and Negaunee was platted in 1865.
Population: 4,568; Growth (since 2000): -0.2%; Density: 337.0 persons per square mile; Race: 96.6% White, 0.1% Black/African American, 0.3% Asian, 1.1% American Indian/Alaska Native, 0.0% Native Hawaiian/Other Pacific Islander, 1.7% Two or more races, 1.1% Hispanic of any race; Average household size: 2.30; Median age: 39.7; Age under 18: 23.9%; Age 65 and over: 16.7%; Males per 100 females: 90.0; Marriage status: 26.6% never married, 50.2% now married, 0.0% separated, 10.0% widowed, 13.2% divorced; Foreign born: 0.6%; Speak English only: 96.1%; With disability: 12.0%; Veterans: 12.5%; Ancestry: 31.5% Finnish, 17.4% English, 13.5% German, 13.3% French, 11.0% Swedish
Employment: 12.2% management, business, and financial, 5.6% computer, engineering, and science, 10.2% education, legal, community service, arts, and media, 5.7% healthcare practitioners, 21.9% service, 23.7% sales and office, 12.3% natural resources, construction, and maintenance, 8.5% production, transportation, and material moving
Income: Per capita: $23,683; Median household: $46,207; Average household: $53,558; Households with income of $100,000 or more: 14.2%; Poverty rate: 10.2%
Educational Attainment: High school diploma or higher: 93.2%; Bachelor's degree or higher: 28.4%; Graduate/professional degree or higher: 7.3%

School District(s)
Negaunee Public Schools (PK-12)
    2012-13 Enrollment: 1,539 . . . . (906) 475-4157
Nice Community SD (PK-12)
    2012-13 Enrollment: 1,175 . . . . (906) 485-1021
Housing: Homeownership rate: 70.8%; Median home value: $107,900; Median year structure built: 1942; Homeowner vacancy rate: 2.3%; Median gross rent: $515 per month; Rental vacancy rate: 7.6%
Health Insurance: 91.0% have insurance; 78.5% have private insurance; 28.1% have public insurance; 9.0% do not have insurance; 2.2% of children under 18 do not have insurance
Safety: Violent crime rate: 4.3 per 10,000 population; Property crime rate: 187.1 per 10,000 population
Transportation: Commute: 94.5% car, 0.0% public transportation, 1.2% walk, 2.9% work from home; Median travel time to work: 21.9 minutes

NEGAUNEE (township). Covers a land area of 42.084 square miles and a water area of 1.578 square miles. Located at 46.55° N. Lat; 87.54° W. Long. Elevation is 1,371 feet.

History: Iron was discovered here in 1844. Michigan Iron Industry Museum. Settled 1846; incorporated as village 1862, as city 1873.

Population: 3,088; Growth (since 2000): 14.1%; Density: 73.4 persons per square mile; Race: 96.0% White, 0.3% Black/African American, 0.4% Asian, 1.9% American Indian/Alaska Native, 0.0% Native Hawaiian/Other Pacific Islander, 1.2% Two or more races, 0.9% Hispanic of any race; Average household size: 2.62; Median age: 41.1; Age under 18: 23.9%; Age 65 and over: 11.5%; Males per 100 females: 109.2; Marriage status: 26.1% never married, 63.9% now married, 0.4% separated, 4.2% widowed, 5.8% divorced; Foreign born: 0.5%; Speak English only: 98.6%; With disability: 10.7%; Veterans: 10.2%; Ancestry: 32.8% Finnish, 15.8% German, 14.3% English, 12.1% Swedish, 11.4% French

Employment: 7.8% management, business, and financial, 3.4% computer, engineering, and science, 6.3% education, legal, community service, arts, and media, 11.3% healthcare practitioners, 18.9% service, 26.0% sales and office, 12.7% natural resources, construction, and maintenance, 13.5% production, transportation, and material moving

Income: Per capita: $26,615; Median household: $66,694; Average household: $73,601; Households with income of $100,000 or more: 26.7%; Poverty rate: 5.0%

Educational Attainment: High school diploma or higher: 95.3%; Bachelor's degree or higher: 26.2%; Graduate/professional degree or higher: 9.3%

School District(s)
Negaunee Public Schools (PK-12)
    2012-13 Enrollment: 1,539 . . . . (906) 475-4157
Nice Community SD (PK-12)
    2012-13 Enrollment: 1,175 . . . . (906) 485-1021

Housing: Homeownership rate: 90.0%; Median home value: $156,600; Median year structure built: 1974; Homeowner vacancy rate: 0.1%; Median gross rent: $642 per month; Rental vacancy rate: 6.3%

Health Insurance: 92.9% have insurance; 84.2% have private insurance; 24.0% have public insurance; 7.1% do not have insurance; 2.9% of children under 18 do not have insurance

Transportation: Commute: 97.8% car, 0.0% public transportation, 0.0% walk, 1.2% work from home; Median travel time to work: 18.0 minutes

PALMER (CDP). Covers a land area of 0.593 square miles and a water area of 0 square miles. Located at 46.44° N. Lat; 87.58° W. Long. Elevation is 1,302 feet.

Population: 418; Growth (since 2000): -6.9%; Density: 705.0 persons per square mile; Race: 97.1% White, 0.0% Black/African American, 0.2% Asian, 1.7% American Indian/Alaska Native, 0.0% Native Hawaiian/Other Pacific Islander, 1.0% Two or more races, 0.5% Hispanic of any race; Average household size: 2.37; Median age: 42.4; Age under 18: 22.5%; Age 65 and over: 12.4%; Males per 100 females: 100.0

Housing: Homeownership rate: 87.7%; Homeowner vacancy rate: 1.3%; Rental vacancy rate: 4.5%

POWELL (township). Covers a land area of 153.697 square miles and a water area of 8.358 square miles. Located at 46.83° N. Lat; 87.81° W. Long.

Population: 816; Growth (since 2000): 12.7%; Density: 5.3 persons per square mile; Race: 95.3% White, 0.1% Black/African American, 1.0% Asian, 2.6% American Indian/Alaska Native, 0.0% Native Hawaiian/Other Pacific Islander, 1.0% Two or more races, 0.4% Hispanic of any race; Average household size: 1.93; Median age: 53.7; Age under 18: 11.9%; Age 65 and over: 22.3%; Males per 100 females: 118.2

Housing: Homeownership rate: 86.3%; Homeowner vacancy rate: 2.4%; Rental vacancy rate: 9.4%

REPUBLIC (CDP). Covers a land area of 3.618 square miles and a water area of 0.315 square miles. Located at 46.41° N. Lat; 87.99° W. Long. Elevation is 1,522 feet.

Population: 570; Growth (since 2000): -7.2%; Density: 157.6 persons per square mile; Race: 97.7% White, 0.5% Black/African American, 0.2% Asian, 0.7% American Indian/Alaska Native, 0.0% Native Hawaiian/Other Pacific Islander, 0.7% Two or more races, 0.2% Hispanic of any race; Average household size: 2.10; Median age: 50.0; Age under 18: 19.1%; Age 65 and over: 25.4%; Males per 100 females: 94.5

School District(s)
Republic-Michigamme Schools (PK-12)
    2012-13 Enrollment: 135 . . . . (906) 376-2277

Housing: Homeownership rate: 80.8%; Homeowner vacancy rate: 3.1%; Rental vacancy rate: 3.7%

REPUBLIC (township). Covers a land area of 111.371 square miles and a water area of 8.171 square miles. Located at 46.39° N. Lat; 88.09° W. Long. Elevation is 1,522 feet.

History: Republic was named for the Republic Mine, which began operation in 1871.

Population: 1,060; Growth (since 2000): -4.2%; Density: 9.5 persons per square mile; Race: 96.9% White, 0.3% Black/African American, 0.2% Asian, 1.6% American Indian/Alaska Native, 0.0% Native Hawaiian/Other Pacific Islander, 0.9% Two or more races, 0.5% Hispanic of any race; Average household size: 2.05; Median age: 52.8; Age under 18: 16.4%; Age 65 and over: 25.2%; Males per 100 females: 105.4

School District(s)
Republic-Michigamme Schools (PK-12)
    2012-13 Enrollment: 135 . . . . (906) 376-2277

Housing: Homeownership rate: 87.4%; Homeowner vacancy rate: 3.2%; Rental vacancy rate: 7.1%

RICHMOND (township). Covers a land area of 55.573 square miles and a water area of 2.043 square miles. Located at 46.40° N. Lat; 87.55° W. Long.

Population: 882; Growth (since 2000): -9.4%; Density: 15.9 persons per square mile; Race: 95.9% White, 0.1% Black/African American, 0.2% Asian, 2.0% American Indian/Alaska Native, 0.0% Native Hawaiian/Other Pacific Islander, 1.5% Two or more races, 1.0% Hispanic of any race; Average household size: 2.32; Median age: 45.7; Age under 18: 19.2%; Age 65 and over: 15.4%; Males per 100 females: 98.2

Housing: Homeownership rate: 88.2%; Homeowner vacancy rate: 1.8%; Rental vacancy rate: 4.3%

SANDS (township). Covers a land area of 66.403 square miles and a water area of 0.354 square miles. Located at 46.42° N. Lat; 87.44° W. Long. Elevation is 1,201 feet.

Population: 2,285; Growth (since 2000): 7.4%; Density: 34.4 persons per square mile; Race: 94.8% White, 0.5% Black/African American, 0.4% Asian, 2.9% American Indian/Alaska Native, 0.0% Native Hawaiian/Other Pacific Islander, 1.4% Two or more races, 1.4% Hispanic of any race; Average household size: 2.59; Median age: 42.0; Age under 18: 23.5%; Age 65 and over: 7.7%; Males per 100 females: 102.8

Housing: Homeownership rate: 92.7%; Homeowner vacancy rate: 2.2%; Rental vacancy rate: 9.9%

SKANDIA (township). Covers a land area of 71.837 square miles and a water area of 0.177 square miles. Located at 46.33° N. Lat; 87.17° W. Long. Elevation is 896 feet.

Population: 826; Growth (since 2000): -8.9%; Density: 11.5 persons per square mile; Race: 93.5% White, 0.1% Black/African American, 0.6% Asian, 2.4% American Indian/Alaska Native, 0.0% Native Hawaiian/Other Pacific Islander, 3.4% Two or more races, 0.6% Hispanic of any race; Average household size: 2.36; Median age: 45.1; Age under 18: 20.6%; Age 65 and over: 14.9%; Males per 100 females: 103.4

Housing: Homeownership rate: 90.3%; Homeowner vacancy rate: 0.6%; Rental vacancy rate: 12.8%

TILDEN (township). Covers a land area of 89.891 square miles and a water area of 6.102 square miles. Located at 46.35° N. Lat; 87.67° W. Long.

Population: 1,013; Growth (since 2000): 1.0%; Density: 11.3 persons per square mile; Race: 97.8% White, 0.2% Black/African American, 0.4% Asian, 1.3% American Indian/Alaska Native, 0.0% Native Hawaiian/Other Pacific Islander, 0.3% Two or more races, 0.5% Hispanic of any race; Average household size: 2.46; Median age: 43.8; Age under 18: 22.3%; Age 65 and over: 13.1%; Males per 100 females: 106.3

Housing: Homeownership rate: 92.5%; Homeowner vacancy rate: 0.5%; Rental vacancy rate: 0.0%

TROWBRIDGE PARK (CDP). Covers a land area of 1.387 square miles and a water area of 0.014 square miles. Located at 46.56° N. Lat; 87.44° W. Long. Elevation is 791 feet.
Population: 2,176; Growth (since 2000): 8.2%; Density: 1,569.0 persons per square mile; Race: 93.9% White, 0.5% Black/African American, 0.4% Asian, 2.8% American Indian/Alaska Native, 0.0% Native Hawaiian/Other Pacific Islander, 2.3% Two or more races, 0.9% Hispanic of any race; Average household size: 2.33; Median age: 38.8; Age under 18: 17.4%; Age 65 and over: 11.8%; Males per 100 females: 101.9
Housing: Homeownership rate: 71.6%; Homeowner vacancy rate: 0.6%; Rental vacancy rate: 1.8%

TURIN (township). Covers a land area of 83.695 square miles and a water area of 0.312 square miles. Located at 46.19° N. Lat; 87.25° W. Long.
Population: 153; Growth (since 2000): 16.8%; Density: 1.8 persons per square mile; Race: 97.4% White, 0.0% Black/African American, 0.0% Asian, 1.3% American Indian/Alaska Native, 0.0% Native Hawaiian/Other Pacific Islander, 0.7% Two or more races, 1.3% Hispanic of any race; Average household size: 2.32; Median age: 50.9; Age under 18: 17.6%; Age 65 and over: 16.3%; Males per 100 females: 98.7
Housing: Homeownership rate: 93.9%; Homeowner vacancy rate: 3.1%; Rental vacancy rate: 0.0%

WELLS (township). Covers a land area of 154.108 square miles and a water area of 0.827 square miles. Located at 46.06° N. Lat; 87.48° W. Long. Elevation is 1,030 feet.
Population: 231; Growth (since 2000): -20.9%; Density: 1.5 persons per square mile; Race: 99.1% White, 0.0% Black/African American, 0.0% Asian, 0.0% American Indian/Alaska Native, 0.0% Native Hawaiian/Other Pacific Islander, 0.9% Two or more races, 0.0% Hispanic of any race; Average household size: 1.93; Median age: 53.9; Age under 18: 12.1%; Age 65 and over: 26.0%; Males per 100 females: 110.0
Housing: Homeownership rate: 94.2%; Homeowner vacancy rate: 1.7%; Rental vacancy rate: 0.0%

WEST BRANCH (township). Covers a land area of 35.484 square miles and a water area of 0.289 square miles. Located at 46.38° N. Lat; 87.29° W. Long.
Population: 1,623; Growth (since 2000): -1.5%; Density: 45.7 persons per square mile; Race: 88.7% White, 2.1% Black/African American, 0.6% Asian, 3.7% American Indian/Alaska Native, 0.0% Native Hawaiian/Other Pacific Islander, 4.7% Two or more races, 1.6% Hispanic of any race; Average household size: 2.53; Median age: 33.9; Age under 18: 26.2%; Age 65 and over: 9.5%; Males per 100 females: 102.9
Housing: Homeownership rate: 50.5%; Homeowner vacancy rate: 1.8%; Rental vacancy rate: 37.5%

WEST ISHPEMING (CDP). Covers a land area of 2.959 square miles and a water area of 0.045 square miles. Located at 46.49° N. Lat; 87.72° W. Long. Elevation is 1,440 feet.
Population: 2,662; Growth (since 2000): -4.7%; Density: 899.6 persons per square mile; Race: 96.7% White, 0.2% Black/African American, 0.4% Asian, 0.8% American Indian/Alaska Native, 0.0% Native Hawaiian/Other Pacific Islander, 1.8% Two or more races, 0.9% Hispanic of any race; Average household size: 2.48; Median age: 43.5; Age under 18: 23.1%; Age 65 and over: 18.7%; Males per 100 females: 93.6; Marriage status: 27.5% never married, 55.4% now married, 0.8% separated, 7.4% widowed, 9.7% divorced; Foreign born: 0.0%; Speak English only: 97.6%; With disability: 10.8%; Veterans: 11.0%; Ancestry: 28.2% Finnish, 18.4% English, 14.1% French, 13.1% German, 12.9% Italian
Employment: 11.5% management, business, and financial, 2.2% computer, engineering, and science, 8.0% education, legal, community service, arts, and media, 13.1% healthcare practitioners, 18.6% service, 21.0% sales and office, 18.4% natural resources, construction, and maintenance, 7.2% production, transportation, and material moving
Income: Per capita: $27,815; Median household: $48,563; Average household: $67,549; Households with income of $100,000 or more: 20.0%; Poverty rate: 8.1%
Educational Attainment: High school diploma or higher: 94.0%; Bachelor's degree or higher: 22.0%; Graduate/professional degree or higher: 3.4%
Housing: Homeownership rate: 91.1%; Median home value: $96,600; Median year structure built: 1966; Homeowner vacancy rate: 0.3%; Median gross rent: n/a per month; Rental vacancy rate: 8.8%

Health Insurance: 90.7% have insurance; 80.1% have private insurance; 28.9% have public insurance; 9.3% do not have insurance; 0.8% of children under 18 do not have insurance
Transportation: Commute: 96.4% car, 0.1% public transportation, 1.2% walk, 1.3% work from home; Median travel time to work: 18.6 minutes

Mason County

Located in western Michigan; bounded on the west by Lake Michigan; drained by the Pere Marquette, Big Sable, and Little Manistee Rivers; includes Hamlin Lake, and Manistee National Forest. Covers a land area of 495.073 square miles, a water area of 747.369 square miles, and is located in the Eastern Time Zone at 44.00° N. Lat., 86.75° W. Long. The county was founded in 1855. County seat is Ludington.

Mason County is part of the Ludington, MI Micropolitan Statistical Area. The entire metro area includes: Mason County, MI

Weather Station: Ludington 4 SE   Elevation: 689 feet

	Jan	Feb	Mar	Apr	May	Jun	Jul	Aug	Sep	Oct	Nov	Dec
High	31	34	43	57	68	77	81	79	72	59	46	35
Low	18	19	25	35	44	53	58	57	51	40	31	22
Precip	1.6	1.1	1.7	2.9	3.4	3.5	2.9	3.6	3.9	3.8	3.6	2.4
Snow	28.7	18.2	8.5	2.7	0.1	0.0	0.0	0.0	0.0	0.2	7.6	25.7

High and Low temperatures in degrees Fahrenheit; Precipitation and Snow in inches

Population: 28,705; Growth (since 2000): 1.5%; Density: 58.0 persons per square mile; Race: 94.8% White, 0.6% Black/African American, 0.5% Asian, 1.0% American Indian/Alaska Native, 0.0% Native Hawaiian/Other Pacific Islander, 1.9% two or more races, 4.0% Hispanic of any race; Average household size: 2.37; Median age: 45.1; Age under 18: 21.7%; Age 65 and over: 19.2%; Males per 100 females: 97.5; Marriage status: 21.8% never married, 59.3% now married, 1.2% separated, 7.1% widowed, 11.8% divorced; Foreign born: 1.8%; Speak English only: 95.6%; With disability: 17.0%; Veterans: 11.5%; Ancestry: 28.9% German, 12.3% Irish, 12.1% Polish, 11.8% English, 7.5% Dutch
Religion: Six largest groups: 15.3% Catholicism, 7.4% Lutheran, 6.0% Methodist/Pietist, 4.8% Presbyterian-Reformed, 3.6% Non-denominational Protestant, 3.0% Baptist
Economy: Unemployment rate: 5.3%; Leading industries: 15.2% retail trade; 12.5% health care and social assistance; 12.1% other services (except public administration); Farms: 440 totaling 79,048 acres; Company size: 0 employ 1,000 or more persons, 2 employ 500 to 999 persons, 10 employ 100 to 499 persons, 732 employ less than 100 persons; Business ownership: 773 women-owned, n/a Black-owned, n/a Hispanic-owned, n/a Asian-owned
Employment: 11.9% management, business, and financial, 2.2% computer, engineering, and science, 10.4% education, legal, community service, arts, and media, 5.6% healthcare practitioners, 19.0% service, 22.0% sales and office, 8.7% natural resources, construction, and maintenance, 20.3% production, transportation, and material moving
Income: Per capita: $23,183; Median household: $41,136; Average household: $53,338; Households with income of $100,000 or more: 12.8%; Poverty rate: 16.2%
Educational Attainment: High school diploma or higher: 89.5%; Bachelor's degree or higher: 19.8%; Graduate/professional degree or higher: 7.2%
Housing: Homeownership rate: 76.5%; Median home value: $117,000; Median year structure built: 1971; Homeowner vacancy rate: 4.0%; Median gross rent: $654 per month; Rental vacancy rate: 9.2%
Vital Statistics: Birth rate: 90.2 per 10,000 population; Death rate: 97.2 per 10,000 population; Age-adjusted cancer mortality rate: 192.5 deaths per 100,000 population
Health Insurance: 86.4% have insurance; 64.8% have private insurance; 40.4% have public insurance; 13.6% do not have insurance; 6.9% of children under 18 do not have insurance
Health Care: Physicians: 18.5 per 10,000 population; Hospital beds: 27.9 per 10,000 population; Hospital admissions: 830.9 per 10,000 population
Air Quality Index: 89.0% good, 11.0% moderate, 0.0% unhealthy for sensitive individuals, 0.0% unhealthy (percent of days)
Transportation: Commute: 91.3% car, 0.6% public transportation, 2.3% walk, 4.3% work from home; Median travel time to work: 17.9 minutes
Presidential Election: 47.0% Obama, 52.0% Romney (2012)
National and State Parks: Ludington State Park

Additional Information Contacts

Additional Information Contacts
Mason Government............................ (231) 843-8202
http://www.masoncounty.net

Mason County Communities

AMBER (township). Covers a land area of 27.554 square miles and a water area of 0.195 square miles. Located at 43.96° N. Lat; 86.35° W. Long. Elevation is 679 feet.
History: Amber Township was formed in 1867, and probably named by Charles W. Jones for his hometown of Amber, Indiana.
Population: 2,535; Growth (since 2000): 23.4%; Density: 92.0 persons per square mile; Race: 94.8% White, 0.5% Black/African American, 0.9% Asian, 0.7% American Indian/Alaska Native, 0.0% Native Hawaiian/Other Pacific Islander, 1.9% Two or more races, 3.5% Hispanic of any race; Average household size: 2.41; Median age: 45.1; Age under 18: 20.5%; Age 65 and over: 17.7%; Males per 100 females: 96.2; Marriage status: 19.8% never married, 64.4% now married, 0.4% separated, 3.8% widowed, 12.0% divorced; Foreign born: 2.6%; Speak English only: 95.8%; With disability: 17.7%; Veterans: 13.0%; Ancestry: 31.9% German, 12.5% Irish, 11.6% Polish, 10.8% English, 5.5% Dutch
Employment: 9.0% management, business, and financial, 0.7% computer, engineering, and science, 11.0% education, legal, community service, arts, and media, 13.3% healthcare practitioners, 16.8% service, 23.6% sales and office, 8.4% natural resources, construction, and maintenance, 17.3% production, transportation, and material moving
Income: Per capita: $24,155; Median household: $48,720; Average household: $55,471; Households with income of $100,000 or more: 12.6%; Poverty rate: 13.9%
Educational Attainment: High school diploma or higher: 93.9%; Bachelor's degree or higher: 20.9%; Graduate/professional degree or higher: 12.2%
Housing: Homeownership rate: 72.1%; Median home value: $151,000; Median year structure built: 1988; Homeowner vacancy rate: 4.2%; Median gross rent: $737 per month; Rental vacancy rate: 11.4%
Health Insurance: 87.1% have insurance; 68.3% have private insurance; 38.5% have public insurance; 12.9% do not have insurance; 3.5% of children under 18 do not have insurance
Transportation: Commute: 96.3% car, 0.0% public transportation, 0.4% walk, 2.9% work from home; Median travel time to work: 13.8 minutes

BRANCH (township). Covers a land area of 35.386 square miles and a water area of 0.579 square miles. Located at 43.95° N. Lat; 86.10° W. Long.
History: Branch was founded in 1875 as a lumber center, established around a station of the Pere Marquette Railway. Besides the sawmills, an early industry was pickle-making.
Population: 1,328; Growth (since 2000): 12.4%; Density: 37.5 persons per square mile; Race: 96.5% White, 0.7% Black/African American, 0.1% Asian, 0.5% American Indian/Alaska Native, 0.0% Native Hawaiian/Other Pacific Islander, 1.7% Two or more races, 2.7% Hispanic of any race; Average household size: 2.35; Median age: 44.3; Age under 18: 23.4%; Age 65 and over: 18.4%; Males per 100 females: 105.9
Housing: Homeownership rate: 86.2%; Homeowner vacancy rate: 5.0%; Rental vacancy rate: 7.1%

CUSTER (township). Covers a land area of 34.879 square miles and a water area of 0.057 square miles. Located at 43.95° N. Lat; 86.22° W. Long. Elevation is 676 feet.
Population: 1,254; Growth (since 2000): -4.1%; Density: 36.0 persons per square mile; Race: 97.0% White, 0.2% Black/African American, 0.0% Asian, 1.1% American Indian/Alaska Native, 0.0% Native Hawaiian/Other Pacific Islander, 1.6% Two or more races, 2.7% Hispanic of any race; Average household size: 2.55; Median age: 45.1; Age under 18: 21.8%; Age 65 and over: 16.5%; Males per 100 females: 103.2
School District(s)
Mason County Eastern Schools (PK-12)
    2012-13 Enrollment: 471...................... (231) 757-3733
Housing: Homeownership rate: 87.6%; Homeowner vacancy rate: 2.7%; Rental vacancy rate: 6.2%

CUSTER (village). Covers a land area of 0.985 square miles and a water area of 0 square miles. Located at 43.95° N. Lat; 86.22° W. Long. Elevation is 676 feet.
History: Custer was founded in 1876 as a station on the Pere Marquette Railroad. The village and township were named for General George A. Custer (1839-1876).
Population: 284; Growth (since 2000): -10.7%; Density: 288.4 persons per square mile; Race: 97.2% White, 0.7% Black/African American, 0.0% Asian, 0.4% American Indian/Alaska Native, 0.0% Native Hawaiian/Other Pacific Islander, 1.8% Two or more races, 3.9% Hispanic of any race; Average household size: 2.58; Median age: 39.0; Age under 18: 23.6%; Age 65 and over: 16.5%; Males per 100 females: 105.8
School District(s)
Mason County Eastern Schools (PK-12)
    2012-13 Enrollment: 471...................... (231) 757-3733
Housing: Homeownership rate: 80.0%; Homeowner vacancy rate: 5.2%; Rental vacancy rate: 12.0%

EDEN (township). Covers a land area of 35.412 square miles and a water area of 0.455 square miles. Located at 43.86° N. Lat; 86.23° W. Long.
Population: 582; Growth (since 2000): 4.9%; Density: 16.4 persons per square mile; Race: 95.0% White, 0.5% Black/African American, 0.5% Asian, 1.4% American Indian/Alaska Native, 0.0% Native Hawaiian/Other Pacific Islander, 1.2% Two or more races, 3.8% Hispanic of any race; Average household size: 2.55; Median age: 43.0; Age under 18: 23.9%; Age 65 and over: 18.7%; Males per 100 females: 104.9
Housing: Homeownership rate: 88.2%; Homeowner vacancy rate: 0.5%; Rental vacancy rate: 0.0%

FOUNTAIN (village). Covers a land area of 1.012 square miles and a water area of 0 square miles. Located at 44.05° N. Lat; 86.18° W. Long. Elevation is 709 feet.
Population: 193; Growth (since 2000): 10.3%; Density: 190.8 persons per square mile; Race: 91.7% White, 0.0% Black/African American, 3.1% Asian, 0.0% American Indian/Alaska Native, 0.0% Native Hawaiian/Other Pacific Islander, 5.2% Two or more races, 3.6% Hispanic of any race; Average household size: 2.72; Median age: 37.8; Age under 18: 26.9%; Age 65 and over: 9.8%; Males per 100 females: 116.9
Housing: Homeownership rate: 80.3%; Homeowner vacancy rate: 3.4%; Rental vacancy rate: 6.7%

FREE SOIL (township). Covers a land area of 38.801 square miles and a water area of 0.420 square miles. Located at 44.13° N. Lat; 86.21° W. Long. Elevation is 686 feet.
Population: 822; Growth (since 2000): 1.6%; Density: 21.2 persons per square mile; Race: 96.7% White, 0.9% Black/African American, 0.1% Asian, 1.6% American Indian/Alaska Native, 0.0% Native Hawaiian/Other Pacific Islander, 0.6% Two or more races, 2.1% Hispanic of any race; Average household size: 2.35; Median age: 47.5; Age under 18: 18.9%; Age 65 and over: 18.4%; Males per 100 females: 115.2
Housing: Homeownership rate: 89.5%; Homeowner vacancy rate: 3.3%; Rental vacancy rate: 5.1%

FREE SOIL (village). Covers a land area of 1.037 square miles and a water area of 0 square miles. Located at 44.11° N. Lat; 86.21° W. Long. Elevation is 686 feet.
Population: 144; Growth (since 2000): -18.6%; Density: 138.9 persons per square mile; Race: 95.8% White, 1.4% Black/African American, 0.0% Asian, 2.8% American Indian/Alaska Native, 0.0% Native Hawaiian/Other Pacific Islander, 0.0% Two or more races, 0.0% Hispanic of any race; Average household size: 2.25; Median age: 44.9; Age under 18: 20.8%; Age 65 and over: 20.8%; Males per 100 females: 105.7
Housing: Homeownership rate: 84.4%; Homeowner vacancy rate: 6.7%; Rental vacancy rate: 0.0%

GRANT (township). Covers a land area of 48.726 square miles and a water area of 0.192 square miles. Located at 44.13° N. Lat; 86.36° W. Long.
History: Grant Township was organized in 1867 and named for Civil War General U.S. Grant.
Population: 909; Growth (since 2000): 6.9%; Density: 18.7 persons per square mile; Race: 95.7% White, 0.0% Black/African American, 0.1% Asian, 1.0% American Indian/Alaska Native, 0.0% Native Hawaiian/Other Pacific Islander, 1.7% Two or more races, 2.5% Hispanic of any race;

Average household size: 2.42; Median age: 48.9; Age under 18: 18.4%; Age 65 and over: 16.4%; Males per 100 females: 107.1
Housing: Homeownership rate: 90.1%; Homeowner vacancy rate: 0.9%; Rental vacancy rate: 9.8%

HAMLIN (township). Covers a land area of 27.435 square miles and a water area of 6.965 square miles. Located at 44.03° N. Lat; 86.45° W. Long.
Population: 3,408; Growth (since 2000): 6.8%; Density: 124.2 persons per square mile; Race: 96.7% White, 0.4% Black/African American, 0.3% Asian, 0.8% American Indian/Alaska Native, 0.0% Native Hawaiian/Other Pacific Islander, 1.4% Two or more races, 2.8% Hispanic of any race; Average household size: 2.37; Median age: 49.7; Age under 18: 19.7%; Age 65 and over: 21.1%; Males per 100 females: 100.4; Marriage status: 17.8% never married, 69.5% now married, 0.0% separated, 4.6% widowed, 8.2% divorced; Foreign born: 0.5%; Speak English only: 98.7%; With disability: 11.6%; Veterans: 12.6%; Ancestry: 32.4% German, 15.6% Irish, 15.2% English, 12.2% Polish, 8.6% Swedish
Employment: 17.9% management, business, and financial, 2.2% computer, engineering, and science, 11.8% education, legal, community service, arts, and media, 6.2% healthcare practitioners, 17.3% service, 23.4% sales and office, 3.7% natural resources, construction, and maintenance, 17.5% production, transportation, and material moving
Income: Per capita: $28,769; Median household: $51,016; Average household: $67,035; Households with income of $100,000 or more: 21.8%; Poverty rate: 7.3%
Educational Attainment: High school diploma or higher: 93.9%; Bachelor's degree or higher: 28.1%; Graduate/professional degree or higher: 9.2%
Housing: Homeownership rate: 92.9%; Median home value: $163,700; Median year structure built: 1978; Homeowner vacancy rate: 3.4%; Median gross rent: $637 per month; Rental vacancy rate: 14.6%
Health Insurance: 91.1% have insurance; 81.1% have private insurance; 29.0% have public insurance; 8.9% do not have insurance; 3.4% of children under 18 do not have insurance
Transportation: Commute: 96.8% car, 0.0% public transportation, 0.0% walk, 3.2% work from home; Median travel time to work: 16.8 minutes

LOGAN (township). Covers a land area of 36.020 square miles and a water area of 0.096 square miles. Located at 43.86° N. Lat; 86.12° W. Long.
Population: 312; Growth (since 2000): -5.2%; Density: 8.7 persons per square mile; Race: 98.1% White, 0.0% Black/African American, 0.0% Asian, 0.3% American Indian/Alaska Native, 0.0% Native Hawaiian/Other Pacific Islander, 1.3% Two or more races, 1.6% Hispanic of any race; Average household size: 2.07; Median age: 55.7; Age under 18: 9.9%; Age 65 and over: 28.2%; Males per 100 females: 119.7
Housing: Homeownership rate: 83.4%; Homeowner vacancy rate: 6.7%; Rental vacancy rate: 0.0%

LUDINGTON (city). County seat. Covers a land area of 3.368 square miles and a water area of 0.335 square miles. Located at 43.96° N. Lat; 86.44° W. Long. Elevation is 591 feet.
History: Ludington was first called Marquette, in honor of Father Jacques Marquette, the missionary and explorer, who died here in 1675. It was later renamed Ludington for James Ludington, a lumberman who lived here in the 1880's. Ludington became an important shipping center, bordering both Lake Michigan and Pere Marquette Lake, which provided a safe harbor for boats, ferries, and lake freighters.
Population: 8,076; Growth (since 2000): -3.4%; Density: 2,398.2 persons per square mile; Race: 92.2% White, 1.1% Black/African American, 0.6% Asian, 1.4% American Indian/Alaska Native, 0.0% Native Hawaiian/Other Pacific Islander, 2.6% Two or more races, 6.3% Hispanic of any race; Average household size: 2.19; Median age: 43.0; Age under 18: 21.8%; Age 65 and over: 21.1%; Males per 100 females: 84.5; Marriage status: 25.6% never married, 49.0% now married, 1.9% separated, 10.2% widowed, 15.2% divorced; Foreign born: 1.8%; Speak English only: 96.2%; With disability: 19.7%; Veterans: 9.8%; Ancestry: 27.7% German, 11.5% English, 10.9% Irish, 10.8% Polish, 7.7% French
Employment: 9.3% management, business, and financial, 2.6% computer, engineering, and science, 14.7% education, legal, community service, arts, and media, 3.4% healthcare practitioners, 19.5% service, 20.6% sales and office, 6.3% natural resources, construction, and maintenance, 23.7% production, transportation, and material moving

Income: Per capita: $21,200; Median household: $32,010; Average household: $44,950; Households with income of $100,000 or more: 9.7%; Poverty rate: 19.5%
Educational Attainment: High school diploma or higher: 88.2%; Bachelor's degree or higher: 21.5%; Graduate/professional degree or higher: 6.5%

School District(s)
Ludington Area SD (PK-12)
    2012-13 Enrollment: 2,211 . . . . (231) 845-7303
West Shore Educational Service District (PK-12)
    2012-13 Enrollment: 99 . . . . (231) 757-3716
Housing: Homeownership rate: 55.8%; Median home value: $104,100; Median year structure built: 1953; Homeowner vacancy rate: 6.7%; Median gross rent: $570 per month; Rental vacancy rate: 7.5%
Health Insurance: 86.4% have insurance; 60.4% have private insurance; 45.1% have public insurance; 13.6% do not have insurance; 3.3% of children under 18 do not have insurance
Hospitals: Memorial Medical Center of West Michigan
Safety: Violent crime rate: 31.1 per 10,000 population; Property crime rate: 245.2 per 10,000 population
Newspapers: Ludington Daily News (daily circulation 8700)
Transportation: Commute: 89.1% car, 1.4% public transportation, 4.2% walk, 2.6% work from home; Median travel time to work: 13.5 minutes
Airports: Mason County (general aviation)
Additional Information Contacts
City of Ludington . . . . (231) 845-6237
    http://www.ludington.mi.us

MEADE (township). Covers a land area of 37.470 square miles and a water area of 0.087 square miles. Located at 44.12° N. Lat; 86.09° W. Long.
Population: 181; Growth (since 2000): -36.9%; Density: 4.8 persons per square mile; Race: 85.1% White, 0.0% Black/African American, 0.0% Asian, 6.6% American Indian/Alaska Native, 0.0% Native Hawaiian/Other Pacific Islander, 6.1% Two or more races, 3.3% Hispanic of any race; Average household size: 2.26; Median age: 49.1; Age under 18: 24.3%; Age 65 and over: 18.2%; Males per 100 females: 126.3
Housing: Homeownership rate: 87.5%; Homeowner vacancy rate: 6.6%; Rental vacancy rate: 0.0%

PERE MARQUETTE (charter township). Covers a land area of 14.088 square miles and a water area of 1.659 square miles. Located at 43.93° N. Lat; 86.42° W. Long.
Population: 2,366; Growth (since 2000): 6.2%; Density: 167.9 persons per square mile; Race: 96.3% White, 0.3% Black/African American, 0.7% Asian, 0.6% American Indian/Alaska Native, 0.0% Native Hawaiian/Other Pacific Islander, 1.4% Two or more races, 2.5% Hispanic of any race; Average household size: 2.50; Median age: 45.3; Age under 18: 23.8%; Age 65 and over: 20.7%; Males per 100 females: 102.7
Housing: Homeownership rate: 87.0%; Homeowner vacancy rate: 2.2%; Rental vacancy rate: 12.5%
Additional Information Contacts
Pere Marquette Charter Township . . . . (231) 845-1277
    http://www.peremarquettetwp.org

RIVERTON (township). Covers a land area of 35.266 square miles and a water area of 0.450 square miles. Located at 43.87° N. Lat; 86.33° W. Long.
Population: 1,153; Growth (since 2000): -13.6%; Density: 32.7 persons per square mile; Race: 95.3% White, 0.2% Black/African American, 0.0% Asian, 0.2% American Indian/Alaska Native, 0.0% Native Hawaiian/Other Pacific Islander, 1.2% Two or more races, 7.5% Hispanic of any race; Average household size: 2.61; Median age: 44.3; Age under 18: 22.6%; Age 65 and over: 13.7%; Males per 100 females: 113.5
Housing: Homeownership rate: 90.1%; Homeowner vacancy rate: 2.1%; Rental vacancy rate: 13.5%

SCOTTVILLE (city). Covers a land area of 1.487 square miles and a water area of 0 square miles. Located at 43.95° N. Lat; 86.28° W. Long. Elevation is 686 feet.
History: Scottville was settled in 1876 and first called Mason Center. In 1881 it was renamed Sweetland in honor of James Sweetland, who platted the community. When it was incorporated as a village in 1889, the name was changed to Scottville to honor Hiram Scott, an early resident. All three

names continued to be used until 1907, when incorporation as a city settled the name of Scottville.

Population: 1,214; Growth (since 2000): -4.1%; Density: 816.5 persons per square mile; Race: 92.9% White, 0.9% Black/African American, 0.5% Asian, 0.9% American Indian/Alaska Native, 0.0% Native Hawaiian/Other Pacific Islander, 2.8% Two or more races, 5.3% Hispanic of any race; Average household size: 2.51; Median age: 35.1; Age under 18: 28.2%; Age 65 and over: 13.8%; Males per 100 females: 92.1

School District(s)
Ludington Area SD (PK-12)
   2012-13 Enrollment: 2,211 . . . . (231) 845-7303
Mason County Central Schools (PK-12)
   2012-13 Enrollment: 1,404 . . . . (231) 757-3713
Two-year College(s)
West Shore Community College (Public)
   Fall 2013 Enrollment: 1,487 . . . . (231) 845-6211
   2013-14 Tuition: In-state $3,978; Out-of-state $5,178
Housing: Homeownership rate: 62.7%; Homeowner vacancy rate: 5.3%; Rental vacancy rate: 15.9%

SHERIDAN (township). Covers a land area of 34.217 square miles and a water area of 1.659 square miles. Located at 44.05° N. Lat; 86.09° W. Long.
Population: 1,072; Growth (since 2000): 10.6%; Density: 31.3 persons per square mile; Race: 96.3% White, 0.0% Black/African American, 0.6% Asian, 1.4% American Indian/Alaska Native, 0.0% Native Hawaiian/Other Pacific Islander, 1.8% Two or more races, 0.8% Hispanic of any race; Average household size: 2.31; Median age: 47.9; Age under 18: 18.1%; Age 65 and over: 21.1%; Males per 100 females: 105.0
Housing: Homeownership rate: 87.5%; Homeowner vacancy rate: 4.5%; Rental vacancy rate: 7.9%

SHERMAN (township). Covers a land area of 36.231 square miles and a water area of 0.055 square miles. Located at 44.04° N. Lat; 86.21° W. Long.
History: Sherman Township was organized in 1867 and named for General William T. Sherman.
Population: 1,186; Growth (since 2000): 8.8%; Density: 32.7 persons per square mile; Race: 94.9% White, 0.3% Black/African American, 0.6% Asian, 0.8% American Indian/Alaska Native, 0.0% Native Hawaiian/Other Pacific Islander, 3.0% Two or more races, 2.9% Hispanic of any race; Average household size: 2.60; Median age: 42.1; Age under 18: 23.5%; Age 65 and over: 14.5%; Males per 100 females: 111.4
Housing: Homeownership rate: 85.8%; Homeowner vacancy rate: 1.8%; Rental vacancy rate: 7.0%

SUMMIT (township). Covers a land area of 12.801 square miles and a water area of 1.490 square miles. Located at 43.86° N. Lat; 86.41° W. Long.
Population: 924; Growth (since 2000): -9.5%; Density: 72.2 persons per square mile; Race: 97.4% White, 0.2% Black/African American, 0.4% Asian, 0.4% American Indian/Alaska Native, 0.0% Native Hawaiian/Other Pacific Islander, 0.5% Two or more races, 2.4% Hispanic of any race; Average household size: 2.32; Median age: 52.3; Age under 18: 17.6%; Age 65 and over: 25.8%; Males per 100 females: 96.6
Housing: Homeownership rate: 90.2%; Homeowner vacancy rate: 3.5%; Rental vacancy rate: 26.4%

VICTORY (township). Covers a land area of 35.933 square miles and a water area of 0.568 square miles. Located at 44.04° N. Lat; 86.34° W. Long.
Population: 1,383; Growth (since 2000): -4.2%; Density: 38.5 persons per square mile; Race: 96.7% White, 0.4% Black/African American, 0.1% Asian, 0.7% American Indian/Alaska Native, 0.0% Native Hawaiian/Other Pacific Islander, 1.4% Two or more races, 2.5% Hispanic of any race; Average household size: 2.64; Median age: 40.9; Age under 18: 26.1%; Age 65 and over: 14.9%; Males per 100 females: 101.9
Housing: Homeownership rate: 86.1%; Homeowner vacancy rate: 2.2%; Rental vacancy rate: 6.3%

WALHALLA (unincorporated postal area)
ZCTA: 49458
   Covers a land area of 7.170 square miles and a water area of 0.057 square miles. Located at 43.92° N. Lat; 86.10° W. Long. Elevation is 699 feet.

Population: 119; Growth (since 2000): -20.1%; Density: 16.6 persons per square mile; Race: 98.3% White, 0.0% Black/African American, 0.0% Asian, 1.7% American Indian/Alaska Native, 0.0% Native Hawaiian/Other Pacific Islander, 0.0% Two or more races, 0.0% Hispanic of any race; Average household size: 2.13; Median age: 50.1; Age under 18: 19.3%; Age 65 and over: 20.2%; Males per 100 females: 105.2
Housing: Homeownership rate: 85.7%; Homeowner vacancy rate: 5.9%; Rental vacancy rate: 11.1%

Mecosta County

Located in central Michigan; drained by the Muskegon, Little Muskegon, Chippewa, and Pine Rivers; includes part of Manistee National Forest. Covers a land area of 555.071 square miles, a water area of 16.123 square miles, and is located in the Eastern Time Zone at 43.64° N. Lat., 85.33° W. Long. The county was founded in 1859. County seat is Big Rapids.

Mecosta County is part of the Big Rapids, MI Micropolitan Statistical Area. The entire metro area includes: Mecosta County, MI

Weather Station: Big Rapids Waterworks										Elevation: 930 feet		
	Jan	Feb	Mar	Apr	May	Jun	Jul	Aug	Sep	Oct	Nov	Dec
High	29	33	43	56	69	78	82	79	72	58	45	33
Low	12	14	20	32	43	53	57	55	47	36	28	18
Precip	2.2	1.7	2.4	3.3	3.4	3.3	3.2	4.0	4.0	3.3	3.2	2.4
Snow	18.1	12.6	8.1	2.0	tr	0.0	0.0	0.0	tr	0.3	5.0	16.4

High and Low temperatures in degrees Fahrenheit; Precipitation and Snow in inches

Population: 42,798; Growth (since 2000): 5.5%; Density: 77.1 persons per square mile; Race: 93.7% White, 2.5% Black/African American, 0.7% Asian, 0.6% American Indian/Alaska Native, 0.0% Native Hawaiian/Other Pacific Islander, 2.1% two or more races, 1.7% Hispanic of any race; Average household size: 2.45; Median age: 34.0; Age under 18: 20.0%; Age 65 and over: 15.4%; Males per 100 females: 100.8; Marriage status: 37.4% never married, 47.6% now married, 1.1% separated, 4.8% widowed, 10.2% divorced; Foreign born: 2.1%; Speak English only: 95.9%; With disability: 15.7%; Veterans: 10.1%; Ancestry: 27.3% German, 12.9% Irish, 12.4% English, 8.5% Polish, 7.2% Dutch
Religion: Six largest groups: 11.2% Catholicism, 4.7% Methodist/Pietist, 4.2% Lutheran, 2.4% Non-denominational Protestant, 2.0% Presbyterian-Reformed, 1.7% European Free-Church
Economy: Unemployment rate: 5.7%; Leading industries: 19.2% retail trade; 13.0% other services (except public administration); 11.2% health care and social assistance; Farms: 779 totaling 123,005 acres; Company size: 0 employ 1,000 or more persons, 0 employ 500 to 999 persons, 19 employ 100 to 499 persons, 720 employ less than 100 persons; Business ownership: n/a women-owned, n/a Black-owned, n/a Hispanic-owned, n/a Asian-owned
Employment: 9.2% management, business, and financial, 2.2% computer, engineering, and science, 11.4% education, legal, community service, arts, and media, 5.2% healthcare practitioners, 21.7% service, 23.2% sales and office, 9.3% natural resources, construction, and maintenance, 17.8% production, transportation, and material moving
Income: Per capita: $19,336; Median household: $39,470; Average household: $50,905; Households with income of $100,000 or more: 11.2%; Poverty rate: 22.9%
Educational Attainment: High school diploma or higher: 89.8%; Bachelor's degree or higher: 21.6%; Graduate/professional degree or higher: 8.5%
Housing: Homeownership rate: 71.6%; Median home value: $112,200; Median year structure built: 1978; Homeowner vacancy rate: 3.7%; Median gross rent: $643 per month; Rental vacancy rate: 7.9%
Vital Statistics: Birth rate: 89.3 per 10,000 population; Death rate: 77.2 per 10,000 population; Age-adjusted cancer mortality rate: 196.8 deaths per 100,000 population
Health Insurance: 86.0% have insurance; 67.1% have private insurance; 34.6% have public insurance; 14.0% do not have insurance; 8.2% of children under 18 do not have insurance
Health Care: Physicians: 9.5 per 10,000 population; Hospital beds: 11.3 per 10,000 population; Hospital admissions: 537.3 per 10,000 population
Transportation: Commute: 88.3% car, 0.7% public transportation, 5.8% walk, 3.7% work from home; Median travel time to work: 22.5 minutes
Presidential Election: 44.5% Obama, 54.4% Romney (2012)

National and State Parks: Fred Meijer White Pine Trail State Park; Haymarsh Lake State Game Area; Martiny Lake State Game Area

Additional Information Contacts

Mecosta Government . . . . (231) 592-0783
http://www.co.mecosta.mi.us

Mecosta County Communities

AETNA (township). Covers a land area of 35.517 square miles and a water area of 0.397 square miles. Located at 43.52° N. Lat; 85.51° W. Long.

Population: 2,299; Growth (since 2000): 12.5%; Density: 64.7 persons per square mile; Race: 96.5% White, 0.6% Black/African American, 0.1% Asian, 0.6% American Indian/Alaska Native, 0.0% Native Hawaiian/Other Pacific Islander, 1.9% Two or more races, 1.9% Hispanic of any race; Average household size: 2.81; Median age: 37.1; Age under 18: 27.8%; Age 65 and over: 11.2%; Males per 100 females: 104.4

Housing: Homeownership rate: 78.9%; Homeowner vacancy rate: 3.3%; Rental vacancy rate: 6.0%

AUSTIN (township). Covers a land area of 35.668 square miles and a water area of 0.085 square miles. Located at 43.60° N. Lat; 85.37° W. Long.

History: Austin Township was organized in 1869.

Population: 1,561; Growth (since 2000): 10.3%; Density: 43.8 persons per square mile; Race: 95.9% White, 0.7% Black/African American, 0.3% Asian, 0.4% American Indian/Alaska Native, 0.0% Native Hawaiian/Other Pacific Islander, 2.4% Two or more races, 2.2% Hispanic of any race; Average household size: 2.77; Median age: 38.0; Age under 18: 28.3%; Age 65 and over: 15.3%; Males per 100 females: 98.6

Housing: Homeownership rate: 88.7%; Homeowner vacancy rate: 4.9%; Rental vacancy rate: 12.3%

BARRYTON (village). Covers a land area of 0.957 square miles and a water area of 0.078 square miles. Located at 43.75° N. Lat; 85.14° W. Long. Elevation is 981 feet.

History: Barryton was founded in 1894 by Frank Barry, who opened a grocery and drug store.

Population: 355; Growth (since 2000): -6.8%; Density: 370.8 persons per square mile; Race: 98.0% White, 0.3% Black/African American, 0.3% Asian, 0.3% American Indian/Alaska Native, 0.0% Native Hawaiian/Other Pacific Islander, 1.1% Two or more races, 0.6% Hispanic of any race; Average household size: 2.31; Median age: 41.2; Age under 18: 22.0%; Age 65 and over: 23.4%; Males per 100 females: 95.1

School District(s)

Chippewa Hills SD (PK-12)
    2012-13 Enrollment: 2,180 . . . . (989) 967-2000

Housing: Homeownership rate: 67.5%; Homeowner vacancy rate: 10.2%; Rental vacancy rate: 9.1%

Safety: Violent crime rate: 0.0 per 10,000 population; Property crime rate: 110.2 per 10,000 population

BIG RAPIDS (charter township). Covers a land area of 30.527 square miles and a water area of 0.426 square miles. Located at 43.68° N. Lat; 85.50° W. Long. Elevation is 928 feet.

History: Incorporated 1869.

Population: 4,208; Growth (since 2000): 29.5%; Density: 137.8 persons per square mile; Race: 93.9% White, 2.4% Black/African American, 1.2% Asian, 0.3% American Indian/Alaska Native, 0.1% Native Hawaiian/Other Pacific Islander, 1.8% Two or more races, 1.9% Hispanic of any race; Average household size: 2.62; Median age: 27.6; Age under 18: 18.3%; Age 65 and over: 12.8%; Males per 100 females: 97.9; Marriage status: 40.2% never married, 48.8% now married, 2.2% separated, 4.8% widowed, 6.2% divorced; Foreign born: 1.3%; Speak English only: 95.8%; With disability: 12.2%; Veterans: 12.1%; Ancestry: 29.7% German, 17.5% Irish, 13.1% English, 8.9% Polish, 8.4% American

Employment: 7.9% management, business, and financial, 0.5% computer, engineering, and science, 18.6% education, legal, community service, arts, and media, 4.6% healthcare practitioners, 24.9% service, 25.3% sales and office, 5.6% natural resources, construction, and maintenance, 12.5% production, transportation, and material moving

Income: Per capita: $26,571; Median household: $43,320; Average household: $63,911; Households with income of $100,000 or more: 16.7%; Poverty rate: 24.0%

Educational Attainment: High school diploma or higher: 97.2%; Bachelor's degree or higher: 33.4%; Graduate/professional degree or higher: 15.1%

School District(s)

Big Rapids Public Schools (KG-12)
    2012-13 Enrollment: 1,893 . . . . (231) 796-2627
Crossroads Charter Academy (PK-12)
    2012-13 Enrollment: 698 . . . . (231) 796-9041
Mecosta-Osceola ISD (PK-12)
    2012-13 Enrollment: 485 . . . . (231) 796-3543

Four-year College(s)

Ferris State University (Public)
    Fall 2013 Enrollment: 14,707 . . . . (231) 591-2000
    2013-14 Tuition: In-state $10,466; Out-of-state $16,722

Housing: Homeownership rate: 62.2%; Median home value: $153,000; Median year structure built: 1989; Homeowner vacancy rate: 1.5%; Median gross rent: $645 per month; Rental vacancy rate: 4.2%

Health Insurance: 92.0% have insurance; 84.7% have private insurance; 22.6% have public insurance; 8.0% do not have insurance; 7.3% of children under 18 do not have insurance

Hospitals: Spectrum Health Big Rapids Hospital (74 beds)

Newspapers: Big Rapids Pioneer (daily circulation 5200); Pioneer Group (weekly circulation 4900)

Transportation: Commute: 98.2% car, 0.1% public transportation, 0.4% walk, 0.9% work from home; Median travel time to work: 17.9 minutes; Amtrak: Bus service available.

Airports: Roben-Hood (general aviation)

BIG RAPIDS (city). County seat. Covers a land area of 4.364 square miles and a water area of 0.122 square miles. Located at 43.70° N. Lat; 85.48° W. Long. Elevation is 928 feet.

History: Big Rapids was first known as Leonard, for an early settler, but the rapids on the Muskegon River became the feature by which the community was known. The first house was built here in 1854. A lumber boom brought early growth to the settlement. When the timber was depleted, Big Rapids became a year-round vacation resort. Natural gas was discovered here in the early 1930's, giving a boost to the economy.

Population: 10,601; Growth (since 2000): -2.3%; Density: 2,429.3 persons per square mile; Race: 88.0% White, 6.8% Black/African American, 1.5% Asian, 0.7% American Indian/Alaska Native, 0.0% Native Hawaiian/Other Pacific Islander, 2.5% Two or more races, 2.4% Hispanic of any race; Average household size: 2.22; Median age: 21.8; Age under 18: 12.5%; Age 65 and over: 6.5%; Males per 100 females: 104.2; Marriage status: 68.4% never married, 20.1% now married, 0.7% separated, 3.5% widowed, 7.9% divorced; Foreign born: 4.3%; Speak English only: 93.8%; With disability: 11.4%; Veterans: 4.8%; Ancestry: 27.8% German, 14.4% Irish, 12.0% Polish, 8.3% Dutch, 7.8% English

Employment: 6.7% management, business, and financial, 2.1% computer, engineering, and science, 13.5% education, legal, community service, arts, and media, 6.0% healthcare practitioners, 28.5% service, 25.7% sales and office, 6.1% natural resources, construction, and maintenance, 11.4% production, transportation, and material moving

Income: Per capita: $12,188; Median household: $24,550; Average household: $35,942; Households with income of $100,000 or more: 7.8%; Poverty rate: 45.6%

Educational Attainment: High school diploma or higher: 88.2%; Bachelor's degree or higher: 32.0%; Graduate/professional degree or higher: 13.4%

School District(s)

Big Rapids Public Schools (KG-12)
    2012-13 Enrollment: 1,893 . . . . (231) 796-2627
Crossroads Charter Academy (PK-12)
    2012-13 Enrollment: 698 . . . . (231) 796-9041
Mecosta-Osceola ISD (PK-12)
    2012-13 Enrollment: 485 . . . . (231) 796-3543

Four-year College(s)

Ferris State University (Public)
    Fall 2013 Enrollment: 14,707 . . . . (231) 591-2000
    2013-14 Tuition: In-state $10,466; Out-of-state $16,722

Housing: Homeownership rate: 34.1%; Median home value: $87,700; Median year structure built: 1966; Homeowner vacancy rate: 3.2%; Median gross rent: $552 per month; Rental vacancy rate: 6.5%

Health Insurance: 84.3% have insurance; 65.8% have private insurance; 25.2% have public insurance; 15.7% do not have insurance; 2.7% of children under 18 do not have insurance

Hospitals: Spectrum Health Big Rapids Hospital (74 beds)
Safety: Violent crime rate: 27.0 per 10,000 population; Property crime rate: 186.3 per 10,000 population
Newspapers: Big Rapids Pioneer (daily circulation 5200); Pioneer Group (weekly circulation 4900)
Transportation: Commute: 73.1% car, 0.8% public transportation, 19.6% walk, 3.5% work from home; Median travel time to work: 14.4 minutes; Amtrak: Bus service available.
Airports: Roben-Hood (general aviation)
Additional Information Contacts
City of Big Rapids . . . . (231) 592-4025
  http://www.ci.big-rapids.mi.us

CANADIAN LAKES (CDP). Covers a land area of 9.491 square miles and a water area of 1.169 square miles. Located at 43.58° N. Lat; 85.30° W. Long. Elevation is 968 feet.
Population: 2,756; Growth (since 2000): 43.4%; Density: 290.4 persons per square mile; Race: 97.2% White, 0.8% Black/African American, 0.4% Asian, 0.5% American Indian/Alaska Native, 0.1% Native Hawaiian/Other Pacific Islander, 1.1% Two or more races, 1.2% Hispanic of any race; Average household size: 2.14; Median age: 60.5; Age under 18: 13.9%; Age 65 and over: 39.3%; Males per 100 females: 98.1; Marriage status: 10.4% never married, 74.1% now married, 0.0% separated, 8.8% widowed, 6.6% divorced; Foreign born: 4.0%; Speak English only: 95.8%; With disability: 12.7%; Veterans: 18.5%; Ancestry: 31.7% German, 23.0% English, 13.2% Irish, 13.0% Polish, 7.0% French
Employment: 14.3% management, business, and financial, 3.0% computer, engineering, and science, 16.5% education, legal, community service, arts, and media, 4.4% healthcare practitioners, 24.8% service, 20.0% sales and office, 2.7% natural resources, construction, and maintenance, 14.3% production, transportation, and material moving
Income: Per capita: $28,572; Median household: $50,385; Average household: $58,916; Households with income of $100,000 or more: 14.0%; Poverty rate: 5.9%
Educational Attainment: High school diploma or higher: 96.4%; Bachelor's degree or higher: 33.4%; Graduate/professional degree or higher: 13.0%
Housing: Homeownership rate: 93.3%; Median home value: $188,300; Median year structure built: 1990; Homeowner vacancy rate: 5.5%; Median gross rent: $839 per month; Rental vacancy rate: 19.1%
Health Insurance: 95.0% have insurance; 86.2% have private insurance; 49.8% have public insurance; 5.0% do not have insurance; 0.0% of children under 18 do not have insurance
Transportation: Commute: 98.8% car, 0.0% public transportation, 0.0% walk, 0.4% work from home; Median travel time to work: 33.1 minutes

CHIPPEWA (township). Covers a land area of 32.981 square miles and a water area of 2.418 square miles. Located at 43.78° N. Lat; 85.26° W. Long.
Population: 1,212; Growth (since 2000): -2.2%; Density: 36.7 persons per square mile; Race: 98.1% White, 0.3% Black/African American, 0.2% Asian, 0.3% American Indian/Alaska Native, 0.0% Native Hawaiian/Other Pacific Islander, 0.7% Two or more races, 1.4% Hispanic of any race; Average household size: 2.24; Median age: 49.3; Age under 18: 18.7%; Age 65 and over: 24.1%; Males per 100 females: 104.4
Housing: Homeownership rate: 83.6%; Homeowner vacancy rate: 6.0%; Rental vacancy rate: 12.0%

CHIPPEWA LAKE (unincorporated postal area)
ZCTA: 49320
  Covers a land area of 0.358 square miles and a water area of 0 square miles. Located at 43.75° N. Lat; 85.28° W. Long. Elevation is 1,106 feet.
  Population: 21; Growth (since 2000): n/a; Density: 58.6 persons per square mile; Race: 100.0% White, 0.0% Black/African American, 0.0% Asian, 0.0% American Indian/Alaska Native, 0.0% Native Hawaiian/Other Pacific Islander, 0.0% Two or more races, 0.0% Hispanic of any race; Average household size: 2.10; Median age: 52.5; Age under 18: 9.5%; Age 65 and over: 23.8%; Males per 100 females: 90.9
  Housing: Homeownership rate: 80.0%; Homeowner vacancy rate: 11.1%; Rental vacancy rate: 0.0%

COLFAX (township). Covers a land area of 35.108 square miles and a water area of 0.737 square miles. Located at 43.68° N. Lat; 85.38° W. Long.
History: Colfax Township was organized in 1869 and named for Vice President Schuyler Colfax.
Population: 1,933; Growth (since 2000): -2.1%; Density: 55.1 persons per square mile; Race: 95.3% White, 1.0% Black/African American, 0.7% Asian, 0.5% American Indian/Alaska Native, 0.0% Native Hawaiian/Other Pacific Islander, 2.2% Two or more races, 1.2% Hispanic of any race; Average household size: 2.53; Median age: 43.5; Age under 18: 24.8%; Age 65 and over: 16.2%; Males per 100 females: 92.9
Housing: Homeownership rate: 89.2%; Homeowner vacancy rate: 2.7%; Rental vacancy rate: 9.7%

DEERFIELD (township). Covers a land area of 35.673 square miles and a water area of 0.222 square miles. Located at 43.51° N. Lat; 85.39° W. Long.
Population: 1,816; Growth (since 2000): 11.4%; Density: 50.9 persons per square mile; Race: 96.3% White, 0.6% Black/African American, 0.0% Asian, 1.5% American Indian/Alaska Native, 0.0% Native Hawaiian/Other Pacific Islander, 1.4% Two or more races, 1.6% Hispanic of any race; Average household size: 3.08; Median age: 34.2; Age under 18: 31.7%; Age 65 and over: 10.4%; Males per 100 females: 102.2
Housing: Homeownership rate: 80.5%; Homeowner vacancy rate: 3.8%; Rental vacancy rate: 5.6%

FORK (township). Covers a land area of 34.781 square miles and a water area of 0.421 square miles. Located at 43.77° N. Lat; 85.15° W. Long.
Population: 1,604; Growth (since 2000): -4.4%; Density: 46.1 persons per square mile; Race: 95.7% White, 1.3% Black/African American, 0.2% Asian, 0.9% American Indian/Alaska Native, 0.0% Native Hawaiian/Other Pacific Islander, 1.8% Two or more races, 1.4% Hispanic of any race; Average household size: 2.41; Median age: 44.8; Age under 18: 22.0%; Age 65 and over: 21.6%; Males per 100 females: 95.8
Housing: Homeownership rate: 84.4%; Homeowner vacancy rate: 6.0%; Rental vacancy rate: 12.7%

GRANT (township). Covers a land area of 32.641 square miles and a water area of 1.377 square miles. Located at 43.77° N. Lat; 85.37° W. Long.
Population: 686; Growth (since 2000): 0.9%; Density: 21.0 persons per square mile; Race: 97.2% White, 0.4% Black/African American, 0.1% Asian, 0.4% American Indian/Alaska Native, 0.0% Native Hawaiian/Other Pacific Islander, 1.5% Two or more races, 0.4% Hispanic of any race; Average household size: 2.47; Median age: 44.5; Age under 18: 22.0%; Age 65 and over: 17.5%; Males per 100 females: 115.0
Housing: Homeownership rate: 85.2%; Homeowner vacancy rate: 2.1%; Rental vacancy rate: 2.4%

GREEN (charter township). Covers a land area of 36.980 square miles and a water area of 0.624 square miles. Located at 43.77° N. Lat; 85.50° W. Long. Elevation is 928 feet.
History: Green Township was organized in 1858 and named for Andrew and Lewis H. Green, who had settled here the year before.
Population: 3,292; Growth (since 2000): 2.6%; Density: 89.0 persons per square mile; Race: 96.5% White, 1.0% Black/African American, 0.4% Asian, 0.5% American Indian/Alaska Native, 0.0% Native Hawaiian/Other Pacific Islander, 1.4% Two or more races, 1.1% Hispanic of any race; Average household size: 2.46; Median age: 42.0; Age under 18: 22.6%; Age 65 and over: 15.9%; Males per 100 females: 97.5; Marriage status: 31.6% never married, 51.3% now married, 3.0% separated, 4.0% widowed, 13.1% divorced; Foreign born: 0.9%; Speak English only: 99.0%; With disability: 18.8%; Veterans: 10.1%; Ancestry: 31.4% German, 19.4% English, 12.9% American, 11.5% Dutch, 11.3% Polish
Employment: 13.1% management, business, and financial, 4.0% computer, engineering, and science, 11.9% education, legal, community service, arts, and media, 5.7% healthcare practitioners, 20.3% service, 23.9% sales and office, 7.2% natural resources, construction, and maintenance, 13.9% production, transportation, and material moving
Income: Per capita: $20,040; Median household: $42,868; Average household: $54,961; Households with income of $100,000 or more: 16.8%; Poverty rate: 14.3%

Educational Attainment: High school diploma or higher: 89.4%; Bachelor's degree or higher: 22.7%; Graduate/professional degree or higher: 6.3%
Housing: Homeownership rate: 82.2%; Median home value: $106,200; Median year structure built: 1977; Homeowner vacancy rate: 2.3%; Median gross rent: $769 per month; Rental vacancy rate: 17.8%
Health Insurance: 80.4% have insurance; 59.7% have private insurance; 36.3% have public insurance; 19.6% do not have insurance; 18.5% of children under 18 do not have insurance
Transportation: Commute: 93.9% car, 2.1% public transportation, 0.7% walk, 2.8% work from home; Median travel time to work: 17.7 minutes

HINTON (township). Covers a land area of 35.729 square miles and a water area of 0.073 square miles. Located at 43.50° N. Lat; 85.26° W. Long.
History: Hinton Township was organized in 1860 and named for John Hinton, who had settled here in 1855.
Population: 1,126; Growth (since 2000): 8.8%; Density: 31.5 persons per square mile; Race: 97.7% White, 0.3% Black/African American, 0.0% Asian, 0.3% American Indian/Alaska Native, 0.0% Native Hawaiian/Other Pacific Islander, 1.5% Two or more races, 1.6% Hispanic of any race; Average household size: 2.78; Median age: 38.0; Age under 18: 26.7%; Age 65 and over: 14.6%; Males per 100 females: 96.9
Housing: Homeownership rate: 82.9%; Homeowner vacancy rate: 2.3%; Rental vacancy rate: 4.2%

MARTINY (township). Covers a land area of 31.977 square miles and a water area of 3.456 square miles. Located at 43.69° N. Lat; 85.27° W. Long.
Population: 1,625; Growth (since 2000): 1.2%; Density: 50.8 persons per square mile; Race: 97.2% White, 0.4% Black/African American, 0.3% Asian, 0.6% American Indian/Alaska Native, 0.0% Native Hawaiian/Other Pacific Islander, 1.3% Two or more races, 0.4% Hispanic of any race; Average household size: 2.18; Median age: 51.8; Age under 18: 16.9%; Age 65 and over: 25.8%; Males per 100 females: 98.4
Housing: Homeownership rate: 87.3%; Homeowner vacancy rate: 5.0%; Rental vacancy rate: 14.4%

MECOSTA (township). Covers a land area of 34.033 square miles and a water area of 1.916 square miles. Located at 43.61° N. Lat; 85.50° W. Long. Elevation is 981 feet.
Population: 2,615; Growth (since 2000): 7.4%; Density: 76.8 persons per square mile; Race: 96.1% White, 0.5% Black/African American, 0.5% Asian, 0.4% American Indian/Alaska Native, 0.0% Native Hawaiian/Other Pacific Islander, 2.1% Two or more races, 2.1% Hispanic of any race; Average household size: 2.54; Median age: 40.1; Age under 18: 23.5%; Age 65 and over: 14.7%; Males per 100 females: 100.5; Marriage status: 26.9% never married, 57.2% now married, 0.3% separated, 4.3% widowed, 11.6% divorced; Foreign born: 1.4%; Speak English only: 93.1%; With disability: 19.2%; Veterans: 10.5%; Ancestry: 25.7% German, 12.6% English, 9.6% Irish, 9.0% Dutch, 8.6% American
Employment: 9.6% management, business, and financial, 2.0% computer, engineering, and science, 9.3% education, legal, community service, arts, and media, 9.5% healthcare practitioners, 14.7% service, 22.5% sales and office, 9.6% natural resources, construction, and maintenance, 22.8% production, transportation, and material moving
Income: Per capita: $20,545; Median household: $40,250; Average household: $50,685; Households with income of $100,000 or more: 10.5%; Poverty rate: 21.8%
Educational Attainment: High school diploma or higher: 88.2%; Bachelor's degree or higher: 19.1%; Graduate/professional degree or higher: 8.6%
School District(s)
Chippewa Hills SD (PK-12)
    2012-13 Enrollment: 2,180 . . . . (989) 967-2000
Housing: Homeownership rate: 76.8%; Median home value: $108,000; Median year structure built: 1981; Homeowner vacancy rate: 4.7%; Median gross rent: $764 per month; Rental vacancy rate: 8.8%
Health Insurance: 83.5% have insurance; 62.3% have private insurance; 34.0% have public insurance; 16.5% do not have insurance; 13.8% of children under 18 do not have insurance
Transportation: Commute: 93.9% car, 0.6% public transportation, 1.1% walk, 3.4% work from home; Median travel time to work: 20.6 minutes

MECOSTA (village). Covers a land area of 1.117 square miles and a water area of <.001 square miles. Located at 43.62° N. Lat; 85.23° W. Long. Elevation is 981 feet.
Population: 457; Growth (since 2000): 3.9%; Density: 409.0 persons per square mile; Race: 88.6% White, 2.0% Black/African American, 0.0% Asian, 0.9% American Indian/Alaska Native, 0.4% Native Hawaiian/Other Pacific Islander, 6.8% Two or more races, 3.1% Hispanic of any race; Average household size: 2.75; Median age: 33.6; Age under 18: 30.9%; Age 65 and over: 11.6%; Males per 100 females: 104.0
School District(s)
Chippewa Hills SD (PK-12)
    2012-13 Enrollment: 2,180 . . . . (989) 967-2000
Housing: Homeownership rate: 72.9%; Homeowner vacancy rate: 3.2%; Rental vacancy rate: 8.2%

MILLBROOK (township). Covers a land area of 35.769 square miles and a water area of 0.085 square miles. Located at 43.51° N. Lat; 85.15° W. Long. Elevation is 948 feet.
Population: 1,113; Growth (since 2000): 3.0%; Density: 31.1 persons per square mile; Race: 96.8% White, 0.4% Black/African American, 0.0% Asian, 0.3% American Indian/Alaska Native, 0.1% Native Hawaiian/Other Pacific Islander, 2.4% Two or more races, 1.3% Hispanic of any race; Average household size: 2.69; Median age: 39.6; Age under 18: 27.0%; Age 65 and over: 14.2%; Males per 100 females: 103.8
Housing: Homeownership rate: 87.9%; Homeowner vacancy rate: 3.1%; Rental vacancy rate: 0.0%

MORLEY (village). Covers a land area of 0.895 square miles and a water area of 0.095 square miles. Located at 43.49° N. Lat; 85.45° W. Long. Elevation is 899 feet.
History: Morley was settled in 1869 as a trading and supply center for the surrounding area.
Population: 493; Growth (since 2000): -0.4%; Density: 550.8 persons per square mile; Race: 94.3% White, 1.0% Black/African American, 0.4% Asian, 0.6% American Indian/Alaska Native, 0.0% Native Hawaiian/Other Pacific Islander, 2.6% Two or more races, 5.7% Hispanic of any race; Average household size: 2.71; Median age: 33.6; Age under 18: 30.0%; Age 65 and over: 14.4%; Males per 100 females: 87.5
School District(s)
Morley Stanwood Community Schools (PK-12)
    2012-13 Enrollment: 1,260 . . . . (231) 856-4392
Housing: Homeownership rate: 62.7%; Homeowner vacancy rate: 11.6%; Rental vacancy rate: 11.5%

MORTON (township). Covers a land area of 33.039 square miles and a water area of 2.591 square miles. Located at 43.60° N. Lat; 85.26° W. Long.
Population: 4,311; Growth (since 2000): 19.8%; Density: 130.5 persons per square mile; Race: 95.2% White, 1.5% Black/African American, 0.3% Asian, 0.4% American Indian/Alaska Native, 0.1% Native Hawaiian/Other Pacific Islander, 2.1% Two or more races, 1.3% Hispanic of any race; Average household size: 2.17; Median age: 56.8; Age under 18: 16.0%; Age 65 and over: 34.5%; Males per 100 females: 97.8; Marriage status: 15.6% never married, 67.8% now married, 0.1% separated, 7.1% widowed, 9.5% divorced; Foreign born: 3.0%; Speak English only: 97.3%; With disability: 16.9%; Veterans: 16.7%; Ancestry: 29.4% German, 19.4% English, 13.1% Irish, 10.5% Polish, 6.5% French
Employment: 14.9% management, business, and financial, 4.0% computer, engineering, and science, 12.2% education, legal, community service, arts, and media, 4.3% healthcare practitioners, 24.5% service, 20.6% sales and office, 3.9% natural resources, construction, and maintenance, 15.7% production, transportation, and material moving
Income: Per capita: $26,477; Median household: $48,154; Average household: $59,778; Households with income of $100,000 or more: 15.7%; Poverty rate: 10.3%
Educational Attainment: High school diploma or higher: 94.8%; Bachelor's degree or higher: 27.9%; Graduate/professional degree or higher: 10.4%
Housing: Homeownership rate: 88.3%; Median home value: $182,900; Median year structure built: 1986; Homeowner vacancy rate: 4.8%; Median gross rent: $680 per month; Rental vacancy rate: 15.3%
Health Insurance: 91.1% have insurance; 74.3% have private insurance; 50.0% have public insurance; 8.9% do not have insurance; 0.6% of children under 18 do not have insurance

Transportation: Commute: 92.9% car, 1.2% public transportation, 0.8% walk, 3.8% work from home; Median travel time to work: 27.8 minutes

REMUS (unincorporated postal area)
ZCTA: 49340

Covers a land area of 86.478 square miles and a water area of 0.776 square miles. Located at 43.62° N. Lat; 85.11° W. Long. Elevation is 1,027 feet.

Population: 2,912; Growth (since 2000): -0.8%; Density: 33.7 persons per square mile; Race: 92.6% White, 1.5% Black/African American, 0.1% Asian, 1.6% American Indian/Alaska Native, 0.0% Native Hawaiian/Other Pacific Islander, 4.1% Two or more races, 1.6% Hispanic of any race; Average household size: 2.59; Median age: 41.3; Age under 18: 23.3%; Age 65 and over: 16.0%; Males per 100 females: 101.1; Marriage status: 25.1% never married, 56.3% now married, 0.4% separated, 5.1% widowed, 13.5% divorced; Foreign born: 0.6%; Speak English only: 98.4%; With disability: 15.1%; Veterans: 9.2%; Ancestry: 30.7% German, 15.6% English, 10.1% Irish, 7.9% American, 5.3% French

Employment: 11.8% management, business, and financial, 2.5% computer, engineering, and science, 9.4% education, legal, community service, arts, and media, 4.3% healthcare practitioners, 15.6% service, 17.8% sales and office, 14.0% natural resources, construction, and maintenance, 24.6% production, transportation, and material moving

Income: Per capita: $20,984; Median household: $42,017; Average household: $52,492; Households with income of $100,000 or more: 10.1%; Poverty rate: 13.9%

Educational Attainment: High school diploma or higher: 88.4%; Bachelor's degree or higher: 15.3%; Graduate/professional degree or higher: 4.8%

School District(s)
Chippewa Hills SD (PK-12)
    2012-13 Enrollment: 2,180 . . . . (989) 967-2000

Housing: Homeownership rate: 81.8%; Median home value: $98,400; Median year structure built: 1980; Homeowner vacancy rate: 2.1%; Median gross rent: $517 per month; Rental vacancy rate: 6.0%

Health Insurance: 92.3% have insurance; 73.0% have private insurance; 34.0% have public insurance; 7.7% do not have insurance; 1.8% of children under 18 do not have insurance

Transportation: Commute: 92.6% car, 0.7% public transportation, 1.8% walk, 4.5% work from home; Median travel time to work: 25.4 minutes

RODNEY (unincorporated postal area)
ZCTA: 49342

Covers a land area of 44.934 square miles and a water area of 1.682 square miles. Located at 43.69° N. Lat; 85.32° W. Long. Elevation is 1,076 feet.

Population: 1,649; Growth (since 2000): -9.0%; Density: 36.7 persons per square mile; Race: 95.6% White, 0.5% Black/African American, 0.5% Asian, 0.4% American Indian/Alaska Native, 0.0% Native Hawaiian/Other Pacific Islander, 2.6% Two or more races, 0.8% Hispanic of any race; Average household size: 2.40; Median age: 41.1; Age under 18: 24.7%; Age 65 and over: 16.8%; Males per 100 females: 96.8

Housing: Homeownership rate: 81.2%; Homeowner vacancy rate: 4.8%; Rental vacancy rate: 16.8%

SHERIDAN (township). Covers a land area of 34.799 square miles and a water area of 0.974 square miles. Located at 43.68° N. Lat; 85.14° W. Long.

History: Sheridan Township was organized in 1867 and named for General Philip H. Sheridan.

Population: 1,393; Growth (since 2000): 2.7%; Density: 40.0 persons per square mile; Race: 91.0% White, 2.4% Black/African American, 0.1% Asian, 1.9% American Indian/Alaska Native, 0.0% Native Hawaiian/Other Pacific Islander, 4.5% Two or more races, 1.7% Hispanic of any race; Average household size: 2.57; Median age: 43.4; Age under 18: 22.3%; Age 65 and over: 16.3%; Males per 100 females: 112.0

Housing: Homeownership rate: 86.4%; Homeowner vacancy rate: 3.5%; Rental vacancy rate: 9.8%

STANWOOD (village). Covers a land area of 0.244 square miles and a water area of <.001 square miles. Located at 43.58° N. Lat; 85.45° W. Long. Elevation is 961 feet.

History: Stanwood was settled in 1870 and named for the plentiful timber in the area. It was incorporated as a village in 1907.

Population: 211; Growth (since 2000): 3.4%; Density: 863.0 persons per square mile; Race: 95.3% White, 2.8% Black/African American, 0.0% Asian, 0.0% American Indian/Alaska Native, 0.0% Native Hawaiian/Other Pacific Islander, 1.9% Two or more races, 2.8% Hispanic of any race; Average household size: 2.78; Median age: 37.4; Age under 18: 26.1%; Age 65 and over: 11.4%; Males per 100 females: 104.9

School District(s)
Morley Stanwood Community Schools (PK-12)
    2012-13 Enrollment: 1,260 . . . . (231) 856-4392

Housing: Homeownership rate: 76.4%; Homeowner vacancy rate: 3.3%; Rental vacancy rate: 5.3%

WHEATLAND (township). Covers a land area of 35.485 square miles and a water area of 0.200 square miles. Located at 43.60° N. Lat; 85.15° W. Long.

Population: 1,403; Growth (since 2000): -4.8%; Density: 39.5 persons per square mile; Race: 92.7% White, 1.2% Black/African American, 0.1% Asian, 1.2% American Indian/Alaska Native, 0.0% Native Hawaiian/Other Pacific Islander, 4.4% Two or more races, 1.3% Hispanic of any race; Average household size: 2.55; Median age: 42.0; Age under 18: 24.9%; Age 65 and over: 16.5%; Males per 100 females: 98.7

Housing: Homeownership rate: 78.7%; Homeowner vacancy rate: 2.3%; Rental vacancy rate: 4.8%

Menominee County

Located in northwestern Michigan on the Upper Peninsula; bounded on the southeast by Green Bay, and on the southwest by Wisconsin; drained by the Menominee, Cedar, and Little Cedar Rivers. Covers a land area of 1,044.079 square miles, a water area of 294.133 square miles, and is located in the Central Time Zone at 45.54° N. Lat., 87.51° W. Long. The county was founded in 1863. County seat is Menominee.

Menominee County is part of the Marinette, WI-MI Micropolitan Statistical Area. The entire metro area includes: Menominee County, MI; Marinette County, WI

Weather Station: Stephenson 8 WNW   Elevation: 709 feet

	Jan	Feb	Mar	Apr	May	Jun	Jul	Aug	Sep	Oct	Nov	Dec
High	26	30	40	54	67	76	80	78	70	57	42	30
Low	5	6	17	30	40	49	54	53	45	34	24	12
Precip	1.1	0.8	1.6	2.4	3.0	3.4	3.4	3.4	3.5	2.9	2.3	1.4
Snow	15.1	8.2	9.5	3.9	0.4	0.0	0.0	0.0	tr	0.6	4.3	12.1

High and Low temperatures in degrees Fahrenheit; Precipitation and Snow in inches

Population: 24,029; Growth (since 2000): -5.1%; Density: 23.0 persons per square mile; Race: 95.3% White, 0.3% Black/African American, 0.3% Asian, 2.7% American Indian/Alaska Native, 0.0% Native Hawaiian/Other Pacific Islander, 1.2% two or more races, 1.2% Hispanic of any race; Average household size: 2.26; Median age: 46.2; Age under 18: 21.0%; Age 65 and over: 19.1%; Males per 100 females: 101.2; Marriage status: 22.8% never married, 56.8% now married, 1.6% separated, 8.6% widowed, 11.8% divorced; Foreign born: 1.0%; Speak English only: 97.3%; With disability: 16.4%; Veterans: 13.7%; Ancestry: 33.4% German, 13.1% French, 9.9% Polish, 9.2% Swedish, 8.9% Irish

Religion: Six largest groups: 33.5% Catholicism, 13.9% Lutheran, 3.9% Methodist/Pietist, 2.2% Baptist, 1.2% Adventist, 1.2% Presbyterian-Reformed

Economy: Unemployment rate: 4.9%; Leading industries: 14.4% retail trade; 10.9% other services (except public administration); 10.1% manufacturing; Farms: 398 totaling 91,900 acres; Company size: 0 employ 1,000 or more persons, 0 employ 500 to 999 persons, 9 employ 100 to 499 persons, 457 employ less than 100 persons; Business ownership: n/a women-owned, n/a Black-owned, n/a Hispanic-owned, n/a Asian-owned

Employment: 12.0% management, business, and financial, 4.1% computer, engineering, and science, 5.6% education, legal, community service, arts, and media, 4.7% healthcare practitioners, 18.4% service, 21.2% sales and office, 11.4% natural resources, construction, and maintenance, 22.6% production, transportation, and material moving

Income: Per capita: $22,331; Median household: $41,739; Average household: $49,147; Households with income of $100,000 or more: 8.2%; Poverty rate: 13.6%

Educational Attainment: High school diploma or higher: 90.2%; Bachelor's degree or higher: 14.4%; Graduate/professional degree or higher: 3.3%

Housing: Homeownership rate: 79.4%; Median home value: $95,300; Median year structure built: 1966; Homeowner vacancy rate: 2.1%; Median gross rent: $513 per month; Rental vacancy rate: 9.1%

Vital Statistics: Birth rate: 81.5 per 10,000 population; Death rate: 98.4 per 10,000 population; Age-adjusted cancer mortality rate: 191.9 deaths per 100,000 population

Health Insurance: 88.0% have insurance; 68.0% have private insurance; 38.7% have public insurance; 12.0% do not have insurance; 5.6% of children under 18 do not have insurance

Health Care: Physicians: 5.9 per 10,000 population; Hospital beds: 0.0 per 10,000 population; Hospital admissions: 0.0 per 10,000 population

Transportation: Commute: 91.7% car, 0.1% public transportation, 2.6% walk, 4.2% work from home; Median travel time to work: 20.2 minutes

Presidential Election: 48.0% Obama, 51.0% Romney (2012)

National and State Parks: Escanaba River State Forest; J W Wells State Park

Additional Information Contacts

Menominee Government. . . . . (906) 863-7779
    http://www.menomineecounty.com

Menominee County Communities

CARNEY (village). Covers a land area of 1.002 square miles and a water area of 0 square miles. Located at 45.59° N. Lat; 87.55° W. Long. Elevation is 797 feet.

History: Carney grew up around a station on the Chicago & Northwestern Railroad in 1879. It was named for Fred Carney, who owned land in the area.

Population: 192; Growth (since 2000): -14.7%; Density: 191.6 persons per square mile; Race: 97.4% White, 0.0% Black/African American, 0.5% Asian, 0.5% American Indian/Alaska Native, 0.0% Native Hawaiian/Other Pacific Islander, 1.0% Two or more races, 0.5% Hispanic of any race; Average household size: 2.24; Median age: 47.0; Age under 18: 16.1%; Age 65 and over: 18.8%; Males per 100 females: 111.0

School District(s)

Carney-Nadeau Public Schools (PK-12)
    2012-13 Enrollment: 231. . . . . (906) 639-2171

Housing: Homeownership rate: 83.2%; Homeowner vacancy rate: 2.8%; Rental vacancy rate: 12.5%

CEDARVILLE (township). Covers a land area of 78.937 square miles and a water area of 0.097 square miles. Located at 45.48° N. Lat; 87.38° W. Long.

Population: 253; Growth (since 2000): -8.3%; Density: 3.2 persons per square mile; Race: 96.8% White, 0.4% Black/African American, 0.0% Asian, 2.0% American Indian/Alaska Native, 0.0% Native Hawaiian/Other Pacific Islander, 0.8% Two or more races, 0.4% Hispanic of any race; Average household size: 2.02; Median age: 57.2; Age under 18: 11.5%; Age 65 and over: 32.0%; Males per 100 females: 123.9

School District(s)

Les Cheneaux Community Schools (KG-12)
    2012-13 Enrollment: 284. . . . . (906) 484-2256

Housing: Homeownership rate: 95.2%; Homeowner vacancy rate: 3.2%; Rental vacancy rate: 0.0%

DAGGETT (township). Covers a land area of 35.943 square miles and a water area of 0.157 square miles. Located at 45.48° N. Lat; 87.55° W. Long. Elevation is 709 feet.

Population: 714; Growth (since 2000): -3.5%; Density: 19.9 persons per square mile; Race: 93.3% White, 2.4% Black/African American, 0.6% Asian, 0.8% American Indian/Alaska Native, 0.0% Native Hawaiian/Other Pacific Islander, 2.1% Two or more races, 5.2% Hispanic of any race; Average household size: 2.63; Median age: 42.4; Age under 18: 25.2%; Age 65 and over: 17.1%; Males per 100 females: 110.0

Housing: Homeownership rate: 90.0%; Homeowner vacancy rate: 1.6%; Rental vacancy rate: 6.9%

DAGGETT (village). Covers a land area of 1.105 square miles and a water area of 0 square miles. Located at 45.46° N. Lat; 87.60° W. Long. Elevation is 709 feet.

Population: 258; Growth (since 2000): -4.4%; Density: 233.5 persons per square mile; Race: 90.3% White, 6.2% Black/African American, 1.2% Asian, 0.0% American Indian/Alaska Native, 0.0% Native Hawaiian/Other Pacific Islander, 0.8% Two or more races, 6.6% Hispanic of any race; Average household size: 2.84; Median age: 36.8; Age under 18: 30.6%; Age 65 and over: 16.3%; Males per 100 females: 104.8

Housing: Homeownership rate: 92.3%; Homeowner vacancy rate: 3.4%; Rental vacancy rate: 22.2%

FAITHORN (township). Covers a land area of 53.711 square miles and a water area of 0.567 square miles. Located at 45.66° N. Lat; 87.73° W. Long. Elevation is 860 feet.

Population: 243; Growth (since 2000): 13.6%; Density: 4.5 persons per square mile; Race: 94.2% White, 0.0% Black/African American, 0.4% Asian, 0.0% American Indian/Alaska Native, 0.0% Native Hawaiian/Other Pacific Islander, 5.3% Two or more races, 0.0% Hispanic of any race; Average household size: 2.31; Median age: 47.4; Age under 18: 23.5%; Age 65 and over: 19.3%; Males per 100 females: 133.7

Housing: Homeownership rate: 96.2%; Homeowner vacancy rate: 0.0%; Rental vacancy rate: 20.0%

GOURLEY (township). Covers a land area of 35.725 square miles and a water area of 0.035 square miles. Located at 45.59° N. Lat; 87.40° W. Long. Elevation is 699 feet.

History: Gourley developed around a mill which was purchased by Arthur Gourley and his partner, Samuel L. Hall. Gourley and Hall founded the village of Gourley. When the township was divided out from Cedarville Township in 1920, the new township was also called Gourley.

Population: 420; Growth (since 2000): 2.7%; Density: 11.8 persons per square mile; Race: 92.6% White, 0.0% Black/African American, 0.2% Asian, 6.7% American Indian/Alaska Native, 0.0% Native Hawaiian/Other Pacific Islander, 0.5% Two or more races, 1.0% Hispanic of any race; Average household size: 2.47; Median age: 42.6; Age under 18: 21.7%; Age 65 and over: 19.0%; Males per 100 females: 113.2

Housing: Homeownership rate: 87.0%; Homeowner vacancy rate: 0.7%; Rental vacancy rate: 0.0%

HARRIS (township). Covers a land area of 143.270 square miles and a water area of 0.141 square miles. Located at 45.81° N. Lat; 87.39° W. Long. Elevation is 781 feet.

History: Harris was named for early settler Michael B. Harris, who came here in 1875 to work in the lumber industry. Harris is credited with saving a group of Potawatomi from starvation by taking food and milk to them when they were quarantined by a smallpox epidemic.

Population: 1,968; Growth (since 2000): 3.9%; Density: 13.7 persons per square mile; Race: 72.9% White, 0.1% Black/African American, 0.1% Asian, 24.2% American Indian/Alaska Native, 0.0% Native Hawaiian/Other Pacific Islander, 2.4% Two or more races, 1.4% Hispanic of any race; Average household size: 2.71; Median age: 38.7; Age under 18: 26.6%; Age 65 and over: 11.8%; Males per 100 females: 102.3

School District(s)

Bark River-Harris SD (KG-12)
    2012-13 Enrollment: 739. . . . . (906) 466-9981

Housing: Homeownership rate: 74.2%; Homeowner vacancy rate: 1.5%; Rental vacancy rate: 5.5%

HERMANSVILLE (unincorporated postal area)
ZCTA: 49847

Covers a land area of 59.084 square miles and a water area of 0.301 square miles. Located at 45.70° N. Lat; 87.64° W. Long. Elevation is 906 feet.

Population: 998; Growth (since 2000): -4.1%; Density: 16.9 persons per square mile; Race: 98.1% White, 0.3% Black/African American, 0.0% Asian, 0.8% American Indian/Alaska Native, 0.0% Native Hawaiian/Other Pacific Islander, 0.7% Two or more races, 1.3% Hispanic of any race; Average household size: 2.30; Median age: 46.1; Age under 18: 20.0%; Age 65 and over: 20.6%; Males per 100 females: 99.6

School District(s)

North Central Area Schools (PK-12)
    2012-13 Enrollment: 465. . . . . (906) 498-7737

Housing: Homeownership rate: 81.5%; Homeowner vacancy rate: 3.8%; Rental vacancy rate: 10.1%

HOLMES (township). Covers a land area of 71.370 square miles and a water area of 1.065 square miles. Located at 45.53° N. Lat; 87.73° W. Long.

Population: 335; Growth (since 2000): 13.2%; Density: 4.7 persons per square mile; Race: 97.0% White, 0.6% Black/African American, 0.6% Asian, 0.3% American Indian/Alaska Native, 0.0% Native Hawaiian/Other Pacific Islander, 1.5% Two or more races, 0.3% Hispanic of any race; Average household size: 2.18; Median age: 50.6; Age under 18: 16.7%; Age 65 and over: 21.5%; Males per 100 females: 120.4

Housing: Homeownership rate: 93.3%; Homeowner vacancy rate: 1.4%; Rental vacancy rate: 0.0%

INGALLS (unincorporated postal area)
ZCTA: 49848

Covers a land area of 4.281 square miles and a water area of 0 square miles. Located at 45.38° N. Lat; 87.64° W. Long. Elevation is 709 feet.

Population: 128; Growth (since 2000): -32.3%; Density: 29.9 persons per square mile; Race: 100.0% White, 0.0% Black/African American, 0.0% Asian, 0.0% American Indian/Alaska Native, 0.0% Native Hawaiian/Other Pacific Islander, 0.0% Two or more races, 0.8% Hispanic of any race; Average household size: 2.06; Median age: 47.3; Age under 18: 14.1%; Age 65 and over: 15.6%; Males per 100 females: 120.7

Housing: Homeownership rate: 90.3%; Homeowner vacancy rate: 0.0%; Rental vacancy rate: 25.0%

INGALLSTON (township). Covers a land area of 70.892 square miles and a water area of 0.824 square miles. Located at 45.28° N. Lat; 87.53° W. Long. Elevation is 591 feet.

History: Ingallston Township was organized in 1863 and named for Eleazer S. and Charles B. Ingalls, brothers who built a sawmill here in 1866.

Population: 935; Growth (since 2000): -10.3%; Density: 13.2 persons per square mile; Race: 98.4% White, 0.0% Black/African American, 0.2% Asian, 0.6% American Indian/Alaska Native, 0.1% Native Hawaiian/Other Pacific Islander, 0.5% Two or more races, 0.2% Hispanic of any race; Average household size: 2.13; Median age: 53.0; Age under 18: 16.1%; Age 65 and over: 22.6%; Males per 100 females: 113.5

Housing: Homeownership rate: 92.7%; Homeowner vacancy rate: 4.2%; Rental vacancy rate: 0.0%

LAKE (township). Covers a land area of 70.736 square miles and a water area of 1.990 square miles. Located at 45.41° N. Lat; 87.76° W. Long.

Population: 556; Growth (since 2000): -3.5%; Density: 7.9 persons per square mile; Race: 98.6% White, 0.2% Black/African American, 0.0% Asian, 0.4% American Indian/Alaska Native, 0.0% Native Hawaiian/Other Pacific Islander, 0.9% Two or more races, 0.0% Hispanic of any race; Average household size: 2.03; Median age: 52.5; Age under 18: 15.8%; Age 65 and over: 23.2%; Males per 100 females: 113.8

Housing: Homeownership rate: 89.2%; Homeowner vacancy rate: 4.1%; Rental vacancy rate: 3.4%

MELLEN (township). Covers a land area of 30.799 square miles and a water area of 0.564 square miles. Located at 45.33° N. Lat; 87.63° W. Long.

Population: 1,150; Growth (since 2000): -8.7%; Density: 37.3 persons per square mile; Race: 98.7% White, 0.1% Black/African American, 0.3% Asian, 0.5% American Indian/Alaska Native, 0.0% Native Hawaiian/Other Pacific Islander, 0.3% Two or more races, 0.9% Hispanic of any race; Average household size: 2.23; Median age: 48.3; Age under 18: 19.2%; Age 65 and over: 19.0%; Males per 100 females: 110.2

Housing: Homeownership rate: 86.6%; Homeowner vacancy rate: 0.9%; Rental vacancy rate: 10.4%

MENOMINEE (city). County seat. Covers a land area of 5.152 square miles and a water area of 0.328 square miles. Located at 45.12° N. Lat; 87.62° W. Long. Elevation is 594 feet.

History: A trading post was established at this spot on the Menominee River in 1796. By the 1830's, a sawmill and dam had been constructed, and soon fish joined lumber as a marketable product. When lumbering declined after 1910, a dairying industry developed. Water power provided

by plants on the Menomnee River later made this a manufacturing city, as well as a destination for vacationers.

Population: 8,599; Growth (since 2000): -5.8%; Density: 1,669.1 persons per square mile; Race: 96.7% White, 0.4% Black/African American, 0.5% Asian, 0.9% American Indian/Alaska Native, 0.0% Native Hawaiian/Other Pacific Islander, 1.2% Two or more races, 1.4% Hispanic of any race; Average household size: 2.13; Median age: 44.0; Age under 18: 21.8%; Age 65 and over: 18.3%; Males per 100 females: 94.8; Marriage status: 28.0% never married, 47.6% now married, 2.7% separated, 10.1% widowed, 14.3% divorced; Foreign born: 0.6%; Speak English only: 97.3%; With disability: 17.0%; Veterans: 14.7%; Ancestry: 36.9% German, 10.9% French, 9.8% Irish, 9.8% Polish, 8.2% Swedish

Employment: 11.9% management, business, and financial, 4.6% computer, engineering, and science, 4.2% education, legal, community service, arts, and media, 4.3% healthcare practitioners, 21.4% service, 20.3% sales and office, 8.9% natural resources, construction, and maintenance, 24.3% production, transportation, and material moving

Income: Per capita: $20,477; Median household: $38,130; Average household: $43,290; Households with income of $100,000 or more: 7.0%; Poverty rate: 17.7%

Educational Attainment: High school diploma or higher: 89.2%; Bachelor's degree or higher: 13.5%; Graduate/professional degree or higher: 2.6%

School District(s)
Menominee Area Public Schools (PK-12)
 2012-13 Enrollment: 1,553 . . . . (906) 863-9951
Menominee ISD (01-12)
 2012-13 Enrollment: 118 . . . . (906) 863-5665

Housing: Homeownership rate: 68.1%; Median home value: $76,500; Median year structure built: 1951; Homeowner vacancy rate: 2.1%; Median gross rent: $509 per month; Rental vacancy rate: 9.6%

Health Insurance: 86.7% have insurance; 61.4% have private insurance; 44.9% have public insurance; 13.3% do not have insurance; 7.9% of children under 18 do not have insurance

Safety: Violent crime rate: 23.6 per 10,000 population; Property crime rate: 225.3 per 10,000 population

Transportation: Commute: 91.2% car, 0.0% public transportation, 3.8% walk, 2.6% work from home; Median travel time to work: 14.1 minutes

Airports: Menominee-Marinette Twin County (general aviation)

Additional Information Contacts
City of Menominee . . . . (906) 863-2656
 http://www.cityofmenominee.org

MENOMINEE (township). Covers a land area of 72.697 square miles and a water area of 0.753 square miles. Located at 45.22° N. Lat; 87.64° W. Long. Elevation is 594 feet.

History: Of interest is the mystery ship, raised (1969) from the bottom of Green Bay, where it sank in 1864. Incorporated 1883.

Population: 3,488; Growth (since 2000): -11.4%; Density: 48.0 persons per square mile; Race: 98.3% White, 0.2% Black/African American, 0.3% Asian, 0.4% American Indian/Alaska Native, 0.1% Native Hawaiian/Other Pacific Islander, 0.7% Two or more races, 0.5% Hispanic of any race; Average household size: 2.28; Median age: 49.0; Age under 18: 18.0%; Age 65 and over: 18.0%; Males per 100 females: 105.3; Marriage status: 18.0% never married, 64.9% now married, 0.8% separated, 7.4% widowed, 9.6% divorced; Foreign born: 1.3%; Speak English only: 98.5%; With disability: 11.7%; Veterans: 12.2%; Ancestry: 38.4% German, 14.3% French, 8.9% Polish, 8.3% Swedish, 7.9% American

Employment: 15.5% management, business, and financial, 5.9% computer, engineering, and science, 6.3% education, legal, community service, arts, and media, 6.5% healthcare practitioners, 11.2% service, 24.2% sales and office, 9.1% natural resources, construction, and maintenance, 21.3% production, transportation, and material moving

Income: Per capita: $28,076; Median household: $54,556; Average household: $60,828; Households with income of $100,000 or more: 11.5%; Poverty rate: 6.4%

Educational Attainment: High school diploma or higher: 95.7%; Bachelor's degree or higher: 18.6%; Graduate/professional degree or higher: 3.2%

School District(s)
Menominee Area Public Schools (PK-12)
 2012-13 Enrollment: 1,553 . . . . (906) 863-9951
Menominee ISD (01-12)
 2012-13 Enrollment: 118 . . . . (906) 863-5665

Housing: Homeownership rate: 92.0%; Median home value: $153,100; Median year structure built: 1976; Homeowner vacancy rate: 1.4%; Median gross rent: $598 per month; Rental vacancy rate: 12.1%
Health Insurance: 92.5% have insurance; 85.0% have private insurance; 26.7% have public insurance; 7.5% do not have insurance; 1.8% of children under 18 do not have insurance
Transportation: Commute: 97.8% car, 0.0% public transportation, 0.0% walk, 2.2% work from home; Median travel time to work: 19.6 minutes
Airports: Menominee-Marinette Twin County (general aviation)

MEYER (township). Covers a land area of 89.694 square miles and a water area of 0.433 square miles. Located at 45.76° N. Lat; 87.64° W. Long.
Population: 1,001; Growth (since 2000): -3.4%; Density: 11.2 persons per square mile; Race: 98.0% White, 0.3% Black/African American, 0.0% Asian, 0.9% American Indian/Alaska Native, 0.1% Native Hawaiian/Other Pacific Islander, 0.7% Two or more races, 1.2% Hispanic of any race; Average household size: 2.31; Median age: 46.0; Age under 18: 20.4%; Age 65 and over: 20.5%; Males per 100 females: 97.8
Housing: Homeownership rate: 82.0%; Homeowner vacancy rate: 3.8%; Rental vacancy rate: 10.3%

NADEAU (township). Covers a land area of 80.751 square miles and a water area of 0.055 square miles. Located at 45.57° N. Lat; 87.54° W. Long. Elevation is 823 feet.
Population: 1,161; Growth (since 2000): 0.1%; Density: 14.4 persons per square mile; Race: 97.2% White, 0.0% Black/African American, 0.1% Asian, 0.6% American Indian/Alaska Native, 0.0% Native Hawaiian/Other Pacific Islander, 2.1% Two or more races, 0.3% Hispanic of any race; Average household size: 2.39; Median age: 45.5; Age under 18: 21.9%; Age 65 and over: 17.4%; Males per 100 females: 108.4
Housing: Homeownership rate: 88.8%; Homeowner vacancy rate: 2.5%; Rental vacancy rate: 10.0%

PERRONVILLE (unincorporated postal area)
ZCTA: 49873
Covers a land area of 168.093 square miles and a water area of 0.285 square miles. Located at 45.89° N. Lat; 87.58° W. Long. Elevation is 810 feet.
Population: 120; Growth (since 2000): 20.0%; Density: 0.7 persons per square mile; Race: 97.5% White, 0.0% Black/African American, 0.0% Asian, 0.0% American Indian/Alaska Native, 0.8% Native Hawaiian/Other Pacific Islander, 1.7% Two or more races, 0.0% Hispanic of any race; Average household size: 2.26; Median age: 46.5; Age under 18: 22.5%; Age 65 and over: 14.2%; Males per 100 females: 114.3
Housing: Homeownership rate: 84.9%; Homeowner vacancy rate: 7.4%; Rental vacancy rate: 0.0%

POWERS (village). Covers a land area of 0.993 square miles and a water area of 0 square miles. Located at 45.69° N. Lat; 87.53° W. Long. Elevation is 873 feet.
History: The village of Powers was platted and named by Edward Powers, a civil engineer with the Chicago & Northwestern Railroad.
Population: 422; Growth (since 2000): -1.9%; Density: 425.1 persons per square mile; Race: 98.3% White, 0.0% Black/African American, 0.2% Asian, 0.9% American Indian/Alaska Native, 0.0% Native Hawaiian/Other Pacific Islander, 0.0% Two or more races, 0.9% Hispanic of any race; Average household size: 1.94; Median age: 65.1; Age under 18: 11.4%; Age 65 and over: 50.2%; Males per 100 females: 70.9
School District(s)
North Central Area Schools (PK-12)
    2012-13 Enrollment: 465. . . . . (906) 498-7737
Housing: Homeownership rate: 60.0%; Homeowner vacancy rate: 3.6%; Rental vacancy rate: 0.0%

SPALDING (township). Covers a land area of 162.588 square miles and a water area of 0.398 square miles. Located at 45.82° N. Lat; 87.55° W. Long. Elevation is 850 feet.
History: Spalding Township was named for Jesse Spalding, who owned land in the area.
Population: 1,674; Growth (since 2000): -4.9%; Density: 10.3 persons per square mile; Race: 98.7% White, 0.1% Black/African American, 0.1% Asian, 0.4% American Indian/Alaska Native, 0.2% Native Hawaiian/Other Pacific Islander, 0.2% Two or more races, 1.0% Hispanic of any race;

Average household size: 2.33; Median age: 48.0; Age under 18: 19.6%; Age 65 and over: 25.3%; Males per 100 females: 95.1
Housing: Homeownership rate: 81.8%; Homeowner vacancy rate: 2.0%; Rental vacancy rate: 6.3%

STEPHENSON (city). Covers a land area of 1.093 square miles and a water area of 0 square miles. Located at 45.41° N. Lat; 87.61° W. Long. Elevation is 669 feet.
History: Stephenson began as a producer of charcoal and tan bark. The Chicago & Northwestern Railroad established a station here in 1872. The town was named for Samuel Stephenson, a member of congress from this district.
Population: 862; Growth (since 2000): -1.5%; Density: 788.7 persons per square mile; Race: 97.3% White, 0.1% Black/African American, 0.3% Asian, 0.0% American Indian/Alaska Native, 0.0% Native Hawaiian/Other Pacific Islander, 1.5% Two or more races, 2.2% Hispanic of any race; Average household size: 2.24; Median age: 47.9; Age under 18: 21.7%; Age 65 and over: 28.7%; Males per 100 females: 86.2
School District(s)
Stephenson Area Public Schools (PK-12)
    2012-13 Enrollment: 614. . . . . (906) 753-2221
Housing: Homeownership rate: 73.2%; Homeowner vacancy rate: 1.5%; Rental vacancy rate: 15.5%
Newspapers: Menominee County Journal (weekly circulation 5400)

STEPHENSON (township). Covers a land area of 40.721 square miles and a water area of 0.467 square miles. Located at 45.42° N. Lat; 87.54° W. Long. Elevation is 669 feet.
Population: 670; Growth (since 2000): -6.4%; Density: 16.5 persons per square mile; Race: 97.9% White, 0.0% Black/African American, 0.1% Asian, 0.4% American Indian/Alaska Native, 0.0% Native Hawaiian/Other Pacific Islander, 1.5% Two or more races, 0.7% Hispanic of any race; Average household size: 2.42; Median age: 45.6; Age under 18: 24.8%; Age 65 and over: 16.9%; Males per 100 females: 106.2
School District(s)
Stephenson Area Public Schools (PK-12)
    2012-13 Enrollment: 614. . . . . (906) 753-2221
Housing: Homeownership rate: 87.0%; Homeowner vacancy rate: 2.0%; Rental vacancy rate: 2.7%
Newspapers: Menominee County Journal (weekly circulation 5400)

WALLACE (unincorporated postal area)
ZCTA: 49893
Covers a land area of 75.060 square miles and a water area of 0.722 square miles. Located at 45.30° N. Lat; 87.61° W. Long. Elevation is 692 feet.
Population: 1,784; Growth (since 2000): 6.3%; Density: 23.8 persons per square mile; Race: 98.0% White, 0.1% Black/African American, 0.4% Asian, 0.4% American Indian/Alaska Native, 0.1% Native Hawaiian/Other Pacific Islander, 0.9% Two or more races, 1.1% Hispanic of any race; Average household size: 2.28; Median age: 48.7; Age under 18: 19.4%; Age 65 and over: 18.1%; Males per 100 females: 108.4
Housing: Homeownership rate: 89.5%; Homeowner vacancy rate: 2.1%; Rental vacancy rate: 9.9%

Midland County

Located in east central Michigan; drained by the Tittabawassee, Pine, and Chippewa Rivers. Covers a land area of 516.253 square miles, a water area of 11.815 square miles, and is located in the Eastern Time Zone at 43.65° N. Lat., 84.38° W. Long. The county was founded in 1850. County seat is Midland.

Midland County is part of the Midland, MI Metropolitan Statistical Area. The entire metro area includes: Midland County, MI

Weather Station: Midland										Elevation: 640 feet	
	Jan	Feb	Mar	Apr	May	Jun	Jul	Aug	Sep	Oct	Nov	Dec
High	30	33	44	58	70	79	83	81	74	60	47	34
Low	17	18	25	36	47	57	61	60	52	41	32	22
Precip	1.6	1.6	2.1	3.1	3.3	3.2	2.6	3.2	3.9	2.8	2.7	1.9
Snow	8.4	5.4	2.2	0.5	0.0	0.0	0.0	0.0	0.0	tr	1.2	5.9

High and Low temperatures in degrees Fahrenheit; Precipitation and Snow in inches

Population: 83,629; Growth (since 2000): 0.9%; Density: 162.0 persons per square mile; Race: 94.5% White, 1.2% Black/African American, 1.9% Asian, 0.4% American Indian/Alaska Native, 0.1% Native Hawaiian/Other Pacific Islander, 1.5% two or more races, 2.0% Hispanic of any race; Average household size: 2.46; Median age: 40.4; Age under 18: 23.7%; Age 65 and over: 14.8%; Males per 100 females: 96.4; Marriage status: 25.8% never married, 57.5% now married, 0.9% separated, 5.8% widowed, 11.0% divorced; Foreign born: 3.8%; Speak English only: 95.1%; With disability: 13.4%; Veterans: 9.3%; Ancestry: 28.4% German, 13.1% Irish, 11.8% English, 7.4% Polish, 7.3% American
Religion: Six largest groups: 14.7% Catholicism, 7.7% Lutheran, 7.6% Methodist/Pietist, 3.4% Pentecostal, 3.1% Holiness, 3.1% Presbyterian-Reformed
Economy: Unemployment rate: 4.7%; Leading industries: 18.1% retail trade; 13.7% health care and social assistance; 12.3% other services (except public administration); Farms: 555 totaling 89,543 acres; Company size: 4 employ 1,000 or more persons, 5 employ 500 to 999 persons, 42 employ 100 to 499 persons, 1,694 employ less than 100 persons; Business ownership: 1,980 women-owned, n/a Black-owned, n/a Hispanic-owned, 150 Asian-owned
Employment: 14.3% management, business, and financial, 8.9% computer, engineering, and science, 10.0% education, legal, community service, arts, and media, 6.1% healthcare practitioners, 16.6% service, 23.0% sales and office, 9.3% natural resources, construction, and maintenance, 11.9% production, transportation, and material moving
Income: Per capita: $29,536; Median household: $53,076; Average household: $73,032; Households with income of $100,000 or more: 20.9%; Poverty rate: 13.4%
Educational Attainment: High school diploma or higher: 92.2%; Bachelor's degree or higher: 32.3%; Graduate/professional degree or higher: 12.5%
Housing: Homeownership rate: 77.1%; Median home value: $128,600; Median year structure built: 1974; Homeowner vacancy rate: 1.8%; Median gross rent: $713 per month; Rental vacancy rate: 6.1%
Vital Statistics: Birth rate: 107.0 per 10,000 population; Death rate: 81.3 per 10,000 population; Age-adjusted cancer mortality rate: 171.9 deaths per 100,000 population
Health Insurance: 90.4% have insurance; 75.7% have private insurance; 30.6% have public insurance; 9.6% do not have insurance; 5.0% of children under 18 do not have insurance
Health Care: Physicians: 26.7 per 10,000 population; Hospital beds: 29.7 per 10,000 population; Hospital admissions: 1,324.6 per 10,000 population
Transportation: Commute: 92.8% car, 0.7% public transportation, 1.4% walk, 3.6% work from home; Median travel time to work: 19.9 minutes
Presidential Election: 41.8% Obama, 57.3% Romney (2012)
National and State Parks: Tittabawassee River State Forest
Additional Information Contacts
Midland Government. . . . . (989) 832-6739
   http://www.co.midland.mi.us

Midland County Communities

COLEMAN (city). Covers a land area of 1.258 square miles and a water area of 0.010 square miles. Located at 43.76° N. Lat; 84.59° W. Long. Elevation is 761 feet.
History: Coleman was surveyed in the 1860's by Seymour Coleman, who donated land for the Pere Marquette Railroad depot in 1871.
Population: 1,243; Growth (since 2000): -4.1%; Density: 988.2 persons per square mile; Race: 96.1% White, 0.7% Black/African American, 0.2% Asian, 0.3% American Indian/Alaska Native, 0.1% Native Hawaiian/Other Pacific Islander, 2.5% Two or more races, 3.1% Hispanic of any race; Average household size: 2.33; Median age: 36.4; Age under 18: 26.5%; Age 65 and over: 17.3%; Males per 100 females: 91.8
School District(s)
Coleman Community Schools (KG-12)
   2012-13 Enrollment: 725. . . . . (989) 465-1891
Housing: Homeownership rate: 59.7%; Homeowner vacancy rate: 3.6%; Rental vacancy rate: 21.1%
Safety: Violent crime rate: 16.2 per 10,000 population; Property crime rate: 414.3 per 10,000 population

EDENVILLE (township). Covers a land area of 34.802 square miles and a water area of 1.109 square miles. Located at 43.77° N. Lat; 84.44° W. Long. Elevation is 692 feet.
Population: 2,551; Growth (since 2000): 0.9%; Density: 73.3 persons per square mile; Race: 97.3% White, 0.2% Black/African American, 0.5% Asian, 0.6% American Indian/Alaska Native, 0.0% Native Hawaiian/Other Pacific Islander, 1.4% Two or more races, 0.7% Hispanic of any race; Average household size: 2.51; Median age: 45.3; Age under 18: 21.1%; Age 65 and over: 15.2%; Males per 100 females: 100.6; Marriage status: 23.1% never married, 64.0% now married, 1.3% separated, 4.0% widowed, 8.8% divorced; Foreign born: 2.2%; Speak English only: 97.2%; With disability: 17.9%; Veterans: 9.6%; Ancestry: 42.3% German, 12.6% English, 12.1% Irish, 9.8% Italian, 8.6% Polish
Employment: 14.8% management, business, and financial, 8.9% computer, engineering, and science, 6.9% education, legal, community service, arts, and media, 3.2% healthcare practitioners, 14.4% service, 25.7% sales and office, 13.0% natural resources, construction, and maintenance, 13.0% production, transportation, and material moving
Income: Per capita: $26,332; Median household: $51,458; Average household: $65,794; Households with income of $100,000 or more: 14.3%; Poverty rate: 15.3%
Educational Attainment: High school diploma or higher: 91.9%; Bachelor's degree or higher: 21.2%; Graduate/professional degree or higher: 6.3%
Housing: Homeownership rate: 89.6%; Median home value: $137,400; Median year structure built: 1979; Homeowner vacancy rate: 3.1%; Median gross rent: $826 per month; Rental vacancy rate: 5.3%
Health Insurance: 86.3% have insurance; 70.5% have private insurance; 30.8% have public insurance; 13.7% do not have insurance; 16.6% of children under 18 do not have insurance
Transportation: Commute: 92.8% car, 2.5% public transportation, 1.5% walk, 3.2% work from home; Median travel time to work: 29.3 minutes

GENEVA (township). Covers a land area of 35.500 square miles and a water area of 0.533 square miles. Located at 43.69° N. Lat; 84.53° W. Long.
Population: 1,056; Growth (since 2000): -7.1%; Density: 29.7 persons per square mile; Race: 98.1% White, 0.2% Black/African American, 0.0% Asian, 0.5% American Indian/Alaska Native, 0.0% Native Hawaiian/Other Pacific Islander, 0.9% Two or more races, 1.9% Hispanic of any race; Average household size: 2.40; Median age: 45.1; Age under 18: 20.1%; Age 65 and over: 15.7%; Males per 100 females: 95.9
Housing: Homeownership rate: 89.8%; Homeowner vacancy rate: 2.4%; Rental vacancy rate: 8.2%

GREENDALE (township). Covers a land area of 35.370 square miles and a water area of 0.701 square miles. Located at 43.60° N. Lat; 84.54° W. Long.
Population: 1,751; Growth (since 2000): -2.1%; Density: 49.5 persons per square mile; Race: 95.5% White, 0.2% Black/African American, 0.3% Asian, 2.0% American Indian/Alaska Native, 0.0% Native Hawaiian/Other Pacific Islander, 1.3% Two or more races, 2.8% Hispanic of any race; Average household size: 2.66; Median age: 39.3; Age under 18: 23.9%; Age 65 and over: 11.5%; Males per 100 females: 100.8
Housing: Homeownership rate: 84.7%; Homeowner vacancy rate: 2.6%; Rental vacancy rate: 12.1%

HOMER (township). Covers a land area of 21.105 square miles and a water area of 0.394 square miles. Located at 43.61° N. Lat; 84.34° W. Long.
Population: 4,009; Growth (since 2000): 2.2%; Density: 190.0 persons per square mile; Race: 96.7% White, 0.6% Black/African American, 0.5% Asian, 0.6% American Indian/Alaska Native, 0.0% Native Hawaiian/Other Pacific Islander, 1.4% Two or more races, 1.5% Hispanic of any race; Average household size: 2.60; Median age: 42.3; Age under 18: 22.9%; Age 65 and over: 14.9%; Males per 100 females: 95.1; Marriage status: 17.9% never married, 68.1% now married, 1.6% separated, 4.4% widowed, 9.7% divorced; Foreign born: 1.0%; Speak English only: 96.7%; With disability: 17.0%; Veterans: 9.0%; Ancestry: 28.9% German, 17.3% English, 16.2% Irish, 10.5% American, 8.3% Polish
Employment: 11.1% management, business, and financial, 5.8% computer, engineering, and science, 10.2% education, legal, community service, arts, and media, 7.0% healthcare practitioners, 13.8% service, 26.0% sales and office, 7.0% natural resources, construction, and maintenance, 19.1% production, transportation, and material moving

Income: Per capita: $24,942; Median household: $60,625; Average household: $68,415; Households with income of $100,000 or more: 22.5%; Poverty rate: 10.5%

Educational Attainment: High school diploma or higher: 90.9%; Bachelor's degree or higher: 24.6%; Graduate/professional degree or higher: 10.7%

Housing: Homeownership rate: 90.0%; Median home value: $129,600; Median year structure built: 1973; Homeowner vacancy rate: 1.8%; Median gross rent: $714 per month; Rental vacancy rate: 3.2%

Health Insurance: 93.5% have insurance; 81.9% have private insurance; 26.3% have public insurance; 6.5% do not have insurance; 1.3% of children under 18 do not have insurance

Transportation: Commute: 94.9% car, 0.0% public transportation, 0.0% walk, 4.0% work from home; Median travel time to work: 21.5 minutes

Additional Information Contacts

Homer Township . . . . (989) 832-0964
http://homertownship.org

HOPE (township). Covers a land area of 23.022 square miles and a water area of 0.332 square miles. Located at 43.78° N. Lat; 84.33° W. Long. Elevation is 679 feet.

History: There were settlers in Hope in the 1850's. The township was organized in 1871, and named by the residents.

Population: 1,361; Growth (since 2000): 5.8%; Density: 59.1 persons per square mile; Race: 97.1% White, 0.7% Black/African American, 0.9% Asian, 0.4% American Indian/Alaska Native, 0.0% Native Hawaiian/Other Pacific Islander, 1.0% Two or more races, 0.9% Hispanic of any race; Average household size: 2.44; Median age: 46.2; Age under 18: 19.9%; Age 65 and over: 17.3%; Males per 100 females: 108.1

Housing: Homeownership rate: 93.1%; Homeowner vacancy rate: 0.6%; Rental vacancy rate: 15.2%

INGERSOLL (township). Covers a land area of 36.462 square miles and a water area of 0.131 square miles. Located at 43.53° N. Lat; 84.23° W. Long.

Population: 2,751; Growth (since 2000): -8.8%; Density: 75.4 persons per square mile; Race: 97.2% White, 0.8% Black/African American, 0.1% Asian, 0.5% American Indian/Alaska Native, 0.0% Native Hawaiian/Other Pacific Islander, 1.1% Two or more races, 2.2% Hispanic of any race; Average household size: 2.67; Median age: 41.8; Age under 18: 24.1%; Age 65 and over: 14.4%; Males per 100 females: 103.2; Marriage status: 25.3% never married, 64.1% now married, 1.5% separated, 2.3% widowed, 8.3% divorced; Foreign born: 1.0%; Speak English only: 98.4%; With disability: 10.5%; Veterans: 10.8%; Ancestry: 34.8% German, 12.9% English, 11.8% Irish, 10.3% Polish, 7.2% American

Employment: 12.5% management, business, and financial, 5.4% computer, engineering, and science, 9.4% education, legal, community service, arts, and media, 5.5% healthcare practitioners, 19.0% service, 25.2% sales and office, 11.0% natural resources, construction, and maintenance, 12.0% production, transportation, and material moving

Income: Per capita: $28,182; Median household: $60,781; Average household: $72,773; Households with income of $100,000 or more: 17.2%; Poverty rate: 6.1%

Educational Attainment: High school diploma or higher: 95.1%; Bachelor's degree or higher: 25.4%; Graduate/professional degree or higher: 9.2%

Housing: Homeownership rate: 89.6%; Median home value: $123,000; Median year structure built: 1970; Homeowner vacancy rate: 1.6%; Median gross rent: $850 per month; Rental vacancy rate: 7.7%

Health Insurance: 89.1% have insurance; 83.7% have private insurance; 20.2% have public insurance; 10.9% do not have insurance; 2.4% of children under 18 do not have insurance

Transportation: Commute: 94.7% car, 0.8% public transportation, 1.1% walk, 3.2% work from home; Median travel time to work: 22.9 minutes

JASPER (township). Covers a land area of 35.920 square miles and a water area of 0.145 square miles. Located at 43.52° N. Lat; 84.54° W. Long.

Population: 1,180; Growth (since 2000): 3.1%; Density: 32.9 persons per square mile; Race: 96.3% White, 0.0% Black/African American, 0.0% Asian, 0.6% American Indian/Alaska Native, 0.0% Native Hawaiian/Other Pacific Islander, 2.2% Two or more races, 3.5% Hispanic of any race; Average household size: 2.66; Median age: 40.9; Age under 18: 25.3%; Age 65 and over: 13.1%; Males per 100 females: 106.3

Housing: Homeownership rate: 88.8%; Homeowner vacancy rate: 1.0%; Rental vacancy rate: 3.8%

JEROME (township). Covers a land area of 31.614 square miles and a water area of 4.054 square miles. Located at 43.68° N. Lat; 84.42° W. Long.

Population: 4,796; Growth (since 2000): -1.9%; Density: 151.7 persons per square mile; Race: 97.7% White, 0.1% Black/African American, 0.3% Asian, 0.5% American Indian/Alaska Native, 0.0% Native Hawaiian/Other Pacific Islander, 1.2% Two or more races, 1.5% Hispanic of any race; Average household size: 2.45; Median age: 44.3; Age under 18: 22.0%; Age 65 and over: 16.3%; Males per 100 females: 100.3; Marriage status: 23.9% never married, 58.4% now married, 1.2% separated, 4.1% widowed, 13.5% divorced; Foreign born: 0.6%; Speak English only: 98.5%; With disability: 17.5%; Veterans: 11.7%; Ancestry: 27.0% German, 11.6% English, 10.4% Irish, 7.7% American, 7.6% Polish

Employment: 13.4% management, business, and financial, 7.2% computer, engineering, and science, 5.0% education, legal, community service, arts, and media, 4.4% healthcare practitioners, 17.0% service, 30.8% sales and office, 10.0% natural resources, construction, and maintenance, 12.1% production, transportation, and material moving

Income: Per capita: $25,676; Median household: $52,965; Average household: $62,407; Households with income of $100,000 or more: 16.2%; Poverty rate: 16.6%

Educational Attainment: High school diploma or higher: 90.5%; Bachelor's degree or higher: 22.6%; Graduate/professional degree or higher: 7.1%

Housing: Homeownership rate: 86.8%; Median home value: $123,900; Median year structure built: 1976; Homeowner vacancy rate: 1.6%; Median gross rent: $770 per month; Rental vacancy rate: 5.8%

Health Insurance: 89.2% have insurance; 71.0% have private insurance; 34.2% have public insurance; 10.8% do not have insurance; 4.0% of children under 18 do not have insurance

Transportation: Commute: 95.1% car, 0.2% public transportation, 0.4% walk, 0.7% work from home; Median travel time to work: 26.3 minutes

LARKIN (charter township). Covers a land area of 32.086 square miles and a water area of 0.073 square miles. Located at 43.71° N. Lat; 84.21° W. Long. Elevation is 669 feet.

History: Larkin Township was organized in 1879 and named for John Larkin, early landowner and lumber camp operator who had petitioned for the township.

Population: 5,136; Growth (since 2000): 13.8%; Density: 160.1 persons per square mile; Race: 95.7% White, 0.9% Black/African American, 1.7% Asian, 0.0% American Indian/Alaska Native, 0.0% Native Hawaiian/Other Pacific Islander, 1.2% Two or more races, 2.0% Hispanic of any race; Average household size: 2.90; Median age: 42.0; Age under 18: 28.9%; Age 65 and over: 10.4%; Males per 100 females: 101.5; Marriage status: 19.9% never married, 74.1% now married, 0.4% separated, 2.5% widowed, 3.5% divorced; Foreign born: 2.7%; Speak English only: 96.5%; With disability: 5.9%; Veterans: 5.7%; Ancestry: 33.1% German, 13.1% Irish, 11.6% English, 10.3% Polish, 7.9% French

Employment: 26.3% management, business, and financial, 11.8% computer, engineering, and science, 8.4% education, legal, community service, arts, and media, 10.5% healthcare practitioners, 9.1% service, 17.9% sales and office, 6.2% natural resources, construction, and maintenance, 9.7% production, transportation, and material moving

Income: Per capita: $48,547; Median household: $108,190; Average household: $143,125; Households with income of $100,000 or more: 51.5%; Poverty rate: 2.8%

Educational Attainment: High school diploma or higher: 95.6%; Bachelor's degree or higher: 52.3%; Graduate/professional degree or higher: 23.5%

Housing: Homeownership rate: 94.2%; Median home value: $227,000; Median year structure built: 1988; Homeowner vacancy rate: 1.1%; Median gross rent: $925 per month; Rental vacancy rate: 3.7%

Health Insurance: 97.3% have insurance; 94.1% have private insurance; 15.9% have public insurance; 2.7% do not have insurance; 0.7% of children under 18 do not have insurance

Transportation: Commute: 95.2% car, 0.6% public transportation, 0.0% walk, 3.4% work from home; Median travel time to work: 17.7 minutes

LEE (township). Covers a land area of 35.618 square miles and a water area of 0.314 square miles. Located at 43.60° N. Lat; 84.43° W. Long.
Population: 4,315; Growth (since 2000): -2.2%; Density: 121.1 persons per square mile; Race: 97.4% White, 0.4% Black/African American, 0.2% Asian, 0.4% American Indian/Alaska Native, 0.0% Native Hawaiian/Other Pacific Islander, 1.4% Two or more races, 1.1% Hispanic of any race; Average household size: 2.73; Median age: 38.6; Age under 18: 25.0%; Age 65 and over: 11.0%; Males per 100 females: 99.6; Marriage status: 23.9% never married, 60.7% now married, 0.6% separated, 4.0% widowed, 11.4% divorced; Foreign born: 0.0%; Speak English only: 97.2%; With disability: 16.0%; Veterans: 8.7%; Ancestry: 19.4% German, 13.1% Irish, 8.2% American, 6.8% English, 6.2% French
Employment: 8.4% management, business, and financial, 6.4% computer, engineering, and science, 10.1% education, legal, community service, arts, and media, 2.9% healthcare practitioners, 17.1% service, 17.8% sales and office, 19.2% natural resources, construction, and maintenance, 18.1% production, transportation, and material moving
Income: Per capita: $22,658; Median household: $51,532; Average household: $61,513; Households with income of $100,000 or more: 15.4%; Poverty rate: 17.9%
Educational Attainment: High school diploma or higher: 88.7%; Bachelor's degree or higher: 13.3%; Graduate/professional degree or higher: 4.8%
Housing: Homeownership rate: 81.9%; Median home value: $101,200; Median year structure built: 1980; Homeowner vacancy rate: 2.0%; Median gross rent: $728 per month; Rental vacancy rate: 6.3%
Health Insurance: 90.7% have insurance; 62.6% have private insurance; 39.1% have public insurance; 9.3% do not have insurance; 0.0% of children under 18 do not have insurance
Transportation: Commute: 97.0% car, 0.1% public transportation, 0.6% walk, 0.5% work from home; Median travel time to work: 25.3 minutes

LINCOLN (township). Covers a land area of 23.312 square miles and a water area of 0.095 square miles. Located at 43.70° N. Lat; 84.32° W. Long.
Population: 2,474; Growth (since 2000): 8.7%; Density: 106.1 persons per square mile; Race: 98.4% White, 0.2% Black/African American, 0.2% Asian, 0.4% American Indian/Alaska Native, 0.0% Native Hawaiian/Other Pacific Islander, 0.7% Two or more races, 1.1% Hispanic of any race; Average household size: 2.46; Median age: 44.4; Age under 18: 21.9%; Age 65 and over: 18.8%; Males per 100 females: 100.0
Housing: Homeownership rate: 87.3%; Homeowner vacancy rate: 1.7%; Rental vacancy rate: 7.2%

MIDLAND (charter township). Covers a land area of 7.635 square miles and a water area of 0.585 square miles. Located at 43.59° N. Lat; 84.24° W. Long. Elevation is 627 feet.
History: Midland owes its development after 1890 to the Dow Chemical Company. Dow Gardens, original gardens at home of Dr. Herbert H. Dow, founder of Dow Chemical Corporation, and Dow Gardens Library and Center for Arts are in Midland; Saginaw Valley State University at University Center, 12 miles east. Incorporated 1887.
Population: 2,287; Growth (since 2000): -0.4%; Density: 299.5 persons per square mile; Race: 97.7% White, 0.7% Black/African American, 0.1% Asian, 0.1% American Indian/Alaska Native, 0.0% Native Hawaiian/Other Pacific Islander, 1.0% Two or more races, 2.1% Hispanic of any race; Average household size: 2.64; Median age: 40.3; Age under 18: 25.1%; Age 65 and over: 13.7%; Males per 100 females: 103.7
School District(s)
Academic and Career Education Academy (KG-12)
    2012-13 Enrollment: 110 . . . . (989) 631-5202
Bullock Creek SD (PK-12)
    2012-13 Enrollment: 1,923 . . . . (989) 631-9022
Midland Academy of Advanced and Creative Studies (KG-12)
    2012-13 Enrollment: 246 . . . . (989) 496-2404
Midland County Educational Service Agency (PK-12)
    2012-13 Enrollment: 133 . . . . (989) 631-5890
Midland Public Schools (PK-12)
    2012-13 Enrollment: 7,989 . . . . (989) 923-5001
Windover High School (KG-12)
    2012-13 Enrollment: 97 . . . . (989) 832-0852
Four-year College(s)
Northwood University-Michigan (Private, Not-for-profit)
    Fall 2013 Enrollment: 3,194 . . . . (989) 837-4200
    2013-14 Tuition: In-state $22,130; Out-of-state $22,130

Housing: Homeownership rate: 93.7%; Homeowner vacancy rate: 0.9%; Rental vacancy rate: 8.3%
Hospitals: Midmichigan Medical Center - Midland (250 beds)
Newspapers: Midland Daily News (daily circulation 16000)

MIDLAND (city). County seat. Covers a land area of 33.695 square miles and a water area of 1.992 square miles. Located at 43.62° N. Lat; 84.23° W. Long. Elevation is 627 feet.
History: Midland developed first as a lumber town, but later became the home of the Dow Chemical Company, organized by Dr. Herbert H. Dow in 1890 as the Midland Chemical Company. Dr. Dow began his experiments in the extraction of bromine and other chemicals from the salt brine underlying the Midland region.
Population: 41,863; Growth (since 2000): 0.4%; Density: 1,242.4 persons per square mile; Race: 92.0% White, 2.0% Black/African American, 3.3% Asian, 0.3% American Indian/Alaska Native, 0.1% Native Hawaiian/Other Pacific Islander, 1.8% Two or more races, 2.4% Hispanic of any race; Average household size: 2.33; Median age: 38.3; Age under 18: 23.4%; Age 65 and over: 15.6%; Males per 100 females: 92.6; Marriage status: 29.8% never married, 51.4% now married, 0.9% separated, 7.2% widowed, 11.7% divorced; Foreign born: 6.5%; Speak English only: 92.4%; With disability: 12.5%; Veterans: 7.9%; Ancestry: 28.0% German, 13.4% Irish, 11.9% English, 7.6% Polish, 6.4% American
Employment: 15.2% management, business, and financial, 11.5% computer, engineering, and science, 11.8% education, legal, community service, arts, and media, 6.6% healthcare practitioners, 17.0% service, 23.1% sales and office, 6.2% natural resources, construction, and maintenance, 8.7% production, transportation, and material moving
Income: Per capita: $31,627; Median household: $50,928; Average household: $74,505; Households with income of $100,000 or more: 21.6%; Poverty rate: 14.3%
Educational Attainment: High school diploma or higher: 93.6%; Bachelor's degree or higher: 42.9%; Graduate/professional degree or higher: 17.0%
School District(s)
Academic and Career Education Academy (KG-12)
    2012-13 Enrollment: 110 . . . . (989) 631-5202
Bullock Creek SD (PK-12)
    2012-13 Enrollment: 1,923 . . . . (989) 631-9022
Midland Academy of Advanced and Creative Studies (KG-12)
    2012-13 Enrollment: 246 . . . . (989) 496-2404
Midland County Educational Service Agency (PK-12)
    2012-13 Enrollment: 133 . . . . (989) 631-5890
Midland Public Schools (PK-12)
    2012-13 Enrollment: 7,989 . . . . (989) 923-5001
Windover High School (KG-12)
    2012-13 Enrollment: 97 . . . . (989) 832-0852
Four-year College(s)
Northwood University-Michigan (Private, Not-for-profit)
    Fall 2013 Enrollment: 3,194 . . . . (989) 837-4200
    2013-14 Tuition: In-state $22,130; Out-of-state $22,130
Housing: Homeownership rate: 67.0%; Median home value: $139,500; Median year structure built: 1971; Homeowner vacancy rate: 1.9%; Median gross rent: $710 per month; Rental vacancy rate: 5.3%
Health Insurance: 90.1% have insurance; 76.5% have private insurance; 29.9% have public insurance; 9.9% do not have insurance; 6.4% of children under 18 do not have insurance
Hospitals: Midmichigan Medical Center - Midland (250 beds)
Newspapers: Midland Daily News (daily circulation 16000)
Transportation: Commute: 90.7% car, 0.8% public transportation, 2.0% walk, 4.6% work from home; Median travel time to work: 15.6 minutes
Additional Information Contacts
City of Midland . . . . (989) 837-3300
    http://www.midland-mi.org

MILLS (township). Covers a land area of 35.556 square miles and a water area of 0.403 square miles. Located at 43.78° N. Lat; 84.23° W. Long.
Population: 1,939; Growth (since 2000): 3.6%; Density: 54.5 persons per square mile; Race: 97.3% White, 0.2% Black/African American, 0.2% Asian, 1.1% American Indian/Alaska Native, 0.0% Native Hawaiian/Other Pacific Islander, 1.2% Two or more races, 0.8% Hispanic of any race; Average household size: 2.75; Median age: 39.6; Age under 18: 25.4%; Age 65 and over: 12.2%; Males per 100 females: 100.1

Housing: Homeownership rate: 89.8%; Homeowner vacancy rate: 1.1%; Rental vacancy rate: 5.3%

MOUNT HALEY (township). Covers a land area of 23.823 square miles and a water area of 0.048 square miles. Located at 43.52° N. Lat; 84.32° W. Long.
Population: 1,678; Growth (since 2000): 1.5%; Density: 70.4 persons per square mile; Race: 97.6% White, 0.0% Black/African American, 0.2% Asian, 1.1% American Indian/Alaska Native, 0.0% Native Hawaiian/Other Pacific Islander, 0.8% Two or more races, 2.0% Hispanic of any race; Average household size: 2.65; Median age: 41.0; Age under 18: 25.0%; Age 65 and over: 12.5%; Males per 100 females: 102.9
Housing: Homeownership rate: 90.7%; Homeowner vacancy rate: 2.0%; Rental vacancy rate: 7.8%

PORTER (township). Covers a land area of 35.168 square miles and a water area of 0.753 square miles. Located at 43.51° N. Lat; 84.42° W. Long. Elevation is 676 feet.
Population: 1,277; Growth (since 2000): 0.6%; Density: 36.3 persons per square mile; Race: 98.0% White, 0.0% Black/African American, 0.3% Asian, 0.9% American Indian/Alaska Native, 0.0% Native Hawaiian/Other Pacific Islander, 0.6% Two or more races, 1.6% Hispanic of any race; Average household size: 2.64; Median age: 40.4; Age under 18: 23.7%; Age 65 and over: 11.8%; Males per 100 females: 100.2
Housing: Homeownership rate: 91.4%; Homeowner vacancy rate: 2.0%; Rental vacancy rate: 6.7%

SANFORD (village). Covers a land area of 1.272 square miles and a water area of 0.276 square miles. Located at 43.68° N. Lat; 84.39° W. Long. Elevation is 627 feet.
History: The village of Sanford was laid out in 1870 by Charles S. Sanford, who had come here from New York.
Population: 859; Growth (since 2000): -8.9%; Density: 675.5 persons per square mile; Race: 97.6% White, 0.1% Black/African American, 0.7% Asian, 0.6% American Indian/Alaska Native, 0.0% Native Hawaiian/Other Pacific Islander, 0.6% Two or more races, 2.6% Hispanic of any race; Average household size: 2.33; Median age: 43.6; Age under 18: 21.4%; Age 65 and over: 16.2%; Males per 100 females: 93.5
School District(s)
Meridian Public Schools (PK-12)
    2012-13 Enrollment: 1,302 . . . . (989) 687-3200
Housing: Homeownership rate: 78.1%; Homeowner vacancy rate: 2.3%; Rental vacancy rate: 12.0%

WARREN (township). Covers a land area of 34.754 square miles and a water area of 0.146 square miles. Located at 43.77° N. Lat; 84.54° W. Long.
Population: 2,119; Growth (since 2000): 0.6%; Density: 61.0 persons per square mile; Race: 97.8% White, 0.0% Black/African American, 0.2% Asian, 0.3% American Indian/Alaska Native, 0.0% Native Hawaiian/Other Pacific Islander, 1.4% Two or more races, 1.1% Hispanic of any race; Average household size: 2.57; Median age: 43.2; Age under 18: 23.4%; Age 65 and over: 15.6%; Males per 100 females: 100.7
Housing: Homeownership rate: 88.5%; Homeowner vacancy rate: 1.3%; Rental vacancy rate: 3.0%

Missaukee County

Located in north central Michigan; drained by the Muskegon River; includes part of Manistee National Forest. Covers a land area of 564.726 square miles, a water area of 9.103 square miles, and is located in the Eastern Time Zone at 44.33° N. Lat., 85.09° W. Long. The county was founded in 1840. County seat is Lake City.

Missaukee County is part of the Cadillac, MI Micropolitan Statistical Area. The entire metro area includes: Missaukee County, MI; Wexford County, MI

Weather Station: Houghton Lake 6 WSW										Elevation: 1,134 feet	
	Jan	Feb	Mar	Apr	May	Jun	Jul	Aug	Sep	Oct	Nov	Dec
High	28	31	40	54	67	77	81	79	71	57	44	32
Low	9	9	16	30	39	48	52	51	42	34	26	16
Precip	1.7	1.3	1.4	2.6	2.9	3.4	2.7	3.5	3.4	3.1	2.6	1.8
Snow	15.4	11.7	na	2.2	0.1	0.0	0.0	0.0	0.0	0.6	5.8	15.2

High and Low temperatures in degrees Fahrenheit; Precipitation and Snow in inches

Weather Station: Lake City Exp Farm										Elevation: 1,240 feet	
	Jan	Feb	Mar	Apr	May	Jun	Jul	Aug	Sep	Oct	Nov	Dec
High	27	30	39	53	66	75	80	77	69	56	43	31
Low	10	10	17	31	41	50	55	53	45	35	27	16
Precip	1.7	1.3	1.9	3.0	3.2	3.4	2.7	3.7	3.6	3.3	2.6	1.9
Snow	18.0	13.0	11.4	4.8	0.5	0.0	0.0	0.0	tr	1.8	9.7	17.0

High and Low temperatures in degrees Fahrenheit; Precipitation and Snow in inches

Population: 14,849; Growth (since 2000): 2.6%; Density: 26.3 persons per square mile; Race: 97.1% White, 0.3% Black/African American, 0.3% Asian, 0.6% American Indian/Alaska Native, 0.0% Native Hawaiian/Other Pacific Islander, 1.2% two or more races, 2.1% Hispanic of any race; Average household size: 2.51; Median age: 42.8; Age under 18: 24.2%; Age 65 and over: 17.4%; Males per 100 females: 103.6; Marriage status: 24.0% never married, 57.4% now married, 1.1% separated, 6.8% widowed, 11.8% divorced; Foreign born: 1.6%; Speak English only: 96.7%; With disability: 17.3%; Veterans: 10.9%; Ancestry: 24.7% German, 18.1% Dutch, 11.6% English, 10.6% Irish, 6.1% American
Religion: Six largest groups: 20.5% Presbyterian-Reformed, 5.6% Catholicism, 3.7% Methodist/Pietist, 3.6% Non-denominational Protestant, 2.5% Lutheran, 1.3% European Free-Church
Economy: Unemployment rate: 6.4%; Leading industries: 17.1% construction; 13.9% retail trade; 12.1% other services (except public administration); Farms: 433 totaling 99,510 acres; Company size: 0 employ 1,000 or more persons, 0 employ 500 to 999 persons, 1 employs 100 to 499 persons, 279 employ less than 100 persons; Business ownership: 280 women-owned, n/a Black-owned, n/a Hispanic-owned, n/a Asian-owned
Employment: 11.1% management, business, and financial, 2.3% computer, engineering, and science, 7.6% education, legal, community service, arts, and media, 3.3% healthcare practitioners, 17.7% service, 22.3% sales and office, 14.9% natural resources, construction, and maintenance, 20.8% production, transportation, and material moving
Income: Per capita: $20,305; Median household: $41,061; Average household: $50,178; Households with income of $100,000 or more: 8.8%; Poverty rate: 15.1%
Educational Attainment: High school diploma or higher: 86.0%; Bachelor's degree or higher: 13.0%; Graduate/professional degree or higher: 4.2%
Housing: Homeownership rate: 81.4%; Median home value: $99,400; Median year structure built: 1976; Homeowner vacancy rate: 3.6%; Median gross rent: $696 per month; Rental vacancy rate: 7.7%
Vital Statistics: Birth rate: 115.6 per 10,000 population; Death rate: 105.0 per 10,000 population; Age-adjusted cancer mortality rate: 211.0 deaths per 100,000 population
Health Insurance: 86.9% have insurance; 62.9% have private insurance; 41.1% have public insurance; 13.1% do not have insurance; 6.2% of children under 18 do not have insurance
Health Care: Physicians: 3.3 per 10,000 population; Hospital beds: 0.0 per 10,000 population; Hospital admissions: 0.0 per 10,000 population
Air Quality Index: 93.1% good, 6.9% moderate, 0.0% unhealthy for sensitive individuals, 0.0% unhealthy (percent of days)
Transportation: Commute: 90.0% car, 0.5% public transportation, 4.0% walk, 4.4% work from home; Median travel time to work: 23.1 minutes
Presidential Election: 32.4% Obama, 66.4% Romney (2012)
Additional Information Contacts
Missaukee Government . . . . (231) 839-4967
    http://www.missaukee.org

Missaukee County Communities

AETNA (township). Covers a land area of 35.877 square miles and a water area of 0.008 square miles. Located at 44.30° N. Lat; 85.04° W. Long.
Population: 413; Growth (since 2000): -15.9%; Density: 11.5 persons per square mile; Race: 98.1% White, 0.0% Black/African American, 0.0% Asian, 0.2% American Indian/Alaska Native, 0.0% Native Hawaiian/Other Pacific Islander, 0.5% Two or more races, 3.9% Hispanic of any race; Average household size: 2.37; Median age: 46.6; Age under 18: 19.4%; Age 65 and over: 20.3%; Males per 100 females: 102.5
Housing: Homeownership rate: 85.1%; Homeowner vacancy rate: 2.0%; Rental vacancy rate: 3.7%

BLOOMFIELD (township). Covers a land area of 35.540 square miles and a water area of 0.146 square miles. Located at 44.47° N. Lat; 85.28° W. Long.
Population: 531; Growth (since 2000): 11.8%; Density: 14.9 persons per square mile; Race: 97.0% White, 0.2% Black/African American, 2.1% Asian, 0.4% American Indian/Alaska Native, 0.0% Native Hawaiian/Other Pacific Islander, 0.4% Two or more races, 1.3% Hispanic of any race; Average household size: 2.52; Median age: 43.3; Age under 18: 23.5%; Age 65 and over: 15.6%; Males per 100 females: 120.3
Housing: Homeownership rate: 87.2%; Homeowner vacancy rate: 5.6%; Rental vacancy rate: 3.4%

BUTTERFIELD (township). Covers a land area of 35.396 square miles and a water area of 0.619 square miles. Located at 44.30° N. Lat; 84.92° W. Long. Elevation is 1,161 feet.
Population: 489; Growth (since 2000): -10.8%; Density: 13.8 persons per square mile; Race: 98.4% White, 0.4% Black/African American, 0.2% Asian, 0.6% American Indian/Alaska Native, 0.0% Native Hawaiian/Other Pacific Islander, 0.4% Two or more races, 0.8% Hispanic of any race; Average household size: 2.43; Median age: 48.0; Age under 18: 20.7%; Age 65 and over: 19.2%; Males per 100 females: 107.2
Housing: Homeownership rate: 85.1%; Homeowner vacancy rate: 3.3%; Rental vacancy rate: 3.1%

CALDWELL (township). Covers a land area of 34.214 square miles and a water area of 1.379 square miles. Located at 44.37° N. Lat; 85.28° W. Long.
History: Caldwell Township was first called Quilna Township, renamed in 1873 for Thomas T. Caldwell. James C. Caldwell was the first postmaster here.
Population: 1,317; Growth (since 2000): -3.4%; Density: 38.5 persons per square mile; Race: 97.2% White, 0.7% Black/African American, 0.0% Asian, 0.7% American Indian/Alaska Native, 0.0% Native Hawaiian/Other Pacific Islander, 1.2% Two or more races, 1.8% Hispanic of any race; Average household size: 2.52; Median age: 43.3; Age under 18: 23.7%; Age 65 and over: 18.0%; Males per 100 females: 112.8
Housing: Homeownership rate: 79.3%; Homeowner vacancy rate: 3.8%; Rental vacancy rate: 5.3%

CLAM UNION (township). Covers a land area of 35.587 square miles and a water area of 0.415 square miles. Located at 44.21° N. Lat; 85.03° W. Long.
Population: 882; Growth (since 2000): 0.0%; Density: 24.8 persons per square mile; Race: 97.1% White, 0.1% Black/African American, 0.2% Asian, 0.2% American Indian/Alaska Native, 0.0% Native Hawaiian/Other Pacific Islander, 1.2% Two or more races, 3.5% Hispanic of any race; Average household size: 2.63; Median age: 39.7; Age under 18: 25.7%; Age 65 and over: 15.8%; Males per 100 females: 100.0
Housing: Homeownership rate: 85.9%; Homeowner vacancy rate: 2.0%; Rental vacancy rate: 4.1%

ENTERPRISE (township). Covers a land area of 34.466 square miles and a water area of 0.551 square miles. Located at 44.39° N. Lat; 84.91° W. Long.
Population: 194; Growth (since 2000): 0.0%; Density: 5.6 persons per square mile; Race: 97.4% White, 0.0% Black/African American, 0.5% Asian, 0.5% American Indian/Alaska Native, 0.0% Native Hawaiian/Other Pacific Islander, 1.5% Two or more races, 0.0% Hispanic of any race; Average household size: 2.55; Median age: 43.0; Age under 18: 23.2%; Age 65 and over: 15.5%; Males per 100 females: 120.5
Housing: Homeownership rate: 85.5%; Homeowner vacancy rate: 12.0%; Rental vacancy rate: 0.0%

FALMOUTH (unincorporated postal area)
ZCTA: 49632
Covers a land area of 84.687 square miles and a water area of 0.508 square miles. Located at 44.24° N. Lat; 84.97° W. Long. Elevation is 1,184 feet.
Population: 1,126; Growth (since 2000): -1.9%; Density: 13.3 persons per square mile; Race: 97.9% White, 0.2% Black/African American, 0.2% Asian, 0.3% American Indian/Alaska Native, 0.0% Native Hawaiian/Other Pacific Islander, 0.6% Two or more races, 3.1% Hispanic of any race; Average household size: 2.40; Median age: 46.0; Age under 18: 22.5%; Age 65 and over: 20.0%; Males per 100 females: 104.4

Housing: Homeownership rate: 85.5%; Homeowner vacancy rate: 1.2%; Rental vacancy rate: 2.9%

FOREST (township). Covers a land area of 35.129 square miles and a water area of 0.033 square miles. Located at 44.38° N. Lat; 85.16° W. Long.
Population: 1,157; Growth (since 2000): 6.9%; Density: 32.9 persons per square mile; Race: 95.8% White, 0.2% Black/African American, 0.0% Asian, 1.2% American Indian/Alaska Native, 0.0% Native Hawaiian/Other Pacific Islander, 1.8% Two or more races, 2.4% Hispanic of any race; Average household size: 2.47; Median age: 41.0; Age under 18: 24.8%; Age 65 and over: 14.3%; Males per 100 females: 91.6
Housing: Homeownership rate: 73.5%; Homeowner vacancy rate: 3.6%; Rental vacancy rate: 5.3%

HOLLAND (township). Covers a land area of 35.620 square miles and a water area of 0.284 square miles. Located at 44.21° N. Lat; 84.92° W. Long.
Population: 248; Growth (since 2000): 11.2%; Density: 7.0 persons per square mile; Race: 96.4% White, 0.0% Black/African American, 0.8% Asian, 0.0% American Indian/Alaska Native, 0.0% Native Hawaiian/Other Pacific Islander, 0.4% Two or more races, 4.0% Hispanic of any race; Average household size: 2.25; Median age: 49.5; Age under 18: 20.2%; Age 65 and over: 21.8%; Males per 100 females: 117.5
Housing: Homeownership rate: 85.5%; Homeowner vacancy rate: 0.0%; Rental vacancy rate: 0.0%

JENNINGS (CDP). Covers a land area of 0.759 square miles and a water area of <.001 square miles. Located at 44.33° N. Lat; 85.30° W. Long. Elevation is 1,306 feet.
Population: 264; Growth (since 2000): n/a; Density: 348.0 persons per square mile; Race: 99.6% White, 0.4% Black/African American, 0.0% Asian, 0.0% American Indian/Alaska Native, 0.0% Native Hawaiian/Other Pacific Islander, 0.0% Two or more races, 1.5% Hispanic of any race; Average household size: 2.75; Median age: 37.0; Age under 18: 28.8%; Age 65 and over: 14.4%; Males per 100 females: 100.0
Housing: Homeownership rate: 68.8%; Homeowner vacancy rate: 1.5%; Rental vacancy rate: 0.0%

LAKE (township). Covers a land area of 31.567 square miles and a water area of 4.469 square miles. Located at 44.30° N. Lat; 85.29° W. Long.
Population: 2,800; Growth (since 2000): 13.5%; Density: 88.7 persons per square mile; Race: 97.1% White, 0.3% Black/African American, 0.2% Asian, 0.4% American Indian/Alaska Native, 0.0% Native Hawaiian/Other Pacific Islander, 1.8% Two or more races, 2.5% Hispanic of any race; Average household size: 2.40; Median age: 45.4; Age under 18: 23.1%; Age 65 and over: 19.6%; Males per 100 females: 99.1; Marriage status: 21.9% never married, 55.8% now married, 0.6% separated, 8.1% widowed, 14.3% divorced; Foreign born: 0.9%; Speak English only: 98.6%; With disability: 19.8%; Veterans: 11.2%; Ancestry: 31.1% German, 16.1% English, 12.6% Irish, 9.6% Polish, 5.6% Dutch
Employment: 13.0% management, business, and financial, 3.4% computer, engineering, and science, 8.5% education, legal, community service, arts, and media, 3.5% healthcare practitioners, 13.7% service, 23.1% sales and office, 9.3% natural resources, construction, and maintenance, 25.5% production, transportation, and material moving
Income: Per capita: $24,611; Median household: $45,938; Average household: $58,707; Households with income of $100,000 or more: 14.1%; Poverty rate: 14.3%
Educational Attainment: High school diploma or higher: 89.5%; Bachelor's degree or higher: 22.2%; Graduate/professional degree or higher: 6.5%
Housing: Homeownership rate: 78.9%; Median home value: $141,500; Median year structure built: 1977; Homeowner vacancy rate: 4.0%; Median gross rent: $795 per month; Rental vacancy rate: 7.4%
Health Insurance: 87.5% have insurance; 63.7% have private insurance; 45.2% have public insurance; 12.5% do not have insurance; 4.5% of children under 18 do not have insurance
Transportation: Commute: 94.7% car, 0.0% public transportation, 0.0% walk, 4.4% work from home; Median travel time to work: 27.7 minutes

LAKE CITY (city). County seat. Covers a land area of 1.048 square miles and a water area of 0 square miles. Located at 44.33° N. Lat; 85.21° W. Long. Elevation is 1,250 feet.

History: Daniel Reeder settled here in 1868. The community was first called Reeder, but was renamed Lake City in 1877, incorporated as a village in 1889 and as a city in 1932.

Population: 836; Growth (since 2000): -9.4%; Density: 797.7 persons per square mile; Race: 95.2% White, 1.2% Black/African American, 0.7% Asian, 1.7% American Indian/Alaska Native, 0.0% Native Hawaiian/Other Pacific Islander, 1.2% Two or more races, 2.9% Hispanic of any race; Average household size: 2.35; Median age: 40.5; Age under 18: 23.4%; Age 65 and over: 19.3%; Males per 100 females: 104.9

School District(s)

Lake City Area SD (KG-12)

    2012-13 Enrollment: 1,148 . . . . (231) 839-4333

Housing: Homeownership rate: 69.2%; Homeowner vacancy rate: 6.7%; Rental vacancy rate: 6.2%

Newspapers: Missaukee Sentinel (weekly circulation 2500)

MCBAIN (city). Covers a land area of 1.251 square miles and a water area of 0 square miles. Located at 44.20° N. Lat; 85.22° W. Long. Elevation is 1,237 feet.

Population: 656; Growth (since 2000): 12.3%; Density: 524.2 persons per square mile; Race: 95.6% White, 0.3% Black/African American, 0.5% Asian, 0.3% American Indian/Alaska Native, 0.0% Native Hawaiian/Other Pacific Islander, 0.8% Two or more races, 3.4% Hispanic of any race; Average household size: 2.29; Median age: 45.9; Age under 18: 22.1%; Age 65 and over: 28.7%; Males per 100 females: 72.6

School District(s)

Mcbain Rural Agricultural Schools (PK-12)

    2012-13 Enrollment: 1,059 . . . . (231) 825-2165

Housing: Homeownership rate: 60.6%; Homeowner vacancy rate: 4.4%; Rental vacancy rate: 9.1%

NORWICH (township). Covers a land area of 71.918 square miles and a water area of 0.679 square miles. Located at 44.47° N. Lat; 84.98° W. Long.

Population: 611; Growth (since 2000): -5.4%; Density: 8.5 persons per square mile; Race: 97.9% White, 0.0% Black/African American, 0.0% Asian, 1.1% American Indian/Alaska Native, 0.0% Native Hawaiian/Other Pacific Islander, 0.8% Two or more races, 0.3% Hispanic of any race; Average household size: 2.25; Median age: 51.0; Age under 18: 16.4%; Age 65 and over: 24.1%; Males per 100 females: 107.1

Housing: Homeownership rate: 88.6%; Homeowner vacancy rate: 6.2%; Rental vacancy rate: 11.4%

PIONEER (township). Covers a land area of 35.909 square miles and a water area of 0.036 square miles. Located at 44.46° N. Lat; 85.15° W. Long. Elevation is 1,329 feet.

Population: 451; Growth (since 2000): -2.0%; Density: 12.6 persons per square mile; Race: 98.4% White, 0.0% Black/African American, 0.0% Asian, 0.7% American Indian/Alaska Native, 0.2% Native Hawaiian/Other Pacific Islander, 0.7% Two or more races, 1.3% Hispanic of any race; Average household size: 2.42; Median age: 45.1; Age under 18: 21.5%; Age 65 and over: 17.3%; Males per 100 females: 112.7

Housing: Homeownership rate: 89.6%; Homeowner vacancy rate: 8.4%; Rental vacancy rate: 4.8%

REEDER (township). Covers a land area of 34.783 square miles and a water area of 0.125 square miles. Located at 44.29° N. Lat; 85.15° W. Long.

Population: 1,128; Growth (since 2000): 1.4%; Density: 32.4 persons per square mile; Race: 96.8% White, 0.4% Black/African American, 0.1% Asian, 0.7% American Indian/Alaska Native, 0.0% Native Hawaiian/Other Pacific Islander, 1.4% Two or more races, 1.4% Hispanic of any race; Average household size: 2.67; Median age: 40.8; Age under 18: 26.0%; Age 65 and over: 16.6%; Males per 100 females: 105.5

Housing: Homeownership rate: 82.0%; Homeowner vacancy rate: 1.4%; Rental vacancy rate: 22.4%

RICHLAND (township). Covers a land area of 35.518 square miles and a water area of 0.072 square miles. Located at 44.21° N. Lat; 85.27° W. Long.

Population: 1,491; Growth (since 2000): 3.2%; Density: 42.0 persons per square mile; Race: 97.9% White, 0.0% Black/African American, 0.5% Asian, 0.3% American Indian/Alaska Native, 0.0% Native Hawaiian/Other Pacific Islander, 1.3% Two or more races, 0.7% Hispanic of any race; Average household size: 2.72; Median age: 38.2; Age under 18: 28.6%; Age 65 and over: 11.5%; Males per 100 females: 109.7

Housing: Homeownership rate: 89.3%; Homeowner vacancy rate: 1.4%; Rental vacancy rate: 6.3%

RIVERSIDE (township). Covers a land area of 35.349 square miles and a water area of 0.204 square miles. Located at 44.22° N. Lat; 85.14° W. Long.

Population: 1,179; Growth (since 2000): 12.3%; Density: 33.4 persons per square mile; Race: 98.3% White, 0.2% Black/African American, 0.4% Asian, 0.1% American Indian/Alaska Native, 0.0% Native Hawaiian/Other Pacific Islander, 0.5% Two or more races, 2.5% Hispanic of any race; Average household size: 3.02; Median age: 34.1; Age under 18: 32.5%; Age 65 and over: 11.3%; Males per 100 females: 105.8

Housing: Homeownership rate: 89.0%; Homeowner vacancy rate: 0.8%; Rental vacancy rate: 6.5%

WEST BRANCH (township). Covers a land area of 35.553 square miles and a water area of 0.082 square miles. Located at 44.38° N. Lat; 85.03° W. Long.

Population: 466; Growth (since 2000): -12.4%; Density: 13.1 persons per square mile; Race: 97.0% White, 0.6% Black/African American, 0.4% Asian, 0.6% American Indian/Alaska Native, 0.0% Native Hawaiian/Other Pacific Islander, 1.1% Two or more races, 1.5% Hispanic of any race; Average household size: 2.38; Median age: 48.5; Age under 18: 17.4%; Age 65 and over: 17.4%; Males per 100 females: 120.9

Housing: Homeownership rate: 88.2%; Homeowner vacancy rate: 4.1%; Rental vacancy rate: 12.0%

Monroe County

Located in southeastern Michigan; bounded on the south by Ohio, on the east by Lake Erie, and on the northeast by the Huron River; drained by the Raisin River. Covers a land area of 549.394 square miles, a water area of 130.625 square miles, and is located in the Eastern Time Zone at 41.92° N. Lat., 83.49° W. Long. The county was founded in 1817. County seat is Monroe.

Monroe County is part of the Monroe, MI Metropolitan Statistical Area. The entire metro area includes: Monroe County, MI

Population: 152,021; Growth (since 2000): 4.2%; Density: 276.7 persons per square mile; Race: 94.4% White, 2.1% Black/African American, 0.6% Asian, 0.3% American Indian/Alaska Native, 0.0% Native Hawaiian/Other Pacific Islander, 1.8% two or more races, 3.1% Hispanic of any race; Average household size: 2.59; Median age: 40.3; Age under 18: 24.1%; Age 65 and over: 13.4%; Males per 100 females: 97.4; Marriage status: 26.5% never married, 55.9% now married, 1.3% separated, 6.3% widowed, 11.3% divorced; Foreign born: 2.0%; Speak English only: 96.3%; With disability: 13.0%; Veterans: 9.9%; Ancestry: 30.8% German, 13.5% Irish, 11.7% American, 10.4% French, 10.3% Polish

Religion: Six largest groups: 21.0% Catholicism, 6.9% Lutheran, 5.4% Baptist, 3.4% Pentecostal, 2.8% Methodist/Pietist, 2.3% Holiness

Economy: Unemployment rate: 5.2%; Leading industries: 16.1% retail trade; 12.2% health care and social assistance; 11.3% accommodation and food services; Farms: 1,144 totaling 214,506 acres; Company size: 1 employs 1,000 or more persons, 5 employ 500 to 999 persons, 50 employ 100 to 499 persons, 2,270 employ less than 100 persons; Business ownership: 3,016 women-owned, 173 Black-owned, 78 Hispanic-owned, 133 Asian-owned

Employment: 10.3% management, business, and financial, 3.7% computer, engineering, and science, 7.4% education, legal, community service, arts, and media, 6.2% healthcare practitioners, 19.5% service, 22.3% sales and office, 9.8% natural resources, construction, and maintenance, 20.8% production, transportation, and material moving

Income: Per capita: $25,939; Median household: $53,972; Average household: $66,063; Households with income of $100,000 or more: 19.5%; Poverty rate: 12.3%

Educational Attainment: High school diploma or higher: 89.3%; Bachelor's degree or higher: 18.0%; Graduate/professional degree or higher: 6.5%

Housing: Homeownership rate: 79.9%; Median home value: $139,100; Median year structure built: 1972; Homeowner vacancy rate: 2.4%; Median gross rent: $777 per month; Rental vacancy rate: 11.8%

Vital Statistics: Birth rate: 103.1 per 10,000 population; Death rate: 86.3 per 10,000 population; Age-adjusted cancer mortality rate: 172.3 deaths per 100,000 population

Health Insurance: 91.0% have insurance; 75.8% have private insurance; 30.3% have public insurance; 9.0% do not have insurance; 3.2% of children under 18 do not have insurance

Health Care: Physicians: 10.4 per 10,000 population; Hospital beds: 11.2 per 10,000 population; Hospital admissions: 633.9 per 10,000 population

Air Quality Index: 91.7% good, 8.3% moderate, 0.0% unhealthy for sensitive individuals, 0.0% unhealthy (percent of days)

Transportation: Commute: 94.1% car, 1.0% public transportation, 1.1% walk, 2.9% work from home; Median travel time to work: 24.7 minutes

Presidential Election: 50.0% Obama, 49.0% Romney (2012)

National and State Parks: Erie State Game Area; Petersburg State Game Management Area; Pointe Mouillee State Game Area; River Raisin National Battlefield Park; Sterling State Park

Additional Information Contacts
Monroe Government . . . . (888) 354-5500
  http://www.co.monroe.mi.us

Monroe County Communities

ASH (township). Covers a land area of 34.602 square miles and a water area of 0.238 square miles. Located at 42.06° N. Lat; 83.37° W. Long.

Population: 7,783; Growth (since 2000): 2.3%; Density: 224.9 persons per square mile; Race: 97.0% White, 0.7% Black/African American, 0.4% Asian, 0.3% American Indian/Alaska Native, 0.0% Native Hawaiian/Other Pacific Islander, 1.4% Two or more races, 2.0% Hispanic of any race; Average household size: 2.59; Median age: 42.4; Age under 18: 22.5%; Age 65 and over: 13.0%; Males per 100 females: 98.9; Marriage status: 23.4% never married, 61.1% now married, 0.9% separated, 5.3% widowed, 10.1% divorced; Foreign born: 2.0%; Speak English only: 96.6%; With disability: 11.7%; Veterans: 11.4%; Ancestry: 26.4% German, 15.0% American, 12.0% Irish, 11.1% French, 10.2% Polish

Employment: 9.7% management, business, and financial, 3.8% computer, engineering, and science, 4.4% education, legal, community service, arts, and media, 6.5% healthcare practitioners, 22.0% service, 23.3% sales and office, 12.2% natural resources, construction, and maintenance, 18.0% production, transportation, and material moving

Income: Per capita: $26,992; Median household: $59,394; Average household: $72,220; Households with income of $100,000 or more: 24.1%; Poverty rate: 11.1%

Educational Attainment: High school diploma or higher: 89.5%; Bachelor's degree or higher: 16.3%; Graduate/professional degree or higher: 6.2%

Housing: Homeownership rate: 88.8%; Median home value: $157,900; Median year structure built: 1980; Homeowner vacancy rate: 2.6%; Median gross rent: $726 per month; Rental vacancy rate: 14.6%

Health Insurance: 91.3% have insurance; 79.1% have private insurance; 28.2% have public insurance; 8.7% do not have insurance; 7.2% of children under 18 do not have insurance

Transportation: Commute: 96.9% car, 0.3% public transportation, 1.0% walk, 1.8% work from home; Median travel time to work: 25.7 minutes

Additional Information Contacts
Ash Township . . . . (734) 654-6992
  http://ashtownship.org

BEDFORD (township). Covers a land area of 39.190 square miles and a water area of 0.172 square miles. Located at 41.77° N. Lat; 83.60° W. Long.

Population: 31,085; Growth (since 2000): 8.7%; Density: 793.2 persons per square mile; Race: 96.5% White, 0.5% Black/African American, 0.8% Asian, 0.2% American Indian/Alaska Native, 0.0% Native Hawaiian/Other Pacific Islander, 1.2% Two or more races, 2.5% Hispanic of any race; Average household size: 2.60; Median age: 42.7; Age under 18: 23.6%; Age 65 and over: 14.9%; Males per 100 females: 95.8; Marriage status: 23.4% never married, 60.4% now married, 0.9% separated, 6.6% widowed, 9.5% divorced; Foreign born: 2.2%; Speak English only: 96.7%;

With disability: 9.0%; Veterans: 9.9%; Ancestry: 35.3% German, 16.4% Polish, 14.0% Irish, 11.1% English, 9.3% French

Employment: 12.1% management, business, and financial, 4.6% computer, engineering, and science, 8.7% education, legal, community service, arts, and media, 6.8% healthcare practitioners, 15.7% service, 24.9% sales and office, 9.2% natural resources, construction, and maintenance, 18.0% production, transportation, and material moving

Income: Per capita: $29,554; Median household: $64,192; Average household: $75,815; Households with income of $100,000 or more: 24.4%; Poverty rate: 7.2%

Educational Attainment: High school diploma or higher: 94.1%; Bachelor's degree or higher: 25.6%; Graduate/professional degree or higher: 9.7%

Housing: Homeownership rate: 85.8%; Median home value: $158,400; Median year structure built: 1978; Homeowner vacancy rate: 1.8%; Median gross rent: $871 per month; Rental vacancy rate: 9.4%

Health Insurance: 93.0% have insurance; 83.3% have private insurance; 24.2% have public insurance; 7.0% do not have insurance; 3.3% of children under 18 do not have insurance

Transportation: Commute: 94.1% car, 0.6% public transportation, 0.1% walk, 4.7% work from home; Median travel time to work: 23.7 minutes

Additional Information Contacts
Bedford Township . . . . (734) 847-6791
  http://www.bedfordmi.org

BERLIN (charter township). Covers a land area of 31.999 square miles and a water area of 5.122 square miles. Located at 42.03° N. Lat; 83.26° W. Long.

Population: 9,299; Growth (since 2000): 34.3%; Density: 290.6 persons per square mile; Race: 96.3% White, 1.3% Black/African American, 0.3% Asian, 0.2% American Indian/Alaska Native, 0.0% Native Hawaiian/Other Pacific Islander, 1.3% Two or more races, 3.2% Hispanic of any race; Average household size: 2.70; Median age: 37.9; Age under 18: 25.6%; Age 65 and over: 9.9%; Males per 100 females: 103.9; Marriage status: 27.8% never married, 53.8% now married, 0.4% separated, 5.9% widowed, 12.6% divorced; Foreign born: 0.7%; Speak English only: 98.3%; With disability: 12.4%; Veterans: 10.1%; Ancestry: 22.2% German, 15.1% American, 13.8% French, 11.6% Irish, 10.5% Polish

Employment: 9.6% management, business, and financial, 4.3% computer, engineering, and science, 5.1% education, legal, community service, arts, and media, 6.5% healthcare practitioners, 20.7% service, 20.1% sales and office, 11.1% natural resources, construction, and maintenance, 22.8% production, transportation, and material moving

Income: Per capita: $27,157; Median household: $61,931; Average household: $75,009; Households with income of $100,000 or more: 25.6%; Poverty rate: 9.2%

Educational Attainment: High school diploma or higher: 88.8%; Bachelor's degree or higher: 14.9%; Graduate/professional degree or higher: 5.4%

Housing: Homeownership rate: 83.5%; Median home value: $142,800; Median year structure built: 1983; Homeowner vacancy rate: 2.7%; Median gross rent: $899 per month; Rental vacancy rate: 16.3%

Health Insurance: 91.8% have insurance; 75.9% have private insurance; 29.1% have public insurance; 8.2% do not have insurance; 1.4% of children under 18 do not have insurance

Transportation: Commute: 97.4% car, 0.7% public transportation, 0.5% walk, 1.3% work from home; Median travel time to work: 27.1 minutes

CARLETON (village). Covers a land area of 0.991 square miles and a water area of 0 square miles. Located at 42.06° N. Lat; 83.39° W. Long. Elevation is 617 feet.

History: Carleton was laid out in 1872 by Daniel A. Matthews, who operated an inn here and became the first postmaster. The village was named for Michigan poet Will Carleton (1845-1912).

Population: 2,345; Growth (since 2000): -8.5%; Density: 2,365.3 persons per square mile; Race: 96.7% White, 0.2% Black/African American, 0.7% Asian, 0.5% American Indian/Alaska Native, 0.1% Native Hawaiian/Other Pacific Islander, 1.7% Two or more races, 2.0% Hispanic of any race; Average household size: 2.46; Median age: 37.2; Age under 18: 25.0%; Age 65 and over: 12.0%; Males per 100 females: 98.6

School District(s)
Airport Community Schools (PK-12)
    2012-13 Enrollment: 2,559 . . . . (734) 654-2414

Housing: Homeownership rate: 83.2%; Homeowner vacancy rate: 3.5%; Rental vacancy rate: 22.7%

Safety: Violent crime rate: 38.7 per 10,000 population; Property crime rate: 124.8 per 10,000 population

DETROIT BEACH (CDP).

Covers a land area of 0.622 square miles and a water area of 0.038 square miles. Located at 41.93° N. Lat; 83.33° W. Long. Elevation is 574 feet.

Population: 2,087; Growth (since 2000): -8.8%; Density: 3,355.0 persons per square mile; Race: 95.9% White, 0.4% Black/African American, 0.0% Asian, 0.2% American Indian/Alaska Native, 0.0% Native Hawaiian/Other Pacific Islander, 2.8% Two or more races, 2.9% Hispanic of any race; Average household size: 2.72; Median age: 37.9; Age under 18: 23.6%; Age 65 and over: 10.3%; Males per 100 females: 104.0

Housing: Homeownership rate: 82.5%; Homeowner vacancy rate: 4.4%; Rental vacancy rate: 12.3%

DUNDEE (township).

Covers a land area of 48.221 square miles and a water area of 0.383 square miles. Located at 41.96° N. Lat; 83.68° W. Long. Elevation is 666 feet.

History: Dundee Township was named by Alonzo Curtis, the postmaster, for the city in Scotland where his forebears had lived.

Population: 6,759; Growth (since 2000): 6.6%; Density: 140.2 persons per square mile; Race: 96.7% White, 0.7% Black/African American, 0.4% Asian, 0.4% American Indian/Alaska Native, 0.0% Native Hawaiian/Other Pacific Islander, 1.3% Two or more races, 2.2% Hispanic of any race; Average household size: 2.62; Median age: 37.7; Age under 18: 25.0%; Age 65 and over: 12.0%; Males per 100 females: 100.5; Marriage status: 25.4% never married, 56.8% now married, 1.6% separated, 4.5% widowed, 13.4% divorced; Foreign born: 1.8%; Speak English only: 95.9%; With disability: 15.0%; Veterans: 8.7%; Ancestry: 33.2% German, 13.4% Irish, 12.2% English, 11.4% American, 8.8% French

Employment: 11.7% management, business, and financial, 3.0% computer, engineering, and science, 13.8% education, legal, community service, arts, and media, 4.8% healthcare practitioners, 29.0% service, 14.9% sales and office, 6.4% natural resources, construction, and maintenance, 16.4% production, transportation, and material moving

Income: Per capita: $23,963; Median household: $49,219; Average household: $58,335; Households with income of $100,000 or more: 14.8%; Poverty rate: 13.3%

Educational Attainment: High school diploma or higher: 88.5%; Bachelor's degree or higher: 16.1%; Graduate/professional degree or higher: 3.7%

School District(s)

Dundee Community Schools (PK-12)

    2012-13 Enrollment: 1,602 . . . . (734) 529-2350

Housing: Homeownership rate: 75.7%; Median home value: $142,100; Median year structure built: 1971; Homeowner vacancy rate: 2.1%; Median gross rent: $638 per month; Rental vacancy rate: 19.3%

Health Insurance: 91.8% have insurance; 75.8% have private insurance; 30.0% have public insurance; 8.2% do not have insurance; 1.5% of children under 18 do not have insurance

Newspapers: The Independent (weekly circulation 2800)

Transportation: Commute: 92.7% car, 0.0% public transportation, 1.4% walk, 2.8% work from home; Median travel time to work: 27.2 minutes

DUNDEE (village).

Covers a land area of 6.040 square miles and a water area of 0.042 square miles. Located at 41.96° N. Lat; 83.67° W. Long. Elevation is 666 feet.

History: The village of Dundee was laid out in the early 1830's by S. Van Ness, when it became known as Van Ness's Mills. The village was incorporated in 1855 under the name of the township.

Population: 3,957; Growth (since 2000): 12.4%; Density: 655.1 persons per square mile; Race: 96.5% White, 0.9% Black/African American, 0.5% Asian, 0.4% American Indian/Alaska Native, 0.0% Native Hawaiian/Other Pacific Islander, 1.2% Two or more races, 2.6% Hispanic of any race; Average household size: 2.55; Median age: 34.3; Age under 18: 27.0%; Age 65 and over: 11.2%; Males per 100 females: 92.8; Marriage status: 25.9% never married, 52.5% now married, 2.4% separated, 3.4% widowed, 18.3% divorced; Foreign born: 3.0%; Speak English only: 94.9%; With disability: 14.8%; Veterans: 9.4%; Ancestry: 33.2% German, 14.4% English, 12.9% Irish, 9.1% French, 8.8% American

Employment: 12.0% management, business, and financial, 2.1% computer, engineering, and science, 15.0% education, legal, community service, arts, and media, 5.4% healthcare practitioners, 29.0% service, 15.0% sales and office, 5.9% natural resources, construction, and maintenance, 15.7% production, transportation, and material moving

Income: Per capita: $21,943; Median household: $41,589; Average household: $52,838; Households with income of $100,000 or more: 14.1%; Poverty rate: 17.0%

Educational Attainment: High school diploma or higher: 88.9%; Bachelor's degree or higher: 17.0%; Graduate/professional degree or higher: 4.4%

School District(s)

Dundee Community Schools (PK-12)

    2012-13 Enrollment: 1,602 . . . . (734) 529-2350

Housing: Homeownership rate: 67.1%; Median home value: $127,600; Median year structure built: 1974; Homeowner vacancy rate: 2.7%; Median gross rent: $635 per month; Rental vacancy rate: 17.6%

Health Insurance: 89.9% have insurance; 70.7% have private insurance; 32.6% have public insurance; 10.1% do not have insurance; 2.4% of children under 18 do not have insurance

Newspapers: The Independent (weekly circulation 2800)

Transportation: Commute: 97.0% car, 0.0% public transportation, 0.6% walk, 0.0% work from home; Median travel time to work: 26.7 minutes

ERIE (township).

Covers a land area of 23.721 square miles and a water area of 5.864 square miles. Located at 41.77° N. Lat; 83.48° W. Long. Elevation is 591 feet.

Population: 4,517; Growth (since 2000): -6.9%; Density: 190.4 persons per square mile; Race: 95.7% White, 0.8% Black/African American, 0.3% Asian, 0.5% American Indian/Alaska Native, 0.0% Native Hawaiian/Other Pacific Islander, 1.6% Two or more races, 4.0% Hispanic of any race; Average household size: 2.53; Median age: 43.0; Age under 18: 22.3%; Age 65 and over: 14.6%; Males per 100 females: 102.4; Marriage status: 25.0% never married, 57.3% now married, 1.7% separated, 6.5% widowed, 11.2% divorced; Foreign born: 1.9%; Speak English only: 95.5%; With disability: 14.6%; Veterans: 9.9%; Ancestry: 21.1% German, 17.0% American, 14.8% French, 9.7% Polish, 9.6% Irish

Employment: 10.1% management, business, and financial, 2.5% computer, engineering, and science, 6.1% education, legal, community service, arts, and media, 3.3% healthcare practitioners, 17.7% service, 21.4% sales and office, 14.2% natural resources, construction, and maintenance, 24.7% production, transportation, and material moving

Income: Per capita: $24,861; Median household: $50,448; Average household: $62,051; Households with income of $100,000 or more: 18.7%; Poverty rate: 10.8%

Educational Attainment: High school diploma or higher: 85.2%; Bachelor's degree or higher: 12.2%; Graduate/professional degree or higher: 2.6%

School District(s)

Mason Consolidated Schools (Monroe) (PK-12)

    2012-13 Enrollment: 1,134 . . . . (734) 848-9304

Housing: Homeownership rate: 86.6%; Median home value: $115,700; Median year structure built: 1962; Homeowner vacancy rate: 4.7%; Median gross rent: $833 per month; Rental vacancy rate: 10.6%

Health Insurance: 85.0% have insurance; 76.2% have private insurance; 27.3% have public insurance; 15.0% do not have insurance; 4.1% of children under 18 do not have insurance

Transportation: Commute: 96.8% car, 0.0% public transportation, 0.0% walk, 1.2% work from home; Median travel time to work: 27.7 minutes

ESTRAL BEACH (village).

Covers a land area of 0.461 square miles and a water area of 0.004 square miles. Located at 41.99° N. Lat; 83.24° W. Long. Elevation is 571 feet.

Population: 418; Growth (since 2000): -14.0%; Density: 907.2 persons per square mile; Race: 99.3% White, 0.0% Black/African American, 0.0% Asian, 0.7% American Indian/Alaska Native, 0.0% Native Hawaiian/Other Pacific Islander, 0.0% Two or more races, 1.0% Hispanic of any race; Average household size: 2.28; Median age: 45.0; Age under 18: 19.9%; Age 65 and over: 13.6%; Males per 100 females: 114.4

Housing: Homeownership rate: 86.3%; Homeowner vacancy rate: 2.4%; Rental vacancy rate: 10.7%

EXETER (township).

Covers a land area of 36.530 square miles and a water area of 0.113 square miles. Located at 42.05° N. Lat; 83.48° W. Long.

Population: 3,968; Growth (since 2000): 6.5%; Density: 108.6 persons per square mile; Race: 93.2% White, 4.9% Black/African American, 0.3% Asian, 0.3% American Indian/Alaska Native, 0.0% Native Hawaiian/Other Pacific Islander, 1.1% Two or more races, 2.0% Hispanic of any race; Average household size: 2.78; Median age: 41.0; Age under 18: 24.2%;

Age 65 and over: 10.7%; Males per 100 females: 100.9; Marriage status: 28.5% never married, 61.9% now married, 1.3% separated, 2.9% widowed, 6.6% divorced; Foreign born: 3.1%; Speak English only: 96.7%; With disability: 15.6%; Veterans: 8.3%; Ancestry: 34.6% German, 15.9% Irish, 11.9% American, 11.6% Polish, 11.0% French

Employment: 9.2% management, business, and financial, 3.2% computer, engineering, and science, 4.9% education, legal, community service, arts, and media, 4.9% healthcare practitioners, 18.4% service, 19.7% sales and office, 17.9% natural resources, construction, and maintenance, 21.8% production, transportation, and material moving

Income: Per capita: $26,040; Median household: $65,293; Average household: $71,883; Households with income of $100,000 or more: 23.7%; Poverty rate: 8.3%

Educational Attainment: High school diploma or higher: 87.8%; Bachelor's degree or higher: 10.8%; Graduate/professional degree or higher: 3.2%

Housing: Homeownership rate: 90.6%; Median home value: $167,500; Median year structure built: 1970; Homeowner vacancy rate: 1.0%; Median gross rent: $874 per month; Rental vacancy rate: 6.2%

Health Insurance: 90.2% have insurance; 78.3% have private insurance; 22.5% have public insurance; 9.8% do not have insurance; 2.9% of children under 18 do not have insurance

Transportation: Commute: 93.8% car, 1.7% public transportation, 0.2% walk, 2.5% work from home; Median travel time to work: 26.5 minutes

FRENCHTOWN (township).
Covers a land area of 41.816 square miles and a water area of 1.303 square miles. Located at 41.96° N. Lat; 83.36° W. Long. Elevation is 591 feet.

Population: 20,428; Growth (since 2000): -1.7%; Density: 488.5 persons per square mile; Race: 93.4% White, 2.1% Black/African American, 0.6% Asian, 0.3% American Indian/Alaska Native, 0.0% Native Hawaiian/Other Pacific Islander, 2.1% Two or more races, 4.1% Hispanic of any race; Average household size: 2.53; Median age: 39.3; Age under 18: 23.2%; Age 65 and over: 13.4%; Males per 100 females: 97.2; Marriage status: 28.7% never married, 51.8% now married, 2.2% separated, 6.7% widowed, 12.8% divorced; Foreign born: 2.4%; Speak English only: 96.1%; With disability: 16.9%; Veterans: 10.3%; Ancestry: 29.3% German, 13.8% Irish, 13.3% American, 10.7% French, 7.6% Polish

Employment: 8.6% management, business, and financial, 3.6% computer, engineering, and science, 7.8% education, legal, community service, arts, and media, 6.1% healthcare practitioners, 19.2% service, 20.8% sales and office, 10.6% natural resources, construction, and maintenance, 23.4% production, transportation, and material moving

Income: Per capita: $23,078; Median household: $46,518; Average household: $57,391; Households with income of $100,000 or more: 12.6%; Poverty rate: 17.7%

Educational Attainment: High school diploma or higher: 83.6%; Bachelor's degree or higher: 13.5%; Graduate/professional degree or higher: 5.7%

Housing: Homeownership rate: 73.8%; Median home value: $113,500; Median year structure built: 1974; Homeowner vacancy rate: 2.8%; Median gross rent: $769 per month; Rental vacancy rate: 14.6%

Health Insurance: 91.1% have insurance; 69.4% have private insurance; 38.1% have public insurance; 8.9% do not have insurance; 0.9% of children under 18 do not have insurance

Transportation: Commute: 94.0% car, 1.9% public transportation, 1.2% walk, 2.3% work from home; Median travel time to work: 24.0 minutes

Additional Information Contacts

Frenchtown Charter Township . . . . (734) 242-3282
   http://www.frenchtowntownship.org

IDA (township).
Covers a land area of 36.745 square miles and a water area of 0.172 square miles. Located at 41.87° N. Lat; 83.60° W. Long. Elevation is 640 feet.

History: Ida Township was organized in 1837 and named for Ida M. Taylor, a community leader.

Population: 4,964; Growth (since 2000): 0.3%; Density: 135.1 persons per square mile; Race: 98.5% White, 0.3% Black/African American, 0.2% Asian, 0.2% American Indian/Alaska Native, 0.0% Native Hawaiian/Other Pacific Islander, 0.6% Two or more races, 1.6% Hispanic of any race; Average household size: 2.83; Median age: 41.5; Age under 18: 24.8%; Age 65 and over: 12.2%; Males per 100 females: 103.7; Marriage status: 23.9% never married, 64.7% now married, 0.3% separated, 3.1% widowed, 8.3% divorced; Foreign born: 0.9%; Speak English only: 98.4%;

With disability: 9.8%; Veterans: 9.0%; Ancestry: 43.7% German, 14.2% French, 9.6% Irish, 9.4% Polish, 8.8% American

Employment: 12.0% management, business, and financial, 3.3% computer, engineering, and science, 7.3% education, legal, community service, arts, and media, 7.1% healthcare practitioners, 13.2% service, 21.9% sales and office, 13.6% natural resources, construction, and maintenance, 21.6% production, transportation, and material moving

Income: Per capita: $31,820; Median household: $73,663; Average household: $85,246; Households with income of $100,000 or more: 30.2%; Poverty rate: 4.9%

Educational Attainment: High school diploma or higher: 94.2%; Bachelor's degree or higher: 19.5%; Graduate/professional degree or higher: 5.1%

School District(s)

Ida Public SD (KG-12)
   2012-13 Enrollment: 1,449 . . . . (734) 269-9003

Housing: Homeownership rate: 91.4%; Median home value: $169,700; Median year structure built: 1975; Homeowner vacancy rate: 1.4%; Median gross rent: $794 per month; Rental vacancy rate: 8.5%

Health Insurance: 93.1% have insurance; 83.2% have private insurance; 22.5% have public insurance; 6.9% do not have insurance; 4.1% of children under 18 do not have insurance

Transportation: Commute: 95.3% car, 0.0% public transportation, 1.1% walk, 3.7% work from home; Median travel time to work: 27.3 minutes

LA SALLE (township).
Covers a land area of 26.571 square miles and a water area of 0.288 square miles. Located at 41.86° N. Lat; 83.48° W. Long. Elevation is 594 feet.

Population: 4,894; Growth (since 2000): -2.1%; Density: 184.2 persons per square mile; Race: 96.7% White, 0.6% Black/African American, 0.3% Asian, 0.4% American Indian/Alaska Native, 0.0% Native Hawaiian/Other Pacific Islander, 1.3% Two or more races, 2.6% Hispanic of any race; Average household size: 2.67; Median age: 44.6; Age under 18: 20.9%; Age 65 and over: 14.0%; Males per 100 females: 104.9; Marriage status: 20.1% never married, 65.2% now married, 0.6% separated, 5.7% widowed, 9.0% divorced; Foreign born: 1.9%; Speak English only: 96.8%; With disability: 10.3%; Veterans: 8.6%; Ancestry: 29.4% German, 15.6% French, 14.0% Irish, 9.7% American, 7.5% English

Employment: 6.0% management, business, and financial, 2.3% computer, engineering, and science, 7.8% education, legal, community service, arts, and media, 9.5% healthcare practitioners, 17.0% service, 24.6% sales and office, 11.9% natural resources, construction, and maintenance, 20.8% production, transportation, and material moving

Income: Per capita: $28,296; Median household: $67,264; Average household: $73,046; Households with income of $100,000 or more: 21.8%; Poverty rate: 13.6%

Educational Attainment: High school diploma or higher: 86.8%; Bachelor's degree or higher: 14.9%; Graduate/professional degree or higher: 4.8%

Housing: Homeownership rate: 91.7%; Median home value: $158,000; Median year structure built: 1967; Homeowner vacancy rate: 1.3%; Median gross rent: $767 per month; Rental vacancy rate: 7.3%

Health Insurance: 92.4% have insurance; 80.7% have private insurance; 26.1% have public insurance; 7.6% do not have insurance; 2.7% of children under 18 do not have insurance

Transportation: Commute: 95.7% car, 0.0% public transportation, 0.0% walk, 3.9% work from home; Median travel time to work: 23.8 minutes

LAMBERTVILLE (CDP).
Covers a land area of 6.075 square miles and a water area of 0.016 square miles. Located at 41.75° N. Lat; 83.62° W. Long. Elevation is 673 feet.

History: Lambertville was founded in 1832 by John Lambert, and named for him.

Population: 9,953; Growth (since 2000): 7.0%; Density: 1,638.3 persons per square mile; Race: 96.9% White, 0.4% Black/African American, 0.9% Asian, 0.3% American Indian/Alaska Native, 0.0% Native Hawaiian/Other Pacific Islander, 1.0% Two or more races, 2.3% Hispanic of any race; Average household size: 2.67; Median age: 42.4; Age under 18: 24.6%; Age 65 and over: 13.6%; Males per 100 females: 98.6; Marriage status: 23.6% never married, 62.6% now married, 0.6% separated, 5.3% widowed, 8.5% divorced; Foreign born: 2.2%; Speak English only: 96.6%; With disability: 6.8%; Veterans: 9.5%; Ancestry: 36.7% German, 17.6% Irish, 14.8% Polish, 9.7% English, 6.5% French

Employment: 12.0% management, business, and financial, 3.6% computer, engineering, and science, 10.7% education, legal, community

service, arts, and media, 6.8% healthcare practitioners, 17.3% service, 26.0% sales and office, 6.4% natural resources, construction, and maintenance, 17.1% production, transportation, and material moving
Income: Per capita: $30,072; Median household: $69,173; Average household: $82,100; Households with income of $100,000 or more: 30.3%; Poverty rate: 4.1%
Educational Attainment: High school diploma or higher: 95.7%; Bachelor's degree or higher: 30.3%; Graduate/professional degree or higher: 12.7%

School District(s)
Bedford Public Schools (KG-12)
   2012-13 Enrollment: 4,659 . . . . (734) 850-6000
New Bedford Academy (KG-12)
   2012-13 Enrollment: 156 . . . . (734) 854-5437
Housing: Homeownership rate: 88.5%; Median home value: $166,800; Median year structure built: 1977; Homeowner vacancy rate: 1.4%; Median gross rent: $1,077 per month; Rental vacancy rate: 8.3%
Health Insurance: 92.5% have insurance; 83.2% have private insurance; 19.0% have public insurance; 7.5% do not have insurance; 3.4% of children under 18 do not have insurance
Newspapers: Bedford Now (weekly circulation 12000); Bedford Press (weekly circulation 15000)
Transportation: Commute: 92.0% car, 0.0% public transportation, 0.0% walk, 7.0% work from home; Median travel time to work: 25.8 minutes
Airports: Toledo Suburban (general aviation)

LONDON (township).
Covers a land area of 35.764 square miles and a water area of 0.110 square miles. Located at 42.04° N. Lat; 83.61° W. Long. Elevation is 669 feet.
History: London Township was organized in 1833.
Population: 3,048; Growth (since 2000): 0.8%; Density: 85.2 persons per square mile; Race: 86.6% White, 9.3% Black/African American, 0.2% Asian, 0.8% American Indian/Alaska Native, 0.1% Native Hawaiian/Other Pacific Islander, 2.7% Two or more races, 1.6% Hispanic of any race; Average household size: 2.77; Median age: 39.7; Age under 18: 25.4%; Age 65 and over: 11.2%; Males per 100 females: 105.5; Marriage status: 31.0% never married, 51.3% now married, 0.0% separated, 5.1% widowed, 12.6% divorced; Foreign born: 0.9%; Speak English only: 97.8%; With disability: 13.6%; Veterans: 8.2%; Ancestry: 34.0% German, 16.6% American, 11.6% Polish, 11.4% Irish, 7.0% English
Employment: 9.2% management, business, and financial, 4.9% computer, engineering, and science, 3.0% education, legal, community service, arts, and media, 7.7% healthcare practitioners, 23.6% service, 18.2% sales and office, 9.2% natural resources, construction, and maintenance, 24.2% production, transportation, and material moving
Income: Per capita: $24,208; Median household: $55,881; Average household: $65,268; Households with income of $100,000 or more: 20.4%; Poverty rate: 9.4%
Educational Attainment: High school diploma or higher: 85.4%; Bachelor's degree or higher: 11.3%; Graduate/professional degree or higher: 2.3%
Housing: Homeownership rate: 89.5%; Median home value: $124,300; Median year structure built: 1972; Homeowner vacancy rate: 2.0%; Median gross rent: $871 per month; Rental vacancy rate: 6.5%
Health Insurance: 92.1% have insurance; 79.2% have private insurance; 30.0% have public insurance; 7.9% do not have insurance; 2.9% of children under 18 do not have insurance
Transportation: Commute: 95.5% car, 2.3% public transportation, 0.0% walk, 1.9% work from home; Median travel time to work: 29.4 minutes

LUNA PIER (city).
Covers a land area of 1.502 square miles and a water area of 0.179 square miles. Located at 41.80° N. Lat; 83.44° W. Long. Elevation is 577 feet.
History: The Luna Pier post office was established in 1929. Luna Pier was incorporated as a city in 1963.
Population: 1,436; Growth (since 2000): -3.2%; Density: 956.3 persons per square mile; Race: 93.2% White, 0.8% Black/African American, 0.5% Asian, 0.8% American Indian/Alaska Native, 0.0% Native Hawaiian/Other Pacific Islander, 3.5% Two or more races, 3.0% Hispanic of any race; Average household size: 2.36; Median age: 41.7; Age under 18: 22.9%; Age 65 and over: 10.5%; Males per 100 females: 93.3
Housing: Homeownership rate: 68.1%; Homeowner vacancy rate: 4.6%; Rental vacancy rate: 7.5%
Safety: Violent crime rate: 7.1 per 10,000 population; Property crime rate: 239.9 per 10,000 population

MAYBEE (village).
Covers a land area of 0.996 square miles and a water area of 0.012 square miles. Located at 42.01° N. Lat; 83.52° W. Long. Elevation is 636 feet.
Population: 562; Growth (since 2000): 11.3%; Density: 564.2 persons per square mile; Race: 96.6% White, 1.4% Black/African American, 0.4% Asian, 0.5% American Indian/Alaska Native, 0.0% Native Hawaiian/Other Pacific Islander, 0.7% Two or more races, 1.8% Hispanic of any race; Average household size: 2.74; Median age: 34.9; Age under 18: 31.0%; Age 65 and over: 5.9%; Males per 100 females: 99.3
Housing: Homeownership rate: 74.1%; Homeowner vacancy rate: 1.9%; Rental vacancy rate: 3.6%

MILAN (township).
Covers a land area of 34.181 square miles and a water area of 0.018 square miles. Located at 42.04° N. Lat; 83.72° W. Long.
Population: 1,601; Growth (since 2000): -4.1%; Density: 46.8 persons per square mile; Race: 96.1% White, 0.2% Black/African American, 0.3% Asian, 0.5% American Indian/Alaska Native, 0.0% Native Hawaiian/Other Pacific Islander, 1.4% Two or more races, 2.9% Hispanic of any race; Average household size: 2.61; Median age: 44.6; Age under 18: 20.9%; Age 65 and over: 15.5%; Males per 100 females: 105.0
School District(s)
Milan Area Schools (PK-12)
   2012-13 Enrollment: 2,420 . . . . (734) 439-5050
Housing: Homeownership rate: 89.4%; Homeowner vacancy rate: 1.1%; Rental vacancy rate: 4.3%

MONROE (charter township).
Covers a land area of 16.900 square miles and a water area of 1.252 square miles. Located at 41.89° N. Lat; 83.42° W. Long. Elevation is 594 feet.
History: Monroe was the scene of the River Raisin massacre during the War of 1812 and the center of the Toledo War. George A. Custer lived here, and the local Museum has a large collection of Custer memorabilia. General Custer Historic Site to northeast. Settled 1778, Incorporated 1837.
Population: 14,568; Growth (since 2000): 8.0%; Density: 862.0 persons per square mile; Race: 92.9% White, 2.5% Black/African American, 0.7% Asian, 0.2% American Indian/Alaska Native, 0.0% Native Hawaiian/Other Pacific Islander, 2.3% Two or more races, 4.0% Hispanic of any race; Average household size: 2.49; Median age: 39.6; Age under 18: 23.8%; Age 65 and over: 14.4%; Males per 100 females: 95.5; Marriage status: 28.9% never married, 49.6% now married, 1.8% separated, 8.6% widowed, 12.9% divorced; Foreign born: 1.9%; Speak English only: 96.2%; With disability: 15.2%; Veterans: 11.6%; Ancestry: 26.0% German, 14.4% Irish, 14.3% American, 9.9% French, 8.6% Italian
Employment: 11.8% management, business, and financial, 3.0% computer, engineering, and science, 7.2% education, legal, community service, arts, and media, 5.4% healthcare practitioners, 23.7% service, 22.1% sales and office, 6.3% natural resources, construction, and maintenance, 20.5% production, transportation, and material moving
Income: Per capita: $24,722; Median household: $43,633; Average household: $60,199; Households with income of $100,000 or more: 16.3%; Poverty rate: 16.1%
Educational Attainment: High school diploma or higher: 85.3%; Bachelor's degree or higher: 16.9%; Graduate/professional degree or higher: 5.7%

School District(s)
Jefferson Schools (Monroe) (PK-12)
   2012-13 Enrollment: 2,018 . . . . (734) 322-2551
Monroe ISD (PK-12)
   2012-13 Enrollment: 1,067 . . . . (734) 242-5799
Monroe Public Schools (PK-12)
   2012-13 Enrollment: 6,065 . . . . (734) 265-3070
Triumph Academy (KG-12)
   2012-13 Enrollment: 645 . . . . (734) 240-2610
Two-year College(s)
Monroe County Community College (Public)
   Fall 2013 Enrollment: 3,777 . . . . (734) 242-7300
   2013-14 Tuition: In-state $5,170; Out-of-state $5,710
Vocational/Technical School(s)
Michigan College of Beauty-Monroe (Private, For-profit)
   Fall 2013 Enrollment: 117 . . . . (734) 241-8877
   2013-14 Tuition: $13,175
Housing: Homeownership rate: 77.1%; Median home value: $100,300; Median year structure built: 1977; Homeowner vacancy rate: 3.0%; Median gross rent: $783 per month; Rental vacancy rate: 9.1%

Health Insurance: 89.9% have insurance; 70.2% have private insurance; 36.6% have public insurance; 10.1% do not have insurance; 3.5% of children under 18 do not have insurance

Hospitals: Mercy Memorial Hospital System (238 beds)

Newspapers: Monroe Evening News (daily circulation 20800)

Transportation: Commute: 93.8% car, 0.7% public transportation, 1.2% walk, 2.5% work from home; Median travel time to work: 24.2 minutes

Airports: Custer (general aviation)

Additional Information Contacts

Monroe Charter Township . . . . (734) 241-5501

MONROE (city). County seat. Covers a land area of 9.166 square miles and a water area of 1.017 square miles. Located at 41.92° N. Lat; 83.38° W. Long. Elevation is 594 feet.

History: First called Frenchtown because of its French settlers, the city was renamed Monroe when a visit from President Monroe was expected. Its location on the River Raisin, a few miles from Lake Erie, placed Monroe in an area where the border was in question. The so-called "Toledo War" dispute between Michigan and Ohio centered in Monroe in 1835, ending with Michigan giving up to Ohio the area to the south that included Toledo, and getting in exchange the Upper Peninsula. An early industry in Monroe was glass making, using local siliceous sand and sandstone. Nurseries and paper plants added to the early economic base. A prominent resident of Monroe was General George A. Custer.

Population: 20,733; Growth (since 2000): -6.1%; Density: 2,262.0 persons per square mile; Race: 88.4% White, 6.2% Black/African American, 0.7% Asian, 0.4% American Indian/Alaska Native, 0.0% Native Hawaiian/Other Pacific Islander, 3.0% Two or more races, 4.1% Hispanic of any race; Average household size: 2.44; Median age: 36.3; Age under 18: 26.2%; Age 65 and over: 13.3%; Males per 100 females: 88.8; Marriage status: 31.3% never married, 46.3% now married, 1.7% separated, 7.7% widowed, 14.6% divorced; Foreign born: 3.0%; Speak English only: 94.5%; With disability: 14.8%; Veterans: 9.5%; Ancestry: 26.4% German, 13.9% Irish, 10.6% American, 9.2% French, 9.2% Italian

Employment: 8.4% management, business, and financial, 3.4% computer, engineering, and science, 8.5% education, legal, community service, arts, and media, 6.1% healthcare practitioners, 21.5% service, 23.6% sales and office, 6.1% natural resources, construction, and maintenance, 22.5% production, transportation, and material moving

Income: Per capita: $22,653; Median household: $42,911; Average household: $54,530; Households with income of $100,000 or more: 13.4%; Poverty rate: 19.5%

Educational Attainment: High school diploma or higher: 88.6%; Bachelor's degree or higher: 17.5%; Graduate/professional degree or higher: 7.8%

School District(s)

Jefferson Schools (Monroe) (PK-12)

    2012-13 Enrollment: 2,018 . . . . (734) 322-2551

Monroe ISD (PK-12)

    2012-13 Enrollment: 1,067 . . . . (734) 242-5799

Monroe Public Schools (PK-12)

    2012-13 Enrollment: 6,065 . . . . (734) 265-3070

Triumph Academy (KG-12)

    2012-13 Enrollment: 645. . . . . (734) 240-2610

Two-year College(s)

Monroe County Community College (Public)

    Fall 2013 Enrollment: 3,777 . . . . (734) 242-7300

    2013-14 Tuition: In-state $5,170; Out-of-state $5,710

Vocational/Technical School(s)

Michigan College of Beauty-Monroe (Private, For-profit)

    Fall 2013 Enrollment: 117 . . . . (734) 241-8877

    2013-14 Tuition: $13,175

Housing: Homeownership rate: 62.1%; Median home value: $107,900; Median year structure built: 1953; Homeowner vacancy rate: 3.5%; Median gross rent: $703 per month; Rental vacancy rate: 12.0%

Health Insurance: 88.6% have insurance; 65.5% have private insurance; 38.3% have public insurance; 11.4% do not have insurance; 2.3% of children under 18 do not have insurance

Hospitals: Mercy Memorial Hospital System (238 beds)

Safety: Violent crime rate: 53.7 per 10,000 population; Property crime rate: 348.7 per 10,000 population

Newspapers: Monroe Evening News (daily circulation 20800)

Transportation: Commute: 91.0% car, 2.4% public transportation, 2.8% walk, 2.2% work from home; Median travel time to work: 20.8 minutes

Airports: Custer (general aviation)

Additional Information Contacts

City of Monroe . . . . (734) 243-0700

    http://www.ci.monroe.mi.us

NEWPORT (unincorporated postal area)

ZCTA: 48166

Covers a land area of 26.568 square miles and a water area of 1.241 square miles. Located at 41.98° N. Lat; 83.29° W. Long. Elevation is 591 feet.

Population: 11,569; Growth (since 2000): 11.0%; Density: 435.5 persons per square mile; Race: 95.8% White, 1.1% Black/African American, 0.4% Asian, 0.4% American Indian/Alaska Native, 0.0% Native Hawaiian/Other Pacific Islander, 1.7% Two or more races, 2.8% Hispanic of any race; Average household size: 2.77; Median age: 35.7; Age under 18: 27.4%; Age 65 and over: 8.5%; Males per 100 females: 101.3; Marriage status: 27.2% never married, 54.2% now married, 1.5% separated, 4.6% widowed, 14.0% divorced; Foreign born: 0.7%; Speak English only: 98.7%; With disability: 14.8%; Veterans: 10.8%; Ancestry: 24.8% German, 14.5% Irish, 13.0% American, 12.2% French, 10.8% Polish

Employment: 7.6% management, business, and financial, 4.0% computer, engineering, and science, 7.6% education, legal, community service, arts, and media, 6.0% healthcare practitioners, 20.4% service, 22.4% sales and office, 8.4% natural resources, construction, and maintenance, 23.5% production, transportation, and material moving

Income: Per capita: $24,162; Median household: $58,017; Average household: $66,717; Households with income of $100,000 or more: 20.7%; Poverty rate: 12.4%

Educational Attainment: High school diploma or higher: 88.1%; Bachelor's degree or higher: 13.7%; Graduate/professional degree or higher: 5.9%

School District(s)

Airport Community Schools (PK-12)

    2012-13 Enrollment: 2,559 . . . . (734) 654-2414

Jefferson Schools (Monroe) (PK-12)

    2012-13 Enrollment: 2,018 . . . . (734) 322-2551

Housing: Homeownership rate: 88.2%; Median home value: $125,400; Median year structure built: 1989; Homeowner vacancy rate: 3.9%; Median gross rent: $812 per month; Rental vacancy rate: 20.8%

Health Insurance: 90.8% have insurance; 71.5% have private insurance; 32.6% have public insurance; 9.2% do not have insurance; 1.3% of children under 18 do not have insurance

Transportation: Commute: 96.2% car, 1.4% public transportation, 0.2% walk, 2.2% work from home; Median travel time to work: 26.9 minutes

---

OTTAWA LAKE (unincorporated postal area)

ZCTA: 49267

Covers a land area of 39.947 square miles and a water area of 0.413 square miles. Located at 41.76° N. Lat; 83.72° W. Long..

Population: 4,072; Growth (since 2000): 0.8%; Density: 101.9 persons per square mile; Race: 96.2% White, 1.7% Black/African American, 0.4% Asian, 0.1% American Indian/Alaska Native, 0.0% Native Hawaiian/Other Pacific Islander, 1.0% Two or more races, 2.0% Hispanic of any race; Average household size: 2.60; Median age: 43.9; Age under 18: 22.8%; Age 65 and over: 15.8%; Males per 100 females: 104.2; Marriage status: 20.2% never married, 66.8% now married, 3.0% separated, 5.9% widowed, 7.1% divorced; Foreign born: 1.4%; Speak English only: 97.0%; With disability: 10.0%; Veterans: 9.5%; Ancestry: 42.7% German, 18.3% Polish, 13.6% Irish, 9.8% English, 9.7% American

Employment: 15.9% management, business, and financial, 2.3% computer, engineering, and science, 6.4% education, legal, community service, arts, and media, 5.9% healthcare practitioners, 17.6% service, 23.1% sales and office, 11.7% natural resources, construction, and maintenance, 17.1% production, transportation, and material moving

Income: Per capita: $28,566; Median household: $55,083; Average household: $72,153; Households with income of $100,000 or more: 18.8%; Poverty rate: 5.1%

Educational Attainment: High school diploma or higher: 95.6%; Bachelor's degree or higher: 20.8%; Graduate/professional degree or higher: 6.9%

School District(s)

Whiteford Agricultural SD (KG-12)

    2012-13 Enrollment: 673. . . . . (734) 856-1443

Housing: Homeownership rate: 86.3%; Median home value: $168,900; Median year structure built: 1964; Homeowner vacancy rate: 1.2%; Median gross rent: $842 per month; Rental vacancy rate: 8.4%
Health Insurance: 91.2% have insurance; 83.8% have private insurance; 23.9% have public insurance; 8.8% do not have insurance; 6.1% of children under 18 do not have insurance
Transportation: Commute: 95.1% car, 0.0% public transportation, 1.3% walk, 2.4% work from home; Median travel time to work: 20.8 minutes

PETERSBURG (city).
Covers a land area of 0.481 square miles and a water area of 0 square miles. Located at 41.90° N. Lat; 83.71° W. Long. Elevation is 679 feet.
History: Petersburg was established on the farm of Richard Peters, who settled here in 1824. Petersburg was incorporated as a village in 1869 and as a city in 1967.
Population: 1,146; Growth (since 2000): -1.0%; Density: 2,384.9 persons per square mile; Race: 97.1% White, 0.3% Black/African American, 0.3% Asian, 0.3% American Indian/Alaska Native, 0.0% Native Hawaiian/Other Pacific Islander, 1.6% Two or more races, 1.7% Hispanic of any race; Average household size: 2.55; Median age: 36.6; Age under 18: 25.0%; Age 65 and over: 12.8%; Males per 100 females: 99.0

School District(s)
Summerfield Schools (PK-12)
    2012-13 Enrollment: 722 . . . . (734) 279-1035
Housing: Homeownership rate: 71.9%; Homeowner vacancy rate: 2.4%; Rental vacancy rate: 5.3%

RAISINVILLE (township).
Covers a land area of 48.144 square miles and a water area of 0.396 square miles. Located at 41.96° N. Lat; 83.51° W. Long.
History: Raisinville Township was organized in 1823, and named for the River Raisin, where wild grapes ("raisin" in French) grew.
Population: 5,816; Growth (since 2000): 18.8%; Density: 120.8 persons per square mile; Race: 96.6% White, 1.0% Black/African American, 0.3% Asian, 0.2% American Indian/Alaska Native, 0.1% Native Hawaiian/Other Pacific Islander, 1.6% Two or more races, 1.8% Hispanic of any race; Average household size: 2.77; Median age: 41.9; Age under 18: 24.6%; Age 65 and over: 13.3%; Males per 100 females: 99.6; Marriage status: 24.1% never married, 63.3% now married, 0.8% separated, 5.8% widowed, 6.8% divorced; Foreign born: 1.5%; Speak English only: 93.5%; With disability: 12.7%; Veterans: 11.1%; Ancestry: 34.5% German, 16.0% Irish, 13.0% French, 9.3% Polish, 9.1% American
Employment: 10.2% management, business, and financial, 3.3% computer, engineering, and science, 6.1% education, legal, community service, arts, and media, 6.4% healthcare practitioners, 17.5% service, 20.1% sales and office, 12.9% natural resources, construction, and maintenance, 23.4% production, transportation, and material moving
Income: Per capita: $25,273; Median household: $61,654; Average household: $71,645; Households with income of $100,000 or more: 24.9%; Poverty rate: 10.6%
Educational Attainment: High school diploma or higher: 92.1%; Bachelor's degree or higher: 16.0%; Graduate/professional degree or higher: 5.5%
Housing: Homeownership rate: 93.2%; Median home value: $158,500; Median year structure built: 1977; Homeowner vacancy rate: 2.1%; Median gross rent: $1,097 per month; Rental vacancy rate: 4.7%
Health Insurance: 92.0% have insurance; 79.3% have private insurance; 30.0% have public insurance; 8.0% do not have insurance; 7.5% of children under 18 do not have insurance
Transportation: Commute: 95.2% car, 1.8% public transportation, 0.5% walk, 2.2% work from home; Median travel time to work: 30.2 minutes

SAMARIA (unincorporated postal area)
ZCTA: 48177
    Covers a land area of 0.622 square miles and a water area of 0 square miles. Located at 41.80° N. Lat; 83.58° W. Long. Elevation is 643 feet.
Population: 218; Growth (since 2000): n/a; Density: 350.7 persons per square mile; Race: 97.2% White, 0.0% Black/African American, 1.8% Asian, 0.0% American Indian/Alaska Native, 0.0% Native Hawaiian/Other Pacific Islander, 0.9% Two or more races, 0.5% Hispanic of any race; Average household size: 2.73; Median age: 36.5; Age under 18: 22.9%; Age 65 and over: 10.6%; Males per 100 females: 80.2
Housing: Homeownership rate: 82.6%; Homeowner vacancy rate: 1.4%; Rental vacancy rate: 12.5%

SOUTH MONROE (CDP).
Covers a land area of 2.371 square miles and a water area of 0 square miles. Located at 41.89° N. Lat; 83.42° W. Long. Elevation is 597 feet.
Population: 6,433; Growth (since 2000): 1.0%; Density: 2,712.7 persons per square mile; Race: 91.6% White, 3.1% Black/African American, 0.7% Asian, 0.2% American Indian/Alaska Native, 0.0% Native Hawaiian/Other Pacific Islander, 2.9% Two or more races, 4.2% Hispanic of any race; Average household size: 2.33; Median age: 41.4; Age under 18: 23.2%; Age 65 and over: 18.6%; Males per 100 females: 84.3; Marriage status: 26.2% never married, 48.7% now married, 1.3% separated, 10.6% widowed, 14.5% divorced; Foreign born: 2.4%; Speak English only: 96.7%; With disability: 18.2%; Veterans: 12.8%; Ancestry: 27.0% German, 15.2% Irish, 12.6% American, 9.1% French, 8.9% Italian
Employment: 13.2% management, business, and financial, 3.2% computer, engineering, and science, 5.8% education, legal, community service, arts, and media, 4.1% healthcare practitioners, 28.0% service, 21.0% sales and office, 5.5% natural resources, construction, and maintenance, 19.2% production, transportation, and material moving
Income: Per capita: $24,941; Median household: $38,571; Average household: $56,427; Households with income of $100,000 or more: 13.6%; Poverty rate: 11.9%
Educational Attainment: High school diploma or higher: 84.8%; Bachelor's degree or higher: 14.7%; Graduate/professional degree or higher: 5.7%
Housing: Homeownership rate: 68.0%; Median home value: $88,200; Median year structure built: 1976; Homeowner vacancy rate: 3.1%; Median gross rent: $693 per month; Rental vacancy rate: 8.6%
Health Insurance: 90.0% have insurance; 72.0% have private insurance; 37.6% have public insurance; 10.0% do not have insurance; 4.6% of children under 18 do not have insurance
Transportation: Commute: 91.6% car, 1.1% public transportation, 0.9% walk, 4.9% work from home; Median travel time to work: 22.7 minutes

SOUTH ROCKWOOD (village).
Covers a land area of 2.348 square miles and a water area of 0.114 square miles. Located at 42.06° N. Lat; 83.26° W. Long. Elevation is 587 feet.
History: South Rockwood was founded in 1863 by John Strong, who operated a store here. He named the village for Rockwood, Ontario.
Population: 1,675; Growth (since 2000): 30.5%; Density: 713.3 persons per square mile; Race: 95.4% White, 2.3% Black/African American, 0.4% Asian, 0.2% American Indian/Alaska Native, 0.0% Native Hawaiian/Other Pacific Islander, 1.3% Two or more races, 4.1% Hispanic of any race; Average household size: 2.44; Median age: 38.9; Age under 18: 20.8%; Age 65 and over: 10.1%; Males per 100 females: 103.0

School District(s)
Airport Community Schools (PK-12)
    2012-13 Enrollment: 2,559 . . . . (734) 654-2414
Housing: Homeownership rate: 62.7%; Homeowner vacancy rate: 1.1%; Rental vacancy rate: 4.1%

STONY POINT (CDP).
Covers a land area of 1.108 square miles and a water area of 0.014 square miles. Located at 41.95° N. Lat; 83.27° W. Long. Elevation is 577 feet.
Population: 1,724; Growth (since 2000): -2.9%; Density: 1,556.0 persons per square mile; Race: 97.0% White, 0.8% Black/African American, 0.3% Asian, 0.4% American Indian/Alaska Native, 0.0% Native Hawaiian/Other Pacific Islander, 1.1% Two or more races, 2.4% Hispanic of any race; Average household size: 2.77; Median age: 36.9; Age under 18: 26.5%; Age 65 and over: 9.1%; Males per 100 females: 103.8
Housing: Homeownership rate: 83.3%; Homeowner vacancy rate: 4.0%; Rental vacancy rate: 12.3%

SUMMERFIELD (township).
Covers a land area of 41.977 square miles and a water area of 0.361 square miles. Located at 41.87° N. Lat; 83.71° W. Long.
Population: 3,308; Growth (since 2000): 2.3%; Density: 78.8 persons per square mile; Race: 97.5% White, 0.2% Black/African American, 0.3% Asian, 0.2% American Indian/Alaska Native, 0.0% Native Hawaiian/Other Pacific Islander, 0.8% Two or more races, 2.1% Hispanic of any race; Average household size: 2.75; Median age: 42.2; Age under 18: 24.1%; Age 65 and over: 13.1%; Males per 100 females: 103.2; Marriage status: 23.9% never married, 63.4% now married, 0.5% separated, 2.9% widowed, 9.8% divorced; Foreign born: 1.7%; Speak English only: 97.2%; With disability: 12.4%; Veterans: 8.8%; Ancestry: 29.2% German, 17.3% American, 15.7% Irish, 8.2% English, 7.7% Polish

Employment: 14.3% management, business, and financial, 3.0% computer, engineering, and science, 5.7% education, legal, community service, arts, and media, 5.7% healthcare practitioners, 16.0% service, 19.9% sales and office, 12.8% natural resources, construction, and maintenance, 22.5% production, transportation, and material moving
Income: Per capita: $25,232; Median household: $59,160; Average household: $69,434; Households with income of $100,000 or more: 23.7%; Poverty rate: 8.8%
Educational Attainment: High school diploma or higher: 91.1%; Bachelor's degree or higher: 22.2%; Graduate/professional degree or higher: 9.3%
Housing: Homeownership rate: 89.8%; Median home value: $161,500; Median year structure built: 1972; Homeowner vacancy rate: 0.9%; Median gross rent: $1,094 per month; Rental vacancy rate: 3.2%
Health Insurance: 93.2% have insurance; 81.6% have private insurance; 26.0% have public insurance; 6.8% do not have insurance; 2.0% of children under 18 do not have insurance
Transportation: Commute: 93.0% car, 0.1% public transportation, 1.0% walk, 4.1% work from home; Median travel time to work: 26.3 minutes

TEMPERANCE (CDP). Covers a land area of 4.608 square miles and a water area of 0.033 square miles. Located at 41.77° N. Lat; 83.57° W. Long. Elevation is 623 feet.
Population: 8,517; Growth (since 2000): 9.8%; Density: 1,848.4 persons per square mile; Race: 97.0% White, 0.4% Black/African American, 0.8% Asian, 0.2% American Indian/Alaska Native, 0.0% Native Hawaiian/Other Pacific Islander, 1.0% Two or more races, 2.2% Hispanic of any race; Average household size: 2.53; Median age: 42.4; Age under 18: 23.9%; Age 65 and over: 15.1%; Males per 100 females: 93.7; Marriage status: 23.3% never married, 59.4% now married, 0.8% separated, 8.2% widowed, 9.1% divorced; Foreign born: 1.4%; Speak English only: 97.1%; With disability: 10.1%; Veterans: 10.4%; Ancestry: 35.7% German, 15.5% Polish, 13.4% English, 10.7% French, 10.3% Irish
Employment: 14.1% management, business, and financial, 3.7% computer, engineering, and science, 9.2% education, legal, community service, arts, and media, 7.1% healthcare practitioners, 15.2% service, 25.9% sales and office, 6.9% natural resources, construction, and maintenance, 18.0% production, transportation, and material moving
Income: Per capita: $29,166; Median household: $58,278; Average household: $73,857; Households with income of $100,000 or more: 20.0%; Poverty rate: 9.3%
Educational Attainment: High school diploma or higher: 92.9%; Bachelor's degree or higher: 27.2%; Graduate/professional degree or higher: 9.5%

School District(s)
Bedford Public Schools (KG-12)
   2012-13 Enrollment: 4,659 . . . . (734) 850-6000
Housing: Homeownership rate: 79.4%; Median home value: $154,300; Median year structure built: 1972; Homeowner vacancy rate: 1.0%; Median gross rent: $787 per month; Rental vacancy rate: 10.1%
Health Insurance: 93.2% have insurance; 82.8% have private insurance; 27.6% have public insurance; 6.8% do not have insurance; 3.8% of children under 18 do not have insurance
Transportation: Commute: 96.0% car, 0.0% public transportation, 0.5% walk, 3.4% work from home; Median travel time to work: 21.6 minutes

WEST MONROE (CDP). Covers a land area of 1.233 square miles and a water area of 0.013 square miles. Located at 41.91° N. Lat; 83.43° W. Long. Elevation is 600 feet.
Population: 3,503; Growth (since 2000): -10.0%; Density: 2,841.6 persons per square mile; Race: 93.7% White, 2.2% Black/African American, 0.3% Asian, 0.2% American Indian/Alaska Native, 0.0% Native Hawaiian/Other Pacific Islander, 2.3% Two or more races, 4.0% Hispanic of any race; Average household size: 2.59; Median age: 34.0; Age under 18: 25.9%; Age 65 and over: 10.2%; Males per 100 females: 98.8; Marriage status: 42.6% never married, 32.4% now married, 2.2% separated, 8.4% widowed, 16.6% divorced; Foreign born: 0.8%; Speak English only: 97.0%; With disability: 14.9%; Veterans: 5.6%; Ancestry: 25.2% German, 16.2% American, 15.1% Irish, 11.6% French, 9.6% Italian
Employment: 0.0% management, business, and financial, 0.0% computer, engineering, and science, 3.4% education, legal, community service, arts, and media, 7.2% healthcare practitioners, 28.3% service, 21.0% sales and office, 9.5% natural resources, construction, and maintenance, 30.6% production, transportation, and material moving

Income: Per capita: $14,372; Median household: $29,446; Average household: $36,948; Households with income of $100,000 or more: 3.3%; Poverty rate: 34.6%
Educational Attainment: High school diploma or higher: 78.0%; Bachelor's degree or higher: 5.5%; Graduate/professional degree or higher: 1.2%
Housing: Homeownership rate: 81.4%; Median home value: $52,800; Median year structure built: 1976; Homeowner vacancy rate: 4.2%; Median gross rent: $1,068 per month; Rental vacancy rate: 7.4%
Health Insurance: 81.9% have insurance; 45.5% have private insurance; 50.7% have public insurance; 18.1% do not have insurance; 2.3% of children under 18 do not have insurance
Transportation: Commute: 93.0% car, 1.0% public transportation, 1.1% walk, 0.5% work from home; Median travel time to work: 24.3 minutes

WHITEFORD (township). Covers a land area of 39.721 square miles and a water area of 0.518 square miles. Located at 41.77° N. Lat; 83.71° W. Long.
Population: 4,602; Growth (since 2000): 4.1%; Density: 115.9 persons per square mile; Race: 96.3% White, 1.5% Black/African American, 0.5% Asian, 0.1% American Indian/Alaska Native, 0.0% Native Hawaiian/Other Pacific Islander, 0.9% Two or more races, 2.1% Hispanic of any race; Average household size: 2.62; Median age: 43.6; Age under 18: 23.3%; Age 65 and over: 15.9%; Males per 100 females: 102.4; Marriage status: 22.3% never married, 64.8% now married, 2.7% separated, 6.0% widowed, 6.9% divorced; Foreign born: 1.4%; Speak English only: 97.1%; With disability: 10.8%; Veterans: 9.0%; Ancestry: 45.5% German, 17.0% Polish, 16.5% Irish, 9.9% English, 9.5% American
Employment: 15.2% management, business, and financial, 2.1% computer, engineering, and science, 5.3% education, legal, community service, arts, and media, 5.5% healthcare practitioners, 17.7% service, 23.1% sales and office, 12.5% natural resources, construction, and maintenance, 18.6% production, transportation, and material moving
Income: Per capita: $26,155; Median household: $53,707; Average household: $68,252; Households with income of $100,000 or more: 18.3%; Poverty rate: 5.6%
Educational Attainment: High school diploma or higher: 95.5%; Bachelor's degree or higher: 21.0%; Graduate/professional degree or higher: 5.9%
Housing: Homeownership rate: 86.6%; Median home value: $169,600; Median year structure built: 1965; Homeowner vacancy rate: 1.2%; Median gross rent: $836 per month; Rental vacancy rate: 8.5%
Health Insurance: 88.8% have insurance; 81.9% have private insurance; 22.7% have public insurance; 11.2% do not have insurance; 9.6% of children under 18 do not have insurance
Transportation: Commute: 96.1% car, 0.0% public transportation, 1.3% walk, 1.6% work from home; Median travel time to work: 20.4 minutes

WOODLAND BEACH (CDP). Covers a land area of 0.520 square miles and a water area of 0.005 square miles. Located at 41.94° N. Lat; 83.31° W. Long. Elevation is 577 feet.
Population: 2,049; Growth (since 2000): -6.0%; Density: 3,941.8 persons per square mile; Race: 96.4% White, 0.4% Black/African American, 0.0% Asian, 0.2% American Indian/Alaska Native, 0.0% Native Hawaiian/Other Pacific Islander, 2.4% Two or more races, 2.5% Hispanic of any race; Average household size: 2.66; Median age: 35.8; Age under 18: 25.3%; Age 65 and over: 8.4%; Males per 100 females: 100.1
Housing: Homeownership rate: 79.6%; Homeowner vacancy rate: 1.4%; Rental vacancy rate: 7.6%

Montcalm County

Located in central Michigan; drained by the Flat, Pine, and Tamarack Rivers; includes several lakes. Covers a land area of 705.399 square miles, a water area of 15.427 square miles, and is located in the Eastern Time Zone at 43.31° N. Lat., 85.15° W. Long. The county was founded in 1831. County seat is Stanton.

Montcalm County is part of the Grand Rapids-Wyoming, MI Metropolitan Statistical Area. The entire metro area includes: Barry County, MI; Kent County, MI; Montcalm County, MI; Ottawa County, MI

Weather Station: Greenville 2 NNE										Elevation: 881 feet	
	Jan	Feb	Mar	Apr	May	Jun	Jul	Aug	Sep	Oct	Nov	Dec
High	30	34	44	59	70	79	83	81	74	61	47	34
Low	14	16	23	34	44	54	58	56	49	38	29	19
Precip	1.8	1.6	2.1	3.1	3.9	3.1	3.2	3.8	3.9	3.2	3.3	2.2
Snow	21.7	15.4	9.9	2.5	tr	0.0	0.0	0.0	0.0	0.5	5.8	19.1

High and Low temperatures in degrees Fahrenheit; Precipitation and Snow in inches

Population: 63,342; Growth (since 2000): 3.4%; Density: 89.8 persons per square mile; Race: 94.3% White, 2.3% Black/African American, 0.4% Asian, 0.5% American Indian/Alaska Native, 0.0% Native Hawaiian/Other Pacific Islander, 1.6% two or more races, 3.1% Hispanic of any race; Average household size: 2.57; Median age: 39.3; Age under 18: 24.1%; Age 65 and over: 14.1%; Males per 100 females: 107.0; Marriage status: 26.7% never married, 54.2% now married, 6.1% widowed, 12.9% divorced; Foreign born: 1.3%; Speak English only: 96.6%; With disability: 17.3%; Veterans: 10.2%; Ancestry: 26.3% German, 15.3% English, 14.9% Irish, 7.6% American, 7.4% Dutch

Religion: Six largest groups: 8.3% Catholicism, 4.9% Methodist/Pietist, 3.6% Non-denominational Protestant, 3.1% Lutheran, 2.9% Holiness, 2.5% Presbyterian-Reformed

Economy: Unemployment rate: 6.6%; Leading industries: 20.8% retail trade; 14.0% other services (except public administration); 10.3% health care and social assistance; Farms: 1,127 totaling 237,252 acres; Company size: 0 employ 1,000 or more persons, 2 employ 500 to 999 persons, 16 employ 100 to 499 persons, 1,002 employ less than 100 persons; Business ownership: 1,246 women-owned, n/a Black-owned, n/a Hispanic-owned, n/a Asian-owned

Employment: 8.3% management, business, and financial, 3.2% computer, engineering, and science, 7.5% education, legal, community service, arts, and media, 5.4% healthcare practitioners, 16.8% service, 24.2% sales and office, 13.0% natural resources, construction, and maintenance, 21.6% production, transportation, and material moving

Income: Per capita: $18,969; Median household: $40,451; Average household: $49,363; Households with income of $100,000 or more: 9.3%; Poverty rate: 18.6%

Educational Attainment: High school diploma or higher: 87.4%; Bachelor's degree or higher: 13.4%; Graduate/professional degree or higher: 5.0%

Housing: Homeownership rate: 79.1%; Median home value: $95,000; Median year structure built: 1973; Homeowner vacancy rate: 2.9%; Median gross rent: $673 per month; Rental vacancy rate: 7.8%

Vital Statistics: Birth rate: 111.1 per 10,000 population; Death rate: 87.0 per 10,000 population; Age-adjusted cancer mortality rate: 199.7 deaths per 100,000 population

Health Insurance: 86.3% have insurance; 64.4% have private insurance; 37.2% have public insurance; 13.7% do not have insurance; 6.2% of children under 18 do not have insurance

Health Care: Physicians: 7.3 per 10,000 population; Hospital beds: 31.8 per 10,000 population; Hospital admissions: 825.5 per 10,000 population

Transportation: Commute: 92.5% car, 0.2% public transportation, 2.1% walk, 3.7% work from home; Median travel time to work: 30.2 minutes

Presidential Election: 45.0% Obama, 53.7% Romney (2012)

National and State Parks: Edmore State Game Area; Flat River State Game Area; Stanton State Game Area

Additional Information Contacts

Montcalm Government . . . . (989) 831-7300
  http://www.montcalm.org

Montcalm County Communities

BELVIDERE (township). Covers a land area of 34.621 square miles and a water area of 1.382 square miles. Located at 43.42° N. Lat; 85.14° W. Long. Elevation is 928 feet.

History: Belvidere Township was established in 1866.

Population: 2,209; Growth (since 2000): -9.4%; Density: 63.8 persons per square mile; Race: 96.7% White, 0.3% Black/African American, 0.0% Asian, 0.7% American Indian/Alaska Native, 0.0% Native Hawaiian/Other Pacific Islander, 1.8% Two or more races, 2.1% Hispanic of any race; Average household size: 2.42; Median age: 44.0; Age under 18: 22.2%; Age 65 and over: 18.5%; Males per 100 females: 102.3

Housing: Homeownership rate: 83.1%; Homeowner vacancy rate: 4.7%; Rental vacancy rate: 4.3%

BLOOMER (township). Covers a land area of 34.773 square miles and a water area of 0.135 square miles. Located at 43.16° N. Lat; 84.90° W. Long.

History: Bloomer Township was organized in 1852, and reportedly named for the shocking new item of ladies' clothing that was coming into vogue at that time.

Population: 3,904; Growth (since 2000): 28.5%; Density: 112.3 persons per square mile; Race: 66.6% White, 32.0% Black/African American, 0.2% Asian, 0.5% American Indian/Alaska Native, 0.0% Native Hawaiian/Other Pacific Islander, 0.5% Two or more races, 1.6% Hispanic of any race; Average household size: 2.86; Median age: 38.6; Age under 18: 10.8%; Age 65 and over: 6.1%; Males per 100 females: 439.2; Marriage status: 44.2% never married, 34.8% now married, 2.5% separated, 2.6% widowed, 18.3% divorced; Foreign born: 2.1%; Speak English only: 91.6%; With disability: 12.3%; Veterans: 9.5%; Ancestry: 20.4% German, 11.3% Irish, 10.5% English, 6.1% Dutch, 5.3% American

Employment: 9.6% management, business, and financial, 1.8% computer, engineering, and science, 6.9% education, legal, community service, arts, and media, 6.4% healthcare practitioners, 26.0% service, 19.8% sales and office, 12.4% natural resources, construction, and maintenance, 17.0% production, transportation, and material moving

Income: Per capita: $11,911; Median household: $51,458; Average household: $60,739; Households with income of $100,000 or more: 14.9%; Poverty rate: 8.7%

Educational Attainment: High school diploma or higher: 87.2%; Bachelor's degree or higher: 8.9%; Graduate/professional degree or higher: 3.8%

Housing: Homeownership rate: 83.8%; Median home value: $109,100; Median year structure built: 1969; Homeowner vacancy rate: 2.4%; Median gross rent: $863 per month; Rental vacancy rate: 9.0%

Health Insurance: 91.6% have insurance; 72.4% have private insurance; 32.9% have public insurance; 8.4% do not have insurance; 5.4% of children under 18 do not have insurance

Transportation: Commute: 88.5% car, 0.0% public transportation, 4.6% walk, 5.8% work from home; Median travel time to work: 29.3 minutes

BUSHNELL (township). Covers a land area of 35.594 square miles and a water area of 0.155 square miles. Located at 43.17° N. Lat; 85.01° W. Long.

History: Bushnell Township was organized in 1850 and named for Daniel P. Bushnell, a clerk of the state legislature.

Population: 1,604; Growth (since 2000): -24.0%; Density: 45.1 persons per square mile; Race: 96.3% White, 0.2% Black/African American, 0.4% Asian, 0.5% American Indian/Alaska Native, 0.0% Native Hawaiian/Other Pacific Islander, 1.7% Two or more races, 2.3% Hispanic of any race; Average household size: 2.73; Median age: 39.6; Age under 18: 25.0%; Age 65 and over: 14.7%; Males per 100 females: 101.5

Housing: Homeownership rate: 86.8%; Homeowner vacancy rate: 2.1%; Rental vacancy rate: 2.5%

CARSON CITY (city). Covers a land area of 1.038 square miles and a water area of 0.028 square miles. Located at 43.18° N. Lat; 84.85° W. Long. Elevation is 761 feet.

History: Carson City developed around a sawmill and a grist mill built in 1868 and 1870. The settlement was named for Carson City, Nevada.

Population: 1,093; Growth (since 2000): -8.2%; Density: 1,053.1 persons per square mile; Race: 96.7% White, 0.4% Black/African American, 0.5% Asian, 0.3% American Indian/Alaska Native, 0.0% Native Hawaiian/Other Pacific Islander, 1.4% Two or more races, 4.2% Hispanic of any race; Average household size: 2.27; Median age: 41.8; Age under 18: 24.4%; Age 65 and over: 24.0%; Males per 100 females: 77.7

School District(s)

Carson City-Crystal Area Schools (KG-12)

  2012-13 Enrollment: 923 . . . . (989) 584-3138

Housing: Homeownership rate: 66.1%; Homeowner vacancy rate: 5.7%; Rental vacancy rate: 11.9%

Hospitals: Carson City Hospital (77 beds)

CATO (township). Covers a land area of 35.138 square miles and a water area of 0.875 square miles. Located at 43.42° N. Lat; 85.27° W. Long.

History: Cato Township was organized in 1857 and named for Cato, New York.

Population: 2,735; Growth (since 2000): -6.3%; Density: 77.8 persons per square mile; Race: 97.5% White, 0.2% Black/African American, 0.4%

Asian, 0.3% American Indian/Alaska Native, 0.1% Native Hawaiian/Other Pacific Islander, 1.1% Two or more races, 3.0% Hispanic of any race; Average household size: 2.41; Median age: 41.3; Age under 18: 23.9%; Age 65 and over: 18.9%; Males per 100 females: 99.1; Marriage status: 22.0% never married, 58.5% now married, 0.8% separated, 6.9% widowed, 12.5% divorced; Foreign born: 1.6%; Speak English only: 95.7%; With disability: 19.1%; Veterans: 10.6%; Ancestry: 27.3% German, 12.3% English, 10.6% American, 10.0% Irish, 7.4% Dutch

Employment: 8.8% management, business, and financial, 6.9% computer, engineering, and science, 7.5% education, legal, community service, arts, and media, 6.1% healthcare practitioners, 15.8% service, 20.1% sales and office, 9.9% natural resources, construction, and maintenance, 24.9% production, transportation, and material moving

Income: Per capita: $17,544; Median household: $31,629; Average household: $43,489; Households with income of $100,000 or more: 6.9%; Poverty rate: 29.3%

Educational Attainment: High school diploma or higher: 84.4%; Bachelor's degree or higher: 13.4%; Graduate/professional degree or higher: 3.9%

Housing: Homeownership rate: 76.3%; Median home value: $87,600; Median year structure built: 1974; Homeowner vacancy rate: 4.0%; Median gross rent: $553 per month; Rental vacancy rate: 5.0%

Health Insurance: 77.7% have insurance; 56.9% have private insurance; 37.9% have public insurance; 22.3% do not have insurance; 22.7% of children under 18 do not have insurance

Transportation: Commute: 87.8% car, 0.0% public transportation, 3.1% walk, 4.7% work from home; Median travel time to work: 30.7 minutes

CORAL (unincorporated postal area)
ZCTA: 49322

Covers a land area of 25.605 square miles and a water area of 0.840 square miles. Located at 43.36° N. Lat; 85.35° W. Long. Elevation is 922 feet.

Population: 1,212; Growth (since 2000): -3.9%; Density: 47.3 persons per square mile; Race: 96.4% White, 0.4% Black/African American, 0.2% Asian, 0.4% American Indian/Alaska Native, 0.2% Native Hawaiian/Other Pacific Islander, 1.7% Two or more races, 2.5% Hispanic of any race; Average household size: 2.75; Median age: 39.0; Age under 18: 25.8%; Age 65 and over: 13.9%; Males per 100 females: 107.9

Housing: Homeownership rate: 84.8%; Homeowner vacancy rate: 1.8%; Rental vacancy rate: 8.3%

CRYSTAL (township). Covers a land area of 34.004 square miles and a water area of 1.806 square miles. Located at 43.25° N. Lat; 84.89° W. Long. Elevation is 820 feet.

Population: 2,689; Growth (since 2000): -4.8%; Density: 79.1 persons per square mile; Race: 97.2% White, 0.3% Black/African American, 0.3% Asian, 0.3% American Indian/Alaska Native, 0.0% Native Hawaiian/Other Pacific Islander, 1.4% Two or more races, 2.3% Hispanic of any race; Average household size: 2.54; Median age: 39.6; Age under 18: 24.4%; Age 65 and over: 15.2%; Males per 100 females: 97.3; Marriage status: 22.7% never married, 61.3% now married, 0.7% separated, 5.1% widowed, 10.9% divorced; Foreign born: 0.9%; Speak English only: 95.5%; With disability: 17.8%; Veterans: 10.3%; Ancestry: 29.2% German, 23.0% English, 10.8% Irish, 8.4% American, 5.7% Scottish

Employment: 11.5% management, business, and financial, 2.1% computer, engineering, and science, 5.9% education, legal, community service, arts, and media, 0.6% healthcare practitioners, 16.6% service, 31.1% sales and office, 12.5% natural resources, construction, and maintenance, 19.5% production, transportation, and material moving

Income: Per capita: $18,583; Median household: $42,218; Average household: $47,935; Households with income of $100,000 or more: 7.4%; Poverty rate: 12.3%

Educational Attainment: High school diploma or higher: 87.1%; Bachelor's degree or higher: 10.9%; Graduate/professional degree or higher: 4.6%

Housing: Homeownership rate: 81.5%; Median home value: $95,200; Median year structure built: 1973; Homeowner vacancy rate: 6.2%; Median gross rent: $704 per month; Rental vacancy rate: 11.6%

Health Insurance: 86.8% have insurance; 63.2% have private insurance; 40.4% have public insurance; 13.2% do not have insurance; 5.8% of children under 18 do not have insurance

Transportation: Commute: 92.2% car, 0.0% public transportation, 0.7% walk, 6.7% work from home; Median travel time to work: 29.8 minutes

DAY (township). Covers a land area of 35.273 square miles and a water area of 0.085 square miles. Located at 43.34° N. Lat; 85.01° W. Long.

Population: 1,172; Growth (since 2000): -8.6%; Density: 33.2 persons per square mile; Race: 96.5% White, 0.3% Black/African American, 0.3% Asian, 0.4% American Indian/Alaska Native, 0.1% Native Hawaiian/Other Pacific Islander, 1.7% Two or more races, 2.2% Hispanic of any race; Average household size: 2.57; Median age: 42.6; Age under 18: 23.0%; Age 65 and over: 16.8%; Males per 100 females: 100.3

Housing: Homeownership rate: 85.5%; Homeowner vacancy rate: 2.2%; Rental vacancy rate: 5.7%

DOUGLASS (township). Covers a land area of 34.739 square miles and a water area of 0.908 square miles. Located at 43.34° N. Lat; 85.15° W. Long.

Population: 2,180; Growth (since 2000): -8.3%; Density: 62.8 persons per square mile; Race: 97.0% White, 0.3% Black/African American, 0.3% Asian, 0.7% American Indian/Alaska Native, 0.0% Native Hawaiian/Other Pacific Islander, 1.0% Two or more races, 2.0% Hispanic of any race; Average household size: 2.45; Median age: 45.1; Age under 18: 21.0%; Age 65 and over: 17.8%; Males per 100 females: 102.2

Housing: Homeownership rate: 84.8%; Homeowner vacancy rate: 3.1%; Rental vacancy rate: 7.5%

EDMORE (village). Covers a land area of 1.512 square miles and a water area of <.001 square miles. Located at 43.41° N. Lat; 85.04° W. Long. Elevation is 968 feet.

History: The village of Edmore was platted in 1878 by Edwin Moore, and named for him. After its heyday as a lumber town, Edmore turned to dairying and milling, and later to gas and oil as its economic base.

Population: 1,201; Growth (since 2000): -3.5%; Density: 794.2 persons per square mile; Race: 94.9% White, 0.5% Black/African American, 0.2% Asian, 0.5% American Indian/Alaska Native, 0.0% Native Hawaiian/Other Pacific Islander, 3.0% Two or more races, 4.1% Hispanic of any race; Average household size: 2.31; Median age: 38.8; Age under 18: 24.6%; Age 65 and over: 16.6%; Males per 100 females: 85.3

Housing: Homeownership rate: 59.0%; Homeowner vacancy rate: 2.2%; Rental vacancy rate: 4.5%

Safety: Violent crime rate: 0.0 per 10,000 population; Property crime rate: 0.0 per 10,000 population

EUREKA (township). Covers a land area of 28.726 square miles and a water area of 0.835 square miles. Located at 43.15° N. Lat; 85.26° W. Long.

Population: 3,959; Growth (since 2000): 21.0%; Density: 137.8 persons per square mile; Race: 93.8% White, 0.5% Black/African American, 0.5% Asian, 0.5% American Indian/Alaska Native, 0.0% Native Hawaiian/Other Pacific Islander, 1.7% Two or more races, 6.0% Hispanic of any race; Average household size: 2.73; Median age: 39.1; Age under 18: 25.7%; Age 65 and over: 12.8%; Males per 100 females: 104.7; Marriage status: 22.4% never married, 67.4% now married, 0.4% separated, 2.1% widowed, 8.1% divorced; Foreign born: 2.2%; Speak English only: 97.1%; With disability: 8.7%; Veterans: 7.3%; Ancestry: 24.0% German, 18.3% English, 17.4% Irish, 8.8% American, 8.4% Dutch

Employment: 13.1% management, business, and financial, 3.2% computer, engineering, and science, 13.4% education, legal, community service, arts, and media, 7.7% healthcare practitioners, 11.6% service, 25.1% sales and office, 7.9% natural resources, construction, and maintenance, 18.0% production, transportation, and material moving

Income: Per capita: $23,694; Median household: $60,533; Average household: $66,970; Households with income of $100,000 or more: 19.7%; Poverty rate: 15.4%

Educational Attainment: High school diploma or higher: 91.4%; Bachelor's degree or higher: 24.4%; Graduate/professional degree or higher: 8.2%

School District(s)
Saint Johns Public Schools (PK-12)
    2012-13 Enrollment: 3,115 . . . . (989) 227-4050

Housing: Homeownership rate: 92.0%; Median home value: $129,400; Median year structure built: 1980; Homeowner vacancy rate: 1.4%; Median gross rent: n/a per month; Rental vacancy rate: 8.0%

Health Insurance: 92.2% have insurance; 74.6% have private insurance; 27.6% have public insurance; 7.8% do not have insurance; 3.1% of children under 18 do not have insurance

Transportation: Commute: 96.4% car, 0.0% public transportation, 0.8% walk, 2.3% work from home; Median travel time to work: 26.0 minutes

EVERGREEN (township). Covers a land area of 34.649 square miles and a water area of 0.687 square miles. Located at 43.25° N. Lat; 85.02° W. Long.
Population: 2,858; Growth (since 2000): -2.2%; Density: 82.5 persons per square mile; Race: 96.9% White, 0.2% Black/African American, 0.5% Asian, 0.6% American Indian/Alaska Native, 0.0% Native Hawaiian/Other Pacific Islander, 1.2% Two or more races, 2.1% Hispanic of any race; Average household size: 2.46; Median age: 42.6; Age under 18: 22.8%; Age 65 and over: 15.6%; Males per 100 females: 99.0; Marriage status: 24.0% never married, 57.7% now married, 1.8% separated, 6.2% widowed, 12.2% divorced; Foreign born: 0.2%; Speak English only: 98.4%; With disability: 19.0%; Veterans: 8.2%; Ancestry: 27.1% German, 20.9% English, 19.2% Irish, 5.7% Dutch, 5.6% American
Employment: 4.4% management, business, and financial, 1.1% computer, engineering, and science, 8.6% education, legal, community service, arts, and media, 5.7% healthcare practitioners, 19.2% service, 27.2% sales and office, 8.2% natural resources, construction, and maintenance, 25.4% production, transportation, and material moving
Income: Per capita: $20,729; Median household: $38,245; Average household: $45,714; Households with income of $100,000 or more: 7.0%; Poverty rate: 17.8%
Educational Attainment: High school diploma or higher: 88.3%; Bachelor's degree or higher: 12.6%; Graduate/professional degree or higher: 6.7%
Housing: Homeownership rate: 79.2%; Median home value: $93,400; Median year structure built: 1975; Homeowner vacancy rate: 3.2%; Median gross rent: $576 per month; Rental vacancy rate: 5.4%
Health Insurance: 84.9% have insurance; 68.6% have private insurance; 35.0% have public insurance; 15.1% do not have insurance; 1.0% of children under 18 do not have insurance
Transportation: Commute: 95.4% car, 0.0% public transportation, 1.2% walk, 3.1% work from home; Median travel time to work: 30.3 minutes

FAIRPLAIN (township). Covers a land area of 35.218 square miles and a water area of 0.735 square miles. Located at 43.16° N. Lat; 85.13° W. Long.
Population: 1,836; Growth (since 2000): 0.5%; Density: 52.1 persons per square mile; Race: 96.7% White, 1.1% Black/African American, 0.2% Asian, 0.2% American Indian/Alaska Native, 0.0% Native Hawaiian/Other Pacific Islander, 0.5% Two or more races, 3.2% Hispanic of any race; Average household size: 2.73; Median age: 40.8; Age under 18: 24.7%; Age 65 and over: 12.5%; Males per 100 females: 102.4
Housing: Homeownership rate: 87.5%; Homeowner vacancy rate: 1.2%; Rental vacancy rate: 8.9%

FENWICK (unincorporated postal area)
ZCTA: 48834
Covers a land area of 46.257 square miles and a water area of 0.865 square miles. Located at 43.13° N. Lat; 85.03° W. Long. Elevation is 837 feet.
Population: 2,090; Growth (since 2000): -13.3%; Density: 45.2 persons per square mile; Race: 97.3% White, 0.4% Black/African American, 0.3% Asian, 0.3% American Indian/Alaska Native, 0.0% Native Hawaiian/Other Pacific Islander, 0.4% Two or more races, 2.6% Hispanic of any race; Average household size: 2.63; Median age: 41.4; Age under 18: 23.8%; Age 65 and over: 14.8%; Males per 100 females: 102.7

School District(s)
Montcalm Area ISD (PK-12)
   2012-13 Enrollment: 454 . . . . (989) 831-5261
Palo Community SD (PK-12)
   2012-13 Enrollment: 74 . . . . (989) 637-4359
   Housing: Homeownership rate: 87.0%; Homeowner vacancy rate: 1.3%; Rental vacancy rate: 5.5%

FERRIS (township). Covers a land area of 36.035 square miles and a water area of 0.073 square miles. Located at 43.33° N. Lat; 84.90° W. Long.
Population: 1,422; Growth (since 2000): 3.1%; Density: 39.5 persons per square mile; Race: 98.3% White, 0.1% Black/African American, 0.1% Asian, 0.6% American Indian/Alaska Native, 0.1% Native Hawaiian/Other Pacific Islander, 0.4% Two or more races, 2.6% Hispanic of any race; Average household size: 2.72; Median age: 39.4; Age under 18: 25.7%; Age 65 and over: 13.6%; Males per 100 females: 104.3

Housing: Homeownership rate: 85.8%; Homeowner vacancy rate: 2.8%; Rental vacancy rate: 1.3%

GREENVILLE (city). Covers a land area of 6.342 square miles and a water area of 0.328 square miles. Located at 43.18° N. Lat; 85.25° W. Long. Elevation is 837 feet.
History: Greenville began as a lumber center, founded by John Green in 1844 and platted in 1853. It later became an important potato market on the Flat River.
Population: 8,481; Growth (since 2000): 6.9%; Density: 1,337.4 persons per square mile; Race: 94.3% White, 0.3% Black/African American, 0.7% Asian, 0.5% American Indian/Alaska Native, 0.1% Native Hawaiian/Other Pacific Islander, 2.4% Two or more races, 4.9% Hispanic of any race; Average household size: 2.39; Median age: 34.7; Age under 18: 26.6%; Age 65 and over: 15.2%; Males per 100 females: 89.3; Marriage status: 28.2% never married, 46.7% now married, 1.4% separated, 8.2% widowed, 16.9% divorced; Foreign born: 1.1%; Speak English only: 97.4%; With disability: 19.2%; Veterans: 10.9%; Ancestry: 27.9% German, 16.4% English, 16.2% Irish, 8.2% Dutch, 5.7% French
Employment: 5.1% management, business, and financial, 8.2% computer, engineering, and science, 10.2% education, legal, community service, arts, and media, 7.6% healthcare practitioners, 18.7% service, 28.1% sales and office, 9.7% natural resources, construction, and maintenance, 12.2% production, transportation, and material moving
Income: Per capita: $17,562; Median household: $30,326; Average household: $42,131; Households with income of $100,000 or more: 5.9%; Poverty rate: 27.8%
Educational Attainment: High school diploma or higher: 87.2%; Bachelor's degree or higher: 20.6%; Graduate/professional degree or higher: 8.4%
School District(s)
Grattan Academy (KG-12)
   2012-13 Enrollment: 271 . . . . (616) 754-9360
Greenville Public Schools (PK-12)
   2012-13 Enrollment: 3,856 . . . . (616) 754-3686
Montcalm Area ISD (PK-12)
   2012-13 Enrollment: 454 . . . . (989) 831-5261
Housing: Homeownership rate: 57.0%; Median home value: $91,100; Median year structure built: 1959; Homeowner vacancy rate: 3.9%; Median gross rent: $680 per month; Rental vacancy rate: 8.7%
Health Insurance: 89.5% have insurance; 60.9% have private insurance; 42.4% have public insurance; 10.5% do not have insurance; 4.3% of children under 18 do not have insurance
Hospitals: Spectrum Health United Memorial - United Campus (105 beds)
Safety: Violent crime rate: 39.2 per 10,000 population; Property crime rate: 409.6 per 10,000 population
Newspapers: Carson City Gazette (weekly circulation 8700); Daily News (daily circulation 8400)
Transportation: Commute: 92.0% car, 0.8% public transportation, 4.4% walk, 2.7% work from home; Median travel time to work: 23.5 minutes
Airports: Greenville Municipal (general aviation)
Additional Information Contacts
City of Greenville . . . . (616) 754-5645
   http://greenvillemi.org

HOME (township). Covers a land area of 36.002 square miles and a water area of 0.120 square miles. Located at 43.44° N. Lat; 85.03° W. Long.
Population: 2,542; Growth (since 2000): -6.1%; Density: 70.6 persons per square mile; Race: 95.7% White, 0.4% Black/African American, 0.2% Asian, 0.5% American Indian/Alaska Native, 0.0% Native Hawaiian/Other Pacific Islander, 2.6% Two or more races, 3.8% Hispanic of any race; Average household size: 2.41; Median age: 41.2; Age under 18: 23.1%; Age 65 and over: 17.3%; Males per 100 females: 94.5; Marriage status: 32.9% never married, 48.0% now married, 0.3% separated, 5.4% widowed, 13.6% divorced; Foreign born: 1.9%; Speak English only: 97.9%; With disability: 19.5%; Veterans: 10.4%; Ancestry: 27.0% German, 13.1% English, 9.7% Irish, 6.8% Dutch, 5.5% American
Employment: 6.4% management, business, and financial, 1.3% computer, engineering, and science, 8.2% education, legal, community service, arts, and media, 6.3% healthcare practitioners, 18.6% service, 21.7% sales and office, 9.6% natural resources, construction, and maintenance, 27.9% production, transportation, and material moving

Income: Per capita: $18,400; Median household: $35,000; Average household: $44,091; Households with income of $100,000 or more: 9.6%; Poverty rate: 16.2%
Educational Attainment: High school diploma or higher: 89.1%; Bachelor's degree or higher: 16.1%; Graduate/professional degree or higher: 6.8%
Housing: Homeownership rate: 69.6%; Median home value: $78,900; Median year structure built: 1964; Homeowner vacancy rate: 2.2%; Median gross rent: $572 per month; Rental vacancy rate: 5.4%
Health Insurance: 85.8% have insurance; 56.3% have private insurance; 43.6% have public insurance; 14.2% do not have insurance; 6.6% of children under 18 do not have insurance
Transportation: Commute: 92.3% car, 0.4% public transportation, 3.8% walk, 0.4% work from home; Median travel time to work: 24.8 minutes

HOWARD CITY (village). Covers a land area of 2.526 square miles and a water area of 0.034 square miles. Located at 43.39° N. Lat; 85.47° W. Long. Elevation is 879 feet.
History: The land on which Howard City was platted in 1868 belonged to Benjamin Ensley. Howard City, formed as a lumber center, turned to farming. Discovery of oil and gas in the 1930's supported the economy.
Population: 1,808; Growth (since 2000): 14.1%; Density: 715.7 persons per square mile; Race: 96.3% White, 0.6% Black/African American, 0.2% Asian, 0.6% American Indian/Alaska Native, 0.0% Native Hawaiian/Other Pacific Islander, 1.5% Two or more races, 2.4% Hispanic of any race; Average household size: 2.63; Median age: 33.6; Age under 18: 29.4%; Age 65 and over: 12.9%; Males per 100 females: 87.4
School District(s)
Tri County Area Schools (PK-12)
    2012-13 Enrollment: 2,181 . . . . (616) 636-5454
Housing: Homeownership rate: 63.5%; Homeowner vacancy rate: 3.1%; Rental vacancy rate: 6.7%
Safety: Violent crime rate: 33.6 per 10,000 population; Property crime rate: 341.5 per 10,000 population

LAKEVIEW (village). Covers a land area of 1.524 square miles and a water area of 0.351 square miles. Located at 43.44° N. Lat; 85.27° W. Long. Elevation is 955 feet.
History: Lakeview was first settled in 1858 on the shore of Tamarck Lake by Albert S. French from New York. It was incorporated as a village in 1881.
Population: 1,007; Growth (since 2000): -9.4%; Density: 660.9 persons per square mile; Race: 96.3% White, 0.4% Black/African American, 0.6% Asian, 0.4% American Indian/Alaska Native, 0.2% Native Hawaiian/Other Pacific Islander, 1.9% Two or more races, 2.6% Hispanic of any race; Average household size: 2.23; Median age: 41.3; Age under 18: 23.1%; Age 65 and over: 21.5%; Males per 100 females: 85.8
School District(s)
Lakeview Community Schools (Montcalm) (KG-12)
    2012-13 Enrollment: 1,289 . . . . (989) 352-6226
Housing: Homeownership rate: 58.7%; Homeowner vacancy rate: 5.1%; Rental vacancy rate: 3.7%
Hospitals: Spectrum Health United Memorial - Kelsey Campus (94 beds)

MAPLE VALLEY (township). Covers a land area of 35.324 square miles and a water area of 0.804 square miles. Located at 43.34° N. Lat; 85.39° W. Long.
Population: 1,944; Growth (since 2000): -6.7%; Density: 55.0 persons per square mile; Race: 95.8% White, 0.6% Black/African American, 0.5% Asian, 0.1% American Indian/Alaska Native, 0.1% Native Hawaiian/Other Pacific Islander, 2.4% Two or more races, 2.4% Hispanic of any race; Average household size: 2.63; Median age: 40.2; Age under 18: 24.6%; Age 65 and over: 15.5%; Males per 100 females: 98.4
Housing: Homeownership rate: 85.9%; Homeowner vacancy rate: 1.8%; Rental vacancy rate: 8.0%

MCBRIDE (village). Covers a land area of 0.383 square miles and a water area of 0 square miles. Located at 43.35° N. Lat; 85.04° W. Long. Elevation is 958 feet.
Population: 205; Growth (since 2000): -11.6%; Density: 535.4 persons per square mile; Race: 98.0% White, 0.0% Black/African American, 0.5% Asian, 0.0% American Indian/Alaska Native, 0.0% Native Hawaiian/Other Pacific Islander, 1.5% Two or more races, 1.0% Hispanic of any race; Average household size: 2.47; Median age: 39.4; Age under 18: 28.8%; Age 65 and over: 15.1%; Males per 100 females: 103.0

Housing: Homeownership rate: 85.5%; Homeowner vacancy rate: 5.3%; Rental vacancy rate: 0.0%

MONTCALM (township). Covers a land area of 35.431 square miles and a water area of 0.983 square miles. Located at 43.24° N. Lat; 85.26° W. Long.
Population: 3,350; Growth (since 2000): 5.4%; Density: 94.6 persons per square mile; Race: 97.3% White, 0.1% Black/African American, 0.1% Asian, 0.4% American Indian/Alaska Native, 0.0% Native Hawaiian/Other Pacific Islander, 1.6% Two or more races, 2.1% Hispanic of any race; Average household size: 2.65; Median age: 40.9; Age under 18: 24.1%; Age 65 and over: 12.6%; Males per 100 females: 104.4; Marriage status: 18.7% never married, 57.7% now married, 0.0% separated, 8.1% widowed, 15.5% divorced; Foreign born: 1.2%; Speak English only: 96.1%; With disability: 15.7%; Veterans: 10.6%; Ancestry: 21.5% German, 15.9% Irish, 15.1% English, 7.9% Danish, 7.5% American
Employment: 7.1% management, business, and financial, 3.4% computer, engineering, and science, 5.4% education, legal, community service, arts, and media, 4.1% healthcare practitioners, 16.7% service, 27.5% sales and office, 12.6% natural resources, construction, and maintenance, 23.2% production, transportation, and material moving
Income: Per capita: $23,096; Median household: $50,320; Average household: $60,578; Households with income of $100,000 or more: 16.3%; Poverty rate: 15.7%
Educational Attainment: High school diploma or higher: 91.3%; Bachelor's degree or higher: 8.9%; Graduate/professional degree or higher: 4.6%
Housing: Homeownership rate: 87.1%; Median home value: $97,100; Median year structure built: 1975; Homeowner vacancy rate: 2.5%; Median gross rent: $724 per month; Rental vacancy rate: 7.8%
Health Insurance: 86.8% have insurance; 67.6% have private insurance; 34.1% have public insurance; 13.2% do not have insurance; 11.5% of children under 18 do not have insurance
Transportation: Commute: 92.2% car, 0.0% public transportation, 1.1% walk, 3.2% work from home; Median travel time to work: 30.1 minutes

PIERSON (township). Covers a land area of 34.638 square miles and a water area of 1.583 square miles. Located at 43.35° N. Lat; 85.50° W. Long. Elevation is 909 feet.
Population: 3,216; Growth (since 2000): 12.2%; Density: 92.8 persons per square mile; Race: 96.4% White, 0.3% Black/African American, 0.3% Asian, 0.8% American Indian/Alaska Native, 0.0% Native Hawaiian/Other Pacific Islander, 1.8% Two or more races, 2.4% Hispanic of any race; Average household size: 2.71; Median age: 39.2; Age under 18: 26.1%; Age 65 and over: 10.7%; Males per 100 females: 103.4; Marriage status: 27.5% never married, 58.5% now married, 1.5% separated, 4.6% widowed, 9.5% divorced; Foreign born: 1.7%; Speak English only: 95.3%; With disability: 14.4%; Veterans: 7.5%; Ancestry: 26.4% German, 15.1% English, 13.6% American, 12.8% Dutch, 12.4% Irish
Employment: 11.6% management, business, and financial, 2.2% computer, engineering, and science, 6.6% education, legal, community service, arts, and media, 3.5% healthcare practitioners, 12.6% service, 25.0% sales and office, 14.6% natural resources, construction, and maintenance, 23.8% production, transportation, and material moving
Income: Per capita: $22,774; Median household: $51,667; Average household: $62,332; Households with income of $100,000 or more: 12.2%; Poverty rate: 12.0%
Educational Attainment: High school diploma or higher: 87.9%; Bachelor's degree or higher: 15.4%; Graduate/professional degree or higher: 6.9%
Housing: Homeownership rate: 88.6%; Median home value: $129,700; Median year structure built: 1980; Homeowner vacancy rate: 1.9%; Median gross rent: $685 per month; Rental vacancy rate: 3.6%
Health Insurance: 89.7% have insurance; 74.1% have private insurance; 28.0% have public insurance; 10.3% do not have insurance; 3.8% of children under 18 do not have insurance
Transportation: Commute: 96.2% car, 0.0% public transportation, 0.0% walk, 3.8% work from home; Median travel time to work: 35.8 minutes

PIERSON (village). Covers a land area of 0.249 square miles and a water area of 0 square miles. Located at 43.32° N. Lat; 85.50° W. Long. Elevation is 909 feet.
History: Pierson was founded in 1856 on land acquired by David S. Pierson. It became a trading center for nearby resorts.

Population: 172; Growth (since 2000): -7.0%; Density: 689.5 persons per square mile; Race: 98.3% White, 0.6% Black/African American, 0.0% Asian, 0.0% American Indian/Alaska Native, 0.0% Native Hawaiian/Other Pacific Islander, 0.0% Two or more races, 1.7% Hispanic of any race; Average household size: 2.77; Median age: 30.3; Age under 18: 29.1%; Age 65 and over: 7.0%; Males per 100 females: 129.3
Housing: Homeownership rate: 71.0%; Homeowner vacancy rate: 6.4%; Rental vacancy rate: 0.0%

PINE (township). Covers a land area of 34.983 square miles and a water area of 1.089 square miles. Located at 43.34° N. Lat; 85.27° W. Long.
Population: 1,834; Growth (since 2000): 10.9%; Density: 52.4 persons per square mile; Race: 97.7% White, 0.4% Black/African American, 0.2% Asian, 0.3% American Indian/Alaska Native, 0.2% Native Hawaiian/Other Pacific Islander, 1.1% Two or more races, 1.5% Hispanic of any race; Average household size: 2.68; Median age: 42.1; Age under 18: 24.7%; Age 65 and over: 15.2%; Males per 100 females: 108.9
Housing: Homeownership rate: 86.6%; Homeowner vacancy rate: 2.0%; Rental vacancy rate: 10.8%

REYNOLDS (township). Covers a land area of 35.694 square miles and a water area of 0.414 square miles. Located at 43.42° N. Lat; 85.53° W. Long.
Population: 5,310; Growth (since 2000): 24.1%; Density: 148.8 persons per square mile; Race: 96.4% White, 0.4% Black/African American, 0.4% Asian, 0.5% American Indian/Alaska Native, 0.0% Native Hawaiian/Other Pacific Islander, 1.9% Two or more races, 1.9% Hispanic of any race; Average household size: 2.75; Median age: 34.7; Age under 18: 28.8%; Age 65 and over: 10.3%; Males per 100 females: 96.4; Marriage status: 28.7% never married, 50.3% now married, 1.4% separated, 9.3% widowed, 11.8% divorced; Foreign born: 1.1%; Speak English only: 98.4%; With disability: 17.1%; Veterans: 9.8%; Ancestry: 32.6% German, 22.0% Irish, 13.7% English, 10.0% Dutch, 5.6% American
Employment: 4.0% management, business, and financial, 3.1% computer, engineering, and science, 3.9% education, legal, community service, arts, and media, 3.4% healthcare practitioners, 13.7% service, 25.6% sales and office, 22.2% natural resources, construction, and maintenance, 24.2% production, transportation, and material moving
Income: Per capita: $19,101; Median household: $41,840; Average household: $48,171; Households with income of $100,000 or more: 8.9%; Poverty rate: 12.9%
Educational Attainment: High school diploma or higher: 82.3%; Bachelor's degree or higher: 8.1%; Graduate/professional degree or higher: 1.5%
Housing: Homeownership rate: 79.0%; Median home value: $90,100; Median year structure built: 1988; Homeowner vacancy rate: 2.5%; Median gross rent: $816 per month; Rental vacancy rate: 8.9%
Health Insurance: 84.6% have insurance; 62.3% have private insurance; 34.8% have public insurance; 15.4% do not have insurance; 6.2% of children under 18 do not have insurance
Transportation: Commute: 95.7% car, 0.0% public transportation, 0.5% walk, 1.5% work from home; Median travel time to work: 38.8 minutes

RICHLAND (township). Covers a land area of 35.633 square miles and a water area of 0.566 square miles. Located at 43.42° N. Lat; 84.90° W. Long.
Population: 2,778; Growth (since 2000): -3.1%; Density: 78.0 persons per square mile; Race: 96.6% White, 0.8% Black/African American, 0.4% Asian, 0.4% American Indian/Alaska Native, 0.0% Native Hawaiian/Other Pacific Islander, 1.1% Two or more races, 3.3% Hispanic of any race; Average household size: 2.61; Median age: 40.7; Age under 18: 24.0%; Age 65 and over: 15.0%; Males per 100 females: 101.6; Marriage status: 22.3% never married, 57.7% now married, 0.7% separated, 9.4% widowed, 10.6% divorced; Foreign born: 1.8%; Speak English only: 95.6%; With disability: 23.0%; Veterans: 15.9%; Ancestry: 19.2% German, 16.3% American, 15.9% Irish, 11.9% English, 7.9% Dutch
Employment: 10.3% management, business, and financial, 2.7% computer, engineering, and science, 9.0% education, legal, community service, arts, and media, 3.8% healthcare practitioners, 23.8% service, 23.8% sales and office, 12.4% natural resources, construction, and maintenance, 14.2% production, transportation, and material moving
Income: Per capita: $20,005; Median household: $41,810; Average household: $49,384; Households with income of $100,000 or more: 10.1%; Poverty rate: 10.6%

Educational Attainment: High school diploma or higher: 89.4%; Bachelor's degree or higher: 12.6%; Graduate/professional degree or higher: 3.6%
Housing: Homeownership rate: 85.5%; Median home value: $87,400; Median year structure built: 1973; Homeowner vacancy rate: 2.7%; Median gross rent: $510 per month; Rental vacancy rate: 4.8%
Health Insurance: 88.8% have insurance; 70.3% have private insurance; 38.5% have public insurance; 11.2% do not have insurance; 5.3% of children under 18 do not have insurance
Transportation: Commute: 91.7% car, 0.4% public transportation, 2.3% walk, 4.7% work from home; Median travel time to work: 31.6 minutes

SHERIDAN (village). Covers a land area of 1.101 square miles and a water area of 0.058 square miles. Located at 43.21° N. Lat; 85.07° W. Long. Elevation is 850 feet.
History: Sheridan grew around a sawmill founded by John W. Winsor in the 1850's. The village was named for General Philip H. Sheridan.
Population: 649; Growth (since 2000): -7.9%; Density: 589.5 persons per square mile; Race: 95.2% White, 0.6% Black/African American, 0.5% Asian, 1.8% American Indian/Alaska Native, 0.0% Native Hawaiian/Other Pacific Islander, 1.7% Two or more races, 1.7% Hispanic of any race; Average household size: 2.34; Median age: 41.9; Age under 18: 23.3%; Age 65 and over: 20.6%; Males per 100 females: 85.4
School District(s)
Central Montcalm Public Schools (PK-12)
    2012-13 Enrollment: 1,714 . . . . (989) 831-2001
Housing: Homeownership rate: 78.3%; Homeowner vacancy rate: 3.9%; Rental vacancy rate: 4.7%
Hospitals: Sheridan Community Hospital (25 beds)

SIDNEY (township). Covers a land area of 33.946 square miles and a water area of 1.094 square miles. Located at 43.25° N. Lat; 85.14° W. Long. Elevation is 896 feet.
History: Sidney Township was organized in 1857 and named for Sidney, Ohio, the former home of some of the early residents.
Population: 2,574; Growth (since 2000): 0.4%; Density: 75.8 persons per square mile; Race: 96.5% White, 0.1% Black/African American, 0.4% Asian, 0.2% American Indian/Alaska Native, 0.0% Native Hawaiian/Other Pacific Islander, 0.8% Two or more races, 4.0% Hispanic of any race; Average household size: 2.55; Median age: 42.7; Age under 18: 23.7%; Age 65 and over: 15.5%; Males per 100 females: 103.8; Marriage status: 19.0% never married, 64.6% now married, 1.9% separated, 3.7% widowed, 12.7% divorced; Foreign born: 1.2%; Speak English only: 98.0%; With disability: 20.1%; Veterans: 13.0%; Ancestry: 31.3% German, 21.8% Irish, 13.6% English, 5.4% Dutch, 5.2% Polish
Employment: 8.1% management, business, and financial, 3.2% computer, engineering, and science, 10.5% education, legal, community service, arts, and media, 4.4% healthcare practitioners, 20.5% service, 21.6% sales and office, 11.2% natural resources, construction, and maintenance, 20.6% production, transportation, and material moving
Income: Per capita: $17,962; Median household: $41,528; Average household: $47,194; Households with income of $100,000 or more: 6.2%; Poverty rate: 15.1%
Educational Attainment: High school diploma or higher: 85.8%; Bachelor's degree or higher: 13.5%; Graduate/professional degree or higher: 1.8%
Two-year College(s)
Montcalm Community College (Public)
    Fall 2013 Enrollment: 1,944 . . . . (989) 328-2111
    2013-14 Tuition: In-state $5,550; Out-of-state $8,040
Housing: Homeownership rate: 87.2%; Median home value: $100,100; Median year structure built: 1977; Homeowner vacancy rate: 2.3%; Median gross rent: $828 per month; Rental vacancy rate: 7.9%
Health Insurance: 84.4% have insurance; 58.7% have private insurance; 42.1% have public insurance; 15.6% do not have insurance; 0.8% of children under 18 do not have insurance
Transportation: Commute: 93.9% car, 0.0% public transportation, 1.6% walk, 2.7% work from home; Median travel time to work: 30.3 minutes

SIX LAKES (unincorporated postal area)
ZCTA: 48886
    Covers a land area of 29.796 square miles and a water area of 1.152 square miles. Located at 43.42° N. Lat; 85.16° W. Long. Elevation is 922 feet.

Population: 2,116; Growth (since 2000): -4.5%; Density: 71.0 persons per square mile; Race: 97.2% White, 0.3% Black/African American, 0.0% Asian, 0.7% American Indian/Alaska Native, 0.0% Native Hawaiian/Other Pacific Islander, 1.6% Two or more races, 2.1% Hispanic of any race; Average household size: 2.48; Median age: 41.5; Age under 18: 23.6%; Age 65 and over: 17.4%; Males per 100 females: 103.5
Housing: Homeownership rate: 83.5%; Homeowner vacancy rate: 4.0%; Rental vacancy rate: 5.3%

STANTON (city). County seat. Covers a land area of 2.145 square miles and a water area of 0.004 square miles. Located at 43.29° N. Lat; 85.08° W. Long. Elevation is 919 feet.
History: Stanton was founded as the seat of Montcalm County in 1860. It was first named Fred, for Fred Hall who had previously owned the land, but was renamed in 1863 for Edwin M. Stanton, secretary of war.
Population: 1,417; Growth (since 2000): -5.8%; Density: 660.5 persons per square mile; Race: 93.8% White, 1.8% Black/African American, 0.2% Asian, 0.7% American Indian/Alaska Native, 0.0% Native Hawaiian/Other Pacific Islander, 1.7% Two or more races, 5.9% Hispanic of any race; Average household size: 2.42; Median age: 33.8; Age under 18: 23.9%; Age 65 and over: 13.8%; Males per 100 females: 102.4
School District(s)
Central Montcalm Public Schools (PK-12)
    2012-13 Enrollment: 1,714 . . . . (989) 831-2001
Montcalm Area ISD (PK-12)
    2012-13 Enrollment: 454 . . . . (989) 831-5261
Housing: Homeownership rate: 60.4%; Homeowner vacancy rate: 1.6%; Rental vacancy rate: 10.2%
Safety: Violent crime rate: 14.2 per 10,000 population; Property crime rate: 92.3 per 10,000 population

TRUFANT (unincorporated postal area)
ZCTA: 49347
    Covers a land area of 18.576 square miles and a water area of 0.791 square miles. Located at 43.32° N. Lat; 85.35° W. Long. Elevation is 899 feet.
Population: 1,257; Growth (since 2000): -2.7%; Density: 67.7 persons per square mile; Race: 96.7% White, 0.6% Black/African American, 0.6% Asian, 0.0% American Indian/Alaska Native, 0.0% Native Hawaiian/Other Pacific Islander, 1.8% Two or more races, 1.8% Hispanic of any race; Average household size: 2.43; Median age: 44.1; Age under 18: 22.3%; Age 65 and over: 18.7%; Males per 100 females: 99.2
Housing: Homeownership rate: 87.8%; Homeowner vacancy rate: 1.7%; Rental vacancy rate: 10.0%

VESTABURG (unincorporated postal area)
ZCTA: 48891
    Covers a land area of 42.785 square miles and a water area of 0.479 square miles. Located at 43.40° N. Lat; 84.91° W. Long. Elevation is 922 feet.
Population: 2,985; Growth (since 2000): -1.5%; Density: 69.8 persons per square mile; Race: 96.5% White, 0.6% Black/African American, 0.4% Asian, 0.6% American Indian/Alaska Native, 0.1% Native Hawaiian/Other Pacific Islander, 1.2% Two or more races, 3.0% Hispanic of any race; Average household size: 2.60; Median age: 40.6; Age under 18: 24.3%; Age 65 and over: 15.2%; Males per 100 females: 102.9; Marriage status: 22.0% never married, 60.1% now married, 1.0% separated, 8.3% widowed, 9.6% divorced; Foreign born: 1.7%; Speak English only: 96.0%; With disability: 20.0%; Veterans: 13.6%; Ancestry: 20.6% German, 15.6% American, 14.6% Irish, 12.5% English, 8.3% Dutch
Employment: 11.2% management, business, and financial, 1.9% computer, engineering, and science, 6.4% education, legal, community service, arts, and media, 4.2% healthcare practitioners, 22.1% service, 22.5% sales and office, 15.8% natural resources, construction, and maintenance, 15.9% production, transportation, and material moving
Income: Per capita: $19,478; Median household: $42,560; Average household: $49,192; Households with income of $100,000 or more: 9.4%; Poverty rate: 11.4%
Educational Attainment: High school diploma or higher: 90.5%; Bachelor's degree or higher: 12.5%; Graduate/professional degree or higher: 3.6%

School District(s)
Vestaburg Community Schools (KG-12)
    2012-13 Enrollment: 692 . . . . (989) 268-5353
Housing: Homeownership rate: 85.0%; Median home value: $86,300; Median year structure built: 1973; Homeowner vacancy rate: 2.7%; Median gross rent: $508 per month; Rental vacancy rate: 3.8%
Health Insurance: 88.4% have insurance; 70.7% have private insurance; 37.1% have public insurance; 11.6% do not have insurance; 7.0% of children under 18 do not have insurance
Transportation: Commute: 92.7% car, 0.3% public transportation, 2.3% walk, 3.1% work from home; Median travel time to work: 31.2 minutes

WINFIELD (township). Covers a land area of 35.457 square miles and a water area of 0.739 square miles. Located at 43.42° N. Lat; 85.37° W. Long. Elevation is 948 feet.
Population: 2,235; Growth (since 2000): 9.1%; Density: 63.0 persons per square mile; Race: 97.2% White, 0.2% Black/African American, 0.0% Asian, 0.8% American Indian/Alaska Native, 0.0% Native Hawaiian/Other Pacific Islander, 1.5% Two or more races, 0.9% Hispanic of any race; Average household size: 2.75; Median age: 38.4; Age under 18: 27.6%; Age 65 and over: 12.8%; Males per 100 females: 106.0
Housing: Homeownership rate: 88.4%; Homeowner vacancy rate: 2.7%; Rental vacancy rate: 7.8%

Montmorency County

Located in northern Michigan; drained by the Thunder Bay, Rainy, and Black Rivers; includes Rush, Long, Grass, Avalon, and East Twin Lakes. Covers a land area of 546.663 square miles, a water area of 15.989 square miles, and is located in the Eastern Time Zone at 45.02° N. Lat., 84.13° W. Long. The county was founded in 1881. County seat is Atlanta.
Population: 9,765; Growth (since 2000): -5.3%; Density: 17.9 persons per square mile; Race: 97.6% White, 0.2% Black/African American, 0.2% Asian, 0.4% American Indian/Alaska Native, 0.0% Native Hawaiian/Other Pacific Islander, 1.5% two or more races, 1.0% Hispanic of any race; Average household size: 2.18; Median age: 52.3; Age under 18: 16.8%; Age 65 and over: 27.0%; Males per 100 females: 101.7; Marriage status: 17.8% never married, 57.1% now married, 2.1% separated, 9.5% widowed, 15.5% divorced; Foreign born: 1.0%; Speak English only: 97.6%; With disability: 25.4%; Veterans: 16.5%; Ancestry: 30.5% German, 14.7% Irish, 14.1% English, 11.5% Polish, 8.5% French
Religion: Six largest groups: 9.1% Lutheran, 7.8% Catholicism, 4.0% Presbyterian-Reformed, 1.7% Methodist/Pietist, 1.4% Non-denominational Protestant, 1.4% Baptist
Economy: Unemployment rate: 8.4%; Leading industries: 19.2% construction; 16.7% retail trade; 11.6% other services (except public administration); Farms: 151 totaling 24,337 acres; Company size: 0 employ 1,000 or more persons, 0 employ 500 to 999 persons, 1 employs 100 to 499 persons, 197 employ less than 100 persons; Business ownership: 257 women-owned, n/a Black-owned, n/a Hispanic-owned, n/a Asian-owned
Employment: 10.3% management, business, and financial, 2.6% computer, engineering, and science, 5.6% education, legal, community service, arts, and media, 5.0% healthcare practitioners, 22.0% service, 23.2% sales and office, 14.2% natural resources, construction, and maintenance, 17.1% production, transportation, and material moving
Income: Per capita: $19,661; Median household: $35,261; Average household: $43,270; Households with income of $100,000 or more: 4.5%; Poverty rate: 18.1%
Educational Attainment: High school diploma or higher: 84.9%; Bachelor's degree or higher: 9.9%; Graduate/professional degree or higher: 3.7%
Housing: Homeownership rate: 85.5%; Median home value: $93,700; Median year structure built: 1973; Homeowner vacancy rate: 4.1%; Median gross rent: $635 per month; Rental vacancy rate: 11.7%
Vital Statistics: Birth rate: 58.8 per 10,000 population; Death rate: 172.2 per 10,000 population; Age-adjusted cancer mortality rate: 138.9 deaths per 100,000 population
Health Insurance: 87.2% have insurance; 60.5% have private insurance; 52.4% have public insurance; 12.8% do not have insurance; 5.1% of children under 18 do not have insurance
Health Care: Physicians: 9.5 per 10,000 population; Hospital beds: 0.0 per 10,000 population; Hospital admissions: 0.0 per 10,000 population
Transportation: Commute: 90.4% car, 0.0% public transportation, 3.6% walk, 5.9% work from home; Median travel time to work: 26.1 minutes

Presidential Election: 40.6% Obama, 58.0% Romney (2012)
National and State Parks: Clear Lake State Park; Presque Isle State Forest
Additional Information Contacts
Montmorency Government . . . . (989) 785-8022
   http://www.montmorencycountymichigan.us

Montmorency County Communities

ALBERT (township). Covers a land area of 65.656 square miles and a water area of 4.708 square miles. Located at 44.89° N. Lat; 84.24° W. Long.
Population: 2,526; Growth (since 2000): -6.3%; Density: 38.5 persons per square mile; Race: 97.6% White, 0.3% Black/African American, 0.0% Asian, 0.2% American Indian/Alaska Native, 0.0% Native Hawaiian/Other Pacific Islander, 1.7% Two or more races, 0.9% Hispanic of any race; Average household size: 2.07; Median age: 54.1; Age under 18: 16.1%; Age 65 and over: 30.8%; Males per 100 females: 98.0; Marriage status: 15.6% never married, 54.4% now married, 2.5% separated, 9.5% widowed, 20.5% divorced; Foreign born: 1.2%; Speak English only: 98.5%; With disability: 20.3%; Veterans: 16.3%; Ancestry: 23.3% German, 12.7% Polish, 12.0% Irish, 10.6% English, 8.3% European
Employment: 3.3% management, business, and financial, 4.8% computer, engineering, and science, 9.4% education, legal, community service, arts, and media, 3.6% healthcare practitioners, 17.2% service, 26.1% sales and office, 11.5% natural resources, construction, and maintenance, 24.2% production, transportation, and material moving
Income: Per capita: $19,390; Median household: $33,585; Average household: $42,595; Households with income of $100,000 or more: 4.3%; Poverty rate: 20.6%
Educational Attainment: High school diploma or higher: 88.2%; Bachelor's degree or higher: 9.8%; Graduate/professional degree or higher: 5.0%
Housing: Homeownership rate: 82.5%; Median home value: $88,300; Median year structure built: 1972; Homeowner vacancy rate: 4.7%; Median gross rent: $672 per month; Rental vacancy rate: 12.2%
Health Insurance: 85.5% have insurance; 55.0% have private insurance; 57.0% have public insurance; 14.5% do not have insurance; 4.6% of children under 18 do not have insurance
Transportation: Commute: 89.8% car, 0.0% public transportation, 4.2% walk, 6.1% work from home; Median travel time to work: 25.9 minutes

ATLANTA (CDP). County seat. Covers a land area of 3.288 square miles and a water area of 0.165 square miles. Located at 45.00° N. Lat; 84.16° W. Long. Elevation is 892 feet.
History: Atlanta was founded by Alfred J. West in 1881. West, a Civil War veteran, named the village after Atlanta, Georgia.
Population: 827; Growth (since 2000): 9.2%; Density: 251.5 persons per square mile; Race: 97.7% White, 0.1% Black/African American, 0.6% Asian, 0.0% American Indian/Alaska Native, 0.0% Native Hawaiian/Other Pacific Islander, 1.6% Two or more races, 1.1% Hispanic of any race; Average household size: 2.20; Median age: 47.1; Age under 18: 18.7%; Age 65 and over: 20.7%; Males per 100 females: 107.3
School District(s)
Atlanta Community Schools (PK-12)
   2012-13 Enrollment: 254 . . . . (989) 785-4877
Housing: Homeownership rate: 75.6%; Homeowner vacancy rate: 7.2%; Rental vacancy rate: 18.0%
Newspapers: Montmorency Tribune (weekly circulation 4500)

AVERY (township). Covers a land area of 35.020 square miles and a water area of 0.298 square miles. Located at 44.98° N. Lat; 84.07° W. Long. Elevation is 801 feet.
Population: 646; Growth (since 2000): -9.9%; Density: 18.4 persons per square mile; Race: 99.1% White, 0.0% Black/African American, 0.2% Asian, 0.0% American Indian/Alaska Native, 0.0% Native Hawaiian/Other Pacific Islander, 0.2% Two or more races, 1.2% Hispanic of any race; Average household size: 2.17; Median age: 54.8; Age under 18: 16.1%; Age 65 and over: 28.3%; Males per 100 females: 103.8
Housing: Homeownership rate: 90.6%; Homeowner vacancy rate: 4.2%; Rental vacancy rate: 3.2%

BRILEY (township). Covers a land area of 68.363 square miles and a water area of 1.978 square miles. Located at 45.02° N. Lat; 84.19° W. Long.
Population: 1,860; Growth (since 2000): -8.3%; Density: 27.2 persons per square mile; Race: 97.4% White, 0.3% Black/African American, 0.3% Asian, 0.4% American Indian/Alaska Native, 0.0% Native Hawaiian/Other Pacific Islander, 1.7% Two or more races, 1.6% Hispanic of any race; Average household size: 2.18; Median age: 50.7; Age under 18: 16.9%; Age 65 and over: 23.5%; Males per 100 females: 104.2
Housing: Homeownership rate: 83.8%; Homeowner vacancy rate: 5.4%; Rental vacancy rate: 13.6%

CANADA CREEK RANCH (CDP). Covers a land area of 3.457 square miles and a water area of 0.256 square miles. Located at 45.18° N. Lat; 84.21° W. Long. Elevation is 820 feet.
Population: 304; Growth (since 2000): -24.9%; Density: 87.9 persons per square mile; Race: 97.4% White, 0.0% Black/African American, 0.3% Asian, 0.7% American Indian/Alaska Native, 0.0% Native Hawaiian/Other Pacific Islander, 1.6% Two or more races, 0.3% Hispanic of any race; Average household size: 1.95; Median age: 64.4; Age under 18: 8.6%; Age 65 and over: 48.7%; Males per 100 females: 100.0
Housing: Homeownership rate: 99.3%; Homeowner vacancy rate: 0.6%; Rental vacancy rate: 75.0%

HILLMAN (township). Covers a land area of 67.629 square miles and a water area of 1.388 square miles. Located at 45.07° N. Lat; 84.00° W. Long. Elevation is 807 feet.
Population: 2,175; Growth (since 2000): -4.1%; Density: 32.2 persons per square mile; Race: 97.7% White, 0.1% Black/African American, 0.1% Asian, 0.5% American Indian/Alaska Native, 0.0% Native Hawaiian/Other Pacific Islander, 1.4% Two or more races, 1.0% Hispanic of any race; Average household size: 2.25; Median age: 50.0; Age under 18: 18.1%; Age 65 and over: 24.3%; Males per 100 females: 99.0
School District(s)
Hillman Community Schools (PK-12)
   2012-13 Enrollment: 516 . . . . (989) 742-2908
Housing: Homeownership rate: 81.1%; Homeowner vacancy rate: 4.0%; Rental vacancy rate: 13.4%

HILLMAN (village). Covers a land area of 1.653 square miles and a water area of 0.048 square miles. Located at 45.06° N. Lat; 83.90° W. Long. Elevation is 807 feet.
History: Hillman was founded in 1880 by John Hillman Stevens, who owned the land. Hillman developed as a popular destination for fishermen in the summer, and for deer hunters in the fall. A number of private hunting clubs were established in this area.
Population: 701; Growth (since 2000): 2.3%; Density: 424.2 persons per square mile; Race: 97.9% White, 0.1% Black/African American, 0.1% Asian, 0.7% American Indian/Alaska Native, 0.0% Native Hawaiian/Other Pacific Islander, 1.0% Two or more races, 1.4% Hispanic of any race; Average household size: 2.02; Median age: 51.4; Age under 18: 17.0%; Age 65 and over: 31.2%; Males per 100 females: 85.9
School District(s)
Hillman Community Schools (PK-12)
   2012-13 Enrollment: 516 . . . . (989) 742-2908
Housing: Homeownership rate: 68.7%; Homeowner vacancy rate: 4.2%; Rental vacancy rate: 21.0%

LEWISTON (CDP). Covers a land area of 6.134 square miles and a water area of 3.330 square miles. Located at 44.87° N. Lat; 84.33° W. Long. Elevation is 1,243 feet.
History: Lewiston grew up around the mill and general store of the Michelson & Hanson Lumber Company. It was named for Lewiston, New York.
Population: 1,392; Growth (since 2000): 40.6%; Density: 226.9 persons per square mile; Race: 97.5% White, 0.2% Black/African American, 0.1% Asian, 0.2% American Indian/Alaska Native, 0.0% Native Hawaiian/Other Pacific Islander, 1.8% Two or more races, 1.3% Hispanic of any race; Average household size: 2.02; Median age: 53.5; Age under 18: 16.7%; Age 65 and over: 30.9%; Males per 100 females: 93.9
School District(s)
Johannesburg-Lewiston Area Schools (KG-12)
   2012-13 Enrollment: 755 . . . . (989) 732-1773
Housing: Homeownership rate: 75.8%; Homeowner vacancy rate: 5.9%; Rental vacancy rate: 10.1%

Airports: Eagle II (general aviation)

LOUD (township). Covers a land area of 35.768 square miles and a water area of 0.094 square miles. Located at 44.91° N. Lat; 84.06° W. Long.
Population: 293; Growth (since 2000): 3.2%; Density: 8.2 persons per square mile; Race: 98.3% White, 0.0% Black/African American, 0.0% Asian, 0.0% American Indian/Alaska Native, 0.0% Native Hawaiian/Other Pacific Islander, 1.7% Two or more races, 0.0% Hispanic of any race; Average household size: 1.95; Median age: 55.8; Age under 18: 10.9%; Age 65 and over: 31.4%; Males per 100 females: 98.0
Housing: Homeownership rate: 91.3%; Homeowner vacancy rate: 6.8%; Rental vacancy rate: 0.0%

MONTMORENCY (township). Covers a land area of 136.610 square miles and a water area of 3.859 square miles. Located at 45.17° N. Lat; 84.13° W. Long.
Population: 1,117; Growth (since 2000): -7.1%; Density: 8.2 persons per square mile; Race: 97.6% White, 0.0% Black/African American, 0.4% Asian, 1.1% American Indian/Alaska Native, 0.0% Native Hawaiian/Other Pacific Islander, 0.9% Two or more races, 0.5% Hispanic of any race; Average household size: 2.12; Median age: 57.4; Age under 18: 13.3%; Age 65 and over: 32.9%; Males per 100 females: 101.3
Housing: Homeownership rate: 93.9%; Homeowner vacancy rate: 2.0%; Rental vacancy rate: 8.3%

RUST (township). Covers a land area of 68.518 square miles and a water area of 3.392 square miles. Located at 44.93° N. Lat; 83.96° W. Long. Elevation is 823 feet.
Population: 561; Growth (since 2000): 2.2%; Density: 8.2 persons per square mile; Race: 95.7% White, 0.0% Black/African American, 0.0% Asian, 0.7% American Indian/Alaska Native, 0.0% Native Hawaiian/Other Pacific Islander, 3.4% Two or more races, 1.1% Hispanic of any race; Average household size: 2.52; Median age: 44.5; Age under 18: 22.5%; Age 65 and over: 21.2%; Males per 100 females: 110.1
Housing: Homeownership rate: 90.6%; Homeowner vacancy rate: 1.9%; Rental vacancy rate: 8.7%

VIENNA (township). Covers a land area of 69.100 square miles and a water area of 0.272 square miles. Located at 45.03° N. Lat; 84.34° W. Long.
Population: 587; Growth (since 2000): 2.6%; Density: 8.5 persons per square mile; Race: 98.0% White, 0.0% Black/African American, 0.0% Asian, 0.7% American Indian/Alaska Native, 0.2% Native Hawaiian/Other Pacific Islander, 1.2% Two or more races, 0.3% Hispanic of any race; Average household size: 2.36; Median age: 48.1; Age under 18: 19.6%; Age 65 and over: 22.5%; Males per 100 females: 114.2
Housing: Homeownership rate: 90.3%; Homeowner vacancy rate: 2.2%; Rental vacancy rate: 3.7%

Muskegon County

Located in southwestern Michigan; bounded on the west by Lake Michigan; drained by the Muskegon and White Rivers; includes part of Manistee National Forest. Covers a land area of 499.246 square miles, a water area of 960.779 square miles, and is located in the Eastern Time Zone at 43.29° N. Lat., 86.75° W. Long. The county was founded in 1859. County seat is Muskegon.

Muskegon County is part of the Muskegon, MI Metropolitan Statistical Area. The entire metro area includes: Muskegon County, MI

Weather Station: Montague 4 NW   Elevation: 649 feet

	Jan	Feb	Mar	Apr	May	Jun	Jul	Aug	Sep	Oct	Nov	Dec
High	30	33	42	56	67	75	79	78	71	59	46	34
Low	18	19	25	34	43	52	57	57	50	40	32	23
Precip	1.5	1.2	2.2	3.3	3.2	2.7	2.7	3.6	3.7	3.6	3.4	1.9
Snow	25.1	14.7	6.6	1.3	tr	0.0	0.0	0.0	0.0	0.2	3.7	20.7

High and Low temperatures in degrees Fahrenheit; Precipitation and Snow in inches

Weather Station: Muskegon County Arpt   Elevation: 625 feet

	Jan	Feb	Mar	Apr	May	Jun	Jul	Aug	Sep	Oct	Nov	Dec
High	31	33	43	56	67	76	80	79	71	59	46	35
Low	19	20	26	36	46	55	61	60	52	41	33	24
Precip	2.1	1.8	2.4	3.0	3.2	2.6	2.4	3.5	3.8	3.1	3.4	2.6
Snow	29.2	18.8	9.2	2.5	tr	tr	tr	tr	tr	0.3	6.3	28.9

High and Low temperatures in degrees Fahrenheit; Precipitation and Snow in inches

Population: 172,188; Growth (since 2000): 1.2%; Density: 344.9 persons per square mile; Race: 80.0% White, 14.5% Black/African American, 0.5% Asian, 0.8% American Indian/Alaska Native, 0.0% Native Hawaiian/Other Pacific Islander, 2.8% two or more races, 4.8% Hispanic of any race; Average household size: 2.53; Median age: 38.2; Age under 18: 24.8%; Age 65 and over: 13.6%; Males per 100 females: 98.5; Marriage status: 30.3% never married, 49.7% now married, 1.6% separated, 6.4% widowed, 13.6% divorced; Foreign born: 1.9%; Speak English only: 95.8%; With disability: 14.8%; Veterans: 10.3%; Ancestry: 20.3% German, 10.6% Dutch, 10.3% Irish, 8.5% English, 6.0% Polish
Religion: Six largest groups: 7.9% Catholicism, 5.1% Presbyterian-Reformed, 3.6% Lutheran, 3.2% Methodist/Pietist, 2.9% Baptist, 1.9% Pentecostal
Economy: Unemployment rate: 5.5%; Leading industries: 17.3% retail trade; 12.3% other services (except public administration); 11.6% health care and social assistance; Farms: 514 totaling 74,246 acres; Company size: 3 employ 1,000 or more persons, 3 employ 500 to 999 persons, 67 employ 100 to 499 persons, 3,120 employ less than 100 persons; Business ownership: 3,068 women-owned, 559 Black-owned, 139 Hispanic-owned, 76 Asian-owned
Employment: 9.5% management, business, and financial, 4.2% computer, engineering, and science, 9.0% education, legal, community service, arts, and media, 5.3% healthcare practitioners, 20.2% service, 23.7% sales and office, 7.3% natural resources, construction, and maintenance, 20.8% production, transportation, and material moving
Income: Per capita: $20,621; Median household: $40,979; Average household: $52,917; Households with income of $100,000 or more: 11.6%; Poverty rate: 19.9%
Educational Attainment: High school diploma or higher: 88.0%; Bachelor's degree or higher: 17.2%; Graduate/professional degree or higher: 5.4%
Housing: Homeownership rate: 75.1%; Median home value: $100,900; Median year structure built: 1966; Homeowner vacancy rate: 2.8%; Median gross rent: $663 per month; Rental vacancy rate: 10.6%
Vital Statistics: Birth rate: 125.0 per 10,000 population; Death rate: 95.2 per 10,000 population; Age-adjusted cancer mortality rate: 212.5 deaths per 100,000 population
Health Insurance: 89.0% have insurance; 62.9% have private insurance; 40.2% have public insurance; 11.0% do not have insurance; 2.7% of children under 18 do not have insurance
Health Care: Physicians: 17.5 per 10,000 population; Hospital beds: 26.6 per 10,000 population; Hospital admissions: 1,162.0 per 10,000 population
Air Quality Index: 79.7% good, 18.9% moderate, 1.4% unhealthy for sensitive individuals, 0.0% unhealthy (percent of days)
Transportation: Commute: 93.6% car, 0.4% public transportation, 1.3% walk, 3.7% work from home; Median travel time to work: 21.0 minutes
Presidential Election: 58.4% Obama, 40.6% Romney (2012)
National and State Parks: Duck Lake State Park; Muskegon State Game Area; Muskegon State Park; P J Hoffmaster State Park
Additional Information Contacts
Muskegon Government . . . . (231) 724-6221
    http://www.co.muskegon.mi.us

Muskegon County Communities

BAILEY (unincorporated postal area)
ZCTA: 49303
    Covers a land area of 15.026 square miles and a water area of 0.053 square miles. Located at 43.27° N. Lat; 85.86° W. Long. Elevation is 837 feet.
    Population: 1,129; Growth (since 2000): 10.3%; Density: 75.1 persons per square mile; Race: 89.3% White, 0.3% Black/African American, 0.2% Asian, 0.4% American Indian/Alaska Native, 0.0% Native Hawaiian/Other Pacific Islander, 2.3% Two or more races, 11.3% Hispanic of any race; Average household size: 3.08; Median age: 34.1; Age under 18: 31.8%; Age 65 and over: 9.8%; Males per 100 females: 104.9

Housing: Homeownership rate: 91.0%; Homeowner vacancy rate: 1.8%; Rental vacancy rate: 13.2%

BLUE LAKE (township).
Covers a land area of 32.246 square miles and a water area of 3.497 square miles. Located at 43.43° N. Lat; 86.20° W. Long.

Population: 2,399; Growth (since 2000): 20.6%; Density: 74.4 persons per square mile; Race: 90.2% White, 3.0% Black/African American, 0.5% Asian, 2.4% American Indian/Alaska Native, 0.0% Native Hawaiian/Other Pacific Islander, 3.6% Two or more races, 2.6% Hispanic of any race; Average household size: 2.91; Median age: 37.8; Age under 18: 29.7%; Age 65 and over: 8.8%; Males per 100 females: 104.0

Housing: Homeownership rate: 85.2%; Homeowner vacancy rate: 2.0%; Rental vacancy rate: 4.7%

CASNOVIA (township).
Covers a land area of 35.597 square miles and a water area of 0.157 square miles. Located at 43.24° N. Lat; 85.84° W. Long. Elevation is 881 feet.

Population: 2,805; Growth (since 2000): 5.8%; Density: 78.8 persons per square mile; Race: 92.5% White, 0.6% Black/African American, 0.2% Asian, 0.2% American Indian/Alaska Native, 0.0% Native Hawaiian/Other Pacific Islander, 2.0% Two or more races, 8.2% Hispanic of any race; Average household size: 2.94; Median age: 35.5; Age under 18: 29.2%; Age 65 and over: 9.9%; Males per 100 females: 105.2; Marriage status: 25.9% never married, 59.1% now married, 2.1% separated, 4.1% widowed, 10.9% divorced; Foreign born: 4.5%; Speak English only: 93.0%; With disability: 14.8%; Veterans: 7.1%; Ancestry: 25.1% German, 12.5% Dutch, 11.6% Irish, 6.2% Swedish, 6.0% English

Employment: 9.9% management, business, and financial, 2.8% computer, engineering, and science, 6.7% education, legal, community service, arts, and media, 5.3% healthcare practitioners, 12.3% service, 21.4% sales and office, 23.3% natural resources, construction, and maintenance, 18.3% production, transportation, and material moving

Income: Per capita: $20,917; Median household: $51,563; Average household: $59,595; Households with income of $100,000 or more: 13.8%; Poverty rate: 14.0%

Educational Attainment: High school diploma or higher: 86.6%; Bachelor's degree or higher: 12.6%; Graduate/professional degree or higher: 1.1%

Housing: Homeownership rate: 87.2%; Median home value: $109,100; Median year structure built: 1971; Homeowner vacancy rate: 1.4%; Median gross rent: $579 per month; Rental vacancy rate: 9.8%

Health Insurance: 84.7% have insurance; 68.9% have private insurance; 25.7% have public insurance; 15.3% do not have insurance; 2.5% of children under 18 do not have insurance

Transportation: Commute: 84.2% car, 0.0% public transportation, 2.2% walk, 13.3% work from home; Median travel time to work: 29.2 minutes

CEDAR CREEK (township).
Covers a land area of 34.699 square miles and a water area of 1.362 square miles. Located at 43.35° N. Lat; 86.09° W. Long.

Population: 3,186; Growth (since 2000): 2.5%; Density: 91.8 persons per square mile; Race: 96.1% White, 1.0% Black/African American, 0.2% Asian, 0.4% American Indian/Alaska Native, 0.0% Native Hawaiian/Other Pacific Islander, 2.0% Two or more races, 2.5% Hispanic of any race; Average household size: 2.62; Median age: 40.9; Age under 18: 24.3%; Age 65 and over: 12.1%; Males per 100 females: 101.0; Marriage status: 16.1% never married, 69.8% now married, 0.7% separated, 5.7% widowed, 8.5% divorced; Foreign born: 0.0%; Speak English only: 99.3%; With disability: 10.8%; Veterans: 15.6%; Ancestry: 19.0% German, 13.4% Dutch, 12.0% American, 9.7% Polish, 8.9% English

Employment: 9.8% management, business, and financial, 3.2% computer, engineering, and science, 4.2% education, legal, community service, arts, and media, 4.4% healthcare practitioners, 18.7% service, 24.5% sales and office, 10.1% natural resources, construction, and maintenance, 25.1% production, transportation, and material moving

Income: Per capita: $25,976; Median household: $47,369; Average household: $59,740; Households with income of $100,000 or more: 18.8%; Poverty rate: 12.9%

Educational Attainment: High school diploma or higher: 91.0%; Bachelor's degree or higher: 12.4%; Graduate/professional degree or higher: 1.8%

Housing: Homeownership rate: 89.5%; Median home value: $110,500; Median year structure built: 1976; Homeowner vacancy rate: 2.5%; Median gross rent: $680 per month; Rental vacancy rate: 27.5%

Health Insurance: 91.1% have insurance; 68.7% have private insurance; 39.3% have public insurance; 8.9% do not have insurance; 4.8% of children under 18 do not have insurance

Transportation: Commute: 95.5% car, 0.0% public transportation, 0.9% walk, 2.3% work from home; Median travel time to work: 29.6 minutes

DALTON (township).
Covers a land area of 35.261 square miles and a water area of 1.024 square miles. Located at 43.35° N. Lat; 86.23° W. Long. Elevation is 659 feet.

Population: 9,300; Growth (since 2000): 15.6%; Density: 263.7 persons per square mile; Race: 94.1% White, 1.8% Black/African American, 0.2% Asian, 0.9% American Indian/Alaska Native, 0.0% Native Hawaiian/Other Pacific Islander, 2.2% Two or more races, 3.4% Hispanic of any race; Average household size: 2.76; Median age: 36.0; Age under 18: 27.5%; Age 65 and over: 9.7%; Males per 100 females: 102.5; Marriage status: 24.9% never married, 57.2% now married, 1.2% separated, 6.3% widowed, 11.6% divorced; Foreign born: 0.8%; Speak English only: 97.3%; With disability: 13.3%; Veterans: 10.9%; Ancestry: 26.2% German, 15.5% Dutch, 14.1% Irish, 8.4% English, 6.9% French

Employment: 8.0% management, business, and financial, 5.5% computer, engineering, and science, 10.1% education, legal, community service, arts, and media, 6.1% healthcare practitioners, 17.6% service, 23.2% sales and office, 6.6% natural resources, construction, and maintenance, 23.1% production, transportation, and material moving

Income: Per capita: $21,195; Median household: $52,544; Average household: $58,392; Households with income of $100,000 or more: 12.3%; Poverty rate: 13.8%

Educational Attainment: High school diploma or higher: 92.1%; Bachelor's degree or higher: 14.1%; Graduate/professional degree or higher: 4.5%

Housing: Homeownership rate: 90.6%; Median home value: $111,900; Median year structure built: 1990; Homeowner vacancy rate: 2.2%; Median gross rent: $708 per month; Rental vacancy rate: 11.8%

Health Insurance: 89.9% have insurance; 71.3% have private insurance; 31.1% have public insurance; 10.1% do not have insurance; 3.6% of children under 18 do not have insurance

Transportation: Commute: 97.0% car, 0.1% public transportation, 0.4% walk, 2.2% work from home; Median travel time to work: 22.4 minutes

Additional Information Contacts

Dalton Township . . . . (231) 766-3043
  http://www.daltontownship.org

EGELSTON (township).
Covers a land area of 31.954 square miles and a water area of 3.836 square miles. Located at 43.26° N. Lat; 86.08° W. Long.

Population: 9,909; Growth (since 2000): 3.9%; Density: 310.1 persons per square mile; Race: 93.1% White, 1.2% Black/African American, 0.4% Asian, 1.1% American Indian/Alaska Native, 0.0% Native Hawaiian/Other Pacific Islander, 3.0% Two or more races, 5.2% Hispanic of any race; Average household size: 2.73; Median age: 37.1; Age under 18: 26.7%; Age 65 and over: 11.8%; Males per 100 females: 96.0; Marriage status: 26.6% never married, 51.8% now married, 1.9% separated, 6.2% widowed, 15.4% divorced; Foreign born: 2.1%; Speak English only: 96.1%; With disability: 16.8%; Veterans: 10.1%; Ancestry: 21.7% German, 10.0% Irish, 9.8% Dutch, 7.6% English, 6.0% French

Employment: 4.3% management, business, and financial, 2.1% computer, engineering, and science, 5.6% education, legal, community service, arts, and media, 3.1% healthcare practitioners, 22.9% service, 27.8% sales and office, 6.2% natural resources, construction, and maintenance, 28.1% production, transportation, and material moving

Income: Per capita: $16,691; Median household: $36,279; Average household: $45,625; Households with income of $100,000 or more: 6.2%; Poverty rate: 19.9%

Educational Attainment: High school diploma or higher: 82.8%; Bachelor's degree or higher: 7.2%; Graduate/professional degree or higher: 2.6%

Housing: Homeownership rate: 88.4%; Median home value: $83,700; Median year structure built: 1980; Homeowner vacancy rate: 2.7%; Median gross rent: $646 per month; Rental vacancy rate: 9.4%

Health Insurance: 87.1% have insurance; 55.7% have private insurance; 43.1% have public insurance; 12.9% do not have insurance; 1.2% of children under 18 do not have insurance

Transportation: Commute: 96.1% car, 0.0% public transportation, 1.1% walk, 2.0% work from home; Median travel time to work: 24.3 minutes

Additional Information Contacts
Egelston Township . . . . (231) 788-2308
    http://www.egelstontwp.org

FRUITLAND (township). Covers a land area of 36.256 square miles and a water area of 3.134 square miles. Located at 43.34° N. Lat; 86.34° W. Long.

Population: 5,543; Growth (since 2000): 5.9%; Density: 152.9 persons per square mile; Race: 95.5% White, 0.7% Black/African American, 0.3% Asian, 1.1% American Indian/Alaska Native, 0.0% Native Hawaiian/Other Pacific Islander, 1.9% Two or more races, 2.0% Hispanic of any race; Average household size: 2.64; Median age: 44.0; Age under 18: 23.2%; Age 65 and over: 14.0%; Males per 100 females: 104.3; Marriage status: 18.7% never married, 65.8% now married, 1.4% separated, 4.0% widowed, 11.4% divorced; Foreign born: 0.5%; Speak English only: 96.8%; With disability: 12.6%; Veterans: 12.7%; Ancestry: 29.0% German, 12.7% Irish, 12.3% Dutch, 10.8% English, 8.0% American
Employment: 16.6% management, business, and financial, 7.3% computer, engineering, and science, 15.2% education, legal, community service, arts, and media, 2.8% healthcare practitioners, 12.5% service, 19.7% sales and office, 11.5% natural resources, construction, and maintenance, 14.5% production, transportation, and material moving
Income: Per capita: $26,742; Median household: $54,944; Average household: $69,869; Households with income of $100,000 or more: 17.6%; Poverty rate: 12.5%
Educational Attainment: High school diploma or higher: 90.5%; Bachelor's degree or higher: 27.6%; Graduate/professional degree or higher: 8.4%
Housing: Homeownership rate: 89.0%; Median home value: $151,900; Median year structure built: 1982; Homeowner vacancy rate: 2.0%; Median gross rent: $952 per month; Rental vacancy rate: 6.0%
Health Insurance: 92.1% have insurance; 74.6% have private insurance; 33.9% have public insurance; 7.9% do not have insurance; 0.0% of children under 18 do not have insurance
Transportation: Commute: 94.6% car, 0.0% public transportation, 1.2% walk, 3.6% work from home; Median travel time to work: 22.6 minutes

FRUITPORT (charter township). Covers a land area of 29.980 square miles and a water area of 0.393 square miles. Located at 43.15° N. Lat; 86.14° W. Long. Elevation is 627 feet.

Population: 13,598; Growth (since 2000): 8.5%; Density: 453.6 persons per square mile; Race: 94.7% White, 1.3% Black/African American, 0.8% Asian, 0.7% American Indian/Alaska Native, 0.0% Native Hawaiian/Other Pacific Islander, 1.7% Two or more races, 3.2% Hispanic of any race; Average household size: 2.65; Median age: 40.8; Age under 18: 24.7%; Age 65 and over: 13.6%; Males per 100 females: 98.1; Marriage status: 24.5% never married, 60.5% now married, 1.6% separated, 5.1% widowed, 9.9% divorced; Foreign born: 2.1%; Speak English only: 95.8%; With disability: 11.1%; Veterans: 10.3%; Ancestry: 24.9% German, 12.8% Dutch, 10.9% Irish, 8.3% Polish, 7.5% English
Employment: 11.4% management, business, and financial, 6.5% computer, engineering, and science, 6.4% education, legal, community service, arts, and media, 6.6% healthcare practitioners, 16.6% service, 21.8% sales and office, 6.1% natural resources, construction, and maintenance, 24.6% production, transportation, and material moving
Income: Per capita: $24,447; Median household: $52,121; Average household: $65,188; Households with income of $100,000 or more: 16.8%; Poverty rate: 8.9%
Educational Attainment: High school diploma or higher: 93.8%; Bachelor's degree or higher: 19.3%; Graduate/professional degree or higher: 5.8%
School District(s)
Fruitport Community Schools (PK-12)
    2012-13 Enrollment: 3,051 . . . . (231) 865-3154
Housing: Homeownership rate: 89.1%; Median home value: $118,900; Median year structure built: 1976; Homeowner vacancy rate: 1.9%; Median gross rent: $854 per month; Rental vacancy rate: 6.1%
Health Insurance: 92.3% have insurance; 76.0% have private insurance; 33.2% have public insurance; 7.7% do not have insurance; 2.1% of children under 18 do not have insurance
Transportation: Commute: 95.9% car, 0.0% public transportation, 0.5% walk, 3.5% work from home; Median travel time to work: 21.3 minutes
Additional Information Contacts
Fruitport Charter Township . . . . (231) 865-3151
    http://www.fruitporttownship-mi.gov

FRUITPORT (village). Covers a land area of 0.907 square miles and a water area of 0.110 square miles. Located at 43.13° N. Lat; 86.16° W. Long. Elevation is 627 feet.

Population: 1,093; Growth (since 2000): -2.8%; Density: 1,204.4 persons per square mile; Race: 95.8% White, 1.5% Black/African American, 0.4% Asian, 0.2% American Indian/Alaska Native, 0.0% Native Hawaiian/Other Pacific Islander, 1.1% Two or more races, 2.0% Hispanic of any race; Average household size: 2.48; Median age: 43.6; Age under 18: 22.5%; Age 65 and over: 16.3%; Males per 100 females: 100.9
School District(s)
Fruitport Community Schools (PK-12)
    2012-13 Enrollment: 3,051 . . . . (231) 865-3154
Housing: Homeownership rate: 82.7%; Homeowner vacancy rate: 1.6%; Rental vacancy rate: 11.4%
Safety: Violent crime rate: 311.9 per 10,000 population; Property crime rate: 4,899.1 per 10,000 population

HOLTON (township). Covers a land area of 34.667 square miles and a water area of 1.051 square miles. Located at 43.43° N. Lat; 86.09° W. Long. Elevation is 728 feet.

Population: 2,515; Growth (since 2000): -0.7%; Density: 72.5 persons per square mile; Race: 95.6% White, 0.4% Black/African American, 0.6% Asian, 1.3% American Indian/Alaska Native, 0.0% Native Hawaiian/Other Pacific Islander, 1.6% Two or more races, 2.3% Hispanic of any race; Average household size: 2.72; Median age: 41.2; Age under 18: 24.0%; Age 65 and over: 12.8%; Males per 100 females: 108.7; Marriage status: 27.9% never married, 56.2% now married, 2.2% separated, 4.6% widowed, 11.3% divorced; Foreign born: 0.2%; Speak English only: 94.1%; With disability: 14.6%; Veterans: 10.3%; Ancestry: 22.2% German, 13.1% Irish, 7.5% English, 6.1% French, 5.7% Dutch
Employment: 7.1% management, business, and financial, 1.8% computer, engineering, and science, 7.0% education, legal, community service, arts, and media, 5.1% healthcare practitioners, 15.4% service, 20.5% sales and office, 15.6% natural resources, construction, and maintenance, 27.4% production, transportation, and material moving
Income: Per capita: $17,824; Median household: $43,661; Average household: $53,864; Households with income of $100,000 or more: 12.8%; Poverty rate: 30.3%
Educational Attainment: High school diploma or higher: 82.2%; Bachelor's degree or higher: 7.6%; Graduate/professional degree or higher: 3.0%
School District(s)
Holton Public Schools (PK-12)
    2012-13 Enrollment: 886 . . . . (231) 821-1700
Housing: Homeownership rate: 84.4%; Median home value: $92,700; Median year structure built: 1983; Homeowner vacancy rate: 2.3%; Median gross rent: $610 per month; Rental vacancy rate: 11.1%
Health Insurance: 82.0% have insurance; 50.2% have private insurance; 42.3% have public insurance; 18.0% do not have insurance; 11.5% of children under 18 do not have insurance
Transportation: Commute: 91.5% car, 0.5% public transportation, 1.2% walk, 2.7% work from home; Median travel time to work: 22.8 minutes

LAKETON (township). Covers a land area of 17.451 square miles and a water area of 1.394 square miles. Located at 43.27° N. Lat; 86.32° W. Long.

History: Laketon Township was created by a division in Muskegon Township in 1865. Its name came from its setting, surrounded on three sides by lakes.
Population: 7,563; Growth (since 2000): 2.7%; Density: 433.4 persons per square mile; Race: 94.6% White, 1.9% Black/African American, 0.6% Asian, 0.5% American Indian/Alaska Native, 0.0% Native Hawaiian/Other Pacific Islander, 2.1% Two or more races, 2.5% Hispanic of any race; Average household size: 2.59; Median age: 42.5; Age under 18: 23.9%; Age 65 and over: 14.8%; Males per 100 females: 99.3; Marriage status: 21.7% never married, 61.2% now married, 0.2% separated, 6.0% widowed, 11.0% divorced; Foreign born: 2.2%; Speak English only: 96.5%; With disability: 11.3%; Veterans: 12.8%; Ancestry: 27.2% German, 15.5% Irish, 13.8% Dutch, 12.5% English, 9.0% Polish
Employment: 18.1% management, business, and financial, 4.2% computer, engineering, and science, 8.7% education, legal, community service, arts, and media, 8.0% healthcare practitioners, 14.9% service, 26.4% sales and office, 5.8% natural resources, construction, and maintenance, 13.9% production, transportation, and material moving

Income: Per capita: $28,612; Median household: $59,668; Average household: $73,816; Households with income of $100,000 or more: 23.3%; Poverty rate: 5.5%
Educational Attainment: High school diploma or higher: 95.9%; Bachelor's degree or higher: 29.5%; Graduate/professional degree or higher: 10.3%
Housing: Homeownership rate: 90.4%; Median home value: $140,200; Median year structure built: 1973; Homeowner vacancy rate: 1.6%; Median gross rent: $784 per month; Rental vacancy rate: 11.7%
Health Insurance: 92.1% have insurance; 80.0% have private insurance; 27.7% have public insurance; 7.9% do not have insurance; 1.0% of children under 18 do not have insurance
Transportation: Commute: 91.0% car, 0.2% public transportation, 1.3% walk, 6.4% work from home; Median travel time to work: 22.6 minutes

LAKEWOOD CLUB (village). Covers a land area of 1.913 square miles and a water area of 0.154 square miles. Located at 43.38° N. Lat; 86.26° W. Long. Elevation is 679 feet.
Population: 1,291; Growth (since 2000): 28.3%; Density: 674.7 persons per square mile; Race: 93.5% White, 1.9% Black/African American, 0.2% Asian, 1.7% American Indian/Alaska Native, 0.1% Native Hawaiian/Other Pacific Islander, 2.0% Two or more races, 3.4% Hispanic of any race; Average household size: 2.82; Median age: 31.7; Age under 18: 30.4%; Age 65 and over: 5.7%; Males per 100 females: 104.3
Housing: Homeownership rate: 93.4%; Homeowner vacancy rate: 2.3%; Rental vacancy rate: 11.8%

MONTAGUE (city). Covers a land area of 2.555 square miles and a water area of 0.710 square miles. Located at 43.41° N. Lat; 86.36° W. Long. Elevation is 630 feet.
History: Montague was established at the head of White Lake. Industries in the early 1900's included a foundry and canning factory. Navy beans, grown in the area, were shipped from Montague.
Population: 2,361; Growth (since 2000): -1.9%; Density: 924.1 persons per square mile; Race: 96.0% White, 0.6% Black/African American, 0.3% Asian, 1.0% American Indian/Alaska Native, 0.0% Native Hawaiian/Other Pacific Islander, 1.6% Two or more races, 3.4% Hispanic of any race; Average household size: 2.35; Median age: 39.9; Age under 18: 25.2%; Age 65 and over: 16.1%; Males per 100 females: 85.3
School District(s)
Montague Area Public Schools (PK-12)
    2012-13 Enrollment: 1,484 . . . . (231) 893-1515
Housing: Homeownership rate: 70.2%; Homeowner vacancy rate: 3.8%; Rental vacancy rate: 9.6%

MONTAGUE (township). Covers a land area of 18.579 square miles and a water area of 0.714 square miles. Located at 43.45° N. Lat; 86.35° W. Long. Elevation is 630 feet.
History: Incorporated as village 1883, as city 1935.
Population: 1,600; Growth (since 2000): -2.3%; Density: 86.1 persons per square mile; Race: 94.3% White, 0.7% Black/African American, 0.3% Asian, 0.8% American Indian/Alaska Native, 0.0% Native Hawaiian/Other Pacific Islander, 2.8% Two or more races, 4.9% Hispanic of any race; Average household size: 2.59; Median age: 43.1; Age under 18: 23.4%; Age 65 and over: 15.4%; Males per 100 females: 96.1
School District(s)
Montague Area Public Schools (PK-12)
    2012-13 Enrollment: 1,484 . . . . (231) 893-1515
Housing: Homeownership rate: 89.2%; Homeowner vacancy rate: 1.6%; Rental vacancy rate: 1.4%

MOORLAND (township). Covers a land area of 35.682 square miles and a water area of 0.852 square miles. Located at 43.25° N. Lat; 85.97° W. Long. Elevation is 682 feet.
Population: 1,575; Growth (since 2000): -2.5%; Density: 44.1 persons per square mile; Race: 96.5% White, 0.3% Black/African American, 0.2% Asian, 0.4% American Indian/Alaska Native, 0.0% Native Hawaiian/Other Pacific Islander, 0.8% Two or more races, 4.7% Hispanic of any race; Average household size: 2.74; Median age: 39.6; Age under 18: 24.4%; Age 65 and over: 11.7%; Males per 100 females: 112.0
Housing: Homeownership rate: 89.5%; Homeowner vacancy rate: 1.9%; Rental vacancy rate: 4.6%

MUSKEGON (charter township). Covers a land area of 22.944 square miles and a water area of 0.868 square miles. Located at 43.26° N. Lat; 86.20° W. Long. Elevation is 617 feet.
History: A fur-trading post was established here c.1810. The first sawmill was built in 1837, and the lumber industry thrived until 1890, when the city was swept by fire. Incorporated as a city 1869.
Population: 17,840; Growth (since 2000): 0.6%; Density: 777.6 persons per square mile; Race: 87.9% White, 6.1% Black/African American, 0.4% Asian, 1.1% American Indian/Alaska Native, 0.0% Native Hawaiian/Other Pacific Islander, 3.2% Two or more races, 5.1% Hispanic of any race; Average household size: 2.58; Median age: 37.2; Age under 18: 26.3%; Age 65 and over: 14.2%; Males per 100 females: 93.1; Marriage status: 28.9% never married, 52.0% now married, 1.3% separated, 7.3% widowed, 11.8% divorced; Foreign born: 0.6%; Speak English only: 97.3%; With disability: 14.7%; Veterans: 12.5%; Ancestry: 22.9% German, 10.9% Dutch, 10.1% Irish, 9.5% Polish, 8.9% English
Employment: 6.2% management, business, and financial, 3.1% computer, engineering, and science, 6.3% education, legal, community service, arts, and media, 4.6% healthcare practitioners, 20.2% service, 27.2% sales and office, 8.5% natural resources, construction, and maintenance, 23.9% production, transportation, and material moving
Income: Per capita: $17,754; Median household: $37,307; Average household: $47,110; Households with income of $100,000 or more: 9.2%; Poverty rate: 21.7%
Educational Attainment: High school diploma or higher: 85.4%; Bachelor's degree or higher: 10.1%; Graduate/professional degree or higher: 3.2%
School District(s)
Fruitport Community Schools (PK-12)
    2012-13 Enrollment: 3,051 . . . . (231) 865-3154
Mona Shores Public SD (PK-12)
    2012-13 Enrollment: 3,791 . . . . (231) 780-4751
Muskegon Area ISD (PK-12)
    2012-13 Enrollment: 869. . . . . (231) 777-2637
Muskegon Heights SD (PK-12)
    2012-13 Enrollment: 2. . . . . (231) 830-3221
Muskegon Public Schools (PK-12)
    2012-13 Enrollment: 4,773 . . . . (231) 720-2000
North Muskegon Public Schools (KG-12)
    2012-13 Enrollment: 987. . . . . (231) 719-4100
Oakridge Public Schools (PK-12)
    2012-13 Enrollment: 1,902 . . . . (231) 788-7100
Orchard View Schools (PK-12)
    2012-13 Enrollment: 2,765 . . . . (231) 760-1309
Ravenna Public Schools (PK-12)
    2012-13 Enrollment: 1,111 . . . . (231) 853-2231
Reeths-Puffer Schools (PK-12)
    2012-13 Enrollment: 3,814 . . . . (231) 719-3101
Three Oaks Public Schools Academy (PK-12)
    2012-13 Enrollment: 323. . . . . (231) 767-3365
Timberland Academy (KG-12)
    2012-13 Enrollment: 490. . . . . (231) 767-9700
Waypoint Academy (KG-12)
    2012-13 Enrollment: 229. . . . . (231) 777-4972
Four-year College(s)
Baker College of Muskegon (Private, Not-for-profit)
    Fall 2013 Enrollment: 4,021 . . . . (231) 777-8800
    2013-14 Tuition: In-state $8,100; Out-of-state $8,100
Two-year College(s)
Muskegon Community College (Public)
    Fall 2013 Enrollment: 4,879 . . . . (231) 773-9131
    2013-14 Tuition: In-state $5,380; Out-of-state $7,180
Housing: Homeownership rate: 78.8%; Median home value: $88,500; Median year structure built: 1969; Homeowner vacancy rate: 1.9%; Median gross rent: $686 per month; Rental vacancy rate: 4.4%
Health Insurance: 88.0% have insurance; 60.3% have private insurance; 39.8% have public insurance; 12.0% do not have insurance; 5.1% of children under 18 do not have insurance
Hospitals: Mercy Health Hackley Campus (181 beds); Mercy Health Partners - Mercy Campus (282 beds)
Newspapers: Muskegon Chronicle (daily circulation 42800); Norton-Lakeshore Examiner (weekly circulation 3000)
Transportation: Commute: 95.5% car, 0.2% public transportation, 0.5% walk, 2.8% work from home; Median travel time to work: 19.0 minutes
Airports: Muskegon County (primary service/non-hub)

Additional Information Contacts

Muskegon Charter Township . . . . (231) 777-2555
http://www.muskegontwp.org

MUSKEGON (city). County seat. Covers a land area of 14.211 square miles and a water area of 3.911 square miles. Located at 43.23° N. Lat; 86.26° W. Long. Elevation is 617 feet.

History: Muskegon's location along the south shore of Muskegon Lake, an arm of Lake Michigan, shaped its development as a lumber center for the Muskegon River valley. In the 1880's, the town had 47 sawmills, earning for it the reputation of Lumber Queen as well as Saloon Queen and Gambling Queen. With the decline of lumbering in the 1890's, Muskegon began to utilize its port for other shipping and more diversified industry. The parent factory of the Continental Motors Corporation was established in Muskegon. In 1927, discovery of oil under the city attracted additional industry.

Population: 38,401; Growth (since 2000): -4.2%; Density: 2,702.2 persons per square mile; Race: 57.0% White, 34.5% Black/African American, 0.4% Asian, 0.9% American Indian/Alaska Native, 0.0% Native Hawaiian/Other Pacific Islander, 4.5% Two or more races, 8.2% Hispanic of any race; Average household size: 2.38; Median age: 34.1; Age under 18: 23.3%; Age 65 and over: 11.6%; Males per 100 females: 108.9; Marriage status: 43.6% never married, 31.7% now married, 2.2% separated, 6.6% widowed, 18.1% divorced; Foreign born: 2.4%; Speak English only: 94.0%; With disability: 19.0%; Veterans: 8.1%; Ancestry: 12.2% German, 6.4% Irish, 6.3% English, 5.3% Dutch, 3.8% Polish

Employment: 5.9% management, business, and financial, 3.4% computer, engineering, and science, 8.3% education, legal, community service, arts, and media, 4.9% healthcare practitioners, 30.4% service, 21.4% sales and office, 5.1% natural resources, construction, and maintenance, 20.6% production, transportation, and material moving

Income: Per capita: $14,699; Median household: $26,079; Average household: $37,030; Households with income of $100,000 or more: 4.5%; Poverty rate: 35.3%

Educational Attainment: High school diploma or higher: 82.3%; Bachelor's degree or higher: 10.9%; Graduate/professional degree or higher: 2.7%

School District(s)

Fruitport Community Schools (PK-12)
    2012-13 Enrollment: 3,051 . . . . (231) 865-3154
Mona Shores Public SD (PK-12)
    2012-13 Enrollment: 3,791 . . . . (231) 780-4751
Muskegon Area ISD (PK-12)
    2012-13 Enrollment: 869 . . . . (231) 777-2637
Muskegon Heights SD (PK-12)
    2012-13 Enrollment: 2 . . . . (231) 830-3221
Muskegon Public Schools (PK-12)
    2012-13 Enrollment: 4,773 . . . . (231) 720-2000
North Muskegon Public Schools (KG-12)
    2012-13 Enrollment: 987 . . . . (231) 719-4100
Oakridge Public Schools (PK-12)
    2012-13 Enrollment: 1,902 . . . . (231) 788-7100
Orchard View Schools (PK-12)
    2012-13 Enrollment: 2,765 . . . . (231) 760-1309
Ravenna Public Schools (PK-12)
    2012-13 Enrollment: 1,111 . . . . (231) 853-2231
Reeths-Puffer Schools (PK-12)
    2012-13 Enrollment: 3,814 . . . . (231) 719-3101
Three Oaks Public Schools Academy (PK-12)
    2012-13 Enrollment: 323 . . . . (231) 767-3365
Timberland Academy (KG-12)
    2012-13 Enrollment: 490 . . . . (231) 767-9700
Waypoint Academy (KG-12)
    2012-13 Enrollment: 229 . . . . (231) 777-4972

Four-year College(s)

Baker College of Muskegon (Private, Not-for-profit)
    Fall 2013 Enrollment: 4,021 . . . . (231) 777-8800
    2013-14 Tuition: In-state $8,100; Out-of-state $8,100

Two-year College(s)

Muskegon Community College (Public)
    Fall 2013 Enrollment: 4,879 . . . . (231) 773-9131
    2013-14 Tuition: In-state $5,380; Out-of-state $7,180

Housing: Homeownership rate: 52.5%; Median home value: $67,500; Median year structure built: 1951; Homeowner vacancy rate: 5.2%; Median gross rent: $603 per month; Rental vacancy rate: 10.5%

Health Insurance: 84.4% have insurance; 44.8% have private insurance; 50.0% have public insurance; 15.6% do not have insurance; 3.4% of children under 18 do not have insurance

Hospitals: Mercy Health Hackley Campus (181 beds); Mercy Health Partners - Mercy Campus (282 beds)

Safety: Violent crime rate: 88.7 per 10,000 population; Property crime rate: 537.4 per 10,000 population

Newspapers: Muskegon Chronicle (daily circulation 42800); Norton-Lakeshore Examiner (weekly circulation 3000)

Transportation: Commute: 90.6% car, 1.2% public transportation, 3.0% walk, 3.8% work from home; Median travel time to work: 17.8 minutes

Airports: Muskegon County (primary service/non-hub)

Additional Information Contacts

City of Muskegon . . . . (231) 724-6705
http://www.muskegon-mi.gov

MUSKEGON HEIGHTS (city). Covers a land area of 3.185 square miles and a water area of <.001 square miles. Located at 43.20° N. Lat; 86.24° W. Long. Elevation is 627 feet.

Population: 10,856; Growth (since 2000): -9.9%; Density: 3,408.2 persons per square mile; Race: 16.0% White, 78.3% Black/African American, 0.1% Asian, 0.3% American Indian/Alaska Native, 0.0% Native Hawaiian/Other Pacific Islander, 3.8% Two or more races, 4.2% Hispanic of any race; Average household size: 2.66; Median age: 30.3; Age under 18: 32.3%; Age 65 and over: 9.6%; Males per 100 females: 86.1; Marriage status: 48.1% never married, 30.0% now married, 3.0% separated, 7.6% widowed, 14.4% divorced; Foreign born: 0.3%; Speak English only: 98.1%; With disability: 19.3%; Veterans: 6.1%; Ancestry: 3.0% Irish, 2.0% American, 1.8% German, 1.7% African, 1.3% English

Employment: 3.7% management, business, and financial, 2.3% computer, engineering, and science, 9.4% education, legal, community service, arts, and media, 2.5% healthcare practitioners, 30.6% service, 12.6% sales and office, 5.3% natural resources, construction, and maintenance, 33.6% production, transportation, and material moving

Income: Per capita: $11,593; Median household: $19,368; Average household: $28,441; Households with income of $100,000 or more: 2.4%; Poverty rate: 46.5%

Educational Attainment: High school diploma or higher: 78.8%; Bachelor's degree or higher: 5.1%; Graduate/professional degree or higher: 1.5%

Housing: Homeownership rate: 51.1%; Median home value: $46,800; Median year structure built: 1948; Homeowner vacancy rate: 5.4%; Median gross rent: $639 per month; Rental vacancy rate: 13.2%

Health Insurance: 88.1% have insurance; 31.3% have private insurance; 67.2% have public insurance; 11.9% do not have insurance; 0.6% of children under 18 do not have insurance

Safety: Violent crime rate: 191.3 per 10,000 population; Property crime rate: 656.6 per 10,000 population

Transportation: Commute: 90.9% car, 0.9% public transportation, 1.6% walk, 4.3% work from home; Median travel time to work: 17.9 minutes

Additional Information Contacts

City of Muskegon Heights . . . . (231) 733-8820
http://www.cityofmuskegonheights.org

NORTH MUSKEGON (city). Covers a land area of 1.760 square miles and a water area of 2.342 square miles. Located at 43.25° N. Lat; 86.27° W. Long. Elevation is 620 feet.

History: Incorporated as village 1881, as city 1891.

Population: 3,786; Growth (since 2000): -6.1%; Density: 2,151.0 persons per square mile; Race: 94.6% White, 2.1% Black/African American, 0.7% Asian, 0.6% American Indian/Alaska Native, 0.1% Native Hawaiian/Other Pacific Islander, 1.8% Two or more races, 2.4% Hispanic of any race; Average household size: 2.30; Median age: 45.0; Age under 18: 22.7%; Age 65 and over: 20.6%; Males per 100 females: 87.6; Marriage status: 23.3% never married, 60.3% now married, 0.8% separated, 7.8% widowed, 8.6% divorced; Foreign born: 4.3%; Speak English only: 95.9%; With disability: 11.3%; Veterans: 9.9%; Ancestry: 24.3% German, 17.4% Irish, 16.6% English, 15.1% Dutch, 6.6% Swedish

Employment: 16.5% management, business, and financial, 6.6% computer, engineering, and science, 15.5% education, legal, community service, arts, and media, 9.7% healthcare practitioners, 12.5% service, 21.9% sales and office, 5.0% natural resources, construction, and maintenance, 12.3% production, transportation, and material moving

Income: Per capita: $34,553; Median household: $57,394; Average household: $76,778; Households with income of $100,000 or more: 26.4%; Poverty rate: 5.8%

Educational Attainment: High school diploma or higher: 91.9%; Bachelor's degree or higher: 40.5%; Graduate/professional degree or higher: 21.4%

Housing: Homeownership rate: 76.1%; Median home value: $133,300; Median year structure built: 1961; Homeowner vacancy rate: 2.7%; Median gross rent: $700 per month; Rental vacancy rate: 13.9%

Health Insurance: 89.4% have insurance; 77.6% have private insurance; 32.4% have public insurance; 10.6% do not have insurance; 7.9% of children under 18 do not have insurance

Safety: Violent crime rate: 13.3 per 10,000 population; Property crime rate: 221.0 per 10,000 population

Transportation: Commute: 94.7% car, 0.0% public transportation, 0.8% walk, 3.0% work from home; Median travel time to work: 17.4 minutes

Additional Information Contacts

City of North Muskegon . . . . (231) 744-1621
  http://www.cityofnorthmuskegon.com

NORTON SHORES (city). Covers a land area of 23.236 square miles and a water area of 1.384 square miles. Located at 43.17° N. Lat; 86.24° W. Long. Elevation is 610 feet.

Population: 23,994; Growth (since 2000): 6.5%; Density: 1,032.6 persons per square mile; Race: 91.8% White, 3.2% Black/African American, 1.2% Asian, 0.8% American Indian/Alaska Native, 0.0% Native Hawaiian/Other Pacific Islander, 2.0% Two or more races, 3.8% Hispanic of any race; Average household size: 2.39; Median age: 43.3; Age under 18: 22.0%; Age 65 and over: 17.8%; Males per 100 females: 94.4; Marriage status: 25.4% never married, 54.6% now married, 1.4% separated, 6.9% widowed, 13.1% divorced; Foreign born: 3.2%; Speak English only: 95.3%; With disability: 12.3%; Veterans: 11.1%; Ancestry: 22.8% German, 15.4% Dutch, 12.6% Irish, 11.2% English, 6.8% Polish

Employment: 12.2% management, business, and financial, 4.3% computer, engineering, and science, 11.0% education, legal, community service, arts, and media, 6.1% healthcare practitioners, 18.1% service, 29.3% sales and office, 4.4% natural resources, construction, and maintenance, 14.5% production, transportation, and material moving

Income: Per capita: $27,325; Median household: $48,536; Average household: $65,147; Households with income of $100,000 or more: 17.4%; Poverty rate: 8.9%

Educational Attainment: High school diploma or higher: 92.5%; Bachelor's degree or higher: 29.2%; Graduate/professional degree or higher: 9.3%

Vocational/Technical School(s)

Nuvo College of Cosmetology (Private, For-profit)
  Fall 2013 Enrollment: 44 . . . . (231) 799-1500
  2013-14 Tuition: $9,445

Housing: Homeownership rate: 81.6%; Median home value: $114,500; Median year structure built: 1970; Homeowner vacancy rate: 2.5%; Median gross rent: $794 per month; Rental vacancy rate: 12.5%

Health Insurance: 92.8% have insurance; 76.9% have private insurance; 34.3% have public insurance; 7.2% do not have insurance; 1.5% of children under 18 do not have insurance

Transportation: Commute: 94.8% car, 0.4% public transportation, 0.4% walk, 3.3% work from home; Median travel time to work: 19.3 minutes

Additional Information Contacts

City of Norton Shores . . . . (231) 798-4391
  http://www.nortonshores.org

RAVENNA (township). Covers a land area of 36.167 square miles and a water area of 0.209 square miles. Located at 43.17° N. Lat; 85.97° W. Long. Elevation is 673 feet.

History: Ravenna grew around a sawmill built in 1844 by E.B. Bostwick. The township was organized in 1848, and named for Ravenna, Ohio, the former home of the surveyor.

Population: 2,905; Growth (since 2000): 1.7%; Density: 80.3 persons per square mile; Race: 95.4% White, 0.2% Black/African American, 0.2% Asian, 0.4% American Indian/Alaska Native, 0.0% Native Hawaiian/Other Pacific Islander, 1.1% Two or more races, 6.0% Hispanic of any race; Average household size: 2.78; Median age: 36.6; Age under 18: 28.3%; Age 65 and over: 12.8%; Males per 100 females: 95.5; Marriage status: 24.7% never married, 64.4% now married, 0.2% separated, 3.7% widowed, 7.2% divorced; Foreign born: 5.0%; Speak English only: 93.4%;

With disability: 10.0%; Veterans: 7.9%; Ancestry: 24.8% German, 21.1% Dutch, 10.6% Irish, 10.1% English, 6.2% American

Employment: 14.3% management, business, and financial, 3.3% computer, engineering, and science, 10.9% education, legal, community service, arts, and media, 4.3% healthcare practitioners, 12.2% service, 22.1% sales and office, 14.5% natural resources, construction, and maintenance, 18.4% production, transportation, and material moving

Income: Per capita: $21,922; Median household: $53,393; Average household: $61,663; Households with income of $100,000 or more: 14.2%; Poverty rate: 8.6%

Educational Attainment: High school diploma or higher: 90.8%; Bachelor's degree or higher: 25.0%; Graduate/professional degree or higher: 6.7%

School District(s)

Ravenna Public Schools (PK-12)
  2012-13 Enrollment: 1,111 . . . . (231) 853-2231

Housing: Homeownership rate: 84.4%; Median home value: $121,700; Median year structure built: 1977; Homeowner vacancy rate: 1.9%; Median gross rent: $671 per month; Rental vacancy rate: 2.4%

Health Insurance: 91.1% have insurance; 79.1% have private insurance; 26.5% have public insurance; 8.9% do not have insurance; 0.7% of children under 18 do not have insurance

Transportation: Commute: 88.3% car, 0.0% public transportation, 0.8% walk, 9.8% work from home; Median travel time to work: 26.7 minutes

RAVENNA (village). Covers a land area of 1.214 square miles and a water area of <.001 square miles. Located at 43.19° N. Lat; 85.94° W. Long. Elevation is 673 feet.

History: The village of Ravenna was first settled in 1847 by Benjamin Smith, and was incorporated in 1922. Ravenna took its name from the township, which was named for Ravenna, Ohio.

Population: 1,219; Growth (since 2000): 1.1%; Density: 1,003.9 persons per square mile; Race: 94.0% White, 0.2% Black/African American, 0.0% Asian, 0.7% American Indian/Alaska Native, 0.0% Native Hawaiian/Other Pacific Islander, 1.7% Two or more races, 6.4% Hispanic of any race; Average household size: 2.67; Median age: 35.2; Age under 18: 29.0%; Age 65 and over: 13.5%; Males per 100 females: 96.0

School District(s)

Ravenna Public Schools (PK-12)
  2012-13 Enrollment: 1,111 . . . . (231) 853-2231

Housing: Homeownership rate: 78.9%; Homeowner vacancy rate: 2.2%; Rental vacancy rate: 2.0%

ROOSEVELT PARK (city). Covers a land area of 1.027 square miles and a water area of 0 square miles. Located at 43.20° N. Lat; 86.27° W. Long. Elevation is 623 feet.

History: Incorporated 1946.

Population: 3,831; Growth (since 2000): -1.5%; Density: 3,728.6 persons per square mile; Race: 85.9% White, 8.4% Black/African American, 1.6% Asian, 0.6% American Indian/Alaska Native, 0.0% Native Hawaiian/Other Pacific Islander, 2.4% Two or more races, 3.9% Hispanic of any race; Average household size: 2.19; Median age: 38.3; Age under 18: 23.8%; Age 65 and over: 17.2%; Males per 100 females: 90.3; Marriage status: 31.8% never married, 41.3% now married, 1.8% separated, 9.4% widowed, 17.6% divorced; Foreign born: 1.5%; Speak English only: 95.7%; With disability: 14.6%; Veterans: 12.9%; Ancestry: 21.6% German, 16.0% Dutch, 13.0% Irish, 9.9% English, 9.5% Polish

Employment: 13.7% management, business, and financial, 4.0% computer, engineering, and science, 11.8% education, legal, community service, arts, and media, 1.9% healthcare practitioners, 20.4% service, 28.3% sales and office, 6.4% natural resources, construction, and maintenance, 13.5% production, transportation, and material moving

Income: Per capita: $19,678; Median household: $39,572; Average household: $45,677; Households with income of $100,000 or more: 6.0%; Poverty rate: 15.5%

Educational Attainment: High school diploma or higher: 95.0%; Bachelor's degree or higher: 20.5%; Graduate/professional degree or higher: 5.8%

Vocational/Technical School(s)

Ross Medical Education Center-Roosevelt Park (Private, For-profit)
  Fall 2013 Enrollment: 186 . . . . (231) 739-1531
  2013-14 Tuition: $15,680

Housing: Homeownership rate: 63.6%; Median home value: $94,800; Median year structure built: 1965; Homeowner vacancy rate: 1.9%; Median gross rent: $711 per month; Rental vacancy rate: 16.1%

Health Insurance: 90.4% have insurance; 68.7% have private insurance; 42.9% have public insurance; 9.6% do not have insurance; 0.7% of children under 18 do not have insurance
Safety: Violent crime rate: 18.4 per 10,000 population; Property crime rate: 700.0 per 10,000 population
Transportation: Commute: 94.0% car, 0.6% public transportation, 1.6% walk, 1.0% work from home; Median travel time to work: 17.1 minutes

---

SULLIVAN (township). Covers a land area of 24.083 square miles and a water area of 0.025 square miles. Located at 43.17° N. Lat; 86.08° W. Long. Elevation is 659 feet.
Population: 2,441; Growth (since 2000): -1.5%; Density: 101.4 persons per square mile; Race: 96.8% White, 0.6% Black/African American, 0.2% Asian, 0.4% American Indian/Alaska Native, 0.0% Native Hawaiian/Other Pacific Islander, 1.3% Two or more races, 2.0% Hispanic of any race; Average household size: 2.62; Median age: 43.3; Age under 18: 22.5%; Age 65 and over: 14.1%; Males per 100 females: 101.6
Housing: Homeownership rate: 93.2%; Homeowner vacancy rate: 1.0%; Rental vacancy rate: 1.5%

TWIN LAKE (CDP). Covers a land area of 2.370 square miles and a water area of 0.557 square miles. Located at 43.37° N. Lat; 86.18° W. Long. Elevation is 686 feet.
Population: 1,720; Growth (since 2000): 6.6%; Density: 725.8 persons per square mile; Race: 94.4% White, 1.0% Black/African American, 0.4% Asian, 1.2% American Indian/Alaska Native, 0.0% Native Hawaiian/Other Pacific Islander, 1.7% Two or more races, 2.6% Hispanic of any race; Average household size: 2.71; Median age: 40.6; Age under 18: 25.5%; Age 65 and over: 13.3%; Males per 100 females: 103.3
School District(s)
Reeths-Puffer Schools (PK-12)
    2012-13 Enrollment: 3,814 . . . . (231) 719-3101
Housing: Homeownership rate: 90.4%; Homeowner vacancy rate: 2.9%; Rental vacancy rate: 8.8%

WHITE RIVER (township). Covers a land area of 15.715 square miles and a water area of 0.200 square miles. Located at 43.44° N. Lat; 86.42° W. Long.
Population: 1,335; Growth (since 2000): -0.2%; Density: 84.9 persons per square mile; Race: 95.5% White, 0.9% Black/African American, 0.0% Asian, 0.9% American Indian/Alaska Native, 0.0% Native Hawaiian/Other Pacific Islander, 1.7% Two or more races, 2.8% Hispanic of any race; Average household size: 2.53; Median age: 48.5; Age under 18: 21.3%; Age 65 and over: 21.0%; Males per 100 females: 96.0
Housing: Homeownership rate: 95.5%; Homeowner vacancy rate: 1.8%; Rental vacancy rate: 36.6%

WHITEHALL (city). Covers a land area of 3.122 square miles and a water area of 0.666 square miles. Located at 43.40° N. Lat; 86.34° W. Long. Elevation is 614 feet.
History: Whitehall, rival of Montague at the head of White Lake, depended on fruit raising for its source of revenue.
Population: 2,706; Growth (since 2000): -6.2%; Density: 866.8 persons per square mile; Race: 95.0% White, 1.4% Black/African American, 0.5% Asian, 0.6% American Indian/Alaska Native, 0.1% Native Hawaiian/Other Pacific Islander, 2.0% Two or more races, 2.7% Hispanic of any race; Average household size: 2.22; Median age: 42.9; Age under 18: 22.7%; Age 65 and over: 20.8%; Males per 100 females: 84.6; Marriage status: 25.7% never married, 46.5% now married, 0.9% separated, 9.3% widowed, 18.5% divorced; Foreign born: 1.5%; Speak English only: 95.1%; With disability: 17.5%; Veterans: 11.5%; Ancestry: 24.5% German, 13.2% English, 10.3% Irish, 8.5% Dutch, 6.8% American
Employment: 8.7% management, business, and financial, 4.4% computer, engineering, and science, 12.1% education, legal, community service, arts, and media, 4.2% healthcare practitioners, 17.3% service, 22.5% sales and office, 12.3% natural resources, construction, and maintenance, 18.5% production, transportation, and material moving
Income: Per capita: $21,413; Median household: $43,700; Average household: $49,347; Households with income of $100,000 or more: 8.0%; Poverty rate: 14.5%
Educational Attainment: High school diploma or higher: 92.5%; Bachelor's degree or higher: 20.9%; Graduate/professional degree or higher: 6.2%

School District(s)
Whitehall District Schools (PK-12)
    2012-13 Enrollment: 2,352 . . . . (231) 893-1005
Housing: Homeownership rate: 64.6%; Median home value: $103,600; Median year structure built: 1960; Homeowner vacancy rate: 3.8%; Median gross rent: $504 per month; Rental vacancy rate: 8.3%
Health Insurance: 90.5% have insurance; 72.9% have private insurance; 37.3% have public insurance; 9.5% do not have insurance; 0.5% of children under 18 do not have insurance
Safety: Violent crime rate: 22.4 per 10,000 population; Property crime rate: 238.5 per 10,000 population
Newspapers: White Lake Beacon (weekly circulation 11000)
Transportation: Commute: 92.8% car, 0.0% public transportation, 2.5% walk, 1.6% work from home; Median travel time to work: 17.9 minutes

---

WHITEHALL (township). Covers a land area of 8.869 square miles and a water area of 0.559 square miles. Located at 43.41° N. Lat; 86.30° W. Long. Elevation is 614 feet.
History: White River Station Museum. Incorporated 1867 as village, as city 1943.
Population: 1,739; Growth (since 2000): 5.5%; Density: 196.1 persons per square mile; Race: 95.3% White, 1.0% Black/African American, 0.3% Asian, 0.6% American Indian/Alaska Native, 0.0% Native Hawaiian/Other Pacific Islander, 2.4% Two or more races, 2.4% Hispanic of any race; Average household size: 2.53; Median age: 43.6; Age under 18: 23.0%; Age 65 and over: 14.2%; Males per 100 females: 98.1
School District(s)
Whitehall District Schools (PK-12)
    2012-13 Enrollment: 2,352 . . . . (231) 893-1005
Housing: Homeownership rate: 91.3%; Homeowner vacancy rate: 1.4%; Rental vacancy rate: 1.6%
Newspapers: White Lake Beacon (weekly circulation 11000)

WOLF LAKE (CDP). Covers a land area of 3.550 square miles and a water area of 0.379 square miles. Located at 43.24° N. Lat; 86.11° W. Long. Elevation is 673 feet.
Population: 4,104; Growth (since 2000): -7.9%; Density: 1,155.9 persons per square mile; Race: 93.8% White, 0.9% Black/African American, 0.1% Asian, 1.0% American Indian/Alaska Native, 0.0% Native Hawaiian/Other Pacific Islander, 2.6% Two or more races, 5.4% Hispanic of any race; Average household size: 2.62; Median age: 37.7; Age under 18: 25.6%; Age 65 and over: 13.1%; Males per 100 females: 94.7; Marriage status: 31.6% never married, 47.8% now married, 3.4% separated, 7.1% widowed, 13.5% divorced; Foreign born: 3.5%; Speak English only: 94.7%; With disability: 16.1%; Veterans: 12.4%; Ancestry: 23.3% German, 10.2% Irish, 10.1% English, 8.2% Dutch, 5.2% Scottish
Employment: 3.9% management, business, and financial, 0.0% computer, engineering, and science, 8.4% education, legal, community service, arts, and media, 2.1% healthcare practitioners, 25.2% service, 28.0% sales and office, 4.9% natural resources, construction, and maintenance, 27.4% production, transportation, and material moving
Income: Per capita: $15,971; Median household: $33,888; Average household: $43,162; Households with income of $100,000 or more: 7.3%; Poverty rate: 21.2%
Educational Attainment: High school diploma or higher: 80.8%; Bachelor's degree or higher: 8.8%; Graduate/professional degree or higher: 5.1%
Housing: Homeownership rate: 86.4%; Median home value: $80,900; Median year structure built: 1970; Homeowner vacancy rate: 3.4%; Median gross rent: $739 per month; Rental vacancy rate: 11.9%
Health Insurance: 84.8% have insurance; 49.9% have private insurance; 46.8% have public insurance; 15.2% do not have insurance; 0.8% of children under 18 do not have insurance
Transportation: Commute: 96.0% car, 0.0% public transportation, 0.0% walk, 2.2% work from home; Median travel time to work: 21.7 minutes

Newaygo County

Located in west central Michigan; drained by the Muskegon, Pere Marquette, and White Rivers; includes part of Manistee National Forest. Covers a land area of 813.204 square miles, a water area of 48.485 square miles, and is located in the Eastern Time Zone at 43.56° N. Lat., 85.79° W. Long. The county was founded in 1840. County seat is White Cloud.

Population: 48,460; Growth (since 2000): 1.2%; Density: 59.6 persons per square mile; Race: 94.1% White, 1.0% Black/African American, 0.4% Asian, 0.8% American Indian/Alaska Native, 0.0% Native Hawaiian/Other Pacific Islander, 1.7% two or more races, 5.5% Hispanic of any race; Average household size: 2.60; Median age: 40.9; Age under 18: 25.0%; Age 65 and over: 15.5%; Males per 100 females: 101.3; Marriage status: 23.9% never married, 56.8% now married, 1.3% separated, 7.2% widowed, 12.1% divorced; Foreign born: 2.3%; Speak English only: 94.8%; With disability: 17.2%; Veterans: 11.3%; Ancestry: 23.6% German, 13.9% Dutch, 10.6% Irish, 10.2% English, 8.2% American
Religion: Six largest groups: 6.9% Presbyterian-Reformed, 6.7% Catholicism, 3.9% Non-denominational Protestant, 3.5% Methodist/Pietist, 2.1% Holiness, 1.6% Pentecostal
Economy: Unemployment rate: 4.9%; Leading industries: 18.9% retail trade; 15.3% other services (except public administration); 10.5% construction; Farms: 923 totaling 125,663 acres; Company size: 0 employ 1,000 or more persons, 4 employ 500 to 999 persons, 9 employ 100 to 499 persons, 769 employ less than 100 persons; Business ownership: 1,275 women-owned, n/a Black-owned, n/a Hispanic-owned, n/a Asian-owned
Employment: 9.4% management, business, and financial, 2.1% computer, engineering, and science, 7.7% education, legal, community service, arts, and media, 5.0% healthcare practitioners, 15.7% service, 23.3% sales and office, 14.9% natural resources, construction, and maintenance, 22.0% production, transportation, and material moving
Income: Per capita: $20,623; Median household: $42,571; Average household: $53,398; Households with income of $100,000 or more: 10.7%; Poverty rate: 18.6%
Educational Attainment: High school diploma or higher: 85.9%; Bachelor's degree or higher: 12.9%; Graduate/professional degree or higher: 4.5%
Housing: Homeownership rate: 82.4%; Median home value: $104,100; Median year structure built: 1977; Homeowner vacancy rate: 2.9%; Median gross rent: $656 per month; Rental vacancy rate: 7.7%
Vital Statistics: Birth rate: 117.5 per 10,000 population; Death rate: 97.3 per 10,000 population; Age-adjusted cancer mortality rate: 211.7 deaths per 100,000 population
Health Insurance: 86.2% have insurance; 61.4% have private insurance; 40.9% have public insurance; 13.8% do not have insurance; 5.6% of children under 18 do not have insurance
Health Care: Physicians: 7.7 per 10,000 population; Hospital beds: 8.3 per 10,000 population; Hospital admissions: 531.0 per 10,000 population
Transportation: Commute: 93.2% car, 0.1% public transportation, 1.5% walk, 4.1% work from home; Median travel time to work: 28.7 minutes
Presidential Election: 40.7% Obama, 58.1% Romney (2012)
National and State Parks: Newaygo State Park; White Cloud State Park
Additional Information Contacts
Newaygo Government. . . . . (231) 689-7200
    http://www.countyofnewaygo.com

Newaygo County Communities

ASHLAND (township). Covers a land area of 34.416 square miles and a water area of 0.930 square miles. Located at 43.34° N. Lat; 85.86° W. Long. Elevation is 791 feet.
History: Ashland Township was organized in 1854 and named for the quantity of white ash timber in the area.
Population: 2,773; Growth (since 2000): 7.9%; Density: 80.6 persons per square mile; Race: 92.3% White, 0.1% Black/African American, 0.3% Asian, 0.6% American Indian/Alaska Native, 0.0% Native Hawaiian/Other Pacific Islander, 1.8% Two or more races, 12.3% Hispanic of any race; Average household size: 2.93; Median age: 36.0; Age under 18: 28.5%; Age 65 and over: 10.5%; Males per 100 females: 109.1; Marriage status: 25.5% never married, 60.7% now married, 0.9% separated, 4.4% widowed, 9.4% divorced; Foreign born: 5.2%; Speak English only: 88.4%; With disability: 13.1%; Veterans: 9.1%; Ancestry: 17.5% German, 10.9% Dutch, 10.3% American, 9.1% English, 8.4% Polish
Employment: 6.2% management, business, and financial, 4.9% computer, engineering, and science, 3.7% education, legal, community service, arts, and media, 7.0% healthcare practitioners, 7.4% service, 20.7% sales and office, 22.8% natural resources, construction, and maintenance, 27.5% production, transportation, and material moving
Income: Per capita: $18,056; Median household: $52,107; Average household: $57,939; Households with income of $100,000 or more: 8.2%; Poverty rate: 19.9%

Educational Attainment: High school diploma or higher: 84.1%; Bachelor's degree or higher: 11.3%; Graduate/professional degree or higher: 1.7%
Housing: Homeownership rate: 86.1%; Median home value: $109,200; Median year structure built: 1990; Homeowner vacancy rate: 2.3%; Median gross rent: $667 per month; Rental vacancy rate: 3.0%
Health Insurance: 88.1% have insurance; 60.8% have private insurance; 40.4% have public insurance; 11.9% do not have insurance; 3.4% of children under 18 do not have insurance
Transportation: Commute: 94.6% car, 0.0% public transportation, 0.0% walk, 4.4% work from home; Median travel time to work: 32.8 minutes

BARTON (township). Covers a land area of 35.065 square miles and a water area of 0.731 square miles. Located at 43.77° N. Lat; 85.63° W. Long.
Population: 717; Growth (since 2000): -12.6%; Density: 20.4 persons per square mile; Race: 97.6% White, 0.1% Black/African American, 0.3% Asian, 0.7% American Indian/Alaska Native, 0.0% Native Hawaiian/Other Pacific Islander, 1.3% Two or more races, 1.0% Hispanic of any race; Average household size: 2.41; Median age: 44.3; Age under 18: 21.2%; Age 65 and over: 15.3%; Males per 100 females: 107.2
Housing: Homeownership rate: 91.2%; Homeowner vacancy rate: 2.5%; Rental vacancy rate: 16.1%

BEAVER (township). Covers a land area of 32.059 square miles and a water area of 3.752 square miles. Located at 43.69° N. Lat; 85.97° W. Long.
Population: 509; Growth (since 2000): -16.3%; Density: 15.9 persons per square mile; Race: 96.1% White, 0.8% Black/African American, 0.2% Asian, 1.4% American Indian/Alaska Native, 0.0% Native Hawaiian/Other Pacific Islander, 1.2% Two or more races, 6.3% Hispanic of any race; Average household size: 2.65; Median age: 41.1; Age under 18: 25.9%; Age 65 and over: 12.2%; Males per 100 females: 106.1
Housing: Homeownership rate: 86.5%; Homeowner vacancy rate: 0.6%; Rental vacancy rate: 0.0%

BIG PRAIRIE (township). Covers a land area of 31.386 square miles and a water area of 4.848 square miles. Located at 43.51° N. Lat; 85.63° W. Long. Elevation is 945 feet.
History: Big Prairie Township was organized in 1852 and named because it was then on prairie land. Later, pine trees were planted here.
Population: 2,573; Growth (since 2000): 4.4%; Density: 82.0 persons per square mile; Race: 96.3% White, 0.2% Black/African American, 0.1% Asian, 1.0% American Indian/Alaska Native, 0.0% Native Hawaiian/Other Pacific Islander, 1.9% Two or more races, 2.6% Hispanic of any race; Average household size: 2.53; Median age: 42.8; Age under 18: 22.2%; Age 65 and over: 17.3%; Males per 100 females: 109.2; Marriage status: 19.4% never married, 57.2% now married, 2.8% separated, 10.1% widowed, 13.4% divorced; Foreign born: 1.1%; Speak English only: 98.6%; With disability: 25.1%; Veterans: 13.3%; Ancestry: 24.4% German, 12.5% English, 12.5% Irish, 11.1% Dutch, 8.3% Polish
Employment: 7.7% management, business, and financial, 1.3% computer, engineering, and science, 2.9% education, legal, community service, arts, and media, 3.8% healthcare practitioners, 22.2% service, 24.6% sales and office, 16.3% natural resources, construction, and maintenance, 21.2% production, transportation, and material moving
Income: Per capita: $17,972; Median household: $32,917; Average household: $42,323; Households with income of $100,000 or more: 7.1%; Poverty rate: 23.2%
Educational Attainment: High school diploma or higher: 79.0%; Bachelor's degree or higher: 9.4%; Graduate/professional degree or higher: 3.8%
Housing: Homeownership rate: 81.1%; Median home value: $69,400; Median year structure built: 1978; Homeowner vacancy rate: 3.8%; Median gross rent: $686 per month; Rental vacancy rate: 3.5%
Health Insurance: 85.0% have insurance; 58.3% have private insurance; 47.2% have public insurance; 15.0% do not have insurance; 3.6% of children under 18 do not have insurance
Transportation: Commute: 97.6% car, 0.0% public transportation, 0.0% walk, 2.4% work from home; Median travel time to work: 34.9 minutes

BITELY (unincorporated postal area)

ZCTA: 49309

Covers a land area of 114.024 square miles and a water area of 11.261 square miles. Located at 43.76° N. Lat; 85.88° W. Long. Elevation is 866 feet.

Population: 1,843; Growth (since 2000): -1.4%; Density: 16.2 persons per square mile; Race: 87.7% White, 7.9% Black/African American, 0.1% Asian, 1.2% American Indian/Alaska Native, 0.0% Native Hawaiian/Other Pacific Islander, 2.6% Two or more races, 2.8% Hispanic of any race; Average household size: 2.17; Median age: 50.9; Age under 18: 18.0%; Age 65 and over: 24.2%; Males per 100 females: 111.8

Housing: Homeownership rate: 84.8%; Homeowner vacancy rate: 3.7%; Rental vacancy rate: 9.7%

BRIDGETON (township). Covers a land area of 35.492 square miles and a water area of 0.616 square miles. Located at 43.34° N. Lat; 85.97° W. Long. Elevation is 633 feet.

History: Bridgeton Township was organized in 1852 and named because of the bridge across the Muskegon River.

Population: 2,141; Growth (since 2000): 2.0%; Density: 60.3 persons per square mile; Race: 96.6% White, 0.3% Black/African American, 0.1% Asian, 0.6% American Indian/Alaska Native, 0.0% Native Hawaiian/Other Pacific Islander, 0.8% Two or more races, 5.0% Hispanic of any race; Average household size: 2.76; Median age: 38.9; Age under 18: 25.6%; Age 65 and over: 11.1%; Males per 100 females: 107.5

Housing: Homeownership rate: 87.5%; Homeowner vacancy rate: 1.9%; Rental vacancy rate: 7.5%

BROHMAN (unincorporated postal area)

ZCTA: 49312

Covers a land area of 27.297 square miles and a water area of 2.033 square miles. Located at 43.69° N. Lat; 85.81° W. Long. Elevation is 965 feet.

Population: 274; Growth (since 2000): 214.9%; Density: 10.0 persons per square mile; Race: 93.1% White, 2.9% Black/African American, 0.0% Asian, 2.2% American Indian/Alaska Native, 0.0% Native Hawaiian/Other Pacific Islander, 1.1% Two or more races, 2.9% Hispanic of any race; Average household size: 2.23; Median age: 49.7; Age under 18: 13.9%; Age 65 and over: 22.3%; Males per 100 females: 104.5

Housing: Homeownership rate: 82.2%; Homeowner vacancy rate: 6.4%; Rental vacancy rate: 4.3%

BROOKS (township). Covers a land area of 31.571 square miles and a water area of 2.397 square miles. Located at 43.42° N. Lat; 85.73° W. Long.

History: Brooks Township was named for John A. Brooks, a lumberman.

Population: 3,510; Growth (since 2000): -4.4%; Density: 111.2 persons per square mile; Race: 94.2% White, 0.3% Black/African American, 0.3% Asian, 0.7% American Indian/Alaska Native, 0.1% Native Hawaiian/Other Pacific Islander, 1.2% Two or more races, 7.2% Hispanic of any race; Average household size: 2.52; Median age: 43.4; Age under 18: 24.1%; Age 65 and over: 16.4%; Males per 100 females: 105.9; Marriage status: 23.1% never married, 57.1% now married, 0.0% separated, 6.4% widowed, 13.3% divorced; Foreign born: 5.7%; Speak English only: 92.0%; With disability: 17.5%; Veterans: 14.8%; Ancestry: 27.7% German, 21.0% Dutch, 13.9% English, 8.6% Irish, 6.8% American

Employment: 15.4% management, business, and financial, 0.6% computer, engineering, and science, 3.8% education, legal, community service, arts, and media, 5.1% healthcare practitioners, 14.8% service, 26.2% sales and office, 18.3% natural resources, construction, and maintenance, 15.8% production, transportation, and material moving

Income: Per capita: $23,930; Median household: $43,269; Average household: $57,415; Households with income of $100,000 or more: 14.1%; Poverty rate: 17.3%

Educational Attainment: High school diploma or higher: 88.8%; Bachelor's degree or higher: 14.0%; Graduate/professional degree or higher: 5.3%

Housing: Homeownership rate: 87.5%; Median home value: $113,500; Median year structure built: 1975; Homeowner vacancy rate: 2.5%; Median gross rent: $701 per month; Rental vacancy rate: 8.4%

Health Insurance: 88.3% have insurance; 62.0% have private insurance; 45.7% have public insurance; 11.7% do not have insurance; 1.6% of children under 18 do not have insurance

Transportation: Commute: 91.1% car, 0.0% public transportation, 1.3% walk, 5.5% work from home; Median travel time to work: 31.6 minutes

Additional Information Contacts

Brooks Township . . . . (231) 652-6763
http://www.brookstownship.org

CROTON (township). Covers a land area of 33.700 square miles and a water area of 2.678 square miles. Located at 43.42° N. Lat; 85.63° W. Long. Elevation is 738 feet.

History: Croton was settled in 1840. First called Stearns Mills after a settler who built a sawmill here, the name was changed in 1850 to Croton, after the Croton Water Works in New York.

Population: 3,228; Growth (since 2000): 6.1%; Density: 95.8 persons per square mile; Race: 96.0% White, 0.3% Black/African American, 0.4% Asian, 1.0% American Indian/Alaska Native, 0.0% Native Hawaiian/Other Pacific Islander, 1.3% Two or more races, 2.9% Hispanic of any race; Average household size: 2.45; Median age: 44.6; Age under 18: 22.0%; Age 65 and over: 16.9%; Males per 100 females: 104.6; Marriage status: 19.2% never married, 53.5% now married, 0.3% separated, 12.0% widowed, 15.4% divorced; Foreign born: 0.3%; Speak English only: 96.6%; With disability: 15.1%; Veterans: 11.8%; Ancestry: 24.6% German, 14.4% Dutch, 10.0% Irish, 8.3% English, 8.1% Polish

Employment: 7.5% management, business, and financial, 1.2% computer, engineering, and science, 10.3% education, legal, community service, arts, and media, 1.4% healthcare practitioners, 11.6% service, 25.5% sales and office, 18.9% natural resources, construction, and maintenance, 23.7% production, transportation, and material moving

Income: Per capita: $21,868; Median household: $42,404; Average household: $53,559; Households with income of $100,000 or more: 12.9%; Poverty rate: 10.5%

Educational Attainment: High school diploma or higher: 90.3%; Bachelor's degree or higher: 14.3%; Graduate/professional degree or higher: 5.0%

Housing: Homeownership rate: 88.3%; Median home value: $118,100; Median year structure built: 1986; Homeowner vacancy rate: 4.7%; Median gross rent: $730 per month; Rental vacancy rate: 12.4%

Health Insurance: 84.4% have insurance; 61.8% have private insurance; 36.2% have public insurance; 15.6% do not have insurance; 0.0% of children under 18 do not have insurance

Transportation: Commute: 96.3% car, 0.0% public transportation, 0.0% walk, 1.3% work from home; Median travel time to work: 40.3 minutes

DAYTON (township). Covers a land area of 32.914 square miles and a water area of 1.218 square miles. Located at 43.51° N. Lat; 85.99° W. Long.

Population: 1,949; Growth (since 2000): -2.6%; Density: 59.2 persons per square mile; Race: 97.1% White, 1.0% Black/African American, 0.3% Asian, 0.2% American Indian/Alaska Native, 0.0% Native Hawaiian/Other Pacific Islander, 1.1% Two or more races, 2.2% Hispanic of any race; Average household size: 2.80; Median age: 42.1; Age under 18: 25.4%; Age 65 and over: 15.7%; Males per 100 females: 100.1

Housing: Homeownership rate: 91.1%; Homeowner vacancy rate: 1.7%; Rental vacancy rate: 4.6%

DENVER (township). Covers a land area of 33.939 square miles and a water area of 1.815 square miles. Located at 43.59° N. Lat; 85.98° W. Long.

Population: 1,928; Growth (since 2000): -2.2%; Density: 56.8 persons per square mile; Race: 94.0% White, 0.3% Black/African American, 0.2% Asian, 1.5% American Indian/Alaska Native, 0.0% Native Hawaiian/Other Pacific Islander, 3.0% Two or more races, 4.6% Hispanic of any race; Average household size: 2.55; Median age: 41.4; Age under 18: 25.0%; Age 65 and over: 16.4%; Males per 100 females: 105.3

Housing: Homeownership rate: 84.9%; Homeowner vacancy rate: 2.8%; Rental vacancy rate: 7.9%

ENSLEY (township). Covers a land area of 35.415 square miles and a water area of 0.817 square miles. Located at 43.33° N. Lat; 85.63° W. Long.

Population: 2,635; Growth (since 2000): 6.5%; Density: 74.4 persons per square mile; Race: 97.0% White, 0.4% Black/African American, 0.3% Asian, 0.6% American Indian/Alaska Native, 0.0% Native Hawaiian/Other Pacific Islander, 1.3% Two or more races, 3.3% Hispanic of any race; Average household size: 2.85; Median age: 38.4; Age under 18: 26.8%; Age 65 and over: 9.6%; Males per 100 females: 102.5; Marriage status:

20.9% never married, 64.5% now married, 1.4% separated, 3.7% widowed, 11.0% divorced; Foreign born: 0.4%; Speak English only: 98.8%; With disability: 12.7%; Veterans: 9.9%; Ancestry: 23.6% German, 18.3% Dutch, 11.5% Irish, 11.3% American, 9.4% Polish

Employment: 9.0% management, business, and financial, 1.0% computer, engineering, and science, 9.0% education, legal, community service, arts, and media, 3.0% healthcare practitioners, 16.5% service, 17.8% sales and office, 15.4% natural resources, construction, and maintenance, 28.3% production, transportation, and material moving

Income: Per capita: $19,632; Median household: $51,000; Average household: $56,310; Households with income of $100,000 or more: 10.6%; Poverty rate: 12.2%

Educational Attainment: High school diploma or higher: 84.7%; Bachelor's degree or higher: 11.1%; Graduate/professional degree or higher: 3.7%

Housing: Homeownership rate: 89.9%; Median home value: $114,700; Median year structure built: 1990; Homeowner vacancy rate: 1.7%; Median gross rent: $621 per month; Rental vacancy rate: 4.1%

Health Insurance: 90.1% have insurance; 76.6% have private insurance; 28.4% have public insurance; 9.9% do not have insurance; 0.8% of children under 18 do not have insurance

Transportation: Commute: 96.7% car, 0.0% public transportation, 0.3% walk, 3.0% work from home; Median travel time to work: 38.5 minutes

EVERETT (township). Covers a land area of 35.238 square miles and a water area of 0.579 square miles. Located at 43.51° N. Lat; 85.73° W. Long.

Population: 1,862; Growth (since 2000): -6.2%; Density: 52.8 persons per square mile; Race: 93.8% White, 1.3% Black/African American, 0.2% Asian, 1.4% American Indian/Alaska Native, 0.0% Native Hawaiian/Other Pacific Islander, 2.3% Two or more races, 2.3% Hispanic of any race; Average household size: 2.59; Median age: 42.0; Age under 18: 25.0%; Age 65 and over: 15.8%; Males per 100 females: 103.1

Housing: Homeownership rate: 84.6%; Homeowner vacancy rate: 3.5%; Rental vacancy rate: 5.8%

FREMONT (city). Covers a land area of 3.424 square miles and a water area of 1.297 square miles. Located at 43.46° N. Lat; 85.95° W. Long. Elevation is 817 feet.

History: Native American village sites and mounds nearby. Settled 1855; incorporated as village 1875, as city 1911.

Population: 4,081; Growth (since 2000): -3.4%; Density: 1,191.9 persons per square mile; Race: 94.5% White, 0.5% Black/African American, 1.1% Asian, 0.3% American Indian/Alaska Native, 0.1% Native Hawaiian/Other Pacific Islander, 1.3% Two or more races, 4.6% Hispanic of any race; Average household size: 2.27; Median age: 39.5; Age under 18: 25.1%; Age 65 and over: 19.4%; Males per 100 females: 80.9; Marriage status: 30.0% never married, 48.9% now married, 1.0% separated, 7.7% widowed, 13.4% divorced; Foreign born: 1.4%; Speak English only: 98.2%; With disability: 16.0%; Veterans: 12.8%; Ancestry: 28.6% German, 18.9% Dutch, 15.0% Irish, 13.1% American, 11.6% English

Employment: 8.4% management, business, and financial, 2.9% computer, engineering, and science, 10.4% education, legal, community service, arts, and media, 7.2% healthcare practitioners, 19.5% service, 28.3% sales and office, 7.4% natural resources, construction, and maintenance, 15.8% production, transportation, and material moving

Income: Per capita: $20,897; Median household: $37,617; Average household: $51,116; Households with income of $100,000 or more: 9.0%; Poverty rate: 21.0%

Educational Attainment: High school diploma or higher: 91.7%; Bachelor's degree or higher: 22.0%; Graduate/professional degree or higher: 8.1%

School District(s)
Fremont Public SD (PK-12)
    2012-13 Enrollment: 2,204 . . . . (231) 924-2350
Newaygo County Resa (PK-12)
    2012-13 Enrollment: 360 . . . . (231) 924-0381

Housing: Homeownership rate: 69.2%; Median home value: $89,000; Median year structure built: 1972; Homeowner vacancy rate: 3.6%; Median gross rent: $596 per month; Rental vacancy rate: 7.7%

Health Insurance: 90.8% have insurance; 63.2% have private insurance; 48.9% have public insurance; 9.2% do not have insurance; 1.0% of children under 18 do not have insurance

Hospitals: Spectrum Health Gerber Memorial (77 beds)

Safety: Violent crime rate: 12.4 per 10,000 population; Property crime rate: 396.6 per 10,000 population

Newspapers: Fremont Times Indicator (weekly circulation 7500)

Transportation: Commute: 89.6% car, 0.0% public transportation, 7.6% walk, 1.8% work from home; Median travel time to work: 15.5 minutes

Airports: Fremont Municipal (general aviation)

Additional Information Contacts
City of Fremont . . . . (231) 924-2101
    http://www.cityoffremont.net

GARFIELD (township). Covers a land area of 31.733 square miles and a water area of 1.914 square miles. Located at 43.43° N. Lat; 85.86° W. Long.

Population: 2,537; Growth (since 2000): 3.0%; Density: 79.9 persons per square mile; Race: 92.3% White, 0.2% Black/African American, 0.3% Asian, 0.5% American Indian/Alaska Native, 0.0% Native Hawaiian/Other Pacific Islander, 1.3% Two or more races, 9.5% Hispanic of any race; Average household size: 2.93; Median age: 42.1; Age under 18: 26.7%; Age 65 and over: 19.0%; Males per 100 females: 95.9; Marriage status: 24.1% never married, 62.4% now married, 2.9% separated, 6.1% widowed, 7.4% divorced; Foreign born: 3.3%; Speak English only: 83.9%; With disability: 12.9%; Veterans: 11.2%; Ancestry: 17.4% German, 13.8% Dutch, 9.5% American, 7.1% English, 7.1% Irish

Employment: 9.1% management, business, and financial, 1.1% computer, engineering, and science, 12.3% education, legal, community service, arts, and media, 3.6% healthcare practitioners, 12.2% service, 18.7% sales and office, 20.7% natural resources, construction, and maintenance, 22.4% production, transportation, and material moving

Income: Per capita: $20,418; Median household: $45,240; Average household: $60,816; Households with income of $100,000 or more: 14.6%; Poverty rate: 29.9%

Educational Attainment: High school diploma or higher: 83.7%; Bachelor's degree or higher: 15.8%; Graduate/professional degree or higher: 7.1%

Housing: Homeownership rate: 86.5%; Median home value: $132,900; Median year structure built: 1976; Homeowner vacancy rate: 2.0%; Median gross rent: $708 per month; Rental vacancy rate: 0.0%

Health Insurance: 73.9% have insurance; 51.3% have private insurance; 34.9% have public insurance; 26.1% do not have insurance; 32.6% of children under 18 do not have insurance

Transportation: Commute: 83.3% car, 0.0% public transportation, 2.3% walk, 11.5% work from home; Median travel time to work: 24.2 minutes

GOODWELL (township). Covers a land area of 33.773 square miles and a water area of 1.963 square miles. Located at 43.60° N. Lat; 85.61° W. Long.

Population: 547; Growth (since 2000): -0.7%; Density: 16.2 persons per square mile; Race: 94.7% White, 1.1% Black/African American, 0.2% Asian, 0.5% American Indian/Alaska Native, 0.0% Native Hawaiian/Other Pacific Islander, 3.5% Two or more races, 1.1% Hispanic of any race; Average household size: 2.64; Median age: 44.0; Age under 18: 21.2%; Age 65 and over: 17.4%; Males per 100 females: 104.1

Housing: Homeownership rate: 89.9%; Homeowner vacancy rate: 2.1%; Rental vacancy rate: 12.5%

GRANT (city). Covers a land area of 0.645 square miles and a water area of 0.020 square miles. Located at 43.33° N. Lat; 85.81° W. Long. Elevation is 833 feet.

History: Andrew J. Squier built a sawmill here in 1882. When the Chicago & Western Michigan Railroad established a station, Squier named it Grant Station, for General Ulysses S. Grant. Grant was incorporated as a village in 1893.

Population: 894; Growth (since 2000): 1.5%; Density: 1,386.4 persons per square mile; Race: 93.8% White, 0.1% Black/African American, 0.3% Asian, 0.4% American Indian/Alaska Native, 0.0% Native Hawaiian/Other Pacific Islander, 0.8% Two or more races, 13.3% Hispanic of any race; Average household size: 2.46; Median age: 31.9; Age under 18: 29.5%; Age 65 and over: 15.7%; Males per 100 females: 85.9

School District(s)
Grant Public SD (PK-12)
    2012-13 Enrollment: 1,934 . . . . (231) 834-5621

Housing: Homeownership rate: 49.0%; Homeowner vacancy rate: 4.8%; Rental vacancy rate: 4.6%

GRANT (township). Covers a land area of 35.435 square miles and a water area of 0.595 square miles. Located at 43.35° N. Lat; 85.75° W. Long. Elevation is 833 feet.
Population: 3,294; Growth (since 2000): 5.2%; Density: 93.0 persons per square mile; Race: 93.5% White, 0.4% Black/African American, 0.3% Asian, 0.4% American Indian/Alaska Native, 0.0% Native Hawaiian/Other Pacific Islander, 1.8% Two or more races, 13.3% Hispanic of any race; Average household size: 2.94; Median age: 37.7; Age under 18: 27.9%; Age 65 and over: 11.0%; Males per 100 females: 104.2; Marriage status: 24.2% never married, 60.1% now married, 0.8% separated, 5.6% widowed, 10.1% divorced; Foreign born: 3.5%; Speak English only: 90.2%; With disability: 15.3%; Veterans: 9.4%; Ancestry: 16.1% German, 14.8% Dutch, 13.3% English, 9.5% Irish, 8.9% American
Employment: 12.3% management, business, and financial, 1.1% computer, engineering, and science, 6.2% education, legal, community service, arts, and media, 8.0% healthcare practitioners, 15.8% service, 21.2% sales and office, 14.3% natural resources, construction, and maintenance, 21.0% production, transportation, and material moving
Income: Per capita: $22,022; Median household: $52,432; Average household: $60,358; Households with income of $100,000 or more: 12.0%; Poverty rate: 13.1%
Educational Attainment: High school diploma or higher: 83.8%; Bachelor's degree or higher: 13.1%; Graduate/professional degree or higher: 4.2%
School District(s)
Grant Public SD (PK-12)
   2012-13 Enrollment: 1,934 . . . . (231) 834-5621
Housing: Homeownership rate: 88.6%; Median home value: $121,100; Median year structure built: 1980; Homeowner vacancy rate: 1.6%; Median gross rent: $783 per month; Rental vacancy rate: 3.7%
Health Insurance: 88.2% have insurance; 66.6% have private insurance; 33.2% have public insurance; 11.8% do not have insurance; 1.1% of children under 18 do not have insurance
Transportation: Commute: 92.1% car, 0.0% public transportation, 2.1% walk, 5.2% work from home; Median travel time to work: 27.6 minutes

HOME (township). Covers a land area of 33.528 square miles and a water area of 2.082 square miles. Located at 43.77° N. Lat; 85.73° W. Long.
Population: 232; Growth (since 2000): -11.1%; Density: 6.9 persons per square mile; Race: 95.3% White, 0.0% Black/African American, 0.0% Asian, 1.3% American Indian/Alaska Native, 0.0% Native Hawaiian/Other Pacific Islander, 3.4% Two or more races, 0.9% Hispanic of any race; Average household size: 2.25; Median age: 50.3; Age under 18: 15.5%; Age 65 and over: 24.6%; Males per 100 females: 121.0
Housing: Homeownership rate: 85.4%; Homeowner vacancy rate: 0.0%; Rental vacancy rate: 0.0%

LILLEY (township). Covers a land area of 30.413 square miles and a water area of 5.215 square miles. Located at 43.77° N. Lat; 85.86° W. Long. Elevation is 863 feet.
Population: 797; Growth (since 2000): 1.1%; Density: 26.2 persons per square mile; Race: 91.3% White, 4.0% Black/African American, 0.1% Asian, 1.5% American Indian/Alaska Native, 0.0% Native Hawaiian/Other Pacific Islander, 2.5% Two or more races, 2.9% Hispanic of any race; Average household size: 2.13; Median age: 52.7; Age under 18: 17.8%; Age 65 and over: 27.0%; Males per 100 females: 112.5
Housing: Homeownership rate: 86.6%; Homeowner vacancy rate: 4.4%; Rental vacancy rate: 19.0%

LINCOLN (township). Covers a land area of 34.346 square miles and a water area of 1.372 square miles. Located at 43.62° N. Lat; 85.87° W. Long.
Population: 1,275; Growth (since 2000): -4.7%; Density: 37.1 persons per square mile; Race: 92.4% White, 1.8% Black/African American, 0.3% Asian, 1.6% American Indian/Alaska Native, 0.1% Native Hawaiian/Other Pacific Islander, 1.9% Two or more races, 4.2% Hispanic of any race; Average household size: 2.55; Median age: 46.0; Age under 18: 22.0%; Age 65 and over: 15.5%; Males per 100 females: 116.5
Housing: Homeownership rate: 88.3%; Homeowner vacancy rate: 3.7%; Rental vacancy rate: 14.7%

MERRILL (township). Covers a land area of 31.925 square miles and a water area of 3.926 square miles. Located at 43.68° N. Lat; 85.87° W. Long.
Population: 667; Growth (since 2000): 13.1%; Density: 20.9 persons per square mile; Race: 76.0% White, 17.2% Black/African American, 0.0% Asian, 2.2% American Indian/Alaska Native, 0.0% Native Hawaiian/Other Pacific Islander, 3.3% Two or more races, 2.1% Hispanic of any race; Average household size: 2.13; Median age: 49.5; Age under 18: 16.5%; Age 65 and over: 22.2%; Males per 100 females: 103.4
Housing: Homeownership rate: 78.4%; Homeowner vacancy rate: 6.1%; Rental vacancy rate: 5.6%

MONROE (township). Covers a land area of 32.837 square miles and a water area of 3.086 square miles. Located at 43.69° N. Lat; 85.73° W. Long.
Population: 320; Growth (since 2000): -1.2%; Density: 9.7 persons per square mile; Race: 94.1% White, 3.8% Black/African American, 0.0% Asian, 0.9% American Indian/Alaska Native, 0.0% Native Hawaiian/Other Pacific Islander, 0.9% Two or more races, 2.2% Hispanic of any race; Average household size: 2.34; Median age: 48.8; Age under 18: 20.0%; Age 65 and over: 20.0%; Males per 100 females: 109.2
Housing: Homeownership rate: 88.3%; Homeowner vacancy rate: 4.7%; Rental vacancy rate: 11.1%

NEWAYGO (city). Covers a land area of 3.744 square miles and a water area of 0.155 square miles. Located at 43.42° N. Lat; 85.80° W. Long. Elevation is 692 feet.
History: Newaygo was settled in 1836 and incorporated as a village in 1867. Industries in the early 1900's included a screw factory and a furniture supply factory.
Population: 1,976; Growth (since 2000): 18.3%; Density: 527.7 persons per square mile; Race: 93.6% White, 0.9% Black/African American, 0.7% Asian, 1.2% American Indian/Alaska Native, 0.1% Native Hawaiian/Other Pacific Islander, 2.0% Two or more races, 7.3% Hispanic of any race; Average household size: 2.51; Median age: 32.4; Age under 18: 29.3%; Age 65 and over: 14.2%; Males per 100 females: 85.4
School District(s)
Newaygo Public SD (KG-12)
   2012-13 Enrollment: 1,738 . . . . (231) 652-6984
Housing: Homeownership rate: 53.3%; Homeowner vacancy rate: 2.6%; Rental vacancy rate: 9.4%
Safety: Violent crime rate: 91.8 per 10,000 population; Property crime rate: 397.8 per 10,000 population

NORWICH (township). Covers a land area of 34.534 square miles and a water area of 0.939 square miles. Located at 43.68° N. Lat; 85.63° W. Long.
Population: 607; Growth (since 2000): 9.0%; Density: 17.6 persons per square mile; Race: 94.7% White, 1.3% Black/African American, 0.3% Asian, 0.7% American Indian/Alaska Native, 0.0% Native Hawaiian/Other Pacific Islander, 2.6% Two or more races, 1.3% Hispanic of any race; Average household size: 2.92; Median age: 41.8; Age under 18: 27.3%; Age 65 and over: 15.0%; Males per 100 females: 106.5
Housing: Homeownership rate: 88.9%; Homeowner vacancy rate: 1.1%; Rental vacancy rate: 14.8%

SHERIDAN (charter township). Covers a land area of 33.038 square miles and a water area of 0.213 square miles. Located at 43.42° N. Lat; 85.99° W. Long.
Population: 2,510; Growth (since 2000): 3.6%; Density: 76.0 persons per square mile; Race: 95.6% White, 0.3% Black/African American, 0.8% Asian, 0.5% American Indian/Alaska Native, 0.0% Native Hawaiian/Other Pacific Islander, 1.2% Two or more races, 3.9% Hispanic of any race; Average household size: 2.75; Median age: 40.5; Age under 18: 25.9%; Age 65 and over: 14.5%; Males per 100 females: 100.3; Marriage status: 24.5% never married, 61.8% now married, 1.2% separated, 8.3% widowed, 5.4% divorced; Foreign born: 2.8%; Speak English only: 95.1%; With disability: 12.7%; Veterans: 10.8%; Ancestry: 21.7% Dutch, 21.1% German, 12.5% American, 9.1% English, 7.1% Irish
Employment: 9.9% management, business, and financial, 1.6% computer, engineering, and science, 9.4% education, legal, community service, arts, and media, 5.6% healthcare practitioners, 16.9% service, 25.9% sales and office, 13.7% natural resources, construction, and maintenance, 17.1% production, transportation, and material moving

Income: Per capita: $22,348; Median household: $53,171; Average household: $61,339; Households with income of $100,000 or more: 10.2%; Poverty rate: 13.2%

Educational Attainment: High school diploma or higher: 89.7%; Bachelor's degree or higher: 17.9%; Graduate/professional degree or higher: 5.0%

Housing: Homeownership rate: 88.2%; Median home value: $140,700; Median year structure built: 1963; Homeowner vacancy rate: 1.8%; Median gross rent: $677 per month; Rental vacancy rate: 13.0%

Health Insurance: 88.5% have insurance; 73.6% have private insurance; 31.6% have public insurance; 11.5% do not have insurance; 3.7% of children under 18 do not have insurance

Transportation: Commute: 94.5% car, 0.0% public transportation, 0.7% walk, 4.3% work from home; Median travel time to work: 18.0 minutes

SHERMAN (township). Covers a land area of 33.415 square miles and a water area of 2.419 square miles. Located at 43.52° N. Lat; 85.86° W. Long.

Population: 2,109; Growth (since 2000): -2.3%; Density: 63.1 persons per square mile; Race: 96.4% White, 0.9% Black/African American, 0.2% Asian, 0.4% American Indian/Alaska Native, 0.0% Native Hawaiian/Other Pacific Islander, 1.3% Two or more races, 1.9% Hispanic of any race; Average household size: 2.58; Median age: 45.4; Age under 18: 23.0%; Age 65 and over: 21.0%; Males per 100 females: 93.1

Housing: Homeownership rate: 87.2%; Homeowner vacancy rate: 2.2%; Rental vacancy rate: 7.3%

TROY (township). Covers a land area of 34.843 square miles and a water area of 1.366 square miles. Located at 43.78° N. Lat; 85.98° W. Long. Elevation is 823 feet.

Population: 283; Growth (since 2000): 16.5%; Density: 8.1 persons per square mile; Race: 96.1% White, 0.7% Black/African American, 0.0% Asian, 0.4% American Indian/Alaska Native, 0.0% Native Hawaiian/Other Pacific Islander, 2.1% Two or more races, 3.2% Hispanic of any race; Average household size: 2.64; Median age: 42.1; Age under 18: 23.7%; Age 65 and over: 14.1%; Males per 100 females: 114.4

Housing: Homeownership rate: 87.0%; Homeowner vacancy rate: 1.1%; Rental vacancy rate: 6.7%

WHITE CLOUD (city). County seat. Covers a land area of 1.950 square miles and a water area of 0.050 square miles. Located at 43.56° N. Lat; 85.77° W. Long. Elevation is 873 feet.

Population: 1,408; Growth (since 2000): -0.8%; Density: 722.1 persons per square mile; Race: 83.7% White, 7.0% Black/African American, 0.5% Asian, 0.6% American Indian/Alaska Native, 0.0% Native Hawaiian/Other Pacific Islander, 5.2% Two or more races, 6.5% Hispanic of any race; Average household size: 2.59; Median age: 32.5; Age under 18: 25.9%; Age 65 and over: 11.6%; Males per 100 females: 116.6

School District(s)

White Cloud Public Schools (PK-12)
    2012-13 Enrollment: 1,059 . . . . (231) 689-3201

Housing: Homeownership rate: 60.6%; Homeowner vacancy rate: 6.6%; Rental vacancy rate: 11.8%

Safety: Violent crime rate: 57.7 per 10,000 population; Property crime rate: 425.4 per 10,000 population

WILCOX (township). Covers a land area of 32.428 square miles and a water area of 1.493 square miles. Located at 43.61° N. Lat; 85.74° W. Long.

Population: 1,098; Growth (since 2000): -4.1%; Density: 33.9 persons per square mile; Race: 94.8% White, 1.1% Black/African American, 0.8% Asian, 1.5% American Indian/Alaska Native, 0.1% Native Hawaiian/Other Pacific Islander, 1.4% Two or more races, 1.5% Hispanic of any race; Average household size: 2.60; Median age: 42.4; Age under 18: 23.1%; Age 65 and over: 14.2%; Males per 100 females: 109.1

Housing: Homeownership rate: 84.9%; Homeowner vacancy rate: 5.5%; Rental vacancy rate: 4.4%

Oakland County

Located in southeastern Michigan; drained by the Shiawassee, Huron, Clinton, and Rogue Rivers; includes many small lakes. Covers a land area of 867.663 square miles, a water area of 39.631 square miles, and is located in the Eastern Time Zone at 42.66° N. Lat., 83.38° W. Long. The county was founded in 1819. County seat is Pontiac.

Oakland County is part of the Detroit-Warren-Dearborn, MI Metropolitan Statistical Area. The entire metro area includes: Detroit-Dearborn-Livonia, MI Metropolitan Division (Wayne County, MI); Warren-Troy-Farmington Hills, MI Metropolitan Division (Lapeer County, MI; Livingston County, MI; Macomb County, MI; Oakland County, MI; Saint Clair County, MI)

Population: 1,202,362; Growth (since 2000): 0.7%; Density: 1,385.7 persons per square mile; Race: 77.3% White, 13.6% Black/African American, 5.6% Asian, 0.3% American Indian/Alaska Native, 0.0% Native Hawaiian/Other Pacific Islander, 2.2% two or more races, 3.5% Hispanic of any race; Average household size: 2.46; Median age: 40.2; Age under 18: 23.5%; Age 65 and over: 13.2%; Males per 100 females: 94.2; Marriage status: 29.4% never married, 53.9% now married, 1.1% separated, 5.7% widowed, 11.0% divorced; Foreign born: 11.4%; Speak English only: 86.0%; With disability: 11.0%; Veterans: 7.3%; Ancestry: 18.5% German, 12.1% Irish, 10.2% Polish, 9.8% English, 6.1% Italian

Religion: Six largest groups: 24.0% Catholicism, 7.6% Non-denominational Protestant, 3.1% Methodist/Pietist, 3.0% Judaism, 2.9% Baptist, 2.7% Lutheran

Economy: Unemployment rate: 6.9%; Leading industries: 16.0% professional, scientific, and technical services; 13.5% health care and social assistance; 12.8% retail trade; Farms: 537 totaling 31,722 acres; Company size: 34 employ 1,000 or more persons, 63 employ 500 to 999 persons, 938 employ 100 to 499 persons, 37,208 employ less than 100 persons; Business ownership: 36,681 women-owned, 10,668 Black-owned, 1,288 Hispanic-owned, 5,990 Asian-owned

Employment: 19.1% management, business, and financial, 9.2% computer, engineering, and science, 11.5% education, legal, community service, arts, and media, 7.2% healthcare practitioners, 14.8% service, 24.7% sales and office, 5.1% natural resources, construction, and maintenance, 8.6% production, transportation, and material moving

Income: Per capita: $36,458; Median household: $65,594; Average household: $89,683; Households with income of $100,000 or more: 31.1%; Poverty rate: 10.3%

Educational Attainment: High school diploma or higher: 92.7%; Bachelor's degree or higher: 43.1%; Graduate/professional degree or higher: 18.1%

Housing: Homeownership rate: 72.6%; Median home value: $170,500; Median year structure built: 1973; Homeowner vacancy rate: 2.5%; Median gross rent: $919 per month; Rental vacancy rate: 11.8%

Vital Statistics: Birth rate: 109.5 per 10,000 population; Death rate: 80.8 per 10,000 population; Age-adjusted cancer mortality rate: 164.0 deaths per 100,000 population

Health Insurance: 90.1% have insurance; 78.1% have private insurance; 25.0% have public insurance; 9.9% do not have insurance; 4.0% of children under 18 do not have insurance

Health Care: Physicians: 58.8 per 10,000 population; Hospital beds: 36.5 per 10,000 population; Hospital admissions: 1,776.6 per 10,000 population

Air Quality Index: 85.1% good, 14.5% moderate, 0.4% unhealthy for sensitive individuals, 0.0% unhealthy (percent of days)

Transportation: Commute: 93.3% car, 0.6% public transportation, 1.1% walk, 4.1% work from home; Median travel time to work: 26.1 minutes

Presidential Election: 53.4% Obama, 45.4% Romney (2012)

National and State Parks: Bald Mountain State Recreation Area; Dodge Brothers State Park Number 2; Highland State Recreation Area; Holly State Recreation Area; Pontiac Lake State Recreation Area; Proud Lake State Recreation Area; Seven Lakes State Park

Additional Information Contacts
Oakland Government . . . . (248) 858-0100
  http://www.oakgov.com

Oakland County Communities

ADDISON (township). Covers a land area of 35.518 square miles and a water area of 1.065 square miles. Located at 42.85° N. Lat; 83.16° W. Long.

History: Addison Township was named for pioneer settler Addison Chamberlain.

Population: 6,351; Growth (since 2000): -1.4%; Density: 178.8 persons per square mile; Race: 96.6% White, 0.6% Black/African American, 0.7% Asian, 0.3% American Indian/Alaska Native, 0.0% Native Hawaiian/Other Pacific Islander, 1.1% Two or more races, 2.9% Hispanic of any race;

Average household size: 2.71; Median age: 44.2; Age under 18: 22.9%; Age 65 and over: 12.4%; Males per 100 females: 105.0; Marriage status: 25.5% never married, 60.3% now married, 1.0% separated, 2.7% widowed, 11.5% divorced; Foreign born: 4.3%; Speak English only: 94.1%; With disability: 8.6%; Veterans: 8.9%; Ancestry: 30.2% German, 14.9% Polish, 14.3% Irish, 10.4% English, 8.6% Italian

Employment: 19.7% management, business, and financial, 8.4% computer, engineering, and science, 11.7% education, legal, community service, arts, and media, 4.4% healthcare practitioners, 12.7% service, 20.2% sales and office, 10.2% natural resources, construction, and maintenance, 12.8% production, transportation, and material moving

Income: Per capita: $33,604; Median household: $79,183; Average household: $92,407; Households with income of $100,000 or more: 37.4%; Poverty rate: 8.4%

Educational Attainment: High school diploma or higher: 90.1%; Bachelor's degree or higher: 30.1%; Graduate/professional degree or higher: 11.1%

Housing: Homeownership rate: 92.5%; Median home value: $236,700; Median year structure built: 1979; Homeowner vacancy rate: 1.9%; Median gross rent: $1,182 per month; Rental vacancy rate: 15.0%

Health Insurance: 91.5% have insurance; 81.7% have private insurance; 20.9% have public insurance; 8.5% do not have insurance; 4.0% of children under 18 do not have insurance

Transportation: Commute: 94.5% car, 0.0% public transportation, 1.9% walk, 2.8% work from home; Median travel time to work: 33.9 minutes

Additional Information Contacts

Addison Township . . . . (248) 648-5409
    http://www.twp.addison.mi.us

AUBURN HILLS (city).
Covers a land area of 16.598 square miles and a water area of 0.042 square miles. Located at 42.67° N. Lat; 83.24° W. Long. Elevation is 958 feet.

History: Auburn Hills, formerly known as Pontiac Township, was settled by Aaron Webster in 1821. He started a saw mill and grist mill to attracted more settlers. Auburn Hills was incorporated as a city in 1983.

Population: 21,412; Growth (since 2000): 7.9%; Density: 1,290.0 persons per square mile; Race: 66.3% White, 18.5% Black/African American, 8.9% Asian, 0.3% American Indian/Alaska Native, 0.0% Native Hawaiian/Other Pacific Islander, 3.4% Two or more races, 7.8% Hispanic of any race; Average household size: 2.24; Median age: 31.4; Age under 18: 19.4%; Age 65 and over: 9.4%; Males per 100 females: 93.8; Marriage status: 37.4% never married, 46.1% now married, 1.0% separated, 4.6% widowed, 11.8% divorced; Foreign born: 15.9%; Speak English only: 80.8%; With disability: 9.8%; Veterans: 7.1%; Ancestry: 18.9% German, 11.0% Irish, 9.2% Polish, 8.4% English, 4.8% Italian

Employment: 13.3% management, business, and financial, 12.8% computer, engineering, and science, 11.7% education, legal, community service, arts, and media, 4.9% healthcare practitioners, 19.0% service, 23.2% sales and office, 5.1% natural resources, construction, and maintenance, 10.1% production, transportation, and material moving

Income: Per capita: $26,843; Median household: $52,509; Average household: $64,158; Households with income of $100,000 or more: 17.4%; Poverty rate: 13.3%

Educational Attainment: High school diploma or higher: 90.0%; Bachelor's degree or higher: 39.9%; Graduate/professional degree or higher: 15.3%

School District(s)
Avondale SD (PK-12)
    2012-13 Enrollment: 3,553 . . . . (248) 537-6002
Gull Lake Community Schools (PK-12)
    2012-13 Enrollment: 2,930 . . . . (269) 488-5000
Pontiac City SD (PK-12)
    2012-13 Enrollment: 5,093 . . . . (248) 451-6883

Four-year College(s)
Baker College of Auburn Hills (Private, Not-for-profit)
    Fall 2013 Enrollment: 3,105 . . . . (248) 340-0600
    2013-14 Tuition: In-state $8,100; Out-of-state $8,100

Housing: Homeownership rate: 51.7%; Median home value: $113,600; Median year structure built: 1983; Homeowner vacancy rate: 3.3%; Median gross rent: $906 per month; Rental vacancy rate: 14.0%

Health Insurance: 84.2% have insurance; 72.5% have private insurance; 21.8% have public insurance; 15.8% do not have insurance; 11.7% of children under 18 do not have insurance

Safety: Violent crime rate: 28.1 per 10,000 population; Property crime rate: 350.1 per 10,000 population

Transportation: Commute: 91.3% car, 0.2% public transportation, 3.2% walk, 3.7% work from home; Median travel time to work: 24.0 minutes

Additional Information Contacts

City of Auburn Hills . . . . (248) 370-9440
    http://www.auburnhills.org

BERKLEY (city).
Covers a land area of 2.615 square miles and a water area of 0 square miles. Located at 42.50° N. Lat; 83.19° W. Long. Elevation is 682 feet.

History: Named for Berkley Road, which ran through a local farm owned by Elmer Cromie. Berkley was incorporated as a village in 1925 and granted a city charter in 1932. The city was established in an area that had been under cultivation until 1913, when it was subdivided by Detroit real estate operators.

Population: 14,970; Growth (since 2000): -3.6%; Density: 5,724.9 persons per square mile; Race: 93.3% White, 3.0% Black/African American, 1.3% Asian, 0.3% American Indian/Alaska Native, 0.1% Native Hawaiian/Other Pacific Islander, 1.8% Two or more races, 1.8% Hispanic of any race; Average household size: 2.27; Median age: 37.9; Age under 18: 21.4%; Age 65 and over: 11.3%; Males per 100 females: 91.8; Marriage status: 31.5% never married, 49.5% now married, 0.3% separated, 7.8% widowed, 11.2% divorced; Foreign born: 5.8%; Speak English only: 95.1%; With disability: 10.7%; Veterans: 7.0%; Ancestry: 26.9% German, 18.2% Irish, 15.4% English, 13.4% Polish, 8.9% Italian

Employment: 16.5% management, business, and financial, 8.6% computer, engineering, and science, 17.3% education, legal, community service, arts, and media, 9.2% healthcare practitioners, 14.6% service, 22.4% sales and office, 3.4% natural resources, construction, and maintenance, 8.0% production, transportation, and material moving

Income: Per capita: $35,635; Median household: $70,023; Average household: $81,276; Households with income of $100,000 or more: 27.2%; Poverty rate: 6.5%

Educational Attainment: High school diploma or higher: 95.5%; Bachelor's degree or higher: 46.0%; Graduate/professional degree or higher: 17.6%

School District(s)
Berkley SD (PK-12)
    2012-13 Enrollment: 4,667 . . . . (248) 837-8000

Housing: Homeownership rate: 81.4%; Median home value: $142,200; Median year structure built: 1949; Homeowner vacancy rate: 2.0%; Median gross rent: $1,067 per month; Rental vacancy rate: 6.0%

Health Insurance: 90.1% have insurance; 82.7% have private insurance; 18.1% have public insurance; 9.9% do not have insurance; 9.3% of children under 18 do not have insurance

Safety: Violent crime rate: 7.9 per 10,000 population; Property crime rate: 97.5 per 10,000 population

Transportation: Commute: 93.3% car, 0.4% public transportation, 2.5% walk, 3.1% work from home; Median travel time to work: 21.9 minutes

Additional Information Contacts

City of Berkley . . . . (248) 658-3300
    http://www.berkleymich.org

BEVERLY HILLS (village).
Covers a land area of 4.000 square miles and a water area of 0.015 square miles. Located at 42.52° N. Lat; 83.24° W. Long. Elevation is 728 feet.

History: Beverly Hills was incorporated as the village of Westwood in 1958, and renamed the next year to reflect the previous referral to the area as the Beverly Hills Subdivisions.

Population: 10,267; Growth (since 2000): -1.6%; Density: 2,567.0 persons per square mile; Race: 89.2% White, 6.6% Black/African American, 2.0% Asian, 0.2% American Indian/Alaska Native, 0.0% Native Hawaiian/Other Pacific Islander, 1.6% Two or more races, 1.7% Hispanic of any race; Average household size: 2.52; Median age: 44.7; Age under 18: 25.1%; Age 65 and over: 17.4%; Males per 100 females: 91.5; Marriage status: 22.5% never married, 62.0% now married, 0.1% separated, 5.7% widowed, 9.9% divorced; Foreign born: 6.1%; Speak English only: 93.8%; With disability: 6.8%; Veterans: 9.0%; Ancestry: 23.6% German, 19.1% Irish, 14.8% English, 11.6% Polish, 9.6% Italian

Employment: 26.0% management, business, and financial, 10.0% computer, engineering, and science, 18.6% education, legal, community service, arts, and media, 4.4% healthcare practitioners, 9.6% service, 25.3% sales and office, 2.2% natural resources, construction, and maintenance, 3.8% production, transportation, and material moving

Income: Per capita: $52,571; Median household: $106,847; Average household: $134,760; Households with income of $100,000 or more: 55.3%; Poverty rate: 2.5%

Educational Attainment: High school diploma or higher: 98.2%; Bachelor's degree or higher: 68.6%; Graduate/professional degree or higher: 32.7%

School District(s)

SD of the City of Birmingham (PK-12)

2012-13 Enrollment: 8,298 . . . . (248) 203-3004

Housing: Homeownership rate: 89.3%; Median home value: $269,400; Median year structure built: 1958; Homeowner vacancy rate: 1.3%; Median gross rent: $1,327 per month; Rental vacancy rate: 4.6%

Health Insurance: 95.0% have insurance; 92.0% have private insurance; 16.4% have public insurance; 5.0% do not have insurance; 2.0% of children under 18 do not have insurance

Safety: Violent crime rate: 5.8 per 10,000 population; Property crime rate: 116.4 per 10,000 population

Transportation: Commute: 93.2% car, 0.2% public transportation, 0.4% walk, 6.1% work from home; Median travel time to work: 23.4 minutes

Additional Information Contacts

Village of Beverly Hills. . . . . (248) 646-6404
http://www.villagebeverlyhills.com

BINGHAM FARMS (village). Covers a land area of 1.208 square miles and a water area of 0 square miles. Located at 42.52° N. Lat; 83.28° W. Long. Elevation is 715 feet.

History: Bingham Farms was founded in 1955, and named for the original owners of the land on which it was established.

Population: 1,111; Growth (since 2000): 7.9%; Density: 919.6 persons per square mile; Race: 85.2% White, 7.6% Black/African American, 4.4% Asian, 0.2% American Indian/Alaska Native, 0.0% Native Hawaiian/Other Pacific Islander, 1.9% Two or more races, 0.9% Hispanic of any race; Average household size: 2.11; Median age: 59.7; Age under 18: 15.2%; Age 65 and over: 39.1%; Males per 100 females: 89.9

School District(s)

SD of the City of Birmingham (PK-12)

2012-13 Enrollment: 8,298 . . . . (248) 203-3004

Housing: Homeownership rate: 87.3%; Homeowner vacancy rate: 2.1%; Rental vacancy rate: 2.9%

Additional Information Contacts

Village of Bingham Farms. . . . . (248) 644-0044
http://www.binghamfarms.org

BIRMINGHAM (city). Covers a land area of 4.792 square miles and a water area of 0.012 square miles. Located at 42.54° N. Lat; 83.22° W. Long. Elevation is 778 feet.

History: Birmingham was founded by John and Rufus Hunter, who built a cabin here in 1817. By 1839, Birmingham was a stagecoach stop on the Saginaw Trail, named by Roswell T. Merrill who believed it would become an industrial leader like Birmingham, England. The village was incorporated in 1864, and became a city in 1933.

Population: 20,103; Growth (since 2000): 4.2%; Density: 4,195.5 persons per square mile; Race: 92.3% White, 3.0% Black/African American, 2.5% Asian, 0.1% American Indian/Alaska Native, 0.0% Native Hawaiian/Other Pacific Islander, 1.6% Two or more races, 2.1% Hispanic of any race; Average household size: 2.22; Median age: 41.1; Age under 18: 24.6%; Age 65 and over: 13.7%; Males per 100 females: 92.7; Marriage status: 24.1% never married, 59.8% now married, 0.3% separated, 4.5% widowed, 11.6% divorced; Foreign born: 8.0%; Speak English only: 89.3%; With disability: 5.9%; Veterans: 5.5%; Ancestry: 20.9% German, 15.2% Irish, 12.9% English, 11.2% Polish, 8.4% Italian

Employment: 30.5% management, business, and financial, 6.5% computer, engineering, and science, 19.4% education, legal, community service, arts, and media, 10.6% healthcare practitioners, 8.2% service, 20.9% sales and office, 2.3% natural resources, construction, and maintenance, 1.7% production, transportation, and material moving

Income: Per capita: $67,663; Median household: $98,750; Average household: $155,185; Households with income of $100,000 or more: 49.4%; Poverty rate: 3.5%

Educational Attainment: High school diploma or higher: 98.8%; Bachelor's degree or higher: 76.9%; Graduate/professional degree or higher: 37.1%

School District(s)

SD of the City of Birmingham (PK-12)

2012-13 Enrollment: 8,298 . . . . (248) 203-3004

Housing: Homeownership rate: 73.0%; Median home value: $347,400; Median year structure built: 1956; Homeowner vacancy rate: 3.4%; Median gross rent: $1,217 per month; Rental vacancy rate: 11.9%

Health Insurance: 95.6% have insurance; 91.3% have private insurance; 15.8% have public insurance; 4.4% do not have insurance; 2.5% of children under 18 do not have insurance

Safety: Violent crime rate: 6.8 per 10,000 population; Property crime rate: 116.3 per 10,000 population

Transportation: Commute: 91.0% car, 0.3% public transportation, 1.6% walk, 6.5% work from home; Median travel time to work: 22.0 minutes; Amtrak: Train service available.

Additional Information Contacts

City of Birmingham . . . . (248) 530-1800
http://www.ci.birmingham.mi.us

BLOOMFIELD (charter township). Covers a land area of 24.628 square miles and a water area of 1.362 square miles. Located at 42.58° N. Lat; 83.27° W. Long. Elevation is 738 feet.

History: Bloomfield Township, referred to as "Bloomfield" by residents and visitors, was organized in 1827 and was the first township to be established in Oakland County.

Population: 41,070; Growth (since 2000): -4.5%; Density: 1,667.6 persons per square mile; Race: 83.7% White, 6.7% Black/African American, 7.2% Asian, 0.1% American Indian/Alaska Native, 0.0% Native Hawaiian/Other Pacific Islander, 1.9% Two or more races, 1.8% Hispanic of any race; Average household size: 2.48; Median age: 48.7; Age under 18: 22.5%; Age 65 and over: 21.7%; Males per 100 females: 93.3; Marriage status: 22.9% never married, 63.6% now married, 0.6% separated, 6.1% widowed, 7.5% divorced; Foreign born: 14.4%; Speak English only: 83.0%; With disability: 8.7%; Veterans: 7.3%; Ancestry: 18.6% German, 14.4% Irish, 10.2% English, 9.3% Polish, 6.6% Italian

Employment: 28.8% management, business, and financial, 6.0% computer, engineering, and science, 15.7% education, legal, community service, arts, and media, 12.2% healthcare practitioners, 9.2% service, 22.2% sales and office, 2.3% natural resources, construction, and maintenance, 3.5% production, transportation, and material moving

Income: Per capita: $62,730; Median household: $105,320; Average household: $157,317; Households with income of $100,000 or more: 52.7%; Poverty rate: 6.1%

Educational Attainment: High school diploma or higher: 97.1%; Bachelor's degree or higher: 68.9%; Graduate/professional degree or higher: 34.5%

Housing: Homeownership rate: 87.3%; Median home value: $328,800; Median year structure built: 1967; Homeowner vacancy rate: 2.4%; Median gross rent: $1,072 per month; Rental vacancy rate: 12.5%

Health Insurance: 95.3% have insurance; 88.6% have private insurance; 25.6% have public insurance; 4.7% do not have insurance; 2.4% of children under 18 do not have insurance

Safety: Violent crime rate: 5.5 per 10,000 population; Property crime rate: 104.1 per 10,000 population

Transportation: Commute: 90.6% car, 0.8% public transportation, 0.5% walk, 7.3% work from home; Median travel time to work: 23.6 minutes

Additional Information Contacts

Bloomfield Township . . . . (248) 433-7700
http://www.bloomfieldtwp.org

BLOOMFIELD HILLS (city). Covers a land area of 4.962 square miles and a water area of 0.077 square miles. Located at 42.58° N. Lat; 83.25° W. Long. Elevation is 830 feet.

History: Bloomfield Hills was first settled by Amasa Bagley, who came to farm the land. A settlement known as Bagley's Corners grew up, but when Bagley moved away the name was changed to Bloomfield Center. For many years a farming town, it gradually became a residential center for city dwellers who wanted privacy and quiet. The name was changed to Bloomfield Hills, and by 1932 it was incorporated as a city.

Population: 3,869; Growth (since 2000): -1.8%; Density: 779.7 persons per square mile; Race: 87.3% White, 4.1% Black/African American, 6.7% Asian, 0.1% American Indian/Alaska Native, 0.0% Native Hawaiian/Other Pacific Islander, 1.6% Two or more races, 1.5% Hispanic of any race; Average household size: 2.44; Median age: 54.1; Age under 18: 19.9%; Age 65 and over: 29.7%; Males per 100 females: 96.0; Marriage status: 22.4% never married, 67.4% now married, 0.2% separated, 6.0% widowed, 4.3% divorced; Foreign born: 18.7%; Speak English only: 79.9%; With disability: 5.4%; Veterans: 6.1%; Ancestry: 21.3% German, 15.2% English, 8.5% Irish, 6.6% American, 6.2% Italian

Employment: 36.2% management, business, and financial, 9.6% computer, engineering, and science, 16.5% education, legal, community service, arts, and media, 12.7% healthcare practitioners, 7.3% service, 16.0% sales and office, 0.6% natural resources, construction, and maintenance, 1.2% production, transportation, and material moving
Income: Per capita: $90,995; Median household: $147,969; Average household: $257,546; Households with income of $100,000 or more: 68.1%; Poverty rate: 3.3%
Educational Attainment: High school diploma or higher: 96.6%; Bachelor's degree or higher: 74.3%; Graduate/professional degree or higher: 37.0%

School District(s)
Bloomfield Hills SD (PK-12)
    2012-13 Enrollment: 5,510 . . . . (248) 341-5405
SD of the City of Birmingham (PK-12)
    2012-13 Enrollment: 8,298 . . . . (248) 203-3004
Four-year College(s)
Cranbrook Academy of Art (Private, Not-for-profit)
    Fall 2013 Enrollment: 149 . . . . (248) 645-3300
Two-year College(s)
Oakland Community College (Public)
    Fall 2013 Enrollment: 26,405 . . . . (248) 341-2000
    2013-14 Tuition: In-state $4,278; Out-of-state $5,961
Housing: Homeownership rate: 90.3%; Median home value: $664,200; Median year structure built: 1974; Homeowner vacancy rate: 3.4%; Median gross rent: $1,761 per month; Rental vacancy rate: 7.6%
Health Insurance: 97.9% have insurance; 93.6% have private insurance; 21.6% have public insurance; 2.1% do not have insurance; 0.0% of children under 18 do not have insurance
Safety: Violent crime rate: 2.5 per 10,000 population; Property crime rate: 91.1 per 10,000 population
Transportation: Commute: 85.5% car, 0.3% public transportation, 2.0% walk, 11.8% work from home; Median travel time to work: 23.4 minutes

BRANDON (charter township). Covers a land area of 35.107 square miles and a water area of 0.870 square miles. Located at 42.84° N. Lat; 83.40° W. Long. Elevation is 1,033 feet.
History: Brandon Township was founded in 1837.
Population: 15,175; Growth (since 2000): 2.8%; Density: 432.3 persons per square mile; Race: 96.0% White, 0.8% Black/African American, 0.9% Asian, 0.4% American Indian/Alaska Native, 0.0% Native Hawaiian/Other Pacific Islander, 1.3% Two or more races, 3.1% Hispanic of any race; Average household size: 2.83; Median age: 40.2; Age under 18: 26.3%; Age 65 and over: 8.5%; Males per 100 females: 100.7; Marriage status: 25.6% never married, 59.5% now married, 1.3% separated, 3.1% widowed, 11.7% divorced; Foreign born: 2.0%; Speak English only: 95.8%; With disability: 9.6%; Veterans: 9.2%; Ancestry: 25.1% German, 17.6% Irish, 16.7% English, 11.2% Polish, 6.7% Italian
Employment: 13.2% management, business, and financial, 8.9% computer, engineering, and science, 9.8% education, legal, community service, arts, and media, 7.4% healthcare practitioners, 17.6% service, 21.7% sales and office, 10.3% natural resources, construction, and maintenance, 11.2% production, transportation, and material moving
Income: Per capita: $28,219; Median household: $67,592; Average household: $77,963; Households with income of $100,000 or more: 29.4%; Poverty rate: 9.7%
Educational Attainment: High school diploma or higher: 92.4%; Bachelor's degree or higher: 26.2%; Graduate/professional degree or higher: 8.3%
Housing: Homeownership rate: 91.5%; Median home value: $165,300; Median year structure built: 1981; Homeowner vacancy rate: 3.2%; Median gross rent: $824 per month; Rental vacancy rate: 12.8%
Health Insurance: 91.1% have insurance; 75.9% have private insurance; 26.8% have public insurance; 8.9% do not have insurance; 2.0% of children under 18 do not have insurance
Transportation: Commute: 94.9% car, 0.0% public transportation, 0.7% walk, 3.5% work from home; Median travel time to work: 32.7 minutes
Additional Information Contacts
Brandon Charter Township . . . . (248) 627-2851
    http://www.brandontownship.us

CLAWSON (city). Covers a land area of 2.199 square miles and a water area of 0 square miles. Located at 42.54° N. Lat; 83.15° W. Long. Elevation is 666 feet.
History: Joshua Fay built a house on this land in 1829, and the settlement that grew up around it was called Pumachug or The Corners. When John Lawson applied for a post office, he asked for it to be named Lawson. An error resulted in the name of Clawson.
Population: 11,825; Growth (since 2000): -7.1%; Density: 5,376.7 persons per square mile; Race: 93.4% White, 1.9% Black/African American, 2.0% Asian, 0.3% American Indian/Alaska Native, 0.0% Native Hawaiian/Other Pacific Islander, 1.9% Two or more races, 2.1% Hispanic of any race; Average household size: 2.14; Median age: 39.9; Age under 18: 17.9%; Age 65 and over: 14.8%; Males per 100 females: 95.9; Marriage status: 31.5% never married, 47.2% now married, 1.9% separated, 7.0% widowed, 14.4% divorced; Foreign born: 8.9%; Speak English only: 90.2%; With disability: 13.5%; Veterans: 7.0%; Ancestry: 25.3% German, 14.6% Polish, 14.5% Irish, 11.7% English, 7.5% French
Employment: 14.3% management, business, and financial, 8.9% computer, engineering, and science, 12.1% education, legal, community service, arts, and media, 4.2% healthcare practitioners, 18.0% service, 26.3% sales and office, 6.2% natural resources, construction, and maintenance, 9.9% production, transportation, and material moving
Income: Per capita: $29,961; Median household: $51,868; Average household: $66,318; Households with income of $100,000 or more: 20.3%; Poverty rate: 7.5%
Educational Attainment: High school diploma or higher: 92.9%; Bachelor's degree or higher: 32.8%; Graduate/professional degree or higher: 10.5%

School District(s)
Clawson Public Schools (PK-12)
    2012-13 Enrollment: 1,771 . . . . (248) 655-4448
Housing: Homeownership rate: 71.9%; Median home value: $126,500; Median year structure built: 1958; Homeowner vacancy rate: 1.8%; Median gross rent: $810 per month; Rental vacancy rate: 7.8%
Health Insurance: 87.2% have insurance; 76.0% have private insurance; 24.0% have public insurance; 12.8% do not have insurance; 5.2% of children under 18 do not have insurance
Safety: Violent crime rate: 8.3 per 10,000 population; Property crime rate: 79.3 per 10,000 population
Transportation: Commute: 95.3% car, 0.4% public transportation, 0.8% walk, 2.7% work from home; Median travel time to work: 22.7 minutes
Additional Information Contacts
City of Clawson . . . . (248) 435-4500
    http://www.cityofclawson.com

COMMERCE (charter township). Covers a land area of 27.451 square miles and a water area of 2.452 square miles. Located at 42.57° N. Lat; 83.50° W. Long. Elevation is 945 feet.
History: Commerce was settled in the 1830's and named by its early residents in the hope that it would become a business center.
Population: 40,186; Growth (since 2000): 15.6%; Density: 1,463.9 persons per square mile; Race: 93.6% White, 1.6% Black/African American, 2.4% Asian, 0.3% American Indian/Alaska Native, 0.0% Native Hawaiian/Other Pacific Islander, 1.6% Two or more races, 2.6% Hispanic of any race; Average household size: 2.68; Median age: 40.2; Age under 18: 26.0%; Age 65 and over: 10.6%; Males per 100 females: 98.9; Marriage status: 22.5% never married, 64.2% now married, 0.9% separated, 4.0% widowed, 9.3% divorced; Foreign born: 8.6%; Speak English only: 88.6%; With disability: 9.5%; Veterans: 7.8%; Ancestry: 25.1% German, 14.4% Irish, 13.2% Polish, 11.7% English, 8.1% Italian
Employment: 20.1% management, business, and financial, 8.2% computer, engineering, and science, 8.6% education, legal, community service, arts, and media, 5.1% healthcare practitioners, 14.0% service, 28.5% sales and office, 5.4% natural resources, construction, and maintenance, 10.0% production, transportation, and material moving
Income: Per capita: $37,091; Median household: $78,514; Average household: $99,428; Households with income of $100,000 or more: 38.5%; Poverty rate: 6.1%
Educational Attainment: High school diploma or higher: 93.6%; Bachelor's degree or higher: 41.0%; Graduate/professional degree or higher: 13.4%
Housing: Homeownership rate: 90.1%; Median home value: $180,300; Median year structure built: 1984; Homeowner vacancy rate: 2.0%; Median gross rent: $1,259 per month; Rental vacancy rate: 8.2%

Health Insurance: 92.1% have insurance; 83.4% have private insurance; 20.3% have public insurance; 7.9% do not have insurance; 3.6% of children under 18 do not have insurance
Transportation: Commute: 94.1% car, 0.1% public transportation, 0.2% walk, 4.8% work from home; Median travel time to work: 29.1 minutes
Additional Information Contacts
Commerce Charter Township . . . . (248) 624-0110
http://www.commercetwp.com

COMMERCE TOWNSHIP (unincorporated postal area)
ZCTA: 48382

Covers a land area of 16.450 square miles and a water area of 1.894 square miles. Located at 42.59° N. Lat; 83.51° W. Long..
Population: 21,945; Growth (since 2000): 15.4%; Density: 1,334.0 persons per square mile; Race: 95.2% White, 1.4% Black/African American, 1.6% Asian, 0.2% American Indian/Alaska Native, 0.0% Native Hawaiian/Other Pacific Islander, 1.3% Two or more races, 1.9% Hispanic of any race; Average household size: 2.85; Median age: 40.2; Age under 18: 28.0%; Age 65 and over: 9.4%; Males per 100 females: 98.6; Marriage status: 20.9% never married, 68.2% now married, 0.6% separated, 3.1% widowed, 7.8% divorced; Foreign born: 6.5%; Speak English only: 90.2%; With disability: 8.6%; Veterans: 7.3%; Ancestry: 25.4% German, 13.7% Polish, 12.8% Irish, 10.9% English, 9.6% Italian
Employment: 21.7% management, business, and financial, 8.3% computer, engineering, and science, 8.9% education, legal, community service, arts, and media, 6.3% healthcare practitioners, 12.2% service, 29.4% sales and office, 5.8% natural resources, construction, and maintenance, 7.3% production, transportation, and material moving
Income: Per capita: $39,583; Median household: $87,835; Average household: $109,956; Households with income of $100,000 or more: 44.5%; Poverty rate: 5.6%
Educational Attainment: High school diploma or higher: 95.3%; Bachelor's degree or higher: 46.9%; Graduate/professional degree or higher: 15.4%

School District(s)
Huron Valley Schools (PK-12)
    2012-13 Enrollment: 9,899 . . . . (248) 684-8234
Walled Lake Consolidated Schools (PK-12)
    2012-13 Enrollment: 15,177 . . . . (248) 956-2000
Housing: Homeownership rate: 93.2%; Median home value: $212,200; Median year structure built: 1980; Homeowner vacancy rate: 1.3%; Median gross rent: $1,268 per month; Rental vacancy rate: 9.6%
Health Insurance: 93.6% have insurance; 86.8% have private insurance; 17.2% have public insurance; 6.4% do not have insurance; 3.0% of children under 18 do not have insurance
Hospitals: Huron Valley - Sinai Hospital (153 beds)
Transportation: Commute: 93.1% car, 0.1% public transportation, 0.4% walk, 5.6% work from home; Median travel time to work: 30.0 minutes

DAVISBURG (unincorporated postal area)
ZCTA: 48350

Covers a land area of 23.787 square miles and a water area of 0.902 square miles. Located at 42.74° N. Lat; 83.53° W. Long. Elevation is 971 feet.
Population: 7,100; Growth (since 2000): 0.3%; Density: 298.5 persons per square mile; Race: 95.7% White, 1.2% Black/African American, 1.0% Asian, 0.2% American Indian/Alaska Native, 0.0% Native Hawaiian/Other Pacific Islander, 1.3% Two or more races, 2.7% Hispanic of any race; Average household size: 2.80; Median age: 42.2; Age under 18: 25.2%; Age 65 and over: 10.2%; Males per 100 females: 102.1; Marriage status: 24.6% never married, 63.5% now married, 0.6% separated, 3.0% widowed, 8.9% divorced; Foreign born: 3.1%; Speak English only: 94.4%; With disability: 9.5%; Veterans: 5.9%; Ancestry: 28.7% German, 17.2% Irish, 15.5% English, 10.6% Polish, 7.3% Italian
Employment: 18.0% management, business, and financial, 7.9% computer, engineering, and science, 8.4% education, legal, community service, arts, and media, 5.4% healthcare practitioners, 19.3% service, 20.1% sales and office, 10.3% natural resources, construction, and maintenance, 10.5% production, transportation, and material moving
Income: Per capita: $30,761; Median household: $75,401; Average household: $84,106; Households with income of $100,000 or more: 33.2%; Poverty rate: 6.1%
Educational Attainment: High school diploma or higher: 94.6%; Bachelor's degree or higher: 32.8%; Graduate/professional degree or higher: 11.7%

School District(s)
Clarkston Community SD (PK-12)
    2012-13 Enrollment: 7,939 . . . . (248) 623-5408
Holly Area SD (PK-12)
    2012-13 Enrollment: 3,415 . . . . (248) 328-3140
Housing: Homeownership rate: 93.6%; Median home value: $208,000; Median year structure built: 1986; Homeowner vacancy rate: 2.9%; Median gross rent: $1,130 per month; Rental vacancy rate: 12.3%
Health Insurance: 89.3% have insurance; 82.2% have private insurance; 18.4% have public insurance; 10.7% do not have insurance; 4.0% of children under 18 do not have insurance
Transportation: Commute: 94.3% car, 0.0% public transportation, 0.6% walk, 4.5% work from home; Median travel time to work: 29.6 minutes

FARMINGTON (city). Covers a land area of 2.660 square miles and a water area of 0 square miles. Located at 42.46° N. Lat; 83.38° W. Long. Elevation is 748 feet.
History: Farmington was settled by Quakers in 1824, when the area was accessible only by a trail. The town was named for the former home in New York of one of the early settlers, but it was often referred to as Quakertown. Farmington later became a residential community for people working in Detroit.
Population: 10,372; Growth (since 2000): -0.5%; Density: 3,899.6 persons per square mile; Race: 71.5% White, 11.4% Black/African American, 13.9% Asian, 0.4% American Indian/Alaska Native, 0.1% Native Hawaiian/Other Pacific Islander, 2.3% Two or more races, 2.1% Hispanic of any race; Average household size: 2.22; Median age: 39.5; Age under 18: 22.0%; Age 65 and over: 15.5%; Males per 100 females: 89.4; Marriage status: 27.7% never married, 53.7% now married, 1.2% separated, 7.1% widowed, 11.5% divorced; Foreign born: 16.8%; Speak English only: 81.5%; With disability: 8.9%; Veterans: 8.2%; Ancestry: 17.7% German, 12.7% Irish, 12.4% English, 9.7% Polish, 5.8% Italian
Employment: 19.4% management, business, and financial, 15.1% computer, engineering, and science, 13.9% education, legal, community service, arts, and media, 5.4% healthcare practitioners, 11.2% service, 24.3% sales and office, 4.4% natural resources, construction, and maintenance, 6.3% production, transportation, and material moving
Income: Per capita: $33,779; Median household: $58,408; Average household: $75,829; Households with income of $100,000 or more: 24.7%; Poverty rate: 7.4%
Educational Attainment: High school diploma or higher: 95.9%; Bachelor's degree or higher: 53.6%; Graduate/professional degree or higher: 23.7%

School District(s)
Farmington Public SD (PK-12)
    2012-13 Enrollment: 11,104 . . . . (248) 489-3339
Housing: Homeownership rate: 62.2%; Median home value: $155,100; Median year structure built: 1966; Homeowner vacancy rate: 2.3%; Median gross rent: $878 per month; Rental vacancy rate: 9.1%
Health Insurance: 93.6% have insurance; 84.0% have private insurance; 21.6% have public insurance; 6.4% do not have insurance; 1.2% of children under 18 do not have insurance
Safety: Violent crime rate: 12.4 per 10,000 population; Property crime rate: 109.4 per 10,000 population
Transportation: Commute: 92.8% car, 0.3% public transportation, 1.0% walk, 4.8% work from home; Median travel time to work: 24.3 minutes
Additional Information Contacts
City of Farmington . . . . (248) 474-5500
http://www.ci.farmington.mi.us

FARMINGTON HILLS (city). Covers a land area of 33.280 square miles and a water area of 0.028 square miles. Located at 42.49° N. Lat; 83.38° W. Long. Elevation is 850 feet.
History: Farmington Hills was settled by Quaker Arthur Power from Farmington, New York who purchased the land in 1823. Farmington was organized in 1827, incorporated as the village of Farmington in 1867, and as a city in 1926.
Population: 79,740; Growth (since 2000): -2.9%; Density: 2,396.0 persons per square mile; Race: 69.7% White, 17.4% Black/African American, 10.1% Asian, 0.2% American Indian/Alaska Native, 0.0% Native Hawaiian/Other Pacific Islander, 2.2% Two or more races, 1.9% Hispanic of any race; Average household size: 2.36; Median age: 42.1; Age under 18: 21.5%; Age 65 and over: 15.9%; Males per 100 females: 89.1; Marriage status: 26.4% never married, 56.3% now married, 1.3% separated, 6.7% widowed, 10.6% divorced; Foreign born: 17.6%; Speak

English only: 78.8%; With disability: 10.9%; Veterans: 7.8%; Ancestry: 12.8% German, 10.5% Polish, 8.4% Irish, 7.2% English, 4.9% Italian
Employment: 19.8% management, business, and financial, 12.3% computer, engineering, and science, 12.1% education, legal, community service, arts, and media, 7.2% healthcare practitioners, 13.6% service, 24.9% sales and office, 3.4% natural resources, construction, and maintenance, 6.8% production, transportation, and material moving
Income: Per capita: $40,604; Median household: $69,700; Average household: $94,395; Households with income of $100,000 or more: 32.6%; Poverty rate: 7.5%
Educational Attainment: High school diploma or higher: 93.9%; Bachelor's degree or higher: 50.8%; Graduate/professional degree or higher: 22.7%

School District(s)
Farmington Public SD (PK-12)
    2012-13 Enrollment: 11,104 . . . . (248) 489-3339
West Bloomfield SD (PK-12)
    2012-13 Enrollment: 6,228 . . . . (248) 865-6485
Four-year College(s)
Michigan School of Professional Psychology (Private, Not-for-profit)
    Fall 2013 Enrollment: 161 . . . . (248) 476-1122
Vocational/Technical School(s)
Dorsey Business Schools-Farmington Hills (Private, For-profit)
    Fall 2013 Enrollment: 97 . . . . (248) 994-0133
    2013-14 Tuition: In-state $17,568; Out-of-state $17,568
Housing: Homeownership rate: 63.6%; Median home value: $201,200; Median year structure built: 1977; Homeowner vacancy rate: 2.1%; Median gross rent: $976 per month; Rental vacancy rate: 9.7%
Health Insurance: 92.4% have insurance; 82.5% have private insurance; 25.2% have public insurance; 7.6% do not have insurance; 3.5% of children under 18 do not have insurance
Hospitals: Botsford Hospital (330 beds)
Safety: Violent crime rate: 8.9 per 10,000 population; Property crime rate: 137.4 per 10,000 population
Transportation: Commute: 92.3% car, 0.6% public transportation, 1.0% walk, 5.2% work from home; Median travel time to work: 23.9 minutes
Additional Information Contacts
City of Farmington Hills . . . . (248) 871-2400
    http://www.ci.farmington-hills.mi.us

FERNDALE (city). Covers a land area of 3.879 square miles and a water area of 0 square miles. Located at 42.46° N. Lat; 83.13° W. Long. Elevation is 646 feet.
History: Named for the many local ferns, by Lovell G. Turnbull. Ferndale was incorporated as a village in 1918, and as a city in 1927.
Population: 19,900; Growth (since 2000): -10.0%; Density: 5,129.6 persons per square mile; Race: 84.7% White, 9.6% Black/African American, 1.3% Asian, 0.5% American Indian/Alaska Native, 0.1% Native Hawaiian/Other Pacific Islander, 3.4% Two or more races, 2.8% Hispanic of any race; Average household size: 2.08; Median age: 35.6; Age under 18: 16.5%; Age 65 and over: 8.9%; Males per 100 females: 99.7; Marriage status: 45.7% never married, 36.9% now married, 2.1% separated, 4.1% widowed, 13.3% divorced; Foreign born: 4.9%; Speak English only: 92.8%; With disability: 14.0%; Veterans: 5.7%; Ancestry: 19.7% German, 16.6% Irish, 12.8% Polish, 9.6% English, 7.0% Italian
Employment: 16.7% management, business, and financial, 5.2% computer, engineering, and science, 17.6% education, legal, community service, arts, and media, 5.1% healthcare practitioners, 17.0% service, 23.8% sales and office, 5.0% natural resources, construction, and maintenance, 9.5% production, transportation, and material moving
Income: Per capita: $28,254; Median household: $47,662; Average household: $58,826; Households with income of $100,000 or more: 15.6%; Poverty rate: 15.1%
Educational Attainment: High school diploma or higher: 93.5%; Bachelor's degree or higher: 40.3%; Graduate/professional degree or higher: 15.5%

School District(s)
Ferndale Public Schools (PK-12)
    2012-13 Enrollment: 3,653 . . . . (248) 586-8651
Hazel Park SD (PK-12)
    2012-13 Enrollment: 4,042 . . . . (248) 658-5220
Housing: Homeownership rate: 65.2%; Median home value: $93,700; Median year structure built: 1946; Homeowner vacancy rate: 3.9%; Median gross rent: $847 per month; Rental vacancy rate: 9.2%

Health Insurance: 78.7% have insurance; 66.0% have private insurance; 21.8% have public insurance; 21.3% do not have insurance; 6.6% of children under 18 do not have insurance
Safety: Violent crime rate: 20.9 per 10,000 population; Property crime rate: 230.3 per 10,000 population
Transportation: Commute: 90.3% car, 1.8% public transportation, 2.6% walk, 3.2% work from home; Median travel time to work: 22.5 minutes
Additional Information Contacts
City of Ferndale . . . . (248) 546-2525
    http://www.ferndale-mi.com

FRANKLIN (village). Covers a land area of 2.660 square miles and a water area of 0 square miles. Located at 42.52° N. Lat; 83.30° W. Long. Elevation is 837 feet.
Population: 3,150; Growth (since 2000): 7.3%; Density: 1,184.2 persons per square mile; Race: 86.2% White, 6.6% Black/African American, 4.8% Asian, 0.1% American Indian/Alaska Native, 0.1% Native Hawaiian/Other Pacific Islander, 1.7% Two or more races, 1.3% Hispanic of any race; Average household size: 2.82; Median age: 45.4; Age under 18: 28.4%; Age 65 and over: 16.2%; Males per 100 females: 102.2; Marriage status: 17.4% never married, 73.5% now married, 0.3% separated, 4.2% widowed, 4.9% divorced; Foreign born: 11.6%; Speak English only: 86.5%; With disability: 8.8%; Veterans: 7.8%; Ancestry: 16.5% German, 11.6% Polish, 9.9% Russian, 9.7% English, 8.1% Italian
Employment: 28.7% management, business, and financial, 3.4% computer, engineering, and science, 18.8% education, legal, community service, arts, and media, 13.3% healthcare practitioners, 5.6% service, 27.8% sales and office, 1.4% natural resources, construction, and maintenance, 1.0% production, transportation, and material moving
Income: Per capita: $80,238; Median household: $139,000; Average household: $229,233; Households with income of $100,000 or more: 65.6%; Poverty rate: 6.4%
Educational Attainment: High school diploma or higher: 97.5%; Bachelor's degree or higher: 72.4%; Graduate/professional degree or higher: 38.0%
Housing: Homeownership rate: 94.8%; Median home value: $467,200; Median year structure built: 1963; Homeowner vacancy rate: 2.3%; Median gross rent: $2,000+ per month; Rental vacancy rate: 7.9%
Health Insurance: 97.9% have insurance; 95.3% have private insurance; 17.0% have public insurance; 2.1% do not have insurance; 0.0% of children under 18 do not have insurance
Safety: Violent crime rate: 6.3 per 10,000 population; Property crime rate: 106.5 per 10,000 population
Transportation: Commute: 84.4% car, 0.6% public transportation, 2.6% walk, 11.2% work from home; Median travel time to work: 21.2 minutes
Additional Information Contacts
Village of Franklin . . . . (248) 626-9666
    http://www.franklin.mi.us

GROVELAND (township). Covers a land area of 35.261 square miles and a water area of 0.776 square miles. Located at 42.84° N. Lat; 83.51° W. Long.
Population: 5,476; Growth (since 2000): -11.0%; Density: 155.3 persons per square mile; Race: 96.0% White, 1.1% Black/African American, 0.9% Asian, 0.3% American Indian/Alaska Native, 0.0% Native Hawaiian/Other Pacific Islander, 1.2% Two or more races, 2.2% Hispanic of any race; Average household size: 2.79; Median age: 43.4; Age under 18: 24.0%; Age 65 and over: 10.2%; Males per 100 females: 107.0; Marriage status: 25.6% never married, 60.9% now married, 0.7% separated, 3.7% widowed, 9.8% divorced; Foreign born: 3.6%; Speak English only: 97.1%; With disability: 12.9%; Veterans: 8.3%; Ancestry: 30.2% German, 17.0% Irish, 12.8% Polish, 12.3% English, 7.3% Italian
Employment: 17.1% management, business, and financial, 9.3% computer, engineering, and science, 10.0% education, legal, community service, arts, and media, 7.4% healthcare practitioners, 16.8% service, 19.9% sales and office, 10.9% natural resources, construction, and maintenance, 8.7% production, transportation, and material moving
Income: Per capita: $30,996; Median household: $81,938; Average household: $87,542; Households with income of $100,000 or more: 36.1%; Poverty rate: 9.9%
Educational Attainment: High school diploma or higher: 93.9%; Bachelor's degree or higher: 26.6%; Graduate/professional degree or higher: 11.5%

Housing: Homeownership rate: 91.3%; Median home value: $196,100; Median year structure built: 1982; Homeowner vacancy rate: 3.1%; Median gross rent: $1,012 per month; Rental vacancy rate: 36.3%
Health Insurance: 91.7% have insurance; 79.4% have private insurance; 24.3% have public insurance; 8.3% do not have insurance; 3.4% of children under 18 do not have insurance
Transportation: Commute: 92.8% car, 0.1% public transportation, 1.8% walk, 4.1% work from home; Median travel time to work: 31.5 minutes

HAZEL PARK (city).
Covers a land area of 2.818 square miles and a water area of 0 square miles. Located at 42.46° N. Lat; 83.10° W. Long. Elevation is 630 feet.
History: Named for the abundance of local hazelnut bushes in the mid-1800s. The land on which Hazel Park was established was once owned by Anthony Neusius. First called Hazel Slump for the hazelnut bushes and water, it was later incorporated as the city of Hazel Park.
Population: 16,422; Growth (since 2000): -13.4%; Density: 5,828.5 persons per square mile; Race: 82.8% White, 9.8% Black/African American, 1.5% Asian, 0.9% American Indian/Alaska Native, 0.0% Native Hawaiian/Other Pacific Islander, 4.6% Two or more races, 2.7% Hispanic of any race; Average household size: 2.47; Median age: 36.1; Age under 18: 24.2%; Age 65 and over: 11.3%; Males per 100 females: 97.5; Marriage status: 38.9% never married, 39.1% now married, 1.0% separated, 8.4% widowed, 13.6% divorced; Foreign born: 6.4%; Speak English only: 93.5%; With disability: 24.8%; Veterans: 8.6%; Ancestry: 16.9% German, 10.7% Irish, 10.6% Polish, 9.6% English, 6.5% Scottish
Employment: 8.3% management, business, and financial, 4.0% computer, engineering, and science, 6.6% education, legal, community service, arts, and media, 3.5% healthcare practitioners, 18.7% service, 27.0% sales and office, 9.5% natural resources, construction, and maintenance, 22.4% production, transportation, and material moving
Income: Per capita: $17,084; Median household: $30,875; Average household: $40,554; Households with income of $100,000 or more: 6.0%; Poverty rate: 27.4%
Educational Attainment: High school diploma or higher: 79.6%; Bachelor's degree or higher: 10.3%; Graduate/professional degree or higher: 1.9%

School District(s)
Hazel Park SD (PK-12)
    2012-13 Enrollment: 4,042 . . . . (248) 658-5220
Michigan Mathematics and Science Academy (KG-12)
    2012-13 Enrollment: 437 . . . . (248) 808-6914
Housing: Homeownership rate: 64.3%; Median home value: $54,700; Median year structure built: 1954; Homeowner vacancy rate: 4.6%; Median gross rent: $879 per month; Rental vacancy rate: 8.8%
Health Insurance: 79.9% have insurance; 48.8% have private insurance; 42.4% have public insurance; 20.1% do not have insurance; 10.1% of children under 18 do not have insurance
Safety: Violent crime rate: 45.7 per 10,000 population; Property crime rate: 262.0 per 10,000 population
Transportation: Commute: 90.2% car, 2.9% public transportation, 3.0% walk, 2.1% work from home; Median travel time to work: 24.3 minutes
Additional Information Contacts
City of Hazel Park . . . . (248) 546-4060
    http://www.hazelpark.org

HIGHLAND (charter township).
Covers a land area of 34.111 square miles and a water area of 2.069 square miles. Located at 42.66° N. Lat; 83.62° W. Long. Elevation is 1,014 feet.
Population: 19,202; Growth (since 2000): 0.2%; Density: 562.9 persons per square mile; Race: 97.1% White, 0.4% Black/African American, 0.5% Asian, 0.3% American Indian/Alaska Native, 0.0% Native Hawaiian/Other Pacific Islander, 1.4% Two or more races, 1.9% Hispanic of any race; Average household size: 2.69; Median age: 42.0; Age under 18: 24.3%; Age 65 and over: 11.4%; Males per 100 females: 100.7; Marriage status: 24.1% never married, 60.0% now married, 0.6% separated, 3.9% widowed, 12.1% divorced; Foreign born: 2.2%; Speak English only: 97.5%; With disability: 11.2%; Veterans: 9.5%; Ancestry: 25.6% German, 17.2% Irish, 14.9% English, 11.7% Polish, 8.7% American
Employment: 16.0% management, business, and financial, 6.0% computer, engineering, and science, 8.8% education, legal, community service, arts, and media, 3.8% healthcare practitioners, 15.8% service, 23.5% sales and office, 11.1% natural resources, construction, and maintenance, 15.0% production, transportation, and material moving

Income: Per capita: $29,575; Median household: $69,085; Average household: $80,691; Households with income of $100,000 or more: 30.5%; Poverty rate: 8.7%
Educational Attainment: High school diploma or higher: 92.6%; Bachelor's degree or higher: 28.2%; Graduate/professional degree or higher: 8.5%

School District(s)
Huron Valley Schools (PK-12)
    2012-13 Enrollment: 9,899 . . . . (248) 684-8234
Housing: Homeownership rate: 89.8%; Median home value: $171,000; Median year structure built: 1977; Homeowner vacancy rate: 2.8%; Median gross rent: $924 per month; Rental vacancy rate: 9.5%
Health Insurance: 90.8% have insurance; 78.8% have private insurance; 24.2% have public insurance; 9.2% do not have insurance; 2.3% of children under 18 do not have insurance
Newspapers: Spinal Column Newsweekly (weekly circulation 50000)
Transportation: Commute: 93.8% car, 0.3% public transportation, 0.8% walk, 4.3% work from home; Median travel time to work: 32.9 minutes
Additional Information Contacts
Highland Charter Township . . . . (248) 887-3791
    http://www.highlandtwp.com

HOLLY (township).
Covers a land area of 34.378 square miles and a water area of 2.042 square miles. Located at 42.83° N. Lat; 83.63° W. Long. Elevation is 925 feet.
History: Settled 1836, incorporated 1865.
Population: 11,362; Growth (since 2000): 13.2%; Density: 330.5 persons per square mile; Race: 93.6% White, 2.1% Black/African American, 1.1% Asian, 0.6% American Indian/Alaska Native, 0.1% Native Hawaiian/Other Pacific Islander, 1.9% Two or more races, 3.2% Hispanic of any race; Average household size: 2.53; Median age: 39.3; Age under 18: 24.2%; Age 65 and over: 12.7%; Males per 100 females: 97.1; Marriage status: 26.7% never married, 52.7% now married, 0.8% separated, 5.6% widowed, 15.0% divorced; Foreign born: 2.2%; Speak English only: 95.3%; With disability: 10.9%; Veterans: 8.7%; Ancestry: 27.9% German, 16.5% English, 14.4% Irish, 9.0% Polish, 5.9% French
Employment: 12.1% management, business, and financial, 7.1% computer, engineering, and science, 9.1% education, legal, community service, arts, and media, 5.1% healthcare practitioners, 16.1% service, 27.5% sales and office, 7.2% natural resources, construction, and maintenance, 15.8% production, transportation, and material moving
Income: Per capita: $26,904; Median household: $62,324; Average household: $72,497; Households with income of $100,000 or more: 22.0%; Poverty rate: 9.3%
Educational Attainment: High school diploma or higher: 90.9%; Bachelor's degree or higher: 20.9%; Graduate/professional degree or higher: 7.2%

School District(s)
Holly Academy (KG-12)
    2012-13 Enrollment: 886 . . . . (248) 634-5554
Holly Area SD (PK-12)
    2012-13 Enrollment: 3,415 . . . . (248) 328-3140
Housing: Homeownership rate: 81.2%; Median home value: $119,000; Median year structure built: 1978; Homeowner vacancy rate: 3.2%; Median gross rent: $861 per month; Rental vacancy rate: 12.3%
Health Insurance: 90.0% have insurance; 76.9% have private insurance; 26.3% have public insurance; 10.0% do not have insurance; 6.0% of children under 18 do not have insurance
Newspapers: Community Voice (weekly circulation 4000)
Transportation: Commute: 96.8% car, 0.0% public transportation, 1.2% walk, 1.4% work from home; Median travel time to work: 30.3 minutes
Additional Information Contacts
Holly Township . . . . (248) 634-9331
    http://www.hollytownship.org

HOLLY (village).
Covers a land area of 2.763 square miles and a water area of 0.285 square miles. Located at 42.80° N. Lat; 83.62° W. Long. Elevation is 925 feet.
History: Holly grew up around a sawmill and a grist mill built by Ira C. Alger in the mid-1840's. The village may have been named Holly because so much holly grew there, or because one of the early settlers was from Mount Holly, New Jersey. Holly had an early reputation as a flower center, encouraged by the Holly Flower Lovers' Club.
Population: 6,086; Growth (since 2000): -0.8%; Density: 2,202.3 persons per square mile; Race: 95.0% White, 1.2% Black/African American, 0.6%

Asian, 0.6% American Indian/Alaska Native, 0.0% Native Hawaiian/Other Pacific Islander, 1.9% Two or more races, 3.6% Hispanic of any race; Average household size: 2.45; Median age: 36.3; Age under 18: 25.5%; Age 65 and over: 12.5%; Males per 100 females: 94.8; Marriage status: 25.0% never married, 53.2% now married, 1.5% separated, 5.3% widowed, 16.5% divorced; Foreign born: 2.2%; Speak English only: 95.4%; With disability: 12.0%; Veterans: 9.2%; Ancestry: 24.6% German, 17.6% English, 12.9% Irish, 6.2% French, 5.9% Polish

Employment: 8.7% management, business, and financial, 7.2% computer, engineering, and science, 9.2% education, legal, community service, arts, and media, 3.3% healthcare practitioners, 16.9% service, 27.1% sales and office, 8.0% natural resources, construction, and maintenance, 19.5% production, transportation, and material moving

Income: Per capita: $23,006; Median household: $60,048; Average household: $60,799; Households with income of $100,000 or more: 12.8%; Poverty rate: 13.8%

Educational Attainment: High school diploma or higher: 87.9%; Bachelor's degree or higher: 13.1%; Graduate/professional degree or higher: 3.3%

School District(s)

Holly Academy (KG-12)
    2012-13 Enrollment: 886 . . . . (248) 634-5554
Holly Area SD (PK-12)
    2012-13 Enrollment: 3,415 . . . . (248) 328-3140

Housing: Homeownership rate: 73.4%; Median home value: $84,400; Median year structure built: 1973; Homeowner vacancy rate: 3.5%; Median gross rent: $761 per month; Rental vacancy rate: 14.3%

Health Insurance: 89.9% have insurance; 74.4% have private insurance; 28.0% have public insurance; 10.1% do not have insurance; 5.1% of children under 18 do not have insurance

Safety: Violent crime rate: 14.6 per 10,000 population; Property crime rate: 149.6 per 10,000 population

Newspapers: Community Voice (weekly circulation 4000)

Transportation: Commute: 95.8% car, 0.0% public transportation, 1.8% walk, 1.3% work from home; Median travel time to work: 30.4 minutes

Additional Information Contacts
Village of Holly. . . . . (248) 634-9571
    http://www.vi.holly.mi.us

HUNTINGTON WOODS (city). Covers a land area of 1.465 square miles and a water area of 0.004 square miles. Located at 42.48° N. Lat; 83.17° W. Long. Elevation is 656 feet.

History: Huntington Woods was established as a residential community in the early 1920's. It was incorporated as a village in 1927 and as a city in 1932.

Population: 6,238; Growth (since 2000): 1.4%; Density: 4,257.9 persons per square mile; Race: 96.0% White, 1.0% Black/African American, 1.3% Asian, 0.2% American Indian/Alaska Native, 0.0% Native Hawaiian/Other Pacific Islander, 1.1% Two or more races, 1.6% Hispanic of any race; Average household size: 2.65; Median age: 42.0; Age under 18: 27.4%; Age 65 and over: 13.6%; Males per 100 females: 96.7; Marriage status: 20.1% never married, 66.6% now married, 0.2% separated, 5.9% widowed, 7.4% divorced; Foreign born: 7.5%; Speak English only: 92.3%; With disability: 8.0%; Veterans: 5.5%; Ancestry: 20.0% Polish, 16.3% German, 13.3% Irish, 10.6% Russian, 9.7% English

Employment: 25.3% management, business, and financial, 6.6% computer, engineering, and science, 27.7% education, legal, community service, arts, and media, 13.8% healthcare practitioners, 9.3% service, 14.0% sales and office, 1.0% natural resources, construction, and maintenance, 2.3% production, transportation, and material moving

Income: Per capita: $53,709; Median household: $112,869; Average household: $143,769; Households with income of $100,000 or more: 59.3%; Poverty rate: 1.8%

Educational Attainment: High school diploma or higher: 99.3%; Bachelor's degree or higher: 79.9%; Graduate/professional degree or higher: 42.6%

School District(s)

Berkley SD (PK-12)
    2012-13 Enrollment: 4,667 . . . . (248) 837-8000

Housing: Homeownership rate: 95.7%; Median home value: $250,500; Median year structure built: 1949; Homeowner vacancy rate: 1.2%; Median gross rent: $1,529 per month; Rental vacancy rate: 3.8%

Health Insurance: 97.1% have insurance; 93.1% have private insurance; 15.1% have public insurance; 2.9% do not have insurance; 2.0% of children under 18 do not have insurance

Safety: Violent crime rate: 1.6 per 10,000 population; Property crime rate: 103.1 per 10,000 population

Transportation: Commute: 89.9% car, 0.8% public transportation, 1.4% walk, 6.8% work from home; Median travel time to work: 21.1 minutes

Additional Information Contacts
City of Huntington Woods . . . . (248) 541-4300
    http://www.ci.huntington-woods.mi.us

INDEPENDENCE (charter township). Covers a land area of 34.992 square miles and a water area of 1.310 square miles. Located at 42.75° N. Lat; 83.39° W. Long.

History: Independence Township was organized in 1837 and named for Independence, New Jersey, the former home of one of its first settlers.

Population: 34,681; Growth (since 2000): 6.4%; Density: 991.1 persons per square mile; Race: 93.0% White, 1.9% Black/African American, 1.5% Asian, 0.3% American Indian/Alaska Native, 0.0% Native Hawaiian/Other Pacific Islander, 2.0% Two or more races, 4.5% Hispanic of any race; Average household size: 2.69; Median age: 40.6; Age under 18: 26.4%; Age 65 and over: 11.5%; Males per 100 females: 97.7; Marriage status: 27.1% never married, 56.8% now married, 0.7% separated, 4.7% widowed, 11.4% divorced; Foreign born: 3.9%; Speak English only: 95.3%; With disability: 9.2%; Veterans: 7.6%; Ancestry: 26.3% German, 17.1% Irish, 13.1% English, 10.0% Polish, 6.4% Italian

Employment: 18.1% management, business, and financial, 9.6% computer, engineering, and science, 9.8% education, legal, community service, arts, and media, 6.4% healthcare practitioners, 14.3% service, 26.3% sales and office, 6.0% natural resources, construction, and maintenance, 9.6% production, transportation, and material moving

Income: Per capita: $34,164; Median household: $72,363; Average household: $89,711; Households with income of $100,000 or more: 33.3%; Poverty rate: 6.3%

Educational Attainment: High school diploma or higher: 94.6%; Bachelor's degree or higher: 38.0%; Graduate/professional degree or higher: 14.5%

Housing: Homeownership rate: 82.1%; Median home value: $184,600; Median year structure built: 1983; Homeowner vacancy rate: 1.9%; Median gross rent: $914 per month; Rental vacancy rate: 13.6%

Health Insurance: 93.6% have insurance; 85.2% have private insurance; 22.7% have public insurance; 6.4% do not have insurance; 1.4% of children under 18 do not have insurance

Transportation: Commute: 94.3% car, 0.1% public transportation, 0.7% walk, 4.4% work from home; Median travel time to work: 28.5 minutes

Additional Information Contacts
Independence Charter Township . . . . (248) 625-5111
    http://www.twp.independence.mi.us

KEEGO HARBOR (city). Covers a land area of 0.504 square miles and a water area of 0.044 square miles. Located at 42.61° N. Lat; 83.35° W. Long. Elevation is 932 feet.

History: In 1902, J.E. Sawyer built a canal connecting Dollar Lake with Cass Lake, thus making Dollar Lake into a harbor which he named Keego Harbor. Keego is the name of a fish.

Population: 2,970; Growth (since 2000): 7.3%; Density: 5,890.8 persons per square mile; Race: 84.1% White, 6.2% Black/African American, 2.3% Asian, 0.3% American Indian/Alaska Native, 0.0% Native Hawaiian/Other Pacific Islander, 3.1% Two or more races, 10.8% Hispanic of any race; Average household size: 2.30; Median age: 35.6; Age under 18: 24.8%; Age 65 and over: 7.6%; Males per 100 females: 101.2; Marriage status: 30.6% never married, 51.2% now married, 2.5% separated, 3.4% widowed, 14.7% divorced; Foreign born: 17.8%; Speak English only: 71.9%; With disability: 11.8%; Veterans: 5.0%; Ancestry: 16.8% German, 10.2% Polish, 9.3% Irish, 8.7% English, 7.6% Assyrian/Chaldean/Syriac

Employment: 17.2% management, business, and financial, 6.4% computer, engineering, and science, 5.6% education, legal, community service, arts, and media, 6.2% healthcare practitioners, 25.3% service, 22.0% sales and office, 5.0% natural resources, construction, and maintenance, 12.3% production, transportation, and material moving

Income: Per capita: $23,628; Median household: $42,596; Average household: $54,647; Households with income of $100,000 or more: 13.2%; Poverty rate: 24.2%

Educational Attainment: High school diploma or higher: 84.6%; Bachelor's degree or higher: 31.4%; Graduate/professional degree or higher: 13.1%

School District(s)
West Bloomfield SD (PK-12)
   2012-13 Enrollment: 6,228 . . . . (248) 865-6485
Housing: Homeownership rate: 62.5%; Median home value: $122,800; Median year structure built: 1965; Homeowner vacancy rate: 4.6%; Median gross rent: $830 per month; Rental vacancy rate: 10.6%
Health Insurance: 74.0% have insurance; 55.9% have private insurance; 25.9% have public insurance; 26.0% do not have insurance; 18.1% of children under 18 do not have insurance
Safety: Violent crime rate: 16.6 per 10,000 population; Property crime rate: 189.2 per 10,000 population
Transportation: Commute: 92.8% car, 0.0% public transportation, 3.9% walk, 2.5% work from home; Median travel time to work: 28.7 minutes

LAKE ANGELUS (city). Covers a land area of 1.066 square miles and a water area of 0.568 square miles. Located at 42.69° N. Lat; 83.33° W. Long. Elevation is 981 feet.
Population: 290; Growth (since 2000): -11.0%; Density: 272.1 persons per square mile; Race: 96.2% White, 0.3% Black/African American, 2.8% Asian, 0.0% American Indian/Alaska Native, 0.0% Native Hawaiian/Other Pacific Islander, 0.7% Two or more races, 0.3% Hispanic of any race; Average household size: 2.23; Median age: 55.3; Age under 18: 12.1%; Age 65 and over: 27.6%; Males per 100 females: 89.5
Housing: Homeownership rate: 92.4%; Homeowner vacancy rate: 2.4%; Rental vacancy rate: 16.7%

LAKE ORION (village). Covers a land area of 0.790 square miles and a water area of 0.514 square miles. Located at 42.79° N. Lat; 83.25° W. Long. Elevation is 984 feet.
History: Lake Orion developed as a country market center, becoming a popular railroad excursion point after 1872. When an electric interurban railway was built between Detroit and Flint in the early 1900's, Lake Orion became a summer resort.
Population: 2,973; Growth (since 2000): 9.5%; Density: 3,764.3 persons per square mile; Race: 94.2% White, 1.6% Black/African American, 1.1% Asian, 0.2% American Indian/Alaska Native, 0.0% Native Hawaiian/Other Pacific Islander, 2.0% Two or more races, 3.5% Hispanic of any race; Average household size: 2.19; Median age: 41.2; Age under 18: 20.6%; Age 65 and over: 16.2%; Males per 100 females: 90.3; Marriage status: 27.5% never married, 50.9% now married, 0.5% separated, 9.3% widowed, 12.3% divorced; Foreign born: 6.2%; Speak English only: 95.2%; With disability: 9.6%; Veterans: 6.6%; Ancestry: 30.3% German, 24.8% Irish, 12.2% English, 7.6% Polish, 6.8% Italian
Employment: 16.5% management, business, and financial, 12.7% computer, engineering, and science, 13.3% education, legal, community service, arts, and media, 6.7% healthcare practitioners, 11.0% service, 20.8% sales and office, 7.8% natural resources, construction, and maintenance, 11.3% production, transportation, and material moving
Income: Per capita: $34,937; Median household: $59,848; Average household: $77,754; Households with income of $100,000 or more: 27.2%; Poverty rate: 9.1%
Educational Attainment: High school diploma or higher: 91.8%; Bachelor's degree or higher: 34.0%; Graduate/professional degree or higher: 11.3%

School District(s)
Lake Orion Community Schools (PK-12)
   2012-13 Enrollment: 7,635 . . . . (248) 693-5413
Housing: Homeownership rate: 58.7%; Median home value: $165,600; Median year structure built: 1959; Homeowner vacancy rate: 3.3%; Median gross rent: $678 per month; Rental vacancy rate: 6.5%
Health Insurance: 91.9% have insurance; 78.8% have private insurance; 23.0% have public insurance; 8.1% do not have insurance; 0.0% of children under 18 do not have insurance
Safety: Violent crime rate: 6.6 per 10,000 population; Property crime rate: 131.1 per 10,000 population
Transportation: Commute: 95.9% car, 0.0% public transportation, 1.3% walk, 2.8% work from home; Median travel time to work: 31.4 minutes

LATHRUP VILLAGE (city). Covers a land area of 1.501 square miles and a water area of 0 square miles. Located at 42.49° N. Lat; 83.23° W. Long. Elevation is 702 feet.
History: Lathrup Village was founded in 1926 by Louise Lathrup, a real estate developer, and promoted by Louise and her husband, Charles D. Kelley, a real estate editor of the Detroit newspaper.

Population: 4,075; Growth (since 2000): -3.8%; Density: 2,715.6 persons per square mile; Race: 34.6% White, 61.2% Black/African American, 0.6% Asian, 0.1% American Indian/Alaska Native, 0.0% Native Hawaiian/Other Pacific Islander, 3.1% Two or more races, 1.5% Hispanic of any race; Average household size: 2.53; Median age: 45.8; Age under 18: 20.9%; Age 65 and over: 15.3%; Males per 100 females: 92.2; Marriage status: 26.1% never married, 56.7% now married, 2.7% separated, 3.5% widowed, 13.6% divorced; Foreign born: 3.7%; Speak English only: 95.4%; With disability: 11.3%; Veterans: 14.0%; Ancestry: 13.5% German, 7.4% English, 4.9% Irish, 4.6% Polish, 3.5% Italian
Employment: 13.5% management, business, and financial, 12.6% computer, engineering, and science, 21.4% education, legal, community service, arts, and media, 6.7% healthcare practitioners, 10.4% service, 25.9% sales and office, 1.0% natural resources, construction, and maintenance, 8.5% production, transportation, and material moving
Income: Per capita: $41,090; Median household: $79,643; Average household: $98,816; Households with income of $100,000 or more: 40.3%; Poverty rate: 5.8%
Educational Attainment: High school diploma or higher: 95.2%; Bachelor's degree or higher: 48.5%; Graduate/professional degree or higher: 24.9%

School District(s)
Southfield Public SD (PK-12)
   2012-13 Enrollment: 7,376 . . . . (248) 746-4366
Housing: Homeownership rate: 93.4%; Median home value: $151,300; Median year structure built: 1959; Homeowner vacancy rate: 2.1%; Median gross rent: $1,523 per month; Rental vacancy rate: 1.8%
Health Insurance: 90.9% have insurance; 83.7% have private insurance; 27.3% have public insurance; 9.1% do not have insurance; 3.0% of children under 18 do not have insurance
Safety: Violent crime rate: 7.3 per 10,000 population; Property crime rate: 169.6 per 10,000 population
Transportation: Commute: 89.8% car, 1.4% public transportation, 1.1% walk, 6.9% work from home; Median travel time to work: 23.6 minutes
Additional Information Contacts
City of Lathrup Village . . . . (248) 557-2600
  http://www.lathrupvillage.org

LEONARD (village). Covers a land area of 0.958 square miles and a water area of 0 square miles. Located at 42.87° N. Lat; 83.14° W. Long. Elevation is 1,001 feet.
History: Leonard was founded in 1882 by Leonard Rowland, and named for him. The town developed after the Pontiac, Oxford & Northern Railroad arrived.
Population: 403; Growth (since 2000): 21.4%; Density: 420.6 persons per square mile; Race: 97.5% White, 0.2% Black/African American, 0.0% Asian, 1.0% American Indian/Alaska Native, 0.0% Native Hawaiian/Other Pacific Islander, 0.5% Two or more races, 2.2% Hispanic of any race; Average household size: 2.63; Median age: 39.9; Age under 18: 24.6%; Age 65 and over: 12.7%; Males per 100 females: 107.7

School District(s)
Oxford Community Schools (PK-12)
   2012-13 Enrollment: 5,226 . . . . (248) 969-5000
Romeo Community Schools (PK-12)
   2012-13 Enrollment: 5,287 . . . . (586) 752-0225
Housing: Homeownership rate: 88.3%; Homeowner vacancy rate: 2.9%; Rental vacancy rate: 10.0%

LYON (charter township). Covers a land area of 30.945 square miles and a water area of 0.803 square miles. Located at 42.48° N. Lat; 83.60° W. Long.
History: Lyon Township was organized in 1832 and named for Lucius Lyon, a member of the state legislature.
Population: 14,545; Growth (since 2000): 31.7%; Density: 470.0 persons per square mile; Race: 94.6% White, 1.4% Black/African American, 1.5% Asian, 0.3% American Indian/Alaska Native, 0.0% Native Hawaiian/Other Pacific Islander, 1.7% Two or more races, 2.9% Hispanic of any race; Average household size: 2.78; Median age: 38.4; Age under 18: 27.2%; Age 65 and over: 9.4%; Males per 100 females: 100.0; Marriage status: 25.3% never married, 61.5% now married, 0.7% separated, 4.6% widowed, 8.5% divorced; Foreign born: 3.6%; Speak English only: 92.6%; With disability: 10.9%; Veterans: 6.9%; Ancestry: 27.1% German, 17.1% Irish, 15.4% Polish, 13.0% English, 10.7% Italian
Employment: 20.7% management, business, and financial, 8.5% computer, engineering, and science, 7.7% education, legal, community

service, arts, and media, 5.8% healthcare practitioners, 16.1% service, 24.7% sales and office, 5.3% natural resources, construction, and maintenance, 11.1% production, transportation, and material moving

Income: Per capita: $33,989; Median household: $75,479; Average household: $93,490; Households with income of $100,000 or more: 35.5%; Poverty rate: 4.7%

Educational Attainment: High school diploma or higher: 93.3%; Bachelor's degree or higher: 35.5%; Graduate/professional degree or higher: 12.0%

Housing: Homeownership rate: 86.1%; Median home value: $215,200; Median year structure built: 1991; Homeowner vacancy rate: 2.5%; Median gross rent: $1,078 per month; Rental vacancy rate: 18.4%

Health Insurance: 92.8% have insurance; 83.7% have private insurance; 19.2% have public insurance; 7.2% do not have insurance; 2.5% of children under 18 do not have insurance

Transportation: Commute: 93.0% car, 0.6% public transportation, 0.9% walk, 5.4% work from home; Median travel time to work: 29.1 minutes

Additional Information Contacts
Lyon Township . . . . (248) 437-2240
    http://www.lyontwp.org

MADISON HEIGHTS (city). Covers a land area of 7.087 square miles and a water area of 0 square miles. Located at 42.51° N. Lat; 83.10° W. Long. Elevation is 630 feet.

History: Named for James Madison, fourth President of the U.S. Incorporated 1955.

Population: 29,694; Growth (since 2000): -4.5%; Density: 4,190.2 persons per square mile; Race: 83.9% White, 6.4% Black/African American, 5.8% Asian, 0.5% American Indian/Alaska Native, 0.1% Native Hawaiian/Other Pacific Islander, 2.7% Two or more races, 2.5% Hispanic of any race; Average household size: 2.32; Median age: 38.3; Age under 18: 20.4%; Age 65 and over: 13.9%; Males per 100 females: 96.3; Marriage status: 31.3% never married, 46.4% now married, 1.1% separated, 7.7% widowed, 14.5% divorced; Foreign born: 17.8%; Speak English only: 80.2%; With disability: 15.4%; Veterans: 7.4%; Ancestry: 18.0% German, 11.8% Irish, 11.7% Polish, 9.7% English, 6.6% American

Employment: 9.4% management, business, and financial, 5.4% computer, engineering, and science, 6.1% education, legal, community service, arts, and media, 5.0% healthcare practitioners, 21.4% service, 29.8% sales and office, 8.2% natural resources, construction, and maintenance, 14.7% production, transportation, and material moving

Income: Per capita: $22,113; Median household: $40,140; Average household: $50,323; Households with income of $100,000 or more: 11.3%; Poverty rate: 18.8%

Educational Attainment: High school diploma or higher: 83.5%; Bachelor's degree or higher: 21.9%; Graduate/professional degree or higher: 5.5%

School District(s)
Clintondale Community Schools (PK-12)
    2012-13 Enrollment: 3,407 . . . . (586) 791-6300
Four Corners Montessori Academy (PK-12)
    2012-13 Enrollment: 325. . . . . (248) 542-7001
Lamphere Public Schools (PK-12)
    2012-13 Enrollment: 2,829 . . . . (248) 589-1990
Madison District Public Schools (KG-12)
    2012-13 Enrollment: 1,298 . . . . (248) 399-7800

Vocational/Technical School(s)
Dorsey Business Schools-Madison Heights (Private, For-profit)
    Fall 2013 Enrollment: 203 . . . . (248) 588-9660
    2013-14 Tuition: In-state $17,568; Out-of-state $17,568
Ross Medical Education Center-Madison Heights (Private, For-profit)
    Fall 2013 Enrollment: 270 . . . . (248) 548-4389
    2013-14 Tuition: $15,680

Housing: Homeownership rate: 64.4%; Median home value: $84,200; Median year structure built: 1960; Homeowner vacancy rate: 2.5%; Median gross rent: $755 per month; Rental vacancy rate: 8.0%

Health Insurance: 86.4% have insurance; 64.2% have private insurance; 34.3% have public insurance; 13.6% do not have insurance; 4.4% of children under 18 do not have insurance

Safety: Violent crime rate: 25.9 per 10,000 population; Property crime rate: 286.6 per 10,000 population

Transportation: Commute: 93.4% car, 1.2% public transportation, 0.9% walk, 4.0% work from home; Median travel time to work: 22.5 minutes

Additional Information Contacts
City of Madison Heights . . . . (248) 583-0826
    http://www.madison-heights.org

MILFORD (charter township). Covers a land area of 32.991 square miles and a water area of 2.177 square miles. Located at 42.57° N. Lat; 83.61° W. Long. Elevation is 961 feet.

History: Incorporated 1869.

Population: 15,736; Growth (since 2000): 3.0%; Density: 477.0 persons per square mile; Race: 95.3% White, 0.9% Black/African American, 1.1% Asian, 0.3% American Indian/Alaska Native, 0.0% Native Hawaiian/Other Pacific Islander, 1.6% Two or more races, 2.2% Hispanic of any race; Average household size: 2.60; Median age: 43.1; Age under 18: 24.0%; Age 65 and over: 13.0%; Males per 100 females: 95.2; Marriage status: 26.1% never married, 58.8% now married, 0.4% separated, 5.2% widowed, 10.0% divorced; Foreign born: 4.1%; Speak English only: 94.0%; With disability: 9.2%; Veterans: 7.6%; Ancestry: 26.7% German, 18.8% Irish, 15.5% Polish, 14.9% English, 8.3% Italian

Employment: 18.3% management, business, and financial, 5.8% computer, engineering, and science, 7.8% education, legal, community service, arts, and media, 8.9% healthcare practitioners, 15.6% service, 25.7% sales and office, 8.3% natural resources, construction, and maintenance, 9.5% production, transportation, and material moving

Income: Per capita: $37,954; Median household: $79,761; Average household: $100,089; Households with income of $100,000 or more: 38.8%; Poverty rate: 6.4%

Educational Attainment: High school diploma or higher: 93.5%; Bachelor's degree or higher: 40.2%; Graduate/professional degree or higher: 13.7%

School District(s)
Huron Valley Schools (PK-12)
    2012-13 Enrollment: 9,899 . . . . (248) 684-8234

Housing: Homeownership rate: 84.6%; Median home value: $207,200; Median year structure built: 1983; Homeowner vacancy rate: 3.3%; Median gross rent: $690 per month; Rental vacancy rate: 12.7%

Health Insurance: 91.3% have insurance; 81.2% have private insurance; 22.7% have public insurance; 8.7% do not have insurance; 1.6% of children under 18 do not have insurance

Safety: Violent crime rate: 7.4 per 10,000 population; Property crime rate: 55.7 per 10,000 population

Transportation: Commute: 93.8% car, 0.0% public transportation, 1.7% walk, 3.7% work from home; Median travel time to work: 32.0 minutes

Additional Information Contacts
Milford Charter Township . . . . (248) 685-8731
    http://www.milfordtownship.com

MILFORD (village). Covers a land area of 2.427 square miles and a water area of 0.092 square miles. Located at 42.59° N. Lat; 83.60° W. Long. Elevation is 961 feet.

Population: 6,175; Growth (since 2000): -1.5%; Density: 2,544.1 persons per square mile; Race: 95.7% White, 0.6% Black/African American, 0.7% Asian, 0.6% American Indian/Alaska Native, 0.0% Native Hawaiian/Other Pacific Islander, 1.7% Two or more races, 2.0% Hispanic of any race; Average household size: 2.38; Median age: 40.8; Age under 18: 23.5%; Age 65 and over: 12.9%; Males per 100 females: 90.3; Marriage status: 29.3% never married, 52.1% now married, 0.6% separated, 6.1% widowed, 12.4% divorced; Foreign born: 2.3%; Speak English only: 94.5%; With disability: 10.4%; Veterans: 6.3%; Ancestry: 26.9% German, 20.5% Irish, 16.0% English, 14.9% Polish, 6.5% Italian

Employment: 18.8% management, business, and financial, 5.7% computer, engineering, and science, 8.3% education, legal, community service, arts, and media, 7.2% healthcare practitioners, 17.9% service, 24.0% sales and office, 7.6% natural resources, construction, and maintenance, 10.5% production, transportation, and material moving

Income: Per capita: $35,614; Median household: $66,626; Average household: $85,612; Households with income of $100,000 or more: 34.7%; Poverty rate: 8.8%

Educational Attainment: High school diploma or higher: 93.3%; Bachelor's degree or higher: 39.1%; Graduate/professional degree or higher: 12.0%

School District(s)
Huron Valley Schools (PK-12)
    2012-13 Enrollment: 9,899 . . . . (248) 684-8234

Housing: Homeownership rate: 73.2%; Median home value: $159,500; Median year structure built: 1967; Homeowner vacancy rate: 2.0%; Median gross rent: $640 per month; Rental vacancy rate: 8.3%
Health Insurance: 91.2% have insurance; 79.1% have private insurance; 26.4% have public insurance; 8.8% do not have insurance; 1.7% of children under 18 do not have insurance
Transportation: Commute: 94.2% car, 0.1% public transportation, 2.4% walk, 2.5% work from home; Median travel time to work: 31.7 minutes

NEW HUDSON (unincorporated postal area)
ZCTA: 48165

Covers a land area of 9.305 square miles and a water area of 0.232 square miles. Located at 42.50° N. Lat; 83.62° W. Long. Elevation is 935 feet.

Population: 6,339; Growth (since 2000): 17.0%; Density: 681.2 persons per square mile; Race: 94.6% White, 1.6% Black/African American, 1.0% Asian, 0.3% American Indian/Alaska Native, 0.0% Native Hawaiian/Other Pacific Islander, 2.0% Two or more races, 3.5% Hispanic of any race; Average household size: 2.60; Median age: 37.2; Age under 18: 25.0%; Age 65 and over: 9.5%; Males per 100 females: 99.6; Marriage status: 30.5% never married, 52.4% now married, 0.6% separated, 5.3% widowed, 11.8% divorced; Foreign born: 2.0%; Speak English only: 92.8%; With disability: 14.3%; Veterans: 6.8%; Ancestry: 29.6% German, 17.8% Irish, 12.6% Polish, 12.5% English, 10.5% Italian
Employment: 16.5% management, business, and financial, 6.3% computer, engineering, and science, 9.7% education, legal, community service, arts, and media, 5.3% healthcare practitioners, 21.3% service, 26.9% sales and office, 5.8% natural resources, construction, and maintenance, 8.1% production, transportation, and material moving
Income: Per capita: $29,372; Median household: $57,339; Average household: $70,808; Households with income of $100,000 or more: 23.6%; Poverty rate: 6.9%
Educational Attainment: High school diploma or higher: 90.7%; Bachelor's degree or higher: 30.2%; Graduate/professional degree or higher: 8.8%

School District(s)
South Lyon Community Schools (PK-12)
    2012-13 Enrollment: 7,325 . . . . (248) 573-8100
Housing: Homeownership rate: 75.9%; Median home value: $176,000; Median year structure built: 1987; Homeowner vacancy rate: 3.4%; Median gross rent: $1,073 per month; Rental vacancy rate: 19.2%
Health Insurance: 90.5% have insurance; 79.6% have private insurance; 21.7% have public insurance; 9.5% do not have insurance; 4.0% of children under 18 do not have insurance
Transportation: Commute: 92.7% car, 0.6% public transportation, 2.3% walk, 4.4% work from home; Median travel time to work: 26.1 minutes

NORTHVILLE (city). Covers a land area of 2.047 square miles and a water area of 0.018 square miles. Located at 42.44° N. Lat; 83.49° W. Long. Elevation is 830 feet.
History: The city was incorporated in 1955 along the boundaries of the Village of Northville. The Village of Northville included portions of Novi Township in Oakland County and Northville Township in Wayne County. Over the next several years, the city boundaries expanded through annexation of portions of Novi Township and the Village of Novi both east and west of the city and north of Baseline Road.
Population: 5,970; Growth (since 2000): -7.6%; Density: 2,916.5 persons per square mile; Race: 93.7% White, 1.6% Black/African American, 2.6% Asian, 0.1% American Indian/Alaska Native, 0.0% Native Hawaiian/Other Pacific Islander, 1.4% Two or more races, 2.2% Hispanic of any race; Average household size: 2.29; Median age: 45.3; Age under 18: 22.0%; Age 65 and over: 16.1%; Males per 100 females: 91.8; Marriage status: 28.6% never married, 52.4% now married, 0.6% separated, 6.2% widowed, 12.8% divorced; Foreign born: 8.1%; Speak English only: 89.2%; With disability: 8.3%; Veterans: 6.7%; Ancestry: 22.6% German, 15.6% Irish, 13.7% English, 9.7% Polish, 8.0% Italian
Employment: 23.5% management, business, and financial, 11.2% computer, engineering, and science, 13.7% education, legal, community service, arts, and media, 8.5% healthcare practitioners, 9.9% service, 23.5% sales and office, 2.7% natural resources, construction, and maintenance, 7.0% production, transportation, and material moving
Income: Per capita: $50,960; Median household: $89,116; Average household: $118,810; Households with income of $100,000 or more: 44.1%; Poverty rate: 4.9%

Educational Attainment: High school diploma or higher: 95.4%; Bachelor's degree or higher: 59.6%; Graduate/professional degree or higher: 24.3%

School District(s)
Northville Public Schools (PK-12)
    2012-13 Enrollment: 7,274 . . . . (248) 349-3400
South Lyon Community Schools (PK-12)
    2012-13 Enrollment: 7,325 . . . . (248) 573-8100
Housing: Homeownership rate: 75.1%; Median home value: $238,300; Median year structure built: 1970; Homeowner vacancy rate: 1.5%; Median gross rent: $903 per month; Rental vacancy rate: 9.6%
Health Insurance: 94.6% have insurance; 89.2% have private insurance; 23.2% have public insurance; 5.4% do not have insurance; 0.0% of children under 18 do not have insurance
Safety: Violent crime rate: 6.7 per 10,000 population; Property crime rate: 85.1 per 10,000 population
Transportation: Commute: 90.0% car, 0.0% public transportation, 2.4% walk, 5.4% work from home; Median travel time to work: 22.4 minutes
Additional Information Contacts
City of Northville . . . . (248) 349-1300
    http://www.ci.northville.mi.us

NOVI (city). Covers a land area of 30.263 square miles and a water area of 1.023 square miles. Located at 42.48° N. Lat; 83.49° W. Long. Elevation is 909 feet.
History: Novi was platted and named in 1830 by the board of supervisors. The name of Novi was reportedly suggested by the wife of one of the supervisors.
Population: 55,224; Growth (since 2000): 16.5%; Density: 1,824.8 persons per square mile; Race: 73.0% White, 8.1% Black/African American, 15.9% Asian, 0.2% American Indian/Alaska Native, 0.0% Native Hawaiian/Other Pacific Islander, 2.1% Two or more races, 3.0% Hispanic of any race; Average household size: 2.46; Median age: 39.1; Age under 18: 25.5%; Age 65 and over: 11.3%; Males per 100 females: 93.7; Marriage status: 25.5% never married, 58.1% now married, 1.2% separated, 6.3% widowed, 10.0% divorced; Foreign born: 19.1%; Speak English only: 77.8%; With disability: 7.7%; Veterans: 6.8%; Ancestry: 17.8% German, 12.4% Irish, 9.9% Polish, 9.7% English, 8.1% Italian
Employment: 23.9% management, business, and financial, 13.6% computer, engineering, and science, 10.3% education, legal, community service, arts, and media, 7.8% healthcare practitioners, 10.5% service, 25.0% sales and office, 2.6% natural resources, construction, and maintenance, 6.4% production, transportation, and material moving
Income: Per capita: $44,390; Median household: $80,108; Average household: $106,754; Households with income of $100,000 or more: 40.3%; Poverty rate: 5.6%
Educational Attainment: High school diploma or higher: 94.7%; Bachelor's degree or higher: 56.2%; Graduate/professional degree or higher: 24.6%

School District(s)
Northville Public Schools (PK-12)
    2012-13 Enrollment: 7,274 . . . . (248) 349-3400
Novi Community SD (PK-12)
    2012-13 Enrollment: 6,283 . . . . (248) 449-1234
Walled Lake Consolidated Schools (PK-12)
    2012-13 Enrollment: 15,177 . . . . (248) 956-2000
Four-year College(s)
South University-Novi (Private, For-profit)
    Fall 2013 Enrollment: 503 . . . . (248) 862-7500
    2013-14 Tuition: In-state $16,360; Out-of-state $16,360
The Art Institute of Michigan (Private, For-profit)
    Fall 2013 Enrollment: 1,003 . . . . (248) 675-3800
    2013-14 Tuition: In-state $17,488; Out-of-state $17,488
Housing: Homeownership rate: 67.2%; Median home value: $235,800; Median year structure built: 1990; Homeowner vacancy rate: 2.4%; Median gross rent: $994 per month; Rental vacancy rate: 13.4%
Health Insurance: 93.0% have insurance; 86.2% have private insurance; 18.3% have public insurance; 7.0% do not have insurance; 2.6% of children under 18 do not have insurance
Safety: Violent crime rate: 8.4 per 10,000 population; Property crime rate: 168.1 per 10,000 population
Transportation: Commute: 95.0% car, 0.4% public transportation, 0.3% walk, 3.7% work from home; Median travel time to work: 26.1 minutes

Additional Information Contacts

City of Novi . . . . (248) 347-0456
> http://www.cityofnovi.org

NOVI (township). Covers a land area of 0.106 square miles and a water area of 0 square miles. Located at 42.46° N. Lat; 83.48° W. Long. Elevation is 909 feet.

Population: 150; Growth (since 2000): -22.3%; Density: 1,411.9 persons per square mile; Race: 94.7% White, 0.0% Black/African American, 3.3% Asian, 0.0% American Indian/Alaska Native, 0.0% Native Hawaiian/Other Pacific Islander, 1.3% Two or more races, 4.0% Hispanic of any race; Average household size: 2.54; Median age: 49.3; Age under 18: 16.7%; Age 65 and over: 14.0%; Males per 100 females: 114.3

School District(s)

Northville Public Schools (PK-12)
> 2012-13 Enrollment: 7,274 . . . . (248) 349-3400

Novi Community SD (PK-12)
> 2012-13 Enrollment: 6,283 . . . . (248) 449-1234

Walled Lake Consolidated Schools (PK-12)
> 2012-13 Enrollment: 15,177 . . . . (248) 956-2000

Four-year College(s)

South University-Novi (Private, For-profit)
> Fall 2013 Enrollment: 503 . . . . (248) 862-7500
> 2013-14 Tuition: In-state $16,360; Out-of-state $16,360

The Art Institute of Michigan (Private, For-profit)
> Fall 2013 Enrollment: 1,003 . . . . (248) 675-3800
> 2013-14 Tuition: In-state $17,488; Out-of-state $17,488

Housing: Homeownership rate: 96.6%; Homeowner vacancy rate: 1.7%; Rental vacancy rate: 0.0%

OAK PARK (city). Covers a land area of 5.164 square miles and a water area of 0 square miles. Located at 42.46° N. Lat; 83.18° W. Long. Elevation is 663 feet.

History: Named for the oak trees. Marian Sandweiss born here. Incorporated 1927.

Population: 29,319; Growth (since 2000): -1.6%; Density: 5,677.2 persons per square mile; Race: 37.4% White, 57.4% Black/African American, 1.4% Asian, 0.2% American Indian/Alaska Native, 0.0% Native Hawaiian/Other Pacific Islander, 3.0% Two or more races, 1.4% Hispanic of any race; Average household size: 2.50; Median age: 37.5; Age under 18: 24.9%; Age 65 and over: 12.9%; Males per 100 females: 82.2; Marriage status: 40.3% never married, 42.2% now married, 1.8% separated, 6.1% widowed, 11.4% divorced; Foreign born: 9.9%; Speak English only: 88.2%; With disability: 15.5%; Veterans: 7.4%; Ancestry: 4.2% Polish, 4.2% German, 3.7% Russian, 3.6% Irish, 2.6% American

Employment: 10.7% management, business, and financial, 5.1% computer, engineering, and science, 13.9% education, legal, community service, arts, and media, 6.1% healthcare practitioners, 22.2% service, 26.1% sales and office, 4.9% natural resources, construction, and maintenance, 10.8% production, transportation, and material moving

Income: Per capita: $21,768; Median household: $48,261; Average household: $55,540; Households with income of $100,000 or more: 12.7%; Poverty rate: 19.4%

Educational Attainment: High school diploma or higher: 91.2%; Bachelor's degree or higher: 28.8%; Graduate/professional degree or higher: 9.6%

School District(s)

Berkley SD (PK-12)
> 2012-13 Enrollment: 4,667 . . . . (248) 837-8000

Clintondale Community Schools (PK-12)
> 2012-13 Enrollment: 3,407 . . . . (586) 791-6300

Ferndale Public Schools (PK-12)
> 2012-13 Enrollment: 3,653 . . . . (248) 586-8651

Oak Park SD (PK-12)
> 2012-13 Enrollment: 4,374 . . . . (248) 336-7706

Four-year College(s)

Yeshiva Gedolah of Greater Detroit (Private, Not-for-profit)
> Fall 2013 Enrollment: 74 . . . . (248) 968-3360
> 2013-14 Tuition: In-state $6,200; Out-of-state $6,200

Housing: Homeownership rate: 60.7%; Median home value: $82,200; Median year structure built: 1957; Homeowner vacancy rate: 3.3%; Median gross rent: $1,014 per month; Rental vacancy rate: 9.3%

Health Insurance: 81.9% have insurance; 60.2% have private insurance; 34.4% have public insurance; 18.1% do not have insurance; 8.3% of children under 18 do not have insurance

Safety: Violent crime rate: 60.6 per 10,000 population; Property crime rate: 272.2 per 10,000 population

Transportation: Commute: 91.8% car, 2.4% public transportation, 2.2% walk, 2.9% work from home; Median travel time to work: 23.2 minutes

Additional Information Contacts

City of Oak Park . . . . (248) 691-7410
> http://www.oakpark-mi.com

OAKLAND (charter township). Covers a land area of 36.300 square miles and a water area of 0.433 square miles. Located at 42.75° N. Lat; 83.15° W. Long.

History: Established in 1827. Schools were built by the first settlers. One was built in 1827 in Section 29. History says it was a log building with a large fireplace that could accommodate six-foot logs.

Population: 16,779; Growth (since 2000): 28.4%; Density: 462.2 persons per square mile; Race: 90.3% White, 2.4% Black/African American, 5.4% Asian, 0.2% American Indian/Alaska Native, 0.0% Native Hawaiian/Other Pacific Islander, 1.3% Two or more races, 2.1% Hispanic of any race; Average household size: 2.90; Median age: 42.5; Age under 18: 27.8%; Age 65 and over: 11.5%; Males per 100 females: 100.1; Marriage status: 22.9% never married, 65.4% now married, 0.6% separated, 3.5% widowed, 8.2% divorced; Foreign born: 10.9%; Speak English only: 87.0%; With disability: 6.4%; Veterans: 6.5%; Ancestry: 23.3% German, 13.0% English, 12.9% Polish, 11.8% Irish, 11.4% Italian

Employment: 29.2% management, business, and financial, 11.8% computer, engineering, and science, 10.5% education, legal, community service, arts, and media, 9.3% healthcare practitioners, 9.4% service, 19.9% sales and office, 4.8% natural resources, construction, and maintenance, 5.0% production, transportation, and material moving

Income: Per capita: $52,093; Median household: $113,654; Average household: $148,462; Households with income of $100,000 or more: 57.2%; Poverty rate: 3.0%

Educational Attainment: High school diploma or higher: 96.2%; Bachelor's degree or higher: 57.2%; Graduate/professional degree or higher: 26.3%

School District(s)

Lake Orion Community Schools (PK-12)
> 2012-13 Enrollment: 7,635 . . . . (248) 693-5413

Rochester Community SD (PK-12)
> 2012-13 Enrollment: 15,007 . . . . (248) 726-3000

Housing: Homeownership rate: 93.3%; Median home value: $313,200; Median year structure built: 1992; Homeowner vacancy rate: 2.1%; Median gross rent: $1,429 per month; Rental vacancy rate: 8.2%

Health Insurance: 94.1% have insurance; 88.8% have private insurance; 17.3% have public insurance; 5.9% do not have insurance; 2.7% of children under 18 do not have insurance

Transportation: Commute: 93.0% car, 0.0% public transportation, 0.8% walk, 6.2% work from home; Median travel time to work: 31.6 minutes

Additional Information Contacts

Oakland Charter Township . . . . (248) 651-4440
> http://www.oaklandtownship.org

ORCHARD LAKE VILLAGE (city). Covers a land area of 2.444 square miles and a water area of 1.681 square miles. Located at 42.59° N. Lat; 83.37° W. Long.

Population: 2,375; Growth (since 2000): 7.2%; Density: 971.8 persons per square mile; Race: 83.9% White, 6.4% Black/African American, 7.4% Asian, 0.0% American Indian/Alaska Native, 0.0% Native Hawaiian/Other Pacific Islander, 2.1% Two or more races, 1.1% Hispanic of any race; Average household size: 2.78; Median age: 46.9; Age under 18: 23.2%; Age 65 and over: 17.5%; Males per 100 females: 115.5

School District(s)

West Bloomfield SD (PK-12)
> 2012-13 Enrollment: 6,228 . . . . (248) 865-6485

Housing: Homeownership rate: 95.1%; Homeowner vacancy rate: 2.5%; Rental vacancy rate: 12.5%

Safety: Violent crime rate: 12.4 per 10,000 population; Property crime rate: 144.4 per 10,000 population

Additional Information Contacts

City of Orchard Lake Village . . . . (248) 682-2400
> http://cityoforchardlake.com

ORION (charter township). Covers a land area of 33.330 square miles and a water area of 2.632 square miles. Located at 42.76° N. Lat; 83.26° W. Long.

Population: 35,394; Growth (since 2000): 5.8%; Density: 1,061.9 persons per square mile; Race: 92.0% White, 2.6% Black/African American, 2.1% Asian, 0.3% American Indian/Alaska Native, 0.0% Native Hawaiian/Other Pacific Islander, 1.8% Two or more races, 4.0% Hispanic of any race; Average household size: 2.71; Median age: 38.6; Age under 18: 27.6%; Age 65 and over: 9.3%; Males per 100 females: 98.3; Marriage status: 25.5% never married, 59.6% now married, 0.8% separated, 4.4% widowed, 10.5% divorced; Foreign born: 6.9%; Speak English only: 91.2%; With disability: 8.3%; Veterans: 6.7%; Ancestry: 26.2% German, 17.6% Irish, 13.0% Polish, 11.5% English, 7.4% Italian

Employment: 18.7% management, business, and financial, 10.4% computer, engineering, and science, 9.7% education, legal, community service, arts, and media, 5.9% healthcare practitioners, 14.1% service, 24.6% sales and office, 5.6% natural resources, construction, and maintenance, 11.1% production, transportation, and material moving

Income: Per capita: $33,721; Median household: $76,769; Average household: $91,114; Households with income of $100,000 or more: 35.6%; Poverty rate: 7.7%

Educational Attainment: High school diploma or higher: 94.9%; Bachelor's degree or higher: 40.3%; Graduate/professional degree or higher: 13.9%

Housing: Homeownership rate: 79.9%; Median home value: $183,000; Median year structure built: 1982; Homeowner vacancy rate: 2.8%; Median gross rent: $858 per month; Rental vacancy rate: 10.7%

Health Insurance: 91.9% have insurance; 83.3% have private insurance; 17.4% have public insurance; 8.1% do not have insurance; 1.3% of children under 18 do not have insurance

Transportation: Commute: 93.9% car, 0.1% public transportation, 0.8% walk, 4.4% work from home; Median travel time to work: 28.4 minutes

Additional Information Contacts

Orion Township . . . . (248) 391-0304
    http://www.oriontownship.org

ORTONVILLE (village). Covers a land area of 0.981 square miles and a water area of 0.003 square miles. Located at 42.85° N. Lat; 83.44° W. Long. Elevation is 938 feet.

Population: 1,442; Growth (since 2000): -6.1%; Density: 1,470.1 persons per square mile; Race: 95.5% White, 0.6% Black/African American, 1.2% Asian, 0.5% American Indian/Alaska Native, 0.0% Native Hawaiian/Other Pacific Islander, 1.8% Two or more races, 2.6% Hispanic of any race; Average household size: 2.76; Median age: 37.5; Age under 18: 27.5%; Age 65 and over: 7.1%; Males per 100 females: 94.9

School District(s)

Brandon SD in the Counties of Oakland and Lapee (PK-12)
    2012-13 Enrollment: 3,177 . . . . (248) 627-1802
Housing: Homeownership rate: 71.4%; Homeowner vacancy rate: 1.6%; Rental vacancy rate: 17.9%

OXFORD (charter township). Covers a land area of 33.781 square miles and a water area of 1.604 square miles. Located at 42.84° N. Lat; 83.28° W. Long. Elevation is 1,056 feet.

Population: 20,526; Growth (since 2000): 28.1%; Density: 607.6 persons per square mile; Race: 94.9% White, 1.4% Black/African American, 1.2% Asian, 0.3% American Indian/Alaska Native, 0.1% Native Hawaiian/Other Pacific Islander, 1.6% Two or more races, 3.1% Hispanic of any race; Average household size: 2.74; Median age: 38.4; Age under 18: 28.1%; Age 65 and over: 10.0%; Males per 100 females: 98.0; Marriage status: 20.7% never married, 64.2% now married, 0.7% separated, 5.8% widowed, 9.3% divorced; Foreign born: 3.9%; Speak English only: 95.7%; With disability: 10.2%; Veterans: 7.2%; Ancestry: 28.6% German, 18.3% Irish, 15.6% English, 12.5% Polish, 7.3% American

Employment: 18.8% management, business, and financial, 8.8% computer, engineering, and science, 10.3% education, legal, community service, arts, and media, 5.4% healthcare practitioners, 14.6% service, 25.5% sales and office, 5.4% natural resources, construction, and maintenance, 11.3% production, transportation, and material moving

Income: Per capita: $32,057; Median household: $72,958; Average household: $88,053; Households with income of $100,000 or more: 37.3%; Poverty rate: 7.5%

Educational Attainment: High school diploma or higher: 93.2%; Bachelor's degree or higher: 34.0%; Graduate/professional degree or higher: 13.6%

School District(s)

Oxford Community Schools (PK-12)
    2012-13 Enrollment: 5,226 . . . . (248) 969-5000
Housing: Homeownership rate: 83.3%; Median home value: $165,300; Median year structure built: 1989; Homeowner vacancy rate: 2.5%; Median gross rent: $875 per month; Rental vacancy rate: 11.8%

Health Insurance: 91.7% have insurance; 82.0% have private insurance; 21.4% have public insurance; 8.3% do not have insurance; 2.4% of children under 18 do not have insurance

Newspapers: Sherman Publications (weekly circulation 62000)

Transportation: Commute: 95.9% car, 0.0% public transportation, 0.4% walk, 2.8% work from home; Median travel time to work: 33.0 minutes

Additional Information Contacts

Oxford Charter Township . . . . (248) 628-9787
    http://www.oxfordtownship.org

OXFORD (village). Covers a land area of 1.252 square miles and a water area of 0.217 square miles. Located at 42.82° N. Lat; 83.25° W. Long. Elevation is 1,056 feet.

History: Settled 1836; incorporated 1876.

Population: 3,436; Growth (since 2000): -2.9%; Density: 2,744.6 persons per square mile; Race: 95.1% White, 1.9% Black/African American, 0.7% Asian, 0.2% American Indian/Alaska Native, 0.0% Native Hawaiian/Other Pacific Islander, 1.3% Two or more races, 4.4% Hispanic of any race; Average household size: 2.49; Median age: 38.5; Age under 18: 25.0%; Age 65 and over: 10.2%; Males per 100 females: 97.1; Marriage status: 30.8% never married, 51.2% now married, 0.0% separated, 5.1% widowed, 12.9% divorced; Foreign born: 2.3%; Speak English only: 96.5%; With disability: 10.2%; Veterans: 6.6%; Ancestry: 35.5% German, 19.8% English, 16.6% Irish, 8.6% Polish, 8.0% American

Employment: 14.0% management, business, and financial, 6.7% computer, engineering, and science, 8.5% education, legal, community service, arts, and media, 2.4% healthcare practitioners, 22.6% service, 24.2% sales and office, 5.0% natural resources, construction, and maintenance, 16.5% production, transportation, and material moving

Income: Per capita: $27,604; Median household: $54,722; Average household: $66,101; Households with income of $100,000 or more: 26.0%; Poverty rate: 12.2%

Educational Attainment: High school diploma or higher: 89.1%; Bachelor's degree or higher: 23.8%; Graduate/professional degree or higher: 8.1%

School District(s)

Oxford Community Schools (PK-12)
    2012-13 Enrollment: 5,226 . . . . (248) 969-5000
Housing: Homeownership rate: 64.0%; Median home value: $128,000; Median year structure built: 1972; Homeowner vacancy rate: 2.3%; Median gross rent: $673 per month; Rental vacancy rate: 12.5%

Health Insurance: 91.9% have insurance; 76.8% have private insurance; 27.5% have public insurance; 8.1% do not have insurance; 4.0% of children under 18 do not have insurance

Safety: Violent crime rate: 17.3 per 10,000 population; Property crime rate: 94.9 per 10,000 population

Newspapers: Sherman Publications (weekly circulation 62000)

Transportation: Commute: 91.0% car, 0.0% public transportation, 1.8% walk, 5.8% work from home; Median travel time to work: 24.5 minutes

PLEASANT RIDGE (city). Covers a land area of 0.569 square miles and a water area of 0 square miles. Located at 42.47° N. Lat; 83.14° W. Long. Elevation is 646 feet.

History: Pleasant Ridge developed as a suburban residential community. It was incorporated as a village in 1919 and as a city in 1938.

Population: 2,526; Growth (since 2000): -2.6%; Density: 4,440.9 persons per square mile; Race: 94.7% White, 1.9% Black/African American, 1.1% Asian, 0.1% American Indian/Alaska Native, 0.0% Native Hawaiian/Other Pacific Islander, 1.9% Two or more races, 1.7% Hispanic of any race; Average household size: 2.27; Median age: 43.4; Age under 18: 20.3%; Age 65 and over: 14.4%; Males per 100 females: 103.1; Marriage status: 28.2% never married, 56.6% now married, 0.9% separated, 4.6% widowed, 10.6% divorced; Foreign born: 8.0%; Speak English only: 93.9%; With disability: 7.5%; Veterans: 7.7%; Ancestry: 27.8% German, 23.0% Irish, 12.7% Polish, 12.4% English, 8.3% Italian

Employment: 27.7% management, business, and financial, 6.5% computer, engineering, and science, 24.1% education, legal, community service, arts, and media, 6.8% healthcare practitioners, 5.0% service,

21.8% sales and office, 5.3% natural resources, construction, and maintenance, 2.7% production, transportation, and material moving
Income: Per capita: $53,652; Median household: $97,670; Average household: $121,384; Households with income of $100,000 or more: 48.2%; Poverty rate: 3.8%
Educational Attainment: High school diploma or higher: 98.9%; Bachelor's degree or higher: 65.0%; Graduate/professional degree or higher: 32.9%
Housing: Homeownership rate: 92.5%; Median home value: $239,900; Median year structure built: Before 1940; Homeowner vacancy rate: 0.6%; Median gross rent: $1,669 per month; Rental vacancy rate: 7.6%
Health Insurance: 94.0% have insurance; 87.2% have private insurance; 19.2% have public insurance; 6.0% do not have insurance; 0.0% of children under 18 do not have insurance
Safety: Violent crime rate: 19.6 per 10,000 population; Property crime rate: 90.2 per 10,000 population
Transportation: Commute: 94.2% car, 0.0% public transportation, 0.5% walk, 5.1% work from home; Median travel time to work: 21.6 minutes

PONTIAC (city). County seat. Covers a land area of 19.971 square miles and a water area of 0.314 square miles. Located at 42.65° N. Lat; 83.29° W. Long. Elevation is 925 feet.

History: Pontiac was established in 1818 by a group of Detroit businessmen known as the Pontiac Company. It was named for Ottawa chief Pontiac. The Pontiac Spring Wagon Works was founded in the mid-1800's, and until the close of the 1800's, carriage manufacture was the chief industry. The early 1900's brought the Oakland Motor Car Company, the Rapid Motor Truck Company, and other automotive firms, including, eventually, the Pontiac Motor Division of the General Motors Corporation.
Population: 59,515; Growth (since 2000): -10.3%; Density: 2,980.0 persons per square mile; Race: 34.4% White, 52.1% Black/African American, 2.3% Asian, 0.6% American Indian/Alaska Native, 0.0% Native Hawaiian/Other Pacific Islander, 4.5% Two or more races, 16.5% Hispanic of any race; Average household size: 2.56; Median age: 33.4; Age under 18: 27.2%; Age 65 and over: 9.3%; Males per 100 females: 96.4; Marriage status: 47.4% never married, 31.4% now married, 2.5% separated, 6.7% widowed, 14.5% divorced; Foreign born: 6.6%; Speak English only: 84.0%; With disability: 18.6%; Veterans: 7.6%; Ancestry: 6.4% German, 5.5% Irish, 3.4% English, 3.1% American, 2.2% Polish
Employment: 5.9% management, business, and financial, 2.8% computer, engineering, and science, 5.9% education, legal, community service, arts, and media, 3.4% healthcare practitioners, 31.0% service, 26.0% sales and office, 9.1% natural resources, construction, and maintenance, 15.9% production, transportation, and material moving
Income: Per capita: $15,906; Median household: $27,528; Average household: $38,462; Households with income of $100,000 or more: 6.3%; Poverty rate: 36.6%
Educational Attainment: High school diploma or higher: 76.4%; Bachelor's degree or higher: 11.8%; Graduate/professional degree or higher: 3.0%

School District(s)
Arts and Technology Academy of Pontiac (KG-12)
    2012-13 Enrollment: 396 . . . . (248) 452-9309
Great Lakes Academy (KG-12)
    2012-13 Enrollment: 233 . . . . (248) 334-6434
Life Skills Center of Pontiac (KG-12)
    2012-13 Enrollment: 173 . . . . (248) 322-1163
Pontiac Academy for Excellence (KG-12)
    2012-13 Enrollment: 1,435 . . . . (248) 745-9420
Pontiac City SD (PK-12)
    2012-13 Enrollment: 5,093 . . . . (248) 451-6883
Walton Charter Academy (KG-12)
    2012-13 Enrollment: 784 . . . . (248) 371-9300
Waterford SD (PK-12)
    2012-13 Enrollment: 10,704 . . . . (248) 682-0554

Vocational/Technical School(s)
Dorsey Business Schools-Waterford Pontiac (Private, For-profit)
    Fall 2013 Enrollment: 229 . . . . (248) 333-1814
    2013-14 Tuition: In-state $17,568; Out-of-state $17,568
Housing: Homeownership rate: 47.7%; Median home value: $61,000; Median year structure built: 1958; Homeowner vacancy rate: 5.7%; Median gross rent: $728 per month; Rental vacancy rate: 15.1%

Health Insurance: 80.8% have insurance; 45.0% have private insurance; 47.5% have public insurance; 19.2% do not have insurance; 5.8% of children under 18 do not have insurance
Hospitals: Doctors' Hospital of Michigan (380 beds); Mclaren Oakland (308 beds); Saint Joseph Mercy Oakland (443 beds)
Newspapers: Oakland Press (daily circulation 66600)
Transportation: Commute: 92.9% car, 1.9% public transportation, 1.9% walk, 1.3% work from home; Median travel time to work: 21.3 minutes; Amtrak: Train service available.
Airports: Oakland County International (general aviation)
Additional Information Contacts
City of Pontiac . . . . (248) 758-3000
    http://www.pontiac.mi.us

ROCHESTER (city). Covers a land area of 3.825 square miles and a water area of 0 square miles. Located at 42.69° N. Lat; 83.12° W. Long. Elevation is 755 feet.

History: Rochester was settled in the early 1800's by families from New York, who named it after the New York town of Rochester. Rochester later developed as a residential community for workers in the Pontiac automobile plants. Industries in the early 1900's in Rochester included a foundry, knitting works, and a paper company.
Population: 12,711; Growth (since 2000): 21.4%; Density: 3,323.2 persons per square mile; Race: 88.6% White, 3.7% Black/African American, 5.5% Asian, 0.2% American Indian/Alaska Native, 0.0% Native Hawaiian/Other Pacific Islander, 1.5% Two or more races, 2.7% Hispanic of any race; Average household size: 2.31; Median age: 38.3; Age under 18: 25.1%; Age 65 and over: 11.5%; Males per 100 females: 92.2; Marriage status: 31.6% never married, 53.6% now married, 0.2% separated, 3.1% widowed, 11.7% divorced; Foreign born: 11.1%; Speak English only: 89.4%; With disability: 6.5%; Veterans: 6.0%; Ancestry: 22.2% German, 15.3% Polish, 14.0% Irish, 12.1% Italian, 10.6% English
Employment: 24.0% management, business, and financial, 10.1% computer, engineering, and science, 12.9% education, legal, community service, arts, and media, 8.3% healthcare practitioners, 12.6% service, 23.4% sales and office, 4.2% natural resources, construction, and maintenance, 4.4% production, transportation, and material moving
Income: Per capita: $47,321; Median household: $77,105; Average household: $109,707; Households with income of $100,000 or more: 42.7%; Poverty rate: 5.4%
Educational Attainment: High school diploma or higher: 98.0%; Bachelor's degree or higher: 61.1%; Graduate/professional degree or higher: 26.4%

School District(s)
Rochester Community SD (PK-12)
    2012-13 Enrollment: 15,007 . . . . (248) 726-3000
Housing: Homeownership rate: 62.5%; Median home value: $266,800; Median year structure built: 1986; Homeowner vacancy rate: 2.5%; Median gross rent: $776 per month; Rental vacancy rate: 10.1%
Health Insurance: 93.6% have insurance; 88.6% have private insurance; 16.8% have public insurance; 6.4% do not have insurance; 1.6% of children under 18 do not have insurance
Hospitals: Crittenton Hospital Medical Center (290 beds)
Safety: Violent crime rate: 7.0 per 10,000 population; Property crime rate: 84.2 per 10,000 population
Transportation: Commute: 93.3% car, 0.0% public transportation, 1.3% walk, 4.5% work from home; Median travel time to work: 29.6 minutes
Additional Information Contacts
City of Rochester . . . . (248) 651-9061
    http://www.ci.rochester.mi.us

ROCHESTER HILLS (city). Covers a land area of 32.820 square miles and a water area of 0.090 square miles. Located at 42.66° N. Lat; 83.16° W. Long. Elevation is 820 feet.

History: Named for Rochester, New York, home of early settlers in the area. Oakland University and Michigan Christian College are here.
Population: 70,995; Growth (since 2000): 3.2%; Density: 2,163.1 persons per square mile; Race: 82.1% White, 4.5% Black/African American, 10.5% Asian, 0.2% American Indian/Alaska Native, 0.0% Native Hawaiian/Other Pacific Islander, 1.9% Two or more races, 3.1% Hispanic of any race; Average household size: 2.53; Median age: 40.9; Age under 18: 23.7%; Age 65 and over: 13.8%; Males per 100 females: 93.7; Marriage status: 26.2% never married, 59.6% now married, 0.6% separated, 5.7% widowed, 8.5% divorced; Foreign born: 15.6%; Speak English only: 82.0%;

With disability: 9.2%; Veterans: 6.3%; Ancestry: 20.5% German, 12.1% Irish, 11.4% Polish, 10.1% English, 7.7% Italian
Employment: 24.0% management, business, and financial, 12.4% computer, engineering, and science, 11.7% education, legal, community service, arts, and media, 7.5% healthcare practitioners, 12.3% service, 23.2% sales and office, 3.8% natural resources, construction, and maintenance, 5.1% production, transportation, and material moving
Income: Per capita: $38,892; Median household: $78,160; Average household: $99,743; Households with income of $100,000 or more: 38.0%; Poverty rate: 6.7%
Educational Attainment: High school diploma or higher: 95.4%; Bachelor's degree or higher: 51.7%; Graduate/professional degree or higher: 22.8%

School District(s)
Avondale SD (PK-12)
    2012-13 Enrollment: 3,553 . . . . (248) 537-6002
Rochester Community SD (PK-12)
    2012-13 Enrollment: 15,007 . . . . (248) 726-3000
Four-year College(s)
Oakland University (Public)
    Fall 2013 Enrollment: 20,169 . . . . (248) 370-2100
    2013-14 Tuition: In-state $10,613; Out-of-state $23,873
Rochester College (Private, Not-for-profit, Churches of Christ)
    Fall 2013 Enrollment: 1,129 . . . . (248) 218-2000
    2013-14 Tuition: In-state $19,920; Out-of-state $19,920
Housing: Homeownership rate: 77.0%; Median home value: $212,700; Median year structure built: 1981; Homeowner vacancy rate: 1.8%; Median gross rent: $1,064 per month; Rental vacancy rate: 12.7%
Health Insurance: 92.2% have insurance; 84.9% have private insurance; 20.2% have public insurance; 7.8% do not have insurance; 3.4% of children under 18 do not have insurance
Transportation: Commute: 93.8% car, 0.1% public transportation, 0.8% walk, 4.3% work from home; Median travel time to work: 26.6 minutes
Additional Information Contacts
City of Rochester Hills . . . . (248) 656-4600
    http://www.rochesterhills.org

ROSE (township). Covers a land area of 34.513 square miles and a water area of 1.615 square miles. Located at 42.74° N. Lat; 83.63° W. Long.
History: Rose Township was organized in 1837. The village of Rose Center grew up around the Pere Marquette Railroad station.
Population: 6,250; Growth (since 2000): 0.6%; Density: 181.1 persons per square mile; Race: 95.9% White, 1.3% Black/African American, 0.9% Asian, 0.4% American Indian/Alaska Native, 0.0% Native Hawaiian/Other Pacific Islander, 1.2% Two or more races, 2.8% Hispanic of any race; Average household size: 2.73; Median age: 44.9; Age under 18: 22.4%; Age 65 and over: 12.1%; Males per 100 females: 104.2; Marriage status: 21.6% never married, 63.9% now married, 1.6% separated, 6.2% widowed, 8.3% divorced; Foreign born: 1.3%; Speak English only: 96.0%; With disability: 10.3%; Veterans: 11.7%; Ancestry: 29.7% German, 16.6% English, 16.4% Irish, 8.0% Polish, 6.4% French
Employment: 11.9% management, business, and financial, 5.3% computer, engineering, and science, 8.1% education, legal, community service, arts, and media, 9.9% healthcare practitioners, 19.1% service, 26.2% sales and office, 10.7% natural resources, construction, and maintenance, 8.8% production, transportation, and material moving
Income: Per capita: $30,281; Median household: $66,082; Average household: $79,387; Households with income of $100,000 or more: 24.6%; Poverty rate: 6.0%
Educational Attainment: High school diploma or higher: 94.3%; Bachelor's degree or higher: 24.9%; Graduate/professional degree or higher: 9.8%
Housing: Homeownership rate: 92.8%; Median home value: $179,400; Median year structure built: 1980; Homeowner vacancy rate: 1.6%; Median gross rent: $795 per month; Rental vacancy rate: 8.4%
Health Insurance: 93.0% have insurance; 82.4% have private insurance; 23.1% have public insurance; 7.0% do not have insurance; 1.0% of children under 18 do not have insurance
Transportation: Commute: 91.4% car, 0.0% public transportation, 0.0% walk, 7.9% work from home; Median travel time to work: 33.8 minutes

ROYAL OAK (charter township). Covers a land area of 0.553 square miles and a water area of 0 square miles. Located at 42.45° N. Lat; 83.16° W. Long. Elevation is 663 feet.
Population: 2,419; Growth (since 2000): -55.6%; Density: 4,376.5 persons per square mile; Race: 1.4% White, 95.3% Black/African American, 0.0% Asian, 0.1% American Indian/Alaska Native, 0.0% Native Hawaiian/Other Pacific Islander, 2.8% Two or more races, 1.3% Hispanic of any race; Average household size: 2.36; Median age: 37.7; Age under 18: 27.4%; Age 65 and over: 17.9%; Males per 100 females: 71.8
School District(s)
SD of the City of Royal Oak (PK-12)
    2012-13 Enrollment: 5,089 . . . . (248) 435-8400
Vocational/Technical School(s)
David Pressley School of Cosmetology (Private, For-profit)
    Fall 2013 Enrollment: 225 . . . . (248) 548-5090
    2013-14 Tuition: $13,150
Housing: Homeownership rate: 35.8%; Homeowner vacancy rate: 2.7%; Rental vacancy rate: 5.4%
Hospitals: Beaumont Health System (1061 beds)
Newspapers: Detroit Daily Press (daily circulation 200000); The New Monitor (weekly circulation 35000)

ROYAL OAK (city). Covers a land area of 11.785 square miles and a water area of 0.001 square miles. Located at 42.51° N. Lat; 83.15° W. Long. Elevation is 663 feet.
History: Named for a large oak tree in the city that reminded Governor Lewis Cass of the Royal Oak in Scotland. The naming of Royal Oak is said to have been by Governor Lewis Cass, who camped under a large oak tree here and exclaimed that it was indeed a royal oak, reminding him of the Royal Oak in Scotland where Prince Charles the Pretender once hid from his enemies. Settlement began here around 1820. For a time, cow bells and sheep bells were manufactured in Royal Oak.
Population: 57,236; Growth (since 2000): -4.7%; Density: 4,856.8 persons per square mile; Race: 90.7% White, 4.3% Black/African American, 2.4% Asian, 0.3% American Indian/Alaska Native, 0.0% Native Hawaiian/Other Pacific Islander, 1.9% Two or more races, 2.3% Hispanic of any race; Average household size: 2.03; Median age: 37.8; Age under 18: 16.7%; Age 65 and over: 13.1%; Males per 100 females: 96.2; Marriage status: 37.8% never married, 44.8% now married, 0.7% separated, 5.4% widowed, 12.1% divorced; Foreign born: 7.3%; Speak English only: 92.7%; With disability: 9.9%; Veterans: 6.3%; Ancestry: 24.0% German, 16.0% Irish, 12.3% English, 12.3% Polish, 7.2% Italian
Employment: 21.7% management, business, and financial, 10.5% computer, engineering, and science, 13.2% education, legal, community service, arts, and media, 8.6% healthcare practitioners, 11.5% service, 24.4% sales and office, 3.6% natural resources, construction, and maintenance, 6.5% production, transportation, and material moving
Income: Per capita: $38,893; Median household: $62,789; Average household: $78,488; Households with income of $100,000 or more: 28.9%; Poverty rate: 6.9%
Educational Attainment: High school diploma or higher: 95.1%; Bachelor's degree or higher: 50.1%; Graduate/professional degree or higher: 20.5%
School District(s)
SD of the City of Royal Oak (PK-12)
    2012-13 Enrollment: 5,089 . . . . (248) 435-8400
Vocational/Technical School(s)
David Pressley School of Cosmetology (Private, For-profit)
    Fall 2013 Enrollment: 225 . . . . (248) 548-5090
    2013-14 Tuition: $13,150
Housing: Homeownership rate: 67.7%; Median home value: $155,700; Median year structure built: 1955; Homeowner vacancy rate: 2.0%; Median gross rent: $882 per month; Rental vacancy rate: 9.3%
Health Insurance: 90.3% have insurance; 82.4% have private insurance; 20.8% have public insurance; 9.7% do not have insurance; 4.5% of children under 18 do not have insurance
Hospitals: Beaumont Health System (1061 beds)
Safety: Violent crime rate: 16.8 per 10,000 population; Property crime rate: 134.5 per 10,000 population
Newspapers: Detroit Daily Press (daily circulation 200000); The New Monitor (weekly circulation 35000)
Transportation: Commute: 93.3% car, 0.8% public transportation, 1.4% walk, 3.7% work from home; Median travel time to work: 23.1 minutes; Amtrak: Train service available.

Additional Information Contacts
City of Royal Oak . . . . (248) 246-3000
  http://www.ci.royal-oak.mi.us

SOUTH LYON (city).
Covers a land area of 3.734 square miles and a water area of 0.002 square miles. Located at 42.46° N. Lat; 83.65° W. Long. Elevation is 925 feet.

History: South Lyon was first settled in 1832 by the widow Thompson and her son William, who operated a store in a part of their home. First called Thompson's Corners, it was later renamed for Lucius Lyon, a member of the legislature.

Population: 11,327; Growth (since 2000): 12.9%; Density: 3,033.4 persons per square mile; Race: 95.2% White, 0.8% Black/African American, 1.7% Asian, 0.3% American Indian/Alaska Native, 0.0% Native Hawaiian/Other Pacific Islander, 1.6% Two or more races, 2.7% Hispanic of any race; Average household size: 2.42; Median age: 38.4; Age under 18: 26.9%; Age 65 and over: 14.1%; Males per 100 females: 87.7; Marriage status: 24.9% never married, 54.3% now married, 0.6% separated, 6.8% widowed, 13.9% divorced; Foreign born: 4.5%; Speak English only: 95.6%; With disability: 11.5%; Veterans: 7.3%; Ancestry: 23.6% German, 18.1% Irish, 14.6% English, 11.0% Polish, 7.7% American

Employment: 19.5% management, business, and financial, 8.7% computer, engineering, and science, 11.1% education, legal, community service, arts, and media, 7.0% healthcare practitioners, 16.7% service, 23.0% sales and office, 6.0% natural resources, construction, and maintenance, 8.0% production, transportation, and material moving

Income: Per capita: $30,843; Median household: $54,895; Average household: $72,630; Households with income of $100,000 or more: 25.8%; Poverty rate: 5.5%

Educational Attainment: High school diploma or higher: 90.8%; Bachelor's degree or higher: 36.4%; Graduate/professional degree or higher: 11.1%

School District(s)
South Lyon Community Schools (PK-12)
  2012-13 Enrollment: 7,325 . . . . (248) 573-8100

Housing: Homeownership rate: 77.7%; Median home value: $151,400; Median year structure built: 1989; Homeowner vacancy rate: 3.7%; Median gross rent: $788 per month; Rental vacancy rate: 15.1%

Health Insurance: 92.2% have insurance; 84.9% have private insurance; 19.3% have public insurance; 7.8% do not have insurance; 1.7% of children under 18 do not have insurance

Safety: Violent crime rate: 14.7 per 10,000 population; Property crime rate: 84.0 per 10,000 population

Newspapers: Milford Times (weekly circulation 7200); Northville Record (weekly circulation 6500); Novi News (weekly circulation 6400); South Lyon Herald (weekly circulation 6600)

Transportation: Commute: 94.9% car, 0.5% public transportation, 1.0% walk, 2.8% work from home; Median travel time to work: 29.7 minutes

Additional Information Contacts
City of South Lyon . . . . (248) 437-1735
  http://www.southlyonmi.org

SOUTHFIELD (city).
Covers a land area of 26.274 square miles and a water area of 0.006 square miles. Located at 42.47° N. Lat; 83.26° W. Long. Elevation is 682 feet.

History: Named for its location in the southern part of the county. Southfield was settled in the 1820's by John Daniels. It was incorporated as a city in 1958.

Population: 71,739; Growth (since 2000): -8.4%; Density: 2,730.5 persons per square mile; Race: 24.9% White, 70.3% Black/African American, 1.7% Asian, 0.2% American Indian/Alaska Native, 0.0% Native Hawaiian/Other Pacific Islander, 2.4% Two or more races, 1.3% Hispanic of any race; Average household size: 2.22; Median age: 42.0; Age under 18: 20.5%; Age 65 and over: 16.9%; Males per 100 females: 80.8; Marriage status: 36.5% never married, 40.5% now married, 2.3% separated, 8.6% widowed, 14.4% divorced; Foreign born: 9.4%; Speak English only: 89.3%; With disability: 15.5%; Veterans: 8.3%; Ancestry: 3.2% German, 3.1% Polish, 2.6% American, 2.2% African, 2.0% Irish

Employment: 15.4% management, business, and financial, 5.9% computer, engineering, and science, 12.4% education, legal, community service, arts, and media, 7.1% healthcare practitioners, 17.7% service, 27.1% sales and office, 3.7% natural resources, construction, and maintenance, 10.6% production, transportation, and material moving

Income: Per capita: $28,635; Median household: $49,841; Average household: $64,219; Households with income of $100,000 or more: 18.9%; Poverty rate: 16.0%

Educational Attainment: High school diploma or higher: 92.4%; Bachelor's degree or higher: 36.2%; Graduate/professional degree or higher: 15.5%

School District(s)
Academy of Southfield (KG-12)
  2012-13 Enrollment: 363 . . . . (248) 557-6121
Agbu Alex-Marie Manoogian School (KG-12)
  2012-13 Enrollment: 375 . . . . (248) 569-2988
Berkley SD (PK-12)
  2012-13 Enrollment: 4,667 . . . . (248) 837-8000
Bradford Academy (KG-12)
  2012-13 Enrollment: 1,084 . . . . (248) 351-0000
Crescent Academy (PK-12)
  2012-13 Enrollment: 935 . . . . (248) 423-4581
Dr. Joseph F. Pollack Academic Center of Excellenc (KG-12)
  2012-13 Enrollment: 867 . . . . (248) 569-1060
Laurus Academy (KG-12)
  2012-13 Enrollment: 715 . . . . (248) 799-8401
Southfield Public SD (PK-12)
  2012-13 Enrollment: 7,376 . . . . (248) 746-4366
Taylor International Academy (KG-12)
  2012-13 Enrollment: 422 . . . . (248) 354-1500

Four-year College(s)
DeVry University-Michigan (Private, For-profit)
  Fall 2013 Enrollment: 304 . . . . (248) 213-1610
  2013-14 Tuition: In-state $16,010; Out-of-state $16,010
ITT Technical Institute-Southfield (Private, For-profit)
  Fall 2013 Enrollment: 143 . . . . (248) 603-6100
  2013-14 Tuition: In-state $18,048; Out-of-state $18,048
Lawrence Technological University (Private, Not-for-profit)
  Fall 2013 Enrollment: 4,002 . . . . (248) 204-4000
  2013-14 Tuition: In-state $28,948; Out-of-state $28,948
University of Phoenix-Detroit Campus (Private, For-profit)
  Fall 2013 Enrollment: 1,249 . . . . (866) 766-0766
  2013-14 Tuition: In-state $12,400; Out-of-state $12,400

Vocational/Technical School(s)
Abcott Institute (Private, For-profit)
  Fall 2013 Enrollment: 151 . . . . (248) 440-6020
  2013-14 Tuition: $9,000
Everest Institute-Southfield (Private, For-profit)
  Fall 2013 Enrollment: 1,003 . . . . (248) 799-9933
  2013-14 Tuition: $17,506
Irene's Myomassology Institute (Private, For-profit)
  Fall 2013 Enrollment: 353 . . . . (248) 350-1400
  2013-14 Tuition: $10,690
Northwestern Technological Institute (Private, For-profit)
  Fall 2013 Enrollment: 406 . . . . (248) 358-4006
  2013-14 Tuition: $15,856
Specs Howard School of Media Arts (Private, For-profit)
  Fall 2013 Enrollment: 597 . . . . (248) 358-9000

Housing: Homeownership rate: 53.7%; Median home value: $108,500; Median year structure built: 1969; Homeowner vacancy rate: 3.2%; Median gross rent: $965 per month; Rental vacancy rate: 12.5%

Health Insurance: 88.2% have insurance; 67.9% have private insurance; 37.2% have public insurance; 11.8% do not have insurance; 4.0% of children under 18 do not have insurance

Hospitals: Oakland Regional Hospital; Providence Hospital & Medical Centers (459 beds); Straith Hospital For Special Surgery (27 beds)

Safety: Violent crime rate: 36.0 per 10,000 population; Property crime rate: 291.4 per 10,000 population

Transportation: Commute: 92.8% car, 2.0% public transportation, 1.7% walk, 3.0% work from home; Median travel time to work: 24.0 minutes

Additional Information Contacts
City of Southfield . . . . (248) 796-5000
  http://www.cityofsouthfield.com

SOUTHFIELD (township).
Covers a land area of 8.046 square miles and a water area of 0.015 square miles. Located at 42.52° N. Lat; 83.26° W. Long. Elevation is 682 feet.

History: Laid out 1817, Incorporated as a city 1958.

Population: 14,547; Growth (since 2000): 0.8%; Density: 1,808.1 persons per square mile; Race: 88.2% White, 6.7% Black/African American, 2.8%

Asian, 0.2% American Indian/Alaska Native, 0.0% Native Hawaiian/Other Pacific Islander, 1.6% Two or more races, 1.5% Hispanic of any race; Average household size: 2.54; Median age: 45.9; Age under 18: 25.1%; Age 65 and over: 18.8%; Males per 100 females: 93.6; Marriage status: 21.2% never married, 64.2% now married, 0.1% separated, 5.7% widowed, 8.9% divorced; Foreign born: 7.3%; Speak English only: 92.3%; With disability: 7.7%; Veterans: 9.1%; Ancestry: 21.6% German, 15.9% Irish, 13.4% English, 11.1% Polish, 9.1% Italian

Employment: 26.6% management, business, and financial, 8.3% computer, engineering, and science, 18.8% education, legal, community service, arts, and media, 6.9% healthcare practitioners, 8.5% service, 25.7% sales and office, 1.9% natural resources, construction, and maintenance, 3.4% production, transportation, and material moving

Income: Per capita: $60,134; Median household: $111,849; Average household: $156,128; Households with income of $100,000 or more: 57.5%; Poverty rate: 3.2%

Educational Attainment: High school diploma or higher: 98.2%; Bachelor's degree or higher: 69.0%; Graduate/professional degree or higher: 33.8%

School District(s)

Academy of Southfield (KG-12)
    2012-13 Enrollment: 363 . . . . (248) 557-6121
Agbu Alex-Marie Manoogian School (KG-12)
    2012-13 Enrollment: 375 . . . . (248) 569-2988
Berkley SD (PK-12)
    2012-13 Enrollment: 4,667 . . . . (248) 837-8000
Bradford Academy (KG-12)
    2012-13 Enrollment: 1,084 . . . . (248) 351-0000
Crescent Academy (PK-12)
    2012-13 Enrollment: 935 . . . . (248) 423-4581
Dr. Joseph F. Pollack Academic Center of Excellenc (KG-12)
    2012-13 Enrollment: 867 . . . . (248) 569-1060
Laurus Academy (KG-12)
    2012-13 Enrollment: 715 . . . . (248) 799-8401
Southfield Public SD (PK-12)
    2012-13 Enrollment: 7,376 . . . . (248) 746-4366
Taylor International Academy (KG-12)
    2012-13 Enrollment: 422 . . . . (248) 354-1500

Four-year College(s)

DeVry University-Michigan (Private, For-profit)
    Fall 2013 Enrollment: 304 . . . . (248) 213-1610
    2013-14 Tuition: In-state $16,010; Out-of-state $16,010
ITT Technical Institute-Southfield (Private, For-profit)
    Fall 2013 Enrollment: 143 . . . . (248) 603-6100
    2013-14 Tuition: In-state $18,048; Out-of-state $18,048
Lawrence Technological University (Private, Not-for-profit)
    Fall 2013 Enrollment: 4,002 . . . . (248) 204-4000
    2013-14 Tuition: In-state $28,948; Out-of-state $28,948
University of Phoenix-Detroit Campus (Private, For-profit)
    Fall 2013 Enrollment: 1,249 . . . . (866) 766-0766
    2013-14 Tuition: In-state $12,400; Out-of-state $12,400

Vocational/Technical School(s)

Abcott Institute (Private, For-profit)
    Fall 2013 Enrollment: 151 . . . . (248) 440-6020
    2013-14 Tuition: $9,000
Everest Institute-Southfield (Private, For-profit)
    Fall 2013 Enrollment: 1,003 . . . . (248) 799-9933
    2013-14 Tuition: $17,506
Irene's Myomassology Institute (Private, For-profit)
    Fall 2013 Enrollment: 353 . . . . (248) 350-1400
    2013-14 Tuition: $10,690
Northwestern Technological Institute (Private, For-profit)
    Fall 2013 Enrollment: 406 . . . . (248) 358-4006
    2013-14 Tuition: $15,856
Specs Howard School of Media Arts (Private, For-profit)
    Fall 2013 Enrollment: 597 . . . . (248) 358-9000

Housing: Homeownership rate: 90.1%; Median home value: $299,100; Median year structure built: 1960; Homeowner vacancy rate: 1.6%; Median gross rent: $1,382 per month; Rental vacancy rate: 4.7%

Health Insurance: 95.4% have insurance; 91.6% have private insurance; 18.5% have public insurance; 4.6% do not have insurance; 1.4% of children under 18 do not have insurance

Hospitals: Oakland Regional Hospital; Providence Hospital & Medical Centers (459 beds); Straith Hospital For Special Surgery (27 beds)

Transportation: Commute: 91.2% car, 0.3% public transportation, 0.8% walk, 7.4% work from home; Median travel time to work: 23.0 minutes

Additional Information Contacts
Southfield Township . . . . (248) 540-3420
    http://www.binghamfarms.org/southfield%20township.html

SPRINGFIELD (charter township). Covers a land area of 35.431 square miles and a water area of 1.214 square miles. Located at 42.75° N. Lat; 83.50° W. Long. Elevation is 1,027 feet.

History: Springfield Township was organized in 1837, after settlement began here in the early 1830's.

Population: 13,940; Growth (since 2000): 4.5%; Density: 393.4 persons per square mile; Race: 95.4% White, 1.1% Black/African American, 1.0% Asian, 0.4% American Indian/Alaska Native, 0.0% Native Hawaiian/Other Pacific Islander, 1.4% Two or more races, 2.9% Hispanic of any race; Average household size: 2.77; Median age: 42.0; Age under 18: 26.0%; Age 65 and over: 10.3%; Males per 100 females: 101.1; Marriage status: 23.4% never married, 64.4% now married, 0.5% separated, 3.5% widowed, 8.7% divorced; Foreign born: 3.8%; Speak English only: 94.8%; With disability: 9.0%; Veterans: 6.0%; Ancestry: 28.0% German, 15.5% English, 15.0% Irish, 11.1% Polish, 7.3% Italian

Employment: 20.7% management, business, and financial, 7.6% computer, engineering, and science, 8.5% education, legal, community service, arts, and media, 8.0% healthcare practitioners, 15.0% service, 22.4% sales and office, 7.6% natural resources, construction, and maintenance, 10.1% production, transportation, and material moving

Income: Per capita: $36,556; Median household: $80,651; Average household: $100,811; Households with income of $100,000 or more: 38.2%; Poverty rate: 4.9%

Educational Attainment: High school diploma or higher: 94.6%; Bachelor's degree or higher: 36.4%; Graduate/professional degree or higher: 13.5%

Housing: Homeownership rate: 90.7%; Median home value: $205,700; Median year structure built: 1984; Homeowner vacancy rate: 2.5%; Median gross rent: <$100 per month; Rental vacancy rate: 15.0%

Health Insurance: 92.1% have insurance; 86.4% have private insurance; 18.5% have public insurance; 7.9% do not have insurance; 2.3% of children under 18 do not have insurance

Transportation: Commute: 93.3% car, 0.1% public transportation, 0.8% walk, 4.8% work from home; Median travel time to work: 30.7 minutes

Additional Information Contacts
Springfield Township . . . . (248) 846-6500
    http://www.springfield-twp.us

SYLVAN LAKE (city). Covers a land area of 0.508 square miles and a water area of 0.315 square miles. Located at 42.62° N. Lat; 83.33° W. Long. Elevation is 958 feet.

History: Sylvan Lake began in 1881 as a station on the Grand Trunk Railroad. A charter commission organized the village in 1921.

Population: 1,720; Growth (since 2000): -0.9%; Density: 3,386.5 persons per square mile; Race: 94.5% White, 2.2% Black/African American, 0.7% Asian, 0.3% American Indian/Alaska Native, 0.0% Native Hawaiian/Other Pacific Islander, 1.7% Two or more races, 1.5% Hispanic of any race; Average household size: 2.13; Median age: 44.8; Age under 18: 20.1%; Age 65 and over: 16.0%; Males per 100 females: 97.2

Housing: Homeownership rate: 79.8%; Homeowner vacancy rate: 2.0%; Rental vacancy rate: 10.9%

Safety: Violent crime rate: 57.2 per 10,000 population; Property crime rate: 274.4 per 10,000 population

Additional Information Contacts
City of Sylvan Lake . . . . (248) 682-1440
    http://www.sylvanlake.org

TROY (city). Covers a land area of 33.473 square miles and a water area of 0.168 square miles. Located at 42.58° N. Lat; 83.15° W. Long. Elevation is 748 feet.

History: Named for Troy, New York, home of the town's early settlers. Troy contains many historic buildings. Settled 1821. Incorporated 1955.

Population: 80,980; Growth (since 2000): 0.0%; Density: 2,419.2 persons per square mile; Race: 74.1% White, 4.0% Black/African American, 19.1% Asian, 0.2% American Indian/Alaska Native, 0.0% Native Hawaiian/Other Pacific Islander, 2.0% Two or more races, 2.1% Hispanic of any race; Average household size: 2.63; Median age: 41.8; Age under 18: 23.8%; Age 65 and over: 13.8%; Males per 100 females: 97.0; Marriage status: 24.4% never married, 63.4% now married, 0.4% separated, 5.1%

widowed, 7.1% divorced; Foreign born: 27.2%; Speak English only: 68.6%; With disability: 8.3%; Veterans: 5.5%; Ancestry: 17.1% German, 11.4% Polish, 10.4% Irish, 8.5% English, 7.0% Italian

Employment: 22.6% management, business, and financial, 16.0% computer, engineering, and science, 12.3% education, legal, community service, arts, and media, 9.3% healthcare practitioners, 11.5% service, 19.1% sales and office, 3.3% natural resources, construction, and maintenance, 5.9% production, transportation, and material moving

Income: Per capita: $40,022; Median household: $85,685; Average household: $106,454; Households with income of $100,000 or more: 40.9%; Poverty rate: 7.2%

Educational Attainment: High school diploma or higher: 94.0%; Bachelor's degree or higher: 57.6%; Graduate/professional degree or higher: 27.0%

School District(s)
Avondale SD (PK-12)
   2012-13 Enrollment: 3,553 . . . . (248) 537-6002
SD of the City of Birmingham (PK-12)
   2012-13 Enrollment: 8,298 . . . . : (248) 203-3004
Troy SD (PK-12)
   2012-13 Enrollment: 12,320 . . . . (248) 823-4000
Warren Consolidated Schools (KG-12)
   2012-13 Enrollment: 15,193 . . . . (586) 825-2400

Four-year College(s)
ITT Technical Institute-Troy (Private, For-profit)
   Fall 2013 Enrollment: 581 . . . . (248) 524-1800
   2013-14 Tuition: In-state $18,048; Out-of-state $18,048
International Academy of Design and Technology-Troy (Private, For-profit)
   Fall 2013 Enrollment: 351 . . . . (248) 457-2700
   2013-14 Tuition: In-state $15,247; Out-of-state $15,247
Walsh College of Accountancy and Business Administration (Private, Not-for-profit)
   Fall 2013 Enrollment: 2,864 . . . . (248) 689-8282

Two-year College(s)
Carnegie Institute (Private, For-profit)
   Fall 2013 Enrollment: 241 . . . . (248) 589-1078
   2013-14 Tuition: In-state $11,765; Out-of-state $11,765

Vocational/Technical School(s)
Michigan College of Beauty-Troy (Private, For-profit)
   Fall 2013 Enrollment: 301 . . . . (248) 528-0303
   2013-14 Tuition: $16,600

Housing: Homeownership rate: 75.9%; Median home value: $219,200; Median year structure built: 1976; Homeowner vacancy rate: 1.4%; Median gross rent: $1,049 per month; Rental vacancy rate: 14.3%

Health Insurance: 91.5% have insurance; 83.5% have private insurance; 20.4% have public insurance; 8.5% do not have insurance; 4.7% of children under 18 do not have insurance

Hospitals: William Beaumont Hospital - Troy (226 beds)

Safety: Violent crime rate: 7.5 per 10,000 population; Property crime rate: 187.6 per 10,000 population

Newspapers: Troy-Somerset Gazette (weekly circulation 25000)

Transportation: Commute: 94.6% car, 0.4% public transportation, 0.8% walk, 3.7% work from home; Median travel time to work: 24.9 minutes

Airports: Oakland/Troy (general aviation)

Additional Information Contacts
City of Troy . . . . (248) 524-3300
   http://troymi.gov

VILLAGE OF CLARKSTON (city). Covers a land area of 0.439 square miles and a water area of 0.073 square miles. Located at 42.73° N. Lat; 83.42° W. Long. Elevation is 1,001 feet.

Population: 882; Growth (since 2000): -8.3%; Density: 2,010.4 persons per square mile; Race: 97.7% White, 0.2% Black/African American, 0.6% Asian, 0.1% American Indian/Alaska Native, 0.0% Native Hawaiian/Other Pacific Islander, 0.9% Two or more races, 1.8% Hispanic of any race; Average household size: 2.19; Median age: 45.4; Age under 18: 21.4%; Age 65 and over: 19.2%; Males per 100 females: 94.7

Housing: Homeownership rate: 63.9%; Homeowner vacancy rate: 4.8%; Rental vacancy rate: 6.3%

WALLED LAKE (city). Covers a land area of 2.176 square miles and a water area of 0.186 square miles. Located at 42.54° N. Lat; 83.47° W. Long. Elevation is 938 feet.

History: The Walled Lake from which the city took its name was called that because it was bordered by a large row of boulders, piled up along the shore by the pressure of expanding ice.

Population: 6,999; Growth (since 2000): 4.3%; Density: 3,216.6 persons per square mile; Race: 88.7% White, 4.4% Black/African American, 2.8% Asian, 0.4% American Indian/Alaska Native, 0.0% Native Hawaiian/Other Pacific Islander, 2.5% Two or more races, 3.9% Hispanic of any race; Average household size: 2.09; Median age: 39.4; Age under 18: 19.9%; Age 65 and over: 13.8%; Males per 100 females: 87.4; Marriage status: 31.9% never married, 45.0% now married, 0.4% separated, 6.3% widowed, 16.8% divorced; Foreign born: 12.4%; Speak English only: 85.1%; With disability: 13.7%; Veterans: 5.9%; Ancestry: 18.7% German, 16.0% Irish, 13.3% English, 9.8% Polish, 8.9% Italian

Employment: 12.6% management, business, and financial, 5.9% computer, engineering, and science, 8.9% education, legal, community service, arts, and media, 5.6% healthcare practitioners, 18.0% service, 29.0% sales and office, 6.6% natural resources, construction, and maintenance, 13.5% production, transportation, and material moving

Income: Per capita: $25,986; Median household: $46,319; Average household: $55,720; Households with income of $100,000 or more: 14.5%; Poverty rate: 13.3%

Educational Attainment: High school diploma or higher: 88.1%; Bachelor's degree or higher: 25.5%; Graduate/professional degree or higher: 8.2%

School District(s)
Walled Lake Consolidated Schools (PK-12)
   2012-13 Enrollment: 15,177 . . . . (248) 956-2000

Housing: Homeownership rate: 61.8%; Median home value: $101,100; Median year structure built: 1982; Homeowner vacancy rate: 4.0%; Median gross rent: $905 per month; Rental vacancy rate: 11.6%

Health Insurance: 84.1% have insurance; 68.2% have private insurance; 27.5% have public insurance; 15.9% do not have insurance; 11.7% of children under 18 do not have insurance

Safety: Violent crime rate: 36.6 per 10,000 population; Property crime rate: 102.8 per 10,000 population

Transportation: Commute: 95.6% car, 0.0% public transportation, 1.2% walk, 2.0% work from home; Median travel time to work: 24.6 minutes

Additional Information Contacts
City of Walled Lake . . . . (248) 624-4847
   http://www.walledlake.com

WATERFORD (charter township). Covers a land area of 30.655 square miles and a water area of 4.538 square miles. Located at 42.66° N. Lat; 83.39° W. Long. Elevation is 968 feet.

Population: 71,707; Growth (since 2000): -2.0%; Density: 2,339.2 persons per square mile; Race: 89.2% White, 4.7% Black/African American, 1.6% Asian, 0.4% American Indian/Alaska Native, 0.0% Native Hawaiian/Other Pacific Islander, 2.4% Two or more races, 6.4% Hispanic of any race; Average household size: 2.40; Median age: 39.1; Age under 18: 23.0%; Age 65 and over: 12.5%; Males per 100 females: 96.1; Marriage status: 30.2% never married, 50.2% now married, 1.5% separated, 5.6% widowed, 13.9% divorced; Foreign born: 5.3%; Speak English only: 92.8%; With disability: 12.8%; Veterans: 8.4%; Ancestry: 23.7% German, 15.0% Irish, 12.2% English, 10.2% Polish, 5.9% American

Employment: 13.2% management, business, and financial, 7.1% computer, engineering, and science, 8.8% education, legal, community service, arts, and media, 4.8% healthcare practitioners, 19.4% service, 27.7% sales and office, 7.9% natural resources, construction, and maintenance, 11.1% production, transportation, and material moving

Income: Per capita: $28,717; Median household: $54,827; Average household: $68,201; Households with income of $100,000 or more: 20.4%; Poverty rate: 13.2%

Educational Attainment: High school diploma or higher: 90.3%; Bachelor's degree or higher: 26.0%; Graduate/professional degree or higher: 9.2%

School District(s)
Academy of Waterford (KG-12)
   2012-13 Enrollment: 228 . . . . (248) 674-1649
Waterford SD (PK-12)
   2012-13 Enrollment: 10,704 . . . . (248) 682-0554

Vocational/Technical School(s)
Marketti Academy of Cosmetology (Private, For-profit)
  Fall 2013 Enrollment: 59 . . . . (248) 618-6394
  2013-14 Tuition: $13,615
Port Huron Cosmetology College (Private, For-profit)
  Fall 2013 Enrollment: 82 . . . . (248) 623-9494
  2013-14 Tuition: $14,825
Housing: Homeownership rate: 73.6%; Median home value: $122,100; Median year structure built: 1970; Homeowner vacancy rate: 2.4%; Median gross rent: $732 per month; Rental vacancy rate: 10.9%
Health Insurance: 87.5% have insurance; 73.3% have private insurance; 27.7% have public insurance; 12.5% do not have insurance; 5.2% of children under 18 do not have insurance
Safety: Violent crime rate: 18.5 per 10,000 population; Property crime rate: 158.6 per 10,000 population
Transportation: Commute: 95.3% car, 0.1% public transportation, 0.8% walk, 2.5% work from home; Median travel time to work: 27.3 minutes
Additional Information Contacts
Waterford Charter Township . . . . (248) 674-3111
  http://www.twp.waterford.mi.us

WEST BLOOMFIELD (charter township). Covers a land area of 27.007 square miles and a water area of 4.262 square miles. Located at 42.57° N. Lat; 83.39° W. Long.
Population: 64,690; Growth (since 2000): -0.3%; Density: 2,395.3 persons per square mile; Race: 77.6% White, 11.4% Black/African American, 8.4% Asian, 0.1% American Indian/Alaska Native, 0.0% Native Hawaiian/Other Pacific Islander, 2.0% Two or more races, 1.6% Hispanic of any race; Average household size: 2.66; Median age: 44.6; Age under 18: 23.6%; Age 65 and over: 17.4%; Males per 100 females: 93.3; Marriage status: 26.4% never married, 58.8% now married, 0.7% separated, 6.0% widowed, 8.9% divorced; Foreign born: 21.3%; Speak English only: 73.2%; With disability: 9.8%; Veterans: 6.4%; Ancestry: 9.8% German, 9.2% Assyrian/Chaldean/Syriac, 9.1% Polish, 6.6% Russian, 6.2% American
Employment: 23.3% management, business, and financial, 8.4% computer, engineering, and science, 13.3% education, legal, community service, arts, and media, 11.0% healthcare practitioners, 8.9% service, 26.6% sales and office, 3.6% natural resources, construction, and maintenance, 4.8% production, transportation, and material moving
Income: Per capita: $47,856; Median household: $90,164; Average household: $126,953; Households with income of $100,000 or more: 45.6%; Poverty rate: 5.5%
Educational Attainment: High school diploma or higher: 94.2%; Bachelor's degree or higher: 56.0%; Graduate/professional degree or higher: 27.4%

School District(s)
Bloomfield Hills SD (PK-12)
  2012-13 Enrollment: 5,510 . . . . (248) 341-5405
Walled Lake Consolidated Schools (PK-12)
  2012-13 Enrollment: 15,177 . . . . (248) 956-2000
West Bloomfield SD (PK-12)
  2012-13 Enrollment: 6,228 . . . . (248) 865-6485
Four-year College(s)
Michigan Jewish Institute (Private, Not-for-profit, Jewish)
  Fall 2013 Enrollment: 1,662 . . . . (248) 414-6900
  2013-14 Tuition: In-state $10,700; Out-of-state $10,700
Housing: Homeownership rate: 82.6%; Median home value: $236,600; Median year structure built: 1979; Homeowner vacancy rate: 1.9%; Median gross rent: $1,534 per month; Rental vacancy rate: 11.1%
Health Insurance: 92.8% have insurance; 84.1% have private insurance; 23.5% have public insurance; 7.2% do not have insurance; 3.1% of children under 18 do not have insurance
Hospitals: Henry Ford West Bloomfield Hospital (300 beds)
Safety: Violent crime rate: 6.5 per 10,000 population; Property crime rate: 107.1 per 10,000 population
Transportation: Commute: 92.7% car, 0.2% public transportation, 0.5% walk, 6.0% work from home; Median travel time to work: 27.3 minutes
Additional Information Contacts
West Bloomfield Charter Township . . . . (248) 451-4800
  http://www.twp.west-bloomfield.mi.us

WHITE LAKE (charter township). Covers a land area of 33.520 square miles and a water area of 3.545 square miles. Located at 42.66° N. Lat; 83.51° W. Long. Elevation is 1,037 feet.
Population: 30,019; Growth (since 2000): 6.4%; Density: 895.6 persons per square mile; Race: 95.3% White, 1.1% Black/African American, 0.9% Asian, 0.4% American Indian/Alaska Native, 0.0% Native Hawaiian/Other Pacific Islander, 1.6% Two or more races, 3.0% Hispanic of any race; Average household size: 2.66; Median age: 41.3; Age under 18: 24.6%; Age 65 and over: 11.4%; Males per 100 females: 98.7; Marriage status: 23.4% never married, 62.1% now married, 1.2% separated, 5.0% widowed, 9.5% divorced; Foreign born: 3.4%; Speak English only: 95.2%; With disability: 11.6%; Veterans: 8.8%; Ancestry: 25.4% German, 19.9% Irish, 13.2% English, 11.4% Polish, 8.7% Italian
Employment: 17.4% management, business, and financial, 8.1% computer, engineering, and science, 8.8% education, legal, community service, arts, and media, 5.6% healthcare practitioners, 16.1% service, 26.5% sales and office, 8.2% natural resources, construction, and maintenance, 9.3% production, transportation, and material moving
Income: Per capita: $31,805; Median household: $72,063; Average household: $83,539; Households with income of $100,000 or more: 32.2%; Poverty rate: 8.0%
Educational Attainment: High school diploma or higher: 93.4%; Bachelor's degree or higher: 31.3%; Graduate/professional degree or higher: 10.1%

School District(s)
Huron Valley Schools (PK-12)
  2012-13 Enrollment: 9,899 . . . . (248) 684-8234
Walled Lake Consolidated Schools (PK-12)
  2012-13 Enrollment: 15,177 . . . . (248) 956-2000
Waterford SD (PK-12)
  2012-13 Enrollment: 10,704 . . . . (248) 682-0554
Housing: Homeownership rate: 87.7%; Median home value: $171,800; Median year structure built: 1979; Homeowner vacancy rate: 1.9%; Median gross rent: $949 per month; Rental vacancy rate: 12.9%
Health Insurance: 90.1% have insurance; 79.1% have private insurance; 23.4% have public insurance; 9.9% do not have insurance; 3.9% of children under 18 do not have insurance
Safety: Violent crime rate: 7.2 per 10,000 population; Property crime rate: 141.9 per 10,000 population
Transportation: Commute: 92.9% car, 0.1% public transportation, 1.5% walk, 4.1% work from home; Median travel time to work: 33.6 minutes
Additional Information Contacts
White Lake Charter Township . . . . (248) 698-3300
  http://www.whitelaketwp.com

WIXOM (city). Covers a land area of 9.154 square miles and a water area of 0.212 square miles. Located at 42.52° N. Lat; 83.53° W. Long. Elevation is 932 feet.
Population: 13,498; Growth (since 2000): 1.8%; Density: 1,474.6 persons per square mile; Race: 79.8% White, 11.1% Black/African American, 4.9% Asian, 0.2% American Indian/Alaska Native, 0.0% Native Hawaiian/Other Pacific Islander, 2.1% Two or more races, 5.1% Hispanic of any race; Average household size: 2.36; Median age: 34.8; Age under 18: 25.4%; Age 65 and over: 7.0%; Males per 100 females: 99.5; Marriage status: 36.1% never married, 49.4% now married, 1.0% separated, 3.0% widowed, 11.5% divorced; Foreign born: 10.7%; Speak English only: 86.5%; With disability: 6.3%; Veterans: 5.3%; Ancestry: 21.0% German, 14.7% Polish, 13.1% Irish, 10.0% English, 5.6% American
Employment: 18.3% management, business, and financial, 8.5% computer, engineering, and science, 6.4% education, legal, community service, arts, and media, 4.3% healthcare practitioners, 18.3% service, 29.9% sales and office, 4.9% natural resources, construction, and maintenance, 9.4% production, transportation, and material moving
Income: Per capita: $30,447; Median household: $46,394; Average household: $67,094; Households with income of $100,000 or more: 23.0%; Poverty rate: 14.5%
Educational Attainment: High school diploma or higher: 92.8%; Bachelor's degree or higher: 38.6%; Graduate/professional degree or higher: 12.2%

School District(s)
Walled Lake Consolidated Schools (PK-12)
  2012-13 Enrollment: 15,177 . . . . (248) 956-2000
Housing: Homeownership rate: 52.3%; Median home value: $179,500; Median year structure built: 1982; Homeowner vacancy rate: 1.4%; Median gross rent: $616 per month; Rental vacancy rate: 20.6%

Health Insurance: 87.8% have insurance; 76.6% have private insurance; 18.5% have public insurance; 12.2% do not have insurance; 5.0% of children under 18 do not have insurance
Safety: Violent crime rate: 14.6 per 10,000 population; Property crime rate: 192.8 per 10,000 population
Transportation: Commute: 94.5% car, 0.1% public transportation, 1.4% walk, 3.7% work from home; Median travel time to work: 25.2 minutes
Additional Information Contacts
City of Wixom . . . . (248) 624-4557
  http://www.ci.wixom.mi.us

WOLVERINE LAKE (village). Covers a land area of 1.269 square miles and a water area of 0.413 square miles. Located at 42.56° N. Lat; 83.49° W. Long. Elevation is 935 feet.
Population: 4,312; Growth (since 2000): -2.3%; Density: 3,397.6 persons per square mile; Race: 95.9% White, 0.7% Black/African American, 1.2% Asian, 0.4% American Indian/Alaska Native, 0.0% Native Hawaiian/Other Pacific Islander, 1.4% Two or more races, 2.4% Hispanic of any race; Average household size: 2.49; Median age: 42.7; Age under 18: 21.6%; Age 65 and over: 11.6%; Males per 100 females: 106.7; Marriage status: 26.4% never married, 59.0% now married, 1.2% separated, 4.3% widowed, 10.3% divorced; Foreign born: 5.5%; Speak English only: 92.3%; With disability: 4.3%; Veterans: 9.9%; Ancestry: 29.8% German, 19.5% Irish, 16.8% English, 14.2% Polish, 7.5% Italian
Employment: 16.4% management, business, and financial, 8.2% computer, engineering, and science, 6.8% education, legal, community service, arts, and media, 1.4% healthcare practitioners, 16.5% service, 26.7% sales and office, 7.4% natural resources, construction, and maintenance, 16.6% production, transportation, and material moving
Income: Per capita: $36,405; Median household: $75,833; Average household: $91,014; Households with income of $100,000 or more: 35.8%; Poverty rate: 4.6%
Educational Attainment: High school diploma or higher: 91.8%; Bachelor's degree or higher: 30.8%; Graduate/professional degree or higher: 8.0%
Housing: Homeownership rate: 86.1%; Median home value: $154,500; Median year structure built: 1968; Homeowner vacancy rate: 1.5%; Median gross rent: $809 per month; Rental vacancy rate: 6.9%
Health Insurance: 90.4% have insurance; 85.1% have private insurance; 17.6% have public insurance; 9.6% do not have insurance; 0.0% of children under 18 do not have insurance
Safety: Violent crime rate: 6.9 per 10,000 population; Property crime rate: 43.5 per 10,000 population
Transportation: Commute: 93.8% car, 0.0% public transportation, 0.0% walk, 5.2% work from home; Median travel time to work: 26.6 minutes
Additional Information Contacts
Village of Wolverine Lake . . . . (248) 624-1710
  http://www.wolverinelake.com

Oceana County

Located in western Michigan; bounded on the west by Lake Michigan; drained by the White and Pentwater Rivers; includes part of Manistee National Forest. Covers a land area of 512.071 square miles, a water area of 793.879 square miles, and is located in the Eastern Time Zone at 43.65° N. Lat., 86.81° W. Long. The county was founded in 1831. County seat is Hart.

Weather Station: Hart | | | | | | | | | | Elevation: 700 feet
	Jan	Feb	Mar	Apr	May	Jun	Jul	Aug	Sep	Oct	Nov	Dec
High	30	32	41	55	66	75	80	78	71	58	46	34
Low	16	17	23	34	44	53	58	58	50	39	31	22
Precip	2.6	1.9	2.1	3.0	3.7	3.2	3.0	3.8	3.9	3.6	3.3	2.7
Snow	25.7	17.3	6.7	1.8	tr	0.0	0.0	0.0	0.0	tr	3.9	22.7

High and Low temperatures in degrees Fahrenheit; Precipitation and Snow in inches

Weather Station: Hesperia 4 WNW | | | | | | | | | | Elevation: 779 feet
	Jan	Feb	Mar	Apr	May	Jun	Jul	Aug	Sep	Oct	Nov	Dec
High	30	33	43	57	68	77	82	80	72	59	46	34
Low	14	15	21	32	42	52	56	55	47	36	28	20
Precip	2.1	1.4	2.1	2.9	3.6	3.3	2.4	3.3	3.7	3.5	3.0	2.5
Snow	21.0	12.0	8.0	1.9	tr	0.0	0.0	0.0	tr	0.3	5.6	21.8

High and Low temperatures in degrees Fahrenheit; Precipitation and Snow in inches

Population: 26,570; Growth (since 2000): -1.1%; Density: 51.9 persons per square mile; Race: 90.1% White, 0.4% Black/African American, 0.2%

Asian, 1.1% American Indian/Alaska Native, 0.0% Native Hawaiian/Other Pacific Islander, 2.0% two or more races, 13.7% Hispanic of any race; Average household size: 2.58; Median age: 41.8; Age under 18: 24.9%; Age 65 and over: 17.0%; Males per 100 females: 100.9; Marriage status: 23.9% never married, 58.5% now married, 1.3% separated, 6.9% widowed, 10.7% divorced; Foreign born: 6.0%; Speak English only: 88.5%; With disability: 17.2%; Veterans: 12.0%; Ancestry: 24.3% German, 12.0% English, 11.2% Irish, 8.7% Dutch, 7.9% American
Religion: Six largest groups: 19.1% Catholicism, 5.4% Presbyterian-Reformed, 3.3% Methodist/Pietist, 2.5% Lutheran, 1.8% Holiness, 1.6% Non-denominational Protestant
Economy: Unemployment rate: 6.1%; Leading industries: 17.6% retail trade; 13.2% construction; 12.4% other services (except public administration); Farms: 609 totaling 127,779 acres; Company size: 0 employ 1,000 or more persons, 0 employ 500 to 999 persons, 6 employ 100 to 499 persons, 493 employ less than 100 persons; Business ownership: 465 women-owned, n/a Black-owned, n/a Hispanic-owned, n/a Asian-owned
Employment: 9.7% management, business, and financial, 3.0% computer, engineering, and science, 7.3% education, legal, community service, arts, and media, 4.4% healthcare practitioners, 18.9% service, 18.2% sales and office, 17.7% natural resources, construction, and maintenance, 20.8% production, transportation, and material moving
Income: Per capita: $18,986; Median household: $40,023; Average household: $50,095; Households with income of $100,000 or more: 9.4%; Poverty rate: 19.9%
Educational Attainment: High school diploma or higher: 84.1%; Bachelor's degree or higher: 15.0%; Graduate/professional degree or higher: 5.9%
Housing: Homeownership rate: 81.3%; Median home value: $106,100; Median year structure built: 1975; Homeowner vacancy rate: 2.8%; Median gross rent: $676 per month; Rental vacancy rate: 8.1%
Vital Statistics: Birth rate: 116.2 per 10,000 population; Death rate: 89.5 per 10,000 population; Age-adjusted cancer mortality rate: 153.4 deaths per 100,000 population
Health Insurance: 85.2% have insurance; 59.8% have private insurance; 42.2% have public insurance; 14.8% do not have insurance; 4.7% of children under 18 do not have insurance
Health Care: Physicians: 8.0 per 10,000 population; Hospital beds: 9.1 per 10,000 population; Hospital admissions: 184.6 per 10,000 population
Transportation: Commute: 85.5% car, 0.1% public transportation, 3.0% walk, 10.2% work from home; Median travel time to work: 23.4 minutes
Presidential Election: 44.3% Obama, 54.5% Romney (2012)
National and State Parks: Charles Mears State Park; Hart-Montague Trail State Park; Rentwater River State Game Area; Silver Lake State Park
Additional Information Contacts
Oceana Government . . . . (231) 873-4835
  http://www.co.oceana.mi.us

Oceana County Communities

BENONA (township). Covers a land area of 40.377 square miles and a water area of 0.845 square miles. Located at 43.60° N. Lat; 86.47° W. Long.
Population: 1,437; Growth (since 2000): -5.5%; Density: 35.6 persons per square mile; Race: 95.3% White, 0.1% Black/African American, 0.6% Asian, 0.4% American Indian/Alaska Native, 0.0% Native Hawaiian/Other Pacific Islander, 1.3% Two or more races, 7.2% Hispanic of any race; Average household size: 2.39; Median age: 48.6; Age under 18: 20.1%; Age 65 and over: 20.3%; Males per 100 females: 105.9
Housing: Homeownership rate: 90.3%; Homeowner vacancy rate: 2.0%; Rental vacancy rate: 10.3%

CLAYBANKS (township). Covers a land area of 23.495 square miles and a water area of 0.502 square miles. Located at 43.52° N. Lat; 86.44° W. Long.
Population: 777; Growth (since 2000): -6.5%; Density: 33.1 persons per square mile; Race: 94.3% White, 0.5% Black/African American, 0.0% Asian, 1.3% American Indian/Alaska Native, 0.0% Native Hawaiian/Other Pacific Islander, 1.8% Two or more races, 5.5% Hispanic of any race; Average household size: 2.38; Median age: 47.8; Age under 18: 20.3%; Age 65 and over: 19.8%; Males per 100 females: 105.6
Housing: Homeownership rate: 88.8%; Homeowner vacancy rate: 2.7%; Rental vacancy rate: 5.3%

COLFAX (township). Covers a land area of 32.713 square miles and a water area of 3.227 square miles. Located at 43.77° N. Lat; 86.10° W. Long. Elevation is 853 feet.

History: Colfax Township was named for Schuyler Colfax, vice president under Ulysses S. Grant.

Population: 462; Growth (since 2000): -19.5%; Density: 14.1 persons per square mile; Race: 93.3% White, 0.4% Black/African American, 0.4% Asian, 2.2% American Indian/Alaska Native, 0.0% Native Hawaiian/Other Pacific Islander, 0.6% Two or more races, 14.7% Hispanic of any race; Average household size: 2.36; Median age: 47.0; Age under 18: 19.3%; Age 65 and over: 20.3%; Males per 100 females: 107.2

Housing: Homeownership rate: 83.7%; Homeowner vacancy rate: 7.3%; Rental vacancy rate: 0.0%

CRYSTAL (township). Covers a land area of 34.704 square miles and a water area of 1.278 square miles. Located at 43.78° N. Lat; 86.22° W. Long.

Population: 838; Growth (since 2000): 0.7%; Density: 24.1 persons per square mile; Race: 82.6% White, 0.0% Black/African American, 0.4% Asian, 1.7% American Indian/Alaska Native, 0.0% Native Hawaiian/Other Pacific Islander, 2.7% Two or more races, 25.7% Hispanic of any race; Average household size: 2.97; Median age: 34.0; Age under 18: 33.3%; Age 65 and over: 12.2%; Males per 100 females: 105.4

Housing: Homeownership rate: 79.7%; Homeowner vacancy rate: 3.0%; Rental vacancy rate: 1.7%

ELBRIDGE (township). Covers a land area of 33.835 square miles and a water area of 2.394 square miles. Located at 43.69° N. Lat; 86.21° W. Long. Elevation is 945 feet.

Population: 971; Growth (since 2000): -21.2%; Density: 28.7 persons per square mile; Race: 88.9% White, 0.3% Black/African American, 0.1% Asian, 0.7% American Indian/Alaska Native, 0.0% Native Hawaiian/Other Pacific Islander, 1.3% Two or more races, 16.1% Hispanic of any race; Average household size: 2.89; Median age: 36.7; Age under 18: 29.6%; Age 65 and over: 12.3%; Males per 100 females: 107.5

Housing: Homeownership rate: 83.4%; Homeowner vacancy rate: 1.8%; Rental vacancy rate: 6.8%

FERRY (township). Covers a land area of 33.291 square miles and a water area of 2.816 square miles. Located at 43.60° N. Lat; 86.22° W. Long. Elevation is 715 feet.

Population: 1,292; Growth (since 2000): -0.3%; Density: 38.8 persons per square mile; Race: 93.0% White, 0.1% Black/African American, 0.5% Asian, 2.2% American Indian/Alaska Native, 0.0% Native Hawaiian/Other Pacific Islander, 2.4% Two or more races, 6.8% Hispanic of any race; Average household size: 2.60; Median age: 41.5; Age under 18: 23.4%; Age 65 and over: 13.4%; Males per 100 females: 112.2

Housing: Homeownership rate: 85.9%; Homeowner vacancy rate: 1.1%; Rental vacancy rate: 10.3%

GOLDEN (township). Covers a land area of 33.466 square miles and a water area of 1.554 square miles. Located at 43.69° N. Lat; 86.45° W. Long.

History: Golden Township was formed in 1864, and named by early settler William J. Haughey. He intended to use his mother's maiden name of Golding, but a clerical error made the name Golden.

Population: 1,742; Growth (since 2000): -3.8%; Density: 52.1 persons per square mile; Race: 94.3% White, 0.2% Black/African American, 0.0% Asian, 1.0% American Indian/Alaska Native, 0.0% Native Hawaiian/Other Pacific Islander, 1.1% Two or more races, 7.5% Hispanic of any race; Average household size: 2.23; Median age: 51.5; Age under 18: 16.5%; Age 65 and over: 25.0%; Males per 100 females: 108.6

Housing: Homeownership rate: 85.0%; Homeowner vacancy rate: 3.3%; Rental vacancy rate: 18.1%

GRANT (township). Covers a land area of 34.095 square miles and a water area of 1.623 square miles. Located at 43.51° N. Lat; 86.34° W. Long.

History: Settled in 1851, Grant Township was organized in 1866 and named for General Ulysses S. Grant.

Population: 2,976; Growth (since 2000): 1.5%; Density: 87.3 persons per square mile; Race: 90.0% White, 1.1% Black/African American, 0.2% Asian, 1.2% American Indian/Alaska Native, 0.1% Native Hawaiian/Other Pacific Islander, 3.0% Two or more races, 12.7% Hispanic of any race; Average household size: 2.68; Median age: 38.3; Age under 18: 26.6%;

Age 65 and over: 12.4%; Males per 100 females: 105.0; Marriage status: 23.9% never married, 60.3% now married, 1.4% separated, 5.9% widowed, 10.0% divorced; Foreign born: 5.4%; Speak English only: 95.1%; With disability: 21.1%; Veterans: 12.7%; Ancestry: 24.6% German, 14.9% Dutch, 12.1% English, 9.1% Irish, 7.4% Polish

Employment: 6.8% management, business, and financial, 2.8% computer, engineering, and science, 4.4% education, legal, community service, arts, and media, 3.4% healthcare practitioners, 26.7% service, 19.6% sales and office, 16.5% natural resources, construction, and maintenance, 19.7% production, transportation, and material moving

Income: Per capita: $18,049; Median household: $40,179; Average household: $51,032; Households with income of $100,000 or more: 11.6%; Poverty rate: 21.8%

Educational Attainment: High school diploma or higher: 87.0%; Bachelor's degree or higher: 9.0%; Graduate/professional degree or higher: 2.7%

Housing: Homeownership rate: 80.9%; Median home value: $85,700; Median year structure built: 1979; Homeowner vacancy rate: 2.3%; Median gross rent: $801 per month; Rental vacancy rate: 5.7%

Health Insurance: 85.0% have insurance; 57.7% have private insurance; 38.6% have public insurance; 15.0% do not have insurance; 1.6% of children under 18 do not have insurance

Transportation: Commute: 87.3% car, 0.0% public transportation, 1.7% walk, 9.7% work from home; Median travel time to work: 23.9 minutes

GREENWOOD (township). Covers a land area of 34.248 square miles and a water area of 1.620 square miles. Located at 43.50° N. Lat; 86.09° W. Long.

History: Greenwood Township was organized in 1858, having been settled three years earlier by Henry D. Clark. It was named for its forests.

Population: 1,184; Growth (since 2000): 2.6%; Density: 34.6 persons per square mile; Race: 96.3% White, 0.8% Black/African American, 0.3% Asian, 0.7% American Indian/Alaska Native, 0.0% Native Hawaiian/Other Pacific Islander, 1.2% Two or more races, 4.0% Hispanic of any race; Average household size: 2.94; Median age: 35.9; Age under 18: 28.8%; Age 65 and over: 12.1%; Males per 100 females: 115.3

Housing: Homeownership rate: 84.6%; Homeowner vacancy rate: 1.7%; Rental vacancy rate: 6.1%

HART (city). County seat. Covers a land area of 1.911 square miles and a water area of 0.163 square miles. Located at 43.70° N. Lat; 86.37° W. Long. Elevation is 676 feet.

History: The town of Hart grew up around a sawmill and grist mill built by Lyman Corbin in the early 1860's. Hart, incorporated as a village in 1885, developed as the center of a region devoted to fruit orchards. It was incorporated as a city in 1946.

Population: 2,126; Growth (since 2000): 9.0%; Density: 1,112.4 persons per square mile; Race: 84.3% White, 0.5% Black/African American, 0.2% Asian, 0.8% American Indian/Alaska Native, 0.0% Native Hawaiian/Other Pacific Islander, 1.6% Two or more races, 25.7% Hispanic of any race; Average household size: 2.58; Median age: 37.3; Age under 18: 26.4%; Age 65 and over: 19.9%; Males per 100 females: 93.1

School District(s)

Hart Public SD (PK-12)
    2012-13 Enrollment: 1,231 . . . . (231) 873-6214
West Shore Educational Service District (PK-12)
    2012-13 Enrollment: 99 . . . . (231) 757-3716

Housing: Homeownership rate: 55.5%; Homeowner vacancy rate: 3.2%; Rental vacancy rate: 6.9%

Safety: Violent crime rate: 19.0 per 10,000 population; Property crime rate: 656.2 per 10,000 population

Newspapers: Oceana's Herald-Journal (weekly circulation 7200)

HART (township). Covers a land area of 32.424 square miles and a water area of 1.819 square miles. Located at 43.69° N. Lat; 86.33° W. Long. Elevation is 676 feet.

History: Hart Township was organized in 1858 and named for Wellington Hart, a pioneer settler.

Population: 1,853; Growth (since 2000): -8.5%; Density: 57.1 persons per square mile; Race: 91.1% White, 0.3% Black/African American, 0.2% Asian, 0.8% American Indian/Alaska Native, 0.0% Native Hawaiian/Other Pacific Islander, 2.5% Two or more races, 14.8% Hispanic of any race; Average household size: 2.64; Median age: 42.8; Age under 18: 25.9%; Age 65 and over: 17.6%; Males per 100 females: 99.0

School District(s)
Hart Public SD (PK-12)
    2012-13 Enrollment: 1,231 . . . . (231) 873-6214
West Shore Educational Service District (PK-12)
    2012-13 Enrollment: 99. . . . . (231) 757-3716
Housing: Homeownership rate: 83.0%; Homeowner vacancy rate: 1.7%; Rental vacancy rate: 8.3%
Newspapers: Oceana's Herald-Journal (weekly circulation 7200)

HESPERIA (village).
Covers a land area of 0.787 square miles and a water area of 0.068 square miles. Located at 43.57° N. Lat; 86.04° W. Long. Elevation is 745 feet.
History: Hesperia was laid out in 1866 by John P. Cook and Daniel Weaver, who operated a sawmill and a general store. There had been settlers in this area since the mid-1850's, including Alexander McLaren, for whom McLaren Lake was named. Cook's daughter suggested the name of Hesperia for the village.
Population: 954; Growth (since 2000): 0.0%; Density: 1,211.5 persons per square mile; Race: 92.2% White, 0.0% Black/African American, 0.1% Asian, 1.4% American Indian/Alaska Native, 0.0% Native Hawaiian/Other Pacific Islander, 3.6% Two or more races, 8.1% Hispanic of any race; Average household size: 2.45; Median age: 35.5; Age under 18: 27.0%; Age 65 and over: 16.1%; Males per 100 females: 78.7
School District(s)
Hesperia Community Schools (KG-12)
    2012-13 Enrollment: 1,115 . . . . (231) 854-6185
Housing: Homeownership rate: 67.8%; Homeowner vacancy rate: 4.3%; Rental vacancy rate: 5.3%

LEAVITT (township).
Covers a land area of 29.325 square miles and a water area of 6.511 square miles. Located at 43.69° N. Lat; 86.10° W. Long.
Population: 891; Growth (since 2000): 5.4%; Density: 30.4 persons per square mile; Race: 87.7% White, 0.9% Black/African American, 0.2% Asian, 1.0% American Indian/Alaska Native, 0.0% Native Hawaiian/Other Pacific Islander, 2.7% Two or more races, 14.6% Hispanic of any race; Average household size: 2.83; Median age: 36.1; Age under 18: 26.6%; Age 65 and over: 13.9%; Males per 100 females: 100.7
Housing: Homeownership rate: 78.0%; Homeowner vacancy rate: 3.6%; Rental vacancy rate: 6.6%

MEARS (unincorporated postal area)
ZCTA: 49436
Covers a land area of 31.267 square miles and a water area of 7.261 square miles. Located at 43.68° N. Lat; 86.47° W. Long. Elevation is 778 feet.
Population: 1,622; Growth (since 2000): -3.2%; Density: 51.9 persons per square mile; Race: 94.2% White, 0.2% Black/African American, 0.1% Asian, 1.0% American Indian/Alaska Native, 0.0% Native Hawaiian/Other Pacific Islander, 1.2% Two or more races, 8.2% Hispanic of any race; Average household size: 2.19; Median age: 52.2; Age under 18: 15.8%; Age 65 and over: 25.4%; Males per 100 females: 107.4
Housing: Homeownership rate: 85.1%; Homeowner vacancy rate: 3.5%; Rental vacancy rate: 18.4%

NEW ERA (village).
Covers a land area of 0.837 square miles and a water area of 0.004 square miles. Located at 43.56° N. Lat; 86.35° W. Long. Elevation is 758 feet.
Population: 451; Growth (since 2000): -2.2%; Density: 539.0 persons per square mile; Race: 96.2% White, 0.2% Black/African American, 0.4% Asian, 1.6% American Indian/Alaska Native, 0.0% Native Hawaiian/Other Pacific Islander, 0.9% Two or more races, 3.1% Hispanic of any race; Average household size: 2.61; Median age: 41.9; Age under 18: 27.1%; Age 65 and over: 17.7%; Males per 100 females: 100.4
School District(s)
Shelby Public Schools (PK-12)
    2012-13 Enrollment: 1,375 . . . . (231) 861-5211
Housing: Homeownership rate: 87.2%; Homeowner vacancy rate: 1.3%; Rental vacancy rate: 0.0%

NEWFIELD (township).
Covers a land area of 32.277 square miles and a water area of 3.422 square miles. Located at 43.60° N. Lat; 86.11° W. Long.
Population: 2,401; Growth (since 2000): -3.3%; Density: 74.4 persons per square mile; Race: 95.2% White, 0.3% Black/African American, 0.3% Asian, 0.6% American Indian/Alaska Native, 0.0% Native Hawaiian/Other Pacific Islander, 2.2% Two or more races, 4.6% Hispanic of any race; Average household size: 2.52; Median age: 43.1; Age under 18: 24.6%; Age 65 and over: 16.7%; Males per 100 females: 96.0
Housing: Homeownership rate: 85.4%; Homeowner vacancy rate: 2.6%; Rental vacancy rate: 4.8%

OTTO (township).
Covers a land area of 33.456 square miles and a water area of 2.387 square miles. Located at 43.51° N. Lat; 86.22° W. Long.
Population: 826; Growth (since 2000): 24.8%; Density: 24.7 persons per square mile; Race: 95.9% White, 1.2% Black/African American, 0.0% Asian, 1.1% American Indian/Alaska Native, 0.0% Native Hawaiian/Other Pacific Islander, 1.1% Two or more races, 7.0% Hispanic of any race; Average household size: 2.66; Median age: 37.1; Age under 18: 26.6%; Age 65 and over: 10.3%; Males per 100 females: 106.0
Housing: Homeownership rate: 90.1%; Homeowner vacancy rate: 2.1%; Rental vacancy rate: 3.1%

PENTWATER (township).
Covers a land area of 12.857 square miles and a water area of 1.313 square miles. Located at 43.76° N. Lat; 86.42° W. Long. Elevation is 600 feet.
History: Incorporated 1867.
Population: 1,515; Growth (since 2000): 0.1%; Density: 117.8 persons per square mile; Race: 97.0% White, 0.1% Black/African American, 0.3% Asian, 0.9% American Indian/Alaska Native, 0.0% Native Hawaiian/Other Pacific Islander, 0.9% Two or more races, 2.1% Hispanic of any race; Average household size: 1.95; Median age: 59.9; Age under 18: 11.6%; Age 65 and over: 35.8%; Males per 100 females: 92.0
School District(s)
Pentwater Public SD (PK-12)
    2012-13 Enrollment: 284. . . . . (231) 869-4100
Housing: Homeownership rate: 86.4%; Homeowner vacancy rate: 4.7%; Rental vacancy rate: 23.6%

PENTWATER (village).
Covers a land area of 1.279 square miles and a water area of 0.338 square miles. Located at 43.78° N. Lat; 86.43° W. Long. Elevation is 600 feet.
History: Pentwater grew up around a sawmill at the mouth of the Pentwater River on Lake Michigan, and later developed as a shipping point for fruit and berries. Many Mennonite farmers settled in this area, and planted orchards. Charles Mears, a Chicago capitalist, built a tile and brick factory here using the clay from the Pentwater River.
Population: 857; Growth (since 2000): -10.5%; Density: 670.2 persons per square mile; Race: 97.3% White, 0.1% Black/African American, 0.0% Asian, 0.2% American Indian/Alaska Native, 0.0% Native Hawaiian/Other Pacific Islander, 1.4% Two or more races, 2.5% Hispanic of any race; Average household size: 1.89; Median age: 60.3; Age under 18: 11.2%; Age 65 and over: 38.3%; Males per 100 females: 83.5
School District(s)
Pentwater Public SD (PK-12)
    2012-13 Enrollment: 284. . . . . (231) 869-4100
Housing: Homeownership rate: 82.7%; Homeowner vacancy rate: 5.6%; Rental vacancy rate: 27.8%
Safety: Violent crime rate: 0.0 per 10,000 population; Property crime rate: 164.9 per 10,000 population

ROTHBURY (village).
Covers a land area of 0.902 square miles and a water area of 0.086 square miles. Located at 43.51° N. Lat; 86.35° W. Long. Elevation is 689 feet.
Population: 432; Growth (since 2000): 3.8%; Density: 478.8 persons per square mile; Race: 86.1% White, 0.9% Black/African American, 0.0% Asian, 3.5% American Indian/Alaska Native, 0.0% Native Hawaiian/Other Pacific Islander, 7.6% Two or more races, 14.8% Hispanic of any race; Average household size: 2.63; Median age: 34.5; Age under 18: 27.5%; Age 65 and over: 11.8%; Males per 100 females: 94.6
School District(s)
Shelby Public Schools (PK-12)
    2012-13 Enrollment: 1,375 . . . . (231) 861-5211

Housing: Homeownership rate: 76.6%; Homeowner vacancy rate: 0.8%; Rental vacancy rate: 7.3%

SHELBY (township). Covers a land area of 35.688 square miles and a water area of 0.398 square miles. Located at 43.61° N. Lat; 86.33° W. Long. Elevation is 817 feet.

History: Shelby Township was named for General Isaac Shelby, leader of the Kentucky Rangers in the War of 1812.

Population: 4,069; Growth (since 2000): 3.0%; Density: 114.0 persons per square mile; Race: 80.3% White, 0.4% Black/African American, 0.2% Asian, 1.4% American Indian/Alaska Native, 0.0% Native Hawaiian/Other Pacific Islander, 2.5% Two or more races, 28.3% Hispanic of any race; Average household size: 2.87; Median age: 35.2; Age under 18: 30.0%; Age 65 and over: 13.4%; Males per 100 females: 93.3; Marriage status: 30.9% never married, 56.1% now married, 2.2% separated, 5.4% widowed, 7.7% divorced; Foreign born: 10.0%; Speak English only: 78.8%; With disability: 12.8%; Veterans: 7.8%; Ancestry: 19.6% German, 10.2% Irish, 9.5% English, 7.7% Norwegian, 6.1% American

Employment: 13.6% management, business, and financial, 7.5% computer, engineering, and science, 11.5% education, legal, community service, arts, and media, 5.7% healthcare practitioners, 11.6% service, 13.0% sales and office, 16.6% natural resources, construction, and maintenance, 20.4% production, transportation, and material moving

Income: Per capita: $17,627; Median household: $45,938; Average household: $50,572; Households with income of $100,000 or more: 9.1%; Poverty rate: 16.7%

Educational Attainment: High school diploma or higher: 79.8%; Bachelor's degree or higher: 15.8%; Graduate/professional degree or higher: 6.9%

School District(s)
Shelby Public Schools (PK-12)
    2012-13 Enrollment: 1,375 . . . . (231) 861-5211

Housing: Homeownership rate: 75.4%; Median home value: $105,400; Median year structure built: 1962; Homeowner vacancy rate: 3.1%; Median gross rent: $669 per month; Rental vacancy rate: 5.4%

Health Insurance: 86.1% have insurance; 62.0% have private insurance; 39.2% have public insurance; 13.9% do not have insurance; 2.4% of children under 18 do not have insurance

Hospitals: Mercy Health Lakeshore Campus

Transportation: Commute: 91.2% car, 0.0% public transportation, 2.8% walk, 3.9% work from home; Median travel time to work: 20.0 minutes

Additional Information Contacts
Shelby Township. . . . . (231) 861-5853

SHELBY (village). Covers a land area of 1.699 square miles and a water area of <.001 square miles. Located at 43.61° N. Lat; 86.36° W. Long. Elevation is 817 feet.

History: Shelby was once on the migration path of thousands of passenger pigeons. The annual slaughter of the birds here led to the extinction of the passenger pigeon. The town of Shelby developed as a center for orchards and dairy farms.

Population: 2,065; Growth (since 2000): 7.9%; Density: 1,215.5 persons per square mile; Race: 68.7% White, 0.4% Black/African American, 0.2% Asian, 1.5% American Indian/Alaska Native, 0.0% Native Hawaiian/Other Pacific Islander, 3.7% Two or more races, 45.6% Hispanic of any race; Average household size: 2.98; Median age: 30.1; Age under 18: 33.2%; Age 65 and over: 12.5%; Males per 100 females: 91.9

School District(s)
Shelby Public Schools (PK-12)
    2012-13 Enrollment: 1,375 . . . . (231) 861-5211

Housing: Homeownership rate: 62.7%; Homeowner vacancy rate: 4.8%; Rental vacancy rate: 6.5%

Hospitals: Mercy Health Lakeshore Campus

WALKERVILLE (village). Covers a land area of 1.083 square miles and a water area of 0.125 square miles. Located at 43.71° N. Lat; 86.13° W. Long. Elevation is 886 feet.

Population: 247; Growth (since 2000): -2.8%; Density: 228.2 persons per square mile; Race: 83.4% White, 1.2% Black/African American, 0.4% Asian, 2.0% American Indian/Alaska Native, 0.0% Native Hawaiian/Other Pacific Islander, 6.5% Two or more races, 17.8% Hispanic of any race; Average household size: 2.94; Median age: 34.2; Age under 18: 27.5%; Age 65 and over: 11.7%; Males per 100 females: 99.2

School District(s)
Walkerville Public Schools (PK-12)
    2012-13 Enrollment: 294 . . . . (231) 873-4850

Housing: Homeownership rate: 70.3%; Homeowner vacancy rate: 3.3%; Rental vacancy rate: 3.8%

WEARE (township). Covers a land area of 33.908 square miles and a water area of 2.152 square miles. Located at 43.77° N. Lat; 86.33° W. Long. Elevation is 738 feet.

Population: 1,210; Growth (since 2000): -4.0%; Density: 35.7 persons per square mile; Race: 92.9% White, 0.0% Black/African American, 0.1% Asian, 1.2% American Indian/Alaska Native, 0.0% Native Hawaiian/Other Pacific Islander, 2.1% Two or more races, 8.1% Hispanic of any race; Average household size: 2.63; Median age: 40.4; Age under 18: 24.3%; Age 65 and over: 16.2%; Males per 100 females: 98.7

Housing: Homeownership rate: 86.6%; Homeowner vacancy rate: 2.9%; Rental vacancy rate: 4.6%

Ogemaw County

Located in northeast central Michigan; drained by the Au Gres and Rifle Rivers; includes many small lakes, and part of Huron National Forest. Covers a land area of 563.487 square miles, a water area of 11.465 square miles, and is located in the Eastern Time Zone at 44.33° N. Lat., 84.13° W. Long. The county was founded in 1875. County seat is West Branch.

Weather Station: West Branch 3 SE   Elevation: 884 feet

	Jan	Feb	Mar	Apr	May	Jun	Jul	Aug	Sep	Oct	Nov	Dec
High	29	32	41	55	68	77	81	79	71	58	45	33
Low	9	10	18	31	42	51	56	54	46	35	27	16
Precip	1.8	1.4	1.8	2.8	3.3	3.1	2.8	3.6	3.5	2.8	2.6	1.9
Snow	14.3	10.0	7.8	2.0	0.2	0.0	0.0	0.0	0.0	0.3	4.2	12.5

High and Low temperatures in degrees Fahrenheit; Precipitation and Snow in inches

Population: 21,699; Growth (since 2000): 0.2%; Density: 38.5 persons per square mile; Race: 97.1% White, 0.2% Black/African American, 0.4% Asian, 0.7% American Indian/Alaska Native, 0.0% Native Hawaiian/Other Pacific Islander, 1.4% two or more races, 1.4% Hispanic of any race; Average household size: 2.31; Median age: 47.6; Age under 18: 20.4%; Age 65 and over: 22.0%; Males per 100 females: 99.3; Marriage status: 22.9% never married, 54.5% now married, 1.3% separated, 9.1% widowed, 13.5% divorced; Foreign born: 1.3%; Speak English only: 97.8%; With disability: 23.1%; Veterans: 13.6%; Ancestry: 30.7% German, 12.9% Irish, 12.1% English, 8.5% American, 7.6% French

Religion: Six largest groups: 13.1% Catholicism, 4.4% Lutheran, 3.5% Pentecostal, 3.3% Methodist/Pietist, 2.0% Non-denominational Protestant, 1.9% Holiness

Economy: Unemployment rate: 6.7%; Leading industries: 20.9% retail trade; 11.6% health care and social assistance; 11.4% accommodation and food services; Farms: 280 totaling 68,162 acres; Company size: 0 employ 1,000 or more persons, 0 employ 500 to 999 persons, 7 employ 100 to 499 persons, 562 employ less than 100 persons; Business ownership: n/a women-owned, n/a Black-owned, n/a Hispanic-owned, n/a Asian-owned

Employment: 9.8% management, business, and financial, 2.1% computer, engineering, and science, 7.5% education, legal, community service, arts, and media, 6.1% healthcare practitioners, 24.1% service, 24.0% sales and office, 11.3% natural resources, construction, and maintenance, 15.1% production, transportation, and material moving

Income: Per capita: $19,634; Median household: $34,619; Average household: $45,186; Households with income of $100,000 or more: 7.5%; Poverty rate: 21.5%

Educational Attainment: High school diploma or higher: 85.1%; Bachelor's degree or higher: 11.3%; Graduate/professional degree or higher: 3.9%

Housing: Homeownership rate: 81.3%; Median home value: $89,500; Median year structure built: 1974; Homeowner vacancy rate: 3.8%; Median gross rent: $642 per month; Rental vacancy rate: 7.6%

Vital Statistics: Birth rate: 89.5 per 10,000 population; Death rate: 127.6 per 10,000 population; Age-adjusted cancer mortality rate: 163.0 deaths per 100,000 population

Health Insurance: 88.0% have insurance; 58.4% have private insurance; 51.0% have public insurance; 12.0% do not have insurance; 4.0% of children under 18 do not have insurance

Health Care: Physicians: 12.1 per 10,000 population; Hospital beds: 36.2 per 10,000 population; Hospital admissions: 1,082.4 per 10,000 population
Transportation: Commute: 93.2% car, 0.3% public transportation, 1.6% walk, 3.6% work from home; Median travel time to work: 23.1 minutes
Presidential Election: 46.2% Obama, 52.5% Romney (2012)
National and State Parks: Ogemaw State Forest; Rifle River State Recreation Area
Additional Information Contacts
Ogemaw Government . . . . (989) 345-0215
   http://www.ogemawcountymi.gov

Ogemaw County Communities

CHURCHILL (township). Covers a land area of 35.532 square miles and a water area of 0.459 square miles. Located at 44.30° N. Lat; 84.07° W. Long.
Population: 1,713; Growth (since 2000): 6.9%; Density: 48.2 persons per square mile; Race: 98.2% White, 0.0% Black/African American, 0.1% Asian, 0.3% American Indian/Alaska Native, 0.3% Native Hawaiian/Other Pacific Islander, 1.0% Two or more races, 1.1% Hispanic of any race; Average household size: 2.40; Median age: 46.0; Age under 18: 21.4%; Age 65 and over: 20.4%; Males per 100 females: 104.2
Housing: Homeownership rate: 86.2%; Homeowner vacancy rate: 3.6%; Rental vacancy rate: 15.5%

CUMMING (township). Covers a land area of 34.493 square miles and a water area of 0.875 square miles. Located at 44.38° N. Lat; 84.07° W. Long.
Population: 698; Growth (since 2000): -12.3%; Density: 20.2 persons per square mile; Race: 98.3% White, 0.0% Black/African American, 0.0% Asian, 1.0% American Indian/Alaska Native, 0.0% Native Hawaiian/Other Pacific Islander, 0.7% Two or more races, 1.7% Hispanic of any race; Average household size: 2.37; Median age: 46.4; Age under 18: 20.8%; Age 65 and over: 19.1%; Males per 100 females: 98.9
Housing: Homeownership rate: 84.4%; Homeowner vacancy rate: 3.9%; Rental vacancy rate: 2.1%

EDWARDS (township). Covers a land area of 34.932 square miles and a water area of 0.746 square miles. Located at 44.20° N. Lat; 84.31° W. Long. Elevation is 843 feet.
Population: 1,413; Growth (since 2000): 1.7%; Density: 40.5 persons per square mile; Race: 98.8% White, 0.1% Black/African American, 0.2% Asian, 0.1% American Indian/Alaska Native, 0.0% Native Hawaiian/Other Pacific Islander, 0.6% Two or more races, 1.3% Hispanic of any race; Average household size: 2.52; Median age: 44.5; Age under 18: 23.2%; Age 65 and over: 18.7%; Males per 100 females: 96.5
Housing: Homeownership rate: 85.3%; Homeowner vacancy rate: 2.5%; Rental vacancy rate: 8.7%

FOSTER (township). Covers a land area of 89.233 square miles and a water area of 0.660 square miles. Located at 44.43° N. Lat; 84.29° W. Long.
Population: 843; Growth (since 2000): 2.7%; Density: 9.4 persons per square mile; Race: 96.9% White, 0.1% Black/African American, 0.1% Asian, 1.2% American Indian/Alaska Native, 0.0% Native Hawaiian/Other Pacific Islander, 0.7% Two or more races, 1.7% Hispanic of any race; Average household size: 2.21; Median age: 53.0; Age under 18: 17.3%; Age 65 and over: 22.4%; Males per 100 females: 109.2
Housing: Homeownership rate: 88.4%; Homeowner vacancy rate: 5.9%; Rental vacancy rate: 12.0%

GOODAR (township). Covers a land area of 35.445 square miles and a water area of 0.693 square miles. Located at 44.47° N. Lat; 83.95° W. Long. Elevation is 1,030 feet.
Population: 398; Growth (since 2000): -19.3%; Density: 11.2 persons per square mile; Race: 97.7% White, 0.3% Black/African American, 0.0% Asian, 0.3% American Indian/Alaska Native, 0.0% Native Hawaiian/Other Pacific Islander, 1.8% Two or more races, 0.5% Hispanic of any race; Average household size: 1.94; Median age: 57.6; Age under 18: 11.8%; Age 65 and over: 32.4%; Males per 100 females: 105.2
Housing: Homeownership rate: 92.7%; Homeowner vacancy rate: 8.1%; Rental vacancy rate: 11.8%

HILL (township). Covers a land area of 32.536 square miles and a water area of 3.574 square miles. Located at 44.38° N. Lat; 83.93° W. Long.
Population: 1,361; Growth (since 2000): -14.1%; Density: 41.8 persons per square mile; Race: 98.8% White, 0.0% Black/African American, 0.2% Asian, 0.4% American Indian/Alaska Native, 0.0% Native Hawaiian/Other Pacific Islander, 0.4% Two or more races, 0.7% Hispanic of any race; Average household size: 2.03; Median age: 57.4; Age under 18: 13.8%; Age 65 and over: 34.9%; Males per 100 females: 107.8
Housing: Homeownership rate: 92.5%; Homeowner vacancy rate: 5.9%; Rental vacancy rate: 3.8%

HORTON (township). Covers a land area of 35.461 square miles and a water area of 0.286 square miles. Located at 44.21° N. Lat; 84.18° W. Long.
Population: 927; Growth (since 2000): -7.0%; Density: 26.1 persons per square mile; Race: 98.4% White, 0.0% Black/African American, 0.4% Asian, 0.6% American Indian/Alaska Native, 0.0% Native Hawaiian/Other Pacific Islander, 0.4% Two or more races, 0.9% Hispanic of any race; Average household size: 2.41; Median age: 44.4; Age under 18: 21.9%; Age 65 and over: 19.5%; Males per 100 females: 98.5
School District(s)
Hanover-Horton SD (PK-12)
   2012-13 Enrollment: 1,222 . . . . (517) 563-0100
Housing: Homeownership rate: 87.0%; Homeowner vacancy rate: 2.3%; Rental vacancy rate: 5.5%

KLACKING (township). Covers a land area of 35.888 square miles and a water area of 0.065 square miles. Located at 44.37° N. Lat; 84.17° W. Long.
Population: 614; Growth (since 2000): -0.5%; Density: 17.1 persons per square mile; Race: 97.7% White, 0.8% Black/African American, 0.0% Asian, 0.2% American Indian/Alaska Native, 0.0% Native Hawaiian/Other Pacific Islander, 1.3% Two or more races, 0.7% Hispanic of any race; Average household size: 2.38; Median age: 50.2; Age under 18: 17.8%; Age 65 and over: 20.5%; Males per 100 females: 98.7
Housing: Homeownership rate: 91.5%; Homeowner vacancy rate: 1.7%; Rental vacancy rate: 0.0%

LOGAN (township). Covers a land area of 35.231 square miles and a water area of 0.759 square miles. Located at 44.30° N. Lat; 83.94° W. Long.
Population: 551; Growth (since 2000): -5.2%; Density: 15.6 persons per square mile; Race: 98.9% White, 0.0% Black/African American, 0.2% Asian, 0.2% American Indian/Alaska Native, 0.0% Native Hawaiian/Other Pacific Islander, 0.4% Two or more races, 1.1% Hispanic of any race; Average household size: 2.20; Median age: 52.7; Age under 18: 15.8%; Age 65 and over: 27.2%; Males per 100 females: 109.5
Housing: Homeownership rate: 88.4%; Homeowner vacancy rate: 3.4%; Rental vacancy rate: 6.5%

LUPTON (CDP). Covers a land area of 3.232 square miles and a water area of 0.030 square miles. Located at 44.43° N. Lat; 84.02° W. Long. Elevation is 922 feet.
Population: 348; Growth (since 2000): n/a; Density: 107.7 persons per square mile; Race: 97.7% White, 0.0% Black/African American, 0.3% Asian, 0.0% American Indian/Alaska Native, 0.0% Native Hawaiian/Other Pacific Islander, 1.4% Two or more races, 1.1% Hispanic of any race; Average household size: 2.38; Median age: 44.7; Age under 18: 21.6%; Age 65 and over: 17.8%; Males per 100 females: 96.6
Housing: Homeownership rate: 83.6%; Homeowner vacancy rate: 1.6%; Rental vacancy rate: 0.0%

MILLS (township). Covers a land area of 34.220 square miles and a water area of 1.352 square miles. Located at 44.20° N. Lat; 84.07° W. Long.
Population: 4,291; Growth (since 2000): 7.1%; Density: 125.4 persons per square mile; Race: 95.1% White, 0.3% Black/African American, 0.3% Asian, 1.4% American Indian/Alaska Native, 0.0% Native Hawaiian/Other Pacific Islander, 2.7% Two or more races, 1.8% Hispanic of any race; Average household size: 2.31; Median age: 46.9; Age under 18: 20.2%; Age 65 and over: 19.8%; Males per 100 females: 104.9; Marriage status: 27.0% never married, 45.4% now married, 1.6% separated, 10.8% widowed, 16.8% divorced; Foreign born: 1.2%; Speak English only: 98.4%; With disability: 28.8%; Veterans: 12.5%; Ancestry: 25.4% German, 11.8% American, 11.5% Irish, 7.3% French, 7.0% English

Employment: 5.8% management, business, and financial, 1.1% computer, engineering, and science, 5.5% education, legal, community service, arts, and media, 7.5% healthcare practitioners, 40.2% service, 18.5% sales and office, 8.9% natural resources, construction, and maintenance, 12.5% production, transportation, and material moving

Income: Per capita: $12,471; Median household: $22,544; Average household: $28,566; Households with income of $100,000 or more: 2.3%; Poverty rate: 42.5%

Educational Attainment: High school diploma or higher: 75.3%; Bachelor's degree or higher: 4.1%; Graduate/professional degree or higher: 1.8%

Housing: Homeownership rate: 80.1%; Median home value: $65,000; Median year structure built: 1972; Homeowner vacancy rate: 4.1%; Median gross rent: $618 per month; Rental vacancy rate: 3.4%

Health Insurance: 89.0% have insurance; 36.9% have private insurance; 71.6% have public insurance; 11.0% do not have insurance; 5.7% of children under 18 do not have insurance

Transportation: Commute: 94.0% car, 0.0% public transportation, 0.0% walk, 6.0% work from home; Median travel time to work: 25.3 minutes

---

OGEMAW (township). Covers a land area of 36.300 square miles and a water area of 0.096 square miles. Located at 44.29° N. Lat; 84.31° W. Long. Elevation is 1,125 feet.

Population: 1,223; Growth (since 2000): 9.4%; Density: 33.7 persons per square mile; Race: 97.6% White, 0.2% Black/African American, 0.7% Asian, 0.3% American Indian/Alaska Native, 0.0% Native Hawaiian/Other Pacific Islander, 0.9% Two or more races, 0.8% Hispanic of any race; Average household size: 2.59; Median age: 43.8; Age under 18: 23.8%; Age 65 and over: 19.1%; Males per 100 females: 104.2

Housing: Homeownership rate: 90.2%; Homeowner vacancy rate: 3.0%; Rental vacancy rate: 9.8%

PRESCOTT (village). Covers a land area of 1.109 square miles and a water area of 0 square miles. Located at 44.19° N. Lat; 83.93° W. Long. Elevation is 797 feet.

History: Prescott was named for C.H. Prescott, who bought the Lake Huron & Southwestern Railroad in 1879.

Population: 266; Growth (since 2000): -7.0%; Density: 239.8 persons per square mile; Race: 96.6% White, 0.0% Black/African American, 0.0% Asian, 0.0% American Indian/Alaska Native, 0.0% Native Hawaiian/Other Pacific Islander, 3.0% Two or more races, 3.8% Hispanic of any race; Average household size: 2.63; Median age: 43.0; Age under 18: 23.7%; Age 65 and over: 18.8%; Males per 100 females: 86.0

Housing: Homeownership rate: 91.1%; Homeowner vacancy rate: 4.1%; Rental vacancy rate: 25.0%

RICHLAND (township). Covers a land area of 34.783 square miles and a water area of 1.066 square miles. Located at 44.21° N. Lat; 83.93° W. Long.

Population: 914; Growth (since 2000): -4.4%; Density: 26.3 persons per square mile; Race: 95.7% White, 0.0% Black/African American, 0.0% Asian, 0.5% American Indian/Alaska Native, 0.0% Native Hawaiian/Other Pacific Islander, 3.6% Two or more races, 3.5% Hispanic of any race; Average household size: 2.43; Median age: 50.1; Age under 18: 19.9%; Age 65 and over: 24.4%; Males per 100 females: 98.7

Housing: Homeownership rate: 91.2%; Homeowner vacancy rate: 2.8%; Rental vacancy rate: 25.5%

ROSE (township). Covers a land area of 52.859 square miles and a water area of 0.248 square miles. Located at 44.46° N. Lat; 84.09° W. Long.

Population: 1,368; Growth (since 2000): -2.9%; Density: 25.9 persons per square mile; Race: 97.4% White, 0.0% Black/African American, 0.5% Asian, 0.4% American Indian/Alaska Native, 0.1% Native Hawaiian/Other Pacific Islander, 1.4% Two or more races, 0.7% Hispanic of any race; Average household size: 2.26; Median age: 49.9; Age under 18: 18.9%; Age 65 and over: 21.6%; Males per 100 females: 103.6

Housing: Homeownership rate: 90.2%; Homeowner vacancy rate: 2.8%; Rental vacancy rate: 1.6%

ROSE CITY (city). Covers a land area of 1.076 square miles and a water area of 0.008 square miles. Located at 44.42° N. Lat; 84.12° W. Long. Elevation is 958 feet.

History: Rose City was settled in the 1870's. The French & Rose Lumber Company was founded here by M.S. French, who negotiatied for the

railroad to build a line in 1892 so lumber could be shipped out. The settlement was first called Churchill, but the name was changed to Rose City in 1892.

Population: 653; Growth (since 2000): -9.4%; Density: 607.0 persons per square mile; Race: 96.9% White, 0.2% Black/African American, 0.3% Asian, 1.2% American Indian/Alaska Native, 0.0% Native Hawaiian/Other Pacific Islander, 0.9% Two or more races, 1.7% Hispanic of any race; Average household size: 2.36; Median age: 44.6; Age under 18: 23.3%; Age 65 and over: 24.8%; Males per 100 females: 93.8

School District(s)

West Branch-Rose City Area Schools (PK-12)

    2012-13 Enrollment: 2,166 . . . . (989) 343-2000

Housing: Homeownership rate: 58.8%; Homeowner vacancy rate: 10.7%; Rental vacancy rate: 7.5%

SKIDWAY LAKE (CDP). Covers a land area of 11.288 square miles and a water area of 0.494 square miles. Located at 44.19° N. Lat; 84.05° W. Long. Elevation is 797 feet.

Population: 3,392; Growth (since 2000): 7.8%; Density: 300.5 persons per square mile; Race: 94.8% White, 0.4% Black/African American, 0.2% Asian, 1.5% American Indian/Alaska Native, 0.0% Native Hawaiian/Other Pacific Islander, 2.9% Two or more races, 2.1% Hispanic of any race; Average household size: 2.33; Median age: 44.9; Age under 18: 21.1%; Age 65 and over: 17.8%; Males per 100 females: 105.1; Marriage status: 31.1% never married, 38.1% now married, 1.5% separated, 11.9% widowed, 18.8% divorced; Foreign born: 0.8%; Speak English only: 98.7%; With disability: 30.6%; Veterans: 12.2%; Ancestry: 28.1% German, 12.6% Irish, 8.5% French, 6.2% English, 6.1% American

Employment: 5.1% management, business, and financial, 0.0% computer, engineering, and science, 4.3% education, legal, community service, arts, and media, 3.8% healthcare practitioners, 42.3% service, 19.1% sales and office, 10.1% natural resources, construction, and maintenance, 15.4% production, transportation, and material moving

Income: Per capita: $12,272; Median household: $22,703; Average household: $27,624; Households with income of $100,000 or more: 1.7%; Poverty rate: 40.2%

Educational Attainment: High school diploma or higher: 73.6%; Bachelor's degree or higher: 3.2%; Graduate/professional degree or higher: 1.5%

Housing: Homeownership rate: 77.4%; Median home value: $57,000; Median year structure built: 1969; Homeowner vacancy rate: 4.0%; Median gross rent: $623 per month; Rental vacancy rate: 3.5%

Health Insurance: 90.6% have insurance; 36.4% have private insurance; 73.2% have public insurance; 9.4% do not have insurance; 3.0% of children under 18 do not have insurance

Transportation: Commute: 98.3% car, 0.0% public transportation, 0.0% walk, 1.7% work from home; Median travel time to work: 25.3 minutes

---

WEST BRANCH (city). County seat. Covers a land area of 1.483 square miles and a water area of <.001 square miles. Located at 44.27° N. Lat; 84.24° W. Long. Elevation is 955 feet.

History: West Branch was settled by farmers along the west branch of the Rifle River. Farming remained the chief source of revenue until oil was discovered here in the 1930's.

Population: 2,139; Growth (since 2000): 11.1%; Density: 1,442.8 persons per square mile; Race: 96.9% White, 0.5% Black/African American, 0.7% Asian, 0.6% American Indian/Alaska Native, 0.0% Native Hawaiian/Other Pacific Islander, 1.1% Two or more races, 1.7% Hispanic of any race; Average household size: 1.99; Median age: 44.3; Age under 18: 20.7%; Age 65 and over: 24.3%; Males per 100 females: 75.0

School District(s)

West Branch-Rose City Area Schools (PK-12)

    2012-13 Enrollment: 2,166 . . . . (989) 343-2000

Housing: Homeownership rate: 44.3%; Homeowner vacancy rate: 4.1%; Rental vacancy rate: 9.4%

Hospitals: West Branch Regional Medical Center (88 beds)

Safety: Violent crime rate: 14.2 per 10,000 population; Property crime rate: 218.0 per 10,000 population

Newspapers: Ogemaw County Herald (weekly circulation 7500)

Airports: West Branch Community (general aviation)

Additional Information Contacts

City of West Branch . . . . (989) 345-0500
    http://www.westbranch.com

WEST BRANCH (township). Covers a land area of 34.016 square miles and a water area of 0.576 square miles. Located at 44.29° N. Lat; 84.18° W. Long. Elevation is 955 feet.

History: Incorporated as village 1885, as city 1905.

Population: 2,593; Growth (since 2000): -1.3%; Density: 76.2 persons per square mile; Race: 97.1% White, 0.1% Black/African American, 0.6% Asian, 0.9% American Indian/Alaska Native, 0.0% Native Hawaiian/Other Pacific Islander, 1.1% Two or more races, 1.6% Hispanic of any race; Average household size: 2.53; Median age: 43.1; Age under 18: 23.4%; Age 65 and over: 18.7%; Males per 100 females: 99.3; Marriage status: 20.1% never married, 63.0% now married, 1.1% separated, 7.0% widowed, 9.9% divorced; Foreign born: 0.7%; Speak English only: 98.9%; With disability: 15.4%; Veterans: 12.6%; Ancestry: 28.1% German, 18.5% English, 17.0% Irish, 10.6% American, 9.3% Polish

Employment: 12.3% management, business, and financial, 2.0% computer, engineering, and science, 14.4% education, legal, community service, arts, and media, 6.9% healthcare practitioners, 17.0% service, 27.9% sales and office, 7.5% natural resources, construction, and maintenance, 12.0% production, transportation, and material moving

Income: Per capita: $25,625; Median household: $38,860; Average household: $61,823; Households with income of $100,000 or more: 14.1%; Poverty rate: 9.9%

Educational Attainment: High school diploma or higher: 91.0%; Bachelor's degree or higher: 19.6%; Graduate/professional degree or higher: 7.4%

School District(s)

West Branch-Rose City Area Schools (PK-12)

    2012-13 Enrollment: 2,166 . . . . (989) 343-2000

Housing: Homeownership rate: 86.9%; Median home value: $105,600; Median year structure built: 1978; Homeowner vacancy rate: 2.3%; Median gross rent: $789 per month; Rental vacancy rate: 3.5%

Health Insurance: 90.3% have insurance; 71.4% have private insurance; 37.9% have public insurance; 9.7% do not have insurance; 3.1% of children under 18 do not have insurance

Hospitals: West Branch Regional Medical Center (88 beds)

Newspapers: Ogemaw County Herald (weekly circulation 7500)

Transportation: Commute: 93.2% car, 0.8% public transportation, 0.0% walk, 4.0% work from home; Median travel time to work: 20.8 minutes

Airports: West Branch Community (general aviation)

Ontonagon County

Located in northwestern Michigan, on the Upper Peninsula; bounded on the north by Lake Superior; drained by the Ontonagon, Iron, and Firesteel Rivers; includes the Porcupine Mountains, and part of Ottawa National Forest and Gogebic Lake. Covers a land area of 1,311.225 square miles, a water area of 2,429.594 square miles, and is located in the Eastern Time Zone at 47.22° N. Lat., 89.50° W. Long. The county was founded in 1843. County seat is Ontonagon.

Weather Station: Bergland Dam   Elevation: 1,299 feet

	Jan	Feb	Mar	Apr	May	Jun	Jul	Aug	Sep	Oct	Nov	Dec
High	21	26	36	50	65	73	78	76	67	53	38	25
Low	2	2	10	26	37	48	52	51	43	32	22	8
Precip	3.0	1.9	2.5	2.7	3.4	3.7	4.0	3.6	3.9	4.1	3.2	3.4
Snow	41.9	25.8	26.0	9.7	1.2	0.0	0.0	0.0	0.2	5.2	25.1	42.7

High and Low temperatures in degrees Fahrenheit; Precipitation and Snow in inches

Weather Station: Ontonagon 6 SE   Elevation: 790 feet

	Jan	Feb	Mar	Apr	May	Jun	Jul	Aug	Sep	Oct	Nov	Dec
High	25	30	40	53	67	75	79	78	70	56	41	29
Low	9	9	17	30	40	49	55	54	47	37	27	14
Precip	2.8	1.6	1.7	2.3	3.0	3.0	3.3	3.0	3.2	3.6	2.6	3.1
Snow	53.3	27.1	18.8	7.5	1.0	0.0	0.0	0.0	0.1	2.4	22.5	55.1

High and Low temperatures in degrees Fahrenheit; Precipitation and Snow in inches

Population: 6,780; Growth (since 2000): -13.3%; Density: 5.2 persons per square mile; Race: 97.3% White, 0.1% Black/African American, 0.2% Asian, 1.1% American Indian/Alaska Native, 0.0% Native Hawaiian/Other Pacific Islander, 1.3% two or more races, 0.9% Hispanic of any race; Average household size: 2.06; Median age: 52.7; Age under 18: 15.8%; Age 65 and over: 26.4%; Males per 100 females: 106.5; Marriage status: 18.9% never married, 58.0% now married, 0.7% separated, 9.8% widowed, 13.4% divorced; Foreign born: 1.7%; Speak English only: 95.0%; With disability: 15.8%; Veterans: 18.1%; Ancestry: 27.8% Finnish, 20.0% German, 10.6% American, 8.9% Irish, 8.5% English

Religion: Six largest groups: 20.9% Catholicism, 20.5% Lutheran, 8.0% Methodist/Pietist, 1.9% Pentecostal, 0.8% Holiness, 0.5% Adventist

Economy: Unemployment rate: 8.7%; Leading industries: 17.0% retail trade; 15.3% accommodation and food services; 13.6% construction; Farms: 109 totaling 29,063 acres; Company size: 0 employ 1,000 or more persons, 0 employ 500 to 999 persons, 1 employs 100 to 499 persons, 175 employ less than 100 persons; Business ownership: 172 women-owned, n/a Black-owned, n/a Hispanic-owned, n/a Asian-owned

Employment: 9.5% management, business, and financial, 1.8% computer, engineering, and science, 9.6% education, legal, community service, arts, and media, 4.5% healthcare practitioners, 24.8% service, 20.8% sales and office, 12.4% natural resources, construction, and maintenance, 16.6% production, transportation, and material moving

Income: Per capita: $21,585; Median household: $34,620; Average household: $42,976; Households with income of $100,000 or more: 6.5%; Poverty rate: 13.8%

Educational Attainment: High school diploma or higher: 88.6%; Bachelor's degree or higher: 15.3%; Graduate/professional degree or higher: 4.7%

Housing: Homeownership rate: 85.9%; Median home value: $72,600; Median year structure built: 1958; Homeowner vacancy rate: 4.1%; Median gross rent: $419 per month; Rental vacancy rate: 14.5%

Vital Statistics: Birth rate: 45.9 per 10,000 population; Death rate: 161.3 per 10,000 population; Age-adjusted cancer mortality rate: 154.3 deaths per 100,000 population

Health Insurance: 86.3% have insurance; 63.8% have private insurance; 46.3% have public insurance; 13.7% do not have insurance; 7.7% of children under 18 do not have insurance

Health Care: Physicians: 7.8 per 10,000 population; Hospital beds: 27.2 per 10,000 population; Hospital admissions: 954.2 per 10,000 population

Transportation: Commute: 90.5% car, 0.2% public transportation, 4.4% walk, 3.9% work from home; Median travel time to work: 24.0 minutes

Presidential Election: 44.8% Obama, 53.9% Romney (2012)

National and State Parks: Mishwabic State Forest; Ottawa National Forest; Porcupine Mountains Wilderness State Park; North Country National Scenic Trail

Additional Information Contacts

Ontonagon Government . . . . (906) 884-4255
    http://www.ontonagonmi.org

Ontonagon County Communities

BERGLAND (township). Covers a land area of 98.504 square miles and a water area of 9.732 square miles. Located at 46.60° N. Lat; 89.66° W. Long. Elevation is 1,329 feet.

History: Bergland was founded by Gunlak A. Bergland of Milwaukee, who opened a sawmill here in 1900.

Population: 467; Growth (since 2000): -15.1%; Density: 4.7 persons per square mile; Race: 97.6% White, 0.0% Black/African American, 0.4% Asian, 0.9% American Indian/Alaska Native, 0.0% Native Hawaiian/Other Pacific Islander, 1.1% Two or more races, 1.1% Hispanic of any race; Average household size: 1.90; Median age: 59.0; Age under 18: 11.1%; Age 65 and over: 32.8%; Males per 100 females: 108.5

School District(s)

Gogebic-Ontonagon ISD (PK-12)

    2012-13 Enrollment: 81 . . . . (906) 575-3438

Housing: Homeownership rate: 89.8%; Homeowner vacancy rate: 4.7%; Rental vacancy rate: 32.4%

BOHEMIA (township). Covers a land area of 91.859 square miles and a water area of 0.429 square miles. Located at 46.84° N. Lat; 88.96° W. Long.

Population: 82; Growth (since 2000): 6.5%; Density: 0.9 persons per square mile; Race: 96.3% White, 0.0% Black/African American, 0.0% Asian, 0.0% American Indian/Alaska Native, 0.0% Native Hawaiian/Other Pacific Islander, 2.4% Two or more races, 3.7% Hispanic of any race; Average household size: 1.61; Median age: 59.8; Age under 18: 4.9%; Age 65 and over: 30.5%; Males per 100 females: 141.2

Housing: Homeownership rate: 92.1%; Homeowner vacancy rate: 0.0%; Rental vacancy rate: 16.7%

BRUCE CROSSING (unincorporated postal area)
ZCTA: 49912

Covers a land area of 214.256 square miles and a water area of 1.625 square miles. Located at 46.50° N. Lat; 89.19° W. Long. Elevation is 1,138 feet.

Population: 1,081; Growth (since 2000): -3.0%; Density: 5.0 persons per square mile; Race: 96.9% White, 0.1% Black/African American, 0.0% Asian, 2.2% American Indian/Alaska Native, 0.0% Native Hawaiian/Other Pacific Islander, 0.7% Two or more races, 1.0% Hispanic of any race; Average household size: 2.10; Median age: 51.9; Age under 18: 14.8%; Age 65 and over: 26.0%; Males per 100 females: 109.1

Housing: Homeownership rate: 88.1%; Homeowner vacancy rate: 2.2%; Rental vacancy rate: 10.4%

CARP LAKE (township).
Covers a land area of 224.838 square miles and a water area of 0.754 square miles. Located at 46.74° N. Lat; 89.67° W. Long.

Population: 722; Growth (since 2000): -19.0%; Density: 3.2 persons per square mile; Race: 96.3% White, 0.1% Black/African American, 0.1% Asian, 1.1% American Indian/Alaska Native, 0.0% Native Hawaiian/Other Pacific Islander, 2.4% Two or more races, 1.2% Hispanic of any race; Average household size: 2.07; Median age: 54.3; Age under 18: 14.1%; Age 65 and over: 29.9%; Males per 100 females: 98.9

Housing: Homeownership rate: 90.2%; Homeowner vacancy rate: 4.8%; Rental vacancy rate: 30.6%

EWEN (unincorporated postal area)
ZCTA: 49925

Covers a land area of 126.703 square miles and a water area of 0.090 square miles. Located at 46.54° N. Lat; 89.37° W. Long. Elevation is 1,135 feet.

Population: 494; Growth (since 2000): -25.4%; Density: 3.9 persons per square mile; Race: 96.6% White, 0.0% Black/African American, 0.4% Asian, 1.4% American Indian/Alaska Native, 0.2% Native Hawaiian/Other Pacific Islander, 1.4% Two or more races, 0.6% Hispanic of any race; Average household size: 1.99; Median age: 53.2; Age under 18: 14.6%; Age 65 and over: 21.5%; Males per 100 females: 109.3

School District(s)
Ewen-Trout Creek Consolidated SD (PK-12)
2012-13 Enrollment: 244 . . . . (906) 988-2364

Housing: Homeownership rate: 80.7%; Homeowner vacancy rate: 3.8%; Rental vacancy rate: 7.4%

GREENLAND (township).
Covers a land area of 113.187 square miles and a water area of 0 square miles. Located at 46.80° N. Lat; 89.06° W. Long. Elevation is 1,138 feet.

History: Greenland was named for Greenland, New Hampshire. A settlement grew up around the mining claim of William W. Spalding, who came here in 1858.

Population: 792; Growth (since 2000): -9.0%; Density: 7.0 persons per square mile; Race: 98.9% White, 0.0% Black/African American, 0.1% Asian, 0.6% American Indian/Alaska Native, 0.0% Native Hawaiian/Other Pacific Islander, 0.4% Two or more races, 0.3% Hispanic of any race; Average household size: 2.15; Median age: 49.1; Age under 18: 18.7%; Age 65 and over: 23.2%; Males per 100 females: 120.6

Housing: Homeownership rate: 91.9%; Homeowner vacancy rate: 5.8%; Rental vacancy rate: 10.3%

HAIGHT (township).
Covers a land area of 105.744 square miles and a water area of 1.297 square miles. Located at 46.41° N. Lat; 89.22° W. Long.

History: Haight Township was organized in 1899 and named for Joseph Haight, the chairman of the board of supervisors at that time.

Population: 212; Growth (since 2000): -7.0%; Density: 2.0 persons per square mile; Race: 98.1% White, 0.5% Black/African American, 0.0% Asian, 0.9% American Indian/Alaska Native, 0.0% Native Hawaiian/Other Pacific Islander, 0.5% Two or more races, 2.8% Hispanic of any race; Average household size: 2.00; Median age: 53.8; Age under 18: 8.5%; Age 65 and over: 27.4%; Males per 100 females: 109.9

Housing: Homeownership rate: 88.7%; Homeowner vacancy rate: 5.1%; Rental vacancy rate: 20.0%

INTERIOR (township).
Covers a land area of 86.419 square miles and a water area of 2.946 square miles. Located at 46.44° N. Lat; 89.05° W. Long.

Population: 336; Growth (since 2000): -10.4%; Density: 3.9 persons per square mile; Race: 96.1% White, 0.0% Black/African American, 0.3% Asian, 2.4% American Indian/Alaska Native, 0.0% Native Hawaiian/Other Pacific Islander, 1.2% Two or more races, 0.3% Hispanic of any race; Average household size: 2.07; Median age: 55.3; Age under 18: 16.4%; Age 65 and over: 30.1%; Males per 100 females: 110.0

Housing: Homeownership rate: 91.9%; Homeowner vacancy rate: 5.1%; Rental vacancy rate: 5.9%

MASS CITY (unincorporated postal area)
ZCTA: 49948

Covers a land area of 132.903 square miles and a water area of 0.489 square miles. Located at 46.71° N. Lat; 89.02° W. Long. Elevation is 1,056 feet.

Population: 590; Growth (since 2000): -14.2%; Density: 4.4 persons per square mile; Race: 98.8% White, 0.0% Black/African American, 0.2% Asian, 0.7% American Indian/Alaska Native, 0.0% Native Hawaiian/Other Pacific Islander, 0.2% Two or more races, 0.8% Hispanic of any race; Average household size: 2.09; Median age: 49.1; Age under 18: 18.6%; Age 65 and over: 23.2%; Males per 100 females: 126.1

Housing: Homeownership rate: 91.2%; Homeowner vacancy rate: 6.5%; Rental vacancy rate: 3.1%

MATCHWOOD (township).
Covers a land area of 109.517 square miles and a water area of 0.018 square miles. Located at 46.60° N. Lat; 89.45° W. Long. Elevation is 1,243 feet.

Population: 94; Growth (since 2000): -18.3%; Density: 0.9 persons per square mile; Race: 98.9% White, 1.1% Black/African American, 0.0% Asian, 0.0% American Indian/Alaska Native, 0.0% Native Hawaiian/Other Pacific Islander, 0.0% Two or more races, 0.0% Hispanic of any race; Average household size: 1.92; Median age: 58.0; Age under 18: 7.4%; Age 65 and over: 29.8%; Males per 100 females: 113.6

Housing: Homeownership rate: 85.7%; Homeowner vacancy rate: 8.7%; Rental vacancy rate: 0.0%

MCMILLAN (township).
Covers a land area of 70.428 square miles and a water area of 0.076 square miles. Located at 46.49° N. Lat; 89.31° W. Long.

Population: 478; Growth (since 2000): -20.5%; Density: 6.8 persons per square mile; Race: 96.2% White, 0.0% Black/African American, 0.4% Asian, 1.5% American Indian/Alaska Native, 0.2% Native Hawaiian/Other Pacific Islander, 1.7% Two or more races, 0.6% Hispanic of any race; Average household size: 1.96; Median age: 52.9; Age under 18: 14.2%; Age 65 and over: 20.9%; Males per 100 females: 115.3

Housing: Homeownership rate: 82.4%; Homeowner vacancy rate: 1.9%; Rental vacancy rate: 8.2%

ONTONAGON (township).
Covers a land area of 192.877 square miles and a water area of 0.703 square miles. Located at 46.84° N. Lat; 89.28° W. Long. Elevation is 617 feet.

History: The Ontonagon boulder, a huge copper mass, was found near the river, and was moved to the Smithsonian Institution. Established on site of Native American village. Incorporated 1885.

Population: 2,579; Growth (since 2000): -12.7%; Density: 13.4 persons per square mile; Race: 97.8% White, 0.1% Black/African American, 0.2% Asian, 0.6% American Indian/Alaska Native, 0.0% Native Hawaiian/Other Pacific Islander, 1.2% Two or more races, 1.0% Hispanic of any race; Average household size: 2.07; Median age: 51.5; Age under 18: 17.3%; Age 65 and over: 25.4%; Males per 100 females: 101.0; Marriage status: 18.8% never married, 55.0% now married, 0.1% separated, 10.8% widowed, 15.4% divorced; Foreign born: 2.9%; Speak English only: 94.9%; With disability: 15.0%; Veterans: 17.2%; Ancestry: 22.1% Finnish, 21.0% German, 13.0% American, 8.6% English, 7.6% Polish

Employment: 5.9% management, business, and financial, 1.9% computer, engineering, and science, 13.0% education, legal, community service, arts, and media, 4.9% healthcare practitioners, 23.6% service, 19.2% sales and office, 12.0% natural resources, construction, and maintenance, 19.6% production, transportation, and material moving

Income: Per capita: $21,517; Median household: $34,274; Average household: $43,388; Households with income of $100,000 or more: 7.9%; Poverty rate: 14.2%

Educational Attainment: High school diploma or higher: 88.6%; Bachelor's degree or higher: 16.9%; Graduate/professional degree or higher: 5.3%

School District(s)
Ontonagon Area Schools (KG-12)
   2012-13 Enrollment: 386 . . . . (906) 884-4963
Housing: Homeownership rate: 80.3%; Median home value: $68,700; Median year structure built: 1956; Homeowner vacancy rate: 4.2%; Median gross rent: $391 per month; Rental vacancy rate: 9.1%
Health Insurance: 84.5% have insurance; 62.2% have private insurance; 43.6% have public insurance; 15.5% do not have insurance; 16.0% of children under 18 do not have insurance
Hospitals: Aspirus Ontonagon Hospital
Newspapers: Ontonagon Herald (weekly circulation 3800)
Transportation: Commute: 92.9% car, 0.0% public transportation, 3.5% walk, 3.0% work from home; Median travel time to work: 19.0 minutes

ONTONAGON (village). County seat. Covers a land area of 3.707 square miles and a water area of 0.151 square miles. Located at 46.87° N. Lat; 89.31° W. Long. Elevation is 617 feet.
History: Ontonagon was first known for the Ontonagon Boulder, a mass of copper that attracted scientists, authors, and the merely curious from the mid-1600's to the mid-1800's, when the boulder ended up in the Smithsonian Institution in Washington, D.C. Attempts at mining in Ontonagon were not successful, and those who settled here turned to lumbering. The Diamond Match Company was the owner of one of the early sawmills.
Population: 1,494; Growth (since 2000): -15.5%; Density: 403.1 persons per square mile; Race: 97.3% White, 0.1% Black/African American, 0.3% Asian, 0.7% American Indian/Alaska Native, 0.0% Native Hawaiian/Other Pacific Islander, 1.5% Two or more races, 1.2% Hispanic of any race; Average household size: 1.99; Median age: 51.1; Age under 18: 17.6%; Age 65 and over: 25.5%; Males per 100 females: 95.8
School District(s)
Ontonagon Area Schools (KG-12)
   2012-13 Enrollment: 386 . . . . (906) 884-4963
Housing: Homeownership rate: 70.8%; Homeowner vacancy rate: 5.4%; Rental vacancy rate: 8.3%
Hospitals: Aspirus Ontonagon Hospital
Newspapers: Ontonagon Herald (weekly circulation 3800)

ROCKLAND (township). Covers a land area of 92.748 square miles and a water area of 1.076 square miles. Located at 46.68° N. Lat; 89.28° W. Long. Elevation is 1,175 feet.
History: A large deposit of pure copper was discovered in the Rockland area in 1856, attracting many Irish and Cornish miners. The village of Rockland was formed in 1864 from the union of Rockland, Rosendale, and Williamsburg. The Minnesota Mining Company was active in this area.
Population: 228; Growth (since 2000): -29.6%; Density: 2.5 persons per square mile; Race: 94.3% White, 0.4% Black/African American, 0.0% Asian, 0.4% American Indian/Alaska Native, 0.0% Native Hawaiian/Other Pacific Islander, 4.8% Two or more races, 1.8% Hispanic of any race; Average household size: 1.97; Median age: 56.1; Age under 18: 15.4%; Age 65 and over: 30.3%; Males per 100 females: 111.1
Housing: Homeownership rate: 96.5%; Homeowner vacancy rate: 1.8%; Rental vacancy rate: 75.0%

STANNARD (township). Covers a land area of 125.104 square miles and a water area of 0.033 square miles. Located at 46.59° N. Lat; 89.14° W. Long.
History: Stannard Township was named for William Stannard, a member of the state legislature.
Population: 790; Growth (since 2000): -5.2%; Density: 6.3 persons per square mile; Race: 96.3% White, 0.0% Black/African American, 0.0% Asian, 2.8% American Indian/Alaska Native, 0.0% Native Hawaiian/Other Pacific Islander, 0.8% Two or more races, 0.6% Hispanic of any race; Average household size: 2.19; Median age: 50.5; Age under 18: 17.6%; Age 65 and over: 25.1%; Males per 100 females: 104.7
Housing: Homeownership rate: 87.0%; Homeowner vacancy rate: 1.6%; Rental vacancy rate: 8.0%

TROUT CREEK (unincorporated postal area)
ZCTA: 49967
Covers a land area of 339.504 square miles and a water area of 7.126 square miles. Located at 46.51° N. Lat; 88.97° W. Long. Elevation is 1,175 feet.
Population: 492; Growth (since 2000): 10.8%; Density: 1.4 persons per square mile; Race: 96.3% White, 0.0% Black/African American, 0.6% Asian, 2.2% American Indian/Alaska Native, 0.0% Native Hawaiian/Other Pacific Islander, 0.8% Two or more races, 0.2% Hispanic of any race; Average household size: 2.00; Median age: 55.8; Age under 18: 13.0%; Age 65 and over: 29.7%; Males per 100 females: 108.5
Housing: Homeownership rate: 92.2%; Homeowner vacancy rate: 6.2%; Rental vacancy rate: 8.0%

WHITE PINE (CDP). Covers a land area of 5.002 square miles and a water area of 0 square miles. Located at 46.74° N. Lat; 89.58° W. Long. Elevation is 899 feet.
Population: 474; Growth (since 2000): n/a; Density: 94.8 persons per square mile; Race: 94.3% White, 0.2% Black/African American, 0.2% Asian, 1.7% American Indian/Alaska Native, 0.0% Native Hawaiian/Other Pacific Islander, 3.6% Two or more races, 1.3% Hispanic of any race; Average household size: 2.11; Median age: 55.1; Age under 18: 15.6%; Age 65 and over: 30.4%; Males per 100 females: 100.0
Housing: Homeownership rate: 88.0%; Homeowner vacancy rate: 6.1%; Rental vacancy rate: 25.0%

Osceola County

Located in central Michigan; crossed by the Muskegon River; drained by the South Branch of the Manistee River; includes part of Manistee National Forest. Covers a land area of 566.391 square miles, a water area of 6.705 square miles, and is located in the Eastern Time Zone at 44.00° N. Lat., 85.32° W. Long. The county was founded in 1869. County seat is Reed City.
Population: 23,528; Growth (since 2000): 1.4%; Density: 41.5 persons per square mile; Race: 96.9% White, 0.6% Black/African American, 0.2% Asian, 0.5% American Indian/Alaska Native, 0.0% Native Hawaiian/Other Pacific Islander, 1.6% two or more races, 1.5% Hispanic of any race; Average household size: 2.50; Median age: 41.8; Age under 18: 24.7%; Age 65 and over: 17.0%; Males per 100 females: 99.2; Marriage status: 23.8% never married, 55.7% now married, 1.4% separated, 7.1% widowed, 13.4% divorced; Foreign born: 0.7%; Speak English only: 95.5%; With disability: 18.0%; Veterans: 12.9%; Ancestry: 28.6% German, 13.5% English, 12.0% Irish, 8.8% American, 7.5% Dutch
Religion: Six largest groups: 9.5% Methodist/Pietist, 6.4% Catholicism, 5.9% Lutheran, 4.6% Holiness, 3.0% Presbyterian-Reformed, 2.5% European Free-Church
Economy: Unemployment rate: 7.6%; Leading industries: 16.4% retail trade; 13.6% other services (except public administration); 11.7% health care and social assistance; Farms: 750 totaling 110,562 acres; Company size: 0 employ 1,000 or more persons, 1 employs 500 to 999 persons, 8 employ 100 to 499 persons, 418 employ less than 100 persons; Business ownership: 543 women-owned, n/a Black-owned, n/a Hispanic-owned, n/a Asian-owned
Employment: 9.8% management, business, and financial, 1.4% computer, engineering, and science, 8.0% education, legal, community service, arts, and media, 5.8% healthcare practitioners, 16.8% service, 19.0% sales and office, 11.6% natural resources, construction, and maintenance, 27.6% production, transportation, and material moving
Income: Per capita: $18,099; Median household: $37,788; Average household: $46,085; Households with income of $100,000 or more: 7.0%; Poverty rate: 21.7%
Educational Attainment: High school diploma or higher: 86.9%; Bachelor's degree or higher: 12.6%; Graduate/professional degree or higher: 4.0%
Housing: Homeownership rate: 79.4%; Median home value: $90,500; Median year structure built: 1976; Homeowner vacancy rate: 3.4%; Median gross rent: $565 per month; Rental vacancy rate: 9.1%
Vital Statistics: Birth rate: 122.5 per 10,000 population; Death rate: 92.4 per 10,000 population; Age-adjusted cancer mortality rate: 207.4 deaths per 100,000 population

Health Insurance: 85.4% have insurance; 60.6% have private insurance; 42.0% have public insurance; 14.6% do not have insurance; 8.9% of children under 18 do not have insurance
Health Care: Physicians: 6.9 per 10,000 population; Hospital beds: 31.6 per 10,000 population; Hospital admissions: 365.9 per 10,000 population
Transportation: Commute: 89.3% car, 0.4% public transportation, 3.0% walk, 5.0% work from home; Median travel time to work: 25.0 minutes
Presidential Election: 38.8% Obama, 59.8% Romney (2012)
National and State Parks: Chippewa River State Forest
Additional Information Contacts
Osceola Government . . . . (231) 832-3261
   http://www.osceola-county.org

Osceola County Communities

BURDELL (township). Covers a land area of 37.331 square miles and a water area of 0.206 square miles. Located at 44.12° N. Lat; 85.50° W. Long.
Population: 1,331; Growth (since 2000): 7.3%; Density: 35.7 persons per square mile; Race: 96.1% White, 0.1% Black/African American, 0.4% Asian, 1.2% American Indian/Alaska Native, 0.0% Native Hawaiian/Other Pacific Islander, 1.9% Two or more races, 2.3% Hispanic of any race; Average household size: 2.61; Median age: 42.3; Age under 18: 24.5%; Age 65 and over: 14.3%; Males per 100 females: 102.6
Housing: Homeownership rate: 89.0%; Homeowner vacancy rate: 3.2%; Rental vacancy rate: 6.6%

CEDAR (township). Covers a land area of 34.478 square miles and a water area of 0.540 square miles. Located at 43.95° N. Lat; 85.39° W. Long.
History: Cedar Township was organized in 1871.
Population: 455; Growth (since 2000): 12.1%; Density: 13.2 persons per square mile; Race: 97.8% White, 0.0% Black/African American, 0.2% Asian, 0.0% American Indian/Alaska Native, 0.0% Native Hawaiian/Other Pacific Islander, 2.0% Two or more races, 1.3% Hispanic of any race; Average household size: 2.40; Median age: 49.3; Age under 18: 21.3%; Age 65 and over: 22.0%; Males per 100 females: 115.6
Housing: Homeownership rate: 90.8%; Homeowner vacancy rate: 3.4%; Rental vacancy rate: 15.0%

EVART (city). Covers a land area of 2.237 square miles and a water area of 0.032 square miles. Located at 43.90° N. Lat; 85.27° W. Long. Elevation is 1,007 feet.
Population: 1,903; Growth (since 2000): 9.5%; Density: 850.8 persons per square mile; Race: 95.7% White, 0.8% Black/African American, 0.1% Asian, 0.8% American Indian/Alaska Native, 0.1% Native Hawaiian/Other Pacific Islander, 2.5% Two or more races, 2.2% Hispanic of any race; Average household size: 2.45; Median age: 33.5; Age under 18: 28.5%; Age 65 and over: 15.9%; Males per 100 females: 82.8
School District(s)
Evart Public Schools (PK-12)
   2012-13 Enrollment: 931 . . . . (231) 734-5594
Mecosta-Osceola ISD (PK-12)
   2012-13 Enrollment: 485 . . . . (231) 796-3543
Housing: Homeownership rate: 48.1%; Homeowner vacancy rate: 4.9%; Rental vacancy rate: 12.2%
Safety: Violent crime rate: 32.0 per 10,000 population; Property crime rate: 287.7 per 10,000 population
Additional Information Contacts
City of Evart. . . . . (231) 734-2181
   http://www.evart.org

EVART (township). Covers a land area of 32.796 square miles and a water area of 1.253 square miles. Located at 43.85° N. Lat; 85.26° W. Long. Elevation is 1,007 feet.
History: Indian mounds nearby. Incorporated as village 1872, as city 1938.
Population: 1,483; Growth (since 2000): -2.0%; Density: 45.2 persons per square mile; Race: 97.1% White, 0.3% Black/African American, 0.1% Asian, 0.7% American Indian/Alaska Native, 0.0% Native Hawaiian/Other Pacific Islander, 1.8% Two or more races, 1.6% Hispanic of any race; Average household size: 2.48; Median age: 46.6; Age under 18: 22.9%; Age 65 and over: 19.2%; Males per 100 females: 106.8

School District(s)
Evart Public Schools (PK-12)
   2012-13 Enrollment: 931 . . . . (231) 734-5594
Mecosta-Osceola ISD (PK-12)
   2012-13 Enrollment: 485 . . . . (231) 796-3543
Housing: Homeownership rate: 83.6%; Homeowner vacancy rate: 4.8%; Rental vacancy rate: 3.0%

HARTWICK (township). Covers a land area of 34.996 square miles and a water area of 0.491 square miles. Located at 44.02° N. Lat; 85.26° W. Long.
History: Hartwick Township was organized in 1870.
Population: 567; Growth (since 2000): -9.9%; Density: 16.2 persons per square mile; Race: 97.5% White, 0.2% Black/African American, 0.2% Asian, 0.7% American Indian/Alaska Native, 0.0% Native Hawaiian/Other Pacific Islander, 1.2% Two or more races, 1.9% Hispanic of any race; Average household size: 2.53; Median age: 47.8; Age under 18: 22.8%; Age 65 and over: 20.3%; Males per 100 females: 107.7
Housing: Homeownership rate: 87.9%; Homeowner vacancy rate: 4.8%; Rental vacancy rate: 10.0%

HERSEY (township). Covers a land area of 35.345 square miles and a water area of 0.556 square miles. Located at 43.86° N. Lat; 85.39° W. Long. Elevation is 974 feet.
Population: 1,950; Growth (since 2000): 5.6%; Density: 55.2 persons per square mile; Race: 96.4% White, 0.5% Black/African American, 0.1% Asian, 0.8% American Indian/Alaska Native, 0.0% Native Hawaiian/Other Pacific Islander, 1.6% Two or more races, 1.9% Hispanic of any race; Average household size: 2.58; Median age: 39.8; Age under 18: 25.4%; Age 65 and over: 15.2%; Males per 100 females: 102.9
School District(s)
Mecosta-Osceola ISD (PK-12)
   2012-13 Enrollment: 485 . . . . (231) 796-3543
Housing: Homeownership rate: 85.0%; Homeowner vacancy rate: 3.8%; Rental vacancy rate: 9.7%

HERSEY (village). Covers a land area of 1.097 square miles and a water area of 0 square miles. Located at 43.85° N. Lat; 85.44° W. Long. Elevation is 974 feet.
History: Hersey was settled in the early 1850's, and named for Nathan Hersey, a trapper who worked in this area in the 1840's.
Population: 350; Growth (since 2000): -6.4%; Density: 319.1 persons per square mile; Race: 96.6% White, 0.3% Black/African American, 0.0% Asian, 0.3% American Indian/Alaska Native, 0.0% Native Hawaiian/Other Pacific Islander, 1.7% Two or more races, 2.6% Hispanic of any race; Average household size: 2.55; Median age: 40.3; Age under 18: 26.3%; Age 65 and over: 14.3%; Males per 100 females: 100.0
School District(s)
Mecosta-Osceola ISD (PK-12)
   2012-13 Enrollment: 485 . . . . (231) 796-3543
Housing: Homeownership rate: 77.3%; Homeowner vacancy rate: 4.5%; Rental vacancy rate: 3.1%

HIGHLAND (township). Covers a land area of 37.378 square miles and a water area of 0.040 square miles. Located at 44.12° N. Lat; 85.26° W. Long. Elevation is 1,348 feet.
Population: 1,250; Growth (since 2000): 3.6%; Density: 33.4 persons per square mile; Race: 98.8% White, 0.2% Black/African American, 0.2% Asian, 0.0% American Indian/Alaska Native, 0.0% Native Hawaiian/Other Pacific Islander, 0.6% Two or more races, 1.3% Hispanic of any race; Average household size: 2.74; Median age: 37.2; Age under 18: 27.1%; Age 65 and over: 15.1%; Males per 100 females: 97.5
Housing: Homeownership rate: 84.5%; Homeowner vacancy rate: 3.0%; Rental vacancy rate: 7.9%

LE ROY (township). Covers a land area of 35.002 square miles and a water area of 0.110 square miles. Located at 44.03° N. Lat; 85.50° W. Long. Elevation is 1,260 feet.
History: Le Roy Township was named for LeRoy Carr, a federal land agent.
Population: 1,212; Growth (since 2000): 4.6%; Density: 34.6 persons per square mile; Race: 96.0% White, 0.3% Black/African American, 0.3% Asian, 0.5% American Indian/Alaska Native, 0.1% Native Hawaiian/Other Pacific Islander, 2.6% Two or more races, 1.0% Hispanic of any race;

Average household size: 2.71; Median age: 38.8; Age under 18: 27.2%; Age 65 and over: 13.8%; Males per 100 females: 101.0

School District(s)
Pine River Area Schools (PK-12)
    2012-13 Enrollment: 1,120 . . . . (231) 829-3141
Housing: Homeownership rate: 89.1%; Homeowner vacancy rate: 2.2%; Rental vacancy rate: 9.3%

LE ROY (village).
Covers a land area of 0.969 square miles and a water area of 0 square miles. Located at 44.04° N. Lat; 85.45° W. Long. Elevation is 1,260 feet.
History: Le Roy was originally settled by a group of Scandinavians, whose immigration was encouraged in the early 1870's by the Grand Rapids & Indiana Railway, which sent an emissary to Norway and Sweden to offer work and free land.
Population: 256; Growth (since 2000): -4.1%; Density: 264.3 persons per square mile; Race: 96.1% White, 1.6% Black/African American, 0.0% Asian, 0.8% American Indian/Alaska Native, 0.0% Native Hawaiian/Other Pacific Islander, 1.6% Two or more races, 0.0% Hispanic of any race; Average household size: 2.64; Median age: 39.6; Age under 18: 25.8%; Age 65 and over: 16.4%; Males per 100 females: 95.4

School District(s)
Pine River Area Schools (PK-12)
    2012-13 Enrollment: 1,120 . . . . (231) 829-3141
Housing: Homeownership rate: 86.6%; Homeowner vacancy rate: 3.4%; Rental vacancy rate: 7.1%

LINCOLN (township).
Covers a land area of 35.125 square miles and a water area of 0.357 square miles. Located at 43.94° N. Lat; 85.50° W. Long.
Population: 1,500; Growth (since 2000): -7.9%; Density: 42.7 persons per square mile; Race: 97.6% White, 0.5% Black/African American, 0.3% Asian, 0.3% American Indian/Alaska Native, 0.0% Native Hawaiian/Other Pacific Islander, 1.2% Two or more races, 0.6% Hispanic of any race; Average household size: 2.51; Median age: 42.5; Age under 18: 23.9%; Age 65 and over: 15.9%; Males per 100 females: 107.5
Housing: Homeownership rate: 87.1%; Homeowner vacancy rate: 3.5%; Rental vacancy rate: 4.8%

MARION (township).
Covers a land area of 37.010 square miles and a water area of 0.041 square miles. Located at 44.12° N. Lat; 85.14° W. Long. Elevation is 1,099 feet.
Population: 1,692; Growth (since 2000): 7.1%; Density: 45.7 persons per square mile; Race: 97.4% White, 0.1% Black/African American, 0.0% Asian, 0.9% American Indian/Alaska Native, 0.0% Native Hawaiian/Other Pacific Islander, 1.5% Two or more races, 1.1% Hispanic of any race; Average household size: 2.56; Median age: 40.4; Age under 18: 27.1%; Age 65 and over: 16.1%; Males per 100 females: 100.2

School District(s)
Marion Public Schools (PK-12)
    2012-13 Enrollment: 542 . . . . (231) 743-2486
Housing: Homeownership rate: 73.1%; Homeowner vacancy rate: 1.8%; Rental vacancy rate: 5.3%
Newspapers: Marion Press (weekly circulation 800)

MARION (village).
Covers a land area of 1.352 square miles and a water area of 0.041 square miles. Located at 44.10° N. Lat; 85.14° W. Long. Elevation is 1,099 feet.
Population: 872; Growth (since 2000): 4.3%; Density: 645.1 persons per square mile; Race: 98.3% White, 0.1% Black/African American, 0.0% Asian, 0.5% American Indian/Alaska Native, 0.0% Native Hawaiian/Other Pacific Islander, 1.0% Two or more races, 1.3% Hispanic of any race; Average household size: 2.48; Median age: 37.4; Age under 18: 27.4%; Age 65 and over: 16.7%; Males per 100 females: 89.2

School District(s)
Marion Public Schools (PK-12)
    2012-13 Enrollment: 542 . . . . (231) 743-2486
Housing: Homeownership rate: 61.0%; Homeowner vacancy rate: 1.8%; Rental vacancy rate: 3.5%
Newspapers: Marion Press (weekly circulation 800)

MIDDLE BRANCH (township).
Covers a land area of 35.499 square miles and a water area of 0.030 square miles. Located at 44.03° N. Lat; 85.15° W. Long.
Population: 843; Growth (since 2000): -1.7%; Density: 23.7 persons per square mile; Race: 97.6% White, 0.4% Black/African American, 0.0% Asian, 0.6% American Indian/Alaska Native, 0.0% Native Hawaiian/Other Pacific Islander, 1.3% Two or more races, 1.7% Hispanic of any race; Average household size: 2.37; Median age: 47.3; Age under 18: 17.4%; Age 65 and over: 19.8%; Males per 100 females: 102.6
Housing: Homeownership rate: 88.4%; Homeowner vacancy rate: 2.2%; Rental vacancy rate: 8.9%

ORIENT (township).
Covers a land area of 34.804 square miles and a water area of 0.612 square miles. Located at 43.86° N. Lat; 85.15° W. Long. Elevation is 1,024 feet.
Population: 773; Growth (since 2000): -3.7%; Density: 22.2 persons per square mile; Race: 98.4% White, 0.1% Black/African American, 0.0% Asian, 0.4% American Indian/Alaska Native, 0.0% Native Hawaiian/Other Pacific Islander, 0.9% Two or more races, 1.6% Hispanic of any race; Average household size: 2.40; Median age: 47.6; Age under 18: 19.8%; Age 65 and over: 22.8%; Males per 100 females: 104.0
Housing: Homeownership rate: 88.7%; Homeowner vacancy rate: 2.7%; Rental vacancy rate: 32.7%

OSCEOLA (township).
Covers a land area of 34.228 square miles and a water area of 0.215 square miles. Located at 43.96° N. Lat; 85.26° W. Long.
Population: 1,076; Growth (since 2000): -3.8%; Density: 31.4 persons per square mile; Race: 94.8% White, 2.6% Black/African American, 0.6% Asian, 0.5% American Indian/Alaska Native, 0.0% Native Hawaiian/Other Pacific Islander, 1.4% Two or more races, 2.0% Hispanic of any race; Average household size: 2.46; Median age: 42.8; Age under 18: 25.9%; Age 65 and over: 17.4%; Males per 100 females: 108.1
Housing: Homeownership rate: 85.7%; Homeowner vacancy rate: 2.8%; Rental vacancy rate: 10.4%

REED CITY (city).
County seat. Covers a land area of 2.078 square miles and a water area of 0.034 square miles. Located at 43.87° N. Lat; 85.51° W. Long. Elevation is 1,037 feet.
History: Many of the early residents of Reed City were immigrants from Germany. Considered a good fishing region, in the early 1900's Reed City had a roller mill, flour mill, and a woolen mill furnishing employment to residents.
Population: 2,425; Growth (since 2000): -0.2%; Density: 1,167.2 persons per square mile; Race: 94.8% White, 1.7% Black/African American, 0.2% Asian, 0.5% American Indian/Alaska Native, 0.0% Native Hawaiian/Other Pacific Islander, 2.5% Two or more races, 2.2% Hispanic of any race; Average household size: 2.26; Median age: 36.1; Age under 18: 26.4%; Age 65 and over: 17.5%; Males per 100 females: 81.4

School District(s)
Reed City Area Public Schools (PK-12)
    2012-13 Enrollment: 1,536 . . . . (231) 832-2201
Housing: Homeownership rate: 54.2%; Homeowner vacancy rate: 4.9%; Rental vacancy rate: 8.7%
Hospitals: Spectrum Health - Reed City Campus (106 beds)
Safety: Violent crime rate: 29.2 per 10,000 population; Property crime rate: 229.5 per 10,000 population

RICHMOND (township).
Covers a land area of 32.887 square miles and a water area of 0.055 square miles. Located at 43.85° N. Lat; 85.49° W. Long.
Population: 1,554; Growth (since 2000): -8.3%; Density: 47.3 persons per square mile; Race: 98.1% White, 0.1% Black/African American, 0.6% Asian, 0.3% American Indian/Alaska Native, 0.1% Native Hawaiian/Other Pacific Islander, 0.8% Two or more races, 0.1% Hispanic of any race; Average household size: 2.53; Median age: 45.8; Age under 18: 21.5%; Age 65 and over: 16.3%; Males per 100 females: 97.2
Housing: Homeownership rate: 91.3%; Homeowner vacancy rate: 1.9%; Rental vacancy rate: 7.0%

ROSE LAKE (township).
Covers a land area of 33.608 square miles and a water area of 1.308 square miles. Located at 44.02° N. Lat; 85.38° W. Long.
Population: 1,373; Growth (since 2000): 11.5%; Density: 40.9 persons per square mile; Race: 98.3% White, 0.2% Black/African American, 0.2%

Asian, 0.3% American Indian/Alaska Native, 0.0% Native Hawaiian/Other Pacific Islander, 0.7% Two or more races, 1.2% Hispanic of any race; Average household size: 2.43; Median age: 45.8; Age under 18: 22.6%; Age 65 and over: 19.7%; Males per 100 females: 100.7
Housing: Homeownership rate: 88.6%; Homeowner vacancy rate: 4.0%; Rental vacancy rate: 4.4%

SEARS (unincorporated postal area)
ZCTA: 49679
Covers a land area of 55.060 square miles and a water area of 0.910 square miles. Located at 43.88° N. Lat; 85.15° W. Long. Elevation is 1,043 feet.
Population: 1,428; Growth (since 2000): 28.6%; Density: 25.9 persons per square mile; Race: 97.1% White, 1.2% Black/African American, 0.0% Asian, 0.4% American Indian/Alaska Native, 0.0% Native Hawaiian/Other Pacific Islander, 1.3% Two or more races, 1.8% Hispanic of any race; Average household size: 2.49; Median age: 45.8; Age under 18: 23.1%; Age 65 and over: 20.6%; Males per 100 females: 104.0
Housing: Homeownership rate: 86.0%; Homeowner vacancy rate: 3.8%; Rental vacancy rate: 17.7%

SHERMAN (township).
Covers a land area of 37.031 square miles and a water area of 0.221 square miles. Located at 44.12° N. Lat; 85.38° W. Long.
Population: 1,042; Growth (since 2000): -3.6%; Density: 28.1 persons per square mile; Race: 97.8% White, 0.0% Black/African American, 0.4% Asian, 0.6% American Indian/Alaska Native, 0.0% Native Hawaiian/Other Pacific Islander, 1.2% Two or more races, 0.3% Hispanic of any race; Average household size: 2.64; Median age: 43.5; Age under 18: 24.3%; Age 65 and over: 16.8%; Males per 100 females: 106.7
Housing: Homeownership rate: 88.2%; Homeowner vacancy rate: 2.0%; Rental vacancy rate: 2.1%

SYLVAN (township).
Covers a land area of 34.559 square miles and a water area of 0.605 square miles. Located at 43.94° N. Lat; 85.15° W. Long.
Population: 1,099; Growth (since 2000): 6.4%; Density: 31.8 persons per square mile; Race: 97.1% White, 0.7% Black/African American, 0.2% Asian, 0.0% American Indian/Alaska Native, 0.0% Native Hawaiian/Other Pacific Islander, 1.9% Two or more races, 1.5% Hispanic of any race; Average household size: 2.54; Median age: 44.3; Age under 18: 26.5%; Age 65 and over: 18.2%; Males per 100 females: 111.3
Housing: Homeownership rate: 85.1%; Homeowner vacancy rate: 5.6%; Rental vacancy rate: 7.6%

TUSTIN (village).
Covers a land area of 0.387 square miles and a water area of 0 square miles. Located at 44.10° N. Lat; 85.46° W. Long. Elevation is 1,224 feet.
Population: 230; Growth (since 2000): -3.0%; Density: 594.1 persons per square mile; Race: 95.2% White, 0.4% Black/African American, 1.3% Asian, 0.0% American Indian/Alaska Native, 0.0% Native Hawaiian/Other Pacific Islander, 2.6% Two or more races, 1.3% Hispanic of any race; Average household size: 2.56; Median age: 37.0; Age under 18: 23.9%; Age 65 and over: 12.6%; Males per 100 females: 101.8
School District(s)
Pine River Area Schools (PK-12)
    2012-13 Enrollment: 1,120 . . . . (231) 829-3141
Housing: Homeownership rate: 76.7%; Homeowner vacancy rate: 0.0%; Rental vacancy rate: 0.0%

Oscoda County

Located in northeast central Michigan; crossed by the Au Sable River; drained by the Upper South Branch of the Thunder Bay River; includes several lakes, and part of Huron National Forest. Covers a land area of 565.731 square miles, a water area of 5.851 square miles, and is located in the Eastern Time Zone at 44.69° N. Lat., 84.12° W. Long. The county was founded in 1840. County seat is Mio.

Weather Station: Mio Hydro Plant									Elevation: 959 feet			
	Jan	Feb	Mar	Apr	May	Jun	Jul	Aug	Sep	Oct	Nov	Dec
High	28	32	41	55	67	77	82	79	71	58	44	33
Low	10	10	18	31	41	51	56	54	46	36	28	17
Precip	1.4	1.1	1.5	2.2	2.6	2.7	2.8	3.3	2.8	2.6	2.1	1.4
Snow	na	4.7	na	1.4	tr	0.0	0.0	0.0	0.0	0.1	2.0	na

High and Low temperatures in degrees Fahrenheit; Precipitation and Snow in inches

Population: 8,640; Growth (since 2000): -8.3%; Density: 15.3 persons per square mile; Race: 97.7% White, 0.2% Black/African American, 0.1% Asian, 0.6% American Indian/Alaska Native, 0.0% Native Hawaiian/Other Pacific Islander, 1.3% two or more races, 0.9% Hispanic of any race; Average household size: 2.27; Median age: 49.7; Age under 18: 20.2%; Age 65 and over: 23.5%; Males per 100 females: 101.6; Marriage status: 21.8% never married, 58.3% now married, 1.1% separated, 7.8% widowed, 12.1% divorced; Foreign born: 1.1%; Speak English only: 92.9%; With disability: 22.0%; Veterans: 15.9%; Ancestry: 30.5% German, 13.9% English, 13.4% Irish, 8.6% American, 7.9% Polish
Religion: Six largest groups: 9.7% Catholicism, 4.9% European Free-Church, 3.4% Methodist/Pietist, 3.0% Holiness, 2.7% Non-denominational Protestant, 1.3% Pentecostal
Economy: Unemployment rate: 8.5%; Leading industries: 19.4% retail trade; 12.0% accommodation and food services; 11.0% other services (except public administration); Farms: 145 totaling 16,748 acres; Company size: 0 employ 1,000 or more persons, 0 employ 500 to 999 persons, 1 employs 100 to 499 persons, 190 employ less than 100 persons; Business ownership: 191 women-owned, n/a Black-owned, n/a Hispanic-owned, n/a Asian-owned
Employment: 7.4% management, business, and financial, 2.2% computer, engineering, and science, 8.5% education, legal, community service, arts, and media, 3.3% healthcare practitioners, 24.5% service, 26.3% sales and office, 10.3% natural resources, construction, and maintenance, 17.6% production, transportation, and material moving
Income: Per capita: $18,057; Median household: $33,239; Average household: $40,991; Households with income of $100,000 or more: 4.4%; Poverty rate: 20.2%
Educational Attainment: High school diploma or higher: 82.6%; Bachelor's degree or higher: 10.4%; Graduate/professional degree or higher: 3.1%
Housing: Homeownership rate: 82.8%; Median home value: $83,000; Median year structure built: 1970; Homeowner vacancy rate: 5.0%; Median gross rent: $589 per month; Rental vacancy rate: 14.0%
Vital Statistics: Birth rate: 88.3 per 10,000 population; Death rate: 128.9 per 10,000 population; Age-adjusted cancer mortality rate: 163.7 deaths per 100,000 population
Health Insurance: 79.7% have insurance; 56.4% have private insurance; 48.0% have public insurance; 20.3% do not have insurance; 19.9% of children under 18 do not have insurance
Health Care: Physicians: 3.5 per 10,000 population; Hospital beds: 0.0 per 10,000 population; Hospital admissions: 0.0 per 10,000 population
Transportation: Commute: 85.3% car, 0.1% public transportation, 3.6% walk, 5.8% work from home; Median travel time to work: 21.2 minutes
Presidential Election: 41.1% Obama, 57.3% Romney (2012)
National and State Parks: Au Sable National Scenic River; Huron National Forest; Oscoda State Forest
Additional Information Contacts
Oscoda Government . . . . (989) 826-1110
    http://www.oscodacountymi.com

Oscoda County Communities

BIG CREEK (township).
Covers a land area of 141.662 square miles and a water area of 1.492 square miles. Located at 44.60° N. Lat; 84.25° W. Long.
Population: 2,827; Growth (since 2000): -16.4%; Density: 20.0 persons per square mile; Race: 96.9% White, 0.2% Black/African American, 0.1% Asian, 0.8% American Indian/Alaska Native, 0.0% Native Hawaiian/Other Pacific Islander, 1.7% Two or more races, 1.3% Hispanic of any race; Average household size: 2.19; Median age: 49.3; Age under 18: 19.1%; Age 65 and over: 22.1%; Males per 100 females: 101.2; Marriage status: 23.7% never married, 53.9% now married, 1.0% separated, 7.8% widowed, 14.6% divorced; Foreign born: 1.0%; Speak English only: 99.0%; With disability: 22.1%; Veterans: 18.0%; Ancestry: 30.3% German, 17.9% English, 14.7% Irish, 11.7% Polish, 9.7% American

Employment: 3.7% management, business, and financial, 1.5% computer, engineering, and science, 10.1% education, legal, community service, arts, and media, 2.7% healthcare practitioners, 30.6% service, 33.2% sales and office, 7.2% natural resources, construction, and maintenance, 11.0% production, transportation, and material moving

Income: Per capita: $17,541; Median household: $32,403; Average household: $38,233; Households with income of $100,000 or more: 4.3%; Poverty rate: 18.4%

Educational Attainment: High school diploma or higher: 89.5%; Bachelor's degree or higher: 11.4%; Graduate/professional degree or higher: 2.3%

Housing: Homeownership rate: 81.6%; Median home value: $72,900; Median year structure built: 1966; Homeowner vacancy rate: 6.7%; Median gross rent: $474 per month; Rental vacancy rate: 13.1%

Health Insurance: 85.9% have insurance; 61.9% have private insurance; 48.6% have public insurance; 14.1% do not have insurance; 0.0% of children under 18 do not have insurance

Transportation: Commute: 88.8% car, 0.0% public transportation, 5.2% walk, 4.3% work from home; Median travel time to work: 22.3 minutes

CLINTON (township).
Covers a land area of 70.505 square miles and a water area of 1.177 square miles. Located at 44.82° N. Lat; 83.99° W. Long.

Population: 441; Growth (since 2000): -13.7%; Density: 6.3 persons per square mile; Race: 98.4% White, 0.0% Black/African American, 0.0% Asian, 0.2% American Indian/Alaska Native, 0.0% Native Hawaiian/Other Pacific Islander, 1.4% Two or more races, 0.2% Hispanic of any race; Average household size: 2.10; Median age: 54.0; Age under 18: 13.2%; Age 65 and over: 24.9%; Males per 100 females: 109.0

Housing: Homeownership rate: 88.0%; Homeowner vacancy rate: 7.9%; Rental vacancy rate: 3.7%

COMINS (township).
Covers a land area of 70.558 square miles and a water area of 1.243 square miles. Located at 44.74° N. Lat; 84.01° W. Long. Elevation is 1,047 feet.

Population: 1,970; Growth (since 2000): -2.3%; Density: 27.9 persons per square mile; Race: 98.4% White, 0.2% Black/African American, 0.1% Asian, 0.5% American Indian/Alaska Native, 0.1% Native Hawaiian/Other Pacific Islander, 0.8% Two or more races, 0.6% Hispanic of any race; Average household size: 2.45; Median age: 49.2; Age under 18: 23.4%; Age 65 and over: 24.3%; Males per 100 females: 93.7

Housing: Homeownership rate: 76.0%; Homeowner vacancy rate: 4.4%; Rental vacancy rate: 17.6%

ELMER (township).
Covers a land area of 70.953 square miles and a water area of 0.417 square miles. Located at 44.76° N. Lat; 84.18° W. Long.

Population: 1,138; Growth (since 2000): 3.9%; Density: 16.0 persons per square mile; Race: 97.5% White, 0.1% Black/African American, 0.3% Asian, 0.4% American Indian/Alaska Native, 0.2% Native Hawaiian/Other Pacific Islander, 1.3% Two or more races, 0.4% Hispanic of any race; Average household size: 2.70; Median age: 41.8; Age under 18: 27.8%; Age 65 and over: 17.6%; Males per 100 females: 106.9

Housing: Homeownership rate: 87.9%; Homeowner vacancy rate: 1.9%; Rental vacancy rate: 17.7%

FAIRVIEW (unincorporated postal area)
ZCTA: 48621

Covers a land area of 55.960 square miles and a water area of 1.209 square miles. Located at 44.74° N. Lat; 84.01° W. Long. Elevation is 1,168 feet.

Population: 1,359; Growth (since 2000): -11.2%; Density: 24.3 persons per square mile; Race: 98.4% White, 0.0% Black/African American, 0.1% Asian, 0.4% American Indian/Alaska Native, 0.0% Native Hawaiian/Other Pacific Islander, 1.0% Two or more races, 0.7% Hispanic of any race; Average household size: 2.33; Median age: 51.0; Age under 18: 20.8%; Age 65 and over: 27.2%; Males per 100 females: 90.9

School District(s)
Fairview Area SD (PK-12)
    2012-13 Enrollment: 318 . . . . (989) 848-7004
Housing: Homeownership rate: 74.7%; Homeowner vacancy rate: 4.7%; Rental vacancy rate: 18.2%

GREENWOOD (township).
Covers a land area of 69.996 square miles and a water area of 0.871 square miles. Located at 44.77° N. Lat; 84.31° W. Long.

Population: 1,121; Growth (since 2000): -6.2%; Density: 16.0 persons per square mile; Race: 97.8% White, 0.1% Black/African American, 0.0% Asian, 0.5% American Indian/Alaska Native, 0.0% Native Hawaiian/Other Pacific Islander, 1.6% Two or more races, 0.7% Hispanic of any race; Average household size: 2.13; Median age: 54.3; Age under 18: 15.9%; Age 65 and over: 29.0%; Males per 100 females: 108.8

Housing: Homeownership rate: 90.8%; Homeowner vacancy rate: 2.7%; Rental vacancy rate: 18.6%

LUZERNE (unincorporated postal area)
ZCTA: 48636

Covers a land area of 87.809 square miles and a water area of 0.208 square miles. Located at 44.60° N. Lat; 84.30° W. Long. Elevation is 1,079 feet.

Population: 864; Growth (since 2000): -26.6%; Density: 9.8 persons per square mile; Race: 96.9% White, 0.1% Black/African American, 0.0% Asian, 0.9% American Indian/Alaska Native, 0.0% Native Hawaiian/Other Pacific Islander, 1.6% Two or more races, 1.4% Hispanic of any race; Average household size: 2.11; Median age: 51.6; Age under 18: 17.1%; Age 65 and over: 25.9%; Males per 100 females: 101.9

Housing: Homeownership rate: 89.3%; Homeowner vacancy rate: 9.5%; Rental vacancy rate: 18.5%

MENTOR (township).
Covers a land area of 142.058 square miles and a water area of 0.651 square miles. Located at 44.61° N. Lat; 84.02° W. Long.

Population: 1,143; Growth (since 2000): -6.3%; Density: 8.0 persons per square mile; Race: 98.1% White, 0.3% Black/African American, 0.0% Asian, 0.4% American Indian/Alaska Native, 0.0% Native Hawaiian/Other Pacific Islander, 0.8% Two or more races, 1.6% Hispanic of any race; Average household size: 2.08; Median age: 51.1; Age under 18: 16.7%; Age 65 and over: 25.7%; Males per 100 females: 102.3

Housing: Homeownership rate: 81.5%; Homeowner vacancy rate: 5.7%; Rental vacancy rate: 6.5%

MIO (CDP).
County seat. Covers a land area of 8.367 square miles and a water area of 0.613 square miles. Located at 44.66° N. Lat; 84.15° W. Long. Elevation is 1,020 feet.

Population: 1,826; Growth (since 2000): -9.4%; Density: 218.2 persons per square mile; Race: 96.5% White, 0.2% Black/African American, 0.1% Asian, 0.8% American Indian/Alaska Native, 0.0% Native Hawaiian/Other Pacific Islander, 1.9% Two or more races, 1.4% Hispanic of any race; Average household size: 2.26; Median age: 43.1; Age under 18: 23.0%; Age 65 and over: 18.1%; Males per 100 females: 93.8

School District(s)
Mio-Ausable Schools (PK-12)
    2012-13 Enrollment: 634 . . . . (989) 826-2401
Housing: Homeownership rate: 70.8%; Homeowner vacancy rate: 5.3%; Rental vacancy rate: 10.3%

Newspapers: Oscoda County Herald (weekly circulation 2600)

Otsego County

Located in northern Michigan; drained by the Sturgeon and Black Rivers and the North Branch of the Au Sable River; includes many small lakes. Covers a land area of 514.971 square miles, a water area of 11.218 square miles, and is located in the Eastern Time Zone at 45.02° N. Lat., 84.58° W. Long. The county was founded in 1875. County seat is Gaylord.

Weather Station: Gaylord   Elevation: 1,350 feet

	Jan	Feb	Mar	Apr	May	Jun	Jul	Aug	Sep	Oct	Nov	Dec
High	26	29	39	54	67	76	79	77	69	55	42	30
Low	11	11	18	30	41	51	56	54	47	37	27	17
Precip	2.9	2.0	2.1	2.4	3.0	2.9	2.9	3.6	3.6	3.7	3.3	3.2
Snow	37.2	26.1	16.4	7.3	0.5	0.0	0.0	0.0	tr	3.3	19.6	36.4

High and Low temperatures in degrees Fahrenheit; Precipitation and Snow in inches

Weather Station: Vanderbilt 11 ENE   Elevation: 924 feet

	Jan	Feb	Mar	Apr	May	Jun	Jul	Aug	Sep	Oct	Nov	Dec
High	26	29	38	53	67	77	81	78	69	55	42	31
Low	7	5	13	27	37	47	51	49	42	33	26	15
Precip	2.2	1.4	1.8	2.6	2.8	2.6	2.8	3.5	3.2	3.1	2.5	2.1
Snow	24.5	15.3	10.9	5.1	0.3	0.0	0.0	0.0	0.0	0.9	9.0	20.2

High and Low temperatures in degrees Fahrenheit; Precipitation and Snow in inches

Population: 24,164; Growth (since 2000): 3.7%; Density: 46.9 persons per square mile; Race: 96.9% White, 0.3% Black/African American, 0.4% Asian, 0.7% American Indian/Alaska Native, 0.0% Native Hawaiian/Other Pacific Islander, 1.5% two or more races, 1.2% Hispanic of any race; Average household size: 2.44; Median age: 43.2; Age under 18: 22.9%; Age 65 and over: 17.0%; Males per 100 females: 96.9; Marriage status: 23.6% never married, 57.7% now married, 1.0% separated, 6.5% widowed, 12.1% divorced; Foreign born: 2.4%; Speak English only: 97.8%; With disability: 15.3%; Veterans: 11.7%; Ancestry: 31.4% German, 18.8% Polish, 14.6% Irish, 13.3% English, 6.7% American
Religion: Six largest groups: 24.0% Catholicism, 6.5% Methodist/Pietist, 2.7% Lutheran, 1.8% Presbyterian-Reformed, 1.7% Non-denominational Protestant, 1.0% Pentecostal
Economy: Unemployment rate: 6.3%; Leading industries: 19.2% retail trade; 10.6% health care and social assistance; 10.2% other services (except public administration); Farms: 180 totaling 32,293 acres; Company size: 0 employ 1,000 or more persons, 0 employ 500 to 999 persons, 6 employ 100 to 499 persons, 771 employs less than 100 persons; Business ownership: 638 women-owned, n/a Black-owned, n/a Hispanic-owned, n/a Asian-owned
Employment: 13.2% management, business, and financial, 2.9% computer, engineering, and science, 8.2% education, legal, community service, arts, and media, 4.9% healthcare practitioners, 19.9% service, 28.1% sales and office, 10.3% natural resources, construction, and maintenance, 12.5% production, transportation, and material moving
Income: Per capita: $24,312; Median household: $47,584; Average household: $59,609; Households with income of $100,000 or more: 14.0%; Poverty rate: 13.5%
Educational Attainment: High school diploma or higher: 91.0%; Bachelor's degree or higher: 19.8%; Graduate/professional degree or higher: 6.3%
Housing: Homeownership rate: 79.7%; Median home value: $116,600; Median year structure built: 1978; Homeowner vacancy rate: 3.2%; Median gross rent: $665 per month; Rental vacancy rate: 10.7%
Vital Statistics: Birth rate: 106.9 per 10,000 population; Death rate: 111.1 per 10,000 population; Age-adjusted cancer mortality rate: 159.6 deaths per 100,000 population
Health Insurance: 87.9% have insurance; 65.9% have private insurance; 38.6% have public insurance; 12.1% do not have insurance; 5.0% of children under 18 do not have insurance
Health Care: Physicians: 19.1 per 10,000 population; Hospital beds: 33.2 per 10,000 population; Hospital admissions: 656.6 per 10,000 population
Transportation: Commute: 93.9% car, 0.4% public transportation, 1.5% walk, 3.4% work from home; Median travel time to work: 20.5 minutes
Presidential Election: 39.6% Obama, 59.2% Romney (2012)
National and State Parks: Otsego Lake State Park; Pigeon River State Forest
Additional Information Contacts
Otsego Government . . . . (989) 731-7520
   http://www.otsegocountymi.gov

Otsego County Communities

BAGLEY (township). Covers a land area of 28.099 square miles and a water area of 2.585 square miles. Located at 44.98° N. Lat; 84.65° W. Long.
History: Bagley Township was named for John J. Bagley, a Republican governor of Michigan.
Population: 5,886; Growth (since 2000): 0.8%; Density: 209.5 persons per square mile; Race: 97.0% White, 0.3% Black/African American, 0.4% Asian, 0.7% American Indian/Alaska Native, 0.0% Native Hawaiian/Other Pacific Islander, 1.3% Two or more races, 1.4% Hispanic of any race; Average household size: 2.55; Median age: 40.4; Age under 18: 25.1%; Age 65 and over: 13.7%; Males per 100 females: 98.6; Marriage status: 26.6% never married, 58.7% now married, 1.3% separated, 4.6% widowed, 10.0% divorced; Foreign born: 4.3%; Speak English only: 97.6%;

With disability: 15.7%; Veterans: 11.9%; Ancestry: 33.7% German, 19.4% Polish, 12.5% Irish, 9.8% English, 8.5% American
Employment: 12.5% management, business, and financial, 1.7% computer, engineering, and science, 7.9% education, legal, community service, arts, and media, 4.3% healthcare practitioners, 26.6% service, 23.8% sales and office, 9.6% natural resources, construction, and maintenance, 13.6% production, transportation, and material moving
Income: Per capita: $23,483; Median household: $43,681; Average household: $60,002; Households with income of $100,000 or more: 12.5%; Poverty rate: 18.0%
Educational Attainment: High school diploma or higher: 92.4%; Bachelor's degree or higher: 18.8%; Graduate/professional degree or higher: 6.2%
Housing: Homeownership rate: 81.5%; Median home value: $115,000; Median year structure built: 1977; Homeowner vacancy rate: 3.3%; Median gross rent: $678 per month; Rental vacancy rate: 12.6%
Health Insurance: 84.6% have insurance; 63.5% have private insurance; 35.3% have public insurance; 15.4% do not have insurance; 9.3% of children under 18 do not have insurance
Transportation: Commute: 98.3% car, 0.0% public transportation, 0.0% walk, 1.3% work from home; Median travel time to work: 17.2 minutes

CHARLTON (township). Covers a land area of 100.368 square miles and a water area of 1.829 square miles. Located at 44.98° N. Lat; 84.43° W. Long.
Population: 1,354; Growth (since 2000): 1.8%; Density: 13.5 persons per square mile; Race: 98.2% White, 0.3% Black/African American, 0.2% Asian, 0.4% American Indian/Alaska Native, 0.0% Native Hawaiian/Other Pacific Islander, 0.9% Two or more races, 0.4% Hispanic of any race; Average household size: 2.28; Median age: 50.7; Age under 18: 17.8%; Age 65 and over: 24.2%; Males per 100 females: 101.8
Housing: Homeownership rate: 93.3%; Homeowner vacancy rate: 1.9%; Rental vacancy rate: 11.1%

CHESTER (township). Covers a land area of 67.565 square miles and a water area of 1.175 square miles. Located at 44.94° N. Lat; 84.54° W. Long.
Population: 1,292; Growth (since 2000): 2.1%; Density: 19.1 persons per square mile; Race: 98.5% White, 0.1% Black/African American, 0.0% Asian, 0.4% American Indian/Alaska Native, 0.0% Native Hawaiian/Other Pacific Islander, 0.9% Two or more races, 0.5% Hispanic of any race; Average household size: 2.44; Median age: 44.0; Age under 18: 20.8%; Age 65 and over: 16.3%; Males per 100 females: 109.4
Housing: Homeownership rate: 88.4%; Homeowner vacancy rate: 4.7%; Rental vacancy rate: 12.7%

CORWITH (township). Covers a land area of 107.481 square miles and a water area of 0.642 square miles. Located at 45.16° N. Lat; 84.55° W. Long.
Population: 1,748; Growth (since 2000): 1.7%; Density: 16.3 persons per square mile; Race: 97.1% White, 0.3% Black/African American, 0.1% Asian, 0.6% American Indian/Alaska Native, 0.0% Native Hawaiian/Other Pacific Islander, 1.7% Two or more races, 1.4% Hispanic of any race; Average household size: 2.36; Median age: 46.0; Age under 18: 20.5%; Age 65 and over: 19.3%; Males per 100 females: 100.2
Housing: Homeownership rate: 81.6%; Homeowner vacancy rate: 6.4%; Rental vacancy rate: 6.2%

DOVER (township). Covers a land area of 35.175 square miles and a water area of 0.049 square miles. Located at 45.07° N. Lat; 84.56° W. Long.
Population: 561; Growth (since 2000): -8.6%; Density: 15.9 persons per square mile; Race: 98.6% White, 0.0% Black/African American, 0.0% Asian, 0.2% American Indian/Alaska Native, 0.0% Native Hawaiian/Other Pacific Islander, 1.2% Two or more races, 0.5% Hispanic of any race; Average household size: 2.60; Median age: 43.3; Age under 18: 23.9%; Age 65 and over: 15.9%; Males per 100 females: 104.7
Housing: Homeownership rate: 88.4%; Homeowner vacancy rate: 3.0%; Rental vacancy rate: 10.7%

ELMIRA (township). Covers a land area of 35.839 square miles and a water area of 0.433 square miles. Located at 45.08° N. Lat; 84.80° W. Long. Elevation is 1,243 feet.
Population: 1,687; Growth (since 2000): 5.6%; Density: 47.1 persons per square mile; Race: 97.3% White, 0.0% Black/African American, 0.1%

Asian, 0.9% American Indian/Alaska Native, 0.1% Native Hawaiian/Other Pacific Islander, 1.3% Two or more races, 0.9% Hispanic of any race; Average household size: 2.60; Median age: 45.0; Age under 18: 22.0%; Age 65 and over: 17.7%; Males per 100 females: 96.6
Housing: Homeownership rate: 92.1%; Homeowner vacancy rate: 1.6%; Rental vacancy rate: 3.8%

GAYLORD (city). County seat. Covers a land area of 4.804 square miles and a water area of 0.025 square miles. Located at 45.02° N. Lat; 84.68° W. Long. Elevation is 1,348 feet.

History: Gaylord was first called Barnes, but when the Jackson, Lansing & Saginaw Railroad arrived in 1874, the name was changed to Gaylord for a railroad attorney. Gaylord was incorporated as a village in 1881 and as a city in 1922. It became the seat of Otsego County in 1878.
Population: 3,645; Growth (since 2000): -1.0%; Density: 758.8 persons per square mile; Race: 94.8% White, 0.9% Black/African American, 1.0% Asian, 0.8% American Indian/Alaska Native, 0.0% Native Hawaiian/Other Pacific Islander, 2.3% Two or more races, 1.8% Hispanic of any race; Average household size: 2.14; Median age: 39.3; Age under 18: 22.7%; Age 65 and over: 20.0%; Males per 100 females: 84.8; Marriage status: 25.6% never married, 39.9% now married, 1.3% separated, 12.8% widowed, 21.7% divorced; Foreign born: 2.4%; Speak English only: 98.9%; With disability: 22.0%; Veterans: 12.2%; Ancestry: 26.7% German, 24.2% Polish, 18.1% Irish, 15.4% English, 9.2% Dutch
Employment: 12.5% management, business, and financial, 2.3% computer, engineering, and science, 10.1% education, legal, community service, arts, and media, 8.6% healthcare practitioners, 24.3% service, 27.8% sales and office, 4.2% natural resources, construction, and maintenance, 10.3% production, transportation, and material moving
Income: Per capita: $21,678; Median household: $37,618; Average household: $45,643; Households with income of $100,000 or more: 10.7%; Poverty rate: 18.3%
Educational Attainment: High school diploma or higher: 87.3%; Bachelor's degree or higher: 17.9%; Graduate/professional degree or higher: 5.5%
School District(s)
Gaylord Community Schools (PK-12)
    2012-13 Enrollment: 3,129 . . . . (989) 705-3009
Housing: Homeownership rate: 45.3%; Median home value: $91,300; Median year structure built: 1973; Homeowner vacancy rate: 3.9%; Median gross rent: $484 per month; Rental vacancy rate: 10.0%
Health Insurance: 86.3% have insurance; 54.1% have private insurance; 47.5% have public insurance; 13.7% do not have insurance; 0.0% of children under 18 do not have insurance
Hospitals: Otsego Memorial Hospital (53 beds)
Safety: Violent crime rate: 22.1 per 10,000 population; Property crime rate: 716.5 per 10,000 population
Newspapers: Gaylord Herald Times (weekly circulation 7000)
Transportation: Commute: 90.6% car, 0.1% public transportation, 6.9% walk, 0.0% work from home; Median travel time to work: 12.1 minutes
Airports: Gaylord Regional (general aviation); Lakes of the North (general aviation)

HAYES (township). Covers a land area of 69.151 square miles and a water area of 1.488 square miles. Located at 44.92° N. Lat; 84.79° W. Long.

Population: 2,619; Growth (since 2000): 9.8%; Density: 37.9 persons per square mile; Race: 96.2% White, 0.2% Black/African American, 0.1% Asian, 0.3% American Indian/Alaska Native, 0.1% Native Hawaiian/Other Pacific Islander, 2.9% Two or more races, 1.0% Hispanic of any race; Average household size: 2.68; Median age: 40.2; Age under 18: 25.8%; Age 65 and over: 12.8%; Males per 100 females: 98.7; Marriage status: 25.3% never married, 61.7% now married, 0.5% separated, 4.4% widowed, 8.7% divorced; Foreign born: 0.7%; Speak English only: 98.3%; With disability: 9.6%; Veterans: 7.4%; Ancestry: 32.2% German, 16.8% English, 15.1% Polish, 11.7% Irish, 9.6% American
Employment: 13.1% management, business, and financial, 2.6% computer, engineering, and science, 4.9% education, legal, community service, arts, and media, 3.7% healthcare practitioners, 22.8% service, 27.3% sales and office, 13.0% natural resources, construction, and maintenance, 12.6% production, transportation, and material moving
Income: Per capita: $21,311; Median household: $53,611; Average household: $64,736; Households with income of $100,000 or more: 14.1%; Poverty rate: 14.5%

Educational Attainment: High school diploma or higher: 90.8%; Bachelor's degree or higher: 18.5%; Graduate/professional degree or higher: 3.6%
Housing: Homeownership rate: 90.9%; Median home value: $125,300; Median year structure built: 1985; Homeowner vacancy rate: 2.8%; Median gross rent: $981 per month; Rental vacancy rate: 9.1%
Health Insurance: 92.2% have insurance; 68.8% have private insurance; 35.4% have public insurance; 7.8% do not have insurance; 0.7% of children under 18 do not have insurance
Transportation: Commute: 92.8% car, 2.0% public transportation, 0.4% walk, 4.4% work from home; Median travel time to work: 27.1 minutes

JOHANNESBURG (unincorporated postal area)
ZCTA: 49751
    Covers a land area of 151.647 square miles and a water area of 2.180 square miles. Located at 44.98° N. Lat; 84.43° W. Long. Elevation is 1,352 feet.
    Population: 2,087; Growth (since 2000): 14.0%; Density: 13.8 persons per square mile; Race: 98.3% White, 0.2% Black/African American, 0.1% Asian, 0.3% American Indian/Alaska Native, 0.0% Native Hawaiian/Other Pacific Islander, 0.8% Two or more races, 0.5% Hispanic of any race; Average household size: 2.36; Median age: 47.4; Age under 18: 19.3%; Age 65 and over: 20.7%; Males per 100 females: 106.4
School District(s)
Johannesburg-Lewiston Area Schools (KG-12)
    2012-13 Enrollment: 755. . . . . (989) 732-1773
    Housing: Homeownership rate: 91.5%; Homeowner vacancy rate: 2.7%; Rental vacancy rate: 12.5%

LIVINGSTON (township). Covers a land area of 33.766 square miles and a water area of 0.295 square miles. Located at 45.08° N. Lat; 84.68° W. Long.

Population: 2,525; Growth (since 2000): 8.0%; Density: 74.8 persons per square mile; Race: 97.1% White, 0.1% Black/African American, 0.6% Asian, 0.8% American Indian/Alaska Native, 0.2% Native Hawaiian/Other Pacific Islander, 1.2% Two or more races, 0.9% Hispanic of any race; Average household size: 2.66; Median age: 41.6; Age under 18: 25.1%; Age 65 and over: 12.7%; Males per 100 females: 95.3; Marriage status: 24.3% never married, 60.1% now married, 0.2% separated, 5.0% widowed, 10.5% divorced; Foreign born: 2.9%; Speak English only: 97.4%; With disability: 13.3%; Veterans: 9.8%; Ancestry: 33.5% German, 20.6% Polish, 14.2% Irish, 12.6% English, 6.0% French
Employment: 11.8% management, business, and financial, 5.9% computer, engineering, and science, 8.7% education, legal, community service, arts, and media, 3.1% healthcare practitioners, 10.8% service, 39.1% sales and office, 12.7% natural resources, construction, and maintenance, 8.0% production, transportation, and material moving
Income: Per capita: $29,011; Median household: $52,083; Average household: $70,820; Households with income of $100,000 or more: 24.5%; Poverty rate: 7.8%
Educational Attainment: High school diploma or higher: 92.3%; Bachelor's degree or higher: 24.9%; Graduate/professional degree or higher: 7.9%
Housing: Homeownership rate: 87.1%; Median home value: $129,300; Median year structure built: 1982; Homeowner vacancy rate: 1.6%; Median gross rent: $738 per month; Rental vacancy rate: 7.0%
Health Insurance: 92.3% have insurance; 79.2% have private insurance; 30.2% have public insurance; 7.7% do not have insurance; 0.0% of children under 18 do not have insurance
Transportation: Commute: 88.0% car, 0.0% public transportation, 2.6% walk, 8.4% work from home; Median travel time to work: 16.1 minutes

OTSEGO LAKE (township). Covers a land area of 32.724 square miles and a water area of 2.695 square miles. Located at 44.91° N. Lat; 84.67° W. Long. Elevation is 1,296 feet.

Population: 2,847; Growth (since 2000): 12.4%; Density: 87.0 persons per square mile; Race: 97.7% White, 0.4% Black/African American, 0.3% Asian, 0.8% American Indian/Alaska Native, 0.0% Native Hawaiian/Other Pacific Islander, 0.5% Two or more races, 1.8% Hispanic of any race; Average household size: 2.29; Median age: 49.4; Age under 18: 19.1%; Age 65 and over: 23.0%; Males per 100 females: 99.0; Marriage status: 16.4% never married, 67.9% now married, 1.0% separated, 6.8% widowed, 8.8% divorced; Foreign born: 3.6%; Speak English only: 97.3%;

With disability: 12.8%; Veterans: 13.7%; Ancestry: 30.1% German, 16.3% Polish, 13.0% English, 9.4% Irish, 8.9% French

Employment: 18.1% management, business, and financial, 2.5% computer, engineering, and science, 9.1% education, legal, community service, arts, and media, 8.9% healthcare practitioners, 9.1% service, 34.9% sales and office, 6.8% natural resources, construction, and maintenance, 10.6% production, transportation, and material moving

Income: Per capita: $28,825; Median household: $51,392; Average household: $67,883; Households with income of $100,000 or more: 15.6%; Poverty rate: 9.1%

Educational Attainment: High school diploma or higher: 96.1%; Bachelor's degree or higher: 26.5%; Graduate/professional degree or higher: 9.0%

Housing: Homeownership rate: 87.6%; Median home value: $140,200; Median year structure built: 1979; Homeowner vacancy rate: 3.4%; Median gross rent: $646 per month; Rental vacancy rate: 17.9%

Health Insurance: 92.1% have insurance; 72.3% have private insurance; 42.4% have public insurance; 7.9% do not have insurance; 0.0% of children under 18 do not have insurance

Transportation: Commute: 94.5% car, 0.8% public transportation, 0.0% walk, 3.8% work from home; Median travel time to work: 24.9 minutes

---

VANDERBILT (village). Covers a land area of 1.127 square miles and a water area of 0 square miles. Located at 45.14° N. Lat; 84.66° W. Long. Elevation is 1,096 feet.

History: Vanderbilt was founded in 1870 and incorporated in 1901. It was named for the prominent Vanderbilt family. The town once had many mills, but later depended on fishing and hunting for its revenue.

Population: 562; Growth (since 2000): -4.3%; Density: 498.7 persons per square mile; Race: 95.6% White, 0.7% Black/African American, 0.0% Asian, 0.9% American Indian/Alaska Native, 0.0% Native Hawaiian/Other Pacific Islander, 2.8% Two or more races, 0.9% Hispanic of any race; Average household size: 2.37; Median age: 44.0; Age under 18: 21.7%; Age 65 and over: 18.1%; Males per 100 females: 95.1

School District(s)
Vanderbilt Area Schools (KG-12)
    2012-13 Enrollment: 121 . . . . (989) 983-4121

Housing: Homeownership rate: 69.6%; Homeowner vacancy rate: 3.5%; Rental vacancy rate: 10.0%

Ottawa County

Located in southwestern Michigan; bounded on the west by Lake Michigan; drained by the Grand and Black Rivers. Covers a land area of 563.467 square miles, a water area of 1,067.942 square miles, and is located in the Eastern Time Zone at 42.94° N. Lat., 86.66° W. Long. The county was founded in 1837. County seat is Grand Haven.

Ottawa County is part of the Grand Rapids-Wyoming, MI Metropolitan Statistical Area. The entire metro area includes: Barry County, MI; Kent County, MI; Montcalm County, MI; Ottawa County, MI

Weather Station: Holland   Elevation: 609 feet

	Jan	Feb	Mar	Apr	May	Jun	Jul	Aug	Sep	Oct	Nov	Dec
High	33	36	45	58	70	79	83	82	74	61	49	37
Low	19	20	26	37	47	56	61	60	52	42	33	24
Precip	na	1.3	1.7	3.0	3.9	3.5	3.4	3.5	3.8	3.7	3.3	2.6
Snow	20.8	13.8	5.2	1.1	tr	0.0	0.0	0.0	0.0	0.2	3.3	20.4

High and Low temperatures in degrees Fahrenheit; Precipitation and Snow in inches

Population: 263,801; Growth (since 2000): 10.7%; Density: 468.2 persons per square mile; Race: 90.1% White, 1.5% Black/African American, 2.6% Asian, 0.4% American Indian/Alaska Native, 0.0% Native Hawaiian/Other Pacific Islander, 2.0% two or more races, 8.6% Hispanic of any race; Average household size: 2.73; Median age: 34.5; Age under 18: 26.1%; Age 65 and over: 11.8%; Males per 100 females: 95.9; Marriage status: 29.2% never married, 58.5% now married, 0.9% separated, 4.5% widowed, 7.8% divorced; Foreign born: 5.8%; Speak English only: 90.2%; With disability: 9.3%; Veterans: 7.2%; Ancestry: 31.0% Dutch, 21.7% German, 9.3% Irish, 8.4% English, 6.1% Polish

Religion: Six largest groups: 28.0% Presbyterian-Reformed, 9.4% Catholicism, 4.9% Non-denominational Protestant, 3.8% Holiness, 2.5% Lutheran, 1.2% Methodist/Pietist

Economy: Unemployment rate: 4.1%; Leading industries: 13.4% retail trade; 12.9% construction; 12.2% other services (except public administration); Farms: 1,363 totaling 186,154 acres; Company size: 7

employ 1,000 or more persons, 13 employ 500 to 999 persons, 123 employ 100 to 499 persons, 5,542 employ less than 100 persons; Business ownership: 5,527 women-owned, n/a Black-owned, 388 Hispanic-owned, 213 Asian-owned

Employment: 13.4% management, business, and financial, 5.3% computer, engineering, and science, 9.8% education, legal, community service, arts, and media, 4.9% healthcare practitioners, 16.2% service, 23.1% sales and office, 8.5% natural resources, construction, and maintenance, 18.7% production, transportation, and material moving

Income: Per capita: $25,371; Median household: $56,453; Average household: $70,918; Households with income of $100,000 or more: 21.1%; Poverty rate: 11.2%

Educational Attainment: High school diploma or higher: 90.9%; Bachelor's degree or higher: 30.0%; Graduate/professional degree or higher: 9.9%

Housing: Homeownership rate: 78.1%; Median home value: $153,200; Median year structure built: 1982; Homeowner vacancy rate: 2.3%; Median gross rent: $767 per month; Rental vacancy rate: 9.9%

Vital Statistics: Birth rate: 126.3 per 10,000 population; Death rate: 61.8 per 10,000 population; Age-adjusted cancer mortality rate: 142.6 deaths per 100,000 population

Health Insurance: 91.7% have insurance; 79.8% have private insurance; 24.2% have public insurance; 8.3% do not have insurance; 3.3% of children under 18 do not have insurance

Health Care: Physicians: 14.8 per 10,000 population; Hospital beds: 8.5 per 10,000 population; Hospital admissions: 382.1 per 10,000 population

Air Quality Index: 87.4% good, 12.6% moderate, 0.0% unhealthy for sensitive individuals, 0.0% unhealthy (percent of days)

Transportation: Commute: 91.9% car, 0.9% public transportation, 2.4% walk, 3.5% work from home; Median travel time to work: 20.2 minutes

Presidential Election: 32.4% Obama, 66.8% Romney (2012)

National and State Parks: Grand Haven State Game Area; Grand Haven State Park; Holland State Park

Additional Information Contacts
Ottawa Government . . . . (616) 738-4000
    http://www.co.ottawa.mi.us

Ottawa County Communities

ALLENDALE (CDP). Covers a land area of 22.726 square miles and a water area of 0.920 square miles. Located at 42.99° N. Lat; 85.95° W. Long. Elevation is 653 feet.

Population: 17,579; Growth (since 2000): 52.1%; Density: 773.5 persons per square mile; Race: 90.7% White, 3.3% Black/African American, 1.5% Asian, 0.4% American Indian/Alaska Native, 0.0% Native Hawaiian/Other Pacific Islander, 2.3% Two or more races, 4.8% Hispanic of any race; Average household size: 3.01; Median age: 20.9; Age under 18: 16.9%; Age 65 and over: 4.2%; Males per 100 females: 84.8; Marriage status: 61.2% never married, 33.0% now married, 0.2% separated, 1.4% widowed, 4.4% divorced; Foreign born: 3.0%; Speak English only: 94.5%; With disability: 4.3%; Veterans: 3.2%; Ancestry: 25.9% German, 23.8% Dutch, 12.9% Irish, 8.5% Polish, 7.7% English

Employment: 7.9% management, business, and financial, 3.7% computer, engineering, and science, 11.3% education, legal, community service, arts, and media, 5.1% healthcare practitioners, 23.5% service, 26.6% sales and office, 9.2% natural resources, construction, and maintenance, 12.6% production, transportation, and material moving

Income: Per capita: $16,327; Median household: $48,487; Average household: $57,680; Households with income of $100,000 or more: 17.0%; Poverty rate: 28.0%

Educational Attainment: High school diploma or higher: 93.5%; Bachelor's degree or higher: 27.0%; Graduate/professional degree or higher: 9.1%

School District(s)
Allendale Public Schools (PK-12)
    2012-13 Enrollment: 2,499 . . . . (616) 892-5570
Ottawa Area ISD (PK-12)
    2012-13 Enrollment: 985 . . . . (616) 738-8940

Four-year College(s)
Grand Valley State University (Public)
    Fall 2013 Enrollment: 24,477 . . . . (616) 331-2020
    2013-14 Tuition: In-state $10,716; Out-of-state $15,388

Housing: Homeownership rate: 54.6%; Median home value: $158,900; Median year structure built: 1994; Homeowner vacancy rate: 2.1%; Median gross rent: $787 per month; Rental vacancy rate: 4.4%

Health Insurance: 91.8% have insurance; 86.9% have private insurance; 9.6% have public insurance; 8.2% do not have insurance; 5.4% of children under 18 do not have insurance
Transportation: Commute: 83.7% car, 5.5% public transportation, 7.3% walk, 1.0% work from home; Median travel time to work: 22.2 minutes

ALLENDALE (charter township). Covers a land area of 31.130 square miles and a water area of 0.925 square miles. Located at 42.98° N. Lat; 85.96° W. Long. Elevation is 653 feet.

History: Allendale Township was organized in 1846, and named for Captain Hannibal Allen, son of Ethan Allen. Agnes Allen, Captain Allen's widow, owned land in the township.
Population: 20,708; Growth (since 2000): 58.8%; Density: 665.2 persons per square mile; Race: 91.1% White, 3.1% Black/African American, 1.4% Asian, 0.4% American Indian/Alaska Native, 0.0% Native Hawaiian/Other Pacific Islander, 2.2% Two or more races, 4.6% Hispanic of any race; Average household size: 3.04; Median age: 21.1; Age under 18: 17.6%; Age 65 and over: 4.2%; Males per 100 females: 86.0; Marriage status: 59.9% never married, 34.0% now married, 0.2% separated, 1.4% widowed, 4.7% divorced; Foreign born: 3.1%; Speak English only: 94.3%; With disability: 4.8%; Veterans: 2.9%; Ancestry: 26.1% German, 25.8% Dutch, 12.3% Irish, 8.1% Polish, 7.8% English
Employment: 7.7% management, business, and financial, 4.6% computer, engineering, and science, 10.7% education, legal, community service, arts, and media, 4.9% healthcare practitioners, 22.7% service, 26.6% sales and office, 9.2% natural resources, construction, and maintenance, 13.6% production, transportation, and material moving
Income: Per capita: $17,125; Median household: $48,489; Average household: $59,380; Households with income of $100,000 or more: 15.1%; Poverty rate: 28.6%
Educational Attainment: High school diploma or higher: 93.6%; Bachelor's degree or higher: 25.0%; Graduate/professional degree or higher: 8.3%

School District(s)
Allendale Public Schools (PK-12)
    2012-13 Enrollment: 2,499 . . . . (616) 892-5570
Ottawa Area ISD (PK-12)
    2012-13 Enrollment: 985. . . . . (616) 738-8940
Four-year College(s)
Grand Valley State University (Public)
    Fall 2013 Enrollment: 24,477 . . . . (616) 331-2020
    2013-14 Tuition: In-state $10,716; Out-of-state $15,388
Housing: Homeownership rate: 56.0%; Median home value: $159,200; Median year structure built: 1995; Homeowner vacancy rate: 1.8%; Median gross rent: $863 per month; Rental vacancy rate: 4.0%
Health Insurance: 91.7% have insurance; 86.9% have private insurance; 10.1% have public insurance; 8.3% do not have insurance; 4.6% of children under 18 do not have insurance
Transportation: Commute: 85.1% car, 5.5% public transportation, 6.3% walk, 0.9% work from home; Median travel time to work: 22.3 minutes
Additional Information Contacts
Allendale Charter Township . . . . (616) 895-6295
    http://www.allendale-twp.org

BEECHWOOD (CDP). Covers a land area of 1.801 square miles and a water area of 0.883 square miles. Located at 42.80° N. Lat; 86.12° W. Long. Elevation is 607 feet.
Population: 3,015; Growth (since 2000): 1.8%; Density: 1,674.3 persons per square mile; Race: 81.7% White, 3.1% Black/African American, 3.9% Asian, 0.4% American Indian/Alaska Native, 0.0% Native Hawaiian/Other Pacific Islander, 4.8% Two or more races, 19.6% Hispanic of any race; Average household size: 2.71; Median age: 35.4; Age under 18: 27.9%; Age 65 and over: 10.5%; Males per 100 females: 108.9; Marriage status: 33.2% never married, 48.9% now married, 2.5% separated, 4.8% widowed, 13.1% divorced; Foreign born: 3.5%; Speak English only: 91.1%; With disability: 11.9%; Veterans: 4.5%; Ancestry: 32.2% Dutch, 21.8% German, 11.9% Irish, 6.1% American, 5.1% French
Employment: 6.4% management, business, and financial, 1.5% computer, engineering, and science, 4.7% education, legal, community service, arts, and media, 4.1% healthcare practitioners, 16.4% service, 27.9% sales and office, 23.6% natural resources, construction, and maintenance, 15.4% production, transportation, and material moving
Income: Per capita: $24,546; Median household: $54,565; Average household: $62,194; Households with income of $100,000 or more: 18.5%; Poverty rate: 12.5%

Educational Attainment: High school diploma or higher: 85.4%; Bachelor's degree or higher: 15.2%; Graduate/professional degree or higher: 6.8%
Housing: Homeownership rate: 73.2%; Median home value: $117,900; Median year structure built: 1967; Homeowner vacancy rate: 2.3%; Median gross rent: $682 per month; Rental vacancy rate: 8.3%
Health Insurance: 89.6% have insurance; 75.5% have private insurance; 27.4% have public insurance; 10.4% do not have insurance; 0.0% of children under 18 do not have insurance
Transportation: Commute: 91.7% car, 0.1% public transportation, 0.0% walk, 3.1% work from home; Median travel time to work: 16.6 minutes

BLENDON (township). Covers a land area of 36.363 square miles and a water area of 0.008 square miles. Located at 42.90° N. Lat; 85.97° W. Long.
History: Blendon Township was named for the Blendon Lumber Company, who owned much land here.
Population: 5,772; Growth (since 2000): 0.9%; Density: 158.7 persons per square mile; Race: 97.3% White, 0.3% Black/African American, 0.6% Asian, 0.1% American Indian/Alaska Native, 0.0% Native Hawaiian/Other Pacific Islander, 0.8% Two or more races, 3.2% Hispanic of any race; Average household size: 2.92; Median age: 38.5; Age under 18: 26.3%; Age 65 and over: 10.0%; Males per 100 females: 102.5; Marriage status: 21.6% never married, 71.3% now married, 0.3% separated, 2.3% widowed, 4.8% divorced; Foreign born: 1.4%; Speak English only: 96.7%; With disability: 7.1%; Veterans: 5.2%; Ancestry: 51.7% Dutch, 14.7% German, 9.0% Irish, 7.1% English, 5.5% American
Employment: 15.8% management, business, and financial, 6.4% computer, engineering, and science, 7.7% education, legal, community service, arts, and media, 8.4% healthcare practitioners, 8.6% service, 25.0% sales and office, 14.7% natural resources, construction, and maintenance, 13.3% production, transportation, and material moving
Income: Per capita: $24,080; Median household: $60,912; Average household: $74,004; Households with income of $100,000 or more: 26.9%; Poverty rate: 2.6%
Educational Attainment: High school diploma or higher: 89.9%; Bachelor's degree or higher: 24.9%; Graduate/professional degree or higher: 10.0%
Housing: Homeownership rate: 87.9%; Median home value: $207,800; Median year structure built: 1980; Homeowner vacancy rate: 0.7%; Median gross rent: <$100 per month; Rental vacancy rate: 6.7%
Health Insurance: 93.2% have insurance; 84.9% have private insurance; 17.5% have public insurance; 6.8% do not have insurance; 7.5% of children under 18 do not have insurance
Transportation: Commute: 89.9% car, 2.3% public transportation, 3.8% walk, 4.0% work from home; Median travel time to work: 20.8 minutes

CHESTER (township). Covers a land area of 35.626 square miles and a water area of 0.191 square miles. Located at 43.17° N. Lat; 85.84° W. Long.
Population: 2,017; Growth (since 2000): -12.9%; Density: 56.6 persons per square mile; Race: 95.9% White, 0.3% Black/African American, 0.3% Asian, 0.5% American Indian/Alaska Native, 0.0% Native Hawaiian/Other Pacific Islander, 1.4% Two or more races, 3.6% Hispanic of any race; Average household size: 2.72; Median age: 41.3; Age under 18: 24.2%; Age 65 and over: 12.4%; Males per 100 females: 106.2
Housing: Homeownership rate: 87.2%; Homeowner vacancy rate: 2.5%; Rental vacancy rate: 10.4%

CONKLIN (unincorporated postal area)
ZCTA: 49403
    Covers a land area of 47.174 square miles and a water area of 0.328 square miles. Located at 43.14° N. Lat; 85.86° W. Long. Elevation is 712 feet.
    Population: 2,473; Growth (since 2000): -0.9%; Density: 52.4 persons per square mile; Race: 95.2% White, 0.1% Black/African American, 0.1% Asian, 0.6% American Indian/Alaska Native, 0.0% Native Hawaiian/Other Pacific Islander, 1.1% Two or more races, 4.7% Hispanic of any race; Average household size: 2.79; Median age: 40.4; Age under 18: 24.7%; Age 65 and over: 12.3%; Males per 100 females: 103.7
    Housing: Homeownership rate: 90.3%; Homeowner vacancy rate: 1.3%; Rental vacancy rate: 4.5%

COOPERSVILLE (city). Covers a land area of 4.810 square miles and a water area of 0.004 square miles. Located at 43.07° N. Lat; 85.93° W. Long. Elevation is 640 feet.

History: Many of the early residents of Coopersville were of Dutch origin. After first being called Polkton, the town was renamed in 1858 for Benjamin F. Cooper, who gave the land for the railroad station. Industries in the early 1900's included a cannery, a flour mill, and a creamery.

Population: 4,275; Growth (since 2000): 9.3%; Density: 888.7 persons per square mile; Race: 95.5% White, 0.5% Black/African American, 0.7% Asian, 0.6% American Indian/Alaska Native, 0.0% Native Hawaiian/Other Pacific Islander, 1.6% Two or more races, 3.7% Hispanic of any race; Average household size: 2.66; Median age: 32.8; Age under 18: 29.3%; Age 65 and over: 11.2%; Males per 100 females: 93.4; Marriage status: 33.9% never married, 52.2% now married, 1.8% separated, 3.9% widowed, 10.0% divorced; Foreign born: 1.7%; Speak English only: 97.3%; With disability: 11.9%; Veterans: 8.6%; Ancestry: 30.0% German, 21.5% Dutch, 10.2% Irish, 8.5% English, 6.6% Polish

Employment: 10.8% management, business, and financial, 5.6% computer, engineering, and science, 5.3% education, legal, community service, arts, and media, 3.5% healthcare practitioners, 12.1% service, 27.5% sales and office, 13.1% natural resources, construction, and maintenance, 22.1% production, transportation, and material moving

Income: Per capita: $21,164; Median household: $54,630; Average household: $57,107; Households with income of $100,000 or more: 12.1%; Poverty rate: 14.8%

Educational Attainment: High school diploma or higher: 91.0%; Bachelor's degree or higher: 18.6%; Graduate/professional degree or higher: 5.9%

School District(s)
Coopersville Area Public SD (PK-12)
    2012-13 Enrollment: 2,477 . . . . (616) 997-3200

Housing: Homeownership rate: 67.9%; Median home value: $118,600; Median year structure built: 1977; Homeowner vacancy rate: 2.1%; Median gross rent: $734 per month; Rental vacancy rate: 14.0%

Health Insurance: 84.9% have insurance; 71.8% have private insurance; 24.3% have public insurance; 15.1% do not have insurance; 7.8% of children under 18 do not have insurance

Newspapers: Coopersville Observer (weekly circulation 8000)

Transportation: Commute: 93.0% car, 0.0% public transportation, 3.2% walk, 2.0% work from home; Median travel time to work: 22.3 minutes

Additional Information Contacts
City of Coopersville . . . . (616) 997-9731
    http://www.cityofcoopersville.com

CROCKERY (township). Covers a land area of 32.446 square miles and a water area of 0.952 square miles. Located at 43.08° N. Lat; 86.08° W. Long.

Population: 3,960; Growth (since 2000): 4.7%; Density: 122.0 persons per square mile; Race: 96.4% White, 0.5% Black/African American, 0.4% Asian, 0.4% American Indian/Alaska Native, 0.1% Native Hawaiian/Other Pacific Islander, 1.5% Two or more races, 2.6% Hispanic of any race; Average household size: 2.59; Median age: 41.1; Age under 18: 23.3%; Age 65 and over: 12.6%; Males per 100 females: 108.5; Marriage status: 19.1% never married, 65.6% now married, 1.5% separated, 3.9% widowed, 11.4% divorced; Foreign born: 1.0%; Speak English only: 97.2%; With disability: 16.8%; Veterans: 9.8%; Ancestry: 29.9% German, 21.6% Dutch, 10.6% English, 9.7% Polish, 7.6% American

Employment: 9.8% management, business, and financial, 4.6% computer, engineering, and science, 10.1% education, legal, community service, arts, and media, 2.5% healthcare practitioners, 14.7% service, 24.5% sales and office, 10.9% natural resources, construction, and maintenance, 22.8% production, transportation, and material moving

Income: Per capita: $21,436; Median household: $46,860; Average household: $55,932; Households with income of $100,000 or more: 13.3%; Poverty rate: 13.1%

Educational Attainment: High school diploma or higher: 87.0%; Bachelor's degree or higher: 15.3%; Graduate/professional degree or higher: 4.6%

Housing: Homeownership rate: 84.3%; Median home value: $153,300; Median year structure built: 1974; Homeowner vacancy rate: 2.2%; Median gross rent: $755 per month; Rental vacancy rate: 6.0%

Health Insurance: 87.4% have insurance; 66.0% have private insurance; 35.9% have public insurance; 12.6% do not have insurance; 4.3% of children under 18 do not have insurance

Transportation: Commute: 91.3% car, 0.5% public transportation, 2.7% walk, 5.1% work from home; Median travel time to work: 23.0 minutes

FERRYSBURG (city). Covers a land area of 2.986 square miles and a water area of 0.603 square miles. Located at 43.09° N. Lat; 86.23° W. Long. Elevation is 597 feet.

Population: 2,892; Growth (since 2000): -4.9%; Density: 968.4 persons per square mile; Race: 95.8% White, 0.5% Black/African American, 0.6% Asian, 0.6% American Indian/Alaska Native, 0.0% Native Hawaiian/Other Pacific Islander, 2.0% Two or more races, 2.5% Hispanic of any race; Average household size: 2.24; Median age: 47.1; Age under 18: 20.0%; Age 65 and over: 20.0%; Males per 100 females: 86.9; Marriage status: 22.4% never married, 53.7% now married, 0.2% separated, 7.9% widowed, 16.0% divorced; Foreign born: 3.5%; Speak English only: 96.2%; With disability: 10.9%; Veterans: 10.3%; Ancestry: 20.4% German, 15.5% Dutch, 15.3% Irish, 12.6% English, 9.3% Polish

Employment: 16.0% management, business, and financial, 3.9% computer, engineering, and science, 15.0% education, legal, community service, arts, and media, 3.6% healthcare practitioners, 16.8% service, 24.8% sales and office, 8.1% natural resources, construction, and maintenance, 11.7% production, transportation, and material moving

Income: Per capita: $42,194; Median household: $58,459; Average household: $90,968; Households with income of $100,000 or more: 21.4%; Poverty rate: 7.4%

Educational Attainment: High school diploma or higher: 90.5%; Bachelor's degree or higher: 35.5%; Graduate/professional degree or higher: 14.4%

Housing: Homeownership rate: 82.6%; Median home value: $149,900; Median year structure built: 1976; Homeowner vacancy rate: 4.4%; Median gross rent: $744 per month; Rental vacancy rate: 8.2%

Health Insurance: 84.8% have insurance; 70.9% have private insurance; 33.8% have public insurance; 15.2% do not have insurance; 11.2% of children under 18 do not have insurance

Transportation: Commute: 95.3% car, 0.0% public transportation, 0.4% walk, 3.8% work from home; Median travel time to work: 19.4 minutes

GEORGETOWN (charter township). Covers a land area of 33.175 square miles and a water area of 0.902 square miles. Located at 42.91° N. Lat; 85.84° W. Long.

Population: 46,985; Growth (since 2000): 12.8%; Density: 1,416.3 persons per square mile; Race: 95.3% White, 1.0% Black/African American, 1.3% Asian, 0.3% American Indian/Alaska Native, 0.0% Native Hawaiian/Other Pacific Islander, 1.5% Two or more races, 2.7% Hispanic of any race; Average household size: 2.81; Median age: 35.3; Age under 18: 27.2%; Age 65 and over: 13.0%; Males per 100 females: 94.7; Marriage status: 25.2% never married, 63.8% now married, 0.9% separated, 5.5% widowed, 5.5% divorced; Foreign born: 3.1%; Speak English only: 96.3%; With disability: 8.7%; Veterans: 7.2%; Ancestry: 38.9% Dutch, 23.6% German, 9.8% Irish, 9.2% English, 6.2% Polish

Employment: 14.0% management, business, and financial, 5.4% computer, engineering, and science, 10.6% education, legal, community service, arts, and media, 6.3% healthcare practitioners, 15.5% service, 26.2% sales and office, 7.5% natural resources, construction, and maintenance, 14.4% production, transportation, and material moving

Income: Per capita: $27,740; Median household: $63,410; Average household: $77,244; Households with income of $100,000 or more: 23.7%; Poverty rate: 6.2%

Educational Attainment: High school diploma or higher: 95.4%; Bachelor's degree or higher: 33.6%; Graduate/professional degree or higher: 10.3%

Housing: Homeownership rate: 83.0%; Median home value: $157,200; Median year structure built: 1983; Homeowner vacancy rate: 1.3%; Median gross rent: $808 per month; Rental vacancy rate: 7.3%

Health Insurance: 94.7% have insurance; 87.5% have private insurance; 21.2% have public insurance; 5.3% do not have insurance; 2.4% of children under 18 do not have insurance

Transportation: Commute: 93.8% car, 0.3% public transportation, 2.0% walk, 3.2% work from home; Median travel time to work: 21.8 minutes

Additional Information Contacts
Georgetown Charter Township . . . . (616) 457-2340
    http://www.georgetown-mi.gov

GRAND HAVEN (charter township). Covers a land area of 28.680 square miles and a water area of 0.838 square miles. Located at 43.00° N. Lat; 86.19° W. Long. Elevation is 604 feet.

History: Tri-City Historical Museum. Incorporated 1867.

Population: 15,178; Growth (since 2000): 14.3%; Density: 529.2 persons per square mile; Race: 95.8% White, 0.3% Black/African American, 1.0% Asian, 0.5% American Indian/Alaska Native, 0.0% Native Hawaiian/Other Pacific Islander, 1.6% Two or more races, 2.9% Hispanic of any race; Average household size: 2.72; Median age: 40.3; Age under 18: 27.1%; Age 65 and over: 11.3%; Males per 100 females: 98.0; Marriage status: 22.8% never married, 63.9% now married, 0.2% separated, 3.8% widowed, 9.6% divorced; Foreign born: 5.3%; Speak English only: 93.1%; With disability: 7.7%; Veterans: 8.4%; Ancestry: 23.5% German, 20.0% Dutch, 10.3% Irish, 10.2% English, 8.7% Polish

Employment: 14.5% management, business, and financial, 6.8% computer, engineering, and science, 13.1% education, legal, community service, arts, and media, 7.0% healthcare practitioners, 17.5% service, 17.7% sales and office, 8.1% natural resources, construction, and maintenance, 15.4% production, transportation, and material moving

Income: Per capita: $31,494; Median household: $67,908; Average household: $85,058; Households with income of $100,000 or more: 30.7%; Poverty rate: 9.6%

Educational Attainment: High school diploma or higher: 94.5%; Bachelor's degree or higher: 41.3%; Graduate/professional degree or higher: 13.0%

School District(s)
Grand Haven Area Public Schools (PK-12)
    2012-13 Enrollment: 6,026 . . . . (616) 850-5015

Housing: Homeownership rate: 85.9%; Median home value: $172,500; Median year structure built: 1990; Homeowner vacancy rate: 1.8%; Median gross rent: $836 per month; Rental vacancy rate: 6.8%

Health Insurance: 91.5% have insurance; 81.1% have private insurance; 22.1% have public insurance; 8.5% do not have insurance; 4.7% of children under 18 do not have insurance

Hospitals: North Ottawa Community Health Center (81 beds)

Newspapers: Grand Haven Tribune (daily circulation 9900); The News-Review (weekly circulation 6000)

Transportation: Commute: 91.5% car, 0.4% public transportation, 1.2% walk, 6.3% work from home; Median travel time to work: 22.6 minutes

Additional Information Contacts
Grand Haven Township. . . . . (616) 842-5988
    http://www.ght.org

GRAND HAVEN (city). County seat. Covers a land area of 5.771 square miles and a water area of 1.592 square miles. Located at 43.06° N. Lat; 86.22° W. Long. Elevation is 604 feet.

History: A trading post was established here in 1833, and in 1834 the New Haven Company was formed to promote the area. Grand Haven, established on Spring Lake which is connected to Lake Michigan by the Grand River, developed as a manufacturing and shipping center as well as a resort.

Population: 10,412; Growth (since 2000): -6.8%; Density: 1,804.1 persons per square mile; Race: 95.0% White, 0.7% Black/African American, 1.0% Asian, 0.9% American Indian/Alaska Native, 0.0% Native Hawaiian/Other Pacific Islander, 1.9% Two or more races, 2.4% Hispanic of any race; Average household size: 2.15; Median age: 42.9; Age under 18: 20.7%; Age 65 and over: 19.1%; Males per 100 females: 90.0; Marriage status: 22.0% never married, 55.8% now married, 1.7% separated, 7.1% widowed, 15.1% divorced; Foreign born: 2.1%; Speak English only: 98.0%; With disability: 11.7%; Veterans: 11.0%; Ancestry: 25.4% German, 20.4% Dutch, 12.1% Irish, 10.3% Polish, 9.7% English

Employment: 16.2% management, business, and financial, 3.5% computer, engineering, and science, 10.6% education, legal, community service, arts, and media, 3.3% healthcare practitioners, 19.3% service, 23.5% sales and office, 6.3% natural resources, construction, and maintenance, 17.3% production, transportation, and material moving

Income: Per capita: $25,978; Median household: $40,967; Average household: $55,235; Households with income of $100,000 or more: 13.5%; Poverty rate: 12.0%

Educational Attainment: High school diploma or higher: 92.6%; Bachelor's degree or higher: 31.2%; Graduate/professional degree or higher: 9.6%

School District(s)
Grand Haven Area Public Schools (PK-12)
    2012-13 Enrollment: 6,026 . . . . (616) 850-5015

Housing: Homeownership rate: 67.9%; Median home value: $117,700; Median year structure built: 1958; Homeowner vacancy rate: 4.9%; Median gross rent: $644 per month; Rental vacancy rate: 13.5%

Health Insurance: 85.3% have insurance; 70.9% have private insurance; 34.4% have public insurance; 14.7% do not have insurance; 4.9% of children under 18 do not have insurance

Hospitals: North Ottawa Community Health Center (81 beds)

Safety: Violent crime rate: 27.0 per 10,000 population; Property crime rate: 257.2 per 10,000 population

Newspapers: Grand Haven Tribune (daily circulation 9900); The News-Review (weekly circulation 6000)

Transportation: Commute: 88.9% car, 1.2% public transportation, 3.2% walk, 2.7% work from home; Median travel time to work: 19.1 minutes

Additional Information Contacts
City of Grand Haven . . . . (616) 842-3210
    http://www.grandhaven.org

HOLLAND (charter township). Covers a land area of 27.028 square miles and a water area of 0.456 square miles. Located at 42.82° N. Lat; 86.08° W. Long. Elevation is 610 feet.

Population: 35,636; Growth (since 2000): 23.3%; Density: 1,318.5 persons per square mile; Race: 73.5% White, 2.6% Black/African American, 9.4% Asian, 0.5% American Indian/Alaska Native, 0.0% Native Hawaiian/Other Pacific Islander, 3.4% Two or more races, 23.4% Hispanic of any race; Average household size: 2.85; Median age: 32.0; Age under 18: 30.3%; Age 65 and over: 8.9%; Males per 100 females: 99.7; Marriage status: 28.6% never married, 58.9% now married, 1.2% separated, 3.7% widowed, 8.8% divorced; Foreign born: 14.7%; Speak English only: 74.4%; With disability: 9.8%; Veterans: 6.1%; Ancestry: 26.5% Dutch, 14.7% German, 7.2% Irish, 6.1% English, 4.3% American

Employment: 11.0% management, business, and financial, 6.3% computer, engineering, and science, 7.7% education, legal, community service, arts, and media, 3.1% healthcare practitioners, 16.7% service, 18.6% sales and office, 9.5% natural resources, construction, and maintenance, 27.1% production, transportation, and material moving

Income: Per capita: $22,015; Median household: $53,499; Average household: $62,344; Households with income of $100,000 or more: 16.1%; Poverty rate: 12.4%

Educational Attainment: High school diploma or higher: 83.2%; Bachelor's degree or higher: 23.9%; Graduate/professional degree or higher: 6.8%

School District(s)
Black River Public Schools (KG-12)
    2012-13 Enrollment: 846 . . . . (616) 355-0055
Eagle Crest Charter Academy (KG-12)
    2012-13 Enrollment: 706 . . . . (616) 786-2400
Hamilton Community Schools (KG-12)
    2012-13 Enrollment: 2,633 . . . . (269) 751-5148
Holland City SD (PK-12)
    2012-13 Enrollment: 4,011 . . . . (616) 494-2005
Ottawa Area ISD (PK-12)
    2012-13 Enrollment: 985 . . . . (616) 738-8940
Vanderbilt Charter Academy (KG-12)
    2012-13 Enrollment: 458 . . . . (616) 820-5050
Wavecrest Career Academy (KG-12)
    2012-13 Enrollment: 152 . . . . (616) 393-7662
West Ottawa Public SD (PK-12)
    2012-13 Enrollment: 7,310 . . . . (616) 738-5795

Four-year College(s)
Hope College (Private, Not-for-profit, Reformed Church in America)
    Fall 2013 Enrollment: 3,388 . . . . (616) 395-7000
    2013-14 Tuition: In-state $28,720; Out-of-state $28,720
Western Theological Seminary (Private, Not-for-profit, Reformed Church in America)
    Fall 2013 Enrollment: 275 . . . . (616) 392-8555

Housing: Homeownership rate: 70.1%; Median home value: $136,200; Median year structure built: 1990; Homeowner vacancy rate: 2.3%; Median gross rent: $734 per month; Rental vacancy rate: 13.4%

Health Insurance: 90.7% have insurance; 74.6% have private insurance; 26.2% have public insurance; 9.3% do not have insurance; 3.0% of children under 18 do not have insurance

Hospitals: Holland Community Hospital (205 beds)

Newspapers: Holland Sentinel (daily circulation 18400)

Transportation: Commute: 95.2% car, 1.0% public transportation, 0.8% walk, 1.9% work from home; Median travel time to work: 17.2 minutes; Amtrak: Train service available.
Airports: Park Township (general aviation); West Michigan Regional (general aviation)
Additional Information Contacts
Holland Charter Township. . . . . (616) 396-2345
　http://www.hct.holland.mi.us

HOLLAND (city). Covers a land area of 16.589 square miles and a water area of 0.762 square miles. Located at 42.77° N. Lat; 86.10° W. Long. Elevation is 610 feet.
History: Holland was founded by 53 members of the Society of Christians for the Holland Emigration to the United States, led by Dr. A.C. Van Raalte in 1847. More Dutch settlers followed, and in 1868 Holland was incorporated as a city. The Dutch Reformed Church founded both Hope College and the Western Theological Seminary in Holland. Industry and commerce developed here, including the Holland Furnace Company established in 1906.
Population: 33,051; Growth (since 2000): -5.7%; Density: 1,992.3 persons per square mile; Race: 80.0% White, 3.6% Black/African American, 3.0% Asian, 0.6% American Indian/Alaska Native, 0.1% Native Hawaiian/Other Pacific Islander, 3.4% Two or more races, 22.7% Hispanic of any race; Average household size: 2.52; Median age: 31.7; Age under 18: 24.0%; Age 65 and over: 13.7%; Males per 100 females: 90.6; Marriage status: 38.8% never married, 46.6% now married, 1.2% separated, 5.7% widowed, 8.9% divorced; Foreign born: 12.5%; Speak English only: 76.2%; With disability: 11.0%; Veterans: 6.1%; Ancestry: 24.1% Dutch, 17.1% German, 7.6% Irish, 7.1% English, 4.7% Polish
Employment: 9.1% management, business, and financial, 4.7% computer, engineering, and science, 11.6% education, legal, community service, arts, and media, 3.3% healthcare practitioners, 19.6% service, 18.4% sales and office, 8.3% natural resources, construction, and maintenance, 25.1% production, transportation, and material moving
Income: Per capita: $20,759; Median household: $43,413; Average household: $58,581; Households with income of $100,000 or more: 13.9%; Poverty rate: 19.2%
Educational Attainment: High school diploma or higher: 84.8%; Bachelor's degree or higher: 31.0%; Graduate/professional degree or higher: 12.3%
School District(s)
Black River Public Schools (KG-12)
　2012-13 Enrollment: 846. . . . . (616) 355-0055
Eagle Crest Charter Academy (KG-12)
　2012-13 Enrollment: 706. . . . . (616) 786-2400
Hamilton Community Schools (KG-12)
　2012-13 Enrollment: 2,633 . . . . (269) 751-5148
Holland City SD (PK-12)
　2012-13 Enrollment: 4,011 . . . . (616) 494-2005
Ottawa Area ISD (PK-12)
　2012-13 Enrollment: 985. . . . . (616) 738-8940
Vanderbilt Charter Academy (KG-12)
　2012-13 Enrollment: 458. . . . . (616) 820-5050
Wavecrest Career Academy (KG-12)
　2012-13 Enrollment: 152. . . . . (616) 393-7662
West Ottawa Public SD (PK-12)
　2012-13 Enrollment: 7,310 . . . . (616) 738-5795
Four-year College(s)
Hope College (Private, Not-for-profit, Reformed Church in America)
　Fall 2013 Enrollment: 3,388 . . . . (616) 395-7000
　2013-14 Tuition: In-state $28,720; Out-of-state $28,720
Western Theological Seminary (Private, Not-for-profit, Reformed Church in America)
　Fall 2013 Enrollment: 275. . . . . (616) 392-8555
Housing: Homeownership rate: 63.7%; Median home value: $117,200; Median year structure built: 1967; Homeowner vacancy rate: 2.9%; Median gross rent: $767 per month; Rental vacancy rate: 9.7%
Health Insurance: 88.7% have insurance; 68.3% have private insurance; 32.9% have public insurance; 11.3% do not have insurance; 3.5% of children under 18 do not have insurance
Hospitals: Holland Community Hospital (205 beds)
Safety: Violent crime rate: 41.1 per 10,000 population; Property crime rate: 320.5 per 10,000 population
Newspapers: Holland Sentinel (daily circulation 18400)

Transportation: Commute: 85.7% car, 1.0% public transportation, 7.2% walk, 3.7% work from home; Median travel time to work: 17.0 minutes; Amtrak: Train service available.
Airports: Park Township (general aviation); West Michigan Regional (general aviation)
Additional Information Contacts
City of Holland. . . . . (616) 355-1300
　http://www.cityofholland.com

HUDSONVILLE (city). Covers a land area of 4.137 square miles and a water area of <.001 square miles. Located at 42.86° N. Lat; 85.86° W. Long. Elevation is 633 feet.
History: Hudsonville was named in 1872 for Homer E. Hudson, the first postmaster of the town that had been called South Georgetown. Another Hudson, Horace A., was the station agent when the Chicago & Western Michigan Railroad arrived here in 1874.
Population: 7,116; Growth (since 2000): -0.6%; Density: 1,720.1 persons per square mile; Race: 94.3% White, 1.5% Black/African American, 0.8% Asian, 0.4% American Indian/Alaska Native, 0.0% Native Hawaiian/Other Pacific Islander, 1.7% Two or more races, 3.2% Hispanic of any race; Average household size: 2.71; Median age: 33.5; Age under 18: 28.4%; Age 65 and over: 14.5%; Males per 100 females: 91.1; Marriage status: 27.8% never married, 59.7% now married, 0.0% separated, 4.7% widowed, 7.7% divorced; Foreign born: 3.1%; Speak English only: 94.2%; With disability: 14.2%; Veterans: 7.3%; Ancestry: 49.8% Dutch, 20.1% German, 8.2% Polish, 7.6% Irish, 4.9% English
Employment: 15.7% management, business, and financial, 3.8% computer, engineering, and science, 8.1% education, legal, community service, arts, and media, 5.8% healthcare practitioners, 17.4% service, 22.9% sales and office, 4.8% natural resources, construction, and maintenance, 21.6% production, transportation, and material moving
Income: Per capita: $23,160; Median household: $54,207; Average household: $64,374; Households with income of $100,000 or more: 16.1%; Poverty rate: 9.7%
Educational Attainment: High school diploma or higher: 89.2%; Bachelor's degree or higher: 23.1%; Graduate/professional degree or higher: 6.1%
School District(s)
Hudsonville Public SD (PK-12)
　2012-13 Enrollment: 6,199 . . . . (616) 669-1740
Housing: Homeownership rate: 82.6%; Median home value: $128,500; Median year structure built: 1979; Homeowner vacancy rate: 2.3%; Median gross rent: $785 per month; Rental vacancy rate: 5.8%
Health Insurance: 92.5% have insurance; 78.4% have private insurance; 26.8% have public insurance; 7.5% do not have insurance; 0.5% of children under 18 do not have insurance
Transportation: Commute: 97.0% car, 0.1% public transportation, 0.8% walk, 1.8% work from home; Median travel time to work: 19.3 minutes
Additional Information Contacts
City of Hudsonville. . . . . (616) 669-0200
　http://www.hudsonville.org

JAMESTOWN (charter township). Covers a land area of 35.376 square miles and a water area of 0.099 square miles. Located at 42.81° N. Lat; 85.84° W. Long. Elevation is 712 feet.
Population: 7,034; Growth (since 2000): 39.0%; Density: 198.8 persons per square mile; Race: 97.2% White, 0.6% Black/African American, 1.0% Asian, 0.2% American Indian/Alaska Native, 0.0% Native Hawaiian/Other Pacific Islander, 0.7% Two or more races, 2.0% Hispanic of any race; Average household size: 3.11; Median age: 33.1; Age under 18: 31.7%; Age 65 and over: 8.1%; Males per 100 females: 101.8; Marriage status: 18.5% never married, 73.1% now married, 0.0% separated, 3.0% widowed, 5.4% divorced; Foreign born: 1.4%; Speak English only: 97.7%; With disability: 7.9%; Veterans: 7.7%; Ancestry: 47.9% Dutch, 20.2% German, 7.1% American, 6.3% English, 4.4% Irish
Employment: 20.3% management, business, and financial, 6.1% computer, engineering, and science, 6.8% education, legal, community service, arts, and media, 8.9% healthcare practitioners, 13.4% service, 22.3% sales and office, 10.0% natural resources, construction, and maintenance, 12.3% production, transportation, and material moving
Income: Per capita: $27,472; Median household: $61,507; Average household: $80,688; Households with income of $100,000 or more: 25.6%; Poverty rate: 5.4%

Educational Attainment: High school diploma or higher: 94.1%; Bachelor's degree or higher: 29.2%; Graduate/professional degree or higher: 7.2%

School District(s)

Hudsonville Public SD (PK-12)

    2012-13 Enrollment: 6,199 . . . . (616) 669-1740

Housing: Homeownership rate: 91.5%; Median home value: $189,900; Median year structure built: 1991; Homeowner vacancy rate: 1.1%; Median gross rent: $702 per month; Rental vacancy rate: 5.9%

Health Insurance: 95.2% have insurance; 88.7% have private insurance; 15.0% have public insurance; 4.8% do not have insurance; 2.9% of children under 18 do not have insurance

Transportation: Commute: 93.3% car, 0.0% public transportation, 0.9% walk, 5.1% work from home; Median travel time to work: 19.2 minutes

JENISON (CDP).

Covers a land area of 5.855 square miles and a water area of 0.076 square miles. Located at 42.90° N. Lat; 85.83° W. Long. Elevation is 604 feet.

History: Jenison grew up around a grist mill built here by Luman and Lucius Jenison in 1864.

Population: 16,538; Growth (since 2000): -3.9%; Density: 2,824.8 persons per square mile; Race: 96.0% White, 0.8% Black/African American, 0.9% Asian, 0.3% American Indian/Alaska Native, 0.0% Native Hawaiian/Other Pacific Islander, 1.5% Two or more races, 2.5% Hispanic of any race; Average household size: 2.64; Median age: 39.7; Age under 18: 25.0%; Age 65 and over: 18.0%; Males per 100 females: 93.0; Marriage status: 23.2% never married, 61.6% now married, 0.8% separated, 7.3% widowed, 7.9% divorced; Foreign born: 1.9%; Speak English only: 96.9%; With disability: 12.2%; Veterans: 8.7%; Ancestry: 41.2% Dutch, 22.9% German, 8.0% English, 7.2% Irish, 6.3% American

Employment: 13.6% management, business, and financial, 5.4% computer, engineering, and science, 7.4% education, legal, community service, arts, and media, 5.0% healthcare practitioners, 17.8% service, 24.0% sales and office, 9.1% natural resources, construction, and maintenance, 17.7% production, transportation, and material moving

Income: Per capita: $24,058; Median household: $54,089; Average household: $64,080; Households with income of $100,000 or more: 14.7%; Poverty rate: 4.8%

Educational Attainment: High school diploma or higher: 93.1%; Bachelor's degree or higher: 26.6%; Graduate/professional degree or higher: 7.3%

School District(s)

Jenison Public Schools (PK-12)

    2012-13 Enrollment: 4,727 . . . . (616) 457-8890

Housing: Homeownership rate: 86.6%; Median home value: $135,000; Median year structure built: 1974; Homeowner vacancy rate: 0.7%; Median gross rent: $1,101 per month; Rental vacancy rate: 6.4%

Health Insurance: 94.9% have insurance; 84.7% have private insurance; 27.7% have public insurance; 5.1% do not have insurance; 2.3% of children under 18 do not have insurance

Newspapers: Advance Newspapers (weekly circulation 189000)

Transportation: Commute: 95.3% car, 0.1% public transportation, 1.6% walk, 2.3% work from home; Median travel time to work: 22.4 minutes

MACATAWA (unincorporated postal area)

ZCTA: 49434

Covers a land area of 0.056 square miles and a water area of 0.316 square miles. Located at 42.77° N. Lat; 86.22° W. Long. Elevation is 591 feet.

Population: 20; Growth (since 2000): -54.5%; Density: 358.8 persons per square mile; Race: 95.0% White, 5.0% Black/African American, 0.0% Asian, 0.0% American Indian/Alaska Native, 0.0% Native Hawaiian/Other Pacific Islander, 0.0% Two or more races, 0.0% Hispanic of any race; Average household size: 1.33; Median age: 69.5; Age under 18: 0.0%; Age 65 and over: 65.0%; Males per 100 females: 150.0

Housing: Homeownership rate: 80.0%; Homeowner vacancy rate: 0.0%; Rental vacancy rate: 0.0%

MARNE (unincorporated postal area)

ZCTA: 49435

Covers a land area of 21.915 square miles and a water area of 0.179 square miles. Located at 43.02° N. Lat; 85.83° W. Long. Elevation is 673 feet.

Population: 3,549; Growth (since 2000): -1.8%; Density: 161.9 persons per square mile; Race: 97.7% White, 0.5% Black/African American, 0.3% Asian, 0.5% American Indian/Alaska Native, 0.0% Native Hawaiian/Other Pacific Islander, 0.7% Two or more races, 2.1% Hispanic of any race; Average household size: 2.84; Median age: 40.5; Age under 18: 25.3%; Age 65 and over: 11.9%; Males per 100 females: 100.4; Marriage status: 27.3% never married, 59.7% now married, 0.3% separated, 6.0% widowed, 7.0% divorced; Foreign born: 1.3%; Speak English only: 97.1%; With disability: 8.8%; Veterans: 9.3%; Ancestry: 24.7% German, 24.6% Dutch, 13.8% Polish, 10.8% Irish, 10.0% American

Employment: 12.9% management, business, and financial, 3.3% computer, engineering, and science, 7.7% education, legal, community service, arts, and media, 3.6% healthcare practitioners, 8.6% service, 32.9% sales and office, 12.6% natural resources, construction, and maintenance, 18.5% production, transportation, and material moving

Income: Per capita: $28,120; Median household: $63,241; Average household: $77,078; Households with income of $100,000 or more: 28.3%; Poverty rate: 8.3%

Educational Attainment: High school diploma or higher: 91.7%; Bachelor's degree or higher: 21.8%; Graduate/professional degree or higher: 5.3%

Housing: Homeownership rate: 92.1%; Median home value: $174,100; Median year structure built: 1972; Homeowner vacancy rate: 0.5%; Median gross rent: $895 per month; Rental vacancy rate: 8.4%

Health Insurance: 93.2% have insurance; 76.6% have private insurance; 24.8% have public insurance; 6.8% do not have insurance; 6.1% of children under 18 do not have insurance

Transportation: Commute: 90.7% car, 0.0% public transportation, 1.0% walk, 7.3% work from home; Median travel time to work: 23.7 minutes

NUNICA (unincorporated postal area)

ZCTA: 49448

Covers a land area of 33.230 square miles and a water area of 0.631 square miles. Located at 43.09° N. Lat; 86.07° W. Long. Elevation is 630 feet.

Population: 3,410; Growth (since 2000): 4.9%; Density: 102.6 persons per square mile; Race: 96.3% White, 0.5% Black/African American, 0.3% Asian, 0.3% American Indian/Alaska Native, 0.1% Native Hawaiian/Other Pacific Islander, 1.7% Two or more races, 2.3% Hispanic of any race; Average household size: 2.60; Median age: 40.5; Age under 18: 23.8%; Age 65 and over: 12.4%; Males per 100 females: 109.3; Marriage status: 19.0% never married, 65.0% now married, 0.7% separated, 4.1% widowed, 11.9% divorced; Foreign born: 1.9%; Speak English only: 95.1%; With disability: 16.7%; Veterans: 10.0%; Ancestry: 27.7% German, 19.4% Dutch, 9.5% English, 8.4% Polish, 6.7% Irish

Employment: 9.4% management, business, and financial, 2.9% computer, engineering, and science, 8.4% education, legal, community service, arts, and media, 4.9% healthcare practitioners, 16.7% service, 21.1% sales and office, 11.4% natural resources, construction, and maintenance, 25.3% production, transportation, and material moving

Income: Per capita: $20,631; Median household: $45,909; Average household: $56,111; Households with income of $100,000 or more: 11.9%; Poverty rate: 15.8%

Educational Attainment: High school diploma or higher: 86.6%; Bachelor's degree or higher: 16.0%; Graduate/professional degree or higher: 6.3%

Housing: Homeownership rate: 85.5%; Median home value: $149,100; Median year structure built: 1975; Homeowner vacancy rate: 1.9%; Median gross rent: $598 per month; Rental vacancy rate: 5.9%

Health Insurance: 85.7% have insurance; 64.4% have private insurance; 36.0% have public insurance; 14.3% do not have insurance; 8.1% of children under 18 do not have insurance

Transportation: Commute: 88.5% car, 0.7% public transportation, 4.2% walk, 5.5% work from home; Median travel time to work: 22.4 minutes

OLIVE (township).

Covers a land area of 36.182 square miles and a water area of 0.041 square miles. Located at 42.90° N. Lat; 86.09° W. Long.

Population: 4,735; Growth (since 2000): 0.9%; Density: 130.9 persons per square mile; Race: 86.2% White, 2.7% Black/African American, 1.4% Asian, 0.6% American Indian/Alaska Native, 0.0% Native Hawaiian/Other Pacific Islander, 1.8% Two or more races, 15.5% Hispanic of any race; Average household size: 3.12; Median age: 32.8; Age under 18: 27.9%; Age 65 and over: 6.7%; Males per 100 females: 119.6; Marriage status:

30.3% never married, 58.1% now married, 1.8% separated, 3.1% widowed, 8.6% divorced; Foreign born: 4.8%; Speak English only: 87.6%; With disability: 9.4%; Veterans: 7.4%; Ancestry: 38.2% Dutch, 15.6% German, 8.1% Irish, 3.4% English, 2.6% French

Employment: 13.4% management, business, and financial, 5.5% computer, engineering, and science, 7.9% education, legal, community service, arts, and media, 4.5% healthcare practitioners, 14.9% service, 25.7% sales and office, 7.7% natural resources, construction, and maintenance, 20.4% production, transportation, and material moving

Income: Per capita: $19,123; Median household: $64,225; Average household: $64,040; Households with income of $100,000 or more: 16.2%; Poverty rate: 12.4%

Educational Attainment: High school diploma or higher: 86.7%; Bachelor's degree or higher: 13.8%; Graduate/professional degree or higher: 2.5%

Housing: Homeownership rate: 88.8%; Median home value: $161,100; Median year structure built: 1984; Homeowner vacancy rate: 5.3%; Median gross rent: $859 per month; Rental vacancy rate: 3.7%

Health Insurance: 90.9% have insurance; 83.0% have private insurance; 21.9% have public insurance; 9.1% do not have insurance; 1.7% of children under 18 do not have insurance

Transportation: Commute: 93.7% car, 1.0% public transportation, 0.6% walk, 4.1% work from home; Median travel time to work: 22.4 minutes

Additional Information Contacts
Olive Township . . . . (616) 786-9996
  http://www.olivetownship.com

PARK (township). Covers a land area of 19.199 square miles and a water area of 2.125 square miles. Located at 42.82° N. Lat; 86.17° W. Long.

History: Park Township is a general law Township established in 1915, consisting of approximately 20 square miles divided by Lake Macatawa with over 90% lying North of the lake.

Population: 17,802; Growth (since 2000): 1.3%; Density: 927.3 persons per square mile; Race: 92.2% White, 0.9% Black/African American, 2.2% Asian, 0.2% American Indian/Alaska Native, 0.0% Native Hawaiian/Other Pacific Islander, 1.8% Two or more races, 8.0% Hispanic of any race; Average household size: 2.70; Median age: 42.1; Age under 18: 26.4%; Age 65 and over: 13.2%; Males per 100 females: 97.9; Marriage status: 22.1% never married, 67.8% now married, 0.7% separated, 3.3% widowed, 6.8% divorced; Foreign born: 3.9%; Speak English only: 91.3%; With disability: 7.1%; Veterans: 6.5%; Ancestry: 31.2% Dutch, 22.9% German, 11.1% English, 9.2% Irish, 5.7% Polish

Employment: 19.2% management, business, and financial, 5.5% computer, engineering, and science, 10.0% education, legal, community service, arts, and media, 5.2% healthcare practitioners, 10.4% service, 27.0% sales and office, 6.1% natural resources, construction, and maintenance, 16.6% production, transportation, and material moving

Income: Per capita: $33,170; Median household: $71,675; Average household: $94,189; Households with income of $100,000 or more: 32.9%; Poverty rate: 6.4%

Educational Attainment: High school diploma or higher: 94.9%; Bachelor's degree or higher: 40.2%; Graduate/professional degree or higher: 16.0%

Housing: Homeownership rate: 91.3%; Median home value: $196,400; Median year structure built: 1982; Homeowner vacancy rate: 2.1%; Median gross rent: $877 per month; Rental vacancy rate: 13.9%

Health Insurance: 94.3% have insurance; 81.5% have private insurance; 25.7% have public insurance; 5.7% do not have insurance; 2.9% of children under 18 do not have insurance

Transportation: Commute: 93.5% car, 0.2% public transportation, 0.3% walk, 4.5% work from home; Median travel time to work: 21.0 minutes

Additional Information Contacts
Park Township. . . . . (616) 399-4520
  http://www.parktownship.org

POLKTON (charter township). Covers a land area of 39.211 square miles and a water area of 0.505 square miles. Located at 43.07° N. Lat; 85.97° W. Long.

Population: 2,423; Growth (since 2000): 3.8%; Density: 61.8 persons per square mile; Race: 98.1% White, 0.1% Black/African American, 0.1% Asian, 0.2% American Indian/Alaska Native, 0.0% Native Hawaiian/Other Pacific Islander, 0.3% Two or more races, 2.6% Hispanic of any race; Average household size: 2.84; Median age: 40.4; Age under 18: 25.2%; Age 65 and over: 13.0%; Males per 100 females: 104.6

Housing: Homeownership rate: 90.1%; Homeowner vacancy rate: 1.3%; Rental vacancy rate: 2.3%

PORT SHELDON (township). Covers a land area of 22.299 square miles and a water area of 0.324 square miles. Located at 42.90° N. Lat; 86.18° W. Long. Elevation is 587 feet.

Population: 4,240; Growth (since 2000): -5.8%; Density: 190.1 persons per square mile; Race: 93.8% White, 0.6% Black/African American, 1.7% Asian, 0.3% American Indian/Alaska Native, 0.0% Native Hawaiian/Other Pacific Islander, 0.8% Two or more races, 6.0% Hispanic of any race; Average household size: 2.61; Median age: 45.3; Age under 18: 22.9%; Age 65 and over: 13.9%; Males per 100 females: 104.6; Marriage status: 20.0% never married, 70.3% now married, 1.7% separated, 3.6% widowed, 6.1% divorced; Foreign born: 3.8%; Speak English only: 94.4%; With disability: 11.2%; Veterans: 10.9%; Ancestry: 37.4% Dutch, 24.1% German, 11.7% English, 9.2% American, 7.2% Irish

Employment: 25.5% management, business, and financial, 6.6% computer, engineering, and science, 9.2% education, legal, community service, arts, and media, 2.6% healthcare practitioners, 19.7% service, 11.0% sales and office, 8.3% natural resources, construction, and maintenance, 17.1% production, transportation, and material moving

Income: Per capita: $31,270; Median household: $61,033; Average household: $78,406; Households with income of $100,000 or more: 26.6%; Poverty rate: 5.4%

Educational Attainment: High school diploma or higher: 90.4%; Bachelor's degree or higher: 34.6%; Graduate/professional degree or higher: 12.2%

Housing: Homeownership rate: 94.5%; Median home value: $204,100; Median year structure built: 1987; Homeowner vacancy rate: 3.3%; Median gross rent: $1,190 per month; Rental vacancy rate: 12.6%

Health Insurance: 94.4% have insurance; 81.8% have private insurance; 23.1% have public insurance; 5.6% do not have insurance; 3.8% of children under 18 do not have insurance

Transportation: Commute: 91.3% car, 0.2% public transportation, 2.3% walk, 5.5% work from home; Median travel time to work: 20.7 minutes

ROBINSON (township). Covers a land area of 38.471 square miles and a water area of 1.058 square miles. Located at 42.99° N. Lat; 86.09° W. Long. Elevation is 627 feet.

History: Robinson was settled by the four Robinson brothers (Ira, John, Lucas, and Rodney) in 1835.

Population: 6,084; Growth (since 2000): 8.9%; Density: 158.1 persons per square mile; Race: 95.4% White, 0.2% Black/African American, 0.6% Asian, 0.6% American Indian/Alaska Native, 0.0% Native Hawaiian/Other Pacific Islander, 1.5% Two or more races, 5.5% Hispanic of any race; Average household size: 2.92; Median age: 37.7; Age under 18: 28.2%; Age 65 and over: 8.5%; Males per 100 females: 107.2; Marriage status: 26.8% never married, 61.3% now married, 1.0% separated, 3.3% widowed, 8.6% divorced; Foreign born: 2.0%; Speak English only: 96.8%; With disability: 8.0%; Veterans: 10.1%; Ancestry: 30.4% Dutch, 24.2% German, 11.8% English, 11.6% Polish, 9.3% Irish

Employment: 10.4% management, business, and financial, 4.4% computer, engineering, and science, 10.5% education, legal, community service, arts, and media, 6.8% healthcare practitioners, 12.0% service, 24.4% sales and office, 8.5% natural resources, construction, and maintenance, 23.1% production, transportation, and material moving

Income: Per capita: $25,469; Median household: $62,200; Average household: $75,061; Households with income of $100,000 or more: 25.2%; Poverty rate: 9.4%

Educational Attainment: High school diploma or higher: 89.3%; Bachelor's degree or higher: 23.6%; Graduate/professional degree or higher: 8.0%

Housing: Homeownership rate: 93.5%; Median home value: $151,800; Median year structure built: 1983; Homeowner vacancy rate: 1.6%; Median gross rent: $894 per month; Rental vacancy rate: 6.3%

Health Insurance: 90.5% have insurance; 78.8% have private insurance; 25.1% have public insurance; 9.5% do not have insurance; 2.9% of children under 18 do not have insurance

Transportation: Commute: 92.9% car, 0.4% public transportation, 0.0% walk, 5.2% work from home; Median travel time to work: 23.1 minutes

Additional Information Contacts
Robinson Township. . . . . (616) 846-2210
  http://www.robinson-twp.org

SPRING LAKE (township). Covers a land area of 16.478 square miles and a water area of 2.254 square miles. Located at 43.07° N. Lat; 86.21° W. Long. Elevation is 597 feet.

History: Native American mounds nearby. Incorporated 1869.

Population: 14,300; Growth (since 2000): 8.8%; Density: 867.8 persons per square mile; Race: 96.0% White, 0.6% Black/African American, 0.8% Asian, 0.5% American Indian/Alaska Native, 0.0% Native Hawaiian/Other Pacific Islander, 1.5% Two or more races, 2.1% Hispanic of any race; Average household size: 2.44; Median age: 42.1; Age under 18: 24.9%; Age 65 and over: 17.0%; Males per 100 females: 93.2; Marriage status: 20.1% never married, 62.1% now married, 1.4% separated, 6.9% widowed, 10.8% divorced; Foreign born: 2.8%; Speak English only: 96.8%; With disability: 11.8%; Veterans: 10.0%; Ancestry: 25.8% German, 18.0% Dutch, 14.3% Irish, 13.8% English, 8.6% Polish

Employment: 15.1% management, business, and financial, 6.6% computer, engineering, and science, 12.8% education, legal, community service, arts, and media, 6.3% healthcare practitioners, 15.1% service, 26.2% sales and office, 6.1% natural resources, construction, and maintenance, 11.8% production, transportation, and material moving

Income: Per capita: $30,482; Median household: $55,815; Average household: $72,895; Households with income of $100,000 or more: 22.3%; Poverty rate: 11.4%

Educational Attainment: High school diploma or higher: 93.7%; Bachelor's degree or higher: 37.0%; Graduate/professional degree or higher: 14.4%

School District(s)
Grand Haven Area Public Schools (PK-12)
    2012-13 Enrollment: 6,026 . . . . (616) 850-5015
Spring Lake Public Schools (PK-12)
    2012-13 Enrollment: 2,455 . . . . (616) 847-7919
Walden Green Montessori (KG-12)
    2012-13 Enrollment: 221 . . . . (616) 842-4523
West Mi Academy of Arts and Academics (KG-12)
    2012-13 Enrollment: 424 . . . . (616) 844-9961

Vocational/Technical School(s)
French Academy of Cosmetology (Private, For-profit)
    Fall 2013 Enrollment: 73 . . . . (616) 844-7070
    2013-14 Tuition: $8,638

Housing: Homeownership rate: 75.8%; Median home value: $171,900; Median year structure built: 1983; Homeowner vacancy rate: 4.2%; Median gross rent: $768 per month; Rental vacancy rate: 14.9%

Health Insurance: 89.6% have insurance; 77.6% have private insurance; 29.4% have public insurance; 10.4% do not have insurance; 2.0% of children under 18 do not have insurance

Transportation: Commute: 93.1% car, 0.0% public transportation, 1.6% walk, 4.5% work from home; Median travel time to work: 21.3 minutes

Additional Information Contacts
Spring Lake Township . . . . (616) 842-1340
    http://www.springlaketwp.org

SPRING LAKE (village). Covers a land area of 1.180 square miles and a water area of 0.560 square miles. Located at 43.07° N. Lat; 86.19° W. Long. Elevation is 597 feet.

History: Spring Lake changed from a milling center, established in 1837 as Hopkins Mill, to a shipping point for fruit. Mineral springs here were popular from 1870 to 1900, attracting visitors seeking cures. The town continued as a resort center.

Population: 2,323; Growth (since 2000): -7.6%; Density: 1,969.3 persons per square mile; Race: 96.7% White, 0.2% Black/African American, 0.3% Asian, 0.8% American Indian/Alaska Native, 0.1% Native Hawaiian/Other Pacific Islander, 1.3% Two or more races, 1.8% Hispanic of any race; Average household size: 2.17; Median age: 44.8; Age under 18: 21.6%; Age 65 and over: 20.5%; Males per 100 females: 88.7

School District(s)
Grand Haven Area Public Schools (PK-12)
    2012-13 Enrollment: 6,026 . . . . (616) 850-5015
Spring Lake Public Schools (PK-12)
    2012-13 Enrollment: 2,455 . . . . (616) 847-7919
Walden Green Montessori (KG-12)
    2012-13 Enrollment: 221 . . . . (616) 842-4523
West Mi Academy of Arts and Academics (KG-12)
    2012-13 Enrollment: 424 . . . . (616) 844-9961

Vocational/Technical School(s)
French Academy of Cosmetology (Private, For-profit)
    Fall 2013 Enrollment: 73 . . . . (616) 844-7070
    2013-14 Tuition: $8,638

Housing: Homeownership rate: 77.1%; Homeowner vacancy rate: 6.9%; Rental vacancy rate: 11.2%

Additional Information Contacts
Village of Spring Lake . . . . (616) 842-1393
    http://www.springlakevillage.org

TALLMADGE (charter township). Covers a land area of 32.211 square miles and a water area of 0.820 square miles. Located at 42.99° N. Lat; 85.84° W. Long. Elevation is 663 feet.

Population: 7,575; Growth (since 2000): 10.1%; Density: 235.2 persons per square mile; Race: 96.6% White, 0.5% Black/African American, 0.7% Asian, 0.5% American Indian/Alaska Native, 0.0% Native Hawaiian/Other Pacific Islander, 1.2% Two or more races, 2.0% Hispanic of any race; Average household size: 2.78; Median age: 40.1; Age under 18: 25.1%; Age 65 and over: 11.5%; Males per 100 females: 98.0; Marriage status: 27.2% never married, 62.7% now married, 0.2% separated, 3.3% widowed, 6.8% divorced; Foreign born: 1.1%; Speak English only: 97.7%; With disability: 8.2%; Veterans: 8.8%; Ancestry: 34.0% Dutch, 24.4% German, 8.9% Polish, 8.6% Irish, 5.7% English

Employment: 15.7% management, business, and financial, 5.0% computer, engineering, and science, 7.6% education, legal, community service, arts, and media, 1.8% healthcare practitioners, 9.3% service, 30.3% sales and office, 12.4% natural resources, construction, and maintenance, 17.9% production, transportation, and material moving

Income: Per capita: $28,181; Median household: $65,026; Average household: $79,600; Households with income of $100,000 or more: 26.8%; Poverty rate: 5.5%

Educational Attainment: High school diploma or higher: 91.3%; Bachelor's degree or higher: 25.3%; Graduate/professional degree or higher: 4.9%

Housing: Homeownership rate: 86.1%; Median home value: $179,600; Median year structure built: 1977; Homeowner vacancy rate: 1.3%; Median gross rent: $956 per month; Rental vacancy rate: 6.2%

Health Insurance: 95.1% have insurance; 83.4% have private insurance; 24.1% have public insurance; 4.9% do not have insurance; 3.6% of children under 18 do not have insurance

Transportation: Commute: 94.6% car, 0.0% public transportation, 0.4% walk, 3.9% work from home; Median travel time to work: 22.9 minutes

Additional Information Contacts
Tallmadge Charter Township . . . . (616) 677-1248
    http://www.tallmadge.com

WEST OLIVE (unincorporated postal area)
ZCTA: 49460
    Covers a land area of 54.626 square miles and a water area of 6.997 square miles. Located at 42.93° N. Lat; 86.15° W. Long. Elevation is 614 feet.

Population: 8,126; Growth (since 2000): 5.6%; Density: 148.8 persons per square mile; Race: 92.1% White, 1.4% Black/African American, 1.2% Asian, 0.5% American Indian/Alaska Native, 0.0% Native Hawaiian/Other Pacific Islander, 1.5% Two or more races, 8.6% Hispanic of any race; Average household size: 2.81; Median age: 38.8; Age under 18: 26.8%; Age 65 and over: 10.3%; Males per 100 females: 111.1; Marriage status: 27.1% never married, 62.4% now married, 1.1% separated, 3.0% widowed, 7.5% divorced; Foreign born: 5.3%; Speak English only: 91.3%; With disability: 9.6%; Veterans: 9.2%; Ancestry: 32.0% Dutch, 21.6% German, 9.3% Irish, 9.1% English, 6.1% Polish

Employment: 18.6% management, business, and financial, 7.7% computer, engineering, and science, 9.5% education, legal, community service, arts, and media, 2.3% healthcare practitioners, 14.1% service, 17.6% sales and office, 9.4% natural resources, construction, and maintenance, 20.7% production, transportation, and material moving

Income: Per capita: $26,379; Median household: $65,230; Average household: $75,955; Households with income of $100,000 or more: 25.6%; Poverty rate: 7.5%

Educational Attainment: High school diploma or higher: 89.6%; Bachelor's degree or higher: 27.2%; Graduate/professional degree or higher: 9.5%

School District(s)
Ottawa Area ISD (PK-12)
    2012-13 Enrollment: 985 . . . . (616) 738-8940

West Ottawa Public SD (PK-12)
  2012-13 Enrollment: 7,310 . . . . (616) 738-5795
  Housing: Homeownership rate: 92.8%; Median home value: $178,300;
  Median year structure built: 1987; Homeowner vacancy rate: 4.5%;
  Median gross rent: $1,026 per month; Rental vacancy rate: 10.0%
  Health Insurance: 90.9% have insurance; 81.5% have private
  insurance; 23.1% have public insurance; 9.1% do not have insurance;
  3.2% of children under 18 do not have insurance
  Transportation: Commute: 93.1% car, 0.3% public transportation, 1.2%
  walk, 5.1% work from home; Median travel time to work: 22.5 minutes

WRIGHT (township). Covers a land area of 36.100 square miles and a
water area of 0.174 square miles. Located at 43.08° N. Lat; 85.85° W.
Long. Elevation is 869 feet.
Population: 3,147; Growth (since 2000): -4.2%; Density: 87.2 persons per
square mile; Race: 96.3% White, 0.5% Black/African American, 0.3%
Asian, 0.6% American Indian/Alaska Native, 0.0% Native Hawaiian/Other
Pacific Islander, 0.7% Two or more races, 3.3% Hispanic of any race;
Average household size: 2.77; Median age: 39.8; Age under 18: 25.0%;
Age 65 and over: 12.5%; Males per 100 females: 101.5; Marriage status:
25.1% never married, 63.7% now married, 0.5% separated, 5.4%
widowed, 5.9% divorced; Foreign born: 3.6%; Speak English only: 92.5%;
With disability: 8.5%; Veterans: 4.8%; Ancestry: 34.0% German, 23.3%
Dutch, 11.6% Polish, 9.8% Irish, 8.5% English
Employment: 12.4% management, business, and financial, 1.2%
computer, engineering, and science, 3.7% education, legal, community
service, arts, and media, 5.6% healthcare practitioners, 18.3% service,
22.3% sales and office, 19.6% natural resources, construction, and
maintenance, 17.0% production, transportation, and material moving
Income: Per capita: $27,018; Median household: $59,911; Average
household: $79,630; Households with income of $100,000 or more: 28.3%;
Poverty rate: 7.4%
Educational Attainment: High school diploma or higher: 90.4%;
Bachelor's degree or higher: 13.8%; Graduate/professional degree or
higher: 2.4%
Housing: Homeownership rate: 90.1%; Median home value: $156,100;
Median year structure built: 1973; Homeowner vacancy rate: 1.0%; Median
gross rent: $810 per month; Rental vacancy rate: 7.5%
Health Insurance: 91.4% have insurance; 78.5% have private insurance;
21.8% have public insurance; 8.6% do not have insurance; 2.3% of
children under 18 do not have insurance
Transportation: Commute: 90.4% car, 0.0% public transportation, 1.0%
walk, 7.7% work from home; Median travel time to work: 22.4 minutes

ZEELAND (charter township). Covers a land area of 34.400 square
miles and a water area of 0.065 square miles. Located at 42.81° N. Lat;
85.96° W. Long. Elevation is 646 feet.
History: Located in Dutch heritage area, Dutch village to northwest.
Settled 1847 by Dutch; Incorporated as village 1875, as city 1907.
Population: 9,971; Growth (since 2000): 31.0%; Density: 289.9 persons
per square mile; Race: 91.5% White, 0.7% Black/African American, 3.2%
Asian, 0.4% American Indian/Alaska Native, 0.0% Native Hawaiian/Other
Pacific Islander, 1.8% Two or more races, 7.0% Hispanic of any race;
Average household size: 2.98; Median age: 33.8; Age under 18: 31.5%;
Age 65 and over: 9.6%; Males per 100 females: 99.8; Marriage status:
23.8% never married, 66.8% now married, 0.4% separated, 2.3%
widowed, 7.1% divorced; Foreign born: 5.5%; Speak English only: 90.3%;
With disability: 8.1%; Veterans: 6.8%; Ancestry: 46.8% Dutch, 19.3%
German, 5.0% Irish, 4.1% English, 2.7% Polish
Employment: 13.2% management, business, and financial, 4.2%
computer, engineering, and science, 5.2% education, legal, community
service, arts, and media, 5.0% healthcare practitioners, 15.1% service,
25.4% sales and office, 8.5% natural resources, construction, and
maintenance, 23.3% production, transportation, and material moving
Income: Per capita: $23,308; Median household: $64,761; Average
household: $72,872; Households with income of $100,000 or more: 27.1%;
Poverty rate: 10.5%
Educational Attainment: High school diploma or higher: 92.5%;
Bachelor's degree or higher: 22.5%; Graduate/professional degree or
higher: 6.8%
School District(s)
Zeeland Public Schools (PK-12)
  2012-13 Enrollment: 5,697 . . . . (616) 748-3000

Housing: Homeownership rate: 93.6%; Median home value: $155,900;
Median year structure built: 1994; Homeowner vacancy rate: 2.0%; Median
gross rent: $585 per month; Rental vacancy rate: 12.7%
Health Insurance: 92.9% have insurance; 82.1% have private insurance;
19.8% have public insurance; 7.1% do not have insurance; 2.0% of
children under 18 do not have insurance
Hospitals: Spectrum Health Zeeland Community Hospital (57 beds)
Newspapers: Zeeland Record (weekly circulation 1500)
Transportation: Commute: 95.0% car, 0.5% public transportation, 0.9%
walk, 3.4% work from home; Median travel time to work: 15.8 minutes
Airports: Ottawa Executive (general aviation)
Additional Information Contacts
Zeeland Charter Township . . . . (616) 772-6701
  http://www.zeelandtwp.org

ZEELAND (city). Covers a land area of 2.992 square miles and a water
area of 0.019 square miles. Located at 42.81° N. Lat; 86.01° W. Long.
Elevation is 646 feet.
History: The site of Zeeland was purchased in 1847 by Johannes Vander
Luyster, and named for the Netherlands province of Zeeland, the former
home of Vander Luyster and his colony of Dutch immigrants. Zeeland was
incorporated in 1904, and became the center of a baby chick industry.
Population: 5,504; Growth (since 2000): -5.2%; Density: 1,839.5 persons
per square mile; Race: 93.8% White, 1.1% Black/African American, 1.3%
Asian, 0.4% American Indian/Alaska Native, 0.0% Native Hawaiian/Other
Pacific Islander, 2.1% Two or more races, 6.4% Hispanic of any race;
Average household size: 2.37; Median age: 38.8; Age under 18: 25.4%;
Age 65 and over: 22.7%; Males per 100 females: 81.2; Marriage status:
22.5% never married, 56.9% now married, 3.9% separated, 12.7%
widowed, 7.9% divorced; Foreign born: 2.8%; Speak English only: 93.5%;
With disability: 14.2%; Veterans: 7.8%; Ancestry: 54.5% Dutch, 15.1%
German, 10.2% Irish, 8.9% French, 6.4% English
Employment: 17.9% management, business, and financial, 4.7%
computer, engineering, and science, 11.0% education, legal, community
service, arts, and media, 2.7% healthcare practitioners, 19.6% service,
18.0% sales and office, 7.2% natural resources, construction, and
maintenance, 18.9% production, transportation, and material moving
Income: Per capita: $23,614; Median household: $41,796; Average
household: $55,134; Households with income of $100,000 or more: 9.6%;
Poverty rate: 15.8%
Educational Attainment: High school diploma or higher: 90.7%;
Bachelor's degree or higher: 31.0%; Graduate/professional degree or
higher: 10.3%
School District(s)
Zeeland Public Schools (PK-12)
  2012-13 Enrollment: 5,697 . . . . (616) 748-3000
Housing: Homeownership rate: 73.1%; Median home value: $125,300;
Median year structure built: 1963; Homeowner vacancy rate: 4.2%; Median
gross rent: $697 per month; Rental vacancy rate: 8.8%
Health Insurance: 93.7% have insurance; 71.5% have private insurance;
40.6% have public insurance; 6.3% do not have insurance; 0.0% of
children under 18 do not have insurance
Hospitals: Spectrum Health Zeeland Community Hospital (57 beds)
Safety: Violent crime rate: 7.2 per 10,000 population; Property crime rate:
218.8 per 10,000 population
Newspapers: Zeeland Record (weekly circulation 1500)
Transportation: Commute: 90.2% car, 0.0% public transportation, 1.8%
walk, 5.6% work from home; Median travel time to work: 14.9 minutes
Airports: Ottawa Executive (general aviation)
Additional Information Contacts
City of Zeeland . . . . (616) 772-6400
  http://www.ci.zeeland.mi.us

Presque Isle County

Located in northeastern Michigan; bounded on the northeast by Lake
Huron; drained by the Black, Rainy, Ocqueoc, and North Branch of the
Thunder Bay Rivers. Covers a land area of 658.719 square miles, a water
area of 1,914.037 square miles, and is located in the Eastern Time Zone at
45.49° N. Lat., 83.38° W. Long. The county was founded in 1840. County
seat is Rogers City.

Weather Station: Onaway State Park — Elevation: 689 feet

	Jan	Feb	Mar	Apr	May	Jun	Jul	Aug	Sep	Oct	Nov	Dec
High	28	32	41	55	69	78	82	80	72	59	44	33
Low	11	12	19	31	42	51	56	55	49	39	29	19
Precip	1.9	1.3	1.8	2.5	2.7	2.7	2.8	3.4	3.2	3.0	2.3	2.0
Snow	23.7	17.1	11.4	5.4	0.2	0.0	0.0	0.0	0.0	0.5	8.4	22.3

High and Low temperatures in degrees Fahrenheit; Precipitation and Snow in inches

Weather Station: Rogers City — Elevation: 615 feet

	Jan	Feb	Mar	Apr	May	Jun	Jul	Aug	Sep	Oct	Nov	Dec
High	28	30	38	51	64	74	79	78	70	56	44	33
Low	13	13	19	31	41	51	57	56	49	39	30	19
Precip	2.0	1.4	1.7	2.4	2.8	2.9	2.9	3.5	3.1	2.8	2.2	2.1
Snow	22.8	15.9	10.6	4.5	0.1	0.0	0.0	0.0	0.0	0.3	6.2	18.4

High and Low temperatures in degrees Fahrenheit; Precipitation and Snow in inches

Population: 13,376; Growth (since 2000): -7.2%; Density: 20.3 persons per square mile; Race: 97.6% White, 0.4% Black/African American, 0.3% Asian, 0.7% American Indian/Alaska Native, 0.0% Native Hawaiian/Other Pacific Islander, 1.0% two or more races, 0.9% Hispanic of any race; Average household size: 2.20; Median age: 51.7; Age under 18: 17.5%; Age 65 and over: 26.2%; Males per 100 females: 100.5; Marriage status: 18.9% never married, 59.8% now married, 1.3% separated, 10.2% widowed, 11.1% divorced; Foreign born: 1.5%; Speak English only: 96.4%; With disability: 18.0%; Veterans: 13.7%; Ancestry: 38.3% German, 28.3% Polish, 11.0% Irish, 10.2% English, 8.2% French

Religion: Six largest groups: 28.9% Catholicism, 18.6% Lutheran, 6.0% Non-denominational Protestant, 2.8% Methodist/Pietist, 1.4% Presbyterian-Reformed, 1.2% Latter-day Saints

Economy: Unemployment rate: 7.9%; Leading industries: 19.1% retail trade; 13.2% construction; 12.4% accommodation and food services; Farms: 323 totaling 81,536 acres; Company size: 0 employ 1,000 or more persons, 0 employ 500 to 999 persons, 3 employ 100 to 499 persons, 337 employ less than 100 persons; Business ownership: 213 women-owned, n/a Black-owned, n/a Hispanic-owned, n/a Asian-owned

Employment: 11.2% management, business, and financial, 2.9% computer, engineering, and science, 8.3% education, legal, community service, arts, and media, 7.4% healthcare practitioners, 18.5% service, 21.9% sales and office, 15.4% natural resources, construction, and maintenance, 14.4% production, transportation, and material moving

Income: Per capita: $22,788; Median household: $39,652; Average household: $48,147; Households with income of $100,000 or more: 6.6%; Poverty rate: 12.9%

Educational Attainment: High school diploma or higher: 86.8%; Bachelor's degree or higher: 16.3%; Graduate/professional degree or higher: 5.5%

Housing: Homeownership rate: 86.6%; Median home value: $95,000; Median year structure built: 1970; Homeowner vacancy rate: 3.8%; Median gross rent: $530 per month; Rental vacancy rate: 17.3%

Vital Statistics: Birth rate: 63.5 per 10,000 population; Death rate: 132.4 per 10,000 population; Age-adjusted cancer mortality rate: 226.0 deaths per 100,000 population

Health Insurance: 87.7% have insurance; 70.4% have private insurance; 43.0% have public insurance; 12.3% do not have insurance; 5.7% of children under 18 do not have insurance

Health Care: Physicians: 3.0 per 10,000 population; Hospital beds: 19.0 per 10,000 population; Hospital admissions: 232.8 per 10,000 population

Transportation: Commute: 91.1% car, 0.1% public transportation, 1.3% walk, 5.6% work from home; Median travel time to work: 23.8 minutes

Presidential Election: 45.1% Obama, 53.6% Romney (2012)

National and State Parks: Onaway State Park; P H Hoeft State Park; Thompson's Harbor State Park

Additional Information Contacts
Presque Isle Government . . . . (989) 734-3288
   http://www.presqueislecounty.org

Presque Isle County Communities

ALLIS (township). Covers a land area of 64.748 square miles and a water area of 1.350 square miles. Located at 45.27° N. Lat; 84.19° W. Long.
Population: 948; Growth (since 2000): -8.4%; Density: 14.6 persons per square mile; Race: 96.5% White, 0.3% Black/African American, 0.1% Asian, 1.9% American Indian/Alaska Native, 0.0% Native Hawaiian/Other Pacific Islander, 1.2% Two or more races, 0.5% Hispanic of any race;

Average household size: 2.39; Median age: 47.5; Age under 18: 21.9%; Age 65 and over: 18.9%; Males per 100 females: 98.7
Housing: Homeownership rate: 90.5%; Homeowner vacancy rate: 2.2%; Rental vacancy rate: 15.9%

BEARINGER (township). Covers a land area of 61.442 square miles and a water area of 2.142 square miles. Located at 45.53° N. Lat; 84.20° W. Long.
Population: 369; Growth (since 2000): 12.2%; Density: 6.0 persons per square mile; Race: 97.6% White, 1.4% Black/African American, 0.0% Asian, 0.5% American Indian/Alaska Native, 0.0% Native Hawaiian/Other Pacific Islander, 0.3% Two or more races, 1.1% Hispanic of any race; Average household size: 2.08; Median age: 58.5; Age under 18: 13.3%; Age 65 and over: 34.1%; Males per 100 females: 101.6
Housing: Homeownership rate: 94.4%; Homeowner vacancy rate: 7.7%; Rental vacancy rate: 16.7%

BELKNAP (township). Covers a land area of 35.703 square miles and a water area of 0.049 square miles. Located at 45.32° N. Lat; 83.84° W. Long. Elevation is 823 feet.
Population: 751; Growth (since 2000): -12.1%; Density: 21.0 persons per square mile; Race: 98.7% White, 0.1% Black/African American, 0.0% Asian, 0.5% American Indian/Alaska Native, 0.0% Native Hawaiian/Other Pacific Islander, 0.7% Two or more races, 0.5% Hispanic of any race; Average household size: 2.27; Median age: 50.6; Age under 18: 17.4%; Age 65 and over: 23.3%; Males per 100 females: 103.5
Housing: Homeownership rate: 94.1%; Homeowner vacancy rate: 1.6%; Rental vacancy rate: 19.2%

BISMARCK (township). Covers a land area of 67.508 square miles and a water area of 2.518 square miles. Located at 45.29° N. Lat; 83.94° W. Long.
Population: 386; Growth (since 2000): -5.4%; Density: 5.7 persons per square mile; Race: 98.2% White, 0.3% Black/African American, 0.3% Asian, 0.8% American Indian/Alaska Native, 0.0% Native Hawaiian/Other Pacific Islander, 0.5% Two or more races, 0.8% Hispanic of any race; Average household size: 2.23; Median age: 51.5; Age under 18: 17.6%; Age 65 and over: 25.6%; Males per 100 females: 106.4
Housing: Homeownership rate: 91.0%; Homeowner vacancy rate: 6.7%; Rental vacancy rate: 4.5%

CASE (township). Covers a land area of 67.203 square miles and a water area of 1.035 square miles. Located at 45.28° N. Lat; 84.07° W. Long.
History: Case Township was named for Charles E. Case, an early resident.
Population: 903; Growth (since 2000): -4.1%; Density: 13.4 persons per square mile; Race: 97.3% White, 0.2% Black/African American, 0.4% Asian, 0.7% American Indian/Alaska Native, 0.0% Native Hawaiian/Other Pacific Islander, 1.3% Two or more races, 1.1% Hispanic of any race; Average household size: 2.43; Median age: 45.8; Age under 18: 24.0%; Age 65 and over: 21.0%; Males per 100 females: 102.5
Housing: Homeownership rate: 89.7%; Homeowner vacancy rate: 4.0%; Rental vacancy rate: 24.5%

HAWKS (unincorporated postal area)
ZCTA: 49743
   Covers a land area of 90.060 square miles and a water area of 1.766 square miles. Located at 45.27° N. Lat; 83.89° W. Long. Elevation is 833 feet.
   Population: 769; Growth (since 2000): -10.6%; Density: 8.5 persons per square mile; Race: 98.2% White, 0.1% Black/African American, 0.3% Asian, 0.4% American Indian/Alaska Native, 0.0% Native Hawaiian/Other Pacific Islander, 1.0% Two or more races, 0.5% Hispanic of any race; Average household size: 2.29; Median age: 50.6; Age under 18: 19.0%; Age 65 and over: 24.3%; Males per 100 females: 107.8
   Housing: Homeownership rate: 93.1%; Homeowner vacancy rate: 4.7%; Rental vacancy rate: 14.7%

KRAKOW (township). Covers a land area of 55.655 square miles and a water area of 5.085 square miles. Located at 45.30° N. Lat; 83.59° W. Long.
Population: 705; Growth (since 2000): 13.3%; Density: 12.7 persons per square mile; Race: 99.7% White, 0.0% Black/African American, 0.0%

Asian, 0.1% American Indian/Alaska Native, 0.0% Native Hawaiian/Other Pacific Islander, 0.1% Two or more races, 0.1% Hispanic of any race; Average household size: 2.20; Median age: 55.3; Age under 18: 13.8%; Age 65 and over: 29.6%; Males per 100 females: 109.2
Housing: Homeownership rate: 94.7%; Homeowner vacancy rate: 5.8%; Rental vacancy rate: 12.5%

METZ (township). Covers a land area of 35.579 square miles and a water area of 0.181 square miles. Located at 45.25° N. Lat; 83.83° W. Long. Elevation is 830 feet.
Population: 302; Growth (since 2000): -8.8%; Density: 8.5 persons per square mile; Race: 99.0% White, 0.0% Black/African American, 0.3% Asian, 0.7% American Indian/Alaska Native, 0.0% Native Hawaiian/Other Pacific Islander, 0.0% Two or more races, 1.3% Hispanic of any race; Average household size: 2.21; Median age: 54.1; Age under 18: 14.6%; Age 65 and over: 25.8%; Males per 100 females: 111.2
Housing: Homeownership rate: 90.3%; Homeowner vacancy rate: 6.2%; Rental vacancy rate: 7.1%

MILLERSBURG (village). Covers a land area of 0.992 square miles and a water area of 0.002 square miles. Located at 45.33° N. Lat; 84.06° W. Long. Elevation is 797 feet.
Population: 206; Growth (since 2000): -21.7%; Density: 207.7 persons per square mile; Race: 97.1% White, 0.0% Black/African American, 0.0% Asian, 1.0% American Indian/Alaska Native, 0.0% Native Hawaiian/Other Pacific Islander, 1.9% Two or more races, 2.4% Hispanic of any race; Average household size: 2.40; Median age: 38.2; Age under 18: 28.6%; Age 65 and over: 18.0%; Males per 100 females: 90.7
Housing: Homeownership rate: 80.2%; Homeowner vacancy rate: 4.2%; Rental vacancy rate: 19.0%

MOLTKE (township). Covers a land area of 33.915 square miles and a water area of 0.027 square miles. Located at 45.41° N. Lat; 83.95° W. Long. Elevation is 912 feet.
Population: 296; Growth (since 2000): -15.9%; Density: 8.7 persons per square mile; Race: 95.3% White, 3.4% Black/African American, 0.0% Asian, 0.0% American Indian/Alaska Native, 0.0% Native Hawaiian/Other Pacific Islander, 1.4% Two or more races, 0.3% Hispanic of any race; Average household size: 2.31; Median age: 50.8; Age under 18: 18.2%; Age 65 and over: 21.3%; Males per 100 females: 122.6
Housing: Homeownership rate: 94.5%; Homeowner vacancy rate: 0.8%; Rental vacancy rate: 0.0%

NORTH ALLIS (township). Covers a land area of 32.716 square miles and a water area of 1.647 square miles. Located at 45.42° N. Lat; 84.19° W. Long.
Population: 521; Growth (since 2000): -15.7%; Density: 15.9 persons per square mile; Race: 96.5% White, 0.0% Black/African American, 0.4% Asian, 0.6% American Indian/Alaska Native, 0.0% Native Hawaiian/Other Pacific Islander, 1.9% Two or more races, 1.9% Hispanic of any race; Average household size: 2.35; Median age: 47.5; Age under 18: 22.1%; Age 65 and over: 21.5%; Males per 100 females: 98.9
Housing: Homeownership rate: 91.9%; Homeowner vacancy rate: 3.3%; Rental vacancy rate: 0.0%

OCQUEOC (township). Covers a land area of 52.148 square miles and a water area of 0.304 square miles. Located at 45.41° N. Lat; 84.05° W. Long. Elevation is 768 feet.
Population: 655; Growth (since 2000): 3.3%; Density: 12.6 persons per square mile; Race: 98.6% White, 0.3% Black/African American, 0.2% Asian, 0.3% American Indian/Alaska Native, 0.0% Native Hawaiian/Other Pacific Islander, 0.6% Two or more races, 0.6% Hispanic of any race; Average household size: 2.20; Median age: 55.9; Age under 18: 15.3%; Age 65 and over: 33.6%; Males per 100 females: 106.0
Housing: Homeownership rate: 92.9%; Homeowner vacancy rate: 4.8%; Rental vacancy rate: 19.2%

ONAWAY (city). Covers a land area of 1.567 square miles and a water area of 0.001 square miles. Located at 45.36° N. Lat; 84.23° W. Long. Elevation is 850 feet.
History: Onaway was founded in 1881 as Shaw Post Office. The town developed as a resort center, depending on tourist trade after its wood-rim plant was destroyed by fire in 1926.
Population: 880; Growth (since 2000): -11.4%; Density: 561.7 persons per square mile; Race: 95.8% White, 0.7% Black/African American, 0.1%

Asian, 0.9% American Indian/Alaska Native, 0.0% Native Hawaiian/Other Pacific Islander, 2.2% Two or more races, 1.6% Hispanic of any race; Average household size: 2.21; Median age: 43.6; Age under 18: 23.2%; Age 65 and over: 19.5%; Males per 100 females: 87.2
School District(s)
Onaway Area Community SD (PK-12)
    2012-13 Enrollment: 667. . . . . (989) 733-4950
Presque Isle Academy II (KG-12)
    2012-13 Enrollment: 61. . . . . (989) 733-6708
Housing: Homeownership rate: 60.9%; Homeowner vacancy rate: 7.5%; Rental vacancy rate: 17.6%
Newspapers: Onaway Outlook (weekly circulation 2000)

POSEN (township). Covers a land area of 35.142 square miles and a water area of 0.373 square miles. Located at 45.25° N. Lat; 83.69° W. Long. Elevation is 797 feet.
History: Posen Township was settled in 1870 by a group of Polish immigrants led by Lawrence Kowalski. They named Posen for the province of Poznan in Poland.
Population: 850; Growth (since 2000): -11.4%; Density: 24.2 persons per square mile; Race: 97.4% White, 0.4% Black/African American, 0.4% Asian, 0.5% American Indian/Alaska Native, 0.1% Native Hawaiian/Other Pacific Islander, 1.1% Two or more races, 1.5% Hispanic of any race; Average household size: 2.29; Median age: 47.5; Age under 18: 19.4%; Age 65 and over: 21.3%; Males per 100 females: 107.8
School District(s)
Posen Consolidated SD No. 9 (KG-12)
    2012-13 Enrollment: 247. . . . . (989) 766-2573
Housing: Homeownership rate: 85.0%; Homeowner vacancy rate: 2.2%; Rental vacancy rate: 27.0%

POSEN (village). Covers a land area of 0.999 square miles and a water area of 0 square miles. Located at 45.26° N. Lat; 83.70° W. Long. Elevation is 797 feet.
History: Many of the early residents of Posen were of Polish ancestry, who settled here about 1870 when it was a thriving lumber town. When the timber was gone, the people turned to farming.
Population: 234; Growth (since 2000): -19.9%; Density: 234.3 persons per square mile; Race: 96.2% White, 0.0% Black/African American, 0.0% Asian, 1.3% American Indian/Alaska Native, 0.4% Native Hawaiian/Other Pacific Islander, 2.1% Two or more races, 0.0% Hispanic of any race; Average household size: 2.07; Median age: 46.0; Age under 18: 22.2%; Age 65 and over: 23.5%; Males per 100 females: 85.7
School District(s)
Posen Consolidated SD No. 9 (KG-12)
    2012-13 Enrollment: 247. . . . . (989) 766-2573
Housing: Homeownership rate: 75.4%; Homeowner vacancy rate: 5.7%; Rental vacancy rate: 38.6%

PRESQUE ISLE (township). Covers a land area of 35.422 square miles and a water area of 11.742 square miles. Located at 45.27° N. Lat; 83.45° W. Long. Elevation is 620 feet.
History: Lighthouse nearby.
Population: 1,656; Growth (since 2000): -2.1%; Density: 46.8 persons per square mile; Race: 99.0% White, 0.1% Black/African American, 0.2% Asian, 0.3% American Indian/Alaska Native, 0.0% Native Hawaiian/Other Pacific Islander, 0.4% Two or more races, 1.0% Hispanic of any race; Average household size: 2.09; Median age: 56.6; Age under 18: 12.7%; Age 65 and over: 31.1%; Males per 100 females: 106.0
Housing: Homeownership rate: 95.9%; Homeowner vacancy rate: 3.2%; Rental vacancy rate: 37.7%

PRESQUE ISLE HARBOR (CDP). Covers a land area of 6.249 square miles and a water area of 0.622 square miles. Located at 45.32° N. Lat; 83.49° W. Long.
Population: 600; Growth (since 2000): n/a; Density: 96.0 persons per square mile; Race: 98.8% White, 0.2% Black/African American, 0.2% Asian, 0.5% American Indian/Alaska Native, 0.0% Native Hawaiian/Other Pacific Islander, 0.3% Two or more races, 1.2% Hispanic of any race; Average household size: 1.95; Median age: 60.7; Age under 18: 9.3%; Age 65 and over: 36.5%; Males per 100 females: 111.3
Housing: Homeownership rate: 96.4%; Homeowner vacancy rate: 3.2%; Rental vacancy rate: 15.4%

PULAWSKI (township). Covers a land area of 41.836 square miles and a water area of 1.984 square miles. Located at 45.36° N. Lat; 83.70° W. Long.
Population: 343; Growth (since 2000): -7.8%; Density: 8.2 persons per square mile; Race: 97.7% White, 0.0% Black/African American, 0.0% Asian, 0.3% American Indian/Alaska Native, 0.0% Native Hawaiian/Other Pacific Islander, 2.0% Two or more races, 0.0% Hispanic of any race; Average household size: 2.49; Median age: 48.1; Age under 18: 21.3%; Age 65 and over: 22.7%; Males per 100 females: 99.4
Housing: Homeownership rate: 94.2%; Homeowner vacancy rate: 1.5%; Rental vacancy rate: 11.1%

ROGERS (township). Covers a land area of 33.611 square miles and a water area of 0.124 square miles. Located at 45.45° N. Lat; 83.88° W. Long.
Population: 984; Growth (since 2000): 3.7%; Density: 29.3 persons per square mile; Race: 96.2% White, 0.4% Black/African American, 0.2% Asian, 1.5% American Indian/Alaska Native, 0.0% Native Hawaiian/Other Pacific Islander, 1.6% Two or more races, 0.5% Hispanic of any race; Average household size: 2.22; Median age: 53.8; Age under 18: 15.9%; Age 65 and over: 28.5%; Males per 100 females: 103.7
Housing: Homeownership rate: 94.1%; Homeowner vacancy rate: 1.9%; Rental vacancy rate: 18.8%

ROGERS CITY (city). County seat. Covers a land area of 4.523 square miles and a water area of 3.824 square miles. Located at 45.42° N. Lat; 83.80° W. Long. Elevation is 600 feet.
History: Rogers City began when Albert Molitor built a dock and mill at this place on Lake Huron. The village that grew up around the mill was named for William E. Rogers, who had come to the area with Molitor. A limestone quarry provided Rogers City with its source of revenue in the early 1900's. The limestone was shipped from the nearby port named Calcite.
Population: 2,827; Growth (since 2000): -14.9%; Density: 625.0 persons per square mile; Race: 97.3% White, 0.6% Black/African American, 0.7% Asian, 0.5% American Indian/Alaska Native, 0.0% Native Hawaiian/Other Pacific Islander, 0.8% Two or more races, 0.8% Hispanic of any race; Average household size: 2.03; Median age: 51.9; Age under 18: 15.7%; Age 65 and over: 29.0%; Males per 100 females: 91.3; Marriage status: 14.9% never married, 55.1% now married, 2.0% separated, 14.8% widowed, 15.2% divorced; Foreign born: 2.1%; Speak English only: 97.4%; With disability: 17.5%; Veterans: 10.8%; Ancestry: 46.8% German, 30.2% Polish, 10.2% Irish, 8.5% French, 7.5% English
Employment: 7.9% management, business, and financial, 2.5% computer, engineering, and science, 13.1% education, legal, community service, arts, and media, 9.7% healthcare practitioners, 20.9% service, 21.7% sales and office, 15.7% natural resources, construction, and maintenance, 8.6% production, transportation, and material moving
Income: Per capita: $23,910; Median household: $38,691; Average household: $47,529; Households with income of $100,000 or more: 7.0%; Poverty rate: 10.2%
Educational Attainment: High school diploma or higher: 87.7%; Bachelor's degree or higher: 19.8%; Graduate/professional degree or higher: 7.6%

School District(s)
Rogers City Area Schools (KG-12)
    2012-13 Enrollment: 557 . . . . (989) 734-9100
Housing: Homeownership rate: 74.6%; Median home value: $75,400; Median year structure built: 1955; Homeowner vacancy rate: 4.1%; Median gross rent: $518 per month; Rental vacancy rate: 14.0%
Health Insurance: 89.9% have insurance; 74.4% have private insurance; 42.9% have public insurance; 10.1% do not have insurance; 1.7% of children under 18 do not have insurance
Safety: Violent crime rate: 10.9 per 10,000 population; Property crime rate: 159.2 per 10,000 population
Newspapers: Presque Isle Co. Advance (weekly circulation 3800)
Transportation: Commute: 92.1% car, 0.0% public transportation, 2.1% walk, 3.2% work from home; Median travel time to work: 16.3 minutes

Roscommon County

Located in north central Michigan; drained by the Muskegon River and branches of the Tittabawassee and Au Sable Rivers; includes Houghton and Higgins Lakes and Lake Saint Helen. Covers a land area of 519.636 square miles, a water area of 60.396 square miles, and is located in the Eastern Time Zone at 44.34° N. Lat., 84.61° W. Long. The county was founded in 1875. County seat is Roscommon.

Weather Station: Houghton Lake Roscommon Co Arpt   Elevation: 1,149 feet

	Jan	Feb	Mar	Apr	May	Jun	Jul	Aug	Sep	Oct	Nov	Dec
High	27	30	40	54	67	76	80	77	69	56	42	31
Low	11	11	19	32	42	51	55	54	47	37	28	18
Precip	1.6	1.2	1.9	2.5	2.8	3.1	2.6	3.4	3.1	2.6	2.3	1.7
Snow	18.0	12.0	8.7	na	na	na	na	tr	tr	0.7	9.2	16.4

High and Low temperatures in degrees Fahrenheit; Precipitation and Snow in inches

Population: 24,449; Growth (since 2000): -4.0%; Density: 47.1 persons per square mile; Race: 97.3% White, 0.4% Black/African American, 0.3% Asian, 0.6% American Indian/Alaska Native, 0.0% Native Hawaiian/Other Pacific Islander, 1.2% two or more races, 1.1% Hispanic of any race; Average household size: 2.11; Median age: 53.3; Age under 18: 16.1%; Age 65 and over: 28.0%; Males per 100 females: 99.5; Marriage status: 20.2% never married, 55.2% now married, 1.2% separated, 9.8% widowed, 14.8% divorced; Foreign born: 2.4%; Speak English only: 97.5%; With disability: 24.5%; Veterans: 15.5%; Ancestry: 27.6% German, 14.5% English, 14.4% Irish, 8.5% Polish, 7.3% French
Religion: Six largest groups: 8.0% Catholicism, 3.6% Lutheran, 3.4% Methodist/Pietist, 3.2% Baptist, 1.1% Non-denominational Protestant, 1.1% Latter-day Saints
Economy: Unemployment rate: 7.2%; Leading industries: 20.6% retail trade; 14.8% other services (except public administration); 13.3% accommodation and food services; Farms: 58 totaling 7,433 acres; Company size: 0 employ 1,000 or more persons, 0 employ 500 to 999 persons, 3 employ 100 to 499 persons, 537 employ less than 100 persons; Business ownership: 411 women-owned, n/a Black-owned, n/a Hispanic-owned, 44 Asian-owned
Employment: 8.6% management, business, and financial, 0.9% computer, engineering, and science, 6.5% education, legal, community service, arts, and media, 5.6% healthcare practitioners, 23.2% service, 30.2% sales and office, 9.7% natural resources, construction, and maintenance, 15.3% production, transportation, and material moving
Income: Per capita: $23,023; Median household: $33,334; Average household: $47,535; Households with income of $100,000 or more: 6.9%; Poverty rate: 22.2%
Educational Attainment: High school diploma or higher: 85.1%; Bachelor's degree or higher: 12.9%; Graduate/professional degree or higher: 4.6%
Housing: Homeownership rate: 82.8%; Median home value: $92,000; Median year structure built: 1975; Homeowner vacancy rate: 5.1%; Median gross rent: $655 per month; Rental vacancy rate: 16.7%
Vital Statistics: Birth rate: 85.4 per 10,000 population; Death rate: 149.5 per 10,000 population; Age-adjusted cancer mortality rate: 222.4 deaths per 100,000 population
Health Insurance: 86.8% have insurance; 57.7% have private insurance; 56.3% have public insurance; 13.2% do not have insurance; 5.1% of children under 18 do not have insurance
Health Care: Physicians: 7.5 per 10,000 population; Hospital beds: 0.0 per 10,000 population; Hospital admissions: 0.0 per 10,000 population
Transportation: Commute: 88.1% car, 1.3% public transportation, 3.7% walk, 5.0% work from home; Median travel time to work: 22.2 minutes
Presidential Election: 47.6% Obama, 51.4% Romney (2012)
National and State Parks: Backus Creek State Game Area; Houghton Lake State Forest; South Higgins Lake State Park
Additional Information Contacts
Roscommon Government . . . . (989) 275-8021
    http://www.roscommoncounty.net

Roscommon County Communities

AU SABLE (township). Covers a land area of 35.659 square miles and a water area of 0.118 square miles. Located at 44.47° N. Lat; 84.43° W. Long.
Population: 255; Growth (since 2000): -9.3%; Density: 7.2 persons per square mile; Race: 97.6% White, 0.8% Black/African American, 0.0% Asian, 0.0% American Indian/Alaska Native, 0.0% Native Hawaiian/Other Pacific Islander, 1.2% Two or more races, 1.2% Hispanic of any race; Average household size: 2.26; Median age: 48.8; Age under 18: 20.0%; Age 65 and over: 16.1%; Males per 100 females: 82.1
Housing: Homeownership rate: 86.7%; Homeowner vacancy rate: 6.6%; Rental vacancy rate: 30.4%

BACKUS (township). Covers a land area of 34.356 square miles and a water area of 1.636 square miles. Located at 44.27° N. Lat; 84.54° W. Long.
Population: 330; Growth (since 2000): -5.7%; Density: 9.6 persons per square mile; Race: 95.2% White, 0.0% Black/African American, 0.3% Asian, 0.6% American Indian/Alaska Native, 0.0% Native Hawaiian/Other Pacific Islander, 3.6% Two or more races, 1.2% Hispanic of any race; Average household size: 2.23; Median age: 49.5; Age under 18: 20.0%; Age 65 and over: 26.1%; Males per 100 females: 101.2
Housing: Homeownership rate: 85.8%; Homeowner vacancy rate: 3.8%; Rental vacancy rate: 8.7%

DENTON (township). Covers a land area of 26.238 square miles and a water area of 9.876 square miles. Located at 44.28° N. Lat; 84.67° W. Long.
Population: 5,557; Growth (since 2000): -4.5%; Density: 211.8 persons per square mile; Race: 97.0% White, 0.5% Black/African American, 0.5% Asian, 0.6% American Indian/Alaska Native, 0.0% Native Hawaiian/Other Pacific Islander, 1.0% Two or more races, 1.4% Hispanic of any race; Average household size: 2.05; Median age: 54.5; Age under 18: 15.0%; Age 65 and over: 29.7%; Males per 100 females: 96.5; Marriage status: 15.9% never married, 56.0% now married, 1.6% separated, 11.1% widowed, 17.0% divorced; Foreign born: 2.1%; Speak English only: 98.4%; With disability: 23.7%; Veterans: 13.1%; Ancestry: 31.0% German, 14.6% Irish, 11.0% English, 9.0% Polish, 7.6% French
Employment: 6.6% management, business, and financial, 0.0% computer, engineering, and science, 9.3% education, legal, community service, arts, and media, 4.8% healthcare practitioners, 24.1% service, 31.7% sales and office, 7.6% natural resources, construction, and maintenance, 15.9% production, transportation, and material moving
Income: Per capita: $21,043; Median household: $32,079; Average household: $41,788; Households with income of $100,000 or more: 6.8%; Poverty rate: 24.0%
Educational Attainment: High school diploma or higher: 86.9%; Bachelor's degree or higher: 11.1%; Graduate/professional degree or higher: 3.9%
Housing: Homeownership rate: 78.4%; Median home value: $99,200; Median year structure built: 1975; Homeowner vacancy rate: 3.9%; Median gross rent: $613 per month; Rental vacancy rate: 14.0%
Health Insurance: 88.0% have insurance; 58.5% have private insurance; 57.7% have public insurance; 12.0% do not have insurance; 12.4% of children under 18 do not have insurance
Safety: Violent crime rate: 16.6 per 10,000 population; Property crime rate: 173.0 per 10,000 population
Transportation: Commute: 89.7% car, 3.7% public transportation, 1.2% walk, 4.8% work from home; Median travel time to work: 19.1 minutes

GERRISH (township). Covers a land area of 27.602 square miles and a water area of 9.626 square miles. Located at 44.47° N. Lat; 84.67° W. Long.
Population: 2,993; Growth (since 2000): -2.6%; Density: 108.4 persons per square mile; Race: 97.9% White, 0.5% Black/African American, 0.3% Asian, 0.3% American Indian/Alaska Native, 0.0% Native Hawaiian/Other Pacific Islander, 0.9% Two or more races, 1.2% Hispanic of any race; Average household size: 2.17; Median age: 55.1; Age under 18: 15.9%; Age 65 and over: 28.6%; Males per 100 females: 102.1; Marriage status: 13.5% never married, 68.3% now married, 0.6% separated, 6.7% widowed, 11.5% divorced; Foreign born: 5.1%; Speak English only: 94.6%; With disability: 18.5%; Veterans: 20.9%; Ancestry: 28.9% German, 17.8% English, 11.0% Italian, 7.8% Irish, 7.0% French
Employment: 16.4% management, business, and financial, 1.4% computer, engineering, and science, 8.1% education, legal, community service, arts, and media, 9.9% healthcare practitioners, 14.3% service, 35.5% sales and office, 6.0% natural resources, construction, and maintenance, 8.4% production, transportation, and material moving
Income: Per capita: $27,878; Median household: $38,026; Average household: $60,839; Households with income of $100,000 or more: 13.7%; Poverty rate: 15.6%
Educational Attainment: High school diploma or higher: 92.0%; Bachelor's degree or higher: 27.9%; Graduate/professional degree or higher: 8.7%
Housing: Homeownership rate: 92.2%; Median home value: $123,600; Median year structure built: 1977; Homeowner vacancy rate: 5.3%; Median gross rent: $665 per month; Rental vacancy rate: 26.3%

Health Insurance: 89.1% have insurance; 61.8% have private insurance; 56.8% have public insurance; 10.9% do not have insurance; 0.0% of children under 18 do not have insurance
Transportation: Commute: 86.2% car, 0.0% public transportation, 3.8% walk, 7.3% work from home; Median travel time to work: 21.8 minutes
Additional Information Contacts
Gerrish Township . . . . (989) 821-9313
  http://www.gerrishtownship.org

HIGGINS (township). Covers a land area of 70.362 square miles and a water area of 2.940 square miles. Located at 44.41° N. Lat; 84.56° W. Long.
Population: 1,932; Growth (since 2000): -6.3%; Density: 27.5 persons per square mile; Race: 97.3% White, 0.2% Black/African American, 0.5% Asian, 0.4% American Indian/Alaska Native, 0.0% Native Hawaiian/Other Pacific Islander, 1.7% Two or more races, 0.6% Hispanic of any race; Average household size: 2.20; Median age: 46.3; Age under 18: 21.3%; Age 65 and over: 23.6%; Males per 100 females: 100.2
Housing: Homeownership rate: 67.6%; Homeowner vacancy rate: 4.6%; Rental vacancy rate: 11.9%

HIGGINS LAKE (unincorporated postal area)
ZCTA: 48627
  Covers a land area of 0.217 square miles and a water area of 0 square miles. Located at 44.46° N. Lat; 84.75° W. Long. Elevation is 1,171 feet.
  Population: 141; Growth (since 2000): -50.0%; Density: 649.0 persons per square mile; Race: 96.5% White, 0.0% Black/African American, 0.0% Asian, 1.4% American Indian/Alaska Native, 0.0% Native Hawaiian/Other Pacific Islander, 2.1% Two or more races, 1.4% Hispanic of any race; Average household size: 1.74; Median age: 60.9; Age under 18: 8.5%; Age 65 and over: 36.2%; Males per 100 females: 98.6
  Housing: Homeownership rate: 92.5%; Homeowner vacancy rate: 2.5%; Rental vacancy rate: 78.4%

HOUGHTON LAKE (CDP). Covers a land area of 5.872 square miles and a water area of 1.629 square miles. Located at 44.31° N. Lat; 84.76° W. Long. Elevation is 1,145 feet.
History: Houghton Lake was named for Douglass Houghton, a pioneer geologist in Michigan. The community developed in the 1870's around the lumber operations of S.C. Hall. It later became a resort area.
Population: 3,427; Growth (since 2000): -8.6%; Density: 583.7 persons per square mile; Race: 97.1% White, 0.8% Black/African American, 0.1% Asian, 0.6% American Indian/Alaska Native, 0.0% Native Hawaiian/Other Pacific Islander, 1.1% Two or more races, 1.3% Hispanic of any race; Average household size: 2.09; Median age: 51.0; Age under 18: 17.4%; Age 65 and over: 25.7%; Males per 100 females: 94.9; Marriage status: 20.4% never married, 50.8% now married, 2.5% separated, 12.2% widowed, 16.6% divorced; Foreign born: 0.4%; Speak English only: 98.3%; With disability: 34.9%; Veterans: 16.0%; Ancestry: 22.4% German, 18.5% Irish, 12.7% English, 8.3% Polish, 4.6% Italian
Employment: 5.7% management, business, and financial, 0.2% computer, engineering, and science, 8.2% education, legal, community service, arts, and media, 4.0% healthcare practitioners, 23.7% service, 33.7% sales and office, 5.7% natural resources, construction, and maintenance, 18.8% production, transportation, and material moving
Income: Per capita: $24,314; Median household: $29,470; Average household: $46,531; Households with income of $100,000 or more: 4.3%; Poverty rate: 22.9%
Educational Attainment: High school diploma or higher: 74.9%; Bachelor's degree or higher: 9.2%; Graduate/professional degree or higher: 2.1%
School District(s)
Houghton Lake Community Schools (KG-12)
  2012-13 Enrollment: 1,529 . . . . (989) 366-2000
Vocational/Technical School(s)
Houghton Lake Institute of Cosmetology (Private, For-profit)
  Fall 2013 Enrollment: 14 . . . . (989) 422-4573
  2013-14 Tuition: $8,475
Housing: Homeownership rate: 72.6%; Median home value: $84,200; Median year structure built: 1966; Homeowner vacancy rate: 6.7%; Median gross rent: $599 per month; Rental vacancy rate: 10.2%
Health Insurance: 84.3% have insurance; 50.0% have private insurance; 60.9% have public insurance; 15.7% do not have insurance; 4.5% of children under 18 do not have insurance

Newspapers: Houghton Lake Resorter (weekly circulation 7400)
Transportation: Commute: 78.8% car, 2.1% public transportation, 7.2% walk, 3.9% work from home; Median travel time to work: 11.8 minutes

HOUGHTON LAKE HEIGHTS (unincorporated postal area)

ZCTA: 48630
Covers a land area of 0.095 square miles and a water area of 0 square miles. Located at 44.32° N. Lat; 84.77° W. Long. Elevation is 1,175 feet.
Population: 69; Growth (since 2000): -74.0%; Density: 722.8 persons per square mile; Race: 100.0% White, 0.0% Black/African American, 0.0% Asian, 0.0% American Indian/Alaska Native, 0.0% Native Hawaiian/Other Pacific Islander, 0.0% Two or more races, 0.0% Hispanic of any race; Average household size: 2.16; Median age: 51.8; Age under 18: 15.9%; Age 65 and over: 26.1%; Males per 100 females: 81.6
Housing: Homeownership rate: 78.2%; Homeowner vacancy rate: 7.4%; Rental vacancy rate: 0.0%

LAKE (township).

Covers a land area of 23.064 square miles and a water area of 12.351 square miles. Located at 44.38° N. Lat; 84.80° W. Long.
Population: 1,215; Growth (since 2000): -10.1%; Density: 52.7 persons per square mile; Race: 95.7% White, 1.1% Black/African American, 0.2% Asian, 1.3% American Indian/Alaska Native, 0.0% Native Hawaiian/Other Pacific Islander, 1.6% Two or more races, 0.9% Hispanic of any race; Average household size: 1.96; Median age: 59.2; Age under 18: 9.6%; Age 65 and over: 36.8%; Males per 100 females: 95.3
Housing: Homeownership rate: 89.5%; Homeowner vacancy rate: 3.8%; Rental vacancy rate: 16.3%

LYON (township).

Covers a land area of 29.977 square miles and a water area of 6.556 square miles. Located at 44.47° N. Lat; 84.79° W. Long. Elevation is 1,171 feet.
Population: 1,370; Growth (since 2000): -6.3%; Density: 45.7 persons per square mile; Race: 97.2% White, 0.8% Black/African American, 0.4% Asian, 0.7% American Indian/Alaska Native, 0.0% Native Hawaiian/Other Pacific Islander, 0.9% Two or more races, 1.0% Hispanic of any race; Average household size: 2.04; Median age: 56.2; Age under 18: 15.0%; Age 65 and over: 30.0%; Males per 100 females: 100.0
Housing: Homeownership rate: 90.4%; Homeowner vacancy rate: 3.0%; Rental vacancy rate: 47.3%

MARKEY (township).

Covers a land area of 28.726 square miles and a water area of 7.375 square miles. Located at 44.38° N. Lat; 84.67° W. Long.
Population: 2,360; Growth (since 2000): -2.6%; Density: 82.2 persons per square mile; Race: 98.5% White, 0.1% Black/African American, 0.3% Asian, 0.5% American Indian/Alaska Native, 0.0% Native Hawaiian/Other Pacific Islander, 0.6% Two or more races, 1.0% Hispanic of any race; Average household size: 2.05; Median age: 55.5; Age under 18: 14.9%; Age 65 and over: 30.3%; Males per 100 females: 102.6
Housing: Homeownership rate: 87.7%; Homeowner vacancy rate: 8.1%; Rental vacancy rate: 33.6%

NESTER (township).

Covers a land area of 71.353 square miles and a water area of 0.905 square miles. Located at 44.20° N. Lat; 84.46° W. Long.
Population: 295; Growth (since 2000): 12.2%; Density: 4.1 persons per square mile; Race: 96.3% White, 0.0% Black/African American, 0.0% Asian, 0.3% American Indian/Alaska Native, 0.0% Native Hawaiian/Other Pacific Islander, 3.4% Two or more races, 1.4% Hispanic of any race; Average household size: 2.06; Median age: 56.6; Age under 18: 9.2%; Age 65 and over: 27.8%; Males per 100 females: 112.2
Housing: Homeownership rate: 92.4%; Homeowner vacancy rate: 5.0%; Rental vacancy rate: 0.0%

PRUDENVILLE (CDP).

Covers a land area of 2.753 square miles and a water area of 0.866 square miles. Located at 44.30° N. Lat; 84.67° W. Long. Elevation is 1,145 feet.
History: Prudenville was founded in 1875 by John Pruden.
Population: 1,682; Growth (since 2000): -3.2%; Density: 611.0 persons per square mile; Race: 96.7% White, 0.5% Black/African American, 1.1% Asian, 0.4% American Indian/Alaska Native, 0.0% Native Hawaiian/Other Pacific Islander, 1.1% Two or more races, 1.4% Hispanic of any race;

Average household size: 2.07; Median age: 54.5; Age under 18: 14.6%; Age 65 and over: 31.1%; Males per 100 females: 97.2
Housing: Homeownership rate: 80.1%; Homeowner vacancy rate: 3.3%; Rental vacancy rate: 25.3%

RICHFIELD (township).

Covers a land area of 68.978 square miles and a water area of 4.018 square miles. Located at 44.34° N. Lat; 84.45° W. Long.
Population: 3,731; Growth (since 2000): -9.9%; Density: 54.1 persons per square mile; Race: 96.8% White, 0.2% Black/African American, 0.2% Asian, 0.8% American Indian/Alaska Native, 0.0% Native Hawaiian/Other Pacific Islander, 1.8% Two or more races, 1.0% Hispanic of any race; Average household size: 2.10; Median age: 52.9; Age under 18: 15.4%; Age 65 and over: 28.1%; Males per 100 females: 101.9; Marriage status: 20.9% never married, 49.9% now married, 1.9% separated, 11.3% widowed, 17.9% divorced; Foreign born: 2.5%; Speak English only: 98.7%; With disability: 29.7%; Veterans: 12.8%; Ancestry: 28.6% German, 18.2% Irish, 14.9% English, 7.7% Polish, 7.1% French
Employment: 6.2% management, business, and financial, 0.5% computer, engineering, and science, 5.8% education, legal, community service, arts, and media, 3.7% healthcare practitioners, 14.7% service, 28.8% sales and office, 21.3% natural resources, construction, and maintenance, 19.1% production, transportation, and material moving
Income: Per capita: $18,672; Median household: $28,275; Average household: $37,587; Households with income of $100,000 or more: 3.8%; Poverty rate: 23.2%
Educational Attainment: High school diploma or higher: 82.2%; Bachelor's degree or higher: 6.6%; Graduate/professional degree or higher: 1.8%
Housing: Homeownership rate: 83.2%; Median home value: $64,800; Median year structure built: 1971; Homeowner vacancy rate: 5.9%; Median gross rent: $561 per month; Rental vacancy rate: 10.3%
Health Insurance: 86.5% have insurance; 54.3% have private insurance; 56.8% have public insurance; 13.5% do not have insurance; 4.6% of children under 18 do not have insurance
Safety: Violent crime rate: 27.3 per 10,000 population; Property crime rate: 139.2 per 10,000 population
Transportation: Commute: 84.6% car, 2.0% public transportation, 6.3% walk, 5.4% work from home; Median travel time to work: 27.4 minutes

ROSCOMMON (township).

Covers a land area of 103.320 square miles and a water area of 4.996 square miles. Located at 44.23° N. Lat; 84.75° W. Long. Elevation is 1,135 feet.
Population: 4,411; Growth (since 2000): 3.8%; Density: 42.7 persons per square mile; Race: 97.9% White, 0.1% Black/African American, 0.2% Asian, 0.7% American Indian/Alaska Native, 0.0% Native Hawaiian/Other Pacific Islander, 1.0% Two or more races, 1.1% Hispanic of any race; Average household size: 2.24; Median age: 48.8; Age under 18: 18.4%; Age 65 and over: 24.0%; Males per 100 females: 99.1; Marriage status: 29.1% never married, 48.3% now married, 1.3% separated, 8.3% widowed, 14.4% divorced; Foreign born: 2.1%; Speak English only: 97.5%; With disability: 28.6%; Veterans: 17.4%; Ancestry: 22.0% German, 16.6% Irish, 16.5% English, 8.3% American, 7.4% Polish
Employment: 5.3% management, business, and financial, 0.0% computer, engineering, and science, 6.5% education, legal, community service, arts, and media, 4.5% healthcare practitioners, 27.0% service, 30.1% sales and office, 4.9% natural resources, construction, and maintenance, 21.7% production, transportation, and material moving
Income: Per capita: $26,980; Median household: $33,258; Average household: $57,009; Households with income of $100,000 or more: 4.6%; Poverty rate: 21.0%
Educational Attainment: High school diploma or higher: 79.2%; Bachelor's degree or higher: 11.5%; Graduate/professional degree or higher: 6.2%

School District(s)

C.o.o.r. ISD (PK-12)
    2012-13 Enrollment: 192 . . . . (989) 275-9520
Houghton Lake Community Schools (KG-12)
    2012-13 Enrollment: 1,529 . . . . (989) 366-2000
Roscommon Area Public Schools (PK-12)
    2012-13 Enrollment: 1,175 . . . . (989) 275-6600

Two-year College(s)

Kirtland Community College (Public)
    Fall 2013 Enrollment: 1,805 . . . . (989) 275-5000
    2013-14 Tuition: In-state $4,495; Out-of-state $7,105

Housing: Homeownership rate: 79.1%; Median home value: $88,500; Median year structure built: 1978; Homeowner vacancy rate: 5.3%; Median gross rent: $770 per month; Rental vacancy rate: 8.1%
Health Insurance: 85.7% have insurance; 54.5% have private insurance; 58.6% have public insurance; 14.3% do not have insurance; 3.7% of children under 18 do not have insurance
Transportation: Commute: 91.0% car, 1.2% public transportation, 3.7% walk, 1.3% work from home; Median travel time to work: 19.6 minutes

ROSCOMMON (village). County seat. Covers a land area of 1.493 square miles and a water area of 0.007 square miles. Located at 44.49° N. Lat; 84.59° W. Long. Elevation is 1,135 feet.
History: Roscommon was founded in 1845 by George C. Robinson of Detroit. It was named for the county, which had been named for a county in Ireland. Roscommon, once a lumber town with one hotel and 14 saloons, became a vacation and resort center.
Population: 1,075; Growth (since 2000): -5.1%; Density: 720.1 persons per square mile; Race: 95.6% White, 0.3% Black/African American, 0.8% Asian, 0.7% American Indian/Alaska Native, 0.0% Native Hawaiian/Other Pacific Islander, 2.6% Two or more races, 0.2% Hispanic of any race; Average household size: 2.13; Median age: 43.6; Age under 18: 22.1%; Age 65 and over: 22.9%; Males per 100 females: 91.6

School District(s)
C.o.o.r. ISD (PK-12)
    2012-13 Enrollment: 192 . . . . (989) 275-9520
Houghton Lake Community Schools (KG-12)
    2012-13 Enrollment: 1,529 . . . . (989) 366-2000
Roscommon Area Public Schools (PK-12)
    2012-13 Enrollment: 1,175 . . . . (989) 275-6600
Two-year College(s)
Kirtland Community College (Public)
    Fall 2013 Enrollment: 1,805 . . . . (989) 275-5000
    2013-14 Tuition: In-state $4,495; Out-of-state $7,105
Housing: Homeownership rate: 50.5%; Homeowner vacancy rate: 4.9%; Rental vacancy rate: 12.2%

SAINT HELEN (CDP). Covers a land area of 5.032 square miles and a water area of 0.892 square miles. Located at 44.36° N. Lat; 84.42° W. Long. Elevation is 1,191 feet.
History: St. Helen was settled in 1870 as a service center for lumbermen working the vast timberlands here. The village was first owned by the Henry L. Stevens & Company lumber firm. It later became a market center for a summer colony.
Population: 2,668; Growth (since 2000): -10.9%; Density: 530.3 persons per square mile; Race: 96.7% White, 0.1% Black/African American, 0.1% Asian, 0.8% American Indian/Alaska Native, 0.0% Native Hawaiian/Other Pacific Islander, 2.1% Two or more races, 1.1% Hispanic of any race; Average household size: 2.08; Median age: 51.3; Age under 18: 15.9%; Age 65 and over: 26.4%; Males per 100 females: 103.5; Marriage status: 20.4% never married, 48.4% now married, 2.6% separated, 12.0% widowed, 19.3% divorced; Foreign born: 2.3%; Speak English only: 98.2%; With disability: 32.3%; Veterans: 13.5%; Ancestry: 30.5% German, 19.9% Irish, 13.5% English, 7.5% Polish, 7.2% French
Employment: 5.9% management, business, and financial, 0.8% computer, engineering, and science, 7.4% education, legal, community service, arts, and media, 4.4% healthcare practitioners, 12.9% service, 32.3% sales and office, 19.1% natural resources, construction, and maintenance, 17.4% production, transportation, and material moving
Income: Per capita: $15,522; Median household: $24,652; Average household: $31,022; Households with income of $100,000 or more: 1.0%; Poverty rate: 27.2%
Educational Attainment: High school diploma or higher: 78.6%; Bachelor's degree or higher: 6.1%; Graduate/professional degree or higher: 1.9%
Housing: Homeownership rate: 80.7%; Median home value: $57,700; Median year structure built: 1969; Homeowner vacancy rate: 6.3%; Median gross rent: $535 per month; Rental vacancy rate: 11.8%
Health Insurance: 85.9% have insurance; 49.5% have private insurance; 60.8% have public insurance; 14.1% do not have insurance; 1.3% of children under 18 do not have insurance
Transportation: Commute: 82.2% car, 1.8% public transportation, 7.2% walk, 7.7% work from home; Median travel time to work: 24.5 minutes

Saginaw County

Located in east central Michigan; drained by the Saginaw, Cass, Flint, Shiawassee, Bad, and Tittabawassee Rivers. Covers a land area of 800.114 square miles, a water area of 15.852 square miles, and is located in the Eastern Time Zone at 43.33° N. Lat., 84.06° W. Long. The county was founded in 1835. County seat is Saginaw.

Saginaw County is part of the Saginaw, MI Metropolitan Statistical Area. The entire metro area includes: Saginaw County, MI

Population: 200,169; Growth (since 2000): -4.7%; Density: 250.2 persons per square mile; Race: 74.6% White, 19.0% Black/African American, 1.1% Asian, 0.4% American Indian/Alaska Native, 0.0% Native Hawaiian/Other Pacific Islander, 2.5% two or more races, 7.8% Hispanic of any race; Average household size: 2.44; Median age: 39.5; Age under 18: 23.4%; Age 65 and over: 15.3%; Males per 100 females: 93.6; Marriage status: 33.4% never married, 47.8% now married, 1.7% separated, 7.2% widowed, 11.6% divorced; Foreign born: 2.3%; Speak English only: 94.9%; With disability: 15.4%; Veterans: 9.9%; Ancestry: 29.6% German, 9.7% Irish, 8.8% Polish, 7.5% English, 5.8% French
Religion: Six largest groups: 17.9% Catholicism, 12.6% Lutheran, 4.7% Baptist, 2.7% Methodist/Pietist, 2.3% Non-denominational Protestant, 1.8% Pentecostal
Economy: Unemployment rate: 5.7%; Leading industries: 19.9% retail trade; 13.4% health care and social assistance; 12.0% other services (except public administration); Farms: 1,318 totaling 309,710 acres; Company size: 7 employ 1,000 or more persons, 8 employ 500 to 999 persons, 78 employ 100 to 499 persons, 4,274 employ less than 100 persons; Business ownership: 4,571 women-owned, 1,628 Black-owned, 351 Hispanic-owned, n/a Asian-owned
Employment: 10.7% management, business, and financial, 3.7% computer, engineering, and science, 8.7% education, legal, community service, arts, and media, 6.5% healthcare practitioners, 21.0% service, 26.4% sales and office, 7.5% natural resources, construction, and maintenance, 15.5% production, transportation, and material moving
Income: Per capita: $22,349; Median household: $42,331; Average household: $55,642; Households with income of $100,000 or more: 13.6%; Poverty rate: 19.2%
Educational Attainment: High school diploma or higher: 87.0%; Bachelor's degree or higher: 19.1%; Graduate/professional degree or higher: 6.3%
Housing: Homeownership rate: 72.3%; Median home value: $97,800; Median year structure built: 1965; Homeowner vacancy rate: 2.4%; Median gross rent: $699 per month; Rental vacancy rate: 10.0%
Vital Statistics: Birth rate: 114.4 per 10,000 population; Death rate: 102.8 per 10,000 population; Age-adjusted cancer mortality rate: 178.0 deaths per 100,000 population
Health Insurance: 89.2% have insurance; 67.0% have private insurance; 38.5% have public insurance; 10.8% do not have insurance; 3.3% of children under 18 do not have insurance
Health Care: Physicians: 28.5 per 10,000 population; Hospital beds: 61.0 per 10,000 population; Hospital admissions: 2,199.8 per 10,000 population
Transportation: Commute: 94.0% car, 0.7% public transportation, 1.6% walk, 2.9% work from home; Median travel time to work: 21.6 minutes
Presidential Election: 55.5% Obama, 43.6% Romney (2012)
National and State Parks: Crow Island State Game Area; Gratiot - Saginaw State Game Management Area; Shiawassee National Wildlife Refuge; Shiawassee River State Game Area
Additional Information Contacts
Saginaw Government . . . . (989) 790-5200
    http://www.saginawcounty.com

Saginaw County Communities

ALBEE (township). Covers a land area of 36.035 square miles and a water area of 0.119 square miles. Located at 43.27° N. Lat; 83.99° W. Long.
History: Albee Township was organized in 1863 and named for William C. Albee, who had settled here in 1855.
Population: 2,160; Growth (since 2000): -7.6%; Density: 59.9 persons per square mile; Race: 94.0% White, 2.1% Black/African American, 0.1% Asian, 0.7% American Indian/Alaska Native, 0.0% Native Hawaiian/Other Pacific Islander, 1.4% Two or more races, 6.5% Hispanic of any race;

Average household size: 2.69; Median age: 40.4; Age under 18: 23.1%; Age 65 and over: 12.6%; Males per 100 females: 101.1

Housing: Homeownership rate: 90.7%; Homeowner vacancy rate: 2.2%; Rental vacancy rate: 3.8%

BIRCH RUN (township).
Covers a land area of 35.506 square miles and a water area of 0.058 square miles. Located at 43.26° N. Lat; 83.76° W. Long. Elevation is 633 feet.

Population: 6,033; Growth (since 2000): -2.6%; Density: 169.9 persons per square mile; Race: 96.5% White, 0.6% Black/African American, 0.1% Asian, 0.7% American Indian/Alaska Native, 0.0% Native Hawaiian/Other Pacific Islander, 1.5% Two or more races, 3.2% Hispanic of any race; Average household size: 2.56; Median age: 41.3; Age under 18: 23.9%; Age 65 and over: 14.7%; Males per 100 females: 96.8; Marriage status: 27.8% never married, 54.8% now married, 0.6% separated, 4.7% widowed, 12.7% divorced; Foreign born: 0.9%; Speak English only: 97.4%; With disability: 11.0%; Veterans: 10.1%; Ancestry: 35.2% German, 16.8% Irish, 9.4% Polish, 8.7% English, 6.1% American

Employment: 9.6% management, business, and financial, 4.2% computer, engineering, and science, 4.3% education, legal, community service, arts, and media, 5.1% healthcare practitioners, 14.5% service, 31.5% sales and office, 8.4% natural resources, construction, and maintenance, 22.4% production, transportation, and material moving

Income: Per capita: $24,944; Median household: $56,745; Average household: $65,721; Households with income of $100,000 or more: 17.7%; Poverty rate: 7.3%

Educational Attainment: High school diploma or higher: 91.2%; Bachelor's degree or higher: 16.2%; Graduate/professional degree or higher: 4.0%

School District(s)
Birch Run Area Schools (PK-12)
    2012-13 Enrollment: 1,792 . . . . (989) 624-9307

Housing: Homeownership rate: 79.2%; Median home value: $123,700; Median year structure built: 1971; Homeowner vacancy rate: 1.9%; Median gross rent: $789 per month; Rental vacancy rate: 10.0%

Health Insurance: 88.6% have insurance; 76.9% have private insurance; 26.6% have public insurance; 11.4% do not have insurance; 4.1% of children under 18 do not have insurance

Transportation: Commute: 94.9% car, 0.0% public transportation, 1.6% walk, 1.7% work from home; Median travel time to work: 22.7 minutes

BIRCH RUN (village).
Covers a land area of 1.886 square miles and a water area of 0.020 square miles. Located at 43.25° N. Lat; 83.79° W. Long. Elevation is 633 feet.

History: Birch Run was founded when the Pere Marquette Railroad needed a station here in 1852. This was first a bean-raising area. Oil was discovered here in 1925.

Population: 1,555; Growth (since 2000): -5.9%; Density: 824.6 persons per square mile; Race: 93.9% White, 1.1% Black/African American, 0.2% Asian, 0.9% American Indian/Alaska Native, 0.0% Native Hawaiian/Other Pacific Islander, 2.8% Two or more races, 5.3% Hispanic of any race; Average household size: 2.37; Median age: 34.6; Age under 18: 25.1%; Age 65 and over: 12.2%; Males per 100 females: 89.9

School District(s)
Birch Run Area Schools (PK-12)
    2012-13 Enrollment: 1,792 . . . . (989) 624-9307

Housing: Homeownership rate: 52.7%; Homeowner vacancy rate: 3.9%; Rental vacancy rate: 9.0%

Safety: Violent crime rate: 39.3 per 10,000 population; Property crime rate: 537.7 per 10,000 population

BLUMFIELD (township).
Covers a land area of 35.648 square miles and a water area of 0.015 square miles. Located at 43.43° N. Lat; 83.76° W. Long.

History: Blumfield Township was organized in 1853 by Germans who fled from the 1848 political turmoil in Germany. It was named for Robert Blum, a political offender who had been killed in 1848.

Population: 1,960; Growth (since 2000): -2.7%; Density: 55.0 persons per square mile; Race: 98.4% White, 0.5% Black/African American, 0.2% Asian, 0.3% American Indian/Alaska Native, 0.1% Native Hawaiian/Other Pacific Islander, 0.5% Two or more races, 1.4% Hispanic of any race; Average household size: 2.56; Median age: 44.9; Age under 18: 21.9%; Age 65 and over: 17.1%; Males per 100 females: 105.0

Housing: Homeownership rate: 91.4%; Homeowner vacancy rate: 1.3%; Rental vacancy rate: 5.8%

BRADY (township).
Covers a land area of 36.749 square miles and a water area of 0.149 square miles. Located at 43.17° N. Lat; 84.22° W. Long.

History: Brady Township was organized in 1856 and named for General Hugh Brady of Detroit.

Population: 2,218; Growth (since 2000): -5.4%; Density: 60.4 persons per square mile; Race: 97.2% White, 0.7% Black/African American, 0.4% Asian, 0.2% American Indian/Alaska Native, 0.0% Native Hawaiian/Other Pacific Islander, 0.9% Two or more races, 4.5% Hispanic of any race; Average household size: 2.59; Median age: 42.2; Age under 18: 23.4%; Age 65 and over: 15.4%; Males per 100 females: 100.5

Housing: Homeownership rate: 88.9%; Homeowner vacancy rate: 2.7%; Rental vacancy rate: 10.4%

BRANT (township).
Covers a land area of 36.838 square miles and a water area of 0.294 square miles. Located at 43.26° N. Lat; 84.22° W. Long. Elevation is 614 feet.

History: Brant Township was founded in 1858.

Population: 2,012; Growth (since 2000): -0.5%; Density: 54.6 persons per square mile; Race: 96.7% White, 0.3% Black/African American, 0.2% Asian, 0.7% American Indian/Alaska Native, 0.0% Native Hawaiian/Other Pacific Islander, 1.4% Two or more races, 3.3% Hispanic of any race; Average household size: 2.71; Median age: 42.3; Age under 18: 22.4%; Age 65 and over: 12.9%; Males per 100 females: 97.8

Housing: Homeownership rate: 92.1%; Homeowner vacancy rate: 1.2%; Rental vacancy rate: 1.7%

BRIDGEPORT (CDP).
Covers a land area of 8.412 square miles and a water area of 0.049 square miles. Located at 43.37° N. Lat; 83.88° W. Long. Elevation is 604 feet.

Population: 6,950; Growth (since 2000): -11.5%; Density: 826.2 persons per square mile; Race: 57.4% White, 35.5% Black/African American, 0.2% Asian, 0.4% American Indian/Alaska Native, 0.0% Native Hawaiian/Other Pacific Islander, 3.2% Two or more races, 10.8% Hispanic of any race; Average household size: 2.42; Median age: 41.5; Age under 18: 24.0%; Age 65 and over: 15.8%; Males per 100 females: 86.1; Marriage status: 31.3% never married, 46.9% now married, 2.5% separated, 6.5% widowed, 15.2% divorced; Foreign born: 0.0%; Speak English only: 96.7%; With disability: 16.8%; Veterans: 12.1%; Ancestry: 19.9% German, 8.5% English, 7.8% Irish, 5.5% American, 4.3% Polish

Employment: 10.2% management, business, and financial, 0.3% computer, engineering, and science, 6.1% education, legal, community service, arts, and media, 5.7% healthcare practitioners, 30.8% service, 25.0% sales and office, 5.0% natural resources, construction, and maintenance, 16.9% production, transportation, and material moving

Income: Per capita: $19,429; Median household: $33,845; Average household: $45,260; Households with income of $100,000 or more: 7.0%; Poverty rate: 23.1%

Educational Attainment: High school diploma or higher: 83.3%; Bachelor's degree or higher: 9.3%; Graduate/professional degree or higher: 3.9%

School District(s)
Bridgeport-Spaulding Community SD (PK-12)
    2012-13 Enrollment: 1,472 . . . . (989) 777-1770

Housing: Homeownership rate: 71.0%; Median home value: $73,100; Median year structure built: 1962; Homeowner vacancy rate: 3.2%; Median gross rent: $634 per month; Rental vacancy rate: 9.5%

Health Insurance: 91.9% have insurance; 63.8% have private insurance; 46.0% have public insurance; 8.1% do not have insurance; 2.5% of children under 18 do not have insurance

Transportation: Commute: 99.9% car, 0.1% public transportation, 0.0% walk, 0.0% work from home; Median travel time to work: 21.2 minutes

BRIDGEPORT (charter township).
Covers a land area of 34.430 square miles and a water area of 0.439 square miles. Located at 43.35° N. Lat; 83.87° W. Long. Elevation is 604 feet.

Population: 10,514; Growth (since 2000): -10.2%; Density: 305.4 persons per square mile; Race: 67.9% White, 25.4% Black/African American, 0.4% Asian, 0.5% American Indian/Alaska Native, 0.0% Native Hawaiian/Other Pacific Islander, 2.8% Two or more races, 9.9% Hispanic of any race; Average household size: 2.42; Median age: 43.4; Age under 18: 22.1%; Age 65 and over: 16.6%; Males per 100 females: 91.8; Marriage status: 29.7% never married, 51.4% now married, 2.6% separated, 5.7% widowed, 13.2% divorced; Foreign born: 0.6%; Speak English only: 96.6%;

With disability: 16.3%; Veterans: 11.5%; Ancestry: 27.2% German, 9.0% English, 8.1% Irish, 7.6% Polish, 5.2% American
Employment: 9.6% management, business, and financial, 1.3% computer, engineering, and science, 7.2% education, legal, community service, arts, and media, 5.7% healthcare practitioners, 26.6% service, 25.1% sales and office, 5.8% natural resources, construction, and maintenance, 18.6% production, transportation, and material moving
Income: Per capita: $20,663; Median household: $39,317; Average household: $48,910; Households with income of $100,000 or more: 7.9%; Poverty rate: 20.8%
Educational Attainment: High school diploma or higher: 84.4%; Bachelor's degree or higher: 9.0%; Graduate/professional degree or higher: 3.0%
School District(s)
Bridgeport-Spaulding Community SD (PK-12)
    2012-13 Enrollment: 1,472 . . . . (989) 777-1770
Housing: Homeownership rate: 77.2%; Median home value: $81,900; Median year structure built: 1963; Homeowner vacancy rate: 2.5%; Median gross rent: $642 per month; Rental vacancy rate: 11.5%
Health Insurance: 91.4% have insurance; 64.8% have private insurance; 45.4% have public insurance; 8.6% do not have insurance; 2.1% of children under 18 do not have insurance
Safety: Violent crime rate: 39.6 per 10,000 population; Property crime rate: 185.7 per 10,000 population
Transportation: Commute: 97.7% car, 0.1% public transportation, 0.7% walk, 1.6% work from home; Median travel time to work: 21.3 minutes
Additional Information Contacts
Bridgeport Charter Township . . . . (989) 777-0940
    http://bridgeportmi.org

BUENA VISTA (CDP). Covers a land area of 4.454 square miles and a water area of 0.054 square miles. Located at 43.42° N. Lat; 83.90° W. Long. Elevation is 607 feet.
Population: 6,816; Growth (since 2000): -13.1%; Density: 1,530.4 persons per square mile; Race: 17.8% White, 74.0% Black/African American, 0.3% Asian, 0.7% American Indian/Alaska Native, 0.0% Native Hawaiian/Other Pacific Islander, 3.4% Two or more races, 10.1% Hispanic of any race; Average household size: 2.46; Median age: 35.7; Age under 18: 28.3%; Age 65 and over: 14.6%; Males per 100 females: 84.4; Marriage status: 43.1% never married, 29.2% now married, 4.6% separated, 11.1% widowed, 16.7% divorced; Foreign born: 2.2%; Speak English only: 93.9%; With disability: 32.1%; Veterans: 15.0%; Ancestry: 5.6% German, 4.3% African, 3.4% American, 2.2% Irish, 1.6% English
Employment: 7.5% management, business, and financial, 1.0% computer, engineering, and science, 7.6% education, legal, community service, arts, and media, 1.2% healthcare practitioners, 41.1% service, 12.2% sales and office, 7.3% natural resources, construction, and maintenance, 22.1% production, transportation, and material moving
Income: Per capita: $14,124; Median household: $21,950; Average household: $30,899; Households with income of $100,000 or more: 3.0%; Poverty rate: 40.2%
Educational Attainment: High school diploma or higher: 78.2%; Bachelor's degree or higher: 6.8%; Graduate/professional degree or higher: 1.7%
Housing: Homeownership rate: 58.9%; Median home value: $39,800; Median year structure built: 1960; Homeowner vacancy rate: 4.4%; Median gross rent: $676 per month; Rental vacancy rate: 9.1%
Health Insurance: 85.5% have insurance; 38.2% have private insurance; 63.8% have public insurance; 14.5% do not have insurance; 7.6% of children under 18 do not have insurance
Transportation: Commute: 81.4% car, 1.5% public transportation, 0.0% walk, 10.3% work from home; Median travel time to work: 18.8 minutes

BUENA VISTA (charter township). Covers a land area of 35.477 square miles and a water area of 0.766 square miles. Located at 43.45° N. Lat; 83.86° W. Long. Elevation is 607 feet.
Population: 8,676; Growth (since 2000): -15.9%; Density: 244.5 persons per square mile; Race: 31.5% White, 61.1% Black/African American, 0.3% Asian, 0.6% American Indian/Alaska Native, 0.0% Native Hawaiian/Other Pacific Islander, 3.2% Two or more races, 9.3% Hispanic of any race; Average household size: 2.44; Median age: 36.5; Age under 18: 27.5%; Age 65 and over: 14.9%; Males per 100 females: 89.5; Marriage status: 42.0% never married, 32.5% now married, 3.9% separated, 9.9% widowed, 15.6% divorced; Foreign born: 1.8%; Speak English only: 95.3%;

With disability: 28.7%; Veterans: 13.2%; Ancestry: 12.9% German, 3.2% American, 3.2% African, 2.9% Irish, 2.8% French
Employment: 7.7% management, business, and financial, 0.9% computer, engineering, and science, 7.1% education, legal, community service, arts, and media, 3.2% healthcare practitioners, 34.4% service, 18.0% sales and office, 7.1% natural resources, construction, and maintenance, 21.7% production, transportation, and material moving
Income: Per capita: $15,239; Median household: $24,100; Average household: $34,830; Households with income of $100,000 or more: 4.8%; Poverty rate: 33.9%
Educational Attainment: High school diploma or higher: 79.7%; Bachelor's degree or higher: 8.6%; Graduate/professional degree or higher: 2.8%
Housing: Homeownership rate: 65.3%; Median home value: $45,600; Median year structure built: 1963; Homeowner vacancy rate: 3.8%; Median gross rent: $674 per month; Rental vacancy rate: 10.0%
Health Insurance: 86.0% have insurance; 44.1% have private insurance; 60.0% have public insurance; 14.0% do not have insurance; 6.8% of children under 18 do not have insurance
Safety: Violent crime rate: 116.5 per 10,000 population; Property crime rate: 311.8 per 10,000 population
Transportation: Commute: 87.1% car, 0.9% public transportation, 0.6% walk, 6.9% work from home; Median travel time to work: 18.5 minutes
Additional Information Contacts
Buena Vista Charter Township . . . . (989) 754-6536
    http://bvct.org

BURT (CDP). Covers a land area of 4.515 square miles and a water area of 0.007 square miles. Located at 43.23° N. Lat; 83.91° W. Long. Elevation is 633 feet.
History: Burt developed around a station on the Cincinnati, Saginaw & Mackinaw Railroad.
Population: 1,228; Growth (since 2000): 9.4%; Density: 272.0 persons per square mile; Race: 93.4% White, 1.5% Black/African American, 0.1% Asian, 0.5% American Indian/Alaska Native, 0.1% Native Hawaiian/Other Pacific Islander, 3.5% Two or more races, 4.2% Hispanic of any race; Average household size: 2.88; Median age: 38.3; Age under 18: 27.8%; Age 65 and over: 9.0%; Males per 100 females: 106.4
Housing: Homeownership rate: 87.6%; Homeowner vacancy rate: 0.8%; Rental vacancy rate: 5.4%

CARROLLTON (township). Covers a land area of 3.337 square miles and a water area of 0.178 square miles. Located at 43.46° N. Lat; 83.94° W. Long. Elevation is 587 feet.
Population: 6,103; Growth (since 2000): -7.6%; Density: 1,829.0 persons per square mile; Race: 80.6% White, 11.7% Black/African American, 0.3% Asian, 0.4% American Indian/Alaska Native, 0.0% Native Hawaiian/Other Pacific Islander, 3.8% Two or more races, 11.9% Hispanic of any race; Average household size: 2.47; Median age: 37.8; Age under 18: 23.7%; Age 65 and over: 15.4%; Males per 100 females: 93.6; Marriage status: 41.0% never married, 34.7% now married, 2.5% separated, 6.5% widowed, 17.8% divorced; Foreign born: 1.6%; Speak English only: 96.5%; With disability: 12.5%; Veterans: 10.1%; Ancestry: 29.4% German, 9.8% Polish, 9.2% French, 8.9% English, 8.0% Irish
Employment: 8.2% management, business, and financial, 2.1% computer, engineering, and science, 8.9% education, legal, community service, arts, and media, 3.9% healthcare practitioners, 18.6% service, 32.9% sales and office, 9.6% natural resources, construction, and maintenance, 15.7% production, transportation, and material moving
Income: Per capita: $18,174; Median household: $33,644; Average household: $43,318; Households with income of $100,000 or more: 7.1%; Poverty rate: 22.4%
Educational Attainment: High school diploma or higher: 87.0%; Bachelor's degree or higher: 13.7%; Graduate/professional degree or higher: 5.3%
Housing: Homeownership rate: 71.0%; Median home value: $69,200; Median year structure built: 1958; Homeowner vacancy rate: 2.1%; Median gross rent: $700 per month; Rental vacancy rate: 9.4%
Health Insurance: 85.1% have insurance; 67.5% have private insurance; 34.1% have public insurance; 14.9% do not have insurance; 0.0% of children under 18 do not have insurance
Safety: Violent crime rate: 33.4 per 10,000 population; Property crime rate: 175.1 per 10,000 population
Transportation: Commute: 97.4% car, 0.1% public transportation, 1.4% walk, 1.1% work from home; Median travel time to work: 17.9 minutes

CHAPIN (township). Covers a land area of 24.645 square miles and a water area of 0.003 square miles. Located at 43.17° N. Lat; 84.34° W. Long. Elevation is 709 feet.

History: Chapin Township was organized in 1867 and named for Austin Chapin, one of the organizers.

Population: 1,060; Growth (since 2000): 1.4%; Density: 43.0 persons per square mile; Race: 96.7% White, 0.1% Black/African American, 0.2% Asian, 0.8% American Indian/Alaska Native, 0.0% Native Hawaiian/Other Pacific Islander, 1.5% Two or more races, 2.5% Hispanic of any race; Average household size: 2.76; Median age: 40.0; Age under 18: 25.3%; Age 65 and over: 12.2%; Males per 100 females: 107.0

Housing: Homeownership rate: 81.8%; Homeowner vacancy rate: 1.9%; Rental vacancy rate: 1.4%

CHESANING (township). Covers a land area of 34.270 square miles and a water area of 0.293 square miles. Located at 43.18° N. Lat; 84.10° W. Long. Elevation is 630 feet.

History: Chesaning Township began as Northampton Township in 1846. It was renamed in 1853. The name is of Indian origin meaning "big rock."

Population: 4,659; Growth (since 2000): -4.2%; Density: 136.0 persons per square mile; Race: 95.9% White, 0.4% Black/African American, 0.2% Asian, 0.4% American Indian/Alaska Native, 0.0% Native Hawaiian/Other Pacific Islander, 1.2% Two or more races, 4.7% Hispanic of any race; Average household size: 2.41; Median age: 42.9; Age under 18: 22.8%; Age 65 and over: 17.3%; Males per 100 females: 96.7; Marriage status: 19.4% never married, 62.0% now married, 0.3% separated, 7.8% widowed, 10.7% divorced; Foreign born: 1.2%; Speak English only: 97.5%; With disability: 14.7%; Veterans: 12.2%; Ancestry: 38.7% German, 9.7% Irish, 9.0% American, 7.1% English, 4.8% Polish

Employment: 11.5% management, business, and financial, 4.0% computer, engineering, and science, 5.9% education, legal, community service, arts, and media, 5.4% healthcare practitioners, 20.8% service, 22.7% sales and office, 8.8% natural resources, construction, and maintenance, 20.9% production, transportation, and material moving

Income: Per capita: $23,473; Median household: $41,926; Average household: $56,304; Households with income of $100,000 or more: 10.9%; Poverty rate: 10.6%

Educational Attainment: High school diploma or higher: 90.2%; Bachelor's degree or higher: 14.2%; Graduate/professional degree or higher: 5.1%

School District(s)

Chesaning Union Schools (PK-12)

    2012-13 Enrollment: 1,616 . . . . (989) 845-7020

Housing: Homeownership rate: 77.1%; Median home value: $100,600; Median year structure built: 1963; Homeowner vacancy rate: 2.4%; Median gross rent: $636 per month; Rental vacancy rate: 12.3%

Health Insurance: 89.8% have insurance; 75.5% have private insurance; 34.0% have public insurance; 10.2% do not have insurance; 0.0% of children under 18 do not have insurance

Newspapers: Tri-County Citizen (weekly circulation 18000)

Transportation: Commute: 93.1% car, 0.0% public transportation, 2.6% walk, 3.7% work from home; Median travel time to work: 29.0 minutes

CHESANING (village). Covers a land area of 3.051 square miles and a water area of 0.092 square miles. Located at 43.18° N. Lat; 84.12° W. Long. Elevation is 630 feet.

History: Chesaning was settled in 1839 by Thomas W. Wright and his family. First called Northampton, the village was renamed Chesaning when the township was renamed.

Population: 2,394; Growth (since 2000): -6.0%; Density: 784.8 persons per square mile; Race: 95.9% White, 0.6% Black/African American, 0.3% Asian, 0.6% American Indian/Alaska Native, 0.0% Native Hawaiian/Other Pacific Islander, 1.1% Two or more races, 4.1% Hispanic of any race; Average household size: 2.32; Median age: 39.7; Age under 18: 24.1%; Age 65 and over: 16.8%; Males per 100 females: 91.2

School District(s)

Chesaning Union Schools (PK-12)

    2012-13 Enrollment: 1,616 . . . . (989) 845-7020

Housing: Homeownership rate: 64.0%; Homeowner vacancy rate: 3.0%; Rental vacancy rate: 13.0%

Safety: Violent crime rate: 12.8 per 10,000 population; Property crime rate: 63.7 per 10,000 population

Newspapers: Tri-County Citizen (weekly circulation 18000)

FRANKENMUTH (city). Covers a land area of 2.994 square miles and a water area of 0.051 square miles. Located at 43.33° N. Lat; 83.74° W. Long. Elevation is 636 feet.

History: Frankenmuth was settled by German immigrants, and became known for its Frankenmuth beer. It was established in 1845 by a group from Bavaria, who were joined by refugees from the German revolution of 1848.

Population: 4,944; Growth (since 2000): 2.2%; Density: 1,651.6 persons per square mile; Race: 97.4% White, 0.5% Black/African American, 0.8% Asian, 0.2% American Indian/Alaska Native, 0.0% Native Hawaiian/Other Pacific Islander, 0.6% Two or more races, 1.9% Hispanic of any race; Average household size: 2.14; Median age: 50.1; Age under 18: 19.3%; Age 65 and over: 28.9%; Males per 100 females: 81.6; Marriage status: 19.0% never married, 54.9% now married, 0.5% separated, 14.0% widowed, 12.1% divorced; Foreign born: 5.2%; Speak English only: 92.2%; With disability: 18.8%; Veterans: 12.3%; Ancestry: 48.3% German, 15.0% Polish, 6.5% English, 5.8% Irish, 5.4% French

Employment: 26.2% management, business, and financial, 8.4% computer, engineering, and science, 6.3% education, legal, community service, arts, and media, 7.8% healthcare practitioners, 15.1% service, 26.3% sales and office, 1.5% natural resources, construction, and maintenance, 8.4% production, transportation, and material moving

Income: Per capita: $31,558; Median household: $49,983; Average household: $66,737; Households with income of $100,000 or more: 20.7%; Poverty rate: 8.0%

Educational Attainment: High school diploma or higher: 93.7%; Bachelor's degree or higher: 34.8%; Graduate/professional degree or higher: 11.4%

School District(s)

Frankenmuth SD (PK-12)

    2012-13 Enrollment: 1,214 . . . . (989) 652-9958

Housing: Homeownership rate: 69.6%; Median home value: $164,100; Median year structure built: 1977; Homeowner vacancy rate: 1.4%; Median gross rent: $693 per month; Rental vacancy rate: 15.3%

Health Insurance: 95.7% have insurance; 89.7% have private insurance; 34.7% have public insurance; 4.3% do not have insurance; 6.5% of children under 18 do not have insurance

Safety: Violent crime rate: 20.3 per 10,000 population; Property crime rate: 190.9 per 10,000 population

Newspapers: Frankenmuth News (weekly circulation 4800)

Transportation: Commute: 91.3% car, 0.3% public transportation, 6.5% walk, 1.9% work from home; Median travel time to work: 23.1 minutes

Additional Information Contacts

City of Frankenmuth . . . . (989) 652-9901

    http://www.frankenmuthcity.com

FRANKENMUTH (township). Covers a land area of 32.293 square miles and a water area of 0.152 square miles. Located at 43.36° N. Lat; 83.77° W..Long. Elevation is 636 feet.

History: Historical Museum, Military and Space Museum, antique-arts village, flour mill (1847), Covered bridge on Cass River, famous German Glockenspiel, 35-bell carillon. Settled 1845 by German Bavarians; incorporated 1904.

Population: 1,959; Growth (since 2000): -4.4%; Density: 60.7 persons per square mile; Race: 97.9% White, 0.3% Black/African American, 0.9% Asian, 0.1% American Indian/Alaska Native, 0.0% Native Hawaiian/Other Pacific Islander, 0.4% Two or more races, 2.0% Hispanic of any race; Average household size: 2.71; Median age: 46.1; Age under 18: 22.8%; Age 65 and over: 19.3%; Males per 100 females: 105.1

School District(s)

Frankenmuth SD (PK-12)

    2012-13 Enrollment: 1,214 . . . . (989) 652-9958

Housing: Homeownership rate: 91.6%; Homeowner vacancy rate: 1.2%; Rental vacancy rate: 12.9%

Newspapers: Frankenmuth News (weekly circulation 4800)

FREELAND (CDP). Covers a land area of 6.584 square miles and a water area of 0.138 square miles. Located at 43.52° N. Lat; 84.11° W. Long. Elevation is 620 feet.

Population: 6,969; Growth (since 2000): 35.4%; Density: 1,058.4 persons per square mile; Race: 84.7% White, 12.5% Black/African American, 0.6% Asian, 0.5% American Indian/Alaska Native, 0.0% Native Hawaiian/Other Pacific Islander, 1.2% Two or more races, 2.9% Hispanic of any race; Average household size: 2.72; Median age: 34.8; Age under 18: 23.3%; Age 65 and over: 8.3%; Males per 100 females: 149.3; Marriage status:

34.2% never married, 51.2% now married, 0.7% separated, 4.2% widowed, 10.3% divorced; Foreign born: 2.1%; Speak English only: 96.9%; With disability: 7.3%; Veterans: 6.7%; Ancestry: 38.3% German, 16.1% Polish, 14.5% Irish, 7.5% English, 6.4% French

Employment: 20.2% management, business, and financial, 7.5% computer, engineering, and science, 8.4% education, legal, community service, arts, and media, 6.8% healthcare practitioners, 13.4% service, 24.6% sales and office, 8.1% natural resources, construction, and maintenance, 10.8% production, transportation, and material moving

Income: Per capita: $23,570; Median household: $73,628; Average household: $79,754; Households with income of $100,000 or more: 29.5%; Poverty rate: 4.8%

Educational Attainment: High school diploma or higher: 88.9%; Bachelor's degree or higher: 30.8%; Graduate/professional degree or higher: 7.3%

School District(s)

Freeland Community SD (KG-12)
    2012-13 Enrollment: 1,821 . . . . (989) 695-5527

Housing: Homeownership rate: 82.5%; Median home value: $158,400; Median year structure built: 1993; Homeowner vacancy rate: 1.9%; Median gross rent: $938 per month; Rental vacancy rate: 4.8%

Health Insurance: 93.0% have insurance; 86.0% have private insurance; 18.1% have public insurance; 7.0% do not have insurance; 5.1% of children under 18 do not have insurance

Transportation: Commute: 96.9% car, 0.0% public transportation, 0.0% walk, 3.1% work from home; Median travel time to work: 22.5 minutes

FREMONT (township). Covers a land area of 36.606 square miles and a water area of 0.154 square miles. Located at 43.35° N. Lat; 84.24° W. Long.

Population: 2,096; Growth (since 2000): -0.1%; Density: 57.3 persons per square mile; Race: 96.7% White, 0.3% Black/African American, 0.2% Asian, 0.8% American Indian/Alaska Native, 0.0% Native Hawaiian/Other Pacific Islander, 1.2% Two or more races, 3.1% Hispanic of any race; Average household size: 2.65; Median age: 43.9; Age under 18: 22.8%; Age 65 and over: 15.1%; Males per 100 females: 105.1

Housing: Homeownership rate: 92.9%; Homeowner vacancy rate: 0.5%; Rental vacancy rate: 5.1%

HEMLOCK (CDP). Covers a land area of 2.519 square miles and a water area of 0.024 square miles. Located at 43.42° N. Lat; 84.24° W. Long. Elevation is 650 feet.

History: Hemlock developed around a sawmill built here in 1868 by W.S. Gillespie. The settlement grew when the Saginaw Valley & St. Louis Railroad arrived in 1869. The town was named for the quantity of hemlock trees in the area.

Population: 1,466; Growth (since 2000): -7.5%; Density: 582.1 persons per square mile; Race: 97.1% White, 0.1% Black/African American, 0.1% Asian, 0.2% American Indian/Alaska Native, 0.0% Native Hawaiian/Other Pacific Islander, 1.7% Two or more races, 3.3% Hispanic of any race; Average household size: 2.47; Median age: 38.4; Age under 18: 25.6%; Age 65 and over: 15.3%; Males per 100 females: 91.1

School District(s)

Hemlock Public SD (PK-12)
    2012-13 Enrollment: 1,245 . . . . (989) 642-5282

Housing: Homeownership rate: 76.8%; Homeowner vacancy rate: 1.5%; Rental vacancy rate: 7.9%

JAMES (township). Covers a land area of 16.735 square miles and a water area of 2.386 square miles. Located at 43.37° N. Lat; 84.05° W. Long.

History: James Township, also known as Jimtown, was organized in 1875 and named for James Murphy, who began making bricks here in 1865.

Population: 2,023; Growth (since 2000): 4.8%; Density: 120.9 persons per square mile; Race: 96.6% White, 0.2% Black/African American, 0.2% Asian, 0.4% American Indian/Alaska Native, 0.0% Native Hawaiian/Other Pacific Islander, 1.3% Two or more races, 3.8% Hispanic of any race; Average household size: 2.60; Median age: 43.7; Age under 18: 22.3%; Age 65 and over: 15.9%; Males per 100 females: 103.9

Housing: Homeownership rate: 92.4%; Homeowner vacancy rate: 0.6%; Rental vacancy rate: 1.7%

JONESFIELD (township). Covers a land area of 25.196 square miles and a water area of 0.024 square miles. Located at 43.44° N. Lat; 84.32° W. Long.

History: The Jonesfield Township was organized in 1873 after the Saginaw Valley & St. Louis Railroad was built here.

Population: 1,667; Growth (since 2000): -2.5%; Density: 66.2 persons per square mile; Race: 97.0% White, 0.6% Black/African American, 0.1% Asian, 0.4% American Indian/Alaska Native, 0.0% Native Hawaiian/Other Pacific Islander, 0.8% Two or more races, 3.9% Hispanic of any race; Average household size: 2.52; Median age: 41.9; Age under 18: 22.4%; Age 65 and over: 17.2%; Males per 100 females: 98.0

Housing: Homeownership rate: 86.2%; Homeowner vacancy rate: 1.6%; Rental vacancy rate: 4.2%

KOCHVILLE (township). Covers a land area of 18.573 square miles and a water area of 0.228 square miles. Located at 43.51° N. Lat; 83.99° W. Long. Elevation is 591 feet.

History: Kochville Township was organized in 1856 and named for Frederick Charles Koch, who had settled here in 1849.

Population: 5,078; Growth (since 2000): 56.7%; Density: 273.4 persons per square mile; Race: 86.4% White, 8.0% Black/African American, 2.8% Asian, 0.6% American Indian/Alaska Native, 0.0% Native Hawaiian/Other Pacific Islander, 1.6% Two or more races, 3.1% Hispanic of any race; Average household size: 2.51; Median age: 20.7; Age under 18: 8.2%; Age 65 and over: 6.8%; Males per 100 females: 79.8; Marriage status: 59.9% never married, 31.0% now married, 1.2% separated, 4.1% widowed, 5.0% divorced; Foreign born: 5.9%; Speak English only: 92.2%; With disability: 6.2%; Veterans: 6.6%; Ancestry: 23.9% German, 12.2% Polish, 8.0% Irish, 5.8% English, 5.6% French

Employment: 10.1% management, business, and financial, 10.3% computer, engineering, and science, 8.2% education, legal, community service, arts, and media, 4.8% healthcare practitioners, 20.0% service, 28.0% sales and office, 8.0% natural resources, construction, and maintenance, 10.5% production, transportation, and material moving

Income: Per capita: $17,435; Median household: $45,811; Average household: $57,802; Households with income of $100,000 or more: 17.3%; Poverty rate: 22.3%

Educational Attainment: High school diploma or higher: 91.6%; Bachelor's degree or higher: 20.0%; Graduate/professional degree or higher: 3.4%

Housing: Homeownership rate: 72.8%; Median home value: $120,500; Median year structure built: 1974; Homeowner vacancy rate: 2.0%; Median gross rent: $763 per month; Rental vacancy rate: 6.8%

Health Insurance: 94.9% have insurance; 87.1% have private insurance; 19.2% have public insurance; 5.1% do not have insurance; 1.1% of children under 18 do not have insurance

Transportation: Commute: 77.3% car, 0.0% public transportation, 14.3% walk, 2.8% work from home; Median travel time to work: 16.6 minutes

LAKEFIELD (township). Covers a land area of 24.083 square miles and a water area of 0.026 square miles. Located at 43.34° N. Lat; 84.32° W. Long. Elevation is 669 feet.

Population: 1,029; Growth (since 2000): -0.1%; Density: 42.7 persons per square mile; Race: 97.0% White, 0.0% Black/African American, 0.2% Asian, 0.0% American Indian/Alaska Native, 0.1% Native Hawaiian/Other Pacific Islander, 1.4% Two or more races, 5.2% Hispanic of any race; Average household size: 2.72; Median age: 41.8; Age under 18: 22.5%; Age 65 and over: 15.0%; Males per 100 females: 99.0

Housing: Homeownership rate: 91.6%; Homeowner vacancy rate: 0.6%; Rental vacancy rate: 0.0%

MAPLE GROVE (township). Covers a land area of 35.798 square miles and a water area of 0.937 square miles. Located at 43.18° N. Lat; 83.99° W. Long. Elevation is 666 feet.

Population: 2,668; Growth (since 2000): 1.1%; Density: 74.5 persons per square mile; Race: 97.3% White, 0.8% Black/African American, 0.0% Asian, 0.5% American Indian/Alaska Native, 0.0% Native Hawaiian/Other Pacific Islander, 0.9% Two or more races, 1.5% Hispanic of any race; Average household size: 2.66; Median age: 41.6; Age under 18: 24.3%; Age 65 and over: 15.0%; Males per 100 females: 103.4; Marriage status: 21.1% never married, 70.3% now married, 1.1% separated, 5.2% widowed, 3.4% divorced; Foreign born: 1.4%; Speak English only: 97.6%; With disability: 9.2%; Veterans: 7.4%; Ancestry: 46.9% German, 15.2% Irish, 6.1% English, 5.2% French, 4.7% Polish

Employment: 14.0% management, business, and financial, 3.6% computer, engineering, and science, 8.0% education, legal, community service, arts, and media, 8.0% healthcare practitioners, 13.0% service, 23.0% sales and office, 13.2% natural resources, construction, and maintenance, 17.1% production, transportation, and material moving
Income: Per capita: $22,733; Median household: $51,742; Average household: $63,567; Households with income of $100,000 or more: 17.6%; Poverty rate: 12.7%
Educational Attainment: High school diploma or higher: 88.8%; Bachelor's degree or higher: 14.6%; Graduate/professional degree or higher: 4.4%
Housing: Homeownership rate: 91.2%; Median home value: $125,400; Median year structure built: 1970; Homeowner vacancy rate: 1.2%; Median gross rent: $850 per month; Rental vacancy rate: 5.4%
Health Insurance: 95.4% have insurance; 83.2% have private insurance; 28.1% have public insurance; 4.6% do not have insurance; 0.0% of children under 18 do not have insurance
Transportation: Commute: 96.5% car, 0.0% public transportation, 0.3% walk, 2.8% work from home; Median travel time to work: 32.4 minutes

MARION (township). Covers a land area of 24.384 square miles and a water area of 0.280 square miles. Located at 43.26° N. Lat; 84.34° W. Long.
Population: 923; Growth (since 2000): -0.2%; Density: 37.9 persons per square mile; Race: 98.0% White, 0.2% Black/African American, 0.0% Asian, 0.7% American Indian/Alaska Native, 0.0% Native Hawaiian/Other Pacific Islander, 0.5% Two or more races, 2.7% Hispanic of any race; Average household size: 2.79; Median age: 37.9; Age under 18: 25.6%; Age 65 and over: 10.4%; Males per 100 females: 100.7
Housing: Homeownership rate: 82.8%; Homeowner vacancy rate: 2.1%; Rental vacancy rate: 9.5%

MERRILL (village). Covers a land area of 0.699 square miles and a water area of 0 square miles. Located at 43.41° N. Lat; 84.33° W. Long. Elevation is 669 feet.
History: Merrill was named for a railroad engineer who assisted the residents of the town in 1881 when a forest fire threatened their community. The town grew up around a wheat, beans, and sugar beet growing area.
Population: 778; Growth (since 2000): -0.5%; Density: 1,113.5 persons per square mile; Race: 95.0% White, 1.2% Black/African American, 0.3% Asian, 0.5% American Indian/Alaska Native, 0.0% Native Hawaiian/Other Pacific Islander, 1.3% Two or more races, 6.7% Hispanic of any race; Average household size: 2.60; Median age: 39.5; Age under 18: 24.6%; Age 65 and over: 17.1%; Males per 100 females: 93.5
School District(s)
Merrill Community Schools (PK-12)
    2012-13 Enrollment: 734 . . . . (989) 643-7261
Housing: Homeownership rate: 79.0%; Homeowner vacancy rate: 1.3%; Rental vacancy rate: 1.6%

OAKLEY (village). Covers a land area of 1.019 square miles and a water area of 0.009 square miles. Located at 43.14° N. Lat; 84.17° W. Long. Elevation is 679 feet.
Population: 290; Growth (since 2000): -14.5%; Density: 284.6 persons per square mile; Race: 95.2% White, 3.8% Black/African American, 0.0% Asian, 0.7% American Indian/Alaska Native, 0.0% Native Hawaiian/Other Pacific Islander, 0.3% Two or more races, 3.8% Hispanic of any race; Average household size: 2.50; Median age: 42.7; Age under 18: 22.1%; Age 65 and over: 17.9%; Males per 100 females: 89.5
Housing: Homeownership rate: 81.0%; Homeowner vacancy rate: 4.1%; Rental vacancy rate: 15.4%
Safety: Violent crime rate: 105.3 per 10,000 population; Property crime rate: 105.3 per 10,000 population

RICHLAND (township). Covers a land area of 36.710 square miles and a water area of 0.359 square miles. Located at 43.44° N. Lat; 84.24° W. Long.
History: Richland Township was first settled in 1857 by Lemuel Cone. The township was organized in 1862, and named by Cone.
Population: 4,144; Growth (since 2000): -3.2%; Density: 112.9 persons per square mile; Race: 97.6% White, 0.3% Black/African American, 0.2% Asian, 0.3% American Indian/Alaska Native, 0.0% Native Hawaiian/Other Pacific Islander, 1.0% Two or more races, 2.8% Hispanic of any race; Average household size: 2.57; Median age: 42.6; Age under 18: 23.4%;

Age 65 and over: 16.2%; Males per 100 females: 96.1; Marriage status: 25.5% never married, 62.1% now married, 0.5% separated, 6.1% widowed, 6.3% divorced; Foreign born: 0.5%; Speak English only: 98.3%; With disability: 10.7%; Veterans: 8.9%; Ancestry: 49.2% German, 17.0% Irish, 10.8% English, 10.4% Polish, 6.7% French
Employment: 8.9% management, business, and financial, 0.8% computer, engineering, and science, 14.4% education, legal, community service, arts, and media, 8.9% healthcare practitioners, 14.0% service, 24.2% sales and office, 11.5% natural resources, construction, and maintenance, 17.2% production, transportation, and material moving
Income: Per capita: $27,976; Median household: $64,121; Average household: $71,373; Households with income of $100,000 or more: 20.0%; Poverty rate: 5.4%
Educational Attainment: High school diploma or higher: 93.7%; Bachelor's degree or higher: 19.6%; Graduate/professional degree or higher: 6.8%
Housing: Homeownership rate: 86.4%; Median home value: $134,800; Median year structure built: 1970; Homeowner vacancy rate: 1.9%; Median gross rent: $639 per month; Rental vacancy rate: 6.7%
Health Insurance: 91.3% have insurance; 77.1% have private insurance; 29.9% have public insurance; 8.7% do not have insurance; 2.1% of children under 18 do not have insurance
Transportation: Commute: 96.9% car, 0.0% public transportation, 1.5% walk, 0.9% work from home; Median travel time to work: 23.6 minutes

ROBIN GLEN-INDIANTOWN (CDP). Covers a land area of 2.075 square miles and a water area of 0 square miles. Located at 43.46° N. Lat; 83.84° W. Long.
Population: 722; Growth (since 2000): -37.7%; Density: 348.0 persons per square mile; Race: 92.4% White, 1.8% Black/African American, 0.6% Asian, 0.4% American Indian/Alaska Native, 0.0% Native Hawaiian/Other Pacific Islander, 3.0% Two or more races, 8.9% Hispanic of any race; Average household size: 2.43; Median age: 35.9; Age under 18: 26.2%; Age 65 and over: 11.5%; Males per 100 females: 90.0
Housing: Homeownership rate: 87.5%; Homeowner vacancy rate: 3.7%; Rental vacancy rate: 30.2%

SAGINAW (charter township). Covers a land area of 24.497 square miles and a water area of 0.378 square miles. Located at 43.45° N. Lat; 84.02° W. Long. Elevation is 581 feet.
History: Native American trails once crossed the site, and local Native American villages were abundant. Lewis Cass negotiated a treaty here (1819) with the indigenous groups, who ceded much of what is now Michigan to the U.S. Fur trade was followed by a great pine-lumbering industry, which thrived until about 1890. The old Schuch Hotel (1868) has an interesting collection of antiques. Saginaw Valley State University. Historical Museum. Settled 1816, Incorporated 1857.
Population: 40,840; Growth (since 2000): 3.0%; Density: 1,667.1 persons per square mile; Race: 83.8% White, 8.8% Black/African American, 3.4% Asian, 0.3% American Indian/Alaska Native, 0.1% Native Hawaiian/Other Pacific Islander, 2.2% Two or more races, 6.4% Hispanic of any race; Average household size: 2.22; Median age: 43.1; Age under 18: 20.0%; Age 65 and over: 19.7%; Males per 100 females: 88.3; Marriage status: 28.4% never married, 53.0% now married, 1.3% separated, 8.4% widowed, 10.2% divorced; Foreign born: 5.0%; Speak English only: 92.6%; With disability: 12.5%; Veterans: 10.1%; Ancestry: 32.5% German, 11.1% Polish, 10.6% Irish, 9.4% English, 7.1% French
Employment: 11.9% management, business, and financial, 4.6% computer, engineering, and science, 11.4% education, legal, community service, arts, and media, 9.2% healthcare practitioners, 17.8% service, 28.6% sales and office, 5.0% natural resources, construction, and maintenance, 11.4% production, transportation, and material moving
Income: Per capita: $29,067; Median household: $48,762; Average household: $65,250; Households with income of $100,000 or more: 19.9%; Poverty rate: 12.3%
Educational Attainment: High school diploma or higher: 92.9%; Bachelor's degree or higher: 32.9%; Graduate/professional degree or higher: 12.0%
School District(s)
Bridgeport-Spaulding Community SD (PK-12)
    2012-13 Enrollment: 1,472 . . . . (989) 777-1770
Buena Vista SD (PK-12)
    2012-13 Enrollment: 428 . . . . (989) 755-2184
Carrollton Public Schools (PK-12)
    2012-13 Enrollment: 1,893 . . . . (989) 754-1475

Francis Reh Psa (PK-12)
2012-13 Enrollment: 409. . . . . (989) 753-2349
International Academy of Saginaw (KG-12)
2012-13 Enrollment: 240. . . . . (989) 921-1000
North Saginaw Charter Academy (KG-12)
2012-13 Enrollment: 317. . . . . (989) 249-5400
Saginaw County Transition Academy (KG-12)
2012-13 Enrollment: 57. . . . . (989) 399-8774
Saginaw ISD (PK-12)
2012-13 Enrollment: 1,130 . . . . (989) 249-8701
Saginaw Learn To Earn Academy (KG-12)
2012-13 Enrollment: 109. . . . . (989) 399-8775
Saginaw Preparatory Academy (PK-12)
2012-13 Enrollment: 413. . . . . (989) 752-9600
Saginaw SD (PK-12)
2012-13 Enrollment: 7,504 . . . . (989) 399-6500
Saginaw Township Community Schools (PK-12)
2012-13 Enrollment: 4,927 . . . . (989) 797-1800
Swan Valley SD (PK-12)
2012-13 Enrollment: 1,804 . . . . (989) 921-3701

Vocational/Technical School(s)
Dorsey Business Schools-Saginaw (Private, For-profit)
Fall 2013 Enrollment: 223. . . . . (989) 249-1926
2013-14 Tuition: In-state $17,568; Out-of-state $17,568
In Session Arts of Cosmetology Beauty School (Private, For-profit)
Fall 2013 Enrollment: 77. . . . . (989) 781-6282
2013-14 Tuition: $7,200
Ross Medical Education Center-Saginaw (Private, For-profit)
Fall 2013 Enrollment: 208. . . . . (989) 791-5192
2013-14 Tuition: $15,680
Housing: Homeownership rate: 64.8%; Median home value: $126,100; Median year structure built: 1973; Homeowner vacancy rate: 1.9%; Median gross rent: $735 per month; Rental vacancy rate: 7.7%
Health Insurance: 91.6% have insurance; 80.7% have private insurance; 31.2% have public insurance; 8.4% do not have insurance; 5.3% of children under 18 do not have insurance
Hospitals: Covenant Medical Center (601 beds); Healthsource Saginaw (317 beds); Saginaw VA Medical Center (238 beds); Saint Mary's of Michigan Medical Center (268 beds)
Safety: Violent crime rate: 23.6 per 10,000 population; Property crime rate: 213.9 per 10,000 population
Newspapers: Saginaw News (weekly circulation 35000); Saginaw Press (weekly circulation 500); The Township Times (weekly circulation 5000)
Transportation: Commute: 96.9% car, 0.1% public transportation, 0.4% walk, 2.0% work from home; Median travel time to work: 18.9 minutes; Amtrak: Train service available.
Airports: MBS International (primary service/non-hub)
Additional Information Contacts
Saginaw Charter Township . . . . (989) 791-9800
http://www.saginawtownship.org

SAGINAW (city). County seat. Covers a land area of 17.336 square miles and a water area of 0.763 square miles. Located at 43.42° N. Lat; 83.95° W. Long. Elevation is 581 feet.
History: In 1816 a fur trading post was built here by Louis Campau of Canada, followed in 1819 by Fort Saginaw, abandoned in 1823. A settlement grew up around the American Fur Company's operation, and was incorporated as the village of Saginaw in 1837. Lumberjacks and steam sawmills became numerous along the Saginaw River, until coal was discovered in the late 1880's. Rivalry between the communities of East and West Saginaw ended in 1889 when the two were united as the City of Saginaw. Saginaw became the center of a large agricultural area, storing and shipping beans, grains, and sugar beets.
Population: 51,508; Growth (since 2000): -16.7%; Density: 2,971.2 persons per square mile; Race: 43.5% White, 46.1% Black/African American, 0.3% Asian, 0.5% American Indian/Alaska Native, 0.0% Native Hawaiian/Other Pacific Islander, 4.4% Two or more races, 14.3% Hispanic of any race; Average household size: 2.52; Median age: 33.5; Age under 18: 28.4%; Age 65 and over: 10.9%; Males per 100 females: 89.1; Marriage status: 45.5% never married, 31.9% now married, 3.1% separated, 7.0% widowed, 15.5% divorced; Foreign born: 1.5%; Speak English only: 93.4%; With disability: 19.8%; Veterans: 8.8%; Ancestry: 14.2% German, 6.3% Irish, 4.6% Polish, 4.3% English, 3.7% French
Employment: 7.1% management, business, and financial, 2.3% computer, engineering, and science, 8.4% education, legal, community service, arts,

and media, 5.2% healthcare practitioners, 30.0% service, 25.0% sales and office, 5.6% natural resources, construction, and maintenance, 16.3% production, transportation, and material moving
Income: Per capita: $14,687; Median household: $27,701; Average household: $36,791; Households with income of $100,000 or more: 5.1%; Poverty rate: 37.4%
Educational Attainment: High school diploma or higher: 77.8%; Bachelor's degree or higher: 11.5%; Graduate/professional degree or higher: 3.8%
School District(s)
Bridgeport-Spaulding Community SD (PK-12)
2012-13 Enrollment: 1,472 . . . . (989) 777-1770
Buena Vista SD (PK-12)
2012-13 Enrollment: 428. . . . . (989) 755-2184
Carrollton Public Schools (PK-12)
2012-13 Enrollment: 1,893 . . . . (989) 754-1475
Francis Reh Psa (PK-12)
2012-13 Enrollment: 409. . . . . (989) 753-2349
International Academy of Saginaw (KG-12)
2012-13 Enrollment: 240. . . . . (989) 921-1000
North Saginaw Charter Academy (KG-12)
2012-13 Enrollment: 317. . . . . (989) 249-5400
Saginaw County Transition Academy (KG-12)
2012-13 Enrollment: 57. . . . . (989) 399-8774
Saginaw ISD (PK-12)
2012-13 Enrollment: 1,130 . . . . (989) 249-8701
Saginaw Learn To Earn Academy (KG-12)
2012-13 Enrollment: 109. . . . . (989) 399-8775
Saginaw Preparatory Academy (PK-12)
2012-13 Enrollment: 413. . . . . (989) 752-9600
Saginaw SD (PK-12)
2012-13 Enrollment: 7,504 . . . . (989) 399-6500
Saginaw Township Community Schools (PK-12)
2012-13 Enrollment: 4,927 . . . . (989) 797-1800
Swan Valley SD (PK-12)
2012-13 Enrollment: 1,804 . . . . (989) 921-3701
Vocational/Technical School(s)
Dorsey Business Schools-Saginaw (Private, For-profit)
Fall 2013 Enrollment: 223. . . . . (989) 249-1926
2013-14 Tuition: In-state $17,568; Out-of-state $17,568
In Session Arts of Cosmetology Beauty School (Private, For-profit)
Fall 2013 Enrollment: 77. . . . . (989) 781-6282
2013-14 Tuition: $7,200
Ross Medical Education Center-Saginaw (Private, For-profit)
Fall 2013 Enrollment: 208. . . . . (989) 791-5192
2013-14 Tuition: $15,680
Housing: Homeownership rate: 60.3%; Median home value: $49,200; Median year structure built: 1947; Homeowner vacancy rate: 4.4%; Median gross rent: $655 per month; Rental vacancy rate: 12.2%
Health Insurance: 84.6% have insurance; 41.5% have private insurance; 54.3% have public insurance; 15.4% do not have insurance; 2.8% of children under 18 do not have insurance
Hospitals: Covenant Medical Center (601 beds); Healthsource Saginaw (317 beds); Saginaw VA Medical Center (238 beds); Saint Mary's of Michigan Medical Center (268 beds)
Safety: Violent crime rate: 194.7 per 10,000 population; Property crime rate: 295.0 per 10,000 population
Newspapers: Saginaw News (weekly circulation 35000); Saginaw Press (weekly circulation 500); The Township Times (weekly circulation 5000)
Transportation: Commute: 91.1% car, 2.6% public transportation, 1.9% walk, 3.3% work from home; Median travel time to work: 19.4 minutes; Amtrak: Train service available.
Airports: MBS International (primary service/non-hub)
Additional Information Contacts
City of Saginaw . . . . (989) 759-1400
http://www.saginaw-mi.com

SAINT CHARLES (township). Covers a land area of 36.490 square miles and a water area of 0.706 square miles. Located at 43.26° N. Lat; 84.11° W. Long. Elevation is 597 feet.
Population: 3,330; Growth (since 2000): -1.9%; Density: 91.3 persons per square mile; Race: 96.7% White, 0.8% Black/African American, 0.2% Asian, 0.4% American Indian/Alaska Native, 0.0% Native Hawaiian/Other Pacific Islander, 1.4% Two or more races, 4.7% Hispanic of any race; Average household size: 2.45; Median age: 40.9; Age under 18: 23.2%;

Age 65 and over: 16.2%; Males per 100 females: 98.1; Marriage status: 25.1% never married, 59.4% now married, 0.9% separated, 6.3% widowed, 9.2% divorced; Foreign born: 0.6%; Speak English only: 97.8%; With disability: 19.5%; Veterans: 9.9%; Ancestry: 37.5% German, 13.2% Polish, 12.5% English, 9.7% French, 8.7% Irish
Employment: 10.8% management, business, and financial, 4.0% computer, engineering, and science, 8.6% education, legal, community service, arts, and media, 5.9% healthcare practitioners, 16.3% service, 24.6% sales and office, 12.1% natural resources, construction, and maintenance, 17.8% production, transportation, and material moving
Income: Per capita: $21,507; Median household: $43,033; Average household: $54,148; Households with income of $100,000 or more: 12.8%; Poverty rate: 12.1%
Educational Attainment: High school diploma or higher: 90.9%; Bachelor's degree or higher: 14.7%; Graduate/professional degree or higher: 3.5%

School District(s)

Saint Charles Community Schools (PK-12)
    2012-13 Enrollment: 1,137 . . . . (989) 865-9961
Housing: Homeownership rate: 76.2%; Median home value: $91,900; Median year structure built: 1961; Homeowner vacancy rate: 1.6%; Median gross rent: $579 per month; Rental vacancy rate: 5.3%
Health Insurance: 88.2% have insurance; 71.4% have private insurance; 35.7% have public insurance; 11.8% do not have insurance; 3.8% of children under 18 do not have insurance
Transportation: Commute: 91.8% car, 0.0% public transportation, 1.8% walk, 3.9% work from home; Median travel time to work: 28.2 minutes

SAINT CHARLES (village). Covers a land area of 2.115 square miles and a water area of 0.076 square miles. Located at 43.30° N. Lat; 84.15° W. Long. Elevation is 597 feet.
History: St. Charles was established in the 1850's on the Bad River, and named for Charles Kimberly who was nicknamed "Saint" Charles.
Population: 2,054; Growth (since 2000): -7.3%; Density: 971.1 persons per square mile; Race: 97.0% White, 0.9% Black/African American, 0.1% Asian, 0.7% American Indian/Alaska Native, 0.0% Native Hawaiian/Other Pacific Islander, 1.1% Two or more races, 5.2% Hispanic of any race; Average household size: 2.36; Median age: 38.7; Age under 18: 24.1%; Age 65 and over: 16.1%; Males per 100 females: 93.8

School District(s)

Saint Charles Community Schools (PK-12)
    2012-13 Enrollment: 1,137 . . . . (989) 865-9961
Housing: Homeownership rate: 69.3%; Homeowner vacancy rate: 2.3%; Rental vacancy rate: 5.0%
Safety: Violent crime rate: 54.4 per 10,000 population; Property crime rate: 193.0 per 10,000 population
Additional Information Contacts
Village of Saint Charles . . . . (989) 865-8287
    http://www.stcmi.com

SHIELDS (CDP). Covers a land area of 6.429 square miles and a water area of 0.157 square miles. Located at 43.42° N. Lat; 84.07° W. Long. Elevation is 597 feet.
Population: 6,587; Growth (since 2000): 0.0%; Density: 1,024.5 persons per square mile; Race: 95.9% White, 1.1% Black/African American, 0.8% Asian, 0.2% American Indian/Alaska Native, 0.0% Native Hawaiian/Other Pacific Islander, 1.2% Two or more races, 4.3% Hispanic of any race; Average household size: 2.34; Median age: 46.6; Age under 18: 20.2%; Age 65 and over: 22.1%; Males per 100 females: 90.7; Marriage status: 26.7% never married, 52.5% now married, 0.6% separated, 11.9% widowed, 8.8% divorced; Foreign born: 2.0%; Speak English only: 96.8%; With disability: 11.9%; Veterans: 9.8%; Ancestry: 37.1% German, 13.7% Irish, 10.7% English, 10.6% Polish, 5.1% French
Employment: 8.6% management, business, and financial, 5.3% computer, engineering, and science, 10.0% education, legal, community service, arts, and media, 9.4% healthcare practitioners, 22.0% service, 23.9% sales and office, 6.4% natural resources, construction, and maintenance, 14.4% production, transportation, and material moving
Income: Per capita: $26,857; Median household: $53,069; Average household: $66,438; Households with income of $100,000 or more: 16.0%; Poverty rate: 4.4%
Educational Attainment: High school diploma or higher: 89.6%; Bachelor's degree or higher: 20.8%; Graduate/professional degree or higher: 7.3%

Housing: Homeownership rate: 81.1%; Median home value: $119,000; Median year structure built: 1972; Homeowner vacancy rate: 2.2%; Median gross rent: $730 per month; Rental vacancy rate: 5.4%
Health Insurance: 90.8% have insurance; 80.4% have private insurance; 31.8% have public insurance; 9.2% do not have insurance; 0.9% of children under 18 do not have insurance
Transportation: Commute: 96.9% car, 0.2% public transportation, 0.8% walk, 2.1% work from home; Median travel time to work: 20.9 minutes

SPAULDING (township). Covers a land area of 25.590 square miles and a water area of 1.844 square miles. Located at 43.34° N. Lat; 83.99° W. Long.
History: Spaulding Township was organized in 1858 and named for Phineas Spaulding, who had come here from New Hampshire in 1835.
Population: 2,153; Growth (since 2000): -10.3%; Density: 84.1 persons per square mile; Race: 76.9% White, 15.7% Black/African American, 0.2% Asian, 0.3% American Indian/Alaska Native, 0.0% Native Hawaiian/Other Pacific Islander, 3.8% Two or more races, 12.8% Hispanic of any race; Average household size: 2.53; Median age: 43.0; Age under 18: 22.8%; Age 65 and over: 17.4%; Males per 100 females: 99.5
Housing: Homeownership rate: 86.1%; Homeowner vacancy rate: 2.0%; Rental vacancy rate: 4.1%

SWAN CREEK (township). Covers a land area of 22.949 square miles and a water area of 0.858 square miles. Located at 43.35° N. Lat; 84.12° W. Long. Elevation is 594 feet.
History: Swan Creek Township was organized in 1860 and named for the stream that traversed it.
Population: 2,456; Growth (since 2000): -3.2%; Density: 107.0 persons per square mile; Race: 97.1% White, 0.3% Black/African American, 0.1% Asian, 0.6% American Indian/Alaska Native, 0.0% Native Hawaiian/Other Pacific Islander, 1.1% Two or more races, 3.9% Hispanic of any race; Average household size: 2.51; Median age: 46.1; Age under 18: 20.7%; Age 65 and over: 16.5%; Males per 100 females: 102.0
Housing: Homeownership rate: 93.6%; Homeowner vacancy rate: 1.2%; Rental vacancy rate: 8.8%

TAYMOUTH (township). Covers a land area of 35.384 square miles and a water area of 0.203 square miles. Located at 43.26° N. Lat; 83.87° W. Long. Elevation is 630 feet.
Population: 4,520; Growth (since 2000): -2.2%; Density: 127.7 persons per square mile; Race: 95.6% White, 0.8% Black/African American, 0.2% Asian, 0.6% American Indian/Alaska Native, 0.1% Native Hawaiian/Other Pacific Islander, 1.8% Two or more races, 3.5% Hispanic of any race; Average household size: 2.74; Median age: 40.9; Age under 18: 24.8%; Age 65 and over: 11.7%; Males per 100 females: 103.0; Marriage status: 25.5% never married, 61.3% now married, 0.9% separated, 5.2% widowed, 7.9% divorced; Foreign born: 0.3%; Speak English only: 98.4%; With disability: 12.3%; Veterans: 11.1%; Ancestry: 36.9% German, 13.2% Polish, 12.4% Irish, 8.0% English, 6.6% American
Employment: 9.6% management, business, and financial, 3.4% computer, engineering, and science, 8.0% education, legal, community service, arts, and media, 2.8% healthcare practitioners, 14.8% service, 31.3% sales and office, 15.5% natural resources, construction, and maintenance, 14.5% production, transportation, and material moving
Income: Per capita: $21,543; Median household: $55,676; Average household: $60,338; Households with income of $100,000 or more: 16.0%; Poverty rate: 11.0%
Educational Attainment: High school diploma or higher: 89.0%; Bachelor's degree or higher: 14.0%; Graduate/professional degree or higher: 4.9%
Housing: Homeownership rate: 90.1%; Median home value: $114,600; Median year structure built: 1974; Homeowner vacancy rate: 0.9%; Median gross rent: $395 per month; Rental vacancy rate: 20.2%
Health Insurance: 88.3% have insurance; 67.1% have private insurance; 34.1% have public insurance; 11.7% do not have insurance; 3.2% of children under 18 do not have insurance
Transportation: Commute: 96.7% car, 0.0% public transportation, 0.0% walk, 3.3% work from home; Median travel time to work: 26.5 minutes

THOMAS (township). Covers a land area of 30.609 square miles and a water area of 1.216 square miles. Located at 43.43° N. Lat; 84.12° W. Long.
Population: 11,985; Growth (since 2000): 0.9%; Density: 391.6 persons per square mile; Race: 95.8% White, 1.1% Black/African American, 1.1%

Asian, 0.2% American Indian/Alaska Native, 0.0% Native Hawaiian/Other Pacific Islander, 1.1% Two or more races, 3.5% Hispanic of any race; Average household size: 2.40; Median age: 47.1; Age under 18: 20.3%; Age 65 and over: 20.4%; Males per 100 females: 93.7; Marriage status: 23.8% never married, 57.0% now married, 1.0% separated, 9.9% widowed, 9.3% divorced; Foreign born: 1.7%; Speak English only: 97.3%; With disability: 12.2%; Veterans: 10.5%; Ancestry: 37.9% German, 15.2% Irish, 11.2% Polish, 10.4% English, 7.4% French

Employment: 10.1% management, business, and financial, 4.8% computer, engineering, and science, 10.3% education, legal, community service, arts, and media, 9.8% healthcare practitioners, 20.2% service, 22.8% sales and office, 8.4% natural resources, construction, and maintenance, 13.6% production, transportation, and material moving

Income: Per capita: $29,779; Median household: $55,203; Average household: $74,800; Households with income of $100,000 or more: 20.1%; Poverty rate: 4.4%

Educational Attainment: High school diploma or higher: 90.3%; Bachelor's degree or higher: 21.8%; Graduate/professional degree or higher: 7.2%

Housing: Homeownership rate: 87.5%; Median home value: $127,400; Median year structure built: 1976; Homeowner vacancy rate: 1.9%; Median gross rent: $726 per month; Rental vacancy rate: 4.7%

Health Insurance: 90.6% have insurance; 80.5% have private insurance; 29.0% have public insurance; 9.4% do not have insurance; 1.2% of children under 18 do not have insurance

Safety: Violent crime rate: 7.6 per 10,000 population; Property crime rate: 140.1 per 10,000 population

Transportation: Commute: 95.7% car, 0.3% public transportation, 0.5% walk, 3.4% work from home; Median travel time to work: 20.9 minutes

Additional Information Contacts
Thomas Township . . . . (989) 781-0150
http://www.thomastwp.org

TITTABAWASSEE (township). Covers a land area of 35.158 square miles and a water area of 0.412 square miles. Located at 43.52° N. Lat; 84.10° W. Long.

Population: 9,726; Growth (since 2000): 26.2%; Density: 276.6 persons per square mile; Race: 88.2% White, 9.1% Black/African American, 0.5% Asian, 0.5% American Indian/Alaska Native, 0.0% Native Hawaiian/Other Pacific Islander, 1.1% Two or more races, 3.0% Hispanic of any race; Average household size: 2.69; Median age: 36.6; Age under 18: 23.5%; Age 65 and over: 9.6%; Males per 100 females: 135.7; Marriage status: 31.1% never married, 53.5% now married, 0.7% separated, 4.9% widowed, 10.5% divorced; Foreign born: 1.6%; Speak English only: 97.1%; With disability: 8.6%; Veterans: 7.0%; Ancestry: 38.8% German, 16.3% Polish, 14.9% Irish, 8.0% English, 6.8% French

Employment: 19.2% management, business, and financial, 6.5% computer, engineering, and science, 7.9% education, legal, community service, arts, and media, 5.2% healthcare practitioners, 12.6% service, 26.4% sales and office, 11.1% natural resources, construction, and maintenance, 11.2% production, transportation, and material moving

Income: Per capita: $24,694; Median household: $68,438; Average household: $77,742; Households with income of $100,000 or more: 27.5%; Poverty rate: 6.8%

Educational Attainment: High school diploma or higher: 90.1%; Bachelor's degree or higher: 29.6%; Graduate/professional degree or higher: 6.7%

Housing: Homeownership rate: 84.6%; Median home value: $156,400; Median year structure built: 1990; Homeowner vacancy rate: 1.7%; Median gross rent: $937 per month; Rental vacancy rate: 6.5%

Health Insurance: 92.2% have insurance; 83.2% have private insurance; 22.1% have public insurance; 7.8% do not have insurance; 4.3% of children under 18 do not have insurance

Safety: Violent crime rate: 15.2 per 10,000 population; Property crime rate: 93.4 per 10,000 population

Transportation: Commute: 96.3% car, 0.0% public transportation, 0.0% walk, 3.7% work from home; Median travel time to work: 22.7 minutes

ZILWAUKEE (city). Covers a land area of 2.214 square miles and a water area of 0.157 square miles. Located at 43.48° N. Lat; 83.92° W. Long. Elevation is 584 feet.

Population: 1,658; Growth (since 2000): -7.8%; Density: 748.7 persons per square mile; Race: 92.3% White, 3.7% Black/African American, 0.3% Asian, 0.5% American Indian/Alaska Native, 0.0% Native Hawaiian/Other Pacific Islander, 1.6% Two or more races, 7.7% Hispanic of any race;

Average household size: 2.47; Median age: 40.0; Age under 18: 22.1%; Age 65 and over: 16.6%; Males per 100 females: 99.0

Housing: Homeownership rate: 83.9%; Homeowner vacancy rate: 1.6%; Rental vacancy rate: 9.1%

Safety: Violent crime rate: 6.1 per 10,000 population; Property crime rate: 55.2 per 10,000 population

ZILWAUKEE (township). Covers a land area of 3.579 square miles and a water area of 2.404 square miles. Located at 43.50° N. Lat; 83.90° W. Long. Elevation is 584 feet.

Population: 67; Growth (since 2000): 9.8%; Density: 18.7 persons per square mile; Race: 82.1% White, 13.4% Black/African American, 0.0% Asian, 0.0% American Indian/Alaska Native, 0.0% Native Hawaiian/Other Pacific Islander, 4.5% Two or more races, 11.9% Hispanic of any race; Average household size: 2.58; Median age: 45.8; Age under 18: 16.4%; Age 65 and over: 20.9%; Males per 100 females: 86.1

Housing: Homeownership rate: 77.0%; Homeowner vacancy rate: 4.8%; Rental vacancy rate: 0.0%

Saint Clair County

Located in eastern Michigan; bounded on the east by Lake Huron and the Saint Clair River, and on the south by Lake Saint Clair; drained by the Belle and Black Rivers. Covers a land area of 721.170 square miles, a water area of 115.336 square miles, and is located in the Eastern Time Zone at 42.93° N. Lat., 82.67° W. Long. The county was founded in 1820. County seat is Port Huron.

Saint Clair County is part of the Detroit-Warren-Dearborn, MI Metropolitan Statistical Area. The entire metro area includes: Detroit-Dearborn-Livonia, MI Metropolitan Division (Wayne County, MI); Warren-Troy-Farmington Hills, MI Metropolitan Division (Lapeer County, MI; Livingston County, MI; Macomb County, MI; Oakland County, MI; Saint Clair County, MI)

Weather Station: Port Huron										Elevation: 589 feet		
	Jan	Feb	Mar	Apr	May	Jun	Jul	Aug	Sep	Oct	Nov	Dec
High	31	34	42	55	67	77	82	80	73	60	48	35
Low	17	18	26	36	46	56	63	62	54	42	33	22
Precip	1.9	1.9	2.1	2.9	3.1	3.4	3.2	3.3	3.8	2.8	3.0	2.2
Snow	10.9	9.0	4.7	0.7	0.0	0.0	0.0	0.0	0.0	0.0	1.3	8.3

High and Low temperatures in degrees Fahrenheit; Precipitation and Snow in inches

Population: 163,040; Growth (since 2000): -0.7%; Density: 226.1 persons per square mile; Race: 93.9% White, 2.4% Black/African American, 0.5% Asian, 0.4% American Indian/Alaska Native, 0.0% Native Hawaiian/Other Pacific Islander, 2.0% two or more races, 2.9% Hispanic of any race; Average household size: 2.52; Median age: 41.3; Age under 18: 23.7%; Age 65 and over: 14.5%; Males per 100 females: 98.1; Marriage status: 26.0% never married, 55.0% now married, 1.2% separated, 6.6% widowed, 12.4% divorced; Foreign born: 2.7%; Speak English only: 96.1%; With disability: 15.7%; Veterans: 10.2%; Ancestry: 31.4% German, 14.9% Irish, 12.5% Polish, 11.1% English, 7.5% French

Religion: Six largest groups: 19.8% Catholicism, 4.8% Lutheran, 2.6% Methodist/Pietist, 2.5% Holiness, 2.5% Non-denominational Protestant, 1.3% Presbyterian-Reformed

Economy: Unemployment rate: 7.8%; Leading industries: 17.3% retail trade; 12.2% health care and social assistance; 10.8% construction; Farms: 1,049 totaling 179,967 acres; Company size: 1 employs 1,000 or more persons, 1 employs 500 to 999 persons, 70 employ 100 to 499 persons, 3,017 employ less than 100 persons; Business ownership: 3,228 women-owned, n/a Black-owned, 97 Hispanic-owned, 124 Asian-owned

Employment: 10.2% management, business, and financial, 3.1% computer, engineering, and science, 7.9% education, legal, community service, arts, and media, 5.5% healthcare practitioners, 19.6% service, 24.8% sales and office, 10.4% natural resources, construction, and maintenance, 18.4% production, transportation, and material moving

Income: Per capita: $24,357; Median household: $48,066; Average household: $60,492; Households with income of $100,000 or more: 15.5%; Poverty rate: 14.9%

Educational Attainment: High school diploma or higher: 89.0%; Bachelor's degree or higher: 16.3%; Graduate/professional degree or higher: 6.2%

Housing: Homeownership rate: 77.3%; Median home value: $121,600; Median year structure built: 1972; Homeowner vacancy rate: 2.4%; Median gross rent: $728 per month; Rental vacancy rate: 11.6%

Vital Statistics: Birth rate: 101.9 per 10,000 population; Death rate: 99.8 per 10,000 population; Age-adjusted cancer mortality rate: 184.7 deaths per 100,000 population

Health Insurance: 88.6% have insurance; 69.9% have private insurance; 34.8% have public insurance; 11.4% do not have insurance; 3.5% of children under 18 do not have insurance

Health Care: Physicians: 14.4 per 10,000 population; Hospital beds: 23.1 per 10,000 population; Hospital admissions: 1,120.7 per 10,000 population

Air Quality Index: 82.7% good, 16.4% moderate, 0.8% unhealthy for sensitive individuals, 0.0% unhealthy (percent of days)

Transportation: Commute: 93.7% car, 0.6% public transportation, 1.7% walk, 2.9% work from home; Median travel time to work: 28.3 minutes

Presidential Election: 45.9% Obama, 53.0% Romney (2012)

National and State Parks: Algonac State Park; Lakeport State Park; Port Huron State Game Area; Saint Clair Flats State Wildlife Area

Additional Information Contacts

Saint Clair Government . . . . (810) 989-6900
 http://www.stclaircounty.org/index.asp

Saint Clair County Communities

ALGONAC (city). Covers a land area of 1.431 square miles and a water area of 0.006 square miles. Located at 42.62° N. Lat; 82.53° W. Long. Elevation is 581 feet.

History: The first settler in Algonac was John Martin, who came in 1805 and called the place Pointe du Chene (Oak Point). After being known as Plainfield and Clay, the town was renamed Algonac, taken from the name of the Algonquin Indians. Algonac developed as a shipbuilding center, with the Chris Craft plant that lead the racing world with its line of "Miss Americas" located here.

Population: 4,110; Growth (since 2000): -10.9%; Density: 2,872.0 persons per square mile; Race: 97.1% White, 0.3% Black/African American, 0.1% Asian, 0.7% American Indian/Alaska Native, 0.0% Native Hawaiian/Other Pacific Islander, 1.6% Two or more races, 1.3% Hispanic of any race; Average household size: 2.33; Median age: 42.3; Age under 18: 21.2%; Age 65 and over: 15.5%; Males per 100 females: 98.3; Marriage status: 26.7% never married, 47.4% now married, 1.8% separated, 8.5% widowed, 17.4% divorced; Foreign born: 1.8%; Speak English only: 97.1%; With disability: 16.7%; Veterans: 10.0%; Ancestry: 29.6% German, 19.4% Irish, 11.7% Polish, 10.2% French, 8.1% English

Employment: 12.7% management, business, and financial, 4.4% computer, engineering, and science, 11.5% education, legal, community service, arts, and media, 5.7% healthcare practitioners, 16.8% service, 21.5% sales and office, 11.9% natural resources, construction, and maintenance, 15.6% production, transportation, and material moving

Income: Per capita: $22,851; Median household: $38,163; Average household: $49,969; Households with income of $100,000 or more: 10.3%; Poverty rate: 14.4%

Educational Attainment: High school diploma or higher: 89.2%; Bachelor's degree or higher: 19.3%; Graduate/professional degree or higher: 8.2%

School District(s)

Algonac Community SD (PK-12)
 2012-13 Enrollment: 1,882 . . . . (810) 794-9364
Blue Water Learning Academy (KG-12)
 2012-13 Enrollment: 33 . . . . (810) 794-8067

Housing: Homeownership rate: 72.8%; Median home value: $98,700; Median year structure built: 1971; Homeowner vacancy rate: 3.8%; Median gross rent: $680 per month; Rental vacancy rate: 14.0%

Health Insurance: 87.6% have insurance; 70.7% have private insurance; 31.8% have public insurance; 12.4% do not have insurance; 4.7% of children under 18 do not have insurance

Transportation: Commute: 94.5% car, 1.2% public transportation, 2.4% walk, 1.8% work from home; Median travel time to work: 35.4 minutes

Additional Information Contacts

City of Algonac . . . . (810) 794-9361
 http://algonac-mi.gov

ALLENTON (unincorporated postal area)

ZCTA: 48002

Covers a land area of 37.125 square miles and a water area of 0.007 square miles. Located at 42.94° N. Lat; 82.92° W. Long. Elevation is 814 feet.

Population: 3,285; Growth (since 2000): 3.9%; Density: 88.5 persons per square mile; Race: 97.3% White, 0.5% Black/African American,

0.4% Asian, 0.3% American Indian/Alaska Native, 0.0% Native Hawaiian/Other Pacific Islander, 0.9% Two or more races, 2.9% Hispanic of any race; Average household size: 2.85; Median age: 41.2; Age under 18: 25.5%; Age 65 and over: 11.1%; Males per 100 females: 106.1; Marriage status: 19.6% never married, 67.5% now married, 0.2% separated, 4.8% widowed, 8.2% divorced; Foreign born: 2.6%; Speak English only: 95.7%; With disability: 12.0%; Veterans: 10.1%; Ancestry: 37.9% German, 12.7% Irish, 12.4% Polish, 9.7% English, 7.4% Belgian

Employment: 8.9% management, business, and financial, 4.7% computer, engineering, and science, 8.4% education, legal, community service, arts, and media, 6.0% healthcare practitioners, 13.1% service, 25.6% sales and office, 11.5% natural resources, construction, and maintenance, 21.9% production, transportation, and material moving

Income: Per capita: $26,939; Median household: $62,958; Average household: $69,875; Households with income of $100,000 or more: 21.0%; Poverty rate: 6.3%

Educational Attainment: High school diploma or higher: 90.5%; Bachelor's degree or higher: 10.0%; Graduate/professional degree or higher: 2.5%

Housing: Homeownership rate: 91.4%; Median home value: $162,200; Median year structure built: 1977; Homeowner vacancy rate: 1.1%; Median gross rent: $1,056 per month; Rental vacancy rate: 3.9%

Health Insurance: 91.1% have insurance; 78.8% have private insurance; 24.9% have public insurance; 8.9% do not have insurance; 0.0% of children under 18 do not have insurance

Transportation: Commute: 97.3% car, 0.0% public transportation, 0.4% walk, 1.2% work from home; Median travel time to work: 41.4 minutes

AVOCA (unincorporated postal area)

ZCTA: 48006

Covers a land area of 71.445 square miles and a water area of 0.374 square miles. Located at 43.08° N. Lat; 82.69° W. Long. Elevation is 764 feet.

Population: 4,007; Growth (since 2000): 5.7%; Density: 56.1 persons per square mile; Race: 97.2% White, 0.2% Black/African American, 0.2% Asian, 0.6% American Indian/Alaska Native, 0.0% Native Hawaiian/Other Pacific Islander, 1.4% Two or more races, 1.5% Hispanic of any race; Average household size: 2.78; Median age: 40.9; Age under 18: 25.6%; Age 65 and over: 12.4%; Males per 100 females: 110.3; Marriage status: 21.8% never married, 62.5% now married, 0.5% separated, 4.2% widowed, 11.5% divorced; Foreign born: 1.1%; Speak English only: 97.5%; With disability: 17.6%; Veterans: 10.0%; Ancestry: 39.1% German, 21.0% Irish, 17.6% Polish, 9.6% English, 7.8% Italian

Employment: 12.0% management, business, and financial, 3.5% computer, engineering, and science, 5.4% education, legal, community service, arts, and media, 4.9% healthcare practitioners, 12.3% service, 22.4% sales and office, 17.4% natural resources, construction, and maintenance, 22.2% production, transportation, and material moving

Income: Per capita: $23,986; Median household: $57,317; Average household: $64,995; Households with income of $100,000 or more: 17.2%; Poverty rate: 8.4%

Educational Attainment: High school diploma or higher: 88.7%; Bachelor's degree or higher: 10.9%; Graduate/professional degree or higher: 3.2%

Housing: Homeownership rate: 92.2%; Median home value: $138,900; Median year structure built: 1978; Homeowner vacancy rate: 2.0%; Median gross rent: $822 per month; Rental vacancy rate: 6.6%

Health Insurance: 91.2% have insurance; 77.9% have private insurance; 28.2% have public insurance; 8.8% do not have insurance; 3.6% of children under 18 do not have insurance

Transportation: Commute: 94.3% car, 0.7% public transportation, 0.0% walk, 4.3% work from home; Median travel time to work: 36.5 minutes

BERLIN (township). Covers a land area of 37.125 square miles and a water area of 0.007 square miles. Located at 42.94° N. Lat; 82.92° W. Long.

Population: 3,285; Growth (since 2000): 3.9%; Density: 88.5 persons per square mile; Race: 97.3% White, 0.5% Black/African American, 0.4% Asian, 0.3% American Indian/Alaska Native, 0.0% Native Hawaiian/Other Pacific Islander, 0.9% Two or more races, 2.9% Hispanic of any race; Average household size: 2.85; Median age: 41.2; Age under 18: 25.5%; Age 65 and over: 11.1%; Males per 100 females: 106.1; Marriage status: 19.6% never married, 67.5% now married, 0.2% separated, 4.8% widowed, 8.2% divorced; Foreign born: 2.6%; Speak English only: 95.7%;

With disability: 12.0%; Veterans: 10.1%; Ancestry: 37.9% German, 12.7% Irish, 12.4% Polish, 9.7% English, 7.4% Belgian
Employment: 8.9% management, business, and financial, 4.7% computer, engineering, and science, 8.4% education, legal, community service, arts, and media, 6.0% healthcare practitioners, 13.1% service, 25.6% sales and office, 11.5% natural resources, construction, and maintenance, 21.9% production, transportation, and material moving
Income: Per capita: $26,939; Median household: $62,958; Average household: $69,875; Households with income of $100,000 or more: 21.0%; Poverty rate: 6.3%
Educational Attainment: High school diploma or higher: 90.5%; Bachelor's degree or higher: 10.0%; Graduate/professional degree or higher: 2.5%
Housing: Homeownership rate: 91.4%; Median home value: $162,200; Median year structure built: 1977; Homeowner vacancy rate: 1.1%; Median gross rent: $1,056 per month; Rental vacancy rate: 3.9%
Health Insurance: 91.1% have insurance; 78.8% have private insurance; 24.9% have public insurance; 8.9% do not have insurance; 0.0% of children under 18 do not have insurance
Transportation: Commute: 97.3% car, 0.0% public transportation, 0.4% walk, 1.2% work from home; Median travel time to work: 41.4 minutes

BROCKWAY (township). Covers a land area of 33.659 square miles and a water area of 0.172 square miles. Located at 43.11° N. Lat; 82.81° W. Long. Elevation is 771 feet.
History: Brockway Township was organized in 1848 and named for Lewis Brockway, who built a grist mill and sawmill here in 1840.
Population: 2,022; Growth (since 2000): 6.4%; Density: 60.1 persons per square mile; Race: 96.9% White, 0.7% Black/African American, 0.0% Asian, 0.6% American Indian/Alaska Native, 0.0% Native Hawaiian/Other Pacific Islander, 1.5% Two or more races, 1.9% Hispanic of any race; Average household size: 2.87; Median age: 39.7; Age under 18: 27.8%; Age 65 and over: 11.5%; Males per 100 females: 106.1
Housing: Homeownership rate: 88.1%; Homeowner vacancy rate: 2.0%; Rental vacancy rate: 5.6%

BURTCHVILLE (township). Covers a land area of 15.549 square miles and a water area of 0.021 square miles. Located at 43.12° N. Lat; 82.52° W. Long.
History: Burtchville Township was named for lumberman Jonathan Burtch, who settled here in 1840. The township was organized in 1862.
Population: 4,008; Growth (since 2000): 1.3%; Density: 257.8 persons per square mile; Race: 96.5% White, 0.3% Black/African American, 0.3% Asian, 0.2% American Indian/Alaska Native, 0.1% Native Hawaiian/Other Pacific Islander, 2.0% Two or more races, 3.2% Hispanic of any race; Average household size: 2.43; Median age: 43.0; Age under 18: 22.6%; Age 65 and over: 15.9%; Males per 100 females: 97.4; Marriage status: 18.1% never married, 63.9% now married, 2.0% separated, 5.3% widowed, 12.6% divorced; Foreign born: 3.6%; Speak English only: 96.5%; With disability: 15.7%; Veterans: 15.0%; Ancestry: 36.8% German, 16.3% English, 11.3% Polish, 10.2% French, 9.6% Irish
Employment: 8.8% management, business, and financial, 2.1% computer, engineering, and science, 11.1% education, legal, community service, arts, and media, 5.8% healthcare practitioners, 15.1% service, 36.3% sales and office, 7.6% natural resources, construction, and maintenance, 13.3% production, transportation, and material moving
Income: Per capita: $26,665; Median household: $53,333; Average household: $66,721; Households with income of $100,000 or more: 17.9%; Poverty rate: 9.2%
Educational Attainment: High school diploma or higher: 91.9%; Bachelor's degree or higher: 17.3%; Graduate/professional degree or higher: 8.0%
Housing: Homeownership rate: 84.5%; Median home value: $117,600; Median year structure built: 1977; Homeowner vacancy rate: 2.6%; Median gross rent: $745 per month; Rental vacancy rate: 26.1%
Health Insurance: 90.8% have insurance; 68.7% have private insurance; 34.9% have public insurance; 9.2% do not have insurance; 0.7% of children under 18 do not have insurance
Transportation: Commute: 95.4% car, 0.0% public transportation, 1.5% walk, 1.6% work from home; Median travel time to work: 25.1 minutes

CAPAC (village). Covers a land area of 1.831 square miles and a water area of 0.051 square miles. Located at 43.00° N. Lat; 82.92° W. Long. Elevation is 817 feet.
History: Capac was founded in 1857 and named for Manco Capac, considered to be the founder of the Inca dynasty in South America. The village was incorporated in 1873.
Population: 1,890; Growth (since 2000): 6.5%; Density: 1,032.4 persons per square mile; Race: 87.7% White, 0.3% Black/African American, 0.1% Asian, 0.6% American Indian/Alaska Native, 0.0% Native Hawaiian/Other Pacific Islander, 3.2% Two or more races, 18.9% Hispanic of any race; Average household size: 2.68; Median age: 33.1; Age under 18: 29.0%; Age 65 and over: 10.5%; Males per 100 females: 92.9
School District(s)
Capac Community Schools (PK-12)
    2012-13 Enrollment: 1,295 . . . . (810) 395-3700
Housing: Homeownership rate: 70.6%; Homeowner vacancy rate: 5.5%; Rental vacancy rate: 16.3%
Safety: Violent crime rate: 21.6 per 10,000 population; Property crime rate: 221.9 per 10,000 population

CASCO (township). Covers a land area of 36.880 square miles and a water area of 0.160 square miles. Located at 42.76° N. Lat; 82.67° W. Long. Elevation is 643 feet.
Population: 4,105; Growth (since 2000): -13.5%; Density: 111.3 persons per square mile; Race: 95.6% White, 0.6% Black/African American, 0.5% Asian, 0.5% American Indian/Alaska Native, 0.0% Native Hawaiian/Other Pacific Islander, 1.7% Two or more races, 2.1% Hispanic of any race; Average household size: 2.73; Median age: 43.1; Age under 18: 23.6%; Age 65 and over: 13.2%; Males per 100 females: 103.3; Marriage status: 25.6% never married, 60.7% now married, 1.6% separated, 5.4% widowed, 8.3% divorced; Foreign born: 1.5%; Speak English only: 95.0%; With disability: 11.9%; Veterans: 9.1%; Ancestry: 28.7% German, 18.7% Polish, 18.3% Irish, 12.8% Italian, 9.1% American
Employment: 12.9% management, business, and financial, 4.4% computer, engineering, and science, 4.6% education, legal, community service, arts, and media, 4.2% healthcare practitioners, 16.3% service, 25.4% sales and office, 12.0% natural resources, construction, and maintenance, 20.3% production, transportation, and material moving
Income: Per capita: $23,084; Median household: $56,250; Average household: $66,830; Households with income of $100,000 or more: 21.0%; Poverty rate: 12.3%
Educational Attainment: High school diploma or higher: 90.2%; Bachelor's degree or higher: 16.4%; Graduate/professional degree or higher: 4.5%
Housing: Homeownership rate: 91.8%; Median home value: $162,400; Median year structure built: 1980; Homeowner vacancy rate: 1.9%; Median gross rent: $748 per month; Rental vacancy rate: 8.8%
Health Insurance: 87.4% have insurance; 69.5% have private insurance; 34.4% have public insurance; 12.6% do not have insurance; 2.8% of children under 18 do not have insurance
Transportation: Commute: 97.5% car, 0.0% public transportation, 0.0% walk, 2.5% work from home; Median travel time to work: 29.3 minutes
Additional Information Contacts
Casco Township . . . . (586) 727-7524
    http://www.cascostclair.org

CHINA (township). Covers a land area of 34.031 square miles and a water area of 0.324 square miles. Located at 42.77° N. Lat; 82.56° W. Long.
History: A dam and a grist mill were built in China Township in 1825. It was named by Captain John Clarke, an early resident, for China Township in Maine where he had previously lived.
Population: 3,551; Growth (since 2000): 6.3%; Density: 104.3 persons per square mile; Race: 98.3% White, 0.2% Black/African American, 0.3% Asian, 0.2% American Indian/Alaska Native, 0.0% Native Hawaiian/Other Pacific Islander, 0.6% Two or more races, 0.8% Hispanic of any race; Average household size: 2.79; Median age: 44.0; Age under 18: 24.5%; Age 65 and over: 12.5%; Males per 100 females: 104.3; Marriage status: 26.9% never married, 61.3% now married, 0.3% separated, 6.5% widowed, 5.3% divorced; Foreign born: 1.4%; Speak English only: 97.2%; With disability: 11.5%; Veterans: 12.3%; Ancestry: 38.2% German, 14.6% Polish, 10.4% French, 9.3% Irish, 8.3% English
Employment: 13.5% management, business, and financial, 3.4% computer, engineering, and science, 7.7% education, legal, community service, arts, and media, 5.6% healthcare practitioners, 16.8% service,

23.6% sales and office, 16.6% natural resources, construction, and maintenance, 12.8% production, transportation, and material moving

Income: Per capita: $31,756; Median household: $69,306; Average household: $91,212; Households with income of $100,000 or more: 24.4%; Poverty rate: 6.6%

Educational Attainment: High school diploma or higher: 94.0%; Bachelor's degree or higher: 18.9%; Graduate/professional degree or higher: 5.5%

School District(s)

East China SD (PK-12)

    2012-13 Enrollment: 4,508 . . . . (810) 676-1018

Housing: Homeownership rate: 95.2%; Median home value: $202,100; Median year structure built: 1985; Homeowner vacancy rate: 1.1%; Median gross rent: $942 per month; Rental vacancy rate: 3.1%

Health Insurance: 89.6% have insurance; 83.0% have private insurance; 19.6% have public insurance; 10.4% do not have insurance; 10.3% of children under 18 do not have insurance

Transportation: Commute: 96.4% car, 0.0% public transportation, 0.3% walk, 3.1% work from home; Median travel time to work: 31.9 minutes

---

CLAY (township). Covers a land area of 35.323 square miles and a water area of 47.145 square miles. Located at 42.60° N. Lat; 82.62° W. Long.

Population: 9,066; Growth (since 2000): -7.7%; Density: 256.7 persons per square mile; Race: 97.8% White, 0.1% Black/African American, 0.3% Asian, 0.5% American Indian/Alaska Native, 0.0% Native Hawaiian/Other Pacific Islander, 1.1% Two or more races, 1.1% Hispanic of any race; Average household size: 2.29; Median age: 48.8; Age under 18: 17.4%; Age 65 and over: 20.1%; Males per 100 females: 104.7; Marriage status: 19.8% never married, 62.8% now married, 1.3% separated, 6.5% widowed, 10.9% divorced; Foreign born: 2.4%; Speak English only: 96.7%; With disability: 15.9%; Veterans: 11.8%; Ancestry: 27.8% German, 20.4% Polish, 15.2% Irish, 9.8% Italian, 9.0% English

Employment: 10.0% management, business, and financial, 7.0% computer, engineering, and science, 6.2% education, legal, community service, arts, and media, 4.7% healthcare practitioners, 14.9% service, 27.7% sales and office, 9.9% natural resources, construction, and maintenance, 19.6% production, transportation, and material moving

Income: Per capita: $29,069; Median household: $52,697; Average household: $65,916; Households with income of $100,000 or more: 17.6%; Poverty rate: 8.8%

Educational Attainment: High school diploma or higher: 89.5%; Bachelor's degree or higher: 17.3%; Graduate/professional degree or higher: 7.2%

School District(s)

Algonac Community SD (PK-12)

    2012-13 Enrollment: 1,882 . . . . (810) 794-9364

Housing: Homeownership rate: 89.3%; Median home value: $151,900; Median year structure built: 1967; Homeowner vacancy rate: 2.0%; Median gross rent: $924 per month; Rental vacancy rate: 10.9%

Health Insurance: 90.6% have insurance; 78.5% have private insurance; 33.6% have public insurance; 9.4% do not have insurance; 3.0% of children under 18 do not have insurance

Safety: Violent crime rate: 12.4 per 10,000 population; Property crime rate: 164.2 per 10,000 population

Transportation: Commute: 91.6% car, 0.2% public transportation, 2.2% walk, 3.8% work from home; Median travel time to work: 35.7 minutes

Additional Information Contacts

Clay Township. . . . . (810) 794-9303

    http://www.claytownship.org

CLYDE (township). Covers a land area of 35.655 square miles and a water area of 0.330 square miles. Located at 43.04° N. Lat; 82.57° W. Long.

Population: 5,579; Growth (since 2000): 1.0%; Density: 156.5 persons per square mile; Race: 97.2% White, 0.6% Black/African American, 0.2% Asian, 0.3% American Indian/Alaska Native, 0.0% Native Hawaiian/Other Pacific Islander, 1.1% Two or more races, 2.2% Hispanic of any race; Average household size: 2.70; Median age: 43.4; Age under 18: 22.6%; Age 65 and over: 12.7%; Males per 100 females: 101.9; Marriage status: 23.4% never married, 64.3% now married, 0.5% separated, 4.5% widowed, 7.8% divorced; Foreign born: 1.9%; Speak English only: 95.7%; With disability: 16.3%; Veterans: 15.0%; Ancestry: 36.8% German, 20.9% Irish, 17.4% English, 7.0% French, 6.4% Polish

Employment: 9.3% management, business, and financial, 2.0% computer, engineering, and science, 7.6% education, legal, community service, arts, and media, 3.3% healthcare practitioners, 18.7% service, 25.9% sales and office, 15.4% natural resources, construction, and maintenance, 17.9% production, transportation, and material moving

Income: Per capita: $26,235; Median household: $58,040; Average household: $70,326; Households with income of $100,000 or more: 20.8%; Poverty rate: 4.3%

Educational Attainment: High school diploma or higher: 92.7%; Bachelor's degree or higher: 18.8%; Graduate/professional degree or higher: 5.0%

Housing: Homeownership rate: 89.7%; Median home value: $119,700; Median year structure built: 1975; Homeowner vacancy rate: 1.8%; Median gross rent: $792 per month; Rental vacancy rate: 7.8%

Health Insurance: 89.2% have insurance; 75.0% have private insurance; 30.1% have public insurance; 10.8% do not have insurance; 6.1% of children under 18 do not have insurance

Transportation: Commute: 95.2% car, 0.1% public transportation, 0.8% walk, 1.7% work from home; Median travel time to work: 26.1 minutes

---

COLUMBUS (township). Covers a land area of 36.641 square miles and a water area of 0.297 square miles. Located at 42.86° N. Lat; 82.68° W. Long. Elevation is 673 feet.

History: Columbus Township was organized in 1837 and named for Christopher Columbus.

Population: 4,070; Growth (since 2000): -11.8%; Density: 111.1 persons per square mile; Race: 96.8% White, 0.4% Black/African American, 0.4% Asian, 0.6% American Indian/Alaska Native, 0.0% Native Hawaiian/Other Pacific Islander, 1.2% Two or more races, 1.6% Hispanic of any race; Average household size: 2.78; Median age: 40.9; Age under 18: 25.3%; Age 65 and over: 11.8%; Males per 100 females: 106.3; Marriage status: 23.0% never married, 56.5% now married, 0.6% separated, 8.4% widowed, 12.0% divorced; Foreign born: 2.2%; Speak English only: 98.8%; With disability: 11.2%; Veterans: 9.4%; Ancestry: 31.3% German, 20.7% Polish, 11.0% French, 10.2% Italian, 8.7% English

Employment: 8.4% management, business, and financial, 2.9% computer, engineering, and science, 7.2% education, legal, community service, arts, and media, 5.8% healthcare practitioners, 19.0% service, 23.7% sales and office, 9.9% natural resources, construction, and maintenance, 23.1% production, transportation, and material moving

Income: Per capita: $27,084; Median household: $57,034; Average household: $73,070; Households with income of $100,000 or more: 19.7%; Poverty rate: 3.3%

Educational Attainment: High school diploma or higher: 92.3%; Bachelor's degree or higher: 11.7%; Graduate/professional degree or higher: 4.5%

Housing: Homeownership rate: 90.1%; Median home value: $141,000; Median year structure built: 1979; Homeowner vacancy rate: 2.1%; Median gross rent: $854 per month; Rental vacancy rate: 8.2%

Health Insurance: 89.3% have insurance; 76.4% have private insurance; 29.5% have public insurance; 10.7% do not have insurance; 3.3% of children under 18 do not have insurance

Transportation: Commute: 98.4% car, 0.0% public transportation, 0.0% walk, 1.0% work from home; Median travel time to work: 35.4 minutes

Additional Information Contacts

Columbus Township . . . . (586) 727-2055

    http://www.stclaircounty.org/townships/columbus

COTTRELLVILLE (township). Covers a land area of 20.861 square miles and a water area of 1.560 square miles. Located at 42.69° N. Lat; 82.56° W. Long.

History: Cottrellville Township was organized in 1822 and named for county commissioner George Cottrell.

Population: 3,559; Growth (since 2000): -6.7%; Density: 170.6 persons per square mile; Race: 97.9% White, 0.4% Black/African American, 0.4% Asian, 0.1% American Indian/Alaska Native, 0.0% Native Hawaiian/Other Pacific Islander, 0.9% Two or more races, 1.2% Hispanic of any race; Average household size: 2.56; Median age: 44.2; Age under 18: 21.8%; Age 65 and over: 13.3%; Males per 100 females: 98.8; Marriage status: 26.5% never married, 54.9% now married, 1.0% separated, 6.5% widowed, 12.1% divorced; Foreign born: 0.2%; Speak English only: 98.5%; With disability: 14.2%; Veterans: 12.4%; Ancestry: 34.2% German, 18.7% French, 14.0% Irish, 13.2% Polish, 8.9% English

Employment: 14.7% management, business, and financial, 1.4% computer, engineering, and science, 1.0% education, legal, community

service, arts, and media, 3.9% healthcare practitioners, 26.4% service, 22.6% sales and office, 15.6% natural resources, construction, and maintenance, 14.4% production, transportation, and material moving
Income: Per capita: $21,771; Median household: $48,897; Average household: $55,088; Households with income of $100,000 or more: 13.3%; Poverty rate: 19.5%
Educational Attainment: High school diploma or higher: 90.0%; Bachelor's degree or higher: 8.1%; Graduate/professional degree or higher: 2.5%
Housing: Homeownership rate: 91.6%; Median home value: $149,000; Median year structure built: 1974; Homeowner vacancy rate: 1.8%; Median gross rent: $865 per month; Rental vacancy rate: 7.8%
Health Insurance: 79.7% have insurance; 64.5% have private insurance; 29.6% have public insurance; 20.3% do not have insurance; 16.5% of children under 18 do not have insurance
Transportation: Commute: 93.0% car, 0.0% public transportation, 1.1% walk, 2.8% work from home; Median travel time to work: 33.7 minutes

EAST CHINA (township). Covers a land area of 6.583 square miles and a water area of 1.259 square miles. Located at 42.76° N. Lat; 82.49° W. Long.
Population: 3,788; Growth (since 2000): 4.4%; Density: 575.4 persons per square mile; Race: 98.1% White, 0.3% Black/African American, 0.3% Asian, 0.4% American Indian/Alaska Native, 0.0% Native Hawaiian/Other Pacific Islander, 0.8% Two or more races, 1.1% Hispanic of any race; Average household size: 2.26; Median age: 50.2; Age under 18: 17.2%; Age 65 and over: 26.2%; Males per 100 females: 90.3; Marriage status: 25.3% never married, 54.1% now married, 2.2% separated, 11.1% widowed, 9.4% divorced; Foreign born: 2.4%; Speak English only: 95.5%; With disability: 17.5%; Veterans: 11.3%; Ancestry: 31.8% German, 17.3% Irish, 13.4% Polish, 9.7% French, 9.5% American
Employment: 10.5% management, business, and financial, 6.6% computer, engineering, and science, 9.7% education, legal, community service, arts, and media, 7.5% healthcare practitioners, 15.3% service, 25.3% sales and office, 6.3% natural resources, construction, and maintenance, 18.7% production, transportation, and material moving
Income: Per capita: $27,747; Median household: $54,224; Average household: $62,567; Households with income of $100,000 or more: 18.3%; Poverty rate: 8.1%
Educational Attainment: High school diploma or higher: 89.7%; Bachelor's degree or higher: 17.8%; Graduate/professional degree or higher: 7.1%
Housing: Homeownership rate: 78.9%; Median home value: $168,500; Median year structure built: 1979; Homeowner vacancy rate: 2.2%; Median gross rent: $646 per month; Rental vacancy rate: 14.2%
Health Insurance: 90.8% have insurance; 79.3% have private insurance; 33.0% have public insurance; 9.2% do not have insurance; 0.0% of children under 18 do not have insurance
Hospitals: Saint John River District Hospital (68 beds)
Transportation: Commute: 98.1% car, 0.4% public transportation, 0.9% walk, 0.0% work from home; Median travel time to work: 31.0 minutes
Additional Information Contacts
East China Charter Township . . . . (810) 765-8879
  http://www.eastchinatownship.org

EMMETT (township). Covers a land area of 35.336 square miles and a water area of 0.022 square miles. Located at 43.02° N. Lat; 82.80° W. Long. Elevation is 778 feet.
Population: 2,654; Growth (since 2000): 5.9%; Density: 75.1 persons per square mile; Race: 96.9% White, 0.4% Black/African American, 0.5% Asian, 0.2% American Indian/Alaska Native, 0.1% Native Hawaiian/Other Pacific Islander, 1.3% Two or more races, 2.8% Hispanic of any race; Average household size: 2.86; Median age: 40.3; Age under 18: 26.8%; Age 65 and over: 11.5%; Males per 100 females: 103.1; Marriage status: 21.3% never married, 66.7% now married, 0.5% separated, 4.6% widowed, 7.5% divorced; Foreign born: 0.5%; Speak English only: 97.0%; With disability: 16.5%; Veterans: 8.5%; Ancestry: 31.9% German, 28.2% Irish, 23.1% Polish, 9.2% English, 6.3% French
Employment: 8.9% management, business, and financial, 3.6% computer, engineering, and science, 4.6% education, legal, community service, arts, and media, 6.0% healthcare practitioners, 13.3% service, 25.1% sales and office, 13.6% natural resources, construction, and maintenance, 24.8% production, transportation, and material moving

Income: Per capita: $23,167; Median household: $61,397; Average household: $63,359; Households with income of $100,000 or more: 13.5%; Poverty rate: 15.0%
Educational Attainment: High school diploma or higher: 93.2%; Bachelor's degree or higher: 9.0%; Graduate/professional degree or higher: 1.9%
School District(s)
Yale Public Schools (PK-12)
  2012-13 Enrollment: 2,082 . . . . (810) 387-3231
Housing: Homeownership rate: 92.4%; Median home value: $144,400; Median year structure built: 1978; Homeowner vacancy rate: 1.6%; Median gross rent: $912 per month; Rental vacancy rate: 4.1%
Health Insurance: 85.7% have insurance; 74.5% have private insurance; 24.1% have public insurance; 14.3% do not have insurance; 6.7% of children under 18 do not have insurance
Transportation: Commute: 92.9% car, 0.0% public transportation, 0.0% walk, 7.1% work from home; Median travel time to work: 45.4 minutes

EMMETT (village). Covers a land area of 1.514 square miles and a water area of 0 square miles. Located at 42.99° N. Lat; 82.77° W. Long. Elevation is 778 feet.
Population: 269; Growth (since 2000): 7.2%; Density: 177.7 persons per square mile; Race: 93.7% White, 0.0% Black/African American, 0.7% Asian, 0.0% American Indian/Alaska Native, 0.7% Native Hawaiian/Other Pacific Islander, 1.5% Two or more races, 3.3% Hispanic of any race; Average household size: 2.96; Median age: 38.4; Age under 18: 29.0%; Age 65 and over: 15.2%; Males per 100 females: 113.5
School District(s)
Yale Public Schools (PK-12)
  2012-13 Enrollment: 2,082 . . . . (810) 387-3231
Housing: Homeownership rate: 87.9%; Homeowner vacancy rate: 2.4%; Rental vacancy rate: 15.4%

FAIR HAVEN (unincorporated postal area)
ZCTA: 48023
  Covers a land area of 17.032 square miles and a water area of 0.110 square miles. Located at 42.70° N. Lat; 82.66° W. Long. Elevation is 577 feet.
  Population: 5,178; Growth (since 2000): -25.9%; Density: 304.0 persons per square mile; Race: 95.6% White, 1.1% Black/African American, 0.4% Asian, 0.3% American Indian/Alaska Native, 0.0% Native Hawaiian/Other Pacific Islander, 1.8% Two or more races, 2.3% Hispanic of any race; Average household size: 2.50; Median age: 42.0; Age under 18: 22.8%; Age 65 and over: 12.8%; Males per 100 females: 102.9; Marriage status: 24.7% never married, 55.1% now married, 1.0% separated, 8.7% widowed, 11.5% divorced; Foreign born: 2.2%; Speak English only: 99.1%; With disability: 14.6%; Veterans: 9.4%; Ancestry: 22.7% German, 19.2% Polish, 12.0% American, 10.4% Irish, 7.7% English
  Employment: 11.9% management, business, and financial, 4.5% computer, engineering, and science, 8.5% education, legal, community service, arts, and media, 3.7% healthcare practitioners, 25.5% service, 24.6% sales and office, 6.3% natural resources, construction, and maintenance, 15.1% production, transportation, and material moving
  Income: Per capita: $25,146; Median household: $44,038; Average household: $62,106; Households with income of $100,000 or more: 18.3%; Poverty rate: 13.8%
  Educational Attainment: High school diploma or higher: 88.9%; Bachelor's degree or higher: 13.6%; Graduate/professional degree or higher: 5.2%
  Housing: Homeownership rate: 80.6%; Median home value: $133,800; Median year structure built: 1975; Homeowner vacancy rate: 1.4%; Median gross rent: $988 per month; Rental vacancy rate: 8.4%
  Health Insurance: 85.8% have insurance; 69.5% have private insurance; 31.2% have public insurance; 14.2% do not have insurance; 0.8% of children under 18 do not have insurance
  Transportation: Commute: 94.7% car, 0.0% public transportation, 1.4% walk, 3.0% work from home; Median travel time to work: 34.3 minutes

FORT GRATIOT (charter township). Covers a land area of 15.959 square miles and a water area of 0.093 square miles. Located at 43.05° N. Lat; 82.49° W. Long.
Population: 11,108; Growth (since 2000): 3.9%; Density: 696.0 persons per square mile; Race: 94.6% White, 1.6% Black/African American, 1.4% Asian, 0.3% American Indian/Alaska Native, 0.0% Native Hawaiian/Other

Pacific Islander, 1.7% Two or more races, 2.5% Hispanic of any race; Average household size: 2.39; Median age: 44.6; Age under 18: 22.3%; Age 65 and over: 19.2%; Males per 100 females: 90.6; Marriage status: 26.6% never married, 53.6% now married, 1.2% separated, 9.1% widowed, 10.7% divorced; Foreign born: 5.4%; Speak English only: 93.1%; With disability: 15.9%; Veterans: 10.2%; Ancestry: 30.2% German, 15.7% Irish, 15.4% English, 7.2% Polish, 6.6% American

Employment: 13.6% management, business, and financial, 3.5% computer, engineering, and science, 9.2% education, legal, community service, arts, and media, 7.4% healthcare practitioners, 16.5% service, 26.7% sales and office, 7.5% natural resources, construction, and maintenance, 15.7% production, transportation, and material moving

Income: Per capita: $30,537; Median household: $49,500; Average household: $72,390; Households with income of $100,000 or more: 21.1%; Poverty rate: 11.0%

Educational Attainment: High school diploma or higher: 91.6%; Bachelor's degree or higher: 26.5%; Graduate/professional degree or higher: 12.0%

School District(s)
Port Huron Area SD (PK-12)
    2012-13 Enrollment: 9,508 . . . . (810) 984-3101

Housing: Homeownership rate: 74.0%; Median home value: $131,800; Median year structure built: 1980; Homeowner vacancy rate: 2.0%; Median gross rent: $730 per month; Rental vacancy rate: 16.9%

Health Insurance: 88.3% have insurance; 72.4% have private insurance; 34.5% have public insurance; 11.7% do not have insurance; 3.9% of children under 18 do not have insurance

Transportation: Commute: 90.6% car, 1.4% public transportation, 3.1% walk, 4.4% work from home; Median travel time to work: 21.7 minutes

Additional Information Contacts
Fort Gratiot Township . . . . (810) 385-4489
    http://www.fortgratiottwp.org

GOODELLS (unincorporated postal area)
ZCTA: 48027
    Covers a land area of 37.373 square miles and a water area of 0.065 square miles. Located at 42.94° N. Lat; 82.69° W. Long. Elevation is 709 feet.

Population: 3,249; Growth (since 2000): 8.8%; Density: 86.9 persons per square mile; Race: 96.2% White, 2.3% Black/African American, 0.1% Asian, 0.2% American Indian/Alaska Native, 0.0% Native Hawaiian/Other Pacific Islander, 1.0% Two or more races, 1.3% Hispanic of any race; Average household size: 2.83; Median age: 40.9; Age under 18: 23.8%; Age 65 and over: 11.8%; Males per 100 females: 104.1; Marriage status: 21.4% never married, 62.9% now married, 0.9% separated, 5.2% widowed, 10.5% divorced; Foreign born: 2.0%; Speak English only: 94.8%; With disability: 17.4%; Veterans: 9.8%; Ancestry: 34.3% German, 17.4% Polish, 14.8% Irish, 9.7% Italian, 8.9% English

Employment: 14.2% management, business, and financial, 1.3% computer, engineering, and science, 5.8% education, legal, community service, arts, and media, 3.0% healthcare practitioners, 18.9% service, 21.0% sales and office, 17.0% natural resources, construction, and maintenance, 18.8% production, transportation, and material moving

Income: Per capita: $24,087; Median household: $56,331; Average household: $61,871; Households with income of $100,000 or more: 15.2%; Poverty rate: 7.1%

Educational Attainment: High school diploma or higher: 91.8%; Bachelor's degree or higher: 17.0%; Graduate/professional degree or higher: 4.5%

Housing: Homeownership rate: 91.9%; Median home value: $133,400; Median year structure built: 1985; Homeowner vacancy rate: 1.9%; Median gross rent: $809 per month; Rental vacancy rate: 7.9%

Health Insurance: 90.8% have insurance; 79.1% have private insurance; 25.8% have public insurance; 9.2% do not have insurance; 1.9% of children under 18 do not have insurance

Transportation: Commute: 97.6% car, 0.0% public transportation, 0.0% walk, 2.4% work from home; Median travel time to work: 34.8 minutes

GRANT (township). Covers a land area of 29.674 square miles and a water area of 0.203 square miles. Located at 43.12° N. Lat; 82.60° W. Long.

Population: 1,891; Growth (since 2000): 13.4%; Density: 63.7 persons per square mile; Race: 96.8% White, 0.2% Black/African American, 0.5% Asian, 0.4% American Indian/Alaska Native, 0.0% Native Hawaiian/Other Pacific Islander, 1.6% Two or more races, 1.2% Hispanic of any race;

Average household size: 2.78; Median age: 42.3; Age under 18: 24.2%; Age 65 and over: 11.8%; Males per 100 females: 105.8

Housing: Homeownership rate: 91.5%; Homeowner vacancy rate: 2.2%; Rental vacancy rate: 3.4%

GREENWOOD (township). Covers a land area of 35.796 square miles and a water area of 0.138 square miles. Located at 43.12° N. Lat; 82.69° W. Long.

Population: 1,538; Growth (since 2000): 12.0%; Density: 43.0 persons per square mile; Race: 96.4% White, 0.3% Black/African American, 0.3% Asian, 0.5% American Indian/Alaska Native, 0.0% Native Hawaiian/Other Pacific Islander, 2.2% Two or more races, 1.9% Hispanic of any race; Average household size: 2.86; Median age: 39.1; Age under 18: 28.5%; Age 65 and over: 11.8%; Males per 100 females: 121.0

Housing: Homeownership rate: 93.1%; Homeowner vacancy rate: 2.3%; Rental vacancy rate: 9.5%

HARSENS ISLAND (unincorporated postal area)
ZCTA: 48028
    Covers a land area of 17.739 square miles and a water area of 15.948 square miles. Located at 42.58° N. Lat; 82.62° W. Long..

Population: 1,190; Growth (since 2000): -7.4%; Density: 67.1 persons per square mile; Race: 99.1% White, 0.1% Black/African American, 0.1% Asian, 0.3% American Indian/Alaska Native, 0.0% Native Hawaiian/Other Pacific Islander, 0.5% Two or more races, 0.3% Hispanic of any race; Average household size: 1.95; Median age: 58.6; Age under 18: 8.8%; Age 65 and over: 35.1%; Males per 100 females: 111.0

Housing: Homeownership rate: 93.6%; Homeowner vacancy rate: 1.7%; Rental vacancy rate: 18.8%

IRA (township). Covers a land area of 17.032 square miles and a water area of 4.602 square miles. Located at 42.70° N. Lat; 82.66° W. Long.

History: Ira Township was organized in 1837 and named for Ira Marks, an early settler here.

Population: 5,178; Growth (since 2000): -25.7%; Density: 304.0 persons per square mile; Race: 95.6% White, 1.1% Black/African American, 0.4% Asian, 0.3% American Indian/Alaska Native, 0.0% Native Hawaiian/Other Pacific Islander, 1.8% Two or more races, 2.3% Hispanic of any race; Average household size: 2.50; Median age: 42.0; Age under 18: 22.8%; Age 65 and over: 12.8%; Males per 100 females: 102.9; Marriage status: 24.7% never married, 55.1% now married, 1.0% separated, 8.7% widowed, 11.5% divorced; Foreign born: 2.2%; Speak English only: 99.1%; With disability: 14.6%; Veterans: 9.4%; Ancestry: 22.7% German, 19.2% Polish, 12.0% American, 10.4% Irish, 7.7% English

Employment: 11.9% management, business, and financial, 4.5% computer, engineering, and science, 8.5% education, legal, community service, arts, and media, 3.7% healthcare practitioners, 25.5% service, 24.6% sales and office, 6.3% natural resources, construction, and maintenance, 15.1% production, transportation, and material moving

Income: Per capita: $25,146; Median household: $44,038; Average household: $62,106; Households with income of $100,000 or more: 18.3%; Poverty rate: 13.8%

Educational Attainment: High school diploma or higher: 88.9%; Bachelor's degree or higher: 13.6%; Graduate/professional degree or higher: 5.2%

School District(s)
Algonac Community SD (PK-12)
    2012-13 Enrollment: 1,882 . . . . (810) 794-9364
Anchor Bay SD (PK-12)
    2012-13 Enrollment: 6,214 . . . . (586) 725-2861
East China SD (PK-12)
    2012-13 Enrollment: 4,508 . . . . (810) 676-1018

Housing: Homeownership rate: 80.6%; Median home value: $133,800; Median year structure built: 1975; Homeowner vacancy rate: 1.4%; Median gross rent: $988 per month; Rental vacancy rate: 8.4%

Health Insurance: 85.8% have insurance; 69.5% have private insurance; 31.2% have public insurance; 14.2% do not have insurance; 0.8% of children under 18 do not have insurance

Transportation: Commute: 94.7% car, 0.0% public transportation, 1.4% walk, 3.0% work from home; Median travel time to work: 34.3 minutes

JEDDO (unincorporated postal area)

ZCTA: 48032

Covers a land area of 37.310 square miles and a water area of 0.318 square miles. Located at 43.13° N. Lat; 82.60° W. Long. Elevation is 715 feet.

Population: 2,322; Growth (since 2000): 12.2%; Density: 62.2 persons per square mile; Race: 96.9% White, 0.3% Black/African American, 0.4% Asian, 0.3% American Indian/Alaska Native, 0.0% Native Hawaiian/Other Pacific Islander, 1.5% Two or more races, 1.2% Hispanic of any race; Average household size: 2.83; Median age: 41.2; Age under 18: 25.1%; Age 65 and over: 11.7%; Males per 100 females: 102.6

Housing: Homeownership rate: 91.6%; Homeowner vacancy rate: 1.8%; Rental vacancy rate: 2.8%

KENOCKEE (township). Covers a land area of 35.652 square miles and a water area of 0.236 square miles. Located at 43.03° N. Lat; 82.69° W. Long.

History: Kenockee Township was organized in 1855. The name is of Chippewa origin, meaning "long-legged."

Population: 2,470; Growth (since 2000): 1.9%; Density: 69.3 persons per square mile; Race: 97.7% White, 0.2% Black/African American, 0.1% Asian, 0.7% American Indian/Alaska Native, 0.0% Native Hawaiian/Other Pacific Islander, 0.9% Two or more races, 1.3% Hispanic of any race; Average household size: 2.74; Median age: 42.7; Age under 18: 23.8%; Age 65 and over: 12.7%; Males per 100 females: 104.3

School District(s)

Yale Public Schools (PK-12)

2012-13 Enrollment: 2,082 . . . . (810) 387-3231

Housing: Homeownership rate: 91.7%; Homeowner vacancy rate: 1.8%; Rental vacancy rate: 5.1%

KIMBALL (township). Covers a land area of 37.142 square miles and a water area of 0.308 square miles. Located at 42.95° N. Lat; 82.56° W. Long. Elevation is 636 feet.

History: Barzillai Wheeler and John S. Kimball settled here about 1840. Kimball Township was organized in 1855 and named for John Kimball.

Population: 9,358; Growth (since 2000): 8.5%; Density: 252.0 persons per square mile; Race: 96.1% White, 1.2% Black/African American, 0.2% Asian, 0.4% American Indian/Alaska Native, 0.0% Native Hawaiian/Other Pacific Islander, 1.7% Two or more races, 2.2% Hispanic of any race; Average household size: 2.61; Median age: 40.9; Age under 18: 23.8%; Age 65 and over: 13.0%; Males per 100 females: 103.3; Marriage status: 23.8% never married, 57.3% now married, 1.0% separated, 4.2% widowed, 14.7% divorced; Foreign born: 2.0%; Speak English only: 97.1%; With disability: 17.8%; Veterans: 8.7%; Ancestry: 29.0% German, 14.7% English, 14.1% Irish, 9.3% French, 8.8% Polish

Employment: 7.6% management, business, and financial, 3.9% computer, engineering, and science, 9.1% education, legal, community service, arts, and media, 5.9% healthcare practitioners, 21.3% service, 23.4% sales and office, 10.9% natural resources, construction, and maintenance, 17.8% production, transportation, and material moving

Income: Per capita: $24,355; Median household: $49,109; Average household: $59,967; Households with income of $100,000 or more: 14.9%; Poverty rate: 12.3%

Educational Attainment: High school diploma or higher: 84.2%; Bachelor's degree or higher: 12.0%; Graduate/professional degree or higher: 6.0%

School District(s)

Landmark Academy (KG-12)

2012-13 Enrollment: 928 . . . . (810) 982-7210

Port Huron Area SD (PK-12)

2012-13 Enrollment: 9,508 . . . . (810) 984-3101

Housing: Homeownership rate: 86.5%; Median home value: $111,900; Median year structure built: 1981; Homeowner vacancy rate: 2.4%; Median gross rent: $796 per month; Rental vacancy rate: 9.1%

Health Insurance: 90.0% have insurance; 72.3% have private insurance; 36.7% have public insurance; 10.0% do not have insurance; 3.9% of children under 18 do not have insurance

Transportation: Commute: 93.6% car, 0.8% public transportation, 1.8% walk, 2.9% work from home; Median travel time to work: 25.5 minutes

Additional Information Contacts

Kimball Township . . . . (810) 987-9797

http://www.kimballtownship.org

LYNN (township). Covers a land area of 35.722 square miles and a water area of 0.343 square miles. Located at 43.11° N. Lat; 82.94° W. Long.

History: Lynn Township was organized in 1850 and named for Edward J. Lynn, a lumber foreman. The settlement grew up around a sawmill established here in 1840.

Population: 1,229; Growth (since 2000): 3.5%; Density: 34.4 persons per square mile; Race: 94.9% White, 1.5% Black/African American, 0.0% Asian, 0.5% American Indian/Alaska Native, 0.0% Native Hawaiian/Other Pacific Islander, 1.8% Two or more races, 5.8% Hispanic of any race; Average household size: 2.83; Median age: 40.2; Age under 18: 25.1%; Age 65 and over: 10.9%; Males per 100 females: 109.7

Housing: Homeownership rate: 89.7%; Homeowner vacancy rate: 1.3%; Rental vacancy rate: 11.8%

MARINE CITY (city). Covers a land area of 2.147 square miles and a water area of 0.311 square miles. Located at 42.71° N. Lat; 82.50° W. Long. Elevation is 584 feet.

History: Marine City began as a lumber town, but turned to shipping from its port on the St. Clair River.

Population: 4,248; Growth (since 2000): -8.7%; Density: 1,978.1 persons per square mile; Race: 96.8% White, 0.3% Black/African American, 0.2% Asian, 0.7% American Indian/Alaska Native, 0.0% Native Hawaiian/Other Pacific Islander, 1.6% Two or more races, 1.7% Hispanic of any race; Average household size: 2.41; Median age: 40.2; Age under 18: 22.9%; Age 65 and over: 15.3%; Males per 100 females: 93.2; Marriage status: 27.1% never married, 51.0% now married, 1.5% separated, 5.0% widowed, 16.8% divorced; Foreign born: 2.4%; Speak English only: 97.4%; With disability: 14.4%; Veterans: 8.4%; Ancestry: 38.4% German, 14.7% French, 13.7% Irish, 11.6% Polish, 10.3% English

Employment: 8.3% management, business, and financial, 3.5% computer, engineering, and science, 4.9% education, legal, community service, arts, and media, 5.2% healthcare practitioners, 18.0% service, 22.4% sales and office, 13.8% natural resources, construction, and maintenance, 24.0% production, transportation, and material moving

Income: Per capita: $22,125; Median household: $45,045; Average household: $53,530; Households with income of $100,000 or more: 10.8%; Poverty rate: 15.0%

Educational Attainment: High school diploma or higher: 90.0%; Bachelor's degree or higher: 12.6%; Graduate/professional degree or higher: 4.5%

School District(s)

East China SD (PK-12)

2012-13 Enrollment: 4,508 . . . . (810) 676-1018

Housing: Homeownership rate: 68.2%; Median home value: $87,800; Median year structure built: 1952; Homeowner vacancy rate: 2.3%; Median gross rent: $653 per month; Rental vacancy rate: 11.6%

Health Insurance: 84.1% have insurance; 66.1% have private insurance; 35.6% have public insurance; 15.9% do not have insurance; 1.0% of children under 18 do not have insurance

Transportation: Commute: 93.2% car, 1.5% public transportation, 3.3% walk, 1.5% work from home; Median travel time to work: 32.4 minutes

Additional Information Contacts

City of Marine City . . . . (810) 765-8846

http://www.marinecity-mi.org

MARYSVILLE (city). Covers a land area of 7.309 square miles and a water area of 0.988 square miles. Located at 42.91° N. Lat; 82.48° W. Long. Elevation is 614 feet.

History: A sawmill was operating in Marysville in 1780, and more sawmills began in 1805, supplying lumber for the growing town of Detroit. Salt beds beneath Marysville provided the material for a Morton Salt Works plant. In 1930, the Gar Wood Boat Works began operations here, founded by Garfield Arthur Wood, speedboat racing champion and inventor of the hydraulic hoist that revolutionized dump trucks.

Population: 9,959; Growth (since 2000): 2.8%; Density: 1,362.5 persons per square mile; Race: 97.5% White, 0.3% Black/African American, 0.6% Asian, 0.2% American Indian/Alaska Native, 0.0% Native Hawaiian/Other Pacific Islander, 0.9% Two or more races, 1.8% Hispanic of any race; Average household size: 2.39; Median age: 42.0; Age under 18: 23.4%; Age 65 and over: 17.5%; Males per 100 females: 92.9; Marriage status: 21.9% never married, 57.6% now married, 0.7% separated, 8.4% widowed, 12.1% divorced; Foreign born: 3.0%; Speak English only: 96.7%; With disability: 11.7%; Veterans: 10.8%; Ancestry: 29.8% German, 14.0% Irish, 12.7% English, 10.7% Polish, 7.0% American

Employment: 10.9% management, business, and financial, 3.4% computer, engineering, and science, 12.1% education, legal, community service, arts, and media, 8.4% healthcare practitioners, 18.8% service, 21.6% sales and office, 10.3% natural resources, construction, and maintenance, 14.5% production, transportation, and material moving
Income: Per capita: $25,982; Median household: $53,237; Average household: $61,226; Households with income of $100,000 or more: 17.6%; Poverty rate: 9.3%
Educational Attainment: High school diploma or higher: 92.8%; Bachelor's degree or higher: 23.9%; Graduate/professional degree or higher: 10.3%

School District(s)
Marysville Public Schools (PK-12)
    2012-13 Enrollment: 2,685 . . . . (810) 364-7731
Saint Clair County Career Prep Academy (KG-12)
    2012-13 Enrollment: n/a . . . . (810) 364-8990
Saint Clair County Resa (PK-12)
    2012-13 Enrollment: 401 . . . . (810) 364-8990
Virtual Learning Academy of Saint Clair County (KG-12)
    2012-13 Enrollment: 174 . . . . (810) 364-8990
Vocational/Technical School(s)
Blue Water College of Cosmetology Inc (Private, For-profit)
    Fall 2013 Enrollment: 57 . . . . (810) 364-9595
    2013-14 Tuition: $15,950
Housing: Homeownership rate: 81.6%; Median home value: $120,700; Median year structure built: 1977; Homeowner vacancy rate: 3.0%; Median gross rent: $713 per month; Rental vacancy rate: 8.8%
Health Insurance: 92.8% have insurance; 81.9% have private insurance; 30.0% have public insurance; 7.2% do not have insurance; 4.4% of children under 18 do not have insurance
Safety: Violent crime rate: 2.0 per 10,000 population; Property crime rate: 189.5 per 10,000 population
Transportation: Commute: 96.0% car, 0.8% public transportation, 1.1% walk, 1.4% work from home; Median travel time to work: 23.9 minutes
Additional Information Contacts
City of Marysville . . . . (810) 364-6613
    http://www.cityofmarysvillemi.com

MUSSEY (township). Covers a land area of 35.676 square miles and a water area of 0.206 square miles. Located at 43.03° N. Lat; 82.93° W. Long. Elevation is 814 feet.
Population: 4,206; Growth (since 2000): 12.5%; Density: 117.9 persons per square mile; Race: 92.0% White, 0.3% Black/African American, 0.4% Asian, 0.5% American Indian/Alaska Native, 0.0% Native Hawaiian/Other Pacific Islander, 2.3% Two or more races, 11.1% Hispanic of any race; Average household size: 2.78; Median age: 36.5; Age under 18: 27.7%; Age 65 and over: 11.0%; Males per 100 females: 100.4; Marriage status: 26.5% never married, 56.2% now married, 0.9% separated, 6.1% widowed, 11.2% divorced; Foreign born: 7.3%; Speak English only: 87.3%; With disability: 12.9%; Veterans: 6.8%; Ancestry: 34.7% German, 15.5% Polish, 10.9% English, 10.6% Irish, 8.2% Italian
Employment: 8.3% management, business, and financial, 1.8% computer, engineering, and science, 5.9% education, legal, community service, arts, and media, 7.5% healthcare practitioners, 21.4% service, 18.5% sales and office, 16.4% natural resources, construction, and maintenance, 20.2% production, transportation, and material moving
Income: Per capita: $18,564; Median household: $47,981; Average household: $53,942; Households with income of $100,000 or more: 11.5%; Poverty rate: 19.5%
Educational Attainment: High school diploma or higher: 80.4%; Bachelor's degree or higher: 8.5%; Graduate/professional degree or higher: 2.6%

School District(s)
Capac Community Schools (PK-12)
    2012-13 Enrollment: 1,295 . . . . (810) 395-3700
Housing: Homeownership rate: 79.9%; Median home value: $111,200; Median year structure built: 1980; Homeowner vacancy rate: 3.9%; Median gross rent: $845 per month; Rental vacancy rate: 14.2%
Health Insurance: 85.2% have insurance; 63.8% have private insurance; 31.5% have public insurance; 14.8% do not have insurance; 10.2% of children under 18 do not have insurance
Transportation: Commute: 91.0% car, 0.0% public transportation, 0.2% walk, 7.8% work from home; Median travel time to work: 36.3 minutes

NORTH STREET (unincorporated postal area)
ZCTA: 48049
Covers a land area of 35.766 square miles and a water area of 0.330 square miles. Located at 43.04° N. Lat; 82.57° W. Long..
Population: 5,582; Growth (since 2000): -3.2%; Density: 156.1 persons per square mile; Race: 97.2% White, 0.6% Black/African American, 0.2% Asian, 0.3% American Indian/Alaska Native, 0.0% Native Hawaiian/Other Pacific Islander, 1.1% Two or more races, 2.2% Hispanic of any race; Average household size: 2.70; Median age: 43.4; Age under 18: 22.6%; Age 65 and over: 12.7%; Males per 100 females: 101.9; Marriage status: 23.4% never married, 64.3% now married, 0.5% separated, 4.5% widowed, 7.8% divorced; Foreign born: 1.9%; Speak English only: 95.7%; With disability: 16.3%; Veterans: 15.0%; Ancestry: 36.8% German, 20.9% Irish, 17.4% English, 7.0% French, 6.4% Polish
Employment: 9.3% management, business, and financial, 2.0% computer, engineering, and science, 7.6% education, legal, community service, arts, and media, 3.3% healthcare practitioners, 18.7% service, 25.9% sales and office, 15.4% natural resources, construction, and maintenance, 17.9% production, transportation, and material moving
Income: Per capita: $26,235; Median household: $58,040; Average household: $70,326; Households with income of $100,000 or more: 20.8%; Poverty rate: 4.3%
Educational Attainment: High school diploma or higher: 92.7%; Bachelor's degree or higher: 18.8%; Graduate/professional degree or higher: 5.0%
Housing: Homeownership rate: 89.8%; Median home value: $119,700; Median year structure built: 1975; Homeowner vacancy rate: 1.8%; Median gross rent: $792 per month; Rental vacancy rate: 7.8%
Health Insurance: 89.2% have insurance; 75.0% have private insurance; 30.1% have public insurance; 10.8% do not have insurance; 6.1% of children under 18 do not have insurance
Transportation: Commute: 95.2% car, 0.1% public transportation, 0.8% walk, 1.7% work from home; Median travel time to work: 26.1 minutes

PEARL BEACH (CDP). Covers a land area of 2.145 square miles and a water area of 0.866 square miles. Located at 42.63° N. Lat; 82.59° W. Long. Elevation is 581 feet.
History: Pearl Beach was settled in the late 1700's. Since the time of the French traders, the village has attracted duck hunters.
Population: 2,829; Growth (since 2000): -12.3%; Density: 1,318.7 persons per square mile; Race: 98.4% White, 0.1% Black/African American, 0.5% Asian, 0.3% American Indian/Alaska Native, 0.0% Native Hawaiian/Other Pacific Islander, 0.6% Two or more races, 0.8% Hispanic of any race; Average household size: 2.11; Median age: 53.8; Age under 18: 12.0%; Age 65 and over: 24.4%; Males per 100 females: 107.6; Marriage status: 11.9% never married, 67.6% now married, 1.6% separated, 9.2% widowed, 11.3% divorced; Foreign born: 1.5%; Speak English only: 98.2%; With disability: 13.9%; Veterans: 14.4%; Ancestry: 29.9% German, 21.3% Polish, 11.4% Irish, 9.2% English, 8.8% Italian
Employment: 9.2% management, business, and financial, 10.2% computer, engineering, and science, 5.4% education, legal, community service, arts, and media, 5.3% healthcare practitioners, 12.9% service, 28.2% sales and office, 12.5% natural resources, construction, and maintenance, 16.3% production, transportation, and material moving
Income: Per capita: $32,280; Median household: $57,700; Average household: $67,418; Households with income of $100,000 or more: 20.5%; Poverty rate: 8.1%
Educational Attainment: High school diploma or higher: 91.4%; Bachelor's degree or higher: 19.0%; Graduate/professional degree or higher: 9.1%
Housing: Homeownership rate: 90.0%; Median home value: $164,900; Median year structure built: 1967; Homeowner vacancy rate: 2.2%; Median gross rent: $958 per month; Rental vacancy rate: 10.5%
Health Insurance: 94.7% have insurance; 85.2% have private insurance; 37.9% have public insurance; 5.3% do not have insurance; 0.0% of children under 18 do not have insurance
Transportation: Commute: 92.6% car, 0.7% public transportation, 2.1% walk, 2.6% work from home; Median travel time to work: 33.8 minutes

PORT HURON (charter township). Covers a land area of 12.838 square miles and a water area of 0.303 square miles. Located at 42.98° N. Lat; 82.48° W. Long. Elevation is 607 feet.
History: The earliest European settlement began (1686) with the French fort, St. Joseph. The town grew after the building (1826) of Fort Gratiot Turnpike (between Port Huron and Detroit), ushering in a lumbering era.

Local deposits of salt, oil, and natural gas were developed. The old Fort Gratiot lighthouse marks the St. Clair straits off Port Huron. Thomas Edison grew up here. Incorporated 1857.

Population: 10,654; Growth (since 2000): 23.7%; Density: 829.9 persons per square mile; Race: 90.9% White, 4.5% Black/African American, 0.4% Asian, 0.7% American Indian/Alaska Native, 0.0% Native Hawaiian/Other Pacific Islander, 2.8% Two or more races, 3.8% Hispanic of any race; Average household size: 2.51; Median age: 38.5; Age under 18: 23.2%; Age 65 and over: 13.0%; Males per 100 females: 99.4; Marriage status: 27.0% never married, 49.8% now married, 1.1% separated, 5.2% widowed, 18.0% divorced; Foreign born: 1.9%; Speak English only: 96.3%; With disability: 19.1%; Veterans: 9.4%; Ancestry: 27.7% German, 14.6% Irish, 12.5% English, 9.7% Polish, 6.6% French

Employment: 9.6% management, business, and financial, 1.1% computer, engineering, and science, 8.0% education, legal, community service, arts, and media, 3.3% healthcare practitioners, 20.4% service, 25.6% sales and office, 9.2% natural resources, construction, and maintenance, 22.9% production, transportation, and material moving

Income: Per capita: $21,557; Median household: $41,238; Average household: $55,025; Households with income of $100,000 or more: 11.1%; Poverty rate: 25.1%

Educational Attainment: High school diploma or higher: 86.0%; Bachelor's degree or higher: 12.6%; Graduate/professional degree or higher: 3.4%

School District(s)
Blue Water Middle College (KG-12)
   2012-13 Enrollment: 247 . . . . (810) 364-8990
Port Huron Area SD (PK-12)
   2012-13 Enrollment: 9,508 . . . . (810) 984-3101
Saint Clair County Intervention Academy (KG-12)
   2012-13 Enrollment: 65 . . . . (810) 966-1649
Saint Clair County Learning Academy (KG-12)
   2012-13 Enrollment: 25 . . . . (810) 364-8990

Four-year College(s)
Baker College of Port Huron (Private, Not-for-profit)
   Fall 2013 Enrollment: 1,039 . . . . (810) 985-7000
   2013-14 Tuition: In-state $8,100; Out-of-state $8,100

Two-year College(s)
St Clair County Community College (Public)
   Fall 2013 Enrollment: 4,324 . . . . (810) 984-3881
   2013-14 Tuition: In-state $6,258; Out-of-state $8,893

Vocational/Technical School(s)
Lakewood School of Therapeutic Massage (Private, For-profit)
   Fall 2013 Enrollment: 22 . . . . (810) 987-3959
Paul Mitchell the School-Great Lakes (Private, For-profit)
   Fall 2013 Enrollment: 87 . . . . (810) 987-8118
   2013-14 Tuition: $11,725
Ross Medical Education Center-Port Huron (Private, For-profit)
   Fall 2013 Enrollment: 62 . . . . (810) 982-0454
   2013-14 Tuition: $15,680

Housing: Homeownership rate: 68.9%; Median home value: $113,400; Median year structure built: 1973; Homeowner vacancy rate: 2.2%; Median gross rent: $761 per month; Rental vacancy rate: 9.5%

Health Insurance: 89.7% have insurance; 61.9% have private insurance; 43.4% have public insurance; 10.3% do not have insurance; 0.9% of children under 18 do not have insurance

Hospitals: Port Huron Hospital (186 beds); Saint Joseph Mercy Port Huron (119 beds)

Newspapers: Times Herald (daily circulation 26100)

Transportation: Commute: 96.5% car, 0.7% public transportation, 1.5% walk, 1.0% work from home; Median travel time to work: 21.1 minutes; Amtrak: Train service available.

Airports: St Clair County International (general aviation)

Additional Information Contacts
Port Huron Charter Township . . . . (810) 987-6600
   http://www.porthurontownship.org

PORT HURON (city). County seat. Covers a land area of 8.081 square miles and a water area of 4.184 square miles. Located at 42.99° N. Lat; 82.43° W. Long. Elevation is 607 feet.

History: Named for the Huron Indians, later known as the Wyandot. Fort St. Joseph, the second fortified post in lower Michigan, was built here in 1686 to protect the French fur trade from English aggression. A permanent colony was founded in 1790, when Frenchman Anselm Petit settled near the mouth of the Black River. In 1814, Fort Gratiot was built on the site of old Fort St. Joseph. It was in 1826, when the Fort Gratiot Turnpike was constructed from Detroit, that the four villages of Peru, Desmond, Huron, and Gratiot, sprang up. They united in 1837 to form the village of Port Huron. Incorporated as a village in 1849 and chartered as a city in 1857, Port Huron became the seat of St. Clair County in 1871. Its location on Lake Huron and the St. Clair River made Port Huron an important port, with access to the Canadian city across the river.

Population: 30,184; Growth (since 2000): -6.7%; Density: 3,735.0 persons per square mile; Race: 84.0% White, 9.1% Black/African American, 0.6% Asian, 0.7% American Indian/Alaska Native, 0.0% Native Hawaiian/Other Pacific Islander, 4.5% Two or more races, 5.4% Hispanic of any race; Average household size: 2.42; Median age: 35.8; Age under 18: 25.6%; Age 65 and over: 13.1%; Males per 100 females: 91.5; Marriage status: 34.4% never married, 42.5% now married, 1.9% separated, 6.9% widowed, 16.2% divorced; Foreign born: 3.7%; Speak English only: 95.7%; With disability: 20.5%; Veterans: 9.8%; Ancestry: 28.8% German, 15.8% Irish, 10.8% English, 6.2% Polish, 5.2% Italian

Employment: 7.2% management, business, and financial, 1.7% computer, engineering, and science, 7.9% education, legal, community service, arts, and media, 4.5% healthcare practitioners, 27.3% service, 25.8% sales and office, 6.2% natural resources, construction, and maintenance, 19.3% production, transportation, and material moving

Income: Per capita: $18,209; Median household: $32,940; Average household: $43,155; Households with income of $100,000 or more: 7.7%; Poverty rate: 28.6%

Educational Attainment: High school diploma or higher: 86.0%; Bachelor's degree or higher: 14.8%; Graduate/professional degree or higher: 5.5%

School District(s)
Blue Water Middle College (KG-12)
   2012-13 Enrollment: 247 . . . . (810) 364-8990
Port Huron Area SD (PK-12)
   2012-13 Enrollment: 9,508 . . . . (810) 984-3101
Saint Clair County Intervention Academy (KG-12)
   2012-13 Enrollment: 65 . . . . (810) 966-1649
Saint Clair County Learning Academy (KG-12)
   2012-13 Enrollment: 25 . . . . (810) 364-8990

Four-year College(s)
Baker College of Port Huron (Private, Not-for-profit)
   Fall 2013 Enrollment: 1,039 . . . . (810) 985-7000
   2013-14 Tuition: In-state $8,100; Out-of-state $8,100

Two-year College(s)
St Clair County Community College (Public)
   Fall 2013 Enrollment: 4,324 . . . . (810) 984-3881
   2013-14 Tuition: In-state $6,258; Out-of-state $8,893

Vocational/Technical School(s)
Lakewood School of Therapeutic Massage (Private, For-profit)
   Fall 2013 Enrollment: 22 . . . . (810) 987-3959
Paul Mitchell the School-Great Lakes (Private, For-profit)
   Fall 2013 Enrollment: 87 . . . . (810) 987-8118
   2013-14 Tuition: $11,725
Ross Medical Education Center-Port Huron (Private, For-profit)
   Fall 2013 Enrollment: 62 . . . . (810) 982-0454
   2013-14 Tuition: $15,680

Housing: Homeownership rate: 54.1%; Median home value: $81,400; Median year structure built: 1951; Homeowner vacancy rate: 3.1%; Median gross rent: $681 per month; Rental vacancy rate: 11.5%

Health Insurance: 86.2% have insurance; 53.2% have private insurance; 47.9% have public insurance; 13.8% do not have insurance; 1.8% of children under 18 do not have insurance

Hospitals: Port Huron Hospital (186 beds); Saint Joseph Mercy Port Huron (119 beds)

Safety: Violent crime rate: 60.6 per 10,000 population; Property crime rate: 308.7 per 10,000 population

Newspapers: Times Herald (daily circulation 26100)

Transportation: Commute: 89.6% car, 1.4% public transportation, 3.8% walk, 3.2% work from home; Median travel time to work: 18.9 minutes; Amtrak: Train service available.

Airports: St Clair County International (general aviation)

Additional Information Contacts
City of Port Huron . . . . (810) 984-9725
   http://www.porthuron.org

RILEY (township). Covers a land area of 38.228 square miles and a water area of 0.091 square miles. Located at 42.95° N. Lat; 82.81° W. Long.

History: Riley Township was organized in 1841 and named for John Riley, a Chippewa who owned land here.

Population: 3,353; Growth (since 2000): 10.1%; Density: 87.7 persons per square mile; Race: 96.5% White, 0.5% Black/African American, 0.4% Asian, 0.4% American Indian/Alaska Native, 0.0% Native Hawaiian/Other Pacific Islander, 1.5% Two or more races, 2.3% Hispanic of any race; Average household size: 2.81; Median age: 41.4; Age under 18: 25.6%; Age 65 and over: 11.2%; Males per 100 females: 110.7; Marriage status: 23.5% never married, 64.8% now married, 1.3% separated, 3.9% widowed, 7.8% divorced; Foreign born: 0.3%; Speak English only: 98.9%; With disability: 9.4%; Veterans: 11.9%; Ancestry: 41.8% German, 31.9% Polish, 13.5% Irish, 9.9% Italian, 9.2% French

Employment: 12.5% management, business, and financial, 2.5% computer, engineering, and science, 6.0% education, legal, community service, arts, and media, 4.5% healthcare practitioners, 14.4% service, 28.5% sales and office, 15.0% natural resources, construction, and maintenance, 16.6% production, transportation, and material moving

Income: Per capita: $26,545; Median household: $57,969; Average household: $70,439; Households with income of $100,000 or more: 20.5%; Poverty rate: 9.9%

Educational Attainment: High school diploma or higher: 91.6%; Bachelor's degree or higher: 10.8%; Graduate/professional degree or higher: 3.9%

Housing: Homeownership rate: 93.4%; Median home value: $167,700; Median year structure built: 1986; Homeowner vacancy rate: 1.4%; Median gross rent: $852 per month; Rental vacancy rate: 4.9%

Health Insurance: 91.3% have insurance; 83.2% have private insurance; 19.5% have public insurance; 8.7% do not have insurance; 4.2% of children under 18 do not have insurance

Transportation: Commute: 92.9% car, 0.1% public transportation, 0.9% walk, 5.9% work from home; Median travel time to work: 45.7 minutes

SAINT CLAIR (city). Covers a land area of 2.931 square miles and a water area of 0.677 square miles. Located at 42.83° N. Lat; 82.49° W. Long. Elevation is 587 feet.

History: St. Clair was laid out in 1818, and a post office was established here in 1826. The name probably came from LaSalle, who entered the lake in 1679 on the feast day of Saint Claire. The name was later applied to the lake, the river, and the village. Between LaSalle and the 19th-century village, a British officer named Patrick Sinclair erected Fort Sinclair as a supply depot in the area. The St. Clair name may have come from him.

Population: 5,485; Growth (since 2000): -5.5%; Density: 1,871.5 persons per square mile; Race: 97.1% White, 0.3% Black/African American, 0.9% Asian, 0.2% American Indian/Alaska Native, 0.0% Native Hawaiian/Other Pacific Islander, 1.2% Two or more races, 1.6% Hispanic of any race; Average household size: 2.37; Median age: 42.5; Age under 18: 23.9%; Age 65 and over: 15.2%; Males per 100 females: 93.5; Marriage status: 27.0% never married, 56.1% now married, 2.1% separated, 7.3% widowed, 9.6% divorced; Foreign born: 3.1%; Speak English only: 96.6%; With disability: 13.0%; Veterans: 7.7%; Ancestry: 35.6% German, 14.1% Polish, 11.4% Irish, 11.3% American, 8.5% English

Employment: 16.8% management, business, and financial, 4.3% computer, engineering, and science, 13.1% education, legal, community service, arts, and media, 7.2% healthcare practitioners, 18.5% service, 22.0% sales and office, 4.1% natural resources, construction, and maintenance, 14.2% production, transportation, and material moving

Income: Per capita: $29,744; Median household: $51,907; Average household: $69,148; Households with income of $100,000 or more: 17.1%; Poverty rate: 9.5%

Educational Attainment: High school diploma or higher: 91.1%; Bachelor's degree or higher: 25.9%; Graduate/professional degree or higher: 11.3%

School District(s)

East China SD (PK-12)
    2012-13 Enrollment: 4,508 . . . . (810) 676-1018

Housing: Homeownership rate: 72.0%; Median home value: $128,400; Median year structure built: 1957; Homeowner vacancy rate: 3.6%; Median gross rent: $635 per month; Rental vacancy rate: 11.3%

Health Insurance: 89.1% have insurance; 78.3% have private insurance; 26.5% have public insurance; 10.9% do not have insurance; 5.9% of children under 18 do not have insurance

Safety: Violent crime rate: 11.2 per 10,000 population; Property crime rate: 161.9 per 10,000 population

Transportation: Commute: 91.7% car, 0.0% public transportation, 1.8% walk, 3.8% work from home; Median travel time to work: 26.4 minutes

SAINT CLAIR (township). Covers a land area of 38.414 square miles and a water area of 0.748 square miles. Located at 42.86° N. Lat; 82.55° W. Long. Elevation is 587 feet.

Population: 6,817; Growth (since 2000): 6.1%; Density: 177.5 persons per square mile; Race: 97.5% White, 0.2% Black/African American, 0.7% Asian, 0.4% American Indian/Alaska Native, 0.0% Native Hawaiian/Other Pacific Islander, 0.9% Two or more races, 1.3% Hispanic of any race; Average household size: 2.69; Median age: 43.6; Age under 18: 24.9%; Age 65 and over: 14.1%; Males per 100 females: 100.9; Marriage status: 23.2% never married, 63.9% now married, 0.9% separated, 4.6% widowed, 8.3% divorced; Foreign born: 2.7%; Speak English only: 96.6%; With disability: 8.7%; Veterans: 10.5%; Ancestry: 31.7% German, 16.9% Polish, 13.2% Irish, 8.9% American, 8.6% English

Employment: 11.2% management, business, and financial, 3.3% computer, engineering, and science, 5.4% education, legal, community service, arts, and media, 7.2% healthcare practitioners, 15.8% service, 27.5% sales and office, 12.3% natural resources, construction, and maintenance, 17.3% production, transportation, and material moving

Income: Per capita: $31,483; Median household: $68,953; Average household: $83,868; Households with income of $100,000 or more: 30.6%; Poverty rate: 7.9%

Educational Attainment: High school diploma or higher: 92.3%; Bachelor's degree or higher: 22.1%; Graduate/professional degree or higher: 8.4%

School District(s)

East China SD (PK-12)
    2012-13 Enrollment: 4,508 . . . . (810) 676-1018

Housing: Homeownership rate: 91.2%; Median home value: $169,300; Median year structure built: 1984; Homeowner vacancy rate: 2.0%; Median gross rent: $814 per month; Rental vacancy rate: 15.4%

Health Insurance: 91.3% have insurance; 81.4% have private insurance; 26.6% have public insurance; 8.7% do not have insurance; 3.0% of children under 18 do not have insurance

Transportation: Commute: 95.9% car, 0.0% public transportation, 0.4% walk, 2.6% work from home; Median travel time to work: 29.2 minutes

SMITHS CREEK (unincorporated postal area)
ZCTA: 48074

Covers a land area of 37.076 square miles and a water area of 0.308 square miles. Located at 42.95° N. Lat; 82.56° W. Long. Elevation is 633 feet.

Population: 9,356; Growth (since 2000): 8.5%; Density: 252.3 persons per square mile; Race: 96.1% White, 1.2% Black/African American, 0.2% Asian, 0.4% American Indian/Alaska Native, 0.0% Native Hawaiian/Other Pacific Islander, 1.7% Two or more races, 2.2% Hispanic of any race; Average household size: 2.61; Median age: 40.9; Age under 18: 23.8%; Age 65 and over: 13.0%; Males per 100 females: 103.3; Marriage status: 23.8% never married, 57.3% now married, 1.0% separated, 4.2% widowed, 14.7% divorced; Foreign born: 2.0%; Speak English only: 97.1%; With disability: 17.8%; Veterans: 8.7%; Ancestry: 29.0% German, 14.7% English, 14.1% Irish, 9.3% French, 8.8% Polish

Employment: 7.6% management, business, and financial, 3.9% computer, engineering, and science, 9.1% education, legal, community service, arts, and media, 5.9% healthcare practitioners, 21.3% service, 23.4% sales and office, 10.9% natural resources, construction, and maintenance, 17.8% production, transportation, and material moving

Income: Per capita: $24,355; Median household: $49,109; Average household: $59,967; Households with income of $100,000 or more: 14.9%; Poverty rate: 12.3%

Educational Attainment: High school diploma or higher: 84.2%; Bachelor's degree or higher: 12.0%; Graduate/professional degree or higher: 6.0%

Housing: Homeownership rate: 86.5%; Median home value: $111,900; Median year structure built: 1981; Homeowner vacancy rate: 2.4%; Median gross rent: $796 per month; Rental vacancy rate: 9.1%

Health Insurance: 90.0% have insurance; 72.3% have private insurance; 36.7% have public insurance; 10.0% do not have insurance; 3.9% of children under 18 do not have insurance

Transportation: Commute: 93.6% car, 0.8% public transportation, 1.8% walk, 2.9% work from home; Median travel time to work: 25.5 minutes

WALES (township). Covers a land area of 37.371 square miles and a water area of 0.065 square miles. Located at 42.94° N. Lat; 82.69° W. Long.

Population: 3,248; Growth (since 2000): 8.8%; Density: 86.9 persons per square mile; Race: 96.2% White, 2.3% Black/African American, 0.1% Asian, 0.2% American Indian/Alaska Native, 0.0% Native Hawaiian/Other Pacific Islander, 1.0% Two or more races, 1.3% Hispanic of any race; Average household size: 2.83; Median age: 40.8; Age under 18: 23.8%; Age 65 and over: 11.8%; Males per 100 females: 104.0; Marriage status: 21.4% never married, 62.9% now married, 0.9% separated, 5.2% widowed, 10.5% divorced; Foreign born: 2.0%; Speak English only: 94.8%; With disability: 17.4%; Veterans: 9.8%; Ancestry: 34.3% German, 17.4% Polish, 14.8% Irish, 9.7% Italian, 8.9% English

Employment: 14.2% management, business, and financial, 1.3% computer, engineering, and science, 5.8% education, legal, community service, arts, and media, 3.0% healthcare practitioners, 18.9% service, 21.0% sales and office, 17.0% natural resources, construction, and maintenance, 18.8% production, transportation, and material moving

Income: Per capita: $24,087; Median household: $56,331; Average household: $61,871; Households with income of $100,000 or more: 15.2%; Poverty rate: 7.1%

Educational Attainment: High school diploma or higher: 91.8%; Bachelor's degree or higher: 17.0%; Graduate/professional degree or higher: 4.5%

Housing: Homeownership rate: 91.9%; Median home value: $133,400; Median year structure built: 1985; Homeowner vacancy rate: 1.9%; Median gross rent: $809 per month; Rental vacancy rate: 7.9%

Health Insurance: 90.8% have insurance; 79.1% have private insurance; 25.8% have public insurance; 9.2% do not have insurance; 1.9% of children under 18 do not have insurance

Transportation: Commute: 97.6% car, 0.0% public transportation, 0.0% walk, 2.4% work from home; Median travel time to work: 34.8 minutes

Additional Information Contacts

Wales Township . . . . (810) 325-1517
http://www.walestownship.org

YALE (city). Covers a land area of 1.383 square miles and a water area of 0.009 square miles. Located at 43.13° N. Lat; 82.80° W. Long. Elevation is 794 feet.

History: Settled 1859; incorporated as village 1885, as city 1905.

Population: 1,955; Growth (since 2000): -5.2%; Density: 1,413.9 persons per square mile; Race: 96.8% White, 0.6% Black/African American, 0.1% Asian, 0.1% American Indian/Alaska Native, 0.0% Native Hawaiian/Other Pacific Islander, 1.6% Two or more races, 1.3% Hispanic of any race; Average household size: 2.56; Median age: 38.2; Age under 18: 27.0%; Age 65 and over: 17.3%; Males per 100 females: 83.7

School District(s)

Yale Public Schools (PK-12)
2012-13 Enrollment: 2,082 . . . . (810) 387-3231

Housing: Homeownership rate: 67.2%; Homeowner vacancy rate: 3.6%; Rental vacancy rate: 10.0%

Safety: Violent crime rate: 26.2 per 10,000 population; Property crime rate: 256.7 per 10,000 population

Newspapers: Yale Expositor (weekly circulation 2700)

Saint Joseph County

Located in southwestern Michigan; bounded on the south by Indiana; drained by the Saint Joseph River; includes several lakes. Covers a land area of 500.591 square miles, a water area of 20.441 square miles, and is located in the Eastern Time Zone at 41.91° N. Lat., 85.52° W. Long. The county was founded in 1829. County seat is Centreville.

Saint Joseph County is part of the Sturgis, MI Micropolitan Statistical Area. The entire metro area includes: Saint Joseph County, MI

Weather Station: Three Rivers   Elevation: 810 feet

	Jan	Feb	Mar	Apr	May	Jun	Jul	Aug	Sep	Oct	Nov	Dec
High	33	36	47	60	71	81	84	82	75	62	49	36
Low	16	18	26	36	46	56	60	58	50	39	31	21
Precip	2.3	1.8	2.4	3.2	4.1	3.5	4.3	4.2	3.9	3.4	3.2	2.6
Snow	9.7	6.4	4.8	0.9	tr	0.0	0.0	0.0	0.0	0.5	2.5	9.5

High and Low temperatures in degrees Fahrenheit; Precipitation and Snow in inches

Population: 61,295; Growth (since 2000): -1.8%; Density: 122.4 persons per square mile; Race: 90.6% White, 2.6% Black/African American, 0.7% Asian, 0.5% American Indian/Alaska Native, 0.0% Native Hawaiian/Other Pacific Islander, 2.2% two or more races, 6.6% Hispanic of any race; Average household size: 2.60; Median age: 38.7; Age under 18: 25.9%; Age 65 and over: 14.9%; Males per 100 females: 97.9; Marriage status: 24.8% never married, 55.3% now married, 1.7% separated, 7.4% widowed, 12.5% divorced; Foreign born: 3.5%; Speak English only: 90.1%; With disability: 12.7%; Veterans: 9.7%; Ancestry: 33.0% German, 11.9% English, 10.0% American, 9.7% Irish, 5.8% Dutch

Religion: Six largest groups: 15.4% Catholicism, 6.1% Non-denominational Protestant, 3.8% Methodist/Pietist, 3.6% European Free-Church, 3.5% Holiness, 3.2% Lutheran

Economy: Unemployment rate: 4.6%; Leading industries: 16.8% retail trade; 13.2% other services (except public administration); 11.4% manufacturing; Farms: 967 totaling 221,745 acres; Company size: 1 employs 1,000 or more persons, 4 employ 500 to 999 persons, 36 employ 100 to 499 persons, 1,122 employ less than 100 persons; Business ownership: 1,137 women-owned, 113 Black-owned, 85 Hispanic-owned, 50 Asian-owned

Employment: 10.5% management, business, and financial, 2.9% computer, engineering, and science, 7.5% education, legal, community service, arts, and media, 4.8% healthcare practitioners, 13.8% service, 21.4% sales and office, 9.5% natural resources, construction, and maintenance, 29.7% production, transportation, and material moving

Income: Per capita: $20,570; Median household: $44,051; Average household: $53,866; Households with income of $100,000 or more: 10.7%; Poverty rate: 17.6%

Educational Attainment: High school diploma or higher: 84.4%; Bachelor's degree or higher: 14.5%; Graduate/professional degree or higher: 5.0%

Housing: Homeownership rate: 75.3%; Median home value: $108,900; Median year structure built: 1972; Homeowner vacancy rate: 2.8%; Median gross rent: $634 per month; Rental vacancy rate: 10.0%

Vital Statistics: Birth rate: 142.7 per 10,000 population; Death rate: 89.4 per 10,000 population; Age-adjusted cancer mortality rate: 170.8 deaths per 100,000 population

Health Insurance: 86.8% have insurance; 65.1% have private insurance; 35.7% have public insurance; 13.2% do not have insurance; 7.9% of children under 18 do not have insurance

Health Care: Physicians: 8.7 per 10,000 population; Hospital beds: 13.8 per 10,000 population; Hospital admissions: 550.9 per 10,000 population

Transportation: Commute: 92.4% car, 0.2% public transportation, 2.9% walk, 3.0% work from home; Median travel time to work: 23.0 minutes

Presidential Election: 43.3% Obama, 55.7% Romney (2012)

National and State Parks: Leidy Lake State Game Area; Three Rivers State Game Area

Additional Information Contacts

Saint Joseph Government . . . . (269) 467-5500
http://www.stjosephcountymi.org

Saint Joseph County Communities

BURR OAK (township). Covers a land area of 35.250 square miles and a water area of 0.697 square miles. Located at 41.85° N. Lat; 85.34° W. Long. Elevation is 879 feet.

Population: 2,611; Growth (since 2000): -4.7%; Density: 74.1 persons per square mile; Race: 97.4% White, 0.5% Black/African American, 0.5% Asian, 0.3% American Indian/Alaska Native, 0.0% Native Hawaiian/Other Pacific Islander, 0.9% Two or more races, 2.5% Hispanic of any race; Average household size: 2.78; Median age: 37.8; Age under 18: 27.1%; Age 65 and over: 14.2%; Males per 100 females: 105.3; Marriage status: 22.2% never married, 59.2% now married, 0.7% separated, 6.5% widowed, 12.1% divorced; Foreign born: 1.8%; Speak English only: 92.5%; With disability: 12.3%; Veterans: 9.7%; Ancestry: 42.8% German, 9.0% English, 8.8% Irish, 5.6% American, 4.9% Dutch

Employment: 11.9% management, business, and financial, 0.8% computer, engineering, and science, 5.1% education, legal, community service, arts, and media, 4.2% healthcare practitioners, 10.0% service, 22.5% sales and office, 11.0% natural resources, construction, and maintenance, 34.5% production, transportation, and material moving

Income: Per capita: $22,026; Median household: $44,866; Average household: $58,039; Households with income of $100,000 or more: 10.2%; Poverty rate: 13.5%

Educational Attainment: High school diploma or higher: 83.1%; Bachelor's degree or higher: 9.1%; Graduate/professional degree or higher: 3.0%

School District(s)
Burr Oak Community SD (KG-12)
    2012-13 Enrollment: 285. . . . . (269) 489-2213
Housing: Homeownership rate: 83.2%; Median home value: $111,200; Median year structure built: 1968; Homeowner vacancy rate: 2.5%; Median gross rent: $786 per month; Rental vacancy rate: 10.2%
Health Insurance: 84.8% have insurance; 64.3% have private insurance; 36.0% have public insurance; 15.2% do not have insurance; 6.3% of children under 18 do not have insurance
Transportation: Commute: 91.2% car, 0.0% public transportation, 3.4% walk, 4.6% work from home; Median travel time to work: 22.0 minutes

BURR OAK (village).
Covers a land area of 1.003 square miles and a water area of <.001 square miles. Located at 41.85° N. Lat; 85.32° W. Long. Elevation is 879 feet.
History: Named for the burr oak trees in the area, Burr Oak was platted in 1851 by William Lock and Henry Weaver. It was first called Lock's Station when the railroad arrived, but was renamed in 1857.
Population: 828; Growth (since 2000): 3.9%; Density: 825.3 persons per square mile; Race: 96.0% White, 0.5% Black/African American, 0.7% Asian, 0.5% American Indian/Alaska Native, 0.0% Native Hawaiian/Other Pacific Islander, 1.7% Two or more races, 3.3% Hispanic of any race; Average household size: 2.91; Median age: 33.1; Age under 18: 29.3%; Age 65 and over: 10.7%; Males per 100 females: 101.5

School District(s)
Burr Oak Community SD (KG-12)
    2012-13 Enrollment: 285. . . . . (269) 489-2213
Housing: Homeownership rate: 74.7%; Homeowner vacancy rate: 5.6%; Rental vacancy rate: 5.3%
Safety: Violent crime rate: 97.6 per 10,000 population; Property crime rate: 97.6 per 10,000 population

CENTREVILLE (village).
County seat. Covers a land area of 1.486 square miles and a water area of 0.007 square miles. Located at 41.92° N. Lat; 85.53° W. Long. Elevation is 823 feet.
History: In Centreville in 1878, the famous Dr. Denton Sleeping Garment Mill had its beginning. The village was settled in the late 1820's, and incorporated in 1837.
Population: 1,425; Growth (since 2000): -9.8%; Density: 959.2 persons per square mile; Race: 93.7% White, 2.9% Black/African American, 0.4% Asian, 0.1% American Indian/Alaska Native, 0.0% Native Hawaiian/Other Pacific Islander, 2.6% Two or more races, 1.5% Hispanic of any race; Average household size: 2.56; Median age: 36.5; Age under 18: 23.6%; Age 65 and over: 15.1%; Males per 100 females: 102.1

School District(s)
Centreville Public Schools (PK-12)
    2012-13 Enrollment: 876. . . . . (269) 467-5220
Saint Joseph County ISD (PK-12)
    2012-13 Enrollment: 389. . . . . (269) 467-5400

Two-year College(s)
Glen Oaks Community College (Public)
    Fall 2013 Enrollment: 1,221 . . . . (269) 467-9945
    2013-14 Tuition: In-state $4,356; Out-of-state $5,124
Housing: Homeownership rate: 71.9%; Homeowner vacancy rate: 3.7%; Rental vacancy rate: 12.2%

COLON (township).
Covers a land area of 34.356 square miles and a water area of 1.976 square miles. Located at 41.95° N. Lat; 85.35° W. Long. Elevation is 863 feet.
Population: 3,329; Growth (since 2000): -2.2%; Density: 96.9 persons per square mile; Race: 98.0% White, 0.2% Black/African American, 0.4% Asian, 0.2% American Indian/Alaska Native, 0.0% Native Hawaiian/Other Pacific Islander, 1.1% Two or more races, 0.9% Hispanic of any race; Average household size: 2.62; Median age: 39.7; Age under 18: 25.7%; Age 65 and over: 15.9%; Males per 100 females: 98.6; Marriage status: 22.9% never married, 56.6% now married, 0.3% separated, 11.3% widowed, 9.1% divorced; Foreign born: 2.3%; Speak English only: 88.2%; With disability: 13.5%; Veterans: 10.5%; Ancestry: 38.2% German, 11.9% American, 11.7% Irish, 9.9% English, 6.6% Dutch
Employment: 6.9% management, business, and financial, 0.2% computer, engineering, and science, 6.9% education, legal, community service, arts, and media, 4.6% healthcare practitioners, 12.7% service, 16.5% sales and

office, 7.6% natural resources, construction, and maintenance, 44.6% production, transportation, and material moving
Income: Per capita: $17,681; Median household: $43,594; Average household: $46,792; Households with income of $100,000 or more: 6.1%; Poverty rate: 13.1%
Educational Attainment: High school diploma or higher: 81.4%; Bachelor's degree or higher: 9.9%; Graduate/professional degree or higher: 3.3%

School District(s)
Colon Community SD (PK-12)
    2012-13 Enrollment: 626. . . . . (269) 386-2239
Housing: Homeownership rate: 81.0%; Median home value: $92,500; Median year structure built: 1968; Homeowner vacancy rate: 1.4%; Median gross rent: $557 per month; Rental vacancy rate: 12.6%
Health Insurance: 85.3% have insurance; 65.5% have private insurance; 38.1% have public insurance; 14.7% do not have insurance; 15.6% of children under 18 do not have insurance
Transportation: Commute: 91.8% car, 0.9% public transportation, 2.5% walk, 3.5% work from home; Median travel time to work: 23.4 minutes

COLON (village).
Covers a land area of 1.366 square miles and a water area of 0.364 square miles. Located at 41.96° N. Lat; 85.32° W. Long. Elevation is 863 feet.
Population: 1,173; Growth (since 2000): -4.4%; Density: 858.8 persons per square mile; Race: 97.3% White, 0.3% Black/African American, 0.2% Asian, 0.3% American Indian/Alaska Native, 0.0% Native Hawaiian/Other Pacific Islander, 1.8% Two or more races, 1.3% Hispanic of any race; Average household size: 2.42; Median age: 39.7; Age under 18: 23.9%; Age 65 and over: 16.7%; Males per 100 females: 92.9

School District(s)
Colon Community SD (PK-12)
    2012-13 Enrollment: 626. . . . . (269) 386-2239
Housing: Homeownership rate: 71.9%; Homeowner vacancy rate: 1.9%; Rental vacancy rate: 14.5%
Safety: Violent crime rate: 17.3 per 10,000 population; Property crime rate: 129.6 per 10,000 population

CONSTANTINE (township).
Covers a land area of 34.470 square miles and a water area of 1.153 square miles. Located at 41.85° N. Lat; 85.70° W. Long. Elevation is 787 feet.
History: Settled 1828; incorporated 1837.
Population: 4,217; Growth (since 2000): 0.9%; Density: 122.3 persons per square mile; Race: 93.9% White, 1.2% Black/African American, 0.6% Asian, 0.6% American Indian/Alaska Native, 0.0% Native Hawaiian/Other Pacific Islander, 2.4% Two or more races, 2.5% Hispanic of any race; Average household size: 2.66; Median age: 37.8; Age under 18: 26.4%; Age 65 and over: 12.2%; Males per 100 females: 101.3; Marriage status: 25.4% never married, 54.7% now married, 2.6% separated, 6.8% widowed, 13.1% divorced; Foreign born: 1.6%; Speak English only: 92.6%; With disability: 14.8%; Veterans: 10.2%; Ancestry: 34.0% German, 15.1% American, 12.6% Irish, 9.0% English, 4.8% French
Employment: 11.3% management, business, and financial, 3.4% computer, engineering, and science, 3.6% education, legal, community service, arts, and media, 4.1% healthcare practitioners, 13.1% service, 19.9% sales and office, 9.0% natural resources, construction, and maintenance, 35.6% production, transportation, and material moving
Income: Per capita: $18,819; Median household: $48,007; Average household: $49,843; Households with income of $100,000 or more: 7.6%; Poverty rate: 19.5%
Educational Attainment: High school diploma or higher: 87.0%; Bachelor's degree or higher: 8.8%; Graduate/professional degree or higher: 1.8%

School District(s)
Constantine Public SD (KG-12)
    2012-13 Enrollment: 1,438 . . . . (269) 435-8900
Housing: Homeownership rate: 77.3%; Median home value: $100,700; Median year structure built: 1973; Homeowner vacancy rate: 2.0%; Median gross rent: $595 per month; Rental vacancy rate: 7.9%
Health Insurance: 89.0% have insurance; 66.2% have private insurance; 35.6% have public insurance; 11.0% do not have insurance; 7.6% of children under 18 do not have insurance
Transportation: Commute: 91.3% car, 0.0% public transportation, 3.3% walk, 3.6% work from home; Median travel time to work: 24.0 minutes

CONSTANTINE (village).
Covers a land area of 1.611 square miles and a water area of 0.161 square miles. Located at 41.84° N. Lat; 85.67° W. Long. Elevation is 787 feet.

History: Constantine grew up in 1830 around a sawmill and gristmill built by Judge William Meek, when the community was known as Meek's Mills. The name was changed in 1835 to honor Constantine the Great. The Constantine Cooperative Creamery was organized here in 1915.

Population: 2,076; Growth (since 2000): -0.9%; Density: 1,288.3 persons per square mile; Race: 91.5% White, 1.8% Black/African American, 0.5% Asian, 0.9% American Indian/Alaska Native, 0.0% Native Hawaiian/Other Pacific Islander, 3.0% Two or more races, 3.3% Hispanic of any race; Average household size: 2.85; Median age: 31.2; Age under 18: 31.6%; Age 65 and over: 8.9%; Males per 100 females: 96.8

School District(s)
Constantine Public SD (KG-12)
　　2012-13 Enrollment: 1,438 . . . . (269) 435-8900
Housing: Homeownership rate: 67.5%; Homeowner vacancy rate: 1.9%; Rental vacancy rate: 8.5%

FABIUS (township).
Covers a land area of 32.034 square miles and a water area of 3.110 square miles. Located at 41.94° N. Lat; 85.70° W. Long. Elevation is 886 feet.

Population: 3,248; Growth (since 2000): -1.1%; Density: 101.4 persons per square mile; Race: 95.9% White, 1.3% Black/African American, 0.6% Asian, 0.3% American Indian/Alaska Native, 0.0% Native Hawaiian/Other Pacific Islander, 1.4% Two or more races, 1.9% Hispanic of any race; Average household size: 2.42; Median age: 48.0; Age under 18: 19.5%; Age 65 and over: 22.0%; Males per 100 females: 101.0; Marriage status: 13.6% never married, 68.5% now married, 1.4% separated, 7.1% widowed, 10.7% divorced; Foreign born: 2.2%; Speak English only: 96.9%; With disability: 8.4%; Veterans: 12.1%; Ancestry: 36.6% German, 20.3% English, 16.4% Irish, 10.4% Polish, 7.4% Dutch
Employment: 16.4% management, business, and financial, 2.5% computer, engineering, and science, 4.2% education, legal, community service, arts, and media, 17.2% healthcare practitioners, 8.9% service, 20.6% sales and office, 8.5% natural resources, construction, and maintenance, 21.6% production, transportation, and material moving
Income: Per capita: $30,417; Median household: $59,779; Average household: $70,458; Households with income of $100,000 or more: 26.0%; Poverty rate: 4.5%
Educational Attainment: High school diploma or higher: 93.1%; Bachelor's degree or higher: 22.4%; Graduate/professional degree or higher: 9.5%
Housing: Homeownership rate: 90.4%; Median home value: $150,000; Median year structure built: 1978; Homeowner vacancy rate: 3.0%; Median gross rent: $544 per month; Rental vacancy rate: 9.5%
Health Insurance: 92.5% have insurance; 81.4% have private insurance; 27.6% have public insurance; 7.5% do not have insurance; 0.0% of children under 18 do not have insurance
Transportation: Commute: 92.9% car, 0.0% public transportation, 2.3% walk, 2.3% work from home; Median travel time to work: 29.2 minutes

FAWN RIVER (township).
Covers a land area of 19.184 square miles and a water area of 0.495 square miles. Located at 41.79° N. Lat; 85.35° W. Long. Elevation is 892 feet.

Population: 1,477; Growth (since 2000): -10.4%; Density: 77.0 persons per square mile; Race: 94.0% White, 0.9% Black/African American, 0.8% Asian, 0.5% American Indian/Alaska Native, 0.0% Native Hawaiian/Other Pacific Islander, 1.7% Two or more races, 5.8% Hispanic of any race; Average household size: 2.64; Median age: 42.4; Age under 18: 24.1%; Age 65 and over: 16.2%; Males per 100 females: 108.6
Housing: Homeownership rate: 84.8%; Homeowner vacancy rate: 1.2%; Rental vacancy rate: 4.5%

FLORENCE (township).
Covers a land area of 33.243 square miles and a water area of 0.564 square miles. Located at 41.86° N. Lat; 85.59° W. Long.

Population: 1,242; Growth (since 2000): -13.5%; Density: 37.4 persons per square mile; Race: 95.4% White, 1.1% Black/African American, 0.1% Asian, 1.2% American Indian/Alaska Native, 0.0% Native Hawaiian/Other Pacific Islander, 1.4% Two or more races, 2.7% Hispanic of any race; Average household size: 2.57; Median age: 41.3; Age under 18: 23.0%; Age 65 and over: 14.7%; Males per 100 females: 108.4
Housing: Homeownership rate: 83.2%; Homeowner vacancy rate: 1.2%; Rental vacancy rate: 5.8%

FLOWERFIELD (township).
Covers a land area of 35.462 square miles and a water area of 0.459 square miles. Located at 42.02° N. Lat; 85.69° W. Long. Elevation is 853 feet.

Population: 1,562; Growth (since 2000): -1.9%; Density: 44.0 persons per square mile; Race: 95.2% White, 1.0% Black/African American, 1.2% Asian, 0.7% American Indian/Alaska Native, 0.0% Native Hawaiian/Other Pacific Islander, 1.4% Two or more races, 1.3% Hispanic of any race; Average household size: 2.57; Median age: 45.4; Age under 18: 21.1%; Age 65 and over: 14.1%; Males per 100 females: 102.6
Housing: Homeownership rate: 89.3%; Homeowner vacancy rate: 1.3%; Rental vacancy rate: 4.4%

LEONIDAS (township).
Covers a land area of 35.507 square miles and a water area of 0.698 square miles. Located at 42.03° N. Lat; 85.35° W. Long. Elevation is 869 feet.

History: Leonidas Township was named for a king of ancient Sparta.
Population: 1,185; Growth (since 2000): -4.4%; Density: 33.4 persons per square mile; Race: 96.6% White, 0.7% Black/African American, 0.2% Asian, 0.5% American Indian/Alaska Native, 0.0% Native Hawaiian/Other Pacific Islander, 1.9% Two or more races, 1.1% Hispanic of any race; Average household size: 2.79; Median age: 39.6; Age under 18: 26.2%; Age 65 and over: 16.6%; Males per 100 females: 94.6
School District(s)
Colon Community SD (PK-12)
　　2012-13 Enrollment: 626 . . . . (269) 386-2239
Housing: Homeownership rate: 85.8%; Homeowner vacancy rate: 1.9%; Rental vacancy rate: 4.8%

LOCKPORT (township).
Covers a land area of 28.601 square miles and a water area of 1.855 square miles. Located at 41.94° N. Lat; 85.58° W. Long.

Population: 3,787; Growth (since 2000): -0.7%; Density: 132.4 persons per square mile; Race: 87.7% White, 7.6% Black/African American, 0.8% Asian, 0.6% American Indian/Alaska Native, 0.0% Native Hawaiian/Other Pacific Islander, 2.3% Two or more races, 2.0% Hispanic of any race; Average household size: 2.65; Median age: 40.5; Age under 18: 25.2%; Age 65 and over: 14.3%; Males per 100 females: 100.3; Marriage status: 23.9% never married, 57.5% now married, 1.4% separated, 6.8% widowed, 11.7% divorced; Foreign born: 3.2%; Speak English only: 94.5%; With disability: 9.5%; Veterans: 9.4%; Ancestry: 25.5% German, 13.4% English, 12.4% Dutch, 8.7% Polish, 6.1% Irish
Employment: 10.1% management, business, and financial, 5.7% computer, engineering, and science, 7.3% education, legal, community service, arts, and media, 6.5% healthcare practitioners, 19.1% service, 19.6% sales and office, 5.7% natural resources, construction, and maintenance, 25.9% production, transportation, and material moving
Income: Per capita: $23,736; Median household: $61,189; Average household: $64,541; Households with income of $100,000 or more: 14.1%; Poverty rate: 4.7%
Educational Attainment: High school diploma or higher: 91.4%; Bachelor's degree or higher: 21.9%; Graduate/professional degree or higher: 7.5%
Housing: Homeownership rate: 87.7%; Median home value: $128,500; Median year structure built: 1973; Homeowner vacancy rate: 2.2%; Median gross rent: $680 per month; Rental vacancy rate: 5.9%
Health Insurance: 93.5% have insurance; 84.5% have private insurance; 29.4% have public insurance; 6.5% do not have insurance; 0.0% of children under 18 do not have insurance
Transportation: Commute: 93.6% car, 0.0% public transportation, 4.8% walk, 1.5% work from home; Median travel time to work: 21.7 minutes

MENDON (township).
Covers a land area of 34.948 square miles and a water area of 1.287 square miles. Located at 42.03° N. Lat; 85.47° W. Long. Elevation is 843 feet.

Population: 2,719; Growth (since 2000): -2.0%; Density: 77.8 persons per square mile; Race: 96.5% White, 1.1% Black/African American, 0.4% Asian, 0.6% American Indian/Alaska Native, 0.0% Native Hawaiian/Other Pacific Islander, 1.1% Two or more races, 1.5% Hispanic of any race; Average household size: 2.57; Median age: 43.8; Age under 18: 24.0%; Age 65 and over: 20.0%; Males per 100 females: 102.3; Marriage status: 23.8% never married, 58.2% now married, 1.1% separated, 7.4% widowed, 10.6% divorced; Foreign born: 1.3%; Speak English only: 94.8%; With disability: 15.2%; Veterans: 13.3%; Ancestry: 32.8% German, 15.6% American, 13.4% English, 11.8% Irish, 6.8% Dutch

Employment: 11.6% management, business, and financial, 3.5% computer, engineering, and science, 9.4% education, legal, community service, arts, and media, 2.3% healthcare practitioners, 12.7% service, 18.6% sales and office, 12.6% natural resources, construction, and maintenance, 29.4% production, transportation, and material moving
Income: Per capita: $19,193; Median household: $43,493; Average household: $51,092; Households with income of $100,000 or more: 9.4%; Poverty rate: 17.2%
Educational Attainment: High school diploma or higher: 85.7%; Bachelor's degree or higher: 15.1%; Graduate/professional degree or higher: 3.5%

School District(s)
Mendon Community SD (PK-12)
    2012-13 Enrollment: 657........................ (269) 496-8491
Housing: Homeownership rate: 87.6%; Median home value: $112,500; Median year structure built: 1974; Homeowner vacancy rate: 3.1%; Median gross rent: $797 per month; Rental vacancy rate: 6.9%
Health Insurance: 90.7% have insurance; 71.2% have private insurance; 39.6% have public insurance; 9.3% do not have insurance; 7.2% of children under 18 do not have insurance
Transportation: Commute: 91.7% car, 0.0% public transportation, 3.1% walk, 4.0% work from home; Median travel time to work: 25.3 minutes

MENDON (village). Covers a land area of 1.015 square miles and a water area of 0.009 square miles. Located at 42.01° N. Lat; 85.45° W. Long. Elevation is 843 feet.
History: A fur-trading post was established here in 1831. Patrice Marantette, a Frenchman, bought the property in 1833 and built a large home on a hill nearby.
Population: 870; Growth (since 2000): -5.1%; Density: 857.2 persons per square mile; Race: 96.9% White, 0.8% Black/African American, 0.3% Asian, 0.3% American Indian/Alaska Native, 0.0% Native Hawaiian/Other Pacific Islander, 1.5% Two or more races, 2.2% Hispanic of any race; Average household size: 2.73; Median age: 37.1; Age under 18: 28.7%; Age 65 and over: 10.9%; Males per 100 females: 97.7

School District(s)
Mendon Community SD (PK-12)
    2012-13 Enrollment: 657........................ (269) 496-8491
Housing: Homeownership rate: 80.5%; Homeowner vacancy rate: 2.3%; Rental vacancy rate: 4.5%

MOTTVILLE (township). Covers a land area of 19.316 square miles and a water area of 0.608 square miles. Located at 41.79° N. Lat; 85.71° W. Long. Elevation is 761 feet.
History: The Mottville area developed around a sawmill erected on the St. Joseph River in the 1820's. The shipping business on the river brought warehouses and businesses, reaching its greatest volume in the 1840's. Mottville declined when the railroad replaced the river as the primary shipping route.
Population: 1,436; Growth (since 2000): -4.2%; Density: 74.3 persons per square mile; Race: 96.5% White, 0.6% Black/African American, 0.1% Asian, 1.0% American Indian/Alaska Native, 0.1% Native Hawaiian/Other Pacific Islander, 0.8% Two or more races, 1.8% Hispanic of any race; Average household size: 2.58; Median age: 42.4; Age under 18: 21.7%; Age 65 and over: 12.7%; Males per 100 females: 110.6
Housing: Homeownership rate: 81.7%; Homeowner vacancy rate: 2.1%; Rental vacancy rate: 8.0%

NOTTAWA (township). Covers a land area of 35.620 square miles and a water area of 2.012 square miles. Located at 41.94° N. Lat; 85.47° W. Long. Elevation is 840 feet.
History: Nottawa Township was settled by a group of Amish colonists, who came from Ohio in 1847. The name of Nottawa comes from that of the Potawatomi chief, Nottawaseepe.
Population: 3,858; Growth (since 2000): -3.5%; Density: 108.3 persons per square mile; Race: 95.3% White, 1.4% Black/African American, 0.9% Asian, 0.2% American Indian/Alaska Native, 0.0% Native Hawaiian/Other Pacific Islander, 1.8% Two or more races, 1.2% Hispanic of any race; Average household size: 2.70; Median age: 39.5; Age under 18: 25.4%; Age 65 and over: 16.1%; Males per 100 females: 98.4; Marriage status: 24.4% never married, 58.0% now married, 0.9% separated, 8.5% widowed, 9.1% divorced; Foreign born: 0.8%; Speak English only: 81.6%; With disability: 12.8%; Veterans: 8.9%; Ancestry: 42.3% German, 11.1% English, 9.0% Irish, 6.8% American, 5.8% Scottish

Employment: 16.1% management, business, and financial, 2.5% computer, engineering, and science, 11.4% education, legal, community service, arts, and media, 5.8% healthcare practitioners, 12.4% service, 16.1% sales and office, 11.2% natural resources, construction, and maintenance, 24.4% production, transportation, and material moving
Income: Per capita: $19,300; Median household: $42,448; Average household: $55,279; Households with income of $100,000 or more: 12.2%; Poverty rate: 18.7%
Educational Attainment: High school diploma or higher: 77.0%; Bachelor's degree or higher: 15.7%; Graduate/professional degree or higher: 6.2%
Housing: Homeownership rate: 81.6%; Median home value: $133,400; Median year structure built: 1975; Homeowner vacancy rate: 2.5%; Median gross rent: $596 per month; Rental vacancy rate: 16.9%
Health Insurance: 75.6% have insurance; 60.0% have private insurance; 29.8% have public insurance; 24.4% do not have insurance; 35.0% of children under 18 do not have insurance
Transportation: Commute: 83.6% car, 0.7% public transportation, 8.2% walk, 4.7% work from home; Median travel time to work: 23.2 minutes

PARK (township). Covers a land area of 34.949 square miles and a water area of 0.744 square miles. Located at 42.02° N. Lat; 85.58° W. Long.
Population: 2,600; Growth (since 2000): -3.7%; Density: 74.4 persons per square mile; Race: 94.7% White, 2.7% Black/African American, 0.2% Asian, 0.4% American Indian/Alaska Native, 0.0% Native Hawaiian/Other Pacific Islander, 1.2% Two or more races, 2.4% Hispanic of any race; Average household size: 2.54; Median age: 45.4; Age under 18: 22.4%; Age 65 and over: 18.5%; Males per 100 females: 103.9; Marriage status: 21.7% never married, 59.9% now married, 4.9% separated, 5.4% widowed, 13.0% divorced; Foreign born: 2.0%; Speak English only: 96.7%; With disability: 15.5%; Veterans: 12.4%; Ancestry: 31.3% German, 14.6% American, 10.7% English, 10.0% Irish, 8.9% Dutch
Employment: 10.3% management, business, and financial, 3.3% computer, engineering, and science, 10.2% education, legal, community service, arts, and media, 4.6% healthcare practitioners, 13.0% service, 25.5% sales and office, 12.3% natural resources, construction, and maintenance, 20.9% production, transportation, and material moving
Income: Per capita: $22,100; Median household: $55,035; Average household: $59,347; Households with income of $100,000 or more: 14.7%; Poverty rate: 10.6%
Educational Attainment: High school diploma or higher: 87.9%; Bachelor's degree or higher: 19.5%; Graduate/professional degree or higher: 6.4%
Housing: Homeownership rate: 87.4%; Median home value: $129,500; Median year structure built: 1972; Homeowner vacancy rate: 1.2%; Median gross rent: $801 per month; Rental vacancy rate: 6.7%
Health Insurance: 89.5% have insurance; 63.4% have private insurance; 39.3% have public insurance; 10.5% do not have insurance; 7.8% of children under 18 do not have insurance
Transportation: Commute: 93.2% car, 0.0% public transportation, 0.5% walk, 5.0% work from home; Median travel time to work: 22.7 minutes

SHERMAN (township). Covers a land area of 32.973 square miles and a water area of 1.973 square miles. Located at 41.86° N. Lat; 85.48° W. Long.
History: Sherman Township was settled in the 1830's, and named for Colonel Benjamin Sherman, an early settler.
Population: 3,205; Growth (since 2000): -1.3%; Density: 97.2 persons per square mile; Race: 96.1% White, 0.4% Black/African American, 0.8% Asian, 0.4% American Indian/Alaska Native, 0.0% Native Hawaiian/Other Pacific Islander, 1.3% Two or more races, 2.2% Hispanic of any race; Average household size: 2.62; Median age: 44.9; Age under 18: 24.1%; Age 65 and over: 15.8%; Males per 100 females: 102.0; Marriage status: 16.3% never married, 70.7% now married, 0.8% separated, 3.5% widowed, 9.5% divorced; Foreign born: 2.9%; Speak English only: 90.5%; With disability: 9.1%; Veterans: 11.2%; Ancestry: 37.9% German, 19.6% American, 11.3% Irish, 8.5% English, 8.3% Dutch
Employment: 12.6% management, business, and financial, 4.4% computer, engineering, and science, 8.6% education, legal, community service, arts, and media, 1.9% healthcare practitioners, 15.5% service, 20.3% sales and office, 9.4% natural resources, construction, and maintenance, 27.2% production, transportation, and material moving

Income: Per capita: $25,320; Median household: $55,469; Average household: $68,519; Households with income of $100,000 or more: 15.6%; Poverty rate: 10.3%

Educational Attainment: High school diploma or higher: 91.5%; Bachelor's degree or higher: 21.8%; Graduate/professional degree or higher: 9.7%

Housing: Homeownership rate: 89.7%; Median home value: $167,100; Median year structure built: 1976; Homeowner vacancy rate: 1.4%; Median gross rent: $947 per month; Rental vacancy rate: 4.6%

Health Insurance: 85.3% have insurance; 72.5% have private insurance; 28.5% have public insurance; 14.7% do not have insurance; 18.6% of children under 18 do not have insurance

Transportation: Commute: 91.4% car, 0.0% public transportation, 2.6% walk, 5.8% work from home; Median travel time to work: 23.9 minutes

STURGIS (city). Covers a land area of 6.494 square miles and a water area of <.001 square miles. Located at 41.80° N. Lat; 85.42° W. Long. Elevation is 915 feet.

History: Sturgis grew up at the junction of the Great Sauk Trail and the Nottawaseepe Trail. Settlement began here in 1827, and the village was established about 1833, named for Judge John Sturgis, the first settler. The manufacture of furniture was an early industry in Sturgis.

Population: 10,994; Growth (since 2000): -2.6%; Density: 1,693.0 persons per square mile; Race: 80.6% White, 1.4% Black/African American, 0.9% Asian, 0.3% American Indian/Alaska Native, 0.0% Native Hawaiian/Other Pacific Islander, 3.2% Two or more races, 22.8% Hispanic of any race; Average household size: 2.65; Median age: 32.3; Age under 18: 30.0%; Age 65 and over: 12.6%; Males per 100 females: 89.8; Marriage status: 25.6% never married, 52.3% now married, 2.3% separated, 9.0% widowed, 13.1% divorced; Foreign born: 8.9%; Speak English only: 78.0%; With disability: 12.6%; Veterans: 8.7%; Ancestry: 25.1% German, 11.4% English, 10.9% American, 7.2% Irish, 5.3% Polish

Employment: 7.4% management, business, and financial, 3.9% computer, engineering, and science, 10.7% education, legal, community service, arts, and media, 5.4% healthcare practitioners, 15.6% service, 19.3% sales and office, 8.7% natural resources, construction, and maintenance, 28.9% production, transportation, and material moving

Income: Per capita: $18,223; Median household: $35,245; Average household: $48,408; Households with income of $100,000 or more: 8.3%; Poverty rate: 25.9%

Educational Attainment: High school diploma or higher: 78.4%; Bachelor's degree or higher: 17.0%; Graduate/professional degree or higher: 5.1%

School District(s)
Nottawa Community School (PK-12)
    2012-13 Enrollment: 140 . . . . (269) 467-7153
Sturgis Public Schools (PK-12)
    2012-13 Enrollment: 3,270 . . . . (269) 659-1500

Housing: Homeownership rate: 57.1%; Median home value: $88,800; Median year structure built: 1965; Homeowner vacancy rate: 5.0%; Median gross rent: $581 per month; Rental vacancy rate: 10.4%

Health Insurance: 87.3% have insurance; 59.4% have private insurance; 40.9% have public insurance; 12.7% do not have insurance; 2.3% of children under 18 do not have insurance

Hospitals: Sturgis Hospital (94 beds)

Newspapers: Sturgis Journal (daily circulation 6300)

Transportation: Commute: 94.8% car, 0.0% public transportation, 1.2% walk, 1.8% work from home; Median travel time to work: 19.3 minutes

Airports: Kirsch Municipal (general aviation)

Additional Information Contacts
City of Sturgis . . . . (269) 651-2321
  http://ci.sturgis.mi.us

STURGIS (township). Covers a land area of 17.681 square miles and a water area of 0.113 square miles. Located at 41.79° N. Lat; 85.48° W. Long. Elevation is 915 feet.

History: Settled 1827; incorporated as village 1855, as city 1895.

Population: 2,261; Growth (since 2000): -5.9%; Density: 127.9 persons per square mile; Race: 88.6% White, 0.7% Black/African American, 0.9% Asian, 0.2% American Indian/Alaska Native, 0.0% Native Hawaiian/Other Pacific Islander, 1.9% Two or more races, 11.3% Hispanic of any race; Average household size: 2.78; Median age: 35.5; Age under 18: 28.0%; Age 65 and over: 12.8%; Males per 100 females: 99.6

School District(s)
Nottawa Community School (PK-12)
    2012-13 Enrollment: 140 . . . . (269) 467-7153
Sturgis Public Schools (PK-12)
    2012-13 Enrollment: 3,270 . . . . (269) 659-1500

Housing: Homeownership rate: 79.9%; Homeowner vacancy rate: 2.4%; Rental vacancy rate: 10.9%

Hospitals: Sturgis Hospital (94 beds)

Newspapers: Sturgis Journal (daily circulation 6300)

Airports: Kirsch Municipal (general aviation)

THREE RIVERS (city). Covers a land area of 5.400 square miles and a water area of 0.263 square miles. Located at 41.95° N. Lat; 85.63° W. Long. Elevation is 804 feet.

History: Three Rivers was established on the site of a 17th-century Jesuit mission.

Population: 7,811; Growth (since 2000): 6.6%; Density: 1,446.5 persons per square mile; Race: 82.6% White, 10.1% Black/African American, 0.9% Asian, 0.6% American Indian/Alaska Native, 0.0% Native Hawaiian/Other Pacific Islander, 4.0% Two or more races, 5.2% Hispanic of any race; Average household size: 2.50; Median age: 31.5; Age under 18: 28.5%; Age 65 and over: 12.0%; Males per 100 females: 91.3; Marriage status: 35.6% never married, 38.6% now married, 1.3% separated, 8.9% widowed, 16.9% divorced; Foreign born: 1.8%; Speak English only: 93.9%; With disability: 14.7%; Veterans: 8.2%; Ancestry: 29.8% German, 15.4% English, 8.3% Irish, 5.9% American, 4.0% Dutch

Employment: 11.0% management, business, and financial, 2.4% computer, engineering, and science, 7.5% education, legal, community service, arts, and media, 3.4% healthcare practitioners, 17.6% service, 26.3% sales and office, 5.3% natural resources, construction, and maintenance, 26.6% production, transportation, and material moving

Income: Per capita: $17,676; Median household: $37,014; Average household: $44,045; Households with income of $100,000 or more: 4.7%; Poverty rate: 27.0%

Educational Attainment: High school diploma or higher: 85.0%; Bachelor's degree or higher: 12.2%; Graduate/professional degree or higher: 3.2%

School District(s)
Three Rivers Community Schools (PK-12)
    2012-13 Enrollment: 2,701 . . . . (269) 279-1100

Housing: Homeownership rate: 55.3%; Median home value: $76,800; Median year structure built: 1963; Homeowner vacancy rate: 5.0%; Median gross rent: $633 per month; Rental vacancy rate: 8.9%

Health Insurance: 85.8% have insurance; 54.6% have private insurance; 40.3% have public insurance; 14.2% do not have insurance; 4.0% of children under 18 do not have insurance

Hospitals: Three Rivers Health (60 beds)

Safety: Violent crime rate: 70.0 per 10,000 population; Property crime rate: 422.7 per 10,000 population

Newspapers: Three Rivers Commercial-News (daily circulation 2000)

Transportation: Commute: 90.8% car, 0.2% public transportation, 5.2% walk, 1.4% work from home; Median travel time to work: 20.7 minutes

Additional Information Contacts
City of Three Rivers . . . . (269) 273-1075
  http://www.threeriversmi.org

WHITE PIGEON (township). Covers a land area of 25.104 square miles and a water area of 2.437 square miles. Located at 41.79° N. Lat; 85.59° W. Long. Elevation is 817 feet.

History: Settled c.1827, incorporated 1837.

Population: 3,753; Growth (since 2000): -2.4%; Density: 149.5 persons per square mile; Race: 95.2% White, 0.3% Black/African American, 0.5% Asian, 0.5% American Indian/Alaska Native, 0.0% Native Hawaiian/Other Pacific Islander, 1.7% Two or more races, 3.2% Hispanic of any race; Average household size: 2.45; Median age: 43.3; Age under 18: 23.2%; Age 65 and over: 17.1%; Males per 100 females: 97.0; Marriage status: 26.3% never married, 53.9% now married, 3.5% separated, 7.1% widowed, 12.8% divorced; Foreign born: 2.4%; Speak English only: 96.0%; With disability: 13.0%; Veterans: 10.3%; Ancestry: 37.5% German, 13.9% English, 10.7% Irish, 9.3% American, 6.2% Polish

Employment: 9.2% management, business, and financial, 0.4% computer, engineering, and science, 6.9% education, legal, community service, arts, and media, 2.0% healthcare practitioners, 6.9% service, 21.4% sales and office, 19.2% natural resources, construction, and maintenance, 33.9% production, transportation, and material moving

Income: Per capita: $19,030; Median household: $42,813; Average household: $51,915; Households with income of $100,000 or more: 12.0%; Poverty rate: 25.4%

Educational Attainment: High school diploma or higher: 81.4%; Bachelor's degree or higher: 9.8%; Graduate/professional degree or higher: 3.0%

School District(s)
White Pigeon Community Schools (PK-12)
    2012-13 Enrollment: 784 . . . . (269) 483-7676

Housing: Homeownership rate: 76.4%; Median home value: $95,300; Median year structure built: 1973; Homeowner vacancy rate: 3.5%; Median gross rent: $652 per month; Rental vacancy rate: 17.0%

Health Insurance: 82.5% have insurance; 51.4% have private insurance; 42.2% have public insurance; 17.5% do not have insurance; 11.7% of children under 18 do not have insurance

Transportation: Commute: 93.8% car, 1.4% public transportation, 0.6% walk, 4.1% work from home; Median travel time to work: 23.5 minutes

WHITE PIGEON (village). Covers a land area of 1.390 square miles and a water area of 0.018 square miles. Located at 41.80° N. Lat; 85.65° W. Long. Elevation is 817 feet.

History: White Pigeon was named for an Indian chief who, according to legend, saved the village from destruction in 1830. The village was settled in 1827, platted in 1830, and incorporated in 1837. The post office was first called Millville, then White Pigeon Prairie, and later shortened to White Pigeon.

Population: 1,522; Growth (since 2000): -6.5%; Density: 1,095.2 persons per square mile; Race: 93.3% White, 0.3% Black/African American, 0.5% Asian, 0.9% American Indian/Alaska Native, 0.0% Native Hawaiian/Other Pacific Islander, 2.4% Two or more races, 5.2% Hispanic of any race; Average household size: 2.45; Median age: 37.1; Age under 18: 27.1%; Age 65 and over: 15.2%; Males per 100 females: 88.8

School District(s)
White Pigeon Community Schools (PK-12)
    2012-13 Enrollment: 784 . . . . (269) 483-7676

Housing: Homeownership rate: 64.4%; Homeowner vacancy rate: 3.1%; Rental vacancy rate: 20.2%

Safety: Violent crime rate: 39.8 per 10,000 population; Property crime rate: 271.9 per 10,000 population

Sanilac County

Located in eastern Michigan; bounded on the east by Lake Huron; drained by the Black and Cass Rivers. Covers a land area of 962.566 square miles, a water area of 627.375 square miles, and is located in the Eastern Time Zone at 43.45° N. Lat., 82.64° W. Long. The county was founded in 1848. County seat is Sandusky.

Weather Station: Sandusky   Elevation: 773 feet

	Jan	Feb	Mar	Apr	May	Jun	Jul	Aug	Sep	Oct	Nov	Dec
High	29	31	41	55	66	76	81	79	72	59	46	34
Low	14	15	23	34	44	54	59	58	50	40	31	21
Precip	1.5	1.4	1.7	2.4	3.2	3.2	3.0	2.9	4.2	2.6	2.3	na
Snow	na	na	5.2	1.0	0.0	0.0	0.0	0.0	0.0	tr	1.0	na

High and Low temperatures in degrees Fahrenheit; Precipitation and Snow in inches

Population: 43,114; Growth (since 2000): -3.2%; Density: 44.8 persons per square mile; Race: 96.6% White, 0.3% Black/African American, 0.3% Asian, 0.5% American Indian/Alaska Native, 0.0% Native Hawaiian/Other Pacific Islander, 1.2% two or more races, 3.3% Hispanic of any race; Average household size: 2.48; Median age: 42.8; Age under 18: 23.6%; Age 65 and over: 17.6%; Males per 100 females: 97.8; Marriage status: 25.5% never married, 55.2% now married, 1.3% separated, 8.2% widowed, 11.1% divorced; Foreign born: 1.1%; Speak English only: 96.3%; With disability: 15.9%; Veterans: 9.8%; Ancestry: 28.4% German, 11.3% English, 11.2% Irish, 10.7% Polish, 5.9% American

Religion: Six largest groups: 17.3% Catholicism, 7.4% Methodist/Pietist, 5.2% Lutheran, 4.0% Holiness, 1.8% Latter-day Saints, 1.4% Presbyterian-Reformed

Economy: Unemployment rate: 6.0%; Leading industries: 18.3% retail trade; 11.7% other services (except public administration); 11.1% construction; Farms: 1,467 totaling 456,877 acres; Company size: 0 employ 1,000 or more persons, 0 employ 500 to 999 persons, 13 employ 100 to 499 persons, 841 employs less than 100 persons; Business

ownership: 1,007 women-owned, n/a Black-owned, n/a Hispanic-owned, n/a Asian-owned

Employment: 13.5% management, business, and financial, 2.4% computer, engineering, and science, 6.2% education, legal, community service, arts, and media, 4.5% healthcare practitioners, 14.7% service, 23.5% sales and office, 13.0% natural resources, construction, and maintenance, 22.1% production, transportation, and material moving

Income: Per capita: $20,713; Median household: $40,478; Average household: $51,159; Households with income of $100,000 or more: 9.7%; Poverty rate: 16.8%

Educational Attainment: High school diploma or higher: 86.8%; Bachelor's degree or higher: 11.4%; Graduate/professional degree or higher: 4.3%

Housing: Homeownership rate: 80.2%; Median home value: $96,500; Median year structure built: 1970; Homeowner vacancy rate: 2.9%; Median gross rent: $619 per month; Rental vacancy rate: 11.3%

Vital Statistics: Birth rate: 97.1 per 10,000 population; Death rate: 113.1 per 10,000 population; Age-adjusted cancer mortality rate: 173.6 deaths per 10,000 population

Health Insurance: 85.5% have insurance; 63.4% have private insurance; 38.9% have public insurance; 14.5% do not have insurance; 8.8% of children under 18 do not have insurance

Health Care: Physicians: 6.4 per 10,000 population; Hospital beds: 26.7 per 10,000 population; Hospital admissions: 428.3 per 10,000 population

Transportation: Commute: 85.5% car, 1.0% public transportation, 4.6% walk, 7.9% work from home; Median travel time to work: 27.8 minutes

Presidential Election: 39.3% Obama, 59.7% Romney (2012)

National and State Parks: Minden City State Game Area; Sanilac Petroglyphs Historic State Park; Sanilac State Game Area

Additional Information Contacts
Sanilac Government . . . . (810) 648-2933
    http://www.sanilaccounty.net

Sanilac County Communities

APPLEGATE (village). Covers a land area of 1.003 square miles and a water area of 0.007 square miles. Located at 43.36° N. Lat; 82.64° W. Long. Elevation is 748 feet.

History: Applegate developed around a sawmill built in 1856 by George Pack. The post office department named the community for Jesse Applegate, leader of the group that opened a route to Oregon in 1845. Applegate was incorporated as a village in 1903.

Population: 248; Growth (since 2000): -13.6%; Density: 247.3 persons per square mile; Race: 93.1% White, 3.2% Black/African American, 2.4% Asian, 0.0% American Indian/Alaska Native, 0.0% Native Hawaiian/Other Pacific Islander, 0.0% Two or more races, 3.2% Hispanic of any race; Average household size: 2.61; Median age: 34.6; Age under 18: 30.6%; Age 65 and over: 12.1%; Males per 100 females: 83.7

Housing: Homeownership rate: 77.9%; Homeowner vacancy rate: 6.3%; Rental vacancy rate: 8.7%

ARGYLE (township). Covers a land area of 36.308 square miles and a water area of 0.020 square miles. Located at 43.56° N. Lat; 82.93° W. Long. Elevation is 791 feet.

History: Argyle Township was organized in 1872 and given its Scottish name by the early residents, who were mostly Scots from Ontario with names like McLachlin, McLean, McIntyre. Alexander McLachlin was the first township supervisor and the first postmaster.

Population: 759; Growth (since 2000): -1.4%; Density: 20.9 persons per square mile; Race: 97.5% White, 0.3% Black/African American, 0.5% Asian, 1.1% American Indian/Alaska Native, 0.0% Native Hawaiian/Other Pacific Islander, 0.4% Two or more races, 2.6% Hispanic of any race; Average household size: 2.67; Median age: 40.0; Age under 18: 26.1%; Age 65 and over: 12.6%; Males per 100 females: 115.0

Housing: Homeownership rate: 85.2%; Homeowner vacancy rate: 2.7%; Rental vacancy rate: 14.3%

AUSTIN (township). Covers a land area of 36.153 square miles and a water area of 0.002 square miles. Located at 43.64° N. Lat; 82.95° W. Long.

History: Austin Township was organized in 1851 and named for William Austin, who had settled here about 1844.

Population: 665; Growth (since 2000): -1.2%; Density: 18.4 persons per square mile; Race: 99.8% White, 0.0% Black/African American, 0.0% Asian, 0.2% American Indian/Alaska Native, 0.0% Native Hawaiian/Other

Pacific Islander, 0.0% Two or more races, 0.0% Hispanic of any race; Average household size: 2.65; Median age: 43.2; Age under 18: 24.5%; Age 65 and over: 17.7%; Males per 100 females: 112.5
Housing: Homeownership rate: 90.4%; Homeowner vacancy rate: 0.9%; Rental vacancy rate: 0.0%

BRIDGEHAMPTON (township). Covers a land area of 36.106 square miles and a water area of 0.083 square miles. Located at 43.47° N. Lat; 82.68° W. Long.
Population: 854; Growth (since 2000): -6.3%; Density: 23.7 persons per square mile; Race: 96.4% White, 0.0% Black/African American, 0.4% Asian, 0.6% American Indian/Alaska Native, 0.0% Native Hawaiian/Other Pacific Islander, 1.6% Two or more races, 3.0% Hispanic of any race; Average household size: 2.54; Median age: 40.8; Age under 18: 24.9%; Age 65 and over: 13.8%; Males per 100 females: 97.2
Housing: Homeownership rate: 80.3%; Homeowner vacancy rate: 1.1%; Rental vacancy rate: 2.9%

BROWN CITY (city). Covers a land area of 1.094 square miles and a water area of 0.002 square miles. Located at 43.21° N. Lat; 82.99° W. Long. Elevation is 827 feet.
History: Brown City was settled by a group of Mennonites when the Port Huron & Northwestern Railroad established a station here. The village was founded by Robert G. and John M. Brown on land belonging to Robert.
Population: 1,325; Growth (since 2000): -0.7%; Density: 1,211.1 persons per square mile; Race: 97.2% White, 0.1% Black/African American, 0.1% Asian, 0.2% American Indian/Alaska Native, 0.0% Native Hawaiian/Other Pacific Islander, 2.0% Two or more races, 2.3% Hispanic of any race; Average household size: 2.49; Median age: 37.3; Age under 18: 27.8%; Age 65 and over: 14.9%; Males per 100 females: 86.4
School District(s)
Brown City Community Schools (PK-12)
    2012-13 Enrollment: 920 . . . . (810) 346-2781
Housing: Homeownership rate: 67.6%; Homeowner vacancy rate: 1.9%; Rental vacancy rate: 7.6%
Safety: Violent crime rate: 23.2 per 10,000 population; Property crime rate: 270.9 per 10,000 population
Newspapers: Brown City Banner (weekly circulation 2900)

BUEL (township). Covers a land area of 37.635 square miles and a water area of 0.019 square miles. Located at 43.30° N. Lat; 82.70° W. Long.
Population: 1,265; Growth (since 2000): 2.3%; Density: 33.6 persons per square mile; Race: 97.9% White, 0.0% Black/African American, 0.1% Asian, 0.2% American Indian/Alaska Native, 0.0% Native Hawaiian/Other Pacific Islander, 0.9% Two or more races, 3.2% Hispanic of any race; Average household size: 2.56; Median age: 42.6; Age under 18: 22.0%; Age 65 and over: 19.2%; Males per 100 females: 101.1
Housing: Homeownership rate: 84.5%; Homeowner vacancy rate: 3.2%; Rental vacancy rate: 2.5%

CARSONVILLE (village). Covers a land area of 1.134 square miles and a water area of 0 square miles. Located at 43.43° N. Lat; 82.67° W. Long. Elevation is 810 feet.
History: Carsonville was first called Hall's Corners for Silas C. Hall, who operated a store. The name was changed to honor another storekeeper, Arthur Carson, who built a store here in 1874 and a grain elevator in 1880.
Population: 527; Growth (since 2000): 5.0%; Density: 464.5 persons per square mile; Race: 94.7% White, 0.2% Black/African American, 0.6% Asian, 0.2% American Indian/Alaska Native, 0.0% Native Hawaiian/Other Pacific Islander, 3.2% Two or more races, 4.7% Hispanic of any race; Average household size: 2.67; Median age: 35.6; Age under 18: 28.7%; Age 65 and over: 10.2%; Males per 100 females: 86.2
School District(s)
Carsonville-Port Sanilac SD (KG-12)
    2012-13 Enrollment: 552 . . . . (810) 657-9393
Housing: Homeownership rate: 70.2%; Homeowner vacancy rate: 3.4%; Rental vacancy rate: 6.5%

CROSWELL (city). Covers a land area of 2.290 square miles and a water area of 0.117 square miles. Located at 43.27° N. Lat; 82.62° W. Long. Elevation is 732 feet.
History: Croswell grew up around a sawmill built by Ephraim Pierce in 1845 on the Black River. The town was named in 1877 for Charles M. Croswell, governor of Michigan.

Population: 2,447; Growth (since 2000): -0.8%; Density: 1,068.4 persons per square mile; Race: 91.7% White, 0.5% Black/African American, 0.2% Asian, 0.7% American Indian/Alaska Native, 0.0% Native Hawaiian/Other Pacific Islander, 1.8% Two or more races, 12.8% Hispanic of any race; Average household size: 2.51; Median age: 38.8; Age under 18: 26.8%; Age 65 and over: 14.2%; Males per 100 females: 91.5
School District(s)
Croswell-Lexington Community Schools (PK-12)
    2012-13 Enrollment: 2,252 . . . . (810) 679-1000
Housing: Homeownership rate: 64.8%; Homeowner vacancy rate: 3.3%; Rental vacancy rate: 18.2%
Safety: Violent crime rate: 37.8 per 10,000 population; Property crime rate: 327.9 per 10,000 population

CUSTER (township). Covers a land area of 35.327 square miles and a water area of 0.012 square miles. Located at 43.47° N. Lat; 82.81° W. Long.
Population: 1,006; Growth (since 2000): -2.9%; Density: 28.5 persons per square mile; Race: 96.1% White, 0.1% Black/African American, 0.6% Asian, 0.4% American Indian/Alaska Native, 0.0% Native Hawaiian/Other Pacific Islander, 1.8% Two or more races, 5.7% Hispanic of any race; Average household size: 2.43; Median age: 45.9; Age under 18: 21.7%; Age 65 and over: 19.6%; Males per 100 females: 93.1
Housing: Homeownership rate: 85.6%; Homeowner vacancy rate: 2.5%; Rental vacancy rate: 0.0%

DECKER (unincorporated postal area)
ZCTA: 48426
    Covers a land area of 39.179 square miles and a water area of 0.095 square miles. Located at 43.51° N. Lat; 83.06° W. Long. Elevation is 771 feet.
    Population: 1,022; Growth (since 2000): -8.5%; Density: 26.1 persons per square mile; Race: 96.9% White, 0.4% Black/African American, 0.1% Asian, 0.6% American Indian/Alaska Native, 0.0% Native Hawaiian/Other Pacific Islander, 1.7% Two or more races, 3.1% Hispanic of any race; Average household size: 2.64; Median age: 39.2; Age under 18: 25.8%; Age 65 and over: 15.9%; Males per 100 females: 110.3
    Housing: Homeownership rate: 86.6%; Homeowner vacancy rate: 0.9%; Rental vacancy rate: 20.3%

DECKERVILLE (village). Covers a land area of 1.246 square miles and a water area of 0 square miles. Located at 43.53° N. Lat; 82.74° W. Long. Elevation is 830 feet.
Population: 830; Growth (since 2000): -12.1%; Density: 666.0 persons per square mile; Race: 94.7% White, 0.2% Black/African American, 0.1% Asian, 1.4% American Indian/Alaska Native, 0.0% Native Hawaiian/Other Pacific Islander, 1.3% Two or more races, 8.7% Hispanic of any race; Average household size: 2.46; Median age: 38.6; Age under 18: 25.7%; Age 65 and over: 21.3%; Males per 100 females: 87.8
School District(s)
Deckerville Community SD (PK-12)
    2012-13 Enrollment: 584 . . . . (810) 376-3615
Housing: Homeownership rate: 65.3%; Homeowner vacancy rate: 9.6%; Rental vacancy rate: 13.6%
Hospitals: Deckerville Community Hospital
Newspapers: Deckerville Recorder (weekly circulation 1500)

DELAWARE (township). Covers a land area of 46.439 square miles and a water area of 0.019 square miles. Located at 43.65° N. Lat; 82.68° W. Long.
Population: 856; Growth (since 2000): -8.0%; Density: 18.4 persons per square mile; Race: 98.9% White, 0.2% Black/African American, 0.0% Asian, 0.2% American Indian/Alaska Native, 0.0% Native Hawaiian/Other Pacific Islander, 0.5% Two or more races, 2.1% Hispanic of any race; Average household size: 2.30; Median age: 49.1; Age under 18: 19.3%; Age 65 and over: 22.3%; Males per 100 females: 105.8
Housing: Homeownership rate: 91.9%; Homeowner vacancy rate: 4.4%; Rental vacancy rate: 6.1%

ELK (township). Covers a land area of 35.666 square miles and a water area of 0.007 square miles. Located at 43.28° N. Lat; 82.83° W. Long.
Population: 1,526; Growth (since 2000): -3.7%; Density: 42.8 persons per square mile; Race: 96.5% White, 0.4% Black/African American, 0.1% Asian, 1.0% American Indian/Alaska Native, 0.0% Native Hawaiian/Other

Pacific Islander, 1.6% Two or more races, 3.7% Hispanic of any race; Average household size: 2.55; Median age: 42.0; Age under 18: 23.3%; Age 65 and over: 15.9%; Males per 100 females: 106.5
Housing: Homeownership rate: 80.0%; Homeowner vacancy rate: 4.2%; Rental vacancy rate: 9.8%

ELMER (township). Covers a land area of 36.332 square miles and a water area of 0.002 square miles. Located at 43.38° N. Lat; 82.93° W. Long. Elevation is 801 feet.
Population: 806; Growth (since 2000): 2.0%; Density: 22.2 persons per square mile; Race: 95.2% White, 0.2% Black/African American, 1.1% Asian, 0.2% American Indian/Alaska Native, 0.0% Native Hawaiian/Other Pacific Islander, 0.7% Two or more races, 3.8% Hispanic of any race; Average household size: 2.55; Median age: 44.1; Age under 18: 20.8%; Age 65 and over: 14.5%; Males per 100 females: 100.0
Housing: Homeownership rate: 84.5%; Homeowner vacancy rate: 0.0%; Rental vacancy rate: 2.0%

EVERGREEN (township). Covers a land area of 35.354 square miles and a water area of 0.132 square miles. Located at 43.54° N. Lat; 83.05° W. Long.
Population: 924; Growth (since 2000): -7.1%; Density: 26.1 persons per square mile; Race: 97.5% White, 0.8% Black/African American, 0.0% Asian, 0.4% American Indian/Alaska Native, 0.0% Native Hawaiian/Other Pacific Islander, 1.0% Two or more races, 1.7% Hispanic of any race; Average household size: 2.84; Median age: 35.8; Age under 18: 30.3%; Age 65 and over: 12.8%; Males per 100 females: 109.5
Housing: Homeownership rate: 87.3%; Homeowner vacancy rate: 2.0%; Rental vacancy rate: 8.9%

FLYNN (township). Covers a land area of 35.815 square miles and a water area of 0.029 square miles. Located at 43.29° N. Lat; 82.94° W. Long.
Population: 1,050; Growth (since 2000): 1.0%; Density: 29.3 persons per square mile; Race: 98.3% White, 0.0% Black/African American, 0.0% Asian, 0.1% American Indian/Alaska Native, 0.0% Native Hawaiian/Other Pacific Islander, 1.0% Two or more races, 1.6% Hispanic of any race; Average household size: 2.90; Median age: 35.8; Age under 18: 29.6%; Age 65 and over: 12.2%; Males per 100 females: 106.3
Housing: Homeownership rate: 83.9%; Homeowner vacancy rate: 1.3%; Rental vacancy rate: 0.0%

FORESTER (township). Covers a land area of 25.238 square miles and a water area of 0.030 square miles. Located at 43.53° N. Lat; 82.61° W. Long. Elevation is 610 feet.
Population: 1,011; Growth (since 2000): -8.8%; Density: 40.1 persons per square mile; Race: 97.8% White, 0.1% Black/African American, 0.4% Asian, 0.6% American Indian/Alaska Native, 0.0% Native Hawaiian/Other Pacific Islander, 0.7% Two or more races, 2.1% Hispanic of any race; Average household size: 2.20; Median age: 52.4; Age under 18: 15.9%; Age 65 and over: 26.6%; Males per 100 females: 99.4
Housing: Homeownership rate: 88.0%; Homeowner vacancy rate: 5.6%; Rental vacancy rate: 6.8%

FORESTVILLE (village). Covers a land area of 0.794 square miles and a water area of 0 square miles. Located at 43.66° N. Lat; 82.61° W. Long. Elevation is 633 feet.
History: Forestville was settled in 1835 as a seaport on Lake Huron.
Population: 136; Growth (since 2000): 7.1%; Density: 171.2 persons per square mile; Race: 97.1% White, 0.0% Black/African American, 0.0% Asian, 1.5% American Indian/Alaska Native, 0.0% Native Hawaiian/Other Pacific Islander, 0.7% Two or more races, 5.1% Hispanic of any race; Average household size: 2.34; Median age: 55.5; Age under 18: 17.6%; Age 65 and over: 25.0%; Males per 100 females: 103.0
Housing: Homeownership rate: 94.8%; Homeowner vacancy rate: 11.3%; Rental vacancy rate: 25.0%

FREMONT (township). Covers a land area of 34.983 square miles and a water area of 0.040 square miles. Located at 43.20° N. Lat; 82.69° W. Long.
Population: 1,051; Growth (since 2000): 15.1%; Density: 30.0 persons per square mile; Race: 96.3% White, 0.1% Black/African American, 0.3% Asian, 0.7% American Indian/Alaska Native, 0.0% Native Hawaiian/Other Pacific Islander, 1.0% Two or more races, 3.2% Hispanic of any race;

Average household size: 2.94; Median age: 38.9; Age under 18: 28.5%; Age 65 and over: 10.8%; Males per 100 females: 116.3
Housing: Homeownership rate: 82.4%; Homeowner vacancy rate: 1.3%; Rental vacancy rate: 1.5%

GREENLEAF (township). Covers a land area of 35.921 square miles and a water area of 0.121 square miles. Located at 43.63° N. Lat; 83.04° W. Long.
Population: 781; Growth (since 2000): -2.9%; Density: 21.7 persons per square mile; Race: 98.5% White, 0.0% Black/African American, 0.0% Asian, 1.2% American Indian/Alaska Native, 0.0% Native Hawaiian/Other Pacific Islander, 0.1% Two or more races, 0.8% Hispanic of any race; Average household size: 2.78; Median age: 41.0; Age under 18: 27.9%; Age 65 and over: 16.8%; Males per 100 females: 112.8
Housing: Homeownership rate: 89.7%; Homeowner vacancy rate: 2.3%; Rental vacancy rate: 23.7%

LAMOTTE (township). Covers a land area of 35.452 square miles and a water area of 0.023 square miles. Located at 43.46° N. Lat; 83.05° W. Long. Elevation is 771 feet.
History: Lamotte Township was organized in 1870. The area had been settled in the late 1850's.
Population: 919; Growth (since 2000): -6.3%; Density: 25.9 persons per square mile; Race: 97.2% White, 0.7% Black/African American, 0.1% Asian, 0.4% American Indian/Alaska Native, 0.0% Native Hawaiian/Other Pacific Islander, 1.4% Two or more races, 2.4% Hispanic of any race; Average household size: 2.64; Median age: 41.1; Age under 18: 24.4%; Age 65 and over: 17.5%; Males per 100 females: 99.8
Housing: Homeownership rate: 84.4%; Homeowner vacancy rate: 0.3%; Rental vacancy rate: 15.6%

LEXINGTON (township). Covers a land area of 36.037 square miles and a water area of 0.151 square miles. Located at 43.30° N. Lat; 82.59° W. Long. Elevation is 617 feet.
Population: 3,658; Growth (since 2000): -0.8%; Density: 101.5 persons per square mile; Race: 96.9% White, 0.2% Black/African American, 0.2% Asian, 0.1% American Indian/Alaska Native, 0.0% Native Hawaiian/Other Pacific Islander, 1.1% Two or more races, 2.4% Hispanic of any race; Average household size: 2.26; Median age: 49.0; Age under 18: 19.4%; Age 65 and over: 24.4%; Males per 100 females: 95.0; Marriage status: 26.8% never married, 54.9% now married, 0.6% separated, 7.9% widowed, 10.3% divorced; Foreign born: 1.6%; Speak English only: 98.1%; With disability: 16.0%; Veterans: 11.7%; Ancestry: 26.8% German, 15.8% Irish, 12.6% English, 8.7% Polish, 7.3% French
Employment: 16.6% management, business, and financial, 1.4% computer, engineering, and science, 8.5% education, legal, community service, arts, and media, 2.1% healthcare practitioners, 15.8% service, 23.8% sales and office, 14.7% natural resources, construction, and maintenance, 17.1% production, transportation, and material moving
Income: Per capita: $25,041; Median household: $35,583; Average household: $54,308; Households with income of $100,000 or more: 11.5%; Poverty rate: 13.3%
Educational Attainment: High school diploma or higher: 88.5%; Bachelor's degree or higher: 12.3%; Graduate/professional degree or higher: 7.4%

School District(s)
Croswell-Lexington Community Schools (PK-12)
    2012-13 Enrollment: 2,252 . . . . (810) 679-1000
Housing: Homeownership rate: 82.6%; Median home value: $105,400; Median year structure built: 1973; Homeowner vacancy rate: 4.0%; Median gross rent: $493 per month; Rental vacancy rate: 12.9%
Health Insurance: 83.7% have insurance; 63.2% have private insurance; 40.4% have public insurance; 16.3% do not have insurance; 2.1% of children under 18 do not have insurance
Transportation: Commute: 75.6% car, 1.3% public transportation, 18.4% walk, 3.6% work from home; Median travel time to work: 22.1 minutes

LEXINGTON (village). Covers a land area of 1.400 square miles and a water area of 0.013 square miles. Located at 43.27° N. Lat; 82.54° W. Long. Elevation is 617 feet.
Population: 1,178; Growth (since 2000): 6.7%; Density: 841.2 persons per square mile; Race: 97.3% White, 0.3% Black/African American, 0.3% Asian, 0.2% American Indian/Alaska Native, 0.0% Native Hawaiian/Other Pacific Islander, 1.3% Two or more races, 1.5% Hispanic of any race;

Average household size: 1.95; Median age: 55.2; Age under 18: 15.2%; Age 65 and over: 33.0%; Males per 100 females: 86.4

School District(s)

Croswell-Lexington Community Schools (PK-12)
  · 2012-13 Enrollment: 2,252 . . . . (810) 679-1000
Housing: Homeownership rate: 74.1%; Homeowner vacancy rate: 2.4%; Rental vacancy rate: 13.8%

MAPLE VALLEY (township). Covers a land area of 34.510 square miles and a water area of 0.048 square miles. Located at 43.19° N. Lat; 82.93° W. Long.
Population: 1,221; Growth (since 2000): 9.6%; Density: 35.4 persons per square mile; Race: 98.9% White, 0.2% Black/African American, 0.2% Asian, 0.3% American Indian/Alaska Native, 0.0% Native Hawaiian/Other Pacific Islander, 0.3% Two or more races, 1.9% Hispanic of any race; Average household size: 2.94; Median age: 35.8; Age under 18: 29.6%; Age 65 and over: 11.6%; Males per 100 females: 102.2
Housing: Homeownership rate: 86.3%; Homeowner vacancy rate: 1.4%; Rental vacancy rate: 1.7%

MARION (township). Covers a land area of 36.078 square miles and a water area of 0.012 square miles. Located at 43.56° N. Lat; 82.69° W. Long.
Population: 1,659; Growth (since 2000): -8.0%; Density: 46.0 persons per square mile; Race: 96.3% White, 0.2% Black/African American, 0.2% Asian, 0.7% American Indian/Alaska Native, 0.0% Native Hawaiian/Other Pacific Islander, 1.3% Two or more races, 5.4% Hispanic of any race; Average household size: 2.49; Median age: 42.0; Age under 18: 24.1%; Age 65 and over: 19.7%; Males per 100 females: 90.7
Housing: Homeownership rate: 76.3%; Homeowner vacancy rate: 5.0%; Rental vacancy rate: 10.6%

MARLETTE (city). Covers a land area of 1.641 square miles and a water area of 0.003 square miles. Located at 43.33° N. Lat; 83.08° W. Long. Elevation is 837 feet.
History: Marlette grew up as the center of a livestock, feed, and dairy products region.
Population: 1,875; Growth (since 2000): -10.9%; Density: 1,142.9 persons per square mile; Race: 95.9% White, 0.3% Black/African American, 0.7% Asian, 0.6% American Indian/Alaska Native, 0.0% Native Hawaiian/Other Pacific Islander, 2.1% Two or more races, 3.4% Hispanic of any race; Average household size: 2.43; Median age: 39.4; Age under 18: 25.2%; Age 65 and over: 17.2%; Males per 100 females: 89.8

School District(s)

Marlette Community Schools (PK-12)
  2012-13 Enrollment: 980 . . . . (989) 635-4900
Housing: Homeownership rate: 58.4%; Homeowner vacancy rate: 3.1%; Rental vacancy rate: 16.1%
Hospitals: Marlette Regional Hospital (97 beds)
Safety: Violent crime rate: 38.3 per 10,000 population; Property crime rate: 147.7 per 10,000 population
Newspapers: Marlette Leader (weekly circulation 2100)

MARLETTE (township). Covers a land area of 52.428 square miles and a water area of 0.031 square miles. Located at 43.35° N. Lat; 83.06° W. Long. Elevation is 837 feet.
History: Incorporated 1881.
Population: 1,763; Growth (since 2000): -14.0%; Density: 33.6 persons per square mile; Race: 96.7% White, 0.3% Black/African American, 0.1% Asian, 0.3% American Indian/Alaska Native, 0.0% Native Hawaiian/Other Pacific Islander, 1.3% Two or more races, 3.2% Hispanic of any race; Average household size: 2.67; Median age: 42.8; Age under 18: 24.7%; Age 65 and over: 15.7%; Males per 100 females: 97.0

School District(s)

Marlette Community Schools (PK-12)
  2012-13 Enrollment: 980 . . . . (989) 635-4900
Housing: Homeownership rate: 86.0%; Homeowner vacancy rate: 2.4%; Rental vacancy rate: 14.7%
Hospitals: Marlette Regional Hospital (97 beds)
Newspapers: Marlette Leader (weekly circulation 2100)

MELVIN (village). Covers a land area of 0.971 square miles and a water area of 0 square miles. Located at 43.19° N. Lat; 82.86° W. Long. Elevation is 833 feet.
Population: 180; Growth (since 2000): 12.5%; Density: 185.4 persons per square mile; Race: 96.1% White, 0.6% Black/African American, 0.0% Asian, 1.7% American Indian/Alaska Native, 0.0% Native Hawaiian/Other Pacific Islander, 1.7% Two or more races, 0.0% Hispanic of any race; Average household size: 2.90; Median age: 36.0; Age under 18: 32.8%; Age 65 and over: 10.6%; Males per 100 females: 109.3
Housing: Homeownership rate: 85.4%; Homeowner vacancy rate: 1.8%; Rental vacancy rate: 30.8%

MINDEN (township). Covers a land area of 36.101 square miles and a water area of 0.022 square miles. Located at 43.64° N. Lat; 82.82° W. Long. Elevation is 778 feet.
History: Also called Minden.
Population: 545; Growth (since 2000): -13.9%; Density: 15.1 persons per square mile; Race: 97.6% White, 0.0% Black/African American, 0.2% Asian, 0.6% American Indian/Alaska Native, 0.0% Native Hawaiian/Other Pacific Islander, 1.1% Two or more races, 1.7% Hispanic of any race; Average household size: 2.45; Median age: 43.0; Age under 18: 20.4%; Age 65 and over: 14.5%; Males per 100 females: 98.2
Housing: Homeownership rate: 87.8%; Homeowner vacancy rate: 3.4%; Rental vacancy rate: 0.0%

MINDEN CITY (village). Covers a land area of 1.096 square miles and a water area of 0.003 square miles. Located at 43.67° N. Lat; 82.78° W. Long. Elevation is 850 feet.
Population: 197; Growth (since 2000): -18.6%; Density: 179.7 persons per square mile; Race: 95.4% White, 0.0% Black/African American, 0.5% Asian, 0.5% American Indian/Alaska Native, 0.0% Native Hawaiian/Other Pacific Islander, 2.0% Two or more races, 1.5% Hispanic of any race; Average household size: 2.43; Median age: 41.5; Age under 18: 21.3%; Age 65 and over: 12.2%; Males per 100 females: 91.3
Housing: Homeownership rate: 80.3%; Homeowner vacancy rate: 8.2%; Rental vacancy rate: 0.0%
Newspapers: Minden City Herald (weekly circulation 1500)

MOORE (township). Covers a land area of 36.296 square miles and a water area of 0.012 square miles. Located at 43.46° N. Lat; 82.93° W. Long.
Population: 1,203; Growth (since 2000): -4.7%; Density: 33.1 persons per square mile; Race: 98.2% White, 0.0% Black/African American, 0.0% Asian, 0.5% American Indian/Alaska Native, 0.2% Native Hawaiian/Other Pacific Islander, 0.7% Two or more races, 3.6% Hispanic of any race; Average household size: 2.68; Median age: 39.0; Age under 18: 26.5%; Age 65 and over: 14.1%; Males per 100 females: 95.6
Housing: Homeownership rate: 86.8%; Homeowner vacancy rate: 2.3%; Rental vacancy rate: 12.1%

PALMS (unincorporated postal area)
ZCTA: 48465
  Covers a land area of 41.057 square miles and a water area of 0.537 square miles. Located at 43.61° N. Lat; 82.71° W. Long. Elevation is 820 feet.
  Population: 629; Growth (since 2000): 0.0%; Density: 15.3 persons per square mile; Race: 97.6% White, 0.3% Black/African American, 0.2% Asian, 1.1% American Indian/Alaska Native, 0.0% Native Hawaiian/Other Pacific Islander, 0.6% Two or more races, 2.4% Hispanic of any race; Average household size: 2.40; Median age: 49.9; Age under 18: 19.9%; Age 65 and over: 21.6%; Males per 100 females: 109.0
  Housing: Homeownership rate: 94.3%; Homeowner vacancy rate: 3.9%; Rental vacancy rate: 6.3%

PECK (village). Covers a land area of 1.050 square miles and a water area of 0 square miles. Located at 43.26° N. Lat; 82.82° W. Long. Elevation is 787 feet.
History: Peck had its beginnings when Nathaniel Vannest built the Globe Hotel here in 1859, followed by a store in 1868. Peck was incorporated as a village in 1903.
Population: 632; Growth (since 2000): 5.5%; Density: 601.8 persons per square mile; Race: 95.1% White, 0.6% Black/African American, 0.2% Asian, 2.2% American Indian/Alaska Native, 0.0% Native Hawaiian/Other Pacific Islander, 1.4% Two or more races, 4.9% Hispanic of any race;

Average household size: 2.54; Median age: 37.1; Age under 18: 25.9%; Age 65 and over: 14.2%; Males per 100 females: 91.5

School District(s)

Peck Community SD (KG-12)

    2012-13 Enrollment: 459 . . . . (810) 378-5171

Housing: Homeownership rate: 74.4%; Homeowner vacancy rate: 6.6%; Rental vacancy rate: 14.7%

PORT SANILAC (village).

Covers a land area of 0.803 square miles and a water area of 0 square miles. Located at 43.43° N. Lat; 82.54° W. Long. Elevation is 610 feet.

History: Port Sanilac was first settled in 1844, when it was known as Bark Shanty Point. For a time, the "Bark Shanty Times" utilized an unusual method of producing its daily newspaper edition, when large sheets of paper were placed on the storekeeper's counter, along with a supply of lead pencils. Customers were invited to write down their news, which was then available for others to read throughout the day. Daily issues were bound and preserved.

Population: 623; Growth (since 2000): -5.3%; Density: 775.8 persons per square mile; Race: 97.3% White, 0.2% Black/African American, 0.3% Asian, 0.3% American Indian/Alaska Native, 0.0% Native Hawaiian/Other Pacific Islander, 1.8% Two or more races, 2.2% Hispanic of any race; Average household size: 2.09; Median age: 51.1; Age under 18: 19.9%; Age 65 and over: 25.4%; Males per 100 females: 83.2

Housing: Homeownership rate: 77.6%; Homeowner vacancy rate: 3.8%; Rental vacancy rate: 25.0%

SANDUSKY (city).

County seat. Covers a land area of 2.144 square miles and a water area of 0.003 square miles. Located at 43.42° N. Lat; 82.83° W. Long. Elevation is 774 feet.

History: Sandusky was founded in 1870 by Wildman Mills and named for his former home of Sandusky, Ohio. Sandusky developed as the center of a livestock area, and as the seat of Sanilac County. For a time it was called Sanilac Center, but was renamed Sandusky when it was incorporated as a city in 1905.

Population: 2,679; Growth (since 2000): -2.4%; Density: 1,249.7 persons per square mile; Race: 94.4% White, 1.5% Black/African American, 1.1% Asian, 0.3% American Indian/Alaska Native, 0.0% Native Hawaiian/Other Pacific Islander, 1.4% Two or more races, 3.5% Hispanic of any race; Average household size: 2.16; Median age: 41.4; Age under 18: 21.3%; Age 65 and over: 18.1%; Males per 100 females: 84.3; Marriage status: 30.4% never married, 43.7% now married, 2.3% separated, 10.8% widowed, 15.1% divorced; Foreign born: 1.3%; Speak English only: 95.8%; With disability: 20.9%; Veterans: 6.5%; Ancestry: 27.3% German, 14.0% English, 9.3% Irish, 7.1% Polish, 6.5% American

Employment: 9.2% management, business, and financial, 3.0% computer, engineering, and science, 7.4% education, legal, community service, arts, and media, 4.2% healthcare practitioners, 17.2% service, 27.8% sales and office, 4.4% natural resources, construction, and maintenance, 26.8% production, transportation, and material moving

Income: Per capita: $22,830; Median household: $31,989; Average household: $50,245; Households with income of $100,000 or more: 7.1%; Poverty rate: 26.2%

Educational Attainment: High school diploma or higher: 84.6%; Bachelor's degree or higher: 12.9%; Graduate/professional degree or higher: 5.7%

School District(s)

Sandusky Community SD (PK-12)

    2012-13 Enrollment: 1,003 . . . . (810) 648-3400

Sanilac ISD (PK-12)

    2012-13 Enrollment: 276 . . . . (810) 648-4700

Housing: Homeownership rate: 52.3%; Median home value: $76,600; Median year structure built: 1967; Homeowner vacancy rate: 4.6%; Median gross rent: $514 per month; Rental vacancy rate: 7.7%

Health Insurance: 88.8% have insurance; 61.3% have private insurance; 47.2% have public insurance; 11.2% do not have insurance; 1.1% of children under 18 do not have insurance

Hospitals: McKenzie Health System (25 beds)

Safety: Violent crime rate: 15.2 per 10,000 population; Property crime rate: 163.9 per 10,000 population

Newspapers: Sanilac County News (weekly circulation 8200)

Transportation: Commute: 82.4% car, 5.3% public transportation, 7.6% walk, 2.9% work from home; Median travel time to work: 18.9 minutes

SANILAC (township).

Covers a land area of 40.772 square miles and a water area of 0.065 square miles. Located at 43.41° N. Lat; 82.58° W. Long.

Population: 2,431; Growth (since 2000): -6.8%; Density: 59.6 persons per square mile; Race: 97.5% White, 0.2% Black/African American, 0.5% Asian, 0.3% American Indian/Alaska Native, 0.0% Native Hawaiian/Other Pacific Islander, 1.1% Two or more races, 1.5% Hispanic of any race; Average household size: 2.19; Median age: 50.9; Age under 18: 18.0%; Age 65 and over: 24.4%; Males per 100 females: 95.3

Housing: Homeownership rate: 86.1%; Homeowner vacancy rate: 4.0%; Rental vacancy rate: 28.1%

SNOVER (CDP).

Covers a land area of 6.873 square miles and a water area of 0.001 square miles. Located at 43.47° N. Lat; 82.97° W. Long. Elevation is 774 feet.

Population: 448; Growth (since 2000): n/a; Density: 65.2 persons per square mile; Race: 97.3% White, 0.0% Black/African American, 0.0% Asian, 1.1% American Indian/Alaska Native, 0.0% Native Hawaiian/Other Pacific Islander, 1.1% Two or more races, 5.1% Hispanic of any race; Average household size: 2.63; Median age: 36.5; Age under 18: 29.0%; Age 65 and over: 13.6%; Males per 100 females: 93.1

Housing: Homeownership rate: 83.2%; Homeowner vacancy rate: 0.7%; Rental vacancy rate: 20.0%

SPEAKER (township).

Covers a land area of 34.551 square miles and a water area of 0.004 square miles. Located at 43.20° N. Lat; 82.81° W. Long. Elevation is 801 feet.

History: Speaker Township was organized in 1858.

Population: 1,483; Growth (since 2000): 5.3%; Density: 42.9 persons per square mile; Race: 97.1% White, 0.7% Black/African American, 0.1% Asian, 0.7% American Indian/Alaska Native, 0.1% Native Hawaiian/Other Pacific Islander, 0.9% Two or more races, 1.1% Hispanic of any race; Average household size: 2.70; Median age: 41.6; Age under 18: 25.5%; Age 65 and over: 12.9%; Males per 100 females: 106.5

Housing: Homeownership rate: 90.3%; Homeowner vacancy rate: 1.2%; Rental vacancy rate: 13.1%

WASHINGTON (township).

Covers a land area of 35.952 square miles and a water area of 0.214 square miles. Located at 43.38° N. Lat; 82.68° W. Long.

Population: 1,659; Growth (since 2000): 1.4%; Density: 46.1 persons per square mile; Race: 95.8% White, 0.6% Black/African American, 0.9% Asian, 0.4% American Indian/Alaska Native, 0.0% Native Hawaiian/Other Pacific Islander, 2.0% Two or more races, 3.0% Hispanic of any race; Average household size: 2.60; Median age: 40.5; Age under 18: 26.2%; Age 65 and over: 16.5%; Males per 100 females: 100.8

Housing: Homeownership rate: 83.9%; Homeowner vacancy rate: 3.2%; Rental vacancy rate: 12.6%

WATERTOWN (township).

Covers a land area of 35.038 square miles and a water area of 0.016 square miles. Located at 43.37° N. Lat; 82.80° W. Long. Elevation is 764 feet.

Population: 1,320; Growth (since 2000): -4.1%; Density: 37.7 persons per square mile; Race: 97.7% White, 0.4% Black/African American, 0.6% Asian, 0.1% American Indian/Alaska Native, 0.0% Native Hawaiian/Other Pacific Islander, 0.8% Two or more races, 2.0% Hispanic of any race; Average household size: 2.53; Median age: 42.4; Age under 18: 23.6%; Age 65 and over: 13.9%; Males per 100 females: 100.3

Housing: Homeownership rate: 85.0%; Homeowner vacancy rate: 0.9%; Rental vacancy rate: 1.3%

WHEATLAND (township).

Covers a land area of 36.342 square miles and a water area of 0.059 square miles. Located at 43.56° N. Lat; 82.81° W. Long.

Population: 488; Growth (since 2000): -7.9%; Density: 13.4 persons per square mile; Race: 93.2% White, 0.0% Black/African American, 0.0% Asian, 1.6% American Indian/Alaska Native, 0.0% Native Hawaiian/Other Pacific Islander, 2.5% Two or more races, 4.3% Hispanic of any race; Average household size: 2.53; Median age: 40.6; Age under 18: 23.4%; Age 65 and over: 18.4%; Males per 100 females: 105.9

Housing: Homeownership rate: 89.1%; Homeowner vacancy rate: 0.6%; Rental vacancy rate: 0.0%

WORTH (township). Covers a land area of 38.596 square miles and a water area of 0.229 square miles. Located at 43.20° N. Lat; 82.58° W. Long.

Population: 3,894; Growth (since 2000): -3.2%; Density: 100.9 persons per square mile; Race: 97.0% White, 0.3% Black/African American, 0.2% Asian, 0.4% American Indian/Alaska Native, 0.1% Native Hawaiian/Other Pacific Islander, 1.0% Two or more races, 2.9% Hispanic of any race; Average household size: 2.41; Median age: 45.3; Age under 18: 22.1%; Age 65 and over: 19.7%; Males per 100 females: 97.1; Marriage status: 23.6% never married, 53.0% now married, 1.7% separated, 12.7% widowed, 10.7% divorced; Foreign born: 1.2%; Speak English only: 98.0%; With disability: 15.1%; Veterans: 11.5%; Ancestry: 38.3% German, 13.5% Irish, 12.4% Polish, 11.4% English, 6.5% French

Employment: 11.3% management, business, and financial, 6.3% computer, engineering, and science, 2.7% education, legal, community service, arts, and media, 9.3% healthcare practitioners, 6.8% service, 32.6% sales and office, 14.4% natural resources, construction, and maintenance, 16.7% production, transportation, and material moving

Income: Per capita: $24,383; Median household: $48,111; Average household: $58,678; Households with income of $100,000 or more: 13.8%; Poverty rate: 12.7%

Educational Attainment: High school diploma or higher: 91.4%; Bachelor's degree or higher: 15.3%; Graduate/professional degree or higher: 4.5%

Housing: Homeownership rate: 87.6%; Median home value: $116,000; Median year structure built: 1965; Homeowner vacancy rate: 2.7%; Median gross rent: $1,083 per month; Rental vacancy rate: 6.8%

Health Insurance: 93.2% have insurance; 72.5% have private insurance; 41.8% have public insurance; 6.8% do not have insurance; 2.2% of children under 18 do not have insurance

Transportation: Commute: 88.1% car, 1.1% public transportation, 0.3% walk, 8.5% work from home; Median travel time to work: 41.3 minutes

Schoolcraft County

Located in northwestern Michigan on the Upper Peninsula; bounded on the south by Lake Michigan; drained by the Indian and Manistique Rivers; includes Indian Lake, and parts of Hiawatha National Forest. Covers a land area of 1,171.358 square miles, a water area of 712.621 square miles, and is located in the Eastern Time Zone at 46.02° N. Lat., 86.20° W. Long. The county was founded in 1843. County seat is Manistique.

Weather Station: Manistique										Elevation: 620 feet	
	Jan	Feb	Mar	Apr	May	Jun	Jul	Aug	Sep	Oct	Nov	Dec
High	26	28	35	47	58	68	73	74	66	53	41	30
Low	10	11	18	31	41	50	56	56	49	38	28	16
Precip	na	0.7	1.3	2.4	2.6	2.9	2.9	2.9	3.4	3.3	2.4	1.5
Snow	21.6	14.3	11.0	2.7	tr	0.0	0.0	0.0	0.0	0.2	4.7	19.6

High and Low temperatures in degrees Fahrenheit; Precipitation and Snow in inches

Population: 8,485; Growth (since 2000): -4.7%; Density: 7.2 persons per square mile; Race: 87.6% White, 0.1% Black/African American, 0.2% Asian, 8.8% American Indian/Alaska Native, 0.0% Native Hawaiian/Other Pacific Islander, 3.3% two or more races, 0.8% Hispanic of any race; Average household size: 2.22; Median age: 48.3; Age under 18: 19.9%; Age 65 and over: 21.2%; Males per 100 females: 98.0; Marriage status: 23.2% never married, 56.2% now married, 1.0% separated, 9.0% widowed, 11.7% divorced; Foreign born: 1.5%; Speak English only: 97.3%; With disability: 19.3%; Veterans: 13.2%; Ancestry: 20.5% German, 9.2% French, 8.8% Irish, 8.5% Swedish, 8.1% English

Religion: Six largest groups: 32.4% Catholicism, 5.3% Lutheran, 4.1% Non-denominational Protestant, 3.9% Baptist, 2.3% Methodist/Pietist, 2.1% Pentecostal

Economy: Unemployment rate: 7.5%; Leading industries: 19.6% retail trade; 15.2% accommodation and food services; 9.6% construction; Farms: 65 totaling 19,423 acres; Company size: 0 employ 1,000 or more persons, 0 employ 500 to 999 persons, 2 employ 100 to 499 persons, 228 employ less than 100 persons; Business ownership: n/a women-owned, n/a Black-owned, n/a Hispanic-owned, n/a Asian-owned

Employment: 13.1% management, business, and financial, 1.6% computer, engineering, and science, 7.5% education, legal, community service, arts, and media, 6.0% healthcare practitioners, 23.7% service, 20.2% sales and office, 13.4% natural resources, construction, and maintenance, 14.7% production, transportation, and material moving

Income: Per capita: $20,892; Median household: $35,260; Average household: $47,071; Households with income of $100,000 or more: 7.8%; Poverty rate: 20.7%

Educational Attainment: High school diploma or higher: 89.9%; Bachelor's degree or higher: 12.4%; Graduate/professional degree or higher: 4.0%

Housing: Homeownership rate: 82.1%; Median home value: $86,200; Median year structure built: 1969; Homeowner vacancy rate: 3.2%; Median gross rent: $512 per month; Rental vacancy rate: 9.5%

Vital Statistics: Birth rate: 81.2 per 10,000 population; Death rate: 123.7 per 10,000 population; Age-adjusted cancer mortality rate: 204.9 deaths per 100,000 population

Health Insurance: 87.9% have insurance; 63.9% have private insurance; 44.0% have public insurance; 12.1% do not have insurance; 1.8% of children under 18 do not have insurance

Health Care: Physicians: 9.6 per 10,000 population; Hospital beds: 21.2 per 10,000 population; Hospital admissions: 396.3 per 10,000 population

Air Quality Index: 92.0% good, 7.5% moderate, 0.5% unhealthy for sensitive individuals, 0.0% unhealthy (percent of days)

Transportation: Commute: 90.2% car, 0.3% public transportation, 4.4% walk, 4.6% work from home; Median travel time to work: 20.0 minutes

Presidential Election: 46.1% Obama, 52.9% Romney (2012)

National and State Parks: Grand Sable State Forest; Indian Lake State Park; Palms Book State Park; Seney National Wildlife Refuge

Additional Information Contacts
Schoolcraft Government . . . . (906) 341-3618
http://www.schoolcraftcountygovernment.com

Schoolcraft County Communities

DOYLE (township). Covers a land area of 146.121 square miles and a water area of 8.071 square miles. Located at 46.16° N. Lat; 86.07° W. Long.

Population: 624; Growth (since 2000): -1.0%; Density: 4.3 persons per square mile; Race: 91.0% White, 0.0% Black/African American, 0.2% Asian, 5.8% American Indian/Alaska Native, 0.0% Native Hawaiian/Other Pacific Islander, 3.0% Two or more races, 0.8% Hispanic of any race; Average household size: 2.24; Median age: 50.7; Age under 18: 17.8%; Age 65 and over: 19.6%; Males per 100 females: 103.9

Housing: Homeownership rate: 92.8%; Homeowner vacancy rate: 5.5%; Rental vacancy rate: 4.8%

GERMFASK (township). Covers a land area of 66.433 square miles and a water area of 5.200 square miles. Located at 46.25° N. Lat; 85.93° W. Long. Elevation is 689 feet.

History: Germfask Township was settled in 1881. The name came from using the first letter of the names of the eight families who founded the town: John Grant, Matthew Edge, George Robinson, Thaddeus Mead, Dr. W.W. French, Ezekiel Ackley, Oscar Shepard, Hezekiah Knaggs.

Population: 486; Growth (since 2000): -1.0%; Density: 7.3 persons per square mile; Race: 90.5% White, 0.0% Black/African American, 0.0% Asian, 7.0% American Indian/Alaska Native, 0.0% Native Hawaiian/Other Pacific Islander, 2.5% Two or more races, 0.4% Hispanic of any race; Average household size: 2.28; Median age: 45.2; Age under 18: 21.4%; Age 65 and over: 20.6%; Males per 100 females: 105.9

Housing: Homeownership rate: 82.7%; Homeowner vacancy rate: 5.9%; Rental vacancy rate: 5.3%

GULLIVER (unincorporated postal area)
ZCTA: 49840

Covers a land area of 180.566 square miles and a water area of 17.159 square miles. Located at 46.10° N. Lat; 86.01° W. Long. Elevation is 623 feet.

Population: 771; Growth (since 2000): -8.5%; Density: 4.3 persons per square mile; Race: 91.2% White, 0.0% Black/African American, 0.0% Asian, 5.8% American Indian/Alaska Native, 0.0% Native Hawaiian/Other Pacific Islander, 3.0% Two or more races, 0.6% Hispanic of any race; Average household size: 2.17; Median age: 51.9; Age under 18: 16.3%; Age 65 and over: 20.9%; Males per 100 females: 105.1

Housing: Homeownership rate: 92.4%; Homeowner vacancy rate: 6.3%; Rental vacancy rate: 3.6%

HIAWATHA (township). Covers a land area of 277.435 square miles and a water area of 13.433 square miles. Located at 46.24° N. Lat; 86.33° W. Long. Elevation is 728 feet.
Population: 1,302; Growth (since 2000): -2.0%; Density: 4.7 persons per square mile; Race: 90.3% White, 0.2% Black/African American, 0.2% Asian, 6.8% American Indian/Alaska Native, 0.0% Native Hawaiian/Other Pacific Islander, 2.2% Two or more races, 0.5% Hispanic of any race; Average household size: 2.21; Median age: 53.1; Age under 18: 15.7%; Age 65 and over: 23.9%; Males per 100 females: 102.5
Housing: Homeownership rate: 95.6%; Homeowner vacancy rate: 3.6%; Rental vacancy rate: 22.9%

INWOOD (township). Covers a land area of 120.224 square miles and a water area of 6.583 square miles. Located at 46.09° N. Lat; 86.47° W. Long.
Population: 733; Growth (since 2000): 1.5%; Density: 6.1 persons per square mile; Race: 90.5% White, 0.0% Black/African American, 0.4% Asian, 6.4% American Indian/Alaska Native, 0.0% Native Hawaiian/Other Pacific Islander, 2.6% Two or more races, 1.4% Hispanic of any race; Average household size: 2.32; Median age: 51.1; Age under 18: 17.9%; Age 65 and over: 20.2%; Males per 100 females: 109.4
Housing: Homeownership rate: 93.1%; Homeowner vacancy rate: 1.7%; Rental vacancy rate: 11.5%

MANISTIQUE (city). County seat. Covers a land area of 3.185 square miles and a water area of 0.323 square miles. Located at 45.96° N. Lat; 86.25° W. Long. Elevation is 600 feet.
History: Manistique began as a lumber town in 1860 and became one of the largest operations on the Upper Peninsula. Around 1900 the supply of pine was gone, and a tannery, chemical factory, lime kilns, and iron furnaces replaced the lumber industry. These were eventually replaced by papermaking, hardwood manufacture, shipping, and commercial fishing.
Population: 3,097; Growth (since 2000): -13.6%; Density: 972.3 persons per square mile; Race: 86.0% White, 0.2% Black/African American, 0.2% Asian, 9.7% American Indian/Alaska Native, 0.0% Native Hawaiian/Other Pacific Islander, 3.9% Two or more races, 1.0% Hispanic of any race; Average household size: 2.15; Median age: 43.0; Age under 18: 23.0%; Age 65 and over: 20.6%; Males per 100 females: 86.3; Marriage status: 30.6% never married, 43.4% now married, 1.8% separated, 13.3% widowed, 12.7% divorced; Foreign born: 1.8%; Speak English only: 96.8%; With disability: 19.7%; Veterans: 9.4%; Ancestry: 16.5% German, 9.1% Swedish, 7.5% Irish, 6.9% French, 5.6% Polish
Employment: 13.7% management, business, and financial, 0.0% computer, engineering, and science, 7.2% education, legal, community service, arts, and media, 4.4% healthcare practitioners, 26.8% service, 19.5% sales and office, 10.6% natural resources, construction, and maintenance, 17.8% production, transportation, and material moving
Income: Per capita: $16,288; Median household: $25,727; Average household: $33,647; Households with income of $100,000 or more: 3.2%; Poverty rate: 28.2%
Educational Attainment: High school diploma or higher: 88.9%; Bachelor's degree or higher: 8.2%; Graduate/professional degree or higher: 1.4%
School District(s)
Manistique Area Schools (PK-12)
    2012-13 Enrollment: 849 . . . . (906) 341-4330
Housing: Homeownership rate: 66.5%; Median home value: $62,500; Median year structure built: 1950; Homeowner vacancy rate: 3.0%; Median gross rent: $489 per month; Rental vacancy rate: 9.4%
Health Insurance: 88.7% have insurance; 56.6% have private insurance; 49.6% have public insurance; 11.3% do not have insurance; 0.0% of children under 18 do not have insurance
Hospitals: Schoolcraft Memorial Hospital (25 beds)
Safety: Violent crime rate: 23.1 per 10,000 population; Property crime rate: 260.6 per 10,000 population
Newspapers: Pioneer Tribune (weekly circulation 3800)
Transportation: Commute: 91.3% car, 0.0% public transportation, 5.9% walk, 2.5% work from home; Median travel time to work: 20.5 minutes
Airports: Schoolcraft County (general aviation)

MANISTIQUE (township). Covers a land area of 149.340 square miles and a water area of 4.350 square miles. Located at 46.13° N. Lat; 86.15° W. Long. Elevation is 600 feet.
History: Incorporated as village 1885, as city 1901.

Population: 1,095; Growth (since 2000): 4.0%; Density: 7.3 persons per square mile; Race: 80.3% White, 0.1% Black/African American, 0.0% Asian, 14.8% American Indian/Alaska Native, 0.0% Native Hawaiian/Other Pacific Islander, 4.7% Two or more races, 0.4% Hispanic of any race; Average household size: 2.37; Median age: 46.9; Age under 18: 21.9%; Age 65 and over: 19.7%; Males per 100 females: 103.5
School District(s)
Manistique Area Schools (PK-12)
    2012-13 Enrollment: 849 . . . . (906) 341-4330
Housing: Homeownership rate: 86.0%; Homeowner vacancy rate: 1.2%; Rental vacancy rate: 5.7%
Hospitals: Schoolcraft Memorial Hospital (25 beds)
Newspapers: Pioneer Tribune (weekly circulation 3800)
Airports: Schoolcraft County (general aviation)

MUELLER (township). Covers a land area of 83.612 square miles and a water area of 4.167 square miles. Located at 46.03° N. Lat; 85.95° W. Long.
Population: 234; Growth (since 2000): -4.5%; Density: 2.8 persons per square mile; Race: 93.6% White, 0.0% Black/African American, 0.0% Asian, 4.3% American Indian/Alaska Native, 0.0% Native Hawaiian/Other Pacific Islander, 2.1% Two or more races, 0.4% Hispanic of any race; Average household size: 1.92; Median age: 58.2; Age under 18: 8.1%; Age 65 and over: 28.2%; Males per 100 females: 107.1
Housing: Homeownership rate: 94.3%; Homeowner vacancy rate: 6.4%; Rental vacancy rate: 0.0%

SENEY (township). Covers a land area of 212.633 square miles and a water area of 2.865 square miles. Located at 46.41° N. Lat; 86.00° W. Long. Elevation is 735 feet.
History: Seney was named for George R. Seney, a railroad director. The township was organized about 1882 around the logging activities of the Alger, Smith Company. Tales of corruption and abuse in Seney made newspaper headlines in the 1880's.
Population: 119; Growth (since 2000): -33.9%; Density: 0.6 persons per square mile; Race: 95.0% White, 0.0% Black/African American, 0.0% Asian, 2.5% American Indian/Alaska Native, 0.0% Native Hawaiian/Other Pacific Islander, 2.5% Two or more races, 0.8% Hispanic of any race; Average household size: 2.04; Median age: 58.1; Age under 18: 10.1%; Age 65 and over: 31.9%; Males per 100 females: 116.4
Housing: Homeownership rate: 88.5%; Homeowner vacancy rate: 6.1%; Rental vacancy rate: 33.3%

THOMPSON (township). Covers a land area of 112.375 square miles and a water area of 5.959 square miles. Located at 45.97° N. Lat; 86.35° W. Long. Elevation is 600 feet.
History: Thompson Township was named for E.L. Thompson of Detroit, president of the Delta Lumber Company which had a mill here. The village of Thompson was first settled by fishermen.
Population: 795; Growth (since 2000): 18.5%; Density: 7.1 persons per square mile; Race: 89.4% White, 0.1% Black/African American, 0.1% Asian, 7.9% American Indian/Alaska Native, 0.0% Native Hawaiian/Other Pacific Islander, 2.4% Two or more races, 0.4% Hispanic of any race; Average household size: 2.29; Median age: 49.8; Age under 18: 19.4%; Age 65 and over: 20.5%; Males per 100 females: 108.1
Housing: Homeownership rate: 92.5%; Homeowner vacancy rate: 2.1%; Rental vacancy rate: 7.1%

Shiawassee County

Located in south central Michigan; drained by the Shiawassee, Maple, and Lookingglass Rivers. Covers a land area of 530.668 square miles, a water area of 10.280 square miles, and is located in the Eastern Time Zone at 42.95° N. Lat., 84.15° W. Long. The county was founded in 1822. County seat is Corunna.

Shiawassee County is part of the Owosso, MI Micropolitan Statistical Area. The entire metro area includes: Shiawassee County, MI

Weather Station: Owosso Wwtp									Elevation: 729 feet		
	Jan	Feb	Mar	Apr	May	Jun	Jul	Aug	Sep	Oct	Nov	Dec
High	30	33	43	57	69	78	82	80	73	60	47	35
Low	14	16	24	35	45	55	59	58	50	39	31	21
Precip	1.6	1.5	1.8	3.0	3.5	3.2	3.1	3.3	3.7	2.9	2.6	2.1
Snow	10.3	7.7	4.3	0.9	tr	0.0	0.0	0.0	0.0	0.2	1.6	10.7

High and Low temperatures in degrees Fahrenheit; Precipitation and Snow in inches

Population: 70,648; Growth (since 2000): -1.4%; Density: 133.1 persons per square mile; Race: 96.7% White, 0.5% Black/African American, 0.4% Asian, 0.5% American Indian/Alaska Native, 0.0% Native Hawaiian/Other Pacific Islander, 1.5% two or more races, 2.4% Hispanic of any race; Average household size: 2.54; Median age: 40.3; Age under 18: 24.1%; Age 65 and over: 14.3%; Males per 100 females: 97.7; Marriage status: 26.4% never married, 55.3% now married, 1.4% separated, 6.3% widowed, 11.9% divorced; Foreign born: 1.0%; Speak English only: 97.6%; With disability: 14.6%; Veterans: 9.8%; Ancestry: 26.9% German, 14.8% English, 13.8% Irish, 8.2% American, 5.6% Polish
Religion: Six largest groups: 12.8% Catholicism, 5.9% Holiness, 4.3% Methodist/Pietist, 2.3% Non-denominational Protestant, 2.3% Lutheran, 1.8% Presbyterian-Reformed
Economy: Unemployment rate: 6.0%; Leading industries: 17.4% retail trade; 13.6% other services (except public administration); 11.8% health care and social assistance; Farms: 1,033 totaling 223,370 acres; Company size: 1 employs 1,000 or more persons, 0 employ 500 to 999 persons, 15 employ 100 to 499 persons, 1,130 employ less than 100 persons; Business ownership: 1,549 women-owned, n/a Black-owned, n/a Hispanic-owned, n/a Asian-owned
Employment: 10.8% management, business, and financial, 3.7% computer, engineering, and science, 7.2% education, legal, community service, arts, and media, 5.6% healthcare practitioners, 19.0% service, 24.4% sales and office, 11.4% natural resources, construction, and maintenance, 17.9% production, transportation, and material moving
Income: Per capita: $22,713; Median household: $46,217; Average household: $56,925; Households with income of $100,000 or more: 13.1%; Poverty rate: 15.3%
Educational Attainment: High school diploma or higher: 90.6%; Bachelor's degree or higher: 14.2%; Graduate/professional degree or higher: 5.2%
Housing: Homeownership rate: 77.5%; Median home value: $108,300; Median year structure built: 1967; Homeowner vacancy rate: 2.5%; Median gross rent: $672 per month; Rental vacancy rate: 9.7%
Vital Statistics: Birth rate: 101.7 per 10,000 population; Death rate: 98.5 per 10,000 population; Age-adjusted cancer mortality rate: 181.6 deaths per 100,000 population
Health Insurance: 88.3% have insurance; 69.6% have private insurance; 34.5% have public insurance; 11.7% do not have insurance; 3.4% of children under 18 do not have insurance
Health Care: Physicians: 10.8 per 10,000 population; Hospital beds: 19.1 per 10,000 population; Hospital admissions: 577.1 per 10,000 population
Transportation: Commute: 92.9% car, 0.3% public transportation, 2.1% walk, 3.5% work from home; Median travel time to work: 28.0 minutes
Presidential Election: 51.1% Obama, 47.4% Romney (2012)
Additional Information Contacts
Shiawassee Government . . . . (989) 743-2242
   http://www.shiawassee.net

Shiawassee County Communities

ANTRIM (township). Covers a land area of 35.334 square miles and a water area of 1.306 square miles. Located at 42.83° N. Lat; 84.11° W. Long.
Population: 2,161; Growth (since 2000): 5.4%; Density: 61.2 persons per square mile; Race: 96.3% White, 0.3% Black/African American, 0.2% Asian, 0.5% American Indian/Alaska Native, 0.1% Native Hawaiian/Other Pacific Islander, 1.7% Two or more races, 2.4% Hispanic of any race; Average household size: 2.70; Median age: 42.5; Age under 18: 22.4%; Age 65 and over: 13.2%; Males per 100 females: 105.8
Housing: Homeownership rate: 90.9%; Homeowner vacancy rate: 1.8%; Rental vacancy rate: 2.7%

BANCROFT (village). Covers a land area of 0.576 square miles and a water area of 0.009 square miles. Located at 42.88° N. Lat; 84.07° W. Long. Elevation is 856 feet.
History: Bancroft became a station on the Chicago & Lake Huron Railroad in 1877. It was incorporated as a village in 1883.
Population: 545; Growth (since 2000): -11.5%; Density: 946.0 persons per square mile; Race: 97.4% White, 0.6% Black/African American, 0.0% Asian, 0.7% American Indian/Alaska Native, 0.0% Native Hawaiian/Other Pacific Islander, 1.1% Two or more races, 1.1% Hispanic of any race;

Average household size: 2.85; Median age: 35.9; Age under 18: 27.2%; Age 65 and over: 9.2%; Males per 100 females: 106.4
Housing: Homeownership rate: 78.5%; Homeowner vacancy rate: 3.8%; Rental vacancy rate: 12.8%

BENNINGTON (township). Covers a land area of 35.482 square miles and a water area of 1.324 square miles. Located at 42.91° N. Lat; 84.22° W. Long. Elevation is 797 feet.
History: Bennington Township was organized in 1838 and named for Bennington, Vermont, the former home of some of the first settlers.
Population: 3,168; Growth (since 2000): 5.0%; Density: 89.3 persons per square mile; Race: 97.5% White, 0.3% Black/African American, 0.3% Asian, 0.3% American Indian/Alaska Native, 0.0% Native Hawaiian/Other Pacific Islander, 0.9% Two or more races, 2.6% Hispanic of any race; Average household size: 2.69; Median age: 43.8; Age under 18: 23.5%; Age 65 and over: 14.9%; Males per 100 females: 100.6; Marriage status: 20.9% never married, 63.3% now married, 0.2% separated, 6.1% widowed, 9.7% divorced; Foreign born: 1.9%; Speak English only: 95.8%; With disability: 11.9%; Veterans: 11.3%; Ancestry: 23.4% German, 20.3% English, 17.0% American, 13.4% Irish, 5.5% Polish
Employment: 10.3% management, business, and financial, 4.0% computer, engineering, and science, 7.8% education, legal, community service, arts, and media, 6.8% healthcare practitioners, 17.8% service, 26.2% sales and office, 11.8% natural resources, construction, and maintenance, 15.4% production, transportation, and material moving
Income: Per capita: $29,046; Median household: $59,408; Average household: $77,821; Households with income of $100,000 or more: 22.0%; Poverty rate: 5.8%
Educational Attainment: High school diploma or higher: 92.9%; Bachelor's degree or higher: 20.3%; Graduate/professional degree or higher: 7.7%
Housing: Homeownership rate: 94.7%; Median home value: $161,000; Median year structure built: 1975; Homeowner vacancy rate: 1.1%; Median gross rent: $1,063 per month; Rental vacancy rate: 6.1%
Health Insurance: 92.4% have insurance; 82.5% have private insurance; 30.6% have public insurance; 7.6% do not have insurance; 0.6% of children under 18 do not have insurance
Transportation: Commute: 96.2% car, 0.0% public transportation, 0.4% walk, 3.4% work from home; Median travel time to work: 37.1 minutes

BURNS (township). Covers a land area of 35.303 square miles and a water area of 0.606 square miles. Located at 42.83° N. Lat; 83.99° W. Long.
Population: 3,457; Growth (since 2000): -1.2%; Density: 97.9 persons per square mile; Race: 97.2% White, 0.2% Black/African American, 0.4% Asian, 0.6% American Indian/Alaska Native, 0.2% Native Hawaiian/Other Pacific Islander, 0.8% Two or more races, 1.6% Hispanic of any race; Average household size: 2.77; Median age: 40.5; Age under 18: 25.7%; Age 65 and over: 12.3%; Males per 100 females: 102.6; Marriage status: 19.1% never married, 63.7% now married, 0.7% separated, 4.1% widowed, 13.1% divorced; Foreign born: 0.8%; Speak English only: 98.0%; With disability: 11.5%; Veterans: 7.3%; Ancestry: 23.7% English, 21.0% German, 13.9% Irish, 9.4% American, 8.3% Polish
Employment: 13.7% management, business, and financial, 5.4% computer, engineering, and science, 5.9% education, legal, community service, arts, and media, 2.2% healthcare practitioners, 18.9% service, 20.7% sales and office, 15.5% natural resources, construction, and maintenance, 17.6% production, transportation, and material moving
Income: Per capita: $21,314; Median household: $51,199; Average household: $58,699; Households with income of $100,000 or more: 12.9%; Poverty rate: 9.2%
Educational Attainment: High school diploma or higher: 89.9%; Bachelor's degree or higher: 12.0%; Graduate/professional degree or higher: 2.8%
Housing: Homeownership rate: 88.0%; Median home value: $126,000; Median year structure built: 1974; Homeowner vacancy rate: 1.9%; Median gross rent: $679 per month; Rental vacancy rate: 7.4%
Health Insurance: 89.7% have insurance; 73.9% have private insurance; 31.0% have public insurance; 10.3% do not have insurance; 6.4% of children under 18 do not have insurance
Transportation: Commute: 95.3% car, 0.0% public transportation, 2.5% walk, 2.0% work from home; Median travel time to work: 35.6 minutes

BYRON (village). Covers a land area of 0.700 square miles and a water area of 0.055 square miles. Located at 42.83° N. Lat; 83.95° W. Long. Elevation is 843 feet.

History: The village of Byron was founded by Judge Samuel W. Dexter in 1824, and was incorporated in 1873.

Population: 581; Growth (since 2000): -2.4%; Density: 829.8 persons per square mile; Race: 95.7% White, 1.0% Black/African American, 0.2% Asian, 1.5% American Indian/Alaska Native, 0.0% Native Hawaiian/Other Pacific Islander, 1.4% Two or more races, 2.1% Hispanic of any race; Average household size: 2.79; Median age: 33.0; Age under 18: 33.9%; Age 65 and over: 8.3%; Males per 100 females: 94.3

School District(s)

Byron Area Schools (PK-12)

    2012-13 Enrollment: 1,105 . . . . (810) 266-4881

Housing: Homeownership rate: 70.7%; Homeowner vacancy rate: 4.5%; Rental vacancy rate: 12.9%

CALEDONIA (charter township). Covers a land area of 31.121 square miles and a water area of 0.271 square miles. Located at 43.00° N. Lat; 84.10° W. Long.

Population: 4,475; Growth (since 2000): 1.1%; Density: 143.8 persons per square mile; Race: 97.6% White, 0.2% Black/African American, 0.4% Asian, 0.4% American Indian/Alaska Native, 0.0% Native Hawaiian/Other Pacific Islander, 1.1% Two or more races, 2.0% Hispanic of any race; Average household size: 2.48; Median age: 43.8; Age under 18: 22.9%; Age 65 and over: 17.4%; Males per 100 females: 95.9; Marriage status: 31.4% never married, 49.0% now married, 1.9% separated, 8.4% widowed, 11.2% divorced; Foreign born: 0.8%; Speak English only: 94.7%; With disability: 17.4%; Veterans: 11.5%; Ancestry: 27.8% German, 15.8% Irish, 11.6% English, 9.1% American, 4.5% Czech

Employment: 13.2% management, business, and financial, 3.9% computer, engineering, and science, 4.6% education, legal, community service, arts, and media, 5.8% healthcare practitioners, 15.5% service, 25.6% sales and office, 10.4% natural resources, construction, and maintenance, 21.0% production, transportation, and material moving

Income: Per capita: $25,581; Median household: $52,594; Average household: $61,218; Households with income of $100,000 or more: 16.7%; Poverty rate: 13.9%

Educational Attainment: High school diploma or higher: 92.1%; Bachelor's degree or higher: 12.7%; Graduate/professional degree or higher: 4.1%

Housing: Homeownership rate: 84.3%; Median home value: $113,500; Median year structure built: 1967; Homeowner vacancy rate: 1.5%; Median gross rent: $757 per month; Rental vacancy rate: 8.7%

Health Insurance: 91.5% have insurance; 75.6% have private insurance; 34.7% have public insurance; 8.5% do not have insurance; 2.4% of children under 18 do not have insurance

Transportation: Commute: 91.7% car, 0.0% public transportation, 2.4% walk, 4.6% work from home; Median travel time to work: 20.0 minutes

Additional Information Contacts

Caledonia Charter Township . . . . (989) 743-5300
    http://caledoniatwp.com

CORUNNA (city). County seat. Covers a land area of 3.193 square miles and a water area of 0.069 square miles. Located at 42.98° N. Lat; 84.12° W. Long. Elevation is 745 feet.

History: Corunna was settled in 1836 around a flour mill, and platted by the Shiawassee County Seat Company in 1837. Industries in the early 1900's included a furniture factory, cigar factory, and some active coal mines.

Population: 3,497; Growth (since 2000): 3.4%; Density: 1,095.1 persons per square mile; Race: 95.0% White, 1.2% Black/African American, 1.3% Asian, 0.4% American Indian/Alaska Native, 0.0% Native Hawaiian/Other Pacific Islander, 1.5% Two or more races, 2.4% Hispanic of any race; Average household size: 2.34; Median age: 36.0; Age under 18: 23.6%; Age 65 and over: 14.7%; Males per 100 females: 91.5; Marriage status: 31.3% never married, 41.6% now married, 2.9% separated, 7.0% widowed, 20.1% divorced; Foreign born: 0.9%; Speak English only: 97.8%; With disability: 14.4%; Veterans: 9.8%; Ancestry: 20.8% German, 19.5% English, 15.7% Irish, 8.9% French, 8.7% American

Employment: 15.5% management, business, and financial, 0.0% computer, engineering, and science, 11.7% education, legal, community service, arts, and media, 4.2% healthcare practitioners, 21.9% service, 26.8% sales and office, 6.1% natural resources, construction, and maintenance, 13.7% production, transportation, and material moving

Income: Per capita: $19,602; Median household: $37,298; Average household: $45,548; Households with income of $100,000 or more: 9.0%; Poverty rate: 22.9%

Educational Attainment: High school diploma or higher: 89.2%; Bachelor's degree or higher: 16.7%; Graduate/professional degree or higher: 7.8%

School District(s)

Corunna Public Schools (PK-12)

    2012-13 Enrollment: 2,114 . . . . (989) 743-6338

Housing: Homeownership rate: 47.1%; Median home value: $87,700; Median year structure built: 1962; Homeowner vacancy rate: 3.2%; Median gross rent: $757 per month; Rental vacancy rate: 7.0%

Health Insurance: 84.7% have insurance; 60.6% have private insurance; 40.3% have public insurance; 15.3% do not have insurance; 3.5% of children under 18 do not have insurance

Safety: Violent crime rate: 14.7 per 10,000 population; Property crime rate: 117.3 per 10,000 population

Transportation: Commute: 92.6% car, 0.8% public transportation, 3.5% walk, 0.5% work from home; Median travel time to work: 22.3 minutes

DURAND (city). Covers a land area of 2.104 square miles and a water area of 0.003 square miles. Located at 42.91° N. Lat; 83.99° W. Long. Elevation is 794 feet.

History: Incorporated as village 1887, as city 1933.

Population: 3,446; Growth (since 2000): -12.4%; Density: 1,637.7 persons per square mile; Race: 96.3% White, 0.6% Black/African American, 0.1% Asian, 1.0% American Indian/Alaska Native, 0.0% Native Hawaiian/Other Pacific Islander, 1.5% Two or more races, 2.9% Hispanic of any race; Average household size: 2.45; Median age: 37.2; Age under 18: 25.8%; Age 65 and over: 15.7%; Males per 100 females: 87.9; Marriage status: 25.0% never married, 47.6% now married, 0.4% separated, 10.5% widowed, 16.8% divorced; Foreign born: 1.0%; Speak English only: 97.4%; With disability: 18.1%; Veterans: 8.9%; Ancestry: 25.7% German, 21.5% Irish, 12.0% English, 6.4% American, 6.3% Polish

Employment: 6.6% management, business, and financial, 6.2% computer, engineering, and science, 10.9% education, legal, community service, arts, and media, 4.6% healthcare practitioners, 21.4% service, 18.2% sales and office, 8.5% natural resources, construction, and maintenance, 23.5% production, transportation, and material moving

Income: Per capita: $19,893; Median household: $42,600; Average household: $46,477; Households with income of $100,000 or more: 6.0%; Poverty rate: 18.9%

Educational Attainment: High school diploma or higher: 87.4%; Bachelor's degree or higher: 12.6%; Graduate/professional degree or higher: 6.7%

School District(s)

Durand Area Schools (PK-12)

    2012-13 Enrollment: 1,602 . . . . (989) 288-2681

Housing: Homeownership rate: 65.5%; Median home value: $78,100; Median year structure built: 1950; Homeowner vacancy rate: 4.2%; Median gross rent: $589 per month; Rental vacancy rate: 17.1%

Health Insurance: 92.5% have insurance; 66.7% have private insurance; 43.7% have public insurance; 7.5% do not have insurance; 0.0% of children under 18 do not have insurance

Transportation: Commute: 89.1% car, 0.0% public transportation, 5.7% walk, 4.6% work from home; Median travel time to work: 29.6 minutes; Amtrak: Train service available.

Additional Information Contacts

City of Durand . . . . (989) 288-3113
    http://www.durandmi.com

FAIRFIELD (township). Covers a land area of 25.062 square miles and a water area of 0.010 square miles. Located at 43.08° N. Lat; 84.34° W. Long.

Population: 755; Growth (since 2000): 1.3%; Density: 30.1 persons per square mile; Race: 97.7% White, 0.3% Black/African American, 0.0% Asian, 0.1% American Indian/Alaska Native, 0.0% Native Hawaiian/Other Pacific Islander, 1.3% Two or more races, 3.2% Hispanic of any race; Average household size: 2.71; Median age: 42.2; Age under 18: 23.3%; Age 65 and over: 15.2%; Males per 100 females: 105.7

Housing: Homeownership rate: 89.9%; Homeowner vacancy rate: 0.8%; Rental vacancy rate: 9.7%

HAZELTON (township). Covers a land area of 37.291 square miles and a water area of 0.035 square miles. Located at 43.09° N. Lat; 83.99° W. Long.
Population: 2,071; Growth (since 2000): -6.1%; Density: 55.5 persons per square mile; Race: 97.2% White, 0.3% Black/African American, 0.6% Asian, 0.1% American Indian/Alaska Native, 0.0% Native Hawaiian/Other Pacific Islander, 1.2% Two or more races, 1.2% Hispanic of any race; Average household size: 2.54; Median age: 44.1; Age under 18: 22.1%; Age 65 and over: 16.9%; Males per 100 females: 94.8
Housing: Homeownership rate: 83.5%; Homeowner vacancy rate: 1.2%; Rental vacancy rate: 9.9%

HENDERSON (CDP). Covers a land area of 3.600 square miles and a water area of 0.066 square miles. Located at 43.09° N. Lat; 84.19° W. Long. Elevation is 732 feet.
Population: 399; Growth (since 2000): n/a; Density: 110.8 persons per square mile; Race: 98.2% White, 0.3% Black/African American, 0.5% Asian, 0.3% American Indian/Alaska Native, 0.3% Native Hawaiian/Other Pacific Islander, 0.5% Two or more races, 0.5% Hispanic of any race; Average household size: 2.56; Median age: 44.6; Age under 18: 20.3%; Age 65 and over: 16.8%; Males per 100 females: 107.8
Housing: Homeownership rate: 87.8%; Homeowner vacancy rate: 4.8%; Rental vacancy rate: 20.8%

LAINGSBURG (city). Covers a land area of 1.473 square miles and a water area of 0.221 square miles. Located at 42.89° N. Lat; 84.35° W. Long. Elevation is 823 feet.
History: Laingsburg was founded in 1836 by Dr. Peter Laing, who operated a tavern here. The village was platted in 1860 when the railroad arrived.
Population: 1,283; Growth (since 2000): 4.9%; Density: 870.8 persons per square mile; Race: 96.6% White, 0.4% Black/African American, 0.4% Asian, 0.4% American Indian/Alaska Native, 0.0% Native Hawaiian/Other Pacific Islander, 1.9% Two or more races, 1.4% Hispanic of any race; Average household size: 2.77; Median age: 33.3; Age under 18: 31.6%; Age 65 and over: 9.5%; Males per 100 females: 101.1
School District(s)
Laingsburg Community Schools (PK-12)
    2012-13 Enrollment: 1,120 . . . . (517) 651-2705
Housing: Homeownership rate: 68.1%; Homeowner vacancy rate: 5.0%; Rental vacancy rate: 16.3%
Safety: Violent crime rate: 15.8 per 10,000 population; Property crime rate: 110.9 per 10,000 population

LENNON (village). Covers a land area of 0.913 square miles and a water area of 0 square miles. Located at 42.99° N. Lat; 83.93° W. Long. Elevation is 794 feet.
History: Lennon was founded by Peter Lennon, Sr., who built a grain elevator here and persuaded the Grand Trunk Railroad to run its line through the town.
Population: 511; Growth (since 2000): -1.2%; Density: 559.5 persons per square mile; Race: 94.5% White, 0.4% Black/African American, 1.0% Asian, 2.3% American Indian/Alaska Native, 0.0% Native Hawaiian/Other Pacific Islander, 1.0% Two or more races, 3.5% Hispanic of any race; Average household size: 2.80; Median age: 40.5; Age under 18: 24.3%; Age 65 and over: 13.7%; Males per 100 females: 107.7
Housing: Homeownership rate: 82.4%; Homeowner vacancy rate: 2.6%; Rental vacancy rate: 3.0%
Safety: Violent crime rate: 0.0 per 10,000 population; Property crime rate: 200.0 per 10,000 population

MIDDLEBURY (township). Covers a land area of 24.757 square miles and a water area of 0.085 square miles. Located at 43.00° N. Lat; 84.32° W. Long.
Population: 1,510; Growth (since 2000): 1.3%; Density: 61.0 persons per square mile; Race: 97.3% White, 0.5% Black/African American, 0.1% Asian, 0.2% American Indian/Alaska Native, 0.0% Native Hawaiian/Other Pacific Islander, 0.7% Two or more races, 3.4% Hispanic of any race; Average household size: 2.50; Median age: 42.6; Age under 18: 22.1%; Age 65 and over: 15.0%; Males per 100 females: 103.5
Housing: Homeownership rate: 86.1%; Homeowner vacancy rate: 0.9%; Rental vacancy rate: 5.6%

MIDDLETOWN (CDP). Covers a land area of 0.468 square miles and a water area of 0.011 square miles. Located at 42.99° N. Lat; 84.14° W. Long. Elevation is 745 feet.
Population: 897; Growth (since 2000): -7.1%; Density: 1,917.8 persons per square mile; Race: 97.5% White, 0.8% Black/African American, 0.1% Asian, 0.0% American Indian/Alaska Native, 0.0% Native Hawaiian/Other Pacific Islander, 0.8% Two or more races, 2.5% Hispanic of any race; Average household size: 2.48; Median age: 38.2; Age under 18: 24.0%; Age 65 and over: 14.9%; Males per 100 females: 98.0
Housing: Homeownership rate: 74.5%; Homeowner vacancy rate: 2.8%; Rental vacancy rate: 7.9%

MORRICE (village). Covers a land area of 1.302 square miles and a water area of 0.082 square miles. Located at 42.84° N. Lat; 84.18° W. Long. Elevation is 889 feet.
Population: 927; Growth (since 2000): 5.1%; Density: 711.8 persons per square mile; Race: 97.0% White, 0.1% Black/African American, 0.1% Asian, 0.6% American Indian/Alaska Native, 0.0% Native Hawaiian/Other Pacific Islander, 1.8% Two or more races, 1.6% Hispanic of any race; Average household size: 2.53; Median age: 32.6; Age under 18: 28.7%; Age 65 and over: 12.4%; Males per 100 females: 103.3
School District(s)
Morrice Area Schools (PK-12)
    2012-13 Enrollment: 622 . . . . (517) 625-3142
Housing: Homeownership rate: 79.0%; Homeowner vacancy rate: 6.4%; Rental vacancy rate: 2.5%
Safety: Violent crime rate: 0.0 per 10,000 population; Property crime rate: 122.4 per 10,000 population

NEW HAVEN (township). Covers a land area of 35.585 square miles and a water area of 0.154 square miles. Located at 43.09° N. Lat; 84.10° W. Long. Elevation is 709 feet.
Population: 1,329; Growth (since 2000): 2.8%; Density: 37.3 persons per square mile; Race: 98.4% White, 0.0% Black/African American, 0.2% Asian, 0.3% American Indian/Alaska Native, 0.0% Native Hawaiian/Other Pacific Islander, 1.0% Two or more races, 0.9% Hispanic of any race; Average household size: 2.66; Median age: 46.3; Age under 18: 21.1%; Age 65 and over: 15.8%; Males per 100 females: 103.2
Housing: Homeownership rate: 90.2%; Homeowner vacancy rate: 1.7%; Rental vacancy rate: 5.7%

NEW LOTHROP (village). Covers a land area of 0.809 square miles and a water area of 0.003 square miles. Located at 43.12° N. Lat; 83.97° W. Long. Elevation is 696 feet.
Population: 581; Growth (since 2000): -3.6%; Density: 718.2 persons per square mile; Race: 95.4% White, 0.2% Black/African American, 1.5% Asian, 0.2% American Indian/Alaska Native, 0.0% Native Hawaiian/Other Pacific Islander, 1.7% Two or more races, 2.8% Hispanic of any race; Average household size: 2.50; Median age: 40.4; Age under 18: 22.9%; Age 65 and over: 15.5%; Males per 100 females: 91.7
School District(s)
New Lothrop Area Public Schools (PK-12)
    2012-13 Enrollment: 912 . . . . (810) 638-5091
Housing: Homeownership rate: 71.1%; Homeowner vacancy rate: 2.3%; Rental vacancy rate: 11.8%

OWOSSO (charter township). Covers a land area of 31.606 square miles and a water area of 0.545 square miles. Located at 43.00° N. Lat; 84.23° W. Long. Elevation is 728 feet.
History: Thomas E. Dewey born here. Incorporated 1859.
Population: 4,821; Growth (since 2000): 3.2%; Density: 152.5 persons per square mile; Race: 97.4% White, 0.1% Black/African American, 0.5% Asian, 0.4% American Indian/Alaska Native, 0.0% Native Hawaiian/Other Pacific Islander, 1.0% Two or more races, 2.0% Hispanic of any race; Average household size: 2.37; Median age: 46.4; Age under 18: 20.8%; Age 65 and over: 20.7%; Males per 100 females: 94.8; Marriage status: 27.7% never married, 57.1% now married, 0.3% separated, 6.5% widowed, 8.7% divorced; Foreign born: 2.6%; Speak English only: 97.6%; With disability: 14.3%; Veterans: 10.0%; Ancestry: 27.8% German, 11.3% English, 10.7% Irish, 5.7% American, 4.7% Polish
Employment: 9.0% management, business, and financial, 1.7% computer, engineering, and science, 6.6% education, legal, community service, arts, and media, 8.6% healthcare practitioners, 23.8% service, 20.6% sales and office, 16.0% natural resources, construction, and maintenance, 13.6% production, transportation, and material moving

Income: Per capita: $26,182; Median household: $47,083; Average household: $66,020; Households with income of $100,000 or more: 16.5%; Poverty rate: 14.1%
Educational Attainment: High school diploma or higher: 90.1%; Bachelor's degree or higher: 14.1%; Graduate/professional degree or higher: 7.3%

School District(s)
Owosso Public Schools (PK-12)
    2012-13 Enrollment: 3,235 . . . . (989) 723-8131
Shiawassee Regional ESD (PK-12)
    2012-13 Enrollment: 476 . . . . (989) 743-3471
Four-year College(s)
Baker College of Owosso (Private, Not-for-profit)
    Fall 2013 Enrollment: 2,828 . . . . (989) 729-3300
    2013-14 Tuition: In-state $8,100; Out-of-state $8,100
Housing: Homeownership rate: 80.1%; Median home value: $101,200; Median year structure built: 1977; Homeowner vacancy rate: 2.3%; Median gross rent: $568 per month; Rental vacancy rate: 8.7%
Health Insurance: 90.6% have insurance; 71.7% have private insurance; 38.0% have public insurance; 9.4% do not have insurance; 4.9% of children under 18 do not have insurance
Hospitals: Memorial Healthcare (143 beds)
Newspapers: Argus-Press (daily circulation 11200); Sunday Independent (weekly circulation 34000)
Transportation: Commute: 96.0% car, 0.0% public transportation, 0.3% walk, 2.9% work from home; Median travel time to work: 28.5 minutes; Amtrak: Train service available.

OWOSSO (city). Covers a land area of 5.228 square miles and a water area of 0.142 square miles. Located at 43.00° N. Lat; 84.18° W. Long. Elevation is 728 feet.
History: Owosso, established on the Shiawassee River, began as a lumber town. Diversified industry replaced lumbering at the turn of the century. Owosso was the home of writer James Oliver Curwood, whose studio and home were both of architectural interest.
Population: 15,194; Growth (since 2000): -3.3%; Density: 2,906.3 persons per square mile; Race: 95.7% White, 0.8% Black/African American, 0.3% Asian, 0.5% American Indian/Alaska Native, 0.0% Native Hawaiian/Other Pacific Islander, 2.1% Two or more races, 3.9% Hispanic of any race; Average household size: 2.41; Median age: 34.8; Age under 18: 25.2%; Age 65 and over: 12.8%; Males per 100 females: 93.7; Marriage status: 32.7% never married, 46.2% now married, 2.6% separated, 6.3% widowed, 14.9% divorced; Foreign born: 0.8%; Speak English only: 97.7%; With disability: 16.2%; Veterans: 8.8%; Ancestry: 27.5% German, 14.0% Irish, 13.8% English, 6.5% Polish, 6.3% American
Employment: 7.5% management, business, and financial, 2.8% computer, engineering, and science, 7.2% education, legal, community service, arts, and media, 5.6% healthcare practitioners, 24.1% service, 24.6% sales and office, 8.8% natural resources, construction, and maintenance, 19.5% production, transportation, and material moving
Income: Per capita: $18,309; Median household: $34,960; Average household: $43,678; Households with income of $100,000 or more: 6.0%; Poverty rate: 22.9%
Educational Attainment: High school diploma or higher: 90.1%; Bachelor's degree or higher: 13.5%; Graduate/professional degree or higher: 4.3%

School District(s)
Owosso Public Schools (PK-12)
    2012-13 Enrollment: 3,235 . . . . (989) 723-8131
Shiawassee Regional ESD (PK-12)
    2012-13 Enrollment: 476 . . . . (989) 743-3471
Four-year College(s)
Baker College of Owosso (Private, Not-for-profit)
    Fall 2013 Enrollment: 2,828 . . . . (989) 729-3300
    2013-14 Tuition: In-state $8,100; Out-of-state $8,100
Housing: Homeownership rate: 62.0%; Median home value: $81,700; Median year structure built: 1952; Homeowner vacancy rate: 3.9%; Median gross rent: $609 per month; Rental vacancy rate: 9.8%
Health Insurance: 83.2% have insurance; 57.9% have private insurance; 39.1% have public insurance; 16.8% do not have insurance; 3.6% of children under 18 do not have insurance
Hospitals: Memorial Healthcare (143 beds)
Safety: Violent crime rate: 37.3 per 10,000 population; Property crime rate: 293.0 per 10,000 population

Newspapers: Argus-Press (daily circulation 11200); Sunday Independent (weekly circulation 34000)
Transportation: Commute: 90.1% car, 0.3% public transportation, 4.4% walk, 3.5% work from home; Median travel time to work: 21.4 minutes; Amtrak: Train service available.
Additional Information Contacts
City of Owosso . . . . (989) 725-0599
    http://ci.owosso.mi.us

PERRY (city). Covers a land area of 2.919 square miles and a water area of 0.255 square miles. Located at 42.83° N. Lat; 84.22° W. Long. Elevation is 889 feet.
History: Perry was founded in 1850 by William P. Laing, who opened a store here. The village was named for Oliver Hazard Perry, American naval hero.
Population: 2,188; Growth (since 2000): 6.0%; Density: 749.6 persons per square mile; Race: 96.8% White, 0.3% Black/African American, 0.3% Asian, 0.4% American Indian/Alaska Native, 0.1% Native Hawaiian/Other Pacific Islander, 1.6% Two or more races, 1.7% Hispanic of any race; Average household size: 2.66; Median age: 34.1; Age under 18: 27.7%; Age 65 and over: 9.0%; Males per 100 females: 93.5
School District(s)
Perry Public Schools (PK-12)
    2012-13 Enrollment: 1,377 . . . . (517) 625-3108
Housing: Homeownership rate: 66.4%; Homeowner vacancy rate: 2.3%; Rental vacancy rate: 12.6%
Safety: Violent crime rate: 9.5 per 10,000 population; Property crime rate: 118.8 per 10,000 population
Additional Information Contacts
City of Perry . . . . (517) 625-6155
    http://www.perry.mi.us

PERRY (township). Covers a land area of 31.139 square miles and a water area of 0.489 square miles. Located at 42.80° N. Lat; 84.19° W. Long. Elevation is 889 feet.
Population: 4,327; Growth (since 2000): -2.5%; Density: 139.0 persons per square mile; Race: 96.5% White, 0.5% Black/African American, 0.3% Asian, 0.6% American Indian/Alaska Native, 0.0% Native Hawaiian/Other Pacific Islander, 1.7% Two or more races, 1.6% Hispanic of any race; Average household size: 2.75; Median age: 36.6; Age under 18: 28.1%; Age 65 and over: 10.8%; Males per 100 females: 101.5; Marriage status: 28.9% never married, 53.7% now married, 1.7% separated, 5.7% widowed, 11.7% divorced; Foreign born: 0.2%; Speak English only: 98.5%; With disability: 15.0%; Veterans: 10.4%; Ancestry: 26.5% German, 14.7% Irish, 8.5% English, 8.2% American, 6.0% French
Employment: 9.9% management, business, and financial, 5.0% computer, engineering, and science, 7.1% education, legal, community service, arts, and media, 8.5% healthcare practitioners, 15.6% service, 25.7% sales and office, 14.6% natural resources, construction, and maintenance, 13.7% production, transportation, and material moving
Income: Per capita: $22,564; Median household: $53,409; Average household: $57,891; Households with income of $100,000 or more: 14.4%; Poverty rate: 19.2%
Educational Attainment: High school diploma or higher: 87.7%; Bachelor's degree or higher: 14.2%; Graduate/professional degree or higher: 6.8%
School District(s)
Perry Public Schools (PK-12)
    2012-13 Enrollment: 1,377 . . . . (517) 625-3108
Housing: Homeownership rate: 84.4%; Median home value: $113,600; Median year structure built: 1987; Homeowner vacancy rate: 3.2%; Median gross rent: $795 per month; Rental vacancy rate: 4.3%
Health Insurance: 87.3% have insurance; 65.7% have private insurance; 33.3% have public insurance; 12.7% do not have insurance; 5.5% of children under 18 do not have insurance
Transportation: Commute: 96.3% car, 0.0% public transportation, 0.0% walk, 2.8% work from home; Median travel time to work: 27.9 minutes

RUSH (township). Covers a land area of 34.901 square miles and a water area of 0.336 square miles. Located at 43.08° N. Lat; 84.23° W. Long.
History: Rush was named for Henry Rush, a settler in the area in the 1840's. The township was organized in 1850.
Population: 1,291; Growth (since 2000): -8.4%; Density: 37.0 persons per square mile; Race: 98.1% White, 0.1% Black/African American, 0.3%

Asian, 0.5% American Indian/Alaska Native, 0.1% Native Hawaiian/Other Pacific Islander, 0.8% Two or more races, 1.3% Hispanic of any race; Average household size: 2.59; Median age: 45.9; Age under 18: 20.1%; Age 65 and over: 16.5%; Males per 100 females: 101.1
Housing: Homeownership rate: 89.7%; Homeowner vacancy rate: 2.6%; Rental vacancy rate: 10.5%

SCIOTA (township). Covers a land area of 25.126 square miles and a water area of 1.683 square miles. Located at 42.91° N. Lat; 84.32° W. Long.
Population: 1,833; Growth (since 2000): 1.8%; Density: 73.0 persons per square mile; Race: 97.4% White, 0.4% Black/African American, 0.7% Asian, 0.4% American Indian/Alaska Native, 0.0% Native Hawaiian/Other Pacific Islander, 0.7% Two or more races, 2.2% Hispanic of any race; Average household size: 2.72; Median age: 42.2; Age under 18: 25.2%; Age 65 and over: 12.2%; Males per 100 females: 98.6
Housing: Homeownership rate: 92.2%; Homeowner vacancy rate: 1.6%; Rental vacancy rate: 3.6%

SHIAWASSEE (township). Covers a land area of 36.388 square miles and a water area of 0.457 square miles. Located at 42.92° N. Lat; 84.10° W. Long.
History: The name of Shiawassee is an Indian word for "the river that twists about." Settlement began here in the 1830's when Charles Bacon of Ohio formed a company to sell land.
Population: 2,840; Growth (since 2000): -2.3%; Density: 78.0 persons per square mile; Race: 97.3% White, 0.2% Black/African American, 0.2% Asian, 0.6% American Indian/Alaska Native, 0.0% Native Hawaiian/Other Pacific Islander, 1.4% Two or more races, 1.3% Hispanic of any race; Average household size: 2.73; Median age: 41.8; Age under 18: 24.1%; Age 65 and over: 12.1%; Males per 100 females: 108.2; Marriage status: 19.4% never married, 66.2% now married, 1.5% separated, 4.7% widowed, 9.8% divorced; Foreign born: 2.1%; Speak English only: 98.0%; With disability: 14.4%; Veterans: 13.8%; Ancestry: 27.1% German, 20.4% English, 11.6% Irish, 10.8% American, 5.4% Polish
Employment: 11.3% management, business, and financial, 3.4% computer, engineering, and science, 6.7% education, legal, community service, arts, and media, 5.1% healthcare practitioners, 14.7% service, 20.0% sales and office, 8.9% natural resources, construction, and maintenance, 29.9% production, transportation, and material moving
Income: Per capita: $23,256; Median household: $49,464; Average household: $61,006; Households with income of $100,000 or more: 16.3%; Poverty rate: 13.1%
Educational Attainment: High school diploma or higher: 92.7%; Bachelor's degree or higher: 13.8%; Graduate/professional degree or higher: 4.7%
Housing: Homeownership rate: 89.2%; Median home value: $122,700; Median year structure built: 1967; Homeowner vacancy rate: 2.2%; Median gross rent: $713 per month; Rental vacancy rate: 9.7%
Health Insurance: 89.7% have insurance; 72.2% have private insurance; 32.3% have public insurance; 10.3% do not have insurance; 1.8% of children under 18 do not have insurance
Transportation: Commute: 95.7% car, 0.0% public transportation, 0.5% walk, 3.7% work from home; Median travel time to work: 33.4 minutes

VENICE (township). Covers a land area of 37.442 square miles and a water area of 0.079 square miles. Located at 43.01° N. Lat; 84.00° W. Long.
Population: 2,578; Growth (since 2000): -0.4%; Density: 68.9 persons per square mile; Race: 97.2% White, 0.2% Black/African American, 0.2% Asian, 0.5% American Indian/Alaska Native, 0.2% Native Hawaiian/Other Pacific Islander, 1.3% Two or more races, 2.7% Hispanic of any race; Average household size: 2.65; Median age: 43.2; Age under 18: 23.4%; Age 65 and over: 16.4%; Males per 100 females: 100.8; Marriage status: 20.2% never married, 61.2% now married, 0.7% separated, 5.4% widowed, 13.1% divorced; Foreign born: 1.9%; Speak English only: 97.6%; With disability: 15.0%; Veterans: 7.2%; Ancestry: 24.8% German, 13.7% English, 8.7% Irish, 7.2% French, 6.5% Polish
Employment: 10.1% management, business, and financial, 0.4% computer, engineering, and science, 7.0% education, legal, community service, arts, and media, 4.3% healthcare practitioners, 15.6% service, 35.5% sales and office, 12.5% natural resources, construction, and maintenance, 14.7% production, transportation, and material moving

Income: Per capita: $23,026; Median household: $46,518; Average household: $59,602; Households with income of $100,000 or more: 11.7%; Poverty rate: 8.7%
Educational Attainment: High school diploma or higher: 92.5%; Bachelor's degree or higher: 10.7%; Graduate/professional degree or higher: 3.6%
Housing: Homeownership rate: 84.2%; Median home value: $105,100; Median year structure built: 1967; Homeowner vacancy rate: 1.3%; Median gross rent: $808 per month; Rental vacancy rate: 4.3%
Health Insurance: 90.7% have insurance; 77.4% have private insurance; 28.1% have public insurance; 9.3% do not have insurance; 2.7% of children under 18 do not have insurance
Transportation: Commute: 96.0% car, 0.4% public transportation, 1.7% walk, 1.9% work from home; Median travel time to work: 27.2 minutes

VERNON (township). Covers a land area of 33.691 square miles and a water area of 0.336 square miles. Located at 42.89° N. Lat; 83.95° W. Long. Elevation is 781 feet.
Population: 4,614; Growth (since 2000): -7.3%; Density: 137.0 persons per square mile; Race: 97.3% White, 0.2% Black/African American, 0.1% Asian, 0.5% American Indian/Alaska Native, 0.0% Native Hawaiian/Other Pacific Islander, 1.4% Two or more races, 2.1% Hispanic of any race; Average household size: 2.52; Median age: 43.6; Age under 18: 22.3%; Age 65 and over: 16.2%; Males per 100 females: 102.3; Marriage status: 21.8% never married, 61.8% now married, 0.0% separated, 6.1% widowed, 10.3% divorced; Foreign born: 0.2%; Speak English only: 98.9%; With disability: 16.2%; Veterans: 13.0%; Ancestry: 31.1% German, 17.2% Irish, 13.7% English, 10.6% American, 4.7% Scottish
Employment: 13.8% management, business, and financial, 4.1% computer, engineering, and science, 5.0% education, legal, community service, arts, and media, 4.2% healthcare practitioners, 20.8% service, 28.3% sales and office, 6.9% natural resources, construction, and maintenance, 16.9% production, transportation, and material moving
Income: Per capita: $21,656; Median household: $40,958; Average household: $52,865; Households with income of $100,000 or more: 10.7%; Poverty rate: 19.8%
Educational Attainment: High school diploma or higher: 90.3%; Bachelor's degree or higher: 8.2%; Graduate/professional degree or higher: 3.3%
School District(s)
Corunna Public Schools (PK-12)
    2012-13 Enrollment: 2,114 . . . . (989) 743-6338
Housing: Homeownership rate: 87.5%; Median home value: $114,400; Median year structure built: 1973; Homeowner vacancy rate: 2.1%; Median gross rent: $842 per month; Rental vacancy rate: 12.3%
Health Insurance: 90.1% have insurance; 71.4% have private insurance; 36.5% have public insurance; 9.9% do not have insurance; 0.3% of children under 18 do not have insurance
Transportation: Commute: 91.5% car, 1.9% public transportation, 1.0% walk, 4.4% work from home; Median travel time to work: 27.9 minutes

VERNON (village). Covers a land area of 0.688 square miles and a water area of 0.022 square miles. Located at 42.94° N. Lat; 84.03° W. Long. Elevation is 781 feet.
Population: 783; Growth (since 2000): -7.6%; Density: 1,137.8 persons per square mile; Race: 97.3% White, 0.1% Black/African American, 0.1% Asian, 0.5% American Indian/Alaska Native, 0.0% Native Hawaiian/Other Pacific Islander, 0.8% Two or more races, 2.6% Hispanic of any race; Average household size: 2.68; Median age: 38.7; Age under 18: 27.2%; Age 65 and over: 13.7%; Males per 100 females: 93.3
School District(s)
Corunna Public Schools (PK-12)
    2012-13 Enrollment: 2,114 . . . . (989) 743-6338
Housing: Homeownership rate: 83.2%; Homeowner vacancy rate: 3.6%; Rental vacancy rate: 5.8%

WOODHULL (township). Covers a land area of 25.521 square miles and a water area of 1.871 square miles. Located at 42.81° N. Lat; 84.32° W. Long.
Population: 3,810; Growth (since 2000): -1.0%; Density: 149.3 persons per square mile; Race: 96.1% White, 0.7% Black/African American, 0.3% Asian, 0.7% American Indian/Alaska Native, 0.1% Native Hawaiian/Other Pacific Islander, 1.7% Two or more races, 1.4% Hispanic of any race; Average household size: 2.60; Median age: 44.5; Age under 18: 22.4%; Age 65 and over: 13.3%; Males per 100 females: 101.2; Marriage status:

23.0% never married, 64.6% now married, 0.5% separated, 4.5% widowed, 7.9% divorced; Foreign born: 0.8%; Speak English only: 97.6%; With disability: 12.1%; Veterans: 8.8%; Ancestry: 26.8% German, 14.7% English, 12.8% Irish, 8.3% American, 6.9% Polish
Employment: 13.2% management, business, and financial, 8.3% computer, engineering, and science, 10.2% education, legal, community service, arts, and media, 5.0% healthcare practitioners, 10.8% service, 28.2% sales and office, 11.6% natural resources, construction, and maintenance, 12.8% production, transportation, and material moving
Income: Per capita: $29,504; Median household: $65,709; Average household: $75,162; Households with income of $100,000 or more: 26.1%; Poverty rate: 8.9%
Educational Attainment: High school diploma or higher: 94.3%; Bachelor's degree or higher: 24.3%; Graduate/professional degree or higher: 8.0%
Housing: Homeownership rate: 91.3%; Median home value: $163,700; Median year structure built: 1978; Homeowner vacancy rate: 2.1%; Median gross rent: $835 per month; Rental vacancy rate: 11.2%
Health Insurance: 88.5% have insurance; 75.2% have private insurance; 27.5% have public insurance; 11.5% do not have insurance; 2.4% of children under 18 do not have insurance
Transportation: Commute: 93.3% car, 0.0% public transportation, 0.0% walk, 4.3% work from home; Median travel time to work: 29.3 minutes

Tuscola County

Located in eastern Michigan; bounded on the northwest by Saginaw Bay; drained by the Cass River and its affluents. Covers a land area of 803.127 square miles, a water area of 110.784 square miles, and is located in the Eastern Time Zone at 43.49° N. Lat., 83.44° W. Long. The county was founded in 1840. County seat is Caro.

Weather Station: Caro Regional Center — Elevation: 669 feet

	Jan	Feb	Mar	Apr	May	Jun	Jul	Aug	Sep	Oct	Nov	Dec
High	30	33	43	58	70	79	83	81	73	60	47	34
Low	15	15	24	34	44	53	59	57	50	39	31	21
Precip	1.9	1.4	2.0	3.2	3.0	3.5	3.1	3.1	4.3	3.0	2.8	2.1
Snow	11.6	7.3	5.2	1.0	tr	0.0	0.0	0.0	0.0	0.1	2.0	9.6

High and Low temperatures in degrees Fahrenheit; Precipitation and Snow in inches

Population: 55,729; Growth (since 2000): -4.4%; Density: 69.4 persons per square mile; Race: 96.1% White, 1.1% Black/African American, 0.3% Asian, 0.5% American Indian/Alaska Native, 0.0% Native Hawaiian/Other Pacific Islander, 1.2% two or more races, 2.8% Hispanic of any race; Average household size: 2.52; Median age: 41.7; Age under 18: 23.5%; Age 65 and over: 15.8%; Males per 100 females: 100.6; Marriage status: 25.7% never married, 56.6% now married, 1.2% separated, 6.7% widowed, 11.0% divorced; Foreign born: 0.8%; Speak English only: 97.3%; With disability: 17.5%; Veterans: 10.5%; Ancestry: 32.8% German, 12.6% Irish, 12.0% English, 9.5% Polish, 7.3% American
Religion: Six largest groups: 16.3% Lutheran, 8.5% Catholicism, 7.0% Methodist/Pietist, 2.3% Non-denominational Protestant, 2.3% Holiness, 1.2% Pentecostal
Economy: Unemployment rate: 6.2%; Leading industries: 18.2% retail trade; 12.7% construction; 12.5% other services (except public administration); Farms: 1,322 totaling 325,372 acres; Company size: 0 employ 1,000 or more persons, 0 employ 500 to 999 persons, 16 employ 100 to 499 persons, 853 employ less than 100 persons; Business ownership: n/a women-owned, n/a Black-owned, n/a Hispanic-owned, 37 Asian-owned
Employment: 9.6% management, business, and financial, 2.7% computer, engineering, and science, 7.7% education, legal, community service, arts, and media, 5.9% healthcare practitioners, 21.3% service, 23.4% sales and office, 11.4% natural resources, construction, and maintenance, 18.0% production, transportation, and material moving
Income: Per capita: $20,767; Median household: $43,039; Average household: $52,430; Households with income of $100,000 or more: 11.5%; Poverty rate: 15.7%
Educational Attainment: High school diploma or higher: 86.8%; Bachelor's degree or higher: 12.7%; Graduate/professional degree or higher: 4.0%
Housing: Homeownership rate: 82.8%; Median home value: $95,700; Median year structure built: 1968; Homeowner vacancy rate: 2.4%; Median gross rent: $642 per month; Rental vacancy rate: 10.4%

Vital Statistics: Birth rate: 94.0 per 10,000 population; Death rate: 111.9 per 10,000 population; Age-adjusted cancer mortality rate: 188.7 deaths per 100,000 population
Health Insurance: 87.5% have insurance; 67.1% have private insurance; 38.4% have public insurance; 12.5% do not have insurance; 4.2% of children under 18 do not have insurance
Health Care: Physicians: 7.5 per 10,000 population; Hospital beds: 43.9 per 10,000 population; Hospital admissions: 252.9 per 10,000 population
Air Quality Index: 96.2% good, 3.8% moderate, 0.0% unhealthy for sensitive individuals, 0.0% unhealthy (percent of days)
Transportation: Commute: 93.1% car, 0.1% public transportation, 2.1% walk, 3.7% work from home; Median travel time to work: 30.2 minutes
Presidential Election: 44.0% Obama, 54.8% Romney (2012)
National and State Parks: Cass City State Game Area; Deford State Game Area; Murphy Lake State Game Area; Tuscola State Game Area; Vassar State Game Area
Additional Information Contacts
Tuscola Government . . . . (989) 672-3700
  http://www.tuscolacounty.org

Tuscola County Communities

AKRON (township). Covers a land area of 52.748 square miles and a water area of 4.114 square miles. Located at 43.63° N. Lat; 83.52° W. Long. Elevation is 640 feet.
Population: 1,503; Growth (since 2000): -5.4%; Density: 28.5 persons per square mile; Race: 96.9% White, 0.1% Black/African American, 0.1% Asian, 0.4% American Indian/Alaska Native, 0.0% Native Hawaiian/Other Pacific Islander, 1.1% Two or more races, 3.9% Hispanic of any race; Average household size: 2.55; Median age: 41.5; Age under 18: 23.1%; Age 65 and over: 17.4%; Males per 100 females: 99.9
School District(s)
Akron-Fairgrove Schools (KG-12)
  2012-13 Enrollment: 277 . . . . (989) 693-6163
Housing: Homeownership rate: 87.2%; Homeowner vacancy rate: 3.2%; Rental vacancy rate: 9.6%

AKRON (village). Covers a land area of 0.942 square miles and a water area of 0 square miles. Located at 43.57° N. Lat; 83.51° W. Long. Elevation is 640 feet.
History: Akron was settled by Charles H. Beach in 1854, and first called Beach's Corners. When the post office was established, it was called Akron, after the township, which had been named for Akron, Ohio. The village was platted in 1882.
Population: 402; Growth (since 2000): -12.8%; Density: 426.8 persons per square mile; Race: 96.3% White, 0.0% Black/African American, 0.0% Asian, 0.2% American Indian/Alaska Native, 0.0% Native Hawaiian/Other Pacific Islander, 3.0% Two or more races, 6.2% Hispanic of any race; Average household size: 2.48; Median age: 34.8; Age under 18: 27.9%; Age 65 and over: 15.7%; Males per 100 females: 94.2
School District(s)
Akron-Fairgrove Schools (KG-12)
  2012-13 Enrollment: 277 . . . . (989) 693-6163
Housing: Homeownership rate: 76.9%; Homeowner vacancy rate: 2.4%; Rental vacancy rate: 9.5%
Safety: Violent crime rate: 25.4 per 10,000 population; Property crime rate: 152.3 per 10,000 population

ALMER (township). Covers a land area of 34.091 square miles and a water area of 0.244 square miles. Located at 43.55° N. Lat; 83.41° W. Long.
Population: 3,101; Growth (since 2000): 2.6%; Density: 91.0 persons per square mile; Race: 96.3% White, 0.7% Black/African American, 0.5% Asian, 0.4% American Indian/Alaska Native, 0.1% Native Hawaiian/Other Pacific Islander, 1.5% Two or more races, 2.5% Hispanic of any race; Average household size: 2.30; Median age: 45.3; Age under 18: 20.7%; Age 65 and over: 23.9%; Males per 100 females: 89.4; Marriage status: 17.1% never married, 64.9% now married, 0.0% separated, 7.0% widowed, 11.0% divorced; Foreign born: 2.4%; Speak English only: 94.4%; With disability: 14.9%; Veterans: 10.3%; Ancestry: 34.7% German, 18.1% English, 10.6% Irish, 9.7% Polish, 8.9% French
Employment: 14.0% management, business, and financial, 1.4% computer, engineering, and science, 5.5% education, legal, community service, arts, and media, 6.6% healthcare practitioners, 9.1% service,

33.7% sales and office, 19.0% natural resources, construction, and maintenance, 10.7% production, transportation, and material moving
Income: Per capita: $27,768; Median household: $57,589; Average household: $66,608; Households with income of $100,000 or more: 24.4%; Poverty rate: 22.9%
Educational Attainment: High school diploma or higher: 85.9%; Bachelor's degree or higher: 19.4%; Graduate/professional degree or higher: 5.6%
Housing: Homeownership rate: 73.9%; Median home value: $97,000; Median year structure built: 1970; Homeowner vacancy rate: 3.3%; Median gross rent: $967 per month; Rental vacancy rate: 7.8%
Health Insurance: 91.4% have insurance; 67.0% have private insurance; 44.4% have public insurance; 8.6% do not have insurance; 0.0% of children under 18 do not have insurance
Transportation: Commute: 95.7% car, 0.0% public transportation, 0.5% walk, 3.0% work from home; Median travel time to work: 29.8 minutes

ARBELA (township).
Covers a land area of 33.458 square miles and a water area of 0.043 square miles. Located at 43.26° N. Lat; 83.64° W. Long.
Population: 3,070; Growth (since 2000): -4.6%; Density: 91.8 persons per square mile; Race: 96.5% White, 0.7% Black/African American, 0.2% Asian, 0.5% American Indian/Alaska Native, 0.0% Native Hawaiian/Other Pacific Islander, 1.6% Two or more races, 1.9% Hispanic of any race; Average household size: 2.69; Median age: 42.5; Age under 18: 22.5%; Age 65 and over: 13.8%; Males per 100 females: 103.2; Marriage status: 21.5% never married, 64.0% now married, 0.7% separated, 4.4% widowed, 10.1% divorced; Foreign born: 1.2%; Speak English only: 96.3%; With disability: 12.2%; Veterans: 9.1%; Ancestry: 30.6% German, 26.3% Irish, 15.9% English, 9.3% American, 7.0% French
Employment: 8.8% management, business, and financial, 1.1% computer, engineering, and science, 5.1% education, legal, community service, arts, and media, 3.5% healthcare practitioners, 17.6% service, 31.2% sales and office, 12.5% natural resources, construction, and maintenance, 20.2% production, transportation, and material moving
Income: Per capita: $20,514; Median household: $45,972; Average household: $54,386; Households with income of $100,000 or more: 13.6%; Poverty rate: 11.6%
Educational Attainment: High school diploma or higher: 86.5%; Bachelor's degree or higher: 10.4%; Graduate/professional degree or higher: 4.5%
Housing: Homeownership rate: 90.1%; Median home value: $102,900; Median year structure built: 1974; Homeowner vacancy rate: 2.0%; Median gross rent: $1,020 per month; Rental vacancy rate: 6.6%
Health Insurance: 91.6% have insurance; 74.9% have private insurance; 33.1% have public insurance; 8.4% do not have insurance; 1.7% of children under 18 do not have insurance
Transportation: Commute: 96.4% car, 0.0% public transportation, 0.2% walk, 2.8% work from home; Median travel time to work: 46.7 minutes

CARO (city).
County seat. Covers a land area of 2.789 square miles and a water area of 0.013 square miles. Located at 43.49° N. Lat; 83.40° W. Long. Elevation is 725 feet.
History: Caro began as a logging camp in 1847. First called Centervillle and later Tuscola Center, the name of Caro was suggested as a form of Egypt's Cairo. Caro developed as the center of an area producing sugar beets, potatoes, and grain. A beet-sugar refinery was opened here.
Population: 4,229; Growth (since 2000): 2.0%; Density: 1,516.4 persons per square mile; Race: 95.5% White, 0.7% Black/African American, 0.8% Asian, 0.4% American Indian/Alaska Native, 0.0% Native Hawaiian/Other Pacific Islander, 1.5% Two or more races, 5.3% Hispanic of any race; Average household size: 2.22; Median age: 39.6; Age under 18: 21.8%; Age 65 and over: 18.8%; Males per 100 females: 86.3; Marriage status: 35.8% never married, 42.6% now married, 1.9% separated, 9.4% widowed, 12.3% divorced; Foreign born: 1.3%; Speak English only: 94.7%; With disability: 21.1%; Veterans: 9.7%; Ancestry: 26.8% German, 11.3% Polish, 11.2% Irish, 8.9% English, 6.6% French
Employment: 5.1% management, business, and financial, 3.6% computer, engineering, and science, 19.8% education, legal, community service, arts, and media, 3.9% healthcare practitioners, 30.8% service, 24.5% sales and office, 4.3% natural resources, construction, and maintenance, 8.0% production, transportation, and material moving
Income: Per capita: $20,359; Median household: $32,639; Average household: $44,983; Households with income of $100,000 or more: 10.2%; Poverty rate: 24.3%

Educational Attainment: High school diploma or higher: 84.6%; Bachelor's degree or higher: 17.2%; Graduate/professional degree or higher: 8.4%
School District(s)
Caro Community Schools (PK-12)
    2012-13 Enrollment: 1,855 . . . . (989) 673-3160
Tuscola ISD (PK-12)
    2012-13 Enrollment: 377. . . . . (989) 673-2144
Housing: Homeownership rate: 59.3%; Median home value: $81,000; Median year structure built: 1962; Homeowner vacancy rate: 3.8%; Median gross rent: $590 per month; Rental vacancy rate: 8.6%
Health Insurance: 86.1% have insurance; 58.8% have private insurance; 44.7% have public insurance; 13.9% do not have insurance; 7.9% of children under 18 do not have insurance
Hospitals: Caro Community Hospital (25 beds)
Safety: Violent crime rate: 62.9 per 10,000 population; Property crime rate: 379.7 per 10,000 population
Newspapers: Tuscola County Advertiser (weekly circulation 10000)
Transportation: Commute: 89.7% car, 0.0% public transportation, 5.7% walk, 2.7% work from home; Median travel time to work: 23.8 minutes
Additional Information Contacts
City of Caro . . . . (989) 673-2226
    http://www.carocity.net

CASS CITY (village).
Covers a land area of 1.777 square miles and a water area of 0.006 square miles. Located at 43.60° N. Lat; 83.18° W. Long. Elevation is 745 feet.
History: Cass City grew up around a lumber mill started in the early 1850's. The town was named for the Cass River, which had been named for General Lewis Cass, territorial governor of Michigan.
Population: 2,428; Growth (since 2000): -8.1%; Density: 1,366.3 persons per square mile; Race: 96.9% White, 0.2% Black/African American, 0.5% Asian, 0.5% American Indian/Alaska Native, 0.0% Native Hawaiian/Other Pacific Islander, 1.7% Two or more races, 2.5% Hispanic of any race; Average household size: 2.26; Median age: 43.7; Age under 18: 21.9%; Age 65 and over: 22.9%; Males per 100 females: 88.7
School District(s)
Cass City Public Schools (PK-12)
    2012-13 Enrollment: 1,060 . . . . (989) 872-2200
Housing: Homeownership rate: 75.3%; Homeowner vacancy rate: 4.8%; Rental vacancy rate: 18.3%
Hospitals: Hills & Dales General Hospital (65 beds)
Safety: Violent crime rate: 12.6 per 10,000 population; Property crime rate: 261.4 per 10,000 population
Newspapers: Cass City Chronicle (weekly circulation 3800)

COLUMBIA (township).
Covers a land area of 35.978 square miles and a water area of 0 square miles. Located at 43.63° N. Lat; 83.41° W. Long.
Population: 1,284; Growth (since 2000): -9.5%; Density: 35.7 persons per square mile; Race: 97.2% White, 0.0% Black/African American, 0.2% Asian, 0.2% American Indian/Alaska Native, 0.2% Native Hawaiian/Other Pacific Islander, 0.8% Two or more races, 3.0% Hispanic of any race; Average household size: 2.50; Median age: 40.4; Age under 18: 24.1%; Age 65 and over: 15.9%; Males per 100 females: 97.2
Housing: Homeownership rate: 89.1%; Homeowner vacancy rate: 0.4%; Rental vacancy rate: 16.2%

DAYTON (township).
Covers a land area of 35.601 square miles and a water area of 0.518 square miles. Located at 43.37° N. Lat; 83.27° W. Long. Elevation is 738 feet.
Population: 1,848; Growth (since 2000): -1.1%; Density: 51.9 persons per square mile; Race: 94.7% White, 2.8% Black/African American, 0.2% Asian, 0.5% American Indian/Alaska Native, 0.0% Native Hawaiian/Other Pacific Islander, 1.3% Two or more races, 1.4% Hispanic of any race; Average household size: 2.57; Median age: 44.7; Age under 18: 23.1%; Age 65 and over: 18.4%; Males per 100 females: 107.6
Housing: Homeownership rate: 88.9%; Homeowner vacancy rate: 3.3%; Rental vacancy rate: 16.8%

DEFORD (unincorporated postal area)
ZCTA: 48729
    Covers a land area of 43.373 square miles and a water area of 0.979 square miles. Located at 43.50° N. Lat; 83.17° W. Long. Elevation is 741 feet.

Population: 1,586; Growth (since 2000): -1.6%; Density: 36.6 persons per square mile; Race: 98.2% White, 0.0% Black/African American, 0.0% Asian, 0.3% American Indian/Alaska Native, 0.0% Native Hawaiian/Other Pacific Islander, 1.3% Two or more races, 0.9% Hispanic of any race; Average household size: 2.67; Median age: 42.3; Age under 18: 25.0%; Age 65 and over: 13.6%; Males per 100 females: 99.7

Housing: Homeownership rate: 87.4%; Homeowner vacancy rate: 1.9%; Rental vacancy rate: 7.4%

DENMARK (township).
Covers a land area of 35.275 square miles and a water area of 0.018 square miles. Located at 43.43° N. Lat; 83.63° W. Long.

Population: 3,068; Growth (since 2000): -5.6%; Density: 87.0 persons per square mile; Race: 96.5% White, 0.5% Black/African American, 1.2% Asian, 0.4% American Indian/Alaska Native, 0.0% Native Hawaiian/Other Pacific Islander, 0.5% Two or more races, 3.8% Hispanic of any race; Average household size: 2.43; Median age: 41.7; Age under 18: 22.8%; Age 65 and over: 16.3%; Males per 100 females: 97.4; Marriage status: 22.3% never married, 57.4% now married, 0.5% separated, 7.1% widowed, 13.2% divorced; Foreign born: 0.7%; Speak English only: 94.9%; With disability: 17.9%; Veterans: 12.2%; Ancestry: 52.6% German, 11.7% English, 7.0% French, 6.6% Irish, 6.3% Polish

Employment: 19.7% management, business, and financial, 3.8% computer, engineering, and science, 7.8% education, legal, community service, arts, and media, 3.8% healthcare practitioners, 15.1% service, 27.0% sales and office, 9.7% natural resources, construction, and maintenance, 13.1% production, transportation, and material moving

Income: Per capita: $25,684; Median household: $45,658; Average household: $57,250; Households with income of $100,000 or more: 12.1%; Poverty rate: 11.3%

Educational Attainment: High school diploma or higher: 91.2%; Bachelor's degree or higher: 19.2%; Graduate/professional degree or higher: 4.8%

Housing: Homeownership rate: 82.9%; Median home value: $110,800; Median year structure built: 1968; Homeowner vacancy rate: 3.1%; Median gross rent: $529 per month; Rental vacancy rate: 12.0%

Health Insurance: 91.6% have insurance; 78.1% have private insurance; 33.2% have public insurance; 8.4% do not have insurance; 1.9% of children under 18 do not have insurance

Transportation: Commute: 94.7% car, 0.0% public transportation, 1.5% walk, 2.8% work from home; Median travel time to work: 23.2 minutes

ELKLAND (township).
Covers a land area of 35.002 square miles and a water area of 0.572 square miles. Located at 43.63° N. Lat; 83.17° W. Long.

Population: 3,528; Growth (since 2000): -3.6%; Density: 100.8 persons per square mile; Race: 97.2% White, 0.3% Black/African American, 0.3% Asian, 0.4% American Indian/Alaska Native, 0.0% Native Hawaiian/Other Pacific Islander, 1.6% Two or more races, 2.2% Hispanic of any race; Average household size: 2.39; Median age: 42.6; Age under 18: 23.4%; Age 65 and over: 20.4%; Males per 100 females: 94.8; Marriage status: 26.9% never married, 54.6% now married, 1.0% separated, 8.4% widowed, 10.1% divorced; Foreign born: 1.3%; Speak English only: 97.3%; With disability: 16.3%; Veterans: 13.3%; Ancestry: 40.3% German, 16.0% Polish, 13.9% English, 11.4% Irish, 7.8% American

Employment: 10.6% management, business, and financial, 0.8% computer, engineering, and science, 6.9% education, legal, community service, arts, and media, 5.9% healthcare practitioners, 20.1% service, 25.9% sales and office, 11.9% natural resources, construction, and maintenance, 18.0% production, transportation, and material moving

Income: Per capita: $21,553; Median household: $40,742; Average household: $51,567; Households with income of $100,000 or more: 12.5%; Poverty rate: 13.8%

Educational Attainment: High school diploma or higher: 87.3%; Bachelor's degree or higher: 14.0%; Graduate/professional degree or higher: 3.9%

Housing: Homeownership rate: 77.9%; Median home value: $84,900; Median year structure built: 1965; Homeowner vacancy rate: 3.9%; Median gross rent: $581 per month; Rental vacancy rate: 15.5%

Health Insurance: 92.5% have insurance; 75.5% have private insurance; 37.9% have public insurance; 7.5% do not have insurance; 0.0% of children under 18 do not have insurance

Transportation: Commute: 93.2% car, 0.0% public transportation, 6.6% walk, 0.3% work from home; Median travel time to work: 23.6 minutes

ELLINGTON (township).
Covers a land area of 35.439 square miles and a water area of 0.224 square miles. Located at 43.54° N. Lat; 83.28° W. Long. Elevation is 787 feet.

Population: 1,332; Growth (since 2000): 2.1%; Density: 37.6 persons per square mile; Race: 98.5% White, 0.0% Black/African American, 0.0% Asian, 0.2% American Indian/Alaska Native, 0.1% Native Hawaiian/Other Pacific Islander, 0.8% Two or more races, 2.6% Hispanic of any race; Average household size: 2.60; Median age: 44.3; Age under 18: 21.9%; Age 65 and over: 15.1%; Males per 100 females: 98.5

Housing: Homeownership rate: 86.6%; Homeowner vacancy rate: 2.0%; Rental vacancy rate: 4.2%

ELMWOOD (township).
Covers a land area of 35.398 square miles and a water area of 0.155 square miles. Located at 43.63° N. Lat; 83.28° W. Long. Elevation is 768 feet.

Population: 1,207; Growth (since 2000): -0.5%; Density: 34.1 persons per square mile; Race: 95.8% White, 0.5% Black/African American, 0.2% Asian, 0.3% American Indian/Alaska Native, 0.0% Native Hawaiian/Other Pacific Islander, 1.2% Two or more races, 5.0% Hispanic of any race; Average household size: 2.52; Median age: 40.9; Age under 18: 24.8%; Age 65 and over: 16.9%; Males per 100 females: 106.0

Housing: Homeownership rate: 80.5%; Homeowner vacancy rate: 2.0%; Rental vacancy rate: 4.0%

FAIRGROVE (township).
Covers a land area of 35.265 square miles and a water area of 0.053 square miles. Located at 43.52° N. Lat; 83.52° W. Long. Elevation is 659 feet.

Population: 1,579; Growth (since 2000): -9.7%; Density: 44.8 persons per square mile; Race: 96.4% White, 0.6% Black/African American, 0.1% Asian, 0.6% American Indian/Alaska Native, 0.0% Native Hawaiian/Other Pacific Islander, 1.6% Two or more races, 4.4% Hispanic of any race; Average household size: 2.47; Median age: 40.4; Age under 18: 25.3%; Age 65 and over: 15.1%; Males per 100 females: 100.6

School District(s)

Akron-Fairgrove Schools (KG-12)
    2012-13 Enrollment: 277. . . . . (989) 693-6163

Housing: Homeownership rate: 82.9%; Homeowner vacancy rate: 1.7%; Rental vacancy rate: 9.6%

FAIRGROVE (village).
Covers a land area of 1.121 square miles and a water area of 0 square miles. Located at 43.52° N. Lat; 83.54° W. Long. Elevation is 659 feet.

Population: 563; Growth (since 2000): -10.2%; Density: 502.1 persons per square mile; Race: 96.4% White, 0.4% Black/African American, 0.0% Asian, 1.1% American Indian/Alaska Native, 0.0% Native Hawaiian/Other Pacific Islander, 0.9% Two or more races, 3.9% Hispanic of any race; Average household size: 2.48; Median age: 37.3; Age under 18: 27.7%; Age 65 and over: 12.8%; Males per 100 females: 103.2

School District(s)

Akron-Fairgrove Schools (KG-12)
    2012-13 Enrollment: 277. . . . . (989) 693-6163

Housing: Homeownership rate: 79.6%; Homeowner vacancy rate: 3.2%; Rental vacancy rate: 7.7%

FOSTORIA (CDP).
Covers a land area of 3.860 square miles and a water area of <.001 square miles. Located at 43.25° N. Lat; 83.37° W. Long. Elevation is 850 feet.

Population: 694; Growth (since 2000): n/a; Density: 179.8 persons per square mile; Race: 96.8% White, 0.0% Black/African American, 0.1% Asian, 2.0% American Indian/Alaska Native, 0.0% Native Hawaiian/Other Pacific Islander, 1.0% Two or more races, 0.7% Hispanic of any race; Average household size: 2.80; Median age: 37.3; Age under 18: 27.4%; Age 65 and over: 12.0%; Males per 100 females: 108.4

Housing: Homeownership rate: 83.1%; Homeowner vacancy rate: 2.4%; Rental vacancy rate: 10.6%

FREMONT (township).
Covers a land area of 35.022 square miles and a water area of 1.059 square miles. Located at 43.36° N. Lat; 83.40° W. Long.

Population: 3,312; Growth (since 2000): -6.9%; Density: 94.6 persons per square mile; Race: 97.1% White, 0.3% Black/African American, 0.3% Asian, 0.4% American Indian/Alaska Native, 0.0% Native Hawaiian/Other Pacific Islander, 1.6% Two or more races, 1.6% Hispanic of any race; Average household size: 2.57; Median age: 42.7; Age under 18: 23.4%; Age 65 and over: 16.6%; Males per 100 females: 99.5; Marriage status:

24.8% never married, 56.9% now married, 1.8% separated, 7.8% widowed, 10.5% divorced; Foreign born: 0.7%; Speak English only: 99.2%; With disability: 20.4%; Veterans: 10.5%; Ancestry: 33.9% German, 13.1% Irish, 11.4% American, 11.2% English, 6.9% Polish

Employment: 8.2% management, business, and financial, 1.7% computer, engineering, and science, 5.5% education, legal, community service, arts, and media, 4.6% healthcare practitioners, 25.9% service, 15.7% sales and office, 13.7% natural resources, construction, and maintenance, 24.7% production, transportation, and material moving

Income: Per capita: $19,596; Median household: $42,281; Average household: $48,104; Households with income of $100,000 or more: 5.8%; Poverty rate: 10.7%

Educational Attainment: High school diploma or higher: 82.9%; Bachelor's degree or higher: 9.8%; Graduate/professional degree or higher: 2.3%

Housing: Homeownership rate: 85.2%; Median home value: $100,400; Median year structure built: 1973; Homeowner vacancy rate: 2.2%; Median gross rent: $800 per month; Rental vacancy rate: 11.8%

Health Insurance: 80.2% have insurance; 64.9% have private insurance; 36.3% have public insurance; 19.8% do not have insurance; 2.8% of children under 18 do not have insurance

Transportation: Commute: 89.3% car, 0.0% public transportation, 3.8% walk, 2.6% work from home; Median travel time to work: 44.2 minutes

GAGETOWN (village).
Covers a land area of 0.981 square miles and a water area of 0.002 square miles. Located at 43.66° N. Lat; 83.24° W. Long. Elevation is 755 feet.

History: Gagetown grew up around a mill and store operated by Joseph Gage in 1869. Gage platted the village in 1871, and it was named for him.

Population: 388; Growth (since 2000): -0.3%; Density: 395.4 persons per square mile; Race: 97.7% White, 0.0% Black/African American, 0.0% Asian, 0.0% American Indian/Alaska Native, 0.0% Native Hawaiian/Other Pacific Islander, 1.3% Two or more races, 3.1% Hispanic of any race; Average household size: 2.59; Median age: 38.2; Age under 18: 27.1%; Age 65 and over: 15.5%; Males per 100 females: 103.1

Housing: Homeownership rate: 68.7%; Homeowner vacancy rate: 1.9%; Rental vacancy rate: 2.0%

GILFORD (township).
Covers a land area of 34.821 square miles and a water area of 0.002 square miles. Located at 43.52° N. Lat; 83.63° W. Long. Elevation is 636 feet.

Population: 741; Growth (since 2000): -11.0%; Density: 21.3 persons per square mile; Race: 96.4% White, 0.4% Black/African American, 0.1% Asian, 0.4% American Indian/Alaska Native, 0.0% Native Hawaiian/Other Pacific Islander, 1.5% Two or more races, 3.5% Hispanic of any race; Average household size: 2.45; Median age: 46.9; Age under 18: 19.6%; Age 65 and over: 19.4%; Males per 100 females: 99.2

Housing: Homeownership rate: 90.7%; Homeowner vacancy rate: 2.8%; Rental vacancy rate: 3.2%

INDIANFIELDS (township).
Covers a land area of 33.751 square miles and a water area of 1.806 square miles. Located at 43.45° N. Lat; 83.40° W. Long.

History: Indianfields Township was organized in 1852 and so named because the earliest inhabitants had used the area to raise corn and potatoes.

Population: 6,048; Growth (since 2000): -5.4%; Density: 179.2 persons per square mile; Race: 93.9% White, 2.4% Black/African American, 0.4% Asian, 0.8% American Indian/Alaska Native, 0.2% Native Hawaiian/Other Pacific Islander, 1.4% Two or more races, 5.3% Hispanic of any race; Average household size: 2.34; Median age: 40.7; Age under 18: 21.1%; Age 65 and over: 14.9%; Males per 100 females: 103.6; Marriage status: 21.8% never married, 56.2% now married, 2.7% separated, 9.7% widowed, 12.2% divorced; Foreign born: 0.9%; Speak English only: 96.9%; With disability: 21.2%; Veterans: 11.6%; Ancestry: 25.7% German, 13.2% Polish, 11.3% English, 9.8% Irish, 5.7% French

Employment: 7.7% management, business, and financial, 3.2% computer, engineering, and science, 9.6% education, legal, community service, arts, and media, 10.6% healthcare practitioners, 19.0% service, 33.2% sales and office, 4.9% natural resources, construction, and maintenance, 11.8% production, transportation, and material moving

Income: Per capita: $20,760; Median household: $40,465; Average household: $48,140; Households with income of $100,000 or more: 10.6%; Poverty rate: 18.6%

Educational Attainment: High school diploma or higher: 85.3%; Bachelor's degree or higher: 12.6%; Graduate/professional degree or higher: 4.0%

Housing: Homeownership rate: 72.3%; Median home value: $84,200; Median year structure built: 1975; Homeowner vacancy rate: 3.0%; Median gross rent: $625 per month; Rental vacancy rate: 8.8%

Health Insurance: 91.9% have insurance; 73.8% have private insurance; 44.3% have public insurance; 8.1% do not have insurance; 0.0% of children under 18 do not have insurance

Transportation: Commute: 94.1% car, 0.0% public transportation, 0.2% walk, 5.7% work from home; Median travel time to work: 24.8 minutes

JUNIATA (township).
Covers a land area of 34.762 square miles and a water area of 0.543 square miles. Located at 43.44° N. Lat; 83.52° W. Long. Elevation is 748 feet.

Population: 1,567; Growth (since 2000): -6.3%; Density: 45.1 persons per square mile; Race: 96.3% White, 1.2% Black/African American, 0.1% Asian, 0.3% American Indian/Alaska Native, 0.0% Native Hawaiian/Other Pacific Islander, 1.3% Two or more races, 3.4% Hispanic of any race; Average household size: 2.44; Median age: 44.9; Age under 18: 21.6%; Age 65 and over: 13.7%; Males per 100 females: 108.4

Housing: Homeownership rate: 90.7%; Homeowner vacancy rate: 1.8%; Rental vacancy rate: 6.3%

KINGSTON (township).
Covers a land area of 34.823 square miles and a water area of 1.033 square miles. Located at 43.45° N. Lat; 83.18° W. Long. Elevation is 804 feet.

Population: 1,574; Growth (since 2000): -2.5%; Density: 45.2 persons per square mile; Race: 97.1% White, 0.3% Black/African American, 0.5% Asian, 0.2% American Indian/Alaska Native, 0.0% Native Hawaiian/Other Pacific Islander, 1.3% Two or more races, 1.7% Hispanic of any race; Average household size: 2.71; Median age: 39.0; Age under 18: 26.4%; Age 65 and over: 13.4%; Males per 100 females: 101.0

School District(s)

Kingston Community SD (PK-12)
  2012-13 Enrollment: 631 . . . . (989) 683-2294

Housing: Homeownership rate: 81.3%; Homeowner vacancy rate: 1.6%; Rental vacancy rate: 6.0%

KINGSTON (village).
Covers a land area of 1.019 square miles and a water area of 0 square miles. Located at 43.41° N. Lat; 83.19° W. Long. Elevation is 804 feet.

History: Alanson K. King settled here in 1857 on the only dry land in an area known as Tag Alder Swamp. First known as Newburg, the settlement was renamed Kingston in 1871, in honor of Alanson King.

Population: 440; Growth (since 2000): -2.2%; Density: 431.7 persons per square mile; Race: 96.1% White, 0.5% Black/African American, 0.0% Asian, 0.7% American Indian/Alaska Native, 0.0% Native Hawaiian/Other Pacific Islander, 2.0% Two or more races, 3.6% Hispanic of any race; Average household size: 2.70; Median age: 35.0; Age under 18: 26.1%; Age 65 and over: 14.3%; Males per 100 females: 100.9

School District(s)

Kingston Community SD (PK-12)
  2012-13 Enrollment: 631 . . . . (989) 683-2294

Housing: Homeownership rate: 67.5%; Homeowner vacancy rate: 4.3%; Rental vacancy rate: 8.6%

KOYLTON (township).
Covers a land area of 34.909 square miles and a water area of 1.266 square miles. Located at 43.37° N. Lat; 83.16° W. Long.

History: Koylton Township was organized in 1859 and named for several settlers of that name who had come here in 1856 and 1857.

Population: 1,585; Growth (since 2000): 0.4%; Density: 45.4 persons per square mile; Race: 97.7% White, 0.6% Black/African American, 0.2% Asian, 0.4% American Indian/Alaska Native, 0.0% Native Hawaiian/Other Pacific Islander, 0.9% Two or more races, 1.9% Hispanic of any race; Average household size: 2.73; Median age: 40.2; Age under 18: 25.2%; Age 65 and over: 13.6%; Males per 100 females: 106.9

Housing: Homeownership rate: 88.3%; Homeowner vacancy rate: 2.6%; Rental vacancy rate: 13.9%

MAYVILLE (village). Covers a land area of 1.134 square miles and a water area of 0.020 square miles. Located at 43.34° N. Lat; 83.35° W. Long. Elevation is 915 feet.

Population: 950; Growth (since 2000): -10.0%; Density: 837.6 persons per square mile; Race: 96.1% White, 0.5% Black/African American, 0.2% Asian, 0.2% American Indian/Alaska Native, 0.0% Native Hawaiian/Other Pacific Islander, 2.4% Two or more races, 2.5% Hispanic of any race; Average household size: 2.43; Median age: 41.1; Age under 18: 25.4%; Age 65 and over: 20.1%; Males per 100 females: 90.0

School District(s)
Mayville Community SD (PK-12)
   2012-13 Enrollment: 729. . . . . (989) 843-6115
Housing: Homeownership rate: 70.8%; Homeowner vacancy rate: 4.4%; Rental vacancy rate: 13.6%
Safety: Violent crime rate: 10.8 per 10,000 population; Property crime rate: 172.4 per 10,000 population

MILLINGTON (township). Covers a land area of 35.440 square miles and a water area of 0.512 square miles. Located at 43.26° N. Lat; 83.52° W. Long. Elevation is 751 feet.

Population: 4,354; Growth (since 2000): -2.4%; Density: 122.9 persons per square mile; Race: 97.1% White, 0.6% Black/African American, 0.3% Asian, 0.6% American Indian/Alaska Native, 0.0% Native Hawaiian/Other Pacific Islander, 0.9% Two or more races, 2.3% Hispanic of any race; Average household size: 2.62; Median age: 41.1; Age under 18: 23.9%; Age 65 and over: 15.8%; Males per 100 females: 99.5; Marriage status: 25.4% never married, 58.4% now married, 1.3% separated, 6.7% widowed, 9.5% divorced; Foreign born: 0.3%; Speak English only: 98.9%; With disability: 18.2%; Veterans: 8.0%; Ancestry: 30.5% German, 14.7% English, 12.7% Irish, 8.1% Polish, 7.7% French
Employment: 4.8% management, business, and financial, 2.8% computer, engineering, and science, 8.0% education, legal, community service, arts, and media, 8.3% healthcare practitioners, 24.1% service, 29.0% sales and office, 13.1% natural resources, construction, and maintenance, 9.8% production, transportation, and material moving
Income: Per capita: $20,040; Median household: $44,265; Average household: $53,916; Households with income of $100,000 or more: 14.0%; Poverty rate: 11.9%
Educational Attainment: High school diploma or higher: 91.9%; Bachelor's degree or higher: 11.0%; Graduate/professional degree or higher: 5.2%

School District(s)
Millington Community Schools (PK-12)
   2012-13 Enrollment: 1,357 . . . . (989) 871-5201
Housing: Homeownership rate: 85.2%; Median home value: $108,100; Median year structure built: 1969; Homeowner vacancy rate: 2.3%; Median gross rent: $664 per month; Rental vacancy rate: 12.1%
Health Insurance: 90.5% have insurance; 75.6% have private insurance; 34.6% have public insurance; 9.5% do not have insurance; 1.8% of children under 18 do not have insurance
Transportation: Commute: 92.6% car, 0.0% public transportation, 0.3% walk, 5.3% work from home; Median travel time to work: 35.9 minutes

MILLINGTON (village). Covers a land area of 1.348 square miles and a water area of 0.002 square miles. Located at 43.28° N. Lat; 83.53° W. Long. Elevation is 751 feet.

Population: 1,072; Growth (since 2000): -5.7%; Density: 795.5 persons per square mile; Race: 94.9% White, 1.5% Black/African American, 0.6% Asian, 0.6% American Indian/Alaska Native, 0.0% Native Hawaiian/Other Pacific Islander, 1.6% Two or more races, 2.5% Hispanic of any race; Average household size: 2.55; Median age: 32.8; Age under 18: 28.5%; Age 65 and over: 14.6%; Males per 100 females: 89.4

School District(s)
Millington Community Schools (PK-12)
   2012-13 Enrollment: 1,357 . . . . (989) 871-5201
Housing: Homeownership rate: 66.4%; Homeowner vacancy rate: 2.8%; Rental vacancy rate: 13.0%

NOVESTA (township). Covers a land area of 35.281 square miles and a water area of 0.598 square miles. Located at 43.54° N. Lat; 83.17° W. Long.

Population: 1,491; Growth (since 2000): -7.2%; Density: 42.3 persons per square mile; Race: 97.9% White, 0.0% Black/African American, 0.0% Asian, 0.4% American Indian/Alaska Native, 0.0% Native Hawaiian/Other Pacific Islander, 1.2% Two or more races, 1.7% Hispanic of any race;

Average household size: 2.64; Median age: 42.9; Age under 18: 24.0%; Age 65 and over: 15.0%; Males per 100 females: 99.6
Housing: Homeownership rate: 89.5%; Homeowner vacancy rate: 1.7%; Rental vacancy rate: 14.5%

REESE (village). Covers a land area of 1.347 square miles and a water area of 0 square miles. Located at 43.45° N. Lat; 83.69° W. Long. Elevation is 630 feet.

History: Reese was settled in the mid-1860's. First called Gates for A.W. Gates, who was responsible for the town receiving a post office in 1871, the town was renamed for G.W. Reese, railroad superintendent, when the Detroit & Bay City Railroad built a station here in 1873.
Population: 1,454; Growth (since 2000): 5.7%; Density: 1,079.3 persons per square mile; Race: 97.2% White, 0.7% Black/African American, 0.7% Asian, 0.2% American Indian/Alaska Native, 0.0% Native Hawaiian/Other Pacific Islander, 0.4% Two or more races, 4.3% Hispanic of any race; Average household size: 2.29; Median age: 42.8; Age under 18: 22.6%; Age 65 and over: 18.1%; Males per 100 females: 89.1

School District(s)
Reese Public Schools (PK-12)
   2012-13 Enrollment: 851. . . . . (989) 868-9864
Housing: Homeownership rate: 76.7%; Homeowner vacancy rate: 3.2%; Rental vacancy rate: 13.7%
Safety: Violent crime rate: 7.0 per 10,000 population; Property crime rate: 147.8 per 10,000 population

SILVERWOOD (unincorporated postal area)
ZCTA: 48760
   Covers a land area of 27.389 square miles and a water area of 0.701 square miles. Located at 43.32° N. Lat; 83.26° W. Long. Elevation is 804 feet.
   Population: 1,351; Growth (since 2000): 19.2%; Density: 49.3 persons per square mile; Race: 94.0% White, 3.1% Black/African American, 0.3% Asian, 0.7% American Indian/Alaska Native, 0.0% Native Hawaiian/Other Pacific Islander, 1.9% Two or more races, 1.6% Hispanic of any race; Average household size: 2.73; Median age: 37.2; Age under 18: 27.5%; Age 65 and over: 13.9%; Males per 100 females: 107.8
   Housing: Homeownership rate: 85.0%; Homeowner vacancy rate: 4.5%; Rental vacancy rate: 20.4%

TUSCOLA (township). Covers a land area of 32.792 square miles and a water area of 0.211 square miles. Located at 43.35° N. Lat; 83.64° W. Long. Elevation is 630 feet.

Population: 2,082; Growth (since 2000): -3.3%; Density: 63.5 persons per square mile; Race: 98.2% White, 0.6% Black/African American, 0.1% Asian, 0.0% American Indian/Alaska Native, 0.0% Native Hawaiian/Other Pacific Islander, 0.6% Two or more races, 1.2% Hispanic of any race; Average household size: 2.56; Median age: 43.3; Age under 18: 24.1%; Age 65 and over: 17.2%; Males per 100 females: 96.0
Housing: Homeownership rate: 87.9%; Homeowner vacancy rate: 1.1%; Rental vacancy rate: 1.0%

UNIONVILLE (village). Covers a land area of 0.939 square miles and a water area of 0 square miles. Located at 43.65° N. Lat; 83.47° W. Long. Elevation is 620 feet.

History: Many of the early residents of Unionville were of German ancestry. The early economy here was based on sugar-beet production, and on coal mining.
Population: 508; Growth (since 2000): -16.0%; Density: 541.0 persons per square mile; Race: 97.6% White, 0.0% Black/African American, 0.2% Asian, 0.0% American Indian/Alaska Native, 0.0% Native Hawaiian/Other Pacific Islander, 1.4% Two or more races, 3.0% Hispanic of any race; Average household size: 2.33; Median age: 43.6; Age under 18: 20.9%; Age 65 and over: 17.1%; Males per 100 females: 96.9

School District(s)
Unionville-Sebewaing Area S.d. (PK-12)
   2012-13 Enrollment: 778. . . . . (989) 883-2360
Housing: Homeownership rate: 85.8%; Homeowner vacancy rate: 0.5%; Rental vacancy rate: 24.4%

VASSAR (city). Covers a land area of 2.122 square miles and a water area of 0.061 square miles. Located at 43.37° N. Lat; 83.58° W. Long. Elevation is 640 feet.

History: Vassar was settled in 1849 on the Cass River, and named for Matthew Vassar, an uncle of one of the early settlers and the founder of Vassar College at Poughkeepsie, New York.

Population: 2,697; Growth (since 2000): -4.5%; Density: 1,271.2 persons per square mile; Race: 87.4% White, 8.8% Black/African American, 0.1% Asian, 0.4% American Indian/Alaska Native, 0.0% Native Hawaiian/Other Pacific Islander, 2.2% Two or more races, 3.0% Hispanic of any race; Average household size: 2.47; Median age: 32.5; Age under 18: 31.6%; Age 65 and over: 11.8%; Males per 100 females: 99.0; Marriage status: 32.1% never married, 50.3% now married, 0.4% separated, 6.1% widowed, 11.6% divorced; Foreign born: 0.4%; Speak English only: 98.7%; With disability: 18.2%; Veterans: 10.2%; Ancestry: 34.7% German, 12.3% English, 11.0% Irish, 9.8% Polish, 7.8% French

Employment: 8.0% management, business, and financial, 7.8% computer, engineering, and science, 11.9% education, legal, community service, arts, and media, 4.7% healthcare practitioners, 23.3% service, 16.2% sales and office, 9.7% natural resources, construction, and maintenance, 18.3% production, transportation, and material moving

Income: Per capita: $18,775; Median household: $42,267; Average household: $52,066; Households with income of $100,000 or more: 11.6%; Poverty rate: 22.2%

Educational Attainment: High school diploma or higher: 82.1%; Bachelor's degree or higher: 17.2%; Graduate/professional degree or higher: 7.1%

School District(s)
Vassar Public Schools (PK-12)
    2012-13 Enrollment: 1,342 . . . . (989) 823-8535

Housing: Homeownership rate: 64.4%; Median home value: $92,500; Median year structure built: 1963; Homeowner vacancy rate: 4.0%; Median gross rent: $562 per month; Rental vacancy rate: 16.4%

Health Insurance: 86.7% have insurance; 59.1% have private insurance; 40.4% have public insurance; 13.3% do not have insurance; 6.7% of children under 18 do not have insurance

Safety: Violent crime rate: 22.8 per 10,000 population; Property crime rate: 102.5 per 10,000 population

Newspapers: Vassar Pioneer-Times (weekly circulation 1800)

Transportation: Commute: 95.3% car, 0.0% public transportation, 1.3% walk, 2.3% work from home; Median travel time to work: 25.4 minutes

Additional Information Contacts

City of Vassar . . . . (989) 823-8517
    http://www.cityofvassar.org

VASSAR (township). Covers a land area of 35.045 square miles and a water area of 0.277 square miles. Located at 43.35° N. Lat; 83.53° W. Long. Elevation is 640 feet.

History: Settled 1849, incorporated 1871 as village, as city 1945.

Population: 4,093; Growth (since 2000): -6.0%; Density: 116.8 persons per square mile; Race: 97.0% White, 0.4% Black/African American, 0.1% Asian, 0.3% American Indian/Alaska Native, 0.0% Native Hawaiian/Other Pacific Islander, 1.3% Two or more races, 2.5% Hispanic of any race; Average household size: 2.65; Median age: 39.5; Age under 18: 23.5%; Age 65 and over: 11.9%; Males per 100 females: 103.4; Marriage status: 26.2% never married, 56.7% now married, 1.9% separated, 3.2% widowed, 13.9% divorced; Foreign born: 1.4%; Speak English only: 99.1%; With disability: 19.5%; Veterans: 9.7%; Ancestry: 19.1% Irish, 15.4% German, 12.7% American, 12.2% English, 4.8% Swedish

Employment: 9.4% management, business, and financial, 5.8% computer, engineering, and science, 5.6% education, legal, community service, arts, and media, 5.9% healthcare practitioners, 20.8% service, 24.8% sales and office, 1.3% natural resources, construction, and maintenance, 26.4% production, transportation, and material moving

Income: Per capita: $17,187; Median household: $36,678; Average household: $46,473; Households with income of $100,000 or more: 8.0%; Poverty rate: 24.8%

Educational Attainment: High school diploma or higher: 85.0%; Bachelor's degree or higher: 9.1%; Graduate/professional degree or higher: 2.1%

School District(s)
Vassar Public Schools (PK-12)
    2012-13 Enrollment: 1,342 . . . . (989) 823-8535

Housing: Homeownership rate: 87.3%; Median home value: $95,100; Median year structure built: 1976; Homeowner vacancy rate: 1.5%; Median gross rent: $702 per month; Rental vacancy rate: 6.3%

Health Insurance: 83.2% have insurance; 50.5% have private insurance; 47.6% have public insurance; 16.8% do not have insurance; 8.3% of children under 18 do not have insurance

Newspapers: Vassar Pioneer-Times (weekly circulation 1800)

Transportation: Commute: 93.7% car, 0.0% public transportation, 2.5% walk, 3.0% work from home; Median travel time to work: 28.9 minutes

Additional Information Contacts

Vassar Township . . . . (989) 823-3541
    http://www.vassartownship.org

WATERTOWN (township). Covers a land area of 32.528 square miles and a water area of 0.415 square miles. Located at 43.28° N. Lat; 83.41° W. Long.

Population: 2,202; Growth (since 2000): -1.3%; Density: 67.7 persons per square mile; Race: 97.9% White, 0.3% Black/African American, 0.1% Asian, 1.0% American Indian/Alaska Native, 0.0% Native Hawaiian/Other Pacific Islander, 0.6% Two or more races, 0.8% Hispanic of any race; Average household size: 2.69; Median age: 42.3; Age under 18: 24.5%; Age 65 and over: 14.6%; Males per 100 females: 107.7

Housing: Homeownership rate: 88.6%; Homeowner vacancy rate: 1.5%; Rental vacancy rate: 7.8%

WELLS (township). Covers a land area of 34.260 square miles and a water area of 1.222 square miles. Located at 43.45° N. Lat; 83.28° W. Long. Elevation is 735 feet.

Population: 1,773; Growth (since 2000): -8.9%; Density: 51.8 persons per square mile; Race: 97.0% White, 0.5% Black/African American, 0.1% Asian, 1.2% American Indian/Alaska Native, 0.0% Native Hawaiian/Other Pacific Islander, 1.0% Two or more races, 3.2% Hispanic of any race; Average household size: 2.70; Median age: 43.4; Age under 18: 23.7%; Age 65 and over: 12.6%; Males per 100 females: 102.2

Housing: Homeownership rate: 90.2%; Homeowner vacancy rate: 1.2%; Rental vacancy rate: 5.9%

WISNER (township). Covers a land area of 19.316 square miles and a water area of 6.365 square miles. Located at 43.60° N. Lat; 83.64° W. Long. Elevation is 584 feet.

Population: 690; Growth (since 2000): -7.9%; Density: 35.7 persons per square mile; Race: 96.4% White, 0.3% Black/African American, 0.1% Asian, 0.9% American Indian/Alaska Native, 0.0% Native Hawaiian/Other Pacific Islander, 1.0% Two or more races, 4.1% Hispanic of any race; Average household size: 2.30; Median age: 49.2; Age under 18: 18.7%; Age 65 and over: 19.6%; Males per 100 females: 106.6

Housing: Homeownership rate: 86.3%; Homeowner vacancy rate: 1.9%; Rental vacancy rate: 8.7%

Van Buren County

Located in southwestern Michigan; bounded on the west by Lake Michigan; drained by the Paw Paw and Black Rivers. Covers a land area of 607.474 square miles, a water area of 482.423 square miles, and is located in the Eastern Time Zone at 42.28° N. Lat., 86.31° W. Long. The county was founded in 1829. County seat is Paw Paw.

Van Buren County is part of the Kalamazoo-Portage, MI Metropolitan Statistical Area. The entire metro area includes: Kalamazoo County, MI; Van Buren County, MI

Weather Station: Bloomingdale   Elevation: 725 feet

	Jan	Feb	Mar	Apr	May	Jun	Jul	Aug	Sep	Oct	Nov	Dec
High	32	35	45	58	69	79	83	81	74	61	48	36
Low	16	17	24	35	44	54	58	57	49	38	30	21
Precip	2.7	2.1	2.5	3.4	3.8	3.1	3.6	3.9	4.2	3.6	3.6	3.2
Snow	29.7	18.1	8.1	1.5	tr	0.0	0.0	0.0	0.0	0.6	7.4	29.1

High and Low temperatures in degrees Fahrenheit; Precipitation and Snow in inches

Weather Station: South Haven   Elevation: 620 feet

	Jan	Feb	Mar	Apr	May	Jun	Jul	Aug	Sep	Oct	Nov	Dec
High	33	35	44	56	66	75	79	79	73	61	49	37
Low	22	23	29	39	49	59	64	64	56	46	37	27
Precip	na	na	1.9	3.1	3.3	2.6	3.1	3.6	3.8	3.3	3.3	na
Snow	na	10.9	4.3	0.7	0.0	0.0	0.0	0.0	0.0	0.1	1.2	na

High and Low temperatures in degrees Fahrenheit; Precipitation and Snow in inches

Population: 76,258; Growth (since 2000): 0.0%; Density: 125.5 persons per square mile; Race: 86.7% White, 4.1% Black/African American, 0.4% Asian, 0.9% American Indian/Alaska Native, 0.0% Native Hawaiian/Other Pacific Islander, 2.7% two or more races, 10.2% Hispanic of any race; Average household size: 2.61; Median age: 39.8; Age under 18: 25.5%; Age 65 and over: 13.8%; Males per 100 females: 98.3; Marriage status: 26.0% never married, 54.8% now married, 1.4% separated, 6.4% widowed, 12.8% divorced; Foreign born: 4.5%; Speak English only: 90.1%; With disability: 14.3%; Veterans: 11.1%; Ancestry: 23.4% German, 12.0% Irish, 11.4% English, 10.4% American, 7.6% Dutch
Religion: Six largest groups: 17.0% Catholicism, 3.5% Lutheran, 3.1% Methodist/Pietist, 2.9% Presbyterian-Reformed, 2.7% Non-denominational Protestant, 2.0% Baptist
Economy: Unemployment rate: 5.4%; Leading industries: 19.3% retail trade; 11.6% accommodation and food services; 11.5% other services (except public administration); Farms: 1,113 totaling 175,121 acres; Company size: 1 employs 1,000 or more persons, 1 employs 500 to 999 persons, 19 employ 100 to 499 persons, 1,268 employ less than 100 persons; Business ownership: 1,587 women-owned, n/a Black-owned, n/a Hispanic-owned, n/a Asian-owned
Employment: 10.8% management, business, and financial, 4.2% computer, engineering, and science, 7.6% education, legal, community service, arts, and media, 4.8% healthcare practitioners, 19.6% service, 21.0% sales and office, 15.1% natural resources, construction, and maintenance, 16.9% production, transportation, and material moving
Income: Per capita: $21,732; Median household: $45,129; Average household: $56,250; Households with income of $100,000 or more: 13.8%; Poverty rate: 19.4%
Educational Attainment: High school diploma or higher: 85.3%; Bachelor's degree or higher: 17.9%; Graduate/professional degree or higher: 6.8%
Housing: Homeownership rate: 77.9%; Median home value: $118,700; Median year structure built: 1975; Homeowner vacancy rate: 3.0%; Median gross rent: $630 per month; Rental vacancy rate: 11.7%
Vital Statistics: Birth rate: 118.3 per 10,000 population; Death rate: 95.8 per 10,000 population; Age-adjusted cancer mortality rate: 182.6 deaths per 100,000 population
Health Insurance: 85.2% have insurance; 62.6% have private insurance; 36.1% have public insurance; 14.8% do not have insurance; 5.3% of children under 18 do not have insurance
Health Care: Physicians: 12.3 per 10,000 population; Hospital beds: 9.0 per 10,000 population; Hospital admissions: 282.0 per 10,000 population
Transportation: Commute: 92.9% car, 0.3% public transportation, 2.1% walk, 3.5% work from home; Median travel time to work: 24.5 minutes
Presidential Election: 49.7% Obama, 49.2% Romney (2012)
National and State Parks: Kal-Haven Trail State Park
Additional Information Contacts
Van Buren Government. . . . . (269) 657-8218
  http://www.vbco.org

Van Buren County Communities

ALMENA (township). Covers a land area of 34.411 square miles and a water area of 0.466 square miles. Located at 42.29° N. Lat; 85.82° W. Long. Elevation is 758 feet.
History: Almena Township was organized in 1842, and named by F.C. Annable for an Indian princess of whom he had heard.
Population: 4,992; Growth (since 2000): 18.1%; Density: 145.1 persons per square mile; Race: 94.3% White, 1.2% Black/African American, 0.9% Asian, 0.5% American Indian/Alaska Native, 0.1% Native Hawaiian/Other Pacific Islander, 2.0% Two or more races, 2.4% Hispanic of any race; Average household size: 2.71; Median age: 41.3; Age under 18: 25.5%; Age 65 and over: 11.3%; Males per 100 females: 104.6; Marriage status: 17.9% never married, 73.2% now married, 0.3% separated, 2.6% widowed, 6.4% divorced; Foreign born: 1.0%; Speak English only: 97.5%; With disability: 9.7%; Veterans: 12.8%; Ancestry: 32.0% German, 18.5% Irish, 13.8% English, 11.4% Dutch, 9.1% French
Employment: 16.2% management, business, and financial, 5.8% computer, engineering, and science, 9.4% education, legal, community service, arts, and media, 9.5% healthcare practitioners, 17.5% service, 16.6% sales and office, 11.8% natural resources, construction, and maintenance, 13.2% production, transportation, and material moving
Income: Per capita: $31,407; Median household: $78,207; Average household: $85,259; Households with income of $100,000 or more: 26.6%; Poverty rate: 6.5%

Educational Attainment: High school diploma or higher: 98.3%; Bachelor's degree or higher: 35.3%; Graduate/professional degree or higher: 15.7%
Housing: Homeownership rate: 92.0%; Median home value: $163,600; Median year structure built: 1988; Homeowner vacancy rate: 1.3%; Median gross rent: n/a per month; Rental vacancy rate: 5.1%
Health Insurance: 94.1% have insurance; 85.4% have private insurance; 22.2% have public insurance; 5.9% do not have insurance; 0.0% of children under 18 do not have insurance
Transportation: Commute: 93.9% car, 0.7% public transportation, 0.8% walk, 4.1% work from home; Median travel time to work: 26.9 minutes

ANTWERP (township). Covers a land area of 34.686 square miles and a water area of 0.300 square miles. Located at 42.20° N. Lat; 85.81° W. Long.
History: Antwerp Township was organized in 1837 and named by its oldest inhabitant at the time, Harmon Van Antwerp, for Antwerp, Belgium.
Population: 12,182; Growth (since 2000): 12.7%; Density: 351.2 persons per square mile; Race: 94.0% White, 1.1% Black/African American, 0.4% Asian, 0.5% American Indian/Alaska Native, 0.0% Native Hawaiian/Other Pacific Islander, 2.1% Two or more races, 5.2% Hispanic of any race; Average household size: 2.70; Median age: 37.3; Age under 18: 27.4%; Age 65 and over: 11.3%; Males per 100 females: 96.2; Marriage status: 25.5% never married, 56.7% now married, 0.6% separated, 5.7% widowed, 12.1% divorced; Foreign born: 2.6%; Speak English only: 95.0%; With disability: 10.5%; Veterans: 9.7%; Ancestry: 27.0% German, 12.8% Irish, 12.4% English, 11.8% American, 10.8% Dutch
Employment: 13.6% management, business, and financial, 6.1% computer, engineering, and science, 8.4% education, legal, community service, arts, and media, 5.8% healthcare practitioners, 19.1% service, 22.7% sales and office, 10.9% natural resources, construction, and maintenance, 13.3% production, transportation, and material moving
Income: Per capita: $25,415; Median household: $57,822; Average household: $68,927; Households with income of $100,000 or more: 20.7%; Poverty rate: 8.2%
Educational Attainment: High school diploma or higher: 92.3%; Bachelor's degree or higher: 26.6%; Graduate/professional degree or higher: 10.1%
Housing: Homeownership rate: 82.7%; Median home value: $142,800; Median year structure built: 1985; Homeowner vacancy rate: 2.4%; Median gross rent: $676 per month; Rental vacancy rate: 7.7%
Health Insurance: 91.3% have insurance; 79.5% have private insurance; 24.1% have public insurance; 8.7% do not have insurance; 2.4% of children under 18 do not have insurance
Transportation: Commute: 95.2% car, 0.1% public transportation, 1.5% walk, 2.6% work from home; Median travel time to work: 23.3 minutes
Additional Information Contacts
Antwerp Township. . . . . (269) 668-2615
  http://antwerptownship.com

ARLINGTON (township). Covers a land area of 34.374 square miles and a water area of 0.523 square miles. Located at 42.29° N. Lat; 86.04° W. Long.
History: Arlington Township was organized in 1842 and named for the town in Vermont.
Population: 2,073; Growth (since 2000): -0.1%; Density: 60.3 persons per square mile; Race: 87.5% White, 2.6% Black/African American, 0.4% Asian, 1.1% American Indian/Alaska Native, 0.1% Native Hawaiian/Other Pacific Islander, 2.2% Two or more races, 12.2% Hispanic of any race; Average household size: 2.70; Median age: 42.2; Age under 18: 23.5%; Age 65 and over: 15.4%; Males per 100 females: 103.4
Housing: Homeownership rate: 85.9%; Homeowner vacancy rate: 3.3%; Rental vacancy rate: 7.8%

BANGOR (city). Covers a land area of 1.826 square miles and a water area of 0.073 square miles. Located at 42.31° N. Lat; 86.11° W. Long. Elevation is 659 feet.
History: The city of Bangor was settled by Charles U. Cross in 1837 and, with the township, was named for Bangor, Maine. Bangor was incorporated as a village in 1877.
Population: 1,885; Growth (since 2000): -2.5%; Density: 1,032.2 persons per square mile; Race: 72.9% White, 11.8% Black/African American, 0.7% Asian, 0.5% American Indian/Alaska Native, 0.0% Native Hawaiian/Other Pacific Islander, 5.4% Two or more races, 14.4% Hispanic of any race;

Average household size: 2.66; Median age: 32.9; Age under 18: 30.0%; Age 65 and over: 11.9%; Males per 100 females: 91.0

School District(s)
Bangor Public Schools (Van Buren) (PK-12)
    2012-13 Enrollment: 1,243 . . . . (269) 427-6800
Bangor Township S/d #8 (KG-12)
    2012-13 Enrollment: 21 . . . . (269) 427-8562
Van Buren ISD (PK-12)
    2012-13 Enrollment: 622 . . . . (269) 674-8091
Housing: Homeownership rate: 59.5%; Homeowner vacancy rate: 5.8%; Rental vacancy rate: 12.0%
Safety: Violent crime rate: 70.0 per 10,000 population; Property crime rate: 366.2 per 10,000 population
Additional Information Contacts
City of Bangor . . . . (269) 427-5831
    http://ci.bangor.mi.us

BANGOR (township). Covers a land area of 33.704 square miles and a water area of 0.845 square miles. Located at 42.29° N. Lat; 86.17° W. Long. Elevation is 659 feet.
History: Bangor Township was organized in 1854 and named for Bangor, Maine.
Population: 2,147; Growth (since 2000): 1.2%; Density: 63.7 persons per square mile; Race: 84.5% White, 4.1% Black/African American, 0.2% Asian, 1.3% American Indian/Alaska Native, 0.1% Native Hawaiian/Other Pacific Islander, 2.4% Two or more races, 14.3% Hispanic of any race; Average household size: 2.67; Median age: 41.3; Age under 18: 23.0%; Age 65 and over: 16.1%; Males per 100 females: 108.4

School District(s)
Bangor Public Schools (Van Buren) (PK-12)
    2012-13 Enrollment: 1,243 . . . . (269) 427-6800
Bangor Township S/d #8 (KG-12)
    2012-13 Enrollment: 21 . . . . (269) 427-8562
Van Buren ISD (PK-12)
    2012-13 Enrollment: 622 . . . . (269) 674-8091
Housing: Homeownership rate: 83.0%; Homeowner vacancy rate: 1.2%; Rental vacancy rate: 10.5%

BLOOMINGDALE (township). Covers a land area of 33.910 square miles and a water area of 1.163 square miles. Located at 42.38° N. Lat; 85.94° W. Long. Elevation is 732 feet.
Population: 3,103; Growth (since 2000): -7.8%; Density: 91.5 persons per square mile; Race: 93.7% White, 1.8% Black/African American, 0.2% Asian, 0.8% American Indian/Alaska Native, 0.0% Native Hawaiian/Other Pacific Islander, 1.9% Two or more races, 3.1% Hispanic of any race; Average household size: 2.53; Median age: 43.7; Age under 18: 22.5%; Age 65 and over: 16.0%; Males per 100 females: 96.0; Marriage status: 22.0% never married, 50.3% now married, 1.2% separated, 7.4% widowed, 20.3% divorced; Foreign born: 0.5%; Speak English only: 97.7%; With disability: 14.3%; Veterans: 15.8%; Ancestry: 21.8% German, 16.5% Irish, 14.5% English, 10.5% Dutch, 5.4% American
Employment: 11.8% management, business, and financial, 2.7% computer, engineering, and science, 5.6% education, legal, community service, arts, and media, 1.1% healthcare practitioners, 22.2% service, 19.9% sales and office, 14.4% natural resources, construction, and maintenance, 22.3% production, transportation, and material moving
Income: Per capita: $21,889; Median household: $39,492; Average household: $49,838; Households with income of $100,000 or more: 11.5%; Poverty rate: 15.7%
Educational Attainment: High school diploma or higher: 82.9%; Bachelor's degree or higher: 11.7%; Graduate/professional degree or higher: 4.0%

School District(s)
Bloomingdale Public SD (PK-12)
    2012-13 Enrollment: 1,180 . . . . (269) 521-3900
Housing: Homeownership rate: 82.5%; Median home value: $91,300; Median year structure built: 1971; Homeowner vacancy rate: 1.9%; Median gross rent: $636 per month; Rental vacancy rate: 10.1%
Health Insurance: 77.3% have insurance; 58.4% have private insurance; 31.3% have public insurance; 22.7% do not have insurance; 8.9% of children under 18 do not have insurance
Transportation: Commute: 90.7% car, 0.0% public transportation, 0.6% walk, 7.7% work from home; Median travel time to work: 27.4 minutes

Additional Information Contacts
Bloomingdale Township . . . . (269) 521-3800
    http://bloomingdaletwp.com

BLOOMINGDALE (village). Covers a land area of 1.135 square miles and a water area of 0.026 square miles. Located at 42.38° N. Lat; 85.96° W. Long. Elevation is 732 feet.
History: Bloomingdale was founded in 1855 by two men who came from Ohio. It was incorporated in 1881.
Population: 454; Growth (since 2000): -14.0%; Density: 399.8 persons per square mile; Race: 93.4% White, 0.2% Black/African American, 0.2% Asian, 0.9% American Indian/Alaska Native, 0.0% Native Hawaiian/Other Pacific Islander, 2.9% Two or more races, 5.1% Hispanic of any race; Average household size: 2.64; Median age: 38.4; Age under 18: 24.4%; Age 65 and over: 12.6%; Males per 100 females: 85.3

School District(s)
Bloomingdale Public SD (PK-12)
    2012-13 Enrollment: 1,180 . . . . (269) 521-3900
Housing: Homeownership rate: 73.9%; Homeowner vacancy rate: 6.5%; Rental vacancy rate: 18.2%
Additional Information Contacts
Village of Bloomingdale . . . . (269) 521-3222

BREEDSVILLE (village). Covers a land area of 0.652 square miles and a water area of 0.013 square miles. Located at 42.35° N. Lat; 86.07° W. Long. Elevation is 663 feet.
History: Breedsville was named for Silas Breed who built a sawmill here in 1835. The village was incorporated in 1883.
Population: 199; Growth (since 2000): -15.3%; Density: 305.0 persons per square mile; Race: 73.9% White, 2.0% Black/African American, 0.0% Asian, 3.0% American Indian/Alaska Native, 0.0% Native Hawaiian/Other Pacific Islander, 2.5% Two or more races, 28.1% Hispanic of any race; Average household size: 3.06; Median age: 34.5; Age under 18: 25.6%; Age 65 and over: 7.0%; Males per 100 females: 107.3
Housing: Homeownership rate: 78.5%; Homeowner vacancy rate: 5.5%; Rental vacancy rate: 0.0%

COLUMBIA (township). Covers a land area of 33.909 square miles and a water area of 1.504 square miles. Located at 42.38° N. Lat; 86.05° W. Long.
Population: 2,588; Growth (since 2000): -4.6%; Density: 76.3 persons per square mile; Race: 85.6% White, 2.6% Black/African American, 0.1% Asian, 1.2% American Indian/Alaska Native, 0.0% Native Hawaiian/Other Pacific Islander, 2.0% Two or more races, 14.4% Hispanic of any race; Average household size: 2.66; Median age: 40.1; Age under 18: 25.7%; Age 65 and over: 14.6%; Males per 100 females: 107.7; Marriage status: 28.7% never married, 54.5% now married, 1.2% separated, 7.1% widowed, 9.7% divorced; Foreign born: 6.8%; Speak English only: 78.8%; With disability: 9.6%; Veterans: 10.3%; Ancestry: 22.3% German, 13.1% American, 12.4% Irish, 9.1% Polish, 5.3% English
Employment: 7.1% management, business, and financial, 2.4% computer, engineering, and science, 6.3% education, legal, community service, arts, and media, 4.1% healthcare practitioners, 7.6% service, 24.6% sales and office, 34.9% natural resources, construction, and maintenance, 12.9% production, transportation, and material moving
Income: Per capita: $17,430; Median household: $40,703; Average household: $51,010; Households with income of $100,000 or more: 8.3%; Poverty rate: 23.3%
Educational Attainment: High school diploma or higher: 74.3%; Bachelor's degree or higher: 5.9%; Graduate/professional degree or higher: 1.6%
Housing: Homeownership rate: 83.0%; Median home value: $89,200; Median year structure built: 1977; Homeowner vacancy rate: 3.9%; Median gross rent: $751 per month; Rental vacancy rate: 11.7%
Health Insurance: 73.8% have insurance; 51.4% have private insurance; 34.9% have public insurance; 26.2% do not have insurance; 14.9% of children under 18 do not have insurance
Transportation: Commute: 97.4% car, 0.0% public transportation, 0.0% walk, 1.9% work from home; Median travel time to work: 29.1 minutes
Additional Information Contacts
Columbia Township . . . . (269) 434-6227
    http://www.columbiatwp.com

COVERT (township). Covers a land area of 34.921 square miles and a water area of 0.058 square miles. Located at 42.28° N. Lat; 86.28° W. Long. Elevation is 692 feet.

Population: 2,888; Growth (since 2000): -8.1%; Density: 82.7 persons per square mile; Race: 50.2% White, 24.2% Black/African American, 0.3% Asian, 1.7% American Indian/Alaska Native, 0.0% Native Hawaiian/Other Pacific Islander, 4.4% Two or more races, 30.5% Hispanic of any race; Average household size: 2.87; Median age: 35.1; Age under 18: 30.3%; Age 65 and over: 12.4%; Males per 100 females: 95.1; Marriage status: 35.9% never married, 47.6% now married, 1.5% separated, 5.8% widowed, 10.8% divorced; Foreign born: 14.7%; Speak English only: 68.0%; With disability: 18.6%; Veterans: 8.8%; Ancestry: 10.3% American, 6.8% German, 4.2% Irish, 4.0% English, 1.6% Dutch

Employment: 9.9% management, business, and financial, 0.5% computer, engineering, and science, 6.8% education, legal, community service, arts, and media, 1.6% healthcare practitioners, 19.1% service, 19.2% sales and office, 16.8% natural resources, construction, and maintenance, 26.0% production, transportation, and material moving

Income: Per capita: $15,922; Median household: $27,500; Average household: $41,574; Households with income of $100,000 or more: 7.3%; Poverty rate: 35.2%

Educational Attainment: High school diploma or higher: 64.3%; Bachelor's degree or higher: 8.3%; Graduate/professional degree or higher: 3.0%

School District(s)
Covert Public Schools (PK-12)
    2012-13 Enrollment: 476. . . . . (269) 764-3701
Housing: Homeownership rate: 69.5%; Median home value: $87,800; Median year structure built: 1966; Homeowner vacancy rate: 3.3%; Median gross rent: $716 per month; Rental vacancy rate: 10.7%
Health Insurance: 77.1% have insurance; 37.8% have private insurance; 49.1% have public insurance; 22.9% do not have insurance; 15.5% of children under 18 do not have insurance
Safety: Violent crime rate: 31.8 per 10,000 population; Property crime rate: 275.3 per 10,000 population
Transportation: Commute: 95.9% car, 0.0% public transportation, 2.5% walk, 1.6% work from home; Median travel time to work: 29.5 minutes

DECATUR (township). Covers a land area of 34.877 square miles and a water area of 0.706 square miles. Located at 42.11° N. Lat; 85.92° W. Long. Elevation is 787 feet.

History: Incorporated 1861.

Population: 3,726; Growth (since 2000): -4.9%; Density: 106.8 persons per square mile; Race: 89.0% White, 2.3% Black/African American, 0.3% Asian, 1.3% American Indian/Alaska Native, 0.0% Native Hawaiian/Other Pacific Islander, 3.6% Two or more races, 8.3% Hispanic of any race; Average household size: 2.63; Median age: 37.7; Age under 18: 26.0%; Age 65 and over: 14.1%; Males per 100 females: 95.9; Marriage status: 30.2% never married, 48.2% now married, 2.5% separated, 8.3% widowed, 13.4% divorced; Foreign born: 1.3%; Speak English only: 95.7%; With disability: 19.1%; Veterans: 8.0%; Ancestry: 21.1% German, 19.8% English, 14.5% Irish, 13.2% Dutch, 8.9% American

Employment: 8.7% management, business, and financial, 1.4% computer, engineering, and science, 8.0% education, legal, community service, arts, and media, 2.8% healthcare practitioners, 30.4% service, 12.5% sales and office, 20.5% natural resources, construction, and maintenance, 15.6% production, transportation, and material moving

Income: Per capita: $18,341; Median household: $35,451; Average household: $47,741; Households with income of $100,000 or more: 8.7%; Poverty rate: 23.2%

Educational Attainment: High school diploma or higher: 82.8%; Bachelor's degree or higher: 10.8%; Graduate/professional degree or higher: 2.9%

School District(s)
Decatur Public Schools (PK-12)
    2012-13 Enrollment: 903. . . . . (269) 423-6800
Housing: Homeownership rate: 73.5%; Median home value: $89,200; Median year structure built: 1963; Homeowner vacancy rate: 4.6%; Median gross rent: $728 per month; Rental vacancy rate: 10.3%
Health Insurance: 87.1% have insurance; 58.8% have private insurance; 44.3% have public insurance; 12.9% do not have insurance; 2.5% of children under 18 do not have insurance
Newspapers: Decatur Republican (weekly circulation 1700)
Transportation: Commute: 94.5% car, 0.8% public transportation, 1.3% walk, 1.7% work from home; Median travel time to work: 23.2 minutes

DECATUR (village). Covers a land area of 1.351 square miles and a water area of 0.078 square miles. Located at 42.11° N. Lat; 85.98° W. Long. Elevation is 787 feet.

Population: 1,819; Growth (since 2000): -1.0%; Density: 1,346.6 persons per square mile; Race: 87.6% White, 2.7% Black/African American, 0.3% Asian, 1.2% American Indian/Alaska Native, 0.1% Native Hawaiian/Other Pacific Islander, 4.0% Two or more races, 9.4% Hispanic of any race; Average household size: 2.55; Median age: 34.6; Age under 18: 28.1%; Age 65 and over: 13.5%; Males per 100 females: 90.9

School District(s)
Decatur Public Schools (PK-12)
    2012-13 Enrollment: 903. . . . . (269) 423-6800
Housing: Homeownership rate: 63.9%; Homeowner vacancy rate: 5.7%; Rental vacancy rate: 6.6%
Newspapers: Decatur Republican (weekly circulation 1700)
Additional Information Contacts
Village of Decatur . . . . (269) 423-6114
    http://www.decaturmi.org

GENEVA (township). Covers a land area of 35.143 square miles and a water area of 0.236 square miles. Located at 42.38° N. Lat; 86.16° W. Long.

Population: 3,573; Growth (since 2000): -10.1%; Density: 101.7 persons per square mile; Race: 80.4% White, 7.0% Black/African American, 0.2% Asian, 1.4% American Indian/Alaska Native, 0.0% Native Hawaiian/Other Pacific Islander, 2.9% Two or more races, 13.5% Hispanic of any race; Average household size: 2.69; Median age: 38.8; Age under 18: 25.7%; Age 65 and over: 13.0%; Males per 100 females: 99.1; Marriage status: 31.2% never married, 47.5% now married, 2.7% separated, 5.4% widowed, 15.9% divorced; Foreign born: 6.0%; Speak English only: 79.1%; With disability: 11.6%; Veterans: 12.3%; Ancestry: 20.7% German, 12.5% American, 8.3% English, 7.0% Polish, 5.8% Irish

Employment: 7.2% management, business, and financial, 2.8% computer, engineering, and science, 4.6% education, legal, community service, arts, and media, 2.7% healthcare practitioners, 21.6% service, 22.4% sales and office, 16.6% natural resources, construction, and maintenance, 22.1% production, transportation, and material moving

Income: Per capita: $17,544; Median household: $39,432; Average household: $53,608; Households with income of $100,000 or more: 13.7%; Poverty rate: 28.1%

Educational Attainment: High school diploma or higher: 78.6%; Bachelor's degree or higher: 11.9%; Graduate/professional degree or higher: 4.4%

Housing: Homeownership rate: 83.7%; Median home value: $102,000; Median year structure built: 1982; Homeowner vacancy rate: 2.9%; Median gross rent: $709 per month; Rental vacancy rate: 13.5%
Health Insurance: 82.9% have insurance; 41.7% have private insurance; 52.5% have public insurance; 17.1% do not have insurance; 2.0% of children under 18 do not have insurance
Transportation: Commute: 95.4% car, 0.8% public transportation, 0.0% walk, 3.8% work from home; Median travel time to work: 22.4 minutes

GOBLES (city). Covers a land area of 1.033 square miles and a water area of 0 square miles. Located at 42.36° N. Lat; 85.88° W. Long. Elevation is 817 feet.

History: Gobles was named for the Gobles. John Goble built a hotel here in the mid-1860's; Hiram E. Goble platted the village in 1870; Warren Goble made an addition to the plat in 1872, when Hiram Goble became the postmaster. Gobles was incorporated as a village in 1893, and as a city in 1957.

Population: 829; Growth (since 2000): 1.7%; Density: 802.6 persons per square mile; Race: 93.1% White, 0.6% Black/African American, 0.0% Asian, 0.2% American Indian/Alaska Native, 0.0% Native Hawaiian/Other Pacific Islander, 4.3% Two or more races, 4.9% Hispanic of any race; Average household size: 2.59; Median age: 37.7; Age under 18: 27.6%; Age 65 and over: 12.7%; Males per 100 females: 91.0

School District(s)
Gobles Public SD (KG-12)
    2012-13 Enrollment: 862. . . . . (269) 628-5618
Housing: Homeownership rate: 65.0%; Homeowner vacancy rate: 1.4%; Rental vacancy rate: 8.1%

GRAND JUNCTION (unincorporated postal area)
ZCTA: 49056

Covers a land area of 56.612 square miles and a water area of 1.914 square miles. Located at 42.40° N. Lat; 86.06° W. Long. Elevation is 679 feet.

Population: 4,016; Growth (since 2000): -2.2%; Density: 70.9 persons per square mile; Race: 85.1% White, 3.2% Black/African American, 0.0% Asian, 1.3% American Indian/Alaska Native, 0.0% Native Hawaiian/Other Pacific Islander, 2.4% Two or more races, 14.0% Hispanic of any race; Average household size: 2.71; Median age: 38.8; Age under 18: 26.0%; Age 65 and over: 13.8%; Males per 100 females: 108.4; Marriage status: 29.7% never married, 57.0% now married, 1.3% separated, 4.2% widowed, 9.1% divorced; Foreign born: 5.4%; Speak English only: 83.4%; With disability: 12.7%; Veterans: 8.7%; Ancestry: 15.3% German, 11.4% American, 9.5% Irish, 7.4% English, 4.9% Polish
Employment: 8.8% management, business, and financial, 1.7% computer, engineering, and science, 4.7% education, legal, community service, arts, and media, 4.5% healthcare practitioners, 13.7% service, 18.4% sales and office, 27.3% natural resources, construction, and maintenance, 20.8% production, transportation, and material moving
Income: Per capita: $19,789; Median household: $40,610; Average household: $59,615; Households with income of $100,000 or more: 10.4%; Poverty rate: 28.9%
Educational Attainment: High school diploma or higher: 76.4%; Bachelor's degree or higher: 8.5%; Graduate/professional degree or higher: 3.4%
Housing: Homeownership rate: 81.7%; Median home value: $100,600; Median year structure built: 1976; Homeowner vacancy rate: 4.1%; Median gross rent: $827 per month; Rental vacancy rate: 11.4%
Health Insurance: 73.1% have insurance; 41.8% have private insurance; 40.1% have public insurance; 26.9% do not have insurance; 9.0% of children under 18 do not have insurance
Transportation: Commute: 92.2% car, 0.7% public transportation, 1.6% walk, 5.0% work from home; Median travel time to work: 30.3 minutes

HAMILTON (township).
Covers a land area of 34.219 square miles and a water area of 1.332 square miles. Located at 42.11° N. Lat; 86.03° W. Long.

History: Hamilton Township was first settled in the early 1830's. When it was organized in 1839, it was called Alpina, but was renamed in 1840 to honor Alexander Hamilton, American statesman.
Population: 1,489; Growth (since 2000): -17.1%; Density: 43.5 persons per square mile; Race: 87.0% White, 2.1% Black/African American, 0.8% Asian, 1.4% American Indian/Alaska Native, 0.0% Native Hawaiian/Other Pacific Islander, 1.9% Two or more races, 11.0% Hispanic of any race; Average household size: 2.68; Median age: 41.5; Age under 18: 24.2%; Age 65 and over: 14.4%; Males per 100 females: 108.0

School District(s)
Hamilton Community Schools (KG-12)
    2012-13 Enrollment: 2,633 . . . . (269) 751-5148
Housing: Homeownership rate: 87.1%; Homeowner vacancy rate: 1.6%; Rental vacancy rate: 12.3%

HARTFORD (city).
Covers a land area of 1.328 square miles and a water area of 0.005 square miles. Located at 42.20° N. Lat; 86.17° W. Long. Elevation is 659 feet.

History: Hartford developed as a shipping center for the fruits and vegetables grown in the area. An industry in Hartford was a foliage factory, where natural foliage was preserved for use in garlands and wreaths.
Population: 2,688; Growth (since 2000): 8.6%; Density: 2,023.4 persons per square mile; Race: 71.9% White, 1.6% Black/African American, 0.5% Asian, 2.8% American Indian/Alaska Native, 0.0% Native Hawaiian/Other Pacific Islander, 4.5% Two or more races, 29.5% Hispanic of any race; Average household size: 2.97; Median age: 31.3; Age under 18: 32.0%; Age 65 and over: 10.0%; Males per 100 females: 96.9; Marriage status: 31.8% never married, 49.5% now married, 1.9% separated, 6.7% widowed, 12.1% divorced; Foreign born: 14.4%; Speak English only: 73.3%; With disability: 11.7%; Veterans: 7.0%; Ancestry: 18.0% German, 10.8% Irish, 10.0% American, 5.5% English, 5.2% Dutch
Employment: 5.8% management, business, and financial, 0.7% computer, engineering, and science, 6.5% education, legal, community service, arts, and media, 4.3% healthcare practitioners, 23.2% service, 18.8% sales and office, 18.1% natural resources, construction, and maintenance, 22.7% production, transportation, and material moving

Income: Per capita: $12,479; Median household: $32,674; Average household: $37,620; Households with income of $100,000 or more: 5.3%; Poverty rate: 26.5%
Educational Attainment: High school diploma or higher: 74.5%; Bachelor's degree or higher: 5.5%; Graduate/professional degree or higher: 2.0%

School District(s)
Hartford Public Schools (PK-12)
    2012-13 Enrollment: 1,369 . . . . (269) 621-7002
Housing: Homeownership rate: 64.1%; Median home value: $68,700; Median year structure built: 1955; Homeowner vacancy rate: 3.1%; Median gross rent: $489 per month; Rental vacancy rate: 10.7%
Health Insurance: 80.1% have insurance; 47.1% have private insurance; 45.4% have public insurance; 19.9% do not have insurance; 7.1% of children under 18 do not have insurance
Safety: Violent crime rate: 38.0 per 10,000 population; Property crime rate: 129.1 per 10,000 population
Transportation: Commute: 96.1% car, 0.0% public transportation, 0.2% walk, 1.1% work from home; Median travel time to work: 27.9 minutes
Additional Information Contacts
City of Hartford . . . . (269) 621-2477
    http://www.cityofhartfordmi.org

HARTFORD (township).
Covers a land area of 33.367 square miles and a water area of 0.516 square miles. Located at 42.17° N. Lat; 86.18° W. Long. Elevation is 659 feet.

History: Hartford Township was settled in 1837 and organized in 1840 under the name of Hartland, for the home town in New York of Ferdino Olds, the first settler here. Since there was already a Hartland in Michigan, the name was changed to Hartford.
Population: 3,274; Growth (since 2000): 3.6%; Density: 98.1 persons per square mile; Race: 82.3% White, 1.1% Black/African American, 0.1% Asian, 1.4% American Indian/Alaska Native, 0.0% Native Hawaiian/Other Pacific Islander, 3.5% Two or more races, 22.2% Hispanic of any race; Average household size: 2.79; Median age: 36.1; Age under 18: 27.6%; Age 65 and over: 11.4%; Males per 100 females: 106.3; Marriage status: 25.6% never married, 55.1% now married, 1.0% separated, 6.0% widowed, 13.4% divorced; Foreign born: 5.0%; Speak English only: 89.6%; With disability: 18.2%; Veterans: 11.0%; Ancestry: 21.3% German, 14.1% American, 9.8% Irish, 6.6% English, 3.9% French
Employment: 7.2% management, business, and financial, 2.4% computer, engineering, and science, 5.1% education, legal, community service, arts, and media, 3.4% healthcare practitioners, 22.4% service, 21.9% sales and office, 12.3% natural resources, construction, and maintenance, 25.3% production, transportation, and material moving
Income: Per capita: $17,872; Median household: $36,108; Average household: $44,825; Households with income of $100,000 or more: 5.8%; Poverty rate: 30.0%
Educational Attainment: High school diploma or higher: 74.5%; Bachelor's degree or higher: 8.8%; Graduate/professional degree or higher: 2.0%

School District(s)
Hartford Public Schools (PK-12)
    2012-13 Enrollment: 1,369 . . . . (269) 621-7002
Housing: Homeownership rate: 76.2%; Median home value: $87,400; Median year structure built: 1978; Homeowner vacancy rate: 1.4%; Median gross rent: $558 per month; Rental vacancy rate: 7.9%
Health Insurance: 81.2% have insurance; 53.0% have private insurance; 44.5% have public insurance; 18.8% do not have insurance; 11.4% of children under 18 do not have insurance
Transportation: Commute: 91.4% car, 0.9% public transportation, 2.5% walk, 3.0% work from home; Median travel time to work: 24.7 minutes

KEELER (township).
Covers a land area of 33.728 square miles and a water area of 1.276 square miles. Located at 42.11° N. Lat; 86.16° W. Long. Elevation is 804 feet.

History: Keeler Township was organized about 1835, and named for Eleazer H. Keeler, tavern operator who became the first postmaster.
Population: 2,169; Growth (since 2000): -16.6%; Density: 64.3 persons per square mile; Race: 84.6% White, 0.2% Black/African American, 0.2% Asian, 1.8% American Indian/Alaska Native, 0.0% Native Hawaiian/Other Pacific Islander, 1.6% Two or more races, 22.0% Hispanic of any race; Average household size: 2.56; Median age: 41.6; Age under 18: 23.3%; Age 65 and over: 16.5%; Males per 100 females: 109.4

Housing: Homeownership rate: 79.8%; Homeowner vacancy rate: 7.4%; Rental vacancy rate: 14.4%

LAWRENCE (township).
Covers a land area of 34.625 square miles and a water area of 1.184 square miles. Located at 42.20° N. Lat; 86.05° W. Long. Elevation is 689 feet.

Population: 3,259; Growth (since 2000): -2.5%; Density: 94.1 persons per square mile; Race: 85.0% White, 1.9% Black/African American, 0.3% Asian, 0.9% American Indian/Alaska Native, 0.0% Native Hawaiian/Other Pacific Islander, 2.5% Two or more races, 17.9% Hispanic of any race; Average household size: 2.65; Median age: 39.3; Age under 18: 26.0%; Age 65 and over: 12.9%; Males per 100 females: 101.9; Marriage status: 27.5% never married, 51.0% now married, 1.7% separated, 7.2% widowed, 14.3% divorced; Foreign born: 5.3%; Speak English only: 86.8%; With disability: 16.4%; Veterans: 9.5%; Ancestry: 21.2% German, 14.1% American, 11.0% Irish, 10.2% English, 5.6% Dutch

Employment: 7.5% management, business, and financial, 2.6% computer, engineering, and science, 9.3% education, legal, community service, arts, and media, 4.5% healthcare practitioners, 21.0% service, 19.7% sales and office, 15.4% natural resources, construction, and maintenance, 19.9% production, transportation, and material moving

Income: Per capita: $19,725; Median household: $43,750; Average household: $49,291; Households with income of $100,000 or more: 9.0%; Poverty rate: 26.0%

Educational Attainment: High school diploma or higher: 84.4%; Bachelor's degree or higher: 13.7%; Graduate/professional degree or higher: 6.9%

School District(s)
Lawrence Public Schools (PK-12)
    2012-13 Enrollment: 670 . . . . (269) 674-8233
Van Buren ISD (PK-12)
    2012-13 Enrollment: 622 . . . . (269) 674-8091

Housing: Homeownership rate: 79.8%; Median home value: $118,100; Median year structure built: 1967; Homeowner vacancy rate: 3.2%; Median gross rent: $526 per month; Rental vacancy rate: 13.6%

Health Insurance: 86.1% have insurance; 59.6% have private insurance; 40.4% have public insurance; 13.9% do not have insurance; 0.5% of children under 18 do not have insurance

Transportation: Commute: 93.4% car, 0.7% public transportation, 0.8% walk, 4.2% work from home; Median travel time to work: 23.4 minutes

LAWRENCE (village).
Covers a land area of 1.713 square miles and a water area of 0.048 square miles. Located at 42.21° N. Lat; 86.06° W. Long. Elevation is 689 feet.

History: Lawrence, founded in 1835 by John Allen, once served as a loading point for flatboats on the Paw Paw River. First known as Mason (for Governor Stevens T. Mason) and later as Brush Creek (for the stream through it), the name of Lawrence was established in 1844. The area produced a variety of fruits and vegetables.

Population: 996; Growth (since 2000): -5.9%; Density: 581.4 persons per square mile; Race: 79.4% White, 1.4% Black/African American, 0.1% Asian, 0.6% American Indian/Alaska Native, 0.0% Native Hawaiian/Other Pacific Islander, 2.9% Two or more races, 27.2% Hispanic of any race; Average household size: 2.65; Median age: 31.7; Age under 18: 32.0%; Age 65 and over: 9.1%; Males per 100 females: 102.0

School District(s)
Lawrence Public Schools (PK-12)
    2012-13 Enrollment: 670 . . . . (269) 674-8233
Van Buren ISD (PK-12)
    2012-13 Enrollment: 622 . . . . (269) 674-8091

Housing: Homeownership rate: 63.6%; Homeowner vacancy rate: 2.5%; Rental vacancy rate: 20.1%

LAWTON (village).
Covers a land area of 2.320 square miles and a water area of 0.035 square miles. Located at 42.17° N. Lat; 85.85° W. Long. Elevation is 791 feet.

History: Lawton developed as a wine making center, surrounded by vineyards. The village was named for Nathan Lawton, who donated land for a railroad depot in 1848.

Population: 1,900; Growth (since 2000): 2.2%; Density: 818.9 persons per square mile; Race: 91.0% White, 0.7% Black/African American, 0.1% Asian, 0.9% American Indian/Alaska Native, 0.0% Native Hawaiian/Other Pacific Islander, 1.7% Two or more races, 9.8% Hispanic of any race; Average household size: 2.45; Median age: 38.9; Age under 18: 25.4%; Age 65 and over: 19.2%; Males per 100 females: 82.0

School District(s)
Lawton Community SD (PK-12)
    2012-13 Enrollment: 990 . . . . (269) 624-7901

Housing: Homeownership rate: 60.2%; Homeowner vacancy rate: 2.4%; Rental vacancy rate: 7.6%

Safety: Violent crime rate: 21.4 per 10,000 population; Property crime rate: 171.1 per 10,000 population

MATTAWAN (village).
Covers a land area of 3.814 square miles and a water area of 0.024 square miles. Located at 42.22° N. Lat; 85.79° W. Long. Elevation is 869 feet.

Population: 1,997; Growth (since 2000): -21.3%; Density: 523.5 persons per square mile; Race: 93.9% White, 2.2% Black/African American, 0.3% Asian, 0.6% American Indian/Alaska Native, 0.0% Native Hawaiian/Other Pacific Islander, 2.7% Two or more races, 3.9% Hispanic of any race; Average household size: 2.53; Median age: 36.5; Age under 18: 27.6%; Age 65 and over: 11.5%; Males per 100 females: 88.8

School District(s)
Mattawan Consolidated School (PK-12)
    2012-13 Enrollment: 3,764 . . . . (269) 668-3361

Housing: Homeownership rate: 77.0%; Homeowner vacancy rate: 5.7%; Rental vacancy rate: 9.8%

Safety: Violent crime rate: 5.1 per 10,000 population; Property crime rate: 142.1 per 10,000 population

PAW PAW (township).
Covers a land area of 34.912 square miles and a water area of 2.106 square miles. Located at 42.20° N. Lat; 85.94° W. Long. Elevation is 732 feet.

History: Paw Paw Township was organized in 1836. It was first called Lafayette, but changed to the name of Paw Paw in 1867.

Population: 7,041; Growth (since 2000): -0.7%; Density: 201.7 persons per square mile; Race: 92.3% White, 2.1% Black/African American, 0.5% Asian, 0.3% American Indian/Alaska Native, 0.0% Native Hawaiian/Other Pacific Islander, 2.9% Two or more races, 5.5% Hispanic of any race; Average household size: 2.38; Median age: 40.7; Age under 18: 22.9%; Age 65 and over: 14.8%; Males per 100 females: 96.6; Marriage status: 30.8% never married, 51.1% now married, 1.7% separated, 6.7% widowed, 11.5% divorced; Foreign born: 3.5%; Speak English only: 95.2%; With disability: 20.2%; Veterans: 12.1%; Ancestry: 22.6% German, 15.5% English, 13.5% American, 11.4% Irish, 7.7% Polish

Employment: 13.4% management, business, and financial, 6.4% computer, engineering, and science, 10.9% education, legal, community service, arts, and media, 6.0% healthcare practitioners, 19.7% service, 21.9% sales and office, 10.7% natural resources, construction, and maintenance, 11.1% production, transportation, and material moving

Income: Per capita: $21,724; Median household: $42,524; Average household: $53,966; Households with income of $100,000 or more: 14.8%; Poverty rate: 26.9%

Educational Attainment: High school diploma or higher: 85.9%; Bachelor's degree or higher: 19.9%; Graduate/professional degree or higher: 5.6%

School District(s)
Paw Paw Public SD (PK-12)
    2012-13 Enrollment: 2,248 . . . . (269) 657-8800
Van Buren ISD (PK-12)
    2012-13 Enrollment: 622 . . . . (269) 674-8091

Housing: Homeownership rate: 67.0%; Median home value: $113,700; Median year structure built: 1972; Homeowner vacancy rate: 3.2%; Median gross rent: $670 per month; Rental vacancy rate: 10.3%

Health Insurance: 87.1% have insurance; 62.5% have private insurance; 38.4% have public insurance; 12.9% do not have insurance; 0.0% of children under 18 do not have insurance

Hospitals: Bronson Lakeview Hospital (174 beds)

Newspapers: The Courier Leader (weekly circulation 3000)

Transportation: Commute: 83.0% car, 0.0% public transportation, 6.1% walk, 7.1% work from home; Median travel time to work: 25.2 minutes

PAW PAW (village).
County seat. Covers a land area of 2.669 square miles and a water area of 0.222 square miles. Located at 42.21° N. Lat; 85.89° W. Long. Elevation is 732 feet.

History: Paw Paw, first settled in 1832, developed as the center of a grape-growing area. The Paw Paw River, as well as the village, was named for the trees that grew along its banks. Paw Paw became the seat of Van Buren County in 1838, and was incorporated as a village in 1859.

Population: 3,534; Growth (since 2000): 5.1%; Density: 1,324.0 persons per square mile; Race: 92.3% White, 2.3% Black/African American, 0.4% Asian, 0.2% American Indian/Alaska Native, 0.0% Native Hawaiian/Other Pacific Islander, 2.7% Two or more races, 5.9% Hispanic of any race; Average household size: 2.27; Median age: 36.4; Age under 18: 24.2%; Age 65 and over: 13.8%; Males per 100 females: 94.3; Marriage status: 38.0% never married, 37.3% now married, 2.6% separated, 7.0% widowed, 17.6% divorced; Foreign born: 3.8%; Speak English only: 93.1%; With disability: 20.0%; Veterans: 10.8%; Ancestry: 20.3% German, 15.4% English, 11.0% Irish, 9.7% American, 6.1% Dutch

Employment: 9.1% management, business, and financial, 2.8% computer, engineering, and science, 11.3% education, legal, community service, arts, and media, 5.8% healthcare practitioners, 30.2% service, 24.2% sales and office, 4.7% natural resources, construction, and maintenance, 12.0% production, transportation, and material moving

Income: Per capita: $16,650; Median household: $25,383; Average household: $42,236; Households with income of $100,000 or more: 12.1%; Poverty rate: 46.3%

Educational Attainment: High school diploma or higher: 81.9%; Bachelor's degree or higher: 14.1%; Graduate/professional degree or higher: 3.7%

School District(s)

Paw Paw Public SD (PK-12)
   2012-13 Enrollment: 2,248 . . . . (269) 657-8800
Van Buren ISD (PK-12)
   2012-13 Enrollment: 622. . . . . (269) 674-8091

Housing: Homeownership rate: 48.5%; Median home value: $86,500; Median year structure built: 1964; Homeowner vacancy rate: 5.1%; Median gross rent: $684 per month; Rental vacancy rate: 10.5%

Health Insurance: 81.5% have insurance; 43.4% have private insurance; 46.6% have public insurance; 18.5% do not have insurance; 0.0% of children under 18 do not have insurance

Hospitals: Bronson Lakeview Hospital (174 beds)

Safety: Violent crime rate: 31.7 per 10,000 population; Property crime rate: 389.0 per 10,000 population

Newspapers: The Courier Leader (weekly circulation 3000)

Transportation: Commute: 80.9% car, 0.0% public transportation, 13.2% walk, 2.6% work from home; Median travel time to work: 17.7 minutes

PINE GROVE (township). Covers a land area of 34.450 square miles and a water area of 0.631 square miles. Located at 42.38° N. Lat; 85.82° W. Long. Elevation is 787 feet.

Population: 2,949; Growth (since 2000): 6.3%; Density: 85.6 persons per square mile; Race: 96.5% White, 0.9% Black/African American, 0.0% Asian, 0.5% American Indian/Alaska Native, 0.0% Native Hawaiian/Other Pacific Islander, 1.8% Two or more races, 1.6% Hispanic of any race; Average household size: 2.62; Median age: 41.9; Age under 18: 23.8%; Age 65 and over: 12.3%; Males per 100 females: 103.2; Marriage status: 17.8% never married, 66.8% now married, 1.3% separated, 4.8% widowed, 10.6% divorced; Foreign born: 2.3%; Speak English only: 94.7%; With disability: 14.0%; Veterans: 11.7%; Ancestry: 25.6% German, 16.4% English, 12.3% Irish, 11.9% Dutch, 11.0% American

Employment: 15.9% management, business, and financial, 7.8% computer, engineering, and science, 8.8% education, legal, community service, arts, and media, 3.8% healthcare practitioners, 8.0% service, 26.7% sales and office, 14.4% natural resources, construction, and maintenance, 14.6% production, transportation, and material moving

Income: Per capita: $24,568; Median household: $57,143; Average household: $63,093; Households with income of $100,000 or more: 16.9%; Poverty rate: 9.5%

Educational Attainment: High school diploma or higher: 91.4%; Bachelor's degree or higher: 19.1%; Graduate/professional degree or higher: 5.8%

Housing: Homeownership rate: 87.2%; Median home value: $130,200; Median year structure built: 1982; Homeowner vacancy rate: 1.7%; Median gross rent: $700 per month; Rental vacancy rate: 3.4%

Health Insurance: 87.6% have insurance; 75.0% have private insurance; 25.1% have public insurance; 12.4% do not have insurance; 1.3% of children under 18 do not have insurance

Transportation: Commute: 96.2% car, 0.0% public transportation, 0.9% walk, 2.9% work from home; Median travel time to work: 27.3 minutes

PORTER (township). Covers a land area of 33.152 square miles and a water area of 2.255 square miles. Located at 42.12° N. Lat; 85.82° W. Long.

History: Porter Township was organized in 1845 and named for Commodore David Porter, American naval hero in the early 1800's.

Population: 2,466; Growth (since 2000): 2.5%; Density: 74.4 persons per square mile; Race: 95.5% White, 1.0% Black/African American, 0.2% Asian, 0.4% American Indian/Alaska Native, 0.0% Native Hawaiian/Other Pacific Islander, 1.5% Two or more races, 4.7% Hispanic of any race; Average household size: 2.55; Median age: 46.1; Age under 18: 22.3%; Age 65 and over: 15.7%; Males per 100 females: 104.0

Housing: Homeownership rate: 88.9%; Homeowner vacancy rate: 1.7%; Rental vacancy rate: 7.8%

SOUTH HAVEN (charter township). Covers a land area of 17.417 square miles and a water area of 0.100 square miles. Located at 42.36° N. Lat; 86.26° W. Long. Elevation is 614 feet.

History: Maritime Museum. Settled before 1840; Incorporated as village 1869, as city 1902.

Population: 3,983; Growth (since 2000): -1.6%; Density: 228.7 persons per square mile; Race: 80.5% White, 10.0% Black/African American, 0.9% Asian, 0.7% American Indian/Alaska Native, 0.0% Native Hawaiian/Other Pacific Islander, 2.8% Two or more races, 10.2% Hispanic of any race; Average household size: 2.45; Median age: 41.9; Age under 18: 24.7%; Age 65 and over: 16.4%; Males per 100 females: 92.8; Marriage status: 18.1% never married, 56.1% now married, 1.4% separated, 9.2% widowed, 16.7% divorced; Foreign born: 4.5%; Speak English only: 91.9%; With disability: 13.6%; Veterans: 12.8%; Ancestry: 29.5% German, 12.8% English, 9.9% Irish, 8.6% American, 7.8% Polish

Employment: 10.5% management, business, and financial, 3.1% computer, engineering, and science, 3.9% education, legal, community service, arts, and media, 7.1% healthcare practitioners, 23.2% service, 25.0% sales and office, 8.3% natural resources, construction, and maintenance, 18.8% production, transportation, and material moving

Income: Per capita: $22,705; Median household: $41,983; Average household: $50,034; Households with income of $100,000 or more: 12.3%; Poverty rate: 13.8%

Educational Attainment: High school diploma or higher: 91.4%; Bachelor's degree or higher: 14.9%; Graduate/professional degree or higher: 8.3%

School District(s)

South Haven Public Schools (PK-12)
   2012-13 Enrollment: 2,134 . . . . (269) 637-0521

Housing: Homeownership rate: 74.1%; Median home value: $115,800; Median year structure built: 1977; Homeowner vacancy rate: 3.5%; Median gross rent: $718 per month; Rental vacancy rate: 15.5%

Health Insurance: 87.4% have insurance; 61.1% have private insurance; 42.3% have public insurance; 12.6% do not have insurance; 3.2% of children under 18 do not have insurance

Hospitals: South Haven Community Hospital (82 beds)

Newspapers: Tribune (weekly circulation 14000)

Transportation: Commute: 93.7% car, 0.7% public transportation, 2.2% walk, 1.3% work from home; Median travel time to work: 17.3 minutes

Airports: South Haven Area Regional (general aviation)

Additional Information Contacts
South Haven Charter Township . . . . (269) 637-3305
   http://www.southhaventownship.com

SOUTH HAVEN (city). Covers a land area of 3.400 square miles and a water area of 0.095 square miles. Located at 42.40° N. Lat; 86.27° W. Long. Elevation is 614 feet.

History: South Haven was laid out in 1851 and named for its location south of Grand Haven. South Haven developed as a port on Lake Michigan, and as a manufacturing city and supply center for resorts on the many small lakes nearby. Peach orchards were planted in South Haven as early as 1826, and continued to be a primary crop.

Population: 4,403; Growth (since 2000): -12.3%; Density: 1,294.8 persons per square mile; Race: 81.7% White, 13.3% Black/African American, 0.5% Asian, 0.7% American Indian/Alaska Native, 0.1% Native Hawaiian/Other Pacific Islander, 2.9% Two or more races, 3.8% Hispanic of any race; Average household size: 2.17; Median age: 47.7; Age under 18: 20.2%; Age 65 and over: 22.5%; Males per 100 females: 81.5; Marriage status: 26.5% never married, 46.4% now married, 3.3% separated, 10.9% widowed, 16.2% divorced; Foreign born: 1.8%; Speak English only: 98.1%;

With disability: 16.4%; Veterans: 13.4%; Ancestry: 27.2% German, 11.7% Irish, 9.7% English, 8.1% American, 6.9% Polish
Employment: 6.9% management, business, and financial, 8.7% computer, engineering, and science, 8.3% education, legal, community service, arts, and media, 5.7% healthcare practitioners, 23.4% service, 28.7% sales and office, 5.1% natural resources, construction, and maintenance, 13.1% production, transportation, and material moving
Income: Per capita: $26,882; Median household: $34,202; Average household: $55,031; Households with income of $100,000 or more: 15.4%; Poverty rate: 22.6%
Educational Attainment: High school diploma or higher: 91.7%; Bachelor's degree or higher: 29.4%; Graduate/professional degree or higher: 13.3%

School District(s)
South Haven Public Schools (PK-12)
    2012-13 Enrollment: 2,134 . . . . (269) 637-0521
Housing: Homeownership rate: 61.4%; Median home value: $167,800; Median year structure built: 1971; Homeowner vacancy rate: 7.0%; Median gross rent: $536 per month; Rental vacancy rate: 19.4%
Health Insurance: 87.7% have insurance; 63.1% have private insurance; 44.2% have public insurance; 12.3% do not have insurance; 0.0% of children under 18 do not have insurance
Hospitals: South Haven Community Hospital (82 beds)
Safety: Violent crime rate: 6.9 per 10,000 population; Property crime rate: 32.1 per 10,000 population
Newspapers: Tribune (weekly circulation 14000)
Transportation: Commute: 91.2% car, 0.0% public transportation, 2.4% walk, 4.8% work from home; Median travel time to work: 14.3 minutes
Airports: South Haven Area Regional (general aviation)
Additional Information Contacts
City of South Haven . . . . (269) 637-0700
    http://www.south-haven.com

WAVERLY (township). Covers a land area of 34.121 square miles and a water area of 0.297 square miles. Located at 42.29° N. Lat; 85.94° W. Long.
Population: 2,554; Growth (since 2000): 3.5%; Density: 74.9 persons per square mile; Race: 94.4% White, 0.9% Black/African American, 0.3% Asian, 0.4% American Indian/Alaska Native, 0.0% Native Hawaiian/Other Pacific Islander, 2.1% Two or more races, 4.8% Hispanic of any race; Average household size: 2.66; Median age: 39.6; Age under 18: 26.7%; Age 65 and over: 11.7%; Males per 100 females: 99.4; Marriage status: 22.6% never married, 57.4% now married, 1.6% separated, 3.9% widowed, 16.1% divorced; Foreign born: 1.9%; Speak English only: 92.0%; With disability: 14.5%; Veterans: 11.2%; Ancestry: 20.9% German, 15.6% Irish, 15.4% American, 10.3% English, 7.2% Dutch
Employment: 6.9% management, business, and financial, 5.6% computer, engineering, and science, 6.1% education, legal, community service, arts, and media, 6.0% healthcare practitioners, 19.1% service, 14.4% sales and office, 21.7% natural resources, construction, and maintenance, 20.2% production, transportation, and material moving
Income: Per capita: $20,176; Median household: $45,625; Average household: $55,112; Households with income of $100,000 or more: 8.8%; Poverty rate: 19.2%
Educational Attainment: High school diploma or higher: 87.6%; Bachelor's degree or higher: 16.1%; Graduate/professional degree or higher: 4.3%
Housing: Homeownership rate: 88.8%; Median home value: $112,100; Median year structure built: 1978; Homeowner vacancy rate: 1.6%; Median gross rent: $695 per month; Rental vacancy rate: 15.2%
Health Insurance: 88.7% have insurance; 66.7% have private insurance; 33.8% have public insurance; 11.3% do not have insurance; 1.1% of children under 18 do not have insurance
Transportation: Commute: 95.1% car, 0.7% public transportation, 0.4% walk, 2.9% work from home; Median travel time to work: 28.8 minutes

Washtenaw County

Located in southeastern Michigan; drained by the Huron and Raisin Rivers. Covers a land area of 705.965 square miles, a water area of 16.454 square miles, and is located in the Eastern Time Zone at 42.25° N. Lat., 83.84° W. Long. The county was founded in 1826. County seat is Ann Arbor.

Washtenaw County is part of the Ann Arbor, MI Metropolitan Statistical Area. The entire metro area includes: Washtenaw County, MI

Weather Station: Ann Arbor Univ of Mich   Elevation: 899 feet

	Jan	Feb	Mar	Apr	May	Jun	Jul	Aug	Sep	Oct	Nov	Dec
High	32	35	46	60	71	80	83	81	74	62	48	35
Low	18	20	27	38	48	58	62	61	53	42	33	23
Precip	2.6	2.4	2.8	3.3	3.3	3.6	3.5	3.8	3.5	2.9	3.0	2.9
Snow	16.2	12.1	9.0	2.7	tr	0.0	0.0	0.0	tr	0.3	3.2	13.5

High and Low temperatures in degrees Fahrenheit; Precipitation and Snow in inches

Weather Station: Detroit Wbap Willow   Elevation: 777 feet

	Jan	Feb	Mar	Apr	May	Jun	Jul	Aug	Sep	Oct	Nov	Dec
High	33	36	47	61	72	81	85	82	75	63	49	37
Low	19	21	28	39	49	59	63	62	54	43	33	24
Precip	1.9	1.8	2.3	3.0	3.6	3.2	3.3	3.5	3.5	2.7	2.9	2.3
Snow	10.8	6.8	5.1	1.0	tr	0.0	0.0	0.0	0.0	0.1	1.3	8.3

High and Low temperatures in degrees Fahrenheit; Precipitation and Snow in inches

Population: 344,791; Growth (since 2000): 6.8%; Density: 488.4 persons per square mile; Race: 74.5% White, 12.7% Black/African American, 7.9% Asian, 0.3% American Indian/Alaska Native, 0.0% Native Hawaiian/Other Pacific Islander, 3.4% two or more races, 4.0% Hispanic of any race; Average household size: 2.38; Median age: 33.3; Age under 18: 20.9%; Age 65 and over: 10.1%; Males per 100 females: 97.4; Marriage status: 41.5% never married, 45.2% now married, 0.9% separated, 4.2% widowed, 9.2% divorced; Foreign born: 11.4%; Speak English only: 85.8%; With disability: 8.5%; Veterans: 6.1%; Ancestry: 21.4% German, 11.5% Irish, 10.9% English, 6.9% Polish, 6.6% American
Religion: Six largest groups: 12.4% Catholicism, 3.1% Methodist/Pietist, 3.0% Presbyterian-Reformed, 2.9% Lutheran, 2.2% Baptist, 1.9% Pentecostal
Economy: Unemployment rate: 4.1%; Leading industries: 16.1% professional, scientific, and technical services; 13.8% retail trade; 12.2% health care and social assistance; Farms: 1,236 totaling 170,154 acres; Company size: 6 employ 1,000 or more persons, 13 employ 500 to 999 persons, 179 employ 100 to 499 persons, 7,759 employ less than 100 persons; Business ownership: 10,811 women-owned, 2,455 Black-owned, n/a Hispanic-owned, 1,605 Asian-owned
Employment: 14.5% management, business, and financial, 11.1% computer, engineering, and science, 17.1% education, legal, community service, arts, and media, 7.7% healthcare practitioners, 16.5% service, 20.7% sales and office, 4.7% natural resources, construction, and maintenance, 7.7% production, transportation, and material moving
Income: Per capita: $33,231; Median household: $59,055; Average household: $81,487; Households with income of $100,000 or more: 28.4%; Poverty rate: 15.4%
Educational Attainment: High school diploma or higher: 94.0%; Bachelor's degree or higher: 51.3%; Graduate/professional degree or higher: 26.3%
Housing: Homeownership rate: 60.9%; Median home value: $198,400; Median year structure built: 1975; Homeowner vacancy rate: 2.1%; Median gross rent: $910 per month; Rental vacancy rate: 7.7%
Vital Statistics: Birth rate: 105.4 per 10,000 population; Death rate: 58.9 per 10,000 population; Age-adjusted cancer mortality rate: 162.3 deaths per 100,000 population
Health Insurance: 92.3% have insurance; 81.3% have private insurance; 22.1% have public insurance; 7.7% do not have insurance; 2.7% of children under 18 do not have insurance
Health Care: Physicians: 98.9 per 10,000 population; Hospital beds: 49.2 per 10,000 population; Hospital admissions: 2,538.5 per 10,000 population
Air Quality Index: 88.2% good, 11.8% moderate, 0.0% unhealthy for sensitive individuals, 0.0% unhealthy (percent of days)
Transportation: Commute: 81.5% car, 4.7% public transportation, 6.3% walk, 5.2% work from home; Median travel time to work: 23.0 minutes
Presidential Election: 67.0% Obama, 31.3% Romney (2012)
National and State Parks: Chelsea State Game Area; Pinckney State Recreation Area
Additional Information Contacts
Washtenaw Government. . . . . (734) 222-6850
    http://www.ewashtenaw.org

Washtenaw County Communities

ANN ARBOR (charter township). Covers a land area of 16.731 square miles and a water area of 0.144 square miles. Located at 42.32° N. Lat; 83.71° W. Long. Elevation is 879 feet.

History: Cobblestone Farm, 19th-century farmhouse, 1837 cabin, gardens. Incorporated 1851.

Population: 4,361; Growth (since 2000): -7.6%; Density: 260.6 persons per square mile; Race: 76.1% White, 2.9% Black/African American, 17.4% Asian, 0.2% American Indian/Alaska Native, 0.0% Native Hawaiian/Other Pacific Islander, 2.3% Two or more races, 2.9% Hispanic of any race; Average household size: 2.30; Median age: 43.5; Age under 18: 20.6%; Age 65 and over: 17.4%; Males per 100 females: 93.6; Marriage status: 24.1% never married, 63.0% now married, 1.1% separated, 4.5% widowed, 8.5% divorced; Foreign born: 20.8%; Speak English only: 74.5%; With disability: 8.5%; Veterans: 5.6%; Ancestry: 16.7% German, 12.0% English, 10.9% Irish, 7.0% Polish, 4.9% French

Employment: 23.3% management, business, and financial, 18.9% computer, engineering, and science, 23.1% education, legal, community service, arts, and media, 10.9% healthcare practitioners, 9.2% service, 8.7% sales and office, 2.6% natural resources, construction, and maintenance, 3.3% production, transportation, and material moving

Income: Per capita: $58,766; Median household: $102,821; Average household: $144,043; Households with income of $100,000 or more: 51.7%; Poverty rate: 6.0%

Educational Attainment: High school diploma or higher: 98.5%; Bachelor's degree or higher: 76.7%; Graduate/professional degree or higher: 53.2%

School District(s)
Ann Arbor Learning Community (KG-12)
    2012-13 Enrollment: 244 . . . . (734) 477-0340
Ann Arbor Public Schools (PK-12)
    2012-13 Enrollment: 16,654 . . . . (734) 994-2230
Central Academy (PK-12)
    2012-13 Enrollment: 543 . . . . (734) 822-1100
Honey Creek Community School (KG-12)
    2012-13 Enrollment: 242 . . . . (734) 994-2636
Multicultural Academy (PK-12)
    2012-13 Enrollment: 289 . . . . (734) 677-0732
Washtenaw ISD (PK-12)
    2012-13 Enrollment: 601 . . . . (734) 994-8100
Washtenaw Technical Middle College (KG-12)
    2012-13 Enrollment: 432 . . . . (734) 973-3410

Four-year College(s)
Cleary University (Private, Not-for-profit)
    Fall 2013 Enrollment: 546 . . . . (800) 686-1883
    2013-14 Tuition: In-state $18,720; Out-of-state $18,720
Concordia University-Ann Arbor (Private, Not-for-profit, Lutheran Church - Missouri Synod)
    Fall 2013 Enrollment: 740 . . . . (734) 995-7300
    2013-14 Tuition: In-state $23,563; Out-of-state $23,563
University of Michigan-Ann Arbor (Public)
    Fall 2013 Enrollment: 43,710 . . . . (734) 764-1817
    2013-14 Tuition: In-state $13,142; Out-of-state $40,392

Two-year College(s)
Washtenaw Community College (Public)
    Fall 2013 Enrollment: 12,327 . . . . (734) 973-3543
    2013-14 Tuition: In-state $3,672; Out-of-state $4,800

Vocational/Technical School(s)
Ann Arbor Institute of Massage Therapy (Private, For-profit)
    Fall 2013 Enrollment: 80 . . . . (734) 677-4430
    2013-14 Tuition: $9,400
Ross Medical Education Center-Ann Arbor (Private, For-profit)
    Fall 2013 Enrollment: 128 . . . . (734) 434-7320
    2013-14 Tuition: $15,680
Scholars Cosmetology University (Private, For-profit)
    Fall 2013 Enrollment: 30 . . . . (734) 971-3001
    2013-14 Tuition: $12,000

Housing: Homeownership rate: 68.7%; Median home value: $380,400; Median year structure built: 1985; Homeowner vacancy rate: 2.3%; Median gross rent: $1,174 per month; Rental vacancy rate: 5.4%

Health Insurance: 96.5% have insurance; 91.8% have private insurance; 21.4% have public insurance; 3.5% do not have insurance; 0.0% of children under 18 do not have insurance

Hospitals: Saint Joseph Mercy Hospital (581 beds); University of Michigan Health System (930 beds); VA Ann Arbor Healthcare System (132 beds)

Transportation: Commute: 82.5% car, 1.8% public transportation, 1.2% walk, 13.4% work from home; Median travel time to work: 22.5 minutes; Amtrak: Train service available.

Airports: Ann Arbor Municipal (general aviation)

Additional Information Contacts
Ann Arbor Charter Township . . . . (734) 663-3418
    http://www.aatwp.org

ANN ARBOR (city). County seat. Covers a land area of 27.830 square miles and a water area of 0.870 square miles. Located at 42.28° N. Lat; 83.73° W. Long. Elevation is 879 feet.

History: The first homes in Ann Arbor were those of John and Ann Allen from Virginia, and Elisha and Ann Rumsey from New York, who settled here in 1824. One version of the naming of the town says that they built an arbor with wild grapevines growing over it, and named the settlement Anns' Arbor for the two wives. Another story attributes the name to a woman named Ann d'Arbeur, who was a wilderness guide in this area in the early 1800's. Allen set up a gristmill when he arrived, and soon other settlers and other mills, a tannery, and a general store followed. In 1837 the young town was successful in its bid to have the University of Michigan moved here from Detroit. One of the early industries in Ann Arbor was the making of watches, followed by the making of organs and pianos. Later industries produced baling machinery, steel balls, radios, and cameras.

Population: 113,934; Growth (since 2000): -0.1%; Density: 4,094.0 persons per square mile; Race: 73.0% White, 7.7% Black/African American, 14.4% Asian, 0.3% American Indian/Alaska Native, 0.0% Native Hawaiian/Other Pacific Islander, 3.6% Two or more races, 4.1% Hispanic of any race; Average household size: 2.17; Median age: 27.8; Age under 18: 14.4%; Age 65 and over: 9.3%; Males per 100 females: 97.2; Marriage status: 55.1% never married, 33.9% now married, 0.6% separated, 3.3% widowed, 7.7% divorced; Foreign born: 17.4%; Speak English only: 78.9%; With disability: 6.5%; Veterans: 4.0%; Ancestry: 18.3% German, 10.5% English, 9.8% Irish, 6.7% Polish, 5.1% American

Employment: 13.2% management, business, and financial, 15.1% computer, engineering, and science, 25.1% education, legal, community service, arts, and media, 7.5% healthcare practitioners, 15.1% service, 17.0% sales and office, 2.5% natural resources, construction, and maintenance, 4.4% production, transportation, and material moving

Income: Per capita: $34,247; Median household: $55,003; Average household: $78,722; Households with income of $100,000 or more: 26.7%; Poverty rate: 22.1%

Educational Attainment: High school diploma or higher: 96.5%; Bachelor's degree or higher: 70.6%; Graduate/professional degree or higher: 41.7%

School District(s)
Ann Arbor Learning Community (KG-12)
    2012-13 Enrollment: 244 . . . . (734) 477-0340
Ann Arbor Public Schools (PK-12)
    2012-13 Enrollment: 16,654 . . . . (734) 994-2230
Central Academy (PK-12)
    2012-13 Enrollment: 543 . . . . (734) 822-1100
Honey Creek Community School (KG-12)
    2012-13 Enrollment: 242 . . . . (734) 994-2636
Multicultural Academy (PK-12)
    2012-13 Enrollment: 289 . . . . (734) 677-0732
Washtenaw ISD (PK-12)
    2012-13 Enrollment: 601 . . . . (734) 994-8100
Washtenaw Technical Middle College (KG-12)
    2012-13 Enrollment: 432 . . . . (734) 973-3410

Four-year College(s)
Cleary University (Private, Not-for-profit)
    Fall 2013 Enrollment: 546 . . . . (800) 686-1883
    2013-14 Tuition: In-state $18,720; Out-of-state $18,720
Concordia University-Ann Arbor (Private, Not-for-profit, Lutheran Church - Missouri Synod)
    Fall 2013 Enrollment: 740 . . . . (734) 995-7300
    2013-14 Tuition: In-state $23,563; Out-of-state $23,563
University of Michigan-Ann Arbor (Public)
    Fall 2013 Enrollment: 43,710 . . . . (734) 764-1817
    2013-14 Tuition: In-state $13,142; Out-of-state $40,392

Two-year College(s)

Washtenaw Community College (Public)

Fall 2013 Enrollment: 12,327 . . . . (734) 973-3543

2013-14 Tuition: In-state $3,672; Out-of-state $4,800

Vocational/Technical School(s)

Ann Arbor Institute of Massage Therapy (Private, For-profit)

Fall 2013 Enrollment: 80. . . . . (734) 677-4430

2013-14 Tuition: $9,400

Ross Medical Education Center-Ann Arbor (Private, For-profit)

Fall 2013 Enrollment: 128. . . . . (734) 434-7320

2013-14 Tuition: $15,680

Scholars Cosmetology University (Private, For-profit)

Fall 2013 Enrollment: 30. . . . . (734) 971-3001

2013-14 Tuition: $12,000

Housing: Homeownership rate: 44.8%; Median home value: $230,700; Median year structure built: 1968; Homeowner vacancy rate: 1.7%; Median gross rent: <$100 per month; Rental vacancy rate: 5.5%

Health Insurance: 93.8% have insurance; 86.2% have private insurance; 17.0% have public insurance; 6.2% do not have insurance; 2.3% of children under 18 do not have insurance

Hospitals: Saint Joseph Mercy Hospital (581 beds); University of Michigan Health System (930 beds); VA Ann Arbor Healthcare System (132 beds)

Safety: Violent crime rate: 21.1 per 10,000 population; Property crime rate: 216.2 per 10,000 population

Transportation: Commute: 64.2% car, 10.2% public transportation, 15.0% walk, 5.7% work from home; Median travel time to work: 19.5 minutes; Amtrak: Train service available.

Airports: Ann Arbor Municipal (general aviation)

Additional Information Contacts

City of Ann Arbor. . . . . (734) 994-2700

http://www.a2gov.org

AUGUSTA (charter township). Covers a land area of 36.699 square miles and a water area of 0.080 square miles. Located at 42.13° N. Lat; 83.59° W. Long.

Population: 6,745; Growth (since 2000): 40.1%; Density: 183.8 persons per square mile; Race: 87.6% White, 7.8% Black/African American, 0.6% Asian, 0.4% American Indian/Alaska Native, 0.0% Native Hawaiian/Other Pacific Islander, 2.5% Two or more races, 2.1% Hispanic of any race; Average household size: 2.77; Median age: 40.3; Age under 18: 25.2%; Age 65 and over: 12.2%; Males per 100 females: 100.2; Marriage status: 25.2% never married, 61.6% now married, 0.5% separated, 5.1% widowed, 8.1% divorced; Foreign born: 0.7%; Speak English only: 98.1%; With disability: 15.3%; Veterans: 8.3%; Ancestry: 30.0% German, 14.9% Irish, 13.5% American, 10.2% English, 8.8% Polish

Employment: 15.8% management, business, and financial, 3.5% computer, engineering, and science, 10.2% education, legal, community service, arts, and media, 4.6% healthcare practitioners, 18.9% service, 20.8% sales and office, 11.6% natural resources, construction, and maintenance, 14.6% production, transportation, and material moving

Income: Per capita: $25,766; Median household: $73,596; Average household: $76,615; Households with income of $100,000 or more: 30.9%; Poverty rate: 8.7%

Educational Attainment: High school diploma or higher: 91.1%; Bachelor's degree or higher: 20.5%; Graduate/professional degree or higher: 8.9%

Housing: Homeownership rate: 90.5%; Median home value: $173,300; Median year structure built: 1979; Homeowner vacancy rate: 2.5%; Median gross rent: $1,263 per month; Rental vacancy rate: 16.6%

Health Insurance: 89.3% have insurance; 79.9% have private insurance; 26.0% have public insurance; 10.7% do not have insurance; 13.1% of children under 18 do not have insurance

Transportation: Commute: 95.6% car, 0.0% public transportation, 1.7% walk, 2.1% work from home; Median travel time to work: 28.0 minutes

---

BARTON HILLS (village). Covers a land area of 0.750 square miles and a water area of 0 square miles. Located at 42.32° N. Lat; 83.76° W. Long. Elevation is 945 feet.

Population: 294; Growth (since 2000): -12.2%; Density: 392.0 persons per square mile; Race: 88.1% White, 1.0% Black/African American, 6.8% Asian, 0.0% American Indian/Alaska Native, 0.0% Native Hawaiian/Other Pacific Islander, 2.4% Two or more races, 5.8% Hispanic of any race; Average household size: 2.39; Median age: 53.7; Age under 18: 21.8%; Age 65 and over: 29.6%; Males per 100 females: 92.2

Housing: Homeownership rate: 93.4%; Homeowner vacancy rate: 4.9%; Rental vacancy rate: 0.0%

BRIDGEWATER (township). Covers a land area of 36.163 square miles and a water area of 0.420 square miles. Located at 42.12° N. Lat; 83.96° W. Long. Elevation is 909 feet.

History: Bridgewater Township was first named Hixon for Colonel Daniel Hixon, who settled here in 1829. It was renamed in 1833.

Population: 1,674; Growth (since 2000): 1.7%; Density: 46.3 persons per square mile; Race: 97.0% White, 0.1% Black/African American, 0.5% Asian, 0.2% American Indian/Alaska Native, 0.0% Native Hawaiian/Other Pacific Islander, 1.2% Two or more races, 2.2% Hispanic of any race; Average household size: 2.67; Median age: 44.7; Age under 18: 23.0%; Age 65 and over: 15.4%; Males per 100 females: 101.9

Housing: Homeownership rate: 91.9%; Homeowner vacancy rate: 1.2%; Rental vacancy rate: 7.3%

CHELSEA (city). Covers a land area of 3.634 square miles and a water area of 0.051 square miles. Located at 42.31° N. Lat; 84.02° W. Long. Elevation is 938 feet.

History: Chelsea came into existence when the Michigan Central Railroad built a station here in 1850. The village was once a leading shipper of wool, as well as the market center for farm produce.

Population: 4,944; Growth (since 2000): 12.4%; Density: 1,360.4 persons per square mile; Race: 96.1% White, 0.4% Black/African American, 1.1% Asian, 0.3% American Indian/Alaska Native, 0.0% Native Hawaiian/Other Pacific Islander, 1.5% Two or more races, 2.5% Hispanic of any race; Average household size: 2.18; Median age: 43.5; Age under 18: 22.7%; Age 65 and over: 22.7%; Males per 100 females: 83.6; Marriage status: 21.2% never married, 52.4% now married, 1.7% separated, 14.0% widowed, 12.4% divorced; Foreign born: 5.1%; Speak English only: 96.0%; With disability: 18.9%; Veterans: 15.0%; Ancestry: 34.8% German, 15.5% English, 12.1% Irish, 8.8% Polish, 8.4% American

Employment: 21.2% management, business, and financial, 9.9% computer, engineering, and science, 14.7% education, legal, community service, arts, and media, 9.7% healthcare practitioners, 9.8% service, 20.9% sales and office, 7.5% natural resources, construction, and maintenance, 6.2% production, transportation, and material moving

Income: Per capita: $32,859; Median household: $53,172; Average household: $71,278; Households with income of $100,000 or more: 23.3%; Poverty rate: 8.7%

Educational Attainment: High school diploma or higher: 93.2%; Bachelor's degree or higher: 45.1%; Graduate/professional degree or higher: 22.0%

School District(s)

Chelsea SD (PK-12)

2012-13 Enrollment: 2,498 . . . . (734) 433-2208

Housing: Homeownership rate: 65.4%; Median home value: $175,100; Median year structure built: 1967; Homeowner vacancy rate: 2.4%; Median gross rent: <$100 per month; Rental vacancy rate: 11.6%

Health Insurance: 91.4% have insurance; 82.9% have private insurance; 31.4% have public insurance; 8.6% do not have insurance; 8.3% of children under 18 do not have insurance

Hospitals: Chelsea Community Hospital (113 beds)

Safety: Violent crime rate: 21.8 per 10,000 population; Property crime rate: 116.7 per 10,000 population

Transportation: Commute: 93.9% car, 0.6% public transportation, 0.0% walk, 4.9% work from home; Median travel time to work: 25.4 minutes

---

DEXTER (township). Covers a land area of 30.357 square miles and a water area of 2.817 square miles. Located at 42.38° N. Lat; 83.94° W. Long. Elevation is 869 feet.

History: Settled 1823; incorporated 1855.

Population: 6,042; Growth (since 2000): 15.1%; Density: 199.0 persons per square mile; Race: 96.5% White, 0.5% Black/African American, 0.7% Asian, 0.2% American Indian/Alaska Native, 0.1% Native Hawaiian/Other Pacific Islander, 1.7% Two or more races, 1.8% Hispanic of any race; Average household size: 2.71; Median age: 43.8; Age under 18: 25.7%; Age 65 and over: 12.1%; Males per 100 females: 102.7; Marriage status: 19.8% never married, 71.1% now married, 0.5% separated, 3.8% widowed, 5.3% divorced; Foreign born: 2.8%; Speak English only: 95.6%; With disability: 7.4%; Veterans: 8.6%; Ancestry: 34.0% German, 21.7% English, 18.4% Irish, 9.3% American, 8.8% Polish

Employment: 21.9% management, business, and financial, 8.7% computer, engineering, and science, 13.5% education, legal, community

service, arts, and media, 9.3% healthcare practitioners, 12.9% service, 22.4% sales and office, 5.6% natural resources, construction, and maintenance, 5.8% production, transportation, and material moving
Income: Per capita: $36,396; Median household: $77,802; Average household: $102,295; Households with income of $100,000 or more: 42.9%; Poverty rate: 4.8%
Educational Attainment: High school diploma or higher: 97.6%; Bachelor's degree or higher: 50.6%; Graduate/professional degree or higher: 22.0%

School District(s)
Dexter Community SD (PK-12)
    2012-13 Enrollment: 3,544 . . . . (734) 424-4100
Housing: Homeownership rate: 92.5%; Median home value: $252,300; Median year structure built: 1976; Homeowner vacancy rate: 1.5%; Median gross rent: $1,243 per month; Rental vacancy rate: 10.5%
Health Insurance: 95.3% have insurance; 88.8% have private insurance; 16.8% have public insurance; 4.7% do not have insurance; 0.0% of children under 18 do not have insurance
Transportation: Commute: 91.7% car, 0.0% public transportation, 0.1% walk, 8.2% work from home; Median travel time to work: 33.1 minutes

DEXTER (village). Covers a land area of 1.866 square miles and a water area of 0.063 square miles. Located at 42.33° N. Lat; 83.88° W. Long. Elevation is 869 feet.
History: Dexter was named for Judge Samuel W. Dexter, who built a home here in the early 1840's.
Population: 4,067; Growth (since 2000): 74.0%; Density: 2,179.1 persons per square mile; Race: 92.7% White, 1.1% Black/African American, 2.8% Asian, 0.4% American Indian/Alaska Native, 0.0% Native Hawaiian/Other Pacific Islander, 2.2% Two or more races, 2.8% Hispanic of any race; Average household size: 2.56; Median age: 36.2; Age under 18: 31.0%; Age 65 and over: 8.6%; Males per 100 females: 89.1; Marriage status: 18.9% never married, 57.2% now married, 0.3% separated, 9.9% widowed, 14.0% divorced; Foreign born: 5.3%; Speak English only: 91.7%; With disability: 7.5%; Veterans: 4.6%; Ancestry: 30.3% German, 17.7% Irish, 17.7% English, 7.8% Polish, 6.8% Italian
Employment: 20.2% management, business, and financial, 15.9% computer, engineering, and science, 19.0% education, legal, community service, arts, and media, 5.5% healthcare practitioners, 9.7% service, 18.7% sales and office, 5.4% natural resources, construction, and maintenance, 5.7% production, transportation, and material moving
Income: Per capita: $30,698; Median household: $71,071; Average household: $78,732; Households with income of $100,000 or more: 29.4%; Poverty rate: 2.3%
Educational Attainment: High school diploma or higher: 94.8%; Bachelor's degree or higher: 56.1%; Graduate/professional degree or higher: 24.4%

School District(s)
Dexter Community SD (PK-12)
    2012-13 Enrollment: 3,544 . . . . (734) 424-4100
Housing: Homeownership rate: 73.7%; Median home value: $217,700; Median year structure built: 1995; Homeowner vacancy rate: 3.4%; Median gross rent: $998 per month; Rental vacancy rate: 9.3%
Health Insurance: 92.3% have insurance; 85.7% have private insurance; 19.3% have public insurance; 7.7% do not have insurance; 3.4% of children under 18 do not have insurance
Transportation: Commute: 92.4% car, 0.5% public transportation, 0.8% walk, 5.6% work from home; Median travel time to work: 22.3 minutes
Additional Information Contacts
Village of Dexter . . . . (734) 426-8303
    http://www.dextermi.gov

FREEDOM (township). Covers a land area of 35.463 square miles and a water area of 0.382 square miles. Located at 42.21° N. Lat; 83.96° W. Long.
Population: 1,428; Growth (since 2000): -8.6%; Density: 40.3 persons per square mile; Race: 97.8% White, 0.3% Black/African American, 0.4% Asian, 0.1% American Indian/Alaska Native, 0.0% Native Hawaiian/Other Pacific Islander, 1.3% Two or more races, 1.5% Hispanic of any race; Average household size: 2.42; Median age: 48.9; Age under 18: 20.4%; Age 65 and over: 17.1%; Males per 100 females: 103.4
Housing: Homeownership rate: 84.5%; Homeowner vacancy rate: 1.2%; Rental vacancy rate: 9.1%

LIMA (township). Covers a land area of 34.534 square miles and a water area of 0.669 square miles. Located at 42.29° N. Lat; 83.95° W. Long.
History: A post office was established in Lima Township in 1832, and was first called Mill Creek, the name being afterwards changed to Lima Center. Asa Williams was the first postmaster and the village was platted here in 1838 by W.A. Shaw, J.E. Freer and Abram Arnold.
Population: 3,307; Growth (since 2000): 2.6%; Density: 95.8 persons per square mile; Race: 94.5% White, 1.5% Black/African American, 1.8% Asian, 0.4% American Indian/Alaska Native, 0.2% Native Hawaiian/Other Pacific Islander, 1.2% Two or more races, 2.2% Hispanic of any race; Average household size: 2.76; Median age: 41.5; Age under 18: 25.8%; Age 65 and over: 12.2%; Males per 100 females: 101.2; Marriage status: 21.4% never married, 66.1% now married, 0.3% separated, 3.3% widowed, 9.2% divorced; Foreign born: 4.5%; Speak English only: 95.1%; With disability: 6.3%; Veterans: 7.9%; Ancestry: 30.3% German, 17.5% Irish, 15.8% English, 7.3% Polish, 6.5% American
Employment: 13.9% management, business, and financial, 9.0% computer, engineering, and science, 9.5% education, legal, community service, arts, and media, 10.3% healthcare practitioners, 14.6% service, 22.9% sales and office, 12.5% natural resources, construction, and maintenance, 7.4% production, transportation, and material moving
Income: Per capita: $36,928; Median household: $91,193; Average household: $96,481; Households with income of $100,000 or more: 38.8%; Poverty rate: 4.1%
Educational Attainment: High school diploma or higher: 96.7%; Bachelor's degree or higher: 41.6%; Graduate/professional degree or higher: 18.8%
Housing: Homeownership rate: 92.8%; Median home value: $244,700; Median year structure built: 1986; Homeowner vacancy rate: 1.0%; Median gross rent: $892 per month; Rental vacancy rate: 3.3%
Health Insurance: 95.2% have insurance; 93.2% have private insurance; 12.5% have public insurance; 4.8% do not have insurance; 3.4% of children under 18 do not have insurance
Transportation: Commute: 96.2% car, 0.4% public transportation, 0.3% walk, 2.0% work from home; Median travel time to work: 24.0 minutes

LODI (township). Covers a land area of 34.269 square miles and a water area of 0.184 square miles. Located at 42.22° N. Lat; 83.85° W. Long.
History: Lodi Township was settled in 1825, and named for Lodi in the Finger Lakes region of New York, the former home of many of the early residents.
Population: 6,058; Growth (since 2000): 6.1%; Density: 176.8 persons per square mile; Race: 90.3% White, 2.4% Black/African American, 2.7% Asian, 0.3% American Indian/Alaska Native, 0.1% Native Hawaiian/Other Pacific Islander, 2.8% Two or more races, 5.0% Hispanic of any race; Average household size: 2.82; Median age: 44.2; Age under 18: 25.3%; Age 65 and over: 12.1%; Males per 100 females: 98.0; Marriage status: 21.0% never married, 70.4% now married, 0.0% separated, 2.7% widowed, 5.9% divorced; Foreign born: 5.8%; Speak English only: 91.9%; With disability: 7.8%; Veterans: 6.7%; Ancestry: 31.5% German, 18.2% English, 13.9% Irish, 11.4% Polish, 6.7% American
Employment: 22.4% management, business, and financial, 9.1% computer, engineering, and science, 15.0% education, legal, community service, arts, and media, 11.9% healthcare practitioners, 8.9% service, 21.9% sales and office, 5.2% natural resources, construction, and maintenance, 5.7% production, transportation, and material moving
Income: Per capita: $46,626; Median household: $107,819; Average household: $126,553; Households with income of $100,000 or more: 54.6%; Poverty rate: 2.8%
Educational Attainment: High school diploma or higher: 97.4%; Bachelor's degree or higher: 58.5%; Graduate/professional degree or higher: 30.6%
Housing: Homeownership rate: 92.8%; Median home value: $302,400; Median year structure built: 1986; Homeowner vacancy rate: 1.9%; Median gross rent: $1,571 per month; Rental vacancy rate: 15.7%
Health Insurance: 95.6% have insurance; 91.6% have private insurance; 17.4% have public insurance; 4.4% do not have insurance; 2.6% of children under 18 do not have insurance
Transportation: Commute: 91.1% car, 0.0% public transportation, 1.5% walk, 6.3% work from home; Median travel time to work: 26.1 minutes

LYNDON (township). Covers a land area of 32.021 square miles and a water area of 3.078 square miles. Located at 42.39° N. Lat; 84.08° W. Long.

Population: 2,720; Growth (since 2000): -0.3%; Density: 84.9 persons per square mile; Race: 93.8% White, 3.1% Black/African American, 0.4% Asian, 0.6% American Indian/Alaska Native, 0.0% Native Hawaiian/Other Pacific Islander, 1.9% Two or more races, 1.7% Hispanic of any race; Average household size: 2.62; Median age: 44.9; Age under 18: 21.3%; Age 65 and over: 12.1%; Males per 100 females: 115.5; Marriage status: 29.6% never married, 57.7% now married, 0.2% separated, 2.7% widowed, 10.0% divorced; Foreign born: 3.3%; Speak English only: 97.1%; With disability: 7.9%; Veterans: 12.9%; Ancestry: 28.6% German, 17.6% English, 10.6% Irish, 7.6% Polish, 6.0% American

Employment: 18.7% management, business, and financial, 9.3% computer, engineering, and science, 11.8% education, legal, community service, arts, and media, 5.1% healthcare practitioners, 10.0% service, 25.4% sales and office, 14.0% natural resources, construction, and maintenance, 5.8% production, transportation, and material moving

Income: Per capita: $33,075; Median household: $85,197; Average household: $91,837; Households with income of $100,000 or more: 35.2%; Poverty rate: 4.8%

Educational Attainment: High school diploma or higher: 93.5%; Bachelor's degree or higher: 43.1%; Graduate/professional degree or higher: 17.3%

Housing: Homeownership rate: 93.3%; Median home value: $209,800; Median year structure built: 1975; Homeowner vacancy rate: 1.3%; Median gross rent: $681 per month; Rental vacancy rate: 11.0%

Health Insurance: 94.9% have insurance; 89.8% have private insurance; 19.8% have public insurance; 5.1% do not have insurance; 0.0% of children under 18 do not have insurance

Transportation: Commute: 89.0% car, 0.0% public transportation, 1.5% walk, 9.3% work from home; Median travel time to work: 29.7 minutes

MANCHESTER (township). Covers a land area of 37.857 square miles and a water area of 0.901 square miles. Located at 42.12° N. Lat; 84.07° W. Long. Elevation is 899 feet.

History: Incorporated 1867.

Population: 4,569; Growth (since 2000): 11.4%; Density: 120.7 persons per square mile; Race: 97.9% White, 0.3% Black/African American, 0.4% Asian, 0.2% American Indian/Alaska Native, 0.0% Native Hawaiian/Other Pacific Islander, 1.1% Two or more races, 1.6% Hispanic of any race; Average household size: 2.45; Median age: 43.3; Age under 18: 23.3%; Age 65 and over: 14.3%; Males per 100 females: 95.8; Marriage status: 22.9% never married, 57.5% now married, 0.8% separated, 5.9% widowed, 13.8% divorced; Foreign born: 0.9%; Speak English only: 96.7%; With disability: 9.6%; Veterans: 7.9%; Ancestry: 40.1% German, 17.5% Irish, 14.0% English, 6.6% Polish, 5.4% French

Employment: 20.1% management, business, and financial, 7.6% computer, engineering, and science, 9.1% education, legal, community service, arts, and media, 4.2% healthcare practitioners, 18.0% service, 20.4% sales and office, 11.0% natural resources, construction, and maintenance, 9.5% production, transportation, and material moving

Income: Per capita: $30,886; Median household: $62,277; Average household: $81,148; Households with income of $100,000 or more: 28.5%; Poverty rate: 10.6%

Educational Attainment: High school diploma or higher: 94.3%; Bachelor's degree or higher: 35.8%; Graduate/professional degree or higher: 11.6%

School District(s)

Manchester Community Schools (PK-12)

 2012-13 Enrollment: 1,186 . . . . (734) 428-9711

Housing: Homeownership rate: 84.9%; Median home value: $164,100; Median year structure built: 1975; Homeowner vacancy rate: 2.0%; Median gross rent: $646 per month; Rental vacancy rate: 11.4%

Health Insurance: 93.5% have insurance; 86.7% have private insurance; 19.4% have public insurance; 6.5% do not have insurance; 1.3% of children under 18 do not have insurance

Transportation: Commute: 89.3% car, 0.0% public transportation, 1.7% walk, 7.1% work from home; Median travel time to work: 31.7 minutes

MANCHESTER (village). Covers a land area of 2.120 square miles and a water area of 0.121 square miles. Located at 42.15° N. Lat; 84.03° W. Long. Elevation is 899 feet.

Population: 2,091; Growth (since 2000): -3.2%; Density: 986.2 persons per square mile; Race: 98.2% White, 0.3% Black/African American, 0.3%

Asian, 0.2% American Indian/Alaska Native, 0.0% Native Hawaiian/Other Pacific Islander, 0.8% Two or more races, 1.6% Hispanic of any race; Average household size: 2.23; Median age: 41.3; Age under 18: 23.3%; Age 65 and over: 15.2%; Males per 100 females: 88.2

School District(s)

Manchester Community Schools (PK-12)

 2012-13 Enrollment: 1,186 . . . . ı (734) 428-9711

Housing: Homeownership rate: 76.1%; Homeowner vacancy rate: 3.3%; Rental vacancy rate: 12.5%

Additional Information Contacts

Village of Manchester . . . . (734) 428-7877

 http://vil-manchester.org

MILAN (city). Covers a land area of 3.318 square miles and a water area of 0.082 square miles. Located at 42.08° N. Lat; 83.68° W. Long. Elevation is 702 feet.

Population: 5,836; Growth (since 2000): 22.2%; Density: 1,759.1 persons per square mile; Race: 92.3% White, 2.8% Black/African American, 0.9% Asian, 0.5% American Indian/Alaska Native, 0.0% Native Hawaiian/Other Pacific Islander, 2.6% Two or more races, 4.6% Hispanic of any race; Average household size: 2.52; Median age: 34.4; Age under 18: 28.0%; Age 65 and over: 9.7%; Males per 100 females: 93.1; Marriage status: 30.1% never married, 50.0% now married, 1.4% separated, 5.1% widowed, 14.8% divorced; Foreign born: 1.4%; Speak English only: 97.0%; With disability: 8.1%; Veterans: 8.8%; Ancestry: 38.7% German, 14.3% Irish, 13.2% English, 12.5% American, 6.2% Polish

Employment: 9.3% management, business, and financial, 6.5% computer, engineering, and science, 9.4% education, legal, community service, arts, and media, 4.1% healthcare practitioners, 25.5% service, 23.3% sales and office, 6.6% natural resources, construction, and maintenance, 15.3% production, transportation, and material moving

Income: Per capita: $28,240; Median household: $62,471; Average household: $68,902; Households with income of $100,000 or more: 22.8%; Poverty rate: 8.1%

Educational Attainment: High school diploma or higher: 94.4%; Bachelor's degree or higher: 29.5%; Graduate/professional degree or higher: 11.6%

School District(s)

Milan Area Schools (PK-12)

 2012-13 Enrollment: 2,420 . . . . (734) 439-5050

Housing: Homeownership rate: 68.5%; Median home value: $124,200; Median year structure built: 1970; Homeowner vacancy rate: 2.3%; Median gross rent: $887 per month; Rental vacancy rate: 7.6%

Health Insurance: 90.0% have insurance; 79.3% have private insurance; 22.7% have public insurance; 10.0% do not have insurance; 3.1% of children under 18 do not have insurance

Safety: Violent crime rate: 18.7 per 10,000 population; Property crime rate: 238.3 per 10,000 population

Transportation: Commute: 89.0% car, 0.0% public transportation, 6.0% walk, 3.9% work from home; Median travel time to work: 24.3 minutes

Additional Information Contacts

City of Milan . . . . (734) 439-1501

 http://milanmich.org

NORTHFIELD (township). Covers a land area of 35.767 square miles and a water area of 0.898 square miles. Located at 42.39° N. Lat; 83.73° W. Long. Elevation is 974 feet.

Population: 8,245; Growth (since 2000): -0.1%; Density: 230.5 persons per square mile; Race: 95.4% White, 1.0% Black/African American, 0.9% Asian, 0.4% American Indian/Alaska Native, 0.0% Native Hawaiian/Other Pacific Islander, 1.8% Two or more races, 2.3% Hispanic of any race; Average household size: 2.49; Median age: 39.7; Age under 18: 23.1%; Age 65 and over: 9.8%; Males per 100 females: 98.3; Marriage status: 26.6% never married, 57.2% now married, 0.5% separated, 4.6% widowed, 11.6% divorced; Foreign born: 4.0%; Speak English only: 95.5%; With disability: 11.1%; Veterans: 8.3%; Ancestry: 25.1% German, 14.3% English, 13.7% Irish, 13.4% Polish, 7.1% American

Employment: 13.0% management, business, and financial, 7.1% computer, engineering, and science, 8.7% education, legal, community service, arts, and media, 6.3% healthcare practitioners, 18.6% service, 26.4% sales and office, 8.0% natural resources, construction, and maintenance, 11.8% production, transportation, and material moving

Income: Per capita: $30,533; Median household: $54,583; Average household: $75,623; Households with income of $100,000 or more: 25.0%; Poverty rate: 7.7%

Educational Attainment: High school diploma or higher: 93.9%; Bachelor's degree or higher: 32.1%; Graduate/professional degree or higher: 10.7%

Housing: Homeownership rate: 78.7%; Median home value: $155,800; Median year structure built: 1986; Homeowner vacancy rate: 3.7%; Median gross rent: $788 per month; Rental vacancy rate: 9.5%

Health Insurance: 93.7% have insurance; 79.4% have private insurance; 28.0% have public insurance; 6.3% do not have insurance; 1.3% of children under 18 do not have insurance

Safety: Violent crime rate: 17.9 per 10,000 population; Property crime rate: 141.9 per 10,000 population

Transportation: Commute: 94.1% car, 0.3% public transportation, 0.9% walk, 3.5% work from home; Median travel time to work: 25.7 minutes

Additional Information Contacts
Northfield Township. . . . . (734) 449-2880
http://twp-northfield.org

PITTSFIELD (charter township). Covers a land area of 27.258 square miles and a water area of 0.068 square miles. Located at 42.21° N. Lat; 83.72° W. Long. Elevation is 833 feet.

History: Settlement began in the 1820's in Pittsfield, which was named for William Pitt, the English prime minister.

Population: 34,663; Growth (since 2000): 14.9%; Density: 1,271.6 persons per square mile; Race: 66.1% White, 13.2% Black/African American, 13.6% Asian, 0.4% American Indian/Alaska Native, 0.0% Native Hawaiian/Other Pacific Islander, 4.0% Two or more races, 6.5% Hispanic of any race; Average household size: 2.43; Median age: 33.8; Age under 18: 24.4%; Age 65 and over: 7.9%; Males per 100 females: 97.5; Marriage status: 38.4% never married, 49.1% now married, 0.9% separated, 3.2% widowed, 9.2% divorced; Foreign born: 18.3%; Speak English only: 77.5%; With disability: 6.4%; Veterans: 5.4%; Ancestry: 18.7% German, 10.9% Irish, 9.9% English, 6.9% American, 5.9% Polish

Employment: 17.3% management, business, and financial, 12.7% computer, engineering, and science, 14.5% education, legal, community service, arts, and media, 9.9% healthcare practitioners, 13.6% service, 21.2% sales and office, 3.0% natural resources, construction, and maintenance, 7.8% production, transportation, and material moving

Income: Per capita: $35,516; Median household: $66,461; Average household: $89,577; Households with income of $100,000 or more: 32.2%; Poverty rate: 10.7%

Educational Attainment: High school diploma or higher: 94.0%; Bachelor's degree or higher: 56.4%; Graduate/professional degree or higher: 27.7%

Housing: Homeownership rate: 57.5%; Median home value: $222,800; Median year structure built: 1991; Homeowner vacancy rate: 1.5%; Median gross rent: $884 per month; Rental vacancy rate: 6.6%

Health Insurance: 92.7% have insurance; 83.6% have private insurance; 17.4% have public insurance; 7.3% do not have insurance; 2.8% of children under 18 do not have insurance

Safety: Violent crime rate: 19.1 per 10,000 population; Property crime rate: 200.6 per 10,000 population

Transportation: Commute: 89.4% car, 3.5% public transportation, 1.0% walk, 4.6% work from home; Median travel time to work: 23.2 minutes

Additional Information Contacts
Pittsfield Charter Township. . . . . (734) 822-3101
http://www.pittsfieldtwp.org

SALEM (township). Covers a land area of 34.287 square miles and a water area of 0.090 square miles. Located at 42.39° N. Lat; 83.61° W. Long. Elevation is 938 feet.

History: Salem was settled in the mid-1820's and named for Salem, Massachusetts, the former home of some of the early residents.

Population: 5,627; Growth (since 2000): 1.2%; Density: 164.1 persons per square mile; Race: 95.3% White, 1.3% Black/African American, 1.2% Asian, 0.3% American Indian/Alaska Native, 0.0% Native Hawaiian/Other Pacific Islander, 1.3% Two or more races, 2.5% Hispanic of any race; Average household size: 2.71; Median age: 45.7; Age under 18: 22.6%; Age 65 and over: 15.1%; Males per 100 females: 103.2; Marriage status: 21.4% never married, 62.4% now married, 1.3% separated, 4.0% widowed, 12.2% divorced; Foreign born: 4.9%; Speak English only: 95.0%; With disability: 8.1%; Veterans: 7.4%; Ancestry: 27.5% German, 21.1% Irish, 13.8% English, 12.2% Polish, 7.4% Italian

Employment: 12.4% management, business, and financial, 9.8% computer, engineering, and science, 13.3% education, legal, community service, arts, and media, 5.9% healthcare practitioners, 14.4% service,

28.9% sales and office, 7.3% natural resources, construction, and maintenance, 8.0% production, transportation, and material moving

Income: Per capita: $34,516; Median household: $69,509; Average household: $91,850; Households with income of $100,000 or more: 33.2%; Poverty rate: 6.2%

Educational Attainment: High school diploma or higher: 95.8%; Bachelor's degree or higher: 27.4%; Graduate/professional degree or higher: 12.9%

Housing: Homeownership rate: 92.7%; Median home value: $242,100; Median year structure built: 1982; Homeowner vacancy rate: 3.4%; Median gross rent: $807 per month; Rental vacancy rate: 3.8%

Health Insurance: 89.9% have insurance; 84.9% have private insurance; 21.4% have public insurance; 10.1% do not have insurance; 1.9% of children under 18 do not have insurance

Transportation: Commute: 90.8% car, 0.0% public transportation, 0.0% walk, 8.5% work from home; Median travel time to work: 28.6 minutes

SALINE (city). Covers a land area of 4.259 square miles and a water area of 0.071 square miles. Located at 42.17° N. Lat; 83.78° W. Long. Elevation is 823 feet.

History: Saline was settled in the mid-1820's and named for the salt springs here, on the Saline River. The old Saline gristmill, built in the 1840's, was purchased by Henry Ford in the early 1900's, who used it to extract oil from soy beans to be used in finishing Ford cars. The Ford Company provided the seed to farmers willing to raise soy beans for this purpose.

Population: 8,810; Growth (since 2000): 9.7%; Density: 2,068.4 persons per square mile; Race: 93.6% White, 1.4% Black/African American, 2.5% Asian, 0.2% American Indian/Alaska Native, 0.0% Native Hawaiian/Other Pacific Islander, 1.8% Two or more races, 2.6% Hispanic of any race; Average household size: 2.34; Median age: 41.1; Age under 18: 24.5%; Age 65 and over: 14.6%; Males per 100 females: 88.5; Marriage status: 26.7% never married, 52.4% now married, 1.0% separated, 8.4% widowed, 12.6% divorced; Foreign born: 4.1%; Speak English only: 95.4%; With disability: 7.4%; Veterans: 8.7%; Ancestry: 31.0% German, 16.0% English, 15.1% Irish, 8.6% Italian, 7.8% American

Employment: 19.9% management, business, and financial, 9.5% computer, engineering, and science, 13.8% education, legal, community service, arts, and media, 9.3% healthcare practitioners, 16.8% service, 22.2% sales and office, 3.8% natural resources, construction, and maintenance, 4.7% production, transportation, and material moving

Income: Per capita: $36,389; Median household: $63,958; Average household: $81,204; Households with income of $100,000 or more: 33.6%; Poverty rate: 3.8%

Educational Attainment: High school diploma or higher: 96.4%; Bachelor's degree or higher: 56.7%; Graduate/professional degree or higher: 20.6%

School District(s)
Saline Area Schools (PK-12)
2012-13 Enrollment: 5,261 . . . . (734) 429-8000

Housing: Homeownership rate: 71.8%; Median home value: $187,200; Median year structure built: 1979; Homeowner vacancy rate: 1.4%; Median gross rent: $792 per month; Rental vacancy rate: 11.3%

Health Insurance: 95.7% have insurance; 89.0% have private insurance; 24.0% have public insurance; 4.3% do not have insurance; 2.0% of children under 18 do not have insurance

Safety: Violent crime rate: 12.2 per 10,000 population; Property crime rate: 142.9 per 10,000 population

Newspapers: Belleville View (weekly circulation 2900); Chelsea Standard (weekly circulation 5000); Heritage Newspapers (weekly circulation 20000); Manchester Enterprise (weekly circulation 2400)

Transportation: Commute: 91.6% car, 1.1% public transportation, 1.1% walk, 4.5% work from home; Median travel time to work: 23.7 minutes

Additional Information Contacts
City of Saline . . . . (734) 429-4907
http://www.city-saline.org

SALINE (township). Covers a land area of 34.693 square miles and a water area of 0.095 square miles. Located at 42.12° N. Lat; 83.84° W. Long. Elevation is 823 feet.

History: Settled 1824; incorporated as city 1931.

Population: 1,896; Growth (since 2000): 45.6%; Density: 54.7 persons per square mile; Race: 93.9% White, 2.1% Black/African American, 0.8% Asian, 0.2% American Indian/Alaska Native, 0.1% Native Hawaiian/Other Pacific Islander, 2.3% Two or more races, 2.5% Hispanic of any race;

Average household size: 2.59; Median age: 43.3; Age under 18: 23.7%; Age 65 and over: 15.1%; Males per 100 females: 95.7

School District(s)
Saline Area Schools (PK-12)
   2012-13 Enrollment: 5,261 . . . . (734) 429-8000
Housing: Homeownership rate: 87.4%; Homeowner vacancy rate: 3.3%; Rental vacancy rate: 14.0%
Newspapers: Belleville View (weekly circulation 2900); Chelsea Standard (weekly circulation 5000); Heritage Newspapers (weekly circulation 20000); Manchester Enterprise (weekly circulation 2400)

SCIO (township).
Covers a land area of 33.730 square miles and a water area of 0.477 square miles. Located at 42.30° N. Lat; 83.86° W. Long. Elevation is 873 feet.
History: Scio was settled in the 1830's. The name is Latin for "I know."
Population: 20,081; Growth (since 2000): 27.4%; Density: 595.4 persons per square mile; Race: 82.5% White, 4.3% Black/African American, 8.6% Asian, 0.3% American Indian/Alaska Native, 0.0% Native Hawaiian/Other Pacific Islander, 3.3% Two or more races, 3.6% Hispanic of any race; Average household size: 2.55; Median age: 40.5; Age under 18: 26.3%; Age 65 and over: 10.9%; Males per 100 females: 93.6; Marriage status: 21.4% never married, 65.3% now married, 0.6% separated, 4.0% widowed, 9.3% divorced; Foreign born: 12.2%; Speak English only: 84.4%; With disability: 6.6%; Veterans: 6.1%; Ancestry: 23.7% German, 14.8% Irish, 13.1% English, 7.6% Italian, 7.2% Polish
Employment: 19.5% management, business, and financial, 12.5% computer, engineering, and science, 20.9% education, legal, community service, arts, and media, 9.2% healthcare practitioners, 11.0% service, 16.9% sales and office, 4.6% natural resources, construction, and maintenance, 5.4% production, transportation, and material moving
Income: Per capita: $44,329; Median household: $90,105; Average household: $114,575; Households with income of $100,000 or more: 44.1%; Poverty rate: 8.7%
Educational Attainment: High school diploma or higher: 97.2%; Bachelor's degree or higher: 63.2%; Graduate/professional degree or higher: 35.8%
Housing: Homeownership rate: 80.1%; Median home value: $268,600; Median year structure built: 1992; Homeowner vacancy rate: 1.7%; Median gross rent: $1,081 per month; Rental vacancy rate: 8.4%
Health Insurance: 95.2% have insurance; 85.8% have private insurance; 19.2% have public insurance; 4.8% do not have insurance; 1.6% of children under 18 do not have insurance
Transportation: Commute: 89.4% car, 0.6% public transportation, 1.4% walk, 7.6% work from home; Median travel time to work: 24.2 minutes
Additional Information Contacts
Scio Township. . . . . (734) 369-9400
  http://www.twp.scio.mi.us

SHARON (township).
Covers a land area of 37.406 square miles and a water area of 0.457 square miles. Located at 42.21° N. Lat; 84.08° W. Long.
History: Settlement began in the 1830's and was known as Peppergrass. The township of Sharon was organized in 1834 and named for Sharon, Connecticut.
Population: 1,737; Growth (since 2000): 3.5%; Density: 46.4 persons per square mile; Race: 98.0% White, 0.3% Black/African American, 0.1% Asian, 0.4% American Indian/Alaska Native, 0.0% Native Hawaiian/Other Pacific Islander, 1.1% Two or more races, 1.8% Hispanic of any race; Average household size: 2.64; Median age: 46.4; Age under 18: 23.3%; Age 65 and over: 15.0%; Males per 100 females: 102.0
Housing: Homeownership rate: 91.1%; Homeowner vacancy rate: 1.8%; Rental vacancy rate: 6.3%

SUPERIOR (charter township).
Covers a land area of 35.211 square miles and a water area of 0.349 square miles. Located at 42.30° N. Lat; 83.60° W. Long. Elevation is 741 feet.
Population: 13,058; Growth (since 2000): 21.6%; Density: 370.9 persons per square mile; Race: 59.0% White, 30.1% Black/African American, 5.7% Asian, 0.2% American Indian/Alaska Native, 0.0% Native Hawaiian/Other Pacific Islander, 3.7% Two or more races, 3.8% Hispanic of any race; Average household size: 2.63; Median age: 37.5; Age under 18: 26.7%; Age 65 and over: 11.7%; Males per 100 females: 91.0; Marriage status: 31.9% never married, 52.7% now married, 0.5% separated, 7.1% widowed, 8.3% divorced; Foreign born: 13.0%; Speak English only: 82.1%;

With disability: 10.6%; Veterans: 5.6%; Ancestry: 15.2% German, 8.9% American, 8.4% Irish, 7.3% English, 4.9% Polish
Employment: 15.3% management, business, and financial, 9.5% computer, engineering, and science, 9.5% education, legal, community service, arts, and media, 8.0% healthcare practitioners, 21.1% service, 21.6% sales and office, 5.1% natural resources, construction, and maintenance, 9.9% production, transportation, and material moving
Income: Per capita: $37,444; Median household: $69,836; Average household: $97,934; Households with income of $100,000 or more: 30.8%; Poverty rate: 10.3%
Educational Attainment: High school diploma or higher: 91.2%; Bachelor's degree or higher: 42.1%; Graduate/professional degree or higher: 19.0%
Housing: Homeownership rate: 79.2%; Median home value: $157,100; Median year structure built: 1984; Homeowner vacancy rate: 3.9%; Median gross rent: $808 per month; Rental vacancy rate: 7.1%
Health Insurance: 92.7% have insurance; 75.8% have private insurance; 31.0% have public insurance; 7.3% do not have insurance; 0.7% of children under 18 do not have insurance
Transportation: Commute: 92.9% car, 2.9% public transportation, 0.8% walk, 2.8% work from home; Median travel time to work: 26.7 minutes
Additional Information Contacts
Superior Township . . . . (734) 482-6099
  http://www.superior-twp.org

SYLVAN (township).
Covers a land area of 32.589 square miles and a water area of 1.373 square miles. Located at 42.29° N. Lat; 84.08° W. Long. Elevation is 951 feet.
History: Sylvan township is adjacent to Chelsea Proving Grounds (Chelsea, Michigan)where Chrysler LLC operates proving grounds for development and validation testing of new vehicles.
Population: 2,833; Growth (since 2000): -55.9%; Density: 86.9 persons per square mile; Race: 94.6% White, 1.1% Black/African American, 0.9% Asian, 0.4% American Indian/Alaska Native, 0.0% Native Hawaiian/Other Pacific Islander, 2.5% Two or more races, 1.9% Hispanic of any race; Average household size: 2.54; Median age: 47.9; Age under 18: 19.9%; Age 65 and over: 13.6%; Males per 100 females: 102.1; Marriage status: 23.8% never married, 60.6% now married, 1.2% separated, 3.5% widowed, 12.2% divorced; Foreign born: 1.6%; Speak English only: 97.1%; With disability: 11.7%; Veterans: 10.0%; Ancestry: 37.7% German, 19.0% Irish, 16.1% English, 13.0% Polish, 6.5% American
Employment: 14.3% management, business, and financial, 6.1% computer, engineering, and science, 10.6% education, legal, community service, arts, and media, 13.0% healthcare practitioners, 13.2% service, 25.9% sales and office, 6.9% natural resources, construction, and maintenance, 9.9% production, transportation, and material moving
Income: Per capita: $37,617; Median household: $80,391; Average household: $94,239; Households with income of $100,000 or more: 35.5%; Poverty rate: 5.9%
Educational Attainment: High school diploma or higher: 94.0%; Bachelor's degree or higher: 43.4%; Graduate/professional degree or higher: 17.8%
Housing: Homeownership rate: 93.5%; Median home value: $217,800; Median year structure built: 1975; Homeowner vacancy rate: 1.3%; Median gross rent: $1,114 per month; Rental vacancy rate: 11.3%
Health Insurance: 95.0% have insurance; 88.6% have private insurance; 22.0% have public insurance; 5.0% do not have insurance; 0.0% of children under 18 do not have insurance
Transportation: Commute: 93.1% car, 1.4% public transportation, 1.2% walk, 3.6% work from home; Median travel time to work: 25.0 minutes

WEBSTER (township).
Covers a land area of 35.091 square miles and a water area of 0.803 square miles. Located at 42.38° N. Lat; 83.86° W. Long. Elevation is 906 feet.
History: At a meeting in a house built by early settler John Williams the township was formally organized in 1833. Up-the-road neighbor Munnis Kenny, who had arrived in 1829 from Massachusetts, proposed the township be named Webster in honor of statesman, Daniel Webster (with whom Kenny was well acquainted).
Population: 6,784; Growth (since 2000): 30.5%; Density: 193.3 persons per square mile; Race: 96.1% White, 0.5% Black/African American, 1.1% Asian, 0.3% American Indian/Alaska Native, 0.0% Native Hawaiian/Other Pacific Islander, 1.6% Two or more races, 1.9% Hispanic of any race; Average household size: 2.88; Median age: 42.8; Age under 18: 27.8%; Age 65 and over: 10.0%; Males per 100 females: 101.8; Marriage status:

21.2% never married, 70.4% now married, 0.0% separated, 4.2% widowed, 4.2% divorced; Foreign born: 8.0%; Speak English only: 91.2%; With disability: 6.9%; Veterans: 6.9%; Ancestry: 29.4% German, 13.8% English, 11.0% Irish, 9.4% Polish, 9.0% Italian

Employment: 17.8% management, business, and financial, 14.3% computer, engineering, and science, 8.0% education, legal, community service, arts, and media, 14.6% healthcare practitioners, 13.7% service, 19.0% sales and office, 7.3% natural resources, construction, and maintenance, 5.3% production, transportation, and material moving

Income: Per capita: $45,020; Median household: $99,803; Average household: $129,512; Households with income of $100,000 or more: 49.6%; Poverty rate: 2.9%

Educational Attainment: High school diploma or higher: 97.0%; Bachelor's degree or higher: 57.8%; Graduate/professional degree or higher: 28.4%

Housing: Homeownership rate: 94.4%; Median home value: $324,000; Median year structure built: 1993; Homeowner vacancy rate: 1.3%; Median gross rent: $1,420 per month; Rental vacancy rate: 8.3%

Health Insurance: 94.7% have insurance; 92.8% have private insurance; 13.8% have public insurance; 5.3% do not have insurance; 4.1% of children under 18 do not have insurance

Transportation: Commute: 90.4% car, 0.8% public transportation, 1.1% walk, 6.9% work from home; Median travel time to work: 27.2 minutes

Additional Information Contacts
Webster Township . . . . (734) 426-5103
http://twp.webster.mi.us

WHITMORE LAKE (CDP). Covers a land area of 4.212 square miles and a water area of 1.078 square miles. Located at 42.42° N. Lat; 83.75° W. Long.

Population: 6,423; Growth (since 2000): -2.3%; Density: 1,524.8 persons per square mile; Race: 95.5% White, 1.0% Black/African American, 0.6% Asian, 0.5% American Indian/Alaska Native, 0.0% Native Hawaiian/Other Pacific Islander, 1.8% Two or more races, 2.3% Hispanic of any race; Average household size: 2.31; Median age: 37.2; Age under 18: 21.4%; Age 65 and over: 9.1%; Males per 100 females: 97.4; Marriage status: 33.8% never married, 45.1% now married, 0.4% separated, 6.0% widowed, 15.1% divorced; Foreign born: 3.3%; Speak English only: 96.9%; With disability: 12.2%; Veterans: 9.7%; Ancestry: 27.4% German, 18.0% Irish, 15.4% Polish, 14.0% English, 7.0% American

Employment: 11.7% management, business, and financial, 4.1% computer, engineering, and science, 10.4% education, legal, community service, arts, and media, 5.3% healthcare practitioners, 20.2% service, 29.6% sales and office, 7.1% natural resources, construction, and maintenance, 11.5% production, transportation, and material moving

Income: Per capita: $28,150; Median household: $50,412; Average household: $61,283; Households with income of $100,000 or more: 18.0%; Poverty rate: 11.1%

Educational Attainment: High school diploma or higher: 94.4%; Bachelor's degree or higher: 31.1%; Graduate/professional degree or higher: 11.5%

School District(s)
Michigan Department of Human Services (KG-12)
    2012-13 Enrollment: 46. . . . . (517) 373-2000
Whitmore Lake Public SD (PK-12)
    2012-13 Enrollment: 1,068 . . . . (734) 449-4464

Housing: Homeownership rate: 70.7%; Median home value: $116,300; Median year structure built: 1984; Homeowner vacancy rate: 4.1%; Median gross rent: $863 per month; Rental vacancy rate: 7.7%

Health Insurance: 91.1% have insurance; 73.7% have private insurance; 32.5% have public insurance; 8.9% do not have insurance; 2.0% of children under 18 do not have insurance

Transportation: Commute: 95.1% car, 0.0% public transportation, 1.1% walk, 3.0% work from home; Median travel time to work: 25.6 minutes

---

WHITTAKER (unincorporated postal area)
ZCTA: 48190
Covers a land area of 0.353 square miles and a water area of 0 square miles. Located at 42.13° N. Lat; 83.59° W. Long. Elevation is 676 feet.
Population: 107; Growth (since 2000): 0.9%; Density: 302.9 persons per square mile; Race: 96.3% White, 2.8% Black/African American, 0.0% Asian, 0.0% American Indian/Alaska Native, 0.0% Native Hawaiian/Other Pacific Islander, 0.9% Two or more races, 1.9% Hispanic of any race; Average household size: 2.33; Median age: 47.3;

Age under 18: 15.9%; Age 65 and over: 15.0%; Males per 100 females: 98.1
Housing: Homeownership rate: 82.6%; Homeowner vacancy rate: 2.6%; Rental vacancy rate: 0.0%

WILLIS (unincorporated postal area)
ZCTA: 48191
Covers a land area of 16.265 square miles and a water area of 0.064 square miles. Located at 42.12° N. Lat; 83.57° W. Long. Elevation is 686 feet.
Population: 4,054; Growth (since 2000): 55.0%; Density: 249.2 persons per square mile; Race: 87.2% White, 7.8% Black/African American, 0.7% Asian, 0.3% American Indian/Alaska Native, 0.0% Native Hawaiian/Other Pacific Islander, 2.7% Two or more races, 2.3% Hispanic of any race; Average household size: 2.75; Median age: 40.0; Age under 18: 25.1%; Age 65 and over: 11.7%; Males per 100 females: 98.3; Marriage status: 25.1% never married, 59.9% now married, 0.9% separated, 5.2% widowed, 9.8% divorced; Foreign born: 0.9%; Speak English only: 99.3%; With disability: 20.7%; Veterans: 6.7%; Ancestry: 35.2% German, 21.4% Irish, 10.0% Polish, 8.2% English, 8.0% American

Employment: 18.2% management, business, and financial, 1.5% computer, engineering, and science, 5.0% education, legal, community service, arts, and media, 5.6% healthcare practitioners, 23.5% service, 18.4% sales and office, 12.8% natural resources, construction, and maintenance, 15.1% production, transportation, and material moving

Income: Per capita: $25,659; Median household: $72,204; Average household: $75,486; Households with income of $100,000 or more: 32.5%; Poverty rate: 10.6%

Educational Attainment: High school diploma or higher: 90.1%; Bachelor's degree or higher: 17.5%; Graduate/professional degree or higher: 7.7%

Housing: Homeownership rate: 89.7%; Median home value: $157,100; Median year structure built: 1991; Homeowner vacancy rate: 3.1%; Median gross rent: $965 per month; Rental vacancy rate: 21.2%

Health Insurance: 91.0% have insurance; 79.3% have private insurance; 31.5% have public insurance; 9.0% do not have insurance; 4.0% of children under 18 do not have insurance

Transportation: Commute: 95.3% car, 0.0% public transportation, 2.3% walk, 2.4% work from home; Median travel time to work: 30.3 minutes

---

YORK (charter township). Covers a land area of 34.698 square miles and a water area of 0.163 square miles. Located at 42.13° N. Lat; 83.72° W. Long.

History: Named for the city on England. When the Vikings captured the city in 866 AD they renamed it J_rv_k and it became the capital of a wider kingdom of the same name covering much of Northern England. After the Norman conquest, the name "York", which was first used in the 13th century, gradually evolved.

Population: 8,708; Growth (since 2000): 17.8%; Density: 251.0 persons per square mile; Race: 84.0% White, 10.1% Black/African American, 1.7% Asian, 0.6% American Indian/Alaska Native, 0.0% Native Hawaiian/Other Pacific Islander, 2.1% Two or more races, 4.9% Hispanic of any race; Average household size: 3.00; Median age: 41.0; Age under 18: 23.1%; Age 65 and over: 9.1%; Males per 100 females: 150.2; Marriage status: 30.5% never married, 57.7% now married, 1.6% separated, 3.1% widowed, 8.7% divorced; Foreign born: 6.2%; Speak English only: 89.2%; With disability: 7.3%; Veterans: 8.2%; Ancestry: 24.8% German, 14.0% English, 12.5% Irish, 11.6% Polish, 5.9% Italian

Employment: 13.6% management, business, and financial, 7.9% computer, engineering, and science, 10.6% education, legal, community service, arts, and media, 12.0% healthcare practitioners, 19.3% service, 20.2% sales and office, 6.2% natural resources, construction, and maintenance, 10.2% production, transportation, and material moving

Income: Per capita: $33,196; Median household: $107,774; Average household: $120,059; Households with income of $100,000 or more: 57.1%; Poverty rate: 2.9%

Educational Attainment: High school diploma or higher: 93.0%; Bachelor's degree or higher: 33.5%; Graduate/professional degree or higher: 13.5%

Housing: Homeownership rate: 93.3%; Median home value: $261,300; Median year structure built: 1984; Homeowner vacancy rate: 1.2%; Median gross rent: $1,125 per month; Rental vacancy rate: 9.2%

Health Insurance: 95.7% have insurance; 91.4% have private insurance; 14.2% have public insurance; 4.3% do not have insurance; 2.9% of children under 18 do not have insurance

Transportation: Commute: 93.9% car, 0.0% public transportation, 0.0% walk, 5.6% work from home; Median travel time to work: 24.6 minutes

YPSILANTI (charter township).
Covers a land area of 29.931 square miles and a water area of 1.794 square miles. Located at 42.21° N. Lat; 83.60° W. Long. Elevation is 725 feet.

History: Native American trails once crossed this site, and a Native American village and a French trading post (1809—c.1819) were here. Eastern Michigan University and Cleary College are here; Historical Museum, Depot Town, pastoral historic district with parks. Incorporated 1832.

Population: 53,362; Growth (since 2000): 8.5%; Density: 1,782.8 persons per square mile; Race: 58.4% White, 32.8% Black/African American, 2.1% Asian, 0.4% American Indian/Alaska Native, 0.1% Native Hawaiian/Other Pacific Islander, 4.6% Two or more races, 4.6% Hispanic of any race; Average household size: 2.49; Median age: 33.3; Age under 18: 26.2%; Age 65 and over: 8.5%; Males per 100 females: 93.4; Marriage status: 41.3% never married, 42.3% now married, 1.7% separated, 4.6% widowed, 11.7% divorced; Foreign born: 5.7%; Speak English only: 92.5%; With disability: 11.7%; Veterans: 7.6%; Ancestry: 15.2% German, 9.8% Irish, 8.7% American, 7.0% English, 4.8% Polish

Employment: 9.9% management, business, and financial, 6.9% computer, engineering, and science, 10.5% education, legal, community service, arts, and media, 6.5% healthcare practitioners, 22.6% service, 24.9% sales and office, 5.9% natural resources, construction, and maintenance, 12.8% production, transportation, and material moving

Income: Per capita: $24,096; Median household: $44,129; Average household: $57,915; Households with income of $100,000 or more: 16.9%; Poverty rate: 20.6%

Educational Attainment: High school diploma or higher: 88.4%; Bachelor's degree or higher: 28.7%; Graduate/professional degree or higher: 10.0%

School District(s)
Ann Arbor Public Schools (PK-12)
    2012-13 Enrollment: 16,654 . . . . (734) 994-2230
Arbor Preparatory High School (KG-12)
    2012-13 Enrollment: 360 . . . . (616) 957-9060
East Arbor Charter Academy (KG-12)
    2012-13 Enrollment: 670 . . . . (734) 484-5506
Fortis Academy (PK-12)
    2012-13 Enrollment: 641 . . . . (734) 572-3623
Lincoln Consolidated SD (PK-12)
    2012-13 Enrollment: 4,355 . . . . (734) 484-7001
New Beginnings Academy (PK-12)
    2012-13 Enrollment: 166 . . . . (734) 481-9001
SD of Ypsilanti (PK-12)
    2012-13 Enrollment: 3,333 . . . . (734) 714-1218
South Arbor Charter Academy (KG-12)
    2012-13 Enrollment: 772 . . . . (734) 528-2821
Van Buren Public Schools (PK-12)
    2012-13 Enrollment: 5,183 . . . . (734) 697-9123
Washtenaw ISD (PK-12)
    2012-13 Enrollment: 601 . . . . (734) 994-8100
Willow Run Community Schools (PK-12)
    2012-13 Enrollment: 1,435 . . . . (734) 961-6310

Four-year College(s)
Eastern Michigan University (Public)
    Fall 2013 Enrollment: 23,447 . . . . (734) 487-1849
    2013-14 Tuition: In-state $9,364; Out-of-state $24,909

Housing: Homeownership rate: 60.1%; Median home value: $112,900; Median year structure built: 1974; Homeowner vacancy rate: 3.0%; Median gross rent: $805 per month; Rental vacancy rate: 10.6%

Health Insurance: 88.1% have insurance; 65.9% have private insurance; 33.8% have public insurance; 11.9% do not have insurance; 2.8% of children under 18 do not have insurance

Transportation: Commute: 93.0% car, 2.6% public transportation, 0.8% walk, 2.9% work from home; Median travel time to work: 24.3 minutes

Additional Information Contacts
Ypsilanti Charter Township . . . . (734) 484-4700
    http://www.twp.ypsilanti.mi.us

YPSILANTI (city).
Covers a land area of 4.329 square miles and a water area of 0.190 square miles. Located at 42.24° N. Lat; 83.62° W. Long. Elevation is 725 feet.

History: In 1809 Ypsilanti was a French trading post. Settlement around it began in 1823, and grew after the railroad arrived in 1838. The city was named by Augustus Woodward, first Chief Justice of the Territorial Supreme Court, for General Demetrios Ypsilanti, a young Greek hero of the early 1800's. The Ypsilanti Monument recognizing the hero was made in Athens by Christopher Natsos, who also designed the Greek monument to the Unknown Soldier.

Population: 19,435; Growth (since 2000): -13.1%; Density: 4,489.0 persons per square mile; Race: 61.5% White, 29.2% Black/African American, 3.4% Asian, 0.6% American Indian/Alaska Native, 0.0% Native Hawaiian/Other Pacific Islander, 4.3% Two or more races, 3.9% Hispanic of any race; Average household size: 2.06; Median age: 25.0; Age under 18: 14.1%; Age 65 and over: 8.3%; Males per 100 females: 98.9; Marriage status: 64.2% never married, 21.3% now married, 1.4% separated, 4.5% widowed, 10.1% divorced; Foreign born: 7.0%; Speak English only: 90.5%; With disability: 10.5%; Veterans: 5.4%; Ancestry: 20.1% German, 10.8% Irish, 7.7% English, 6.9% Polish, 6.2% American

Employment: 9.5% management, business, and financial, 5.6% computer, engineering, and science, 15.9% education, legal, community service, arts, and media, 1.8% healthcare practitioners, 23.2% service, 29.1% sales and office, 4.7% natural resources, construction, and maintenance, 10.1% production, transportation, and material moving

Income: Per capita: $21,350; Median household: $33,406; Average household: $47,038; Households with income of $100,000 or more: 10.5%; Poverty rate: 30.2%

Educational Attainment: High school diploma or higher: 89.1%; Bachelor's degree or higher: 36.9%; Graduate/professional degree or higher: 17.4%

School District(s)
Ann Arbor Public Schools (PK-12)
    2012-13 Enrollment: 16,654 . . . . (734) 994-2230
Arbor Preparatory High School (KG-12)
    2012-13 Enrollment: 360 . . . . (616) 957-9060
East Arbor Charter Academy (KG-12)
    2012-13 Enrollment: 670 . . . . (734) 484-5506
Fortis Academy (PK-12)
    2012-13 Enrollment: 641 . . . . (734) 572-3623
Lincoln Consolidated SD (PK-12)
    2012-13 Enrollment: 4,355 . . . . (734) 484-7001
New Beginnings Academy (PK-12)
    2012-13 Enrollment: 166 . . . . (734) 481-9001
SD of Ypsilanti (PK-12)
    2012-13 Enrollment: 3,333 . . . . (734) 714-1218
South Arbor Charter Academy (KG-12)
    2012-13 Enrollment: 772 . . . . (734) 528-2821
Van Buren Public Schools (PK-12)
    2012-13 Enrollment: 5,183 . . . . (734) 697-9123
Washtenaw ISD (PK-12)
    2012-13 Enrollment: 601 . . . . (734) 994-8100
Willow Run Community Schools (PK-12)
    2012-13 Enrollment: 1,435 . . . . (734) 961-6310

Four-year College(s)
Eastern Michigan University (Public)
    Fall 2013 Enrollment: 23,447 . . . . (734) 487-1849
    2013-14 Tuition: In-state $9,364; Out-of-state $24,909

Housing: Homeownership rate: 33.3%; Median home value: $123,100; Median year structure built: 1954; Homeowner vacancy rate: 2.7%; Median gross rent: $720 per month; Rental vacancy rate: 12.4%

Health Insurance: 85.5% have insurance; 64.4% have private insurance; 29.6% have public insurance; 14.5% do not have insurance; 2.7% of children under 18 do not have insurance

Safety: Violent crime rate: 82.8 per 10,000 population; Property crime rate: 341.0 per 10,000 population

Transportation: Commute: 77.9% car, 5.4% public transportation, 10.8% walk, 4.6% work from home; Median travel time to work: 20.3 minutes

Additional Information Contacts
City of Ypsilanti . . . . (734) 483-1100
    http://www.cityofypsilanti.com

Wayne County

Located in southeastern Michigan; bounded on the east by the Detroit River, Lakes Saint Clair and Erie, and the Canadian province of Ontario; drained by the Huron River and the River Rogue. Covers a land area of 612.080 square miles, a water area of 60.597 square miles, and is located in the Eastern Time Zone at 42.28° N. Lat., 83.26° W. Long. The county was founded in 1796. County seat is Detroit.

Wayne County is part of the Detroit-Warren-Dearborn, MI Metropolitan Statistical Area. The entire metro area includes: Detroit-Dearborn-Livonia, MI Metropolitan Division (Wayne County, MI); Warren-Troy-Farmington Hills, MI Metropolitan Division (Lapeer County, MI; Livingston County, MI; Macomb County, MI; Oakland County, MI; Saint Clair County, MI)

Weather Station: Dearborn   Elevation: 604 feet

	Jan	Feb	Mar	Apr	May	Jun	Jul	Aug	Sep	Oct	Nov	Dec
High	33	36	46	59	71	80	84	83	76	62	49	37
Low	17	19	26	37	47	57	62	60	52	41	32	22
Precip	2.0	2.0	2.4	3.0	3.1	3.3	3.3	2.8	3.4	3.0	2.8	2.5
Snow	10.6	8.0	5.3	0.7	0.0	0.0	0.0	0.0	0.0	0.1	1.0	7.1

High and Low temperatures in degrees Fahrenheit; Precipitation and Snow in inches

Weather Station: Detroit Metropolitan Arpt   Elevation: 632 feet

	Jan	Feb	Mar	Apr	May	Jun	Jul	Aug	Sep	Oct	Nov	Dec
High	32	35	45	59	70	79	83	81	74	61	49	36
Low	18	20	28	39	49	59	63	62	54	43	34	24
Precip	2.0	2.0	2.4	3.0	3.3	3.6	3.3	3.2	3.3	2.5	2.7	2.5
Snow	12.3	10.1	7.3	1.8	tr	tr	0.0	0.0	tr	0.3	1.5	9.8

High and Low temperatures in degrees Fahrenheit; Precipitation and Snow in inches

Weather Station: Grosse Pointe Farms   Elevation: 612 feet

	Jan	Feb	Mar	Apr	May	Jun	Jul	Aug	Sep	Oct	Nov	Dec
High	33	35	44	58	69	79	83	81	74	61	49	36
Low	19	21	28	38	49	58	64	63	55	44	34	24
Precip	1.9	2.0	2.4	3.1	3.3	3.6	3.5	3.5	3.5	2.9	2.8	2.6
Snow	8.7	6.9	3.6	0.6	0.0	0.0	0.0	0.0	0.0	tr	0.6	6.5

High and Low temperatures in degrees Fahrenheit; Precipitation and Snow in inches

Population: 1,820,584; Growth (since 2000): -11.7%; Density: 2,974.4 persons per square mile; Race: 52.3% White, 40.5% Black/African American, 2.5% Asian, 0.4% American Indian/Alaska Native, 0.0% Native Hawaiian/Other Pacific Islander, 2.4% two or more races, 5.2% Hispanic of any race; Average household size: 2.56; Median age: 37.3; Age under 18: 25.4%; Age 65 and over: 12.7%; Males per 100 females: 92.4; Marriage status: 40.0% never married, 41.0% now married, 2.4% separated, 7.0% widowed, 11.9% divorced; Foreign born: 7.8%; Speak English only: 87.4%; With disability: 16.0%; Veterans: 7.8%; Ancestry: 11.1% German, 8.1% Polish, 8.0% Irish, 5.2% English, 4.1% American

Religion: Six largest groups: 16.3% Catholicism, 7.8% Baptist, 5.1% Non-denominational Protestant, 3.7% Muslim Estimate, 2.3% Lutheran, 2.0% Methodist/Pietist

Economy: Unemployment rate: 9.3%; Leading industries: 19.0% retail trade; 12.9% health care and social assistance; 11.3% other services (except public administration); Farms: 287 totaling 15,767 acres; Company size: 53 employ 1,000 or more persons, 57 employ 500 to 999 persons, 770 employ 100 to 499 persons, 31,134 employ less than 100 persons; Business ownership: 50,570 women-owned, 39,325 Black-owned, 2,635 Hispanic-owned, 5,093 Asian-owned

Employment: 11.7% management, business, and financial, 4.9% computer, engineering, and science, 9.1% education, legal, community service, arts, and media, 5.7% healthcare practitioners, 21.2% service, 24.9% sales and office, 6.9% natural resources, construction, and maintenance, 15.5% production, transportation, and material moving

Income: Per capita: $22,308; Median household: $41,184; Average household: $57,369; Households with income of $100,000 or more: 15.6%; Poverty rate: 24.5%

Educational Attainment: High school diploma or higher: 84.1%; Bachelor's degree or higher: 21.3%; Graduate/professional degree or higher: 8.3%

Housing: Homeownership rate: 64.7%; Median home value: $86,800; Median year structure built: 1955; Homeowner vacancy rate: 2.9%; Median gross rent: $792 per month; Rental vacancy rate: 14.4%

Vital Statistics: Birth rate: 131.9 per 10,000 population; Death rate: 100.2 per 10,000 population; Age-adjusted cancer mortality rate: 200.3 deaths per 100,000 population

Health Insurance: 85.3% have insurance; 58.5% have private insurance; 39.4% have public insurance; 14.7% do not have insurance; 4.7% of children under 18 do not have insurance

Health Care: Physicians: 27.7 per 10,000 population; Hospital beds: 33.6 per 10,000 population; Hospital admissions: 1,498.5 per 10,000 population

Air Quality Index: 48.2% good, 51.2% moderate, 0.5% unhealthy for sensitive individuals, 0.0% unhealthy (percent of days)

Transportation: Commute: 90.9% car, 3.2% public transportation, 1.8% walk, 2.7% work from home; Median travel time to work: 25.0 minutes

Presidential Election: 72.8% Obama, 26.1% Romney (2012)

National and State Parks: Marbury State Park; Maybury State Park; William G Milliken State Park and Harbor; Wyandotte National Wildlife Refuge

Additional Information Contacts

Wayne Government . . . . (313) 224-6262
   http://www.waynecounty.com

Wayne County Communities

ALLEN PARK (city). Covers a land area of 7.004 square miles and a water area of 0.047 square miles. Located at 42.26° N. Lat; 83.21° W. Long. Elevation is 594 feet.

History: Allen Park was incorporated as a village in 1927 and as a city in 1957. It was named for Lewis Allen, a lawyer and lumberman who came to the area as a child in 1819, and later owned the land on which Allen Park was established.

Population: 28,210; Growth (since 2000): -4.0%; Density: 4,027.8 persons per square mile; Race: 92.9% White, 2.1% Black/African American, 0.8% Asian, 0.5% American Indian/Alaska Native, 0.0% Native Hawaiian/Other Pacific Islander, 1.6% Two or more races, 8.1% Hispanic of any race; Average household size: 2.42; Median age: 41.7; Age under 18: 21.7%; Age 65 and over: 17.2%; Males per 100 females: 92.7; Marriage status: 29.2% never married, 50.0% now married, 0.6% separated, 9.8% widowed, 11.0% divorced; Foreign born: 4.8%; Speak English only: 90.9%; With disability: 14.5%; Veterans: 9.8%; Ancestry: 22.6% German, 17.6% Polish, 13.8% Irish, 11.5% English, 9.4% Italian

Employment: 11.3% management, business, and financial, 5.6% computer, engineering, and science, 8.9% education, legal, community service, arts, and media, 7.6% healthcare practitioners, 17.5% service, 24.8% sales and office, 9.2% natural resources, construction, and maintenance, 15.0% production, transportation, and material moving

Income: Per capita: $27,082; Median household: $58,654; Average household: $67,322; Households with income of $100,000 or more: 20.4%; Poverty rate: 7.8%

Educational Attainment: High school diploma or higher: 90.2%; Bachelor's degree or higher: 22.7%; Graduate/professional degree or higher: 7.7%

School District(s)

Allen Park Public Schools (PK-12)
   2012-13 Enrollment: 3,784 . . . . (313) 827-2150
Melvindale-North Allen Park Schools (KG-12)
   2012-13 Enrollment: 2,824 . . . . (313) 389-3300

Four-year College(s)

Baker College of Allen Park (Private, Not-for-profit)
   Fall 2013 Enrollment: 3,800 . . . . (313) 425-3700
   2013-14 Tuition: In-state $8,100; Out-of-state $8,100

Vocational/Technical School(s)

Stautzenberger Institute-Allen Park (Private, For-profit)
   Fall 2013 Enrollment: 106 . . . . (313) 294-9715
   2013-14 Tuition: In-state $10,170; Out-of-state $10,170

Housing: Homeownership rate: 85.5%; Median home value: $101,500; Median year structure built: 1955; Homeowner vacancy rate: 1.6%; Median gross rent: $855 per month; Rental vacancy rate: 7.1%

Health Insurance: 90.8% have insurance; 80.5% have private insurance; 26.9% have public insurance; 9.2% do not have insurance; 2.9% of children under 18 do not have insurance

Safety: Violent crime rate: 12.7 per 10,000 population; Property crime rate: 239.8 per 10,000 population

Transportation: Commute: 97.2% car, 0.1% public transportation, 0.7% walk, 1.4% work from home; Median travel time to work: 22.5 minutes

Additional Information Contacts

City of Allen Park . . . . (313) 928-1400
   http://www.cityofallenpark.org

BELLEVILLE (city). Covers a land area of 1.136 square miles and a water area of 0.064 square miles. Located at 42.20° N. Lat; 83.48° W. Long. Elevation is 676 feet.

History: Belleville was first settled in 1826. The village was platted in 1848, and incorporated in 1905. In 1946 it received city status.

Population: 3,991; Growth (since 2000): -0.2%; Density: 3,511.8 persons per square mile; Race: 80.6% White, 14.1% Black/African American, 0.8% Asian, 0.4% American Indian/Alaska Native, 0.0% Native Hawaiian/Other Pacific Islander, 3.2% Two or more races, 3.8% Hispanic of any race; Average household size: 2.26; Median age: 40.0; Age under 18: 21.9%; Age 65 and over: 14.6%; Males per 100 females: 87.6; Marriage status: 30.5% never married, 44.1% now married, 4.4% separated, 6.4% widowed, 19.1% divorced; Foreign born: 3.1%; Speak English only: 90.7%; With disability: 14.5%; Veterans: 14.9%; Ancestry: 18.3% German, 18.1% Irish, 11.4% English, 10.6% Polish, 8.6% American

Employment: 10.3% management, business, and financial, 7.0% computer, engineering, and science, 8.1% education, legal, community service, arts, and media, 3.4% healthcare practitioners, 29.0% service, 23.7% sales and office, 6.9% natural resources, construction, and maintenance, 11.6% production, transportation, and material moving

Income: Per capita: $26,919; Median household: $45,473; Average household: $61,226; Households with income of $100,000 or more: 14.4%; Poverty rate: 14.7%

Educational Attainment: High school diploma or higher: 84.5%; Bachelor's degree or higher: 18.0%; Graduate/professional degree or higher: 7.4%

School District(s)
Keystone Academy (KG-12)
   2012-13 Enrollment: 753 . . . . (734) 697-9470
Lincoln Consolidated SD (PK-12)
   2012-13 Enrollment: 4,355 . . . . (734) 484-7001
Van Buren Public Schools (PK-12)
   2012-13 Enrollment: 5,183 . . . . (734) 697-9123

Housing: Homeownership rate: 65.2%; Median home value: $113,100; Median year structure built: 1977; Homeowner vacancy rate: 4.0%; Median gross rent: $716 per month; Rental vacancy rate: 14.2%

Health Insurance: 92.2% have insurance; 78.9% have private insurance; 25.1% have public insurance; 7.8% do not have insurance; 2.2% of children under 18 do not have insurance

Safety: Violent crime rate: 10.3 per 10,000 population; Property crime rate: 215.4 per 10,000 population

Newspapers: Belleville Area Independent (weekly circulation 7000); Ypsilanti Courier (weekly circulation 7000)

Transportation: Commute: 96.4% car, 0.1% public transportation, 1.2% walk, 0.4% work from home; Median travel time to work: 33.1 minutes

Additional Information Contacts
City of Belleville. . . . . (734) 697-9323
   http://www.belleville.mi.us

BROWNSTOWN (charter township). Covers a land area of 22.191 square miles and a water area of 8.450 square miles. Located at 42.11° N. Lat; 83.23° W. Long.

History: Brownstown Township was named for Adam Brown, adopted by a group of Virginia Indians as a child, who later became a chief when the group migrated to Michigan.

Population: 30,627; Growth (since 2000): 33.2%; Density: 1,380.2 persons per square mile; Race: 82.4% White, 8.6% Black/African American, 5.2% Asian, 0.4% American Indian/Alaska Native, 0.0% Native Hawaiian/Other Pacific Islander, 2.1% Two or more races, 5.2% Hispanic of any race; Average household size: 2.69; Median age: 37.6; Age under 18: 26.4%; Age 65 and over: 9.7%; Males per 100 females: 95.6; Marriage status: 25.7% never married, 57.8% now married, 1.7% separated, 5.6% widowed, 10.9% divorced; Foreign born: 8.7%; Speak English only: 87.9%; With disability: 12.0%; Veterans: 9.1%; Ancestry: 17.3% German, 12.6% Polish, 10.8% Irish, 9.1% English, 8.1% American

Employment: 14.7% management, business, and financial, 5.1% computer, engineering, and science, 8.2% education, legal, community service, arts, and media, 7.5% healthcare practitioners, 14.8% service, 26.0% sales and office, 9.2% natural resources, construction, and maintenance, 14.6% production, transportation, and material moving

Income: Per capita: $28,431; Median household: $64,396; Average household: $77,203; Households with income of $100,000 or more: 26.8%; Poverty rate: 8.1%

Educational Attainment: High school diploma or higher: 89.5%; Bachelor's degree or higher: 23.3%; Graduate/professional degree or higher: 8.5%

School District(s)
Gibraltar SD (KG-12)
   2012-13 Enrollment: 3,730 . . . . (734) 379-6350
Woodhaven-Brownstown SD (PK-12)
   2012-13 Enrollment: 5,043 . . . . (734) 789-2357

Housing: Homeownership rate: 76.2%; Median home value: $153,700; Median year structure built: 1991; Homeowner vacancy rate: 2.5%; Median gross rent: $821 per month; Rental vacancy rate: 10.1%

Health Insurance: 91.2% have insurance; 80.1% have private insurance; 21.6% have public insurance; 8.8% do not have insurance; 4.3% of children under 18 do not have insurance

Safety: Violent crime rate: 18.4 per 10,000 population; Property crime rate: 137.9 per 10,000 population

Transportation: Commute: 96.3% car, 0.7% public transportation, 0.3% walk, 2.0% work from home; Median travel time to work: 26.1 minutes

Additional Information Contacts
Brownstown Charter Township . . . . (734) 675-0071
   http://www.brownstown-mi.org

CANTON (charter township). Covers a land area of 36.109 square miles and a water area of 0.029 square miles. Located at 42.31° N. Lat; 83.49° W. Long. Elevation is 679 feet.

Population: 90,173; Growth (since 2000): 18.1%; Density: 2,497.2 persons per square mile; Race: 72.2% White, 10.2% Black/African American, 14.1% Asian, 0.2% American Indian/Alaska Native, 0.0% Native Hawaiian/Other Pacific Islander, 2.5% Two or more races, 3.1% Hispanic of any race; Average household size: 2.75; Median age: 36.9; Age under 18: 27.2%; Age 65 and over: 8.9%; Males per 100 females: 95.5; Marriage status: 28.0% never married, 59.8% now married, 1.2% separated, 4.2% widowed, 8.0% divorced; Foreign born: 15.8%; Speak English only: 80.4%; With disability: 7.2%; Veterans: 7.1%; Ancestry: 17.3% German, 12.3% Polish, 10.4% Irish, 9.2% American, 7.8% English

Employment: 18.9% management, business, and financial, 12.2% computer, engineering, and science, 10.0% education, legal, community service, arts, and media, 8.4% healthcare practitioners, 13.5% service, 22.7% sales and office, 4.7% natural resources, construction, and maintenance, 9.6% production, transportation, and material moving

Income: Per capita: $34,409; Median household: $81,667; Average household: $97,079; Households with income of $100,000 or more: 38.6%; Poverty rate: 6.0%

Educational Attainment: High school diploma or higher: 94.5%; Bachelor's degree or higher: 46.7%; Graduate/professional degree or higher: 18.5%

School District(s)
Achieve Charter Academy (KG-12)
   2012-13 Enrollment: 721. . . . . (734) 397-0960
Canton Charter Academy (KG-12)
   2012-13 Enrollment: 737. . . . . (734) 453-9517
Plymouth-Canton Community Schools (PK-12)
   2012-13 Enrollment: 17,997 . . . . (734) 416-2700
South Canton Scholars Charter Academy (KG-12)
   2012-13 Enrollment: 655 . . . . (734) 398-5658
Wayne-Westland Community SD (PK-12)
   2012-13 Enrollment: 12,030 . . . . (734) 419-2000

Four-year College(s)
ITT Technical Institute-Canton (Private, For-profit)
   Fall 2013 Enrollment: 442 . . . . (734) 397-7800
   2013-14 Tuition: In-state $18,048; Out-of-state $18,048

Two-year College(s)
MIAT College of Technology (Private, For-profit)
   Fall 2013 Enrollment: 498 . . . . (734) 423-2100
   2013-14 Tuition: In-state $14,428; Out-of-state $14,428

Vocational/Technical School(s)
Ross Medical Education Center-Canton (Private, For-profit)
   Fall 2013 Enrollment: 131 . . . . (734) 459-1723
   2013-14 Tuition: $15,680

Housing: Homeownership rate: 76.2%; Median home value: $190,900; Median year structure built: 1987; Homeowner vacancy rate: 2.6%; Median gross rent: $965 per month; Rental vacancy rate: 9.6%

Health Insurance: 91.5% have insurance; 84.2% have private insurance; 16.5% have public insurance; 8.5% do not have insurance; 3.3% of children under 18 do not have insurance

Safety: Violent crime rate: 10.6 per 10,000 population; Property crime rate: 140.5 per 10,000 population
Transportation: Commute: 94.1% car, 0.4% public transportation, 0.4% walk, 4.1% work from home; Median travel time to work: 26.8 minutes
Additional Information Contacts
Canton Charter Township . . . . (734) 394-5100
  http://www.canton-mi.org

DEARBORN (city). Covers a land area of 24.225 square miles and a water area of 0.247 square miles. Located at 42.31° N. Lat; 83.21° W. Long. Elevation is 591 feet.

History: Among the first to settle in Dearborn were A.J. Bucklin and the Thomas brothers from Ohio, whose homesteads later became part of the Ford estate. Pekin Township, established when many settlers came after the War of 1812, later became Dearborn, renamed to honor General Henry Dearborn (1751-1829), secretary of war under President Andrew Jackson. Dearborn later encompassed Greenfield and Springwells Townships as well. A local legend claims that Michigan's nickname of the Wolverine State originated at Conrad "Old Coon" Ten Eyck's Tavern in Dearborn, where visitors were told they had been served wolf steaks and were then wolverines. Henry Ford was born in Dearborn in 1863. When he founded a plant to build small iron ships here on the River Rouge in 1917, his Ford Motor Company had already made him wealthy. Soon the entire plant was moved from Highland Park, and the City of Springwells was incorporated. Its name was changed to Fordson in 1925, and in 1928 Fordson and Dearborn were united as one municipality.

Population: 98,153; Growth (since 2000): 0.4%; Density: 4,051.8 persons per square mile; Race: 89.1% White, 4.0% Black/African American, 1.7% Asian, 0.2% American Indian/Alaska Native, 0.0% Native Hawaiian/Other Pacific Islander, 4.0% Two or more races, 3.4% Hispanic of any race; Average household size: 2.85; Median age: 33.0; Age under 18: 29.7%; Age 65 and over: 12.0%; Males per 100 females: 97.8; Marriage status: 30.7% never married, 53.3% now married, 1.3% separated, 6.7% widowed, 9.4% divorced; Foreign born: 26.9%; Speak English only: 53.2%; With disability: 12.3%; Veterans: 6.0%; Ancestry: 19.4% Lebanese, 10.0% German, 10.0% Polish, 9.5% Other Arab, 7.6% Irish
Employment: 13.0% management, business, and financial, 8.1% computer, engineering, and science, 11.9% education, legal, community service, arts, and media, 6.6% healthcare practitioners, 15.2% service, 25.0% sales and office, 6.1% natural resources, construction, and maintenance, 14.0% production, transportation, and material moving
Income: Per capita: $21,262; Median household: $46,739; Average household: $62,138; Households with income of $100,000 or more: 18.8%; Poverty rate: 27.5%
Educational Attainment: High school diploma or higher: 81.1%; Bachelor's degree or higher: 28.9%; Graduate/professional degree or higher: 11.4%

School District(s)
Academy for Business and Technology (KG-12)
  2012-13 Enrollment: 709 . . . . (313) 383-3422
Advanced Technology Academy (PK-12)
  2012-13 Enrollment: 1,476 . . . . (313) 625-4700
Clintondale Community Schools (PK-12)
  2012-13 Enrollment: 3,407 . . . . (586) 791-6300
Dearborn City SD (PK-12)
  2012-13 Enrollment: 18,915 . . . . (313) 827-3022
Henry Ford Academy (KG-12)
  2012-13 Enrollment: 525 . . . . (313) 982-6193
Riverside Academy (PK-12)
  2012-13 Enrollment: 1,073 . . . . (734) 662-7050
The Dearborn Academy (KG-12)
  2012-13 Enrollment: 452 . . . . (313) 271-0644
West Village Academy (KG-12)
  2012-13 Enrollment: 407 . . . . (313) 274-9200
Westwood Community SD (PK-12)
  2012-13 Enrollment: 2,502 . . . . (313) 565-1901

Four-year College(s)
ITT Technical Institute-Dearborn (Private, For-profit)
  Fall 2013 Enrollment: 438 . . . . (313) 278-5208
  2013-14 Tuition: In-state $18,048; Out-of-state $18,048
University of Michigan-Dearborn (Public)
  Fall 2013 Enrollment: 8,748 . . . . (313) 593-5000
  2013-14 Tuition: In-state $10,614; Out-of-state $23,124

Two-year College(s)
Henry Ford Community College (Public)
  Fall 2013 Enrollment: 13,836 . . . . (313) 845-9600
  2013-14 Tuition: In-state $3,958; Out-of-state $4,078
Sanford-Brown College-Dearborn (Private, For-profit)
  Fall 2013 Enrollment: 107 . . . . (313) 203-3541

Vocational/Technical School(s)
Everest Institute-Dearborn (Private, For-profit)
  Fall 2013 Enrollment: 666 . . . . (313) 562-4228
  2013-14 Tuition: $18,556

Housing: Homeownership rate: 69.0%; Median home value: $103,300; Median year structure built: 1950; Homeowner vacancy rate: 2.3%; Median gross rent: $962 per month; Rental vacancy rate: 8.2%
Health Insurance: 85.4% have insurance; 56.4% have private insurance; 40.2% have public insurance; 14.6% do not have insurance; 4.9% of children under 18 do not have insurance
Hospitals: Oakwood Hospital - Dearborn (632 beds)
Safety: Violent crime rate: 36.1 per 10,000 population; Property crime rate: 323.3 per 10,000 population
Newspapers: Times Herald (weekly circulation 27000)
Transportation: Commute: 94.5% car, 0.5% public transportation, 1.8% walk, 2.5% work from home; Median travel time to work: 21.6 minutes; Amtrak: Train service available.
Additional Information Contacts
City of Dearborn . . . . (313) 943-2000
  http://www.cityofdearborn.org

DEARBORN HEIGHTS (city). Covers a land area of 11.743 square miles and a water area of 0.009 square miles. Located at 42.34° N. Lat; 83.29° W. Long. Elevation is 620 feet.

Population: 57,774; Growth (since 2000): -0.8%; Density: 4,919.9 persons per square mile; Race: 86.1% White, 7.9% Black/African American, 1.7% Asian, 0.4% American Indian/Alaska Native, 0.0% Native Hawaiian/Other Pacific Islander, 2.8% Two or more races, 4.7% Hispanic of any race; Average household size: 2.57; Median age: 38.3; Age under 18: 25.0%; Age 65 and over: 16.1%; Males per 100 females: 93.6; Marriage status: 31.0% never married, 50.0% now married, 1.6% separated, 8.0% widowed, 11.0% divorced; Foreign born: 17.1%; Speak English only: 72.6%; With disability: 14.0%; Veterans: 8.0%; Ancestry: 14.6% Polish, 13.8% Lebanese, 12.5% German, 9.6% Irish, 6.1% English
Employment: 10.0% management, business, and financial, 5.5% computer, engineering, and science, 9.9% education, legal, community service, arts, and media, 6.1% healthcare practitioners, 19.3% service, 26.9% sales and office, 6.4% natural resources, construction, and maintenance, 15.9% production, transportation, and material moving
Income: Per capita: $21,433; Median household: $43,001; Average household: $55,405; Households with income of $100,000 or more: 13.2%; Poverty rate: 19.0%
Educational Attainment: High school diploma or higher: 85.2%; Bachelor's degree or higher: 19.9%; Graduate/professional degree or higher: 7.9%

School District(s)
Clara B. Ford Academy (Sda) (KG-12)
  2012-13 Enrollment: 158 . . . . (313) 240-4347
Crestwood SD (PK-12)
  2012-13 Enrollment: 3,436 . . . . (313) 274-6320
Dearborn City SD (PK-12)
  2012-13 Enrollment: 18,915 . . . . (313) 827-3022
Dearborn Heights SD #7 (PK-12)
  2012-13 Enrollment: 2,799 . . . . (313) 278-1900
Global Heights Academy (KG-12)
  2012-13 Enrollment: 178 . . . . (734) 369-9500
Star International Academy (PK-12)
  2012-13 Enrollment: 1,509 . . . . (313) 724-8990
Vista Meadows Academy (KG-12)
  2012-13 Enrollment: 171 . . . . (313) 240-4347
Westwood Community SD (PK-12)
  2012-13 Enrollment: 2,502 . . . . (313) 565-1901

Housing: Homeownership rate: 77.9%; Median home value: $85,600; Median year structure built: 1957; Homeowner vacancy rate: 2.4%; Median gross rent: $975 per month; Rental vacancy rate: 7.2%
Health Insurance: 84.3% have insurance; 62.7% have private insurance; 37.0% have public insurance; 15.7% do not have insurance; 6.8% of children under 18 do not have insurance

Safety: Violent crime rate: 37.5 per 10,000 population; Property crime rate: 236.5 per 10,000 population

Transportation: Commute: 95.5% car, 0.6% public transportation, 0.7% walk, 2.2% work from home; Median travel time to work: 23.5 minutes

Additional Information Contacts

City of Dearborn Heights . . . . (313) 791-3400
  http://www.ci.dearborn-heights.mi.us

DETROIT (city). County seat. Covers a land area of 138.750 square miles and a water area of 4.119 square miles. Located at 42.38° N. Lat; 83.10° W. Long. Elevation is 597 feet.

History: Detroit began as a trading post founded in 1701 by Antoine de la Mothe Cadillac, in the service of Louis XIV of France. The post became an important fur depot and a military site for the British, who acquired it at the end of the French and Indian War and held it until 1796. The settlement that then came under American rule was named for the river, "detroit" being French for "the strait." Growth in Detroit was slowed by political dissension and reports of the swampy and sandy soil, which discouraged settlers until after the Erie Canal was completed. Between 1830 and 1860 the town grew rapidly, becoming an industrial center that continued to expand after the Civil War. The automobile changed Detroit as it changed America. Not only Ford came to Detroit, but also Buick, Durant, R.E. Olds, the Fisher brothers, and numerous others connected with the automobile industry.

Population: 713,777; Growth (since 2000): -25.0%; Density: 5,144.3 persons per square mile; Race: 10.6% White, 82.7% Black/African American, 1.1% Asian, 0.4% American Indian/Alaska Native, 0.0% Native Hawaiian/Other Pacific Islander, 2.2% Two or more races, 6.8% Hispanic of any race; Average household size: 2.59; Median age: 34.8; Age under 18: 26.7%; Age 65 and over: 11.5%; Males per 100 females: 89.8; Marriage status: 53.2% never married, 27.1% now married, 3.7% separated, 7.5% widowed, 12.3% divorced; Foreign born: 5.1%; Speak English only: 90.4%; With disability: 19.5%; Veterans: 6.8%; Ancestry: 1.5% American, 1.5% German, 1.4% Irish, 1.4% Polish, 1.3% African

Employment: 7.9% management, business, and financial, 2.0% computer, engineering, and science, 8.8% education, legal, community service, arts, and media, 3.9% healthcare practitioners, 28.9% service, 24.7% sales and office, 6.3% natural resources, construction, and maintenance, 17.4% production, transportation, and material moving

Income: Per capita: $14,870; Median household: $26,325; Average household: $37,887; Households with income of $100,000 or more: 6.4%; Poverty rate: 39.3%

Educational Attainment: High school diploma or higher: 77.6%; Bachelor's degree or higher: 12.7%; Graduate/professional degree or higher: 5.2%

School District(s)

Aisha Shule/Web Dubois Prep. Academy School (KG-12)
  2012-13 Enrollment: 111 . . . . (313) 345-6050
Allen Academy (KG-12)
  2012-13 Enrollment: 1,000 . . . . (313) 898-6444
American International Academy (KG-12)
  2012-13 Enrollment: 272 . . . . (810) 750-3007
Blanche Kelso Bruce Academy (PK-12)
  2012-13 Enrollment: 475 . . . . (313) 656-2600
Bridge Academy (PK-12)
  2012-13 Enrollment: 650 . . . . (313) 887-8100
Casa Richard Academy (KG-12)
  2012-13 Enrollment: 84 . . . . (313) 963-7757
Center for Literacy and Creativity (KG-12)
  2012-13 Enrollment: 89 . . . . (313) 537-9400
Cesar Chavez Academy (KG-12)
  2012-13 Enrollment: 2,169 . . . . (313) 361-1083
Covenant House Academy Central (KG-12)
  2012-13 Enrollment: 315 . . . . (313) 463-2023
Covenant House Academy East (KG-12)
  2012-13 Enrollment: 249 . . . . (313) 463-2023
Covenant House Academy Southwest (KG-12)
  2012-13 Enrollment: 262 . . . . (313) 463-2023
David Ellis Academy (KG-12)
  2012-13 Enrollment: 343 . . . . (313) 927-5395
Detroit Academy of Arts and Sciences (KG-12)
  2012-13 Enrollment: 1,018 . . . . (313) 259-1744
Detroit City SD (PK-12)
  2012-13 Enrollment: 49,239 . . . . (313) 873-6205

Detroit Community Schools (KG-12)
  2012-13 Enrollment: 938 . . . . (313) 537-3570
Detroit Enterprise Academy (KG-12)
  2012-13 Enrollment: 672 . . . . (313) 823-5799
Detroit Innovation Academy
  2012-13 Enrollment: 149 . . . . (313) 242-1500
Detroit Leadership Academy (KG-12)
  2012-13 Enrollment: 364 . . . . (313) 242-1500
Detroit Merit Charter Academy (KG-12)
  2012-13 Enrollment: 713 . . . . (313) 331-3328
Detroit Premier Academy (KG-12)
  2012-13 Enrollment: 730 . . . . (313) 945-1472
Detroit Service Learning Academy (KG-12)
  2012-13 Enrollment: 1,113 . . . . (313) 541-7619
Dove Academy of Detroit (KG-12)
  2012-13 Enrollment: 419 . . . . (313) 366-9110
Edison Public Schools Academy (PK-12)
  2012-13 Enrollment: 1,311 . . . . (313) 833-1100
Eman Hamilton Academy (KG-12)
  2012-13 Enrollment: 407 . . . . (586) 576-0885
Flagship Charter Academy (KG-12)
  2012-13 Enrollment: 652 . . . . (313) 933-7933
Gee Edmonson Academy (PK-12)
  2012-13 Enrollment: 270 . . . . (734) 369-9500
Gee White Academy (PK-12)
  2012-13 Enrollment: 406 . . . . (734) 369-9500
George Crockett Academy (KG-12)
  2012-13 Enrollment: 358 . . . . (313) 896-6078
Henry Ford Academy: School for Creative Studies (P (KG-12)
  2012-13 Enrollment: 1,135 . . . . (313) 481-4000
Hope Academy (KG-12)
  2012-13 Enrollment: 788 . . . . (313) 934-0054
Hope of Detroit Academy (KG-12)
  2012-13 Enrollment: n/a . . . . (313) 897-8720
Jalen Rose Leadership Academy (KG-12)
  2012-13 Enrollment: 205 . . . . (313) 397-3333
Joy Preparatory Academy (KG-12)
  2012-13 Enrollment: 384 . . . . (313) 340-0023
Legacy Charter Academy (KG-12)
  2012-13 Enrollment: 603 . . . . (877) 223-6402
Martin Luther King Jr. Education Center Academy (KG-12)
  2012-13 Enrollment: 343 . . . . (313) 341-4944
Marvin L. Winans Academy of Performing Arts (KG-12)
  2012-13 Enrollment: 1,181 . . . . (313) 365-5578
Michigan Connections Academy (KG-12)
  2012-13 Enrollment: 813 . . . . (517) 507-5390
Michigan Technical Academy (PK-12)
  2012-13 Enrollment: 1,042 . . . . (313) 537-8820
Nataki Talibah Schoolhouse of Detroit (KG-12)
  2012-13 Enrollment: 326 . . . . (313) 531-3720
New Paradigm Glazer Academy (KG-12)
  2012-13 Enrollment: 167 . . . . (313) 833-1100
New Paradigm Loving Academy (KG-12)
  2012-13 Enrollment: 235 . . . . (313) 833-1100
Nsoroma Institute (KG-12)
  2012-13 Enrollment: 175 . . . . (313) 521-0400
Oakland International Academy (KG-12)
  2012-13 Enrollment: 684 . . . . (313) 925-1000
Old Redford Academy (PK-12)
  2012-13 Enrollment: 2,055 . . . . (248) 799-2780
Pierre Toussaint Academy (KG-12)
  2012-13 Enrollment: 357 . . . . (313) 383-1485
Plymouth Educational Center (KG-12)
  2012-13 Enrollment: 1,328 . . . . (313) 831-3280
Regent Park Scholars Charter Academy (KG-12)
  2012-13 Enrollment: 546 . . . . (313) 371-1300
Ross-Hill Academy (KG-12)
  2012-13 Enrollment: 95 . . . . (313) 922-8088
Timbuktu Academy of Science and Technology (KG-12)
  2012-13 Enrollment: 294 . . . . (313) 823-6000
Universal Academy (KG-12)
  2012-13 Enrollment: 599 . . . . (313) 581-5006
University Preparatory Academy (PSAD) (KG-12)
  2012-13 Enrollment: 1,685 . . . . (313) 874-4340
University Preparatory Science and Math (Psad) (KG-12)
  2012-13 Enrollment: 750 . . . . (313) 324-0140

University Yes Academy (KG-12)
2012-13 Enrollment: 364 . . . . (281) 543-8894
University Yes East Academy
2012-13 Enrollment: n/a . . . . (313) 618-3551
Voyageur Academy (KG-12)
2012-13 Enrollment: 996 . . . . (313) 361-4180
Warrendale Charter Academy (KG-12)
2012-13 Enrollment: 711 . . . . (313) 240-4200
Weston Preparatory Academy (KG-12)
2012-13 Enrollment: 298 . . . . (313) 387-6038
Woodward Academy (PK-12)
2012-13 Enrollment: 740 . . . . (313) 961-2108

Four-year College(s)

College for Creative Studies (Private, Not-for-profit)
Fall 2013 Enrollment: 1,423 . . . . (313) 664-7400
2013-14 Tuition: In-state $35,710; Out-of-state $35,710
Ecumenical Theological Seminary (Private, Not-for-profit)
Fall 2013 Enrollment: 81 . . . . (313) 831-5200
Marygrove College (Private, Not-for-profit, Roman Catholic)
Fall 2013 Enrollment: 1,960 . . . . (313) 927-1200
2013-14 Tuition: In-state $19,850; Out-of-state $19,850
Sacred Heart Major Seminary (Private, Not-for-profit, Roman Catholic)
Fall 2013 Enrollment: 436 . . . . (313) 883-8500
2013-14 Tuition: In-state $17,000; Out-of-state $17,000
University of Detroit Mercy (Private, Not-for-profit, Roman Catholic)
Fall 2013 Enrollment: 5,112 . . . . (313) 993-1000
2013-14 Tuition: In-state $35,920; Out-of-state $35,920
Wayne State University (Public)
Fall 2013 Enrollment: 27,897 . . . . (313) 577-2424
2013-14 Tuition: In-state $11,094; Out-of-state $23,714

Two-year College(s)

Kaplan Career Institute-Dearborn (Private, For-profit)
Fall 2013 Enrollment: 36 . . . . (313) 425-4300
Michigan Barber School Inc (Private, Not-for-profit)
Fall 2013 Enrollment: 163 . . . . (313) 894-2300
Wayne County Community College District (Public)
Fall 2013 Enrollment: 18,119 . . . . (313) 496-2600
2013-14 Tuition: In-state $2,980; Out-of-state $3,700

Vocational/Technical School(s)

Everest Institute-Detroit (Private, For-profit)
Fall 2013 Enrollment: 494 . . . . (313) 567-5350
2013-14 Tuition: $18,556
Focus-Hope Information Technologies Center (Private, Not-for-profit)
Fall 2013 Enrollment: 17 . . . . (313) 494-5500
2013-14 Tuition: $6,500
P&A Scholars Beauty School (Private, For-profit)
Fall 2013 Enrollment: 241 . . . . (248) 262-7309
2013-14 Tuition: $13,500

Housing: Homeownership rate: 51.1%; Median home value: $50,400; Median year structure built: 1947; Homeowner vacancy rate: 3.8%; Median gross rent: $761 per month; Rental vacancy rate: 18.0%
Health Insurance: 80.6% have insurance; 39.5% have private insurance; 51.7% have public insurance; 19.4% do not have insurance; 5.7% of children under 18 do not have insurance
Hospitals: Children's Hospital of Michigan (240 beds); Detroit (John D. Dingell) VA Medical Center (372 beds); Detroit Receiving Hospital & University Health Center (258 beds); Harper University Hospital (658 beds); Henry Ford Hospital (903 beds); Karmanos Cancer Center (123 beds); Saint John Hospital & Medical Center (772 beds); Sinai - Grace Hospital (404 beds)
Safety: Violent crime rate: 207.2 per 10,000 population; Property crime rate: 583.5 per 10,000 population
Newspapers: Detroit Free Press (daily circulation 291000); Detroit News (daily circulation 202000); Metro Times (weekly circulation 100000)
Transportation: Commute: 82.5% car, 8.7% public transportation, 3.4% walk, 3.1% work from home; Median travel time to work: 26.6 minutes; Amtrak: Train service available.
Airports: Coleman A. Young Municipal (general aviation); Detroit Metropolitan Wayne County (primary service/large hub); Willow Run (general aviation)
Additional Information Contacts
City of Detroit . . . . (313) 224-3260
http://www.detroitmi.gov

ECORSE (city). Covers a land area of 2.804 square miles and a water area of 0.887 square miles. Located at 42.25° N. Lat; 83.14° W. Long. Elevation is 584 feet.
History: Named for the French name for the river, " Riviere aux Ecorces," by early French settlers. First called Grandport, the village of Ecorse was established at the mouth of a stream known to the French as the Riviere Aux Ecorses. The French who first settled here were descendants of the early fur trappers and traders. During prohibition times, Ecorse was known as a rumrunners' paradise, outside the control of the Detroit authorities and with the river islands giving hiding places from the Federal authorities.
Population: 9,512; Growth (since 2000): -15.3%; Density: 3,391.7 persons per square mile; Race: 44.0% White, 46.4% Black/African American, 0.3% Asian, 0.8% American Indian/Alaska Native, 0.0% Native Hawaiian/Other Pacific Islander, 4.6% Two or more races, 13.4% Hispanic of any race; Average household size: 2.60; Median age: 35.4; Age under 18: 27.1%; Age 65 and over: 12.8%; Males per 100 females: 89.7; Marriage status: 41.3% never married, 33.7% now married, 4.1% separated, 9.6% widowed, 15.4% divorced; Foreign born: 6.8%; Speak English only: 86.7%; With disability: 18.7%; Veterans: 6.8%; Ancestry: 6.1% Polish, 5.5% German, 4.2% Italian, 4.1% French, 4.0% Irish
Employment: 6.6% management, business, and financial, 2.9% computer, engineering, and science, 3.8% education, legal, community service, arts, and media, 4.2% healthcare practitioners, 24.0% service, 24.1% sales and office, 11.2% natural resources, construction, and maintenance, 23.1% production, transportation, and material moving
Income: Per capita: $15,564; Median household: $28,013; Average household: $38,531; Households with income of $100,000 or more: 4.4%; Poverty rate: 32.5%
Educational Attainment: High school diploma or higher: 72.1%; Bachelor's degree or higher: 11.6%; Graduate/professional degree or higher: 3.6%

School District(s)

Dr. Charles Drew Academy (KG-12)
2012-13 Enrollment: 346 . . . . (313) 383-7501
Ecorse Public Schools (PK-12)
2012-13 Enrollment: 1,029 . . . . (313) 294-4750

Housing: Homeownership rate: 57.9%; Median home value: $50,200; Median year structure built: 1946; Homeowner vacancy rate: 5.5%; Median gross rent: $731 per month; Rental vacancy rate: 12.8%
Health Insurance: 83.3% have insurance; 41.9% have private insurance; 54.7% have public insurance; 16.7% do not have insurance; 1.2% of children under 18 do not have insurance
Transportation: Commute: 93.1% car, 1.6% public transportation, 2.2% walk, 1.8% work from home; Median travel time to work: 21.4 minutes
Additional Information Contacts
City of Ecorse . . . . (313) 386-2520
http://www.city-ecorse.org

FLAT ROCK (city). Covers a land area of 6.533 square miles and a water area of 0.144 square miles. Located at 42.10° N. Lat; 83.27° W. Long. Elevation is 600 feet.
History: A community was first settled here in 1824, and later grew around a branch plant of the Ford Motor Company where headlights and taillights were manufactured. The name of Flat Rock came from the smooth rock bed of the Huron River at this point.
Population: 9,878; Growth (since 2000): 16.4%; Density: 1,512.0 persons per square mile; Race: 91.1% White, 4.1% Black/African American, 0.8% Asian, 0.5% American Indian/Alaska Native, 0.0% Native Hawaiian/Other Pacific Islander, 2.9% Two or more races, 4.4% Hispanic of any race; Average household size: 2.62; Median age: 36.9; Age under 18: 27.4%; Age 65 and over: 10.4%; Males per 100 females: 92.8; Marriage status: 31.6% never married, 48.6% now married, 1.0% separated, 4.9% widowed, 14.8% divorced; Foreign born: 1.9%; Speak English only: 96.3%; With disability: 14.0%; Veterans: 9.3%; Ancestry: 18.9% German, 15.3% Irish, 10.2% Polish, 9.5% Italian, 9.4% English
Employment: 12.9% management, business, and financial, 6.0% computer, engineering, and science, 8.1% education, legal, community service, arts, and media, 6.2% healthcare practitioners, 18.3% service, 24.2% sales and office, 5.2% natural resources, construction, and maintenance, 19.2% production, transportation, and material moving
Income: Per capita: $23,212; Median household: $50,494; Average household: $61,387; Households with income of $100,000 or more: 17.7%; Poverty rate: 15.0%

Educational Attainment: High school diploma or higher: 89.9%; Bachelor's degree or higher: 16.3%; Graduate/professional degree or higher: 7.0%

School District(s)

Flat Rock Community Schools (PK-12)
    2012-13 Enrollment: 1,886 . . . . (734) 535-6500
Summit Academy (KG-12)
    2012-13 Enrollment: 454. . . . . (734) 379-9766
Woodhaven-Brownstown SD (PK-12)
    2012-13 Enrollment: 5,043 . . . . (734) 789-2357

Housing: Homeownership rate: 74.9%; Median home value: $99,400; Median year structure built: 1979; Homeowner vacancy rate: 3.2%; Median gross rent: $716 per month; Rental vacancy rate: 6.8%

Health Insurance: 88.9% have insurance; 67.0% have private insurance; 31.4% have public insurance; 11.1% do not have insurance; 3.1% of children under 18 do not have insurance

Safety: Violent crime rate: 17.4 per 10,000 population; Property crime rate: 144.3 per 10,000 population

Transportation: Commute: 96.9% car, 1.6% public transportation, 0.4% walk, 1.1% work from home; Median travel time to work: 22.3 minutes

Additional Information Contacts

City of Flat Rock . . . . (734) 782-2455
    http://www.flatrockmi.org

GARDEN CITY (city).
Covers a land area of 5.869 square miles and a water area of 0 square miles. Located at 42.32° N. Lat; 83.34° W. Long. Elevation is 633 feet.

History: Named for its small, garden-sized lots, that were designed to grow into large vegetable gardens. Garden City was laid out in 1921, with the plots purposely being large enough so that each owner could have a vegetable garden.

Population: 27,692; Growth (since 2000): -7.8%; Density: 4,718.1 persons per square mile; Race: 92.5% White, 3.4% Black/African American, 0.8% Asian, 0.4% American Indian/Alaska Native, 0.0% Native Hawaiian/Other Pacific Islander, 2.1% Two or more races, 3.3% Hispanic of any race; Average household size: 2.54; Median age: 39.9; Age under 18: 22.4%; Age 65 and over: 14.0%; Males per 100 females: 96.4; Marriage status: 30.7% never married, 49.1% now married, 1.1% separated, 7.6% widowed, 12.6% divorced; Foreign born: 3.2%; Speak English only: 95.8%; With disability: 14.4%; Veterans: 10.2%; Ancestry: 24.5% German, 19.4% Polish, 17.0% Irish, 10.7% English, 7.0% Italian

Employment: 10.1% management, business, and financial, 3.1% computer, engineering, and science, 6.6% education, legal, community service, arts, and media, 3.9% healthcare practitioners, 17.6% service, 25.8% sales and office, 10.8% natural resources, construction, and maintenance, 22.1% production, transportation, and material moving

Income: Per capita: $23,997; Median household: $52,425; Average household: $61,126; Households with income of $100,000 or more: 14.5%; Poverty rate: 9.4%

Educational Attainment: High school diploma or higher: 89.4%; Bachelor's degree or higher: 12.3%; Graduate/professional degree or higher: 3.2%

School District(s)

Garden City SD (PK-12)
    2012-13 Enrollment: 4,640 . . . . (734) 762-6311

Housing: Homeownership rate: 82.5%; Median home value: $83,100; Median year structure built: 1956; Homeowner vacancy rate: 2.0%; Median gross rent: $989 per month; Rental vacancy rate: 6.8%

Health Insurance: 86.9% have insurance; 73.1% have private insurance; 28.5% have public insurance; 13.1% do not have insurance; 4.8% of children under 18 do not have insurance

Hospitals: Garden City Hospital (323 beds)

Safety: Violent crime rate: 29.5 per 10,000 population; Property crime rate: 199.6 per 10,000 population

Newspapers: The Citizen (weekly circulation 13000)

Transportation: Commute: 95.5% car, 0.4% public transportation, 1.0% walk, 2.1% work from home; Median travel time to work: 23.6 minutes

Additional Information Contacts

City of Garden City . . . . (734) 793-1600
    http://www.gardencitymi.org

GIBRALTAR (city).
Covers a land area of 3.780 square miles and a water area of 0.632 square miles. Located at 42.11° N. Lat; 83.20° W. Long. Elevation is 574 feet.

History: Gibraltar was first settled in 1811. The settlement was platted in 1837, but prospered only after the suburban growth of Wayne County in the 1900's.

Population: 4,656; Growth (since 2000): 9.2%; Density: 1,231.9 persons per square mile; Race: 94.7% White, 2.0% Black/African American, 0.7% Asian, 0.4% American Indian/Alaska Native, 0.1% Native Hawaiian/Other Pacific Islander, 1.6% Two or more races, 2.9% Hispanic of any race; Average household size: 2.39; Median age: 41.4; Age under 18: 22.0%; Age 65 and over: 14.2%; Males per 100 females: 99.7; Marriage status: 24.4% never married, 53.7% now married, 0.4% separated, 5.7% widowed, 16.2% divorced; Foreign born: 1.3%; Speak English only: 98.1%; With disability: 15.6%; Veterans: 12.5%; Ancestry: 21.7% German, 19.9% Irish, 12.7% Polish, 10.9% American, 10.3% English

Employment: 11.2% management, business, and financial, 2.3% computer, engineering, and science, 8.7% education, legal, community service, arts, and media, 6.9% healthcare practitioners, 24.3% service, 18.0% sales and office, 12.2% natural resources, construction, and maintenance, 16.5% production, transportation, and material moving

Income: Per capita: $29,209; Median household: $67,636; Average household: $72,447; Households with income of $100,000 or more: 24.5%; Poverty rate: 11.2%

Educational Attainment: High school diploma or higher: 90.8%; Bachelor's degree or higher: 21.3%; Graduate/professional degree or higher: 8.3%

Housing: Homeownership rate: 75.8%; Median home value: $116,200; Median year structure built: 1974; Homeowner vacancy rate: 5.0%; Median gross rent: $853 per month; Rental vacancy rate: 19.6%

Health Insurance: 91.3% have insurance; 82.8% have private insurance; 26.3% have public insurance; 8.7% do not have insurance; 1.6% of children under 18 do not have insurance

Safety: Violent crime rate: 17.5 per 10,000 population; Property crime rate: 144.6 per 10,000 population

Transportation: Commute: 95.1% car, 2.2% public transportation, 2.0% walk, 0.0% work from home; Median travel time to work: 26.9 minutes

GROSSE ILE (township).
Covers a land area of 9.200 square miles and a water area of 9.468 square miles. Located at 42.13° N. Lat; 83.15° W. Long. Elevation is 597 feet.

Population: 10,371; Growth (since 2000): -4.8%; Density: 1,127.2 persons per square mile; Race: 95.5% White, 0.4% Black/African American, 2.4% Asian, 0.4% American Indian/Alaska Native, 0.0% Native Hawaiian/Other Pacific Islander, 1.1% Two or more races, 2.6% Hispanic of any race; Average household size: 2.50; Median age: 49.0; Age under 18: 21.6%; Age 65 and over: 19.2%; Males per 100 females: 96.0; Marriage status: 18.2% never married, 66.7% now married, 0.1% separated, 6.1% widowed, 8.9% divorced; Foreign born: 7.1%; Speak English only: 91.9%; With disability: 9.7%; Veterans: 9.3%; Ancestry: 25.2% German, 14.3% Irish, 14.2% Polish, 13.6% English, 7.8% French

Employment: 20.5% management, business, and financial, 5.4% computer, engineering, and science, 12.7% education, legal, community service, arts, and media, 9.5% healthcare practitioners, 13.5% service, 23.4% sales and office, 4.8% natural resources, construction, and maintenance, 10.1% production, transportation, and material moving

Income: Per capita: $42,685; Median household: $88,238; Average household: $106,095; Households with income of $100,000 or more: 44.3%; Poverty rate: 3.7%

Educational Attainment: High school diploma or higher: 96.8%; Bachelor's degree or higher: 46.8%; Graduate/professional degree or higher: 20.7%

School District(s)

Grosse Ile Township Schools (KG-12)
    2012-13 Enrollment: 1,831 . . . . (734) 362-2581

Housing: Homeownership rate: 91.1%; Median home value: $239,500; Median year structure built: 1968; Homeowner vacancy rate: 2.4%; Median gross rent: $1,201 per month; Rental vacancy rate: 14.0%

Health Insurance: 96.2% have insurance; 90.6% have private insurance; 23.2% have public insurance; 3.8% do not have insurance; 1.8% of children under 18 do not have insurance

Safety: Violent crime rate: 3.9 per 10,000 population; Property crime rate: 43.2 per 10,000 population

Transportation: Commute: 93.3% car, 0.0% public transportation, 1.0% walk, 4.7% work from home; Median travel time to work: 29.3 minutes

GROSSE POINTE (city).
Covers a land area of 1.059 square miles and a water area of 1.194 square miles. Located at 42.38° N. Lat; 82.90° W. Long. Elevation is 587 feet.

History: Grosse Pointe developed as one of the Gold Coast communities along the shore of Lake St. Clair.

Population: 5,421; Growth (since 2000): -4.4%; Density: 5,118.1 persons per square mile; Race: 93.2% White, 3.3% Black/African American, 1.6% Asian, 0.1% American Indian/Alaska Native, 0.1% Native Hawaiian/Other Pacific Islander, 1.5% Two or more races, 1.8% Hispanic of any race; Average household size: 2.42; Median age: 44.7; Age under 18: 26.4%; Age 65 and over: 16.1%; Males per 100 females: 86.7; Marriage status: 25.2% never married, 57.1% now married, 0.7% separated, 6.9% widowed, 10.8% divorced; Foreign born: 5.1%; Speak English only: 91.2%; With disability: 7.1%; Veterans: 7.4%; Ancestry: 25.6% German, 15.6% Irish, 15.3% English, 14.3% Italian, 10.7% Polish

Employment: 23.6% management, business, and financial, 7.4% computer, engineering, and science, 25.3% education, legal, community service, arts, and media, 11.2% healthcare practitioners, 7.4% service, 20.4% sales and office, 1.8% natural resources, construction, and maintenance, 2.8% production, transportation, and material moving

Income: Per capita: $55,166; Median household: $99,698; Average household: $135,201; Households with income of $100,000 or more: 49.9%; Poverty rate: 3.2%

Educational Attainment: High school diploma or higher: 98.9%; Bachelor's degree or higher: 69.8%; Graduate/professional degree or higher: 35.5%

School District(s)
Grosse Pointe Public Schools (PK-12)
    2012-13 Enrollment: 8,348 . . . . (313) 432-3000

Housing: Homeownership rate: 81.2%; Median home value: $242,700; Median year structure built: Before 1940; Homeowner vacancy rate: 2.4%; Median gross rent: $1,244 per month; Rental vacancy rate: 12.2%

Health Insurance: 95.9% have insurance; 89.5% have private insurance; 20.3% have public insurance; 4.1% do not have insurance; 3.4% of children under 18 do not have insurance

Hospitals: Beaumont Health System (289 beds)

Safety: Violent crime rate: 9.4 per 10,000 population; Property crime rate: 183.0 per 10,000 population

Transportation: Commute: 91.4% car, 1.4% public transportation, 0.4% walk, 2.9% work from home; Median travel time to work: 27.3 minutes

Additional Information Contacts
City of Grosse Pointe . . . . (313) 885-5800
http://www.grossepointecity.org

GROSSE POINTE FARMS (city).
Covers a land area of 2.750 square miles and a water area of 9.574 square miles. Located at 42.40° N. Lat; 82.89° W. Long. Elevation is 610 feet.

History: Named for the point of land projecting into Lake St. Clair, settled by the French. Grosse Pointe Farms was the first settled of the Gold Coast communities. Captain Alexander Grant, Commodore of the British Navy on the Great Lakes, purchased land here during the time of English occupation, and erected a large home known as Grant's Castle, a gathering place for British officers and Detroit society of the day. Grosse Pointe Farms was incorporated as a village in 1879.

Population: 9,479; Growth (since 2000): -2.9%; Density: 3,446.6 persons per square mile; Race: 95.4% White, 1.8% Black/African American, 1.3% Asian, 0.2% American Indian/Alaska Native, 0.0% Native Hawaiian/Other Pacific Islander, 1.0% Two or more races, 2.0% Hispanic of any race; Average household size: 2.55; Median age: 45.1; Age under 18: 25.8%; Age 65 and over: 17.5%; Males per 100 females: 95.2; Marriage status: 20.3% never married, 65.2% now married, 0.3% separated, 7.9% widowed, 6.5% divorced; Foreign born: 3.7%; Speak English only: 93.6%; With disability: 7.9%; Veterans: 6.8%; Ancestry: 27.3% German, 17.5% Irish, 15.4% English, 12.1% Italian, 10.7% Polish

Employment: 28.7% management, business, and financial, 5.0% computer, engineering, and science, 17.6% education, legal, community service, arts, and media, 13.1% healthcare practitioners, 8.3% service, 22.0% sales and office, 2.3% natural resources, construction, and maintenance, 2.9% production, transportation, and material moving

Income: Per capita: $57,860; Median household: $107,152; Average household: $145,649; Households with income of $100,000 or more: 54.8%; Poverty rate: 4.3%

Educational Attainment: High school diploma or higher: 99.1%; Bachelor's degree or higher: 69.6%; Graduate/professional degree or higher: 31.1%

School District(s)
Grosse Pointe Public Schools (PK-12)
    2012-13 Enrollment: 8,348 . . . . (313) 432-3000

Housing: Homeownership rate: 94.2%; Median home value: $247,300; Median year structure built: 1948; Homeowner vacancy rate: 1.9%; Median gross rent: $599 per month; Rental vacancy rate: 7.7%

Health Insurance: 97.8% have insurance; 95.7% have private insurance; 19.7% have public insurance; 2.2% do not have insurance; 2.1% of children under 18 do not have insurance

Safety: Violent crime rate: 7.6 per 10,000 population; Property crime rate: 96.0 per 10,000 population

Newspapers: Grosse Pointe News (weekly circulation 15000)

Transportation: Commute: 94.3% car, 1.0% public transportation, 1.3% walk, 2.8% work from home; Median travel time to work: 25.0 minutes

Additional Information Contacts
City of Grosse Pointe Farms . . . . (313) 885-6600
http://www.ci.grosse-pointe-farms.mi.us

GROSSE POINTE PARK (city).
Covers a land area of 2.169 square miles and a water area of 1.542 square miles. Located at 42.37° N. Lat; 82.92° W. Long. Elevation is 581 feet.

History: Named for the point of land projecting into Lake St. Clair, settled by the French. Grosse Pointe Park grew as the Gold Coast community closest to the industrial outskirts of Detroit.

Population: 11,555; Growth (since 2000): -7.1%; Density: 5,327.5 persons per square mile; Race: 85.0% White, 10.5% Black/African American, 1.8% Asian, 0.2% American Indian/Alaska Native, 0.0% Native Hawaiian/Other Pacific Islander, 1.9% Two or more races, 2.5% Hispanic of any race; Average household size: 2.56; Median age: 41.8; Age under 18: 26.5%; Age 65 and over: 12.8%; Males per 100 females: 93.9; Marriage status: 29.5% never married, 59.2% now married, 0.8% separated, 3.6% widowed, 7.7% divorced; Foreign born: 7.3%; Speak English only: 90.7%; With disability: 8.3%; Veterans: 7.2%; Ancestry: 23.0% German, 16.9% Irish, 11.9% English, 11.6% Polish, 8.5% Italian

Employment: 21.2% management, business, and financial, 8.1% computer, engineering, and science, 22.3% education, legal, community service, arts, and media, 12.4% healthcare practitioners, 12.0% service, 17.2% sales and office, 2.6% natural resources, construction, and maintenance, 4.2% production, transportation, and material moving

Income: Per capita: $50,430; Median household: $93,415; Average household: $132,884; Households with income of $100,000 or more: 48.7%; Poverty rate: 6.2%

Educational Attainment: High school diploma or higher: 95.5%; Bachelor's degree or higher: 64.7%; Graduate/professional degree or higher: 35.7%

School District(s)
Grosse Pointe Public Schools (PK-12)
    2012-13 Enrollment: 8,348 . . . . (313) 432-3000

Housing: Homeownership rate: 72.9%; Median home value: $253,700; Median year structure built: Before 1940; Homeowner vacancy rate: 2.8%; Median gross rent: $928 per month; Rental vacancy rate: 10.5%

Health Insurance: 93.8% have insurance; 85.5% have private insurance; 20.8% have public insurance; 6.2% do not have insurance; 1.7% of children under 18 do not have insurance

Safety: Violent crime rate: 15.9 per 10,000 population; Property crime rate: 220.6 per 10,000 population

Transportation: Commute: 89.1% car, 1.3% public transportation, 2.4% walk, 5.0% work from home; Median travel time to work: 25.1 minutes

Additional Information Contacts
City of Grosse Pointe Park . . . . (313) 822-6200
http://www.grossepointepark.org

GROSSE POINTE WOODS (city).
Covers a land area of 3.249 square miles and a water area of 0.001 square miles. Located at 42.44° N. Lat; 82.90° W. Long. Elevation is 587 feet.

History: Named for the point of land projecting into Lake St. Clair, settled by the French. Grosse Pointe Woods was first known as the village of Lochmoor. It was incorporated as Grosse Pointe Woods in 1939, becoming part of the Gold Coast development.

Population: 16,135; Growth (since 2000): -5.5%; Density: 4,965.6 persons per square mile; Race: 91.4% White, 4.5% Black/African American, 2.4% Asian, 0.1% American Indian/Alaska Native, 0.0% Native Hawaiian/Other Pacific Islander, 1.3% Two or more races, 1.7% Hispanic of any race; Average household size: 2.51; Median age: 45.1; Age under 18: 23.7%; Age 65 and over: 17.7%; Males per 100 females: 91.8; Marriage status: 25.8% never married, 59.0% now married, 0.4% separated, 7.7% widowed, 7.4% divorced; Foreign born: 3.8%; Speak English only: 92.9%; With disability: 7.9%; Veterans: 7.7%; Ancestry: 26.5% German, 16.1% Irish, 13.1% Polish, 11.9% Italian, 10.7% English

Employment: 18.4% management, business, and financial, 5.9% computer, engineering, and science, 20.6% education, legal, community service, arts, and media, 9.9% healthcare practitioners, 11.3% service, 26.1% sales and office, 4.5% natural resources, construction, and maintenance, 3.3% production, transportation, and material moving

Income: Per capita: $39,736; Median household: $87,123; Average household: $100,396; Households with income of $100,000 or more: 42.1%; Poverty rate: 4.6%

Educational Attainment: High school diploma or higher: 97.3%; Bachelor's degree or higher: 57.1%; Graduate/professional degree or higher: 25.0%

School District(s)
Grosse Pointe Public Schools (PK-12)
    2012-13 Enrollment: 8,348 . . . . (313) 432-3000

Housing: Homeownership rate: 90.4%; Median home value: $186,300; Median year structure built: 1953; Homeowner vacancy rate: 2.4%; Median gross rent: $1,275 per month; Rental vacancy rate: 9.5%

Health Insurance: 94.5% have insurance; 90.3% have private insurance; 21.6% have public insurance; 5.5% do not have insurance; 3.6% of children under 18 do not have insurance

Safety: Violent crime rate: 12.1 per 10,000 population; Property crime rate: 139.6 per 10,000 population

Transportation: Commute: 93.2% car, 0.8% public transportation, 0.6% walk, 3.7% work from home; Median travel time to work: 24.2 minutes

Additional Information Contacts
City of Grosse Pointe Woods . . . . (313) 343-2440
    http://www.gpwmi.us

HAMTRAMCK (city).
Covers a land area of 2.086 square miles and a water area of 0 square miles. Located at 42.40° N. Lat; 83.06° W. Long. Elevation is 630 feet.

History: Hamtramck Township was named for Colonel John Francis Hamtramck, a German-French Canadian who became General Anthony Wayne's strategist after the Revolutionary War, and the first military commander of Detroit. In 1901 Hamtramck was organized as a village settled by German-American farmers. The Dodge Brothers Company established an automobile plant here in 1910, which attracted the Polish migration to Hamtramck. It was incorporated as a city in 1922. Though surrounded by Detroit, Hamtramck has maintained its city status, partly because the large number of Polish residents relished political autonomy.

Population: 22,423; Growth (since 2000): -2.4%; Density: 10,751.0 persons per square mile; Race: 53.6% White, 19.3% Black/African American, 21.5% Asian, 0.3% American Indian/Alaska Native, 0.0% Native Hawaiian/Other Pacific Islander, 4.7% Two or more races, 1.5% Hispanic of any race; Average household size: 3.09; Median age: 28.8; Age under 18: 31.7%; Age 65 and over: 7.7%; Males per 100 females: 106.5; Marriage status: 37.2% never married, 49.4% now married, 2.4% separated, 6.1% widowed, 7.2% divorced; Foreign born: 44.4%; Speak English only: 36.2%; With disability: 15.2%; Veterans: 3.0%; Ancestry: 13.3% Arab, 10.6% Polish, 10.0% Other Arab, 6.6% Yugoslavian, 3.0% German

Employment: 5.4% management, business, and financial, 2.7% computer, engineering, and science, 7.3% education, legal, community service, arts, and media, 3.3% healthcare practitioners, 26.4% service, 21.7% sales and office, 6.1% natural resources, construction, and maintenance, 27.0% production, transportation, and material moving

Income: Per capita: $10,890; Median household: $25,659; Average household: $34,304; Households with income of $100,000 or more: 4.7%; Poverty rate: 43.4%

Educational Attainment: High school diploma or higher: 64.8%; Bachelor's degree or higher: 12.4%; Graduate/professional degree or higher: 4.4%

School District(s)
Academy of International Studies
    2012-13 Enrollment: 69 . . . . (313) 873-9900

Bridge Academy (PK-12)
    2012-13 Enrollment: 650 . . . . (313) 887-8100
Commonwealth Community Devel. Academy (KG-12)
    2012-13 Enrollment: 239 . . . . (313) 366-9470
Frontier International Academy (KG-12)
    2012-13 Enrollment: 368 . . . . (313) 887-7500
Hamtramck Academy (KG-12)
    2012-13 Enrollment: 490 . . . . (313) 368-7312
Hamtramck SD (PK-12)
    2012-13 Enrollment: 2,868 . . . . (313) 872-9270
Hanley International Academy (PK-12)
    2012-13 Enrollment: 612 . . . . (586) 731-5300

Housing: Homeownership rate: 49.4%; Median home value: $46,600; Median year structure built: Before 1940; Homeowner vacancy rate: 4.0%; Median gross rent: $610 per month; Rental vacancy rate: 12.2%

Health Insurance: 76.6% have insurance; 34.5% have private insurance; 53.1% have public insurance; 23.4% do not have insurance; 6.0% of children under 18 do not have insurance

Safety: Violent crime rate: 166.2 per 10,000 population; Property crime rate: 369.7 per 10,000 population

Transportation: Commute: 89.8% car, 2.0% public transportation, 1.5% walk, 2.5% work from home; Median travel time to work: 25.8 minutes

Additional Information Contacts
City of Hamtramck . . . . (313) 876-7700
    http://www.hamtramck.us

HARPER WOODS (city).
Covers a land area of 2.610 square miles and a water area of 0 square miles. Located at 42.44° N. Lat; 82.93° W. Long. Elevation is 587 feet.

History: There was settlement in the Harper Woods area in the 1850's, and a plat was recorded in 1920 calling it Manchester Park. After the 1929 depression, however, the area returned to wilderness. A new community was developed in 1934 by subdividers, who named it Harper Woods.

Population: 14,236; Growth (since 2000): -0.1%; Density: 5,455.1 persons per square mile; Race: 49.6% White, 45.6% Black/African American, 1.5% Asian, 0.2% American Indian/Alaska Native, 0.0% Native Hawaiian/Other Pacific Islander, 2.7% Two or more races, 2.0% Hispanic of any race; Average household size: 2.42; Median age: 37.5; Age under 18: 25.9%; Age 65 and over: 12.8%; Males per 100 females: 85.9; Marriage status: 43.2% never married, 36.9% now married, 1.6% separated, 6.6% widowed, 13.3% divorced; Foreign born: 4.2%; Speak English only: 94.1%; With disability: 12.6%; Veterans: 5.8%; Ancestry: 13.0% German, 11.3% Irish, 8.6% Polish, 7.4% Italian, 4.1% American

Employment: 10.6% management, business, and financial, 1.9% computer, engineering, and science, 10.8% education, legal, community service, arts, and media, 6.1% healthcare practitioners, 25.1% service, 26.9% sales and office, 5.7% natural resources, construction, and maintenance, 13.0% production, transportation, and material moving

Income: Per capita: $21,286; Median household: $44,778; Average household: $54,117; Households with income of $100,000 or more: 10.2%; Poverty rate: 16.5%

Educational Attainment: High school diploma or higher: 87.3%; Bachelor's degree or higher: 25.1%; Graduate/professional degree or higher: 8.9%

School District(s)
Chandler Park Academy (KG-12)
    2012-13 Enrollment: 2,419 . . . . (248) 905-5030
Grosse Pointe Public Schools (PK-12)
    2012-13 Enrollment: 8,348 . . . . (313) 432-3000
Harper Woods the SD of The City of (PK-12)
    2012-13 Enrollment: 1,505 . . . . (313) 245-3000
Heart Academy (KG-12)
    2012-13 Enrollment: 166 . . . . (313) 882-4631
Starr Detroit Academy
    2012-13 Enrollment: 499 . . . . (313) 980-9819

Housing: Homeownership rate: 71.2%; Median home value: $68,100; Median year structure built: 1953; Homeowner vacancy rate: 4.5%; Median gross rent: $1,020 per month; Rental vacancy rate: 8.2%

Health Insurance: 84.9% have insurance; 67.0% have private insurance; 29.9% have public insurance; 15.1% do not have insurance; 5.8% of children under 18 do not have insurance

Safety: Violent crime rate: 121.4 per 10,000 population; Property crime rate: 703.2 per 10,000 population

Transportation: Commute: 91.4% car, 2.8% public transportation, 1.5% walk, 2.3% work from home; Median travel time to work: 25.8 minutes

Additional Information Contacts
City of Harper Woods . . . . (313) 343-2500
    http://www.harperwoodscity.citymax.com

HIGHLAND PARK (city). Covers a land area of 2.971 square miles and a water area of 0 square miles. Located at 42.41° N. Lat; 83.10° W. Long. Elevation is 636 feet.

History: Named for the ridge, or high land, on which the town was built. About a hundred years before Henry Ford brought prosperity to Highland Park with his Ford Motor Company plant in 1909, another Ford, Richard (not related to Henry) had settled here. He built his farm on the ridge, since leveled, that was the "highland" for which the town was named. Several attempts at creating a town failed, until 1887 when Captain William H. Stevens, who had made a fortune in the Colorado silver mines, attracted investors in a promotional scheme. The village of Highland Park was organized in 1889, and in 1918 it was incorporated as a city. When Ford moved his plant to Dearborn in 1920, Highland Park's population declined, but later grew as it became a residential suburb for Detroit.

Population: 11,776; Growth (since 2000): -29.7%; Density: 3,963.9 persons per square mile; Race: 3.2% White, 93.5% Black/African American, 0.4% Asian, 0.3% American Indian/Alaska Native, 0.0% Native Hawaiian/Other Pacific Islander, 2.3% Two or more races, 1.3% Hispanic of any race; Average household size: 2.36; Median age: 40.5; Age under 18: 23.7%; Age 65 and over: 14.4%; Males per 100 females: 96.8; Marriage status: 52.5% never married, 21.3% now married, 6.8% separated, 11.1% widowed, 15.0% divorced; Foreign born: 0.7%; Speak English only: 97.4%; With disability: 28.3%; Veterans: 8.3%; Ancestry: 1.7% Irish, 1.7% African, 1.2% American, 1.1% German, 0.5% English

Employment: 6.4% management, business, and financial, 0.7% computer, engineering, and science, 12.1% education, legal, community service, arts, and media, 4.5% healthcare practitioners, 32.7% service, 22.2% sales and office, 3.1% natural resources, construction, and maintenance, 18.3% production, transportation, and material moving

Income: Per capita: $13,539; Median household: $18,981; Average household: $29,656; Households with income of $100,000 or more: 1.7%; Poverty rate: 51.1%

Educational Attainment: High school diploma or higher: 73.8%; Bachelor's degree or higher: 9.9%; Graduate/professional degree or higher: 3.8%

School District(s)
Ace Academy (Sda) (KG-12)
    2012-13 Enrollment: 132 . . . . (248) 582-8100
Clintondale Community Schools (PK-12)
    2012-13 Enrollment: 3,407 . . . . (586) 791-6300
George Washington Carver Academy (KG-12)
    2012-13 Enrollment: 420 . . . . (313) 865-6024
Highland Park City Schools (PK-12)
    2012-13 Enrollment: n/a . . . . (313) 957-3000
Northpointe Academy (KG-12)
    2012-13 Enrollment: 307 . . . . (313) 577-8411

Housing: Homeownership rate: 37.0%; Median home value: $42,200; Median year structure built: 1947; Homeowner vacancy rate: 3.7%; Median gross rent: $582 per month; Rental vacancy rate: 14.2%

Health Insurance: 82.4% have insurance; 35.5% have private insurance; 59.0% have public insurance; 17.6% do not have insurance; 1.2% of children under 18 do not have insurance

Safety: Violent crime rate: 161.3 per 10,000 population; Property crime rate: 497.8 per 10,000 population

Transportation: Commute: 71.5% car, 17.9% public transportation, 2.4% walk, 5.1% work from home; Median travel time to work: 28.0 minutes

Additional Information Contacts
City of Highland Park . . . . (313) 252-0050
    http://www.highlandparkcity.us

HURON (charter township). Covers a land area of 35.352 square miles and a water area of 0.482 square miles. Located at 42.14° N. Lat; 83.36° W. Long.

History: Huron Charter Township was named for the Huron River, which flows through the township from northwest to southeast. It was organized in 1827 and originally included the land that now contains the cities of Romulus and Belleville as well as the townships of Van Buren and Sumpter.

Population: 15,879; Growth (since 2000): 15.6%; Density: 449.2 persons per square mile; Race: 93.1% White, 2.5% Black/African American, 0.7% Asian, 0.7% American Indian/Alaska Native, 0.0% Native Hawaiian/Other

Pacific Islander, 2.5% Two or more races, 3.2% Hispanic of any race; Average household size: 2.73; Median age: 39.4; Age under 18: 25.2%; Age 65 and over: 10.4%; Males per 100 females: 100.8; Marriage status: 25.4% never married, 60.1% now married, 1.4% separated, 3.7% widowed, 10.8% divorced; Foreign born: 2.2%; Speak English only: 96.9%; With disability: 12.3%; Veterans: 9.8%; Ancestry: 25.8% German, 13.4% Irish, 12.4% Polish, 9.0% English, 9.0% French

Employment: 13.4% management, business, and financial, 2.6% computer, engineering, and science, 7.5% education, legal, community service, arts, and media, 5.7% healthcare practitioners, 15.7% service, 24.0% sales and office, 11.1% natural resources, construction, and maintenance, 20.1% production, transportation, and material moving

Income: Per capita: $27,177; Median household: $65,480; Average household: $74,227; Households with income of $100,000 or more: 29.0%; Poverty rate: 11.8%

Educational Attainment: High school diploma or higher: 88.0%; Bachelor's degree or higher: 18.6%; Graduate/professional degree or higher: 5.6%

School District(s)
Summit Academy North (KG-12)
    2012-13 Enrollment: 1,951 . . . . (734) 379-9766

Housing: Homeownership rate: 90.6%; Median home value: $152,600; Median year structure built: 1990; Homeowner vacancy rate: 2.8%; Median gross rent: $927 per month; Rental vacancy rate: 5.4%

Health Insurance: 91.6% have insurance; 78.9% have private insurance; 24.5% have public insurance; 8.4% do not have insurance; 3.7% of children under 18 do not have insurance

Safety: Violent crime rate: 24.3 per 10,000 population; Property crime rate: 130.1 per 10,000 population

Transportation: Commute: 92.1% car, 1.8% public transportation, 1.1% walk, 2.9% work from home; Median travel time to work: 27.4 minutes

Additional Information Contacts
Huron Charter Township . . . . (734) 753-4466
    http://www.hurontownship-mi.gov

INKSTER (city). Covers a land area of 6.253 square miles and a water area of <.001 square miles. Located at 42.29° N. Lat; 83.32° W. Long. Elevation is 627 feet.

History: Named for Robert Inkster, who operated a steam sawmill here in the early 1860s. A post office was established here in 1857, when it was known as Moulin Rouge. In the early 1860's, Robert Inkster operated a steam sawmill in the area, and the name was changed to Inkster. Inkster grew in the 1900's as a residential community for workers in the factories of neighboring Dearborn and Detroit. The economic depression of the early 1930's had a disastrous effect here.

Population: 25,369; Growth (since 2000): -15.8%; Density: 4,057.1 persons per square mile; Race: 20.5% White, 73.2% Black/African American, 1.6% Asian, 0.3% American Indian/Alaska Native, 0.1% Native Hawaiian/Other Pacific Islander, 3.6% Two or more races, 2.6% Hispanic of any race; Average household size: 2.56; Median age: 34.2; Age under 18: 27.9%; Age 65 and over: 11.3%; Males per 100 females: 88.1; Marriage status: 47.2% never married, 30.4% now married, 4.1% separated, 6.8% widowed, 15.6% divorced; Foreign born: 3.2%; Speak English only: 94.5%; With disability: 22.2%; Veterans: 7.4%; Ancestry: 2.8% German, 2.1% Irish, 2.0% Polish, 2.0% American, 1.9% African

Employment: 4.4% management, business, and financial, 2.6% computer, engineering, and science, 7.9% education, legal, community service, arts, and media, 4.4% healthcare practitioners, 28.3% service, 25.4% sales and office, 5.6% natural resources, construction, and maintenance, 21.4% production, transportation, and material moving

Income: Per capita: $14,259; Median household: $26,512; Average household: $35,501; Households with income of $100,000 or more: 3.9%; Poverty rate: 38.2%

Educational Attainment: High school diploma or higher: 79.3%; Bachelor's degree or higher: 10.1%; Graduate/professional degree or higher: 2.6%

School District(s)
Discovery Arts and Technology Psa (PK-12)
    2012-13 Enrollment: 226 . . . . (313) 827-0762
Gaudior Academy (PK-12)
    2012-13 Enrollment: 225 . . . . (313) 792-9444
SD of the City of Inkster (PK-12)
    2012-13 Enrollment: 2,247 . . . . (734) 722-5310
Wayne-Westland Community SD (PK-12)
    2012-13 Enrollment: 12,030 . . . . (734) 419-2000

Westwood Community SD (PK-12)
2012-13 Enrollment: 2,502 . . . . (313) 565-1901
Housing: Homeownership rate: 52.4%; Median home value: $55,400;
Median year structure built: 1958; Homeowner vacancy rate: 4.0%; Median
gross rent: $741 per month; Rental vacancy rate: 11.8%
Health Insurance: 84.5% have insurance; 41.8% have private insurance;
54.1% have public insurance; 15.5% do not have insurance; 4.5% of
children under 18 do not have insurance
Safety: Violent crime rate: 159.4 per 10,000 population; Property crime
rate: 416.1 per 10,000 population
Transportation: Commute: 94.5% car, 3.2% public transportation, 0.7%
walk, 0.9% work from home; Median travel time to work: 24.5 minutes
Additional Information Contacts
City of Inkster . . . . (313) 563-4232
http://www.cityofinkster.com

LINCOLN PARK (city). Covers a land area of 5.888 square miles
and a water area of <.001 square miles. Located at 42.24° N. Lat; 83.18°
W. Long. Elevation is 587 feet.
History: Named for a community in Illinois, by the developer. Lincoln Park
developed as a residential suburb for workers in the Ford Motor
Company's Dearborn plant or in the other industries in the south section of
Detroit. The town was laid out in 1906, incorporated as a village in 1921
and as a city in 1925.
Population: 38,144; Growth (since 2000): -4.7%; Density: 6,478.3 persons
per square mile; Race: 84.2% White, 5.9% Black/African American, 0.5%
Asian, 0.7% American Indian/Alaska Native, 0.0% Native Hawaiian/Other
Pacific Islander, 3.2% Two or more races, 14.9% Hispanic of any race;
Average household size: 2.55; Median age: 36.7; Age under 18: 24.8%;
Age 65 and over: 11.5%; Males per 100 females: 96.2; Marriage status:
34.3% never married, 43.9% now married, 2.2% separated, 7.1%
widowed, 14.7% divorced; Foreign born: 6.3%; Speak English only: 86.9%;
With disability: 19.0%; Veterans: 9.1%; Ancestry: 18.8% German, 15.3%
Irish, 11.1% Polish, 8.3% Italian, 8.3% English
Employment: 6.3% management, business, and financial, 3.3% computer,
engineering, and science, 6.3% education, legal, community service, arts,
and media, 3.9% healthcare practitioners, 22.1% service, 27.2% sales and
office, 10.2% natural resources, construction, and maintenance, 20.7%
production, transportation, and material moving
Income: Per capita: $19,385; Median household: $40,589; Average
household: $48,800; Households with income of $100,000 or more: 8.6%;
Poverty rate: 18.3%
Educational Attainment: High school diploma or higher: 80.4%;
Bachelor's degree or higher: 8.1%; Graduate/professional degree or
higher: 2.3%
School District(s)
Lincoln Park SD (PK-12)
2012-13 Enrollment: 4,786 . . . . (313) 389-0200
Housing: Homeownership rate: 73.9%; Median home value: $62,500;
Median year structure built: 1954; Homeowner vacancy rate: 2.8%; Median
gross rent: $787 per month; Rental vacancy rate: 9.5%
Health Insurance: 83.8% have insurance; 58.7% have private insurance;
37.5% have public insurance; 16.2% do not have insurance; 4.6% of
children under 18 do not have insurance
Safety: Violent crime rate: 62.2 per 10,000 population; Property crime rate:
360.1 per 10,000 population
Transportation: Commute: 96.4% car, 0.8% public transportation, 0.5%
walk, 1.7% work from home; Median travel time to work: 23.0 minutes
Additional Information Contacts
City of Lincoln Park . . . . (313) 386-1800
http://lincolnpark.govoffice.com

LIVONIA (city). Covers a land area of 35.695 square miles and a water
area of 0.159 square miles. Located at 42.40° N. Lat; 83.37° W. Long.
Elevation is 640 feet.
History: Livonia was named for Livonia, New York, the former home of
several of the early residents. The area was first settled in 1832, and was
incorporated as the city of Livonia in 1950.
Population: 96,942; Growth (since 2000): -3.6%; Density: 2,715.8 persons
per square mile; Race: 92.0% White, 3.4% Black/African American, 2.5%
Asian, 0.2% American Indian/Alaska Native, 0.0% Native Hawaiian/Other
Pacific Islander, 1.4% Two or more races, 2.5% Hispanic of any race;
Average household size: 2.47; Median age: 44.5; Age under 18: 20.8%;
Age 65 and over: 17.7%; Males per 100 females: 93.6; Marriage status:
27.2% never married, 55.4% now married, 0.5% separated, 7.2%

widowed, 10.2% divorced; Foreign born: 7.0%; Speak English only: 91.1%;
With disability: 11.6%; Veterans: 9.2%; Ancestry: 20.7% German, 17.5%
Polish, 15.2% Irish, 10.7% English, 8.7% American
Employment: 15.8% management, business, and financial, 8.8%
computer, engineering, and science, 10.3% education, legal, community
service, arts, and media, 7.6% healthcare practitioners, 15.5% service,
25.4% sales and office, 7.0% natural resources, construction, and
maintenance, 9.7% production, transportation, and material moving
Income: Per capita: $32,249; Median household: $68,973; Average
household: $80,865; Households with income of $100,000 or more: 29.5%;
Poverty rate: 6.1%
Educational Attainment: High school diploma or higher: 93.2%;
Bachelor's degree or higher: 35.4%; Graduate/professional degree or
higher: 11.8%
School District(s)
American Montessori Academy (KG-12)
2012-13 Enrollment: 503 . . . . (734) 525-7100
Clarenceville SD (PK-12)
2012-13 Enrollment: 1,880 . . . . (248) 919-0400
Japanese American School of South East Michigan (KG-12)
2012-13 Enrollment: 73 . . . . (734) 422-5931
Livonia Public Schools SD (PK-12)
2012-13 Enrollment: 15,176 . . . . (734) 744-2525
Universal Learning Academy (PK-12)
2012-13 Enrollment: 624 . . . . (734) 402-5900
Four-year College(s)
Madonna University (Private, Not-for-profit, Roman Catholic)
Fall 2013 Enrollment: 4,399 . . . . (734) 432-5300
2013-14 Tuition: In-state $16,340; Out-of-state $16,340
Two-year College(s)
Schoolcraft College (Public)
Fall 2013 Enrollment: 12,385 . . . . (734) 462-4400
2013-14 Tuition: In-state $4,370; Out-of-state $6,290
Vocational/Technical School(s)
L'esprit Academy (Private, For-profit)
Fall 2013 Enrollment: 129 . . . . (734) 762-0200
2013-14 Tuition: $13,665
Housing: Homeownership rate: 86.2%; Median home value: $154,900;
Median year structure built: 1963; Homeowner vacancy rate: 1.1%; Median
gross rent: $968 per month; Rental vacancy rate: 7.5%
Health Insurance: 92.5% have insurance; 84.1% have private insurance;
25.2% have public insurance; 7.5% do not have insurance; 3.1% of
children under 18 do not have insurance
Hospitals: Saint Mary Mercy Hospital (304 beds)
Safety: Violent crime rate: 15.5 per 10,000 population; Property crime rate:
205.9 per 10,000 population
Newspapers: Observer & Eccentric Newspapers (weekly circulation
172000)
Transportation: Commute: 95.6% car, 0.3% public transportation, 0.6%
walk, 3.0% work from home; Median travel time to work: 23.9 minutes
Additional Information Contacts
City of Livonia . . . . (734) 466-2200
http://www.ci.livonia.mi.us

MELVINDALE (city). Covers a land area of 2.720 square miles and a
water area of 0.038 square miles. Located at 42.28° N. Lat; 83.18° W.
Long. Elevation is 591 feet.
History: Named for Melvin Wilkinson who plotted the village. Melvindale
grew up as a residential suburb for workers in the Dearborn and Detroit
factories.
Population: 10,715; Growth (since 2000): -0.2%; Density: 3,938.7 persons
per square mile; Race: 76.8% White, 11.3% Black/African American, 0.8%
Asian, 0.7% American Indian/Alaska Native, 0.0% Native Hawaiian/Other
Pacific Islander, 3.9% Two or more races, 18.3% Hispanic of any race;
Average household size: 2.42; Median age: 36.5; Age under 18: 24.7%;
Age 65 and over: 11.8%; Males per 100 females: 92.6; Marriage status:
36.2% never married, 43.5% now married, 2.8% separated, 6.1%
widowed, 14.1% divorced; Foreign born: 14.2%; Speak English only:
75.9%; With disability: 18.0%; Veterans: 8.9%; Ancestry: 14.6% German,
10.7% Irish, 9.2% Polish, 7.6% Other Arab, 4.2% Italian
Employment: 7.7% management, business, and financial, 2.1% computer,
engineering, and science, 9.1% education, legal, community service, arts,
and media, 3.5% healthcare practitioners, 26.2% service, 18.1% sales and
office, 11.3% natural resources, construction, and maintenance, 21.9%
production, transportation, and material moving

Income: Per capita: $18,171; Median household: $33,302; Average household: $42,374; Households with income of $100,000 or more: 6.6%; Poverty rate: 22.8%

Educational Attainment: High school diploma or higher: 76.8%; Bachelor's degree or higher: 11.7%; Graduate/professional degree or higher: 4.4%

School District(s)

Academy for Business and Technology (KG-12)
   2012-13 Enrollment: 709 . . . . (313) 383-3422
Melvindale-North Allen Park Schools (KG-12)
   2012-13 Enrollment: 2,824 . . . . (313) 389-3300

Housing: Homeownership rate: 62.8%; Median home value: $59,000; Median year structure built: 1954; Homeowner vacancy rate: 2.3%; Median gross rent: $734 per month; Rental vacancy rate: 7.2%

Health Insurance: 85.2% have insurance; 59.4% have private insurance; 40.0% have public insurance; 14.8% do not have insurance; 4.3% of children under 18 do not have insurance

Safety: Violent crime rate: 32.5 per 10,000 population; Property crime rate: 293.1 per 10,000 population

Transportation: Commute: 96.2% car, 0.0% public transportation, 2.3% walk, 1.5% work from home; Median travel time to work: 20.1 minutes

Additional Information Contacts

City of Melvindale . . . . (313) 429-1040
   http://www.melvindale.org

NEW BOSTON (unincorporated postal area)

ZCTA: 48164

Covers a land area of 29.390 square miles and a water area of 0.147 square miles. Located at 42.12° N. Lat; 83.39° W. Long. Elevation is 636 feet.

Population: 9,175; Growth (since 2000): 17.7%; Density: 312.2 persons per square mile; Race: 92.9% White, 3.5% Black/African American, 0.8% Asian, 0.5% American Indian/Alaska Native, 0.0% Native Hawaiian/Other Pacific Islander, 1.9% Two or more races, 2.3% Hispanic of any race; Average household size: 2.73; Median age: 42.0; Age under 18: 23.9%; Age 65 and over: 10.9%; Males per 100 females: 103.2; Marriage status: 23.3% never married, 64.7% now married, 1.2% separated, 3.7% widowed, 8.2% divorced; Foreign born: 2.9%; Speak English only: 95.8%; With disability: 9.6%; Veterans: 8.1%; Ancestry: 24.7% German, 14.7% Polish, 13.1% Irish, 9.1% English, 9.0% Italian

Employment: 15.8% management, business, and financial, 3.3% computer, engineering, and science, 8.7% education, legal, community service, arts, and media, 5.9% healthcare practitioners, 16.2% service, 22.1% sales and office, 12.2% natural resources, construction, and maintenance, 15.8% production, transportation, and material moving

Income: Per capita: $29,096; Median household: $75,034; Average household: $85,007; Households with income of $100,000 or more: 31.8%; Poverty rate: 7.3%

Educational Attainment: High school diploma or higher: 90.3%; Bachelor's degree or higher: 21.9%; Graduate/professional degree or higher: 7.7%

School District(s)

Huron SD (KG-12)
   2012-13 Enrollment: 2,431 . . . . (734) 782-2441

Housing: Homeownership rate: 91.0%; Median home value: $175,600; Median year structure built: 1989; Homeowner vacancy rate: 2.4%; Median gross rent: $892 per month; Rental vacancy rate: 5.9%

Health Insurance: 93.4% have insurance; 86.0% have private insurance; 18.9% have public insurance; 6.6% do not have insurance; 2.5% of children under 18 do not have insurance

Transportation: Commute: 92.9% car, 2.4% public transportation, 1.0% walk, 3.4% work from home; Median travel time to work: 28.8 minutes

NORTHVILLE (township). Covers a land area of 16.192 square miles and a water area of 0.378 square miles. Located at 42.42° N. Lat; 83.49° W. Long. Elevation is 827 feet.

Population: 28,497; Growth (since 2000): 35.5%; Density: 1,759.9 persons per square mile; Race: 82.7% White, 3.6% Black/African American, 11.3% Asian, 0.1% American Indian/Alaska Native, 0.0% Native Hawaiian/Other Pacific Islander, 1.8% Two or more races, 2.4% Hispanic of any race; Average household size: 2.47; Median age: 42.4; Age under 18: 24.4%; Age 65 and over: 15.3%; Males per 100 females: 91.8; Marriage status: 25.3% never married, 61.0% now married, 0.6% separated, 5.7% widowed, 8.0% divorced; Foreign born: 15.6%; Speak

English only: 79.9%; With disability: 8.0%; Veterans: 7.7%; Ancestry: 18.4% German, 13.6% Polish, 11.6% Irish, 10.4% English, 8.3% Italian

Employment: 28.3% management, business, and financial, 13.4% computer, engineering, and science, 11.1% education, legal, community service, arts, and media, 10.2% healthcare practitioners, 10.6% service, 18.3% sales and office, 3.4% natural resources, construction, and maintenance, 4.7% production, transportation, and material moving

Income: Per capita: $51,883; Median household: $97,161; Average household: $133,341; Households with income of $100,000 or more: 48.5%; Poverty rate: 3.2%

Educational Attainment: High school diploma or higher: 96.2%; Bachelor's degree or higher: 58.7%; Graduate/professional degree or higher: 30.1%

School District(s)

Northville Public Schools (PK-12)
   2012-13 Enrollment: 7,274 . . . . (248) 349-3400

Housing: Homeownership rate: 76.5%; Median home value: $315,900; Median year structure built: 1988; Homeowner vacancy rate: 1.9%; Median gross rent: $1,058 per month; Rental vacancy rate: 9.5%

Health Insurance: 94.3% have insurance; 88.6% have private insurance; 20.0% have public insurance; 5.7% do not have insurance; 2.1% of children under 18 do not have insurance

Safety: Violent crime rate: 6.3 per 10,000 population; Property crime rate: 126.7 per 10,000 population

Transportation: Commute: 94.7% car, 0.3% public transportation, 0.7% walk, 3.8% work from home; Median travel time to work: 28.4 minutes

Additional Information Contacts

Northville Township . . . . (248) 348-5800
   http://www.northvillemich.com

PLYMOUTH (charter township). Covers a land area of 15.930 square miles and a water area of 0.095 square miles. Located at 42.37° N. Lat; 83.50° W. Long. Elevation is 725 feet.

Population: 27,524; Growth (since 2000): -1.0%; Density: 1,727.8 persons per square mile; Race: 92.1% White, 2.2% Black/African American, 3.5% Asian, 0.3% American Indian/Alaska Native, 0.0% Native Hawaiian/Other Pacific Islander, 1.5% Two or more races, 2.4% Hispanic of any race; Average household size: 2.45; Median age: 44.5; Age under 18: 22.3%; Age 65 and over: 16.5%; Males per 100 females: 94.5; Marriage status: 24.2% never married, 62.7% now married, 0.2% separated, 5.3% widowed, 7.7% divorced; Foreign born: 7.5%; Speak English only: 91.1%; With disability: 7.9%; Veterans: 8.5%; Ancestry: 24.3% German, 15.4% Polish, 14.7% Irish, 12.7% English, 8.2% Italian

Employment: 24.7% management, business, and financial, 10.2% computer, engineering, and science, 12.5% education, legal, community service, arts, and media, 7.9% healthcare practitioners, 11.6% service, 23.1% sales and office, 3.0% natural resources, construction, and maintenance, 7.0% production, transportation, and material moving

Income: Per capita: $43,889; Median household: $86,217; Average household: $112,110; Households with income of $100,000 or more: 43.2%; Poverty rate: 4.1%

Educational Attainment: High school diploma or higher: 96.4%; Bachelor's degree or higher: 51.1%; Graduate/professional degree or higher: 22.7%

School District(s)

Plymouth-Canton Community Schools (PK-12)
   2012-13 Enrollment: 17,997 . . . . (734) 416-2700

Housing: Homeownership rate: 83.2%; Median home value: $240,400; Median year structure built: 1977; Homeowner vacancy rate: 1.2%; Median gross rent: $783 per month; Rental vacancy rate: 9.2%

Health Insurance: 94.2% have insurance; 88.1% have private insurance; 21.2% have public insurance; 5.8% do not have insurance; 2.8% of children under 18 do not have insurance

Safety: Violent crime rate: 6.6 per 10,000 population; Property crime rate: 109.3 per 10,000 population

Newspapers: Associated Newspapers (weekly circulation 32000)

Transportation: Commute: 94.7% car, 0.2% public transportation, 0.6% walk, 3.7% work from home; Median travel time to work: 25.1 minutes

Additional Information Contacts

Plymouth Charter Township . . . . (734) 453-3840
   http://www.plymouthtwp.org

PLYMOUTH (city). Covers a land area of 2.211 square miles and a water area of 0.012 square miles. Located at 42.37° N. Lat; 83.47° W. Long. Elevation is 725 feet.

History: Plymouth was settled in 1825 by descendants of the Pilgrims, who named it for the landing place in Massachusetts. It developed as an industrial town around two air rifle factories.

Population: 9,132; Growth (since 2000): 1.2%; Density: 4,130.5 persons per square mile; Race: 94.2% White, 1.6% Black/African American, 2.2% Asian, 0.3% American Indian/Alaska Native, 0.0% Native Hawaiian/Other Pacific Islander, 1.4% Two or more races, 1.8% Hispanic of any race; Average household size: 2.08; Median age: 39.2; Age under 18: 21.5%; Age 65 and over: 14.0%; Males per 100 females: 92.2; Marriage status: 34.2% never married, 46.6% now married, 1.7% separated, 4.4% widowed, 14.8% divorced; Foreign born: 4.7%; Speak English only: 94.0%; With disability: 6.6%; Veterans: 6.9%; Ancestry: 20.9% German, 15.6% Irish, 14.7% Polish, 13.2% English, 13.1% American

Employment: 17.7% management, business, and financial, 9.1% computer, engineering, and science, 17.6% education, legal, community service, arts, and media, 5.8% healthcare practitioners, 14.2% service, 23.2% sales and office, 5.5% natural resources, construction, and maintenance, 6.8% production, transportation, and material moving

Income: Per capita: $38,864; Median household: $73,389; Average household: $82,818; Households with income of $100,000 or more: 31.8%; Poverty rate: 5.8%

Educational Attainment: High school diploma or higher: 95.7%; Bachelor's degree or higher: 52.9%; Graduate/professional degree or higher: 22.0%

School District(s)

Plymouth-Canton Community Schools (PK-12)

    2012-13 Enrollment: 17,997 . . . . (734) 416-2700

Housing: Homeownership rate: 63.7%; Median home value: $195,700; Median year structure built: 1955; Homeowner vacancy rate: 2.4%; Median gross rent: $848 per month; Rental vacancy rate: 9.9%

Health Insurance: 91.0% have insurance; 82.2% have private insurance; 20.0% have public insurance; 9.0% do not have insurance; 0.0% of children under 18 do not have insurance

Safety: Violent crime rate: 15.6 per 10,000 population; Property crime rate: 99.5 per 10,000 population

Newspapers: Associated Newspapers (weekly circulation 32000)

Transportation: Commute: 91.5% car, 0.0% public transportation, 2.8% walk, 5.7% work from home; Median travel time to work: 22.9 minutes

Additional Information Contacts

City of Plymouth . . . . (734) 453-1234
    http://www.ci.plymouth.mi.us

REDFORD (charter township). Covers a land area of 11.239 square miles and a water area of 0.003 square miles. Located at 42.39° N. Lat; 83.29° W. Long. Elevation is 623 feet.

Population: 48,362; Growth (since 2000): -6.3%; Density: 4,303.1 persons per square mile; Race: 66.4% White, 28.9% Black/African American, 0.8% Asian, 0.5% American Indian/Alaska Native, 0.0% Native Hawaiian/Other Pacific Islander, 2.5% Two or more races, 2.9% Hispanic of any race; Average household size: 2.51; Median age: 38.0; Age under 18: 23.9%; Age 65 and over: 12.0%; Males per 100 females: 94.8; Marriage status: 36.2% never married, 43.2% now married, 1.9% separated, 7.0% widowed, 13.5% divorced; Foreign born: 2.3%; Speak English only: 95.7%; With disability: 15.0%; Veterans: 9.8%; Ancestry: 16.8% German, 12.9% Polish, 12.0% Irish, 7.5% English, 7.1% American

Employment: 10.0% management, business, and financial, 4.5% computer, engineering, and science, 8.6% education, legal, community service, arts, and media, 4.3% healthcare practitioners, 18.0% service, 28.3% sales and office, 8.2% natural resources, construction, and maintenance, 18.1% production, transportation, and material moving

Income: Per capita: $22,853; Median household: $49,188; Average household: $57,032; Households with income of $100,000 or more: 12.1%; Poverty rate: 13.4%

Educational Attainment: High school diploma or higher: 89.2%; Bachelor's degree or higher: 18.2%; Graduate/professional degree or higher: 6.3%

School District(s)

American Montessori Academy (KG-12)

    2012-13 Enrollment: 503 . . . . (734) 525-7100

David Ellis Academy West (KG-12)

    2012-13 Enrollment: 802 . . . . (313) 450-0300

Detroit City SD (PK-12)

    2012-13 Enrollment: 49,239 . . . . (313) 873-6205

Detroit West Preparatory Academy (KG-12)

    2012-13 Enrollment: 289 . . . . (313) 387-9238

Michigan Technical Academy (PK-12)

    2012-13 Enrollment: 1,042 . . . . (313) 537-8820

Redford Union Schools District No. 1 (PK-12)

    2012-13 Enrollment: 2,863 . . . . (313) 242-6000

South Redford SD (PK-12)

    2012-13 Enrollment: 3,231 . . . . (313) 535-4000

Washington-Parks Academy (KG-12)

    2012-13 Enrollment: 1,017 . . . . (313) 592-6061

Housing: Homeownership rate: 82.3%; Median home value: $69,800; Median year structure built: 1955; Homeowner vacancy rate: 2.5%; Median gross rent: $1,046 per month; Rental vacancy rate: 8.1%

Health Insurance: 86.3% have insurance; 69.9% have private insurance; 30.7% have public insurance; 13.7% do not have insurance; 5.4% of children under 18 do not have insurance

Safety: Violent crime rate: 51.4 per 10,000 population; Property crime rate: 324.3 per 10,000 population

Transportation: Commute: 94.9% car, 1.1% public transportation, 1.2% walk, 2.0% work from home; Median travel time to work: 23.0 minutes

Additional Information Contacts

Redford Charter Township . . . . (313) 387-2751
    http://www.redfordtwp.com

RIVER ROUGE (city). Covers a land area of 2.653 square miles and a water area of 0.593 square miles. Located at 42.27° N. Lat; 83.12° W. Long. Elevation is 584 feet.

History: Named for the river, called River Rouge by early French settlers for its reddish clay banks. The River Rouge area was settled by French immigrant farmers in the late 1700's. River Rouge became a village in 1899, and was incorporated as a city in 1921. It developed as an industrial area, particularly influenced by the Ford Motor Company and by the Great Lakes Engineering Works (formerly S.F. Hodge & Company), builders of machinery and marine engines.

Population: 7,903; Growth (since 2000): -20.3%; Density: 2,978.4 persons per square mile; Race: 39.4% White, 50.5% Black/African American, 0.2% Asian, 0.6% American Indian/Alaska Native, 0.1% Native Hawaiian/Other Pacific Islander, 5.0% Two or more races, 11.2% Hispanic of any race; Average household size: 2.73; Median age: 33.0; Age under 18: 29.2%; Age 65 and over: 11.2%; Males per 100 females: 88.8; Marriage status: 50.1% never married, 27.0% now married, 2.6% separated, 6.8% widowed, 16.0% divorced; Foreign born: 3.2%; Speak English only: 90.7%; With disability: 19.1%; Veterans: 7.8%; Ancestry: 7.1% Irish, 5.9% German, 4.7% Polish, 4.0% French, 3.3% English

Employment: 4.3% management, business, and financial, 1.8% computer, engineering, and science, 6.8% education, legal, community service, arts, and media, 3.4% healthcare practitioners, 29.7% service, 20.3% sales and office, 7.9% natural resources, construction, and maintenance, 25.8% production, transportation, and material moving

Income: Per capita: $13,819; Median household: $26,185; Average household: $35,349; Households with income of $100,000 or more: 5.9%; Poverty rate: 38.5%

Educational Attainment: High school diploma or higher: 74.0%; Bachelor's degree or higher: 6.7%; Graduate/professional degree or higher: 2.8%

School District(s)

River Rouge SD of the City of (PK-12)

    2012-13 Enrollment: 1,239 . . . . (313) 297-9600

Southgate Community SD (PK-12)

    2012-13 Enrollment: 5,175 . . . . (734) 246-4600

Housing: Homeownership rate: 54.4%; Median home value: $38,600; Median year structure built: Before 1940; Homeowner vacancy rate: 6.7%; Median gross rent: $723 per month; Rental vacancy rate: 11.7%

Health Insurance: 82.4% have insurance; 32.6% have private insurance; 59.7% have public insurance; 17.6% do not have insurance; 3.9% of children under 18 do not have insurance

Safety: Violent crime rate: 108.8 per 10,000 population; Property crime rate: 363.8 per 10,000 population

Transportation: Commute: 91.4% car, 5.3% public transportation, 2.2% walk, 0.0% work from home; Median travel time to work: 24.2 minutes

Additional Information Contacts

City of River Rouge . . . . (313) 842-4200
    http://www.cityofriverrouge.com

RIVERVIEW (city). Covers a land area of 4.395 square miles and a water area of 0.087 square miles. Located at 42.17° N. Lat; 83.19° W. Long. Elevation is 600 feet.

History: Named for its view of the Detroit River. Riverview came into existence in 1906 when the Detroit, Monroe & Toledo Railroad built a station here. The river that was in view was the Detroit River.

Population: 12,486; Growth (since 2000): -5.9%; Density: 2,840.8 persons per square mile; Race: 93.0% White, 3.1% Black/African American, 1.6% Asian, 0.4% American Indian/Alaska Native, 0.0% Native Hawaiian/Other Pacific Islander, 1.3% Two or more races, 4.1% Hispanic of any race; Average household size: 2.31; Median age: 45.4; Age under 18: 19.6%; Age 65 and over: 22.6%; Males per 100 females: 86.6; Marriage status: 26.9% never married, 47.7% now married, 1.7% separated, 11.2% widowed, 14.2% divorced; Foreign born: 3.0%; Speak English only: 93.2%; With disability: 17.3%; Veterans: 10.1%; Ancestry: 17.9% German, 15.8% Irish, 12.5% Polish, 12.4% English, 8.0% Italian

Employment: 14.3% management, business, and financial, 2.3% computer, engineering, and science, 7.9% education, legal, community service, arts, and media, 7.1% healthcare practitioners, 22.8% service, 26.3% sales and office, 5.7% natural resources, construction, and maintenance, 13.6% production, transportation, and material moving

Income: Per capita: $24,982; Median household: $48,575; Average household: $61,132; Households with income of $100,000 or more: 17.7%; Poverty rate: 12.1%

Educational Attainment: High school diploma or higher: 86.7%; Bachelor's degree or higher: 23.2%; Graduate/professional degree or higher: 7.2%

School District(s)
Riverview Community SD (KG-12)
    2012-13 Enrollment: 2,839 . . . . (734) 285-9660
Vocational/Technical School(s)
Detroit Business Institute-Downriver (Private, For-profit)
    Fall 2013 Enrollment: 76 . . . . (734) 479-0660
    2013-14 Tuition: $26,400

Housing: Homeownership rate: 63.3%; Median home value: $117,200; Median year structure built: 1970; Homeowner vacancy rate: 1.8%; Median gross rent: $713 per month; Rental vacancy rate: 8.8%

Health Insurance: 89.9% have insurance; 75.6% have private insurance; 32.9% have public insurance; 10.1% do not have insurance; 1.6% of children under 18 do not have insurance

Safety: Violent crime rate: 15.5 per 10,000 population; Property crime rate: 121.5 per 10,000 population

Transportation: Commute: 97.6% car, 0.7% public transportation, 0.7% walk, 0.2% work from home; Median travel time to work: 23.2 minutes

Additional Information Contacts
City of Riverview . . . . (734) 281-4239
    http://www.cityofriverview.com

ROCKWOOD (city). Covers a land area of 2.521 square miles and a water area of 0.127 square miles. Located at 42.07° N. Lat; 83.24° W. Long. Elevation is 584 feet.

History: Incorporated 1926.

Population: 3,289; Growth (since 2000): -4.4%; Density: 1,304.6 persons per square mile; Race: 94.6% White, 1.7% Black/African American, 0.9% Asian, 0.9% American Indian/Alaska Native, 0.0% Native Hawaiian/Other Pacific Islander, 1.5% Two or more races, 2.7% Hispanic of any race; Average household size: 2.52; Median age: 40.9; Age under 18: 23.0%; Age 65 and over: 12.0%; Males per 100 females: 100.3; Marriage status: 32.9% never married, 46.8% now married, 1.9% separated, 4.2% widowed, 16.1% divorced; Foreign born: 6.3%; Speak English only: 91.1%; With disability: 16.7%; Veterans: 8.8%; Ancestry: 23.7% German, 15.4% Polish, 14.0% French, 13.4% American, 10.8% Irish

Employment: 10.2% management, business, and financial, 4.2% computer, engineering, and science, 3.1% education, legal, community service, arts, and media, 5.5% healthcare practitioners, 24.9% service, 16.7% sales and office, 10.3% natural resources, construction, and maintenance, 25.2% production, transportation, and material moving

Income: Per capita: $26,794; Median household: $55,944; Average household: $70,566; Households with income of $100,000 or more: 19.5%; Poverty rate: 8.4%

Educational Attainment: High school diploma or higher: 86.0%; Bachelor's degree or higher: 10.0%; Graduate/professional degree or higher: 2.8%

School District(s)
Gibraltar SD (KG-12)
    2012-13 Enrollment: 3,730 . . . . (734) 379-6350
Housing: Homeownership rate: 72.0%; Median home value: $121,100; Median year structure built: 1968; Homeowner vacancy rate: 2.2%; Median gross rent: $710 per month; Rental vacancy rate: 11.0%

Health Insurance: 87.9% have insurance; 76.9% have private insurance; 26.4% have public insurance; 12.1% do not have insurance; 4.2% of children under 18 do not have insurance

Safety: Violent crime rate: 6.2 per 10,000 population; Property crime rate: 99.3 per 10,000 population

Transportation: Commute: 97.2% car, 0.9% public transportation, 0.0% walk, 1.5% work from home; Median travel time to work: 21.7 minutes

ROMULUS (city). Covers a land area of 35.608 square miles and a water area of 0.346 square miles. Located at 42.22° N. Lat; 83.37° W. Long. Elevation is 659 feet.

History: Romulus was named for Romulus, New York, the former home of Samuel McMath whose family settled here in the 1820's.

Population: 23,989; Growth (since 2000): 4.4%; Density: 673.7 persons per square mile; Race: 50.5% White, 43.0% Black/African American, 1.1% Asian, 0.5% American Indian/Alaska Native, 0.1% Native Hawaiian/Other Pacific Islander, 3.9% Two or more races, 3.0% Hispanic of any race; Average household size: 2.64; Median age: 36.2; Age under 18: 26.8%; Age 65 and over: 9.8%; Males per 100 females: 93.6; Marriage status: 39.3% never married, 41.9% now married, 1.7% separated, 4.9% widowed, 14.0% divorced; Foreign born: 4.4%; Speak English only: 93.5%; With disability: 20.0%; Veterans: 9.8%; Ancestry: 14.5% German, 11.6% Irish, 6.5% Polish, 4.2% English, 3.7% Italian

Employment: 8.2% management, business, and financial, 1.7% computer, engineering, and science, 3.6% education, legal, community service, arts, and media, 3.9% healthcare practitioners, 23.3% service, 24.5% sales and office, 9.0% natural resources, construction, and maintenance, 25.7% production, transportation, and material moving

Income: Per capita: $20,537; Median household: $44,119; Average household: $51,920; Households with income of $100,000 or more: 10.4%; Poverty rate: 21.4%

Educational Attainment: High school diploma or higher: 85.7%; Bachelor's degree or higher: 10.1%; Graduate/professional degree or higher: 3.1%

School District(s)
Metro Charter Academy (KG-12)
    2012-13 Enrollment: 729 . . . . (734) 641-3200
Romulus Community Schools (PK-12)
    2012-13 Enrollment: 2,934 . . . . (734) 532-1610
Woodhaven-Brownstown SD (PK-12)
    2012-13 Enrollment: 5,043 . . . . (734) 789-2357
Housing: Homeownership rate: 67.1%; Median home value: $73,100; Median year structure built: 1971; Homeowner vacancy rate: 4.0%; Median gross rent: $743 per month; Rental vacancy rate: 10.6%

Health Insurance: 84.9% have insurance; 60.0% have private insurance; 37.1% have public insurance; 15.1% do not have insurance; 3.1% of children under 18 do not have insurance

Safety: Violent crime rate: 58.8 per 10,000 population; Property crime rate: 297.2 per 10,000 population

Transportation: Commute: 95.5% car, 0.9% public transportation, 0.8% walk, 1.7% work from home; Median travel time to work: 24.5 minutes

Additional Information Contacts
City of Romulus . . . . (734) 942-7540
    http://www.romulusgov.com

SOUTHGATE (city). Covers a land area of 6.846 square miles and a water area of 0.005 square miles. Located at 42.20° N. Lat; 83.21° W. Long. Elevation is 591 feet.

History: Named for its location as a southern gateway to the Detroit metropolitan area. Pierre Michel Campau settled here in 1795. The village later became a gateway to the metropolitan Detroit area, and was incorporated in the 1950's.

Population: 30,047; Growth (since 2000): -0.3%; Density: 4,389.0 persons per square mile; Race: 88.7% White, 5.5% Black/African American, 1.6% Asian, 0.5% American Indian/Alaska Native, 0.0% Native Hawaiian/Other Pacific Islander, 2.0% Two or more races, 6.5% Hispanic of any race; Average household size: 2.29; Median age: 40.8; Age under 18: 20.3%; Age 65 and over: 16.3%; Males per 100 females: 91.5; Marriage status: 33.2% never married, 44.8% now married, 1.6% separated, 7.8%

widowed, 14.2% divorced; Foreign born: 5.3%; Speak English only: 91.3%; With disability: 15.5%; Veterans: 9.5%; Ancestry: 20.9% German, 15.5% Polish, 14.8% Irish, 10.0% English, 8.0% Italian

Employment: 11.0% management, business, and financial, 5.3% computer, engineering, and science, 6.8% education, legal, community service, arts, and media, 6.5% healthcare practitioners, 17.8% service, 28.1% sales and office, 9.4% natural resources, construction, and maintenance, 15.0% production, transportation, and material moving

Income: Per capita: $25,903; Median household: $48,439; Average household: $59,513; Households with income of $100,000 or more: 16.5%; Poverty rate: 10.5%

Educational Attainment: High school diploma or higher: 88.4%; Bachelor's degree or higher: 16.6%; Graduate/professional degree or higher: 6.0%

School District(s)
Creative Montessori Academy (PK-12)
    2012-13 Enrollment: 619 . . . . (734) 284-5600
Southgate Community SD (PK-12)
    2012-13 Enrollment: 5,175 . . . . (734) 246-4600

Vocational/Technical School(s)
Dorsey Business Schools-Southgate (Private, For-profit)
    Fall 2013 Enrollment: 145 . . . . (734) 285-5400
    2013-14 Tuition: In-state $17,568; Out-of-state $17,568
Regency Beauty Institute-Detroit Southgate (Private, For-profit)
    Fall 2013 Enrollment: 163 . . . . (800) 787-6456
    2013-14 Tuition: $17,300

Housing: Homeownership rate: 66.0%; Median home value: $88,200; Median year structure built: 1960; Homeowner vacancy rate: 1.7%; Median gross rent: $794 per month; Rental vacancy rate: 7.6%

Health Insurance: 90.5% have insurance; 77.8% have private insurance; 29.4% have public insurance; 9.5% do not have insurance; 4.0% of children under 18 do not have insurance

Safety: Violent crime rate: 28.9 per 10,000 population; Property crime rate: 357.1 per 10,000 population

Newspapers: Dearborn Press & Guide (weekly circulation 19000); Heritage Newspapers (weekly circulation 123000); The Ile Camera (weekly circulation 3700)

Transportation: Commute: 97.1% car, 0.5% public transportation, 0.9% walk, 1.0% work from home; Median travel time to work: 24.0 minutes

Additional Information Contacts
City of Southgate . . . . (734) 258-3010
    http://www.southgatemi.org

SUMPTER (township).
Covers a land area of 37.358 square miles and a water area of 0.085 square miles. Located at 42.13° N. Lat; 83.47° W. Long.

Population: 9,549; Growth (since 2000): -19.5%; Density: 255.6 persons per square mile; Race: 83.8% White, 12.0% Black/African American, 0.3% Asian, 0.6% American Indian/Alaska Native, 0.0% Native Hawaiian/Other Pacific Islander, 2.9% Two or more races, 2.6% Hispanic of any race; Average household size: 2.71; Median age: 40.3; Age under 18: 23.9%; Age 65 and over: 11.0%; Males per 100 females: 102.6; Marriage status: 29.1% never married, 53.4% now married, 3.0% separated, 4.8% widowed, 12.8% divorced; Foreign born: 2.4%; Speak English only: 95.4%; With disability: 17.8%; Veterans: 13.2%; Ancestry: 24.5% German, 16.9% Irish, 13.8% English, 9.5% Polish, 6.4% American

Employment: 6.6% management, business, and financial, 2.5% computer, engineering, and science, 5.1% education, legal, community service, arts, and media, 7.1% healthcare practitioners, 17.1% service, 29.9% sales and office, 14.5% natural resources, construction, and maintenance, 17.1% production, transportation, and material moving

Income: Per capita: $25,543; Median household: $53,109; Average household: $65,360; Households with income of $100,000 or more: 19.9%; Poverty rate: 17.4%

Educational Attainment: High school diploma or higher: 88.6%; Bachelor's degree or higher: 11.9%; Graduate/professional degree or higher: 4.6%

Housing: Homeownership rate: 89.6%; Median home value: $118,700; Median year structure built: 1976; Homeowner vacancy rate: 7.2%; Median gross rent: $820 per month; Rental vacancy rate: 13.9%

Health Insurance: 90.6% have insurance; 71.5% have private insurance; 35.9% have public insurance; 9.4% do not have insurance; 0.9% of children under 18 do not have insurance

Safety: Violent crime rate: 15.0 per 10,000 population; Property crime rate: 116.0 per 10,000 population

Transportation: Commute: 96.7% car, 0.0% public transportation, 1.8% walk, 1.3% work from home; Median travel time to work: 29.6 minutes

Additional Information Contacts
Sumpter Township . . . . (734) 461-6201
    http://www.sumptertwp.com

TAYLOR (city).
Covers a land area of 23.597 square miles and a water area of 0.037 square miles. Located at 42.23° N. Lat; 83.27° W. Long. Elevation is 614 feet.

History: Named for General Zachary Taylor, in 1849, who had just distinguished himself in the Mexican War. A small rural village until World War II, it grew from a population of c.5,000 to its present size. Its growth has been commercial as well as residential. Founded 1847 as a township. Incorporated as a city 1968.

Population: 63,131; Growth (since 2000): -4.2%; Density: 2,675.3 persons per square mile; Race: 78.0% White, 15.8% Black/African American, 1.8% Asian, 0.5% American Indian/Alaska Native, 0.0% Native Hawaiian/Other Pacific Islander, 2.6% Two or more races, 5.1% Hispanic of any race; Average household size: 2.56; Median age: 36.9; Age under 18: 24.7%; Age 65 and over: 12.8%; Males per 100 females: 91.8; Marriage status: 35.4% never married, 44.1% now married, 1.9% separated, 6.6% widowed, 13.9% divorced; Foreign born: 4.5%; Speak English only: 93.5%; With disability: 18.0%; Veterans: 9.1%; Ancestry: 16.8% German, 14.8% Irish, 10.6% Polish, 6.6% English, 5.6% French

Employment: 8.8% management, business, and financial, 2.8% computer, engineering, and science, 5.1% education, legal, community service, arts, and media, 3.8% healthcare practitioners, 21.6% service, 26.6% sales and office, 9.9% natural resources, construction, and maintenance, 21.4% production, transportation, and material moving

Income: Per capita: $20,101; Median household: $41,933; Average household: $51,473; Households with income of $100,000 or more: 10.3%; Poverty rate: 21.2%

Educational Attainment: High school diploma or higher: 82.3%; Bachelor's degree or higher: 9.7%; Graduate/professional degree or higher: 2.8%

School District(s)
Quest Charter Academy (KG-12)
    2012-13 Enrollment: 691 . . . . (313) 299-0534
Taylor Exemplar Academy (KG-12)
    2012-13 Enrollment: 694 . . . . (734) 941-7742
Taylor SD (PK-12)
    2012-13 Enrollment: 7,206 . . . . (734) 374-1200
Trillium Academy (KG-12)
    2012-13 Enrollment: 682 . . . . (734) 374-8222

Vocational/Technical School(s)
Ross Medical Education Center-Taylor (Private, For-profit)
    Fall 2013 Enrollment: 80 . . . . (734) 374-8260
    2013-14 Tuition: $15,680
Taylortown School of Beauty Inc (Private, For-profit)
    Fall 2013 Enrollment: 204 . . . . (248) 585-9200
    2013-14 Tuition: $16,969

Housing: Homeownership rate: 67.4%; Median home value: $77,800; Median year structure built: 1962; Homeowner vacancy rate: 2.8%; Median gross rent: $787 per month; Rental vacancy rate: 7.8%

Health Insurance: 85.4% have insurance; 60.3% have private insurance; 39.5% have public insurance; 14.6% do not have insurance; 5.3% of children under 18 do not have insurance

Hospitals: Oakwood Hospital - Taylor (248 beds)

Safety: Violent crime rate: 56.1 per 10,000 population; Property crime rate: 336.9 per 10,000 population

Transportation: Commute: 96.0% car, 0.9% public transportation, 1.0% walk, 1.2% work from home; Median travel time to work: 22.5 minutes

Additional Information Contacts
City of Taylor . . . . (734) 287-6550
    http://www.cityoftaylor.com

TRENTON (city).
Covers a land area of 7.276 square miles and a water area of 0.229 square miles. Located at 42.14° N. Lat; 83.19° W. Long. Elevation is 597 feet.

History: Named for a strata of limestone (called trentonian) underlying the town. The site of Trenton was acquired by Major Caleb Truax, who came from New York in 1816. He built a sawmill, church, and store, and platted a village in 1827 with the name of Truaxton. Truaxton became a shipping and shipbuilding center in the days of wooden vessels. With the opening of the Erie Canal in 1825, industry in Truaxton expanded to include

commercial fishing and the production of lime and building stone from quarries nearby. In 1875, Truaxton was incorporated as a village and the name was changed to Trenton.

Population: 18,853; Growth (since 2000): -3.7%; Density: 2,591.2 persons per square mile; Race: 95.5% White, 1.3% Black/African American, 0.7% Asian, 0.5% American Indian/Alaska Native, 0.0% Native Hawaiian/Other Pacific Islander, 1.4% Two or more races, 3.2% Hispanic of any race; Average household size: 2.33; Median age: 45.0; Age under 18: 21.3%; Age 65 and over: 19.8%; Males per 100 females: 92.6; Marriage status: 25.0% never married, 50.8% now married, 1.4% separated, 9.7% widowed, 14.4% divorced; Foreign born: 3.6%; Speak English only: 94.7%; With disability: 14.3%; Veterans: 10.9%; Ancestry: 23.6% German, 14.9% Polish, 14.3% Irish, 12.9% English, 9.5% French

Employment: 13.8% management, business, and financial, 4.1% computer, engineering, and science, 10.3% education, legal, community service, arts, and media, 6.6% healthcare practitioners, 18.4% service, 25.4% sales and office, 9.8% natural resources, construction, and maintenance, 11.5% production, transportation, and material moving

Income: Per capita: $27,790; Median household: $53,101; Average household: $65,104; Households with income of $100,000 or more: 21.5%; Poverty rate: 9.8%

Educational Attainment: High school diploma or higher: 90.1%; Bachelor's degree or higher: 24.1%; Graduate/professional degree or higher: 9.4%

School District(s)
Trenton Public Schools (PK-12)
    2012-13 Enrollment: 2,615 . . . . (734) 676-8600

Housing: Homeownership rate: 79.1%; Median home value: $118,300; Median year structure built: 1960; Homeowner vacancy rate: 2.6%; Median gross rent: $676 per month; Rental vacancy rate: 9.4%

Health Insurance: 92.7% have insurance; 80.0% have private insurance; 31.5% have public insurance; 7.3% do not have insurance; 1.8% of children under 18 do not have insurance

Hospitals: Oakwood Hospital - Southshore (203 beds)

Safety: Violent crime rate: 13.5 per 10,000 population; Property crime rate: 134.7 per 10,000 population

Transportation: Commute: 95.1% car, 0.5% public transportation, 0.7% walk, 3.2% work from home; Median travel time to work: 23.9 minutes

Additional Information Contacts
City of Trenton. . . . . (734) 675-8600
    http://www.trentonmi.org

VAN BUREN (charter township). Covers a land area of 33.969 square miles and a water area of 2.089 square miles. Located at 42.22° N. Lat; 83.48° W. Long. Elevation is 679 feet.

Population: 28,821; Growth (since 2000): 22.3%; Density: 848.4 persons per square mile; Race: 64.6% White, 28.7% Black/African American, 2.5% Asian, 0.5% American Indian/Alaska Native, 0.0% Native Hawaiian/Other Pacific Islander, 2.9% Two or more races, 2.7% Hispanic of any race; Average household size: 2.42; Median age: 36.5; Age under 18: 23.9%; Age 65 and over: 8.8%; Males per 100 females: 93.7; Marriage status: 37.2% never married, 46.8% now married, 1.0% separated, 4.7% widowed, 11.3% divorced; Foreign born: 4.2%; Speak English only: 94.7%; With disability: 12.0%; Veterans: 9.0%; Ancestry: 18.0% German, 11.8% Irish, 8.2% English, 8.1% Polish, 4.5% Italian

Employment: 13.2% management, business, and financial, 5.5% computer, engineering, and science, 7.5% education, legal, community service, arts, and media, 5.8% healthcare practitioners, 18.7% service, 25.3% sales and office, 6.7% natural resources, construction, and maintenance, 17.3% production, transportation, and material moving

Income: Per capita: $27,997; Median household: $52,572; Average household: $67,676; Households with income of $100,000 or more: 20.2%; Poverty rate: 12.4%

Educational Attainment: High school diploma or higher: 91.1%; Bachelor's degree or higher: 27.8%; Graduate/professional degree or higher: 9.8%

Housing: Homeownership rate: 65.7%; Median home value: $129,300; Median year structure built: 1983; Homeowner vacancy rate: 3.2%; Median gross rent: $823 per month; Rental vacancy rate: 17.1%

Health Insurance: 87.8% have insurance; 72.8% have private insurance; 26.8% have public insurance; 12.2% do not have insurance; 3.2% of children under 18 do not have insurance

Safety: Violent crime rate: 22.3 per 10,000 population; Property crime rate: 234.8 per 10,000 population

Transportation: Commute: 94.7% car, 0.5% public transportation, 2.7% walk, 1.5% work from home; Median travel time to work: 25.4 minutes

Additional Information Contacts
Van Buren Charter Township . . . . (734) 699-8900
    http://www.vanburen-mi.org

VILLAGE OF GROSSE POINTE SHORES (city). Covers a land area of 1.149 square miles and a water area of 18.076 square miles. Located at 42.45° N. Lat; 82.87° W. Long.

Population: 3,008; Growth (since 2000): n/a; Density: 2,617.4 persons per square mile; Race: 92.8% White, 1.9% Black/African American, 3.8% Asian, 0.3% American Indian/Alaska Native, 0.0% Native Hawaiian/Other Pacific Islander, 1.0% Two or more races, 1.9% Hispanic of any race; Average household size: 2.50; Median age: 52.2; Age under 18: 19.6%; Age 65 and over: 27.6%; Males per 100 females: 100.3; Marriage status: 21.7% never married, 64.8% now married, 0.0% separated, 8.3% widowed, 5.2% divorced; Foreign born: 16.2%; Speak English only: 79.7%; With disability: 10.3%; Veterans: 6.5%; Ancestry: 16.1% Italian, 15.3% German, 13.5% Polish, 11.2% Lebanese, 7.3% English

Employment: 25.4% management, business, and financial, 4.3% computer, engineering, and science, 12.1% education, legal, community service, arts, and media, 21.4% healthcare practitioners, 4.2% service, 25.5% sales and office, 3.5% natural resources, construction, and maintenance, 3.6% production, transportation, and material moving

Income: Per capita: $81,540; Median household: $137,303; Average household: $207,710; Households with income of $100,000 or more: 61.2%; Poverty rate: 2.8%

Educational Attainment: High school diploma or higher: 98.4%; Bachelor's degree or higher: 66.3%; Graduate/professional degree or higher: 38.1%

Housing: Homeownership rate: 96.4%; Median home value: $400,900; Median year structure built: 1960; Homeowner vacancy rate: 3.9%; Median gross rent: $1,750 per month; Rental vacancy rate: 57.4%

Health Insurance: 96.0% have insurance; 91.9% have private insurance; 23.5% have public insurance; 4.0% do not have insurance; 4.8% of children under 18 do not have insurance

Transportation: Commute: 95.7% car, 0.0% public transportation, 0.0% walk, 3.6% work from home; Median travel time to work: 24.6 minutes

Additional Information Contacts
Village of Grosse Pointe Shores . . . . (313) 881-6565
    http://www.gpshoresmi.gov

WAYNE (city). Covers a land area of 6.020 square miles and a water area of <.001 square miles. Located at 42.28° N. Lat; 83.39° W. Long. Elevation is 656 feet.

History: Wayne was settled in 1836 and named for General "Mad Anthony" Wayne, the Revolutionary War hero. Situated near the highly industrialized west-side corridor of Dearborn and Detroit, Wayne developed several industries of its own, including an aircraft plant.

Population: 17,593; Growth (since 2000): -7.7%; Density: 2,922.6 persons per square mile; Race: 76.3% White, 17.1% Black/African American, 2.1% Asian, 0.5% American Indian/Alaska Native, 0.0% Native Hawaiian/Other Pacific Islander, 3.0% Two or more races, 3.4% Hispanic of any race; Average household size: 2.45; Median age: 38.6; Age under 18: 23.5%; Age 65 and over: 12.5%; Males per 100 females: 93.1; Marriage status: 31.9% never married, 44.2% now married, 2.0% separated, 7.3% widowed, 16.6% divorced; Foreign born: 4.0%; Speak English only: 94.6%; With disability: 16.8%; Veterans: 9.3%; Ancestry: 21.2% German, 14.4% Irish, 10.6% English, 8.8% Polish, 7.4% American

Employment: 8.5% management, business, and financial, 3.2% computer, engineering, and science, 6.7% education, legal, community service, arts, and media, 3.3% healthcare practitioners, 23.1% service, 26.6% sales and office, 7.6% natural resources, construction, and maintenance, 21.1% production, transportation, and material moving

Income: Per capita: $19,874; Median household: $39,566; Average household: $48,511; Households with income of $100,000 or more: 9.2%; Poverty rate: 17.5%

Educational Attainment: High school diploma or higher: 84.1%; Bachelor's degree or higher: 11.6%; Graduate/professional degree or higher: 3.1%

School District(s)
Wayne Resa (PK-12)
    2012-13 Enrollment: 5,260 . . . . (734) 334-1300
Wayne-Westland Community SD (PK-12)
    2012-13 Enrollment: 12,030 . . . . (734) 419-2000

Vocational/Technical School(s)
Dorsey Business Schools-Wayne (Private, For-profit)
Fall 2013 Enrollment: 191 . . . . (734) 595-1540
2013-14 Tuition: In-state $14,688; Out-of-state $14,688
Housing: Homeownership rate: 61.7%; Median home value: $74,000; Median year structure built: 1957; Homeowner vacancy rate: 2.4%; Median gross rent: $649 per month; Rental vacancy rate: 10.3%
Health Insurance: 86.3% have insurance; 66.9% have private insurance; 33.4% have public insurance; 13.7% do not have insurance; 4.6% of children under 18 do not have insurance
Hospitals: Oakwood Hospital - Wayne (247 beds)
Safety: Violent crime rate: 70.2 per 10,000 population; Property crime rate: 278.0 per 10,000 population
Transportation: Commute: 93.8% car, 1.1% public transportation, 2.5% walk, 1.9% work from home; Median travel time to work: 23.6 minutes
Additional Information Contacts
City of Wayne . . . . (734) 722-2000
http://www.ci.wayne.mi.us

WESTLAND (city). Covers a land area of 20.425 square miles and a water area of 0.015 square miles. Located at 42.32° N. Lat; 83.38° W. Long. Elevation is 666 feet.
Population: 84,094; Growth (since 2000): -2.9%; Density: 4,117.3 persons per square mile; Race: 75.8% White, 17.2% Black/African American, 3.0% Asian, 0.5% American Indian/Alaska Native, 0.0% Native Hawaiian/Other Pacific Islander, 2.4% Two or more races, 3.8% Hispanic of any race; Average household size: 2.31; Median age: 38.3; Age under 18: 22.1%; Age 65 and over: 14.0%; Males per 100 females: 90.4; Marriage status: 35.3% never married, 43.0% now married, 1.8% separated, 7.6% widowed, 14.1% divorced; Foreign born: 6.5%; Speak English only: 91.3%; With disability: 15.6%; Veterans: 8.3%; Ancestry: 18.2% German, 13.1% Irish, 12.1% Polish, 7.3% English, 7.3% American
Employment: 10.6% management, business, and financial, 4.8% computer, engineering, and science, 6.3% education, legal, community service, arts, and media, 5.0% healthcare practitioners, 21.8% service, 27.5% sales and office, 7.2% natural resources, construction, and maintenance, 16.8% production, transportation, and material moving
Income: Per capita: $23,993; Median household: $43,993; Average household: $55,754; Households with income of $100,000 or more: 13.0%; Poverty rate: 15.5%
Educational Attainment: High school diploma or higher: 87.7%; Bachelor's degree or higher: 17.8%; Graduate/professional degree or higher: 5.0%
School District(s)
Livonia Public Schools SD (PK-12)
2012-13 Enrollment: 15,176 . . . . (734) 744-2525
Wayne-Westland Community SD (PK-12)
2012-13 Enrollment: 12,030 . . . . (734) 419-2000
Four-year College(s)
Manthano Christian College (Private, Not-for-profit)
Fall 2013 Enrollment: 28 . . . . (734) 895-3280
2013-14 Tuition: In-state $5,100; Out-of-state $5,100
Housing: Homeownership rate: 61.5%; Median home value: $90,600; Median year structure built: 1966; Homeowner vacancy rate: 2.3%; Median gross rent: $781 per month; Rental vacancy rate: 10.4%
Health Insurance: 86.5% have insurance; 67.2% have private insurance; 34.5% have public insurance; 13.5% do not have insurance; 4.1% of children under 18 do not have insurance
Safety: Violent crime rate: 44.0 per 10,000 population; Property crime rate: 290.6 per 10,000 population
Transportation: Commute: 95.0% car, 0.6% public transportation, 1.2% walk, 2.2% work from home; Median travel time to work: 25.0 minutes
Additional Information Contacts
City of Westland . . . . (734) 467-3185
http://www.cityofwestland.com

WOODHAVEN (city). Covers a land area of 6.387 square miles and a water area of 0.058 square miles. Located at 42.13° N. Lat; 83.24° W. Long. Elevation is 604 feet.
Population: 12,875; Growth (since 2000): 2.8%; Density: 2,015.7 persons per square mile; Race: 88.9% White, 5.3% Black/African American, 2.3% Asian, 0.3% American Indian/Alaska Native, 0.0% Native Hawaiian/Other Pacific Islander, 1.9% Two or more races, 5.5% Hispanic of any race; Average household size: 2.46; Median age: 40.3; Age under 18: 22.3%; Age 65 and over: 11.9%; Males per 100 females: 98.0; Marriage status:

29.4% never married, 50.7% now married, 2.9% separated, 5.7% widowed, 14.2% divorced; Foreign born: 4.1%; Speak English only: 92.9%; With disability: 12.0%; Veterans: 9.7%; Ancestry: 24.8% German, 17.4% Polish, 12.1% Irish, 10.3% American, 8.8% English
Employment: 12.5% management, business, and financial, 3.6% computer, engineering, and science, 11.3% education, legal, community service, arts, and media, 8.1% healthcare practitioners, 14.7% service, 25.4% sales and office, 6.8% natural resources, construction, and maintenance, 17.7% production, transportation, and material moving
Income: Per capita: $30,686; Median household: $58,953; Average household: $75,917; Households with income of $100,000 or more: 25.0%; Poverty rate: 9.3%
Educational Attainment: High school diploma or higher: 95.6%; Bachelor's degree or higher: 22.9%; Graduate/professional degree or higher: 7.5%
School District(s)
Gibraltar SD (KG-12)
2012-13 Enrollment: 3,730 . . . . (734) 379-6350
Woodhaven-Brownstown SD (PK-12)
2012-13 Enrollment: 5,043 . . . . (734) 789-2357
Housing: Homeownership rate: 72.4%; Median home value: $123,100; Median year structure built: 1979; Homeowner vacancy rate: 2.4%; Median gross rent: $713 per month; Rental vacancy rate: 9.4%
Health Insurance: 91.2% have insurance; 79.8% have private insurance; 25.2% have public insurance; 8.8% do not have insurance; 2.8% of children under 18 do not have insurance
Safety: Violent crime rate: 13.4 per 10,000 population; Property crime rate: 144.6 per 10,000 population
Transportation: Commute: 93.1% car, 4.4% public transportation, 0.8% walk, 1.5% work from home; Median travel time to work: 23.1 minutes
Additional Information Contacts
City of Woodhaven . . . . (734) 675-3000
http://www.woodhavenmi.org

WYANDOTTE (city). Covers a land area of 5.274 square miles and a water area of 1.737 square miles. Located at 42.21° N. Lat; 83.16° W. Long. Elevation is 581 feet.
History: Named for the Indian tribe who once had a village here. Major John Biddle purchased land and settled here in 1818. In 1853, Captain Eber B. Ward purchased the Biddle estate and founded the Eureka Iron and Steel Company, with a blast furnace and rolling mill. The settlement of Wyandotte was platted then, and grew up around the steel plant. It was incorporated as a city in 1867. In 1891, salt replaced steel in Wyandotte, and many products such as baking soda, soaps, and cleaners were developed from the soda ash mined here.
Population: 25,883; Growth (since 2000): -7.6%; Density: 4,908.1 persons per square mile; Race: 94.7% White, 1.3% Black/African American, 0.5% Asian, 0.7% American Indian/Alaska Native, 0.0% Native Hawaiian/Other Pacific Islander, 1.9% Two or more races, 5.1% Hispanic of any race; Average household size: 2.35; Median age: 40.4; Age under 18: 21.4%; Age 65 and over: 13.8%; Males per 100 females: 95.8; Marriage status: 30.5% never married, 47.4% now married, 1.2% separated, 8.3% widowed, 13.8% divorced; Foreign born: 2.3%; Speak English only: 92.6%; With disability: 17.1%; Veterans: 8.6%; Ancestry: 21.5% German, 21.0% Polish, 17.4% Irish, 8.1% Italian, 8.1% English
Employment: 9.2% management, business, and financial, 4.7% computer, engineering, and science, 8.3% education, legal, community service, arts, and media, 6.3% healthcare practitioners, 21.7% service, 24.9% sales and office, 9.1% natural resources, construction, and maintenance, 15.8% production, transportation, and material moving
Income: Per capita: $25,287; Median household: $48,664; Average household: $59,280; Households with income of $100,000 or more: 15.8%; Poverty rate: 11.7%
Educational Attainment: High school diploma or higher: 86.6%; Bachelor's degree or higher: 15.8%; Graduate/professional degree or higher: 5.5%
School District(s)
Wyandotte SD (KG-12)
2012-13 Enrollment: 4,466 . . . . (734) 759-6002
Housing: Homeownership rate: 72.4%; Median home value: $87,600; Median year structure built: 1949; Homeowner vacancy rate: 2.8%; Median gross rent: $697 per month; Rental vacancy rate: 10.0%
Health Insurance: 87.9% have insurance; 71.7% have private insurance; 31.3% have public insurance; 12.1% do not have insurance; 4.2% of children under 18 do not have insurance

Hospitals: Henry Ford Wyandotte Hospital (162 beds)
Safety: Violent crime rate: 22.1 per 10,000 population; Property crime rate: 224.6 per 10,000 population
Transportation: Commute: 92.2% car, 1.4% public transportation, 3.4% walk, 1.7% work from home; Median travel time to work: 22.5 minutes
Additional Information Contacts
City of Wyandotte . . . . (734) 324-4500
  http://www.wyandotte.net

Wexford County

Located in northwestern Michigan; crossed by the Manistee River; drained by the Clam River; includes Lakes Mitchell and Cadillac, and part of Manistee National Forest. Covers a land area of 565.002 square miles, a water area of 10.464 square miles, and is located in the Eastern Time Zone at 44.33° N. Lat., 85.57° W. Long. The county was founded in 1840. County seat is Cadillac.

Wexford County is part of the Cadillac, MI Micropolitan Statistical Area. The entire metro area includes: Missaukee County, MI; Wexford County, MI

Weather Station: Cadillac   Elevation: 1,294 feet

	Jan	Feb	Mar	Apr	May	Jun	Jul	Aug	Sep	Oct	Nov	Dec
High	27	30	39	53	66	75	79	77	69	56	43	31
Low	11	11	18	31	41	51	55	54	45	36	27	17
Precip	2.0	1.4	2.0	2.9	3.3	3.5	3.1	3.8	3.8	3.6	2.7	2.1
Snow	na	na	na	2.7	0.0	0.0	0.0	0.0	0.0	0.4	na	na

High and Low temperatures in degrees Fahrenheit; Precipitation and Snow in inches

Population: 32,735; Growth (since 2000): 7.4%; Density: 57.9 persons per square mile; Race: 96.5% White, 0.4% Black/African American, 0.6% Asian, 0.6% American Indian/Alaska Native, 0.1% Native Hawaiian/Other Pacific Islander, 1.5% two or more races, 1.6% Hispanic of any race; Average household size: 2.48; Median age: 40.9; Age under 18: 24.3%; Age 65 and over: 15.9%; Males per 100 females: 99.3; Marriage status: 23.6% never married, 55.3% now married, 1.5% separated, 7.0% widowed, 14.1% divorced; Foreign born: 1.0%; Speak English only: 96.9%; With disability: 16.0%; Veterans: 11.8%; Ancestry: 23.4% German, 12.4% Irish, 11.8% English, 9.8% American, 6.8% Dutch
Religion: Six largest groups: 9.7% Non-denominational Protestant, 6.2% Catholicism, 4.2% Methodist/Pietist, 3.7% Baptist, 3.6% Lutheran, 3.3% Holiness
Economy: Unemployment rate: 7.5%; Leading industries: 20.1% retail trade; 11.7% health care and social assistance; 11.4% other services (except public administration); Farms: 357 totaling 40,333 acres; Company size: 0 employ 1,000 or more persons, 2 employ 500 to 999 persons, 19 employ 100 to 499 persons, 810 employ less than 100 persons; Business ownership: n/a women-owned, n/a Black-owned, n/a Hispanic-owned, n/a Asian-owned
Employment: 9.9% management, business, and financial, 2.6% computer, engineering, and science, 7.1% education, legal, community service, arts, and media, 6.3% healthcare practitioners, 17.6% service, 21.6% sales and office, 9.2% natural resources, construction, and maintenance, 25.7% production, transportation, and material moving
Income: Per capita: $20,573; Median household: $40,965; Average household: $51,923; Households with income of $100,000 or more: 9.5%; Poverty rate: 18.6%
Educational Attainment: High school diploma or higher: 88.0%; Bachelor's degree or higher: 16.8%; Graduate/professional degree or higher: 6.0%
Housing: Homeownership rate: 75.9%; Median home value: $100,100; Median year structure built: 1976; Homeowner vacancy rate: 3.9%; Median gross rent: $698 per month; Rental vacancy rate: 10.2%
Vital Statistics: Birth rate: 127.4 per 10,000 population; Death rate: 92.2 per 10,000 population; Age-adjusted cancer mortality rate: 224.6 deaths per 100,000 population
Health Insurance: 86.4% have insurance; 62.9% have private insurance; 39.9% have public insurance; 13.6% do not have insurance; 7.3% of children under 18 do not have insurance
Health Care: Physicians: 20.2 per 10,000 population; Hospital beds: 19.9 per 10,000 population; Hospital admissions: 1,236.4 per 10,000 population
Air Quality Index: 93.9% good, 6.1% moderate, 0.0% unhealthy for sensitive individuals, 0.0% unhealthy (percent of days)
Transportation: Commute: 91.8% car, 0.1% public transportation, 2.4% walk, 4.5% work from home; Median travel time to work: 20.5 minutes

Presidential Election: 41.3% Obama, 57.5% Romney (2012)
National and State Parks: White Pine Trail State Park; William Mitchell State Park
Additional Information Contacts
Wexford Government . . . . (231) 779-9453
  http://www.wexfordcounty.org

Wexford County Communities

ANTIOCH (township). Covers a land area of 35.221 square miles and a water area of 0.037 square miles. Located at 44.38° N. Lat; 85.64° W. Long.
Population: 815; Growth (since 2000): 0.6%; Density: 23.1 persons per square mile; Race: 96.0% White, 0.1% Black/African American, 0.9% Asian, 1.0% American Indian/Alaska Native, 0.2% Native Hawaiian/Other Pacific Islander, 1.8% Two or more races, 0.6% Hispanic of any race; Average household size: 2.48; Median age: 44.3; Age under 18: 22.9%; Age 65 and over: 19.1%; Males per 100 females: 111.1
Housing: Homeownership rate: 86.2%; Homeowner vacancy rate: 2.7%; Rental vacancy rate: 10.0%

BOON (CDP). Covers a land area of 1.756 square miles and a water area of 0 square miles. Located at 44.29° N. Lat; 85.60° W. Long. Elevation is 1,378 feet.
Population: 167; Growth (since 2000): n/a; Density: 95.1 persons per square mile; Race: 98.2% White, 0.0% Black/African American, 0.6% Asian, 0.0% American Indian/Alaska Native, 0.0% Native Hawaiian/Other Pacific Islander, 1.2% Two or more races, 0.0% Hispanic of any race; Average household size: 2.46; Median age: 39.6; Age under 18: 21.6%; Age 65 and over: 9.0%; Males per 100 females: 116.9
School District(s)
Cadillac Area Public Schools (PK-12)
  2012-13 Enrollment: 3,020 . . . . (231) 876-5000
Housing: Homeownership rate: 78.0%; Homeowner vacancy rate: 1.8%; Rental vacancy rate: 0.0%

BOON (township). Covers a land area of 36.007 square miles and a water area of 0 square miles. Located at 44.29° N. Lat; 85.64° W. Long. Elevation is 1,378 feet.
Population: 687; Growth (since 2000): 2.5%; Density: 19.1 persons per square mile; Race: 96.7% White, 0.9% Black/African American, 0.1% Asian, 0.3% American Indian/Alaska Native, 0.0% Native Hawaiian/Other Pacific Islander, 2.0% Two or more races, 1.5% Hispanic of any race; Average household size: 2.59; Median age: 42.4; Age under 18: 24.0%; Age 65 and over: 14.7%; Males per 100 females: 112.0
School District(s)
Cadillac Area Public Schools (PK-12)
  2012-13 Enrollment: 3,020 . . . . (231) 876-5000
Housing: Homeownership rate: 87.5%; Homeowner vacancy rate: 4.1%; Rental vacancy rate: 24.4%

BUCKLEY (village). Covers a land area of 1.777 square miles and a water area of 0.060 square miles. Located at 44.50° N. Lat; 85.67° W. Long. Elevation is 1,050 feet.
History: Buckley was founded in 1905 by G.A. Brigham and named for the Buckley & Douglas Lumber Company.
Population: 697; Growth (since 2000): 26.7%; Density: 392.2 persons per square mile; Race: 95.3% White, 0.7% Black/African American, 0.1% Asian, 0.9% American Indian/Alaska Native, 0.9% Native Hawaiian/Other Pacific Islander, 2.0% Two or more races, 2.0% Hispanic of any race; Average household size: 2.83; Median age: 30.2; Age under 18: 31.3%; Age 65 and over: 7.2%; Males per 100 females: 100.9
School District(s)
Buckley Community Schools (PK-12)
  2012-13 Enrollment: 425. . . . . (231) 269-3325
Housing: Homeownership rate: 69.5%; Homeowner vacancy rate: 8.5%; Rental vacancy rate: 7.3%

CABERFAE (CDP). Covers a land area of 0.345 square miles and a water area of 0 square miles. Located at 44.25° N. Lat; 85.72° W. Long.
Population: 64; Growth (since 2000): n/a; Density: 185.3 persons per square mile; Race: 98.4% White, 0.0% Black/African American, 0.0% Asian, 0.0% American Indian/Alaska Native, 0.0% Native Hawaiian/Other Pacific Islander, 1.6% Two or more races, 0.0% Hispanic of any race;

Average household size: 2.13; Median age: 57.5; Age under 18: 15.6%; Age 65 and over: 37.5%; Males per 100 females: 106.5
Housing: Homeownership rate: 90.0%; Homeowner vacancy rate: 10.0%; Rental vacancy rate: 25.0%

CADILLAC (city). County seat. Covers a land area of 7.164 square miles and a water area of 1.864 square miles. Located at 44.25° N. Lat; 85.41° W. Long. Elevation is 1,306 feet.

History: Cadillac was settled by timber operators, and incorporated in 1877. It was named for Antoine de la Mothe Cadillac, the founder of Detroit. When two railroad lines were built through Cadillac, it developed as an industrial center.
Population: 10,355; Growth (since 2000): 3.6%; Density: 1,445.4 persons per square mile; Race: 95.6% White, 0.5% Black/African American, 1.0% Asian, 0.6% American Indian/Alaska Native, 0.0% Native Hawaiian/Other Pacific Islander, 1.8% Two or more races, 1.8% Hispanic of any race; Average household size: 2.34; Median age: 36.5; Age under 18: 24.7%; Age 65 and over: 17.1%; Males per 100 females: 90.2; Marriage status: 24.2% never married, 48.3% now married, 1.6% separated, 8.4% widowed, 19.1% divorced; Foreign born: 0.8%; Speak English only: 97.2%; With disability: 18.2%; Veterans: 12.1%; Ancestry: 22.1% German, 14.3% Irish, 10.3% American, 8.0% English, 6.3% Polish
Employment: 7.7% management, business, and financial, 0.9% computer, engineering, and science, 5.0% education, legal, community service, arts, and media, 8.9% healthcare practitioners, 19.8% service, 20.7% sales and office, 6.4% natural resources, construction, and maintenance, 30.7% production, transportation, and material moving
Income: Per capita: $19,589; Median household: $32,963; Average household: $46,050; Households with income of $100,000 or more: 6.3%; Poverty rate: 22.6%
Educational Attainment: High school diploma or higher: 89.2%; Bachelor's degree or higher: 15.5%; Graduate/professional degree or higher: 6.1%

School District(s)
Cadillac Area Public Schools (PK-12)
    2012-13 Enrollment: 3,020 . . . . (231) 876-5000
Wexford-Missaukee ISD (PK-12)
    2012-13 Enrollment: 420 . . . . (231) 876-2260
Four-year College(s)
Baker College of Cadillac (Private, Not-for-profit)
    Fall 2013 Enrollment: 1,549 . . . . (231) 876-3101
    2013-14 Tuition: In-state $8,100; Out-of-state $8,100
Vocational/Technical School(s)
Cadillac Institute of Cosmetology (Private, For-profit)
    Fall 2013 Enrollment: 39 . . . . (231) 775-3642
    2013-14 Tuition: $8,475
Housing: Homeownership rate: 58.8%; Median home value: $80,200; Median year structure built: 1959; Homeowner vacancy rate: 5.9%; Median gross rent: $679 per month; Rental vacancy rate: 9.8%
Health Insurance: 87.6% have insurance; 61.9% have private insurance; 43.7% have public insurance; 12.4% do not have insurance; 5.3% of children under 18 do not have insurance
Hospitals: Mercy Hospital - Cadillac (174 beds)
Safety: Violent crime rate: 44.9 per 10,000 population; Property crime rate: 413.1 per 10,000 population
Newspapers: Cadillac News (daily circulation 10200); Northern Michigan News (weekly circulation 22000)
Transportation: Commute: 89.4% car, 0.1% public transportation, 4.8% walk, 4.2% work from home; Median travel time to work: 14.3 minutes; Amtrak: Bus service available.
Airports: Wexford County (general aviation)
Additional Information Contacts
City of Cadillac . . . . (231) 775-0181
    http://www.cadillac-mi.net

CEDAR CREEK (township). Covers a land area of 34.118 square miles and a water area of 0.023 square miles. Located at 44.38° N. Lat; 85.40° W. Long.
Population: 1,757; Growth (since 2000): 18.0%; Density: 51.5 persons per square mile; Race: 96.9% White, 0.2% Black/African American, 0.2% Asian, 0.4% American Indian/Alaska Native, 0.1% Native Hawaiian/Other Pacific Islander, 1.9% Two or more races, 2.0% Hispanic of any race; Average household size: 2.88; Median age: 36.8; Age under 18: 29.2%; Age 65 and over: 11.4%; Males per 100 females: 98.8

Housing: Homeownership rate: 87.9%; Homeowner vacancy rate: 2.7%; Rental vacancy rate: 5.1%

CHERRY GROVE (township). Covers a land area of 33.368 square miles and a water area of 2.843 square miles. Located at 44.21° N. Lat; 85.53° W. Long.
Population: 2,377; Growth (since 2000): 2.1%; Density: 71.2 persons per square mile; Race: 96.8% White, 0.2% Black/African American, 0.9% Asian, 0.7% American Indian/Alaska Native, 0.0% Native Hawaiian/Other Pacific Islander, 1.1% Two or more races, 1.4% Hispanic of any race; Average household size: 2.44; Median age: 46.8; Age under 18: 20.5%; Age 65 and over: 18.4%; Males per 100 females: 101.4
Housing: Homeownership rate: 85.6%; Homeowner vacancy rate: 3.3%; Rental vacancy rate: 16.2%

CLAM LAKE (township). Covers a land area of 30.708 square miles and a water area of 0.142 square miles. Located at 44.20° N. Lat; 85.39° W. Long.
Population: 2,467; Growth (since 2000): 10.2%; Density: 80.3 persons per square mile; Race: 97.3% White, 0.6% Black/African American, 0.6% Asian, 0.3% American Indian/Alaska Native, 0.0% Native Hawaiian/Other Pacific Islander, 1.1% Two or more races, 0.6% Hispanic of any race; Average household size: 2.57; Median age: 45.1; Age under 18: 23.9%; Age 65 and over: 16.7%; Males per 100 females: 102.0
Housing: Homeownership rate: 86.8%; Homeowner vacancy rate: 2.4%; Rental vacancy rate: 13.1%

COLFAX (township). Covers a land area of 35.265 square miles and a water area of 0.139 square miles. Located at 44.40° N. Lat; 85.53° W. Long.
History: Colfax County was named for Schuyler Colfax, vice president under Ulysses S. Grant.
Population: 840; Growth (since 2000): 10.1%; Density: 23.8 persons per square mile; Race: 98.3% White, 0.5% Black/African American, 0.5% Asian, 0.0% American Indian/Alaska Native, 0.0% Native Hawaiian/Other Pacific Islander, 0.4% Two or more races, 1.8% Hispanic of any race; Average household size: 2.58; Median age: 42.8; Age under 18: 25.6%; Age 65 and over: 15.4%; Males per 100 females: 111.6
Housing: Homeownership rate: 93.2%; Homeowner vacancy rate: 2.3%; Rental vacancy rate: 17.2%

GREENWOOD (township). Covers a land area of 35.356 square miles and a water area of 0.019 square miles. Located at 44.48° N. Lat; 85.53° W. Long.
Population: 587; Growth (since 2000): 8.3%; Density: 16.6 persons per square mile; Race: 97.6% White, 0.3% Black/African American, 0.2% Asian, 0.7% American Indian/Alaska Native, 0.0% Native Hawaiian/Other Pacific Islander, 1.2% Two or more races, 1.2% Hispanic of any race; Average household size: 2.78; Median age: 39.5; Age under 18: 29.0%; Age 65 and over: 10.4%; Males per 100 females: 120.7
Housing: Homeownership rate: 87.7%; Homeowner vacancy rate: 4.1%; Rental vacancy rate: 6.9%

HANOVER (township). Covers a land area of 35.986 square miles and a water area of 0.162 square miles. Located at 44.48° N. Lat; 85.65° W. Long.
Population: 1,560; Growth (since 2000): 30.0%; Density: 43.4 persons per square mile; Race: 96.5% White, 0.4% Black/African American, 0.1% Asian, 0.9% American Indian/Alaska Native, 0.4% Native Hawaiian/Other Pacific Islander, 1.5% Two or more races, 1.7% Hispanic of any race; Average household size: 2.66; Median age: 34.5; Age under 18: 27.8%; Age 65 and over: 11.3%; Males per 100 females: 103.7
Housing: Homeownership rate: 77.9%; Homeowner vacancy rate: 5.1%; Rental vacancy rate: 7.0%

HARING (CDP). Covers a land area of 2.233 square miles and a water area of 0 square miles. Located at 44.28° N. Lat; 85.40° W. Long. Elevation is 1,325 feet.
Population: 328; Growth (since 2000): n/a; Density: 146.9 persons per square mile; Race: 95.4% White, 0.0% Black/African American, 0.6% Asian, 0.6% American Indian/Alaska Native, 0.3% Native Hawaiian/Other Pacific Islander, 2.7% Two or more races, 1.5% Hispanic of any race; Average household size: 2.62; Median age: 47.2; Age under 18: 17.4%; Age 65 and over: 18.3%; Males per 100 females: 101.2

Housing: Homeownership rate: 78.4%; Homeowner vacancy rate: 1.9%; Rental vacancy rate: 3.6%

HARING (charter township).
Covers a land area of 32.357 square miles and a water area of 0.420 square miles. Located at 44.30° N. Lat; 85.40° W. Long. Elevation is 1,325 feet.
Population: 3,173; Growth (since 2000): 7.1%; Density: 98.1 persons per square mile; Race: 97.1% White, 0.3% Black/African American, 0.3% Asian, 0.6% American Indian/Alaska Native, 0.1% Native Hawaiian/Other Pacific Islander, 1.4% Two or more races, 1.9% Hispanic of any race; Average household size: 2.58; Median age: 43.0; Age under 18: 22.5%; Age 65 and over: 15.0%; Males per 100 females: 101.6; Marriage status: 23.0% never married, 53.7% now married, 2.3% separated, 7.2% widowed, 16.1% divorced; Foreign born: 1.2%; Speak English only: 98.0%; With disability: 12.6%; Veterans: 10.8%; Ancestry: 21.6% German, 14.8% English, 13.0% Irish, 10.4% American, 9.4% Dutch
Employment: 9.2% management, business, and financial, 0.5% computer, engineering, and science, 10.2% education, legal, community service, arts, and media, 5.0% healthcare practitioners, 12.9% service, 23.5% sales and office, 11.8% natural resources, construction, and maintenance, 26.9% production, transportation, and material moving
Income: Per capita: $21,785; Median household: $49,052; Average household: $60,308; Households with income of $100,000 or more: 12.3%; Poverty rate: 18.9%
Educational Attainment: High school diploma or higher: 88.9%; Bachelor's degree or higher: 21.8%; Graduate/professional degree or higher: 7.7%
Housing: Homeownership rate: 86.6%; Median home value: $101,900; Median year structure built: 1981; Homeowner vacancy rate: 2.5%; Median gross rent: $636 per month; Rental vacancy rate: 8.7%
Health Insurance: 88.4% have insurance; 67.8% have private insurance; 36.7% have public insurance; 11.6% do not have insurance; 6.2% of children under 18 do not have insurance
Transportation: Commute: 96.6% car, 0.0% public transportation, 1.5% walk, 0.9% work from home; Median travel time to work: 13.2 minutes

HARRIETTA (village).
Covers a land area of 0.933 square miles and a water area of 0 square miles. Located at 44.31° N. Lat; 85.70° W. Long. Elevation is 1,135 feet.
History: There was a post office here as early as 1874, called Springdale. The village of Harrietta was platted in 1889 by James M. Ashley and named by combining his father's name of Harry and his fiancee's name of Henriette.
Population: 143; Growth (since 2000): -15.4%; Density: 153.3 persons per square mile; Race: 94.4% White, 0.7% Black/African American, 0.7% Asian, 0.0% American Indian/Alaska Native, 0.0% Native Hawaiian/Other Pacific Islander, 4.2% Two or more races, 4.2% Hispanic of any race; Average household size: 2.38; Median age: 46.1; Age under 18: 21.0%; Age 65 and over: 17.5%; Males per 100 females: 116.7
Housing: Homeownership rate: 80.0%; Homeowner vacancy rate: 9.3%; Rental vacancy rate: 36.8%

HENDERSON (township).
Covers a land area of 36.214 square miles and a water area of 0.001 square miles. Located at 44.21° N. Lat; 85.63° W. Long.
Population: 163; Growth (since 2000): -7.4%; Density: 4.5 persons per square mile; Race: 100.0% White, 0.0% Black/African American, 0.0% Asian, 0.0% American Indian/Alaska Native, 0.0% Native Hawaiian/Other Pacific Islander, 0.0% Two or more races, 0.0% Hispanic of any race; Average household size: 2.14; Median age: 52.9; Age under 18: 13.5%; Age 65 and over: 23.3%; Males per 100 females: 129.6
Housing: Homeownership rate: 96.0%; Homeowner vacancy rate: 5.2%; Rental vacancy rate: 25.0%

LIBERTY (township).
Covers a land area of 36.510 square miles and a water area of 0.021 square miles. Located at 44.47° N. Lat; 85.40° W. Long.
Population: 861; Growth (since 2000): 7.6%; Density: 23.6 persons per square mile; Race: 96.3% White, 0.0% Black/African American, 0.5% Asian, 0.7% American Indian/Alaska Native, 0.0% Native Hawaiian/Other Pacific Islander, 2.6% Two or more races, 0.9% Hispanic of any race; Average household size: 2.64; Median age: 42.6; Age under 18: 25.0%; Age 65 and over: 15.6%; Males per 100 females: 97.0
Housing: Homeownership rate: 89.2%; Homeowner vacancy rate: 2.4%; Rental vacancy rate: 10.3%

MANTON (city).
Covers a land area of 1.559 square miles and a water area of 0.054 square miles. Located at 44.41° N. Lat; 85.40° W. Long. Elevation is 1,119 feet.
History: Manton was settled in 1871. It developed as a lumber town with a sawmill and planing mill.
Population: 1,287; Growth (since 2000): 5.4%; Density: 825.7 persons per square mile; Race: 96.3% White, 0.5% Black/African American, 0.0% Asian, 0.9% American Indian/Alaska Native, 0.0% Native Hawaiian/Other Pacific Islander, 1.9% Two or more races, 2.3% Hispanic of any race; Average household size: 2.54; Median age: 31.9; Age under 18: 30.0%; Age 65 and over: 14.4%; Males per 100 females: 90.4
School District(s)
Manton Consolidated Schools (PK-12)
    2012-13 Enrollment: 907. . . . . (231) 824-6411
Housing: Homeownership rate: 59.7%; Homeowner vacancy rate: 3.8%; Rental vacancy rate: 10.2%

MESICK (village).
Covers a land area of 1.295 square miles and a water area of 0.005 square miles. Located at 44.40° N. Lat; 85.72° W. Long. Elevation is 922 feet.
History: Annual mushroom festival.
Population: 394; Growth (since 2000): -11.9%; Density: 304.3 persons per square mile; Race: 96.7% White, 0.3% Black/African American, 0.0% Asian, 1.0% American Indian/Alaska Native, 0.3% Native Hawaiian/Other Pacific Islander, 1.0% Two or more races, 3.3% Hispanic of any race; Average household size: 2.45; Median age: 37.8; Age under 18: 25.9%; Age 65 and over: 15.7%; Males per 100 females: 96.0
School District(s)
Mesick Consolidated Schools (KG-12)
    2012-13 Enrollment: 652. . . . . (231) 885-2727
Housing: Homeownership rate: 69.0%; Homeowner vacancy rate: 4.3%; Rental vacancy rate: 10.7%

SELMA (township).
Covers a land area of 34.314 square miles and a water area of 1.678 square miles. Located at 44.29° N. Lat; 85.51° W. Long.
Population: 2,093; Growth (since 2000): 9.3%; Density: 61.0 persons per square mile; Race: 96.7% White, 0.7% Black/African American, 0.5% Asian, 0.2% American Indian/Alaska Native, 0.0% Native Hawaiian/Other Pacific Islander, 1.1% Two or more races, 1.3% Hispanic of any race; Average household size: 2.45; Median age: 44.1; Age under 18: 21.3%; Age 65 and over: 16.5%; Males per 100 females: 105.6
Housing: Homeownership rate: 85.1%; Homeowner vacancy rate: 2.9%; Rental vacancy rate: 5.9%

SLAGLE (township).
Covers a land area of 35.790 square miles and a water area of 0 square miles. Located at 44.29° N. Lat; 85.76° W. Long.
Population: 503; Growth (since 2000): -11.6%; Density: 14.1 persons per square mile; Race: 98.6% White, 0.0% Black/African American, 0.2% Asian, 0.6% American Indian/Alaska Native, 0.0% Native Hawaiian/Other Pacific Islander, 0.6% Two or more races, 2.6% Hispanic of any race; Average household size: 2.22; Median age: 50.8; Age under 18: 16.3%; Age 65 and over: 21.7%; Males per 100 females: 107.0
Housing: Homeownership rate: 89.0%; Homeowner vacancy rate: 5.6%; Rental vacancy rate: 21.9%

SOUTH BRANCH (township).
Covers a land area of 36.026 square miles and a water area of 0.024 square miles. Located at 44.20° N. Lat; 85.76° W. Long.
Population: 383; Growth (since 2000): 16.1%; Density: 10.6 persons per square mile; Race: 96.1% White, 0.3% Black/African American, 0.3% Asian, 1.3% American Indian/Alaska Native, 0.5% Native Hawaiian/Other Pacific Islander, 1.3% Two or more races, 0.8% Hispanic of any race; Average household size: 2.24; Median age: 50.2; Age under 18: 15.9%; Age 65 and over: 22.5%; Males per 100 females: 114.0
Housing: Homeownership rate: 89.5%; Homeowner vacancy rate: 3.8%; Rental vacancy rate: 5.3%

SPRINGVILLE (township).
Covers a land area of 32.499 square miles and a water area of 3.031 square miles. Located at 44.38° N. Lat; 85.76° W. Long.
Population: 1,755; Growth (since 2000): 4.9%; Density: 54.0 persons per square mile; Race: 96.1% White, 0.1% Black/African American, 0.3% Asian, 1.5% American Indian/Alaska Native, 0.2% Native Hawaiian/Other

Pacific Islander, 1.7% Two or more races, 1.6% Hispanic of any race;
Average household size: 2.45; Median age: 41.1; Age under 18: 24.8%;
Age 65 and over: 14.5%; Males per 100 females: 104.1
Housing: Homeownership rate: 79.2%; Homeowner vacancy rate: 4.5%;
Rental vacancy rate: 9.1%

WEDGEWOOD (CDP). Covers a land area of 0.623 square miles and
a water area of 0.030 square miles. Located at 44.19° N. Lat; 85.49° W.
Long.
Population: 237; Growth (since 2000): n/a; Density: 380.3 persons per
square mile; Race: 98.7% White, 0.0% Black/African American, 1.3%
Asian, 0.0% American Indian/Alaska Native, 0.0% Native Hawaiian/Other
Pacific Islander, 0.0% Two or more races, 1.3% Hispanic of any race;
Average household size: 2.58; Median age: 49.2; Age under 18: 19.8%;
Age 65 and over: 13.9%; Males per 100 females: 109.7
Housing: Homeownership rate: 94.5%; Homeowner vacancy rate: 5.4%;
Rental vacancy rate: 0.0%

WEXFORD (township). Covers a land area of 36.538 square miles and
a water area of 0.006 square miles. Located at 44.47° N. Lat; 85.76° W.
Long.
Population: 1,072; Growth (since 2000): 34.3%; Density: 29.3 persons per
square mile; Race: 97.8% White, 0.0% Black/African American, 0.3%
Asian, 1.0% American Indian/Alaska Native, 0.0% Native Hawaiian/Other
Pacific Islander, 0.7% Two or more races, 1.6% Hispanic of any race;
Average household size: 2.67; Median age: 38.9; Age under 18: 27.3%;
Age 65 and over: 11.9%; Males per 100 females: 114.4
Housing: Homeownership rate: 87.0%; Homeowner vacancy rate: 3.3%;
Rental vacancy rate: 10.3%

Place Name Index

Acme (township) Grand Traverse County, 171
Ada (township) Kent County, 232
Adams (township) Arenac County, 81
Adams (township) Hillsdale County, 180
Adams (township) Houghton County, 184
Addison (village) Lenawee County, 257
Addison (township) Oakland County, 332
Adrian (township) Lenawee County, 257
Adrian (city) Lenawee County, 257
Advance (CDP) Charlevoix County, 121
Aetna (township) Mecosta County, 294
Aetna (township) Missaukee County, 304
Afton (unincorporated) Cheboygan County, 125
Ahmeek (village) Keweenaw County, 244
Akron (township) Tuscola County, 415
Akron (village) Tuscola County, 415
Alabaster (township) Iosco County, 206
Alaiedon (township) Ingham County, 194
Alamo (township) Kalamazoo County, 223
Alanson (village) Emmet County, 153
Alba (CDP) Antrim County, 77
Albee (township) Saginaw County, 380
Albert (township) Montmorency County, 320
Albion (township) Calhoun County, 111
Albion (city) Calhoun County, 111
Alcona (township) Alcona County, 63
Alcona County, 63
Alden (CDP) Antrim County, 78
Algansee (township) Branch County, 108
Alger (unincorporated) Arenac County, 81
Alger County, 65
Algoma (township) Kent County, 232
Algonac (city) Saint Clair County, 389
Allegan (township) Allegan County, 68
Allegan (city) Allegan County, 68
Allegan County, 67
Allen (township) Hillsdale County, 180
Allen (village) Hillsdale County, 180
Allen Park (city) Wayne County, 436
Allendale (charter township) Ottawa County, 367
Allendale (CDP) Ottawa County, 366
Allenton (unincorporated) Saint Clair County, 389
Allis (township) Presque Isle County, 375
Allouez (township) Keweenaw County, 245
Alma (city) Gratiot County, 176
Almena (township) Van Buren County, 421
Almer (township) Tuscola County, 415
Almira (township) Benzie County, 95
Almont (township) Lapeer County, 248
Almont (village) Lapeer County, 248
Aloha (township) Cheboygan County, 125
Alpena (township) Alpena County, 76
Alpena (city) Alpena County, 75
Alpena County, 75
Alpha (village) Iron County, 209
Alpine (township) Kent County, 233
Alto (unincorporated) Kent County, 233
Amasa (CDP) Iron County, 209
Amber (township) Mason County, 291
Amboy (township) Hillsdale County, 180
Ann Arbor (charter township) Washtenaw County, 428
Ann Arbor (city) Washtenaw County, 428
Antioch (township) Wexford County, 452
Antrim (township) Shiawassee County, 410
Antrim County, 77
Antwerp (township) Van Buren County, 421
Applegate (village) Sanilac County, 403
Arbela (township) Tuscola County, 416
Arcada (township) Gratiot County, 176
Arcadia (township) Lapeer County, 249
Arcadia (township) Manistee County, 282
Arcadia (CDP) Manistee County, 282

Arenac (township) Arenac County, 81
Arenac County, 80
Argentine (township) Genesee County, 157
Argentine (CDP) Genesee County, 157
Argyle (township) Sanilac County, 403
Arlington (township) Van Buren County, 421
Armada (township) Macomb County, 273
Armada (village) Macomb County, 273
Arnold (unincorporated) Marquette County, 285
Arthur (township) Clare County, 132
Arvon (township) Baraga County, 83
Ash (township) Monroe County, 307
Ashland (township) Newaygo County, 328
Ashley (village) Gratiot County, 176
Assyria (township) Barry County, 85
Athens (township) Calhoun County, 111
Athens (village) Calhoun County, 112
Atlanta (CDP) Montmorency County, 320
Atlantic Mine (unincorporated) Houghton County, 184
Atlas (township) Genesee County, 157
Attica (township) Lapeer County, 249
Attica (CDP) Lapeer County, 249
Au Gres (township) Arenac County, 81
Au Gres (city) Arenac County, 81
Au Sable (charter township) Iosco County, 206
Au Sable (CDP) Iosco County, 206
Au Sable (township) Roscommon County, 377
Au Train (township) Alger County, 65
Auburn (city) Bay County, 90
Auburn Hills (city) Oakland County, 333
Augusta (village) Kalamazoo County, 223
Augusta (charter township) Washtenaw County, 429
Aurelius (township) Ingham County, 194
Austin (township) Mecosta County, 294
Austin (township) Sanilac County, 403
Avery (township) Montmorency County, 320
Avoca (unincorporated) Saint Clair County, 389
Backus (township) Roscommon County, 378
Bad Axe (city) Huron County, 189
Bagley (township) Otsego County, 364
Bailey (unincorporated) Muskegon County, 321
Bainbridge (township) Berrien County, 98
Baldwin (township) Delta County, 141
Baldwin (township) Iosco County, 206
Baldwin (village) Lake County, 246
Baltimore (township) Barry County, 85
Bancroft (village) Shiawassee County, 410
Bangor (charter township) Bay County, 90
Bangor (township) Van Buren County, 422
Bangor (city) Van Buren County, 421
Banks (township) Antrim County, 78
Bannister (unincorporated) Gratiot County, 176
Baraga (township) Baraga County, 83
Baraga (village) Baraga County, 83
Baraga County, 83
Barbeau (unincorporated) Chippewa County, 128
Bark River (township) Delta County, 141
Barnes Lake-Millers Lake (CDP) Lapeer County, 249
Baroda (township) Berrien County, 98
Baroda (village) Berrien County, 98
Barry (township) Barry County, 85
Barry County, 85
Barryton (village) Mecosta County, 294
Barton (township) Newaygo County, 328
Barton City (unincorporated) Alcona County, 63
Barton Hills (village) Washtenaw County, 429
Batavia (township) Branch County, 108
Bates (township) Iron County, 209
Bath (charter township) Clinton County, 135
Bath (CDP) Clinton County, 135
Battle Creek (city) Calhoun County, 112

Bay (township) Charlevoix County, 121
Bay City (city) Bay County, 90
Bay County, 90
Bay de Noc (township) Delta County, 141
Bay Mills (township) Chippewa County, 128
Bay Port (CDP) Huron County, 189
Bay Shore (CDP) Charlevoix County, 122
Bay View (CDP) Emmet County, 153
Beal City (CDP) Isabella County, 211
Bear Creek (township) Emmet County, 153
Bear Lake (township) Kalkaska County, 230
Bear Lake (CDP) Kalkaska County, 230
Bear Lake (township) Manistee County, 282
Bear Lake (village) Manistee County, 282
Bearinger (township) Presque Isle County, 375
Beaugrand (township) Cheboygan County, 125
Beaver (township) Bay County, 91
Beaver (township) Newaygo County, 328
Beaver Creek (township) Crawford County, 140
Beaver Island (unincorporated) Charlevoix County, 122
Beaverton (township) Gladwin County, 167
Beaverton (city) Gladwin County, 167
Bedford (charter township) Calhoun County, 112
Bedford (township) Monroe County, 307
Beecher (CDP) Genesee County, 157
Beechwood (CDP) Ottawa County, 367
Belding (city) Ionia County, 201
Belknap (township) Presque Isle County, 375
Bellaire (village) Antrim County, 78
Belleville (city) Wayne County, 437
Bellevue (township) Eaton County, 147
Bellevue (village) Eaton County, 147
Belmont (unincorporated) Kent County, 233
Belvidere (township) Montcalm County, 314
Bendon (CDP) Benzie County, 95
Bengal (township) Clinton County, 136
Bennington (township) Shiawassee County, 410
Benona (township) Oceana County, 351
Bentley (township) Gladwin County, 167
Benton (charter township) Berrien County, 98
Benton (township) Cheboygan County, 125
Benton (township) Eaton County, 147
Benton Harbor (city) Berrien County, 99
Benton Heights (CDP) Berrien County, 99
Benzie County, 94
Benzonia (township) Benzie County, 95
Benzonia (village) Benzie County, 95
Bergland (township) Ontonagon County, 357
Berkley (city) Oakland County, 333
Berlin (township) Ionia County, 201
Berlin (charter township) Monroe County, 307
Berlin (township) Saint Clair County, 389
Berrien (township) Berrien County, 99
Berrien Center (unincorporated) Berrien County, 100
Berrien County, 97
Berrien Springs (village) Berrien County, 100
Bertrand (township) Berrien County, 100
Bessemer (township) Gogebic County, 169
Bessemer (city) Gogebic County, 169
Bethany (township) Gratiot County, 176
Bethel (township) Branch County, 108
Beulah (village) Benzie County, 95
Beverly Hills (village) Oakland County, 333
Big Bay (CDP) Marquette County, 285
Big Creek (township) Oscoda County, 362
Big Prairie (township) Newaygo County, 328
Big Rapids (charter township) Mecosta County, 294
Big Rapids (city) Mecosta County, 294
Billings (township) Gladwin County, 167
Bingham (township) Clinton County, 136
Bingham (township) Huron County, 189

CDP = Census Designated Place

Bingham (township) Leelanau County, 254
Bingham Farms (village) Oakland County, 334
Birch Run (township) Saginaw County, 381
Birch Run (village) Saginaw County, 381
Birmingham (city) Oakland County, 334
Bismarck (township) Presque Isle County, 375
Bitely (unincorporated) Newaygo County, 329
Black River (unincorporated) Alcona County, 63
Blackman (charter township) Jackson County, 215
Blaine (township) Benzie County, 95
Blair (township) Grand Traverse County, 171
Blanchard (unincorporated) Isabella County, 211
Blendon (township) Ottawa County, 367
Bliss (township) Emmet County, 153
Blissfield (township) Lenawee County, 258
Blissfield (village) Lenawee County, 258
Bloomer (township) Montcalm County, 314
Bloomfield (township) Huron County, 189
Bloomfield (township) Missaukee County, 305
Bloomfield (charter township) Oakland County, 334
Bloomfield Hills (city) Oakland County, 334
Bloomingdale (township) Van Buren County, 422
Bloomingdale (village) Van Buren County, 422
Blue Lake (township) Kalkaska County, 230
Blue Lake (township) Muskegon County, 322
Blumfield (township) Saginaw County, 381
Boardman (township) Kalkaska County, 230
Bohemia (township) Ontonagon County, 357
Bois Blanc (township) Mackinac County, 271
Boon (township) Wexford County, 452
Boon (CDP) Wexford County, 452
Boston (township) Ionia County, 201
Bourret (township) Gladwin County, 167
Bowne (township) Kent County, 234
Boyne City (city) Charlevoix County, 122
Boyne Falls (village) Charlevoix County, 122
Boyne Valley (township) Charlevoix County, 122
Brady (township) Kalamazoo County, 223
Brady (township) Saginaw County, 381
Brampton (township) Delta County, 141
Branch (township) Mason County, 291
Branch County, 107
Brandon (charter township) Oakland County, 335
Brant (township) Saginaw County, 381
Breckenridge (village) Gratiot County, 176
Breedsville (village) Van Buren County, 422
Breen (township) Dickinson County, 144
Breitung (charter township) Dickinson County, 144
Brethren (CDP) Manistee County, 282
Brevort (township) Mackinac County, 271
Bridgehampton (township) Sanilac County, 404
Bridgeport (charter township) Saginaw County, 381
Bridgeport (CDP) Saginaw County, 381
Bridgeton (township) Newaygo County, 329
Bridgewater (township) Washtenaw County, 429
Bridgman (city) Berrien County, 100
Brighton (township) Livingston County, 264
Brighton (city) Livingston County, 263
Briley (township) Montmorency County, 320
Brimley (unincorporated) Chippewa County, 129
Britton (village) Lenawee County, 258
Brockway (township) Saint Clair County, 390
Brohman (unincorporated) Newaygo County, 329
Bronson (township) Branch County, 108
Bronson (city) Branch County, 108
Brookfield (township) Eaton County, 148
Brookfield (township) Huron County, 189

Brooklyn (village) Jackson County, 215
Brooks (township) Newaygo County, 329
Broomfield (township) Isabella County, 211
Brown (township) Manistee County, 282
Brown City (city) Sanilac County, 404
Brownlee Park (CDP) Calhoun County, 113
Brownstown (charter township) Wayne County, 437
Bruce (township) Chippewa County, 129
Bruce (township) Macomb County, 274
Bruce Crossing (unincorporated) Ontonagon County, 358
Brutus (CDP) Emmet County, 153
Buchanan (township) Berrien County, 101
Buchanan (city) Berrien County, 100
Buckeye (township) Gladwin County, 167
Buckley (village) Wexford County, 452
Buel (township) Sanilac County, 404
Buena Vista (charter township) Saginaw County, 382
Buena Vista (CDP) Saginaw County, 382
Bunker Hill (township) Ingham County, 195
Burdell (township) Osceola County, 360
Burleigh (township) Iosco County, 206
Burlington (township) Calhoun County, 113
Burlington (village) Calhoun County, 113
Burlington (township) Lapeer County, 249
Burns (township) Shiawassee County, 410
Burnside (township) Lapeer County, 249
Burr Oak (township) Saint Joseph County, 398
Burr Oak (village) Saint Joseph County, 399
Burt (township) Alger County, 65
Burt (township) Cheboygan County, 125
Burt (CDP) Saginaw County, 382
Burt Lake (unincorporated) Cheboygan County, 125
Burtchville (township) Saint Clair County, 390
Burton (city) Genesee County, 157
Bushnell (township) Montcalm County, 314
Butler (township) Branch County, 108
Butman (township) Gladwin County, 167
Butterfield (township) Missaukee County, 305
Byron (township) Kent County, 234
Byron (village) Shiawassee County, 411
Byron Center (CDP) Kent County, 234
Caberfae (CDP) Wexford County, 452
Cadillac (city) Wexford County, 453
Caldwell (township) Missaukee County, 305
Caledonia (township) Alcona County, 63
Caledonia (township) Kent County, 234
Caledonia (village) Kent County, 235
Caledonia (charter township) Shiawassee County, 411
Calhoun County, 111
California (township) Branch County, 108
Calumet (charter township) Houghton County, 184
Calumet (village) Houghton County, 185
Calvin (township) Cass County, 117
Cambria (township) Hillsdale County, 180
Cambridge (township) Lenawee County, 258
Camden (township) Hillsdale County, 180
Camden (village) Hillsdale County, 180
Campbell (township) Ionia County, 202
Canada Creek Ranch (CDP) Montmorency County, 320
Canadian Lakes (CDP) Mecosta County, 295
Cannon (township) Kent County, 235
Canton (charter township) Wayne County, 437
Capac (village) Saint Clair County, 390
Carleton (village) Monroe County, 307
Carlton (township) Barry County, 86
Carmel (township) Eaton County, 148
Carney (village) Menominee County, 298

Caro (city) Tuscola County, 416
Carp Lake (township) Emmet County, 153
Carp Lake (CDP) Emmet County, 153
Carp Lake (township) Ontonagon County, 358
Carrollton (township) Saginaw County, 382
Carson City (city) Montcalm County, 314
Carsonville (village) Sanilac County, 404
Cascade (charter township) Kent County, 235
Casco (township) Allegan County, 68
Casco (township) Saint Clair County, 390
Case (township) Presque Isle County, 375
Caseville (township) Huron County, 190
Caseville (city) Huron County, 190
Casnovia (village) Kent County, 235
Casnovia (township) Muskegon County, 322
Caspian (city) Iron County, 209
Cass City (village) Tuscola County, 416
Cass County, 117
Cassopolis (village) Cass County, 117
Castleton (township) Barry County, 86
Cato (township) Montcalm County, 314
Cedar (CDP) Leelanau County, 254
Cedar (township) Osceola County, 360
Cedar Creek (township) Muskegon County, 322
Cedar Creek (township) Wexford County, 453
Cedar Springs (city) Kent County, 235
Cedarville (township) Menominee County, 298
Cement City (village) Lenawee County, 259
Center (township) Emmet County, 154
Center Line (city) Macomb County, 274
Centerville (township) Leelanau County, 254
Central Lake (township) Antrim County, 78
Central Lake (village) Antrim County, 78
Centreville (village) Saint Joseph County, 399
Ceresco (unincorporated) Calhoun County, 113
Champion (township) Marquette County, 285
Chandler (township) Charlevoix County, 122
Chandler (township) Huron County, 190
Channing (unincorporated) Dickinson County, 145
Chapin (township) Saginaw County, 383
Charleston (township) Kalamazoo County, 224
Charlevoix (township) Charlevoix County, 123
Charlevoix (city) Charlevoix County, 122
Charlevoix County, 121
Charlotte (city) Eaton County, 148
Charlton (township) Otsego County, 364
Chase (township) Lake County, 246
Chassell (township) Houghton County, 185
Chatham (village) Alger County, 65
Cheboygan (city) Cheboygan County, 126
Cheboygan County, 124
Chelsea (city) Washtenaw County, 429
Cherry Grove (township) Wexford County, 453
Cherry Valley (township) Lake County, 246
Chesaning (township) Saginaw County, 383
Chesaning (village) Saginaw County, 383
Cheshire (township) Allegan County, 69
Chester (township) Eaton County, 148
Chester (township) Otsego County, 364
Chester (township) Ottawa County, 367
Chesterfield (township) Macomb County, 274
Chestonia (township) Antrim County, 78
Chikaming (township) Berrien County, 101
China (township) Saint Clair County, 390
Chippewa (township) Chippewa County, 129
Chippewa (township) Isabella County, 211
Chippewa (township) Mecosta County, 295
Chippewa County, 128
Chippewa Lake (unincorporated) Mecosta County, 295
Chocolay (charter township) Marquette County, 285

CDP = Census Designated Place

Chums Corner (CDP) Grand Traverse County, 172

Churchill (township) Ogemaw County, 355

Clam Lake (township) Wexford County, 453

Clam Union (township) Missaukee County, 305

Clare (city) Clare County, 132

Clare County, 132

Clarence (township) Calhoun County, 113

Clarendon (township) Calhoun County, 113

Clark (township) Mackinac County, 271

Clarklake (unincorporated) Jackson County, 215

Clarksville (village) Ionia County, 202

Clawson (city) Oakland County, 335

Clay (township) Saint Clair County, 391

Claybanks (township) Oceana County, 351

Clayton (township) Arenac County, 81

Clayton (charter township) Genesee County, 158

Clayton (village) Lenawee County, 259

Clearwater (township) Kalkaska County, 230

Clement (township) Gladwin County, 167

Cleon (township) Manistee County, 282

Cleveland (township) Leelanau County, 254

Clifford (village) Lapeer County, 249

Climax (township) Kalamazoo County, 224

Climax (village) Kalamazoo County, 224

Clinton (township) Lenawee County, 259

Clinton (village) Lenawee County, 259

Clinton (charter township) Macomb County, 274

Clinton (township) Oscoda County, 363

Clinton County, 135

Clio (city) Genesee County, 158

Clyde (township) Allegan County, 69

Clyde (township) Saint Clair County, 391

Coe (township) Isabella County, 212

Cohoctah (township) Livingston County, 264

Coldsprings (township) Kalkaska County, 230

Coldwater (township) Branch County, 109

Coldwater (city) Branch County, 108

Coldwater (township) Isabella County, 212

Coleman (city) Midland County, 301

Colfax (township) Benzie County, 95

Colfax (township) Huron County, 190

Colfax (township) Mecosta County, 295

Colfax (township) Oceana County, 352

Colfax (township) Wexford County, 453

Coloma (charter township) Berrien County, 101

Coloma (city) Berrien County, 101

Colon (township) Saint Joseph County, 399

Colon (village) Saint Joseph County, 399

Columbia (township) Jackson County, 216

Columbia (township) Tuscola County, 416

Columbia (township) Van Buren County, 422

Columbiaville (village) Lapeer County, 250

Columbus (township) Luce County, 269

Columbus (township) Saint Clair County, 391

Comins (township) Oscoda County, 363

Commerce (charter township) Oakland County, 335

Commerce Township (unincorporated) Oakland County, 336

Comstock (charter township) Kalamazoo County, 224

Comstock Northwest (CDP) Kalamazoo County, 224

Comstock Park (CDP) Kent County, 236

Concord (township) Jackson County, 216

Concord (village) Jackson County, 216

Conklin (unincorporated) Ottawa County, 367

Constantine (township) Saint Joseph County, 399

Constantine (village) Saint Joseph County, 400

Convis (township) Calhoun County, 113

Conway (CDP) Emmet County, 154

Conway (township) Livingston County, 264

Cooks (unincorporated) Delta County, 141

Cooper (charter township) Kalamazoo County, 224

Coopersville (city) Ottawa County, 368

Copemish (village) Manistee County, 282

Copper City (village) Houghton County, 185

Copper Harbor (CDP) Keweenaw County, 245

Coral (unincorporated) Montcalm County, 315

Cornell (township) Delta County, 142

Corunna (city) Shiawassee County, 411

Corwith (township) Otsego County, 364

Cottrellville (township) Saint Clair County, 391

Courtland (township) Kent County, 236

Covert (township) Van Buren County, 423

Covington (township) Baraga County, 84

Crawford County, 139

Crockery (township) Ottawa County, 368

Cross Village (township) Emmet County, 154

Cross Village (CDP) Emmet County, 154

Croswell (city) Sanilac County, 404

Croton (township) Newaygo County, 329

Crystal (township) Montcalm County, 315

Crystal (township) Oceana County, 352

Crystal Downs Country Club (CDP) Benzie County, 96

Crystal Falls (township) Iron County, 210

Crystal Falls (city) Iron County, 209

Crystal Lake (township) Benzie County, 96

Crystal Mountain (CDP) Benzie County, 96

Cumming (township) Ogemaw County, 355

Curran (unincorporated) Alcona County, 63

Curtis (township) Alcona County, 63

Custer (township) Antrim County, 78

Custer (township) Mason County, 291

Custer (village) Mason County, 291

Custer (township) Sanilac County, 404

Cutlerville (CDP) Kent County, 236

Dafter (township) Chippewa County, 129

Daggett (township) Menominee County, 298

Daggett (village) Menominee County, 298

Dallas (township) Clinton County, 136

Dalton (township) Muskegon County, 322

Danby (township) Ionia County, 202

Dansville (village) Ingham County, 195

Davisburg (unincorporated) Oakland County, 336

Davison (township) Genesee County, 159

Davison (city) Genesee County, 158

Day (township) Montcalm County, 315

Dayton (township) Newaygo County, 329

Dayton (township) Tuscola County, 416

De Tour Village (village) Chippewa County, 129

Dearborn (city) Wayne County, 438

Dearborn Heights (city) Wayne County, 438

Decatur (township) Van Buren County, 423

Decatur (village) Van Buren County, 423

Decker (unincorporated) Sanilac County, 404

Deckerville (village) Sanilac County, 404

Deep River (township) Arenac County, 81

Deerfield (township) Isabella County, 212

Deerfield (township) Lapeer County, 250

Deerfield (township) Lenawee County, 259

Deerfield (village) Lenawee County, 259

Deerfield (township) Livingston County, 265

Deerfield (township) Mecosta County, 295

Deerton (unincorporated) Alger County, 66

Deford (unincorporated) Tuscola County, 416

Delaware (township) Sanilac County, 404

Delhi (charter township) Ingham County, 195

Delta (charter township) Eaton County, 148

Delta County, 141

Delton (CDP) Barry County, 86

Denmark (township) Tuscola County, 417

Denton (township) Roscommon County, 378

Denver (township) Isabella County, 212

Denver (township) Newaygo County, 329

Detour (township) Chippewa County, 129

Detroit (city) Wayne County, 439

Detroit Beach (CDP) Monroe County, 308

DeWitt (charter township) Clinton County, 136

DeWitt (city) Clinton County, 136

Dexter (township) Washtenaw County, 429

Dexter (village) Washtenaw County, 430

Dickinson County, 144

Dickson (township) Manistee County, 282

Dimondale (village) Eaton County, 149

Dodgeville (unincorporated) Houghton County, 185

Dollar Bay (CDP) Houghton County, 185

Dorr (township) Allegan County, 69

Douglas (city) Allegan County, 69

Douglass (township) Montcalm County, 315

Dover (township) Lake County, 246

Dover (township) Lenawee County, 259

Dover (township) Otsego County, 364

Dowagiac (city) Cass County, 117

Dowling (CDP) Barry County, 86

Doyle (township) Schoolcraft County, 408

Drummond (township) Chippewa County, 129

Drummond Island (unincorporated) Chippewa County, 130

Dryden (township) Lapeer County, 250

Dryden (village) Lapeer County, 250

Duncan (township) Houghton County, 185

Dundee (township) Monroe County, 308

Dundee (village) Monroe County, 308

Duplain (township) Clinton County, 137

Durand (city) Shiawassee County, 411

Dwight (township) Huron County, 190

Eagle (township) Clinton County, 137

Eagle (village) Clinton County, 137

Eagle Harbor (township) Keweenaw County, 245

Eagle Harbor (CDP) Keweenaw County, 245

Eagle River (CDP) Keweenaw County, 245

East Bay (township) Grand Traverse County, 172

East China (township) Saint Clair County, 392

East Grand Rapids (city) Kent County, 236

East Jordan (city) Charlevoix County, 123

East Lansing (city) Ingham County, 195

East Leroy (unincorporated) Calhoun County, 113

East Tawas (city) Iosco County, 207

Eastlake (village) Manistee County, 282

Easton (township) Ionia County, 202

Eastpointe (city) Macomb County, 275

Eastport (CDP) Antrim County, 78

Eastwood (CDP) Kalamazoo County, 225

Eaton (township) Eaton County, 149

Eaton County, 147

Eaton Rapids (township) Eaton County, 149

Eaton Rapids (city) Eaton County, 149

Eau Claire (village) Berrien County, 101

Eben Junction (unincorporated) Alger County, 66

Echo (township) Antrim County, 78

Eckerman (unincorporated) Chippewa County, 130

Eckford (township) Calhoun County, 113

Ecorse (city) Wayne County, 440

Eden (township) Lake County, 246

Eden (township) Mason County, 291

Edenville (township) Midland County, 301

Edgemont Park (CDP) Ingham County, 195

Edmore (village) Montcalm County, 315

Edwards (township) Ogemaw County, 355

Edwardsburg (village) Cass County, 118

Egelston (township) Muskegon County, 322

Elba (township) Gratiot County, 176

CDP = Census Designated Place

Elba (township) Lapeer County, 250
Elberta (village) Benzie County, 96
Elbridge (township) Oceana County, 352
Elk (township) Lake County, 246
Elk (township) Sanilac County, 404
Elk Rapids (township) Antrim County, 78
Elk Rapids (village) Antrim County, 79
Elkland (township) Tuscola County, 417
Elkton (village) Huron County, 190
Ellington (township) Tuscola County, 417
Ellis (township) Cheboygan County, 126
Ellsworth (village) Antrim County, 79
Ellsworth (township) Lake County, 246
Elm River (township) Houghton County, 185
Elmer (township) Oscoda County, 363
Elmer (township) Sanilac County, 405
Elmira (township) Otsego County, 364
Elmwood (charter township) Leelanau County, 254
Elmwood (township) Tuscola County, 417
Elsie (village) Clinton County, 137
Elwell (unincorporated) Gratiot County, 177
Ely (township) Marquette County, 286
Emerson (township) Gratiot County, 177
Emmet County, 152
Emmett (charter township) Calhoun County, 114
Emmett (township) Saint Clair County, 392
Emmett (village) Saint Clair County, 392
Empire (township) Leelanau County, 255
Empire (village) Leelanau County, 255
Engadine (unincorporated) Mackinac County, 271
Ensign (township) Delta County, 142
Ensley (township) Newaygo County, 329
Enterprise (township) Missaukee County, 305
Erie (township) Monroe County, 308
Erwin (township) Gogebic County, 169
Escanaba (township) Delta County, 142
Escanaba (city) Delta County, 142
Essex (township) Clinton County, 137
Essexville (city) Bay County, 91
Estral Beach (village) Monroe County, 308
Eureka (township) Montcalm County, 315
Evangeline (township) Charlevoix County, 123
Evart (township) Osceola County, 360
Evart (city) Osceola County, 360
Eveline (township) Charlevoix County, 123
Everett (township) Newaygo County, 330
Evergreen (township) Montcalm County, 316
Evergreen (township) Sanilac County, 405
Ewen (unincorporated) Ontonagon County, 358
Ewing (township) Marquette County, 286
Excelsior (township) Kalkaska County, 230
Exeter (township) Monroe County, 308
Fabius (township) Saint Joseph County, 400
Fair Haven (unincorporated) Saint Clair County, 392
Fair Plain (CDP) Berrien County, 102
Fairbanks (township) Delta County, 142
Fairfield (township) Lenawee County, 260
Fairfield (township) Shiawassee County, 411
Fairgrove (township) Tuscola County, 417
Fairgrove (village) Tuscola County, 417
Fairhaven (township) Huron County, 190
Fairplain (township) Montcalm County, 316
Fairview (unincorporated) Oscoda County, 363
Faithorn (township) Menominee County, 298
Falmouth (unincorporated) Missaukee County, 305
Farmington (city) Oakland County, 336
Farmington Hills (city) Oakland County, 336
Farwell (village) Clare County, 133
Fawn River (township) Saint Joseph County, 400
Fayette (township) Hillsdale County, 180

Felch (township) Dickinson County, 145
Fennville (city) Allegan County, 69
Fenton (charter township) Genesee County, 159
Fenton (city) Genesee County, 159
Fenwick (unincorporated) Montcalm County, 316
Ferndale (city) Oakland County, 337
Ferris (township) Montcalm County, 316
Ferry (township) Oceana County, 352
Ferrysburg (city) Ottawa County, 368
Fife Lake (township) Grand Traverse County, 172
Fife Lake (village) Grand Traverse County, 172
Filer (charter township) Manistee County, 282
Filer City (CDP) Manistee County, 283
Filion (unincorporated) Huron County, 190
Fillmore (township) Allegan County, 69
Flat Rock (city) Wayne County, 440
Flint (charter township) Genesee County, 160
Flint (city) Genesee County, 160
Florence (township) Saint Joseph County, 400
Flowerfield (township) Saint Joseph County, 400
Flushing (charter township) Genesee County, 161
Flushing (city) Genesee County, 161
Flynn (township) Sanilac County, 405
Ford River (township) Delta County, 143
Forest (township) Cheboygan County, 126
Forest (township) Genesee County, 162
Forest (township) Missaukee County, 305
Forest Hills (CDP) Kent County, 237
Forest Home (township) Antrim County, 79
Forester (township) Sanilac County, 405
Forestville (village) Sanilac County, 405
Fork (township) Mecosta County, 295
Forsyth (township) Marquette County, 286
Fort Gratiot (charter township) Saint Clair County, 392
Foster (township) Ogemaw County, 355
Foster City (unincorporated) Dickinson County, 145
Fostoria (CDP) Tuscola County, 417
Fountain (village) Mason County, 291
Fowler (village) Clinton County, 137
Fowlerville (village) Livingston County, 265
Frankenlust (township) Bay County, 91
Frankenmuth (township) Saginaw County, 383
Frankenmuth (city) Saginaw County, 383
Frankfort (city) Benzie County, 96
Franklin (township) Clare County, 133
Franklin (township) Houghton County, 185
Franklin (township) Lenawee County, 260
Franklin (village) Oakland County, 337
Fraser (township) Bay County, 92
Fraser (city) Macomb County, 275
Frederic (township) Crawford County, 140
Fredonia (township) Calhoun County, 114
Free Soil (township) Mason County, 291
Free Soil (village) Mason County, 291
Freedom (township) Washtenaw County, 430
Freeland (CDP) Saginaw County, 383
Freeman (township) Clare County, 133
Freeport (village) Barry County, 86
Fremont (township) Isabella County, 212
Fremont (city) Newaygo County, 330
Fremont (township) Saginaw County, 384
Fremont (township) Sanilac County, 405
Fremont (township) Tuscola County, 417
Frenchtown (township) Monroe County, 309
Friendship (township) Emmet County, 154
Frost (township) Clare County, 133
Fruitland (township) Muskegon County, 323
Fruitport (charter township) Muskegon County, 323
Fruitport (village) Muskegon County, 323

Fulton (township) Gratiot County, 177
Gaastra (city) Iron County, 210
Gagetown (village) Tuscola County, 418
Gaines (township) Genesee County, 162
Gaines (village) Genesee County, 162
Gaines (charter township) Kent County, 237
Galesburg (city) Kalamazoo County, 225
Galien (township) Berrien County, 102
Galien (village) Berrien County, 102
Ganges (township) Allegan County, 69
Garden (township) Delta County, 143
Garden (village) Delta County, 143
Garden City (city) Wayne County, 441
Garfield (township) Bay County, 92
Garfield (township) Clare County, 133
Garfield (charter township) Grand Traverse County, 172
Garfield (township) Kalkaska County, 231
Garfield (township) Mackinac County, 271
Garfield (township) Newaygo County, 330
Gaylord (city) Otsego County, 365
Genesee (charter township) Genesee County, 162
Genesee County, 156
Geneva (township) Midland County, 301
Geneva (township) Van Buren County, 423
Genoa (township) Livingston County, 265
Georgetown (charter township) Ottawa County, 368
Germfask (township) Schoolcraft County, 408
Gerrish (township) Roscommon County, 378
Gibraltar (city) Wayne County, 441
Gibson (township) Bay County, 92
Gilead (township) Branch County, 109
Gilford (township) Tuscola County, 418
Gilmore (township) Benzie County, 96
Gilmore (township) Isabella County, 212
Girard (township) Branch County, 109
Gladstone (city) Delta County, 143
Gladwin (township) Gladwin County, 168
Gladwin (city) Gladwin County, 167
Gladwin County, 166
Glen Arbor (township) Leelanau County, 255
Glen Arbor (CDP) Leelanau County, 255
Glennie (unincorporated) Alcona County, 64
Gobles (city) Van Buren County, 423
Goetzville (unincorporated) Chippewa County, 130
Gogebic County, 169
Golden (township) Oceana County, 352
Goodar (township) Ogemaw County, 355
Goodells (unincorporated) Saint Clair County, 393
Goodland (township) Lapeer County, 250
Goodrich (village) Genesee County, 162
Goodwell (township) Newaygo County, 330
Gore (township) Huron County, 190
Gould City (unincorporated) Mackinac County, 271
Gourley (township) Menominee County, 298
Gowen (unincorporated) Kent County, 237
Grand Beach (village) Berrien County, 102
Grand Blanc (charter township) Genesee County, 163
Grand Blanc (city) Genesee County, 163
Grand Haven (charter township) Ottawa County, 369
Grand Haven (city) Ottawa County, 369
Grand Island (township) Alger County, 66
Grand Junction (unincorporated) Van Buren County, 424
Grand Ledge (city) Eaton County, 150
Grand Marais (unincorporated) Alger County, 66

Grand Rapids (charter township) Kent County, 237
Grand Rapids (city) Kent County, 238
Grand Traverse County, 171
Grandville (city) Kent County, 239
Grant (township) Cheboygan County, 126
Grant (township) Clare County, 133
Grant (township) Grand Traverse County, 173
Grant (township) Huron County, 191
Grant (township) Iosco County, 207
Grant (township) Keweenaw County, 245
Grant (township) Mason County, 291
Grant (township) Mecosta County, 295
Grant (township) Newaygo County, 331
Grant (city) Newaygo County, 330
Grant (township) Oceana County, 352
Grant (township) Saint Clair County, 393
Grass Lake (charter township) Jackson County, 216
Grass Lake (village) Jackson County, 216
Gratiot County, 175
Grattan (township) Kent County, 239
Grawn (CDP) Grand Traverse County, 173
Grayling (charter township) Crawford County, 140
Grayling (city) Crawford County, 140
Green (township) Alpena County, 76
Green (charter township) Mecosta County, 295
Green Lake (township) Grand Traverse County, 173
Green Oak (township) Livingston County, 265
Greenbush (township) Alcona County, 64
Greenbush (township) Clinton County, 137
Greendale (township) Midland County, 301
Greenland (township) Ontonagon County, 358
Greenleaf (township) Sanilac County, 405
Greenville (city) Montcalm County, 316
Greenwood (township) Clare County, 133
Greenwood (township) Oceana County, 352
Greenwood (township) Oscoda County, 363
Greenwood (township) Saint Clair County, 393
Greenwood (township) Wexford County, 453
Gregory (unincorporated) Livingston County, 266
Greilickville (CDP) Leelanau County, 255
Grim (township) Gladwin County, 168
Grosse Ile (township) Wayne County, 441
Grosse Pointe (city) Wayne County, 442
Grosse Pointe Farms (city) Wayne County, 442
Grosse Pointe Park (city) Wayne County, 442
Grosse Pointe Woods (city) Wayne County, 442
Grout (township) Gladwin County, 168
Groveland (township) Oakland County, 337
Gulliver (unincorporated) Schoolcraft County, 408
Gun Plain (township) Allegan County, 70
Gustin (township) Alcona County, 64
Gwinn (CDP) Marquette County, 286
Hadley (township) Lapeer County, 251
Hagar (township) Berrien County, 102
Haight (township) Ontonagon County, 358
Hale (unincorporated) Iosco County, 207
Hamburg (township) Livingston County, 266
Hamilton (township) Clare County, 133
Hamilton (township) Gratiot County, 177
Hamilton (township) Van Buren County, 424
Hamlin (township) Eaton County, 150
Hamlin (township) Mason County, 292
Hampton (charter township) Bay County, 92
Hamtramck (city) Wayne County, 443
Hancock (township) Houghton County, 186
Hancock (city) Houghton County, 185
Handy (township) Livingston County, 266
Hanover (township) Jackson County, 217
Hanover (village) Jackson County, 217

Hanover (township) Wexford County, 453
Harbor Beach (city) Huron County, 191
Harbor Springs (city) Emmet County, 154
Hardwood Acres (CDP) Benzie County, 96
Haring (charter township) Wexford County, 454
Haring (CDP) Wexford County, 453
Harper Woods (city) Wayne County, 443
Harrietta (village) Wexford County, 454
Harris (township) Menominee County, 298
Harrison (city) Clare County, 134
Harrison (charter township) Macomb County, 275
Harrison Township (unincorporated) Macomb County, 276
Harrisville (township) Alcona County, 64
Harrisville (city) Alcona County, 64
Harsens Island (unincorporated) Saint Clair County, 393
Hart (township) Oceana County, 352
Hart (city) Oceana County, 352
Hartford (township) Van Buren County, 424
Hartford (city) Van Buren County, 424
Hartland (township) Livingston County, 266
Hartwick (township) Osceola County, 360
Harvey (CDP) Marquette County, 286
Haslett (CDP) Ingham County, 196
Hastings (charter township) Barry County, 86
Hastings (city) Barry County, 86
Hatton (township) Clare County, 134
Hawes (township) Alcona County, 64
Hawks (unincorporated) Presque Isle County, 375
Hay (township) Gladwin County, 168
Hayes (township) Charlevoix County, 123
Hayes (township) Clare County, 134
Hayes (township) Otsego County, 365
Haynes (township) Alcona County, 64
Hazel Park (city) Oakland County, 338
Hazelton (township) Shiawassee County, 412
Heath (township) Allegan County, 70
Hebron (township) Cheboygan County, 126
Helena (township) Antrim County, 79
Hematite (township) Iron County, 210
Hemlock (CDP) Saginaw County, 384
Henderson (CDP) Shiawassee County, 412
Henderson (township) Wexford County, 454
Hendricks (township) Mackinac County, 271
Henrietta (township) Jackson County, 217
Hermansville (unincorporated) Menominee County, 298
Herron (unincorporated) Alpena County, 76
Hersey (township) Osceola County, 360
Hersey (village) Osceola County, 360
Hesperia (village) Oceana County, 353
Hessel (unincorporated) Mackinac County, 271
Hiawatha (township) Schoolcraft County, 409
Hickory Corners (CDP) Barry County, 87
Higgins (township) Roscommon County, 378
Higgins Lake (unincorporated) Roscommon County, 378
Highland (charter township) Oakland County, 338
Highland (township) Osceola County, 360
Highland Park (city) Wayne County, 444
Hill (township) Ogemaw County, 355
Hillman (township) Montmorency County, 320
Hillman (village) Montmorency County, 320
Hillsdale (township) Hillsdale County, 181
Hillsdale (city) Hillsdale County, 181
Hillsdale County, 179
Hinton (township) Mecosta County, 296
Holland (township) Missaukee County, 305
Holland (charter township) Ottawa County, 369
Holland (city) Ottawa County, 370

Holly (township) Oakland County, 338
Holly (village) Oakland County, 338
Holmes (township) Menominee County, 299
Holt (CDP) Ingham County, 196
Holton (township) Muskegon County, 323
Home (township) Montcalm County, 316
Home (township) Newaygo County, 331
Homer (township) Calhoun County, 114
Homer (village) Calhoun County, 114
Homer (township) Midland County, 301
Homestead (township) Benzie County, 96
Honor (village) Benzie County, 96
Hope (township) Barry County, 87
Hope (township) Midland County, 302
Hopkins (township) Allegan County, 70
Hopkins (village) Allegan County, 70
Horton (township) Ogemaw County, 355
Horton Bay (CDP) Charlevoix County, 123
Houghton (city) Houghton County, 186
Houghton (township) Keweenaw County, 245
Houghton County, 184
Houghton Lake (CDP) Roscommon County, 378
Houghton Lake Heights (unincorporated) Roscommon County, 379
Howard (township) Cass County, 118
Howard City (village) Montcalm County, 317
Howell (township) Livingston County, 267
Howell (city) Livingston County, 267
Hubbard Lake (CDP) Alcona County, 64
Hubbardston (village) Ionia County, 202
Hubbell (CDP) Houghton County, 186
Hudson (township) Charlevoix County, 123
Hudson (township) Lenawee County, 260
Hudson (city) Lenawee County, 260
Hudson (township) Mackinac County, 271
Hudsonville (city) Ottawa County, 370
Hulbert (township) Chippewa County, 130
Humboldt (township) Marquette County, 286
Hume (township) Huron County, 191
Huntington Woods (city) Oakland County, 339
Huron (township) Huron County, 191
Huron (charter township) Wayne County, 444
Huron County, 188
Ida (township) Monroe County, 309
Idlewild (unincorporated) Lake County, 246
Imlay (township) Lapeer County, 251
Imlay City (city) Lapeer County, 251
Independence (charter township) Oakland County, 339
Indian River (CDP) Cheboygan County, 126
Indianfields (township) Tuscola County, 418
Ingalls (unincorporated) Menominee County, 299
Ingallston (township) Menominee County, 299
Ingersoll (township) Midland County, 302
Ingham (township) Ingham County, 196
Ingham County, 194
Inkster (city) Wayne County, 444
Inland (township) Benzie County, 96
Interior (township) Ontonagon County, 358
Interlochen (CDP) Grand Traverse County, 173
Inverness (township) Cheboygan County, 126
Inwood (township) Schoolcraft County, 409
Ionia (township) Ionia County, 203
Ionia (city) Ionia County, 202
Ionia County, 200
Iosco (township) Livingston County, 267
Iosco County, 205
Ira (township) Saint Clair County, 393
Iron County, 209
Iron Mountain (city) Dickinson County, 145
Iron River (township) Iron County, 210
Iron River (city) Iron County, 210
Irons (unincorporated) Lake County, 247
Ironton (CDP) Charlevoix County, 123

CDP = Census Designated Place

CDP = Census Designated Place

Manistee Lake (CDP) Kalkaska County, 231
Manistique (township) Schoolcraft County, 409
Manistique (city) Schoolcraft County, 409
Manitou Beach-Devils Lake (CDP) Lenawee County, 261
Manlius (township) Allegan County, 71
Mansfield (township) Iron County, 210
Manton (city) Wexford County, 454
Maple City (CDP) Leelanau County, 256
Maple Forest (township) Crawford County, 140
Maple Grove (township) Barry County, 88
Maple Grove (CDP) Benzie County, 97
Maple Grove (township) Manistee County, 283
Maple Grove (township) Saginaw County, 384
Maple Rapids (village) Clinton County, 138
Maple Ridge (township) Alpena County, 77
Maple Ridge (township) Delta County, 143
Maple River (township) Emmet County, 155
Maple Valley (township) Montcalm County, 317
Maple Valley (township) Sanilac County, 406
Marathon (township) Lapeer County, 252
Marcellus (township) Cass County, 119
Marcellus (village) Cass County, 119
Marengo (township) Calhoun County, 115
Marenisco (township) Gogebic County, 170
Marenisco (CDP) Gogebic County, 170
Marilla (township) Manistee County, 283
Marine City (city) Saint Clair County, 394
Marion (township) Charlevoix County, 124
Marion (township) Livingston County, 268
Marion (township) Osceola County, 361
Marion (village) Osceola County, 361
Marion (township) Saginaw County, 385
Marion (township) Sanilac County, 406
Markey (township) Roscommon County, 379
Marlette (township) Sanilac County, 406
Marlette (city) Sanilac County, 406
Marne (unincorporated) Ottawa County, 371
Marquette (township) Mackinac County, 272
Marquette (charter township) Marquette County, 287
Marquette (city) Marquette County, 288
Marquette County, 284
Marshall (township) Calhoun County, 115
Marshall (city) Calhoun County, 115
Martin (township) Allegan County, 71
Martin (village) Allegan County, 72
Martiny (township) Mecosta County, 296
Marysville (city) Saint Clair County, 394
Mason (township) Arenac County, 81
Mason (township) Cass County, 119
Mason (city) Ingham County, 198
Mason County, 290
Masonville (township) Delta County, 143
Mass City (unincorporated) Ontonagon County, 358
Mastodon (township) Iron County, 210
Matchwood (township) Ontonagon County, 358
Mathias (township) Alger County, 66
Mattawan (village) Van Buren County, 425
Matteson (township) Branch County, 109
Maybee (village) Monroe County, 310
Mayfield (township) Grand Traverse County, 174
Mayfield (township) Lapeer County, 252
Mayville (village) Tuscola County, 419
McBain (city) Missaukee County, 306
McBride (village) Montcalm County, 317
McKinley (township) Emmet County, 155
McKinley (township) Huron County, 191
McMillan (township) Luce County, 270
McMillan (township) Ontonagon County, 358
Meade (township) Huron County, 191
Meade (township) Mason County, 292
Mears (unincorporated) Oceana County, 353

Mecosta (township) Mecosta County, 296
Mecosta (village) Mecosta County, 296
Mecosta County, 293
Medina (township) Lenawee County, 261
Mellen (township) Menominee County, 299
Melrose (township) Charlevoix County, 124
Melvin (village) Sanilac County, 406
Melvindale (city) Wayne County, 445
Memphis (city) Macomb County, 276
Mendon (township) Saint Joseph County, 400
Mendon (village) Saint Joseph County, 401
Menominee (township) Menominee County, 299
Menominee (city) Menominee County, 299
Menominee County, 297
Mentor (township) Cheboygan County, 127
Mentor (township) Oscoda County, 363
Meridian (charter township) Ingham County, 198
Merrill (township) Newaygo County, 331
Merrill (village) Saginaw County, 385
Merritt (township) Bay County, 93
Mesick (village) Wexford County, 454
Metamora (township) Lapeer County, 252
Metamora (village) Lapeer County, 253
Metz (township) Presque Isle County, 376
Meyer (township) Menominee County, 300
Michiana (village) Berrien County, 103
Michigamme (township) Marquette County, 288
Michigamme (CDP) Marquette County, 288
Michigan Center (CDP) Jackson County, 218
Middle Branch (township) Osceola County, 361
Middlebury (township) Shiawassee County, 412
Middleton (unincorporated) Gratiot County, 177
Middletown (CDP) Shiawassee County, 412
Middleville (village) Barry County, 88
Midland (charter township) Midland County, 303
Midland (city) Midland County, 303
Midland County, 300
Mikado (township) Alcona County, 64
Milan (township) Monroe County, 310
Milan (city) Washtenaw County, 431
Milford (charter township) Oakland County, 341
Milford (village) Oakland County, 341
Millbrook (township) Mecosta County, 296
Millen (township) Alcona County, 65
Millersburg (village) Presque Isle County, 376
Millington (township) Tuscola County, 419
Millington (village) Tuscola County, 419
Mills (township) Midland County, 303
Mills (township) Ogemaw County, 355
Milton (township) Antrim County, 80
Milton (township) Cass County, 119
Minden (township) Sanilac County, 406
Minden City (village) Sanilac County, 406
Mio (CDP) Oscoda County, 363
Missaukee County, 304
Mitchell (township) Alcona County, 65
Moffatt (township) Arenac County, 82
Mohawk (unincorporated) Keweenaw County, 245
Moline (unincorporated) Allegan County, 72
Moltke (township) Presque Isle County, 376
Monitor (charter township) Bay County, 93
Monroe (charter township) Monroe County, 310
Monroe (city) Monroe County, 311
Monroe (township) Newaygo County, 331
Monroe County, 306
Montague (township) Muskegon County, 324
Montague (city) Muskegon County, 324
Montcalm (township) Montcalm County, 317
Montcalm County, 313
Monterey (township) Allegan County, 72
Montgomery (village) Hillsdale County, 182
Montmorency (township) Montmorency County, 321

Montmorency County, 319
Montrose (charter township) Genesee County, 164
Montrose (city) Genesee County, 164
Moore (township) Sanilac County, 406
Moorland (township) Muskegon County, 324
Moran (township) Mackinac County, 272
Morenci (city) Lenawee County, 261
Morley (village) Mecosta County, 296
Morrice (village) Shiawassee County, 412
Morton (township) Mecosta County, 296
Moscow (township) Hillsdale County, 182
Mottville (township) Saint Joseph County, 401
Mount Clemens (city) Macomb County, 277
Mount Forest (township) Bay County, 93
Mount Haley (township) Midland County, 304
Mount Morris (township) Genesee County, 164
Mount Morris (city) Genesee County, 164
Mount Pleasant (city) Isabella County, 213
Mueller (township) Schoolcraft County, 409
Muir (village) Ionia County, 204
Mullett (township) Cheboygan County, 127
Mulliken (village) Eaton County, 150
Mundy (township) Genesee County, 165
Munger (unincorporated) Bay County, 93
Munising (township) Alger County, 66
Munising (city) Alger County, 66
Munith (unincorporated) Jackson County, 219
Munro (township) Cheboygan County, 127
Muskegon (charter township) Muskegon County, 324
Muskegon (city) Muskegon County, 325
Muskegon County, 321
Muskegon Heights (city) Muskegon County, 325
Mussey (township) Saint Clair County, 395
Nadeau (township) Menominee County, 300
Nahma (township) Delta County, 143
Napoleon (township) Jackson County, 219
Napoleon (CDP) Jackson County, 219
Nashville (village) Barry County, 88
National City (unincorporated) Iosco County, 207
Naubinway (unincorporated) Mackinac County, 272
Nazareth (unincorporated) Kalamazoo County, 226
Negaunee (township) Marquette County, 289
Negaunee (city) Marquette County, 288
Nelson (township) Kent County, 241
Nessen City (CDP) Benzie County, 97
Nester (township) Roscommon County, 379
New Baltimore (city) Macomb County, 277
New Boston (unincorporated) Wayne County, 446
New Buffalo (township) Berrien County, 103
New Buffalo (city) Berrien County, 103
New Era (village) Oceana County, 353
New Haven (township) Gratiot County, 178
New Haven (village) Macomb County, 277
New Haven (township) Shiawassee County, 412
New Hudson (unincorporated) Oakland County, 342
New Lothrop (village) Shiawassee County, 412
New Troy (CDP) Berrien County, 103
Newark (township) Gratiot County, 178
Newaygo (city) Newaygo County, 331
Newaygo County, 327
Newberg (township) Cass County, 119
Newberry (village) Luce County, 270
Newfield (township) Oceana County, 353
Newkirk (township) Lake County, 247
Newport (unincorporated) Monroe County, 311
Newton (township) Calhoun County, 116
Newton (township) Mackinac County, 272

CDP = Census Designated Place

Niles (township) Berrien County, 104
Niles (city) Berrien County, 103
Nisula (unincorporated) Houghton County, 187
Noble (township) Branch County, 109
Norman (township) Manistee County, 284
North Adams (village) Hillsdale County, 182
North Allis (township) Presque Isle County, 376
North Branch (township) Lapeer County, 253
North Branch (village) Lapeer County, 253
North Muskegon (city) Muskegon County, 325
North Plains (township) Ionia County, 204
North Shade (township) Gratiot County, 178
North Star (township) Gratiot County, 178
North Street (unincorporated) Saint Clair County, 395
Northfield (township) Washtenaw County, 431
Northport (village) Leelanau County, 256
Northview (CDP) Kent County, 241
Northville (city) Oakland County, 342
Northville (township) Wayne County, 446
Norton Shores (city) Muskegon County, 326
Norvell (township) Jackson County, 219
Norway (township) Dickinson County, 146
Norway (city) Dickinson County, 146
Norwich (township) Missaukee County, 306
Norwich (township) Newaygo County, 331
Norwood (township) Charlevoix County, 124
Norwood (CDP) Charlevoix County, 124
Nottawa (township) Isabella County, 213
Nottawa (township) Saint Joseph County, 401
Novesta (township) Tuscola County, 419
Novi (township) Oakland County, 343
Novi (city) Oakland County, 342
Nunda (township) Cheboygan County, 127
Nunica (unincorporated) Ottawa County, 371
Oak Hill (CDP) Manistee County, 284
Oak Park (city) Oakland County, 343
Oakfield (township) Kent County, 241
Oakland (charter township) Oakland County, 343
Oakland County, 332
Oakley (village) Saginaw County, 385
Oceana County, 351
Oceola (township) Livingston County, 268
Ocqueoc (township) Presque Isle County, 376
Oden (CDP) Emmet County, 155
Odessa (township) Ionia County, 204
Ogden (township) Lenawee County, 261
Ogemaw (township) Ogemaw County, 356
Ogemaw County, 354
Okemos (CDP) Ingham County, 198
Olive (township) Clinton County, 138
Olive (township) Ottawa County, 371
Oliver (township) Huron County, 192
Oliver (township) Kalkaska County, 231
Olivet (city) Eaton County, 150
Omena (CDP) Leelanau County, 256
Omer (city) Arenac County, 82
Onaway (city) Presque Isle County, 376
Oneida (charter township) Eaton County, 151
Onekama (township) Manistee County, 284
Onekama (village) Manistee County, 284
Onondaga (township) Ingham County, 199
Onota (township) Alger County, 67
Onsted (village) Lenawee County, 261
Ontonagon (township) Ontonagon County, 358
Ontonagon (village) Ontonagon County, 359
Ontonagon County, 357
Ontwa (township) Cass County, 120
Orange (township) Ionia County, 204
Orange (township) Kalkaska County, 231
Orangeville (township) Barry County, 88
Orchard Lake Village (city) Oakland County, 343
Oregon (township) Lapeer County, 253

Orient (township) Osceola County, 361
Orion (charter township) Oakland County, 344
Orleans (township) Ionia County, 204
Oronoko (charter township) Berrien County, 104
Ortonville (village) Oakland County, 344
Osceola (township) Houghton County, 187
Osceola (township) Osceola County, 361
Osceola County, 359
Oscoda (charter township) Iosco County, 207
Oscoda (CDP) Iosco County, 207
Oscoda County, 362
Oshtemo (charter township) Kalamazoo County, 226
Osseo (unincorporated) Hillsdale County, 182
Ossineke (township) Alpena County, 77
Ossineke (CDP) Alpena County, 77
Otisco (township) Ionia County, 204
Otisville (village) Genesee County, 165
Otsego (township) Allegan County, 72
Otsego (city) Allegan County, 72
Otsego County, 363
Otsego Lake (township) Otsego County, 365
Ottawa County, 366
Ottawa Lake (unincorporated) Monroe County, 311
Otter Lake (village) Lapeer County, 253
Otto (township) Oceana County, 353
Overisel (township) Allegan County, 72
Ovid (township) Branch County, 110
Ovid (township) Clinton County, 138
Ovid (village) Clinton County, 138
Owendale (village) Huron County, 192
Owosso (charter township) Shiawassee County, 412
Owosso (city) Shiawassee County, 413
Oxford (charter township) Oakland County, 344
Oxford (village) Oakland County, 344
Painesdale (unincorporated) Houghton County, 187
Palmer (CDP) Marquette County, 289
Palms (unincorporated) Sanilac County, 406
Palmyra (township) Lenawee County, 261
Palo (unincorporated) Ionia County, 204
Paradise (township) Grand Traverse County, 174
Parchment (city) Kalamazoo County, 227
Paris (township) Huron County, 192
Park (township) Ottawa County, 372
Park (township) Saint Joseph County, 401
Parkdale (CDP) Manistee County, 284
Parma (township) Jackson County, 219
Parma (village) Jackson County, 220
Pavilion (township) Kalamazoo County, 227
Paw Paw (township) Van Buren County, 425
Paw Paw (village) Van Buren County, 425
Paw Paw Lake (CDP) Berrien County, 104
Peacock (township) Lake County, 247
Peaine (township) Charlevoix County, 124
Pearl Beach (CDP) Saint Clair County, 395
Peck (village) Sanilac County, 406
Pelkie (unincorporated) Houghton County, 187
Pellston (village) Emmet County, 155
Peninsula (township) Grand Traverse County, 174
Penn (township) Cass County, 120
Pennfield (charter township) Calhoun County, 116
Pentland (township) Luce County, 270
Pentwater (township) Oceana County, 353
Pentwater (village) Oceana County, 353
Pere Marquette (charter township) Mason County, 292
Perkins (unincorporated) Delta County, 143
Perrinton (village) Gratiot County, 178

Perronville (unincorporated) Menominee County, 300
Perry (township) Shiawassee County, 413
Perry (city) Shiawassee County, 413
Petersburg (city) Monroe County, 312
Petoskey (city) Emmet County, 155
Pewamo (village) Ionia County, 205
Pickford (township) Chippewa County, 130
Pierson (township) Montcalm County, 317
Pierson (village) Montcalm County, 317
Pigeon (village) Huron County, 192
Pilgrim (CDP) Benzie County, 97
Pinckney (village) Livingston County, 268
Pinconning (township) Bay County, 94
Pinconning (city) Bay County, 93
Pine (township) Montcalm County, 318
Pine Grove (township) Van Buren County, 426
Pine River (township) Gratiot County, 178
Pinora (township) Lake County, 247
Pioneer (township) Missaukee County, 306
Pipestone (township) Berrien County, 105
Pittsfield (charter township) Washtenaw County, 432
Pittsford (township) Hillsdale County, 182
Plainfield (township) Iosco County, 208
Plainfield (charter township) Kent County, 241
Plainwell (city) Allegan County, 73
Platte (township) Benzie County, 97
Pleasant Lake (unincorporated) Jackson County, 220
Pleasant Plains (township) Lake County, 247
Pleasant Ridge (city) Oakland County, 344
Pleasanton (township) Manistee County, 284
Pleasantview (township) Emmet County, 155
Plymouth (charter township) Wayne County, 446
Plymouth (city) Wayne County, 447
Pointe Aux Barques (township) Huron County, 192
Pointe Aux Pins (unincorporated) Mackinac County, 272
Pokagon (township) Cass County, 120
Polkton (charter township) Ottawa County, 372
Pompeii (unincorporated) Gratiot County, 178
Ponshewaing (CDP) Emmet County, 155
Pontiac (city) Oakland County, 345
Port Austin (township) Huron County, 192
Port Austin (village) Huron County, 192
Port Hope (village) Huron County, 192
Port Huron (charter township) Saint Clair County, 395
Port Huron (city) Saint Clair County, 396
Port Sanilac (village) Sanilac County, 407
Port Sheldon (township) Ottawa County, 372
Portage (charter township) Houghton County, 187
Portage (city) Kalamazoo County, 227
Portage (township) Mackinac County, 272
Porter (township) Cass County, 120
Porter (township) Midland County, 304
Porter (township) Van Buren County, 426
Portland (township) Ionia County, 205
Portland (city) Ionia County, 205
Portsmouth (charter township) Bay County, 94
Posen (township) Presque Isle County, 376
Posen (village) Presque Isle County, 376
Potterville (city) Eaton County, 151
Powell (township) Marquette County, 289
Powers (village) Menominee County, 300
Prairie Ronde (township) Kalamazoo County, 227
Prairieville (township) Barry County, 88
Prescott (village) Ogemaw County, 356
Presque Isle (township) Presque Isle County, 376

CDP = Census Designated Place

CDP = Census Designated Place

CDP = Census Designated Place

Comparative Statistics

This section compares the 100 largest cities by population in the state, by the following data points:

Population

Place	2000 Census	2010 Census	Growth 2000–2010 (%)
Adrian city *Lenawee Co.*	21,574	21,133	-2.0
Allen Park city *Wayne Co.*	29,376	28,210	-3.9
Allendale charter twp *Ottawa Co.*	13,042	20,708	58.7
Ann Arbor city *Washtenaw Co.*	114,024	113,934	-0.0
Auburn Hills city *Oakland Co.*	19,837	21,412	7.9
Battle Creek city *Calhoun Co.*	53,364	52,347	-1.9
Bay City city *Bay Co.*	36,817	34,932	-5.1
Bedford township *Monroe Co.*	28,606	31,085	8.6
Blackman charter twp *Jackson Co.*	22,800	24,051	5.4
Bloomfield charter twp *Oakland Co.*	43,023	41,070	-4.5
Brownstown charter twp *Wayne Co.*	22,989	30,627	33.2
Burton city *Genesee Co.*	30,308	29,999	-1.0
Byron township *Kent Co.*	17,553	20,317	15.7
Canton charter twp *Wayne Co.*	76,366	90,173	18.0
Chesterfield township *Macomb Co.*	37,405	43,381	15.9
Clinton charter twp *Macomb Co.*	95,648	96,796	1.2
Commerce charter twp *Oakland Co.*	34,764	40,186	15.6
Dearborn city *Wayne Co.*	97,775	98,153	0.3
Dearborn Heights city *Wayne Co.*	58,264	57,774	-0.8
Delhi charter twp *Ingham Co.*	22,569	25,877	14.6
Delta charter twp *Eaton Co.*	29,682	32,408	9.1
Detroit city *Wayne Co.*	951,270	713,777	-24.9
East Lansing city *Ingham Co.*	46,525	48,579	4.4
Eastpointe city *Macomb Co.*	34,077	32,442	-4.8
Farmington Hills city *Oakland Co.*	82,111	79,740	-2.8
Flint city *Genesee Co.*	124,943	102,434	-18.0
Flint charter twp *Genesee Co.*	33,691	31,929	-5.2
Forest Hills cdp *Kent Co.*	20,942	25,867	23.5
Frenchtown township *Monroe Co.*	20,777	20,428	-1.6
Gaines charter twp *Kent Co.*	20,112	25,146	25.0
Garden City city *Wayne Co.*	30,047	27,692	-7.8
Genesee charter twp *Genesee Co.*	24,125	21,581	-10.5
Georgetown charter twp *Ottawa Co.*	41,658	46,985	12.7
Grand Blanc charter twp *Genesee Co.*	29,827	37,508	25.7
Grand Rapids city *Kent Co.*	197,800	188,040	-4.9
Hamburg township *Livingston Co.*	20,627	21,165	2.6
Hamtramck city *Wayne Co.*	22,976	22,423	-2.4
Harrison charter twp *Macomb Co.*	24,461	24,587	0.5
Holland charter twp *Ottawa Co.*	28,911	35,636	23.2
Holland city *Ottawa Co.*	35,048	33,051	-5.7
Holt cdp *Ingham Co.*	11,315	23,973	111.8
Independence charter twp *Oakland Co.*	32,581	34,681	6.4
Inkster city *Wayne Co.*	30,115	25,369	-15.7
Jackson city *Jackson Co.*	36,316	33,534	-7.6
Kalamazoo city *Kalamazoo Co.*	77,145	74,262	-3.7
Kalamazoo charter twp *Kalamazoo Co.*	21,675	21,918	1.1
Kentwood city *Kent Co.*	45,255	48,707	7.6
Lansing city *Ingham Co.*	119,128	114,297	-4.0
Lincoln Park city *Wayne Co.*	40,008	38,144	-4.6
Livonia city *Wayne Co.*	100,545	96,942	-3.5

Place	2000 Census	2010 Census	Growth 2000–2010 (%)
Macomb township *Macomb Co.*	50,478	79,580	57.6
Madison Heights city *Oakland Co.*	31,101	29,694	-4.5
Marquette city *Marquette Co.*	19,661	21,355	8.6
Meridian charter twp *Ingham Co.*	39,116	39,688	1.4
Midland city *Midland Co.*	41,685	41,863	0.4
Monroe city *Monroe Co.*	22,076	20,733	-6.0
Mount Morris township *Genesee Co.*	23,725	21,501	-9.3
Mount Pleasant city *Isabella Co.*	25,946	26,016	0.2
Muskegon city *Muskegon Co.*	40,105	38,401	-4.2
Northville township *Wayne Co.*	21,036	28,497	35.4
Norton Shores city *Muskegon Co.*	22,527	23,994	6.5
Novi city *Oakland Co.*	47,386	55,224	16.5
Oak Park city *Oakland Co.*	29,793	29,319	-1.5
Okemos cdp *Ingham Co.*	22,805	21,369	-6.3
Orion charter twp *Oakland Co.*	33,463	35,394	5.7
Oshtemo charter twp *Kalamazoo Co.*	17,003	21,705	27.6
Oxford charter twp *Oakland Co.*	16,025	20,526	28.0
Pittsfield charter twp *Washtenaw Co.*	30,167	34,663	14.9
Plainfield charter twp *Kent Co.*	30,195	30,952	2.5
Plymouth charter twp *Wayne Co.*	27,798	27,524	-0.9
Pontiac city *Oakland Co.*	66,337	59,515	-10.2
Port Huron city *Saint Clair Co.*	32,338	30,184	-6.6
Portage city *Kalamazoo Co.*	44,897	46,292	3.1
Redford charter twp *Wayne Co.*	51,622	48,362	-6.3
Rochester Hills city *Oakland Co.*	68,825	70,995	3.1
Romulus city *Wayne Co.*	22,979	23,989	4.4
Roseville city *Macomb Co.*	48,129	47,299	-1.7
Royal Oak city *Oakland Co.*	60,062	57,236	-4.7
Saginaw city *Saginaw Co.*	61,799	51,508	-16.6
Saginaw charter twp *Saginaw Co.*	39,657	40,840	2.9
Saint Clair Shores city *Macomb Co.*	63,096	59,715	-5.3
Shelby charter twp *Macomb Co.*	65,159	73,804	13.2
Southfield city *Oakland Co.*	78,296	71,739	-8.3
Southgate city *Wayne Co.*	30,136	30,047	-0.3
Sterling Heights city *Macomb Co.*	124,471	129,699	4.2
Summit township *Jackson Co.*	21,534	22,508	4.5
Taylor city *Wayne Co.*	65,868	63,131	-4.1
Troy city *Oakland Co.*	80,959	80,980	0.0
Van Buren charter twp *Wayne Co.*	23,559	28,821	22.3
Walker city *Kent Co.*	21,842	23,537	7.7
Warren city *Macomb Co.*	138,247	134,056	-3.0
Washington township *Macomb Co.*	19,080	25,139	31.7
Waterford charter twp *Oakland Co.*	73,150	71,707	-1.9
Waverly cdp *Eaton Co.*	16,194	23,925	47.7
West Bloomfield charter twp *Oakland Co.*	64,860	64,690	-0.2
Westland city *Wayne Co.*	86,602	84,094	-2.9
White Lake charter twp *Oakland Co.*	28,219	30,019	6.3
Wyandotte city *Wayne Co.*	28,006	25,883	-7.5
Wyoming city *Kent Co.*	69,368	72,125	3.9
Ypsilanti charter twp *Washtenaw Co.*	49,182	53,362	8.5

SOURCE: U.S. Census Bureau, Census 2010, Census 2000

Physical Characteristics

Place	Density (persons per square mile)	Land Area (square miles)	Water Area (square miles)	Elevation (feet)
Adrian city *Lenawee Co.*	2,657.1	7.95	0.15	774
Allen Park city *Wayne Co.*	4,027.8	7.00	0.05	594
Allendale charter twp *Ottawa Co.*	665.2	31.13	0.93	653
Ann Arbor city *Washtenaw Co.*	4,094.0	27.83	0.87	879
Auburn Hills city *Oakland Co.*	1,290.0	16.60	0.04	958
Battle Creek city *Calhoun Co.*	1,228.6	42.61	1.12	840
Bay City city *Bay Co.*	3,436.0	10.17	1.04	594
Bedford township *Monroe Co.*	793.2	39.19	0.17	n/a
Blackman charter twp *Jackson Co.*	758.5	31.71	0.19	n/a
Bloomfield charter twp *Oakland Co.*	1,667.6	24.63	1.36	738
Brownstown charter twp *Wayne Co.*	1,380.2	22.19	8.45	n/a
Burton city *Genesee Co.*	1,284.5	23.36	0.07	774
Byron township *Kent Co.*	562.8	36.10	0.07	748
Canton charter twp *Wayne Co.*	2,497.2	36.11	0.03	679
Chesterfield township *Macomb Co.*	1,573.1	27.58	3.03	607
Clinton charter twp *Macomb Co.*	3,445.0	28.10	0.27	607
Commerce charter twp *Oakland Co.*	1,463.9	27.45	2.45	945
Dearborn city *Wayne Co.*	4,051.8	24.22	0.25	591
Dearborn Heights city *Wayne Co.*	4,919.9	11.74	0.01	620
Delhi charter twp *Ingham Co.*	904.5	28.61	0.42	883
Delta charter twp *Eaton Co.*	998.3	32.46	0.75	866
Detroit city *Wayne Co.*	5,144.3	138.75	4.12	597
East Lansing city *Ingham Co.*	3,573.5	13.59	0.08	856
Eastpointe city *Macomb Co.*	6,307.4	5.14	0.00	614
Farmington Hills city *Oakland Co.*	2,396.0	33.28	0.03	850
Flint city *Genesee Co.*	3,065.4	33.42	0.64	751
Flint charter twp *Genesee Co.*	1,371.4	23.28	0.22	751
Forest Hills cdp *Kent Co.*	525.0	49.27	1.53	630
Frenchtown township *Monroe Co.*	488.5	41.82	1.30	591
Gaines charter twp *Kent Co.*	704.3	35.70	0.06	n/a
Garden City city *Wayne Co.*	4,718.1	5.87	0.00	633
Genesee charter twp *Genesee Co.*	742.6	29.06	1.21	755
Georgetown charter twp *Ottawa Co.*	1,416.3	33.17	0.90	n/a
Grand Blanc charter twp *Genesee Co.*	1,147.0	32.70	0.34	840
Grand Rapids city *Kent Co.*	4,235.6	44.40	0.87	640
Hamburg township *Livingston Co.*	656.5	32.24	3.78	899
Hamtramck city *Wayne Co.*	10,751.0	2.09	0.00	630
Harrison charter twp *Macomb Co.*	1,700.9	14.46	9.31	n/a
Holland charter twp *Ottawa Co.*	1,318.5	27.03	0.46	610
Holland city *Ottawa Co.*	1,992.3	16.59	0.76	610
Holt cdp *Ingham Co.*	1,529.5	15.67	0.20	889
Independence charter twp *Oakland Co.*	991.1	34.99	1.31	n/a
Inkster city *Wayne Co.*	4,057.1	6.25	0.00	627
Jackson city *Jackson Co.*	3,086.6	10.86	0.12	932
Kalamazoo city *Kalamazoo Co.*	3,008.5	24.68	0.43	787
Kalamazoo charter twp *Kalamazoo Co.*	1,876.6	11.68	0.11	787
Kentwood city *Kent Co.*	2,330.1	20.90	0.05	689
Lansing city *Ingham Co.*	3,170.6	36.05	0.63	853
Lincoln Park city *Wayne Co.*	6,478.3	5.89	0.00	587
Livonia city *Wayne Co.*	2,715.8	35.70	0.16	640

Place	Density (persons per square mile)	Land Area (square miles)	Water Area (square miles)	Elevation (feet)
Macomb township *Macomb Co.*	2,196.8	36.23	0.12	627
Madison Heights city *Oakland Co.*	4,190.2	7.09	0.00	630
Marquette city *Marquette Co.*	1,874.4	11.39	8.06	666
Meridian charter twp *Ingham Co.*	1,301.9	30.49	1.08	896
Midland city *Midland Co.*	1,242.4	33.69	1.99	627
Monroe city *Monroe Co.*	2,262.0	9.17	1.02	594
Mount Morris township *Genesee Co.*	682.4	31.51	0.11	771
Mount Pleasant city *Isabella Co.*	3,360.8	7.74	0.09	771
Muskegon city *Muskegon Co.*	2,702.2	14.21	3.91	617
Northville township *Wayne Co.*	1,759.9	16.19	0.38	827
Norton Shores city *Muskegon Co.*	1,032.6	23.24	1.38	610
Novi city *Oakland Co.*	1,824.8	30.26	1.02	909
Oak Park city *Oakland Co.*	5,677.2	5.16	0.00	663
Okemos cdp *Ingham Co.*	1,274.8	16.76	0.15	840
Orion charter twp *Oakland Co.*	1,061.9	33.33	2.63	n/a
Oshtemo charter twp *Kalamazoo Co.*	605.1	35.87	0.13	968
Oxford charter twp *Oakland Co.*	607.6	33.78	1.60	1,056
Pittsfield charter twp *Washtenaw Co.*	1,271.6	27.26	0.07	833
Plainfield charter twp *Kent Co.*	883.2	35.04	1.69	n/a
Plymouth charter twp *Wayne Co.*	1,727.8	15.93	0.10	725
Pontiac city *Oakland Co.*	2,980.0	19.97	0.31	925
Port Huron city *Saint Clair Co.*	3,735.0	8.08	4.18	607
Portage city *Kalamazoo Co.*	1,436.5	32.22	2.94	879
Redford charter twp *Wayne Co.*	4,303.1	11.24	0.00	623
Rochester Hills city *Oakland Co.*	2,163.1	32.82	0.09	820
Romulus city *Wayne Co.*	673.7	35.61	0.35	659
Roseville city *Macomb Co.*	4,813.9	9.83	0.03	617
Royal Oak city *Oakland Co.*	4,856.8	11.78	0.00	663
Saginaw city *Saginaw Co.*	2,971.2	17.34	0.76	581
Saginaw charter twp *Saginaw Co.*	1,667.1	24.50	0.38	581
Saint Clair Shores city *Macomb Co.*	5,139.5	11.62	2.66	581
Shelby charter twp *Macomb Co.*	2,154.4	34.26	0.89	682
Southfield city *Oakland Co.*	2,730.5	26.27	0.01	682
Southgate city *Wayne Co.*	4,389.0	6.85	0.00	591
Sterling Heights city *Macomb Co.*	3,552.9	36.50	0.29	614
Summit township *Jackson Co.*	773.7	29.09	0.92	n/a
Taylor city *Wayne Co.*	2,675.3	23.60	0.04	614
Troy city *Oakland Co.*	2,419.2	33.47	0.17	748
Van Buren charter twp *Wayne Co.*	848.4	33.97	2.09	679
Walker city *Kent Co.*	943.7	24.94	0.54	748
Warren city *Macomb Co.*	3,899.2	34.38	0.08	623
Washington township *Macomb Co.*	708.6	35.48	1.28	702
Waterford charter twp *Oakland Co.*	2,339.2	30.66	4.54	968
Waverly cdp *Eaton Co.*	2,638.5	9.07	0.06	860
West Bloomfield charter twp *Oakland Co.*	2,395.3	27.01	4.26	n/a
Westland city *Wayne Co.*	4,117.3	20.42	0.02	666
White Lake charter twp *Oakland Co.*	895.6	33.52	3.55	1,037
Wyandotte city *Wayne Co.*	4,908.1	5.27	1.74	581
Wyoming city *Kent Co.*	2,927.3	24.64	0.23	643
Ypsilanti charter twp *Washtenaw Co.*	1,782.8	29.93	1.79	725

SOURCE: U.S. Census Bureau, Census 2010

Population by Race/Hispanic Origin

Place	White[1] (%)	Black[1] (%)	Asian[1] (%)	AIAN[1,2] (%)	NHOPI[1,3] (%)	Two or More Races (%)	Hispanic[4] (%)
Adrian city *Lenawee Co.*	84.1	4.4	0.9	0.6	0.0	4.0	18.8
Allen Park city *Wayne Co.*	92.9	2.1	0.8	0.5	0.0	1.6	8.1
Allendale charter twp *Ottawa Co.*	91.1	3.1	1.4	0.4	0.0	2.2	4.6
Ann Arbor city *Washtenaw Co.*	73.0	7.7	14.4	0.3	0.0	3.6	4.1
Auburn Hills city *Oakland Co.*	66.3	18.5	8.9	0.3	0.0	3.4	7.8
Battle Creek city *Calhoun Co.*	71.7	18.2	2.4	0.7	0.0	4.3	6.7
Bay City city *Bay Co.*	89.7	3.5	0.5	0.6	0.0	3.9	8.5
Bedford township *Monroe Co.*	96.5	0.5	0.8	0.2	0.0	1.2	2.5
Blackman charter twp *Jackson Co.*	79.1	16.6	1.0	0.5	0.0	1.9	3.6
Bloomfield charter twp *Oakland Co.*	83.7	6.7	7.2	0.1	0.0	1.9	1.8
Brownstown charter twp *Wayne Co.*	82.4	8.6	5.2	0.4	0.0	2.1	5.2
Burton city *Genesee Co.*	88.1	7.3	0.6	0.6	0.0	2.5	3.1
Byron township *Kent Co.*	92.8	1.6	1.6	0.5	0.0	1.9	4.2
Canton charter twp *Wayne Co.*	72.2	10.2	14.1	0.2	0.0	2.5	3.1
Chesterfield township *Macomb Co.*	90.8	5.3	1.0	0.4	0.0	1.8	2.4
Clinton charter twp *Macomb Co.*	82.1	13.0	1.8	0.3	0.0	2.2	2.4
Commerce charter twp *Oakland Co.*	93.6	1.6	2.4	0.3	0.0	1.6	2.6
Dearborn city *Wayne Co.*	89.1	4.0	1.7	0.2	0.0	4.0	3.4
Dearborn Heights city *Wayne Co.*	86.1	7.9	1.7	0.4	0.0	2.8	4.7
Delhi charter twp *Ingham Co.*	86.8	5.2	2.9	0.5	0.0	3.1	5.3
Delta charter twp *Eaton Co.*	78.6	11.6	3.8	0.5	0.0	3.6	6.2
Detroit city *Wayne Co.*	10.6	82.7	1.1	0.4	0.0	2.2	6.8
East Lansing city *Ingham Co.*	78.4	6.8	10.6	0.3	0.0	2.9	3.4
Eastpointe city *Macomb Co.*	65.6	29.5	1.1	0.4	0.0	2.9	2.1
Farmington Hills city *Oakland Co.*	69.7	17.4	10.1	0.2	0.0	2.2	1.9
Flint city *Genesee Co.*	37.4	56.6	0.5	0.5	0.0	3.9	3.9
Flint charter twp *Genesee Co.*	68.0	25.7	1.9	0.5	0.0	3.1	2.9
Forest Hills cdp *Kent Co.*	93.4	1.2	3.4	0.2	0.0	1.3	1.7
Frenchtown township *Monroe Co.*	93.4	2.1	0.6	0.3	0.0	2.1	4.1
Gaines charter twp *Kent Co.*	80.5	9.3	4.6	0.5	0.0	2.7	6.1
Garden City city *Wayne Co.*	92.5	3.4	0.8	0.4	0.0	2.1	3.3
Genesee charter twp *Genesee Co.*	87.2	8.6	0.2	0.8	0.0	2.5	3.8
Georgetown charter twp *Ottawa Co.*	95.3	1.0	1.3	0.3	0.0	1.5	2.7
Grand Blanc charter twp *Genesee Co.*	82.6	10.7	3.4	0.4	0.0	2.3	3.1
Grand Rapids city *Kent Co.*	64.6	20.9	1.9	0.7	0.1	4.2	15.6
Hamburg township *Livingston Co.*	97.2	0.3	0.6	0.3	0.0	1.3	1.3
Hamtramck city *Wayne Co.*	53.6	19.3	21.5	0.3	0.0	4.7	1.5
Harrison charter twp *Macomb Co.*	89.0	7.4	0.7	0.3	0.0	1.8	2.6
Holland charter twp *Ottawa Co.*	73.5	2.6	9.4	0.5	0.0	3.4	23.4
Holland city *Ottawa Co.*	80.0	3.6	3.0	0.6	0.1	3.4	22.7
Holt cdp *Ingham Co.*	86.3	5.6	3.1	0.5	0.0	3.2	5.4
Independence charter twp *Oakland Co.*	93.0	1.9	1.5	0.3	0.0	2.0	4.5
Inkster city *Wayne Co.*	20.5	73.2	1.6	0.3	0.1	3.6	2.6
Jackson city *Jackson Co.*	71.4	20.4	0.7	0.4	0.0	5.5	5.3
Kalamazoo city *Kalamazoo Co.*	68.1	22.2	1.7	0.5	0.0	4.6	6.4
Kalamazoo charter twp *Kalamazoo Co.*	75.7	16.4	1.3	0.4	0.0	4.1	4.6
Kentwood city *Kent Co.*	70.1	15.4	6.6	0.4	0.1	3.9	8.5
Lansing city *Ingham Co.*	61.2	23.7	3.7	0.8	0.0	6.2	12.5
Lincoln Park city *Wayne Co.*	84.2	5.9	0.5	0.7	0.0	3.2	14.9
Livonia city *Wayne Co.*	92.0	3.4	2.5	0.2	0.0	1.4	2.5

Place	White[1] (%)	Black[1] (%)	Asian[1] (%)	AIAN[1,2] (%)	NHOPI[1,3] (%)	Two or More Races (%)	Hispanic[4] (%)
Macomb township *Macomb Co.*	90.5	3.9	3.1	0.2	0.0	1.6	2.3
Madison Heights city *Oakland Co.*	83.9	6.4	5.8	0.5	0.1	2.7	2.5
Marquette city *Marquette Co.*	91.1	4.4	0.9	1.5	0.0	1.8	1.4
Meridian charter twp *Ingham Co.*	80.0	4.9	10.9	0.4	0.0	2.8	3.8
Midland city *Midland Co.*	92.0	2.0	3.3	0.3	0.1	1.8	2.4
Monroe city *Monroe Co.*	88.4	6.2	0.7	0.4	0.0	3.0	4.1
Mount Morris township *Genesee Co.*	51.7	42.8	0.3	0.7	0.0	3.5	3.3
Mount Pleasant city *Isabella Co.*	87.6	3.9	3.0	2.0	0.0	2.8	3.3
Muskegon city *Muskegon Co.*	57.0	34.5	0.4	0.9	0.0	4.5	8.2
Northville township *Wayne Co.*	82.7	3.6	11.3	0.1	0.0	1.8	2.4
Norton Shores city *Muskegon Co.*	91.8	3.2	1.2	0.8	0.0	2.0	3.8
Novi city *Oakland Co.*	73.0	8.1	15.9	0.2	0.0	2.1	3.0
Oak Park city *Oakland Co.*	37.4	57.4	1.4	0.2	0.0	3.0	1.4
Okemos cdp *Ingham Co.*	76.5	5.1	14.4	0.3	0.1	2.6	3.3
Orion charter twp *Oakland Co.*	92.0	2.6	2.1	0.3	0.0	1.8	4.0
Oshtemo charter twp *Kalamazoo Co.*	80.0	12.2	2.8	0.3	0.0	3.3	4.0
Oxford charter twp *Oakland Co.*	94.9	1.4	1.2	0.3	0.1	1.6	3.1
Pittsfield charter twp *Washtenaw Co.*	66.1	13.2	13.6	0.4	0.0	4.0	6.5
Plainfield charter twp *Kent Co.*	93.7	2.1	1.2	0.3	0.0	2.1	2.6
Plymouth charter twp *Wayne Co.*	92.1	2.2	3.5	0.3	0.0	1.5	2.4
Pontiac city *Oakland Co.*	34.4	52.1	2.3	0.6	0.0	4.5	16.5
Port Huron city *Saint Clair Co.*	84.0	9.1	0.6	0.7	0.0	4.5	5.4
Portage city *Kalamazoo Co.*	86.9	4.9	3.8	0.4	0.0	3.0	3.1
Redford charter twp *Wayne Co.*	66.4	28.9	0.8	0.5	0.0	2.5	2.9
Rochester Hills city *Oakland Co.*	82.1	4.5	10.5	0.2	0.0	1.9	3.1
Romulus city *Wayne Co.*	50.5	43.0	1.1	0.5	0.1	3.9	3.0
Roseville city *Macomb Co.*	83.1	11.8	1.6	0.4	0.0	2.6	2.0
Royal Oak city *Oakland Co.*	90.7	4.3	2.4	0.3	0.0	1.9	2.3
Saginaw city *Saginaw Co.*	43.5	46.1	0.3	0.5	0.0	4.4	14.3
Saginaw charter twp *Saginaw Co.*	83.8	8.8	3.4	0.3	0.1	2.2	6.4
Saint Clair Shores city *Macomb Co.*	92.7	3.9	1.0	0.3	0.0	1.7	1.7
Shelby charter twp *Macomb Co.*	90.9	3.2	3.3	0.3	0.0	1.7	2.4
Southfield city *Oakland Co.*	24.9	70.3	1.7	0.2	0.0	2.4	1.3
Southgate city *Wayne Co.*	88.7	5.5	1.6	0.5	0.0	2.0	6.5
Sterling Heights city *Macomb Co.*	85.1	5.2	6.7	0.2	0.0	2.2	1.9
Summit township *Jackson Co.*	89.6	5.3	1.5	0.3	0.1	2.5	2.7
Taylor city *Wayne Co.*	78.0	15.8	1.8	0.5	0.0	2.6	5.1
Troy city *Oakland Co.*	74.1	4.0	19.1	0.2	0.0	2.0	2.1
Van Buren charter twp *Wayne Co.*	64.6	28.7	2.5	0.5	0.0	2.9	2.7
Walker city *Kent Co.*	91.3	2.8	1.9	0.5	0.0	2.1	4.1
Warren city *Macomb Co.*	78.4	13.5	4.6	0.4	0.0	2.6	2.1
Washington township *Macomb Co.*	94.8	1.6	1.0	0.2	0.0	1.3	3.9
Waterford charter twp *Oakland Co.*	89.2	4.7	1.6	0.4	0.0	2.4	6.4
Waverly cdp *Eaton Co.*	75.2	13.8	4.2	0.5	0.0	4.0	6.9
West Bloomfield charter twp *Oakland Co.*	77.6	11.4	8.4	0.1	0.0	2.0	1.6
Westland city *Wayne Co.*	75.8	17.2	3.0	0.5	0.0	2.4	3.8
White Lake charter twp *Oakland Co.*	95.3	1.1	0.9	0.4	0.0	1.6	3.0
Wyandotte city *Wayne Co.*	94.7	1.3	0.5	0.7	0.0	1.9	5.1
Wyoming city *Kent Co.*	75.8	7.2	2.8	0.6	0.0	3.8	19.4
Ypsilanti charter twp *Washtenaw Co.*	58.4	32.8	2.1	0.4	0.1	4.6	4.6

NOTE: (1) Exclude multiple race combinations; (2) American Indian/Alaska Native; (3) Native Hawaiian/Other Pacific Islander; (4) May be of any race
SOURCE: U.S. Census Bureau, Census 2010

Average Household Size, Age, and Male/Female Ratio

Place	Average Household Size (persons)	Median Age (years)	Age Under 18 (%)	Age 65 and Over (%)	Males per 100 Females
Adrian city *Lenawee Co.*	2.37	32.5	23.0	14.2	91.4
Allen Park city *Wayne Co.*	2.42	41.7	21.7	17.2	92.7
Allendale charter twp *Ottawa Co.*	3.04	21.1	17.6	4.2	86.0
Ann Arbor city *Washtenaw Co.*	2.17	27.8	14.4	9.3	97.2
Auburn Hills city *Oakland Co.*	2.24	31.4	19.4	9.4	93.8
Battle Creek city *Calhoun Co.*	2.41	36.3	26.1	13.4	91.9
Bay City city *Bay Co.*	2.38	35.8	24.9	12.3	95.0
Bedford township *Monroe Co.*	2.60	42.7	23.6	14.9	95.8
Blackman charter twp *Jackson Co.*	2.23	39.2	16.2	13.7	164.4
Bloomfield charter twp *Oakland Co.*	2.48	48.7	22.5	21.7	93.3
Brownstown charter twp *Wayne Co.*	2.69	37.6	26.4	9.7	95.6
Burton city *Genesee Co.*	2.50	38.6	24.0	13.2	95.3
Byron township *Kent Co.*	2.68	38.8	26.3	14.1	98.4
Canton charter twp *Wayne Co.*	2.75	36.9	27.2	8.9	95.5
Chesterfield township *Macomb Co.*	2.66	38.2	26.1	9.4	96.1
Clinton charter twp *Macomb Co.*	2.29	40.7	20.9	16.2	88.6
Commerce charter twp *Oakland Co.*	2.68	40.2	26.0	10.6	98.9
Dearborn city *Wayne Co.*	2.85	33.0	29.7	12.0	97.8
Dearborn Heights city *Wayne Co.*	2.57	38.3	25.0	16.1	93.6
Delhi charter twp *Ingham Co.*	2.52	37.7	25.5	10.9	93.2
Delta charter twp *Eaton Co.*	2.26	41.4	20.9	15.9	91.5
Detroit city *Wayne Co.*	2.59	34.8	26.7	11.5	89.8
East Lansing city *Ingham Co.*	2.23	21.6	7.5	6.4	94.3
Eastpointe city *Macomb Co.*	2.58	36.3	25.7	11.3	93.8
Farmington Hills city *Oakland Co.*	2.36	42.1	21.5	15.9	89.1
Flint city *Genesee Co.*	2.45	33.6	27.3	10.7	92.2
Flint charter twp *Genesee Co.*	2.34	40.6	23.0	17.2	86.8
Forest Hills cdp *Kent Co.*	2.87	41.2	30.1	11.2	98.0
Frenchtown township *Monroe Co.*	2.53	39.3	23.2	13.4	97.2
Gaines charter twp *Kent Co.*	2.69	34.8	27.5	10.5	96.4
Garden City city *Wayne Co.*	2.54	39.9	22.4	14.0	96.4
Genesee charter twp *Genesee Co.*	2.55	40.8	24.0	15.0	94.9
Georgetown charter twp *Ottawa Co.*	2.81	35.3	27.2	13.0	94.7
Grand Blanc charter twp *Genesee Co.*	2.52	36.8	26.5	12.3	93.3
Grand Rapids city *Kent Co.*	2.49	30.8	24.7	11.1	94.9
Hamburg township *Livingston Co.*	2.69	42.6	25.3	11.0	101.8
Hamtramck city *Wayne Co.*	3.09	28.8	31.7	7.7	106.5
Harrison charter twp *Macomb Co.*	2.21	43.5	19.2	13.7	97.1
Holland charter twp *Ottawa Co.*	2.85	32.0	30.3	8.9	99.7
Holland city *Ottawa Co.*	2.52	31.7	24.0	13.7	90.6
Holt cdp *Ingham Co.*	2.52	37.0	25.7	10.6	92.6
Independence charter twp *Oakland Co.*	2.69	40.6	26.4	11.5	97.7
Inkster city *Wayne Co.*	2.56	34.2	27.9	11.3	88.1
Jackson city *Jackson Co.*	2.46	32.2	28.5	10.3	91.2
Kalamazoo city *Kalamazoo Co.*	2.29	26.2	20.5	9.4	97.4
Kalamazoo charter twp *Kalamazoo Co.*	2.32	33.3	22.3	12.9	96.0
Kentwood city *Kent Co.*	2.45	34.3	25.4	11.5	92.2
Lansing city *Ingham Co.*	2.33	32.2	24.2	9.7	93.8
Lincoln Park city *Wayne Co.*	2.55	36.7	24.8	11.5	96.2
Livonia city *Wayne Co.*	2.47	44.5	20.8	17.7	93.6

Place	Average Household Size (persons)	Median Age (years)	Age Under 18 (%)	Age 65 and Over (%)	Males per 100 Females
Macomb township *Macomb Co.*	2.99	37.4	29.1	9.3	98.1
Madison Heights city *Oakland Co.*	2.32	38.3	20.4	13.9	96.3
Marquette city *Marquette Co.*	2.05	29.1	12.2	13.0	107.7
Meridian charter twp *Ingham Co.*	2.26	38.2	20.8	13.3	90.7
Midland city *Midland Co.*	2.33	38.3	23.4	15.6	92.6
Monroe city *Monroe Co.*	2.44	36.3	26.2	13.3	88.8
Mount Morris township *Genesee Co.*	2.61	37.0	27.4	14.3	92.2
Mount Pleasant city *Isabella Co.*	2.35	22.0	11.0	7.2	90.0
Muskegon city *Muskegon Co.*	2.38	34.1	23.3	11.6	108.9
Northville township *Wayne Co.*	2.47	42.4	24.4	15.3	91.8
Norton Shores city *Muskegon Co.*	2.39	43.3	22.0	17.8	94.4
Novi city *Oakland Co.*	2.46	39.1	25.5	11.3	93.7
Oak Park city *Oakland Co.*	2.50	37.5	24.9	12.9	82.2
Okemos cdp *Ingham Co.*	2.38	37.9	21.3	12.3	92.8
Orion charter twp *Oakland Co.*	2.71	38.6	27.6	9.3	98.3
Oshtemo charter twp *Kalamazoo Co.*	2.21	32.0	18.4	15.2	90.9
Oxford charter twp *Oakland Co.*	2.74	38.4	28.1	10.0	98.0
Pittsfield charter twp *Washtenaw Co.*	2.43	33.8	24.4	7.9	97.5
Plainfield charter twp *Kent Co.*	2.59	39.7	25.1	12.3	94.6
Plymouth charter twp *Wayne Co.*	2.45	44.5	22.3	16.5	94.5
Pontiac city *Oakland Co.*	2.56	33.4	27.2	9.3	96.4
Port Huron city *Saint Clair Co.*	2.42	35.8	25.6	13.1	91.5
Portage city *Kalamazoo Co.*	2.40	38.1	24.8	13.6	92.1
Redford charter twp *Wayne Co.*	2.51	38.0	23.9	12.0	94.8
Rochester Hills city *Oakland Co.*	2.53	40.9	23.7	13.8	93.7
Romulus city *Wayne Co.*	2.64	36.2	26.8	9.8	93.6
Roseville city *Macomb Co.*	2.41	37.9	23.0	13.1	93.8
Royal Oak city *Oakland Co.*	2.03	37.8	16.7	13.1	96.2
Saginaw city *Saginaw Co.*	2.52	33.5	28.4	10.9	89.1
Saginaw charter twp *Saginaw Co.*	2.22	43.1	20.0	19.7	88.3
Saint Clair Shores city *Macomb Co.*	2.24	44.2	19.0	19.2	91.5
Shelby charter twp *Macomb Co.*	2.60	41.0	22.7	14.5	96.5
Southfield city *Oakland Co.*	2.22	42.0	20.5	16.9	80.8
Southgate city *Wayne Co.*	2.29	40.8	20.3	16.3	91.5
Sterling Heights city *Macomb Co.*	2.61	40.4	21.7	15.2	94.1
Summit township *Jackson Co.*	2.42	42.8	23.1	18.5	91.9
Taylor city *Wayne Co.*	2.56	36.9	24.7	12.8	91.8
Troy city *Oakland Co.*	2.63	41.8	23.8	13.8	97.0
Van Buren charter twp *Wayne Co.*	2.42	36.5	23.9	8.8	93.7
Walker city *Kent Co.*	2.40	34.6	22.9	12.1	95.0
Warren city *Macomb Co.*	2.49	39.4	22.7	16.1	93.8
Washington township *Macomb Co.*	2.70	41.3	25.0	14.1	95.9
Waterford charter twp *Oakland Co.*	2.40	39.1	23.0	12.5	96.1
Waverly cdp *Eaton Co.*	2.15	40.7	19.7	16.4	89.6
West Bloomfield charter twp *Oakland Co.*	2.66	44.6	23.6	17.4	93.3
Westland city *Wayne Co.*	2.31	38.3	22.1	14.0	90.4
White Lake charter twp *Oakland Co.*	2.66	41.3	24.6	11.4	98.7
Wyandotte city *Wayne Co.*	2.35	40.4	21.4	13.8	95.8
Wyoming city *Kent Co.*	2.66	32.1	27.1	9.0	97.3
Ypsilanti charter twp *Washtenaw Co.*	2.49	33.3	26.2	8.5	93.4

SOURCE: U.S. Census Bureau, Census 2010

Foreign Born, Language Spoken, Disabled Persons, and Veterans

Place	Foreign Born (%)	Speak English Only at Home (%)	With a Disability (%)	Veterans (%)
Adrian city *Lenawee Co.*	2.80	90.7	18.4	8.9
Allen Park city *Wayne Co.*	4.80	90.9	14.5	9.8
Allendale charter twp *Ottawa Co.*	3.10	94.3	4.8	2.9
Ann Arbor city *Washtenaw Co.*	17.40	78.9	6.5	4.0
Auburn Hills city *Oakland Co.*	15.90	80.8	9.8	7.1
Battle Creek city *Calhoun Co.*	6.00	90.5	16.2	11.1
Bay City city *Bay Co.*	1.20	96.0	16.5	9.9
Bedford township *Monroe Co.*	2.20	96.7	9.0	9.9
Blackman charter twp *Jackson Co.*	0.90	95.7	19.0	10.7
Bloomfield charter twp *Oakland Co.*	14.40	83.0	8.7	7.3
Brownstown charter twp *Wayne Co.*	8.70	87.9	12.0	9.1
Burton city *Genesee Co.*	1.20	97.9	17.4	9.6
Byron township *Kent Co.*	4.20	93.4	10.0	9.6
Canton charter twp *Wayne Co.*	15.80	80.4	7.2	7.1
Chesterfield township *Macomb Co.*	4.40	93.8	10.2	8.6
Clinton charter twp *Macomb Co.*	7.30	90.2	15.1	9.2
Commerce charter twp *Oakland Co.*	8.60	88.6	9.5	7.8
Dearborn city *Wayne Co.*	26.90	53.2	12.3	6.0
Dearborn Heights city *Wayne Co.*	17.10	72.6	14.0	8.0
Delhi charter twp *Ingham Co.*	5.20	92.2	11.4	10.3
Delta charter twp *Eaton Co.*	6.50	89.3	12.4	9.9
Detroit city *Wayne Co.*	5.10	90.4	19.5	6.8
East Lansing city *Ingham Co.*	14.90	82.8	5.1	2.4
Eastpointe city *Macomb Co.*	3.20	94.1	16.2	7.4
Farmington Hills city *Oakland Co.*	17.60	78.8	10.9	7.8
Flint city *Genesee Co.*	1.20	97.4	20.6	7.9
Flint charter twp *Genesee Co.*	4.20	94.2	17.0	8.9
Forest Hills cdp *Kent Co.*	5.50	93.8	5.2	6.7
Frenchtown township *Monroe Co.*	2.40	96.1	16.9	10.3
Gaines charter twp *Kent Co.*	4.90	91.8	12.0	8.7
Garden City city *Wayne Co.*	3.20	95.8	14.4	10.2
Genesee charter twp *Genesee Co.*	1.50	97.5	19.4	12.0
Georgetown charter twp *Ottawa Co.*	3.10	96.3	8.7	7.2
Grand Blanc charter twp *Genesee Co.*	6.30	92.5	9.9	9.6
Grand Rapids city *Kent Co.*	10.10	84.5	11.9	6.7
Hamburg township *Livingston Co.*	2.60	96.0	9.7	8.3
Hamtramck city *Wayne Co.*	44.40	36.2	15.2	3.0
Harrison charter twp *Macomb Co.*	4.20	94.1	13.7	11.4
Holland charter twp *Ottawa Co.*	14.70	74.4	9.8	6.1
Holland city *Ottawa Co.*	12.50	76.2	11.0	6.1
Holt cdp *Ingham Co.*	4.80	92.7	11.3	10.3
Independence charter twp *Oakland Co.*	3.90	95.3	9.2	7.6
Inkster city *Wayne Co.*	3.20	94.5	22.2	7.4
Jackson city *Jackson Co.*	1.90	96.0	17.8	7.5
Kalamazoo city *Kalamazoo Co.*	6.30	89.3	13.1	5.4
Kalamazoo charter twp *Kalamazoo Co.*	3.40	94.2	13.9	9.0
Kentwood city *Kent Co.*	13.50	81.4	11.7	7.4
Lansing city *Ingham Co.*	8.10	87.0	16.5	7.5
Lincoln Park city *Wayne Co.*	6.30	86.9	19.0	9.1
Livonia city *Wayne Co.*	7.00	91.1	11.6	9.2

Place	Foreign Born (%)	Speak English Only at Home (%)	With a Disability (%)	Veterans (%)
Macomb township *Macomb Co.*	10.40	85.3	7.8	6.9
Madison Heights city *Oakland Co.*	17.80	80.2	15.4	7.4
Marquette city *Marquette Co.*	1.50	95.4	10.0	8.8
Meridian charter twp *Ingham Co.*	12.80	84.9	8.5	8.1
Midland city *Midland Co.*	6.50	92.4	12.5	7.9
Monroe city *Monroe Co.*	3.00	94.5	14.8	9.5
Mount Morris township *Genesee Co.*	1.80	97.6	19.6	9.7
Mount Pleasant city *Isabella Co.*	5.60	92.2	10.1	4.0
Muskegon city *Muskegon Co.*	2.40	94.0	19.0	8.1
Northville township *Wayne Co.*	15.60	79.9	8.0	7.7
Norton Shores city *Muskegon Co.*	3.20	95.3	12.3	11.1
Novi city *Oakland Co.*	19.10	77.8	7.7	6.8
Oak Park city *Oakland Co.*	9.90	88.2	15.5	7.4
Okemos cdp *Ingham Co.*	14.60	82.3	7.4	7.8
Orion charter twp *Oakland Co.*	6.90	91.2	8.3	6.7
Oshtemo charter twp *Kalamazoo Co.*	6.50	91.9	12.7	7.9
Oxford charter twp *Oakland Co.*	3.90	95.7	10.2	7.2
Pittsfield charter twp *Washtenaw Co.*	18.30	77.5	6.4	5.4
Plainfield charter twp *Kent Co.*	2.30	95.9	10.1	9.0
Plymouth charter twp *Wayne Co.*	7.50	91.1	7.9	8.5
Pontiac city *Oakland Co.*	6.60	84.0	18.6	7.6
Port Huron city *Saint Clair Co.*	3.70	95.7	20.5	9.8
Portage city *Kalamazoo Co.*	5.00	93.8	11.3	8.4
Redford charter twp *Wayne Co.*	2.30	95.7	15.0	9.8
Rochester Hills city *Oakland Co.*	15.60	82.0	9.2	6.3
Romulus city *Wayne Co.*	4.40	93.5	20.0	9.8
Roseville city *Macomb Co.*	3.60	93.7	17.1	7.9
Royal Oak city *Oakland Co.*	7.30	92.7	9.9	6.3
Saginaw city *Saginaw Co.*	1.50	93.4	19.8	8.8
Saginaw charter twp *Saginaw Co.*	5.00	92.6	12.5	10.1
Saint Clair Shores city *Macomb Co.*	4.90	93.4	15.1	10.6
Shelby charter twp *Macomb Co.*	13.20	83.9	10.6	8.4
Southfield city *Oakland Co.*	9.40	89.3	15.5	8.3
Southgate city *Wayne Co.*	5.30	91.3	15.5	9.5
Sterling Heights city *Macomb Co.*	24.20	69.6	12.8	7.4
Summit township *Jackson Co.*	3.80	94.8	13.8	10.8
Taylor city *Wayne Co.*	4.50	93.5	18.0	9.1
Troy city *Oakland Co.*	27.20	68.6	8.3	5.5
Van Buren charter twp *Wayne Co.*	4.20	94.7	12.0	9.0
Walker city *Kent Co.*	3.80	93.9	11.1	7.6
Warren city *Macomb Co.*	11.40	85.0	15.9	8.7
Washington township *Macomb Co.*	10.50	87.1	9.3	8.1
Waterford charter twp *Oakland Co.*	5.30	92.8	12.8	8.4
Waverly cdp *Eaton Co.*	6.50	88.9	13.7	10.3
West Bloomfield charter twp *Oakland Co.*	21.30	73.2	9.8	6.4
Westland city *Wayne Co.*	6.50	91.3	15.6	8.3
White Lake charter twp *Oakland Co.*	3.40	95.2	11.6	8.8
Wyandotte city *Wayne Co.*	2.30	92.6	17.1	8.6
Wyoming city *Kent Co.*	10.80	81.5	10.9	6.8
Ypsilanti charter twp *Washtenaw Co.*	5.70	92.5	11.7	7.6

SOURCE: U.S. Census Bureau, American Community Survey, 2009-2013 Five-Year Estimates

Five Largest Ancestry Groups

Place	Group 1	Group 2	Group 3	Group 4	Group 5
Adrian city *Lenawee Co.*	German (23.6%)	Irish (12.6%)	English (9.0%)	Polish (5.0%)	American (4.6%)
Allen Park city *Wayne Co.*	German (22.6%)	Polish (17.6%)	Irish (13.8%)	English (11.5%)	Italian (9.4%)
Allendale charter twp *Ottawa Co.*	German (26.1%)	Dutch (25.8%)	Irish (12.3%)	Polish (8.1%)	English (7.8%)
Ann Arbor city *Washtenaw Co.*	German (18.3%)	English (10.5%)	Irish (9.8%)	Polish (6.7%)	American (5.1%)
Auburn Hills city *Oakland Co.*	German (18.9%)	Irish (11.0%)	Polish (9.2%)	English (8.4%)	Italian (4.8%)
Battle Creek city *Calhoun Co.*	German (19.2%)	English (11.9%)	Irish (10.9%)	American (6.0%)	Polish (3.8%)
Bay City city *Bay Co.*	German (26.7%)	Polish (19.5%)	French (12.3%)	Irish (10.7%)	English (6.7%)
Bedford township *Monroe Co.*	German (35.3%)	Polish (16.4%)	Irish (14.0%)	English (11.1%)	French (9.3%)
Blackman charter twp *Jackson Co.*	German (23.2%)	Irish (14.7%)	English (12.5%)	Polish (8.5%)	American (7.6%)
Bloomfield charter twp *Oakland Co.*	German (18.6%)	Irish (14.4%)	English (10.2%)	Polish (9.3%)	Italian (6.6%)
Brownstown charter twp *Wayne Co.*	German (17.3%)	Polish (12.6%)	Irish (10.8%)	English (9.1%)	American (8.1%)
Burton city *Genesee Co.*	German (19.6%)	Irish (12.6%)	English (10.1%)	American (7.2%)	French (5.9%)
Byron township *Kent Co.*	Dutch (37.3%)	German (23.4%)	Irish (11.7%)	English (8.5%)	Polish (5.1%)
Canton charter twp *Wayne Co.*	German (17.3%)	Polish (12.3%)	Irish (10.4%)	American (9.2%)	English (7.8%)
Chesterfield township *Macomb Co.*	German (26.6%)	Polish (20.4%)	Italian (14.4%)	Irish (12.4%)	American (7.7%)
Clinton charter twp *Macomb Co.*	German (20.4%)	Polish (16.7%)	Italian (14.1%)	Irish (10.3%)	English (6.5%)
Commerce charter twp *Oakland Co.*	German (25.1%)	Irish (14.4%)	Polish (13.2%)	English (11.7%)	Italian (8.1%)
Dearborn city *Wayne Co.*	Lebanese (19.4%)	German (10.0%)	Polish (10.0%)	Other Arab (9.5%)	Irish (7.6%)
Dearborn Heights city *Wayne Co.*	Polish (14.6%)	Lebanese (13.8%)	German (12.5%)	Irish (9.6%)	English (6.1%)
Delhi charter twp *Ingham Co.*	German (26.1%)	English (12.6%)	Irish (11.7%)	American (7.4%)	Polish (5.7%)
Delta charter twp *Eaton Co.*	German (25.6%)	English (13.3%)	Irish (12.1%)	Polish (5.8%)	American (4.7%)
Detroit city *Wayne Co.*	American (1.5%)	German (1.5%)	Irish (1.4%)	Polish (1.4%)	African (1.3%)
East Lansing city *Ingham Co.*	German (22.4%)	Irish (15.1%)	English (10.6%)	Polish (9.6%)	Italian (8.3%)
Eastpointe city *Macomb Co.*	German (16.7%)	Polish (11.0%)	Irish (10.3%)	Italian (10.2%)	English (4.5%)
Farmington Hills city *Oakland Co.*	German (12.8%)	Polish (10.5%)	Irish (8.4%)	English (7.2%)	Italian (4.9%)
Flint city *Genesee Co.*	German (6.3%)	Irish (5.4%)	English (4.1%)	American (3.7%)	French (1.8%)
Flint charter twp *Genesee Co.*	German (13.6%)	English (8.8%)	Irish (8.4%)	American (4.7%)	Polish (4.0%)
Forest Hills cdp *Kent Co.*	German (27.5%)	Dutch (20.7%)	Irish (16.1%)	English (15.0%)	Polish (6.3%)
Frenchtown township *Monroe Co.*	German (29.3%)	Irish (13.8%)	American (13.3%)	French (10.7%)	Polish (7.6%)
Gaines charter twp *Kent Co.*	Dutch (28.0%)	German (20.4%)	Irish (9.8%)	English (9.0%)	Polish (7.0%)
Garden City city *Wayne Co.*	German (24.5%)	Polish (19.4%)	Irish (17.0%)	English (10.7%)	Italian (7.0%)
Genesee charter twp *Genesee Co.*	German (19.0%)	Irish (13.2%)	English (10.1%)	American (7.6%)	French (6.2%)
Georgetown charter twp *Ottawa Co.*	Dutch (38.9%)	German (23.6%)	Irish (9.8%)	English (9.2%)	Polish (6.2%)
Grand Blanc charter twp *Genesee Co.*	German (19.5%)	English (10.5%)	Irish (10.0%)	Polish (8.0%)	American (6.0%)
Grand Rapids city *Kent Co.*	German (15.6%)	Dutch (14.7%)	Irish (8.8%)	Polish (7.5%)	English (6.8%)
Hamburg township *Livingston Co.*	German (28.2%)	Irish (18.5%)	English (17.1%)	Polish (13.0%)	Italian (7.1%)
Hamtramck city *Wayne Co.*	Arab (13.3%)	Polish (10.6%)	Other Arab (10.0%)	Yugoslavian (6.6%)	German (3.0%)
Harrison charter twp *Macomb Co.*	German (23.6%)	Polish (17.4%)	Italian (12.7%)	Irish (11.0%)	American (10.6%)
Holland charter twp *Ottawa Co.*	Dutch (26.5%)	German (14.7%)	Irish (7.2%)	English (6.1%)	American (4.3%)
Holland city *Ottawa Co.*	Dutch (24.1%)	German (17.1%)	Irish (7.6%)	English (7.1%)	Polish (4.7%)
Holt cdp *Ingham Co.*	German (26.1%)	English (12.7%)	Irish (12.0%)	American (7.0%)	Polish (6.0%)
Independence charter twp *Oakland Co.*	German (26.3%)	Irish (17.1%)	English (13.1%)	Polish (10.0%)	Italian (6.4%)
Inkster city *Wayne Co.*	German (2.8%)	Irish (2.1%)	Polish (2.0%)	American (2.0%)	African (1.9%)
Jackson city *Jackson Co.*	German (18.6%)	Irish (13.2%)	English (13.1%)	Polish (7.9%)	African (7.9%)
Kalamazoo city *Kalamazoo Co.*	German (18.9%)	Irish (10.9%)	English (9.6%)	Dutch (8.4%)	Polish (5.7%)
Kalamazoo charter twp *Kalamazoo Co.*	German (21.6%)	Irish (13.6%)	Dutch (13.1%)	English (11.0%)	Polish (4.9%)
Kentwood city *Kent Co.*	German (17.0%)	Dutch (15.0%)	Irish (10.0%)	English (7.6%)	Polish (5.0%)
Lansing city *Ingham Co.*	German (18.7%)	Irish (10.0%)	English (8.3%)	Polish (4.4%)	American (4.2%)
Lincoln Park city *Wayne Co.*	German (18.8%)	Irish (15.3%)	Polish (11.1%)	Italian (8.3%)	English (8.3%)
Livonia city *Wayne Co.*	German (20.7%)	Polish (17.5%)	Irish (15.2%)	English (10.7%)	American (8.7%)

Place	Group 1	Group 2	Group 3	Group 4	Group 5
Macomb township *Macomb Co.*	German (20.7%)	Italian (20.7%)	Polish (19.0%)	Irish (9.2%)	American (7.0%)
Madison Heights city *Oakland Co.*	German (18.0%)	Irish (11.8%)	Polish (11.7%)	English (9.7%)	American (6.6%)
Marquette city *Marquette Co.*	German (20.1%)	Irish (11.2%)	English (10.7%)	Finnish (10.7%)	French (8.5%)
Meridian charter twp *Ingham Co.*	German (25.0%)	Irish (14.0%)	English (13.6%)	Polish (6.1%)	American (4.2%)
Midland city *Midland Co.*	German (28.0%)	Irish (13.4%)	English (11.9%)	Polish (7.6%)	American (6.4%)
Monroe city *Monroe Co.*	German (26.4%)	Irish (13.9%)	American (10.6%)	French (9.2%)	Italian (9.2%)
Mount Morris township *Genesee Co.*	German (11.5%)	Irish (7.2%)	English (6.7%)	American (4.4%)	Polish (4.1%)
Mount Pleasant city *Isabella Co.*	German (27.4%)	Irish (15.4%)	Polish (10.8%)	English (10.0%)	Italian (6.4%)
Muskegon city *Muskegon Co.*	German (12.2%)	Irish (6.4%)	English (6.3%)	Dutch (5.3%)	Polish (3.8%)
Northville township *Wayne Co.*	German (18.4%)	Polish (13.6%)	Irish (11.6%)	English (10.4%)	Italian (8.3%)
Norton Shores city *Muskegon Co.*	German (22.8%)	Dutch (15.4%)	Irish (12.6%)	English (11.2%)	Polish (6.8%)
Novi city *Oakland Co.*	German (17.8%)	Irish (12.4%)	Polish (9.9%)	English (9.7%)	Italian (8.1%)
Oak Park city *Oakland Co.*	Polish (4.2%)	German (4.2%)	Russian (3.7%)	Irish (3.6%)	American (2.6%)
Okemos cdp *Ingham Co.*	German (25.4%)	English (13.4%)	Irish (12.9%)	Polish (7.5%)	American (4.5%)
Orion charter twp *Oakland Co.*	German (26.2%)	Irish (17.6%)	Polish (13.0%)	English (11.5%)	Italian (7.4%)
Oshtemo charter twp *Kalamazoo Co.*	German (24.4%)	English (14.3%)	Irish (12.3%)	Dutch (12.2%)	Polish (4.9%)
Oxford charter twp *Oakland Co.*	German (28.6%)	Irish (18.3%)	English (15.6%)	Polish (12.5%)	American (7.3%)
Pittsfield charter twp *Washtenaw Co.*	German (18.7%)	Irish (10.9%)	English (9.9%)	American (6.9%)	Polish (5.9%)
Plainfield charter twp *Kent Co.*	German (26.8%)	Dutch (21.4%)	Irish (15.5%)	English (12.4%)	Polish (11.1%)
Plymouth charter twp *Wayne Co.*	German (24.3%)	Polish (15.4%)	Irish (14.7%)	English (12.7%)	Italian (8.2%)
Pontiac city *Oakland Co.*	German (6.4%)	Irish (5.5%)	English (3.4%)	American (3.1%)	Polish (2.2%)
Port Huron city *Saint Clair Co.*	German (28.8%)	Irish (15.8%)	English (10.8%)	Polish (6.2%)	Italian (5.2%)
Portage city *Kalamazoo Co.*	German (25.4%)	Irish (15.9%)	English (13.8%)	Dutch (12.1%)	Polish (6.1%)
Redford charter twp *Wayne Co.*	German (16.8%)	Polish (12.9%)	Irish (12.0%)	English (7.5%)	American (7.1%)
Rochester Hills city *Oakland Co.*	German (20.5%)	Irish (12.1%)	Polish (11.4%)	English (10.1%)	Italian (7.7%)
Romulus city *Wayne Co.*	German (14.5%)	Irish (11.6%)	Polish (6.5%)	English (4.2%)	Italian (3.7%)
Roseville city *Macomb Co.*	German (23.9%)	Polish (17.2%)	Italian (11.8%)	Irish (11.7%)	English (6.5%)
Royal Oak city *Oakland Co.*	German (24.0%)	Irish (16.0%)	English (12.3%)	Polish (12.3%)	Italian (7.2%)
Saginaw city *Saginaw Co.*	German (14.2%)	Irish (6.3%)	Polish (4.6%)	English (4.3%)	French (3.7%)
Saginaw charter twp *Saginaw Co.*	German (32.5%)	Polish (11.1%)	Irish (10.6%)	English (9.4%)	French (7.1%)
Saint Clair Shores city *Macomb Co.*	German (24.0%)	Polish (18.2%)	Irish (15.2%)	Italian (14.3%)	English (8.4%)
Shelby charter twp *Macomb Co.*	German (19.0%)	Polish (14.9%)	Italian (13.7%)	Irish (10.2%)	American (9.2%)
Southfield city *Oakland Co.*	German (3.2%)	Polish (3.1%)	American (2.6%)	African (2.2%)	Irish (2.0%)
Southgate city *Wayne Co.*	German (20.9%)	Polish (15.5%)	Irish (14.8%)	English (10.0%)	Italian (8.0%)
Sterling Heights city *Macomb Co.*	German (16.3%)	Polish (15.6%)	Italian (9.8%)	Irish (8.6%)	Assyrian (8.0%)
Summit township *Jackson Co.*	German (23.9%)	English (17.1%)	Irish (16.1%)	American (10.5%)	Polish (7.6%)
Taylor city *Wayne Co.*	German (16.8%)	Irish (14.8%)	Polish (10.6%)	English (6.6%)	French (5.6%)
Troy city *Oakland Co.*	German (17.1%)	Polish (11.4%)	Irish (10.4%)	English (8.5%)	Italian (7.0%)
Van Buren charter twp *Wayne Co.*	German (18.0%)	Irish (11.8%)	English (8.2%)	Polish (8.1%)	Italian (4.5%)
Walker city *Kent Co.*	Dutch (25.9%)	German (23.4%)	Polish (16.1%)	Irish (14.4%)	English (9.8%)
Warren city *Macomb Co.*	Polish (17.8%)	German (17.8%)	Irish (10.5%)	Italian (8.9%)	English (6.3%)
Washington township *Macomb Co.*	German (23.7%)	Polish (17.2%)	Italian (14.6%)	Irish (10.7%)	English (8.7%)
Waterford charter twp *Oakland Co.*	German (23.7%)	Irish (15.0%)	English (12.2%)	Polish (10.2%)	American (5.9%)
Waverly cdp *Eaton Co.*	German (23.5%)	English (12.5%)	Irish (11.8%)	Polish (5.1%)	Dutch (4.6%)
West Bloomfield charter twp *Oakland Co.*	German (9.8%)	Assyrian (9.2%)	Polish (9.1%)	Russian (6.6%)	American (6.2%)
Westland city *Wayne Co.*	German (18.2%)	Irish (13.1%)	Polish (12.1%)	English (7.3%)	American (7.3%)
White Lake charter twp *Oakland Co.*	German (25.4%)	Irish (19.9%)	English (13.2%)	Polish (11.4%)	Italian (8.7%)
Wyandotte city *Wayne Co.*	German (21.5%)	Polish (21.0%)	Irish (17.4%)	Italian (8.1%)	English (8.1%)
Wyoming city *Kent Co.*	Dutch (21.1%)	German (18.0%)	Irish (10.8%)	English (7.7%)	Polish (7.1%)
Ypsilanti charter twp *Washtenaw Co.*	German (15.2%)	Irish (9.8%)	American (8.7%)	English (7.0%)	Polish (4.8%)

NOTE: "French" excludes Basque; Assyrian includes Assyrian, Chaldean and Syriac; Please refer to the User Guide for more information.
SOURCE: U.S. Census Bureau, American Community Survey, 2009-2013 Five-Year Estimates

Marriage Status

Place	Never Married (%)	Now Married[1] (%)	Separated (%)	Widowed (%)	Divorced (%)
Adrian city *Lenawee Co.*	43.7	37.6	3.5	6.2	12.4
Allen Park city *Wayne Co.*	29.2	50.0	0.6	9.8	11.0
Allendale charter twp *Ottawa Co.*	59.9	34.0	0.2	1.4	4.7
Ann Arbor city *Washtenaw Co.*	55.1	33.9	0.6	3.3	7.7
Auburn Hills city *Oakland Co.*	37.4	46.1	1.0	4.6	11.8
Battle Creek city *Calhoun Co.*	32.2	45.6	2.5	7.1	15.1
Bay City city *Bay Co.*	36.2	42.3	1.4	6.9	14.6
Bedford township *Monroe Co.*	23.4	60.4	0.9	6.6	9.5
Blackman charter twp *Jackson Co.*	34.3	38.4	2.0	7.6	19.7
Bloomfield charter twp *Oakland Co.*	22.9	63.6	0.6	6.1	7.5
Brownstown charter twp *Wayne Co.*	25.7	57.8	1.7	5.6	10.9
Burton city *Genesee Co.*	30.9	47.9	1.5	7.5	13.7
Byron township *Kent Co.*	23.7	62.7	1.2	4.8	8.7
Canton charter twp *Wayne Co.*	28.0	59.8	1.2	4.2	8.0
Chesterfield township *Macomb Co.*	26.3	57.2	1.2	5.3	11.2
Clinton charter twp *Macomb Co.*	32.0	47.0	1.5	8.1	13.0
Commerce charter twp *Oakland Co.*	22.5	64.2	0.9	4.0	9.3
Dearborn city *Wayne Co.*	30.7	53.3	1.3	6.7	9.4
Dearborn Heights city *Wayne Co.*	31.0	50.0	1.6	8.0	11.0
Delhi charter twp *Ingham Co.*	23.9	59.0	1.0	4.8	12.3
Delta charter twp *Eaton Co.*	29.2	52.0	1.2	6.3	12.5
Detroit city *Wayne Co.*	53.2	27.1	3.7	7.5	12.3
East Lansing city *Ingham Co.*	76.7	17.6	0.5	2.2	3.5
Eastpointe city *Macomb Co.*	38.7	39.6	2.1	7.3	14.4
Farmington Hills city *Oakland Co.*	26.4	56.3	1.3	6.7	10.6
Flint city *Genesee Co.*	48.0	30.1	3.2	6.3	15.7
Flint charter twp *Genesee Co.*	32.9	44.4	3.0	8.7	14.1
Forest Hills cdp *Kent Co.*	18.9	72.3	0.2	3.3	5.5
Frenchtown township *Monroe Co.*	28.7	51.8	2.2	6.7	12.8
Gaines charter twp *Kent Co.*	28.2	57.6	1.6	3.9	10.3
Garden City city *Wayne Co.*	30.7	49.1	1.1	7.6	12.6
Genesee charter twp *Genesee Co.*	29.8	50.3	2.0	6.8	13.2
Georgetown charter twp *Ottawa Co.*	25.2	63.8	0.9	5.5	5.5
Grand Blanc charter twp *Genesee Co.*	26.9	56.6	1.6	5.5	11.1
Grand Rapids city *Kent Co.*	43.7	40.0	2.4	5.4	10.9
Hamburg township *Livingston Co.*	21.4	65.6	0.7	4.1	8.8
Hamtramck city *Wayne Co.*	37.2	49.4	2.4	6.1	7.2
Harrison charter twp *Macomb Co.*	29.4	50.7	1.7	6.4	13.5
Holland charter twp *Ottawa Co.*	28.6	58.9	1.2	3.7	8.8
Holland city *Ottawa Co.*	38.8	46.6	1.2	5.7	8.9
Holt cdp *Ingham Co.*	24.0	58.7	1.0	4.6	12.7
Independence charter twp *Oakland Co.*	27.1	56.8	0.7	4.7	11.4
Inkster city *Wayne Co.*	47.2	30.4	4.1	6.8	15.6
Jackson city *Jackson Co.*	40.1	38.1	2.6	6.4	15.4
Kalamazoo city *Kalamazoo Co.*	55.5	27.9	1.7	4.6	12.1
Kalamazoo charter twp *Kalamazoo Co.*	32.7	45.4	1.4	5.9	15.9
Kentwood city *Kent Co.*	34.9	49.6	1.3	4.8	10.7
Lansing city *Ingham Co.*	43.3	38.3	2.1	4.4	13.9
Lincoln Park city *Wayne Co.*	34.3	43.9	2.2	7.1	14.7
Livonia city *Wayne Co.*	27.2	55.4	0.5	7.2	10.2

Place	Never Married (%)	Now Married[1] (%)	Separated (%)	Widowed (%)	Divorced (%)
Macomb township *Macomb Co.*	25.4	64.2	0.8	4.2	6.3
Madison Heights city *Oakland Co.*	31.3	46.4	1.1	7.7	14.5
Marquette city *Marquette Co.*	51.1	34.6	0.8	4.6	9.7
Meridian charter twp *Ingham Co.*	32.5	52.1	0.8	6.1	9.3
Midland city *Midland Co.*	29.8	51.4	0.9	7.2	11.7
Monroe city *Monroe Co.*	31.3	46.3	1.7	7.7	14.6
Mount Morris township *Genesee Co.*	37.1	40.4	1.7	7.6	14.9
Mount Pleasant city *Isabella Co.*	67.9	21.5	0.5	3.2	7.4
Muskegon city *Muskegon Co.*	43.6	31.7	2.2	6.6	18.1
Northville township *Wayne Co.*	25.3	61.0	0.6	5.7	8.0
Norton Shores city *Muskegon Co.*	25.4	54.6	1.4	6.9	13.1
Novi city *Oakland Co.*	25.5	58.1	1.2	6.3	10.0
Oak Park city *Oakland Co.*	40.3	42.2	1.8	6.1	11.4
Okemos cdp *Ingham Co.*	32.8	54.4	0.6	4.4	8.4
Orion charter twp *Oakland Co.*	25.5	59.6	0.8	4.4	10.5
Oshtemo charter twp *Kalamazoo Co.*	41.0	43.8	1.7	6.4	8.8
Oxford charter twp *Oakland Co.*	20.7	64.2	0.7	5.8	9.3
Pittsfield charter twp *Washtenaw Co.*	38.4	49.1	0.9	3.2	9.2
Plainfield charter twp *Kent Co.*	26.8	58.8	0.8	4.7	9.7
Plymouth charter twp *Wayne Co.*	24.2	62.7	0.2	5.3	7.7
Pontiac city *Oakland Co.*	47.4	31.4	2.5	6.7	14.5
Port Huron city *Saint Clair Co.*	34.4	42.5	1.9	6.9	16.2
Portage city *Kalamazoo Co.*	28.7	55.8	1.6	5.2	10.2
Redford charter twp *Wayne Co.*	36.2	43.2	1.9	7.0	13.5
Rochester Hills city *Oakland Co.*	26.2	59.6	0.6	5.7	8.5
Romulus city *Wayne Co.*	39.3	41.9	1.7	4.9	14.0
Roseville city *Macomb Co.*	36.1	41.7	1.2	7.6	14.6
Royal Oak city *Oakland Co.*	37.8	44.8	0.7	5.4	12.1
Saginaw city *Saginaw Co.*	45.5	31.9	3.1	7.0	15.5
Saginaw charter twp *Saginaw Co.*	28.4	53.0	1.3	8.4	10.2
Saint Clair Shores city *Macomb Co.*	29.1	49.1	0.8	9.0	12.8
Shelby charter twp *Macomb Co.*	26.8	57.8	0.7	6.5	8.9
Southfield city *Oakland Co.*	36.5	40.5	2.3	8.6	14.4
Southgate city *Wayne Co.*	33.2	44.8	1.6	7.8	14.2
Sterling Heights city *Macomb Co.*	29.3	54.8	1.0	7.3	8.5
Summit township *Jackson Co.*	24.9	58.8	1.4	6.5	9.7
Taylor city *Wayne Co.*	35.4	44.1	1.9	6.6	13.9
Troy city *Oakland Co.*	24.4	63.4	0.4	5.1	7.1
Van Buren charter twp *Wayne Co.*	37.2	46.8	1.0	4.7	11.3
Walker city *Kent Co.*	32.6	50.1	0.8	5.8	11.4
Warren city *Macomb Co.*	34.4	46.0	1.4	8.6	11.0
Washington township *Macomb Co.*	23.9	62.3	0.5	3.7	10.2
Waterford charter twp *Oakland Co.*	30.2	50.2	1.5	5.6	13.9
Waverly cdp *Eaton Co.*	30.4	49.7	1.5	6.5	13.4
West Bloomfield charter twp *Oakland Co.*	26.4	58.8	0.7	6.0	8.9
Westland city *Wayne Co.*	35.3	43.0	1.8	7.6	14.1
White Lake charter twp *Oakland Co.*	23.4	62.1	1.2	5.0	9.5
Wyandotte city *Wayne Co.*	30.5	47.4	1.2	8.3	13.8
Wyoming city *Kent Co.*	33.5	51.1	1.9	4.3	11.1
Ypsilanti charter twp *Washtenaw Co.*	41.3	42.3	1.7	4.6	11.7

NOTE: (1) Includes separated.
SOURCE: U.S. Census Bureau, American Community Survey, 2009-2013 Five-Year Estimates

Employment by Occupation

Place	MBF[1] (%)	CES[2] (%)	ELCAM[3] (%)	HPT[4] (%)	S[5] (%)	SO[6] (%)	NRCM[7] (%)	PTMM[8] (%)
Adrian city *Lenawee Co.*	8.7	2.9	10.0	3.9	27.1	24.3	5.4	17.8
Allen Park city *Wayne Co.*	11.3	5.6	8.9	7.6	17.5	24.8	9.2	15.0
Allendale charter twp *Ottawa Co.*	7.7	4.6	10.7	4.9	22.7	26.6	9.2	13.6
Ann Arbor city *Washtenaw Co.*	13.2	15.1	25.1	7.5	15.1	17.0	2.5	4.4
Auburn Hills city *Oakland Co.*	13.3	12.8	11.7	4.9	19.0	23.2	5.1	10.1
Battle Creek city *Calhoun Co.*	11.5	3.6	8.1	5.1	20.4	24.3	6.6	20.4
Bay City city *Bay Co.*	8.7	2.4	7.4	5.5	25.7	27.3	7.2	15.7
Bedford township *Monroe Co.*	12.1	4.6	8.7	6.8	15.7	24.9	9.2	18.0
Blackman charter twp *Jackson Co.*	11.3	3.3	8.6	2.8	23.4	26.1	6.5	18.1
Bloomfield charter twp *Oakland Co.*	28.8	6.0	15.7	12.2	9.2	22.2	2.3	3.5
Brownstown charter twp *Wayne Co.*	14.7	5.1	8.2	7.5	14.8	26.0	9.2	14.6
Burton city *Genesee Co.*	8.5	2.8	8.8	5.9	20.3	26.3	7.6	19.7
Byron township *Kent Co.*	15.4	5.6	8.3	4.3	13.5	26.1	10.8	16.0
Canton charter twp *Wayne Co.*	18.9	12.2	10.0	8.4	13.5	22.7	4.7	9.6
Chesterfield township *Macomb Co.*	13.8	6.5	7.7	5.5	16.7	26.3	7.4	16.0
Clinton charter twp *Macomb Co.*	12.1	4.6	8.4	5.7	20.6	27.2	6.8	14.8
Commerce charter twp *Oakland Co.*	20.1	8.2	8.6	5.1	14.0	28.5	5.4	10.0
Dearborn city *Wayne Co.*	13.0	8.1	11.9	6.6	15.2	25.0	6.1	14.0
Dearborn Heights city *Wayne Co.*	10.0	5.5	9.9	6.1	19.3	26.9	6.4	15.9
Delhi charter twp *Ingham Co.*	17.4	6.5	8.6	7.4	17.2	27.7	4.5	10.6
Delta charter twp *Eaton Co.*	17.2	9.2	10.3	5.4	15.8	27.4	3.8	10.8
Detroit city *Wayne Co.*	7.9	2.0	8.8	3.9	28.9	24.7	6.3	17.4
East Lansing city *Ingham Co.*	11.0	8.1	20.7	3.7	27.4	22.7	2.7	3.7
Eastpointe city *Macomb Co.*	6.4	3.2	6.4	4.0	21.9	32.2	6.6	19.4
Farmington Hills city *Oakland Co.*	19.8	12.3	12.1	7.2	13.6	24.9	3.4	6.8
Flint city *Genesee Co.*	6.1	2.2	9.0	4.4	28.3	24.4	7.0	18.7
Flint charter twp *Genesee Co.*	7.6	3.2	9.8	6.5	25.0	23.8	6.6	17.4
Forest Hills cdp *Kent Co.*	28.2	6.1	12.8	11.5	9.3	23.6	2.4	6.0
Frenchtown township *Monroe Co.*	8.6	3.6	7.8	6.1	19.2	20.8	10.6	23.4
Gaines charter twp *Kent Co.*	13.0	5.3	8.7	5.7	17.4	26.8	5.1	17.9
Garden City city *Wayne Co.*	10.1	3.1	6.6	3.9	17.6	25.8	10.8	22.1
Genesee charter twp *Genesee Co.*	6.8	2.6	4.8	5.6	20.5	28.1	12.5	19.2
Georgetown charter twp *Ottawa Co.*	14.0	5.4	10.6	6.3	15.5	26.2	7.5	14.4
Grand Blanc charter twp *Genesee Co.*	15.4	6.5	11.2	12.3	15.1	23.8	5.0	10.6
Grand Rapids city *Kent Co.*	11.7	4.1	12.6	4.5	19.6	23.4	7.1	17.1
Hamburg township *Livingston Co.*	17.9	7.7	8.8	7.9	13.8	24.0	8.8	11.2
Hamtramck city *Wayne Co.*	5.4	2.7	7.3	3.3	26.4	21.7	6.1	27.0
Harrison charter twp *Macomb Co.*	13.1	5.5	9.5	6.5	17.3	25.5	10.0	12.7
Holland charter twp *Ottawa Co.*	11.0	6.3	7.7	3.1	16.7	18.6	9.5	27.1
Holland city *Ottawa Co.*	9.1	4.7	11.6	3.3	19.6	18.4	8.3	25.1
Holt cdp *Ingham Co.*	18.3	6.7	8.7	7.7	16.2	27.1	4.4	10.8
Independence charter twp *Oakland Co.*	18.1	9.6	9.8	6.4	14.3	26.3	6.0	9.6
Inkster city *Wayne Co.*	4.4	2.6	7.9	4.4	28.3	25.4	5.6	21.4
Jackson city *Jackson Co.*	7.6	2.3	6.8	4.1	26.0	27.5	6.7	19.0
Kalamazoo city *Kalamazoo Co.*	11.1	4.2	12.3	4.7	26.1	25.2	4.8	11.6
Kalamazoo charter twp *Kalamazoo Co.*	11.4	6.0	11.0	4.9	24.3	22.4	7.0	12.8
Kentwood city *Kent Co.*	12.8	6.3	8.6	5.3	16.1	27.7	4.5	18.7
Lansing city *Ingham Co.*	10.4	5.1	11.1	3.8	23.4	25.2	6.1	14.9
Lincoln Park city *Wayne Co.*	6.3	3.3	6.3	3.9	22.1	27.2	10.2	20.7
Livonia city *Wayne Co.*	15.8	8.8	10.3	7.6	15.5	25.4	7.0	9.7

Place	MBF[1] (%)	CES[2] (%)	ELCAM[3] (%)	HPT[4] (%)	S[5] (%)	SO[6] (%)	NRCM[7] (%)	PTMM[8] (%)
Macomb township *Macomb Co.*	17.8	8.6	9.6	6.8	13.7	26.7	5.9	11.0
Madison Heights city *Oakland Co.*	9.4	5.4	6.1	5.0	21.4	29.8	8.2	14.7
Marquette city *Marquette Co.*	9.6	4.5	9.7	8.5	29.7	23.8	7.6	6.7
Meridian charter twp *Ingham Co.*	19.1	11.1	21.2	6.8	13.5	21.7	2.3	4.2
Midland city *Midland Co.*	15.2	11.5	11.8	6.6	17.0	23.1	6.2	8.7
Monroe city *Monroe Co.*	8.4	3.4	8.5	6.1	21.5	23.6	6.1	22.5
Mount Morris township *Genesee Co.*	9.6	1.4	7.3	4.6	26.1	26.9	6.8	17.4
Mount Pleasant city *Isabella Co.*	9.1	3.0	15.9	2.7	32.5	27.6	3.2	6.1
Muskegon city *Muskegon Co.*	5.9	3.4	8.3	4.9	30.4	21.4	5.1	20.6
Northville township *Wayne Co.*	28.3	13.4	11.1	10.2	10.6	18.3	3.4	4.7
Norton Shores city *Muskegon Co.*	12.2	4.3	11.0	6.1	18.1	29.3	4.4	14.5
Novi city *Oakland Co.*	23.9	13.6	10.3	7.8	10.5	25.0	2.6	6.4
Oak Park city *Oakland Co.*	10.7	5.1	13.9	6.1	22.2	26.1	4.9	10.8
Okemos cdp *Ingham Co.*	18.3	12.8	23.4	6.1	14.6	17.7	3.6	3.6
Orion charter twp *Oakland Co.*	18.7	10.4	9.7	5.9	14.1	24.6	5.6	11.1
Oshtemo charter twp *Kalamazoo Co.*	11.5	5.4	13.9	6.8	24.9	23.0	4.4	10.1
Oxford charter twp *Oakland Co.*	18.8	8.8	10.3	5.4	14.6	25.5	5.4	11.3
Pittsfield charter twp *Washtenaw Co.*	17.3	12.7	14.5	9.9	13.6	21.2	3.0	7.8
Plainfield charter twp *Kent Co.*	18.1	4.7	10.8	6.7	16.3	25.7	5.3	12.4
Plymouth charter twp *Wayne Co.*	24.7	10.2	12.5	7.9	11.6	23.1	3.0	7.0
Pontiac city *Oakland Co.*	5.9	2.8	5.9	3.4	31.0	26.0	9.1	15.9
Port Huron city *Saint Clair Co.*	7.2	1.7	7.9	4.5	27.3	25.8	6.2	19.3
Portage city *Kalamazoo Co.*	18.7	7.5	11.1	8.3	12.7	25.2	5.9	10.6
Redford charter twp *Wayne Co.*	10.0	4.5	8.6	4.3	18.0	28.3	8.2	18.1
Rochester Hills city *Oakland Co.*	24.0	12.4	11.7	7.5	12.3	23.2	3.8	5.1
Romulus city *Wayne Co.*	8.2	1.7	3.6	3.9	23.3	24.5	9.0	25.7
Roseville city *Macomb Co.*	8.3	4.2	5.9	3.1	22.8	27.0	9.1	19.5
Royal Oak city *Oakland Co.*	21.7	10.5	13.2	8.6	11.5	24.4	3.6	6.5
Saginaw city *Saginaw Co.*	7.1	2.3	8.4	5.2	30.0	25.0	5.6	16.3
Saginaw charter twp *Saginaw Co.*	11.9	4.6	11.4	9.2	17.8	28.6	5.0	11.4
Saint Clair Shores city *Macomb Co.*	13.7	4.4	8.9	7.3	17.5	26.6	8.8	12.8
Shelby charter twp *Macomb Co.*	17.0	7.5	9.3	5.9	15.3	26.6	6.3	11.9
Southfield city *Oakland Co.*	15.4	5.9	12.4	7.1	17.7	27.1	3.7	10.6
Southgate city *Wayne Co.*	11.0	5.3	6.8	6.5	17.8	28.1	9.4	15.0
Sterling Heights city *Macomb Co.*	13.3	7.4	8.6	5.9	18.0	26.4	6.5	13.9
Summit township *Jackson Co.*	16.2	6.4	11.9	7.2	15.4	22.7	6.3	14.0
Taylor city *Wayne Co.*	8.8	2.8	5.1	3.8	21.6	26.6	9.9	21.4
Troy city *Oakland Co.*	22.6	16.0	12.3	9.3	11.5	19.1	3.3	5.9
Van Buren charter twp *Wayne Co.*	13.2	5.5	7.5	5.8	18.7	25.3	6.7	17.3
Walker city *Kent Co.*	14.3	7.0	10.9	6.9	14.7	24.9	7.6	13.6
Warren city *Macomb Co.*	10.9	4.4	6.2	4.9	20.4	28.4	8.0	16.9
Washington township *Macomb Co.*	18.7	7.3	9.3	6.9	12.0	24.7	8.2	12.8
Waterford charter twp *Oakland Co.*	13.2	7.1	8.8	4.8	19.4	27.7	7.9	11.1
Waverly cdp *Eaton Co.*	17.4	8.9	8.8	4.9	16.1	28.3	3.9	11.8
West Bloomfield charter twp *Oakland Co.*	23.3	8.4	13.3	11.0	8.9	26.6	3.6	4.8
Westland city *Wayne Co.*	10.6	4.8	6.3	5.0	21.8	27.5	7.2	16.8
White Lake charter twp *Oakland Co.*	17.4	8.1	8.8	5.6	16.1	26.5	8.2	9.3
Wyandotte city *Wayne Co.*	9.2	4.7	8.3	6.3	21.7	24.9	9.1	15.8
Wyoming city *Kent Co.*	9.8	3.8	6.6	3.8	18.5	27.8	8.2	21.5
Ypsilanti charter twp *Washtenaw Co.*	9.9	6.9	10.5	6.5	22.6	24.9	5.9	12.8

NOTES: (1) Management, business, and financial occupations; (2) Computer, engineering, and science occupations; (3) Education, legal, community service, arts, and media occupations; (4) Healthcare practitioners and technical occupations; (5) Service occupations; (6) Sales and office occupations; (7) Natural resources, construction, and maintenance occupations; (8) Production, transportation, and material moving occupations
SOURCE: U.S. Census Bureau, American Community Survey, 2009-2013 Five-Year Estimates

Educational Attainment

Place	Percent of Population 25 Years and Over with:		
	High School Diploma or Higher[1]	Bachelor's Degree or Higher	Graduate/Professional Degree or Higher
Adrian city Lenawee Co.	81.2	19.9	8.1
Allen Park city Wayne Co.	90.2	22.7	7.7
Allendale charter twp Ottawa Co.	93.6	25.0	8.3
Ann Arbor city Washtenaw Co.	96.5	70.6	41.7
Auburn Hills city Oakland Co.	90.0	39.9	15.3
Battle Creek city Calhoun Co.	88.3	21.9	8.2
Bay City city Bay Co.	86.1	15.9	4.9
Bedford township Monroe Co.	94.1	25.6	9.7
Blackman charter twp Jackson Co.	86.4	13.0	3.8
Bloomfield charter twp Oakland Co.	97.1	68.9	34.5
Brownstown charter twp Wayne Co.	89.5	23.3	8.5
Burton city Genesee Co.	88.8	14.2	4.3
Byron township Kent Co.	90.7	28.4	8.0
Canton charter twp Wayne Co.	94.5	46.7	18.5
Chesterfield township Macomb Co.	90.1	21.8	6.1
Clinton charter twp Macomb Co.	89.3	20.5	7.2
Commerce charter twp Oakland Co.	93.6	41.0	13.4
Dearborn city Wayne Co.	81.1	28.9	11.4
Dearborn Heights city Wayne Co.	85.2	19.9	7.9
Delhi charter twp Ingham Co.	93.5	32.2	10.7
Delta charter twp Eaton Co.	95.2	36.6	14.0
Detroit city Wayne Co.	77.6	12.7	5.2
East Lansing city Ingham Co.	97.2	68.5	38.3
Eastpointe city Macomb Co.	84.8	13.0	4.9
Farmington Hills city Oakland Co.	93.9	50.8	22.7
Flint city Genesee Co.	81.7	11.0	4.0
Flint charter twp Genesee Co.	87.2	19.1	7.1
Forest Hills cdp Kent Co.	98.2	63.8	27.9
Frenchtown township Monroe Co.	83.6	13.5	5.7
Gaines charter twp Kent Co.	90.6	29.9	10.2
Garden City city Wayne Co.	89.4	12.3	3.2
Genesee charter twp Genesee Co.	85.2	11.6	3.2
Georgetown charter twp Ottawa Co.	95.4	33.6	10.3
Grand Blanc charter twp Genesee Co.	94.8	34.5	13.7
Grand Rapids city Kent Co.	83.9	29.4	10.1
Hamburg township Livingston Co.	95.1	36.8	13.2
Hamtramck city Wayne Co.	64.8	12.4	4.4
Harrison charter twp Macomb Co.	92.0	24.8	10.0
Holland charter twp Ottawa Co.	83.2	23.9	6.8
Holland city Ottawa Co.	84.8	31.0	12.3
Holt cdp Ingham Co.	93.6	32.5	10.8
Independence charter twp Oakland Co.	94.6	38.0	14.5
Inkster city Wayne Co.	79.3	10.1	2.6
Jackson city Jackson Co.	82.9	13.5	4.0
Kalamazoo city Kalamazoo Co.	89.4	31.9	13.4
Kalamazoo charter twp Kalamazoo Co.	90.2	29.8	10.8
Kentwood city Kent Co.	90.9	33.1	10.3
Lansing city Ingham Co.	86.2	24.7	9.0
Lincoln Park city Wayne Co.	80.4	8.1	2.3
Livonia city Wayne Co.	93.2	35.4	11.8

Place	Percent of Population 25 Years and Over with:		
	High School Diploma or Higher[1]	Bachelor's Degree or Higher	Graduate/Professional Degree or Higher
Macomb township *Macomb Co.*	92.2	33.8	11.7
Madison Heights city *Oakland Co.*	83.5	21.9	5.5
Marquette city *Marquette Co.*	93.2	37.0	12.2
Meridian charter twp *Ingham Co.*	97.1	64.8	33.6
Midland city *Midland Co.*	93.6	42.9	17.0
Monroe city *Monroe Co.*	88.6	17.5	7.8
Mount Morris township *Genesee Co.*	84.1	11.5	2.8
Mount Pleasant city *Isabella Co.*	92.7	39.1	20.5
Muskegon city *Muskegon Co.*	82.3	10.9	2.7
Northville township *Wayne Co.*	96.2	58.7	30.1
Norton Shores city *Muskegon Co.*	92.5	29.2	9.3
Novi city *Oakland Co.*	94.7	56.2	24.6
Oak Park city *Oakland Co.*	91.2	28.8	9.6
Okemos cdp *Ingham Co.*	97.9	70.0	37.2
Orion charter twp *Oakland Co.*	94.9	40.3	13.9
Oshtemo charter twp *Kalamazoo Co.*	95.7	44.1	18.3
Oxford charter twp *Oakland Co.*	93.2	34.0	13.6
Pittsfield charter twp *Washtenaw Co.*	94.0	56.4	27.7
Plainfield charter twp *Kent Co.*	95.0	33.2	10.5
Plymouth charter twp *Wayne Co.*	96.4	51.1	22.7
Pontiac city *Oakland Co.*	76.4	11.8	3.0
Port Huron city *Saint Clair Co.*	86.0	14.8	5.5
Portage city *Kalamazoo Co.*	95.7	39.8	14.7
Redford charter twp *Wayne Co.*	89.2	18.2	6.3
Rochester Hills city *Oakland Co.*	95.4	51.7	22.8
Romulus city *Wayne Co.*	85.7	10.1	3.1
Roseville city *Macomb Co.*	85.3	9.8	2.4
Royal Oak city *Oakland Co.*	95.1	50.1	20.5
Saginaw city *Saginaw Co.*	77.8	11.5	3.8
Saginaw charter twp *Saginaw Co.*	92.9	32.9	12.0
Saint Clair Shores city *Macomb Co.*	91.8	24.1	7.4
Shelby charter twp *Macomb Co.*	90.6	30.2	11.5
Southfield city *Oakland Co.*	92.4	36.2	15.5
Southgate city *Wayne Co.*	88.4	16.6	6.0
Sterling Heights city *Macomb Co.*	85.8	25.8	9.2
Summit township *Jackson Co.*	93.9	30.5	10.5
Taylor city *Wayne Co.*	82.3	9.7	2.8
Troy city *Oakland Co.*	94.0	57.6	27.0
Van Buren charter twp *Wayne Co.*	91.1	27.8	9.8
Walker city *Kent Co.*	92.8	28.5	7.7
Warren city *Macomb Co.*	83.8	16.3	4.9
Washington township *Macomb Co.*	93.1	30.7	10.8
Waterford charter twp *Oakland Co.*	90.3	26.0	9.2
Waverly cdp *Eaton Co.*	95.2	35.2	12.1
West Bloomfield charter twp *Oakland Co.*	94.2	56.0	27.4
Westland city *Wayne Co.*	87.7	17.8	5.0
White Lake charter twp *Oakland Co.*	93.4	31.3	10.1
Wyandotte city *Wayne Co.*	86.6	15.8	5.5
Wyoming city *Kent Co.*	85.2	19.4	5.1
Ypsilanti charter twp *Washtenaw Co.*	88.4	28.7	10.0

NOTE: (1) Includes General Equivalency Diploma (GED)
SOURCE: U.S. Census Bureau, American Community Survey, 2009-2013 Five-Year Estimates

Health Insurance

Place	Percent of Total Population with:				Percent of Population[1] Under Age 18 without Health Insurance
	Any Insurance	Private Insurance	Public Insurance	No Insurance	
Adrian city *Lenawee Co.*	84.7	55.3	44.2	15.3	4.8
Allen Park city *Wayne Co.*	90.8	80.5	26.9	9.2	2.9
Allendale charter twp *Ottawa Co.*	91.7	86.9	10.1	8.3	4.6
Ann Arbor city *Washtenaw Co.*	93.8	86.2	17.0	6.2	2.3
Auburn Hills city *Oakland Co.*	84.2	72.5	21.8	15.8	11.7
Battle Creek city *Calhoun Co.*	86.5	58.5	43.0	13.5	3.4
Bay City city *Bay Co.*	86.3	57.2	43.0	13.7	3.1
Bedford township *Monroe Co.*	93.0	83.3	24.2	7.0	3.3
Blackman charter twp *Jackson Co.*	87.4	67.5	37.0	12.6	2.3
Bloomfield charter twp *Oakland Co.*	95.3	88.6	25.6	4.7	2.4
Brownstown charter twp *Wayne Co.*	91.2	80.1	21.6	8.8	4.3
Burton city *Genesee Co.*	89.0	65.4	38.6	11.0	6.7
Byron township *Kent Co.*	93.3	79.2	27.4	6.7	2.9
Canton charter twp *Wayne Co.*	91.5	84.2	16.5	8.5	3.3
Chesterfield township *Macomb Co.*	91.2	78.4	23.9	8.8	1.5
Clinton charter twp *Macomb Co.*	87.4	71.0	33.5	12.6	5.3
Commerce charter twp *Oakland Co.*	92.1	83.4	20.3	7.9	3.6
Dearborn city *Wayne Co.*	85.4	56.4	40.2	14.6	4.9
Dearborn Heights city *Wayne Co.*	84.3	62.7	37.0	15.7	6.8
Delhi charter twp *Ingham Co.*	91.6	80.7	24.7	8.4	2.3
Delta charter twp *Eaton Co.*	92.3	82.8	26.2	7.7	1.7
Detroit city *Wayne Co.*	80.6	39.5	51.7	19.4	5.7
East Lansing city *Ingham Co.*	93.8	88.0	12.9	6.2	2.2
Eastpointe city *Macomb Co.*	87.3	59.8	39.6	12.7	1.9
Farmington Hills city *Oakland Co.*	92.4	82.5	25.2	7.6	3.5
Flint city *Genesee Co.*	86.7	39.3	60.2	13.3	3.0
Flint charter twp *Genesee Co.*	89.9	63.7	44.0	10.1	3.4
Forest Hills cdp *Kent Co.*	96.6	91.7	15.4	3.4	1.7
Frenchtown township *Monroe Co.*	91.1	69.4	38.1	8.9	0.9
Gaines charter twp *Kent Co.*	91.6	75.9	26.1	8.4	2.5
Garden City city *Wayne Co.*	86.9	73.1	28.5	13.1	4.8
Genesee charter twp *Genesee Co.*	89.9	62.8	45.2	10.1	4.9
Georgetown charter twp *Ottawa Co.*	94.7	87.5	21.2	5.3	2.4
Grand Blanc charter twp *Genesee Co.*	92.4	79.8	26.5	7.6	1.7
Grand Rapids city *Kent Co.*	86.4	60.1	37.6	13.6	3.0
Hamburg township *Livingston Co.*	94.8	87.7	18.7	5.2	1.6
Hamtramck city *Wayne Co.*	76.6	34.5	53.1	23.4	6.0
Harrison charter twp *Macomb Co.*	88.7	74.3	29.7	11.3	3.9
Holland charter twp *Ottawa Co.*	90.7	74.6	26.2	9.3	3.0
Holland city *Ottawa Co.*	88.7	68.3	32.9	11.3	3.5
Holt cdp *Ingham Co.*	92.0	80.9	24.3	8.0	2.4
Independence charter twp *Oakland Co.*	93.6	85.2	22.7	6.4	1.4
Inkster city *Wayne Co.*	84.5	41.8	54.1	15.5	4.5
Jackson city *Jackson Co.*	81.4	44.1	47.3	18.6	5.9
Kalamazoo city *Kalamazoo Co.*	85.8	62.7	33.4	14.2	5.2
Kalamazoo charter twp *Kalamazoo Co.*	86.1	66.4	34.0	13.9	5.0
Kentwood city *Kent Co.*	89.0	72.1	27.7	11.0	5.0
Lansing city *Ingham Co.*	87.1	55.8	42.7	12.9	3.6
Lincoln Park city *Wayne Co.*	83.8	58.7	37.5	16.2	4.6
Livonia city *Wayne Co.*	92.5	84.1	25.2	7.5	3.1

Place	Percent of Total Population with:				Percent of Population[1] Under Age 18 without Health Insurance
	Any Insurance	Private Insurance	Public Insurance	No Insurance	
Macomb township *Macomb Co.*	94.3	86.5	18.2	5.7	1.5
Madison Heights city *Oakland Co.*	86.4	64.2	34.3	13.6	4.4
Marquette city *Marquette Co.*	85.6	73.4	25.1	14.4	1.4
Meridian charter twp *Ingham Co.*	92.4	84.3	21.5	7.6	2.5
Midland city *Midland Co.*	90.1	76.5	29.9	9.9	6.4
Monroe city *Monroe Co.*	88.6	65.5	38.3	11.4	2.3
Mount Morris township *Genesee Co.*	88.0	49.8	54.9	12.0	2.9
Mount Pleasant city *Isabella Co.*	87.8	74.4	21.3	12.2	3.1
Muskegon city *Muskegon Co.*	84.4	44.8	50.0	15.6	3.4
Northville township *Wayne Co.*	94.3	88.6	20.0	5.7	2.1
Norton Shores city *Muskegon Co.*	92.8	76.9	34.3	7.2	1.5
Novi city *Oakland Co.*	93.0	86.2	18.3	7.0	2.6
Oak Park city *Oakland Co.*	81.9	60.2	34.4	18.1	8.3
Okemos cdp *Ingham Co.*	94.2	86.5	20.7	5.8	1.6
Orion charter twp *Oakland Co.*	91.9	83.3	17.4	8.1	1.3
Oshtemo charter twp *Kalamazoo Co.*	90.5	74.6	30.3	9.5	4.5
Oxford charter twp *Oakland Co.*	91.7	82.0	21.4	8.3	2.4
Pittsfield charter twp *Washtenaw Co.*	92.7	83.6	17.4	7.3	2.8
Plainfield charter twp *Kent Co.*	92.1	81.4	23.6	7.9	1.4
Plymouth charter twp *Wayne Co.*	94.2	88.1	21.2	5.8	2.8
Pontiac city *Oakland Co.*	80.8	45.0	47.5	19.2	5.8
Port Huron city *Saint Clair Co.*	86.2	53.2	47.9	13.8	1.8
Portage city *Kalamazoo Co.*	90.7	77.7	26.8	9.3	2.5
Redford charter twp *Wayne Co.*	86.3	69.9	30.7	13.7	5.4
Rochester Hills city *Oakland Co.*	92.2	84.9	20.2	7.8	3.4
Romulus city *Wayne Co.*	84.9	60.0	37.1	15.1	3.1
Roseville city *Macomb Co.*	85.7	64.3	35.8	14.3	3.4
Royal Oak city *Oakland Co.*	90.3	82.4	20.8	9.7	4.5
Saginaw city *Saginaw Co.*	84.6	41.5	54.3	15.4	2.8
Saginaw charter twp *Saginaw Co.*	91.6	80.7	31.2	8.4	5.3
Saint Clair Shores city *Macomb Co.*	89.0	77.4	29.6	11.0	3.4
Shelby charter twp *Macomb Co.*	90.4	79.8	25.6	9.6	4.4
Southfield city *Oakland Co.*	88.2	67.9	37.2	11.8	4.0
Southgate city *Wayne Co.*	90.5	77.8	29.4	9.5	4.0
Sterling Heights city *Macomb Co.*	87.7	71.2	30.1	12.3	4.3
Summit township *Jackson Co.*	91.3	73.3	35.3	8.7	2.4
Taylor city *Wayne Co.*	85.4	60.3	39.5	14.6	5.3
Troy city *Oakland Co.*	91.5	83.5	20.4	8.5	4.7
Van Buren charter twp *Wayne Co.*	87.8	72.8	26.8	12.2	3.2
Walker city *Kent Co.*	91.0	80.5	21.6	9.0	4.5
Warren city *Macomb Co.*	85.7	63.7	36.5	14.3	4.3
Washington township *Macomb Co.*	90.4	78.8	25.6	9.6	3.1
Waterford charter twp *Oakland Co.*	87.5	73.3	27.7	12.5	5.2
Waverly cdp *Eaton Co.*	91.5	80.8	28.2	8.5	1.4
West Bloomfield charter twp *Oakland Co.*	92.8	84.1	23.5	7.2	3.1
Westland city *Wayne Co.*	86.5	67.2	34.5	13.5	4.1
White Lake charter twp *Oakland Co.*	90.1	79.1	23.4	9.9	3.9
Wyandotte city *Wayne Co.*	87.9	71.7	31.3	12.1	4.2
Wyoming city *Kent Co.*	84.6	67.4	26.9	15.4	6.0
Ypsilanti charter twp *Washtenaw Co.*	88.1	65.9	33.8	11.9	2.8

NOTE: (1) Civilian noninstitutionalized population.
SOURCE: U.S. Census Bureau, American Community Survey, 2009-2013 Five-Year Estimates

Income and Poverty

Place	Average Household Income ($)	Median Household Income ($)	Per Capita Income ($)	Households w/$100,000+ Income (%)	Poverty Rate (%)
Adrian city Lenawee Co.	42,195	30,094	16,604	8.5	30.9
Allen Park city Wayne Co.	67,322	58,654	27,082	20.4	7.8
Allendale charter twp Ottawa Co.	59,380	48,489	17,125	15.1	28.6
Ann Arbor city Washtenaw Co.	78,722	55,003	34,247	26.7	22.1
Auburn Hills city Oakland Co.	64,158	52,509	26,843	17.4	13.3
Battle Creek city Calhoun Co.	55,091	37,814	22,154	12.1	22.1
Bay City city Bay Co.	44,981	35,352	18,922	7.7	22.4
Bedford township Monroe Co.	75,815	64,192	29,554	24.4	7.2
Blackman charter twp Jackson Co.	49,380	36,324	18,389	10.5	16.4
Bloomfield charter twp Oakland Co.	157,317	105,320	62,730	52.7	6.1
Brownstown charter twp Wayne Co.	77,203	64,396	28,431	26.8	8.1
Burton city Genesee Co.	54,482	43,983	21,804	11.5	19.7
Byron township Kent Co.	74,324	57,310	26,917	22.4	9.9
Canton charter twp Wayne Co.	97,079	81,667	34,409	38.6	6.0
Chesterfield township Macomb Co.	76,805	65,392	29,221	27.3	8.8
Clinton charter twp Macomb Co.	60,107	47,609	26,168	15.4	11.8
Commerce charter twp Oakland Co.	99,428	78,514	37,091	38.5	6.1
Dearborn city Wayne Co.	62,138	46,739	21,262	18.8	27.5
Dearborn Heights city Wayne Co.	55,405	43,001	21,433	13.2	19.0
Delhi charter twp Ingham Co.	73,493	61,273	29,064	26.1	10.0
Delta charter twp Eaton Co.	70,139	60,902	32,290	22.1	7.9
Detroit city Wayne Co.	37,887	26,325	14,870	6.4	39.3
East Lansing city Ingham Co.	62,193	32,953	18,650	18.7	41.1
Eastpointe city Macomb Co.	48,863	43,207	18,940	8.4	22.6
Farmington Hills city Oakland Co.	94,395	69,700	40,604	32.6	7.5
Flint city Genesee Co.	34,085	24,834	14,360	4.4	41.5
Flint charter twp Genesee Co.	53,009	40,888	22,347	11.1	19.2
Forest Hills cdp Kent Co.	148,079	112,454	50,807	56.1	2.3
Frenchtown township Monroe Co.	57,391	46,518	23,078	12.6	17.7
Gaines charter twp Kent Co.	68,186	55,929	26,485	20.6	11.5
Garden City city Wayne Co.	61,126	52,425	23,997	14.5	9.4
Genesee charter twp Genesee Co.	49,467	39,429	20,455	10.6	19.2
Georgetown charter twp Ottawa Co.	77,244	63,410	27,740	23.7	6.2
Grand Blanc charter twp Genesee Co.	76,603	58,521	30,084	24.5	9.8
Grand Rapids city Kent Co.	50,908	39,227	20,214	10.6	26.8
Hamburg township Livingston Co.	93,123	78,191	35,101	34.0	3.8
Hamtramck city Wayne Co.	34,304	25,659	10,890	4.7	43.4
Harrison charter twp Macomb Co.	68,293	52,125	31,259	23.1	12.1
Holland charter twp Ottawa Co.	62,344	53,499	22,015	16.1	12.4
Holland city Ottawa Co.	58,581	43,413	20,759	13.9	19.2
Holt cdp Ingham Co.	73,150	60,237	28,740	26.1	9.7
Independence charter twp Oakland Co.	89,711	72,363	34,164	33.3	6.3
Inkster city Wayne Co.	35,501	26,512	14,259	3.9	38.2
Jackson city Jackson Co.	38,176	28,309	15,336	5.8	34.7
Kalamazoo city Kalamazoo Co.	46,381	31,893	18,468	10.1	34.3
Kalamazoo charter twp Kalamazoo Co.	48,208	38,685	22,097	9.3	18.9
Kentwood city Kent Co.	60,855	48,368	24,851	15.6	13.5
Lansing city Ingham Co.	44,652	36,054	19,440	7.1	28.7
Lincoln Park city Wayne Co.	48,800	40,589	19,385	8.6	18.3
Livonia city Wayne Co.	80,865	68,973	32,249	29.5	6.1

Place	Average Household Income ($)	Median Household Income ($)	Per Capita Income ($)	Households w/$100,000+ Income (%)	Poverty Rate (%)
Macomb township *Macomb Co.*	93,655	82,957	31,715	39.6	5.1
Madison Heights city *Oakland Co.*	50,323	40,140	22,113	11.3	18.8
Marquette city *Marquette Co.*	55,470	37,770	21,764	14.6	25.5
Meridian charter twp *Ingham Co.*	85,330	62,145	37,732	30.6	13.1
Midland city *Midland Co.*	74,505	50,928	31,627	21.6	14.3
Monroe city *Monroe Co.*	54,530	42,911	22,653	13.4	19.5
Mount Morris township *Genesee Co.*	47,275	34,697	18,211	8.0	30.8
Mount Pleasant city *Isabella Co.*	45,515	28,336	15,945	10.6	45.3
Muskegon city *Muskegon Co.*	37,030	26,079	14,699	4.5	35.3
Northville township *Wayne Co.*	133,341	97,161	51,883	48.5	3.2
Norton Shores city *Muskegon Co.*	65,147	48,536	27,325	17.4	8.9
Novi city *Oakland Co.*	106,754	80,108	44,390	40.3	5.6
Oak Park city *Oakland Co.*	55,540	48,261	21,768	12.7	19.4
Okemos cdp *Ingham Co.*	94,266	70,781	39,889	35.8	11.6
Orion charter twp *Oakland Co.*	91,114	76,769	33,721	35.6	7.7
Oshtemo charter twp *Kalamazoo Co.*	61,155	41,675	27,918	18.8	23.5
Oxford charter twp *Oakland Co.*	88,053	72,958	32,057	37.3	7.5
Pittsfield charter twp *Washtenaw Co.*	89,577	66,461	35,516	32.2	10.7
Plainfield charter twp *Kent Co.*	75,963	60,218	29,375	22.7	7.4
Plymouth charter twp *Wayne Co.*	112,110	86,217	43,889	43.2	4.1
Pontiac city *Oakland Co.*	38,462	27,528	15,906	6.3	36.6
Port Huron city *Saint Clair Co.*	43,155	32,940	18,209	7.7	28.6
Portage city *Kalamazoo Co.*	71,816	55,036	29,738	21.8	11.7
Redford charter twp *Wayne Co.*	57,032	49,188	22,853	12.1	13.4
Rochester Hills city *Oakland Co.*	99,743	78,160	38,892	38.0	6.7
Romulus city *Wayne Co.*	51,920	44,119	20,537	10.4	21.4
Roseville city *Macomb Co.*	48,564	40,337	20,578	8.2	16.3
Royal Oak city *Oakland Co.*	78,488	62,789	38,893	28.9	6.9
Saginaw city *Saginaw Co.*	36,791	27,701	14,687	5.1	37.4
Saginaw charter twp *Saginaw Co.*	65,250	48,762	29,067	19.9	12.3
Saint Clair Shores city *Macomb Co.*	64,420	53,069	29,479	17.8	10.3
Shelby charter twp *Macomb Co.*	79,646	63,212	30,947	27.9	9.6
Southfield city *Oakland Co.*	64,219	49,841	28,635	18.9	16.0
Southgate city *Wayne Co.*	59,513	48,439	25,903	16.5	10.5
Sterling Heights city *Macomb Co.*	68,810	57,075	26,691	22.1	13.0
Summit township *Jackson Co.*	70,595	56,103	28,578	20.2	11.7
Taylor city *Wayne Co.*	51,473	41,933	20,101	10.3	21.2
Troy city *Oakland Co.*	106,454	85,685	40,022	40.9	7.2
Van Buren charter twp *Wayne Co.*	67,676	52,572	27,997	20.2	12.4
Walker city *Kent Co.*	61,898	50,828	26,694	17.3	11.7
Warren city *Macomb Co.*	53,776	43,962	21,744	11.8	18.2
Washington township *Macomb Co.*	94,759	75,449	35,562	33.5	6.6
Waterford charter twp *Oakland Co.*	68,201	54,827	28,717	20.4	13.2
Waverly cdp *Eaton Co.*	64,392	53,520	31,100	17.6	9.1
West Bloomfield charter twp *Oakland Co.*	126,953	90,164	47,856	45.6	5.5
Westland city *Wayne Co.*	55,754	43,993	23,993	13.0	15.5
White Lake charter twp *Oakland Co.*	83,539	72,063	31,805	32.2	8.0
Wyandotte city *Wayne Co.*	59,280	48,664	25,287	15.8	11.7
Wyoming city *Kent Co.*	55,718	45,477	21,246	11.7	16.7
Ypsilanti charter twp *Washtenaw Co.*	57,915	44,129	24,096	16.9	20.6

SOURCE: U.S. Census Bureau, American Community Survey, 2009-2013 Five-Year Estimates

Housing

Place	Homeownership Rate (%)	Median Home Value ($)	Median Year Structure Built	Homeowner Vacancy Rate (%)	Median Gross Rent ($/month)	Rental Vacancy Rate (%)
Adrian city *Lenawee Co.*	55.1	$74,200	1955	4.1	$679	14.2
Allen Park city *Wayne Co.*	85.5	$101,500	1955	1.6	$855	7.1
Allendale charter twp *Ottawa Co.*	56.0	$159,200	1995	1.8	$863	4.0
Ann Arbor city *Washtenaw Co.*	44.8	$230,700	1968	1.7	<$101	5.5
Auburn Hills city *Oakland Co.*	51.7	$113,600	1983	3.3	$906	14.0
Battle Creek city *Calhoun Co.*	60.6	$84,400	1955	4.0	$689	12.8
Bay City city *Bay Co.*	68.1	$69,200	1942	3.2	$563	8.6
Bedford township *Monroe Co.*	85.8	$158,400	1978	1.8	$871	9.4
Blackman charter twp *Jackson Co.*	55.5	$100,500	1975	2.5	$728	17.5
Bloomfield charter twp *Oakland Co.*	87.3	$328,800	1967	2.4	$1,072	12.5
Brownstown charter twp *Wayne Co.*	76.2	$153,700	1991	2.5	$821	10.1
Burton city *Genesee Co.*	74.7	$74,600	1962	3.5	$766	8.1
Byron township *Kent Co.*	83.1	$160,800	1991	1.7	$804	12.0
Canton charter twp *Wayne Co.*	76.2	$190,900	1987	2.6	$965	9.6
Chesterfield township *Macomb Co.*	83.3	$150,600	1991	2.7	$936	13.1
Clinton charter twp *Macomb Co.*	67.1	$119,100	1979	2.2	$784	10.5
Commerce charter twp *Oakland Co.*	90.1	$180,300	1984	2.0	$1,259	8.2
Dearborn city *Wayne Co.*	69.0	$103,300	1950	2.3	$962	8.2
Dearborn Heights city *Wayne Co.*	77.9	$85,600	1957	2.4	$975	7.2
Delhi charter twp *Ingham Co.*	74.0	$151,200	1983	2.1	$914	6.6
Delta charter twp *Eaton Co.*	64.0	$150,500	1978	2.0	$783	8.3
Detroit city *Wayne Co.*	51.1	$50,400	1947	3.8	$761	18.0
East Lansing city *Ingham Co.*	33.6	$177,000	1970	2.8	$856	6.0
Eastpointe city *Macomb Co.*	78.0	$62,500	1954	3.5	$1,025	7.6
Farmington Hills city *Oakland Co.*	63.6	$201,200	1977	2.1	$976	9.7
Flint city *Genesee Co.*	55.2	$41,700	1954	3.9	$668	16.5
Flint charter twp *Genesee Co.*	65.1	$85,300	1969	2.7	$716	14.5
Forest Hills cdp *Kent Co.*	93.3	$262,700	1985	1.2	$1,336	7.4
Frenchtown township *Monroe Co.*	73.8	$113,500	1974	2.8	$769	14.6
Gaines charter twp *Kent Co.*	71.6	$153,400	1990	1.8	$743	11.6
Garden City city *Wayne Co.*	82.5	$83,100	1956	2.0	$989	6.8
Genesee charter twp *Genesee Co.*	79.6	$72,300	1968	4.1	$798	19.6
Georgetown charter twp *Ottawa Co.*	83.0	$157,200	1983	1.3	$808	7.3
Grand Blanc charter twp *Genesee Co.*	68.6	$130,800	1981	3.3	$744	10.9
Grand Rapids city *Kent Co.*	56.0	$109,400	1952	3.3	$758	10.2
Hamburg township *Livingston Co.*	91.9	$193,800	1984	1.9	$938	6.3
Hamtramck city *Wayne Co.*	49.4	$46,600	Before 1940	4.0	$610	12.2
Harrison charter twp *Macomb Co.*	69.3	$150,200	1977	3.0	$798	14.3
Holland charter twp *Ottawa Co.*	70.1	$136,200	1990	2.3	$734	13.4
Holland city *Ottawa Co.*	63.7	$117,200	1967	2.9	$767	9.7
Holt cdp *Ingham Co.*	72.8	$148,700	1985	2.2	$910	6.7
Independence charter twp *Oakland Co.*	82.1	$184,600	1983	1.9	$914	13.6
Inkster city *Wayne Co.*	52.4	$55,400	1958	4.0	$741	11.8
Jackson city *Jackson Co.*	52.7	$66,900	Before 1940	4.6	$636	12.4
Kalamazoo city *Kalamazoo Co.*	43.6	$97,600	1957	3.9	$707	9.0
Kalamazoo charter twp *Kalamazoo Co.*	65.6	$97,600	1961	2.4	$737	11.9
Kentwood city *Kent Co.*	61.1	$129,200	1980	2.5	$762	13.1
Lansing city *Ingham Co.*	53.7	$85,000	1959	3.9	$729	10.3
Lincoln Park city *Wayne Co.*	73.9	$62,500	1954	2.8	$787	9.5
Livonia city *Wayne Co.*	86.2	$154,900	1963	1.1	$968	7.5

Place	Homeownership Rate (%)	Median Home Value ($)	Median Year Structure Built	Homeowner Vacancy Rate (%)	Median Gross Rent ($/month)	Rental Vacancy Rate (%)
Macomb township *Macomb Co.*	93.5	$204,000	1998	1.9	$1,142	8.1
Madison Heights city *Oakland Co.*	64.4	$84,200	1960	2.5	$755	8.0
Marquette city *Marquette Co.*	48.0	$159,600	1963	1.9	$648	3.8
Meridian charter twp *Ingham Co.*	60.9	$184,400	1979	2.0	$794	7.6
Midland city *Midland Co.*	67.0	$139,500	1971	1.9	$710	5.3
Monroe city *Monroe Co.*	62.1	$107,900	1953	3.5	$703	12.0
Mount Morris township *Genesee Co.*	72.1	$65,500	1964	3.4	$796	17.0
Mount Pleasant city *Isabella Co.*	34.7	$123,400	1974	2.1	$687	6.6
Muskegon city *Muskegon Co.*	52.5	$67,500	1951	5.2	$603	10.5
Northville township *Wayne Co.*	76.5	$315,900	1988	1.9	$1,058	9.5
Norton Shores city *Muskegon Co.*	81.6	$114,500	1970	2.5	$794	12.5
Novi city *Oakland Co.*	67.2	$235,800	1990	2.4	$994	13.4
Oak Park city *Oakland Co.*	60.7	$82,200	1957	3.3	$1,014	9.3
Okemos cdp *Ingham Co.*	63.8	$193,300	1977	1.7	$822	7.8
Orion charter twp *Oakland Co.*	79.9	$183,000	1982	2.8	$858	10.7
Oshtemo charter twp *Kalamazoo Co.*	50.5	$167,200	1986	2.5	$695	11.9
Oxford charter twp *Oakland Co.*	83.3	$165,300	1989	2.5	$875	11.8
Pittsfield charter twp *Washtenaw Co.*	57.5	$222,800	1991	1.5	$884	6.6
Plainfield charter twp *Kent Co.*	83.0	$155,000	1981	1.6	$696	9.5
Plymouth charter twp *Wayne Co.*	83.2	$240,400	1977	1.2	$783	9.2
Pontiac city *Oakland Co.*	47.7	$61,000	1958	5.7	$728	15.1
Port Huron city *Saint Clair Co.*	54.1	$81,400	1951	3.1	$681	11.5
Portage city *Kalamazoo Co.*	68.9	$148,100	1975	2.1	$712	10.4
Redford charter twp *Wayne Co.*	82.3	$69,800	1955	2.5	$1,046	8.1
Rochester Hills city *Oakland Co.*	77.0	$212,700	1981	1.8	$1,064	12.7
Romulus city *Wayne Co.*	67.1	$73,100	1971	4.0	$743	10.6
Roseville city *Macomb Co.*	70.3	$66,100	1959	2.8	$846	8.8
Royal Oak city *Oakland Co.*	67.7	$155,700	1955	2.0	$882	9.3
Saginaw city *Saginaw Co.*	60.3	$49,200	1947	4.4	$655	12.2
Saginaw charter twp *Saginaw Co.*	64.8	$126,100	1973	1.9	$735	7.7
Saint Clair Shores city *Macomb Co.*	81.9	$94,600	1957	2.1	$865	10.2
Shelby charter twp *Macomb Co.*	78.3	$182,300	1986	1.8	$909	14.0
Southfield city *Oakland Co.*	53.7	$108,500	1969	3.2	$965	12.5
Southgate city *Wayne Co.*	66.0	$88,200	1960	1.7	$794	7.6
Sterling Heights city *Macomb Co.*	76.2	$144,200	1976	1.7	$856	8.7
Summit township *Jackson Co.*	79.3	$118,400	1964	3.0	$889	11.5
Taylor city *Wayne Co.*	67.4	$77,800	1962	2.8	$787	7.8
Troy city *Oakland Co.*	75.9	$219,200	1976	1.4	$1,049	14.3
Van Buren charter twp *Wayne Co.*	65.7	$129,300	1983	3.2	$823	17.1
Walker city *Kent Co.*	62.8	$145,900	1982	1.3	$694	12.3
Warren city *Macomb Co.*	74.4	$89,500	1964	2.2	$804	9.0
Washington township *Macomb Co.*	84.0	$216,100	1992	2.1	$941	13.0
Waterford charter twp *Oakland Co.*	73.6	$122,100	1970	2.4	$732	10.9
Waverly cdp *Eaton Co.*	56.0	$142,700	1978	1.8	$779	8.2
West Bloomfield charter twp *Oakland Co.*	82.6	$236,600	1979	1.9	$1,534	11.1
Westland city *Wayne Co.*	61.5	$90,600	1966	2.3	$781	10.4
White Lake charter twp *Oakland Co.*	87.7	$171,800	1979	1.9	$949	12.9
Wyandotte city *Wayne Co.*	72.4	$87,600	1949	2.8	$697	10.0
Wyoming city *Kent Co.*	66.0	$103,500	1966	2.9	$714	7.7
Ypsilanti charter twp *Washtenaw Co.*	60.1	$112,900	1974	3.0	$805	10.6

SOURCE: *U.S. Census Bureau, Census 2010; U.S. Census Bureau, American Community Survey, 2009-2013 Five-Year Estimates*

Commute to Work

Place	Automobile (%)	Public Transportation (%)	Walk (%)	Work from Home (%)	Median Travel Time to Work (minutes)
Adrian city *Lenawee Co.*	84.0	0.2	11.7	2.1	16.5
Allen Park city *Wayne Co.*	97.2	0.1	0.7	1.4	22.5
Allendale charter twp *Ottawa Co.*	85.1	5.5	6.3	0.9	22.3
Ann Arbor city *Washtenaw Co.*	64.2	10.2	15.0	5.7	19.5
Auburn Hills city *Oakland Co.*	91.3	0.2	3.2	3.7	24.0
Battle Creek city *Calhoun Co.*	91.0	1.4	3.5	2.7	18.8
Bay City city *Bay Co.*	93.1	0.7	2.3	2.3	18.4
Bedford township *Monroe Co.*	94.1	0.6	0.1	4.7	23.7
Blackman charter twp *Jackson Co.*	92.8	0.6	1.8	1.6	20.2
Bloomfield charter twp *Oakland Co.*	90.6	0.8	0.5	7.3	23.6
Brownstown charter twp *Wayne Co.*	96.3	0.7	0.3	2.0	26.1
Burton city *Genesee Co.*	96.1	0.2	0.4	2.4	23.2
Byron township *Kent Co.*	94.5	0.2	0.9	2.9	21.6
Canton charter twp *Wayne Co.*	94.1	0.4	0.4	4.1	26.8
Chesterfield township *Macomb Co.*	95.7	0.5	0.3	2.9	29.5
Clinton charter twp *Macomb Co.*	95.2	1.4	0.5	2.3	26.9
Commerce charter twp *Oakland Co.*	94.1	0.1	0.2	4.8	29.1
Dearborn city *Wayne Co.*	94.5	0.5	1.8	2.5	21.6
Dearborn Heights city *Wayne Co.*	95.5	0.6	0.7	2.2	23.5
Delhi charter twp *Ingham Co.*	92.2	1.5	0.7	4.0	20.6
Delta charter twp *Eaton Co.*	95.6	0.3	1.0	2.6	19.0
Detroit city *Wayne Co.*	82.5	8.7	3.4	3.1	26.6
East Lansing city *Ingham Co.*	58.5	5.5	22.2	5.6	15.3
Eastpointe city *Macomb Co.*	94.1	0.9	2.2	1.4	23.6
Farmington Hills city *Oakland Co.*	92.3	0.6	1.0	5.2	23.9
Flint city *Genesee Co.*	88.0	4.4	3.0	3.5	21.7
Flint charter twp *Genesee Co.*	93.8	0.9	1.6	2.9	22.0
Forest Hills cdp *Kent Co.*	92.7	0.5	0.6	5.5	20.2
Frenchtown township *Monroe Co.*	94.0	1.9	1.2	2.3	24.0
Gaines charter twp *Kent Co.*	94.6	1.7	0.9	2.3	20.3
Garden City city *Wayne Co.*	95.5	0.4	1.0	2.1	23.6
Genesee charter twp *Genesee Co.*	93.8	1.2	0.8	2.8	29.6
Georgetown charter twp *Ottawa Co.*	93.8	0.3	2.0	3.2	21.8
Grand Blanc charter twp *Genesee Co.*	96.1	0.1	0.3	3.3	25.2
Grand Rapids city *Kent Co.*	86.7	3.5	3.3	4.9	19.5
Hamburg township *Livingston Co.*	91.9	0.1	0.7	6.9	32.7
Hamtramck city *Wayne Co.*	89.8	2.0	1.5	2.5	25.8
Harrison charter twp *Macomb Co.*	94.3	0.5	1.1	2.6	28.8
Holland charter twp *Ottawa Co.*	95.2	1.0	0.8	1.9	17.2
Holland city *Ottawa Co.*	85.7	1.0	7.2	3.7	17.0
Holt cdp *Ingham Co.*	92.2	1.6	0.7	4.0	20.2
Independence charter twp *Oakland Co.*	94.3	0.1	0.7	4.4	28.5
Inkster city *Wayne Co.*	94.5	3.2	0.7	0.9	24.5
Jackson city *Jackson Co.*	90.1	1.4	3.2	2.9	18.3
Kalamazoo city *Kalamazoo Co.*	85.6	2.4	7.6	3.3	18.0
Kalamazoo charter twp *Kalamazoo Co.*	90.6	3.2	1.6	2.5	18.9
Kentwood city *Kent Co.*	93.3	1.3	1.1	2.9	18.8
Lansing city *Ingham Co.*	88.5	4.4	2.7	2.7	19.1
Lincoln Park city *Wayne Co.*	96.4	0.8	0.5	1.7	23.0
Livonia city *Wayne Co.*	95.6	0.3	0.6	3.0	23.9

Place	Automobile (%)	Public Transportation (%)	Walk (%)	Work from Home (%)	Median Travel Time to Work (minutes)
Macomb township *Macomb Co.*	95.9	0.2	0.2	3.3	31.0
Madison Heights city *Oakland Co.*	93.4	1.2	0.9	4.0	22.5
Marquette city *Marquette Co.*	78.2	0.8	13.5	4.4	11.7
Meridian charter twp *Ingham Co.*	89.7	1.7	2.1	4.9	19.8
Midland city *Midland Co.*	90.7	0.8	2.0	4.6	15.6
Monroe city *Monroe Co.*	91.0	2.4	2.8	2.2	20.8
Mount Morris township *Genesee Co.*	93.1	2.2	0.6	3.1	24.0
Mount Pleasant city *Isabella Co.*	76.3	1.1	16.2	2.9	14.4
Muskegon city *Muskegon Co.*	90.6	1.2	3.0	3.8	17.8
Northville township *Wayne Co.*	94.7	0.3	0.7	3.8	28.4
Norton Shores city *Muskegon Co.*	94.8	0.4	0.4	3.3	19.3
Novi city *Oakland Co.*	95.0	0.4	0.3	3.7	26.1
Oak Park city *Oakland Co.*	91.8	2.4	2.2	2.9	23.2
Okemos cdp *Ingham Co.*	88.1	1.9	3.0	5.0	20.1
Orion charter twp *Oakland Co.*	93.9	0.1	0.8	4.4	28.4
Oshtemo charter twp *Kalamazoo Co.*	92.9	0.9	1.3	3.3	20.9
Oxford charter twp *Oakland Co.*	95.9	0.0	0.4	2.8	33.0
Pittsfield charter twp *Washtenaw Co.*	89.4	3.5	1.0	4.6	23.2
Plainfield charter twp *Kent Co.*	92.0	0.4	0.9	5.7	20.0
Plymouth charter twp *Wayne Co.*	94.7	0.2	0.6	3.7	25.1
Pontiac city *Oakland Co.*	92.9	1.9	1.9	1.3	21.3
Port Huron city *Saint Clair Co.*	89.6	1.4	3.8	3.2	18.9
Portage city *Kalamazoo Co.*	94.1	0.5	1.2	3.2	20.0
Redford charter twp *Wayne Co.*	94.9	1.1	1.2	2.0	23.0
Rochester Hills city *Oakland Co.*	93.8	0.1	0.8	4.3	26.6
Romulus city *Wayne Co.*	95.5	0.9	0.8	1.7	24.5
Roseville city *Macomb Co.*	93.7	1.7	1.4	2.3	24.7
Royal Oak city *Oakland Co.*	93.3	0.8	1.4	3.7	23.1
Saginaw city *Saginaw Co.*	91.1	2.6	1.9	3.3	19.4
Saginaw charter twp *Saginaw Co.*	96.9	0.1	0.4	2.0	18.9
Saint Clair Shores city *Macomb Co.*	94.9	1.5	0.6	2.4	26.6
Shelby charter twp *Macomb Co.*	96.3	0.3	0.5	2.6	27.6
Southfield city *Oakland Co.*	92.8	2.0	1.7	3.0	24.0
Southgate city *Wayne Co.*	97.1	0.5	0.9	1.0	24.0
Sterling Heights city *Macomb Co.*	96.3	0.4	0.6	2.2	25.7
Summit township *Jackson Co.*	93.6	0.1	1.1	4.3	21.1
Taylor city *Wayne Co.*	96.0	0.9	1.0	1.2	22.5
Troy city *Oakland Co.*	94.6	0.4	0.8	3.7	24.9
Van Buren charter twp *Wayne Co.*	94.7	0.5	2.7	1.5	25.4
Walker city *Kent Co.*	95.0	1.2	0.9	2.2	19.2
Warren city *Macomb Co.*	94.8	1.0	0.9	1.9	23.8
Washington township *Macomb Co.*	93.2	0.0	1.0	4.5	28.4
Waterford charter twp *Oakland Co.*	95.3	0.1	0.8	2.5	27.3
Waverly cdp *Eaton Co.*	95.2	0.2	1.0	2.9	18.4
West Bloomfield charter twp *Oakland Co.*	92.7	0.2	0.5	6.0	27.3
Westland city *Wayne Co.*	95.0	0.6	1.2	2.2	25.0
White Lake charter twp *Oakland Co.*	92.9	0.1	1.5	4.1	33.6
Wyandotte city *Wayne Co.*	92.2	1.4	3.4	1.7	22.5
Wyoming city *Kent Co.*	93.4	1.6	0.8	3.0	20.3
Ypsilanti charter twp *Washtenaw Co.*	93.0	2.6	0.8	2.9	24.3

SOURCE: U.S. Census Bureau, American Community Survey, 2009-2013 Five-Year Estimates

Crime

Place	Violent Crime Rate (crimes per 10,000 population)	Property Crime Rate (crimes per 10,000 population)
Adrian city Lenawee Co.	n/a	n/a
Allen Park city Wayne Co.	12.7	239.8
Allendale charter twp Ottawa Co.	n/a	n/a
Ann Arbor city Washtenaw Co.	21.1	216.2
Auburn Hills city Oakland Co.	28.1	350.1
Battle Creek city Calhoun Co.	n/a	n/a
Bay City city Bay Co.	63.1	272.7
Bedford township Monroe Co.	n/a	n/a
Blackman charter twp Jackson Co.	n/a	n/a
Bloomfield charter twp Oakland Co.	5.5	104.1
Brownstown charter twp Wayne Co.	18.4	137.9
Burton city Genesee Co.	40.7	423.4
Byron township Kent Co.	n/a	n/a
Canton charter twp Wayne Co.	10.6	140.5
Chesterfield township Macomb Co.	27.2	165.8
Clinton charter twp Macomb Co.	29.1	217.6
Commerce charter twp Oakland Co.	n/a	n/a
Dearborn city Wayne Co.	36.1	323.3
Dearborn Heights city Wayne Co.	37.5	236.5
Delhi charter twp Ingham Co.	n/a	n/a
Delta charter twp Eaton Co.	n/a	n/a
Detroit city Wayne Co.	207.2	583.5
East Lansing city Ingham Co.	22.5	164.7
Eastpointe city Macomb Co.	91.0	359.9
Farmington Hills city Oakland Co.	8.9	137.4
Flint city Genesee Co.	190.8	426.4
Flint charter twp Genesee Co.	107.8	629.9
Forest Hills cdp Kent Co.	n/a	n/a
Frenchtown township Monroe Co.	n/a	n/a
Gaines charter twp Kent Co.	n/a	n/a
Garden City city Wayne Co.	29.5	199.6
Genesee charter twp Genesee Co.	56.3	187.3
Georgetown charter twp Ottawa Co.	n/a	n/a
Grand Blanc charter twp Genesee Co.	17.1	165.5
Grand Rapids city Kent Co.	69.3	323.6
Hamburg township Livingston Co.	2.3	75.5
Hamtramck city Wayne Co.	166.2	369.7
Harrison charter twp Macomb Co.	n/a	n/a
Holland charter twp Ottawa Co.	n/a	n/a
Holland city Ottawa Co.	41.1	320.5
Holt cdp Ingham Co.	n/a	n/a
Independence charter twp Oakland Co.	n/a	n/a
Inkster city Wayne Co.	159.4	416.1
Jackson city Jackson Co.	110.9	518.9
Kalamazoo city Kalamazoo Co.	n/a	n/a
Kalamazoo charter twp Kalamazoo Co.	n/a	n/a
Kentwood city Kent Co.	28.2	242.5
Lansing city Ingham Co.	105.7	347.7
Lincoln Park city Wayne Co.	62.2	360.1
Livonia city Wayne Co.	15.5	205.9

Place	Violent Crime Rate (crimes per 10,000 population)	Property Crime Rate (crimes per 10,000 population)
Macomb township *Macomb Co.*	n/a	n/a
Madison Heights city *Oakland Co.*	25.9	286.6
Marquette city *Marquette Co.*	8.8	148.7
Meridian charter twp *Ingham Co.*	28.6	229.3
Midland city *Midland Co.*	n/a	n/a
Monroe city *Monroe Co.*	53.7	348.7
Mount Morris township *Genesee Co.*	71.0	426.9
Mount Pleasant city *Isabella Co.*	22.1	187.1
Muskegon city *Muskegon Co.*	88.7	537.4
Northville township *Wayne Co.*	6.3	126.7
Norton Shores city *Muskegon Co.*	n/a	n/a
Novi city *Oakland Co.*	8.4	168.1
Oak Park city *Oakland Co.*	60.6	272.2
Okemos cdp *Ingham Co.*	n/a	n/a
Orion charter twp *Oakland Co.*	n/a	n/a
Oshtemo charter twp *Kalamazoo Co.*	n/a	n/a
Oxford charter twp *Oakland Co.*	n/a	n/a
Pittsfield charter twp *Washtenaw Co.*	19.1	200.6
Plainfield charter twp *Kent Co.*	n/a	n/a
Plymouth charter twp *Wayne Co.*	6.6	109.3
Pontiac city *Oakland Co.*	n/a	n/a
Port Huron city *Saint Clair Co.*	60.6	308.7
Portage city *Kalamazoo Co.*	18.6	338.9
Redford charter twp *Wayne Co.*	51.4	324.3
Rochester Hills city *Oakland Co.*	n/a	n/a
Romulus city *Wayne Co.*	58.8	297.2
Roseville city *Macomb Co.*	46.1	416.7
Royal Oak city *Oakland Co.*	16.8	134.5
Saginaw city *Saginaw Co.*	194.7	295.0
Saginaw charter twp *Saginaw Co.*	23.6	213.9
Saint Clair Shores city *Macomb Co.*	n/a	n/a
Shelby charter twp *Macomb Co.*	n/a	n/a
Southfield city *Oakland Co.*	36.0	291.4
Southgate city *Wayne Co.*	28.9	357.1
Sterling Heights city *Macomb Co.*	18.7	190.3
Summit township *Jackson Co.*	n/a	n/a
Taylor city *Wayne Co.*	56.1	336.9
Troy city *Oakland Co.*	7.5	187.6
Van Buren charter twp *Wayne Co.*	22.3	234.8
Walker city *Kent Co.*	16.6	280.7
Warren city *Macomb Co.*	50.6	261.5
Washington township *Macomb Co.*	n/a	n/a
Waterford charter twp *Oakland Co.*	18.5	158.6
Waverly cdp *Eaton Co.*	n/a	n/a
West Bloomfield charter twp *Oakland Co.*	6.5	107.1
Westland city *Wayne Co.*	44.0	290.6
White Lake charter twp *Oakland Co.*	7.2	141.9
Wyandotte city *Wayne Co.*	22.1	224.6
Wyoming city *Kent Co.*	41.9	223.2
Ypsilanti charter twp *Washtenaw Co.*	n/a	n/a

NOTE: n/a not available.
SOURCE: Federal Bureau of Investigation, Uniform Crime Reports, 2013

Community Rankings

This section ranks incorporated places and CDPs (Census Designated Places) with populations of 10,000 or more. Unincorporated postal areas were not considered. For each topic below, you will find two tables, one in Descending Order—highest to lowest, and one in Ascending Order—lowest to highest. Four topics are exceptions to this rule, and only include Descending Order—Water Area, Ancestry (five tables), Native Hawaiian/Other Pacific Islander, and Commute to Work: Public Transportation. This is because there are an extraordinarily large number of places that place at the bottom of these topics with zero numbers.

Land Area

Top 150 Places Ranked in *Descending* Order

State Rank	Nat'l Rank	Sq. Miles	Place	State Rank	Nat'l Rank	Sq. Miles	Place
1	62	138.750	**Detroit** (city) Wayne County	76	935	30.945	**Lyon** (charter township) Oakland County
2	373	49.270	**Forest Hills** (CDP) Kent County	77	951	30.655	**Waterford** (charter township) Oakland County
3	384	48.544	**Leoni** (township) Jackson County	78	953	30.609	**Thomas** (township) Saginaw County
4	456	44.395	**Grand Rapids** (city) Kent County	79	959	30.485	**Meridian** (charter township) Ingham County
5	488	42.606	**Battle Creek** (city) Calhoun County	80	967	30.263	**Novi** (city) Oakland County
6	514	41.816	**Frenchtown** (township) Monroe County	81	976	29.980	**Fruitport** (charter township) Muskegon County
7	560	39.928	**East Bay** (township) Grand Traverse County	82	981	29.931	**Ypsilanti** (charter township) Washtenaw County
8	577	39.190	**Bedford** (township) Monroe County	83	1019	29.090	**Summit** (township) Jackson County
9	590	38.706	**Lenox** (township) Macomb County	84	1020	29.061	**Genesee** (charter township) Genesee County
10	623	37.316	**Niles** (township) Berrien County	85	1041	28.680	**Grand Haven** (charter township) Ottawa County
11	638	36.779	**Monitor** (charter township) Bay County	86	1046	28.610	**Delhi** (charter township) Ingham County
12	643	36.505	**Sterling Heights** (city) Macomb County	87	1073	28.157	**Union** (charter township) Isabella County
13	652	36.335	**Cooper** (charter township) Kalamazoo County	88	1076	28.097	**Clinton** (charter township) Macomb County
14	654	36.300	**Oakland** (charter township) Oakland County	89	1090	27.830	**Ann Arbor** (city) Washtenaw County
15	657	36.225	**Macomb** (township) Macomb County	90	1106	27.577	**Chesterfield** (township) Macomb County
16	665	36.119	**Oceola** (township) Livingston County	91	1109	27.451	**Commerce** (charter township) Oakland County
17	666	36.109	**Canton** (charter township) Wayne County	92	1123	27.258	**Pittsfield** (charter township) Washtenaw County
18	667	36.098	**Byron** (township) Kent County	93	1138	27.028	**Holland** (charter township) Ottawa County
19	669	36.049	**Lansing** (city) Ingham County	94	1139	27.007	**West Bloomfield** (charter township) Oakland County
20	671	36.036	**Ada** (township) Kent County	95	1170	26.592	**Garfield** (charter township) Grand Traverse County
21	672	36.033	**Mundy** (township) Genesee County	96	1189	26.274	**Southfield** (city) Oakland County
22	678	35.903	**Alpine** (township) Kent County	97	1252	24.942	**Walker** (city) Kent County
23	680	35.869	**Oshtemo** (charter township) Kalamazoo County	98	1264	24.684	**Kalamazoo** (city) Kalamazoo County
24	682	35.857	**Hartland** (township) Livingston County	99	1267	24.639	**Wyoming** (city) Kent County
25	693	35.703	**Gaines** (charter township) Kent County	100	1269	24.628	**Bloomfield** (charter township) Oakland County
26	694	35.695	**Livonia** (city) Wayne County	101	1277	24.497	**Saginaw** (charter township) Saginaw County
27	700	35.608	**Romulus** (city) Wayne County	102	1295	24.225	**Dearborn** (city) Wayne County
28	710	35.476	**Washington** (township) Macomb County	103	1323	23.803	**Fenton** (charter township) Genesee County
29	713	35.431	**Springfield** (charter township) Oakland County	104	1336	23.597	**Taylor** (city) Wayne County
30	715	35.405	**Tyrone** (township) Livingston County	105	1348	23.355	**Burton** (city) Genesee County
31	716	35.352	**Huron** (charter township) Wayne County	106	1354	23.281	**Flint** (charter township) Genesee County
32	718	35.260	**Cannon** (township) Kent County	107	1359	23.236	**Norton Shores** (city) Muskegon County
33	719	35.211	**Superior** (charter township) Washtenaw County	108	1386	22.944	**Muskegon** (charter township) Muskegon County
34	726	35.107	**Brandon** (charter township) Oakland County	109	1404	22.726	**Allendale** (CDP) Ottawa County
35	731	35.045	**Plainfield** (charter township) Kent County	110	1443	22.191	**Brownstown** (charter township) Wayne County
36	733	35.006	**Vienna** (charter township) Genesee County	111	1526	20.904	**Kentwood** (city) Kent County
37	735	34.992	**Independence** (charter township) Oakland County	112	1573	20.425	**Westland** (city) Wayne County
38	738	34.913	**Caledonia** (township) Kent County	113	1606	19.971	**Pontiac** (city) Oakland County
39	746	34.686	**Antwerp** (township) Van Buren County	114	1668	19.199	**Park** (township) Ottawa County
40	757	34.430	**Bridgeport** (charter township) Saginaw County	115	1776	17.911	**Lincoln** (charter township) Berrien County
41	761	34.383	**Texas** (charter township) Kalamazoo County	116	1824	17.336	**Saginaw** (city) Saginaw County
42	762	34.381	**Warren** (city) Macomb County	117	1865	16.900	**Monroe** (charter township) Monroe County
43	763	34.378	**Holly** (charter township) Oakland County	118	1881	16.763	**Okemos** (CDP) Ingham County
44	766	34.300	**Green Oak** (township) Livingston County	119	1896	16.598	**Auburn Hills** (city) Oakland County
45	769	34.257	**Shelby** (charter township) Macomb County	120	1898	16.589	**Holland** (city) Ottawa County
46	776	34.111	**Highland** (charter township) Oakland County	121	1905	16.478	**Spring Lake** (township) Ottawa County
47	783	34.048	**Genoa** (township) Livingston County	122	1943	16.192	**Northville** (township) Wayne County
48	786	33.969	**Van Buren** (charter township) Wayne County	123	1969	15.959	**Fort Gratiot** (charter township) Saint Clair County
49	790	33.884	**Cascade** (charter township) Kent County	124	1973	15.930	**Plymouth** (charter township) Wayne County
50	799	33.781	**Oxford** (charter township) Oakland County	125	2001	15.674	**Holt** (CDP) Ingham County
51	801	33.730	**Scio** (township) Washtenaw County	126	2041	15.370	**Haslett** (CDP) Ingham County
52	804	33.695	**Midland** (city) Midland County	127	2043	15.342	**Grand Rapids** (charter township) Kent County
53	813	33.520	**White Lake** (charter township) Oakland County	128	2113	14.774	**Sault Sainte Marie** (city) Chippewa County
54	815	33.473	**Troy** (city) Oakland County	129	2149	14.456	**Harrison** (charter township) Macomb County
55	818	33.416	**Flint** (city) Genesee County	130	2183	14.211	**Muskegon** (city) Muskegon County
56	821	33.330	**Orion** (charter township) Oakland County	131	2194	14.100	**Bangor** (charter township) Bay County
57	823	33.318	**Davison** (township) Genesee County	132	2252	13.594	**East Lansing** (city) Ingham County
58	824	33.314	**Comstock** (charter township) Kalamazoo County	133	2353	12.875	**Escanaba** (city) Delta County
59	825	33.280	**Farmington Hills** (city) Oakland County	134	2355	12.838	**Port Huron** (charter township) Saint Clair County
60	830	33.175	**Georgetown** (charter township) Ottawa County	135	2493	11.785	**Royal Oak** (city) Oakland County
61	839	32.991	**Milford** (charter township) Oakland County	136	2499	11.743	**Dearborn Heights** (city) Wayne County
62	843	32.958	**Brighton** (township) Livingston County	137	2506	11.680	**Kalamazoo** (charter township) Kalamazoo County
63	852	32.820	**Rochester Hills** (city) Oakland County	138	2522	11.619	**Saint Clair Shores** (city) Macomb County
64	857	32.700	**Grand Blanc** (charter township) Genesee County	139	2560	11.393	**Marquette** (city) Marquette County
65	866	32.464	**Delta** (charter township) Eaton County	140	2583	11.239	**Redford** (charter township) Wayne County
66	871	32.370	**Benton** (township) Berrien County	141	2635	10.865	**Jackson** (city) Jackson County
67	879	32.241	**Hamburg** (township) Livingston County	142	2714	10.336	**Northview** (CDP) Kent County
68	880	32.225	**Portage** (city) Kalamazoo County	143	2745	10.166	**Bay City** (city) Bay County
69	890	32.000	**Emmett** (charter township) Calhoun County	144	2839	9.826	**Roseville** (city) Macomb County
70	901	31.835	**Bath** (charter township) Clinton County	145	2938	9.200	**Grosse Ile** (township) Wayne County
71	905	31.709	**Blackman** (charter township) Jackson County	146	2947	9.166	**Monroe** (city) Monroe County
72	915	31.506	**Mount Morris** (charter township) Genesee County	147	2952	9.154	**Wixom** (city) Oakland County
73	919	31.366	**Flushing** (charter township) Genesee County	148	2968	9.068	**Waverly** (CDP) Eaton County
74	929	31.130	**Allendale** (charter township) Ottawa County	149	3075	8.541	**Alpena** (city) Alpena County
75	934	31.030	**DeWitt** (charter township) Clinton County	150	3111	8.326	**Traverse City** (city) Grand Traverse County

Note: The state column ranks the top/bottom 150 places from all places in the state with population of 10,000 or more. The national column ranks the top/bottom 150 places from all places in the country with population of 10,000 or more. Places that are unincorporated were not considered in the rankings. Please refer to the User Guide for additional information.

Land Area

Top 150 Places Ranked in *Ascending* Order

State Rank	Nat'l Rank	Sq. Miles	Place	State Rank	Nat'l Rank	Sq. Miles	Place
1	122	2.086	**Hamtramck** (city) Wayne County	76	2507	14.456	**Harrison** (charter township) Macomb County
2	131	2.169	**Grosse Pointe Park** (city) Wayne County	77	2543	14.774	**Sault Sainte Marie** (city) Chippewa County
3	139	2.199	**Clawson** (city) Oakland County	78	2613	15.342	**Grand Rapids** (charter township) Kent County
4	214	2.610	**Harper Woods** (city) Wayne County	79	2615	15.370	**Haslett** (CDP) Ingham County
5	217	2.615	**Berkley** (city) Oakland County	80	2655	15.674	**Holt** (CDP) Ingham County
6	229	2.660	**Farmington** (city) Oakland County	81	2683	15.930	**Plymouth** (charter township) Wayne County
7	248	2.720	**Melvindale** (city) Wayne County	82	2687	15.959	**Fort Gratiot** (charter township) Saint Clair County
8	277	2.818	**Hazel Park** (city) Oakland County	83	2713	16.192	**Northville** (township) Wayne County
9	306	2.934	**East Grand Rapids** (city) Kent County	84	2751	16.478	**Spring Lake** (township) Ottawa County
10	314	2.971	**Highland Park** (city) Wayne County	85	2758	16.589	**Holland** (city) Ottawa County
11	355	3.185	**Muskegon Heights** (city) Muskegon County	86	2760	16.598	**Auburn Hills** (city) Oakland County
12	369	3.249	**Grosse Pointe Woods** (city) Wayne County	87	2775	16.763	**Okemos** (CDP) Ingham County
13	465	3.734	**South Lyon** (city) Oakland County	88	2791	16.900	**Monroe** (charter township) Monroe County
14	488	3.825	**Rochester** (city) Oakland County	89	2832	17.336	**Saginaw** (city) Saginaw County
15	501	3.879	**Ferndale** (city) Oakland County	90	2880	17.911	**Lincoln** (charter township) Berrien County
16	502	3.880	**Comstock Park** (CDP) Kent County	91	2988	19.199	**Park** (township) Ottawa County
17	536	4.000	**Beverly Hills** (village) Oakland County	92	3050	19.971	**Pontiac** (city) Oakland County
18	552	4.069	**Mount Clemens** (city) Macomb County	93	3083	20.425	**Westland** (city) Wayne County
19	568	4.141	**Fraser** (city) Macomb County	94	3130	20.904	**Kentwood** (city) Kent County
20	619	4.329	**Ypsilanti** (city) Washtenaw County	95	3213	22.191	**Brownstown** (charter township) Wayne County
21	628	4.364	**Big Rapids** (city) Mecosta County	96	3252	22.726	**Allendale** (CDP) Ottawa County
22	638	4.395	**Riverview** (city) Wayne County	97	3270	22.944	**Muskegon** (charter township) Muskegon County
23	646	4.427	**Benton Harbor** (city) Berrien County	98	3297	23.236	**Norton Shores** (city) Muskegon County
24	692	4.608	**New Baltimore** (city) Macomb County	99	3302	23.281	**Flint** (charter township) Genesee County
25	738	4.792	**Birmingham** (city) Oakland County	100	3308	23.355	**Burton** (city) Genesee County
26	823	5.143	**Eastpointe** (city) Macomb County	101	3320	23.597	**Taylor** (city) Wayne County
27	830	5.164	**Oak Park** (city) Oakland County	102	3333	23.803	**Fenton** (charter township) Genesee County
28	844	5.228	**Owosso** (city) Shiawassee County	103	3361	24.225	**Dearborn** (city) Wayne County
29	851	5.274	**Wyandotte** (city) Wayne County	104	3379	24.497	**Saginaw** (charter township) Saginaw County
30	870	5.346	**Ionia** (city) Ionia County	105	3387	24.628	**Bloomfield** (charter township) Oakland County
31	968	5.771	**Grand Haven** (city) Ottawa County	106	3389	24.639	**Wyoming** (city) Kent County
32	971	5.791	**Niles** (city) Berrien County	107	3392	24.684	**Kalamazoo** (city) Kalamazoo County
33	992	5.855	**Jenison** (CDP) Ottawa County	108	3404	24.942	**Walker** (city) Kent County
34	998	5.869	**Garden City** (city) Wayne County	109	3467	26.274	**Southfield** (city) Oakland County
35	999	5.869	**Cutlerville** (CDP) Kent County	110	3486	26.592	**Garfield** (charter township) Grand Traverse County
36	1003	5.882	**Beecher** (CDP) Genesee County	111	3517	27.007	**West Bloomfield** (charter township) Oakland County
37	1005	5.888	**Lincoln Park** (city) Wayne County	112	3518	27.028	**Holland** (charter township) Ottawa County
38	1039	6.020	**Wayne** (city) Wayne County	113	3533	27.258	**Pittsfield** (charter township) Washtenaw County
39	1086	6.253	**Inkster** (city) Wayne County	114	3547	27.451	**Commerce** (charter township) Oakland County
40	1115	6.387	**Woodhaven** (city) Wayne County	115	3550	27.577	**Chesterfield** (township) Macomb County
41	1135	6.494	**Sturgis** (city) Saint Joseph County	116	3566	27.830	**Ann Arbor** (city) Washtenaw County
42	1174	6.648	**Saint Joseph** (charter township) Berrien County	117	3580	28.097	**Clinton** (charter township) Macomb County
43	1186	6.678	**Fenton** (city) Genesee County	118	3583	28.157	**Union** (charter township) Isabella County
44	1220	6.846	**Southgate** (city) Wayne County	119	3610	28.610	**Delhi** (charter township) Ingham County
45	1268	7.004	**Allen Park** (city) Wayne County	120	3615	28.680	**Grand Haven** (charter township) Ottawa County
46	1284	7.087	**Madison Heights** (city) Oakland County	121	3636	29.061	**Genesee** (charter township) Genesee County
47	1299	7.164	**Cadillac** (city) Wexford County	122	3637	29.090	**Summit** (township) Jackson County
48	1327	7.273	**Grandville** (city) Kent County	123	3675	29.931	**Ypsilanti** (charter township) Washtenaw County
49	1328	7.276	**Trenton** (city) Wayne County	124	3680	29.980	**Fruitport** (charter township) Muskegon County
50	1422	7.741	**Mount Pleasant** (city) Isabella County	125	3689	30.263	**Novi** (city) Oakland County
51	1477	7.953	**Adrian** (city) Lenawee County	126	3697	30.485	**Meridian** (charter township) Ingham County
52	1489	8.033	**Coldwater** (city) Branch County	127	3703	30.609	**Thomas** (township) Saginaw County
53	1491	8.046	**Southfield** (township) Oakland County	128	3705	30.655	**Waterford** (charter township) Oakland County
54	1496	8.081	**Port Huron** (city) Saint Clair County	129	3721	30.945	**Lyon** (charter township) Oakland County
55	1545	8.326	**Traverse City** (city) Grand Traverse County	130	3722	31.030	**DeWitt** (charter township) Clinton County
56	1581	8.541	**Alpena** (city) Alpena County	131	3727	31.130	**Allendale** (charter township) Ottawa County
57	1688	9.068	**Waverly** (CDP) Eaton County	132	3737	31.366	**Flushing** (charter township) Genesee County
58	1704	9.154	**Wixom** (city) Oakland County	133	3741	31.506	**Mount Morris** (township) Genesee County
59	1709	9.166	**Monroe** (city) Monroe County	134	3751	31.709	**Blackman** (charter township) Jackson County
60	1718	9.200	**Grosse Ile** (township) Wayne County	135	3755	31.835	**Bath** (charter township) Clinton County
61	1817	9.826	**Roseville** (city) Macomb County	136	3766	32.000	**Emmett** (charter township) Calhoun County
62	1911	10.166	**Bay City** (city) Bay County	137	3776	32.225	**Portage** (city) Kalamazoo County
63	1942	10.336	**Northview** (CDP) Kent County	138	3777	32.241	**Hamburg** (township) Livingston County
64	2021	10.865	**Jackson** (city) Jackson County	139	3785	32.370	**Benton** (charter township) Berrien County
65	2073	11.239	**Redford** (charter township) Wayne County	140	3790	32.464	**Delta** (charter township) Eaton County
66	2096	11.393	**Marquette** (city) Marquette County	141	3799	32.700	**Grand Blanc** (charter township) Genesee County
67	2134	11.619	**Saint Clair Shores** (city) Macomb County	142	3804	32.820	**Rochester Hills** (city) Oakland County
68	2150	11.680	**Kalamazoo** (charter township) Kalamazoo County	143	3813	32.958	**Brighton** (township) Livingston County
69	2157	11.743	**Dearborn Heights** (city) Wayne County	144	3817	32.991	**Milford** (charter township) Oakland County
70	2163	11.785	**Royal Oak** (city) Oakland County	145	3826	33.175	**Georgetown** (charter township) Ottawa County
71	2301	12.838	**Port Huron** (charter township) Saint Clair County	146	3831	33.280	**Farmington Hills** (city) Oakland County
72	2303	12.875	**Escanaba** (city) Delta County	147	3832	33.314	**Comstock** (charter township) Kalamazoo County
73	2404	13.594	**East Lansing** (city) Ingham County	148	3833	33.318	**Davison** (township) Genesee County
74	2462	14.100	**Bangor** (charter township) Bay County	149	3835	33.330	**Orion** (charter township) Oakland County
75	2473	14.211	**Muskegon** (city) Muskegon County	150	3838	33.416	**Flint** (city) Genesee County

Note: The state column ranks the top/bottom 150 places from all places in the state with population of 10,000 or more. The national column ranks the top/bottom 150 places from all places in the country with population of 10,000 or more. Places that are unincorporated were not considered in the rankings. Please refer to the User Guide for additional information.

Water Area

Top 150 Places Ranked in *Descending* Order

State Rank	Nat'l Rank	Sq. Miles	Place
1	161	9.468	**Grosse Ile** (township) Wayne County
2	163	9.311	**Harrison** (charter township) Macomb County
3	176	8.450	**Brownstown** (charter township) Wayne County
4	183	8.063	**Marquette** (city) Marquette County
5	186	8.000	**Bangor** (charter township) Bay County
6	256	5.388	**Sault Sainte Marie** (city) Chippewa County
7	290	4.538	**Waterford** (charter township) Oakland County
8	299	4.262	**West Bloomfield** (charter township) Oakland County
9	305	4.184	**Port Huron** (city) Saint Clair County
10	312	4.119	**Detroit** (city) Wayne County
11	325	3.911	**Muskegon** (city) Muskegon County
12	336	3.779	**Hamburg** (township) Livingston County
13	344	3.728	**Fenton** (charter township) Genesee County
14	355	3.622	**Escanaba** (city) Delta County
15	364	3.545	**White Lake** (charter township) Oakland County
16	402	3.197	**Bath** (charter township) Clinton County
17	419	3.026	**Chesterfield** (township) Macomb County
18	424	2.941	**Portage** (city) Kalamazoo County
19	455	2.678	**Leoni** (township) Jackson County
20	456	2.668	**Green Oak** (township) Livingston County
21	458	2.659	**Saint Clair Shores** (city) Macomb County
22	465	2.632	**Orion** (charter township) Oakland County
23	486	2.466	**East Bay** (township) Grand Traverse County
24	490	2.452	**Commerce** (charter township) Oakland County
25	510	2.341	**Genoa** (township) Livingston County
26	526	2.254	**Spring Lake** (township) Ottawa County
27	545	2.177	**Milford** (charter township) Oakland County
28	550	2.125	**Park** (township) Ottawa County
29	551	2.124	**New Baltimore** (city) Macomb County
30	556	2.089	**Van Buren** (charter township) Wayne County
31	563	2.069	**Highland** (charter township) Oakland County
32	566	2.042	**Holly** (township) Oakland County
33	581	1.992	**Midland** (city) Midland County
34	588	1.937	**Comstock** (charter township) Kalamazoo County
35	595	1.915	**Texas** (charter township) Kalamazoo County
36	609	1.864	**Cadillac** (city) Wexford County
37	630	1.794	**Ypsilanti** (charter township) Washtenaw County
38	649	1.737	**Wyandotte** (city) Wayne County
39	652	1.712	**Cannon** (township) Kent County
40	660	1.687	**Plainfield** (charter township) Kent County
41	673	1.641	**Brighton** (township) Livingston County
42	686	1.604	**Oxford** (charter township) Oakland County
43	688	1.592	**Grand Haven** (city) Ottawa County
44	700	1.542	**Grosse Pointe Park** (city) Wayne County
45	701	1.531	**Forest Hills** (CDP) Kent County
46	741	1.438	**Hartland** (township) Livingston County
47	769	1.384	**Norton Shores** (city) Muskegon County
48	779	1.362	**Bloomfield** (charter township) Oakland County
49	806	1.310	**Independence** (charter township) Oakland County
50	809	1.303	**Frenchtown** (township) Monroe County
51	822	1.282	**Tyrone** (township) Livingston County
52	825	1.276	**Washington** (township) Macomb County
53	842	1.252	**Monroe** (charter township) Monroe County
54	857	1.216	**Thomas** (township) Saginaw County
55	859	1.214	**Springfield** (charter township) Oakland County
56	863	1.207	**Genesee** (charter township) Genesee County
57	898	1.117	**Battle Creek** (city) Calhoun County
58	903	1.101	**Garfield** (charter township) Grand Traverse County
59	915	1.084	**Meridian** (charter township) Ingham County
60	918	1.077	**Ada** (township) Kent County
61	921	1.072	**Niles** (township) Berrien County
62	944	1.039	**Bay City** (city) Bay County
63	953	1.023	**Novi** (city) Oakland County
64	960	1.017	**Monroe** (city) Monroe County
65	985	0.972	**Cascade** (charter township) Kent County
66	1014	0.925	**Allendale** (charter township) Ottawa County
67	1018	0.920	**Allendale** (CDP) Ottawa County
68	1019	0.919	**Summit** (township) Jackson County
69	1027	0.902	**Georgetown** (charter township) Ottawa County
70	1033	0.895	**Haslett** (CDP) Ingham County
71	1039	0.887	**Shelby** (charter township) Macomb County
72	1052	0.870	**Ann Arbor** (city) Washtenaw County
73	1053	0.870	**Brandon** (charter township) Oakland County
74	1055	0.870	**Grand Rapids** (city) Kent County
75	1057	0.868	**Muskegon** (charter township) Muskegon County
76	1077	0.838	**Grand Haven** (charter township) Ottawa County
77	1109	0.803	**Lyon** (charter township) Oakland County
78	1126	0.784	**Caledonia** (township) Kent County
79	1145	0.763	**Saginaw** (city) Saginaw County
80	1146	0.762	**Holland** (city) Ottawa County
81	1157	0.749	**Delta** (charter township) Eaton County
82	1200	0.699	**Northview** (CDP) Kent County
83	1209	0.689	**Alpena** (city) Alpena County
84	1260	0.636	**Flint** (city) Genesee County
85	1261	0.636	**Oceola** (township) Livingston County
86	1271	0.626	**Lansing** (city) Ingham County
87	1366	0.544	**Walker** (city) Kent County
88	1423	0.501	**Emmett** (charter township) Calhoun County
89	1449	0.482	**Huron** (charter township) Wayne County
90	1459	0.477	**Scio** (township) Washtenaw County
91	1473	0.468	**East Grand Rapids** (city) Kent County
92	1486	0.456	**Holland** (charter township) Ottawa County
93	1496	0.446	**Benton** (charter township) Berrien County
94	1506	0.439	**Bridgeport** (charter township) Saginaw County
95	1517	0.433	**Oakland** (charter township) Oakland County
96	1521	0.432	**Kalamazoo** (city) Kalamazoo County
97	1546	0.417	**Delhi** (charter township) Ingham County
98	1576	0.398	**Grandville** (city) Kent County
99	1582	0.393	**Fruitport** (charter township) Muskegon County
100	1609	0.378	**Northville** (township) Wayne County
101	1610	0.378	**Saginaw** (charter township) Saginaw County
102	1667	0.349	**Superior** (charter township) Washtenaw County
103	1675	0.346	**Romulus** (city) Wayne County
104	1695	0.339	**Grand Blanc** (charter township) Genesee County
105	1711	0.332	**Traverse City** (city) Grand Traverse County
106	1718	0.330	**Union** (charter township) Isabella County
107	1741	0.324	**Fenton** (city) Genesee County
108	1756	0.318	**Saint Joseph** (charter township) Berrien County
109	1763	0.315	**Davison** (township) Genesee County
110	1769	0.314	**Pontiac** (city) Oakland County
111	1774	0.310	**Alpine** (township) Kent County
112	1778	0.309	**Cooper** (charter township) Kalamazoo County
113	1783	0.306	**Flushing** (charter township) Genesee County
114	1786	0.305	**Lincoln** (charter township) Berrien County
115	1793	0.303	**Port Huron** (charter township) Saint Clair County
116	1800	0.300	**Antwerp** (township) Van Buren County
117	1821	0.294	**Sterling Heights** (city) Macomb County
118	1881	0.272	**Clinton** (charter township) Macomb County
119	1936	0.254	**Benton Harbor** (city) Berrien County
120	1960	0.247	**Dearborn** (city) Wayne County
121	2002	0.236	**DeWitt** (charter township) Clinton County
122	2003	0.236	**Coldwater** (city) Branch County
123	2013	0.234	**Wyoming** (city) Kent County
124	2024	0.229	**Trenton** (city) Wayne County
125	2047	0.222	**Lenox** (township) Macomb County
126	2049	0.221	**Grand Rapids** (charter township) Kent County
127	2070	0.217	**Flint** (charter township) Genesee County
128	2081	0.212	**Wixom** (city) Oakland County
129	2148	0.198	**Holt** (CDP) Ingham County
130	2152	0.197	**Monitor** (charter township) Bay County
131	2159	0.195	**Blackman** (charter township) Jackson County
132	2180	0.190	**Ypsilanti** (city) Washtenaw County
133	2250	0.172	**Bedford** (township) Monroe County
134	2277	0.168	**Troy** (city) Oakland County
135	2319	0.159	**Livonia** (city) Wayne County
136	2325	0.158	**Niles** (city) Berrien County
137	2366	0.149	**Adrian** (city) Lenawee County
138	2372	0.148	**Okemos** (CDP) Ingham County
139	2377	0.147	**Mundy** (township) Genesee County
140	2393	0.142	**Owosso** (city) Shiawassee County
141	2454	0.135	**Oshtemo** (charter township) Kalamazoo County
142	2476	0.131	**Mount Clemens** (city) Macomb County
143	2489	0.130	**Ionia** (city) Ionia County
144	2532	0.122	**Big Rapids** (city) Mecosta County
145	2552	0.119	**Macomb** (township) Macomb County
146	2559	0.118	**Jackson** (city) Jackson County
147	2593	0.113	**Mount Morris** (township) Genesee County
148	2609	0.112	**Kalamazoo** (charter township) Kalamazoo County
149	2627	0.110	**Vienna** (charter township) Genesee County
150	2729	0.095	**Plymouth** (charter township) Wayne County

Note: The state column ranks the top/bottom 150 places from all places in the state with population of 10,000 or more. The national column ranks the top/bottom 150 places from all places in the country with population of 10,000 or more. Places that are unincorporated were not considered in the rankings. Please refer to the User Guide for additional information.

Elevation

Top 150 Places Ranked in *Descending* Order

State Rank	Nat'l Rank	Feet	Place
1	395	1,306	**Cadillac** (city) Wexford County
2	600	1,056	**Oxford** (charter township) Oakland County
3	628	1,037	**White Lake** (charter township) Oakland County
4	635	1,033	**Brandon** (charter township) Oakland County
5	649	1,027	**Springfield** (charter township) Oakland County
6	670	1,014	**Highland** (charter township) Oakland County
7	714	984	**Leoni** (township) Jackson County
8	748	968	**Coldwater** (city) Branch County
8	748	968	**Oshtemo** (charter township) Kalamazoo County
8	748	968	**Waterford** (charter township) Oakland County
11	762	961	**Milford** (charter township) Oakland County
12	764	958	**Auburn Hills** (city) Oakland County
13	780	948	**Hartland** (township) Livingston County
14	789	945	**Commerce** (charter township) Oakland County
15	816	932	**Jackson** (city) Jackson County
15	816	932	**Wixom** (city) Oakland County
17	824	928	**Big Rapids** (city) Mecosta County
17	824	928	**Green Oak** (township) Livingston County
19	831	925	**Brighton** (township) Livingston County
19	831	925	**Holly** (township) Oakland County
19	831	925	**Pontiac** (city) Oakland County
19	831	925	**South Lyon** (city) Oakland County
23	846	915	**Sturgis** (city) Saint Joseph County
24	862	909	**Novi** (city) Oakland County
25	869	906	**Fenton** (charter township) Genesee County
25	869	906	**Fenton** (city) Genesee County
27	889	899	**Hamburg** (township) Livingston County
28	900	896	**Meridian** (charter township) Ingham County
29	913	889	**Holt** (CDP) Ingham County
30	932	883	**Delhi** (charter township) Ingham County
31	940	879	**Ann Arbor** (city) Washtenaw County
31	940	879	**Portage** (city) Kalamazoo County
33	955	876	**Haslett** (CDP) Ingham County
34	961	873	**Cooper** (charter township) Kalamazoo County
34	961	873	**Scio** (township) Washtenaw County
36	981	866	**Delta** (charter township) Eaton County
37	990	863	**Bath** (charter township) Clinton County
38	999	860	**Waverly** (CDP) Eaton County
39	1007	856	**East Lansing** (city) Ingham County
40	1013	853	**Lansing** (city) Ingham County
41	1021	850	**Farmington Hills** (city) Oakland County
42	1037	840	**Battle Creek** (city) Calhoun County
42	1037	840	**Grand Blanc** (charter township) Genesee County
42	1037	840	**Okemos** (CDP) Ingham County
45	1050	837	**DeWitt** (charter township) Clinton County
46	1055	833	**Pittsfield** (charter township) Washtenaw County
47	1073	827	**Northville** (township) Wayne County
48	1088	820	**Rochester Hills** (city) Oakland County
49	1100	814	**Caledonia** (township) Kent County
50	1131	801	**Beecher** (CDP) Genesee County
51	1150	794	**Davison** (township) Genesee County
52	1163	787	**Kalamazoo** (charter township) Kalamazoo County
52	1163	787	**Kalamazoo** (city) Kalamazoo County
54	1188	778	**Birmingham** (city) Oakland County
54	1188	778	**Comstock** (charter township) Kalamazoo County
56	1195	774	**Adrian** (city) Lenawee County
56	1195	774	**Burton** (city) Genesee County
58	1202	771	**Mount Morris** (township) Genesee County
58	1202	771	**Mount Pleasant** (city) Isabella County
60	1243	758	**Alpine** (township) Kent County
61	1251	755	**Genesee** (charter township) Genesee County
61	1251	755	**Rochester** (city) Oakland County
63	1264	751	**East Grand Rapids** (city) Kent County
63	1264	751	**Flint** (charter township) Genesee County
63	1264	751	**Flint** (city) Genesee County
66	1273	748	**Byron** (township) Kent County
66	1273	748	**Farmington** (city) Oakland County
66	1273	748	**Troy** (city) Oakland County
66	1273	748	**Walker** (city) Kent County
70	1284	745	**Northview** (CDP) Kent County
71	1290	741	**Superior** (charter township) Washtenaw County
72	1302	738	**Bloomfield** (charter township) Oakland County
73	1330	728	**Beverly Hills** (village) Oakland County
73	1330	728	**Owosso** (city) Shiawassee County
75	1343	725	**Plymouth** (charter township) Wayne County
75	1343	725	**Ypsilanti** (charter township) Washtenaw County
75	1343	725	**Ypsilanti** (city) Washtenaw County
78	1363	718	**Ionia** (city) Ionia County
79	1411	702	**Washington** (township) Macomb County
80	1424	699	**Flushing** (charter township) Genesee County
81	1443	692	**Niles** (city) Berrien County
81	1443	692	**Niles** (township) Berrien County
83	1453	689	**Kentwood** (city) Kent County
84	1466	682	**Berkley** (city) Oakland County
84	1466	682	**Shelby** (charter township) Macomb County
84	1466	682	**Southfield** (city) Oakland County
84	1466	682	**Southfield** (township) Oakland County
88	1479	679	**Canton** (charter township) Wayne County
88	1479	679	**Van Buren** (charter township) Wayne County
90	1491	676	**Cutlerville** (CDP) Kent County
91	1524	666	**Cascade** (charter township) Kent County
91	1524	666	**Clawson** (city) Oakland County
91	1524	666	**Marquette** (city) Marquette County
91	1524	666	**Westland** (city) Wayne County
95	1538	663	**Oak Park** (city) Oakland County
95	1538	663	**Royal Oak** (city) Oakland County
97	1546	659	**Comstock Park** (CDP) Kent County
97	1546	659	**Romulus** (city) Wayne County
99	1560	656	**Wayne** (city) Wayne County
100	1566	653	**Allendale** (CDP) Ottawa County
100	1566	653	**Allendale** (charter township) Ottawa County
102	1593	646	**Ferndale** (city) Oakland County
103	1606	643	**Wyoming** (city) Kent County
104	1618	640	**Ada** (township) Kent County
104	1618	640	**Grand Rapids** (charter township) Kent County
104	1618	640	**Grand Rapids** (city) Kent County
104	1618	640	**Livonia** (city) Wayne County
108	1633	636	**Highland Park** (city) Wayne County
109	1642	633	**Garden City** (city) Wayne County
109	1642	633	**Saint Joseph** (charter township) Berrien County
111	1654	630	**Forest Hills** (CDP) Kent County
111	1654	630	**Hamtramck** (city) Wayne County
111	1654	630	**Hazel Park** (city) Oakland County
111	1654	630	**Madison Heights** (city) Oakland County
115	1671	627	**Fruitport** (charter township) Muskegon County
115	1671	627	**Inkster** (city) Wayne County
115	1671	627	**Macomb** (township) Macomb County
115	1671	627	**Midland** (city) Midland County
115	1671	627	**Muskegon Heights** (city) Muskegon County
120	1686	623	**Redford** (charter township) Wayne County
120	1686	623	**Warren** (city) Macomb County
122	1703	620	**Dearborn Heights** (city) Wayne County
123	1714	617	**Muskegon** (charter township) Muskegon County
123	1714	617	**Muskegon** (city) Muskegon County
123	1714	617	**Roseville** (city) Macomb County
123	1714	617	**Sault Sainte Marie** (city) Chippewa County
127	1729	614	**Eastpointe** (city) Macomb County
127	1729	614	**Fraser** (city) Macomb County
127	1729	614	**Sterling Heights** (city) Macomb County
127	1729	614	**Taylor** (city) Wayne County
131	1749	610	**Holland** (charter township) Ottawa County
131	1749	610	**Holland** (city) Ottawa County
131	1749	610	**Mount Clemens** (city) Macomb County
131	1749	610	**Norton Shores** (city) Muskegon County
135	1770	607	**Chesterfield** (township) Macomb County
135	1770	607	**Clinton** (charter township) Macomb County
135	1770	607	**Escanaba** (city) Delta County
135	1770	607	**Port Huron** (charter township) Saint Clair County
135	1770	607	**Port Huron** (city) Saint Clair County
140	1786	604	**Bridgeport** (charter township) Saginaw County
140	1786	604	**Grand Haven** (charter township) Ottawa County
140	1786	604	**Grand Haven** (city) Ottawa County
140	1786	604	**Grandville** (city) Kent County
140	1786	604	**Jenison** (CDP) Ottawa County
140	1786	604	**Woodhaven** (city) Wayne County
146	1812	600	**Riverview** (city) Wayne County
147	1833	597	**Detroit** (city) Wayne County
147	1833	597	**Grosse Ile** (township) Wayne County
147	1833	597	**Spring Lake** (township) Ottawa County
147	1833	597	**Traverse City** (city) Grand Traverse County

Note: *The state column ranks the top/bottom 150 places from all places in the state with population of 10,000 or more. The national column ranks the top/bottom 150 places from all places in the country with population of 10,000 or more. Places that are unincorporated were not considered in the rankings. Please refer to the User Guide for additional information.*

Elevation

Top 150 Places Ranked in *Ascending* Order

State Rank	Nat'l Rank	Feet	Place
1	2463	581	**Grosse Pointe Park** (city) Wayne County
1	2463	581	**Saginaw** (charter township) Saginaw County
1	2463	581	**Saginaw** (city) Saginaw County
1	2463	581	**Saint Clair Shores** (city) Macomb County
1	2463	581	**Wyandotte** (city) Wayne County
6	2484	587	**Grosse Pointe Woods** (city) Wayne County
6	2484	587	**Harper Woods** (city) Wayne County
6	2484	587	**Lincoln Park** (city) Wayne County
6	2484	587	**New Baltimore** (city) Macomb County
10	2492	591	**Alpena** (city) Alpena County
10	2492	591	**Dearborn** (city) Wayne County
10	2492	591	**Frenchtown** (township) Monroe County
10	2492	591	**Melvindale** (city) Wayne County
10	2492	591	**Southgate** (city) Wayne County
15	2503	594	**Allen Park** (city) Wayne County
15	2503	594	**Bay City** (city) Bay County
15	2503	594	**Benton Harbor** (city) Berrien County
15	2503	594	**Monroe** (charter township) Monroe County
15	2503	594	**Monroe** (city) Monroe County
20	2517	597	**Detroit** (city) Wayne County
20	2517	597	**Grosse Ile** (township) Wayne County
20	2517	597	**Spring Lake** (township) Ottawa County
20	2517	597	**Traverse City** (city) Grand Traverse County
20	2517	597	**Trenton** (city) Wayne County
25	2535	600	**Riverview** (city) Wayne County
26	2556	604	**Bridgeport** (charter township) Saginaw County
26	2556	604	**Grand Haven** (charter township) Ottawa County
26	2556	604	**Grand Haven** (city) Ottawa County
26	2556	604	**Grandville** (city) Kent County
26	2556	604	**Jenison** (CDP) Ottawa County
26	2556	604	**Woodhaven** (city) Wayne County
32	2582	607	**Chesterfield** (township) Macomb County
32	2582	607	**Clinton** (charter township) Macomb County
32	2582	607	**Escanaba** (city) Delta County
32	2582	607	**Port Huron** (charter township) Saint Clair County
32	2582	607	**Port Huron** (city) Saint Clair County
37	2598	610	**Holland** (charter township) Ottawa County
37	2598	610	**Holland** (city) Ottawa County
37	2598	610	**Mount Clemens** (city) Macomb County
37	2598	610	**Norton Shores** (city) Muskegon County
41	2619	614	**Eastpointe** (city) Macomb County
41	2619	614	**Fraser** (city) Macomb County
41	2619	614	**Sterling Heights** (city) Macomb County
41	2619	614	**Taylor** (city) Wayne County
45	2639	617	**Muskegon** (charter township) Muskegon County
45	2639	617	**Muskegon** (city) Muskegon County
45	2639	617	**Roseville** (city) Macomb County
45	2639	617	**Sault Sainte Marie** (city) Chippewa County
49	2654	620	**Dearborn Heights** (city) Wayne County
50	2665	623	**Redford** (charter township) Wayne County
50	2665	623	**Warren** (city) Macomb County
52	2682	627	**Fruitport** (charter township) Muskegon County
52	2682	627	**Inkster** (city) Wayne County
52	2682	627	**Macomb** (township) Macomb County
52	2682	627	**Midland** (city) Midland County
52	2682	627	**Muskegon Heights** (city) Muskegon County
57	2697	630	**Forest Hills** (CDP) Kent County
57	2697	630	**Hamtramck** (city) Wayne County
57	2697	630	**Hazel Park** (city) Oakland County
57	2697	630	**Madison Heights** (city) Oakland County
61	2714	633	**Garden City** (city) Wayne County
61	2714	633	**Saint Joseph** (charter township) Berrien County
63	2726	636	**Highland Park** (city) Wayne County
64	2735	640	**Ada** (township) Kent County
64	2735	640	**Grand Rapids** (charter township) Kent County
64	2735	640	**Grand Rapids** (city) Kent County
64	2735	640	**Livonia** (city) Wayne County
68	2750	643	**Wyoming** (city) Kent County
69	2762	646	**Ferndale** (city) Oakland County
70	2788	653	**Allendale** (CDP) Ottawa County
70	2788	653	**Allendale** (charter township) Ottawa County
72	2802	656	**Wayne** (city) Wayne County
73	2808	659	**Comstock Park** (CDP) Kent County
73	2808	659	**Romulus** (city) Wayne County
75	2822	663	**Oak Park** (city) Oakland County
75	2822	663	**Royal Oak** (city) Oakland County
77	2830	666	**Cascade** (charter township) Kent County
77	2830	666	**Clawson** (city) Oakland County
77	2830	666	**Marquette** (city) Marquette County
77	2830	666	**Westland** (city) Wayne County
81	2865	676	**Cutlerville** (CDP) Kent County
82	2877	679	**Canton** (charter township) Wayne County
82	2877	679	**Van Buren** (charter township) Wayne County
84	2889	682	**Berkley** (city) Oakland County
84	2889	682	**Shelby** (charter township) Macomb County
84	2889	682	**Southfield** (city) Oakland County
84	2889	682	**Southfield** (township) Oakland County
88	2910	689	**Kentwood** (city) Kent County
89	2915	692	**Niles** (city) Berrien County
89	2915	692	**Niles** (township) Berrien County
91	2933	699	**Flushing** (charter township) Genesee County
92	2944	702	**Washington** (township) Macomb County
93	2993	718	**Ionia** (city) Ionia County
94	3014	725	**Plymouth** (charter township) Wayne County
94	3014	725	**Ypsilanti** (charter township) Washtenaw County
94	3014	725	**Ypsilanti** (city) Washtenaw County
97	3025	728	**Beverly Hills** (village) Oakland County
97	3025	728	**Owosso** (city) Shiawassee County
99	3053	738	**Bloomfield** (charter township) Oakland County
100	3066	741	**Superior** (charter township) Washtenaw County
101	3078	745	**Northview** (CDP) Kent County
102	3084	748	**Byron** (township) Kent County
102	3084	748	**Farmington** (city) Oakland County
102	3084	748	**Troy** (city) Oakland County
102	3084	748	**Walker** (city) Kent County
106	3095	751	**East Grand Rapids** (city) Kent County
106	3095	751	**Flint** (charter township) Genesee County
106	3095	751	**Flint** (city) Genesee County
109	3104	755	**Genesee** (charter township) Genesee County
109	3104	755	**Rochester** (city) Oakland County
111	3117	758	**Alpine** (township) Kent County
112	3157	771	**Mount Morris** (township) Genesee County
112	3157	771	**Mount Pleasant** (city) Isabella County
114	3166	774	**Adrian** (city) Lenawee County
114	3166	774	**Burton** (city) Genesee County
116	3173	778	**Birmingham** (city) Oakland County
116	3173	778	**Comstock** (charter township) Kalamazoo County
118	3194	787	**Kalamazoo** (charter township) Kalamazoo County
118	3194	787	**Kalamazoo** (city) Kalamazoo County
120	3208	794	**Davison** (township) Genesee County
121	3228	801	**Beecher** (CDP) Genesee County
122	3259	814	**Caledonia** (township) Kent County
123	3273	820	**Rochester Hills** (city) Oakland County
124	3283	827	**Northville** (township) Wayne County
125	3306	833	**Pittsfield** (charter township) Washtenaw County
126	3313	837	**DeWitt** (charter township) Clinton County
127	3318	840	**Battle Creek** (city) Calhoun County
127	3318	840	**Grand Blanc** (charter township) Genesee County
127	3318	840	**Okemos** (CDP) Ingham County
130	3339	850	**Farmington Hills** (city) Oakland County
131	3347	853	**Lansing** (city) Ingham County
132	3355	856	**East Lansing** (city) Ingham County
133	3361	860	**Waverly** (CDP) Eaton County
134	3369	863	**Bath** (charter township) Clinton County
135	3378	866	**Delta** (charter township) Eaton County
136	3395	873	**Cooper** (charter township) Kalamazoo County
136	3395	873	**Scio** (township) Washtenaw County
138	3407	876	**Haslett** (CDP) Ingham County
139	3413	879	**Ann Arbor** (city) Washtenaw County
139	3413	879	**Portage** (city) Kalamazoo County
141	3428	883	**Delhi** (charter township) Ingham County
142	3444	889	**Holt** (CDP) Ingham County
143	3458	896	**Meridian** (charter township) Ingham County
144	3468	899	**Hamburg** (township) Livingston County
145	3488	906	**Fenton** (charter township) Genesee County
145	3488	906	**Fenton** (city) Genesee County
147	3499	909	**Novi** (city) Oakland County
148	3516	915	**Sturgis** (city) Saint Joseph County
149	3530	925	**Brighton** (township) Livingston County
149	3530	925	**Holly** (township) Oakland County

Note: The state column ranks the top/bottom 150 places from all places in the state with population of 10,000 or more. The national column ranks the top/bottom 150 places from all places in the country with population of 10,000 or more. Places that are unincorporated were not considered in the rankings. Please refer to the User Guide for additional information.

Population

Top 150 Places Ranked in *Descending* Order

State Rank	Nat'l Rank	Number	Place
1	23	713,777	**Detroit** (city) Wayne County
2	138	188,040	**Grand Rapids** (city) Kent County
3	201	134,056	**Warren** (city) Macomb County
4	206	129,699	**Sterling Heights** (city) Macomb County
5	247	114,297	**Lansing** (city) Ingham County
6	248	113,934	**Ann Arbor** (city) Washtenaw County
7	291	102,434	**Flint** (city) Genesee County
8	313	98,153	**Dearborn** (city) Wayne County
9	321	96,942	**Livonia** (city) Wayne County
10	324	96,796	**Clinton** (charter township) Macomb County
11	359	90,173	**Canton** (charter township) Wayne County
12	404	84,094	**Westland** (city) Wayne County
13	424	80,980	**Troy** (city) Oakland County
14	435	79,740	**Farmington Hills** (city) Oakland County
15	436	79,580	**Macomb** (township) Macomb County
16	486	74,262	**Kalamazoo** (city) Kalamazoo County
17	491	73,804	**Shelby** (charter township) Macomb County
18	502	72,125	**Wyoming** (city) Kent County
19	506	71,739	**Southfield** (city) Oakland County
20	507	71,707	**Waterford** (charter township) Oakland County
21	513	70,995	**Rochester Hills** (city) Oakland County
22	582	64,690	**West Bloomfield** (charter township) Oakland County
23	600	63,131	**Taylor** (city) Wayne County
24	653	59,715	**Saint Clair Shores** (city) Macomb County
25	656	59,515	**Pontiac** (city) Oakland County
26	684	57,774	**Dearborn Heights** (city) Wayne County
27	693	57,236	**Royal Oak** (city) Oakland County
28	738	55,224	**Novi** (city) Oakland County
29	772	53,362	**Ypsilanti** (charter township) Washtenaw County
30	789	52,347	**Battle Creek** (city) Calhoun County
31	804	51,508	**Saginaw** (city) Saginaw County
32	864	48,707	**Kentwood** (city) Kent County
33	866	48,579	**East Lansing** (city) Ingham County
34	875	48,362	**Redford** (charter township) Wayne County
35	908	47,299	**Roseville** (city) Macomb County
36	913	46,985	**Georgetown** (charter township) Ottawa County
37	925	46,292	**Portage** (city) Kalamazoo County
38	988	43,381	**Chesterfield** (township) Macomb County
39	1030	41,863	**Midland** (city) Midland County
40	1059	41,070	**Bloomfield** (charter township) Oakland County
41	1068	40,840	**Saginaw** (charter township) Saginaw County
42	1083	40,186	**Commerce** (charter township) Oakland County
43	1097	39,688	**Meridian** (charter township) Ingham County
44	1137	38,401	**Muskegon** (city) Muskegon County
45	1143	38,144	**Lincoln Park** (city) Wayne County
46	1167	37,508	**Grand Blanc** (charter township) Genesee County
47	1250	35,636	**Holland** (charter township) Ottawa County
48	1262	35,394	**Orion** (charter township) Oakland County
49	1281	34,932	**Bay City** (city) Bay County
50	1292	34,681	**Independence** (charter township) Oakland County
51	1294	34,663	**Pittsfield** (charter township) Washtenaw County
52	1341	33,534	**Jackson** (city) Jackson County
53	1374	33,051	**Holland** (city) Ottawa County
54	1402	32,442	**Eastpointe** (city) Macomb County
55	1406	32,408	**Delta** (charter township) Eaton County
56	1427	31,929	**Flint** (charter township) Genesee County
57	1464	31,085	**Bedford** (township) Monroe County
58	1471	30,952	**Plainfield** (charter township) Kent County
59	1485	30,627	**Brownstown** (charter township) Wayne County
60	1516	30,184	**Port Huron** (city) Saint Clair County
61	1523	30,047	**Southgate** (city) Wayne County
62	1526	30,019	**White Lake** (charter township) Oakland County
63	1528	29,999	**Burton** (city) Genesee County
64	1548	29,694	**Madison Heights** (city) Oakland County
65	1579	29,319	**Oak Park** (city) Oakland County
66	1616	28,821	**Van Buren** (charter township) Wayne County
67	1633	28,497	**Northville** (township) Wayne County
68	1655	28,210	**Allen Park** (city) Wayne County
69	1693	27,692	**Garden City** (city) Wayne County
70	1707	27,524	**Plymouth** (charter township) Wayne County
71	1823	26,016	**Mount Pleasant** (city) Isabella County
72	1829	25,883	**Wyandotte** (city) Wayne County
73	1830	25,877	**Delhi** (charter township) Ingham County
74	1831	25,867	**Forest Hills** (CDP) Kent County
75	1873	25,369	**Inkster** (city) Wayne County
76	1892	25,146	**Gaines** (charter township) Kent County
77	1893	25,139	**Washington** (township) Macomb County
78	1939	24,587	**Harrison** (charter township) Macomb County
79	1987	24,051	**Blackman** (charter township) Jackson County
80	1996	23,994	**Norton Shores** (city) Muskegon County
81	1997	23,989	**Romulus** (city) Wayne County
82	1998	23,973	**Holt** (CDP) Ingham County
83	2002	23,925	**Waverly** (CDP) Eaton County
84	2041	23,537	**Walker** (city) Kent County
85	2150	22,508	**Summit** (township) Jackson County
86	2156	22,423	**Hamtramck** (city) Wayne County
87	2204	21,918	**Kalamazoo** (charter township) Kalamazoo County
88	2223	21,705	**Oshtemo** (charter township) Kalamazoo County
89	2234	21,581	**Genesee** (charter township) Genesee County
90	2244	21,501	**Mount Morris** (township) Genesee County
91	2255	21,412	**Auburn Hills** (city) Oakland County
92	2262	21,369	**Okemos** (CDP) Ingham County
93	2264	21,355	**Marquette** (city) Marquette County
94	2286	21,165	**Hamburg** (township) Livingston County
95	2290	21,133	**Adrian** (city) Lenawee County
96	2327	20,733	**Monroe** (city) Monroe County
97	2331	20,708	**Allendale** (charter township) Ottawa County
98	2351	20,526	**Oxford** (charter township) Oakland County
99	2360	20,428	**Frenchtown** (township) Monroe County
100	2378	20,317	**Byron** (township) Kent County
101	2407	20,103	**Birmingham** (city) Oakland County
102	2409	20,081	**Scio** (township) Washtenaw County
103	2434	19,900	**Ferndale** (city) Oakland County
104	2442	19,821	**Genoa** (township) Livingston County
105	2470	19,575	**Davison** (township) Genesee County
106	2493	19,435	**Ypsilanti** (city) Washtenaw County
107	2523	19,220	**Haslett** (CDP) Ingham County
108	2530	19,202	**Highland** (charter township) Oakland County
109	2588	18,853	**Trenton** (city) Wayne County
110	2744	17,840	**Muskegon** (charter township) Muskegon County
111	2750	17,802	**Park** (township) Ottawa County
112	2752	17,791	**Brighton** (township) Livingston County
113	2778	17,593	**Wayne** (city) Wayne County
114	2780	17,579	**Allendale** (CDP) Ottawa County
115	2804	17,476	**Green Oak** (township) Livingston County
116	2860	17,134	**Cascade** (charter township) Kent County
117	2901	16,779	**Oakland** (charter township) Oakland County
118	2924	16,661	**Grand Rapids** (charter township) Kent County
119	2941	16,538	**Jenison** (CDP) Ottawa County
120	2957	16,422	**Hazel Park** (city) Oakland County
121	2983	16,314	**Mount Clemens** (city) Macomb County
122	2993	16,256	**Garfield** (charter township) Grand Traverse County
123	3015	16,135	**Grosse Pointe Woods** (city) Wayne County
124	3062	15,879	**Huron** (charter township) Wayne County
125	3095	15,736	**Milford** (charter township) Oakland County
126	3130	15,552	**Fenton** (charter township) Genesee County
127	3165	15,378	**Grandville** (city) Kent County
128	3206	15,194	**Owosso** (city) Shiawassee County
129	3211	15,178	**Grand Haven** (charter township) Ottawa County
130	3214	15,175	**Brandon** (charter township) Oakland County
131	3236	15,082	**Mundy** (township) Genesee County
132	3257	14,970	**Berkley** (city) Oakland County
133	3283	14,854	**Comstock** (charter township) Kalamazoo County
134	3307	14,749	**Benton** (charter township) Berrien County
135	3317	14,697	**Texas** (charter township) Kalamazoo County
136	3318	14,691	**Lincoln** (charter township) Berrien County
137	3321	14,674	**Traverse City** (city) Grand Traverse County
138	3324	14,663	**Hartland** (township) Livingston County
139	3330	14,641	**Bangor** (township) Bay County
140	3344	14,568	**Monroe** (charter township) Monroe County
141	3348	14,547	**Southfield** (township) Oakland County
142	3350	14,545	**Lyon** (charter township) Oakland County
143	3354	14,497	**Northview** (CDP) Kent County
144	3370	14,480	**Fraser** (city) Macomb County
145	3392	14,370	**Cutlerville** (CDP) Kent County
146	3399	14,321	**DeWitt** (charter township) Clinton County
147	3406	14,300	**Spring Lake** (township) Ottawa County
148	3419	14,236	**Harper Woods** (city) Wayne County
149	3441	14,164	**Niles** (township) Berrien County
150	3446	14,144	**Sault Sainte Marie** (city) Chippewa County

Note: The state column ranks the top/bottom 150 places from all places in the state with population of 10,000 or more. The national column ranks the top/bottom 150 places from all places in the country with population of 10,000 or more. Places that are unincorporated were not considered in the rankings. Please refer to the User Guide for additional information.

Population

Top 150 Places Ranked in *Ascending* Order

State Rank	Nat'l Rank	Number	Place
1	6	10,020	**Tyrone** (township) Livingston County
2	10	10,028	**Saint Joseph** (charter township) Berrien County
3	14	10,038	**Benton Harbor** (city) Berrien County
4	24	10,088	**Comstock Park** (CDP) Kent County
5	36	10,111	**Cooper** (charter township) Kalamazoo County
6	83	10,232	**Beecher** (CDP) Genesee County
7	97	10,267	**Beverly Hills** (village) Oakland County
8	130	10,355	**Cadillac** (city) Wexford County
9	133	10,371	**Grosse Ile** (township) Wayne County
10	134	10,372	**Farmington** (city) Oakland County
11	148	10,412	**Grand Haven** (city) Ottawa County
12	163	10,470	**Lenox** (township) Macomb County
13	169	10,483	**Alpena** (city) Alpena County
14	185	10,514	**Bridgeport** (charter township) Saginaw County
15	218	10,601	**Big Rapids** (city) Mecosta County
16	232	10,640	**Flushing** (charter township) Genesee County
17	240	10,654	**Port Huron** (charter township) Saint Clair County
18	243	10,663	**East Bay** (township) Grand Traverse County
19	256	10,694	**East Grand Rapids** (city) Kent County
20	265	10,715	**Melvindale** (city) Wayne County
21	268	10,735	**Monitor** (charter township) Bay County
22	309	10,856	**Muskegon Heights** (city) Muskegon County
23	342	10,945	**Coldwater** (city) Branch County
24	355	10,994	**Sturgis** (city) Saint Joseph County
25	392	11,108	**Fort Gratiot** (charter township) Saint Clair County
26	471	11,327	**South Lyon** (city) Oakland County
27	480	11,362	**Holly** (township) Oakland County
28	493	11,394	**Ionia** (city) Ionia County
29	552	11,555	**Grosse Pointe Park** (city) Wayne County
30	570	11,598	**Bath** (charter township) Clinton County
31	571	11,600	**Niles** (city) Berrien County
32	600	11,756	**Fenton** (city) Genesee County
33	605	11,770	**Emmett** (charter township) Calhoun County
34	610	11,776	**Highland Park** (city) Wayne County
35	623	11,825	**Clawson** (city) Oakland County
36	651	11,936	**Oceola** (township) Livingston County
37	668	11,985	**Thomas** (township) Saginaw County
38	696	12,084	**New Baltimore** (city) Macomb County
39	722	12,182	**Antwerp** (township) Van Buren County
40	760	12,332	**Caledonia** (township) Kent County
41	801	12,486	**Riverview** (city) Wayne County
42	831	12,616	**Escanaba** (city) Delta County
43	857	12,711	**Rochester** (city) Oakland County
44	894	12,875	**Woodhaven** (city) Wayne County
45	902	12,927	**Union** (charter township) Isabella County
46	933	13,058	**Superior** (charter township) Washtenaw County
47	955	13,142	**Ada** (township) Kent County
48	984	13,255	**Vienna** (charter township) Genesee County
49	1004	13,336	**Alpine** (township) Kent County
49	1004	13,336	**Cannon** (township) Kent County
51	1047	13,498	**Wixom** (city) Oakland County
52	1077	13,598	**Fruitport** (charter township) Muskegon County
53	1131	13,807	**Leoni** (township) Jackson County
54	1159	13,940	**Springfield** (charter township) Oakland County
55	1210	14,144	**Sault Sainte Marie** (city) Chippewa County
56	1215	14,164	**Niles** (township) Berrien County
57	1236	14,236	**Harper Woods** (city) Wayne County
58	1250	14,300	**Spring Lake** (township) Ottawa County
59	1256	14,321	**DeWitt** (charter township) Clinton County
60	1264	14,370	**Cutlerville** (CDP) Kent County
61	1286	14,480	**Fraser** (city) Macomb County
62	1301	14,541	**Northview** (CDP) Kent County
63	1304	14,545	**Lyon** (charter township) Oakland County
64	1308	14,547	**Southfield** (township) Oakland County
65	1311	14,568	**Monroe** (charter township) Monroe County
66	1326	14,641	**Bangor** (charter township) Bay County
67	1331	14,663	**Hartland** (township) Livingston County
68	1335	14,674	**Traverse City** (city) Grand Traverse County
69	1337	14,691	**Lincoln** (charter township) Berrien County
70	1339	14,697	**Texas** (charter township) Kalamazoo County
71	1349	14,749	**Benton** (charter township) Berrien County
72	1373	14,854	**Comstock** (charter township) Kalamazoo County
73	1399	14,970	**Berkley** (city) Oakland County
74	1420	15,082	**Mundy** (township) Genesee County
75	1441	15,175	**Brandon** (charter township) Oakland County
76	1445	15,178	**Grand Haven** (charter township) Ottawa County
77	1450	15,194	**Owosso** (city) Shiawassee County
78	1491	15,378	**Grandville** (city) Kent County
79	1525	15,552	**Fenton** (charter township) Genesee County
80	1561	15,736	**Milford** (charter township) Oakland County
81	1594	15,879	**Huron** (charter township) Wayne County
82	1641	16,135	**Grosse Pointe Woods** (city) Wayne County
83	1662	16,256	**Garfield** (charter township) Grand Traverse County
84	1673	16,314	**Mount Clemens** (city) Macomb County
85	1698	16,422	**Hazel Park** (city) Oakland County
86	1715	16,538	**Jenison** (CDP) Ottawa County
87	1732	16,661	**Grand Rapids** (charter township) Kent County
88	1755	16,779	**Oakland** (charter township) Oakland County
89	1796	17,134	**Cascade** (charter township) Kent County
90	1852	17,476	**Green Oak** (township) Livingston County
91	1876	17,579	**Allendale** (CDP) Ottawa County
92	1878	17,593	**Wayne** (city) Wayne County
93	1904	17,791	**Brighton** (township) Livingston County
94	1906	17,802	**Park** (township) Ottawa County
95	1912	17,840	**Muskegon** (charter township) Muskegon County
96	2068	18,853	**Trenton** (city) Wayne County
97	2126	19,202	**Highland** (charter township) Oakland County
98	2133	19,220	**Haslett** (CDP) Ingham County
99	2162	19,435	**Ypsilanti** (city) Washtenaw County
100	2186	19,575	**Davison** (township) Genesee County
101	2214	19,821	**Genoa** (township) Livingston County
102	2222	19,900	**Ferndale** (city) Oakland County
103	2247	20,081	**Scio** (township) Washtenaw County
104	2249	20,103	**Birmingham** (city) Oakland County
105	2278	20,317	**Byron** (township) Kent County
106	2296	20,428	**Frenchtown** (township) Monroe County
107	2305	20,526	**Oxford** (charter township) Oakland County
108	2325	20,708	**Allendale** (charter township) Ottawa County
109	2329	20,733	**Monroe** (city) Monroe County
110	2366	21,133	**Adrian** (city) Lenawee County
111	2369	21,165	**Hamburg** (township) Livingston County
112	2392	21,355	**Marquette** (city) Marquette County
113	2394	21,369	**Okemos** (CDP) Ingham County
114	2401	21,412	**Auburn Hills** (city) Oakland County
115	2412	21,501	**Mount Morris** (township) Genesee County
116	2422	21,581	**Genesee** (charter township) Genesee County
117	2432	21,705	**Oshtemo** (charter township) Kalamazoo County
118	2452	21,918	**Kalamazoo** (charter township) Kalamazoo County
119	2500	22,423	**Hamtramck** (city) Wayne County
120	2506	22,508	**Summit** (township) Jackson County
121	2615	23,537	**Walker** (city) Kent County
122	2654	23,925	**Waverly** (CDP) Eaton County
123	2658	23,973	**Holt** (CDP) Ingham County
124	2659	23,989	**Romulus** (city) Wayne County
125	2660	23,994	**Norton Shores** (city) Muskegon County
126	2669	24,051	**Blackman** (charter township) Jackson County
127	2717	24,587	**Harrison** (charter township) Macomb County
128	2763	25,139	**Washington** (township) Macomb County
129	2764	25,146	**Gaines** (charter township) Kent County
130	2783	25,369	**Inkster** (city) Wayne County
131	2825	25,867	**Forest Hills** (CDP) Kent County
132	2826	25,877	**Delhi** (charter township) Ingham County
133	2827	25,883	**Wyandotte** (city) Wayne County
134	2833	26,016	**Mount Pleasant** (city) Isabella County
135	2949	27,524	**Plymouth** (charter township) Wayne County
136	2963	27,692	**Garden City** (city) Wayne County
137	3001	28,210	**Allen Park** (city) Wayne County
138	3023	28,497	**Northville** (township) Wayne County
139	3040	28,821	**Van Buren** (charter township) Wayne County
140	3077	29,319	**Oak Park** (city) Oakland County
141	3108	29,694	**Madison Heights** (city) Oakland County
142	3128	29,999	**Burton** (city) Genesee County
143	3130	30,019	**White Lake** (charter township) Oakland County
144	3133	30,047	**Southgate** (city) Wayne County
145	3140	30,184	**Port Huron** (city) Saint Clair County
146	3171	30,627	**Brownstown** (charter township) Wayne County
147	3185	30,952	**Plainfield** (charter township) Kent County
148	3192	31,085	**Bedford** (township) Monroe County
149	3229	31,929	**Flint** (charter township) Genesee County
150	3250	32,408	**Delta** (charter township) Eaton County

Note: The state column ranks the top/bottom 150 places from all places in the state with population of 10,000 or more. The national column ranks the top/bottom 150 places from all places in the country with population of 10,000 or more. Places that are unincorporated were not considered in the rankings. Please refer to the User Guide for additional information.

Population Growth

Top 150 Places Ranked in *Descending* Order

State Rank	Nat'l Rank	Percent	Place	State Rank	Nat'l Rank	Percent	Place
1	142	111.9	Holt (CDP) Ingham County	76	2187	6.3	Niles (township) Berrien County
2	268	70.3	Haslett (CDP) Ingham County	77	2253	5.8	Orion (charter township) Oakland County
3	270	69.8	Union (charter township) Isabella County	78	2287	5.5	Blackman (charter township) Jackson County
4	309	63.2	New Baltimore (city) Macomb County	79	2324	5.3	Lincoln (charter township) Berrien County
5	335	58.8	Allendale (charter township) Ottawa County	80	2469	4.5	Springfield (charter township) Oakland County
6	346	57.7	Macomb (township) Macomb County	80	2469	4.5	Summit (township) Jackson County
7	377	53.8	Bath (charter township) Clinton County	82	2481	4.4	East Lansing (city) Ingham County
8	393	52.1	Allendale (CDP) Ottawa County	82	2481	4.4	Romulus (city) Wayne County
9	435	47.7	Waverly (CDP) Eaton County	84	2515	4.2	Birmingham (city) Oakland County
10	495	42.7	Oceola (township) Livingston County	84	2515	4.2	Sterling Heights (city) Macomb County
11	588	37.6	Caledonia (township) Kent County	86	2547	4.0	Flushing (charter township) Genesee County
12	629	35.5	Northville (township) Wayne County	86	2547	4.0	Wyoming (city) Kent County
13	649	34.6	Texas (charter township) Kalamazoo County	88	2573	3.9	Fort Gratiot (charter township) Saint Clair County
14	673	33.3	Hartland (township) Livingston County	89	2638	3.6	Cadillac (city) Wexford County
15	675	33.2	Brownstown (charter township) Wayne County	90	2723	3.2	Rochester Hills (city) Oakland County
16	678	33.0	Ada (township) Kent County	91	2747	3.1	Portage (city) Kalamazoo County
17	708	31.8	Washington (township) Macomb County	92	2773	3.0	Milford (charter township) Oakland County
18	710	31.7	Lyon (charter township) Oakland County	92	2773	3.0	Saginaw (charter township) Saginaw County
19	779	28.4	Oakland (charter township) Oakland County	94	2812	2.8	Brandon (charter township) Oakland County
20	788	28.1	Oxford (charter township) Oakland County	94	2812	2.8	Woodhaven (city) Wayne County
21	798	27.7	Oshtemo (charter township) Kalamazoo County	96	2846	2.6	Hamburg (township) Livingston County
22	809	27.4	Scio (township) Washtenaw County	96	2846	2.6	Leoni (township) Jackson County
23	858	25.8	Grand Blanc (charter township) Genesee County	98	2869	2.5	Plainfield (charter township) Kent County
24	882	25.0	Gaines (charter township) Kent County	99	3030	1.8	Wixom (city) Oakland County
25	891	24.7	Genoa (township) Livingston County	100	3092	1.5	Meridian (charter township) Ingham County
26	916	24.2	Lenox (township) Macomb County	101	3133	1.3	Park (township) Ottawa County
27	933	23.7	Mundy (township) Genesee County	102	3156	1.2	Clinton (charter township) Macomb County
27	933	23.7	Port Huron (charter township) Saint Clair County	103	3175	1.1	Kalamazoo (charter township) Kalamazoo County
29	945	23.5	Forest Hills (CDP) Kent County	103	3175	1.1	Vienna (charter township) Genesee County
30	951	23.3	Holland (charter township) Ottawa County	105	3190	1.0	Traverse City (city) Grand Traverse County
31	991	22.3	Van Buren (charter township) Wayne County	106	3211	0.9	Thomas (township) Saginaw County
32	1019	21.6	Superior (charter township) Washtenaw County	107	3237	0.8	Southfield (township) Oakland County
33	1027	21.4	Rochester (city) Oakland County	108	3256	0.7	Brighton (township) Livingston County
34	1092	19.9	Fenton (charter township) Genesee County	109	3281	0.6	Muskegon (charter township) Muskegon County
35	1152	18.5	Grand Rapids (charter township) Kent County	110	3296	0.5	Harrison (charter township) Macomb County
35	1152	18.5	Tyrone (township) Livingston County	111	3318	0.4	Dearborn (city) Wayne County
37	1167	18.1	Canton (charter township) Wayne County	111	3318	0.4	Midland (city) Midland County
38	1172	17.9	DeWitt (charter township) Clinton County	113	3342	0.3	Mount Pleasant (city) Isabella County
39	1197	17.5	Garfield (charter township) Grand Traverse County	114	3367	0.2	Highland (charter township) Oakland County
40	1250	16.5	Novi (city) Oakland County	115	3406	0.0	Troy (city) Oakland County
41	1283	16.0	Chesterfield (township) Macomb County	116	3428	-0.1	Ann Arbor (city) Washtenaw County
42	1308	15.7	Byron (township) Kent County	116	3428	-0.1	Harper Woods (city) Wayne County
43	1318	15.6	Commerce (charter township) Oakland County	116	3428	-0.1	Saint Joseph (charter township) Berrien County
43	1318	15.6	Huron (charter township) Wayne County	119	3452	-0.2	Melvindale (city) Wayne County
45	1323	15.5	Cooper (charter township) Kalamazoo County	120	3468	-0.3	Southgate (city) Wayne County
46	1363	14.9	Pittsfield (charter township) Washtenaw County	120	3468	-0.3	West Bloomfield (charter township) Oakland County
47	1373	14.7	Delhi (charter township) Ingham County	122	3507	-0.5	Farmington (city) Oakland County
48	1396	14.3	Grand Haven (charter township) Ottawa County	123	3550	-0.7	East Grand Rapids (city) Kent County
49	1462	13.4	Cascade (charter township) Kent County	124	3569	-0.8	Dearborn Heights (city) Wayne County
50	1471	13.3	Shelby (charter township) Macomb County	125	3607	-1.0	Burton (city) Genesee County
51	1478	13.2	Holly (charter township) Oakland County	125	3607	-1.0	Plymouth (charter township) Wayne County
52	1503	12.9	South Lyon (city) Oakland County	127	3820	-1.3	Northview (CDP) Kent County
53	1513	12.8	Georgetown (charter township) Ottawa County	128	3866	-1.6	Beverly Hills (village) Oakland County
54	1523	12.7	Antwerp (township) Van Buren County	128	3866	-1.6	Oak Park (city) Oakland County
55	1585	11.9	Green Oak (charter township) Livingston County	130	3884	-1.7	Emmett (charter township) Calhoun County
56	1642	11.1	Fenton (city) Genesee County	130	3884	-1.7	Frenchtown (township) Monroe County
57	1689	10.5	Davison (township) Genesee County	130	3884	-1.7	Roseville (city) Macomb County
58	1696	10.4	Cannon (township) Kent County	133	3913	-1.9	Battle Creek (city) Calhoun County
59	1828	9.2	Delta (charter township) Eaton County	134	3933	-2.0	Adrian (city) Lenawee County
60	1877	8.8	Spring Lake (township) Ottawa County	134	3933	-2.0	Waterford (charter township) Oakland County
61	1888	8.7	Bedford (township) Monroe County	136	3977	-2.3	Big Rapids (city) Mecosta County
62	1898	8.6	Marquette (city) Marquette County	137	3992	-2.4	Hamtramck (city) Wayne County
63	1909	8.5	Fruitport (charter township) Muskegon County	138	4015	-2.6	Sturgis (city) Saint Joseph County
63	1909	8.5	Ypsilanti (charter township) Washtenaw County	139	4053	-2.9	Farmington Hills (city) Oakland County
65	1968	8.0	Monroe (charter township) Monroe County	139	4053	-2.9	Westland (city) Wayne County
66	1981	7.9	Auburn Hills (city) Oakland County	141	4064	-3.0	Warren (city) Macomb County
67	1991	7.8	Ionia (city) Ionia County	142	4099	-3.3	Owosso (city) Shiawassee County
67	1991	7.8	Walker (city) Kent County	143	4136	-3.6	Berkley (city) Oakland County
69	2010	7.6	Kentwood (city) Kent County	143	4136	-3.6	Livonia (city) Wayne County
70	2024	7.5	East Bay (township) Grand Traverse County	145	4149	-3.7	Kalamazoo (city) Kalamazoo County
71	2060	7.2	Comstock (charter township) Kalamazoo County	145	4149	-3.7	Trenton (city) Wayne County
72	2093	7.0	Monitor (charter township) Bay County	147	4172	-3.9	Jenison (CDP) Ottawa County
73	2162	6.5	Norton Shores (city) Muskegon County	148	4180	-4.0	Allen Park (city) Wayne County
74	2174	6.4	Independence (charter township) Oakland County	148	4180	-4.0	Escanaba (city) Delta County
74	2174	6.4	White Lake (charter township) Oakland County	150	4191	-4.1	Lansing (city) Ingham County

Note: The state column ranks the top/bottom 150 places from all places in the state with population of 10,000 or more. The national column ranks the top/bottom 150 places from all places in the country with population of 10,000 or more. Places that are unincorporated were not considered in the rankings. Please refer to the User Guide for additional information.

Population Growth

Top 150 Places Ranked in *Ascending* Order

State Rank	Nat'l Rank	Percent	Place
1	13	-29.7	**Highland Park** (city) Wayne County
2	24	-25.0	**Detroit** (city) Wayne County
3	33	-20.0	**Beecher** (CDP) Genesee County
4	40	-18.0	**Flint** (city) Genesee County
5	49	-16.7	**Saginaw** (city) Saginaw County
6	53	-15.8	**Inkster** (city) Wayne County
7	61	-14.5	**Sault Sainte Marie** (city) Chippewa County
8	71	-13.8	**Coldwater** (city) Branch County
9	73	-13.4	**Hazel Park** (city) Oakland County
10	76	-13.1	**Ypsilanti** (city) Washtenaw County
11	104	-10.5	**Genesee** (charter township) Genesee County
12	109	-10.3	**Pontiac** (city) Oakland County
13	111	-10.2	**Benton Harbor** (city) Berrien County
13	111	-10.2	**Bridgeport** (charter township) Saginaw County
15	115	-10.1	**Benton** (charter township) Berrien County
16	116	-10.0	**Ferndale** (city) Oakland County
17	121	-9.9	**Muskegon Heights** (city) Muskegon County
18	136	-9.4	**Mount Morris** (township) Genesee County
19	156	-8.4	**Southfield** (city) Oakland County
20	185	-7.8	**Garden City** (city) Wayne County
21	190	-7.7	**Jackson** (city) Jackson County
21	190	-7.7	**Wayne** (city) Wayne County
23	195	-7.6	**Wyandotte** (city) Wayne County
24	209	-7.3	**Alpena** (city) Alpena County
25	215	-7.1	**Clawson** (city) Oakland County
25	215	-7.1	**Grosse Pointe Park** (city) Wayne County
27	233	-6.8	**Grand Haven** (city) Ottawa County
28	238	-6.7	**Port Huron** (city) Saint Clair County
29	257	-6.3	**Okemos** (CDP) Ingham County
29	257	-6.3	**Redford** (charter township) Wayne County
31	275	-6.1	**Monroe** (city) Monroe County
32	286	-5.9	**Riverview** (city) Wayne County
33	294	-5.8	**Bangor** (charter township) Bay County
33	294	-5.8	**Mount Clemens** (city) Macomb County
35	301	-5.7	**Holland** (city) Ottawa County
36	316	-5.5	**Comstock Park** (CDP) Kent County
36	316	-5.5	**Grosse Pointe Woods** (city) Wayne County
38	324	-5.4	**Grandville** (city) Kent County
38	324	-5.4	**Saint Clair Shores** (city) Macomb County
40	331	-5.3	**Fraser** (city) Macomb County
41	336	-5.2	**Flint** (charter township) Genesee County
42	342	-5.1	**Bay City** (city) Bay County
43	354	-4.9	**Cutlerville** (CDP) Kent County
43	354	-4.9	**Grand Rapids** (city) Kent County
43	354	-4.9	**Niles** (city) Berrien County
46	370	-4.8	**Eastpointe** (city) Macomb County
46	370	-4.8	**Grosse Ile** (township) Wayne County
48	382	-4.7	**Lincoln Park** (city) Wayne County
48	382	-4.7	**Royal Oak** (city) Oakland County
50	393	-4.6	**Alpine** (township) Kent County
51	407	-4.5	**Bloomfield** (charter township) Oakland County
51	407	-4.5	**Madison Heights** (city) Oakland County
53	442	-4.2	**Muskegon** (city) Muskegon County
53	442	-4.2	**Taylor** (city) Wayne County
55	455	-4.1	**Lansing** (city) Ingham County
56	466	-4.0	**Allen Park** (city) Wayne County
56	466	-4.0	**Escanaba** (city) Delta County
58	477	-3.9	**Jenison** (CDP) Ottawa County
59	493	-3.7	**Kalamazoo** (city) Kalamazoo County
59	493	-3.7	**Trenton** (city) Wayne County
61	508	-3.6	**Berkley** (city) Oakland County
61	508	-3.6	**Livonia** (city) Wayne County
63	546	-3.3	**Owosso** (city) Shiawassee County
64	578	-3.0	**Warren** (city) Macomb County
65	593	-2.9	**Farmington Hills** (city) Oakland County
65	593	-2.9	**Westland** (city) Wayne County
67	629	-2.6	**Sturgis** (city) Saint Joseph County
68	653	-2.4	**Hamtramck** (city) Wayne County
69	665	-2.3	**Big Rapids** (city) Mecosta County
70	709	-2.0	**Adrian** (city) Lenawee County
70	709	-2.0	**Waterford** (charter township) Oakland County
72	724	-1.9	**Battle Creek** (city) Calhoun County
73	760	-1.7	**Emmett** (charter township) Calhoun County
73	760	-1.7	**Frenchtown** (township) Monroe County
73	760	-1.7	**Roseville** (city) Macomb County
76	773	-1.6	**Beverly Hills** (village) Oakland County
76	773	-1.6	**Oak Park** (city) Oakland County
78	821	-1.3	**Northview** (CDP) Kent County
79	863	-1.0	**Burton** (city) Genesee County
79	863	-1.0	**Plymouth** (charter township) Wayne County
81	905	-0.8	**Dearborn Heights** (city) Wayne County
82	924	-0.7	**East Grand Rapids** (city) Kent County
83	962	-0.5	**Farmington** (city) Oakland County
84	1006	-0.3	**Southgate** (city) Wayne County
84	1006	-0.3	**West Bloomfield** (charter township) Oakland County
86	1025	-0.2	**Melvindale** (city) Wayne County
87	1041	-0.1	**Ann Arbor** (city) Washtenaw County
87	1041	-0.1	**Harper Woods** (city) Wayne County
87	1041	-0.1	**Saint Joseph** (charter township) Berrien County
90	1065	0.0	**Troy** (city) Oakland County
91	1104	0.2	**Highland** (charter township) Oakland County
92	1126	0.3	**Mount Pleasant** (city) Isabella County
93	1151	0.4	**Dearborn** (city) Wayne County
93	1151	0.4	**Midland** (city) Midland County
95	1175	0.5	**Harrison** (charter township) Macomb County
96	1197	0.6	**Muskegon** (charter township) Muskegon County
97	1212	0.7	**Brighton** (township) Livingston County
98	1237	0.8	**Southfield** (township) Oakland County
99	1256	0.9	**Thomas** (township) Saginaw County
100	1282	1.0	**Traverse City** (city) Grand Traverse County
101	1303	1.1	**Kalamazoo** (charter township) Kalamazoo County
101	1303	1.1	**Vienna** (charter township) Genesee County
103	1318	1.2	**Clinton** (charter township) Macomb County
104	1337	1.3	**Park** (township) Ottawa County
105	1381	1.5	**Meridian** (charter township) Ingham County
106	1438	1.8	**Wixom** (city) Oakland County
107	1596	2.5	**Plainfield** (charter township) Kent County
108	1624	2.6	**Hamburg** (township) Livingston County
108	1624	2.6	**Leoni** (township) Jackson County
110	1663	2.8	**Brandon** (charter township) Oakland County
110	1663	2.8	**Woodhaven** (city) Wayne County
112	1702	3.0	**Milford** (charter township) Oakland County
112	1702	3.0	**Saginaw** (charter township) Saginaw County
114	1720	3.1	**Portage** (city) Kalamazoo County
115	1746	3.2	**Rochester Hills** (city) Oakland County
116	1824	3.6	**Cadillac** (city) Wexford County
117	1901	3.9	**Fort Gratiot** (charter township) Saint Clair County
118	1920	4.0	**Flushing** (charter township) Genesee County
118	1920	4.0	**Wyoming** (city) Kent County
120	1964	4.2	**Birmingham** (city) Oakland County
120	1964	4.2	**Sterling Heights** (city) Macomb County
122	1992	4.4	**East Lansing** (city) Ingham County
122	1992	4.4	**Romulus** (city) Wayne County
124	2012	4.5	**Springfield** (charter township) Oakland County
124	2012	4.5	**Summit** (township) Jackson County
126	2152	5.3	**Lincoln** (charter township) Berrien County
127	2186	5.5	**Blackman** (charter township) Jackson County
128	2229	5.8	**Orion** (charter township) Oakland County
129	2289	6.3	**Niles** (township) Berrien County
130	2306	6.4	**Independence** (charter township) Oakland County
130	2306	6.4	**White Lake** (charter township) Oakland County
132	2319	6.5	**Norton Shores** (city) Muskegon County
133	2381	7.0	**Monitor** (charter township) Bay County
134	2415	7.2	**Comstock** (charter township) Kalamazoo County
135	2456	7.5	**East Bay** (township) Grand Traverse County
136	2469	7.6	**Kentwood** (city) Kent County
137	2490	7.8	**Ionia** (city) Ionia County
137	2490	7.8	**Walker** (city) Kent County
139	2502	7.9	**Auburn Hills** (city) Oakland County
140	2512	8.0	**Monroe** (charter township) Monroe County
141	2571	8.5	**Fruitport** (charter township) Muskegon County
141	2571	8.5	**Ypsilanti** (charter township) Washtenaw County
143	2584	8.6	**Marquette** (city) Marquette County
144	2595	8.7	**Bedford** (township) Monroe County
145	2605	8.8	**Spring Lake** (township) Ottawa County
146	2656	9.2	**Delta** (charter township) Eaton County
147	2781	10.4	**Cannon** (township) Kent County
148	2797	10.5	**Davison** (township) Genesee County
149	2839	11.1	**Fenton** (city) Genesee County
150	2898	11.9	**Green Oak** (township) Livingston County

Note: The state column ranks the top/bottom 150 places from all places in the state with population of 10,000 or more. The national column ranks the top/bottom 150 places from all places in the country with population of 10,000 or more. Places that are unincorporated were not considered in the rankings. Please refer to the User Guide for additional information.

Population Density

Top 150 Places Ranked in *Descending* Order

State Rank	Nat'l Rank	Pop./ Sq. Mi.	Place
1	112	10,751.0	**Hamtramck** (city) Wayne County
2	350	6,478.3	**Lincoln Park** (city) Wayne County
3	377	6,307.4	**Eastpointe** (city) Macomb County
4	455	5,828.5	**Hazel Park** (city) Oakland County
5	470	5,724.9	**Berkley** (city) Oakland County
6	479	5,677.2	**Oak Park** (city) Oakland County
7	517	5,455.1	**Harper Woods** (city) Wayne County
8	525	5,376.7	**Clawson** (city) Oakland County
9	532	5,327.5	**Grosse Pointe Park** (city) Wayne County
10	568	5,144.3	**Detroit** (city) Wayne County
11	570	5,139.5	**Saint Clair Shores** (city) Macomb County
12	575	5,129.6	**Ferndale** (city) Oakland County
13	610	4,965.6	**Grosse Pointe Woods** (city) Wayne County
14	619	4,919.9	**Dearborn Heights** (city) Wayne County
15	628	4,908.1	**Wyandotte** (city) Wayne County
16	638	4,856.8	**Royal Oak** (city) Oakland County
17	653	4,813.9	**Roseville** (city) Macomb County
18	680	4,718.1	**Garden City** (city) Wayne County
19	763	4,489.0	**Ypsilanti** (city) Washtenaw County
20	790	4,389.0	**Southgate** (city) Wayne County
21	810	4,303.1	**Redford** (charter township) Wayne County
22	829	4,235.6	**Grand Rapids** (city) Kent County
23	842	4,195.5	**Birmingham** (city) Oakland County
24	846	4,190.2	**Madison Heights** (city) Oakland County
25	864	4,117.3	**Westland** (city) Wayne County
26	876	4,094.0	**Ann Arbor** (city) Washtenaw County
27	892	4,057.1	**Inkster** (city) Wayne County
28	894	4,051.8	**Dearborn** (city) Wayne County
29	902	4,027.8	**Allen Park** (city) Wayne County
30	913	4,009.1	**Mount Clemens** (city) Macomb County
31	934	3,963.9	**Highland Park** (city) Wayne County
32	945	3,938.7	**Melvindale** (city) Wayne County
33	963	3,899.6	**Farmington** (city) Oakland County
34	964	3,899.2	**Warren** (city) Macomb County
35	1043	3,735.0	**Port Huron** (city) Saint Clair County
36	1079	3,645.3	**East Grand Rapids** (city) Kent County
37	1113	3,573.5	**East Lansing** (city) Ingham County
38	1128	3,552.9	**Sterling Heights** (city) Macomb County
39	1155	3,496.6	**Fraser** (city) Macomb County
40	1183	3,445.0	**Clinton** (charter township) Macomb County
41	1191	3,436.0	**Bay City** (city) Bay County
42	1218	3,408.2	**Muskegon Heights** (city) Muskegon County
43	1241	3,360.8	**Mount Pleasant** (city) Isabella County
44	1268	3,323.2	**Rochester** (city) Oakland County
45	1365	3,170.6	**Lansing** (city) Ingham County
46	1415	3,086.6	**Jackson** (city) Jackson County
47	1429	3,065.4	**Flint** (city) Genesee County
48	1451	3,033.4	**South Lyon** (city) Oakland County
49	1470	3,008.5	**Kalamazoo** (city) Kalamazoo County
50	1493	2,980.0	**Pontiac** (city) Oakland County
51	1501	2,971.2	**Saginaw** (city) Saginaw County
52	1525	2,927.3	**Wyoming** (city) Kent County
53	1528	2,922.6	**Wayne** (city) Wayne County
54	1548	2,906.3	**Owosso** (city) Shiawassee County
55	1583	2,840.8	**Riverview** (city) Wayne County
56	1604	2,824.8	**Jenison** (CDP) Ottawa County
57	1665	2,730.5	**Southfield** (city) Oakland County
58	1674	2,715.8	**Livonia** (city) Wayne County
59	1686	2,702.2	**Muskegon** (city) Muskegon County
60	1710	2,675.3	**Taylor** (city) Wayne County
61	1722	2,657.1	**Adrian** (city) Lenawee County
62	1738	2,638.5	**Waverly** (CDP) Eaton County
63	1749	2,622.2	**New Baltimore** (city) Macomb County
64	1775	2,600.2	**Comstock Park** (CDP) Kent County
65	1789	2,591.2	**Trenton** (city) Wayne County
66	1807	2,567.0	**Beverly Hills** (village) Oakland County
67	1856	2,497.2	**Canton** (charter township) Wayne County
68	1895	2,448.3	**Cutlerville** (CDP) Kent County
69	1920	2,429.3	**Big Rapids** (city) Mecosta County
70	1931	2,419.2	**Troy** (city) Oakland County
71	1949	2,396.0	**Farmington Hills** (city) Oakland County
72	1951	2,395.3	**West Bloomfield** (charter township) Oakland County
73	2005	2,339.2	**Waterford** (charter township) Oakland County
74	2022	2,330.1	**Kentwood** (city) Kent County
75	2089	2,267.5	**Benton Harbor** (city) Berrien County
76	2097	2,262.0	**Monroe** (city) Monroe County
77	2149	2,196.8	**Macomb** (township) Macomb County
78	2185	2,163.1	**Rochester Hills** (city) Oakland County
79	2193	2,154.4	**Shelby** (charter township) Macomb County
80	2219	2,131.3	**Ionia** (city) Ionia County
81	2239	2,114.4	**Grandville** (city) Kent County
82	2343	2,015.7	**Woodhaven** (city) Wayne County
83	2353	2,003.0	**Niles** (city) Berrien County
84	2364	1,992.3	**Holland** (city) Ottawa County
85	2491	1,876.6	**Kalamazoo** (charter township) Kalamazoo County
86	2494	1,874.4	**Marquette** (city) Marquette County
87	2552	1,824.8	**Novi** (city) Oakland County
88	2574	1,808.1	**Southfield** (township) Oakland County
89	2580	1,804.1	**Grand Haven** (city) Ottawa County
90	2612	1,782.8	**Ypsilanti** (charter township) Washtenaw County
91	2638	1,762.5	**Traverse City** (city) Grand Traverse County
92	2642	1,760.5	**Fenton** (city) Genesee County
93	2645	1,759.9	**Northville** (township) Wayne County
94	2669	1,739.5	**Beecher** (CDP) Genesee County
95	2684	1,727.8	**Plymouth** (charter township) Wayne County
96	2719	1,700.9	**Harrison** (charter township) Macomb County
97	2725	1,693.0	**Sturgis** (city) Saint Joseph County
98	2769	1,667.6	**Bloomfield** (charter township) Oakland County
99	2770	1,667.1	**Saginaw** (charter township) Saginaw County
100	2880	1,573.1	**Chesterfield** (township) Macomb County
101	2936	1,529.5	**Holt** (CDP) Ingham County
102	2967	1,508.4	**Saint Joseph** (charter township) Berrien County
103	3006	1,474.6	**Wixom** (city) Oakland County
104	3020	1,463.9	**Commerce** (charter township) Oakland County
105	3045	1,445.4	**Cadillac** (city) Wexford County
106	3064	1,436.5	**Portage** (city) Kalamazoo County
107	3095	1,416.3	**Georgetown** (charter township) Ottawa County
108	3106	1,406.8	**Northview** (CDP) Kent County
109	3148	1,380.2	**Brownstown** (charter township) Wayne County
110	3157	1,371.4	**Flint** (charter township) Genesee County
111	3173	1,362.5	**Coldwater** (city) Branch County
112	3235	1,318.5	**Holland** (charter township) Ottawa County
113	3253	1,301.9	**Meridian** (charter township) Ingham County
114	3263	1,290.0	**Auburn Hills** (city) Oakland County
115	3271	1,284.5	**Burton** (city) Genesee County
116	3286	1,274.8	**Okemos** (CDP) Ingham County
117	3293	1,271.6	**Pittsfield** (charter township) Washtenaw County
118	3320	1,250.5	**Haslett** (CDP) Ingham County
119	3328	1,242.4	**Midland** (city) Midland County
120	3350	1,228.6	**Battle Creek** (city) Calhoun County
121	3352	1,227.3	**Alpena** (city) Alpena County
122	3478	1,147.0	**Grand Blanc** (charter township) Genesee County
123	3503	1,127.2	**Grosse Ile** (township) Wayne County
124	3559	1,086.0	**Grand Rapids** (charter township) Kent County
125	3594	1,061.9	**Orion** (charter township) Oakland County
126	3626	1,038.4	**Bangor** (charter township) Bay County
127	3633	1,032.6	**Norton Shores** (city) Muskegon County
128	3679	998.3	**Delta** (charter township) Eaton County
129	3693	991.1	**Independence** (charter township) Oakland County
130	3709	979.9	**Escanaba** (city) Delta County
131	3737	957.3	**Sault Sainte Marie** (city) Chippewa County
132	3755	943.7	**Walker** (city) Kent County
133	3780	927.3	**Park** (township) Ottawa County
134	3803	904.5	**Delhi** (charter township) Ingham County
135	3819	895.6	**White Lake** (charter township) Oakland County
136	3834	883.2	**Plainfield** (charter township) Kent County
137	3853	867.8	**Spring Lake** (township) Ottawa County
138	3860	862.0	**Monroe** (charter township) Monroe County
139	3895	848.4	**Van Buren** (charter township) Wayne County
140	3895	829.9	**Port Huron** (charter township) Saint Clair County
141	3908	820.2	**Lincoln** (charter township) Berrien County
142	3948	793.2	**Bedford** (township) Monroe County
143	3965	777.6	**Muskegon** (charter township) Muskegon County
144	3970	773.7	**Summit** (township) Jackson County
145	3972	773.5	**Allendale** (CDP) Ottawa County
146	3991	758.5	**Blackman** (charter township) Jackson County
147	4012	742.6	**Genesee** (charter township) Genesee County
148	4048	708.6	**Washington** (township) Macomb County
149	4053	704.3	**Gaines** (charter township) Kent County
150	4063	696.0	**Fort Gratiot** (charter township) Saint Clair County

Note: The state column ranks the top/bottom 150 places from all places in the state with population of 10,000 or more. The national column ranks the top/bottom 150 places from all places in the country with population of 10,000 or more. Places that are unincorporated were not considered in the rankings. Please refer to the User Guide for additional information.

Population Density

Top 150 Places Ranked in *Ascending* Order

State Rank	Nat'l Rank	Pop./ Sq. Mi.	Place	State Rank	Nat'l Rank	Pop./ Sq. Mi.	Place
1	76	267.1	**East Bay** (township) Grand Traverse County	76	963	991.1	**Independence** (charter township) Oakland County
2	81	270.5	**Lenox** (township) Macomb County	77	977	998.3	**Delta** (charter township) Eaton County
3	85	278.3	**Cooper** (charter township) Kalamazoo County	78	1023	1,032.6	**Norton Shores** (city) Muskegon County
4	87	283.0	**Tyrone** (township) Livingston County	79	1030	1,038.4	**Bangor** (charter township) Bay County
5	88	284.4	**Leoni** (township) Jackson County	80	1062	1,061.9	**Orion** (charter township) Oakland County
6	102	291.9	**Monitor** (charter township) Bay County	81	1097	1,086.0	**Grand Rapids** (charter township) Kent County
7	117	305.4	**Bridgeport** (charter township) Saginaw County	82	1153	1,127.2	**Grosse Ile** (township) Wayne County
8	143	330.5	**Holly** (township) Oakland County	83	1178	1,147.0	**Grand Blanc** (charter township) Genesee County
8	143	330.5	**Oceola** (township) Livingston County	84	1303	1,227.3	**Alpena** (city) Alpena County
10	154	339.2	**Flushing** (charter township) Genesee County	85	1306	1,228.6	**Battle Creek** (city) Calhoun County
11	168	351.2	**Antwerp** (township) Van Buren County	86	1328	1,242.4	**Midland** (city) Midland County
12	173	353.2	**Caledonia** (township) Kent County	87	1336	1,250.5	**Haslett** (CDP) Ingham County
13	186	364.3	**Bath** (charter township) Clinton County	88	1363	1,271.6	**Pittsfield** (charter township) Washtenaw County
14	187	364.7	**Ada** (township) Kent County	89	1370	1,274.8	**Okemos** (CDP) Ingham County
15	189	367.8	**Emmett** (charter township) Calhoun County	90	1384	1,284.5	**Burton** (city) Genesee County
16	192	370.9	**Superior** (charter township) Washtenaw County	91	1393	1,290.0	**Auburn Hills** (city) Oakland County
17	194	371.4	**Alpine** (township) Kent County	92	1403	1,301.9	**Meridian** (charter township) Ingham County
18	203	378.2	**Cannon** (township) Kent County	93	1421	1,318.5	**Holland** (charter township) Ottawa County
19	205	378.7	**Vienna** (charter township) Genesee County	94	1483	1,362.5	**Coldwater** (city) Branch County
20	207	379.6	**Niles** (township) Berrien County	95	1499	1,371.4	**Flint** (charter township) Genesee County
21	221	391.6	**Thomas** (township) Saginaw County	96	1508	1,380.2	**Brownstown** (charter township) Wayne County
22	222	393.4	**Springfield** (charter township) Oakland County	97	1550	1,406.8	**Northview** (CDP) Kent County
23	239	408.9	**Hartland** (township) Livingston County	98	1561	1,416.3	**Georgetown** (charter township) Ottawa County
24	246	418.6	**Mundy** (township) Genesee County	99	1592	1,436.5	**Portage** (city) Kalamazoo County
25	256	427.4	**Texas** (charter township) Kalamazoo County	100	1611	1,445.4	**Cadillac** (city) Wexford County
26	259	432.3	**Brandon** (charter township) Oakland County	101	1636	1,463.9	**Commerce** (charter township) Oakland County
27	271	445.9	**Comstock** (charter township) Kalamazoo County	102	1650	1,474.6	**Wixom** (city) Oakland County
28	274	449.2	**Huron** (charter township) Wayne County	103	1689	1,508.4	**Saint Joseph** (charter township) Berrien County
29	280	453.6	**Fruitport** (charter township) Muskegon County	104	1720	1,529.5	**Holt** (CDP) Ingham County
30	283	455.6	**Benton** (charter township) Berrien County	105	1776	1,573.1	**Chesterfield** (township) Macomb County
31	290	459.1	**Union** (charter township) Isabella County	106	1886	1,667.1	**Saginaw** (charter township) Saginaw County
32	293	461.5	**DeWitt** (charter township) Clinton County	107	1887	1,667.6	**Bloomfield** (charter township) Oakland County
33	294	462.2	**Oakland** (charter township) Oakland County	108	1931	1,693.0	**Sturgis** (city) Saint Joseph County
34	300	470.0	**Lyon** (charter township) Oakland County	109	1937	1,700.9	**Harrison** (charter township) Macomb County
35	307	477.0	**Milford** (charter township) Oakland County	110	1972	1,727.8	**Plymouth** (charter township) Wayne County
36	328	488.5	**Frenchtown** (township) Monroe County	111	1986	1,739.5	**Beecher** (CDP) Genesee County
37	352	505.7	**Cascade** (charter township) Kent County	112	2011	1,759.9	**Northville** (township) Wayne County
38	358	509.5	**Green Oak** (township) Livingston County	113	2014	1,760.5	**Fenton** (city) Genesee County
39	380	525.0	**Forest Hills** (CDP) Kent County	114	2018	1,762.5	**Traverse City** (city) Grand Traverse County
40	385	529.2	**Grand Haven** (charter township) Ottawa County	115	2044	1,782.8	**Ypsilanti** (charter township) Washtenaw County
41	392	539.8	**Brighton** (township) Livingston County	116	2076	1,804.1	**Grand Haven** (city) Ottawa County
42	424	562.8	**Byron** (township) Kent County	117	2082	1,808.1	**Southfield** (township) Oakland County
43	425	562.9	**Highland** (charter township) Oakland County	118	2104	1,824.8	**Novi** (city) Oakland County
44	449	582.1	**Genoa** (township) Livingston County	119	2162	1,874.4	**Marquette** (city) Marquette County
45	454	587.5	**Davison** (township) Genesee County	120	2165	1,876.6	**Kalamazoo** (charter township) Kalamazoo County
46	463	595.4	**Scio** (township) Washtenaw County	121	2292	1,992.3	**Holland** (city) Ottawa County
47	475	605.1	**Oshtemo** (charter township) Kalamazoo County	122	2302	2,003.0	**Niles** (city) Berrien County
48	479	607.6	**Oxford** (charter township) Oakland County	123	2313	2,015.7	**Woodhaven** (city) Wayne County
49	485	611.3	**Garfield** (charter township) Grand Traverse County	124	2417	2,114.4	**Grandville** (city) Kent County
50	524	653.4	**Fenton** (charter township) Genesee County	125	2437	2,131.3	**Ionia** (city) Ionia County
51	531	656.5	**Hamburg** (township) Livingston County	126	2463	2,154.4	**Shelby** (charter township) Macomb County
52	543	665.2	**Allendale** (charter township) Ottawa County	127	2471	2,163.1	**Rochester Hills** (city) Oakland County
53	553	673.7	**Romulus** (city) Wayne County	128	2507	2,196.8	**Macomb** (township) Macomb County
54	570	682.4	**Mount Morris** (township) Genesee County	129	2559	2,262.0	**Monroe** (city) Monroe County
55	593	696.0	**Fort Gratiot** (charter township) Saint Clair County	130	2567	2,267.5	**Benton Harbor** (city) Berrien County
56	602	704.3	**Gaines** (charter township) Kent County	131	2634	2,330.1	**Kentwood** (city) Kent County
57	608	708.6	**Washington** (township) Macomb County	132	2651	2,339.2	**Waterford** (charter township) Oakland County
58	644	742.6	**Genesee** (charter township) Genesee County	133	2705	2,395.3	**West Bloomfield** (charter township) Oakland County
59	665	758.5	**Blackman** (charter township) Jackson County	134	2707	2,396.0	**Farmington Hills** (city) Oakland County
60	684	773.5	**Allendale** (CDP) Ottawa County	135	2725	2,419.2	**Troy** (city) Oakland County
61	685	773.7	**Summit** (township) Jackson County	136	2736	2,429.3	**Big Rapids** (city) Mecosta County
62	691	777.6	**Muskegon** (charter township) Muskegon County	137	2761	2,448.3	**Cutlerville** (CDP) Kent County
63	708	793.2	**Bedford** (township) Monroe County	138	2800	2,497.2	**Canton** (charter township) Wayne County
64	748	820.2	**Lincoln** (charter township) Berrien County	139	2849	2,567.0	**Beverly Hills** (village) Oakland County
65	761	829.9	**Port Huron** (charter township) Saint Clair County	140	2867	2,591.2	**Trenton** (city) Wayne County
66	787	848.4	**Van Buren** (charter township) Wayne County	141	2880	2,600.2	**Comstock Park** (CDP) Kent County
67	796	862.0	**Monroe** (charter township) Monroe County	142	2907	2,622.2	**New Baltimore** (city) Macomb County
68	803	867.8	**Spring Lake** (township) Ottawa County	143	2918	2,638.5	**Waverly** (CDP) Eaton County
69	822	883.2	**Plainfield** (charter township) Kent County	144	2934	2,657.1	**Adrian** (city) Lenawee County
70	837	895.6	**White Lake** (charter township) Oakland County	145	2946	2,675.3	**Taylor** (city) Wayne County
71	852	904.5	**Delhi** (charter township) Ingham County	146	2970	2,702.2	**Muskegon** (city) Muskegon County
72	876	927.3	**Park** (township) Ottawa County	147	2982	2,715.8	**Livonia** (city) Wayne County
73	901	943.7	**Walker** (city) Kent County	148	2991	2,730.5	**Southfield** (city) Oakland County
74	919	957.3	**Sault Sainte Marie** (city) Chippewa County	149	3052	2,824.8	**Jenison** (CDP) Ottawa County
75	947	979.9	**Escanaba** (city) Delta County	150	3073	2,840.8	**Riverview** (city) Wayne County

Note: The state column ranks the top/bottom 150 places from all places in the state with population of 10,000 or more. The national column ranks the top/bottom 150 places from all places in the country with population of 10,000 or more. Places that are unincorporated were not considered in the rankings. Please refer to the User Guide for additional information.

White Population

Top 150 Places Ranked in *Descending* Order

State Rank	Nat'l Rank	Percent	Place		State Rank	Nat'l Rank	Percent	Place
1	35	97.2	Hamburg (township) Livingston County		73	896	92.0	Midland (city) Midland County
2	43	97.1	Highland (charter township) Oakland County		73	896	92.0	Orion (charter township) Oakland County
2	43	97.1	Monitor (charter township) Bay County		78	943	91.8	Norton Shores (city) Muskegon County
4	49	97.0	Brighton (township) Livingston County		79	994	91.5	Grand Rapids (charter township) Kent County
5	68	96.8	Alpena (city) Alpena County		79	994	91.5	Northview (CDP) Kent County
6	77	96.7	Oceola (township) Livingston County		81	1011	91.4	Emmett (charter township) Calhoun County
7	88	96.6	Green Oak (township) Livingston County		81	1011	91.4	Grosse Pointe Woods (city) Wayne County
7	88	96.6	Hartland (township) Livingston County		83	1024	91.3	Walker (city) Kent County
9	103	96.5	Bedford (township) Monroe County		84	1053	91.1	Allendale (charter township) Ottawa County
9	103	96.5	Fenton (charter township) Genesee County		84	1053	91.1	Marquette (city) Marquette County
11	114	96.4	Tyrone (township) Livingston County		86	1087	90.9	Port Huron (charter township) Saint Clair County
12	124	96.3	Cannon (township) Kent County		86	1087	90.9	Shelby (charter township) Macomb County
13	154	96.1	East Bay (township) Grand Traverse County		88	1106	90.8	Chesterfield (township) Macomb County
13	154	96.1	Genoa (township) Livingston County		88	1106	90.8	DeWitt (charter township) Clinton County
15	170	96.0	Brandon (charter township) Oakland County		90	1127	90.7	Allendale (CDP) Ottawa County
15	170	96.0	Jenison (CDP) Ottawa County		90	1127	90.7	Royal Oak (city) Oakland County
15	170	96.0	Spring Lake (township) Ottawa County		92	1142	90.6	Texas (charter township) Kalamazoo County
18	210	95.8	Grand Haven (charter township) Ottawa County		93	1161	90.5	Macomb (township) Macomb County
18	210	95.8	Thomas (township) Saginaw County		94	1188	90.3	Oakland (charter township) Oakland County
20	224	95.7	Owosso (city) Shiawassee County		95	1235	90.0	Niles (township) Berrien County
21	244	95.6	Cadillac (city) Wexford County		96	1280	89.7	Bay City (city) Bay County
22	258	95.5	Grosse Ile (township) Wayne County		97	1294	89.6	Summit (township) Jackson County
22	258	95.5	Trenton (city) Wayne County		98	1361	89.2	Beverly Hills (village) Oakland County
24	276	95.4	East Grand Rapids (city) Kent County		98	1361	89.2	Waterford (charter township) Oakland County
24	276	95.4	Springfield (charter township) Oakland County		100	1371	89.1	Dearborn (city) Wayne County
26	291	95.3	Georgetown (charter township) Ottawa County		101	1385	89.0	Harrison (charter township) Macomb County
26	291	95.3	Leoni (township) Jackson County		102	1400	88.9	Woodhaven (city) Wayne County
26	291	95.3	Milford (charter township) Oakland County		103	1435	88.7	Southgate (city) Wayne County
26	291	95.3	White Lake (charter township) Oakland County		104	1451	88.6	Rochester (city) Oakland County
30	307	95.2	Bangor (charter township) Bay County		105	1482	88.4	Monroe (city) Monroe County
30	307	95.2	Caledonia (township) Kent County		106	1507	88.2	Southfield (township) Oakland County
30	307	95.2	South Lyon (city) Oakland County		107	1520	88.1	Burton (city) Genesee County
33	328	95.1	Fenton (city) Genesee County		107	1520	88.1	Comstock (charter township) Kalamazoo County
34	347	95.0	Grand Haven (city) Ottawa County		109	1541	88.0	Big Rapids (city) Mecosta County
35	362	94.9	Oxford (charter township) Oakland County		110	1555	87.9	Muskegon (charter township) Muskegon County
36	380	94.8	Washington (township) Macomb County		111	1594	87.6	Mount Pleasant (city) Isabella County
37	402	94.7	Fruitport (charter township) Muskegon County		111	1594	87.6	Union (charter township) Isabella County
37	402	94.7	Vienna (charter township) Genesee County		113	1608	87.5	Bath (charter township) Clinton County
37	402	94.7	Wyandotte (city) Wayne County		114	1648	87.2	Genesee (charter township) Genesee County
40	427	94.6	Fort Gratiot (charter township) Saint Clair County		115	1693	86.9	Portage (city) Kalamazoo County
40	427	94.6	Lyon (charter township) Oakland County		116	1707	86.8	Delhi (charter township) Ingham County
42	461	94.4	Flushing (charter township) Genesee County		117	1783	86.3	Holt (CDP) Ingham County
42	461	94.4	New Baltimore (city) Macomb County		118	1811	86.1	Dearborn Heights (city) Wayne County
42	461	94.4	Traverse City (city) Grand Traverse County		119	1932	85.1	Sterling Heights (city) Macomb County
45	516	94.0	Antwerp (township) Van Buren County		120	1953	85.0	Grosse Pointe Park (city) Wayne County
46	536	93.9	Garfield (charter township) Grand Traverse County		121	1982	84.7	Ferndale (city) Oakland County
47	577	93.7	Plainfield (charter township) Kent County		121	1982	84.7	Haslett (CDP) Ingham County
48	590	93.6	Commerce (charter township) Oakland County		123	2037	84.2	Lincoln Park (city) Wayne County
48	590	93.6	Holly (township) Oakland County		124	2053	84.1	Adrian (city) Lenawee County
50	610	93.5	Cascade (charter township) Kent County		125	2064	84.0	Port Huron (city) Saint Clair County
50	610	93.5	Escanaba (city) Delta County		126	2077	83.9	Madison Heights (city) Oakland County
52	632	93.4	Clawson (city) Oakland County		127	2092	83.8	Saginaw (charter township) Saginaw County
52	632	93.4	Forest Hills (CDP) Kent County		128	2101	83.7	Bloomfield (charter township) Oakland County
52	632	93.4	Frenchtown (township) Monroe County		129	2165	83.1	Roseville (city) Macomb County
55	655	93.3	Ada (township) Kent County		130	2198	82.8	Hazel Park (city) Oakland County
55	655	93.3	Berkley (city) Oakland County		131	2208	82.7	Northville (township) Wayne County
55	655	93.3	Davison (township) Genesee County		132	2214	82.6	Grand Blanc (charter township) Genesee County
58	675	93.2	Cooper (charter township) Kalamazoo County		133	2223	82.5	Scio (township) Washtenaw County
59	693	93.1	Huron (charter township) Wayne County		134	2238	82.4	Brownstown (charter township) Wayne County
60	715	93.0	Independence (charter township) Oakland County		135	2264	82.2	Cutlerville (CDP) Kent County
60	715	93.0	Riverview (city) Wayne County		136	2275	82.1	Clinton (charter township) Macomb County
62	732	92.9	Allen Park (city) Wayne County		136	2275	82.1	Rochester Hills (city) Oakland County
62	732	92.9	Monroe (charter township) Monroe County		138	2294	81.9	Alpine (township) Kent County
64	749	92.8	Byron (township) Kent County		139	2323	81.6	Saint Joseph (charter township) Berrien County
65	770	92.7	Saint Clair Shores (city) Macomb County		140	2375	81.0	Lenox (township) Macomb County
66	807	92.5	Coldwater (city) Branch County		141	2418	80.6	Sturgis (city) Saint Joseph County
66	807	92.5	Garden City (city) Wayne County		142	2430	80.5	Gaines (charter township) Kent County
68	817	92.4	Lincoln (charter township) Berrien County		143	2453	80.3	Niles (city) Berrien County
69	836	92.3	Birmingham (city) Oakland County		144	2475	80.0	Holland (city) Ottawa County
70	854	92.2	Park (township) Ottawa County		144	2475	80.0	Meridian (charter township) Ingham County
71	870	92.1	Mundy (township) Genesee County		144	2475	80.0	Oshtemo (charter township) Kalamazoo County
71	870	92.1	Plymouth (charter township) Wayne County		147	2497	79.8	Wixom (city) Oakland County
73	896	92.0	Fraser (city) Macomb County		148	2561	79.1	Blackman (charter township) Jackson County
73	896	92.0	Grandville (city) Kent County		149	2594	78.7	Comstock Park (CDP) Kent County
73	896	92.0	Livonia (city) Wayne County		150	2606	78.6	Delta (charter township) Eaton County

Note: The state column ranks the top/bottom 150 places from all places in the state with population of 10,000 or more. The national column ranks the top/bottom 150 places from all places in the country with population of 10,000 or more. Places that are unincorporated were not considered in the rankings. Please refer to the User Guide for additional information.

White Population

Top 150 Places Ranked in *Ascending* Order

State Rank	Nat'l Rank	Percent	Place
1	7	3.2	**Highland Park** (city) Wayne County
2	24	7.0	**Benton Harbor** (city) Berrien County
3	37	10.6	**Detroit** (city) Wayne County
4	66	16.0	**Muskegon Heights** (city) Muskegon County
5	106	20.5	**Inkster** (city) Wayne County
6	143	24.9	**Southfield** (city) Oakland County
7	147	25.3	**Beecher** (CDP) Genesee County
8	240	34.4	**Pontiac** (city) Oakland County
9	277	37.4	**Flint** (city) Genesee County
9	277	37.4	**Oak Park** (city) Oakland County
11	355	42.0	**Benton** (charter township) Berrien County
12	385	43.5	**Saginaw** (city) Saginaw County
13	537	49.6	**Harper Woods** (city) Wayne County
14	563	50.5	**Romulus** (city) Wayne County
15	598	51.7	**Mount Morris** (township) Genesee County
16	654	53.6	**Hamtramck** (city) Wayne County
17	763	57.0	**Muskegon** (city) Muskegon County
18	814	58.4	**Ypsilanti** (charter township) Washtenaw County
19	840	59.0	**Superior** (charter township) Washtenaw County
20	935	61.2	**Lansing** (city) Ingham County
21	944	61.5	**Ypsilanti** (city) Washtenaw County
22	1097	64.6	**Grand Rapids** (city) Kent County
22	1097	64.6	**Van Buren** (charter township) Wayne County
24	1146	65.6	**Eastpointe** (city) Macomb County
25	1178	66.1	**Pittsfield** (charter township) Washtenaw County
26	1188	66.3	**Auburn Hills** (city) Oakland County
27	1194	66.4	**Redford** (charter township) Wayne County
28	1278	67.9	**Bridgeport** (charter township) Saginaw County
29	1284	68.0	**Flint** (charter township) Genesee County
30	1293	68.1	**Kalamazoo** (city) Kalamazoo County
31	1387	69.7	**Farmington Hills** (city) Oakland County
32	1411	70.0	**Mount Clemens** (city) Macomb County
33	1419	70.1	**Kentwood** (city) Kent County
34	1468	70.9	**Ionia** (city) Ionia County
35	1504	71.4	**Jackson** (city) Jackson County
36	1514	71.5	**Farmington** (city) Oakland County
37	1528	71.7	**Battle Creek** (city) Calhoun County
38	1567	72.2	**Canton** (charter township) Wayne County
39	1613	73.0	**Ann Arbor** (city) Washtenaw County
39	1613	73.0	**Novi** (city) Oakland County
41	1642	73.5	**Holland** (charter township) Ottawa County
42	1676	74.1	**Troy** (city) Oakland County
43	1735	74.8	**Sault Sainte Marie** (city) Chippewa County
44	1765	75.2	**Waverly** (CDP) Eaton County
45	1806	75.7	**Kalamazoo** (charter township) Kalamazoo County
46	1815	75.8	**Westland** (city) Wayne County
46	1815	75.8	**Wyoming** (city) Kent County
48	1864	76.3	**Wayne** (city) Wayne County
49	1871	76.5	**Okemos** (CDP) Ingham County
50	1896	76.8	**Melvindale** (city) Wayne County
51	1963	77.6	**West Bloomfield** (charter township) Oakland County
52	1994	78.0	**Taylor** (city) Wayne County
53	2023	78.4	**East Lansing** (city) Ingham County
53	2023	78.4	**Warren** (city) Macomb County
55	2041	78.6	**Delta** (charter township) Eaton County
56	2051	78.7	**Comstock Park** (CDP) Kent County
57	2089	79.1	**Blackman** (charter township) Jackson County
58	2151	79.8	**Wixom** (city) Oakland County
59	2169	80.0	**Holland** (city) Ottawa County
59	2169	80.0	**Meridian** (charter township) Ingham County
59	2169	80.0	**Oshtemo** (charter township) Kalamazoo County
62	2198	80.3	**Niles** (city) Berrien County
63	2221	80.5	**Gaines** (charter township) Kent County
64	2227	80.6	**Sturgis** (city) Saint Joseph County
65	2271	81.0	**Lenox** (township) Macomb County
66	2325	81.6	**Saint Joseph** (charter township) Berrien County
67	2353	81.9	**Alpine** (township) Kent County
68	2377	82.1	**Clinton** (charter township) Macomb County
68	2377	82.1	**Rochester Hills** (city) Oakland County
70	2382	82.2	**Cutlerville** (CDP) Kent County
71	2406	82.4	**Brownstown** (charter township) Wayne County
72	2419	82.5	**Scio** (township) Washtenaw County
73	2434	82.6	**Grand Blanc** (charter township) Genesee County
74	2443	82.7	**Northville** (township) Wayne County
75	2449	82.8	**Hazel Park** (city) Oakland County
76	2480	83.1	**Roseville** (city) Macomb County
77	2550	83.7	**Bloomfield** (charter township) Oakland County
78	2556	83.8	**Saginaw** (charter township) Saginaw County
79	2565	83.9	**Madison Heights** (city) Oakland County
80	2580	84.0	**Port Huron** (city) Saint Clair County
81	2593	84.1	**Adrian** (city) Lenawee County
82	2604	84.2	**Lincoln Park** (city) Wayne County
83	2667	84.7	**Ferndale** (city) Oakland County
83	2667	84.7	**Haslett** (CDP) Ingham County
85	2693	85.0	**Grosse Pointe Park** (city) Wayne County
86	2704	85.1	**Sterling Heights** (city) Macomb County
87	2826	86.1	**Dearborn Heights** (city) Wayne County
88	2859	86.3	**Holt** (CDP) Ingham County
89	2928	86.8	**Delhi** (charter township) Ingham County
90	2950	86.9	**Portage** (city) Kalamazoo County
91	2994	87.2	**Genesee** (charter township) Genesee County
92	3031	87.5	**Bath** (charter township) Clinton County
93	3049	87.6	**Mount Pleasant** (city) Isabella County
93	3049	87.6	**Union** (charter township) Isabella County
95	3088	87.9	**Muskegon** (charter township) Muskegon County
96	3102	88.0	**Big Rapids** (city) Mecosta County
97	3116	88.1	**Burton** (city) Genesee County
97	3116	88.1	**Comstock** (charter township) Kalamazoo County
99	3137	88.2	**Southfield** (township) Oakland County
100	3163	88.4	**Monroe** (city) Monroe County
101	3188	88.6	**Rochester** (city) Oakland County
102	3206	88.7	**Southgate** (city) Wayne County
103	3242	88.9	**Woodhaven** (city) Wayne County
104	3257	89.0	**Harrison** (charter township) Macomb County
105	3272	89.1	**Dearborn** (city) Wayne County
106	3286	89.2	**Beverly Hills** (village) Oakland County
106	3286	89.2	**Waterford** (charter township) Oakland County
108	3348	89.6	**Summit** (township) Jackson County
109	3363	89.7	**Bay City** (city) Bay County
110	3407	90.0	**Niles** (township) Berrien County
111	3451	90.3	**Oakland** (charter township) Oakland County
112	3484	90.5	**Macomb** (township) Macomb County
113	3496	90.6	**Texas** (charter township) Kalamazoo County
114	3515	90.7	**Allendale** (CDP) Ottawa County
114	3515	90.7	**Royal Oak** (city) Oakland County
116	3530	90.8	**Chesterfield** (township) Macomb County
116	3530	90.8	**DeWitt** (charter township) Clinton County
118	3551	90.9	**Port Huron** (charter township) Saint Clair County
118	3551	90.9	**Shelby** (charter township) Macomb County
120	3587	91.1	**Allendale** (charter township) Ottawa County
120	3587	91.1	**Marquette** (city) Marquette County
122	3621	91.3	**Walker** (city) Kent County
123	3633	91.4	**Emmett** (charter township) Calhoun County
123	3633	91.4	**Grosse Pointe Woods** (city) Wayne County
125	3646	91.5	**Grand Rapids** (charter township) Kent County
125	3646	91.5	**Northview** (CDP) Kent County
127	3695	91.8	**Norton Shores** (city) Muskegon County
128	3738	92.0	**Fraser** (city) Macomb County
128	3738	92.0	**Grandville** (city) Kent County
128	3738	92.0	**Livonia** (city) Wayne County
128	3738	92.0	**Midland** (city) Midland County
128	3738	92.0	**Orion** (charter township) Oakland County
133	3761	92.1	**Mundy** (township) Genesee County
133	3761	92.1	**Plymouth** (charter township) Wayne County
135	3787	92.2	**Park** (township) Ottawa County
136	3803	92.3	**Birmingham** (city) Oakland County
137	3821	92.4	**Lincoln** (charter township) Berrien County
138	3840	92.5	**Coldwater** (city) Branch County
138	3840	92.5	**Garden City** (city) Wayne County
140	3872	92.7	**Saint Clair Shores** (city) Macomb County
141	3887	92.8	**Byron** (township) Kent County
142	3908	92.9	**Allen Park** (city) Wayne County
142	3908	92.9	**Monroe** (charter township) Monroe County
144	3925	93.0	**Independence** (charter township) Oakland County
144	3925	93.0	**Riverview** (city) Wayne County
146	3942	93.1	**Huron** (charter township) Wayne County
147	3964	93.2	**Cooper** (charter township) Kalamazoo County
148	3982	93.3	**Ada** (township) Kent County
148	3982	93.3	**Berkley** (city) Oakland County
148	3982	93.3	**Davison** (township) Genesee County

Note: The state column ranks the top/bottom 150 places from all places in the state with population of 10,000 or more. The national column ranks the top/bottom 150 places from all places in the country with population of 10,000 or more. Places that are unincorporated were not considered in the rankings. Please refer to the User Guide for additional information.

Black/African American Population

Top 150 Places Ranked in *Descending* Order

State Rank	Nat'l Rank	Percent	Place
1	6	93.5	**Highland Park** (city) Wayne County
2	17	89.2	**Benton Harbor** (city) Berrien County
3	31	82.7	**Detroit** (city) Wayne County
4	53	78.3	**Muskegon Heights** (city) Muskegon County
5	78	73.2	**Inkster** (city) Wayne County
6	89	70.3	**Southfield** (city) Oakland County
7	92	69.1	**Beecher** (CDP) Genesee County
8	153	57.4	**Oak Park** (city) Oakland County
9	155	56.6	**Flint** (city) Genesee County
10	190	52.1	**Pontiac** (city) Oakland County
11	196	51.7	**Benton** (charter township) Berrien County
12	249	46.1	**Saginaw** (city) Saginaw County
13	255	45.6	**Harper Woods** (city) Wayne County
14	275	43.0	**Romulus** (city) Wayne County
15	278	42.8	**Mount Morris** (township) Genesee County
16	380	34.5	**Muskegon** (city) Muskegon County
17	410	32.8	**Ypsilanti** (charter township) Washtenaw County
18	469	30.1	**Superior** (charter township) Washtenaw County
19	485	29.5	**Eastpointe** (city) Macomb County
20	491	29.2	**Ypsilanti** (city) Washtenaw County
21	494	28.9	**Redford** (charter township) Wayne County
22	498	28.7	**Van Buren** (charter township) Wayne County
23	574	25.7	**Flint** (charter township) Genesee County
24	584	25.4	**Bridgeport** (charter township) Saginaw County
25	598	25.0	**Ionia** (city) Ionia County
26	602	24.8	**Mount Clemens** (city) Macomb County
27	623	23.7	**Lansing** (city) Ingham County
28	675	22.2	**Kalamazoo** (city) Kalamazoo County
29	712	20.9	**Grand Rapids** (city) Kent County
30	728	20.4	**Jackson** (city) Jackson County
31	771	19.3	**Hamtramck** (city) Wayne County
32	804	18.5	**Auburn Hills** (city) Oakland County
33	824	18.2	**Battle Creek** (city) Calhoun County
34	856	17.4	**Farmington Hills** (city) Oakland County
35	864	17.2	**Westland** (city) Wayne County
36	867	17.1	**Wayne** (city) Wayne County
37	897	16.6	**Blackman** (charter township) Jackson County
38	907	16.4	**Kalamazoo** (charter township) Kalamazoo County
39	946	15.8	**Taylor** (city) Wayne County
40	970	15.4	**Kentwood** (city) Kent County
41	1028	14.5	**Lenox** (township) Macomb County
42	1070	13.8	**Waverly** (CDP) Eaton County
43	1088	13.5	**Warren** (city) Macomb County
44	1107	13.3	**Saint Joseph** (charter township) Berrien County
45	1111	13.2	**Pittsfield** (charter township) Washtenaw County
46	1121	13.0	**Clinton** (charter township) Macomb County
47	1165	12.4	**Niles** (city) Berrien County
48	1180	12.2	**Oshtemo** (charter township) Kalamazoo County
49	1214	11.8	**Roseville** (city) Macomb County
50	1229	11.6	**Delta** (charter township) Eaton County
51	1244	11.4	**Farmington** (city) Oakland County
51	1244	11.4	**West Bloomfield** (charter township) Oakland County
53	1256	11.3	**Melvindale** (city) Wayne County
54	1273	11.1	**Wixom** (city) Oakland County
55	1312	10.7	**Grand Blanc** (charter township) Genesee County
56	1333	10.5	**Grosse Pointe Park** (city) Wayne County
57	1363	10.2	**Canton** (charter township) Wayne County
58	1415	9.8	**Hazel Park** (city) Oakland County
59	1436	9.6	**Ferndale** (city) Oakland County
60	1464	9.3	**Gaines** (charter township) Kent County
61	1482	9.1	**Port Huron** (city) Saint Clair County
62	1510	8.8	**Saginaw** (charter township) Saginaw County
63	1529	8.6	**Brownstown** (charter township) Wayne County
63	1529	8.6	**Genesee** (charter township) Genesee County
65	1586	8.1	**Novi** (city) Oakland County
66	1598	8.0	**Comstock Park** (CDP) Kent County
67	1613	7.9	**Dearborn Heights** (city) Wayne County
68	1640	7.7	**Ann Arbor** (city) Washtenaw County
69	1684	7.4	**Harrison** (charter township) Macomb County
70	1696	7.3	**Burton** (city) Genesee County
71	1712	7.2	**Cutlerville** (CDP) Kent County
71	1712	7.2	**Wyoming** (city) Kent County
73	1780	6.8	**Big Rapids** (city) Mecosta County
73	1780	6.8	**East Lansing** (city) Ingham County
75	1793	6.7	**Bloomfield** (charter township) Oakland County
75	1793	6.7	**Southfield** (township) Oakland County
77	1808	6.6	**Beverly Hills** (village) Oakland County
78	1840	6.4	**Madison Heights** (city) Oakland County
79	1890	6.2	**Alpine** (township) Kent County
79	1890	6.2	**Monroe** (city) Monroe County
81	1911	6.1	**Muskegon** (charter township) Muskegon County
82	1947	5.9	**Lincoln Park** (city) Wayne County
83	2001	5.6	**Comstock** (charter township) Kalamazoo County
83	2001	5.6	**Holt** (CDP) Ingham County
85	2026	5.5	**Southgate** (city) Wayne County
86	2066	5.3	**Chesterfield** (township) Macomb County
86	2066	5.3	**Summit** (township) Jackson County
86	2066	5.3	**Woodhaven** (city) Wayne County
89	2090	5.2	**Bath** (charter township) Clinton County
89	2090	5.2	**Delhi** (charter township) Ingham County
89	2090	5.2	**Sterling Heights** (city) Macomb County
92	2116	5.1	**Okemos** (CDP) Ingham County
93	2156	4.9	**Meridian** (charter township) Ingham County
93	2156	4.9	**Portage** (city) Kalamazoo County
95	2206	4.7	**Waterford** (charter township) Oakland County
96	2253	4.5	**Grosse Pointe Woods** (city) Wayne County
96	2253	4.5	**Port Huron** (charter township) Saint Clair County
96	2253	4.5	**Rochester Hills** (city) Oakland County
99	2278	4.4	**Adrian** (city) Lenawee County
99	2278	4.4	**Haslett** (CDP) Ingham County
99	2278	4.4	**Marquette** (city) Marquette County
102	2302	4.3	**Mundy** (township) Genesee County
102	2302	4.3	**Royal Oak** (city) Oakland County
102	2302	4.3	**Scio** (township) Washtenaw County
105	2390	4.0	**Dearborn** (city) Wayne County
105	2390	4.0	**Troy** (city) Oakland County
107	2415	3.9	**Fraser** (city) Macomb County
107	2415	3.9	**Macomb** (township) Macomb County
107	2415	3.9	**Mount Pleasant** (city) Isabella County
107	2415	3.9	**Saint Clair Shores** (city) Macomb County
111	2446	3.8	**Union** (charter township) Isabella County
112	2480	3.7	**Niles** (township) Berrien County
112	2480	3.7	**Rochester** (city) Oakland County
114	2510	3.6	**Holland** (city) Ottawa County
114	2510	3.6	**Northview** (CDP) Kent County
114	2510	3.6	**Northville** (township) Wayne County
117	2534	3.5	**Bay City** (city) Bay County
118	2568	3.4	**Garden City** (city) Wayne County
118	2568	3.4	**Livonia** (city) Wayne County
120	2602	3.3	**Allendale** (CDP) Ottawa County
121	2654	3.2	**Norton Shores** (city) Muskegon County
121	2654	3.2	**Shelby** (charter township) Macomb County
123	2693	3.1	**Allendale** (charter township) Ottawa County
123	2693	3.1	**Emmett** (charter township) Calhoun County
123	2693	3.1	**Riverview** (city) Wayne County
126	2726	3.0	**Berkley** (city) Oakland County
126	2726	3.0	**Birmingham** (city) Oakland County
126	2726	3.0	**Cooper** (charter township) Kalamazoo County
129	2768	2.9	**Davison** (township) Genesee County
130	2800	2.8	**Walker** (city) Kent County
131	2839	2.7	**New Baltimore** (city) Macomb County
132	2884	2.6	**DeWitt** (charter township) Clinton County
132	2884	2.6	**Holland** (charter township) Ottawa County
132	2884	2.6	**Orion** (charter township) Oakland County
135	2925	2.5	**Huron** (charter township) Wayne County
135	2925	2.5	**Monroe** (charter township) Monroe County
135	2925	2.5	**Texas** (charter township) Kalamazoo County
138	2973	2.4	**Oakland** (charter township) Oakland County
139	3070	2.2	**Grandville** (city) Kent County
139	3070	2.2	**Lincoln** (charter township) Berrien County
139	3070	2.2	**Plymouth** (charter township) Wayne County
142	3124	2.1	**Allen Park** (city) Wayne County
142	3124	2.1	**Flushing** (charter township) Genesee County
142	3124	2.1	**Frenchtown** (township) Monroe County
142	3124	2.1	**Holly** (township) Oakland County
142	3124	2.1	**Plainfield** (charter township) Kent County
147	3175	2.0	**Midland** (city) Midland County
148	3239	1.9	**Clawson** (city) Oakland County
148	3239	1.9	**Independence** (charter township) Oakland County
150	3304	1.8	**Grand Rapids** (charter township) Kent County

Note: The state column ranks the top/bottom 150 places from all places in the state with population of 10,000 or more. The national column ranks the top/bottom 150 places from all places in the country with population of 10,000 or more. Places that are unincorporated were not considered in the rankings. Please refer to the User Guide for additional information.

Black/African American Population

Top 150 Places Ranked in *Ascending* Order

State Rank	Nat'l Rank	Percent	Place
1	15	0.3	**East Bay** (township) Grand Traverse County
1	15	0.3	**Grand Haven** (charter township) Ottawa County
1	15	0.3	**Hamburg** (township) Livingston County
4	56	0.4	**Escanaba** (city) Delta County
4	56	0.4	**Fenton** (charter township) Genesee County
4	56	0.4	**Grosse Ile** (township) Wayne County
4	56	0.4	**Highland** (charter township) Oakland County
4	56	0.4	**Monitor** (charter township) Bay County
4	56	0.4	**Oceola** (township) Livingston County
10	131	0.5	**Alpena** (city) Alpena County
10	131	0.5	**Bedford** (township) Monroe County
10	131	0.5	**Cadillac** (city) Wexford County
10	131	0.5	**Hartland** (township) Livingston County
10	131	0.5	**Tyrone** (township) Livingston County
15	234	0.6	**Brighton** (township) Livingston County
15	234	0.6	**Coldwater** (city) Branch County
15	234	0.6	**Genoa** (township) Livingston County
15	234	0.6	**Spring Lake** (township) Ottawa County
19	327	0.7	**Cannon** (township) Kent County
19	327	0.7	**Grand Haven** (city) Ottawa County
19	327	0.7	**Green Oak** (township) Livingston County
19	327	0.7	**Sault Sainte Marie** (city) Chippewa County
19	327	0.7	**Traverse City** (city) Grand Traverse County
24	424	0.8	**Brandon** (charter township) Oakland County
24	424	0.8	**Garfield** (charter township) Grand Traverse County
24	424	0.8	**Jenison** (CDP) Ottawa County
24	424	0.8	**Owosso** (city) Shiawassee County
24	424	0.8	**South Lyon** (city) Oakland County
29	548	0.9	**Bangor** (charter township) Bay County
29	548	0.9	**Milford** (charter township) Oakland County
29	548	0.9	**Park** (township) Ottawa County
32	640	1.0	**Ada** (township) Kent County
32	640	1.0	**Georgetown** (charter township) Ottawa County
34	745	1.1	**Antwerp** (township) Van Buren County
34	745	1.1	**East Grand Rapids** (city) Kent County
34	745	1.1	**Springfield** (charter township) Oakland County
34	745	1.1	**Thomas** (township) Saginaw County
34	745	1.1	**White Lake** (charter township) Oakland County
39	830	1.2	**Caledonia** (township) Kent County
39	830	1.2	**Forest Hills** (CDP) Kent County
39	830	1.2	**Leoni** (township) Jackson County
42	919	1.3	**Fenton** (city) Genesee County
42	919	1.3	**Fruitport** (charter township) Muskegon County
42	919	1.3	**Trenton** (city) Wayne County
42	919	1.3	**Wyandotte** (city) Wayne County
46	994	1.4	**Lyon** (charter township) Oakland County
46	994	1.4	**Oxford** (charter township) Oakland County
46	994	1.4	**Sturgis** (city) Saint Joseph County
49	1071	1.5	**Cascade** (charter township) Kent County
50	1155	1.6	**Byron** (township) Kent County
50	1155	1.6	**Commerce** (charter township) Oakland County
50	1155	1.6	**Fort Gratiot** (charter township) Saint Clair County
50	1155	1.6	**Washington** (township) Macomb County
54	1298	1.8	**Grand Rapids** (charter township) Kent County
54	1298	1.8	**Vienna** (charter township) Genesee County
56	1353	1.9	**Clawson** (city) Oakland County
56	1353	1.9	**Independence** (charter township) Oakland County
58	1418	2.0	**Midland** (city) Midland County
59	1482	2.1	**Allen Park** (city) Wayne County
59	1482	2.1	**Flushing** (charter township) Genesee County
59	1482	2.1	**Frenchtown** (township) Monroe County
59	1482	2.1	**Holly** (township) Oakland County
59	1482	2.1	**Plainfield** (charter township) Kent County
64	1533	2.2	**Grandville** (city) Kent County
64	1533	2.2	**Lincoln** (charter township) Berrien County
64	1533	2.2	**Plymouth** (charter township) Wayne County
67	1638	2.4	**Oakland** (charter township) Oakland County
68	1684	2.5	**Huron** (charter township) Wayne County
68	1684	2.5	**Monroe** (charter township) Monroe County
68	1684	2.5	**Texas** (charter township) Kalamazoo County
71	1732	2.6	**DeWitt** (charter township) Clinton County
71	1732	2.6	**Holland** (charter township) Ottawa County
71	1732	2.6	**Orion** (charter township) Oakland County
74	1773	2.7	**New Baltimore** (city) Macomb County
75	1818	2.8	**Walker** (city) Kent County
76	1857	2.9	**Davison** (township) Genesee County
77	1889	3.0	**Berkley** (city) Oakland County
77	1889	3.0	**Birmingham** (city) Oakland County
77	1889	3.0	**Cooper** (charter township) Kalamazoo County
80	1931	3.1	**Allendale** (charter township) Ottawa County
80	1931	3.1	**Emmett** (charter township) Calhoun County
80	1931	3.1	**Riverview** (city) Wayne County
83	1964	3.2	**Norton Shores** (city) Muskegon County
83	1964	3.2	**Shelby** (charter township) Macomb County
85	2003	3.3	**Allendale** (CDP) Ottawa County
86	2055	3.4	**Garden City** (city) Wayne County
86	2055	3.4	**Livonia** (city) Wayne County
88	2089	3.5	**Bay City** (city) Bay County
89	2123	3.6	**Holland** (city) Ottawa County
89	2123	3.6	**Northview** (CDP) Kent County
89	2123	3.6	**Northville** (township) Wayne County
92	2147	3.7	**Niles** (township) Berrien County
92	2147	3.7	**Rochester** (city) Oakland County
94	2177	3.8	**Union** (charter township) Isabella County
95	2211	3.9	**Fraser** (city) Macomb County
95	2211	3.9	**Macomb** (township) Macomb County
95	2211	3.9	**Mount Pleasant** (city) Isabella County
95	2211	3.9	**Saint Clair Shores** (city) Macomb County
99	2242	4.0	**Dearborn** (city) Wayne County
99	2242	4.0	**Troy** (city) Oakland County
101	2319	4.3	**Mundy** (township) Genesee County
101	2319	4.3	**Royal Oak** (city) Oakland County
101	2319	4.3	**Scio** (township) Washtenaw County
104	2355	4.4	**Adrian** (city) Lenawee County
104	2355	4.4	**Haslett** (CDP) Ingham County
104	2355	4.4	**Marquette** (city) Marquette County
107	2379	4.5	**Grosse Pointe Woods** (city) Wayne County
107	2379	4.5	**Port Huron** (charter township) Saint Clair County
107	2379	4.5	**Rochester Hills** (city) Oakland County
110	2426	4.7	**Waterford** (charter township) Oakland County
111	2475	4.9	**Meridian** (charter township) Ingham County
111	2475	4.9	**Portage** (city) Kalamazoo County
113	2518	5.1	**Okemos** (CDP) Ingham County
114	2541	5.2	**Bath** (charter township) Clinton County
114	2541	5.2	**Delhi** (charter township) Ingham County
114	2541	5.2	**Sterling Heights** (city) Macomb County
117	2567	5.3	**Chesterfield** (township) Macomb County
117	2567	5.3	**Summit** (township) Jackson County
117	2567	5.3	**Woodhaven** (city) Wayne County
120	2607	5.5	**Southgate** (city) Wayne County
121	2631	5.6	**Comstock** (charter township) Kalamazoo County
121	2631	5.6	**Holt** (CDP) Ingham County
123	2686	5.9	**Lincoln Park** (city) Wayne County
124	2731	6.1	**Muskegon** (charter township) Muskegon County
125	2746	6.2	**Alpine** (township) Kent County
125	2746	6.2	**Monroe** (city) Monroe County
127	2784	6.4	**Madison Heights** (city) Oakland County
128	2829	6.6	**Beverly Hills** (village) Oakland County
129	2849	6.7	**Bloomfield** (charter township) Oakland County
129	2849	6.7	**Southfield** (township) Oakland County
131	2864	6.8	**Big Rapids** (city) Mecosta County
131	2864	6.8	**East Lansing** (city) Ingham County
133	2928	7.2	**Cutlerville** (CDP) Kent County
133	2928	7.2	**Wyoming** (city) Kent County
135	2945	7.3	**Burton** (city) Genesee County
136	2961	7.4	**Harrison** (charter township) Macomb County
137	3004	7.7	**Ann Arbor** (city) Washtenaw County
138	3032	7.9	**Dearborn Heights** (city) Wayne County
139	3044	8.0	**Comstock Park** (CDP) Kent County
140	3059	8.1	**Novi** (city) Oakland County
141	3112	8.6	**Brownstown** (charter township) Wayne County
141	3112	8.6	**Genesee** (charter township) Genesee County
143	3140	8.8	**Saginaw** (charter township) Saginaw County
144	3168	9.1	**Port Huron** (city) Saint Clair County
145	3186	9.3	**Gaines** (charter township) Kent County
146	3208	9.6	**Ferndale** (city) Oakland County
147	3235	9.8	**Hazel Park** (city) Oakland County
148	3276	10.2	**Canton** (charter township) Wayne County
149	3314	10.5	**Grosse Pointe Park** (city) Wayne County
150	3332	10.7	**Grand Blanc** (charter township) Genesee County

Note: The state column ranks the top/bottom 150 places from all places in the state with population of 10,000 or more. The national column ranks the top/bottom 150 places from all places in the country with population of 10,000 or more. Places that are unincorporated were not considered in the rankings. Please refer to the User Guide for additional information.

Asian Population

Top 150 Places Ranked in *Descending* Order

State Rank	Nat'l Rank	Percent	Place
1	163	21.5	**Hamtramck** (city) Wayne County
2	198	19.1	**Troy** (city) Oakland County
3	260	15.9	**Novi** (city) Oakland County
4	325	14.4	**Ann Arbor** (city) Washtenaw County
4	325	14.4	**Okemos** (CDP) Ingham County
6	338	14.1	**Canton** (charter township) Wayne County
7	344	13.9	**Farmington** (city) Oakland County
8	351	13.6	**Pittsfield** (charter township) Washtenaw County
9	452	11.3	**Northville** (township) Wayne County
10	481	10.9	**Meridian** (charter township) Ingham County
11	505	10.6	**East Lansing** (city) Ingham County
12	512	10.5	**Rochester Hills** (city) Oakland County
13	550	10.1	**Farmington Hills** (city) Oakland County
14	593	9.4	**Holland** (charter township) Ottawa County
15	630	8.9	**Auburn Hills** (city) Oakland County
16	655	8.6	**Scio** (township) Washtenaw County
17	674	8.4	**West Bloomfield** (charter township) Oakland County
18	814	7.2	**Bloomfield** (charter township) Oakland County
19	882	6.7	**Sterling Heights** (city) Macomb County
20	892	6.6	**Kentwood** (city) Kent County
21	911	6.5	**Haslett** (CDP) Ingham County
22	1022	5.8	**Madison Heights** (city) Oakland County
23	1036	5.7	**Superior** (charter township) Washtenaw County
24	1080	5.5	**Rochester** (city) Oakland County
25	1103	5.4	**Oakland** (charter township) Oakland County
26	1135	5.2	**Brownstown** (charter township) Wayne County
27	1206	4.9	**Wixom** (city) Oakland County
28	1266	4.6	**Gaines** (charter township) Kent County
28	1266	4.6	**Warren** (city) Macomb County
30	1326	4.4	**Grand Rapids** (charter township) Kent County
31	1388	4.2	**Waverly** (CDP) Eaton County
32	1423	4.1	**Texas** (charter township) Kalamazoo County
33	1521	3.8	**Delta** (charter township) Eaton County
33	1521	3.8	**Portage** (city) Kalamazoo County
35	1569	3.7	**Lansing** (city) Ingham County
36	1618	3.6	**Ada** (township) Kent County
36	1618	3.6	**Bath** (charter township) Clinton County
38	1659	3.5	**Plymouth** (charter township) Wayne County
39	1700	3.4	**Forest Hills** (CDP) Kent County
39	1700	3.4	**Grand Blanc** (charter township) Genesee County
39	1700	3.4	**Saginaw** (charter township) Saginaw County
39	1700	3.4	**Ypsilanti** (city) Washtenaw County
43	1745	3.3	**Midland** (city) Midland County
43	1745	3.3	**Shelby** (charter township) Macomb County
45	1850	3.1	**Cascade** (charter township) Kent County
45	1850	3.1	**Holt** (CDP) Ingham County
45	1850	3.1	**Macomb** (township) Macomb County
48	1902	3.0	**Cutlerville** (CDP) Kent County
48	1902	3.0	**Holland** (city) Ottawa County
48	1902	3.0	**Mount Pleasant** (city) Isabella County
48	1902	3.0	**Westland** (city) Wayne County
52	1953	2.9	**Delhi** (charter township) Ingham County
53	2010	2.8	**Oshtemo** (charter township) Kalamazoo County
53	2010	2.8	**Southfield** (township) Oakland County
53	2010	2.8	**Wyoming** (city) Kent County
56	2114	2.6	**Saint Joseph** (charter township) Berrien County
57	2173	2.5	**Birmingham** (city) Oakland County
57	2173	2.5	**Livonia** (city) Wayne County
57	2173	2.5	**Van Buren** (charter township) Wayne County
60	2237	2.4	**Battle Creek** (city) Calhoun County
60	2237	2.4	**Commerce** (charter township) Oakland County
60	2237	2.4	**Grosse Ile** (township) Wayne County
60	2237	2.4	**Grosse Pointe Woods** (city) Wayne County
60	2237	2.4	**Lincoln** (charter township) Berrien County
60	2237	2.4	**Royal Oak** (city) Oakland County
66	2314	2.3	**Pontiac** (city) Oakland County
66	2314	2.3	**Woodhaven** (city) Wayne County
68	2384	2.2	**Park** (township) Ottawa County
69	2465	2.1	**Orion** (charter township) Oakland County
69	2465	2.1	**Wayne** (city) Wayne County
69	2465	2.1	**Ypsilanti** (charter township) Washtenaw County
72	2527	2.0	**Beverly Hills** (village) Oakland County
72	2527	2.0	**Clawson** (city) Oakland County
74	2598	1.9	**Comstock** (charter township) Kalamazoo County
74	2598	1.9	**Flint** (charter township) Genesee County
74	2598	1.9	**Grand Rapids** (city) Kent County
74	2598	1.9	**Union** (charter township) Isabella County
74	2598	1.9	**Walker** (city) Kent County
79	2688	1.8	**Clinton** (charter township) Macomb County
79	2688	1.8	**Grosse Pointe Park** (city) Wayne County
79	2688	1.8	**Taylor** (city) Wayne County
82	2801	1.7	**Dearborn** (city) Wayne County
82	2801	1.7	**Dearborn Heights** (city) Wayne County
82	2801	1.7	**Kalamazoo** (city) Kalamazoo County
82	2801	1.7	**South Lyon** (city) Oakland County
82	2801	1.7	**Southfield** (city) Oakland County
87	2898	1.6	**Byron** (township) Kent County
87	2898	1.6	**Inkster** (city) Wayne County
87	2898	1.6	**Riverview** (city) Wayne County
87	2898	1.6	**Roseville** (city) Macomb County
87	2898	1.6	**Southgate** (city) Wayne County
87	2898	1.6	**Waterford** (charter township) Oakland County
93	3009	1.5	**Allendale** (CDP) Ottawa County
93	3009	1.5	**Big Rapids** (city) Mecosta County
93	3009	1.5	**East Grand Rapids** (city) Kent County
93	3009	1.5	**Fraser** (city) Macomb County
93	3009	1.5	**Grandville** (city) Kent County
93	3009	1.5	**Harper Woods** (city) Wayne County
93	3009	1.5	**Hazel Park** (city) Oakland County
93	3009	1.5	**Independence** (charter township) Oakland County
93	3009	1.5	**Lyon** (charter township) Oakland County
93	3009	1.5	**Summit** (township) Jackson County
103	3111	1.4	**Allendale** (charter township) Ottawa County
103	3111	1.4	**DeWitt** (charter township) Clinton County
103	3111	1.4	**Fort Gratiot** (charter township) Saint Clair County
103	3111	1.4	**Oak Park** (city) Oakland County
107	3229	1.3	**Berkley** (city) Oakland County
107	3229	1.3	**Ferndale** (city) Oakland County
107	3229	1.3	**Georgetown** (charter township) Ottawa County
107	3229	1.3	**Kalamazoo** (charter township) Kalamazoo County
107	3229	1.3	**Northview** (CDP) Kent County
112	3327	1.2	**Caledonia** (township) Kent County
112	3327	1.2	**Comstock Park** (CDP) Kent County
112	3327	1.2	**Emmett** (charter township) Calhoun County
112	3327	1.2	**Norton Shores** (city) Muskegon County
112	3327	1.2	**Oxford** (charter township) Oakland County
112	3327	1.2	**Plainfield** (charter township) Kent County
118	3443	1.1	**Detroit** (city) Wayne County
118	3443	1.1	**Eastpointe** (city) Macomb County
118	3443	1.1	**Garfield** (charter township) Grand Traverse County
118	3443	1.1	**Holly** (township) Oakland County
118	3443	1.1	**Milford** (charter township) Oakland County
118	3443	1.1	**Romulus** (city) Wayne County
118	3443	1.1	**Thomas** (township) Saginaw County
125	3560	1.0	**Alpine** (township) Kent County
125	3560	1.0	**Blackman** (charter township) Jackson County
125	3560	1.0	**Cadillac** (city) Wexford County
125	3560	1.0	**Chesterfield** (township) Macomb County
125	3560	1.0	**Cooper** (charter township) Kalamazoo County
125	3560	1.0	**Fenton** (charter township) Genesee County
125	3560	1.0	**Genoa** (township) Livingston County
125	3560	1.0	**Grand Haven** (charter township) Ottawa County
125	3560	1.0	**Grand Haven** (city) Ottawa County
125	3560	1.0	**Hartland** (township) Livingston County
125	3560	1.0	**Mundy** (township) Genesee County
125	3560	1.0	**Saint Clair Shores** (city) Macomb County
125	3560	1.0	**Springfield** (charter township) Oakland County
125	3560	1.0	**Washington** (township) Macomb County
139	3694	0.9	**Adrian** (charter township) Lenawee County
139	3694	0.9	**Brandon** (charter township) Oakland County
139	3694	0.9	**Brighton** (township) Livingston County
139	3694	0.9	**Green Oak** (township) Livingston County
139	3694	0.9	**Jenison** (CDP) Ottawa County
139	3694	0.9	**Marquette** (city) Marquette County
139	3694	0.9	**New Baltimore** (city) Macomb County
139	3694	0.9	**Oceola** (township) Livingston County
139	3694	0.9	**Sault Sainte Marie** (city) Chippewa County
139	3694	0.9	**Sturgis** (city) Saint Joseph County
139	3694	0.9	**White Lake** (charter township) Oakland County
150	3856	0.8	**Allen Park** (city) Wayne County

Note: *The state column ranks the top/bottom 150 places from all places in the state with population of 10,000 or more. The national column ranks the top/bottom 150 places from all places in the country with population of 10,000 or more. Places that are unincorporated were not considered in the rankings. Please refer to the User Guide for additional information.*

Asian Population

Top 150 Places Ranked in *Ascending* Order

State Rank	Nat'l Rank	Percent	Place
1	4	0.1	**Beecher** (CDP) Genesee County
1	4	0.1	**Benton Harbor** (city) Berrien County
1	4	0.1	**Muskegon Heights** (city) Muskegon County
4	20	0.2	**Genesee** (charter township) Genesee County
5	61	0.3	**Mount Morris** (township) Genesee County
5	61	0.3	**Owosso** (city) Shiawassee County
5	61	0.3	**Saginaw** (city) Saginaw County
8	108	0.4	**Antwerp** (township) Van Buren County
8	108	0.4	**Benton** (charter township) Berrien County
8	108	0.4	**Bridgeport** (charter township) Saginaw County
8	108	0.4	**Highland Park** (city) Wayne County
8	108	0.4	**Ionia** (city) Ionia County
8	108	0.4	**Muskegon** (charter township) Muskegon County
8	108	0.4	**Muskegon** (city) Muskegon County
8	108	0.4	**Port Huron** (charter township) Saint Clair County
8	108	0.4	**Vienna** (charter township) Genesee County
17	198	0.5	**Bay City** (city) Bay County
17	198	0.5	**Flint** (city) Genesee County
17	198	0.5	**Highland** (charter township) Oakland County
17	198	0.5	**Lenox** (township) Macomb County
17	198	0.5	**Leoni** (township) Jackson County
17	198	0.5	**Lincoln Park** (city) Wayne County
17	198	0.5	**Mount Clemens** (city) Macomb County
17	198	0.5	**Wyandotte** (city) Wayne County
25	321	0.6	**Burton** (city) Genesee County
25	321	0.6	**Escanaba** (city) Delta County
25	321	0.6	**Frenchtown** (township) Monroe County
25	321	0.6	**Hamburg** (township) Livingston County
25	321	0.6	**Monitor** (charter township) Bay County
25	321	0.6	**Niles** (city) Berrien County
25	321	0.6	**Port Huron** (city) Saint Clair County
32	452	0.7	**Alpena** (city) Alpena County
32	452	0.7	**East Bay** (township) Grand Traverse County
32	452	0.7	**Fenton** (city) Genesee County
32	452	0.7	**Harrison** (charter township) Macomb County
32	452	0.7	**Huron** (charter township) Wayne County
32	452	0.7	**Jackson** (city) Jackson County
32	452	0.7	**Monroe** (charter township) Monroe County
32	452	0.7	**Monroe** (city) Monroe County
32	452	0.7	**Niles** (township) Berrien County
32	452	0.7	**Traverse City** (city) Grand Traverse County
32	452	0.7	**Trenton** (city) Wayne County
32	452	0.7	**Tyrone** (township) Livingston County
44	629	0.8	**Allen Park** (city) Wayne County
44	629	0.8	**Bangor** (charter township) Bay County
44	629	0.8	**Bedford** (township) Monroe County
44	629	0.8	**Cannon** (township) Kent County
44	629	0.8	**Coldwater** (city) Branch County
44	629	0.8	**Davison** (township) Genesee County
44	629	0.8	**Flushing** (charter township) Genesee County
44	629	0.8	**Fruitport** (charter township) Muskegon County
44	629	0.8	**Garden City** (city) Wayne County
44	629	0.8	**Melvindale** (city) Wayne County
44	629	0.8	**Redford** (charter township) Wayne County
44	629	0.8	**Spring Lake** (township) Ottawa County
56	801	0.9	**Adrian** (city) Lenawee County
56	801	0.9	**Brandon** (charter township) Oakland County
56	801	0.9	**Brighton** (township) Livingston County
56	801	0.9	**Green Oak** (township) Livingston County
56	801	0.9	**Jenison** (CDP) Ottawa County
56	801	0.9	**Marquette** (city) Marquette County
56	801	0.9	**New Baltimore** (city) Macomb County
56	801	0.9	**Oceola** (township) Livingston County
56	801	0.9	**Sault Sainte Marie** (city) Chippewa County
56	801	0.9	**Sturgis** (city) Saint Joseph County
56	801	0.9	**White Lake** (charter township) Oakland County
67	963	1.0	**Alpine** (township) Kent County
67	963	1.0	**Blackman** (charter township) Jackson County
67	963	1.0	**Cadillac** (city) Wexford County
67	963	1.0	**Chesterfield** (township) Macomb County
67	963	1.0	**Cooper** (charter township) Kalamazoo County
67	963	1.0	**Fenton** (charter township) Genesee County
67	963	1.0	**Genoa** (township) Livingston County
67	963	1.0	**Grand Haven** (charter township) Ottawa County
67	963	1.0	**Grand Haven** (city) Ottawa County
67	963	1.0	**Hartland** (township) Livingston County
67	963	1.0	**Mundy** (township) Genesee County
67	963	1.0	**Saint Clair Shores** (city) Macomb County
67	963	1.0	**Springfield** (charter township) Oakland County
67	963	1.0	**Washington** (township) Macomb County
81	1097	1.1	**Detroit** (city) Wayne County
81	1097	1.1	**Eastpointe** (city) Macomb County
81	1097	1.1	**Garfield** (charter township) Grand Traverse County
81	1097	1.1	**Holly** (township) Oakland County
81	1097	1.1	**Milford** (charter township) Oakland County
81	1097	1.1	**Romulus** (city) Wayne County
81	1097	1.1	**Thomas** (township) Saginaw County
88	1214	1.2	**Caledonia** (township) Kent County
88	1214	1.2	**Comstock Park** (CDP) Kent County
88	1214	1.2	**Emmett** (charter township) Calhoun County
88	1214	1.2	**Norton Shores** (city) Muskegon County
88	1214	1.2	**Oxford** (charter township) Oakland County
88	1214	1.2	**Plainfield** (charter township) Kent County
94	1330	1.3	**Berkley** (city) Oakland County
94	1330	1.3	**Ferndale** (city) Oakland County
94	1330	1.3	**Georgetown** (charter township) Ottawa County
94	1330	1.3	**Kalamazoo** (charter township) Kalamazoo County
94	1330	1.3	**Northview** (CDP) Kent County
99	1428	1.4	**Allendale** (charter township) Ottawa County
99	1428	1.4	**DeWitt** (charter township) Clinton County
99	1428	1.4	**Fort Gratiot** (charter township) Saint Clair County
99	1428	1.4	**Oak Park** (city) Oakland County
103	1546	1.5	**Allendale** (CDP) Ottawa County
103	1546	1.5	**Big Rapids** (city) Mecosta County
103	1546	1.5	**East Grand Rapids** (city) Kent County
103	1546	1.5	**Fraser** (city) Macomb County
103	1546	1.5	**Grandville** (city) Kent County
103	1546	1.5	**Harper Woods** (city) Wayne County
103	1546	1.5	**Hazel Park** (city) Oakland County
103	1546	1.5	**Independence** (charter township) Oakland County
103	1546	1.5	**Lyon** (charter township) Oakland County
103	1546	1.5	**Summit** (township) Jackson County
113	1648	1.6	**Byron** (township) Kent County
113	1648	1.6	**Inkster** (city) Wayne County
113	1648	1.6	**Riverview** (city) Wayne County
113	1648	1.6	**Roseville** (city) Macomb County
113	1648	1.6	**Southgate** (city) Wayne County
113	1648	1.6	**Waterford** (charter township) Oakland County
119	1759	1.7	**Dearborn** (city) Wayne County
119	1759	1.7	**Dearborn Heights** (city) Wayne County
119	1759	1.7	**Kalamazoo** (city) Kalamazoo County
119	1759	1.7	**South Lyon** (city) Oakland County
119	1759	1.7	**Southfield** (city) Oakland County
124	1856	1.8	**Clinton** (charter township) Macomb County
124	1856	1.8	**Grosse Pointe Park** (city) Wayne County
124	1856	1.8	**Taylor** (city) Wayne County
127	1969	1.9	**Comstock** (charter township) Kalamazoo County
127	1969	1.9	**Flint** (charter township) Genesee County
127	1969	1.9	**Grand Rapids** (city) Kent County
127	1969	1.9	**Union** (charter township) Isabella County
127	1969	1.9	**Walker** (city) Kent County
132	2059	2.0	**Beverly Hills** (village) Oakland County
132	2059	2.0	**Clawson** (city) Oakland County
134	2130	2.1	**Orion** (charter township) Oakland County
134	2130	2.1	**Wayne** (city) Wayne County
134	2130	2.1	**Ypsilanti** (charter township) Washtenaw County
137	2192	2.2	**Park** (township) Ottawa County
138	2273	2.3	**Pontiac** (city) Oakland County
138	2273	2.3	**Woodhaven** (city) Wayne County
140	2343	2.4	**Battle Creek** (city) Calhoun County
140	2343	2.4	**Commerce** (charter township) Oakland County
140	2343	2.4	**Grosse Ile** (township) Wayne County
140	2343	2.4	**Grosse Pointe Woods** (city) Wayne County
140	2343	2.4	**Lincoln** (charter township) Berrien County
140	2343	2.4	**Royal Oak** (city) Oakland County
146	2420	2.5	**Birmingham** (city) Oakland County
146	2420	2.5	**Livonia** (city) Wayne County
146	2420	2.5	**Van Buren** (charter township) Wayne County
149	2484	2.6	**Saint Joseph** (charter township) Berrien County
150	2593	2.8	**Oshtemo** (charter township) Kalamazoo County

Note: The state column ranks the top/bottom 150 places from all places in the state with population of 10,000 or more. The national column ranks the top/bottom 150 places from all places in the country with population of 10,000 or more. Places that are unincorporated were not considered in the rankings. Please refer to the User Guide for additional information.

American Indian/Alaska Native Population

Top 150 Places Ranked in *Descending* Order

State Rank	Nat'l Rank	Percent	Place
1	5	17.7	**Sault Sainte Marie** (city) Chippewa County
2	92	3.2	**Union** (charter township) Isabella County
3	121	2.6	**Escanaba** (city) Delta County
4	164	2.0	**Mount Pleasant** (city) Isabella County
5	187	1.8	**Traverse City** (city) Grand Traverse County
6	251	1.5	**Marquette** (city) Marquette County
7	390	1.2	**Garfield** (charter township) Grand Traverse County
8	474	1.1	**Muskegon** (charter township) Muskegon County
9	553	1.0	**East Bay** (township) Grand Traverse County
10	667	0.9	**Grand Haven** (city) Ottawa County
10	667	0.9	**Hazel Park** (city) Oakland County
10	667	0.9	**Muskegon** (city) Muskegon County
13	795	0.8	**Beecher** (CDP) Genesee County
13	795	0.8	**Cutlerville** (CDP) Kent County
13	795	0.8	**Genesee** (charter township) Genesee County
13	795	0.8	**Lansing** (city) Ingham County
13	795	0.8	**Norton Shores** (city) Muskegon County
18	954	0.7	**Battle Creek** (city) Calhoun County
18	954	0.7	**Big Rapids** (city) Mecosta County
18	954	0.7	**Comstock Park** (CDP) Kent County
18	954	0.7	**Fruitport** (charter township) Muskegon County
18	954	0.7	**Grand Rapids** (city) Kent County
18	954	0.7	**Huron** (charter township) Wayne County
18	954	0.7	**Ionia** (city) Ionia County
18	954	0.7	**Lincoln Park** (city) Wayne County
18	954	0.7	**Melvindale** (city) Wayne County
18	954	0.7	**Mount Morris** (township) Genesee County
18	954	0.7	**Niles** (township) Berrien County
18	954	0.7	**Port Huron** (charter township) Saint Clair County
18	954	0.7	**Port Huron** (city) Saint Clair County
18	954	0.7	**Wyandotte** (city) Wayne County
32	1134	0.6	**Adrian** (city) Lenawee County
32	1134	0.6	**Alpine** (township) Kent County
32	1134	0.6	**Bangor** (charter township) Bay County
32	1134	0.6	**Bay City** (city) Bay County
32	1134	0.6	**Burton** (city) Genesee County
32	1134	0.6	**Cadillac** (city) Wexford County
32	1134	0.6	**Davison** (township) Genesee County
32	1134	0.6	**DeWitt** (charter township) Clinton County
32	1134	0.6	**Emmett** (charter township) Calhoun County
32	1134	0.6	**Flushing** (charter township) Genesee County
32	1134	0.6	**Holland** (city) Ottawa County
32	1134	0.6	**Holly** (township) Oakland County
32	1134	0.6	**Niles** (city) Berrien County
32	1134	0.6	**Pontiac** (city) Oakland County
32	1134	0.6	**Vienna** (charter township) Genesee County
32	1134	0.6	**Wyoming** (city) Kent County
32	1134	0.6	**Ypsilanti** (city) Washtenaw County
49	1413	0.5	**Allen Park** (city) Wayne County
49	1413	0.5	**Antwerp** (township) Van Buren County
49	1413	0.5	**Benton** (charter township) Berrien County
49	1413	0.5	**Blackman** (charter township) Jackson County
49	1413	0.5	**Bridgeport** (charter township) Saginaw County
49	1413	0.5	**Byron** (township) Kent County
49	1413	0.5	**Comstock** (charter township) Kalamazoo County
49	1413	0.5	**Delhi** (charter township) Ingham County
49	1413	0.5	**Delta** (charter township) Eaton County
49	1413	0.5	**Ferndale** (city) Oakland County
49	1413	0.5	**Flint** (charter township) Genesee County
49	1413	0.5	**Flint** (city) Genesee County
49	1413	0.5	**Fraser** (city) Macomb County
49	1413	0.5	**Gaines** (charter township) Kent County
49	1413	0.5	**Grand Haven** (charter township) Ottawa County
49	1413	0.5	**Green Oak** (charter township) Livingston County
49	1413	0.5	**Holland** (charter township) Ottawa County
49	1413	0.5	**Holt** (CDP) Ingham County
49	1413	0.5	**Kalamazoo** (city) Kalamazoo County
49	1413	0.5	**Lenox** (township) Macomb County
49	1413	0.5	**Madison Heights** (city) Oakland County
49	1413	0.5	**Owosso** (city) Shiawassee County
49	1413	0.5	**Redford** (charter township) Wayne County
49	1413	0.5	**Romulus** (city) Wayne County
49	1413	0.5	**Saginaw** (city) Saginaw County
49	1413	0.5	**Southgate** (city) Wayne County
49	1413	0.5	**Spring Lake** (township) Ottawa County
49	1413	0.5	**Taylor** (city) Wayne County
49	1413	0.5	**Trenton** (city) Wayne County
49	1413	0.5	**Van Buren** (charter township) Wayne County
49	1413	0.5	**Walker** (city) Kent County
49	1413	0.5	**Waverly** (CDP) Eaton County
49	1413	0.5	**Wayne** (city) Wayne County
49	1413	0.5	**Westland** (city) Wayne County
83	1783	0.4	**Allendale** (CDP) Ottawa County
83	1783	0.4	**Allendale** (charter township) Ottawa County
83	1783	0.4	**Alpena** (city) Alpena County
83	1783	0.4	**Bath** (charter township) Clinton County
83	1783	0.4	**Brandon** (charter township) Oakland County
83	1783	0.4	**Brownstown** (charter township) Wayne County
83	1783	0.4	**Chesterfield** (township) Macomb County
83	1783	0.4	**Cooper** (charter township) Kalamazoo County
83	1783	0.4	**Dearborn Heights** (city) Wayne County
83	1783	0.4	**Detroit** (city) Wayne County
83	1783	0.4	**Eastpointe** (city) Macomb County
83	1783	0.4	**Farmington** (city) Oakland County
83	1783	0.4	**Fenton** (charter township) Genesee County
83	1783	0.4	**Garden City** (city) Wayne County
83	1783	0.4	**Genoa** (township) Livingston County
83	1783	0.4	**Grand Blanc** (charter township) Genesee County
83	1783	0.4	**Grosse Ile** (township) Wayne County
83	1783	0.4	**Haslett** (CDP) Ingham County
83	1783	0.4	**Jackson** (city) Jackson County
83	1783	0.4	**Kalamazoo** (charter township) Kalamazoo County
83	1783	0.4	**Kentwood** (city) Kent County
83	1783	0.4	**Leoni** (township) Jackson County
83	1783	0.4	**Meridian** (charter township) Ingham County
83	1783	0.4	**Monroe** (city) Monroe County
83	1783	0.4	**New Baltimore** (city) Macomb County
83	1783	0.4	**Oceola** (township) Livingston County
83	1783	0.4	**Pittsfield** (charter township) Washtenaw County
83	1783	0.4	**Portage** (city) Kalamazoo County
83	1783	0.4	**Riverview** (city) Wayne County
83	1783	0.4	**Roseville** (city) Macomb County
83	1783	0.4	**Springfield** (charter township) Oakland County
83	1783	0.4	**Tyrone** (township) Livingston County
83	1783	0.4	**Warren** (city) Macomb County
83	1783	0.4	**Waterford** (charter township) Oakland County
83	1783	0.4	**White Lake** (charter township) Oakland County
83	1783	0.4	**Ypsilanti** (charter township) Washtenaw County
119	2288	0.3	**Ann Arbor** (city) Washtenaw County
119	2288	0.3	**Auburn Hills** (city) Oakland County
119	2288	0.3	**Benton Harbor** (city) Berrien County
119	2288	0.3	**Berkley** (city) Oakland County
119	2288	0.3	**Brighton** (township) Livingston County
119	2288	0.3	**Caledonia** (township) Kent County
119	2288	0.3	**Clawson** (city) Oakland County
119	2288	0.3	**Clinton** (charter township) Macomb County
119	2288	0.3	**Commerce** (charter township) Oakland County
119	2288	0.3	**East Lansing** (city) Ingham County
119	2288	0.3	**Fenton** (city) Genesee County
119	2288	0.3	**Fort Gratiot** (charter township) Saint Clair County
119	2288	0.3	**Frenchtown** (township) Monroe County
119	2288	0.3	**Georgetown** (charter township) Ottawa County
119	2288	0.3	**Hamburg** (township) Livingston County
119	2288	0.3	**Hamtramck** (city) Wayne County
119	2288	0.3	**Harrison** (charter township) Macomb County
119	2288	0.3	**Hartland** (township) Livingston County
119	2288	0.3	**Highland** (charter township) Oakland County
119	2288	0.3	**Highland Park** (city) Wayne County
119	2288	0.3	**Independence** (charter township) Oakland County
119	2288	0.3	**Inkster** (city) Wayne County
119	2288	0.3	**Jenison** (CDP) Ottawa County
119	2288	0.3	**Lincoln** (charter township) Berrien County
119	2288	0.3	**Lyon** (charter township) Oakland County
119	2288	0.3	**Midland** (city) Midland County
119	2288	0.3	**Milford** (charter township) Oakland County
119	2288	0.3	**Monitor** (charter township) Bay County
119	2288	0.3	**Mount Clemens** (city) Macomb County
119	2288	0.3	**Mundy** (township) Genesee County
119	2288	0.3	**Muskegon Heights** (city) Muskegon County
119	2288	0.3	**Northview** (CDP) Kent County

Note: The state column ranks the top/bottom 150 places from all places in the state with population of 10,000 or more. The national column ranks the top/bottom 150 places from all places in the country with population of 10,000 or more. Places that are unincorporated were not considered in the rankings. Please refer to the User Guide for additional information.

American Indian/Alaska Native Population

Top 150 Places Ranked in *Ascending* Order

State Rank	Nat'l Rank	Percent	Place
1	61	0.1	**Birmingham** (city) Oakland County
1	61	0.1	**Bloomfield** (charter township) Oakland County
1	61	0.1	**East Grand Rapids** (city) Kent County
1	61	0.1	**Grosse Pointe Woods** (city) Wayne County
1	61	0.1	**Northville** (township) Wayne County
1	61	0.1	**West Bloomfield** (charter township) Oakland County
7	722	0.2	**Ada** (township) Kent County
7	722	0.2	**Bedford** (township) Monroe County
7	722	0.2	**Beverly Hills** (village) Oakland County
7	722	0.2	**Cannon** (township) Kent County
7	722	0.2	**Canton** (charter township) Wayne County
7	722	0.2	**Cascade** (charter township) Kent County
7	722	0.2	**Coldwater** (city) Branch County
7	722	0.2	**Dearborn** (city) Wayne County
7	722	0.2	**Farmington Hills** (city) Oakland County
7	722	0.2	**Forest Hills** (CDP) Kent County
7	722	0.2	**Grand Rapids** (charter township) Kent County
7	722	0.2	**Grandville** (city) Kent County
7	722	0.2	**Grosse Pointe Park** (city) Wayne County
7	722	0.2	**Harper Woods** (city) Wayne County
7	722	0.2	**Livonia** (city) Wayne County
7	722	0.2	**Macomb** (township) Macomb County
7	722	0.2	**Monroe** (charter township) Monroe County
7	722	0.2	**Novi** (city) Oakland County
7	722	0.2	**Oak Park** (city) Oakland County
7	722	0.2	**Oakland** (charter township) Oakland County
7	722	0.2	**Park** (township) Ottawa County
7	722	0.2	**Rochester** (city) Oakland County
7	722	0.2	**Rochester Hills** (city) Oakland County
7	722	0.2	**Southfield** (city) Oakland County
7	722	0.2	**Southfield** (township) Oakland County
7	722	0.2	**Sterling Heights** (city) Macomb County
7	722	0.2	**Superior** (charter township) Washtenaw County
7	722	0.2	**Thomas** (township) Saginaw County
7	722	0.2	**Troy** (city) Oakland County
7	722	0.2	**Washington** (township) Macomb County
7	722	0.2	**Wixom** (city) Oakland County
38	1626	0.3	**Ann Arbor** (city) Washtenaw County
38	1626	0.3	**Auburn Hills** (city) Oakland County
38	1626	0.3	**Benton Harbor** (city) Berrien County
38	1626	0.3	**Berkley** (city) Oakland County
38	1626	0.3	**Brighton** (township) Livingston County
38	1626	0.3	**Caledonia** (township) Kent County
38	1626	0.3	**Clawson** (city) Oakland County
38	1626	0.3	**Clinton** (charter township) Macomb County
38	1626	0.3	**Commerce** (charter township) Oakland County
38	1626	0.3	**East Lansing** (city) Ingham County
38	1626	0.3	**Fenton** (city) Genesee County
38	1626	0.3	**Fort Gratiot** (charter township) Saint Clair County
38	1626	0.3	**Frenchtown** (township) Monroe County
38	1626	0.3	**Georgetown** (charter township) Ottawa County
38	1626	0.3	**Hamburg** (township) Livingston County
38	1626	0.3	**Hamtramck** (city) Wayne County
38	1626	0.3	**Harrison** (charter township) Macomb County
38	1626	0.3	**Hartland** (township) Livingston County
38	1626	0.3	**Highland** (charter township) Oakland County
38	1626	0.3	**Highland Park** (city) Wayne County
38	1626	0.3	**Independence** (charter township) Oakland County
38	1626	0.3	**Inkster** (city) Wayne County
38	1626	0.3	**Jenison** (CDP) Ottawa County
38	1626	0.3	**Lincoln** (charter township) Berrien County
38	1626	0.3	**Lyon** (charter township) Oakland County
38	1626	0.3	**Midland** (city) Midland County
38	1626	0.3	**Milford** (charter township) Oakland County
38	1626	0.3	**Monitor** (charter township) Bay County
38	1626	0.3	**Mount Clemens** (city) Macomb County
38	1626	0.3	**Mundy** (township) Genesee County
38	1626	0.3	**Muskegon Heights** (city) Muskegon County
38	1626	0.3	**Northview** (CDP) Kent County
38	1626	0.3	**Okemos** (CDP) Ingham County
38	1626	0.3	**Orion** (charter township) Oakland County
38	1626	0.3	**Oshtemo** (charter township) Kalamazoo County
38	1626	0.3	**Oxford** (charter township) Oakland County
38	1626	0.3	**Plainfield** (charter township) Kent County
38	1626	0.3	**Plymouth** (charter township) Wayne County
38	1626	0.3	**Royal Oak** (city) Oakland County
38	1626	0.3	**Saginaw** (charter township) Saginaw County
38	1626	0.3	**Saint Clair Shores** (city) Macomb County
38	1626	0.3	**Saint Joseph** (charter township) Berrien County
38	1626	0.3	**Scio** (township) Washtenaw County
38	1626	0.3	**Shelby** (charter township) Macomb County
38	1626	0.3	**South Lyon** (city) Oakland County
38	1626	0.3	**Sturgis** (city) Saint Joseph County
38	1626	0.3	**Summit** (township) Jackson County
38	1626	0.3	**Texas** (charter township) Kalamazoo County
38	1626	0.3	**Woodhaven** (city) Wayne County
87	2369	0.4	**Allendale** (CDP) Ottawa County
87	2369	0.4	**Allendale** (charter township) Ottawa County
87	2369	0.4	**Alpena** (city) Alpena County
87	2369	0.4	**Bath** (charter township) Clinton County
87	2369	0.4	**Brandon** (charter township) Oakland County
87	2369	0.4	**Brownstown** (charter township) Wayne County
87	2369	0.4	**Chesterfield** (township) Macomb County
87	2369	0.4	**Cooper** (charter township) Kalamazoo County
87	2369	0.4	**Dearborn Heights** (city) Wayne County
87	2369	0.4	**Detroit** (city) Wayne County
87	2369	0.4	**Eastpointe** (city) Macomb County
87	2369	0.4	**Farmington** (city) Oakland County
87	2369	0.4	**Fenton** (charter township) Genesee County
87	2369	0.4	**Garden City** (city) Wayne County
87	2369	0.4	**Genoa** (township) Livingston County
87	2369	0.4	**Grand Blanc** (charter township) Genesee County
87	2369	0.4	**Grosse Ile** (township) Wayne County
87	2369	0.4	**Haslett** (CDP) Ingham County
87	2369	0.4	**Jackson** (city) Jackson County
87	2369	0.4	**Kalamazoo** (charter township) Kalamazoo County
87	2369	0.4	**Kentwood** (city) Kent County
87	2369	0.4	**Leoni** (township) Jackson County
87	2369	0.4	**Meridian** (charter township) Ingham County
87	2369	0.4	**Monroe** (city) Monroe County
87	2369	0.4	**New Baltimore** (city) Macomb County
87	2369	0.4	**Oceola** (township) Livingston County
87	2369	0.4	**Pittsfield** (charter township) Washtenaw County
87	2369	0.4	**Portage** (city) Kalamazoo County
87	2369	0.4	**Riverview** (city) Wayne County
87	2369	0.4	**Roseville** (city) Macomb County
87	2369	0.4	**Springfield** (charter township) Oakland County
87	2369	0.4	**Tyrone** (township) Livingston County
87	2369	0.4	**Warren** (city) Macomb County
87	2369	0.4	**Waterford** (charter township) Oakland County
87	2369	0.4	**White Lake** (charter township) Oakland County
87	2369	0.4	**Ypsilanti** (charter township) Washtenaw County
123	2874	0.5	**Allen Park** (city) Wayne County
123	2874	0.5	**Antwerp** (township) Van Buren County
123	2874	0.5	**Benton** (charter township) Berrien County
123	2874	0.5	**Blackman** (charter township) Jackson County
123	2874	0.5	**Bridgeport** (charter township) Saginaw County
123	2874	0.5	**Byron** (township) Kent County
123	2874	0.5	**Comstock** (charter township) Kalamazoo County
123	2874	0.5	**Delhi** (charter township) Ingham County
123	2874	0.5	**Delta** (charter township) Eaton County
123	2874	0.5	**Ferndale** (city) Oakland County
123	2874	0.5	**Flint** (charter township) Genesee County
123	2874	0.5	**Flint** (city) Genesee County
123	2874	0.5	**Fraser** (city) Macomb County
123	2874	0.5	**Gaines** (charter township) Kent County
123	2874	0.5	**Grand Haven** (charter township) Ottawa County
123	2874	0.5	**Green Oak** (township) Livingston County
123	2874	0.5	**Holland** (charter township) Ottawa County
123	2874	0.5	**Holt** (CDP) Ingham County
123	2874	0.5	**Kalamazoo** (city) Kalamazoo County
123	2874	0.5	**Lenox** (township) Macomb County
123	2874	0.5	**Madison Heights** (city) Oakland County
123	2874	0.5	**Owosso** (city) Shiawassee County
123	2874	0.5	**Redford** (charter township) Wayne County
123	2874	0.5	**Romulus** (city) Wayne County
123	2874	0.5	**Saginaw** (city) Saginaw County
123	2874	0.5	**Southgate** (city) Wayne County
123	2874	0.5	**Spring Lake** (township) Ottawa County
123	2874	0.5	**Taylor** (city) Wayne County

Note: The state column ranks the top/bottom 150 places from all places in the state with population of 10,000 or more. The national column ranks the top/bottom 150 places from all places in the country with population of 10,000 or more. Places that are unincorporated were not considered in the rankings. Please refer to the User Guide for additional information.

Native Hawaiian/Other Pacific Islander Population

Top 150 Places Ranked in *Descending* Order

State Rank	Nat'l Rank	Percent	Place
1	820	0.1	**Alpena** (city) Alpena County
1	820	0.1	**Berkley** (city) Oakland County
1	820	0.1	**Cannon** (township) Kent County
1	820	0.1	**Comstock** (charter township) Kalamazoo County
1	820	0.1	**Farmington** (city) Oakland County
1	820	0.1	**Ferndale** (city) Oakland County
1	820	0.1	**Grand Rapids** (city) Kent County
1	820	0.1	**Holland** (city) Ottawa County
1	820	0.1	**Holly** (township) Oakland County
1	820	0.1	**Inkster** (city) Wayne County
1	820	0.1	**Kentwood** (city) Kent County
1	820	0.1	**Madison Heights** (city) Oakland County
1	820	0.1	**Midland** (city) Midland County
1	820	0.1	**Mundy** (township) Genesee County
1	820	0.1	**Niles** (city) Berrien County
1	820	0.1	**Northview** (CDP) Kent County
1	820	0.1	**Oceola** (township) Livingston County
1	820	0.1	**Okemos** (CDP) Ingham County
1	820	0.1	**Oxford** (charter township) Oakland County
1	820	0.1	**Romulus** (city) Wayne County
1	820	0.1	**Saginaw** (charter township) Saginaw County
1	820	0.1	**Sault Sainte Marie** (city) Chippewa County
1	820	0.1	**Summit** (township) Jackson County
1	820	0.1	**Ypsilanti** (charter township) Washtenaw County
25	2061	0.0	**Ada** (township) Kent County
25	2061	0.0	**Adrian** (city) Lenawee County
25	2061	0.0	**Allen Park** (city) Wayne County
25	2061	0.0	**Allendale** (CDP) Ottawa County
25	2061	0.0	**Allendale** (charter township) Ottawa County
25	2061	0.0	**Alpine** (township) Kent County
25	2061	0.0	**Ann Arbor** (city) Washtenaw County
25	2061	0.0	**Antwerp** (township) Van Buren County
25	2061	0.0	**Auburn Hills** (city) Oakland County
25	2061	0.0	**Bangor** (charter township) Bay County
25	2061	0.0	**Bath** (charter township) Clinton County
25	2061	0.0	**Battle Creek** (city) Calhoun County
25	2061	0.0	**Bay City** (city) Bay County
25	2061	0.0	**Bedford** (township) Monroe County
25	2061	0.0	**Beecher** (CDP) Genesee County
25	2061	0.0	**Benton** (charter township) Berrien County
25	2061	0.0	**Benton Harbor** (city) Berrien County
25	2061	0.0	**Beverly Hills** (village) Oakland County
25	2061	0.0	**Big Rapids** (city) Mecosta County
25	2061	0.0	**Birmingham** (city) Oakland County
25	2061	0.0	**Blackman** (charter township) Jackson County
25	2061	0.0	**Bloomfield** (charter township) Oakland County
25	2061	0.0	**Brandon** (charter township) Oakland County
25	2061	0.0	**Bridgeport** (charter township) Saginaw County
25	2061	0.0	**Brighton** (township) Livingston County
25	2061	0.0	**Brownstown** (charter township) Wayne County
25	2061	0.0	**Burton** (city) Genesee County
25	2061	0.0	**Byron** (township) Kent County
25	2061	0.0	**Cadillac** (city) Wexford County
25	2061	0.0	**Caledonia** (township) Kent County
25	2061	0.0	**Canton** (charter township) Wayne County
25	2061	0.0	**Cascade** (charter township) Kent County
25	2061	0.0	**Chesterfield** (township) Macomb County
25	2061	0.0	**Clawson** (city) Oakland County
25	2061	0.0	**Clinton** (charter township) Macomb County
25	2061	0.0	**Coldwater** (city) Branch County
25	2061	0.0	**Commerce** (charter township) Oakland County
25	2061	0.0	**Comstock Park** (CDP) Kent County
25	2061	0.0	**Cooper** (charter township) Kalamazoo County
25	2061	0.0	**Cutlerville** (CDP) Kent County
25	2061	0.0	**Davison** (township) Genesee County
25	2061	0.0	**DeWitt** (charter township) Clinton County
25	2061	0.0	**Dearborn** (city) Wayne County
25	2061	0.0	**Dearborn Heights** (city) Wayne County
25	2061	0.0	**Delhi** (charter township) Ingham County
25	2061	0.0	**Delta** (charter township) Eaton County
25	2061	0.0	**Detroit** (city) Wayne County
25	2061	0.0	**East Bay** (township) Grand Traverse County
25	2061	0.0	**East Grand Rapids** (city) Kent County
25	2061	0.0	**East Lansing** (city) Ingham County
25	2061	0.0	**Eastpointe** (city) Macomb County
25	2061	0.0	**Emmett** (charter township) Calhoun County
25	2061	0.0	**Escanaba** (city) Delta County
25	2061	0.0	**Farmington Hills** (city) Oakland County
25	2061	0.0	**Fenton** (charter township) Genesee County
25	2061	0.0	**Fenton** (city) Genesee County
25	2061	0.0	**Flint** (charter township) Genesee County
25	2061	0.0	**Flint** (city) Genesee County
25	2061	0.0	**Flushing** (charter township) Genesee County
25	2061	0.0	**Forest Hills** (CDP) Kent County
25	2061	0.0	**Fort Gratiot** (charter township) Saint Clair County
25	2061	0.0	**Fraser** (city) Macomb County
25	2061	0.0	**Frenchtown** (township) Monroe County
25	2061	0.0	**Fruitport** (charter township) Muskegon County
25	2061	0.0	**Gaines** (charter township) Kent County
25	2061	0.0	**Garden City** (city) Wayne County
25	2061	0.0	**Garfield** (charter township) Grand Traverse County
25	2061	0.0	**Genesee** (charter township) Genesee County
25	2061	0.0	**Genoa** (township) Livingston County
25	2061	0.0	**Georgetown** (charter township) Ottawa County
25	2061	0.0	**Grand Blanc** (charter township) Genesee County
25	2061	0.0	**Grand Haven** (charter township) Ottawa County
25	2061	0.0	**Grand Haven** (city) Ottawa County
25	2061	0.0	**Grand Rapids** (charter township) Kent County
25	2061	0.0	**Grandville** (city) Kent County
25	2061	0.0	**Green Oak** (township) Livingston County
25	2061	0.0	**Grosse Ile** (township) Wayne County
25	2061	0.0	**Grosse Pointe Park** (city) Wayne County
25	2061	0.0	**Grosse Pointe Woods** (city) Wayne County
25	2061	0.0	**Hamburg** (township) Livingston County
25	2061	0.0	**Hamtramck** (city) Wayne County
25	2061	0.0	**Harper Woods** (city) Wayne County
25	2061	0.0	**Harrison** (charter township) Macomb County
25	2061	0.0	**Hartland** (township) Livingston County
25	2061	0.0	**Haslett** (CDP) Ingham County
25	2061	0.0	**Hazel Park** (city) Oakland County
25	2061	0.0	**Highland** (charter township) Oakland County
25	2061	0.0	**Highland Park** (city) Wayne County
25	2061	0.0	**Holland** (charter township) Ottawa County
25	2061	0.0	**Holt** (CDP) Ingham County
25	2061	0.0	**Huron** (charter township) Wayne County
25	2061	0.0	**Independence** (charter township) Oakland County
25	2061	0.0	**Ionia** (city) Ionia County
25	2061	0.0	**Jackson** (city) Jackson County
25	2061	0.0	**Jenison** (CDP) Ottawa County
25	2061	0.0	**Kalamazoo** (charter township) Kalamazoo County
25	2061	0.0	**Kalamazoo** (city) Kalamazoo County
25	2061	0.0	**Lansing** (city) Ingham County
25	2061	0.0	**Lenox** (township) Macomb County
25	2061	0.0	**Leoni** (township) Jackson County
25	2061	0.0	**Lincoln** (charter township) Berrien County
25	2061	0.0	**Lincoln Park** (city) Wayne County
25	2061	0.0	**Livonia** (city) Wayne County
25	2061	0.0	**Lyon** (charter township) Oakland County
25	2061	0.0	**Macomb** (township) Macomb County
25	2061	0.0	**Marquette** (city) Marquette County
25	2061	0.0	**Melvindale** (city) Wayne County
25	2061	0.0	**Meridian** (charter township) Ingham County
25	2061	0.0	**Milford** (charter township) Oakland County
25	2061	0.0	**Monitor** (charter township) Bay County
25	2061	0.0	**Monroe** (charter township) Monroe County
25	2061	0.0	**Monroe** (city) Monroe County
25	2061	0.0	**Mount Clemens** (city) Macomb County
25	2061	0.0	**Mount Morris** (township) Genesee County
25	2061	0.0	**Mount Pleasant** (city) Isabella County
25	2061	0.0	**Muskegon** (charter township) Muskegon County
25	2061	0.0	**Muskegon** (city) Muskegon County
25	2061	0.0	**Muskegon Heights** (city) Muskegon County
25	2061	0.0	**New Baltimore** (city) Macomb County
25	2061	0.0	**Niles** (township) Berrien County
25	2061	0.0	**Northville** (township) Wayne County
25	2061	0.0	**Norton Shores** (city) Muskegon County
25	2061	0.0	**Novi** (city) Oakland County
25	2061	0.0	**Oak Park** (city) Oakland County
25	2061	0.0	**Oakland** (charter township) Oakland County
25	2061	0.0	**Orion** (charter township) Oakland County

Note: The state column ranks the top/bottom 150 places from all places in the state with population of 10,000 or more. The national column ranks the top/bottom 150 places from all places in the country with population of 10,000 or more. Places that are unincorporated were not considered in the rankings. Please refer to the User Guide for additional information.

Two or More Races

Top 150 Places Ranked in *Descending* Order

State Rank	Nat'l Rank	Percent	Place
1	157	6.2	**Lansing** (city) Ingham County
2	259	5.5	**Jackson** (city) Jackson County
2	259	5.5	**Sault Sainte Marie** (city) Chippewa County
4	496	4.7	**Hamtramck** (city) Wayne County
5	537	4.6	**Hazel Park** (city) Oakland County
5	537	4.6	**Kalamazoo** (city) Kalamazoo County
5	537	4.6	**Ypsilanti** (charter township) Washtenaw County
8	577	4.5	**Muskegon** (city) Muskegon County
8	577	4.5	**Niles** (city) Berrien County
8	577	4.5	**Pontiac** (city) Oakland County
8	577	4.5	**Port Huron** (city) Saint Clair County
12	625	4.4	**Saginaw** (city) Saginaw County
13	681	4.3	**Battle Creek** (city) Calhoun County
13	681	4.3	**Ypsilanti** (city) Washtenaw County
15	735	4.2	**Grand Rapids** (city) Kent County
16	790	4.1	**Kalamazoo** (charter township) Kalamazoo County
17	854	4.0	**Adrian** (city) Lenawee County
17	854	4.0	**Comstock Park** (CDP) Kent County
17	854	4.0	**Dearborn** (city) Wayne County
17	854	4.0	**Pittsfield** (charter township) Washtenaw County
17	854	4.0	**Waverly** (CDP) Eaton County
22	915	3.9	**Bay City** (city) Bay County
22	915	3.9	**Flint** (city) Genesee County
22	915	3.9	**Kentwood** (city) Kent County
22	915	3.9	**Melvindale** (city) Wayne County
22	915	3.9	**Romulus** (city) Wayne County
27	972	3.8	**Muskegon Heights** (city) Muskegon County
27	972	3.8	**Wyoming** (city) Kent County
29	1030	3.7	**Superior** (charter township) Washtenaw County
30	1109	3.6	**Alpine** (township) Kent County
30	1109	3.6	**Ann Arbor** (city) Washtenaw County
30	1109	3.6	**Delta** (charter township) Eaton County
30	1109	3.6	**Inkster** (city) Wayne County
30	1109	3.6	**Mount Clemens** (city) Macomb County
35	1191	3.5	**Mount Morris** (township) Genesee County
36	1272	3.4	**Auburn Hills** (city) Oakland County
36	1272	3.4	**Beecher** (CDP) Genesee County
36	1272	3.4	**Ferndale** (city) Oakland County
36	1272	3.4	**Holland** (charter township) Ottawa County
36	1272	3.4	**Holland** (city) Ottawa County
41	1354	3.3	**Oshtemo** (charter township) Kalamazoo County
41	1354	3.3	**Scio** (township) Washtenaw County
43	1439	3.2	**Holt** (CDP) Ingham County
43	1439	3.2	**Lincoln Park** (city) Wayne County
43	1439	3.2	**Muskegon** (charter township) Muskegon County
43	1439	3.2	**Sturgis** (city) Saint Joseph County
47	1517	3.1	**Cutlerville** (CDP) Kent County
47	1517	3.1	**Delhi** (charter township) Ingham County
47	1517	3.1	**Flint** (charter township) Genesee County
50	1610	3.0	**Haslett** (CDP) Ingham County
50	1610	3.0	**Monroe** (city) Monroe County
50	1610	3.0	**Oak Park** (city) Oakland County
50	1610	3.0	**Portage** (city) Kalamazoo County
50	1610	3.0	**Wayne** (city) Wayne County
55	1717	2.9	**Comstock** (charter township) Kalamazoo County
55	1717	2.9	**East Lansing** (city) Ingham County
55	1717	2.9	**Eastpointe** (city) Macomb County
55	1717	2.9	**Union** (charter township) Isabella County
55	1717	2.9	**Van Buren** (charter township) Wayne County
60	1828	2.8	**Bridgeport** (charter township) Saginaw County
60	1828	2.8	**DeWitt** (charter township) Clinton County
60	1828	2.8	**Dearborn Heights** (city) Wayne County
60	1828	2.8	**Meridian** (charter township) Ingham County
60	1828	2.8	**Mount Pleasant** (city) Isabella County
60	1828	2.8	**Port Huron** (charter township) Saint Clair County
66	1935	2.7	**Coldwater** (city) Branch County
66	1935	2.7	**Escanaba** (city) Delta County
66	1935	2.7	**Gaines** (charter township) Kent County
66	1935	2.7	**Harper Woods** (city) Wayne County
66	1935	2.7	**Madison Heights** (city) Oakland County
71	2062	2.6	**Benton Harbor** (city) Berrien County
71	2062	2.6	**Lenox** (township) Macomb County
71	2062	2.6	**Niles** (township) Berrien County
71	2062	2.6	**Northview** (CDP) Kent County
71	2062	2.6	**Okemos** (CDP) Ingham County
71	2062	2.6	**Roseville** (city) Macomb County
71	2062	2.6	**Taylor** (city) Wayne County
71	2062	2.6	**Warren** (city) Macomb County
79	2209	2.5	**Benton** (charter township) Berrien County
79	2209	2.5	**Big Rapids** (city) Mecosta County
79	2209	2.5	**Burton** (city) Genesee County
79	2209	2.5	**Canton** (charter township) Wayne County
79	2209	2.5	**Emmett** (charter township) Calhoun County
79	2209	2.5	**Genesee** (charter township) Genesee County
79	2209	2.5	**Huron** (charter township) Wayne County
79	2209	2.5	**Redford** (charter township) Wayne County
79	2209	2.5	**Summit** (township) Jackson County
88	2357	2.4	**Garfield** (charter township) Grand Traverse County
88	2357	2.4	**Grandville** (city) Kent County
88	2357	2.4	**Southfield** (city) Oakland County
88	2357	2.4	**Waterford** (charter township) Oakland County
88	2357	2.4	**Westland** (city) Wayne County
93	2489	2.3	**Allendale** (CDP) Ottawa County
93	2489	2.3	**Bath** (charter township) Clinton County
93	2489	2.3	**Farmington** (city) Oakland County
93	2489	2.3	**Grand Blanc** (charter township) Genesee County
93	2489	2.3	**Highland Park** (city) Wayne County
93	2489	2.3	**Monroe** (charter township) Monroe County
99	2642	2.2	**Allendale** (charter township) Ottawa County
99	2642	2.2	**Clinton** (charter township) Macomb County
99	2642	2.2	**Detroit** (city) Wayne County
99	2642	2.2	**Farmington Hills** (city) Oakland County
99	2642	2.2	**Saginaw** (charter township) Saginaw County
99	2642	2.2	**Sterling Heights** (city) Macomb County
105	2791	2.1	**Antwerp** (township) Van Buren County
105	2791	2.1	**Brownstown** (charter township) Wayne County
105	2791	2.1	**Cooper** (charter township) Kalamazoo County
105	2791	2.1	**Frenchtown** (township) Monroe County
105	2791	2.1	**Garden City** (city) Wayne County
105	2791	2.1	**Leoni** (township) Jackson County
105	2791	2.1	**Novi** (city) Oakland County
105	2791	2.1	**Owosso** (city) Shiawassee County
105	2791	2.1	**Plainfield** (charter township) Kent County
105	2791	2.1	**Walker** (city) Kent County
105	2791	2.1	**Wixom** (city) Oakland County
116	2950	2.0	**Fenton** (city) Genesee County
116	2950	2.0	**Independence** (charter township) Oakland County
116	2950	2.0	**Norton Shores** (city) Muskegon County
116	2950	2.0	**Southgate** (city) Wayne County
116	2950	2.0	**Texas** (charter township) Kalamazoo County
116	2950	2.0	**Troy** (city) Oakland County
116	2950	2.0	**West Bloomfield** (charter township) Oakland County
123	3098	1.9	**Blackman** (charter township) Jackson County
123	3098	1.9	**Bloomfield** (charter township) Oakland County
123	3098	1.9	**Byron** (township) Kent County
123	3098	1.9	**Clawson** (city) Oakland County
123	3098	1.9	**Davison** (township) Genesee County
123	3098	1.9	**Grand Haven** (city) Ottawa County
123	3098	1.9	**Grosse Pointe Park** (city) Wayne County
123	3098	1.9	**Holly** (township) Oakland County
123	3098	1.9	**Rochester Hills** (city) Oakland County
123	3098	1.9	**Royal Oak** (city) Oakland County
123	3098	1.9	**Traverse City** (city) Grand Traverse County
123	3098	1.9	**Vienna** (charter township) Genesee County
123	3098	1.9	**Woodhaven** (city) Wayne County
123	3098	1.9	**Wyandotte** (city) Wayne County
137	3250	1.8	**Berkley** (city) Oakland County
137	3250	1.8	**Cadillac** (city) Wexford County
137	3250	1.8	**Chesterfield** (township) Macomb County
137	3250	1.8	**Fraser** (city) Macomb County
137	3250	1.8	**Harrison** (charter township) Macomb County
137	3250	1.8	**Lincoln** (charter township) Berrien County
137	3250	1.8	**Marquette** (city) Marquette County
137	3250	1.8	**Midland** (city) Midland County
137	3250	1.8	**Mundy** (township) Genesee County
137	3250	1.8	**Northville** (township) Wayne County
137	3250	1.8	**Orion** (charter township) Oakland County
137	3250	1.8	**Park** (township) Ottawa County
149	3438	1.7	**Bangor** (charter township) Bay County
149	3438	1.7	**Fort Gratiot** (charter township) Saint Clair County

Note: The state column ranks the top/bottom 150 places from all places in the state with population of 10,000 or more. The national column ranks the top/bottom 150 places from all places in the country with population of 10,000 or more. Places that are unincorporated were not considered in the rankings. Please refer to the User Guide for additional information.

Two or More Races

Top 150 Places Ranked in *Ascending* Order

State Rank	Nat'l Rank	Percent	Place
1	124	1.0	**Brighton** (township) Livingston County
2	192	1.1	**Green Oak** (township) Livingston County
2	192	1.1	**Grosse Ile** (township) Wayne County
2	192	1.1	**Thomas** (township) Saginaw County
5	295	1.2	**Bedford** (township) Monroe County
6	415	1.3	**Brandon** (charter township) Oakland County
6	415	1.3	**Cascade** (charter township) Kent County
6	415	1.3	**Forest Hills** (CDP) Kent County
6	415	1.3	**Grosse Pointe Woods** (city) Wayne County
6	415	1.3	**Hamburg** (township) Livingston County
6	415	1.3	**Hartland** (township) Livingston County
6	415	1.3	**Oakland** (charter township) Oakland County
6	415	1.3	**Riverview** (city) Wayne County
6	415	1.3	**Washington** (township) Macomb County
15	549	1.4	**Alpena** (city) Alpena County
15	549	1.4	**Fenton** (charter township) Genesee County
15	549	1.4	**Genoa** (township) Livingston County
15	549	1.4	**Highland** (charter township) Oakland County
15	549	1.4	**Ionia** (city) Ionia County
15	549	1.4	**Livonia** (city) Wayne County
15	549	1.4	**Monitor** (charter township) Bay County
15	549	1.4	**New Baltimore** (city) Macomb County
15	549	1.4	**Oceola** (township) Livingston County
15	549	1.4	**Springfield** (charter township) Oakland County
15	549	1.4	**Trenton** (city) Wayne County
26	724	1.5	**Cannon** (township) Kent County
26	724	1.5	**East Bay** (township) Grand Traverse County
26	724	1.5	**Georgetown** (charter township) Ottawa County
26	724	1.5	**Jenison** (CDP) Ottawa County
26	724	1.5	**Plymouth** (charter township) Wayne County
26	724	1.5	**Rochester** (city) Oakland County
26	724	1.5	**Spring Lake** (township) Ottawa County
33	861	1.6	**Ada** (township) Kent County
33	861	1.6	**Allen Park** (city) Wayne County
33	861	1.6	**Beverly Hills** (village) Oakland County
33	861	1.6	**Birmingham** (city) Oakland County
33	861	1.6	**Caledonia** (township) Kent County
33	861	1.6	**Commerce** (charter township) Oakland County
33	861	1.6	**East Grand Rapids** (city) Kent County
33	861	1.6	**Flushing** (charter township) Genesee County
33	861	1.6	**Grand Haven** (charter township) Ottawa County
33	861	1.6	**Macomb** (township) Macomb County
33	861	1.6	**Milford** (charter township) Oakland County
33	861	1.6	**Oxford** (charter township) Oakland County
33	861	1.6	**Saint Joseph** (charter township) Berrien County
33	861	1.6	**South Lyon** (city) Oakland County
33	861	1.6	**Southfield** (township) Oakland County
33	861	1.6	**Tyrone** (township) Livingston County
33	861	1.6	**White Lake** (charter township) Oakland County
50	1050	1.7	**Bangor** (charter township) Bay County
50	1050	1.7	**Fort Gratiot** (charter township) Saint Clair County
50	1050	1.7	**Fruitport** (charter township) Muskegon County
50	1050	1.7	**Grand Rapids** (charter township) Kent County
50	1050	1.7	**Lyon** (charter township) Oakland County
50	1050	1.7	**Saint Clair Shores** (city) Macomb County
50	1050	1.7	**Shelby** (charter township) Macomb County
57	1219	1.8	**Berkley** (city) Oakland County
57	1219	1.8	**Cadillac** (city) Wexford County
57	1219	1.8	**Chesterfield** (township) Macomb County
57	1219	1.8	**Fraser** (city) Macomb County
57	1219	1.8	**Harrison** (charter township) Macomb County
57	1219	1.8	**Lincoln** (charter township) Berrien County
57	1219	1.8	**Marquette** (city) Marquette County
57	1219	1.8	**Midland** (city) Midland County
57	1219	1.8	**Mundy** (township) Genesee County
57	1219	1.8	**Northville** (township) Wayne County
57	1219	1.8	**Orion** (charter township) Oakland County
57	1219	1.8	**Park** (township) Ottawa County
69	1407	1.9	**Blackman** (charter township) Jackson County
69	1407	1.9	**Bloomfield** (charter township) Oakland County
69	1407	1.9	**Byron** (township) Kent County
69	1407	1.9	**Clawson** (city) Oakland County
69	1407	1.9	**Davison** (township) Genesee County
69	1407	1.9	**Grand Haven** (city) Ottawa County
69	1407	1.9	**Grosse Pointe Park** (city) Wayne County
69	1407	1.9	**Holly** (township) Oakland County
69	1407	1.9	**Rochester Hills** (city) Oakland County
69	1407	1.9	**Royal Oak** (city) Oakland County
69	1407	1.9	**Traverse City** (city) Grand Traverse County
69	1407	1.9	**Vienna** (charter township) Genesee County
69	1407	1.9	**Woodhaven** (city) Wayne County
69	1407	1.9	**Wyandotte** (city) Wayne County
83	1559	2.0	**Fenton** (city) Genesee County
83	1559	2.0	**Independence** (charter township) Oakland County
83	1559	2.0	**Norton Shores** (city) Muskegon County
83	1559	2.0	**Southgate** (city) Wayne County
83	1559	2.0	**Texas** (charter township) Kalamazoo County
83	1559	2.0	**Troy** (city) Oakland County
83	1559	2.0	**West Bloomfield** (charter township) Oakland County
90	1707	2.1	**Antwerp** (township) Van Buren County
90	1707	2.1	**Brownstown** (charter township) Wayne County
90	1707	2.1	**Cooper** (charter township) Kalamazoo County
90	1707	2.1	**Frenchtown** (township) Monroe County
90	1707	2.1	**Garden City** (city) Wayne County
90	1707	2.1	**Leoni** (township) Jackson County
90	1707	2.1	**Novi** (city) Oakland County
90	1707	2.1	**Owosso** (city) Shiawassee County
90	1707	2.1	**Plainfield** (charter township) Kent County
90	1707	2.1	**Walker** (city) Kent County
90	1707	2.1	**Wixom** (city) Oakland County
101	1866	2.2	**Allendale** (charter township) Ottawa County
101	1866	2.2	**Clinton** (charter township) Macomb County
101	1866	2.2	**Detroit** (city) Wayne County
101	1866	2.2	**Farmington Hills** (city) Oakland County
101	1866	2.2	**Saginaw** (charter township) Saginaw County
101	1866	2.2	**Sterling Heights** (city) Macomb County
107	2015	2.3	**Allendale** (CDP) Ottawa County
107	2015	2.3	**Bath** (charter township) Clinton County
107	2015	2.3	**Farmington** (city) Oakland County
107	2015	2.3	**Grand Blanc** (charter township) Genesee County
107	2015	2.3	**Highland Park** (city) Wayne County
107	2015	2.3	**Monroe** (charter township) Monroe County
113	2168	2.4	**Garfield** (charter township) Grand Traverse County
113	2168	2.4	**Grandville** (city) Kent County
113	2168	2.4	**Southfield** (city) Oakland County
113	2168	2.4	**Waterford** (charter township) Oakland County
113	2168	2.4	**Westland** (city) Wayne County
118	2300	2.5	**Benton** (charter township) Berrien County
118	2300	2.5	**Big Rapids** (city) Mecosta County
118	2300	2.5	**Burton** (city) Genesee County
118	2300	2.5	**Canton** (charter township) Wayne County
118	2300	2.5	**Emmett** (charter township) Calhoun County
118	2300	2.5	**Genesee** (charter township) Genesee County
118	2300	2.5	**Huron** (charter township) Wayne County
118	2300	2.5	**Redford** (charter township) Wayne County
118	2300	2.5	**Summit** (township) Jackson County
127	2448	2.6	**Benton Harbor** (city) Berrien County
127	2448	2.6	**Lenox** (township) Macomb County
127	2448	2.6	**Niles** (township) Berrien County
127	2448	2.6	**Northview** (CDP) Kent County
127	2448	2.6	**Okemos** (CDP) Ingham County
127	2448	2.6	**Roseville** (city) Macomb County
127	2448	2.6	**Taylor** (city) Wayne County
127	2448	2.6	**Warren** (city) Macomb County
135	2595	2.7	**Coldwater** (city) Branch County
135	2595	2.7	**Escanaba** (city) Delta County
135	2595	2.7	**Gaines** (charter township) Kent County
135	2595	2.7	**Harper Woods** (city) Wayne County
135	2595	2.7	**Madison Heights** (city) Oakland County
140	2722	2.8	**Bridgeport** (charter township) Saginaw County
140	2722	2.8	**DeWitt** (charter township) Clinton County
140	2722	2.8	**Dearborn Heights** (city) Wayne County
140	2722	2.8	**Meridian** (charter township) Ingham County
140	2722	2.8	**Mount Pleasant** (city) Isabella County
140	2722	2.8	**Port Huron** (charter township) Saint Clair County
146	2829	2.9	**Comstock** (charter township) Kalamazoo County
146	2829	2.9	**East Lansing** (city) Ingham County
146	2829	2.9	**Eastpointe** (city) Macomb County
146	2829	2.9	**Union** (charter township) Isabella County
146	2829	2.9	**Van Buren** (charter township) Wayne County

Note: *The state column ranks the top/bottom 150 places from all places in the state with population of 10,000 or more. The national column ranks the top/bottom 150 places from all places in the country with population of 10,000 or more. Places that are unincorporated were not considered in the rankings. Please refer to the User Guide for additional information.*

Hispanic Population

Top 150 Places Ranked in *Descending* Order

State Rank	Nat'l Rank	Percent	Place
1	856	23.4	**Holland** (charter township) Ottawa County
2	876	22.8	**Sturgis** (city) Saint Joseph County
3	883	22.7	**Holland** (city) Ottawa County
4	1031	19.4	**Wyoming** (city) Kent County
5	1056	18.8	**Adrian** (city) Lenawee County
6	1086	18.3	**Melvindale** (city) Wayne County
7	1190	16.5	**Pontiac** (city) Oakland County
8	1259	15.6	**Grand Rapids** (city) Kent County
9	1310	14.9	**Lincoln Park** (city) Wayne County
10	1368	14.3	**Comstock Park** (CDP) Kent County
10	1368	14.3	**Saginaw** (city) Saginaw County
12	1491	13.0	**Alpine** (township) Kent County
13	1549	12.5	**Lansing** (city) Ingham County
14	1846	9.9	**Bridgeport** (charter township) Saginaw County
15	2034	8.5	**Bay City** (city) Bay County
15	2034	8.5	**Kentwood** (city) Kent County
17	2081	8.2	**Cutlerville** (CDP) Kent County
17	2081	8.2	**Muskegon** (city) Muskegon County
19	2099	8.1	**Allen Park** (city) Wayne County
20	2117	8.0	**Park** (township) Ottawa County
21	2145	7.8	**Auburn Hills** (city) Oakland County
22	2166	7.7	**Ionia** (city) Ionia County
23	2334	6.9	**Waverly** (CDP) Eaton County
24	2357	6.8	**Detroit** (city) Wayne County
25	2382	6.7	**Battle Creek** (city) Calhoun County
26	2406	6.6	**Coldwater** (city) Branch County
27	2428	6.5	**Pittsfield** (charter township) Washtenaw County
27	2428	6.5	**Southgate** (city) Wayne County
29	2462	6.4	**Kalamazoo** (city) Kalamazoo County
29	2462	6.4	**Saginaw** (charter township) Saginaw County
29	2462	6.4	**Waterford** (charter township) Oakland County
32	2522	6.2	**Delta** (charter township) Eaton County
32	2522	6.2	**Grandville** (city) Kent County
34	2544	6.1	**DeWitt** (charter township) Clinton County
34	2544	6.1	**Gaines** (charter township) Kent County
36	2564	6.0	**Benton** (charter township) Berrien County
37	2640	5.7	**Niles** (city) Berrien County
38	2687	5.5	**Woodhaven** (city) Wayne County
39	2712	5.4	**Holt** (CDP) Ingham County
39	2712	5.4	**Port Huron** (city) Saint Clair County
41	2736	5.3	**Delhi** (charter township) Ingham County
41	2736	5.3	**Jackson** (city) Jackson County
43	2770	5.2	**Antwerp** (township) Van Buren County
43	2770	5.2	**Brownstown** (charter township) Wayne County
45	2801	5.1	**Muskegon** (charter township) Muskegon County
45	2801	5.1	**Taylor** (city) Wayne County
45	2801	5.1	**Wixom** (city) Oakland County
45	2801	5.1	**Wyandotte** (city) Wayne County
49	2904	4.8	**Allendale** (CDP) Ottawa County
50	2931	4.7	**Dearborn Heights** (city) Wayne County
51	2961	4.6	**Allendale** (charter township) Ottawa County
51	2961	4.6	**Kalamazoo** (charter township) Kalamazoo County
51	2961	4.6	**Ypsilanti** (charter township) Washtenaw County
54	2995	4.5	**Independence** (charter township) Oakland County
54	2995	4.5	**Niles** (township) Berrien County
56	3060	4.3	**Haslett** (CDP) Ingham County
57	3098	4.2	**Byron** (township) Kent County
57	3098	4.2	**Muskegon Heights** (city) Muskegon County
59	3122	4.1	**Ann Arbor** (city) Washtenaw County
59	3122	4.1	**Frenchtown** (township) Monroe County
59	3122	4.1	**Monroe** (city) Monroe County
59	3122	4.1	**Riverview** (city) Wayne County
59	3122	4.1	**Walker** (city) Kent County
64	3169	4.0	**Monroe** (charter township) Monroe County
64	3169	4.0	**Orion** (charter township) Oakland County
64	3169	4.0	**Oshtemo** (charter township) Kalamazoo County
67	3198	3.9	**Bangor** (charter township) Bay County
67	3198	3.9	**Emmett** (charter township) Calhoun County
67	3198	3.9	**Flint** (city) Genesee County
67	3198	3.9	**Owosso** (city) Shiawassee County
67	3198	3.9	**Washington** (township) Macomb County
67	3198	3.9	**Ypsilanti** (city) Washtenaw County
73	3229	3.8	**Genesee** (charter township) Genesee County
73	3229	3.8	**Lenox** (township) Macomb County
73	3229	3.8	**Meridian** (charter township) Ingham County
73	3229	3.8	**Norton Shores** (city) Muskegon County
73	3229	3.8	**Port Huron** (charter township) Saint Clair County
73	3229	3.8	**Superior** (charter township) Washtenaw County
73	3229	3.8	**Westland** (city) Wayne County
80	3297	3.6	**Blackman** (charter township) Jackson County
80	3297	3.6	**Scio** (township) Washtenaw County
82	3334	3.5	**Beecher** (CDP) Genesee County
82	3334	3.5	**Thomas** (township) Saginaw County
84	3377	3.4	**Bath** (charter township) Clinton County
84	3377	3.4	**Dearborn** (city) Wayne County
84	3377	3.4	**East Lansing** (city) Ingham County
84	3377	3.4	**Wayne** (city) Wayne County
88	3421	3.3	**Garden City** (city) Wayne County
88	3421	3.3	**Mount Morris** (township) Genesee County
88	3421	3.3	**Mount Pleasant** (city) Isabella County
88	3421	3.3	**Okemos** (CDP) Ingham County
92	3462	3.2	**Davison** (township) Genesee County
92	3462	3.2	**Fruitport** (charter township) Muskegon County
92	3462	3.2	**Holly** (township) Oakland County
92	3462	3.2	**Huron** (charter township) Wayne County
92	3462	3.2	**Trenton** (city) Wayne County
92	3462	3.2	**Union** (charter township) Isabella County
98	3505	3.1	**Brandon** (charter township) Oakland County
98	3505	3.1	**Burton** (city) Genesee County
98	3505	3.1	**Canton** (charter township) Wayne County
98	3505	3.1	**Grand Blanc** (charter township) Genesee County
98	3505	3.1	**Oxford** (charter township) Oakland County
98	3505	3.1	**Portage** (city) Kalamazoo County
98	3505	3.1	**Rochester Hills** (city) Oakland County
105	3560	3.0	**Comstock** (charter township) Kalamazoo County
105	3560	3.0	**Novi** (city) Oakland County
105	3560	3.0	**Romulus** (city) Wayne County
105	3560	3.0	**White Lake** (charter township) Oakland County
109	3607	2.9	**Flint** (charter township) Genesee County
109	3607	2.9	**Grand Haven** (charter township) Ottawa County
109	3607	2.9	**Lyon** (charter township) Oakland County
109	3607	2.9	**Mount Clemens** (city) Macomb County
109	3607	2.9	**Northview** (CDP) Kent County
109	3607	2.9	**Redford** (charter township) Wayne County
109	3607	2.9	**Springfield** (charter township) Oakland County
116	3660	2.8	**Ferndale** (city) Oakland County
116	3660	2.8	**Lincoln** (charter township) Berrien County
118	3711	2.7	**Georgetown** (charter township) Ottawa County
118	3711	2.7	**Hazel Park** (city) Oakland County
118	3711	2.7	**Rochester** (city) Oakland County
118	3711	2.7	**South Lyon** (city) Oakland County
118	3711	2.7	**Summit** (township) Jackson County
118	3711	2.7	**Van Buren** (charter township) Wayne County
124	3754	2.6	**Commerce** (charter township) Oakland County
124	3754	2.6	**Grosse Ile** (township) Wayne County
124	3754	2.6	**Harrison** (charter township) Macomb County
124	3754	2.6	**Inkster** (city) Wayne County
124	3754	2.6	**Plainfield** (charter township) Kent County
124	3754	2.6	**Vienna** (charter township) Genesee County
130	3812	2.5	**Bedford** (township) Monroe County
130	3812	2.5	**Fenton** (city) Genesee County
130	3812	2.5	**Fort Gratiot** (charter township) Saint Clair County
130	3812	2.5	**Grosse Pointe Park** (city) Wayne County
130	3812	2.5	**Jenison** (CDP) Ottawa County
130	3812	2.5	**Livonia** (city) Wayne County
130	3812	2.5	**Madison Heights** (city) Oakland County
137	3857	2.4	**Big Rapids** (city) Mecosta County
137	3857	2.4	**Chesterfield** (township) Macomb County
137	3857	2.4	**Clinton** (charter township) Macomb County
137	3857	2.4	**Flushing** (charter township) Genesee County
137	3857	2.4	**Garfield** (charter township) Grand Traverse County
137	3857	2.4	**Grand Haven** (city) Ottawa County
137	3857	2.4	**Leoni** (township) Jackson County
137	3857	2.4	**Midland** (city) Midland County
137	3857	2.4	**Monitor** (charter township) Bay County
137	3857	2.4	**Mundy** (township) Genesee County
137	3857	2.4	**Northville** (township) Wayne County
137	3857	2.4	**Plymouth** (charter township) Wayne County
137	3857	2.4	**Saint Joseph** (charter township) Berrien County
137	3857	2.4	**Shelby** (charter township) Macomb County

Note: The state column ranks the top/bottom 150 places from all places in the state with population of 10,000 or more. The national column ranks the top/bottom 150 places from all places in the country with population of 10,000 or more. Places that are unincorporated were not considered in the rankings. Please refer to the User Guide for additional information.

Hispanic Population

Top 150 Places Ranked in *Ascending* Order

State Rank	Nat'l Rank	Percent	Place
1	58	1.0	**Alpena** (city) Alpena County
2	107	1.2	**Escanaba** (city) Delta County
3	144	1.3	**Hamburg** (township) Livingston County
3	144	1.3	**Highland Park** (city) Wayne County
3	144	1.3	**Southfield** (city) Oakland County
6	172	1.4	**Marquette** (city) Marquette County
6	172	1.4	**Oak Park** (city) Oakland County
8	215	1.5	**East Grand Rapids** (city) Kent County
8	215	1.5	**Hamtramck** (city) Wayne County
8	215	1.5	**Sault Sainte Marie** (city) Chippewa County
8	215	1.5	**Southfield** (township) Oakland County
12	263	1.6	**Cooper** (charter township) Kalamazoo County
12	263	1.6	**East Bay** (township) Grand Traverse County
12	263	1.6	**West Bloomfield** (charter township) Oakland County
15	317	1.7	**Ada** (township) Kent County
15	317	1.7	**Beverly Hills** (village) Oakland County
15	317	1.7	**Brighton** (township) Livingston County
15	317	1.7	**Forest Hills** (CDP) Kent County
15	317	1.7	**Grosse Pointe Woods** (city) Wayne County
15	317	1.7	**Saint Clair Shores** (city) Macomb County
21	370	1.8	**Berkley** (city) Oakland County
21	370	1.8	**Bloomfield** (charter township) Oakland County
21	370	1.8	**Cadillac** (city) Wexford County
21	370	1.8	**Cannon** (township) Kent County
21	370	1.8	**Fenton** (charter township) Genesee County
21	370	1.8	**New Baltimore** (city) Macomb County
27	444	1.9	**Cascade** (charter township) Kent County
27	444	1.9	**Farmington Hills** (city) Oakland County
27	444	1.9	**Green Oak** (township) Livingston County
27	444	1.9	**Highland** (charter township) Oakland County
27	444	1.9	**Oceola** (township) Livingston County
27	444	1.9	**Sterling Heights** (city) Macomb County
27	444	1.9	**Traverse City** (city) Grand Traverse County
34	501	2.0	**Grand Rapids** (charter township) Kent County
34	501	2.0	**Harper Woods** (city) Wayne County
34	501	2.0	**Roseville** (city) Macomb County
37	563	2.1	**Birmingham** (city) Oakland County
37	563	2.1	**Clawson** (city) Oakland County
37	563	2.1	**Eastpointe** (city) Macomb County
37	563	2.1	**Farmington** (city) Oakland County
37	563	2.1	**Fraser** (city) Macomb County
37	563	2.1	**Genoa** (township) Livingston County
37	563	2.1	**Oakland** (charter township) Oakland County
37	563	2.1	**Spring Lake** (township) Ottawa County
37	563	2.1	**Texas** (charter township) Kalamazoo County
37	563	2.1	**Troy** (city) Oakland County
37	563	2.1	**Warren** (city) Macomb County
48	612	2.2	**Benton Harbor** (city) Berrien County
48	612	2.2	**Milford** (charter township) Oakland County
48	612	2.2	**Tyrone** (township) Livingston County
51	669	2.3	**Caledonia** (township) Kent County
51	669	2.3	**Hartland** (township) Livingston County
51	669	2.3	**Macomb** (township) Macomb County
51	669	2.3	**Royal Oak** (city) Oakland County
55	726	2.4	**Big Rapids** (city) Mecosta County
55	726	2.4	**Chesterfield** (township) Macomb County
55	726	2.4	**Clinton** (charter township) Macomb County
55	726	2.4	**Flushing** (charter township) Genesee County
55	726	2.4	**Garfield** (charter township) Grand Traverse County
55	726	2.4	**Grand Haven** (city) Ottawa County
55	726	2.4	**Leoni** (township) Jackson County
55	726	2.4	**Midland** (city) Midland County
55	726	2.4	**Monitor** (charter township) Bay County
55	726	2.4	**Mundy** (township) Genesee County
55	726	2.4	**Northville** (township) Wayne County
55	726	2.4	**Plymouth** (charter township) Wayne County
55	726	2.4	**Saint Joseph** (charter township) Berrien County
55	726	2.4	**Shelby** (charter township) Macomb County
69	800	2.5	**Bedford** (township) Monroe County
69	800	2.5	**Fenton** (city) Genesee County
69	800	2.5	**Fort Gratiot** (charter township) Saint Clair County
69	800	2.5	**Grosse Pointe Park** (city) Wayne County
69	800	2.5	**Jenison** (CDP) Ottawa County
69	800	2.5	**Livonia** (city) Wayne County
69	800	2.5	**Madison Heights** (city) Oakland County
76	845	2.6	**Commerce** (charter township) Oakland County
76	845	2.6	**Grosse Ile** (township) Wayne County
76	845	2.6	**Harrison** (charter township) Macomb County
76	845	2.6	**Inkster** (city) Wayne County
76	845	2.6	**Plainfield** (charter township) Kent County
76	845	2.6	**Vienna** (charter township) Genesee County
82	903	2.7	**Georgetown** (charter township) Ottawa County
82	903	2.7	**Hazel Park** (city) Oakland County
82	903	2.7	**Rochester** (city) Oakland County
82	903	2.7	**South Lyon** (city) Oakland County
82	903	2.7	**Summit** (township) Jackson County
82	903	2.7	**Van Buren** (charter township) Wayne County
88	946	2.8	**Ferndale** (city) Oakland County
88	946	2.8	**Lincoln** (charter township) Berrien County
90	997	2.9	**Flint** (charter township) Genesee County
90	997	2.9	**Grand Haven** (charter township) Ottawa County
90	997	2.9	**Lyon** (charter township) Oakland County
90	997	2.9	**Mount Clemens** (city) Macomb County
90	997	2.9	**Northview** (CDP) Kent County
90	997	2.9	**Redford** (charter township) Wayne County
90	997	2.9	**Springfield** (charter township) Oakland County
97	1050	3.0	**Comstock** (charter township) Kalamazoo County
97	1050	3.0	**Novi** (city) Oakland County
97	1050	3.0	**Romulus** (city) Wayne County
97	1050	3.0	**White Lake** (charter township) Oakland County
101	1097	3.1	**Brandon** (charter township) Oakland County
101	1097	3.1	**Burton** (city) Genesee County
101	1097	3.1	**Canton** (charter township) Wayne County
101	1097	3.1	**Grand Blanc** (charter township) Genesee County
101	1097	3.1	**Oxford** (charter township) Oakland County
101	1097	3.1	**Portage** (city) Kalamazoo County
101	1097	3.1	**Rochester Hills** (city) Oakland County
108	1152	3.2	**Davison** (township) Genesee County
108	1152	3.2	**Fruitport** (charter township) Muskegon County
108	1152	3.2	**Holly** (township) Oakland County
108	1152	3.2	**Huron** (charter township) Wayne County
108	1152	3.2	**Trenton** (city) Wayne County
108	1152	3.2	**Union** (charter township) Isabella County
114	1195	3.3	**Garden City** (city) Wayne County
114	1195	3.3	**Mount Morris** (township) Genesee County
114	1195	3.3	**Mount Pleasant** (city) Isabella County
114	1195	3.3	**Okemos** (CDP) Ingham County
118	1236	3.4	**Bath** (charter township) Clinton County
118	1236	3.4	**Dearborn** (city) Wayne County
118	1236	3.4	**East Lansing** (city) Ingham County
118	1236	3.4	**Wayne** (city) Wayne County
122	1280	3.5	**Beecher** (CDP) Genesee County
122	1280	3.5	**Thomas** (township) Saginaw County
124	1323	3.6	**Blackman** (charter township) Jackson County
124	1323	3.6	**Scio** (township) Washtenaw County
126	1396	3.8	**Genesee** (charter township) Genesee County
126	1396	3.8	**Lenox** (township) Macomb County
126	1396	3.8	**Meridian** (charter township) Ingham County
126	1396	3.8	**Norton Shores** (city) Muskegon County
126	1396	3.8	**Port Huron** (charter township) Saint Clair County
126	1396	3.8	**Superior** (charter township) Washtenaw County
126	1396	3.8	**Westland** (city) Wayne County
133	1428	3.9	**Bangor** (charter township) Bay County
133	1428	3.9	**Emmett** (charter township) Calhoun County
133	1428	3.9	**Flint** (city) Genesee County
133	1428	3.9	**Owosso** (city) Shiawassee County
133	1428	3.9	**Washington** (township) Macomb County
133	1428	3.9	**Ypsilanti** (city) Washtenaw County
139	1459	4.0	**Monroe** (charter township) Monroe County
139	1459	4.0	**Orion** (charter township) Oakland County
139	1459	4.0	**Oshtemo** (charter township) Kalamazoo County
142	1488	4.1	**Ann Arbor** (city) Washtenaw County
142	1488	4.1	**Frenchtown** (township) Monroe County
142	1488	4.1	**Monroe** (city) Monroe County
142	1488	4.1	**Riverview** (city) Wayne County
142	1488	4.1	**Walker** (city) Kent County
147	1535	4.2	**Byron** (township) Kent County
147	1535	4.2	**Muskegon Heights** (city) Muskegon County
149	1559	4.3	**Haslett** (CDP) Ingham County
150	1626	4.5	**Independence** (charter township) Oakland County

Note: The state column ranks the top/bottom 150 places from all places in the state with population of 10,000 or more. The national column ranks the top/bottom 150 places from all places in the country with population of 10,000 or more. Places that are unincorporated were not considered in the rankings. Please refer to the User Guide for additional information.

Average Household Size

Top 150 Places Ranked in *Descending* Order

State Rank	Nat'l Rank	Persons	Place	State Rank	Nat'l Rank	Persons	Place
1	441	3.0	**Hamtramck** (city) Wayne County	74	2334	2.5	**Grandville** (city) Kent County
2	516	3.0	**Allendale** (charter township) Ottawa County	74	2334	2.5	**Southfield** (township) Oakland County
3	579	3.0	**Allendale** (CDP) Ottawa County	78	2398	2.5	**Cooper** (charter township) Kalamazoo County
4	619	2.9	**Macomb** (township) Macomb County	78	2398	2.5	**DeWitt** (charter township) Clinton County
5	704	2.9	**Ada** (township) Kent County	78	2398	2.5	**Frenchtown** (township) Monroe County
6	761	2.9	**Oceola** (township) Livingston County	78	2398	2.5	**Holly** (township) Oakland County
7	823	2.9	**Cannon** (township) Kent County	78	2398	2.5	**Ionia** (city) Ionia County
8	845	2.9	**Oakland** (charter township) Oakland County	78	2398	2.5	**Rochester Hills** (city) Oakland County
9	931	2.8	**Forest Hills** (CDP) Kent County	84	2464	2.5	**Alpine** (township) Kent County
10	989	2.8	**Dearborn** (city) Wayne County	84	2464	2.5	**Beverly Hills** (village) Oakland County
10	989	2.8	**Holland** (charter township) Ottawa County	84	2464	2.5	**Delhi** (charter township) Ingham County
12	1018	2.8	**Hartland** (township) Livingston County	84	2464	2.5	**Grand Blanc** (charter township) Genesee County
12	1018	2.8	**Tyrone** (township) Livingston County	84	2464	2.5	**Holland** (city) Ottawa County
14	1049	2.8	**Brandon** (charter township) Oakland County	84	2464	2.5	**Holt** (CDP) Ingham County
14	1049	2.8	**Lenox** (township) Macomb County	84	2464	2.5	**Leoni** (township) Jackson County
16	1118	2.8	**Georgetown** (charter township) Ottawa County	84	2464	2.5	**Saginaw** (city) Saginaw County
16	1118	2.8	**Texas** (charter township) Kalamazoo County	84	2464	2.5	**Vienna** (charter township) Genesee County
18	1151	2.8	**Caledonia** (township) Kent County	93	2518	2.5	**Grosse Pointe Woods** (city) Wayne County
18	1151	2.8	**East Grand Rapids** (city) Kent County	93	2518	2.5	**Port Huron** (charter township) Saint Clair County
20	1213	2.7	**Lyon** (charter township) Oakland County	93	2518	2.5	**Redford** (charter township) Wayne County
21	1246	2.7	**Benton Harbor** (city) Berrien County	96	2568	2.5	**Burton** (city) Genesee County
21	1246	2.7	**Springfield** (charter township) Oakland County	96	2568	2.5	**Grosse Ile** (township) Wayne County
23	1283	2.7	**Brighton** (township) Livingston County	96	2568	2.5	**Oak Park** (city) Oakland County
24	1314	2.7	**Canton** (charter township) Wayne County	99	2630	2.4	**Coldwater** (city) Branch County
25	1353	2.7	**Beecher** (CDP) Genesee County	99	2630	2.4	**Grand Rapids** (city) Kent County
25	1353	2.7	**Oxford** (charter township) Oakland County	99	2630	2.4	**Monroe** (charter township) Monroe County
27	1394	2.7	**Huron** (charter township) Wayne County	99	2630	2.4	**Warren** (city) Macomb County
28	1433	2.7	**Cascade** (charter township) Kent County	99	2630	2.4	**Ypsilanti** (charter township) Washtenaw County
28	1433	2.7	**Grand Haven** (charter township) Ottawa County	104	2698	2.4	**Bloomfield** (charter township) Oakland County
28	1433	2.7	**Grand Rapids** (charter township) Kent County	104	2698	2.4	**East Bay** (township) Grand Traverse County
28	1433	2.7	**New Baltimore** (city) Macomb County	106	2768	2.4	**Hazel Park** (city) Oakland County
32	1483	2.7	**Orion** (charter township) Oakland County	106	2768	2.4	**Livonia** (city) Wayne County
33	1528	2.7	**Antwerp** (township) Van Buren County	106	2768	2.4	**Northville** (township) Wayne County
33	1528	2.7	**Park** (township) Ottawa County	109	2829	2.4	**Benton** (charter township) Berrien County
33	1528	2.7	**Washington** (township) Macomb County	109	2829	2.4	**Jackson** (city) Jackson County
36	1563	2.6	**Brownstown** (charter township) Wayne County	109	2829	2.4	**Lincoln** (charter township) Berrien County
36	1563	2.6	**Gaines** (charter township) Kent County	109	2829	2.4	**Niles** (township) Berrien County
36	1563	2.6	**Green Oak** (township) Livingston County	109	2829	2.4	**Novi** (city) Oakland County
36	1563	2.6	**Hamburg** (township) Livingston County	109	2829	2.4	**Union** (charter township) Isabella County
36	1563	2.6	**Highland** (charter township) Oakland County	109	2829	2.4	**Woodhaven** (city) Wayne County
36	1563	2.6	**Independence** (charter township) Oakland County	116	2893	2.4	**Bath** (charter township) Clinton County
42	1617	2.6	**Byron** (township) Kent County	116	2893	2.4	**Comstock** (charter township) Kalamazoo County
42	1617	2.6	**Commerce** (charter township) Oakland County	116	2893	2.4	**Cutlerville** (CDP) Kent County
44	1738	2.6	**Chesterfield** (township) Macomb County	116	2893	2.4	**Flint** (city) Genesee County
44	1738	2.6	**Muskegon Heights** (city) Muskegon County	116	2893	2.4	**Kentwood** (city) Kent County
44	1738	2.6	**West Bloomfield** (charter township) Oakland County	116	2893	2.4	**Mundy** (township) Genesee County
44	1738	2.6	**White Lake** (charter township) Oakland County	116	2893	2.4	**Plymouth** (charter township) Wayne County
44	1738	2.6	**Wyoming** (city) Kent County	116	2893	2.4	**Wayne** (city) Wayne County
49	1788	2.6	**Fruitport** (charter township) Muskegon County	124	2968	2.4	**Monroe** (city) Monroe County
49	1788	2.6	**Sturgis** (city) Saint Joseph County	124	2968	2.4	**Northview** (CDP) Kent County
51	1833	2.6	**Flushing** (charter township) Genesee County	124	2968	2.4	**Spring Lake** (township) Ottawa County
51	1833	2.6	**Jenison** (CDP) Ottawa County	127	3032	2.4	**Pittsfield** (charter township) Washtenaw County
51	1833	2.6	**Romulus** (city) Wayne County	128	3107	2.4	**Allen Park** (city) Wayne County
54	1900	2.6	**Superior** (charter township) Washtenaw County	128	3107	2.4	**Bridgeport** (charter township) Saginaw County
54	1900	2.6	**Troy** (city) Oakland County	128	3107	2.4	**Comstock Park** (CDP) Kent County
56	2001	2.6	**Mount Morris** (township) Genesee County	128	3107	2.4	**Emmett** (charter township) Calhoun County
56	2001	2.6	**Sterling Heights** (city) Macomb County	128	3107	2.4	**Harper Woods** (city) Wayne County
58	2049	2.6	**Bedford** (township) Monroe County	128	3107	2.4	**Melvindale** (city) Wayne County
58	2049	2.6	**Milford** (charter township) Oakland County	128	3107	2.4	**Port Huron** (city) Saint Clair County
58	2049	2.6	**Shelby** (charter township) Macomb County	128	3107	2.4	**Saint Joseph** (charter township) Berrien County
61	2093	2.5	**Detroit** (city) Wayne County	128	3107	2.4	**South Lyon** (city) Oakland County
61	2093	2.5	**Fenton** (charter township) Genesee County	128	3107	2.4	**Summit** (township) Jackson County
61	2093	2.5	**Plainfield** (charter township) Kent County	128	3107	2.4	**Van Buren** (charter township) Wayne County
64	2136	2.5	**Eastpointe** (city) Macomb County	139	3179	2.4	**Battle Creek** (city) Calhoun County
64	2136	2.5	**Muskegon** (charter township) Muskegon County	139	3179	2.4	**Owosso** (city) Shiawassee County
66	2188	2.5	**Dearborn Heights** (city) Wayne County	139	3179	2.4	**Roseville** (city) Macomb County
67	2234	2.5	**Grosse Pointe Park** (city) Wayne County	142	3241	2.4	**Portage** (city) Kalamazoo County
67	2234	2.5	**Inkster** (city) Wayne County	142	3241	2.4	**Thomas** (township) Saginaw County
67	2234	2.5	**Pontiac** (city) Oakland County	142	3241	2.4	**Walker** (city) Kent County
67	2234	2.5	**Taylor** (city) Wayne County	142	3241	2.4	**Waterford** (charter township) Oakland County
71	2282	2.5	**Genesee** (charter township) Genesee County	146	3296	2.3	**Fort Gratiot** (charter township) Saint Clair County
71	2282	2.5	**Lincoln Park** (city) Wayne County	146	3296	2.3	**Norton Shores** (city) Muskegon County
71	2282	2.5	**Scio** (township) Washtenaw County	148	3347	2.3	**Bay City** (city) Bay County
74	2334	2.5	**Garden City** (city) Wayne County	148	3347	2.3	**Davison** (township) Genesee County
74	2334	2.5	**Genoa** (township) Livingston County	148	3347	2.3	**Monitor** (charter township) Bay County

Note: The state column ranks the top/bottom 150 places from all places in the state with population of 10,000 or more. The national column ranks the top/bottom 150 places from all places in the country with population of 10,000 or more. Places that are unincorporated were not considered in the rankings. Please refer to the User Guide for additional information.

Average Household Size

Top 150 Places Ranked in *Ascending* Order

State Rank	Nat'l Rank	Persons	Place		State Rank	Nat'l Rank	Persons	Place
1	65	2.0	**Royal Oak** (city) Oakland County		67	1478	2.4	**Summit** (township) Jackson County
2	80	2.0	**Marquette** (city) Marquette County		67	1478	2.4	**Van Buren** (charter township) Wayne County
3	88	2.0	**Ypsilanti** (city) Washtenaw County		78	1550	2.4	**Pittsfield** (charter township) Washtenaw County
4	102	2.0	**Ferndale** (city) Oakland County		79	1625	2.4	**Monroe** (city) Monroe County
4	102	2.0	**Traverse City** (city) Grand Traverse County		79	1625	2.4	**Northview** (CDP) Kent County
6	170	2.1	**Alpena** (city) Alpena County		79	1625	2.4	**Spring Lake** (township) Ottawa County
7	183	2.1	**Clawson** (city) Oakland County		82	1689	2.4	**Bath** (charter township) Clinton County
7	183	2.1	**Escanaba** (city) Delta County		82	1689	2.4	**Comstock** (charter township) Kalamazoo County
9	199	2.1	**Grand Haven** (city) Ottawa County		82	1689	2.4	**Cutlerville** (CDP) Kent County
9	199	2.1	**Haslett** (CDP) Ingham County		82	1689	2.4	**Flint** (city) Genesee County
9	199	2.1	**Waverly** (CDP) Eaton County		82	1689	2.4	**Kentwood** (city) Kent County
12	223	2.1	**Garfield** (charter township) Grand Traverse County		82	1689	2.4	**Mundy** (township) Genesee County
13	244	2.1	**Ann Arbor** (city) Washtenaw County		82	1689	2.4	**Plymouth** (charter township) Wayne County
14	312	2.1	**Mount Clemens** (city) Macomb County		82	1689	2.4	**Wayne** (city) Wayne County
15	364	2.2	**Harrison** (charter township) Macomb County		90	1764	2.4	**Benton** (charter township) Berrien County
15	364	2.2	**Oshtemo** (charter township) Kalamazoo County		90	1764	2.4	**Jackson** (city) Jackson County
17	405	2.2	**Big Rapids** (city) Mecosta County		90	1764	2.4	**Lincoln** (charter township) Berrien County
17	405	2.2	**Birmingham** (city) Oakland County		90	1764	2.4	**Niles** (township) Berrien County
17	405	2.2	**Farmington** (city) Oakland County		90	1764	2.4	**Novi** (city) Oakland County
17	405	2.2	**Saginaw** (charter township) Saginaw County		90	1764	2.4	**Union** (charter township) Isabella County
17	405	2.2	**Sault Sainte Marie** (city) Chippewa County		90	1764	2.4	**Woodhaven** (city) Wayne County
17	405	2.2	**Southfield** (city) Oakland County		97	1828	2.4	**Hazel Park** (city) Oakland County
23	453	2.2	**Blackman** (charter township) Jackson County		97	1828	2.4	**Livonia** (city) Wayne County
23	453	2.2	**East Lansing** (city) Ingham County		97	1828	2.4	**Northville** (township) Wayne County
25	493	2.2	**Auburn Hills** (city) Oakland County		100	1889	2.4	**Bloomfield** (charter township) Oakland County
25	493	2.2	**Saint Clair Shores** (city) Macomb County		100	1889	2.4	**East Bay** (township) Grand Traverse County
27	573	2.2	**Delta** (charter township) Eaton County		102	1959	2.4	**Coldwater** (city) Branch County
27	573	2.2	**Meridian** (charter township) Ingham County		102	1959	2.4	**Grand Rapids** (city) Kent County
29	623	2.2	**Berkley** (city) Oakland County		102	1959	2.4	**Monroe** (charter township) Monroe County
29	623	2.2	**Fenton** (city) Genesee County		102	1959	2.4	**Warren** (city) Macomb County
31	720	2.2	**Bangor** (charter township) Bay County		102	1959	2.4	**Ypsilanti** (charter township) Washtenaw County
31	720	2.2	**Clinton** (charter township) Macomb County		107	2027	2.5	**Burton** (city) Genesee County
31	720	2.2	**Kalamazoo** (city) Kalamazoo County		107	2027	2.5	**Grosse Ile** (township) Wayne County
31	720	2.2	**Southgate** (city) Wayne County		107	2027	2.5	**Oak Park** (city) Oakland County
35	837	2.3	**Riverview** (city) Wayne County		110	2089	2.5	**Grosse Pointe Woods** (city) Wayne County
35	837	2.3	**Rochester** (city) Oakland County		110	2089	2.5	**Port Huron** (charter township) Saint Clair County
35	837	2.3	**Westland** (city) Wayne County		110	2089	2.5	**Redford** (charter township) Wayne County
38	892	2.3	**Kalamazoo** (charter township) Kalamazoo County		113	2139	2.5	**Alpine** (township) Kent County
38	892	2.3	**Madison Heights** (city) Oakland County		113	2139	2.5	**Beverly Hills** (village) Oakland County
40	944	2.3	**Lansing** (city) Ingham County		113	2139	2.5	**Delhi** (charter township) Ingham County
40	944	2.3	**Midland** (city) Midland County		113	2139	2.5	**Grand Blanc** (charter township) Genesee County
40	944	2.3	**Trenton** (city) Wayne County		113	2139	2.5	**Holland** (city) Ottawa County
43	997	2.3	**Cadillac** (city) Wexford County		113	2139	2.5	**Holt** (CDP) Ingham County
43	997	2.3	**Flint** (charter township) Genesee County		113	2139	2.5	**Leoni** (township) Jackson County
45	1049	2.3	**Mount Pleasant** (city) Isabella County		113	2139	2.5	**Saginaw** (city) Saginaw County
45	1049	2.3	**Wyandotte** (city) Wayne County		113	2139	2.5	**Vienna** (charter township) Genesee County
47	1107	2.3	**Farmington Hills** (city) Oakland County		122	2193	2.5	**Cooper** (charter township) Kalamazoo County
47	1107	2.3	**Fraser** (city) Macomb County		122	2193	2.5	**DeWitt** (charter township) Clinton County
47	1107	2.3	**Highland Park** (city) Wayne County		122	2193	2.5	**Frenchtown** (township) Monroe County
47	1107	2.3	**Wixom** (city) Oakland County		122	2193	2.5	**Holly** (township) Oakland County
51	1172	2.3	**Adrian** (city) Lenawee County		122	2193	2.5	**Ionia** (city) Ionia County
51	1172	2.3	**Niles** (city) Berrien County		122	2193	2.5	**Rochester Hills** (city) Oakland County
53	1234	2.3	**Bay City** (city) Bay County		128	2259	2.5	**Garden City** (city) Wayne County
53	1234	2.3	**Davison** (township) Genesee County		128	2259	2.5	**Genoa** (township) Livingston County
53	1234	2.3	**Monitor** (charter township) Bay County		128	2259	2.5	**Grandville** (city) Kent County
53	1234	2.3	**Muskegon** (city) Muskegon County		128	2259	2.5	**Southfield** (township) Oakland County
53	1234	2.3	**Okemos** (CDP) Ingham County		132	2323	2.5	**Genesee** (charter township) Genesee County
58	1310	2.3	**Fort Gratiot** (charter township) Saint Clair County		132	2323	2.5	**Lincoln Park** (city) Wayne County
58	1310	2.3	**Norton Shores** (city) Muskegon County		132	2323	2.5	**Scio** (township) Washtenaw County
60	1361	2.4	**Portage** (city) Kalamazoo County		135	2375	2.5	**Grosse Pointe Park** (city) Wayne County
60	1361	2.4	**Thomas** (township) Saginaw County		135	2375	2.5	**Inkster** (city) Wayne County
60	1361	2.4	**Walker** (city) Kent County		135	2375	2.5	**Pontiac** (city) Oakland County
60	1361	2.4	**Waterford** (charter township) Oakland County		135	2375	2.5	**Taylor** (city) Wayne County
64	1416	2.4	**Battle Creek** (city) Calhoun County		139	2423	2.5	**Dearborn Heights** (city) Wayne County
64	1416	2.4	**Owosso** (city) Shiawassee County		140	2469	2.5	**Eastpointe** (city) Macomb County
64	1416	2.4	**Roseville** (city) Macomb County		140	2469	2.5	**Muskegon** (charter township) Muskegon County
67	1478	2.4	**Allen Park** (city) Wayne County		142	2521	2.5	**Detroit** (city) Wayne County
67	1478	2.4	**Bridgeport** (charter township) Saginaw County		142	2521	2.5	**Fenton** (township) Genesee County
67	1478	2.4	**Comstock Park** (CDP) Kent County		142	2521	2.5	**Plainfield** (charter township) Kent County
67	1478	2.4	**Emmett** (charter township) Calhoun County		145	2564	2.6	**Bedford** (township) Monroe County
67	1478	2.4	**Harper Woods** (city) Wayne County		145	2564	2.6	**Milford** (charter township) Oakland County
67	1478	2.4	**Melvindale** (city) Wayne County		145	2564	2.6	**Shelby** (charter township) Macomb County
67	1478	2.4	**Port Huron** (city) Saint Clair County		148	2608	2.6	**Mount Morris** (township) Genesee County
67	1478	2.4	**Saint Joseph** (charter township) Berrien County		148	2608	2.6	**Sterling Heights** (city) Macomb County
67	1478	2.4	**South Lyon** (city) Oakland County		150	2696	2.6	**Superior** (charter township) Washtenaw County

Note: The state column ranks the top/bottom 150 places from all places in the state with population of 10,000 or more. The national column ranks the top/bottom 150 places from all places in the country with population of 10,000 or more. Places that are unincorporated were not considered in the rankings. Please refer to the User Guide for additional information.

Median Age

Top 150 Places Ranked in *Descending* Order

State Rank	Nat'l Rank	Years	Place		State Rank	Nat'l Rank	Years	Place
1	92	49.0	**Grosse Ile** (township) Wayne County		75	1472	40.4	**Sterling Heights** (city) Macomb County
2	104	48.7	**Bloomfield** (charter township) Oakland County		75	1472	40.4	**Wyandotte** (city) Wayne County
3	161	47.1	**Thomas** (township) Saginaw County		78	1505	40.3	**Grand Haven** (charter township) Ottawa County
4	173	46.9	**Monitor** (charter township) Bay County		78	1505	40.3	**Woodhaven** (city) Wayne County
5	216	46.2	**Saint Joseph** (charter township) Berrien County		80	1538	40.2	**Brandon** (charter township) Oakland County
6	236	45.9	**Southfield** (township) Oakland County		80	1538	40.2	**Commerce** (charter township) Oakland County
7	262	45.6	**Bangor** (charter township) Bay County		82	1635	39.9	**Clawson** (city) Oakland County
8	291	45.4	**Riverview** (city) Wayne County		82	1635	39.9	**Garden City** (city) Wayne County
9	335	45.1	**Grosse Pointe Woods** (city) Wayne County		84	1673	39.8	**Ada** (township) Kent County
10	351	45.0	**Trenton** (city) Wayne County		84	1673	39.8	**East Grand Rapids** (city) Kent County
11	398	44.7	**Beverly Hills** (village) Oakland County		84	1673	39.8	**Northview** (CDP) Kent County
12	413	44.6	**Fort Gratiot** (charter township) Saint Clair County		87	1710	39.7	**Jenison** (CDP) Ottawa County
12	413	44.6	**West Bloomfield** (charter township) Oakland County		87	1710	39.7	**Plainfield** (charter township) Kent County
14	429	44.5	**Livonia** (city) Wayne County		89	1736	39.6	**Monroe** (charter township) Monroe County
14	429	44.5	**Plymouth** (charter township) Wayne County		90	1770	39.5	**Farmington** (city) Oakland County
16	471	44.2	**Saint Clair Shores** (city) Macomb County		90	1770	39.5	**Texas** (charter township) Kalamazoo County
17	533	43.8	**Brighton** (township) Livingston County		92	1808	39.4	**Haslett** (CDP) Ingham County
18	588	43.5	**Harrison** (charter township) Macomb County		92	1808	39.4	**Huron** (charter township) Wayne County
19	613	43.4	**Bridgeport** (charter township) Saginaw County		92	1808	39.4	**Warren** (city) Macomb County
20	632	43.3	**Cascade** (charter township) Kent County		95	1839	39.3	**Frenchtown** (township) Monroe County
20	632	43.3	**Norton Shores** (city) Muskegon County		95	1839	39.3	**Hartland** (township) Livingston County
22	677	43.1	**Milford** (charter township) Oakland County		95	1839	39.3	**Holly** (township) Oakland County
22	677	43.1	**Saginaw** (charter township) Saginaw County		98	1872	39.2	**Blackman** (charter township) Jackson County
24	699	43.0	**Garfield** (charter township) Grand Traverse County		99	1904	39.1	**Novi** (city) Oakland County
25	720	42.9	**Flushing** (charter township) Genesee County		99	1904	39.1	**Waterford** (charter township) Oakland County
25	720	42.9	**Fraser** (city) Macomb County		101	1961	38.9	**Comstock** (charter township) Kalamazoo County
25	720	42.9	**Grand Haven** (city) Ottawa County		102	1994	38.8	**Byron** (township) Kent County
28	755	42.8	**Summit** (township) Jackson County		103	2042	38.6	**Burton** (city) Genesee County
29	787	42.7	**Bedford** (township) Monroe County		103	2042	38.6	**Orion** (charter township) Oakland County
29	787	42.7	**Fenton** (charter township) Genesee County		103	2042	38.6	**Wayne** (city) Wayne County
29	787	42.7	**Genoa** (township) Livingston County		106	2066	38.5	**Port Huron** (charter township) Saint Clair County
32	810	42.6	**Hamburg** (township) Livingston County		107	2107	38.4	**Davison** (township) Genesee County
33	843	42.5	**Alpena** (city) Alpena County		107	2107	38.4	**Lyon** (charter township) Oakland County
33	843	42.5	**Oakland** (charter township) Oakland County		107	2107	38.4	**Oxford** (charter township) Oakland County
33	843	42.5	**Vienna** (charter township) Genesee County		107	2107	38.4	**South Lyon** (city) Oakland County
36	876	42.4	**Northville** (township) Wayne County		111	2137	38.3	**Dearborn Heights** (city) Wayne County
36	876	42.4	**Tyrone** (township) Livingston County		111	2137	38.3	**Madison Heights** (city) Oakland County
38	905	42.3	**Green Oak** (township) Livingston County		111	2137	38.3	**Midland** (city) Midland County
38	905	42.3	**Lincoln** (charter township) Berrien County		111	2137	38.3	**Mount Clemens** (city) Macomb County
40	955	42.1	**Farmington Hills** (city) Oakland County		111	2137	38.3	**Rochester** (city) Oakland County
40	955	42.1	**Park** (township) Ottawa County		111	2137	38.3	**Westland** (city) Wayne County
40	955	42.1	**Spring Lake** (township) Ottawa County		117	2175	38.2	**Chesterfield** (township) Macomb County
43	980	42.0	**Highland** (charter township) Oakland County		117	2175	38.2	**Meridian** (charter township) Ingham County
43	980	42.0	**Southfield** (city) Oakland County		119	2205	38.1	**Portage** (city) Kalamazoo County
43	980	42.0	**Springfield** (charter township) Oakland County		120	2234	38.0	**Redford** (charter township) Wayne County
46	1008	41.9	**Niles** (township) Berrien County		121	2272	37.9	**Berkley** (city) Oakland County
47	1043	41.8	**Grosse Pointe Park** (city) Wayne County		121	2272	37.9	**Okemos** (CDP) Ingham County
47	1043	41.8	**Troy** (city) Oakland County		121	2272	37.9	**Roseville** (city) Macomb County
49	1073	41.7	**Allen Park** (city) Wayne County		124	2309	37.8	**Caledonia** (township) Kent County
50	1132	41.5	**Mundy** (township) Genesee County		124	2309	37.8	**Royal Oak** (city) Oakland County
51	1167	41.4	**Delta** (charter township) Eaton County		126	2342	37.7	**Delhi** (charter township) Ingham County
51	1167	41.4	**Escanaba** (city) Delta County		127	2367	37.6	**Brownstown** (charter township) Wayne County
53	1204	41.3	**Grand Rapids** (charter township) Kent County		128	2398	37.5	**Harper Woods** (city) Wayne County
53	1204	41.3	**Washington** (township) Macomb County		128	2398	37.5	**Oak Park** (city) Oakland County
53	1204	41.3	**White Lake** (charter township) Oakland County		128	2398	37.5	**Oceola** (township) Livingston County
56	1244	41.2	**Forest Hills** (CDP) Kent County		128	2398	37.5	**Superior** (charter township) Washtenaw County
56	1244	41.2	**Leoni** (township) Jackson County		132	2432	37.4	**Macomb** (township) Macomb County
58	1274	41.1	**Birmingham** (city) Oakland County		133	2466	37.3	**Antwerp** (township) Van Buren County
58	1274	41.1	**East Bay** (township) Grand Traverse County		134	2496	37.2	**Benton** (charter township) Berrien County
60	1296	41.0	**Shelby** (charter township) Macomb County		134	2496	37.2	**Muskegon** (charter township) Muskegon County
61	1321	40.9	**Rochester Hills** (city) Oakland County		136	2534	37.1	**New Baltimore** (city) Macomb County
62	1349	40.8	**Fruitport** (charter township) Muskegon County		137	2575	37.0	**Holt** (CDP) Ingham County
62	1349	40.8	**Genesee** (charter township) Genesee County		137	2575	37.0	**Mount Morris** (township) Genesee County
62	1349	40.8	**Southgate** (city) Wayne County		139	2615	36.9	**Canton** (charter township) Wayne County
62	1349	40.8	**Traverse City** (city) Grand Traverse County		139	2615	36.9	**Taylor** (city) Wayne County
66	1373	40.7	**Clinton** (charter township) Macomb County		141	2641	36.8	**Grand Blanc** (charter township) Genesee County
66	1373	40.7	**Waverly** (CDP) Eaton County		141	2641	36.8	**Lenox** (township) Macomb County
68	1404	40.6	**Emmett** (charter township) Calhoun County		143	2681	36.7	**Lincoln Park** (city) Wayne County
68	1404	40.6	**Flint** (charter township) Genesee County		144	2742	36.5	**Cadillac** (city) Wexford County
68	1404	40.6	**Independence** (charter township) Oakland County		144	2742	36.5	**Melvindale** (city) Wayne County
71	1437	40.5	**Cannon** (township) Kent County		144	2742	36.5	**Van Buren** (charter township) Wayne County
71	1437	40.5	**Cooper** (charter township) Kalamazoo County		147	2802	36.3	**Battle Creek** (city) Calhoun County
71	1437	40.5	**Highland Park** (city) Wayne County		147	2802	36.3	**Eastpointe** (city) Macomb County
71	1437	40.5	**Scio** (township) Washtenaw County		147	2802	36.3	**Grandville** (city) Kent County
75	1472	40.4	**DeWitt** (charter township) Clinton County		147	2802	36.3	**Monroe** (city) Monroe County

Note: The state column ranks the top/bottom 150 places from all places in the state with population of 10,000 or more. The national column ranks the top/bottom 150 places from all places in the country with population of 10,000 or more. Places that are unincorporated were not considered in the rankings. Please refer to the User Guide for additional information.

Median Age

Top 150 Places Ranked in *Ascending* Order

State Rank	Nat'l Rank	Years	Place
1	10	20.9	**Allendale** (CDP) Ottawa County
2	12	21.1	**Allendale** (charter township) Ottawa County
3	22	21.6	**East Lansing** (city) Ingham County
4	28	21.8	**Big Rapids** (city) Mecosta County
5	35	22.0	**Mount Pleasant** (city) Isabella County
6	57	22.8	**Union** (charter township) Isabella County
7	116	25.0	**Ypsilanti** (city) Washtenaw County
8	160	26.2	**Kalamazoo** (city) Kalamazoo County
9	221	27.8	**Ann Arbor** (city) Washtenaw County
10	254	28.3	**Benton Harbor** (city) Berrien County
11	292	28.8	**Hamtramck** (city) Wayne County
12	322	29.1	**Marquette** (city) Marquette County
13	421	30.1	**Bath** (charter township) Clinton County
14	446	30.3	**Muskegon Heights** (city) Muskegon County
15	513	30.8	**Comstock Park** (CDP) Kent County
15	513	30.8	**Grand Rapids** (city) Kent County
17	608	31.4	**Auburn Hills** (city) Oakland County
18	658	31.7	**Holland** (city) Ottawa County
19	715	32.0	**Holland** (charter township) Ottawa County
19	715	32.0	**Oshtemo** (charter township) Kalamazoo County
21	733	32.1	**Wyoming** (city) Kent County
22	755	32.2	**Jackson** (city) Jackson County
22	755	32.2	**Lansing** (city) Ingham County
24	777	32.3	**Ionia** (city) Ionia County
24	777	32.3	**Sturgis** (city) Saint Joseph County
26	818	32.5	**Adrian** (city) Lenawee County
27	851	32.6	**Alpine** (township) Kent County
28	910	32.9	**Beecher** (CDP) Genesee County
29	929	33.0	**Dearborn** (city) Wayne County
30	1006	33.3	**Kalamazoo** (charter township) Kalamazoo County
30	1006	33.3	**Ypsilanti** (charter township) Washtenaw County
32	1027	33.4	**Pontiac** (city) Oakland County
33	1055	33.5	**Saginaw** (city) Saginaw County
34	1080	33.6	**Flint** (city) Genesee County
35	1141	33.8	**Pittsfield** (charter township) Washtenaw County
35	1141	33.8	**Sault Sainte Marie** (city) Chippewa County
37	1225	34.1	**Muskegon** (city) Muskegon County
38	1249	34.2	**Inkster** (city) Wayne County
39	1279	34.3	**Kentwood** (city) Kent County
40	1339	34.6	**Walker** (city) Kent County
41	1410	34.8	**Detroit** (city) Wayne County
41	1410	34.8	**Gaines** (charter township) Kent County
41	1410	34.8	**Owosso** (city) Shiawassee County
41	1410	34.8	**Wixom** (city) Oakland County
45	1512	35.2	**Coldwater** (city) Branch County
46	1533	35.3	**Georgetown** (charter township) Ottawa County
47	1618	35.6	**Ferndale** (city) Oakland County
48	1679	35.8	**Bay City** (city) Bay County
48	1679	35.8	**Cutlerville** (CDP) Kent County
48	1679	35.8	**Port Huron** (city) Saint Clair County
51	1728	36.0	**Fenton** (city) Genesee County
52	1764	36.1	**Hazel Park** (city) Oakland County
52	1764	36.1	**Niles** (city) Berrien County
54	1796	36.2	**Romulus** (city) Wayne County
55	1831	36.3	**Battle Creek** (city) Calhoun County
55	1831	36.3	**Eastpointe** (city) Macomb County
55	1831	36.3	**Grandville** (city) Kent County
55	1831	36.3	**Monroe** (city) Monroe County
59	1889	36.5	**Cadillac** (city) Wexford County
59	1889	36.5	**Melvindale** (city) Wayne County
59	1889	36.5	**Van Buren** (charter township) Wayne County
62	1941	36.7	**Lincoln Park** (city) Wayne County
63	1976	36.8	**Grand Blanc** (charter township) Genesee County
63	1976	36.8	**Lenox** (township) Macomb County
65	2016	36.9	**Canton** (charter township) Wayne County
65	2016	36.9	**Taylor** (city) Wayne County
67	2042	37.0	**Holt** (CDP) Ingham County
67	2042	37.0	**Mount Morris** (township) Genesee County
69	2082	37.1	**New Baltimore** (city) Macomb County
70	2123	37.2	**Benton** (charter township) Berrien County
70	2123	37.2	**Muskegon** (charter township) Muskegon County
72	2161	37.3	**Antwerp** (township) Van Buren County
73	2191	37.4	**Macomb** (township) Macomb County
74	2225	37.5	**Harper Woods** (city) Wayne County
74	2225	37.5	**Oak Park** (city) Oakland County
74	2225	37.5	**Oceola** (township) Livingston County
74	2225	37.5	**Superior** (charter township) Washtenaw County
78	2259	37.6	**Brownstown** (charter township) Wayne County
79	2290	37.7	**Delhi** (charter township) Ingham County
80	2315	37.8	**Caledonia** (township) Kent County
80	2315	37.8	**Royal Oak** (city) Oakland County
82	2348	37.9	**Berkley** (city) Oakland County
82	2348	37.9	**Okemos** (CDP) Ingham County
82	2348	37.9	**Roseville** (city) Macomb County
85	2385	38.0	**Redford** (charter township) Wayne County
86	2423	38.1	**Portage** (city) Kalamazoo County
87	2452	38.2	**Chesterfield** (township) Macomb County
87	2452	38.2	**Meridian** (charter township) Ingham County
89	2482	38.3	**Dearborn Heights** (city) Wayne County
89	2482	38.3	**Madison Heights** (city) Oakland County
89	2482	38.3	**Midland** (city) Midland County
89	2482	38.3	**Mount Clemens** (city) Macomb County
89	2482	38.3	**Rochester** (city) Oakland County
89	2482	38.3	**Westland** (city) Wayne County
95	2520	38.4	**Davison** (township) Genesee County
95	2520	38.4	**Lyon** (charter township) Oakland County
95	2520	38.4	**Oxford** (charter township) Oakland County
95	2520	38.4	**South Lyon** (city) Oakland County
99	2550	38.5	**Port Huron** (charter township) Saint Clair County
100	2591	38.6	**Burton** (city) Genesee County
100	2591	38.6	**Orion** (charter township) Oakland County
100	2591	38.6	**Wayne** (city) Wayne County
103	2639	38.8	**Byron** (township) Kent County
104	2663	38.9	**Comstock** (charter township) Kalamazoo County
105	2723	39.1	**Novi** (city) Oakland County
105	2723	39.1	**Waterford** (charter township) Oakland County
107	2753	39.2	**Blackman** (charter township) Jackson County
108	2785	39.3	**Frenchtown** (township) Monroe County
108	2785	39.3	**Hartland** (township) Livingston County
108	2785	39.3	**Holly** (township) Oakland County
111	2818	39.4	**Haslett** (CDP) Ingham County
111	2818	39.4	**Huron** (charter township) Wayne County
111	2818	39.4	**Warren** (city) Macomb County
114	2849	39.5	**Farmington** (city) Oakland County
114	2849	39.5	**Texas** (charter township) Kalamazoo County
116	2887	39.6	**Monroe** (charter township) Monroe County
117	2921	39.7	**Jenison** (CDP) Ottawa County
117	2921	39.7	**Plainfield** (charter township) Kent County
119	2947	39.8	**Ada** (township) Kent County
119	2947	39.8	**East Grand Rapids** (city) Kent County
119	2947	39.8	**Northview** (CDP) Kent County
122	2984	39.9	**Clawson** (city) Oakland County
122	2984	39.9	**Garden City** (city) Wayne County
124	3081	40.2	**Brandon** (charter township) Oakland County
124	3081	40.2	**Commerce** (charter township) Oakland County
126	3119	40.3	**Grand Haven** (charter township) Ottawa County
126	3119	40.3	**Woodhaven** (city) Wayne County
128	3152	40.4	**DeWitt** (charter township) Clinton County
128	3152	40.4	**Sterling Heights** (city) Macomb County
128	3152	40.4	**Wyandotte** (city) Wayne County
131	3185	40.5	**Cannon** (township) Kent County
131	3185	40.5	**Cooper** (charter township) Kalamazoo County
131	3185	40.5	**Highland Park** (city) Wayne County
131	3185	40.5	**Scio** (township) Washtenaw County
135	3220	40.6	**Emmett** (charter township) Calhoun County
135	3220	40.6	**Flint** (charter township) Genesee County
135	3220	40.6	**Independence** (charter township) Oakland County
138	3253	40.7	**Clinton** (charter township) Macomb County
138	3253	40.7	**Waverly** (CDP) Eaton County
140	3284	40.8	**Fruitport** (charter township) Muskegon County
140	3284	40.8	**Genesee** (charter township) Genesee County
140	3284	40.8	**Southgate** (city) Wayne County
140	3284	40.8	**Traverse City** (city) Grand Traverse County
144	3308	40.9	**Rochester Hills** (city) Oakland County
145	3336	41.0	**Shelby** (charter township) Macomb County
146	3361	41.1	**Birmingham** (city) Oakland County
146	3361	41.1	**East Bay** (township) Grand Traverse County
148	3383	41.2	**Forest Hills** (CDP) Kent County
148	3383	41.2	**Leoni** (township) Jackson County
150	3413	41.3	**Grand Rapids** (charter township) Kent County

Note: *The state column ranks the top/bottom 150 places from all places in the state with population of 10,000 or more. The national column ranks the top/bottom 150 places from all places in the country with population of 10,000 or more. Places that are unincorporated were not considered in the rankings. Please refer to the User Guide for additional information.*

Population Under Age 18

Top 150 Places Ranked in *Descending* Order

State Rank	Nat'l Rank	Percent	Place
1	79	35.1	**Benton Harbor** (city) Berrien County
2	222	32.3	**Muskegon Heights** (city) Muskegon County
3	279	31.7	**Hamtramck** (city) Wayne County
4	287	31.6	**East Grand Rapids** (city) Kent County
5	318	31.3	**Ada** (township) Kent County
6	408	30.5	**Beecher** (CDP) Genesee County
7	443	30.3	**Holland** (charter township) Ottawa County
8	468	30.1	**Cannon** (township) Kent County
8	468	30.1	**Forest Hills** (CDP) Kent County
10	485	30.0	**Sturgis** (city) Saint Joseph County
11	509	29.9	**Oceola** (township) Livingston County
12	539	29.7	**Dearborn** (city) Wayne County
13	632	29.1	**Macomb** (township) Macomb County
14	674	28.8	**New Baltimore** (city) Macomb County
14	674	28.8	**Texas** (charter township) Kalamazoo County
16	717	28.6	**Hartland** (township) Livingston County
17	737	28.5	**Jackson** (city) Jackson County
18	760	28.4	**Saginaw** (city) Saginaw County
19	846	28.1	**Oxford** (charter township) Oakland County
20	867	28.0	**Caledonia** (township) Kent County
20	867	28.0	**Cascade** (charter township) Kent County
22	889	27.9	**Inkster** (city) Wayne County
23	925	27.8	**Oakland** (charter township) Oakland County
24	972	27.6	**Orion** (charter township) Oakland County
25	995	27.5	**Gaines** (charter township) Kent County
26	1018	27.4	**Antwerp** (township) Van Buren County
26	1018	27.4	**Mount Morris** (township) Genesee County
28	1041	27.3	**Flint** (city) Genesee County
28	1041	27.3	**Grand Rapids** (charter township) Kent County
30	1069	27.2	**Canton** (charter township) Wayne County
30	1069	27.2	**Coldwater** (city) Branch County
30	1069	27.2	**Georgetown** (charter township) Ottawa County
30	1069	27.2	**Lyon** (charter township) Oakland County
30	1069	27.2	**Pontiac** (city) Oakland County
35	1097	27.1	**Grand Haven** (charter township) Ottawa County
35	1097	27.1	**Wyoming** (city) Kent County
37	1156	26.9	**Benton** (charter township) Berrien County
37	1156	26.9	**South Lyon** (city) Oakland County
39	1194	26.8	**Romulus** (city) Wayne County
40	1221	26.7	**Detroit** (city) Wayne County
40	1221	26.7	**Superior** (charter township) Washtenaw County
42	1290	26.5	**Grand Blanc** (charter township) Genesee County
42	1290	26.5	**Grosse Pointe Park** (city) Wayne County
42	1290	26.5	**Tyrone** (township) Livingston County
45	1328	26.4	**Brownstown** (charter township) Wayne County
45	1328	26.4	**Independence** (charter township) Oakland County
45	1328	26.4	**Park** (township) Ottawa County
48	1371	26.3	**Brandon** (charter township) Oakland County
48	1371	26.3	**Byron** (township) Kent County
48	1371	26.3	**Muskegon** (charter township) Muskegon County
48	1371	26.3	**Scio** (township) Washtenaw County
52	1403	26.2	**Monroe** (city) Monroe County
52	1403	26.2	**Ypsilanti** (charter township) Washtenaw County
54	1440	26.1	**Battle Creek** (city) Calhoun County
54	1440	26.1	**Chesterfield** (township) Macomb County
56	1461	26.0	**Commerce** (charter township) Oakland County
56	1461	26.0	**Springfield** (charter township) Oakland County
58	1496	25.9	**Harper Woods** (city) Wayne County
59	1530	25.8	**Alpine** (township) Kent County
59	1530	25.8	**Comstock Park** (CDP) Kent County
61	1567	25.7	**Eastpointe** (city) Macomb County
61	1567	25.7	**Holt** (CDP) Ingham County
63	1602	25.6	**Niles** (city) Berrien County
63	1602	25.6	**Port Huron** (city) Saint Clair County
65	1643	25.5	**Delhi** (charter township) Ingham County
65	1643	25.5	**Novi** (city) Oakland County
67	1682	25.4	**Kentwood** (city) Kent County
67	1682	25.4	**Wixom** (city) Oakland County
69	1718	25.3	**DeWitt** (charter township) Clinton County
69	1718	25.3	**Hamburg** (township) Livingston County
71	1762	25.2	**Huron** (charter township) Wayne County
71	1762	25.2	**Owosso** (city) Shiawassee County
73	1797	25.1	**Beverly Hills** (village) Oakland County
73	1797	25.1	**Green Oak** (township) Livingston County
73	1797	25.1	**Plainfield** (charter township) Kent County
73	1797	25.1	**Rochester** (city) Oakland County
73	1797	25.1	**Southfield** (township) Oakland County
78	1841	25.0	**Dearborn Heights** (city) Wayne County
78	1841	25.0	**Jenison** (CDP) Ottawa County
78	1841	25.0	**Washington** (township) Macomb County
81	1891	24.9	**Bay City** (city) Bay County
81	1891	24.9	**Oak Park** (city) Oakland County
81	1891	24.9	**Spring Lake** (township) Ottawa County
84	1934	24.8	**Grandville** (city) Kent County
84	1934	24.8	**Lincoln Park** (city) Wayne County
84	1934	24.8	**Portage** (city) Kalamazoo County
87	1977	24.7	**Cadillac** (city) Wexford County
87	1977	24.7	**Fruitport** (charter township) Muskegon County
87	1977	24.7	**Grand Rapids** (city) Kent County
87	1977	24.7	**Lenox** (township) Macomb County
87	1977	24.7	**Melvindale** (city) Wayne County
87	1977	24.7	**Taylor** (city) Wayne County
93	2025	24.6	**Birmingham** (city) Oakland County
93	2025	24.6	**Brighton** (township) Livingston County
93	2025	24.6	**White Lake** (charter township) Oakland County
96	2122	24.4	**Northville** (township) Wayne County
96	2122	24.4	**Pittsfield** (charter township) Washtenaw County
98	2158	24.3	**Fenton** (charter township) Genesee County
98	2158	24.3	**Highland** (charter township) Oakland County
100	2205	24.2	**Genoa** (township) Livingston County
100	2205	24.2	**Hazel Park** (city) Oakland County
100	2205	24.2	**Holly** (township) Oakland County
100	2205	24.2	**Lansing** (city) Ingham County
104	2255	24.1	**Cutlerville** (CDP) Kent County
104	2255	24.1	**Fenton** (city) Genesee County
104	2255	24.1	**Lincoln** (charter township) Berrien County
107	2302	24.0	**Burton** (city) Genesee County
107	2302	24.0	**Genesee** (charter township) Genesee County
107	2302	24.0	**Holland** (city) Ottawa County
107	2302	24.0	**Milford** (charter township) Oakland County
111	2343	23.9	**Flushing** (charter township) Genesee County
111	2343	23.9	**Redford** (charter township) Wayne County
111	2343	23.9	**Van Buren** (charter township) Wayne County
114	2389	23.8	**Monroe** (charter township) Monroe County
114	2389	23.8	**Troy** (city) Oakland County
116	2423	23.7	**Davison** (township) Genesee County
116	2423	23.7	**Grosse Pointe Woods** (city) Wayne County
116	2423	23.7	**Highland Park** (city) Wayne County
116	2423	23.7	**Rochester Hills** (city) Oakland County
120	2483	23.6	**Bedford** (township) Monroe County
120	2483	23.6	**Comstock** (charter township) Kalamazoo County
120	2483	23.6	**West Bloomfield** (charter township) Oakland County
123	2525	23.5	**Leoni** (township) Jackson County
123	2525	23.5	**Northview** (CDP) Kent County
123	2525	23.5	**Wayne** (city) Wayne County
126	2577	23.4	**Midland** (city) Midland County
127	2624	23.3	**Muskegon** (city) Muskegon County
128	2676	23.2	**Frenchtown** (township) Monroe County
128	2676	23.2	**Port Huron** (charter township) Saint Clair County
130	2724	23.1	**East Bay** (township) Grand Traverse County
130	2724	23.1	**Summit** (township) Jackson County
132	2776	23.0	**Adrian** (city) Lenawee County
132	2776	23.0	**Emmett** (charter township) Calhoun County
132	2776	23.0	**Flint** (charter township) Genesee County
132	2776	23.0	**Roseville** (city) Macomb County
132	2776	23.0	**Waterford** (charter township) Oakland County
137	2824	22.9	**Mundy** (township) Genesee County
137	2824	22.9	**Walker** (city) Kent County
139	2913	22.7	**Shelby** (charter township) Macomb County
139	2913	22.7	**Warren** (city) Macomb County
141	2957	22.6	**Cooper** (charter township) Kalamazoo County
141	2957	22.6	**Niles** (township) Berrien County
143	3007	22.5	**Bloomfield** (charter township) Oakland County
144	3047	22.4	**Garden City** (city) Wayne County
145	3092	22.3	**Fort Gratiot** (charter township) Saint Clair County
145	3092	22.3	**Kalamazoo** (charter township) Kalamazoo County
145	3092	22.3	**Plymouth** (charter township) Wayne County
145	3092	22.3	**Vienna** (charter township) Genesee County
145	3092	22.3	**Woodhaven** (city) Wayne County
150	3185	22.1	**Bridgeport** (charter township) Saginaw County

Note: The state column ranks the top/bottom 150 places from all places in the state with population of 10,000 or more. The national column ranks the top/bottom 150 places from all places in the country with population of 10,000 or more. Places that are unincorporated were not considered in the rankings. Please refer to the User Guide for additional information.

Population Under Age 18

Top 150 Places Ranked in *Ascending* Order

State Rank	Nat'l Rank	Percent	Place
1	23	7.5	**East Lansing** (city) Ingham County
2	51	11.0	**Mount Pleasant** (city) Isabella County
3	67	12.2	**Marquette** (city) Marquette County
4	73	12.5	**Big Rapids** (city) Mecosta County
5	112	14.1	**Ypsilanti** (city) Washtenaw County
6	118	14.3	**Union** (charter township) Isabella County
7	123	14.4	**Ann Arbor** (city) Washtenaw County
8	168	15.7	**Ionia** (city) Ionia County
9	192	16.2	**Blackman** (charter township) Jackson County
10	216	16.5	**Ferndale** (city) Oakland County
11	226	16.7	**Royal Oak** (city) Oakland County
12	238	16.9	**Allendale** (CDP) Ottawa County
13	294	17.6	**Allendale** (charter township) Ottawa County
14	318	17.9	**Clawson** (city) Oakland County
15	348	18.2	**Traverse City** (city) Grand Traverse County
16	368	18.4	**Oshtemo** (charter township) Kalamazoo County
17	471	19.0	**Saint Clair Shores** (city) Macomb County
18	487	19.1	**Bath** (charter township) Clinton County
19	514	19.2	**Harrison** (charter township) Macomb County
20	555	19.4	**Auburn Hills** (city) Oakland County
21	605	19.6	**Bangor** (charter township) Bay County
21	605	19.6	**Riverview** (city) Wayne County
23	631	19.7	**Waverly** (CDP) Eaton County
24	680	19.9	**Monitor** (charter township) Bay County
25	696	20.0	**Saginaw** (charter township) Saginaw County
26	719	20.1	**Garfield** (charter township) Grand Traverse County
26	719	20.1	**Haslett** (CDP) Ingham County
28	776	20.3	**Southgate** (city) Wayne County
28	776	20.3	**Thomas** (township) Saginaw County
30	807	20.4	**Madison Heights** (city) Oakland County
31	840	20.5	**Kalamazoo** (city) Kalamazoo County
31	840	20.5	**Southfield** (city) Oakland County
33	867	20.6	**Mount Clemens** (city) Macomb County
34	891	20.7	**Alpena** (city) Alpena County
34	891	20.7	**Grand Haven** (city) Ottawa County
36	928	20.8	**Livonia** (city) Wayne County
36	928	20.8	**Meridian** (charter township) Ingham County
38	967	20.9	**Clinton** (charter township) Macomb County
38	967	20.9	**Delta** (charter township) Eaton County
40	1121	21.3	**Okemos** (CDP) Ingham County
40	1121	21.3	**Sault Sainte Marie** (city) Chippewa County
40	1121	21.3	**Trenton** (city) Wayne County
43	1158	21.4	**Berkley** (city) Oakland County
43	1158	21.4	**Escanaba** (city) Delta County
43	1158	21.4	**Fraser** (city) Macomb County
43	1158	21.4	**Wyandotte** (city) Wayne County
47	1195	21.5	**Farmington Hills** (city) Oakland County
48	1235	21.6	**Grosse Ile** (township) Wayne County
49	1271	21.7	**Allen Park** (city) Wayne County
49	1271	21.7	**Saint Joseph** (charter township) Berrien County
49	1271	21.7	**Sterling Heights** (city) Macomb County
52	1390	22.0	**Farmington** (city) Oakland County
52	1390	22.0	**Norton Shores** (city) Muskegon County
54	1435	22.1	**Bridgeport** (charter township) Saginaw County
54	1435	22.1	**Westland** (city) Wayne County
56	1516	22.3	**Fort Gratiot** (charter township) Saint Clair County
56	1516	22.3	**Kalamazoo** (charter township) Kalamazoo County
56	1516	22.3	**Plymouth** (charter township) Wayne County
56	1516	22.3	**Vienna** (charter township) Genesee County
56	1516	22.3	**Woodhaven** (city) Wayne County
61	1565	22.4	**Garden City** (city) Wayne County
62	1610	22.5	**Bloomfield** (charter township) Oakland County
63	1650	22.6	**Cooper** (charter township) Kalamazoo County
63	1650	22.6	**Niles** (township) Berrien County
65	1700	22.7	**Shelby** (charter township) Macomb County
65	1700	22.7	**Warren** (city) Macomb County
67	1787	22.9	**Mundy** (township) Genesee County
67	1787	22.9	**Walker** (city) Kent County
69	1833	23.0	**Adrian** (city) Lenawee County
69	1833	23.0	**Emmett** (charter township) Calhoun County
69	1833	23.0	**Flint** (charter township) Genesee County
69	1833	23.0	**Roseville** (city) Macomb County
69	1833	23.0	**Waterford** (charter township) Oakland County
74	1881	23.1	**East Bay** (township) Grand Traverse County
74	1881	23.1	**Summit** (township) Jackson County
76	1933	23.2	**Frenchtown** (township) Monroe County
76	1933	23.2	**Port Huron** (charter township) Saint Clair County
78	1981	23.3	**Muskegon** (city) Muskegon County
79	2033	23.4	**Midland** (city) Midland County
80	2080	23.5	**Leoni** (township) Jackson County
80	2080	23.5	**Northview** (CDP) Kent County
80	2080	23.5	**Wayne** (city) Wayne County
83	2132	23.6	**Bedford** (township) Monroe County
83	2132	23.6	**Comstock** (charter township) Kalamazoo County
83	2132	23.6	**West Bloomfield** (charter township) Oakland County
86	2174	23.7	**Davison** (township) Genesee County
86	2174	23.7	**Grosse Pointe Woods** (city) Wayne County
86	2174	23.7	**Highland Park** (city) Wayne County
86	2174	23.7	**Rochester Hills** (city) Oakland County
90	2234	23.8	**Monroe** (charter township) Monroe County
90	2234	23.8	**Troy** (city) Oakland County
92	2268	23.9	**Flushing** (charter township) Genesee County
92	2268	23.9	**Redford** (charter township) Wayne County
92	2268	23.9	**Van Buren** (charter township) Wayne County
95	2314	24.0	**Burton** (city) Genesee County
95	2314	24.0	**Genesee** (charter township) Genesee County
95	2314	24.0	**Holland** (city) Ottawa County
95	2314	24.0	**Milford** (charter township) Oakland County
99	2355	24.1	**Cutlerville** (CDP) Kent County
99	2355	24.1	**Fenton** (city) Genesee County
99	2355	24.1	**Lincoln** (charter township) Berrien County
102	2402	24.2	**Genoa** (township) Livingston County
102	2402	24.2	**Hazel Park** (city) Oakland County
102	2402	24.2	**Holly** (township) Oakland County
102	2402	24.2	**Lansing** (city) Ingham County
106	2452	24.3	**Fenton** (charter township) Genesee County
106	2452	24.3	**Highland** (charter township) Oakland County
108	2499	24.4	**Northville** (township) Wayne County
108	2499	24.4	**Pittsfield** (charter township) Washtenaw County
110	2582	24.6	**Birmingham** (city) Oakland County
110	2582	24.6	**Brighton** (township) Livingston County
110	2582	24.6	**White Lake** (charter township) Oakland County
113	2632	24.7	**Cadillac** (city) Wexford County
113	2632	24.7	**Fruitport** (charter township) Muskegon County
113	2632	24.7	**Grand Rapids** (city) Kent County
113	2632	24.7	**Lenox** (township) Macomb County
113	2632	24.7	**Melvindale** (city) Wayne County
113	2632	24.7	**Taylor** (city) Wayne County
119	2680	24.8	**Grandville** (city) Kent County
119	2680	24.8	**Lincoln Park** (city) Wayne County
119	2680	24.8	**Portage** (city) Kalamazoo County
122	2723	24.9	**Bay City** (city) Bay County
122	2723	24.9	**Oak Park** (city) Oakland County
122	2723	24.9	**Spring Lake** (township) Ottawa County
125	2766	25.0	**Dearborn Heights** (city) Wayne County
125	2766	25.0	**Jenison** (CDP) Ottawa County
125	2766	25.0	**Washington** (township) Macomb County
128	2816	25.1	**Beverly Hills** (village) Oakland County
128	2816	25.1	**Green Oak** (township) Livingston County
128	2816	25.1	**Plainfield** (charter township) Kent County
128	2816	25.1	**Rochester** (city) Oakland County
128	2816	25.1	**Southfield** (township) Oakland County
133	2860	25.2	**Huron** (charter township) Wayne County
133	2860	25.2	**Owosso** (city) Shiawassee County
135	2895	25.3	**DeWitt** (charter township) Clinton County
135	2895	25.3	**Hamburg** (township) Livingston County
137	2939	25.4	**Kentwood** (city) Kent County
137	2939	25.4	**Wixom** (city) Oakland County
139	2975	25.5	**Delhi** (charter township) Ingham County
139	2975	25.5	**Novi** (city) Oakland County
141	3014	25.6	**Niles** (city) Berrien County
141	3014	25.6	**Port Huron** (city) Saint Clair County
143	3055	25.7	**Eastpointe** (city) Macomb County
143	3055	25.7	**Holt** (CDP) Ingham County
145	3090	25.8	**Alpine** (township) Kent County
145	3090	25.8	**Comstock Park** (CDP) Kent County
147	3127	25.9	**Harper Woods** (city) Wayne County
148	3161	26.0	**Commerce** (charter township) Oakland County
148	3161	26.0	**Springfield** (charter township) Oakland County
150	3196	26.1	**Battle Creek** (city) Calhoun County

Note: The state column ranks the top/bottom 150 places from all places in the state with population of 10,000 or more. The national column ranks the top/bottom 150 places from all places in the country with population of 10,000 or more. Places that are unincorporated were not considered in the rankings. Please refer to the User Guide for additional information.

Population Age 65 and Over

Top 150 Places Ranked in *Descending* Order

State Rank	Nat'l Rank	Percent	Place	State Rank	Nat'l Rank	Percent	Place
1	161	22.6	**Riverview** (city) Wayne County	76	1911	13.9	**Davison** (township) Genesee County
2	191	22.0	**Monitor** (charter township) Bay County	76	1911	13.9	**Madison Heights** (city) Oakland County
3	204	21.7	**Bloomfield** (charter township) Oakland County	76	1911	13.9	**Sault Sainte Marie** (city) Chippewa County
4	269	20.4	**Garfield** (charter township) Grand Traverse County	79	1964	13.8	**Rochester Hills** (city) Oakland County
4	269	20.4	**Thomas** (township) Saginaw County	79	1964	13.8	**Troy** (city) Oakland County
6	320	19.9	**Saint Joseph** (charter township) Berrien County	79	1964	13.8	**Wyandotte** (city) Wayne County
7	331	19.8	**Trenton** (city) Wayne County	82	2011	13.7	**Birmingham** (city) Oakland County
8	341	19.7	**Saginaw** (charter township) Saginaw County	82	2011	13.7	**Blackman** (charter township) Jackson County
9	350	19.6	**Escanaba** (city) Delta County	82	2011	13.7	**Fenton** (charter township) Genesee County
10	373	19.4	**Alpena** (city) Alpena County	82	2011	13.7	**Harrison** (charter township) Macomb County
11	392	19.2	**Fort Gratiot** (charter township) Saint Clair County	82	2011	13.7	**Holland** (city) Ottawa County
11	392	19.2	**Grosse Ile** (township) Wayne County	82	2011	13.7	**Northview** (CDP) Kent County
11	392	19.2	**Saint Clair Shores** (city) Macomb County	88	2052	13.6	**Cooper** (charter township) Kalamazoo County
14	404	19.1	**Bangor** (charter township) Bay County	88	2052	13.6	**Fruitport** (charter township) Muskegon County
14	404	19.1	**Grand Haven** (city) Ottawa County	88	2052	13.6	**Portage** (city) Kalamazoo County
16	467	18.8	**Southfield** (township) Oakland County	91	2143	13.4	**Battle Creek** (city) Calhoun County
17	508	18.5	**Summit** (township) Jackson County	91	2143	13.4	**Frenchtown** (township) Monroe County
18	595	18.0	**Jenison** (CDP) Ottawa County	93	2183	13.3	**Comstock** (charter township) Kalamazoo County
19	635	17.8	**Norton Shores** (city) Muskegon County	93	2183	13.3	**Meridian** (charter township) Ingham County
20	659	17.7	**Grosse Pointe Woods** (city) Wayne County	93	2183	13.3	**Monroe** (city) Monroe County
20	659	17.7	**Livonia** (city) Wayne County	96	2220	13.2	**Burton** (city) Genesee County
22	741	17.4	**Beverly Hills** (village) Oakland County	96	2220	13.2	**Park** (township) Ottawa County
22	741	17.4	**West Bloomfield** (charter township) Oakland County	98	2260	13.1	**Port Huron** (city) Saint Clair County
24	762	17.3	**Niles** (township) Berrien County	98	2260	13.1	**Roseville** (city) Macomb County
25	786	17.2	**Allen Park** (city) Wayne County	98	2260	13.1	**Royal Oak** (city) Oakland County
25	786	17.2	**Flint** (charter township) Genesee County	101	2304	13.0	**Georgetown** (charter township) Ottawa County
27	820	17.1	**Cadillac** (city) Wexford County	101	2304	13.0	**Marquette** (city) Marquette County
28	848	17.0	**Spring Lake** (township) Ottawa County	101	2304	13.0	**Milford** (charter township) Oakland County
29	874	16.9	**Southfield** (city) Oakland County	101	2304	13.0	**Mount Clemens** (city) Macomb County
30	918	16.7	**Traverse City** (city) Grand Traverse County	101	2304	13.0	**Port Huron** (charter township) Saint Clair County
30	918	16.7	**Vienna** (charter township) Genesee County	106	2344	12.9	**Cutlerville** (CDP) Kent County
32	939	16.6	**Bridgeport** (charter township) Saginaw County	106	2344	12.9	**Kalamazoo** (charter township) Kalamazoo County
33	971	16.5	**Plymouth** (charter township) Wayne County	106	2344	12.9	**Oak Park** (city) Oakland County
34	1004	16.4	**Waverly** (CDP) Eaton County	109	2390	12.8	**Grosse Pointe Park** (city) Wayne County
35	1033	16.3	**Southgate** (city) Wayne County	109	2390	12.8	**Harper Woods** (city) Wayne County
36	1062	16.2	**Clinton** (charter township) Macomb County	109	2390	12.8	**Owosso** (city) Shiawassee County
36	1062	16.2	**Fraser** (city) Macomb County	109	2390	12.8	**Taylor** (city) Wayne County
38	1091	16.1	**Dearborn Heights** (city) Wayne County	113	2436	12.7	**Holly** (township) Oakland County
38	1091	16.1	**Warren** (city) Macomb County	114	2486	12.6	**Sturgis** (city) Saint Joseph County
40	1150	15.9	**Delta** (charter township) Eaton County	115	2538	12.5	**Waterford** (charter township) Oakland County
40	1150	15.9	**Farmington Hills** (city) Oakland County	115	2538	12.5	**Wayne** (city) Wayne County
42	1222	15.7	**Lincoln** (charter township) Berrien County	117	2582	12.4	**Beecher** (CDP) Genesee County
43	1258	15.6	**Midland** (city) Midland County	118	2628	12.3	**Bay City** (city) Bay County
44	1295	15.5	**Farmington** (city) Oakland County	118	2628	12.3	**Grand Blanc** (charter township) Genesee County
45	1355	15.3	**Grand Rapids** (charter township) Kent County	118	2628	12.3	**Okemos** (CDP) Ingham County
45	1355	15.3	**Northville** (township) Wayne County	118	2628	12.3	**Plainfield** (charter township) Kent County
47	1386	15.2	**Flushing** (charter township) Genesee County	122	2699	12.1	**Walker** (city) Kent County
47	1386	15.2	**Oshtemo** (charter township) Kalamazoo County	123	2738	12.0	**Dearborn** (city) Wayne County
47	1386	15.2	**Sterling Heights** (city) Macomb County	123	2738	12.0	**Redford** (charter township) Wayne County
50	1466	15.0	**Coldwater** (city) Branch County	123	2738	12.0	**Tyrone** (township) Livingston County
50	1466	15.0	**Genesee** (charter township) Genesee County	126	2780	11.9	**East Bay** (township) Grand Traverse County
50	1466	15.0	**Mundy** (township) Genesee County	126	2780	11.9	**Woodhaven** (city) Wayne County
53	1502	14.9	**Bedford** (township) Monroe County	128	2823	11.8	**Melvindale** (city) Wayne County
54	1532	14.8	**Clawson** (city) Oakland County	129	2868	11.7	**Brighton** (township) Livingston County
54	1532	14.8	**Emmett** (charter township) Calhoun County	129	2868	11.7	**Green Oak** (township) Livingston County
56	1615	14.6	**Benton** (charter township) Berrien County	129	2868	11.7	**Superior** (charter township) Washtenaw County
56	1615	14.6	**Grandville** (city) Kent County	132	2924	11.6	**Muskegon** (city) Muskegon County
58	1653	14.5	**Cascade** (charter township) Kent County	133	2957	11.5	**Detroit** (city) Wayne County
58	1653	14.5	**Haslett** (CDP) Ingham County	133	2957	11.5	**Independence** (charter township) Oakland County
58	1653	14.5	**Shelby** (charter township) Macomb County	133	2957	11.5	**Kentwood** (city) Kent County
61	1691	14.4	**Fenton** (city) Genesee County	133	2957	11.5	**Lincoln Park** (city) Wayne County
61	1691	14.4	**Genoa** (township) Livingston County	133	2957	11.5	**Oakland** (charter township) Oakland County
61	1691	14.4	**Highland Park** (city) Wayne County	133	2957	11.5	**Rochester** (city) Oakland County
61	1691	14.4	**Leoni** (township) Jackson County	139	2991	11.4	**Highland** (charter township) Oakland County
61	1691	14.4	**Monroe** (charter township) Monroe County	139	2991	11.4	**White Lake** (charter township) Oakland County
61	1691	14.4	**Niles** (city) Berrien County	141	3031	11.3	**Antwerp** (township) Van Buren County
67	1740	14.3	**Mount Morris** (township) Genesee County	141	3031	11.3	**Berkley** (city) Oakland County
68	1781	14.2	**Adrian** (city) Lenawee County	141	3031	11.3	**Eastpointe** (city) Macomb County
68	1781	14.2	**Muskegon** (charter township) Muskegon County	141	3031	11.3	**Grand Haven** (charter township) Ottawa County
70	1832	14.1	**Byron** (township) Kent County	141	3031	11.3	**Hazel Park** (city) Oakland County
70	1832	14.1	**South Lyon** (city) Oakland County	141	3031	11.3	**Inkster** (city) Wayne County
70	1832	14.1	**Washington** (township) Macomb County	141	3031	11.3	**Novi** (city) Oakland County
73	1865	14.0	**DeWitt** (charter township) Clinton County	148	3081	11.2	**Forest Hills** (CDP) Kent County
73	1865	14.0	**Garden City** (city) Wayne County	149	3125	11.1	**Grand Rapids** (city) Kent County
73	1865	14.0	**Westland** (city) Wayne County	150	3159	11.0	**Hamburg** (township) Livingston County

Note: The state column ranks the top/bottom 150 places from all places in the state with population of 10,000 or more. The national column ranks the top/bottom 150 places from all places in the country with population of 10,000 or more. Places that are unincorporated were not considered in the rankings. Please refer to the User Guide for additional information.

Population Age 65 and Over

Top 150 Places Ranked in *Ascending* Order

State Rank	Nat'l Rank	Percent	Place
1	41	4.2	**Allendale** (CDP) Ottawa County
1	41	4.2	**Allendale** (charter township) Ottawa County
3	222	6.3	**Union** (charter township) Isabella County
4	242	6.4	**East Lansing** (city) Ingham County
4	242	6.4	**Ionia** (city) Ionia County
6	258	6.5	**Big Rapids** (city) Mecosta County
7	348	7.0	**Wixom** (city) Oakland County
8	383	7.2	**Mount Pleasant** (city) Isabella County
9	481	7.7	**Benton Harbor** (city) Berrien County
9	481	7.7	**Hamtramck** (city) Wayne County
11	525	7.9	**Pittsfield** (charter township) Washtenaw County
12	614	8.3	**Ypsilanti** (city) Washtenaw County
13	671	8.5	**Brandon** (charter township) Oakland County
13	671	8.5	**Ypsilanti** (charter township) Washtenaw County
15	767	8.8	**Cannon** (township) Kent County
15	767	8.8	**Lenox** (township) Macomb County
15	767	8.8	**Van Buren** (charter township) Wayne County
18	801	8.9	**Canton** (charter township) Wayne County
18	801	8.9	**Ferndale** (city) Oakland County
18	801	8.9	**Holland** (charter township) Ottawa County
21	835	9.0	**Wyoming** (city) Kent County
22	861	9.1	**Oceola** (township) Livingston County
23	884	9.2	**Ada** (township) Kent County
24	912	9.3	**Ann Arbor** (city) Washtenaw County
24	912	9.3	**Macomb** (township) Macomb County
24	912	9.3	**Orion** (charter township) Oakland County
24	912	9.3	**Pontiac** (city) Oakland County
28	944	9.4	**Auburn Hills** (city) Oakland County
28	944	9.4	**Chesterfield** (township) Macomb County
28	944	9.4	**Kalamazoo** (city) Kalamazoo County
28	944	9.4	**Lyon** (charter township) Oakland County
32	976	9.5	**Comstock Park** (CDP) Kent County
33	997	9.6	**Muskegon Heights** (city) Muskegon County
34	1026	9.7	**Brownstown** (charter township) Wayne County
34	1026	9.7	**East Grand Rapids** (city) Kent County
34	1026	9.7	**Lansing** (city) Ingham County
37	1046	9.8	**New Baltimore** (city) Macomb County
37	1046	9.8	**Romulus** (city) Wayne County
39	1072	9.9	**Bath** (charter township) Clinton County
40	1094	10.0	**Oxford** (charter township) Oakland County
41	1137	10.1	**Caledonia** (township) Kent County
42	1195	10.3	**Jackson** (city) Jackson County
42	1195	10.3	**Springfield** (charter township) Oakland County
44	1230	10.4	**Huron** (charter township) Wayne County
45	1269	10.5	**Gaines** (charter township) Kent County
45	1269	10.5	**Texas** (charter township) Kalamazoo County
47	1306	10.6	**Commerce** (charter township) Oakland County
47	1306	10.6	**Hartland** (township) Livingston County
47	1306	10.6	**Holt** (CDP) Ingham County
50	1351	10.7	**Alpine** (township) Kent County
50	1351	10.7	**Flint** (city) Genesee County
52	1427	10.9	**Delhi** (charter township) Ingham County
52	1427	10.9	**Saginaw** (city) Saginaw County
52	1427	10.9	**Scio** (township) Washtenaw County
55	1467	11.0	**Hamburg** (township) Livingston County
56	1498	11.1	**Grand Rapids** (city) Kent County
57	1532	11.2	**Forest Hills** (CDP) Kent County
58	1576	11.3	**Antwerp** (township) Van Buren County
58	1576	11.3	**Berkley** (city) Oakland County
58	1576	11.3	**Eastpointe** (city) Macomb County
58	1576	11.3	**Grand Haven** (charter township) Ottawa County
58	1576	11.3	**Hazel Park** (city) Oakland County
58	1576	11.3	**Inkster** (city) Wayne County
58	1576	11.3	**Novi** (city) Oakland County
65	1626	11.4	**Highland** (charter township) Oakland County
65	1626	11.4	**White Lake** (charter township) Oakland County
67	1666	11.5	**Detroit** (city) Wayne County
67	1666	11.5	**Independence** (charter township) Oakland County
67	1666	11.5	**Kentwood** (city) Kent County
67	1666	11.5	**Lincoln Park** (city) Wayne County
67	1666	11.5	**Oakland** (charter township) Oakland County
67	1666	11.5	**Rochester** (city) Oakland County
73	1700	11.6	**Muskegon** (city) Muskegon County
74	1733	11.7	**Brighton** (township) Livingston County
74	1733	11.7	**Green Oak** (township) Livingston County
74	1733	11.7	**Superior** (charter township) Washtenaw County
77	1789	11.8	**Melvindale** (city) Wayne County
78	1834	11.9	**East Bay** (township) Grand Traverse County
78	1834	11.9	**Woodhaven** (city) Wayne County
80	1877	12.0	**Dearborn** (city) Wayne County
80	1877	12.0	**Redford** (charter township) Wayne County
80	1877	12.0	**Tyrone** (township) Livingston County
83	1919	12.1	**Walker** (city) Kent County
84	1992	12.3	**Bay City** (city) Bay County
84	1992	12.3	**Grand Blanc** (charter township) Genesee County
84	1992	12.3	**Okemos** (CDP) Ingham County
84	1992	12.3	**Plainfield** (charter township) Kent County
88	2029	12.4	**Beecher** (CDP) Genesee County
89	2075	12.5	**Waterford** (charter township) Oakland County
89	2075	12.5	**Wayne** (city) Wayne County
91	2119	12.6	**Sturgis** (city) Saint Joseph County
92	2171	12.7	**Holly** (township) Oakland County
93	2221	12.8	**Grosse Pointe Park** (city) Wayne County
93	2221	12.8	**Harper Woods** (city) Wayne County
93	2221	12.8	**Owosso** (city) Shiawassee County
93	2221	12.8	**Taylor** (city) Wayne County
97	2267	12.9	**Cutlerville** (CDP) Kent County
97	2267	12.9	**Kalamazoo** (charter township) Kalamazoo County
97	2267	12.9	**Oak Park** (city) Oakland County
100	2313	13.0	**Georgetown** (charter township) Ottawa County
100	2313	13.0	**Marquette** (city) Marquette County
100	2313	13.0	**Milford** (charter township) Oakland County
100	2313	13.0	**Mount Clemens** (city) Macomb County
100	2313	13.0	**Port Huron** (charter township) Saint Clair County
105	2353	13.1	**Port Huron** (city) Saint Clair County
105	2353	13.1	**Roseville** (city) Macomb County
105	2353	13.1	**Royal Oak** (city) Oakland County
108	2397	13.2	**Burton** (city) Genesee County
108	2397	13.2	**Park** (township) Ottawa County
110	2437	13.3	**Comstock** (charter township) Kalamazoo County
110	2437	13.3	**Meridian** (charter township) Ingham County
110	2437	13.3	**Monroe** (city) Monroe County
113	2474	13.4	**Battle Creek** (city) Calhoun County
113	2474	13.4	**Frenchtown** (township) Monroe County
115	2562	13.6	**Cooper** (charter township) Kalamazoo County
115	2562	13.6	**Fruitport** (charter township) Muskegon County
115	2562	13.6	**Portage** (city) Kalamazoo County
118	2605	13.7	**Birmingham** (city) Oakland County
118	2605	13.7	**Blackman** (charter township) Jackson County
118	2605	13.7	**Fenton** (charter township) Genesee County
118	2605	13.7	**Harrison** (charter township) Macomb County
118	2605	13.7	**Holland** (city) Ottawa County
118	2605	13.7	**Northview** (CDP) Kent County
124	2646	13.8	**Rochester Hills** (city) Oakland County
124	2646	13.8	**Troy** (city) Oakland County
124	2646	13.8	**Wyandotte** (city) Wayne County
127	2693	13.9	**Davison** (township) Genesee County
127	2693	13.9	**Madison Heights** (city) Oakland County
127	2693	13.9	**Sault Sainte Marie** (city) Chippewa County
130	2746	14.0	**DeWitt** (charter township) Clinton County
130	2746	14.0	**Garden City** (city) Wayne County
130	2746	14.0	**Westland** (city) Wayne County
133	2792	14.1	**Byron** (township) Kent County
133	2792	14.1	**South Lyon** (city) Oakland County
133	2792	14.1	**Washington** (township) Macomb County
136	2825	14.2	**Adrian** (city) Lenawee County
136	2825	14.2	**Muskegon** (charter township) Muskegon County
138	2876	14.3	**Mount Morris** (township) Genesee County
139	2917	14.4	**Fenton** (city) Genesee County
139	2917	14.4	**Genoa** (township) Livingston County
139	2917	14.4	**Highland Park** (city) Wayne County
139	2917	14.4	**Leoni** (township) Jackson County
139	2917	14.4	**Monroe** (charter township) Monroe County
139	2917	14.4	**Niles** (city) Berrien County
145	2966	14.5	**Cascade** (charter township) Kent County
145	2966	14.5	**Haslett** (CDP) Ingham County
145	2966	14.5	**Shelby** (charter township) Macomb County
148	3004	14.6	**Benton** (charter township) Berrien County
148	3004	14.6	**Grandville** (city) Kent County
150	3083	14.8	**Clawson** (city) Oakland County

Note: The state column ranks the top/bottom 150 places from all places in the state with population of 10,000 or more. The national column ranks the top/bottom 150 places from all places in the country with population of 10,000 or more. Places that are unincorporated were not considered in the rankings. Please refer to the User Guide for additional information.

Males per 100 Females

Top 150 Places Ranked in *Descending* Order

State Rank	Nat'l Rank	Ratio	Place
1	6	246.1	**Ionia** (city) Ionia County
2	17	164.4	**Blackman** (charter township) Jackson County
3	68	123.5	**Lenox** (township) Macomb County
4	159	108.9	**Muskegon** (city) Muskegon County
5	179	107.7	**Marquette** (city) Marquette County
6	206	106.5	**Hamtramck** (city) Wayne County
7	214	106.2	**Mount Clemens** (city) Macomb County
8	285	104.2	**Big Rapids** (city) Mecosta County
9	297	103.8	**Brighton** (township) Livingston County
10	391	102.4	**Caledonia** (township) Kent County
11	413	102.1	**Tyrone** (township) Livingston County
12	441	101.8	**Hamburg** (township) Livingston County
13	457	101.6	**Hartland** (township) Livingston County
14	501	101.1	**Green Oak** (township) Livingston County
14	501	101.1	**Springfield** (charter township) Oakland County
16	538	100.8	**Huron** (charter township) Wayne County
17	548	100.7	**Brandon** (charter township) Oakland County
17	548	100.7	**Highland** (charter township) Oakland County
19	560	100.6	**Oceola** (township) Livingston County
20	638	100.1	**Oakland** (charter township) Oakland County
21	653	100.0	**Lyon** (charter township) Oakland County
22	683	99.8	**Leoni** (township) Jackson County
23	697	99.7	**Ferndale** (city) Oakland County
23	697	99.7	**Holland** (charter township) Ottawa County
25	715	99.6	**Cannon** (township) Kent County
26	736	99.5	**Wixom** (city) Oakland County
27	753	99.4	**Emmett** (charter township) Calhoun County
27	753	99.4	**Port Huron** (charter township) Saint Clair County
29	830	99.0	**Fenton** (charter township) Genesee County
29	830	99.0	**Texas** (charter township) Kalamazoo County
31	851	98.9	**Commerce** (charter township) Oakland County
31	851	98.9	**Ypsilanti** (city) Washtenaw County
33	893	98.7	**White Lake** (charter township) Oakland County
34	921	98.6	**East Bay** (township) Grand Traverse County
35	974	98.4	**Byron** (township) Kent County
36	995	98.3	**Orion** (charter township) Oakland County
37	1043	98.1	**Fruitport** (charter township) Muskegon County
37	1043	98.1	**Macomb** (township) Macomb County
39	1070	98.0	**Forest Hills** (CDP) Kent County
39	1070	98.0	**Grand Haven** (charter township) Ottawa County
39	1070	98.0	**Oxford** (charter township) Oakland County
39	1070	98.0	**Woodhaven** (city) Wayne County
43	1086	97.9	**Park** (township) Ottawa County
44	1115	97.8	**Ada** (township) Kent County
44	1115	97.8	**Dearborn** (city) Wayne County
46	1140	97.7	**Independence** (charter township) Oakland County
47	1187	97.5	**Hazel Park** (city) Oakland County
47	1187	97.5	**Pittsfield** (charter township) Washtenaw County
49	1217	97.4	**Kalamazoo** (city) Kalamazoo County
50	1244	97.3	**Cascade** (charter township) Kent County
50	1244	97.3	**Wyoming** (city) Kent County
52	1281	97.2	**Ann Arbor** (city) Washtenaw County
52	1281	97.2	**Frenchtown** (township) Monroe County
54	1311	97.1	**Harrison** (charter township) Macomb County
54	1311	97.1	**Holly** (township) Oakland County
56	1345	97.0	**Flushing** (charter township) Genesee County
56	1345	97.0	**Troy** (city) Oakland County
58	1382	96.9	**Vienna** (charter township) Genesee County
59	1413	96.8	**Comstock** (charter township) Kalamazoo County
59	1413	96.8	**Highland Park** (city) Wayne County
61	1504	96.5	**Shelby** (charter township) Macomb County
62	1532	96.4	**Gaines** (charter township) Kent County
62	1532	96.4	**Garden City** (city) Wayne County
62	1532	96.4	**Pontiac** (city) Oakland County
65	1574	96.3	**Cooper** (charter township) Kalamazoo County
65	1574	96.3	**Madison Heights** (city) Oakland County
67	1598	96.2	**Antwerp** (township) Van Buren County
67	1598	96.2	**Lincoln Park** (city) Wayne County
67	1598	96.2	**Royal Oak** (city) Oakland County
70	1647	96.1	**Chesterfield** (township) Macomb County
70	1647	96.1	**DeWitt** (charter township) Clinton County
70	1647	96.1	**Genoa** (township) Livingston County
70	1647	96.1	**Waterford** (charter township) Oakland County
74	1685	96.0	**Grosse Ile** (township) Wayne County
74	1685	96.0	**Kalamazoo** (charter township) Kalamazoo County
76	1730	95.9	**Clawson** (city) Oakland County
76	1730	95.9	**New Baltimore** (city) Macomb County
76	1730	95.9	**Washington** (township) Macomb County
79	1769	95.8	**Bedford** (township) Monroe County
79	1769	95.8	**Wyandotte** (city) Wayne County
81	1809	95.7	**Cutlerville** (CDP) Kent County
82	1839	95.6	**Alpine** (township) Kent County
82	1839	95.6	**Brownstown** (charter township) Wayne County
84	1882	95.5	**Canton** (charter township) Wayne County
84	1882	95.5	**Monroe** (charter township) Monroe County
86	1923	95.4	**Mundy** (township) Genesee County
87	1954	95.3	**Burton** (city) Genesee County
88	2001	95.2	**Lincoln** (charter township) Berrien County
88	2001	95.2	**Milford** (charter township) Oakland County
90	2089	95.0	**Bay City** (city) Bay County
90	2089	95.0	**Walker** (city) Kent County
92	2117	94.9	**Genesee** (charter township) Genesee County
92	2117	94.9	**Grand Rapids** (city) Kent County
94	2171	94.8	**Redford** (charter township) Wayne County
95	2207	94.7	**Georgetown** (charter township) Ottawa County
96	2254	94.6	**Plainfield** (charter township) Kent County
97	2299	94.5	**Plymouth** (charter township) Wayne County
98	2330	94.4	**Norton Shores** (city) Muskegon County
99	2363	94.3	**East Lansing** (city) Ingham County
100	2431	94.1	**Sault Sainte Marie** (city) Chippewa County
100	2431	94.1	**Sterling Heights** (city) Macomb County
102	2526	93.9	**Grosse Pointe Park** (city) Wayne County
103	2575	93.8	**Auburn Hills** (city) Oakland County
103	2575	93.8	**Eastpointe** (city) Macomb County
103	2575	93.8	**Grand Rapids** (charter township) Kent County
103	2575	93.8	**Lansing** (city) Ingham County
103	2575	93.8	**Roseville** (city) Macomb County
103	2575	93.8	**Warren** (city) Macomb County
109	2620	93.7	**Novi** (city) Oakland County
109	2620	93.7	**Owosso** (city) Shiawassee County
109	2620	93.7	**Rochester Hills** (city) Oakland County
109	2620	93.7	**Thomas** (township) Saginaw County
109	2620	93.7	**Van Buren** (charter township) Wayne County
114	2672	93.6	**Dearborn Heights** (city) Wayne County
114	2672	93.6	**East Grand Rapids** (city) Kent County
114	2672	93.6	**Grandville** (city) Kent County
114	2672	93.6	**Livonia** (city) Wayne County
114	2672	93.6	**Niles** (township) Berrien County
114	2672	93.6	**Romulus** (city) Wayne County
114	2672	93.6	**Scio** (township) Washtenaw County
114	2672	93.6	**Southfield** (township) Oakland County
122	2760	93.4	**Comstock Park** (CDP) Kent County
122	2760	93.4	**Ypsilanti** (charter township) Washtenaw County
124	2806	93.3	**Bloomfield** (charter township) Oakland County
124	2806	93.3	**Grand Blanc** (charter township) Genesee County
124	2806	93.3	**West Bloomfield** (charter township) Oakland County
127	2846	93.2	**Delhi** (charter township) Ingham County
127	2846	93.2	**Spring Lake** (township) Ottawa County
129	2894	93.1	**Muskegon** (charter township) Muskegon County
129	2894	93.1	**Wayne** (city) Wayne County
131	2929	93.0	**Jenison** (CDP) Ottawa County
132	2989	92.8	**Okemos** (CDP) Ingham County
132	2989	92.8	**Saint Joseph** (charter township) Berrien County
134	3028	92.7	**Allen Park** (city) Wayne County
134	3028	92.7	**Birmingham** (city) Oakland County
136	3076	92.6	**Holt** (CDP) Ingham County
136	3076	92.6	**Melvindale** (city) Wayne County
136	3076	92.6	**Midland** (city) Midland County
136	3076	92.6	**Trenton** (city) Wayne County
140	3144	92.4	**Monitor** (charter township) Bay County
141	3199	92.2	**Flint** (city) Genesee County
141	3199	92.2	**Kentwood** (city) Kent County
141	3199	92.2	**Mount Morris** (township) Genesee County
141	3199	92.2	**Rochester** (city) Oakland County
145	3243	92.1	**Portage** (city) Kalamazoo County
145	3243	92.1	**Union** (charter township) Isabella County
147	3314	91.9	**Battle Creek** (city) Calhoun County
147	3314	91.9	**Summit** (township) Jackson County
149	3357	91.8	**Beecher** (CDP) Genesee County
149	3357	91.8	**Berkley** (city) Oakland County

Note: The state column ranks the top/bottom 150 places from all places in the state with population of 10,000 or more. The national column ranks the top/bottom 150 places from all places in the country with population of 10,000 or more. Places that are unincorporated were not considered in the rankings. Please refer to the User Guide for additional information.

Males per 100 Females

Top 150 Places Ranked in *Ascending* Order

State Rank	Nat'l Rank	Ratio	Place	State Rank	Nat'l Rank	Ratio	Place
1	43	80.8	**Southfield** (city) Oakland County	75	1728	93.1	**Wayne** (city) Wayne County
2	73	82.2	**Oak Park** (city) Oakland County	77	1763	93.2	**Delhi** (charter township) Ingham County
3	137	84.4	**Garfield** (charter township) Grand Traverse County	77	1763	93.2	**Spring Lake** (township) Ottawa County
4	165	84.8	**Allendale** (CDP) Ottawa County	79	1811	93.3	**Bloomfield** (charter township) Oakland County
5	237	85.9	**Harper Woods** (city) Wayne County	79	1811	93.3	**Grand Blanc** (charter township) Genesee County
6	245	86.0	**Allendale** (charter township) Ottawa County	79	1811	93.3	**West Bloomfield** (charter township) Oakland County
7	253	86.1	**Muskegon Heights** (city) Muskegon County	82	1851	93.4	**Comstock Park** (CDP) Kent County
8	286	86.6	**Fraser** (city) Macomb County	82	1851	93.4	**Ypsilanti** (charter township) Washtenaw County
8	286	86.6	**Riverview** (city) Wayne County	84	1940	93.6	**Dearborn Heights** (city) Wayne County
10	313	86.8	**Flint** (charter township) Genesee County	84	1940	93.6	**East Grand Rapids** (city) Kent County
11	328	86.9	**Benton Harbor** (city) Berrien County	84	1940	93.6	**Grandville** (city) Kent County
12	401	87.7	**South Lyon** (city) Oakland County	84	1940	93.6	**Livonia** (city) Wayne County
13	452	88.1	**Fenton** (city) Genesee County	84	1940	93.6	**Niles** (township) Berrien County
13	452	88.1	**Inkster** (city) Wayne County	84	1940	93.6	**Romulus** (city) Wayne County
15	478	88.3	**Saginaw** (charter township) Saginaw County	84	1940	93.6	**Scio** (township) Washtenaw County
16	521	88.6	**Clinton** (charter township) Macomb County	84	1940	93.6	**Southfield** (township) Oakland County
17	549	88.8	**Monroe** (city) Monroe County	92	1985	93.7	**Novi** (city) Oakland County
18	587	89.0	**Escanaba** (city) Delta County	92	1985	93.7	**Owosso** (city) Shiawassee County
18	587	89.0	**Haslett** (CDP) Ingham County	92	1985	93.7	**Rochester Hills** (city) Oakland County
20	606	89.1	**Farmington Hills** (city) Oakland County	92	1985	93.7	**Thomas** (township) Saginaw County
20	606	89.1	**Niles** (city) Berrien County	92	1985	93.7	**Van Buren** (charter township) Wayne County
20	606	89.1	**Saginaw** (city) Saginaw County	97	2037	93.8	**Auburn Hills** (city) Oakland County
23	655	89.4	**Farmington** (city) Oakland County	97	2037	93.8	**Eastpointe** (city) Macomb County
24	689	89.6	**Waverly** (CDP) Eaton County	97	2037	93.8	**Grand Rapids** (charter township) Kent County
25	734	89.8	**Detroit** (city) Wayne County	97	2037	93.8	**Lansing** (city) Ingham County
25	734	89.8	**Sturgis** (city) Saint Joseph County	97	2037	93.8	**Roseville** (city) Macomb County
27	774	90.0	**Grand Haven** (city) Ottawa County	97	2037	93.8	**Warren** (city) Macomb County
27	774	90.0	**Mount Pleasant** (city) Isabella County	103	2082	93.9	**Grosse Pointe Park** (city) Wayne County
27	774	90.0	**Traverse City** (city) Grand Traverse County	104	2182	94.1	**Sault Sainte Marie** (city) Chippewa County
30	822	90.2	**Cadillac** (city) Wexford County	104	2182	94.1	**Sterling Heights** (city) Macomb County
31	838	90.3	**Bath** (charter township) Clinton County	106	2258	94.3	**East Lansing** (city) Ingham County
32	869	90.4	**Westland** (city) Wayne County	107	2294	94.4	**Norton Shores** (city) Muskegon County
33	921	90.6	**Fort Gratiot** (charter township) Saint Clair County	108	2327	94.5	**Plymouth** (charter township) Wayne County
33	921	90.6	**Holland** (city) Ottawa County	109	2358	94.6	**Plainfield** (charter township) Kent County
35	951	90.7	**Meridian** (charter township) Ingham County	110	2403	94.7	**Georgetown** (charter township) Ottawa County
36	999	90.9	**Oshtemo** (charter township) Kalamazoo County	111	2450	94.8	**Redford** (charter township) Wayne County
37	1024	91.0	**Benton** (charter township) Berrien County	112	2486	94.9	**Genesee** (charter township) Genesee County
37	1024	91.0	**Superior** (charter township) Washtenaw County	112	2486	94.9	**Grand Rapids** (city) Kent County
39	1059	91.1	**Alpena** (city) Alpena County	114	2540	95.0	**Bay City** (city) Bay County
39	1059	91.1	**Northview** (CDP) Kent County	114	2540	95.0	**Walker** (city) Kent County
41	1091	91.2	**Davison** (township) Genesee County	116	2609	95.2	**Lincoln** (charter township) Berrien County
41	1091	91.2	**Jackson** (city) Jackson County	116	2609	95.2	**Milford** (charter township) Oakland County
43	1142	91.4	**Adrian** (city) Lenawee County	118	2656	95.3	**Burton** (city) Genesee County
43	1142	91.4	**Coldwater** (city) Branch County	119	2703	95.4	**Mundy** (township) Genesee County
45	1176	91.5	**Beverly Hills** (village) Oakland County	120	2734	95.5	**Canton** (charter township) Wayne County
45	1176	91.5	**Delta** (charter township) Eaton County	120	2734	95.5	**Monroe** (charter township) Monroe County
45	1176	91.5	**Port Huron** (city) Saint Clair County	122	2775	95.6	**Alpine** (township) Kent County
45	1176	91.5	**Saint Clair Shores** (city) Macomb County	122	2775	95.6	**Brownstown** (charter township) Wayne County
45	1176	91.5	**Southgate** (city) Wayne County	124	2818	95.7	**Cutlerville** (CDP) Kent County
50	1206	91.6	**Bangor** (charter township) Bay County	125	2848	95.8	**Bedford** (township) Monroe County
51	1264	91.8	**Beecher** (CDP) Genesee County	125	2848	95.8	**Wyandotte** (city) Wayne County
51	1264	91.8	**Berkley** (city) Oakland County	127	2888	95.9	**Clawson** (city) Oakland County
51	1264	91.8	**Bridgeport** (charter township) Saginaw County	127	2888	95.9	**New Baltimore** (city) Macomb County
51	1264	91.8	**Grosse Pointe Woods** (city) Wayne County	127	2888	95.9	**Washington** (township) Macomb County
51	1264	91.8	**Northville** (township) Wayne County	130	2927	96.0	**Grosse Ile** (township) Wayne County
51	1264	91.8	**Taylor** (city) Wayne County	130	2927	96.0	**Kalamazoo** (charter township) Kalamazoo County
57	1300	91.9	**Battle Creek** (city) Calhoun County	132	2972	96.1	**Chesterfield** (township) Macomb County
57	1300	91.9	**Summit** (township) Jackson County	132	2972	96.1	**DeWitt** (charter township) Clinton County
59	1381	92.1	**Portage** (city) Kalamazoo County	132	2972	96.1	**Genoa** (township) Livingston County
59	1381	92.1	**Union** (charter township) Isabella County	132	2972	96.1	**Waterford** (charter township) Oakland County
61	1414	92.2	**Flint** (city) Genesee County	136	3010	96.2	**Antwerp** (township) Van Buren County
61	1414	92.2	**Kentwood** (city) Kent County	136	3010	96.2	**Lincoln Park** (city) Wayne County
61	1414	92.2	**Mount Morris** (township) Genesee County	136	3010	96.2	**Royal Oak** (city) Oakland County
61	1414	92.2	**Rochester** (city) Oakland County	139	3059	96.3	**Cooper** (charter township) Kalamazoo County
65	1487	92.4	**Monitor** (charter township) Bay County	139	3059	96.3	**Madison Heights** (city) Oakland County
66	1546	92.6	**Holt** (CDP) Ingham County	141	3083	96.4	**Gaines** (charter township) Kent County
66	1546	92.6	**Melvindale** (city) Wayne County	141	3083	96.4	**Garden City** (city) Wayne County
66	1546	92.6	**Midland** (city) Midland County	141	3083	96.4	**Pontiac** (city) Oakland County
66	1546	92.6	**Trenton** (city) Wayne County	144	3125	96.5	**Shelby** (charter township) Macomb County
70	1581	92.7	**Allen Park** (city) Wayne County	145	3216	96.8	**Comstock** (charter township) Kalamazoo County
70	1581	92.7	**Birmingham** (city) Oakland County	145	3216	96.8	**Highland Park** (city) Wayne County
72	1629	92.8	**Okemos** (CDP) Ingham County	147	3244	96.9	**Vienna** (charter township) Genesee County
72	1629	92.8	**Saint Joseph** (charter township) Berrien County	148	3275	97.0	**Flushing** (charter township) Genesee County
74	1695	93.0	**Jenison** (CDP) Ottawa County	148	3275	97.0	**Troy** (city) Oakland County
75	1728	93.1	**Muskegon** (charter township) Muskegon County	150	3312	97.1	**Harrison** (charter township) Macomb County

Note: The state column ranks the top/bottom 150 places from all places in the state with population of 10,000 or more. The national column ranks the top/bottom 150 places from all places in the country with population of 10,000 or more. Places that are unincorporated were not considered in the rankings. Please refer to the User Guide for additional information.

Marriage Status: Never Married

Top 150 Places Ranked in *Descending* Order

State Rank	Nat'l Rank	Percent	Place	State Rank	Nat'l Rank	Percent	Place
1	11	76.7	**East Lansing** (city) Ingham County	76	1847	31.8	**Haslett** (CDP) Ingham County
2	22	68.4	**Big Rapids** (city) Mecosta County	77	1905	31.6	**Rochester** (city) Oakland County
3	25	67.9	**Mount Pleasant** (city) Isabella County	78	1929	31.5	**Berkley** (city) Oakland County
4	31	66.2	**Union** (charter township) Isabella County	78	1929	31.5	**Clawson** (city) Oakland County
5	38	64.2	**Ypsilanti** (city) Washtenaw County	78	1929	31.5	**Coldwater** (city) Branch County
6	46	61.2	**Allendale** (CDP) Ottawa County	81	1984	31.3	**Madison Heights** (city) Oakland County
7	54	59.9	**Allendale** (charter township) Ottawa County	81	1984	31.3	**Monroe** (city) Monroe County
8	68	57.6	**Benton Harbor** (city) Berrien County	83	2048	31.0	**Dearborn Heights** (city) Wayne County
9	97	55.5	**Kalamazoo** (city) Kalamazoo County	84	2072	30.9	**Burton** (city) Genesee County
10	100	55.1	**Ann Arbor** (city) Washtenaw County	84	2072	30.9	**Davison** (township) Genesee County
11	127	53.2	**Detroit** (city) Wayne County	86	2130	30.7	**Dearborn** (city) Wayne County
12	145	52.5	**Highland Park** (city) Wayne County	86	2130	30.7	**Garden City** (city) Wayne County
13	169	51.1	**Marquette** (city) Marquette County	88	2173	30.5	**Niles** (township) Berrien County
14	187	50.2	**Beecher** (CDP) Genesee County	88	2173	30.5	**Wyandotte** (city) Wayne County
15	190	49.9	**Ionia** (city) Ionia County	90	2192	30.4	**Waverly** (CDP) Eaton County
16	228	48.1	**Muskegon Heights** (city) Muskegon County	91	2241	30.2	**Waterford** (charter township) Oakland County
17	233	48.0	**Flint** (city) Genesee County	92	2357	29.8	**Genesee** (charter township) Genesee County
18	254	47.4	**Pontiac** (city) Oakland County	92	2357	29.8	**Midland** (city) Midland County
19	265	47.2	**Inkster** (city) Wayne County	94	2380	29.7	**Alpena** (city) Alpena County
20	306	45.7	**Ferndale** (city) Oakland County	94	2380	29.7	**Bridgeport** (charter township) Saginaw County
21	315	45.5	**Saginaw** (city) Saginaw County	96	2423	29.5	**Fenton** (city) Genesee County
22	385	43.7	**Adrian** (city) Lenawee County	96	2423	29.5	**Grosse Pointe Park** (city) Wayne County
22	385	43.7	**Grand Rapids** (city) Kent County	98	2459	29.4	**Harrison** (charter township) Macomb County
24	394	43.6	**Muskegon** (city) Muskegon County	98	2459	29.4	**Woodhaven** (city) Wayne County
25	412	43.3	**Lansing** (city) Ingham County	100	2491	29.3	**Sterling Heights** (city) Macomb County
26	416	43.2	**Harper Woods** (city) Wayne County	101	2512	29.2	**Allen Park** (city) Wayne County
27	508	41.7	**Mount Clemens** (city) Macomb County	101	2512	29.2	**Delta** (charter township) Eaton County
28	532	41.3	**Ypsilanti** (charter township) Washtenaw County	103	2541	29.1	**Saint Clair Shores** (city) Macomb County
29	553	41.0	**Oshtemo** (charter township) Kalamazoo County	104	2567	29.0	**Comstock** (charter township) Kalamazoo County
30	576	40.8	**Bath** (charter township) Clinton County	104	2567	29.0	**Grandville** (city) Kent County
31	614	40.3	**Oak Park** (city) Oakland County	104	2567	29.0	**Leoni** (township) Jackson County
32	633	40.1	**Jackson** (city) Jackson County	107	2587	28.9	**Garfield** (charter township) Grand Traverse County
33	689	39.3	**Romulus** (city) Wayne County	107	2587	28.9	**Monroe** (charter township) Monroe County
34	714	39.0	**Comstock Park** (CDP) Kent County	107	2587	28.9	**Muskegon** (charter township) Muskegon County
35	730	38.9	**Hazel Park** (city) Oakland County	107	2587	28.9	**Northview** (CDP) Kent County
36	743	38.8	**Holland** (city) Ottawa County	111	2646	28.7	**Cooper** (charter township) Kalamazoo County
37	754	38.7	**Eastpointe** (city) Macomb County	111	2646	28.7	**Frenchtown** (township) Monroe County
38	783	38.4	**Pittsfield** (charter township) Washtenaw County	111	2646	28.7	**Portage** (city) Kalamazoo County
39	793	38.3	**Alpine** (township) Kent County	114	2681	28.6	**Holland** (charter township) Ottawa County
39	793	38.3	**Sault Sainte Marie** (city) Chippewa County	115	2746	28.4	**East Bay** (township) Grand Traverse County
41	839	37.8	**Royal Oak** (city) Oakland County	115	2746	28.4	**Saginaw** (charter township) Saginaw County
42	894	37.4	**Auburn Hills** (city) Oakland County	117	2776	28.3	**Fraser** (city) Macomb County
43	913	37.2	**Hamtramck** (city) Wayne County	118	2802	28.2	**Gaines** (charter township) Kent County
43	913	37.2	**Van Buren** (charter township) Wayne County	119	2834	28.1	**Escanaba** (city) Delta County
45	924	37.1	**Mount Morris** (township) Genesee County	120	2866	28.0	**Canton** (charter township) Wayne County
46	1001	36.5	**Southfield** (city) Oakland County	121	2954	27.7	**Farmington** (city) Oakland County
47	1040	36.2	**Bay City** (city) Bay County	122	2984	27.6	**Emmett** (charter township) Calhoun County
47	1040	36.2	**Melvindale** (city) Wayne County	123	3022	27.5	**Vienna** (charter township) Genesee County
47	1040	36.2	**Redford** (charter township) Wayne County	124	3100	27.2	**Livonia** (city) Wayne County
50	1058	36.1	**Roseville** (city) Macomb County	125	3134	27.1	**Independence** (charter township) Oakland County
50	1058	36.1	**Wixom** (city) Oakland County	126	3155	27.0	**Port Huron** (charter township) Saint Clair County
52	1141	35.4	**Taylor** (city) Wayne County	127	3174	26.9	**Grand Blanc** (charter township) Genesee County
53	1158	35.3	**Benton** (charter township) Berrien County	127	3174	26.9	**Riverview** (city) Wayne County
53	1158	35.3	**Westland** (city) Wayne County	129	3201	26.8	**Plainfield** (charter township) Kent County
55	1192	35.1	**Lenox** (township) Macomb County	129	3201	26.8	**Shelby** (charter township) Macomb County
56	1228	34.9	**Kentwood** (city) Kent County	131	3238	26.7	**Holly** (township) Oakland County
57	1312	34.4	**Port Huron** (city) Saint Clair County	132	3265	26.6	**Fort Gratiot** (charter township) Saint Clair County
57	1312	34.4	**Warren** (city) Macomb County	133	3330	26.4	**Farmington Hills** (city) Oakland County
59	1342	34.3	**Blackman** (charter township) Jackson County	133	3330	26.4	**West Bloomfield** (charter township) Oakland County
59	1342	34.3	**Lincoln Park** (city) Wayne County	135	3359	26.3	**Chesterfield** (township) Macomb County
61	1388	34.1	**Niles** (city) Berrien County	136	3376	26.2	**Rochester Hills** (city) Oakland County
62	1471	33.6	**Traverse City** (city) Grand Traverse County	137	3403	26.1	**Milford** (charter township) Oakland County
63	1488	33.5	**Wyoming** (city) Kent County	138	3430	26.0	**DeWitt** (charter township) Clinton County
64	1544	33.2	**Southgate** (city) Wayne County	139	3469	25.8	**Brighton** (township) Livingston County
65	1597	32.9	**Flint** (charter township) Genesee County	139	3469	25.8	**Grosse Pointe Woods** (city) Wayne County
66	1619	32.8	**Okemos** (CDP) Ingham County	141	3493	25.7	**Brownstown** (charter township) Wayne County
67	1639	32.7	**Kalamazoo** (charter township) Kalamazoo County	142	3516	25.6	**Brandon** (charter township) Oakland County
67	1639	32.7	**Owosso** (city) Shiawassee County	142	3516	25.6	**Sturgis** (city) Saint Joseph County
69	1661	32.6	**Walker** (city) Kent County	144	3551	25.5	**Antwerp** (township) Van Buren County
70	1679	32.5	**Meridian** (charter township) Ingham County	144	3551	25.5	**Novi** (city) Oakland County
71	1742	32.2	**Battle Creek** (city) Calhoun County	144	3551	25.5	**Orion** (charter township) Oakland County
72	1768	32.1	**Cutlerville** (CDP) Kent County	147	3574	25.4	**Huron** (charter township) Wayne County
73	1793	32.0	**Clinton** (charter township) Macomb County	147	3574	25.4	**Macomb** (township) Macomb County
74	1810	31.9	**Superior** (charter township) Washtenaw County	147	3574	25.4	**Norton Shores** (city) Muskegon County
74	1810	31.9	**Wayne** (city) Wayne County	150	3602	25.3	**Lyon** (charter township) Oakland County

Note: The state column ranks the top/bottom 150 places from all places in the state with population of 10,000 or more. The national column ranks the top/bottom 150 places from all places in the country with population of 10,000 or more. Places that are unincorporated were not considered in the rankings. Please refer to the User Guide for additional information.

Marriage Status: Never Married

Top 150 Places Ranked in *Ascending* Order

State Rank	Nat'l Rank	Percent	Place	State Rank	Nat'l Rank	Percent	Place
1	47	17.8	Cascade (charter township) Kent County	75	1419	26.8	Shelby (charter township) Macomb County
2	49	17.9	Saint Joseph (charter township) Berrien County	77	1456	26.9	Grand Blanc (charter township) Genesee County
3	60	18.2	Grosse Ile (township) Wayne County	77	1456	26.9	Riverview (city) Wayne County
4	86	18.9	Forest Hills (CDP) Kent County	79	1483	27.0	Port Huron (charter township) Saint Clair County
5	104	19.4	East Grand Rapids (city) Kent County	80	1502	27.1	Independence (charter township) Oakland County
5	104	19.4	New Baltimore (city) Macomb County	81	1523	27.2	Livonia (city) Wayne County
7	117	19.6	Ada (township) Kent County	82	1615	27.5	Vienna (charter township) Genesee County
8	151	20.1	Spring Lake (township) Ottawa County	83	1635	27.6	Emmett (charter township) Calhoun County
9	176	20.5	Lincoln (charter township) Berrien County	84	1673	27.7	Farmington (city) Oakland County
10	194	20.7	Fenton (charter township) Genesee County	85	1756	28.0	Canton (charter township) Wayne County
10	194	20.7	Oxford (charter township) Oakland County	86	1791	28.1	Escanaba (city) Delta County
12	234	21.1	Texas (charter township) Kalamazoo County	87	1823	28.2	Gaines (charter township) Kent County
13	243	21.2	Southfield (township) Oakland County	88	1855	28.3	Fraser (city) Macomb County
14	262	21.4	Hamburg (township) Livingston County	89	1881	28.4	East Bay (township) Grand Traverse County
14	262	21.4	Scio (township) Washtenaw County	89	1881	28.4	Saginaw (charter township) Saginaw County
16	334	22.0	Grand Haven (city) Ottawa County	91	1944	28.6	Holland (charter township) Ottawa County
17	347	22.1	Park (township) Ottawa County	92	1976	28.7	Cooper (charter township) Kalamazoo County
18	385	22.3	Genoa (township) Livingston County	92	1976	28.7	Frenchtown (township) Monroe County
19	401	22.4	Caledonia (township) Kent County	92	1976	28.7	Portage (city) Kalamazoo County
20	423	22.5	Beverly Hills (village) Oakland County	95	2039	28.9	Garfield (charter township) Grand Traverse County
20	423	22.5	Commerce (charter township) Oakland County	95	2039	28.9	Monroe (charter township) Monroe County
22	440	22.6	Cannon (township) Kent County	95	2039	28.9	Muskegon (charter township) Muskegon County
22	440	22.6	Flushing (charter township) Genesee County	95	2039	28.9	Northview (CDP) Kent County
24	482	22.8	Grand Haven (charter township) Ottawa County	99	2070	29.0	Comstock (charter township) Kalamazoo County
25	501	22.9	Bloomfield (charter township) Oakland County	99	2070	29.0	Grandville (city) Kent County
25	501	22.9	Oakland (charter township) Oakland County	99	2070	29.0	Leoni (township) Jackson County
27	520	23.0	Grand Rapids (charter township) Kent County	102	2090	29.1	Saint Clair Shores (city) Macomb County
27	520	23.0	Oceola (township) Livingston County	103	2116	29.2	Allen Park (city) Wayne County
29	540	23.1	Monitor (charter township) Bay County	103	2116	29.2	Delta (charter township) Eaton County
29	540	23.1	Tyrone (township) Livingston County	105	2145	29.3	Sterling Heights (city) Macomb County
31	565	23.2	Bangor (charter township) Bay County	106	2166	29.4	Harrison (charter township) Macomb County
31	565	23.2	Jenison (CDP) Ottawa County	106	2166	29.4	Woodhaven (city) Wayne County
33	613	23.4	Bedford (township) Monroe County	108	2198	29.5	Fenton (city) Genesee County
33	613	23.4	Springfield (charter township) Oakland County	108	2198	29.5	Grosse Pointe Park (city) Wayne County
33	613	23.4	White Lake (charter township) Oakland County	110	2258	29.7	Alpena (city) Alpena County
36	691	23.7	Byron (township) Kent County	110	2258	29.7	Bridgeport (charter township) Saginaw County
37	713	23.8	Thomas (township) Saginaw County	112	2277	29.8	Genesee (charter township) Genesee County
38	733	23.9	Delhi (charter township) Ingham County	112	2277	29.8	Midland (city) Midland County
38	733	23.9	Washington (township) Macomb County	114	2380	30.2	Waterford (charter township) Oakland County
40	748	24.0	Hartland (township) Livingston County	115	2438	30.4	Waverly (CDP) Eaton County
40	748	24.0	Holt (CDP) Ingham County	116	2465	30.5	Niles (township) Berrien County
42	766	24.1	Birmingham (city) Oakland County	116	2465	30.5	Wyandotte (city) Wayne County
42	766	24.1	Highland (charter township) Oakland County	118	2499	30.7	Dearborn (city) Wayne County
44	794	24.2	Cadillac (city) Wexford County	118	2499	30.7	Garden City (city) Wayne County
44	794	24.2	Plymouth (charter township) Wayne County	120	2555	30.9	Burton (city) Genesee County
46	831	24.4	Troy (city) Oakland County	120	2555	30.9	Davison (township) Genesee County
47	862	24.5	Fruitport (charter township) Muskegon County	122	2585	31.0	Dearborn Heights (city) Wayne County
48	884	24.6	Green Oak (township) Livingston County	123	2645	31.3	Madison Heights (city) Oakland County
49	928	24.8	Mundy (township) Genesee County	123	2645	31.3	Monroe (city) Monroe County
50	947	24.9	South Lyon (city) Oakland County	125	2694	31.5	Berkley (city) Oakland County
50	947	24.9	Summit (township) Jackson County	125	2694	31.5	Clawson (city) Oakland County
52	965	25.0	Trenton (city) Wayne County	125	2694	31.5	Coldwater (city) Branch County
53	1007	25.2	Georgetown (charter township) Ottawa County	128	2728	31.6	Rochester (city) Oakland County
54	1025	25.3	Lyon (charter township) Oakland County	129	2781	31.8	Haslett (CDP) Ingham County
54	1025	25.3	Northville (township) Wayne County	130	2810	31.9	Superior (charter township) Washtenaw County
56	1055	25.4	Huron (charter township) Wayne County	130	2810	31.9	Wayne (city) Wayne County
56	1055	25.4	Macomb (township) Macomb County	132	2847	32.0	Clinton (charter township) Macomb County
56	1055	25.4	Norton Shores (city) Muskegon County	133	2864	32.1	Cutlerville (CDP) Kent County
59	1083	25.5	Antwerp (township) Van Buren County	134	2889	32.2	Battle Creek (city) Calhoun County
59	1083	25.5	Novi (city) Oakland County	135	2951	32.5	Meridian (charter township) Ingham County
59	1083	25.5	Orion (charter township) Oakland County	136	2978	32.6	Walker (city) Kent County
62	1106	25.6	Brandon (charter township) Oakland County	137	2996	32.7	Kalamazoo (charter township) Kalamazoo County
62	1106	25.6	Sturgis (city) Saint Joseph County	137	2996	32.7	Owosso (city) Shiawassee County
64	1141	25.7	Brownstown (charter township) Wayne County	139	3018	32.8	Okemos (CDP) Ingham County
65	1164	25.8	Brighton (township) Livingston County	140	3038	32.9	Flint (charter township) Genesee County
65	1164	25.8	Grosse Pointe Woods (city) Wayne County	141	3095	33.2	Southgate (city) Wayne County
67	1203	26.0	DeWitt (charter township) Clinton County	142	3148	33.5	Wyoming (city) Kent County
68	1227	26.1	Milford (charter township) Oakland County	143	3169	33.6	Traverse City (city) Grand Traverse County
69	1254	26.2	Rochester Hills (city) Oakland County	144	3249	34.1	Niles (city) Berrien County
70	1281	26.3	Chesterfield (township) Macomb County	145	3287	34.3	Blackman (charter township) Jackson County
71	1298	26.4	Farmington Hills (city) Oakland County	145	3287	34.3	Lincoln Park (city) Wayne County
71	1298	26.4	West Bloomfield (charter township) Oakland County	147	3315	34.4	Port Huron (city) Saint Clair County
73	1355	26.6	Fort Gratiot (charter township) Saint Clair County	147	3315	34.4	Warren (city) Macomb County
74	1392	26.7	Holly (township) Oakland County	149	3412	34.9	Kentwood (city) Kent County
75	1419	26.8	Plainfield (charter township) Kent County	150	3445	35.1	Lenox (township) Macomb County

Note: The state column ranks the top/bottom 150 places from all places in the state with population of 10,000 or more. The national column ranks the top/bottom 150 places from all places in the country with population of 10,000 or more. Places that are unincorporated were not considered in the rankings. Please refer to the User Guide for additional information.

Marriage Status: Now Married

Top 150 Places Ranked in *Descending* Order

State Rank	Nat'l Rank	Percent	Place
1	18	72.7	**Ada** (township) Kent County
2	24	72.3	**Forest Hills** (CDP) Kent County
3	37	71.4	**Cascade** (charter township) Kent County
4	98	68.3	**Texas** (charter township) Kalamazoo County
5	128	67.8	**Park** (township) Ottawa County
6	150	67.3	**East Grand Rapids** (city) Kent County
7	181	66.7	**Cannon** (township) Kent County
7	181	66.7	**Grosse Ile** (township) Wayne County
9	203	66.2	**Tyrone** (township) Livingston County
10	233	65.8	**Caledonia** (township) Kent County
10	233	65.8	**Saint Joseph** (charter township) Berrien County
12	246	65.6	**Hamburg** (township) Livingston County
13	256	65.4	**Oakland** (charter township) Oakland County
14	262	65.3	**Scio** (township) Washtenaw County
15	336	64.4	**Hartland** (township) Livingston County
15	336	64.4	**Lincoln** (charter township) Berrien County
15	336	64.4	**Springfield** (charter township) Oakland County
18	347	64.3	**Oceola** (township) Livingston County
19	360	64.2	**Commerce** (charter township) Oakland County
19	360	64.2	**Macomb** (township) Macomb County
19	360	64.2	**Oxford** (charter township) Oakland County
19	360	64.2	**Southfield** (township) Oakland County
23	390	63.9	**Grand Haven** (charter township) Ottawa County
24	399	63.8	**Georgetown** (charter township) Ottawa County
25	416	63.6	**Bloomfield** (charter township) Oakland County
25	416	63.6	**New Baltimore** (city) Macomb County
27	428	63.4	**Troy** (city) Oakland County
28	485	62.7	**Byron** (township) Kent County
28	485	62.7	**Plymouth** (charter township) Wayne County
30	525	62.4	**Brighton** (township) Livingston County
30	525	62.4	**Fenton** (charter township) Genesee County
32	535	62.3	**Washington** (township) Macomb County
33	548	62.1	**Spring Lake** (township) Ottawa County
33	548	62.1	**White Lake** (charter township) Oakland County
35	565	62.0	**Beverly Hills** (village) Oakland County
35	565	62.0	**Genoa** (township) Livingston County
37	621	61.6	**Jenison** (CDP) Ottawa County
38	634	61.5	**Lyon** (charter township) Oakland County
39	664	61.2	**Grand Rapids** (charter township) Kent County
40	706	61.0	**Northville** (township) Wayne County
41	764	60.5	**Fruitport** (charter township) Muskegon County
42	783	60.4	**Bedford** (township) Monroe County
43	829	60.1	**Huron** (charter township) Wayne County
44	843	60.0	**Highland** (charter township) Oakland County
45	871	59.8	**Birmingham** (city) Oakland County
45	871	59.8	**Canton** (charter township) Wayne County
47	885	59.7	**Monitor** (charter township) Bay County
48	901	59.6	**Orion** (charter township) Oakland County
48	901	59.6	**Rochester Hills** (city) Oakland County
50	919	59.5	**Brandon** (charter township) Oakland County
51	930	59.4	**Green Oak** (township) Livingston County
52	959	59.2	**Grosse Pointe Park** (city) Wayne County
53	991	59.0	**Delhi** (charter township) Ingham County
53	991	59.0	**Grosse Pointe Woods** (city) Wayne County
55	1006	58.9	**Holland** (charter township) Ottawa County
56	1025	58.8	**Flushing** (charter township) Genesee County
56	1025	58.8	**Milford** (charter township) Oakland County
56	1025	58.8	**Plainfield** (charter township) Kent County
56	1025	58.8	**Summit** (township) Jackson County
56	1025	58.8	**West Bloomfield** (charter township) Oakland County
61	1046	58.7	**Holt** (CDP) Ingham County
62	1129	58.1	**Mundy** (township) Genesee County
62	1129	58.1	**Novi** (city) Oakland County
64	1180	57.8	**Brownstown** (charter township) Wayne County
64	1180	57.8	**Shelby** (charter township) Macomb County
66	1211	57.6	**Gaines** (charter township) Kent County
67	1276	57.2	**Chesterfield** (township) Macomb County
68	1311	57.0	**Thomas** (township) Saginaw County
69	1339	56.8	**Independence** (charter township) Oakland County
70	1352	56.7	**Antwerp** (township) Van Buren County
70	1352	56.7	**DeWitt** (charter township) Clinton County
72	1376	56.6	**Grand Blanc** (charter township) Genesee County
73	1443	56.3	**East Bay** (township) Grand Traverse County
73	1443	56.3	**Farmington Hills** (city) Oakland County
75	1531	55.8	**Grand Haven** (city) Ottawa County
75	1531	55.8	**Portage** (city) Kalamazoo County
77	1595	55.5	**Cooper** (charter township) Kalamazoo County
78	1618	55.4	**Livonia** (city) Wayne County
79	1671	55.1	**Bangor** (charter township) Bay County
80	1697	55.0	**Grandville** (city) Kent County
81	1733	54.8	**Sterling Heights** (city) Macomb County
82	1773	54.6	**Norton Shores** (city) Muskegon County
83	1809	54.4	**Okemos** (CDP) Ingham County
84	1829	54.3	**South Lyon** (city) Oakland County
85	1847	54.2	**Comstock** (charter township) Kalamazoo County
85	1847	54.2	**Emmett** (charter township) Calhoun County
87	1958	53.7	**Farmington** (city) Oakland County
87	1958	53.7	**Vienna** (charter township) Genesee County
89	1976	53.6	**Fort Gratiot** (charter township) Saint Clair County
89	1976	53.6	**Rochester** (city) Oakland County
91	2053	53.3	**Dearborn** (city) Wayne County
91	2053	53.3	**Northview** (CDP) Kent County
93	2109	53.0	**Saginaw** (charter township) Saginaw County
94	2170	52.7	**Holly** (township) Oakland County
94	2170	52.7	**Superior** (charter township) Washtenaw County
96	2242	52.3	**Sturgis** (city) Saint Joseph County
97	2291	52.1	**Meridian** (charter township) Ingham County
98	2306	52.0	**Delta** (charter township) Eaton County
98	2306	52.0	**Muskegon** (charter township) Muskegon County
100	2347	51.8	**Frenchtown** (township) Monroe County
101	2422	51.4	**Bridgeport** (charter township) Saginaw County
101	2422	51.4	**Midland** (city) Midland County
103	2435	51.3	**Fraser** (city) Macomb County
104	2482	51.1	**Wyoming** (city) Kent County
105	2535	50.8	**Trenton** (city) Wayne County
106	2557	50.7	**Harrison** (charter township) Macomb County
106	2557	50.7	**Woodhaven** (city) Wayne County
108	2607	50.5	**Lenox** (township) Macomb County
109	2631	50.4	**Haslett** (CDP) Ingham County
110	2651	50.3	**Genesee** (charter township) Genesee County
111	2671	50.2	**Waterford** (charter township) Oakland County
112	2697	50.1	**Walker** (city) Kent County
113	2720	50.0	**Allen Park** (city) Wayne County
113	2720	50.0	**Dearborn Heights** (city) Wayne County
115	2753	49.8	**Port Huron** (charter township) Saint Clair County
116	2774	49.7	**Waverly** (CDP) Eaton County
117	2803	49.6	**Kentwood** (city) Kent County
117	2803	49.6	**Monroe** (charter township) Monroe County
119	2820	49.5	**Berkley** (city) Oakland County
120	2849	49.4	**Hamtramck** (city) Wayne County
120	2849	49.4	**Wixom** (city) Oakland County
122	2901	49.1	**Cutlerville** (CDP) Kent County
122	2901	49.1	**Garden City** (city) Wayne County
122	2901	49.1	**Pittsfield** (charter township) Washtenaw County
122	2901	49.1	**Saint Clair Shores** (city) Macomb County
126	3005	48.6	**Davison** (township) Genesee County
126	3005	48.6	**Niles** (township) Berrien County
128	3042	48.4	**Alpena** (city) Alpena County
129	3067	48.3	**Cadillac** (city) Wexford County
129	3067	48.3	**Fenton** (city) Genesee County
131	3138	47.9	**Burton** (city) Genesee County
131	3138	47.9	**Garfield** (charter township) Grand Traverse County
133	3172	47.7	**Riverview** (city) Wayne County
134	3237	47.4	**Wyandotte** (city) Wayne County
135	3268	47.2	**Clawson** (city) Oakland County
136	3286	47.1	**Bath** (charter township) Clinton County
136	3286	47.1	**Escanaba** (city) Delta County
138	3296	47.0	**Clinton** (charter township) Macomb County
139	3311	46.9	**Leoni** (township) Jackson County
140	3330	46.8	**Van Buren** (charter township) Wayne County
141	3370	46.6	**Holland** (city) Ottawa County
142	3408	46.4	**Madison Heights** (city) Oakland County
143	3426	46.3	**Monroe** (city) Monroe County
144	3444	46.2	**Owosso** (city) Shiawassee County
145	3459	46.1	**Auburn Hills** (city) Oakland County
146	3478	46.0	**Warren** (city) Macomb County
147	3538	45.6	**Battle Creek** (city) Calhoun County
148	3579	45.4	**Kalamazoo** (charter township) Kalamazoo County
149	3606	45.2	**Alpine** (township) Kent County
150	3651	44.8	**Royal Oak** (city) Oakland County

Note: The state column ranks the top/bottom 150 places from all places in the state with population of 10,000 or more. The national column ranks the top/bottom 150 places from all places in the country with population of 10,000 or more. Places that are unincorporated were not considered in the rankings. Please refer to the User Guide for additional information.

Marriage Status: Now Married

Top 150 Places Ranked in *Ascending* Order

State Rank	Nat'l Rank	Percent	Place		State Rank	Nat'l Rank	Percent	Place
1	12	17.6	**East Lansing** (city) Ingham County		75	1570	48.3	**Fenton** (city) Genesee County
2	17	20.1	**Big Rapids** (city) Mecosta County		77	1590	48.4	**Alpena** (city) Alpena County
3	22	21.3	**Highland Park** (city) Wayne County		78	1634	48.6	**Davison** (township) Genesee County
3	22	21.3	**Ypsilanti** (city) Washtenaw County		78	1634	48.6	**Niles** (township) Berrien County
5	24	21.5	**Mount Pleasant** (city) Isabella County		80	1733	49.1	**Cutlerville** (CDP) Kent County
6	25	21.6	**Benton Harbor** (city) Berrien County		80	1733	49.1	**Garden City** (city) Wayne County
7	37	24.5	**Union** (charter township) Isabella County		80	1733	49.1	**Pittsfield** (charter township) Washtenaw County
8	55	27.1	**Detroit** (city) Wayne County		80	1733	49.1	**Saint Clair Shores** (city) Macomb County
9	60	27.9	**Kalamazoo** (city) Kalamazoo County		84	1788	49.4	**Hamtramck** (city) Wayne County
10	62	28.3	**Ionia** (city) Ionia County		84	1788	49.4	**Wixom** (city) Oakland County
11	74	29.0	**Beecher** (CDP) Genesee County		86	1808	49.5	**Berkley** (city) Oakland County
12	88	30.0	**Muskegon Heights** (city) Muskegon County		87	1837	49.6	**Kentwood** (city) Kent County
13	90	30.1	**Flint** (city) Genesee County		87	1837	49.6	**Monroe** (charter township) Monroe County
14	100	30.4	**Inkster** (city) Wayne County		89	1854	49.7	**Waverly** (CDP) Eaton County
15	120	31.4	**Pontiac** (city) Oakland County		90	1883	49.8	**Port Huron** (charter township) Saint Clair County
16	128	31.7	**Muskegon** (city) Muskegon County		91	1918	50.0	**Allen Park** (city) Wayne County
17	131	31.9	**Saginaw** (city) Saginaw County		91	1918	50.0	**Dearborn Heights** (city) Wayne County
18	158	33.0	**Allendale** (CDP) Ottawa County		93	1937	50.1	**Walker** (city) Kent County
19	190	33.9	**Ann Arbor** (city) Washtenaw County		94	1960	50.2	**Waterford** (charter township) Oakland County
20	194	34.0	**Allendale** (charter township) Ottawa County		95	1986	50.3	**Genesee** (charter township) Genesee County
21	202	34.4	**Mount Clemens** (city) Macomb County		96	2006	50.4	**Haslett** (CDP) Ingham County
22	210	34.6	**Marquette** (city) Marquette County		97	2026	50.5	**Lenox** (township) Macomb County
23	304	36.9	**Ferndale** (city) Oakland County		98	2075	50.7	**Harrison** (charter township) Macomb County
23	304	36.9	**Harper Woods** (city) Wayne County		98	2075	50.7	**Woodhaven** (city) Wayne County
25	337	37.6	**Adrian** (city) Lenawee County		100	2100	50.8	**Trenton** (city) Wayne County
26	368	38.1	**Jackson** (city) Jackson County		101	2157	51.1	**Wyoming** (city) Kent County
27	381	38.3	**Lansing** (city) Ingham County		102	2190	51.3	**Fraser** (city) Macomb County
28	390	38.4	**Blackman** (charter township) Jackson County		103	2222	51.4	**Bridgeport** (charter township) Saginaw County
29	436	39.1	**Hazel Park** (city) Oakland County		103	2222	51.4	**Midland** (city) Midland County
30	461	39.6	**Eastpointe** (city) Macomb County		105	2282	51.8	**Frenchtown** (township) Monroe County
31	489	40.0	**Benton** (charter township) Berrien County		106	2332	52.0	**Delta** (charter township) Eaton County
31	489	40.0	**Grand Rapids** (city) Kent County		106	2332	52.0	**Muskegon** (charter township) Muskegon County
33	526	40.4	**Mount Morris** (township) Genesee County		108	2351	52.1	**Meridian** (charter township) Ingham County
34	535	40.5	**Southfield** (city) Oakland County		109	2393	52.3	**Sturgis** (city) Saint Joseph County
35	599	41.4	**Sault Sainte Marie** (city) Chippewa County		110	2467	52.7	**Holly** (township) Oakland County
36	626	41.7	**Roseville** (city) Macomb County		110	2467	52.7	**Superior** (charter township) Washtenaw County
37	638	41.9	**Romulus** (city) Wayne County		112	2526	53.0	**Saginaw** (charter township) Saginaw County
38	666	42.2	**Oak Park** (city) Oakland County		113	2587	53.3	**Dearborn** (city) Wayne County
39	676	42.3	**Bay City** (city) Bay County		113	2587	53.3	**Northview** (CDP) Kent County
39	676	42.3	**Ypsilanti** (charter township) Washtenaw County		115	2654	53.6	**Fort Gratiot** (charter township) Saint Clair County
41	701	42.5	**Port Huron** (city) Saint Clair County		115	2654	53.6	**Rochester** (city) Oakland County
42	760	43.0	**Westland** (city) Wayne County		117	2681	53.7	**Farmington** (city) Oakland County
43	777	43.2	**Redford** (charter township) Wayne County		117	2681	53.7	**Vienna** (charter township) Genesee County
44	788	43.3	**Comstock Park** (CDP) Kent County		119	2786	54.2	**Comstock** (charter township) Kalamazoo County
45	818	43.5	**Melvindale** (city) Wayne County		119	2786	54.2	**Emmett** (charter township) Calhoun County
46	858	43.8	**Oshtemo** (charter township) Kalamazoo County		121	2810	54.3	**South Lyon** (city) Oakland County
47	871	43.9	**Lincoln Park** (city) Wayne County		122	2828	54.4	**Okemos** (CDP) Ingham County
48	896	44.1	**Niles** (city) Berrien County		123	2865	54.6	**Norton Shores** (city) Muskegon County
48	896	44.1	**Taylor** (city) Wayne County		124	2901	54.8	**Sterling Heights** (city) Macomb County
48	896	44.1	**Traverse City** (city) Grand Traverse County		125	2946	55.0	**Grandville** (city) Kent County
51	910	44.2	**Wayne** (city) Wayne County		126	2960	55.1	**Bangor** (charter township) Bay County
52	931	44.4	**Flint** (charter township) Genesee County		127	3019	55.4	**Livonia** (city) Wayne County
53	975	44.7	**Coldwater** (city) Branch County		128	3039	55.5	**Cooper** (charter township) Kalamazoo County
54	998	44.8	**Royal Oak** (city) Oakland County		129	3103	55.8	**Grand Haven** (city) Ottawa County
54	998	44.8	**Southgate** (city) Wayne County		129	3103	55.8	**Portage** (city) Kalamazoo County
56	1043	45.2	**Alpine** (township) Kent County		131	3193	56.3	**East Bay** (township) Grand Traverse County
57	1067	45.4	**Kalamazoo** (charter township) Kalamazoo County		131	3193	56.3	**Farmington Hills** (city) Oakland County
58	1099	45.6	**Battle Creek** (city) Calhoun County		133	3258	56.6	**Grand Blanc** (charter township) Genesee County
59	1167	46.0	**Warren** (city) Macomb County		134	3281	56.7	**Antwerp** (township) Van Buren County
60	1179	46.1	**Auburn Hills** (city) Oakland County		134	3281	56.7	**DeWitt** (charter township) Clinton County
61	1198	46.2	**Owosso** (city) Shiawassee County		136	3305	56.8	**Independence** (charter township) Oakland County
62	1213	46.3	**Monroe** (city) Monroe County		137	3334	57.0	**Thomas** (township) Saginaw County
63	1231	46.4	**Madison Heights** (city) Oakland County		138	3360	57.2	**Chesterfield** (township) Macomb County
64	1264	46.6	**Holland** (city) Ottawa County		139	3428	57.6	**Gaines** (charter township) Kent County
65	1307	46.8	**Van Buren** (charter township) Wayne County		140	3462	57.8	**Brownstown** (charter township) Wayne County
66	1327	46.9	**Leoni** (township) Jackson County		140	3462	57.8	**Shelby** (charter township) Macomb County
67	1346	47.0	**Clinton** (charter township) Macomb County		142	3512	58.1	**Mundy** (township) Genesee County
68	1361	47.1	**Bath** (charter township) Clinton County		142	3512	58.1	**Novi** (city) Oakland County
68	1361	47.1	**Escanaba** (city) Delta County		144	3597	58.7	**Holt** (CDP) Ingham County
70	1371	47.2	**Clawson** (city) Oakland County		145	3611	58.8	**Flushing** (charter township) Genesee County
71	1404	47.4	**Wyandotte** (city) Wayne County		145	3611	58.8	**Milford** (charter township) Oakland County
72	1458	47.7	**Riverview** (city) Wayne County		145	3611	58.8	**Plainfield** (charter township) Kent County
73	1504	47.9	**Burton** (city) Genesee County		145	3611	58.8	**Summit** (township) Jackson County
73	1504	47.9	**Garfield** (charter township) Grand Traverse County		145	3611	58.8	**West Bloomfield** (charter township) Oakland County
75	1570	48.3	**Cadillac** (city) Wexford County		150	3632	58.9	**Holland** (charter township) Ottawa County

Note: The state column ranks the top/bottom 150 places from all places in the state with population of 10,000 or more. The national column ranks the top/bottom 150 places from all places in the country with population of 10,000 or more. Places that are unincorporated were not considered in the rankings. Please refer to the User Guide for additional information.

Marriage Status: Separated

Top 150 Places Ranked in *Descending* Order

State Rank	Nat'l Rank	Percent	Place
1	7	6.8	**Highland Park** (city) Wayne County
2	236	4.1	**Inkster** (city) Wayne County
3	305	3.9	**Benton Harbor** (city) Berrien County
4	387	3.7	**Detroit** (city) Wayne County
5	487	3.5	**Adrian** (city) Lenawee County
6	686	3.2	**Flint** (city) Genesee County
7	747	3.1	**Saginaw** (city) Saginaw County
8	815	3.0	**Coldwater** (city) Branch County
8	815	3.0	**Flint** (charter township) Genesee County
8	815	3.0	**Muskegon Heights** (city) Muskegon County
11	906	2.9	**Mount Clemens** (city) Macomb County
11	906	2.9	**Woodhaven** (city) Wayne County
13	1005	2.8	**Melvindale** (city) Wayne County
14	1100	2.7	**Benton** (charter township) Berrien County
15	1195	2.6	**Bridgeport** (charter township) Saginaw County
15	1195	2.6	**Jackson** (city) Jackson County
15	1195	2.6	**Owosso** (city) Shiawassee County
18	1300	2.5	**Battle Creek** (city) Calhoun County
18	1300	2.5	**Niles** (city) Berrien County
18	1300	2.5	**Pontiac** (city) Oakland County
21	1419	2.4	**Beecher** (CDP) Genesee County
21	1419	2.4	**Grand Rapids** (city) Kent County
21	1419	2.4	**Hamtramck** (city) Wayne County
24	1550	2.3	**Southfield** (city) Oakland County
24	1550	2.3	**Sturgis** (city) Saint Joseph County
26	1676	2.2	**Frenchtown** (township) Monroe County
26	1676	2.2	**Lincoln Park** (city) Wayne County
26	1676	2.2	**Muskegon** (city) Muskegon County
29	1816	2.1	**Eastpointe** (city) Macomb County
29	1816	2.1	**Ferndale** (city) Oakland County
29	1816	2.1	**Lansing** (city) Ingham County
32	1961	2.0	**Blackman** (charter township) Jackson County
32	1961	2.0	**Fenton** (city) Genesee County
32	1961	2.0	**Genesee** (charter township) Genesee County
32	1961	2.0	**Ionia** (city) Ionia County
32	1961	2.0	**Wayne** (city) Wayne County
37	2118	1.9	**Clawson** (city) Oakland County
37	2118	1.9	**Cutlerville** (CDP) Kent County
37	2118	1.9	**Port Huron** (city) Saint Clair County
37	2118	1.9	**Redford** (charter township) Wayne County
37	2118	1.9	**Taylor** (city) Wayne County
37	2118	1.9	**Wyoming** (city) Kent County
43	2275	1.8	**Monroe** (charter township) Monroe County
43	2275	1.8	**Oak Park** (city) Oakland County
43	2275	1.8	**Westland** (city) Wayne County
46	2422	1.7	**Brownstown** (charter township) Wayne County
46	2422	1.7	**Grand Haven** (city) Ottawa County
46	2422	1.7	**Harrison** (charter township) Macomb County
46	2422	1.7	**Kalamazoo** (city) Kalamazoo County
46	2422	1.7	**Monroe** (city) Monroe County
46	2422	1.7	**Mount Morris** (township) Genesee County
46	2422	1.7	**Oshtemo** (charter township) Kalamazoo County
46	2422	1.7	**Riverview** (city) Wayne County
46	2422	1.7	**Romulus** (city) Wayne County
46	2422	1.7	**Ypsilanti** (charter township) Washtenaw County
56	2603	1.6	**Cadillac** (city) Wexford County
56	2603	1.6	**Comstock** (charter township) Kalamazoo County
56	2603	1.6	**Dearborn Heights** (city) Wayne County
56	2603	1.6	**Fruitport** (charter township) Muskegon County
56	2603	1.6	**Gaines** (charter township) Kent County
56	2603	1.6	**Grand Blanc** (charter township) Genesee County
56	2603	1.6	**Harper Woods** (city) Wayne County
56	2603	1.6	**Niles** (township) Berrien County
56	2603	1.6	**Portage** (city) Kalamazoo County
56	2603	1.6	**Southgate** (city) Wayne County
66	2791	1.5	**Bangor** (charter township) Bay County
66	2791	1.5	**Burton** (city) Genesee County
66	2791	1.5	**Clinton** (charter township) Macomb County
66	2791	1.5	**Northview** (CDP) Kent County
66	2791	1.5	**Sault Sainte Marie** (city) Chippewa County
66	2791	1.5	**Waterford** (charter township) Oakland County
66	2791	1.5	**Waverly** (CDP) Eaton County
73	2983	1.4	**Bay City** (city) Bay County
73	2983	1.4	**Fraser** (city) Macomb County
73	2983	1.4	**Huron** (charter township) Wayne County
73	2983	1.4	**Kalamazoo** (charter township) Kalamazoo County
73	2983	1.4	**Norton Shores** (city) Muskegon County
73	2983	1.4	**Spring Lake** (township) Ottawa County
73	2983	1.4	**Summit** (township) Jackson County
73	2983	1.4	**Trenton** (city) Wayne County
73	2983	1.4	**Warren** (city) Macomb County
73	2983	1.4	**Ypsilanti** (city) Washtenaw County
83	3167	1.3	**Brandon** (charter township) Oakland County
83	3167	1.3	**Dearborn** (city) Wayne County
83	3167	1.3	**Farmington Hills** (city) Oakland County
83	3167	1.3	**Kentwood** (city) Kent County
83	3167	1.3	**Muskegon** (charter township) Muskegon County
83	3167	1.3	**Saginaw** (charter township) Saginaw County
83	3167	1.3	**Vienna** (charter township) Genesee County
90	3376	1.2	**Byron** (township) Kent County
90	3376	1.2	**Canton** (charter township) Wayne County
90	3376	1.2	**Chesterfield** (township) Macomb County
90	3376	1.2	**Delta** (charter township) Eaton County
90	3376	1.2	**Farmington** (city) Oakland County
90	3376	1.2	**Fort Gratiot** (charter township) Saint Clair County
90	3376	1.2	**Garfield** (charter township) Grand Traverse County
90	3376	1.2	**Holland** (charter township) Ottawa County
90	3376	1.2	**Holland** (city) Ottawa County
90	3376	1.2	**Lenox** (township) Macomb County
90	3376	1.2	**Novi** (city) Oakland County
90	3376	1.2	**Roseville** (city) Macomb County
90	3376	1.2	**White Lake** (charter township) Oakland County
90	3376	1.2	**Wyandotte** (city) Wayne County
104	3561	1.1	**Alpena** (city) Alpena County
104	3561	1.1	**Garden City** (city) Wayne County
104	3561	1.1	**Haslett** (CDP) Ingham County
104	3561	1.1	**Lincoln** (charter township) Berrien County
104	3561	1.1	**Madison Heights** (city) Oakland County
104	3561	1.1	**Monitor** (charter township) Bay County
104	3561	1.1	**Port Huron** (charter township) Saint Clair County
104	3561	1.1	**Traverse City** (city) Grand Traverse County
112	3734	1.0	**Auburn Hills** (city) Oakland County
112	3734	1.0	**Bath** (charter township) Clinton County
112	3734	1.0	**Delhi** (charter township) Ingham County
112	3734	1.0	**Emmett** (charter township) Calhoun County
112	3734	1.0	**Hazel Park** (city) Oakland County
112	3734	1.0	**Holt** (CDP) Ingham County
112	3734	1.0	**Sterling Heights** (city) Macomb County
112	3734	1.0	**Thomas** (township) Saginaw County
112	3734	1.0	**Van Buren** (charter township) Wayne County
112	3734	1.0	**Wixom** (city) Oakland County
122	3894	0.9	**Bedford** (township) Monroe County
122	3894	0.9	**Commerce** (charter township) Oakland County
122	3894	0.9	**Comstock Park** (CDP) Kent County
122	3894	0.9	**Georgetown** (charter township) Ottawa County
122	3894	0.9	**Hartland** (township) Livingston County
122	3894	0.9	**Leoni** (township) Jackson County
122	3894	0.9	**Midland** (city) Midland County
122	3894	0.9	**Mundy** (township) Genesee County
122	3894	0.9	**New Baltimore** (city) Macomb County
122	3894	0.9	**Pittsfield** (charter township) Washtenaw County
132	4037	0.8	**Davison** (township) Genesee County
132	4037	0.8	**DeWitt** (charter township) Clinton County
132	4037	0.8	**Flushing** (charter township) Genesee County
132	4037	0.8	**Grosse Pointe Park** (city) Wayne County
132	4037	0.8	**Holly** (township) Oakland County
132	4037	0.8	**Jenison** (CDP) Ottawa County
132	4037	0.8	**Macomb** (township) Macomb County
132	4037	0.8	**Marquette** (city) Marquette County
132	4037	0.8	**Meridian** (charter township) Ingham County
132	4037	0.8	**Orion** (charter township) Oakland County
132	4037	0.8	**Plainfield** (charter township) Kent County
132	4037	0.8	**Saint Clair Shores** (city) Macomb County
132	4037	0.8	**Walker** (city) Kent County
145	4190	0.7	**Alpine** (township) Kent County
145	4190	0.7	**Big Rapids** (city) Mecosta County
145	4190	0.7	**Hamburg** (township) Livingston County
145	4190	0.7	**Independence** (charter township) Oakland County
145	4190	0.7	**Lyon** (charter township) Oakland County
145	4190	0.7	**Oceola** (township) Livingston County

Note: The state column ranks the top/bottom 150 places from all places in the state with population of 10,000 or more. The national column ranks the top/bottom 150 places from all places in the country with population of 10,000 or more. Places that are unincorporated were not considered in the rankings. Please refer to the User Guide for additional information.

Marriage Status: Separated

Top 150 Places Ranked in *Ascending* Order

State Rank	Nat'l Rank	Percent	Place
1	1	0.0	**Ada** (township) Kent County
2	6	0.1	**Beverly Hills** (village) Oakland County
2	6	0.1	**Brighton** (township) Livingston County
2	6	0.1	**East Grand Rapids** (city) Kent County
2	6	0.1	**Grosse Ile** (township) Wayne County
2	6	0.1	**Southfield** (township) Oakland County
2	6	0.1	**Texas** (charter township) Kalamazoo County
8	24	0.2	**Allendale** (CDP) Ottawa County
8	24	0.2	**Allendale** (charter township) Ottawa County
8	24	0.2	**East Bay** (township) Grand Traverse County
8	24	0.2	**Forest Hills** (CDP) Kent County
8	24	0.2	**Genoa** (township) Livingston County
8	24	0.2	**Grand Haven** (charter township) Ottawa County
8	24	0.2	**Plymouth** (charter township) Wayne County
8	24	0.2	**Rochester** (city) Oakland County
16	50	0.3	**Berkley** (city) Oakland County
16	50	0.3	**Birmingham** (city) Oakland County
16	50	0.3	**Grand Rapids** (charter township) Kent County
16	50	0.3	**Green Oak** (township) Livingston County
20	80	0.4	**Cannon** (township) Kent County
20	80	0.4	**Cascade** (charter township) Kent County
20	80	0.4	**Grandville** (city) Kent County
20	80	0.4	**Grosse Pointe Woods** (city) Wayne County
20	80	0.4	**Milford** (charter township) Oakland County
20	80	0.4	**Troy** (city) Oakland County
26	133	0.5	**Caledonia** (township) Kent County
26	133	0.5	**Cooper** (charter township) Kalamazoo County
26	133	0.5	**East Lansing** (city) Ingham County
26	133	0.5	**Fenton** (charter township) Genesee County
26	133	0.5	**Livonia** (city) Wayne County
26	133	0.5	**Mount Pleasant** (city) Isabella County
26	133	0.5	**Saint Joseph** (charter township) Berrien County
26	133	0.5	**Springfield** (charter township) Oakland County
26	133	0.5	**Superior** (charter township) Washtenaw County
26	133	0.5	**Washington** (township) Macomb County
36	212	0.6	**Allen Park** (city) Wayne County
36	212	0.6	**Ann Arbor** (city) Washtenaw County
36	212	0.6	**Antwerp** (township) Van Buren County
36	212	0.6	**Bloomfield** (charter township) Oakland County
36	212	0.6	**Escanaba** (city) Delta County
36	212	0.6	**Highland** (charter township) Oakland County
36	212	0.6	**Northville** (township) Wayne County
36	212	0.6	**Oakland** (charter township) Oakland County
36	212	0.6	**Okemos** (CDP) Ingham County
36	212	0.6	**Rochester Hills** (city) Oakland County
36	212	0.6	**Scio** (township) Washtenaw County
36	212	0.6	**South Lyon** (city) Oakland County
36	212	0.6	**Union** (charter township) Isabella County
49	344	0.7	**Alpine** (township) Kent County
49	344	0.7	**Big Rapids** (city) Mecosta County
49	344	0.7	**Hamburg** (township) Livingston County
49	344	0.7	**Independence** (charter township) Oakland County
49	344	0.7	**Lyon** (charter township) Oakland County
49	344	0.7	**Oceola** (township) Livingston County
49	344	0.7	**Oxford** (charter township) Oakland County
49	344	0.7	**Park** (township) Ottawa County
49	344	0.7	**Royal Oak** (city) Oakland County
49	344	0.7	**Shelby** (charter township) Macomb County
49	344	0.7	**Tyrone** (township) Livingston County
49	344	0.7	**West Bloomfield** (charter township) Oakland County
61	467	0.8	**Davison** (township) Genesee County
61	467	0.8	**DeWitt** (charter township) Clinton County
61	467	0.8	**Flushing** (charter township) Genesee County
61	467	0.8	**Grosse Pointe Park** (city) Wayne County
61	467	0.8	**Holly** (township) Oakland County
61	467	0.8	**Jenison** (CDP) Ottawa County
61	467	0.8	**Macomb** (township) Macomb County
61	467	0.8	**Marquette** (city) Marquette County
61	467	0.8	**Meridian** (charter township) Ingham County
61	467	0.8	**Orion** (charter township) Oakland County
61	467	0.8	**Plainfield** (charter township) Kent County
61	467	0.8	**Saint Clair Shores** (city) Macomb County
61	467	0.8	**Walker** (city) Kent County
74	620	0.9	**Bedford** (township) Monroe County
74	620	0.9	**Commerce** (charter township) Oakland County
74	620	0.9	**Comstock Park** (CDP) Kent County
74	620	0.9	**Georgetown** (charter township) Ottawa County
74	620	0.9	**Hartland** (township) Livingston County
74	620	0.9	**Leoni** (township) Jackson County
74	620	0.9	**Midland** (city) Midland County
74	620	0.9	**Mundy** (township) Genesee County
74	620	0.9	**New Baltimore** (city) Macomb County
74	620	0.9	**Pittsfield** (charter township) Washtenaw County
84	763	1.0	**Auburn Hills** (city) Oakland County
84	763	1.0	**Bath** (charter township) Clinton County
84	763	1.0	**Delhi** (charter township) Ingham County
84	763	1.0	**Emmett** (charter township) Calhoun County
84	763	1.0	**Hazel Park** (city) Oakland County
84	763	1.0	**Holt** (CDP) Ingham County
84	763	1.0	**Sterling Heights** (city) Macomb County
84	763	1.0	**Thomas** (township) Saginaw County
84	763	1.0	**Van Buren** (charter township) Wayne County
84	763	1.0	**Wixom** (city) Oakland County
94	923	1.1	**Alpena** (city) Alpena County
94	923	1.1	**Garden City** (city) Wayne County
94	923	1.1	**Haslett** (CDP) Ingham County
94	923	1.1	**Lincoln** (charter township) Berrien County
94	923	1.1	**Madison Heights** (city) Oakland County
94	923	1.1	**Monitor** (charter township) Bay County
94	923	1.1	**Port Huron** (charter township) Saint Clair County
94	923	1.1	**Traverse City** (city) Grand Traverse County
102	1096	1.2	**Byron** (township) Kent County
102	1096	1.2	**Canton** (charter township) Wayne County
102	1096	1.2	**Chesterfield** (township) Macomb County
102	1096	1.2	**Delta** (charter township) Eaton County
102	1096	1.2	**Farmington** (city) Oakland County
102	1096	1.2	**Fort Gratiot** (charter township) Saint Clair County
102	1096	1.2	**Garfield** (charter township) Grand Traverse County
102	1096	1.2	**Holland** (charter township) Ottawa County
102	1096	1.2	**Holland** (city) Ottawa County
102	1096	1.2	**Lenox** (township) Macomb County
102	1096	1.2	**Novi** (city) Oakland County
102	1096	1.2	**Roseville** (city) Macomb County
102	1096	1.2	**White Lake** (charter township) Oakland County
102	1096	1.2	**Wyandotte** (city) Wayne County
116	1281	1.3	**Brandon** (charter township) Oakland County
116	1281	1.3	**Dearborn** (city) Wayne County
116	1281	1.3	**Farmington Hills** (city) Oakland County
116	1281	1.3	**Kentwood** (city) Kent County
116	1281	1.3	**Muskegon** (charter township) Muskegon County
116	1281	1.3	**Saginaw** (charter township) Saginaw County
116	1281	1.3	**Vienna** (charter township) Genesee County
123	1490	1.4	**Bay City** (city) Bay County
123	1490	1.4	**Fraser** (city) Macomb County
123	1490	1.4	**Huron** (charter township) Wayne County
123	1490	1.4	**Kalamazoo** (charter township) Kalamazoo County
123	1490	1.4	**Norton Shores** (city) Muskegon County
123	1490	1.4	**Spring Lake** (township) Ottawa County
123	1490	1.4	**Summit** (township) Jackson County
123	1490	1.4	**Trenton** (city) Wayne County
123	1490	1.4	**Warren** (city) Macomb County
123	1490	1.4	**Ypsilanti** (city) Washtenaw County
133	1674	1.5	**Bangor** (charter township) Bay County
133	1674	1.5	**Burton** (city) Genesee County
133	1674	1.5	**Clinton** (charter township) Macomb County
133	1674	1.5	**Northview** (CDP) Kent County
133	1674	1.5	**Sault Sainte Marie** (city) Chippewa County
133	1674	1.5	**Waterford** (charter township) Oakland County
133	1674	1.5	**Waverly** (CDP) Eaton County
140	1866	1.6	**Cadillac** (city) Wexford County
140	1866	1.6	**Comstock** (charter township) Kalamazoo County
140	1866	1.6	**Dearborn Heights** (city) Wayne County
140	1866	1.6	**Fruitport** (charter township) Muskegon County
140	1866	1.6	**Gaines** (charter township) Kent County
140	1866	1.6	**Grand Blanc** (charter township) Genesee County
140	1866	1.6	**Harper Woods** (city) Wayne County
140	1866	1.6	**Niles** (township) Berrien County
140	1866	1.6	**Portage** (city) Kalamazoo County
140	1866	1.6	**Southgate** (city) Wayne County
150	2054	1.7	**Brownstown** (charter township) Wayne County

Note: The state column ranks the top/bottom 150 places from all places in the state with population of 10,000 or more. The national column ranks the top/bottom 150 places from all places in the country with population of 10,000 or more. Places that are unincorporated were not considered in the rankings. Please refer to the User Guide for additional information.

Marriage Status: Widowed

Top 150 Places Ranked in *Descending* Order

State Rank	Nat'l Rank	Percent	Place	State Rank	Nat'l Rank	Percent	Place
1	69	11.2	**Riverview** (city) Wayne County	75	1706	6.7	**Farmington Hills** (city) Oakland County
2	72	11.1	**Highland Park** (city) Wayne County	75	1706	6.7	**Frenchtown** (township) Monroe County
3	144	10.3	**Escanaba** (city) Delta County	75	1706	6.7	**Leoni** (township) Jackson County
4	217	9.9	**Garfield** (charter township) Grand Traverse County	75	1706	6.7	**Pontiac** (city) Oakland County
4	217	9.9	**Thomas** (township) Saginaw County	80	1779	6.6	**Bedford** (township) Monroe County
6	234	9.8	**Allen Park** (city) Wayne County	80	1779	6.6	**Harper Woods** (city) Wayne County
7	250	9.7	**Trenton** (city) Wayne County	80	1779	6.6	**Muskegon** (city) Muskegon County
8	304	9.5	**Benton** (charter township) Berrien County	80	1779	6.6	**Taylor** (city) Wayne County
9	403	9.1	**Bangor** (charter township) Bay County	84	1858	6.5	**Shelby** (charter township) Macomb County
9	403	9.1	**Fort Gratiot** (charter township) Saint Clair County	84	1858	6.5	**Summit** (township) Jackson County
11	433	9.0	**Fenton** (city) Genesee County	84	1858	6.5	**Waverly** (CDP) Eaton County
11	433	9.0	**Saint Clair Shores** (city) Macomb County	87	1936	6.4	**Harrison** (charter township) Macomb County
11	433	9.0	**Sturgis** (city) Saint Joseph County	87	1936	6.4	**Jackson** (city) Jackson County
14	480	8.8	**Monitor** (charter township) Bay County	87	1936	6.4	**Oshtemo** (charter township) Kalamazoo County
15	514	8.7	**Flint** (charter township) Genesee County	90	2038	6.3	**Delta** (township) Eaton County
16	560	8.6	**Coldwater** (city) Branch County	90	2038	6.3	**Flint** (city) Genesee County
16	560	8.6	**Monroe** (charter township) Monroe County	90	2038	6.3	**Novi** (city) Oakland County
16	560	8.6	**Niles** (township) Berrien County	90	2038	6.3	**Owosso** (city) Shiawassee County
16	560	8.6	**Southfield** (city) Oakland County	94	2119	6.2	**Adrian** (city) Lenawee County
16	560	8.6	**Warren** (city) Macomb County	95	2198	6.1	**Bloomfield** (charter township) Oakland County
21	648	8.4	**Cadillac** (city) Wexford County	95	2198	6.1	**Grosse Ile** (township) Wayne County
21	648	8.4	**Hazel Park** (city) Oakland County	95	2198	6.1	**Hamtramck** (city) Wayne County
21	648	8.4	**Saginaw** (charter township) Saginaw County	95	2198	6.1	**Melvindale** (city) Wayne County
24	696	8.3	**Fraser** (city) Macomb County	95	2198	6.1	**Meridian** (charter township) Ingham County
24	696	8.3	**Wyandotte** (city) Wayne County	95	2198	6.1	**Oak Park** (city) Oakland County
26	743	8.2	**Alpena** (city) Alpena County	101	2296	6.0	**Davison** (township) Genesee County
27	786	8.1	**Clinton** (charter township) Macomb County	101	2296	6.0	**Green Oak** (township) Livingston County
28	833	8.0	**Dearborn Heights** (city) Wayne County	101	2296	6.0	**Lincoln** (charter township) Berrien County
29	942	7.8	**Berkley** (city) Oakland County	101	2296	6.0	**West Bloomfield** (charter township) Oakland County
29	942	7.8	**Southgate** (city) Wayne County	105	2383	5.9	**Kalamazoo** (charter township) Kalamazoo County
31	986	7.7	**Grand Rapids** (charter township) Kent County	105	2383	5.9	**Mundy** (township) Genesee County
31	986	7.7	**Grosse Pointe Woods** (city) Wayne County	107	2479	5.8	**New Baltimore** (city) Macomb County
31	986	7.7	**Haslett** (CDP) Ingham County	107	2479	5.8	**Northview** (CDP) Kent County
31	986	7.7	**Madison Heights** (city) Oakland County	107	2479	5.8	**Oxford** (charter township) Oakland County
31	986	7.7	**Monroe** (city) Monroe County	107	2479	5.8	**Walker** (city) Kent County
36	1048	7.6	**Blackman** (charter township) Jackson County	111	2574	5.7	**Antwerp** (township) Van Buren County
36	1048	7.6	**Garden City** (city) Wayne County	111	2574	5.7	**Beverly Hills** (village) Oakland County
36	1048	7.6	**Mount Clemens** (city) Macomb County	111	2574	5.7	**Bridgeport** (charter township) Saginaw County
36	1048	7.6	**Mount Morris** (township) Genesee County	111	2574	5.7	**Holland** (city) Ottawa County
36	1048	7.6	**Muskegon Heights** (city) Muskegon County	111	2574	5.7	**Northville** (township) Wayne County
36	1048	7.6	**Roseville** (city) Macomb County	111	2574	5.7	**Rochester Hills** (city) Oakland County
36	1048	7.6	**Westland** (city) Wayne County	111	2574	5.7	**Southfield** (township) Oakland County
43	1110	7.5	**Burton** (city) Genesee County	111	2574	5.7	**Woodhaven** (city) Wayne County
43	1110	7.5	**Detroit** (city) Wayne County	119	2683	5.6	**Brownstown** (charter township) Wayne County
43	1110	7.5	**Traverse City** (city) Grand Traverse County	119	2683	5.6	**DeWitt** (charter township) Clinton County
46	1250	7.3	**Eastpointe** (city) Macomb County	119	2683	5.6	**Holly** (township) Oakland County
46	1250	7.3	**Jenison** (CDP) Ottawa County	119	2683	5.6	**Waterford** (charter township) Oakland County
46	1250	7.3	**Muskegon** (charter township) Muskegon County	123	2766	5.5	**Georgetown** (charter township) Ottawa County
46	1250	7.3	**Sterling Heights** (city) Macomb County	123	2766	5.5	**Grand Blanc** (charter township) Genesee County
46	1250	7.3	**Wayne** (city) Wayne County	123	2766	5.5	**Lenox** (township) Macomb County
51	1323	7.2	**Livonia** (city) Wayne County	126	2863	5.4	**Comstock** (charter township) Kalamazoo County
51	1323	7.2	**Midland** (city) Midland County	126	2863	5.4	**Grand Rapids** (city) Kent County
51	1323	7.2	**Vienna** (charter township) Genesee County	126	2863	5.4	**Royal Oak** (city) Oakland County
54	1398	7.1	**Battle Creek** (city) Calhoun County	129	2953	5.3	**Alpine** (township) Kent County
54	1398	7.1	**Farmington** (city) Oakland County	129	2953	5.3	**Chesterfield** (township) Macomb County
54	1398	7.1	**Grand Haven** (city) Ottawa County	129	2953	5.3	**Cutlerville** (CDP) Kent County
54	1398	7.1	**Lincoln Park** (city) Wayne County	129	2953	5.3	**Grandville** (city) Kent County
54	1398	7.1	**Sault Sainte Marie** (city) Chippewa County	129	2953	5.3	**Plymouth** (charter township) Wayne County
54	1398	7.1	**Superior** (charter township) Washtenaw County	134	3051	5.2	**Cooper** (charter township) Kalamazoo County
60	1478	7.0	**Clawson** (city) Oakland County	134	3051	5.2	**Emmett** (charter township) Calhoun County
60	1478	7.0	**Flushing** (city) Genesee County	134	3051	5.2	**Fenton** (charter township) Genesee County
60	1478	7.0	**Niles** (city) Berrien County	134	3051	5.2	**Milford** (charter township) Oakland County
60	1478	7.0	**Redford** (charter township) Wayne County	134	3051	5.2	**Port Huron** (charter township) Saint Clair County
60	1478	7.0	**Saginaw** (city) Saginaw County	134	3051	5.2	**Portage** (city) Kalamazoo County
65	1553	6.9	**Bay City** (city) Bay County	140	3126	5.1	**Comstock Park** (CDP) Kent County
65	1553	6.9	**Benton Harbor** (city) Berrien County	140	3126	5.1	**Fruitport** (charter township) Muskegon County
65	1553	6.9	**Norton Shores** (city) Muskegon County	140	3126	5.1	**Troy** (city) Oakland County
65	1553	6.9	**Port Huron** (city) Saint Clair County	143	3200	5.0	**White Lake** (charter township) Oakland County
65	1553	6.9	**Saint Joseph** (charter township) Berrien County	144	3273	4.9	**Romulus** (city) Wayne County
65	1553	6.9	**Spring Lake** (township) Ottawa County	145	3362	4.8	**Byron** (township) Kent County
71	1628	6.8	**Beecher** (CDP) Genesee County	145	3362	4.8	**Delhi** (charter township) Ingham County
71	1628	6.8	**Genesee** (charter township) Genesee County	145	3362	4.8	**Ionia** (city) Ionia County
71	1628	6.8	**Inkster** (city) Wayne County	145	3362	4.8	**Kentwood** (city) Kent County
71	1628	6.8	**South Lyon** (city) Oakland County	149	3439	4.7	**Independence** (charter township) Oakland County
75	1706	6.7	**Dearborn** (city) Wayne County	149	3439	4.7	**Plainfield** (charter township) Kent County

Note: The state column ranks the top/bottom 150 places from all places in the state with population of 10,000 or more. The national column ranks the top/bottom 150 places from all places in the country with population of 10,000 or more. Places that are unincorporated were not considered in the rankings. Please refer to the User Guide for additional information.

Marriage Status: Widowed

Top 150 Places Ranked in *Ascending* Order

State Rank	Nat'l Rank	Percent	Place
1	21	1.4	**Allendale** (CDP) Ottawa County
1	21	1.4	**Allendale** (charter township) Ottawa County
3	67	2.1	**Union** (charter township) Isabella County
4	75	2.2	**East Lansing** (city) Ingham County
5	92	2.4	**Cannon** (township) Kent County
5	92	2.4	**Tyrone** (township) Livingston County
7	156	2.7	**Bath** (charter township) Clinton County
8	187	2.8	**Ada** (township) Kent County
9	246	3.0	**East Bay** (township) Grand Traverse County
9	246	3.0	**East Grand Rapids** (city) Kent County
9	246	3.0	**Wixom** (city) Oakland County
12	281	3.1	**Brandon** (charter township) Oakland County
12	281	3.1	**Rochester** (city) Oakland County
14	307	3.2	**Mount Pleasant** (city) Isabella County
14	307	3.2	**Pittsfield** (charter township) Washtenaw County
16	347	3.3	**Ann Arbor** (city) Washtenaw County
16	347	3.3	**Forest Hills** (CDP) Kent County
16	347	3.3	**Park** (township) Ottawa County
19	424	3.5	**Big Rapids** (city) Mecosta County
19	424	3.5	**Oakland** (charter township) Oakland County
19	424	3.5	**Springfield** (charter township) Oakland County
22	478	3.6	**Caledonia** (township) Kent County
22	478	3.6	**Grosse Pointe Park** (city) Wayne County
24	519	3.7	**Holland** (charter township) Ottawa County
24	519	3.7	**Huron** (charter township) Wayne County
24	519	3.7	**Washington** (township) Macomb County
27	571	3.8	**Grand Haven** (charter township) Ottawa County
27	571	3.8	**Hartland** (township) Livingston County
29	629	3.9	**Gaines** (charter township) Kent County
29	629	3.9	**Highland** (charter township) Oakland County
31	676	4.0	**Brighton** (township) Livingston County
31	676	4.0	**Commerce** (charter township) Oakland County
31	676	4.0	**Oceola** (township) Livingston County
31	676	4.0	**Scio** (township) Washtenaw County
35	718	4.1	**Ferndale** (city) Oakland County
35	718	4.1	**Hamburg** (township) Livingston County
35	718	4.1	**Texas** (charter township) Kalamazoo County
38	768	4.2	**Canton** (charter township) Wayne County
38	768	4.2	**Macomb** (township) Macomb County
40	840	4.3	**Wyoming** (city) Kent County
41	904	4.4	**Lansing** (city) Ingham County
41	904	4.4	**Okemos** (CDP) Ingham County
41	904	4.4	**Orion** (charter township) Oakland County
44	965	4.5	**Birmingham** (city) Oakland County
44	965	4.5	**Genoa** (township) Livingston County
44	965	4.5	**Ypsilanti** (city) Washtenaw County
47	1039	4.6	**Auburn Hills** (city) Oakland County
47	1039	4.6	**Cascade** (charter township) Kent County
47	1039	4.6	**Holt** (CDP) Ingham County
47	1039	4.6	**Kalamazoo** (city) Kalamazoo County
47	1039	4.6	**Lyon** (charter township) Oakland County
47	1039	4.6	**Marquette** (city) Marquette County
47	1039	4.6	**Ypsilanti** (charter township) Washtenaw County
54	1132	4.7	**Independence** (charter township) Oakland County
54	1132	4.7	**Plainfield** (charter township) Kent County
54	1132	4.7	**Van Buren** (charter township) Wayne County
57	1218	4.8	**Byron** (township) Kent County
57	1218	4.8	**Delhi** (charter township) Ingham County
57	1218	4.8	**Ionia** (city) Ionia County
57	1218	4.8	**Kentwood** (city) Kent County
61	1295	4.9	**Romulus** (city) Wayne County
62	1384	5.0	**White Lake** (charter township) Oakland County
63	1457	5.1	**Comstock Park** (CDP) Kent County
63	1457	5.1	**Fruitport** (charter township) Muskegon County
63	1457	5.1	**Troy** (city) Oakland County
66	1531	5.2	**Cooper** (charter township) Kalamazoo County
66	1531	5.2	**Emmett** (charter township) Calhoun County
66	1531	5.2	**Fenton** (charter township) Genesee County
66	1531	5.2	**Milford** (charter township) Oakland County
66	1531	5.2	**Port Huron** (charter township) Saint Clair County
66	1531	5.2	**Portage** (city) Kalamazoo County
72	1606	5.3	**Alpine** (charter township) Kent County
72	1606	5.3	**Chesterfield** (township) Macomb County
72	1606	5.3	**Cutlerville** (CDP) Kent County
72	1606	5.3	**Grandville** (city) Kent County
72	1606	5.3	**Plymouth** (charter township) Wayne County
77	1704	5.4	**Comstock** (charter township) Kalamazoo County
77	1704	5.4	**Grand Rapids** (city) Kent County
77	1704	5.4	**Royal Oak** (city) Oakland County
80	1794	5.5	**Georgetown** (charter township) Ottawa County
80	1794	5.5	**Grand Blanc** (charter township) Genesee County
80	1794	5.5	**Lenox** (township) Macomb County
83	1891	5.6	**Brownstown** (charter township) Wayne County
83	1891	5.6	**DeWitt** (charter township) Clinton County
83	1891	5.6	**Holly** (township) Oakland County
83	1891	5.6	**Waterford** (charter township) Oakland County
87	1974	5.7	**Antwerp** (township) Van Buren County
87	1974	5.7	**Beverly Hills** (village) Oakland County
87	1974	5.7	**Bridgeport** (charter township) Saginaw County
87	1974	5.7	**Holland** (city) Ottawa County
87	1974	5.7	**Northville** (township) Wayne County
87	1974	5.7	**Rochester Hills** (city) Oakland County
87	1974	5.7	**Southfield** (township) Oakland County
87	1974	5.7	**Woodhaven** (city) Wayne County
95	2083	5.8	**New Baltimore** (city) Macomb County
95	2083	5.8	**Northview** (CDP) Kent County
95	2083	5.8	**Oxford** (charter township) Oakland County
95	2083	5.8	**Walker** (city) Kent County
99	2178	5.9	**Kalamazoo** (charter township) Kalamazoo County
99	2178	5.9	**Mundy** (township) Genesee County
101	2274	6.0	**Davison** (township) Genesee County
101	2274	6.0	**Green Oak** (township) Livingston County
101	2274	6.0	**Lincoln** (charter township) Berrien County
101	2274	6.0	**West Bloomfield** (charter township) Oakland County
105	2361	6.1	**Bloomfield** (charter township) Oakland County
105	2361	6.1	**Grosse Ile** (township) Wayne County
105	2361	6.1	**Hamtramck** (city) Wayne County
105	2361	6.1	**Melvindale** (city) Wayne County
105	2361	6.1	**Meridian** (charter township) Ingham County
105	2361	6.1	**Oak Park** (city) Oakland County
111	2459	6.2	**Adrian** (city) Lenawee County
112	2538	6.3	**Delta** (charter township) Eaton County
112	2538	6.3	**Flint** (city) Genesee County
112	2538	6.3	**Novi** (city) Oakland County
112	2538	6.3	**Owosso** (city) Shiawassee County
116	2619	6.4	**Harrison** (charter township) Macomb County
116	2619	6.4	**Jackson** (city) Jackson County
116	2619	6.4	**Oshtemo** (charter township) Kalamazoo County
119	2721	6.5	**Shelby** (charter township) Macomb County
119	2721	6.5	**Summit** (township) Jackson County
119	2721	6.5	**Waverly** (CDP) Eaton County
122	2799	6.6	**Bedford** (township) Monroe County
122	2799	6.6	**Harper Woods** (city) Wayne County
122	2799	6.6	**Muskegon** (city) Muskegon County
122	2799	6.6	**Taylor** (city) Wayne County
126	2878	6.7	**Dearborn** (city) Wayne County
126	2878	6.7	**Farmington Hills** (city) Oakland County
126	2878	6.7	**Frenchtown** (township) Monroe County
126	2878	6.7	**Leoni** (township) Jackson County
126	2878	6.7	**Pontiac** (city) Oakland County
131	2951	6.8	**Beecher** (CDP) Genesee County
131	2951	6.8	**Genesee** (charter township) Genesee County
131	2951	6.8	**Inkster** (city) Wayne County
131	2951	6.8	**South Lyon** (city) Oakland County
135	3029	6.9	**Bay City** (city) Bay County
135	3029	6.9	**Benton Harbor** (city) Berrien County
135	3029	6.9	**Norton Shores** (city) Muskegon County
135	3029	6.9	**Port Huron** (city) Saint Clair County
135	3029	6.9	**Saint Joseph** (charter township) Berrien County
135	3029	6.9	**Spring Lake** (township) Ottawa County
141	3104	7.0	**Clawson** (city) Oakland County
141	3104	7.0	**Flushing** (charter township) Genesee County
141	3104	7.0	**Niles** (city) Berrien County
141	3104	7.0	**Redford** (charter township) Wayne County
141	3104	7.0	**Saginaw** (city) Saginaw County
146	3179	7.1	**Battle Creek** (city) Calhoun County
146	3179	7.1	**Farmington** (city) Oakland County
146	3179	7.1	**Grand Haven** (city) Ottawa County
146	3179	7.1	**Lincoln Park** (city) Wayne County
146	3179	7.1	**Sault Sainte Marie** (city) Chippewa County

Note: The state column ranks the top/bottom 150 places from all places in the state with population of 10,000 or more. The national column ranks the top/bottom 150 places from all places in the country with population of 10,000 or more. Places that are unincorporated were not considered in the rankings. Please refer to the User Guide for additional information.

Marriage Status: Divorced

Top 150 Places Ranked in *Descending* Order

State Rank	Nat'l Rank	Percent	Place	State Rank	Nat'l Rank	Percent	Place
1	15	19.7	**Blackman** (charter township) Jackson County	74	1312	12.6	**Garden City** (city) Wayne County
2	27	19.1	**Cadillac** (city) Wexford County	77	1361	12.5	**Delta** (charter township) Eaton County
3	46	18.1	**Muskegon** (city) Muskegon County	78	1398	12.4	**Adrian** (city) Lenawee County
4	53	18.0	**Port Huron** (charter township) Saint Clair County	78	1398	12.4	**East Bay** (township) Grand Traverse County
5	85	17.4	**Leoni** (township) Jackson County	80	1444	12.3	**Delhi** (charter township) Ingham County
6	115	17.0	**Ionia** (city) Ionia County	80	1444	12.3	**Detroit** (city) Wayne County
7	159	16.6	**Wayne** (city) Wayne County	80	1444	12.3	**Niles** (township) Berrien County
8	194	16.3	**Mount Clemens** (city) Macomb County	83	1545	12.1	**Antwerp** (township) Van Buren County
9	204	16.2	**Port Huron** (city) Saint Clair County	83	1545	12.1	**Fraser** (city) Macomb County
10	258	15.9	**Kalamazoo** (charter township) Kalamazoo County	83	1545	12.1	**Highland** (charter township) Oakland County
11	285	15.7	**Flint** (city) Genesee County	83	1545	12.1	**Kalamazoo** (city) Kalamazoo County
12	306	15.6	**Inkster** (city) Wayne County	83	1545	12.1	**Royal Oak** (city) Oakland County
13	321	15.5	**Saginaw** (city) Saginaw County	88	1646	11.9	**Northview** (CDP) Kent County
14	339	15.4	**Jackson** (city) Jackson County	89	1695	11.8	**Auburn Hills** (city) Oakland County
15	366	15.3	**Coldwater** (city) Branch County	89	1695	11.8	**Muskegon** (charter township) Muskegon County
16	386	15.2	**Benton** (charter township) Berrien County	91	1750	11.7	**Brandon** (charter township) Oakland County
17	413	15.1	**Battle Creek** (city) Calhoun County	91	1750	11.7	**DeWitt** (charter township) Clinton County
17	413	15.1	**Grand Haven** (city) Ottawa County	91	1750	11.7	**Midland** (city) Midland County
19	437	15.0	**Highland Park** (city) Wayne County	91	1750	11.7	**Rochester** (city) Oakland County
19	437	15.0	**Holly** (township) Oakland County	91	1750	11.7	**Ypsilanti** (charter township) Washtenaw County
21	464	14.9	**Mount Morris** (township) Genesee County	96	1804	11.6	**Birmingham** (city) Oakland County
21	464	14.9	**Owosso** (city) Shiawassee County	96	1804	11.6	**Fenton** (charter township) Genesee County
23	494	14.8	**Niles** (city) Berrien County	96	1804	11.6	**Flushing** (charter township) Genesee County
24	514	14.7	**Lincoln Park** (city) Wayne County	96	1804	11.6	**Vienna** (charter township) Genesee County
24	514	14.7	**Traverse City** (city) Grand Traverse County	100	1859	11.5	**Farmington** (city) Oakland County
26	543	14.6	**Bay City** (city) Bay County	100	1859	11.5	**Wixom** (city) Oakland County
26	543	14.6	**Monroe** (city) Monroe County	102	1910	11.4	**Comstock** (charter township) Kalamazoo County
26	543	14.6	**Roseville** (city) Macomb County	102	1910	11.4	**Independence** (charter township) Oakland County
29	573	14.5	**Davison** (township) Genesee County	102	1910	11.4	**Oak Park** (city) Oakland County
29	573	14.5	**Escanaba** (city) Delta County	102	1910	11.4	**Walker** (city) Kent County
29	573	14.5	**Madison Heights** (city) Oakland County	106	1954	11.3	**Van Buren** (charter township) Wayne County
29	573	14.5	**Pontiac** (city) Oakland County	107	2009	11.2	**Alpine** (township) Kent County
33	613	14.4	**Clawson** (city) Oakland County	107	2009	11.2	**Berkley** (city) Oakland County
33	613	14.4	**Eastpointe** (city) Macomb County	107	2009	11.2	**Chesterfield** (township) Macomb County
33	613	14.4	**Muskegon Heights** (city) Muskegon County	107	2009	11.2	**Genoa** (township) Livingston County
33	613	14.4	**Southfield** (city) Oakland County	107	2009	11.2	**Mundy** (township) Genesee County
33	613	14.4	**Trenton** (city) Wayne County	107	2009	11.2	**New Baltimore** (city) Macomb County
38	667	14.2	**Riverview** (city) Wayne County	113	2066	11.1	**Grand Blanc** (charter township) Genesee County
38	667	14.2	**Southgate** (city) Wayne County	113	2066	11.1	**Wyoming** (city) Kent County
38	667	14.2	**Woodhaven** (city) Wayne County	115	2111	11.0	**Allen Park** (city) Wayne County
41	698	14.1	**Flint** (charter township) Genesee County	115	2111	11.0	**Dearborn Heights** (city) Wayne County
41	698	14.1	**Melvindale** (city) Wayne County	115	2111	11.0	**Warren** (city) Macomb County
41	698	14.1	**Westland** (city) Wayne County	118	2168	10.9	**Brownstown** (charter township) Wayne County
44	738	14.0	**Beecher** (CDP) Genesee County	118	2168	10.9	**Grand Rapids** (city) Kent County
44	738	14.0	**Romulus** (city) Wayne County	120	2216	10.8	**Huron** (charter township) Wayne County
46	766	13.9	**Benton Harbor** (city) Berrien County	120	2216	10.8	**Spring Lake** (township) Ottawa County
46	766	13.9	**Lansing** (city) Ingham County	122	2277	10.7	**Fort Gratiot** (charter township) Saint Clair County
46	766	13.9	**South Lyon** (city) Oakland County	122	2277	10.7	**Kentwood** (city) Kent County
46	766	13.9	**Taylor** (city) Wayne County	124	2339	10.6	**Cooper** (charter township) Kalamazoo County
46	766	13.9	**Waterford** (charter township) Oakland County	124	2339	10.6	**Farmington Hills** (city) Oakland County
51	809	13.8	**Wyandotte** (city) Wayne County	124	2339	10.6	**Grandville** (city) Kent County
52	850	13.7	**Alpena** (city) Alpena County	127	2394	10.5	**Orion** (charter township) Oakland County
52	850	13.7	**Burton** (city) Genesee County	128	2487	10.3	**East Grand Rapids** (city) Kent County
54	889	13.6	**Hazel Park** (city) Oakland County	128	2487	10.3	**Gaines** (charter township) Kent County
55	920	13.5	**Cutlerville** (CDP) Kent County	130	2536	10.2	**Livonia** (city) Wayne County
55	920	13.5	**Harrison** (charter township) Macomb County	130	2536	10.2	**Portage** (city) Kalamazoo County
55	920	13.5	**Redford** (charter township) Wayne County	130	2536	10.2	**Saginaw** (charter township) Saginaw County
58	969	13.4	**Waverly** (CDP) Eaton County	130	2536	10.2	**Washington** (township) Macomb County
59	1025	13.3	**Ferndale** (city) Oakland County	134	2602	10.1	**Haslett** (CDP) Ingham County
59	1025	13.3	**Garfield** (charter township) Grand Traverse County	134	2602	10.1	**Ypsilanti** (city) Washtenaw County
59	1025	13.3	**Harper Woods** (city) Wayne County	136	2675	10.0	**Green Oak** (township) Livingston County
62	1051	13.2	**Bridgeport** (charter township) Saginaw County	136	2675	10.0	**Milford** (charter township) Oakland County
62	1051	13.2	**Fenton** (city) Genesee County	136	2675	10.0	**Novi** (city) Oakland County
62	1051	13.2	**Genesee** (charter township) Genesee County	139	2726	9.9	**Beverly Hills** (village) Oakland County
62	1051	13.2	**Sault Sainte Marie** (city) Chippewa County	139	2726	9.9	**Fruitport** (charter township) Muskegon County
66	1090	13.1	**Norton Shores** (city) Muskegon County	141	2834	9.7	**Marquette** (city) Marquette County
66	1090	13.1	**Sturgis** (city) Saint Joseph County	141	2834	9.7	**Plainfield** (charter township) Kent County
68	1134	13.0	**Clinton** (charter township) Macomb County	141	2834	9.7	**Summit** (township) Jackson County
68	1134	13.0	**Emmett** (charter township) Calhoun County	144	2882	9.6	**Grand Haven** (charter township) Ottawa County
70	1186	12.9	**Monroe** (charter township) Monroe County	145	2927	9.5	**Bedford** (township) Monroe County
71	1223	12.8	**Frenchtown** (township) Monroe County	145	2927	9.5	**White Lake** (charter township) Oakland County
71	1223	12.8	**Saint Clair Shores** (city) Macomb County	147	2980	9.4	**Bath** (charter township) Clinton County
73	1270	12.7	**Holt** (CDP) Ingham County	147	2980	9.4	**Dearborn** (city) Wayne County
74	1312	12.6	**Bangor** (charter township) Bay County	147	2980	9.4	**Saint Joseph** (charter township) Berrien County
74	1312	12.6	**Comstock Park** (CDP) Kent County	150	3032	9.3	**Commerce** (charter township) Oakland County

Note: The state column ranks the top/bottom 150 places from all places in the state with population of 10,000 or more. The national column ranks the top/bottom 150 places from all places in the country with population of 10,000 or more. Places that are unincorporated were not considered in the rankings. Please refer to the User Guide for additional information.

Marriage Status: Divorced

Top 150 Places Ranked in *Ascending* Order

State Rank	Nat'l Rank	Percent	Place
1	35	3.5	**East Lansing** (city) Ingham County
2	73	4.4	**Allendale** (CDP) Ottawa County
3	99	4.7	**Allendale** (charter township) Ottawa County
4	125	5.0	**Ada** (township) Kent County
5	199	5.5	**Forest Hills** (CDP) Kent County
5	199	5.5	**Georgetown** (charter township) Ottawa County
7	348	6.2	**Cascade** (charter township) Kent County
8	368	6.3	**Macomb** (township) Macomb County
9	420	6.5	**Texas** (charter township) Kalamazoo County
10	493	6.8	**Park** (township) Ottawa County
11	587	7.1	**Troy** (city) Oakland County
12	620	7.2	**Hamtramck** (city) Wayne County
12	620	7.2	**Union** (charter township) Isabella County
14	689	7.4	**Grosse Pointe Woods** (city) Wayne County
14	689	7.4	**Mount Pleasant** (city) Isabella County
16	729	7.5	**Bloomfield** (charter township) Oakland County
17	808	7.7	**Ann Arbor** (city) Washtenaw County
17	808	7.7	**Grosse Pointe Park** (city) Wayne County
17	808	7.7	**Plymouth** (charter township) Wayne County
20	849	7.8	**Brighton** (township) Livingston County
20	849	7.8	**Hartland** (township) Livingston County
22	902	7.9	**Big Rapids** (city) Mecosta County
22	902	7.9	**Jenison** (CDP) Ottawa County
24	949	8.0	**Canton** (charter township) Wayne County
24	949	8.0	**Northville** (township) Wayne County
26	1044	8.2	**Caledonia** (township) Kent County
26	1044	8.2	**Grand Rapids** (charter township) Kent County
26	1044	8.2	**Oakland** (charter township) Oakland County
26	1044	8.2	**Tyrone** (township) Livingston County
30	1092	8.3	**Superior** (charter township) Washtenaw County
31	1135	8.4	**Cannon** (township) Kent County
31	1135	8.4	**Okemos** (CDP) Ingham County
33	1178	8.5	**Lyon** (charter township) Oakland County
33	1178	8.5	**Monitor** (charter township) Bay County
33	1178	8.5	**Rochester Hills** (city) Oakland County
33	1178	8.5	**Sterling Heights** (city) Macomb County
37	1273	8.7	**Byron** (township) Kent County
37	1273	8.7	**Oceola** (township) Livingston County
37	1273	8.7	**Springfield** (charter township) Oakland County
40	1324	8.8	**Hamburg** (township) Livingston County
40	1324	8.8	**Holland** (charter township) Ottawa County
40	1324	8.8	**Oshtemo** (charter township) Kalamazoo County
43	1372	8.9	**Grosse Ile** (township) Wayne County
43	1372	8.9	**Holland** (city) Ottawa County
43	1372	8.9	**Lenox** (township) Macomb County
43	1372	8.9	**Shelby** (charter township) Macomb County
43	1372	8.9	**Southfield** (charter township) Oakland County
43	1372	8.9	**West Bloomfield** (charter township) Oakland County
49	1471	9.1	**Lincoln** (charter township) Berrien County
50	1512	9.2	**Pittsfield** (charter township) Washtenaw County
51	1570	9.3	**Commerce** (charter township) Oakland County
51	1570	9.3	**Meridian** (charter township) Ingham County
51	1570	9.3	**Oxford** (charter township) Oakland County
51	1570	9.3	**Scio** (township) Washtenaw County
51	1570	9.3	**Thomas** (township) Saginaw County
56	1625	9.4	**Bath** (charter township) Clinton County
56	1625	9.4	**Dearborn** (city) Wayne County
56	1625	9.4	**Saint Joseph** (charter township) Berrien County
59	1677	9.5	**Bedford** (township) Monroe County
59	1677	9.5	**White Lake** (charter township) Oakland County
61	1730	9.6	**Grand Haven** (charter township) Ottawa County
62	1775	9.7	**Marquette** (city) Marquette County
62	1775	9.7	**Plainfield** (charter township) Kent County
62	1775	9.7	**Summit** (township) Jackson County
65	1878	9.9	**Beverly Hills** (village) Oakland County
65	1878	9.9	**Fruitport** (charter township) Muskegon County
67	1931	10.0	**Green Oak** (township) Livingston County
67	1931	10.0	**Milford** (charter township) Oakland County
67	1931	10.0	**Novi** (city) Oakland County
70	1982	10.1	**Haslett** (CDP) Ingham County
70	1982	10.1	**Ypsilanti** (city) Washtenaw County
72	2055	10.2	**Livonia** (city) Wayne County
72	2055	10.2	**Portage** (city) Kalamazoo County
72	2055	10.2	**Saginaw** (charter township) Saginaw County
72	2055	10.2	**Washington** (township) Macomb County
76	2121	10.3	**East Grand Rapids** (city) Kent County
76	2121	10.3	**Gaines** (charter township) Kent County
78	2216	10.5	**Orion** (charter township) Oakland County
79	2263	10.6	**Cooper** (charter township) Kalamazoo County
79	2263	10.6	**Farmington Hills** (city) Oakland County
79	2263	10.6	**Grandville** (city) Kent County
82	2318	10.7	**Fort Gratiot** (charter township) Saint Clair County
82	2318	10.7	**Kentwood** (city) Kent County
84	2380	10.8	**Huron** (charter township) Wayne County
84	2380	10.8	**Spring Lake** (township) Ottawa County
86	2441	10.9	**Brownstown** (charter township) Wayne County
86	2441	10.9	**Grand Rapids** (city) Kent County
88	2489	11.0	**Allen Park** (city) Wayne County
88	2489	11.0	**Dearborn Heights** (city) Wayne County
88	2489	11.0	**Warren** (city) Macomb County
91	2546	11.1	**Grand Blanc** (charter township) Genesee County
91	2546	11.1	**Wyoming** (city) Kent County
93	2591	11.2	**Alpine** (township) Kent County
93	2591	11.2	**Berkley** (city) Oakland County
93	2591	11.2	**Chesterfield** (township) Macomb County
93	2591	11.2	**Genoa** (township) Livingston County
93	2591	11.2	**Mundy** (township) Genesee County
93	2591	11.2	**New Baltimore** (city) Macomb County
99	2648	11.3	**Van Buren** (charter township) Wayne County
100	2703	11.4	**Comstock** (charter township) Kalamazoo County
100	2703	11.4	**Independence** (charter township) Oakland County
100	2703	11.4	**Oak Park** (city) Oakland County
100	2703	11.4	**Walker** (city) Kent County
104	2747	11.5	**Farmington** (city) Oakland County
104	2747	11.5	**Wixom** (city) Oakland County
106	2798	11.6	**Birmingham** (city) Oakland County
106	2798	11.6	**Fenton** (charter township) Genesee County
106	2798	11.6	**Flushing** (charter township) Genesee County
106	2798	11.6	**Vienna** (charter township) Genesee County
110	2853	11.7	**Brandon** (charter township) Oakland County
110	2853	11.7	**DeWitt** (charter township) Clinton County
110	2853	11.7	**Midland** (city) Midland County
110	2853	11.7	**Rochester** (city) Oakland County
110	2853	11.7	**Ypsilanti** (charter township) Washtenaw County
115	2907	11.8	**Auburn Hills** (city) Oakland County
115	2907	11.8	**Muskegon** (charter township) Muskegon County
117	2962	11.9	**Northview** (CDP) Kent County
118	3053	12.1	**Antwerp** (township) Van Buren County
118	3053	12.1	**Fraser** (city) Macomb County
118	3053	12.1	**Highland** (charter township) Oakland County
118	3053	12.1	**Kalamazoo** (city) Kalamazoo County
118	3053	12.1	**Royal Oak** (city) Oakland County
123	3160	12.3	**Delhi** (charter township) Ingham County
123	3160	12.3	**Detroit** (city) Wayne County
123	3160	12.3	**Niles** (township) Berrien County
126	3213	12.4	**Adrian** (city) Lenawee County
126	3213	12.4	**East Bay** (township) Grand Traverse County
128	3259	12.5	**Delta** (charter township) Eaton County
129	3296	12.6	**Bangor** (charter township) Bay County
129	3296	12.6	**Comstock Park** (CDP) Kent County
129	3296	12.6	**Garden City** (city) Wayne County
132	3345	12.7	**Holt** (CDP) Ingham County
133	3387	12.8	**Frenchtown** (township) Monroe County
133	3387	12.8	**Saint Clair Shores** (city) Macomb County
135	3434	12.9	**Monroe** (charter township) Monroe County
136	3471	13.0	**Clinton** (charter township) Macomb County
136	3471	13.0	**Emmett** (charter township) Calhoun County
138	3523	13.1	**Norton Shores** (city) Muskegon County
138	3523	13.1	**Sturgis** (city) Saint Joseph County
140	3567	13.2	**Bridgeport** (charter township) Saginaw County
140	3567	13.2	**Fenton** (city) Genesee County
140	3567	13.2	**Genesee** (charter township) Genesee County
140	3567	13.2	**Sault Sainte Marie** (city) Chippewa County
144	3606	13.3	**Ferndale** (city) Oakland County
144	3606	13.3	**Garfield** (charter township) Grand Traverse County
144	3606	13.3	**Harper Woods** (city) Wayne County
147	3632	13.4	**Waverly** (CDP) Eaton County
148	3688	13.5	**Cutlerville** (CDP) Kent County
148	3688	13.5	**Harrison** (charter township) Macomb County
148	3688	13.5	**Redford** (charter township) Wayne County

Note: The state column ranks the top/bottom 150 places from all places in the state with population of 10,000 or more. The national column ranks the top/bottom 150 places from all places in the country with population of 10,000 or more. Places that are unincorporated were not considered in the rankings. Please refer to the User Guide for additional information.

Foreign Born

Top 150 Places Ranked in *Descending* Order

State Rank	Nat'l Rank	Percent	Place
1	91	44.4	**Hamtramck** (city) Wayne County
2	516	27.2	**Troy** (city) Oakland County
3	535	26.9	**Dearborn** (city) Wayne County
4	672	24.2	**Sterling Heights** (city) Macomb County
5	818	21.3	**West Bloomfield** (charter township) Oakland County
6	956	19.1	**Novi** (city) Oakland County
7	1024	18.3	**Pittsfield** (charter township) Washtenaw County
8	1066	17.8	**Madison Heights** (city) Oakland County
9	1090	17.6	**Farmington Hills** (city) Oakland County
10	1105	17.4	**Ann Arbor** (city) Washtenaw County
11	1122	17.1	**Dearborn Heights** (city) Wayne County
12	1148	16.8	**Farmington** (city) Oakland County
13	1215	15.9	**Auburn Hills** (city) Oakland County
14	1220	15.8	**Canton** (charter township) Wayne County
15	1241	15.6	**Northville** (township) Wayne County
15	1241	15.6	**Rochester Hills** (city) Oakland County
17	1323	14.9	**East Lansing** (city) Ingham County
18	1349	14.7	**Holland** (charter township) Ottawa County
19	1363	14.6	**Okemos** (CDP) Ingham County
20	1385	14.4	**Bloomfield** (charter township) Oakland County
21	1400	14.2	**Melvindale** (city) Wayne County
22	1479	13.5	**Kentwood** (city) Kent County
23	1520	13.2	**Shelby** (charter township) Macomb County
24	1538	13.0	**Superior** (charter township) Washtenaw County
25	1560	12.8	**Meridian** (charter township) Ingham County
26	1589	12.5	**Holland** (city) Ottawa County
27	1633	12.2	**Scio** (township) Washtenaw County
28	1750	11.4	**Warren** (city) Macomb County
29	1799	11.1	**Rochester** (city) Oakland County
30	1842	10.9	**Oakland** (charter township) Oakland County
31	1856	10.8	**Wyoming** (city) Kent County
32	1871	10.7	**Wixom** (city) Oakland County
33	1907	10.5	**Washington** (township) Macomb County
34	1931	10.4	**Macomb** (township) Macomb County
35	1987	10.1	**Grand Rapids** (city) Kent County
36	2031	9.9	**Haslett** (CDP) Ingham County
36	2031	9.9	**Oak Park** (city) Oakland County
38	2138	9.4	**Southfield** (city) Oakland County
39	2201	9.1	**Comstock Park** (CDP) Kent County
40	2240	8.9	**Clawson** (city) Oakland County
40	2240	8.9	**Sturgis** (city) Saint Joseph County
42	2283	8.7	**Brownstown** (charter township) Wayne County
43	2302	8.6	**Commerce** (charter township) Oakland County
44	2402	8.1	**Lansing** (city) Ingham County
45	2429	8.0	**Birmingham** (city) Oakland County
46	2497	7.7	**Alpine** (township) Kent County
47	2565	7.5	**Plymouth** (charter township) Wayne County
48	2588	7.4	**Lincoln** (charter township) Berrien County
49	2615	7.3	**Clinton** (charter township) Macomb County
49	2615	7.3	**Grosse Pointe Park** (city) Wayne County
49	2615	7.3	**Royal Oak** (city) Oakland County
49	2615	7.3	**Southfield** (township) Oakland County
53	2669	7.1	**Grosse Ile** (township) Wayne County
54	2696	7.0	**Livonia** (city) Wayne County
54	2696	7.0	**Ypsilanti** (city) Washtenaw County
56	2729	6.9	**Orion** (charter township) Oakland County
57	2755	6.8	**Grand Rapids** (charter township) Kent County
58	2806	6.6	**Pontiac** (city) Oakland County
59	2839	6.5	**Delta** (charter township) Eaton County
59	2839	6.5	**Midland** (city) Midland County
59	2839	6.5	**Oshtemo** (charter township) Kalamazoo County
59	2839	6.5	**Waverly** (CDP) Eaton County
59	2839	6.5	**Westland** (city) Wayne County
64	2869	6.4	**Hazel Park** (city) Oakland County
65	2904	6.3	**Grand Blanc** (charter township) Genesee County
65	2904	6.3	**Kalamazoo** (city) Kalamazoo County
65	2904	6.3	**Lincoln Park** (city) Wayne County
68	2955	6.1	**Beverly Hills** (village) Oakland County
68	2955	6.1	**Cascade** (charter township) Kent County
70	2990	6.0	**Battle Creek** (city) Calhoun County
71	3011	5.9	**Texas** (charter township) Kalamazoo County
72	3039	5.8	**Berkley** (city) Oakland County
73	3070	5.7	**Ypsilanti** (charter township) Washtenaw County
74	3093	5.6	**Bath** (charter township) Clinton County
74	3093	5.6	**Mount Pleasant** (city) Isabella County
76	3128	5.5	**Ada** (township) Kent County
76	3128	5.5	**Comstock** (charter township) Kalamazoo County
76	3128	5.5	**Forest Hills** (CDP) Kent County
79	3165	5.4	**Fort Gratiot** (charter township) Saint Clair County
80	3191	5.3	**Grand Haven** (charter township) Ottawa County
80	3191	5.3	**Southgate** (city) Wayne County
80	3191	5.3	**Waterford** (charter township) Oakland County
83	3225	5.2	**Delhi** (charter township) Ingham County
84	3257	5.1	**Coldwater** (city) Branch County
84	3257	5.1	**Detroit** (city) Wayne County
86	3295	5.0	**Portage** (city) Kalamazoo County
86	3295	5.0	**Saginaw** (charter township) Saginaw County
88	3329	4.9	**Cutlerville** (CDP) Kent County
88	3329	4.9	**Ferndale** (city) Oakland County
88	3329	4.9	**Gaines** (charter township) Kent County
88	3329	4.9	**Saint Clair Shores** (city) Macomb County
92	3363	4.8	**Allen Park** (city) Wayne County
92	3363	4.8	**Holt** (CDP) Ingham County
94	3401	4.7	**East Grand Rapids** (city) Kent County
94	3401	4.7	**Fraser** (city) Macomb County
96	3455	4.5	**South Lyon** (city) Oakland County
96	3455	4.5	**Taylor** (city) Wayne County
98	3489	4.4	**Chesterfield** (township) Macomb County
98	3489	4.4	**Romulus** (city) Wayne County
98	3489	4.4	**Saint Joseph** (charter township) Berrien County
101	3522	4.3	**Big Rapids** (city) Mecosta County
102	3554	4.2	**Byron** (township) Kent County
102	3554	4.2	**Flint** (charter township) Genesee County
102	3554	4.2	**Harper Woods** (city) Wayne County
102	3554	4.2	**Harrison** (charter township) Macomb County
102	3554	4.2	**Van Buren** (charter township) Wayne County
107	3592	4.1	**Milford** (charter township) Oakland County
107	3592	4.1	**Woodhaven** (city) Wayne County
109	3625	4.0	**Benton** (charter township) Berrien County
109	3625	4.0	**Brighton** (township) Livingston County
109	3625	4.0	**Wayne** (city) Wayne County
112	3661	3.9	**Genoa** (township) Livingston County
112	3661	3.9	**Independence** (charter township) Oakland County
112	3661	3.9	**Oxford** (charter township) Oakland County
112	3661	3.9	**Park** (township) Ottawa County
116	3689	3.8	**Grosse Pointe Woods** (city) Wayne County
116	3689	3.8	**Springfield** (charter township) Oakland County
116	3689	3.8	**Summit** (township) Jackson County
116	3689	3.8	**Walker** (city) Kent County
120	3723	3.7	**Niles** (city) Berrien County
120	3723	3.7	**Niles** (township) Berrien County
120	3723	3.7	**Port Huron** (city) Saint Clair County
120	3723	3.7	**Sault Sainte Marie** (city) Chippewa County
124	3755	3.6	**Caledonia** (township) Kent County
124	3755	3.6	**Grandville** (city) Kent County
124	3755	3.6	**Lyon** (charter township) Oakland County
124	3755	3.6	**Roseville** (city) Macomb County
124	3755	3.6	**Trenton** (city) Wayne County
129	3831	3.4	**Fenton** (city) Genesee County
129	3831	3.4	**Kalamazoo** (charter township) Kalamazoo County
129	3831	3.4	**White Lake** (charter township) Oakland County
132	3896	3.2	**Eastpointe** (city) Macomb County
132	3896	3.2	**Garden City** (city) Wayne County
132	3896	3.2	**Inkster** (city) Wayne County
132	3896	3.2	**Norton Shores** (city) Muskegon County
136	3933	3.1	**Allendale** (charter township) Ottawa County
136	3933	3.1	**Cannon** (township) Kent County
136	3933	3.1	**Georgetown** (charter township) Ottawa County
139	3969	3.0	**Allendale** (CDP) Ottawa County
139	3969	3.0	**Green Oak** (township) Livingston County
139	3969	3.0	**Monroe** (city) Monroe County
139	3969	3.0	**Oceola** (township) Livingston County
139	3969	3.0	**Riverview** (city) Wayne County
139	3969	3.0	**Tyrone** (township) Livingston County
145	4035	2.8	**Adrian** (city) Lenawee County
145	4035	2.8	**Spring Lake** (township) Ottawa County
147	4085	2.7	**Emmett** (charter township) Calhoun County
147	4085	2.7	**Mount Clemens** (city) Macomb County
149	4119	2.6	**Antwerp** (township) Van Buren County
149	4119	2.6	**DeWitt** (charter township) Clinton County

Note: The state column ranks the top/bottom 150 places from all places in the state with population of 10,000 or more. The national column ranks the top/bottom 150 places from all places in the country with population of 10,000 or more. Places that are unincorporated were not considered in the rankings. Please refer to the User Guide for additional information.

Foreign Born

Top 150 Places Ranked in *Ascending* Order

State Rank	Nat'l Rank	Percent	Place
1	4	0.3	**Muskegon Heights** (city) Muskegon County
2	11	0.5	**Beecher** (CDP) Genesee County
3	17	0.6	**Benton Harbor** (city) Berrien County
3	17	0.6	**Bridgeport** (charter township) Saginaw County
3	17	0.6	**Muskegon** (charter township) Muskegon County
6	30	0.7	**Highland Park** (city) Wayne County
7	41	0.8	**Cadillac** (city) Wexford County
7	41	0.8	**Owosso** (city) Shiawassee County
9	58	0.9	**Alpena** (city) Alpena County
9	58	0.9	**Blackman** (charter township) Jackson County
9	58	0.9	**Escanaba** (city) Delta County
12	75	1.0	**Monitor** (charter township) Bay County
13	96	1.1	**Ionia** (city) Ionia County
14	119	1.2	**Bay City** (city) Bay County
14	119	1.2	**Burton** (city) Genesee County
14	119	1.2	**Flint** (city) Genesee County
17	162	1.4	**East Bay** (township) Grand Traverse County
18	182	1.5	**Davison** (township) Genesee County
18	182	1.5	**Genesee** (charter township) Genesee County
18	182	1.5	**Marquette** (city) Marquette County
18	182	1.5	**Saginaw** (city) Saginaw County
22	212	1.6	**Leoni** (township) Jackson County
23	236	1.7	**Thomas** (township) Saginaw County
24	261	1.8	**Garfield** (charter township) Grand Traverse County
24	261	1.8	**Mount Morris** (township) Genesee County
26	292	1.9	**Jackson** (city) Jackson County
26	292	1.9	**Jenison** (CDP) Ottawa County
26	292	1.9	**Monroe** (charter township) Monroe County
26	292	1.9	**Port Huron** (charter township) Saint Clair County
30	319	2.0	**Brandon** (charter township) Oakland County
30	319	2.0	**Traverse City** (city) Grand Traverse County
32	352	2.1	**Bangor** (charter township) Bay County
32	352	2.1	**Cooper** (charter township) Kalamazoo County
32	352	2.1	**Flushing** (charter township) Genesee County
32	352	2.1	**Fruitport** (charter township) Muskegon County
32	352	2.1	**Grand Haven** (city) Ottawa County
32	352	2.1	**New Baltimore** (city) Macomb County
38	381	2.2	**Bedford** (township) Monroe County
38	381	2.2	**Highland** (charter township) Oakland County
38	381	2.2	**Holly** (township) Oakland County
38	381	2.2	**Huron** (charter township) Wayne County
38	381	2.2	**Mundy** (township) Genesee County
38	381	2.2	**Vienna** (charter township) Genesee County
44	418	2.3	**Fenton** (charter township) Genesee County
44	418	2.3	**Hartland** (township) Livingston County
44	418	2.3	**Northview** (CDP) Kent County
44	418	2.3	**Plainfield** (charter township) Kent County
44	418	2.3	**Redford** (charter township) Wayne County
44	418	2.3	**Wyandotte** (city) Wayne County
50	459	2.4	**Frenchtown** (township) Monroe County
50	459	2.4	**Lenox** (township) Macomb County
50	459	2.4	**Muskegon** (city) Muskegon County
53	481	2.5	**Union** (charter township) Isabella County
54	506	2.6	**Antwerp** (township) Van Buren County
54	506	2.6	**DeWitt** (charter township) Clinton County
54	506	2.6	**Hamburg** (township) Livingston County
57	538	2.7	**Emmett** (charter township) Calhoun County
57	538	2.7	**Mount Clemens** (city) Macomb County
59	572	2.8	**Adrian** (city) Lenawee County
59	572	2.8	**Spring Lake** (township) Ottawa County
61	648	3.0	**Allendale** (CDP) Ottawa County
61	648	3.0	**Green Oak** (township) Livingston County
61	648	3.0	**Monroe** (city) Monroe County
61	648	3.0	**Oceola** (township) Livingston County
61	648	3.0	**Riverview** (city) Wayne County
61	648	3.0	**Tyrone** (township) Livingston County
67	688	3.1	**Allendale** (charter township) Ottawa County
67	688	3.1	**Cannon** (township) Kent County
67	688	3.1	**Georgetown** (charter township) Ottawa County
70	724	3.2	**Eastpointe** (city) Macomb County
70	724	3.2	**Garden City** (city) Wayne County
70	724	3.2	**Inkster** (city) Wayne County
70	724	3.2	**Norton Shores** (city) Muskegon County
74	791	3.4	**Fenton** (city) Genesee County
74	791	3.4	**Kalamazoo** (charter township) Kalamazoo County

State Rank	Nat'l Rank	Percent	Place
74	791	3.4	**White Lake** (charter township) Oakland County
77	865	3.6	**Caledonia** (township) Kent County
77	865	3.6	**Grandville** (city) Kent County
77	865	3.6	**Lyon** (charter township) Oakland County
77	865	3.6	**Roseville** (city) Macomb County
77	865	3.6	**Trenton** (city) Wayne County
82	902	3.7	**Niles** (city) Berrien County
82	902	3.7	**Niles** (township) Berrien County
82	902	3.7	**Port Huron** (city) Saint Clair County
82	902	3.7	**Sault Sainte Marie** (city) Chippewa County
86	934	3.8	**Grosse Pointe Woods** (city) Wayne County
86	934	3.8	**Springfield** (charter township) Oakland County
86	934	3.8	**Summit** (township) Jackson County
86	934	3.8	**Walker** (city) Kent County
90	968	3.9	**Genoa** (township) Livingston County
90	968	3.9	**Independence** (charter township) Oakland County
90	968	3.9	**Oxford** (charter township) Oakland County
90	968	3.9	**Park** (township) Ottawa County
94	996	4.0	**Benton** (charter township) Berrien County
94	996	4.0	**Brighton** (township) Livingston County
94	996	4.0	**Wayne** (city) Wayne County
97	1032	4.1	**Milford** (charter township) Oakland County
97	1032	4.1	**Woodhaven** (city) Wayne County
99	1065	4.2	**Byron** (township) Kent County
99	1065	4.2	**Flint** (charter township) Genesee County
99	1065	4.2	**Harper Woods** (city) Wayne County
99	1065	4.2	**Harrison** (charter township) Macomb County
99	1065	4.2	**Van Buren** (charter township) Wayne County
104	1103	4.3	**Big Rapids** (city) Mecosta County
105	1135	4.4	**Chesterfield** (township) Macomb County
105	1135	4.4	**Romulus** (city) Wayne County
105	1135	4.4	**Saint Joseph** (charter township) Berrien County
108	1168	4.5	**South Lyon** (city) Oakland County
108	1168	4.5	**Taylor** (city) Wayne County
110	1224	4.7	**East Grand Rapids** (city) Kent County
110	1224	4.7	**Fraser** (city) Macomb County
112	1256	4.8	**Allen Park** (city) Wayne County
112	1256	4.8	**Holt** (CDP) Ingham County
114	1294	4.9	**Cutlerville** (CDP) Kent County
114	1294	4.9	**Ferndale** (city) Oakland County
114	1294	4.9	**Gaines** (township) Kent County
114	1294	4.9	**Saint Clair Shores** (city) Macomb County
118	1328	5.0	**Portage** (city) Kalamazoo County
118	1328	5.0	**Saginaw** (charter township) Saginaw County
120	1362	5.1	**Coldwater** (city) Branch County
120	1362	5.1	**Detroit** (city) Wayne County
122	1400	5.2	**Delhi** (charter township) Ingham County
123	1432	5.3	**Grand Haven** (charter township) Ottawa County
123	1432	5.3	**Southgate** (city) Wayne County
123	1432	5.3	**Waterford** (charter township) Oakland County
126	1466	5.4	**Fort Gratiot** (charter township) Saint Clair County
127	1492	5.5	**Ada** (township) Kent County
127	1492	5.5	**Comstock** (charter township) Kalamazoo County
127	1492	5.5	**Forest Hills** (CDP) Kent County
130	1529	5.6	**Bath** (charter township) Clinton County
130	1529	5.6	**Mount Pleasant** (city) Isabella County
132	1564	5.7	**Ypsilanti** (charter township) Washtenaw County
133	1587	5.8	**Berkley** (city) Oakland County
134	1618	5.9	**Texas** (charter township) Kalamazoo County
135	1646	6.0	**Battle Creek** (city) Calhoun County
136	1667	6.1	**Beverly Hills** (village) Oakland County
136	1667	6.1	**Cascade** (charter township) Kent County
138	1728	6.3	**Grand Blanc** (charter township) Genesee County
138	1728	6.3	**Kalamazoo** (city) Kalamazoo County
138	1728	6.3	**Lincoln Park** (city) Wayne County
141	1753	6.4	**Hazel Park** (city) Oakland County
142	1788	6.5	**Delta** (charter township) Eaton County
142	1788	6.5	**Midland** (city) Midland County
142	1788	6.5	**Oshtemo** (charter township) Kalamazoo County
142	1788	6.5	**Waverly** (CDP) Eaton County
142	1788	6.5	**Westland** (city) Wayne County
147	1818	6.6	**Pontiac** (city) Oakland County
148	1875	6.8	**Grand Rapids** (charter township) Kent County
149	1902	6.9	**Orion** (charter township) Oakland County
150	1928	7.0	**Livonia** (city) Wayne County

Note: *The state column ranks the top/bottom 150 places from all places in the state with population of 10,000 or more. The national column ranks the top/bottom 150 places from all places in the country with population of 10,000 or more. Places that are unincorporated were not considered in the rankings. Please refer to the User Guide for additional information.*

Speak English Only at Home

Top 150 Places Ranked in *Descending* Order

State Rank	Nat'l Rank	Percent	Place
1	15	98.7	**Beecher** (CDP) Genesee County
2	49	98.1	**Muskegon Heights** (city) Muskegon County
3	60	98.0	**Grand Haven** (city) Ottawa County
4	65	97.9	**Burton** (city) Genesee County
4	65	97.9	**East Bay** (township) Grand Traverse County
6	89	97.7	**Benton Harbor** (city) Berrien County
6	89	97.7	**Owosso** (city) Shiawassee County
8	106	97.6	**Mount Morris** (township) Genesee County
9	116	97.5	**Alpena** (city) Alpena County
9	116	97.5	**Genesee** (charter township) Genesee County
9	116	97.5	**Highland** (charter township) Oakland County
12	126	97.4	**Flint** (city) Genesee County
12	126	97.4	**Highland Park** (city) Wayne County
14	144	97.3	**Cooper** (charter township) Kalamazoo County
14	144	97.3	**Muskegon** (charter township) Muskegon County
14	144	97.3	**Thomas** (township) Saginaw County
14	144	97.3	**Vienna** (charter township) Genesee County
18	162	97.2	**Cadillac** (city) Wexford County
18	162	97.2	**Hartland** (township) Livingston County
20	179	97.1	**Escanaba** (city) Delta County
20	179	97.1	**Garfield** (charter township) Grand Traverse County
22	191	97.0	**Monitor** (charter township) Bay County
23	210	96.9	**Huron** (charter township) Wayne County
23	210	96.9	**Jenison** (CDP) Ottawa County
23	210	96.9	**Tyrone** (township) Livingston County
26	240	96.8	**Spring Lake** (township) Ottawa County
27	254	96.7	**Bangor** (charter township) Bay County
27	254	96.7	**Bedford** (township) Monroe County
27	254	96.7	**Fenton** (charter township) Genesee County
27	254	96.7	**Fenton** (city) Genesee County
27	254	96.7	**Flushing** (charter township) Genesee County
32	282	96.6	**Bridgeport** (charter township) Saginaw County
33	301	96.5	**Brighton** (township) Livingston County
34	318	96.4	**Green Oak** (township) Livingston County
34	318	96.4	**Mundy** (township) Genesee County
36	338	96.3	**Davison** (township) Genesee County
36	338	96.3	**Georgetown** (charter township) Ottawa County
36	338	96.3	**Port Huron** (charter township) Saint Clair County
39	363	96.2	**Emmett** (charter township) Calhoun County
39	363	96.2	**Monroe** (charter township) Monroe County
41	386	96.1	**Frenchtown** (township) Monroe County
41	386	96.1	**Saint Joseph** (charter township) Berrien County
41	386	96.1	**Traverse City** (city) Grand Traverse County
44	412	96.0	**Bay City** (city) Bay County
44	412	96.0	**Hamburg** (township) Livingston County
44	412	96.0	**Jackson** (city) Jackson County
44	412	96.0	**Mount Clemens** (city) Macomb County
48	436	95.9	**Plainfield** (charter township) Kent County
49	456	95.8	**Brandon** (charter township) Oakland County
49	456	95.8	**Fruitport** (charter township) Muskegon County
49	456	95.8	**Garden City** (city) Wayne County
49	456	95.8	**Leoni** (township) Jackson County
49	456	95.8	**Sault Sainte Marie** (city) Chippewa County
54	492	95.7	**Blackman** (charter township) Jackson County
54	492	95.7	**Genoa** (township) Livingston County
54	492	95.7	**Oxford** (charter township) Oakland County
54	492	95.7	**Port Huron** (city) Saint Clair County
54	492	95.7	**Redford** (charter township) Wayne County
59	520	95.6	**DeWitt** (charter township) Clinton County
59	520	95.6	**South Lyon** (city) Oakland County
61	551	95.5	**New Baltimore** (city) Macomb County
61	551	95.5	**Union** (charter township) Isabella County
63	579	95.4	**Grandville** (city) Kent County
63	579	95.4	**Marquette** (city) Marquette County
65	594	95.3	**Holly** (township) Oakland County
65	594	95.3	**Independence** (charter township) Oakland County
65	594	95.3	**Norton Shores** (city) Muskegon County
68	629	95.2	**Northview** (CDP) Kent County
68	629	95.2	**White Lake** (charter township) Oakland County
70	658	95.1	**Berkley** (city) Oakland County
70	658	95.1	**Lenox** (township) Macomb County
72	688	95.0	**Antwerp** (township) Van Buren County
73	742	94.8	**Caledonia** (township) Kent County
73	742	94.8	**Fraser** (city) Macomb County
73	742	94.8	**Oceola** (township) Livingston County
73	742	94.8	**Springfield** (charter township) Oakland County
73	742	94.8	**Summit** (township) Jackson County
78	768	94.7	**Cannon** (township) Kent County
78	768	94.7	**Trenton** (city) Wayne County
78	768	94.7	**Van Buren** (charter township) Wayne County
81	794	94.6	**Wayne** (city) Wayne County
82	814	94.5	**Allendale** (CDP) Ottawa County
82	814	94.5	**Inkster** (city) Wayne County
82	814	94.5	**Monroe** (city) Monroe County
85	854	94.3	**Allendale** (charter township) Ottawa County
85	854	94.3	**Ionia** (city) Ionia County
87	882	94.2	**Flint** (charter township) Genesee County
87	882	94.2	**Kalamazoo** (charter township) Kalamazoo County
89	904	94.1	**Eastpointe** (city) Macomb County
89	904	94.1	**Harper Woods** (city) Wayne County
89	904	94.1	**Harrison** (charter township) Macomb County
92	931	94.0	**East Grand Rapids** (city) Kent County
92	931	94.0	**Milford** (charter township) Oakland County
92	931	94.0	**Muskegon** (city) Muskegon County
92	931	94.0	**Niles** (township) Berrien County
96	954	93.9	**Walker** (city) Kent County
97	975	93.8	**Beverly Hills** (village) Oakland County
97	975	93.8	**Big Rapids** (city) Mecosta County
97	975	93.8	**Chesterfield** (township) Macomb County
97	975	93.8	**Forest Hills** (CDP) Kent County
97	975	93.8	**Portage** (city) Kalamazoo County
102	998	93.7	**Comstock** (charter township) Kalamazoo County
102	998	93.7	**Roseville** (city) Macomb County
104	1025	93.6	**Benton** (charter township) Berrien County
105	1047	93.5	**Hazel Park** (city) Oakland County
105	1047	93.5	**Romulus** (city) Wayne County
105	1047	93.5	**Taylor** (city) Wayne County
108	1071	93.4	**Ada** (township) Kent County
108	1071	93.4	**Byron** (township) Kent County
108	1071	93.4	**Saginaw** (city) Saginaw County
108	1071	93.4	**Saint Clair Shores** (city) Macomb County
112	1124	93.2	**Cascade** (charter township) Kent County
112	1124	93.2	**Grand Rapids** (charter township) Kent County
112	1124	93.2	**Riverview** (city) Wayne County
115	1144	93.1	**Fort Gratiot** (charter township) Saint Clair County
115	1144	93.1	**Grand Haven** (charter township) Ottawa County
117	1194	92.9	**Grosse Pointe Woods** (city) Wayne County
117	1194	92.9	**Woodhaven** (city) Wayne County
119	1210	92.8	**Ferndale** (city) Oakland County
119	1210	92.8	**Waterford** (charter township) Oakland County
121	1240	92.7	**Holt** (CDP) Ingham County
121	1240	92.7	**Royal Oak** (city) Oakland County
121	1240	92.7	**Texas** (charter township) Kalamazoo County
124	1271	92.6	**Lyon** (charter township) Oakland County
124	1271	92.6	**Saginaw** (charter township) Saginaw County
124	1271	92.6	**Wyandotte** (city) Wayne County
127	1296	92.5	**Grand Blanc** (charter township) Genesee County
127	1296	92.5	**Ypsilanti** (charter township) Washtenaw County
129	1325	92.4	**Midland** (city) Midland County
130	1346	92.3	**Southfield** (township) Oakland County
131	1370	92.2	**Delhi** (charter township) Ingham County
131	1370	92.2	**Mount Pleasant** (city) Isabella County
133	1441	91.9	**Grosse Ile** (township) Wayne County
133	1441	91.9	**Oshtemo** (charter township) Kalamazoo County
135	1457	91.8	**Gaines** (charter township) Kent County
135	1457	91.8	**Lincoln** (charter township) Berrien County
137	1481	91.7	**Cutlerville** (CDP) Kent County
138	1502	91.6	**Bath** (charter township) Clinton County
139	1566	91.3	**Park** (township) Ottawa County
139	1566	91.3	**Southgate** (city) Wayne County
139	1566	91.3	**Westland** (city) Wayne County
142	1583	91.2	**Orion** (charter township) Oakland County
143	1605	91.1	**Livonia** (city) Wayne County
143	1605	91.1	**Plymouth** (charter township) Wayne County
145	1639	90.9	**Allen Park** (city) Wayne County
146	1674	90.7	**Adrian** (city) Lenawee County
146	1674	90.7	**Grosse Pointe Park** (city) Wayne County
148	1719	90.5	**Battle Creek** (city) Calhoun County
148	1719	90.5	**Ypsilanti** (city) Washtenaw County
150	1736	90.4	**Detroit** (city) Wayne County

Note: The state column ranks the top/bottom 150 places from all places in the state with population of 10,000 or more. The national column ranks the top/bottom 150 places from all places in the country with population of 10,000 or more. Places that are unincorporated were not considered in the rankings. Please refer to the User Guide for additional information.

Speak English Only at Home

Top 150 Places Ranked in *Ascending* Order

State Rank	Nat'l Rank	Percent	Place
1	188	36.2	**Hamtramck** (city) Wayne County
2	418	53.2	**Dearborn** (city) Wayne County
3	868	68.6	**Troy** (city) Oakland County
4	900	69.6	**Sterling Heights** (city) Macomb County
5	1030	72.6	**Dearborn Heights** (city) Wayne County
6	1067	73.2	**West Bloomfield** (charter township) Oakland County
7	1131	74.4	**Holland** (charter township) Ottawa County
8	1218	75.9	**Melvindale** (city) Wayne County
9	1242	76.2	**Holland** (city) Ottawa County
10	1332	77.5	**Pittsfield** (charter township) Washtenaw County
11	1349	77.8	**Novi** (city) Oakland County
12	1360	78.0	**Sturgis** (city) Saint Joseph County
13	1423	78.8	**Farmington Hills** (city) Oakland County
14	1427	78.9	**Ann Arbor** (city) Washtenaw County
15	1505	79.9	**Northville** (township) Wayne County
16	1522	80.2	**Madison Heights** (city) Oakland County
17	1539	80.4	**Canton** (charter township) Wayne County
18	1586	80.8	**Auburn Hills** (city) Oakland County
19	1640	81.4	**Kentwood** (city) Kent County
20	1648	81.5	**Farmington** (city) Oakland County
20	1648	81.5	**Wyoming** (city) Kent County
22	1694	82.0	**Rochester Hills** (city) Oakland County
23	1705	82.1	**Superior** (charter township) Washtenaw County
24	1724	82.3	**Okemos** (CDP) Ingham County
25	1787	82.8	**Comstock Park** (CDP) Kent County
25	1787	82.8	**East Lansing** (city) Ingham County
27	1817	83.0	**Bloomfield** (charter township) Oakland County
28	1906	83.9	**Shelby** (charter township) Macomb County
29	1918	84.0	**Pontiac** (city) Oakland County
30	1965	84.4	**Scio** (township) Washtenaw County
31	1973	84.5	**Grand Rapids** (city) Kent County
32	2021	84.9	**Meridian** (charter township) Ingham County
33	2032	85.0	**Warren** (city) Macomb County
34	2086	85.3	**Macomb** (township) Macomb County
35	2157	85.9	**Alpine** (township) Kent County
36	2251	86.5	**Wixom** (city) Oakland County
37	2304	86.9	**Lincoln Park** (city) Wayne County
38	2320	87.0	**Lansing** (city) Ingham County
38	2320	87.0	**Oakland** (charter township) Oakland County
40	2333	87.1	**Washington** (township) Macomb County
41	2440	87.9	**Brownstown** (charter township) Wayne County
42	2492	88.2	**Oak Park** (city) Oakland County
43	2511	88.3	**Coldwater** (city) Branch County
44	2563	88.6	**Commerce** (charter township) Oakland County
45	2598	88.8	**Haslett** (CDP) Ingham County
46	2617	88.9	**Waverly** (CDP) Eaton County
47	2689	89.3	**Birmingham** (city) Oakland County
47	2689	89.3	**Delta** (charter township) Eaton County
47	2689	89.3	**Kalamazoo** (city) Kalamazoo County
47	2689	89.3	**Southfield** (city) Oakland County
51	2708	89.4	**Rochester** (city) Oakland County
52	2849	90.2	**Clawson** (city) Oakland County
52	2849	90.2	**Clinton** (charter township) Macomb County
54	2897	90.4	**Detroit** (city) Wayne County
54	2897	90.4	**Niles** (city) Berrien County
56	2921	90.5	**Battle Creek** (city) Calhoun County
56	2921	90.5	**Ypsilanti** (city) Washtenaw County
58	2963	90.7	**Adrian** (city) Lenawee County
58	2963	90.7	**Grosse Pointe Park** (city) Wayne County
60	2998	90.9	**Allen Park** (city) Wayne County
61	3035	91.1	**Livonia** (city) Wayne County
61	3035	91.1	**Plymouth** (charter township) Wayne County
63	3052	91.2	**Orion** (charter township) Oakland County
64	3074	91.3	**Park** (township) Ottawa County
64	3074	91.3	**Southgate** (city) Wayne County
64	3074	91.3	**Westland** (city) Wayne County
67	3128	91.6	**Bath** (charter township) Clinton County
68	3155	91.7	**Cutlerville** (CDP) Kent County
69	3176	91.8	**Gaines** (charter township) Kent County
69	3176	91.8	**Lincoln** (charter township) Berrien County
71	3200	91.9	**Grosse Ile** (township) Wayne County
71	3200	91.9	**Oshtemo** (charter township) Kalamazoo County
73	3262	92.2	**Delhi** (charter township) Ingham County
73	3262	92.2	**Mount Pleasant** (city) Isabella County
75	3287	92.3	**Southfield** (township) Oakland County
76	3311	92.4	**Midland** (city) Midland County
77	3332	92.5	**Grand Blanc** (charter township) Genesee County
77	3332	92.5	**Ypsilanti** (charter township) Washtenaw County
79	3361	92.6	**Lyon** (charter township) Oakland County
79	3361	92.6	**Saginaw** (charter township) Saginaw County
79	3361	92.6	**Wyandotte** (city) Wayne County
82	3386	92.7	**Holt** (CDP) Ingham County
82	3386	92.7	**Royal Oak** (city) Oakland County
82	3386	92.7	**Texas** (charter township) Kalamazoo County
85	3417	92.8	**Ferndale** (city) Oakland County
85	3417	92.8	**Waterford** (charter township) Oakland County
87	3447	92.9	**Grosse Pointe Woods** (city) Wayne County
87	3447	92.9	**Woodhaven** (city) Wayne County
89	3489	93.1	**Fort Gratiot** (charter township) Saint Clair County
89	3489	93.1	**Grand Haven** (charter township) Ottawa County
91	3513	93.2	**Cascade** (charter township) Kent County
91	3513	93.2	**Grand Rapids** (charter township) Kent County
91	3513	93.2	**Riverview** (city) Wayne County
94	3560	93.4	**Ada** (township) Kent County
94	3560	93.4	**Byron** (township) Kent County
94	3560	93.4	**Saginaw** (city) Saginaw County
94	3560	93.4	**Saint Clair Shores** (city) Macomb County
98	3586	93.5	**Hazel Park** (city) Oakland County
98	3586	93.5	**Romulus** (city) Wayne County
98	3586	93.5	**Taylor** (city) Wayne County
101	3610	93.6	**Benton** (charter township) Berrien County
102	3632	93.7	**Comstock** (charter township) Kalamazoo County
102	3632	93.7	**Roseville** (city) Macomb County
104	3659	93.8	**Beverly Hills** (village) Oakland County
104	3659	93.8	**Big Rapids** (city) Mecosta County
104	3659	93.8	**Chesterfield** (township) Macomb County
104	3659	93.8	**Forest Hills** (CDP) Kent County
104	3659	93.8	**Portage** (city) Kalamazoo County
109	3682	93.9	**Walker** (city) Kent County
110	3703	94.0	**East Grand Rapids** (city) Kent County
110	3703	94.0	**Milford** (charter township) Oakland County
110	3703	94.0	**Muskegon** (city) Muskegon County
110	3703	94.0	**Niles** (township) Berrien County
114	3726	94.1	**Eastpointe** (city) Macomb County
114	3726	94.1	**Harper Woods** (city) Wayne County
114	3726	94.1	**Harrison** (charter township) Macomb County
117	3753	94.2	**Flint** (charter township) Genesee County
117	3753	94.2	**Kalamazoo** (charter township) Kalamazoo County
119	3775	94.3	**Allendale** (charter township) Ottawa County
119	3775	94.3	**Ionia** (city) Ionia County
121	3825	94.5	**Allendale** (CDP) Ottawa County
121	3825	94.5	**Inkster** (city) Wayne County
121	3825	94.5	**Monroe** (city) Monroe County
124	3843	94.6	**Wayne** (city) Wayne County
125	3863	94.7	**Cannon** (township) Kent County
125	3863	94.7	**Trenton** (city) Wayne County
125	3863	94.7	**Van Buren** (charter township) Wayne County
128	3889	94.8	**Caledonia** (township) Kent County
128	3889	94.8	**Fraser** (city) Macomb County
128	3889	94.8	**Oceola** (township) Livingston County
128	3889	94.8	**Springfield** (charter township) Oakland County
128	3889	94.8	**Summit** (township) Jackson County
133	3943	95.0	**Antwerp** (township) Van Buren County
134	3969	95.1	**Berkley** (city) Oakland County
134	3969	95.1	**Lenox** (township) Macomb County
136	3999	95.2	**Northview** (CDP) Kent County
136	3999	95.2	**White Lake** (charter township) Oakland County
138	4028	95.3	**Holly** (township) Oakland County
138	4028	95.3	**Independence** (charter township) Oakland County
138	4028	95.3	**Norton Shores** (city) Muskegon County
141	4063	95.4	**Grandville** (city) Kent County
141	4063	95.4	**Marquette** (city) Marquette County
143	4078	95.5	**New Baltimore** (city) Macomb County
143	4078	95.5	**Union** (charter township) Isabella County
145	4106	95.6	**DeWitt** (charter township) Clinton County
145	4106	95.6	**South Lyon** (city) Oakland County
147	4137	95.7	**Blackman** (charter township) Jackson County
147	4137	95.7	**Genoa** (township) Livingston County
147	4137	95.7	**Oxford** (charter township) Oakland County
147	4137	95.7	**Port Huron** (city) Saint Clair County

Note: *The state column ranks the top/bottom 150 places from all places in the state with population of 10,000 or more. The national column ranks the top/bottom 150 places from all places in the country with population of 10,000 or more. Places that are unincorporated were not considered in the rankings. Please refer to the User Guide for additional information.*

Population with a Disability

Top 150 Places Ranked in *Descending* Order

State Rank	Nat'l Rank	Percent	Place
1	4	28.3	**Highland Park** (city) Wayne County
2	18	24.8	**Hazel Park** (city) Oakland County
3	28	23.6	**Beecher** (CDP) Genesee County
4	49	22.2	**Inkster** (city) Wayne County
5	80	21.3	**Benton Harbor** (city) Berrien County
5	80	21.3	**Mount Clemens** (city) Macomb County
7	84	21.2	**Escanaba** (city) Delta County
8	109	20.6	**Flint** (city) Genesee County
9	112	20.5	**Port Huron** (city) Saint Clair County
10	148	20.0	**Romulus** (city) Wayne County
11	165	19.8	**Alpena** (city) Alpena County
11	165	19.8	**Saginaw** (city) Saginaw County
13	188	19.6	**Mount Morris** (township) Genesee County
14	195	19.5	**Detroit** (city) Wayne County
15	206	19.4	**Genesee** (charter township) Genesee County
16	211	19.3	**Muskegon Heights** (city) Muskegon County
17	228	19.1	**Port Huron** (charter township) Saint Clair County
18	239	19.0	**Blackman** (charter township) Jackson County
18	239	19.0	**Lincoln Park** (city) Wayne County
18	239	19.0	**Muskegon** (city) Muskegon County
21	280	18.6	**Pontiac** (city) Oakland County
22	300	18.4	**Adrian** (city) Lenawee County
23	310	18.3	**Niles** (city) Berrien County
23	310	18.3	**Sault Sainte Marie** (city) Chippewa County
25	318	18.2	**Cadillac** (city) Wexford County
26	332	18.0	**Melvindale** (city) Wayne County
26	332	18.0	**Taylor** (city) Wayne County
28	349	17.9	**Ionia** (city) Ionia County
29	357	17.8	**Benton** (charter township) Berrien County
29	357	17.8	**Jackson** (city) Jackson County
31	414	17.4	**Burton** (city) Genesee County
32	425	17.3	**Riverview** (city) Wayne County
33	451	17.1	**Roseville** (city) Macomb County
33	451	17.1	**Wyandotte** (city) Wayne County
35	466	17.0	**Flint** (charter township) Genesee County
36	481	16.9	**Frenchtown** (township) Monroe County
36	481	16.9	**Leoni** (township) Jackson County
38	499	16.8	**Wayne** (city) Wayne County
39	515	16.7	**Bangor** (charter township) Bay County
40	555	16.5	**Bay City** (city) Bay County
40	555	16.5	**Lansing** (city) Ingham County
42	593	16.3	**Bridgeport** (charter township) Saginaw County
43	610	16.2	**Battle Creek** (city) Calhoun County
43	610	16.2	**Eastpointe** (city) Macomb County
43	610	16.2	**Owosso** (city) Shiawassee County
46	632	16.1	**Niles** (township) Berrien County
47	681	15.9	**Fort Gratiot** (charter township) Saint Clair County
47	681	15.9	**Warren** (city) Macomb County
49	699	15.8	**Monitor** (charter township) Bay County
50	740	15.6	**Garfield** (charter township) Grand Traverse County
50	740	15.6	**Westland** (city) Wayne County
52	774	15.5	**Oak Park** (city) Oakland County
52	774	15.5	**Southfield** (city) Oakland County
52	774	15.5	**Southgate** (city) Wayne County
55	791	15.4	**Comstock** (charter township) Kalamazoo County
55	791	15.4	**Madison Heights** (city) Oakland County
57	839	15.2	**Hamtramck** (city) Wayne County
57	839	15.2	**Monroe** (charter township) Monroe County
57	839	15.2	**Mundy** (township) Genesee County
60	869	15.1	**Clinton** (charter township) Macomb County
60	869	15.1	**Coldwater** (city) Branch County
60	869	15.1	**Saint Clair Shores** (city) Macomb County
63	899	15.0	**Redford** (charter township) Wayne County
64	943	14.8	**Monroe** (city) Monroe County
65	957	14.7	**Muskegon** (charter township) Muskegon County
66	1007	14.5	**Allen Park** (city) Wayne County
67	1031	14.4	**Garden City** (city) Wayne County
68	1058	14.3	**Flushing** (city) Genesee County
68	1058	14.3	**Trenton** (city) Wayne County
70	1086	14.2	**Cutlerville** (CDP) Kent County
71	1145	14.0	**Dearborn Heights** (city) Wayne County
71	1145	14.0	**Ferndale** (city) Oakland County
73	1177	13.9	**Kalamazoo** (charter township) Kalamazoo County
74	1201	13.8	**Lenox** (township) Macomb County
74	1201	13.8	**Summit** (township) Jackson County
76	1228	13.7	**Harrison** (charter township) Macomb County
76	1228	13.7	**Waverly** (CDP) Eaton County
78	1298	13.5	**Clawson** (city) Oakland County
79	1426	13.1	**Kalamazoo** (city) Kalamazoo County
79	1426	13.1	**Vienna** (charter township) Genesee County
81	1489	12.9	**Fraser** (city) Macomb County
82	1522	12.8	**Cooper** (charter township) Kalamazoo County
82	1522	12.8	**Sterling Heights** (city) Macomb County
82	1522	12.8	**Waterford** (charter township) Oakland County
85	1554	12.7	**Oshtemo** (charter township) Kalamazoo County
86	1580	12.6	**Harper Woods** (city) Wayne County
86	1580	12.6	**Sturgis** (city) Saint Joseph County
86	1580	12.6	**Traverse City** (city) Grand Traverse County
89	1618	12.5	**Davison** (township) Genesee County
89	1618	12.5	**Midland** (city) Midland County
89	1618	12.5	**Saginaw** (charter township) Saginaw County
92	1655	12.4	**Delta** (charter township) Eaton County
93	1705	12.3	**Dearborn** (city) Wayne County
93	1705	12.3	**Huron** (charter township) Wayne County
93	1705	12.3	**Norton Shores** (city) Muskegon County
96	1744	12.2	**Jenison** (CDP) Ottawa County
96	1744	12.2	**Thomas** (township) Saginaw County
98	1788	12.1	**Emmett** (charter township) Calhoun County
99	1824	12.0	**Brownstown** (charter township) Wayne County
99	1824	12.0	**Gaines** (charter township) Kent County
99	1824	12.0	**Van Buren** (charter township) Wayne County
99	1824	12.0	**Woodhaven** (city) Wayne County
103	1872	11.9	**DeWitt** (charter township) Clinton County
103	1872	11.9	**Grand Rapids** (city) Kent County
105	1912	11.8	**Spring Lake** (township) Ottawa County
106	1952	11.7	**Grand Haven** (city) Ottawa County
106	1952	11.7	**Kentwood** (city) Kent County
106	1952	11.7	**Ypsilanti** (charter township) Washtenaw County
109	1996	11.6	**Grandville** (city) Kent County
109	1996	11.6	**Livonia** (city) Wayne County
109	1996	11.6	**White Lake** (charter township) Oakland County
112	2049	11.5	**Saint Joseph** (charter township) Berrien County
112	2049	11.5	**South Lyon** (city) Oakland County
114	2082	11.4	**Big Rapids** (city) Mecosta County
114	2082	11.4	**Delhi** (charter township) Ingham County
114	2082	11.4	**Northview** (CDP) Kent County
117	2134	11.3	**Holt** (CDP) Ingham County
117	2134	11.3	**Portage** (city) Kalamazoo County
119	2178	11.2	**Highland** (charter township) Oakland County
120	2220	11.1	**Comstock Park** (CDP) Kent County
120	2220	11.1	**Fruitport** (charter township) Muskegon County
120	2220	11.1	**Walker** (city) Kent County
123	2256	11.0	**Holland** (city) Ottawa County
124	2307	10.9	**Alpine** (township) Kent County
124	2307	10.9	**Farmington Hills** (city) Oakland County
124	2307	10.9	**Holly** (township) Oakland County
124	2307	10.9	**Lyon** (charter township) Oakland County
124	2307	10.9	**Wyoming** (city) Kent County
129	2395	10.7	**Berkley** (city) Oakland County
130	2439	10.6	**Shelby** (charter township) Macomb County
130	2439	10.6	**Superior** (charter township) Washtenaw County
132	2495	10.5	**Antwerp** (township) Van Buren County
132	2495	10.5	**Ypsilanti** (city) Washtenaw County
134	2599	10.3	**Fenton** (city) Genesee County
134	2599	10.3	**Genoa** (township) Livingston County
136	2645	10.2	**Chesterfield** (township) Macomb County
136	2645	10.2	**Oxford** (charter township) Oakland County
138	2684	10.1	**Mount Pleasant** (city) Isabella County
138	2684	10.1	**Plainfield** (charter township) Kent County
138	2684	10.1	**Union** (charter township) Isabella County
141	2731	10.0	**Byron** (township) Kent County
141	2731	10.0	**Marquette** (city) Marquette County
143	2772	9.9	**Grand Blanc** (charter township) Genesee County
143	2772	9.9	**Royal Oak** (city) Oakland County
145	2831	9.8	**Auburn Hills** (city) Oakland County
145	2831	9.8	**Holland** (charter township) Ottawa County
145	2831	9.8	**West Bloomfield** (charter township) Oakland County
148	2884	9.7	**Bath** (charter township) Clinton County
148	2884	9.7	**Grosse Ile** (township) Wayne County
148	2884	9.7	**Hamburg** (township) Livingston County

Note: The state column ranks the top/bottom 150 places from all places in the state with population of 10,000 or more. The national column ranks the top/bottom 150 places from all places in the country with population of 10,000 or more. Places that are unincorporated were not considered in the rankings. Please refer to the User Guide for additional information.

Population with a Disability

Top 150 Places Ranked in *Ascending* Order

State Rank	Nat'l Rank	Percent	Place
1	34	4.3	**Allendale** (CDP) Ottawa County
2	71	4.8	**Allendale** (charter township) Ottawa County
3	91	5.0	**Ada** (township) Kent County
4	104	5.1	**East Lansing** (city) Ingham County
5	119	5.2	**East Grand Rapids** (city) Kent County
5	119	5.2	**Forest Hills** (CDP) Kent County
7	179	5.6	**Cannon** (township) Kent County
8	237	5.9	**Birmingham** (city) Oakland County
8	237	5.9	**Hartland** (township) Livingston County
10	305	6.3	**Wixom** (city) Oakland County
11	333	6.4	**Oakland** (charter township) Oakland County
11	333	6.4	**Pittsfield** (charter township) Washtenaw County
13	358	6.5	**Ann Arbor** (city) Washtenaw County
13	358	6.5	**Rochester** (city) Oakland County
15	386	6.6	**Scio** (township) Washtenaw County
16	408	6.7	**Cascade** (charter township) Kent County
17	435	6.8	**Beverly Hills** (village) Oakland County
18	486	7.0	**Texas** (charter township) Kalamazoo County
19	520	7.1	**Park** (township) Ottawa County
20	550	7.2	**Canton** (charter township) Wayne County
21	624	7.4	**Brighton** (township) Livingston County
21	624	7.4	**Okemos** (CDP) Ingham County
23	749	7.7	**Grand Haven** (charter township) Ottawa County
23	749	7.7	**Novi** (city) Oakland County
23	749	7.7	**Oceola** (township) Livingston County
23	749	7.7	**Southfield** (township) Oakland County
27	797	7.8	**Macomb** (township) Macomb County
28	853	7.9	**Grosse Pointe Woods** (city) Wayne County
28	853	7.9	**Plymouth** (charter township) Wayne County
30	903	8.0	**Northville** (township) Wayne County
31	953	8.1	**Caledonia** (township) Kent County
31	953	8.1	**Grand Rapids** (charter township) Kent County
33	1041	8.3	**Grosse Pointe Park** (city) Wayne County
33	1041	8.3	**Orion** (charter township) Oakland County
33	1041	8.3	**Troy** (city) Oakland County
36	1127	8.5	**Meridian** (charter township) Ingham County
37	1228	8.7	**Bloomfield** (charter township) Oakland County
37	1228	8.7	**Georgetown** (charter township) Ottawa County
37	1228	8.7	**Tyrone** (township) Livingston County
40	1327	8.9	**East Bay** (township) Grand Traverse County
40	1327	8.9	**Farmington** (city) Oakland County
40	1327	8.9	**Green Oak** (township) Livingston County
43	1373	9.0	**Bedford** (township) Monroe County
43	1373	9.0	**Fenton** (charter township) Genesee County
43	1373	9.0	**New Baltimore** (city) Macomb County
43	1373	9.0	**Springfield** (charter township) Oakland County
47	1468	9.2	**Independence** (charter township) Oakland County
47	1468	9.2	**Milford** (charter township) Oakland County
47	1468	9.2	**Rochester Hills** (city) Oakland County
50	1527	9.3	**Washington** (township) Macomb County
51	1567	9.4	**Lincoln** (charter township) Berrien County
52	1625	9.5	**Commerce** (charter township) Oakland County
53	1680	9.6	**Brandon** (charter township) Oakland County
53	1680	9.6	**Haslett** (CDP) Ingham County
55	1740	9.7	**Bath** (charter township) Clinton County
55	1740	9.7	**Grosse Ile** (township) Wayne County
55	1740	9.7	**Hamburg** (township) Livingston County
58	1773	9.8	**Auburn Hills** (city) Oakland County
58	1773	9.8	**Holland** (charter township) Ottawa County
58	1773	9.8	**West Bloomfield** (charter township) Oakland County
61	1826	9.9	**Grand Blanc** (charter township) Genesee County
61	1826	9.9	**Royal Oak** (city) Oakland County
63	1885	10.0	**Byron** (township) Kent County
63	1885	10.0	**Marquette** (city) Marquette County
65	1926	10.1	**Mount Pleasant** (city) Isabella County
65	1926	10.1	**Plainfield** (charter township) Kent County
65	1926	10.1	**Union** (charter township) Isabella County
68	1973	10.2	**Chesterfield** (township) Macomb County
68	1973	10.2	**Oxford** (charter township) Oakland County
70	2012	10.3	**Fenton** (city) Genesee County
70	2012	10.3	**Genoa** (township) Livingston County
72	2113	10.5	**Antwerp** (township) Van Buren County
72	2113	10.5	**Ypsilanti** (township) Washtenaw County
74	2162	10.6	**Shelby** (charter township) Macomb County
74	2162	10.6	**Superior** (charter township) Washtenaw County
76	2218	10.7	**Berkley** (city) Oakland County
77	2305	10.9	**Alpine** (township) Kent County
77	2305	10.9	**Farmington Hills** (city) Oakland County
77	2305	10.9	**Holly** (township) Oakland County
77	2305	10.9	**Lyon** (charter township) Oakland County
77	2305	10.9	**Wyoming** (city) Kent County
82	2350	11.0	**Holland** (city) Ottawa County
83	2401	11.1	**Comstock Park** (CDP) Kent County
83	2401	11.1	**Fruitport** (charter township) Muskegon County
83	2401	11.1	**Walker** (city) Kent County
86	2437	11.2	**Highland** (charter township) Oakland County
87	2479	11.3	**Holt** (CDP) Ingham County
87	2479	11.3	**Portage** (city) Kalamazoo County
89	2523	11.4	**Big Rapids** (city) Mecosta County
89	2523	11.4	**Delhi** (charter township) Ingham County
89	2523	11.4	**Northview** (CDP) Kent County
92	2575	11.5	**Saint Joseph** (charter township) Berrien County
92	2575	11.5	**South Lyon** (city) Oakland County
94	2608	11.6	**Grandville** (city) Kent County
94	2608	11.6	**Livonia** (city) Wayne County
94	2608	11.6	**White Lake** (charter township) Oakland County
97	2661	11.7	**Grand Haven** (city) Ottawa County
97	2661	11.7	**Kentwood** (city) Kent County
97	2661	11.7	**Ypsilanti** (charter township) Washtenaw County
100	2705	11.8	**Spring Lake** (township) Ottawa County
101	2745	11.9	**DeWitt** (charter township) Clinton County
101	2745	11.9	**Grand Rapids** (city) Kent County
103	2785	12.0	**Brownstown** (charter township) Wayne County
103	2785	12.0	**Gaines** (charter township) Kent County
103	2785	12.0	**Van Buren** (charter township) Wayne County
103	2785	12.0	**Woodhaven** (city) Wayne County
107	2833	12.1	**Emmett** (charter township) Calhoun County
108	2869	12.2	**Jenison** (CDP) Ottawa County
108	2869	12.2	**Thomas** (township) Saginaw County
110	2913	12.3	**Dearborn** (city) Wayne County
110	2913	12.3	**Huron** (charter township) Wayne County
110	2913	12.3	**Norton Shores** (city) Muskegon County
113	2952	12.4	**Delta** (charter township) Eaton County
114	3002	12.5	**Davison** (township) Genesee County
114	3002	12.5	**Midland** (city) Midland County
114	3002	12.5	**Saginaw** (charter township) Saginaw County
117	3039	12.6	**Harper Woods** (city) Wayne County
117	3039	12.6	**Sturgis** (city) Saint Joseph County
117	3039	12.6	**Traverse City** (city) Grand Traverse County
120	3077	12.7	**Oshtemo** (charter township) Kalamazoo County
121	3103	12.8	**Cooper** (charter township) Kalamazoo County
121	3103	12.8	**Sterling Heights** (city) Macomb County
121	3103	12.8	**Waterford** (charter township) Oakland County
124	3135	12.9	**Fraser** (city) Macomb County
125	3199	13.1	**Kalamazoo** (city) Kalamazoo County
125	3199	13.1	**Vienna** (charter township) Genesee County
127	3333	13.5	**Clawson** (city) Oakland County
128	3399	13.7	**Harrison** (charter township) Macomb County
128	3399	13.7	**Waverly** (CDP) Eaton County
130	3429	13.8	**Lenox** (township) Macomb County
130	3429	13.8	**Summit** (township) Jackson County
132	3456	13.9	**Kalamazoo** (charter township) Kalamazoo County
133	3480	14.0	**Dearborn Heights** (city) Wayne County
133	3480	14.0	**Ferndale** (city) Oakland County
135	3538	14.2	**Cutlerville** (CDP) Kent County
136	3571	14.3	**Flushing** (charter township) Genesee County
136	3571	14.3	**Trenton** (city) Wayne County
138	3599	14.4	**Garden City** (city) Wayne County
139	3626	14.5	**Allen Park** (city) Wayne County
140	3678	14.7	**Muskegon** (charter township) Muskegon County
141	3700	14.8	**Monroe** (city) Monroe County
142	3737	15.0	**Redford** (charter township) Wayne County
143	3758	15.1	**Clinton** (charter township) Macomb County
143	3758	15.1	**Coldwater** (city) Branch County
143	3758	15.1	**Saint Clair Shores** (city) Macomb County
146	3788	15.2	**Hamtramck** (city) Wayne County
146	3788	15.2	**Monroe** (charter township) Monroe County
146	3788	15.2	**Mundy** (township) Genesee County
149	3837	15.4	**Comstock** (charter township) Kalamazoo County
149	3837	15.4	**Madison Heights** (city) Oakland County

Note: The state column ranks the top/bottom 150 places from all places in the state with population of 10,000 or more. The national column ranks the top/bottom 150 places from all places in the country with population of 10,000 or more. Places that are unincorporated were not considered in the rankings. Please refer to the User Guide for additional information.

Veterans

Top 150 Places Ranked in *Descending* Order

State Rank	Nat'l Rank	Percent	Place	State Rank	Nat'l Rank	Percent	Place
1	542	12.5	**Muskegon** (charter township) Muskegon County	76	2103	9.1	**Brownstown** (charter township) Wayne County
2	629	12.1	**Cadillac** (city) Wexford County	76	2103	9.1	**Lincoln Park** (city) Wayne County
3	652	12.0	**Genesee** (charter township) Genesee County	76	2103	9.1	**Southfield** (township) Oakland County
4	675	11.9	**Bangor** (charter township) Bay County	76	2103	9.1	**Taylor** (city) Wayne County
4	675	11.9	**Garfield** (charter township) Grand Traverse County	80	2178	9.0	**Beverly Hills** (village) Oakland County
6	697	11.8	**Escanaba** (city) Delta County	80	2178	9.0	**Kalamazoo** (charter township) Kalamazoo County
7	720	11.7	**Monitor** (charter township) Bay County	80	2178	9.0	**Plainfield** (charter township) Kent County
8	756	11.6	**Monroe** (charter township) Monroe County	80	2178	9.0	**Van Buren** (charter township) Wayne County
9	796	11.5	**Bridgeport** (charter township) Saginaw County	84	2253	8.9	**Adrian** (city) Lenawee County
10	831	11.4	**Emmett** (charter township) Calhoun County	84	2253	8.9	**Brighton** (township) Livingston County
10	831	11.4	**Harrison** (charter township) Macomb County	84	2253	8.9	**Flint** (charter township) Genesee County
12	933	11.1	**Battle Creek** (city) Calhoun County	84	2253	8.9	**Melvindale** (city) Wayne County
12	933	11.1	**Leoni** (township) Jackson County	88	2312	8.8	**Ionia** (city) Ionia County
12	933	11.1	**Norton Shores** (city) Muskegon County	88	2312	8.8	**Marquette** (city) Marquette County
15	976	11.0	**Grand Haven** (city) Ottawa County	88	2312	8.8	**Owosso** (city) Shiawassee County
16	1016	10.9	**DeWitt** (charter township) Clinton County	88	2312	8.8	**Saginaw** (city) Saginaw County
16	1016	10.9	**Trenton** (city) Wayne County	88	2312	8.8	**White Lake** (charter township) Oakland County
18	1065	10.8	**Alpena** (city) Alpena County	93	2383	8.7	**Fraser** (city) Macomb County
18	1065	10.8	**Summit** (township) Jackson County	93	2383	8.7	**Gaines** (charter township) Kent County
20	1118	10.7	**Blackman** (charter township) Jackson County	93	2383	8.7	**Grand Rapids** (charter township) Kent County
21	1169	10.6	**Flushing** (charter township) Genesee County	93	2383	8.7	**Holly** (township) Oakland County
21	1169	10.6	**Lincoln** (charter township) Berrien County	93	2383	8.7	**Jenison** (CDP) Ottawa County
21	1169	10.6	**Saint Clair Shores** (city) Macomb County	93	2383	8.7	**Sturgis** (city) Saint Joseph County
24	1222	10.5	**Thomas** (township) Saginaw County	93	2383	8.7	**Warren** (city) Macomb County
25	1272	10.4	**Sault Sainte Marie** (city) Chippewa County	100	2468	8.6	**Caledonia** (township) Kent County
26	1328	10.3	**Comstock** (charter township) Kalamazoo County	100	2468	8.6	**Chesterfield** (township) Macomb County
26	1328	10.3	**Delhi** (charter township) Ingham County	100	2468	8.6	**Haslett** (CDP) Ingham County
26	1328	10.3	**Frenchtown** (township) Monroe County	100	2468	8.6	**Hazel Park** (city) Oakland County
26	1328	10.3	**Fruitport** (charter township) Muskegon County	100	2468	8.6	**Northview** (CDP) Kent County
26	1328	10.3	**Holt** (CDP) Ingham County	100	2468	8.6	**Wyandotte** (city) Wayne County
26	1328	10.3	**Waverly** (CDP) Eaton County	106	2535	8.5	**Hartland** (township) Livingston County
32	1386	10.2	**Cutlerville** (CDP) Kent County	106	2535	8.5	**Plymouth** (charter township) Wayne County
32	1386	10.2	**Fort Gratiot** (charter township) Saint Clair County	108	2599	8.4	**Grand Haven** (charter township) Ottawa County
32	1386	10.2	**Garden City** (city) Wayne County	108	2599	8.4	**Portage** (city) Kalamazoo County
32	1386	10.2	**Vienna** (charter township) Genesee County	108	2599	8.4	**Shelby** (charter township) Macomb County
36	1445	10.1	**Mundy** (township) Genesee County	108	2599	8.4	**Waterford** (charter township) Oakland County
36	1445	10.1	**New Baltimore** (city) Macomb County	112	2666	8.3	**Hamburg** (township) Livingston County
36	1445	10.1	**Riverview** (city) Wayne County	112	2666	8.3	**Highland Park** (city) Wayne County
36	1445	10.1	**Saginaw** (charter township) Saginaw County	112	2666	8.3	**Southfield** (city) Oakland County
40	1492	10.0	**Niles** (township) Berrien County	112	2666	8.3	**Westland** (city) Wayne County
40	1492	10.0	**Saint Joseph** (charter township) Berrien County	116	2727	8.2	**Farmington** (city) Oakland County
40	1492	10.0	**Spring Lake** (township) Ottawa County	117	2781	8.1	**Cascade** (charter township) Kent County
43	1565	9.9	**Bay City** (city) Bay County	117	2781	8.1	**Meridian** (charter township) Ingham County
43	1565	9.9	**Bedford** (township) Monroe County	117	2781	8.1	**Muskegon** (city) Muskegon County
43	1565	9.9	**Delta** (charter township) Eaton County	117	2781	8.1	**Niles** (city) Berrien County
46	1640	9.8	**Allen Park** (city) Wayne County	117	2781	8.1	**Washington** (township) Macomb County
46	1640	9.8	**Huron** (charter township) Wayne County	122	2835	8.0	**Dearborn Heights** (city) Wayne County
46	1640	9.8	**Port Huron** (city) Saint Clair County	123	2894	7.9	**Beecher** (CDP) Genesee County
46	1640	9.8	**Redford** (charter township) Wayne County	123	2894	7.9	**Coldwater** (city) Branch County
46	1640	9.8	**Romulus** (city) Wayne County	123	2894	7.9	**Flint** (city) Genesee County
51	1706	9.7	**Antwerp** (township) Van Buren County	123	2894	7.9	**Midland** (city) Midland County
51	1706	9.7	**Davison** (township) Genesee County	123	2894	7.9	**Oshtemo** (charter township) Kalamazoo County
51	1706	9.7	**East Bay** (township) Grand Traverse County	123	2894	7.9	**Roseville** (city) Macomb County
51	1706	9.7	**Fenton** (charter township) Genesee County	129	2947	7.8	**Commerce** (charter township) Oakland County
51	1706	9.7	**Lenox** (township) Macomb County	129	2947	7.8	**Farmington Hills** (city) Oakland County
51	1706	9.7	**Mount Morris** (township) Genesee County	129	2947	7.8	**Okemos** (CDP) Ingham County
51	1706	9.7	**Oceola** (township) Livingston County	132	2996	7.7	**Benton** (charter township) Berrien County
51	1706	9.7	**Woodhaven** (city) Wayne County	132	2996	7.7	**Grandville** (city) Kent County
59	1770	9.6	**Burton** (city) Genesee County	132	2996	7.7	**Grosse Pointe Woods** (city) Wayne County
59	1770	9.6	**Byron** (township) Kent County	132	2996	7.7	**Northville** (township) Wayne County
59	1770	9.6	**Cooper** (charter township) Kalamazoo County	132	2996	7.7	**Texas** (charter township) Kalamazoo County
59	1770	9.6	**Grand Blanc** (charter township) Genesee County	137	3058	7.6	**Independence** (charter township) Oakland County
63	1832	9.5	**Highland** (charter township) Oakland County	137	3058	7.6	**Milford** (charter township) Oakland County
63	1832	9.5	**Monroe** (city) Monroe County	137	3058	7.6	**Pontiac** (city) Oakland County
63	1832	9.5	**Southgate** (city) Wayne County	137	3058	7.6	**Walker** (city) Kent County
66	1897	9.4	**Port Huron** (charter township) Saint Clair County	137	3058	7.6	**Ypsilanti** (charter township) Washtenaw County
67	1977	9.3	**Fenton** (city) Genesee County	142	3105	7.5	**Alpine** (township) Kent County
67	1977	9.3	**Grosse Ile** (township) Wayne County	142	3105	7.5	**Jackson** (city) Jackson County
67	1977	9.3	**Wayne** (city) Wayne County	142	3105	7.5	**Lansing** (city) Ingham County
70	2042	9.2	**Brandon** (charter township) Oakland County	145	3150	7.4	**Comstock Park** (CDP) Kent County
70	2042	9.2	**Clinton** (charter township) Macomb County	145	3150	7.4	**Eastpointe** (city) Macomb County
70	2042	9.2	**Genoa** (township) Livingston County	145	3150	7.4	**Inkster** (city) Wayne County
70	2042	9.2	**Livonia** (city) Wayne County	145	3150	7.4	**Kentwood** (city) Kent County
70	2042	9.2	**Traverse City** (city) Grand Traverse County	145	3150	7.4	**Madison Heights** (city) Oakland County
70	2042	9.2	**Tyrone** (township) Livingston County	145	3150	7.4	**Oak Park** (city) Oakland County

Note: The state column ranks the top/bottom 150 places from all places in the state with population of 10,000 or more. The national column ranks the top/bottom 150 places from all places in the country with population of 10,000 or more. Places that are unincorporated were not considered in the rankings. Please refer to the User Guide for additional information.

Veterans

Top 150 Places Ranked in *Ascending* Order

State Rank	Nat'l Rank	Percent	Place
1	70	2.4	**East Lansing** (city) Ingham County
2	101	2.9	**Allendale** (charter township) Ottawa County
3	111	3.0	**Hamtramck** (city) Wayne County
4	133	3.2	**Allendale** (CDP) Ottawa County
5	200	3.8	**Union** (charter township) Isabella County
6	229	4.0	**Ann Arbor** (city) Washtenaw County
6	229	4.0	**Mount Pleasant** (city) Isabella County
8	337	4.6	**Benton Harbor** (city) Berrien County
9	382	4.8	**Big Rapids** (city) Mecosta County
10	520	5.3	**Wixom** (city) Oakland County
11	558	5.4	**Kalamazoo** (city) Kalamazoo County
11	558	5.4	**Pittsfield** (charter township) Washtenaw County
11	558	5.4	**Ypsilanti** (city) Washtenaw County
14	586	5.5	**Bath** (charter township) Clinton County
14	586	5.5	**Birmingham** (city) Oakland County
14	586	5.5	**Troy** (city) Oakland County
17	631	5.6	**Superior** (charter township) Washtenaw County
18	669	5.7	**Ferndale** (city) Oakland County
19	703	5.8	**Harper Woods** (city) Wayne County
20	780	6.0	**Dearborn** (city) Wayne County
20	780	6.0	**Rochester** (city) Oakland County
20	780	6.0	**Springfield** (charter township) Oakland County
23	826	6.1	**Holland** (charter township) Ottawa County
23	826	6.1	**Holland** (city) Ottawa County
23	826	6.1	**Muskegon Heights** (city) Muskegon County
23	826	6.1	**Scio** (township) Washtenaw County
27	868	6.2	**Ada** (township) Kent County
28	904	6.3	**Rochester Hills** (city) Oakland County
28	904	6.3	**Royal Oak** (city) Oakland County
30	952	6.4	**West Bloomfield** (charter township) Oakland County
31	991	6.5	**Oakland** (charter township) Oakland County
31	991	6.5	**Park** (township) Ottawa County
33	1032	6.6	**East Grand Rapids** (city) Kent County
34	1064	6.7	**Forest Hills** (CDP) Kent County
34	1064	6.7	**Grand Rapids** (city) Kent County
34	1064	6.7	**Orion** (charter township) Oakland County
37	1119	6.8	**Cannon** (township) Kent County
37	1119	6.8	**Detroit** (city) Wayne County
37	1119	6.8	**Novi** (city) Oakland County
37	1119	6.8	**Wyoming** (city) Kent County
41	1179	6.9	**Lyon** (charter township) Oakland County
41	1179	6.9	**Macomb** (township) Macomb County
43	1230	7.0	**Berkley** (city) Oakland County
43	1230	7.0	**Clawson** (city) Oakland County
43	1230	7.0	**Mount Clemens** (city) Macomb County
46	1286	7.1	**Auburn Hills** (city) Oakland County
46	1286	7.1	**Canton** (charter township) Wayne County
48	1344	7.2	**Georgetown** (charter township) Ottawa County
48	1344	7.2	**Grosse Pointe Park** (city) Wayne County
48	1344	7.2	**Oxford** (charter township) Oakland County
51	1398	7.3	**Bloomfield** (charter township) Oakland County
51	1398	7.3	**Green Oak** (township) Livingston County
51	1398	7.3	**South Lyon** (city) Oakland County
54	1443	7.4	**Comstock Park** (CDP) Kent County
54	1443	7.4	**Eastpointe** (city) Macomb County
54	1443	7.4	**Inkster** (city) Wayne County
54	1443	7.4	**Kentwood** (city) Kent County
54	1443	7.4	**Madison Heights** (city) Oakland County
54	1443	7.4	**Oak Park** (city) Oakland County
54	1443	7.4	**Sterling Heights** (city) Macomb County
61	1507	7.5	**Alpine** (township) Kent County
61	1507	7.5	**Jackson** (city) Jackson County
61	1507	7.5	**Lansing** (city) Ingham County
64	1552	7.6	**Independence** (charter township) Oakland County
64	1552	7.6	**Milford** (charter township) Oakland County
64	1552	7.6	**Pontiac** (city) Oakland County
64	1552	7.6	**Walker** (city) Kent County
64	1552	7.6	**Ypsilanti** (charter township) Washtenaw County
69	1599	7.7	**Benton** (charter township) Berrien County
69	1599	7.7	**Grandville** (city) Kent County
69	1599	7.7	**Grosse Pointe Woods** (city) Wayne County
69	1599	7.7	**Northville** (township) Wayne County
69	1599	7.7	**Texas** (charter township) Kalamazoo County
74	1661	7.8	**Commerce** (charter township) Oakland County
74	1661	7.8	**Farmington Hills** (city) Oakland County
74	1661	7.8	**Okemos** (CDP) Ingham County
77	1710	7.9	**Beecher** (CDP) Genesee County
77	1710	7.9	**Coldwater** (city) Branch County
77	1710	7.9	**Flint** (city) Genesee County
77	1710	7.9	**Midland** (city) Midland County
77	1710	7.9	**Oshtemo** (charter township) Kalamazoo County
77	1710	7.9	**Roseville** (city) Macomb County
83	1763	8.0	**Dearborn Heights** (city) Wayne County
84	1822	8.1	**Cascade** (charter township) Kent County
84	1822	8.1	**Meridian** (charter township) Ingham County
84	1822	8.1	**Muskegon** (city) Muskegon County
84	1822	8.1	**Niles** (city) Berrien County
84	1822	8.1	**Washington** (township) Macomb County
89	1876	8.2	**Farmington** (city) Oakland County
90	1930	8.3	**Hamburg** (township) Livingston County
90	1930	8.3	**Highland Park** (city) Wayne County
90	1930	8.3	**Southfield** (city) Oakland County
90	1930	8.3	**Westland** (city) Wayne County
94	1991	8.4	**Grand Haven** (charter township) Ottawa County
94	1991	8.4	**Portage** (city) Kalamazoo County
94	1991	8.4	**Shelby** (charter township) Macomb County
94	1991	8.4	**Waterford** (charter township) Oakland County
98	2058	8.5	**Hartland** (township) Livingston County
98	2058	8.5	**Plymouth** (charter township) Wayne County
100	2122	8.6	**Caledonia** (township) Kent County
100	2122	8.6	**Chesterfield** (township) Macomb County
100	2122	8.6	**Haslett** (CDP) Ingham County
100	2122	8.6	**Hazel Park** (city) Oakland County
100	2122	8.6	**Northview** (CDP) Kent County
100	2122	8.6	**Wyandotte** (city) Wayne County
106	2189	8.7	**Fraser** (city) Macomb County
106	2189	8.7	**Gaines** (charter township) Kent County
106	2189	8.7	**Grand Rapids** (charter township) Kent County
106	2189	8.7	**Holly** (township) Oakland County
106	2189	8.7	**Jenison** (CDP) Ottawa County
106	2189	8.7	**Sturgis** (city) Saint Joseph County
106	2189	8.7	**Warren** (city) Macomb County
113	2274	8.8	**Ionia** (city) Ionia County
113	2274	8.8	**Marquette** (city) Marquette County
113	2274	8.8	**Owosso** (city) Shiawassee County
113	2274	8.8	**Saginaw** (city) Saginaw County
113	2274	8.8	**White Lake** (charter township) Oakland County
118	2345	8.9	**Adrian** (city) Lenawee County
118	2345	8.9	**Brighton** (township) Livingston County
118	2345	8.9	**Flint** (charter township) Genesee County
118	2345	8.9	**Melvindale** (city) Wayne County
122	2404	9.0	**Beverly Hills** (village) Oakland County
122	2404	9.0	**Kalamazoo** (charter township) Kalamazoo County
122	2404	9.0	**Plainfield** (charter township) Kent County
122	2404	9.0	**Van Buren** (charter township) Wayne County
126	2479	9.1	**Brownstown** (charter township) Wayne County
126	2479	9.1	**Lincoln Park** (city) Wayne County
126	2479	9.1	**Southfield** (township) Oakland County
126	2479	9.1	**Taylor** (city) Wayne County
130	2554	9.2	**Brandon** (charter township) Oakland County
130	2554	9.2	**Clinton** (charter township) Macomb County
130	2554	9.2	**Genoa** (township) Livingston County
130	2554	9.2	**Livonia** (city) Wayne County
130	2554	9.2	**Traverse City** (city) Grand Traverse County
130	2554	9.2	**Tyrone** (township) Livingston County
136	2615	9.3	**Fenton** (city) Genesee County
136	2615	9.3	**Grosse Ile** (township) Wayne County
136	2615	9.3	**Wayne** (city) Wayne County
139	2680	9.4	**Port Huron** (charter township) Saint Clair County
140	2760	9.5	**Highland** (charter township) Oakland County
140	2760	9.5	**Monroe** (city) Monroe County
140	2760	9.5	**Southgate** (city) Wayne County
143	2825	9.6	**Burton** (city) Genesee County
143	2825	9.6	**Byron** (township) Kent County
143	2825	9.6	**Cooper** (charter township) Kalamazoo County
143	2825	9.6	**Grand Blanc** (charter township) Genesee County
147	2887	9.7	**Antwerp** (township) Van Buren County
147	2887	9.7	**Davison** (township) Genesee County
147	2887	9.7	**East Bay** (township) Grand Traverse County
147	2887	9.7	**Fenton** (charter township) Genesee County

Note: *The state column ranks the top/bottom 150 places from all places in the state with population of 10,000 or more. The national column ranks the top/bottom 150 places from all places in the country with population of 10,000 or more. Places that are unincorporated were not considered in the rankings. Please refer to the User Guide for additional information.*

Ancestry: German

Top 150 Places Ranked in *Descending* Order

State Rank	Nat'l Rank	Percent	Place
1	1	76.8	**Chilton** (city) Calumet County
2	2	73.3	**Barton** (town) Washington County
3	3	73.0	**Addison** (town) Washington County
4	4	72.6	**Dyersville** (city) Dubuque County
5	5	70.9	**Jackson** (town) Washington County
6	6	70.5	**Howards Grove** (village) Sheboygan County
7	7	70.3	**Mayville** (city) Dodge County
8	8	69.9	**Minster** (village) Auglaize County
9	9	69.1	**Hartford** (town) Washington County
9	9	69.1	**Polk** (town) Washington County
11	11	68.4	**Medford** (town) Taylor County
12	12	68.1	**Brillion** (city) Calumet County
13	13	67.8	**Kiel** (city) Manitowoc County
14	14	67.7	**Hortonville** (village) Outagamie County
15	15	66.9	**Wakefield** (township) Stearns County
16	16	66.1	**Center** (town) Outagamie County
17	17	66.0	**Plymouth** (town) Sheboygan County
17	17	66.0	**Sheboygan** (town) Sheboygan County
17	17	66.0	**Trenton** (town) Washington County
20	20	65.8	**Fayette** (township) Juniata County
20	20	65.8	**Wheatland** (town) Kenosha County
22	22	65.5	**Kewaskum** (village) Washington County
23	23	65.4	**Springfield** (town) Dane County
24	24	65.2	**Empire** (town) Fond du Lac County
25	25	64.8	**Mukwa** (town) Waupaca County
26	26	64.2	**Albany** (city) Stearns County
27	27	64.0	**Jackson** (village) Washington County
28	28	63.9	**New Bremen** (village) Auglaize County
29	29	63.8	**New Ulm** (city) Brown County
30	30	63.0	**Coldwater** (village) Mercer County
30	30	63.0	**West Bend** (town) Washington County
32	32	62.3	**Breese** (city) Clinton County
33	33	61.9	**Taycheedah** (town) Fond du Lac County
34	34	61.4	**Merrill** (town) Lincoln County
34	34	61.4	**New Holstein** (city) Calumet County
36	36	60.9	**Beaver Dam** (town) Dodge County
36	36	60.9	**Friendship** (town) Fond du Lac County
36	36	60.9	**Mandan** (city) Morton County
39	39	60.8	**Miami Heights** (CDP) Hamilton County
40	40	60.6	**Plymouth** (city) Sheboygan County
40	40	60.6	**Sheboygan Falls** (city) Sheboygan County
42	42	60.4	**Medford** (city) Taylor County
43	43	60.3	**Merrill** (city) Lincoln County
43	43	60.3	**Saint Marys** (city) Elk County
45	45	60.2	**Elizabeth** (township) Lancaster County
46	46	59.7	**Stettin** (town) Marathon County
47	47	59.6	**Merton** (village) Waukesha County
48	48	59.5	**Wales** (village) Waukesha County
49	49	59.4	**Dale** (town) Outagamie County
49	49	59.4	**Germantown** (village) Washington County
49	49	59.4	**Grundy Center** (city) Grundy County
49	49	59.4	**Saint Augusta** (city) Stearns County
53	53	59.3	**Columbus** (city) Columbia County
53	53	59.3	**Farmington** (town) Washington County
55	55	59.2	**Fond du Lac** (town) Fond du Lac County
55	55	59.2	**Wayne** (city) Wayne County
57	57	59.1	**Caledonia** (city) Houston County
58	58	58.9	**Ixonia** (town) Jefferson County
58	58	58.9	**Lodi** (town) Columbia County
60	60	58.3	**Horicon** (city) Dodge County
61	61	58.2	**Johnson Creek** (village) Jefferson County
62	62	58.0	**Oakland** (town) Jefferson County
62	62	58.0	**Sauk Centre** (city) Stearns County
64	64	57.8	**Richfield** (village) Washington County
65	65	57.7	**Harrison** (town) Calumet County
65	65	57.7	**Sebewaing** (township) Huron County
67	67	57.6	**Fox** (township) Elk County
67	67	57.6	**West Bend** (city) Washington County
69	69	57.4	**Grafton** (town) Ozaukee County
69	69	57.4	**Ripon** (city) Fond du Lac County
71	71	57.3	**Harrison** (city) Hamilton County
72	72	57.2	**Carroll** (city) Carroll County
72	72	57.2	**Washington** (township) Schuylkill County
74	74	57.1	**Kronenwetter** (village) Marathon County
75	75	56.9	**Ellington** (town) Outagamie County
76	76	56.8	**Norwood Young America** (city) Carver County
76	76	56.8	**Saukville** (village) Ozaukee County
78	78	56.5	**Sherwood** (village) Calumet County
78	78	56.5	**Slinger** (village) Washington County
80	80	56.4	**Delphos** (city) Allen County
80	80	56.4	**Oregon** (town) Dane County
80	80	56.4	**Shelby** (town) La Crosse County
83	83	56.3	**Lisbon** (town) Waukesha County
83	83	56.3	**Sussex** (village) Waukesha County
85	85	56.2	**Bismarck** (city) Burleigh County
85	85	56.2	**Poynette** (village) Columbia County
87	87	56.0	**Alsace** (township) Berks County
87	87	56.0	**Jordan** (city) Scott County
89	89	55.9	**Eagle** (town) Waukesha County
90	90	55.8	**Waukesha** (town) Waukesha County
91	91	55.7	**Clayton** (town) Winnebago County
91	91	55.7	**Pine Grove** (township) Schuylkill County
93	93	55.6	**Ashippun** (town) Dodge County
93	93	55.6	**Rockland** (township) Berks County
95	95	55.5	**Clintonville** (city) Waupaca County
95	95	55.5	**Pewaukee** (city) Waukesha County
95	95	55.5	**Sevastopol** (town) Door County
98	98	55.3	**Lake Crystal** (city) Blue Earth County
98	98	55.3	**Plainview** (city) Wabasha County
98	98	55.3	**Rock Rapids** (city) Lyon County
101	101	55.2	**De Witt** (city) Clinton County
101	101	55.2	**Merton** (town) Waukesha County
101	101	55.2	**Watertown** (city) Jefferson County
104	104	55.1	**Hartford** (city) Washington County
105	105	55.0	**Upper Augusta** (township) Northumberland County
106	106	54.9	**Delhi Hills** (CDP) Hamilton County
107	107	54.8	**Aberdeen** (city) Brown County
107	107	54.8	**Delafield** (town) Waukesha County
109	109	54.7	**Jamestown** (city) Stutsman County
110	110	54.6	**Cottage Grove** (town) Dane County
110	110	54.6	**Hallam** (borough) York County
110	110	54.6	**Vernon** (town) Waukesha County
113	113	54.5	**Monticello** (city) Jones County
113	113	54.5	**Mukwonago** (town) Waukesha County
115	115	54.4	**Milbank** (city) Grant County
116	116	54.3	**Beulah** (city) Mercer County
116	116	54.3	**Cross Plains** (village) Dane County
116	116	54.3	**Lima** (town) Sheboygan County
119	119	54.2	**Algoma** (city) Kewaunee County
119	119	54.2	**Cold Spring** (city) Stearns County
119	119	54.2	**Lodi** (city) Columbia County
119	119	54.2	**Monfort Heights** (CDP) Hamilton County
123	123	54.1	**Mack** (CDP) Hamilton County
123	123	54.1	**North Mankato** (city) Nicollet County
125	125	54.0	**Menasha** (town) Winnebago County
125	125	54.0	**Rome** (town) Adams County
127	127	53.9	**Hays** (city) Ellis County
128	128	53.8	**Brockway** (township) Stearns County
128	128	53.8	**Dent** (CDP) Hamilton County
128	128	53.8	**Lake Wazeecha** (CDP) Wood County
128	128	53.8	**Sleepy Eye** (city) Brown County
132	132	53.7	**Zumbrota** (city) Goodhue County
133	133	53.6	**Dickinson** (city) Stark County
134	134	53.5	**Beaver Dam** (city) Dodge County
134	134	53.5	**Fond du Lac** (city) Fond du Lac County
134	134	53.5	**Wescott** (town) Shawano County
137	137	53.4	**Eagle Point** (town) Chippewa County
137	137	53.4	**Grafton** (village) Ozaukee County
139	139	53.3	**Freeburg** (village) Saint Clair County
140	140	53.2	**Lake Wisconsin** (CDP) Columbia County
140	140	53.2	**Marshfield** (city) Wood County
142	142	53.1	**Dell Rapids** (city) Minnehaha County
142	142	53.1	**Lake Mills** (city) Jefferson County
142	142	53.1	**Muskego** (city) Waukesha County
142	142	53.1	**Oregon** (village) Dane County
142	142	53.1	**Portage** (city) Columbia County
147	147	53.0	**Hereford** (township) Berks County
147	147	53.0	**Marysville** (city) Marshall County
147	147	53.0	**North Fond du Lac** (village) Fond du Lac County
150	150	52.9	**Blackhawk** (CDP) Meade County

Note: The state column ranks the top/bottom 150 places from all places in the state with population of 10,000 or more. The national column ranks the top/bottom 150 places from all places in the country with population of 10,000 or more. Places that are unincorporated were not considered in the rankings. Please refer to the User Guide for additional information.

Ancestry: English

Top 150 Places Ranked in *Descending* Order

State Rank	Nat'l Rank	Percent	Place
1	1	84.4	**Hildale** (city) Washington County
2	2	66.2	**Colorado City** (town) Mohave County
3	3	42.2	**Alpine** (city) Utah County
4	4	41.5	**Fruit Heights** (city) Davis County
4	4	41.5	**Manti** (city) Sanpete County
6	6	40.8	**Highland** (city) Utah County
7	7	40.5	**Mapleton** (city) Utah County
8	8	39.1	**Beaver** (city) Beaver County
9	9	38.4	**Centerville** (city) Davis County
10	10	38.2	**Hooper** (city) Weber County
10	10	38.2	**Hopkinton** (town) Merrimack County
12	12	37.8	**Sheridan** (city) Grant County
13	13	36.9	**Santa Clara** (city) Washington County
14	14	36.0	**Saint George** (town) Knox County
15	15	35.9	**Farmingdale** (town) Kennebec County
16	16	35.7	**Bountiful** (city) Davis County
17	17	35.6	**Rockport** (town) Knox County
18	18	35.4	**Kanab** (city) Kane County
18	18	35.4	**McCall** (city) Valley County
20	20	35.0	**Wolfeboro** (CDP) Carroll County
21	21	34.8	**Farr West** (city) Weber County
21	21	34.8	**Providence** (city) Cache County
23	23	34.6	**Bristol** (town) Lincoln County
23	23	34.6	**Rexburg** (city) Madison County
25	25	34.5	**North Logan** (city) Cache County
26	26	34.3	**Boothbay** (town) Lincoln County
26	26	34.3	**Parowan** (city) Iron County
28	28	34.2	**Pleasant View** (city) Weber County
29	29	33.8	**Wellsville** (city) Cache County
30	30	33.6	**Monmouth** (town) Kennebec County
31	31	33.5	**Holladay** (city) Salt Lake County
32	32	33.4	**Hyde Park** (city) Cache County
32	32	33.4	**Trent Woods** (town) Craven County
34	34	33.0	**Salem** (city) Utah County
35	35	32.9	**Delta** (city) Millard County
36	36	32.8	**Freeport** (town) Cumberland County
36	36	32.8	**Midway** (city) Wasatch County
36	36	32.8	**West Bountiful** (city) Davis County
39	39	32.6	**Farmington** (city) Davis County
39	39	32.6	**Kaysville** (city) Davis County
41	41	32.5	**Kennebunkport** (town) York County
42	42	32.4	**Wolfeboro** (town) Carroll County
43	43	32.2	**Woodstock** (town) Windsor County
44	44	32.0	**Santaquin** (city) Utah County
45	45	31.9	**Chichester** (town) Merrimack County
46	46	31.8	**American Fork** (city) Utah County
46	46	31.8	**Anson** (town) Somerset County
46	46	31.8	**Camden** (town) Knox County
46	46	31.8	**Hyrum** (city) Cache County
50	50	31.6	**Spring Arbor** (township) Jackson County
51	51	31.5	**Poland** (town) Androscoggin County
52	52	31.4	**Herriman** (city) Salt Lake County
53	53	31.3	**Morgan** (city) Morgan County
54	54	31.1	**Alamo** (town) Wheeler County
54	54	31.1	**Charlestown** (town) Sullivan County
56	56	31.0	**Spanish Fork** (city) Utah County
56	56	31.0	**Waldoboro** (town) Lincoln County
58	58	30.9	**Ivins** (city) Washington County
59	59	30.8	**Yarmouth** (town) Cumberland County
60	60	30.7	**Cedar Hills** (city) Utah County
61	61	30.6	**Bethel** (town) Oxford County
61	61	30.6	**Bridgton** (town) Cumberland County
61	61	30.6	**Lake San Marcos** (CDP) San Diego County
61	61	30.6	**Rockland** (city) Knox County
61	61	30.6	**Saint George** (city) Washington County
61	61	30.6	**Woods Cross** (city) Davis County
67	67	30.5	**Cedar City** (city) Iron County
68	68	30.3	**North Salt Lake** (city) Davis County
68	68	30.3	**South Jordan** (city) Salt Lake County
70	70	30.2	**Eagle Mountain** (city) Utah County
71	71	30.1	**Preston** (city) Franklin County
72	72	29.9	**Camden** (CDP) Knox County
73	73	29.8	**South Beach** (CDP) Indian River County
74	74	29.7	**Harpswell** (town) Cumberland County
74	74	29.7	**Indian River Shores** (town) Indian River County
76	76	29.5	**Helena** (city) Telfair County
76	76	29.5	**Manchester** (town) Kennebec County
76	76	29.5	**Nephi** (city) Juab County
76	76	29.5	**Washington Terrace** (city) Weber County
80	80	29.4	**Yarmouth** (CDP) Cumberland County
81	81	29.3	**Springville** (city) Utah County
82	82	29.2	**Clinton** (town) Kennebec County
82	82	29.2	**Grantsville** (city) Tooele County
84	84	29.1	**Little Compton** (town) Newport County
84	84	29.1	**Plain City** (city) Weber County
86	86	29.0	**Cottonwood Heights** (city) Salt Lake County
86	86	29.0	**Warren** (town) Knox County
88	88	28.9	**Madison** (town) Carroll County
88	88	28.9	**Washington** (city) Washington County
90	90	28.8	**Lindon** (city) Utah County
90	90	28.8	**Livermore Falls** (town) Androscoggin County
90	90	28.8	**Nibley** (city) Cache County
93	93	28.7	**Orem** (city) Utah County
93	93	28.7	**Woolwich** (town) Sagadahoc County
95	95	28.6	**Pleasant Grove** (city) Utah County
96	96	28.5	**Arundel** (town) York County
96	96	28.5	**China** (town) Kennebec County
98	98	28.4	**Lehi** (city) Utah County
98	98	28.4	**Tamworth** (town) Carroll County
100	100	28.3	**Bradford** (town) Orange County
100	100	28.3	**Enoch** (city) Iron County
102	102	28.2	**Oneida** (town) Scott County
102	102	28.2	**Oxford** (town) Oxford County
102	102	28.2	**South Weber** (city) Davis County
105	105	28.1	**Maeser** (CDP) Uintah County
105	105	28.1	**Walpole** (town) Cheshire County
107	107	28.0	**Hampden** (CDP) Penobscot County
107	107	28.0	**Sandy** (city) Salt Lake County
109	109	27.9	**Northfield** (town) Franklin County
109	109	27.9	**Perry** (city) Box Elder County
111	111	27.8	**Limerick** (town) York County
111	111	27.8	**Orleans** (town) Barnstable County
111	111	27.8	**Riverton** (city) Salt Lake County
114	114	27.7	**Draper** (city) Salt Lake County
114	114	27.7	**Hartland** (town) Windsor County
114	114	27.7	**Otisco** (town) Onondaga County
114	114	27.7	**Saratoga Springs** (city) Utah County
114	114	27.7	**Smithfield** (city) Cache County
119	119	27.6	**Bluffdale** (city) Salt Lake County
119	119	27.6	**Bowdoin** (town) Sagadahoc County
119	119	27.6	**East Bloomfield** (town) Ontario County
119	119	27.6	**North Yarmouth** (town) Cumberland County
119	119	27.6	**Syracuse** (city) Davis County
124	124	27.5	**Harrison** (town) Cumberland County
124	124	27.5	**Highland Park** (town) Dallas County
124	124	27.5	**South Eliot** (CDP) York County
127	127	27.4	**Hampden** (town) Penobscot County
127	127	27.4	**Montpelier** (city) Bear Lake County
127	127	27.4	**Winston** (city) Douglas County
130	130	27.3	**Buxton** (town) York County
130	130	27.3	**North Ogden** (city) Weber County
130	130	27.3	**White Hall** (city) Jefferson County
133	133	27.2	**Thetford** (town) Orange County
134	134	27.1	**Greene** (town) Chenango County
134	134	27.1	**Wakefield** (town) Carroll County
136	136	26.9	**New Durham** (town) Strafford County
136	136	26.9	**Stansbury Park** (CDP) Tooele County
136	136	26.9	**Surfside Beach** (town) Horry County
139	139	26.8	**Stratham** (town) Rockingham County
140	140	26.6	**Concord** (township) Jackson County
140	140	26.6	**Millcreek** (CDP) Salt Lake County
140	140	26.6	**Peterborough** (CDP) Hillsborough County
140	140	26.6	**Turner** (town) Androscoggin County
144	144	26.5	**Foster** (town) Providence County
144	144	26.5	**Hope** (township) Barry County
144	144	26.5	**Norwich** (town) Windsor County
147	147	26.4	**Belle Meade** (city) Davidson County
148	148	26.3	**Belfast** (city) Waldo County
149	149	26.2	**Richfield** (city) Sevier County
149	149	26.2	**South Duxbury** (CDP) Plymouth County

Note: *The state column ranks the top/bottom 150 places from all places in the state with population of 10,000 or more. The national column ranks the top/bottom 150 places from all places in the country with population of 10,000 or more. Places that are unincorporated were not considered in the rankings. Please refer to the User Guide for additional information.*

Ancestry: American

Top 150 Places Ranked in *Descending* Order

State Rank	Nat'l Rank	Percent	Place
1	1	66.4	**La Follette** (city) Campbell County
2	2	60.0	**Gloverville** (CDP) Aiken County
3	3	54.6	**Clearwater** (CDP) Aiken County
4	4	54.4	**Treasure Lake** (CDP) Clearfield County
5	5	51.7	**Healdton** (city) Carter County
6	6	45.9	**Bonifay** (city) Holmes County
7	7	45.8	**Harlem** (CDP) Hendry County
8	8	45.5	**Bean Station** (city) Grainger County
8	8	45.5	**Stanford** (city) Lincoln County
10	10	44.5	**Pell City** (city) Saint Clair County
11	11	44.3	**New Tazewell** (town) Claiborne County
12	12	43.9	**Dresden** (town) Weakley County
13	13	43.6	**Hartford** (city) Ohio County
14	14	43.2	**Blue Hill** (town) Hancock County
15	15	43.1	**Eaton** (town) Madison County
16	16	43.0	**Church Hill** (city) Hawkins County
17	17	42.6	**Middlesborough** (city) Bell County
18	18	42.1	**Temple** (city) Carroll County
19	19	41.1	**Georgetown** (city) Vermilion County
20	20	40.9	**Grantville** (city) Coweta County
20	20	40.9	**Summerville** (city) Chattooga County
22	22	40.6	**Morehead** (city) Rowan County
23	23	40.5	**Bayou Vista** (CDP) Saint Mary Parish
24	24	40.4	**Lone Grove** (city) Carter County
24	24	40.4	**Wilkesboro** (town) Wilkes County
26	26	39.9	**Chincoteague** (town) Accomack County
27	27	39.8	**Bremen** (city) Haralson County
28	28	39.7	**Cullowhee** (CDP) Jackson County
29	29	39.4	**Nassau Village-Ratliff** (CDP) Nassau County
30	30	38.8	**Crab Orchard** (CDP) Raleigh County
31	31	38.7	**Stanton** (city) Powell County
32	32	38.4	**Rogersville** (town) Hawkins County
33	33	38.2	**Cookeville** (city) Putnam County
34	34	38.0	**Livingston** (town) Overton County
35	35	37.6	**Gray Summit** (CDP) Franklin County
35	35	37.6	**Harrogate** (city) Claiborne County
37	37	37.4	**North Terre Haute** (CDP) Vigo County
38	38	37.3	**Mount Carmel** (CDP) Clermont County
39	39	36.9	**Atkins** (city) Pope County
39	39	36.9	**Burnettown** (town) Aiken County
39	39	36.9	**De Funiak Springs** (city) Walton County
42	42	36.8	**Lake of the Woods** (CDP) Champaign County
42	42	36.8	**Suncoast Estates** (CDP) Lee County
44	44	36.7	**Lancaster** (city) Garrard County
44	44	36.7	**Sandy** (township) Clearfield County
46	46	36.6	**Donalsonville** (city) Seminole County
47	47	36.3	**Bradford** (township) Clearfield County
47	47	36.3	**Broadway** (town) Rockingham County
47	47	36.3	**Jena** (town) La Salle Parish
50	50	36.2	**Algood** (city) Putnam County
50	50	36.2	**Sylva** (town) Jackson County
52	52	36.0	**Unicoi** (town) Unicoi County
53	53	35.6	**Bloomingdale** (CDP) Sullivan County
53	53	35.6	**Somerset** (city) Pulaski County
53	53	35.6	**Timberville** (town) Rockingham County
56	56	35.5	**Beaver Dam** (city) Ohio County
56	56	35.5	**Oliver Springs** (town) Anderson County
58	58	35.4	**Bucksport** (CDP) Hancock County
59	59	35.1	**England** (city) Lonoke County
59	59	35.1	**Fairview** (CDP) Walker County
59	59	35.1	**LaFayette** (city) Walker County
62	62	34.9	**Bucksport** (town) Hancock County
62	62	34.9	**Mountain City** (town) Johnson County
62	62	34.9	**Shepherdsville** (city) Bullitt County
65	65	34.8	**Blennerhassett** (CDP) Wood County
66	66	34.7	**South Lebanon** (village) Warren County
67	67	34.5	**Mount Carmel** (town) Hawkins County
68	68	34.3	**Hannahs Mill** (CDP) Upson County
69	69	34.2	**Mills** (town) Natrona County
69	69	34.2	**Rockwood** (city) Roane County
71	71	33.5	**North Wilkesboro** (town) Wilkes County
71	71	33.5	**Odenville** (town) Saint Clair County
73	73	33.3	**Ward** (city) Lonoke County
74	74	33.2	**Bawcomville** (CDP) Ouachita Parish
75	75	33.1	**Bethel** (village) Clermont County
75	75	33.1	**Grottoes** (town) Rockingham County
77	77	33.0	**Shelbyville** (city) Bedford County
78	78	32.7	**Dawson Springs** (city) Hopkins County
78	78	32.7	**Galena** (city) Cherokee County
78	78	32.7	**Pike Road** (town) Montgomery County
81	81	32.6	**Erwin** (town) Unicoi County
81	81	32.6	**Honea Path** (town) Anderson County
83	83	32.5	**West Tisbury** (town) Dukes County
84	84	32.3	**Pearisburg** (town) Giles County
85	85	32.2	**Evansville** (town) Natrona County
86	86	32.0	**Moody** (city) Saint Clair County
86	86	32.0	**Pittsburg** (city) Crawford County
88	88	31.9	**Woodbury** (town) Cannon County
89	89	31.8	**Dandridge** (town) Jefferson County
90	90	31.7	**Withamsville** (CDP) Clermont County
91	91	31.5	**Margaret** (town) Saint Clair County
92	92	31.4	**Pigeon Forge** (city) Sevier County
93	93	31.3	**Alva** (CDP) Lee County
94	94	31.1	**Hilliard** (town) Nassau County
95	95	30.8	**Monterey** (town) Putnam County
96	96	30.7	**Icard** (CDP) Burke County
97	97	30.5	**Flemingsburg** (city) Fleming County
97	97	30.5	**Shady Spring** (CDP) Raleigh County
99	99	30.4	**Irvine** (city) Estill County
100	100	30.3	**Cloverdale** (CDP) Botetourt County
100	100	30.3	**Hamilton** (town) Madison County
100	100	30.3	**Sylacauga** (city) Talladega County
100	100	30.3	**Underwood-Petersville** (CDP) Lauderdale County
104	104	30.2	**Central City** (city) Muhlenberg County
104	104	30.2	**Harriman** (city) Roane County
104	104	30.2	**Prestonsburg** (city) Floyd County
107	107	30.1	**Stuarts Draft** (CDP) Augusta County
108	108	30.0	**Madison** (town) Madison County
108	108	30.0	**Verona** (CDP) Augusta County
108	108	30.0	**Waynesville** (town) Haywood County
111	111	29.8	**Granville** (town) Washington County
111	111	29.8	**Paris** (city) Bourbon County
111	111	29.8	**Winchester** (city) Clark County
114	114	29.7	**Byron** (city) Peach County
114	114	29.7	**Emmett** (city) Gem County
114	114	29.7	**Hillview** (city) Bullitt County
114	114	29.7	**Oak Grove** (CDP) Washington County
114	114	29.7	**Sunnyvale** (town) Dallas County
114	114	29.7	**Wickenburg** (town) Maricopa County
120	120	29.6	**Jefferson City** (city) Jefferson County
121	121	29.5	**Ball** (town) Rapides Parish
121	121	29.5	**Corinth** (town) Penobscot County
121	121	29.5	**Lincoln** (city) Talladega County
124	124	29.4	**Manchester** (city) Coffee County
124	124	29.4	**Owensboro** (city) Daviess County
126	126	29.3	**Kings Mountain** (city) Cleveland County
127	127	29.2	**Buckner** (CDP) Oldham County
127	127	29.2	**Malabar** (town) Brevard County
129	129	29.1	**Baxter Springs** (city) Cherokee County
130	130	28.9	**Kingston** (city) Roane County
130	130	28.9	**Morristown** (city) Hamblen County
132	132	28.8	**Bayshore** (CDP) New Hanover County
132	132	28.8	**Buena Vista** (independent city)
134	134	28.7	**Grissom AFB** (CDP) Miami County
134	134	28.7	**Hodgenville** (city) Larue County
136	136	28.5	**Claiborne** (CDP) Ouachita Parish
136	136	28.5	**Inwood** (CDP) Polk County
136	136	28.5	**Moyock** (CDP) Currituck County
136	136	28.5	**Richlands** (town) Tazewell County
136	136	28.5	**Tabor City** (town) Columbus County
141	141	28.4	**Dundee** (town) Polk County
141	141	28.4	**Jan Phyl Village** (CDP) Polk County
141	141	28.4	**Morgan** (city) Morgan County
144	144	28.3	**West Liberty** (city) Morgan County
145	145	28.2	**Bicknell** (city) Knox County
145	145	28.2	**Fort Scott** (city) Bourbon County
145	145	28.2	**Putney** (CDP) Dougherty County
148	148	28.1	**Berwick** (town) Saint Mary Parish
148	148	28.1	**Corinth** (town) Saratoga County
148	148	28.1	**Middleton** (city) Canyon County

Note: The state column ranks the top/bottom 150 places from all places in the state with population of 10,000 or more. The national column ranks the top/bottom 150 places from all places in the country with population of 10,000 or more. Places that are unincorporated were not considered in the rankings. Please refer to the User Guide for additional information.

Ancestry: Irish

Top 150 Places Ranked in *Descending* Order

State Rank	Nat'l Rank	Percent	Place
1	1	52.0	**Pearl River** (CDP) Rockland County
2	2	51.7	**Ocean Bluff-Brant Rock** (CDP) Plymouth County
3	3	50.6	**Green Harbor-Cedar Crest** (CDP) Plymouth County
4	4	49.4	**Rockledge** (borough) Montgomery County
5	5	48.3	**Walpole** (CDP) Norfolk County
6	6	47.4	**North Scituate** (CDP) Plymouth County
7	7	47.0	**Scituate** (CDP) Plymouth County
8	8	46.9	**Marshfield** (town) Plymouth County
9	9	46.2	**Scituate** (town) Plymouth County
10	10	45.8	**Ridley Park** (borough) Delaware County
11	11	45.5	**Spring Lake Heights** (borough) Monmouth County
12	12	45.3	**Oak Valley** (CDP) Gloucester County
13	13	45.2	**Hanover** (town) Plymouth County
14	14	44.7	**Norwell** (town) Plymouth County
15	15	44.2	**Glenside** (CDP) Montgomery County
15	15	44.2	**Manasquan** (borough) Monmouth County
17	17	43.8	**Norwood** (borough) Delaware County
18	18	42.9	**Walpole** (CDP) Norfolk County
18	18	42.9	**Wynantskill** (CDP) Rensselaer County
20	20	42.8	**Springfield** (township) Delaware County
21	21	42.6	**Folsom** (CDP) Delaware County
21	21	42.6	**Glenolden** (borough) Delaware County
21	21	42.6	**Highlands** (borough) Monmouth County
24	24	42.2	**Marshfield** (CDP) Plymouth County
25	25	41.7	**North Middletown** (CDP) Monmouth County
26	26	41.6	**Braintree Town** (city) Norfolk County
27	27	41.4	**Weymouth Town** (city) Norfolk County
28	28	41.1	**Littleton Common** (CDP) Middlesex County
28	28	41.1	**North Wildwood** (city) Cape May County
30	30	41.0	**Bridgewater** (CDP) Plymouth County
31	31	40.9	**Abington** (cdp/town) Plymouth County
31	31	40.9	**Nahant** (cdp/town) Essex County
31	31	40.9	**Spring Lake** (borough) Monmouth County
34	34	40.6	**Whitman** (town) Plymouth County
35	35	40.5	**Cohasset** (town) Norfolk County
35	35	40.5	**Hopedale** (CDP) Worcester County
35	35	40.5	**Sayville** (CDP) Suffolk County
38	38	40.4	**Brielle** (borough) Monmouth County
39	39	40.3	**Hull** (cdp/town) Plymouth County
40	40	40.2	**Gloucester City** (city) Camden County
41	41	39.9	**Churchville** (CDP) Bucks County
42	42	39.7	**Haddon Heights** (borough) Camden County
43	43	39.6	**Notre Dame** (CDP) Saint Joseph County
44	44	39.5	**Ashland** (borough) Schuylkill County
44	44	39.5	**Hingham** (town) Plymouth County
46	46	39.4	**Avon** (town) Norfolk County
47	47	39.3	**Garden City** (village) Nassau County
47	47	39.3	**Tinicum** (township) Delaware County
49	49	39.2	**Milton** (cdp/town) Norfolk County
49	49	39.2	**Ramtown** (CDP) Monmouth County
51	51	39.1	**Ridley** (township) Delaware County
52	52	38.8	**Bridgewater** (town) Plymouth County
53	53	38.5	**Hanson** (town) Plymouth County
53	53	38.5	**North Reading** (town) Middlesex County
53	53	38.5	**Prospect Park** (borough) Delaware County
53	53	38.5	**Rockland** (CDP) Plymouth County
57	57	38.4	**Hingham** (CDP) Plymouth County
58	58	38.3	**Foxborough** (town) Norfolk County
59	59	38.1	**Foxborough** (CDP) Norfolk County
60	60	38.0	**Barrington** (borough) Camden County
61	61	37.9	**Aldan** (borough) Delaware County
61	61	37.9	**Mansfield Center** (CDP) Bristol County
61	61	37.9	**National Park** (borough) Gloucester County
64	64	37.8	**East Sandwich** (CDP) Barnstable County
65	65	37.6	**Haverford** (township) Delaware County
65	65	37.6	**West Brandywine** (township) Chester County
67	67	37.5	**East Bridgewater** (town) Plymouth County
68	68	37.4	**Buzzards Bay** (CDP) Barnstable County
69	69	37.3	**Blauvelt** (CDP) Rockland County
69	69	37.3	**East Quogue** (CDP) Suffolk County
71	71	37.2	**Canton** (town) Norfolk County
71	71	37.2	**North Falmouth** (CDP) Barnstable County
73	73	37.1	**Pembroke** (town) Plymouth County
73	73	37.1	**Upton** (CDP) Worcester County
73	73	37.1	**Woodbury Heights** (borough) Gloucester County
76	76	36.9	**Fair Haven** (borough) Monmouth County
77	77	36.8	**Clementon** (borough) Camden County
77	77	36.8	**Duxbury** (town) Plymouth County
79	79	36.7	**Fairview** (CDP) Monmouth County
79	79	36.7	**Folcroft** (borough) Delaware County
79	79	36.7	**Newtown** (township) Delaware County
82	82	36.6	**Rockville Centre** (village) Nassau County
83	83	36.5	**Oceanport** (borough) Monmouth County
83	83	36.5	**West Bridgewater** (town) Plymouth County
85	85	36.2	**Audubon** (borough) Camden County
85	85	36.2	**Campo** (CDP) San Diego County
87	87	36.0	**Orleans** (town) Jefferson County
87	87	36.0	**Shark River Hills** (CDP) Monmouth County
89	89	35.8	**Drexel Hill** (CDP) Delaware County
89	89	35.8	**Trappe** (borough) Montgomery County
89	89	35.8	**West Sayville** (CDP) Suffolk County
92	92	35.5	**Leonardo** (CDP) Monmouth County
92	92	35.5	**Little Silver** (borough) Monmouth County
94	94	35.3	**Bethlehem** (township) Hunterdon County
95	95	35.2	**East Islip** (CDP) Suffolk County
95	95	35.2	**Kingston** (town) Plymouth County
97	97	35.1	**Dedham** (cdp/town) Norfolk County
97	97	35.1	**Hopedale** (town) Worcester County
97	97	35.1	**Wilmington** (cdp/town) Middlesex County
100	100	35.0	**Green Island** (town/village) Albany County
100	100	35.0	**Medford Lakes** (borough) Burlington County
102	102	34.9	**Holbrook** (cdp/town) Plymouth County
102	102	34.9	**Mansfield** (town) Bristol County
104	104	34.8	**LaFayette** (town) Onondaga County
104	104	34.8	**North Plymouth** (CDP) Plymouth County
104	104	34.8	**Norton** (town) Bristol County
104	104	34.8	**Tuckerton** (borough) Ocean County
104	104	34.8	**Wakefield** (cdp/town) Middlesex County
109	109	34.7	**Cape Neddick** (CDP) York County
109	109	34.7	**Tewksbury** (town) Middlesex County
109	109	34.7	**Woodlyn** (CDP) Delaware County
109	109	34.7	**Woolwich** (township) Gloucester County
113	113	34.6	**Wanamassa** (CDP) Monmouth County
114	114	34.5	**East Shoreham** (CDP) Suffolk County
114	114	34.5	**Horsham** (CDP) Montgomery County
114	114	34.5	**Skippack** (CDP) Montgomery County
117	117	34.4	**Plymouth** (town) Plymouth County
117	117	34.4	**Western Springs** (village) Cook County
119	119	34.3	**Bethel** (township) Delaware County
119	119	34.3	**Melrose** (city) Middlesex County
119	119	34.3	**Point Pleasant** (borough) Ocean County
122	122	34.2	**Aston** (township) Delaware County
122	122	34.2	**North Seekonk** (CDP) Bristol County
122	122	34.2	**Wanakah** (CDP) Erie County
122	122	34.2	**Westvale** (CDP) Onondaga County
126	126	34.1	**Reading** (cdp/town) Middlesex County
126	126	34.1	**Winthrop Town** (city) Suffolk County
128	128	34.0	**Atkinson** (town) Rockingham County
128	128	34.0	**Bella Vista** (CDP) Shasta County
128	128	34.0	**Hopkinton** (CDP) Middlesex County
128	128	34.0	**Plymouth** (CDP) Plymouth County
128	128	34.0	**Washington** (town) Dutchess County
128	128	34.0	**Williston Park** (village) Nassau County
134	134	33.9	**Norwood** (cdp/town) Norfolk County
135	135	33.8	**Clinton** (town) Worcester County
135	135	33.8	**Halifax** (town) Plymouth County
135	135	33.8	**Mystic Island** (CDP) Ocean County
135	135	33.8	**Wall** (township) Monmouth County
139	139	33.7	**Massapequa Park** (village) Nassau County
140	140	33.6	**Cold Spring Harbor** (CDP) Suffolk County
140	140	33.6	**Dalton** (town) Berkshire County
142	142	33.5	**Colonie** (village) Albany County
142	142	33.5	**Middletown** (township) Monmouth County
142	142	33.5	**Seabrook** (town) Rockingham County
142	142	33.5	**Waterford** (township) Camden County
146	146	33.4	**Medfield** (CDP) Norfolk County
146	146	33.4	**Montgomery** (village) Orange County
146	146	33.4	**Mount Ephraim** (borough) Camden County
149	149	33.3	**Dover** (town) Dutchess County
149	149	33.3	**Fort Salonga** (CDP) Suffolk County

Note: The state column ranks the top/bottom 150 places from all places in the state with population of 10,000 or more. The national column ranks the top/bottom 150 places from all places in the country with population of 10,000 or more. Places that are unincorporated were not considered in the rankings. Please refer to the User Guide for additional information.

Ancestry: Italian

Top 150 Places Ranked in *Descending* Order

State Rank	Nat'l Rank	Percent	Place
1	1	51.2	**Johnston** (town) Providence County
2	2	50.9	**Fairfield** (township) Essex County
3	3	49.0	**North Massapequa** (CDP) Nassau County
4	4	47.7	**East Haven** (cdp/town) New Haven County
5	5	47.3	**Watertown** (CDP) Litchfield County
6	6	46.3	**Massapequa** (CDP) Nassau County
7	7	45.4	**Eastchester** (CDP) Westchester County
8	8	45.3	**Thornwood** (CDP) Westchester County
9	9	44.4	**Glendora** (CDP) Camden County
10	10	44.0	**Frankfort** (village) Herkimer County
11	11	43.5	**Hawthorne** (CDP) Westchester County
12	12	43.4	**Hammonton** (town) Atlantic County
13	13	43.3	**North Branford** (town) New Haven County
13	13	43.3	**Turnersville** (CDP) Gloucester County
15	15	42.8	**West Islip** (CDP) Suffolk County
16	16	42.6	**Massapequa Park** (village) Nassau County
17	17	42.1	**Franklin Square** (CDP) Nassau County
18	18	41.9	**Islip Terrace** (CDP) Suffolk County
19	19	41.6	**Watertown** (town) Litchfield County
20	20	41.4	**Nesconset** (CDP) Suffolk County
21	21	41.1	**Lake Grove** (village) Suffolk County
22	22	40.4	**North Haven** (cdp/town) New Haven County
23	23	40.3	**Gibbstown** (CDP) Gloucester County
24	24	40.2	**Saint James** (CDP) Suffolk County
24	24	40.2	**Seaford** (CDP) Nassau County
26	26	40.1	**East Hanover** (township) Morris County
26	26	40.1	**Saugus** (cdp/town) Essex County
28	28	39.9	**Marlboro** (CDP) Ulster County
29	29	39.7	**Beach Haven West** (CDP) Ocean County
30	30	39.5	**East Islip** (CDP) Suffolk County
30	30	39.5	**Smithtown** (CDP) Suffolk County
32	32	39.3	**Jefferson Valley-Yorktown** (CDP) Westchester County
33	33	39.2	**Jessup** (borough) Lackawanna County
33	33	39.2	**Monmouth Beach** (borough) Monmouth County
35	35	39.0	**Brightwaters** (village) Suffolk County
36	36	38.7	**South Farmingdale** (CDP) Nassau County
37	37	38.1	**Frankfort** (town) Herkimer County
37	37	38.1	**Richwood** (CDP) Gloucester County
39	39	38.0	**Bayville** (village) Nassau County
39	39	38.0	**Malverne** (village) Nassau County
39	39	38.0	**North Providence** (town) Providence County
42	42	37.9	**Cedar Grove** (township) Essex County
43	43	37.8	**Plainedge** (CDP) Nassau County
44	44	37.7	**Holtsville** (CDP) Suffolk County
44	44	37.7	**Oakville** (CDP) Litchfield County
46	46	37.6	**Blackwood** (CDP) Camden County
46	46	37.6	**Holbrook** (CDP) Suffolk County
48	48	37.4	**Center Moriches** (CDP) Suffolk County
48	48	37.4	**Dunmore** (borough) Lackawanna County
48	48	37.4	**Smithtown** (town) Suffolk County
51	51	37.2	**North Great River** (CDP) Suffolk County
52	52	37.1	**Blue Point** (CDP) Suffolk County
52	52	37.1	**East Norwich** (CDP) Nassau County
52	52	37.1	**Ronkonkoma** (CDP) Suffolk County
52	52	37.1	**West Pittston** (borough) Luzerne County
56	56	36.9	**Hauppauge** (CDP) Suffolk County
57	57	36.8	**Bohemia** (CDP) Suffolk County
57	57	36.8	**Farmingville** (CDP) Suffolk County
57	57	36.8	**Old Forge** (borough) Lackawanna County
57	57	36.8	**Pemberwick** (CDP) Fairfield County
61	61	36.7	**Mechanicville** (city) Saratoga County
61	61	36.7	**Miller Place** (CDP) Suffolk County
61	61	36.7	**Nutley** (township) Essex County
61	61	36.7	**Selden** (CDP) Suffolk County
61	61	36.7	**Wood-Ridge** (borough) Bergen County
66	66	36.6	**Glen Head** (CDP) Nassau County
67	67	36.5	**Pittston** (city) Luzerne County
68	68	36.4	**Centerport** (CDP) Suffolk County
69	69	36.2	**Barnegat** (CDP) Ocean County
70	70	36.1	**Mahopac** (CDP) Putnam County
70	70	36.1	**Ocean Acres** (CDP) Ocean County
72	72	36.0	**Lindenhurst** (village) Suffolk County
72	72	36.0	**Lyncourt** (CDP) Onondaga County
72	72	36.0	**Union Vale** (town) Dutchess County
72	72	36.0	**Washington** (township) Gloucester County
76	76	35.9	**Eastchester** (town) Westchester County
77	77	35.8	**Garden City South** (CDP) Nassau County
77	77	35.8	**Greenwich** (township) Gloucester County
77	77	35.8	**Manorville** (CDP) Suffolk County
80	80	35.7	**Lake Pocotopaug** (CDP) Middlesex County
80	80	35.7	**Moonachie** (borough) Bergen County
80	80	35.7	**Oyster Bay** (CDP) Nassau County
83	83	35.6	**East Freehold** (CDP) Monmouth County
83	83	35.6	**Oakdale** (CDP) Suffolk County
83	83	35.6	**Ramtown** (CDP) Monmouth County
86	86	35.5	**Kensington** (CDP) Hartford County
86	86	35.5	**Pelham Manor** (village) Westchester County
88	88	35.4	**Holiday City-Berkeley** (CDP) Ocean County
88	88	35.4	**Yaphank** (CDP) Suffolk County
90	90	35.2	**Carmel** (town) Putnam County
91	91	35.1	**Commack** (CDP) Suffolk County
92	92	34.9	**Hazlet** (township) Monmouth County
92	92	34.9	**Somers** (town) Westchester County
94	94	34.5	**Bethpage** (CDP) Nassau County
94	94	34.5	**Middle Island** (CDP) Suffolk County
94	94	34.5	**Port Jefferson Station** (CDP) Suffolk County
97	97	34.4	**Lynnfield** (cdp/town) Essex County
98	98	34.3	**Kings Park** (CDP) Suffolk County
98	98	34.3	**North Babylon** (CDP) Suffolk County
98	98	34.3	**West Babylon** (CDP) Suffolk County
101	101	34.2	**Totowa** (borough) Passaic County
102	102	34.1	**Ellwood City** (borough) Lawrence County
102	102	34.1	**Stoneham** (cdp/town) Middlesex County
104	104	34.0	**Cranston** (city) Providence County
104	104	34.0	**Shirley** (CDP) Suffolk County
106	106	33.9	**Pequannock** (township) Morris County
106	106	33.9	**Pine Lake Park** (CDP) Ocean County
108	108	33.8	**East Fishkill** (town) Dutchess County
108	108	33.8	**Montrose** (CDP) Westchester County
110	110	33.7	**Locust Valley** (CDP) Nassau County
110	110	33.7	**Neshannock** (township) Lawrence County
110	110	33.7	**West Bay Shore** (CDP) Suffolk County
110	110	33.7	**Yorktown** (town) Westchester County
114	114	33.6	**Holiday City South** (CDP) Ocean County
114	114	33.6	**Kenmore** (village) Erie County
114	114	33.6	**Lacey** (township) Ocean County
114	114	33.6	**Prospect** (town) New Haven County
114	114	33.6	**Roseland** (borough) Essex County
114	114	33.6	**Wantagh** (CDP) Nassau County
120	120	33.5	**Waldwick** (borough) Bergen County
120	120	33.5	**Wolcott** (town) New Haven County
122	122	33.4	**East Shoreham** (CDP) Suffolk County
122	122	33.4	**South Huntington** (CDP) Suffolk County
122	122	33.4	**West Sayville** (CDP) Suffolk County
125	125	33.3	**Exeter** (borough) Luzerne County
125	125	33.3	**Toms River** (township) Ocean County
127	127	33.2	**East Williston** (village) Nassau County
127	127	33.2	**Lyndhurst** (township) Bergen County
129	129	33.1	**Lake Ronkonkoma** (CDP) Suffolk County
129	129	33.1	**Toms River** (CDP) Ocean County
129	129	33.1	**Westerly** (CDP) Washington County
132	132	33.0	**Cold Spring Harbor** (CDP) Suffolk County
132	132	33.0	**Mount Sinai** (CDP) Suffolk County
134	134	32.9	**Hasbrouck Heights** (borough) Bergen County
134	134	32.9	**Stafford** (township) Ocean County
136	136	32.8	**Berlin** (town) Hartford County
136	136	32.8	**Galeville** (CDP) Onondaga County
136	136	32.8	**West Caldwell** (township) Essex County
139	139	32.7	**Putnam Valley** (town) Putnam County
139	139	32.7	**Sound Beach** (CDP) Suffolk County
141	141	32.6	**Babylon** (village) Suffolk County
141	141	32.6	**Centereach** (CDP) Suffolk County
141	141	32.6	**Elwood** (CDP) Suffolk County
141	141	32.6	**Middletown** (township) Monmouth County
141	141	32.6	**North Patchogue** (CDP) Suffolk County
146	146	32.5	**Lincroft** (CDP) Monmouth County
147	147	32.4	**Barnegat** (township) Ocean County
147	147	32.4	**Caldwell** (borough) Essex County
147	147	32.4	**Levittown** (CDP) Nassau County
147	147	32.4	**Oceanport** (borough) Monmouth County

Note: The state column ranks the top/bottom 150 places from all places in the state with population of 10,000 or more. The national column ranks the top/bottom 150 places from all places in the country with population of 10,000 or more. Places that are unincorporated were not considered in the rankings. Please refer to the User Guide for additional information.

Employment: Management, Business, and Financial Occupations

Top 150 Places Ranked in *Descending* Order

State Rank	Nat'l Rank	Percent	Place
1	84	30.5	**Birmingham** (city) Oakland County
2	112	29.2	**Oakland** (charter township) Oakland County
3	125	28.8	**Bloomfield** (charter township) Oakland County
4	147	28.3	**Northville** (township) Wayne County
5	151	28.2	**Ada** (township) Kent County
5	151	28.2	**Forest Hills** (CDP) Kent County
7	234	26.6	**Cascade** (charter township) Kent County
7	234	26.6	**Southfield** (township) Oakland County
9	268	26.0	**Beverly Hills** (village) Oakland County
10	354	24.7	**Plymouth** (charter township) Wayne County
11	413	24.0	**Rochester** (city) Oakland County
11	413	24.0	**Rochester Hills** (city) Oakland County
13	422	23.9	**Novi** (city) Oakland County
14	435	23.8	**Texas** (charter township) Kalamazoo County
15	477	23.3	**West Bloomfield** (charter township) Oakland County
16	495	23.1	**Cannon** (township) Kent County
17	546	22.7	**East Grand Rapids** (city) Kent County
18	555	22.6	**Troy** (city) Oakland County
19	619	21.9	**Oceola** (township) Livingston County
20	646	21.7	**Royal Oak** (city) Oakland County
21	701	21.2	**Grosse Pointe Park** (city) Wayne County
22	767	20.7	**Lyon** (charter township) Oakland County
22	767	20.7	**Springfield** (charter township) Oakland County
24	781	20.6	**Grand Rapids** (charter township) Kent County
25	800	20.5	**Grosse Ile** (township) Wayne County
26	852	20.1	**Commerce** (charter township) Oakland County
27	869	20.0	**Lincoln** (charter township) Berrien County
28	888	19.8	**Farmington Hills** (city) Oakland County
28	888	19.8	**Haslett** (CDP) Ingham County
30	940	19.5	**Northview** (CDP) Kent County
30	940	19.5	**Scio** (township) Washtenaw County
30	940	19.5	**South Lyon** (city) Oakland County
33	959	19.4	**Farmington** (city) Oakland County
34	993	19.2	**Park** (township) Ottawa County
35	1004	19.1	**Meridian** (charter township) Ingham County
36	1036	18.9	**Canton** (charter township) Wayne County
37	1058	18.8	**Oxford** (charter township) Oakland County
38	1072	18.7	**Orion** (charter township) Oakland County
38	1072	18.7	**Portage** (city) Kalamazoo County
38	1072	18.7	**Washington** (township) Macomb County
41	1141	18.4	**Grosse Pointe Woods** (city) Wayne County
42	1156	18.3	**Holt** (CDP) Ingham County
42	1156	18.3	**Milford** (charter township) Oakland County
42	1156	18.3	**Okemos** (CDP) Ingham County
42	1156	18.3	**Wixom** (city) Oakland County
46	1194	18.1	**Independence** (charter township) Oakland County
46	1194	18.1	**Plainfield** (charter township) Kent County
48	1214	18.0	**Brighton** (township) Livingston County
48	1214	18.0	**Caledonia** (township) Kent County
50	1231	17.9	**Hamburg** (township) Livingston County
51	1256	17.8	**Bath** (charter township) Clinton County
51	1256	17.8	**Macomb** (township) Macomb County
53	1293	17.6	**Hartland** (township) Livingston County
54	1311	17.5	**Tyrone** (township) Livingston County
55	1336	17.4	**Delhi** (charter township) Ingham County
55	1336	17.4	**Waverly** (CDP) Eaton County
55	1336	17.4	**White Lake** (charter township) Oakland County
58	1361	17.3	**Pittsfield** (charter township) Washtenaw County
59	1375	17.2	**Delta** (charter township) Eaton County
60	1401	17.1	**Traverse City** (city) Grand Traverse County
61	1419	17.0	**Shelby** (charter township) Macomb County
62	1457	16.8	**New Baltimore** (city) Macomb County
63	1479	16.7	**Ferndale** (city) Oakland County
63	1479	16.7	**Genoa** (township) Livingston County
63	1479	16.7	**Green Oak** (township) Livingston County
66	1535	16.5	**Berkley** (city) Oakland County
67	1559	16.4	**DeWitt** (charter township) Clinton County
68	1600	16.2	**Grand Haven** (city) Ottawa County
68	1600	16.2	**Summit** (township) Jackson County
70	1618	16.1	**Saint Joseph** (charter township) Berrien County
71	1644	16.0	**Highland** (charter township) Oakland County
72	1695	15.8	**Livonia** (city) Wayne County
73	1802	15.4	**Byron** (township) Kent County
73	1802	15.4	**Grand Blanc** (charter township) Genesee County
73	1802	15.4	**Southfield** (city) Oakland County
76	1841	15.3	**Superior** (charter township) Washtenaw County
77	1870	15.2	**Midland** (city) Midland County
78	1894	15.1	**Fenton** (charter township) Genesee County
78	1894	15.1	**Spring Lake** (township) Ottawa County
80	1983	14.7	**Brownstown** (charter township) Wayne County
81	2028	14.5	**Garfield** (charter township) Grand Traverse County
81	2028	14.5	**Grand Haven** (charter township) Ottawa County
83	2085	14.3	**Clawson** (city) Oakland County
83	2085	14.3	**Riverview** (city) Wayne County
83	2085	14.3	**Walker** (city) Kent County
86	2195	14.0	**Georgetown** (charter township) Ottawa County
87	2245	13.8	**Chesterfield** (township) Macomb County
87	2245	13.8	**Flushing** (charter township) Genesee County
87	2245	13.8	**Trenton** (city) Wayne County
90	2274	13.7	**Saint Clair Shores** (city) Macomb County
91	2311	13.6	**Antwerp** (township) Van Buren County
91	2311	13.6	**Comstock** (charter township) Kalamazoo County
91	2311	13.6	**Fort Gratiot** (charter township) Saint Clair County
91	2311	13.6	**Jenison** (CDP) Ottawa County
95	2341	13.5	**Lenox** (township) Macomb County
96	2363	13.4	**East Bay** (township) Grand Traverse County
96	2363	13.4	**Huron** (charter township) Wayne County
98	2393	13.3	**Auburn Hills** (city) Oakland County
98	2393	13.3	**Sterling Heights** (city) Macomb County
100	2436	13.2	**Ann Arbor** (city) Washtenaw County
100	2436	13.2	**Brandon** (charter township) Oakland County
100	2436	13.2	**Grandville** (city) Kent County
100	2436	13.2	**Van Buren** (charter township) Wayne County
100	2436	13.2	**Waterford** (charter township) Oakland County
105	2476	13.1	**Emmett** (charter township) Calhoun County
105	2476	13.1	**Harrison** (charter township) Macomb County
107	2520	13.0	**Dearborn** (city) Wayne County
107	2520	13.0	**Gaines** (charter township) Kent County
109	2551	12.9	**Fraser** (city) Macomb County
110	2579	12.8	**Kentwood** (city) Kent County
111	2645	12.6	**Cooper** (charter township) Kalamazoo County
111	2645	12.6	**Fenton** (city) Genesee County
113	2673	12.5	**Mount Clemens** (city) Macomb County
113	2673	12.5	**Mundy** (township) Genesee County
113	2673	12.5	**Woodhaven** (city) Wayne County
116	2733	12.3	**Leoni** (township) Jackson County
116	2733	12.3	**Monitor** (charter township) Bay County
118	2771	12.2	**Davison** (township) Genesee County
118	2771	12.2	**Norton Shores** (city) Muskegon County
120	2808	12.1	**Bedford** (township) Monroe County
120	2808	12.1	**Clinton** (charter township) Macomb County
120	2808	12.1	**Holly** (township) Oakland County
123	2882	11.9	**Saginaw** (charter township) Saginaw County
124	2927	11.8	**Monroe** (charter township) Monroe County
125	2963	11.7	**Grand Rapids** (city) Kent County
126	3023	11.5	**Battle Creek** (city) Calhoun County
126	3023	11.5	**Oshtemo** (charter township) Kalamazoo County
128	3061	11.4	**Fruitport** (charter township) Muskegon County
128	3061	11.4	**Kalamazoo** (charter township) Kalamazoo County
130	3101	11.3	**Allen Park** (city) Wayne County
130	3101	11.3	**Blackman** (charter township) Jackson County
132	3167	11.1	**Kalamazoo** (city) Kalamazoo County
133	3202	11.0	**East Lansing** (city) Ingham County
133	3202	11.0	**Holland** (charter township) Ottawa County
133	3202	11.0	**Southgate** (city) Wayne County
136	3235	10.9	**Warren** (city) Macomb County
137	3270	10.8	**Niles** (township) Berrien County
138	3303	10.7	**Oak Park** (city) Oakland County
139	3336	10.6	**Harper Woods** (city) Wayne County
139	3336	10.6	**Westland** (city) Wayne County
141	3397	10.4	**Lansing** (city) Ingham County
141	3397	10.4	**Sault Sainte Marie** (city) Chippewa County
143	3480	10.2	**Bangor** (charter township) Bay County
144	3512	10.1	**Garden City** (city) Wayne County
144	3512	10.1	**Thomas** (township) Saginaw County
146	3549	10.0	**Dearborn Heights** (city) Wayne County
146	3549	10.0	**Redford** (charter township) Wayne County
148	3590	9.9	**Cutlerville** (CDP) Kent County
148	3590	9.9	**Ypsilanti** (charter township) Washtenaw County
150	3616	9.8	**Wyoming** (city) Kent County

Note: *The state column ranks the top/bottom 150 places from all places in the state with population of 10,000 or more. The national column ranks the top/bottom 150 places from all places in the country with population of 10,000 or more. Places that are unincorporated were not considered in the rankings. Please refer to the User Guide for additional information.*

Employment: Management, Business, and Financial Occupations

Top 150 Places Ranked in *Ascending* Order

State Rank	Nat'l Rank	Percent	Place		State Rank	Nat'l Rank	Percent	Place
1	23	3.4	**Beecher** (CDP) Genesee County		76	1556	11.4	**Fruitport** (charter township) Muskegon County
2	30	3.7	**Muskegon Heights** (city) Muskegon County		76	1556	11.4	**Kalamazoo** (charter township) Kalamazoo County
3	47	4.4	**Inkster** (city) Wayne County		78	1596	11.5	**Battle Creek** (city) Calhoun County
4	62	4.8	**Benton Harbor** (city) Berrien County		78	1596	11.5	**Oshtemo** (charter township) Kalamazoo County
5	96	5.4	**Hamtramck** (city) Wayne County		80	1656	11.7	**Grand Rapids** (city) Kent County
6	139	5.9	**Muskegon** (city) Muskegon County		81	1694	11.8	**Monroe** (charter township) Monroe County
6	139	5.9	**Pontiac** (city) Oakland County		82	1730	11.9	**Saginaw** (charter township) Saginaw County
8	157	6.1	**Flint** (city) Genesee County		83	1815	12.1	**Bedford** (township) Monroe County
9	166	6.2	**Muskegon** (charter township) Muskegon County		83	1815	12.1	**Clinton** (charter township) Macomb County
10	184	6.3	**Lincoln Park** (city) Wayne County		83	1815	12.1	**Holly** (township) Oakland County
10	184	6.3	**Niles** (city) Berrien County		86	1849	12.2	**Davison** (township) Genesee County
12	193	6.4	**Eastpointe** (city) Macomb County		86	1849	12.2	**Norton Shores** (city) Muskegon County
12	193	6.4	**Highland Park** (city) Wayne County		88	1886	12.3	**Leoni** (township) Jackson County
14	224	6.7	**Big Rapids** (city) Mecosta County		88	1886	12.3	**Monitor** (charter township) Bay County
15	239	6.8	**Alpena** (city) Alpena County		90	1960	12.5	**Mount Clemens** (city) Macomb County
15	239	6.8	**Genesee** (charter township) Genesee County		90	1960	12.5	**Mundy** (township) Genesee County
17	248	6.9	**Benton** (charter township) Berrien County		90	1960	12.5	**Woodhaven** (city) Wayne County
18	288	7.1	**Saginaw** (city) Saginaw County		93	1984	12.6	**Cooper** (charter township) Kalamazoo County
19	311	7.2	**Escanaba** (city) Delta County		93	1984	12.6	**Fenton** (city) Genesee County
19	311	7.2	**Port Huron** (city) Saint Clair County		95	2044	12.8	**Kentwood** (city) Kent County
21	344	7.4	**Sturgis** (city) Saint Joseph County		96	2078	12.9	**Fraser** (city) Macomb County
22	357	7.5	**Comstock Park** (CDP) Kent County		97	2106	13.0	**Dearborn** (city) Wayne County
22	357	7.5	**Owosso** (city) Shiawassee County		97	2106	13.0	**Gaines** (charter township) Kent County
24	380	7.6	**Flint** (charter township) Genesee County		99	2137	13.1	**Emmett** (charter township) Calhoun County
24	380	7.6	**Ionia** (city) Ionia County		99	2137	13.1	**Harrison** (charter township) Macomb County
24	380	7.6	**Jackson** (city) Jackson County		101	2181	13.2	**Ann Arbor** (city) Washtenaw County
27	406	7.7	**Allendale** (charter township) Ottawa County		101	2181	13.2	**Brandon** (charter township) Oakland County
27	406	7.7	**Cadillac** (city) Wexford County		101	2181	13.2	**Grandville** (city) Kent County
27	406	7.7	**Melvindale** (city) Wayne County		101	2181	13.2	**Van Buren** (charter township) Wayne County
30	419	7.8	**Union** (charter township) Isabella County		101	2181	13.2	**Waterford** (charter township) Oakland County
31	439	7.9	**Allendale** (CDP) Ottawa County		106	2221	13.3	**Auburn Hills** (city) Oakland County
31	439	7.9	**Detroit** (city) Wayne County		106	2221	13.3	**Sterling Heights** (city) Macomb County
33	456	8.0	**Coldwater** (city) Branch County		108	2264	13.4	**East Bay** (township) Grand Traverse County
34	497	8.2	**Romulus** (city) Wayne County		108	2264	13.4	**Huron** (charter township) Wayne County
35	519	8.3	**Alpine** (township) Kent County		110	2294	13.5	**Lenox** (township) Macomb County
35	519	8.3	**Hazel Park** (city) Oakland County		111	2316	13.6	**Antwerp** (township) Van Buren County
35	519	8.3	**Roseville** (city) Macomb County		111	2316	13.6	**Comstock** (charter township) Kalamazoo County
38	546	8.4	**Monroe** (city) Monroe County		111	2316	13.6	**Fort Gratiot** (charter township) Saint Clair County
39	569	8.5	**Burton** (city) Genesee County		111	2316	13.6	**Jenison** (CDP) Ottawa County
39	569	8.5	**Wayne** (city) Wayne County		115	2346	13.7	**Saint Clair Shores** (city) Macomb County
41	602	8.6	**Frenchtown** (township) Monroe County		116	2383	13.8	**Chesterfield** (township) Macomb County
42	627	8.7	**Adrian** (city) Lenawee County		116	2383	13.8	**Flushing** (charter township) Genesee County
42	627	8.7	**Bay City** (city) Bay County		116	2383	13.8	**Trenton** (city) Wayne County
44	653	8.8	**Taylor** (city) Wayne County		119	2433	14.0	**Georgetown** (charter township) Ottawa County
45	757	9.1	**Holland** (city) Ottawa County		120	2531	14.3	**Clawson** (city) Oakland County
45	757	9.1	**Mount Pleasant** (city) Isabella County		120	2531	14.3	**Riverview** (city) Wayne County
47	789	9.2	**Wyandotte** (city) Wayne County		120	2531	14.3	**Walker** (city) Kent County
48	832	9.3	**Vienna** (charter township) Genesee County		123	2596	14.5	**Garfield** (charter township) Grand Traverse County
49	863	9.4	**Madison Heights** (city) Oakland County		123	2596	14.5	**Grand Haven** (charter township) Ottawa County
50	904	9.5	**Ypsilanti** (city) Washtenaw County		125	2649	14.7	**Brownstown** (charter township) Wayne County
51	940	9.6	**Bridgeport** (charter township) Saginaw County		126	2747	15.1	**Fenton** (charter township) Genesee County
51	940	9.6	**Marquette** (city) Marquette County		126	2747	15.1	**Spring Lake** (township) Ottawa County
51	940	9.6	**Mount Morris** (township) Genesee County		128	2763	15.2	**Midland** (city) Midland County
51	940	9.6	**Port Huron** (charter township) Saint Clair County		129	2787	15.3	**Superior** (charter township) Washtenaw County
55	1004	9.8	**Wyoming** (city) Kent County		130	2816	15.4	**Byron** (township) Kent County
56	1041	9.9	**Cutlerville** (CDP) Kent County		130	2816	15.4	**Grand Blanc** (charter township) Genesee County
56	1041	9.9	**Ypsilanti** (charter township) Washtenaw County		130	2816	15.4	**Southfield** (city) Oakland County
58	1067	10.0	**Dearborn Heights** (city) Wayne County		133	2935	15.8	**Livonia** (city) Wayne County
58	1067	10.0	**Redford** (charter township) Wayne County		134	2986	16.0	**Highland** (charter township) Oakland County
60	1108	10.1	**Garden City** (city) Wayne County		135	3013	16.1	**Saint Joseph** (charter township) Berrien County
60	1108	10.1	**Thomas** (township) Saginaw County		136	3039	16.2	**Grand Haven** (city) Ottawa County
62	1145	10.2	**Bangor** (charter township) Bay County		136	3039	16.2	**Summit** (township) Jackson County
63	1224	10.4	**Lansing** (city) Ingham County		138	3080	16.4	**DeWitt** (charter township) Clinton County
63	1224	10.4	**Sault Sainte Marie** (city) Chippewa County		139	3098	16.5	**Berkley** (city) Oakland County
65	1285	10.6	**Harper Woods** (city) Wayne County		140	3150	16.7	**Ferndale** (city) Oakland County
65	1285	10.6	**Westland** (city) Wayne County		140	3150	16.7	**Genoa** (township) Livingston County
67	1321	10.7	**Oak Park** (city) Oakland County		140	3150	16.7	**Green Oak** (township) Livingston County
68	1354	10.8	**Niles** (township) Berrien County		143	3178	16.8	**New Baltimore** (city) Macomb County
69	1387	10.9	**Warren** (city) Macomb County		144	3217	17.0	**Shelby** (charter township) Macomb County
70	1422	11.0	**East Lansing** (city) Ingham County		145	3238	17.1	**Traverse City** (city) Grand Traverse County
70	1422	11.0	**Holland** (charter township) Ottawa County		146	3256	17.2	**Delta** (charter township) Eaton County
70	1422	11.0	**Southgate** (city) Wayne County		147	3282	17.3	**Pittsfield** (charter township) Washtenaw County
73	1455	11.1	**Kalamazoo** (city) Kalamazoo County		148	3296	17.4	**Delhi** (charter township) Ingham County
74	1524	11.3	**Allen Park** (city) Wayne County		148	3296	17.4	**Waverly** (CDP) Eaton County
74	1524	11.3	**Blackman** (charter township) Jackson County		148	3296	17.4	**White Lake** (charter township) Oakland County

Note: The state column ranks the top/bottom 150 places from all places in the state with population of 10,000 or more. The national column ranks the top/bottom 150 places from all places in the country with population of 10,000 or more. Places that are unincorporated were not considered in the rankings. Please refer to the User Guide for additional information.

Employment: Computer, Engineering, and Science Occupations

Top 150 Places Ranked in *Descending* Order

State Rank	Nat'l Rank	Percent	Place	State Rank	Nat'l Rank	Percent	Place
1	78	16.0	Troy (city) Oakland County	75	1484	6.3	Holland (charter township) Ottawa County
2	100	15.1	Ann Arbor (city) Washtenaw County	75	1484	6.3	Kentwood (city) Kent County
2	100	15.1	Farmington (city) Oakland County	78	1535	6.2	Cascade (charter township) Kent County
4	143	13.6	Novi (city) Oakland County	79	1579	6.1	Antwerp (township) Van Buren County
5	152	13.4	Northville (township) Wayne County	79	1579	6.1	Forest Hills (CDP) Kent County
6	190	12.8	Auburn Hills (city) Oakland County	79	1579	6.1	Fraser (city) Macomb County
6	190	12.8	Okemos (CDP) Ingham County	82	1624	6.0	Bloomfield (charter township) Oakland County
8	197	12.7	Pittsfield (charter township) Washtenaw County	82	1624	6.0	Highland (charter township) Oakland County
9	210	12.5	Scio (township) Washtenaw County	82	1624	6.0	Kalamazoo (charter township) Kalamazoo County
10	220	12.4	Rochester Hills (city) Oakland County	85	1682	5.9	Caledonia (township) Kent County
11	226	12.3	Farmington Hills (city) Oakland County	85	1682	5.9	Grosse Pointe Woods (city) Wayne County
12	229	12.2	Canton (charter township) Wayne County	85	1682	5.9	Southfield (city) Oakland County
13	262	11.8	Oakland (charter township) Oakland County	88	1735	5.8	Cannon (township) Kent County
14	287	11.5	Midland (city) Midland County	88	1735	5.8	Milford (charter township) Oakland County
15	318	11.1	Meridian (charter township) Ingham County	90	1790	5.7	Fenton (city) Genesee County
16	374	10.5	Royal Oak (city) Oakland County	91	1837	5.6	Allen Park (city) Wayne County
17	393	10.4	Orion (charter township) Oakland County	91	1837	5.6	Byron (township) Kent County
18	424	10.2	Plymouth (charter township) Wayne County	91	1837	5.6	Ypsilanti (city) Washtenaw County
19	439	10.1	Rochester (city) Oakland County	94	1895	5.5	Ada (township) Kent County
20	453	10.0	Beverly Hills (village) Oakland County	94	1895	5.5	Dearborn Heights (city) Wayne County
21	514	9.6	Independence (charter township) Oakland County	94	1895	5.5	Harrison (charter township) Macomb County
22	524	9.5	Superior (charter township) Washtenaw County	94	1895	5.5	Park (township) Ottawa County
23	550	9.3	Saint Joseph (charter township) Berrien County	94	1895	5.5	Van Buren (charter township) Wayne County
24	566	9.2	Delta (charter township) Eaton County	99	1952	5.4	Georgetown (charter township) Ottawa County
24	566	9.2	Haslett (CDP) Ingham County	99	1952	5.4	Grosse Ile (township) Wayne County
24	566	9.2	Lincoln (township) Berrien County	99	1952	5.4	Jenison (CDP) Ottawa County
27	622	8.9	Brandon (charter township) Oakland County	99	1952	5.4	Madison Heights (city) Oakland County
27	622	8.9	Clawson (city) Oakland County	99	1952	5.4	Oshtemo (charter township) Kalamazoo County
27	622	8.9	Waverly (CDP) Eaton County	104	2011	5.3	Cutlerville (CDP) Kent County
30	642	8.8	Livonia (city) Wayne County	104	2011	5.3	Gaines (charter township) Kent County
30	642	8.8	Oxford (charter township) Oakland County	104	2011	5.3	Southgate (city) Wayne County
32	667	8.7	South Lyon (city) Oakland County	107	2067	5.2	Bath (charter township) Clinton County
32	667	8.7	Texas (charter township) Kalamazoo County	107	2067	5.2	Ferndale (city) Oakland County
34	695	8.6	Berkley (city) Oakland County	109	2126	5.1	Brownstown (charter township) Wayne County
34	695	8.6	Brighton (township) Livingston County	109	2126	5.1	Lansing (city) Ingham County
34	695	8.6	Macomb (township) Macomb County	109	2126	5.1	Oak Park (city) Oakland County
37	715	8.5	Lyon (charter township) Oakland County	112	2178	5.0	Leoni (township) Jackson County
37	715	8.5	Wixom (city) Oakland County	113	2311	4.8	Thomas (township) Saginaw County
39	744	8.4	West Bloomfield (charter township) Oakland County	113	2311	4.8	Westland (city) Wayne County
40	767	8.3	Comstock (charter township) Kalamazoo County	115	2376	4.7	Holland (city) Ottawa County
40	767	8.3	Southfield (township) Oakland County	115	2376	4.7	Monitor (charter township) Bay County
42	794	8.2	Commerce (charter township) Oakland County	115	2376	4.7	Plainfield (charter township) Kent County
43	821	8.1	Dearborn (city) Wayne County	115	2376	4.7	Wyandotte (city) Wayne County
43	821	8.1	East Lansing (city) Ingham County	119	2428	4.6	Allendale (charter township) Ottawa County
43	821	8.1	Grosse Pointe Park (city) Wayne County	119	2428	4.6	Bangor (charter township) Bay County
43	821	8.1	Hartland (township) Livingston County	119	2428	4.6	Bedford (township) Monroe County
43	821	8.1	White Lake (charter township) Oakland County	119	2428	4.6	Clinton (charter township) Macomb County
48	874	7.9	East Grand Rapids (city) Kent County	119	2428	4.6	Mount Clemens (city) Macomb County
49	924	7.7	Hamburg (township) Livingston County	119	2428	4.6	Mundy (township) Genesee County
49	924	7.7	Tyrone (township) Livingston County	119	2428	4.6	Saginaw (charter township) Saginaw County
51	957	7.6	Springfield (charter township) Oakland County	126	2496	4.5	Flushing (charter township) Genesee County
52	992	7.5	Fenton (charter township) Genesee County	126	2496	4.5	Marquette (city) Marquette County
52	992	7.5	Portage (city) Kalamazoo County	126	2496	4.5	Redford (charter township) Wayne County
52	992	7.5	Shelby (charter township) Macomb County	129	2583	4.4	Grandville (city) Kent County
55	1022	7.4	Sterling Heights (city) Macomb County	129	2583	4.4	Saint Clair Shores (city) Macomb County
56	1061	7.3	Green Oak (township) Livingston County	129	2583	4.4	Warren (city) Macomb County
56	1061	7.3	Washington (township) Macomb County	132	2627	4.3	Davison (township) Genesee County
58	1097	7.2	Genoa (township) Livingston County	132	2627	4.3	Norton Shores (city) Muskegon County
59	1137	7.1	Grand Rapids (charter township) Kent County	134	2703	4.2	Kalamazoo (city) Kalamazoo County
59	1137	7.1	Holly (township) Oakland County	134	2703	4.2	Roseville (city) Macomb County
59	1137	7.1	Waterford (charter township) Oakland County	136	2777	4.1	Grand Rapids (city) Kent County
62	1190	7.0	Walker (city) Kent County	136	2777	4.1	Lenox (township) Macomb County
63	1224	6.9	Ypsilanti (charter township) Washtenaw County	136	2777	4.1	Trenton (city) Wayne County
64	1267	6.8	Grand Haven (charter township) Ottawa County	139	2835	4.0	Hazel Park (city) Oakland County
65	1303	6.7	Holt (CDP) Ingham County	140	2899	3.9	Comstock Park (CDP) Kent County
65	1303	6.7	Oceola (township) Livingston County	140	2899	3.9	Northview (CDP) Kent County
67	1354	6.6	DeWitt (charter township) Clinton County	140	2899	3.9	Sturgis (city) Saint Joseph County
67	1354	6.6	Spring Lake (township) Ottawa County	143	2972	3.8	Wyoming (city) Kent County
69	1402	6.5	Birmingham (city) Oakland County	144	3030	3.7	Allendale (CDP) Ottawa County
69	1402	6.5	Chesterfield (township) Macomb County	145	3093	3.6	Battle Creek (city) Calhoun County
69	1402	6.5	Delhi (charter township) Ingham County	145	3093	3.6	Frenchtown (township) Monroe County
69	1402	6.5	Fruitport (charter township) Muskegon County	145	3093	3.6	Woodhaven (city) Wayne County
69	1402	6.5	Grand Blanc (charter township) Genesee County	148	3157	3.5	Fort Gratiot (charter township) Saint Clair County
74	1445	6.4	Summit (township) Jackson County	148	3157	3.5	Grand Haven (city) Ottawa County
75	1484	6.3	Cooper (charter township) Kalamazoo County	150	3220	3.4	Monroe (city) Monroe County

Note: The state column ranks the top/bottom 150 places from all places in the state with population of 10,000 or more. The national column ranks the top/bottom 150 places from all places in the country with population of 10,000 or more. Places that are unincorporated were not considered in the rankings. Please refer to the User Guide for additional information.

Employment: Computer, Engineering, and Science Occupations

Top 150 Places Ranked in *Ascending* Order

State Rank	Nat'l Rank	Percent	Place	State Rank	Nat'l Rank	Percent	Place
1	9	0.2	Beecher (CDP) Genesee County	74	2030	4.4	Warren (city) Macomb County
2	46	0.7	Highland Park (city) Wayne County	77	2074	4.5	Flushing (charter township) Genesee County
3	80	0.9	Cadillac (city) Wexford County	77	2074	4.5	Marquette (city) Marquette County
4	120	1.1	Port Huron (charter township) Saint Clair County	77	2074	4.5	Redford (charter township) Wayne County
5	172	1.3	Bridgeport (charter township) Saginaw County	80	2161	4.6	Allendale (charter township) Ottawa County
5	172	1.3	Sault Sainte Marie (city) Chippewa County	80	2161	4.6	Bangor (charter township) Bay County
7	202	1.4	Mount Morris (township) Genesee County	80	2161	4.6	Bedford (township) Monroe County
8	239	1.5	Benton Harbor (city) Berrien County	80	2161	4.6	Clinton (charter township) Macomb County
8	239	1.5	Ionia (city) Ionia County	80	2161	4.6	Mount Clemens (city) Macomb County
10	283	1.6	Niles (township) Berrien County	80	2161	4.6	Mundy (township) Genesee County
11	325	1.7	Port Huron (city) Saint Clair County	80	2161	4.6	Saginaw (charter township) Saginaw County
11	325	1.7	Romulus (city) Wayne County	87	2229	4.7	Holland (city) Ottawa County
13	360	1.8	Emmett (charter township) Calhoun County	87	2229	4.7	Monitor (charter township) Bay County
14	425	1.9	Harper Woods (city) Wayne County	87	2229	4.7	Plainfield (charter township) Kent County
15	479	2.0	Coldwater (city) Branch County	87	2229	4.7	Wyandotte (city) Wayne County
15	479	2.0	Detroit (city) Wayne County	91	2281	4.8	Thomas (township) Saginaw County
17	536	2.1	Big Rapids (city) Mecosta County	91	2281	4.8	Westland (city) Wayne County
17	536	2.1	Melvindale (city) Wayne County	93	2413	5.0	Leoni (township) Jackson County
19	586	2.2	Flint (city) Genesee County	94	2479	5.1	Brownstown (charter township) Wayne County
19	586	2.2	Vienna (charter township) Genesee County	94	2479	5.1	Lansing (city) Ingham County
21	649	2.3	Benton (charter township) Berrien County	94	2479	5.1	Oak Park (city) Oakland County
21	649	2.3	Jackson (city) Jackson County	97	2531	5.2	Bath (charter township) Clinton County
21	649	2.3	Muskegon Heights (city) Muskegon County	97	2531	5.2	Ferndale (city) Oakland County
21	649	2.3	Riverview (city) Wayne County	99	2590	5.3	Cutlerville (CDP) Kent County
21	649	2.3	Saginaw (city) Saginaw County	99	2590	5.3	Gaines (charter township) Kent County
26	704	2.4	Bay City (city) Bay County	99	2590	5.3	Southgate (city) Wayne County
27	820	2.6	Genesee (charter township) Genesee County	102	2646	5.4	Georgetown (charter township) Ottawa County
27	820	2.6	Huron (charter township) Wayne County	102	2646	5.4	Grosse Ile (township) Wayne County
27	820	2.6	Inkster (city) Wayne County	102	2646	5.4	Jenison (CDP) Ottawa County
30	893	2.7	Escanaba (city) Delta County	102	2646	5.4	Madison Heights (city) Oakland County
30	893	2.7	Garfield (charter township) Grand Traverse County	102	2646	5.4	Oshtemo (charter township) Kalamazoo County
30	893	2.7	Hamtramck (city) Wayne County	107	2705	5.5	Ada (township) Kent County
33	952	2.8	Burton (city) Genesee County	107	2705	5.5	Dearborn Heights (city) Wayne County
33	952	2.8	East Bay (township) Grand Traverse County	107	2705	5.5	Harrison (charter township) Macomb County
33	952	2.8	Owosso (city) Shiawassee County	107	2705	5.5	Park (township) Ottawa County
33	952	2.8	Pontiac (city) Oakland County	107	2705	5.5	Van Buren (charter township) Wayne County
33	952	2.8	Taylor (city) Wayne County	112	2762	5.6	Allen Park (city) Wayne County
38	1025	2.9	Adrian (city) Lenawee County	112	2762	5.6	Byron (township) Kent County
38	1025	2.9	Niles (city) Berrien County	112	2762	5.6	Ypsilanti (city) Washtenaw County
40	1089	3.0	Monroe (charter township) Monroe County	115	2820	5.7	Fenton (city) Genesee County
40	1089	3.0	Mount Pleasant (city) Isabella County	116	2867	5.8	Cannon (township) Kent County
40	1089	3.0	Union (charter township) Isabella County	116	2867	5.8	Milford (charter township) Oakland County
43	1168	3.1	Alpena (city) Alpena County	118	2922	5.9	Caledonia (township) Kent County
43	1168	3.1	Garden City (city) Wayne County	118	2922	5.9	Grosse Pointe Woods (city) Wayne County
43	1168	3.1	Muskegon (charter township) Muskegon County	118	2922	5.9	Southfield (city) Oakland County
43	1168	3.1	Traverse City (city) Grand Traverse County	121	2975	6.0	Bloomfield (charter township) Oakland County
47	1222	3.2	Eastpointe (city) Macomb County	121	2975	6.0	Highland (charter township) Oakland County
47	1222	3.2	Flint (charter township) Genesee County	121	2975	6.0	Kalamazoo (charter township) Kalamazoo County
47	1222	3.2	Wayne (city) Wayne County	124	3033	6.1	Antwerp (township) Van Buren County
50	1299	3.3	Alpine (township) Kent County	124	3033	6.1	Forest Hills (CDP) Kent County
50	1299	3.3	Blackman (charter township) Jackson County	124	3033	6.1	Fraser (city) Macomb County
50	1299	3.3	Lincoln Park (city) Wayne County	127	3078	6.2	Cascade (charter township) Kent County
50	1299	3.3	New Baltimore (city) Macomb County	128	3122	6.3	Cooper (charter township) Kalamazoo County
54	1360	3.4	Monroe (city) Monroe County	128	3122	6.3	Holland (charter township) Ottawa County
54	1360	3.4	Muskegon (city) Muskegon County	128	3122	6.3	Kentwood (city) Kent County
56	1437	3.5	Fort Gratiot (charter township) Saint Clair County	131	3173	6.4	Summit (township) Jackson County
56	1437	3.5	Grand Haven (city) Ottawa County	132	3212	6.5	Birmingham (city) Oakland County
58	1500	3.6	Battle Creek (city) Calhoun County	132	3212	6.5	Chesterfield (township) Macomb County
58	1500	3.6	Frenchtown (township) Monroe County	132	3212	6.5	Delhi (charter township) Ingham County
58	1500	3.6	Woodhaven (city) Wayne County	132	3212	6.5	Fruitport (charter township) Muskegon County
61	1564	3.7	Allendale (CDP) Ottawa County	132	3212	6.5	Grand Blanc (charter township) Genesee County
62	1627	3.8	Wyoming (city) Kent County	137	3255	6.6	DeWitt (charter township) Clinton County
63	1685	3.9	Comstock Park (CDP) Kent County	137	3255	6.6	Spring Lake (township) Ottawa County
63	1685	3.9	Northview (CDP) Kent County	139	3303	6.7	Holt (CDP) Ingham County
63	1685	3.9	Sturgis (city) Saint Joseph County	139	3303	6.7	Oceola (township) Livingston County
66	1758	4.0	Hazel Park (city) Oakland County	141	3354	6.8	Grand Haven (charter township) Ottawa County
67	1822	4.1	Grand Rapids (city) Kent County	142	3390	6.9	Ypsilanti (charter township) Washtenaw County
67	1822	4.1	Lenox (township) Macomb County	143	3433	7.0	Walker (city) Kent County
67	1822	4.1	Trenton (city) Wayne County	144	3467	7.1	Grand Rapids (charter township) Kent County
70	1880	4.2	Kalamazoo (city) Kalamazoo County	144	3467	7.1	Holly (township) Oakland County
70	1880	4.2	Roseville (city) Macomb County	144	3467	7.1	Waterford (charter township) Oakland County
72	1954	4.3	Davison (township) Genesee County	147	3520	7.2	Genoa (township) Livingston County
72	1954	4.3	Norton Shores (city) Muskegon County	148	3560	7.3	Green Oak (township) Livingston County
74	2030	4.4	Grandville (city) Kent County	148	3560	7.3	Washington (township) Macomb County
74	2030	4.4	Saint Clair Shores (city) Macomb County	150	3596	7.4	Sterling Heights (city) Macomb County

Note: *The state column ranks the top/bottom 150 places from all places in the state with population of 10,000 or more. The national column ranks the top/bottom 150 places from all places in the country with population of 10,000 or more. Places that are unincorporated were not considered in the rankings. Please refer to the User Guide for additional information.*

Employment: Education, Legal, Community Service, Arts, and Media Occupations

Top 150 Places Ranked in *Descending* Order

State Rank	Nat'l Rank	Percent	Place	State Rank	Nat'l Rank	Percent	Place
1	35	25.1	**Ann Arbor** (city) Washtenaw County	75	2283	10.6	**Grand Haven** (city) Ottawa County
2	40	24.8	**East Grand Rapids** (city) Kent County	77	2350	10.5	**Oakland** (charter township) Oakland County
3	64	23.4	**Okemos** (CDP) Ingham County	77	2350	10.5	**Ypsilanti** (charter township) Washtenaw County
4	86	22.3	**Grosse Pointe Park** (city) Wayne County	79	2414	10.4	**DeWitt** (charter township) Clinton County
5	122	21.2	**Meridian** (charter township) Ingham County	80	2466	10.3	**Delta** (charter township) Eaton County
6	130	20.9	**Scio** (township) Washtenaw County	80	2466	10.3	**Genoa** (township) Livingston County
7	134	20.7	**East Lansing** (city) Ingham County	80	2466	10.3	**Livonia** (city) Wayne County
8	138	20.6	**Grosse Pointe Woods** (city) Wayne County	80	2466	10.3	**Novi** (city) Oakland County
9	193	19.4	**Birmingham** (city) Oakland County	80	2466	10.3	**Oxford** (charter township) Oakland County
10	227	18.8	**Southfield** (township) Oakland County	80	2466	10.3	**Thomas** (township) Saginaw County
11	239	18.6	**Beverly Hills** (village) Oakland County	80	2466	10.3	**Trenton** (city) Wayne County
12	258	18.3	**Haslett** (CDP) Ingham County	87	2529	10.2	**Alpena** (city) Alpena County
13	302	17.6	**Ferndale** (city) Oakland County	87	2529	10.2	**Mount Clemens** (city) Macomb County
14	327	17.3	**Berkley** (city) Oakland County	89	2588	10.1	**Davison** (township) Genesee County
15	471	15.9	**Mount Pleasant** (city) Isabella County	90	2650	10.0	**Adrian** (city) Lenawee County
15	471	15.9	**Ypsilanti** (city) Washtenaw County	90	2650	10.0	**Canton** (charter township) Wayne County
17	500	15.7	**Bloomfield** (charter township) Oakland County	90	2650	10.0	**Park** (township) Ottawa County
18	718	14.5	**Pittsfield** (charter township) Washtenaw County	93	2719	9.9	**Dearborn Heights** (city) Wayne County
19	744	14.4	**Bath** (charter township) Clinton County	94	2775	9.8	**Brandon** (charter township) Oakland County
20	824	14.1	**Cascade** (charter township) Kent County	94	2775	9.8	**Flint** (charter township) Genesee County
21	851	14.0	**Saint Joseph** (charter township) Berrien County	94	2775	9.8	**Independence** (charter township) Oakland County
22	878	13.9	**Farmington** (city) Oakland County	97	2823	9.7	**Marquette** (city) Marquette County
22	878	13.9	**Oak Park** (city) Oakland County	97	2823	9.7	**Orion** (charter township) Oakland County
22	878	13.9	**Oshtemo** (charter township) Kalamazoo County	97	2823	9.7	**Union** (charter township) Isabella County
25	931	13.7	**Grand Rapids** (charter township) Kent County	100	2888	9.6	**Macomb** (township) Macomb County
26	993	13.5	**Big Rapids** (city) Mecosta County	101	2942	9.5	**Caledonia** (township) Kent County
27	1045	13.3	**West Bloomfield** (charter township) Oakland County	101	2942	9.5	**Harrison** (charter township) Macomb County
28	1079	13.2	**Royal Oak** (city) Oakland County	101	2942	9.5	**Superior** (charter township) Washtenaw County
29	1117	13.1	**Grand Haven** (charter township) Ottawa County	104	2993	9.4	**Muskegon Heights** (city) Muskegon County
30	1188	12.9	**Flushing** (charter township) Genesee County	105	3049	9.3	**Shelby** (charter township) Macomb County
30	1188	12.9	**Rochester** (city) Oakland County	105	3049	9.3	**Washington** (township) Macomb County
32	1228	12.8	**Forest Hills** (CDP) Kent County	107	3111	9.2	**Fort Gratiot** (charter township) Saint Clair County
32	1228	12.8	**Spring Lake** (township) Ottawa County	107	3111	9.2	**Northview** (CDP) Kent County
34	1263	12.7	**Grosse Ile** (township) Wayne County	109	3168	9.1	**Fraser** (city) Macomb County
35	1307	12.6	**Grand Rapids** (city) Kent County	109	3168	9.1	**Holly** (township) Oakland County
36	1346	12.5	**Plymouth** (charter township) Wayne County	109	3168	9.1	**Melvindale** (city) Wayne County
37	1380	12.4	**Southfield** (city) Oakland County	109	3168	9.1	**Tyrone** (township) Livingston County
37	1380	12.4	**Texas** (charter township) Kalamazoo County	113	3217	9.0	**Flint** (city) Genesee County
39	1421	12.3	**Kalamazoo** (city) Kalamazoo County	113	3217	9.0	**Monitor** (charter township) Bay County
39	1421	12.3	**Troy** (city) Oakland County	115	3269	8.9	**Allen Park** (city) Wayne County
41	1505	12.1	**Clawson** (city) Oakland County	115	3269	8.9	**Cooper** (charter township) Kalamazoo County
41	1505	12.1	**Farmington Hills** (city) Oakland County	115	3269	8.9	**Saint Clair Shores** (city) Macomb County
41	1505	12.1	**Highland Park** (city) Wayne County	118	3328	8.8	**Burton** (city) Genesee County
44	1586	11.9	**Dearborn** (city) Wayne County	118	3328	8.8	**Detroit** (city) Wayne County
44	1586	11.9	**Summit** (township) Jackson County	118	3328	8.8	**Hamburg** (township) Livingston County
46	1642	11.8	**Cannon** (township) Kent County	118	3328	8.8	**Highland** (charter township) Oakland County
46	1642	11.8	**Midland** (city) Midland County	118	3328	8.8	**Waterford** (charter township) Oakland County
48	1698	11.7	**Auburn Hills** (city) Oakland County	118	3328	8.8	**Waverly** (CDP) Eaton County
48	1698	11.7	**Fenton** (charter township) Genesee County	118	3328	8.8	**White Lake** (charter township) Oakland County
48	1698	11.7	**Rochester Hills** (city) Oakland County	125	3397	8.7	**Bedford** (township) Monroe County
51	1745	11.6	**Holland** (city) Ottawa County	125	3397	8.7	**Gaines** (charter township) Kent County
52	1841	11.4	**Mundy** (township) Genesee County	125	3397	8.7	**Holt** (CDP) Ingham County
52	1841	11.4	**Saginaw** (charter township) Saginaw County	128	3441	8.6	**Blackman** (charter township) Jackson County
54	1897	11.3	**Allendale** (CDP) Ottawa County	128	3441	8.6	**Commerce** (charter township) Oakland County
54	1897	11.3	**Brighton** (township) Livingston County	128	3441	8.6	**Delhi** (charter township) Ingham County
54	1897	11.3	**Woodhaven** (city) Wayne County	128	3441	8.6	**Kentwood** (city) Kent County
57	1945	11.2	**Ada** (township) Kent County	128	3441	8.6	**Redford** (charter township) Wayne County
57	1945	11.2	**Grand Blanc** (charter township) Genesee County	128	3441	8.6	**Sterling Heights** (city) Macomb County
57	1945	11.2	**Traverse City** (city) Grand Traverse County	134	3485	8.5	**Monroe** (city) Monroe County
60	1998	11.1	**Grandville** (city) Kent County	134	3485	8.5	**New Baltimore** (city) Macomb County
60	1998	11.1	**Lansing** (city) Ingham County	134	3485	8.5	**Springfield** (charter township) Oakland County
60	1998	11.1	**Lincoln** (charter township) Berrien County	137	3539	8.4	**Antwerp** (township) Van Buren County
60	1998	11.1	**Northville** (township) Wayne County	137	3539	8.4	**Clinton** (charter township) Macomb County
60	1998	11.1	**Portage** (city) Kalamazoo County	137	3539	8.4	**Hartland** (township) Livingston County
60	1998	11.1	**Sault Sainte Marie** (city) Chippewa County	137	3539	8.4	**Saginaw** (city) Saginaw County
60	1998	11.1	**South Lyon** (city) Oakland County	141	3590	8.3	**Byron** (township) Kent County
67	2048	11.0	**Kalamazoo** (charter township) Kalamazoo County	141	3590	8.3	**Fenton** (city) Genesee County
67	2048	11.0	**Norton Shores** (city) Muskegon County	141	3590	8.3	**Muskegon** (city) Muskegon County
69	2104	10.9	**Walker** (city) Kent County	141	3590	8.3	**Wyandotte** (city) Wayne County
70	2158	10.8	**Harper Woods** (city) Wayne County	145	3634	8.2	**Brownstown** (charter township) Wayne County
70	2158	10.8	**Plainfield** (charter township) Kent County	146	3680	8.1	**Battle Creek** (city) Calhoun County
72	2211	10.7	**Allendale** (charter township) Ottawa County	147	3721	8.0	**Port Huron** (charter township) Saint Clair County
72	2211	10.7	**Green Oak** (township) Livingston County	148	3764	7.9	**Inkster** (city) Wayne County
72	2211	10.7	**Sturgis** (city) Saint Joseph County	148	3764	7.9	**Niles** (township) Berrien County
75	2283	10.6	**Georgetown** (charter township) Ottawa County	148	3764	7.9	**Port Huron** (city) Saint Clair County

Note: The state column ranks the top/bottom 150 places from all places in the state with population of 10,000 or more. The national column ranks the top/bottom 150 places from all places in the country with population of 10,000 or more. Places that are unincorporated were not considered in the rankings. Please refer to the User Guide for additional information.

Employment: Education, Legal, Community Service, Arts, and Media Occupations

Top 150 Places Ranked in *Ascending* Order

State Rank	Nat'l Rank	Percent	Place
1	22	3.6	**Romulus** (city) Wayne County
2	35	4.0	**Leoni** (township) Jackson County
3	73	4.7	**Lenox** (township) Macomb County
4	81	4.8	**Comstock Park** (CDP) Kent County
4	81	4.8	**Genesee** (charter township) Genesee County
6	97	5.0	**Cadillac** (city) Wexford County
7	110	5.1	**Taylor** (city) Wayne County
8	136	5.3	**Alpine** (township) Kent County
9	175	5.6	**Cutlerville** (CDP) Kent County
10	220	5.9	**Pontiac** (city) Oakland County
10	220	5.9	**Roseville** (city) Macomb County
12	235	6.0	**Niles** (city) Berrien County
13	257	6.1	**Madison Heights** (city) Oakland County
14	292	6.2	**Warren** (city) Macomb County
15	312	6.3	**Ionia** (city) Ionia County
15	312	6.3	**Lincoln Park** (city) Wayne County
15	312	6.3	**Muskegon** (charter township) Muskegon County
15	312	6.3	**Westland** (city) Wayne County
19	331	6.4	**Eastpointe** (city) Macomb County
19	331	6.4	**Fruitport** (charter township) Muskegon County
19	331	6.4	**Wixom** (city) Oakland County
22	353	6.5	**Benton** (charter township) Berrien County
23	384	6.6	**Garden City** (city) Wayne County
23	384	6.6	**Hazel Park** (city) Oakland County
23	384	6.6	**Wyoming** (city) Kent County
26	409	6.7	**Benton Harbor** (city) Berrien County
26	409	6.7	**Wayne** (city) Wayne County
28	433	6.8	**Jackson** (city) Jackson County
28	433	6.8	**Southgate** (city) Wayne County
30	461	6.9	**Comstock** (charter township) Kalamazoo County
31	507	7.0	**Beecher** (CDP) Genesee County
31	507	7.0	**Emmett** (charter township) Calhoun County
33	573	7.2	**Bangor** (charter township) Bay County
33	573	7.2	**Bridgeport** (charter township) Saginaw County
33	573	7.2	**Monroe** (charter township) Monroe County
33	573	7.2	**Owosso** (city) Shiawassee County
33	573	7.2	**Vienna** (charter township) Genesee County
38	606	7.3	**Coldwater** (city) Branch County
38	606	7.3	**East Bay** (township) Grand Traverse County
38	606	7.3	**Garfield** (charter township) Grand Traverse County
38	606	7.3	**Hamtramck** (city) Wayne County
38	606	7.3	**Mount Morris** (township) Genesee County
43	646	7.4	**Bay City** (city) Bay County
43	646	7.4	**Jenison** (CDP) Ottawa County
45	682	7.5	**Huron** (charter township) Wayne County
45	682	7.5	**Van Buren** (charter township) Wayne County
47	759	7.7	**Chesterfield** (township) Macomb County
47	759	7.7	**Holland** (charter township) Ottawa County
47	759	7.7	**Lyon** (charter township) Oakland County
50	794	7.8	**Escanaba** (city) Delta County
50	794	7.8	**Frenchtown** (township) Monroe County
50	794	7.8	**Milford** (charter township) Oakland County
50	794	7.8	**Oceola** (township) Livingston County
54	845	7.9	**Inkster** (city) Wayne County
54	845	7.9	**Niles** (township) Berrien County
54	845	7.9	**Port Huron** (city) Saint Clair County
54	845	7.9	**Riverview** (city) Wayne County
58	893	8.0	**Port Huron** (charter township) Saint Clair County
59	936	8.1	**Battle Creek** (city) Calhoun County
60	977	8.2	**Brownstown** (charter township) Wayne County
61	1023	8.3	**Byron** (township) Kent County
61	1023	8.3	**Fenton** (city) Genesee County
61	1023	8.3	**Muskegon** (city) Muskegon County
61	1023	8.3	**Wyandotte** (city) Wayne County
65	1067	8.4	**Antwerp** (township) Van Buren County
65	1067	8.4	**Clinton** (charter township) Macomb County
65	1067	8.4	**Hartland** (township) Livingston County
65	1067	8.4	**Saginaw** (city) Saginaw County
69	1118	8.5	**Monroe** (city) Monroe County
69	1118	8.5	**New Baltimore** (city) Macomb County
69	1118	8.5	**Springfield** (charter township) Oakland County
72	1172	8.6	**Blackman** (charter township) Jackson County
72	1172	8.6	**Commerce** (charter township) Oakland County
72	1172	8.6	**Delhi** (charter township) Ingham County
72	1172	8.6	**Kentwood** (city) Kent County
72	1172	8.6	**Redford** (charter township) Wayne County
72	1172	8.6	**Sterling Heights** (city) Macomb County
78	1216	8.7	**Bedford** (township) Monroe County
78	1216	8.7	**Gaines** (charter township) Kent County
78	1216	8.7	**Holt** (CDP) Ingham County
81	1260	8.8	**Burton** (city) Genesee County
81	1260	8.8	**Detroit** (city) Wayne County
81	1260	8.8	**Hamburg** (township) Livingston County
81	1260	8.8	**Highland** (charter township) Oakland County
81	1260	8.8	**Waterford** (charter township) Oakland County
81	1260	8.8	**Waverly** (CDP) Eaton County
81	1260	8.8	**White Lake** (charter township) Oakland County
88	1329	8.9	**Allen Park** (city) Wayne County
88	1329	8.9	**Cooper** (charter township) Kalamazoo County
88	1329	8.9	**Saint Clair Shores** (city) Macomb County
91	1388	9.0	**Flint** (city) Genesee County
91	1388	9.0	**Monitor** (charter township) Bay County
93	1440	9.1	**Fraser** (city) Macomb County
93	1440	9.1	**Holly** (township) Oakland County
93	1440	9.1	**Melvindale** (city) Wayne County
93	1440	9.1	**Tyrone** (township) Livingston County
97	1489	9.2	**Fort Gratiot** (charter township) Saint Clair County
97	1489	9.2	**Northview** (CDP) Kent County
99	1546	9.3	**Shelby** (charter township) Macomb County
99	1546	9.3	**Washington** (township) Macomb County
101	1608	9.4	**Muskegon Heights** (city) Muskegon County
102	1664	9.5	**Caledonia** (township) Kent County
102	1664	9.5	**Harrison** (charter township) Macomb County
102	1664	9.5	**Superior** (charter township) Washtenaw County
105	1715	9.6	**Macomb** (township) Macomb County
106	1769	9.7	**Marquette** (city) Marquette County
106	1769	9.7	**Orion** (charter township) Oakland County
106	1769	9.7	**Union** (charter township) Isabella County
109	1834	9.8	**Brandon** (charter township) Oakland County
109	1834	9.8	**Flint** (charter township) Genesee County
109	1834	9.8	**Independence** (charter township) Oakland County
112	1882	9.9	**Dearborn Heights** (city) Wayne County
113	1938	10.0	**Adrian** (city) Lenawee County
113	1938	10.0	**Canton** (charter township) Wayne County
113	1938	10.0	**Park** (township) Ottawa County
116	2007	10.1	**Davison** (township) Genesee County
117	2069	10.2	**Alpena** (city) Alpena County
117	2069	10.2	**Mount Clemens** (city) Macomb County
119	2128	10.3	**Delta** (charter township) Eaton County
119	2128	10.3	**Genoa** (township) Livingston County
119	2128	10.3	**Livonia** (city) Wayne County
119	2128	10.3	**Novi** (city) Oakland County
119	2128	10.3	**Oxford** (charter township) Oakland County
119	2128	10.3	**Thomas** (township) Saginaw County
119	2128	10.3	**Trenton** (city) Wayne County
126	2191	10.4	**DeWitt** (charter township) Clinton County
127	2243	10.5	**Oakland** (charter township) Oakland County
127	2243	10.5	**Ypsilanti** (charter township) Washtenaw County
129	2307	10.6	**Georgetown** (charter township) Ottawa County
129	2307	10.6	**Grand Haven** (city) Ottawa County
131	2374	10.7	**Allendale** (charter township) Ottawa County
131	2374	10.7	**Green Oak** (township) Livingston County
131	2374	10.7	**Sturgis** (city) Saint Joseph County
134	2446	10.8	**Harper Woods** (city) Wayne County
134	2446	10.8	**Plainfield** (charter township) Kent County
136	2499	10.9	**Walker** (city) Kent County
137	2553	11.0	**Kalamazoo** (charter township) Kalamazoo County
137	2553	11.0	**Norton Shores** (city) Muskegon County
139	2609	11.1	**Grandville** (city) Kent County
139	2609	11.1	**Lansing** (city) Ingham County
139	2609	11.1	**Lincoln** (charter township) Berrien County
139	2609	11.1	**Northville** (township) Wayne County
139	2609	11.1	**Portage** (city) Kalamazoo County
139	2609	11.1	**Sault Sainte Marie** (city) Chippewa County
139	2609	11.1	**South Lyon** (city) Oakland County
146	2659	11.2	**Ada** (township) Kent County
146	2659	11.2	**Grand Blanc** (charter township) Genesee County
146	2659	11.2	**Traverse City** (city) Grand Traverse County
149	2712	11.3	**Allendale** (CDP) Ottawa County
149	2712	11.3	**Brighton** (township) Livingston County

Note: The state column ranks the top/bottom 150 places from all places in the state with population of 10,000 or more. The national column ranks the top/bottom 150 places from all places in the country with population of 10,000 or more. Places that are unincorporated were not considered in the rankings. Please refer to the User Guide for additional information.

Employment: Healthcare Practitioners

Top 150 Places Ranked in *Descending* Order

State Rank	Nat'l Rank	Percent	Place
1	43	12.4	**Grosse Pointe Park** (city) Wayne County
2	47	12.3	**Grand Blanc** (charter township) Genesee County
3	50	12.2	**Bloomfield** (charter township) Oakland County
4	73	11.5	**Forest Hills** (CDP) Kent County
5	99	11.1	**Cascade** (charter township) Kent County
6	101	11.0	**West Bloomfield** (charter township) Oakland County
7	106	10.8	**East Grand Rapids** (city) Kent County
8	129	10.6	**Ada** (township) Kent County
8	129	10.6	**Birmingham** (city) Oakland County
10	144	10.4	**Grand Rapids** (charter township) Kent County
11	164	10.2	**Northville** (township) Wayne County
12	180	10.0	**Caledonia** (township) Kent County
13	193	9.9	**Grosse Pointe Woods** (city) Wayne County
13	193	9.9	**Pittsfield** (charter township) Washtenaw County
15	206	9.8	**Thomas** (township) Saginaw County
16	253	9.5	**Grosse Ile** (township) Wayne County
17	279	9.4	**Mundy** (township) Genesee County
18	294	9.3	**Oakland** (charter township) Oakland County
18	294	9.3	**Troy** (city) Oakland County
20	315	9.2	**Berkley** (city) Oakland County
20	315	9.2	**Saginaw** (charter township) Saginaw County
20	315	9.2	**Scio** (township) Washtenaw County
23	377	8.9	**Cadillac** (city) Wexford County
23	377	8.9	**Milford** (charter township) Oakland County
23	377	8.9	**Oceola** (township) Livingston County
26	412	8.7	**East Bay** (township) Grand Traverse County
26	412	8.7	**Texas** (charter township) Kalamazoo County
28	441	8.6	**Bangor** (charter township) Bay County
28	441	8.6	**Royal Oak** (city) Oakland County
30	465	8.5	**Marquette** (city) Marquette County
31	491	8.4	**Canton** (charter township) Wayne County
31	491	8.4	**Cooper** (charter township) Kalamazoo County
33	519	8.3	**Portage** (city) Kalamazoo County
33	519	8.3	**Rochester** (city) Oakland County
35	597	8.1	**Hartland** (township) Livingston County
35	597	8.1	**Woodhaven** (city) Wayne County
37	636	8.0	**Flushing** (charter township) Genesee County
37	636	8.0	**Springfield** (charter township) Oakland County
37	636	8.0	**Superior** (charter township) Washtenaw County
40	668	7.9	**Fenton** (charter township) Genesee County
40	668	7.9	**Hamburg** (township) Livingston County
40	668	7.9	**Plymouth** (charter township) Wayne County
43	718	7.8	**Novi** (city) Oakland County
44	755	7.7	**Brighton** (township) Livingston County
44	755	7.7	**Cannon** (township) Kent County
44	755	7.7	**Holt** (CDP) Ingham County
47	804	7.6	**Allen Park** (city) Wayne County
47	804	7.6	**Livonia** (city) Wayne County
49	848	7.5	**Ann Arbor** (city) Washtenaw County
49	848	7.5	**Brownstown** (charter township) Wayne County
49	848	7.5	**Rochester Hills** (city) Oakland County
52	903	7.4	**Brandon** (charter township) Oakland County
52	903	7.4	**Delhi** (charter township) Ingham County
52	903	7.4	**Fort Gratiot** (charter township) Saint Clair County
55	954	7.3	**Escanaba** (city) Delta County
55	954	7.3	**Monitor** (charter township) Bay County
55	954	7.3	**Saint Clair Shores** (city) Macomb County
58	1026	7.2	**Farmington Hills** (city) Oakland County
58	1026	7.2	**Haslett** (CDP) Ingham County
58	1026	7.2	**Summit** (township) Jackson County
58	1026	7.2	**Traverse City** (city) Grand Traverse County
62	1083	7.1	**Riverview** (city) Wayne County
62	1083	7.1	**Southfield** (city) Oakland County
64	1138	7.0	**Comstock** (charter township) Kalamazoo County
64	1138	7.0	**Grand Haven** (charter township) Ottawa County
64	1138	7.0	**Ionia** (city) Ionia County
64	1138	7.0	**South Lyon** (city) Oakland County
68	1192	6.9	**Northview** (CDP) Kent County
68	1192	6.9	**Southfield** (township) Oakland County
68	1192	6.9	**Walker** (city) Kent County
68	1192	6.9	**Washington** (township) Macomb County
72	1253	6.8	**Bedford** (township) Monroe County
72	1253	6.8	**Macomb** (township) Macomb County
72	1253	6.8	**Meridian** (charter township) Ingham County
72	1253	6.8	**Oshtemo** (charter township) Kalamazoo County
76	1339	6.7	**Plainfield** (charter township) Kent County
77	1404	6.6	**Dearborn** (city) Wayne County
77	1404	6.6	**Fruitport** (charter township) Muskegon County
77	1404	6.6	**Midland** (city) Midland County
77	1404	6.6	**Trenton** (city) Wayne County
81	1488	6.5	**Bath** (charter township) Clinton County
81	1488	6.5	**Flint** (charter township) Genesee County
81	1488	6.5	**Harrison** (charter township) Macomb County
81	1488	6.5	**Southgate** (city) Wayne County
81	1488	6.5	**Ypsilanti** (charter township) Washtenaw County
86	1560	6.4	**Davison** (township) Genesee County
86	1560	6.4	**Independence** (charter township) Oakland County
86	1560	6.4	**Saint Joseph** (charter township) Berrien County
89	1625	6.3	**Georgetown** (charter township) Ottawa County
89	1625	6.3	**Grandville** (city) Kent County
89	1625	6.3	**New Baltimore** (city) Macomb County
89	1625	6.3	**Spring Lake** (township) Ottawa County
89	1625	6.3	**Wyandotte** (city) Wayne County
94	1723	6.2	**Coldwater** (city) Branch County
95	1812	6.1	**Dearborn Heights** (city) Wayne County
95	1812	6.1	**Frenchtown** (township) Monroe County
95	1812	6.1	**Harper Woods** (city) Wayne County
95	1812	6.1	**Monroe** (city) Monroe County
95	1812	6.1	**Norton Shores** (city) Muskegon County
95	1812	6.1	**Oak Park** (city) Oakland County
95	1812	6.1	**Okemos** (CDP) Ingham County
102	1919	6.0	**Big Rapids** (city) Mecosta County
103	2017	5.9	**Alpena** (city) Alpena County
103	2017	5.9	**Burton** (city) Genesee County
103	2017	5.9	**Orion** (charter township) Oakland County
103	2017	5.9	**Shelby** (charter township) Macomb County
103	2017	5.9	**Sterling Heights** (city) Macomb County
108	2114	5.8	**Antwerp** (township) Van Buren County
108	2114	5.8	**Garfield** (charter township) Grand Traverse County
108	2114	5.8	**Lyon** (charter township) Oakland County
108	2114	5.8	**Sault Sainte Marie** (city) Chippewa County
108	2114	5.8	**Van Buren** (charter township) Wayne County
113	2211	5.7	**Bridgeport** (charter township) Saginaw County
113	2211	5.7	**Clinton** (charter township) Macomb County
113	2211	5.7	**Gaines** (charter township) Kent County
113	2211	5.7	**Huron** (charter township) Wayne County
113	2211	5.7	**Vienna** (charter township) Genesee County
118	2328	5.6	**DeWitt** (charter township) Clinton County
118	2328	5.6	**Emmett** (charter township) Calhoun County
118	2328	5.6	**Genesee** (charter township) Genesee County
118	2328	5.6	**Owosso** (city) Shiawassee County
118	2328	5.6	**White Lake** (charter township) Oakland County
123	2423	5.5	**Bay City** (city) Bay County
123	2423	5.5	**Chesterfield** (township) Macomb County
123	2423	5.5	**Genoa** (township) Livingston County
123	2423	5.5	**Green Oak** (township) Livingston County
123	2423	5.5	**Niles** (township) Berrien County
128	2519	5.4	**Delta** (charter township) Eaton County
128	2519	5.4	**Farmington** (city) Oakland County
128	2519	5.4	**Monroe** (charter township) Monroe County
128	2519	5.4	**Oxford** (charter township) Oakland County
128	2519	5.4	**Sturgis** (city) Saint Joseph County
133	2614	5.3	**Kentwood** (city) Kent County
133	2614	5.3	**Leoni** (township) Jackson County
133	2614	5.3	**Tyrone** (township) Livingston County
136	2696	5.2	**Park** (township) Ottawa County
136	2696	5.2	**Saginaw** (city) Saginaw County
138	2789	5.1	**Allendale** (CDP) Ottawa County
138	2789	5.1	**Battle Creek** (city) Calhoun County
138	2789	5.1	**Commerce** (charter township) Oakland County
138	2789	5.1	**Ferndale** (city) Oakland County
138	2789	5.1	**Holly** (township) Oakland County
143	2895	5.0	**Jenison** (CDP) Ottawa County
143	2895	5.0	**Lincoln** (charter township) Berrien County
143	2895	5.0	**Madison Heights** (city) Oakland County
143	2895	5.0	**Westland** (city) Wayne County
147	2977	4.9	**Allendale** (charter township) Ottawa County
147	2977	4.9	**Auburn Hills** (city) Oakland County
147	2977	4.9	**Kalamazoo** (charter township) Kalamazoo County
147	2977	4.9	**Muskegon** (city) Muskegon County

Note: The state column ranks the top/bottom 150 places from all places in the state with population of 10,000 or more. The national column ranks the top/bottom 150 places from all places in the country with population of 10,000 or more. Places that are unincorporated were not considered in the rankings. Please refer to the User Guide for additional information.

Employment: Healthcare Practitioners

Top 150 Places Ranked in *Ascending* Order

State Rank	Nat'l Rank	Percent	Place	State Rank	Nat'l Rank	Percent	Place
1	71	1.7	**Comstock Park** (CDP) Kent County	73	2043	5.4	**Oxford** (charter township) Oakland County
2	80	1.8	**Ypsilanti** (city) Washtenaw County	73	2043	5.4	**Sturgis** (city) Saint Joseph County
3	156	2.3	**Lenox** (township) Macomb County	78	2138	5.5	**Bay City** (city) Bay County
4	198	2.5	**Muskegon Heights** (city) Muskegon County	78	2138	5.5	**Chesterfield** (township) Macomb County
5	253	2.7	**Alpine** (township) Kent County	78	2138	5.5	**Genoa** (township) Livingston County
5	253	2.7	**Benton** (charter township) Berrien County	78	2138	5.5	**Green Oak** (township) Livingston County
5	253	2.7	**Mount Pleasant** (city) Isabella County	78	2138	5.5	**Niles** (township) Berrien County
8	280	2.8	**Blackman** (charter township) Jackson County	83	2234	5.6	**DeWitt** (charter township) Clinton County
8	280	2.8	**Union** (charter township) Isabella County	83	2234	5.6	**Emmett** (charter township) Calhoun County
10	396	3.1	**Holland** (charter township) Ottawa County	83	2234	5.6	**Genesee** (charter township) Genesee County
10	396	3.1	**Roseville** (city) Macomb County	83	2234	5.6	**Owosso** (city) Shiawassee County
12	480	3.3	**Grand Haven** (city) Ottawa County	83	2234	5.6	**White Lake** (charter township) Oakland County
12	480	3.3	**Hamtramck** (city) Wayne County	88	2329	5.7	**Bridgeport** (charter township) Saginaw County
12	480	3.3	**Holland** (city) Ottawa County	88	2329	5.7	**Clinton** (charter township) Macomb County
12	480	3.3	**Port Huron** (charter township) Saint Clair County	88	2329	5.7	**Gaines** (charter township) Kent County
12	480	3.3	**Wayne** (city) Wayne County	88	2329	5.7	**Huron** (charter township) Wayne County
17	529	3.4	**Pontiac** (city) Oakland County	88	2329	5.7	**Vienna** (charter township) Genesee County
18	595	3.5	**Cutlerville** (CDP) Kent County	93	2446	5.8	**Antwerp** (township) Van Buren County
18	595	3.5	**Hazel Park** (city) Oakland County	93	2446	5.8	**Garfield** (charter township) Grand Traverse County
18	595	3.5	**Melvindale** (city) Wayne County	93	2446	5.8	**Lyon** (charter township) Oakland County
21	706	3.7	**East Lansing** (city) Ingham County	93	2446	5.8	**Sault Sainte Marie** (city) Chippewa County
22	760	3.8	**Highland** (charter township) Oakland County	93	2446	5.8	**Van Buren** (charter township) Wayne County
22	760	3.8	**Lansing** (city) Ingham County	98	2543	5.9	**Alpena** (city) Alpena County
22	760	3.8	**Taylor** (city) Wayne County	98	2543	5.9	**Burton** (city) Genesee County
22	760	3.8	**Wyoming** (city) Kent County	98	2543	5.9	**Orion** (charter township) Oakland County
26	823	3.9	**Adrian** (city) Lenawee County	98	2543	5.9	**Shelby** (charter township) Macomb County
26	823	3.9	**Beecher** (CDP) Genesee County	98	2543	5.9	**Sterling Heights** (city) Macomb County
26	823	3.9	**Detroit** (city) Wayne County	103	2640	6.0	**Big Rapids** (city) Mecosta County
26	823	3.9	**Garden City** (city) Wayne County	104	2738	6.1	**Dearborn Heights** (city) Wayne County
26	823	3.9	**Lincoln Park** (city) Wayne County	104	2738	6.1	**Frenchtown** (township) Monroe County
26	823	3.9	**Romulus** (city) Wayne County	104	2738	6.1	**Harper Woods** (city) Wayne County
32	876	4.0	**Eastpointe** (city) Macomb County	104	2738	6.1	**Monroe** (city) Monroe County
33	935	4.1	**Jackson** (city) Jackson County	104	2738	6.1	**Norton Shores** (city) Muskegon County
34	1004	4.2	**Benton Harbor** (city) Berrien County	104	2738	6.1	**Oak Park** (city) Oakland County
34	1004	4.2	**Clawson** (city) Oakland County	104	2738	6.1	**Okemos** (CDP) Ingham County
36	1076	4.3	**Byron** (township) Kent County	111	2845	6.2	**Coldwater** (city) Branch County
36	1076	4.3	**Redford** (charter township) Wayne County	112	2934	6.3	**Georgetown** (charter township) Ottawa County
36	1076	4.3	**Wixom** (city) Oakland County	112	2934	6.3	**Grandville** (city) Kent County
39	1151	4.4	**Beverly Hills** (village) Oakland County	112	2934	6.3	**New Baltimore** (city) Macomb County
39	1151	4.4	**Flint** (city) Genesee County	112	2934	6.3	**Spring Lake** (township) Ottawa County
39	1151	4.4	**Inkster** (city) Wayne County	112	2934	6.3	**Wyandotte** (city) Wayne County
42	1248	4.5	**Fraser** (city) Macomb County	117	3032	6.4	**Davison** (township) Genesee County
42	1248	4.5	**Grand Rapids** (city) Kent County	117	3032	6.4	**Independence** (charter township) Oakland County
42	1248	4.5	**Highland Park** (city) Wayne County	117	3032	6.4	**Saint Joseph** (charter township) Berrien County
42	1248	4.5	**Port Huron** (city) Saint Clair County	120	3097	6.5	**Bath** (charter township) Clinton County
46	1345	4.6	**Fenton** (city) Genesee County	120	3097	6.5	**Flint** (charter township) Genesee County
46	1345	4.6	**Mount Clemens** (city) Macomb County	120	3097	6.5	**Harrison** (charter township) Macomb County
46	1345	4.6	**Mount Morris** (township) Genesee County	120	3097	6.5	**Southgate** (city) Wayne County
46	1345	4.6	**Muskegon** (charter township) Muskegon County	120	3097	6.5	**Ypsilanti** (charter township) Washtenaw County
46	1345	4.6	**Niles** (city) Berrien County	125	3169	6.6	**Dearborn** (city) Wayne County
51	1418	4.7	**Kalamazoo** (city) Kalamazoo County	125	3169	6.6	**Fruitport** (charter township) Muskegon County
52	1502	4.8	**Waterford** (charter township) Oakland County	125	3169	6.6	**Midland** (city) Midland County
53	1586	4.9	**Allendale** (charter township) Ottawa County	125	3169	6.6	**Trenton** (city) Wayne County
53	1586	4.9	**Auburn Hills** (city) Oakland County	129	3253	6.7	**Plainfield** (charter township) Kent County
53	1586	4.9	**Kalamazoo** (charter township) Kalamazoo County	130	3318	6.8	**Bedford** (township) Monroe County
53	1586	4.9	**Muskegon** (city) Muskegon County	130	3318	6.8	**Macomb** (township) Macomb County
53	1586	4.9	**Warren** (city) Macomb County	130	3318	6.8	**Meridian** (charter township) Ingham County
53	1586	4.9	**Waverly** (CDP) Eaton County	130	3318	6.8	**Oshtemo** (charter township) Kalamazoo County
59	1680	5.0	**Jenison** (CDP) Ottawa County	134	3404	6.9	**Northview** (CDP) Kent County
59	1680	5.0	**Lincoln** (charter township) Berrien County	134	3404	6.9	**Southfield** (township) Oakland County
59	1680	5.0	**Madison Heights** (city) Oakland County	134	3404	6.9	**Walker** (city) Kent County
59	1680	5.0	**Westland** (city) Wayne County	134	3404	6.9	**Washington** (township) Macomb County
63	1762	5.1	**Allendale** (CDP) Ottawa County	138	3465	7.0	**Comstock** (charter township) Kalamazoo County
63	1762	5.1	**Battle Creek** (city) Calhoun County	138	3465	7.0	**Grand Haven** (charter township) Ottawa County
63	1762	5.1	**Commerce** (charter township) Oakland County	138	3465	7.0	**Ionia** (city) Ionia County
63	1762	5.1	**Ferndale** (city) Oakland County	138	3465	7.0	**South Lyon** (city) Oakland County
63	1762	5.1	**Holly** (township) Oakland County	142	3519	7.1	**Riverview** (city) Wayne County
68	1868	5.2	**Park** (township) Ottawa County	142	3519	7.1	**Southfield** (city) Oakland County
68	1868	5.2	**Saginaw** (city) Saginaw County	144	3574	7.2	**Farmington Hills** (city) Oakland County
70	1961	5.3	**Kentwood** (city) Kent County	144	3574	7.2	**Haslett** (CDP) Ingham County
70	1961	5.3	**Leoni** (township) Jackson County	144	3574	7.2	**Summit** (township) Jackson County
70	1961	5.3	**Tyrone** (township) Livingston County	144	3574	7.2	**Traverse City** (city) Grand Traverse County
73	2043	5.4	**Delta** (charter township) Eaton County	148	3631	7.3	**Escanaba** (city) Delta County
73	2043	5.4	**Farmington** (city) Oakland County	148	3631	7.3	**Monitor** (charter township) Bay County
73	2043	5.4	**Monroe** (charter township) Monroe County	148	3631	7.3	**Saint Clair Shores** (city) Macomb County

Note: The state column ranks the top/bottom 150 places from all places in the state with population of 10,000 or more. The national column ranks the top/bottom 150 places from all places in the country with population of 10,000 or more. Places that are unincorporated were not considered in the rankings. Please refer to the User Guide for additional information.

Employment: Service Occupations

Top 150 Places Ranked in *Descending* Order

State Rank	Nat'l Rank	Percent	Place
1	41	33.9	**Beecher** (CDP) Genesee County
2	46	33.7	**Benton Harbor** (city) Berrien County
3	51	33.5	**Union** (charter township) Isabella County
4	62	32.7	**Highland Park** (city) Wayne County
5	70	32.5	**Mount Pleasant** (city) Isabella County
6	98	31.0	**Pontiac** (city) Oakland County
7	107	30.6	**Muskegon Heights** (city) Muskegon County
8	110	30.4	**Muskegon** (city) Muskegon County
9	117	30.0	**Saginaw** (city) Saginaw County
10	132	29.7	**Marquette** (city) Marquette County
11	161	28.9	**Detroit** (city) Wayne County
12	181	28.5	**Big Rapids** (city) Mecosta County
13	192	28.3	**Benton** (charter township) Berrien County
13	192	28.3	**Flint** (city) Genesee County
13	192	28.3	**Inkster** (city) Wayne County
16	205	28.1	**Sault Sainte Marie** (city) Chippewa County
17	241	27.4	**East Lansing** (city) Ingham County
18	248	27.3	**Port Huron** (city) Saint Clair County
19	261	27.1	**Adrian** (city) Lenawee County
20	285	26.6	**Bridgeport** (charter township) Saginaw County
21	299	26.4	**Hamtramck** (city) Wayne County
22	319	26.2	**Melvindale** (city) Wayne County
23	325	26.1	**Kalamazoo** (city) Kalamazoo County
23	325	26.1	**Mount Morris** (township) Genesee County
25	338	26.0	**Jackson** (city) Jackson County
26	347	25.9	**Niles** (city) Berrien County
27	367	25.7	**Bay City** (city) Bay County
28	407	25.3	**Escanaba** (city) Delta County
29	432	25.1	**Harper Woods** (city) Wayne County
30	446	25.0	**Flint** (charter township) Genesee County
31	460	24.9	**Oshtemo** (charter township) Kalamazoo County
32	495	24.7	**Comstock Park** (CDP) Kent County
33	553	24.3	**Kalamazoo** (charter township) Kalamazoo County
34	590	24.1	**Owosso** (city) Shiawassee County
35	617	23.9	**Traverse City** (city) Grand Traverse County
36	651	23.7	**Monroe** (charter township) Monroe County
37	676	23.5	**Allendale** (CDP) Ottawa County
38	693	23.4	**Blackman** (charter township) Jackson County
38	693	23.4	**Lansing** (city) Ingham County
40	710	23.3	**Romulus** (city) Wayne County
41	734	23.2	**Ypsilanti** (city) Washtenaw County
42	752	23.1	**Wayne** (city) Wayne County
43	794	22.9	**Mount Clemens** (city) Macomb County
44	822	22.8	**Riverview** (city) Wayne County
44	822	22.8	**Roseville** (city) Macomb County
46	841	22.7	**Allendale** (charter township) Ottawa County
47	859	22.6	**Ypsilanti** (charter township) Washtenaw County
48	892	22.4	**Garfield** (charter township) Grand Traverse County
49	940	22.2	**Alpena** (city) Alpena County
49	940	22.2	**Oak Park** (city) Oakland County
51	963	22.1	**Lincoln Park** (city) Wayne County
52	1007	21.9	**DeWitt** (charter township) Clinton County
52	1007	21.9	**Eastpointe** (city) Macomb County
54	1035	21.8	**Westland** (city) Wayne County
55	1060	21.7	**Wyandotte** (city) Wayne County
56	1083	21.6	**Taylor** (city) Wayne County
57	1108	21.5	**Monroe** (city) Monroe County
58	1138	21.4	**Madison Heights** (city) Oakland County
59	1192	21.2	**Bath** (charter township) Clinton County
59	1192	21.2	**Coldwater** (city) Branch County
61	1222	21.1	**Alpine** (township) Kent County
61	1222	21.1	**Superior** (charter township) Washtenaw County
63	1252	21.0	**Vienna** (charter township) Genesee County
64	1361	20.6	**Clinton** (charter township) Macomb County
65	1386	20.5	**Genesee** (charter township) Genesee County
66	1413	20.4	**Battle Creek** (city) Calhoun County
66	1413	20.4	**Port Huron** (charter township) Saint Clair County
66	1413	20.4	**Warren** (city) Macomb County
69	1443	20.3	**Burton** (city) Genesee County
69	1443	20.3	**Fenton** (city) Genesee County
71	1475	20.2	**Muskegon** (charter township) Muskegon County
71	1475	20.2	**Thomas** (township) Saginaw County
73	1530	20.0	**Bangor** (charter township) Bay County
74	1565	19.9	**Ionia** (city) Ionia County
75	1592	19.8	**Cadillac** (city) Wexford County
75	1592	19.8	**East Bay** (township) Grand Traverse County
77	1662	19.6	**Grand Rapids** (city) Kent County
77	1662	19.6	**Holland** (city) Ottawa County
79	1732	19.4	**Waterford** (charter township) Oakland County
80	1763	19.3	**Dearborn Heights** (city) Wayne County
80	1763	19.3	**Grand Haven** (city) Ottawa County
82	1792	19.2	**Frenchtown** (township) Monroe County
83	1833	19.1	**Antwerp** (township) Van Buren County
84	1875	19.0	**Auburn Hills** (city) Oakland County
85	1940	18.8	**Leoni** (township) Jackson County
86	1971	18.7	**Hazel Park** (city) Oakland County
86	1971	18.7	**Van Buren** (charter township) Wayne County
88	2037	18.5	**Wyoming** (city) Kent County
89	2067	18.4	**Trenton** (city) Wayne County
90	2095	18.3	**Niles** (township) Berrien County
90	2095	18.3	**Wixom** (city) Oakland County
92	2158	18.1	**Norton Shores** (city) Muskegon County
93	2185	18.0	**Clawson** (city) Oakland County
93	2185	18.0	**Genoa** (township) Livingston County
93	2185	18.0	**Redford** (charter township) Wayne County
93	2185	18.0	**Sterling Heights** (city) Macomb County
97	2260	17.8	**Cutlerville** (CDP) Kent County
97	2260	17.8	**Jenison** (CDP) Ottawa County
97	2260	17.8	**Monitor** (charter township) Bay County
97	2260	17.8	**Saginaw** (charter township) Saginaw County
97	2260	17.8	**Southgate** (city) Wayne County
102	2291	17.7	**Southfield** (city) Oakland County
103	2317	17.6	**Brandon** (charter township) Oakland County
103	2317	17.6	**Garden City** (city) Wayne County
105	2361	17.5	**Allen Park** (city) Wayne County
105	2361	17.5	**Grand Haven** (charter township) Ottawa County
105	2361	17.5	**Saint Clair Shores** (city) Macomb County
108	2396	17.4	**Comstock** (charter township) Kalamazoo County
108	2396	17.4	**Gaines** (charter township) Kent County
110	2429	17.3	**Harrison** (charter township) Macomb County
111	2468	17.2	**Delhi** (charter township) Ingham County
112	2496	17.1	**Saint Joseph** (charter township) Berrien County
113	2519	17.0	**Ferndale** (city) Oakland County
113	2519	17.0	**Midland** (city) Midland County
115	2554	16.9	**Fraser** (city) Macomb County
116	2607	16.7	**Chesterfield** (township) Macomb County
116	2607	16.7	**Holland** (charter township) Ottawa County
116	2607	16.7	**South Lyon** (city) Oakland County
119	2651	16.6	**Fruitport** (charter township) Muskegon County
120	2692	16.5	**Emmett** (charter township) Calhoun County
120	2692	16.5	**Fort Gratiot** (charter township) Saint Clair County
122	2722	16.4	**Cooper** (charter township) Kalamazoo County
123	2763	16.3	**Northview** (CDP) Kent County
123	2763	16.3	**Plainfield** (charter township) Kent County
125	2797	16.2	**Holt** (CDP) Ingham County
126	2828	16.1	**Holly** (township) Oakland County
126	2828	16.1	**Kentwood** (city) Kent County
126	2828	16.1	**Lincoln** (charter township) Berrien County
126	2828	16.1	**Lyon** (charter township) Oakland County
126	2828	16.1	**Waverly** (CDP) Eaton County
126	2828	16.1	**White Lake** (charter township) Oakland County
132	2865	16.0	**Davison** (township) Genesee County
133	2929	15.8	**Delta** (charter township) Eaton County
133	2929	15.8	**Highland** (charter township) Oakland County
135	2962	15.7	**Bedford** (township) Monroe County
135	2962	15.7	**Huron** (charter township) Wayne County
137	3000	15.6	**Milford** (charter township) Oakland County
137	3000	15.6	**New Baltimore** (city) Macomb County
137	3000	15.6	**Sturgis** (city) Saint Joseph County
140	3032	15.5	**Georgetown** (charter township) Ottawa County
140	3032	15.5	**Livonia** (city) Wayne County
142	3065	15.4	**Grandville** (city) Kent County
142	3065	15.4	**Summit** (township) Jackson County
144	3090	15.3	**Shelby** (charter township) Macomb County
145	3128	15.2	**Dearborn** (city) Wayne County
146	3151	15.1	**Ann Arbor** (city) Washtenaw County
146	3151	15.1	**Grand Blanc** (charter township) Genesee County
146	3151	15.1	**Spring Lake** (township) Ottawa County
149	3182	15.0	**Fenton** (charter township) Genesee County
149	3182	15.0	**Springfield** (charter township) Oakland County

Note: The state column ranks the top/bottom 150 places from all places in the state with population of 10,000 or more. The national column ranks the top/bottom 150 places from all places in the country with population of 10,000 or more. Places that are unincorporated were not considered in the rankings. Please refer to the User Guide for additional information.

Employment: Service Occupations

Top 150 Places Ranked in *Ascending* Order

State Rank	Nat'l Rank	Percent	Place
1	37	6.2	**East Grand Rapids** (city) Kent County
2	135	8.2	**Birmingham** (city) Oakland County
2	135	8.2	**Cascade** (charter township) Kent County
4	158	8.5	**Southfield** (township) Oakland County
5	199	8.9	**West Bloomfield** (charter township) Oakland County
6	235	9.2	**Bloomfield** (charter township) Oakland County
7	246	9.3	**Forest Hills** (CDP) Kent County
8	256	9.4	**Oakland** (charter township) Oakland County
9	276	9.6	**Beverly Hills** (village) Oakland County
10	378	10.4	**Park** (township) Ottawa County
11	396	10.5	**Novi** (city) Oakland County
12	408	10.6	**Northville** (township) Wayne County
13	468	11.0	**Ada** (township) Kent County
13	468	11.0	**Scio** (township) Washtenaw County
15	509	11.2	**Farmington** (city) Oakland County
16	535	11.3	**Grosse Pointe Woods** (city) Wayne County
17	571	11.5	**Caledonia** (township) Kent County
17	571	11.5	**Royal Oak** (city) Oakland County
17	571	11.5	**Troy** (city) Oakland County
20	594	11.6	**Oceola** (township) Livingston County
20	594	11.6	**Plymouth** (charter township) Wayne County
22	634	11.8	**Texas** (charter township) Kalamazoo County
23	651	11.9	**Grand Rapids** (charter township) Kent County
24	680	12.0	**Grosse Pointe Park** (city) Wayne County
24	680	12.0	**Washington** (township) Macomb County
26	738	12.3	**Rochester Hills** (city) Oakland County
27	796	12.6	**Rochester** (city) Oakland County
28	822	12.7	**Brighton** (township) Livingston County
28	822	12.7	**Portage** (city) Kalamazoo County
30	846	12.8	**Cannon** (township) Kent County
31	864	12.9	**Haslett** (CDP) Ingham County
32	1010	13.5	**Byron** (township) Kent County
32	1010	13.5	**Canton** (charter township) Wayne County
32	1010	13.5	**Grosse Ile** (township) Wayne County
32	1010	13.5	**Meridian** (charter township) Ingham County
36	1040	13.6	**Farmington Hills** (city) Oakland County
36	1040	13.6	**Green Oak** (township) Livingston County
36	1040	13.6	**Pittsfield** (charter township) Washtenaw County
39	1061	13.7	**Macomb** (township) Macomb County
40	1085	13.8	**Hamburg** (township) Livingston County
41	1114	13.9	**Flushing** (charter township) Genesee County
42	1143	14.0	**Commerce** (charter township) Oakland County
43	1167	14.1	**Orion** (charter township) Oakland County
44	1223	14.3	**Independence** (charter township) Oakland County
44	1223	14.3	**Mundy** (township) Genesee County
46	1312	14.6	**Berkley** (city) Oakland County
46	1312	14.6	**Okemos** (CDP) Ingham County
46	1312	14.6	**Oxford** (charter township) Oakland County
49	1345	14.7	**Lenox** (township) Macomb County
49	1345	14.7	**Walker** (city) Kent County
49	1345	14.7	**Woodhaven** (city) Wayne County
52	1375	14.8	**Brownstown** (charter township) Wayne County
52	1375	14.8	**Hartland** (township) Livingston County
52	1375	14.8	**Tyrone** (township) Livingston County
55	1442	15.0	**Fenton** (charter township) Genesee County
55	1442	15.0	**Springfield** (charter township) Oakland County
57	1475	15.1	**Ann Arbor** (city) Washtenaw County
57	1475	15.1	**Grand Blanc** (charter township) Genesee County
57	1475	15.1	**Spring Lake** (township) Ottawa County
60	1506	15.2	**Dearborn** (city) Wayne County
61	1529	15.3	**Shelby** (charter township) Macomb County
62	1567	15.4	**Grandville** (city) Kent County
62	1567	15.4	**Summit** (township) Jackson County
64	1592	15.5	**Georgetown** (charter township) Ottawa County
64	1592	15.5	**Livonia** (city) Wayne County
66	1625	15.6	**Milford** (charter township) Oakland County
66	1625	15.6	**New Baltimore** (city) Macomb County
66	1625	15.6	**Sturgis** (city) Saint Joseph County
69	1657	15.7	**Bedford** (township) Monroe County
69	1657	15.7	**Huron** (charter township) Wayne County
71	1695	15.8	**Delta** (charter township) Eaton County
71	1695	15.8	**Highland** (charter township) Oakland County
73	1764	16.0	**Davison** (township) Genesee County
74	1792	16.1	**Holly** (township) Oakland County
74	1792	16.1	**Kentwood** (city) Kent County
74	1792	16.1	**Lincoln** (charter township) Berrien County
74	1792	16.1	**Lyon** (charter township) Oakland County
74	1792	16.1	**Waverly** (CDP) Eaton County
74	1792	16.1	**White Lake** (charter township) Oakland County
80	1829	16.2	**Holt** (CDP) Ingham County
81	1860	16.3	**Northview** (CDP) Kent County
81	1860	16.3	**Plainfield** (charter township) Kent County
83	1894	16.4	**Cooper** (charter township) Kalamazoo County
84	1935	16.5	**Emmett** (charter township) Calhoun County
84	1935	16.5	**Fort Gratiot** (charter township) Saint Clair County
86	1965	16.6	**Fruitport** (charter township) Muskegon County
87	2006	16.7	**Chesterfield** (township) Macomb County
87	2006	16.7	**Holland** (charter township) Ottawa County
87	2006	16.7	**South Lyon** (city) Oakland County
90	2072	16.9	**Fraser** (city) Macomb County
91	2103	17.0	**Ferndale** (city) Oakland County
91	2103	17.0	**Midland** (city) Midland County
93	2138	17.1	**Saint Joseph** (charter township) Berrien County
94	2161	17.2	**Delhi** (charter township) Ingham County
95	2189	17.3	**Harrison** (charter township) Macomb County
96	2228	17.4	**Comstock** (charter township) Kalamazoo County
96	2228	17.4	**Gaines** (charter township) Kent County
98	2261	17.5	**Allen Park** (city) Wayne County
98	2261	17.5	**Grand Haven** (charter township) Ottawa County
98	2261	17.5	**Saint Clair Shores** (city) Macomb County
101	2296	17.6	**Brandon** (charter township) Oakland County
101	2296	17.6	**Garden City** (city) Wayne County
103	2340	17.7	**Southfield** (city) Oakland County
104	2366	17.8	**Cutlerville** (CDP) Kent County
104	2366	17.8	**Jenison** (CDP) Ottawa County
104	2366	17.8	**Monitor** (charter township) Bay County
104	2366	17.8	**Saginaw** (charter township) Saginaw County
104	2366	17.8	**Southgate** (city) Wayne County
109	2436	18.0	**Clawson** (city) Oakland County
109	2436	18.0	**Genoa** (township) Livingston County
109	2436	18.0	**Redford** (charter township) Wayne County
109	2436	18.0	**Sterling Heights** (city) Macomb County
113	2472	18.1	**Norton Shores** (city) Muskegon County
114	2523	18.3	**Niles** (township) Berrien County
114	2523	18.3	**Wixom** (city) Oakland County
116	2562	18.4	**Trenton** (city) Wayne County
117	2590	18.5	**Wyoming** (city) Kent County
118	2652	18.7	**Hazel Park** (city) Oakland County
118	2652	18.7	**Van Buren** (charter township) Wayne County
120	2686	18.8	**Leoni** (township) Jackson County
121	2747	19.0	**Auburn Hills** (city) Oakland County
122	2782	19.1	**Antwerp** (township) Van Buren County
123	2824	19.2	**Frenchtown** (township) Monroe County
124	2865	19.3	**Dearborn Heights** (city) Wayne County
124	2865	19.3	**Grand Haven** (city) Ottawa County
126	2894	19.4	**Waterford** (charter township) Oakland County
127	2961	19.6	**Grand Rapids** (city) Kent County
127	2961	19.6	**Holland** (city) Ottawa County
129	3031	19.8	**Cadillac** (city) Wexford County
129	3031	19.8	**East Bay** (township) Grand Traverse County
131	3065	19.9	**Ionia** (city) Ionia County
132	3092	20.0	**Bangor** (charter township) Bay County
133	3152	20.2	**Muskegon** (charter township) Muskegon County
133	3152	20.2	**Thomas** (township) Saginaw County
135	3182	20.3	**Burton** (city) Genesee County
135	3182	20.3	**Fenton** (city) Genesee County
137	3214	20.4	**Battle Creek** (city) Calhoun County
137	3214	20.4	**Port Huron** (charter township) Saint Clair County
137	3214	20.4	**Warren** (city) Macomb County
140	3244	20.5	**Genesee** (charter township) Genesee County
141	3271	20.6	**Clinton** (charter township) Macomb County
142	3385	21.0	**Vienna** (charter township) Genesee County
143	3405	21.1	**Alpine** (township) Kent County
143	3405	21.1	**Superior** (charter township) Washtenaw County
145	3435	21.2	**Bath** (charter township) Clinton County
145	3435	21.2	**Coldwater** (city) Branch County
147	3495	21.4	**Madison Heights** (city) Oakland County
148	3519	21.5	**Monroe** (city) Monroe County
149	3549	21.6	**Taylor** (city) Wayne County
150	3574	21.7	**Wyandotte** (city) Wayne County

Note: The state column ranks the top/bottom 150 places from all places in the state with population of 10,000 or more. The national column ranks the top/bottom 150 places from all places in the country with population of 10,000 or more. Places that are unincorporated were not considered in the rankings. Please refer to the User Guide for additional information.

Employment: Sales and Office Occupations

Top 150 Places Ranked in *Descending* Order

State Rank	Nat'l Rank	Percent	Place
1	76	32.8	**Alpena** (city) Alpena County
2	88	32.6	**Union** (charter township) Isabella County
3	114	32.2	**Eastpointe** (city) Macomb County
4	209	31.1	**Comstock Park** (CDP) Kent County
4	209	31.1	**Vienna** (charter township) Genesee County
6	229	31.0	**Alpine** (township) Kent County
7	262	30.7	**Garfield** (charter township) Grand Traverse County
8	376	29.9	**Wixom** (city) Oakland County
9	395	29.8	**East Bay** (township) Grand Traverse County
9	395	29.8	**Madison Heights** (city) Oakland County
11	524	29.3	**Norton Shores** (city) Muskegon County
12	583	29.1	**Fraser** (city) Macomb County
12	583	29.1	**Lenox** (township) Macomb County
12	583	29.1	**Ypsilanti** (city) Washtenaw County
15	624	28.9	**New Baltimore** (city) Macomb County
16	674	28.7	**Sault Sainte Marie** (city) Chippewa County
17	701	28.6	**Saginaw** (charter township) Saginaw County
18	733	28.5	**Commerce** (charter township) Oakland County
18	733	28.5	**Emmett** (charter township) Calhoun County
20	771	28.4	**Warren** (city) Macomb County
21	800	28.3	**Redford** (charter township) Wayne County
21	800	28.3	**Waverly** (CDP) Eaton County
23	860	28.1	**Genesee** (charter township) Genesee County
23	860	28.1	**Southgate** (city) Wayne County
25	939	27.9	**Davison** (township) Genesee County
26	972	27.8	**Wyoming** (city) Kent County
27	1015	27.7	**Delhi** (charter township) Ingham County
27	1015	27.7	**Kentwood** (city) Kent County
27	1015	27.7	**Waterford** (charter township) Oakland County
30	1062	27.6	**Mount Pleasant** (city) Isabella County
31	1110	27.5	**Holly** (township) Oakland County
31	1110	27.5	**Jackson** (city) Jackson County
31	1110	27.5	**Westland** (city) Wayne County
34	1156	27.4	**Delta** (charter township) Eaton County
35	1198	27.3	**Bay City** (city) Bay County
36	1236	27.2	**Clinton** (charter township) Macomb County
36	1236	27.2	**Lincoln Park** (city) Wayne County
36	1236	27.2	**Muskegon** (charter township) Muskegon County
39	1286	27.1	**Holt** (CDP) Ingham County
39	1286	27.1	**Southfield** (city) Oakland County
41	1337	27.0	**Hazel Park** (city) Oakland County
41	1337	27.0	**Park** (township) Ottawa County
41	1337	27.0	**Roseville** (city) Macomb County
44	1394	26.9	**Dearborn Heights** (city) Wayne County
44	1394	26.9	**Harper Woods** (city) Wayne County
44	1394	26.9	**Mount Morris** (township) Genesee County
47	1464	26.8	**Ada** (township) Kent County
47	1464	26.8	**Gaines** (charter township) Kent County
47	1464	26.8	**Green Oak** (township) Livingston County
50	1515	26.7	**Benton Harbor** (city) Berrien County
50	1515	26.7	**Fort Gratiot** (charter township) Saint Clair County
50	1515	26.7	**Macomb** (township) Macomb County
53	1565	26.6	**Allendale** (CDP) Ottawa County
53	1565	26.6	**Allendale** (charter township) Ottawa County
53	1565	26.6	**Flushing** (charter township) Genesee County
53	1565	26.6	**Saint Clair Shores** (city) Macomb County
53	1565	26.6	**Shelby** (charter township) Macomb County
53	1565	26.6	**Taylor** (city) Wayne County
53	1565	26.6	**Wayne** (city) Wayne County
53	1565	26.6	**West Bloomfield** (charter township) Oakland County
61	1625	26.5	**Grandville** (city) Kent County
61	1625	26.5	**White Lake** (charter township) Oakland County
63	1681	26.4	**Sterling Heights** (city) Macomb County
64	1738	26.3	**Burton** (city) Genesee County
64	1738	26.3	**Chesterfield** (township) Macomb County
64	1738	26.3	**Clawson** (city) Oakland County
64	1738	26.3	**Independence** (charter township) Oakland County
64	1738	26.3	**Riverview** (city) Wayne County
69	1799	26.2	**Bangor** (charter township) Bay County
69	1799	26.2	**Georgetown** (charter township) Ottawa County
69	1799	26.2	**Monitor** (charter township) Bay County
69	1799	26.2	**Spring Lake** (township) Ottawa County
73	1873	26.1	**Blackman** (charter township) Jackson County
73	1873	26.1	**Byron** (township) Kent County
73	1873	26.1	**Grosse Pointe Woods** (city) Wayne County

State Rank	Nat'l Rank	Percent	Place
73	1873	26.1	**Oak Park** (city) Oakland County
77	1930	26.0	**Beecher** (CDP) Genesee County
77	1930	26.0	**Brownstown** (charter township) Wayne County
77	1930	26.0	**Haslett** (CDP) Ingham County
77	1930	26.0	**Pontiac** (city) Oakland County
81	1997	25.9	**Cannon** (township) Kent County
81	1997	25.9	**Niles** (city) Berrien County
83	2060	25.8	**Garden City** (city) Wayne County
83	2060	25.8	**Port Huron** (city) Saint Clair County
85	2116	25.7	**Big Rapids** (city) Mecosta County
85	2116	25.7	**Cutlerville** (CDP) Kent County
85	2116	25.7	**Milford** (charter township) Oakland County
85	2116	25.7	**Plainfield** (charter township) Kent County
85	2116	25.7	**Southfield** (township) Oakland County
90	2172	25.6	**Port Huron** (charter township) Saint Clair County
91	2226	25.5	**Harrison** (charter township) Macomb County
91	2226	25.5	**Oxford** (charter township) Oakland County
93	2276	25.4	**Inkster** (city) Wayne County
93	2276	25.4	**Livonia** (city) Wayne County
93	2276	25.4	**Trenton** (city) Wayne County
93	2276	25.4	**Woodhaven** (city) Wayne County
97	2327	25.3	**Beverly Hills** (village) Oakland County
97	2327	25.3	**Van Buren** (charter township) Wayne County
99	2385	25.2	**Benton** (charter township) Berrien County
99	2385	25.2	**Kalamazoo** (city) Kalamazoo County
99	2385	25.2	**Lansing** (city) Ingham County
99	2385	25.2	**Oceola** (township) Livingston County
99	2385	25.2	**Portage** (city) Kalamazoo County
104	2441	25.1	**Bridgeport** (charter township) Saginaw County
104	2441	25.1	**Northview** (CDP) Kent County
106	2489	25.0	**Brighton** (township) Livingston County
106	2489	25.0	**Dearborn** (city) Wayne County
106	2489	25.0	**Genoa** (township) Livingston County
106	2489	25.0	**Ionia** (city) Ionia County
106	2489	25.0	**Novi** (city) Oakland County
106	2489	25.0	**Saginaw** (city) Saginaw County
112	2554	24.9	**Bedford** (township) Monroe County
112	2554	24.9	**Farmington Hills** (city) Oakland County
112	2554	24.9	**Walker** (city) Kent County
112	2554	24.9	**Wyandotte** (city) Wayne County
112	2554	24.9	**Ypsilanti** (charter township) Washtenaw County
117	2612	24.8	**Allen Park** (city) Wayne County
118	2671	24.7	**Detroit** (city) Wayne County
118	2671	24.7	**Lyon** (charter township) Oakland County
118	2671	24.7	**Washington** (township) Macomb County
121	2724	24.6	**Caledonia** (township) Kent County
121	2724	24.6	**Coldwater** (city) Branch County
121	2724	24.6	**Leoni** (township) Jackson County
121	2724	24.6	**Orion** (charter township) Oakland County
121	2724	24.6	**Owosso** (city) Shiawassee County
126	2790	24.5	**Romulus** (city) Wayne County
126	2790	24.5	**Tyrone** (township) Livingston County
128	2857	24.4	**Flint** (city) Genesee County
128	2857	24.4	**Royal Oak** (city) Oakland County
128	2857	24.4	**Traverse City** (city) Grand Traverse County
131	2911	24.3	**Adrian** (city) Lenawee County
131	2911	24.3	**Battle Creek** (city) Calhoun County
131	2911	24.3	**Farmington** (city) Oakland County
134	2964	24.2	**Escanaba** (city) Delta County
135	3009	24.1	**Hartland** (township) Livingston County
136	3051	24.0	**Hamburg** (township) Livingston County
136	3051	24.0	**Huron** (charter township) Wayne County
136	3051	24.0	**Jenison** (CDP) Ottawa County
136	3051	24.0	**Mundy** (township) Genesee County
140	3142	23.8	**Ferndale** (city) Oakland County
140	3142	23.8	**Flint** (charter township) Genesee County
140	3142	23.8	**Grand Blanc** (charter township) Genesee County
140	3142	23.8	**Marquette** (city) Marquette County
144	3190	23.7	**Grand Rapids** (charter township) Kent County
145	3236	23.6	**Cascade** (charter township) Kent County
145	3236	23.6	**Forest Hills** (CDP) Kent County
145	3236	23.6	**Monroe** (city) Monroe County
148	3282	23.5	**Fenton** (charter township) Genesee County
148	3282	23.5	**Grand Haven** (city) Ottawa County
148	3282	23.5	**Highland** (charter township) Oakland County

Note: The state column ranks the top/bottom 150 places from all places in the state with population of 10,000 or more. The national column ranks the top/bottom 150 places from all places in the country with population of 10,000 or more. Places that are unincorporated were not considered in the rankings. Please refer to the User Guide for additional information.

Employment: Sales and Office Occupations

Top 150 Places Ranked in *Ascending* Order

State Rank	Nat'l Rank	Percent	Place
1	8	12.6	**Muskegon Heights** (city) Muskegon County
2	76	16.9	**Scio** (township) Washtenaw County
3	82	17.0	**Ann Arbor** (city) Washtenaw County
4	92	17.2	**Grosse Pointe Park** (city) Wayne County
5	115	17.7	**Grand Haven** (charter township) Ottawa County
5	115	17.7	**Okemos** (CDP) Ingham County
7	146	18.1	**Melvindale** (city) Wayne County
8	157	18.3	**Northville** (township) Wayne County
9	167	18.4	**Holland** (city) Ottawa County
10	181	18.6	**Holland** (charter township) Ottawa County
11	222	19.1	**Troy** (city) Oakland County
12	244	19.3	**Sturgis** (city) Saint Joseph County
13	321	19.9	**Oakland** (charter township) Oakland County
14	464	20.7	**Cadillac** (city) Wexford County
15	482	20.8	**Frenchtown** (township) Monroe County
16	507	20.9	**Birmingham** (city) Oakland County
17	545	21.1	**Cooper** (charter township) Kalamazoo County
18	571	21.2	**Pittsfield** (charter township) Washtenaw County
19	618	21.4	**Muskegon** (city) Muskegon County
19	618	21.4	**Saint Joseph** (charter township) Berrien County
19	618	21.4	**Texas** (charter township) Kalamazoo County
22	675	21.6	**Superior** (charter township) Washtenaw County
23	707	21.7	**Brandon** (charter township) Oakland County
23	707	21.7	**Hamtramck** (city) Wayne County
23	707	21.7	**Meridian** (charter township) Ingham County
26	729	21.8	**Fruitport** (charter township) Muskegon County
27	812	22.1	**Monroe** (charter township) Monroe County
28	836	22.2	**Bloomfield** (charter township) Oakland County
28	836	22.2	**Highland Park** (city) Wayne County
30	906	22.4	**Berkley** (city) Oakland County
30	906	22.4	**Kalamazoo** (charter township) Kalamazoo County
30	906	22.4	**Niles** (township) Berrien County
30	906	22.4	**Springfield** (charter township) Oakland County
34	940	22.5	**Lincoln** (charter township) Berrien County
35	1004	22.7	**Antwerp** (township) Van Buren County
35	1004	22.7	**Bath** (charter township) Clinton County
35	1004	22.7	**Canton** (charter township) Wayne County
35	1004	22.7	**East Lansing** (city) Ingham County
35	1004	22.7	**Summit** (township) Jackson County
40	1041	22.8	**Comstock** (charter township) Kalamazoo County
40	1041	22.8	**Thomas** (township) Saginaw County
42	1126	23.0	**East Grand Rapids** (city) Kent County
42	1126	23.0	**Oshtemo** (charter township) Kalamazoo County
42	1126	23.0	**South Lyon** (city) Oakland County
45	1162	23.1	**Midland** (city) Midland County
45	1162	23.1	**Plymouth** (charter township) Wayne County
47	1198	23.2	**Auburn Hills** (city) Oakland County
47	1198	23.2	**Rochester Hills** (city) Oakland County
49	1239	23.3	**Fenton** (city) Genesee County
50	1275	23.4	**DeWitt** (charter township) Clinton County
50	1275	23.4	**Grand Rapids** (city) Kent County
50	1275	23.4	**Grosse Ile** (township) Wayne County
50	1275	23.4	**Rochester** (city) Oakland County
54	1320	23.5	**Fenton** (charter township) Genesee County
54	1320	23.5	**Grand Haven** (city) Ottawa County
54	1320	23.5	**Highland** (charter township) Oakland County
54	1320	23.5	**Mount Clemens** (city) Macomb County
58	1375	23.6	**Cascade** (charter township) Kent County
58	1375	23.6	**Forest Hills** (CDP) Kent County
58	1375	23.6	**Monroe** (city) Monroe County
61	1421	23.7	**Grand Rapids** (charter township) Kent County
62	1467	23.8	**Ferndale** (city) Oakland County
62	1467	23.8	**Flint** (charter township) Genesee County
62	1467	23.8	**Grand Blanc** (charter township) Genesee County
62	1467	23.8	**Marquette** (city) Marquette County
66	1555	24.0	**Hamburg** (township) Livingston County
66	1555	24.0	**Huron** (charter township) Wayne County
66	1555	24.0	**Jenison** (CDP) Ottawa County
66	1555	24.0	**Mundy** (township) Genesee County
70	1606	24.1	**Hartland** (township) Livingston County
71	1648	24.2	**Escanaba** (city) Delta County
72	1693	24.3	**Adrian** (city) Lenawee County
72	1693	24.3	**Battle Creek** (city) Calhoun County
72	1693	24.3	**Farmington** (city) Oakland County
75	1746	24.4	**Flint** (city) Genesee County
75	1746	24.4	**Royal Oak** (city) Oakland County
75	1746	24.4	**Traverse City** (city) Grand Traverse County
78	1800	24.5	**Romulus** (city) Wayne County
78	1800	24.5	**Tyrone** (township) Livingston County
80	1867	24.6	**Caledonia** (township) Kent County
80	1867	24.6	**Coldwater** (city) Branch County
80	1867	24.6	**Leoni** (township) Jackson County
80	1867	24.6	**Orion** (charter township) Oakland County
80	1867	24.6	**Owosso** (city) Shiawassee County
85	1933	24.7	**Detroit** (city) Wayne County
85	1933	24.7	**Lyon** (charter township) Oakland County
85	1933	24.7	**Washington** (township) Macomb County
88	1986	24.8	**Allen Park** (city) Wayne County
89	2045	24.9	**Bedford** (township) Monroe County
89	2045	24.9	**Farmington Hills** (city) Oakland County
89	2045	24.9	**Walker** (city) Kent County
89	2045	24.9	**Wyandotte** (city) Wayne County
89	2045	24.9	**Ypsilanti** (charter township) Washtenaw County
94	2103	25.0	**Brighton** (township) Livingston County
94	2103	25.0	**Dearborn** (city) Wayne County
94	2103	25.0	**Genoa** (township) Livingston County
94	2103	25.0	**Ionia** (city) Ionia County
94	2103	25.0	**Novi** (city) Oakland County
94	2103	25.0	**Saginaw** (city) Saginaw County
100	2168	25.1	**Bridgeport** (charter township) Saginaw County
100	2168	25.1	**Northview** (CDP) Kent County
102	2216	25.2	**Benton** (charter township) Berrien County
102	2216	25.2	**Kalamazoo** (city) Kalamazoo County
102	2216	25.2	**Lansing** (city) Ingham County
102	2216	25.2	**Oceola** (township) Livingston County
102	2216	25.2	**Portage** (city) Kalamazoo County
107	2272	25.3	**Beverly Hills** (village) Oakland County
107	2272	25.3	**Van Buren** (charter township) Wayne County
109	2330	25.4	**Inkster** (city) Wayne County
109	2330	25.4	**Livonia** (city) Wayne County
109	2330	25.4	**Trenton** (city) Wayne County
109	2330	25.4	**Woodhaven** (city) Wayne County
113	2381	25.5	**Harrison** (charter township) Macomb County
113	2381	25.5	**Oxford** (charter township) Oakland County
115	2431	25.6	**Port Huron** (charter township) Saint Clair County
116	2485	25.7	**Big Rapids** (city) Mecosta County
116	2485	25.7	**Cutlerville** (CDP) Kent County
116	2485	25.7	**Milford** (charter township) Oakland County
116	2485	25.7	**Plainfield** (charter township) Kent County
116	2485	25.7	**Southfield** (township) Oakland County
121	2541	25.8	**Garden City** (city) Wayne County
121	2541	25.8	**Port Huron** (city) Saint Clair County
123	2597	25.9	**Cannon** (township) Kent County
123	2597	25.9	**Niles** (city) Berrien County
125	2660	26.0	**Beecher** (CDP) Genesee County
125	2660	26.0	**Brownstown** (charter township) Wayne County
125	2660	26.0	**Haslett** (CDP) Ingham County
125	2660	26.0	**Pontiac** (city) Oakland County
129	2727	26.1	**Blackman** (charter township) Jackson County
129	2727	26.1	**Byron** (township) Kent County
129	2727	26.1	**Grosse Pointe Woods** (city) Wayne County
129	2727	26.1	**Oak Park** (city) Oakland County
133	2784	26.2	**Bangor** (charter township) Bay County
133	2784	26.2	**Georgetown** (charter township) Ottawa County
133	2784	26.2	**Monitor** (charter township) Bay County
133	2784	26.2	**Spring Lake** (township) Ottawa County
137	2858	26.3	**Burton** (city) Genesee County
137	2858	26.3	**Chesterfield** (township) Macomb County
137	2858	26.3	**Clawson** (city) Oakland County
137	2858	26.3	**Independence** (charter township) Oakland County
137	2858	26.3	**Riverview** (city) Wayne County
142	2919	26.4	**Sterling Heights** (city) Macomb County
143	2976	26.5	**Grandville** (city) Kent County
143	2976	26.5	**White Lake** (charter township) Oakland County
145	3032	26.6	**Allendale** (CDP) Ottawa County
145	3032	26.6	**Allendale** (charter township) Ottawa County
145	3032	26.6	**Flushing** (charter township) Genesee County
145	3032	26.6	**Saint Clair Shores** (city) Macomb County
145	3032	26.6	**Shelby** (charter township) Macomb County
145	3032	26.6	**Taylor** (city) Wayne County

Note: The state column ranks the top/bottom 150 places from all places in the state with population of 10,000 or more. The national column ranks the top/bottom 150 places from all places in the country with population of 10,000 or more. Places that are unincorporated were not considered in the rankings. Please refer to the User Guide for additional information.

Employment: Natural Resources, Construction, and Maintenance Occupations

Top 150 Places Ranked in *Descending* Order

State Rank	Nat'l Rank	Percent	Place
1	475	12.5	**Genesee** (charter township) Genesee County
2	513	12.3	**Lenox** (township) Macomb County
3	715	11.3	**Melvindale** (city) Wayne County
4	762	11.1	**Highland** (charter township) Oakland County
4	762	11.1	**Huron** (charter township) Wayne County
6	819	10.9	**Antwerp** (township) Van Buren County
6	819	10.9	**Cooper** (charter township) Kalamazoo County
8	847	10.8	**Byron** (township) Kent County
8	847	10.8	**Garden City** (city) Wayne County
10	904	10.6	**Frenchtown** (township) Monroe County
11	1009	10.3	**Brandon** (charter township) Oakland County
12	1044	10.2	**Lincoln Park** (city) Wayne County
12	1044	10.2	**Oceola** (township) Livingston County
14	1124	10.0	**Harrison** (charter township) Macomb County
15	1163	9.9	**Taylor** (city) Wayne County
15	1163	9.9	**Vienna** (charter township) Genesee County
17	1202	9.8	**Trenton** (city) Wayne County
18	1289	9.6	**Ionia** (city) Ionia County
18	1289	9.6	**New Baltimore** (city) Macomb County
20	1329	9.5	**East Bay** (township) Grand Traverse County
20	1329	9.5	**Hazel Park** (city) Oakland County
20	1329	9.5	**Holland** (charter township) Ottawa County
20	1329	9.5	**Niles** (township) Berrien County
24	1370	9.4	**Cutlerville** (CDP) Kent County
24	1370	9.4	**Southgate** (city) Wayne County
26	1465	9.2	**Allen Park** (city) Wayne County
26	1465	9.2	**Allendale** (CDP) Ottawa County
26	1465	9.2	**Allendale** (charter township) Ottawa County
26	1465	9.2	**Bedford** (township) Monroe County
26	1465	9.2	**Brownstown** (charter township) Wayne County
26	1465	9.2	**Comstock** (charter township) Kalamazoo County
26	1465	9.2	**Port Huron** (charter township) Saint Clair County
33	1514	9.1	**Jenison** (CDP) Ottawa County
33	1514	9.1	**Pontiac** (city) Oakland County
33	1514	9.1	**Roseville** (city) Macomb County
33	1514	9.1	**Wyandotte** (city) Wayne County
37	1566	9.0	**Alpine** (township) Kent County
37	1566	9.0	**Romulus** (city) Wayne County
37	1566	9.0	**Tyrone** (township) Livingston County
40	1624	8.9	**Bangor** (charter township) Bay County
40	1624	8.9	**Benton** (charter township) Berrien County
40	1624	8.9	**Emmett** (charter township) Calhoun County
43	1683	8.8	**Hamburg** (township) Livingston County
43	1683	8.8	**Owosso** (city) Shiawassee County
43	1683	8.8	**Saint Clair Shores** (city) Macomb County
46	1748	8.7	**Hartland** (township) Livingston County
46	1748	8.7	**Sturgis** (city) Saint Joseph County
48	1835	8.5	**Green Oak** (township) Livingston County
48	1835	8.5	**Muskegon** (charter township) Muskegon County
50	1887	8.4	**Fenton** (city) Genesee County
50	1887	8.4	**Thomas** (township) Saginaw County
52	1931	8.3	**Holland** (city) Ottawa County
52	1931	8.3	**Milford** (charter township) Oakland County
54	1984	8.2	**Leoni** (township) Jackson County
54	1984	8.2	**Madison Heights** (city) Oakland County
54	1984	8.2	**Redford** (charter township) Wayne County
54	1984	8.2	**Washington** (township) Macomb County
54	1984	8.2	**White Lake** (charter township) Oakland County
54	1984	8.2	**Wyoming** (city) Kent County
60	2041	8.1	**Fraser** (city) Macomb County
60	2041	8.1	**Grand Haven** (charter township) Ottawa County
62	2093	8.0	**Warren** (city) Macomb County
63	2142	7.9	**Flushing** (charter township) Genesee County
63	2142	7.9	**Monitor** (charter township) Bay County
63	2142	7.9	**Waterford** (charter township) Oakland County
66	2189	7.8	**Escanaba** (city) Delta County
67	2240	7.7	**Mundy** (township) Genesee County
68	2306	7.6	**Burton** (city) Genesee County
68	2306	7.6	**Marquette** (city) Marquette County
68	2306	7.6	**Springfield** (charter township) Oakland County
68	2306	7.6	**Walker** (city) Kent County
68	2306	7.6	**Wayne** (city) Wayne County
73	2372	7.5	**Fort Gratiot** (charter township) Saint Clair County
73	2372	7.5	**Georgetown** (charter township) Ottawa County
75	2439	7.4	**Chesterfield** (township) Macomb County
76	2570	7.2	**Bay City** (city) Bay County
76	2570	7.2	**Coldwater** (city) Branch County
76	2570	7.2	**Holly** (township) Oakland County
76	2570	7.2	**Westland** (city) Wayne County
80	2639	7.1	**Grand Rapids** (city) Kent County
81	2692	7.0	**Comstock Park** (CDP) Kent County
81	2692	7.0	**Flint** (city) Genesee County
81	2692	7.0	**Kalamazoo** (charter township) Kalamazoo County
81	2692	7.0	**Livonia** (city) Wayne County
85	2750	6.9	**Caledonia** (township) Kent County
86	2807	6.8	**Clinton** (charter township) Macomb County
86	2807	6.8	**Mount Morris** (township) Genesee County
86	2807	6.8	**Woodhaven** (city) Wayne County
89	2855	6.7	**Jackson** (city) Jackson County
89	2855	6.7	**Van Buren** (charter township) Wayne County
91	2904	6.6	**Battle Creek** (city) Calhoun County
91	2904	6.6	**Eastpointe** (city) Macomb County
91	2904	6.6	**Flint** (charter township) Genesee County
91	2904	6.6	**Genoa** (township) Livingston County
91	2904	6.6	**Grandville** (city) Kent County
91	2904	6.6	**Mount Clemens** (city) Macomb County
97	2974	6.5	**Blackman** (charter township) Jackson County
97	2974	6.5	**Fenton** (charter township) Genesee County
97	2974	6.5	**Sault Sainte Marie** (city) Chippewa County
97	2974	6.5	**Sterling Heights** (city) Macomb County
101	3035	6.4	**Cadillac** (city) Wexford County
101	3035	6.4	**Dearborn Heights** (city) Wayne County
103	3112	6.3	**Detroit** (city) Wayne County
103	3112	6.3	**Grand Haven** (city) Ottawa County
103	3112	6.3	**Monroe** (charter township) Monroe County
103	3112	6.3	**Shelby** (charter township) Macomb County
103	3112	6.3	**Summit** (township) Jackson County
108	3158	6.2	**Beecher** (CDP) Genesee County
108	3158	6.2	**Clawson** (city) Oakland County
108	3158	6.2	**Midland** (city) Midland County
108	3158	6.2	**Port Huron** (city) Saint Clair County
112	3207	6.1	**Big Rapids** (city) Mecosta County
112	3207	6.1	**Brighton** (township) Livingston County
112	3207	6.1	**Davison** (township) Genesee County
112	3207	6.1	**Dearborn** (city) Wayne County
112	3207	6.1	**Fruitport** (charter township) Muskegon County
112	3207	6.1	**Hamtramck** (city) Wayne County
112	3207	6.1	**Lansing** (township) Ingham County
112	3207	6.1	**Monroe** (city) Monroe County
112	3207	6.1	**Park** (township) Ottawa County
112	3207	6.1	**Spring Lake** (township) Ottawa County
122	3276	6.0	**Independence** (charter township) Oakland County
122	3276	6.0	**South Lyon** (city) Oakland County
124	3341	5.9	**Macomb** (township) Macomb County
124	3341	5.9	**Portage** (city) Kalamazoo County
124	3341	5.9	**Ypsilanti** (charter township) Washtenaw County
127	3411	5.8	**Bridgeport** (charter township) Saginaw County
128	3458	5.7	**Harper Woods** (city) Wayne County
128	3458	5.7	**Niles** (city) Berrien County
128	3458	5.7	**Riverview** (city) Wayne County
131	3508	5.6	**Cannon** (township) Kent County
131	3508	5.6	**Inkster** (city) Wayne County
131	3508	5.6	**Lincoln** (charter township) Berrien County
131	3508	5.6	**Orion** (charter township) Oakland County
131	3508	5.6	**Saginaw** (city) Saginaw County
136	3584	5.4	**Adrian** (city) Lenawee County
136	3584	5.4	**Commerce** (charter township) Oakland County
136	3584	5.4	**Oxford** (charter township) Oakland County
139	3634	5.3	**Garfield** (charter township) Grand Traverse County
139	3634	5.3	**Lyon** (charter township) Oakland County
139	3634	5.3	**Muskegon Heights** (city) Muskegon County
139	3634	5.3	**Plainfield** (charter township) Kent County
139	3634	5.3	**Traverse City** (city) Grand Traverse County
144	3710	5.1	**Auburn Hills** (city) Oakland County
144	3710	5.1	**DeWitt** (charter township) Clinton County
144	3710	5.1	**Gaines** (charter township) Kent County
144	3710	5.1	**Muskegon** (city) Muskegon County
144	3710	5.1	**Superior** (charter township) Washtenaw County
149	3766	5.0	**Ferndale** (city) Oakland County
149	3766	5.0	**Grand Blanc** (charter township) Genesee County

Note: *The state column ranks the top/bottom 150 places from all places in the state with population of 10,000 or more. The national column ranks the top/bottom 150 places from all places in the country with population of 10,000 or more. Places that are unincorporated were not considered in the rankings. Please refer to the User Guide for additional information.*

Employment: Natural Resources, Construction, and Maintenance Occupations

Top 150 Places Ranked in *Ascending* Order

State Rank	Nat'l Rank	Percent	Place	State Rank	Nat'l Rank	Percent	Place
1	24	1.3	**East Grand Rapids** (city) Kent County	75	1149	5.7	**Niles** (city) Berrien County
2	37	1.5	**Haslett** (CDP) Ingham County	75	1149	5.7	**Riverview** (city) Wayne County
3	71	1.9	**Southfield** (township) Oakland County	78	1199	5.8	**Bridgeport** (charter township) Saginaw County
4	99	2.1	**Cascade** (charter township) Kent County	79	1246	5.9	**Macomb** (township) Macomb County
5	112	2.2	**Beverly Hills** (village) Oakland County	79	1246	5.9	**Portage** (city) Kalamazoo County
6	127	2.3	**Birmingham** (city) Oakland County	79	1246	5.9	**Ypsilanti** (charter township) Washtenaw County
6	127	2.3	**Bloomfield** (charter township) Oakland County	82	1316	6.0	**Independence** (charter township) Oakland County
6	127	2.3	**Meridian** (charter township) Ingham County	82	1316	6.0	**South Lyon** (city) Oakland County
9	138	2.4	**Forest Hills** (CDP) Kent County	84	1381	6.1	**Big Rapids** (city) Mecosta County
10	151	2.5	**Ann Arbor** (city) Washtenaw County	84	1381	6.1	**Brighton** (township) Livingston County
11	169	2.6	**Grosse Pointe Park** (city) Wayne County	84	1381	6.1	**Davison** (township) Genesee County
11	169	2.6	**Novi** (city) Oakland County	84	1381	6.1	**Dearborn** (city) Wayne County
13	187	2.7	**East Lansing** (city) Ingham County	84	1381	6.1	**Fruitport** (charter township) Muskegon County
14	236	3.0	**Pittsfield** (charter township) Washtenaw County	84	1381	6.1	**Hamtramck** (city) Wayne County
14	236	3.0	**Plymouth** (charter township) Wayne County	84	1381	6.1	**Lansing** (city) Ingham County
14	236	3.0	**Saint Joseph** (charter township) Berrien County	84	1381	6.1	**Monroe** (city) Monroe County
17	257	3.1	**Ada** (township) Kent County	84	1381	6.1	**Park** (township) Ottawa County
17	257	3.1	**Highland Park** (city) Wayne County	84	1381	6.1	**Spring Lake** (township) Ottawa County
19	281	3.2	**Mount Pleasant** (city) Isabella County	94	1450	6.2	**Beecher** (CDP) Genesee County
20	308	3.3	**Troy** (city) Oakland County	94	1450	6.2	**Clawson** (city) Oakland County
21	324	3.4	**Berkley** (city) Oakland County	94	1450	6.2	**Midland** (city) Midland County
21	324	3.4	**Farmington Hills** (city) Oakland County	94	1450	6.2	**Port Huron** (city) Saint Clair County
21	324	3.4	**Northville** (township) Wayne County	98	1499	6.3	**Detroit** (city) Wayne County
24	377	3.6	**Okemos** (CDP) Ingham County	98	1499	6.3	**Grand Haven** (city) Ottawa County
24	377	3.6	**Royal Oak** (city) Oakland County	98	1499	6.3	**Monroe** (charter township) Monroe County
24	377	3.6	**West Bloomfield** (charter township) Oakland County	98	1499	6.3	**Shelby** (charter township) Macomb County
27	407	3.7	**Southfield** (city) Oakland County	98	1499	6.3	**Summit** (township) Jackson County
28	442	3.8	**Delta** (charter township) Eaton County	103	1545	6.4	**Cadillac** (city) Wexford County
28	442	3.8	**Rochester Hills** (city) Oakland County	103	1545	6.4	**Dearborn Heights** (city) Wayne County
30	466	3.9	**Waverly** (CDP) Eaton County	105	1622	6.5	**Blackman** (charter township) Jackson County
31	518	4.1	**Benton Harbor** (city) Berrien County	105	1622	6.5	**Fenton** (charter township) Genesee County
32	553	4.2	**Rochester** (city) Oakland County	105	1622	6.5	**Sault Sainte Marie** (city) Chippewa County
33	608	4.4	**Farmington** (city) Oakland County	105	1622	6.5	**Sterling Heights** (city) Macomb County
33	608	4.4	**Holt** (CDP) Ingham County	109	1683	6.6	**Battle Creek** (city) Calhoun County
33	608	4.4	**Norton Shores** (city) Muskegon County	109	1683	6.6	**Eastpointe** (city) Macomb County
33	608	4.4	**Oshtemo** (charter township) Kalamazoo County	109	1683	6.6	**Flint** (charter township) Genesee County
37	641	4.5	**Delhi** (charter township) Ingham County	109	1683	6.6	**Genoa** (township) Livingston County
37	641	4.5	**Grosse Pointe Woods** (city) Wayne County	109	1683	6.6	**Grandville** (city) Kent County
37	641	4.5	**Kentwood** (city) Kent County	109	1683	6.6	**Mount Clemens** (city) Macomb County
40	692	4.6	**Bath** (charter township) Clinton County	115	1753	6.7	**Jackson** (city) Jackson County
40	692	4.6	**Scio** (township) Washtenaw County	115	1753	6.7	**Van Buren** (charter township) Wayne County
40	692	4.6	**Union** (charter township) Isabella County	117	1802	6.8	**Clinton** (charter township) Macomb County
43	729	4.7	**Canton** (charter township) Wayne County	117	1802	6.8	**Mount Morris** (township) Genesee County
43	729	4.7	**Ypsilanti** (city) Washtenaw County	117	1802	6.8	**Woodhaven** (city) Wayne County
45	765	4.8	**Alpena** (city) Alpena County	120	1850	6.9	**Caledonia** (township) Kent County
45	765	4.8	**Grand Rapids** (charter township) Kent County	121	1907	7.0	**Comstock Park** (CDP) Kent County
45	765	4.8	**Grosse Ile** (township) Wayne County	121	1907	7.0	**Flint** (city) Genesee County
45	765	4.8	**Kalamazoo** (city) Kalamazoo County	121	1907	7.0	**Kalamazoo** (charter township) Kalamazoo County
45	765	4.8	**Oakland** (charter township) Oakland County	121	1907	7.0	**Livonia** (city) Wayne County
50	813	4.9	**Northview** (CDP) Kent County	125	1965	7.1	**Grand Rapids** (city) Kent County
50	813	4.9	**Oak Park** (city) Oakland County	126	2018	7.2	**Bay City** (city) Bay County
50	813	4.9	**Wixom** (city) Oakland County	126	2018	7.2	**Coldwater** (city) Branch County
53	846	5.0	**Ferndale** (city) Oakland County	126	2018	7.2	**Holly** (township) Oakland County
53	846	5.0	**Grand Blanc** (charter township) Genesee County	126	2018	7.2	**Westland** (city) Wayne County
53	846	5.0	**Saginaw** (charter township) Saginaw County	130	2145	7.4	**Chesterfield** (township) Macomb County
53	846	5.0	**Texas** (charter township) Kalamazoo County	131	2218	7.5	**Fort Gratiot** (charter township) Saint Clair County
57	891	5.1	**Auburn Hills** (city) Oakland County	131	2218	7.5	**Georgetown** (charter township) Ottawa County
57	891	5.1	**DeWitt** (charter township) Clinton County	133	2285	7.6	**Burton** (city) Genesee County
57	891	5.1	**Gaines** (charter township) Kent County	133	2285	7.6	**Marquette** (city) Marquette County
57	891	5.1	**Muskegon** (city) Muskegon County	133	2285	7.6	**Springfield** (charter township) Oakland County
57	891	5.1	**Superior** (charter township) Washtenaw County	133	2285	7.6	**Walker** (city) Kent County
62	987	5.3	**Garfield** (charter township) Grand Traverse County	133	2285	7.6	**Wayne** (city) Wayne County
62	987	5.3	**Lyon** (charter township) Oakland County	138	2351	7.7	**Mundy** (township) Genesee County
62	987	5.3	**Muskegon Heights** (city) Muskegon County	139	2417	7.8	**Escanaba** (city) Delta County
62	987	5.3	**Plainfield** (charter township) Kent County	140	2468	7.9	**Flushing** (charter township) Genesee County
62	987	5.3	**Traverse City** (city) Grand Traverse County	140	2468	7.9	**Monitor** (charter township) Bay County
67	1023	5.4	**Adrian** (city) Lenawee County	140	2468	7.9	**Waterford** (charter township) Oakland County
67	1023	5.4	**Commerce** (charter township) Oakland County	143	2515	8.0	**Warren** (city) Macomb County
67	1023	5.4	**Oxford** (charter township) Oakland County	144	2564	8.1	**Fraser** (city) Macomb County
70	1109	5.6	**Cannon** (township) Kent County	144	2564	8.1	**Grand Haven** (charter township) Ottawa County
70	1109	5.6	**Inkster** (city) Wayne County	146	2616	8.2	**Leoni** (township) Jackson County
70	1109	5.6	**Lincoln** (charter township) Berrien County	146	2616	8.2	**Madison Heights** (city) Oakland County
70	1109	5.6	**Orion** (charter township) Oakland County	146	2616	8.2	**Redford** (charter township) Wayne County
70	1109	5.6	**Saginaw** (city) Saginaw County	146	2616	8.2	**Washington** (township) Macomb County
75	1149	5.7	**Harper Woods** (city) Wayne County	146	2616	8.2	**White Lake** (charter township) Oakland County

Note: The state column ranks the top/bottom 150 places from all places in the state with population of 10,000 or more. The national column ranks the top/bottom 150 places from all places in the country with population of 10,000 or more. Places that are unincorporated were not considered in the rankings. Please refer to the User Guide for additional information.

Employment: Production, Transportation, and Material Moving Occupations

Top 150 Places Ranked in *Descending* Order

State Rank	Nat'l Rank	Percent	Place
1	14	33.6	**Muskegon Heights** (city) Muskegon County
2	33	30.7	**Cadillac** (city) Wexford County
3	54	28.9	**Sturgis** (city) Saint Joseph County
4	85	27.1	**Holland** (charter township) Ottawa County
5	86	27.0	**Hamtramck** (city) Wayne County
6	116	25.7	**Romulus** (city) Wayne County
7	128	25.1	**Holland** (city) Ottawa County
8	137	24.6	**Fruitport** (charter township) Muskegon County
9	173	23.9	**Muskegon** (charter township) Muskegon County
9	173	23.9	**Niles** (township) Berrien County
11	184	23.5	**Coldwater** (city) Branch County
12	186	23.4	**Frenchtown** (township) Monroe County
13	193	23.2	**Ionia** (city) Ionia County
14	208	22.9	**Port Huron** (charter township) Saint Clair County
15	210	22.8	**Cutlerville** (CDP) Kent County
15	210	22.8	**Niles** (city) Berrien County
17	221	22.5	**Monroe** (city) Monroe County
18	227	22.4	**Hazel Park** (city) Oakland County
19	240	22.1	**Garden City** (city) Wayne County
20	246	22.0	**Leoni** (township) Jackson County
21	254	21.9	**Melvindale** (city) Wayne County
22	270	21.5	**Wyoming** (city) Kent County
23	278	21.4	**Inkster** (city) Wayne County
23	278	21.4	**Taylor** (city) Wayne County
25	301	21.1	**Wayne** (city) Wayne County
26	332	20.7	**Lincoln Park** (city) Wayne County
27	346	20.6	**Muskegon** (city) Muskegon County
28	356	20.5	**Monroe** (charter township) Monroe County
29	368	20.4	**Battle Creek** (city) Calhoun County
30	391	20.1	**Huron** (charter township) Wayne County
31	423	19.7	**Burton** (city) Genesee County
32	438	19.5	**Owosso** (city) Shiawassee County
32	438	19.5	**Roseville** (city) Macomb County
34	453	19.4	**Beecher** (CDP) Genesee County
34	453	19.4	**Eastpointe** (city) Macomb County
36	459	19.3	**Port Huron** (city) Saint Clair County
37	468	19.2	**Alpine** (township) Kent County
37	468	19.2	**Comstock Park** (CDP) Kent County
37	468	19.2	**Genesee** (charter township) Genesee County
37	468	19.2	**Lenox** (township) Macomb County
41	476	19.1	**Benton** (charter township) Berrien County
42	488	19.0	**Jackson** (city) Jackson County
43	512	18.7	**Flint** (city) Genesee County
43	512	18.7	**Kentwood** (city) Kent County
45	522	18.6	**Bridgeport** (charter township) Saginaw County
45	522	18.6	**Emmett** (charter township) Calhoun County
47	556	18.3	**Benton Harbor** (city) Berrien County
47	556	18.3	**Highland Park** (city) Wayne County
49	591	18.1	**Blackman** (charter township) Jackson County
49	591	18.1	**Redford** (charter township) Wayne County
51	610	18.0	**Bedford** (township) Monroe County
52	627	17.9	**Gaines** (charter township) Kent County
53	639	17.8	**Adrian** (city) Lenawee County
53	639	17.8	**Escanaba** (city) Delta County
55	651	17.7	**Jenison** (CDP) Ottawa County
55	651	17.7	**Woodhaven** (city) Wayne County
57	691	17.4	**Detroit** (city) Wayne County
57	691	17.4	**Flint** (charter township) Genesee County
57	691	17.4	**Mount Morris** (township) Genesee County
60	707	17.3	**Grand Haven** (city) Ottawa County
60	707	17.3	**Van Buren** (charter township) Wayne County
62	739	17.1	**Grand Rapids** (city) Kent County
63	754	17.0	**Davison** (township) Genesee County
64	770	16.9	**Warren** (city) Macomb County
65	787	16.8	**Fenton** (city) Genesee County
65	787	16.8	**Westland** (city) Wayne County
67	808	16.6	**Park** (township) Ottawa County
68	825	16.5	**Grandville** (city) Kent County
69	860	16.3	**Saginaw** (city) Saginaw County
70	876	16.2	**Mundy** (township) Genesee County
71	909	16.0	**Byron** (township) Kent County
71	909	16.0	**Chesterfield** (township) Macomb County
73	929	15.9	**Dearborn Heights** (city) Wayne County
73	929	15.9	**Pontiac** (city) Oakland County
75	949	15.8	**Holly** (township) Oakland County
75	949	15.8	**Wyandotte** (city) Wayne County
77	972	15.7	**Bay City** (city) Bay County
77	972	15.7	**Fort Gratiot** (charter township) Saint Clair County
79	1035	15.4	**Cooper** (charter township) Kalamazoo County
79	1035	15.4	**Grand Haven** (charter township) Ottawa County
81	1107	15.0	**Allen Park** (city) Wayne County
81	1107	15.0	**Highland** (charter township) Oakland County
81	1107	15.0	**Mount Clemens** (city) Macomb County
81	1107	15.0	**Southgate** (city) Wayne County
85	1128	14.9	**Lansing** (city) Ingham County
86	1152	14.8	**Clinton** (charter township) Macomb County
86	1152	14.8	**Monitor** (charter township) Bay County
88	1163	14.7	**Comstock** (charter township) Kalamazoo County
88	1163	14.7	**Madison Heights** (city) Oakland County
90	1184	14.6	**Brownstown** (charter township) Wayne County
91	1203	14.5	**Norton Shores** (city) Muskegon County
92	1224	14.4	**Georgetown** (charter township) Ottawa County
93	1249	14.3	**Bangor** (charter township) Bay County
94	1288	14.1	**Alpena** (city) Alpena County
94	1288	14.1	**Northview** (CDP) Kent County
96	1316	14.0	**Dearborn** (city) Wayne County
96	1316	14.0	**Summit** (township) Jackson County
98	1337	13.9	**Sterling Heights** (city) Macomb County
99	1416	13.6	**Allendale** (charter township) Ottawa County
99	1416	13.6	**Riverview** (city) Wayne County
99	1416	13.6	**Thomas** (township) Saginaw County
99	1416	13.6	**Vienna** (charter township) Genesee County
99	1416	13.6	**Walker** (city) Kent County
104	1442	13.5	**Caledonia** (township) Kent County
105	1483	13.3	**Antwerp** (township) Van Buren County
105	1483	13.3	**Fraser** (city) Macomb County
107	1552	13.0	**Harper Woods** (city) Wayne County
108	1582	12.9	**Fenton** (charter township) Genesee County
109	1608	12.8	**Kalamazoo** (charter township) Kalamazoo County
109	1608	12.8	**Saint Clair Shores** (city) Macomb County
109	1608	12.8	**Saint Joseph** (charter township) Berrien County
109	1608	12.8	**Washington** (township) Macomb County
109	1608	12.8	**Ypsilanti** (charter township) Washtenaw County
114	1633	12.7	**Harrison** (charter township) Macomb County
115	1665	12.6	**Allendale** (CDP) Ottawa County
116	1723	12.4	**Flushing** (charter township) Genesee County
116	1723	12.4	**Plainfield** (charter township) Kent County
118	1815	12.1	**Tyrone** (township) Livingston County
119	1868	11.9	**Shelby** (charter township) Macomb County
120	1893	11.8	**Spring Lake** (township) Ottawa County
120	1893	11.8	**Waverly** (CDP) Eaton County
122	1958	11.6	**Kalamazoo** (city) Kalamazoo County
123	1994	11.5	**Trenton** (city) Wayne County
124	2015	11.4	**Big Rapids** (city) Mecosta County
124	2015	11.4	**Saginaw** (charter township) Saginaw County
126	2043	11.3	**Garfield** (charter township) Grand Traverse County
126	2043	11.3	**Oxford** (charter township) Oakland County
128	2080	11.2	**Brandon** (charter township) Oakland County
128	2080	11.2	**Hamburg** (township) Livingston County
130	2115	11.1	**Green Oak** (township) Livingston County
130	2115	11.1	**Lyon** (charter township) Oakland County
130	2115	11.1	**New Baltimore** (city) Macomb County
130	2115	11.1	**Orion** (charter township) Oakland County
130	2115	11.1	**Waterford** (charter township) Oakland County
135	2146	11.0	**Macomb** (township) Macomb County
136	2211	10.8	**Delta** (charter township) Eaton County
136	2211	10.8	**Holt** (CDP) Ingham County
136	2211	10.8	**Oak Park** (city) Oakland County
139	2253	10.7	**Genoa** (township) Livingston County
140	2288	10.6	**Brighton** (township) Livingston County
140	2288	10.6	**DeWitt** (charter township) Clinton County
140	2288	10.6	**Delhi** (charter township) Ingham County
140	2288	10.6	**Grand Blanc** (charter township) Genesee County
140	2288	10.6	**Lincoln** (charter township) Berrien County
140	2288	10.6	**Portage** (city) Kalamazoo County
140	2288	10.6	**Southfield** (city) Oakland County
147	2415	10.2	**Hartland** (township) Livingston County
148	2450	10.1	**Auburn Hills** (city) Oakland County
148	2450	10.1	**Grosse Ile** (township) Wayne County
148	2450	10.1	**Oshtemo** (charter township) Kalamazoo County

Note: *The state column ranks the top/bottom 150 places from all places in the state with population of 10,000 or more. The national column ranks the top/bottom 150 places from all places in the country with population of 10,000 or more. Places that are unincorporated were not considered in the rankings. Please refer to the User Guide for additional information.*

Employment: Production, Transportation, and Material Moving Occupations

Top 150 Places Ranked in *Ascending* Order

State Rank	Nat'l Rank	Percent	Place	State Rank	Nat'l Rank	Percent	Place
1	26	1.7	**Birmingham** (city) Oakland County	76	2542	11.2	**Brandon** (charter township) Oakland County
2	168	3.2	**East Grand Rapids** (city) Kent County	76	2542	11.2	**Hamburg** (township) Livingston County
3	188	3.3	**Grosse Pointe Woods** (city) Wayne County	78	2577	11.3	**Garfield** (charter township) Grand Traverse County
4	197	3.4	**Southfield** (township) Oakland County	78	2577	11.3	**Oxford** (charter township) Oakland County
5	214	3.5	**Bloomfield** (charter township) Oakland County	80	2614	11.4	**Big Rapids** (city) Mecosta County
6	235	3.6	**Ada** (township) Kent County	80	2614	11.4	**Saginaw** (charter township) Saginaw County
6	235	3.6	**Okemos** (CDP) Ingham County	82	2642	11.5	**Trenton** (city) Wayne County
8	254	3.7	**East Lansing** (city) Ingham County	83	2663	11.6	**Kalamazoo** (city) Kalamazoo County
9	269	3.8	**Beverly Hills** (village) Oakland County	84	2734	11.8	**Spring Lake** (township) Ottawa County
10	352	4.2	**Grosse Pointe Park** (city) Wayne County	84	2734	11.8	**Waverly** (CDP) Eaton County
10	352	4.2	**Meridian** (charter township) Ingham County	86	2764	11.9	**Shelby** (charter township) Macomb County
12	398	4.4	**Ann Arbor** (city) Washtenaw County	87	2816	12.1	**Tyrone** (township) Livingston County
12	398	4.4	**Rochester** (city) Oakland County	88	2898	12.4	**Flushing** (charter township) Genesee County
14	470	4.7	**Northville** (township) Wayne County	88	2898	12.4	**Plainfield** (charter township) Kent County
15	491	4.8	**West Bloomfield** (charter township) Oakland County	90	2964	12.6	**Allendale** (CDP) Ottawa County
16	548	5.0	**Oakland** (charter township) Oakland County	91	2992	12.7	**Harrison** (charter township) Macomb County
17	569	5.1	**Haslett** (CDP) Ingham County	92	3024	12.8	**Kalamazoo** (charter township) Kalamazoo County
17	569	5.1	**Rochester Hills** (city) Oakland County	92	3024	12.8	**Saint Clair Shores** (city) Macomb County
19	664	5.4	**Scio** (township) Washtenaw County	92	3024	12.8	**Saint Joseph** (charter township) Berrien County
20	792	5.9	**Troy** (city) Oakland County	92	3024	12.8	**Washington** (township) Macomb County
21	817	6.0	**Forest Hills** (CDP) Kent County	92	3024	12.8	**Ypsilanti** (charter township) Washtenaw County
21	817	6.0	**Union** (charter township) Isabella County	97	3049	12.9	**Fenton** (charter township) Genesee County
23	853	6.1	**Mount Pleasant** (city) Isabella County	98	3075	13.0	**Harper Woods** (city) Wayne County
24	916	6.3	**Farmington** (city) Oakland County	99	3149	13.3	**Antwerp** (township) Van Buren County
25	942	6.4	**Novi** (city) Oakland County	99	3149	13.3	**Fraser** (city) Macomb County
26	970	6.5	**Royal Oak** (city) Oakland County	101	3200	13.5	**Caledonia** (township) Kent County
27	1020	6.7	**Marquette** (city) Marquette County	102	3215	13.6	**Allendale** (charter township) Ottawa County
28	1049	6.8	**Farmington Hills** (city) Oakland County	102	3215	13.6	**Riverview** (city) Wayne County
29	1123	7.0	**Plymouth** (charter township) Wayne County	102	3215	13.6	**Thomas** (township) Saginaw County
30	1193	7.3	**Cannon** (township) Kent County	102	3215	13.6	**Vienna** (charter township) Genesee County
31	1301	7.6	**Bath** (charter township) Clinton County	102	3215	13.6	**Walker** (city) Kent County
32	1325	7.7	**Oceola** (township) Livingston County	107	3294	13.9	**Sterling Heights** (city) Macomb County
32	1325	7.7	**Traverse City** (city) Grand Traverse County	108	3320	14.0	**Dearborn** (city) Wayne County
34	1362	7.8	**Grand Rapids** (charter township) Kent County	108	3320	14.0	**Summit** (township) Jackson County
34	1362	7.8	**Pittsfield** (charter township) Washtenaw County	110	3341	14.1	**Alpena** (city) Alpena County
36	1444	8.0	**Berkley** (city) Oakland County	110	3341	14.1	**Northview** (CDP) Kent County
36	1444	8.0	**Sault Sainte Marie** (city) Chippewa County	112	3388	14.3	**Bangor** (charter township) Bay County
36	1444	8.0	**South Lyon** (city) Oakland County	113	3408	14.4	**Georgetown** (charter township) Ottawa County
39	1479	8.1	**Cascade** (charter township) Kent County	114	3433	14.5	**Norton Shores** (city) Muskegon County
40	1515	8.2	**Texas** (charter township) Kalamazoo County	115	3454	14.6	**Brownstown** (charter township) Wayne County
41	1684	8.7	**Midland** (city) Midland County	116	3473	14.7	**Comstock** (charter township) Kalamazoo County
42	1718	8.8	**East Bay** (township) Grand Traverse County	116	3473	14.7	**Madison Heights** (city) Oakland County
43	1898	9.3	**White Lake** (charter township) Oakland County	118	3494	14.8	**Clinton** (charter township) Macomb County
44	1926	9.4	**Wixom** (city) Oakland County	118	3494	14.8	**Monitor** (charter township) Bay County
45	1957	9.5	**Ferndale** (city) Oakland County	120	3505	14.9	**Lansing** (city) Ingham County
45	1957	9.5	**Milford** (charter township) Oakland County	121	3529	15.0	**Allen Park** (city) Wayne County
47	1997	9.6	**Canton** (charter township) Wayne County	121	3529	15.0	**Highland** (charter township) Oakland County
47	1997	9.6	**Independence** (charter township) Oakland County	121	3529	15.0	**Mount Clemens** (city) Macomb County
49	2032	9.7	**Livonia** (city) Wayne County	121	3529	15.0	**Southgate** (city) Wayne County
50	2106	9.9	**Clawson** (city) Oakland County	125	3607	15.4	**Cooper** (charter township) Kalamazoo County
50	2106	9.9	**Superior** (charter township) Washtenaw County	125	3607	15.4	**Grand Haven** (charter township) Ottawa County
52	2134	10.0	**Commerce** (charter township) Oakland County	127	3661	15.7	**Bay City** (city) Bay County
53	2173	10.1	**Auburn Hills** (city) Oakland County	127	3661	15.7	**Fort Gratiot** (charter township) Saint Clair County
53	2173	10.1	**Grosse Ile** (township) Wayne County	129	3685	15.8	**Holly** (township) Oakland County
53	2173	10.1	**Oshtemo** (charter township) Kalamazoo County	129	3685	15.8	**Wyandotte** (city) Wayne County
53	2173	10.1	**Springfield** (charter township) Oakland County	131	3708	15.9	**Dearborn Heights** (city) Wayne County
53	2173	10.1	**Ypsilanti** (city) Washtenaw County	131	3708	15.9	**Pontiac** (city) Oakland County
58	2207	10.2	**Hartland** (township) Livingston County	133	3728	16.0	**Byron** (township) Kent County
59	2322	10.6	**Brighton** (township) Livingston County	133	3728	16.0	**Chesterfield** (township) Macomb County
59	2322	10.6	**DeWitt** (charter township) Clinton County	135	3767	16.2	**Mundy** (township) Genesee County
59	2322	10.6	**Delhi** (charter township) Ingham County	136	3781	16.3	**Saginaw** (city) Saginaw County
59	2322	10.6	**Grand Blanc** (charter township) Genesee County	137	3818	16.5	**Grandville** (city) Kent County
59	2322	10.6	**Lincoln** (charter township) Berrien County	138	3832	16.6	**Park** (township) Ottawa County
59	2322	10.6	**Portage** (city) Kalamazoo County	139	3860	16.8	**Fenton** (city) Genesee County
59	2322	10.6	**Southfield** (city) Oakland County	139	3860	16.8	**Westland** (city) Wayne County
66	2369	10.7	**Genoa** (township) Livingston County	141	3870	16.9	**Warren** (city) Macomb County
67	2404	10.8	**Delta** (charter township) Eaton County	142	3887	17.0	**Davison** (township) Genesee County
67	2404	10.8	**Holt** (CDP) Ingham County	143	3903	17.1	**Grand Rapids** (city) Kent County
67	2404	10.8	**Oak Park** (city) Oakland County	144	3939	17.3	**Grand Haven** (city) Ottawa County
70	2477	11.0	**Macomb** (township) Macomb County	144	3939	17.3	**Van Buren** (charter township) Wayne County
71	2511	11.1	**Green Oak** (township) Livingston County	146	3950	17.4	**Detroit** (city) Wayne County
71	2511	11.1	**Lyon** (charter township) Oakland County	146	3950	17.4	**Flint** (charter township) Genesee County
71	2511	11.1	**New Baltimore** (city) Macomb County	146	3950	17.4	**Mount Morris** (township) Genesee County
71	2511	11.1	**Orion** (charter township) Oakland County	149	3989	17.7	**Jenison** (CDP) Ottawa County
71	2511	11.1	**Waterford** (charter township) Oakland County	149	3989	17.7	**Woodhaven** (city) Wayne County

Note: The state column ranks the top/bottom 150 places from all places in the state with population of 10,000 or more. The national column ranks the top/bottom 150 places from all places in the country with population of 10,000 or more. Places that are unincorporated were not considered in the rankings. Please refer to the User Guide for additional information.

Per Capita Income

Top 150 Places Ranked in *Descending* Order

State Rank	Nat'l Rank	Dollars	Place
1	79	67,663	**Birmingham** (city) Oakland County
2	110	62,730	**Bloomfield** (charter township) Oakland County
3	129	60,134	**Southfield** (township) Oakland County
4	211	54,452	**East Grand Rapids** (city) Kent County
5	250	52,571	**Beverly Hills** (village) Oakland County
6	262	52,093	**Oakland** (charter township) Oakland County
7	267	51,883	**Northville** (township) Wayne County
8	283	50,936	**Cascade** (charter township) Kent County
9	288	50,807	**Forest Hills** (CDP) Kent County
10	296	50,430	**Grosse Pointe Park** (city) Wayne County
11	367	47,925	**Ada** (township) Kent County
12	373	47,856	**West Bloomfield** (charter township) Oakland County
13	394	47,321	**Rochester** (city) Oakland County
14	511	44,390	**Novi** (city) Oakland County
15	515	44,329	**Scio** (township) Washtenaw County
16	541	43,889	**Plymouth** (charter township) Wayne County
17	618	42,685	**Grosse Ile** (township) Wayne County
18	723	40,837	**Texas** (charter township) Kalamazoo County
19	733	40,604	**Farmington Hills** (city) Oakland County
20	778	40,022	**Troy** (city) Oakland County
21	792	39,889	**Okemos** (CDP) Ingham County
22	809	39,736	**Grosse Pointe Woods** (city) Wayne County
23	855	39,086	**Grand Rapids** (charter township) Kent County
24	870	38,893	**Royal Oak** (city) Oakland County
25	871	38,892	**Rochester Hills** (city) Oakland County
26	945	37,954	**Milford** (charter township) Oakland County
27	964	37,732	**Meridian** (charter township) Ingham County
28	994	37,444	**Superior** (charter township) Washtenaw County
29	1004	37,350	**Brighton** (township) Livingston County
30	1025	37,091	**Commerce** (charter township) Oakland County
31	1063	36,579	**Genoa** (township) Livingston County
32	1067	36,556	**Springfield** (charter township) Oakland County
33	1165	35,635	**Berkley** (city) Oakland County
34	1174	35,562	**Washington** (township) Macomb County
35	1179	35,516	**Pittsfield** (charter township) Washtenaw County
36	1216	35,195	**Haslett** (CDP) Ingham County
37	1225	35,101	**Hamburg** (township) Livingston County
38	1242	34,959	**Cannon** (township) Kent County
39	1314	34,409	**Canton** (charter township) Wayne County
40	1337	34,247	**Ann Arbor** (city) Washtenaw County
41	1349	34,164	**Independence** (charter township) Oakland County
42	1369	33,989	**Lyon** (charter township) Oakland County
43	1394	33,779	**Farmington** (city) Oakland County
44	1399	33,721	**Orion** (charter township) Oakland County
45	1453	33,258	**Green Oak** (township) Livingston County
46	1468	33,170	**Park** (township) Ottawa County
47	1483	33,053	**Lincoln** (charter township) Berrien County
48	1484	33,046	**Saint Joseph** (charter township) Berrien County
49	1530	32,730	**Tyrone** (township) Livingston County
50	1581	32,290	**Delta** (charter township) Eaton County
51	1589	32,249	**Livonia** (city) Wayne County
52	1617	32,057	**Oxford** (charter township) Oakland County
53	1629	31,948	**Fenton** (charter township) Genesee County
54	1658	31,805	**White Lake** (charter township) Oakland County
55	1661	31,775	**Hartland** (township) Livingston County
56	1668	31,715	**Macomb** (township) Macomb County
57	1678	31,627	**Midland** (city) Midland County
58	1691	31,547	**Oceola** (township) Livingston County
59	1700	31,494	**Grand Haven** (charter township) Ottawa County
60	1736	31,259	**Harrison** (charter township) Macomb County
61	1758	31,100	**Waverly** (CDP) Eaton County
62	1770	30,972	**New Baltimore** (city) Macomb County
63	1774	30,947	**Shelby** (charter township) Macomb County
64	1793	30,843	**South Lyon** (city) Oakland County
65	1821	30,686	**Woodhaven** (city) Wayne County
66	1852	30,537	**Fort Gratiot** (charter township) Saint Clair County
67	1863	30,482	**Spring Lake** (township) Ottawa County
68	1870	30,447	**Wixom** (city) Oakland County
69	1897	30,241	**DeWitt** (charter township) Clinton County
70	1917	30,084	**Grand Blanc** (charter township) Genesee County
71	1938	29,961	**Clawson** (city) Oakland County
72	1939	29,959	**Caledonia** (township) Kent County
73	1954	29,779	**Thomas** (township) Saginaw County
74	1961	29,738	**Portage** (city) Kalamazoo County
75	1984	29,593	**Traverse City** (city) Grand Traverse County
76	1987	29,575	**Highland** (charter township) Oakland County
77	1993	29,554	**Bedford** (township) Monroe County
78	1994	29,546	**Bath** (charter township) Clinton County
79	2006	29,479	**Saint Clair Shores** (city) Macomb County
80	2020	29,375	**Plainfield** (charter township) Kent County
81	2049	29,221	**Chesterfield** (charter township) Macomb County
82	2071	29,067	**Saginaw** (charter township) Saginaw County
83	2073	29,064	**Delhi** (charter township) Ingham County
84	2080	29,038	**Northview** (CDP) Kent County
85	2102	28,915	**Monitor** (charter township) Bay County
86	2133	28,740	**Holt** (CDP) Ingham County
87	2139	28,717	**Waterford** (charter township) Oakland County
88	2149	28,635	**Southfield** (city) Oakland County
89	2164	28,578	**Summit** (township) Jackson County
90	2188	28,474	**Fraser** (city) Macomb County
91	2200	28,431	**Brownstown** (charter township) Wayne County
92	2227	28,254	**Ferndale** (city) Oakland County
93	2232	28,219	**Brandon** (charter township) Oakland County
94	2273	27,997	**Van Buren** (charter township) Wayne County
95	2286	27,918	**Oshtemo** (charter township) Kalamazoo County
96	2304	27,790	**Trenton** (city) Wayne County
97	2317	27,740	**Georgetown** (charter township) Ottawa County
98	2382	27,325	**Norton Shores** (city) Muskegon County
99	2396	27,243	**Flushing** (charter township) Genesee County
100	2407	27,177	**Huron** (charter township) Wayne County
101	2415	27,082	**Allen Park** (city) Wayne County
102	2436	26,996	**Bangor** (charter township) Bay County
103	2456	26,917	**Byron** (township) Kent County
104	2460	26,904	**Holly** (township) Oakland County
105	2476	26,843	**Auburn Hills** (city) Oakland County
106	2496	26,704	**East Bay** (township) Grand Traverse County
107	2499	26,694	**Walker** (city) Kent County
108	2500	26,691	**Sterling Heights** (city) Macomb County
109	2521	26,597	**Cooper** (charter township) Kalamazoo County
110	2542	26,485	**Gaines** (charter township) Kent County
111	2578	26,261	**Comstock** (charter township) Kalamazoo County
112	2586	26,217	**Garfield** (charter township) Grand Traverse County
113	2593	26,168	**Clinton** (charter township) Macomb County
114	2620	26,056	**Emmett** (charter township) Calhoun County
115	2624	26,014	**Mundy** (township) Genesee County
116	2634	25,978	**Grand Haven** (city) Ottawa County
117	2639	25,953	**Davison** (township) Genesee County
118	2646	25,903	**Southgate** (city) Wayne County
119	2742	25,415	**Antwerp** (township) Van Buren County
120	2762	25,287	**Wyandotte** (city) Wayne County
121	2808	24,982	**Riverview** (city) Wayne County
122	2842	24,851	**Kentwood** (city) Kent County
123	2877	24,722	**Monroe** (charter township) Monroe County
124	2920	24,447	**Fruitport** (charter township) Muskegon County
125	2974	24,141	**Grandville** (city) Kent County
126	2984	24,096	**Ypsilanti** (charter township) Washtenaw County
127	2991	24,058	**Jenison** (CDP) Ottawa County
128	3000	23,997	**Garden City** (city) Wayne County
129	3003	23,993	**Westland** (city) Wayne County
130	3037	23,841	**Fenton** (city) Genesee County
131	3123	23,386	**Vienna** (charter township) Genesee County
132	3190	23,078	**Frenchtown** (township) Monroe County
133	3241	22,853	**Redford** (charter township) Wayne County
134	3277	22,653	**Monroe** (city) Monroe County
135	3305	22,538	**Alpine** (township) Kent County
136	3312	22,522	**Niles** (township) Berrien County
137	3349	22,347	**Flint** (charter township) Genesee County
138	3384	22,154	**Battle Creek** (city) Calhoun County
139	3397	22,113	**Madison Heights** (city) Oakland County
140	3399	22,097	**Kalamazoo** (charter township) Kalamazoo County
141	3411	22,018	**Leoni** (township) Jackson County
142	3412	22,015	**Holland** (charter township) Ottawa County
143	3445	21,847	**Lenox** (township) Macomb County
144	3450	21,804	**Burton** (city) Genesee County
145	3458	21,768	**Oak Park** (city) Oakland County
146	3459	21,764	**Marquette** (city) Marquette County
147	3464	21,744	**Warren** (city) Macomb County
148	3470	21,725	**Mount Clemens** (city) Macomb County
149	3508	21,557	**Port Huron** (charter township) Saint Clair County
150	3536	21,433	**Dearborn Heights** (city) Wayne County

Note: The state column ranks the top/bottom 150 places from all places in the state with population of 10,000 or more. The national column ranks the top/bottom 150 places from all places in the country with population of 10,000 or more. Places that are unincorporated were not considered in the rankings. Please refer to the User Guide for additional information.

Per Capita Income

Top 150 Places Ranked in *Ascending* Order

State Rank	Nat'l Rank	Dollars	Place
1	16	10,083	**Benton Harbor** (city) Berrien County
2	25	10,890	**Hamtramck** (city) Wayne County
3	38	11,593	**Muskegon Heights** (city) Muskegon County
4	59	12,188	**Big Rapids** (city) Mecosta County
5	64	12,270	**Ionia** (city) Ionia County
6	98	13,539	**Highland Park** (city) Wayne County
7	108	13,813	**Beecher** (CDP) Genesee County
8	122	14,259	**Inkster** (city) Wayne County
9	128	14,360	**Flint** (city) Genesee County
10	143	14,687	**Saginaw** (city) Saginaw County
11	144	14,699	**Muskegon** (city) Muskegon County
12	157	14,870	**Detroit** (city) Wayne County
13	183	15,336	**Jackson** (city) Jackson County
14	214	15,906	**Pontiac** (city) Oakland County
15	218	15,928	**Benton** (charter township) Berrien County
16	222	15,945	**Mount Pleasant** (city) Isabella County
17	253	16,327	**Allendale** (CDP) Ottawa County
18	286	16,604	**Adrian** (city) Lenawee County
19	319	16,976	**Union** (charter township) Isabella County
20	337	17,084	**Hazel Park** (city) Oakland County
21	342	17,125	**Allendale** (charter township) Ottawa County
22	349	17,186	**Niles** (city) Berrien County
23	427	17,754	**Muskegon** (charter township) Muskegon County
24	498	18,171	**Melvindale** (city) Wayne County
25	504	18,209	**Port Huron** (city) Saint Clair County
26	505	18,211	**Mount Morris** (township) Genesee County
27	509	18,223	**Sturgis** (city) Saint Joseph County
28	512	18,244	**Coldwater** (city) Branch County
29	522	18,309	**Owosso** (city) Shiawassee County
30	532	18,389	**Blackman** (charter township) Jackson County
31	539	18,468	**Kalamazoo** (city) Kalamazoo County
32	578	18,650	**East Lansing** (city) Ingham County
33	627	18,922	**Bay City** (city) Bay County
34	631	18,940	**Eastpointe** (city) Macomb County
35	700	19,385	**Lincoln Park** (city) Wayne County
36	708	19,440	**Lansing** (city) Ingham County
37	732	19,556	**Escanaba** (city) Delta County
38	739	19,589	**Cadillac** (city) Wexford County
39	794	19,874	**Wayne** (city) Wayne County
40	842	20,101	**Alpena** (city) Alpena County
40	842	20,101	**Taylor** (city) Wayne County
42	868	20,214	**Grand Rapids** (city) Kent County
43	910	20,455	**Genesee** (charter township) Genesee County
44	928	20,537	**Romulus** (city) Wayne County
45	939	20,578	**Roseville** (city) Macomb County
46	957	20,663	**Bridgeport** (charter township) Saginaw County
47	975	20,759	**Holland** (city) Ottawa County
48	998	20,851	**Cutlerville** (CDP) Kent County
49	1047	21,095	**Comstock Park** (CDP) Kent County
50	1078	21,246	**Wyoming** (city) Kent County
51	1085	21,262	**Dearborn** (city) Wayne County
52	1089	21,265	**Sault Sainte Marie** (city) Chippewa County
53	1098	21,286	**Harper Woods** (city) Wayne County
54	1106	21,350	**Ypsilanti** (city) Washtenaw County
55	1120	21,433	**Dearborn Heights** (city) Wayne County
56	1148	21,557	**Port Huron** (charter township) Saint Clair County
57	1186	21,725	**Mount Clemens** (city) Macomb County
58	1192	21,744	**Warren** (city) Macomb County
59	1197	21,764	**Marquette** (city) Marquette County
60	1198	21,768	**Oak Park** (city) Oakland County
61	1206	21,804	**Burton** (city) Genesee County
62	1211	21,847	**Lenox** (township) Macomb County
63	1244	22,015	**Holland** (charter township) Ottawa County
64	1245	22,018	**Leoni** (township) Jackson County
65	1256	22,097	**Kalamazoo** (charter township) Kalamazoo County
66	1259	22,113	**Madison Heights** (city) Oakland County
67	1272	22,154	**Battle Creek** (city) Calhoun County
68	1307	22,347	**Flint** (charter township) Genesee County
69	1344	22,522	**Niles** (township) Berrien County
70	1351	22,538	**Alpine** (township) Kent County
71	1379	22,653	**Monroe** (city) Monroe County
72	1415	22,853	**Redford** (charter township) Wayne County
73	1466	23,078	**Frenchtown** (township) Monroe County
74	1533	23,386	**Vienna** (charter township) Genesee County
75	1619	23,841	**Fenton** (city) Genesee County
76	1653	23,993	**Westland** (city) Wayne County
77	1656	23,997	**Garden City** (city) Wayne County
78	1665	24,058	**Jenison** (CDP) Ottawa County
79	1672	24,096	**Ypsilanti** (charter township) Washtenaw County
80	1681	24,141	**Grandville** (city) Kent County
81	1736	24,447	**Fruitport** (charter township) Muskegon County
82	1778	24,722	**Monroe** (charter township) Monroe County
83	1814	24,851	**Kentwood** (city) Kent County
84	1847	24,982	**Riverview** (city) Wayne County
85	1894	25,287	**Wyandotte** (city) Wayne County
86	1914	25,415	**Antwerp** (township) Van Buren County
87	2010	25,903	**Southgate** (city) Wayne County
88	2017	25,953	**Davison** (township) Genesee County
89	2021	25,978	**Grand Haven** (city) Ottawa County
90	2031	26,014	**Mundy** (township) Genesee County
91	2036	26,056	**Emmett** (charter township) Calhoun County
92	2063	26,168	**Clinton** (charter township) Macomb County
93	2070	26,217	**Garfield** (charter township) Grand Traverse County
94	2077	26,261	**Comstock** (charter township) Kalamazoo County
95	2114	26,485	**Gaines** (charter township) Kent County
96	2135	26,597	**Cooper** (charter township) Kalamazoo County
97	2156	26,691	**Sterling Heights** (city) Macomb County
98	2157	26,694	**Walker** (city) Kent County
99	2160	26,704	**East Bay** (township) Grand Traverse County
100	2180	26,843	**Auburn Hills** (city) Oakland County
101	2196	26,904	**Holly** (township) Oakland County
102	2199	26,917	**Byron** (township) Kent County
103	2220	26,996	**Bangor** (charter township) Bay County
104	2240	27,082	**Allen Park** (city) Wayne County
105	2249	27,177	**Huron** (charter township) Wayne County
106	2260	27,243	**Flushing** (charter township) Genesee County
107	2274	27,325	**Norton Shores** (city) Muskegon County
108	2339	27,740	**Georgetown** (charter township) Ottawa County
109	2352	27,790	**Trenton** (city) Wayne County
110	2370	27,918	**Oshtemo** (charter township) Kalamazoo County
111	2383	27,997	**Van Buren** (charter township) Wayne County
112	2424	28,219	**Brandon** (charter township) Oakland County
113	2429	28,254	**Ferndale** (city) Oakland County
114	2456	28,431	**Brownstown** (charter township) Wayne County
115	2468	28,474	**Fraser** (city) Macomb County
116	2491	28,578	**Summit** (township) Jackson County
117	2507	28,635	**Southfield** (city) Oakland County
118	2517	28,717	**Waterford** (charter township) Oakland County
119	2523	28,740	**Holt** (CDP) Ingham County
120	2554	28,915	**Monitor** (charter township) Bay County
121	2576	29,038	**Northview** (CDP) Kent County
122	2583	29,064	**Delhi** (charter township) Ingham County
123	2584	29,067	**Saginaw** (charter township) Saginaw County
124	2607	29,221	**Chesterfield** (township) Macomb County
125	2636	29,375	**Plainfield** (charter township) Kent County
126	2650	29,479	**Saint Clair Shores** (city) Macomb County
127	2662	29,546	**Bath** (charter township) Clinton County
128	2663	29,554	**Bedford** (township) Monroe County
129	2669	29,575	**Highland** (charter township) Oakland County
130	2672	29,593	**Traverse City** (city) Grand Traverse County
131	2695	29,738	**Portage** (city) Kalamazoo County
132	2702	29,779	**Thomas** (township) Saginaw County
133	2717	29,959	**Caledonia** (township) Kent County
134	2718	29,961	**Clawson** (city) Oakland County
135	2739	30,084	**Grand Blanc** (charter township) Genesee County
136	2759	30,241	**DeWitt** (charter township) Clinton County
137	2786	30,447	**Wixom** (city) Oakland County
138	2793	30,482	**Spring Lake** (township) Ottawa County
139	2804	30,537	**Fort Gratiot** (charter township) Saint Clair County
140	2835	30,686	**Woodhaven** (city) Wayne County
141	2863	30,843	**South Lyon** (city) Oakland County
142	2882	30,947	**Shelby** (charter township) Macomb County
143	2886	30,972	**New Baltimore** (city) Macomb County
144	2898	31,100	**Waverly** (CDP) Eaton County
145	2920	31,259	**Harrison** (charter township) Macomb County
146	2955	31,494	**Grand Haven** (charter township) Ottawa County
147	2965	31,547	**Oceola** (township) Livingston County
148	2978	31,627	**Midland** (city) Midland County
149	2988	31,715	**Macomb** (township) Macomb County
150	2995	31,775	**Hartland** (township) Livingston County

Note: The state column ranks the top/bottom 150 places from all places in the state with population of 10,000 or more. The national column ranks the top/bottom 150 places from all places in the country with population of 10,000 or more. Places that are unincorporated were not considered in the rankings. Please refer to the User Guide for additional information.

Median Household Income

Top 150 Places Ranked in *Descending* Order

State Rank	Nat'l Rank	Dollars	Place
1	224	113,654	**Oakland** (charter township) Oakland County
2	243	112,466	**Ada** (township) Kent County
3	244	112,454	**Forest Hills** (CDP) Kent County
4	250	111,849	**Southfield** (township) Oakland County
5	333	106,847	**Beverly Hills** (village) Oakland County
6	356	105,320	**Bloomfield** (charter township) Oakland County
7	413	101,875	**East Grand Rapids** (city) Kent County
8	421	101,273	**Cascade** (charter township) Kent County
9	475	98,750	**Birmingham** (city) Oakland County
10	502	97,161	**Northville** (township) Wayne County
11	599	93,415	**Grosse Pointe Park** (city) Wayne County
12	664	90,882	**Texas** (charter township) Kalamazoo County
13	682	90,164	**West Bloomfield** (charter township) Oakland County
14	685	90,105	**Scio** (township) Washtenaw County
15	691	89,919	**Brighton** (township) Livingston County
16	705	89,452	**Cannon** (township) Kent County
17	746	88,238	**Grosse Ile** (township) Wayne County
18	779	87,123	**Grosse Pointe Woods** (city) Wayne County
19	812	86,217	**Plymouth** (charter township) Wayne County
20	839	85,685	**Troy** (city) Oakland County
21	915	82,957	**Macomb** (township) Macomb County
22	961	81,706	**Hartland** (township) Livingston County
23	963	81,667	**Canton** (charter township) Wayne County
24	976	81,351	**Tyrone** (township) Livingston County
25	1005	80,731	**Oceola** (township) Livingston County
26	1008	80,651	**Springfield** (charter township) Oakland County
27	1041	80,108	**Novi** (city) Oakland County
28	1057	79,761	**Milford** (charter township) Oakland County
29	1077	79,267	**New Baltimore** (city) Macomb County
30	1096	78,690	**Caledonia** (township) Kent County
31	1101	78,514	**Commerce** (charter township) Oakland County
32	1111	78,191	**Hamburg** (township) Livingston County
33	1114	78,160	**Rochester Hills** (city) Oakland County
34	1118	78,071	**Grand Rapids** (charter township) Kent County
35	1166	77,105	**Rochester** (city) Oakland County
36	1182	76,769	**Orion** (charter township) Oakland County
37	1241	75,479	**Lyon** (charter township) Oakland County
38	1243	75,449	**Washington** (township) Macomb County
39	1279	74,510	**Green Oak** (township) Livingston County
40	1320	73,574	**Genoa** (township) Livingston County
41	1350	72,958	**Oxford** (charter township) Oakland County
42	1389	72,363	**Independence** (charter township) Oakland County
43	1404	72,063	**White Lake** (charter township) Oakland County
44	1428	71,675	**Park** (township) Ottawa County
45	1429	71,667	**Fenton** (charter township) Genesee County
46	1476	70,781	**Okemos** (CDP) Ingham County
47	1523	70,023	**Berkley** (city) Oakland County
48	1530	69,836	**Superior** (charter township) Washtenaw County
49	1543	69,700	**Farmington Hills** (city) Oakland County
50	1562	69,085	**Highland** (charter township) Oakland County
51	1571	68,973	**Livonia** (city) Wayne County
52	1620	67,908	**Grand Haven** (charter township) Ottawa County
53	1641	67,592	**Brandon** (charter township) Oakland County
54	1702	66,461	**Pittsfield** (charter township) Washtenaw County
55	1769	65,480	**Huron** (charter township) Wayne County
56	1775	65,392	**Chesterfield** (township) Macomb County
57	1801	65,023	**Lincoln** (charter township) Berrien County
58	1842	64,396	**Brownstown** (charter township) Wayne County
59	1852	64,192	**Bedford** (township) Monroe County
60	1902	63,410	**Georgetown** (charter township) Ottawa County
61	1910	63,212	**Shelby** (charter township) Macomb County
62	1938	62,789	**Royal Oak** (city) Oakland County
63	1976	62,324	**Holly** (township) Oakland County
64	1985	62,145	**Meridian** (charter township) Ingham County
65	1988	62,088	**Saint Joseph** (charter township) Berrien County
66	2049	61,273	**Delhi** (charter township) Ingham County
67	2052	61,224	**Flushing** (charter township) Genesee County
68	2072	60,902	**Delta** (charter township) Eaton County
69	2080	60,815	**DeWitt** (charter township) Clinton County
70	2125	60,237	**Holt** (CDP) Ingham County
71	2129	60,218	**Plainfield** (charter township) Kent County
72	2203	58,953	**Woodhaven** (city) Wayne County
73	2220	58,654	**Allen Park** (city) Wayne County
74	2231	58,521	**Grand Blanc** (charter township) Genesee County
75	2240	58,408	**Farmington** (city) Oakland County
76	2283	57,822	**Antwerp** (township) Van Buren County
77	2318	57,310	**Byron** (township) Kent County
78	2329	57,075	**Sterling Heights** (city) Macomb County
79	2343	56,844	**Bath** (charter township) Clinton County
80	2355	56,621	**East Bay** (township) Grand Traverse County
81	2373	56,424	**Cooper** (charter township) Kalamazoo County
82	2382	56,319	**Lenox** (township) Macomb County
83	2394	56,103	**Summit** (township) Jackson County
84	2408	55,929	**Gaines** (charter township) Kent County
85	2416	55,815	**Spring Lake** (township) Ottawa County
86	2418	55,785	**Haslett** (CDP) Ingham County
87	2437	55,470	**Monitor** (charter township) Bay County
88	2448	55,203	**Thomas** (township) Saginaw County
89	2461	55,041	**Mundy** (township) Genesee County
90	2463	55,036	**Portage** (city) Kalamazoo County
91	2466	55,003	**Ann Arbor** (city) Washtenaw County
92	2478	54,895	**South Lyon** (city) Oakland County
93	2484	54,827	**Waterford** (charter township) Oakland County
94	2542	54,089	**Jenison** (CDP) Ottawa County
95	2580	53,701	**Grandville** (city) Kent County
96	2596	53,520	**Waverly** (CDP) Eaton County
97	2597	53,499	**Holland** (charter township) Ottawa County
98	2626	53,101	**Trenton** (city) Wayne County
99	2629	53,090	**Northview** (CDP) Kent County
100	2631	53,069	**Saint Clair Shores** (city) Macomb County
101	2664	52,684	**Vienna** (charter township) Genesee County
102	2678	52,572	**Van Buren** (charter township) Wayne County
103	2681	52,509	**Auburn Hills** (city) Oakland County
104	2687	52,425	**Garden City** (city) Wayne County
105	2715	52,125	**Harrison** (charter township) Macomb County
106	2716	52,121	**Fruitport** (charter township) Muskegon County
107	2732	51,868	**Clawson** (city) Oakland County
108	2751	51,585	**Fraser** (city) Macomb County
109	2793	50,928	**Midland** (city) Midland County
110	2801	50,828	**Walker** (city) Kent County
111	2810	50,739	**Davison** (township) Genesee County
112	2869	50,041	**Comstock** (charter township) Kalamazoo County
113	2889	49,841	**Southfield** (city) Oakland County
114	2910	49,500	**Fort Gratiot** (charter township) Saint Clair County
115	2936	49,188	**Redford** (charter township) Wayne County
116	2974	48,762	**Saginaw** (charter township) Saginaw County
117	2983	48,664	**Wyandotte** (city) Wayne County
118	2990	48,575	**Riverview** (city) Wayne County
119	2994	48,536	**Norton Shores** (city) Muskegon County
120	3003	48,489	**Allendale** (charter township) Ottawa County
121	3004	48,487	**Allendale** (CDP) Ottawa County
122	3008	48,439	**Southgate** (city) Wayne County
123	3016	48,368	**Kentwood** (city) Kent County
124	3021	48,261	**Oak Park** (city) Oakland County
125	3079	47,662	**Ferndale** (city) Oakland County
126	3081	47,652	**Emmett** (charter township) Calhoun County
127	3085	47,609	**Clinton** (charter township) Macomb County
128	3161	46,739	**Dearborn** (city) Wayne County
129	3173	46,518	**Frenchtown** (township) Monroe County
130	3178	46,394	**Wixom** (city) Oakland County
131	3249	45,497	**Traverse City** (city) Grand Traverse County
132	3253	45,477	**Wyoming** (city) Kent County
133	3290	44,947	**Bangor** (charter township) Bay County
134	3304	44,778	**Harper Woods** (city) Wayne County
135	3362	44,152	**Garfield** (charter township) Grand Traverse County
136	3365	44,129	**Ypsilanti** (charter township) Washtenaw County
137	3366	44,119	**Romulus** (city) Wayne County
138	3379	43,993	**Westland** (city) Wayne County
139	3380	43,983	**Burton** (city) Genesee County
140	3384	43,962	**Warren** (city) Macomb County
141	3392	43,852	**Fenton** (city) Genesee County
142	3409	43,633	**Monroe** (charter township) Monroe County
143	3429	43,413	**Holland** (city) Ottawa County
144	3452	43,252	**Alpine** (township) Kent County
145	3455	43,245	**Leoni** (township) Jackson County
146	3463	43,207	**Eastpointe** (city) Macomb County
147	3479	43,001	**Dearborn Heights** (city) Wayne County
148	3488	42,911	**Monroe** (city) Monroe County
149	3511	42,672	**Niles** (township) Berrien County
150	3531	42,453	**Cutlerville** (CDP) Kent County

Note: *The state column ranks the top/bottom 150 places from all places in the state with population of 10,000 or more. The national column ranks the top/bottom 150 places from all places in the country with population of 10,000 or more. Places that are unincorporated were not considered in the rankings. Please refer to the User Guide for additional information.*

Median Household Income

Top 150 Places Ranked in *Ascending* Order

State Rank	Nat'l Rank	Dollars	Place
1	4	18,208	**Benton Harbor** (city) Berrien County
2	5	18,981	**Highland Park** (city) Wayne County
3	9	19,368	**Muskegon Heights** (city) Muskegon County
4	30	24,550	**Big Rapids** (city) Mecosta County
5	37	24,834	**Flint** (city) Genesee County
6	43	25,083	**Benton** (charter township) Berrien County
7	51	25,568	**Beecher** (CDP) Genesee County
8	52	25,590	**Union** (charter township) Isabella County
9	53	25,659	**Hamtramck** (city) Wayne County
10	60	26,079	**Muskegon** (city) Muskegon County
11	67	26,325	**Detroit** (city) Wayne County
12	73	26,512	**Inkster** (city) Wayne County
13	98	27,328	**Escanaba** (city) Delta County
14	106	27,528	**Pontiac** (city) Oakland County
15	111	27,701	**Saginaw** (city) Saginaw County
16	133	28,309	**Jackson** (city) Jackson County
17	135	28,336	**Mount Pleasant** (city) Isabella County
18	190	30,094	**Adrian** (city) Lenawee County
19	224	30,875	**Hazel Park** (city) Oakland County
20	281	31,841	**Niles** (city) Berrien County
21	284	31,893	**Kalamazoo** (city) Kalamazoo County
22	346	32,940	**Port Huron** (city) Saint Clair County
23	348	32,953	**East Lansing** (city) Ingham County
24	350	32,963	**Cadillac** (city) Wexford County
25	363	33,208	**Mount Clemens** (city) Macomb County
26	370	33,302	**Melvindale** (city) Wayne County
27	372	33,311	**Alpena** (city) Alpena County
28	376	33,406	**Ypsilanti** (city) Washtenaw County
29	393	33,620	**Sault Sainte Marie** (city) Chippewa County
30	459	34,697	**Mount Morris** (township) Genesee County
31	479	34,960	**Owosso** (city) Shiawassee County
32	502	35,245	**Sturgis** (city) Saint Joseph County
33	505	35,352	**Bay City** (city) Bay County
34	553	36,014	**Coldwater** (city) Branch County
35	557	36,054	**Lansing** (city) Ingham County
36	582	36,324	**Blackman** (charter township) Jackson County
37	588	36,419	**Ionia** (city) Ionia County
38	651	37,307	**Muskegon** (charter township) Muskegon County
39	690	37,770	**Marquette** (city) Marquette County
40	693	37,814	**Battle Creek** (city) Calhoun County
41	772	38,685	**Kalamazoo** (charter township) Kalamazoo County
42	813	39,177	**Comstock Park** (CDP) Kent County
43	819	39,227	**Grand Rapids** (city) Kent County
44	825	39,317	**Bridgeport** (charter township) Saginaw County
45	837	39,429	**Genesee** (charter township) Genesee County
46	854	39,566	**Wayne** (city) Wayne County
47	897	40,140	**Madison Heights** (city) Oakland County
48	915	40,337	**Roseville** (city) Macomb County
49	933	40,589	**Lincoln Park** (city) Wayne County
50	974	40,888	**Flint** (charter township) Genesee County
51	981	40,967	**Grand Haven** (city) Ottawa County
52	1007	41,238	**Port Huron** (charter township) Saint Clair County
53	1051	41,675	**Oshtemo** (charter township) Kalamazoo County
54	1071	41,933	**Taylor** (city) Wayne County
55	1125	42,453	**Cutlerville** (CDP) Kent County
56	1145	42,672	**Niles** (township) Berrien County
57	1168	42,911	**Monroe** (city) Monroe County
58	1177	43,001	**Dearborn Heights** (city) Wayne County
59	1193	43,207	**Eastpointe** (city) Macomb County
60	1201	43,245	**Leoni** (township) Jackson County
61	1204	43,252	**Alpine** (township) Kent County
62	1227	43,413	**Holland** (city) Ottawa County
63	1247	43,633	**Monroe** (charter township) Monroe County
64	1264	43,852	**Fenton** (city) Genesee County
65	1272	43,962	**Warren** (city) Macomb County
66	1276	43,983	**Burton** (city) Genesee County
67	1277	43,993	**Westland** (city) Wayne County
68	1290	44,119	**Romulus** (city) Wayne County
69	1291	44,129	**Ypsilanti** (charter township) Washtenaw County
70	1294	44,152	**Garfield** (charter township) Grand Traverse County
71	1352	44,778	**Harper Woods** (city) Wayne County
72	1366	44,947	**Bangor** (charter township) Bay County
73	1403	45,477	**Wyoming** (city) Kent County
74	1407	45,497	**Traverse City** (city) Grand Traverse County
75	1478	46,394	**Wixom** (city) Oakland County
76	1483	46,518	**Frenchtown** (township) Monroe County
77	1495	46,739	**Dearborn** (city) Wayne County
78	1571	47,609	**Clinton** (charter township) Macomb County
79	1575	47,652	**Emmett** (charter township) Calhoun County
80	1577	47,662	**Ferndale** (city) Oakland County
81	1635	48,261	**Oak Park** (city) Oakland County
82	1640	48,368	**Kentwood** (city) Kent County
83	1648	48,439	**Southgate** (city) Wayne County
84	1652	48,487	**Allendale** (CDP) Ottawa County
85	1653	48,489	**Allendale** (charter township) Ottawa County
86	1662	48,536	**Norton Shores** (city) Muskegon County
87	1666	48,575	**Riverview** (city) Wayne County
88	1673	48,664	**Wyandotte** (city) Wayne County
89	1682	48,762	**Saginaw** (charter township) Saginaw County
90	1720	49,188	**Redford** (charter township) Wayne County
91	1746	49,500	**Fort Gratiot** (charter township) Saint Clair County
92	1767	49,841	**Southfield** (city) Oakland County
93	1787	50,041	**Comstock** (charter township) Kalamazoo County
94	1846	50,739	**Davison** (township) Genesee County
95	1855	50,828	**Walker** (city) Kent County
96	1862	50,928	**Midland** (city) Midland County
97	1905	51,585	**Fraser** (city) Macomb County
98	1924	51,868	**Clawson** (city) Oakland County
99	1940	52,121	**Fruitport** (charter township) Muskegon County
100	1941	52,125	**Harrison** (charter township) Macomb County
101	1969	52,425	**Garden City** (city) Wayne County
102	1975	52,509	**Auburn Hills** (city) Oakland County
103	1978	52,572	**Van Buren** (charter township) Wayne County
104	1992	52,684	**Vienna** (charter township) Genesee County
105	2025	53,069	**Saint Clair Shores** (city) Macomb County
106	2027	53,090	**Northview** (CDP) Kent County
107	2029	53,101	**Trenton** (city) Wayne County
108	2059	53,499	**Holland** (charter township) Ottawa County
109	2060	53,520	**Waverly** (CDP) Eaton County
110	2076	53,701	**Grandville** (city) Kent County
111	2114	54,089	**Jenison** (CDP) Ottawa County
112	2172	54,827	**Waterford** (charter township) Oakland County
113	2178	54,895	**South Lyon** (city) Oakland County
114	2190	55,003	**Ann Arbor** (city) Washtenaw County
115	2193	55,036	**Portage** (city) Kalamazoo County
116	2195	55,041	**Mundy** (township) Genesee County
117	2208	55,203	**Thomas** (township) Saginaw County
118	2219	55,470	**Monitor** (charter township) Bay County
119	2238	55,785	**Haslett** (CDP) Ingham County
120	2240	55,815	**Spring Lake** (township) Ottawa County
121	2248	55,929	**Gaines** (charter township) Kent County
122	2262	56,103	**Summit** (township) Jackson County
123	2274	56,319	**Lenox** (township) Macomb County
124	2283	56,424	**Cooper** (charter township) Kalamazoo County
125	2300	56,621	**East Bay** (township) Grand Traverse County
126	2313	56,844	**Bath** (charter township) Clinton County
127	2327	57,075	**Sterling Heights** (city) Macomb County
128	2338	57,310	**Byron** (township) Kent County
129	2373	57,822	**Antwerp** (township) Van Buren County
130	2416	58,408	**Farmington** (city) Oakland County
131	2425	58,521	**Grand Blanc** (charter township) Genesee County
132	2436	58,654	**Allen Park** (city) Wayne County
133	2453	58,953	**Woodhaven** (city) Wayne County
134	2527	60,218	**Plainfield** (charter township) Kent County
135	2531	60,237	**Holt** (CDP) Ingham County
136	2576	60,815	**DeWitt** (charter township) Clinton County
137	2583	60,902	**Delta** (charter township) Eaton County
138	2603	61,224	**Flushing** (charter township) Genesee County
139	2607	61,273	**Delhi** (charter township) Ingham County
140	2668	62,088	**Saint Joseph** (charter township) Berrien County
141	2671	62,145	**Meridian** (charter township) Ingham County
142	2680	62,324	**Holly** (township) Oakland County
143	2718	62,789	**Royal Oak** (city) Oakland County
144	2746	63,212	**Shelby** (charter township) Macomb County
145	2754	63,410	**Georgetown** (charter township) Ottawa County
146	2804	64,192	**Bedford** (township) Monroe County
147	2814	64,396	**Brownstown** (charter township) Wayne County
148	2855	65,023	**Lincoln** (charter township) Berrien County
149	2881	65,392	**Chesterfield** (township) Macomb County
150	2887	65,480	**Huron** (charter township) Wayne County

Note: The state column ranks the top/bottom 150 places from all places in the state with population of 10,000 or more. The national column ranks the top/bottom 150 places from all places in the country with population of 10,000 or more. Places that are unincorporated were not considered in the rankings. Please refer to the User Guide for additional information.

Average Household Income

Top 150 Places Ranked in *Descending* Order

State Rank	Nat'l Rank	Dollars	Place
1	154	157,317	**Bloomfield** (charter township) Oakland County
2	156	156,128	**Southfield** (township) Oakland County
3	165	155,185	**Birmingham** (city) Oakland County
4	207	148,462	**Oakland** (charter township) Oakland County
5	211	148,079	**Forest Hills** (CDP) Kent County
6	212	147,979	**East Grand Rapids** (city) Kent County
7	231	144,485	**Ada** (township) Kent County
8	276	139,009	**Cascade** (charter township) Kent County
9	316	134,760	**Beverly Hills** (village) Oakland County
10	331	133,341	**Northville** (township) Wayne County
11	335	132,884	**Grosse Pointe Park** (city) Wayne County
12	398	126,953	**West Bloomfield** (charter township) Oakland County
13	492	120,156	**Texas** (charter township) Kalamazoo County
14	584	114,575	**Scio** (township) Washtenaw County
15	652	112,110	**Plymouth** (charter township) Wayne County
16	700	109,707	**Rochester** (city) Oakland County
17	721	108,890	**Grand Rapids** (charter township) Kent County
18	765	106,754	**Novi** (city) Oakland County
19	769	106,454	**Troy** (city) Oakland County
20	779	106,137	**Cannon** (township) Kent County
21	781	106,095	**Grosse Ile** (township) Wayne County
22	826	104,412	**Brighton** (township) Livingston County
23	941	100,811	**Springfield** (charter township) Oakland County
24	957	100,396	**Grosse Pointe Woods** (city) Wayne County
25	967	100,089	**Milford** (charter township) Oakland County
26	978	99,743	**Rochester Hills** (city) Oakland County
27	990	99,428	**Commerce** (charter township) Oakland County
28	1042	97,934	**Superior** (charter township) Washtenaw County
29	1074	97,079	**Canton** (charter township) Wayne County
30	1121	95,800	**Hartland** (township) Livingston County
31	1140	95,257	**Tyrone** (township) Livingston County
32	1155	94,759	**Washington** (township) Macomb County
33	1168	94,395	**Farmington Hills** (city) Oakland County
34	1175	94,266	**Okemos** (CDP) Ingham County
35	1177	94,189	**Park** (township) Ottawa County
36	1199	93,655	**Macomb** (township) Macomb County
37	1205	93,490	**Lyon** (charter township) Oakland County
38	1226	93,123	**Hamburg** (township) Livingston County
39	1247	92,616	**Genoa** (township) Livingston County
40	1301	91,114	**Orion** (charter township) Oakland County
41	1339	90,321	**Oceola** (township) Livingston County
42	1363	89,711	**Independence** (charter township) Oakland County
43	1371	89,577	**Pittsfield** (charter township) Washtenaw County
44	1427	88,053	**Oxford** (charter township) Oakland County
45	1471	87,048	**Green Oak** (township) Livingston County
46	1515	85,635	**Caledonia** (township) Kent County
47	1527	85,330	**Meridian** (charter township) Ingham County
48	1544	85,058	**Grand Haven** (charter township) Ottawa County
49	1564	84,543	**New Baltimore** (city) Macomb County
50	1608	83,539	**White Lake** (charter township) Oakland County
51	1621	83,193	**Fenton** (charter township) Genesee County
52	1724	81,276	**Berkley** (city) Oakland County
53	1739	80,865	**Livonia** (city) Wayne County
54	1749	80,691	**Highland** (charter township) Oakland County
55	1809	79,795	**Saint Joseph** (charter township) Berrien County
56	1815	79,646	**Shelby** (charter township) Macomb County
57	1821	79,529	**Lincoln** (charter township) Berrien County
58	1867	78,722	**Ann Arbor** (city) Washtenaw County
59	1885	78,488	**Royal Oak** (city) Oakland County
60	1899	78,242	**Bath** (charter township) Clinton County
61	1913	77,963	**Brandon** (charter township) Oakland County
62	1958	77,244	**Georgetown** (charter township) Ottawa County
63	1959	77,203	**Brownstown** (charter township) Wayne County
64	1996	76,805	**Chesterfield** (charter township) Macomb County
65	2002	76,603	**Grand Blanc** (charter township) Genesee County
66	2012	76,467	**Haslett** (CDP) Ingham County
67	2032	75,963	**Plainfield** (charter township) Kent County
68	2035	75,917	**Woodhaven** (city) Wayne County
69	2039	75,829	**Farmington** (city) Oakland County
70	2040	75,815	**Bedford** (township) Monroe County
71	2085	75,009	**DeWitt** (charter township) Clinton County
72	2099	74,800	**Thomas** (township) Saginaw County
73	2117	74,505	**Midland** (city) Midland County
74	2134	74,324	**Byron** (township) Kent County
75	2138	74,227	**Huron** (charter township) Wayne County
76	2179	73,493	**Delhi** (charter township) Ingham County
77	2196	73,150	**Holt** (CDP) Ingham County
78	2208	72,895	**Spring Lake** (township) Ottawa County
79	2224	72,630	**South Lyon** (city) Oakland County
80	2230	72,497	**Holly** (township) Oakland County
81	2240	72,390	**Fort Gratiot** (charter township) Saint Clair County
82	2275	71,816	**Portage** (city) Kalamazoo County
83	2313	71,192	**Flushing** (charter township) Genesee County
84	2358	70,622	**Northview** (CDP) Kent County
85	2361	70,595	**Summit** (township) Jackson County
86	2393	70,139	**Delta** (charter township) Eaton County
87	2425	69,611	**Monitor** (charter township) Bay County
88	2466	68,927	**Antwerp** (township) Van Buren County
89	2477	68,810	**Sterling Heights** (city) Macomb County
90	2508	68,293	**Harrison** (charter township) Macomb County
91	2512	68,201	**Waterford** (charter township) Oakland County
92	2514	68,186	**Gaines** (charter township) Kent County
93	2554	67,676	**Van Buren** (charter township) Wayne County
94	2579	67,343	**Fraser** (city) Macomb County
95	2581	67,322	**Allen Park** (city) Wayne County
96	2586	67,255	**East Bay** (township) Grand Traverse County
97	2601	67,094	**Wixom** (city) Oakland County
98	2630	66,781	**Cooper** (charter township) Kalamazoo County
99	2640	66,696	**Lenox** (township) Macomb County
100	2671	66,318	**Clawson** (city) Oakland County
101	2678	66,223	**Traverse City** (city) Grand Traverse County
102	2713	65,806	**Emmett** (charter township) Calhoun County
103	2736	65,414	**Mundy** (township) Genesee County
104	2752	65,250	**Saginaw** (charter township) Saginaw County
105	2758	65,188	**Fruitport** (charter township) Muskegon County
106	2761	65,147	**Norton Shores** (city) Muskegon County
107	2763	65,104	**Trenton** (city) Wayne County
108	2807	64,420	**Saint Clair Shores** (city) Macomb County
109	2810	64,392	**Waverly** (CDP) Eaton County
110	2822	64,219	**Southfield** (city) Oakland County
111	2825	64,158	**Auburn Hills** (city) Oakland County
112	2828	64,080	**Jenison** (CDP) Ottawa County
113	2906	62,901	**Comstock** (charter township) Kalamazoo County
114	2925	62,653	**Grandville** (city) Kent County
115	2934	62,579	**Davison** (township) Genesee County
116	2957	62,344	**Holland** (charter township) Ottawa County
117	2972	62,193	**East Lansing** (city) Ingham County
118	2978	62,138	**Dearborn** (city) Wayne County
119	2998	61,898	**Walker** (city) Kent County
120	3052	61,155	**Oshtemo** (charter township) Kalamazoo County
121	3053	61,132	**Riverview** (city) Wayne County
122	3056	61,126	**Garden City** (city) Wayne County
123	3082	60,855	**Kentwood** (city) Kent County
124	3103	60,558	**Vienna** (charter township) Genesee County
125	3123	60,199	**Monroe** (charter township) Monroe County
126	3133	60,107	**Clinton** (charter township) Macomb County
127	3147	59,855	**Bangor** (charter township) Bay County
128	3166	59,513	**Southgate** (city) Wayne County
129	3179	59,380	**Allendale** (charter township) Ottawa County
130	3190	59,280	**Wyandotte** (city) Wayne County
131	3224	58,826	**Ferndale** (city) Oakland County
132	3242	58,581	**Holland** (city) Ottawa County
133	3304	57,915	**Ypsilanti** (charter township) Washtenaw County
134	3326	57,680	**Allendale** (CDP) Ottawa County
135	3331	57,391	**Garfield** (charter township) Grand Traverse County
136	3351	57,391	**Frenchtown** (township) Monroe County
137	3385	57,032	**Redford** (charter township) Wayne County
138	3389	56,977	**Alpine** (township) Kent County
139	3444	56,285	**Fenton** (city) Genesee County
140	3494	55,754	**Westland** (city) Wayne County
141	3498	55,718	**Wyoming** (city) Kent County
142	3517	55,540	**Oak Park** (city) Oakland County
143	3520	55,470	**Marquette** (city) Marquette County
144	3525	55,405	**Dearborn Heights** (city) Wayne County
145	3539	55,242	**Niles** (township) Berrien County
146	3541	55,235	**Grand Haven** (city) Ottawa County
147	3552	55,091	**Battle Creek** (city) Calhoun County
148	3556	55,025	**Port Huron** (charter township) Saint Clair County
149	3599	54,530	**Monroe** (city) Monroe County
150	3606	54,482	**Burton** (city) Genesee County

Note: The state column ranks the top/bottom 150 places from all places in the state with population of 10,000 or more. The national column ranks the top/bottom 150 places from all places in the country with population of 10,000 or more. Places that are unincorporated were not considered in the rankings. Please refer to the User Guide for additional information.

Average Household Income

Top 150 Places Ranked in *Ascending* Order

State Rank	Nat'l Rank	Dollars	Place	State Rank	Nat'l Rank	Dollars	Place
1	2	25,566	Benton Harbor (city) Berrien County	76	1477	59,380	Allendale (charter township) Ottawa County
2	5	28,441	Muskegon Heights (city) Muskegon County	77	1490	59,513	Southgate (city) Wayne County
3	8	29,656	Highland Park (city) Wayne County	78	1509	59,855	Bangor (charter township) Bay County
4	23	34,085	Flint (city) Genesee County	79	1523	60,107	Clinton (charter township) Macomb County
5	24	34,304	Hamtramck (city) Wayne County	80	1533	60,199	Monroe (city) Monroe County
6	34	35,501	Inkster (city) Wayne County	81	1553	60,558	Vienna (charter township) Genesee County
7	36	35,942	Big Rapids (city) Mecosta County	82	1574	60,855	Kentwood (city) Kent County
8	43	36,791	Saginaw (city) Saginaw County	83	1600	61,126	Garden City (city) Wayne County
9	46	37,030	Muskegon (city) Muskegon County	84	1603	61,132	Riverview (city) Wayne County
10	58	37,765	Benton (charter township) Berrien County	85	1604	61,155	Oshtemo (charter township) Kalamazoo County
11	60	37,887	Detroit (city) Wayne County	86	1658	61,898	Walker (city) Kent County
12	68	38,175	Beecher (CDP) Genesee County	87	1677	62,138	Dearborn (city) Wayne County
13	69	38,176	Jackson (city) Jackson County	88	1684	62,193	East Lansing (city) Ingham County
14	73	38,462	Pontiac (city) Oakland County	89	1699	62,344	Holland (charter township) Ottawa County
15	127	40,554	Hazel Park (city) Oakland County	90	1722	62,579	Davison (township) Genesee County
16	140	40,949	Ionia (city) Ionia County	91	1731	62,653	Grandville (city) Kent County
17	166	41,797	Escanaba (city) Delta County	92	1750	62,901	Comstock (charter township) Kalamazoo County
18	173	41,976	Niles (city) Berrien County	93	1828	64,080	Jenison (CDP) Ottawa County
19	180	42,195	Adrian (city) Lenawee County	94	1831	64,158	Auburn Hills (city) Oakland County
20	189	42,374	Melvindale (city) Wayne County	95	1834	64,219	Southfield (city) Oakland County
21	210	42,880	Union (charter township) Isabella County	96	1846	64,392	Waverly (CDP) Eaton County
22	218	43,155	Port Huron (city) Saint Clair County	97	1849	64,420	Saint Clair Shores (city) Macomb County
23	234	43,561	Alpena (city) Alpena County	98	1893	65,104	Trenton (city) Wayne County
24	238	43,678	Owosso (city) Shiawassee County	99	1895	65,147	Norton Shores (city) Muskegon County
25	287	44,652	Lansing (city) Ingham County	100	1898	65,188	Fruitport (charter township) Muskegon County
26	309	44,981	Bay City (city) Bay County	101	1904	65,250	Saginaw (charter township) Saginaw County
27	344	45,515	Mount Pleasant (city) Isabella County	102	1920	65,414	Mundy (township) Genesee County
28	382	46,050	Cadillac (city) Wexford County	103	1943	65,806	Emmett (charter township) Calhoun County
29	404	46,381	Kalamazoo (city) Kalamazoo County	104	1978	66,223	Traverse City (city) Grand Traverse County
30	450	46,917	Mount Clemens (city) Macomb County	105	1985	66,318	Clawson (city) Oakland County
31	462	47,038	Ypsilanti (city) Washtenaw County	106	2016	66,696	Lenox (township) Macomb County
32	467	47,110	Muskegon (charter township) Muskegon County	107	2026	66,781	Cooper (charter township) Kalamazoo County
33	477	47,275	Mount Morris (township) Genesee County	108	2055	67,094	Wixom (city) Oakland County
34	541	48,208	Kalamazoo (charter township) Kalamazoo County	109	2070	67,255	East Bay (township) Grand Traverse County
35	558	48,408	Sturgis (city) Saint Joseph County	110	2075	67,322	Allen Park (city) Wayne County
36	566	48,511	Wayne (city) Wayne County	111	2077	67,343	Fraser (city) Macomb County
37	570	48,564	Roseville (city) Macomb County	112	2101	67,676	Van Buren (charter township) Wayne County
38	582	48,706	Coldwater (city) Branch County	113	2142	68,186	Gaines (charter township) Kent County
39	593	48,800	Lincoln Park (city) Wayne County	114	2144	68,201	Waterford (charter township) Oakland County
40	605	48,863	Eastpointe (city) Macomb County	115	2148	68,293	Harrison (charter township) Macomb County
41	610	48,910	Bridgeport (charter township) Saginaw County	116	2179	68,810	Sterling Heights (city) Macomb County
42	627	49,086	Sault Sainte Marie (city) Chippewa County	117	2190	68,927	Antwerp (township) Van Buren County
43	648	49,380	Blackman (charter township) Jackson County	118	2231	69,611	Monitor (charter township) Bay County
44	653	49,467	Genesee (charter township) Genesee County	119	2263	70,139	Delta (charter township) Eaton County
45	715	50,323	Madison Heights (city) Oakland County	120	2295	70,595	Summit (township) Jackson County
46	754	50,908	Grand Rapids (city) Kent County	121	2298	70,622	Northview (CDP) Kent County
47	800	51,460	Comstock Park (CDP) Kent County	122	2343	71,192	Flushing (charter township) Genesee County
48	801	51,473	Taylor (city) Wayne County	123	2381	71,816	Portage (city) Kalamazoo County
49	829	51,920	Romulus (city) Wayne County	124	2416	72,390	Fort Gratiot (charter township) Saint Clair County
50	891	52,696	Cutlerville (CDP) Kent County	125	2426	72,497	Holly (township) Oakland County
51	921	53,009	Flint (charter township) Genesee County	126	2432	72,630	South Lyon (city) Oakland County
52	942	53,207	Leoni (township) Jackson County	127	2448	72,895	Spring Lake (township) Ottawa County
53	981	53,776	Warren (city) Macomb County	128	2460	73,150	Holt (CDP) Ingham County
54	1008	54,117	Harper Woods (city) Wayne County	129	2477	73,493	Delhi (charter township) Ingham County
55	1050	54,482	Burton (city) Genesee County	130	2518	74,227	Huron (charter township) Wayne County
56	1057	54,530	Monroe (city) Monroe County	131	2522	74,324	Byron (township) Kent County
57	1100	55,025	Port Huron (charter township) Saint Clair County	132	2539	74,505	Midland (city) Midland County
58	1104	55,091	Battle Creek (city) Calhoun County	133	2557	74,800	Thomas (township) Saginaw County
59	1115	55,235	Grand Haven (city) Ottawa County	134	2571	75,009	DeWitt (charter township) Clinton County
60	1117	55,242	Niles (township) Berrien County	135	2616	75,815	Bedford (township) Monroe County
61	1131	55,405	Dearborn Heights (city) Wayne County	136	2617	75,829	Farmington (city) Oakland County
62	1136	55,470	Marquette (city) Marquette County	137	2621	75,917	Woodhaven (city) Wayne County
63	1139	55,540	Oak Park (city) Oakland County	138	2624	75,963	Plainfield (charter township) Kent County
64	1158	55,718	Wyoming (city) Kent County	139	2644	76,467	Haslett (CDP) Ingham County
65	1161	55,754	Westland (city) Wayne County	140	2653	76,603	Grand Blanc (charter township) Genesee County
66	1212	56,285	Fenton (city) Genesee County	141	2660	76,805	Chesterfield (township) Macomb County
67	1267	56,977	Alpine (township) Kent County	142	2697	77,203	Brownstown (charter township) Wayne County
68	1271	57,032	Redford (charter township) Wayne County	143	2698	77,244	Georgetown (charter township) Ottawa County
69	1305	57,391	Frenchtown (township) Monroe County	144	2743	77,963	Brandon (charter township) Oakland County
70	1325	57,602	Garfield (charter township) Grand Traverse County	145	2757	78,242	Bath (charter township) Clinton County
71	1330	57,680	Allendale (CDP) Ottawa County	146	2771	78,488	Royal Oak (city) Oakland County
72	1352	57,915	Ypsilanti (charter township) Washtenaw County	147	2789	78,722	Ann Arbor (city) Washtenaw County
73	1414	58,581	Holland (city) Ottawa County	148	2835	79,529	Lincoln (charter township) Berrien County
74	1432	58,826	Ferndale (city) Oakland County	149	2841	79,646	Shelby (charter township) Macomb County
75	1465	59,280	Wyandotte (city) Wayne County	150	2847	79,795	Saint Joseph (charter township) Berrien County

Note: The state column ranks the top/bottom 150 places from all places in the state with population of 10,000 or more. The national column ranks the top/bottom 150 places from all places in the country with population of 10,000 or more. Places that are unincorporated were not considered in the rankings. Please refer to the User Guide for additional information.

Households with Income of $100,000 or More

Top 150 Places Ranked in *Descending* Order

State Rank	Nat'l Rank	Percent	Place
1	205	57.5	**Southfield** (township) Oakland County
2	215	57.2	**Oakland** (charter township) Oakland County
3	222	56.8	**Ada** (township) Kent County
4	238	56.1	**Forest Hills** (CDP) Kent County
5	265	55.3	**Beverly Hills** (village) Oakland County
6	353	52.7	**Bloomfield** (charter township) Oakland County
7	406	51.3	**Cascade** (charter township) Kent County
8	420	50.7	**East Grand Rapids** (city) Kent County
9	472	49.4	**Birmingham** (city) Oakland County
10	497	48.7	**Grosse Pointe Park** (city) Wayne County
11	507	48.5	**Northville** (township) Wayne County
12	630	45.6	**West Bloomfield** (charter township) Oakland County
13	646	45.2	**Texas** (charter township) Kalamazoo County
14	655	45.0	**Cannon** (township) Kent County
15	680	44.3	**Grosse Ile** (township) Wayne County
16	693	44.1	**Scio** (township) Washtenaw County
17	717	43.7	**Brighton** (township) Livingston County
18	738	43.2	**Plymouth** (charter township) Wayne County
19	767	42.7	**Rochester** (city) Oakland County
20	805	42.1	**Grosse Pointe Woods** (city) Wayne County
21	874	40.9	**Troy** (city) Oakland County
22	910	40.3	**Novi** (city) Oakland County
23	942	39.6	**Macomb** (township) Macomb County
24	1000	38.8	**Milford** (charter township) Oakland County
25	1010	38.6	**Canton** (charter township) Wayne County
26	1018	38.5	**Commerce** (charter township) Oakland County
27	1034	38.2	**Springfield** (charter township) Oakland County
28	1040	38.1	**Hartland** (township) Livingston County
29	1049	38.0	**Rochester Hills** (city) Oakland County
30	1105	37.3	**Oxford** (charter township) Oakland County
31	1131	36.8	**Grand Rapids** (charter township) Kent County
32	1210	35.8	**Okemos** (CDP) Ingham County
33	1226	35.6	**Orion** (charter township) Oakland County
33	1226	35.6	**Tyrone** (township) Livingston County
35	1234	35.5	**Lyon** (charter township) Oakland County
36	1257	35.2	**Green Oak** (township) Livingston County
37	1267	35.1	**New Baltimore** (city) Macomb County
38	1297	34.7	**Oceola** (township) Livingston County
39	1342	34.0	**Hamburg** (township) Livingston County
40	1374	33.5	**Washington** (township) Macomb County
41	1387	33.3	**Independence** (charter township) Oakland County
42	1402	33.1	**Genoa** (township) Livingston County
43	1419	32.9	**Park** (township) Ottawa County
44	1435	32.6	**Farmington Hills** (city) Oakland County
45	1456	32.2	**Pittsfield** (charter township) Washtenaw County
45	1456	32.2	**White Lake** (charter township) Oakland County
47	1534	31.0	**Fenton** (charter township) Genesee County
48	1546	30.8	**Superior** (charter township) Washtenaw County
49	1554	30.7	**Caledonia** (township) Kent County
49	1554	30.7	**Grand Haven** (charter township) Ottawa County
51	1562	30.6	**Meridian** (charter township) Ingham County
52	1569	30.5	**Highland** (charter township) Oakland County
53	1636	29.5	**Livonia** (city) Wayne County
54	1644	29.4	**Brandon** (charter township) Oakland County
55	1683	29.0	**Huron** (charter township) Wayne County
56	1688	28.9	**Royal Oak** (city) Oakland County
57	1777	27.9	**Shelby** (charter township) Macomb County
58	1822	27.3	**Chesterfield** (township) Macomb County
59	1831	27.2	**Berkley** (city) Oakland County
60	1861	26.8	**Brownstown** (charter township) Wayne County
61	1873	26.7	**Ann Arbor** (city) Washtenaw County
62	1895	26.4	**Haslett** (CDP) Ingham County
63	1926	26.1	**Delhi** (charter township) Ingham County
63	1926	26.1	**Holt** (CDP) Ingham County
63	1926	26.1	**Lincoln** (charter township) Berrien County
66	1963	25.8	**South Lyon** (city) Oakland County
67	2051	25.0	**Woodhaven** (city) Wayne County
68	2080	24.7	**Farmington** (city) Oakland County
69	2088	24.6	**Bath** (charter township) Clinton County
70	2095	24.5	**Grand Blanc** (charter township) Genesee County
71	2107	24.4	**Bedford** (township) Monroe County
72	2123	24.2	**DeWitt** (charter township) Clinton County
73	2165	23.7	**Georgetown** (charter township) Ottawa County
74	2219	23.1	**Harrison** (charter township) Macomb County
75	2233	23.0	**Wixom** (city) Oakland County
76	2259	22.7	**Plainfield** (charter township) Kent County
76	2259	22.7	**Saint Joseph** (charter township) Berrien County
78	2284	22.4	**Byron** (township) Kent County
79	2298	22.3	**Spring Lake** (township) Ottawa County
80	2319	22.1	**Delta** (charter township) Eaton County
80	2319	22.1	**Sterling Heights** (city) Macomb County
82	2331	22.0	**Holly** (township) Oakland County
83	2350	21.8	**Portage** (city) Kalamazoo County
84	2371	21.6	**Midland** (city) Midland County
85	2383	21.5	**Trenton** (city) Wayne County
86	2426	21.1	**Fort Gratiot** (charter township) Saint Clair County
87	2466	20.7	**Antwerp** (township) Van Buren County
88	2479	20.6	**Gaines** (charter township) Kent County
89	2504	20.4	**Allen Park** (city) Wayne County
89	2504	20.4	**Waterford** (charter township) Oakland County
91	2516	20.3	**Clawson** (city) Oakland County
92	2531	20.2	**Summit** (township) Jackson County
92	2531	20.2	**Van Buren** (charter township) Wayne County
94	2547	20.1	**Thomas** (township) Saginaw County
95	2562	20.0	**Fraser** (city) Macomb County
96	2579	19.9	**Monitor** (charter township) Bay County
96	2579	19.9	**Saginaw** (charter township) Saginaw County
98	2697	18.9	**Flushing** (charter township) Genesee County
98	2697	18.9	**Southfield** (city) Oakland County
100	2710	18.8	**Dearborn** (city) Wayne County
100	2710	18.8	**Oshtemo** (charter township) Kalamazoo County
102	2722	18.7	**East Lansing** (city) Ingham County
103	2748	18.5	**Lenox** (township) Macomb County
104	2772	18.3	**Cooper** (charter township) Kalamazoo County
104	2772	18.3	**Northview** (CDP) Kent County
104	2772	18.3	**Traverse City** (city) Grand Traverse County
107	2801	18.1	**Davison** (township) Genesee County
108	2842	17.8	**Saint Clair Shores** (city) Macomb County
109	2853	17.7	**Riverview** (city) Wayne County
110	2865	17.6	**Waverly** (CDP) Eaton County
111	2888	17.4	**Auburn Hills** (city) Oakland County
111	2888	17.4	**Norton Shores** (city) Muskegon County
113	2901	17.3	**Mundy** (township) Genesee County
113	2901	17.3	**Walker** (city) Kent County
115	2938	17.0	**Allendale** (CDP) Ottawa County
116	2950	16.9	**Emmett** (charter township) Calhoun County
116	2950	16.9	**Ypsilanti** (charter township) Washtenaw County
118	2964	16.8	**Fruitport** (charter township) Muskegon County
119	2996	16.5	**Southgate** (city) Wayne County
120	3023	16.3	**Monroe** (charter township) Monroe County
121	3047	16.1	**Holland** (charter township) Ottawa County
122	3089	15.8	**Wyandotte** (city) Wayne County
123	3112	15.6	**Ferndale** (city) Oakland County
123	3112	15.6	**Kentwood** (city) Kent County
125	3126	15.5	**Bangor** (charter township) Bay County
125	3126	15.5	**Comstock** (charter township) Kalamazoo County
127	3136	15.4	**Clinton** (charter township) Macomb County
128	3178	15.1	**Allendale** (charter township) Ottawa County
129	3220	14.8	**Alpine** (township) Kent County
130	3234	14.7	**Fenton** (city) Genesee County
130	3234	14.7	**Jenison** (CDP) Ottawa County
132	3254	14.6	**East Bay** (township) Grand Traverse County
132	3254	14.6	**Marquette** (city) Marquette County
134	3268	14.5	**Garden City** (city) Wayne County
135	3303	14.2	**Vienna** (charter township) Genesee County
136	3317	14.1	**Grandville** (city) Kent County
137	3333	14.0	**Garfield** (charter township) Grand Traverse County
138	3347	13.9	**Holland** (city) Ottawa County
139	3392	13.5	**Grand Haven** (city) Ottawa County
140	3414	13.4	**Monroe** (city) Monroe County
141	3448	13.2	**Dearborn Heights** (city) Wayne County
142	3478	13.0	**Westland** (city) Wayne County
143	3512	12.7	**Oak Park** (city) Oakland County
144	3531	12.6	**Comstock Park** (CDP) Kent County
144	3531	12.6	**Frenchtown** (township) Monroe County
146	3632	12.1	**Battle Creek** (city) Calhoun County
146	3632	12.1	**Redford** (charter township) Wayne County
148	3653	12.0	**Cutlerville** (CDP) Kent County
149	3691	11.8	**Warren** (city) Macomb County
150	3706	11.7	**Niles** (township) Berrien County

Note: The state column ranks the top/bottom 150 places from all places in the state with population of 10,000 or more. The national column ranks the top/bottom 150 places from all places in the country with population of 10,000 or more. Places that are unincorporated were not considered in the rankings. Please refer to the User Guide for additional information.

Households with Income of $100,000 or More

Top 150 Places Ranked in *Ascending* Order

State Rank	Nat'l Rank	Percent	Place
1	2	1.4	Benton Harbor (city) Berrien County
2	4	1.7	Highland Park (city) Wayne County
3	9	2.4	Muskegon Heights (city) Muskegon County
4	11	2.5	Beecher (CDP) Genesee County
5	37	3.9	Inkster (city) Wayne County
6	47	4.4	Flint (city) Genesee County
7	48	4.5	Muskegon (city) Muskegon County
8	59	4.7	Hamtramck (city) Wayne County
9	69	4.9	Ionia (city) Ionia County
10	74	5.1	Saginaw (city) Saginaw County
11	87	5.3	Benton (charter township) Berrien County
12	123	5.8	Jackson (city) Jackson County
13	134	6.0	Hazel Park (city) Oakland County
13	134	6.0	Owosso (city) Shiawassee County
15	154	6.3	Cadillac (city) Wexford County
15	154	6.3	Pontiac (city) Oakland County
17	167	6.4	Detroit (city) Wayne County
18	182	6.6	Alpena (city) Alpena County
18	182	6.6	Melvindale (city) Wayne County
20	227	7.1	Escanaba (city) Delta County
20	227	7.1	Lansing (city) Ingham County
20	227	7.1	Niles (city) Berrien County
23	270	7.5	Coldwater (city) Branch County
24	294	7.7	Bay City (city) Bay County
24	294	7.7	Port Huron (city) Saint Clair County
26	305	7.8	Big Rapids (city) Mecosta County
27	317	7.9	Bridgeport (charter township) Saginaw County
28	334	8.0	Mount Morris (township) Genesee County
29	362	8.2	Roseville (city) Macomb County
30	375	8.3	Sturgis (city) Saint Joseph County
31	386	8.4	Eastpointe (city) Macomb County
32	401	8.5	Adrian (city) Lenawee County
33	414	8.6	Lincoln Park (city) Wayne County
34	449	8.8	Union (charter township) Isabella County
35	504	9.2	Mount Clemens (city) Macomb County
35	504	9.2	Muskegon (charter township) Muskegon County
35	504	9.2	Sault Sainte Marie (city) Chippewa County
35	504	9.2	Wayne (city) Wayne County
39	519	9.3	Kalamazoo (charter township) Kalamazoo County
40	650	10.1	Kalamazoo (city) Kalamazoo County
41	666	10.2	Harper Woods (city) Wayne County
42	689	10.3	Taylor (city) Wayne County
43	704	10.4	Romulus (city) Wayne County
44	719	10.5	Blackman (charter township) Jackson County
44	719	10.5	Ypsilanti (city) Washtenaw County
46	741	10.6	Genesee (charter township) Genesee County
46	741	10.6	Grand Rapids (city) Kent County
46	741	10.6	Mount Pleasant (city) Isabella County
49	826	11.1	Flint (charter township) Genesee County
49	826	11.1	Port Huron (charter township) Saint Clair County
51	862	11.3	Madison Heights (city) Oakland County
52	894	11.5	Burton (city) Genesee County
52	894	11.5	Leoni (township) Jackson County
54	937	11.7	Niles (township) Berrien County
54	937	11.7	Wyoming (city) Kent County
56	951	11.8	Warren (city) Macomb County
57	986	12.0	Cutlerville (CDP) Kent County
58	1004	12.1	Battle Creek (city) Calhoun County
58	1004	12.1	Redford (charter township) Wayne County
60	1105	12.6	Comstock Park (CDP) Kent County
60	1105	12.6	Frenchtown (township) Monroe County
62	1126	12.7	Oak Park (city) Oakland County
63	1163	13.0	Westland (city) Wayne County
64	1194	13.2	Dearborn Heights (city) Wayne County
65	1223	13.4	Monroe (city) Monroe County
66	1243	13.5	Grand Haven (city) Ottawa County
67	1300	13.9	Holland (city) Ottawa County
68	1310	14.0	Garfield (charter township) Grand Traverse County
69	1324	14.1	Grandville (city) Kent County
70	1340	14.2	Vienna (charter township) Genesee County
71	1377	14.5	Garden City (city) Wayne County
72	1389	14.6	East Bay (township) Grand Traverse County
72	1389	14.6	Marquette (city) Marquette County
74	1403	14.7	Fenton (city) Genesee County
74	1403	14.7	Jenison (CDP) Ottawa County
76	1423	14.8	Alpine (township) Kent County
77	1465	15.1	Allendale (charter township) Ottawa County
78	1504	15.4	Clinton (charter township) Macomb County
79	1521	15.5	Bangor (charter township) Bay County
79	1521	15.5	Comstock (charter township) Kalamazoo County
81	1531	15.6	Ferndale (city) Oakland County
81	1531	15.6	Kentwood (city) Kent County
83	1554	15.8	Wyandotte (city) Wayne County
84	1600	16.1	Holland (charter township) Ottawa County
85	1626	16.3	Monroe (charter township) Monroe County
86	1643	16.5	Southgate (city) Wayne County
87	1682	16.8	Fruitport (charter township) Muskegon County
88	1693	16.9	Emmett (charter township) Calhoun County
88	1693	16.9	Ypsilanti (charter township) Washtenaw County
90	1707	17.0	Allendale (CDP) Ottawa County
91	1743	17.3	Mundy (township) Genesee County
91	1743	17.3	Walker (city) Kent County
93	1756	17.4	Auburn Hills (city) Oakland County
93	1756	17.4	Norton Shores (city) Muskegon County
95	1781	17.6	Waverly (CDP) Eaton County
96	1792	17.7	Riverview (city) Wayne County
97	1804	17.8	Saint Clair Shores (city) Macomb County
98	1841	18.1	Davison (township) Genesee County
99	1873	18.3	Cooper (charter township) Kalamazoo County
99	1873	18.3	Northview (CDP) Kent County
99	1873	18.3	Traverse City (city) Grand Traverse County
102	1897	18.5	Lenox (township) Macomb County
103	1927	18.7	East Lansing (city) Ingham County
104	1935	18.8	Dearborn (city) Wayne County
104	1935	18.8	Oshtemo (charter township) Kalamazoo County
106	1947	18.9	Flushing (charter township) Genesee County
106	1947	18.9	Southfield (city) Oakland County
108	2062	19.9	Monitor (charter township) Bay County
108	2062	19.9	Saginaw (township) Saginaw County
110	2078	20.0	Fraser (city) Macomb County
111	2095	20.1	Thomas (township) Saginaw County
112	2110	20.2	Summit (township) Jackson County
112	2110	20.2	Van Buren (charter township) Wayne County
114	2126	20.3	Clawson (city) Oakland County
115	2141	20.4	Allen Park (city) Wayne County
115	2141	20.4	Waterford (charter township) Oakland County
117	2165	20.6	Gaines (charter township) Kent County
118	2178	20.7	Antwerp (township) Van Buren County
119	2220	21.1	Fort Gratiot (charter township) Saint Clair County
120	2262	21.5	Trenton (city) Wayne County
121	2274	21.6	Midland (city) Midland County
122	2295	21.8	Portage (city) Kalamazoo County
123	2313	22.0	Holly (township) Oakland County
124	2326	22.1	Delta (charter township) Eaton County
124	2326	22.1	Sterling Heights (city) Macomb County
126	2347	22.3	Spring Lake (township) Ottawa County
127	2359	22.4	Byron (township) Kent County
128	2391	22.7	Plainfield (charter township) Kent County
128	2391	22.7	Saint Joseph (charter township) Berrien County
130	2417	23.0	Wixom (city) Oakland County
131	2424	23.1	Harrison (charter township) Macomb County
132	2482	23.7	Georgetown (charter township) Ottawa County
133	2524	24.2	DeWitt (charter township) Clinton County
134	2542	24.4	Bedford (township) Monroe County
135	2550	24.5	Grand Blanc (charter township) Genesee County
136	2562	24.6	Bath (charter township) Clinton County
137	2569	24.7	Farmington (city) Oakland County
138	2591	25.0	Woodhaven (city) Wayne County
139	2683	25.8	South Lyon (city) Oakland County
140	2717	26.1	Delhi (charter township) Ingham County
140	2717	26.1	Holt (CDP) Ingham County
140	2717	26.1	Lincoln (charter township) Berrien County
143	2750	26.4	Haslett (CDP) Ingham County
144	2775	26.7	Ann Arbor (city) Washtenaw County
145	2784	26.8	Brownstown (charter township) Wayne County
146	2818	27.2	Berkley (city) Oakland County
147	2826	27.3	Chesterfield (township) Macomb County
148	2868	27.9	Shelby (charter township) Macomb County
149	2959	28.9	Royal Oak (city) Oakland County
150	2969	29.0	Huron (charter township) Wayne County

Note: The state column ranks the top/bottom 150 places from all places in the state with population of 10,000 or more. The national column ranks the top/bottom 150 places from all places in the country with population of 10,000 or more. Places that are unincorporated were not considered in the rankings. Please refer to the User Guide for additional information.

Poverty Rate

Top 150 Places Ranked in *Descending* Order

State Rank	Nat'l Rank	Percent	Place
1	7	51.1	**Highland Park** (city) Wayne County
2	10	48.4	**Benton Harbor** (city) Berrien County
3	17	46.5	**Muskegon Heights** (city) Muskegon County
3	17	46.5	**Union** (charter township) Isabella County
5	23	45.6	**Big Rapids** (city) Mecosta County
6	25	45.3	**Mount Pleasant** (city) Isabella County
7	33	43.4	**Hamtramck** (city) Wayne County
8	37	42.2	**Beecher** (CDP) Genesee County
9	42	41.5	**Flint** (city) Genesee County
10	46	41.1	**East Lansing** (city) Ingham County
11	56	39.3	**Detroit** (city) Wayne County
12	68	38.2	**Inkster** (city) Wayne County
13	77	37.4	**Saginaw** (city) Saginaw County
14	86	36.6	**Pontiac** (city) Oakland County
15	117	35.3	**Muskegon** (city) Muskegon County
16	127	34.7	**Jackson** (city) Jackson County
17	136	34.3	**Kalamazoo** (city) Kalamazoo County
18	141	34.2	**Benton** (charter township) Berrien County
19	235	30.9	**Adrian** (city) Lenawee County
20	237	30.8	**Mount Morris** (township) Genesee County
21	266	30.2	**Ypsilanti** (city) Washtenaw County
22	338	28.7	**Lansing** (city) Ingham County
23	341	28.6	**Allendale** (charter township) Ottawa County
23	341	28.6	**Port Huron** (city) Saint Clair County
25	362	28.0	**Allendale** (CDP) Ottawa County
26	386	27.6	**Niles** (city) Berrien County
27	391	27.5	**Dearborn** (city) Wayne County
28	398	27.4	**Hazel Park** (city) Oakland County
29	432	26.8	**Escanaba** (city) Delta County
29	432	26.8	**Grand Rapids** (city) Kent County
31	498	25.9	**Sturgis** (city) Saint Joseph County
32	523	25.5	**Marquette** (city) Marquette County
33	556	25.1	**Port Huron** (charter township) Saint Clair County
34	601	24.4	**Ionia** (city) Ionia County
35	662	23.8	**Sault Sainte Marie** (city) Chippewa County
36	690	23.5	**Oshtemo** (charter township) Kalamazoo County
37	721	23.2	**Bath** (charter township) Clinton County
38	752	22.9	**Owosso** (city) Shiawassee County
39	762	22.8	**Melvindale** (city) Wayne County
40	781	22.6	**Cadillac** (city) Wexford County
40	781	22.6	**Eastpointe** (city) Macomb County
42	797	22.4	**Alpena** (city) Alpena County
42	797	22.4	**Bay City** (city) Bay County
44	814	22.3	**Comstock Park** (CDP) Kent County
45	832	22.1	**Ann Arbor** (city) Washtenaw County
45	832	22.1	**Battle Creek** (city) Calhoun County
47	867	21.8	**Mount Clemens** (city) Macomb County
48	872	21.7	**Muskegon** (charter township) Muskegon County
49	905	21.4	**Romulus** (city) Wayne County
50	924	21.2	**Taylor** (city) Wayne County
51	964	20.8	**Bridgeport** (charter township) Saginaw County
52	982	20.6	**Ypsilanti** (charter township) Washtenaw County
53	1041	20.1	**Coldwater** (city) Branch County
54	1065	19.9	**Alpine** (township) Kent County
55	1091	19.7	**Burton** (city) Genesee County
56	1115	19.5	**Monroe** (city) Monroe County
57	1131	19.4	**Oak Park** (city) Oakland County
58	1157	19.2	**Cutlerville** (CDP) Kent County
58	1157	19.2	**Flint** (charter township) Genesee County
58	1157	19.2	**Genesee** (charter township) Genesee County
58	1157	19.2	**Holland** (city) Ottawa County
62	1193	19.0	**Dearborn Heights** (city) Wayne County
63	1205	18.9	**Kalamazoo** (charter township) Kalamazoo County
64	1215	18.8	**Madison Heights** (city) Oakland County
65	1273	18.3	**Lincoln Park** (city) Wayne County
66	1282	18.2	**Warren** (city) Macomb County
67	1352	17.7	**Frenchtown** (township) Monroe County
68	1387	17.5	**Wayne** (city) Wayne County
69	1487	16.7	**Wyoming** (city) Kent County
70	1520	16.5	**Harper Woods** (city) Wayne County
71	1532	16.4	**Blackman** (charter township) Jackson County
71	1532	16.4	**Niles** (township) Berrien County
73	1545	16.3	**Roseville** (city) Macomb County
74	1561	16.2	**Leoni** (township) Jackson County
75	1573	16.1	**Monroe** (charter township) Monroe County
76	1589	16.0	**Southfield** (city) Oakland County
77	1630	15.7	**Traverse City** (city) Grand Traverse County
78	1638	15.6	**Fenton** (city) Genesee County
79	1652	15.5	**Westland** (city) Wayne County
80	1715	15.1	**Ferndale** (city) Oakland County
81	1773	14.7	**Comstock** (charter township) Kalamazoo County
82	1808	14.5	**Wixom** (city) Oakland County
83	1837	14.3	**Garfield** (charter township) Grand Traverse County
83	1837	14.3	**Midland** (city) Midland County
85	1901	13.9	**Haslett** (CDP) Ingham County
86	1954	13.5	**Bangor** (charter township) Bay County
86	1954	13.5	**Emmett** (charter township) Calhoun County
86	1954	13.5	**Kentwood** (city) Kent County
89	1979	13.4	**Redford** (charter township) Wayne County
90	1995	13.3	**Auburn Hills** (city) Oakland County
91	2008	13.2	**Waterford** (charter township) Oakland County
92	2027	13.1	**Meridian** (charter township) Ingham County
93	2035	13.0	**Sterling Heights** (city) Macomb County
94	2109	12.4	**Holland** (charter township) Ottawa County
94	2109	12.4	**Van Buren** (charter township) Wayne County
96	2127	12.3	**Saginaw** (charter township) Saginaw County
97	2161	12.1	**Harrison** (charter township) Macomb County
97	2161	12.1	**Riverview** (city) Wayne County
99	2185	12.0	**Grand Haven** (city) Ottawa County
100	2214	11.8	**Clinton** (charter township) Macomb County
100	2214	11.8	**Huron** (charter township) Wayne County
102	2230	11.7	**Portage** (city) Kalamazoo County
102	2230	11.7	**Summit** (township) Jackson County
102	2230	11.7	**Walker** (city) Kent County
102	2230	11.7	**Wyandotte** (city) Wayne County
106	2255	11.6	**Okemos** (CDP) Ingham County
107	2274	11.5	**Gaines** (charter township) Kent County
108	2295	11.4	**Spring Lake** (township) Ottawa County
109	2327	11.2	**Northview** (CDP) Kent County
110	2369	11.0	**Fort Gratiot** (charter township) Saint Clair County
111	2415	10.7	**Pittsfield** (charter township) Washtenaw County
112	2433	10.6	**Vienna** (charter township) Genesee County
113	2453	10.5	**Southgate** (city) Wayne County
114	2498	10.3	**Lenox** (township) Macomb County
114	2498	10.3	**Saint Clair Shores** (city) Macomb County
114	2498	10.3	**Superior** (charter township) Washtenaw County
117	2553	10.0	**Delhi** (charter township) Ingham County
118	2575	9.9	**Byron** (township) Kent County
118	2575	9.9	**Grandville** (city) Kent County
120	2599	9.8	**Cooper** (charter township) Kalamazoo County
120	2599	9.8	**Grand Blanc** (charter township) Genesee County
120	2599	9.8	**Trenton** (city) Wayne County
123	2626	9.7	**Brandon** (charter township) Oakland County
123	2626	9.7	**Fraser** (city) Macomb County
123	2626	9.7	**Holt** (CDP) Ingham County
126	2648	9.6	**Grand Haven** (charter township) Ottawa County
126	2648	9.6	**Shelby** (charter township) Macomb County
128	2691	9.4	**Garden City** (city) Wayne County
129	2711	9.3	**Holly** (township) Oakland County
129	2711	9.3	**Woodhaven** (city) Wayne County
131	2730	9.2	**Davison** (township) Genesee County
132	2747	9.1	**Flushing** (charter township) Genesee County
132	2747	9.1	**Waverly** (CDP) Eaton County
134	2792	8.9	**Fenton** (charter township) Genesee County
134	2792	8.9	**Fruitport** (charter township) Muskegon County
134	2792	8.9	**Norton Shores** (city) Muskegon County
137	2816	8.8	**Chesterfield** (township) Macomb County
138	2834	8.7	**Highland** (charter township) Oakland County
138	2834	8.7	**Scio** (township) Washtenaw County
140	2952	8.2	**Antwerp** (township) Van Buren County
141	2973	8.1	**Brownstown** (charter township) Wayne County
141	2973	8.1	**East Bay** (township) Grand Traverse County
143	3006	8.0	**White Lake** (charter township) Oakland County
144	3028	7.9	**Delta** (charter township) Eaton County
145	3056	7.8	**Allen Park** (city) Wayne County
145	3056	7.8	**DeWitt** (charter township) Clinton County
147	3085	7.7	**Mundy** (township) Genesee County
147	3085	7.7	**Orion** (charter township) Oakland County
149	3148	7.5	**Clawson** (city) Oakland County
149	3148	7.5	**Farmington Hills** (city) Oakland County

Note: The state column ranks the top/bottom 150 places from all places in the state with population of 10,000 or more. The national column ranks the top/bottom 150 places from all places in the country with population of 10,000 or more. Places that are unincorporated were not considered in the rankings. Please refer to the User Guide for additional information.

Poverty Rate

Top 150 Places Ranked in *Ascending* Order

State Rank	Nat'l Rank	Percent	Place
1	83	2.3	**Forest Hills** (CDP) Kent County
2	93	2.4	**Cascade** (charter township) Kent County
3	105	2.5	**Beverly Hills** (village) Oakland County
4	144	2.7	**Ada** (township) Kent County
5	157	2.8	**Grand Rapids** (charter township) Kent County
6	197	3.0	**Oakland** (charter township) Oakland County
7	247	3.2	**East Grand Rapids** (city) Kent County
7	247	3.2	**Northville** (township) Wayne County
7	247	3.2	**Oceola** (township) Livingston County
7	247	3.2	**Southfield** (township) Oakland County
11	330	3.5	**Birmingham** (city) Oakland County
12	365	3.6	**Hartland** (township) Livingston County
13	391	3.7	**Grosse Ile** (township) Wayne County
14	428	3.8	**Hamburg** (township) Livingston County
15	520	4.1	**Caledonia** (township) Kent County
15	520	4.1	**Plymouth** (charter township) Wayne County
17	546	4.2	**Brighton** (township) Livingston County
18	618	4.4	**Genoa** (township) Livingston County
18	618	4.4	**Thomas** (township) Saginaw County
20	680	4.6	**Grosse Pointe Woods** (city) Wayne County
20	680	4.6	**Saint Joseph** (charter township) Berrien County
22	710	4.7	**Lyon** (charter township) Oakland County
23	745	4.8	**Jenison** (CDP) Ottawa County
24	773	4.9	**Cannon** (township) Kent County
24	773	4.9	**Springfield** (charter township) Oakland County
26	821	5.1	**Macomb** (township) Macomb County
26	821	5.1	**Texas** (charter township) Kalamazoo County
28	909	5.4	**Lincoln** (charter township) Berrien County
28	909	5.4	**Rochester** (city) Oakland County
30	937	5.5	**South Lyon** (city) Oakland County
30	937	5.5	**West Bloomfield** (charter township) Oakland County
32	964	5.6	**Novi** (city) Oakland County
33	988	5.7	**Tyrone** (township) Livingston County
34	1020	5.8	**Green Oak** (township) Livingston County
35	1071	6.0	**Canton** (charter township) Wayne County
36	1095	6.1	**Bloomfield** (charter township) Oakland County
36	1095	6.1	**Commerce** (charter township) Oakland County
36	1095	6.1	**Livonia** (city) Wayne County
39	1134	6.2	**Georgetown** (charter township) Ottawa County
39	1134	6.2	**Grosse Pointe Park** (city) Wayne County
41	1157	6.3	**Independence** (charter township) Oakland County
42	1184	6.4	**Milford** (charter township) Oakland County
42	1184	6.4	**Park** (township) Ottawa County
44	1212	6.5	**Berkley** (city) Oakland County
45	1235	6.6	**New Baltimore** (city) Macomb County
45	1235	6.6	**Washington** (township) Macomb County
47	1275	6.7	**Rochester Hills** (city) Oakland County
48	1329	6.9	**Royal Oak** (city) Oakland County
49	1383	7.1	**Monitor** (charter township) Bay County
50	1407	7.2	**Bedford** (township) Monroe County
50	1407	7.2	**Troy** (city) Oakland County
52	1453	7.4	**Farmington** (city) Oakland County
52	1453	7.4	**Plainfield** (charter township) Kent County
54	1482	7.5	**Clawson** (city) Oakland County
54	1482	7.5	**Farmington Hills** (city) Oakland County
54	1482	7.5	**Oxford** (charter township) Oakland County
57	1533	7.7	**Mundy** (township) Genesee County
57	1533	7.7	**Orion** (charter township) Oakland County
59	1572	7.8	**Allen Park** (city) Wayne County
59	1572	7.8	**DeWitt** (charter township) Clinton County
61	1601	7.9	**Delta** (charter township) Eaton County
62	1629	8.0	**White Lake** (charter township) Oakland County
63	1651	8.1	**Brownstown** (charter township) Wayne County
63	1651	8.1	**East Bay** (township) Grand Traverse County
65	1684	8.2	**Antwerp** (township) Van Buren County
66	1804	8.7	**Highland** (charter township) Oakland County
66	1804	8.7	**Scio** (township) Washtenaw County
68	1823	8.8	**Chesterfield** (township) Macomb County
69	1841	8.9	**Fenton** (charter township) Genesee County
69	1841	8.9	**Fruitport** (charter township) Muskegon County
69	1841	8.9	**Norton Shores** (city) Muskegon County
72	1889	9.1	**Flushing** (charter township) Genesee County
72	1889	9.1	**Waverly** (CDP) Eaton County
74	1910	9.2	**Davison** (township) Genesee County
75	1927	9.3	**Holly** (township) Oakland County
75	1927	9.3	**Woodhaven** (city) Wayne County
77	1946	9.4	**Garden City** (city) Wayne County
78	1982	9.6	**Grand Haven** (charter township) Ottawa County
78	1982	9.6	**Shelby** (charter township) Macomb County
80	2009	9.7	**Brandon** (charter township) Oakland County
80	2009	9.7	**Fraser** (city) Macomb County
80	2009	9.7	**Holt** (CDP) Ingham County
83	2031	9.8	**Cooper** (charter township) Kalamazoo County
83	2031	9.8	**Grand Blanc** (charter township) Genesee County
83	2031	9.8	**Trenton** (city) Wayne County
86	2058	9.9	**Byron** (township) Kent County
86	2058	9.9	**Grandville** (city) Kent County
88	2082	10.0	**Delhi** (charter township) Ingham County
89	2136	10.3	**Lenox** (township) Macomb County
89	2136	10.3	**Saint Clair Shores** (city) Macomb County
89	2136	10.3	**Superior** (charter township) Washtenaw County
92	2178	10.5	**Southgate** (city) Wayne County
93	2204	10.6	**Vienna** (charter township) Genesee County
94	2224	10.7	**Pittsfield** (charter township) Washtenaw County
95	2273	11.0	**Fort Gratiot** (charter township) Saint Clair County
96	2308	11.2	**Northview** (CDP) Kent County
97	2343	11.4	**Spring Lake** (township) Ottawa County
98	2362	11.5	**Gaines** (charter township) Kent County
99	2383	11.6	**Okemos** (CDP) Ingham County
100	2402	11.7	**Portage** (city) Kalamazoo County
100	2402	11.7	**Summit** (township) Jackson County
100	2402	11.7	**Walker** (city) Kent County
100	2402	11.7	**Wyandotte** (city) Wayne County
104	2427	11.8	**Clinton** (charter township) Macomb County
104	2427	11.8	**Huron** (charter township) Wayne County
106	2455	12.0	**Grand Haven** (city) Ottawa County
107	2472	12.1	**Harrison** (charter township) Macomb County
107	2472	12.1	**Riverview** (city) Wayne County
109	2517	12.3	**Saginaw** (charter township) Saginaw County
110	2530	12.4	**Holland** (charter township) Ottawa County
110	2530	12.4	**Van Buren** (charter township) Wayne County
112	2614	13.0	**Sterling Heights** (city) Macomb County
113	2622	13.1	**Meridian** (charter township) Ingham County
114	2630	13.2	**Waterford** (charter township) Oakland County
115	2649	13.3	**Auburn Hills** (city) Oakland County
116	2662	13.4	**Redford** (charter township) Wayne County
117	2678	13.5	**Bangor** (charter township) Bay County
117	2678	13.5	**Emmett** (charter township) Calhoun County
117	2678	13.5	**Kentwood** (city) Kent County
120	2743	13.9	**Haslett** (CDP) Ingham County
121	2804	14.3	**Garfield** (charter township) Grand Traverse County
121	2804	14.3	**Midland** (city) Midland County
123	2836	14.5	**Wixom** (city) Oakland County
124	2866	14.7	**Comstock** (charter township) Kalamazoo County
125	2924	15.1	**Ferndale** (city) Oakland County
126	2987	15.5	**Westland** (city) Wayne County
127	3005	15.6	**Fenton** (city) Genesee County
128	3019	15.7	**Traverse City** (city) Grand Traverse County
129	3050	16.0	**Southfield** (city) Oakland County
130	3068	16.1	**Monroe** (charter township) Monroe County
131	3084	16.2	**Leoni** (township) Jackson County
132	3096	16.3	**Roseville** (city) Macomb County
133	3112	16.4	**Blackman** (charter township) Jackson County
133	3112	16.4	**Niles** (township) Berrien County
135	3125	16.5	**Harper Woods** (city) Wayne County
136	3153	16.7	**Wyoming** (city) Kent County
137	3258	17.5	**Wayne** (city) Wayne County
138	3289	17.7	**Frenchtown** (township) Monroe County
139	3362	18.2	**Warren** (city) Macomb County
140	3375	18.3	**Lincoln Park** (city) Wayne County
141	3435	18.8	**Madison Heights** (city) Oakland County
142	3442	18.9	**Kalamazoo** (charter township) Kalamazoo County
143	3452	19.0	**Dearborn Heights** (city) Wayne County
144	3482	19.2	**Cutlerville** (CDP) Kent County
144	3482	19.2	**Flint** (charter township) Genesee County
144	3482	19.2	**Genesee** (charter township) Genesee County
144	3482	19.2	**Holland** (city) Ottawa County
148	3512	19.4	**Oak Park** (city) Oakland County
149	3526	19.5	**Monroe** (city) Monroe County
150	3557	19.7	**Burton** (city) Genesee County

Note: The state column ranks the top/bottom 150 places from all places in the state with population of 10,000 or more. The national column ranks the top/bottom 150 places from all places in the country with population of 10,000 or more. Places that are unincorporated were not considered in the rankings. Please refer to the User Guide for additional information.

Educational Attainment: High School Diploma or Higher

Top 150 Places Ranked in *Descending* Order

State Rank	Nat'l Rank	Percent	Place
1	6	99.2	**East Grand Rapids** (city) Kent County
2	9	99.0	**Ada** (township) Kent County
3	17	98.8	**Birmingham** (city) Oakland County
4	61	98.2	**Beverly Hills** (village) Oakland County
4	61	98.2	**Forest Hills** (CDP) Kent County
4	61	98.2	**Southfield** (township) Oakland County
7	89	98.0	**Rochester** (city) Oakland County
8	100	97.9	**Okemos** (CDP) Ingham County
9	116	97.8	**Cascade** (charter township) Kent County
10	202	97.3	**Grosse Pointe Woods** (city) Wayne County
11	229	97.2	**East Lansing** (city) Ingham County
11	229	97.2	**Scio** (township) Washtenaw County
13	252	97.1	**Bloomfield** (charter township) Oakland County
13	252	97.1	**Meridian** (charter township) Ingham County
13	252	97.1	**Texas** (charter township) Kalamazoo County
16	287	96.9	**Cannon** (township) Kent County
17	306	96.8	**Brighton** (township) Livingston County
17	306	96.8	**Grand Rapids** (charter township) Kent County
17	306	96.8	**Grosse Ile** (township) Wayne County
20	372	96.5	**Ann Arbor** (city) Washtenaw County
21	391	96.4	**Haslett** (CDP) Ingham County
21	391	96.4	**Oceola** (township) Livingston County
21	391	96.4	**Plymouth** (charter township) Wayne County
24	453	96.2	**Northville** (township) Wayne County
24	453	96.2	**Oakland** (charter township) Oakland County
26	524	95.9	**Farmington** (city) Oakland County
27	558	95.8	**Genoa** (township) Livingston County
28	580	95.7	**Flushing** (charter township) Genesee County
28	580	95.7	**Oshtemo** (charter township) Kalamazoo County
28	580	95.7	**Portage** (city) Kalamazoo County
28	580	95.7	**Tyrone** (township) Livingston County
32	615	95.6	**Saint Joseph** (charter township) Berrien County
32	615	95.6	**Woodhaven** (city) Wayne County
34	644	95.5	**Berkley** (city) Oakland County
34	644	95.5	**Grosse Pointe Park** (city) Wayne County
36	668	95.4	**Georgetown** (charter township) Ottawa County
36	668	95.4	**Northview** (CDP) Kent County
36	668	95.4	**Rochester Hills** (city) Oakland County
39	732	95.2	**Delta** (charter township) Eaton County
39	732	95.2	**Waverly** (CDP) Eaton County
41	766	95.1	**Hamburg** (township) Livingston County
41	766	95.1	**Royal Oak** (city) Oakland County
41	766	95.1	**Traverse City** (city) Grand Traverse County
44	790	95.0	**Plainfield** (charter township) Kent County
45	823	94.9	**Hartland** (township) Livingston County
45	823	94.9	**Orion** (charter township) Oakland County
45	823	94.9	**Park** (township) Ottawa County
48	852	94.8	**Grand Blanc** (charter township) Genesee County
48	852	94.8	**Green Oak** (township) Livingston County
50	881	94.7	**Caledonia** (township) Kent County
50	881	94.7	**Davison** (township) Genesee County
50	881	94.7	**Novi** (city) Oakland County
53	910	94.6	**Independence** (charter township) Oakland County
53	910	94.6	**Springfield** (charter township) Oakland County
55	937	94.5	**Canton** (charter township) Wayne County
55	937	94.5	**Grand Haven** (charter township) Ottawa County
57	970	94.4	**Fenton** (charter township) Genesee County
58	1043	94.2	**West Bloomfield** (charter township) Oakland County
59	1077	94.1	**Bedford** (township) Monroe County
60	1118	94.0	**Bath** (charter township) Clinton County
60	1118	94.0	**Mundy** (township) Genesee County
60	1118	94.0	**Pittsfield** (charter township) Washtenaw County
60	1118	94.0	**Troy** (city) Oakland County
64	1160	93.9	**Farmington Hills** (city) Oakland County
64	1160	93.9	**Summit** (township) Jackson County
66	1192	93.8	**Fruitport** (charter township) Muskegon County
67	1224	93.7	**Spring Lake** (township) Ottawa County
68	1264	93.6	**Allendale** (charter township) Ottawa County
68	1264	93.6	**Commerce** (charter township) Oakland County
68	1264	93.6	**Holt** (CDP) Ingham County
68	1264	93.6	**Midland** (city) Midland County
68	1264	93.6	**New Baltimore** (city) Macomb County
73	1301	93.5	**Allendale** (CDP) Ottawa County
73	1301	93.5	**Delhi** (charter township) Ingham County
73	1301	93.5	**Ferndale** (city) Oakland County
73	1301	93.5	**Grandville** (city) Kent County
73	1301	93.5	**Milford** (charter township) Oakland County
78	1330	93.4	**White Lake** (charter township) Oakland County
79	1369	93.3	**Lincoln** (charter township) Berrien County
79	1369	93.3	**Lyon** (charter township) Oakland County
81	1399	93.2	**East Bay** (township) Grand Traverse County
81	1399	93.2	**Livonia** (city) Wayne County
81	1399	93.2	**Marquette** (city) Marquette County
81	1399	93.2	**Oxford** (charter township) Oakland County
85	1431	93.1	**Jenison** (CDP) Ottawa County
85	1431	93.1	**Washington** (township) Macomb County
87	1494	92.9	**Clawson** (city) Oakland County
87	1494	92.9	**Saginaw** (charter township) Saginaw County
89	1532	92.8	**Garfield** (charter township) Grand Traverse County
89	1532	92.8	**Walker** (city) Kent County
89	1532	92.8	**Wixom** (city) Oakland County
92	1569	92.7	**Mount Pleasant** (city) Isabella County
93	1595	92.6	**Grand Haven** (city) Ottawa County
93	1595	92.6	**Highland** (charter township) Oakland County
95	1629	92.5	**Norton Shores** (city) Muskegon County
96	1670	92.4	**Brandon** (charter township) Oakland County
96	1670	92.4	**DeWitt** (charter township) Clinton County
96	1670	92.4	**Southfield** (city) Oakland County
99	1702	92.3	**Antwerp** (township) Van Buren County
99	1702	92.3	**Union** (charter township) Isabella County
101	1734	92.2	**Macomb** (township) Macomb County
102	1799	92.0	**Harrison** (charter township) Macomb County
103	1856	91.8	**Monitor** (charter township) Bay County
103	1856	91.8	**Saint Clair Shores** (city) Macomb County
105	1906	91.6	**Fort Gratiot** (charter township) Saint Clair County
106	2024	91.2	**Cooper** (charter township) Kalamazoo County
106	2024	91.2	**Oak Park** (city) Oakland County
106	2024	91.2	**Superior** (charter township) Washtenaw County
109	2050	91.1	**Van Buren** (charter township) Wayne County
110	2102	90.9	**Holly** (township) Oakland County
110	2102	90.9	**Kentwood** (city) Kent County
112	2137	90.8	**South Lyon** (city) Oakland County
113	2160	90.7	**Bangor** (charter township) Bay County
113	2160	90.7	**Byron** (township) Kent County
115	2184	90.6	**Gaines** (charter township) Kent County
115	2184	90.6	**Shelby** (charter township) Macomb County
117	2239	90.4	**Emmett** (charter township) Calhoun County
117	2239	90.4	**Fenton** (city) Genesee County
119	2264	90.3	**Thomas** (township) Saginaw County
119	2264	90.3	**Waterford** (charter township) Oakland County
121	2293	90.2	**Allen Park** (city) Wayne County
121	2293	90.2	**Kalamazoo** (charter township) Kalamazoo County
123	2321	90.1	**Chesterfield** (township) Macomb County
123	2321	90.1	**Owosso** (city) Shiawassee County
123	2321	90.1	**Trenton** (city) Wayne County
126	2342	90.0	**Auburn Hills** (city) Oakland County
126	2342	90.0	**Fraser** (city) Macomb County
128	2389	89.8	**Comstock** (charter township) Kalamazoo County
129	2407	89.7	**Escanaba** (city) Delta County
130	2454	89.5	**Brownstown** (charter township) Wayne County
131	2476	89.4	**Garden City** (city) Wayne County
131	2476	89.4	**Kalamazoo** (city) Kalamazoo County
133	2501	89.3	**Clinton** (charter township) Macomb County
134	2525	89.2	**Cadillac** (city) Wexford County
134	2525	89.2	**Redford** (charter township) Wayne County
134	2525	89.2	**Sault Sainte Marie** (city) Chippewa County
137	2551	89.1	**Ypsilanti** (city) Washtenaw County
138	2614	88.8	**Burton** (city) Genesee County
139	2654	88.6	**Alpena** (city) Alpena County
139	2654	88.6	**Lenox** (township) Macomb County
139	2654	88.6	**Monroe** (city) Monroe County
142	2710	88.4	**Southgate** (city) Wayne County
142	2710	88.4	**Vienna** (charter township) Genesee County
142	2710	88.4	**Ypsilanti** (charter township) Washtenaw County
145	2739	88.3	**Battle Creek** (city) Calhoun County
146	2764	88.2	**Big Rapids** (city) Mecosta County
147	2805	88.0	**Huron** (charter township) Wayne County
148	2873	87.7	**Westland** (city) Wayne County
149	2947	87.3	**Harper Woods** (city) Wayne County
150	2968	87.2	**Flint** (charter township) Genesee County

Note: *The state column ranks the top/bottom 150 places from all places in the state with population of 10,000 or more. The national column ranks the top/bottom 150 places from all places in the country with population of 10,000 or more. Places that are unincorporated were not considered in the rankings. Please refer to the User Guide for additional information.*

Educational Attainment: High School Diploma or Higher

Top 150 Places Ranked in *Ascending* Order

State Rank	Nat'l Rank	Percent	Place
1	122	64.8	**Hamtramck** (city) Wayne County
2	246	71.8	**Benton Harbor** (city) Berrien County
3	311	73.8	**Highland Park** (city) Wayne County
4	395	75.7	**Benton** (charter township) Berrien County
5	427	76.4	**Pontiac** (city) Oakland County
6	446	76.8	**Melvindale** (city) Wayne County
7	498	77.6	**Detroit** (city) Wayne County
8	510	77.8	**Saginaw** (city) Saginaw County
9	549	78.4	**Sturgis** (city) Saint Joseph County
10	576	78.8	**Muskegon Heights** (city) Muskegon County
11	595	79.0	**Beecher** (CDP) Genesee County
12	621	79.3	**Inkster** (city) Wayne County
13	646	79.6	**Hazel Park** (city) Oakland County
14	710	80.4	**Lincoln Park** (city) Wayne County
15	755	80.9	**Niles** (city) Berrien County
16	774	81.1	**Dearborn** (city) Wayne County
17	787	81.2	**Adrian** (city) Lenawee County
18	847	81.7	**Flint** (city) Genesee County
19	899	82.3	**Muskegon** (city) Muskegon County
19	899	82.3	**Taylor** (city) Wayne County
21	974	82.9	**Jackson** (city) Jackson County
22	1007	83.2	**Holland** (charter township) Ottawa County
22	1007	83.2	**Mount Clemens** (city) Macomb County
24	1048	83.5	**Madison Heights** (city) Oakland County
25	1065	83.6	**Frenchtown** (township) Monroe County
26	1086	83.7	**Ionia** (city) Ionia County
27	1103	83.8	**Warren** (city) Macomb County
28	1121	83.9	**Grand Rapids** (city) Kent County
29	1157	84.1	**Mount Morris** (township) Genesee County
29	1157	84.1	**Wayne** (city) Wayne County
31	1196	84.4	**Bridgeport** (charter township) Saginaw County
32	1206	84.5	**Niles** (township) Berrien County
33	1235	84.7	**Comstock Park** (CDP) Kent County
34	1250	84.8	**Eastpointe** (city) Macomb County
34	1250	84.8	**Holland** (city) Ottawa County
36	1307	85.2	**Alpine** (township) Kent County
36	1307	85.2	**Dearborn Heights** (city) Wayne County
36	1307	85.2	**Genesee** (charter township) Genesee County
36	1307	85.2	**Wyoming** (city) Kent County
40	1333	85.3	**Monroe** (charter township) Monroe County
40	1333	85.3	**Roseville** (city) Macomb County
42	1350	85.4	**Coldwater** (city) Branch County
42	1350	85.4	**Muskegon** (charter township) Muskegon County
44	1403	85.7	**Romulus** (city) Wayne County
45	1424	85.8	**Sterling Heights** (city) Macomb County
46	1445	85.9	**Leoni** (township) Jackson County
47	1463	86.0	**Port Huron** (charter township) Saint Clair County
47	1463	86.0	**Port Huron** (city) Saint Clair County
49	1486	86.1	**Bay City** (city) Bay County
50	1502	86.2	**Lansing** (city) Ingham County
51	1537	86.4	**Blackman** (charter township) Jackson County
52	1569	86.6	**Wyandotte** (city) Wayne County
53	1580	86.7	**Riverview** (city) Wayne County
54	1626	87.0	**Cutlerville** (CDP) Kent County
55	1670	87.2	**Flint** (charter township) Genesee County
56	1689	87.3	**Harper Woods** (city) Wayne County
57	1758	87.7	**Westland** (city) Wayne County
58	1827	88.0	**Huron** (charter township) Wayne County
59	1872	88.2	**Big Rapids** (city) Mecosta County
60	1893	88.3	**Battle Creek** (city) Calhoun County
61	1918	88.4	**Southgate** (city) Wayne County
61	1918	88.4	**Vienna** (charter township) Genesee County
61	1918	88.4	**Ypsilanti** (charter township) Washtenaw County
64	1973	88.6	**Alpena** (city) Alpena County
64	1973	88.6	**Lenox** (township) Macomb County
64	1973	88.6	**Monroe** (city) Monroe County
67	2021	88.8	**Burton** (city) Genesee County
68	2086	89.1	**Ypsilanti** (city) Washtenaw County
69	2106	89.2	**Cadillac** (city) Wexford County
69	2106	89.2	**Redford** (charter township) Wayne County
69	2106	89.2	**Sault Sainte Marie** (city) Chippewa County
72	2132	89.3	**Clinton** (charter township) Macomb County
73	2156	89.4	**Garden City** (city) Wayne County
73	2156	89.4	**Kalamazoo** (city) Kalamazoo County
75	2181	89.5	**Brownstown** (charter township) Wayne County
76	2227	89.7	**Escanaba** (city) Delta County
77	2250	89.8	**Comstock** (charter township) Kalamazoo County
78	2288	90.0	**Auburn Hills** (city) Oakland County
78	2288	90.0	**Fraser** (city) Macomb County
80	2315	90.1	**Chesterfield** (township) Macomb County
80	2315	90.1	**Owosso** (city) Shiawassee County
80	2315	90.1	**Trenton** (city) Wayne County
83	2336	90.2	**Allen Park** (city) Wayne County
83	2336	90.2	**Kalamazoo** (charter township) Kalamazoo County
85	2364	90.3	**Thomas** (township) Saginaw County
85	2364	90.3	**Waterford** (charter township) Oakland County
87	2393	90.4	**Emmett** (charter township) Calhoun County
87	2393	90.4	**Fenton** (city) Genesee County
89	2441	90.6	**Gaines** (charter township) Kent County
89	2441	90.6	**Shelby** (charter township) Macomb County
91	2473	90.7	**Bangor** (charter township) Bay County
91	2473	90.7	**Byron** (township) Kent County
93	2497	90.8	**South Lyon** (city) Oakland County
94	2520	90.9	**Holly** (township) Oakland County
94	2520	90.9	**Kentwood** (city) Kent County
96	2586	91.1	**Van Buren** (charter township) Wayne County
97	2607	91.2	**Cooper** (charter township) Kalamazoo County
97	2607	91.2	**Oak Park** (city) Oakland County
97	2607	91.2	**Superior** (charter township) Washtenaw County
100	2713	91.6	**Fort Gratiot** (charter township) Saint Clair County
101	2773	91.8	**Monitor** (charter township) Bay County
101	2773	91.8	**Saint Clair Shores** (city) Macomb County
103	2827	92.0	**Harrison** (charter township) Macomb County
104	2889	92.2	**Macomb** (township) Macomb County
105	2923	92.3	**Antwerp** (township) Van Buren County
105	2923	92.3	**Union** (charter township) Isabella County
107	2955	92.4	**Brandon** (charter township) Oakland County
107	2955	92.4	**DeWitt** (charter township) Clinton County
107	2955	92.4	**Southfield** (city) Oakland County
110	2987	92.5	**Norton Shores** (city) Muskegon County
111	3028	92.6	**Grand Haven** (city) Ottawa County
111	3028	92.6	**Highland** (charter township) Oakland County
113	3062	92.7	**Mount Pleasant** (city) Isabella County
114	3088	92.8	**Garfield** (charter township) Grand Traverse County
114	3088	92.8	**Walker** (city) Kent County
114	3088	92.8	**Wixom** (city) Oakland County
117	3125	92.9	**Clawson** (city) Oakland County
117	3125	92.9	**Saginaw** (charter township) Saginaw County
119	3189	93.1	**Jenison** (CDP) Ottawa County
119	3189	93.1	**Washington** (township) Macomb County
121	3226	93.2	**East Bay** (township) Grand Traverse County
121	3226	93.2	**Livonia** (city) Wayne County
121	3226	93.2	**Marquette** (city) Marquette County
121	3226	93.2	**Oxford** (charter township) Oakland County
125	3258	93.3	**Lincoln** (charter township) Berrien County
125	3258	93.3	**Lyon** (charter township) Oakland County
127	3288	93.4	**White Lake** (charter township) Oakland County
128	3327	93.5	**Allendale** (CDP) Ottawa County
128	3327	93.5	**Delhi** (charter township) Ingham County
128	3327	93.5	**Ferndale** (city) Oakland County
128	3327	93.5	**Grandville** (city) Kent County
128	3327	93.5	**Milford** (charter township) Oakland County
133	3356	93.6	**Allendale** (charter township) Ottawa County
133	3356	93.6	**Commerce** (charter township) Oakland County
133	3356	93.6	**Holt** (CDP) Ingham County
133	3356	93.6	**Midland** (city) Midland County
133	3356	93.6	**New Baltimore** (city) Macomb County
138	3393	93.7	**Spring Lake** (township) Ottawa County
139	3433	93.8	**Fruitport** (charter township) Muskegon County
140	3465	93.9	**Farmington Hills** (city) Oakland County
140	3465	93.9	**Summit** (township) Jackson County
142	3497	94.0	**Bath** (charter township) Clinton County
142	3497	94.0	**Mundy** (township) Genesee County
142	3497	94.0	**Pittsfield** (charter township) Washtenaw County
142	3497	94.0	**Troy** (city) Oakland County
146	3539	94.1	**Bedford** (township) Monroe County
147	3580	94.2	**West Bloomfield** (charter township) Oakland County
148	3653	94.4	**Fenton** (charter township) Genesee County
149	3687	94.5	**Canton** (charter township) Wayne County
149	3687	94.5	**Grand Haven** (charter township) Ottawa County

Note: The state column ranks the top/bottom 150 places from all places in the state with population of 10,000 or more. The national column ranks the top/bottom 150 places from all places in the country with population of 10,000 or more. Places that are unincorporated were not considered in the rankings. Please refer to the User Guide for additional information.

Educational Attainment: Bachelor's Degree or Higher

Top 150 Places Ranked in *Descending* Order

State Rank	Nat'l Rank	Percent	Place	State Rank	Nat'l Rank	Percent	Place
1	30	77.9	**East Grand Rapids** (city) Kent County	76	1831	33.1	**Kentwood** (city) Kent County
2	37	76.9	**Birmingham** (city) Oakland County	77	1841	33.0	**Fenton** (charter township) Genesee County
3	113	70.6	**Ann Arbor** (city) Washtenaw County	78	1852	32.9	**Saginaw** (charter township) Saginaw County
4	123	70.0	**Okemos** (CDP) Ingham County	79	1861	32.8	**Clawson** (city) Oakland County
5	131	69.0	**Southfield** (township) Oakland County	80	1874	32.7	**Grandville** (city) Kent County
6	132	68.9	**Bloomfield** (charter township) Oakland County	81	1895	32.5	**Holt** (CDP) Ingham County
7	136	68.6	**Beverly Hills** (village) Oakland County	82	1919	32.2	**Delhi** (charter township) Ingham County
8	138	68.5	**East Lansing** (city) Ingham County	83	1935	32.0	**Big Rapids** (city) Mecosta County
9	212	64.8	**Meridian** (charter township) Ingham County	84	1948	31.9	**Kalamazoo** (city) Kalamazoo County
10	215	64.7	**Grosse Pointe Park** (city) Wayne County	85	2002	31.3	**White Lake** (charter township) Oakland County
11	238	63.8	**Cascade** (charter township) Kent County	86	2011	31.2	**Grand Haven** (city) Ottawa County
11	238	63.8	**Forest Hills** (CDP) Kent County	87	2032	31.0	**Holland** (city) Ottawa County
13	257	63.2	**Scio** (township) Washtenaw County	88	2065	30.7	**Washington** (township) Macomb County
14	307	61.1	**Rochester** (city) Oakland County	89	2090	30.5	**Summit** (township) Jackson County
15	353	59.1	**Ada** (township) Kent County	90	2103	30.4	**Northview** (CDP) Kent County
16	361	58.7	**Northville** (township) Wayne County	91	2109	30.3	**Flushing** (charter township) Genesee County
17	375	58.1	**Haslett** (CDP) Ingham County	92	2122	30.2	**Shelby** (charter township) Macomb County
18	388	57.6	**Troy** (city) Oakland County	93	2158	29.9	**Gaines** (charter township) Kent County
19	402	57.2	**Oakland** (charter township) Oakland County	94	2174	29.8	**East Bay** (township) Grand Traverse County
20	407	57.1	**Grosse Pointe Woods** (city) Wayne County	94	2174	29.8	**Kalamazoo** (charter township) Kalamazoo County
21	433	56.4	**Pittsfield** (charter township) Washtenaw County	96	2187	29.7	**DeWitt** (charter township) Clinton County
22	437	56.2	**Novi** (city) Oakland County	96	2187	29.7	**Union** (charter township) Isabella County
23	448	56.0	**West Bloomfield** (charter township) Oakland County	98	2216	29.4	**Grand Rapids** (city) Kent County
24	523	54.2	**Grand Rapids** (charter township) Kent County	99	2236	29.2	**Norton Shores** (city) Muskegon County
25	550	53.6	**Farmington** (city) Oakland County	100	2275	28.9	**Dearborn** (city) Wayne County
26	569	52.9	**Texas** (charter township) Kalamazoo County	101	2291	28.8	**Garfield** (charter township) Grand Traverse County
27	619	51.7	**Rochester Hills** (city) Oakland County	101	2291	28.8	**Oak Park** (city) Oakland County
28	643	51.1	**Plymouth** (charter township) Wayne County	103	2297	28.7	**Ypsilanti** (charter township) Washtenaw County
29	656	50.8	**Farmington Hills** (city) Oakland County	104	2316	28.5	**Walker** (city) Kent County
30	683	50.1	**Royal Oak** (city) Oakland County	105	2327	28.4	**Byron** (township) Kent County
31	758	48.6	**Cannon** (township) Kent County	106	2348	28.2	**Highland** (charter township) Oakland County
32	841	46.8	**Grosse Ile** (township) Wayne County	107	2366	28.0	**Cooper** (charter township) Kalamazoo County
33	847	46.7	**Canton** (charter township) Wayne County	108	2387	27.8	**Van Buren** (charter township) Wayne County
34	883	46.0	**Berkley** (city) Oakland County	109	2442	27.3	**Fenton** (city) Genesee County
35	942	45.0	**Bath** (charter township) Clinton County	110	2484	27.0	**Allendale** (CDP) Ottawa County
36	989	44.1	**Oshtemo** (charter township) Kalamazoo County	111	2529	26.6	**Antwerp** (township) Van Buren County
37	1051	43.1	**Brighton** (township) Livingston County	111	2529	26.6	**Jenison** (CDP) Ottawa County
38	1058	42.9	**Midland** (city) Midland County	111	2529	26.6	**New Baltimore** (city) Macomb County
39	1102	42.1	**Superior** (charter township) Washtenaw County	114	2542	26.5	**Fort Gratiot** (charter township) Saint Clair County
40	1150	41.3	**Grand Haven** (charter township) Ottawa County	115	2582	26.2	**Brandon** (charter township) Oakland County
41	1163	41.0	**Commerce** (charter township) Oakland County	116	2597	26.1	**Comstock** (charter township) Kalamazoo County
42	1219	40.3	**Ferndale** (city) Oakland County	117	2605	26.0	**Waterford** (charter township) Oakland County
42	1219	40.3	**Orion** (charter township) Oakland County	118	2632	25.8	**Sterling Heights** (city) Macomb County
42	1219	40.3	**Traverse City** (city) Grand Traverse County	119	2658	25.6	**Bedford** (township) Monroe County
45	1229	40.2	**Milford** (charter township) Oakland County	120	2711	25.1	**Harper Woods** (city) Wayne County
45	1229	40.2	**Park** (township) Ottawa County	121	2722	25.0	**Allendale** (charter township) Ottawa County
47	1252	39.9	**Auburn Hills** (city) Oakland County	122	2747	24.8	**Harrison** (charter township) Macomb County
48	1258	39.8	**Portage** (city) Kalamazoo County	123	2759	24.7	**Lansing** (city) Ingham County
49	1306	39.1	**Mount Pleasant** (city) Isabella County	124	2835	24.1	**Saint Clair Shores** (city) Macomb County
50	1323	38.9	**Lincoln** (charter township) Berrien County	124	2835	24.1	**Trenton** (city) Wayne County
51	1344	38.6	**Wixom** (city) Oakland County	126	2840	24.0	**Monitor** (charter township) Bay County
52	1361	38.4	**Genoa** (township) Livingston County	127	2852	23.9	**Holland** (charter township) Ottawa County
53	1374	38.2	**Saint Joseph** (charter township) Berrien County	128	2932	23.3	**Brownstown** (charter township) Wayne County
54	1390	38.0	**Independence** (charter township) Oakland County	129	2946	23.2	**Riverview** (city) Wayne County
55	1400	37.9	**Hartland** (township) Livingston County	130	2978	22.9	**Woodhaven** (city) Wayne County
56	1437	37.4	**Caledonia** (township) Kent County	131	2998	22.7	**Allen Park** (city) Wayne County
57	1464	37.0	**Marquette** (city) Marquette County	132	3098	21.9	**Battle Creek** (city) Calhoun County
57	1464	37.0	**Spring Lake** (township) Ottawa County	132	3098	21.9	**Madison Heights** (city) Oakland County
59	1473	36.9	**Ypsilanti** (city) Washtenaw County	134	3111	21.8	**Chesterfield** (township) Macomb County
60	1479	36.8	**Hamburg** (township) Livingston County	134	3111	21.8	**Thomas** (township) Saginaw County
61	1495	36.6	**Delta** (charter township) Eaton County	136	3120	21.7	**Davison** (township) Genesee County
62	1514	36.4	**South Lyon** (city) Oakland County	137	3150	21.5	**Mundy** (township) Genesee County
62	1514	36.4	**Springfield** (charter township) Oakland County	138	3229	20.9	**Holly** (township) Oakland County
64	1529	36.2	**Southfield** (city) Oakland County	138	3229	20.9	**Sault Sainte Marie** (city) Chippewa County
65	1564	35.8	**Oceola** (township) Livingston County	140	3301	20.5	**Clinton** (charter township) Macomb County
66	1592	35.5	**Lyon** (charter township) Oakland County	141	3385	19.9	**Adrian** (city) Lenawee County
67	1600	35.4	**Livonia** (city) Wayne County	141	3385	19.9	**Dearborn Heights** (city) Wayne County
68	1617	35.2	**Tyrone** (township) Livingston County	143	3445	19.4	**Wyoming** (city) Kent County
68	1617	35.2	**Waverly** (CDP) Eaton County	144	3460	19.3	**Fruitport** (charter township) Muskegon County
70	1629	35.1	**Green Oak** (township) Livingston County	145	3488	19.1	**Flint** (charter township) Genesee County
71	1696	34.5	**Grand Blanc** (charter township) Genesee County	146	3516	18.9	**Fraser** (city) Macomb County
72	1745	34.0	**Oxford** (charter township) Oakland County	147	3527	18.8	**Emmett** (charter township) Calhoun County
73	1763	33.8	**Macomb** (township) Macomb County	148	3557	18.6	**Comstock Park** (CDP) Kent County
74	1789	33.6	**Georgetown** (township) Ottawa County	148	3557	18.6	**Huron** (charter township) Wayne County
75	1817	33.2	**Plainfield** (charter township) Kent County	150	3590	18.4	**Cutlerville** (CDP) Kent County

Note: The state column ranks the top/bottom 150 places from all places in the state with population of 10,000 or more. The national column ranks the top/bottom 150 places from all places in the country with population of 10,000 or more. Places that are unincorporated were not considered in the rankings. Please refer to the User Guide for additional information.

Educational Attainment: Bachelor's Degree or Higher

Top 150 Places Ranked in *Ascending* Order

State Rank	Nat'l Rank	Percent	Place	State Rank	Nat'l Rank	Percent	Place
1	24	4.8	**Benton Harbor** (city) Berrien County	76	1704	23.2	**Riverview** (city) Wayne County
2	28	5.1	**Muskegon Heights** (city) Muskegon County	77	1711	23.3	**Brownstown** (charter township) Wayne County
3	44	6.0	**Beecher** (CDP) Genesee County	78	1790	23.9	**Holland** (charter township) Ottawa County
4	90	8.1	**Lincoln Park** (city) Wayne County	79	1805	24.0	**Monitor** (charter township) Bay County
5	109	9.0	**Bridgeport** (charter township) Saginaw County	80	1817	24.1	**Saint Clair Shores** (city) Macomb County
5	109	9.0	**Ionia** (city) Ionia County	80	1817	24.1	**Trenton** (city) Wayne County
7	138	9.7	**Taylor** (city) Wayne County	82	1883	24.7	**Lansing** (city) Ingham County
8	143	9.8	**Roseville** (city) Macomb County	83	1898	24.8	**Harrison** (charter township) Macomb County
9	149	9.9	**Highland Park** (city) Wayne County	84	1920	25.0	**Allendale** (charter township) Ottawa County
10	165	10.1	**Inkster** (city) Wayne County	85	1935	25.1	**Harper Woods** (city) Wayne County
10	165	10.1	**Muskegon** (charter township) Muskegon County	86	1993	25.6	**Bedford** (township) Monroe County
10	165	10.1	**Romulus** (city) Wayne County	87	2010	25.8	**Sterling Heights** (city) Macomb County
13	184	10.3	**Hazel Park** (city) Oakland County	88	2039	26.0	**Waterford** (charter township) Oakland County
14	218	10.8	**Benton** (charter township) Berrien County	89	2052	26.1	**Comstock** (charter township) Kalamazoo County
15	225	10.9	**Muskegon** (city) Muskegon County	90	2060	26.2	**Brandon** (charter township) Oakland County
16	231	11.0	**Flint** (city) Genesee County	91	2095	26.5	**Fort Gratiot** (charter township) Saint Clair County
17	269	11.5	**Mount Morris** (township) Genesee County	92	2115	26.6	**Antwerp** (township) Van Buren County
17	269	11.5	**Saginaw** (city) Saginaw County	92	2115	26.6	**Jenison** (CDP) Ottawa County
19	276	11.6	**Genesee** (charter township) Genesee County	92	2115	26.6	**New Baltimore** (city) Macomb County
19	276	11.6	**Niles** (city) Berrien County	95	2160	27.0	**Allendale** (CDP) Ottawa County
19	276	11.6	**Wayne** (city) Wayne County	96	2197	27.3	**Fenton** (city) Genesee County
22	286	11.7	**Melvindale** (city) Wayne County	97	2253	27.8	**Van Buren** (charter township) Wayne County
23	295	11.8	**Pontiac** (city) Oakland County	98	2280	28.0	**Cooper** (charter township) Kalamazoo County
24	328	12.3	**Garden City** (city) Wayne County	99	2298	28.2	**Highland** (charter township) Oakland County
25	340	12.4	**Hamtramck** (city) Wayne County	100	2318	28.4	**Byron** (township) Kent County
26	348	12.5	**Lenox** (township) Macomb County	101	2330	28.5	**Walker** (city) Kent County
27	356	12.6	**Port Huron** (charter township) Saint Clair County	102	2349	28.7	**Ypsilanti** (charter township) Washtenaw County
28	366	12.7	**Detroit** (city) Wayne County	103	2360	28.8	**Garfield** (charter township) Grand Traverse County
29	394	13.0	**Blackman** (charter township) Jackson County	103	2360	28.8	**Oak Park** (city) Oakland County
29	394	13.0	**Coldwater** (city) Branch County	105	2366	28.9	**Dearborn** (city) Wayne County
29	394	13.0	**Eastpointe** (city) Macomb County	106	2403	29.2	**Norton Shores** (city) Muskegon County
32	440	13.5	**Frenchtown** (township) Monroe County	107	2426	29.4	**Grand Rapids** (city) Kent County
32	440	13.5	**Jackson** (city) Jackson County	108	2462	29.7	**DeWitt** (charter township) Clinton County
32	440	13.5	**Owosso** (city) Shiawassee County	108	2462	29.7	**Union** (charter township) Isabella County
35	499	14.2	**Burton** (city) Genesee County	110	2470	29.8	**East Bay** (township) Grand Traverse County
36	564	14.8	**Port Huron** (city) Saint Clair County	110	2470	29.8	**Kalamazoo** (charter township) Kalamazoo County
37	668	15.5	**Cadillac** (city) Wexford County	112	2483	29.9	**Gaines** (charter township) Kent County
38	703	15.8	**Wyandotte** (city) Wayne County	113	2523	30.2	**Shelby** (charter township) Macomb County
39	719	15.9	**Bay City** (city) Bay County	114	2535	30.3	**Flushing** (charter township) Genesee County
40	733	16.0	**Escanaba** (city) Delta County	115	2548	30.4	**Northview** (CDP) Kent County
40	733	16.0	**Leoni** (township) Jackson County	116	2554	30.5	**Summit** (township) Jackson County
42	762	16.2	**Vienna** (charter township) Genesee County	117	2583	30.7	**Washington** (township) Macomb County
43	774	16.3	**Warren** (city) Macomb County	118	2611	31.0	**Holland** (city) Ottawa County
44	812	16.6	**Southgate** (city) Wayne County	119	2635	31.2	**Grand Haven** (city) Ottawa County
45	842	16.9	**Monroe** (charter township) Monroe County	120	2646	31.3	**White Lake** (charter township) Oakland County
46	857	17.0	**Sturgis** (city) Saint Joseph County	121	2695	31.9	**Kalamazoo** (city) Kalamazoo County
47	905	17.4	**Bangor** (charter township) Bay County	122	2709	32.0	**Big Rapids** (city) Mecosta County
48	922	17.5	**Monroe** (city) Monroe County	123	2731	32.2	**Delhi** (charter township) Ingham County
48	922	17.5	**Niles** (township) Berrien County	124	2754	32.5	**Holt** (CDP) Ingham County
50	958	17.8	**Westland** (city) Wayne County	125	2768	32.7	**Grandville** (city) Kent County
51	985	18.0	**Alpena** (city) Alpena County	126	2783	32.8	**Clawson** (city) Oakland County
52	1025	18.2	**Mount Clemens** (city) Macomb County	127	2796	32.9	**Saginaw** (charter township) Saginaw County
52	1025	18.2	**Redford** (charter township) Wayne County	128	2805	33.0	**Fenton** (charter township) Genesee County
54	1042	18.3	**Alpine** (township) Kent County	129	2816	33.1	**Kentwood** (city) Kent County
55	1051	18.4	**Cutlerville** (CDP) Kent County	130	2826	33.2	**Plainfield** (charter township) Kent County
56	1080	18.6	**Comstock Park** (CDP) Kent County	131	2857	33.6	**Georgetown** (charter township) Ottawa County
56	1080	18.6	**Huron** (charter township) Wayne County	132	2882	33.8	**Macomb** (township) Macomb County
58	1116	18.8	**Emmett** (charter township) Calhoun County	133	2905	34.0	**Oxford** (charter township) Oakland County
59	1130	18.9	**Fraser** (city) Macomb County	134	2952	34.5	**Grand Blanc** (charter township) Genesee County
60	1150	19.1	**Flint** (charter township) Genesee County	135	3008	35.1	**Green Oak** (township) Livingston County
61	1185	19.3	**Fruitport** (charter township) Muskegon County	136	3028	35.2	**Tyrone** (township) Livingston County
62	1197	19.4	**Wyoming** (city) Kent County	136	3028	35.2	**Waverly** (CDP) Eaton County
63	1261	19.9	**Adrian** (city) Lenawee County	138	3048	35.4	**Livonia** (city) Wayne County
63	1261	19.9	**Dearborn Heights** (city) Wayne County	139	3057	35.5	**Lyon** (charter township) Oakland County
65	1343	20.5	**Clinton** (charter township) Macomb County	140	3084	35.8	**Oceola** (township) Livingston County
66	1404	20.9	**Holly** (township) Oakland County	141	3117	36.2	**Southfield** (city) Oakland County
66	1404	20.9	**Sault Sainte Marie** (city) Chippewa County	142	3133	36.4	**South Lyon** (city) Oakland County
68	1491	21.5	**Mundy** (township) Genesee County	142	3133	36.4	**Springfield** (charter township) Oakland County
69	1522	21.7	**Davison** (township) Genesee County	144	3149	36.6	**Delta** (charter township) Eaton County
70	1537	21.8	**Chesterfield** (township) Macomb County	145	3167	36.8	**Hamburg** (township) Livingston County
70	1537	21.8	**Thomas** (township) Saginaw County	146	3178	36.9	**Ypsilanti** (city) Washtenaw County
72	1546	21.9	**Battle Creek** (city) Calhoun County	147	3184	37.0	**Marquette** (city) Marquette County
72	1546	21.9	**Madison Heights** (city) Oakland County	147	3184	37.0	**Spring Lake** (township) Ottawa County
74	1643	22.7	**Allen Park** (city) Wayne County	149	3212	37.4	**Caledonia** (township) Kent County
75	1667	22.9	**Woodhaven** (city) Wayne County	150	3249	37.9	**Hartland** (township) Livingston County

Note: The state column ranks the top/bottom 150 places from all places in the state with population of 10,000 or more. The national column ranks the top/bottom 150 places from all places in the country with population of 10,000 or more. Places that are unincorporated were not considered in the rankings. Please refer to the User Guide for additional information.

590   Community Rankings

Educational Attainment: Graduate/Professional Degree or Higher

Top 150 Places Ranked in *Descending* Order

State Rank	Nat'l Rank	Percent	Place
1	51	41.7	**Ann Arbor** (city) Washtenaw County
2	72	38.3	**East Lansing** (city) Ingham County
3	89	37.2	**Okemos** (CDP) Ingham County
4	92	37.1	**Birmingham** (city) Oakland County
5	110	35.8	**Scio** (township) Washtenaw County
6	112	35.7	**Grosse Pointe Park** (city) Wayne County
7	131	34.5	**Bloomfield** (charter township) Oakland County
8	135	34.2	**East Grand Rapids** (city) Kent County
9	149	33.8	**Southfield** (township) Oakland County
10	152	33.6	**Meridian** (charter township) Ingham County
11	168	32.7	**Beverly Hills** (village) Oakland County
12	237	30.1	**Northville** (township) Wayne County
13	275	28.8	**Haslett** (CDP) Ingham County
14	288	28.5	**Cascade** (charter township) Kent County
15	308	27.9	**Forest Hills** (CDP) Kent County
16	318	27.7	**Pittsfield** (charter township) Washtenaw County
17	334	27.4	**West Bloomfield** (charter township) Oakland County
18	354	27.0	**Troy** (city) Oakland County
19	369	26.4	**Rochester** (city) Oakland County
20	373	26.3	**Oakland** (charter township) Oakland County
21	418	25.0	**Grosse Pointe Woods** (city) Wayne County
22	435	24.6	**Novi** (city) Oakland County
23	441	24.5	**Ada** (township) Kent County
24	453	24.2	**Texas** (charter township) Kalamazoo County
25	475	23.7	**Farmington** (city) Oakland County
26	512	22.8	**Rochester Hills** (city) Oakland County
27	519	22.7	**Farmington Hills** (city) Oakland County
27	519	22.7	**Plymouth** (charter township) Wayne County
29	643	20.8	**Grand Rapids** (charter township) Kent County
30	653	20.7	**Grosse Ile** (township) Wayne County
31	667	20.5	**Mount Pleasant** (city) Isabella County
31	667	20.5	**Royal Oak** (city) Oakland County
33	804	19.0	**Superior** (charter township) Washtenaw County
34	811	18.9	**Cannon** (township) Kent County
35	850	18.5	**Canton** (charter township) Wayne County
36	868	18.3	**Oshtemo** (charter township) Kalamazoo County
37	886	18.1	**Bath** (charter township) Clinton County
38	938	17.6	**Berkley** (city) Oakland County
39	966	17.4	**Ypsilanti** (city) Washtenaw County
40	1020	17.0	**Midland** (city) Midland County
41	1134	16.0	**Park** (township) Ottawa County
42	1145	15.9	**Saint Joseph** (charter township) Berrien County
43	1199	15.5	**Ferndale** (city) Oakland County
43	1199	15.5	**Southfield** (city) Oakland County
45	1218	15.3	**Auburn Hills** (city) Oakland County
45	1218	15.3	**Brighton** (township) Livingston County
47	1292	14.7	**Portage** (city) Kalamazoo County
48	1302	14.6	**Traverse City** (city) Grand Traverse County
49	1314	14.5	**Independence** (charter township) Oakland County
50	1326	14.4	**Genoa** (township) Livingston County
50	1326	14.4	**Spring Lake** (township) Ottawa County
52	1360	14.2	**Lincoln** (charter township) Berrien County
53	1389	14.0	**Delta** (charter township) Eaton County
54	1412	13.9	**Orion** (charter township) Oakland County
55	1443	13.7	**Grand Blanc** (charter township) Genesee County
55	1443	13.7	**Milford** (charter township) Oakland County
57	1460	13.6	**Green Oak** (township) Livingston County
57	1460	13.6	**Oxford** (charter township) Oakland County
59	1476	13.5	**Springfield** (charter township) Oakland County
60	1497	13.4	**Big Rapids** (city) Mecosta County
60	1497	13.4	**Commerce** (charter township) Oakland County
60	1497	13.4	**Kalamazoo** (city) Kalamazoo County
63	1527	13.2	**Hamburg** (township) Livingston County
64	1561	13.0	**Grand Haven** (charter township) Ottawa County
65	1663	12.5	**Union** (charter township) Isabella County
66	1692	12.3	**East Bay** (township) Grand Traverse County
66	1692	12.3	**Holland** (city) Ottawa County
68	1719	12.2	**Fenton** (charter township) Genesee County
68	1719	12.2	**Marquette** (city) Marquette County
68	1719	12.2	**Wixom** (city) Oakland County
71	1741	12.1	**Oceola** (township) Livingston County
71	1741	12.1	**Waverly** (CDP) Eaton County
73	1765	12.0	**Caledonia** (township) Kent County
73	1765	12.0	**Fort Gratiot** (charter township) Saint Clair County
73	1765	12.0	**Lyon** (charter township) Oakland County
73	1765	12.0	**Saginaw** (charter township) Saginaw County
77	1813	11.8	**Livonia** (city) Wayne County
78	1834	11.7	**Macomb** (township) Macomb County
79	1870	11.5	**New Baltimore** (city) Macomb County
79	1870	11.5	**Shelby** (charter township) Macomb County
81	1897	11.4	**Dearborn** (city) Wayne County
81	1897	11.4	**Hartland** (township) Livingston County
83	1960	11.1	**South Lyon** (city) Oakland County
84	2008	10.9	**Tyrone** (township) Livingston County
85	2028	10.8	**Holt** (CDP) Ingham County
85	2028	10.8	**Kalamazoo** (charter township) Kalamazoo County
85	2028	10.8	**Washington** (township) Macomb County
88	2059	10.7	**Delhi** (charter township) Ingham County
89	2101	10.5	**Clawson** (city) Oakland County
89	2101	10.5	**Plainfield** (charter township) Kent County
89	2101	10.5	**Summit** (township) Jackson County
92	2148	10.3	**Georgetown** (charter township) Ottawa County
92	2148	10.3	**Kentwood** (city) Kent County
94	2183	10.2	**Gaines** (charter township) Kent County
95	2213	10.1	**Antwerp** (township) Van Buren County
95	2213	10.1	**Cooper** (charter township) Kalamazoo County
95	2213	10.1	**Garfield** (charter township) Grand Traverse County
95	2213	10.1	**Grand Rapids** (city) Kent County
95	2213	10.1	**White Lake** (charter township) Oakland County
100	2241	10.0	**Harrison** (charter township) Macomb County
100	2241	10.0	**Northview** (CDP) Kent County
100	2241	10.0	**Ypsilanti** (charter township) Washtenaw County
103	2271	9.9	**Comstock** (charter township) Kalamazoo County
104	2294	9.8	**Fenton** (city) Genesee County
104	2294	9.8	**Van Buren** (charter township) Wayne County
106	2317	9.7	**Bedford** (township) Monroe County
107	2345	9.6	**Grand Haven** (city) Ottawa County
107	2345	9.6	**Grandville** (city) Kent County
107	2345	9.6	**Oak Park** (city) Oakland County
110	2374	9.5	**Mundy** (township) Genesee County
111	2412	9.4	**Trenton** (city) Wayne County
112	2445	9.3	**DeWitt** (charter township) Clinton County
112	2445	9.3	**Norton Shores** (city) Muskegon County
114	2471	9.2	**Sterling Heights** (city) Macomb County
114	2471	9.2	**Waterford** (charter township) Oakland County
116	2501	9.1	**Allendale** (CDP) Ottawa County
116	2501	9.1	**Flushing** (charter township) Genesee County
118	2534	9.0	**Lansing** (city) Ingham County
119	2565	8.9	**Harper Woods** (city) Wayne County
120	2615	8.7	**Sault Sainte Marie** (city) Chippewa County
121	2683	8.5	**Brownstown** (charter township) Wayne County
121	2683	8.5	**Highland** (charter township) Oakland County
123	2749	8.3	**Allendale** (charter township) Ottawa County
123	2749	8.3	**Brandon** (charter township) Oakland County
125	2785	8.2	**Battle Creek** (city) Calhoun County
126	2814	8.1	**Adrian** (city) Lenawee County
126	2814	8.1	**Alpena** (city) Alpena County
128	2851	8.0	**Byron** (township) Kent County
129	2882	7.9	**Davison** (township) Genesee County
129	2882	7.9	**Dearborn Heights** (city) Wayne County
131	2917	7.8	**Monitor** (charter township) Bay County
131	2917	7.8	**Monroe** (city) Monroe County
133	2960	7.7	**Allen Park** (city) Wayne County
133	2960	7.7	**Walker** (city) Kent County
135	3022	7.5	**Woodhaven** (city) Wayne County
136	3055	7.4	**Saint Clair Shores** (city) Macomb County
137	3086	7.3	**Jenison** (CDP) Ottawa County
138	3128	7.2	**Clinton** (charter township) Macomb County
138	3128	7.2	**Holly** (township) Oakland County
138	3128	7.2	**Riverview** (city) Wayne County
138	3128	7.2	**Thomas** (township) Saginaw County
142	3171	7.1	**Flint** (charter township) Genesee County
143	3266	6.8	**Holland** (charter township) Ottawa County
143	3266	6.8	**Mount Clemens** (city) Macomb County
145	3449	6.3	**Niles** (township) Berrien County
145	3449	6.3	**Redford** (charter township) Wayne County
147	3486	6.2	**Vienna** (charter township) Genesee County
148	3519	6.1	**Cadillac** (city) Wexford County
148	3519	6.1	**Chesterfield** (township) Macomb County
150	3558	6.0	**Southgate** (city) Wayne County

Note: *The state column ranks the top/bottom 150 places from all places in the state with population of 10,000 or more. The national column ranks the top/bottom 150 places from all places in the country with population of 10,000 or more. Places that are unincorporated were not considered in the rankings. Please refer to the User Guide for additional information.*

Educational Attainment: Graduate/Professional Degree or Higher

Top 150 Places Ranked in *Ascending* Order

State Rank	Nat'l Rank	Percent	Place	State Rank	Nat'l Rank	Percent	Place
1	32	1.3	**Beecher** (CDP) Genesee County	75	1740	7.9	**Dearborn Heights** (city) Wayne County
2	46	1.5	**Muskegon Heights** (city) Muskegon County	77	1775	8.0	**Byron** (township) Kent County
3	75	1.9	**Hazel Park** (city) Oakland County	78	1806	8.1	**Adrian** (city) Lenawee County
4	106	2.3	**Lincoln Park** (city) Wayne County	78	1806	8.1	**Alpena** (city) Alpena County
5	120	2.4	**Roseville** (city) Macomb County	80	1843	8.2	**Battle Creek** (city) Calhoun County
6	133	2.5	**Ionia** (city) Ionia County	81	1872	8.3	**Allendale** (charter township) Ottawa County
7	144	2.6	**Inkster** (city) Wayne County	81	1872	8.3	**Brandon** (charter township) Oakland County
8	163	2.7	**Muskegon** (city) Muskegon County	83	1941	8.5	**Brownstown** (charter township) Wayne County
9	180	2.8	**Mount Morris** (township) Genesee County	83	1941	8.5	**Highland** (charter township) Oakland County
9	180	2.8	**Taylor** (city) Wayne County	85	2011	8.7	**Sault Sainte Marie** (city) Chippewa County
11	205	3.0	**Benton Harbor** (city) Berrien County	86	2071	8.9	**Harper Woods** (city) Wayne County
11	205	3.0	**Bridgeport** (charter township) Saginaw County	87	2092	9.0	**Lansing** (city) Ingham County
11	205	3.0	**Pontiac** (city) Oakland County	88	2123	9.1	**Allendale** (CDP) Ottawa County
14	229	3.1	**Romulus** (city) Wayne County	88	2123	9.1	**Flushing** (charter township) Genesee County
14	229	3.1	**Wayne** (city) Wayne County	90	2156	9.2	**Sterling Heights** (city) Macomb County
16	248	3.2	**Escanaba** (city) Delta County	90	2156	9.2	**Waterford** (charter township) Oakland County
16	248	3.2	**Garden City** (city) Wayne County	92	2186	9.3	**DeWitt** (charter township) Clinton County
16	248	3.2	**Genesee** (charter township) Genesee County	92	2186	9.3	**Norton Shores** (city) Muskegon County
16	248	3.2	**Muskegon** (charter township) Muskegon County	94	2212	9.4	**Trenton** (city) Wayne County
20	284	3.4	**Port Huron** (charter township) Saint Clair County	95	2245	9.5	**Mundy** (township) Genesee County
21	351	3.7	**Niles** (city) Berrien County	96	2283	9.6	**Grand Haven** (city) Ottawa County
22	378	3.8	**Blackman** (charter township) Jackson County	96	2283	9.6	**Grandville** (city) Kent County
22	378	3.8	**Highland Park** (city) Wayne County	96	2283	9.6	**Oak Park** (city) Oakland County
22	378	3.8	**Saginaw** (city) Saginaw County	99	2312	9.7	**Bedford** (township) Monroe County
25	415	4.0	**Flint** (city) Genesee County	100	2340	9.8	**Fenton** (city) Genesee County
25	415	4.0	**Jackson** (city) Jackson County	100	2340	9.8	**Van Buren** (charter township) Wayne County
27	481	4.2	**Benton** (charter township) Berrien County	102	2363	9.9	**Comstock** (charter township) Kalamazoo County
27	481	4.2	**Lenox** (township) Macomb County	103	2386	10.0	**Harrison** (charter township) Macomb County
29	497	4.3	**Burton** (city) Genesee County	103	2386	10.0	**Northview** (CDP) Kent County
29	497	4.3	**Owosso** (city) Shiawassee County	103	2386	10.0	**Ypsilanti** (charter township) Washtenaw County
31	525	4.4	**Hamtramck** (city) Wayne County	106	2416	10.1	**Antwerp** (township) Van Buren County
31	525	4.4	**Melvindale** (city) Wayne County	106	2416	10.1	**Cooper** (charter township) Kalamazoo County
33	551	4.5	**Bangor** (charter township) Bay County	106	2416	10.1	**Garfield** (charter township) Grand Traverse County
34	646	4.8	**Leoni** (township) Jackson County	106	2416	10.1	**Grand Rapids** (city) Kent County
35	679	4.9	**Bay City** (city) Bay County	106	2416	10.1	**White Lake** (charter township) Oakland County
35	679	4.9	**Cutlerville** (CDP) Kent County	111	2444	10.2	**Gaines** (charter township) Kent County
35	679	4.9	**Eastpointe** (city) Macomb County	112	2474	10.3	**Georgetown** (charter township) Ottawa County
35	679	4.9	**Warren** (city) Macomb County	112	2474	10.3	**Kentwood** (city) Kent County
39	726	5.0	**Emmett** (charter township) Calhoun County	114	2530	10.5	**Clawson** (city) Oakland County
39	726	5.0	**Westland** (city) Wayne County	114	2530	10.5	**Plainfield** (charter township) Kent County
41	758	5.1	**Comstock Park** (CDP) Kent County	114	2530	10.5	**Summit** (township) Jackson County
41	758	5.1	**Sturgis** (city) Saint Joseph County	117	2575	10.7	**Delhi** (charter township) Ingham County
41	758	5.1	**Wyoming** (city) Kent County	118	2598	10.8	**Holt** (CDP) Ingham County
44	791	5.2	**Coldwater** (city) Branch County	118	2598	10.8	**Kalamazoo** (charter township) Kalamazoo County
44	791	5.2	**Detroit** (city) Wayne County	118	2598	10.8	**Washington** (township) Macomb County
46	863	5.4	**Alpine** (township) Kent County	121	2629	10.9	**Tyrone** (township) Livingston County
47	892	5.5	**Madison Heights** (city) Oakland County	122	2672	11.1	**South Lyon** (city) Oakland County
47	892	5.5	**Port Huron** (city) Saint Clair County	123	2743	11.4	**Dearborn** (city) Wayne County
47	892	5.5	**Wyandotte** (city) Wayne County	123	2743	11.4	**Hartland** (township) Livingston County
50	922	5.6	**Huron** (charter township) Wayne County	125	2760	11.5	**New Baltimore** (city) Macomb County
51	960	5.7	**Frenchtown** (township) Monroe County	125	2760	11.5	**Shelby** (charter township) Macomb County
51	960	5.7	**Monroe** (charter township) Monroe County	127	2804	11.7	**Macomb** (township) Macomb County
53	991	5.8	**Fruitport** (charter township) Muskegon County	128	2823	11.8	**Livonia** (city) Wayne County
54	1028	5.9	**Fraser** (city) Macomb County	129	2866	12.0	**Caledonia** (township) Kent County
55	1064	6.0	**Southgate** (city) Wayne County	129	2866	12.0	**Fort Gratiot** (charter township) Saint Clair County
56	1099	6.1	**Cadillac** (city) Wexford County	129	2866	12.0	**Lyon** (charter township) Oakland County
56	1099	6.1	**Chesterfield** (township) Macomb County	129	2866	12.0	**Saginaw** (charter township) Saginaw County
58	1138	6.2	**Vienna** (charter township) Genesee County	133	2892	12.1	**Oceola** (township) Livingston County
59	1171	6.3	**Niles** (township) Berrien County	133	2892	12.1	**Waverly** (CDP) Eaton County
59	1171	6.3	**Redford** (charter township) Wayne County	135	2916	12.2	**Fenton** (charter township) Genesee County
61	1360	6.8	**Holland** (charter township) Ottawa County	135	2916	12.2	**Marquette** (city) Marquette County
61	1360	6.8	**Mount Clemens** (city) Macomb County	135	2916	12.2	**Wixom** (city) Oakland County
63	1460	7.1	**Flint** (charter township) Genesee County	138	2938	12.3	**East Bay** (township) Grand Traverse County
64	1486	7.2	**Clinton** (charter township) Macomb County	138	2938	12.3	**Holland** (city) Ottawa County
64	1486	7.2	**Holly** (township) Oakland County	140	2977	12.5	**Union** (charter township) Isabella County
64	1486	7.2	**Riverview** (city) Wayne County	141	3078	13.0	**Grand Haven** (charter township) Ottawa County
64	1486	7.2	**Thomas** (township) Saginaw County	142	3114	13.2	**Hamburg** (township) Livingston County
68	1529	7.3	**Jenison** (CDP) Ottawa County	143	3147	13.4	**Big Rapids** (city) Mecosta County
69	1571	7.4	**Saint Clair Shores** (city) Macomb County	143	3147	13.4	**Commerce** (charter township) Oakland County
70	1602	7.5	**Woodhaven** (city) Wayne County	143	3147	13.4	**Kalamazoo** (city) Kalamazoo County
71	1660	7.7	**Allen Park** (city) Wayne County	146	3160	13.5	**Springfield** (charter township) Oakland County
71	1660	7.7	**Walker** (city) Kent County	147	3181	13.6	**Green Oak** (township) Livingston County
73	1697	7.8	**Monitor** (charter township) Bay County	147	3181	13.6	**Oxford** (charter township) Oakland County
73	1697	7.8	**Monroe** (city) Monroe County	149	3197	13.7	**Grand Blanc** (charter township) Genesee County
75	1740	7.9	**Davison** (township) Genesee County	149	3197	13.7	**Milford** (charter township) Oakland County

Note: The state column ranks the top/bottom 150 places from all places in the state with population of 10,000 or more. The national column ranks the top/bottom 150 places from all places in the country with population of 10,000 or more. Places that are unincorporated were not considered in the rankings. Please refer to the User Guide for additional information.

Homeownership Rate

Top 150 Places Ranked in *Descending* Order

State Rank	Nat'l Rank	Percent	Place
1	49	93.5	**Flushing** (charter township) Genesee County
1	49	93.5	**Macomb** (township) Macomb County
3	57	93.3	**Forest Hills** (CDP) Kent County
3	57	93.3	**Oakland** (charter township) Oakland County
5	73	93.0	**Cannon** (township) Kent County
6	78	92.7	**Brighton** (township) Livingston County
7	86	92.3	**Monitor** (charter township) Bay County
8	91	92.2	**Cascade** (charter township) Kent County
9	104	92.0	**Ada** (township) Kent County
10	107	91.9	**Hamburg** (township) Livingston County
11	125	91.5	**Brandon** (charter township) Oakland County
11	125	91.5	**East Grand Rapids** (city) Kent County
13	138	91.3	**Park** (township) Ottawa County
14	150	91.1	**Grosse Ile** (township) Wayne County
15	156	91.0	**Oceola** (township) Livingston County
16	168	90.8	**Texas** (charter township) Kalamazoo County
16	168	90.8	**Tyrone** (township) Livingston County
18	175	90.7	**Springfield** (charter township) Oakland County
19	180	90.6	**Huron** (charter township) Wayne County
20	184	90.4	**Grosse Pointe Woods** (city) Wayne County
21	195	90.1	**Commerce** (charter township) Oakland County
21	195	90.1	**Southfield** (township) Oakland County
23	213	89.8	**Highland** (charter township) Oakland County
24	217	89.7	**Fenton** (charter township) Genesee County
25	245	89.3	**Beverly Hills** (village) Oakland County
26	250	89.1	**Caledonia** (township) Kent County
26	250	89.1	**Fruitport** (charter township) Muskegon County
28	259	89.0	**Green Oak** (township) Livingston County
29	291	88.5	**Grand Rapids** (charter township) Kent County
30	320	88.0	**Saint Joseph** (charter township) Berrien County
31	344	87.7	**White Lake** (charter township) Oakland County
32	365	87.5	**Thomas** (township) Saginaw County
33	373	87.4	**Hartland** (township) Livingston County
34	379	87.3	**Bloomfield** (charter township) Oakland County
35	423	86.6	**Jenison** (CDP) Ottawa County
36	451	86.2	**Livonia** (city) Wayne County
37	461	86.1	**Lyon** (charter township) Oakland County
38	470	85.9	**Grand Haven** (charter township) Ottawa County
39	474	85.8	**Bedford** (township) Monroe County
40	496	85.5	**Allen Park** (city) Wayne County
41	537	84.9	**Lenox** (township) Macomb County
42	563	84.6	**Milford** (charter township) Oakland County
43	608	84.0	**Washington** (township) Macomb County
44	668	83.3	**Chesterfield** (township) Macomb County
44	668	83.3	**Oxford** (charter township) Oakland County
46	678	83.2	**Plymouth** (charter township) Wayne County
47	686	83.1	**Byron** (township) Kent County
48	695	83.0	**Georgetown** (charter township) Ottawa County
48	695	83.0	**Plainfield** (charter township) Kent County
50	703	82.9	**Leoni** (township) Jackson County
51	709	82.8	**Mundy** (township) Genesee County
52	718	82.7	**Antwerp** (township) Van Buren County
53	724	82.6	**West Bloomfield** (charter township) Oakland County
54	733	82.5	**Garden City** (city) Wayne County
54	733	82.5	**Genoa** (township) Livingston County
56	753	82.3	**Redford** (charter township) Wayne County
57	774	82.1	**Independence** (charter township) Oakland County
58	786	82.0	**Vienna** (charter township) Genesee County
59	794	81.9	**Saint Clair Shores** (city) Macomb County
60	807	81.8	**East Bay** (township) Grand Traverse County
61	828	81.6	**Norton Shores** (city) Muskegon County
62	842	81.4	**Berkley** (city) Oakland County
63	858	81.2	**Holly** (township) Oakland County
64	931	80.3	**Niles** (township) Berrien County
65	959	80.1	**Scio** (township) Washtenaw County
66	972	80.0	**DeWitt** (charter township) Clinton County
66	972	80.0	**Lincoln** (charter township) Berrien County
68	980	79.9	**Orion** (charter township) Oakland County
69	986	79.8	**Cooper** (charter township) Kalamazoo County
70	1004	79.6	**Genesee** (charter township) Genesee County
71	1034	79.3	**Summit** (township) Jackson County
72	1040	79.2	**Superior** (charter township) Washtenaw County
73	1046	79.1	**Trenton** (city) Wayne County
74	1056	79.0	**New Baltimore** (city) Macomb County
75	1075	78.8	**Muskegon** (charter township) Muskegon County
76	1124	78.3	**Shelby** (charter township) Macomb County
77	1156	78.0	**Eastpointe** (city) Macomb County
78	1169	77.9	**Dearborn Heights** (city) Wayne County
79	1183	77.7	**South Lyon** (city) Oakland County
80	1226	77.2	**Bridgeport** (charter township) Saginaw County
81	1238	77.1	**Monroe** (charter township) Monroe County
82	1248	77.0	**Rochester Hills** (city) Oakland County
83	1275	76.8	**Bangor** (charter township) Bay County
84	1297	76.5	**Northville** (township) Wayne County
85	1337	76.2	**Brownstown** (charter township) Wayne County
85	1337	76.2	**Canton** (charter township) Wayne County
85	1337	76.2	**Sterling Heights** (city) Macomb County
88	1368	75.9	**Troy** (city) Oakland County
89	1377	75.8	**Spring Lake** (township) Ottawa County
90	1469	74.7	**Burton** (city) Genesee County
90	1469	74.7	**Northview** (CDP) Kent County
92	1505	74.4	**Warren** (city) Macomb County
93	1546	74.0	**Delhi** (charter township) Ingham County
93	1546	74.0	**Fort Gratiot** (charter township) Saint Clair County
95	1552	73.9	**Lincoln Park** (city) Wayne County
96	1559	73.8	**Frenchtown** (township) Monroe County
97	1576	73.6	**Waterford** (charter township) Oakland County
98	1638	73.0	**Birmingham** (city) Oakland County
99	1650	72.9	**Grosse Pointe Park** (city) Wayne County
100	1655	72.8	**Holt** (CDP) Ingham County
101	1700	72.4	**Woodhaven** (city) Wayne County
101	1700	72.4	**Wyandotte** (city) Wayne County
103	1715	72.3	**Emmett** (charter township) Calhoun County
104	1748	72.1	**Mount Morris** (township) Genesee County
105	1776	71.9	**Clawson** (city) Oakland County
105	1776	71.9	**Grandville** (city) Kent County
107	1809	71.6	**Gaines** (charter township) Kent County
108	1852	71.2	**Harper Woods** (city) Wayne County
109	1906	70.7	**Comstock** (charter township) Kalamazoo County
110	1923	70.5	**Fraser** (city) Macomb County
111	1942	70.3	**Roseville** (city) Macomb County
112	1958	70.1	**Holland** (charter township) Ottawa County
113	2032	69.4	**Cutlerville** (CDP) Kent County
114	2042	69.3	**Harrison** (charter township) Macomb County
115	2075	69.0	**Dearborn** (city) Wayne County
116	2088	68.9	**Port Huron** (charter township) Saint Clair County
116	2088	68.9	**Portage** (city) Kalamazoo County
118	2120	68.6	**Grand Blanc** (charter township) Genesee County
119	2170	68.1	**Bay City** (city) Bay County
120	2190	67.9	**Grand Haven** (city) Ottawa County
121	2215	67.7	**Royal Oak** (city) Oakland County
122	2243	67.4	**Taylor** (city) Wayne County
123	2267	67.2	**Novi** (city) Oakland County
124	2278	67.1	**Clinton** (charter township) Macomb County
124	2278	67.1	**Romulus** (city) Wayne County
126	2292	67.0	**Midland** (city) Midland County
127	2360	66.4	**Alpena** (city) Alpena County
128	2404	66.0	**Southgate** (city) Wayne County
128	2404	66.0	**Wyoming** (city) Kent County
130	2435	65.7	**Davison** (township) Genesee County
130	2435	65.7	**Van Buren** (charter township) Wayne County
132	2448	65.6	**Kalamazoo** (charter township) Kalamazoo County
133	2499	65.2	**Ferndale** (city) Oakland County
134	2512	65.1	**Flint** (charter township) Genesee County
135	2534	64.8	**Saginaw** (charter township) Saginaw County
136	2567	64.4	**Madison Heights** (city) Oakland County
137	2577	64.3	**Hazel Park** (city) Oakland County
138	2602	64.0	**Delta** (charter township) Eaton County
139	2620	63.8	**Okemos** (CDP) Ingham County
140	2628	63.7	**Holland** (city) Ottawa County
141	2639	63.6	**Farmington Hills** (city) Oakland County
142	2670	63.3	**Riverview** (city) Wayne County
143	2726	62.8	**Melvindale** (city) Wayne County
143	2726	62.8	**Walker** (city) Kent County
145	2747	62.6	**Beecher** (CDP) Genesee County
146	2761	62.5	**Rochester** (city) Oakland County
147	2795	62.2	**Farmington** (city) Oakland County
148	2802	62.1	**Bath** (charter township) Clinton County
148	2802	62.1	**Monroe** (city) Monroe County
150	2817	62.0	**Owosso** (city) Shiawassee County

Note: The state column ranks the top/bottom 150 places from all places in the state with population of 10,000 or more. The national column ranks the top/bottom 150 places from all places in the country with population of 10,000 or more. Places that are unincorporated were not considered in the rankings. Please refer to the User Guide for additional information.

Homeownership Rate

Top 150 Places Ranked in *Ascending* Order

State Rank	Nat'l Rank	Percent	Place
1	82	33.3	**Ypsilanti** (city) Washtenaw County
2	86	33.5	**Benton Harbor** (city) Berrien County
3	89	33.6	**East Lansing** (city) Ingham County
4	95	34.1	**Big Rapids** (city) Mecosta County
5	105	34.7	**Mount Pleasant** (city) Isabella County
5	105	34.7	**Union** (charter township) Isabella County
7	132	37.0	**Highland Park** (city) Wayne County
8	322	43.6	**Kalamazoo** (city) Kalamazoo County
9	351	44.8	**Ann Arbor** (city) Washtenaw County
10	462	47.5	**Comstock Park** (CDP) Kent County
11	470	47.7	**Pontiac** (city) Oakland County
12	492	48.0	**Marquette** (city) Marquette County
13	582	49.4	**Hamtramck** (city) Wayne County
14	637	50.5	**Oshtemo** (charter township) Kalamazoo County
15	677	51.1	**Detroit** (city) Wayne County
15	677	51.1	**Muskegon Heights** (city) Muskegon County
17	717	51.7	**Auburn Hills** (city) Oakland County
18	767	52.3	**Wixom** (city) Oakland County
19	781	52.4	**Inkster** (city) Wayne County
20	795	52.5	**Muskegon** (city) Muskegon County
21	813	52.7	**Jackson** (city) Jackson County
22	896	53.7	**Lansing** (city) Ingham County
22	896	53.7	**Southfield** (city) Oakland County
24	907	53.8	**Ionia** (city) Ionia County
25	932	54.1	**Port Huron** (city) Saint Clair County
26	973	54.6	**Allendale** (CDP) Ottawa County
27	1015	55.1	**Adrian** (city) Lenawee County
28	1025	55.2	**Flint** (city) Genesee County
28	1025	55.2	**Sault Sainte Marie** (city) Chippewa County
30	1063	55.5	**Blackman** (charter township) Jackson County
31	1112	56.0	**Allendale** (charter township) Ottawa County
31	1112	56.0	**Grand Rapids** (city) Kent County
31	1112	56.0	**Waverly** (CDP) Eaton County
34	1135	56.2	**Benton** (charter township) Berrien County
35	1236	57.1	**Sturgis** (city) Saint Joseph County
36	1251	57.2	**Niles** (city) Berrien County
37	1289	57.5	**Pittsfield** (charter township) Washtenaw County
38	1334	57.9	**Mount Clemens** (city) Macomb County
39	1367	58.2	**Traverse City** (city) Grand Traverse County
40	1378	58.3	**Alpine** (township) Kent County
41	1443	58.8	**Cadillac** (city) Wexford County
42	1457	58.9	**Fenton** (city) Genesee County
43	1504	59.3	**Haslett** (CDP) Ingham County
44	1595	60.1	**Ypsilanti** (charter township) Washtenaw County
45	1614	60.3	**Saginaw** (city) Saginaw County
46	1659	60.6	**Battle Creek** (city) Calhoun County
46	1659	60.6	**Coldwater** (city) Branch County
48	1674	60.7	**Garfield** (charter township) Grand Traverse County
48	1674	60.7	**Oak Park** (city) Oakland County
50	1713	60.9	**Meridian** (charter township) Ingham County
51	1734	61.1	**Kentwood** (city) Kent County
52	1757	61.3	**Escanaba** (city) Delta County
53	1782	61.5	**Westland** (city) Wayne County
54	1803	61.7	**Wayne** (city) Wayne County
55	1832	62.0	**Owosso** (city) Shiawassee County
56	1840	62.1	**Bath** (charter township) Clinton County
56	1840	62.1	**Monroe** (city) Monroe County
58	1855	62.2	**Farmington** (city) Oakland County
59	1882	62.5	**Rochester** (city) Oakland County
60	1896	62.6	**Beecher** (CDP) Genesee County
61	1916	62.8	**Melvindale** (city) Wayne County
61	1916	62.8	**Walker** (city) Kent County
63	1975	63.3	**Riverview** (city) Wayne County
64	2010	63.6	**Farmington Hills** (city) Oakland County
65	2018	63.7	**Holland** (city) Ottawa County
66	2029	63.8	**Okemos** (CDP) Ingham County
67	2046	64.0	**Delta** (charter township) Eaton County
68	2075	64.3	**Hazel Park** (city) Oakland County
69	2080	64.4	**Madison Heights** (city) Oakland County
70	2111	64.8	**Saginaw** (charter township) Saginaw County
71	2136	65.1	**Flint** (charter township) Genesee County
72	2145	65.2	**Ferndale** (city) Oakland County
73	2196	65.6	**Kalamazoo** (charter township) Kalamazoo County
74	2209	65.7	**Davison** (township) Genesee County
74	2209	65.7	**Van Buren** (charter township) Wayne County
76	2241	66.0	**Southgate** (city) Wayne County
76	2241	66.0	**Wyoming** (city) Kent County
78	2284	66.4	**Alpena** (city) Alpena County
79	2350	67.0	**Midland** (city) Midland County
80	2365	67.1	**Clinton** (charter township) Macomb County
80	2365	67.1	**Romulus** (city) Wayne County
82	2379	67.2	**Novi** (city) Oakland County
83	2402	67.4	**Taylor** (city) Wayne County
84	2432	67.7	**Royal Oak** (city) Oakland County
85	2451	67.9	**Grand Haven** (city) Ottawa County
86	2475	68.1	**Bay City** (city) Bay County
87	2525	68.6	**Grand Blanc** (charter township) Genesee County
88	2549	68.9	**Port Huron** (charter township) Saint Clair County
88	2549	68.9	**Portage** (city) Kalamazoo County
90	2569	69.0	**Dearborn** (city) Wayne County
91	2606	69.3	**Harrison** (charter township) Macomb County
92	2615	69.4	**Cutlerville** (CDP) Kent County
93	2691	70.1	**Holland** (charter township) Ottawa County
94	2710	70.3	**Roseville** (city) Macomb County
95	2720	70.5	**Fraser** (city) Macomb County
96	2741	70.7	**Comstock** (charter township) Kalamazoo County
97	2792	71.2	**Harper Woods** (city) Wayne County
98	2834	71.6	**Gaines** (charter township) Kent County
99	2865	71.9	**Clawson** (city) Oakland County
99	2865	71.9	**Grandville** (city) Kent County
101	2889	72.1	**Mount Morris** (township) Genesee County
102	2921	72.3	**Emmett** (charter township) Calhoun County
103	2942	72.4	**Woodhaven** (city) Wayne County
103	2942	72.4	**Wyandotte** (city) Wayne County
105	2989	72.8	**Holt** (CDP) Ingham County
106	3002	72.9	**Grosse Pointe Park** (city) Wayne County
107	3007	73.0	**Birmingham** (city) Oakland County
108	3071	73.6	**Waterford** (charter township) Oakland County
109	3090	73.8	**Frenchtown** (township) Monroe County
110	3098	73.9	**Lincoln Park** (city) Wayne County
111	3105	74.0	**Delhi** (charter township) Ingham County
111	3105	74.0	**Fort Gratiot** (charter township) Saint Clair County
113	3142	74.4	**Warren** (city) Macomb County
114	3177	74.7	**Burton** (city) Genesee County
114	3177	74.7	**Northview** (CDP) Kent County
116	3274	75.8	**Spring Lake** (township) Ottawa County
117	3280	75.9	**Troy** (city) Oakland County
118	3305	76.2	**Brownstown** (charter township) Wayne County
118	3305	76.2	**Canton** (charter township) Wayne County
118	3305	76.2	**Sterling Heights** (city) Macomb County
121	3348	76.5	**Northville** (township) Wayne County
122	3370	76.8	**Bangor** (charter township) Bay County
123	3396	77.0	**Rochester Hills** (city) Oakland County
124	3409	77.1	**Monroe** (charter township) Monroe County
125	3419	77.2	**Bridgeport** (charter township) Saginaw County
126	3464	77.7	**South Lyon** (city) Oakland County
127	3479	77.9	**Dearborn Heights** (city) Wayne County
128	3488	78.0	**Eastpointe** (city) Macomb County
129	3520	78.3	**Shelby** (charter township) Macomb County
130	3566	78.8	**Muskegon** (charter township) Muskegon County
131	3594	79.0	**New Baltimore** (city) Macomb County
132	3601	79.1	**Trenton** (city) Wayne County
133	3611	79.2	**Superior** (charter township) Washtenaw County
134	3617	79.3	**Summit** (township) Jackson County
135	3642	79.6	**Genesee** (charter township) Genesee County
136	3662	79.8	**Cooper** (charter township) Kalamazoo County
137	3671	79.9	**Orion** (charter township) Oakland County
138	3677	80.0	**DeWitt** (charter township) Clinton County
138	3677	80.0	**Lincoln** (charter township) Berrien County
140	3685	80.1	**Scio** (township) Washtenaw County
141	3707	80.3	**Niles** (township) Berrien County
142	3790	81.2	**Holly** (township) Oakland County
143	3806	81.4	**Berkley** (city) Oakland County
144	3822	81.6	**Norton Shores** (city) Muskegon County
145	3842	81.8	**East Bay** (township) Grand Traverse County
146	3850	81.9	**Saint Clair Shores** (city) Macomb County
147	3863	82.0	**Vienna** (charter township) Genesee County
148	3871	82.1	**Independence** (charter township) Oakland County
149	3894	82.3	**Redford** (charter township) Wayne County
150	3912	82.5	**Garden City** (city) Wayne County

Note: The state column ranks the top/bottom 150 places from all places in the state with population of 10,000 or more. The national column ranks the top/bottom 150 places from all places in the country with population of 10,000 or more. Places that are unincorporated were not considered in the rankings. Please refer to the User Guide for additional information.

Median Home Value

Top 150 Places Ranked in *Descending* Order

State Rank	Nat'l Rank	Dollars	Place
1	839	347,400	**Birmingham** (city) Oakland County
2	965	328,800	**Bloomfield** (charter township) Oakland County
3	1059	315,900	**Northville** (township) Wayne County
4	1082	313,200	**Oakland** (charter township) Oakland County
5	1171	299,100	**Southfield** (township) Oakland County
6	1413	269,400	**Beverly Hills** (village) Oakland County
7	1421	268,600	**Scio** (township) Washtenaw County
8	1440	266,800	**Rochester** (city) Oakland County
9	1480	262,700	**Forest Hills** (CDP) Kent County
10	1511	260,000	**Ada** (township) Kent County
11	1534	258,500	**Cascade** (charter township) Kent County
12	1566	253,700	**Grosse Pointe Park** (city) Wayne County
13	1637	246,100	**East Grand Rapids** (city) Kent County
14	1687	242,200	**Texas** (charter township) Kalamazoo County
15	1710	240,400	**Plymouth** (charter township) Wayne County
16	1715	239,500	**Grosse Ile** (township) Wayne County
17	1760	236,600	**West Bloomfield** (charter township) Oakland County
18	1768	235,800	**Novi** (city) Oakland County
19	1821	230,700	**Ann Arbor** (city) Washtenaw County
20	1886	224,100	**Brighton** (township) Livingston County
21	1895	223,300	**Cannon** (township) Kent County
22	1898	222,800	**Pittsfield** (charter township) Washtenaw County
23	1939	219,200	**Troy** (city) Oakland County
24	1977	216,100	**Washington** (township) Macomb County
25	1987	215,200	**Lyon** (charter township) Oakland County
26	2020	212,700	**Rochester Hills** (city) Oakland County
27	2048	211,000	**Grand Rapids** (charter township) Kent County
28	2102	207,200	**Milford** (charter township) Oakland County
29	2125	205,700	**Springfield** (charter township) Oakland County
30	2139	204,000	**Macomb** (township) Macomb County
31	2167	201,200	**Farmington Hills** (city) Oakland County
32	2184	200,100	**Genoa** (township) Livingston County
33	2203	199,000	**Hartland** (township) Livingston County
34	2217	198,000	**Caledonia** (township) Kent County
35	2230	196,400	**Park** (township) Ottawa County
36	2246	195,400	**Tyrone** (township) Livingston County
37	2268	194,000	**Green Oak** (township) Livingston County
38	2272	193,800	**Hamburg** (township) Livingston County
39	2281	193,300	**Okemos** (CDP) Ingham County
40	2314	190,900	**Canton** (charter township) Wayne County
41	2375	187,000	**Oceola** (township) Livingston County
42	2391	186,300	**Grosse Pointe Woods** (city) Wayne County
43	2414	184,600	**Independence** (charter township) Oakland County
44	2416	184,400	**Meridian** (charter township) Ingham County
45	2428	183,000	**Orion** (charter township) Oakland County
46	2435	182,300	**Shelby** (charter township) Macomb County
47	2465	180,300	**Commerce** (charter township) Oakland County
48	2482	179,500	**Wixom** (city) Oakland County
49	2516	177,000	**East Lansing** (city) Ingham County
50	2578	173,700	**Lincoln** (charter township) Berrien County
51	2582	173,500	**Fenton** (charter township) Genesee County
52	2597	172,500	**Grand Haven** (charter township) Ottawa County
53	2611	171,900	**Spring Lake** (township) Ottawa County
54	2614	171,800	**White Lake** (charter township) Oakland County
55	2631	171,000	**Highland** (charter township) Oakland County
56	2650	169,900	**Haslett** (CDP) Ingham County
57	2666	168,900	**Traverse City** (city) Grand Traverse County
58	2674	168,700	**New Baltimore** (city) Macomb County
59	2690	167,800	**Bath** (charter township) Clinton County
60	2711	167,200	**Oshtemo** (charter township) Kalamazoo County
61	2748	165,300	**Brandon** (charter township) Oakland County
61	2748	165,300	**Oxford** (charter township) Oakland County
63	2774	163,900	**East Bay** (township) Grand Traverse County
64	2835	160,800	**Byron** (township) Kent County
65	2859	159,600	**Garfield** (charter township) Grand Traverse County
65	2859	159,600	**Marquette** (city) Marquette County
67	2870	159,200	**Allendale** (charter township) Ottawa County
68	2879	158,900	**Allendale** (CDP) Ottawa County
69	2891	158,400	**Bedford** (township) Monroe County
70	2919	157,200	**Georgetown** (charter township) Ottawa County
71	2925	157,100	**Superior** (charter township) Washtenaw County
72	2953	155,700	**Royal Oak** (city) Oakland County
73	2964	155,100	**Farmington** (city) Oakland County
74	2968	155,000	**Plainfield** (charter township) Kent County
75	2970	154,900	**Livonia** (city) Wayne County
76	2989	153,700	**Brownstown** (charter township) Wayne County
77	2997	153,400	**Gaines** (charter township) Kent County
78	3013	152,600	**Huron** (charter township) Wayne County
79	3041	151,400	**South Lyon** (city) Oakland County
80	3049	151,200	**Delhi** (charter township) Ingham County
81	3063	150,600	**Chesterfield** (township) Macomb County
82	3067	150,500	**Delta** (charter township) Eaton County
83	3074	150,200	**Harrison** (charter township) Macomb County
84	3109	148,700	**Holt** (CDP) Ingham County
85	3129	148,100	**Portage** (city) Kalamazoo County
86	3143	147,400	**Saint Joseph** (charter township) Berrien County
87	3160	146,200	**DeWitt** (charter township) Clinton County
88	3167	145,900	**Walker** (city) Kent County
89	3193	144,200	**Sterling Heights** (city) Macomb County
90	3222	142,800	**Antwerp** (township) Van Buren County
91	3225	142,700	**Waverly** (CDP) Eaton County
92	3240	142,200	**Berkley** (city) Oakland County
93	3262	140,900	**Northview** (CDP) Kent County
94	3266	140,800	**Cooper** (charter township) Kalamazoo County
95	3283	139,500	**Midland** (city) Midland County
96	3349	136,200	**Holland** (charter township) Ottawa County
97	3370	135,000	**Grandville** (city) Kent County
97	3370	135,000	**Jenison** (CDP) Ottawa County
99	3436	132,000	**Lenox** (township) Macomb County
100	3447	131,800	**Fort Gratiot** (charter township) Saint Clair County
101	3459	130,800	**Grand Blanc** (charter township) Genesee County
102	3465	130,500	**Comstock** (charter township) Kalamazoo County
103	3483	129,700	**Union** (charter township) Isabella County
104	3498	129,300	**Van Buren** (charter township) Wayne County
105	3505	129,200	**Kentwood** (city) Kent County
106	3538	127,400	**Thomas** (township) Saginaw County
107	3541	127,200	**Alpine** (township) Kent County
108	3553	126,500	**Clawson** (city) Oakland County
109	3559	126,100	**Saginaw** (charter township) Saginaw County
110	3567	125,500	**Monitor** (charter township) Bay County
111	3603	123,400	**Mount Pleasant** (city) Isabella County
112	3607	123,100	**Woodhaven** (city) Wayne County
112	3607	123,100	**Ypsilanti** (city) Washtenaw County
114	3617	122,600	**Comstock Park** (CDP) Kent County
115	3624	122,100	**Waterford** (charter township) Oakland County
116	3671	120,200	**Davison** (township) Genesee County
117	3688	119,100	**Clinton** (charter township) Macomb County
118	3693	119,000	**Holly** (township) Oakland County
119	3696	118,900	**Fruitport** (charter township) Muskegon County
120	3709	118,400	**Summit** (township) Jackson County
121	3711	118,300	**Trenton** (city) Wayne County
122	3732	117,900	**Emmett** (charter township) Calhoun County
123	3738	117,700	**Grand Haven** (city) Ottawa County
124	3749	117,200	**Holland** (city) Ottawa County
124	3749	117,200	**Riverview** (city) Wayne County
126	3767	116,200	**Mundy** (township) Genesee County
127	3780	115,600	**Cutlerville** (CDP) Kent County
128	3809	114,500	**Norton Shores** (city) Muskegon County
129	3826	113,900	**Fraser** (city) Macomb County
130	3829	113,700	**Flushing** (charter township) Genesee County
131	3832	113,600	**Auburn Hills** (city) Oakland County
132	3834	113,500	**Frenchtown** (township) Monroe County
133	3835	113,400	**Port Huron** (charter township) Saint Clair County
134	3841	113,200	**Vienna** (charter township) Genesee County
135	3847	112,900	**Ypsilanti** (charter township) Washtenaw County
136	3913	109,400	**Grand Rapids** (city) Kent County
137	3919	109,100	**Leoni** (township) Jackson County
138	3928	108,500	**Southfield** (city) Oakland County
139	3934	108,100	**Bangor** (charter township) Bay County
140	3938	107,900	**Monroe** (city) Monroe County
141	3974	105,800	**Fenton** (city) Genesee County
142	4010	103,500	**Wyoming** (city) Kent County
143	4013	103,300	**Dearborn** (city) Wayne County
144	4048	101,500	**Allen Park** (city) Wayne County
145	4065	100,500	**Blackman** (charter township) Jackson County
146	4072	100,300	**Monroe** (charter township) Monroe County
147	4117	97,600	**Kalamazoo** (charter township) Kalamazoo County
147	4117	97,600	**Kalamazoo** (city) Kalamazoo County
149	4155	95,600	**Niles** (township) Berrien County
150	4168	94,600	**Saint Clair Shores** (city) Macomb County

Note: *The state column ranks the top/bottom 150 places from all places in the state with population of 10,000 or more. The national column ranks the top/bottom 150 places from all places in the country with population of 10,000 or more. Places that are unincorporated were not considered in the rankings. Please refer to the User Guide for additional information.*

Median Home Value

Top 150 Places Ranked in *Ascending* Order

State Rank	Nat'l Rank	Dollars	Place
1	2	41,700	**Flint** (city) Genesee County
2	3	42,200	**Highland Park** (city) Wayne County
3	7	45,600	**Beecher** (CDP) Genesee County
4	9	46,600	**Hamtramck** (city) Wayne County
5	11	46,800	**Muskegon Heights** (city) Muskegon County
6	12	49,200	**Saginaw** (city) Saginaw County
7	14	49,800	**Benton Harbor** (city) Berrien County
8	15	50,400	**Detroit** (city) Wayne County
9	17	54,700	**Hazel Park** (city) Oakland County
10	20	55,400	**Inkster** (city) Wayne County
11	34	59,000	**Melvindale** (city) Wayne County
12	43	61,000	**Pontiac** (city) Oakland County
13	47	62,500	**Eastpointe** (city) Macomb County
13	47	62,500	**Lincoln Park** (city) Wayne County
15	63	65,500	**Mount Morris** (township) Genesee County
16	66	66,100	**Roseville** (city) Macomb County
17	72	66,900	**Jackson** (city) Jackson County
18	77	67,500	**Muskegon** (city) Muskegon County
19	82	68,100	**Harper Woods** (city) Wayne County
20	95	69,200	**Bay City** (city) Bay County
21	99	69,800	**Redford** (charter township) Wayne County
22	110	72,300	**Genesee** (charter township) Genesee County
23	114	73,100	**Romulus** (city) Wayne County
24	124	74,000	**Wayne** (city) Wayne County
25	127	74,200	**Adrian** (city) Lenawee County
26	135	74,600	**Burton** (city) Genesee County
27	156	76,800	**Mount Clemens** (city) Macomb County
28	165	77,500	**Alpena** (city) Alpena County
29	170	77,800	**Taylor** (city) Wayne County
30	180	78,700	**Niles** (city) Berrien County
31	201	80,200	**Cadillac** (city) Wexford County
32	203	80,300	**Coldwater** (city) Branch County
33	206	80,400	**Benton** (charter township) Berrien County
34	222	81,400	**Port Huron** (city) Saint Clair County
34	222	81,400	**Sault Sainte Marie** (city) Chippewa County
36	231	81,700	**Owosso** (city) Shiawassee County
37	235	81,900	**Bridgeport** (charter township) Saginaw County
38	241	82,200	**Oak Park** (city) Oakland County
39	246	82,500	**Escanaba** (city) Delta County
40	249	82,600	**Ionia** (city) Ionia County
41	253	83,100	**Garden City** (city) Wayne County
42	269	84,200	**Madison Heights** (city) Oakland County
43	272	84,400	**Battle Creek** (city) Calhoun County
44	283	85,000	**Lansing** (city) Ingham County
45	291	85,300	**Flint** (charter township) Genesee County
46	295	85,600	**Dearborn Heights** (city) Wayne County
47	335	87,600	**Wyandotte** (city) Wayne County
48	336	87,700	**Big Rapids** (city) Mecosta County
49	350	88,200	**Southgate** (city) Wayne County
50	353	88,500	**Muskegon** (charter township) Muskegon County
51	362	88,800	**Sturgis** (city) Saint Joseph County
52	376	89,500	**Warren** (city) Macomb County
53	393	90,600	**Westland** (city) Wayne County
54	465	93,700	**Ferndale** (city) Oakland County
55	479	94,600	**Saint Clair Shores** (city) Macomb County
56	490	95,600	**Niles** (township) Berrien County
57	527	97,600	**Kalamazoo** (charter township) Kalamazoo County
57	527	97,600	**Kalamazoo** (city) Kalamazoo County
59	575	100,300	**Monroe** (charter township) Monroe County
60	579	100,500	**Blackman** (charter township) Jackson County
61	598	101,500	**Allen Park** (city) Wayne County
62	633	103,300	**Dearborn** (city) Wayne County
63	636	103,500	**Wyoming** (city) Kent County
64	673	105,800	**Fenton** (city) Genesee County
65	709	107,900	**Monroe** (city) Monroe County
66	713	108,100	**Bangor** (charter township) Bay County
67	717	108,500	**Southfield** (city) Oakland County
68	728	109,100	**Leoni** (township) Jackson County
69	731	109,400	**Grand Rapids** (city) Kent County
70	800	112,900	**Ypsilanti** (charter township) Washtenaw County
71	804	113,200	**Vienna** (charter township) Genesee County
72	811	113,400	**Port Huron** (charter township) Saint Clair County
73	814	113,500	**Frenchtown** (township) Monroe County
74	815	113,600	**Auburn Hills** (city) Oakland County
75	817	113,700	**Flushing** (charter township) Genesee County
76	821	113,900	**Fraser** (city) Macomb County
77	837	114,500	**Norton Shores** (city) Muskegon County
78	864	115,600	**Cutlerville** (CDP) Kent County
79	877	116,200	**Mundy** (township) Genesee County
80	897	117,200	**Holland** (city) Ottawa County
80	897	117,200	**Riverview** (city) Wayne County
82	908	117,700	**Grand Haven** (city) Ottawa County
83	913	117,900	**Emmett** (charter township) Calhoun County
84	936	118,300	**Trenton** (city) Wayne County
85	938	118,400	**Summit** (township) Jackson County
86	951	118,900	**Fruitport** (charter township) Muskegon County
87	953	119,000	**Holly** (township) Oakland County
88	956	119,100	**Clinton** (charter township) Macomb County
89	974	120,200	**Davison** (township) Genesee County
90	1020	122,100	**Waterford** (charter township) Oakland County
91	1030	122,600	**Comstock Park** (CDP) Kent County
92	1039	123,100	**Woodhaven** (city) Wayne County
92	1039	123,100	**Ypsilanti** (city) Washtenaw County
94	1044	123,400	**Mount Pleasant** (city) Isabella County
95	1079	125,500	**Monitor** (charter township) Bay County
96	1088	126,100	**Saginaw** (charter township) Saginaw County
97	1095	126,500	**Clawson** (city) Oakland County
98	1105	127,200	**Alpine** (township) Kent County
99	1108	127,400	**Thomas** (township) Saginaw County
100	1141	129,200	**Kentwood** (city) Kent County
101	1144	129,300	**Van Buren** (charter township) Wayne County
102	1161	129,700	**Union** (charter township) Isabella County
103	1182	130,500	**Comstock** (charter township) Kalamazoo County
104	1188	130,800	**Grand Blanc** (charter township) Genesee County
105	1201	131,800	**Fort Gratiot** (charter township) Saint Clair County
106	1209	132,000	**Lenox** (township) Macomb County
107	1277	135,000	**Grandville** (city) Kent County
107	1277	135,000	**Jenison** (CDP) Ottawa County
109	1297	136,200	**Holland** (charter township) Ottawa County
110	1363	139,500	**Midland** (city) Midland County
111	1382	140,800	**Cooper** (charter township) Kalamazoo County
112	1383	140,900	**Northview** (CDP) Kent County
113	1407	142,200	**Berkley** (city) Oakland County
114	1420	142,700	**Waverly** (CDP) Eaton County
115	1424	142,800	**Antwerp** (township) Van Buren County
116	1455	144,200	**Sterling Heights** (city) Macomb County
117	1480	145,900	**Walker** (city) Kent County
118	1485	146,200	**DeWitt** (charter township) Clinton County
119	1502	147,400	**Saint Joseph** (charter township) Berrien County
120	1518	148,100	**Portage** (city) Kalamazoo County
121	1538	148,700	**Holt** (CDP) Ingham County
122	1573	150,200	**Harrison** (charter township) Macomb County
123	1579	150,500	**Delta** (charter township) Eaton County
124	1582	150,600	**Chesterfield** (township) Macomb County
125	1596	151,200	**Delhi** (charter township) Ingham County
126	1605	151,400	**South Lyon** (city) Oakland County
127	1633	152,600	**Huron** (charter township) Wayne County
128	1651	153,400	**Gaines** (charter township) Kent County
129	1656	153,700	**Brownstown** (charter township) Wayne County
130	1678	154,900	**Livonia** (city) Wayne County
131	1679	155,000	**Plainfield** (charter township) Kent County
132	1681	155,100	**Farmington** (city) Oakland County
133	1693	155,700	**Royal Oak** (city) Oakland County
134	1720	157,100	**Superior** (charter township) Washtenaw County
135	1724	157,200	**Georgetown** (charter township) Ottawa County
136	1755	158,400	**Bedford** (township) Monroe County
137	1767	158,900	**Allendale** (CDP) Ottawa County
138	1773	159,200	**Allendale** (charter township) Ottawa County
139	1785	159,600	**Garfield** (charter township) Grand Traverse County
139	1785	159,600	**Marquette** (city) Marquette County
141	1811	160,800	**Byron** (township) Kent County
142	1870	163,900	**East Bay** (township) Grand Traverse County
143	1896	165,300	**Brandon** (charter township) Oakland County
143	1896	165,300	**Oxford** (charter township) Oakland County
145	1935	167,200	**Oshtemo** (charter township) Kalamazoo County
146	1954	167,800	**Bath** (charter township) Clinton County
147	1969	168,700	**New Baltimore** (city) Macomb County
148	1980	168,900	**Traverse City** (city) Grand Traverse County
149	1998	169,900	**Haslett** (CDP) Ingham County
150	2015	171,000	**Highland** (charter township) Oakland County

Note: The state column ranks the top/bottom 150 places from all places in the state with population of 10,000 or more. The national column ranks the top/bottom 150 places from all places in the country with population of 10,000 or more. Places that are unincorporated were not considered in the rankings. Please refer to the User Guide for additional information.

Median Year Structure Built

Top 150 Places Ranked in *Descending* Order

State Rank	Nat'l Rank	Year	Place
1	181	1998	**Macomb** (township) Macomb County
2	220	1997	**Bath** (charter township) Clinton County
3	312	1995	**Allendale** (charter township) Ottawa County
3	312	1995	**Oceola** (township) Livingston County
5	369	1994	**Allendale** (CDP) Ottawa County
5	369	1994	**Union** (charter township) Isabella County
7	435	1993	**New Baltimore** (city) Macomb County
8	501	1992	**Caledonia** (township) Kent County
8	501	1992	**Genoa** (township) Livingston County
8	501	1992	**Hartland** (township) Livingston County
8	501	1992	**Oakland** (charter township) Oakland County
8	501	1992	**Scio** (township) Washtenaw County
8	501	1992	**Washington** (township) Macomb County
14	566	1991	**Brownstown** (charter township) Wayne County
14	566	1991	**Byron** (township) Kent County
14	566	1991	**Cannon** (township) Kent County
14	566	1991	**Chesterfield** (township) Macomb County
14	566	1991	**Lyon** (charter township) Oakland County
14	566	1991	**Pittsfield** (charter township) Washtenaw County
14	566	1991	**Texas** (charter township) Kalamazoo County
21	651	1990	**Gaines** (charter township) Kent County
21	651	1990	**Garfield** (charter township) Grand Traverse County
21	651	1990	**Grand Haven** (charter township) Ottawa County
21	651	1990	**Holland** (charter township) Ottawa County
21	651	1990	**Huron** (charter township) Wayne County
21	651	1990	**Novi** (city) Oakland County
27	715	1989	**Oxford** (charter township) Oakland County
27	715	1989	**South Lyon** (city) Oakland County
29	778	1988	**Ada** (township) Kent County
29	778	1988	**Northville** (township) Wayne County
31	851	1987	**Canton** (charter township) Wayne County
31	851	1987	**Fenton** (charter township) Genesee County
31	851	1987	**Lenox** (township) Macomb County
34	933	1986	**Oshtemo** (charter township) Kalamazoo County
34	933	1986	**Rochester** (city) Oakland County
34	933	1986	**Shelby** (charter township) Macomb County
37	1031	1985	**Antwerp** (township) Van Buren County
37	1031	1985	**Cutlerville** (CDP) Kent County
37	1031	1985	**Forest Hills** (CDP) Kent County
37	1031	1985	**Holt** (CDP) Ingham County
41	1133	1984	**Commerce** (charter township) Oakland County
41	1133	1984	**Green Oak** (township) Livingston County
41	1133	1984	**Hamburg** (township) Livingston County
41	1133	1984	**Springfield** (charter township) Oakland County
41	1133	1984	**Superior** (charter township) Washtenaw County
41	1133	1984	**Tyrone** (township) Livingston County
47	1238	1983	**Auburn Hills** (city) Oakland County
47	1238	1983	**Cascade** (charter township) Kent County
47	1238	1983	**Delhi** (charter township) Ingham County
47	1238	1983	**Fenton** (city) Genesee County
47	1238	1983	**Georgetown** (charter township) Ottawa County
47	1238	1983	**Grand Rapids** (charter township) Kent County
47	1238	1983	**Independence** (charter township) Oakland County
47	1238	1983	**Milford** (charter township) Oakland County
47	1238	1983	**Spring Lake** (township) Ottawa County
47	1238	1983	**Van Buren** (charter township) Wayne County
57	1344	1982	**East Bay** (township) Grand Traverse County
57	1344	1982	**Orion** (charter township) Oakland County
57	1344	1982	**Park** (township) Ottawa County
57	1344	1982	**Walker** (city) Kent County
57	1344	1982	**Wixom** (city) Oakland County
62	1463	1981	**Brandon** (charter township) Oakland County
62	1463	1981	**Brighton** (township) Livingston County
62	1463	1981	**Grand Blanc** (charter township) Genesee County
62	1463	1981	**Plainfield** (charter township) Kent County
62	1463	1981	**Rochester Hills** (city) Oakland County
67	1563	1980	**Fort Gratiot** (charter township) Saint Clair County
67	1563	1980	**Haslett** (CDP) Ingham County
67	1563	1980	**Kentwood** (city) Kent County
70	1668	1979	**Alpine** (township) Kent County
70	1668	1979	**Clinton** (charter township) Macomb County
70	1668	1979	**Davison** (township) Genesee County
70	1668	1979	**Meridian** (charter township) Ingham County
70	1668	1979	**Mundy** (township) Genesee County
70	1668	1979	**West Bloomfield** (charter township) Oakland County
70	1668	1979	**White Lake** (charter township) Oakland County
70	1668	1979	**Woodhaven** (city) Wayne County
78	1795	1978	**Bedford** (township) Monroe County
78	1795	1978	**Comstock Park** (CDP) Kent County
78	1795	1978	**DeWitt** (charter township) Clinton County
78	1795	1978	**Delta** (charter township) Eaton County
78	1795	1978	**Holly** (township) Oakland County
78	1795	1978	**Waverly** (CDP) Eaton County
84	1932	1977	**Farmington Hills** (city) Oakland County
84	1932	1977	**Harrison** (charter township) Macomb County
84	1932	1977	**Highland** (charter township) Oakland County
84	1932	1977	**Monroe** (charter township) Monroe County
84	1932	1977	**Okemos** (CDP) Ingham County
84	1932	1977	**Plymouth** (charter township) Wayne County
90	2051	1976	**Flushing** (charter township) Genesee County
90	2051	1976	**Fruitport** (charter township) Muskegon County
90	2051	1976	**Lincoln** (charter township) Berrien County
90	2051	1976	**Sterling Heights** (city) Macomb County
90	2051	1976	**Thomas** (township) Saginaw County
90	2051	1976	**Troy** (city) Oakland County
96	2191	1975	**Blackman** (charter township) Jackson County
96	2191	1975	**Comstock** (charter township) Kalamazoo County
96	2191	1975	**Grandville** (city) Kent County
96	2191	1975	**Northview** (CDP) Kent County
96	2191	1975	**Portage** (city) Kalamazoo County
101	2330	1974	**Frenchtown** (township) Monroe County
101	2330	1974	**Jenison** (CDP) Ottawa County
101	2330	1974	**Mount Pleasant** (city) Isabella County
101	2330	1974	**Ypsilanti** (charter township) Washtenaw County
105	2449	1973	**Cooper** (charter township) Kalamazoo County
105	2449	1973	**Port Huron** (charter township) Saint Clair County
105	2449	1973	**Saginaw** (charter township) Saginaw County
105	2449	1973	**Vienna** (charter township) Genesee County
109	2560	1972	**Monitor** (charter township) Bay County
110	2668	1971	**Fraser** (city) Macomb County
110	2668	1971	**Midland** (city) Midland County
110	2668	1971	**Romulus** (city) Wayne County
113	2810	1970	**East Lansing** (city) Ingham County
113	2810	1970	**Norton Shores** (city) Muskegon County
113	2810	1970	**Riverview** (city) Wayne County
113	2810	1970	**Waterford** (charter township) Oakland County
117	2903	1969	**Flint** (charter township) Genesee County
117	2903	1969	**Muskegon** (charter township) Muskegon County
117	2903	1969	**Southfield** (city) Oakland County
120	3015	1968	**Ann Arbor** (city) Washtenaw County
120	3015	1968	**Bangor** (charter township) Bay County
120	3015	1968	**Genesee** (charter township) Genesee County
120	3015	1968	**Grosse Ile** (township) Wayne County
120	3015	1968	**Niles** (township) Berrien County
125	3117	1967	**Bloomfield** (charter township) Oakland County
125	3117	1967	**Holland** (city) Ottawa County
127	3213	1966	**Big Rapids** (city) Mecosta County
127	3213	1966	**Farmington** (city) Oakland County
127	3213	1966	**Westland** (city) Wayne County
127	3213	1966	**Wyoming** (city) Kent County
131	3323	1965	**Sturgis** (city) Saint Joseph County
132	3399	1964	**Emmett** (charter township) Calhoun County
132	3399	1964	**Leoni** (township) Jackson County
132	3399	1964	**Mount Morris** (township) Genesee County
132	3399	1964	**Saint Joseph** (charter township) Berrien County
132	3399	1964	**Summit** (township) Jackson County
132	3399	1964	**Warren** (city) Macomb County
138	3485	1963	**Bridgeport** (charter township) Saginaw County
138	3485	1963	**Livonia** (city) Wayne County
138	3485	1963	**Marquette** (city) Marquette County
141	3560	1962	**Benton** (charter township) Berrien County
141	3560	1962	**Burton** (city) Genesee County
141	3560	1962	**Coldwater** (city) Branch County
141	3560	1962	**Taylor** (city) Wayne County
145	3639	1961	**Kalamazoo** (charter township) Kalamazoo County
146	3696	1960	**Beecher** (CDP) Genesee County
146	3696	1960	**Madison Heights** (city) Oakland County
146	3696	1960	**Southfield** (township) Oakland County
146	3696	1960	**Southgate** (city) Wayne County
146	3696	1960	**Trenton** (city) Wayne County

Note: *The state column ranks the top/bottom 150 places from all places in the state with population of 10,000 or more. The national column ranks the top/bottom 150 places from all places in the country with population of 10,000 or more. Places that are unincorporated were not considered in the rankings. Please refer to the User Guide for additional information.*

Median Year Structure Built

Top 150 Places Ranked in *Ascending* Order

State Rank	Nat'l Rank	Year	Place
1	1	<1940	**Grosse Pointe Park** (city) Wayne County
1	1	<1940	**Hamtramck** (city) Wayne County
1	1	<1940	**Ionia** (city) Ionia County
1	1	<1940	**Jackson** (city) Jackson County
5	130	1942	**Bay City** (city) Bay County
6	156	1944	**Benton Harbor** (city) Berrien County
7	179	1946	**Ferndale** (city) Oakland County
8	202	1947	**Detroit** (city) Wayne County
8	202	1947	**Escanaba** (city) Delta County
8	202	1947	**Highland Park** (city) Wayne County
8	202	1947	**Saginaw** (city) Saginaw County
12	224	1948	**Muskegon Heights** (city) Muskegon County
13	245	1949	**Berkley** (city) Oakland County
13	245	1949	**Wyandotte** (city) Wayne County
15	270	1950	**Dearborn** (city) Wayne County
16	306	1951	**Muskegon** (city) Muskegon County
16	306	1951	**Port Huron** (city) Saint Clair County
18	344	1952	**Alpena** (city) Alpena County
18	344	1952	**Grand Rapids** (city) Kent County
18	344	1952	**Owosso** (city) Shiawassee County
21	383	1953	**East Grand Rapids** (city) Kent County
21	383	1953	**Grosse Pointe Woods** (city) Wayne County
21	383	1953	**Harper Woods** (city) Wayne County
21	383	1953	**Monroe** (city) Monroe County
21	383	1953	**Niles** (city) Berrien County
26	425	1954	**Eastpointe** (city) Macomb County
26	425	1954	**Flint** (city) Genesee County
26	425	1954	**Hazel Park** (city) Oakland County
26	425	1954	**Lincoln Park** (city) Wayne County
26	425	1954	**Melvindale** (city) Wayne County
26	425	1954	**Ypsilanti** (city) Washtenaw County
32	482	1955	**Adrian** (city) Lenawee County
32	482	1955	**Allen Park** (city) Wayne County
32	482	1955	**Battle Creek** (city) Calhoun County
32	482	1955	**Redford** (charter township) Wayne County
32	482	1955	**Royal Oak** (city) Oakland County
37	544	1956	**Birmingham** (city) Oakland County
37	544	1956	**Garden City** (city) Wayne County
37	544	1956	**Mount Clemens** (city) Macomb County
40	630	1957	**Dearborn Heights** (city) Wayne County
40	630	1957	**Kalamazoo** (city) Kalamazoo County
40	630	1957	**Oak Park** (city) Oakland County
40	630	1957	**Saint Clair Shores** (city) Macomb County
40	630	1957	**Sault Sainte Marie** (city) Chippewa County
40	630	1957	**Wayne** (city) Wayne County
46	725	1958	**Beverly Hills** (village) Oakland County
46	725	1958	**Clawson** (city) Oakland County
46	725	1958	**Grand Haven** (city) Ottawa County
46	725	1958	**Inkster** (city) Wayne County
46	725	1958	**Pontiac** (city) Oakland County
46	725	1958	**Traverse City** (city) Grand Traverse County
52	808	1959	**Cadillac** (city) Wexford County
52	808	1959	**Lansing** (city) Ingham County
52	808	1959	**Roseville** (city) Macomb County
55	886	1960	**Beecher** (CDP) Genesee County
55	886	1960	**Madison Heights** (city) Oakland County
55	886	1960	**Southfield** (township) Oakland County
55	886	1960	**Southgate** (city) Wayne County
55	886	1960	**Trenton** (city) Wayne County
60	961	1961	**Kalamazoo** (charter township) Kalamazoo County
61	1018	1962	**Benton** (charter township) Berrien County
61	1018	1962	**Burton** (city) Genesee County
61	1018	1962	**Coldwater** (city) Branch County
61	1018	1962	**Taylor** (city) Wayne County
65	1097	1963	**Bridgeport** (charter township) Saginaw County
65	1097	1963	**Livonia** (city) Wayne County
65	1097	1963	**Marquette** (city) Marquette County
68	1172	1964	**Emmett** (charter township) Calhoun County
68	1172	1964	**Leoni** (township) Jackson County
68	1172	1964	**Mount Morris** (township) Genesee County
68	1172	1964	**Saint Joseph** (charter township) Berrien County
68	1172	1964	**Summit** (township) Jackson County
68	1172	1964	**Warren** (city) Macomb County
74	1258	1965	**Sturgis** (city) Saint Joseph County
75	1334	1966	**Big Rapids** (city) Mecosta County
75	1334	1966	**Farmington** (city) Oakland County
75	1334	1966	**Westland** (city) Wayne County
75	1334	1966	**Wyoming** (city) Kent County
79	1444	1967	**Bloomfield** (charter township) Oakland County
79	1444	1967	**Holland** (city) Ottawa County
81	1540	1968	**Ann Arbor** (city) Washtenaw County
81	1540	1968	**Bangor** (charter township) Bay County
81	1540	1968	**Genesee** (charter township) Genesee County
81	1540	1968	**Grosse Ile** (township) Wayne County
81	1540	1968	**Niles** (township) Berrien County
86	1642	1969	**Flint** (charter township) Genesee County
86	1642	1969	**Muskegon** (charter township) Muskegon County
86	1642	1969	**Southfield** (city) Oakland County
89	1754	1970	**East Lansing** (city) Ingham County
89	1754	1970	**Norton Shores** (city) Muskegon County
89	1754	1970	**Riverview** (city) Wayne County
89	1754	1970	**Waterford** (charter township) Oakland County
93	1847	1971	**Fraser** (city) Macomb County
93	1847	1971	**Midland** (city) Midland County
93	1847	1971	**Romulus** (city) Wayne County
96	1989	1972	**Monitor** (charter township) Bay County
97	2097	1973	**Cooper** (charter township) Kalamazoo County
97	2097	1973	**Port Huron** (charter township) Saint Clair County
97	2097	1973	**Saginaw** (charter township) Saginaw County
97	2097	1973	**Vienna** (charter township) Genesee County
101	2208	1974	**Frenchtown** (township) Monroe County
101	2208	1974	**Jenison** (CDP) Ottawa County
101	2208	1974	**Mount Pleasant** (city) Isabella County
101	2208	1974	**Ypsilanti** (charter township) Washtenaw County
105	2327	1975	**Blackman** (charter township) Jackson County
105	2327	1975	**Comstock** (charter township) Kalamazoo County
105	2327	1975	**Grandville** (city) Kent County
105	2327	1975	**Northview** (CDP) Kent County
105	2327	1975	**Portage** (city) Kalamazoo County
110	2466	1976	**Flushing** (charter township) Genesee County
110	2466	1976	**Fruitport** (charter township) Muskegon County
110	2466	1976	**Lincoln** (charter township) Berrien County
110	2466	1976	**Sterling Heights** (city) Macomb County
110	2466	1976	**Thomas** (township) Saginaw County
110	2466	1976	**Troy** (city) Oakland County
116	2606	1977	**Farmington Hills** (city) Oakland County
116	2606	1977	**Harrison** (charter township) Macomb County
116	2606	1977	**Highland** (charter township) Oakland County
116	2606	1977	**Monroe** (charter township) Monroe County
116	2606	1977	**Okemos** (CDP) Ingham County
116	2606	1977	**Plymouth** (charter township) Wayne County
122	2725	1978	**Bedford** (township) Monroe County
122	2725	1978	**Comstock Park** (CDP) Kent County
122	2725	1978	**DeWitt** (charter township) Clinton County
122	2725	1978	**Delta** (charter township) Eaton County
122	2725	1978	**Holly** (township) Oakland County
122	2725	1978	**Waverly** (CDP) Eaton County
128	2862	1979	**Alpine** (township) Kent County
128	2862	1979	**Clinton** (charter township) Macomb County
128	2862	1979	**Davison** (township) Genesee County
128	2862	1979	**Meridian** (charter township) Ingham County
128	2862	1979	**Mundy** (township) Genesee County
128	2862	1979	**West Bloomfield** (charter township) Oakland County
128	2862	1979	**White Lake** (charter township) Oakland County
128	2862	1979	**Woodhaven** (city) Wayne County
136	2989	1980	**Fort Gratiot** (charter township) Saint Clair County
136	2989	1980	**Haslett** (CDP) Ingham County
136	2989	1980	**Kentwood** (city) Kent County
139	3094	1981	**Brandon** (charter township) Oakland County
139	3094	1981	**Brighton** (township) Livingston County
139	3094	1981	**Grand Blanc** (charter township) Genesee County
139	3094	1981	**Plainfield** (charter township) Kent County
139	3094	1981	**Rochester Hills** (city) Oakland County
144	3194	1982	**East Bay** (township) Grand Traverse County
144	3194	1982	**Orion** (charter township) Oakland County
144	3194	1982	**Park** (township) Ottawa County
144	3194	1982	**Walker** (city) Kent County
144	3194	1982	**Wixom** (city) Oakland County
149	3313	1983	**Auburn Hills** (city) Oakland County
149	3313	1983	**Cascade** (charter township) Kent County

Note: The state column ranks the top/bottom 150 places from all places in the state with population of 10,000 or more. The national column ranks the top/bottom 150 places from all places in the country with population of 10,000 or more. Places that are unincorporated were not considered in the rankings. Please refer to the User Guide for additional information.

Homeowner Vacancy Rate

Top 150 Places Ranked in *Descending* Order

State Rank	Nat'l Rank	Percent	Place
1	97	5.9	**Cadillac** (city) Wexford County
2	109	5.7	**Ionia** (city) Ionia County
2	109	5.7	**Pontiac** (city) Oakland County
4	136	5.4	**Muskegon Heights** (city) Muskegon County
5	158	5.2	**Muskegon** (city) Muskegon County
6	185	5.0	**Sturgis** (city) Saint Joseph County
7	206	4.9	**Coldwater** (city) Branch County
7	206	4.9	**Grand Haven** (city) Ottawa County
9	263	4.6	**Hazel Park** (city) Oakland County
9	263	4.6	**Jackson** (city) Jackson County
11	287	4.5	**Harper Woods** (city) Wayne County
12	318	4.4	**Niles** (city) Berrien County
12	318	4.4	**Saginaw** (city) Saginaw County
14	340	4.3	**Lenox** (township) Macomb County
15	367	4.2	**Spring Lake** (township) Ottawa County
16	403	4.1	**Adrian** (city) Lenawee County
16	403	4.1	**Genesee** (charter township) Genesee County
18	444	4.0	**Battle Creek** (city) Calhoun County
18	444	4.0	**Hamtramck** (city) Wayne County
18	444	4.0	**Inkster** (city) Wayne County
18	444	4.0	**Romulus** (city) Wayne County
22	485	3.9	**Fenton** (city) Genesee County
22	485	3.9	**Ferndale** (city) Oakland County
22	485	3.9	**Flint** (city) Genesee County
22	485	3.9	**Kalamazoo** (city) Kalamazoo County
22	485	3.9	**Lansing** (city) Ingham County
22	485	3.9	**Owosso** (city) Shiawassee County
22	485	3.9	**Superior** (charter township) Washtenaw County
29	539	3.8	**Detroit** (city) Wayne County
30	589	3.7	**Highland Park** (city) Wayne County
30	589	3.7	**South Lyon** (city) Oakland County
32	641	3.6	**Beecher** (CDP) Genesee County
33	702	3.5	**Burton** (city) Genesee County
33	702	3.5	**Eastpointe** (city) Macomb County
33	702	3.5	**Monroe** (city) Monroe County
33	702	3.5	**Mount Clemens** (city) Macomb County
37	765	3.4	**Birmingham** (city) Oakland County
37	765	3.4	**Garfield** (charter township) Grand Traverse County
37	765	3.4	**Mount Morris** (township) Genesee County
40	841	3.3	**Auburn Hills** (city) Oakland County
40	841	3.3	**Grand Blanc** (charter township) Genesee County
40	841	3.3	**Grand Rapids** (city) Kent County
40	841	3.3	**Milford** (charter township) Oakland County
40	841	3.3	**Oak Park** (city) Oakland County
45	932	3.2	**Alpena** (city) Alpena County
45	932	3.2	**Bay City** (city) Bay County
45	932	3.2	**Big Rapids** (city) Mecosta County
45	932	3.2	**Brandon** (charter township) Oakland County
45	932	3.2	**Holly** (township) Oakland County
45	932	3.2	**Southfield** (city) Oakland County
45	932	3.2	**Van Buren** (charter township) Wayne County
52	1014	3.1	**Benton Harbor** (city) Berrien County
52	1014	3.1	**Niles** (township) Berrien County
52	1014	3.1	**Port Huron** (city) Saint Clair County
55	1083	3.0	**Harrison** (charter township) Macomb County
55	1083	3.0	**Monroe** (charter township) Monroe County
55	1083	3.0	**Summit** (township) Jackson County
55	1083	3.0	**Ypsilanti** (charter township) Washtenaw County
59	1191	2.9	**Holland** (city) Ottawa County
59	1191	2.9	**Wyoming** (city) Kent County
61	1296	2.8	**East Lansing** (city) Ingham County
61	1296	2.8	**Frenchtown** (township) Monroe County
61	1296	2.8	**Grosse Pointe Park** (city) Wayne County
61	1296	2.8	**Highland** (charter township) Oakland County
61	1296	2.8	**Huron** (charter township) Wayne County
61	1296	2.8	**Lincoln Park** (city) Wayne County
61	1296	2.8	**Orion** (charter township) Oakland County
61	1296	2.8	**Roseville** (city) Macomb County
61	1296	2.8	**Taylor** (city) Wayne County
61	1296	2.8	**Traverse City** (city) Grand Traverse County
61	1296	2.8	**Wyandotte** (city) Wayne County
72	1413	2.7	**Benton** (charter township) Berrien County
72	1413	2.7	**Chesterfield** (township) Macomb County
72	1413	2.7	**Flint** (charter township) Genesee County
72	1413	2.7	**Ypsilanti** (city) Washtenaw County
76	1548	2.6	**Canton** (charter township) Wayne County
76	1548	2.6	**Trenton** (city) Wayne County
76	1548	2.6	**Vienna** (charter township) Genesee County
79	1665	2.5	**Blackman** (charter township) Jackson County
79	1665	2.5	**Bridgeport** (charter township) Saginaw County
79	1665	2.5	**Brownstown** (charter township) Wayne County
79	1665	2.5	**Cutlerville** (CDP) Kent County
79	1665	2.5	**Davison** (township) Genesee County
79	1665	2.5	**Kentwood** (city) Kent County
79	1665	2.5	**Lyon** (charter township) Oakland County
79	1665	2.5	**Madison Heights** (city) Oakland County
79	1665	2.5	**Mundy** (township) Genesee County
79	1665	2.5	**Norton Shores** (city) Muskegon County
79	1665	2.5	**Oshtemo** (charter township) Kalamazoo County
79	1665	2.5	**Oxford** (charter township) Oakland County
79	1665	2.5	**Redford** (charter township) Wayne County
79	1665	2.5	**Rochester** (city) Oakland County
79	1665	2.5	**Springfield** (charter township) Oakland County
94	1799	2.4	**Antwerp** (township) Van Buren County
94	1799	2.4	**Bath** (charter township) Clinton County
94	1799	2.4	**Bloomfield** (charter township) Oakland County
94	1799	2.4	**Comstock Park** (CDP) Kent County
94	1799	2.4	**DeWitt** (charter township) Clinton County
94	1799	2.4	**Dearborn Heights** (city) Wayne County
94	1799	2.4	**East Bay** (township) Grand Traverse County
94	1799	2.4	**Fenton** (charter township) Genesee County
94	1799	2.4	**Grosse Ile** (township) Wayne County
94	1799	2.4	**Grosse Pointe Woods** (city) Wayne County
94	1799	2.4	**Kalamazoo** (charter township) Kalamazoo County
94	1799	2.4	**Leoni** (township) Jackson County
94	1799	2.4	**Novi** (city) Oakland County
94	1799	2.4	**Waterford** (charter township) Oakland County
94	1799	2.4	**Wayne** (city) Wayne County
94	1799	2.4	**Woodhaven** (city) Wayne County
110	1955	2.3	**Dearborn** (city) Wayne County
110	1955	2.3	**Emmett** (charter township) Calhoun County
110	1955	2.3	**Escanaba** (city) Delta County
110	1955	2.3	**Farmington** (city) Oakland County
110	1955	2.3	**Holland** (charter township) Ottawa County
110	1955	2.3	**Melvindale** (city) Wayne County
110	1955	2.3	**Westland** (city) Wayne County
117	2126	2.2	**Clinton** (charter township) Macomb County
117	2126	2.2	**Fraser** (city) Macomb County
117	2126	2.2	**Green Oak** (township) Livingston County
117	2126	2.2	**Haslett** (CDP) Ingham County
117	2126	2.2	**Holt** (CDP) Ingham County
117	2126	2.2	**Port Huron** (charter township) Saint Clair County
117	2126	2.2	**Warren** (city) Macomb County
124	2268	2.1	**Allendale** (CDP) Ottawa County
124	2268	2.1	**Delhi** (charter township) Ingham County
124	2268	2.1	**Farmington Hills** (city) Oakland County
124	2268	2.1	**Mount Pleasant** (city) Isabella County
124	2268	2.1	**Oakland** (charter township) Oakland County
124	2268	2.1	**Park** (township) Ottawa County
124	2268	2.1	**Portage** (city) Kalamazoo County
124	2268	2.1	**Saint Clair Shores** (city) Macomb County
124	2268	2.1	**Sault Sainte Marie** (city) Chippewa County
124	2268	2.1	**Texas** (charter township) Kalamazoo County
124	2268	2.1	**Washington** (township) Macomb County
135	2443	2.0	**Berkley** (city) Oakland County
135	2443	2.0	**Commerce** (charter township) Oakland County
135	2443	2.0	**Delta** (charter township) Eaton County
135	2443	2.0	**Fort Gratiot** (charter township) Saint Clair County
135	2443	2.0	**Garden City** (city) Wayne County
135	2443	2.0	**Genoa** (township) Livingston County
135	2443	2.0	**Lincoln** (charter township) Berrien County
135	2443	2.0	**Meridian** (charter township) Ingham County
135	2443	2.0	**Royal Oak** (city) Oakland County
144	2621	1.9	**Alpine** (township) Kent County
144	2621	1.9	**Fruitport** (charter township) Muskegon County
144	2621	1.9	**Hamburg** (township) Livingston County
144	2621	1.9	**Independence** (charter township) Oakland County
144	2621	1.9	**Macomb** (township) Macomb County
144	2621	1.9	**Marquette** (city) Marquette County
144	2621	1.9	**Midland** (city) Midland County

Note: The state column ranks the top/bottom 150 places from all places in the state with population of 10,000 or more. The national column ranks the top/bottom 150 places from all places in the country with population of 10,000 or more. Places that are unincorporated were not considered in the rankings. Please refer to the User Guide for additional information.

Homeowner Vacancy Rate

Top 150 Places Ranked in *Ascending* Order

State Rank	Nat'l Rank	Percent	Place	State Rank	Nat'l Rank	Percent	Place
1	85	0.7	**Jenison** (CDP) Ottawa County	71	2214	2.1	**Park** (township) Ottawa County
2	519	1.1	**Livonia** (city) Wayne County	71	2214	2.1	**Portage** (city) Kalamazoo County
3	672	1.2	**Ada** (township) Kent County	71	2214	2.1	**Saint Clair Shores** (city) Macomb County
3	672	1.2	**Cannon** (township) Kent County	71	2214	2.1	**Sault Sainte Marie** (city) Chippewa County
3	672	1.2	**Forest Hills** (CDP) Kent County	71	2214	2.1	**Texas** (charter township) Kalamazoo County
3	672	1.2	**Plymouth** (charter township) Wayne County	71	2214	2.1	**Washington** (township) Macomb County
7	842	1.3	**Beverly Hills** (village) Oakland County	82	2389	2.2	**Clinton** (charter township) Macomb County
7	842	1.3	**Cooper** (charter township) Kalamazoo County	82	2389	2.2	**Fraser** (city) Macomb County
7	842	1.3	**East Grand Rapids** (city) Kent County	82	2389	2.2	**Green Oak** (township) Livingston County
7	842	1.3	**Georgetown** (charter township) Ottawa County	82	2389	2.2	**Haslett** (CDP) Ingham County
7	842	1.3	**Walker** (city) Kent County	82	2389	2.2	**Holt** (CDP) Ingham County
12	1011	1.4	**Cascade** (charter township) Kent County	82	2389	2.2	**Port Huron** (charter township) Saint Clair County
12	1011	1.4	**Oceola** (township) Livingston County	82	2389	2.2	**Warren** (city) Macomb County
12	1011	1.4	**Troy** (city) Oakland County	89	2531	2.3	**Dearborn** (city) Wayne County
12	1011	1.4	**Wixom** (city) Oakland County	89	2531	2.3	**Emmett** (charter township) Calhoun County
16	1168	1.5	**Grand Rapids** (charter township) Kent County	89	2531	2.3	**Escanaba** (city) Delta County
16	1168	1.5	**Pittsfield** (charter township) Washtenaw County	89	2531	2.3	**Farmington** (city) Oakland County
18	1342	1.6	**Allen Park** (city) Wayne County	89	2531	2.3	**Holland** (charter township) Ottawa County
18	1342	1.6	**Grandville** (city) Kent County	89	2531	2.3	**Melvindale** (city) Wayne County
18	1342	1.6	**Monitor** (charter township) Bay County	89	2531	2.3	**Westland** (city) Wayne County
18	1342	1.6	**New Baltimore** (city) Macomb County	96	2702	2.4	**Antwerp** (township) Van Buren County
18	1342	1.6	**Plainfield** (charter township) Kent County	96	2702	2.4	**Bath** (charter township) Clinton County
18	1342	1.6	**Southfield** (township) Oakland County	96	2702	2.4	**Bloomfield** (charter township) Oakland County
18	1342	1.6	**Union** (charter township) Isabella County	96	2702	2.4	**Comstock Park** (CDP) Kent County
25	1503	1.7	**Ann Arbor** (city) Washtenaw County	96	2702	2.4	**DeWitt** (charter township) Clinton County
25	1503	1.7	**Brighton** (township) Livingston County	96	2702	2.4	**Dearborn Heights** (city) Wayne County
25	1503	1.7	**Byron** (township) Kent County	96	2702	2.4	**East Bay** (township) Grand Traverse County
25	1503	1.7	**Flushing** (charter township) Genesee County	96	2702	2.4	**Fenton** (charter township) Genesee County
25	1503	1.7	**Northview** (CDP) Kent County	96	2702	2.4	**Grosse Ile** (township) Wayne County
25	1503	1.7	**Okemos** (CDP) Ingham County	96	2702	2.4	**Grosse Pointe Woods** (city) Wayne County
25	1503	1.7	**Scio** (township) Washtenaw County	96	2702	2.4	**Kalamazoo** (charter township) Kalamazoo County
25	1503	1.7	**Southgate** (city) Wayne County	96	2702	2.4	**Leoni** (township) Jackson County
25	1503	1.7	**Sterling Heights** (city) Macomb County	96	2702	2.4	**Novi** (city) Oakland County
25	1503	1.7	**Tyrone** (township) Livingston County	96	2702	2.4	**Waterford** (charter township) Oakland County
35	1694	1.8	**Allendale** (charter township) Ottawa County	96	2702	2.4	**Wayne** (city) Wayne County
35	1694	1.8	**Bangor** (charter township) Bay County	96	2702	2.4	**Woodhaven** (city) Wayne County
35	1694	1.8	**Bedford** (township) Monroe County	112	2858	2.5	**Blackman** (charter township) Jackson County
35	1694	1.8	**Caledonia** (township) Kent County	112	2858	2.5	**Bridgeport** (charter township) Saginaw County
35	1694	1.8	**Clawson** (city) Oakland County	112	2858	2.5	**Brownstown** (charter township) Wayne County
35	1694	1.8	**Comstock** (charter township) Kalamazoo County	112	2858	2.5	**Cutlerville** (CDP) Kent County
35	1694	1.8	**Gaines** (charter township) Kent County	112	2858	2.5	**Davison** (township) Genesee County
35	1694	1.8	**Grand Haven** (charter township) Ottawa County	112	2858	2.5	**Kentwood** (city) Kent County
35	1694	1.8	**Hartland** (township) Livingston County	112	2858	2.5	**Lyon** (charter township) Oakland County
35	1694	1.8	**Riverview** (city) Wayne County	112	2858	2.5	**Madison Heights** (city) Oakland County
35	1694	1.8	**Rochester Hills** (city) Oakland County	112	2858	2.5	**Mundy** (township) Genesee County
35	1694	1.8	**Shelby** (charter township) Macomb County	112	2858	2.5	**Norton Shores** (city) Muskegon County
35	1694	1.8	**Waverly** (CDP) Eaton County	112	2858	2.5	**Oshtemo** (charter township) Kalamazoo County
48	1847	1.9	**Alpine** (township) Kent County	112	2858	2.5	**Oxford** (charter township) Oakland County
48	1847	1.9	**Fruitport** (charter township) Muskegon County	112	2858	2.5	**Redford** (charter township) Wayne County
48	1847	1.9	**Hamburg** (township) Livingston County	112	2858	2.5	**Rochester** (city) Oakland County
48	1847	1.9	**Independence** (charter township) Oakland County	112	2858	2.5	**Springfield** (charter township) Oakland County
48	1847	1.9	**Macomb** (township) Macomb County	127	2992	2.6	**Canton** (charter township) Wayne County
48	1847	1.9	**Marquette** (city) Marquette County	127	2992	2.6	**Trenton** (city) Wayne County
48	1847	1.9	**Midland** (city) Midland County	127	2992	2.6	**Vienna** (charter township) Genesee County
48	1847	1.9	**Muskegon** (charter township) Muskegon County	130	3109	2.7	**Benton** (charter township) Berrien County
48	1847	1.9	**Northville** (township) Wayne County	130	3109	2.7	**Chesterfield** (township) Macomb County
48	1847	1.9	**Saginaw** (charter township) Saginaw County	130	3109	2.7	**Flint** (charter township) Genesee County
48	1847	1.9	**Saint Joseph** (charter township) Berrien County	130	3109	2.7	**Ypsilanti** (city) Washtenaw County
48	1847	1.9	**Thomas** (township) Saginaw County	134	3244	2.8	**East Lansing** (city) Ingham County
48	1847	1.9	**West Bloomfield** (charter township) Oakland County	134	3244	2.8	**Frenchtown** (township) Monroe County
48	1847	1.9	**White Lake** (charter township) Oakland County	134	3244	2.8	**Grosse Pointe Park** (city) Wayne County
62	2036	2.0	**Berkley** (city) Oakland County	134	3244	2.8	**Highland** (charter township) Oakland County
62	2036	2.0	**Commerce** (charter township) Oakland County	134	3244	2.8	**Huron** (charter township) Wayne County
62	2036	2.0	**Delta** (charter township) Eaton County	134	3244	2.8	**Lincoln Park** (city) Wayne County
62	2036	2.0	**Fort Gratiot** (charter township) Saint Clair County	134	3244	2.8	**Orion** (charter township) Oakland County
62	2036	2.0	**Garden City** (city) Wayne County	134	3244	2.8	**Roseville** (city) Macomb County
62	2036	2.0	**Genoa** (township) Livingston County	134	3244	2.8	**Taylor** (city) Wayne County
62	2036	2.0	**Lincoln** (charter township) Berrien County	134	3244	2.8	**Traverse City** (city) Grand Traverse County
62	2036	2.0	**Meridian** (charter township) Ingham County	134	3244	2.8	**Wyandotte** (city) Wayne County
62	2036	2.0	**Royal Oak** (city) Oakland County	145	3361	2.9	**Holland** (city) Ottawa County
71	2214	2.1	**Allendale** (CDP) Ottawa County	145	3361	2.9	**Wyoming** (city) Kent County
71	2214	2.1	**Delhi** (charter township) Ingham County	147	3466	3.0	**Harrison** (charter township) Macomb County
71	2214	2.1	**Farmington Hills** (city) Oakland County	147	3466	3.0	**Monroe** (charter township) Monroe County
71	2214	2.1	**Mount Pleasant** (city) Isabella County	147	3466	3.0	**Summit** (township) Jackson County
71	2214	2.1	**Oakland** (charter township) Oakland County	147	3466	3.0	**Ypsilanti** (charter township) Washtenaw County

Note: The state column ranks the top/bottom 150 places from all places in the state with population of 10,000 or more. The national column ranks the top/bottom 150 places from all places in the country with population of 10,000 or more. Places that are unincorporated were not considered in the rankings. Please refer to the User Guide for additional information.

Median Gross Rent

Top 150 Places Ranked in *Descending* Order

State Rank	Nat'l Rank	Dollars	Place
1	434	1,534	**West Bloomfield** (charter township) Oakland County
2	513	1,474	**Ada** (township) Kent County
3	603	1,429	**Oakland** (charter township) Oakland County
4	706	1,382	**Southfield** (township) Oakland County
5	821	1,336	**Forest Hills** (CDP) Kent County
6	854	1,327	**Beverly Hills** (village) Oakland County
7	952	1,281	**Cascade** (charter township) Kent County
8	970	1,275	**Grosse Pointe Woods** (city) Wayne County
9	1019	1,259	**Commerce** (charter township) Oakland County
10	1160	1,217	**Birmingham** (city) Oakland County
11	1217	1,201	**Grosse Ile** (township) Wayne County
12	1255	1,187	**Grand Rapids** (charter township) Kent County
13	1296	1,178	**Flushing** (charter township) Genesee County
14	1316	1,174	**Brighton** (township) Livingston County
15	1438	1,142	**Macomb** (township) Macomb County
16	1462	1,137	**Cannon** (township) Kent County
17	1469	1,135	**East Grand Rapids** (city) Kent County
18	1616	1,101	**Jenison** (CDP) Ottawa County
19	1706	1,081	**Scio** (township) Washtenaw County
20	1725	1,078	**Lyon** (charter township) Oakland County
21	1749	1,072	**Bloomfield** (charter township) Oakland County
22	1778	1,067	**Berkley** (city) Oakland County
23	1791	1,064	**Rochester Hills** (city) Oakland County
24	1811	1,059	**Hartland** (township) Livingston County
25	1816	1,058	**Northville** (township) Wayne County
26	1859	1,049	**Troy** (city) Oakland County
27	1867	1,046	**Redford** (charter township) Wayne County
28	1949	1,025	**Eastpointe** (city) Macomb County
29	1958	1,020	**Harper Woods** (city) Wayne County
30	1977	1,014	**Oak Park** (city) Oakland County
31	1997	1,008	**Ann Arbor** (city) Washtenaw County
32	2000	1,006	**Springfield** (charter township) Oakland County
33	2074	994	**Novi** (city) Oakland County
34	2081	993	**Tyrone** (township) Livingston County
35	2105	989	**Garden City** (city) Wayne County
36	2114	988	**Oceola** (township) Livingston County
37	2158	981	**Bath** (charter township) Clinton County
38	2197	976	**Farmington Hills** (city) Oakland County
39	2202	975	**Dearborn Heights** (city) Wayne County
40	2220	972	**Green Oak** (township) Livingston County
41	2231	971	**Genoa** (township) Livingston County
42	2250	968	**Livonia** (city) Wayne County
43	2275	965	**Canton** (charter township) Wayne County
43	2275	965	**Southfield** (city) Oakland County
45	2293	962	**Dearborn** (city) Wayne County
46	2378	949	**White Lake** (charter township) Oakland County
47	2425	941	**Washington** (township) Macomb County
48	2440	938	**Hamburg** (township) Livingston County
49	2451	936	**Chesterfield** (township) Macomb County
50	2497	928	**Grosse Pointe Park** (city) Wayne County
51	2507	927	**Huron** (charter township) Wayne County
52	2521	924	**Highland** (charter township) Oakland County
53	2552	920	**Saint Joseph** (charter township) Berrien County
54	2581	914	**Delhi** (charter township) Ingham County
54	2581	914	**Independence** (charter township) Oakland County
56	2596	911	**Lenox** (township) Macomb County
57	2603	910	**Holt** (CDP) Ingham County
58	2614	909	**Shelby** (charter township) Macomb County
59	2631	906	**Auburn Hills** (city) Oakland County
60	2730	891	**Fenton** (charter township) Genesee County
61	2740	889	**Cooper** (charter township) Kalamazoo County
61	2740	889	**Summit** (township) Jackson County
63	2770	884	**Pittsfield** (charter township) Washtenaw County
64	2785	882	**Royal Oak** (city) Oakland County
65	2805	879	**Hazel Park** (city) Oakland County
66	2814	878	**Farmington** (city) Oakland County
67	2822	877	**Park** (township) Ottawa County
68	2835	875	**Oxford** (charter township) Oakland County
69	2858	871	**Bedford** (township) Monroe County
70	2876	869	**Texas** (charter township) Kalamazoo County
71	2898	865	**Saint Clair Shores** (city) Macomb County
72	2911	863	**Allendale** (charter township) Ottawa County
73	2916	861	**Holly** (township) Oakland County
74	2936	858	**Orion** (charter township) Oakland County
75	2951	856	**East Lansing** (city) Ingham County
75	2951	856	**Garfield** (charter township) Grand Traverse County
75	2951	856	**Sterling Heights** (city) Macomb County
78	2961	855	**Allen Park** (city) Wayne County
79	2968	854	**Fruitport** (charter township) Muskegon County
80	3016	847	**Ferndale** (city) Oakland County
81	3026	846	**Roseville** (city) Macomb County
82	3084	837	**Leoni** (township) Jackson County
83	3087	836	**Grand Haven** (charter township) Ottawa County
84	3156	824	**Brandon** (charter township) Oakland County
84	3156	824	**East Bay** (township) Grand Traverse County
86	3163	823	**Van Buren** (charter township) Wayne County
87	3169	822	**Okemos** (CDP) Ingham County
88	3177	821	**Brownstown** (charter township) Wayne County
89	3234	810	**Clawson** (city) Oakland County
90	3245	808	**Georgetown** (charter township) Ottawa County
90	3245	808	**Mundy** (township) Genesee County
90	3245	808	**Superior** (charter township) Washtenaw County
90	3245	808	**Traverse City** (city) Grand Traverse County
94	3263	805	**Ypsilanti** (charter township) Washtenaw County
95	3265	804	**Byron** (township) Kent County
95	3265	804	**Warren** (city) Macomb County
97	3292	799	**Lincoln** (charter township) Berrien County
98	3298	798	**Caledonia** (township) Kent County
98	3298	798	**Genesee** (charter township) Genesee County
98	3298	798	**Harrison** (charter township) Macomb County
101	3309	796	**Mount Morris** (township) Genesee County
102	3320	794	**Meridian** (charter township) Ingham County
102	3320	794	**Norton Shores** (city) Muskegon County
102	3320	794	**Southgate** (city) Wayne County
105	3357	788	**South Lyon** (city) Oakland County
106	3365	787	**Allendale** (CDP) Ottawa County
106	3365	787	**Lincoln Park** (city) Wayne County
106	3365	787	**Taylor** (city) Wayne County
109	3378	784	**Clinton** (charter township) Macomb County
110	3385	783	**Delta** (charter township) Eaton County
110	3385	783	**Monroe** (charter township) Monroe County
110	3385	783	**Plymouth** (charter township) Wayne County
113	3398	781	**Fenton** (city) Genesee County
113	3398	781	**Westland** (city) Wayne County
115	3412	779	**Waverly** (CDP) Eaton County
116	3423	777	**Beecher** (CDP) Genesee County
116	3423	777	**Haslett** (CDP) Ingham County
118	3433	776	**Rochester** (city) Oakland County
119	3473	769	**Frenchtown** (township) Monroe County
120	3479	768	**Spring Lake** (township) Ottawa County
121	3485	767	**Holland** (city) Ottawa County
122	3488	766	**Burton** (city) Genesee County
123	3505	763	**Cutlerville** (CDP) Kent County
124	3511	762	**Kentwood** (city) Kent County
125	3517	761	**Detroit** (city) Wayne County
125	3517	761	**Port Huron** (charter township) Saint Clair County
127	3536	758	**Grand Rapids** (city) Kent County
128	3550	755	**Madison Heights** (city) Oakland County
129	3624	744	**Grand Blanc** (charter township) Genesee County
130	3631	743	**Gaines** (charter township) Kent County
130	3631	743	**Romulus** (city) Wayne County
132	3652	741	**Inkster** (city) Wayne County
133	3670	737	**Kalamazoo** (charter township) Kalamazoo County
134	3682	735	**Saginaw** (charter township) Saginaw County
135	3687	734	**Holland** (charter township) Ottawa County
135	3687	734	**Melvindale** (city) Wayne County
137	3700	732	**Waterford** (charter township) Oakland County
138	3715	730	**Fort Gratiot** (charter township) Saint Clair County
139	3723	729	**Lansing** (city) Ingham County
140	3728	728	**Blackman** (charter township) Jackson County
140	3728	728	**Pontiac** (city) Oakland County
142	3740	726	**Thomas** (township) Saginaw County
143	3770	721	**DeWitt** (charter township) Clinton County
144	3781	720	**Ypsilanti** (city) Washtenaw County
145	3797	716	**Flint** (charter township) Genesee County
146	3808	714	**Wyoming** (city) Kent County
147	3812	713	**Riverview** (city) Wayne County
147	3812	713	**Woodhaven** (city) Wayne County
149	3819	712	**Portage** (city) Kalamazoo County
150	3827	711	**Bangor** (charter township) Bay County

Note: The state column ranks the top/bottom 150 places from all places in the state with population of 10,000 or more. The national column ranks the top/bottom 150 places from all places in the country with population of 10,000 or more. Places that are unincorporated were not considered in the rankings. Please refer to the User Guide for additional information.

Median Gross Rent

Top 150 Places Ranked in *Ascending* Order

State Rank	Nat'l Rank	Dollars	Place
1	17	519	**Alpena** (city) Alpena County
2	19	521	**Escanaba** (city) Delta County
3	54	552	**Big Rapids** (city) Mecosta County
4	62	557	**Benton** (charter township) Berrien County
5	85	563	**Bay City** (city) Bay County
6	95	566	**Benton Harbor** (city) Berrien County
7	136	579	**Monitor** (charter township) Bay County
8	144	581	**Sturgis** (city) Saint Joseph County
9	149	582	**Highland Park** (city) Wayne County
10	175	588	**Niles** (city) Berrien County
11	183	591	**Mount Clemens** (city) Macomb County
12	192	593	**Sault Sainte Marie** (city) Chippewa County
13	238	603	**Muskegon** (city) Muskegon County
14	262	609	**Owosso** (city) Shiawassee County
15	265	610	**Hamtramck** (city) Wayne County
16	299	616	**Wixom** (city) Oakland County
17	374	632	**Davison** (township) Genesee County
18	398	636	**Jackson** (city) Jackson County
19	418	639	**Muskegon Heights** (city) Muskegon County
20	439	642	**Bridgeport** (charter township) Saginaw County
20	439	642	**Ionia** (city) Ionia County
22	452	644	**Grand Haven** (city) Ottawa County
23	468	647	**New Baltimore** (city) Macomb County
24	472	648	**Marquette** (city) Marquette County
25	480	649	**Emmett** (charter township) Calhoun County
25	480	649	**Wayne** (city) Wayne County
27	513	655	**Saginaw** (city) Saginaw County
28	574	668	**Flint** (city) Genesee County
29	608	674	**Grandville** (city) Kent County
30	616	675	**Coldwater** (city) Branch County
31	622	676	**Antwerp** (township) Van Buren County
31	622	676	**Trenton** (city) Wayne County
33	627	677	**Niles** (township) Berrien County
34	637	679	**Adrian** (city) Lenawee County
34	637	679	**Cadillac** (city) Wexford County
34	637	679	**Comstock Park** (CDP) Kent County
37	650	681	**Port Huron** (city) Saint Clair County
38	656	682	**Alpine** (township) Kent County
39	679	686	**Muskegon** (charter township) Muskegon County
40	683	687	**Mount Pleasant** (city) Isabella County
41	698	689	**Battle Creek** (city) Calhoun County
41	698	689	**Fraser** (city) Macomb County
41	698	689	**Northview** (CDP) Kent County
44	705	690	**Milford** (charter township) Oakland County
45	710	691	**Vienna** (charter township) Genesee County
46	722	693	**Comstock** (charter township) Kalamazoo County
47	728	694	**Walker** (city) Kent County
48	735	695	**Oshtemo** (charter township) Kalamazoo County
49	740	696	**Plainfield** (charter township) Kent County
50	744	697	**Wyandotte** (city) Wayne County
51	771	702	**Union** (charter township) Isabella County
52	775	703	**Monroe** (city) Monroe County
53	798	707	**Kalamazoo** (city) Kalamazoo County
54	818	710	**Midland** (city) Midland County
55	824	711	**Bangor** (charter township) Bay County
56	830	712	**Portage** (city) Kalamazoo County
57	838	713	**Riverview** (city) Wayne County
57	838	713	**Woodhaven** (city) Wayne County
59	845	714	**Wyoming** (city) Kent County
60	853	716	**Flint** (charter township) Genesee County
61	871	720	**Ypsilanti** (city) Washtenaw County
62	876	721	**DeWitt** (charter township) Clinton County
63	910	726	**Thomas** (township) Saginaw County
64	921	728	**Blackman** (charter township) Jackson County
64	921	728	**Pontiac** (city) Oakland County
66	929	729	**Lansing** (city) Ingham County
67	934	730	**Fort Gratiot** (charter township) Saint Clair County
68	945	732	**Waterford** (charter township) Oakland County
69	962	734	**Holland** (charter township) Ottawa County
69	962	734	**Melvindale** (city) Wayne County
71	970	735	**Saginaw** (charter township) Saginaw County
72	982	737	**Kalamazoo** (charter township) Kalamazoo County
73	998	741	**Inkster** (city) Wayne County
74	1019	743	**Gaines** (charter township) Kent County
74	1019	743	**Romulus** (city) Wayne County
76	1026	744	**Grand Blanc** (charter township) Genesee County
77	1097	755	**Madison Heights** (city) Oakland County
78	1117	758	**Grand Rapids** (city) Kent County
79	1135	761	**Detroit** (city) Wayne County
79	1135	761	**Port Huron** (charter township) Saint Clair County
81	1140	762	**Kentwood** (city) Kent County
82	1146	763	**Cutlerville** (CDP) Kent County
83	1163	766	**Burton** (city) Genesee County
84	1169	767	**Holland** (city) Ottawa County
85	1172	768	**Spring Lake** (township) Ottawa County
86	1178	769	**Frenchtown** (township) Monroe County
87	1214	776	**Rochester** (city) Oakland County
88	1224	777	**Beecher** (CDP) Genesee County
88	1224	777	**Haslett** (CDP) Ingham County
90	1238	779	**Waverly** (CDP) Eaton County
91	1252	781	**Fenton** (city) Genesee County
91	1252	781	**Westland** (city) Wayne County
93	1261	783	**Delta** (charter township) Eaton County
93	1261	783	**Monroe** (charter township) Monroe County
93	1261	783	**Plymouth** (charter township) Wayne County
96	1272	784	**Clinton** (charter township) Macomb County
97	1285	787	**Allendale** (CDP) Ottawa County
97	1285	787	**Lincoln Park** (city) Wayne County
97	1285	787	**Taylor** (city) Wayne County
100	1292	788	**South Lyon** (city) Oakland County
101	1326	794	**Meridian** (charter township) Ingham County
101	1326	794	**Norton Shores** (city) Muskegon County
101	1326	794	**Southgate** (city) Wayne County
104	1341	796	**Mount Morris** (township) Genesee County
105	1353	798	**Caledonia** (township) Kent County
105	1353	798	**Genesee** (charter township) Genesee County
105	1353	798	**Harrison** (charter township) Macomb County
108	1359	799	**Lincoln** (charter township) Berrien County
109	1383	804	**Byron** (township) Kent County
109	1383	804	**Warren** (city) Macomb County
111	1392	805	**Ypsilanti** (charter township) Washtenaw County
112	1404	808	**Georgetown** (charter township) Ottawa County
112	1404	808	**Mundy** (township) Genesee County
112	1404	808	**Superior** (charter township) Washtenaw County
112	1404	808	**Traverse City** (city) Grand Traverse County
116	1418	810	**Clawson** (city) Oakland County
117	1473	821	**Brownstown** (charter township) Wayne County
118	1480	822	**Okemos** (CDP) Ingham County
119	1488	823	**Van Buren** (charter township) Wayne County
120	1494	824	**Brandon** (charter township) Oakland County
120	1494	824	**East Bay** (township) Grand Traverse County
122	1565	836	**Grand Haven** (charter township) Ottawa County
123	1570	837	**Leoni** (township) Jackson County
124	1622	846	**Roseville** (city) Macomb County
125	1631	847	**Ferndale** (city) Oakland County
126	1680	854	**Fruitport** (charter township) Muskegon County
127	1689	855	**Allen Park** (city) Wayne County
128	1696	856	**East Lansing** (city) Ingham County
128	1696	856	**Garfield** (charter township) Grand Traverse County
128	1696	856	**Sterling Heights** (city) Macomb County
131	1713	858	**Orion** (charter township) Oakland County
132	1734	861	**Holly** (township) Oakland County
133	1744	863	**Allendale** (charter township) Ottawa County
134	1751	865	**Saint Clair Shores** (city) Macomb County
135	1775	869	**Texas** (charter township) Kalamazoo County
136	1794	871	**Bedford** (township) Monroe County
137	1814	875	**Oxford** (charter township) Oakland County
138	1828	877	**Park** (township) Ottawa County
139	1835	878	**Farmington** (city) Oakland County
140	1843	879	**Hazel Park** (city) Oakland County
141	1863	882	**Royal Oak** (city) Oakland County
142	1880	884	**Pittsfield** (charter township) Washtenaw County
143	1904	889	**Cooper** (charter township) Kalamazoo County
143	1904	889	**Summit** (township) Jackson County
145	1924	891	**Fenton** (charter township) Genesee County
146	2022	906	**Auburn Hills** (city) Oakland County
147	2040	909	**Shelby** (charter township) Macomb County
148	2043	910	**Holt** (CDP) Ingham County
149	2054	911	**Lenox** (township) Macomb County
150	2069	914	**Delhi** (charter township) Ingham County

Note: The state column ranks the top/bottom 150 places from all places in the state with population of 10,000 or more. The national column ranks the top/bottom 150 places from all places in the country with population of 10,000 or more. Places that are unincorporated were not considered in the rankings. Please refer to the User Guide for additional information.

Rental Vacancy Rate

Top 150 Places Ranked in *Descending* Order

State Rank	Nat'l Rank	Percent	Place
1	32	22.0	**Flushing** (charter township) Genesee County
2	41	20.8	**Beecher** (CDP) Genesee County
3	43	20.6	**Wixom** (city) Oakland County
4	52	19.6	**Genesee** (charter township) Genesee County
5	76	18.4	**Lyon** (charter township) Oakland County
6	85	18.0	**Detroit** (city) Wayne County
7	102	17.5	**Blackman** (charter township) Jackson County
8	117	17.1	**Van Buren** (charter township) Wayne County
9	121	17.0	**Mount Morris** (township) Genesee County
10	124	16.9	**Fort Gratiot** (charter township) Saint Clair County
11	135	16.5	**Flint** (city) Genesee County
12	181	15.7	**Comstock** (charter township) Kalamazoo County
13	211	15.1	**Pontiac** (city) Oakland County
13	211	15.1	**South Lyon** (city) Oakland County
15	219	15.0	**Springfield** (charter township) Oakland County
16	225	14.9	**Spring Lake** (township) Ottawa County
17	239	14.7	**Alpine** (township) Kent County
18	246	14.6	**Frenchtown** (township) Monroe County
18	246	14.6	**Niles** (township) Berrien County
20	259	14.5	**Comstock Park** (CDP) Kent County
20	259	14.5	**Flint** (charter township) Genesee County
22	275	14.3	**Harrison** (charter township) Macomb County
22	275	14.3	**Leoni** (township) Jackson County
22	275	14.3	**Troy** (city) Oakland County
25	283	14.2	**Adrian** (city) Lenawee County
25	283	14.2	**Highland Park** (city) Wayne County
27	303	14.0	**Auburn Hills** (city) Oakland County
27	303	14.0	**Grosse Ile** (township) Wayne County
27	303	14.0	**Shelby** (charter township) Macomb County
30	316	13.9	**Park** (township) Ottawa County
31	321	13.8	**Emmett** (charter township) Calhoun County
32	352	13.6	**Independence** (charter township) Oakland County
33	363	13.5	**Grand Haven** (city) Ottawa County
34	370	13.4	**Holland** (charter township) Ottawa County
34	370	13.4	**Novi** (city) Oakland County
36	385	13.3	**East Bay** (township) Grand Traverse County
37	400	13.2	**Muskegon Heights** (city) Muskegon County
38	409	13.1	**Chesterfield** (township) Macomb County
38	409	13.1	**Kentwood** (city) Kent County
40	428	13.0	**Washington** (township) Macomb County
41	446	12.9	**White Lake** (charter township) Oakland County
42	459	12.8	**Battle Creek** (city) Calhoun County
42	459	12.8	**Brandon** (charter township) Oakland County
44	480	12.7	**Milford** (charter township) Oakland County
44	480	12.7	**Rochester Hills** (city) Oakland County
46	512	12.5	**Bloomfield** (charter township) Oakland County
46	512	12.5	**Norton Shores** (city) Muskegon County
46	512	12.5	**Southfield** (city) Oakland County
49	530	12.4	**Jackson** (city) Jackson County
49	530	12.4	**Ypsilanti** (city) Washtenaw County
51	543	12.3	**Holly** (township) Oakland County
51	543	12.3	**Walker** (city) Kent County
53	561	12.2	**DeWitt** (charter township) Clinton County
53	561	12.2	**Hamtramck** (city) Wayne County
53	561	12.2	**Saginaw** (city) Saginaw County
56	605	12.0	**Byron** (township) Kent County
56	605	12.0	**Grand Rapids** (charter township) Kent County
56	605	12.0	**Monroe** (city) Monroe County
56	605	12.0	**New Baltimore** (city) Macomb County
60	635	11.9	**Birmingham** (city) Oakland County
60	635	11.9	**Kalamazoo** (charter township) Kalamazoo County
60	635	11.9	**Mount Clemens** (city) Macomb County
60	635	11.9	**Oshtemo** (charter township) Kalamazoo County
64	656	11.8	**Bath** (charter township) Clinton County
64	656	11.8	**Cascade** (charter township) Kent County
64	656	11.8	**Inkster** (city) Wayne County
64	656	11.8	**Oxford** (charter township) Oakland County
68	706	11.6	**Gaines** (charter township) Kent County
68	706	11.6	**Ionia** (city) Ionia County
70	731	11.5	**Bridgeport** (charter township) Saginaw County
70	731	11.5	**Fenton** (charter township) Genesee County
70	731	11.5	**Lenox** (township) Macomb County
70	731	11.5	**Port Huron** (city) Saint Clair County
70	731	11.5	**Summit** (township) Jackson County
75	756	11.4	**Coldwater** (city) Branch County
75	756	11.4	**Cutlerville** (CDP) Kent County
77	831	11.1	**West Bloomfield** (charter township) Oakland County
78	860	11.0	**Garfield** (charter township) Grand Traverse County
79	896	10.9	**Grand Blanc** (charter township) Genesee County
79	896	10.9	**Niles** (city) Berrien County
79	896	10.9	**Waterford** (charter township) Oakland County
82	930	10.8	**Benton** (charter township) Berrien County
83	960	10.7	**Orion** (charter township) Oakland County
84	991	10.6	**Romulus** (city) Wayne County
84	991	10.6	**Ypsilanti** (charter township) Washtenaw County
86	1024	10.5	**Clinton** (charter township) Macomb County
86	1024	10.5	**Grosse Pointe Park** (city) Wayne County
86	1024	10.5	**Muskegon** (city) Muskegon County
89	1061	10.4	**Portage** (city) Kalamazoo County
89	1061	10.4	**Sturgis** (city) Saint Joseph County
89	1061	10.4	**Westland** (city) Wayne County
92	1107	10.3	**Lansing** (city) Ingham County
92	1107	10.3	**Wayne** (city) Wayne County
94	1151	10.2	**Grand Rapids** (city) Kent County
94	1151	10.2	**Saint Clair Shores** (city) Macomb County
94	1151	10.2	**Vienna** (charter township) Genesee County
97	1185	10.1	**Brownstown** (charter township) Wayne County
97	1185	10.1	**Northview** (CDP) Kent County
97	1185	10.1	**Rochester** (city) Oakland County
100	1220	10.0	**Wyandotte** (city) Wayne County
101	1291	9.8	**Cadillac** (city) Wexford County
101	1291	9.8	**Lincoln** (charter township) Berrien County
101	1291	9.8	**Owosso** (city) Shiawassee County
104	1340	9.7	**Farmington Hills** (city) Oakland County
104	1340	9.7	**Holland** (city) Ottawa County
106	1384	9.6	**Canton** (charter township) Wayne County
107	1415	9.5	**Green Oak** (township) Livingston County
107	1415	9.5	**Grosse Pointe Woods** (city) Wayne County
107	1415	9.5	**Highland** (charter township) Oakland County
107	1415	9.5	**Lincoln Park** (city) Wayne County
107	1415	9.5	**Northville** (township) Wayne County
107	1415	9.5	**Plainfield** (charter township) Kent County
107	1415	9.5	**Port Huron** (charter township) Saint Clair County
114	1455	9.4	**Bedford** (township) Monroe County
114	1455	9.4	**Trenton** (city) Wayne County
114	1455	9.4	**Tyrone** (township) Livingston County
114	1455	9.4	**Woodhaven** (city) Wayne County
118	1496	9.3	**Oak Park** (city) Oakland County
118	1496	9.3	**Royal Oak** (city) Oakland County
120	1541	9.2	**Bangor** (charter township) Bay County
120	1541	9.2	**Ferndale** (city) Oakland County
120	1541	9.2	**Plymouth** (charter township) Wayne County
123	1583	9.1	**Ada** (township) Kent County
123	1583	9.1	**Farmington** (city) Oakland County
123	1583	9.1	**Monroe** (charter township) Monroe County
126	1625	9.0	**Kalamazoo** (city) Kalamazoo County
126	1625	9.0	**Mundy** (township) Genesee County
126	1625	9.0	**Warren** (city) Macomb County
129	1710	8.8	**Alpena** (city) Alpena County
129	1710	8.8	**Hazel Park** (city) Oakland County
129	1710	8.8	**Riverview** (city) Wayne County
129	1710	8.8	**Roseville** (city) Macomb County
133	1755	8.7	**Sterling Heights** (city) Macomb County
134	1792	8.6	**Bay City** (city) Bay County
135	1833	8.5	**Benton Harbor** (city) Berrien County
135	1833	8.5	**Davison** (township) Genesee County
135	1833	8.5	**Fenton** (city) Genesee County
138	1892	8.4	**Scio** (township) Washtenaw County
139	1940	8.3	**Delta** (charter township) Eaton County
139	1940	8.3	**Genoa** (township) Livingston County
141	1993	8.2	**Commerce** (charter township) Oakland County
141	1993	8.2	**Dearborn** (city) Wayne County
141	1993	8.2	**Harper Woods** (city) Wayne County
141	1993	8.2	**Oakland** (charter township) Oakland County
141	1993	8.2	**Waverly** (CDP) Eaton County
146	2058	8.1	**Burton** (city) Genesee County
146	2058	8.1	**Macomb** (township) Macomb County
146	2058	8.1	**Redford** (charter township) Wayne County
149	2115	8.0	**Grandville** (city) Kent County
149	2115	8.0	**Madison Heights** (city) Oakland County

Note: *The state column ranks the top/bottom 150 places from all places in the state with population of 10,000 or more. The national column ranks the top/bottom 150 places from all places in the country with population of 10,000 or more. Places that are unincorporated were not considered in the rankings. Please refer to the User Guide for additional information.*

Rental Vacancy Rate

Top 150 Places Ranked in *Ascending* Order

State Rank	Nat'l Rank	Percent	Place
1	240	3.8	**Marquette** (city) Marquette County
1	240	3.8	**Union** (charter township) Isabella County
3	304	4.0	**Allendale** (charter township) Ottawa County
4	452	4.4	**Allendale** (CDP) Ottawa County
4	452	4.4	**Muskegon** (charter township) Muskegon County
6	537	4.6	**Beverly Hills** (village) Oakland County
7	593	4.7	**Southfield** (township) Oakland County
7	593	4.7	**Thomas** (township) Saginaw County
9	900	5.3	**Midland** (city) Midland County
10	949	5.4	**Huron** (charter township) Wayne County
11	1010	5.5	**Ann Arbor** (city) Washtenaw County
11	1010	5.5	**Texas** (charter township) Kalamazoo County
13	1198	5.8	**Cannon** (township) Kent County
14	1305	6.0	**Berkley** (city) Oakland County
14	1305	6.0	**Brighton** (township) Livingston County
14	1305	6.0	**East Lansing** (city) Ingham County
17	1364	6.1	**Fraser** (city) Macomb County
17	1364	6.1	**Fruitport** (charter township) Muskegon County
17	1364	6.1	**Sault Sainte Marie** (city) Chippewa County
20	1423	6.2	**Caledonia** (township) Kent County
20	1423	6.2	**Cooper** (charter township) Kalamazoo County
22	1480	6.3	**Escanaba** (city) Delta County
22	1480	6.3	**Hamburg** (township) Livingston County
22	1480	6.3	**Monitor** (charter township) Bay County
22	1480	6.3	**Traverse City** (city) Grand Traverse County
26	1540	6.4	**Hartland** (township) Livingston County
26	1540	6.4	**Jenison** (CDP) Ottawa County
28	1614	6.5	**Big Rapids** (city) Mecosta County
29	1680	6.6	**Delhi** (charter township) Ingham County
29	1680	6.6	**Mount Pleasant** (city) Isabella County
29	1680	6.6	**Oceola** (township) Livingston County
29	1680	6.6	**Pittsfield** (charter township) Washtenaw County
33	1726	6.7	**Holt** (CDP) Ingham County
34	1792	6.8	**Garden City** (city) Wayne County
34	1792	6.8	**Grand Haven** (charter township) Ottawa County
36	1960	7.1	**Allen Park** (city) Wayne County
36	1960	7.1	**Superior** (charter township) Washtenaw County
38	2026	7.2	**Dearborn Heights** (city) Wayne County
38	2026	7.2	**Melvindale** (city) Wayne County
38	2026	7.2	**Saint Joseph** (charter township) Berrien County
41	2099	7.3	**Georgetown** (charter township) Ottawa County
42	2153	7.4	**East Grand Rapids** (city) Kent County
42	2153	7.4	**Forest Hills** (CDP) Kent County
42	2153	7.4	**Haslett** (CDP) Ingham County
45	2217	7.5	**Livonia** (city) Wayne County
46	2268	7.6	**Eastpointe** (city) Macomb County
46	2268	7.6	**Meridian** (charter township) Ingham County
46	2268	7.6	**Southgate** (city) Wayne County
49	2332	7.7	**Antwerp** (township) Van Buren County
49	2332	7.7	**Saginaw** (charter township) Saginaw County
49	2332	7.7	**Wyoming** (city) Kent County
52	2372	7.8	**Clawson** (city) Oakland County
52	2372	7.8	**Okemos** (CDP) Ingham County
52	2372	7.8	**Taylor** (city) Wayne County
55	2481	8.0	**Grandville** (city) Kent County
55	2481	8.0	**Madison Heights** (city) Oakland County
57	2542	8.1	**Burton** (city) Genesee County
57	2542	8.1	**Macomb** (township) Macomb County
57	2542	8.1	**Redford** (charter township) Wayne County
60	2599	8.2	**Commerce** (charter township) Oakland County
60	2599	8.2	**Dearborn** (city) Wayne County
60	2599	8.2	**Harper Woods** (city) Wayne County
60	2599	8.2	**Oakland** (charter township) Oakland County
60	2599	8.2	**Waverly** (CDP) Eaton County
65	2664	8.3	**Delta** (charter township) Eaton County
65	2664	8.3	**Genoa** (township) Livingston County
67	2717	8.4	**Scio** (township) Washtenaw County
68	2765	8.5	**Benton Harbor** (city) Berrien County
68	2765	8.5	**Davison** (township) Genesee County
68	2765	8.5	**Fenton** (city) Genesee County
71	2824	8.6	**Bay City** (city) Bay County
72	2865	8.7	**Sterling Heights** (city) Macomb County
73	2902	8.8	**Alpena** (city) Alpena County
73	2902	8.8	**Hazel Park** (city) Oakland County
73	2902	8.8	**Riverview** (city) Wayne County
73	2902	8.8	**Roseville** (city) Macomb County
77	2983	9.0	**Kalamazoo** (city) Kalamazoo County
77	2983	9.0	**Mundy** (township) Genesee County
77	2983	9.0	**Warren** (city) Macomb County
80	3032	9.1	**Ada** (township) Kent County
80	3032	9.1	**Farmington** (city) Oakland County
80	3032	9.1	**Monroe** (charter township) Monroe County
83	3074	9.2	**Bangor** (charter township) Bay County
83	3074	9.2	**Ferndale** (city) Oakland County
83	3074	9.2	**Plymouth** (charter township) Wayne County
86	3116	9.3	**Oak Park** (city) Oakland County
86	3116	9.3	**Royal Oak** (city) Oakland County
88	3161	9.4	**Bedford** (township) Monroe County
88	3161	9.4	**Trenton** (city) Wayne County
88	3161	9.4	**Tyrone** (township) Livingston County
88	3161	9.4	**Woodhaven** (city) Wayne County
92	3202	9.5	**Green Oak** (township) Livingston County
92	3202	9.5	**Grosse Pointe Woods** (city) Wayne County
92	3202	9.5	**Highland** (charter township) Oakland County
92	3202	9.5	**Lincoln Park** (city) Wayne County
92	3202	9.5	**Northville** (township) Wayne County
92	3202	9.5	**Plainfield** (charter township) Kent County
92	3202	9.5	**Port Huron** (charter township) Saint Clair County
99	3242	9.6	**Canton** (charter township) Wayne County
100	3273	9.7	**Farmington Hills** (city) Oakland County
100	3273	9.7	**Holland** (city) Ottawa County
102	3317	9.8	**Cadillac** (city) Wexford County
102	3317	9.8	**Lincoln** (charter township) Berrien County
102	3317	9.8	**Owosso** (city) Shiawassee County
105	3399	10.0	**Wyandotte** (city) Wayne County
106	3437	10.1	**Brownstown** (charter township) Wayne County
106	3437	10.1	**Northview** (CDP) Kent County
106	3437	10.1	**Rochester** (city) Oakland County
109	3472	10.2	**Grand Rapids** (city) Kent County
109	3472	10.2	**Saint Clair Shores** (city) Macomb County
109	3472	10.2	**Vienna** (charter township) Genesee County
112	3506	10.3	**Lansing** (city) Ingham County
112	3506	10.3	**Wayne** (city) Wayne County
114	3550	10.4	**Portage** (city) Kalamazoo County
114	3550	10.4	**Sturgis** (city) Saint Joseph County
114	3550	10.4	**Westland** (city) Wayne County
117	3596	10.5	**Clinton** (charter township) Macomb County
117	3596	10.5	**Grosse Pointe Park** (city) Wayne County
117	3596	10.5	**Muskegon** (city) Muskegon County
120	3633	10.6	**Romulus** (city) Wayne County
120	3633	10.6	**Ypsilanti** (charter township) Washtenaw County
122	3666	10.7	**Orion** (charter township) Oakland County
123	3697	10.8	**Benton** (charter township) Berrien County
124	3727	10.9	**Grand Blanc** (charter township) Genesee County
124	3727	10.9	**Niles** (city) Berrien County
124	3727	10.9	**Waterford** (charter township) Oakland County
127	3761	11.0	**Garfield** (charter township) Grand Traverse County
128	3797	11.1	**West Bloomfield** (charter township) Oakland County
129	3879	11.4	**Coldwater** (city) Branch County
129	3879	11.4	**Cutlerville** (CDP) Kent County
131	3901	11.5	**Bridgeport** (charter township) Saginaw County
131	3901	11.5	**Fenton** (charter township) Genesee County
131	3901	11.5	**Lenox** (township) Macomb County
131	3901	11.5	**Port Huron** (city) Saint Clair County
131	3901	11.5	**Summit** (township) Jackson County
136	3926	11.6	**Gaines** (charter township) Kent County
136	3926	11.6	**Ionia** (city) Ionia County
138	3975	11.8	**Bath** (charter township) Clinton County
138	3975	11.8	**Cascade** (charter township) Kent County
138	3975	11.8	**Inkster** (city) Wayne County
138	3975	11.8	**Oxford** (charter township) Oakland County
142	4001	11.9	**Birmingham** (city) Oakland County
142	4001	11.9	**Kalamazoo** (charter township) Kalamazoo County
142	4001	11.9	**Mount Clemens** (city) Macomb County
142	4001	11.9	**Oshtemo** (charter township) Kalamazoo County
146	4022	12.0	**Byron** (township) Kent County
146	4022	12.0	**Grand Rapids** (charter township) Kent County
146	4022	12.0	**Monroe** (city) Monroe County
146	4022	12.0	**New Baltimore** (city) Macomb County
150	4075	12.2	**DeWitt** (charter township) Clinton County

Note: The state column ranks the top/bottom 150 places from all places in the state with population of 10,000 or more. The national column ranks the top/bottom 150 places from all places in the country with population of 10,000 or more. Places that are unincorporated were not considered in the rankings. Please refer to the User Guide for additional information.

Population with Health Insurance

Top 150 Places Ranked in *Descending* Order

State Rank	Nat'l Rank	Percent	Place
1	121	97.4	**Ada** (township) Kent County
2	134	97.3	**East Grand Rapids** (city) Kent County
3	245	96.6	**Forest Hills** (CDP) Kent County
4	314	96.2	**Grosse Ile** (township) Wayne County
5	412	95.8	**Cannon** (township) Kent County
5	412	95.8	**Texas** (charter township) Kalamazoo County
7	456	95.6	**Birmingham** (city) Oakland County
8	519	95.4	**Southfield** (township) Oakland County
9	542	95.3	**Bloomfield** (charter township) Oakland County
9	542	95.3	**Cascade** (charter township) Kent County
11	559	95.2	**Caledonia** (township) Kent County
11	559	95.2	**Scio** (township) Washtenaw County
13	597	95.0	**Beverly Hills** (village) Oakland County
14	622	94.9	**Grand Rapids** (charter township) Kent County
14	622	94.9	**Jenison** (CDP) Ottawa County
16	651	94.8	**Hamburg** (township) Livingston County
17	680	94.7	**Georgetown** (charter township) Ottawa County
18	730	94.5	**Grosse Pointe Woods** (city) Wayne County
19	779	94.3	**Macomb** (township) Macomb County
19	779	94.3	**Northville** (township) Wayne County
19	779	94.3	**Park** (township) Ottawa County
22	801	94.2	**Okemos** (CDP) Ingham County
22	801	94.2	**Plymouth** (charter township) Wayne County
24	828	94.1	**Flushing** (charter township) Genesee County
24	828	94.1	**Hartland** (township) Livingston County
24	828	94.1	**Oakland** (charter township) Oakland County
24	828	94.1	**Oceola** (township) Livingston County
28	886	93.9	**New Baltimore** (city) Macomb County
28	886	93.9	**Saint Joseph** (charter township) Berrien County
30	902	93.8	**Ann Arbor** (city) Washtenaw County
30	902	93.8	**East Lansing** (city) Ingham County
30	902	93.8	**Grosse Pointe Park** (city) Wayne County
33	926	93.7	**Tyrone** (township) Livingston County
34	959	93.6	**Farmington** (city) Oakland County
34	959	93.6	**Independence** (charter township) Oakland County
34	959	93.6	**Rochester** (city) Oakland County
37	1046	93.3	**Byron** (township) Kent County
38	1063	93.2	**Cooper** (charter township) Kalamazoo County
39	1087	93.1	**Brighton** (township) Livingston County
40	1109	93.0	**Bedford** (township) Monroe County
40	1109	93.0	**Novi** (city) Oakland County
42	1134	92.9	**Mundy** (township) Genesee County
43	1161	92.8	**Lyon** (charter township) Oakland County
43	1161	92.8	**Norton Shores** (city) Muskegon County
43	1161	92.8	**West Bloomfield** (charter township) Oakland County
46	1199	92.7	**Fenton** (charter township) Genesee County
46	1199	92.7	**Pittsfield** (charter township) Washtenaw County
46	1199	92.7	**Superior** (charter township) Washtenaw County
46	1199	92.7	**Trenton** (city) Wayne County
50	1266	92.5	**Livonia** (city) Wayne County
51	1286	92.4	**Farmington Hills** (city) Oakland County
51	1286	92.4	**Grand Blanc** (charter township) Genesee County
51	1286	92.4	**Meridian** (charter township) Ingham County
54	1315	92.3	**Delta** (charter township) Eaton County
54	1315	92.3	**Fruitport** (charter township) Muskegon County
56	1343	92.2	**Monitor** (charter township) Bay County
56	1343	92.2	**Rochester Hills** (city) Oakland County
56	1343	92.2	**South Lyon** (city) Oakland County
59	1366	92.1	**Commerce** (charter township) Oakland County
59	1366	92.1	**Plainfield** (charter township) Kent County
59	1366	92.1	**Springfield** (charter township) Oakland County
62	1391	92.0	**Green Oak** (township) Livingston County
62	1391	92.0	**Holt** (CDP) Ingham County
62	1391	92.0	**Lincoln** (charter township) Berrien County
65	1428	91.9	**Orion** (charter township) Oakland County
66	1454	91.8	**Allendale** (CDP) Ottawa County
67	1478	91.7	**Allendale** (charter township) Ottawa County
67	1478	91.7	**Oxford** (charter township) Oakland County
69	1499	91.6	**Delhi** (charter township) Ingham County
69	1499	91.6	**Gaines** (charter township) Kent County
69	1499	91.6	**Huron** (charter township) Wayne County
69	1499	91.6	**Saginaw** (charter township) Saginaw County
73	1525	91.5	**Canton** (charter township) Wayne County
73	1525	91.5	**Grand Haven** (charter township) Ottawa County
73	1525	91.5	**Troy** (city) Oakland County
73	1525	91.5	**Waverly** (CDP) Eaton County
77	1552	91.4	**Bridgeport** (charter township) Saginaw County
78	1579	91.3	**Antwerp** (township) Van Buren County
78	1579	91.3	**Milford** (charter township) Oakland County
78	1579	91.3	**Summit** (township) Jackson County
81	1606	91.2	**Brownstown** (charter township) Wayne County
81	1606	91.2	**Chesterfield** (township) Macomb County
81	1606	91.2	**Davison** (township) Genesee County
81	1606	91.2	**Genoa** (township) Livingston County
81	1606	91.2	**Woodhaven** (city) Wayne County
86	1634	91.1	**Brandon** (charter township) Oakland County
86	1634	91.1	**Frenchtown** (township) Monroe County
88	1655	91.0	**Walker** (city) Kent County
89	1675	90.9	**Comstock** (charter township) Kalamazoo County
90	1703	90.8	**Allen Park** (city) Wayne County
90	1703	90.8	**Highland** (charter township) Oakland County
92	1728	90.7	**Holland** (charter township) Ottawa County
92	1728	90.7	**Portage** (city) Kalamazoo County
94	1759	90.6	**Cutlerville** (CDP) Kent County
94	1759	90.6	**Fraser** (city) Macomb County
94	1759	90.6	**Thomas** (township) Saginaw County
97	1781	90.5	**Haslett** (CDP) Ingham County
97	1781	90.5	**Oshtemo** (charter township) Kalamazoo County
97	1781	90.5	**Southgate** (city) Wayne County
100	1807	90.4	**Shelby** (charter township) Macomb County
100	1807	90.4	**Washington** (township) Macomb County
102	1830	90.3	**Royal Oak** (city) Oakland County
103	1847	90.2	**Grandville** (city) Kent County
104	1876	90.1	**Berkley** (city) Oakland County
104	1876	90.1	**Midland** (city) Midland County
104	1876	90.1	**White Lake** (charter township) Oakland County
107	1898	90.0	**Holly** (township) Oakland County
108	1919	89.9	**Coldwater** (city) Branch County
108	1919	89.9	**DeWitt** (charter township) Clinton County
108	1919	89.9	**Flint** (charter township) Genesee County
108	1919	89.9	**Genesee** (charter township) Genesee County
108	1919	89.9	**Monroe** (charter township) Monroe County
108	1919	89.9	**Northview** (CDP) Kent County
108	1919	89.9	**Riverview** (city) Wayne County
115	1948	89.8	**Bath** (charter township) Clinton County
116	1978	89.7	**Port Huron** (charter township) Saint Clair County
117	2004	89.6	**Spring Lake** (township) Ottawa County
118	2117	89.1	**East Bay** (township) Grand Traverse County
118	2117	89.1	**Lenox** (township) Macomb County
120	2144	89.0	**Beecher** (CDP) Genesee County
120	2144	89.0	**Burton** (city) Genesee County
120	2144	89.0	**Kentwood** (city) Kent County
120	2144	89.0	**Saint Clair Shores** (city) Macomb County
120	2144	89.0	**Vienna** (charter township) Genesee County
125	2171	88.9	**Emmett** (charter township) Calhoun County
126	2223	88.7	**Harrison** (charter township) Macomb County
126	2223	88.7	**Holland** (city) Ottawa County
128	2245	88.6	**Monroe** (city) Monroe County
129	2264	88.5	**Bangor** (charter township) Bay County
129	2264	88.5	**Garfield** (charter township) Grand Traverse County
131	2303	88.3	**Fort Gratiot** (charter township) Saint Clair County
132	2326	88.2	**Southfield** (city) Oakland County
133	2351	88.1	**Muskegon Heights** (city) Muskegon County
133	2351	88.1	**Ypsilanti** (charter township) Washtenaw County
135	2375	88.0	**Leoni** (township) Jackson County
135	2375	88.0	**Mount Morris** (township) Genesee County
135	2375	88.0	**Muskegon** (charter township) Muskegon County
135	2375	88.0	**Niles** (city) Berrien County
139	2405	87.9	**Wyandotte** (city) Wayne County
140	2425	87.8	**Mount Pleasant** (city) Isabella County
140	2425	87.8	**Van Buren** (charter township) Wayne County
140	2425	87.8	**Wixom** (city) Oakland County
143	2456	87.7	**Sterling Heights** (city) Macomb County
144	2482	87.6	**Cadillac** (city) Wexford County
145	2504	87.5	**Waterford** (charter township) Oakland County
146	2527	87.4	**Blackman** (charter township) Jackson County
146	2527	87.4	**Clinton** (charter township) Macomb County
148	2546	87.3	**Eastpointe** (city) Macomb County
148	2546	87.3	**Sturgis** (city) Saint Joseph County
150	2574	87.2	**Clawson** (city) Oakland County

Note: The state column ranks the top/bottom 150 places from all places in the state with population of 10,000 or more. The national column ranks the top/bottom 150 places from all places in the country with population of 10,000 or more. Places that are unincorporated were not considered in the rankings. Please refer to the User Guide for additional information.

Population with Health Insurance

Top 150 Places Ranked in *Ascending* Order

State Rank	Nat'l Rank	Percent	Place
1	414	76.6	**Hamtramck** (city) Wayne County
2	577	78.7	**Ferndale** (city) Oakland County
3	707	79.9	**Hazel Park** (city) Oakland County
4	795	80.6	**Detroit** (city) Wayne County
5	822	80.8	**Pontiac** (city) Oakland County
6	922	81.4	**Jackson** (city) Jackson County
7	952	81.6	**Union** (charter township) Isabella County
8	1000	81.9	**Oak Park** (city) Oakland County
9	1020	82.0	**Comstock Park** (CDP) Kent County
10	1033	82.1	**Benton** (charter township) Berrien County
11	1074	82.4	**Highland Park** (city) Wayne County
12	1225	83.2	**Owosso** (city) Shiawassee County
13	1286	83.5	**Escanaba** (city) Delta County
13	1286	83.5	**Sault Sainte Marie** (city) Chippewa County
15	1311	83.6	**Benton Harbor** (city) Berrien County
16	1355	83.8	**Alpine** (township) Kent County
16	1355	83.8	**Lincoln Park** (city) Wayne County
18	1373	83.9	**Mount Clemens** (city) Macomb County
19	1429	84.2	**Auburn Hills** (city) Oakland County
20	1452	84.3	**Big Rapids** (city) Mecosta County
20	1452	84.3	**Dearborn Heights** (city) Wayne County
22	1472	84.4	**Muskegon** (city) Muskegon County
23	1490	84.5	**Inkster** (city) Wayne County
24	1511	84.6	**Saginaw** (city) Saginaw County
24	1511	84.6	**Wyoming** (city) Kent County
26	1529	84.7	**Adrian** (city) Lenawee County
27	1557	84.9	**Harper Woods** (city) Wayne County
27	1557	84.9	**Romulus** (city) Wayne County
29	1603	85.2	**Melvindale** (city) Wayne County
30	1624	85.3	**Grand Haven** (city) Ottawa County
31	1643	85.4	**Dearborn** (city) Wayne County
31	1643	85.4	**Taylor** (city) Wayne County
33	1663	85.5	**Ypsilanti** (city) Washtenaw County
34	1683	85.6	**Marquette** (city) Marquette County
35	1713	85.7	**Roseville** (city) Macomb County
35	1713	85.7	**Warren** (city) Macomb County
37	1736	85.8	**Kalamazoo** (city) Kalamazoo County
38	1813	86.1	**Kalamazoo** (charter township) Kalamazoo County
39	1835	86.2	**Ionia** (city) Ionia County
39	1835	86.2	**Port Huron** (city) Saint Clair County
41	1855	86.3	**Bay City** (city) Bay County
41	1855	86.3	**Niles** (township) Berrien County
41	1855	86.3	**Redford** (charter township) Wayne County
41	1855	86.3	**Wayne** (city) Wayne County
45	1884	86.4	**Grand Rapids** (city) Kent County
45	1884	86.4	**Madison Heights** (city) Oakland County
47	1897	86.5	**Battle Creek** (city) Calhoun County
47	1897	86.5	**Fenton** (city) Genesee County
47	1897	86.5	**Westland** (city) Wayne County
50	1918	86.6	**Traverse City** (city) Grand Traverse County
51	1942	86.7	**Flint** (city) Genesee County
52	1991	86.9	**Garden City** (city) Wayne County
53	2019	87.0	**Alpena** (city) Alpena County
54	2045	87.1	**Lansing** (city) Ingham County
55	2063	87.2	**Clawson** (city) Oakland County
56	2083	87.3	**Eastpointe** (city) Macomb County
56	2083	87.3	**Sturgis** (city) Saint Joseph County
58	2111	87.4	**Blackman** (charter township) Jackson County
58	2111	87.4	**Clinton** (charter township) Macomb County
60	2130	87.5	**Waterford** (charter township) Oakland County
61	2153	87.6	**Cadillac** (city) Wexford County
62	2175	87.7	**Sterling Heights** (city) Macomb County
63	2201	87.8	**Mount Pleasant** (city) Isabella County
63	2201	87.8	**Van Buren** (charter township) Wayne County
63	2201	87.8	**Wixom** (city) Oakland County
66	2232	87.9	**Wyandotte** (city) Wayne County
67	2252	88.0	**Leoni** (township) Jackson County
67	2252	88.0	**Mount Morris** (township) Genesee County
67	2252	88.0	**Muskegon** (charter township) Muskegon County
67	2252	88.0	**Niles** (city) Berrien County
71	2282	88.1	**Muskegon Heights** (city) Muskegon County
71	2282	88.1	**Ypsilanti** (charter township) Washtenaw County
73	2306	88.2	**Southfield** (city) Oakland County
74	2331	88.3	**Fort Gratiot** (charter township) Saint Clair County
75	2372	88.5	**Bangor** (charter township) Bay County
75	2372	88.5	**Garfield** (charter township) Grand Traverse County
77	2393	88.6	**Monroe** (city) Monroe County
78	2412	88.7	**Harrison** (charter township) Macomb County
78	2412	88.7	**Holland** (city) Ottawa County
80	2463	88.9	**Emmett** (charter township) Calhoun County
81	2486	89.0	**Beecher** (CDP) Genesee County
81	2486	89.0	**Burton** (city) Genesee County
81	2486	89.0	**Kentwood** (city) Kent County
81	2486	89.0	**Saint Clair Shores** (city) Macomb County
81	2486	89.0	**Vienna** (charter township) Genesee County
86	2513	89.1	**East Bay** (township) Grand Traverse County
86	2513	89.1	**Lenox** (township) Macomb County
88	2636	89.6	**Spring Lake** (township) Ottawa County
89	2653	89.7	**Port Huron** (charter township) Saint Clair County
90	2679	89.8	**Bath** (charter township) Clinton County
91	2709	89.9	**Coldwater** (city) Branch County
91	2709	89.9	**DeWitt** (charter township) Clinton County
91	2709	89.9	**Flint** (charter township) Genesee County
91	2709	89.9	**Genesee** (charter township) Genesee County
91	2709	89.9	**Monroe** (charter township) Monroe County
91	2709	89.9	**Northview** (CDP) Kent County
91	2709	89.9	**Riverview** (city) Wayne County
98	2738	90.0	**Holly** (township) Oakland County
99	2759	90.1	**Berkley** (city) Oakland County
99	2759	90.1	**Midland** (city) Midland County
99	2759	90.1	**White Lake** (charter township) Oakland County
102	2781	90.2	**Grandville** (city) Kent County
103	2810	90.3	**Royal Oak** (city) Oakland County
104	2827	90.4	**Shelby** (charter township) Macomb County
104	2827	90.4	**Washington** (township) Macomb County
106	2850	90.5	**Haslett** (CDP) Ingham County
106	2850	90.5	**Oshtemo** (charter township) Kalamazoo County
106	2850	90.5	**Southgate** (city) Wayne County
109	2876	90.6	**Cutlerville** (CDP) Kent County
109	2876	90.6	**Fraser** (city) Macomb County
109	2876	90.6	**Thomas** (township) Saginaw County
112	2898	90.7	**Holland** (charter township) Ottawa County
112	2898	90.7	**Portage** (city) Kalamazoo County
114	2929	90.8	**Allen Park** (city) Wayne County
114	2929	90.8	**Highland** (charter township) Oakland County
116	2954	90.9	**Comstock** (charter township) Kalamazoo County
117	2982	91.0	**Walker** (city) Kent County
118	3002	91.1	**Brandon** (charter township) Oakland County
118	3002	91.1	**Frenchtown** (township) Monroe County
120	3023	91.2	**Brownstown** (charter township) Wayne County
120	3023	91.2	**Chesterfield** (township) Macomb County
120	3023	91.2	**Davison** (township) Genesee County
120	3023	91.2	**Genoa** (township) Livingston County
120	3023	91.2	**Woodhaven** (city) Wayne County
125	3051	91.3	**Antwerp** (township) Van Buren County
125	3051	91.3	**Milford** (charter township) Oakland County
125	3051	91.3	**Summit** (township) Jackson County
128	3078	91.4	**Bridgeport** (charter township) Saginaw County
129	3105	91.5	**Canton** (charter township) Wayne County
129	3105	91.5	**Grand Haven** (charter township) Ottawa County
129	3105	91.5	**Troy** (city) Oakland County
129	3105	91.5	**Waverly** (CDP) Eaton County
133	3132	91.6	**Delhi** (charter township) Ingham County
133	3132	91.6	**Gaines** (charter township) Kent County
133	3132	91.6	**Huron** (charter township) Wayne County
133	3132	91.6	**Saginaw** (charter township) Saginaw County
137	3158	91.7	**Allendale** (charter township) Ottawa County
137	3158	91.7	**Oxford** (charter township) Oakland County
139	3179	91.8	**Allendale** (CDP) Ottawa County
140	3203	91.9	**Orion** (charter township) Oakland County
141	3229	92.0	**Green Oak** (township) Livingston County
141	3229	92.0	**Holt** (CDP) Ingham County
141	3229	92.0	**Lincoln** (charter township) Berrien County
144	3266	92.1	**Commerce** (charter township) Oakland County
144	3266	92.1	**Plainfield** (charter township) Kent County
144	3266	92.1	**Springfield** (charter township) Oakland County
147	3291	92.2	**Monitor** (charter township) Bay County
147	3291	92.2	**Rochester Hills** (city) Oakland County
147	3291	92.2	**South Lyon** (city) Oakland County
150	3314	92.3	**Delta** (charter township) Eaton County

Note: The state column ranks the top/bottom 150 places from all places in the state with population of 10,000 or more. The national column ranks the top/bottom 150 places from all places in the country with population of 10,000 or more. Places that are unincorporated were not considered in the rankings. Please refer to the User Guide for additional information.

Population with Private Health Insurance

Top 150 Places Ranked in *Descending* Order

State Rank	Nat'l Rank	Percent	Place
1	56	93.1	**Ada** (township) Kent County
2	103	92.0	**Beverly Hills** (village) Oakland County
3	120	91.7	**Forest Hills** (CDP) Kent County
4	123	91.6	**East Grand Rapids** (city) Kent County
4	123	91.6	**Southfield** (township) Oakland County
6	138	91.4	**Cannon** (township) Kent County
7	146	91.3	**Birmingham** (city) Oakland County
8	185	90.6	**Grosse Ile** (township) Wayne County
9	217	90.3	**Grosse Pointe Woods** (city) Wayne County
10	286	89.5	**Hartland** (township) Livingston County
11	315	89.1	**Cascade** (charter township) Kent County
12	336	88.9	**Grand Rapids** (charter township) Kent County
13	343	88.8	**Caledonia** (township) Kent County
13	343	88.8	**Oakland** (charter township) Oakland County
15	361	88.6	**Bloomfield** (charter township) Oakland County
15	361	88.6	**Northville** (township) Wayne County
15	361	88.6	**Rochester** (city) Oakland County
18	413	88.2	**Oceola** (township) Livingston County
19	427	88.1	**Plymouth** (charter township) Wayne County
20	437	88.0	**East Lansing** (city) Ingham County
21	475	87.7	**Hamburg** (township) Livingston County
22	510	87.5	**Georgetown** (charter township) Ottawa County
23	529	87.3	**New Baltimore** (city) Macomb County
24	559	87.0	**Brighton** (township) Livingston County
24	559	87.0	**Texas** (charter township) Kalamazoo County
26	577	86.9	**Allendale** (CDP) Ottawa County
26	577	86.9	**Allendale** (charter township) Ottawa County
28	622	86.5	**Macomb** (township) Macomb County
28	622	86.5	**Okemos** (CDP) Ingham County
30	635	86.4	**Springfield** (charter township) Oakland County
31	655	86.2	**Ann Arbor** (city) Washtenaw County
31	655	86.2	**Novi** (city) Oakland County
33	711	85.8	**Scio** (township) Washtenaw County
34	754	85.5	**Grosse Pointe Park** (city) Wayne County
35	797	85.2	**Independence** (charter township) Oakland County
36	826	84.9	**Rochester Hills** (city) Oakland County
36	826	84.9	**South Lyon** (city) Oakland County
38	844	84.8	**Fenton** (charter township) Genesee County
39	858	84.7	**Jenison** (CDP) Ottawa County
39	858	84.7	**Tyrone** (township) Livingston County
41	902	84.3	**Meridian** (charter township) Ingham County
42	918	84.2	**Canton** (charter township) Wayne County
43	927	84.1	**Livonia** (city) Wayne County
43	927	84.1	**West Bloomfield** (charter township) Oakland County
45	938	84.0	**Farmington** (city) Oakland County
46	957	83.9	**Green Oak** (township) Livingston County
47	979	83.7	**Genoa** (township) Livingston County
47	979	83.7	**Lyon** (charter township) Oakland County
49	991	83.6	**Pittsfield** (charter township) Washtenaw County
50	1002	83.5	**Troy** (city) Oakland County
51	1018	83.4	**Commerce** (charter township) Oakland County
52	1030	83.3	**Bedford** (township) Monroe County
52	1030	83.3	**Orion** (charter township) Oakland County
54	1060	83.1	**Saint Joseph** (charter township) Berrien County
55	1096	82.8	**Delta** (charter township) Eaton County
56	1110	82.7	**Berkley** (city) Oakland County
57	1131	82.5	**Farmington Hills** (city) Oakland County
58	1143	82.4	**Royal Oak** (city) Oakland County
59	1155	82.3	**Haslett** (CDP) Ingham County
60	1195	82.0	**Oxford** (charter township) Oakland County
61	1244	81.5	**Park** (township) Ottawa County
62	1253	81.4	**Plainfield** (charter township) Kent County
63	1276	81.2	**Milford** (charter township) Oakland County
64	1290	81.1	**Grand Haven** (charter township) Ottawa County
65	1321	80.9	**Holt** (CDP) Ingham County
66	1334	80.8	**Waverly** (CDP) Eaton County
67	1347	80.7	**Delhi** (charter township) Ingham County
67	1347	80.7	**Saginaw** (charter township) Saginaw County
69	1384	80.5	**Allen Park** (city) Wayne County
69	1384	80.5	**Monitor** (charter township) Bay County
69	1384	80.5	**Thomas** (township) Saginaw County
69	1384	80.5	**Walker** (city) Kent County
73	1399	80.4	**Lincoln** (charter township) Berrien County
74	1419	80.2	**Cooper** (charter township) Kalamazoo County
75	1440	80.1	**Brownstown** (charter township) Wayne County
76	1451	80.0	**Trenton** (city) Wayne County
77	1474	79.8	**Grand Blanc** (charter township) Genesee County
77	1474	79.8	**Shelby** (charter township) Macomb County
77	1474	79.8	**Woodhaven** (city) Wayne County
80	1514	79.5	**Antwerp** (township) Van Buren County
80	1514	79.5	**Bath** (charter township) Clinton County
82	1553	79.2	**Byron** (township) Kent County
83	1566	79.1	**White Lake** (charter township) Oakland County
84	1594	78.9	**Huron** (charter township) Wayne County
85	1603	78.8	**Highland** (charter township) Oakland County
85	1603	78.8	**Washington** (township) Macomb County
87	1650	78.4	**Chesterfield** (township) Macomb County
87	1650	78.4	**DeWitt** (charter township) Clinton County
89	1671	78.2	**Flushing** (charter township) Genesee County
90	1689	78.0	**Mundy** (township) Genesee County
91	1708	77.8	**Southgate** (city) Wayne County
92	1722	77.7	**Portage** (city) Kalamazoo County
93	1729	77.6	**Spring Lake** (township) Ottawa County
94	1745	77.4	**Saint Clair Shores** (city) Macomb County
95	1761	77.2	**Fraser** (city) Macomb County
96	1805	76.9	**Holly** (township) Oakland County
96	1805	76.9	**Norton Shores** (city) Muskegon County
98	1836	76.6	**Wixom** (city) Oakland County
99	1847	76.5	**Midland** (city) Midland County
100	1887	76.2	**East Bay** (township) Grand Traverse County
101	1912	76.0	**Clawson** (city) Oakland County
101	1912	76.0	**Davison** (township) Genesee County
101	1912	76.0	**Fruitport** (charter township) Muskegon County
101	1912	76.0	**Northview** (CDP) Kent County
105	1921	75.9	**Brandon** (charter township) Oakland County
105	1921	75.9	**Gaines** (charter township) Kent County
107	1937	75.8	**Superior** (charter township) Washtenaw County
108	1955	75.6	**Riverview** (city) Wayne County
109	1978	75.4	**Grandville** (city) Kent County
110	2020	75.0	**Vienna** (charter township) Genesee County
111	2068	74.6	**Emmett** (charter township) Calhoun County
111	2068	74.6	**Holland** (charter township) Ottawa County
111	2068	74.6	**Oshtemo** (charter township) Kalamazoo County
114	2094	74.4	**Mount Pleasant** (city) Isabella County
115	2109	74.3	**Harrison** (charter township) Macomb County
116	2201	73.4	**Marquette** (city) Marquette County
117	2208	73.3	**Summit** (township) Jackson County
117	2208	73.3	**Waterford** (charter township) Oakland County
119	2227	73.1	**Garden City** (city) Wayne County
120	2254	72.8	**Van Buren** (charter township) Wayne County
121	2289	72.5	**Auburn Hills** (city) Oakland County
122	2299	72.4	**Fort Gratiot** (charter township) Saint Clair County
122	2299	72.4	**Lenox** (township) Macomb County
124	2319	72.1	**Kentwood** (city) Kent County
125	2329	72.0	**Comstock** (charter township) Kalamazoo County
126	2354	71.7	**Bangor** (charter township) Bay County
126	2354	71.7	**Wyandotte** (city) Wayne County
128	2408	71.2	**Sterling Heights** (city) Macomb County
129	2426	71.0	**Clinton** (charter township) Macomb County
130	2442	70.9	**Grand Haven** (city) Ottawa County
131	2462	70.7	**Traverse City** (city) Grand Traverse County
132	2513	70.2	**Monroe** (charter township) Monroe County
133	2553	69.9	**Redford** (charter township) Wayne County
134	2578	69.7	**Coldwater** (city) Branch County
134	2578	69.7	**Union** (charter township) Isabella County
136	2607	69.4	**Frenchtown** (township) Monroe County
137	2617	69.3	**Fenton** (city) Genesee County
138	2685	68.6	**Leoni** (township) Jackson County
139	2718	68.3	**Holland** (city) Ottawa County
140	2751	67.9	**Southfield** (city) Oakland County
141	2788	67.5	**Blackman** (charter township) Jackson County
142	2799	67.4	**Wyoming** (city) Kent County
143	2817	67.2	**Westland** (city) Wayne County
144	2836	67.0	**Harper Woods** (city) Wayne County
145	2854	66.9	**Wayne** (city) Wayne County
146	2878	66.7	**Cutlerville** (CDP) Kent County
147	2902	66.4	**Kalamazoo** (charter township) Kalamazoo County
148	2934	66.0	**Ferndale** (city) Oakland County
149	2941	65.9	**Ypsilanti** (charter township) Washtenaw County
150	2949	65.8	**Big Rapids** (city) Mecosta County

Note: The state column ranks the top/bottom 150 places from all places in the state with population of 10,000 or more. The national column ranks the top/bottom 150 places from all places in the country with population of 10,000 or more. Places that are unincorporated were not considered in the rankings. Please refer to the User Guide for additional information.

Population with Private Health Insurance

Top 150 Places Ranked in *Ascending* Order

State Rank	Nat'l Rank	Percent	Place	State Rank	Nat'l Rank	Percent	Place
1	25	26.3	**Benton Harbor** (city) Berrien County	76	2215	71.0	**Clinton** (charter township) Macomb County
2	54	31.3	**Muskegon Heights** (city) Muskegon County	77	2241	71.2	**Sterling Heights** (city) Macomb County
3	76	33.8	**Beecher** (CDP) Genesee County	78	2283	71.7	**Bangor** (charter township) Bay County
4	87	34.5	**Hamtramck** (city) Wayne County	78	2283	71.7	**Wyandotte** (city) Wayne County
5	100	35.5	**Highland Park** (city) Wayne County	80	2316	72.0	**Comstock** (charter township) Kalamazoo County
6	152	39.3	**Flint** (city) Genesee County	81	2328	72.1	**Kentwood** (city) Kent County
7	155	39.5	**Detroit** (city) Wayne County	82	2351	72.4	**Fort Gratiot** (charter township) Saint Clair County
8	184	41.5	**Saginaw** (city) Saginaw County	82	2351	72.4	**Lenox** (township) Macomb County
9	189	41.7	**Benton** (charter township) Berrien County	84	2358	72.5	**Auburn Hills** (city) Oakland County
10	193	41.8	**Inkster** (city) Wayne County	85	2394	72.8	**Van Buren** (charter township) Wayne County
11	247	44.1	**Jackson** (city) Jackson County	86	2420	73.1	**Garden City** (city) Wayne County
12	276	44.8	**Muskegon** (city) Muskegon County	87	2440	73.3	**Summit** (township) Jackson County
13	286	45.0	**Pontiac** (city) Oakland County	87	2440	73.3	**Waterford** (charter township) Oakland County
14	434	48.8	**Hazel Park** (city) Oakland County	89	2449	73.4	**Marquette** (city) Marquette County
15	487	49.8	**Mount Morris** (township) Genesee County	90	2537	74.3	**Harrison** (charter township) Macomb County
16	653	53.2	**Port Huron** (city) Saint Clair County	91	2548	74.4	**Mount Pleasant** (city) Isabella County
17	755	54.9	**Niles** (city) Berrien County	92	2568	74.6	**Emmett** (charter township) Calhoun County
18	796	55.3	**Adrian** (city) Lenawee County	92	2568	74.6	**Holland** (charter township) Ottawa County
19	831	55.8	**Lansing** (city) Ingham County	92	2568	74.6	**Oshtemo** (charter township) Kalamazoo County
20	879	56.4	**Dearborn** (city) Wayne County	95	2628	75.0	**Vienna** (charter township) Genesee County
21	918	56.8	**Escanaba** (city) Delta County	96	2668	75.4	**Grandville** (city) Kent County
22	935	57.1	**Ionia** (city) Ionia County	97	2687	75.6	**Riverview** (city) Wayne County
23	946	57.2	**Bay City** (city) Bay County	98	2714	75.8	**Superior** (charter township) Washtenaw County
24	966	57.4	**Mount Clemens** (city) Macomb County	99	2720	75.9	**Brandon** (charter township) Oakland County
25	1011	57.9	**Owosso** (city) Shiawassee County	99	2720	75.9	**Gaines** (charter township) Kent County
26	1028	58.1	**Comstock Park** (CDP) Kent County	101	2736	76.0	**Clawson** (city) Oakland County
27	1058	58.5	**Battle Creek** (city) Calhoun County	101	2736	76.0	**Davison** (township) Genesee County
28	1071	58.7	**Lincoln Park** (city) Wayne County	101	2736	76.0	**Fruitport** (charter township) Muskegon County
29	1126	59.4	**Melvindale** (city) Wayne County	101	2736	76.0	**Northview** (CDP) Kent County
29	1126	59.4	**Sturgis** (city) Saint Joseph County	105	2756	76.2	**East Bay** (township) Grand Traverse County
31	1159	59.8	**Eastpointe** (city) Macomb County	106	2800	76.5	**Midland** (city) Midland County
32	1178	60.0	**Romulus** (city) Wayne County	107	2810	76.6	**Wixom** (city) Oakland County
33	1186	60.1	**Grand Rapids** (city) Kent County	108	2841	76.9	**Holly** (township) Oakland County
34	1199	60.2	**Oak Park** (city) Oakland County	108	2841	76.9	**Norton Shores** (city) Muskegon County
35	1206	60.3	**Muskegon** (charter township) Muskegon County	110	2880	77.2	**Fraser** (city) Macomb County
35	1206	60.3	**Taylor** (city) Wayne County	111	2901	77.4	**Saint Clair Shores** (city) Macomb County
37	1290	61.4	**Alpine** (township) Kent County	112	2921	77.6	**Spring Lake** (township) Ottawa County
38	1332	61.9	**Cadillac** (city) Wexford County	113	2928	77.7	**Portage** (city) Kalamazoo County
38	1332	61.9	**Port Huron** (charter township) Saint Clair County	114	2935	77.8	**Southgate** (city) Wayne County
40	1366	62.4	**Sault Sainte Marie** (city) Chippewa County	115	2958	78.0	**Mundy** (township) Genesee County
41	1396	62.7	**Dearborn Heights** (city) Wayne County	116	2975	78.2	**Flushing** (charter township) Genesee County
41	1396	62.7	**Kalamazoo** (city) Kalamazoo County	117	2995	78.4	**Chesterfield** (township) Macomb County
43	1405	62.8	**Genesee** (charter township) Genesee County	117	2995	78.4	**DeWitt** (charter township) Clinton County
44	1450	63.3	**Alpena** (city) Alpena County	119	3042	78.8	**Highland** (charter township) Oakland County
45	1498	63.7	**Flint** (charter township) Genesee County	119	3042	78.8	**Washington** (township) Macomb County
45	1498	63.7	**Warren** (city) Macomb County	121	3054	78.9	**Huron** (charter township) Wayne County
47	1507	63.8	**Niles** (township) Berrien County	122	3080	79.1	**White Lake** (charter township) Oakland County
48	1544	64.2	**Madison Heights** (city) Oakland County	123	3091	79.2	**Byron** (township) Kent County
49	1553	64.3	**Roseville** (city) Macomb County	124	3124	79.5	**Antwerp** (township) Van Buren County
50	1559	64.4	**Ypsilanti** (city) Washtenaw County	124	3124	79.5	**Bath** (charter township) Clinton County
51	1604	64.8	**Bridgeport** (charter township) Saginaw County	126	3164	79.8	**Grand Blanc** (charter township) Genesee County
52	1661	65.4	**Burton** (city) Genesee County	126	3164	79.8	**Shelby** (charter township) Macomb County
53	1672	65.5	**Monroe** (city) Monroe County	126	3164	79.8	**Woodhaven** (city) Wayne County
54	1697	65.8	**Big Rapids** (city) Mecosta County	129	3195	80.0	**Trenton** (city) Wayne County
54	1697	65.8	**Garfield** (charter township) Grand Traverse County	130	3206	80.1	**Brownstown** (charter township) Wayne County
56	1708	65.9	**Ypsilanti** (charter township) Washtenaw County	131	3217	80.2	**Cooper** (charter township) Kalamazoo County
57	1716	66.0	**Ferndale** (city) Oakland County	132	3252	80.4	**Lincoln** (charter township) Berrien County
58	1744	66.4	**Kalamazoo** (charter township) Kalamazoo County	133	3258	80.5	**Allen Park** (city) Wayne County
59	1774	66.7	**Cutlerville** (CDP) Kent County	133	3258	80.5	**Monitor** (charter township) Bay County
60	1792	66.9	**Wayne** (city) Wayne County	133	3258	80.5	**Thomas** (township) Saginaw County
61	1803	67.0	**Harper Woods** (city) Wayne County	133	3258	80.5	**Walker** (city) Kent County
62	1829	67.2	**Westland** (city) Wayne County	137	3289	80.7	**Delhi** (charter township) Ingham County
63	1846	67.4	**Wyoming** (city) Kent County	137	3289	80.7	**Saginaw** (charter township) Saginaw County
64	1858	67.5	**Blackman** (charter township) Jackson County	139	3310	80.8	**Waverly** (CDP) Eaton County
65	1900	67.9	**Southfield** (city) Oakland County	140	3323	80.9	**Holt** (CDP) Ingham County
66	1931	68.3	**Holland** (city) Ottawa County	141	3351	81.1	**Grand Haven** (charter township) Ottawa County
67	1963	68.6	**Leoni** (township) Jackson County	142	3367	81.2	**Milford** (charter township) Oakland County
68	2031	69.3	**Fenton** (city) Genesee County	143	3387	81.4	**Plainfield** (charter township) Kent County
69	2040	69.4	**Frenchtown** (township) Monroe County	144	3404	81.5	**Park** (township) Ottawa County
70	2063	69.7	**Coldwater** (city) Branch County	145	3451	82.0	**Oxford** (charter township) Oakland County
70	2063	69.7	**Union** (charter township) Isabella County	146	3487	82.3	**Haslett** (CDP) Ingham County
72	2090	69.9	**Redford** (charter township) Wayne County	147	3502	82.4	**Royal Oak** (city) Oakland County
73	2128	70.2	**Monroe** (charter township) Monroe County	148	3514	82.5	**Farmington Hills** (city) Oakland County
74	2186	70.7	**Traverse City** (city) Grand Traverse County	149	3532	82.7	**Berkley** (city) Oakland County
75	2205	70.9	**Grand Haven** (city) Ottawa County	150	3547	82.8	**Delta** (charter township) Eaton County

Note: The state column ranks the top/bottom 150 places from all places in the state with population of 10,000 or more. The national column ranks the top/bottom 150 places from all places in the country with population of 10,000 or more. Places that are unincorporated were not considered in the rankings. Please refer to the User Guide for additional information.

Population with Public Health Insurance

Top 150 Places Ranked in *Descending* Order

State Rank	Nat'l Rank	Percent	Place	State Rank	Nat'l Rank	Percent	Place
1	10	70.0	**Beecher** (CDP) Genesee County	75	1456	32.9	**Riverview** (city) Wayne County
2	11	67.2	**Muskegon Heights** (city) Muskegon County	77	1484	32.7	**Mundy** (township) Genesee County
3	15	63.3	**Benton Harbor** (city) Berrien County	78	1516	32.5	**Comstock Park** (CDP) Kent County
4	18	60.2	**Flint** (city) Genesee County	79	1588	31.9	**Vienna** (charter township) Genesee County
5	24	59.0	**Highland Park** (city) Wayne County	80	1653	31.5	**Trenton** (city) Wayne County
6	38	54.9	**Mount Morris** (township) Genesee County	81	1688	31.3	**Wyandotte** (city) Wayne County
7	44	54.3	**Saginaw** (city) Saginaw County	82	1702	31.2	**Saginaw** (charter township) Saginaw County
8	47	54.1	**Inkster** (city) Wayne County	83	1727	31.0	**Superior** (charter township) Washtenaw County
9	56	53.1	**Hamtramck** (city) Wayne County	84	1776	30.7	**Redford** (charter township) Wayne County
10	66	52.3	**Benton** (charter township) Berrien County	85	1830	30.4	**Fraser** (city) Macomb County
11	73	51.7	**Detroit** (city) Wayne County	86	1844	30.3	**Oshtemo** (charter township) Kalamazoo County
12	110	50.0	**Muskegon** (city) Muskegon County	87	1857	30.2	**Fenton** (city) Genesee County
13	158	47.9	**Port Huron** (city) Saint Clair County	88	1878	30.1	**Sterling Heights** (city) Macomb County
14	172	47.5	**Pontiac** (city) Oakland County	89	1921	29.9	**Harper Woods** (city) Wayne County
15	178	47.3	**Jackson** (city) Jackson County	89	1921	29.9	**Midland** (city) Midland County
16	200	46.8	**Niles** (city) Berrien County	89	1921	29.9	**Traverse City** (city) Grand Traverse County
17	256	45.4	**Bridgeport** (charter township) Saginaw County	92	1949	29.7	**Grandville** (city) Kent County
18	263	45.2	**Genesee** (charter township) Genesee County	92	1949	29.7	**Harrison** (charter township) Macomb County
19	278	44.9	**Escanaba** (city) Delta County	94	1966	29.6	**Saint Clair Shores** (city) Macomb County
20	320	44.2	**Adrian** (city) Lenawee County	94	1966	29.6	**Ypsilanti** (city) Washtenaw County
21	336	44.0	**Flint** (charter township) Genesee County	96	1999	29.4	**Southgate** (city) Wayne County
22	354	43.7	**Cadillac** (city) Wexford County	96	1999	29.4	**Spring Lake** (township) Ottawa County
23	373	43.4	**Port Huron** (charter township) Saint Clair County	98	2010	29.3	**Lenox** (township) Macomb County
24	401	43.0	**Battle Creek** (city) Calhoun County	99	2056	29.0	**Thomas** (township) Saginaw County
24	401	43.0	**Bay City** (city) Bay County	100	2078	28.9	**Emmett** (charter township) Calhoun County
26	419	42.7	**Alpena** (city) Alpena County	101	2094	28.8	**Saint Joseph** (charter township) Berrien County
26	419	42.7	**Lansing** (city) Ingham County	102	2142	28.5	**Garden City** (city) Wayne County
28	433	42.4	**Hazel Park** (city) Oakland County	103	2176	28.3	**Cooper** (charter township) Kalamazoo County
29	526	41.2	**Garfield** (charter township) Grand Traverse County	104	2195	28.2	**Waverly** (CDP) Eaton County
30	550	40.9	**Sturgis** (city) Saint Joseph County	105	2283	27.7	**Jenison** (CDP) Ottawa County
31	564	40.6	**Mount Clemens** (city) Macomb County	105	2283	27.7	**Kentwood** (city) Kent County
32	595	40.2	**Dearborn** (city) Wayne County	105	2283	27.7	**Northview** (CDP) Kent County
32	595	40.2	**Ionia** (city) Ionia County	105	2283	27.7	**Waterford** (charter township) Oakland County
34	615	40.0	**Melvindale** (city) Wayne County	109	2335	27.4	**Byron** (township) Kent County
35	629	39.8	**Muskegon** (charter township) Muskegon County	110	2352	27.3	**DeWitt** (charter township) Clinton County
36	647	39.6	**Eastpointe** (city) Macomb County	111	2425	26.9	**Allen Park** (city) Wayne County
37	655	39.5	**Taylor** (city) Wayne County	111	2425	26.9	**East Bay** (township) Grand Traverse County
38	695	39.1	**Owosso** (city) Shiawassee County	111	2425	26.9	**Wyoming** (city) Kent County
39	736	38.6	**Burton** (city) Genesee County	114	2451	26.8	**Brandon** (charter township) Oakland County
40	754	38.4	**Niles** (township) Berrien County	114	2451	26.8	**Portage** (city) Kalamazoo County
41	765	38.3	**Monroe** (city) Monroe County	114	2451	26.8	**Van Buren** (charter township) Wayne County
42	779	38.1	**Frenchtown** (township) Monroe County	117	2504	26.6	**Lincoln** (charter township) Berrien County
43	834	37.6	**Cutlerville** (CDP) Kent County	118	2529	26.5	**Grand Blanc** (charter township) Genesee County
43	834	37.6	**Grand Rapids** (city) Kent County	119	2569	26.3	**Holly** (township) Oakland County
43	834	37.6	**Leoni** (township) Jackson County	120	2582	26.2	**Delta** (charter township) Eaton County
46	847	37.5	**Bangor** (charter township) Bay County	120	2582	26.2	**Holland** (charter township) Ottawa County
46	847	37.5	**Lincoln Park** (city) Wayne County	122	2602	26.1	**Gaines** (charter township) Kent County
48	878	37.2	**Southfield** (city) Oakland County	123	2674	25.7	**Park** (township) Ottawa County
49	891	37.1	**Romulus** (city) Wayne County	124	2692	25.6	**Bloomfield** (charter township) Oakland County
50	907	37.0	**Blackman** (charter township) Jackson County	124	2692	25.6	**Shelby** (charter township) Macomb County
50	907	37.0	**Dearborn Heights** (city) Wayne County	124	2692	25.6	**Washington** (township) Macomb County
52	939	36.6	**Monroe** (charter township) Monroe County	127	2774	25.2	**Big Rapids** (city) Mecosta County
53	950	36.5	**Warren** (city) Macomb County	127	2774	25.2	**Farmington Hills** (city) Oakland County
54	1040	35.8	**Roseville** (city) Macomb County	127	2774	25.2	**Livonia** (city) Wayne County
55	1066	35.6	**Coldwater** (city) Branch County	127	2774	25.2	**Woodhaven** (city) Wayne County
56	1095	35.3	**Summit** (township) Jackson County	131	2791	25.1	**Marquette** (city) Marquette County
57	1204	34.5	**Comstock** (charter township) Kalamazoo County	132	2865	24.7	**Delhi** (charter township) Ingham County
57	1204	34.5	**Fort Gratiot** (charter township) Saint Clair County	133	2906	24.5	**Huron** (charter township) Wayne County
57	1204	34.5	**Westland** (city) Wayne County	134	2934	24.3	**Holt** (CDP) Ingham County
60	1218	34.4	**Grand Haven** (city) Ottawa County	135	2954	24.2	**Bedford** (township) Monroe County
60	1218	34.4	**Oak Park** (city) Oakland County	135	2954	24.2	**Highland** (charter township) Oakland County
62	1235	34.3	**Madison Heights** (city) Oakland County	137	2974	24.1	**Antwerp** (township) Van Buren County
62	1235	34.3	**Norton Shores** (city) Muskegon County	138	3004	24.0	**Clawson** (city) Oakland County
64	1253	34.2	**Sault Sainte Marie** (city) Chippewa County	139	3019	23.9	**Chesterfield** (township) Macomb County
65	1279	34.0	**Flushing** (charter township) Genesee County	140	3069	23.6	**Plainfield** (charter township) Kent County
65	1279	34.0	**Kalamazoo** (charter township) Kalamazoo County	141	3090	23.5	**West Bloomfield** (charter township) Oakland County
67	1310	33.8	**Ypsilanti** (charter township) Washtenaw County	142	3117	23.4	**Genoa** (township) Livingston County
68	1330	33.7	**Alpine** (township) Kent County	142	3117	23.4	**White Lake** (charter township) Oakland County
69	1360	33.5	**Clinton** (charter township) Macomb County	144	3166	23.2	**Grosse Ile** (township) Wayne County
70	1376	33.4	**Kalamazoo** (city) Kalamazoo County	145	3253	22.7	**Independence** (charter township) Oakland County
70	1376	33.4	**Wayne** (city) Wayne County	145	3253	22.7	**Milford** (township) Oakland County
72	1410	33.2	**Fruitport** (charter township) Muskegon County	145	3253	22.7	**Tyrone** (township) Livingston County
73	1426	33.1	**Monitor** (charter township) Bay County	148	3277	22.6	**Fenton** (charter township) Genesee County
74	1441	33.0	**Davison** (township) Genesee County	149	3293	22.5	**Haslett** (CDP) Ingham County
75	1456	32.9	**Holland** (city) Ottawa County	150	3360	22.1	**Grand Haven** (charter township) Ottawa County

Note: The state column ranks the top/bottom 150 places from all places in the state with population of 10,000 or more. The national column ranks the top/bottom 150 places from all places in the country with population of 10,000 or more. Places that are unincorporated were not considered in the rankings. Please refer to the User Guide for additional information.

Population with Public Health Insurance

Top 150 Places Ranked in *Ascending* Order

State Rank	Nat'l Rank	Percent	Place
1	45	9.6	**Allendale** (CDP) Ottawa County
2	52	10.1	**Allendale** (charter township) Ottawa County
3	150	12.9	**East Lansing** (city) Ingham County
4	178	13.5	**Ada** (township) Kent County
5	215	14.1	**East Grand Rapids** (city) Kent County
6	287	15.1	**Cannon** (township) Kent County
7	315	15.4	**Forest Hills** (CDP) Kent County
8	347	15.8	**Birmingham** (city) Oakland County
9	358	15.9	**Hartland** (township) Livingston County
10	390	16.4	**Beverly Hills** (village) Oakland County
11	405	16.5	**Caledonia** (township) Kent County
11	405	16.5	**Canton** (charter township) Wayne County
13	441	16.8	**Rochester** (city) Oakland County
14	460	17.0	**Ann Arbor** (city) Washtenaw County
15	499	17.3	**Oakland** (charter township) Oakland County
16	512	17.4	**Orion** (charter township) Oakland County
16	512	17.4	**Pittsfield** (charter township) Washtenaw County
18	553	17.8	**Oceola** (township) Livingston County
19	588	18.1	**Berkley** (city) Oakland County
20	603	18.2	**Macomb** (township) Macomb County
21	624	18.3	**Novi** (city) Oakland County
22	655	18.5	**Southfield** (township) Oakland County
22	655	18.5	**Springfield** (charter township) Oakland County
22	655	18.5	**Union** (charter township) Isabella County
22	655	18.5	**Wixom** (city) Oakland County
26	668	18.6	**Brighton** (township) Livingston County
27	681	18.7	**Cascade** (charter township) Kent County
27	681	18.7	**Hamburg** (township) Livingston County
29	763	19.2	**Lyon** (charter township) Oakland County
29	763	19.2	**Scio** (township) Washtenaw County
31	779	19.3	**South Lyon** (city) Oakland County
32	797	19.4	**Texas** (charter township) Kalamazoo County
33	850	19.7	**Green Oak** (township) Livingston County
34	897	20.0	**Northville** (township) Wayne County
35	936	20.2	**New Baltimore** (city) Macomb County
35	936	20.2	**Rochester Hills** (city) Oakland County
37	954	20.3	**Commerce** (charter township) Oakland County
38	973	20.4	**Troy** (city) Oakland County
39	1007	20.6	**Bath** (charter township) Clinton County
40	1025	20.7	**Okemos** (CDP) Ingham County
41	1040	20.8	**Grand Rapids** (charter township) Kent County
41	1040	20.8	**Grosse Pointe Park** (city) Wayne County
41	1040	20.8	**Royal Oak** (city) Oakland County
44	1104	21.2	**Georgetown** (charter township) Ottawa County
44	1104	21.2	**Plymouth** (charter township) Wayne County
46	1133	21.3	**Mount Pleasant** (city) Isabella County
47	1151	21.4	**Oxford** (charter township) Oakland County
48	1170	21.5	**Meridian** (charter township) Ingham County
49	1187	21.6	**Brownstown** (charter township) Wayne County
49	1187	21.6	**Farmington** (city) Oakland County
49	1187	21.6	**Grosse Pointe Woods** (city) Wayne County
49	1187	21.6	**Walker** (city) Kent County
53	1219	21.8	**Auburn Hills** (city) Oakland County
53	1219	21.8	**Ferndale** (city) Oakland County
55	1272	22.1	**Grand Haven** (charter township) Ottawa County
56	1352	22.5	**Haslett** (CDP) Ingham County
57	1364	22.6	**Fenton** (charter township) Genesee County
58	1380	22.7	**Independence** (charter township) Oakland County
58	1380	22.7	**Milford** (charter township) Oakland County
58	1380	22.7	**Tyrone** (township) Livingston County
61	1466	23.2	**Grosse Ile** (township) Wayne County
62	1515	23.4	**Genoa** (township) Livingston County
62	1515	23.4	**White Lake** (charter township) Oakland County
64	1540	23.5	**West Bloomfield** (charter township) Oakland County
65	1567	23.6	**Plainfield** (charter township) Kent County
66	1623	23.9	**Chesterfield** (township) Macomb County
67	1638	24.0	**Clawson** (city) Oakland County
68	1653	24.1	**Antwerp** (township) Van Buren County
69	1683	24.2	**Bedford** (township) Monroe County
69	1683	24.2	**Highland** (charter township) Oakland County
71	1703	24.3	**Holt** (CDP) Ingham County
72	1740	24.5	**Huron** (charter township) Wayne County
73	1768	24.7	**Delhi** (charter township) Ingham County
74	1848	25.1	**Marquette** (city) Marquette County
75	1866	25.2	**Big Rapids** (city) Mecosta County
75	1866	25.2	**Farmington Hills** (city) Oakland County
75	1866	25.2	**Livonia** (city) Wayne County
75	1866	25.2	**Woodhaven** (city) Wayne County
79	1944	25.6	**Bloomfield** (charter township) Oakland County
79	1944	25.6	**Shelby** (charter township) Macomb County
79	1944	25.6	**Washington** (township) Macomb County
82	1965	25.7	**Park** (township) Ottawa County
83	2035	26.1	**Gaines** (charter township) Kent County
84	2055	26.2	**Delta** (charter township) Eaton County
84	2055	26.2	**Holland** (charter township) Ottawa County
86	2075	26.3	**Holly** (township) Oakland County
87	2114	26.5	**Grand Blanc** (charter township) Genesee County
88	2128	26.6	**Lincoln** (charter township) Berrien County
89	2174	26.8	**Brandon** (charter township) Oakland County
89	2174	26.8	**Portage** (city) Kalamazoo County
89	2174	26.8	**Van Buren** (charter township) Wayne County
92	2206	26.9	**Allen Park** (city) Wayne County
92	2206	26.9	**East Bay** (township) Grand Traverse County
92	2206	26.9	**Wyoming** (city) Kent County
95	2286	27.3	**DeWitt** (charter township) Clinton County
96	2305	27.4	**Byron** (township) Kent County
97	2358	27.7	**Jenison** (CDP) Ottawa County
97	2358	27.7	**Kentwood** (city) Kent County
97	2358	27.7	**Northview** (CDP) Kent County
97	2358	27.7	**Waterford** (charter township) Oakland County
101	2446	28.2	**Waverly** (CDP) Eaton County
102	2462	28.3	**Cooper** (charter township) Kalamazoo County
103	2502	28.5	**Garden City** (city) Wayne County
104	2545	28.8	**Saint Joseph** (charter township) Berrien County
105	2563	28.9	**Emmett** (charter township) Calhoun County
106	2579	29.0	**Thomas** (township) Saginaw County
107	2636	29.3	**Lenox** (township) Macomb County
108	2647	29.4	**Southgate** (city) Wayne County
108	2647	29.4	**Spring Lake** (township) Ottawa County
110	2671	29.6	**Saint Clair Shores** (city) Macomb County
110	2671	29.6	**Ypsilanti** (city) Washtenaw County
112	2691	29.7	**Grandville** (city) Kent County
112	2691	29.7	**Harrison** (charter township) Macomb County
114	2723	29.9	**Harper Woods** (city) Wayne County
114	2723	29.9	**Midland** (city) Midland County
114	2723	29.9	**Traverse City** (city) Grand Traverse County
117	2761	30.1	**Sterling Heights** (city) Macomb County
118	2779	30.2	**Fenton** (city) Genesee County
119	2800	30.3	**Oshtemo** (charter township) Kalamazoo County
120	2813	30.4	**Fraser** (city) Macomb County
121	2862	30.7	**Redford** (charter township) Wayne County
122	2917	31.0	**Superior** (charter township) Washtenaw County
123	2944	31.2	**Saginaw** (charter township) Saginaw County
124	2955	31.3	**Wyandotte** (city) Wayne County
125	2989	31.5	**Trenton** (city) Wayne County
126	3052	31.9	**Vienna** (charter township) Genesee County
127	3125	32.5	**Comstock Park** (CDP) Kent County
128	3152	32.7	**Mundy** (township) Genesee County
129	3185	32.9	**Holland** (city) Ottawa County
129	3185	32.9	**Riverview** (city) Wayne County
131	3201	33.0	**Davison** (township) Genesee County
132	3216	33.1	**Monitor** (charter township) Bay County
133	3231	33.2	**Fruitport** (charter township) Muskegon County
134	3262	33.4	**Kalamazoo** (city) Kalamazoo County
134	3262	33.4	**Wayne** (city) Wayne County
136	3281	33.5	**Clinton** (charter township) Macomb County
137	3309	33.7	**Alpine** (township) Kent County
138	3327	33.8	**Ypsilanti** (charter township) Washtenaw County
139	3365	34.0	**Flushing** (charter township) Genesee County
139	3365	34.0	**Kalamazoo** (charter township) Kalamazoo County
141	3394	34.2	**Sault Sainte Marie** (city) Chippewa County
142	3404	34.3	**Madison Heights** (city) Oakland County
142	3404	34.3	**Norton Shores** (city) Muskegon County
144	3422	34.4	**Grand Haven** (city) Ottawa County
144	3422	34.4	**Oak Park** (city) Oakland County
146	3439	34.5	**Comstock** (charter township) Kalamazoo County
146	3439	34.5	**Fort Gratiot** (charter township) Saint Clair County
146	3439	34.5	**Westland** (city) Wayne County
149	3545	35.3	**Summit** (township) Jackson County
150	3580	35.6	**Coldwater** (city) Branch County

Note: The state column ranks the top/bottom 150 places from all places in the state with population of 10,000 or more. The national column ranks the top/bottom 150 places from all places in the country with population of 10,000 or more. Places that are unincorporated were not considered in the rankings. Please refer to the User Guide for additional information.

Population with No Health Insurance

Top 150 Places Ranked in *Descending* Order

State Rank	Nat'l Rank	Percent	Place
1	414	23.4	Hamtramck (city) Wayne County
2	577	21.3	Ferndale (city) Oakland County
3	707	20.1	Hazel Park (city) Oakland County
4	795	19.4	Detroit (city) Wayne County
5	822	19.2	Pontiac (city) Oakland County
6	922	18.6	Jackson (city) Jackson County
7	952	18.4	Union (charter township) Isabella County
8	1000	18.1	Oak Park (city) Oakland County
9	1020	18.0	Comstock Park (CDP) Kent County
10	1033	17.9	Benton (charter township) Berrien County
11	1074	17.6	Highland Park (city) Wayne County
12	1225	16.8	Owosso (city) Shiawassee County
13	1286	16.5	Escanaba (city) Delta County
13	1286	16.5	Sault Sainte Marie (city) Chippewa County
15	1311	16.4	Benton Harbor (city) Berrien County
16	1355	16.2	Alpine (township) Kent County
16	1355	16.2	Lincoln Park (city) Wayne County
18	1373	16.1	Mount Clemens (city) Macomb County
19	1429	15.8	Auburn Hills (city) Oakland County
20	1452	15.7	Big Rapids (city) Mecosta County
20	1452	15.7	Dearborn Heights (city) Wayne County
22	1472	15.6	Muskegon (city) Muskegon County
23	1490	15.5	Inkster (city) Wayne County
24	1511	15.4	Saginaw (city) Saginaw County
24	1511	15.4	Wyoming (city) Kent County
26	1529	15.3	Adrian (city) Lenawee County
27	1557	15.1	Harper Woods (city) Wayne County
27	1557	15.1	Romulus (city) Wayne County
29	1603	14.8	Melvindale (city) Wayne County
30	1624	14.7	Grand Haven (city) Ottawa County
31	1643	14.6	Dearborn (city) Wayne County
31	1643	14.6	Taylor (city) Wayne County
33	1663	14.5	Ypsilanti (city) Washtenaw County
34	1683	14.4	Marquette (city) Marquette County
35	1713	14.3	Roseville (city) Macomb County
35	1713	14.3	Warren (city) Macomb County
37	1736	14.2	Kalamazoo (city) Kalamazoo County
38	1813	13.9	Kalamazoo (charter township) Kalamazoo County
39	1835	13.8	Ionia (city) Ionia County
39	1835	13.8	Port Huron (city) Saint Clair County
41	1855	13.7	Bay City (city) Bay County
41	1855	13.7	Niles (township) Berrien County
41	1855	13.7	Redford (charter township) Wayne County
41	1855	13.7	Wayne (city) Wayne County
45	1884	13.6	Grand Rapids (city) Kent County
45	1884	13.6	Madison Heights (city) Oakland County
47	1897	13.5	Battle Creek (city) Calhoun County
47	1897	13.5	Fenton (city) Genesee County
47	1897	13.5	Westland (city) Wayne County
50	1918	13.4	Traverse City (city) Grand Traverse County
51	1942	13.3	Flint (city) Genesee County
52	1991	13.1	Garden City (city) Wayne County
53	2019	13.0	Alpena (city) Alpena County
54	2045	12.9	Lansing (city) Ingham County
55	2063	12.8	Clawson (city) Oakland County
56	2083	12.7	Eastpointe (city) Macomb County
56	2083	12.7	Sturgis (city) Saint Joseph County
58	2111	12.6	Blackman (charter township) Jackson County
58	2111	12.6	Clinton (charter township) Macomb County
60	2130	12.5	Waterford (charter township) Oakland County
61	2153	12.4	Cadillac (city) Wexford County
62	2175	12.3	Sterling Heights (city) Macomb County
63	2201	12.2	Mount Pleasant (city) Isabella County
63	2201	12.2	Van Buren (charter township) Wayne County
63	2201	12.2	Wixom (city) Oakland County
66	2232	12.1	Wyandotte (city) Wayne County
67	2252	12.0	Leoni (township) Jackson County
67	2252	12.0	Mount Morris (township) Genesee County
67	2252	12.0	Muskegon (charter township) Muskegon County
67	2252	12.0	Niles (city) Berrien County
71	2282	11.9	Muskegon Heights (city) Muskegon County
71	2282	11.9	Ypsilanti (charter township) Washtenaw County
73	2306	11.8	Southfield (city) Oakland County
74	2331	11.7	Fort Gratiot (charter township) Saint Clair County
75	2372	11.5	Bangor (charter township) Bay County
75	2372	11.5	Garfield (charter township) Grand Traverse County
77	2393	11.4	Monroe (city) Monroe County
78	2412	11.3	Harrison (charter township) Macomb County
78	2412	11.3	Holland (city) Ottawa County
80	2463	11.1	Emmett (charter township) Calhoun County
81	2486	11.0	Beecher (CDP) Genesee County
81	2486	11.0	Burton (city) Genesee County
81	2486	11.0	Kentwood (city) Kent County
81	2486	11.0	Saint Clair Shores (city) Macomb County
81	2486	11.0	Vienna (charter township) Genesee County
86	2513	10.9	East Bay (township) Grand Traverse County
86	2513	10.9	Lenox (township) Macomb County
88	2636	10.4	Spring Lake (township) Ottawa County
89	2653	10.3	Port Huron (charter township) Saint Clair County
90	2679	10.2	Bath (charter township) Clinton County
91	2709	10.1	Coldwater (city) Branch County
91	2709	10.1	DeWitt (charter township) Clinton County
91	2709	10.1	Flint (charter township) Genesee County
91	2709	10.1	Genesee (charter township) Genesee County
91	2709	10.1	Monroe (charter township) Monroe County
91	2709	10.1	Northview (CDP) Kent County
91	2709	10.1	Riverview (city) Wayne County
98	2738	10.0	Holly (township) Oakland County
99	2759	9.9	Berkley (city) Oakland County
99	2759	9.9	Midland (city) Midland County
99	2759	9.9	White Lake (charter township) Oakland County
102	2781	9.8	Grandville (city) Kent County
103	2810	9.7	Royal Oak (city) Oakland County
104	2827	9.6	Shelby (charter township) Macomb County
104	2827	9.6	Washington (township) Macomb County
106	2850	9.5	Haslett (CDP) Ingham County
106	2850	9.5	Oshtemo (charter township) Kalamazoo County
106	2850	9.5	Southgate (city) Wayne County
109	2876	9.4	Cutlerville (CDP) Kent County
109	2876	9.4	Fraser (city) Macomb County
109	2876	9.4	Thomas (township) Saginaw County
112	2898	9.3	Holland (charter township) Ottawa County
112	2898	9.3	Portage (city) Kalamazoo County
114	2929	9.2	Allen Park (city) Wayne County
114	2929	9.2	Highland (charter township) Oakland County
116	2954	9.1	Comstock (charter township) Kalamazoo County
117	2982	9.0	Walker (city) Kent County
118	3002	8.9	Brandon (charter township) Oakland County
118	3002	8.9	Frenchtown (township) Monroe County
120	3023	8.8	Brownstown (charter township) Wayne County
120	3023	8.8	Chesterfield (township) Macomb County
120	3023	8.8	Davison (township) Genesee County
120	3023	8.8	Genoa (township) Livingston County
120	3023	8.8	Woodhaven (city) Wayne County
125	3051	8.7	Antwerp (township) Van Buren County
125	3051	8.7	Milford (charter township) Oakland County
125	3051	8.7	Summit (township) Jackson County
128	3078	8.6	Bridgeport (charter township) Saginaw County
129	3105	8.5	Canton (charter township) Wayne County
129	3105	8.5	Grand Haven (charter township) Ottawa County
129	3105	8.5	Troy (city) Oakland County
129	3105	8.5	Waverly (CDP) Eaton County
133	3132	8.4	Delhi (charter township) Ingham County
133	3132	8.4	Gaines (charter township) Kent County
133	3132	8.4	Huron (charter township) Wayne County
133	3132	8.4	Saginaw (charter township) Saginaw County
137	3158	8.3	Allendale (charter township) Ottawa County
137	3158	8.3	Oxford (charter township) Oakland County
139	3179	8.2	Allendale (CDP) Ottawa County
140	3203	8.1	Orion (charter township) Oakland County
141	3229	8.0	Green Oak (township) Livingston County
141	3229	8.0	Holt (CDP) Ingham County
141	3229	8.0	Lincoln (charter township) Berrien County
144	3266	7.9	Commerce (charter township) Oakland County
144	3266	7.9	Plainfield (charter township) Kent County
144	3266	7.9	Springfield (charter township) Oakland County
147	3291	7.8	Monitor (charter township) Bay County
147	3291	7.8	Rochester Hills (city) Oakland County
147	3291	7.8	South Lyon (city) Oakland County
150	3314	7.7	Delta (charter township) Eaton County

Note: *The state column ranks the top/bottom 150 places from all places in the state with population of 10,000 or more. The national column ranks the top/bottom 150 places from all places in the country with population of 10,000 or more. Places that are unincorporated were not considered in the rankings. Please refer to the User Guide for additional information.*

Population with No Health Insurance

Top 150 Places Ranked in *Ascending* Order

State Rank	Nat'l Rank	Percent	Place
1	121	2.6	**Ada** (township) Kent County
2	134	2.7	**East Grand Rapids** (city) Kent County
3	245	3.4	**Forest Hills** (CDP) Kent County
4	314	3.8	**Grosse Ile** (township) Wayne County
5	412	4.2	**Cannon** (township) Kent County
5	412	4.2	**Texas** (charter township) Kalamazoo County
7	456	4.4	**Birmingham** (city) Oakland County
8	519	4.6	**Southfield** (township) Oakland County
9	542	4.7	**Bloomfield** (charter township) Oakland County
9	542	4.7	**Cascade** (charter township) Kent County
11	559	4.8	**Caledonia** (township) Kent County
11	559	4.8	**Scio** (township) Washtenaw County
13	597	5.0	**Beverly Hills** (village) Oakland County
14	622	5.1	**Grand Rapids** (charter township) Kent County
14	622	5.1	**Jenison** (CDP) Ottawa County
16	651	5.2	**Hamburg** (township) Livingston County
17	680	5.3	**Georgetown** (charter township) Ottawa County
18	730	5.5	**Grosse Pointe Woods** (city) Wayne County
19	779	5.7	**Macomb** (township) Macomb County
19	779	5.7	**Northville** (township) Wayne County
19	779	5.7	**Park** (township) Ottawa County
22	801	5.8	**Okemos** (CDP) Ingham County
22	801	5.8	**Plymouth** (charter township) Wayne County
24	828	5.9	**Flushing** (charter township) Genesee County
24	828	5.9	**Hartland** (township) Livingston County
24	828	5.9	**Oakland** (charter township) Oakland County
24	828	5.9	**Oceola** (township) Livingston County
28	886	6.1	**New Baltimore** (city) Macomb County
28	886	6.1	**Saint Joseph** (charter township) Berrien County
30	902	6.2	**Ann Arbor** (city) Washtenaw County
30	902	6.2	**East Lansing** (city) Ingham County
30	902	6.2	**Grosse Pointe Park** (city) Wayne County
33	926	6.3	**Tyrone** (township) Livingston County
34	959	6.4	**Farmington** (city) Oakland County
34	959	6.4	**Independence** (charter township) Oakland County
34	959	6.4	**Rochester** (city) Oakland County
37	1046	6.7	**Byron** (township) Kent County
38	1063	6.8	**Cooper** (charter township) Kalamazoo County
39	1087	6.9	**Brighton** (township) Livingston County
40	1109	7.0	**Bedford** (township) Monroe County
40	1109	7.0	**Novi** (city) Oakland County
42	1134	7.1	**Mundy** (township) Genesee County
43	1161	7.2	**Lyon** (charter township) Oakland County
43	1161	7.2	**Norton Shores** (city) Muskegon County
43	1161	7.2	**West Bloomfield** (charter township) Oakland County
46	1199	7.3	**Fenton** (charter township) Genesee County
46	1199	7.3	**Pittsfield** (charter township) Washtenaw County
46	1199	7.3	**Superior** (charter township) Washtenaw County
46	1199	7.3	**Trenton** (city) Wayne County
50	1266	7.5	**Livonia** (city) Wayne County
51	1286	7.6	**Farmington Hills** (city) Oakland County
51	1286	7.6	**Grand Blanc** (charter township) Genesee County
51	1286	7.6	**Meridian** (charter township) Ingham County
54	1315	7.7	**Delta** (charter township) Eaton County
54	1315	7.7	**Fruitport** (charter township) Muskegon County
56	1343	7.8	**Monitor** (charter township) Bay County
56	1343	7.8	**Rochester Hills** (city) Oakland County
56	1343	7.8	**South Lyon** (city) Oakland County
59	1366	7.9	**Commerce** (charter township) Oakland County
59	1366	7.9	**Plainfield** (charter township) Kent County
59	1366	7.9	**Springfield** (charter township) Oakland County
62	1391	8.0	**Green Oak** (township) Livingston County
62	1391	8.0	**Holt** (CDP) Ingham County
62	1391	8.0	**Lincoln** (charter township) Berrien County
65	1428	8.1	**Orion** (charter township) Oakland County
66	1454	8.2	**Allendale** (CDP) Ottawa County
67	1478	8.3	**Allendale** (charter township) Ottawa County
67	1478	8.3	**Oxford** (charter township) Oakland County
69	1499	8.4	**Delhi** (charter township) Ingham County
69	1499	8.4	**Gaines** (charter township) Kent County
69	1499	8.4	**Huron** (charter township) Wayne County
69	1499	8.4	**Saginaw** (charter township) Saginaw County
73	1525	8.5	**Canton** (charter township) Wayne County
73	1525	8.5	**Grand Haven** (charter township) Ottawa County
73	1525	8.5	**Troy** (city) Oakland County
73	1525	8.5	**Waverly** (CDP) Eaton County
77	1552	8.6	**Bridgeport** (charter township) Saginaw County
78	1579	8.7	**Antwerp** (township) Van Buren County
78	1579	8.7	**Milford** (charter township) Oakland County
78	1579	8.7	**Summit** (township) Jackson County
81	1606	8.8	**Brownstown** (charter township) Wayne County
81	1606	8.8	**Chesterfield** (township) Macomb County
81	1606	8.8	**Davison** (township) Genesee County
81	1606	8.8	**Genoa** (township) Livingston County
81	1606	8.8	**Woodhaven** (city) Wayne County
86	1634	8.9	**Brandon** (charter township) Oakland County
86	1634	8.9	**Frenchtown** (township) Monroe County
88	1655	9.0	**Walker** (city) Kent County
89	1675	9.1	**Comstock** (charter township) Kalamazoo County
90	1703	9.2	**Allen Park** (city) Wayne County
90	1703	9.2	**Highland** (charter township) Oakland County
92	1728	9.3	**Holland** (charter township) Ottawa County
92	1728	9.3	**Portage** (city) Kalamazoo County
94	1759	9.4	**Cutlerville** (CDP) Kent County
94	1759	9.4	**Fraser** (city) Macomb County
94	1759	9.4	**Thomas** (township) Saginaw County
97	1781	9.5	**Haslett** (CDP) Ingham County
97	1781	9.5	**Oshtemo** (charter township) Kalamazoo County
97	1781	9.5	**Southgate** (city) Wayne County
100	1807	9.6	**Shelby** (charter township) Macomb County
100	1807	9.6	**Washington** (township) Macomb County
102	1830	9.7	**Royal Oak** (city) Oakland County
103	1847	9.8	**Grandville** (city) Kent County
104	1876	9.9	**Berkley** (city) Oakland County
104	1876	9.9	**Midland** (city) Midland County
104	1876	9.9	**White Lake** (charter township) Oakland County
107	1898	10.0	**Holly** (township) Oakland County
108	1919	10.1	**Coldwater** (city) Branch County
108	1919	10.1	**DeWitt** (charter township) Clinton County
108	1919	10.1	**Flint** (charter township) Genesee County
108	1919	10.1	**Genesee** (charter township) Genesee County
108	1919	10.1	**Monroe** (charter township) Monroe County
108	1919	10.1	**Northview** (CDP) Kent County
108	1919	10.1	**Riverview** (city) Wayne County
115	1948	10.2	**Bath** (charter township) Clinton County
116	1978	10.3	**Port Huron** (charter township) Saint Clair County
117	2004	10.4	**Spring Lake** (township) Ottawa County
118	2117	10.9	**East Bay** (township) Grand Traverse County
118	2117	10.9	**Lenox** (township) Macomb County
120	2144	11.0	**Beecher** (CDP) Genesee County
120	2144	11.0	**Burton** (city) Genesee County
120	2144	11.0	**Kentwood** (city) Kent County
120	2144	11.0	**Saint Clair Shores** (city) Macomb County
120	2144	11.0	**Vienna** (charter township) Genesee County
125	2171	11.1	**Emmett** (charter township) Calhoun County
126	2223	11.3	**Harrison** (charter township) Macomb County
126	2223	11.3	**Holland** (city) Ottawa County
128	2245	11.4	**Monroe** (city) Monroe County
129	2264	11.5	**Bangor** (charter township) Bay County
129	2264	11.5	**Garfield** (charter township) Grand Traverse County
131	2303	11.7	**Fort Gratiot** (charter township) Saint Clair County
132	2326	11.8	**Southfield** (city) Oakland County
133	2351	11.9	**Muskegon Heights** (city) Muskegon County
133	2351	11.9	**Ypsilanti** (charter township) Washtenaw County
135	2375	12.0	**Leoni** (township) Jackson County
135	2375	12.0	**Mount Morris** (township) Genesee County
135	2375	12.0	**Muskegon** (charter township) Muskegon County
135	2375	12.0	**Niles** (city) Berrien County
139	2405	12.1	**Wyandotte** (city) Wayne County
140	2425	12.2	**Mount Pleasant** (city) Isabella County
140	2425	12.2	**Van Buren** (charter township) Wayne County
140	2425	12.2	**Wixom** (city) Oakland County
143	2456	12.3	**Sterling Heights** (city) Macomb County
144	2482	12.4	**Cadillac** (city) Wexford County
145	2504	12.5	**Waterford** (charter township) Oakland County
146	2527	12.6	**Blackman** (charter township) Jackson County
146	2527	12.6	**Clinton** (charter township) Macomb County
148	2546	12.7	**Eastpointe** (city) Macomb County
148	2546	12.7	**Sturgis** (city) Saint Joseph County
150	2574	12.8	**Clawson** (city) Oakland County

Note: The state column ranks the top/bottom 150 places from all places in the state with population of 10,000 or more. The national column ranks the top/bottom 150 places from all places in the country with population of 10,000 or more. Places that are unincorporated were not considered in the rankings. Please refer to the User Guide for additional information.

Population Under 18 Years Old with No Health Insurance

Top 150 Places Ranked in *Descending* Order

State Rank	Nat'l Rank	Percent	Place
1	532	12.1	**Union** (charter township) Isabella County
2	588	11.7	**Auburn Hills** (city) Oakland County
3	823	10.1	**Hazel Park** (city) Oakland County
4	881	9.8	**Sault Sainte Marie** (city) Chippewa County
5	1004	9.3	**Berkley** (city) Oakland County
6	1164	8.5	**Escanaba** (city) Delta County
7	1205	8.3	**Oak Park** (city) Oakland County
8	1227	8.2	**Benton** (charter township) Berrien County
9	1335	7.8	**Vienna** (charter township) Genesee County
10	1361	7.7	**Bath** (charter township) Clinton County
11	1650	6.8	**Dearborn Heights** (city) Wayne County
12	1687	6.7	**Burton** (city) Genesee County
13	1719	6.6	**Ferndale** (city) Oakland County
14	1785	6.4	**Midland** (city) Midland County
15	1849	6.2	**Leoni** (township) Jackson County
16	1922	6.0	**Hamtramck** (city) Wayne County
16	1922	6.0	**Holly** (township) Oakland County
16	1922	6.0	**Wyoming** (city) Kent County
19	1955	5.9	**Jackson** (city) Jackson County
20	1989	5.8	**Fraser** (city) Macomb County
20	1989	5.8	**Harper Woods** (city) Wayne County
20	1989	5.8	**Pontiac** (city) Oakland County
23	2025	5.7	**Detroit** (city) Wayne County
24	2147	5.4	**Allendale** (CDP) Ottawa County
24	2147	5.4	**Grandville** (city) Kent County
24	2147	5.4	**Redford** (charter township) Wayne County
27	2193	5.3	**Cadillac** (city) Wexford County
27	2193	5.3	**Clinton** (charter township) Macomb County
27	2193	5.3	**Saginaw** (charter township) Saginaw County
27	2193	5.3	**Taylor** (city) Wayne County
31	2239	5.2	**Clawson** (city) Oakland County
31	2239	5.2	**Fenton** (city) Genesee County
31	2239	5.2	**Kalamazoo** (city) Kalamazoo County
31	2239	5.2	**Waterford** (charter township) Oakland County
35	2289	5.1	**Muskegon** (charter township) Muskegon County
36	2330	5.0	**Kalamazoo** (charter township) Kalamazoo County
36	2330	5.0	**Kentwood** (city) Kent County
36	2330	5.0	**Wixom** (city) Oakland County
39	2378	4.9	**Dearborn** (city) Wayne County
39	2378	4.9	**Genesee** (charter township) Genesee County
39	2378	4.9	**Grand Haven** (city) Ottawa County
42	2419	4.8	**Adrian** (city) Lenawee County
42	2419	4.8	**Garden City** (city) Wayne County
44	2465	4.7	**DeWitt** (charter township) Clinton County
44	2465	4.7	**Grand Haven** (charter township) Ottawa County
44	2465	4.7	**Troy** (city) Oakland County
47	2503	4.6	**Allendale** (charter township) Ottawa County
47	2503	4.6	**Lincoln Park** (city) Wayne County
47	2503	4.6	**Wayne** (city) Wayne County
50	2540	4.5	**Inkster** (city) Wayne County
50	2540	4.5	**Oshtemo** (charter township) Kalamazoo County
50	2540	4.5	**Royal Oak** (city) Oakland County
50	2540	4.5	**Walker** (city) Kent County
54	2578	4.4	**Madison Heights** (city) Oakland County
54	2578	4.4	**Shelby** (charter township) Macomb County
56	2616	4.3	**Brownstown** (charter township) Wayne County
56	2616	4.3	**Melvindale** (city) Wayne County
56	2616	4.3	**Sterling Heights** (city) Macomb County
56	2616	4.3	**Warren** (city) Macomb County
60	2675	4.2	**Lenox** (township) Macomb County
60	2675	4.2	**Wyandotte** (city) Wayne County
62	2719	4.1	**Flushing** (charter township) Genesee County
62	2719	4.1	**Traverse City** (city) Grand Traverse County
62	2719	4.1	**Westland** (city) Wayne County
65	2765	4.0	**Southfield** (city) Oakland County
65	2765	4.0	**Southgate** (city) Wayne County
67	2825	3.9	**Fort Gratiot** (charter township) Saint Clair County
67	2825	3.9	**Harrison** (charter township) Macomb County
67	2825	3.9	**White Lake** (charter township) Oakland County
70	2871	3.8	**Comstock** (charter township) Kalamazoo County
71	2926	3.7	**Alpine** (township) Kent County
71	2926	3.7	**Huron** (charter township) Wayne County
73	2975	3.6	**Commerce** (charter township) Oakland County
73	2975	3.6	**Fenton** (charter township) Genesee County
73	2975	3.6	**Grosse Pointe Woods** (city) Wayne County
73	2975	3.6	**Lansing** (city) Ingham County
73	2975	3.6	**Mount Clemens** (city) Macomb County
73	2975	3.6	**Owosso** (city) Shiawassee County
79	3036	3.5	**Farmington Hills** (city) Oakland County
79	3036	3.5	**Holland** (city) Ottawa County
79	3036	3.5	**Monroe** (charter township) Monroe County
82	3084	3.4	**Battle Creek** (city) Calhoun County
82	3084	3.4	**Flint** (charter township) Genesee County
82	3084	3.4	**Haslett** (CDP) Ingham County
82	3084	3.4	**Muskegon** (city) Muskegon County
82	3084	3.4	**Rochester Hills** (city) Oakland County
82	3084	3.4	**Roseville** (city) Macomb County
82	3084	3.4	**Saint Clair Shores** (city) Macomb County
89	3151	3.3	**Bedford** (township) Monroe County
89	3151	3.3	**Canton** (charter township) Wayne County
91	3196	3.2	**Comstock Park** (CDP) Kent County
91	3196	3.2	**Garfield** (charter township) Grand Traverse County
91	3196	3.2	**Van Buren** (charter township) Wayne County
94	3246	3.1	**Bay City** (city) Bay County
94	3246	3.1	**Livonia** (city) Wayne County
94	3246	3.1	**Mount Pleasant** (city) Isabella County
94	3246	3.1	**Romulus** (city) Wayne County
94	3246	3.1	**Washington** (township) Macomb County
94	3246	3.1	**West Bloomfield** (charter township) Oakland County
100	3306	3.0	**Brighton** (township) Livingston County
100	3306	3.0	**Flint** (city) Genesee County
100	3306	3.0	**Grand Rapids** (city) Kent County
100	3306	3.0	**Holland** (charter township) Ottawa County
100	3306	3.0	**Mundy** (township) Genesee County
105	3371	2.9	**Allen Park** (city) Wayne County
105	3371	2.9	**Bangor** (charter township) Bay County
105	3371	2.9	**Byron** (township) Kent County
105	3371	2.9	**Mount Morris** (township) Genesee County
105	3371	2.9	**Park** (township) Ottawa County
110	3429	2.8	**Coldwater** (city) Branch County
110	3429	2.8	**Genoa** (township) Livingston County
110	3429	2.8	**Pittsfield** (charter township) Washtenaw County
110	3429	2.8	**Plymouth** (charter township) Wayne County
110	3429	2.8	**Saginaw** (city) Saginaw County
110	3429	2.8	**Woodhaven** (city) Wayne County
110	3429	2.8	**Ypsilanti** (charter township) Washtenaw County
117	3472	2.7	**Big Rapids** (city) Mecosta County
117	3472	2.7	**Oakland** (charter township) Oakland County
117	3472	2.7	**Ypsilanti** (city) Washtenaw County
120	3524	2.6	**Ionia** (city) Ionia County
120	3524	2.6	**Novi** (city) Oakland County
122	3571	2.5	**Beecher** (CDP) Genesee County
122	3571	2.5	**Birmingham** (city) Oakland County
122	3571	2.5	**Cutlerville** (CDP) Kent County
122	3571	2.5	**Gaines** (charter township) Kent County
122	3571	2.5	**Lyon** (charter township) Oakland County
122	3571	2.5	**Meridian** (charter township) Ingham County
122	3571	2.5	**Portage** (city) Kalamazoo County
129	3623	2.4	**Antwerp** (township) Van Buren County
129	3623	2.4	**Bloomfield** (charter township) Oakland County
129	3623	2.4	**Davison** (township) Genesee County
129	3623	2.4	**Georgetown** (charter township) Ottawa County
129	3623	2.4	**Holt** (CDP) Ingham County
129	3623	2.4	**New Baltimore** (city) Macomb County
129	3623	2.4	**Oxford** (charter township) Oakland County
129	3623	2.4	**Summit** (township) Jackson County
137	3677	2.3	**Ann Arbor** (city) Washtenaw County
137	3677	2.3	**Blackman** (charter township) Jackson County
137	3677	2.3	**Cooper** (charter township) Kalamazoo County
137	3677	2.3	**Delhi** (charter township) Ingham County
137	3677	2.3	**Highland** (charter township) Oakland County
137	3677	2.3	**Jenison** (CDP) Ottawa County
137	3677	2.3	**Monroe** (city) Monroe County
137	3677	2.3	**Springfield** (charter township) Oakland County
137	3677	2.3	**Sturgis** (city) Saint Joseph County
146	3730	2.2	**East Grand Rapids** (city) Kent County
146	3730	2.2	**East Lansing** (city) Ingham County
146	3730	2.2	**Grand Rapids** (charter township) Kent County
146	3730	2.2	**Lincoln** (charter township) Berrien County
150	3781	2.1	**Bridgeport** (charter township) Saginaw County

Note: The state column ranks the top/bottom 150 places from all places in the state with population of 10,000 or more. The national column ranks the top/bottom 150 places from all places in the country with population of 10,000 or more. Places that are unincorporated were not considered in the rankings. Please refer to the User Guide for additional information.

Population Under 18 Years Old with No Health Insurance

Top 150 Places Ranked in *Ascending* Order

State Rank	Nat'l Rank	Percent	Place	State Rank	Nat'l Rank	Percent	Place
1	1	0.0	**Texas** (charter township) Kalamazoo County	69	980	2.4	**Summit** (township) Jackson County
2	89	0.2	**Northview** (CDP) Kent County	77	1034	2.5	**Beecher** (CDP) Genesee County
3	153	0.5	**Emmett** (charter township) Calhoun County	77	1034	2.5	**Birmingham** (city) Oakland County
4	177	0.6	**Muskegon Heights** (city) Muskegon County	77	1034	2.5	**Cutlerville** (CDP) Kent County
5	210	0.7	**Superior** (charter township) Washtenaw County	77	1034	2.5	**Gaines** (charter township) Kent County
6	264	0.9	**Frenchtown** (township) Monroe County	77	1034	2.5	**Lyon** (charter township) Oakland County
6	264	0.9	**Port Huron** (charter township) Saint Clair County	77	1034	2.5	**Meridian** (charter township) Ingham County
6	264	0.9	**Tyrone** (township) Livingston County	77	1034	2.5	**Portage** (city) Kalamazoo County
9	300	1.0	**East Bay** (township) Grand Traverse County	84	1086	2.6	**Ionia** (city) Ionia County
10	344	1.1	**Alpena** (city) Alpena County	84	1086	2.6	**Novi** (city) Oakland County
11	382	1.2	**Cannon** (township) Kent County	86	1133	2.7	**Big Rapids** (city) Mecosta County
11	382	1.2	**Farmington** (city) Oakland County	86	1133	2.7	**Oakland** (charter township) Oakland County
11	382	1.2	**Hartland** (township) Livingston County	86	1133	2.7	**Ypsilanti** (city) Washtenaw County
11	382	1.2	**Highland Park** (city) Wayne County	89	1185	2.8	**Coldwater** (city) Branch County
11	382	1.2	**Thomas** (township) Saginaw County	89	1185	2.8	**Genoa** (township) Livingston County
16	424	1.3	**Orion** (charter township) Oakland County	89	1185	2.8	**Pittsfield** (charter township) Washtenaw County
17	469	1.4	**Independence** (charter township) Oakland County	89	1185	2.8	**Plymouth** (charter township) Wayne County
17	469	1.4	**Marquette** (city) Marquette County	89	1185	2.8	**Saginaw** (city) Saginaw County
17	469	1.4	**Plainfield** (charter township) Kent County	89	1185	2.8	**Woodhaven** (city) Wayne County
17	469	1.4	**Saint Joseph** (charter township) Berrien County	89	1185	2.8	**Ypsilanti** (charter township) Washtenaw County
17	469	1.4	**Southfield** (township) Oakland County	96	1228	2.9	**Allen Park** (city) Wayne County
17	469	1.4	**Waverly** (CDP) Eaton County	96	1228	2.9	**Bangor** (township) Bay County
23	528	1.5	**Chesterfield** (township) Macomb County	96	1228	2.9	**Byron** (township) Kent County
23	528	1.5	**Macomb** (township) Macomb County	96	1228	2.9	**Mount Morris** (township) Genesee County
23	528	1.5	**Monitor** (charter township) Bay County	96	1228	2.9	**Park** (township) Ottawa County
23	528	1.5	**Niles** (city) Berrien County	101	1286	3.0	**Brighton** (township) Livingston County
23	528	1.5	**Norton Shores** (city) Muskegon County	101	1286	3.0	**Flint** (city) Genesee County
28	577	1.6	**Hamburg** (township) Livingston County	101	1286	3.0	**Grand Rapids** (city) Kent County
28	577	1.6	**Milford** (charter township) Oakland County	101	1286	3.0	**Holland** (charter township) Ottawa County
28	577	1.6	**Okemos** (CDP) Ingham County	101	1286	3.0	**Mundy** (township) Genesee County
28	577	1.6	**Riverview** (city) Wayne County	106	1351	3.1	**Bay City** (city) Bay County
28	577	1.6	**Rochester** (city) Oakland County	106	1351	3.1	**Livonia** (city) Wayne County
28	577	1.6	**Scio** (township) Washtenaw County	106	1351	3.1	**Mount Pleasant** (city) Isabella County
34	627	1.7	**Caledonia** (township) Kent County	106	1351	3.1	**Romulus** (city) Wayne County
34	627	1.7	**Delta** (charter township) Eaton County	106	1351	3.1	**Washington** (township) Macomb County
34	627	1.7	**Forest Hills** (CDP) Kent County	106	1351	3.1	**West Bloomfield** (charter township) Oakland County
34	627	1.7	**Grand Blanc** (charter township) Genesee County	112	1411	3.2	**Comstock Park** (CDP) Kent County
34	627	1.7	**Green Oak** (township) Livingston County	112	1411	3.2	**Garfield** (charter township) Grand Traverse County
34	627	1.7	**Grosse Pointe Park** (city) Wayne County	112	1411	3.2	**Van Buren** (charter township) Wayne County
34	627	1.7	**South Lyon** (city) Oakland County	115	1461	3.3	**Bedford** (township) Monroe County
41	681	1.8	**Grosse Ile** (township) Wayne County	115	1461	3.3	**Canton** (charter township) Wayne County
41	681	1.8	**Port Huron** (city) Saint Clair County	117	1506	3.4	**Battle Creek** (city) Calhoun County
41	681	1.8	**Trenton** (city) Wayne County	117	1506	3.4	**Flint** (charter township) Genesee County
44	729	1.9	**Benton Harbor** (city) Berrien County	117	1506	3.4	**Haslett** (CDP) Ingham County
44	729	1.9	**Cascade** (charter township) Kent County	117	1506	3.4	**Muskegon** (city) Muskegon County
44	729	1.9	**Eastpointe** (city) Macomb County	117	1506	3.4	**Rochester Hills** (city) Oakland County
44	729	1.9	**Oceola** (township) Livingston County	117	1506	3.4	**Roseville** (city) Macomb County
48	783	2.0	**Ada** (township) Kent County	117	1506	3.4	**Saint Clair Shores** (city) Macomb County
48	783	2.0	**Beverly Hills** (village) Oakland County	124	1573	3.5	**Farmington Hills** (city) Oakland County
48	783	2.0	**Brandon** (charter township) Oakland County	124	1573	3.5	**Holland** (city) Ottawa County
48	783	2.0	**Niles** (township) Berrien County	124	1573	3.5	**Monroe** (charter township) Monroe County
48	783	2.0	**Spring Lake** (township) Ottawa County	127	1621	3.6	**Commerce** (charter township) Oakland County
53	835	2.1	**Bridgeport** (charter township) Saginaw County	127	1621	3.6	**Fenton** (charter township) Genesee County
53	835	2.1	**Fruitport** (charter township) Muskegon County	127	1621	3.6	**Grosse Pointe Woods** (city) Wayne County
53	835	2.1	**Northville** (township) Wayne County	127	1621	3.6	**Lansing** (city) Ingham County
56	876	2.2	**East Grand Rapids** (city) Kent County	127	1621	3.6	**Mount Clemens** (city) Macomb County
56	876	2.2	**East Lansing** (city) Ingham County	127	1621	3.6	**Owosso** (city) Shiawassee County
56	876	2.2	**Grand Rapids** (charter township) Kent County	133	1682	3.7	**Alpine** (township) Kent County
56	876	2.2	**Lincoln** (charter township) Berrien County	133	1682	3.7	**Huron** (charter township) Wayne County
60	927	2.3	**Ann Arbor** (city) Washtenaw County	135	1731	3.8	**Comstock** (charter township) Kalamazoo County
60	927	2.3	**Blackman** (charter township) Jackson County	136	1786	3.9	**Fort Gratiot** (charter township) Saint Clair County
60	927	2.3	**Cooper** (charter township) Kalamazoo County	136	1786	3.9	**Harrison** (charter township) Macomb County
60	927	2.3	**Delhi** (charter township) Ingham County	136	1786	3.9	**White Lake** (charter township) Oakland County
60	927	2.3	**Highland** (charter township) Oakland County	139	1832	4.0	**Southfield** (city) Oakland County
60	927	2.3	**Jenison** (CDP) Ottawa County	139	1832	4.0	**Southgate** (city) Wayne County
60	927	2.3	**Monroe** (city) Monroe County	141	1892	4.1	**Flushing** (charter township) Genesee County
60	927	2.3	**Springfield** (charter township) Oakland County	141	1892	4.1	**Traverse City** (city) Grand Traverse County
60	927	2.3	**Sturgis** (city) Saint Joseph County	141	1892	4.1	**Westland** (city) Wayne County
69	980	2.4	**Antwerp** (township) Van Buren County	144	1938	4.2	**Lenox** (township) Macomb County
69	980	2.4	**Bloomfield** (charter township) Oakland County	144	1938	4.2	**Wyandotte** (city) Wayne County
69	980	2.4	**Davison** (township) Genesee County	146	1982	4.3	**Brownstown** (charter township) Wayne County
69	980	2.4	**Georgetown** (charter township) Ottawa County	146	1982	4.3	**Melvindale** (city) Wayne County
69	980	2.4	**Holt** (CDP) Ingham County	146	1982	4.3	**Sterling Heights** (city) Macomb County
69	980	2.4	**New Baltimore** (city) Macomb County	146	1982	4.3	**Warren** (city) Macomb County
69	980	2.4	**Oxford** (charter township) Oakland County	150	2041	4.4	**Madison Heights** (city) Oakland County

Note: The state column ranks the top/bottom 150 places from all places in the state with population of 10,000 or more. The national column ranks the top/bottom 150 places from all places in the country with population of 10,000 or more. Places that are unincorporated were not considered in the rankings. Please refer to the User Guide for additional information.

Commute to Work: Car

Top 150 Places Ranked in *Descending* Order

State Rank	Nat'l Rank	Percent	Place
1	15	97.7	**Bridgeport** (charter township) Saginaw County
2	20	97.6	**Riverview** (city) Wayne County
3	34	97.2	**Allen Park** (city) Wayne County
3	34	97.2	**New Baltimore** (city) Macomb County
5	39	97.1	**Southgate** (city) Wayne County
6	53	96.9	**Saginaw** (charter township) Saginaw County
7	62	96.8	**Holly** (township) Oakland County
8	73	96.7	**Leoni** (township) Jackson County
9	102	96.5	**Port Huron** (charter township) Saint Clair County
10	115	96.4	**Lincoln Park** (city) Wayne County
11	123	96.3	**Brownstown** (charter township) Wayne County
11	123	96.3	**Shelby** (charter township) Macomb County
11	123	96.3	**Sterling Heights** (city) Macomb County
14	138	96.2	**Melvindale** (city) Wayne County
15	150	96.1	**Burton** (city) Genesee County
15	150	96.1	**Grand Blanc** (charter township) Genesee County
17	168	96.0	**Taylor** (city) Wayne County
18	177	95.9	**Fruitport** (charter township) Muskegon County
18	177	95.9	**Macomb** (township) Macomb County
18	177	95.9	**Oxford** (charter township) Oakland County
21	228	95.7	**Chesterfield** (township) Macomb County
21	228	95.7	**Davison** (township) Genesee County
21	228	95.7	**Thomas** (township) Saginaw County
21	228	95.7	**Vienna** (charter township) Genesee County
25	252	95.6	**Delta** (charter township) Eaton County
25	252	95.6	**Lincoln** (charter township) Berrien County
25	252	95.6	**Livonia** (city) Wayne County
25	252	95.6	**Mundy** (township) Genesee County
29	278	95.5	**Dearborn Heights** (city) Wayne County
29	278	95.5	**Garden City** (city) Wayne County
29	278	95.5	**Muskegon** (charter township) Muskegon County
29	278	95.5	**Romulus** (city) Wayne County
33	306	95.4	**Fenton** (charter township) Genesee County
33	306	95.4	**Fraser** (city) Macomb County
35	333	95.3	**Clawson** (city) Oakland County
35	333	95.3	**DeWitt** (charter township) Clinton County
35	333	95.3	**Jenison** (CDP) Ottawa County
35	333	95.3	**Waterford** (charter township) Oakland County
39	365	95.2	**Antwerp** (township) Van Buren County
39	365	95.2	**Clinton** (charter township) Macomb County
39	365	95.2	**Holland** (charter township) Ottawa County
39	365	95.2	**Waverly** (CDP) Eaton County
43	390	95.1	**Trenton** (city) Wayne County
44	412	95.0	**Novi** (city) Oakland County
44	412	95.0	**Walker** (city) Kent County
44	412	95.0	**Westland** (city) Wayne County
47	437	94.9	**Brandon** (charter township) Oakland County
47	437	94.9	**Redford** (charter township) Wayne County
47	437	94.9	**Saint Clair Shores** (city) Macomb County
47	437	94.9	**South Lyon** (city) Oakland County
51	469	94.8	**Cooper** (charter township) Kalamazoo County
51	469	94.8	**Lenox** (township) Macomb County
51	469	94.8	**Norton Shores** (city) Muskegon County
51	469	94.8	**Sturgis** (city) Saint Joseph County
51	469	94.8	**Warren** (city) Macomb County
56	500	94.7	**Northville** (township) Wayne County
56	500	94.7	**Plymouth** (charter township) Wayne County
56	500	94.7	**Van Buren** (charter township) Wayne County
59	539	94.6	**Gaines** (charter township) Kent County
59	539	94.6	**Troy** (city) Oakland County
61	574	94.5	**Byron** (township) Kent County
61	574	94.5	**Dearborn** (city) Wayne County
61	574	94.5	**Green Oak** (township) Livingston County
61	574	94.5	**Inkster** (city) Wayne County
61	574	94.5	**Ionia** (city) Ionia County
61	574	94.5	**Wixom** (city) Oakland County
67	609	94.4	**Emmett** (charter township) Calhoun County
67	609	94.4	**Hartland** (township) Livingston County
69	649	94.3	**Flushing** (charter township) Genesee County
69	649	94.3	**Garfield** (charter township) Grand Traverse County
69	649	94.3	**Harrison** (charter township) Macomb County
69	649	94.3	**Independence** (charter township) Oakland County
73	722	94.1	**Bedford** (township) Monroe County
73	722	94.1	**Canton** (charter township) Wayne County
73	722	94.1	**Commerce** (charter township) Oakland County
73	722	94.1	**Eastpointe** (city) Macomb County
73	722	94.1	**Portage** (city) Kalamazoo County
78	767	94.0	**Frenchtown** (township) Monroe County
78	767	94.0	**Monitor** (charter township) Bay County
80	816	93.9	**Orion** (charter township) Oakland County
80	816	93.9	**Tyrone** (township) Livingston County
82	865	93.8	**Fenton** (city) Genesee County
82	865	93.8	**Flint** (charter township) Genesee County
82	865	93.8	**Genesee** (charter township) Genesee County
82	865	93.8	**Georgetown** (charter township) Ottawa County
82	865	93.8	**Highland** (charter township) Oakland County
82	865	93.8	**Milford** (charter township) Oakland County
82	865	93.8	**Monroe** (charter township) Monroe County
82	865	93.8	**Rochester Hills** (city) Oakland County
82	865	93.8	**Wayne** (city) Wayne County
91	917	93.7	**East Bay** (township) Grand Traverse County
91	917	93.7	**Niles** (township) Berrien County
91	917	93.7	**Roseville** (city) Macomb County
94	964	93.6	**Summit** (township) Jackson County
95	1000	93.5	**Comstock** (charter township) Kalamazoo County
95	1000	93.5	**Genoa** (township) Livingston County
95	1000	93.5	**Park** (township) Ottawa County
98	1043	93.4	**Cannon** (township) Kent County
98	1043	93.4	**Madison Heights** (city) Oakland County
98	1043	93.4	**Wyoming** (city) Kent County
101	1086	93.3	**Berkley** (city) Oakland County
101	1086	93.3	**Brighton** (township) Livingston County
101	1086	93.3	**Grosse Ile** (township) Wayne County
101	1086	93.3	**Kentwood** (city) Kent County
101	1086	93.3	**Rochester** (city) Oakland County
101	1086	93.3	**Royal Oak** (city) Oakland County
101	1086	93.3	**Springfield** (charter township) Oakland County
108	1147	93.2	**Ada** (township) Kent County
108	1147	93.2	**Beverly Hills** (village) Oakland County
108	1147	93.2	**Grosse Pointe Woods** (city) Wayne County
108	1147	93.2	**Washington** (township) Macomb County
112	1193	93.1	**Bay City** (city) Bay County
112	1193	93.1	**Mount Morris** (township) Genesee County
112	1193	93.1	**Spring Lake** (township) Ottawa County
112	1193	93.1	**Woodhaven** (city) Wayne County
116	1237	93.0	**Lyon** (charter township) Oakland County
116	1237	93.0	**Oakland** (charter township) Oakland County
116	1237	93.0	**Saint Joseph** (charter township) Berrien County
116	1237	93.0	**Ypsilanti** (charter township) Washtenaw County
120	1277	92.9	**Cutlerville** (CDP) Kent County
120	1277	92.9	**Oshtemo** (charter township) Kalamazoo County
120	1277	92.9	**Pontiac** (city) Oakland County
120	1277	92.9	**Superior** (charter township) Washtenaw County
120	1277	92.9	**White Lake** (charter township) Oakland County
125	1322	92.8	**Blackman** (charter township) Jackson County
125	1322	92.8	**Farmington** (city) Oakland County
125	1322	92.8	**Southfield** (city) Oakland County
128	1371	92.7	**Benton** (charter township) Berrien County
128	1371	92.7	**Forest Hills** (CDP) Kent County
128	1371	92.7	**West Bloomfield** (charter township) Oakland County
131	1563	92.3	**Bangor** (charter township) Bay County
131	1563	92.3	**Caledonia** (township) Kent County
131	1563	92.3	**Comstock Park** (CDP) Kent County
131	1563	92.3	**Farmington Hills** (city) Oakland County
131	1563	92.3	**Northview** (CDP) Kent County
136	1608	92.2	**Delhi** (charter township) Ingham County
136	1608	92.2	**Holt** (CDP) Ingham County
136	1608	92.2	**Texas** (charter township) Kalamazoo County
136	1608	92.2	**Wyandotte** (city) Wayne County
140	1644	92.1	**Benton Harbor** (city) Berrien County
140	1644	92.1	**Haslett** (CDP) Ingham County
140	1644	92.1	**Huron** (charter township) Wayne County
140	1644	92.1	**Oceola** (township) Livingston County
144	1695	92.0	**Cascade** (charter township) Kent County
144	1695	92.0	**Plainfield** (charter township) Kent County
146	1744	91.9	**Hamburg** (township) Livingston County
147	1782	91.8	**Oak Park** (city) Oakland County
147	1782	91.8	**Union** (charter township) Isabella County
149	1819	91.7	**Grandville** (city) Kent County
150	1892	91.5	**Grand Haven** (charter township) Ottawa County

Note: The state column ranks the top/bottom 150 places from all places in the state with population of 10,000 or more. The national column ranks the top/bottom 150 places from all places in the country with population of 10,000 or more. Places that are unincorporated were not considered in the rankings. Please refer to the User Guide for additional information.

Commute to Work: Car

Top 150 Places Ranked in *Ascending* Order

State Rank	Nat'l Rank	Percent	Place
1	57	58.5	**East Lansing** (city) Ingham County
2	110	64.2	**Ann Arbor** (city) Washtenaw County
3	213	71.5	**Highland Park** (city) Wayne County
4	252	73.1	**Big Rapids** (city) Mecosta County
5	339	76.3	**Mount Pleasant** (city) Isabella County
6	396	77.9	**Ypsilanti** (city) Washtenaw County
7	410	78.2	**Marquette** (city) Marquette County
8	576	81.4	**Sault Sainte Marie** (city) Chippewa County
9	647	82.3	**Traverse City** (city) Grand Traverse County
10	667	82.5	**Detroit** (city) Wayne County
11	796	83.7	**Allendale** (CDP) Ottawa County
12	833	84.0	**Adrian** (city) Lenawee County
13	972	85.1	**Allendale** (charter township) Ottawa County
14	1041	85.6	**Kalamazoo** (city) Kalamazoo County
15	1060	85.7	**Holland** (city) Ottawa County
16	1095	85.9	**Beecher** (CDP) Genesee County
17	1111	86.0	**East Grand Rapids** (city) Kent County
18	1241	86.7	**Grand Rapids** (city) Kent County
19	1509	88.0	**Flint** (city) Genesee County
20	1535	88.1	**Okemos** (CDP) Ingham County
21	1664	88.5	**Lansing** (city) Ingham County
22	1763	88.9	**Bath** (charter township) Clinton County
22	1763	88.9	**Coldwater** (city) Branch County
22	1763	88.9	**Grand Haven** (city) Ottawa County
25	1826	89.1	**Grosse Pointe Park** (city) Wayne County
26	1887	89.3	**Escanaba** (city) Delta County
27	1916	89.4	**Cadillac** (city) Wexford County
27	1916	89.4	**Pittsfield** (charter township) Washtenaw County
27	1916	89.4	**Scio** (township) Washtenaw County
30	2000	89.6	**Port Huron** (city) Saint Clair County
31	2028	89.7	**Meridian** (charter township) Ingham County
32	2053	89.8	**Hamtramck** (city) Wayne County
33	2086	89.9	**Mount Clemens** (city) Macomb County
34	2170	90.1	**Jackson** (city) Jackson County
34	2170	90.1	**Owosso** (city) Shiawassee County
36	2204	90.2	**Hazel Park** (city) Oakland County
37	2234	90.3	**Ferndale** (city) Oakland County
38	2310	90.5	**Alpena** (city) Alpena County
39	2349	90.6	**Alpine** (township) Kent County
39	2349	90.6	**Bloomfield** (charter township) Oakland County
39	2349	90.6	**Fort Gratiot** (charter township) Saint Clair County
39	2349	90.6	**Kalamazoo** (charter township) Kalamazoo County
39	2349	90.6	**Muskegon** (city) Muskegon County
44	2381	90.7	**Midland** (city) Midland County
45	2457	90.9	**Grand Rapids** (charter township) Kent County
45	2457	90.9	**Muskegon Heights** (city) Muskegon County
47	2508	91.0	**Battle Creek** (city) Calhoun County
47	2508	91.0	**Birmingham** (city) Oakland County
47	2508	91.0	**Monroe** (city) Monroe County
50	2545	91.1	**Saginaw** (city) Saginaw County
51	2590	91.2	**Southfield** (township) Oakland County
52	2634	91.3	**Auburn Hills** (city) Oakland County
53	2676	91.4	**Harper Woods** (city) Wayne County
53	2676	91.4	**Niles** (city) Berrien County
55	2720	91.5	**Grand Haven** (charter township) Ottawa County
56	2800	91.7	**Grandville** (city) Kent County
57	2838	91.8	**Oak Park** (city) Oakland County
57	2838	91.8	**Union** (charter township) Isabella County
59	2875	91.9	**Hamburg** (township) Livingston County
60	2913	92.0	**Cascade** (charter township) Kent County
60	2913	92.0	**Plainfield** (charter township) Kent County
62	2962	92.1	**Benton Harbor** (city) Berrien County
62	2962	92.1	**Haslett** (CDP) Ingham County
62	2962	92.1	**Huron** (charter township) Wayne County
62	2962	92.1	**Oceola** (township) Livingston County
66	3013	92.2	**Delhi** (charter township) Ingham County
66	3013	92.2	**Holt** (CDP) Ingham County
66	3013	92.2	**Texas** (charter township) Kalamazoo County
66	3013	92.2	**Wyandotte** (city) Wayne County
70	3049	92.3	**Bangor** (charter township) Bay County
70	3049	92.3	**Caledonia** (township) Kent County
70	3049	92.3	**Comstock Park** (CDP) Kent County
70	3049	92.3	**Farmington Hills** (city) Oakland County
70	3049	92.3	**Northview** (CDP) Kent County
75	3241	92.7	**Benton** (charter township) Berrien County
75	3241	92.7	**Forest Hills** (CDP) Kent County
75	3241	92.7	**West Bloomfield** (charter township) Oakland County
78	3286	92.8	**Blackman** (charter township) Jackson County
78	3286	92.8	**Farmington** (city) Oakland County
78	3286	92.8	**Southfield** (city) Oakland County
81	3335	92.9	**Cutlerville** (CDP) Kent County
81	3335	92.9	**Oshtemo** (charter township) Kalamazoo County
81	3335	92.9	**Pontiac** (city) Oakland County
81	3335	92.9	**Superior** (charter township) Washtenaw County
81	3335	92.9	**White Lake** (charter township) Oakland County
86	3380	93.0	**Lyon** (charter township) Oakland County
86	3380	93.0	**Oakland** (charter township) Oakland County
86	3380	93.0	**Saint Joseph** (charter township) Berrien County
86	3380	93.0	**Ypsilanti** (charter township) Washtenaw County
90	3420	93.1	**Bay City** (city) Bay County
90	3420	93.1	**Mount Morris** (township) Genesee County
90	3420	93.1	**Spring Lake** (township) Ottawa County
90	3420	93.1	**Woodhaven** (city) Wayne County
94	3464	93.2	**Ada** (township) Kent County
94	3464	93.2	**Beverly Hills** (village) Oakland County
94	3464	93.2	**Grosse Pointe Woods** (city) Wayne County
94	3464	93.2	**Washington** (township) Macomb County
98	3510	93.3	**Berkley** (city) Oakland County
98	3510	93.3	**Brighton** (township) Livingston County
98	3510	93.3	**Grosse Ile** (township) Wayne County
98	3510	93.3	**Kentwood** (city) Kent County
98	3510	93.3	**Rochester** (city) Oakland County
98	3510	93.3	**Royal Oak** (city) Oakland County
98	3510	93.3	**Springfield** (charter township) Oakland County
105	3571	93.4	**Cannon** (township) Kent County
105	3571	93.4	**Madison Heights** (city) Oakland County
105	3571	93.4	**Wyoming** (city) Kent County
108	3614	93.5	**Comstock** (charter township) Kalamazoo County
108	3614	93.5	**Genoa** (township) Livingston County
108	3614	93.5	**Park** (township) Ottawa County
111	3657	93.6	**Summit** (township) Jackson County
112	3693	93.7	**East Bay** (township) Grand Traverse County
112	3693	93.7	**Niles** (township) Berrien County
112	3693	93.7	**Roseville** (city) Macomb County
115	3740	93.8	**Fenton** (city) Genesee County
115	3740	93.8	**Flint** (charter township) Genesee County
115	3740	93.8	**Genesee** (charter township) Genesee County
115	3740	93.8	**Georgetown** (charter township) Ottawa County
115	3740	93.8	**Highland** (charter township) Oakland County
115	3740	93.8	**Milford** (charter township) Oakland County
115	3740	93.8	**Monroe** (charter township) Monroe County
115	3740	93.8	**Rochester Hills** (city) Oakland County
115	3740	93.8	**Wayne** (city) Wayne County
124	3792	93.9	**Orion** (charter township) Oakland County
124	3792	93.9	**Tyrone** (township) Livingston County
126	3841	94.0	**Frenchtown** (township) Monroe County
126	3841	94.0	**Monitor** (charter township) Bay County
128	3890	94.1	**Bedford** (township) Monroe County
128	3890	94.1	**Canton** (charter township) Wayne County
128	3890	94.1	**Commerce** (charter township) Oakland County
128	3890	94.1	**Eastpointe** (city) Macomb County
128	3890	94.1	**Portage** (city) Kalamazoo County
133	3979	94.3	**Flushing** (charter township) Genesee County
133	3979	94.3	**Garfield** (charter township) Grand Traverse County
133	3979	94.3	**Harrison** (charter township) Macomb County
133	3979	94.3	**Independence** (charter township) Oakland County
137	4008	94.4	**Emmett** (charter township) Calhoun County
137	4008	94.4	**Hartland** (township) Livingston County
139	4048	94.5	**Byron** (township) Kent County
139	4048	94.5	**Dearborn** (city) Wayne County
139	4048	94.5	**Green Oak** (township) Livingston County
139	4048	94.5	**Inkster** (city) Wayne County
139	4048	94.5	**Ionia** (city) Ionia County
139	4048	94.5	**Wixom** (city) Oakland County
145	4083	94.6	**Gaines** (charter township) Kent County
145	4083	94.6	**Troy** (city) Oakland County
147	4118	94.7	**Northville** (township) Wayne County
147	4118	94.7	**Plymouth** (charter township) Wayne County
147	4118	94.7	**Van Buren** (charter township) Wayne County
150	4157	94.8	**Cooper** (charter township) Kalamazoo County

Note: The state column ranks the top/bottom 150 places from all places in the state with population of 10,000 or more. The national column ranks the top/bottom 150 places from all places in the country with population of 10,000 or more. Places that are unincorporated were not considered in the rankings. Please refer to the User Guide for additional information.

Commute to Work: Public Transportation

Top 150 Places Ranked in *Descending* Order

State Rank	Nat'l Rank	Percent	Place
1	141	17.9	**Highland Park** (city) Wayne County
2	385	10.2	**Ann Arbor** (city) Washtenaw County
3	508	8.7	**Detroit** (city) Wayne County
4	854	5.5	**Allendale** (CDP) Ottawa County
4	854	5.5	**Allendale** (charter township) Ottawa County
4	854	5.5	**East Lansing** (city) Ingham County
7	872	5.4	**Ypsilanti** (city) Washtenaw County
8	1060	4.4	**Flint** (city) Genesee County
8	1060	4.4	**Lansing** (city) Ingham County
8	1060	4.4	**Woodhaven** (city) Wayne County
11	1107	4.2	**Beecher** (CDP) Genesee County
12	1311	3.5	**Grand Rapids** (city) Kent County
12	1311	3.5	**Pittsfield** (charter township) Washtenaw County
14	1411	3.2	**Inkster** (city) Wayne County
14	1411	3.2	**Kalamazoo** (charter township) Kalamazoo County
16	1513	2.9	**Hazel Park** (city) Oakland County
16	1513	2.9	**Mount Clemens** (city) Macomb County
16	1513	2.9	**Superior** (charter township) Washtenaw County
19	1549	2.8	**Bath** (charter township) Clinton County
19	1549	2.8	**Harper Woods** (city) Wayne County
21	1596	2.7	**East Grand Rapids** (city) Kent County
22	1635	2.6	**Saginaw** (city) Saginaw County
22	1635	2.6	**Ypsilanti** (charter township) Washtenaw County
24	1685	2.5	**Cutlerville** (CDP) Kent County
25	1739	2.4	**Kalamazoo** (city) Kalamazoo County
25	1739	2.4	**Monroe** (city) Monroe County
25	1739	2.4	**Oak Park** (city) Oakland County
28	1855	2.2	**Mount Morris** (township) Genesee County
29	1897	2.1	**Grandville** (city) Kent County
30	1948	2.0	**Hamtramck** (city) Wayne County
30	1948	2.0	**Southfield** (city) Oakland County
30	1948	2.0	**Union** (charter township) Isabella County
33	2005	1.9	**Frenchtown** (township) Monroe County
33	2005	1.9	**Okemos** (CDP) Ingham County
33	2005	1.9	**Pontiac** (city) Oakland County
36	2054	1.8	**Ferndale** (city) Oakland County
36	2054	1.8	**Huron** (charter township) Wayne County
38	2111	1.7	**Gaines** (charter township) Kent County
38	2111	1.7	**Meridian** (charter township) Ingham County
38	2111	1.7	**Roseville** (city) Macomb County
41	2157	1.6	**Holt** (CDP) Ingham County
41	2157	1.6	**Sault Sainte Marie** (city) Chippewa County
41	2157	1.6	**Wyoming** (city) Kent County
44	2239	1.5	**Cooper** (charter township) Kalamazoo County
44	2239	1.5	**Delhi** (charter township) Ingham County
44	2239	1.5	**Haslett** (CDP) Ingham County
44	2239	1.5	**Saint Clair Shores** (city) Macomb County
48	2324	1.4	**Battle Creek** (city) Calhoun County
48	2324	1.4	**Benton Harbor** (city) Berrien County
48	2324	1.4	**Clinton** (charter township) Macomb County
48	2324	1.4	**Fort Gratiot** (charter township) Saint Clair County
48	2324	1.4	**Jackson** (city) Jackson County
48	2324	1.4	**Port Huron** (city) Saint Clair County
48	2324	1.4	**Wyandotte** (city) Wayne County
55	2411	1.3	**Grosse Pointe Park** (city) Wayne County
55	2411	1.3	**Kentwood** (city) Kent County
57	2496	1.2	**Benton** (charter township) Berrien County
57	2496	1.2	**Genesee** (charter township) Genesee County
57	2496	1.2	**Grand Haven** (city) Ottawa County
57	2496	1.2	**Madison Heights** (city) Oakland County
57	2496	1.2	**Muskegon** (city) Muskegon County
57	2496	1.2	**Traverse City** (city) Grand Traverse County
57	2496	1.2	**Walker** (city) Kent County
64	2599	1.1	**Comstock Park** (CDP) Kent County
64	2599	1.1	**Mount Pleasant** (city) Isabella County
64	2599	1.1	**Redford** (charter township) Wayne County
64	2599	1.1	**Wayne** (city) Wayne County
68	2684	1.0	**Holland** (charter township) Ottawa County
68	2684	1.0	**Holland** (city) Ottawa County
68	2684	1.0	**Monitor** (charter township) Bay County
68	2684	1.0	**Warren** (city) Macomb County
72	2793	0.9	**Alpena** (city) Alpena County
72	2793	0.9	**Alpine** (township) Kent County
72	2793	0.9	**Eastpointe** (city) Macomb County
72	2793	0.9	**Flint** (charter township) Genesee County
72	2793	0.9	**Muskegon Heights** (city) Muskegon County
72	2793	0.9	**Oshtemo** (charter township) Kalamazoo County
72	2793	0.9	**Romulus** (city) Wayne County
72	2793	0.9	**Taylor** (city) Wayne County
80	2912	0.8	**Big Rapids** (city) Mecosta County
80	2912	0.8	**Bloomfield** (charter township) Oakland County
80	2912	0.8	**Grosse Pointe Woods** (city) Wayne County
80	2912	0.8	**Lincoln Park** (city) Wayne County
80	2912	0.8	**Marquette** (city) Marquette County
80	2912	0.8	**Midland** (city) Midland County
80	2912	0.8	**Royal Oak** (city) Oakland County
87	3031	0.7	**Ada** (township) Kent County
87	3031	0.7	**Bay City** (city) Bay County
87	3031	0.7	**Brownstown** (charter township) Wayne County
87	3031	0.7	**Monroe** (charter township) Monroe County
87	3031	0.7	**Niles** (city) Berrien County
87	3031	0.7	**Northview** (CDP) Kent County
87	3031	0.7	**Port Huron** (charter township) Saint Clair County
87	3031	0.7	**Riverview** (city) Wayne County
95	3184	0.6	**Bedford** (township) Monroe County
95	3184	0.6	**Blackman** (charter township) Jackson County
95	3184	0.6	**Coldwater** (city) Branch County
95	3184	0.6	**Comstock** (charter township) Kalamazoo County
95	3184	0.6	**Dearborn Heights** (city) Wayne County
95	3184	0.6	**Farmington Hills** (city) Oakland County
95	3184	0.6	**Fraser** (city) Macomb County
95	3184	0.6	**Lyon** (charter township) Oakland County
95	3184	0.6	**Oceola** (township) Livingston County
95	3184	0.6	**Scio** (township) Washtenaw County
95	3184	0.6	**Westland** (city) Wayne County
106	3338	0.5	**Chesterfield** (township) Macomb County
106	3338	0.5	**DeWitt** (charter township) Clinton County
106	3338	0.5	**Dearborn** (city) Wayne County
106	3338	0.5	**Escanaba** (city) Delta County
106	3338	0.5	**Fenton** (city) Genesee County
106	3338	0.5	**Forest Hills** (CDP) Kent County
106	3338	0.5	**Harrison** (charter township) Macomb County
106	3338	0.5	**Portage** (city) Kalamazoo County
106	3338	0.5	**South Lyon** (city) Oakland County
106	3338	0.5	**Southgate** (city) Wayne County
106	3338	0.5	**Trenton** (city) Wayne County
106	3338	0.5	**Van Buren** (charter township) Wayne County
118	3488	0.4	**Bangor** (charter township) Bay County
118	3488	0.4	**Berkley** (city) Oakland County
118	3488	0.4	**Canton** (charter township) Wayne County
118	3488	0.4	**Clawson** (city) Oakland County
118	3488	0.4	**Garden City** (city) Wayne County
118	3488	0.4	**Grand Haven** (charter township) Ottawa County
118	3488	0.4	**Lenox** (township) Macomb County
118	3488	0.4	**Norton Shores** (city) Muskegon County
118	3488	0.4	**Novi** (city) Oakland County
118	3488	0.4	**Plainfield** (charter township) Kent County
118	3488	0.4	**Sterling Heights** (city) Macomb County
118	3488	0.4	**Troy** (city) Oakland County
130	3669	0.3	**Birmingham** (city) Oakland County
130	3669	0.3	**Delta** (charter township) Eaton County
130	3669	0.3	**Emmett** (charter township) Calhoun County
130	3669	0.3	**Farmington** (city) Oakland County
130	3669	0.3	**Fenton** (charter township) Genesee County
130	3669	0.3	**Georgetown** (charter township) Ottawa County
130	3669	0.3	**Highland** (charter township) Oakland County
130	3669	0.3	**Ionia** (city) Ionia County
130	3669	0.3	**Livonia** (city) Wayne County
130	3669	0.3	**Northville** (township) Wayne County
130	3669	0.3	**Owosso** (city) Shiawassee County
130	3669	0.3	**Shelby** (charter township) Macomb County
130	3669	0.3	**Southfield** (township) Oakland County
130	3669	0.3	**Thomas** (township) Saginaw County
144	3876	0.2	**Adrian** (city) Lenawee County
144	3876	0.2	**Auburn Hills** (city) Oakland County
144	3876	0.2	**Beverly Hills** (village) Oakland County
144	3876	0.2	**Burton** (city) Genesee County
144	3876	0.2	**Byron** (township) Kent County
144	3876	0.2	**Cannon** (township) Kent County
144	3876	0.2	**Davison** (township) Genesee County

Note: The state column ranks the top/bottom 150 places from all places in the state with population of 10,000 or more. The national column ranks the top/bottom 150 places from all places in the country with population of 10,000 or more. Places that are unincorporated were not considered in the rankings. Please refer to the User Guide for additional information.

Commute to Work: Walk

Top 150 Places Ranked in *Descending* Order

State Rank	Nat'l Rank	Percent	Place	State Rank	Nat'l Rank	Percent	Place
1	24	22.2	**East Lansing** (city) Ingham County	76	2500	1.4	**Bath** (charter township) Clinton County
2	32	19.6	**Big Rapids** (city) Mecosta County	76	2500	1.4	**Fraser** (city) Macomb County
3	55	16.2	**Mount Pleasant** (city) Isabella County	76	2500	1.4	**Oceola** (township) Livingston County
4	68	15.0	**Ann Arbor** (city) Washtenaw County	76	2500	1.4	**Roseville** (city) Macomb County
5	86	13.5	**Marquette** (city) Marquette County	76	2500	1.4	**Royal Oak** (city) Oakland County
6	111	11.7	**Adrian** (city) Lenawee County	76	2500	1.4	**Scio** (township) Washtenaw County
7	122	11.1	**Sault Sainte Marie** (city) Chippewa County	76	2500	1.4	**Wixom** (city) Oakland County
8	126	10.8	**Ypsilanti** (city) Washtenaw County	83	2661	1.3	**Oshtemo** (charter township) Kalamazoo County
9	256	7.6	**Kalamazoo** (city) Kalamazoo County	83	2661	1.3	**Rochester** (city) Oakland County
10	278	7.3	**Allendale** (CDP) Ottawa County	85	2817	1.2	**Cooper** (charter township) Kalamazoo County
11	285	7.2	**Holland** (city) Ottawa County	85	2817	1.2	**Davison** (township) Genesee County
12	353	6.3	**Allendale** (charter township) Ottawa County	85	2817	1.2	**Emmett** (charter township) Calhoun County
13	427	5.5	**Traverse City** (city) Grand Traverse County	85	2817	1.2	**Frenchtown** (township) Monroe County
14	483	5.1	**Escanaba** (city) Delta County	85	2817	1.2	**Grand Haven** (charter township) Ottawa County
15	520	4.8	**Cadillac** (city) Wexford County	85	2817	1.2	**Holly** (township) Oakland County
16	589	4.4	**Owosso** (city) Shiawassee County	85	2817	1.2	**Monroe** (charter township) Monroe County
17	637	4.2	**Union** (charter township) Isabella County	85	2817	1.2	**Niles** (township) Berrien County
18	731	3.8	**Port Huron** (city) Saint Clair County	85	2817	1.2	**Portage** (city) Kalamazoo County
19	799	3.6	**Mount Clemens** (city) Macomb County	85	2817	1.2	**Redford** (charter township) Wayne County
20	839	3.5	**Battle Creek** (city) Calhoun County	85	2817	1.2	**Sturgis** (city) Saint Joseph County
20	839	3.5	**Niles** (city) Berrien County	85	2817	1.2	**Westland** (city) Wayne County
22	879	3.4	**Detroit** (city) Wayne County	97	2976	1.1	**Cutlerville** (CDP) Kent County
22	879	3.4	**Wyandotte** (city) Wayne County	97	2976	1.1	**East Bay** (township) Grand Traverse County
24	925	3.3	**Coldwater** (city) Branch County	97	2976	1.1	**Fenton** (city) Genesee County
24	925	3.3	**Grand Rapids** (city) Kent County	97	2976	1.1	**Harrison** (charter township) Macomb County
26	965	3.2	**Auburn Hills** (city) Oakland County	97	2976	1.1	**Hartland** (township) Livingston County
26	965	3.2	**Grand Haven** (city) Ottawa County	97	2976	1.1	**Haslett** (CDP) Ingham County
26	965	3.2	**Jackson** (city) Jackson County	97	2976	1.1	**Huron** (charter township) Wayne County
29	1009	3.1	**Fort Gratiot** (charter township) Saint Clair County	97	2976	1.1	**Kentwood** (city) Kent County
30	1053	3.0	**Flint** (city) Genesee County	97	2976	1.1	**Summit** (township) Jackson County
30	1053	3.0	**Hazel Park** (city) Oakland County	97	2976	1.1	**Vienna** (charter township) Genesee County
30	1053	3.0	**Muskegon** (city) Muskegon County	107	3154	1.0	**Delta** (charter township) Eaton County
30	1053	3.0	**Okemos** (CDP) Ingham County	107	3154	1.0	**Farmington** (city) Oakland County
34	1164	2.8	**Caledonia** (township) Kent County	107	3154	1.0	**Farmington Hills** (city) Oakland County
34	1164	2.8	**Monroe** (city) Monroe County	107	3154	1.0	**Garden City** (city) Wayne County
36	1218	2.7	**Bangor** (charter township) Bay County	107	3154	1.0	**Grosse Ile** (township) Wayne County
36	1218	2.7	**Lansing** (city) Ingham County	107	3154	1.0	**Leoni** (township) Jackson County
36	1218	2.7	**Van Buren** (charter township) Wayne County	107	3154	1.0	**Pittsfield** (charter township) Washtenaw County
39	1289	2.6	**Ferndale** (city) Oakland County	107	3154	1.0	**South Lyon** (city) Oakland County
40	1347	2.5	**Berkley** (city) Oakland County	107	3154	1.0	**Taylor** (city) Wayne County
40	1347	2.5	**East Grand Rapids** (city) Kent County	107	3154	1.0	**Washington** (township) Macomb County
40	1347	2.5	**Wayne** (city) Wayne County	107	3154	1.0	**Waverly** (CDP) Eaton County
43	1439	2.4	**Grosse Pointe Park** (city) Wayne County	118	3333	0.9	**Byron** (township) Kent County
43	1439	2.4	**Highland Park** (city) Wayne County	118	3333	0.9	**Cannon** (township) Kent County
45	1513	2.3	**Bay City** (city) Bay County	118	3333	0.9	**Gaines** (charter township) Kent County
45	1513	2.3	**Melvindale** (city) Wayne County	118	3333	0.9	**Lyon** (charter township) Oakland County
47	1584	2.2	**Eastpointe** (city) Macomb County	118	3333	0.9	**Madison Heights** (city) Oakland County
47	1584	2.2	**Oak Park** (city) Oakland County	118	3333	0.9	**Plainfield** (charter township) Kent County
49	1686	2.1	**Meridian** (charter township) Ingham County	118	3333	0.9	**Southgate** (city) Wayne County
50	1781	2.0	**Benton Harbor** (city) Berrien County	118	3333	0.9	**Walker** (city) Kent County
50	1781	2.0	**Comstock Park** (CDP) Kent County	118	3333	0.9	**Warren** (city) Macomb County
50	1781	2.0	**Georgetown** (charter township) Ottawa County	127	3503	0.8	**Beecher** (CDP) Genesee County
50	1781	2.0	**Midland** (city) Midland County	127	3503	0.8	**Clawson** (city) Oakland County
54	1886	1.9	**Grandville** (city) Kent County	127	3503	0.8	**Genesee** (charter township) Genesee County
54	1886	1.9	**Lenox** (township) Macomb County	127	3503	0.8	**Highland** (charter township) Oakland County
54	1886	1.9	**Pontiac** (city) Oakland County	127	3503	0.8	**Holland** (charter township) Ottawa County
54	1886	1.9	**Saginaw** (city) Saginaw County	127	3503	0.8	**Oakland** (charter township) Oakland County
58	1994	1.8	**Blackman** (charter township) Jackson County	127	3503	0.8	**Orion** (charter township) Oakland County
58	1994	1.8	**Dearborn** (city) Wayne County	127	3503	0.8	**Rochester Hills** (city) Oakland County
60	2120	1.7	**Milford** (charter township) Oakland County	127	3503	0.8	**Romulus** (city) Wayne County
60	2120	1.7	**Monitor** (charter township) Bay County	127	3503	0.8	**Southfield** (township) Oakland County
60	2120	1.7	**Southfield** (city) Oakland County	127	3503	0.8	**Springfield** (charter township) Oakland County
63	2230	1.6	**Alpine** (township) Kent County	127	3503	0.8	**Superior** (charter township) Washtenaw County
63	2230	1.6	**Birmingham** (city) Oakland County	127	3503	0.8	**Troy** (city) Oakland County
63	2230	1.6	**Flint** (charter township) Genesee County	127	3503	0.8	**Waterford** (charter township) Oakland County
63	2230	1.6	**Ionia** (city) Ionia County	127	3503	0.8	**Woodhaven** (city) Wayne County
63	2230	1.6	**Jenison** (CDP) Ottawa County	127	3503	0.8	**Wyoming** (city) Kent County
63	2230	1.6	**Kalamazoo** (charter township) Kalamazoo County	127	3503	0.8	**Ypsilanti** (charter township) Washtenaw County
63	2230	1.6	**Muskegon Heights** (city) Muskegon County	144	3687	0.7	**Allen Park** (city) Wayne County
63	2230	1.6	**Spring Lake** (township) Ottawa County	144	3687	0.7	**Brandon** (charter township) Oakland County
71	2367	1.5	**Antwerp** (township) Van Buren County	144	3687	0.7	**Bridgeport** (charter township) Saginaw County
71	2367	1.5	**Hamtramck** (city) Wayne County	144	3687	0.7	**Brighton** (township) Livingston County
71	2367	1.5	**Harper Woods** (city) Wayne County	144	3687	0.7	**Comstock** (charter township) Kalamazoo County
71	2367	1.5	**Port Huron** (charter township) Saint Clair County	144	3687	0.7	**Dearborn Heights** (city) Wayne County
71	2367	1.5	**White Lake** (charter township) Oakland County	144	3687	0.7	**Delhi** (charter township) Ingham County

Note: The state column ranks the top/bottom 150 places from all places in the state with population of 10,000 or more. The national column ranks the top/bottom 150 places from all places in the country with population of 10,000 or more. Places that are unincorporated were not considered in the rankings. Please refer to the User Guide for additional information.

Commute to Work: Walk

Top 150 Places Ranked in *Ascending* Order

State Rank	Nat'l Rank	Percent	Place	State Rank	Nat'l Rank	Percent	Place
1	1	0.0	**DeWitt** (charter township) Clinton County	62	970	0.8	**Woodhaven** (city) Wayne County
1	1	0.0	**Flushing** (charter township) Genesee County	62	970	0.8	**Wyoming** (city) Kent County
3	93	0.1	**Bedford** (township) Monroe County	62	970	0.8	**Ypsilanti** (charter township) Washtenaw County
3	93	0.1	**Lincoln** (charter township) Berrien County	79	1154	0.9	**Byron** (township) Kent County
5	151	0.2	**Commerce** (charter township) Oakland County	79	1154	0.9	**Cannon** (township) Kent County
5	151	0.2	**Green Oak** (township) Livingston County	79	1154	0.9	**Gaines** (charter township) Kent County
5	151	0.2	**Macomb** (township) Macomb County	79	1154	0.9	**Lyon** (charter township) Oakland County
5	151	0.2	**Texas** (charter township) Kalamazoo County	79	1154	0.9	**Madison Heights** (city) Oakland County
9	246	0.3	**Brownstown** (charter township) Wayne County	79	1154	0.9	**Plainfield** (charter township) Kent County
9	246	0.3	**Chesterfield** (township) Macomb County	79	1154	0.9	**Southgate** (city) Wayne County
9	246	0.3	**Grand Blanc** (charter township) Genesee County	79	1154	0.9	**Walker** (city) Kent County
9	246	0.3	**Novi** (city) Oakland County	79	1154	0.9	**Warren** (city) Macomb County
9	246	0.3	**Park** (township) Ottawa County	88	1324	1.0	**Delta** (charter township) Eaton County
9	246	0.3	**Tyrone** (township) Livingston County	88	1324	1.0	**Farmington** (city) Oakland County
15	358	0.4	**Benton** (charter township) Berrien County	88	1324	1.0	**Farmington Hills** (city) Oakland County
15	358	0.4	**Beverly Hills** (village) Oakland County	88	1324	1.0	**Garden City** (city) Wayne County
15	358	0.4	**Burton** (city) Genesee County	88	1324	1.0	**Grosse Ile** (township) Wayne County
15	358	0.4	**Canton** (charter township) Wayne County	88	1324	1.0	**Leoni** (township) Jackson County
15	358	0.4	**Genoa** (township) Livingston County	88	1324	1.0	**Pittsfield** (charter township) Washtenaw County
15	358	0.4	**Norton Shores** (city) Muskegon County	88	1324	1.0	**South Lyon** (city) Oakland County
15	358	0.4	**Oxford** (charter township) Oakland County	88	1324	1.0	**Taylor** (city) Wayne County
15	358	0.4	**Saginaw** (charter township) Saginaw County	88	1324	1.0	**Washington** (township) Macomb County
23	497	0.5	**Alpena** (city) Alpena County	88	1324	1.0	**Waverly** (CDP) Eaton County
23	497	0.5	**Bloomfield** (charter township) Oakland County	99	1503	1.1	**Cutlerville** (CDP) Kent County
23	497	0.5	**Cascade** (charter township) Kent County	99	1503	1.1	**East Bay** (township) Grand Traverse County
23	497	0.5	**Clinton** (charter township) Macomb County	99	1503	1.1	**Fenton** (city) Genesee County
23	497	0.5	**Fruitport** (charter township) Muskegon County	99	1503	1.1	**Harrison** (charter township) Macomb County
23	497	0.5	**Grand Rapids** (charter township) Kent County	99	1503	1.1	**Hartland** (township) Livingston County
23	497	0.5	**Lincoln Park** (city) Wayne County	99	1503	1.1	**Haslett** (CDP) Ingham County
23	497	0.5	**Muskegon** (charter township) Muskegon County	99	1503	1.1	**Huron** (charter township) Wayne County
23	497	0.5	**Shelby** (charter township) Macomb County	99	1503	1.1	**Kentwood** (city) Kent County
23	497	0.5	**Thomas** (township) Saginaw County	99	1503	1.1	**Summit** (township) Jackson County
23	497	0.5	**West Bloomfield** (charter township) Oakland County	99	1503	1.1	**Vienna** (charter township) Genesee County
34	651	0.6	**Ada** (township) Kent County	109	1681	1.2	**Cooper** (charter township) Kalamazoo County
34	651	0.6	**Fenton** (township) Genesee County	109	1681	1.2	**Davison** (township) Genesee County
34	651	0.6	**Forest Hills** (CDP) Kent County	109	1681	1.2	**Emmett** (charter township) Calhoun County
34	651	0.6	**Garfield** (charter township) Grand Traverse County	109	1681	1.2	**Frenchtown** (township) Monroe County
34	651	0.6	**Grosse Pointe Woods** (city) Wayne County	109	1681	1.2	**Grand Haven** (charter township) Ottawa County
34	651	0.6	**Livonia** (city) Wayne County	109	1681	1.2	**Holly** (township) Oakland County
34	651	0.6	**Mount Morris** (township) Genesee County	109	1681	1.2	**Monroe** (charter township) Monroe County
34	651	0.6	**Mundy** (township) Genesee County	109	1681	1.2	**Niles** (township) Berrien County
34	651	0.6	**Northview** (CDP) Kent County	109	1681	1.2	**Portage** (city) Kalamazoo County
34	651	0.6	**Plymouth** (charter township) Wayne County	109	1681	1.2	**Redford** (charter township) Wayne County
34	651	0.6	**Saint Clair Shores** (city) Macomb County	109	1681	1.2	**Sturgis** (city) Saint Joseph County
34	651	0.6	**Saint Joseph** (charter township) Berrien County	109	1681	1.2	**Westland** (city) Wayne County
34	651	0.6	**Sterling Heights** (city) Macomb County	121	1840	1.3	**Oshtemo** (charter township) Kalamazoo County
47	802	0.7	**Allen Park** (city) Wayne County	121	1840	1.3	**Rochester** (city) Oakland County
47	802	0.7	**Brandon** (charter township) Oakland County	123	1996	1.4	**Bath** (charter township) Clinton County
47	802	0.7	**Bridgeport** (charter township) Saginaw County	123	1996	1.4	**Fraser** (city) Macomb County
47	802	0.7	**Brighton** (township) Livingston County	123	1996	1.4	**Oceola** (township) Livingston County
47	802	0.7	**Comstock** (charter township) Kalamazoo County	123	1996	1.4	**Roseville** (city) Macomb County
47	802	0.7	**Dearborn Heights** (city) Wayne County	123	1996	1.4	**Royal Oak** (city) Oakland County
47	802	0.7	**Delhi** (charter township) Ingham County	123	1996	1.4	**Scio** (township) Washtenaw County
47	802	0.7	**Hamburg** (township) Livingston County	123	1996	1.4	**Wixom** (city) Oakland County
47	802	0.7	**Holt** (CDP) Ingham County	130	2157	1.5	**Antwerp** (township) Van Buren County
47	802	0.7	**Independence** (charter township) Oakland County	130	2157	1.5	**Hamtramck** (city) Wayne County
47	802	0.7	**Inkster** (city) Wayne County	130	2157	1.5	**Harper Woods** (city) Wayne County
47	802	0.7	**New Baltimore** (city) Macomb County	130	2157	1.5	**Port Huron** (charter township) Saint Clair County
47	802	0.7	**Northville** (township) Wayne County	130	2157	1.5	**White Lake** (charter township) Oakland County
47	802	0.7	**Riverview** (city) Wayne County	135	2290	1.6	**Alpine** (township) Kent County
47	802	0.7	**Trenton** (city) Wayne County	135	2290	1.6	**Birmingham** (city) Oakland County
62	970	0.8	**Beecher** (CDP) Genesee County	135	2290	1.6	**Flint** (charter township) Genesee County
62	970	0.8	**Clawson** (city) Oakland County	135	2290	1.6	**Ionia** (city) Ionia County
62	970	0.8	**Genesee** (charter township) Genesee County	135	2290	1.6	**Jenison** (CDP) Ottawa County
62	970	0.8	**Highland** (charter township) Oakland County	135	2290	1.6	**Kalamazoo** (charter township) Kalamazoo County
62	970	0.8	**Holland** (charter township) Ottawa County	135	2290	1.6	**Muskegon Heights** (city) Muskegon County
62	970	0.8	**Oakland** (charter township) Oakland County	135	2290	1.6	**Spring Lake** (township) Ottawa County
62	970	0.8	**Orion** (charter township) Oakland County	143	2427	1.7	**Milford** (charter township) Oakland County
62	970	0.8	**Rochester Hills** (city) Oakland County	143	2427	1.7	**Monitor** (charter township) Bay County
62	970	0.8	**Romulus** (city) Wayne County	143	2427	1.7	**Southfield** (city) Oakland County
62	970	0.8	**Southfield** (township) Oakland County	146	2537	1.8	**Blackman** (charter township) Jackson County
62	970	0.8	**Springfield** (charter township) Oakland County	146	2537	1.8	**Dearborn** (city) Wayne County
62	970	0.8	**Superior** (charter township) Washtenaw County	148	2663	1.9	**Grandville** (city) Kent County
62	970	0.8	**Troy** (city) Oakland County	148	2663	1.9	**Lenox** (township) Macomb County
62	970	0.8	**Waterford** (charter township) Oakland County	148	2663	1.9	**Pontiac** (city) Oakland County

Note: The state column ranks the top/bottom 150 places from all places in the state with population of 10,000 or more. The national column ranks the top/bottom 150 places from all places in the country with population of 10,000 or more. Places that are unincorporated were not considered in the rankings. Please refer to the User Guide for additional information.

Commute to Work: Work from Home

Top 150 Places Ranked in *Descending* Order

State Rank	Nat'l Rank	Percent	Place	State Rank	Nat'l Rank	Percent	Place
1	366	7.6	**Scio** (township) Washtenaw County	76	2137	3.7	**Auburn Hills** (city) Oakland County
2	387	7.5	**Grand Rapids** (charter township) Kent County	76	2137	3.7	**Grosse Pointe Woods** (city) Wayne County
3	404	7.4	**East Grand Rapids** (city) Kent County	76	2137	3.7	**Holland** (city) Ottawa County
3	404	7.4	**Southfield** (township) Oakland County	76	2137	3.7	**Lincoln** (charter township) Berrien County
5	426	7.3	**Bloomfield** (charter township) Oakland County	76	2137	3.7	**Milford** (charter township) Oakland County
6	515	6.9	**Hamburg** (township) Livingston County	76	2137	3.7	**Niles** (township) Berrien County
7	548	6.8	**Texas** (charter township) Kalamazoo County	76	2137	3.7	**Novi** (city) Oakland County
8	572	6.7	**Bath** (charter township) Clinton County	76	2137	3.7	**Plymouth** (charter township) Wayne County
9	600	6.6	**Cascade** (charter township) Kent County	76	2137	3.7	**Royal Oak** (city) Oakland County
10	623	6.5	**Birmingham** (city) Oakland County	76	2137	3.7	**Troy** (city) Oakland County
11	676	6.3	**Grand Haven** (charter township) Ottawa County	76	2137	3.7	**Wixom** (city) Oakland County
12	701	6.2	**Oakland** (charter township) Oakland County	87	2227	3.6	**Benton** (charter township) Berrien County
13	739	6.1	**Beverly Hills** (village) Oakland County	88	2321	3.5	**Big Rapids** (city) Mecosta County
14	769	6.0	**West Bloomfield** (charter township) Oakland County	88	2321	3.5	**Brandon** (charter township) Oakland County
15	845	5.8	**Tyrone** (township) Livingston County	88	2321	3.5	**Flint** (city) Genesee County
16	887	5.7	**Ann Arbor** (city) Washtenaw County	88	2321	3.5	**Fruitport** (charter township) Muskegon County
16	887	5.7	**Flushing** (charter township) Genesee County	88	2321	3.5	**Owosso** (city) Shiawassee County
16	887	5.7	**Plainfield** (charter township) Kent County	93	2433	3.4	**Bangor** (charter township) Bay County
16	887	5.7	**Saint Joseph** (charter township) Berrien County	93	2433	3.4	**Comstock Park** (CDP) Kent County
20	931	5.6	**East Lansing** (city) Ingham County	93	2433	3.4	**Thomas** (township) Saginaw County
21	967	5.5	**Brighton** (township) Livingston County	96	2522	3.3	**Grand Blanc** (charter township) Genesee County
21	967	5.5	**Forest Hills** (CDP) Kent County	96	2522	3.3	**Kalamazoo** (city) Kalamazoo County
23	1010	5.4	**Alpine** (township) Kent County	96	2522	3.3	**Macomb** (township) Macomb County
23	1010	5.4	**Lyon** (charter township) Oakland County	96	2522	3.3	**Norton Shores** (city) Muskegon County
25	1060	5.3	**Alpena** (city) Alpena County	96	2522	3.3	**Oshtemo** (charter township) Kalamazoo County
26	1109	5.2	**Farmington Hills** (city) Oakland County	96	2522	3.3	**Saginaw** (city) Saginaw County
26	1109	5.2	**Genoa** (township) Livingston County	102	2621	3.2	**Ferndale** (city) Oakland County
28	1163	5.1	**Cannon** (township) Kent County	102	2621	3.2	**Georgetown** (charter township) Ottawa County
28	1163	5.1	**Highland Park** (city) Wayne County	102	2621	3.2	**Mundy** (township) Genesee County
28	1163	5.1	**Northview** (CDP) Kent County	102	2621	3.2	**Port Huron** (city) Saint Clair County
31	1209	5.0	**Grosse Pointe Park** (city) Wayne County	102	2621	3.2	**Portage** (city) Kalamazoo County
31	1209	5.0	**Okemos** (CDP) Ingham County	102	2621	3.2	**Trenton** (city) Wayne County
33	1254	4.9	**Grand Rapids** (city) Kent County	108	2729	3.1	**Berkley** (city) Oakland County
33	1254	4.9	**Meridian** (charter township) Ingham County	108	2729	3.1	**Detroit** (city) Wayne County
33	1254	4.9	**Oceola** (township) Livingston County	108	2729	3.1	**Escanaba** (city) Delta County
36	1316	4.8	**Beecher** (CDP) Genesee County	108	2729	3.1	**Garfield** (charter township) Grand Traverse County
36	1316	4.8	**Commerce** (charter township) Oakland County	108	2729	3.1	**Monitor** (charter township) Bay County
36	1316	4.8	**Farmington** (city) Oakland County	108	2729	3.1	**Mount Morris** (township) Genesee County
36	1316	4.8	**Green Oak** (township) Livingston County	114	2821	3.0	**DeWitt** (charter township) Clinton County
36	1316	4.8	**Springfield** (charter township) Oakland County	114	2821	3.0	**Livonia** (city) Wayne County
36	1316	4.8	**Traverse City** (city) Grand Traverse County	114	2821	3.0	**Southfield** (city) Oakland County
42	1372	4.7	**Ada** (township) Kent County	114	2821	3.0	**Wyoming** (city) Kent County
42	1372	4.7	**Bedford** (township) Monroe County	118	2913	2.9	**Byron** (township) Kent County
42	1372	4.7	**Coldwater** (city) Branch County	118	2913	2.9	**Chesterfield** (township) Macomb County
42	1372	4.7	**Grosse Ile** (township) Wayne County	118	2913	2.9	**Fenton** (charter township) Genesee County
46	1429	4.6	**Midland** (city) Midland County	118	2913	2.9	**Flint** (charter township) Genesee County
46	1429	4.6	**Pittsfield** (charter township) Washtenaw County	118	2913	2.9	**Hartland** (township) Livingston County
46	1429	4.6	**Ypsilanti** (city) Washtenaw County	118	2913	2.9	**Huron** (charter township) Wayne County
49	1495	4.5	**Caledonia** (township) Kent County	118	2913	2.9	**Jackson** (city) Jackson County
49	1495	4.5	**Fenton** (city) Genesee County	118	2913	2.9	**Kentwood** (city) Kent County
49	1495	4.5	**Haslett** (CDP) Ingham County	118	2913	2.9	**Mount Pleasant** (city) Isabella County
49	1495	4.5	**Park** (township) Ottawa County	118	2913	2.9	**Oak Park** (city) Oakland County
49	1495	4.5	**Rochester** (city) Oakland County	118	2913	2.9	**Waverly** (CDP) Eaton County
49	1495	4.5	**Spring Lake** (township) Ottawa County	118	2913	2.9	**Ypsilanti** (charter township) Washtenaw County
49	1495	4.5	**Washington** (township) Macomb County	130	3026	2.8	**Emmett** (charter township) Calhoun County
56	1566	4.4	**Fort Gratiot** (charter township) Saint Clair County	130	3026	2.8	**Genesee** (charter township) Genesee County
56	1566	4.4	**Independence** (charter township) Oakland County	130	3026	2.8	**Muskegon** (charter township) Muskegon County
56	1566	4.4	**Marquette** (city) Marquette County	130	3026	2.8	**Oxford** (charter township) Oakland County
56	1566	4.4	**Orion** (charter township) Oakland County	130	3026	2.8	**South Lyon** (city) Oakland County
60	1650	4.3	**Highland** (charter township) Oakland County	130	3026	2.8	**Superior** (charter township) Washtenaw County
60	1650	4.3	**Muskegon Heights** (city) Muskegon County	136	3110	2.7	**Battle Creek** (city) Calhoun County
60	1650	4.3	**Rochester Hills** (city) Oakland County	136	3110	2.7	**Clawson** (city) Oakland County
60	1650	4.3	**Summit** (township) Jackson County	136	3110	2.7	**Grand Haven** (city) Ottawa County
64	1720	4.2	**Cadillac** (city) Wexford County	136	3110	2.7	**Lansing** (city) Ingham County
65	1790	4.1	**Canton** (charter township) Wayne County	140	3231	2.6	**Antwerp** (township) Van Buren County
65	1790	4.1	**Comstock** (charter township) Kalamazoo County	140	3231	2.6	**Davison** (township) Genesee County
65	1790	4.1	**East Bay** (township) Grand Traverse County	140	3231	2.6	**Delta** (charter township) Eaton County
65	1790	4.1	**Sault Sainte Marie** (city) Chippewa County	140	3231	2.6	**Harrison** (charter township) Macomb County
65	1790	4.1	**White Lake** (charter township) Oakland County	140	3231	2.6	**Lenox** (township) Macomb County
70	1884	4.0	**Delhi** (charter township) Ingham County	140	3231	2.6	**Shelby** (charter township) Macomb County
70	1884	4.0	**Holt** (CDP) Ingham County	146	3336	2.5	**Cutlerville** (CDP) Kent County
70	1884	4.0	**Madison Heights** (city) Oakland County	146	3336	2.5	**Dearborn** (city) Wayne County
73	2046	3.8	**Grandville** (city) Kent County	146	3336	2.5	**Hamtramck** (city) Wayne County
73	2046	3.8	**Muskegon** (city) Muskegon County	146	3336	2.5	**Kalamazoo** (charter township) Kalamazoo County
73	2046	3.8	**Northville** (township) Wayne County	146	3336	2.5	**Monroe** (charter township) Monroe County

Note: The state column ranks the top/bottom 150 places from all places in the state with population of 10,000 or more. The national column ranks the top/bottom 150 places from all places in the country with population of 10,000 or more. Places that are unincorporated were not considered in the rankings. Please refer to the User Guide for additional information.

Commute to Work: Work from Home

Top 150 Places Ranked in *Ascending* Order

State Rank	Nat'l Rank	Percent	Place	State Rank	Nat'l Rank	Percent	Place
1	5	0.2	**Riverview** (city) Wayne County	76	1631	2.9	**Byron** (township) Kent County
2	59	0.8	**Union** (charter township) Isabella County	76	1631	2.9	**Chesterfield** (township) Macomb County
3	86	0.9	**Allendale** (charter township) Ottawa County	76	1631	2.9	**Fenton** (charter township) Genesee County
3	86	0.9	**Inkster** (city) Wayne County	76	1631	2.9	**Flint** (charter township) Genesee County
5	110	1.0	**Allendale** (CDP) Ottawa County	76	1631	2.9	**Hartland** (township) Livingston County
5	110	1.0	**Port Huron** (charter township) Saint Clair County	76	1631	2.9	**Huron** (charter township) Wayne County
5	110	1.0	**Southgate** (city) Wayne County	76	1631	2.9	**Jackson** (city) Jackson County
8	180	1.2	**Taylor** (city) Wayne County	76	1631	2.9	**Kentwood** (city) Kent County
9	225	1.3	**Pontiac** (city) Oakland County	76	1631	2.9	**Mount Pleasant** (city) Isabella County
9	225	1.3	**Vienna** (charter township) Genesee County	76	1631	2.9	**Oak Park** (city) Oakland County
11	272	1.4	**Allen Park** (city) Wayne County	76	1631	2.9	**Waverly** (CDP) Eaton County
11	272	1.4	**Eastpointe** (city) Macomb County	76	1631	2.9	**Ypsilanti** (charter township) Washtenaw County
11	272	1.4	**Holly** (township) Oakland County	88	1744	3.0	**DeWitt** (charter township) Clinton County
14	327	1.5	**Melvindale** (city) Wayne County	88	1744	3.0	**Livonia** (city) Wayne County
14	327	1.5	**Van Buren** (charter township) Wayne County	88	1744	3.0	**Southfield** (city) Oakland County
14	327	1.5	**Woodhaven** (city) Wayne County	88	1744	3.0	**Wyoming** (city) Kent County
17	398	1.6	**Blackman** (charter township) Jackson County	92	1836	3.1	**Berkley** (city) Oakland County
17	398	1.6	**Bridgeport** (charter township) Saginaw County	92	1836	3.1	**Detroit** (city) Wayne County
17	398	1.6	**Cooper** (charter township) Kalamazoo County	92	1836	3.1	**Escanaba** (city) Delta County
17	398	1.6	**Leoni** (township) Jackson County	92	1836	3.1	**Garfield** (charter township) Grand Traverse County
21	467	1.7	**Lincoln Park** (city) Wayne County	92	1836	3.1	**Monitor** (charter township) Bay County
21	467	1.7	**Romulus** (city) Wayne County	92	1836	3.1	**Mount Morris** (township) Genesee County
21	467	1.7	**Wyandotte** (city) Wayne County	98	1928	3.2	**Ferndale** (city) Oakland County
24	539	1.8	**Fraser** (city) Macomb County	98	1928	3.2	**Georgetown** (charter township) Ottawa County
24	539	1.8	**Ionia** (city) Ionia County	98	1928	3.2	**Mundy** (township) Genesee County
24	539	1.8	**Sturgis** (city) Saint Joseph County	98	1928	3.2	**Port Huron** (city) Saint Clair County
27	634	1.9	**Benton Harbor** (city) Berrien County	98	1928	3.2	**Portage** (city) Kalamazoo County
27	634	1.9	**Holland** (charter township) Ottawa County	98	1928	3.2	**Trenton** (city) Wayne County
27	634	1.9	**Warren** (city) Macomb County	104	2036	3.3	**Grand Blanc** (charter township) Genesee County
27	634	1.9	**Wayne** (city) Wayne County	104	2036	3.3	**Kalamazoo** (city) Kalamazoo County
31	710	2.0	**Brownstown** (charter township) Wayne County	104	2036	3.3	**Macomb** (township) Macomb County
31	710	2.0	**New Baltimore** (city) Macomb County	104	2036	3.3	**Norton Shores** (city) Muskegon County
31	710	2.0	**Redford** (charter township) Wayne County	104	2036	3.3	**Oshtemo** (charter township) Kalamazoo County
31	710	2.0	**Saginaw** (charter township) Saginaw County	104	2036	3.3	**Saginaw** (city) Saginaw County
35	818	2.1	**Adrian** (city) Lenawee County	110	2135	3.4	**Bangor** (charter township) Bay County
35	818	2.1	**Garden City** (city) Wayne County	110	2135	3.4	**Comstock Park** (CDP) Kent County
35	818	2.1	**Hazel Park** (city) Oakland County	110	2135	3.4	**Thomas** (township) Saginaw County
38	905	2.2	**Dearborn Heights** (city) Wayne County	113	2224	3.5	**Big Rapids** (city) Mecosta County
38	905	2.2	**Monroe** (city) Monroe County	113	2224	3.5	**Brandon** (charter township) Oakland County
38	905	2.2	**Sterling Heights** (city) Macomb County	113	2224	3.5	**Flint** (city) Genesee County
38	905	2.2	**Walker** (city) Kent County	113	2224	3.5	**Fruitport** (charter township) Muskegon County
38	905	2.2	**Westland** (city) Wayne County	113	2224	3.5	**Owosso** (city) Shiawassee County
43	1012	2.3	**Bay City** (city) Bay County	118	2336	3.6	**Benton** (charter township) Berrien County
43	1012	2.3	**Clinton** (charter township) Macomb County	119	2430	3.7	**Auburn Hills** (city) Oakland County
43	1012	2.3	**Frenchtown** (township) Monroe County	119	2430	3.7	**Grosse Pointe Woods** (city) Wayne County
43	1012	2.3	**Gaines** (charter township) Kent County	119	2430	3.7	**Holland** (city) Ottawa County
43	1012	2.3	**Harper Woods** (city) Wayne County	119	2430	3.7	**Lincoln** (charter township) Berrien County
43	1012	2.3	**Jenison** (CDP) Ottawa County	119	2430	3.7	**Milford** (charter township) Oakland County
43	1012	2.3	**Roseville** (city) Macomb County	119	2430	3.7	**Niles** (township) Berrien County
50	1104	2.4	**Burton** (city) Genesee County	119	2430	3.7	**Novi** (city) Oakland County
50	1104	2.4	**Mount Clemens** (city) Macomb County	119	2430	3.7	**Plymouth** (charter township) Wayne County
50	1104	2.4	**Saint Clair Shores** (city) Macomb County	119	2430	3.7	**Royal Oak** (city) Oakland County
53	1206	2.5	**Cutlerville** (CDP) Kent County	119	2430	3.7	**Troy** (city) Oakland County
53	1206	2.5	**Dearborn** (city) Wayne County	119	2430	3.7	**Wixom** (city) Oakland County
53	1206	2.5	**Hamtramck** (city) Wayne County	130	2520	3.8	**Grandville** (city) Kent County
53	1206	2.5	**Kalamazoo** (charter township) Kalamazoo County	130	2520	3.8	**Muskegon** (city) Muskegon County
53	1206	2.5	**Monroe** (charter township) Monroe County	130	2520	3.8	**Northville** (township) Wayne County
53	1206	2.5	**Niles** (city) Berrien County	133	2705	4.0	**Delhi** (charter township) Ingham County
53	1206	2.5	**Waterford** (charter township) Oakland County	133	2705	4.0	**Holt** (CDP) Ingham County
60	1321	2.6	**Antwerp** (township) Van Buren County	133	2705	4.0	**Madison Heights** (city) Oakland County
60	1321	2.6	**Davison** (township) Genesee County	136	2773	4.1	**Canton** (charter township) Wayne County
60	1321	2.6	**Delta** (charter township) Eaton County	136	2773	4.1	**Comstock** (charter township) Kalamazoo County
60	1321	2.6	**Harrison** (charter township) Macomb County	136	2773	4.1	**East Bay** (township) Grand Traverse County
60	1321	2.6	**Lenox** (township) Macomb County	136	2773	4.1	**Sault Sainte Marie** (city) Chippewa County
60	1321	2.6	**Shelby** (charter township) Macomb County	136	2773	4.1	**White Lake** (charter township) Oakland County
66	1426	2.7	**Battle Creek** (city) Calhoun County	141	2867	4.2	**Cadillac** (city) Wexford County
66	1426	2.7	**Clawson** (city) Oakland County	142	2937	4.3	**Highland** (charter township) Oakland County
66	1426	2.7	**Grand Haven** (city) Ottawa County	142	2937	4.3	**Muskegon Heights** (city) Muskegon County
66	1426	2.7	**Lansing** (city) Ingham County	142	2937	4.3	**Rochester Hills** (city) Oakland County
70	1547	2.8	**Emmett** (charter township) Calhoun County	142	2937	4.3	**Summit** (township) Jackson County
70	1547	2.8	**Genesee** (charter township) Genesee County	146	3007	4.4	**Fort Gratiot** (charter township) Saint Clair County
70	1547	2.8	**Muskegon** (charter township) Muskegon County	146	3007	4.4	**Independence** (charter township) Oakland County
70	1547	2.8	**Oxford** (charter township) Oakland County	146	3007	4.4	**Marquette** (city) Marquette County
70	1547	2.8	**South Lyon** (city) Oakland County	146	3007	4.4	**Orion** (charter township) Oakland County
70	1547	2.8	**Superior** (charter township) Washtenaw County	150	3091	4.5	**Caledonia** (township) Kent County

Note: The state column ranks the top/bottom 150 places from all places in the state with population of 10,000 or more. The national column ranks the top/bottom 150 places from all places in the country with population of 10,000 or more. Places that are unincorporated were not considered in the rankings. Please refer to the User Guide for additional information.

Median Travel Time to Work

Top 150 Places Ranked in *Descending* Order

State Rank	Nat'l Rank	Minutes	Place
1	387	33.6	**White Lake** (charter township) Oakland County
2	449	33.0	**Oceola** (township) Livingston County
2	449	33.0	**Oxford** (charter township) Oakland County
4	459	32.9	**Highland** (charter township) Oakland County
5	489	32.7	**Brandon** (charter township) Oakland County
5	489	32.7	**Hamburg** (township) Livingston County
7	515	32.5	**Lenox** (township) Macomb County
8	542	32.3	**Hartland** (township) Livingston County
9	602	32.0	**Milford** (charter township) Oakland County
10	650	31.6	**Oakland** (charter township) Oakland County
11	670	31.5	**New Baltimore** (city) Macomb County
12	737	31.1	**Tyrone** (township) Livingston County
13	755	31.0	**Macomb** (township) Macomb County
14	812	30.7	**Springfield** (charter township) Oakland County
15	892	30.3	**Holly** (township) Oakland County
16	974	29.9	**Green Oak** (township) Livingston County
17	1018	29.7	**Brighton** (township) Livingston County
17	1018	29.7	**South Lyon** (city) Oakland County
19	1044	29.6	**Genesee** (charter township) Genesee County
19	1044	29.6	**Rochester** (city) Oakland County
21	1068	29.5	**Chesterfield** (township) Macomb County
22	1082	29.4	**Genoa** (township) Livingston County
23	1101	29.3	**Flushing** (charter township) Genesee County
23	1101	29.3	**Grosse Ile** (township) Wayne County
25	1152	29.1	**Commerce** (charter township) Oakland County
25	1152	29.1	**Lyon** (charter township) Oakland County
27	1211	28.8	**Harrison** (charter township) Macomb County
28	1279	28.5	**Fenton** (charter township) Genesee County
28	1279	28.5	**Independence** (charter township) Oakland County
30	1306	28.4	**Northville** (township) Wayne County
30	1306	28.4	**Orion** (charter township) Oakland County
30	1306	28.4	**Washington** (township) Macomb County
33	1399	28.0	**Highland Park** (city) Wayne County
34	1498	27.6	**Shelby** (charter township) Macomb County
35	1545	27.4	**Huron** (charter township) Wayne County
36	1559	27.3	**Waterford** (charter township) Oakland County
36	1559	27.3	**West Bloomfield** (charter township) Oakland County
38	1622	27.0	**Fenton** (city) Genesee County
39	1656	26.9	**Clinton** (charter township) Macomb County
40	1674	26.8	**Canton** (charter township) Wayne County
41	1696	26.7	**Superior** (charter township) Washtenaw County
42	1718	26.6	**Detroit** (city) Wayne County
42	1718	26.6	**Rochester Hills** (city) Oakland County
42	1718	26.6	**Saint Clair Shores** (city) Macomb County
45	1799	26.3	**Davison** (township) Genesee County
46	1851	26.1	**Brownstown** (charter township) Wayne County
46	1851	26.1	**Mundy** (township) Genesee County
46	1851	26.1	**Novi** (city) Oakland County
49	1939	25.8	**Hamtramck** (city) Wayne County
49	1939	25.8	**Harper Woods** (city) Wayne County
51	1966	25.7	**Cannon** (township) Kent County
51	1966	25.7	**Sterling Heights** (city) Macomb County
53	1997	25.6	**Fraser** (city) Macomb County
54	2037	25.4	**Van Buren** (charter township) Wayne County
55	2097	25.2	**Grand Blanc** (charter township) Genesee County
55	2097	25.2	**Wixom** (city) Oakland County
57	2124	25.1	**Grosse Pointe Park** (city) Wayne County
57	2124	25.1	**Plymouth** (charter township) Wayne County
57	2124	25.1	**Vienna** (charter township) Genesee County
60	2149	25.0	**Westland** (city) Wayne County
61	2187	24.9	**Troy** (city) Oakland County
62	2239	24.7	**Roseville** (city) Macomb County
63	2284	24.5	**Inkster** (city) Wayne County
63	2284	24.5	**Romulus** (city) Wayne County
65	2313	24.4	**Ionia** (city) Ionia County
66	2350	24.3	**Farmington** (city) Oakland County
66	2350	24.3	**Hazel Park** (city) Oakland County
66	2350	24.3	**Ypsilanti** (charter township) Washtenaw County
69	2386	24.2	**Grosse Pointe Woods** (city) Wayne County
69	2386	24.2	**Monroe** (charter township) Monroe County
69	2386	24.2	**Scio** (township) Washtenaw County
72	2445	24.0	**Auburn Hills** (city) Oakland County
72	2445	24.0	**Beecher** (CDP) Genesee County
72	2445	24.0	**Frenchtown** (township) Monroe County
72	2445	24.0	**Mount Morris** (township) Genesee County
72	2445	24.0	**Southfield** (city) Oakland County
72	2445	24.0	**Southgate** (city) Wayne County
78	2483	23.9	**Farmington Hills** (city) Oakland County
78	2483	23.9	**Livonia** (city) Wayne County
78	2483	23.9	**Trenton** (city) Wayne County
81	2510	23.8	**Warren** (city) Macomb County
82	2543	23.7	**Bedford** (township) Monroe County
83	2577	23.6	**Bloomfield** (charter township) Oakland County
83	2577	23.6	**Eastpointe** (city) Macomb County
83	2577	23.6	**Garden City** (city) Wayne County
83	2577	23.6	**Wayne** (city) Wayne County
87	2614	23.5	**Dearborn Heights** (city) Wayne County
87	2614	23.5	**Mount Clemens** (city) Macomb County
89	2641	23.4	**Beverly Hills** (village) Oakland County
90	2664	23.3	**Antwerp** (township) Van Buren County
91	2697	23.2	**Burton** (city) Genesee County
91	2697	23.2	**Niles** (township) Berrien County
91	2697	23.2	**Oak Park** (city) Oakland County
91	2697	23.2	**Pittsfield** (charter township) Washtenaw County
91	2697	23.2	**Riverview** (city) Wayne County
96	2725	23.1	**Royal Oak** (city) Oakland County
96	2725	23.1	**Woodhaven** (city) Wayne County
98	2741	23.0	**Lincoln Park** (city) Wayne County
98	2741	23.0	**Redford** (charter township) Wayne County
98	2741	23.0	**Southfield** (township) Oakland County
101	2760	22.9	**Caledonia** (township) Kent County
102	2818	22.7	**Clawson** (city) Oakland County
102	2818	22.7	**Leoni** (township) Jackson County
104	2845	22.6	**Grand Haven** (charter township) Ottawa County
105	2871	22.5	**Allen Park** (city) Wayne County
105	2871	22.5	**Ferndale** (city) Oakland County
105	2871	22.5	**Madison Heights** (city) Oakland County
105	2871	22.5	**Taylor** (city) Wayne County
105	2871	22.5	**Wyandotte** (city) Wayne County
110	2911	22.4	**Jenison** (CDP) Ottawa County
111	2943	22.3	**Allendale** (charter township) Ottawa County
112	2977	22.2	**Allendale** (CDP) Ottawa County
113	3005	22.1	**Grandville** (city) Kent County
114	3038	22.0	**Birmingham** (city) Oakland County
114	3038	22.0	**Flint** (charter township) Genesee County
116	3064	21.9	**Berkley** (city) Oakland County
117	3095	21.8	**Georgetown** (charter township) Ottawa County
118	3114	21.7	**Flint** (city) Genesee County
118	3114	21.7	**Fort Gratiot** (charter township) Saint Clair County
120	3142	21.6	**Byron** (township) Kent County
120	3142	21.6	**Cooper** (charter township) Kalamazoo County
120	3142	21.6	**Dearborn** (city) Wayne County
123	3200	21.4	**Owosso** (city) Shiawassee County
124	3222	21.3	**Bridgeport** (charter township) Saginaw County
124	3222	21.3	**Fruitport** (charter township) Muskegon County
124	3222	21.3	**Pontiac** (city) Oakland County
124	3222	21.3	**Spring Lake** (township) Ottawa County
128	3272	21.1	**Cutlerville** (CDP) Kent County
128	3272	21.1	**DeWitt** (charter township) Clinton County
128	3272	21.1	**Port Huron** (charter township) Saint Clair County
128	3272	21.1	**Summit** (township) Jackson County
132	3309	21.0	**Park** (township) Ottawa County
132	3309	21.0	**Texas** (charter township) Kalamazoo County
134	3334	20.9	**Oshtemo** (charter township) Kalamazoo County
134	3334	20.9	**Thomas** (township) Saginaw County
136	3359	20.8	**Monroe** (city) Monroe County
137	3410	20.6	**Delhi** (charter township) Ingham County
137	3410	20.6	**Monitor** (charter township) Bay County
139	3453	20.4	**Ada** (township) Kent County
140	3478	20.3	**Coldwater** (city) Branch County
140	3478	20.3	**Gaines** (charter township) Kent County
140	3478	20.3	**Niles** (city) Berrien County
140	3478	20.3	**Wyoming** (city) Kent County
140	3478	20.3	**Ypsilanti** (city) Washtenaw County
145	3506	20.2	**Bath** (charter township) Clinton County
145	3506	20.2	**Blackman** (charter township) Jackson County
145	3506	20.2	**Forest Hills** (CDP) Kent County
145	3506	20.2	**Haslett** (CDP) Ingham County
145	3506	20.2	**Holt** (CDP) Ingham County
150	3541	20.1	**Melvindale** (city) Wayne County

Note: The state column ranks the top/bottom 150 places from all places in the state with population of 10,000 or more. The national column ranks the top/bottom 150 places from all places in the country with population of 10,000 or more. Places that are unincorporated were not considered in the rankings. Please refer to the User Guide for additional information.

Median Travel Time to Work

Top 150 Places Ranked in *Ascending* Order

State Rank	Nat'l Rank	Minutes	Place
1	6	10.4	**Sault Sainte Marie** (city) Chippewa County
2	17	11.7	**Marquette** (city) Marquette County
3	43	12.8	**Alpena** (city) Alpena County
4	69	13.4	**Escanaba** (city) Delta County
5	77	13.6	**Benton Harbor** (city) Berrien County
6	84	13.7	**Union** (charter township) Isabella County
7	119	14.3	**Cadillac** (city) Wexford County
8	125	14.4	**Big Rapids** (city) Mecosta County
8	125	14.4	**Mount Pleasant** (city) Isabella County
10	185	15.0	**Traverse City** (city) Grand Traverse County
11	214	15.3	**East Lansing** (city) Ingham County
12	254	15.6	**Midland** (city) Midland County
13	306	16.0	**Saint Joseph** (charter township) Berrien County
14	372	16.5	**Adrian** (city) Lenawee County
15	455	17.0	**Holland** (city) Ottawa County
16	468	17.1	**Garfield** (charter township) Grand Traverse County
17	484	17.2	**Benton** (charter township) Berrien County
17	484	17.2	**Holland** (charter township) Ottawa County
19	551	17.6	**Grand Rapids** (charter township) Kent County
20	568	17.7	**East Grand Rapids** (city) Kent County
20	568	17.7	**Emmett** (charter township) Calhoun County
22	590	17.8	**Muskegon** (city) Muskegon County
23	611	17.9	**Muskegon Heights** (city) Muskegon County
24	630	18.0	**Kalamazoo** (city) Kalamazoo County
25	643	18.1	**Lincoln** (charter township) Berrien County
26	686	18.3	**Jackson** (city) Jackson County
27	701	18.4	**Bay City** (city) Bay County
27	701	18.4	**Northview** (CDP) Kent County
27	701	18.4	**Waverly** (CDP) Eaton County
30	781	18.8	**Battle Creek** (city) Calhoun County
30	781	18.8	**Kentwood** (city) Kent County
32	798	18.9	**Kalamazoo** (charter township) Kalamazoo County
32	798	18.9	**Port Huron** (city) Saint Clair County
32	798	18.9	**Saginaw** (charter township) Saginaw County
35	811	19.0	**Delta** (charter township) Eaton County
35	811	19.0	**Muskegon** (charter township) Muskegon County
37	833	19.1	**Comstock** (charter township) Kalamazoo County
37	833	19.1	**Grand Haven** (city) Ottawa County
37	833	19.1	**Lansing** (city) Ingham County
40	862	19.2	**Comstock Park** (CDP) Kent County
40	862	19.2	**Walker** (city) Kent County
42	883	19.3	**Norton Shores** (city) Muskegon County
42	883	19.3	**Sturgis** (city) Saint Joseph County
44	909	19.4	**Saginaw** (city) Saginaw County
45	937	19.5	**Ann Arbor** (city) Washtenaw County
45	937	19.5	**Grand Rapids** (city) Kent County
47	973	19.6	**Alpine** (township) Kent County
48	1019	19.8	**Bangor** (charter township) Bay County
48	1019	19.8	**Meridian** (charter township) Ingham County
50	1065	20.0	**Cascade** (charter township) Kent County
50	1065	20.0	**East Bay** (township) Grand Traverse County
50	1065	20.0	**Plainfield** (charter township) Kent County
50	1065	20.0	**Portage** (city) Kalamazoo County
54	1085	20.1	**Melvindale** (city) Wayne County
54	1085	20.1	**Okemos** (CDP) Ingham County
56	1116	20.2	**Bath** (charter township) Clinton County
56	1116	20.2	**Blackman** (charter township) Jackson County
56	1116	20.2	**Forest Hills** (CDP) Kent County
56	1116	20.2	**Haslett** (CDP) Ingham County
56	1116	20.2	**Holt** (CDP) Ingham County
61	1151	20.3	**Coldwater** (city) Branch County
61	1151	20.3	**Gaines** (charter township) Kent County
61	1151	20.3	**Niles** (city) Berrien County
61	1151	20.3	**Wyoming** (city) Kent County
61	1151	20.3	**Ypsilanti** (city) Washtenaw County
66	1179	20.4	**Ada** (township) Kent County
67	1223	20.6	**Delhi** (charter township) Ingham County
67	1223	20.6	**Monitor** (charter township) Bay County
69	1266	20.8	**Monroe** (city) Monroe County
70	1298	20.9	**Oshtemo** (charter township) Kalamazoo County
70	1298	20.9	**Thomas** (township) Saginaw County
72	1323	21.0	**Park** (township) Ottawa County
72	1323	21.0	**Texas** (charter township) Kalamazoo County
74	1348	21.1	**Cutlerville** (CDP) Kent County
74	1348	21.1	**DeWitt** (charter township) Clinton County
74	1348	21.1	**Port Huron** (charter township) Saint Clair County
74	1348	21.1	**Summit** (township) Jackson County
78	1406	21.3	**Bridgeport** (charter township) Saginaw County
78	1406	21.3	**Fruitport** (charter township) Muskegon County
78	1406	21.3	**Pontiac** (city) Oakland County
78	1406	21.3	**Spring Lake** (township) Ottawa County
82	1435	21.4	**Owosso** (city) Shiawassee County
83	1491	21.6	**Byron** (township) Kent County
83	1491	21.6	**Cooper** (charter township) Kalamazoo County
83	1491	21.6	**Dearborn** (city) Wayne County
86	1515	21.7	**Flint** (city) Genesee County
86	1515	21.7	**Fort Gratiot** (charter township) Saint Clair County
88	1543	21.8	**Georgetown** (charter township) Ottawa County
89	1562	21.9	**Berkley** (city) Oakland County
90	1593	22.0	**Birmingham** (city) Oakland County
90	1593	22.0	**Flint** (charter township) Genesee County
92	1619	22.1	**Grandville** (city) Kent County
93	1652	22.2	**Allendale** (CDP) Ottawa County
94	1680	22.3	**Allendale** (charter township) Ottawa County
95	1714	22.4	**Jenison** (CDP) Ottawa County
96	1746	22.5	**Allen Park** (city) Wayne County
96	1746	22.5	**Ferndale** (city) Oakland County
96	1746	22.5	**Madison Heights** (city) Oakland County
96	1746	22.5	**Taylor** (city) Wayne County
96	1746	22.5	**Wyandotte** (city) Wayne County
101	1786	22.6	**Grand Haven** (charter township) Ottawa County
102	1812	22.7	**Clawson** (city) Oakland County
102	1812	22.7	**Leoni** (township) Jackson County
104	1861	22.9	**Caledonia** (township) Kent County
105	1897	23.0	**Lincoln Park** (city) Wayne County
105	1897	23.0	**Redford** (charter township) Wayne County
105	1897	23.0	**Southfield** (township) Oakland County
108	1916	23.1	**Royal Oak** (city) Oakland County
108	1916	23.1	**Woodhaven** (city) Wayne County
110	1932	23.2	**Burton** (city) Genesee County
110	1932	23.2	**Niles** (township) Berrien County
110	1932	23.2	**Oak Park** (city) Oakland County
110	1932	23.2	**Pittsfield** (charter township) Washtenaw County
110	1932	23.2	**Riverview** (city) Wayne County
115	1960	23.3	**Antwerp** (township) Van Buren County
116	1993	23.4	**Beverly Hills** (village) Oakland County
117	2016	23.5	**Dearborn Heights** (city) Wayne County
117	2016	23.5	**Mount Clemens** (city) Macomb County
119	2043	23.6	**Bloomfield** (charter township) Oakland County
119	2043	23.6	**Eastpointe** (city) Macomb County
119	2043	23.6	**Garden City** (city) Wayne County
119	2043	23.6	**Wayne** (city) Wayne County
123	2080	23.7	**Bedford** (township) Monroe County
124	2114	23.8	**Warren** (city) Macomb County
125	2147	23.9	**Farmington Hills** (city) Oakland County
125	2147	23.9	**Livonia** (city) Wayne County
125	2147	23.9	**Trenton** (city) Wayne County
128	2174	24.0	**Auburn Hills** (city) Oakland County
128	2174	24.0	**Beecher** (CDP) Genesee County
128	2174	24.0	**Frenchtown** (township) Monroe County
128	2174	24.0	**Mount Morris** (township) Genesee County
128	2174	24.0	**Southfield** (city) Oakland County
128	2174	24.0	**Southgate** (city) Wayne County
134	2236	24.2	**Grosse Pointe Woods** (city) Wayne County
134	2236	24.2	**Monroe** (charter township) Monroe County
134	2236	24.2	**Scio** (township) Washtenaw County
137	2271	24.3	**Farmington** (city) Oakland County
137	2271	24.3	**Hazel Park** (city) Oakland County
137	2271	24.3	**Ypsilanti** (charter township) Washtenaw County
140	2307	24.4	**Ionia** (city) Ionia County
141	2344	24.5	**Inkster** (city) Wayne County
141	2344	24.5	**Romulus** (city) Wayne County
143	2392	24.7	**Roseville** (city) Macomb County
144	2448	24.9	**Troy** (city) Oakland County
145	2470	25.0	**Westland** (city) Wayne County
146	2508	25.1	**Grosse Pointe Park** (city) Wayne County
146	2508	25.1	**Plymouth** (charter township) Wayne County
146	2508	25.1	**Vienna** (charter township) Genesee County
149	2533	25.2	**Grand Blanc** (charter township) Genesee County
149	2533	25.2	**Wixom** (city) Oakland County

Note: The state column ranks the top/bottom 150 places from all places in the state with population of 10,000 or more. The national column ranks the top/bottom 150 places from all places in the country with population of 10,000 or more. Places that are unincorporated were not considered in the rankings. Please refer to the User Guide for additional information.

Violent Crime Rate per 10,000 Population

Top 150 Places Ranked in *Descending* Order

State Rank	Nat'l Rank	Rate	Place
1	4	224.1	**Benton Harbor** (city) Berrien County
2	9	207.2	**Detroit** (city) Wayne County
3	13	194.7	**Saginaw** (city) Saginaw County
4	16	191.3	**Muskegon Heights** (city) Muskegon County
5	17	190.8	**Flint** (city) Genesee County
6	24	166.2	**Hamtramck** (city) Wayne County
7	30	161.3	**Highland Park** (city) Wayne County
8	32	159.4	**Inkster** (city) Wayne County
9	84	121.4	**Harper Woods** (city) Wayne County
10	98	110.9	**Jackson** (city) Jackson County
11	102	107.8	**Flint** (charter township) Genesee County
12	105	107.7	**Benton** (charter township) Berrien County
13	110	105.7	**Lansing** (city) Ingham County
14	174	91.0	**Eastpointe** (city) Macomb County
15	182	88.7	**Muskegon** (city) Muskegon County
16	216	82.8	**Ypsilanti** (city) Washtenaw County
17	311	71.0	**Mount Morris** (township) Genesee County
18	318	70.2	**Wayne** (city) Wayne County
19	327	69.3	**Grand Rapids** (city) Kent County
20	396	63.1	**Bay City** (city) Bay County
21	409	62.2	**Lincoln Park** (city) Wayne County
22	439	60.6	**Oak Park** (city) Oakland County
22	439	60.6	**Port Huron** (city) Saint Clair County
24	462	58.8	**Romulus** (city) Wayne County
25	496	56.3	**Genesee** (charter township) Genesee County
26	497	56.1	**Taylor** (city) Wayne County
27	527	53.7	**Monroe** (city) Monroe County
28	576	51.4	**Redford** (charter township) Wayne County
29	590	50.6	**Warren** (city) Macomb County
30	655	47.1	**Niles** (city) Berrien County
31	678	46.4	**Emmett** (charter township) Calhoun County
32	686	46.1	**Roseville** (city) Macomb County
33	698	45.7	**Hazel Park** (city) Oakland County
34	725	44.9	**Cadillac** (city) Wexford County
35	731	44.7	**Alpena** (city) Alpena County
36	737	44.0	**Westland** (city) Wayne County
37	787	41.9	**Wyoming** (city) Kent County
38	799	41.1	**Holland** (city) Ottawa County
39	813	40.7	**Burton** (city) Genesee County
40	845	39.6	**Bridgeport** (charter township) Saginaw County
41	906	37.5	**Dearborn Heights** (city) Wayne County
42	914	37.3	**Owosso** (city) Shiawassee County
43	951	36.1	**Dearborn** (city) Wayne County
44	957	36.0	**Southfield** (city) Oakland County
45	1080	32.5	**Melvindale** (city) Wayne County
46	1199	29.5	**Garden City** (city) Wayne County
47	1220	29.1	**Clinton** (charter township) Macomb County
48	1231	28.9	**Southgate** (city) Wayne County
49	1246	28.6	**Meridian** (charter township) Ingham County
50	1263	28.2	**Kentwood** (city) Kent County
51	1266	28.1	**Auburn Hills** (city) Oakland County
52	1309	27.2	**Chesterfield** (township) Macomb County
53	1322	27.0	**Big Rapids** (city) Mecosta County
53	1322	27.0	**Grand Haven** (city) Ottawa County
55	1366	25.9	**Madison Heights** (city) Oakland County
56	1392	25.3	**Sault Sainte Marie** (city) Chippewa County
57	1441	24.3	**Huron** (charter township) Wayne County
58	1481	23.6	**Saginaw** (charter township) Saginaw County
59	1518	22.5	**East Lansing** (city) Ingham County
60	1526	22.3	**Van Buren** (charter township) Wayne County
61	1535	22.1	**Mount Pleasant** (city) Isabella County
61	1535	22.1	**Wyandotte** (city) Wayne County
63	1606	21.1	**Ann Arbor** (city) Washtenaw County
64	1620	20.9	**Ferndale** (city) Oakland County
65	1632	20.7	**Escanaba** (city) Delta County
66	1668	20.0	**Fraser** (city) Macomb County
67	1724	19.1	**Pittsfield** (charter township) Washtenaw County
67	1724	19.1	**Saint Joseph** (charter township) Berrien County
69	1753	18.7	**Sterling Heights** (city) Macomb County
70	1764	18.6	**Portage** (city) Kalamazoo County
71	1769	18.5	**Waterford** (charter township) Oakland County
72	1780	18.4	**Brownstown** (charter township) Wayne County
72	1780	18.4	**Ionia** (city) Ionia County
74	1855	17.1	**Grand Blanc** (charter township) Genesee County
75	1885	16.8	**Royal Oak** (city) Oakland County
76	1893	16.6	**Grandville** (city) Kent County
76	1893	16.6	**Walker** (city) Kent County
78	1924	16.2	**Bath** (charter township) Clinton County
79	1951	15.9	**Grosse Pointe Park** (city) Wayne County
80	1973	15.6	**Mundy** (township) Genesee County
81	1985	15.5	**Livonia** (city) Wayne County
81	1985	15.5	**Riverview** (city) Wayne County
83	2034	14.8	**Fenton** (city) Genesee County
84	2041	14.7	**South Lyon** (city) Oakland County
85	2050	14.6	**Wixom** (city) Oakland County
86	2096	14.1	**Davison** (township) Genesee County
87	2144	13.5	**Trenton** (city) Wayne County
88	2153	13.4	**Woodhaven** (city) Wayne County
89	2208	12.7	**Allen Park** (city) Wayne County
90	2232	12.4	**Farmington** (city) Oakland County
91	2240	12.3	**Lincoln** (charter township) Berrien County
92	2247	12.2	**Green Oak** (township) Livingston County
93	2259	12.1	**Grosse Pointe Woods** (city) Wayne County
94	2363	10.6	**Canton** (charter township) Wayne County
95	2509	8.9	**Farmington Hills** (city) Oakland County
96	2520	8.8	**Marquette** (city) Marquette County
97	2557	8.4	**Novi** (city) Oakland County
98	2568	8.3	**Clawson** (city) Oakland County
99	2606	7.9	**Berkley** (city) Oakland County
100	2646	7.6	**Thomas** (township) Saginaw County
101	2656	7.5	**Troy** (city) Oakland County
102	2669	7.4	**Milford** (charter township) Oakland County
102	2669	7.4	**New Baltimore** (city) Macomb County
104	2693	7.2	**White Lake** (charter township) Oakland County
105	2719	7.0	**Rochester** (city) Oakland County
106	2741	6.8	**Birmingham** (city) Oakland County
107	2770	6.6	**Plymouth** (charter township) Wayne County
108	2780	6.5	**West Bloomfield** (charter township) Oakland County
109	2798	6.3	**Northville** (township) Wayne County
110	2855	5.8	**Beverly Hills** (village) Oakland County
111	2888	5.5	**Bloomfield** (charter township) Oakland County
112	3040	3.9	**Grosse Ile** (township) Wayne County
113	3124	2.7	**East Grand Rapids** (city) Kent County
114	3159	2.3	**Hamburg** (township) Livingston County

Note: The state column ranks the top/bottom 150 places from all places in the state with population of 10,000 or more. The national column ranks the top/bottom 150 places from all places in the country with population of 10,000 or more. Places that are unincorporated were not considered in the rankings. Please refer to the User Guide for additional information.

Violent Crime Rate per 10,000 Population

Top 150 Places Ranked in *Ascending* Order

State Rank	Nat'l Rank	Rate	Place
1	107	2.3	**Hamburg** (township) Livingston County
2	143	2.7	**East Grand Rapids** (city) Kent County
3	220	3.9	**Grosse Ile** (township) Wayne County
4	373	5.5	**Bloomfield** (charter township) Oakland County
5	407	5.8	**Beverly Hills** (village) Oakland County
6	462	6.3	**Northville** (township) Wayne County
7	483	6.5	**West Bloomfield** (charter township) Oakland County
8	492	6.6	**Plymouth** (charter township) Wayne County
9	516	6.8	**Birmingham** (city) Oakland County
10	542	7.0	**Rochester** (city) Oakland County
11	564	7.2	**White Lake** (charter township) Oakland County
12	590	7.4	**Milford** (charter township) Oakland County
12	590	7.4	**New Baltimore** (city) Macomb County
14	603	7.5	**Troy** (city) Oakland County
15	616	7.6	**Thomas** (township) Saginaw County
16	651	7.9	**Berkley** (city) Oakland County
17	689	8.3	**Clawson** (city) Oakland County
18	704	8.4	**Novi** (city) Oakland County
19	743	8.8	**Marquette** (city) Marquette County
20	752	8.9	**Farmington Hills** (city) Oakland County
21	900	10.6	**Canton** (charter township) Wayne County
22	1003	12.1	**Grosse Pointe Woods** (city) Wayne County
23	1013	12.2	**Green Oak** (township) Livingston County
24	1025	12.3	**Lincoln** (charter township) Berrien County
25	1032	12.4	**Farmington** (city) Oakland County
26	1052	12.7	**Allen Park** (city) Wayne County
27	1113	13.4	**Woodhaven** (city) Wayne County
28	1119	13.5	**Trenton** (city) Wayne County
29	1162	14.1	**Davison** (township) Genesee County
30	1209	14.6	**Wixom** (city) Oakland County
31	1222	14.7	**South Lyon** (city) Oakland County
32	1231	14.8	**Fenton** (city) Genesee County
33	1280	15.5	**Livonia** (city) Wayne County
33	1280	15.5	**Riverview** (city) Wayne County
35	1287	15.6	**Mundy** (township) Genesee County
36	1315	15.9	**Grosse Pointe Park** (city) Wayne County
37	1337	16.2	**Bath** (charter township) Clinton County
38	1370	16.6	**Grandville** (city) Kent County
38	1370	16.6	**Walker** (city) Kent County
40	1384	16.8	**Royal Oak** (city) Oakland County
41	1404	17.1	**Grand Blanc** (charter township) Genesee County
42	1480	18.4	**Brownstown** (charter township) Wayne County
42	1480	18.4	**Ionia** (city) Ionia County
44	1492	18.5	**Waterford** (charter township) Oakland County
45	1503	18.6	**Portage** (city) Kalamazoo County
46	1508	18.7	**Sterling Heights** (city) Macomb County
47	1541	19.1	**Pittsfield** (charter township) Washtenaw County
47	1541	19.1	**Saint Joseph** (charter township) Berrien County
49	1593	20.0	**Fraser** (city) Macomb County
50	1629	20.7	**Escanaba** (city) Delta County
51	1648	20.9	**Ferndale** (city) Oakland County
52	1657	21.1	**Ann Arbor** (city) Washtenaw County
53	1730	22.1	**Mount Pleasant** (city) Isabella County
53	1730	22.1	**Wyandotte** (city) Wayne County
55	1741	22.3	**Van Buren** (charter township) Wayne County
56	1751	22.5	**East Lansing** (city) Ingham County
57	1789	23.6	**Saginaw** (charter township) Saginaw County
58	1828	24.3	**Huron** (charter township) Wayne County
59	1873	25.3	**Sault Sainte Marie** (city) Chippewa County
60	1899	25.9	**Madison Heights** (city) Oakland County
61	1944	27.0	**Big Rapids** (city) Mecosta County
61	1944	27.0	**Grand Haven** (city) Ottawa County
63	1954	27.2	**Chesterfield** (township) Macomb County
64	1999	28.1	**Auburn Hills** (city) Oakland County
65	2006	28.2	**Kentwood** (city) Kent County
66	2020	28.6	**Meridian** (charter township) Ingham County
67	2037	28.9	**Southgate** (city) Wayne County
68	2046	29.1	**Clinton** (charter township) Macomb County
69	2067	29.5	**Garden City** (city) Wayne County
70	2187	32.5	**Melvindale** (city) Wayne County
71	2310	36.0	**Southfield** (city) Oakland County
72	2315	36.1	**Dearborn** (city) Wayne County
73	2352	37.3	**Owosso** (city) Shiawassee County
74	2361	37.5	**Dearborn Heights** (city) Wayne County
75	2423	39.6	**Bridgeport** (charter township) Saginaw County
76	2453	40.7	**Burton** (city) Genesee County
77	2469	41.1	**Holland** (city) Ottawa County
78	2484	41.9	**Wyoming** (city) Kent County
79	2533	44.0	**Westland** (city) Wayne County
80	2538	44.7	**Alpena** (city) Alpena County
81	2545	44.9	**Cadillac** (city) Wexford County
82	2568	45.7	**Hazel Park** (city) Oakland County
83	2581	46.1	**Roseville** (city) Macomb County
84	2590	46.4	**Emmett** (charter township) Calhoun County
85	2612	47.1	**Niles** (city) Berrien County
86	2681	50.6	**Warren** (city) Macomb County
87	2693	51.4	**Redford** (charter township) Wayne County
88	2740	53.7	**Monroe** (city) Monroe County
89	2774	56.1	**Taylor** (city) Wayne County
90	2775	56.3	**Genesee** (charter township) Genesee County
91	2808	58.8	**Romulus** (city) Wayne County
92	2831	60.6	**Oak Park** (city) Oakland County
92	2831	60.6	**Port Huron** (city) Saint Clair County
94	2862	62.2	**Lincoln Park** (city) Wayne County
95	2873	63.1	**Bay City** (city) Bay County
96	2943	69.3	**Grand Rapids** (city) Kent County
97	2952	70.2	**Wayne** (city) Wayne County
98	2960	71.0	**Mount Morris** (township) Genesee County
99	3055	82.8	**Ypsilanti** (city) Washtenaw County
100	3088	88.7	**Muskegon** (city) Muskegon County
101	3097	91.0	**Eastpointe** (city) Macomb County
102	3161	105.7	**Lansing** (city) Ingham County
103	3166	107.7	**Benton** (charter township) Berrien County
104	3167	107.8	**Flint** (charter township) Genesee County
105	3173	110.9	**Jackson** (city) Jackson County
106	3187	121.4	**Harper Woods** (city) Wayne County
107	3237	159.4	**Inkster** (city) Wayne County
108	3241	161.3	**Highland Park** (city) Wayne County
109	3247	166.2	**Hamtramck** (city) Wayne County
110	3254	190.8	**Flint** (city) Genesee County
111	3255	191.3	**Muskegon Heights** (city) Muskegon County
112	3258	194.7	**Saginaw** (city) Saginaw County
113	3262	207.2	**Detroit** (city) Wayne County
114	3267	224.1	**Benton Harbor** (city) Berrien County

Note: The state column ranks the top/bottom 150 places from all places in the state with population of 10,000 or more. The national column ranks the top/bottom 150 places from all places in the country with population of 10,000 or more. Places that are unincorporated were not considered in the rankings. Please refer to the User Guide for additional information.

Property Crime Rate per 10,000 Population

Top 150 Places Ranked in *Descending* Order

State Rank	Nat'l Rank	Rate	Place
1	33	825.9	**Benton** (charter township) Berrien County
2	82	703.3	**Benton Harbor** (city) Berrien County
3	83	703.2	**Harper Woods** (city) Wayne County
4	115	656.6	**Muskegon Heights** (city) Muskegon County
5	146	629.9	**Flint** (charter township) Genesee County
6	202	583.5	**Detroit** (city) Wayne County
7	249	552.9	**Emmett** (charter township) Calhoun County
8	278	537.4	**Muskegon** (city) Muskegon County
9	317	518.9	**Jackson** (city) Jackson County
10	364	501.2	**Escanaba** (city) Delta County
11	375	497.8	**Highland Park** (city) Wayne County
12	507	458.2	**Grandville** (city) Kent County
13	617	426.9	**Mount Morris** (township) Genesee County
14	619	426.4	**Flint** (city) Genesee County
15	634	423.4	**Burton** (city) Genesee County
16	659	416.7	**Roseville** (city) Macomb County
17	662	416.1	**Inkster** (city) Wayne County
18	674	413.1	**Cadillac** (city) Wexford County
19	851	369.7	**Hamtramck** (city) Wayne County
20	905	360.1	**Lincoln Park** (city) Wayne County
21	906	359.9	**Eastpointe** (city) Macomb County
22	917	357.1	**Southgate** (city) Wayne County
23	951	350.1	**Auburn Hills** (city) Oakland County
24	959	348.7	**Monroe** (city) Monroe County
25	962	347.7	**Lansing** (city) Ingham County
26	992	341.0	**Ypsilanti** (city) Washtenaw County
27	1006	338.9	**Portage** (city) Kalamazoo County
28	1013	336.9	**Taylor** (city) Wayne County
29	1091	324.3	**Redford** (charter township) Wayne County
30	1097	323.6	**Grand Rapids** (city) Kent County
31	1099	323.3	**Dearborn** (city) Wayne County
32	1120	320.5	**Holland** (city) Ottawa County
33	1184	308.7	**Port Huron** (city) Saint Clair County
34	1265	297.2	**Romulus** (city) Wayne County
35	1276	295.0	**Saginaw** (city) Saginaw County
36	1287	293.1	**Melvindale** (city) Wayne County
37	1288	293.0	**Owosso** (city) Shiawassee County
38	1304	291.4	**Southfield** (city) Oakland County
39	1311	290.6	**Westland** (city) Wayne County
40	1333	287.1	**Fenton** (city) Genesee County
41	1337	286.6	**Madison Heights** (city) Oakland County
42	1376	280.7	**Walker** (city) Kent County
43	1389	279.5	**Sault Sainte Marie** (city) Chippewa County
44	1401	278.0	**Wayne** (city) Wayne County
45	1448	272.7	**Bay City** (city) Bay County
46	1450	272.2	**Oak Park** (city) Oakland County
47	1465	270.5	**Fraser** (city) Macomb County
48	1510	265.0	**Niles** (city) Berrien County
49	1536	262.0	**Hazel Park** (city) Oakland County
50	1542	261.5	**Warren** (city) Macomb County
51	1580	257.2	**Grand Haven** (city) Ottawa County
52	1618	252.5	**Alpena** (city) Alpena County
53	1694	242.5	**Kentwood** (city) Kent County
54	1718	239.8	**Allen Park** (city) Wayne County
55	1747	236.5	**Dearborn Heights** (city) Wayne County
56	1751	236.1	**Mundy** (township) Genesee County
57	1762	234.8	**Van Buren** (charter township) Wayne County
58	1799	230.3	**Ferndale** (city) Oakland County
59	1804	229.3	**Meridian** (charter township) Ingham County
60	1844	224.6	**Wyandotte** (city) Wayne County
61	1858	223.2	**Wyoming** (city) Kent County
62	1883	220.6	**Grosse Pointe Park** (city) Wayne County
63	1903	217.6	**Clinton** (charter township) Macomb County
64	1920	216.2	**Ann Arbor** (city) Washtenaw County
65	1950	213.9	**Saginaw** (charter township) Saginaw County
66	2024	205.9	**Livonia** (city) Wayne County
67	2048	204.0	**Davison** (township) Genesee County
68	2090	200.6	**Pittsfield** (charter township) Washtenaw County
69	2101	199.6	**Garden City** (city) Wayne County
70	2153	192.8	**Wixom** (city) Oakland County
71	2170	190.3	**Sterling Heights** (city) Macomb County
72	2208	187.6	**Troy** (city) Oakland County
73	2212	187.3	**Genesee** (charter township) Genesee County
74	2215	187.1	**Mount Pleasant** (city) Isabella County
75	2226	186.3	**Big Rapids** (city) Mecosta County
76	2235	185.7	**Bridgeport** (charter township) Saginaw County
77	2260	181.9	**Ionia** (city) Ionia County
78	2367	168.1	**Novi** (city) Oakland County
79	2389	165.8	**Chesterfield** (township) Macomb County
80	2392	165.5	**Grand Blanc** (charter township) Genesee County
81	2401	164.7	**East Lansing** (city) Ingham County
82	2448	158.6	**Waterford** (charter township) Oakland County
83	2531	148.7	**Marquette** (city) Marquette County
84	2563	144.6	**Woodhaven** (city) Wayne County
85	2568	143.7	**Saint Joseph** (charter township) Berrien County
86	2589	141.9	**White Lake** (charter township) Oakland County
87	2603	140.5	**Canton** (charter township) Wayne County
88	2609	140.1	**Thomas** (township) Saginaw County
89	2614	139.6	**Grosse Pointe Woods** (city) Wayne County
90	2627	137.9	**Brownstown** (charter township) Wayne County
91	2628	137.4	**Farmington Hills** (city) Oakland County
92	2642	134.7	**Trenton** (city) Wayne County
93	2644	134.5	**Royal Oak** (city) Oakland County
94	2683	130.1	**Huron** (charter township) Wayne County
95	2706	128.5	**Green Oak** (township) Livingston County
96	2716	126.7	**Northville** (township) Wayne County
97	2734	124.3	**East Grand Rapids** (city) Kent County
98	2744	123.3	**Bath** (charter township) Clinton County
99	2760	121.5	**Riverview** (city) Wayne County
100	2782	118.3	**Lincoln** (charter township) Berrien County
101	2798	116.4	**Beverly Hills** (village) Oakland County
102	2802	116.3	**Birmingham** (city) Oakland County
103	2855	109.4	**Farmington** (city) Oakland County
104	2857	109.3	**Plymouth** (charter township) Wayne County
105	2875	107.1	**West Bloomfield** (charter township) Oakland County
106	2902	104.1	**Bloomfield** (charter township) Oakland County
107	2961	97.5	**Berkley** (city) Oakland County
108	3055	84.2	**Rochester** (city) Oakland County
109	3058	84.0	**South Lyon** (city) Oakland County
110	3090	79.3	**Clawson** (city) Oakland County
111	3111	75.5	**Hamburg** (township) Livingston County
112	3196	56.0	**New Baltimore** (city) Macomb County
113	3198	55.7	**Milford** (charter township) Oakland County
114	3238	43.2	**Grosse Ile** (township) Wayne County

Note: The state column ranks the top/bottom 150 places from all places in the state with population of 10,000 or more. The national column ranks the top/bottom 150 places from all places in the country with population of 10,000 or more. Places that are unincorporated were not considered in the rankings. Please refer to the User Guide for additional information.

Property Crime Rate per 10,000 Population

Top 150 Places Ranked in *Ascending* Order

State Rank	Nat'l Rank	Rate	Place
1	32	43.2	**Grosse Ile** (township) Wayne County
2	72	55.7	**Milford** (charter township) Oakland County
3	74	56.0	**New Baltimore** (city) Macomb County
4	158	75.5	**Hamburg** (township) Livingston County
5	180	79.3	**Clawson** (city) Oakland County
6	210	84.0	**South Lyon** (city) Oakland County
7	214	84.2	**Rochester** (city) Oakland County
8	309	97.5	**Berkley** (city) Oakland County
9	367	104.1	**Bloomfield** (charter township) Oakland County
10	393	107.1	**West Bloomfield** (charter township) Oakland County
11	412	109.3	**Plymouth** (charter township) Wayne County
12	414	109.4	**Farmington** (city) Oakland County
13	467	116.3	**Birmingham** (city) Oakland County
14	469	116.4	**Beverly Hills** (village) Oakland County
15	485	118.3	**Lincoln** (charter township) Berrien County
16	510	121.5	**Riverview** (city) Wayne County
17	525	123.3	**Bath** (charter township) Clinton County
18	535	124.3	**East Grand Rapids** (city) Kent County
19	554	126.7	**Northville** (township) Wayne County
20	563	128.5	**Green Oak** (township) Livingston County
21	585	130.1	**Huron** (charter township) Wayne County
22	626	134.5	**Royal Oak** (city) Oakland County
23	628	134.7	**Trenton** (city) Wayne County
24	641	137.4	**Farmington Hills** (city) Oakland County
25	643	137.9	**Brownstown** (charter township) Wayne County
26	655	139.6	**Grosse Pointe Woods** (city) Wayne County
27	660	140.1	**Thomas** (township) Saginaw County
28	666	140.5	**Canton** (charter township) Wayne County
29	679	141.9	**White Lake** (charter township) Oakland County
30	701	143.7	**Saint Joseph** (charter township) Berrien County
31	707	144.6	**Woodhaven** (city) Wayne County
32	739	148.7	**Marquette** (city) Marquette County
33	821	158.6	**Waterford** (charter township) Oakland County
34	868	164.7	**East Lansing** (city) Ingham County
35	877	165.5	**Grand Blanc** (charter township) Genesee County
36	881	165.8	**Chesterfield** (township) Macomb County
37	901	168.1	**Novi** (city) Oakland County
38	1009	181.9	**Ionia** (city) Ionia County
39	1035	185.7	**Bridgeport** (charter township) Saginaw County
40	1042	186.3	**Big Rapids** (city) Mecosta County
41	1052	187.1	**Mount Pleasant** (city) Isabella County
42	1058	187.3	**Genesee** (charter township) Genesee County
43	1060	187.6	**Troy** (city) Oakland County
44	1099	190.3	**Sterling Heights** (city) Macomb County
45	1115	192.8	**Wixom** (city) Oakland County
46	1168	199.6	**Garden City** (city) Wayne County
47	1180	200.6	**Pittsfield** (charter township) Washtenaw County
48	1222	204.0	**Davison** (township) Genesee County
49	1244	205.9	**Livonia** (city) Wayne County
50	1319	213.9	**Saginaw** (charter township) Saginaw County
51	1349	216.2	**Ann Arbor** (city) Washtenaw County
52	1366	217.6	**Clinton** (charter township) Macomb County
53	1387	220.6	**Grosse Pointe Park** (city) Wayne County
54	1410	223.2	**Wyoming** (city) Kent County
55	1425	224.6	**Wyandotte** (city) Wayne County
56	1463	229.3	**Meridian** (charter township) Ingham County
57	1471	230.3	**Ferndale** (city) Oakland County
58	1508	234.8	**Van Buren** (charter township) Wayne County
59	1519	236.1	**Mundy** (township) Genesee County
60	1523	236.5	**Dearborn Heights** (city) Wayne County
61	1552	239.8	**Allen Park** (city) Wayne County
62	1575	242.5	**Kentwood** (city) Kent County
63	1650	252.5	**Alpena** (city) Alpena County
64	1688	257.2	**Grand Haven** (city) Ottawa County
65	1728	261.5	**Warren** (city) Macomb County
66	1733	262.0	**Hazel Park** (city) Oakland County
67	1758	265.0	**Niles** (city) Berrien County
68	1805	270.5	**Fraser** (city) Macomb County
69	1819	272.2	**Oak Park** (city) Oakland County
70	1822	272.7	**Bay City** (city) Bay County
71	1868	278.0	**Wayne** (city) Wayne County
72	1881	279.5	**Sault Sainte Marie** (city) Chippewa County
73	1892	280.7	**Walker** (city) Kent County
74	1933	286.6	**Madison Heights** (city) Oakland County
75	1937	287.1	**Fenton** (city) Genesee County
76	1959	290.6	**Westland** (city) Wayne County
77	1965	291.4	**Southfield** (city) Oakland County
78	1982	293.0	**Owosso** (city) Shiawassee County
79	1983	293.1	**Melvindale** (city) Wayne County
80	1994	295.0	**Saginaw** (city) Saginaw County
81	2005	297.2	**Romulus** (city) Wayne County
82	2084	308.7	**Port Huron** (city) Saint Clair County
83	2149	320.5	**Holland** (city) Ottawa County
84	2169	323.3	**Dearborn** (city) Wayne County
85	2173	323.6	**Grand Rapids** (city) Kent County
86	2178	324.3	**Redford** (charter township) Wayne County
87	2257	336.9	**Taylor** (city) Wayne County
88	2263	338.9	**Portage** (city) Kalamazoo County
89	2276	341.0	**Ypsilanti** (city) Washtenaw County
90	2308	347.7	**Lansing** (city) Ingham County
91	2311	348.7	**Monroe** (city) Monroe County
92	2319	350.1	**Auburn Hills** (city) Oakland County
93	2353	357.1	**Southgate** (city) Wayne County
94	2364	359.9	**Eastpointe** (city) Macomb County
95	2365	360.1	**Lincoln Park** (city) Wayne County
96	2419	369.7	**Hamtramck** (city) Wayne County
97	2596	413.1	**Cadillac** (city) Wexford County
98	2608	416.1	**Inkster** (city) Wayne County
99	2611	416.7	**Roseville** (city) Macomb County
100	2636	423.4	**Burton** (city) Genesee County
101	2651	426.4	**Flint** (city) Genesee County
102	2653	426.9	**Mount Morris** (township) Genesee County
103	2763	458.2	**Grandville** (city) Kent County
104	2894	497.8	**Highland Park** (city) Wayne County
105	2906	501.2	**Escanaba** (city) Delta County
106	2953	518.9	**Jackson** (city) Jackson County
107	2992	537.4	**Muskegon** (city) Muskegon County
108	3021	552.9	**Emmett** (charter township) Calhoun County
109	3068	583.5	**Detroit** (city) Wayne County
110	3123	629.9	**Flint** (charter township) Genesee County
111	3155	656.6	**Muskegon Heights** (city) Muskegon County
112	3187	703.2	**Harper Woods** (city) Wayne County
113	3188	703.3	**Benton Harbor** (city) Berrien County
114	3237	825.9	**Benton** (charter township) Berrien County

Note: *The state column ranks the top/bottom 150 places from all places in the state with population of 10,000 or more. The national column ranks the top/bottom 150 places from all places in the country with population of 10,000 or more. Places that are unincorporated were not considered in the rankings. Please refer to the User Guide for additional information.*

Education

Michigan Public School Educational Profile

Category	Value	Category	Value
Schools (2011-2012)	3,565	**Diploma Recipients** (2009-2010)	110,682
Instructional Level		White, Non-Hispanic	83,188
Primary	1,773	Black, Non-Hispanic	19,278
Middle	573	Asian/Pacific Islander, Non-Hispanic	2,808
High	865	American Indian/Alaskan Native, Non-Hispanic	891
Other/Not Reported	354	Hawaiian Native/Pacific Islander, Non-Hispanic	n/a
Curriculum		Two or More Races, Non-Hispanic	n/a
Regular	3,081	Hispanic of Any Race	3,721
Special Education	197	**Staff** (2011-2012)	
Vocational	9	Teachers (FTE)	86,819.1
Alternative	278	Salary[1] ($)	61,866
Type		Librarians/Media Specialists (FTE)	631.5
Magnet	436	Guidance Counselors (FTE)	2,197.1
Charter	310	**Ratios** (2011-2012)	
Title I Eligible	2,775	Number of Students per Teacher	18.0 to 1
School-wide Title I	1,739	Number of Students per Librarian	2,476.4 to 1
Students (2011-2012)	1,563,827	Number of Students per Guidance Counselor	711.8 to 1
Gender (%)		**Finances** (2010-2011)	
Male	51.5	Current Expenditures ($ per student)	
Female	48.5	Total	10,577
Race/Ethnicity (%)		Instruction	6,095
White, Non-Hispanic	69.2	Support Services	4,118
Black, Non-Hispanic	18.8	Other	364
Asian, Non-Hispanic	2.7	General Revenue ($ per student)	
American Indian/Alaskan Native, Non-Hisp.	0.8	Total	12,266
Hawaiian Native/Pacific Islander, Non-Hisp.	0.1	From Federal Sources	1,705
Two or More Races, Non-Hispanic	2.2	From State Sources	6,753
Hispanic of Any Race	6.2	From Local Sources	3,808
Special Programs (%)		Long-Term Debt Outstanding ($ per student)	
Individual Education Program (IEP)	13.3	At Beginning of Fiscal Year	9,574
English Language Learner (ELL)	3.8	Issued During Fiscal Year	929
Eligible for Free Lunch Program	42.4	Retired During Fiscal Year	696
Eligible for Reduced-Price Lunch Program	5.5	At End of Fiscal Year	9,912
Average Freshman Grad. Rate (%) (2009-2010)	75.9	**College Entrance Exam Scores**	
White, Non-Hispanic	81.5	SAT Reasoning Test™ (2013)	
Black, Non-Hispanic	59.2	Participation Rate (%)	4
Asian/Pacific Islander, Non-Hispanic	92.6	Mean Critical Reading Score	590
American Indian/Alaskan Native, Non-Hispanic	62.7	Mean Math Score	610
Hispanic of Any Race	62.9	Mean Writing Score	582
High School Drop-out Rate (%) (2009-2010)	4.3	ACT (2013)	
White, Non-Hispanic	2.7	Participation Rate (%)	100
Black, Non-Hispanic	9.2	Mean Composite Score	19.9
Asian/Pacific Islander, Non-Hispanic	3.1	Mean English Score	19.1
American Indian/Alaskan Native, Non-Hispanic	5.4	Mean Math Score	19.9
Hawaiian Native/Pacific Islander, Non-Hispanic	n/a	Mean Reading Score	20.0
Two or More Races, Non-Hispanic	n/a	Mean Science Score	20.2
Hispanic of Any Race	6.2		

Note: For an explanation of data, please refer to the User's Guide in the front of the book; (1) Average salary for classroom teachers in 2013-14

Number of Schools

Rank	Number	District Name	City
1	132	Detroit City SD	Detroit
2	64	Grand Rapids Public Schools	Grand Rapids
3	38	Utica Community Schools	Sterling Hgts
4	33	Dearborn City SD	Dearborn
5	32	Ann Arbor Public Schools	Ann Arbor
6	31	Lansing Public SD	Lansing
7	26	Livonia Public Schools SD	Livonia
8	25	Kalamazoo Public Schools	Kalamazoo
8	25	Plymouth-Canton Comm Schools	Plymouth
8	25	Warren Consolidated Schools	Warren
11	24	Flint SD	Flint
12	23	Saginaw SD	Saginaw
13	22	Rochester Community SD	Rochester
13	22	Walled Lake Consolidated Schools	Walled Lake
15	21	Waterford SD	Waterford
16	20	Chippewa Valley Schools	Clinton Twp
16	20	L'anse Creuse Public Schools	Harrison Twp
16	20	Traverse City Area Public Schools	Traverse City
16	20	Troy SD	Troy
16	20	Wayne-Westland Community SD	Westland
21	19	Farmington Public SD	Farmington
22	17	Forest Hills Public Schools	Grand Rapids
22	17	Kentwood Public Schools	Grand Rapids
22	17	Port Huron Area SD	Port Huron
25	15	Bay City SD	Bay City
25	15	Huron Valley Schools	Highland
27	14	Grosse Pointe Public Schools	Grosse Pointe
27	14	Niles Community Schools	Niles
27	14	Portage Public Schools	Portage
27	14	Rockford Public Schools	Rockford
27	14	Taylor SD	Taylor
27	14	Zeeland Public Schools	Zeeland
33	13	Battle Creek Public Schools	Battle Creek
33	13	Grand Blanc Community Schools	Grand Blanc
33	13	SD of the City of Birmingham	Birmingham
33	13	Southfield Public SD	Southfield
33	13	West Ottawa Public SD	Holland
38	12	Clarkston Community SD	Clarkston
38	12	Grand Haven Area Public Schools	Grand Haven
38	12	Holt Public Schools	Holt
38	12	Lake Orion Community Schools	Lake Orion
38	12	Lapeer Community Schools	Lapeer
38	12	Midland Public Schools	Midland
38	12	Muskegon Public Schools	Muskegon
38	12	Northville Public Schools	Northville
38	12	Southgate Community SD	Southgate
47	11	Anchor Bay SD	Casco
47	11	Bloomfield Hls SD	Bloomfield Hls
47	11	Caledonia Community Schools	Caledonia
47	11	Clintondale Community Schools	Clinton Twp
47	11	Hazel Park SD	Hazel Park
47	11	Hudsonville Public SD	Hudsonville
47	11	Jackson Public Schools	Jackson
47	11	Oxford Community Schools	Oxford
47	11	South Lyon Community Schools	South Lyon
47	11	West Bloomfield SD	West Bloomfield
57	10	East China SD	East China
57	10	Howell Public Schools	Howell
57	10	Mt. Pleasant City SD	Mount Pleasant
57	10	Pontiac City SD	Pontiac
57	10	Roseville Community Schools	Roseville
57	10	Woodhaven-Brownstown SD	Woodhaven
63	9	Alpena Public Schools	Alpena
63	9	Benton Harbor Area Schools	Benton Harbor
63	9	Davison Community Schools	Davison
63	9	Grandville Public Schools	Grandville
63	9	Jenison Public Schools	Jenison
63	9	Lincoln Park SD	Lincoln Park
63	9	Monroe Public Schools	Monroe
63	9	Novi Community SD	Novi
63	9	SD of the City of Royal Oak	Royal Oak
63	9	Van Buren Public Schools	Belleville
63	9	Wyandotte SD	Wyandotte
63	9	Wyoming Public Schools	Wyoming
75	8	Adrian SD	Adrian
75	8	Berkley SD	Oak Park
75	8	Brighton Area Schools	Brighton
75	8	Cadillac Area Public Schools	Cadillac
75	8	Cedar Springs Public Schools	Cedar Springs
75	8	East Lansing SD	East Lansing
75	8	Fraser Public Schools	Fraser
75	8	Garden City SD	Garden City
75	8	Grand Ledge Public Schools	Grand Ledge
75	8	Hartland Consolidated Schools	Hartland
75	8	Ionia Public Schools	Ionia
75	8	Lincoln Consolidated SD	Ypsilanti
75	8	Macomb ISD	Clinton Twp
75	8	Reeths-Puffer Schools	Muskegon
75	8	Romeo Community Schools	Romeo
75	8	Romulus Community Schools	Romulus
75	8	Saginaw Township Comm. Schools	Saginaw
75	8	Saint Johns Public Schools	Saint Johns
75	8	SD of Ypsilanti	Ypsilanti
75	8	Swartz Creek Community Schools	Swartz Creek
75	8	Warren Woods Public Schools	Warren
96	7	Allegan Public Schools	Allegan
96	7	Avondale SD	Auburn Hills
96	7	Bendle Public Schools	Burton
96	7	Benzie County Central Schools	Benzonia
96	7	Brandon SD	Ortonville
96	7	Carman-Ainsworth Comm. Schools	Flint
96	7	Chippewa Hills SD	Remus
96	7	Coldwater Community Schools	Coldwater
96	7	Dearborn Hgts SD #7	Dearborn Hgts
96	7	Dowagiac Union SD	Dowagiac
96	7	East Detroit Public Schools	Eastpointe
96	7	Eaton Rapids Public Schools	Eaton Rapids
96	7	Ferndale Public Schools	Ferndale
96	7	Flushing Community Schools	Flushing
96	7	Fruitport Community Schools	Fruitport
96	7	Gibraltar SD	Woodhaven
96	7	Gull Lake Community Schools	Richland
96	7	Hamilton Community Schools	Hamilton
96	7	Hamtramck SD	Hamtramck
96	7	Holland City SD	Holland
96	7	Holly Area SD	Holly
96	7	Lamphere Public Schools	Madison Heights
96	7	Lowell Area Schools	Lowell
96	7	Marquette Area Public Schools	Marquette
96	7	Northview Public Schools	Grand Rapids
96	7	Oak Park SD	Oak Park
96	7	Okemos Public Schools	Okemos
96	7	Pinckney Community Schools	Pinckney
96	7	Public Schools of Petoskey	Petoskey
96	7	Saline Area Schools	Saline
96	7	Shelby Public Schools	Shelby
96	7	Sturgis Public Schools	Sturgis
96	7	Tecumseh Public Schools	Tecumseh
96	7	Three Rivers Community Schools	Three Rivers
96	7	Van Dyke Public Schools	Warren
96	7	Westwood Community SD	Dearborn Hgts
132	6	Airport Community Schools	Carleton
132	6	Allen Park Public Schools	Allen Park
132	6	Alma Public Schools	Alma
132	6	Bedford Public Schools	Temperance
132	6	Byron Center Public Schools	Byron Center
132	6	Center Line Public Schools	Center Line
132	6	Charlotte Public Schools	Charlotte
132	6	Clio Area SD	Clio
132	6	Coloma Community Schools	Coloma
132	6	Comstock Public Schools	Kalamazoo
132	6	Crestwood SD	Dearborn Hgts
132	6	Croswell-Lexington Comm. Schools	Croswell
132	6	Dewitt Public Schools	Dewitt
132	6	Dexter Community SD	Dexter
132	6	Escanaba Area Public Schools	Escanaba
132	6	Fenton Area Public Schools	Fenton
132	6	Fitzgerald Public Schools	Warren
132	6	Fremont Public SD	Fremont
132	6	Gaylord Community Schools	Gaylord
132	6	Greenville Public Schools	Greenville
132	6	Hastings Area SD	Hastings
132	6	Kalkaska Public Schools	Kalkaska
132	6	Kelloggsville Public Schools	Grand Rapids
132	6	Kenowa Hills Public Schools	Grand Rapids
132	6	Lake Shore Public Schls (Macomb)	St Clair Shores
132	6	Lakeview Public Schools (Macomb)	St Clair Shores
132	6	Lakeview SD (Calhoun)	Battle Creek
132	6	Lakeville Community SD	Otisville
132	6	Lakewood Public Schools	Woodland
132	6	Ludington Area SD	Ludington
132	6	Manistee Area Public Schools	Manistee
132	6	Marshall Public Schools	Marshall
132	6	Mona Shores Public SD	Muskegon
132	6	Mt. Morris Consolidated Schools	Mount Morris
132	6	Oakridge Public Schools	Muskegon
132	6	Otsego Public Schools	Otsego
132	6	Owosso Public Schools	Owosso
132	6	Parchment SD	Kalamazoo
132	6	Plainwell Community Schools	Plainwell
132	6	Redford Union Schools Dist. No. 1	Redford
132	6	Sault Ste Marie Area Schools	Sault Ste Marie
132	6	South Redford SD	Redford
132	6	Spring Lake Public Schools	Spring Lake
132	6	Thornapple Kellogg SD	Middleville
132	6	Waverly Community Schools	Lansing
132	6	Wayland Union Schools	Wayland
132	6	West Branch-Rose City Area Schls	Rose City
132	6	Western SD	Parma
132	6	Whitehall District Schools	Whitehall
132	6	Yale Public Schools	Yale
182	5	Algonac Community SD	Algonac
182	5	Allendale Public Schools	Allendale
182	5	Armada Area Schools	Armada
182	5	Bangor Township Schools	Bay City
182	5	Beecher Community SD	Flint
182	5	Belding Area SD	Belding
182	5	Berrien Springs Public Schools	Berrien Springs
182	5	Big Rapids Public Schools	Big Rapids
182	5	Bullock Creek SD	Midland
182	5	Caro Community Schools	Caro
182	5	Central Montcalm Public Schools	Stanton
182	5	Cheboygan Area Schools	Cheboygan
182	5	Comstock Park Public Schools	Comstock Park
182	5	Coopersville Area Public SD	Coopersville
182	5	Corunna Public Schools	Corunna
182	5	E Grand Rapids Public Schools	Grand Rapids
182	5	Edwardsburg Public Schools	Edwardsburg
182	5	Essexville-Hampton Public Schools	Essexville
182	5	Fowlerville Community Schools	Fowlerville
182	5	Gladwin Community Schools	Gladwin
182	5	Godfrey-Lee Public Schools	Wyoming
182	5	Godwin Heights Public Schools	Grand Rapids
182	5	Grant Public SD	Grant
182	5	Harper Creek Community Schools	Battle Creek
182	5	Harrison Community Schools	Harrison
182	5	Haslett Public Schools	Haslett
182	5	Hillsdale Community Schools	Hillsdale
182	5	Houghton Lake Community Schools	Houghton Lake
182	5	Imlay City Community Schools	Imlay City
182	5	Jefferson Schools (Monroe)	Monroe
182	5	Kearsley Community SD	Flint
182	5	Lakeshore SD (Berrien)	Stevensville
182	5	Linden Community Schools	Linden
182	5	Marysville Public Schools	Marysville
182	5	Mason Public Schools (Ingham)	Mason
182	5	Menominee Area Public Schools	Menominee
182	5	Mount Clemens Community SD	Mount Clemens
182	5	Muskegon Hgts SD	Muskegon
182	5	Newaygo Public SD	Newaygo
182	5	North Branch Area Schools	North Branch
182	5	Northwest Community Schools	Jackson
182	5	Ovid-Elsie Area Schools	Elsie
182	5	Paw Paw Public SD	Paw Paw
182	5	Pennfield Schools	Battle Creek
182	5	Perry Public Schools	Perry
182	5	Riverview Community SD	Riverview
182	5	Saginaw ISD	Saginaw
182	5	Saint Joseph Public Schools	Saint Joseph
182	5	Shepherd Public Schools	Shepherd
182	5	South Haven Public Schools	South Haven
182	5	South Lake Schools	St Clair Shores
182	5	Sparta Area Schools	Sparta
182	5	Stockbridge Community Schools	Stockbridge
182	5	Swan Valley SD	Saginaw
182	5	Vicksburg Community Schools	Vicksburg
237	4	Birch Run Area Schools	Birch Run
237	4	Buchanan Community Schools	Buchanan
237	4	Carrollton Public Schools	Saginaw
237	4	Cesar Chavez Academy	Detroit
237	4	Chelsea SD	Chelsea
237	4	Clare Public Schools	Clare
237	4	Clarenceville SD	Livonia
237	4	Clawson Public Schools	Clawson
237	4	Columbia SD	Brooklyn
237	4	Crawford Ausable Schools	Grayling
237	4	Delton Kellogg Schools	Delton
237	4	Dundee Community Schools	Dundee
237	4	Durand Area Schools	Durand
237	4	Flat Rock Community Schools	Flat Rock
237	4	Gladstone Area Schools	Gladstone
237	4	Goodrich Area Schools	Goodrich

Note: This section only includes districts with 1,500 or more students; All categories are ranked from high to low

237	4	Grosse Ile Township Schools	Grosse Ile
237	4	Hopkins Public Schools	Hopkins
237	4	Huron SD	New Boston
237	4	Lake Fenton Community Schools	Fenton
237	4	Mattawan Consolidated School	Mattawan
237	4	Melvindale-North Allen Park Schools	Melvindale
237	4	Milan Area Schools	Milan
237	4	Napoleon Community Schools	Napoleon
237	4	Orchard View Schools	Muskegon
237	4	Portland Public Schools	Portland
237	4	SD of the City of Inkster	Inkster
237	4	Standish-Sterling Community Schls	Standish
237	4	Trenton Public Schools	Trenton
237	4	Tri County Area Schools	Sand Lake
237	4	University Preparatory Acad. (PSAD)	Detroit
237	4	Williamston Community Schools	Williamston
237	4	Willow Run Community Schools	Ypsilanti
270	3	Almont Community Schools	Almont
270	3	Breitung Township SD	Kingsford
270	3	Chandler Park Academy	Harper Woods
270	3	Chesaning Union Schools	Chesaning
270	3	Freeland Community SD	Freeland
270	3	Old Redford Academy	Detroit
270	3	Olivet Community Schools	Olivet
270	3	Onsted Community Schools	Onsted
270	3	Reed City Area Public Schools	Reed City
270	3	Richmond Community Schools	Richmond
270	3	Summit Academy North	Romulus
281	1	Kent ISD	Grand Rapids
281	1	Wayne Resa	Wayne

Number of Teachers

Rank	Number	District Name	City
1	4,204.0	Detroit City SD	Detroit
2	1,330.9	Utica Community Schools	Sterling Hgts
3	1,161.0	Grand Rapids Public Schools	Grand Rapids
4	1,127.6	Dearborn City SD	Dearborn
5	966.7	Ann Arbor Public Schools	Ann Arbor
6	931.7	Plymouth-Canton Comm Schools	Plymouth
7	823.4	Livonia Public Schools SD	Livonia
8	817.5	Rochester Community SD	Rochester
9	783.7	Chippewa Valley Schools	Clinton Twp
10	781.1	Walled Lake Consolidated Schools	Walled Lake
11	780.0	Warren Consolidated Schools	Warren
12	759.7	Kalamazoo Public Schools	Kalamazoo
13	740.6	Lansing Public SD	Lansing
14	698.3	Flint SD	Flint
15	680.8	Wayne-Westland Community SD	Westland
16	680.1	Troy SD	Troy
17	674.3	Farmington Public SD	Farmington
18	633.7	Waterford SD	Waterford
19	592.4	L'anse Creuse Public Schools	Harrison Twp
20	563.4	Forest Hills Public Schools	Grand Rapids
21	552.4	Port Huron Area SD	Port Huron
22	522.2	Huron Valley Schools	Highland
23	520.4	Grosse Pointe Public Schools	Grosse Pointe
24	514.9	SD of the City of Birmingham	Birmingham
25	503.1	Traverse City Area Public Schools	Traverse City
26	501.3	Saginaw SD	Saginaw
27	462.1	Taylor SD	Taylor
28	444.0	Southfield Public SD	Southfield
29	443.9	Kentwood Public Schools	Grand Rapids
30	440.7	Portage Public Schools	Portage
31	440.6	Grand Blanc Community Schools	Grand Blanc
32	427.9	Midland Public Schools	Midland
33	421.1	Rockford Public Schools	Rockford
34	411.4	Bay City SD	Bay City
35	410.2	Howell Public Schools	Howell
36	410.1	Lake Orion Community Schools	Lake Orion
37	410.0	Bloomfield Hls SD	Bloomfield Hls
38	397.6	Clarkston Community SD	Clarkston
39	393.0	West Ottawa Public SD	Holland
40	368.0	Northville Public Schools	Northville
41	363.1	Novi Community SD	Novi
42	360.6	West Bloomfield SD	West Bloomfield
43	359.1	Jackson Public Schools	Jackson
44	353.5	Pontiac City SD	Pontiac
45	350.6	South Lyon Community Schools	South Lyon
46	348.6	Battle Creek Public Schools	Battle Creek
47	328.3	Grand Haven Area Public Schools	Grand Haven
48	317.7	Hudsonville Public SD	Hudsonville
49	314.2	Holt Public Schools	Holt
50	309.3	Lapeer Community Schools	Lapeer
51	308.0	Garden City SD	Garden City
52	306.8	Brighton Area Schools	Brighton
53	296.0	Monroe Public Schools	Monroe
54	288.9	Anchor Bay SD	Casco
55	286.2	Muskegon Public Schools	Muskegon
56	284.2	Zeeland Public Schools	Zeeland
57	283.3	Grandville Public Schools	Grandville
58	276.0	Southgate Community SD	Southgate
59	275.7	SD of the City of Royal Oak	Royal Oak
60	275.5	Fraser Public Schools	Fraser
61	275.0	Hartland Consolidated Schools	Hartland
62	272.9	Romeo Community Schools	Romeo
63	270.2	Roseville Community Schools	Roseville
64	269.0	Woodhaven-Brownstown SD	Woodhaven
65	263.4	Carman-Ainsworth Comm. Schools	Flint
66	262.8	Grand Ledge Public Schools	Grand Ledge
67	261.3	Saline Area Schools	Saline
68	259.5	Van Buren Public Schools	Belleville
69	258.8	Wyandotte SD	Wyandotte
70	258.4	Davison Community Schools	Davison
71	257.3	Saginaw Township Comm. Schools	Saginaw
72	252.0	Hazel Park SD	Hazel Park
73	250.4	Lincoln Park SD	Lincoln Park
74	248.1	Berkley SD	Oak Park
75	247.6	Lincoln Consolidated SD	Ypsilanti
76	241.0	Jenison Public Schools	Jenison
77	239.6	Wyoming Public Schools	Wyoming
78	239.1	Oxford Community Schools	Oxford
79	238.4	East China SD	East China
80	236.4	SD of Ypsilanti	Ypsilanti
81	235.1	Bedford Public Schools	Temperance
82	222.4	Mt. Pleasant City SD	Mount Pleasant
83	221.8	Caledonia Community Schools	Caledonia
84	220.0	Okemos Public Schools	Okemos
85	217.1	Holland City SD	Holland
86	215.0	Lakeview SD (Calhoun)	Battle Creek
86	215.0	Pinckney Community Schools	Pinckney
88	211.3	Niles Community Schools	Niles
89	209.5	Adrian SD	Adrian
90	207.5	Macomb ISD	Clinton Twp
91	206.0	Swartz Creek Community Schools	Swartz Creek
92	203.7	Flushing Community Schools	Flushing
93	203.4	Reeths-Puffer Schools	Muskegon
94	201.4	Alpena Public Schools	Alpena
95	200.0	Holly Area SD	Holly
96	199.9	Avondale SD	Auburn Hills
97	199.5	Mona Shores Public SD	Muskegon
98	197.3	Warren Woods Public Schools	Warren
99	196.6	Ferndale Public Schools	Ferndale
100	194.4	Dexter Community SD	Dexter
101	194.0	East Detroit Public Schools	Eastpointe
102	192.8	East Lansing SD	East Lansing
103	191.9	Greenville Public Schools	Greenville
104	188.1	Lowell Area Schools	Lowell
105	187.1	Redford Union Schools Dist. No. 1	Redford
106	187.0	Oak Park SD	Oak Park
107	185.5	Lakeview Public Schools (Macomb)	St Clair Shores
108	183.8	Mattawan Consolidated School	Mattawan
109	182.5	Romulus Community Schools	Romulus
110	182.2	Northview Public Schools	Grand Rapids
111	178.9	Lake Shore Public Schls (Macomb)	St Clair Shores
112	178.8	Allen Park Public Schools	Allen Park
112	178.8	Benton Harbor Area Schools	Benton Harbor
114	178.6	Gibraltar SD	Woodhaven
115	176.8	Fenton Area Public Schools	Fenton
116	174.1	Fruitport Community Schools	Fruitport
117	172.5	Sturgis Public Schools	Sturgis
118	171.3	Cedar Springs Public Schools	Cedar Springs
119	170.9	Owosso Public Schools	Owosso
120	169.7	Kenowa Hills Public Schools	Grand Rapids
121	169.3	Clio Area SD	Clio
122	169.2	Crestwood SD	Dearborn Hgts
123	168.2	Marquette Area Public Schools	Marquette
124	166.8	Van Dyke Public Schools	Warren
125	166.0	Saint Johns Public Schools	Saint Johns
126	165.7	Brandon SD	Ortonville
127	163.2	Lamphere Public Schools	Madison Heights
127	163.2	South Redford SD	Redford
129	162.6	Cadillac Area Public Schools	Cadillac
129	162.6	Mason Public Schools (Ingham)	Mason
131	158.9	Gull Lake Community Schools	Richland
132	158.7	Byron Center Public Schools	Byron Center
133	158.5	Hamtramck SD	Hamtramck
134	157.4	Harper Creek Community Schools	Battle Creek
135	155.8	Saginaw ISD	Saginaw
136	155.4	E Grand Rapids Public Schools	Grand Rapids
137	154.0	Gaylord Community Schools	Gaylord
138	153.9	Ionia Public Schools	Ionia
139	153.8	Fitzgerald Public Schools	Warren
139	153.8	Tecumseh Public Schools	Tecumseh
141	153.1	Trenton Public Schools	Trenton
142	152.8	Waverly Community Schools	Lansing
143	151.7	Three Rivers Community Schools	Three Rivers
144	151.5	Lakeshore SD (Berrien)	Stevensville
145	151.4	Dewitt Public Schools	Dewitt
146	151.2	Fowlerville Community Schools	Fowlerville
147	149.2	Public Schools of Petoskey	Petoskey
148	147.9	Clintondale Community Schools	Clinton Twp
149	147.3	Charlotte Public Schools	Charlotte
149	147.3	Western SD	Parma
151	146.1	Sparta Area Schools	Sparta
152	145.4	Kearsley Community SD	Flint
153	145.1	Wayland Union Schools	Wayland
154	144.2	Plainwell Community Schools	Plainwell
155	143.5	Coldwater Community Schools	Coldwater
156	143.4	Hastings Area SD	Hastings
157	142.4	Northwest Community Schools	Jackson
158	142.0	Thornapple Kellogg SD	Middleville
159	141.1	Eaton Rapids Public Schools	Eaton Rapids
160	140.9	Saint Joseph Public Schools	Saint Joseph
161	140.1	Center Line Public Schools	Center Line
162	140.0	Dearborn Hgts SD #7	Dearborn Hgts
162	140.0	Linden Community Schools	Linden
164	138.5	Haslett Public Schools	Haslett
165	138.2	Chelsea SD	Chelsea
166	138.1	Hamilton Community Schools	Hamilton
167	137.3	Milan Area Schools	Milan
168	137.1	Allegan Public Schools	Allegan
169	136.7	Airport Community Schools	Carleton
170	136.3	Marshall Public Schools	Marshall
171	132.1	Sault Ste Marie Area Schools	Sault Ste Marie
172	131.2	Marysville Public Schools	Marysville
173	130.5	University Preparatory Acad. (PSAD)	Detroit
174	129.3	South Haven Public Schools	South Haven
175	128.6	Alma Public Schools	Alma
176	128.3	Corunna Public Schools	Corunna
177	127.7	Comstock Park Public Schools	Comstock Park
177	127.7	Westwood Community SD	Dearborn Hgts
179	127.6	Mt. Morris Consolidated Schools	Mount Morris
179	127.6	Riverview Community SD	Riverview
181	127.1	Vicksburg Community Schools	Vicksburg
182	126.7	Huron SD	New Boston
183	126.4	Edwardsburg Public Schools	Edwardsburg
184	124.6	Dowagiac Union SD	Dowagiac
185	124.5	SD of the City of Inkster	Inkster
186	123.5	Orchard View Schools	Muskegon
187	123.0	Otsego Public Schools	Otsego
188	122.5	Spring Lake Public Schools	Spring Lake
189	120.4	Cesar Chavez Academy	Detroit
190	120.3	North Branch Area Schools	North Branch
191	120.1	Kelloggsville Public Schools	Grand Rapids
192	120.0	Escanaba Area Public Schools	Escanaba
193	119.7	Croswell-Lexington Comm. Schools	Croswell
194	119.2	Comstock Public Schools	Kalamazoo
194	119.2	West Branch-Rose City Area Schls	Rose City
196	118.5	Coopersville Area Public SD	Coopersville
197	118.4	Bangor Township Schools	Bay City
198	117.5	Paw Paw Public SD	Paw Paw
199	117.1	Melvindale-North Allen Park Schools	Melvindale
200	117.0	Clawson Public Schools	Clawson
201	116.0	Old Redford Academy	Detroit
202	115.5	Tri County Area Schools	Sand Lake
202	115.5	Whitehall District Schools	Whitehall
204	115.1	Chippewa Hills SD	Remus
204	115.1	Ludington Area SD	Ludington
206	115.0	Godwin Heights Public Schools	Grand Rapids
206	115.0	Jefferson Schools (Monroe)	Monroe
208	114.8	Allendale Public Schools	Allendale
209	113.8	Berrien Springs Public Schools	Berrien Springs
210	113.1	South Lake Schools	St Clair Shores
211	112.9	Belding Area SD	Belding
212	111.7	Fremont Public SD	Fremont
213	110.7	Carrollton Public Schools	Saginaw
214	109.0	Chandler Park Academy	Harper Woods
215	108.5	Coloma Community Schools	Coloma
216	106.2	Pennfield Schools	Battle Creek
217	104.5	Lakewood Public Schools	Woodland
218	104.1	Portland Public Schools	Portland
219	103.0	Cheboygan Area Schools	Cheboygan
220	102.3	Williamston Community Schools	Williamston

Note: This section only includes districts with 1,500 or more students; All categories are ranked from high to low

221	102.2	Yale Public Schools	Yale
222	102.0	Crawford Ausable Schools	Grayling
223	101.0	Goodrich Area Schools	Goodrich
224	100.8	Armada Area Schools	Armada
225	100.5	Godfrey-Lee Public Schools	Wyoming
225	100.5	Mount Clemens Community SD	Mount Clemens
227	100.0	Willow Run Community Schools	Ypsilanti
228	99.8	Bullock Creek SD	Midland
229	99.1	Menominee Area Public Schools	Menominee
230	99.0	Grant Public SD	Grant
231	98.9	Flat Rock Community Schools	Flat Rock
232	98.4	Shepherd Public Schools	Shepherd
233	97.9	Imlay City Community Schools	Imlay City
234	97.8	Kent ISD	Grand Rapids
235	97.0	Algonac Community SD	Algonac
236	96.5	Muskegon Hgts SD	Muskegon
236	96.5	Oakridge Public Schools	Muskegon
238	96.1	Clarenceville SD	Livonia
239	96.0	Caro Community Schools	Caro
240	95.6	Gladwin Community Schools	Gladwin
241	95.5	Parchment SD	Kalamazoo
242	95.2	Newaygo Public SD	Newaygo
243	92.3	Freeland Community SD	Freeland
244	91.9	Central Montcalm Public Schools	Stanton
245	91.7	Birch Run Area Schools	Birch Run
246	90.9	Houghton Lake Community Schools	Houghton Lake
247	90.7	Grosse Ile Township Schools	Grosse Ile
247	90.7	Swan Valley SD	Saginaw
249	88.7	Olivet Community Schools	Olivet
250	87.9	Kalkaska Public Schools	Kalkaska
251	87.2	Ovid-Elsie Area Schools	Elsie
252	86.7	Essexville-Hampton Public Schools	Essexville
253	86.1	Lake Fenton Community Schools	Fenton
254	86.0	Reed City Area Public Schools	Reed City
255	85.3	Lakeville Community SD	Otisville
256	85.0	Beecher Community SD	Flint
256	85.0	Perry Public Schools	Perry
258	84.9	Big Rapids Public Schools	Big Rapids
259	84.4	Buchanan Community Schools	Buchanan
259	84.4	Chesaning Union Schools	Chesaning
261	83.6	Stockbridge Community Schools	Stockbridge
262	83.4	Benzie County Central Schools	Benzonia
263	83.0	Durand Area Schools	Durand
264	81.9	Shelby Public Schools	Shelby
265	81.7	Breitung Township SD	Kingsford
266	81.0	Standish-Sterling Community Schls	Standish
267	79.3	Bendle Public Schools	Burton
268	78.9	Clare Public Schools	Clare
268	78.9	Dundee Community Schools	Dundee
270	78.5	Hopkins Public Schools	Hopkins
271	78.3	Napoleon Community Schools	Napoleon
272	77.9	Hillsdale Community Schools	Hillsdale
273	77.6	Delton Kellogg Schools	Delton
274	77.5	Almont Community Schools	Almont
275	77.2	Richmond Community Schools	Richmond
276	76.7	Columbia SD	Brooklyn
277	75.8	Summit Academy North	Romulus
278	75.6	Onsted Community Schools	Onsted
279	74.9	Manistee Area Public Schools	Manistee
280	74.0	Gladstone Area Schools	Gladstone
281	73.6	Harrison Community Schools	Harrison
282	0.0	Wayne Resa	Wayne

Number of Students

Rank	Number	District Name	City
1	67,064	Detroit City SD	Detroit
2	28,606	Utica Community Schools	Sterling Hgts
3	18,736	Dearborn City SD	Dearborn
4	18,426	Plymouth-Canton Comm Schools	Plymouth
5	17,606	Grand Rapids Public Schools	Grand Rapids
6	16,635	Ann Arbor Public Schools	Ann Arbor
7	16,178	Chippewa Valley Schools	Clinton Twp
8	15,467	Walled Lake Consolidated Schools	Walled Lake
9	15,426	Livonia Public Schools SD	Livonia
10	15,414	Warren Consolidated Schools	Warren
11	14,922	Rochester Community SD	Rochester
12	12,957	Lansing Public SD	Lansing
13	12,414	Kalamazoo Public Schools	Kalamazoo
14	12,413	Wayne-Westland Community SD	Westland
15	12,262	Troy SD	Troy
16	11,786	L'anse Creuse Public Schools	Harrison Twp
17	11,288	Farmington Public SD	Farmington
18	10,889	Waterford SD	Waterford
19	10,114	Flint SD	Flint
20	10,112	Forest Hills Public Schools	Grand Rapids
21	9,969	Huron Valley Schools	Highland
22	9,807	Port Huron Area SD	Port Huron
23	9,793	Traverse City Area Public Schools	Traverse City
24	8,761	Kentwood Public Schools	Grand Rapids
25	8,691	Grand Blanc Community Schools	Grand Blanc
26	8,639	Portage Public Schools	Portage
27	8,463	Bay City SD	Bay City
28	8,399	Grosse Pointe Public Schools	Grosse Pointe
29	8,274	SD of the City of Birmingham	Birmingham
30	8,117	Midland Public Schools	Midland
31	8,056	Clarkston Community SD	Clarkston
32	8,001	Howell Public Schools	Howell
33	7,951	Saginaw SD	Saginaw
34	7,880	Rockford Public Schools	Rockford
35	7,765	Lake Orion Community Schools	Lake Orion
36	7,640	Southfield Public SD	Southfield
37	7,400	Taylor SD	Taylor
38	7,340	West Ottawa Public SD	Holland
39	7,172	Northville Public Schools	Northville
40	7,040	South Lyon Community Schools	South Lyon
41	6,504	West Bloomfield SD	West Bloomfield
42	6,268	Anchor Bay SD	Casco
43	6,242	Novi Community SD	Novi
44	6,158	Monroe Public Schools	Monroe
45	6,086	Brighton Area Schools	Brighton
46	6,048	Hudsonville Public SD	Hudsonville
47	6,019	Lapeer Community Schools	Lapeer
48	5,985	Jackson Public Schools	Jackson
49	5,882	Grand Haven Area Public Schools	Grand Haven
50	5,844	Holt Public Schools	Holt
51	5,757	Zeeland Public Schools	Zeeland
52	5,690	Grandville Public Schools	Grandville
53	5,558	Hartland Consolidated Schools	Hartland
54	5,502	Davison Community Schools	Davison
55	5,491	Pontiac City SD	Pontiac
56	5,463	Bloomfield Hls SD	Bloomfield Hls
57	5,425	Romeo Community Schools	Romeo
58	5,393	Southgate Community SD	Southgate
59	5,358	Battle Creek Public Schools	Battle Creek
60	5,282	Van Buren Public Schools	Belleville
61	5,243	Fraser Public Schools	Fraser
62	5,239	Roseville Community Schools	Roseville
63	5,235	Saline Area Schools	Saline
64	5,170	SD of the City of Royal Oak	Royal Oak
65	5,115	Grand Ledge Public Schools	Grand Ledge
66	5,062	Saginaw Township Comm. Schools	Saginaw
67	4,941	Muskegon Public Schools	Muskegon
68	4,914	Woodhaven-Brownstown SD	Woodhaven
69	4,866	Oxford Community Schools	Oxford
70	4,793	Garden City SD	Garden City
71	4,781	Bedford Public Schools	Temperance
72	4,735	Lincoln Park SD	Lincoln Park
73	4,698	East China SD	East China
74	4,639	Berkley SD	Oak Park
75	4,628	Jenison Public Schools	Jenison
76	4,621	Carman-Ainsworth Comm. Schools	Flint
76	4,621	Wyoming Public Schools	Wyoming
78	4,604	Hazel Park SD	Hazel Park
79	4,540	Lincoln Consolidated SD	Ypsilanti
80	4,486	Wyandotte SD	Wyandotte
81	4,212	Flushing Community Schools	Flushing
82	4,167	Oak Park SD	Oak Park
83	4,166	Caledonia Community Schools	Caledonia
84	4,128	Pinckney Community Schools	Pinckney
85	4,094	Wayne Resa	Wayne
86	4,053	Holland City SD	Holland
87	4,033	Alpena Public Schools	Alpena
88	3,937	Swartz Creek Community Schools	Swartz Creek
89	3,884	Lakeview SD (Calhoun)	Battle Creek
90	3,877	Okemos Public Schools	Okemos
91	3,863	Niles Community Schools	Niles
92	3,813	Reeths-Puffer Schools	Muskegon
93	3,795	Greenville Public Schools	Greenville
94	3,794	Lowell Area Schools	Lowell
95	3,788	Ferndale Public Schools	Ferndale
96	3,772	Mona Shores Public SD	Muskegon
97	3,770	Clintondale Community Schools	Clinton Twp
97	3,770	Lakeview Public Schools (Macomb)	St Clair Shores
99	3,755	Mattawan Consolidated School	Mattawan
100	3,752	Allen Park Public Schools	Allen Park
101	3,746	Gibraltar SD	Woodhaven
102	3,674	East Detroit Public Schools	Eastpointe
103	3,635	SD of Ypsilanti	Ypsilanti
104	3,612	Clio Area SD	Clio
105	3,578	Dexter Community SD	Dexter
106	3,571	Avondale SD	Auburn Hills
107	3,551	Lake Shore Public Schls (Macomb)	St Clair Shores
108	3,528	Holly Area SD	Holly
109	3,511	Fenton Area Public Schools	Fenton
110	3,497	Mt. Pleasant City SD	Mount Pleasant
111	3,483	Byron Center Public Schools	Byron Center
112	3,456	Northview Public Schools	Grand Rapids
113	3,411	East Lansing SD	East Lansing
114	3,402	Warren Woods Public Schools	Warren
115	3,395	Cedar Springs Public Schools	Cedar Springs
116	3,391	Crestwood SD	Dearborn Hgts
117	3,330	Owosso Public Schools	Owosso
118	3,319	Romulus Community Schools	Romulus
119	3,318	Kenowa Hills Public Schools	Grand Rapids
120	3,264	Brandon SD	Ortonville
121	3,263	Sturgis Public Schools	Sturgis
122	3,259	South Redford SD	Redford
123	3,181	Saint Johns Public Schools	Saint Johns
124	3,153	Adrian SD	Adrian
125	3,137	Benton Harbor Area Schools	Benton Harbor
126	3,135	Fruitport Community Schools	Fruitport
127	3,129	Kearsley Community SD	Flint
128	3,114	Ionia Public Schools	Ionia
129	3,084	Gaylord Community Schools	Gaylord
130	3,081	Van Dyke Public Schools	Warren
131	3,048	Thornapple Kellogg SD	Middleville
132	3,029	Cadillac Area Public Schools	Cadillac
133	3,024	Marquette Area Public Schools	Marquette
134	2,993	Mason Public Schools (Ingham)	Mason
135	2,979	Dewitt Public Schools	Dewitt
136	2,976	E Grand Rapids Public Schools	Grand Rapids
136	2,976	Fowlerville Community Schools	Fowlerville
138	2,959	Redford Union Schools Dist. No. 1	Redford
139	2,945	Linden Community Schools	Linden
140	2,943	Hamtramck SD	Hamtramck
141	2,940	Tecumseh Public Schools	Tecumseh
142	2,936	Coldwater Community Schools	Coldwater
143	2,927	Public Schools of Petoskey	Petoskey
144	2,920	Lakeshore SD (Berrien)	Stevensville
145	2,913	Gull Lake Community Schools	Richland
146	2,898	Dearborn Hgts SD #7	Dearborn Hgts
147	2,894	Western SD	Parma
148	2,865	Fitzgerald Public Schools	Warren
149	2,860	Sparta Area Schools	Sparta
150	2,837	Northwest Community Schools	Jackson
151	2,834	Hastings Area SD	Hastings
152	2,827	Orchard View Schools	Muskegon
153	2,820	Melvindale-North Allen Park Schools	Melvindale
154	2,809	Riverview Community SD	Riverview
154	2,809	Waverly Community Schools	Lansing
156	2,802	Wayland Union Schools	Wayland
157	2,780	Lamphere Public Schools	Madison Heights
158	2,775	Saint Joseph Public Schools	Saint Joseph
159	2,737	Westwood Community SD	Dearborn Hgts
160	2,736	Center Line Public Schools	Center Line
161	2,706	Haslett Public Schools	Haslett
162	2,703	Plainwell Community Schools	Plainwell
163	2,702	Edwardsburg Public Schools	Edwardsburg
164	2,688	Allegan Public Schools	Allegan
165	2,685	Three Rivers Community Schools	Three Rivers
166	2,679	Charlotte Public Schools	Charlotte
167	2,639	Hamilton Community Schools	Hamilton
168	2,635	Marysville Public Schools	Marysville
169	2,631	SD of the City of Inkster	Inkster
170	2,626	Airport Community Schools	Carleton
171	2,613	Eaton Rapids Public Schools	Eaton Rapids
172	2,611	Trenton Public Schools	Trenton
173	2,585	Milan Area Schools	Milan
174	2,555	Escanaba Area Public Schools	Escanaba
175	2,520	Harper Creek Community Schools	Battle Creek
176	2,519	Vicksburg Community Schools	Vicksburg
177	2,515	Bangor Township Schools	Bay City
178	2,501	Sault Ste Marie Area Schools	Sault Ste Marie
179	2,492	Chelsea SD	Chelsea
180	2,490	Mt. Morris Consolidated Schools	Mount Morris
181	2,488	Coopersville Area Public SD	Coopersville
182	2,452	Spring Lake Public Schools	Spring Lake
183	2,431	North Branch Area Schools	North Branch
184	2,398	Dowagiac Union SD	Dowagiac
185	2,396	Huron SD	New Boston
186	2,390	Chandler Park Academy	Harper Woods
187	2,369	Allendale Public Schools	Allendale
188	2,357	Whitehall District Schools	Whitehall

Note: This section only includes districts with 1,500 or more students; All categories are ranked from high to low

189	2,351	Comstock Park Public Schools	Comstock Park
190	2,339	Otsego Public Schools	Otsego
191	2,314	Marshall Public Schools	Marshall
192	2,289	Fremont Public SD	Fremont
193	2,287	Paw Paw Public SD	Paw Paw
194	2,284	Kelloggsville Public Schools	Grand Rapids
195	2,255	Tri County Area Schools	Sand Lake
196	2,250	Corunna Public Schools	Corunna
197	2,214	Alma Public Schools	Alma
198	2,200	Ludington Area SD	Ludington
198	2,200	South Haven Public Schools	South Haven
200	2,196	Bendle Public Schools	Burton
201	2,190	Chippewa Hills SD	Remus
201	2,190	West Branch-Rose City Area Schls	Rose City
203	2,184	Imlay City Community Schools	Imlay City
204	2,168	Macomb ISD	Clinton Twp
205	2,164	Cesar Chavez Academy	Detroit
206	2,154	South Lake Schools	St Clair Shores
207	2,147	Godwin Heights Public Schools	Grand Rapids
208	2,133	Croswell-Lexington Comm. Schools	Croswell
208	2,133	Goodrich Area Schools	Goodrich
210	2,122	Berrien Springs Public Schools	Berrien Springs
211	2,096	Comstock Public Schools	Kalamazoo
212	2,090	Yale Public Schools	Yale
213	2,076	Pennfield Schools	Battle Creek
214	2,074	Belding Area SD	Belding
215	2,067	Lakewood Public Schools	Woodland
216	2,056	Grant Public SD	Grant
216	2,056	Jefferson Schools (Monroe)	Monroe
218	2,021	Old Redford Academy	Detroit
218	2,021	Portland Public Schools	Portland
220	1,996	Armada Area Schools	Armada
221	1,969	Carrollton Public Schools	Saginaw
222	1,954	Bullock Creek SD	Midland
223	1,917	Big Rapids Public Schools	Big Rapids
224	1,910	Cheboygan Area Schools	Cheboygan
225	1,904	Algonac Community SD	Algonac
226	1,877	Birch Run Area Schools	Birch Run
227	1,874	Flat Rock Community Schools	Flat Rock
228	1,866	Oakridge Public Schools	Muskegon
229	1,862	Williamston Community Schools	Williamston
230	1,859	Clarenceville SD	Livonia
231	1,858	Caro Community Schools	Caro
232	1,857	Lake Fenton Community Schools	Fenton
233	1,852	Grosse Ile Township Schools	Grosse Ile
234	1,843	Beecher Community SD	Flint
234	1,843	Central Montcalm Public Schools	Stanton
236	1,834	Saginaw ISD	Saginaw
237	1,830	Freeland Community SD	Freeland
238	1,820	Coloma Community Schools	Coloma
239	1,810	Gladwin Community Schools	Gladwin
240	1,802	Swan Valley SD	Saginaw
241	1,792	Clawson Public Schools	Clawson
242	1,786	Shepherd Public Schools	Shepherd
243	1,777	Godfrey-Lee Public Schools	Wyoming
244	1,765	Essexville-Hampton Public Schools	Essexville
245	1,751	Summit Academy North	Romulus
246	1,734	Parchment SD	Kalamazoo
247	1,709	Benzie County Central Schools	Benzonia
248	1,706	University Preparatory Acad. (PSAD)	Detroit
249	1,699	Richmond Community Schools	Richmond
250	1,698	Newaygo Public SD	Newaygo
251	1,697	Ovid-Elsie Area Schools	Elsie
252	1,688	Standish-Sterling Community Schls	Standish
253	1,678	Manistee Area Public Schools	Manistee
254	1,664	Menominee Area Public Schools	Menominee
255	1,662	Willow Run Community Schools	Ypsilanti
256	1,661	Crawford Ausable Schools	Grayling
257	1,657	Breitung Township SD	Kingsford
258	1,635	Durand Area Schools	Durand
259	1,623	Chesaning Union Schools	Chesaning
260	1,616	Almont Community Schools	Almont
260	1,616	Lakeville Community SD	Otisville
262	1,604	Dundee Community Schools	Dundee
263	1,603	Houghton Lake Community Schools	Houghton Lake
264	1,591	Mount Clemens Community SD	Mount Clemens
265	1,578	Hopkins Public Schools	Hopkins
266	1,574	Kalkaska Public Schools	Kalkaska
267	1,568	Buchanan Community Schools	Buchanan
268	1,567	Harrison Community Schools	Harrison
269	1,559	Olivet Community Schools	Olivet
269	1,559	Stockbridge Community Schools	Stockbridge
271	1,558	Kent ISD	Grand Rapids
272	1,550	Gladstone Area Schools	Gladstone
273	1,549	Hillsdale Community Schools	Hillsdale
274	1,546	Shelby Public Schools	Shelby
275	1,541	Onsted Community Schools	Onsted
276	1,533	Clare Public Schools	Clare
277	1,524	Reed City Area Public Schools	Reed City
278	1,520	Columbia SD	Brooklyn
279	1,519	Napoleon Community Schools	Napoleon
280	1,516	Delton Kellogg Schools	Delton
281	1,514	Muskegon Hgts SD	Muskegon
282	1,500	Perry Public Schools	Perry

Male Students

Rank	Percent	District Name	City
1	62.0	Macomb ISD	Clinton Twp
2	56.1	Hamtramck SD	Hamtramck
3	55.2	Almont Community Schools	Almont
4	54.7	Redford Union Schools Dist. No. 1	Redford
5	54.5	Grant Public SD	Grant
6	54.4	East Detroit Public Schools	Eastpointe
7	54.2	Fowlerville Community Schools	Fowlerville
8	54.0	Garden City SD	Garden City
9	53.8	Swan Valley SD	Saginaw
10	53.7	Saint Joseph Public Schools	Saint Joseph
11	53.5	Clare Public Schools	Clare
11	53.5	Columbia SD	Brooklyn
11	53.5	Crestwood SD	Dearborn Hgts
11	53.5	Public Schools of Petoskey	Petoskey
15	53.4	Chelsea SD	Chelsea
15	53.4	Hazel Park SD	Hazel Park
15	53.4	Lakeshore SD (Berrien)	Stevensville
15	53.4	Van Dyke Public Schools	Warren
19	53.3	Kelloggsville Public Schools	Grand Rapids
19	53.3	Mt. Morris Consolidated Schools	Mount Morris
19	53.3	South Lake Schools	St Clair Shores
22	53.2	Napoleon Community Schools	Napoleon
23	53.1	Caledonia Community Schools	Caledonia
24	53.0	Bullock Creek SD	Midland
24	53.0	Coloma Community Schools	Coloma
24	53.0	Hopkins Public Schools	Hopkins
24	53.0	Kearsley Community SD	Flint
24	53.0	Lowell Area Schools	Lowell
24	53.0	Saginaw ISD	Saginaw
24	53.0	Sault Ste Marie Area Schools	Sault Ste Marie
31	52.9	Benton Harbor Area Schools	Benton Harbor
31	52.9	Clarkston Community SD	Clarkston
31	52.9	Godwin Heights Public Schools	Grand Rapids
31	52.9	Pontiac City SD	Pontiac
31	52.9	Wyandotte SD	Wyandotte
36	52.8	Big Rapids Public Schools	Big Rapids
36	52.8	Jefferson Schools (Monroe)	Monroe
36	52.8	Lake Fenton Community Schools	Fenton
36	52.8	Stockbridge Community Schools	Stockbridge
40	52.7	Comstock Park Public Schools	Comstock Park
40	52.7	Gladstone Area Schools	Gladstone
40	52.7	Hamilton Community Schools	Hamilton
40	52.7	Milan Area Schools	Milan
40	52.7	Oak Park SD	Oak Park
40	52.7	Reed City Area Public Schools	Reed City
46	52.6	Allegan Public Schools	Allegan
46	52.6	Berrien Springs Public Schools	Berrien Springs
46	52.6	Dundee Community Schools	Dundee
46	52.6	Grand Rapids Public Schools	Grand Rapids
46	52.6	Lapeer Community Schools	Lapeer
46	52.6	North Branch Area Schools	North Branch
46	52.6	SD of Ypsilanti	Ypsilanti
46	52.6	Willow Run Community Schools	Ypsilanti
54	52.5	Clio Area SD	Clio
54	52.5	Corunna Public Schools	Corunna
54	52.5	Freeland Community SD	Freeland
54	52.5	Grand Blanc Community Schools	Grand Blanc
54	52.5	Grand Haven Area Public Schools	Grand Haven
54	52.5	Holly Area SD	Holly
54	52.5	Lakewood Public Schools	Woodland
54	52.5	Lincoln Park SD	Lincoln Park
54	52.5	Muskegon Hgts SD	Muskegon
54	52.5	Owosso Public Schools	Owosso
64	52.4	Benzie County Central Schools	Benzonia
64	52.4	Ferndale Public Schools	Ferndale
64	52.4	Niles Community Schools	Niles
64	52.4	Otsego Public Schools	Otsego
64	52.4	South Redford SD	Redford
64	52.4	Troy SD	Troy
70	52.3	Bay City SD	Bay City
70	52.3	Clarenceville SD	Livonia
70	52.3	Grand Ledge Public Schools	Grand Ledge
70	52.3	Greenville Public Schools	Greenville
70	52.3	Hillsdale Community Schools	Hillsdale
70	52.3	Romulus Community Schools	Romulus
70	52.3	Taylor SD	Taylor
77	52.2	Dearborn City SD	Dearborn
77	52.2	Harrison Community Schools	Harrison
77	52.2	Richmond Community Schools	Richmond
77	52.2	Shelby Public Schools	Shelby
81	52.1	Alma Public Schools	Alma
81	52.1	Harper Creek Community Schools	Battle Creek
81	52.1	Spring Lake Public Schools	Spring Lake
81	52.1	Waverly Community Schools	Lansing
81	52.1	Yale Public Schools	Yale
86	52.0	Allendale Public Schools	Allendale
86	52.0	Birch Run Area Schools	Birch Run
86	52.0	Byron Center Public Schools	Byron Center
86	52.0	Onsted Community Schools	Onsted
86	52.0	Portage Public Schools	Portage
86	52.0	Rockford Public Schools	Rockford
86	52.0	Saint Johns Public Schools	Saint Johns
86	52.0	Three Rivers Community Schools	Three Rivers
86	52.0	Waterford SD	Waterford
86	52.0	Whitehall District Schools	Whitehall
96	51.9	Avondale SD	Auburn Hills
96	51.9	Battle Creek Public Schools	Battle Creek
96	51.9	Cedar Springs Public Schools	Cedar Springs
96	51.9	Chesaning Union Schools	Chesaning
96	51.9	Flint SD	Flint
96	51.9	Goodrich Area Schools	Goodrich
96	51.9	Hartland Consolidated Schools	Hartland
96	51.9	Kenowa Hills Public Schools	Grand Rapids
96	51.9	Lansing Public SD	Lansing
96	51.9	Marquette Area Public Schools	Marquette
96	51.9	Okemos Public Schools	Okemos
96	51.9	Orchard View Schools	Muskegon
96	51.9	Paw Paw Public SD	Paw Paw
96	51.9	Standish-Sterling Community Schls	Standish
110	51.8	Central Montcalm Public Schools	Stanton
110	51.8	Clintondale Community Schools	Clinton Twp
110	51.8	Gladwin Community Schools	Gladwin
110	51.8	Holland City SD	Holland
110	51.8	Linden Community Schools	Linden
110	51.8	Marysville Public Schools	Marysville
110	51.8	Portland Public Schools	Portland
110	51.8	SD of the City of Birmingham	Birmingham
110	51.8	Sparta Area Schools	Sparta
119	51.7	Chippewa Hills SD	Remus
119	51.7	Chippewa Valley Schools	Clinton Twp
119	51.7	Essexville-Hampton Public Schools	Essexville
119	51.7	Fitzgerald Public Schools	Warren
119	51.7	Grosse Pointe Public Schools	Grosse Pointe
119	51.7	L'anse Creuse Public Schools	Harrison Twp
119	51.7	Livonia Public Schools SD	Livonia
119	51.7	Northville Public Schools	Northville
119	51.7	Oxford Community Schools	Oxford
119	51.7	Roseville Community Schools	Roseville
119	51.7	Southfield Public SD	Southfield
119	51.7	Wayne-Westland Community SD	Westland
119	51.7	West Ottawa Public SD	Holland
119	51.7	Wyoming Public Schools	Wyoming
119	51.7	Zeeland Public Schools	Zeeland
134	51.6	Ann Arbor Public Schools	Ann Arbor
134	51.6	Forest Hills Public Schools	Grand Rapids
134	51.6	Howell Public Schools	Howell
134	51.6	Ionia Public Schools	Ionia
134	51.6	Novi Community SD	Novi
134	51.6	Oakridge Public Schools	Muskegon
134	51.6	Port Huron Area SD	Port Huron
134	51.6	Saline Area Schools	Saline
142	51.5	Belding Area SD	Belding
142	51.5	Coopersville Area Public SD	Coopersville
142	51.5	Kalamazoo Public Schools	Kalamazoo
142	51.5	Kentwood Public Schools	Grand Rapids
142	51.5	Olivet Community Schools	Olivet
142	51.5	Rochester Community SD	Rochester
142	51.5	Thornapple Kellogg SD	Middleville
142	51.5	Utica Community Schools	Sterling Hgts
142	51.5	Woodhaven-Brownstown SD	Woodhaven
151	51.4	Fraser Public Schools	Fraser
151	51.4	Fremont Public SD	Fremont
151	51.4	Gull Lake Community Schools	Richland
151	51.4	Huron SD	New Boston
151	51.4	Lamphere Public Schools	Madison Heights
151	51.4	Reeths-Puffer Schools	Muskegon
151	51.4	SD of the City of Royal Oak	Royal Oak

Note: This section only includes districts with 1,500 or more students; All categories are ranked from high to low

151	51.4	Southgate Community SD	Southgate
151	51.4	Traverse City Area Public Schools	Traverse City
151	51.4	Warren Consolidated Schools	Warren
161	51.3	Buchanan Community Schools	Buchanan
161	51.3	Dewitt Public Schools	Dewitt
161	51.3	E Grand Rapids Public Schools	Grand Rapids
161	51.3	Farmington Public SD	Farmington
161	51.3	Houghton Lake Community Schools	Houghton Lake
161	51.3	Midland Public Schools	Midland
161	51.3	Plainwell Community Schools	Plainwell
161	51.3	Tecumseh Public Schools	Tecumseh
161	51.3	Trenton Public Schools	Trenton
170	51.2	Algonac Community SD	Algonac
170	51.2	Center Line Public Schools	Center Line
170	51.2	Fruitport Community Schools	Fruitport
170	51.2	Lake Orion Community Schools	Lake Orion
170	51.2	Lincoln Consolidated SD	Ypsilanti
170	51.2	Walled Lake Consolidated Schools	Walled Lake
176	51.1	Adrian SD	Adrian
176	51.1	Allen Park Public Schools	Allen Park
176	51.1	Armada Area Schools	Armada
176	51.1	Holt Public Schools	Holt
176	51.1	Huron Valley Schools	Highland
176	51.1	Kent ISD	Grand Rapids
176	51.1	Monroe Public Schools	Monroe
176	51.1	Northwest Community Schools	Jackson
176	51.1	Pinckney Community Schools	Pinckney
176	51.1	Summit Academy North	Romulus
186	51.0	Anchor Bay SD	Casco
186	51.0	Carrollton Public Schools	Saginaw
186	51.0	Gibraltar SD	Woodhaven
186	51.0	Mattawan Consolidated School	Mattawan
186	51.0	Northview Public Schools	Grand Rapids
186	51.0	Sturgis Public Schools	Sturgis
186	51.0	Van Buren Public Schools	Belleville
186	51.0	Westwood Community SD	Dearborn Hgts
194	50.9	Brighton Area Schools	Brighton
194	50.9	Grosse Ile Township Schools	Grosse Ile
194	50.9	Jenison Public Schools	Jenison
194	50.9	Perry Public Schools	Perry
194	50.9	Romeo Community Schools	Romeo
199	50.8	Detroit City SD	Detroit
199	50.8	Escanaba Area Public Schools	Escanaba
199	50.8	Imlay City Community Schools	Imlay City
199	50.8	Ludington Area SD	Ludington
199	50.8	West Branch-Rose City Area Schls	Rose City
204	50.7	Airport Community Schools	Carleton
204	50.7	Berkley SD	Oak Park
204	50.7	Cadillac Area Public Schools	Cadillac
204	50.7	Crawford Ausable Schools	Grayling
204	50.7	Haslett Public Schools	Haslett
204	50.7	Hastings Area SD	Hastings
204	50.7	Mason Public Schools (Ingham)	Mason
204	50.7	Muskegon Public Schools	Muskegon
204	50.7	Ovid-Elsie Area Schools	Elsie
204	50.7	Plymouth-Canton Comm Schools	Plymouth
204	50.7	Vicksburg Community Schools	Vicksburg
215	50.6	Bloomfield Hls SD	Bloomfield Hls
215	50.6	Cheboygan Area Schools	Cheboygan
215	50.6	Croswell-Lexington Comm. Schools	Croswell
215	50.6	Fenton Area Public Schools	Fenton
215	50.6	Hudsonville Public SD	Hudsonville
215	50.6	Kalkaska Public Schools	Kalkaska
215	50.6	Lakeville Community SD	Otisville
215	50.6	Mount Clemens Community SD	Mount Clemens
215	50.6	Mt. Pleasant City SD	Mount Pleasant
215	50.6	Saginaw Township Comm. Schools	Saginaw
225	50.5	Alpena Public Schools	Alpena
225	50.5	Brandon SD	Ortonville
225	50.5	Charlotte Public Schools	Charlotte
225	50.5	East China SD	East China
225	50.5	Godfrey-Lee Public Schools	Wyoming
225	50.5	Jackson Public Schools	Jackson
225	50.5	Manistee Area Public Schools	Manistee
225	50.5	SD of the City of Inkster	Inkster
225	50.5	South Lyon Community Schools	South Lyon
225	50.5	Swartz Creek Community Schools	Swartz Creek
225	50.5	Warren Woods Public Schools	Warren
236	50.4	Dexter Community SD	Dexter
236	50.4	Dowagiac Union SD	Dowagiac
236	50.4	Newaygo Public SD	Newaygo
236	50.4	Shepherd Public Schools	Shepherd
236	50.4	South Haven Public Schools	South Haven
241	50.3	Grandville Public Schools	Grandville
241	50.3	Marshall Public Schools	Marshall
241	50.3	Wayland Union Schools	Wayland
244	50.2	Caro Community Schools	Caro
244	50.2	East Lansing SD	East Lansing
244	50.2	Edwardsburg Public Schools	Edwardsburg
244	50.2	Lake Shore Public Schls (Macomb)	St Clair Shores
244	50.2	Saginaw SD	Saginaw
249	50.1	Beecher Community SD	Flint
249	50.1	Eaton Rapids Public Schools	Eaton Rapids
249	50.1	Flat Rock Community Schools	Flat Rock
249	50.1	Flushing Community Schools	Flushing
249	50.1	Mona Shores Public SD	Muskegon
249	50.1	Tri County Area Schools	Sand Lake
255	50.0	Breitung Township SD	Kingsford
255	50.0	Durand Area Schools	Durand
257	49.9	Carman-Ainsworth Comm. Schools	Flint
257	49.9	Davison Community Schools	Davison
257	49.9	Delton Kellogg Schools	Delton
257	49.9	University Preparatory Acad. (PSAD)	Detroit
261	49.8	Bedford Public Schools	Temperance
261	49.8	Comstock Public Schools	Kalamazoo
263	49.7	Coldwater Community Schools	Coldwater
263	49.7	Lakeview SD (Calhoun)	Battle Creek
263	49.7	Riverview Community SD	Riverview
263	49.7	West Bloomfield SD	West Bloomfield
267	49.6	Lakeview Public Schools (Macomb)	St Clair Shores
267	49.6	Western SD	Parma
267	49.6	Williamston Community Schools	Williamston
270	49.4	Gaylord Community Schools	Gaylord
270	49.4	Melvindale-North Allen Park Schools	Melvindale
272	49.3	Cesar Chavez Academy	Detroit
273	49.2	Menominee Area Public Schools	Menominee
273	49.2	Pennfield Schools	Battle Creek
275	49.1	Parchment SD	Kalamazoo
276	48.9	Bangor Township Schools	Bay City
277	48.8	Dearborn Hgts SD #7	Dearborn Hgts
278	48.6	Clawson Public Schools	Clawson
279	48.5	Old Redford Academy	Detroit
279	48.5	Wayne Resa	Wayne
281	47.3	Bendle Public Schools	Burton
282	45.7	Chandler Park Academy	Harper Woods

Female Students

Rank	Percent	District Name	City
1	54.3	Chandler Park Academy	Harper Woods
2	52.7	Bendle Public Schools	Burton
3	51.5	Old Redford Academy	Detroit
3	51.5	Wayne Resa	Wayne
5	51.4	Clawson Public Schools	Clawson
6	51.2	Dearborn Hgts SD #7	Dearborn Hgts
7	51.1	Bangor Township Schools	Bay City
8	50.9	Parchment SD	Kalamazoo
9	50.8	Menominee Area Public Schools	Menominee
9	50.8	Pennfield Schools	Battle Creek
11	50.7	Cesar Chavez Academy	Detroit
12	50.6	Gaylord Community Schools	Gaylord
12	50.6	Melvindale-North Allen Park Schools	Melvindale
14	50.4	Lakeview Public Schools (Macomb)	St Clair Shores
14	50.4	Western SD	Parma
14	50.4	Williamston Community Schools	Williamston
17	50.3	Coldwater Community Schools	Coldwater
17	50.3	Lakeview SD (Calhoun)	Battle Creek
17	50.3	Riverview Community SD	Riverview
17	50.3	West Bloomfield SD	West Bloomfield
21	50.2	Bedford Public Schools	Temperance
21	50.2	Comstock Public Schools	Kalamazoo
23	50.1	Carman-Ainsworth Comm. Schools	Flint
23	50.1	Davison Community Schools	Davison
23	50.1	Delton Kellogg Schools	Delton
23	50.1	University Preparatory Acad. (PSAD)	Detroit
27	50.0	Breitung Township SD	Kingsford
27	50.0	Durand Area Schools	Durand
29	49.9	Beecher Community SD	Flint
29	49.9	Eaton Rapids Public Schools	Eaton Rapids
29	49.9	Flat Rock Community Schools	Flat Rock
29	49.9	Flushing Community Schools	Flushing
29	49.9	Mona Shores Public SD	Muskegon
29	49.9	Tri County Area Schools	Sand Lake
35	49.8	Caro Community Schools	Caro
35	49.8	East Lansing SD	East Lansing
35	49.8	Edwardsburg Public Schools	Edwardsburg
35	49.8	Lake Shore Public Schls (Macomb)	St Clair Shores
35	49.8	Saginaw SD	Saginaw
40	49.7	Grandville Public Schools	Grandville
40	49.7	Marshall Public Schools	Marshall
40	49.7	Wayland Union Schools	Wayland
43	49.6	Dexter Community SD	Dexter
43	49.6	Dowagiac Union SD	Dowagiac
43	49.6	Newaygo Public SD	Newaygo
43	49.6	Shepherd Public Schools	Shepherd
43	49.6	South Haven Public Schools	South Haven
48	49.5	Alpena Public Schools	Alpena
48	49.5	Brandon SD	Ortonville
48	49.5	Charlotte Public Schools	Charlotte
48	49.5	East China SD	East China
48	49.5	Godfrey-Lee Public Schools	Wyoming
48	49.5	Jackson Public Schools	Jackson
48	49.5	Manistee Area Public Schools	Manistee
48	49.5	SD of the City of Inkster	Inkster
48	49.5	South Lyon Community Schools	South Lyon
48	49.5	Swartz Creek Community Schools	Swartz Creek
48	49.5	Warren Woods Public Schools	Warren
59	49.4	Bloomfield Hls SD	Bloomfield Hls
59	49.4	Cheboygan Area Schools	Cheboygan
59	49.4	Croswell-Lexington Comm. Schools	Croswell
59	49.4	Fenton Area Public Schools	Fenton
59	49.4	Hudsonville Public SD	Hudsonville
59	49.4	Kalkaska Public Schools	Kalkaska
59	49.4	Lakeville Community SD	Otisville
59	49.4	Mount Clemens Community SD	Mount Clemens
59	49.4	Mt. Pleasant City SD	Mount Pleasant
59	49.4	Saginaw Township Comm. Schools	Saginaw
69	49.3	Airport Community Schools	Carleton
69	49.3	Berkley SD	Oak Park
69	49.3	Cadillac Area Public Schools	Cadillac
69	49.3	Crawford Ausable Schools	Grayling
69	49.3	Haslett Public Schools	Haslett
69	49.3	Hastings Area SD	Hastings
69	49.3	Mason Public Schools (Ingham)	Mason
69	49.3	Muskegon Public Schools	Muskegon
69	49.3	Ovid-Elsie Area Schools	Elsie
69	49.3	Plymouth-Canton Comm Schools	Plymouth
69	49.3	Vicksburg Community Schools	Vicksburg
80	49.2	Detroit City SD	Detroit
80	49.2	Escanaba Area Public Schools	Escanaba
80	49.2	Imlay City Community Schools	Imlay City
80	49.2	Ludington Area SD	Ludington
80	49.2	West Branch-Rose City Area Schls	Rose City
85	49.1	Brighton Area Schools	Brighton
85	49.1	Grosse Ile Township Schools	Grosse Ile
85	49.1	Jenison Public Schools	Jenison
85	49.1	Perry Public Schools	Perry
85	49.1	Romeo Community Schools	Romeo
90	49.0	Anchor Bay SD	Casco
90	49.0	Carrollton Public Schools	Saginaw
90	49.0	Gibraltar SD	Woodhaven
90	49.0	Mattawan Consolidated School	Mattawan
90	49.0	Northview Public Schools	Grand Rapids
90	49.0	Sturgis Public Schools	Sturgis
90	49.0	Van Buren Public Schools	Belleville
90	49.0	Westwood Community SD	Dearborn Hgts
98	48.9	Adrian SD	Adrian
98	48.9	Allen Park Public Schools	Allen Park
98	48.9	Armada Area Schools	Armada
98	48.9	Holt Public Schools	Holt
98	48.9	Huron Valley Schools	Highland
98	48.9	Kent ISD	Grand Rapids
98	48.9	Monroe Public Schools	Monroe
98	48.9	Northwest Community Schools	Jackson
98	48.9	Pinckney Community Schools	Pinckney
98	48.9	Summit Academy North	Romulus
108	48.8	Algonac Community SD	Algonac
108	48.8	Center Line Public Schools	Center Line
108	48.8	Fruitport Community Schools	Fruitport
108	48.8	Lake Orion Community Schools	Lake Orion
108	48.8	Lincoln Consolidated SD	Ypsilanti
108	48.8	Walled Lake Consolidated Schools	Walled Lake
114	48.7	Buchanan Community Schools	Buchanan
114	48.7	Dewitt Public Schools	Dewitt
114	48.7	E Grand Rapids Public Schools	Grand Rapids
114	48.7	Farmington Public SD	Farmington
114	48.7	Houghton Lake Community Schools	Houghton Lake
114	48.7	Midland Public Schools	Midland
114	48.7	Plainwell Community Schools	Plainwell
114	48.7	Tecumseh Public Schools	Tecumseh
114	48.7	Trenton Public Schools	Trenton
123	48.6	Fraser Public Schools	Fraser
123	48.6	Fremont Public SD	Fremont
123	48.6	Gull Lake Community Schools	Richland
123	48.6	Huron SD	New Boston

Note: This section only includes districts with 1,500 or more students; All categories are ranked from high to low

123	48.6	Lamphere Public Schools	Madison Heights
123	48.6	Reeths-Puffer Schools	Muskegon
123	48.6	SD of the City of Royal Oak	Royal Oak
123	48.6	Southgate Community SD	Southgate
123	48.6	Traverse City Area Public Schools	Traverse City
123	48.6	Warren Consolidated Schools	Warren
133	48.5	Belding Area SD	Belding
133	48.5	Coopersville Area Public SD	Coopersville
133	48.5	Kalamazoo Public Schools	Kalamazoo
133	48.5	Kentwood Public Schools	Grand Rapids
133	48.5	Olivet Community Schools	Olivet
133	48.5	Rochester Community SD	Rochester
133	48.5	Thornapple Kellogg SD	Middleville
133	48.5	Utica Community Schools	Sterling Hgts
133	48.5	Woodhaven-Brownstown SD	Woodhaven
142	48.4	Ann Arbor Public Schools	Ann Arbor
142	48.4	Forest Hills Public Schools	Grand Rapids
142	48.4	Howell Public Schools	Howell
142	48.4	Ionia Public Schools	Ionia
142	48.4	Novi Community SD	Novi
142	48.4	Oakridge Public Schools	Muskegon
142	48.4	Port Huron Area SD	Port Huron
142	48.4	Saline Area Schools	Saline
150	48.3	Chippewa Hills SD	Remus
150	48.3	Chippewa Valley Schools	Clinton Twp
150	48.3	Essexville-Hampton Public Schools	Essexville
150	48.3	Fitzgerald Public Schools	Warren
150	48.3	Grosse Pointe Public Schools	Grosse Pointe
150	48.3	L'anse Creuse Public Schools	Harrison Twp
150	48.3	Livonia Public Schools SD	Livonia
150	48.3	Northville Public Schools	Northville
150	48.3	Oxford Community Schools	Oxford
150	48.3	Roseville Community Schools	Roseville
150	48.3	Southfield Public SD	Southfield
150	48.3	Wayne-Westland Community SD	Westland
150	48.3	West Ottawa Public SD	Holland
150	48.3	Wyoming Public Schools	Wyoming
150	48.3	Zeeland Public Schools	Zeeland
165	48.2	Central Montcalm Public Schools	Stanton
165	48.2	Clintondale Community Schools	Clinton Twp
165	48.2	Gladwin Community Schools	Gladwin
165	48.2	Holland City SD	Holland
165	48.2	Linden Community Schools	Linden
165	48.2	Marysville Public Schools	Marysville
165	48.2	Portland Public Schools	Portland
165	48.2	SD of the City of Birmingham	Birmingham
165	48.2	Sparta Area Schools	Sparta
174	48.1	Avondale SD	Auburn Hills
174	48.1	Battle Creek Public Schools	Battle Creek
174	48.1	Cedar Springs Public Schools	Cedar Springs
174	48.1	Chesaning Union Schools	Chesaning
174	48.1	Flint SD	Flint
174	48.1	Goodrich Area Schools	Goodrich
174	48.1	Hartland Consolidated Schools	Hartland
174	48.1	Kenowa Hills Public Schools	Grand Rapids
174	48.1	Lansing Public SD	Lansing
174	48.1	Marquette Area Public Schools	Marquette
174	48.1	Okemos Public Schools	Okemos
174	48.1	Orchard View Schools	Muskegon
174	48.1	Paw Paw Public SD	Paw Paw
174	48.1	Standish-Sterling Community Schls	Standish
188	48.0	Allendale Public Schools	Allendale
188	48.0	Birch Run Area Schools	Birch Run
188	48.0	Byron Center Public Schools	Byron Center
188	48.0	Onsted Community Schools	Onsted
188	48.0	Portage Public Schools	Portage
188	48.0	Rockford Public Schools	Rockford
188	48.0	Saint Johns Public Schools	Saint Johns
188	48.0	Three Rivers Community Schools	Three Rivers
188	48.0	Waterford SD	Waterford
188	48.0	Whitehall District Schools	Whitehall
198	47.9	Alma Public Schools	Alma
198	47.9	Harper Creek Community Schools	Battle Creek
198	47.9	Spring Lake Public Schools	Spring Lake
198	47.9	Waverly Community Schools	Lansing
198	47.9	Yale Public Schools	Yale
203	47.8	Dearborn City SD	Dearborn
203	47.8	Harrison Community Schools	Harrison
203	47.8	Richmond Community Schools	Richmond
203	47.8	Shelby Public Schools	Shelby
207	47.7	Bay City SD	Bay City
207	47.7	Clarenceville SD	Livonia
207	47.7	Grand Ledge Public Schools	Grand Ledge
207	47.7	Greenville Public Schools	Greenville
207	47.7	Hillsdale Community Schools	Hillsdale
207	47.7	Romulus Community Schools	Romulus
207	47.7	Taylor SD	Taylor
214	47.6	Benzie County Central Schools	Benzonia
214	47.6	Ferndale Public Schools	Ferndale
214	47.6	Niles Community Schools	Niles
214	47.6	Otsego Public Schools	Otsego
214	47.6	South Redford SD	Redford
214	47.6	Troy SD	Troy
220	47.5	Clio Area SD	Clio
220	47.5	Corunna Public Schools	Corunna
220	47.5	Freeland Community SD	Freeland
220	47.5	Grand Blanc Community Schools	Grand Blanc
220	47.5	Grand Haven Area Public Schools	Grand Haven
220	47.5	Holly Area SD	Holly
220	47.5	Lakewood Public Schools	Woodland
220	47.5	Lincoln Park SD	Lincoln Park
220	47.5	Muskegon Hgts SD	Muskegon
220	47.5	Owosso Public Schools	Owosso
230	47.4	Allegan Public Schools	Allegan
230	47.4	Berrien Springs Public Schools	Berrien Springs
230	47.4	Dundee Community Schools	Dundee
230	47.4	Grand Rapids Public Schools	Grand Rapids
230	47.4	Lapeer Community Schools	Lapeer
230	47.4	North Branch Area Schools	North Branch
230	47.4	SD of Ypsilanti	Ypsilanti
230	47.4	Willow Run Community Schools	Ypsilanti
238	47.3	Comstock Park Public Schools	Comstock Park
238	47.3	Gladstone Area Schools	Gladstone
238	47.3	Hamilton Community Schools	Hamilton
238	47.3	Milan Area Schools	Milan
238	47.3	Oak Park SD	Oak Park
238	47.3	Reed City Area Public Schools	Reed City
244	47.2	Big Rapids Public Schools	Big Rapids
244	47.2	Jefferson Schools (Monroe)	Monroe
244	47.2	Lake Fenton Community Schools	Fenton
244	47.2	Stockbridge Community Schools	Stockbridge
248	47.1	Benton Harbor Area Schools	Benton Harbor
248	47.1	Clarkston Community SD	Clarkston
248	47.1	Godwin Heights Public Schools	Grand Rapids
248	47.1	Pontiac City SD	Pontiac
248	47.1	Wyandotte SD	Wyandotte
253	47.0	Bullock Creek SD	Midland
253	47.0	Coloma Community Schools	Coloma
253	47.0	Hopkins Public Schools	Hopkins
253	47.0	Kearsley Community SD	Flint
253	47.0	Lowell Area Schools	Lowell
253	47.0	Saginaw ISD	Saginaw
253	47.0	Sault Ste Marie Area Schools	Sault Ste Marie
260	46.9	Caledonia Community Schools	Caledonia
261	46.8	Napoleon Community Schools	Napoleon
262	46.7	Kelloggsville Public Schools	Grand Rapids
262	46.7	Mt. Morris Consolidated Schools	Mount Morris
262	46.7	South Lake Schools	St Clair Shores
265	46.6	Chelsea SD	Chelsea
265	46.6	Hazel Park SD	Hazel Park
265	46.6	Lakeshore SD (Berrien)	Stevensville
265	46.6	Van Dyke Public Schools	Warren
269	46.5	Clare Public Schools	Clare
269	46.5	Columbia SD	Brooklyn
269	46.5	Crestwood SD	Dearborn Hgts
269	46.5	Public Schools of Petoskey	Petoskey
273	46.3	Saint Joseph Public Schools	Saint Joseph
274	46.2	Swan Valley SD	Saginaw
275	46.0	Garden City SD	Garden City
276	45.8	Fowlerville Community Schools	Fowlerville
277	45.6	East Detroit Public Schools	Eastpointe
278	45.5	Grant Public SD	Grant
279	45.3	Redford Union Schools Dist. No. 1	Redford
280	44.8	Almont Community Schools	Almont
281	43.9	Hamtramck SD	Hamtramck
282	38.0	Macomb ISD	Clinton Twp

Individual Education Program Students

Rank	Percent	District Name	City
1	61.2	Macomb ISD	Clinton Twp
2	29.5	Redford Union Schools Dist. No. 1	Redford
3	25.1	Wyandotte SD	Wyandotte
4	22.8	Willow Run Community Schools	Ypsilanti
5	22.5	Mount Clemens Community SD	Mount Clemens
6	21.8	Grand Rapids Public Schools	Grand Rapids
7	21.2	Carrollton Public Schools	Saginaw
8	19.1	Holly Area SD	Holly
8	19.1	Van Dyke Public Schools	Warren
10	18.9	Alma Public Schools	Alma
10	18.9	Ionia Public Schools	Ionia
12	18.7	Garden City SD	Garden City
13	18.5	Holland City SD	Holland
14	18.4	Muskegon Public Schools	Muskegon
14	18.4	Saginaw ISD	Saginaw
16	17.9	Mt. Pleasant City SD	Mount Pleasant
17	17.7	East Detroit Public Schools	Eastpointe
18	17.6	Lansing Public SD	Lansing
19	17.5	Harrison Community Schools	Harrison
19	17.5	Lincoln Consolidated SD	Ypsilanti
19	17.5	Taylor SD	Taylor
22	17.4	Muskegon Hgts SD	Muskegon
23	17.3	Pontiac City SD	Pontiac
23	17.3	Southgate Community SD	Southgate
23	17.3	Warren Woods Public Schools	Warren
26	17.2	SD of Ypsilanti	Ypsilanti
27	17.1	Detroit City SD	Detroit
27	17.1	Monroe Public Schools	Monroe
29	17.0	Crawford Ausable Schools	Grayling
29	17.0	Shepherd Public Schools	Shepherd
31	16.9	Chippewa Hills SD	Remus
32	16.8	Bloomfield Hls SD	Bloomfield Hls
33	16.7	Marquette Area Public Schools	Marquette
33	16.7	Roseville Community Schools	Roseville
33	16.7	Trenton Public Schools	Trenton
33	16.7	Waverly Community Schools	Lansing
37	16.6	Linden Community Schools	Linden
38	16.5	Bay City SD	Bay City
38	16.5	Chesaning Union Schools	Chesaning
40	16.4	Clawson Public Schools	Clawson
40	16.4	Jefferson Schools (Monroe)	Monroe
40	16.4	Livonia Public Schools SD	Livonia
43	16.1	Breitung Township SD	Kingsford
43	16.1	Owosso Public Schools	Owosso
45	15.8	Carman-Ainsworth Comm. Schools	Flint
46	15.7	Belding Area SD	Belding
46	15.7	Houghton Lake Community Schools	Houghton Lake
46	15.7	Lakewood Public Schools	Woodland
49	15.6	Reed City Area Public Schools	Reed City
49	15.6	Saginaw SD	Saginaw
51	15.4	Battle Creek Public Schools	Battle Creek
51	15.4	Flat Rock Community Schools	Flat Rock
51	15.4	Sault Ste Marie Area Schools	Sault Ste Marie
51	15.4	Van Buren Public Schools	Belleville
55	15.3	Grand Ledge Public Schools	Grand Ledge
55	15.3	Perry Public Schools	Perry
55	15.3	Wayne-Westland Community SD	Westland
58	15.2	Caro Community Schools	Caro
58	15.2	Lamphere Public Schools	Madison Heights
58	15.2	Reeths-Puffer Schools	Muskegon
61	15.0	Durand Area Schools	Durand
61	15.0	Gladwin Community Schools	Gladwin
61	15.0	Greenville Public Schools	Greenville
61	15.0	Lakeville Community SD	Otisville
61	15.0	Niles Community Schools	Niles
61	15.0	Sparta Area Schools	Sparta
67	14.9	Bedford Public Schools	Temperance
67	14.9	Eaton Rapids Public Schools	Eaton Rapids
67	14.9	Westwood Community SD	Dearborn Hgts
70	14.8	Bullock Creek SD	Midland
70	14.8	Escanaba Area Public Schools	Escanaba
70	14.8	Flint SD	Flint
70	14.8	Mt. Morris Consolidated Schools	Mount Morris
70	14.8	Stockbridge Community Schools	Stockbridge
70	14.8	Wyoming Public Schools	Wyoming
76	14.7	Coldwater Community Schools	Coldwater
77	14.6	Cedar Springs Public Schools	Cedar Springs
78	14.5	Bangor Township Schools	Bay City
78	14.5	Fowlerville Community Schools	Fowlerville
78	14.5	Fremont Public SD	Fremont
78	14.5	Gibraltar SD	Woodhaven
78	14.5	Huron SD	New Boston
78	14.5	Port Huron Area SD	Port Huron
84	14.4	Clarenceville SD	Livonia
85	14.3	Columbia SD	Brooklyn
85	14.3	Godwin Heights Public Schools	Grand Rapids
85	14.3	Ludington Area SD	Ludington
88	14.2	Airport Community Schools	Carleton
88	14.2	Benton Harbor Area Schools	Benton Harbor
88	14.2	Kalkaska Public Schools	Kalkaska
88	14.2	Kearsley Community SD	Flint
88	14.2	Lapeer Community Schools	Lapeer
88	14.2	Saginaw Township Comm. Schools	Saginaw
94	14.1	Big Rapids Public Schools	Big Rapids
94	14.1	Hillsdale Community Schools	Hillsdale

Note: This section only includes districts with 1,500 or more students; All categories are ranked from high to low

94	14.1	Lincoln Park SD	Lincoln Park
97	14.0	Benzie County Central Schools	Benzonia
97	14.0	South Lake Schools	St Clair Shores
99	13.9	Coopersville Area Public SD	Coopersville
99	13.9	Menominee Area Public Schools	Menominee
99	13.9	Romeo Community Schools	Romeo
99	13.9	Traverse City Area Public Schools	Traverse City
103	13.8	Kalamazoo Public Schools	Kalamazoo
103	13.8	Kentwood Public Schools	Grand Rapids
103	13.8	South Redford SD	Redford
106	13.7	Allegan Public Schools	Allegan
106	13.7	Birch Run Area Schools	Birch Run
106	13.7	Delton Kellogg Schools	Delton
106	13.7	Swartz Creek Community Schools	Swartz Creek
110	13.6	Almont Community Schools	Almont
110	13.6	Northwest Community Schools	Jackson
112	13.5	Midland Public Schools	Midland
112	13.5	Northview Public Schools	Grand Rapids
112	13.5	Swan Valley SD	Saginaw
115	13.4	Algonac Community SD	Algonac
115	13.4	Brighton Area Schools	Brighton
115	13.4	Grosse Pointe Public Schools	Grosse Pointe
115	13.4	Hazel Park SD	Hazel Park
115	13.4	Portland Public Schools	Portland
115	13.4	Shelby Public Schools	Shelby
115	13.4	Standish-Sterling Community Schls	Standish
122	13.3	Hastings Area SD	Hastings
122	13.3	Holt Public Schools	Holt
122	13.3	Jackson Public Schools	Jackson
122	13.3	West Branch-Rose City Area Schls	Rose City
126	13.2	Mason Public Schools (Ingham)	Mason
126	13.2	Romulus Community Schools	Romulus
128	13.1	Marshall Public Schools	Marshall
128	13.1	Saline Area Schools	Saline
130	13.0	Anchor Bay SD	Casco
130	13.0	Howell Public Schools	Howell
130	13.0	Southfield Public SD	Southfield
130	13.0	Whitehall District Schools	Whitehall
134	12.9	Three Rivers Community Schools	Three Rivers
135	12.8	Comstock Public Schools	Kalamazoo
135	12.8	Dowagiac Union SD	Dowagiac
135	12.8	Fruitport Community Schools	Fruitport
135	12.8	Orchard View Schools	Muskegon
139	12.7	Lake Shore Public Schls (Macomb)	St Clair Shores
139	12.7	Pinckney Community Schools	Pinckney
139	12.7	Waterford SD	Waterford
142	12.6	Comstock Park Public Schools	Comstock Park
142	12.6	Tri County Area Schools	Sand Lake
142	12.6	Woodhaven-Brownstown SD	Woodhaven
145	12.5	Charlotte Public Schools	Charlotte
145	12.5	Huron Valley Schools	Highland
145	12.5	Milan Area Schools	Milan
148	12.4	Clarkston Community SD	Clarkston
148	12.4	Corunna Public Schools	Corunna
148	12.4	Gladstone Area Schools	Gladstone
148	12.4	Grandville Public Schools	Grandville
148	12.4	Harper Creek Community Schools	Battle Creek
148	12.4	SD of the City of Inkster	Inkster
148	12.4	South Lyon Community Schools	South Lyon
155	12.3	Chelsea SD	Chelsea
155	12.3	Western SD	Parma
155	12.3	Yale Public Schools	Yale
158	12.2	Fenton Area Public Schools	Fenton
158	12.2	Freeland Community SD	Freeland
158	12.2	Hamilton Community Schools	Hamilton
158	12.2	Manistee Area Public Schools	Manistee
158	12.2	Newaygo Public SD	Newaygo
163	12.1	Coloma Community Schools	Coloma
163	12.1	Haslett Public Schools	Haslett
163	12.1	Richmond Community Schools	Richmond
166	12.0	Grand Haven Area Public Schools	Grand Haven
166	12.0	Lakeview SD (Calhoun)	Battle Creek
166	12.0	Utica Community Schools	Sterling Hgts
169	11.9	Alpena Public Schools	Alpena
169	11.9	Godfrey-Lee Public Schools	Wyoming
169	11.9	Wayland Union Schools	Wayland
172	11.8	Brandon SD	Ortonville
172	11.8	Fitzgerald Public Schools	Warren
172	11.8	Grant Public SD	Grant
172	11.8	North Branch Area Schools	North Branch
172	11.8	Rochester Community SD	Rochester
172	11.8	West Bloomfield SD	West Bloomfield
178	11.7	Cadillac Area Public Schools	Cadillac
178	11.7	Central Montcalm Public Schools	Stanton
178	11.7	Essexville-Hampton Public Schools	Essexville
178	11.7	Flushing Community Schools	Flushing
178	11.7	Oakridge Public Schools	Muskegon
178	11.7	Paw Paw Public SD	Paw Paw
184	11.6	Adrian SD	Adrian
184	11.6	SD of the City of Birmingham	Birmingham
184	11.6	Zeeland Public Schools	Zeeland
187	11.4	Buchanan Community Schools	Buchanan
187	11.4	Marysville Public Schools	Marysville
187	11.4	South Haven Public Schools	South Haven
190	11.3	Ann Arbor Public Schools	Ann Arbor
190	11.3	Lake Orion Community Schools	Lake Orion
192	11.2	Kelloggsville Public Schools	Grand Rapids
192	11.2	Okemos Public Schools	Okemos
194	11.1	Caledonia Community Schools	Caledonia
194	11.1	Crestwood SD	Dearborn Hgts
194	11.1	Dexter Community SD	Dexter
194	11.1	East China SD	East China
194	11.1	L'anse Creuse Public Schools	Harrison Twp
194	11.1	Walled Lake Consolidated Schools	Walled Lake
200	11.0	Center Line Public Schools	Center Line
200	11.0	Clio Area SD	Clio
200	11.0	Farmington Public SD	Farmington
200	11.0	Fraser Public Schools	Fraser
200	11.0	Lake Fenton Community Schools	Fenton
200	11.0	Tecumseh Public Schools	Tecumseh
206	10.9	Allen Park Public Schools	Allen Park
206	10.9	Chippewa Valley Schools	Clinton Twp
206	10.9	Davison Community Schools	Davison
206	10.9	Jenison Public Schools	Jenison
206	10.9	Portage Public Schools	Portage
211	10.8	Dearborn City SD	Dearborn
212	10.7	Avondale SD	Auburn Hills
212	10.7	Ovid-Elsie Area Schools	Elsie
212	10.7	Warren Consolidated Schools	Warren
215	10.6	Cesar Chavez Academy	Detroit
215	10.6	Clintondale Community Schools	Clinton Twp
215	10.6	Kenowa Hills Public Schools	Grand Rapids
215	10.6	Public Schools of Petoskey	Petoskey
219	10.5	Croswell-Lexington Comm. Schools	Croswell
219	10.5	Dearborn Hgts SD #7	Dearborn Hgts
219	10.5	Edwardsburg Public Schools	Edwardsburg
219	10.5	Hudsonville Public SD	Hudsonville
219	10.5	Plainwell Community Schools	Plainwell
224	10.4	Dundee Community Schools	Dundee
225	10.3	Beecher Community SD	Flint
225	10.3	Lakeview Public Schools (Macomb)	St Clair Shores
225	10.3	Onsted Community Schools	Onsted
225	10.3	Oxford Community Schools	Oxford
225	10.3	Summit Academy North	Romulus
225	10.3	Williamston Community Schools	Williamston
231	10.2	SD of the City of Royal Oak	Royal Oak
232	10.1	Berrien Springs Public Schools	Berrien Springs
232	10.1	Byron Center Public Schools	Byron Center
232	10.1	Gaylord Community Schools	Gaylord
232	10.1	Grand Blanc Community Schools	Grand Blanc
232	10.1	Imlay City Community Schools	Imlay City
232	10.1	West Ottawa Public SD	Holland
238	10.0	Parchment SD	Kalamazoo
239	9.9	Plymouth-Canton Comm Schools	Plymouth
240	9.8	Allendale Public Schools	Allendale
240	9.8	Lowell Area Schools	Lowell
240	9.8	Thornapple Kellogg SD	Middleville
243	9.7	Berkley SD	Oak Park
243	9.7	Grosse Ile Township Schools	Grosse Ile
243	9.7	Melvindale-North Allen Park Schools	Melvindale
246	9.6	Bendle Public Schools	Burton
246	9.6	Napoleon Community Schools	Napoleon
246	9.6	Northville Public Schools	Northville
246	9.6	Riverview Community SD	Riverview
250	9.4	Hopkins Public Schools	Hopkins
250	9.4	Pennfield Schools	Battle Creek
250	9.4	Vicksburg Community Schools	Vicksburg
253	9.3	Spring Lake Public Schools	Spring Lake
254	9.2	Oak Park SD	Oak Park
255	9.1	Cheboygan Area Schools	Cheboygan
255	9.1	East Lansing SD	East Lansing
257	9.0	Forest Hills Public Schools	Grand Rapids
257	9.0	Mona Shores Public SD	Muskegon
259	8.9	Hamtramck SD	Hamtramck
259	8.9	Saint Johns Public Schools	Saint Johns
261	8.8	Troy SD	Troy
262	8.7	Novi Community SD	Novi
263	8.6	Armada Area Schools	Armada
263	8.6	Clare Public Schools	Clare
265	8.5	Hartland Consolidated Schools	Hartland
266	8.4	Ferndale Public Schools	Ferndale
266	8.4	Goodrich Area Schools	Goodrich
266	8.4	Lakeshore SD (Berrien)	Stevensville
269	8.3	Olivet Community Schools	Olivet
269	8.3	Sturgis Public Schools	Sturgis
269	8.3	University Preparatory Acad. (PSAD)	Detroit
272	8.1	Gull Lake Community Schools	Richland
272	8.1	Mattawan Consolidated School	Mattawan
274	7.4	Rockford Public Schools	Rockford
275	7.2	Old Redford Academy	Detroit
276	7.0	Saint Joseph Public Schools	Saint Joseph
277	6.7	Otsego Public Schools	Otsego
278	6.2	Dewitt Public Schools	Dewitt
279	6.0	E Grand Rapids Public Schools	Grand Rapids
280	2.4	Chandler Park Academy	Harper Woods
281	0.3	Wayne Resa	Wayne
282	0.0	Kent ISD	Grand Rapids

English Language Learner Students

Rank	Percent	District Name	City
1	39.1	Dearborn City SD	Dearborn
2	33.9	Godfrey-Lee Public Schools	Wyoming
3	27.4	Hamtramck SD	Hamtramck
4	22.1	Shelby Public Schools	Shelby
5	20.7	Grand Rapids Public Schools	Grand Rapids
6	19.7	Lamphere Public Schools	Madison Heights
7	18.4	Cesar Chavez Academy	Detroit
8	17.2	West Ottawa Public SD	Holland
9	16.2	Melvindale-North Allen Park Schools	Melvindale
10	14.7	Wyoming Public Schools	Wyoming
11	13.9	Warren Consolidated Schools	Warren
12	13.8	Sturgis Public Schools	Sturgis
13	13.3	Godwin Heights Public Schools	Grand Rapids
14	11.9	Kentwood Public Schools	Grand Rapids
14	11.9	Pontiac City SD	Pontiac
16	11.2	Kelloggsville Public Schools	Grand Rapids
17	10.9	Berrien Springs Public Schools	Berrien Springs
18	10.8	Troy SD	Troy
19	10.4	Farmington Public SD	Farmington
20	9.7	Detroit City SD	Detroit
21	9.6	Lansing Public SD	Lansing
22	9.3	Lincoln Park SD	Lincoln Park
22	9.3	Walled Lake Consolidated Schools	Walled Lake
24	9.1	Novi Community SD	Novi
25	8.9	Dowagiac Union SD	Dowagiac
25	8.9	Sparta Area Schools	Sparta
27	8.7	Grant Public SD	Grant
28	8.6	Fitzgerald Public Schools	Warren
29	8.4	Coldwater Community Schools	Coldwater
30	8.3	Imlay City Community Schools	Imlay City
31	8.2	Crestwood SD	Dearborn Hgts
32	7.9	Hazel Park SD	Hazel Park
33	7.6	Comstock Park Public Schools	Comstock Park
34	7.4	Kalamazoo Public Schools	Kalamazoo
35	6.6	Holland City SD	Holland
36	6.5	Battle Creek Public Schools	Battle Creek
36	6.5	West Bloomfield SD	West Bloomfield
38	5.7	Adrian SD	Adrian
39	5.3	Avondale SD	Auburn Hills
40	5.2	East Lansing SD	East Lansing
41	5.0	Chippewa Valley Schools	Clinton Twp
42	4.9	Belding Area SD	Belding
42	4.9	Center Line Public Schools	Center Line
44	4.5	Muskegon Public Schools	Muskegon
45	4.4	Kenowa Hills Public Schools	Grand Rapids
46	4.0	Ann Arbor Public Schools	Ann Arbor
47	3.8	Dearborn Hgts SD #7	Dearborn Hgts
48	3.7	Plymouth-Canton Comm Schools	Plymouth
48	3.7	SD of Ypsilanti	Ypsilanti
48	3.7	Waterford SD	Waterford
51	3.6	Utica Community Schools	Sterling Hgts
52	3.5	Brandon SD	Ortonville
52	3.5	Lakeview SD (Calhoun)	Battle Creek
54	3.3	Almont Community Schools	Almont
54	3.3	Clawson Public Schools	Clawson
56	3.2	Clarenceville SD	Livonia
56	3.2	Saginaw SD	Saginaw
58	3.0	Allendale Public Schools	Allendale
58	3.0	Bloomfield Hls SD	Bloomfield Hls
58	3.0	Niles Community Schools	Niles
61	2.9	Paw Paw Public SD	Paw Paw
61	2.9	Taylor SD	Taylor
63	2.8	Northville Public Schools	Northville
63	2.8	Oak Park SD	Oak Park

Note: This section only includes districts with 1,500 or more students; All categories are ranked from high to low

65	2.5	Rochester Community SD	Rochester
66	2.4	Coopersville Area Public SD	Coopersville
66	2.4	L'anse Creuse Public Schools	Harrison Twp
66	2.4	Warren Woods Public Schools	Warren
66	2.4	Wayne-Westland Community SD	Westland
70	2.3	Bay City SD	Bay City
70	2.3	SD of the City of Birmingham	Birmingham
70	2.3	Willow Run Community Schools	Ypsilanti
73	2.2	Forest Hills Public Schools	Grand Rapids
73	2.2	Monroe Public Schools	Monroe
73	2.2	SD of the City of Royal Oak	Royal Oak
73	2.2	Waverly Community Schools	Lansing
73	2.2	Woodhaven-Brownstown SD	Woodhaven
78	2.1	Jackson Public Schools	Jackson
78	2.1	Newaygo Public SD	Newaygo
78	2.1	Summit Academy North	Romulus
81	2.0	Byron Center Public Schools	Byron Center
81	2.0	Richmond Community Schools	Richmond
83	1.9	Lake Orion Community Schools	Lake Orion
83	1.9	Romeo Community Schools	Romeo
83	1.9	Van Dyke Public Schools	Warren
86	1.7	Clarkston Community SD	Clarkston
86	1.7	East Detroit Public Schools	Eastpointe
86	1.7	Flint SD	Flint
89	1.6	Milan Area Schools	Milan
89	1.6	South Redford SD	Redford
89	1.6	Zeeland Public Schools	Zeeland
92	1.5	Grandville Public Schools	Grandville
92	1.5	Oxford Community Schools	Oxford
92	1.5	Southfield Public SD	Southfield
92	1.5	Southgate Community SD	Southgate
96	1.4	Grand Haven Area Public Schools	Grand Haven
96	1.4	Greenville Public Schools	Greenville
96	1.4	Mount Clemens Community SD	Mount Clemens
96	1.4	Saline Area Schools	Saline
100	1.3	Grand Blanc Community Schools	Grand Blanc
100	1.3	Huron Valley Schools	Highland
100	1.3	Romulus Community Schools	Romulus
103	1.2	Fowlerville Community Schools	Fowlerville
103	1.2	Fraser Public Schools	Fraser
103	1.2	Garden City SD	Garden City
103	1.2	Ionia Public Schools	Ionia
103	1.2	Northview Public Schools	Grand Rapids
103	1.2	Van Buren Public Schools	Belleville
109	1.1	Airport Community Schools	Carleton
109	1.1	Berkley SD	Oak Park
109	1.1	Comstock Public Schools	Kalamazoo
109	1.1	Ferndale Public Schools	Ferndale
109	1.1	Holt Public Schools	Holt
109	1.1	Hudsonville Public SD	Hudsonville
109	1.1	Lincoln Consolidated SD	Ypsilanti
109	1.1	Traverse City Area Public Schools	Traverse City
117	1.0	Central Montcalm Public Schools	Stanton
117	1.0	Holly Area SD	Holly
117	1.0	Huron SD	New Boston
120	0.9	Carman-Ainsworth Comm. Schools	Flint
120	0.9	Hastings Area SD	Hastings
122	0.8	Buchanan Community Schools	Buchanan
122	0.8	Chelsea SD	Chelsea
122	0.8	Grand Ledge Public Schools	Grand Ledge
122	0.8	Okemos Public Schools	Okemos
122	0.8	Ovid-Elsie Area Schools	Elsie
122	0.8	Roseville Community Schools	Roseville
122	0.8	SD of the City of Inkster	Inkster
122	0.8	Westwood Community SD	Dearborn Hgts
130	0.7	Allen Park Public Schools	Allen Park
130	0.7	Anchor Bay SD	Casco
130	0.7	Caledonia Community Schools	Caledonia
130	0.7	Clintondale Community Schools	Clinton Twp
130	0.7	E Grand Rapids Public Schools	Grand Rapids
130	0.7	Haslett Public Schools	Haslett
130	0.7	Midland Public Schools	Midland
130	0.7	Saint Johns Public Schools	Saint Johns
138	0.6	Lake Fenton Community Schools	Fenton
138	0.6	Port Huron Area SD	Port Huron
138	0.6	Riverview Community SD	Riverview
138	0.6	Swartz Creek Community Schools	Swartz Creek
138	0.6	Thornapple Kellogg SD	Middleville
138	0.6	Wayland Union Schools	Wayland
144	0.5	Alma Public Schools	Alma
144	0.5	Bedford Public Schools	Temperance
144	0.5	Beecher Community SD	Flint
144	0.5	Eaton Rapids Public Schools	Eaton Rapids
144	0.5	Gibraltar SD	Woodhaven
144	0.5	Goodrich Area Schools	Goodrich
144	0.5	Grosse Pointe Public Schools	Grosse Pointe
144	0.5	Hillsdale Community Schools	Hillsdale
144	0.5	Howell Public Schools	Howell
144	0.5	Mattawan Consolidated School	Mattawan
144	0.5	Saginaw Township Comm. Schools	Saginaw
155	0.4	Davison Community Schools	Davison
155	0.4	Dexter Community SD	Dexter
155	0.4	Hamilton Community Schools	Hamilton
155	0.4	Lake Shore Public Schls (Macomb)	St Clair Shores
155	0.4	Lakeview Public Schools (Macomb)	St Clair Shores
155	0.4	Lakewood Public Schools	Woodland
155	0.4	Mason Public Schools (Ingham)	Mason
155	0.4	Mona Shores Public SD	Muskegon
155	0.4	South Lyon Community Schools	South Lyon
164	0.3	Delton Kellogg Schools	Delton
164	0.3	Flushing Community Schools	Flushing
164	0.3	Gladwin Community Schools	Gladwin
164	0.3	Kearsley Community SD	Flint
164	0.3	Lapeer Community Schools	Lapeer
164	0.3	Linden Community Schools	Linden
164	0.3	Lowell Area Schools	Lowell
164	0.3	Mt. Pleasant City SD	Mount Pleasant
164	0.3	Redford Union Schools Dist. No. 1	Redford
164	0.3	South Lake Schools	St Clair Shores
164	0.3	Three Rivers Community Schools	Three Rivers
164	0.3	Trenton Public Schools	Trenton
164	0.3	Western SD	Parma
177	0.2	Armada Area Schools	Armada
177	0.2	Bullock Creek SD	Midland
177	0.2	Cedar Springs Public Schools	Cedar Springs
177	0.2	Dewitt Public Schools	Dewitt
177	0.2	Edwardsburg Public Schools	Edwardsburg
177	0.2	Flat Rock Community Schools	Flat Rock
177	0.2	Freeland Community SD	Freeland
177	0.2	Jenison Public Schools	Jenison
177	0.2	Marquette Area Public Schools	Marquette
177	0.2	Mt. Morris Consolidated Schools	Mount Morris
177	0.2	Pinckney Community Schools	Pinckney
177	0.2	Reeths-Puffer Schools	Muskegon
177	0.2	Rockford Public Schools	Rockford
177	0.2	Tri County Area Schools	Sand Lake
177	0.2	Williamston Community Schools	Williamston
177	0.2	Wyandotte SD	Wyandotte
193	0.1	Algonac Community SD	Algonac
193	0.1	Alpena Public Schools	Alpena
193	0.1	Bendle Public Schools	Burton
193	0.1	Breitung Township SD	Kingsford
193	0.1	Clio Area SD	Clio
193	0.1	Coloma Community Schools	Coloma
193	0.1	Columbia SD	Brooklyn
193	0.1	Hartland Consolidated Schools	Hartland
193	0.1	Macomb ISD	Clinton Twp
193	0.1	Sault Ste Marie Area Schools	Sault Ste Marie
203	0.0	Allegan Public Schools	Allegan
203	0.0	Bangor Township Schools	Bay City
203	0.0	Benton Harbor Area Schools	Benton Harbor
203	0.0	Benzie County Central Schools	Benzonia
203	0.0	Big Rapids Public Schools	Big Rapids
203	0.0	Birch Run Area Schools	Birch Run
203	0.0	Brighton Area Schools	Brighton
203	0.0	Cadillac Area Public Schools	Cadillac
203	0.0	Caro Community Schools	Caro
203	0.0	Carrollton Public Schools	Saginaw
203	0.0	Chandler Park Academy	Harper Woods
203	0.0	Charlotte Public Schools	Charlotte
203	0.0	Cheboygan Area Schools	Cheboygan
203	0.0	Chesaning Union Schools	Chesaning
203	0.0	Chippewa Hills SD	Remus
203	0.0	Clare Public Schools	Clare
203	0.0	Corunna Public Schools	Corunna
203	0.0	Crawford Ausable Schools	Grayling
203	0.0	Croswell-Lexington Comm. Schools	Croswell
203	0.0	Dundee Community Schools	Dundee
203	0.0	Durand Area Schools	Durand
203	0.0	East China SD	East China
203	0.0	Escanaba Area Public Schools	Escanaba
203	0.0	Essexville-Hampton Public Schools	Essexville
203	0.0	Fenton Area Public Schools	Fenton
203	0.0	Fremont Public SD	Fremont
203	0.0	Fruitport Community Schools	Fruitport
203	0.0	Gaylord Community Schools	Gaylord
203	0.0	Gladstone Area Schools	Gladstone
203	0.0	Grosse Ile Township Schools	Grosse Ile
203	0.0	Gull Lake Community Schools	Richland
203	0.0	Harper Creek Community Schools	Battle Creek
203	0.0	Harrison Community Schools	Harrison
203	0.0	Hopkins Public Schools	Hopkins
203	0.0	Houghton Lake Community Schools	Houghton Lake
203	0.0	Jefferson Schools (Monroe)	Monroe
203	0.0	Kalkaska Public Schools	Kalkaska
203	0.0	Kent ISD	Grand Rapids
203	0.0	Lakeshore SD (Berrien)	Stevensville
203	0.0	Lakeville Community SD	Otisville
203	0.0	Livonia Public Schools SD	Livonia
203	0.0	Ludington Area SD	Ludington
203	0.0	Manistee Area Public Schools	Manistee
203	0.0	Marshall Public Schools	Marshall
203	0.0	Marysville Public Schools	Marysville
203	0.0	Menominee Area Public Schools	Menominee
203	0.0	Muskegon Hgts SD	Muskegon
203	0.0	Napoleon Community Schools	Napoleon
203	0.0	North Branch Area Schools	North Branch
203	0.0	Northwest Community Schools	Jackson
203	0.0	Oakridge Public Schools	Muskegon
203	0.0	Old Redford Academy	Detroit
203	0.0	Olivet Community Schools	Olivet
203	0.0	Onsted Community Schools	Onsted
203	0.0	Orchard View Schools	Muskegon
203	0.0	Otsego Public Schools	Otsego
203	0.0	Owosso Public Schools	Owosso
203	0.0	Parchment SD	Kalamazoo
203	0.0	Pennfield Schools	Battle Creek
203	0.0	Perry Public Schools	Perry
203	0.0	Plainwell Community Schools	Plainwell
203	0.0	Portage Public Schools	Portage
203	0.0	Portland Public Schools	Portland
203	0.0	Public Schools of Petoskey	Petoskey
203	0.0	Reed City Area Public Schools	Reed City
203	0.0	Saginaw ISD	Saginaw
203	0.0	Saint Joseph Public Schools	Saint Joseph
203	0.0	Shepherd Public Schools	Shepherd
203	0.0	South Haven Public Schools	South Haven
203	0.0	Spring Lake Public Schools	Spring Lake
203	0.0	Standish-Sterling Community Schls	Standish
203	0.0	Stockbridge Community Schools	Stockbridge
203	0.0	Swan Valley SD	Saginaw
203	0.0	Tecumseh Public Schools	Tecumseh
203	0.0	University Preparatory Acad. (PSAD)	Detroit
203	0.0	Vicksburg Community Schools	Vicksburg
203	0.0	Wayne Resa	Wayne
203	0.0	West Branch-Rose City Area Schls	Rose City
203	0.0	Whitehall District Schools	Whitehall
203	0.0	Yale Public Schools	Yale

Students Eligible for Free Lunch

Rank	Percent	District Name	City
1	93.5	Cesar Chavez Academy	Detroit
2	90.1	Benton Harbor Area Schools	Benton Harbor
3	88.5	Hamtramck SD	Hamtramck
4	87.3	SD of the City of Inkster	Inkster
5	87.1	Muskegon Hgts SD	Muskegon
6	84.5	Chandler Park Academy	Harper Woods
7	81.8	Beecher Community SD	Flint
8	81.7	Grand Rapids Public Schools	Grand Rapids
8	81.7	Muskegon Public Schools	Muskegon
10	80.6	Flint SD	Flint
11	80.4	Detroit City SD	Detroit
12	80.2	Mount Clemens Community SD	Mount Clemens
13	80.0	Saginaw SD	Saginaw
14	79.4	Godfrey-Lee Public Schools	Wyoming
15	78.2	Van Dyke Public Schools	Warren
16	76.5	Battle Creek Public Schools	Battle Creek
17	75.8	Godwin Heights Public Schools	Grand Rapids
18	74.9	Old Redford Academy	Detroit
19	74.3	Pontiac City SD	Pontiac
20	73.2	Oak Park SD	Oak Park
21	72.5	Fitzgerald Public Schools	Warren
22	72.1	Bendle Public Schools	Burton
23	71.7	University Preparatory Acad. (PSAD)	Detroit
24	70.9	Clintondale Community Schools	Clinton Twp
25	70.4	East Detroit Public Schools	Eastpointe
26	69.7	Mt. Morris Consolidated Schools	Mount Morris
27	68.8	Lincoln Park SD	Lincoln Park
28	68.6	Kelloggsville Public Schools	Grand Rapids
29	68.2	Jackson Public Schools	Jackson
30	68.1	Willow Run Community Schools	Ypsilanti
31	67.0	Harrison Community Schools	Harrison
32	66.6	Westwood Community SD	Dearborn Hgts

Note: This section only includes districts with 1,500 or more students; All categories are ranked from high to low

33	66.5	Houghton Lake Community Schools	Houghton Lake
34	65.8	Dearborn City SD	Dearborn
34	65.8	Hazel Park SD	Hazel Park
36	65.1	Carrollton Public Schools	Saginaw
37	64.8	Romulus Community Schools	Romulus
38	64.6	Orchard View Schools	Muskegon
39	64.3	Kalamazoo Public Schools	Kalamazoo
40	64.1	Roseville Community Schools	Roseville
41	63.8	Dowagiac Union SD	Dowagiac
42	63.0	Taylor SD	Taylor
43	62.8	Carman-Ainsworth Comm. Schools	Flint
44	62.4	Lansing Public SD	Lansing
45	62.1	Wyoming Public Schools	Wyoming
46	61.9	Comstock Public Schools	Kalamazoo
47	60.7	SD of Ypsilanti	Ypsilanti
48	59.7	Holland City SD	Holland
49	58.8	Shelby Public Schools	Shelby
50	58.5	Chippewa Hills SD	Remus
51	58.2	Center Line Public Schools	Center Line
52	57.8	Sturgis Public Schools	Sturgis
53	57.4	Melvindale-North Allen Park Schools	Melvindale
54	57.0	Adrian SD	Adrian
55	56.3	Coloma Community Schools	Coloma
55	56.3	Kalkaska Public Schools	Kalkaska
57	55.9	Kentwood Public Schools	Grand Rapids
58	55.8	Dearborn Hgts SD #7	Dearborn Hgts
59	55.5	Hillsdale Community Schools	Hillsdale
60	54.6	Wayne-Westland Community SD	Westland
61	54.2	Ferndale Public Schools	Ferndale
62	54.0	Redford Union Schools Dist. No. 1	Redford
63	53.9	Cheboygan Area Schools	Cheboygan
64	53.3	Niles Community Schools	Niles
65	53.2	Crestwood SD	Dearborn Hgts
65	53.2	Newaygo Public SD	Newaygo
67	53.0	Benzie County Central Schools	Benzonia
68	52.8	Crawford Ausable Schools	Grayling
69	52.6	South Haven Public Schools	South Haven
70	52.5	Owosso Public Schools	Owosso
71	52.4	Central Montcalm Public Schools	Stanton
72	51.9	Berrien Springs Public Schools	Berrien Springs
73	51.8	Ionia Public Schools	Ionia
74	51.7	Belding Area SD	Belding
75	51.5	Oakridge Public Schools	Muskegon
75	51.5	West Branch-Rose City Area Schls	Rose City
77	50.5	Three Rivers Community Schools	Three Rivers
78	50.2	Port Huron Area SD	Port Huron
79	50.1	Reed City Area Public Schools	Reed City
80	49.9	Gladwin Community Schools	Gladwin
81	49.8	Caro Community Schools	Caro
82	49.6	Southfield Public SD	Southfield
83	49.3	Saginaw ISD	Saginaw
84	48.9	Kearsley Community SD	Flint
85	48.7	Cadillac Area Public Schools	Cadillac
86	48.4	Monroe Public Schools	Monroe
87	47.9	Alma Public Schools	Alma
87	47.9	Coldwater Community Schools	Coldwater
89	47.3	Grant Public SD	Grant
90	46.5	Warren Consolidated Schools	Warren
91	46.3	Clarenceville SD	Livonia
92	46.0	South Lake Schools	St Clair Shores
93	45.9	Delton Kellogg Schools	Delton
93	45.9	South Redford SD	Redford
95	45.8	Ludington Area SD	Ludington
96	45.6	Van Buren Public Schools	Belleville
97	45.1	Summit Academy North	Romulus
98	45.0	Parchment SD	Kalamazoo
99	44.6	Standish-Sterling Community Schls	Standish
100	44.5	Gaylord Community Schools	Gaylord
101	44.3	Greenville Public Schools	Greenville
102	44.2	Alpena Public Schools	Alpena
103	44.1	Croswell-Lexington Comm. Schools	Croswell
104	44.0	Lakeville Community SD	Otisville
105	43.9	Warren Woods Public Schools	Warren
106	43.8	Lincoln Consolidated SD	Ypsilanti
107	43.7	Big Rapids Public Schools	Big Rapids
108	43.6	West Ottawa Public SD	Holland
109	43.4	Clare Public Schools	Clare
109	43.4	Lamphere Public Schools	Madison Heights
111	43.2	Imlay City Community Schools	Imlay City
112	43.1	Clio Area SD	Clio
112	43.1	Durand Area Schools	Durand
114	42.9	Wyandotte SD	Wyandotte
115	42.8	North Branch Area Schools	North Branch
116	42.6	Bay City SD	Bay City
117	42.3	Bangor Township Schools	Bay City
118	42.1	Pennfield Schools	Battle Creek
119	42.0	Corunna Public Schools	Corunna
120	41.7	Napoleon Community Schools	Napoleon
121	41.5	Waterford SD	Waterford
122	41.4	Cedar Springs Public Schools	Cedar Springs
123	40.9	Buchanan Community Schools	Buchanan
124	40.6	Garden City SD	Garden City
125	40.5	Northwest Community Schools	Jackson
125	40.5	Paw Paw Public SD	Paw Paw
125	40.5	Waverly Community Schools	Lansing
128	40.4	Manistee Area Public Schools	Manistee
129	40.3	Macomb ISD	Clinton Twp
130	40.1	Reeths-Puffer Schools	Muskegon
131	40.0	Lapeer Community Schools	Lapeer
132	39.9	Tri County Area Schools	Sand Lake
133	39.5	Comstock Park Public Schools	Comstock Park
134	39.4	Southgate Community SD	Southgate
135	39.2	Fraser Public Schools	Fraser
135	39.2	Shepherd Public Schools	Shepherd
137	39.1	Fruitport Community Schools	Fruitport
137	39.1	Sault Ste Marie Area Schools	Sault Ste Marie
139	38.9	Columbia SD	Brooklyn
140	38.7	Menominee Area Public Schools	Menominee
141	38.3	Sparta Area Schools	Sparta
142	38.1	Escanaba Area Public Schools	Escanaba
142	38.1	Swartz Creek Community Schools	Swartz Creek
144	38.0	Algonac Community SD	Algonac
145	37.9	Airport Community Schools	Carleton
146	37.5	Charlotte Public Schools	Charlotte
147	36.8	Mt. Pleasant City SD	Mount Pleasant
148	36.7	Kenowa Hills Public Schools	Grand Rapids
149	36.6	Lakeview SD (Calhoun)	Battle Creek
150	36.5	L'anse Creuse Public Schools	Harrison Twp
151	36.2	Davison Community Schools	Davison
152	36.0	Eaton Rapids Public Schools	Eaton Rapids
153	35.8	Hastings Area SD	Hastings
154	35.5	Whitehall District Schools	Whitehall
155	35.3	Otsego Public Schools	Otsego
156	35.2	Lake Shore Public Schls (Macomb)	St Clair Shores
156	35.2	Northview Public Schools	Grand Rapids
156	35.2	Saginaw Township Comm. Schools	Saginaw
159	34.7	Wayland Union Schools	Wayland
160	34.3	Birch Run Area Schools	Birch Run
161	34.2	Holly Area SD	Holly
161	34.2	Perry Public Schools	Perry
163	34.0	Edwardsburg Public Schools	Edwardsburg
164	33.9	Traverse City Area Public Schools	Traverse City
165	33.5	Western SD	Parma
166	33.4	Stockbridge Community Schools	Stockbridge
167	33.2	Flat Rock Community Schools	Flat Rock
167	33.2	Lakewood Public Schools	Woodland
167	33.2	Olivet Community Schools	Olivet
170	32.7	Brandon SD	Ortonville
171	32.5	Public Schools of Petoskey	Petoskey
172	32.2	Chesaning Union Schools	Chesaning
172	32.2	Harper Creek Community Schools	Battle Creek
172	32.2	Holt Public Schools	Holt
172	32.2	Yale Public Schools	Yale
176	32.0	Woodhaven-Brownstown SD	Woodhaven
177	31.9	Mona Shores Public SD	Muskegon
177	31.9	Plainwell Community Schools	Plainwell
179	31.7	Ovid-Elsie Area Schools	Elsie
180	31.6	Bullock Creek SD	Midland
181	31.4	Breitung Township SD	Kingsford
182	31.3	Allegan Public Schools	Allegan
183	31.2	Hopkins Public Schools	Hopkins
184	31.1	Jefferson Schools (Monroe)	Monroe
185	30.5	Riverview Community SD	Riverview
185	30.5	Swan Valley SD	Saginaw
187	29.9	Essexville-Hampton Public Schools	Essexville
187	29.9	Onsted Community Schools	Onsted
189	29.5	Flushing Community Schools	Flushing
190	29.4	Clawson Public Schools	Clawson
190	29.4	Grand Haven Area Public Schools	Grand Haven
192	28.8	Gladstone Area Schools	Gladstone
193	28.6	Coopersville Area Public SD	Coopersville
194	28.4	Fowlerville Community Schools	Fowlerville
194	28.4	Marshall Public Schools	Marshall
196	27.4	Almont Community Schools	Almont
197	27.3	Gibraltar SD	Woodhaven
198	27.2	Lakeview Public Schools (Macomb)	St Clair Shores
198	27.2	Milan Area Schools	Milan
198	27.2	Richmond Community Schools	Richmond
201	27.0	Vicksburg Community Schools	Vicksburg
202	26.9	East China SD	East China
202	26.9	Thornapple Kellogg SD	Middleville
204	26.8	Linden Community Schools	Linden
205	26.6	Allendale Public Schools	Allendale
206	26.4	East Lansing SD	East Lansing
207	26.1	Avondale SD	Auburn Hills
208	25.9	Dundee Community Schools	Dundee
209	25.8	Allen Park Public Schools	Allen Park
209	25.8	Howell Public Schools	Howell
211	25.6	Fenton Area Public Schools	Fenton
212	25.1	Portland Public Schools	Portland
213	25.0	Berkley SD	Oak Park
213	25.0	Huron SD	New Boston
215	24.8	Grandville Public Schools	Grandville
216	24.6	Marquette Area Public Schools	Marquette
217	24.5	Huron Valley Schools	Highland
218	24.3	Lowell Area Schools	Lowell
218	24.3	Utica Community Schools	Sterling Hgts
220	24.0	Grand Blanc Community Schools	Grand Blanc
220	24.0	Saint Johns Public Schools	Saint Johns
222	23.9	Lakeshore SD (Berrien)	Stevensville
222	23.9	SD of the City of Royal Oak	Royal Oak
224	23.8	Marysville Public Schools	Marysville
225	23.7	Romeo Community Schools	Romeo
226	23.3	Mason Public Schools (Ingham)	Mason
227	22.8	Midland Public Schools	Midland
228	22.7	Walled Lake Consolidated Schools	Walled Lake
229	22.4	Chippewa Valley Schools	Clinton Twp
230	22.3	Farmington Public SD	Farmington
231	22.0	Trenton Public Schools	Trenton
232	21.7	Grand Ledge Public Schools	Grand Ledge
233	21.4	Portage Public Schools	Portage
234	21.3	Anchor Bay SD	Casco
235	21.0	Livonia Public Schools SD	Livonia
236	20.6	Ann Arbor Public Schools	Ann Arbor
237	20.4	Pinckney Community Schools	Pinckney
237	20.4	Tecumseh Public Schools	Tecumseh
239	20.2	West Bloomfield SD	West Bloomfield
240	20.1	Hamilton Community Schools	Hamilton
241	20.0	Oxford Community Schools	Oxford
242	19.8	Byron Center Public Schools	Byron Center
243	19.6	Jenison Public Schools	Jenison
244	19.5	Williamston Community Schools	Williamston
245	19.0	Clarkston Community SD	Clarkston
246	18.9	Bedford Public Schools	Temperance
246	18.9	Zeeland Public Schools	Zeeland
248	18.6	Gull Lake Community Schools	Richland
249	18.1	Spring Lake Public Schools	Spring Lake
250	17.9	South Lyon Community Schools	South Lyon
251	17.7	Freeland Community SD	Freeland
252	17.4	Hudsonville Public SD	Hudsonville
253	17.3	Goodrich Area Schools	Goodrich
254	17.0	Haslett Public Schools	Haslett
255	16.7	Wayne Resa	Wayne
256	16.0	Lake Fenton Community Schools	Fenton
257	15.7	Lake Orion Community Schools	Lake Orion
258	14.9	Armada Area Schools	Armada
259	14.4	Saint Joseph Public Schools	Saint Joseph
260	14.0	Caledonia Community Schools	Caledonia
261	13.9	Mattawan Consolidated School	Mattawan
262	13.8	Okemos Public Schools	Okemos
263	13.3	Grosse Pointe Public Schools	Grosse Pointe
264	12.8	Rockford Public Schools	Rockford
265	12.6	Rochester Community SD	Rochester
266	12.5	Hartland Consolidated Schools	Hartland
267	12.0	Plymouth-Canton Comm Schools	Plymouth
268	10.9	Troy SD	Troy
269	10.8	Brighton Area Schools	Brighton
270	9.4	Forest Hills Public Schools	Grand Rapids
271	9.1	Bloomfield Hls SD	Bloomfield Hls
271	9.1	Chelsea SD	Chelsea
273	9.0	Dewitt Public Schools	Dewitt
274	8.4	Grosse Ile Township Schools	Grosse Ile
275	7.8	Novi Community SD	Novi
276	7.7	Dexter Community SD	Dexter
277	7.6	E Grand Rapids Public Schools	Grand Rapids
278	7.5	Saline Area Schools	Saline
279	7.3	SD of the City of Birmingham	Birmingham
280	5.6	Northville Public Schools	Northville
n/a	n/a	Fremont Public SD	Fremont
n/a	n/a	Kent ISD	Grand Rapids

Note: This section only includes districts with 1,500 or more students; All categories are ranked from high to low

Students Eligible for Reduced-Price Lunch

Rank	Percent	District Name	City
1	39.2	Lakeview Public Schools (Macomb)	St Clair Shores
2	33.3	Wayne Resa	Wayne
3	12.2	Oakridge Public Schools	Muskegon
4	11.8	Lake Shore Public Schls (Macomb)	St Clair Shores
4	11.8	Wayland Union Schools	Wayland
6	11.3	Imlay City Community Schools	Imlay City
7	10.7	Tri County Area Schools	Sand Lake
7	10.7	Warren Woods Public Schools	Warren
9	10.5	Belding Area SD	Belding
9	10.5	Croswell-Lexington Comm. Schools	Croswell
9	10.5	Manistee Area Public Schools	Manistee
12	10.4	Crawford Ausable Schools	Grayling
12	10.4	Durand Area Schools	Durand
12	10.4	West Ottawa Public SD	Holland
15	10.3	Kelloggsville Public Schools	Grand Rapids
16	10.2	Crestwood SD	Dearborn Hgts
17	10.1	Corunna Public Schools	Corunna
18	9.9	Standish-Sterling Community Schls	Standish
19	9.8	Benzie County Central Schools	Benzonia
19	9.8	Clawson Public Schools	Clawson
21	9.6	Lakewood Public Schools	Woodland
21	9.6	Wyoming Public Schools	Wyoming
23	9.5	West Branch-Rose City Area Schls	Rose City
24	9.4	Roseville Community Schools	Roseville
25	9.2	Reeths-Puffer Schools	Muskegon
25	9.2	Shelby Public Schools	Shelby
27	9.0	Big Rapids Public Schools	Big Rapids
27	9.0	Dearborn Hgts SD #7	Dearborn Hgts
29	8.9	Hopkins Public Schools	Hopkins
29	8.9	Lincoln Park SD	Lincoln Park
29	8.9	Olivet Community Schools	Olivet
32	8.8	Gladstone Area Schools	Gladstone
32	8.8	Kenowa Hills Public Schools	Grand Rapids
32	8.8	North Branch Area Schools	North Branch
35	8.7	Kalkaska Public Schools	Kalkaska
36	8.6	Greenville Public Schools	Greenville
36	8.6	Lapeer Community Schools	Lapeer
36	8.6	Northview Public Schools	Grand Rapids
36	8.6	Wayne-Westland Community SD	Westland
40	8.5	Central Montcalm Public Schools	Stanton
40	8.5	Lakeville Community SD	Otisville
40	8.5	Western SD	Parma
43	8.4	Buchanan Community Schools	Buchanan
43	8.4	Grand Haven Area Public Schools	Grand Haven
45	8.3	Coldwater Community Schools	Coldwater
45	8.3	Escanaba Area Public Schools	Escanaba
45	8.3	Grandville Public Schools	Grandville
45	8.3	Niles Community Schools	Niles
45	8.3	Summit Academy North	Romulus
45	8.3	Waterford SD	Waterford
51	8.2	Cadillac Area Public Schools	Cadillac
51	8.2	Caro Community Schools	Caro
51	8.2	Hillsdale Community Schools	Hillsdale
51	8.2	Melvindale-North Allen Park Schools	Melvindale
51	8.2	Swartz Creek Community Schools	Swartz Creek
56	8.1	Allendale Public Schools	Allendale
56	8.1	Cheboygan Area Schools	Cheboygan
56	8.1	Comstock Park Public Schools	Comstock Park
56	8.1	Fowlerville Community Schools	Fowlerville
56	8.1	Menominee Area Public Schools	Menominee
61	8.0	Three Rivers Community Schools	Three Rivers
61	8.0	University Preparatory Acad. (PSAD)	Detroit
63	7.9	Alpena Public Schools	Alpena
63	7.9	Hamilton Community Schools	Hamilton
63	7.9	Lowell Area Schools	Lowell
63	7.9	Orchard View Schools	Muskegon
63	7.9	Public Schools of Petoskey	Petoskey
68	7.8	Cedar Springs Public Schools	Cedar Springs
68	7.8	Harrison Community Schools	Harrison
68	7.8	Holland City SD	Holland
68	7.8	Southfield Public SD	Southfield
72	7.7	Bangor Township Schools	Bay City
72	7.7	Carman-Ainsworth Comm. Schools	Flint
72	7.7	Ionia Public Schools	Ionia
72	7.7	Shepherd Public Schools	Shepherd
76	7.6	Byron Center Public Schools	Byron Center
76	7.6	Fraser Public Schools	Fraser
76	7.6	Romulus Community Schools	Romulus
79	7.5	Jenison Public Schools	Jenison
80	7.4	Breitung Township SD	Kingsford
80	7.4	Delton Kellogg Schools	Delton
80	7.4	Eaton Rapids Public Schools	Eaton Rapids
80	7.4	Hastings Area SD	Hastings
80	7.4	Kearsley Community SD	Flint
80	7.4	Kentwood Public Schools	Grand Rapids
80	7.4	Warren Consolidated Schools	Warren
87	7.3	Godfrey-Lee Public Schools	Wyoming
87	7.3	Swan Valley SD	Saginaw
89	7.2	Chippewa Hills SD	Remus
89	7.2	Fenton Area Public Schools	Fenton
89	7.2	Holly Area SD	Holly
89	7.2	Parchment SD	Kalamazoo
89	7.2	Reed City Area Public Schools	Reed City
94	7.1	Coloma Community Schools	Coloma
94	7.1	Houghton Lake Community Schools	Houghton Lake
94	7.1	Zeeland Public Schools	Zeeland
97	7.0	Algonac Community SD	Algonac
97	7.0	Alma Public Schools	Alma
97	7.0	Pennfield Schools	Battle Creek
97	7.0	Stockbridge Community Schools	Stockbridge
97	7.0	Wyandotte SD	Wyandotte
102	6.9	Allen Park Public Schools	Allen Park
102	6.9	Bedford Public Schools	Temperance
102	6.9	Fruitport Community Schools	Fruitport
105	6.8	Charlotte Public Schools	Charlotte
105	6.8	Clarenceville SD	Livonia
105	6.8	South Redford SD	Redford
105	6.8	Tecumseh Public Schools	Tecumseh
109	6.7	Sault Ste Marie Area Schools	Sault Ste Marie
109	6.7	Taylor SD	Taylor
111	6.6	Center Line Public Schools	Center Line
111	6.6	Dowagiac Union SD	Dowagiac
111	6.6	Jackson Public Schools	Jackson
111	6.6	Yale Public Schools	Yale
115	6.5	Davison Community Schools	Davison
115	6.5	Godwin Heights Public Schools	Grand Rapids
115	6.5	Traverse City Area Public Schools	Traverse City
118	6.4	Bay City SD	Bay City
118	6.4	Berrien Springs Public Schools	Berrien Springs
118	6.4	Jefferson Schools (Monroe)	Monroe
118	6.4	Ovid-Elsie Area Schools	Elsie
118	6.4	Sturgis Public Schools	Sturgis
123	6.3	Carrollton Public Schools	Saginaw
123	6.3	East Detroit Public Schools	Eastpointe
123	6.3	Fitzgerald Public Schools	Warren
123	6.3	Mason Public Schools (Ingham)	Mason
123	6.3	Southgate Community SD	Southgate
128	6.2	Garden City SD	Garden City
128	6.2	Gladwin Community Schools	Gladwin
128	6.2	Northwest Community Schools	Jackson
128	6.2	Perry Public Schools	Perry
132	6.1	Adrian SD	Adrian
132	6.1	South Lake Schools	St Clair Shores
132	6.1	Thornapple Kellogg SD	Middleville
135	6.0	Clare Public Schools	Clare
135	6.0	Lincoln Consolidated SD	Ypsilanti
135	6.0	Mona Shores Public SD	Muskegon
135	6.0	Owosso Public Schools	Owosso
135	6.0	Whitehall District Schools	Whitehall
140	5.9	Comstock Public Schools	Kalamazoo
140	5.9	Flat Rock Community Schools	Flat Rock
140	5.9	Vicksburg Community Schools	Vicksburg
143	5.8	Sparta Area Schools	Sparta
144	5.7	Birch Run Area Schools	Birch Run
144	5.7	East China SD	East China
144	5.7	Flushing Community Schools	Flushing
144	5.7	Mt. Morris Consolidated Schools	Mount Morris
144	5.7	Newaygo Public SD	Newaygo
144	5.7	Van Buren Public Schools	Belleville
150	5.6	Caledonia Community Schools	Caledonia
150	5.6	Monroe Public Schools	Monroe
150	5.6	Otsego Public Schools	Otsego
150	5.6	Saint Johns Public Schools	Saint Johns
154	5.5	Lamphere Public Schools	Madison Heights
155	5.4	Columbia SD	Brooklyn
155	5.4	Ferndale Public Schools	Ferndale
155	5.4	Onsted Community Schools	Onsted
155	5.4	Redford Union Schools Dist. No. 1	Redford
159	5.3	Kalamazoo Public Schools	Kalamazoo
159	5.3	Riverview Community SD	Riverview
159	5.3	Waverly Community Schools	Lansing
162	5.2	Airport Community Schools	Carleton
162	5.2	Huron Valley Schools	Highland
162	5.2	Lakeview SD (Calhoun)	Battle Creek
162	5.2	Milan Area Schools	Milan
162	5.2	Port Huron Area SD	Port Huron
162	5.2	SD of Ypsilanti	Ypsilanti
168	5.1	Clio Area SD	Clio
168	5.1	Dundee Community Schools	Dundee
168	5.1	Edwardsburg Public Schools	Edwardsburg
168	5.1	Essexville-Hampton Public Schools	Essexville
168	5.1	Hudsonville Public SD	Hudsonville
168	5.1	Huron SD	New Boston
168	5.1	Linden Community Schools	Linden
168	5.1	Mount Clemens Community SD	Mount Clemens
168	5.1	Old Redford Academy	Detroit
177	5.0	Coopersville Area Public SD	Coopersville
177	5.0	Howell Public Schools	Howell
177	5.0	Lakeshore SD (Berrien)	Stevensville
177	5.0	Paw Paw Public SD	Paw Paw
177	5.0	Woodhaven-Brownstown SD	Woodhaven
182	4.9	Grant Public SD	Grant
182	4.9	Holt Public Schools	Holt
182	4.9	Napoleon Community Schools	Napoleon
185	4.8	Anchor Bay SD	Casco
185	4.8	Portage Public Schools	Portage
185	4.8	Spring Lake Public Schools	Spring Lake
188	4.7	Farmington Public SD	Farmington
188	4.7	Portland Public Schools	Portland
190	4.6	Brandon SD	Ortonville
190	4.6	Hazel Park SD	Hazel Park
190	4.6	Ludington Area SD	Ludington
190	4.6	Marysville Public Schools	Marysville
190	4.6	Plainwell Community Schools	Plainwell
190	4.6	South Haven Public Schools	South Haven
196	4.5	Van Dyke Public Schools	Warren
197	4.4	Almont Community Schools	Almont
197	4.4	Mt. Pleasant City SD	Mount Pleasant
199	4.3	Bendle Public Schools	Burton
199	4.3	Grand Blanc Community Schools	Grand Blanc
199	4.3	Romeo Community Schools	Romeo
199	4.3	Saginaw Township Comm. Schools	Saginaw
199	4.3	Utica Community Schools	Sterling Hgts
204	4.2	Gibraltar SD	Woodhaven
204	4.2	Midland Public Schools	Midland
206	4.1	Gaylord Community Schools	Gaylord
206	4.1	Livonia Public Schools SD	Livonia
208	4.0	Avondale SD	Auburn Hills
208	4.0	Bullock Creek SD	Midland
208	4.0	Richmond Community Schools	Richmond
208	4.0	SD of the City of Royal Oak	Royal Oak
212	3.9	Armada Area Schools	Armada
212	3.9	Battle Creek Public Schools	Battle Creek
212	3.9	Chandler Park Academy	Harper Woods
212	3.9	Dearborn City SD	Dearborn
212	3.9	Hartland Consolidated Schools	Hartland
212	3.9	Mattawan Consolidated School	Mattawan
212	3.9	Muskegon Public Schools	Muskegon
212	3.9	Saint Joseph Public Schools	Saint Joseph
212	3.9	Walled Lake Consolidated Schools	Walled Lake
221	3.8	East Lansing SD	East Lansing
221	3.8	Harper Creek Community Schools	Battle Creek
221	3.8	Macomb ISD	Clinton Twp
224	3.7	Clarkston Community SD	Clarkston
224	3.7	Lake Orion Community Schools	Lake Orion
224	3.7	Marshall Public Schools	Marshall
227	3.6	Clintondale Community Schools	Clinton Twp
227	3.6	Marquette Area Public Schools	Marquette
227	3.6	Oxford Community Schools	Oxford
227	3.6	South Lyon Community Schools	South Lyon
231	3.5	Chippewa Valley Schools	Clinton Twp
231	3.5	Goodrich Area Schools	Goodrich
231	3.5	Grand Rapids Public Schools	Grand Rapids
234	3.4	Berkley SD	Oak Park
234	3.4	Oak Park SD	Oak Park
236	3.3	West Bloomfield SD	West Bloomfield
237	3.2	Haslett Public Schools	Haslett
238	3.1	Brighton Area Schools	Brighton
238	3.1	Chelsea SD	Chelsea
240	3.0	Freeland Community SD	Freeland
241	2.9	Chesaning Union Schools	Chesaning
241	2.9	Grand Ledge Public Schools	Grand Ledge
241	2.9	Gull Lake Community Schools	Richland
241	2.9	Okemos Public Schools	Okemos
241	2.9	Pinckney Community Schools	Pinckney
241	2.9	Williamston Community Schools	Williamston
247	2.8	Benton Harbor Area Schools	Benton Harbor
247	2.8	Cesar Chavez Academy	Detroit
247	2.8	Plymouth-Canton Comm Schools	Plymouth
250	2.7	Lansing Public SD	Lansing
251	2.6	Ann Arbor Public Schools	Ann Arbor

Note: This section only includes districts with 1,500 or more students; All categories are ranked from high to low

251	2.6	Rockford Public Schools	Rockford
253	2.3	Rochester Community SD	Rochester
253	2.3	Trenton Public Schools	Trenton
255	2.2	Dexter Community SD	Dexter
255	2.2	Westwood Community SD	Dearborn Hgts
257	2.1	Grosse Pointe Public Schools	Grosse Pointe
258	2.0	Hamtramck SD	Hamtramck
258	2.0	Troy SD	Troy
260	1.9	Forest Hills Public Schools	Grand Rapids
261	1.8	Saginaw ISD	Saginaw
262	1.7	Novi Community SD	Novi
263	1.6	SD of the City of Birmingham	Birmingham
264	1.5	Saline Area Schools	Saline
265	1.4	Beecher Community SD	Flint
265	1.4	Dewitt Public Schools	Dewitt
265	1.4	Flint SD	Flint
265	1.4	Pontiac City SD	Pontiac
269	1.3	Bloomfield Hls SD	Bloomfield Hls
269	1.3	Detroit City SD	Detroit
269	1.3	Grosse Ile Township Schools	Grosse Ile
272	1.1	Muskegon Hgts SD	Muskegon
273	1.0	SD of the City of Inkster	Inkster
274	0.9	Willow Run Community Schools	Ypsilanti
275	0.8	Northville Public Schools	Northville
275	0.8	Saginaw SD	Saginaw
277	0.5	E Grand Rapids Public Schools	Grand Rapids
278	0.0	Allegan Public Schools	Allegan
278	0.0	L'anse Creuse Public Schools	Harrison Twp
278	0.0	Lake Fenton Community Schools	Fenton
n/a	n/a	Fremont Public SD	Fremont
n/a	n/a	Kent ISD	Grand Rapids

Student/Teacher Ratio

(number of students per teacher)

Rank	Number	District Name	City
1	10.4	Macomb ISD	Clinton Twp
2	11.8	Saginaw ISD	Saginaw
3	13.1	University Preparatory Acad. (PSAD)	Detroit
4	13.3	Bloomfield Hls SD	Bloomfield Hls
5	14.5	Flint SD	Flint
6	15.0	Adrian SD	Adrian
7	15.2	Grand Rapids Public Schools	Grand Rapids
8	15.3	Clawson Public Schools	Clawson
9	15.4	Battle Creek Public Schools	Battle Creek
9	15.4	SD of Ypsilanti	Ypsilanti
11	15.5	Pontiac City SD	Pontiac
12	15.6	Garden City SD	Garden City
13	15.7	Mt. Pleasant City SD	Mount Pleasant
13	15.7	Muskegon Hgts SD	Muskegon
15	15.8	Mount Clemens Community SD	Mount Clemens
15	15.8	Redford Union Schools Dist. No. 1	Redford
17	15.9	Kent ISD	Grand Rapids
17	15.9	Saginaw SD	Saginaw
19	16.0	Detroit City SD	Detroit
19	16.0	Harper Creek Community Schools	Battle Creek
19	16.0	Taylor SD	Taylor
22	16.1	Grosse Pointe Public Schools	Grosse Pointe
22	16.1	SD of the City of Birmingham	Birmingham
24	16.3	Crawford Ausable Schools	Grayling
24	16.3	Kalamazoo Public Schools	Kalamazoo
26	16.6	Dearborn City SD	Dearborn
26	16.6	Willow Run Community Schools	Ypsilanti
28	16.7	Farmington Public SD	Farmington
28	16.7	Jackson Public Schools	Jackson
30	16.8	Coloma Community Schools	Coloma
30	16.8	Menominee Area Public Schools	Menominee
32	17.0	Lamphere Public Schools	Madison Heights
32	17.0	Marshall Public Schools	Marshall
32	17.0	South Haven Public Schools	South Haven
35	17.1	Trenton Public Schools	Trenton
36	17.2	Alma Public Schools	Alma
36	17.2	Ann Arbor Public Schools	Ann Arbor
36	17.2	Novi Community SD	Novi
36	17.2	Southfield Public SD	Southfield
36	17.2	Warren Woods Public Schools	Warren
36	17.2	Waterford SD	Waterford
42	17.3	Muskegon Public Schools	Muskegon
42	17.3	Wyandotte SD	Wyandotte
44	17.4	Old Redford Academy	Detroit
45	17.5	Benton Harbor Area Schools	Benton Harbor
45	17.5	Carman-Ainsworth Comm. Schools	Flint
45	17.5	Corunna Public Schools	Corunna
45	17.5	Lansing Public SD	Lansing
49	17.6	Comstock Public Schools	Kalamazoo
49	17.6	Holly Area SD	Holly
49	17.6	Houghton Lake Community Schools	Houghton Lake
49	17.6	Okemos Public Schools	Okemos
49	17.6	Olivet Community Schools	Olivet
49	17.6	Perry Public Schools	Perry
55	17.7	East Lansing SD	East Lansing
55	17.7	Godfrey-Lee Public Schools	Wyoming
55	17.7	Reed City Area Public Schools	Reed City
55	17.7	Three Rivers Community Schools	Three Rivers
59	17.8	Carrollton Public Schools	Saginaw
59	17.8	Croswell-Lexington Comm. Schools	Croswell
59	17.8	Newaygo Public SD	Newaygo
59	17.8	Port Huron Area SD	Port Huron
63	17.9	Avondale SD	Auburn Hills
63	17.9	Forest Hills Public Schools	Grand Rapids
63	17.9	Grand Haven Area Public Schools	Grand Haven
63	17.9	Jefferson Schools (Monroe)	Monroe
63	17.9	Kalkaska Public Schools	Kalkaska
68	18.0	Cesar Chavez Academy	Detroit
68	18.0	Chelsea SD	Chelsea
68	18.0	Fruitport Community Schools	Fruitport
68	18.0	Marquette Area Public Schools	Marquette
68	18.0	Troy SD	Troy
68	18.0	West Bloomfield SD	West Bloomfield
74	18.1	Lakeview SD (Calhoun)	Battle Creek
75	18.2	Charlotte Public Schools	Charlotte
75	18.2	Parchment SD	Kalamazoo
75	18.2	Romulus Community Schools	Romulus
75	18.2	Shepherd Public Schools	Shepherd
75	18.2	Wayne-Westland Community SD	Westland
75	18.2	Williamston Community Schools	Williamston
81	18.3	Gull Lake Community Schools	Richland
81	18.3	Hazel Park SD	Hazel Park
81	18.3	Lincoln Consolidated SD	Ypsilanti
81	18.3	Niles Community Schools	Niles
81	18.3	Rochester Community SD	Rochester
81	18.3	Woodhaven-Brownstown SD	Woodhaven
87	18.4	Belding Area SD	Belding
87	18.4	Comstock Park Public Schools	Comstock Park
87	18.4	Dexter Community SD	Dexter
87	18.4	Mason Public Schools (Ingham)	Mason
87	18.4	Waverly Community Schools	Lansing
87	18.4	West Branch-Rose City Area Schls	Rose City
93	18.5	Cheboygan Area Schools	Cheboygan
93	18.5	Eaton Rapids Public Schools	Eaton Rapids
93	18.5	Van Dyke Public Schools	Warren
96	18.6	Berrien Springs Public Schools	Berrien Springs
96	18.6	Buchanan Community Schools	Buchanan
96	18.6	Cadillac Area Public Schools	Cadillac
96	18.6	Fitzgerald Public Schools	Warren
96	18.6	Hamtramck SD	Hamtramck
96	18.6	Holt Public Schools	Holt
102	18.7	Berkley SD	Oak Park
102	18.7	Godwin Heights Public Schools	Grand Rapids
102	18.7	Holland City SD	Holland
102	18.7	Livonia Public Schools SD	Livonia
102	18.7	Plainwell Community Schools	Plainwell
102	18.7	Rockford Public Schools	Rockford
102	18.7	Stockbridge Community Schools	Stockbridge
102	18.7	West Ottawa Public SD	Holland
110	18.8	Caledonia Community Schools	Caledonia
110	18.8	Milan Area Schools	Milan
110	18.8	Reeths-Puffer Schools	Muskegon
110	18.8	SD of the City of Royal Oak	Royal Oak
114	18.9	East Detroit Public Schools	Eastpointe
114	18.9	Gladwin Community Schools	Gladwin
114	18.9	Huron SD	New Boston
114	18.9	Lake Orion Community Schools	Lake Orion
114	18.9	Lakeville Community SD	Otisville
114	18.9	Lincoln Park SD	Lincoln Park
114	18.9	Mona Shores Public SD	Muskegon
114	18.9	Sault Ste Marie Area Schools	Sault Ste Marie
114	18.9	Shelby Public Schools	Shelby
114	18.9	Sturgis Public Schools	Sturgis
124	19.0	Chippewa Hills SD	Remus
124	19.0	Flat Rock Community Schools	Flat Rock
124	19.0	Fraser Public Schools	Fraser
124	19.0	Hudsonville Public SD	Hudsonville
124	19.0	Kelloggsville Public Schools	Grand Rapids
124	19.0	Midland Public Schools	Midland
124	19.0	Northview Public Schools	Grand Rapids
124	19.0	Otsego Public Schools	Otsego
124	19.0	South Lake Schools	St Clair Shores
133	19.1	E Grand Rapids Public Schools	Grand Rapids
133	19.1	Hamilton Community Schools	Hamilton
133	19.1	Huron Valley Schools	Highland
133	19.1	Ludington Area SD	Ludington
133	19.1	Swartz Creek Community Schools	Swartz Creek
133	19.1	Tecumseh Public Schools	Tecumseh
139	19.2	Airport Community Schools	Carleton
139	19.2	Chesaning Union Schools	Chesaning
139	19.2	Dowagiac Union SD	Dowagiac
139	19.2	Jenison Public Schools	Jenison
139	19.2	Pinckney Community Schools	Pinckney
139	19.2	Saint Johns Public Schools	Saint Johns
145	19.3	Ferndale Public Schools	Ferndale
145	19.3	Lakeshore SD (Berrien)	Stevensville
145	19.3	Oakridge Public Schools	Muskegon
145	19.3	Wayland Union Schools	Wayland
145	19.3	Wyoming Public Schools	Wyoming
150	19.4	Caro Community Schools	Caro
150	19.4	Clare Public Schools	Clare
150	19.4	Clarenceville SD	Livonia
150	19.4	Napoleon Community Schools	Napoleon
150	19.4	Portland Public Schools	Portland
150	19.4	Roseville Community Schools	Roseville
156	19.5	Center Line Public Schools	Center Line
156	19.5	Delton Kellogg Schools	Delton
156	19.5	Grand Ledge Public Schools	Grand Ledge
156	19.5	Haslett Public Schools	Haslett
156	19.5	Howell Public Schools	Howell
156	19.5	Lapeer Community Schools	Lapeer
156	19.5	Mt. Morris Consolidated Schools	Mount Morris
156	19.5	Northville Public Schools	Northville
156	19.5	Ovid-Elsie Area Schools	Elsie
156	19.5	Owosso Public Schools	Owosso
156	19.5	Paw Paw Public SD	Paw Paw
156	19.5	Southgate Community SD	Southgate
156	19.5	Traverse City Area Public Schools	Traverse City
156	19.5	Tri County Area Schools	Sand Lake
170	19.6	Algonac Community SD	Algonac
170	19.6	Allegan Public Schools	Allegan
170	19.6	Bullock Creek SD	Midland
170	19.6	Kenowa Hills Public Schools	Grand Rapids
170	19.6	Pennfield Schools	Battle Creek
170	19.6	Portage Public Schools	Portage
170	19.6	Public Schools of Petoskey	Petoskey
170	19.6	Sparta Area Schools	Sparta
170	19.6	Western SD	Parma
179	19.7	Brandon SD	Ortonville
179	19.7	Dewitt Public Schools	Dewitt
179	19.7	Durand Area Schools	Durand
179	19.7	East China SD	East China
179	19.7	Fowlerville Community Schools	Fowlerville
179	19.7	Grand Blanc Community Schools	Grand Blanc
179	19.7	Kentwood Public Schools	Grand Rapids
179	19.7	Saginaw Township Comm. Schools	Saginaw
179	19.7	Saint Joseph Public Schools	Saint Joseph
188	19.8	Armada Area Schools	Armada
188	19.8	Brighton Area Schools	Brighton
188	19.8	Cedar Springs Public Schools	Cedar Springs
188	19.8	Columbia SD	Brooklyn
188	19.8	Freeland Community SD	Freeland
188	19.8	Greenville Public Schools	Greenville
188	19.8	Hastings Area SD	Hastings
188	19.8	Lakewood Public Schools	Woodland
188	19.8	Plymouth-Canton Comm Schools	Plymouth
188	19.8	Vicksburg Community Schools	Vicksburg
188	19.8	Walled Lake Consolidated Schools	Walled Lake
188	19.8	Warren Consolidated Schools	Warren
200	19.9	Fenton Area Public Schools	Fenton
200	19.9	Hillsdale Community Schools	Hillsdale
200	19.9	L'anse Creuse Public Schools	Harrison Twp
200	19.9	Lake Shore Public Schls (Macomb)	St Clair Shores
200	19.9	Northwest Community Schools	Jackson
200	19.9	Romeo Community Schools	Romeo
200	19.9	Swan Valley SD	Saginaw
207	20.0	Alpena Public Schools	Alpena
207	20.0	Crestwood SD	Dearborn Hgts
207	20.0	Gaylord Community Schools	Gaylord
207	20.0	Saline Area Schools	Saline
207	20.0	South Redford SD	Redford
207	20.0	Spring Lake Public Schools	Spring Lake
213	20.1	Central Montcalm Public Schools	Stanton
213	20.1	Grandville Public Schools	Grandville
213	20.1	Hopkins Public Schools	Hopkins
213	20.1	Marysville Public Schools	Marysville
213	20.1	South Lyon Community Schools	South Lyon
218	20.2	Hartland Consolidated Schools	Hartland

Note: This section only includes districts with 1,500 or more students; All categories are ranked from high to low

218	20.2	Ionia Public Schools	Ionia
218	20.2	Lowell Area Schools	Lowell
218	20.2	North Branch Area Schools	North Branch
222	20.3	Bedford Public Schools	Temperance
222	20.3	Breitung Township SD	Kingsford
222	20.3	Clarkston Community SD	Clarkston
222	20.3	Dundee Community Schools	Dundee
222	20.3	Lakeview Public Schools (Macomb)	St Clair Shores
222	20.3	Zeeland Public Schools	Zeeland
228	20.4	Essexville-Hampton Public Schools	Essexville
228	20.4	Grosse Ile Township Schools	Grosse Ile
228	20.4	Mattawan Consolidated School	Mattawan
228	20.4	Onsted Community Schools	Onsted
228	20.4	Oxford Community Schools	Oxford
228	20.4	Van Buren Public Schools	Belleville
228	20.4	Whitehall District Schools	Whitehall
235	20.5	Benzie County Central Schools	Benzonia
235	20.5	Birch Run Area Schools	Birch Run
235	20.5	Coldwater Community Schools	Coldwater
235	20.5	Fremont Public SD	Fremont
235	20.5	Yale Public Schools	Yale
240	20.6	Allendale Public Schools	Allendale
240	20.6	Bay City SD	Bay City
240	20.6	Chippewa Valley Schools	Clinton Twp
243	20.7	Dearborn Hgts SD #7	Dearborn Hgts
243	20.7	Flushing Community Schools	Flushing
245	20.8	Almont Community Schools	Almont
245	20.8	Grant Public SD	Grant
245	20.8	Monroe Public Schools	Monroe
245	20.8	Standish-Sterling Community Schls	Standish
249	21.0	Allen Park Public Schools	Allen Park
249	21.0	Coopersville Area Public SD	Coopersville
249	21.0	Gibraltar SD	Woodhaven
249	21.0	Gladstone Area Schools	Gladstone
249	21.0	Linden Community Schools	Linden
254	21.1	Goodrich Area Schools	Goodrich
254	21.1	SD of the City of Inkster	Inkster
256	21.2	Bangor Township Schools	Bay City
257	21.3	Clio Area SD	Clio
257	21.3	Davison Community Schools	Davison
257	21.3	Escanaba Area Public Schools	Escanaba
257	21.3	Harrison Community Schools	Harrison
261	21.4	Edwardsburg Public Schools	Edwardsburg
261	21.4	Westwood Community SD	Dearborn Hgts
263	21.5	Kearsley Community SD	Flint
263	21.5	Thornapple Kellogg SD	Middleville
263	21.5	Utica Community Schools	Sterling Hgts
266	21.6	Lake Fenton Community Schools	Fenton
267	21.7	Anchor Bay SD	Casco
267	21.7	Beecher Community SD	Flint
269	21.9	Chandler Park Academy	Harper Woods
270	22.0	Byron Center Public Schools	Byron Center
270	22.0	Richmond Community Schools	Richmond
270	22.0	Riverview Community SD	Riverview
273	22.3	Imlay City Community Schools	Imlay City
273	22.3	Oak Park SD	Oak Park
275	22.4	Manistee Area Public Schools	Manistee
276	22.6	Big Rapids Public Schools	Big Rapids
277	22.9	Orchard View Schools	Muskegon
278	23.1	Summit Academy North	Romulus
279	24.1	Melvindale-North Allen Park Schools	Melvindale
280	25.5	Clintondale Community Schools	Clinton Twp
281	27.7	Bendle Public Schools	Burton
n/a	n/a	Wayne Resa	Wayne

Student/Librarian Ratio

(number of students per librarian)

Rank	Number	District Name	City
1	483.0	Dearborn Hgts SD #7	Dearborn Hgts
2	588.8	Ann Arbor Public Schools	Ann Arbor
3	591.0	SD of the City of Birmingham	Birmingham
4	596.3	Dexter Community SD	Dexter
5	607.0	Bloomfield Hls SD	Bloomfield Hls
6	647.9	Lansing Public SD	Lansing
7	710.2	Lake Shore Public Schls (Macomb)	St Clair Shores
8	712.3	Rochester Community SD	Rochester
9	734.6	Livonia Public Schools SD	Livonia
10	767.8	Plymouth-Canton Comm Schools	Plymouth
11	770.3	Van Dyke Public Schools	Warren
12	780.3	Novi Community SD	Novi
13	813.9	Berkley SD	Oak Park
14	868.3	Farmington Public SD	Farmington
15	900.7	Edwardsburg Public Schools	Edwardsburg
16	908.0	Lincoln Consolidated SD	Ypsilanti
17	911.5	Lamphere Public Schools	Madison Heights
18	922.3	Parchment SD	Kalamazoo
19	929.5	Clarenceville SD	Livonia
20	938.0	Allen Park Public Schools	Allen Park
21	938.8	Mattawan Consolidated School	Mattawan
22	980.3	Grand Haven Area Public Schools	Grand Haven
23	998.0	Armada Area Schools	Armada
24	1,008.4	Lake Orion Community Schools	Lake Orion
25	1,009.7	SD of Ypsilanti	Ypsilanti
26	1,038.2	Grosse Pointe Public Schools	Grosse Pointe
27	1,056.4	Van Buren Public Schools	Belleville
28	1,057.8	Algonac Community SD	Algonac
29	1,084.0	West Bloomfield SD	West Bloomfield
30	1,110.4	West Ottawa Public SD	Holland
31	1,111.6	Hartland Consolidated Schools	Hartland
32	1,136.7	Portage Public Schools	Portage
33	1,151.0	Hazel Park SD	Hazel Park
34	1,157.0	Marshall Public Schools	Marshall
35	1,167.8	Troy SD	Troy
36	1,174.5	East China SD	East China
37	1,224.7	East Detroit Public Schools	Eastpointe
38	1,228.5	Woodhaven-Brownstown SD	Woodhaven
39	1,253.2	Warren Consolidated Schools	Warren
40	1,261.0	Jenison Public Schools	Jenison
41	1,305.5	Saline Area Schools	Saline
42	1,315.5	SD of the City of Inkster	Inkster
43	1,356.3	Romeo Community Schools	Romeo
44	1,360.8	Warren Woods Public Schools	Warren
45	1,387.5	Saint Joseph Public Schools	Saint Joseph
46	1,410.5	Bay City SD	Bay City
47	1,417.0	Hastings Area SD	Hastings
48	1,436.0	South Lake Schools	St Clair Shores
49	1,456.5	Gull Lake Community Schools	Richland
50	1,461.0	Holt Public Schools	Holt
51	1,464.7	Clarkston Community SD	Clarkston
52	1,471.5	Hamtramck SD	Hamtramck
53	1,488.0	Fowlerville Community Schools	Fowlerville
54	1,500.0	Perry Public Schools	Perry
55	1,520.0	Columbia SD	Brooklyn
56	1,521.5	Brighton Area Schools	Brighton
57	1,541.0	Onsted Community Schools	Onsted
58	1,546.0	Shelby Public Schools	Shelby
59	1,568.0	Buchanan Community Schools	Buchanan
60	1,574.0	Kalkaska Public Schools	Kalkaska
61	1,591.0	Mount Clemens Community SD	Mount Clemens
62	1,593.8	Northville Public Schools	Northville
63	1,597.7	Garden City SD	Garden City
64	1,603.0	Houghton Lake Community Schools	Houghton Lake
65	1,631.9	Trenton Public Schools	Trenton
66	1,635.0	Durand Area Schools	Durand
67	1,635.5	Mason Public Schools (Ingham)	Mason
68	1,662.0	Willow Run Community Schools	Ypsilanti
69	1,679.3	Vicksburg Community Schools	Vicksburg
70	1,760.0	South Lyon Community Schools	South Lyon
71	1,773.4	Kalamazoo Public Schools	Kalamazoo
72	1,786.0	Shepherd Public Schools	Shepherd
73	1,790.6	Fitzgerald Public Schools	Warren
74	1,792.0	Clawson Public Schools	Clawson
75	1,802.0	Swan Valley SD	Saginaw
76	1,806.0	Clio Area SD	Clio
77	1,825.0	Lakeshore SD (Berrien)	Stevensville
78	1,830.0	Freeland Community SD	Freeland
79	1,843.0	Beecher Community SD	Flint
80	1,852.0	Grosse Ile Township Schools	Grosse Ile
81	1,857.0	Lake Fenton Community Schools	Fenton
82	1,866.0	Oakridge Public Schools	Muskegon
83	1,873.0	Gibraltar SD	Woodhaven
84	1,875.6	Standish-Sterling Community Schls	Standish
85	1,886.0	Mona Shores Public SD	Muskegon
86	1,910.0	Cheboygan Area Schools	Cheboygan
87	1,938.5	Okemos Public Schools	Okemos
88	1,954.0	Bullock Creek SD	Midland
89	1,958.6	Traverse City Area Public Schools	Traverse City
90	1,969.0	Carrollton Public Schools	Saginaw
91	1,987.8	Saginaw SD	Saginaw
92	2,005.0	Dundee Community Schools	Dundee
93	2,009.1	Carman-Ainsworth Comm. Schools	Flint
94	2,021.0	Old Redford Academy	Detroit
95	2,022.4	Forest Hills Public Schools	Grand Rapids
96	2,074.0	Belding Area SD	Belding
97	2,076.9	Huron Valley Schools	Highland
98	2,122.2	Southfield Public SD	Southfield
99	2,147.0	Godwin Heights Public Schools	Grand Rapids
100	2,179.3	Port Huron Area SD	Port Huron
101	2,190.0	West Branch-Rose City Area Schls	Rose City
102	2,209.6	Walled Lake Consolidated Schools	Walled Lake
103	2,214.0	Alma Public Schools	Alma
104	2,284.0	Kelloggsville Public Schools	Grand Rapids
105	2,310.5	Wyoming Public Schools	Wyoming
106	2,339.0	Otsego Public Schools	Otsego
107	2,370.0	Kenowa Hills Public Schools	Grand Rapids
108	2,396.0	Huron SD	New Boston
109	2,398.0	Dowagiac Union SD	Dowagiac
110	2,424.7	Tri County Area Schools	Sand Lake
111	2,433.0	Oxford Community Schools	Oxford
112	2,452.0	Spring Lake Public Schools	Spring Lake
113	2,466.7	Taylor SD	Taylor
114	2,520.0	Harper Creek Community Schools	Battle Creek
115	2,528.5	Flint SD	Flint
116	2,540.0	Thornapple Kellogg SD	Middleville
117	2,566.6	Dearborn City SD	Dearborn
118	2,621.5	Fraser Public Schools	Fraser
119	2,626.0	Airport Community Schools	Carleton
120	2,626.7	Rockford Public Schools	Rockford
121	2,685.0	Three Rivers Community Schools	Three Rivers
122	2,703.0	Plainwell Community Schools	Plainwell
123	2,706.0	Haslett Public Schools	Haslett
124	2,722.3	Waterford SD	Waterford
125	2,737.0	Westwood Community SD	Dearborn Hgts
126	2,745.5	Pontiac City SD	Pontiac
127	2,751.0	Davison Community Schools	Davison
128	2,765.6	Southgate Community SD	Southgate
129	2,802.0	Wayland Union Schools	Wayland
130	2,809.0	Riverview Community SD	Riverview
130	2,809.0	Waverly Community Schools	Lansing
132	2,827.0	Orchard View Schools	Muskegon
133	2,897.0	Grand Blanc Community Schools	Grand Blanc
134	2,930.1	Kentwood Public Schools	Grand Rapids
135	2,936.0	Coldwater Community Schools	Coldwater
136	2,959.0	Redford Union Schools Dist. No. 1	Redford
137	3,009.5	Lapeer Community Schools	Lapeer
138	3,029.0	Cadillac Area Public Schools	Cadillac
139	3,128.3	Birch Run Area Schools	Birch Run
140	3,137.0	Benton Harbor Area Schools	Benton Harbor
141	3,153.0	Adrian SD	Adrian
142	3,259.0	South Redford SD	Redford
143	3,294.0	Muskegon Public Schools	Muskegon
144	3,319.0	Romulus Community Schools	Romulus
145	3,330.0	Owosso Public Schools	Owosso
146	3,356.0	Manistee Area Public Schools	Manistee
147	3,411.0	East Lansing SD	East Lansing
148	3,497.0	Mt. Pleasant City SD	Mount Pleasant
149	3,788.0	Ferndale Public Schools	Ferndale
150	3,794.0	Lowell Area Schools	Lowell
151	3,795.0	Greenville Public Schools	Greenville
152	3,797.5	Napoleon Community Schools	Napoleon
153	3,813.0	Reeths-Puffer Schools	Muskegon
154	3,884.0	Lakeview SD (Calhoun)	Battle Creek
155	4,000.5	Howell Public Schools	Howell
156	4,137.7	Wayne-Westland Community SD	Westland
157	4,166.0	Caledonia Community Schools	Caledonia
158	4,167.0	Oak Park SD	Oak Park
159	4,212.0	Flushing Community Schools	Flushing
160	4,320.0	Hudsonville Public SD	Hudsonville
161	4,398.3	Hamilton Community Schools	Hamilton
162	4,578.0	Fremont Public SD	Fremont
163	4,735.0	Lincoln Park SD	Lincoln Park
164	4,781.0	Bedford Public Schools	Temperance
165	4,943.9	Sturgis Public Schools	Sturgis
166	5,062.0	Saginaw Township Comm. Schools	Saginaw
167	5,170.0	SD of the City of Royal Oak	Royal Oak
168	5,358.0	Charlotte Public Schools	Charlotte
169	5,690.0	Grandville Public Schools	Grandville
170	5,757.0	Zeeland Public Schools	Zeeland
171	6,158.0	Monroe Public Schools	Monroe
172	6,528.0	Brandon SD	Ortonville
173	6,706.4	Detroit City SD	Detroit
174	7,750.0	Gladstone Area Schools	Gladstone
175	8,089.0	Chippewa Valley Schools	Clinton Twp
176	9,975.0	Jackson Public Schools	Jackson
177	15,080.0	Clintondale Community Schools	Clinton Twp
178	16,970.0	Ovid-Elsie Area Schools	Elsie
179	17,606.0	Grand Rapids Public Schools	Grand Rapids
180	19,685.0	Swartz Creek Community Schools	Swartz Creek
181	31,340.0	Anchor Bay SD	Casco
n/a	n/a	Allegan Public Schools	Allegan
n/a	n/a	Allendale Public Schools	Allendale
n/a	n/a	Almont Community Schools	Almont
n/a	n/a	Alpena Public Schools	Alpena

Note: This section only includes districts with 1,500 or more students; All categories are ranked from high to low

n/a	n/a	Avondale SD	Auburn Hills
n/a	n/a	Bangor Township Schools	Bay City
n/a	n/a	Battle Creek Public Schools	Battle Creek
n/a	n/a	Bendle Public Schools	Burton
n/a	n/a	Benzie County Central Schools	Benzonia
n/a	n/a	Berrien Springs Public Schools	Berrien Springs
n/a	n/a	Big Rapids Public Schools	Big Rapids
n/a	n/a	Breitung Township SD	Kingsford
n/a	n/a	Byron Center Public Schools	Byron Center
n/a	n/a	Caro Community Schools	Caro
n/a	n/a	Cedar Springs Public Schools	Cedar Springs
n/a	n/a	Center Line Public Schools	Center Line
n/a	n/a	Central Montcalm Public Schools	Stanton
n/a	n/a	Cesar Chavez Academy	Detroit
n/a	n/a	Chandler Park Academy	Harper Woods
n/a	n/a	Chelsea SD	Chelsea
n/a	n/a	Chesaning Union Schools	Chesaning
n/a	n/a	Chippewa Hills SD	Remus
n/a	n/a	Clare Public Schools	Clare
n/a	n/a	Coloma Community Schools	Coloma
n/a	n/a	Comstock Park Public Schools	Comstock Park
n/a	n/a	Comstock Public Schools	Kalamazoo
n/a	n/a	Coopersville Area Public SD	Coopersville
n/a	n/a	Corunna Public Schools	Corunna
n/a	n/a	Crawford Ausable Schools	Grayling
n/a	n/a	Crestwood SD	Dearborn Hgts
n/a	n/a	Croswell-Lexington Comm. Schools	Croswell
n/a	n/a	Delton Kellogg Schools	Delton
n/a	n/a	Dewitt Public Schools	Dewitt
n/a	n/a	E Grand Rapids Public Schools	Grand Rapids
n/a	n/a	Eaton Rapids Public Schools	Eaton Rapids
n/a	n/a	Escanaba Area Public Schools	Escanaba
n/a	n/a	Essexville-Hampton Public Schools	Essexville
n/a	n/a	Fenton Area Public Schools	Fenton
n/a	n/a	Flat Rock Community Schools	Flat Rock
n/a	n/a	Fruitport Community Schools	Fruitport
n/a	n/a	Gaylord Community Schools	Gaylord
n/a	n/a	Gladwin Community Schools	Gladwin
n/a	n/a	Godfrey-Lee Public Schools	Wyoming
n/a	n/a	Goodrich Area Schools	Goodrich
n/a	n/a	Grand Ledge Public Schools	Grand Ledge
n/a	n/a	Grant Public SD	Grant
n/a	n/a	Harrison Community Schools	Harrison
n/a	n/a	Hillsdale Community Schools	Hillsdale
n/a	n/a	Holland City SD	Holland
n/a	n/a	Holly Area SD	Holly
n/a	n/a	Hopkins Public Schools	Hopkins
n/a	n/a	Imlay City Community Schools	Imlay City
n/a	n/a	Ionia Public Schools	Ionia
n/a	n/a	Jefferson Schools (Monroe)	Monroe
n/a	n/a	Kearsley Community SD	Flint
n/a	n/a	Kent ISD	Grand Rapids
n/a	n/a	L'anse Creuse Public Schools	Harrison Twp
n/a	n/a	Lakeview Public Schools (Macomb)	St Clair Shores
n/a	n/a	Lakeville Community SD	Otisville
n/a	n/a	Lakewood Public Schools	Woodland
n/a	n/a	Linden Community Schools	Linden
n/a	n/a	Ludington Area SD	Ludington
n/a	n/a	Macomb ISD	Clinton Twp
n/a	n/a	Marquette Area Public Schools	Marquette
n/a	n/a	Marysville Public Schools	Marysville
n/a	n/a	Melvindale-North Allen Park Schools	Melvindale
n/a	n/a	Menominee Area Public Schools	Menominee
n/a	n/a	Midland Public Schools	Midland
n/a	n/a	Milan Area Schools	Milan
n/a	n/a	Mt. Morris Consolidated Schools	Mount Morris
n/a	n/a	Muskegon Hgts SD	Muskegon
n/a	n/a	Newaygo Public SD	Newaygo
n/a	n/a	Niles Community Schools	Niles
n/a	n/a	North Branch Area Schools	North Branch
n/a	n/a	Northview Public Schools	Grand Rapids
n/a	n/a	Northwest Community Schools	Jackson
n/a	n/a	Olivet Community Schools	Olivet
n/a	n/a	Paw Paw Public SD	Paw Paw
n/a	n/a	Pennfield Schools	Battle Creek
n/a	n/a	Pinckney Community Schools	Pinckney
n/a	n/a	Portland Public Schools	Portland
n/a	n/a	Public Schools of Petoskey	Petoskey
n/a	n/a	Reed City Area Public Schools	Reed City
n/a	n/a	Richmond Community Schools	Richmond
n/a	n/a	Roseville Community Schools	Roseville
n/a	n/a	Saginaw ISD	Saginaw
n/a	n/a	Saint Johns Public Schools	Saint Johns
n/a	n/a	Sault Ste Marie Area Schools	Sault Ste Marie
n/a	n/a	South Haven Public Schools	South Haven
n/a	n/a	Sparta Area Schools	Sparta
n/a	n/a	Stockbridge Community Schools	Stockbridge
n/a	n/a	Summit Academy North	Romulus
n/a	n/a	Tecumseh Public Schools	Tecumseh
n/a	n/a	University Preparatory Acad. (PSAD)	Detroit
n/a	n/a	Utica Community Schools	Sterling Hgts
n/a	n/a	Wayne Resa	Wayne
n/a	n/a	Western SD	Parma
n/a	n/a	Whitehall District Schools	Whitehall
n/a	n/a	Williamston Community Schools	Williamston
n/a	n/a	Wyandotte SD	Wyandotte
n/a	n/a	Yale Public Schools	Yale

Student/Counselor Ratio

(number of students per counselor)

Rank	Number	District Name	City
1	327.9	Kalkaska Public Schools	Kalkaska
2	385.7	Marshall Public Schools	Marshall
3	388.6	Mt. Pleasant City SD	Mount Pleasant
4	390.2	Bloomfield Hls SD	Bloomfield Hls
5	407.9	Sturgis Public Schools	Sturgis
6	415.0	Mt. Morris Consolidated Schools	Mount Morris
7	417.1	Lakeshore SD (Berrien)	Stevensville
8	420.1	Carman-Ainsworth Comm. Schools	Flint
9	423.0	Kelloggsville Public Schools	Grand Rapids
10	424.5	Newaygo Public SD	Newaygo
11	430.8	South Lake Schools	St Clair Shores
12	438.0	West Branch-Rose City Area Schls	Rose City
13	440.4	Buchanan Community Schools	Buchanan
14	441.3	Essexville-Hampton Public Schools	Essexville
15	443.5	Forest Hills Public Schools	Grand Rapids
16	447.0	Kearsley Community SD	Flint
17	447.9	Fruitport Community Schools	Fruitport
18	449.6	Ann Arbor Public Schools	Ann Arbor
19	453.2	Onsted Community Schools	Onsted
20	459.3	East Detroit Public Schools	Eastpointe
20	459.3	Houghton Lake Community Schools	Houghton Lake
22	467.1	Warren Consolidated Schools	Warren
23	467.8	Otsego Public Schools	Otsego
24	479.1	Ionia Public Schools	Ionia
25	487.2	Vicksburg Community Schools	Vicksburg
26	488.5	Bullock Creek SD	Midland
27	490.7	Rochester Community SD	Rochester
28	493.1	Detroit City SD	Detroit
29	495.0	Waterford SD	Waterford
30	500.0	Perry Public Schools	Perry
31	501.5	Berkley SD	Oak Park
32	504.0	Harper Creek Community Schools	Battle Creek
32	504.0	Marquette Area Public Schools	Marquette
34	504.7	Muskegon Hgts SD	Muskegon
35	505.3	Delton Kellogg Schools	Delton
36	510.1	Avondale SD	Auburn Hills
37	513.5	Van Dyke Public Schools	Warren
38	515.3	Shelby Public Schools	Shelby
39	515.8	Northwest Community Schools	Jackson
40	516.2	Southfield Public SD	Southfield
41	517.0	Milan Area Schools	Milan
42	519.0	Pennfield Schools	Battle Creek
43	522.5	Yale Public Schools	Yale
44	524.9	Grosse Pointe Public Schools	Grosse Pointe
45	526.0	Hopkins Public Schools	Hopkins
46	526.2	SD of the City of Inkster	Inkster
47	527.1	Allegan Public Schools	Allegan
48	532.4	Huron SD	New Boston
49	533.8	SD of the City of Birmingham	Birmingham
50	537.4	Warren Woods Public Schools	Warren
51	540.4	Holland City SD	Holland
52	541.1	Ferndale Public Schools	Ferndale
53	541.6	Dewitt Public Schools	Dewitt
54	544.9	Spring Lake Public Schools	Spring Lake
55	545.0	Durand Area Schools	Durand
56	547.2	Center Line Public Schools	Center Line
57	548.6	Fenton Area Public Schools	Fenton
58	549.0	Bendle Public Schools	Burton
59	550.0	Ludington Area SD	Ludington
59	550.0	Sparta Area Schools	Sparta
61	553.2	Romulus Community Schools	Romulus
62	562.7	Standish-Sterling Community Schls	Standish
63	563.5	Dexter Community SD	Dexter
64	569.2	Taylor SD	Taylor
65	571.2	Lakeview SD (Calhoun)	Battle Creek
66	572.3	Dowagiac Union SD	Dowagiac
67	575.9	Central Montcalm Public Schools	Stanton
68	576.7	Livonia Public Schools SD	Livonia
69	579.6	Dearborn Hgts SD #7	Dearborn Hgts
70	580.2	Trenton Public Schools	Trenton
71	581.3	Grand Ledge Public Schools	Grand Ledge
72	582.6	Gull Lake Community Schools	Richland
73	583.9	Stockbridge Community Schools	Stockbridge
74	587.1	Coloma Community Schools	Coloma
75	588.0	Holly Area SD	Holly
76	588.6	Wayne-Westland Community SD	Westland
77	594.1	Farmington Public SD	Farmington
78	595.3	Shepherd Public Schools	Shepherd
79	597.5	Chandler Park Academy	Harper Woods
80	599.4	Armada Area Schools	Armada
81	601.9	Lapeer Community Schools	Lapeer
82	602.4	Fremont Public SD	Fremont
83	604.5	Bay City SD	Bay City
84	605.8	SD of Ypsilanti	Ypsilanti
85	609.6	Thornapple Kellogg SD	Middleville
86	611.3	Davison Community Schools	Davison
87	611.7	Coldwater Community Schools	Coldwater
88	614.5	Garden City SD	Garden City
89	616.8	Gaylord Community Schools	Gaylord
90	617.1	Northview Public Schools	Grand Rapids
91	617.3	Grosse Ile Township Schools	Grosse Ile
92	617.6	Hartland Consolidated Schools	Hartland
92	617.6	Muskegon Public Schools	Muskegon
94	622.0	Oakridge Public Schools	Muskegon
95	622.8	Belding Area SD	Belding
96	625.1	Carrollton Public Schools	Saginaw
97	625.3	Sault Ste Marie Area Schools	Sault Ste Marie
98	625.7	Birch Run Area Schools	Birch Run
99	625.8	Kentwood Public Schools	Grand Rapids
100	626.9	L'anse Creuse Public Schools	Harrison Twp
101	628.8	Bangor Township Schools	Bay City
102	632.1	Flint SD	Flint
103	633.8	Crestwood SD	Dearborn Hgts
104	636.2	Saint Johns Public Schools	Saint Johns
105	637.6	Plymouth-Canton Comm Schools	Plymouth
106	639.2	Willow Run Community Schools	Ypsilanti
107	640.1	Howell Public Schools	Howell
108	646.0	Pontiac City SD	Pontiac
109	646.2	Godfrey-Lee Public Schools	Wyoming
110	646.4	Almont Community Schools	Almont
111	648.6	Lincoln Consolidated SD	Ypsilanti
112	649.9	Walled Lake Consolidated Schools	Walled Lake
113	650.4	West Bloomfield SD	West Bloomfield
114	653.1	Comstock Park Public Schools	Comstock Park
115	653.5	Richmond Community Schools	Richmond
116	656.5	Airport Community Schools	Carleton
117	658.8	Marysville Public Schools	Marysville
118	663.7	Huron Valley Schools	Highland
119	668.4	Okemos Public Schools	Okemos
120	669.8	Charlotte Public Schools	Charlotte
121	673.7	Portland Public Schools	Portland
122	675.2	Lake Orion Community Schools	Lake Orion
123	675.8	Plainwell Community Schools	Plainwell
124	676.5	Haslett Public Schools	Haslett
125	677.7	Greenville Public Schools	Greenville
126	678.8	Ovid-Elsie Area Schools	Elsie
127	683.5	Monroe Public Schools	Monroe
128	685.3	Jefferson Schools (Monroe)	Monroe
129	689.0	Lakewood Public Schools	Woodland
130	689.3	SD of the City of Royal Oak	Royal Oak
131	693.6	Novi Community SD	Novi
132	693.8	Saint Joseph Public Schools	Saint Joseph
133	694.3	Caledonia Community Schools	Caledonia
134	695.3	Alpena Public Schools	Alpena
135	697.3	Chippewa Valley Schools	Clinton Twp
136	702.0	Woodhaven-Brownstown SD	Woodhaven
137	702.3	Riverview Community SD	Riverview
138	706.4	Portage Public Schools	Portage
139	706.8	Orchard View Schools	Muskegon
140	707.3	Berrien Springs Public Schools	Berrien Springs
141	710.2	Lake Shore Public Schls (Macomb)	St Clair Shores
142	711.0	Croswell-Lexington Comm. Schools	Croswell
142	711.0	Goodrich Area Schools	Goodrich
144	712.0	Chelsea SD	Chelsea
145	716.2	Williamston Community Schools	Williamston
146	716.3	Fitzgerald Public Schools	Warren
147	716.4	Rockford Public Schools	Rockford
148	721.3	Troy SD	Troy
149	722.4	Clio Area SD	Clio
150	723.1	Saginaw Township Comm. Schools	Saginaw
151	723.5	Western SD	Parma
152	727.9	Lansing Public SD	Lansing

Note: This section only includes districts with 1,500 or more students; All categories are ranked from high to low

153	730.2	Kalamazoo Public Schools	Kalamazoo
154	731.8	Public Schools of Petoskey	Petoskey
155	732.0	Freeland Community SD	Freeland
156	733.3	South Haven Public Schools	South Haven
157	734.5	Lakeville Community SD	Otisville
158	735.0	Tecumseh Public Schools	Tecumseh
159	739.8	Redford Union Schools Dist. No. 1	Redford
160	744.0	E Grand Rapids Public Schools	Grand Rapids
161	748.3	Mason Public Schools (Ingham)	Mason
162	750.0	Corunna Public Schools	Corunna
163	750.4	Allen Park Public Schools	Allen Park
164	750.8	Utica Community Schools	Sterling Hgts
165	751.0	Mattawan Consolidated School	Mattawan
166	754.0	Lakeview Public Schools (Macomb)	St Clair Shores
167	754.4	Mona Shores Public SD	Muskegon
168	757.3	Cadillac Area Public Schools	Cadillac
169	758.8	Lowell Area Schools	Lowell
170	759.5	Napoleon Community Schools	Napoleon
171	761.7	Flushing Community Schools	Flushing
172	762.0	Reed City Area Public Schools	Reed City
173	762.3	Paw Paw Public SD	Paw Paw
174	762.6	Reeths-Puffer Schools	Muskegon
175	765.0	Bedford Public Schools	Temperance
176	779.0	Kent ISD	Grand Rapids
177	783.0	East China SD	East China
178	787.4	Swartz Creek Community Schools	Swartz Creek
179	789.5	Grand Haven Area Public Schools	Grand Haven
180	789.8	Traverse City Area Public Schools	Traverse City
181	790.9	Port Huron Area SD	Port Huron
182	796.9	Northville Public Schools	Northville
183	810.3	North Branch Area Schools	North Branch
184	811.1	Chippewa Hills SD	Remus
185	811.5	Chesaning Union Schools	Chesaning
186	814.8	South Redford SD	Redford
187	829.5	Kenowa Hills Public Schools	Grand Rapids
188	832.5	Owosso Public Schools	Owosso
189	833.4	Oak Park SD	Oak Park
190	834.8	Clarkston Community SD	Clarkston
191	834.9	Holt Public Schools	Holt
192	836.5	Hudsonville Public SD	Hudsonville
193	849.5	Byron Center Public Schools	Byron Center
194	852.8	East Lansing SD	East Lansing
195	854.5	Benzie County Central Schools	Benzonia
196	858.8	Grand Rapids Public Schools	Grand Rapids
197	869.1	Grand Blanc Community Schools	Grand Blanc
198	869.4	Brighton Area Schools	Brighton
199	871.0	Eaton Rapids Public Schools	Eaton Rapids
200	872.5	Saline Area Schools	Saline
201	873.8	Fraser Public Schools	Fraser
202	879.6	Dearborn City SD	Dearborn
203	883.4	Saginaw SD	Saginaw
204	884.7	Oxford Community Schools	Oxford
205	896.0	Clawson Public Schools	Clawson
206	900.7	Edwardsburg Public Schools	Edwardsburg
207	900.9	Adrian SD	Adrian
208	901.8	Clare Public Schools	Clare
209	904.2	Romeo Community Schools	Romeo
210	905.0	Gladwin Community Schools	Gladwin
211	909.3	Menominee Area Public Schools	Menominee
212	912.3	Westwood Community SD	Dearborn Hgts
213	915.7	Columbia SD	Brooklyn
214	920.8	Hazel Park SD	Hazel Park
215	926.7	Lamphere Public Schools	Madison Heights
216	928.5	Lake Fenton Community Schools	Fenton
217	929.0	Caro Community Schools	Caro
218	934.0	Wayland Union Schools	Wayland
219	936.5	Gibraltar SD	Woodhaven
220	937.0	Flat Rock Community Schools	Flat Rock
221	938.7	South Lyon Community Schools	South Lyon
222	947.0	Lincoln Park SD	Lincoln Park
223	948.3	Grandville Public Schools	Grandville
224	964.2	Jenison Public Schools	Jenison
225	981.7	Linden Community Schools	Linden
226	992.0	Fowlerville Community Schools	Fowlerville
227	992.2	Breitung Township SD	Kingsford
228	994.4	Three Rivers Community Schools	Three Rivers
229	997.5	Jackson Public Schools	Jackson
230	1,014.6	Midland Public Schools	Midland
231	1,028.0	Zeeland Public Schools	Zeeland
232	1,045.7	Benton Harbor Area Schools	Benton Harbor
233	1,047.8	Roseville Community Schools	Roseville
234	1,048.6	West Ottawa Public SD	Holland
235	1,055.6	Hamilton Community Schools	Hamilton
236	1,056.4	Van Buren Public Schools	Belleville
237	1,062.3	Clarenceville SD	Livonia
238	1,071.6	Battle Creek Public Schools	Battle Creek
239	1,088.0	Brandon SD	Ortonville
240	1,092.0	Imlay City Community Schools	Imlay City
241	1,107.0	Alma Public Schools	Alma
242	1,118.7	Manistee Area Public Schools	Manistee
243	1,178.5	Whitehall District Schools	Whitehall
244	1,214.9	Allendale Public Schools	Allendale
245	1,253.6	Harrison Community Schools	Harrison
246	1,256.7	Clintondale Community Schools	Clinton Twp
247	1,348.3	Southgate Community SD	Southgate
248	1,360.0	Algonac Community SD	Algonac
249	1,410.0	Melvindale-North Allen Park Schools	Melvindale
250	1,417.0	Hastings Area SD	Hastings
251	1,471.5	Hamtramck SD	Hamtramck
252	1,495.3	Wyandotte SD	Wyandotte
253	1,512.0	Godwin Heights Public Schools	Grand Rapids
254	1,540.3	Wyoming Public Schools	Wyoming
255	1,549.0	Hillsdale Community Schools	Hillsdale
256	1,559.0	Olivet Community Schools	Olivet
257	1,567.0	Anchor Bay SD	Casco
258	1,591.0	Mount Clemens Community SD	Mount Clemens
259	1,661.0	Crawford Ausable Schools	Grayling
260	1,697.5	Cedar Springs Public Schools	Cedar Springs
261	1,706.0	University Preparatory Acad. (PSAD)	Detroit
262	1,734.0	Parchment SD	Kalamazoo
263	1,775.0	Big Rapids Public Schools	Big Rapids
264	1,802.0	Swan Valley SD	Saginaw
265	1,834.0	Saginaw ISD	Saginaw
266	1,843.0	Beecher Community SD	Flint
267	1,879.2	Tri County Area Schools	Sand Lake
268	1,910.0	Cheboygan Area Schools	Cheboygan
269	1,931.5	Niles Community Schools	Niles
270	1,937.5	Gladstone Area Schools	Gladstone
271	2,021.0	Old Redford Academy	Detroit
272	2,064.0	Pinckney Community Schools	Pinckney
273	2,168.0	Macomb ISD	Clinton Twp
274	2,488.0	Coopersville Area Public SD	Coopersville
275	2,555.0	Escanaba Area Public Schools	Escanaba
276	2,570.0	Grant Public SD	Grant
277	2,809.0	Waverly Community Schools	Lansing
n/a	n/a	Cesar Chavez Academy	Detroit
n/a	n/a	Comstock Public Schools	Kalamazoo
n/a	n/a	Dundee Community Schools	Dundee
n/a	n/a	Summit Academy North	Romulus
n/a	n/a	Wayne Resa	Wayne

Current Expenditures per Student

Rank	Dollars	District Name	City
1	15,852	Bloomfield Hls SD	Bloomfield Hls
2	15,092	Flint SD	Flint
3	14,471	Muskegon Hgts SD	Muskegon
4	14,434	Pontiac City SD	Pontiac
5	13,932	Mount Clemens Community SD	Mount Clemens
6	13,735	SD of Ypsilanti	Ypsilanti
7	13,655	SD of the City of Birmingham	Birmingham
8	13,578	Beecher Community SD	Flint
9	13,416	Detroit City SD	Detroit
10	13,175	Farmington Public SD	Farmington
11	12,577	Southfield Public SD	Southfield
12	12,471	Grand Rapids Public Schools	Grand Rapids
13	12,426	Lansing Public SD	Lansing
14	12,355	Battle Creek Public Schools	Battle Creek
15	12,192	Grosse Pointe Public Schools	Grosse Pointe
16	12,167	Redford Union Schools Dist. No. 1	Redford
17	12,125	Oak Park SD	Oak Park
18	12,117	Van Dyke Public Schools	Warren
19	12,031	Wyandotte SD	Wyandotte
20	11,959	Willow Run Community Schools	Ypsilanti
21	11,865	Center Line Public Schools	Center Line
22	11,829	Lamphere Public Schools	Madison Heights
23	11,771	Clawson Public Schools	Clawson
24	11,684	Garden City SD	Garden City
25	11,600	Hamtramck SD	Hamtramck
26	11,596	Romulus Community Schools	Romulus
27	11,502	Fitzgerald Public Schools	Warren
28	11,500	Benton Harbor Area Schools	Benton Harbor
29	11,459	Taylor SD	Taylor
30	11,439	Saginaw SD	Saginaw
31	11,386	Ann Arbor Public Schools	Ann Arbor
32	11,384	Muskegon Public Schools	Muskegon
33	11,334	South Lake Schools	St Clair Shores
34	11,305	Trenton Public Schools	Trenton
35	11,257	Jackson Public Schools	Jackson
36	11,145	Lincoln Park SD	Lincoln Park
37	11,134	Northville Public Schools	Northville
38	11,052	Dearborn City SD	Dearborn
39	11,046	Westwood Community SD	Dearborn Hgts
40	10,975	Troy SD	Troy
41	10,956	Hazel Park SD	Hazel Park
42	10,872	Livonia Public Schools SD	Livonia
43	10,870	SD of the City of Inkster	Inkster
44	10,772	West Bloomfield SD	West Bloomfield
45	10,767	Novi Community SD	Novi
46	10,726	Adrian SD	Adrian
47	10,720	Kalamazoo Public Schools	Kalamazoo
48	10,673	Wayne-Westland Community SD	Westland
49	10,666	Holland City SD	Holland
50	10,601	Carman-Ainsworth Comm. Schools	Flint
51	10,573	Warren Consolidated Schools	Warren
52	10,490	Warren Woods Public Schools	Warren
53	10,421	Okemos Public Schools	Okemos
54	10,408	Waterford SD	Waterford
55	10,318	Waverly Community Schools	Lansing
56	10,270	Avondale SD	Auburn Hills
57	10,253	Walled Lake Consolidated Schools	Walled Lake
58	10,185	Rochester Community SD	Rochester
59	10,155	Lincoln Consolidated SD	Ypsilanti
60	10,099	Lake Orion Community Schools	Lake Orion
61	10,020	SD of the City of Royal Oak	Royal Oak
62	9,997	South Redford SD	Redford
63	9,974	Holly Area SD	Holly
64	9,959	Saline Area Schools	Saline
65	9,936	Grosse Ile Township Schools	Grosse Ile
66	9,895	Roseville Community Schools	Roseville
67	9,894	East Lansing SD	East Lansing
68	9,875	East Detroit Public Schools	Eastpointe
69	9,868	Clarenceville SD	Livonia
70	9,818	Chelsea SD	Chelsea
71	9,805	Jefferson Schools (Monroe)	Monroe
72	9,780	Lake Shore Public Schls (Macomb)	St Clair Shores
73	9,779	Dexter Community SD	Dexter
74	9,717	Berkley SD	Oak Park
75	9,715	Port Huron Area SD	Port Huron
76	9,699	Mt. Morris Consolidated Schools	Mount Morris
77	9,675	West Ottawa Public SD	Holland
78	9,661	Jenison Public Schools	Jenison
79	9,637	Shelby Public Schools	Shelby
80	9,589	Caledonia Community Schools	Caledonia
81	9,585	University Preparatory Acad. (PSAD)	Detroit
82	9,550	Grand Haven Area Public Schools	Grand Haven
83	9,548	Forest Hills Public Schools	Grand Rapids
84	9,528	Huron SD	New Boston
85	9,523	Fruitport Community Schools	Fruitport
86	9,512	Mt. Pleasant City SD	Mount Pleasant
87	9,492	Midland Public Schools	Midland
88	9,483	Godwin Heights Public Schools	Grand Rapids
89	9,470	Kentwood Public Schools	Grand Rapids
90	9,443	Godfrey-Lee Public Schools	Wyoming
91	9,436	Van Buren Public Schools	Belleville
92	9,428	Ionia Public Schools	Ionia
92	9,428	Northview Public Schools	Grand Rapids
94	9,414	Ferndale Public Schools	Ferndale
95	9,385	Ludington Area SD	Ludington
96	9,372	Spring Lake Public Schools	Spring Lake
97	9,362	Woodhaven-Brownstown SD	Woodhaven
98	9,346	Wyoming Public Schools	Wyoming
99	9,338	Hamilton Community Schools	Hamilton
100	9,319	Southgate Community SD	Southgate
101	9,300	Fraser Public Schools	Fraser
102	9,297	West Branch-Rose City Area Schls	Rose City
103	9,283	Clarkston Community SD	Clarkston
104	9,266	Lakeview Public Schools (Macomb)	St Clair Shores
105	9,262	Harrison Community Schools	Harrison
106	9,243	Belding Area SD	Belding
107	9,239	Holt Public Schools	Holt
108	9,220	L'anse Creuse Public Schools	Harrison Twp
109	9,204	Coloma Community Schools	Coloma
110	9,194	Parchment SD	Kalamazoo
111	9,183	Comstock Public Schools	Kalamazoo
112	9,164	Cheboygan Area Schools	Cheboygan
113	9,148	Williamston Community Schools	Williamston
114	9,144	Coopersville Area Public SD	Coopersville
115	9,136	East China SD	East China
116	9,130	Berrien Springs Public Schools	Berrien Springs
117	9,128	Huron Valley Schools	Highland
118	9,115	Marquette Area Public Schools	Marquette
119	9,107	Owosso Public Schools	Owosso
120	9,093	Anchor Bay SD	Casco
120	9,093	Reed City Area Public Schools	Reed City

Note: This section only includes districts with 1,500 or more students; All categories are ranked from high to low

122	9,091	Haslett Public Schools	Haslett
122	9,091	Standish-Sterling Community Schls	Standish
124	9,089	Mason Public Schools (Ingham)	Mason
125	9,088	Crestwood SD	Dearborn Hgts
126	9,087	Lapeer Community Schools	Lapeer
127	9,060	E Grand Rapids Public Schools	Grand Rapids
128	9,043	Allendale Public Schools	Allendale
129	9,026	Plymouth-Canton Comm Schools	Plymouth
130	9,023	Chesaning Union Schools	Chesaning
131	9,010	Public Schools of Petoskey	Petoskey
132	8,988	Chippewa Hills SD	Remus
133	8,981	Kelloggsville Public Schools	Grand Rapids
134	8,980	Oxford Community Schools	Oxford
135	8,977	Benzie County Central Schools	Benzonia
136	8,973	Escanaba Area Public Schools	Escanaba
137	8,968	Newaygo Public SD	Newaygo
138	8,965	Traverse City Area Public Schools	Traverse City
139	8,960	Swartz Creek Community Schools	Swartz Creek
140	8,937	Sparta Area Schools	Sparta
141	8,927	Utica Community Schools	Sterling Hgts
142	8,917	Gaylord Community Schools	Gaylord
143	8,905	Lakeshore SD (Berrien)	Stevensville
144	8,900	Sault Ste Marie Area Schools	Sault Ste Marie
145	8,892	Zeeland Public Schools	Zeeland
146	8,889	Old Redford Academy	Detroit
147	8,880	Milan Area Schools	Milan
148	8,867	Alpena Public Schools	Alpena
148	8,867	South Haven Public Schools	South Haven
150	8,866	Gull Lake Community Schools	Richland
151	8,860	Brandon SD	Ortonville
152	8,831	Stockbridge Community Schools	Stockbridge
153	8,830	Fenton Area Public Schools	Fenton
154	8,827	Kenowa Hills Public Schools	Grand Rapids
155	8,822	Fremont Public SD	Fremont
156	8,818	Orchard View Schools	Muskegon
157	8,815	Harper Creek Community Schools	Battle Creek
158	8,811	Riverview Community SD	Riverview
159	8,806	Olivet Community Schools	Olivet
160	8,789	Kearsley Community SD	Flint
161	8,787	Dearborn Hgts SD #7	Dearborn Hgts
162	8,776	Alma Public Schools	Alma
163	8,773	Columbia SD	Brooklyn
164	8,759	Napoleon Community Schools	Napoleon
165	8,752	Lakeville Community SD	Otisville
166	8,746	Gibraltar SD	Woodhaven
167	8,739	Cedar Springs Public Schools	Cedar Springs
168	8,730	Portage Public Schools	Portage
169	8,727	Crawford Ausable Schools	Grayling
170	8,715	Dundee Community Schools	Dundee
171	8,708	Gladwin Community Schools	Gladwin
172	8,707	Reeths-Puffer Schools	Muskegon
173	8,706	Clintondale Community Schools	Clinton Twp
174	8,682	Romeo Community Schools	Romeo
175	8,681	Mona Shores Public SD	Muskegon
176	8,679	Carrollton Public Schools	Saginaw
177	8,669	Northwest Community Schools	Jackson
178	8,668	Bedford Public Schools	Temperance
179	8,646	Byron Center Public Schools	Byron Center
179	8,646	Dowagiac Union SD	Dowagiac
181	8,614	Big Rapids Public Schools	Big Rapids
182	8,610	Central Montcalm Public Schools	Stanton
183	8,608	Kalkaska Public Schools	Kalkaska
184	8,603	Brighton Area Schools	Brighton
184	8,603	Niles Community Schools	Niles
186	8,602	Manistee Area Public Schools	Manistee
187	8,595	Grant Public SD	Grant
188	8,593	Buchanan Community Schools	Buchanan
189	8,586	Saint Joseph Public Schools	Saint Joseph
190	8,575	Grandville Public Schools	Grandville
191	8,563	Hudsonville Public SD	Hudsonville
192	8,558	Airport Community Schools	Carleton
193	8,547	Marshall Public Schools	Marshall
194	8,546	Cadillac Area Public Schools	Cadillac
195	8,532	Greenville Public Schools	Greenville
196	8,530	Houghton Lake Community Schools	Houghton Lake
197	8,526	Goodrich Area Schools	Goodrich
198	8,517	Grand Blanc Community Schools	Grand Blanc
199	8,516	Ovid-Elsie Area Schools	Elsie
200	8,508	Caro Community Schools	Caro
201	8,491	Allen Park Public Schools	Allen Park
202	8,487	Corunna Public Schools	Corunna
203	8,486	Melvindale-North Allen Park Schools	Melvindale
204	8,473	Perry Public Schools	Perry
205	8,468	Clio Area SD	Clio
206	8,460	Yale Public Schools	Yale
207	8,446	Chippewa Valley Schools	Clinton Twp
208	8,443	Oakridge Public Schools	Muskegon
209	8,439	Almont Community Schools	Almont
210	8,425	Onsted Community Schools	Onsted
211	8,420	North Branch Area Schools	North Branch
212	8,418	Hastings Area SD	Hastings
213	8,417	Lakewood Public Schools	Woodland
214	8,413	Menominee Area Public Schools	Menominee
215	8,410	Algonac Community SD	Algonac
216	8,406	Allegan Public Schools	Allegan
217	8,400	Lakeview SD (Calhoun)	Battle Creek
218	8,396	Hillsdale Community Schools	Hillsdale
219	8,395	Charlotte Public Schools	Charlotte
220	8,356	Flat Rock Community Schools	Flat Rock
221	8,355	Armada Area Schools	Armada
221	8,355	Comstock Park Public Schools	Comstock Park
223	8,352	Lake Fenton Community Schools	Fenton
224	8,351	Richmond Community Schools	Richmond
225	8,336	Rockford Public Schools	Rockford
226	8,325	Hopkins Public Schools	Hopkins
227	8,295	Monroe Public Schools	Monroe
228	8,273	Wayland Union Schools	Wayland
229	8,270	Western SD	Parma
230	8,262	Breitung Township SD	Kingsford
231	8,236	Linden Community Schools	Linden
232	8,230	Lowell Area Schools	Lowell
233	8,228	Delton Kellogg Schools	Delton
234	8,223	Essexville-Hampton Public Schools	Essexville
235	8,222	Thornapple Kellogg SD	Middleville
236	8,216	Clare Public Schools	Clare
236	8,216	Marysville Public Schools	Marysville
238	8,203	Bay City SD	Bay City
239	8,199	Croswell-Lexington Comm. Schools	Croswell
240	8,197	Fowlerville Community Schools	Fowlerville
240	8,197	Three Rivers Community Schools	Three Rivers
242	8,170	Paw Paw Public SD	Paw Paw
243	8,152	Bullock Creek SD	Midland
244	8,148	Saginaw Township Comm. Schools	Saginaw
245	8,140	Plainwell Community Schools	Plainwell
246	8,131	Durand Area Schools	Durand
247	8,125	Eaton Rapids Public Schools	Eaton Rapids
248	8,123	Tecumseh Public Schools	Tecumseh
249	8,113	Bangor Township Schools	Bay City
250	8,103	Vicksburg Community Schools	Vicksburg
251	8,085	Saint Johns Public Schools	Saint Johns
252	8,076	Davison Community Schools	Davison
253	8,066	Grand Ledge Public Schools	Grand Ledge
254	8,048	Mattawan Consolidated School	Mattawan
254	8,048	Otsego Public Schools	Otsego
256	7,999	Gladstone Area Schools	Gladstone
257	7,966	Imlay City Community Schools	Imlay City
258	7,959	Flushing Community Schools	Flushing
259	7,934	Tri County Area Schools	Sand Lake
260	7,928	Sturgis Public Schools	Sturgis
261	7,916	South Lyon Community Schools	South Lyon
262	7,913	Pinckney Community Schools	Pinckney
263	7,900	Birch Run Area Schools	Birch Run
264	7,834	Cesar Chavez Academy	Detroit
265	7,831	Coldwater Community Schools	Coldwater
266	7,787	Dewitt Public Schools	Dewitt
267	7,750	Portland Public Schools	Portland
268	7,737	Hartland Consolidated Schools	Hartland
269	7,628	Howell Public Schools	Howell
270	7,627	Chandler Park Academy	Harper Woods
271	7,524	Pennfield Schools	Battle Creek
272	7,470	Shepherd Public Schools	Shepherd
273	7,442	Whitehall District Schools	Whitehall
274	7,426	Freeland Community SD	Freeland
275	7,390	Edwardsburg Public Schools	Edwardsburg
276	7,248	Swan Valley SD	Saginaw
277	5,607	Summit Academy North	Romulus
n/a	n/a	Bendle Public Schools	Burton
n/a	n/a	Kent ISD	Grand Rapids
n/a	n/a	Macomb ISD	Clinton Twp
n/a	n/a	Saginaw ISD	Saginaw
n/a	n/a	Wayne Resa	Wayne

Total General Revenue per Student

Rank	Dollars	District Name	City
1	18,736	Bloomfield Hls SD	Bloomfield Hls
2	16,603	SD of the City of Birmingham	Birmingham
3	16,214	Mount Clemens Community SD	Mount Clemens
4	16,087	Detroit City SD	Detroit
5	16,035	Willow Run Community Schools	Ypsilanti
6	15,641	SD of Ypsilanti	Ypsilanti
7	15,238	Flint SD	Flint
8	15,211	Southfield Public SD	Southfield
9	14,783	Grand Rapids Public Schools	Grand Rapids
10	14,367	Farmington Public SD	Farmington
11	14,238	Beecher Community SD	Flint
12	13,996	Lamphere Public Schools	Madison Heights
13	13,841	Pontiac City SD	Pontiac
14	13,813	Novi Community SD	Novi
15	13,786	Clawson Public Schools	Clawson
16	13,714	Battle Creek Public Schools	Battle Creek
17	13,640	Oak Park SD	Oak Park
18	13,614	Ann Arbor Public Schools	Ann Arbor
19	13,598	Wyandotte SD	Wyandotte
20	13,555	Garden City SD	Garden City
21	13,461	Avondale SD	Auburn Hills
22	13,432	West Bloomfield SD	West Bloomfield
23	13,292	SD of the City of Royal Oak	Royal Oak
24	13,280	Muskegon Hgts SD	Muskegon
25	13,267	Troy SD	Troy
26	13,239	Holland City SD	Holland
27	13,188	Okemos Public Schools	Okemos
28	13,172	Center Line Public Schools	Center Line
29	13,107	Romulus Community Schools	Romulus
30	12,910	Dexter Community SD	Dexter
31	12,870	Grosse Pointe Public Schools	Grosse Pointe
32	12,838	Redford Union Schools Dist. No. 1	Redford
33	12,822	Northville Public Schools	Northville
34	12,817	East Lansing SD	East Lansing
35	12,801	Van Dyke Public Schools	Warren
36	12,744	Benton Harbor Area Schools	Benton Harbor
37	12,652	Rochester Community SD	Rochester
38	12,604	Saline Area Schools	Saline
39	12,585	South Lake Schools	St Clair Shores
40	12,564	Muskegon Public Schools	Muskegon
41	12,343	Jackson Public Schools	Jackson
42	12,323	Warren Woods Public Schools	Warren
43	12,290	Chelsea SD	Chelsea
44	12,264	Forest Hills Public Schools	Grand Rapids
45	12,259	Coopersville Area Public SD	Coopersville
46	12,199	Lansing Public SD	Lansing
47	12,150	Adrian SD	Adrian
47	12,150	Byron Center Public Schools	Byron Center
49	12,119	Grosse Ile Township Schools	Grosse Ile
50	12,103	Dearborn City SD	Dearborn
51	12,060	Waterford SD	Waterford
52	12,059	Kalamazoo Public Schools	Kalamazoo
53	12,054	Orchard View Schools	Muskegon
54	12,053	Waverly Community Schools	Lansing
55	11,998	Warren Consolidated Schools	Warren
56	11,984	Lake Orion Community Schools	Lake Orion
57	11,959	Hazel Park SD	Hazel Park
58	11,952	Fitzgerald Public Schools	Warren
59	11,938	Haslett Public Schools	Haslett
60	11,871	Wayne-Westland Community SD	Westland
61	11,840	Caledonia Community Schools	Caledonia
62	11,744	Trenton Public Schools	Trenton
63	11,733	Walled Lake Consolidated Schools	Walled Lake
64	11,708	Melvindale-North Allen Park Schools	Melvindale
65	11,695	West Ottawa Public SD	Holland
66	11,647	Lincoln Park SD	Lincoln Park
67	11,632	Saginaw SD	Saginaw
68	11,620	Livonia Public Schools SD	Livonia
68	11,620	South Redford SD	Redford
70	11,591	Holly Area SD	Holly
71	11,572	Comstock Public Schools	Kalamazoo
72	11,496	Lake Shore Public Schls (Macomb)	St Clair Shores
73	11,462	Holt Public Schools	Holt
74	11,425	Williamston Community Schools	Williamston
75	11,407	Mt. Pleasant City SD	Mount Pleasant
76	11,398	Ferndale Public Schools	Ferndale
77	11,397	Lincoln Consolidated SD	Ypsilanti
78	11,395	Belding Area SD	Belding
79	11,369	Carman-Ainsworth Comm. Schools	Flint
80	11,344	Godwin Heights Public Schools	Grand Rapids
81	11,338	Roseville Community Schools	Roseville
82	11,323	Van Buren Public Schools	Belleville
83	11,257	Huron Valley Schools	Highland
84	11,254	Wyoming Public Schools	Wyoming
85	11,207	Berkley SD	Oak Park
86	11,198	Kentwood Public Schools	Grand Rapids
87	11,176	Allendale Public Schools	Allendale
88	11,175	Clarkston Community SD	Clarkston
89	11,148	Marshall Public Schools	Marshall
90	11,140	Fremont Public SD	Fremont

Note: This section only includes districts with 1,500 or more students; All categories are ranked from high to low

90	11,140	Jenison Public Schools	Jenison
92	11,136	Berrien Springs Public Schools	Berrien Springs
93	11,133	Taylor SD	Taylor
94	11,125	SD of the City of Inkster	Inkster
95	11,100	Hamtramck SD	Hamtramck
96	11,083	Zeeland Public Schools	Zeeland
97	11,073	Woodhaven-Brownstown SD	Woodhaven
98	11,064	Oxford Community Schools	Oxford
99	11,063	Kenowa Hills Public Schools	Grand Rapids
100	11,022	Fraser Public Schools	Fraser
101	10,968	South Lyon Community Schools	South Lyon
102	10,962	Grand Haven Area Public Schools	Grand Haven
103	10,932	Spring Lake Public Schools	Spring Lake
104	10,924	Milan Area Schools	Milan
105	10,923	Kalkaska Public Schools	Kalkaska
106	10,910	Lakeview Public Schools (Macomb)	St Clair Shores
107	10,884	E Grand Rapids Public Schools	Grand Rapids
108	10,878	Huron SD	New Boston
109	10,858	Clarenceville SD	Livonia
110	10,848	Godfrey-Lee Public Schools	Wyoming
111	10,839	Hamilton Community Schools	Hamilton
112	10,824	Saint Johns Public Schools	Saint Johns
113	10,815	Kelloggsville Public Schools	Grand Rapids
114	10,763	Dundee Community Schools	Dundee
115	10,733	East Detroit Public Schools	Eastpointe
116	10,706	Harper Creek Community Schools	Battle Creek
117	10,683	Gibraltar SD	Woodhaven
118	10,678	Rockford Public Schools	Rockford
119	10,671	Westwood Community SD	Dearborn Hgts
120	10,664	L'anse Creuse Public Schools	Harrison Twp
121	10,662	Public Schools of Petoskey	Petoskey
122	10,640	Grand Ledge Public Schools	Grand Ledge
123	10,635	Brighton Area Schools	Brighton
124	10,634	Comstock Park Public Schools	Comstock Park
125	10,627	Pinckney Community Schools	Pinckney
126	10,596	Grandville Public Schools	Grandville
127	10,586	Breitung Township SD	Kingsford
127	10,586	Northview Public Schools	Grand Rapids
129	10,542	Clintondale Community Schools	Clinton Twp
130	10,541	Chippewa Valley Schools	Clinton Twp
131	10,526	Shelby Public Schools	Shelby
131	10,526	Traverse City Area Public Schools	Traverse City
133	10,516	Cedar Springs Public Schools	Cedar Springs
134	10,510	Lake Fenton Community Schools	Fenton
135	10,501	Saint Joseph Public Schools	Saint Joseph
136	10,496	Mason Public Schools (Ingham)	Mason
137	10,490	Hartland Consolidated Schools	Hartland
138	10,478	Fenton Area Public Schools	Fenton
139	10,465	Gull Lake Community Schools	Richland
140	10,463	Ionia Public Schools	Ionia
141	10,452	Escanaba Area Public Schools	Escanaba
142	10,445	Charlotte Public Schools	Charlotte
143	10,439	Parchment SD	Kalamazoo
144	10,429	Portage Public Schools	Portage
145	10,428	Midland Public Schools	Midland
146	10,420	Mona Shores Public SD	Muskegon
147	10,416	Sparta Area Schools	Sparta
148	10,407	Flat Rock Community Schools	Flat Rock
149	10,356	Lowell Area Schools	Lowell
150	10,332	East China SD	East China
151	10,327	Jefferson Schools (Monroe)	Monroe
151	10,327	Southgate Community SD	Southgate
153	10,312	Alma Public Schools	Alma
154	10,299	Newaygo Public SD	Newaygo
155	10,290	Romeo Community Schools	Romeo
156	10,270	Cheboygan Area Schools	Cheboygan
157	10,262	South Haven Public Schools	South Haven
158	10,254	Allegan Public Schools	Allegan
159	10,251	Reeths-Puffer Schools	Muskegon
160	10,245	Crawford Ausable Schools	Grayling
161	10,236	Ovid-Elsie Area Schools	Elsie
162	10,233	Stockbridge Community Schools	Stockbridge
163	10,208	Greenville Public Schools	Greenville
164	10,179	Hopkins Public Schools	Hopkins
165	10,176	Plymouth-Canton Comm Schools	Plymouth
166	10,164	Standish-Sterling Community Schls	Standish
167	10,162	Dewitt Public Schools	Dewitt
168	10,123	Harrison Community Schools	Harrison
169	10,119	Tecumseh Public Schools	Tecumseh
170	10,112	Wayland Union Schools	Wayland
171	10,110	Goodrich Area Schools	Goodrich
172	10,094	Anchor Bay SD	Casco
173	10,083	Gaylord Community Schools	Gaylord
174	10,079	University Preparatory Acad. (PSAD)	Detroit
175	10,067	Bullock Creek SD	Midland
176	10,063	Eaton Rapids Public Schools	Eaton Rapids
177	10,058	Algonac Community SD	Algonac
177	10,058	Fowlerville Community Schools	Fowlerville
179	10,044	Brandon SD	Ortonville
180	10,037	Manistee Area Public Schools	Manistee
181	10,011	Big Rapids Public Schools	Big Rapids
182	9,974	Armada Area Schools	Armada
183	9,962	Buchanan Community Schools	Buchanan
184	9,959	Ludington Area SD	Ludington
185	9,954	West Branch-Rose City Area Schls	Rose City
186	9,953	Howell Public Schools	Howell
187	9,950	Otsego Public Schools	Otsego
188	9,945	Mt. Morris Consolidated Schools	Mount Morris
189	9,927	Portland Public Schools	Portland
189	9,927	Whitehall District Schools	Whitehall
191	9,922	Lakewood Public Schools	Woodland
192	9,861	Richmond Community Schools	Richmond
193	9,845	Grand Blanc Community Schools	Grand Blanc
194	9,836	Utica Community Schools	Sterling Hgts
195	9,832	Lakeview SD (Calhoun)	Battle Creek
196	9,812	Three Rivers Community Schools	Three Rivers
197	9,798	Chesaning Union Schools	Chesaning
198	9,782	Vicksburg Community Schools	Vicksburg
199	9,770	Dowagiac Union SD	Dowagiac
200	9,766	Paw Paw Public SD	Paw Paw
201	9,765	Almont Community Schools	Almont
202	9,764	Port Huron Area SD	Port Huron
203	9,760	Sturgis Public Schools	Sturgis
204	9,751	Reed City Area Public Schools	Reed City
205	9,744	Fruitport Community Schools	Fruitport
206	9,713	Onsted Community Schools	Onsted
206	9,713	Yale Public Schools	Yale
208	9,712	Hudsonville Public SD	Hudsonville
209	9,703	Olivet Community Schools	Olivet
210	9,686	Central Montcalm Public Schools	Stanton
211	9,661	Airport Community Schools	Carleton
212	9,657	Hillsdale Community Schools	Hillsdale
213	9,650	Allen Park Public Schools	Allen Park
214	9,643	Cadillac Area Public Schools	Cadillac
215	9,629	Perry Public Schools	Perry
216	9,625	Lakeville Community SD	Otisville
217	9,619	Chippewa Hills SD	Remus
218	9,614	Gladstone Area Schools	Gladstone
219	9,604	Marysville Public Schools	Marysville
220	9,598	Essexville-Hampton Public Schools	Essexville
221	9,593	Bedford Public Schools	Temperance
222	9,582	Carrollton Public Schools	Saginaw
223	9,578	Bay City SD	Bay City
224	9,575	Columbia SD	Brooklyn
225	9,574	Marquette Area Public Schools	Marquette
226	9,570	Plainwell Community Schools	Plainwell
227	9,567	Thornapple Kellogg SD	Middleville
228	9,565	Coloma Community Schools	Coloma
229	9,558	Benzie County Central Schools	Benzonia
230	9,550	Monroe Public Schools	Monroe
231	9,540	Oakridge Public Schools	Muskegon
232	9,528	Linden Community Schools	Linden
233	9,527	Coldwater Community Schools	Coldwater
233	9,527	Crestwood SD	Dearborn Hgts
235	9,522	Lakeshore SD (Berrien)	Stevensville
236	9,511	Sault Ste Marie Area Schools	Sault Ste Marie
237	9,476	Alpena Public Schools	Alpena
238	9,466	Delton Kellogg Schools	Delton
239	9,440	Hastings Area SD	Hastings
240	9,430	Owosso Public Schools	Owosso
241	9,404	Lapeer Community Schools	Lapeer
242	9,402	Shepherd Public Schools	Shepherd
243	9,399	Grant Public SD	Grant
244	9,352	Cesar Chavez Academy	Detroit
245	9,349	Imlay City Community Schools	Imlay City
246	9,290	Caro Community Schools	Caro
247	9,277	Croswell-Lexington Comm. Schools	Croswell
248	9,251	Gladwin Community Schools	Gladwin
249	9,238	Durand Area Schools	Durand
249	9,238	Riverview Community SD	Riverview
251	9,208	Niles Community Schools	Niles
252	9,203	Houghton Lake Community Schools	Houghton Lake
253	9,191	Napoleon Community Schools	Napoleon
254	9,179	Northwest Community Schools	Jackson
255	9,165	Birch Run Area Schools	Birch Run
256	9,145	Kearsley Community SD	Flint
257	9,135	North Branch Area Schools	North Branch
258	9,133	Corunna Public Schools	Corunna
259	9,127	Western SD	Parma
260	9,107	Dearborn Hgts SD #7	Dearborn Hgts
261	9,093	Clare Public Schools	Clare
261	9,093	Swartz Creek Community Schools	Swartz Creek
263	9,092	Swan Valley SD	Saginaw
264	9,087	Old Redford Academy	Detroit
265	9,079	Pennfield Schools	Battle Creek
266	9,073	Tri County Area Schools	Sand Lake
267	9,058	Freeland Community SD	Freeland
268	9,053	Saginaw Township Comm. Schools	Saginaw
269	8,980	Menominee Area Public Schools	Menominee
270	8,969	Flushing Community Schools	Flushing
271	8,954	Clio Area SD	Clio
272	8,907	Mattawan Consolidated School	Mattawan
273	8,885	Bangor Township Schools	Bay City
274	8,878	Davison Community Schools	Davison
275	8,756	Edwardsburg Public Schools	Edwardsburg
276	8,527	Chandler Park Academy	Harper Woods
277	8,081	Summit Academy North	Romulus
n/a	n/a	Bendle Public Schools	Burton
n/a	n/a	Kent ISD	Grand Rapids
n/a	n/a	Macomb ISD	Clinton Twp
n/a	n/a	Saginaw ISD	Saginaw
n/a	n/a	Wayne Resa	Wayne

Long-Term Debt per Student (end of FY)

Rank	Dollars	District Name	City
1	239,916	Oxford Community Schools	Oxford
2	106,187	Hazel Park SD	Hazel Park
3	43,748	Allendale Public Schools	Allendale
4	41,556	Mount Clemens Community SD	Mount Clemens
5	40,008	Willow Run Community Schools	Ypsilanti
6	37,973	Milan Area Schools	Milan
7	32,907	Byron Center Public Schools	Byron Center
8	32,145	Brandon SD	Ortonville
9	31,679	Coopersville Area Public SD	Coopersville
10	30,861	Marysville Public Schools	Marysville
11	30,672	Chippewa Valley Schools	Clinton Twp
12	30,668	Avondale SD	Auburn Hills
13	30,370	Dexter Community SD	Dexter
14	29,786	Hartland Consolidated Schools	Hartland
15	28,781	Pinckney Community Schools	Pinckney
16	28,464	Fowlerville Community Schools	Fowlerville
17	27,820	Thornapple Kellogg SD	Middleville
18	26,859	Saint Johns Public Schools	Saint Johns
19	26,381	Charlotte Public Schools	Charlotte
20	26,361	Comstock Park Public Schools	Comstock Park
21	26,055	Otsego Public Schools	Otsego
22	25,996	SD of the City of Birmingham	Birmingham
23	25,473	Caledonia Community Schools	Caledonia
24	25,057	Harper Creek Community Schools	Battle Creek
25	24,552	Hudsonville Public SD	Hudsonville
26	24,444	Detroit City SD	Detroit
27	24,423	Lincoln Consolidated SD	Ypsilanti
28	24,348	Saline Area Schools	Saline
29	23,419	Marshall Public Schools	Marshall
30	22,326	Reeths-Puffer Schools	Muskegon
31	22,320	Goodrich Area Schools	Goodrich
32	21,933	Saint Joseph Public Schools	Saint Joseph
33	20,903	Almont Community Schools	Almont
34	20,746	Paw Paw Public SD	Paw Paw
35	19,975	Parchment SD	Kalamazoo
36	19,962	North Branch Area Schools	North Branch
37	19,840	Forest Hills Public Schools	Grand Rapids
38	19,514	Allen Park Public Schools	Allen Park
39	19,382	Lakewood Public Schools	Woodland
40	19,102	Clarkston Community SD	Clarkston
41	19,090	Perry Public Schools	Perry
42	18,991	Roseville Community Schools	Roseville
43	18,967	Flat Rock Community Schools	Flat Rock
44	18,593	Lake Orion Community Schools	Lake Orion
45	18,362	Chelsea SD	Chelsea
46	18,324	Dewitt Public Schools	Dewitt
47	18,095	Jenison Public Schools	Jenison
48	18,066	Muskegon Hgts SD	Muskegon
49	17,693	Fraser Public Schools	Fraser
50	16,964	East Lansing SD	East Lansing
51	16,777	Pennfield Schools	Battle Creek
52	16,749	Allegan Public Schools	Allegan
53	16,591	Whitehall District Schools	Whitehall
54	16,156	Shepherd Public Schools	Shepherd
55	16,140	Novi Community SD	Novi
56	15,944	Brighton Area Schools	Brighton
57	15,727	Grosse Ile Township Schools	Grosse Ile
58	15,269	Tecumseh Public Schools	Tecumseh
59	15,158	Holt Public Schools	Holt

Note: This section only includes districts with 1,500 or more students; All categories are ranked from high to low

60	15,013	Clawson Public Schools	Clawson
61	14,891	Greenville Public Schools	Greenville
62	14,819	Romulus Community Schools	Romulus
63	14,366	Onsted Community Schools	Onsted
64	14,363	Ionia Public Schools	Ionia
65	14,169	Woodhaven-Brownstown SD	Woodhaven
66	14,135	Rockford Public Schools	Rockford
67	14,134	Orchard View Schools	Muskegon
68	14,131	Grand Ledge Public Schools	Grand Ledge
69	14,083	Alma Public Schools	Alma
70	13,760	Portland Public Schools	Portland
71	13,713	SD of the City of Royal Oak	Royal Oak
72	13,603	Lakeview SD (Calhoun)	Battle Creek
73	13,591	Adrian SD	Adrian
74	13,461	Spring Lake Public Schools	Spring Lake
75	13,158	Hamilton Community Schools	Hamilton
76	13,046	Fenton Area Public Schools	Fenton
77	13,007	Gull Lake Community Schools	Richland
78	12,872	Warren Woods Public Schools	Warren
79	12,641	Kenowa Hills Public Schools	Grand Rapids
80	12,609	Gibraltar SD	Woodhaven
81	12,338	Dowagiac Union SD	Dowagiac
82	12,306	Okemos Public Schools	Okemos
83	11,975	Durand Area Schools	Durand
84	11,970	Fitzgerald Public Schools	Warren
85	11,966	South Haven Public Schools	South Haven
86	11,772	Huron Valley Schools	Highland
87	11,771	Walled Lake Consolidated Schools	Walled Lake
88	11,685	SD of the City of Inkster	Inkster
89	11,546	Waverly Community Schools	Lansing
90	11,475	Kalamazoo Public Schools	Kalamazoo
91	11,400	Rochester Community SD	Rochester
92	11,301	Sparta Area Schools	Sparta
93	10,961	Huron SD	New Boston
94	10,799	Lakeview Public Schools (Macomb)	St Clair Shores
95	10,472	Plymouth-Canton Comm Schools	Plymouth
96	10,211	Richmond Community Schools	Richmond
97	10,088	Ann Arbor Public Schools	Ann Arbor
98	10,033	Linden Community Schools	Linden
99	9,894	Mt. Pleasant City SD	Mount Pleasant
100	9,844	Waterford SD	Waterford
101	9,593	Grand Haven Area Public Schools	Grand Haven
102	9,581	Newaygo Public SD	Newaygo
103	9,572	Reed City Area Public Schools	Reed City
104	9,536	Grand Blanc Community Schools	Grand Blanc
105	9,285	Warren Consolidated Schools	Warren
106	9,179	Big Rapids Public Schools	Big Rapids
107	9,028	Crawford Ausable Schools	Grayling
108	8,744	Troy SD	Troy
109	8,734	Jackson Public Schools	Jackson
110	8,663	Lapeer Community Schools	Lapeer
111	8,545	Carman-Ainsworth Comm. Schools	Flint
112	8,402	Redford Union Schools Dist. No. 1	Redford
113	8,393	Traverse City Area Public Schools	Traverse City
114	8,328	East Detroit Public Schools	Eastpointe
115	8,324	Stockbridge Community Schools	Stockbridge
116	8,148	Lake Shore Public Schls (Macomb)	St Clair Shores
117	8,025	Kentwood Public Schools	Grand Rapids
118	7,874	Oak Park SD	Oak Park
119	7,835	Mona Shores Public SD	Muskegon
120	7,735	Gaylord Community Schools	Gaylord
121	7,544	Utica Community Schools	Sterling Hgts
122	7,378	Grand Rapids Public Schools	Grand Rapids
123	7,272	Dearborn City SD	Dearborn
124	7,214	Bay City SD	Bay City
125	7,201	Fruitport Community Schools	Fruitport
126	7,199	East China SD	East China
127	7,098	Hastings Area SD	Hastings
128	6,906	Western SD	Parma
129	6,738	Southgate Community SD	Southgate
130	6,693	Wyandotte SD	Wyandotte
131	6,669	Grosse Pointe Public Schools	Grosse Pointe
132	6,664	Garden City SD	Garden City
133	6,605	Mason Public Schools (Ingham)	Mason
134	6,508	West Branch-Rose City Area Schls	Rose City
135	6,316	Muskegon Public Schools	Muskegon
136	6,094	Lincoln Park SD	Lincoln Park
137	6,067	Mattawan Consolidated School	Mattawan
138	6,055	Cadillac Area Public Schools	Cadillac
139	5,972	Bullock Creek SD	Midland
140	5,962	Coldwater Community Schools	Coldwater
141	5,893	Clare Public Schools	Clare
142	5,710	Gladwin Community Schools	Gladwin
143	5,672	Chippewa Hills SD	Remus
144	5,592	Carrollton Public Schools	Saginaw
145	5,509	Livonia Public Schools SD	Livonia
146	5,487	Bangor Township Schools	Bay City
147	5,105	Cheboygan Area Schools	Cheboygan
148	4,931	Romeo Community Schools	Romeo
149	4,916	Public Schools of Petoskey	Petoskey
150	4,879	Berkley SD	Oak Park
150	4,879	Lamphere Public Schools	Madison Heights
152	4,850	Melvindale-North Allen Park Schools	Melvindale
153	4,779	Oakridge Public Schools	Muskegon
154	4,775	Napoleon Community Schools	Napoleon
155	4,752	Wayne-Westland Community SD	Westland
156	4,633	Shelby Public Schools	Shelby
157	4,608	Flushing Community Schools	Flushing
158	4,558	Benzie County Central Schools	Benzonia
159	4,509	Comstock Public Schools	Kalamazoo
160	4,482	Lansing Public SD	Lansing
161	4,433	Grant Public SD	Grant
162	4,368	Escanaba Area Public Schools	Escanaba
163	4,294	Center Line Public Schools	Center Line
164	4,208	Buchanan Community Schools	Buchanan
165	4,037	Port Huron Area SD	Port Huron
166	3,864	Riverview Community SD	Riverview
167	3,801	Swartz Creek Community Schools	Swartz Creek
168	3,741	Lakeville Community SD	Otisville
169	3,713	Alpena Public Schools	Alpena
170	3,609	Farmington Public SD	Farmington
171	3,574	Menominee Area Public Schools	Menominee
172	3,453	Saginaw SD	Saginaw
173	3,441	Lakeshore SD (Berrien)	Stevensville
174	3,240	Grandville Public Schools	Grandville
175	2,992	Sault Ste Marie Area Schools	Sault Ste Marie
176	2,932	Ludington Area SD	Ludington
177	2,679	Summit Academy North	Romulus
178	2,563	E Grand Rapids Public Schools	Grand Rapids
179	2,531	Cedar Springs Public Schools	Cedar Springs
180	2,440	Lake Fenton Community Schools	Fenton
181	2,420	Tri County Area Schools	Sand Lake
182	2,364	Breitung Township SD	Kingsford
183	2,335	Flint SD	Flint
184	2,310	Davison Community Schools	Davison
185	2,205	Berrien Springs Public Schools	Berrien Springs
186	2,128	Central Montcalm Public Schools	Stanton
187	1,992	Chandler Park Academy	Harper Woods
188	1,860	Howell Public Schools	Howell
189	1,805	Coloma Community Schools	Coloma
190	1,803	Bloomfield Hls SD	Bloomfield Hls
191	1,636	Airport Community Schools	Carleton
192	1,628	Marquette Area Public Schools	Marquette
193	1,593	Chesaning Union Schools	Chesaning
194	1,393	Croswell-Lexington Comm. Schools	Croswell
195	1,232	Corunna Public Schools	Corunna
196	1,129	Birch Run Area Schools	Birch Run
197	1,114	Columbia SD	Brooklyn
198	998	Bedford Public Schools	Temperance
199	893	Crestwood SD	Dearborn Hgts
200	620	Westwood Community SD	Dearborn Hgts
201	564	Godwin Heights Public Schools	Grand Rapids
202	221	Kearsley Community SD	Flint
203	174	Monroe Public Schools	Monroe
204	146	Belding Area SD	Belding
205	118	Clarenceville SD	Livonia
206	87	Mt. Morris Consolidated Schools	Mount Morris
207	86	Jefferson Schools (Monroe)	Monroe
208	67	Benton Harbor Area Schools	Benton Harbor
209	52	Clio Area SD	Clio
210	15	West Bloomfield SD	West Bloomfield
211	9	Owosso Public Schools	Owosso
212	3	Midland Public Schools	Midland
213	0	Algonac Community SD	Algonac
213	0	Anchor Bay SD	Casco
213	0	Armada Area Schools	Armada
213	0	Battle Creek Public Schools	Battle Creek
213	0	Beecher Community SD	Flint
213	0	Caro Community Schools	Caro
213	0	Cesar Chavez Academy	Detroit
213	0	Clintondale Community Schools	Clinton Twp
213	0	Dearborn Hgts SD #7	Dearborn Hgts
213	0	Delton Kellogg Schools	Delton
213	0	Dundee Community Schools	Dundee
213	0	Eaton Rapids Public Schools	Eaton Rapids
213	0	Edwardsburg Public Schools	Edwardsburg
213	0	Essexville-Hampton Public Schools	Essexville
213	0	Ferndale Public Schools	Ferndale
213	0	Freeland Community SD	Freeland
213	0	Fremont Public SD	Fremont
213	0	Gladstone Area Schools	Gladstone
213	0	Godfrey-Lee Public Schools	Wyoming
213	0	Hamtramck SD	Hamtramck
213	0	Harrison Community Schools	Harrison
213	0	Haslett Public Schools	Haslett
213	0	Hillsdale Community Schools	Hillsdale
213	0	Holland City SD	Holland
213	0	Holly Area SD	Holly
213	0	Hopkins Public Schools	Hopkins
213	0	Houghton Lake Community Schools	Houghton Lake
213	0	Imlay City Community Schools	Imlay City
213	0	Kalkaska Public Schools	Kalkaska
213	0	Kelloggsville Public Schools	Grand Rapids
213	0	L'anse Creuse Public Schools	Harrison Twp
213	0	Lowell Area Schools	Lowell
213	0	Manistee Area Public Schools	Manistee
213	0	Niles Community Schools	Niles
213	0	Northview Public Schools	Grand Rapids
213	0	Northville Public Schools	Northville
213	0	Northwest Community Schools	Jackson
213	0	Old Redford Academy	Detroit
213	0	Olivet Community Schools	Olivet
213	0	Ovid-Elsie Area Schools	Elsie
213	0	Plainwell Community Schools	Plainwell
213	0	Pontiac City SD	Pontiac
213	0	Portage Public Schools	Portage
213	0	Saginaw Township Comm. Schools	Saginaw
213	0	SD of Ypsilanti	Ypsilanti
213	0	South Lake Schools	St Clair Shores
213	0	South Lyon Community Schools	South Lyon
213	0	South Redford SD	Redford
213	0	Southfield Public SD	Southfield
213	0	Standish-Sterling Community Schls	Standish
213	0	Sturgis Public Schools	Sturgis
213	0	Swan Valley SD	Saginaw
213	0	Taylor SD	Taylor
213	0	Three Rivers Community Schools	Three Rivers
213	0	Trenton Public Schools	Trenton
213	0	University Preparatory Acad. (PSAD)	Detroit
213	0	Van Buren Public Schools	Belleville
213	0	Van Dyke Public Schools	Warren
213	0	Vicksburg Community Schools	Vicksburg
213	0	Wayland Union Schools	Wayland
213	0	West Ottawa Public SD	Holland
213	0	Williamston Community Schools	Williamston
213	0	Wyoming Public Schools	Wyoming
213	0	Yale Public Schools	Yale
213	0	Zeeland Public Schools	Zeeland
n/a	n/a	Bendle Public Schools	Burton
n/a	n/a	Kent ISD	Grand Rapids
n/a	n/a	Macomb ISD	Clinton Twp
n/a	n/a	Saginaw ISD	Saginaw
n/a	n/a	Wayne Resa	Wayne

Number of Diploma Recipients

Rank	Number	District Name	City
1	5,634	Detroit City SD	Detroit
2	2,236	Utica Community Schools	Sterling Hgts
3	1,393	Livonia Public Schools SD	Livonia
4	1,379	Plymouth-Canton Comm Schools	Plymouth
5	1,289	Ann Arbor Public Schools	Ann Arbor
6	1,220	Dearborn City SD	Dearborn
7	1,193	Walled Lake Consolidated Schools	Walled Lake
8	1,182	Rochester Community SD	Rochester
9	1,136	Warren Consolidated Schools	Warren
10	1,124	Chippewa Valley Schools	Clinton Twp
11	1,002	Troy SD	Troy
12	990	Farmington Public SD	Farmington
13	878	Wayne-Westland Community SD	Westland
14	849	Traverse City Area Public Schools	Traverse City
15	826	Lansing Public SD	Lansing
16	812	L'anse Creuse Public Schools	Harrison Twp
17	808	Grand Rapids Public Schools	Grand Rapids
18	781	Huron Valley Schools	Highland
19	777	Forest Hills Public Schools	Grand Rapids
20	762	Grosse Pointe Public Schools	Grosse Pointe
21	757	Southfield Public SD	Southfield
22	728	Flint SD	Flint
23	723	Portage Public Schools	Portage
24	711	Waterford SD	Waterford
25	700	Midland Public Schools	Midland
26	698	Port Huron Area SD	Port Huron
27	634	Rockford Public Schools	Rockford
28	632	Clarkston Community SD	Clarkston

Note: This section only includes districts with 1,500 or more students; All categories are ranked from high to low

29	631	Taylor SD	Taylor
30	627	SD of the City of Birmingham	Birmingham
31	621	Bay City SD	Bay City
32	593	Brighton Area Schools	Brighton
33	590	Kentwood Public Schools	Grand Rapids
34	572	Lapeer Community Schools	Lapeer
35	565	Howell Public Schools	Howell
36	563	Northville Public Schools	Northville
37	556	Lake Orion Community Schools	Lake Orion
38	546	Grand Blanc Community Schools	Grand Blanc
39	524	Ferndale Public Schools	Ferndale
40	504	Southgate Community SD	Southgate
41	499	Bloomfield Hls SD	Bloomfield Hls
42	498	Kalamazoo Public Schools	Kalamazoo
43	483	West Bloomfield SD	West Bloomfield
44	482	Van Buren Public Schools	Belleville
45	474	Hartland Consolidated Schools	Hartland
46	473	Monroe Public Schools	Monroe
47	464	Saginaw SD	Saginaw
48	459	South Lyon Community Schools	South Lyon
49	451	West Ottawa Public SD	Holland
50	450	Roseville Community Schools	Roseville
51	445	Anchor Bay SD	Casco
52	444	Grand Haven Area Public Schools	Grand Haven
53	441	East China SD	East China
54	439	Grand Ledge Public Schools	Grand Ledge
54	439	Novi Community SD	Novi
56	435	Grandville Public Schools	Grandville
57	434	Jackson Public Schools	Jackson
58	423	Romeo Community Schools	Romeo
59	419	Bedford Public Schools	Temperance
60	418	Pontiac City SD	Pontiac
61	416	SD of the City of Royal Oak	Royal Oak
62	413	Wyoming Public Schools	Wyoming
63	410	Holt Public Schools	Holt
63	410	Saline Area Schools	Saline
65	406	Zeeland Public Schools	Zeeland
66	405	Saginaw Township Comm. Schools	Saginaw
67	383	Garden City SD	Garden City
68	369	Davison Community Schools	Davison
69	363	Flushing Community Schools	Flushing
70	360	Woodhaven-Brownstown SD	Woodhaven
71	356	Jenison Public Schools	Jenison
71	356	Romulus Community Schools	Romulus
73	351	Fraser Public Schools	Fraser
74	349	Berkley SD	Oak Park
75	340	Battle Creek Public Schools	Battle Creek
76	337	Oak Park SD	Oak Park
76	337	Pinckney Community Schools	Pinckney
78	329	Clintondale Community Schools	Clinton Twp
79	325	Allen Park Public Schools	Allen Park
80	324	Carman-Ainsworth Comm. Schools	Flint
80	324	Northview Public Schools	Grand Rapids
82	317	Mt. Pleasant City SD	Mount Pleasant
83	315	Alpena Public Schools	Alpena
84	314	Okemos Public Schools	Okemos
85	309	Lowell Area Schools	Lowell
85	309	Swartz Creek Community Schools	Swartz Creek
87	305	East Detroit Public Schools	Eastpointe
87	305	Warren Woods Public Schools	Warren
89	304	Holly Area SD	Holly
90	300	Brandon SD	Ortonville
91	292	Kearsley Community SD	Flint
92	291	Mona Shores Public SD	Muskegon
93	289	Lincoln Consolidated SD	Ypsilanti
93	289	Reeths-Puffer Schools	Muskegon
95	288	Wyandotte SD	Wyandotte
96	285	Hazel Park SD	Hazel Park
96	285	Kenowa Hills Public Schools	Grand Rapids
98	283	Marquette Area Public Schools	Marquette
99	281	Avondale SD	Auburn Hills
99	281	Greenville Public Schools	Greenville
101	279	Lake Shore Public Schls (Macomb)	St Clair Shores
101	279	Owosso Public Schools	Owosso
101	279	Redford Union Schools Dist. No. 1	Redford
101	279	Saint Johns Public Schools	Saint Johns
105	278	Oxford Community Schools	Oxford
106	277	Caledonia Community Schools	Caledonia
106	277	Muskegon Public Schools	Muskegon
108	275	Hudsonville Public SD	Hudsonville
109	270	Gibraltar SD	Woodhaven
110	265	Lakeview SD (Calhoun)	Battle Creek
111	260	Holland City SD	Holland
112	257	Saint Joseph Public Schools	Saint Joseph
113	255	Adrian SD	Adrian
114	254	Fowlerville Community Schools	Fowlerville
115	251	Niles Community Schools	Niles
116	250	Cedar Springs Public Schools	Cedar Springs
116	250	Lincoln Park SD	Lincoln Park
116	250	Mt. Morris Consolidated Schools	Mount Morris
119	246	Clio Area SD	Clio
120	245	Wayland Union Schools	Wayland
121	244	Lakeshore SD (Berrien)	Stevensville
121	244	Public Schools of Petoskey	Petoskey
123	241	Plainwell Community Schools	Plainwell
124	240	Dexter Community SD	Dexter
125	239	Sturgis Public Schools	Sturgis
125	239	Tecumseh Public Schools	Tecumseh
127	238	Waverly Community Schools	Lansing
128	236	Haslett Public Schools	Haslett
128	236	Ionia Public Schools	Ionia
130	235	Airport Community Schools	Carleton
130	235	Coldwater Community Schools	Coldwater
130	235	E Grand Rapids Public Schools	Grand Rapids
130	235	Fenton Area Public Schools	Fenton
130	235	Mattawan Consolidated School	Mattawan
135	234	Cadillac Area Public Schools	Cadillac
135	234	Ludington Area SD	Ludington
137	233	Northwest Community Schools	Jackson
138	232	Lakeview Public Schools (Macomb)	St Clair Shores
138	232	Mason Public Schools (Ingham)	Mason
140	231	Chelsea SD	Chelsea
141	230	East Lansing SD	East Lansing
141	230	Gaylord Community Schools	Gaylord
141	230	South Redford SD	Redford
144	229	Benton Harbor Area Schools	Benton Harbor
145	228	Crestwood SD	Dearborn Hgts
145	228	Gull Lake Community Schools	Richland
147	226	Fitzgerald Public Schools	Warren
148	225	Western SD	Parma
149	222	Escanaba Area Public Schools	Escanaba
149	222	Fruitport Community Schools	Fruitport
151	219	Dewitt Public Schools	Dewitt
151	219	Hastings Area SD	Hastings
151	219	Sault Ste Marie Area Schools	Sault Ste Marie
154	215	Milan Area Schools	Milan
154	215	North Branch Area Schools	North Branch
156	211	Bangor Township Schools	Bay City
156	211	SD of Ypsilanti	Ypsilanti
158	210	Marshall Public Schools	Marshall
159	209	Riverview Community SD	Riverview
159	209	Thornapple Kellogg SD	Middleville
161	207	Alma Public Schools	Alma
162	206	Croswell-Lexington Comm. Schools	Croswell
163	205	Ovid-Elsie Area Schools	Elsie
163	205	Sparta Area Schools	Sparta
165	204	Trenton Public Schools	Trenton
166	202	Charlotte Public Schools	Charlotte
166	202	Huron SD	New Boston
168	201	Orchard View Schools	Muskegon
169	199	Linden Community Schools	Linden
169	199	Three Rivers Community Schools	Three Rivers
171	197	Center Line Public Schools	Center Line
172	194	Byron Center Public Schools	Byron Center
172	194	Coopersville Area Public SD	Coopersville
174	193	SD of the City of Inkster	Inkster
175	192	Lakewood Public Schools	Woodland
175	192	Vicksburg Community Schools	Vicksburg
177	188	Harper Creek Community Schools	Battle Creek
177	188	Imlay City Community Schools	Imlay City
177	188	Otsego Public Schools	Otsego
180	186	Corunna Public Schools	Corunna
180	186	Paw Paw Public SD	Paw Paw
182	185	Cheboygan Area Schools	Cheboygan
183	184	Marysville Public Schools	Marysville
183	184	West Branch-Rose City Area Schls	Rose City
183	184	Whitehall District Schools	Whitehall
186	181	Algonac Community SD	Algonac
186	181	Spring Lake Public Schools	Spring Lake
188	180	Goodrich Area Schools	Goodrich
189	178	Hamilton Community Schools	Hamilton
190	175	Comstock Public Schools	Kalamazoo
191	173	Berrien Springs Public Schools	Berrien Springs
191	173	Breitung Township SD	Kingsford
193	171	Eaton Rapids Public Schools	Eaton Rapids
193	171	Richmond Community Schools	Richmond
195	170	Allegan Public Schools	Allegan
195	170	Allendale Public Schools	Allendale
197	169	Fremont Public SD	Fremont
198	167	Delton Kellogg Schools	Delton
198	167	Melvindale-North Allen Park Schools	Melvindale
198	167	Tri County Area Schools	Sand Lake
201	166	Grant Public SD	Grant
202	165	Portland Public Schools	Portland
203	163	Comstock Park Public Schools	Comstock Park
203	163	South Lake Schools	St Clair Shores
205	160	Big Rapids Public Schools	Big Rapids
205	160	Yale Public Schools	Yale
207	159	Lamphere Public Schools	Madison Heights
208	158	Bendle Public Schools	Burton
209	157	Reed City Area Public Schools	Reed City
210	156	Jefferson Schools (Monroe)	Monroe
210	156	Standish-Sterling Community Schls	Standish
212	155	Clare Public Schools	Clare
213	154	Van Dyke Public Schools	Warren
214	152	Newaygo Public SD	Newaygo
215	151	Belding Area SD	Belding
215	151	Chippewa Hills SD	Remus
215	151	Dowagiac Union SD	Dowagiac
215	151	Westwood Community SD	Dearborn Hgts
219	150	Birch Run Area Schools	Birch Run
219	150	Swan Valley SD	Saginaw
221	149	Columbia SD	Brooklyn
221	149	Kelloggsville Public Schools	Grand Rapids
221	149	Onsted Community Schools	Onsted
224	147	Parchment SD	Kalamazoo
225	146	Grosse Ile Township Schools	Grosse Ile
226	145	Lakeville Community SD	Otisville
227	143	Edwardsburg Public Schools	Edwardsburg
228	142	Manistee Area Public Schools	Manistee
229	141	Armada Area Schools	Armada
229	141	Godwin Heights Public Schools	Grand Rapids
229	141	Perry Public Schools	Perry
232	140	Freeland Community SD	Freeland
232	140	Houghton Lake Community Schools	Houghton Lake
234	139	Hamtramck SD	Hamtramck
234	139	Williamston Community Schools	Williamston
236	138	Bullock Creek SD	Midland
236	138	Gladwin Community Schools	Gladwin
236	138	South Haven Public Schools	South Haven
236	138	Stockbridge Community Schools	Stockbridge
240	136	Central Montcalm Public Schools	Stanton
240	136	Pennfield Schools	Battle Creek
242	135	Clarenceville SD	Livonia
242	135	Coloma Community Schools	Coloma
244	134	Caro Community Schools	Caro
244	134	Dearborn Hgts SD #7	Dearborn Hgts
244	134	Hopkins Public Schools	Hopkins
244	134	Shelby Public Schools	Shelby
248	133	Napoleon Community Schools	Napoleon
249	131	Crawford Ausable Schools	Grayling
250	129	Almont Community Schools	Almont
251	128	Oakridge Public Schools	Muskegon
252	126	Lake Fenton Community Schools	Fenton
253	125	Chesaning Union Schools	Chesaning
254	123	Durand Area Schools	Durand
254	123	Gladstone Area Schools	Gladstone
256	122	University Preparatory Acad. (PSAD)	Detroit
257	121	Shepherd Public Schools	Shepherd
258	120	Menominee Area Public Schools	Menominee
259	119	Essexville-Hampton Public Schools	Essexville
260	112	Kalkaska Public Schools	Kalkaska
261	111	Hillsdale Community Schools	Hillsdale
262	110	Muskegon Hgts SD	Muskegon
263	108	Flat Rock Community Schools	Flat Rock
263	108	Godfrey-Lee Public Schools	Wyoming
263	108	Harrison Community Schools	Harrison
263	108	Mount Clemens Community SD	Mount Clemens
267	106	Clawson Public Schools	Clawson
267	106	Dundee Community Schools	Dundee
269	105	Beecher Community SD	Flint
270	103	Buchanan Community Schools	Buchanan
271	100	Old Redford Academy	Detroit
272	97	Olivet Community Schools	Olivet
273	96	Carrollton Public Schools	Saginaw
274	93	Cesar Chavez Academy	Detroit
275	85	Willow Run Community Schools	Ypsilanti
276	83	Summit Academy North	Romulus
277	7	Benzie County Central Schools	Benzonia
278	3	Macomb ISD	Clinton Twp
279	1	Kent ISD	Grand Rapids
n/a	n/a	Chandler Park Academy	Harper Woods
n/a	n/a	Saginaw ISD	Saginaw
n/a	n/a	Wayne Resa	Wayne

Note: This section only includes districts with 1,500 or more students; All categories are ranked from high to low

High School Drop-out Rate

Rank	Percent	District Name	City
1	44.3	Clintondale Community Schools	Clinton Twp
2	24.3	Bendle Public Schools	Burton
3	17.6	Hazel Park SD	Hazel Park
4	16.8	Ferndale Public Schools	Ferndale
5	16.3	Godwin Heights Public Schools	Grand Rapids
6	15.5	Wayne Resa	Wayne
7	14.5	Van Dyke Public Schools	Warren
8	13.7	Mt. Morris Consolidated Schools	Mount Morris
9	12.9	Godfrey-Lee Public Schools	Wyoming
10	12.8	Beecher Community SD	Flint
11	12.1	Battle Creek Public Schools	Battle Creek
12	9.4	Kelloggsville Public Schools	Grand Rapids
13	9.3	Muskegon Hgts SD	Muskegon
14	8.8	Comstock Public Schools	Kalamazoo
14	8.8	Wyoming Public Schools	Wyoming
16	8.4	Hamtramck SD	Hamtramck
17	8.1	Newaygo Public SD	Newaygo
17	8.1	Parchment SD	Kalamazoo
19	8.0	Coldwater Community Schools	Coldwater
20	7.7	Clare Public Schools	Clare
21	7.6	Flint SD	Flint
21	7.6	Jackson Public Schools	Jackson
23	7.4	Muskegon Public Schools	Muskegon
23	7.4	Three Rivers Community Schools	Three Rivers
23	7.4	Whitehall District Schools	Whitehall
26	7.2	Caro Community Schools	Caro
26	7.2	Kearsley Community SD	Flint
28	7.0	SD of the City of Inkster	Inkster
29	6.9	Holt Public Schools	Holt
30	6.7	Ludington Area SD	Ludington
31	6.6	Fitzgerald Public Schools	Warren
31	6.6	SD of Ypsilanti	Ypsilanti
33	6.5	Grand Rapids Public Schools	Grand Rapids
34	6.4	Lansing Public SD	Lansing
35	6.3	Willow Run Community Schools	Ypsilanti
36	6.1	Carrollton Public Schools	Saginaw
37	6.0	Cadillac Area Public Schools	Cadillac
37	6.0	Detroit City SD	Detroit
37	6.0	Pontiac City SD	Pontiac
40	5.9	Dundee Community Schools	Dundee
40	5.9	Western SD	Parma
42	5.6	Bay City SD	Bay City
42	5.6	Kentwood Public Schools	Grand Rapids
42	5.6	Mount Clemens Community SD	Mount Clemens
42	5.6	Saginaw Township Comm. Schools	Saginaw
46	5.5	Shelby Public Schools	Shelby
47	5.4	Wayne-Westland Community SD	Westland
48	5.2	Dowagiac Union SD	Dowagiac
49	5.0	Kalamazoo Public Schools	Kalamazoo
50	4.9	Alpena Public Schools	Alpena
50	4.9	Belding Area SD	Belding
50	4.9	Crawford Ausable Schools	Grayling
53	4.8	Berkley SD	Oak Park
53	4.8	Reed City Area Public Schools	Reed City
53	4.8	Taylor SD	Taylor
56	4.7	Port Huron Area SD	Port Huron
57	4.6	Adrian SD	Adrian
57	4.6	Charlotte Public Schools	Charlotte
57	4.6	Northwest Community Schools	Jackson
60	4.5	Westwood Community SD	Dearborn Hgts
61	4.4	Garden City SD	Garden City
61	4.4	Kalkaska Public Schools	Kalkaska
61	4.4	Menominee Area Public Schools	Menominee
61	4.4	Mt. Pleasant City SD	Mount Pleasant
65	4.3	Comstock Park Public Schools	Comstock Park
65	4.3	Fremont Public SD	Fremont
65	4.3	Romulus Community Schools	Romulus
65	4.3	Southgate Community SD	Southgate
65	4.3	West Branch-Rose City Area Schls	Rose City
70	4.2	Benton Harbor Area Schools	Benton Harbor
70	4.2	Flat Rock Community Schools	Flat Rock
70	4.2	Holland City SD	Holland
70	4.2	Owosso Public Schools	Owosso
74	4.0	Delton Kellogg Schools	Delton
74	4.0	Marshall Public Schools	Marshall
74	4.0	Niles Community Schools	Niles
74	4.0	Redford Union Schools Dist. No. 1	Redford
74	4.0	Sault Ste Marie Area Schools	Sault Ste Marie
79	3.9	Cedar Springs Public Schools	Cedar Springs
79	3.9	Dearborn Hgts SD #7	Dearborn Hgts
79	3.9	East Detroit Public Schools	Eastpointe
79	3.9	Eaton Rapids Public Schools	Eaton Rapids
79	3.9	Ionia Public Schools	Ionia
79	3.9	L'anse Creuse Public Schools	Harrison Twp
79	3.9	Standish-Sterling Community Schls	Standish
86	3.8	Oakridge Public Schools	Muskegon
86	3.8	Paw Paw Public SD	Paw Paw
88	3.6	Chesaning Union Schools	Chesaning
88	3.6	Clio Area SD	Clio
88	3.6	Durand Area Schools	Durand
88	3.6	Mason Public Schools (Ingham)	Mason
92	3.5	Haslett Public Schools	Haslett
92	3.5	Saginaw ISD	Saginaw
94	3.4	Fowlerville Community Schools	Fowlerville
94	3.4	Saginaw SD	Saginaw
96	3.3	Sturgis Public Schools	Sturgis
97	3.2	Brighton Area Schools	Brighton
97	3.2	Holly Area SD	Holly
97	3.2	Lakeville Community SD	Otisville
97	3.2	Macomb ISD	Clinton Twp
97	3.2	Summit Academy North	Romulus
97	3.2	Traverse City Area Public Schools	Traverse City
103	3.1	Allen Park Public Schools	Allen Park
103	3.1	Chelsea SD	Chelsea
103	3.1	Chippewa Hills SD	Remus
103	3.1	Northview Public Schools	Grand Rapids
107	3.0	Fruitport Community Schools	Fruitport
107	3.0	Hastings Area SD	Hastings
107	3.0	Hillsdale Community Schools	Hillsdale
107	3.0	Imlay City Community Schools	Imlay City
107	3.0	Roseville Community Schools	Roseville
112	2.9	Houghton Lake Community Schools	Houghton Lake
112	2.9	West Ottawa Public SD	Holland
114	2.8	Coloma Community Schools	Coloma
114	2.8	Fenton Area Public Schools	Fenton
114	2.8	Grandville Public Schools	Grandville
114	2.8	Jefferson Schools (Monroe)	Monroe
118	2.7	Big Rapids Public Schools	Big Rapids
118	2.7	Columbia SD	Brooklyn
120	2.6	Cesar Chavez Academy	Detroit
120	2.6	Davison Community Schools	Davison
120	2.6	Grand Ledge Public Schools	Grand Ledge
120	2.6	Howell Public Schools	Howell
124	2.5	Airport Community Schools	Carleton
124	2.5	Escanaba Area Public Schools	Escanaba
124	2.5	Orchard View Schools	Muskegon
124	2.5	South Redford SD	Redford
128	2.4	Allegan Public Schools	Allegan
128	2.4	Bangor Township Schools	Bay City
128	2.4	Perry Public Schools	Perry
128	2.4	Portland Public Schools	Portland
128	2.4	Walled Lake Consolidated Schools	Walled Lake
128	2.4	Woodhaven-Brownstown SD	Woodhaven
134	2.3	Lake Fenton Community Schools	Fenton
134	2.3	Lapeer Community Schools	Lapeer
134	2.3	Lincoln Park SD	Lincoln Park
134	2.3	Oak Park SD	Oak Park
134	2.3	Onsted Community Schools	Onsted
134	2.3	South Haven Public Schools	South Haven
134	2.3	Van Buren Public Schools	Belleville
134	2.3	Warren Woods Public Schools	Warren
134	2.3	Waverly Community Schools	Lansing
143	2.2	Algonac Community SD	Algonac
143	2.2	Plainwell Community Schools	Plainwell
143	2.2	Warren Consolidated Schools	Warren
143	2.2	Waterford SD	Waterford
147	2.1	Birch Run Area Schools	Birch Run
147	2.1	Cheboygan Area Schools	Cheboygan
147	2.1	Corunna Public Schools	Corunna
147	2.1	Lincoln Consolidated SD	Ypsilanti
147	2.1	Mona Shores Public SD	Muskegon
147	2.1	Oxford Community Schools	Oxford
153	2.0	Alma Public Schools	Alma
153	2.0	Brandon SD	Ortonville
153	2.0	East China SD	East China
153	2.0	Gaylord Community Schools	Gaylord
153	2.0	Grand Blanc Community Schools	Grand Blanc
153	2.0	Plymouth-Canton Comm Schools	Plymouth
153	2.0	Zeeland Public Schools	Zeeland
160	1.9	Dearborn City SD	Dearborn
160	1.9	Gibraltar SD	Woodhaven
160	1.9	Kenowa Hills Public Schools	Grand Rapids
160	1.9	Olivet Community Schools	Olivet
164	1.8	Berrien Springs Public Schools	Berrien Springs
164	1.8	Greenville Public Schools	Greenville
164	1.8	Lamphere Public Schools	Madison Heights
164	1.8	Manistee Area Public Schools	Manistee
164	1.8	Sparta Area Schools	Sparta
164	1.8	Swartz Creek Community Schools	Swartz Creek
164	1.8	Wayland Union Schools	Wayland
171	1.7	Anchor Bay SD	Casco
171	1.7	Ann Arbor Public Schools	Ann Arbor
171	1.7	Bullock Creek SD	Midland
171	1.7	Chippewa Valley Schools	Clinton Twp
171	1.7	Clarkston Community SD	Clarkston
171	1.7	Gladwin Community Schools	Gladwin
171	1.7	Goodrich Area Schools	Goodrich
171	1.7	Grant Public SD	Grant
171	1.7	Harper Creek Community Schools	Battle Creek
171	1.7	Lakewood Public Schools	Woodland
171	1.7	Marquette Area Public Schools	Marquette
171	1.7	South Lyon Community Schools	South Lyon
171	1.7	Vicksburg Community Schools	Vicksburg
184	1.6	Buchanan Community Schools	Buchanan
184	1.6	Central Montcalm Public Schools	Stanton
184	1.6	Melvindale-North Allen Park Schools	Melvindale
184	1.6	Okemos Public Schools	Okemos
184	1.6	Old Redford Academy	Detroit
184	1.6	Otsego Public Schools	Otsego
184	1.6	Wyandotte SD	Wyandotte
191	1.5	Avondale SD	Auburn Hills
191	1.5	Carman-Ainsworth Comm. Schools	Flint
191	1.5	Clarenceville SD	Livonia
191	1.5	Huron SD	New Boston
191	1.5	Portage Public Schools	Portage
191	1.5	Public Schools of Petoskey	Petoskey
191	1.5	SD of the City of Royal Oak	Royal Oak
191	1.5	Stockbridge Community Schools	Stockbridge
191	1.5	Swan Valley SD	Saginaw
191	1.5	Troy SD	Troy
201	1.4	Allendale Public Schools	Allendale
201	1.4	Coopersville Area Public SD	Coopersville
201	1.4	Croswell-Lexington Comm. Schools	Croswell
201	1.4	Farmington Public SD	Farmington
201	1.4	Flushing Community Schools	Flushing
201	1.4	Grand Haven Area Public Schools	Grand Haven
201	1.4	Huron Valley Schools	Highland
201	1.4	Mattawan Consolidated School	Mattawan
201	1.4	Milan Area Schools	Milan
201	1.4	Reeths-Puffer Schools	Muskegon
201	1.4	Richmond Community Schools	Richmond
212	1.3	Byron Center Public Schools	Byron Center
212	1.3	Crestwood SD	Dearborn Hgts
212	1.3	Edwardsburg Public Schools	Edwardsburg
212	1.3	Hopkins Public Schools	Hopkins
212	1.3	Lake Orion Community Schools	Lake Orion
212	1.3	North Branch Area Schools	North Branch
212	1.3	Riverview Community SD	Riverview
212	1.3	Rockford Public Schools	Rockford
212	1.3	Saint Johns Public Schools	Saint Johns
212	1.3	Tecumseh Public Schools	Tecumseh
212	1.3	University Preparatory Acad. (PSAD)	Detroit
223	1.2	Caledonia Community Schools	Caledonia
223	1.2	East Lansing SD	East Lansing
223	1.2	Jenison Public Schools	Jenison
223	1.2	Linden Community Schools	Linden
223	1.2	Lowell Area Schools	Lowell
223	1.2	Yale Public Schools	Yale
229	1.1	Almont Community Schools	Almont
229	1.1	Bedford Public Schools	Temperance
229	1.1	Gladstone Area Schools	Gladstone
229	1.1	Napoleon Community Schools	Napoleon
229	1.1	Shepherd Public Schools	Shepherd
229	1.1	Southfield Public SD	Southfield
235	1.0	Breitung Township SD	Kingsford
235	1.0	Hartland Consolidated Schools	Hartland
235	1.0	Hudsonville Public SD	Hudsonville
235	1.0	Lakeshore SD (Berrien)	Stevensville
235	1.0	Livonia Public Schools SD	Livonia
235	1.0	Midland Public Schools	Midland
235	1.0	Romeo Community Schools	Romeo
235	1.0	South Lake Schools	St Clair Shores
243	0.9	Clawson Public Schools	Clawson
243	0.9	Gull Lake Community Schools	Richland
243	0.9	Harrison Community Schools	Harrison
243	0.9	Lakeview Public Schools (Macomb)	St Clair Shores
243	0.9	Thornapple Kellogg SD	Middleville
243	0.9	Tri County Area Schools	Sand Lake
243	0.9	Utica Community Schools	Sterling Hgts
250	0.8	Marysville Public Schools	Marysville
250	0.8	Monroe Public Schools	Monroe
250	0.8	Ovid-Elsie Area Schools	Elsie

Note: This section only includes districts with 1,500 or more students; All categories are ranked from high to low

250	0.8	Saline Area Schools	Saline
250	0.8	Spring Lake Public Schools	Spring Lake
255	0.7	Armada Area Schools	Armada
255	0.7	Freeland Community SD	Freeland
255	0.7	Lakeview SD (Calhoun)	Battle Creek
255	0.7	Pennfield Schools	Battle Creek
255	0.7	Trenton Public Schools	Trenton
260	0.6	Forest Hills Public Schools	Grand Rapids
260	0.6	Grosse Ile Township Schools	Grosse Ile
260	0.6	Lake Shore Public Schls (Macomb)	St Clair Shores
260	0.6	Novi Community SD	Novi
260	0.6	Pinckney Community Schools	Pinckney
260	0.6	West Bloomfield SD	West Bloomfield
266	0.5	Dexter Community SD	Dexter
266	0.5	Grosse Pointe Public Schools	Grosse Pointe
266	0.5	Hamilton Community Schools	Hamilton
266	0.5	Saint Joseph Public Schools	Saint Joseph
270	0.4	Bloomfield Hls SD	Bloomfield Hls
270	0.4	Northville Public Schools	Northville
270	0.4	Rochester Community SD	Rochester
273	0.3	SD of the City of Birmingham	Birmingham
n/a	n/a	Center Line Public Schools	Center Line
n/a	n/a	Dewitt Public Schools	Dewitt
n/a	n/a	Fraser Public Schools	Fraser
n/a	n/a	Chandler Park Academy	Harper Woods
n/a	n/a	Kent ISD	Grand Rapids
n/a	n/a	Benzie County Central Schools	Benzonia
n/a	n/a	E Grand Rapids Public Schools	Grand Rapids
n/a	n/a	Essexville-Hampton Public Schools	Essexville
n/a	n/a	Williamston Community Schools	Williamston

Average Freshman Graduation Rate

Rank	Percent	District Name	City
1	100.0	Berkley SD	Oak Park
1	100.0	Berrien Springs Public Schools	Berrien Springs
1	100.0	Clare Public Schools	Clare
1	100.0	Clintondale Community Schools	Clinton Twp
1	100.0	Ferndale Public Schools	Ferndale
1	100.0	Forest Hills Public Schools	Grand Rapids
1	100.0	Mt. Pleasant City SD	Mount Pleasant
1	100.0	Northview Public Schools	Grand Rapids
1	100.0	Ovid-Elsie Area Schools	Elsie
1	100.0	SD of the City of Inkster	Inkster
11	99.6	Plainwell Community Schools	Plainwell
12	98.9	Spring Lake Public Schools	Spring Lake
13	98.8	Delton Kellogg Schools	Delton
14	98.4	Northville Public Schools	Northville
14	98.4	Troy SD	Troy
16	97.5	E Grand Rapids Public Schools	Grand Rapids
16	97.5	Hartland Consolidated Schools	Hartland
18	97.3	Manistee Area Public Schools	Manistee
19	97.2	Caledonia Community Schools	Caledonia
19	97.2	Farmington Public SD	Farmington
19	97.2	Rochester Community SD	Rochester
22	97.1	Bloomfield Hls SD	Bloomfield Hls
22	97.1	Portland Public Schools	Portland
24	96.9	Paw Paw Public SD	Paw Paw
25	96.7	Grosse Pointe Public Schools	Grosse Pointe
26	96.4	Otsego Public Schools	Otsego
27	96.1	Dewitt Public Schools	Dewitt
28	95.9	Rockford Public Schools	Rockford
29	95.7	Lakeshore SD (Berrien)	Stevensville
30	95.6	Allen Park Public Schools	Allen Park
31	95.5	Allendale Public Schools	Allendale
31	95.5	Saint Joseph Public Schools	Saint Joseph
33	95.3	Clarkston Community SD	Clarkston
34	95.0	Warren Woods Public Schools	Warren
35	94.9	Brighton Area Schools	Brighton
35	94.9	SD of the City of Birmingham	Birmingham
37	94.7	North Branch Area Schools	North Branch
38	94.4	Novi Community SD	Novi
39	94.1	Thornapple Kellogg SD	Middleville
40	93.8	Traverse City Area Public Schools	Traverse City
41	93.7	Plymouth-Canton Comm Schools	Plymouth
42	93.6	Ludington Area SD	Ludington
43	93.5	Breitung Township SD	Kingsford
44	93.1	Hopkins Public Schools	Hopkins
44	93.1	Lake Orion Community Schools	Lake Orion
44	93.1	Marquette Area Public Schools	Marquette
44	93.1	Utica Community Schools	Sterling Hgts
48	93.0	Saint Johns Public Schools	Saint Johns
49	92.8	Alma Public Schools	Alma
49	92.8	Ann Arbor Public Schools	Ann Arbor
51	92.7	Lake Shore Public Schls (Macomb)	St Clair Shores
52	92.5	East China SD	East China
52	92.5	Whitehall District Schools	Whitehall
54	92.4	Grosse Ile Township Schools	Grosse Ile
54	92.4	Napoleon Community Schools	Napoleon
54	92.4	Public Schools of Petoskey	Petoskey
57	92.0	Swan Valley SD	Saginaw
58	91.9	Gull Lake Community Schools	Richland
58	91.9	Lakewood Public Schools	Woodland
58	91.9	Sparta Area Schools	Sparta
61	91.8	Gladstone Area Schools	Gladstone
61	91.8	Haslett Public Schools	Haslett
61	91.8	Huron SD	New Boston
61	91.8	Kalkaska Public Schools	Kalkaska
61	91.8	Shelby Public Schools	Shelby
66	91.7	Lowell Area Schools	Lowell
67	91.6	Corunna Public Schools	Corunna
68	91.4	Goodrich Area Schools	Goodrich
68	91.4	Onsted Community Schools	Onsted
70	91.3	Chelsea SD	Chelsea
70	91.3	Sault Ste Marie Area Schools	Sault Ste Marie
72	91.1	Saline Area Schools	Saline
73	90.9	Portage Public Schools	Portage
74	90.5	Chippewa Valley Schools	Clinton Twp
75	90.4	Big Rapids Public Schools	Big Rapids
75	90.4	Coldwater Community Schools	Coldwater
75	90.4	West Bloomfield SD	West Bloomfield
78	90.3	Grand Ledge Public Schools	Grand Ledge
79	90.1	Walled Lake Consolidated Schools	Walled Lake
80	89.9	Livonia Public Schools SD	Livonia
81	89.6	Milan Area Schools	Milan
82	89.4	Cheboygan Area Schools	Cheboygan
83	89.3	Riverview Community SD	Riverview
84	89.2	Columbia SD	Brooklyn
84	89.2	Perry Public Schools	Perry
86	89.1	Williamston Community Schools	Williamston
87	89.0	Zeeland Public Schools	Zeeland
88	88.9	Southgate Community SD	Southgate
89	88.8	Sturgis Public Schools	Sturgis
89	88.8	Warren Consolidated Schools	Warren
91	88.6	Owosso Public Schools	Owosso
92	88.5	Brandon SD	Ortonville
92	88.5	Fowlerville Community Schools	Fowlerville
92	88.5	Okemos Public Schools	Okemos
95	88.1	Flushing Community Schools	Flushing
96	88.0	Croswell-Lexington Comm. Schools	Croswell
97	87.9	Imlay City Community Schools	Imlay City
97	87.9	Jenison Public Schools	Jenison
99	87.7	Grandville Public Schools	Grandville
100	87.5	Lakeview Public Schools (Macomb)	St Clair Shores
100	87.5	Wayland Union Schools	Wayland
102	87.4	Yale Public Schools	Yale
103	87.2	Standish-Sterling Community Schls	Standish
103	87.2	Western SD	Parma
105	87.1	Escanaba Area Public Schools	Escanaba
105	87.1	Grand Blanc Community Schools	Grand Blanc
107	87.0	Dexter Community SD	Dexter
107	87.0	Freeland Community SD	Freeland
109	86.9	Romeo Community Schools	Romeo
110	86.7	Howell Public Schools	Howell
111	86.6	Almont Community Schools	Almont
112	86.5	Avondale SD	Auburn Hills
112	86.5	Three Rivers Community Schools	Three Rivers
114	86.3	Lake Fenton Community Schools	Fenton
114	86.3	Stockbridge Community Schools	Stockbridge
116	86.2	Birch Run Area Schools	Birch Run
117	86.1	Kelloggsville Public Schools	Grand Rapids
118	86.0	Oak Park SD	Oak Park
119	85.9	Bedford Public Schools	Temperance
119	85.9	Garden City SD	Garden City
121	85.8	Comstock Park Public Schools	Comstock Park
121	85.8	Fremont Public SD	Fremont
121	85.8	Midland Public Schools	Midland
121	85.8	Van Buren Public Schools	Belleville
125	85.6	SD of the City of Royal Oak	Royal Oak
126	85.5	Coopersville Area Public SD	Coopersville
127	85.4	Marshall Public Schools	Marshall
128	85.1	Huron Valley Schools	Highland
129	85.0	Chesaning Union Schools	Chesaning
129	85.0	Romulus Community Schools	Romulus
131	84.8	Mattawan Consolidated School	Mattawan
132	84.6	L'anse Creuse Public Schools	Harrison Twp
132	84.6	Shepherd Public Schools	Shepherd
134	84.4	Bangor Township Schools	Bay City
134	84.4	Lakeview SD (Calhoun)	Battle Creek
136	84.3	Lakeville Community SD	Otisville
137	84.1	Mason Public Schools (Ingham)	Mason
138	84.0	Swartz Creek Community Schools	Swartz Creek
139	83.9	Grand Haven Area Public Schools	Grand Haven
140	83.5	Clawson Public Schools	Clawson
141	83.3	Davison Community Schools	Davison
142	83.2	South Lyon Community Schools	South Lyon
143	83.1	Gibraltar SD	Woodhaven
144	83.0	Fraser Public Schools	Fraser
144	83.0	Pinckney Community Schools	Pinckney
144	83.0	Tecumseh Public Schools	Tecumseh
147	82.9	Mona Shores Public SD	Muskegon
148	82.6	Anchor Bay SD	Casco
148	82.6	Trenton Public Schools	Trenton
150	82.5	Saginaw Township Comm. Schools	Saginaw
151	82.4	Kenowa Hills Public Schools	Grand Rapids
152	82.2	Woodhaven-Brownstown SD	Woodhaven
153	82.0	Oxford Community Schools	Oxford
154	81.9	Bendle Public Schools	Burton
155	81.8	Reed City Area Public Schools	Reed City
156	81.7	Harper Creek Community Schools	Battle Creek
156	81.7	Hastings Area SD	Hastings
158	81.5	Durand Area Schools	Durand
159	81.4	Marysville Public Schools	Marysville
160	81.2	Greenville Public Schools	Greenville
161	81.1	Lamphere Public Schools	Madison Heights
162	81.0	Oakridge Public Schools	Muskegon
162	81.0	Richmond Community Schools	Richmond
164	80.9	Crestwood SD	Dearborn Hgts
165	80.8	Clarenceville SD	Livonia
166	80.7	Vicksburg Community Schools	Vicksburg
167	80.6	Holt Public Schools	Holt
167	80.6	Lapeer Community Schools	Lapeer
169	80.5	Ionia Public Schools	Ionia
170	80.4	Crawford Ausable Schools	Grayling
171	80.2	Bullock Creek SD	Midland
171	80.2	Byron Center Public Schools	Byron Center
173	79.7	West Branch-Rose City Area Schls	Rose City
174	79.5	Menominee Area Public Schools	Menominee
175	79.3	Fruitport Community Schools	Fruitport
175	79.3	Gaylord Community Schools	Gaylord
177	79.1	Tri County Area Schools	Sand Lake
178	78.8	East Lansing SD	East Lansing
179	78.6	Parchment SD	Kalamazoo
180	78.3	Linden Community Schools	Linden
181	78.0	South Redford SD	Redford
182	77.9	Orchard View Schools	Muskegon
183	77.6	Olivet Community Schools	Olivet
184	77.5	Armada Area Schools	Armada
185	77.3	Airport Community Schools	Carleton
185	77.3	Reeths-Puffer Schools	Muskegon
187	77.2	Cadillac Area Public Schools	Cadillac
187	77.2	Newaygo Public SD	Newaygo
189	77.1	Gladwin Community Schools	Gladwin
190	77.0	Algonac Community SD	Algonac
191	76.9	South Lake Schools	St Clair Shores
192	76.8	Dundee Community Schools	Dundee
193	76.6	Clio Area SD	Clio
194	76.4	Northwest Community Schools	Jackson
195	76.2	Cedar Springs Public Schools	Cedar Springs
195	76.2	Godwin Heights Public Schools	Grand Rapids
197	75.8	Kearsley Community SD	Flint
198	75.7	Southfield Public SD	Southfield
199	75.5	Wyoming Public Schools	Wyoming
200	75.4	Dearborn City SD	Dearborn
201	74.6	Adrian SD	Adrian
202	74.5	Hamilton Community Schools	Hamilton
203	74.3	Fitzgerald Public Schools	Warren
204	74.1	Monroe Public Schools	Monroe
204	74.1	Roseville Community Schools	Roseville
206	74.0	Westwood Community SD	Dearborn Hgts
207	73.9	Jefferson Schools (Monroe)	Monroe
208	73.7	Belding Area SD	Belding
209	73.5	Flat Rock Community Schools	Flat Rock
209	73.5	Hillsdale Community Schools	Hillsdale
209	73.5	Waverly Community Schools	Lansing
212	73.2	Niles Community Schools	Niles
213	73.0	Center Line Public Schools	Center Line
214	72.9	Comstock Public Schools	Kalamazoo
215	72.7	Central Montcalm Public Schools	Stanton
216	71.9	Charlotte Public Schools	Charlotte
216	71.9	Port Huron Area SD	Port Huron
218	71.6	Pennfield Schools	Battle Creek
219	71.4	Fenton Area Public Schools	Fenton
219	71.4	Old Redford Academy	Detroit

Note: This section only includes districts with 1,500 or more students; All categories are ranked from high to low

221	71.1	Godfrey-Lee Public Schools	Wyoming
222	70.9	Kentwood Public Schools	Grand Rapids
223	70.8	Edwardsburg Public Schools	Edwardsburg
223	70.8	Essexville-Hampton Public Schools	Essexville
225	70.0	Holly Area SD	Holly
226	69.9	Wyandotte SD	Wyandotte
227	69.8	Hudsonville Public SD	Hudsonville
228	69.1	Caro Community Schools	Caro
229	68.5	Wayne-Westland Community SD	Westland
230	68.4	Bay City SD	Bay City
231	68.3	Houghton Lake Community Schools	Houghton Lake
232	67.9	Alpena Public Schools	Alpena
233	67.6	Waterford SD	Waterford
234	67.0	West Ottawa Public SD	Holland
235	66.4	Cesar Chavez Academy	Detroit
236	66.1	Taylor SD	Taylor
237	65.9	Allegan Public Schools	Allegan
238	65.7	Jackson Public Schools	Jackson
239	65.6	Grant Public SD	Grant
240	65.1	Chippewa Hills SD	Remus
241	64.9	Carrollton Public Schools	Saginaw
242	64.8	Dowagiac Union SD	Dowagiac
243	64.3	Harrison Community Schools	Harrison
244	64.0	Buchanan Community Schools	Buchanan
245	63.4	SD of Ypsilanti	Ypsilanti
246	63.0	Lincoln Consolidated SD	Ypsilanti
247	62.9	Muskegon Hgts SD	Muskegon
248	62.7	South Haven Public Schools	South Haven
249	61.9	Melvindale-North Allen Park Schools	Melvindale
250	61.5	Redford Union Schools Dist. No. 1	Redford
251	61.1	Benton Harbor Area Schools	Benton Harbor
251	61.1	Coloma Community Schools	Coloma
253	60.7	Beecher Community SD	Flint
254	59.9	Carman-Ainsworth Comm. Schools	Flint
255	59.8	Lansing Public SD	Lansing
256	58.8	Eaton Rapids Public Schools	Eaton Rapids
257	58.0	Holland City SD	Holland
258	57.4	Kalamazoo Public Schools	Kalamazoo
259	56.5	East Detroit Public Schools	Eastpointe
259	56.5	Summit Academy North	Romulus
261	55.7	Mount Clemens Community SD	Mount Clemens
262	55.3	Lincoln Park SD	Lincoln Park
263	53.0	Dearborn Hgts SD #7	Dearborn Hgts
264	48.6	Mt. Morris Consolidated Schools	Mount Morris
265	48.4	Pontiac City SD	Pontiac
266	47.4	Battle Creek Public Schools	Battle Creek
267	46.9	Saginaw SD	Saginaw
268	46.6	Hamtramck SD	Hamtramck
269	46.1	Muskegon Public Schools	Muskegon
270	45.8	Hazel Park SD	Hazel Park
271	45.7	Grand Rapids Public Schools	Grand Rapids
272	45.1	Detroit City SD	Detroit
273	41.3	Willow Run Community Schools	Ypsilanti
274	40.9	Flint SD	Flint
275	40.1	Van Dyke Public Schools	Warren
276	3.8	Benzie County Central Schools	Benzonia
277	2.1	Macomb ISD	Clinton Twp
n/a	n/a	Chandler Park Academy	Harper Woods
n/a	n/a	Kent ISD	Grand Rapids
n/a	n/a	Saginaw ISD	Saginaw
n/a	n/a	University Preparatory Acad. (PSAD)	Detroit
n/a	n/a	Wayne Resa	Wayne

Note: This section only includes districts with 1,500 or more students; All categories are ranked from high to low

The Nation's Report Card
Mathematics
2013 State Snapshot Report

Michigan
Grade 4
Public Schools

Overall Results

- In 2013, the average score of fourth-grade students in Michigan was 237. This was lower than the average score of 241 for public school students in the nation.
- The average score for students in Michigan in 2013 (237) was not significantly different from their average score in 2011 (236) and was higher than their average score in 1992 (220).
- The score gap between higher performing students in Michigan (those at the 75th percentile) and lower performing students (those at the 25th percentile) was 43 points in 2013. This performance gap was not significantly different from that in 1992 (43 points).
- The percentage of students in Michigan who performed at or above the NAEP *Proficient* level was 37 percent in 2013. This percentage was not significantly different from that in 2011 (35 percent) and was greater than that in 1992 (18 percent).
- The percentage of students in Michigan who performed at or above the NAEP *Basic* level was 77 percent in 2013. This percentage was not significantly different from that in 2011 (78 percent) and was greater than that in 1992 (61 percent).

Achievement-Level Percentages and Average Score Results

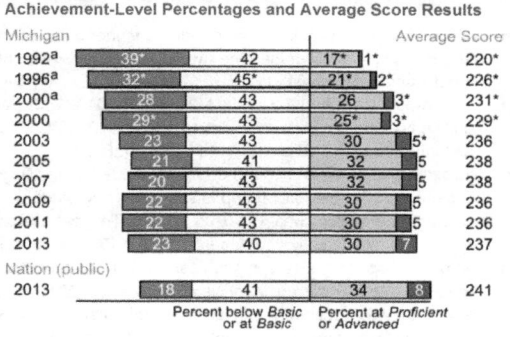

Michigan				Average Score
1992[a]	39*	42	17* 1*	220*
1996[a]	32*	45*	21* 2*	226*
2000[a]	28	43	26 3*	231*
2000	29*	43	25* 3*	229*
2003	23	43	30 5*	236
2005	21	41	32 5	238
2007	20	43	32 5	238
2009	22	43	30 5	236
2011	22	43	30 5	236
2013	23	40	30 7	237
Nation (public)				
2013	18	41	34 8	241

Percent below *Basic* or at *Basic*   Percent at *Proficient* or *Advanced*

■ Below *Basic* □ *Basic* □ *Proficient* ■ *Advanced*

* Significantly different (*p* < .05) from state's results in 2013. Significance tests were performed using unrounded numbers.
a Accommodations not permitted. For information about NAEP accommodations, see http://nces.ed.gov/nationsreportcard/about/inclusion.aspx.

NOTE: Detail may not sum to totals because of rounding.

Compare the Average Score in 2013 to Other States/Jurisdictions

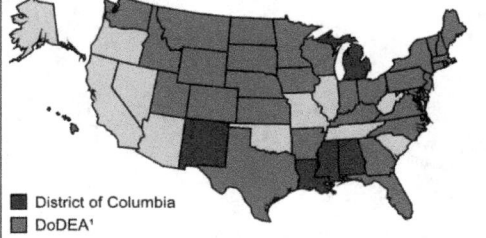

■ District of Columbia
■ DoDEA[']

[']Department of Defense Education Activity (overseas and domestic schools).

In 2013, the average score in Michigan (237) was
- lower than those in 35 states/jurisdictions
- higher than those in 5 states/jurisdictions
- not significantly different from those in 11 states/jurisdictions

Average Scores for State/Jurisdiction and Nation (public)

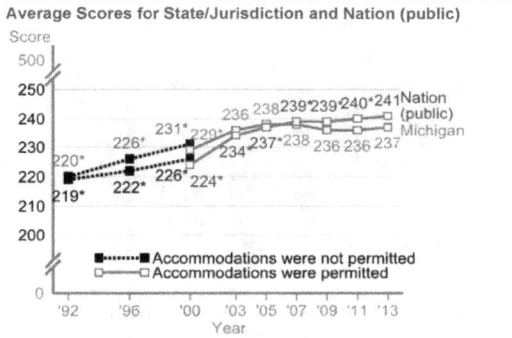

Nation (public): 236 238 239* 239* 240* 241
Michigan: 220* 226* 231* 229* 234 237* 238 236 236 237
219* 222* 226* 224*

■⋯⋯■ Accommodations were not permitted
□—□ Accommodations were permitted

* Significantly different (*p* < .05) from 2013. Significance tests were performed using unrounded numbers.

NOTE: For information about NAEP accommodations, see http://nces.ed.gov/nationsreportcard/about/inclusion.aspx.

Results for Student Groups in 2013

Reporting Groups	Percent of students	Avg. score	Percentages at or above *Basic*	*Proficient*	Percent at *Advanced*
Race/Ethnicity					
White	66	244	86	45	7
Black	19	212	47	10	1
Hispanic	9	226	64	22	4
Asian	3	262	91	65	31
American Indian/Alaska Native	#	‡	‡	‡	‡
Native Hawaiian/Pacific Islander	#	‡	‡	‡	‡
Two or more races	2	241	84	34	10
Gender					
Male	52	237	76	38	7
Female	48	236	77	36	6
National School Lunch Program					
Eligible	54	224	65	20	2
Not eligible	46	252	91	57	12

\# Rounds to zero.   ‡ Reporting standards not met.

NOTE: Detail may not sum to totals because of rounding, and because the "Information not available" category for the National School Lunch Program, which provides free/reduced-price lunches, is not displayed. Black includes African American and Hispanic includes Latino. Race categories exclude Hispanic origin.

Score Gaps for Student Groups

- In 2013, Black students had an average score that was 32 points lower than White students. This performance gap was narrower than that in 1992 (42 points).
- In 2013, Hispanic students had an average score that was 18 points lower than White students. Data are not reported for Hispanic students in 1992, because reporting standards were not met.
- In 2013, male students in Michigan had an average score that was not significantly different from female students.
- In 2013, students who were eligible for free/reduced-price school lunch, an indicator of low family income, had an average score that was 28 points lower than students who were not eligible for free/reduced-price school lunch. This performance gap was not significantly different from that in 1996 (24 points).

NOTE: Statistical comparisons are calculated on the basis of unrounded scale scores or percentages.
SOURCE: U.S. Department of Education, Institute of Education Sciences, National Center for Education Statistics, National Assessment of Educational Progress (NAEP), various years, 1992–2013 Mathematics Assessments.

2013 State Snapshot Report

Michigan
Grade 8
Public Schools

Overall Results

- In 2013, the average score of eighth-grade students in Michigan was 280. This was lower than the average score of 284 for public school students in the nation.
- The average score for students in Michigan in 2013 (280) was not significantly different from their average score in 2011 (280) and was higher than their average score in 1990 (264).
- The score gap between higher performing students in Michigan (those at the 75th percentile) and lower performing students (those at the 25th percentile) was 48 points in 2013. This performance gap was not significantly different from that in 1990 (47 points).
- The percentage of students in Michigan who performed at or above the NAEP *Proficient* level was 30 percent in 2013. This percentage was not significantly different from that in 2011 (31 percent) and was greater than that in 1990 (16 percent).
- The percentage of students in Michigan who performed at or above the NAEP *Basic* level was 70 percent in 2013. This percentage was not significantly different from that in 2011 (71 percent) and was greater than that in 1990 (53 percent).

Achievement-Level Percentages and Average Score Results

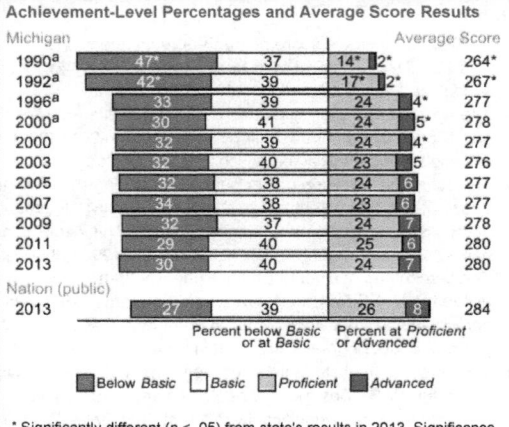

* Significantly different ($p < .05$) from state's results in 2013. Significance tests were performed using unrounded numbers.
a Accommodations not permitted. For information about NAEP accommodations, see http://nces.ed.gov/nationsreportcard/about/inclusion.aspx.

NOTE: Detail may not sum to totals because of rounding.

Compare the Average Score in 2013 to Other States/Jurisdictions

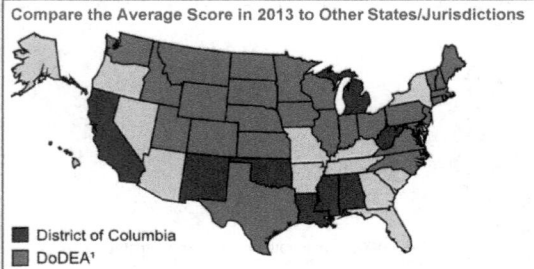

- District of Columbia
- DoDEA[1]

[1] Department of Defense Education Activity (overseas and domestic schools).

In 2013, the average score in **Michigan** (280) was
- lower than those in 29 states/jurisdictions
- higher than those in 8 states/jurisdictions
- not significantly different from those in 14 states/jurisdictions

Average Scores for State/Jurisdiction and Nation (public)

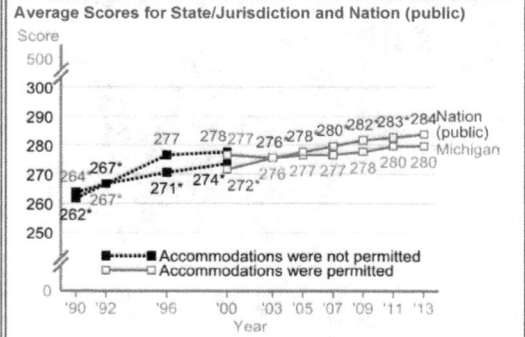

* Significantly different ($p < .05$) from 2013. Significance tests were performed using unrounded numbers.

NOTE: For information about NAEP accommodations, see http://nces.ed.gov/nationsreportcard/about/inclusion.aspx.

Results for Student Groups in 2013

Reporting Groups	Percent of students	Avg. score	Percentages at or above Basic	Percentages at or above Proficient	Percent at Advanced
Race/Ethnicity					
White	72	287	79	36	7
Black	16	251	36	7	1
Hispanic	6	261	49	14	1
Asian	3	310	88	61	30
American Indian/Alaska Native	1	‡	‡	‡	‡
Native Hawaiian/Pacific Islander	#	‡	‡	‡	‡
Two or more races	2	‡	‡	‡	‡
Gender					
Male	52	280	69	31	8
Female	48	281	72	30	6
National School Lunch Program					
Eligible	46	265	54	16	2
Not eligible	54	293	84	42	10

Rounds to zero.   ‡ Reporting standards not met.

NOTE: Detail may not sum to totals because of rounding, and because the "Information not available" category for the National School Lunch Program, which provides free/reduced-price lunches, is not displayed. Black includes African American and Hispanic includes Latino. Race categories exclude Hispanic origin.

Score Gaps for Student Groups

- In 2013, Black students had an average score that was 36 points lower than White students. This performance gap was not significantly different from that in 1990 (39 points).
- In 2013, Hispanic students had an average score that was 26 points lower than White students. Data are not reported for Hispanic students in 1990, because reporting standards were not met.
- In 2013, male students in Michigan had an average score that was not significantly different from female students.
- In 2013, students who were eligible for free/reduced-price school lunch, an indicator of low family income, had an average score that was 27 points lower than students who were not eligible for free/reduced-price school lunch. This performance gap was not significantly different from that in 1996 (27 points).

NOTE: Statistical comparisons are calculated on the basis of unrounded scale scores or percentages.
SOURCE: U.S. Department of Education, Institute of Education Sciences, National Center for Education Statistics, National Assessment of Educational Progress (NAEP), various years, 1990–2013 Mathematics Assessments.

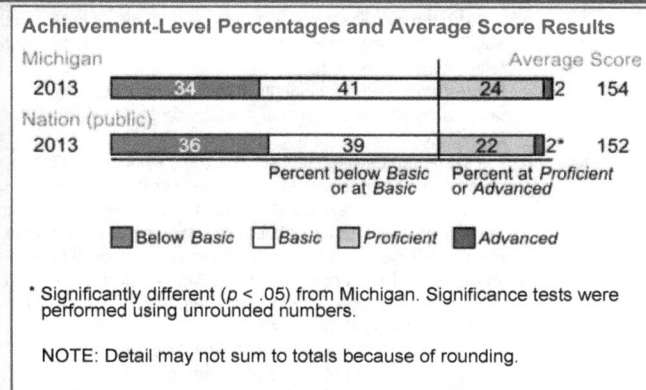

The Nation's Report Card

Mathematics
2013 State Snapshot Report

Michigan
Grade 12
Public Schools

Overall Results

- In 2013, the average score of twelfth-grade students in Michigan was 154. This was not significantly different from the average score of 152 for public school students in the nation.
- The percentage of students in Michigan who performed at or above the NAEP *Proficient* level was 25 percent in 2013. This percentage was not significantly different from the nation (25 percent).
- The percentage of students in Michigan who performed at or above the NAEP *Basic* level was 66 percent in 2013. This percentage was not significantly different from the nation (64 percent).

Achievement-Level Percentages and Average Score Results

Michigan   Average Score

2013	34	41	24	2	154

Nation (public)

2013	36	39	22	2*	152

Percent below *Basic*   Percent at *Proficient*
or at *Basic*   or *Advanced*

☐ Below *Basic*   ☐ *Basic*   ☐ *Proficient*   ☐ *Advanced*

* Significantly different (*p* < .05) from Michigan. Significance tests were performed using unrounded numbers.

NOTE: Detail may not sum to totals because of rounding.

Compare the Average Score in 2013 to Other States/Jurisdictions

☐ District of Columbia
☐ DoDEA[1]

[1] Department of Defense Education Activity (overseas and domestic schools).

In 2013, the average score in Michigan (154) was
- lower than those in 5 states/jurisdictions
- higher than those in 4 states/jurisdictions
- not significantly different from those in 3 states/jurisdictions

Average Scores for State/Jurisdiction and Nation (public)

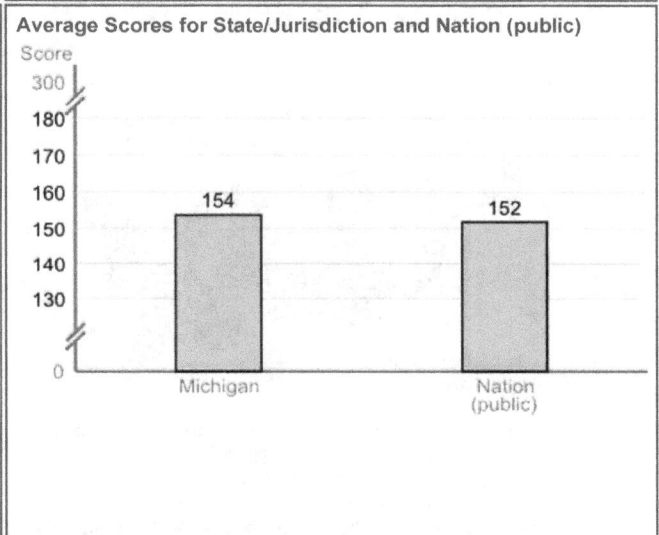

Results for Student Groups in 2013

Reporting Groups	Percent of students	Avg. score	Percentages at or above		Percent at Advanced
			Basic	*Proficient*	
Race/Ethnicity					
White	76	159	73	30	2
Black	14	129	32	5	#
Hispanic	5	135	42	9	#
Asian	3	166	73	42	7
American Indian/Alaska Native	1	‡	‡	‡	‡
Native Hawaiian/Pacific Islander	#	‡	‡	‡	‡
Two or more races	1	‡	‡	‡	‡
Gender					
Male	51	156	68	27	2
Female	49	152	65	23	1

\# Rounds to zero.   ‡ Reporting standards not met.

NOTE: Detail may not sum to totals because of rounding. Black includes African American and Hispanic includes Latino. Race categories exclude Hispanic origin.

Score Gaps for Student Groups

- In 2013, Black students had an average score that was 31 points lower than White students. This performance gap was not significantly different from the nation (29 points).
- In 2013, Hispanic students had an average score that was 24 points lower than White students. This performance gap was not significantly different from the nation (21 points).
- In 2013, male students in Michigan had an average score that was not significantly different from female students.

NOTE: Statistical comparisons are calculated on the basis of unrounded scale scores or percentages.
SOURCE: U.S. Department of Education, Institute of Education Sciences, National Center for Education Statistics, National Assessment of Educational Progress (NAEP), 2013 Mathematics Assessment.

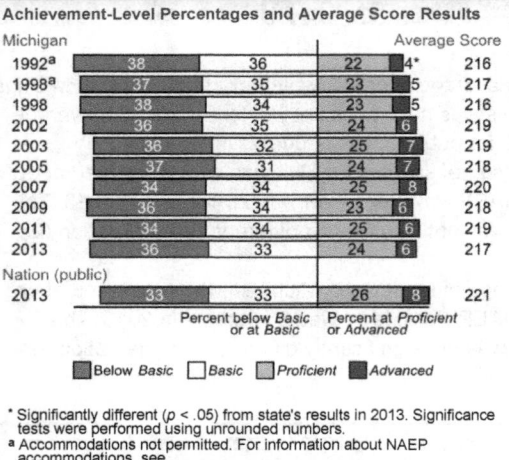

The Nation's Report Card Reading
2013 State Snapshot Report

Michigan
Grade 4
Public Schools

Overall Results

- In 2013, the average score of fourth-grade students in Michigan was 217. This was lower than the average score of 221 for public school students in the nation.
- The average score for students in Michigan in 2013 (217) was not significantly different from their average score in 2011 (219) and in 1992 (216).
- The score gap between higher performing students in Michigan (those at the 75th percentile) and lower performing students (those at the 25th percentile) was 47 points in 2013. This performance gap was not significantly different from that in 1992 (44 points).
- The percentage of students in Michigan who performed at or above the NAEP *Proficient* level was 31 percent in 2013. This percentage was not significantly different from that in 2011 (31 percent) and in 1992 (26 percent).
- The percentage of students in Michigan who performed at or above the NAEP *Basic* level was 64 percent in 2013. This percentage was not significantly different from that in 2011 (66 percent) and in 1992 (62 percent).

Achievement-Level Percentages and Average Score Results

Michigan					Average Score
1992[a]	38	36	22	4*	216
1998[a]	37	35	23	5	217
1998	38	34	23	5	216
2002	36	35	24	6	219
2003	36	32	25	7	219
2005	37	31	24	7	218
2007	34	34	25	8	220
2009	36	34	23	6	218
2011	34	34	25	6	219
2013	36	33	24	6	217

Nation (public)					
2013	33	33	26	8	221

Percent below *Basic* or at *Basic*   Percent at *Proficient* or *Advanced*

■ Below *Basic*   □ *Basic*   ▨ *Proficient*   ■ *Advanced*

* Significantly different (*p* < .05) from state's results in 2013. Significance tests were performed using unrounded numbers.
[a] Accommodations not permitted. For information about NAEP accommodations, see http://nces.ed.gov/nationsreportcard/about/inclusion.aspx.

NOTE: Detail may not sum to totals because of rounding.

Compare the Average Score in 2013 to Other States/Jurisdictions

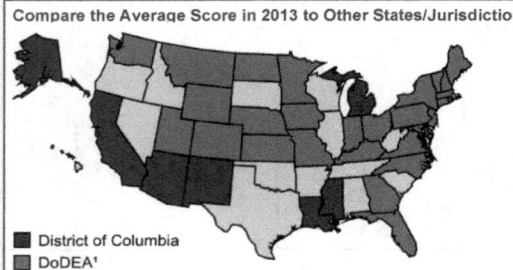

■ District of Columbia
▨ DoDEA[1]

[1] Department of Defense Education Activity (overseas and domestic schools).

In 2013, the average score in Michigan (217) was
- lower than those in 30 states/jurisdictions
- higher than those in 7 states/jurisdictions
- not significantly different from those in 14 states/jurisdictions

Average Scores for State/Jurisdiction and Nation (public)

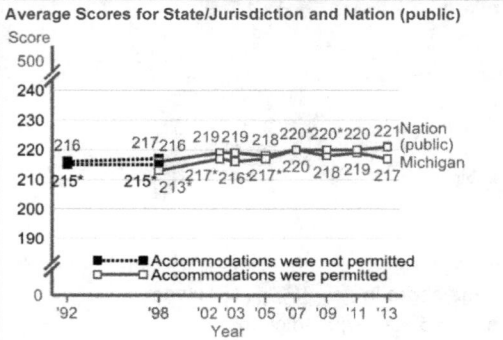

■ Accommodations were not permitted
□ Accommodations were permitted

* Significantly different (*p* < .05) from 2013. Significance tests were performed using unrounded numbers.

NOTE: For information about NAEP accommodations, see http://nces.ed.gov/nationsreportcard/about/inclusion.aspx.

Results for Student Groups in 2013

Reporting Groups	Percent of students	Avg. score	Percentages at or above *Basic*	Percentages at or above *Proficient*	Percent at *Advanced*
Race/Ethnicity					
White	66	224	72	37	8
Black	18	196	39	12	1
Hispanic	9	209	53	21	3
Asian	3	228	78	46	13
American Indian/Alaska Native	1	‡	‡	‡	‡
Native Hawaiian/Pacific Islander	#	‡	‡	‡	‡
Two or more races	2	203	47	16	2
Gender					
Male	52	214	61	28	5
Female	48	221	67	33	8
National School Lunch Program					
Eligible	54	206	51	19	3
Not eligible	46	231	79	44	10

Rounds to zero.   ‡ Reporting standards not met.

NOTE: Detail may not sum to totals because of rounding, and because the "Information not available" category for the National School Lunch Program, which provides free/reduced-price lunches, is not displayed. Black includes African American and Hispanic includes Latino. Race categories exclude Hispanic origin.

Score Gaps for Student Groups

- In 2013, Black students had an average score that was 28 points lower than White students. This performance gap was not significantly different from that in 1992 (35 points).
- In 2013, Hispanic students had an average score that was 15 points lower than White students. Data are not reported for Hispanic students in 1992, because reporting standards were not met.
- In 2013, female students in Michigan had an average score that was higher than male students by 7 points.
- In 2013, students who were eligible for free/reduced-price school lunch, an indicator of low family income, had an average score that was 25 points lower than students who were not eligible for free/reduced-price school lunch. This performance gap was not significantly different from that in 1998 (24 points).

ies NATIONAL CENTER FOR EDUCATION STATISTICS   Institute of Education Sciences

NOTE: Statistical comparisons are calculated on the basis of unrounded scale scores or percentages.
SOURCE: U.S. Department of Education, Institute of Education Sciences, National Center for Education Statistics, National Assessment of Educational Progress (NAEP), various years, 1992–2013 Reading Assessments.

The Nation's Report Card — Reading
2013 State Snapshot Report

Michigan
Grade 8
Public Schools

Overall Results

- In 2013, the average score of eighth-grade students in Michigan was 266. This was not significantly different from the average score of 266 for public school students in the nation.
- The average score for students in Michigan in 2013 (266) was not significantly different from their average score in 2011 (265) and in 2002 (265).
- The score gap between higher performing students in Michigan (those at the 75th percentile) and lower performing students (those at the 25th percentile) was 42 points in 2013. This performance gap was not significantly different from that in 2002 (43 points).
- The percentage of students in Michigan who performed at or above the NAEP *Proficient* level was 33 percent in 2013. This percentage was not significantly different from that in 2011 (32 percent) and in 2002 (32 percent).
- The percentage of students in Michigan who performed at or above the NAEP *Basic* level was 77 percent in 2013. This percentage was not significantly different from that in 2011 (77 percent) and in 2002 (77 percent).

Achievement-Level Percentages and Average Score Results

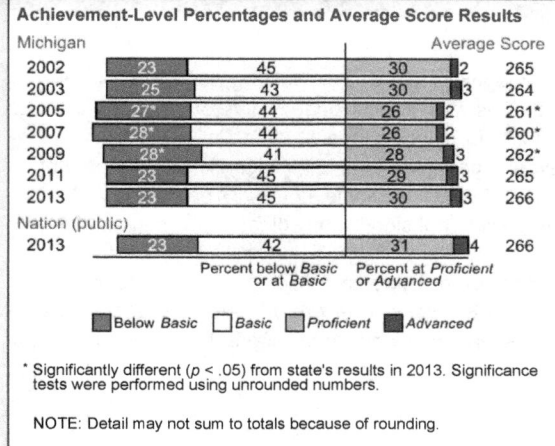

* Significantly different (*p* < .05) from state's results in 2013. Significance tests were performed using unrounded numbers.

NOTE: Detail may not sum to totals because of rounding.

Compare the Average Score in 2013 to Other States/Jurisdictions

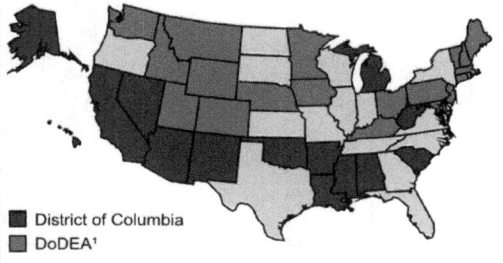

- District of Columbia
- DoDEA¹

¹ Department of Defense Education Activity (overseas and domestic schools).

In 2013, the average score in Michigan (266) was
- lower than those in 20 states/jurisdictions
- higher than those in 14 states/jurisdictions
- not significantly different from those in 17 states/jurisdictions

Average Scores for State/Jurisdiction and Nation (public)

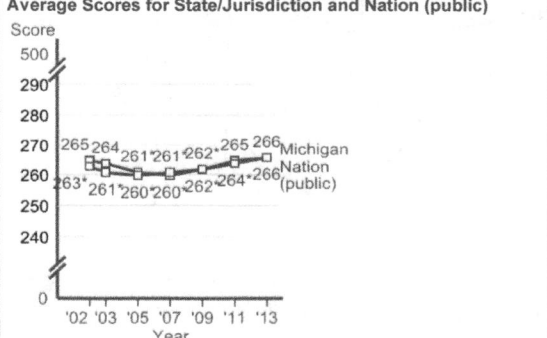

* Significantly different (*p* < .05) from 2013. Significance tests were performed using unrounded numbers.

Results for Student Groups in 2013

Reporting Groups	Percent of students	Avg. score	Percentages at or above Basic	Proficient	Percent at Advanced
Race/Ethnicity					
White	72	271	83	37	3
Black	15	246	54	12	#
Hispanic	6	257	69	22	2
Asian	3	280	83	53	14
American Indian/Alaska Native	1	‡	‡	‡	‡
Native Hawaiian/Pacific Islander	#	‡	‡	‡	‡
Two or more races	2	‡	‡	‡	‡
Gender					
Male	52	262	74	27	2
Female	48	271	81	39	4
National School Lunch Program					
Eligible	46	254	66	19	1
Not eligible	54	276	87	45	5

Rounds to zero.   ‡ Reporting standards not met.

NOTE: Detail may not sum to totals because of rounding, and because the "Information not available" category for the National School Lunch Program, which provides free/reduced-price lunches, is not displayed. Black includes African American and Hispanic includes Latino. Race categories exclude Hispanic origin.

Score Gaps for Student Groups

- In 2013, Black students had an average score that was 25 points lower than White students. This performance gap was not significantly different from that in 2002 (28 points).
- In 2013, Hispanic students had an average score that was 14 points lower than White students. Data are not reported for Hispanic students in 2002, because reporting standards were not met.
- In 2013, female students in Michigan had an average score that was higher than male students by 9 points.
- In 2013, students who were eligible for free/reduced-price school lunch, an indicator of low family income, had an average score that was 22 points lower than students who were not eligible for free/reduced-price school lunch. This performance gap was wider than that in 2002 (13 points).

ies NATIONAL CENTER FOR EDUCATION STATISTICS
Institute of Education Sciences

NOTE: Statistical comparisons are calculated on the basis of unrounded scale scores or percentages.
SOURCE: U.S. Department of Education, Institute of Education Sciences, National Center for Education Statistics, National Assessment of Educational Progress (NAEP), various years, 2002–2013 Reading Assessments.

The **Nation's** Reading
Report Card 2013 State Snapshot Report

Overall Results

- In 2013, the average score of twelfth-grade students in Michigan was 288. This was not significantly different from the average score of 287 for public school students in the nation.
- The percentage of students in Michigan who performed at or above the NAEP *Proficient* level was 37 percent in 2013. This percentage was not significantly different from the nation (36 percent).
- The percentage of students in Michigan who performed at or above the NAEP *Basic* level was 74 percent in 2013. This percentage was not significantly different from the nation (73 percent).

Achievement-Level Percentages and Average Score Results

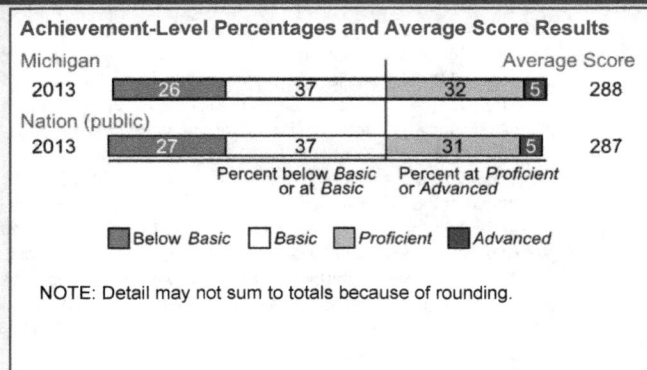

Michigan   Average Score
2013 | 26 | 37 | 32 | 5 | 288
Nation (public)
2013 | 27 | 37 | 31 | 5 | 287

Percent below *Basic*   Percent at *Proficient*
or at *Basic*   or *Advanced*

■ Below *Basic*   □ *Basic*   ▨ *Proficient*   ■ *Advanced*

NOTE: Detail may not sum to totals because of rounding.

Compare the Average Score in 2013 to Other States/Jurisdictions

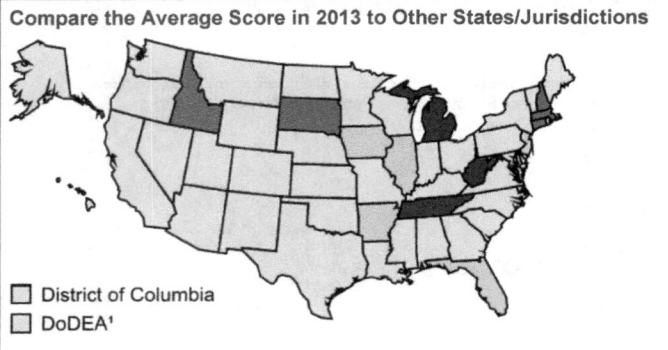

☐ District of Columbia
☐ DoDEA¹

¹ Department of Defense Education Activity (overseas and domestic schools).

In 2013, the average score in Michigan (288) was
- lower than those in 5 states/jurisdictions
- higher than those in 2 states/jurisdictions
- not significantly different from those in 5 states/jurisdictions

Average Scores for State/Jurisdiction and Nation (public)

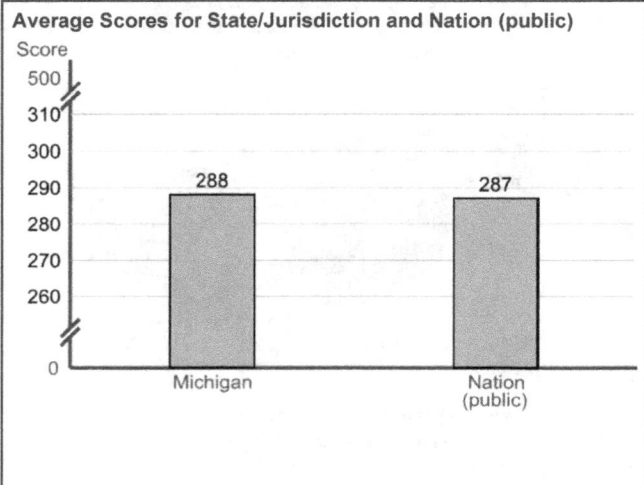

	Michigan	Nation (public)
Score	288	287

Results for Student Groups in 2013

Reporting Groups	Percent of students	Avg. score	Percentages at or above Basic	Percentages at or above Proficient	Percent at Advanced
Race/Ethnicity					
White	76	293	80	42	6
Black	14	262	48	12	#
Hispanic	5	276	66	22	1
Asian	3	296	78	53	12
American Indian/Alaska Native	1	‡	‡	‡	‡
Native Hawaiian/Pacific Islander	#	‡	‡	‡	‡
Two or more races	1	‡	‡	‡	‡
Gender					
Male	50	282	69	32	4
Female	50	294	80	43	6

Rounds to zero.   ‡ Reporting standards not met.
NOTE: Detail may not sum to totals because of rounding. Black includes African American and Hispanic includes Latino. Race categories exclude Hispanic origin.

Score Gaps for Student Groups

- In 2013, Black students had an average score that was 31 points lower than White students. This performance gap was not significantly different from the nation (29 points).
- In 2013, Hispanic students had an average score that was 18 points lower than White students. This performance gap was not significantly different from the nation (21 points).
- In 2013, female students in Michigan had an average score that was higher than male students by 12 points.

 NATIONAL CENTER FOR EDUCATION STATISTICS
Institute of Education Sciences

NOTE: Statistical comparisons are calculated on the basis of unrounded scale scores or percentages.
SOURCE: U.S. Department of Education, Institute of Education Sciences, National Center for Education Statistics, National Assessment of Educational Progress (NAEP), 2013 Reading Assessment.

NATIONAL CENTER FOR EDUCATION STATISTICS
Institute of Education Sciences

The Nation's Report Card

Science 2009
State Snapshot Report

Michigan
Grade 4
Public Schools

2009 Science Assessment Content

Guided by a new framework, the NAEP science assessment was updated in 2009 to keep the content current with key developments in science, curriculum standards, assessments, and research. The 2009 framework organizes science content into three broad content areas. **Physical science** includes concepts related to properties and changes of matter, forms of energy, energy transfer and conservation, position and motion of objects, and forces affecting motion. **Life science** includes concepts related to organization and development, matter and energy transformations, interdependence, heredity and reproduction, and evolution and diversity. **Earth and space sciences** includes concepts related to objects in the universe, the history of the Earth, properties of Earth materials, tectonics, energy in Earth systems, climate and weather, and biogeochemical cycles.

The 2009 science assessment was composed of 143 questions at grade 4, 162 at grade 8, and 179 at grade 12. Students responded to only a portion of the questions, which included both multiple-choice questions and questions that required a written response.

Compare the Average Score in 2009 to Other States/Jurisdictions

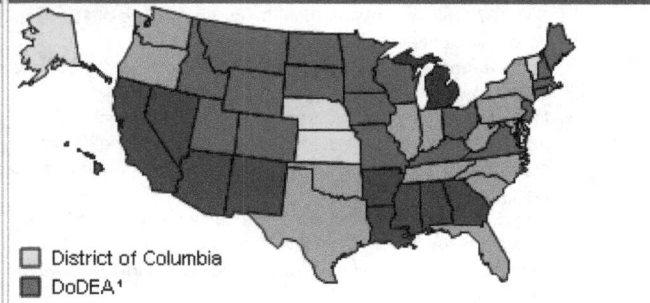

☐ District of Columbia
◼ DoDEA[1]

[1] Department of Defense Education Activity (overseas and domestic schools).

In 2009, the average score in **Michigan** was
- lower than those in 20 states/jurisdictions
- higher than those in 10 states/jurisdictions
- not significantly different from those in 16 states/jurisdictions

    5 states/jurisdictions did not participate

Overall Results

- In 2009, the average score of fourth-grade students in Michigan was 150. This was not significantly different from the average score of 149 for public school students in the nation.
- The percentage of students in Michigan who performed at or above the NAEP *Proficient* level was 34 percent in 2009. This percentage was not significantly different from the nation (32 percent).
- The percentage of students in Michigan who performed at or above the NAEP *Basic* level was 72 percent in 2009. This percentage was not significantly different from the nation (71 percent).

Achievement-Level Percentages and Average Score Results

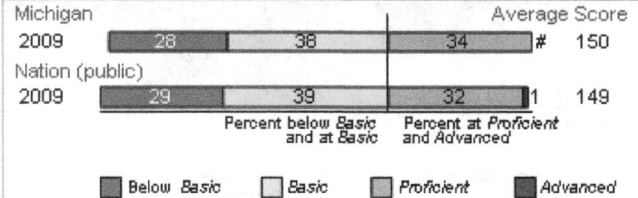

	Average Score
Michigan 2009	28 / 38 / 34 / # — 150
Nation (public) 2009	29 / 39 / 32 / 1 — 149

Percent below *Basic* and at *Basic*   Percent at *Proficient* and *Advanced*

◼ Below *Basic*   ☐ *Basic*   ▨ *Proficient*   ◼ *Advanced*

Rounds to zero.

NOTE: Detail may not sum to totals because of rounding.

Results for Student Groups in 2009

Reporting Groups	Percent of students	Avg. score	Percentages at or above — Basic	Proficient	Percent at Advanced
Gender					
Male	50	151	73	37	#
Female	50	149	72	32	1
Race/Ethnicity					
White	71	160	83	43	1
Black	20	118	34	6	#
Hispanic	5	138	60	20	#
Asian/Pacific Islander	3	162	79	49	2
American Indian/Alaska Native	#	‡	‡	‡	‡
National School Lunch Program					
Eligible	43	134	55	18	#
Not eligible	56	163	86	47	1

Rounds to zero.   ‡ Reporting standards not met.

NOTE: Detail may not sum to totals because of rounding, and because the "Information not available" category for the National School Lunch Program, which provides free/reduced-price lunches, and the "Unclassified" category for race/ethnicity are not displayed.

Score Gaps for Student Groups

- In 2009, male students in Michigan had an average score that was not significantly different from female students.
- In 2009, Black students had an average score that was 42 points lower than White students. This performance gap was wider than the nation (35 points).
- In 2009, Hispanic students had an average score that was 22 points lower than White students. This performance gap was narrower than the nation (32 points).
- In 2009, students who were eligible for free/reduced-price school lunch, an indicator of low family income, had an average score that was 29 points lower than students who were not eligible for free/reduced-price school lunch. This performance gap was not significantly different from the nation (29 points).

NOTE: Statistical comparisons are calculated on the basis of unrounded scale scores or percentages.
SOURCE: U.S. Department of Education, Institute of Education Sciences, National Center for Education Statistics, National Assessment of Educational Progress (NAEP), 2009 Science Assessment.

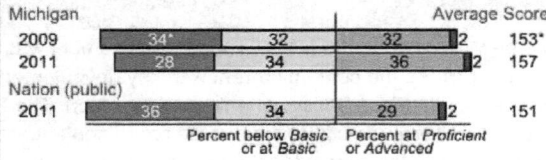

The Nation's Science Report Card 2011 State Snapshot Report

Michigan
Grade 8
Public Schools

Overall Results

- In 2011, the average score of eighth-grade students in Michigan was 157. This was higher than the average score of 151 for public school students in the nation.
- The average score for students in Michigan in 2011 (157) was higher than their average score in 2009 (153).
- In 2011, the score gap between students in Michigan at the 75th percentile and students at the 25th percentile was 43 points. This performance gap was not significantly different from that of 2009 (48 points).
- The percentage of students in Michigan who performed at or above the NAEP *Proficient* level was 38 percent in 2011. This percentage was not significantly different from that in 2009 (35 percent).
- The percentage of students in Michigan who performed at or above the NAEP *Basic* level was 72 percent in 2011. This percentage was greater than that in 2009 (66 percent).

Achievement-Level Percentages and Average Score Results

Michigan	Below Basic	Basic	Proficient	Advanced	Average Score
2009	34*	32	32	2	153*
2011	28	34	36	2	157
Nation (public)					
2011	36	34	29	2	151

Percent below *Basic* or at *Basic*　　Percent at *Proficient* or *Advanced*

■ Below *Basic*　　□ *Basic*　　▨ *Proficient*　　■ *Advanced*

* Significantly different (*p* < .05) from state's results in 2011. Significance tests were performed using unrounded numbers.

NOTE: Detail may not sum to totals because of rounding.

Compare the Average Score in 2011 to Other States/Jurisdictions

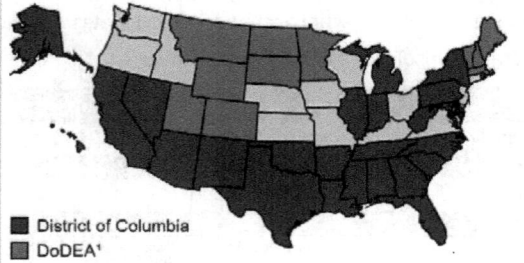

■ District of Columbia
▨ DoDEA[1]

[1] Department of Defense Education Activity (overseas and domestic schools).

In 2011, the average score in Michigan (157) was
- lower than those in 12 states/jurisdictions
- higher than those in 26 states/jurisdictions
- not significantly different from those in 13 states/jurisdictions

Average Scores for State/Jurisdiction and Nation (public)

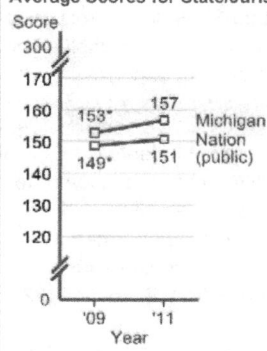

Michigan: 153* (2009), 157 (2011)
Nation (public): 149* (2009), 151 (2011)

* Significantly different (*p* < .05) from 2011. Significance tests were performed using unrounded numbers.

Results for Student Groups in 2011

Reporting Groups	Percent of students	Avg. score	Percentages at or above Basic	Percentages at or above Proficient	Percent at Advanced
Race/Ethnicity					
White	75	165	81	45	3
Black	16	124	31	6	#
Hispanic	4	146	60	24	#
Asian	3	166	77	50	3
American Indian/Alaska Native	1	‡	‡	‡	‡
Native Hawaiian/Pacific Islander	#	‡	‡	‡	‡
Two or more races	1	‡	‡	‡	‡
Gender					
Male	51	160	74	42	3
Female	49	154	69	34	1
National School Lunch Program					
Eligible	42	143	55	22	1
Not eligible	57	168	84	50	3

Rounds to zero.　　　　‡ Reporting standards not met.

NOTE: Detail may not sum to totals because of rounding, and because the "Information not available" category for the National School Lunch Program, which provides free/reduced-price lunches, is not displayed. Black includes African American and Hispanic includes Latino. Race categories exclude Hispanic origin.

Score Gaps for Student Groups

- In 2011, Black students had an average score that was 41 points lower than White students. This performance gap was not significantly different from that in 2009 (41 points).
- In 2011, Hispanic students had an average score that was 19 points lower than White students. This performance gap was not significantly different from that in 2009 (23 points).
- In 2011, male students in Michigan had an average score that was higher than female students by 5 points.
- In 2011, students who were eligible for free/reduced-price school lunch, an indicator of low family income, had an average score that was 24 points lower than students who were not eligible for free/reduced-price school lunch. This performance gap was not significantly different from that in 2009 (24 points).

ies NATIONAL CENTER FOR EDUCATION STATISTICS Institute of Education Sciences

NOTE: Statistical comparisons are calculated on the basis of unrounded scale scores or percentages.
SOURCE: U.S. Department of Education, Institute of Education Sciences, National Center for Education Statistics, National Assessment of Educational Progress (NAEP), 2009 and 2011 Science Assessments.

The writing assessment of the National Assessment of Educational Progress (NAEP) measures narrative, informative, and persuasive writing–three purposes identified in the NAEP framework. The NAEP writing scale ranges from 0 to 300.

Overall Writing Results for Michigan

- The average scale score for fourth-grade students in Michigan was 147.

- Michigan's average score (147) was lower[1] than that of the nation's public schools (153).

- Students' average scale scores in Michigan were higher than those in 9 jurisdictions[2], not significantly different from those in 16 jurisdictions, and lower than those in 22 jurisdictions.

- The percentage of students who performed at or above the NAEP *Proficient* level was 19 percent. The percentage of students who performed at or above the *Basic* level was 84 percent.

Student Percentage at Each Achievement Level

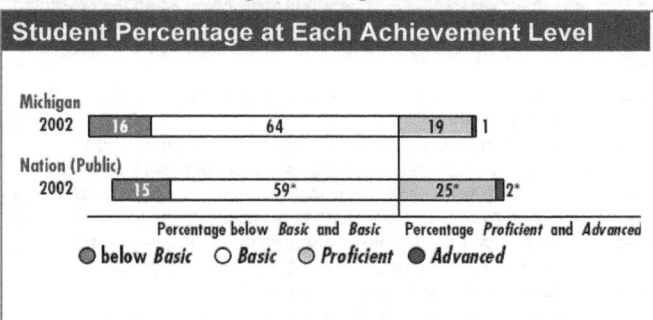

Michigan
2002 | 16 | 64 | 19 | 1 |

Nation (Public)
2002 | 15 | 59* | 25* | 2* |

Percentage below *Basic* and *Basic*   Percentage *Proficient* and *Advanced*

● below *Basic*   ○ *Basic*   ○ *Proficient*   ● *Advanced*

Performance of NAEP Reporting Groups in Michigan

Reporting groups	Percentage of students	Average Score	Below *Basic*	*Basic*	*Proficient*	*Advanced*
Male	51	138 ↓	22	67 ↑	11 ↓	#
Female	49	156 ↓	11	61 ↑	27 ↓	1 ↓
White	72	152 ↓	12	65 ↑	22 ↓	1 ↓
Black	20	131 ↓	30	61	8 ↓	#
Hispanic	4	139	23	66	11	1
Asian/Pacific Islander	2	---	---	---	---	---
American Indian/Alaska Native	2	---	---	---	---	---
Free/reduced-priced school lunch						
Eligible	38	134 ↓	27	65	8 ↓	#
Not eligible	57	157 ↓	9	63 ↑	26 ↓	1 ↓
Information not available	5	141 ↓	18	70 ↑	12 ↓	0

Average Score Gaps Between Selected Groups

- Female students in Michigan had an average score that was higher than that of male students (18 points). This performance gap was not significantly different from that of the Nation (18 points).

- White students had an average score that was higher than that of Black students (21 points). This performance gap was not significantly different from that of the Nation (20 points).

- White students had an average score that was higher than that of Hispanic students (13 points). This performance gap was not significantly different from that of the Nation (19 points).

- Students who were not eligible for free/reduced-price school lunch had an average score that was higher than that of students who were eligible (23 points). This performance gap was not significantly different from that of the Nation (22 points).

Writing Scale Scores at Selected Percentiles

Scale Score Distribution

	25th Percentile	50th Percentile	75th Percentile
Michigan	125 ↓	147 ↓	170 ↓
Nation (Public)	128	153	178

An examination of scores at different percentiles on the 0-300 NAEP writing scale at each grade indicates how well students at lower, middle, and higher levels of the distribution performed. For example, the data above shows that 75 percent of students in public schools nationally scored below *178*, while 75 percent of students in Michigan scored below *170*.

Percentage rounds to zero.   --- Reporting standards not met; sample size insufficient to permit a reliable estimate.
* Significantly different from Michigan.   ↑ Significantly higher than, ↓ lower than appropriate subgroup in the nation (public).
[1] Comparisons (higher/lower/not different) are based on statistical tests. The .05 level was used for testing statistical significance.
[2] "Jurisdictions" includes participating states and other jurisdictions (such as Guam or the District of Columbia).
NOTE: Detail may not sum to totals because of rounding. Score gaps are calculated based on differences between unrounded average scale scores.
Visit http://nces.ed.gov/nationsreportcard/states/ for additional results and detailed information.
SOURCE: U.S. Department of Education, Institute of Education Sciences, National Center for Education Statistics, National Assessment of Educational Progress (NAEP), 2002 Writing Assessment.

:ies NATIONAL CENTER FOR EDUCATION STATISTICS
Institute of Education Sciences
NCES 2008-470MI8

The Nation's Report Card

Writing **2007**
State Snapshot Report

Michigan
Grade 8
Public Schools

The National Assessment of Educational Progress (NAEP) assesses writing for three purposes identified in the NAEP framework: narrative, informative, and persuasive. The NAEP writing scale ranges from 0 to 300.

Overall Writing Results for Michigan

- In 2007, the average scale score for eighth-grade students in Michigan was 151. This was not significantly different from their average score in 2002 (147).[1]
- Michigan's average score (151) in 2007 was lower than that of the nation's public schools (154).
- Of the 45 states and one other jurisdiction that participated in the 2007 eighth-grade assessment, students' average scale score in Michigan was higher than those in 7 jurisdictions, not significantly different from those in 15 jurisdictions, and lower than those in 23 jurisdictions.[2]
- The percentage of students in Michigan who performed at or above the NAEP *Proficient* level was 27 percent in 2007. This percentage was not significantly different from that in 2002 (24 percent).
- The percentage of students in Michigan who performed at or above the NAEP *Basic* level was 86 percent in 2007. This percentage was not significantly different from that in 2002 (83 percent).

Percentages at NAEP Achievement Levels and Average Score

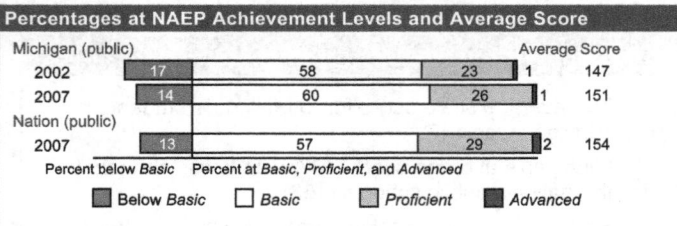

Michigan (public)   Average Score
2002   17   58   23   1   147
2007   14   60   26   1   151
Nation (public)
2007   13   57   29   2   154

Percent below *Basic*   Percent at *Basic, Proficient,* and *Advanced*

■ Below *Basic*   □ *Basic*   ▨ *Proficient*   ■ *Advanced*

NOTE: The NAEP grade 8 writing achievement levels correspond to the following scale points: Below *Basic*, 113 or lower; *Basic*, 114–172; *Proficient*, 173–223; *Advanced*, 224 or above.

Performance of NAEP Reporting Groups in Michigan: 2007

Reporting groups	Percent of students	Average score	Percent below *Basic*	Percent of students at or above		Percent *Advanced*
				Basic	*Proficient*	
Male	50	140	20	80	14	#
Female	50	162	7	93	39	2
White	75	156	10↓	90↑	30	1
Black	19	132	27	73	10	#
Hispanic	3	135	32	68	17	1
Asian/Pacific Islander	2	‡	‡	‡	‡	‡
American Indian/Alaska Native	1	‡	‡	‡	‡	‡
Eligible for National School Lunch Program	32	137	23	77	14	#
Not eligible for National School Lunch Program	68	158	9	91	33	1

Average Score Gaps Between Selected Groups

- In 2007, male students in Michigan had an average score that was lower than that of female students by 23 points. This performance gap was not significantly different from that of 2002 (21 points).
- In 2007, Black students had an average score that was lower than that of White students by 24 points. This performance gap was not significantly different from that of 2002 (22 points).
- In 2007, Hispanic students had an average score that was lower than that of White students by 21 points. Data are not reported for Hispanic students in 2002, because reporting standards were not met. Therefore, the performance gap results are not reported.
- In 2007, students who were eligible for free/reduced-price school lunch, an indicator of poverty, had an average score that was lower than that of students who were not eligible for free/reduced-price school lunch by 20 points. This performance gap was not significantly different from that of 2002 (17 points).
- In 2007, the score gap between students at the 75th percentile and students at the 25th percentile was 45 points. This performance gap was not significantly different from that of 2002 (49 points).

Writing Scores at Selected Percentiles in Michigan

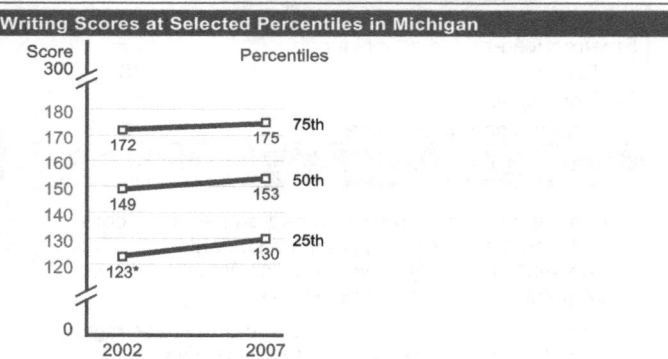

Score
Percentiles
172 → 175 75th
149 → 153 50th
123* → 130 25th
2002   2007

NOTE: Scores at selected percentiles on the NAEP writing scale indicate how well students at lower, middle, and higher levels performed.

Rounds to zero.
‡ Reporting standards not met.
* Significantly different from 2007.
↑ Significantly higher than 2002. ↓ Significantly lower than 2002.
[1] Comparisons (higher/lower/narrower/wider/not different) are based on statistical tests. The .05 level with appropriate adjustments for multiple comparisons was used for testing statistical significance. Statistical comparisons are calculated on the basis of unrounded scale scores or percentages. Comparisons across jurisdictions and comparisons with the nation or within a jurisdiction across years may be affected by differences in exclusion rates for students with disabilities (SD) and English language learners (ELL). The exclusion rates for SD and ELL in Michigan were 4 percent and "percentage rounds to zero" in 2007, respectively. For more information on NAEP significance testing, see http://nces.ed.gov/nationsreportcard/writing/interpret-results.asp#statistical.
[2] "Jurisdiction" refers to states, the District of Columbia, and the Department of Defense Education Activity schools.
NOTE: Detail may not sum to totals because of rounding and because the "Information not available" category for the National School Lunch Program, which provides free and reduced-price lunches, and the "Unclassified" category for race/ethnicity are not displayed. Visit http://nces.ed.gov/nationsreportcard/states/ for additional results and detailed information.
SOURCE: U.S. Department of Education, Institute of Education Sciences, National Center for Education Statistics, National Assessment of Educational Progress (NAEP), 2002 and 2007 Writing Assessments.

MI School Data

06/03/2015

Annual Education Report

Statewide

Michigan Educational Assessment Program (MEAP)

Subject	Grade	Testing Group	School Year	State % Students Proficient	% Advanced (Level 1)	% Proficient (Level 2)	% Partially Proficient (Level 3)	% Not Proficient (Level 4)
Mathematics	3rd	All Students	2012-13	40.9%	4%	36.9%	23.4%	35.7%
Mathematics	3rd	All Students	2013-14	40.1%	7.8%	32.3%	23.9%	36%
Mathematics	3rd	American Indian	2012-13	30.6%	1.8%	28.8%	27.1%	42.3%
Mathematics	3rd	American Indian	2013-14	33.7%	4.5%	29.3%	24.7%	41.6%
Mathematics	3rd	African American	2012-13	18%	1%	16.9%	19.4%	62.6%
Mathematics	3rd	African American	2013-14	18.2%	2%	16.2%	19.5%	62.3%
Mathematics	3rd	Asian	2012-13	65.6%	14.5%	51%	16.3%	18.1%
Mathematics	3rd	Asian	2013-14	66%	24.1%	41.9%	17.1%	16.9%
Mathematics	3rd	Hispanic of Any Race	2012-13	25.7%	1.6%	24.1%	25%	49.3%
Mathematics	3rd	Hispanic of Any Race	2013-14	26.3%	3.5%	22.9%	24.2%	49.5%
Mathematics	3rd	Migrant	2012-13	10.1%	0.7%	9.5%	31.1%	58.8%
Mathematics	3rd	Migrant	2013-14	18.6%	1.4%	17.3%	21.4%	60%
Mathematics	3rd	Native Hawaiian or Other Pacific Islander	2012-13	40.2%	6.5%	33.6%	25.2%	34.6%
Mathematics	3rd	Native Hawaiian or Other Pacific Islander	2013-14	30.1%	2.7%	27.4%	24.7%	45.2%
Mathematics	3rd	Two or More Races	2012-13	40%	4.6%	35.4%	22.7%	37.3%
Mathematics	3rd	Two or More Races	2013-14	38.1%	7.1%	31%	24.6%	37.2%
Mathematics	3rd	White	2012-13	47.4%	4.6%	42.8%	24.6%	28%
Mathematics	3rd	White	2013-14	46.6%	9.2%	37.4%	25.3%	28.1%

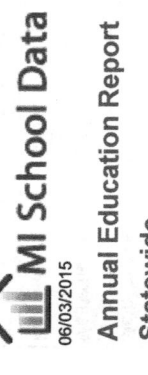

MI School Data
06/03/2015
Annual Education Report
Statewide

Michigan Educational Assessment Program (MEAP)

Subject	Grade	Testing Group	School Year	State % Students Proficient	% Advanced (Level 1)	% Proficient (Level 2)	% Partially Proficient (Level 3)	% Not Proficient (Level 4)
Mathematics	3rd	Female	2012-13	39.8%	3.5%	36.3%	24.2%	36%
Mathematics	3rd	Female	2013-14	39.7%	7.3%	32.5%	24.6%	35.7%
Mathematics	3rd	Male	2012-13	42%	4.6%	37.4%	22.5%	35.5%
Mathematics	3rd	Male	2013-14	40.6%	8.4%	32.2%	23.2%	36.2%
Mathematics	3rd	Economically Disadvantaged	2012-13	26.8%	1.5%	25.3%	23.8%	49.5%
Mathematics	3rd	Economically Disadvantaged	2013-14	26.9%	3.5%	23.4%	24%	49.1%
Mathematics	3rd	English Language Learners	2012-13	23%	1.7%	21.4%	23%	53.9%
Mathematics	3rd	English Language Learners	2013-14	26.4%	4.1%	22.3%	22.5%	51.1%
Mathematics	3rd	Students With Disabilities	2012-13	21.5%	1.4%	20.1%	20.5%	58.1%
Mathematics	3rd	Students With Disabilities	2013-14	22.2%	3.1%	19.1%	20.2%	57.6%
Mathematics	4th	All Students	2012-13	46.1%	8.3%	37.8%	15.4%	38.5%
Mathematics	4th	All Students	2013-14	45.3%	9.7%	35.6%	16.5%	38.2%
Mathematics	4th	American Indian	2012-13	39.8%	3.8%	36%	16.4%	43.8%
Mathematics	4th	American Indian	2013-14	37.6%	4.2%	33.4%	17.5%	44.9%
Mathematics	4th	African American	2012-13	20%	1.7%	18.4%	13.4%	66.5%
Mathematics	4th	African American	2013-14	18.2%	1.8%	16.4%	14.6%	67.2%
Mathematics	4th	Asian	2012-13	71.4%	27.9%	43.5%	10.7%	17.9%
Mathematics	4th	Asian	2013-14	69.2%	28.1%	41.1%	11.9%	19%

MI School Data
06/03/2015

Annual Education Report

Statewide

Michigan Educational Assessment Program (MEAP)

Subject	Grade	Testing Group	School Year	State % Students Proficient	% Advanced (Level 1)	% Proficient (Level 2)	% Partially Proficient (Level 3)	% Not Proficient (Level 4)
Mathematics	4th	Hispanic of Any Race	2012-13	33.3%	3.4%	29.9%	16.6%	50.1%
Mathematics	4th	Hispanic of Any Race	2013-14	29.3%	3.8%	25.5%	18.2%	52.5%
Mathematics	4th	Migrant	2012-13	38.6%	1.6%	37%	18.1%	43.3%
Mathematics	4th	Migrant	2013-14	24.4%	1%	23.4%	18.8%	56.9%
Mathematics	4th	Native Hawaiian or Other Pacific Islander	2012-13	53.1%	7.3%	45.8%	11.5%	35.4%
Mathematics	4th	Native Hawaiian or Other Pacific Islander	2013-14	46.5%	11.1%	35.4%	17.2%	36.4%
Mathematics	4th	Two or More Races	2012-13	44.3%	7.9%	36.5%	15.5%	40.2%
Mathematics	4th	Two or More Races	2013-14	43.8%	9%	34.8%	16.3%	39.9%
Mathematics	4th	White	2012-13	53%	9.6%	43.3%	16%	31%
Mathematics	4th	White	2013-14	52.9%	11.5%	41.4%	17.1%	30%
Mathematics	4th	Female	2012-13	45.7%	7.8%	37.9%	15.9%	38.3%
Mathematics	4th	Female	2013-14	43.4%	8.3%	35.1%	17.3%	39.3%
Mathematics	4th	Male	2012-13	46.4%	8.8%	37.6%	14.9%	38.7%
Mathematics	4th	Male	2013-14	47.2%	11.1%	36.1%	15.8%	37.1%
Mathematics	4th	Economically Disadvantaged	2012-13	31.1%	3.1%	28%	16.1%	52.9%
Mathematics	4th	Economically Disadvantaged	2013-14	29.5%	3.8%	25.7%	17.3%	53.2%

MI School Data

06/03/2015

Annual Education Report

Statewide

Michigan Educational Assessment Program (MEAP)

Subject	Grade	Testing Group	School Year	State % Students Proficient	% Advanced (Level 1)	% Proficient (Level 2)	% Partially Proficient (Level 3)	% Not Proficient (Level 4)
Mathematics	4th	English Language Learners	2012-13	24.4%	2.2%	22.2%	15.3%	60.3%
Mathematics	4th	English Language Learners	2013-14	23.1%	2.7%	20.4%	17.2%	59.8%
Mathematics	4th	Students With Disabilities	2012-13	23%	3.2%	19.8%	11.8%	65.2%
Mathematics	4th	Students With Disabilities	2013-14	23.2%	4%	19.2%	13.9%	62.9%
Mathematics	5th	All Students	2012-13	45.7%	5.6%	40.1%	17.1%	37.2%
Mathematics	5th	All Students	2013-14	45.2%	5.8%	39.4%	18.8%	35.9%
Mathematics	5th	American Indian	2012-13	34.7%	2.3%	32.5%	19.9%	45.4%
Mathematics	5th	American Indian	2013-14	35.9%	4.2%	31.7%	20.8%	43.3%
Mathematics	5th	African American	2012-13	20.5%	1.1%	19.4%	15.6%	63.9%
Mathematics	5th	African American	2013-14	20%	1.1%	18.9%	17.4%	62.7%
Mathematics	5th	Asian	2012-13	74.7%	25.8%	48.9%	9.7%	15.6%
Mathematics	5th	Asian	2013-14	73.6%	26.4%	47.1%	11.6%	14.8%
Mathematics	5th	Hispanic of Any Race	2012-13	31.7%	2.2%	29.5%	19.2%	49.1%
Mathematics	5th	Hispanic of Any Race	2013-14	32.3%	2.3%	29.9%	20.4%	47.3%
Mathematics	5th	Migrant	2012-13	32%	0%	32%	19.7%	48.4%
Mathematics	5th	Migrant	2013-14	40.7%	1.2%	39.5%	26.2%	33.1%
Mathematics	5th	Native Hawaiian or Other Pacific Islander	2012-13	67.2%	6%	61.2%	13.4%	19.4%

MI School Data
06/03/2015
Annual Education Report
Statewide

Michigan Educational Assessment Program (MEAP)

Subject	Grade	Testing Group	School Year	State % Students Proficient	% Advanced (Level 1)	% Proficient (Level 2)	% Partially Proficient (Level 3)	% Not Proficient (Level 4)
Mathematics	5th	Native Hawaiian or Other Pacific Islander	2013-14	38.2%	5.6%	32.6%	21.3%	40.4%
Mathematics	5th	Two or More Races	2012-13	42.7%	5.9%	36.8%	17.5%	39.8%
Mathematics	5th	Two or More Races	2013-14	43.2%	6.2%	37%	19.6%	37.3%
Mathematics	5th	White	2012-13	52.4%	6.2%	46.1%	17.6%	30%
Mathematics	5th	White	2013-14	51.7%	6.4%	45.3%	19.3%	29%
Mathematics	5th	Female	2012-13	43.9%	4.6%	39.2%	18.1%	38%
Mathematics	5th	Female	2013-14	44.7%	5%	39.7%	19.4%	35.9%
Mathematics	5th	Male	2012-13	47.5%	6.6%	40.9%	16.1%	36.3%
Mathematics	5th	Male	2013-14	45.7%	6.7%	39%	18.3%	36%
Mathematics	5th	Economically Disadvantaged	2012-13	30.3%	1.8%	28.5%	17.9%	51.8%
Mathematics	5th	Economically Disadvantaged	2013-14	29.5%	1.9%	27.6%	20%	50.6%
Mathematics	5th	English Language Learners	2012-13	22.9%	1.5%	21.4%	17.1%	59.9%
Mathematics	5th	English Language Learners	2013-14	23.1%	1.8%	21.3%	19.8%	57.1%
Mathematics	5th	Students With Disabilities	2012-13	19.9%	1.8%	18.1%	12.2%	67.9%
Mathematics	5th	Students With Disabilities	2013-14	20%	2.2%	17.8%	14.6%	65.3%
Mathematics	6th	All Students	2012-13	40.2%	5.5%	34.6%	20.7%	39.2%
Mathematics	6th	All Students	2013-14	41.5%	8.9%	32.5%	18.8%	39.7%

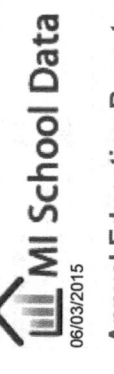

MI School Data
06/03/2015

Annual Education Report

Statewide

Michigan Educational Assessment Program (MEAP)

Subject	Grade	Testing Group	School Year	State % Students Proficient	% Advanced (Level 1)	% Proficient (Level 2)	% Partially Proficient (Level 3)	% Not Proficient (Level 4)
Mathematics	6th	American Indian	2012-13	29.4%	1.9%	27.4%	22.2%	48.4%
Mathematics	6th	American Indian	2013-14	27.7%	3.5%	24.2%	22.2%	50.1%
Mathematics	6th	African American	2012-13	15.9%	0.7%	15.2%	18.4%	65.7%
Mathematics	6th	African American	2013-14	17.6%	1.7%	15.9%	16%	66.4%
Mathematics	6th	Asian	2012-13	70.8%	27.5%	43.3%	12.7%	16.5%
Mathematics	6th	Asian	2013-14	73.2%	37.5%	35.7%	10.8%	16%
Mathematics	6th	Hispanic of Any Race	2012-13	26.3%	2.1%	24.1%	22.1%	51.6%
Mathematics	6th	Hispanic of Any Race	2013-14	27.6%	3.3%	24.3%	20.4%	52%
Mathematics	6th	Migrant	2012-13	19.1%	0.9%	18.2%	21.8%	59.1%
Mathematics	6th	Migrant	2013-14	26.1%	0.6%	25.5%	25.5%	48.5%
Mathematics	6th	Native Hawaiian or Other Pacific Islander	2012-13	55.8%	8.1%	47.7%	18.6%	25.6%
Mathematics	6th	Native Hawaiian or Other Pacific Islander	2013-14	58.3%	11.7%	46.7%	21.7%	20%
Mathematics	6th	Two or More Races	2012-13	36.1%	5.4%	30.7%	20.9%	43%
Mathematics	6th	Two or More Races	2013-14	39.1%	9%	30.1%	18.6%	42.3%
Mathematics	6th	White	2012-13	46.6%	6.1%	40.4%	21.5%	32%
Mathematics	6th	White	2013-14	47.6%	10%	37.6%	19.7%	32.7%
Mathematics	6th	Female	2012-13	38.8%	4.6%	34.2%	22.1%	39.1%
Mathematics	6th	Female	2013-14	40.9%	8.1%	32.8%	19.8%	39.2%

MI School Data
06/03/2015
Annual Education Report
Statewide

Michigan Educational Assessment Program (MEAP)

Subject	Grade	Testing Group	School Year	State % Students Proficient	% Advanced (Level 1)	% Proficient (Level 2)	% Partially Proficient (Level 3)	% Not Proficient (Level 4)
Mathematics	6th	Male	2012-13	41.4%	6.4%	35%	19.3%	39.3%
Mathematics	6th	Male	2013-14	42%	9.8%	32.3%	17.8%	40.2%
Mathematics	6th	Economically Disadvantaged	2012-13	24.6%	1.6%	23%	21.2%	54.2%
Mathematics	6th	Economically Disadvantaged	2013-14	25.9%	3%	22.9%	19.1%	54.9%
Mathematics	6th	English Language Learners	2012-13	18.2%	1.3%	16.9%	18.2%	63.6%
Mathematics	6th	English Language Learners	2013-14	18.2%	2.5%	15.7%	18.1%	63.6%
Mathematics	6th	Students With Disabilities	2012-13	13.2%	1.2%	12%	12.7%	74.1%
Mathematics	6th	Students With Disabilities	2013-14	14.3%	2.3%	12%	12%	73.7%
Mathematics	7th	All Students	2012-13	38.1%	6%	32.1%	24.1%	37.8%
Mathematics	7th	All Students	2013-14	39.2%	5.2%	33.9%	23.2%	37.6%
Mathematics	7th	American Indian	2012-13	26.4%	2.2%	24.2%	24.2%	49.4%
Mathematics	7th	American Indian	2013-14	26.8%	1.8%	25.1%	23.3%	49.9%
Mathematics	7th	African American	2012-13	15.4%	1%	14.5%	20.9%	63.7%
Mathematics	7th	African American	2013-14	15.3%	1%	14.3%	19.9%	64.8%
Mathematics	7th	Asian	2012-13	70.4%	32.4%	38%	14.1%	15.5%
Mathematics	7th	Asian	2013-14	69.6%	29.1%	40.5%	13.7%	16.7%
Mathematics	7th	Hispanic of Any Race	2012-13	23.8%	2.1%	21.7%	24.6%	51.6%

MI School Data
06/03/2015
Annual Education Report
Statewide

Michigan Educational Assessment Program (MEAP)

Subject	Grade	Testing Group	School Year	State % Students Proficient	% Advanced (Level 1)	% Proficient (Level 2)	% Partially Proficient (Level 3)	% Not Proficient (Level 4)
Mathematics	7th	Hispanic of Any Race	2013-14	25.4%	1.6%	23.7%	24.5%	50.1%
Mathematics	7th	Migrant	2012-13	22.2%	0%	22.2%	28.2%	49.6%
Mathematics	7th	Migrant	2013-14	19.7%	0%	19.7%	23.2%	57%
Mathematics	7th	Native Hawaiian or Other Pacific Islander	2012-13	53.3%	12.5%	40.8%	23.3%	23.3%
Mathematics	7th	Native Hawaiian or Other Pacific Islander	2013-14	50%	7.6%	42.4%	23.9%	26.1%
Mathematics	7th	Two or More Races	2012-13	34.5%	5.4%	29.1%	23.5%	42%
Mathematics	7th	Two or More Races	2013-14	34.8%	4.9%	29.9%	22.8%	42.4%
Mathematics	7th	White	2012-13	44.2%	6.6%	37.6%	25.4%	30.5%
Mathematics	7th	White	2013-14	45.4%	5.6%	39.8%	24.3%	30.2%
Mathematics	7th	Female	2012-13	38.8%	5.6%	33.1%	25.7%	35.5%
Mathematics	7th	Female	2013-14	39.9%	5%	34.9%	24.3%	35.8%
Mathematics	7th	Male	2012-13	37.5%	6.4%	31.1%	22.5%	40%
Mathematics	7th	Male	2013-14	38.5%	5.4%	33%	22.1%	39.4%
Mathematics	7th	Economically Disadvantaged	2012-13	22.5%	1.7%	20.8%	24.4%	53.1%
Mathematics	7th	Economically Disadvantaged	2013-14	23.5%	1.5%	22%	23.3%	53.3%
Mathematics	7th	English Language Learners	2012-13	14%	1.4%	12.6%	20.3%	65.7%

MI School Data

06/03/2015

Annual Education Report

Statewide

Michigan Educational Assessment Program (MEAP)

Subject	Grade	Testing Group	School Year	State % Students Proficient	% Advanced (Level 1)	% Proficient (Level 2)	% Partially Proficient (Level 3)	% Not Proficient (Level 4)
Mathematics	7th	English Language Learners	2013-14	14.5%	1.2%	13.3%	19.6%	65.9%
Mathematics	7th	Students With Disabilities	2012-13	9.8%	0.9%	8.8%	13.5%	76.7%
Mathematics	7th	Students With Disabilities	2013-14	10.4%	0.7%	9.7%	14.3%	75.3%
Mathematics	8th	All Students	2012-13	34.5%	8.2%	26.4%	26.3%	39.2%
Mathematics	8th	All Students	2013-14	34.5%	7.1%	27.4%	23.6%	41.8%
Mathematics	8th	American Indian	2012-13	22.7%	3.3%	19.5%	29.5%	47.8%
Mathematics	8th	American Indian	2013-14	21.5%	2.7%	18.8%	27.3%	51.2%
Mathematics	8th	African American	2012-13	11.9%	1.4%	10.5%	21.4%	66.7%
Mathematics	8th	African American	2013-14	11.4%	1.3%	10.1%	17.4%	71.2%
Mathematics	8th	Asian	2012-13	66.7%	33.2%	33.4%	17.7%	15.7%
Mathematics	8th	Asian	2013-14	66.7%	32.3%	34.4%	15.3%	18%
Mathematics	8th	Hispanic of Any Race	2012-13	19.9%	3%	16.9%	27%	53.2%
Mathematics	8th	Hispanic of Any Race	2013-14	20.4%	2.6%	17.8%	24.1%	55.5%
Mathematics	8th	Migrant	2012-13	19%	0%	19%	23%	58%
Mathematics	8th	Migrant	2013-14	14.8%	0%	14.8%	27.1%	58.1%
Mathematics	8th	Native Hawaiian or Other Pacific Islander	2012-13	49.5%	12.1%	37.4%	25.3%	25.3%

MI School Data

06/03/2015

Annual Education Report

Statewide

Michigan Educational Assessment Program (MEAP)

Subject	Grade	Testing Group	School Year	State % Students Proficient	% Advanced (Level 1)	% Proficient (Level 2)	% Partially Proficient (Level 3)	% Not Proficient (Level 4)
Mathematics	8th	Native Hawaiian or Other Pacific Islander	2013-14	46.4%	8%	38.4%	18.4%	35.2%
Mathematics	8th	Two or More Races	2012-13	31.2%	9.1%	22.1%	26.3%	42.6%
Mathematics	8th	Two or More Races	2013-14	31.5%	7%	24.5%	22.5%	46%
Mathematics	8th	White	2012-13	40.4%	9.3%	31.1%	27.8%	31.8%
Mathematics	8th	White	2013-14	40.5%	8%	32.5%	25.5%	33.9%
Mathematics	8th	Female	2012-13	34.1%	7.1%	27%	27.5%	38.4%
Mathematics	8th	Female	2013-14	33.8%	6.5%	27.2%	24.7%	41.5%
Mathematics	8th	Male	2012-13	34.9%	9.2%	25.7%	25.2%	39.9%
Mathematics	8th	Male	2013-14	35.3%	7.7%	27.5%	22.6%	42.1%
Mathematics	8th	Economically Disadvantaged	2012-13	18.7%	2.5%	16.3%	26%	55.2%
Mathematics	8th	Economically Disadvantaged	2013-14	18.7%	2.1%	16.6%	22.8%	58.5%
Mathematics	8th	English Language Learners	2012-13	11%	2%	9%	21.6%	67.4%
Mathematics	8th	English Language Learners	2013-14	12.3%	1.9%	10.4%	18.3%	69.4%
Mathematics	8th	Students With Disabilities	2012-13	6.9%	1.3%	5.7%	15.4%	77.7%
Mathematics	8th	Students With Disabilities	2013-14	8.2%	1.1%	7.1%	12.5%	79.3%
Reading	3rd	All Students	2012-13	66.5%	9.2%	57.3%	21.9%	11.6%
Reading	3rd	All Students	2013-14	61.3%	8.3%	53%	29.4%	9.2%

MI School Data

06/03/2015

Annual Education Report

Statewide

Michigan Educational Assessment Program (MEAP)

Subject	Grade	Testing Group	School Year	State % Students Proficient	% Advanced (Level 1)	% Proficient (Level 2)	% Partially Proficient (Level 3)	% Not Proficient (Level 4)
Reading	3rd	American Indian	2012-13	60.9%	6%	54.9%	24.6%	14.6%
Reading	3rd	American Indian	2013-14	58.4%	6.8%	51.6%	33%	8.6%
Reading	3rd	African American	2012-13	44.8%	3.1%	41.7%	31.4%	23.8%
Reading	3rd	African American	2013-14	37.3%	2.3%	35%	43.2%	19.5%
Reading	3rd	Asian	2012-13	79%	16%	62.9%	14.4%	6.6%
Reading	3rd	Asian	2013-14	76.2%	16.4%	59.8%	19%	4.8%
Reading	3rd	Hispanic of Any Race	2012-13	53.5%	4.6%	48.9%	30.2%	16.3%
Reading	3rd	Hispanic of Any Race	2013-14	46.9%	3.9%	43%	40.4%	12.7%
Reading	3rd	Migrant	2012-13	43.9%	2.3%	41.6%	35.3%	20.8%
Reading	3rd	Migrant	2013-14	32.9%	1.8%	31.1%	45.9%	21.2%
Reading	3rd	Native Hawaiian or Other Pacific Islander	2012-13	68.2%	15.9%	52.3%	18.7%	13.1%
Reading	3rd	Native Hawaiian or Other Pacific Islander	2013-14	54.9%	2.8%	52.1%	33.8%	11.3%
Reading	3rd	Two or More Races	2012-13	67.6%	9.9%	57.7%	22.1%	10.2%
Reading	3rd	Two or More Races	2013-14	61.8%	8.4%	53.5%	29.6%	8.6%
Reading	3rd	White	2012-13	73%	10.9%	62.1%	18.8%	8.2%
Reading	3rd	White	2013-14	68.8%	10.1%	58.7%	24.8%	6.3%
Reading	3rd	Female	2012-13	70.2%	10.9%	59.3%	20.2%	9.6%
Reading	3rd	Female	2013-14	64.1%	9.4%	54.8%	28.1%	7.7%

MI School Data
06/03/2015

Annual Education Report

Statewide

Michigan Educational Assessment Program (MEAP)

Subject	Grade	Testing Group	School Year	State % Students Proficient	% Advanced (Level 1)	% Proficient (Level 2)	% Partially Proficient (Level 3)	% Not Proficient (Level 4)
Reading	3rd	Male	2012-13	63%	7.6%	55.4%	23.4%	13.6%
Reading	3rd	Male	2013-14	58.6%	7.4%	51.2%	30.6%	10.8%
Reading	3rd	Economically Disadvantaged	2012-13	53.8%	4.3%	49.5%	28.4%	17.8%
Reading	3rd	Economically Disadvantaged	2013-14	47.9%	4%	44%	38.1%	13.9%
Reading	3rd	English Language Learners	2012-13	41.5%	2.2%	39.4%	35.5%	23%
Reading	3rd	English Language Learners	2013-14	37.2%	2.2%	35%	45.7%	17.1%
Reading	3rd	Students With Disabilities	2012-13	37.9%	3.1%	34.7%	30.3%	31.9%
Reading	3rd	Students With Disabilities	2013-14	35.1%	3.1%	32%	41.6%	23.3%
Reading	4th	All Students	2012-13	68.1%	5%	63.1%	24.9%	7.1%
Reading	4th	All Students	2013-14	70%	7.1%	62.9%	19.8%	10.2%
Reading	4th	American Indian	2012-13	66.4%	2.9%	63.6%	25.5%	8.1%
Reading	4th	American Indian	2013-14	64.3%	2.6%	61.7%	22.8%	12.9%
Reading	4th	African American	2012-13	43%	0.9%	42.1%	40.8%	16.2%
Reading	4th	African American	2013-14	47.6%	2.1%	45.5%	29.3%	23.1%
Reading	4th	Asian	2012-13	79.2%	8.9%	70.3%	17.3%	3.5%
Reading	4th	Asian	2013-14	81.1%	12.2%	68.9%	13.9%	5%
Reading	4th	Hispanic of Any Race	2012-13	57.5%	2.1%	55.4%	33.5%	9%

06/03/2015

MI School Data

Annual Education Report

Statewide

Michigan Educational Assessment Program (MEAP)

Subject	Grade	Testing Group	School Year	State % Students Proficient	% Advanced (Level 1)	% Proficient (Level 2)	% Partially Proficient (Level 3)	% Not Proficient (Level 4)
Reading	4th	Hispanic of Any Race	2013-14	57.8%	3.4%	54.4%	28%	14.3%
Reading	4th	Migrant	2012-13	57.4%	1.4%	56%	36.2%	6.4%
Reading	4th	Migrant	2013-14	46.2%	0%	46.2%	34.9%	19%
Reading	4th	Native Hawaiian or Other Pacific Islander	2012-13	71.6%	4.2%	67.4%	18.9%	9.5%
Reading	4th	Native Hawaiian or Other Pacific Islander	2013-14	76.8%	10.1%	66.7%	15.2%	8.1%
Reading	4th	Two or More Races	2012-13	68.7%	5%	63.7%	24.4%	7%
Reading	4th	Two or More Races	2013-14	71.2%	6.9%	64.3%	19.3%	9.5%
Reading	4th	White	2012-13	75.1%	6.2%	68.9%	20.3%	4.7%
Reading	4th	White	2013-14	76.5%	8.5%	67.9%	16.7%	6.8%
Reading	4th	Female	2012-13	71.1%	5.6%	65.6%	23.3%	5.5%
Reading	4th	Female	2013-14	73%	8%	65.1%	18.4%	8.5%
Reading	4th	Male	2012-13	65.1%	4.5%	60.6%	26.4%	8.6%
Reading	4th	Male	2013-14	67%	6.2%	60.8%	21.1%	11.9%
Reading	4th	Economically Disadvantaged	2012-13	55.1%	1.8%	53.3%	33.8%	11.1%
Reading	4th	Economically Disadvantaged	2013-14	57.3%	3%	54.3%	26.5%	16.2%
Reading	4th	English Language Learners	2012-13	39.1%	0.4%	38.6%	45.4%	15.5%

MI School Data

06/03/2015

Annual Education Report

Statewide

Michigan Educational Assessment Program (MEAP)

Subject	Grade	Testing Group	School Year	State % Students Proficient	% Advanced (Level 1)	% Proficient (Level 2)	% Partially Proficient (Level 3)	% Not Proficient (Level 4)
Reading	4th	English Language Learners	2013-14	42.9%	0.9%	42%	35.3%	21.8%
Reading	4th	Students With Disabilities	2012-13	38.3%	1.7%	36.5%	39.4%	22.3%
Reading	4th	Students With Disabilities	2013-14	41.6%	2.4%	39.2%	28.9%	29.5%
Reading	5th	All Students	2012-13	70.4%	12.6%	57.8%	18%	11.6%
Reading	5th	All Students	2013-14	71.7%	18.1%	53.6%	19.2%	9.1%
Reading	5th	American Indian	2012-13	64.1%	7.8%	56.4%	24.2%	11.6%
Reading	5th	American Indian	2013-14	70.2%	14.1%	56.1%	22%	7.8%
Reading	5th	African American	2012-13	47.8%	3.7%	44.2%	27.7%	24.5%
Reading	5th	African American	2013-14	48.7%	5.5%	43.1%	31.1%	20.3%
Reading	5th	Asian	2012-13	81.5%	24.3%	57.2%	11.4%	7.1%
Reading	5th	Asian	2013-14	80%	29.7%	50.3%	13.8%	6.2%
Reading	5th	Hispanic of Any Race	2012-13	58.1%	6.6%	51.5%	24.8%	17.1%
Reading	5th	Hispanic of Any Race	2013-14	60.8%	9.5%	51.3%	26.1%	13%
Reading	5th	Migrant	2012-13	46.6%	1.5%	45.1%	31.6%	21.8%
Reading	5th	Migrant	2013-14	55.4%	3%	52.4%	32.1%	12.5%
Reading	5th	Native Hawaiian or Other Pacific Islander	2012-13	83.6%	11.9%	71.6%	13.4%	3%

MI School Data
06/03/2015
Annual Education Report
Statewide

Michigan Educational Assessment Program (MEAP)

Subject	Grade	Testing Group	School Year	State % Students Proficient	% Advanced (Level 1)	% Proficient (Level 2)	% Partially Proficient (Level 3)	% Not Proficient (Level 4)
Reading	5th	Native Hawaiian or Other Pacific Islander	2013-14	70.9%	17.4%	53.5%	25.6%	3.5%
Reading	5th	Two or More Races	2012-13	70.4%	12.7%	57.6%	18.5%	11.1%
Reading	5th	Two or More Races	2013-14	72.6%	17.4%	55.2%	18.9%	8.4%
Reading	5th	White	2012-13	76.9%	14.9%	61.9%	15.1%	8%
Reading	5th	White	2013-14	78.2%	21.6%	56.5%	15.8%	6%
Reading	5th	Female	2012-13	74.1%	14.7%	59.4%	16.8%	9.2%
Reading	5th	Female	2013-14	74.2%	20%	54.1%	18.4%	7.5%
Reading	5th	Male	2012-13	66.8%	10.5%	56.3%	19.3%	13.9%
Reading	5th	Male	2013-14	69.2%	16.1%	53.1%	20.1%	10.7%
Reading	5th	Economically Disadvantaged	2012-13	57.9%	5.9%	52%	24.3%	17.9%
Reading	5th	Economically Disadvantaged	2013-14	59.4%	9%	50.4%	26.3%	14.3%
Reading	5th	English Language Learners	2012-13	36.3%	1.4%	34.9%	33.3%	30.4%
Reading	5th	English Language Learners	2013-14	39.2%	2%	37.2%	36.5%	24.4%
Reading	5th	Students With Disabilities	2012-13	36.6%	3.5%	33.1%	26.2%	37.2%
Reading	5th	Students With Disabilities	2013-14	41.1%	5.8%	35.3%	30.1%	28.8%
Reading	6th	All Students	2012-13	68.2%	22.7%	45.5%	17.4%	14.4%
Reading	6th	All Students	2013-14	71.5%	22.7%	48.8%	16.4%	12.1%

MI School Data
06/03/2015

Annual Education Report

Statewide

Michigan Educational Assessment Program (MEAP)

Subject	Grade	Testing Group	School Year	State % Students Proficient	% Advanced (Level 1)	% Proficient (Level 2)	% Partially Proficient (Level 3)	% Not Proficient (Level 4)
Reading	6th	American Indian	2012-13	61.1%	16%	45.1%	21.4%	17.5%
Reading	6th	American Indian	2013-14	64.6%	15.9%	48.7%	21%	14.4%
Reading	6th	African American	2012-13	46.4%	8.8%	37.6%	24.5%	29.1%
Reading	6th	African American	2013-14	50%	9.7%	40.4%	24.6%	25.4%
Reading	6th	Asian	2012-13	82.3%	40.9%	41.4%	9.7%	8%
Reading	6th	Asian	2013-14	82.4%	38.7%	43.7%	9.9%	7.6%
Reading	6th	Hispanic of Any Race	2012-13	57.6%	13.5%	44.1%	22.6%	19.7%
Reading	6th	Hispanic of Any Race	2013-14	60.1%	13.3%	46.7%	21.5%	18.5%
Reading	6th	Migrant	2012-13	49.2%	11.9%	37.3%	20.3%	30.5%
Reading	6th	Migrant	2013-14	53.3%	8.4%	44.9%	25.1%	21.6%
Reading	6th	Native Hawaiian or Other Pacific Islander	2012-13	75%	30.7%	44.3%	13.6%	11.4%
Reading	6th	Native Hawaiian or Other Pacific Islander	2013-14	83.1%	25.4%	57.6%	15.3%	1.7%
Reading	6th	Two or More Races	2012-13	67%	22.6%	44.4%	18.4%	14.6%
Reading	6th	Two or More Races	2013-14	70.4%	22.1%	48.3%	18.3%	11.3%
Reading	6th	White	2012-13	74.3%	26.4%	47.9%	15.3%	10.4%
Reading	6th	White	2013-14	77.7%	26.2%	51.4%	14%	8.3%
Reading	6th	Female	2012-13	71.2%	25.1%	46%	16.8%	12.1%
Reading	6th	Female	2013-14	74.7%	24.7%	50%	15.6%	9.8%

MI School Data

06/03/2015

Annual Education Report

Statewide

Michigan Educational Assessment Program (MEAP)

Subject	Grade	Testing Group	School Year	State % Students Proficient	% Advanced (Level 1)	% Proficient (Level 2)	% Partially Proficient (Level 3)	% Not Proficient (Level 4)
Reading	6th	Male	2012-13	65.4%	20.3%	45.1%	17.9%	16.7%
Reading	6th	Male	2013-14	68.4%	20.7%	47.7%	17.2%	14.3%
Reading	6th	Economically Disadvantaged	2012-13	56.4%	13.2%	43.2%	22.1%	21.5%
Reading	6th	Economically Disadvantaged	2013-14	59.2%	12.9%	46.3%	22%	18.8%
Reading	6th	English Language Learners	2012-13	36.7%	4.8%	31.9%	27.8%	35.5%
Reading	6th	English Language Learners	2013-14	36.8%	3.8%	32.9%	28.8%	34.4%
Reading	6th	Students With Disabilities	2012-13	32.8%	6.5%	26.3%	23.1%	44.1%
Reading	6th	Students With Disabilities	2013-14	33.6%	5.5%	28.1%	25.4%	40.9%
Reading	7th	All Students	2012-13	62%	14.1%	47.9%	22.1%	15.9%
Reading	7th	All Students	2013-14	60.4%	15.8%	44.7%	24.4%	15.1%
Reading	7th	American Indian	2012-13	53.1%	8.4%	44.7%	26.3%	20.6%
Reading	7th	American Indian	2013-14	48.9%	8.9%	39.9%	31.3%	19.8%
Reading	7th	African American	2012-13	36.8%	4.5%	32.3%	30.3%	32.9%
Reading	7th	African American	2013-14	34.6%	4.4%	30.1%	32.7%	32.7%
Reading	7th	Asian	2012-13	75.4%	26.6%	48.8%	14.8%	9.8%
Reading	7th	Asian	2013-14	75.2%	33.2%	42.1%	15.3%	9.5%
Reading	7th	Hispanic of Any Race	2012-13	47%	6.7%	40.3%	28.6%	24.3%

MI School Data

06/03/2015

Annual Education Report

Statewide

Michigan Educational Assessment Program (MEAP)

Subject	Grade	Testing Group	School Year	State % Students Proficient	% Advanced (Level 1)	% Proficient (Level 2)	% Partially Proficient (Level 3)	% Not Proficient (Level 4)
Reading	7th	Hispanic of Any Race	2013-14	46.8%	8.2%	38.6%	31.9%	21.4%
Reading	7th	Migrant	2012-13	35.2%	1.6%	33.6%	35.2%	29.6%
Reading	7th	Migrant	2013-14	28.9%	3.5%	25.4%	40.1%	31%
Reading	7th	Native Hawaiian or Other Pacific Islander	2012-13	68.3%	16.7%	51.7%	20%	11.7%
Reading	7th	Native Hawaiian or Other Pacific Islander	2013-14	72.3%	21.3%	51.1%	14.9%	12.8%
Reading	7th	Two or More Races	2012-13	61.8%	13.6%	48.1%	23%	15.2%
Reading	7th	Two or More Races	2013-14	59%	14.7%	44.3%	26.5%	14.5%
Reading	7th	White	2012-13	69.5%	16.8%	52.7%	19.6%	10.9%
Reading	7th	White	2013-14	67.8%	18.7%	49.1%	21.9%	10.3%
Reading	7th	Female	2012-13	65.3%	16.1%	49.1%	21.3%	13.4%
Reading	7th	Female	2013-14	62.5%	17.1%	45.4%	24.3%	13.2%
Reading	7th	Male	2012-13	58.8%	12.1%	46.8%	22.9%	18.3%
Reading	7th	Male	2013-14	58.4%	14.5%	44%	24.6%	17%
Reading	7th	Economically Disadvantaged	2012-13	47.4%	6.7%	40.7%	28%	24.7%
Reading	7th	Economically Disadvantaged	2013-14	45.4%	7.5%	37.9%	30.9%	23.7%
Reading	7th	English Language Learners	2012-13	20.9%	1.2%	19.7%	31.2%	47.9%

MI School Data

06/03/2015

Annual Education Report

Statewide

Michigan Educational Assessment Program (MEAP)

Subject	Grade	Testing Group	School Year	State % Students Proficient	% Advanced (Level 1)	% Proficient (Level 2)	% Partially Proficient (Level 3)	% Not Proficient (Level 4)
Reading	7th	English Language Learners	2013-14	23%	2%	21%	35.7%	41.3%
Reading	7th	Students With Disabilities	2012-13	23%	2.3%	20.6%	27.8%	49.2%
Reading	7th	Students With Disabilities	2013-14	22.9%	3.1%	19.8%	29.8%	47.3%
Reading	8th	All Students	2012-13	65.7%	12.4%	53.3%	24.6%	9.7%
Reading	8th	All Students	2013-14	72.7%	28%	44.7%	17.3%	9.9%
Reading	8th	American Indian	2012-13	58.1%	8.6%	49.4%	29%	12.9%
Reading	8th	American Indian	2013-14	68.7%	18.8%	49.8%	20.8%	10.6%
Reading	8th	African American	2012-13	45.2%	4.3%	40.9%	36.3%	18.6%
Reading	8th	African American	2013-14	49.7%	11.3%	38.5%	28.2%	22%
Reading	8th	Asian	2012-13	79.9%	28.3%	51.6%	13.9%	6.2%
Reading	8th	Asian	2013-14	84.2%	47.3%	36.9%	9.5%	6.3%
Reading	8th	Hispanic of Any Race	2012-13	56.5%	6.9%	49.6%	31.2%	12.3%
Reading	8th	Hispanic of Any Race	2013-14	61.8%	16.7%	45%	23.1%	15.1%
Reading	8th	Migrant	2012-13	50.5%	7.3%	43.1%	29.4%	20.2%
Reading	8th	Migrant	2013-14	49.3%	6.6%	42.8%	28.9%	21.7%
Reading	8th	Native Hawaiian or Other Pacific Islander	2012-13	78.6%	14.3%	64.3%	17.3%	4.1%

MI School Data

06/03/2015

Annual Education Report

Statewide

Michigan Educational Assessment Program (MEAP)

Subject	Grade	Testing Group	School Year	State % Students Proficient	% Advanced (Level 1)	% Proficient (Level 2)	% Partially Proficient (Level 3)	% Not Proficient (Level 4)
Reading	8th	Native Hawaiian or Other Pacific Islander	2013-14	72.2%	32.5%	39.7%	16.7%	11.1%
Reading	8th	Two or More Races	2012-13	65.6%	12.6%	53%	25.4%	9%
Reading	8th	Two or More Races	2013-14	72.5%	27.7%	44.8%	17.4%	10.1%
Reading	8th	White	2012-13	71.2%	14.3%	56.9%	21.4%	7.4%
Reading	8th	White	2013-14	79.2%	32.6%	46.6%	14.3%	6.5%
Reading	8th	Female	2012-13	70.1%	14.4%	55.7%	23%	6.9%
Reading	8th	Female	2013-14	74.6%	28.9%	45.7%	17.1%	8.4%
Reading	8th	Male	2012-13	61.5%	10.4%	51.1%	26.1%	12.5%
Reading	8th	Male	2013-14	70.9%	27.2%	43.7%	17.6%	11.5%
Reading	8th	Economically Disadvantaged	2012-13	53%	6.3%	46.7%	32%	15%
Reading	8th	Economically Disadvantaged	2013-14	60.1%	16.2%	43.8%	23.9%	16%
Reading	8th	English Language Learners	2012-13	31.6%	2.1%	29.5%	41.2%	27.2%
Reading	8th	English Language Learners	2013-14	35.5%	4.9%	30.6%	32.8%	31.7%
Reading	8th	Students With Disabilities	2012-13	26.4%	2%	24.4%	37.3%	36.3%
Reading	8th	Students With Disabilities	2013-14	33.9%	6%	27.8%	29.2%	36.9%
Science	5th	All Students	2012-13	13.1%	4.9%	8.2%	34.7%	52.3%
Science	5th	All Students	2013-14	16.8%	5.9%	10.9%	31.5%	51.7%

MI School Data
06/03/2015

Annual Education Report

Statewide

Michigan Educational Assessment Program (MEAP)

Subject	Grade	Testing Group	School Year	State % Students Proficient	% Advanced (Level 1)	% Proficient (Level 2)	% Partially Proficient (Level 3)	% Not Proficient (Level 4)
Science	5th	American Indian	2012-13	8.4%	2.7%	5.7%	34.1%	57.5%
Science	5th	American Indian	2013-14	12.6%	4.6%	8%	31.1%	56.3%
Science	5th	African American	2012-13	2.6%	0.9%	1.8%	16.4%	81%
Science	5th	African American	2013-14	3.3%	0.8%	2.5%	15.3%	81.4%
Science	5th	Asian	2012-13	26.6%	12.6%	14%	37.9%	35.5%
Science	5th	Asian	2013-14	30.1%	14.3%	15.9%	33.4%	36.4%
Science	5th	Hispanic of Any Race	2012-13	5.4%	1.5%	3.8%	25.9%	68.8%
Science	5th	Hispanic of Any Race	2013-14	7.7%	2.2%	5.5%	23.9%	68.3%
Science	5th	Migrant	2012-13	2.4%	0%	2.4%	20%	77.6%
Science	5th	Migrant	2013-14	1.1%	0%	1.1%	20.6%	78.3%
Science	5th	Native Hawaiian or Other Pacific Islander	2012-13	13%	2.9%	10.1%	36.2%	50.7%
Science	5th	Native Hawaiian or Other Pacific Islander	2013-14	14.6%	9%	5.6%	31.5%	53.9%
Science	5th	Two or More Races	2012-13	12.2%	4.9%	7.3%	34.3%	53.6%
Science	5th	Two or More Races	2013-14	15.2%	5.3%	9.9%	30.8%	54%
Science	5th	White	2012-13	16%	5.9%	10.1%	40.1%	43.9%
Science	5th	White	2013-14	20.7%	7.2%	13.4%	36.3%	43%
Science	5th	Female	2012-13	11.6%	4.2%	7.5%	35.4%	53%
Science	5th	Female	2013-14	15.9%	5.2%	10.7%	32.5%	51.6%

MI School Data
06/03/2015

Annual Education Report

Statewide

Michigan Educational Assessment Program (MEAP)

Subject	Grade	Testing Group	School Year	State % Students Proficient	% Advanced (Level 1)	% Proficient (Level 2)	% Partially Proficient (Level 3)	% Not Proficient (Level 4)
Science	5th	Male	2012-13	14.5%	5.6%	8.9%	33.9%	51.6%
Science	5th	Male	2013-14	17.7%	6.6%	11.1%	30.5%	51.8%
Science	5th	Economically Disadvantaged	2012-13	5.8%	1.8%	4%	26.6%	67.6%
Science	5th	Economically Disadvantaged	2013-14	8%	2.2%	5.8%	24.3%	67.7%
Science	5th	English Language Learners	2012-13	1.4%	0.4%	1.1%	13.2%	85.4%
Science	5th	English Language Learners	2013-14	2.9%	0.9%	1.9%	14.3%	82.8%
Science	5th	Students With Disabilities	2012-13	4.1%	1.6%	2.5%	17.6%	78.3%
Science	5th	Students With Disabilities	2013-14	5.6%	1.9%	3.7%	15.8%	78.7%
Science	8th	All Students	2012-13	15.9%	4%	11.9%	26%	58.1%
Science	8th	All Students	2013-14	19.8%	6.3%	13.5%	25.7%	54.6%
Science	8th	American Indian	2012-13	10.1%	2.1%	7.9%	21.7%	68.2%
Science	8th	American Indian	2013-14	12.8%	2.7%	10.1%	25.1%	62%
Science	8th	African American	2012-13	3.3%	0.5%	2.8%	12.9%	83.8%
Science	8th	African American	2013-14	3.9%	0.8%	3.1%	13.2%	82.9%
Science	8th	Asian	2012-13	31.5%	11.1%	20.4%	30.3%	38.2%
Science	8th	Asian	2013-14	35.6%	15.7%	19.9%	29.6%	34.9%
Science	8th	Hispanic of Any Race	2012-13	7.1%	1.3%	5.7%	20.4%	72.5%

MI School Data

06/03/2015

Annual Education Report

Statewide

Michigan Educational Assessment Program (MEAP)

Subject	Grade	Testing Group	School Year	State % Students Proficient	% Advanced (Level 1)	% Proficient (Level 2)	% Partially Proficient (Level 3)	% Not Proficient (Level 4)
Science	8th	Hispanic of Any Race	2013-14	9.7%	2.4%	7.3%	20%	70.2%
Science	8th	Migrant	2012-13	4.8%	0%	4.8%	14.4%	80.8%
Science	8th	Migrant	2013-14	5.2%	0.6%	4.5%	12.3%	82.6%
Science	8th	Native Hawaiian or Other Pacific Islander	2012-13	22.8%	5.9%	16.8%	34.7%	42.6%
Science	8th	Native Hawaiian or Other Pacific Islander	2013-14	26.8%	7.1%	19.7%	23.6%	49.6%
Science	8th	Two or More Races	2012-13	15.3%	4.1%	11.1%	24.3%	60.4%
Science	8th	Two or More Races	2013-14	17.9%	5.6%	12.3%	25.7%	56.4%
Science	8th	White	2012-13	19.3%	4.9%	14.4%	29.8%	50.9%
Science	8th	White	2013-14	24.2%	7.7%	16.5%	29.2%	46.6%
Science	8th	Female	2012-13	13.7%	3%	10.7%	27.1%	59.2%
Science	8th	Female	2013-14	17.5%	4.9%	12.6%	26.7%	55.8%
Science	8th	Male	2012-13	18%	5%	13%	25%	57%
Science	8th	Male	2013-14	22%	7.6%	14.4%	24.6%	53.4%
Science	8th	Economically Disadvantaged	2012-13	7.4%	1.4%	6%	19.1%	73.5%
Science	8th	Economically Disadvantaged	2013-14	9.4%	2.2%	7.1%	19.7%	70.9%
Science	8th	English Language Learners	2012-13	2.1%	0.2%	1.8%	8.9%	89.1%

MI School Data

06/03/2015

Annual Education Report

Statewide

Michigan Educational Assessment Program (MEAP)

Subject	Grade	Testing Group	School Year	State % Students Proficient	% Advanced (Level 1)	% Proficient (Level 2)	% Partially Proficient (Level 3)	% Not Proficient (Level 4)
Science	8th	English Language Learners	2013-14	2.1%	0.3%	1.8%	9%	88.9%
Science	8th	Students With Disabilities	2012-13	3.5%	0.9%	2.6%	8.5%	88%
Science	8th	Students With Disabilities	2013-14	4.5%	1.2%	3.2%	8.4%	87.1%

Ancestry and Ethnicity

Michigan State Profile

Population: 9,883,640

Ancestry	Population	%
Afghan (108)	174	<0.01
African, Sub-Saharan (43,840)	54,355	0.55
African (31,011)	39,842	0.40
Cape Verdean (124)	177	<0.01
Ethiopian (1,455)	1,696	0.02
Ghanaian (513)	563	0.01
Kenyan (849)	876	0.01
Liberian (780)	830	0.01
Nigerian (3,981)	4,487	0.05
Senegalese (323)	396	<0.01
Sierra Leonean (23)	23	<0.01
Somalian (936)	981	0.01
South African (763)	1,042	0.01
Sudanese (812)	846	0.01
Ugandan (101)	129	<0.01
Zimbabwean (437)	446	0.01
Other Sub-Saharan African (1,732)	2,021	0.02
Albanian (21,347)	22,903	0.23
Alsatian (17)	147	<0.01
American (473,397)	473,397	4.76
Arab (118,517)	152,212	1.53
Arab (30,035)	34,741	0.35
Egyptian (2,685)	3,275	0.03
Iraqi (16,327)	19,942	0.20
Jordanian (3,332)	3,841	0.04
Lebanese (40,452)	57,876	0.58
Moroccan (1,268)	1,643	0.02
Palestinian (3,810)	4,576	0.05
Syrian (4,118)	8,240	0.08
Other Arab (16,490)	18,078	0.18
Armenian (9,378)	17,345	0.17
Assyrian/Chaldean/Syriac (27,439)	33,051	0.33
Australian (1,225)	2,822	0.03
Austrian (4,829)	22,990	0.23
Basque (59)	301	<0.01
Belgian (13,825)	56,212	0.56
Brazilian (1,520)	2,563	0.03
British (15,371)	33,670	0.34
Bulgarian (1,869)	3,473	0.03
Cajun (260)	547	0.01
Canadian (21,090)	50,490	0.51
Carpatho Rusyn (54)	269	<0.01
Celtic (800)	1,510	0.02
Croatian (6,713)	20,547	0.21
Cypriot (53)	82	<0.01
Czech (12,666)	52,092	0.52
Czechoslovakian (7,065)	16,698	0.17
Danish (10,543)	44,243	0.44
Dutch (210,571)	515,229	5.18
Eastern European (7,249)	8,444	0.08
English (287,286)	1,034,184	10.39
Estonian (292)	461	<0.01
European (76,047)	86,424	0.87
Finnish (42,350)	111,010	1.12
French, ex. Basque (74,075)	509,548	5.12
French Canadian (60,597)	177,875	1.79
German (672,071)	2,254,107	22.65
German Russian (176)	417	<0.01
Greek (19,573)	46,165	0.46
Guyanese (142)	366	<0.01
Hungarian (31,666)	104,987	1.05
Icelander (221)	1,022	0.01
Iranian (3,448)	4,305	0.04
Irish (260,092)	1,186,068	11.92
Israeli (1,469)	1,908	0.02
Italian (167,367)	478,974	4.81
Latvian (2,240)	4,265	0.04
Lithuanian (10,723)	31,966	0.32
Luxemburger (265)	781	0.01
Macedonian (6,976)	10,155	0.10
Maltese (5,113)	12,447	0.13
New Zealander (228)	286	<0.01
Northern European (4,876)	5,448	0.05

Ancestry	Population	%
Norwegian (22,747)	87,020	0.87
Pennsylvania German (5,245)	9,478	0.10
Polish (326,853)	900,446	9.05
Portuguese (1,989)	6,093	0.06
Romanian (17,284)	30,320	0.30
Russian (26,497)	78,153	0.79
Scandinavian (5,797)	14,042	0.14
Scotch-Irish (52,590)	156,935	1.58
Scottish (61,687)	245,563	2.47
Serbian (4,264)	9,458	0.10
Slavic (1,896)	6,334	0.06
Slovak (9,078)	27,400	0.28
Slovene (1,407)	4,617	0.05
Soviet Union (52)	52	<0.01
Swedish (39,339)	172,043	1.73
Swiss (4,874)	24,617	0.25
Turkish (1,774)	2,589	0.03
Ukrainian (16,914)	41,842	0.42
Welsh (7,900)	51,799	0.52
West Indian, ex. Hispanic (7,948)	13,682	0.14
Bahamian (221)	326	<0.01
Barbadian (176)	356	<0.01
Belizean (133)	188	<0.01
Bermudan (50)	153	<0.01
British West Indian (177)	301	<0.01
Dutch West Indian (127)	284	<0.01
Haitian (1,351)	2,376	0.02
Jamaican (4,598)	7,188	0.07
Trinidadian/Tobagonian (509)	980	0.01
U.S. Virgin Islander (32)	108	<0.01
West Indian (553)	1,380	0.01
Other West Indian (21)	42	<0.01
Yugoslavian (12,894)	20,532	0.21

Hispanic Origin	Population	%
Hispanic or Latino (of any race)	436,358	4.41
Central American, ex. Mexican	17,785	0.18
Costa Rican	903	0.01
Guatemalan	8,428	0.09
Honduran	2,694	0.03
Nicaraguan	870	0.01
Panamanian	1,359	0.01
Salvadoran	3,401	0.03
Other Central American	130	<0.01
Cuban	9,922	0.10
Dominican Republic	5,012	0.05
Mexican	317,903	3.22
Puerto Rican	37,267	0.38
South American	13,243	0.13
Argentinean	2,113	0.02
Bolivian	512	0.01
Chilean	1,160	0.01
Colombian	3,991	0.04
Ecuadorian	1,312	0.01
Paraguayan	225	<0.01
Peruvian	2,040	0.02
Uruguayan	224	<0.01
Venezuelan	1,496	0.02
Other South American	170	<0.01
Other Hispanic or Latino	35,226	0.36

Race*	Population	%
African-American/Black (1,400,362)	1,505,514	15.23
Not Hispanic (1,383,756)	1,477,071	14.94
Hispanic (16,606)	28,443	0.29
American Indian/Alaska Native (62,007)	139,095	1.41
Not Hispanic (54,665)	123,267	1.25
Hispanic (7,342)	15,828	0.16
Alaska Athabascan (Ala. Nat.) (64)	113	<0.01
Aleut (Alaska Native) (54)	107	<0.01
Apache (379)	1,246	0.01
Arapaho (28)	67	<0.01
Blackfeet (496)	3,911	0.04
Canadian/French Am. Ind. (683)	1,366	0.01
Central American Ind. (137)	194	<0.01
Cherokee (3,396)	17,821	0.18

	Population	%
Cheyenne (39)	175	<0.01
Chickasaw (92)	261	<0.01
Chippewa (23,564)	36,296	0.37
Choctaw (366)	1,463	0.01
Colville (7)	15	<0.01
Comanche (94)	214	<0.01
Cree (82)	358	<0.01
Creek (238)	620	0.01
Crow (18)	169	<0.01
Delaware (127)	308	<0.01
Hopi (21)	66	<0.01
Houma (9)	15	<0.01
Inupiat (Alaska Native) (50)	150	<0.01
Iroquois (1,260)	2,803	0.03
Kiowa (15)	44	<0.01
Lumbee (629)	1,130	0.01
Menominee (103)	212	<0.01
Mexican American Ind. (1,402)	2,219	0.02
Navajo (292)	646	0.01
Osage (30)	110	<0.01
Ottawa (4,297)	7,499	0.08
Paiute (10)	41	<0.01
Pima (18)	36	<0.01
Potawatomi (2,881)	4,901	0.05
Pueblo (78)	150	<0.01
Puget Sound Salish (32)	46	<0.01
Seminole (58)	375	<0.01
Shoshone (29)	77	<0.01
Sioux (614)	1,856	0.02
South American Ind. (141)	348	<0.01
Spanish American Ind. (93)	143	<0.01
Tlingit-Haida (Alaska Native) (67)	123	<0.01
Tohono O'Odham (13)	22	<0.01
Tsimshian (Alaska Native) (10)	22	<0.01
Ute (17)	43	<0.01
Yakama (6)	17	<0.01
Yaqui (61)	119	<0.01
Yuman (5)	22	<0.01
Yup'ik (Alaska Native) (36)	62	<0.01
Asian (238,199)	289,607	2.93
Not Hispanic (236,490)	284,695	2.88
Hispanic (1,709)	4,912	0.05
Bangladeshi (7,965)	8,730	0.09
Bhutanese (360)	443	<0.01
Burmese (1,652)	1,856	0.02
Cambodian (1,658)	2,219	0.02
Chinese, ex. Taiwanese (41,451)	48,302	0.49
Filipino (22,047)	32,324	0.33
Hmong (5,580)	5,924	0.06
Indian (77,132)	84,750	0.86
Indonesian (641)	1,148	0.01
Japanese (10,911)	17,412	0.18
Korean (24,186)	30,292	0.31
Laotian (2,646)	3,380	0.03
Malaysian (447)	629	0.01
Nepalese (722)	847	0.01
Pakistani (9,931)	11,056	0.11
Sri Lankan (757)	887	0.01
Taiwanese (2,926)	3,347	0.03
Thai (1,972)	3,212	0.03
Vietnamese (16,787)	19,456	0.20
Hawaii Native/Pacific Islander (2,604)	9,348	0.09
Not Hispanic (2,170)	7,917	0.08
Hispanic (434)	1,431	0.01
Fijian (36)	77	<0.01
Guamanian/Chamorro (521)	1,072	0.01
Marshallese (28)	47	<0.01
Native Hawaiian (753)	2,708	0.03
Samoan (359)	848	0.01
Tongan (54)	108	<0.01
White (7,803,120)	8,006,969	81.01
Not Hispanic (7,569,939)	7,740,156	78.31
Hispanic (233,181)	266,813	2.70

*Notes: † The Census 2010 population figure is used to calculate the percentages in the Hispanic Origin and Race categories. Ancestry percentages are based on the 2006-2010 American Community Survey population (not shown); ‡ Numbers in parentheses indicate the number of people reporting a single ancestry; * Numbers in parentheses indicate the number of persons reporting this race alone, not in combination with any other race; Please refer to the User Guide for more information.*

County Profiles

Allegan County
Population: 111,408

Ancestry	Population	%
Afghan (0)	0	<0.01
African, Sub-Saharan (67)	90	0.08
African (54)	77	0.07
Cape Verdean (0)	0	<0.01
Ethiopian (13)	13	0.01
Ghanaian (0)	0	<0.01
Kenyan (0)	0	<0.01
Liberian (0)	0	<0.01
Nigerian (0)	0	<0.01
Senegalese (0)	0	<0.01
Sierra Leonean (0)	0	<0.01
Somalian (0)	0	<0.01
South African (0)	0	<0.01
Sudanese (0)	0	<0.01
Ugandan (0)	0	<0.01
Zimbabwean (0)	0	<0.01
Other Sub-Saharan African (0)	0	<0.01
Albanian (29)	37	0.03
Alsatian (0)	0	<0.01
American (6,556)	6,556	5.89
Arab (29)	176	0.16
Arab (6)	6	0.01
Egyptian (0)	0	<0.01
Iraqi (0)	49	0.04
Jordanian (0)	0	<0.01
Lebanese (23)	90	0.08
Moroccan (0)	0	<0.01
Palestinian (0)	0	<0.01
Syrian (0)	31	0.03
Other Arab (0)	0	<0.01
Armenian (39)	59	0.05
Assyrian/Chaldean/Syriac (0)	49	0.04
Australian (19)	27	0.02
Austrian (75)	281	0.25
Basque (0)	0	<0.01
Belgian (58)	162	0.15
Brazilian (0)	0	<0.01
British (125)	259	0.23
Bulgarian (0)	0	<0.01
Cajun (0)	10	0.01
Canadian (109)	194	0.17
Carpatho Rusyn (0)	0	<0.01
Celtic (14)	14	0.01
Croatian (76)	199	0.18
Cypriot (0)	0	<0.01
Czech (185)	626	0.56
Czechoslovakian (69)	113	0.10
Danish (82)	510	0.46
Dutch (14,263)	26,238	23.56
Eastern European (28)	28	0.03
English (3,226)	11,968	10.74
Estonian (0)	0	<0.01
European (991)	1,143	1.03
Finnish (165)	362	0.32
French, ex. Basque (730)	4,262	3.83
French Canadian (464)	1,016	0.91
German (6,365)	26,100	23.43
German Russian (0)	19	0.02
Greek (29)	204	0.18
Guyanese (0)	0	<0.01
Hungarian (188)	779	0.70
Icelander (0)	0	<0.01
Iranian (0)	0	<0.01
Irish (2,308)	12,090	10.85
Israeli (0)	0	<0.01
Italian (603)	2,314	2.08
Latvian (33)	33	0.03
Lithuanian (142)	284	0.25
Luxemburger (0)	0	<0.01
Macedonian (0)	0	<0.01
Maltese (0)	15	0.01
New Zealander (0)	0	<0.01
Northern European (22)	26	0.02
Norwegian (196)	702	0.63
Pennsylvania German (35)	111	0.10
Polish (1,859)	6,025	5.41
Portuguese (0)	64	0.06
Romanian (22)	22	0.02
Russian (51)	383	0.34
Scandinavian (73)	189	0.17
Scotch-Irish (442)	1,399	1.26
Scottish (433)	1,998	1.79
Serbian (0)	0	<0.01
Slavic (28)	71	0.06
Slovak (85)	262	0.24
Slovene (29)	67	0.06
Soviet Union (0)	0	<0.01
Swedish (588)	1,862	1.67
Swiss (20)	168	0.15
Turkish (12)	12	0.01
Ukrainian (21)	118	0.11
Welsh (52)	559	0.50
West Indian, ex. Hispanic (0)	0	<0.01
Bahamian (0)	0	<0.01
Barbadian (0)	0	<0.01
Belizean (0)	0	<0.01
Bermudan (0)	0	<0.01
British West Indian (0)	0	<0.01
Dutch West Indian (0)	0	<0.01
Haitian (0)	0	<0.01
Jamaican (0)	0	<0.01
Trinidadian/Tobagonian (0)	0	<0.01
U.S. Virgin Islander (0)	0	<0.01
West Indian (0)	0	<0.01
Other West Indian (0)	0	<0.01
Yugoslavian (11)	28	0.03

Hispanic Origin	Population	%
Hispanic or Latino (of any race)	7,454	6.69
Central American, ex. Mexican	149	0.13
Costa Rican	3	<0.01
Guatemalan	80	0.07
Honduran	30	0.03
Nicaraguan	5	<0.01
Panamanian	6	0.01
Salvadoran	25	0.02
Other Central American	0	<0.01
Cuban	55	0.05
Dominican Republic	21	0.02
Mexican	6,320	5.67
Puerto Rican	342	0.31
South American	87	0.08
Argentinean	3	<0.01
Bolivian	0	<0.01
Chilean	7	0.01
Colombian	41	0.04
Ecuadorian	15	0.01
Paraguayan	2	<0.01
Peruvian	13	0.01
Uruguayan	3	<0.01
Venezuelan	2	<0.01
Other South American	1	<0.01
Other Hispanic or Latino	480	0.43

Race*	Population	%
African-American/Black (1,358)	2,062	1.85
Not Hispanic (1,264)	1,878	1.69
Hispanic (94)	184	0.17
American Indian/Alaska Native (636)	1,439	1.29
Not Hispanic (543)	1,218	1.09
Hispanic (93)	221	0.20
Alaska Athabascan (Ala. Nat.) (0)	0	<0.01
Aleut (Alaska Native) (0)	0	<0.01
Apache (2)	24	0.02
Arapaho (0)	0	<0.01
Blackfeet (5)	28	0.03
Canadian/French Am. Ind. (1)	3	<0.01
Central American Ind. (2)	3	<0.01

	Population	%
Cherokee (44)	158	0.14
Cheyenne (1)	1	<0.01
Chickasaw (2)	5	<0.01
Chippewa (161)	259	0.23
Choctaw (1)	21	0.02
Colville (0)	0	<0.01
Comanche (0)	0	<0.01
Cree (2)	5	<0.01
Creek (1)	2	<0.01
Crow (0)	2	<0.01
Delaware (0)	0	<0.01
Hopi (0)	0	<0.01
Houma (0)	0	<0.01
Inupiat (Alaska Native) (0)	0	<0.01
Iroquois (6)	11	0.01
Kiowa (0)	0	<0.01
Lumbee (2)	5	<0.01
Menominee (0)	0	<0.01
Mexican American Ind. (13)	25	0.02
Navajo (0)	6	0.01
Osage (1)	6	0.01
Ottawa (52)	98	0.09
Paiute (0)	0	<0.01
Pima (0)	3	<0.01
Potawatomi (123)	206	0.18
Pueblo (0)	0	<0.01
Puget Sound Salish (0)	0	<0.01
Seminole (0)	0	<0.01
Shoshone (1)	2	<0.01
Sioux (17)	33	0.03
South American Ind. (1)	1	<0.01
Spanish American Ind. (0)	0	<0.01
Tlingit-Haida (Alaska Native) (0)	0	<0.01
Tohono O'Odham (0)	0	<0.01
Tsimshian (Alaska Native) (2)	2	<0.01
Ute (0)	0	<0.01
Yakama (0)	0	<0.01
Yaqui (0)	0	<0.01
Yuman (0)	0	<0.01
Yup'ik (Alaska Native) (0)	0	<0.01
Asian (648)	942	0.85
Not Hispanic (620)	878	0.79
Hispanic (28)	64	0.06
Bangladeshi (1)	1	<0.01
Bhutanese (0)	0	<0.01
Burmese (7)	11	0.01
Cambodian (55)	70	0.06
Chinese, ex. Taiwanese (87)	117	0.11
Filipino (68)	126	0.11
Hmong (0)	0	<0.01
Indian (55)	72	0.06
Indonesian (4)	12	0.01
Japanese (19)	61	0.05
Korean (136)	173	0.16
Laotian (76)	99	0.09
Malaysian (0)	0	<0.01
Nepalese (0)	0	<0.01
Pakistani (2)	5	<0.01
Sri Lankan (0)	0	<0.01
Taiwanese (2)	2	<0.01
Thai (16)	25	0.02
Vietnamese (82)	113	0.10
Hawaii Native/Pacific Islander (22)	86	0.08
Not Hispanic (21)	68	0.06
Hispanic (1)	18	0.02
Fijian (0)	0	<0.01
Guamanian/Chamorro (1)	2	<0.01
Marshallese (2)	2	<0.01
Native Hawaiian (7)	39	0.04
Samoan (7)	10	0.01
Tongan (0)	0	<0.01
White (103,513)	105,552	94.74
Not Hispanic (99,945)	101,384	91.00
Hispanic (3,568)	4,168	3.74

*Notes: † The Census 2010 population figure is used to calculate the percentages in the Hispanic Origin and Race categories. Ancestry percentages are based on the 2006-2010 American Community Survey population (not shown); ‡ Numbers in parentheses indicate the number of people reporting a single ancestry; * Numbers in parentheses indicate the number of persons reporting this race alone, not in combination with any other race; Please refer to the User Guide for more information.*

Barry County

Population: 59,173

Ancestry	Population	%
Afghan (0)	0	<0.01
African, Sub-Saharan (97)	97	0.16
African (97)	97	0.16
Cape Verdean (0)	0	<0.01
Ethiopian (0)	0	<0.01
Ghanaian (0)	0	<0.01
Kenyan (0)	0	<0.01
Liberian (0)	0	<0.01
Nigerian (0)	0	<0.01
Senegalese (0)	0	<0.01
Sierra Leonean (0)	0	<0.01
Somalian (0)	0	<0.01
South African (0)	0	<0.01
Sudanese (0)	0	<0.01
Ugandan (0)	0	<0.01
Zimbabwean (0)	0	<0.01
Other Sub-Saharan African (0)	0	<0.01
Albanian (0)	0	<0.01
Alsatian (0)	0	<0.01
American (9,231)	9,231	15.49
Arab (49)	61	0.10
Arab (9)	9	0.02
Egyptian (0)	0	<0.01
Iraqi (0)	0	<0.01
Jordanian (0)	0	<0.01
Lebanese (37)	40	0.07
Moroccan (0)	0	<0.01
Palestinian (3)	3	0.01
Syrian (0)	1	<0.01
Other Arab (0)	8	0.01
Armenian (11)	11	0.02
Assyrian/Chaldean/Syriac (0)	0	<0.01
Australian (0)	29	0.05
Austrian (36)	51	0.09
Basque (0)	0	<0.01
Belgian (15)	58	0.10
Brazilian (0)	0	<0.01
British (93)	186	0.31
Bulgarian (65)	65	0.11
Cajun (0)	0	<0.01
Canadian (43)	95	0.16
Carpatho Rusyn (0)	0	<0.01
Celtic (0)	0	<0.01
Croatian (22)	146	0.25
Cypriot (0)	0	<0.01
Czech (36)	184	0.31
Czechoslovakian (8)	61	0.10
Danish (182)	681	1.14
Dutch (3,313)	7,543	12.66
Eastern European (30)	43	0.07
English (2,831)	8,532	14.32
Estonian (0)	0	<0.01
European (470)	504	0.85
Finnish (89)	194	0.33
French, ex. Basque (319)	3,134	5.26
French Canadian (275)	730	1.23
German (4,776)	14,469	24.29
German Russian (0)	0	<0.01
Greek (7)	106	0.18
Guyanese (0)	0	<0.01
Hungarian (60)	177	0.30
Icelander (0)	0	<0.01
Iranian (0)	0	<0.01
Irish (1,594)	7,118	11.95
Israeli (0)	0	<0.01
Italian (515)	1,371	2.30
Latvian (9)	9	0.02
Lithuanian (102)	192	0.32
Luxemburger (3)	3	0.01
Macedonian (0)	0	<0.01
Maltese (0)	27	0.05
New Zealander (0)	0	<0.01
Northern European (37)	37	0.06
Norwegian (132)	579	0.97
Pennsylvania German (20)	84	0.14

Ancestry	Population	%
Polish (720)	2,252	3.78
Portuguese (19)	33	0.06
Romanian (3)	16	0.03
Russian (24)	78	0.13
Scandinavian (0)	9	0.02
Scotch-Irish (322)	871	1.46
Scottish (383)	1,395	2.34
Serbian (0)	0	<0.01
Slavic (0)	13	0.02
Slovak (0)	18	0.03
Slovene (0)	26	0.04
Soviet Union (0)	0	<0.01
Swedish (226)	1,017	1.71
Swiss (18)	229	0.38
Turkish (0)	0	<0.01
Ukrainian (20)	20	0.03
Welsh (88)	461	0.77
West Indian, ex. Hispanic (0)	0	<0.01
Bahamian (0)	0	<0.01
Barbadian (0)	0	<0.01
Belizean (0)	0	<0.01
Bermudan (0)	0	<0.01
British West Indian (0)	0	<0.01
Dutch West Indian (0)	0	<0.01
Haitian (0)	0	<0.01
Jamaican (0)	0	<0.01
Trinidadian/Tobagonian (0)	0	<0.01
U.S. Virgin Islander (0)	0	<0.01
West Indian (0)	0	<0.01
Other West Indian (0)	0	<0.01
Yugoslavian (0)	0	<0.01

Hispanic Origin	Population	%
Hispanic or Latino (of any race)	1,336	2.26
Central American, ex. Mexican	46	0.08
Costa Rican	1	<0.01
Guatemalan	16	0.03
Honduran	9	0.02
Nicaraguan	7	0.01
Panamanian	2	<0.01
Salvadoran	11	0.02
Other Central American	0	<0.01
Cuban	12	0.02
Dominican Republic	8	0.01
Mexican	977	1.65
Puerto Rican	117	0.20
South American	45	0.08
Argentinean	4	0.01
Bolivian	0	<0.01
Chilean	2	<0.01
Colombian	34	0.06
Ecuadorian	2	<0.01
Paraguayan	0	<0.01
Peruvian	0	<0.01
Uruguayan	1	<0.01
Venezuelan	2	<0.01
Other South American	0	<0.01
Other Hispanic or Latino	131	0.22

Race*	Population	%
African-American/Black (219)	459	0.78
Not Hispanic (205)	430	0.73
Hispanic (14)	29	0.05
American Indian/Alaska Native (272)	654	1.11
Not Hispanic (251)	591	1.00
Hispanic (21)	63	0.11
Alaska Athabascan (Ala. Nat.) (0)	0	<0.01
Aleut (Alaska Native) (1)	1	<0.01
Apache (0)	7	0.01
Arapaho (0)	0	<0.01
Blackfeet (1)	14	0.02
Canadian/French Am. Ind. (2)	3	0.01
Central American Ind. (0)	0	<0.01
Cherokee (22)	92	0.16
Cheyenne (0)	0	<0.01
Chickasaw (0)	0	<0.01
Chippewa (77)	118	0.20
Choctaw (3)	4	0.01
Colville (0)	0	<0.01

Race*	Population	%
Comanche (1)	1	<0.01
Cree (4)	5	0.01
Creek (0)	1	<0.01
Crow (0)	1	<0.01
Delaware (3)	3	0.01
Hopi (0)	1	<0.01
Houma (0)	0	<0.01
Inupiat (Alaska Native) (0)	0	<0.01
Iroquois (5)	15	0.03
Kiowa (0)	0	<0.01
Lumbee (2)	2	<0.01
Menominee (0)	0	<0.01
Mexican American Ind. (3)	8	0.01
Navajo (1)	3	<0.01
Osage (0)	0	<0.01
Ottawa (18)	40	0.07
Paiute (0)	0	<0.01
Pima (0)	0	<0.01
Potawatomi (39)	72	0.12
Pueblo (0)	0	<0.01
Puget Sound Salish (0)	0	<0.01
Seminole (0)	1	<0.01
Shoshone (0)	0	<0.01
Sioux (8)	14	0.02
South American Ind. (0)	0	<0.01
Spanish American Ind. (0)	0	<0.01
Tlingit-Haida (Alaska Native) (0)	0	<0.01
Tohono O'Odham (0)	0	<0.01
Tsimshian (Alaska Native) (0)	0	<0.01
Ute (0)	0	<0.01
Yakama (0)	0	<0.01
Yaqui (1)	1	<0.01
Yuman (0)	0	<0.01
Yup'ik (Alaska Native) (0)	0	<0.01
Asian (219)	342	0.58
Not Hispanic (212)	322	0.54
Hispanic (7)	20	0.03
Bangladeshi (2)	2	<0.01
Bhutanese (0)	0	<0.01
Burmese (7)	7	0.01
Cambodian (1)	3	0.01
Chinese, ex. Taiwanese (32)	47	0.08
Filipino (39)	63	0.11
Hmong (2)	2	<0.01
Indian (23)	30	0.05
Indonesian (4)	4	0.01
Japanese (17)	37	0.06
Korean (59)	95	0.16
Laotian (6)	6	0.01
Malaysian (0)	0	<0.01
Nepalese (0)	0	<0.01
Pakistani (0)	7	0.01
Sri Lankan (0)	0	<0.01
Taiwanese (0)	0	<0.01
Thai (2)	4	0.01
Vietnamese (15)	26	0.04
Hawaii Native/Pacific Islander (6)	18	0.03
Not Hispanic (5)	14	0.02
Hispanic (1)	4	0.01
Fijian (0)	0	<0.01
Guamanian/Chamorro (2)	4	0.01
Marshallese (0)	0	<0.01
Native Hawaiian (2)	7	0.01
Samoan (0)	0	<0.01
Tongan (0)	0	<0.01
White (57,350)	58,105	98.20
Not Hispanic (56,487)	57,130	96.55
Hispanic (863)	975	1.65

*Notes: † The Census 2010 population figure is used to calculate the percentages in the Hispanic Origin and Race categories. Ancestry percentages are based on the 2006-2010 American Community Survey population (not shown); ‡ Numbers in parentheses indicate the number of people reporting a single ancestry; * Numbers in parentheses indicate the number of persons reporting this race alone, not in combination with any other race; Please refer to the User Guide for more information.*

Bay County

Population: 107,771

Ancestry	Population	%
Afghan (0)	0	<0.01
African, Sub-Saharan (189)	249	0.23
African (128)	188	0.17
Cape Verdean (0)	0	<0.01
Ethiopian (9)	9	0.01
Ghanaian (0)	0	<0.01
Kenyan (52)	52	0.05
Liberian (0)	0	<0.01
Nigerian (0)	0	<0.01
Senegalese (0)	0	<0.01
Sierra Leonean (0)	0	<0.01
Somalian (0)	0	<0.01
South African (0)	0	<0.01
Sudanese (0)	0	<0.01
Ugandan (0)	0	<0.01
Zimbabwean (0)	0	<0.01
Other Sub-Saharan African (0)	0	<0.01
Albanian (18)	33	0.03
Alsatian (0)	0	<0.01
American (4,302)	4,302	3.98
Arab (152)	290	0.27
Arab (64)	82	0.08
Egyptian (0)	12	0.01
Iraqi (0)	0	<0.01
Jordanian (0)	0	<0.01
Lebanese (80)	169	0.16
Moroccan (0)	0	<0.01
Palestinian (0)	11	0.01
Syrian (0)	8	0.01
Other Arab (8)	8	0.01
Armenian (53)	64	0.06
Assyrian/Chaldean/Syriac (2)	2	<0.01
Australian (0)	21	0.02
Austrian (44)	159	0.15
Basque (0)	0	<0.01
Belgian (66)	451	0.42
Brazilian (0)	0	<0.01
British (78)	210	0.19
Bulgarian (29)	46	0.04
Cajun (0)	0	<0.01
Canadian (333)	608	0.56
Carpatho Rusyn (0)	0	<0.01
Celtic (0)	0	<0.01
Croatian (28)	78	0.07
Cypriot (0)	0	<0.01
Czech (84)	626	0.58
Czechoslovakian (75)	114	0.11
Danish (50)	118	0.11
Dutch (662)	3,180	2.94
Eastern European (13)	24	0.02
English (2,383)	9,254	8.56
Estonian (13)	13	0.01
European (250)	270	0.25
Finnish (185)	479	0.44
French, ex. Basque (3,133)	14,792	13.68
French Canadian (2,017)	4,293	3.97
German (13,746)	34,862	32.23
German Russian (11)	11	0.01
Greek (60)	361	0.33
Guyanese (0)	0	<0.01
Hungarian (517)	1,593	1.47
Icelander (0)	0	<0.01
Iranian (6)	6	0.01
Irish (4,067)	13,856	12.81
Israeli (0)	0	<0.01
Italian (1,072)	2,802	2.59
Latvian (0)	0	<0.01
Lithuanian (105)	238	0.22
Luxemburger (0)	0	<0.01
Macedonian (0)	0	<0.01
Maltese (0)	0	<0.01
New Zealander (0)	0	<0.01
Northern European (30)	30	0.03
Norwegian (112)	459	0.42
Pennsylvania German (26)	71	0.07

Ancestry (cont.)	Population	%
Polish (10,027)	22,193	20.52
Portuguese (13)	13	0.01
Romanian (10)	68	0.06
Russian (205)	566	0.52
Scandinavian (91)	151	0.14
Scotch-Irish (476)	1,479	1.37
Scottish (695)	2,242	2.07
Serbian (0)	12	0.01
Slavic (0)	16	0.01
Slovak (24)	91	0.08
Slovene (13)	36	0.03
Soviet Union (0)	0	<0.01
Swedish (237)	1,213	1.12
Swiss (81)	531	0.49
Turkish (0)	0	<0.01
Ukrainian (37)	202	0.19
Welsh (109)	422	0.39
West Indian, ex. Hispanic (0)	0	<0.01
Bahamian (0)	0	<0.01
Barbadian (0)	0	<0.01
Belizean (0)	0	<0.01
Bermudan (0)	0	<0.01
British West Indian (0)	0	<0.01
Dutch West Indian (0)	0	<0.01
Haitian (0)	0	<0.01
Jamaican (0)	0	<0.01
Trinidadian/Tobagonian (0)	0	<0.01
U.S. Virgin Islander (0)	0	<0.01
West Indian (0)	0	<0.01
Other West Indian (0)	0	<0.01
Yugoslavian (42)	89	0.08

Hispanic Origin	Population	%
Hispanic or Latino (of any race)	5,093	4.73
Central American, ex. Mexican	32	0.03
Costa Rican	5	<0.01
Guatemalan	7	0.01
Honduran	7	0.01
Nicaraguan	2	<0.01
Panamanian	7	0.01
Salvadoran	4	<0.01
Other Central American	0	<0.01
Cuban	37	0.03
Dominican Republic	20	0.02
Mexican	4,376	4.06
Puerto Rican	95	0.09
South American	59	0.05
Argentinean	7	0.01
Bolivian	1	<0.01
Chilean	7	0.01
Colombian	23	0.02
Ecuadorian	9	0.01
Paraguayan	3	<0.01
Peruvian	4	<0.01
Uruguayan	0	<0.01
Venezuelan	5	<0.01
Other South American	0	<0.01
Other Hispanic or Latino	474	0.44

Race*	Population	%
African-American/Black (1,702)	2,751	2.55
Not Hispanic (1,574)	2,498	2.32
Hispanic (128)	253	0.23
American Indian/Alaska Native (564)	1,390	1.29
Not Hispanic (476)	1,152	1.07
Hispanic (88)	238	0.22
Alaska Athabascan (Ala. Nat.) (1)	5	<0.01
Aleut (Alaska Native) (1)	4	<0.01
Apache (1)	15	0.01
Arapaho (0)	1	<0.01
Blackfeet (0)	26	0.02
Canadian/French Am. Ind. (5)	18	0.02
Central American Ind. (0)	0	<0.01
Cherokee (30)	128	0.12
Cheyenne (0)	1	<0.01
Chickasaw (0)	3	<0.01
Chippewa (253)	497	0.46
Choctaw (3)	10	0.01
Colville (0)	0	<0.01

Race* (cont.)	Population	%
Comanche (0)	3	<0.01
Cree (1)	4	<0.01
Creek (0)	0	<0.01
Crow (1)	2	<0.01
Delaware (0)	0	<0.01
Hopi (4)	8	0.01
Houma (0)	0	<0.01
Inupiat (Alaska Native) (0)	0	<0.01
Iroquois (10)	18	0.02
Kiowa (4)	4	<0.01
Lumbee (1)	4	<0.01
Menominee (1)	1	<0.01
Mexican American Ind. (9)	15	0.01
Navajo (2)	5	<0.01
Osage (0)	0	<0.01
Ottawa (17)	54	0.05
Paiute (0)	0	<0.01
Pima (0)	0	<0.01
Potawatomi (15)	21	0.02
Pueblo (0)	5	<0.01
Puget Sound Salish (0)	0	<0.01
Seminole (0)	1	<0.01
Shoshone (0)	0	<0.01
Sioux (4)	16	0.01
South American Ind. (0)	1	<0.01
Spanish American Ind. (0)	0	<0.01
Tlingit-Haida (Alaska Native) (1)	1	<0.01
Tohono O'Odham (0)	0	<0.01
Tsimshian (Alaska Native) (2)	2	<0.01
Ute (0)	0	<0.01
Yakama (0)	0	<0.01
Yaqui (0)	0	<0.01
Yuman (0)	1	<0.01
Yup'ik (Alaska Native) (0)	0	<0.01
Asian (578)	806	0.75
Not Hispanic (566)	763	0.71
Hispanic (12)	43	0.04
Bangladeshi (2)	2	<0.01
Bhutanese (0)	0	<0.01
Burmese (0)	0	<0.01
Cambodian (7)	7	0.01
Chinese, ex. Taiwanese (78)	105	0.10
Filipino (81)	149	0.14
Hmong (30)	32	0.03
Indian (116)	132	0.12
Indonesian (4)	7	0.01
Japanese (20)	51	0.05
Korean (89)	132	0.12
Laotian (10)	13	0.01
Malaysian (3)	3	<0.01
Nepalese (11)	14	0.01
Pakistani (39)	41	0.04
Sri Lankan (0)	0	<0.01
Taiwanese (0)	0	<0.01
Thai (11)	21	0.02
Vietnamese (55)	63	0.06
Hawaii Native/Pacific Islander (14)	38	0.04
Not Hispanic (13)	34	0.03
Hispanic (1)	4	<0.01
Fijian (0)	0	<0.01
Guamanian/Chamorro (0)	0	<0.01
Marshallese (0)	0	<0.01
Native Hawaiian (7)	17	0.02
Samoan (3)	10	0.01
Tongan (0)	0	<0.01
White (101,451)	103,772	96.29
Not Hispanic (98,241)	99,952	92.74
Hispanic (3,210)	3,820	3.54

*Notes: † The Census 2010 population figure is used to calculate the percentages in the Hispanic Origin and Race categories. Ancestry percentages are based on the 2006-2010 American Community Survey population (not shown); ‡ Numbers in parentheses indicate the number of people reporting a single ancestry; * Numbers in parentheses indicate the number of persons reporting this race alone, not in combination with any other race; Please refer to the User Guide for more information.*

Berrien County

Population: 156,813

Ancestry	Population	%
Afghan (0)	0	<0.01
African, Sub-Saharan (881)	1,114	0.71
African (769)	981	0.62
Cape Verdean (0)	0	<0.01
Ethiopian (0)	0	<0.01
Ghanaian (11)	11	0.01
Kenyan (15)	15	0.01
Liberian (0)	0	<0.01
Nigerian (0)	15	0.01
Senegalese (0)	0	<0.01
Sierra Leonean (0)	0	<0.01
Somalian (0)	0	<0.01
South African (25)	25	0.02
Sudanese (0)	0	<0.01
Ugandan (0)	0	<0.01
Zimbabwean (8)	8	0.01
Other Sub-Saharan African (53)	59	0.04
Albanian (0)	9	0.01
Alsatian (0)	0	<0.01
American (8,561)	8,561	5.44
Arab (89)	172	0.11
Arab (6)	51	0.03
Egyptian (12)	12	0.01
Iraqi (8)	8	0.01
Jordanian (21)	21	0.01
Lebanese (11)	33	0.02
Moroccan (0)	0	<0.01
Palestinian (0)	0	<0.01
Syrian (31)	47	0.03
Other Arab (0)	0	<0.01
Armenian (69)	124	0.08
Assyrian/Chaldean/Syriac (43)	43	0.03
Australian (129)	151	0.10
Austrian (144)	469	0.30
Basque (0)	0	<0.01
Belgian (130)	390	0.25
Brazilian (91)	174	0.11
British (205)	430	0.27
Bulgarian (11)	22	0.01
Cajun (0)	0	<0.01
Canadian (207)	451	0.29
Carpatho Rusyn (0)	0	<0.01
Celtic (5)	38	0.02
Croatian (224)	554	0.35
Cypriot (0)	0	<0.01
Czech (495)	1,367	0.87
Czechoslovakian (94)	242	0.15
Danish (292)	866	0.55
Dutch (1,682)	7,003	4.45
Eastern European (53)	60	0.04
English (4,060)	15,346	9.76
Estonian (25)	25	0.02
European (1,278)	1,475	0.94
Finnish (176)	523	0.33
French, ex. Basque (676)	4,606	2.93
French Canadian (282)	1,014	0.64
German (22,693)	51,419	32.70
German Russian (9)	12	0.01
Greek (156)	322	0.20
Guyanese (0)	16	0.01
Hungarian (441)	1,457	0.93
Icelander (0)	6	<0.01
Iranian (8)	25	0.02
Irish (4,393)	20,430	12.99
Israeli (6)	18	0.01
Italian (2,002)	6,486	4.13
Latvian (0)	94	0.06
Lithuanian (394)	745	0.47
Luxemburger (0)	13	0.01
Macedonian (0)	12	0.01
Maltese (12)	12	0.01
New Zealander (0)	0	<0.01
Northern European (38)	46	0.03
Norwegian (317)	1,394	0.89
Pennsylvania German (101)	253	0.16

Ancestry	Population	%
Polish (2,743)	7,899	5.02
Portuguese (23)	72	0.05
Romanian (63)	103	0.07
Russian (278)	1,291	0.82
Scandinavian (127)	429	0.27
Scotch-Irish (934)	2,243	1.43
Scottish (677)	2,754	1.75
Serbian (61)	129	0.08
Slavic (25)	100	0.06
Slovak (84)	174	0.11
Slovene (47)	94	0.06
Soviet Union (0)	0	<0.01
Swedish (963)	3,184	2.03
Swiss (63)	315	0.20
Turkish (0)	9	0.01
Ukrainian (210)	474	0.30
Welsh (105)	886	0.56
West Indian, ex. Hispanic (518)	769	0.49
Bahamian (0)	13	0.01
Barbadian (11)	13	0.01
Belizean (15)	18	0.01
Bermudan (0)	0	<0.01
British West Indian (51)	62	0.04
Dutch West Indian (0)	0	<0.01
Haitian (200)	215	0.14
Jamaican (173)	321	0.20
Trinidadian/Tobagonian (16)	57	0.04
U.S. Virgin Islander (0)	5	<0.01
West Indian (40)	53	0.03
Other West Indian (12)	12	0.01
Yugoslavian (100)	185	0.12

Hispanic Origin	Population	%
Hispanic or Latino (of any race)	7,054	4.50
Central American, ex. Mexican	256	0.16
Costa Rican	28	0.02
Guatemalan	51	0.03
Honduran	35	0.02
Nicaraguan	40	0.03
Panamanian	55	0.04
Salvadoran	45	0.03
Other Central American	2	<0.01
Cuban	162	0.10
Dominican Republic	136	0.09
Mexican	4,759	3.03
Puerto Rican	700	0.45
South American	479	0.31
Argentinean	70	0.04
Bolivian	17	0.01
Chilean	71	0.05
Colombian	132	0.08
Ecuadorian	36	0.02
Paraguayan	4	<0.01
Peruvian	77	0.05
Uruguayan	13	0.01
Venezuelan	54	0.03
Other South American	5	<0.01
Other Hispanic or Latino	562	0.36

Race*	Population	%
African-American/Black (24,037)	25,882	16.51
Not Hispanic (23,766)	25,455	16.23
Hispanic (271)	427	0.27
American Indian/Alaska Native (834)	2,077	1.32
Not Hispanic (765)	1,898	1.21
Hispanic (69)	179	0.11
Alaska Athabascan (Ala. Nat.) (0)	0	<0.01
Aleut (Alaska Native) (3)	3	<0.01
Apache (4)	17	0.01
Arapaho (0)	1	<0.01
Blackfeet (4)	70	0.04
Canadian/French Am. Ind. (9)	16	0.01
Central American Ind. (0)	2	<0.01
Cherokee (81)	426	0.27
Cheyenne (0)	0	<0.01
Chickasaw (2)	4	<0.01
Chippewa (108)	163	0.10
Choctaw (10)	30	0.02
Colville (0)	0	<0.01

Race*	Population	%
Comanche (5)	5	<0.01
Cree (1)	9	0.01
Creek (2)	4	<0.01
Crow (0)	1	<0.01
Delaware (2)	3	<0.01
Hopi (0)	0	<0.01
Houma (1)	2	<0.01
Inupiat (Alaska Native) (1)	1	<0.01
Iroquois (10)	19	0.01
Kiowa (0)	0	<0.01
Lumbee (0)	1	<0.01
Menominee (1)	3	<0.01
Mexican American Ind. (11)	16	0.01
Navajo (2)	4	<0.01
Osage (0)	0	<0.01
Ottawa (19)	39	0.02
Paiute (0)	0	<0.01
Pima (0)	0	<0.01
Potawatomi (299)	453	0.29
Pueblo (3)	4	<0.01
Puget Sound Salish (0)	5	<0.01
Seminole (0)	5	<0.01
Shoshone (0)	0	<0.01
Sioux (6)	31	0.02
South American Ind. (5)	6	<0.01
Spanish American Ind. (2)	2	<0.01
Tlingit-Haida (Alaska Native) (0)	1	<0.01
Tohono O'Odham (0)	0	<0.01
Tsimshian (Alaska Native) (0)	0	<0.01
Ute (0)	0	<0.01
Yakama (0)	0	<0.01
Yaqui (1)	3	<0.01
Yuman (0)	0	<0.01
Yup'ik (Alaska Native) (0)	0	<0.01
Asian (2,451)	3,196	2.04
Not Hispanic (2,410)	3,072	1.96
Hispanic (41)	124	0.08
Bangladeshi (48)	53	0.03
Bhutanese (0)	0	<0.01
Burmese (7)	15	0.01
Cambodian (1)	1	<0.01
Chinese, ex. Taiwanese (357)	478	0.30
Filipino (300)	492	0.31
Hmong (5)	5	<0.01
Indian (720)	848	0.54
Indonesian (82)	104	0.07
Japanese (72)	192	0.12
Korean (608)	693	0.44
Laotian (22)	27	0.02
Malaysian (29)	37	0.02
Nepalese (1)	2	<0.01
Pakistani (41)	43	0.03
Sri Lankan (0)	4	<0.01
Taiwanese (9)	10	0.01
Thai (24)	40	0.03
Vietnamese (63)	96	0.06
Hawaii Native/Pacific Islander (118)	239	0.15
Not Hispanic (115)	211	0.13
Hispanic (3)	28	0.02
Fijian (3)	9	0.01
Guamanian/Chamorro (4)	11	0.01
Marshallese (0)	0	<0.01
Native Hawaiian (21)	67	0.04
Samoan (63)	89	0.06
Tongan (20)	23	0.01
White (122,804)	126,169	80.46
Not Hispanic (119,389)	122,248	77.96
Hispanic (3,415)	3,921	2.50

*Notes: † The Census 2010 population figure is used to calculate the percentages in the Hispanic Origin and Race categories. Ancestry percentages are based on the 2006-2010 American Community Survey population (not shown); ‡ Numbers in parentheses indicate the number of people reporting a single ancestry; * Numbers in parentheses indicate the number of persons reporting this race alone, not in combination with any other race; Please refer to the User Guide for more information.*

Calhoun County

Population: 136,146

Ancestry	Population	%
Afghan (0)	0	<0.01
African, Sub-Saharan (134)	196	0.14
African (58)	120	0.09
Cape Verdean (4)	4	<0.01
Ethiopian (0)	0	<0.01
Ghanaian (0)	0	<0.01
Kenyan (9)	9	0.01
Liberian (0)	0	<0.01
Nigerian (0)	0	<0.01
Senegalese (0)	0	<0.01
Sierra Leonean (0)	0	<0.01
Somalian (0)	0	<0.01
South African (31)	31	0.02
Sudanese (0)	0	<0.01
Ugandan (9)	9	0.01
Zimbabwean (23)	23	0.02
Other Sub-Saharan African (0)	0	<0.01
Albanian (20)	20	0.01
Alsatian (0)	0	<0.01
American (10,604)	10,604	7.73
Arab (160)	218	0.16
Arab (59)	80	0.06
Egyptian (0)	0	<0.01
Iraqi (0)	0	<0.01
Jordanian (0)	0	<0.01
Lebanese (73)	98	0.07
Moroccan (9)	9	0.01
Palestinian (10)	22	0.02
Syrian (9)	9	0.01
Other Arab (0)	0	<0.01
Armenian (45)	144	0.11
Assyrian/Chaldean/Syriac (0)	0	<0.01
Australian (10)	92	0.07
Austrian (20)	136	0.10
Basque (10)	10	0.01
Belgian (72)	344	0.25
Brazilian (34)	34	0.02
British (199)	477	0.35
Bulgarian (52)	60	0.04
Cajun (0)	0	<0.01
Canadian (217)	458	0.33
Carpatho Rusyn (0)	0	<0.01
Celtic (6)	54	0.04
Croatian (84)	195	0.14
Cypriot (0)	0	<0.01
Czech (64)	266	0.19
Czechoslovakian (32)	73	0.05
Danish (54)	357	0.26
Dutch (1,965)	6,258	4.56
Eastern European (0)	0	<0.01
English (6,993)	18,388	13.41
Estonian (0)	0	<0.01
European (1,167)	1,333	0.97
Finnish (102)	441	0.32
French, ex. Basque (993)	5,014	3.66
French Canadian (529)	1,334	0.97
German (12,214)	31,303	22.83
German Russian (0)	0	<0.01
Greek (231)	384	0.28
Guyanese (0)	0	<0.01
Hungarian (343)	821	0.60
Icelander (0)	8	0.01
Iranian (6)	6	<0.01
Irish (4,583)	15,541	11.33
Israeli (0)	0	<0.01
Italian (1,098)	2,903	2.12
Latvian (16)	39	0.03
Lithuanian (106)	249	0.18
Luxemburger (0)	0	<0.01
Macedonian (150)	311	0.23
Maltese (16)	53	0.04
New Zealander (0)	0	<0.01
Northern European (41)	57	0.04
Norwegian (334)	1,056	0.77
Pennsylvania German (361)	462	0.34
Polish (1,666)	4,836	3.53
Portuguese (130)	173	0.13
Romanian (21)	31	0.02
Russian (211)	563	0.41
Scandinavian (86)	211	0.15
Scotch-Irish (766)	2,016	1.47
Scottish (620)	2,966	2.16
Serbian (22)	100	0.07
Slavic (0)	41	0.03
Slovak (18)	202	0.15
Slovene (7)	15	0.01
Soviet Union (0)	0	<0.01
Swedish (468)	1,556	1.13
Swiss (78)	218	0.16
Turkish (16)	24	0.02
Ukrainian (71)	202	0.15
Welsh (147)	920	0.67
West Indian, ex. Hispanic (154)	187	0.14
Bahamian (0)	0	<0.01
Barbadian (57)	57	0.04
Belizean (0)	0	<0.01
Bermudan (0)	0	<0.01
British West Indian (0)	0	<0.01
Dutch West Indian (0)	0	<0.01
Haitian (0)	0	<0.01
Jamaican (32)	40	0.03
Trinidadian/Tobagonian (50)	50	0.04
U.S. Virgin Islander (0)	0	<0.01
West Indian (15)	40	0.03
Other West Indian (0)	0	<0.01
Yugoslavian (97)	187	0.14

Hispanic Origin	Population	%
Hispanic or Latino (of any race)	6,177	4.54
Central American, ex. Mexican	96	0.07
Costa Rican	18	0.01
Guatemalan	26	0.02
Honduran	10	0.01
Nicaraguan	4	<0.01
Panamanian	22	0.02
Salvadoran	15	0.01
Other Central American	1	<0.01
Cuban	91	0.07
Dominican Republic	43	0.03
Mexican	4,700	3.45
Puerto Rican	469	0.34
South American	137	0.10
Argentinean	10	0.01
Bolivian	3	<0.01
Chilean	4	<0.01
Colombian	61	0.04
Ecuadorian	7	0.01
Paraguayan	3	<0.01
Peruvian	36	0.03
Uruguayan	4	<0.01
Venezuelan	9	0.01
Other South American	0	<0.01
Other Hispanic or Latino	641	0.47

Race*	Population	%
African-American/Black (14,872)	17,375	12.76
Not Hispanic (14,630)	16,916	12.42
Hispanic (242)	459	0.34
American Indian/Alaska Native (831)	2,114	1.55
Not Hispanic (714)	1,884	1.38
Hispanic (117)	230	0.17
Alaska Athabascan *(Ala. Nat.)* (7)	11	0.01
Aleut *(Alaska Native)* (0)	3	<0.01
Apache (9)	37	0.03
Arapaho (0)	0	<0.01
Blackfeet (6)	107	0.08
Canadian/French Am. Ind. (6)	15	0.01
Central American Ind. (1)	1	<0.01
Cherokee (83)	409	0.30
Cheyenne (0)	6	<0.01
Chickasaw (4)	5	<0.01
Chippewa (123)	186	0.14
Choctaw (3)	14	0.01
Colville (0)	0	<0.01
Comanche (0)	7	0.01
Cree (0)	6	<0.01
Creek (0)	3	<0.01
Crow (0)	6	<0.01
Delaware (0)	1	<0.01
Hopi (1)	2	<0.01
Houma (1)	1	<0.01
Inupiat *(Alaska Native)* (0)	0	<0.01
Iroquois (8)	21	0.02
Kiowa (1)	1	<0.01
Lumbee (2)	8	0.01
Menominee (0)	0	<0.01
Mexican American Ind. (15)	24	0.02
Navajo (7)	11	0.01
Osage (2)	2	<0.01
Ottawa (57)	82	0.06
Paiute (0)	0	<0.01
Pima (1)	1	<0.01
Potawatomi (117)	208	0.15
Pueblo (1)	1	<0.01
Puget Sound Salish (3)	3	<0.01
Seminole (0)	4	<0.01
Shoshone (0)	0	<0.01
Sioux (12)	33	0.02
South American Ind. (2)	3	<0.01
Spanish American Ind. (3)	6	<0.01
Tlingit-Haida *(Alaska Native)* (0)	1	<0.01
Tohono O'Odham (0)	0	<0.01
Tsimshian *(Alaska Native)* (0)	0	<0.01
Ute (1)	1	<0.01
Yakama (0)	0	<0.01
Yaqui (5)	5	<0.01
Yuman (0)	0	<0.01
Yup'ik *(Alaska Native)* (0)	0	<0.01
Asian (2,179)	2,705	1.99
Not Hispanic (2,154)	2,651	1.95
Hispanic (25)	54	0.04
Bangladeshi (5)	5	<0.01
Bhutanese (0)	0	<0.01
Burmese (600)	674	0.50
Cambodian (2)	2	<0.01
Chinese, ex. Taiwanese (205)	253	0.19
Filipino (211)	332	0.24
Hmong (5)	5	<0.01
Indian (462)	556	0.41
Indonesian (8)	22	0.02
Japanese (304)	403	0.30
Korean (157)	242	0.18
Laotian (1)	6	<0.01
Malaysian (0)	0	<0.01
Nepalese (6)	6	<0.01
Pakistani (6)	7	0.01
Sri Lankan (0)	0	<0.01
Taiwanese (3)	3	<0.01
Thai (17)	31	0.02
Vietnamese (63)	86	0.06
Hawaii Native/Pacific Islander (56)	198	0.15
Not Hispanic (45)	169	0.12
Hispanic (11)	29	0.02
Fijian (0)	1	<0.01
Guamanian/Chamorro (8)	18	0.01
Marshallese (0)	0	<0.01
Native Hawaiian (11)	52	0.04
Samoan (4)	17	0.01
Tongan (1)	6	<0.01
White (111,915)	115,733	85.01
Not Hispanic (108,664)	111,993	82.26
Hispanic (3,251)	3,740	2.75

*Notes: † The Census 2010 population figure is used to calculate the percentages in the Hispanic Origin and Race categories. Ancestry percentages are based on the 2006-2010 American Community Survey population (not shown); ‡ Numbers in parentheses indicate the number of people reporting a single ancestry; * Numbers in parentheses indicate the number of persons reporting this race alone, not in combination with any other race; Please refer to the User Guide for more information.*

Cass County

Population: 52,293

Ancestry	Population	%
Afghan (0)	0	<0.01
African, Sub-Saharan (58)	96	0.18
African (35)	56	0.11
Cape Verdean (0)	0	<0.01
Ethiopian (0)	0	<0.01
Ghanaian (0)	0	<0.01
Kenyan (9)	9	0.02
Liberian (14)	14	0.03
Nigerian (0)	17	0.03
Senegalese (0)	0	<0.01
Sierra Leonean (0)	0	<0.01
Somalian (0)	0	<0.01
South African (0)	0	<0.01
Sudanese (0)	0	<0.01
Ugandan (0)	0	<0.01
Zimbabwean (0)	0	<0.01
Other Sub-Saharan African (0)	0	<0.01
Albanian (0)	0	<0.01
Alsatian (0)	0	<0.01
American (3,841)	3,841	7.33
Arab (15)	83	0.16
Arab (0)	12	0.02
Egyptian (0)	0	<0.01
Iraqi (0)	0	<0.01
Jordanian (0)	0	<0.01
Lebanese (10)	53	0.10
Moroccan (0)	0	<0.01
Palestinian (0)	0	<0.01
Syrian (5)	18	0.03
Other Arab (0)	0	<0.01
Armenian (0)	23	0.04
Assyrian/Chaldean/Syriac (0)	0	<0.01
Australian (0)	3	0.01
Austrian (11)	67	0.13
Basque (0)	0	<0.01
Belgian (85)	179	0.34
Brazilian (10)	10	0.02
British (49)	101	0.19
Bulgarian (0)	68	0.13
Cajun (0)	0	<0.01
Canadian (55)	141	0.27
Carpatho Rusyn (0)	0	<0.01
Celtic (3)	3	0.01
Croatian (27)	85	0.16
Cypriot (0)	0	<0.01
Czech (67)	220	0.42
Czechoslovakian (12)	19	0.04
Danish (72)	215	0.41
Dutch (607)	2,984	5.69
Eastern European (52)	52	0.10
English (2,051)	6,291	12.00
Estonian (0)	0	<0.01
European (295)	366	0.70
Finnish (0)	79	0.15
French, ex. Basque (276)	2,136	4.07
French Canadian (218)	389	0.74
German (5,933)	16,139	30.78
German Russian (2)	2	<0.01
Greek (44)	118	0.23
Guyanese (0)	0	<0.01
Hungarian (322)	1,017	1.94
Icelander (0)	0	<0.01
Iranian (0)	0	<0.01
Irish (1,772)	7,434	14.18
Israeli (0)	0	<0.01
Italian (366)	1,128	2.15
Latvian (6)	17	0.03
Lithuanian (176)	249	0.47
Luxemburger (0)	4	0.01
Macedonian (0)	0	<0.01
Maltese (7)	7	0.01
New Zealander (0)	0	<0.01
Northern European (28)	28	0.05
Norwegian (176)	779	1.49
Pennsylvania German (124)	205	0.39

Ancestry	Population	%
Polish (1,316)	3,721	7.10
Portuguese (15)	30	0.06
Romanian (44)	80	0.15
Russian (26)	226	0.43
Scandinavian (217)	230	0.44
Scotch-Irish (291)	718	1.37
Scottish (322)	865	1.65
Serbian (11)	25	0.05
Slavic (6)	81	0.15
Slovak (28)	87	0.17
Slovene (12)	14	0.03
Soviet Union (0)	0	<0.01
Swedish (284)	1,181	2.25
Swiss (58)	302	0.58
Turkish (0)	0	<0.01
Ukrainian (40)	132	0.25
Welsh (47)	309	0.59
West Indian, ex. Hispanic (22)	68	0.13
Bahamian (3)	3	0.01
Barbadian (0)	0	<0.01
Belizean (0)	0	<0.01
Bermudan (0)	0	<0.01
British West Indian (0)	0	<0.01
Dutch West Indian (17)	17	0.03
Haitian (0)	0	<0.01
Jamaican (2)	48	0.09
Trinidadian/Tobagonian (0)	0	<0.01
U.S. Virgin Islander (0)	0	<0.01
West Indian (0)	0	<0.01
Other West Indian (0)	0	<0.01
Yugoslavian (6)	34	0.06

Hispanic Origin	Population	%
Hispanic or Latino (of any race)	1,570	3.00
Central American, ex. Mexican	30	0.06
Costa Rican	6	0.01
Guatemalan	9	0.02
Honduran	2	<0.01
Nicaraguan	2	<0.01
Panamanian	3	0.01
Salvadoran	8	0.02
Other Central American	0	<0.01
Cuban	20	0.04
Dominican Republic	3	0.01
Mexican	1,200	2.29
Puerto Rican	168	0.32
South American	36	0.07
Argentinean	0	<0.01
Bolivian	0	<0.01
Chilean	7	0.01
Colombian	3	0.01
Ecuadorian	13	0.02
Paraguayan	0	<0.01
Peruvian	6	0.01
Uruguayan	0	<0.01
Venezuelan	7	0.01
Other South American	0	<0.01
Other Hispanic or Latino	113	0.22

Race*	Population	%
African-American/Black (2,821)	3,639	6.96
Not Hispanic (2,776)	3,551	6.79
Hispanic (45)	88	0.17
American Indian/Alaska Native (504)	1,119	2.14
Not Hispanic (476)	1,068	2.04
Hispanic (28)	51	0.10
Alaska Athabascan (Ala. Nat.) (0)	0	<0.01
Aleut (Alaska Native) (0)	1	<0.01
Apache (4)	8	0.02
Arapaho (0)	0	<0.01
Blackfeet (1)	52	0.10
Canadian/French Am. Ind. (0)	1	<0.01
Central American Ind. (0)	0	<0.01
Cherokee (22)	150	0.29
Cheyenne (0)	0	<0.01
Chickasaw (2)	2	<0.01
Chippewa (59)	72	0.14
Choctaw (1)	19	0.04
Colville (0)	0	<0.01

	Population	%
Comanche (0)	0	<0.01
Cree (1)	1	<0.01
Creek (0)	2	<0.01
Crow (0)	3	0.01
Delaware (0)	0	<0.01
Hopi (0)	0	<0.01
Houma (0)	1	<0.01
Inupiat (Alaska Native) (0)	4	0.01
Iroquois (1)	5	0.01
Kiowa (0)	0	<0.01
Lumbee (1)	2	<0.01
Menominee (0)	0	<0.01
Mexican American Ind. (10)	11	0.02
Navajo (1)	3	0.01
Osage (0)	0	<0.01
Ottawa (20)	35	0.07
Paiute (0)	0	<0.01
Pima (0)	0	<0.01
Potawatomi (255)	367	0.70
Pueblo (1)	2	<0.01
Puget Sound Salish (1)	1	<0.01
Seminole (0)	4	0.01
Shoshone (0)	1	<0.01
Sioux (2)	13	0.02
South American Ind. (1)	1	<0.01
Spanish American Ind. (0)	0	<0.01
Tlingit-Haida (Alaska Native) (0)	0	<0.01
Tohono O'Odham (0)	0	<0.01
Tsimshian (Alaska Native) (0)	0	<0.01
Ute (0)	0	<0.01
Yakama (0)	0	<0.01
Yaqui (0)	0	<0.01
Yuman (0)	0	<0.01
Yup'ik (Alaska Native) (0)	0	<0.01
Asian (339)	477	0.91
Not Hispanic (334)	470	0.90
Hispanic (5)	7	0.01
Bangladeshi (2)	9	0.02
Bhutanese (0)	0	<0.01
Burmese (0)	0	<0.01
Cambodian (1)	2	<0.01
Chinese, ex. Taiwanese (29)	38	0.07
Filipino (59)	88	0.17
Hmong (0)	0	<0.01
Indian (39)	69	0.13
Indonesian (0)	2	<0.01
Japanese (12)	40	0.08
Korean (55)	89	0.17
Laotian (90)	95	0.18
Malaysian (0)	0	<0.01
Nepalese (0)	0	<0.01
Pakistani (1)	1	<0.01
Sri Lankan (5)	5	0.01
Taiwanese (2)	2	<0.01
Thai (11)	15	0.03
Vietnamese (11)	15	0.03
Hawaii Native/Pacific Islander (10)	26	0.05
Not Hispanic (6)	21	0.04
Hispanic (4)	5	0.01
Fijian (0)	0	<0.01
Guamanian/Chamorro (5)	7	0.01
Marshallese (0)	0	<0.01
Native Hawaiian (4)	8	0.02
Samoan (1)	3	0.01
Tongan (0)	2	<0.01
White (46,496)	47,966	91.73
Not Hispanic (45,704)	46,992	89.86
Hispanic (792)	974	1.86

Notes: † The Census 2010 population figure is used to calculate the percentages in the Hispanic Origin and Race categories. Ancestry percentages are based on the 2006-2010 American Community Survey population (not shown); ‡ Numbers in parentheses indicate the number of people reporting a single ancestry; * Numbers in parentheses indicate the number of persons reporting this race alone, not in combination with any other race; Please refer to the User Guide for more information.

Clinton County

Population: 75,382

Ancestry	Population	%
Afghan (0)	0	<0.01
African, Sub-Saharan (194)	331	0.45
African (194)	295	0.40
Cape Verdean (0)	0	<0.01
Ethiopian (0)	0	<0.01
Ghanaian (0)	0	<0.01
Kenyan (0)	0	<0.01
Liberian (0)	0	<0.01
Nigerian (0)	0	<0.01
Senegalese (0)	0	<0.01
Sierra Leonean (0)	0	<0.01
Somalian (0)	0	<0.01
South African (0)	36	0.05
Sudanese (0)	0	<0.01
Ugandan (0)	0	<0.01
Zimbabwean (0)	0	<0.01
Other Sub-Saharan African (0)	0	<0.01
Albanian (19)	19	0.03
Alsatian (0)	0	<0.01
American (9,929)	9,929	13.38
Arab (58)	239	0.32
Arab (0)	0	<0.01
Egyptian (0)	0	<0.01
Iraqi (15)	27	0.04
Jordanian (0)	0	<0.01
Lebanese (29)	156	0.21
Moroccan (0)	0	<0.01
Palestinian (0)	0	<0.01
Syrian (14)	56	0.08
Other Arab (0)	0	<0.01
Armenian (58)	76	0.10
Assyrian/Chaldean/Syriac (25)	25	0.03
Australian (0)	45	0.06
Austrian (31)	145	0.20
Basque (0)	0	<0.01
Belgian (64)	203	0.27
Brazilian (0)	0	<0.01
British (58)	164	0.22
Bulgarian (0)	0	<0.01
Cajun (0)	0	<0.01
Canadian (156)	427	0.58
Carpatho Rusyn (13)	27	0.04
Celtic (0)	0	<0.01
Croatian (24)	103	0.14
Cypriot (0)	0	<0.01
Czech (229)	1,067	1.44
Czechoslovakian (174)	393	0.53
Danish (41)	337	0.45
Dutch (600)	2,643	3.56
Eastern European (14)	26	0.04
English (3,163)	11,126	14.99
Estonian (0)	0	<0.01
European (467)	567	0.76
Finnish (96)	452	0.61
French, ex. Basque (326)	3,182	4.29
French Canadian (340)	1,028	1.38
German (11,185)	27,439	36.96
German Russian (0)	0	<0.01
Greek (65)	157	0.21
Guyanese (0)	0	<0.01
Hungarian (120)	605	0.81
Icelander (0)	0	<0.01
Iranian (0)	0	<0.01
Irish (2,158)	10,001	13.47
Israeli (0)	0	<0.01
Italian (789)	2,327	3.13
Latvian (12)	37	0.05
Lithuanian (19)	140	0.19
Luxemburger (0)	16	0.02
Macedonian (14)	19	0.03
Maltese (0)	23	0.03
New Zealander (0)	0	<0.01
Northern European (85)	85	0.11
Norwegian (187)	624	0.84
Pennsylvania German (19)	24	0.03

Ancestry	Population	%
Polish (935)	3,683	4.96
Portuguese (22)	62	0.08
Romanian (3)	33	0.04
Russian (76)	314	0.42
Scandinavian (10)	59	0.08
Scotch-Irish (185)	1,462	1.97
Scottish (384)	2,005	2.70
Serbian (22)	81	0.11
Slavic (0)	27	0.04
Slovak (111)	328	0.44
Slovene (20)	29	0.04
Soviet Union (0)	0	<0.01
Swedish (185)	1,292	1.74
Swiss (31)	330	0.44
Turkish (0)	0	<0.01
Ukrainian (12)	66	0.09
Welsh (64)	502	0.68
West Indian, ex. Hispanic (0)	18	0.02
Bahamian (0)	0	<0.01
Barbadian (0)	0	<0.01
Belizean (0)	0	<0.01
Bermudan (0)	0	<0.01
British West Indian (0)	0	<0.01
Dutch West Indian (0)	0	<0.01
Haitian (0)	0	<0.01
Jamaican (0)	18	0.02
Trinidadian/Tobagonian (0)	0	<0.01
U.S. Virgin Islander (0)	0	<0.01
West Indian (0)	0	<0.01
Other West Indian (0)	0	<0.01
Yugoslavian (23)	35	0.05

Hispanic Origin	Population	%
Hispanic or Latino (of any race)	2,947	3.91
Central American, ex. Mexican	78	0.10
Costa Rican	10	0.01
Guatemalan	33	0.04
Honduran	17	0.02
Nicaraguan	7	0.01
Panamanian	3	<0.01
Salvadoran	8	0.01
Other Central American	0	<0.01
Cuban	115	0.15
Dominican Republic	19	0.03
Mexican	2,245	2.98
Puerto Rican	102	0.14
South American	83	0.11
Argentinean	16	0.02
Bolivian	1	<0.01
Chilean	3	<0.01
Colombian	19	0.03
Ecuadorian	15	0.02
Paraguayan	2	<0.01
Peruvian	9	0.01
Uruguayan	3	<0.01
Venezuelan	10	0.01
Other South American	5	0.01
Other Hispanic or Latino	305	0.40

Race*	Population	%
African-American/Black (1,549)	2,128	2.82
Not Hispanic (1,506)	2,024	2.68
Hispanic (43)	104	0.14
American Indian/Alaska Native (333)	819	1.09
Not Hispanic (309)	748	0.99
Hispanic (24)	71	0.09
Alaska Athabascan (Ala. Nat.) (1)	1	<0.01
Aleut (Alaska Native) (0)	0	<0.01
Apache (0)	2	<0.01
Arapaho (0)	0	<0.01
Blackfeet (0)	8	0.01
Canadian/French Am. Ind. (10)	17	0.02
Central American Ind. (0)	0	<0.01
Cherokee (22)	81	0.11
Cheyenne (1)	3	<0.01
Chickasaw (0)	0	<0.01
Chippewa (130)	219	0.29
Choctaw (0)	1	<0.01
Colville (0)	0	<0.01

	Population	%
Comanche (1)	1	<0.01
Cree (0)	1	<0.01
Creek (0)	1	<0.01
Crow (0)	0	<0.01
Delaware (1)	1	<0.01
Hopi (0)	1	<0.01
Houma (0)	0	<0.01
Inupiat (Alaska Native) (1)	1	<0.01
Iroquois (13)	24	0.03
Kiowa (0)	4	0.01
Lumbee (0)	1	<0.01
Menominee (1)	1	<0.01
Mexican American Ind. (3)	7	0.01
Navajo (0)	2	<0.01
Osage (0)	0	<0.01
Ottawa (46)	76	0.10
Paiute (0)	0	<0.01
Pima (1)	1	<0.01
Potawatomi (6)	16	0.02
Pueblo (0)	1	<0.01
Puget Sound Salish (0)	0	<0.01
Seminole (0)	1	<0.01
Shoshone (0)	0	<0.01
Sioux (3)	13	0.02
South American Ind. (1)	3	<0.01
Spanish American Ind. (0)	0	<0.01
Tlingit-Haida (Alaska Native) (2)	2	<0.01
Tohono O'Odham (0)	0	<0.01
Tsimshian (Alaska Native) (0)	0	<0.01
Ute (0)	0	<0.01
Yakama (0)	0	<0.01
Yaqui (0)	4	0.01
Yuman (0)	0	<0.01
Yup'ik (Alaska Native) (0)	0	<0.01
Asian (1,115)	1,427	1.89
Not Hispanic (1,105)	1,404	1.86
Hispanic (10)	23	0.03
Bangladeshi (0)	0	<0.01
Bhutanese (0)	0	<0.01
Burmese (13)	13	0.02
Cambodian (0)	0	<0.01
Chinese, ex. Taiwanese (349)	396	0.53
Filipino (85)	161	0.21
Hmong (79)	81	0.11
Indian (183)	218	0.29
Indonesian (1)	2	<0.01
Japanese (33)	72	0.10
Korean (224)	295	0.39
Laotian (9)	11	0.01
Malaysian (1)	7	0.01
Nepalese (3)	3	<0.01
Pakistani (22)	27	0.04
Sri Lankan (4)	4	0.01
Taiwanese (9)	14	0.02
Thai (8)	15	0.02
Vietnamese (48)	73	0.10
Hawaii Native/Pacific Islander (15)	51	0.07
Not Hispanic (12)	41	0.05
Hispanic (3)	10	0.01
Fijian (0)	0	<0.01
Guamanian/Chamorro (3)	4	0.01
Marshallese (0)	0	<0.01
Native Hawaiian (5)	16	0.02
Samoan (3)	14	0.02
Tongan (0)	0	<0.01
White (70,018)	71,415	94.74
Not Hispanic (68,243)	69,383	92.04
Hispanic (1,775)	2,032	2.70

Notes: † The Census 2010 population figure is used to calculate the percentages in the Hispanic Origin and Race categories. Ancestry percentages are based on the 2006-2010 American Community Survey population (not shown); ‡ Numbers in parentheses indicate the number of people reporting a single ancestry; * Numbers in parentheses indicate the number of persons reporting this race alone, not in combination with any other race; Please refer to the User Guide for more information.

Eaton County

Population: 107,759

Ancestry	Population	%
Afghan (0)	0	<0.01
African, Sub-Saharan (162)	284	0.26
African (103)	222	0.21
Cape Verdean (0)	0	<0.01
Ethiopian (59)	59	0.05
Ghanaian (0)	0	<0.01
Kenyan (0)	0	<0.01
Liberian (0)	0	<0.01
Nigerian (0)	0	<0.01
Senegalese (0)	0	<0.01
Sierra Leonean (0)	0	<0.01
Somalian (0)	3	<0.01
South African (0)	0	<0.01
Sudanese (0)	0	<0.01
Ugandan (0)	0	<0.01
Zimbabwean (0)	0	<0.01
Other Sub-Saharan African (0)	0	<0.01
Albanian (179)	179	0.17
Alsatian (0)	0	<0.01
American (5,987)	5,987	5.54
Arab (260)	470	0.44
Arab (0)	0	<0.01
Egyptian (0)	0	<0.01
Iraqi (0)	0	<0.01
Jordanian (0)	0	<0.01
Lebanese (252)	434	0.40
Moroccan (0)	0	<0.01
Palestinian (8)	8	0.01
Syrian (0)	11	0.01
Other Arab (0)	17	0.02
Armenian (12)	79	0.07
Assyrian/Chaldean/Syriac (410)	410	0.38
Australian (11)	36	0.03
Austrian (27)	160	0.15
Basque (0)	0	<0.01
Belgian (61)	312	0.29
Brazilian (0)	0	<0.01
British (258)	471	0.44
Bulgarian (0)	0	<0.01
Cajun (0)	3	<0.01
Canadian (84)	231	0.21
Carpatho Rusyn (0)	0	<0.01
Celtic (0)	25	0.02
Croatian (84)	175	0.16
Cypriot (0)	0	<0.01
Czech (163)	853	0.79
Czechoslovakian (77)	140	0.13
Danish (77)	633	0.59
Dutch (1,049)	5,240	4.85
Eastern European (38)	77	0.07
English (5,618)	17,657	16.35
Estonian (0)	0	<0.01
European (983)	1,102	1.02
Finnish (200)	581	0.54
French, ex. Basque (618)	5,874	5.44
French Canadian (442)	1,502	1.39
German (9,982)	32,093	29.72
German Russian (0)	0	<0.01
Greek (116)	316	0.29
Guyanese (0)	8	0.01
Hungarian (216)	592	0.55
Icelander (3)	3	<0.01
Iranian (0)	0	<0.01
Irish (3,290)	15,902	14.72
Israeli (0)	0	<0.01
Italian (1,343)	4,011	3.71
Latvian (16)	46	0.04
Lithuanian (68)	164	0.15
Luxemburger (0)	0	<0.01
Macedonian (36)	86	0.08
Maltese (0)	0	<0.01
New Zealander (0)	0	<0.01
Northern European (123)	123	0.11
Norwegian (298)	1,387	1.28
Pennsylvania German (191)	295	0.27

Ancestry	Population	%
Polish (1,471)	5,581	5.17
Portuguese (49)	118	0.11
Romanian (20)	88	0.08
Russian (80)	583	0.54
Scandinavian (68)	257	0.24
Scotch-Irish (563)	1,937	1.79
Scottish (819)	2,913	2.70
Serbian (6)	67	0.06
Slavic (71)	271	0.25
Slovak (83)	324	0.30
Slovene (11)	27	0.02
Soviet Union (0)	0	<0.01
Swedish (442)	2,172	2.01
Swiss (42)	328	0.30
Turkish (7)	27	0.02
Ukrainian (79)	193	0.18
Welsh (74)	719	0.67
West Indian, ex. Hispanic (132)	143	0.13
Bahamian (0)	0	<0.01
Barbadian (0)	0	<0.01
Belizean (0)	0	<0.01
Bermudan (0)	0	<0.01
British West Indian (0)	0	<0.01
Dutch West Indian (27)	27	0.02
Haitian (45)	45	0.04
Jamaican (28)	39	0.04
Trinidadian/Tobagonian (0)	0	<0.01
U.S. Virgin Islander (0)	0	<0.01
West Indian (32)	32	0.03
Other West Indian (0)	0	<0.01
Yugoslavian (98)	150	0.14

Hispanic Origin	Population	%
Hispanic or Latino (of any race)	5,101	4.73
Central American, ex. Mexican	118	0.11
Costa Rican	11	0.01
Guatemalan	43	0.04
Honduran	17	0.02
Nicaraguan	9	0.01
Panamanian	28	0.03
Salvadoran	10	0.01
Other Central American	0	<0.01
Cuban	268	0.25
Dominican Republic	18	0.02
Mexican	3,927	3.64
Puerto Rican	227	0.21
South American	113	0.10
Argentinean	12	0.01
Bolivian	17	0.02
Chilean	3	<0.01
Colombian	22	0.02
Ecuadorian	28	0.03
Paraguayan	0	<0.01
Peruvian	11	0.01
Uruguayan	5	<0.01
Venezuelan	12	0.01
Other South American	3	<0.01
Other Hispanic or Latino	430	0.40

Race*	Population	%
African-American/Black (6,811)	8,081	7.50
Not Hispanic (6,661)	7,759	7.20
Hispanic (150)	322	0.30
American Indian/Alaska Native (466)	1,393	1.29
Not Hispanic (407)	1,209	1.12
Hispanic (59)	184	0.17
Alaska Athabascan (Ala. Nat.) (0)	1	<0.01
Aleut (Alaska Native) (1)	1	<0.01
Apache (5)	14	0.01
Arapaho (1)	1	<0.01
Blackfeet (10)	50	0.05
Canadian/French Am. Ind. (6)	9	0.01
Central American Ind. (3)	3	<0.01
Cherokee (28)	197	0.18
Cheyenne (0)	0	<0.01
Chickasaw (0)	1	<0.01
Chippewa (118)	242	0.22
Choctaw (3)	17	0.02
Colville (0)	0	<0.01

	Population	%
Comanche (0)	1	<0.01
Cree (3)	9	0.01
Creek (1)	7	0.01
Crow (0)	2	<0.01
Delaware (4)	4	<0.01
Hopi (0)	0	<0.01
Houma (0)	0	<0.01
Inupiat (Alaska Native) (0)	0	<0.01
Iroquois (8)	26	0.02
Kiowa (0)	0	<0.01
Lumbee (0)	0	<0.01
Menominee (1)	8	0.01
Mexican American Ind. (10)	14	0.01
Navajo (4)	7	0.01
Osage (0)	3	<0.01
Ottawa (71)	112	0.10
Paiute (0)	0	<0.01
Pima (0)	0	<0.01
Potawatomi (11)	43	0.04
Pueblo (0)	2	<0.01
Puget Sound Salish (0)	0	<0.01
Seminole (0)	1	<0.01
Shoshone (0)	0	<0.01
Sioux (13)	31	0.03
South American Ind. (1)	3	<0.01
Spanish American Ind. (1)	1	<0.01
Tlingit-Haida (Alaska Native) (1)	2	<0.01
Tohono O'Odham (0)	1	<0.01
Tsimshian (Alaska Native) (0)	1	<0.01
Ute (0)	0	<0.01
Yakama (0)	0	<0.01
Yaqui (2)	3	<0.01
Yuman (0)	0	<0.01
Yup'ik (Alaska Native) (0)	0	<0.01
Asian (1,809)	2,254	2.09
Not Hispanic (1,790)	2,205	2.05
Hispanic (19)	49	0.05
Bangladeshi (2)	2	<0.01
Bhutanese (0)	0	<0.01
Burmese (18)	18	0.02
Cambodian (6)	12	0.01
Chinese, ex. Taiwanese (199)	269	0.25
Filipino (102)	190	0.18
Hmong (144)	165	0.15
Indian (599)	669	0.62
Indonesian (7)	11	0.01
Japanese (28)	75	0.07
Korean (140)	199	0.18
Laotian (19)	27	0.03
Malaysian (2)	2	<0.01
Nepalese (1)	2	<0.01
Pakistani (61)	68	0.06
Sri Lankan (6)	8	0.01
Taiwanese (3)	6	0.01
Thai (12)	27	0.03
Vietnamese (395)	443	0.41
Hawaii Native/Pacific Islander (18)	74	0.07
Not Hispanic (13)	52	0.05
Hispanic (5)	22	0.02
Fijian (0)	0	<0.01
Guamanian/Chamorro (4)	11	0.01
Marshallese (0)	0	<0.01
Native Hawaiian (6)	22	0.02
Samoan (1)	2	<0.01
Tongan (0)	6	0.01
White (94,561)	97,066	90.08
Not Hispanic (91,540)	93,489	86.76
Hispanic (3,021)	3,577	3.32

Notes: † The Census 2010 population figure is used to calculate the percentages in the Hispanic Origin and Race categories. Ancestry percentages are based on the 2006-2010 American Community Survey population (not shown); ‡ Numbers in parentheses indicate the number of people reporting a single ancestry; * Numbers in parentheses indicate the number of persons reporting this race alone, not in combination with any other race; Please refer to the User Guide for more information.

Genesee County

Population: 425,790

Ancestry	Population	%
Afghan (0)	0	<0.01
African, Sub-Saharan (2,232)	2,694	0.62
African (1,828)	2,267	0.52
Cape Verdean (0)	0	<0.01
Ethiopian (95)	95	0.02
Ghanaian (0)	0	<0.01
Kenyan (0)	0	<0.01
Liberian (0)	0	<0.01
Nigerian (164)	187	0.04
Senegalese (0)	0	<0.01
Sierra Leonean (13)	13	<0.01
Somalian (0)	0	<0.01
South African (52)	52	0.01
Sudanese (31)	31	0.01
Ugandan (0)	0	<0.01
Zimbabwean (0)	0	<0.01
Other Sub-Saharan African (49)	49	0.01
Albanian (15)	15	<0.01
Alsatian (0)	9	<0.01
American (23,305)	23,305	5.38
Arab (3,130)	4,246	0.98
Arab (754)	933	0.22
Egyptian (67)	67	0.02
Iraqi (68)	87	0.02
Jordanian (0)	0	<0.01
Lebanese (1,220)	1,892	0.44
Moroccan (63)	93	0.02
Palestinian (218)	241	0.06
Syrian (494)	635	0.15
Other Arab (246)	298	0.07
Armenian (47)	153	0.04
Assyrian/Chaldean/Syriac (802)	970	0.22
Australian (29)	86	0.02
Austrian (129)	647	0.15
Basque (0)	11	<0.01
Belgian (228)	973	0.22
Brazilian (15)	15	<0.01
British (718)	1,429	0.33
Bulgarian (20)	91	0.02
Cajun (38)	38	0.01
Canadian (1,017)	2,140	0.49
Carpatho Rusyn (0)	93	0.02
Celtic (42)	120	0.03
Croatian (148)	590	0.14
Cypriot (0)	0	<0.01
Czech (742)	2,309	0.53
Czechoslovakian (447)	1,011	0.23
Danish (271)	1,164	0.27
Dutch (2,039)	9,361	2.16
Eastern European (108)	170	0.04
English (14,619)	45,857	10.59
Estonian (0)	0	<0.01
European (3,054)	3,658	0.84
Finnish (962)	2,795	0.65
French, ex. Basque (3,315)	20,770	4.80
French Canadian (3,566)	9,892	2.28
German (22,195)	77,993	18.01
German Russian (0)	6	<0.01
Greek (566)	1,216	0.28
Guyanese (0)	58	0.01
Hungarian (1,714)	4,786	1.11
Icelander (14)	54	0.01
Iranian (124)	132	0.03
Irish (10,935)	47,731	11.02
Israeli (375)	375	0.09
Italian (4,157)	12,629	2.92
Latvian (24)	43	0.01
Lithuanian (127)	540	0.12
Luxemburger (35)	45	0.01
Macedonian (108)	271	0.06
Maltese (118)	184	0.04
New Zealander (17)	17	<0.01
Northern European (146)	190	0.04
Norwegian (1,104)	3,456	0.80
Pennsylvania German (152)	264	0.06

Ancestry	Population	%
Polish (7,604)	23,616	5.45
Portuguese (68)	124	0.03
Romanian (254)	456	0.11
Russian (581)	2,268	0.52
Scandinavian (271)	593	0.14
Scotch-Irish (2,297)	6,794	1.57
Scottish (2,835)	10,832	2.50
Serbian (121)	305	0.07
Slavic (76)	246	0.06
Slovak (459)	1,349	0.31
Slovene (23)	55	0.01
Soviet Union (0)	0	<0.01
Swedish (1,137)	4,600	1.06
Swiss (110)	596	0.14
Turkish (11)	11	<0.01
Ukrainian (503)	1,372	0.32
Welsh (289)	1,880	0.43
West Indian, ex. Hispanic (133)	329	0.08
Bahamian (7)	7	<0.01
Barbadian (0)	0	<0.01
Belizean (0)	0	<0.01
Bermudan (0)	0	<0.01
British West Indian (0)	0	<0.01
Dutch West Indian (0)	32	0.01
Haitian (15)	52	0.01
Jamaican (45)	138	0.03
Trinidadian/Tobagonian (55)	76	0.02
U.S. Virgin Islander (0)	0	<0.01
West Indian (11)	24	0.01
Other West Indian (0)	0	<0.01
Yugoslavian (179)	296	0.07

Hispanic Origin	Population	%
Hispanic or Latino (of any race)	12,983	3.05
Central American, ex. Mexican	266	0.06
Costa Rican	27	0.01
Guatemalan	84	0.02
Honduran	48	0.01
Nicaraguan	12	<0.01
Panamanian	50	0.01
Salvadoran	45	0.01
Other Central American	0	<0.01
Cuban	248	0.06
Dominican Republic	43	0.01
Mexican	10,080	2.37
Puerto Rican	893	0.21
South American	299	0.07
Argentinean	20	<0.01
Bolivian	13	<0.01
Chilean	10	<0.01
Colombian	117	0.03
Ecuadorian	19	<0.01
Paraguayan	6	<0.01
Peruvian	63	0.01
Uruguayan	5	<0.01
Venezuelan	39	0.01
Other South American	7	<0.01
Other Hispanic or Latino	1,154	0.27

Race*	Population	%
African-American/Black (88,127)	94,278	22.14
Not Hispanic (87,352)	92,991	21.84
Hispanic (775)	1,287	0.30
American Indian/Alaska Native (2,252)	6,254	1.47
Not Hispanic (1,961)	5,644	1.33
Hispanic (291)	610	0.14
Alaska Athabascan (Ala. Nat.) (2)	4	<0.01
Aleut (Alaska Native) (5)	6	<0.01
Apache (37)	98	0.02
Arapaho (0)	3	<0.01
Blackfeet (34)	310	0.07
Canadian/French Am. Ind. (13)	33	0.01
Central American Ind. (3)	6	<0.01
Cherokee (262)	1,238	0.29
Cheyenne (5)	20	<0.01
Chickasaw (8)	26	0.01
Chippewa (641)	1,167	0.27
Choctaw (35)	130	0.03
Colville (0)	0	<0.01

Comanche (5)	12	<0.01
Cree (6)	24	0.01
Creek (14)	38	0.01
Crow (1)	20	<0.01
Delaware (0)	5	<0.01
Hopi (0)	1	<0.01
Houma (2)	2	<0.01
Inupiat (Alaska Native) (1)	7	<0.01
Iroquois (34)	102	0.02
Kiowa (3)	3	<0.01
Lumbee (12)	19	<0.01
Menominee (2)	7	<0.01
Mexican American Ind. (47)	96	0.02
Navajo (16)	28	0.01
Osage (2)	10	<0.01
Ottawa (93)	174	0.04
Paiute (0)	2	<0.01
Pima (1)	1	<0.01
Potawatomi (32)	79	0.02
Pueblo (2)	5	<0.01
Puget Sound Salish (8)	9	<0.01
Seminole (2)	23	0.01
Shoshone (2)	4	<0.01
Sioux (26)	62	0.01
South American Ind. (6)	15	<0.01
Spanish American Ind. (1)	4	<0.01
Tlingit-Haida (Alaska Native) (0)	7	<0.01
Tohono O'Odham (0)	1	<0.01
Tsimshian (Alaska Native) (0)	0	<0.01
Ute (1)	1	<0.01
Yakama (0)	2	<0.01
Yaqui (4)	7	<0.01
Yuman (0)	1	<0.01
Yup'ik (Alaska Native) (0)	4	<0.01
Asian (3,879)	5,502	1.29
Not Hispanic (3,834)	5,332	1.25
Hispanic (45)	170	0.04
Bangladeshi (22)	24	0.01
Bhutanese (0)	0	<0.01
Burmese (5)	9	<0.01
Cambodian (14)	19	<0.01
Chinese, ex. Taiwanese (547)	747	0.18
Filipino (525)	826	0.19
Hmong (107)	117	0.03
Indian (1,370)	1,575	0.37
Indonesian (3)	21	<0.01
Japanese (110)	331	0.08
Korean (485)	735	0.17
Laotian (11)	26	0.01
Malaysian (2)	6	<0.01
Nepalese (18)	18	<0.01
Pakistani (145)	177	0.04
Sri Lankan (14)	16	<0.01
Taiwanese (22)	40	0.01
Thai (69)	134	0.03
Vietnamese (248)	316	0.07
Hawaii Native/Pacific Islander (79)	342	0.08
Not Hispanic (74)	307	0.07
Hispanic (5)	35	0.01
Fijian (7)	14	<0.01
Guamanian/Chamorro (14)	53	0.01
Marshallese (0)	0	<0.01
Native Hawaiian (35)	134	0.03
Samoan (5)	25	0.01
Tongan (0)	0	<0.01
White (317,393)	327,057	76.81
Not Hispanic (309,683)	318,053	74.70
Hispanic (7,710)	9,004	2.11

*Notes: † The Census 2010 population figure is used to calculate the percentages in the Hispanic Origin and Race categories. Ancestry percentages are based on the 2006-2010 American Community Survey population (not shown); ‡ Numbers in parentheses indicate the number of people reporting a single ancestry; * Numbers in parentheses indicate the number of persons reporting this race alone, not in combination with any other race; Please refer to the User Guide for more information.*

Grand Traverse County

Population: 86,986

Ancestry	Population	%
Afghan (0)	0	<0.01
African, Sub-Saharan (422)	490	0.57
African (414)	464	0.54
Cape Verdean (0)	0	<0.01
Ethiopian (0)	0	<0.01
Ghanaian (0)	0	<0.01
Kenyan (0)	0	<0.01
Liberian (0)	0	<0.01
Nigerian (0)	0	<0.01
Senegalese (0)	0	<0.01
Sierra Leonean (0)	0	<0.01
Somalian (0)	0	<0.01
South African (0)	18	0.02
Sudanese (0)	0	<0.01
Ugandan (0)	0	<0.01
Zimbabwean (0)	0	<0.01
Other Sub-Saharan African (8)	8	0.01
Albanian (0)	0	<0.01
Alsatian (0)	0	<0.01
American (5,942)	5,942	6.90
Arab (80)	135	0.16
Arab (11)	14	0.02
Egyptian (0)	0	<0.01
Iraqi (16)	44	0.05
Jordanian (0)	0	<0.01
Lebanese (43)	67	0.08
Moroccan (10)	10	0.01
Palestinian (0)	0	<0.01
Syrian (0)	0	<0.01
Other Arab (0)	0	<0.01
Armenian (33)	105	0.12
Assyrian/Chaldean/Syriac (10)	21	0.02
Australian (0)	7	0.01
Austrian (53)	326	0.38
Basque (0)	74	0.09
Belgian (35)	406	0.47
Brazilian (0)	0	<0.01
British (157)	499	0.58
Bulgarian (21)	21	0.02
Cajun (0)	0	<0.01
Canadian (103)	370	0.43
Carpatho Rusyn (0)	0	<0.01
Celtic (7)	10	0.01
Croatian (56)	130	0.15
Cypriot (0)	0	<0.01
Czech (227)	1,437	1.67
Czechoslovakian (145)	212	0.25
Danish (107)	856	0.99
Dutch (1,486)	4,237	4.92
Eastern European (54)	110	0.13
English (3,307)	12,474	14.49
Estonian (0)	0	<0.01
European (1,086)	1,141	1.33
Finnish (409)	1,126	1.31
French, ex. Basque (818)	6,684	7.77
French Canadian (636)	2,058	2.39
German (8,061)	27,008	31.38
German Russian (0)	0	<0.01
Greek (128)	407	0.47
Guyanese (0)	0	<0.01
Hungarian (114)	459	0.53
Icelander (14)	14	0.02
Iranian (0)	0	<0.01
Irish (2,661)	12,743	14.81
Israeli (0)	0	<0.01
Italian (924)	3,565	4.14
Latvian (7)	44	0.05
Lithuanian (52)	228	0.26
Luxemburger (0)	0	<0.01
Macedonian (0)	14	0.02
Maltese (38)	69	0.08
New Zealander (8)	8	0.01
Northern European (156)	156	0.18
Norwegian (442)	1,549	1.80
Pennsylvania German (42)	82	0.10
Polish (2,338)	7,841	9.11
Portuguese (0)	45	0.05
Romanian (83)	178	0.21
Russian (164)	439	0.51
Scandinavian (116)	376	0.44
Scotch-Irish (501)	1,934	2.25
Scottish (1,002)	3,386	3.93
Serbian (12)	122	0.14
Slavic (83)	106	0.12
Slovak (3)	74	0.09
Slovene (15)	15	0.02
Soviet Union (52)	52	0.06
Swedish (507)	2,428	2.82
Swiss (95)	320	0.37
Turkish (0)	0	<0.01
Ukrainian (156)	379	0.44
Welsh (21)	591	0.69
West Indian, ex. Hispanic (0)	16	0.02
Bahamian (0)	11	0.01
Barbadian (0)	0	<0.01
Belizean (0)	0	<0.01
Bermudan (0)	0	<0.01
British West Indian (0)	0	<0.01
Dutch West Indian (0)	0	<0.01
Haitian (0)	0	<0.01
Jamaican (0)	5	0.01
Trinidadian/Tobagonian (0)	0	<0.01
U.S. Virgin Islander (0)	0	<0.01
West Indian (0)	0	<0.01
Other West Indian (0)	0	<0.01
Yugoslavian (3)	53	0.06

Hispanic Origin	Population	%
Hispanic or Latino (of any race)	1,874	2.15
Central American, ex. Mexican	58	0.07
Costa Rican	7	0.01
Guatemalan	22	0.03
Honduran	3	<0.01
Nicaraguan	3	<0.01
Panamanian	8	0.01
Salvadoran	15	0.02
Other Central American	0	<0.01
Cuban	53	0.06
Dominican Republic	2	<0.01
Mexican	1,227	1.41
Puerto Rican	136	0.16
South American	72	0.08
Argentinean	6	0.01
Bolivian	2	<0.01
Chilean	1	<0.01
Colombian	37	0.04
Ecuadorian	10	0.01
Paraguayan	2	<0.01
Peruvian	6	0.01
Uruguayan	0	<0.01
Venezuelan	8	0.01
Other South American	0	<0.01
Other Hispanic or Latino	326	0.37

Race*	Population	%
African-American/Black (1,033)	1,468	1.69
Not Hispanic (1,023)	1,436	1.65
Hispanic (10)	32	0.04
American Indian/Alaska Native (1,010)	1,707	1.96
Not Hispanic (941)	1,595	1.83
Hispanic (69)	112	0.13
Alaska Athabascan (Ala. Nat.) (3)	4	<0.01
Aleut (Alaska Native) (2)	4	<0.01
Apache (1)	10	0.01
Arapaho (0)	4	<0.01
Blackfeet (4)	23	0.03
Canadian/French Am. Ind. (14)	27	0.03
Central American Ind. (1)	1	<0.01
Cherokee (17)	71	0.08
Cheyenne (0)	0	<0.01
Chickasaw (1)	1	<0.01
Chippewa (500)	769	0.88
Choctaw (4)	13	0.01
Colville (0)	0	<0.01
Comanche (0)	2	<0.01
Cree (0)	1	<0.01
Creek (2)	2	<0.01
Crow (0)	0	<0.01
Delaware (6)	7	0.01
Hopi (0)	0	<0.01
Houma (0)	0	<0.01
Inupiat (Alaska Native) (1)	3	<0.01
Iroquois (9)	14	0.02
Kiowa (0)	0	<0.01
Lumbee (1)	2	<0.01
Menominee (1)	3	<0.01
Mexican American Ind. (11)	18	0.02
Navajo (9)	14	0.02
Osage (0)	0	<0.01
Ottawa (86)	228	0.26
Paiute (0)	0	<0.01
Pima (2)	2	<0.01
Potawatomi (15)	26	0.03
Pueblo (0)	0	<0.01
Puget Sound Salish (0)	0	<0.01
Seminole (1)	1	<0.01
Shoshone (0)	2	<0.01
Sioux (14)	28	0.03
South American Ind. (2)	2	<0.01
Spanish American Ind. (2)	2	<0.01
Tlingit-Haida (Alaska Native) (0)	0	<0.01
Tohono O'Odham (0)	0	<0.01
Tsimshian (Alaska Native) (0)	0	<0.01
Ute (0)	1	<0.01
Yakama (0)	0	<0.01
Yaqui (0)	0	<0.01
Yuman (0)	0	<0.01
Yup'ik (Alaska Native) (1)	1	<0.01
Asian (601)	906	1.04
Not Hispanic (588)	869	1.00
Hispanic (13)	37	0.04
Bangladeshi (3)	3	<0.01
Bhutanese (0)	0	<0.01
Burmese (1)	1	<0.01
Cambodian (1)	4	<0.01
Chinese, ex. Taiwanese (125)	179	0.21
Filipino (84)	156	0.18
Hmong (23)	26	0.03
Indian (47)	80	0.09
Indonesian (1)	4	<0.01
Japanese (19)	63	0.07
Korean (90)	139	0.16
Laotian (62)	75	0.09
Malaysian (2)	2	<0.01
Nepalese (0)	1	<0.01
Pakistani (8)	9	0.01
Sri Lankan (1)	3	<0.01
Taiwanese (6)	7	0.01
Thai (11)	25	0.03
Vietnamese (65)	81	0.09
Hawaii Native/Pacific Islander (38)	113	0.13
Not Hispanic (25)	92	0.11
Hispanic (13)	21	0.02
Fijian (3)	10	0.01
Guamanian/Chamorro (4)	11	0.01
Marshallese (1)	1	<0.01
Native Hawaiian (13)	40	0.05
Samoan (2)	6	0.01
Tongan (0)	1	<0.01
White (82,334)	83,749	96.28
Not Hispanic (81,188)	82,441	94.78
Hispanic (1,146)	1,308	1.50

*Notes: † The Census 2010 population figure is used to calculate the percentages in the Hispanic Origin and Race categories. Ancestry percentages are based on the 2006-2010 American Community Survey population (not shown); ‡ Numbers in parentheses indicate the number of people reporting a single ancestry; * Numbers in parentheses indicate the number of persons reporting this race alone, not in combination with any other race; Please refer to the User Guide for more information.*

Ingham County

Population: 280,895

Ancestry	Population	%
Afghan (0)	0	<0.01
African, Sub-Saharan (2,904)	3,453	1.23
African (1,224)	1,737	0.62
Cape Verdean (0)	0	<0.01
Ethiopian (158)	158	0.06
Ghanaian (23)	23	0.01
Kenyan (108)	118	0.04
Liberian (0)	0	<0.01
Nigerian (224)	232	0.08
Senegalese (84)	84	0.03
Sierra Leonean (0)	0	<0.01
Somalian (350)	361	0.13
South African (43)	50	0.02
Sudanese (297)	297	0.11
Ugandan (0)	0	<0.01
Zimbabwean (68)	68	0.02
Other Sub-Saharan African (325)	325	0.12
Albanian (267)	279	0.10
Alsatian (0)	0	<0.01
American (19,551)	19,551	6.95
Arab (1,678)	2,509	0.89
Arab (208)	284	0.10
Egyptian (121)	121	0.04
Iraqi (277)	290	0.10
Jordanian (0)	0	<0.01
Lebanese (723)	1,290	0.46
Moroccan (0)	14	<0.01
Palestinian (45)	79	0.03
Syrian (85)	151	0.05
Other Arab (219)	280	0.10
Armenian (345)	508	0.18
Assyrian/Chaldean/Syriac (42)	52	0.02
Australian (133)	153	0.05
Austrian (67)	526	0.19
Basque (13)	13	<0.01
Belgian (183)	1,219	0.43
Brazilian (26)	127	0.05
British (715)	1,733	0.62
Bulgarian (124)	195	0.07
Cajun (0)	0	<0.01
Canadian (276)	1,015	0.36
Carpatho Rusyn (0)	15	0.01
Celtic (17)	54	0.02
Croatian (277)	749	0.27
Cypriot (9)	9	<0.01
Czech (317)	1,452	0.52
Czechoslovakian (177)	423	0.15
Danish (269)	1,265	0.45
Dutch (2,798)	10,085	3.58
Eastern European (254)	286	0.10
English (10,082)	34,870	12.39
Estonian (0)	23	0.01
European (3,227)	3,701	1.32
Finnish (613)	2,024	0.72
French, ex. Basque (1,530)	11,083	3.94
French Canadian (946)	3,755	1.33
German (17,742)	64,422	22.90
German Russian (6)	6	<0.01
Greek (538)	1,289	0.46
Guyanese (0)	0	<0.01
Hungarian (733)	2,355	0.84
Icelander (0)	0	<0.01
Iranian (166)	213	0.08
Irish (7,727)	36,494	12.97
Israeli (14)	14	<0.01
Italian (3,507)	11,179	3.97
Latvian (86)	150	0.05
Lithuanian (312)	793	0.28
Luxemburger (0)	16	0.01
Macedonian (110)	176	0.06
Maltese (35)	240	0.09
New Zealander (0)	19	0.01
Northern European (249)	296	0.11
Norwegian (702)	2,790	0.99
Pennsylvania German (67)	150	0.05

Ancestry	Population	%
Polish (4,685)	15,493	5.51
Portuguese (65)	133	0.05
Romanian (199)	551	0.20
Russian (940)	2,732	0.97
Scandinavian (126)	478	0.17
Scotch-Irish (1,617)	4,762	1.69
Scottish (2,068)	7,574	2.69
Serbian (154)	195	0.07
Slavic (45)	113	0.04
Slovak (266)	713	0.25
Slovene (61)	176	0.06
Soviet Union (0)	0	<0.01
Swedish (831)	4,638	1.65
Swiss (98)	806	0.29
Turkish (195)	209	0.07
Ukrainian (417)	1,178	0.42
Welsh (212)	1,962	0.70
West Indian, ex. Hispanic (574)	843	0.30
Bahamian (0)	0	<0.01
Barbadian (0)	37	0.01
Belizean (11)	21	0.01
Bermudan (0)	0	<0.01
British West Indian (13)	13	<0.01
Dutch West Indian (0)	0	<0.01
Haitian (320)	344	0.12
Jamaican (170)	242	0.09
Trinidadian/Tobagonian (47)	47	0.02
U.S. Virgin Islander (0)	0	<0.01
West Indian (13)	123	0.04
Other West Indian (0)	16	0.01
Yugoslavian (145)	305	0.11

Hispanic Origin	Population	%
Hispanic or Latino (of any race)	20,526	7.31
Central American, ex. Mexican	448	0.16
Costa Rican	41	0.01
Guatemalan	202	0.07
Honduran	58	0.02
Nicaraguan	33	0.01
Panamanian	48	0.02
Salvadoran	56	0.02
Other Central American	10	<0.01
Cuban	1,492	0.53
Dominican Republic	103	0.04
Mexican	15,106	5.38
Puerto Rican	1,112	0.40
South American	660	0.23
Argentinean	85	0.03
Bolivian	27	0.01
Chilean	39	0.01
Colombian	237	0.08
Ecuadorian	72	0.03
Paraguayan	18	0.01
Peruvian	91	0.03
Uruguayan	8	<0.01
Venezuelan	77	0.03
Other South American	6	<0.01
Other Hispanic or Latino	1,605	0.57

Race*	Population	%
African-American/Black (33,047)	39,361	14.01
Not Hispanic (31,931)	37,227	13.25
Hispanic (1,116)	2,134	0.76
American Indian/Alaska Native (1,546)	4,314	1.54
Not Hispanic (1,239)	3,538	1.26
Hispanic (307)	776	0.28
Alaska Athabascan (Ala. Nat.) (0)	1	<0.01
Aleut (Alaska Native) (0)	2	<0.01
Apache (21)	60	0.02
Arapaho (1)	2	<0.01
Blackfeet (24)	213	0.08
Canadian/French Am. Ind. (29)	51	0.02
Central American Ind. (3)	3	<0.01
Cherokee (83)	465	0.17
Cheyenne (1)	5	<0.01
Chickasaw (4)	9	<0.01
Chippewa (376)	764	0.27
Choctaw (13)	44	0.02
Colville (0)	0	<0.01

	Population	%
Comanche (3)	5	<0.01
Cree (2)	11	<0.01
Creek (10)	22	0.01
Crow (0)	3	<0.01
Delaware (2)	3	<0.01
Hopi (2)	2	<0.01
Houma (1)	1	<0.01
Inupiat (Alaska Native) (4)	6	<0.01
Iroquois (38)	94	0.03
Kiowa (0)	0	<0.01
Lumbee (1)	7	<0.01
Menominee (3)	5	<0.01
Mexican American Ind. (79)	141	0.05
Navajo (7)	21	0.01
Osage (0)	3	<0.01
Ottawa (159)	280	0.10
Paiute (1)	4	<0.01
Pima (3)	3	<0.01
Potawatomi (53)	109	0.04
Pueblo (5)	5	<0.01
Puget Sound Salish (0)	0	<0.01
Seminole (2)	19	0.01
Shoshone (2)	5	<0.01
Sioux (11)	71	0.03
South American Ind. (9)	19	0.01
Spanish American Ind. (6)	8	<0.01
Tlingit-Haida (Alaska Native) (4)	5	<0.01
Tohono O'Odham (2)	3	<0.01
Tsimshian (Alaska Native) (0)	0	<0.01
Ute (0)	1	<0.01
Yakama (0)	0	<0.01
Yaqui (1)	7	<0.01
Yuman (0)	0	<0.01
Yup'ik (Alaska Native) (4)	4	<0.01
Asian (14,599)	16,791	5.98
Not Hispanic (14,504)	16,565	5.90
Hispanic (95)	226	0.08
Bangladeshi (40)	45	0.02
Bhutanese (226)	288	0.10
Burmese (368)	402	0.14
Cambodian (19)	25	0.01
Chinese, ex. Taiwanese (3,604)	3,992	1.42
Filipino (484)	848	0.30
Hmong (668)	712	0.25
Indian (3,278)	3,597	1.28
Indonesian (82)	104	0.04
Japanese (356)	676	0.24
Korean (2,312)	2,575	0.92
Laotian (54)	82	0.03
Malaysian (94)	102	0.04
Nepalese (111)	159	0.06
Pakistani (352)	408	0.15
Sri Lankan (64)	80	0.03
Taiwanese (302)	336	0.12
Thai (173)	210	0.07
Vietnamese (1,510)	1,642	0.58
Hawaii Native/Pacific Islander (114)	381	0.14
Not Hispanic (88)	317	0.11
Hispanic (26)	64	0.02
Fijian (2)	2	<0.01
Guamanian/Chamorro (19)	37	0.01
Marshallese (2)	2	<0.01
Native Hawaiian (32)	141	0.05
Samoan (17)	52	0.02
Tongan (1)	1	<0.01
White (213,913)	223,731	79.65
Not Hispanic (203,459)	211,344	75.24
Hispanic (10,454)	12,387	4.41

*Notes: † The Census 2010 population figure is used to calculate the percentages in the Hispanic Origin and Race categories. Ancestry percentages are based on the 2006-2010 American Community Survey population (not shown); ‡ Numbers in parentheses indicate the number of people reporting a single ancestry; * Numbers in parentheses indicate the number of persons reporting this race alone, not in combination with any other race; Please refer to the User Guide for more information.*

Ionia County

Population: 63,905

Ancestry	Population	%
Afghan (0)	0	<0.01
African, Sub-Saharan (128)	241	0.37
African (128)	238	0.37
Cape Verdean (0)	3	<0.01
Ethiopian (0)	0	<0.01
Ghanaian (0)	0	<0.01
Kenyan (0)	0	<0.01
Liberian (0)	0	<0.01
Nigerian (0)	0	<0.01
Senegalese (0)	0	<0.01
Sierra Leonean (0)	0	<0.01
Somalian (0)	0	<0.01
South African (0)	0	<0.01
Sudanese (0)	0	<0.01
Ugandan (0)	0	<0.01
Zimbabwean (0)	0	<0.01
Other Sub-Saharan African (0)	0	<0.01
Albanian (0)	0	<0.01
Alsatian (0)	0	<0.01
American (4,608)	4,608	7.13
Arab (125)	191	0.30
Arab (0)	17	0.03
Egyptian (13)	13	0.02
Iraqi (9)	9	0.01
Jordanian (0)	0	<0.01
Lebanese (25)	54	0.08
Moroccan (72)	72	0.11
Palestinian (0)	0	<0.01
Syrian (6)	26	0.04
Other Arab (0)	0	<0.01
Armenian (1)	6	0.01
Assyrian/Chaldean/Syriac (80)	80	0.12
Australian (8)	17	0.03
Austrian (6)	29	0.04
Basque (2)	2	<0.01
Belgian (94)	184	0.28
Brazilian (3)	3	<0.01
British (64)	139	0.22
Bulgarian (0)	0	<0.01
Cajun (6)	6	0.01
Canadian (21)	135	0.21
Carpatho Rusyn (0)	0	<0.01
Celtic (0)	0	<0.01
Croatian (10)	17	0.03
Cypriot (0)	0	<0.01
Czech (83)	390	0.60
Czechoslovakian (37)	65	0.10
Danish (100)	710	1.10
Dutch (1,632)	4,995	7.73
Eastern European (0)	0	<0.01
English (2,617)	8,580	13.27
Estonian (0)	3	<0.01
European (541)	582	0.90
Finnish (156)	394	0.61
French, ex. Basque (381)	2,742	4.24
French Canadian (197)	993	1.54
German (7,160)	19,615	30.34
German Russian (0)	0	<0.01
Greek (3)	47	0.07
Guyanese (0)	0	<0.01
Hungarian (52)	166	0.26
Icelander (0)	19	0.03
Iranian (0)	0	<0.01
Irish (2,046)	8,840	13.67
Israeli (0)	0	<0.01
Italian (391)	1,363	2.11
Latvian (13)	13	0.02
Lithuanian (54)	146	0.23
Luxemburger (0)	0	<0.01
Macedonian (0)	0	<0.01
Maltese (0)	9	0.01
New Zealander (71)	71	0.11
Northern European (6)	6	0.01
Norwegian (105)	647	1.00
Pennsylvania German (43)	125	0.19

Ancestry (cont.)	Population	%
Polish (697)	2,919	4.52
Portuguese (43)	53	0.08
Romanian (22)	39	0.06
Russian (35)	189	0.29
Scandinavian (23)	52	0.08
Scotch-Irish (246)	710	1.10
Scottish (407)	1,407	2.18
Serbian (8)	8	0.01
Slavic (9)	9	0.01
Slovak (3)	66	0.10
Slovene (0)	6	0.01
Soviet Union (0)	0	<0.01
Swedish (255)	1,086	1.68
Swiss (61)	177	0.27
Turkish (0)	0	<0.01
Ukrainian (2)	8	0.01
Welsh (11)	202	0.31
West Indian, ex. Hispanic (12)	33	0.05
Bahamian (0)	0	<0.01
Barbadian (0)	12	0.02
Belizean (0)	0	<0.01
Bermudan (0)	0	<0.01
British West Indian (0)	0	<0.01
Dutch West Indian (0)	0	<0.01
Haitian (0)	0	<0.01
Jamaican (12)	21	0.03
Trinidadian/Tobagonian (0)	0	<0.01
U.S. Virgin Islander (0)	0	<0.01
West Indian (0)	0	<0.01
Other West Indian (0)	0	<0.01
Yugoslavian (12)	23	0.04

Hispanic Origin	Population	%
Hispanic or Latino (of any race)	2,791	4.37
Central American, ex. Mexican	47	0.07
Costa Rican	1	<0.01
Guatemalan	27	0.04
Honduran	12	0.02
Nicaraguan	1	<0.01
Panamanian	0	<0.01
Salvadoran	5	0.01
Other Central American	1	<0.01
Cuban	30	0.05
Dominican Republic	16	0.03
Mexican	2,216	3.47
Puerto Rican	113	0.18
South American	13	0.02
Argentinean	0	<0.01
Bolivian	1	<0.01
Chilean	0	<0.01
Colombian	6	0.01
Ecuadorian	4	0.01
Paraguayan	0	<0.01
Peruvian	0	<0.01
Uruguayan	0	<0.01
Venezuelan	2	<0.01
Other South American	0	<0.01
Other Hispanic or Latino	356	0.56

Race*	Population	%
African-American/Black (3,019)	3,313	5.18
Not Hispanic (2,962)	3,214	5.03
Hispanic (57)	99	0.15
American Indian/Alaska Native (289)	653	1.02
Not Hispanic (230)	549	0.86
Hispanic (59)	104	0.16
Alaska Athabascan (Ala. Nat.) (0)	0	<0.01
Aleut (Alaska Native) (0)	0	<0.01
Apache (4)	15	0.02
Arapaho (0)	0	<0.01
Blackfeet (4)	20	0.03
Canadian/French Am. Ind. (1)	5	0.01
Central American Ind. (0)	0	<0.01
Cherokee (16)	66	0.10
Cheyenne (0)	0	<0.01
Chickasaw (0)	0	<0.01
Chippewa (73)	128	0.20
Choctaw (0)	3	<0.01
Colville (0)	0	<0.01

Race* (cont.)	Population	%
Comanche (0)	0	<0.01
Cree (1)	3	<0.01
Creek (0)	0	<0.01
Crow (0)	0	<0.01
Delaware (0)	0	<0.01
Hopi (1)	1	<0.01
Houma (0)	0	<0.01
Inupiat (Alaska Native) (0)	0	<0.01
Iroquois (1)	16	0.03
Kiowa (0)	0	<0.01
Lumbee (2)	2	<0.01
Menominee (0)	0	<0.01
Mexican American Ind. (8)	9	0.01
Navajo (1)	3	<0.01
Osage (0)	0	<0.01
Ottawa (25)	38	0.06
Paiute (0)	0	<0.01
Pima (0)	0	<0.01
Potawatomi (12)	39	0.06
Pueblo (1)	1	<0.01
Puget Sound Salish (0)	0	<0.01
Seminole (0)	1	<0.01
Shoshone (0)	0	<0.01
Sioux (2)	11	0.02
South American Ind. (0)	0	<0.01
Spanish American Ind. (0)	0	<0.01
Tlingit-Haida (Alaska Native) (0)	1	<0.01
Tohono O'Odham (0)	0	<0.01
Tsimshian (Alaska Native) (0)	0	<0.01
Ute (0)	0	<0.01
Yakama (1)	1	<0.01
Yaqui (2)	2	<0.01
Yuman (0)	0	<0.01
Yup'ik (Alaska Native) (0)	0	<0.01
Asian (248)	401	0.63
Not Hispanic (241)	384	0.60
Hispanic (7)	17	0.03
Bangladeshi (0)	0	<0.01
Bhutanese (0)	0	<0.01
Burmese (8)	9	0.01
Cambodian (0)	0	<0.01
Chinese, ex. Taiwanese (36)	63	0.10
Filipino (38)	68	0.11
Hmong (10)	18	0.03
Indian (41)	61	0.10
Indonesian (2)	2	<0.01
Japanese (8)	14	0.02
Korean (63)	97	0.15
Laotian (4)	4	0.01
Malaysian (1)	2	<0.01
Nepalese (0)	1	<0.01
Pakistani (0)	0	<0.01
Sri Lankan (0)	0	<0.01
Taiwanese (3)	7	0.01
Thai (6)	13	0.02
Vietnamese (10)	26	0.04
Hawaii Native/Pacific Islander (7)	30	0.05
Not Hispanic (6)	22	0.03
Hispanic (1)	8	0.01
Fijian (0)	0	<0.01
Guamanian/Chamorro (3)	10	0.02
Marshallese (0)	0	<0.01
Native Hawaiian (0)	7	0.01
Samoan (3)	5	0.01
Tongan (0)	0	<0.01
White (58,563)	59,460	93.04
Not Hispanic (56,962)	57,629	90.18
Hispanic (1,601)	1,831	2.87

Notes: † The Census 2010 population figure is used to calculate the percentages in the Hispanic Origin and Race categories. Ancestry percentages are based on the 2006-2010 American Community Survey population (not shown); ‡ Numbers in parentheses indicate the number of people reporting a single ancestry; * Numbers in parentheses indicate the number of persons reporting this race alone, not in combination with any other race; Please refer to the User Guide for more information.

Isabella County

Population: 70,311

Ancestry	Population	%
Afghan (0)	0	<0.01
African, Sub-Saharan (159)	213	0.31
African (127)	156	0.22
Cape Verdean (0)	0	<0.01
Ethiopian (0)	0	<0.01
Ghanaian (14)	14	0.02
Kenyan (0)	0	<0.01
Liberian (0)	0	<0.01
Nigerian (0)	0	<0.01
Senegalese (0)	0	<0.01
Sierra Leonean (0)	0	<0.01
Somalian (0)	0	<0.01
South African (2)	2	<0.01
Sudanese (0)	0	<0.01
Ugandan (0)	0	<0.01
Zimbabwean (0)	0	<0.01
Other Sub-Saharan African (16)	41	0.06
Albanian (3)	12	0.02
Alsatian (0)	3	<0.01
American (2,943)	2,943	4.24
Arab (116)	409	0.59
Arab (62)	65	0.09
Egyptian (0)	49	0.07
Iraqi (0)	0	<0.01
Jordanian (0)	0	<0.01
Lebanese (42)	223	0.32
Moroccan (0)	0	<0.01
Palestinian (0)	0	<0.01
Syrian (12)	72	0.10
Other Arab (0)	0	<0.01
Armenian (50)	82	0.12
Assyrian/Chaldean/Syriac (7)	7	0.01
Australian (0)	0	<0.01
Austrian (24)	167	0.24
Basque (0)	0	<0.01
Belgian (96)	302	0.43
Brazilian (15)	15	0.02
British (98)	347	0.50
Bulgarian (16)	25	0.04
Cajun (3)	8	0.01
Canadian (124)	357	0.51
Carpatho Rusyn (0)	0	<0.01
Celtic (3)	3	<0.01
Croatian (13)	40	0.06
Cypriot (0)	0	<0.01
Czech (123)	516	0.74
Czechoslovakian (45)	151	0.22
Danish (123)	597	0.86
Dutch (571)	2,638	3.80
Eastern European (25)	25	0.04
English (3,682)	9,973	14.36
Estonian (0)	0	<0.01
European (526)	566	0.81
Finnish (101)	536	0.77
French, ex. Basque (633)	3,905	5.62
French Canadian (622)	1,742	2.51
German (7,188)	21,954	31.61
German Russian (0)	0	<0.01
Greek (106)	255	0.37
Guyanese (0)	0	<0.01
Hungarian (152)	474	0.68
Icelander (0)	43	0.06
Iranian (42)	42	0.06
Irish (2,593)	11,618	16.73
Israeli (8)	8	0.01
Italian (932)	2,855	4.11
Latvian (15)	59	0.08
Lithuanian (13)	117	0.17
Luxemburger (0)	0	<0.01
Macedonian (12)	12	0.02
Maltese (2)	10	0.01
New Zealander (0)	0	<0.01
Northern European (37)	37	0.05
Norwegian (107)	635	0.91
Pennsylvania German (25)	72	0.10

Ancestry (cont.)	Population	%
Polish (1,448)	4,924	7.09
Portuguese (11)	63	0.09
Romanian (27)	138	0.20
Russian (256)	532	0.77
Scandinavian (64)	92	0.13
Scotch-Irish (469)	1,411	2.03
Scottish (682)	2,412	3.47
Serbian (4)	7	0.01
Slavic (3)	51	0.07
Slovak (40)	128	0.18
Slovene (0)	3	<0.01
Soviet Union (0)	0	<0.01
Swedish (298)	1,105	1.59
Swiss (28)	214	0.31
Turkish (3)	6	0.01
Ukrainian (34)	229	0.33
Welsh (45)	389	0.56
West Indian, ex. Hispanic (60)	60	0.09
Bahamian (0)	0	<0.01
Barbadian (0)	0	<0.01
Belizean (0)	0	<0.01
Bermudan (0)	0	<0.01
British West Indian (0)	0	<0.01
Dutch West Indian (0)	0	<0.01
Haitian (0)	0	<0.01
Jamaican (60)	60	0.09
Trinidadian/Tobagonian (0)	0	<0.01
U.S. Virgin Islander (0)	0	<0.01
West Indian (0)	0	<0.01
Other West Indian (0)	0	<0.01
Yugoslavian (55)	89	0.13

Hispanic Origin	Population	%
Hispanic or Latino (of any race)	2,197	3.12
Central American, ex. Mexican	63	0.09
Costa Rican	7	0.01
Guatemalan	12	0.02
Honduran	15	0.02
Nicaraguan	3	<0.01
Panamanian	11	0.02
Salvadoran	15	0.02
Other Central American	0	<0.01
Cuban	29	0.04
Dominican Republic	12	0.02
Mexican	1,660	2.36
Puerto Rican	139	0.20
South American	81	0.12
Argentinean	16	0.02
Bolivian	1	<0.01
Chilean	10	0.01
Colombian	19	0.03
Ecuadorian	5	0.01
Paraguayan	1	<0.01
Peruvian	21	0.03
Uruguayan	1	<0.01
Venezuelan	4	0.01
Other South American	3	<0.01
Other Hispanic or Latino	213	0.30

Race*	Population	%
African-American/Black (1,676)	2,339	3.33
Not Hispanic (1,643)	2,244	3.19
Hispanic (33)	95	0.14
American Indian/Alaska Native (2,414)	3,437	4.89
Not Hispanic (2,161)	3,000	4.27
Hispanic (253)	437	0.62
Alaska Athabascan (Ala. Nat.) (0)	1	<0.01
Aleut (Alaska Native) (1)	2	<0.01
Apache (2)	3	<0.01
Arapaho (0)	0	<0.01
Blackfeet (0)	6	0.01
Canadian/French Am. Ind. (31)	47	0.07
Central American Ind. (0)	0	<0.01
Cherokee (31)	110	0.16
Cheyenne (0)	0	<0.01
Chickasaw (1)	1	<0.01
Chippewa (1,619)	2,094	2.98
Choctaw (3)	10	0.01
Colville (0)	0	<0.01

Race* (cont.)	Population	%
Comanche (0)	3	<0.01
Cree (2)	2	<0.01
Creek (0)	2	<0.01
Crow (1)	1	<0.01
Delaware (0)	0	<0.01
Hopi (1)	1	<0.01
Houma (1)	1	<0.01
Inupiat (Alaska Native) (0)	1	<0.01
Iroquois (21)	34	0.05
Kiowa (0)	0	<0.01
Lumbee (3)	3	<0.01
Menominee (5)	7	0.01
Mexican American Ind. (17)	20	0.03
Navajo (12)	16	0.02
Osage (0)	1	<0.01
Ottawa (90)	133	0.19
Paiute (0)	0	<0.01
Pima (0)	0	<0.01
Potawatomi (53)	68	0.10
Pueblo (0)	4	<0.01
Puget Sound Salish (0)	0	<0.01
Seminole (0)	1	<0.01
Shoshone (0)	0	<0.01
Sioux (6)	9	0.01
South American Ind. (1)	1	<0.01
Spanish American Ind. (5)	6	0.01
Tlingit-Haida (Alaska Native) (0)	1	<0.01
Tohono O'Odham (0)	0	<0.01
Tsimshian (Alaska Native) (0)	0	<0.01
Ute (1)	1	<0.01
Yakama (0)	0	<0.01
Yaqui (0)	0	<0.01
Yuman (0)	0	<0.01
Yup'ik (Alaska Native) (0)	1	<0.01
Asian (1,148)	1,441	2.05
Not Hispanic (1,141)	1,415	2.01
Hispanic (7)	26	0.04
Bangladeshi (4)	5	0.01
Bhutanese (0)	0	<0.01
Burmese (2)	2	<0.01
Cambodian (7)	8	0.01
Chinese, ex. Taiwanese (368)	403	0.57
Filipino (80)	145	0.21
Hmong (11)	12	0.02
Indian (267)	315	0.45
Indonesian (1)	4	0.01
Japanese (77)	121	0.17
Korean (179)	222	0.32
Laotian (1)	1	<0.01
Malaysian (2)	4	0.01
Nepalese (8)	8	0.01
Pakistani (12)	19	0.03
Sri Lankan (13)	14	0.02
Taiwanese (17)	21	0.03
Thai (2)	18	0.03
Vietnamese (50)	69	0.10
Hawaii Native/Pacific Islander (18)	80	0.11
Not Hispanic (14)	68	0.10
Hispanic (4)	12	0.02
Fijian (0)	0	<0.01
Guamanian/Chamorro (3)	8	0.01
Marshallese (0)	0	<0.01
Native Hawaiian (10)	32	0.05
Samoan (1)	17	0.02
Tongan (0)	1	<0.01
White (62,697)	64,476	91.70
Not Hispanic (61,514)	63,000	89.60
Hispanic (1,183)	1,476	2.10

*Notes: † The Census 2010 population figure is used to calculate the percentages in the Hispanic Origin and Race categories. Ancestry percentages are based on the 2006-2010 American Community Survey population (not shown); ‡ Numbers in parentheses indicate the number of people reporting a single ancestry; * Numbers in parentheses indicate the number of persons reporting this race alone, not in combination with any other race; Please refer to the User Guide for more information.*

Jackson County

Population: 160,248

Ancestry	Population	%
Afghan (0)	0	<0.01
African, Sub-Saharan (1,802)	1,971	1.22
African (1,765)	1,921	1.19
Cape Verdean (0)	0	<0.01
Ethiopian (27)	27	0.02
Ghanaian (0)	0	<0.01
Kenyan (0)	0	<0.01
Liberian (0)	0	<0.01
Nigerian (0)	0	<0.01
Senegalese (0)	13	0.01
Sierra Leonean (10)	10	0.01
Somalian (0)	0	<0.01
South African (0)	0	<0.01
Sudanese (0)	0	<0.01
Ugandan (0)	0	<0.01
Zimbabwean (0)	0	<0.01
Other Sub-Saharan African (0)	0	<0.01
Albanian (0)	0	<0.01
Alsatian (0)	0	<0.01
American (13,406)	13,406	8.30
Arab (282)	463	0.29
Arab (0)	43	0.03
Egyptian (3)	3	<0.01
Iraqi (9)	9	0.01
Jordanian (0)	0	<0.01
Lebanese (76)	178	0.11
Moroccan (72)	72	0.04
Palestinian (0)	0	<0.01
Syrian (0)	36	0.02
Other Arab (122)	122	0.08
Armenian (55)	81	0.05
Assyrian/Chaldean/Syriac (0)	0	<0.01
Australian (0)	10	0.01
Austrian (52)	207	0.13
Basque (0)	0	<0.01
Belgian (282)	789	0.49
Brazilian (19)	19	0.01
British (149)	368	0.23
Bulgarian (51)	75	0.05
Cajun (0)	0	<0.01
Canadian (241)	475	0.29
Carpatho Rusyn (0)	0	<0.01
Celtic (5)	43	0.03
Croatian (102)	235	0.15
Cypriot (0)	0	<0.01
Czech (161)	562	0.35
Czechoslovakian (8)	165	0.10
Danish (115)	329	0.20
Dutch (1,026)	5,737	3.55
Eastern European (18)	27	0.02
English (11,241)	28,571	17.68
Estonian (0)	0	<0.01
European (1,280)	1,343	0.83
Finnish (246)	577	0.36
French, ex. Basque (804)	6,567	4.06
French Canadian (792)	1,791	1.11
German (13,718)	41,461	25.66
German Russian (0)	0	<0.01
Greek (240)	639	0.40
Guyanese (0)	0	<0.01
Hungarian (183)	981	0.61
Icelander (0)	0	<0.01
Iranian (0)	0	<0.01
Irish (5,539)	24,545	15.19
Israeli (31)	59	0.04
Italian (1,687)	4,467	2.76
Latvian (0)	0	<0.01
Lithuanian (105)	334	0.21
Luxemburger (0)	0	<0.01
Macedonian (136)	322	0.20
Maltese (10)	28	0.02
New Zealander (0)	0	<0.01
Northern European (117)	117	0.07
Norwegian (270)	1,297	0.80
Pennsylvania German (80)	200	0.12

Ancestry (cont.)	Population	%
Polish (4,416)	11,543	7.14
Portuguese (34)	189	0.12
Romanian (75)	326	0.20
Russian (165)	647	0.40
Scandinavian (117)	268	0.17
Scotch-Irish (1,156)	3,150	1.95
Scottish (1,129)	4,075	2.52
Serbian (11)	38	0.02
Slavic (25)	28	0.02
Slovak (33)	241	0.15
Slovene (0)	21	0.01
Soviet Union (0)	0	<0.01
Swedish (555)	1,824	1.13
Swiss (39)	463	0.29
Turkish (0)	9	0.01
Ukrainian (103)	248	0.15
Welsh (196)	963	0.60
West Indian, ex. Hispanic (68)	171	0.11
Bahamian (0)	0	<0.01
Barbadian (0)	14	0.01
Belizean (0)	0	<0.01
Bermudan (0)	0	<0.01
British West Indian (0)	0	<0.01
Dutch West Indian (0)	0	<0.01
Haitian (19)	38	0.02
Jamaican (49)	106	0.07
Trinidadian/Tobagonian (0)	0	<0.01
U.S. Virgin Islander (0)	13	0.01
West Indian (0)	0	<0.01
Other West Indian (0)	0	<0.01
Yugoslavian (36)	65	0.04

Hispanic Origin	Population	%
Hispanic or Latino (of any race)	4,837	3.02
Central American, ex. Mexican	109	0.07
Costa Rican	16	0.01
Guatemalan	36	0.02
Honduran	24	0.01
Nicaraguan	13	0.01
Panamanian	16	0.01
Salvadoran	4	<0.01
Other Central American	0	<0.01
Cuban	59	0.04
Dominican Republic	15	0.01
Mexican	3,641	2.27
Puerto Rican	386	0.24
South American	101	0.06
Argentinean	5	<0.01
Bolivian	9	0.01
Chilean	6	<0.01
Colombian	32	0.02
Ecuadorian	1	<0.01
Paraguayan	1	<0.01
Peruvian	24	0.01
Uruguayan	0	<0.01
Venezuelan	16	0.01
Other South American	7	<0.01
Other Hispanic or Latino	526	0.33

Race*	Population	%
African-American/Black (12,739)	15,199	9.48
Not Hispanic (12,560)	14,806	9.24
Hispanic (179)	393	0.25
American Indian/Alaska Native (592)	1,838	1.15
Not Hispanic (521)	1,621	1.01
Hispanic (71)	217	0.14
Alaska Athabascan (Ala. Nat.) (1)	2	<0.01
Aleut (Alaska Native) (0)	1	<0.01
Apache (4)	19	0.01
Arapaho (0)	0	<0.01
Blackfeet (14)	76	0.05
Canadian/French Am. Ind. (16)	25	0.02
Central American Ind. (0)	0	<0.01
Cherokee (53)	353	0.22
Cheyenne (1)	5	<0.01
Chickasaw (0)	1	<0.01
Chippewa (109)	250	0.16
Choctaw (3)	14	0.01
Colville (0)	0	<0.01

Race* (cont.)	Population	%
Comanche (4)	5	<0.01
Cree (0)	3	<0.01
Creek (3)	9	0.01
Crow (0)	6	<0.01
Delaware (0)	10	0.01
Hopi (1)	1	<0.01
Houma (0)	0	<0.01
Inupiat (Alaska Native) (0)	0	<0.01
Iroquois (12)	29	0.02
Kiowa (0)	0	<0.01
Lumbee (16)	26	0.02
Menominee (0)	3	<0.01
Mexican American Ind. (13)	23	0.01
Navajo (3)	7	<0.01
Osage (0)	0	<0.01
Ottawa (27)	54	0.03
Paiute (0)	0	<0.01
Pima (0)	0	<0.01
Potawatomi (20)	62	0.04
Pueblo (0)	4	<0.01
Puget Sound Salish (0)	0	<0.01
Seminole (1)	9	0.01
Shoshone (1)	2	<0.01
Sioux (10)	38	0.02
South American Ind. (1)	8	<0.01
Spanish American Ind. (0)	0	<0.01
Tlingit-Haida (Alaska Native) (2)	2	<0.01
Tohono O'Odham (0)	0	<0.01
Tsimshian (Alaska Native) (0)	0	<0.01
Ute (1)	1	<0.01
Yakama (0)	0	<0.01
Yaqui (0)	1	<0.01
Yuman (0)	0	<0.01
Yup'ik (Alaska Native) (0)	0	<0.01
Asian (1,137)	1,524	0.95
Not Hispanic (1,122)	1,485	0.93
Hispanic (15)	39	0.02
Bangladeshi (2)	2	<0.01
Bhutanese (0)	0	<0.01
Burmese (0)	0	<0.01
Cambodian (2)	2	<0.01
Chinese, ex. Taiwanese (156)	184	0.11
Filipino (127)	230	0.14
Hmong (6)	6	<0.01
Indian (356)	400	0.25
Indonesian (6)	8	<0.01
Japanese (90)	165	0.10
Korean (119)	209	0.13
Laotian (4)	4	<0.01
Malaysian (2)	2	<0.01
Nepalese (3)	3	<0.01
Pakistani (70)	73	0.05
Sri Lankan (3)	3	<0.01
Taiwanese (5)	7	<0.01
Thai (26)	36	0.02
Vietnamese (89)	117	0.07
Hawaii Native/Pacific Islander (33)	90	0.06
Not Hispanic (27)	72	0.04
Hispanic (6)	18	0.01
Fijian (0)	0	<0.01
Guamanian/Chamorro (9)	10	0.01
Marshallese (0)	0	<0.01
Native Hawaiian (14)	29	0.02
Samoan (3)	6	<0.01
Tongan (3)	9	0.01
White (140,507)	144,245	90.01
Not Hispanic (137,588)	140,848	87.89
Hispanic (2,919)	3,397	2.12

Notes: † The Census 2010 population figure is used to calculate the percentages in the Hispanic Origin and Race categories. Ancestry percentages are based on the 2006-2010 American Community Survey population (not shown); ‡ Numbers in parentheses indicate the number of people reporting a single ancestry; * Numbers in parentheses indicate the number of persons reporting this race alone, not in combination with any other race; Please refer to the User Guide for more information.

Kalamazoo County

Population: 250,331

Ancestry	Population	%
Afghan (0)	32	0.01
African, Sub-Saharan (1,373)	1,499	0.61
African (922)	1,032	0.42
Cape Verdean (0)	0	<0.01
Ethiopian (0)	0	<0.01
Ghanaian (21)	29	0.01
Kenyan (23)	23	0.01
Liberian (0)	0	<0.01
Nigerian (50)	58	0.02
Senegalese (0)	0	<0.01
Sierra Leonean (0)	0	<0.01
Somalian (0)	0	<0.01
South African (58)	58	0.02
Sudanese (0)	0	<0.01
Ugandan (61)	61	0.02
Zimbabwean (221)	221	0.09
Other Sub-Saharan African (17)	17	0.01
Albanian (24)	58	0.02
Alsatian (0)	0	<0.01
American (10,889)	10,889	4.40
Arab (712)	973	0.39
Arab (219)	324	0.13
Egyptian (57)	57	0.02
Iraqi (82)	92	0.04
Jordanian (41)	41	0.02
Lebanese (151)	210	0.08
Moroccan (0)	0	<0.01
Palestinian (0)	48	0.02
Syrian (0)	22	0.01
Other Arab (162)	179	0.07
Armenian (39)	160	0.06
Assyrian/Chaldean/Syriac (76)	90	0.04
Australian (7)	66	0.03
Austrian (157)	595	0.24
Basque (0)	0	<0.01
Belgian (75)	727	0.29
Brazilian (40)	49	0.02
British (504)	1,144	0.46
Bulgarian (29)	84	0.03
Cajun (17)	50	0.02
Canadian (403)	914	0.37
Carpatho Rusyn (0)	0	<0.01
Celtic (85)	101	0.04
Croatian (225)	471	0.19
Cypriot (0)	0	<0.01
Czech (389)	1,277	0.52
Czechoslovakian (162)	373	0.15
Danish (316)	1,081	0.44
Dutch (13,447)	30,684	12.41
Eastern European (262)	270	0.11
English (9,255)	32,989	13.34
Estonian (0)	0	<0.01
European (2,369)	2,805	1.13
Finnish (289)	1,285	0.52
French, ex. Basque (1,041)	9,781	3.96
French Canadian (669)	2,903	1.17
German (17,738)	61,050	24.69
German Russian (11)	11	<0.01
Greek (266)	935	0.38
Guyanese (0)	0	<0.01
Hungarian (709)	2,152	0.87
Icelander (25)	65	0.03
Iranian (78)	127	0.05
Irish (7,000)	33,185	13.42
Israeli (145)	145	0.06
Italian (2,394)	8,787	3.55
Latvian (328)	553	0.22
Lithuanian (100)	799	0.32
Luxemburger (41)	104	0.04
Macedonian (59)	75	0.03
Maltese (23)	62	0.03
New Zealander (4)	4	<0.01
Northern European (255)	260	0.11
Norwegian (783)	2,881	1.17
Pennsylvania German (186)	419	0.17

Ancestry	Population	%
Polish (4,028)	14,325	5.79
Portuguese (27)	124	0.05
Romanian (116)	225	0.09
Russian (243)	1,164	0.47
Scandinavian (127)	330	0.13
Scotch-Irish (1,416)	4,211	1.70
Scottish (2,133)	7,448	3.01
Serbian (28)	74	0.03
Slavic (52)	146	0.06
Slovak (146)	583	0.24
Slovene (27)	116	0.05
Soviet Union (0)	0	<0.01
Swedish (1,130)	4,620	1.87
Swiss (147)	679	0.27
Turkish (29)	60	0.02
Ukrainian (160)	540	0.22
Welsh (308)	1,652	0.67
West Indian, ex. Hispanic (14)	60	0.02
Bahamian (0)	0	<0.01
Barbadian (0)	0	<0.01
Belizean (0)	7	<0.01
Bermudan (0)	0	<0.01
British West Indian (0)	10	<0.01
Dutch West Indian (0)	0	<0.01
Haitian (0)	0	<0.01
Jamaican (0)	29	0.01
Trinidadian/Tobagonian (14)	14	0.01
U.S. Virgin Islander (0)	0	<0.01
West Indian (0)	0	<0.01
Other West Indian (0)	0	<0.01
Yugoslavian (173)	388	0.16

Hispanic Origin	Population	%
Hispanic or Latino (of any race)	9,959	3.98
Central American, ex. Mexican	391	0.16
Costa Rican	25	0.01
Guatemalan	186	0.07
Honduran	37	0.01
Nicaraguan	18	0.01
Panamanian	64	0.03
Salvadoran	61	0.02
Other Central American	0	<0.01
Cuban	258	0.10
Dominican Republic	250	0.10
Mexican	7,021	2.80
Puerto Rican	778	0.31
South American	411	0.16
Argentinean	64	0.03
Bolivian	18	0.01
Chilean	32	0.01
Colombian	129	0.05
Ecuadorian	43	0.02
Paraguayan	4	<0.01
Peruvian	34	0.01
Uruguayan	2	<0.01
Venezuelan	81	0.03
Other South American	4	<0.01
Other Hispanic or Latino	850	0.34

Race*	Population	%
African-American/Black (27,266)	32,118	12.83
Not Hispanic (26,677)	31,060	12.41
Hispanic (589)	1,058	0.42
American Indian/Alaska Native (1,059)	3,479	1.39
Not Hispanic (923)	3,069	1.23
Hispanic (136)	410	0.16
Alaska Athabascan (Ala. Nat.) (4)	5	<0.01
Aleut (Alaska Native) (1)	1	<0.01
Apache (8)	32	0.01
Arapaho (4)	4	<0.01
Blackfeet (21)	133	0.05
Canadian/French Am. Ind. (4)	12	<0.01
Central American Ind. (3)	7	<0.01
Cherokee (105)	572	0.23
Cheyenne (5)	7	<0.01
Chickasaw (7)	8	<0.01
Chippewa (187)	376	0.15
Choctaw (12)	60	0.02
Colville (0)	0	<0.01

Race*	Population	%
Comanche (2)	7	<0.01
Cree (4)	5	<0.01
Creek (5)	16	0.01
Crow (2)	3	<0.01
Delaware (1)	8	<0.01
Hopi (1)	1	<0.01
Houma (0)	0	<0.01
Inupiat (Alaska Native) (1)	1	<0.01
Iroquois (21)	53	0.02
Kiowa (0)	1	<0.01
Lumbee (2)	7	<0.01
Menominee (1)	3	<0.01
Mexican American Ind. (34)	68	0.03
Navajo (14)	26	0.01
Osage (0)	0	<0.01
Ottawa (75)	107	0.04
Paiute (0)	0	<0.01
Pima (0)	0	<0.01
Potawatomi (118)	276	0.11
Pueblo (7)	11	<0.01
Puget Sound Salish (0)	0	<0.01
Seminole (2)	11	<0.01
Shoshone (1)	4	<0.01
Sioux (21)	52	0.02
South American Ind. (2)	4	<0.01
Spanish American Ind. (0)	1	<0.01
Tlingit-Haida (Alaska Native) (3)	5	<0.01
Tohono O'Odham (1)	1	<0.01
Tsimshian (Alaska Native) (0)	0	<0.01
Ute (0)	0	<0.01
Yakama (0)	0	<0.01
Yaqui (8)	13	0.01
Yuman (0)	0	<0.01
Yup'ik (Alaska Native) (0)	0	<0.01
Asian (5,212)	6,809	2.72
Not Hispanic (5,186)	6,669	2.66
Hispanic (26)	140	0.06
Bangladeshi (32)	38	0.02
Bhutanese (0)	0	<0.01
Burmese (12)	21	0.01
Cambodian (22)	40	0.02
Chinese, ex. Taiwanese (927)	1,150	0.46
Filipino (415)	695	0.28
Hmong (13)	15	0.01
Indian (1,804)	2,049	0.82
Indonesian (19)	44	0.02
Japanese (210)	434	0.17
Korean (619)	839	0.34
Laotian (34)	51	0.02
Malaysian (68)	83	0.03
Nepalese (53)	59	0.02
Pakistani (250)	271	0.11
Sri Lankan (35)	37	0.01
Taiwanese (80)	97	0.04
Thai (62)	137	0.05
Vietnamese (368)	436	0.17
Hawaii Native/Pacific Islander (88)	287	0.11
Not Hispanic (73)	234	0.09
Hispanic (15)	53	0.02
Fijian (1)	1	<0.01
Guamanian/Chamorro (18)	24	0.01
Marshallese (4)	4	<0.01
Native Hawaiian (25)	81	0.03
Samoan (8)	28	0.01
Tongan (0)	1	<0.01
White (204,644)	211,987	84.68
Not Hispanic (200,047)	206,464	82.48
Hispanic (4,597)	5,523	2.21

*Notes: † The Census 2010 population figure is used to calculate the percentages in the Hispanic Origin and Race categories. Ancestry percentages are based on the 2006-2010 American Community Survey population (not shown); ‡ Numbers in parentheses indicate the number of people reporting a single ancestry; * Numbers in parentheses indicate the number of persons reporting this race alone, not in combination with any other race; Please refer to the User Guide for more information.*

Kent County

Population: 602,622

Ancestry	Population	%
Afghan (0)	0	<0.01
African, Sub-Saharan (3,335)	3,957	0.66
African (1,743)	2,223	0.37
Cape Verdean (72)	72	0.01
Ethiopian (449)	504	0.08
Ghanaian (2)	2	<0.01
Kenyan (101)	118	0.02
Liberian (338)	374	0.06
Nigerian (18)	18	<0.01
Senegalese (0)	0	<0.01
Sierra Leonean (0)	0	<0.01
Somalian (86)	86	0.01
South African (53)	67	0.01
Sudanese (318)	318	0.05
Ugandan (0)	11	<0.01
Zimbabwean (12)	12	<0.01
Other Sub-Saharan African (143)	152	0.03
Albanian (83)	135	0.02
Alsatian (0)	0	<0.01
American (19,778)	19,778	3.30
Arab (1,616)	3,276	0.55
Arab (393)	607	0.10
Egyptian (18)	18	<0.01
Iraqi (0)	0	<0.01
Jordanian (211)	223	0.04
Lebanese (555)	1,233	0.21
Moroccan (0)	0	<0.01
Palestinian (43)	53	0.01
Syrian (143)	758	0.13
Other Arab (253)	384	0.06
Armenian (192)	429	0.07
Assyrian/Chaldean/Syriac (83)	129	0.02
Australian (64)	142	0.02
Austrian (167)	1,089	0.18
Basque (0)	0	<0.01
Belgian (347)	1,466	0.24
Brazilian (69)	144	0.02
British (789)	2,193	0.37
Bulgarian (87)	141	0.02
Cajun (0)	62	0.01
Canadian (877)	1,995	0.33
Carpatho Rusyn (0)	0	<0.01
Celtic (23)	66	0.01
Croatian (296)	811	0.14
Cypriot (0)	0	<0.01
Czech (485)	2,379	0.40
Czechoslovakian (433)	1,047	0.17
Danish (1,154)	5,124	0.85
Dutch (61,302)	117,723	19.64
Eastern European (285)	356	0.06
English (15,330)	64,695	10.79
Estonian (30)	30	0.01
European (6,118)	6,936	1.16
Finnish (846)	3,033	0.51
French, ex. Basque (2,330)	21,025	3.51
French Canadian (1,891)	6,219	1.04
German (31,965)	131,340	21.91
German Russian (0)	0	<0.01
Greek (572)	1,574	0.26
Guyanese (0)	7	<0.01
Hungarian (846)	3,085	0.51
Icelander (26)	39	0.01
Iranian (115)	182	0.03
Irish (13,528)	71,811	11.98
Israeli (13)	13	<0.01
Italian (5,395)	18,005	3.00
Latvian (347)	722	0.12
Lithuanian (1,163)	3,568	0.60
Luxemburger (59)	98	0.02
Macedonian (41)	236	0.04
Maltese (37)	65	0.01
New Zealander (15)	15	<0.01
Northern European (300)	327	0.05
Norwegian (1,508)	5,986	1.00
Pennsylvania German (217)	546	0.09

Ancestry	Population	%
Polish (16,134)	49,004	8.18
Portuguese (68)	410	0.07
Romanian (533)	790	0.13
Russian (911)	3,075	0.51
Scandinavian (384)	1,158	0.19
Scotch-Irish (2,606)	8,751	1.46
Scottish (2,558)	11,750	1.96
Serbian (54)	198	0.03
Slavic (77)	236	0.04
Slovak (237)	795	0.13
Slovene (0)	82	0.01
Soviet Union (0)	0	<0.01
Swedish (2,953)	13,783	2.30
Swiss (276)	2,074	0.35
Turkish (7)	18	<0.01
Ukrainian (412)	1,111	0.19
Welsh (478)	2,730	0.46
West Indian, ex. Hispanic (271)	587	0.10
Bahamian (13)	13	<0.01
Barbadian (14)	14	<0.01
Belizean (0)	0	<0.01
Bermudan (0)	12	<0.01
British West Indian (13)	13	<0.01
Dutch West Indian (26)	26	<0.01
Haitian (63)	73	0.01
Jamaican (111)	298	0.05
Trinidadian/Tobagonian (0)	0	<0.01
U.S. Virgin Islander (0)	11	<0.01
West Indian (22)	118	0.02
Other West Indian (9)	9	<0.01
Yugoslavian (2,270)	2,588	0.43

Hispanic Origin	Population	%
Hispanic or Latino (of any race)	58,437	9.70
Central American, ex. Mexican	6,036	1.00
Costa Rican	69	0.01
Guatemalan	4,536	0.75
Honduran	472	0.08
Nicaraguan	115	0.02
Panamanian	72	0.01
Salvadoran	734	0.12
Other Central American	38	0.01
Cuban	1,789	0.30
Dominican Republic	2,394	0.40
Mexican	38,006	6.31
Puerto Rican	5,739	0.95
South American	1,065	0.18
Argentinean	98	0.02
Bolivian	81	0.01
Chilean	100	0.02
Colombian	319	0.05
Ecuadorian	100	0.02
Paraguayan	23	<0.01
Peruvian	220	0.04
Uruguayan	10	<0.01
Venezuelan	109	0.02
Other South American	5	<0.01
Other Hispanic or Latino	3,408	0.57

Race*	Population	%
African-American/Black (58,648)	68,281	11.33
Not Hispanic (56,372)	64,312	10.67
Hispanic (2,276)	3,969	0.66
American Indian/Alaska Native (3,056)	7,581	1.26
Not Hispanic (2,075)	5,834	0.97
Hispanic (981)	1,747	0.29
Alaska Athabascan (Ala. Nat.) (5)	8	<0.01
Aleut (Alaska Native) (0)	4	<0.01
Apache (21)	66	0.01
Arapaho (3)	3	<0.01
Blackfeet (20)	197	0.03
Canadian/French Am. Ind. (30)	52	0.01
Central American Ind. (78)	83	0.01
Cherokee (116)	695	0.12
Cheyenne (1)	12	<0.01
Chickasaw (7)	15	<0.01
Chippewa (618)	1,217	0.20
Choctaw (10)	51	0.01
Colville (1)	3	<0.01

Race*	Population	%
Comanche (2)	13	<0.01
Cree (1)	11	<0.01
Creek (10)	34	0.01
Crow (0)	5	<0.01
Delaware (1)	7	<0.01
Hopi (1)	1	<0.01
Houma (0)	0	<0.01
Inupiat (Alaska Native) (6)	17	<0.01
Iroquois (15)	92	0.02
Kiowa (0)	0	<0.01
Lumbee (10)	23	<0.01
Menominee (0)	2	<0.01
Mexican American Ind. (201)	281	0.05
Navajo (26)	52	0.01
Osage (0)	6	<0.01
Ottawa (368)	703	0.12
Paiute (0)	0	<0.01
Pima (1)	1	<0.01
Potawatomi (213)	436	0.07
Pueblo (3)	10	<0.01
Puget Sound Salish (1)	3	<0.01
Seminole (0)	26	<0.01
Shoshone (1)	2	<0.01
Sioux (24)	105	0.02
South American Ind. (20)	41	0.01
Spanish American Ind. (23)	30	<0.01
Tlingit-Haida (Alaska Native) (5)	11	<0.01
Tohono O'Odham (1)	1	<0.01
Tsimshian (Alaska Native) (1)	5	<0.01
Ute (0)	2	<0.01
Yakama (0)	0	<0.01
Yaqui (3)	5	<0.01
Yuman (1)	3	<0.01
Yup'ik (Alaska Native) (0)	0	<0.01
Asian (14,053)	17,261	2.86
Not Hispanic (13,932)	16,855	2.80
Hispanic (121)	406	0.07
Bangladeshi (79)	84	0.01
Bhutanese (105)	117	0.02
Burmese (468)	505	0.08
Cambodian (39)	73	0.01
Chinese, ex. Taiwanese (1,798)	2,390	0.40
Filipino (843)	1,506	0.25
Hmong (80)	88	0.01
Indian (2,032)	2,381	0.40
Indonesian (63)	149	0.02
Japanese (303)	707	0.12
Korean (1,897)	2,496	0.41
Laotian (62)	89	0.01
Malaysian (16)	21	<0.01
Nepalese (62)	76	0.01
Pakistani (220)	258	0.04
Sri Lankan (30)	46	0.01
Taiwanese (59)	73	0.01
Thai (106)	230	0.04
Vietnamese (5,314)	5,803	0.96
Hawaii Native/Pacific Islander (249)	755	0.13
Not Hispanic (163)	541	0.09
Hispanic (86)	214	0.04
Fijian (4)	11	<0.01
Guamanian/Chamorro (78)	121	0.02
Marshallese (3)	8	<0.01
Native Hawaiian (67)	221	0.04
Samoan (20)	38	0.01
Tongan (1)	2	<0.01
White (481,594)	497,445	82.55
Not Hispanic (457,769)	469,631	77.93
Hispanic (23,825)	27,814	4.62

Notes: † The Census 2010 population figure is used to calculate the percentages in the Hispanic Origin and Race categories. Ancestry percentages are based on the 2006-2010 American Community Survey population (not shown); ‡ Numbers in parentheses indicate the number of people reporting a single ancestry; * Numbers in parentheses indicate the number of persons reporting this race alone, not in combination with any other race; Please refer to the User Guide for more information.

Lapeer County

Population: 88,319

Ancestry	Population	%
Afghan (0)	0	<0.01
African, Sub-Saharan (31)	34	0.04
African (20)	23	0.03
Cape Verdean (0)	0	<0.01
Ethiopian (0)	0	<0.01
Ghanaian (0)	0	<0.01
Kenyan (0)	0	<0.01
Liberian (0)	0	<0.01
Nigerian (0)	0	<0.01
Senegalese (0)	0	<0.01
Sierra Leonean (0)	0	<0.01
Somalian (0)	0	<0.01
South African (0)	0	<0.01
Sudanese (0)	0	<0.01
Ugandan (0)	0	<0.01
Zimbabwean (11)	11	0.01
Other Sub-Saharan African (0)	0	<0.01
Albanian (9)	36	0.04
Alsatian (0)	0	<0.01
American (6,281)	6,281	6.98
Arab (331)	384	0.43
Arab (13)	13	0.01
Egyptian (0)	0	<0.01
Iraqi (9)	9	0.01
Jordanian (0)	0	<0.01
Lebanese (157)	200	0.22
Moroccan (27)	27	0.03
Palestinian (63)	63	0.07
Syrian (45)	55	0.06
Other Arab (17)	17	0.02
Armenian (25)	65	0.07
Assyrian/Chaldean/Syriac (0)	0	<0.01
Australian (17)	39	0.04
Austrian (24)	277	0.31
Basque (0)	0	<0.01
Belgian (112)	644	0.72
Brazilian (0)	0	<0.01
British (121)	459	0.51
Bulgarian (25)	70	0.08
Cajun (0)	0	<0.01
Canadian (418)	712	0.79
Carpatho Rusyn (12)	12	0.01
Celtic (0)	0	<0.01
Croatian (129)	174	0.19
Cypriot (0)	0	<0.01
Czech (129)	373	0.41
Czechoslovakian (70)	125	0.14
Danish (147)	423	0.47
Dutch (626)	2,391	2.66
Eastern European (43)	43	0.05
English (3,667)	12,118	13.47
Estonian (0)	0	<0.01
European (772)	823	0.92
Finnish (219)	531	0.59
French, ex. Basque (941)	5,733	6.37
French Canadian (1,026)	2,536	2.82
German (8,004)	25,506	28.36
German Russian (0)	0	<0.01
Greek (60)	264	0.29
Guyanese (0)	0	<0.01
Hungarian (128)	753	0.84
Icelander (0)	10	0.01
Iranian (0)	0	<0.01
Irish (3,543)	13,640	15.16
Israeli (0)	0	<0.01
Italian (1,493)	4,187	4.66
Latvian (30)	30	0.03
Lithuanian (115)	247	0.27
Luxemburger (0)	0	<0.01
Macedonian (7)	20	0.02
Maltese (28)	103	0.11
New Zealander (0)	0	<0.01
Northern European (56)	72	0.08
Norwegian (161)	564	0.63
Pennsylvania German (9)	43	0.05

	Population	%
Polish (2,899)	8,859	9.85
Portuguese (29)	163	0.18
Romanian (106)	284	0.32
Russian (156)	481	0.53
Scandinavian (15)	120	0.13
Scotch-Irish (699)	1,960	2.18
Scottish (1,080)	3,800	4.22
Serbian (0)	23	0.03
Slavic (6)	19	0.02
Slovak (196)	254	0.28
Slovene (30)	101	0.11
Soviet Union (0)	0	<0.01
Swedish (205)	1,268	1.41
Swiss (110)	273	0.30
Turkish (8)	8	0.01
Ukrainian (108)	304	0.34
Welsh (95)	458	0.51
West Indian, ex. Hispanic (0)	38	0.04
Bahamian (0)	0	<0.01
Barbadian (0)	14	0.02
Belizean (0)	0	<0.01
Bermudan (0)	24	0.03
British West Indian (0)	0	<0.01
Dutch West Indian (0)	0	<0.01
Haitian (0)	0	<0.01
Jamaican (0)	0	<0.01
Trinidadian/Tobagonian (0)	0	<0.01
U.S. Virgin Islander (0)	0	<0.01
West Indian (0)	0	<0.01
Other West Indian (0)	0	<0.01
Yugoslavian (40)	45	0.05

Hispanic Origin	Population	%
Hispanic or Latino (of any race)	3,622	4.10
Central American, ex. Mexican	52	0.06
Costa Rican	1	<0.01
Guatemalan	22	0.02
Honduran	1	<0.01
Nicaraguan	12	0.01
Panamanian	10	0.01
Salvadoran	6	0.01
Other Central American	0	<0.01
Cuban	27	0.03
Dominican Republic	2	<0.01
Mexican	2,954	3.34
Puerto Rican	334	0.38
South American	41	0.05
Argentinean	10	0.01
Bolivian	0	<0.01
Chilean	5	0.01
Colombian	15	0.02
Ecuadorian	2	<0.01
Paraguayan	0	<0.01
Peruvian	5	0.01
Uruguayan	1	<0.01
Venezuelan	3	<0.01
Other South American	0	<0.01
Other Hispanic or Latino	212	0.24

Race*	Population	%
African-American/Black (922)	1,242	1.41
Not Hispanic (896)	1,180	1.34
Hispanic (26)	62	0.07
American Indian/Alaska Native (403)	954	1.08
Not Hispanic (348)	851	0.96
Hispanic (55)	103	0.12
Alaska Athabascan (Ala. Nat.) (0)	1	<0.01
Aleut (Alaska Native) (0)	0	<0.01
Apache (2)	9	0.01
Arapaho (0)	0	<0.01
Blackfeet (3)	28	0.03
Canadian/French Am. Ind. (4)	6	0.01
Central American Ind. (0)	0	<0.01
Cherokee (31)	168	0.19
Cheyenne (1)	8	0.01
Chickasaw (5)	6	0.01
Chippewa (141)	252	0.29
Choctaw (6)	19	0.02
Colville (0)	0	<0.01

	Population	%
Comanche (0)	1	<0.01
Cree (0)	0	<0.01
Creek (0)	5	0.01
Crow (1)	3	<0.01
Delaware (2)	4	<0.01
Hopi (0)	1	<0.01
Houma (0)	0	<0.01
Inupiat (Alaska Native) (0)	0	<0.01
Iroquois (7)	25	0.03
Kiowa (2)	2	<0.01
Lumbee (7)	10	0.01
Menominee (0)	0	<0.01
Mexican American Ind. (2)	11	0.01
Navajo (5)	11	0.01
Osage (0)	0	<0.01
Ottawa (23)	43	0.05
Paiute (0)	0	<0.01
Pima (0)	0	<0.01
Potawatomi (8)	12	0.01
Pueblo (1)	1	<0.01
Puget Sound Salish (0)	0	<0.01
Seminole (0)	0	<0.01
Shoshone (0)	1	<0.01
Sioux (3)	7	0.01
South American Ind. (2)	4	<0.01
Spanish American Ind. (1)	2	<0.01
Tlingit-Haida (Alaska Native) (0)	0	<0.01
Tohono O'Odham (0)	0	<0.01
Tsimshian (Alaska Native) (0)	0	<0.01
Ute (0)	0	<0.01
Yakama (0)	0	<0.01
Yaqui (1)	1	<0.01
Yuman (0)	0	<0.01
Yup'ik (Alaska Native) (1)	1	<0.01
Asian (309)	520	0.59
Not Hispanic (308)	507	0.57
Hispanic (1)	13	0.01
Bangladeshi (0)	0	<0.01
Bhutanese (0)	0	<0.01
Burmese (0)	0	<0.01
Cambodian (0)	3	<0.01
Chinese, ex. Taiwanese (43)	74	0.08
Filipino (62)	110	0.12
Hmong (10)	13	0.01
Indian (36)	63	0.07
Indonesian (4)	13	0.01
Japanese (35)	77	0.09
Korean (66)	92	0.10
Laotian (2)	9	0.01
Malaysian (0)	0	<0.01
Nepalese (0)	0	<0.01
Pakistani (6)	22	0.02
Sri Lankan (0)	0	<0.01
Taiwanese (1)	1	<0.01
Thai (10)	17	0.02
Vietnamese (14)	22	0.02
Hawaii Native/Pacific Islander (9)	25	0.03
Not Hispanic (9)	23	0.03
Hispanic (0)	2	<0.01
Fijian (0)	0	<0.01
Guamanian/Chamorro (0)	0	<0.01
Marshallese (1)	1	<0.01
Native Hawaiian (2)	7	0.01
Samoan (1)	1	<0.01
Tongan (0)	0	<0.01
White (84,351)	85,548	96.86
Not Hispanic (82,147)	83,094	94.08
Hispanic (2,204)	2,454	2.78

*Notes: † The Census 2010 population figure is used to calculate the percentages in the Hispanic Origin and Race categories. Ancestry percentages are based on the 2006-2010 American Community Survey population (not shown); ‡ Numbers in parentheses indicate the number of people reporting a single ancestry; * Numbers in parentheses indicate the number of persons reporting this race alone, not in combination with any other race; Please refer to the User Guide for more information.*

Lenawee County

Population: 99,892

Ancestry	Population	%
Afghan (0)	0	<0.01
African, Sub-Saharan (262)	306	0.30
African (175)	219	0.22
Cape Verdean (0)	0	<0.01
Ethiopian (0)	0	<0.01
Ghanaian (0)	0	<0.01
Kenyan (87)	87	0.09
Liberian (0)	0	<0.01
Nigerian (0)	0	<0.01
Senegalese (0)	0	<0.01
Sierra Leonean (0)	0	<0.01
Somalian (0)	0	<0.01
South African (0)	0	<0.01
Sudanese (0)	0	<0.01
Ugandan (0)	0	<0.01
Zimbabwean (0)	0	<0.01
Other Sub-Saharan African (0)	0	<0.01
Albanian (0)	0	<0.01
Alsatian (4)	10	0.01
American (6,756)	6,756	6.70
Arab (196)	272	0.27
Arab (31)	49	0.05
Egyptian (0)	0	<0.01
Iraqi (0)	0	<0.01
Jordanian (0)	0	<0.01
Lebanese (156)	199	0.20
Moroccan (9)	9	0.01
Palestinian (0)	0	<0.01
Syrian (0)	15	0.01
Other Arab (0)	0	<0.01
Armenian (22)	84	0.08
Assyrian/Chaldean/Syriac (0)	0	<0.01
Australian (0)	26	0.03
Austrian (22)	54	0.05
Basque (0)	0	<0.01
Belgian (179)	398	0.39
Brazilian (0)	29	0.03
British (169)	310	0.31
Bulgarian (0)	18	0.02
Cajun (0)	52	0.05
Canadian (217)	479	0.47
Carpatho Rusyn (0)	0	<0.01
Celtic (9)	9	0.01
Croatian (5)	29	0.03
Cypriot (0)	0	<0.01
Czech (283)	643	0.64
Czechoslovakian (129)	195	0.19
Danish (81)	271	0.27
Dutch (635)	3,558	3.53
Eastern European (15)	15	0.01
English (5,071)	15,033	14.90
Estonian (6)	30	0.03
European (694)	830	0.82
Finnish (137)	440	0.44
French, ex. Basque (1,034)	6,012	5.96
French Canadian (456)	1,757	1.74
German (11,782)	32,371	32.08
German Russian (0)	0	<0.01
Greek (64)	258	0.26
Guyanese (0)	0	<0.01
Hungarian (528)	1,285	1.27
Icelander (0)	0	<0.01
Iranian (19)	19	0.02
Irish (3,484)	14,728	14.60
Israeli (0)	0	<0.01
Italian (1,135)	3,146	3.12
Latvian (0)	0	<0.01
Lithuanian (41)	142	0.14
Luxemburger (18)	18	0.02
Macedonian (16)	16	0.02
Maltese (65)	150	0.15
New Zealander (0)	0	<0.01
Northern European (26)	29	0.03
Norwegian (182)	690	0.68
Pennsylvania German (70)	155	0.15

Ancestry	Population	%
Polish (1,425)	5,517	5.47
Portuguese (8)	52	0.05
Romanian (23)	70	0.07
Russian (126)	375	0.37
Scandinavian (68)	171	0.17
Scotch-Irish (551)	1,566	1.55
Scottish (627)	2,300	2.28
Serbian (0)	34	0.03
Slavic (37)	52	0.05
Slovak (56)	181	0.18
Slovene (0)	0	<0.01
Soviet Union (0)	0	<0.01
Swedish (152)	850	0.84
Swiss (62)	420	0.42
Turkish (0)	55	0.05
Ukrainian (98)	349	0.35
Welsh (80)	661	0.66
West Indian, ex. Hispanic (43)	55	0.05
Bahamian (0)	0	<0.01
Barbadian (0)	0	<0.01
Belizean (0)	0	<0.01
Bermudan (0)	0	<0.01
British West Indian (0)	0	<0.01
Dutch West Indian (40)	40	0.04
Haitian (0)	0	<0.01
Jamaican (0)	12	0.01
Trinidadian/Tobagonian (0)	0	<0.01
U.S. Virgin Islander (0)	0	<0.01
West Indian (3)	3	<0.01
Other West Indian (0)	0	<0.01
Yugoslavian (22)	81	0.08

Hispanic Origin	Population	%
Hispanic or Latino (of any race)	7,614	7.62
Central American, ex. Mexican	65	0.07
Costa Rican	11	0.01
Guatemalan	40	0.04
Honduran	1	<0.01
Nicaraguan	3	<0.01
Panamanian	3	<0.01
Salvadoran	7	0.01
Other Central American	0	<0.01
Cuban	54	0.05
Dominican Republic	23	0.02
Mexican	6,330	6.34
Puerto Rican	445	0.45
South American	103	0.10
Argentinean	5	0.01
Bolivian	5	0.01
Chilean	13	0.01
Colombian	38	0.04
Ecuadorian	12	0.01
Paraguayan	9	0.01
Peruvian	13	0.01
Uruguayan	2	<0.01
Venezuelan	3	<0.01
Other South American	3	<0.01
Other Hispanic or Latino	594	0.59

Race*	Population	%
African-American/Black (2,539)	3,376	3.38
Not Hispanic (2,397)	3,050	3.05
Hispanic (142)	326	0.33
American Indian/Alaska Native (475)	1,200	1.20
Not Hispanic (379)	1,005	1.01
Hispanic (96)	195	0.20
Alaska Athabascan *(Ala. Nat.)* (1)	2	<0.01
Aleut *(Alaska Native)* (0)	3	<0.01
Apache (2)	17	0.02
Arapaho (0)	0	<0.01
Blackfeet (7)	41	0.04
Canadian/French Am. Ind. (4)	5	0.01
Central American Ind. (1)	1	<0.01
Cherokee (65)	221	0.22
Cheyenne (0)	4	<0.01
Chickasaw (1)	5	0.01
Chippewa (105)	181	0.18
Choctaw (16)	29	0.03
Colville (0)	0	<0.01

Race*	Population	%
Comanche (1)	2	<0.01
Cree (1)	5	0.01
Creek (3)	9	0.01
Crow (0)	1	<0.01
Delaware (1)	2	<0.01
Hopi (0)	0	<0.01
Houma (1)	2	<0.01
Inupiat *(Alaska Native)* (2)	2	<0.01
Iroquois (5)	21	0.02
Kiowa (1)	1	<0.01
Lumbee (5)	8	0.01
Menominee (2)	2	<0.01
Mexican American Ind. (21)	29	0.03
Navajo (2)	8	0.01
Osage (1)	2	<0.01
Ottawa (8)	23	0.02
Paiute (0)	0	<0.01
Pima (0)	0	<0.01
Potawatomi (8)	26	0.03
Pueblo (0)	0	<0.01
Puget Sound Salish (0)	0	<0.01
Seminole (0)	0	<0.01
Shoshone (0)	0	<0.01
Sioux (5)	34	0.03
South American Ind. (1)	2	<0.01
Spanish American Ind. (0)	3	<0.01
Tlingit-Haida *(Alaska Native)* (1)	2	<0.01
Tohono O'Odham (0)	0	<0.01
Tsimshian *(Alaska Native)* (0)	0	<0.01
Ute (0)	0	<0.01
Yakama (0)	0	<0.01
Yaqui (0)	6	0.01
Yuman (0)	0	<0.01
Yup'ik *(Alaska Native)* (2)	2	<0.01
Asian (519)	794	0.79
Not Hispanic (492)	726	0.73
Hispanic (27)	68	0.07
Bangladeshi (2)	2	<0.01
Bhutanese (0)	0	<0.01
Burmese (0)	0	<0.01
Cambodian (4)	4	<0.01
Chinese, ex. Taiwanese (67)	100	0.10
Filipino (89)	168	0.17
Hmong (12)	12	0.01
Indian (96)	110	0.11
Indonesian (2)	6	0.01
Japanese (52)	112	0.11
Korean (99)	147	0.15
Laotian (0)	2	<0.01
Malaysian (0)	3	<0.01
Nepalese (0)	0	<0.01
Pakistani (15)	18	0.02
Sri Lankan (0)	0	<0.01
Taiwanese (3)	5	0.01
Thai (8)	14	0.01
Vietnamese (43)	57	0.06
Hawaii Native/Pacific Islander (26)	59	0.06
Not Hispanic (21)	47	0.05
Hispanic (5)	12	0.01
Fijian (0)	0	<0.01
Guamanian/Chamorro (5)	10	0.01
Marshallese (0)	0	<0.01
Native Hawaiian (9)	24	0.02
Samoan (2)	2	<0.01
Tongan (4)	5	0.01
White (92,174)	94,261	94.36
Not Hispanic (87,483)	88,904	89.00
Hispanic (4,691)	5,357	5.36

*Notes: † The Census 2010 population figure is used to calculate the percentages in the Hispanic Origin and Race categories. Ancestry percentages are based on the 2006-2010 American Community Survey population (not shown); ‡ Numbers in parentheses indicate the number of people reporting a single ancestry; * Numbers in parentheses indicate the number of persons reporting this race alone, not in combination with any other race; Please refer to the User Guide for more information.*

Livingston County

Population: 180,967

Ancestry	Population	%
Afghan (0)	0	<0.01
African, Sub-Saharan (67)	90	0.05
African (0)	23	0.01
Cape Verdean (0)	0	<0.01
Ethiopian (0)	0	<0.01
Ghanaian (0)	0	<0.01
Kenyan (0)	0	<0.01
Liberian (0)	0	<0.01
Nigerian (0)	0	<0.01
Senegalese (0)	0	<0.01
Sierra Leonean (0)	0	<0.01
Somalian (0)	0	<0.01
South African (67)	67	0.04
Sudanese (0)	0	<0.01
Ugandan (0)	0	<0.01
Zimbabwean (0)	0	<0.01
Other Sub-Saharan African (0)	0	<0.01
Albanian (75)	130	0.07
Alsatian (0)	0	<0.01
American (10,630)	10,630	5.86
Arab (454)	1,249	0.69
Arab (104)	119	0.07
Egyptian (0)	0	<0.01
Iraqi (10)	56	0.03
Jordanian (18)	26	0.01
Lebanese (146)	642	0.35
Moroccan (10)	10	0.01
Palestinian (83)	132	0.07
Syrian (83)	264	0.15
Other Arab (0)	0	<0.01
Armenian (122)	488	0.27
Assyrian/Chaldean/Syriac (16)	115	0.06
Australian (21)	72	0.04
Austrian (142)	644	0.36
Basque (0)	0	<0.01
Belgian (183)	1,027	0.57
Brazilian (25)	44	0.02
British (597)	1,128	0.62
Bulgarian (0)	0	<0.01
Cajun (8)	8	<0.01
Canadian (563)	1,625	0.90
Carpatho Rusyn (0)	0	<0.01
Celtic (23)	23	0.01
Croatian (193)	492	0.27
Cypriot (0)	0	<0.01
Czech (242)	1,267	0.70
Czechoslovakian (200)	484	0.27
Danish (288)	991	0.55
Dutch (1,138)	5,232	2.89
Eastern European (111)	111	0.06
English (8,321)	27,307	15.06
Estonian (0)	0	<0.01
European (1,772)	1,968	1.09
Finnish (2,084)	4,218	2.33
French, ex. Basque (1,570)	11,200	6.18
French Canadian (1,273)	5,064	2.79
German (13,723)	51,505	28.40
German Russian (0)	0	<0.01
Greek (558)	1,234	0.68
Guyanese (0)	0	<0.01
Hungarian (887)	2,686	1.48
Icelander (0)	33	0.02
Iranian (21)	31	0.02
Irish (7,689)	31,970	17.63
Israeli (0)	9	<0.01
Italian (3,506)	12,122	6.68
Latvian (20)	60	0.03
Lithuanian (367)	978	0.54
Luxemburger (0)	0	<0.01
Macedonian (164)	445	0.25
Maltese (254)	665	0.37
New Zealander (0)	0	<0.01
Northern European (249)	304	0.17
Norwegian (611)	1,796	0.99
Pennsylvania German (115)	158	0.09

Ancestry	Population	%
Polish (8,499)	23,567	13.00
Portuguese (56)	167	0.09
Romanian (271)	531	0.29
Russian (451)	1,481	0.82
Scandinavian (201)	295	0.16
Scotch-Irish (1,587)	4,112	2.27
Scottish (2,155)	7,459	4.11
Serbian (31)	172	0.09
Slavic (27)	143	0.08
Slovak (173)	674	0.37
Slovene (45)	158	0.09
Soviet Union (0)	0	<0.01
Swedish (945)	3,918	2.16
Swiss (234)	593	0.33
Turkish (7)	64	0.04
Ukrainian (493)	1,213	0.67
Welsh (262)	1,221	0.67
West Indian, ex. Hispanic (14)	14	0.01
Bahamian (0)	0	<0.01
Barbadian (0)	0	<0.01
Belizean (0)	0	<0.01
Bermudan (0)	0	<0.01
British West Indian (0)	0	<0.01
Dutch West Indian (0)	0	<0.01
Haitian (0)	0	<0.01
Jamaican (0)	0	<0.01
Trinidadian/Tobagonian (14)	14	0.01
U.S. Virgin Islander (0)	0	<0.01
West Indian (0)	0	<0.01
Other West Indian (0)	0	<0.01
Yugoslavian (52)	215	0.12

Hispanic Origin	Population	%
Hispanic or Latino (of any race)	3,460	1.91
Central American, ex. Mexican	143	0.08
Costa Rican	11	0.01
Guatemalan	82	0.05
Honduran	18	0.01
Nicaraguan	11	0.01
Panamanian	7	<0.01
Salvadoran	10	0.01
Other Central American	4	<0.01
Cuban	133	0.07
Dominican Republic	24	0.01
Mexican	2,229	1.23
Puerto Rican	267	0.15
South American	255	0.14
Argentinean	55	0.03
Bolivian	3	<0.01
Chilean	22	0.01
Colombian	74	0.04
Ecuadorian	12	0.01
Paraguayan	2	<0.01
Peruvian	55	0.03
Uruguayan	1	<0.01
Venezuelan	26	0.01
Other South American	5	<0.01
Other Hispanic or Latino	409	0.23

Race*	Population	%
African-American/Black (809)	1,239	0.68
Not Hispanic (776)	1,163	0.64
Hispanic (33)	76	0.04
American Indian/Alaska Native (707)	1,756	0.97
Not Hispanic (648)	1,595	0.88
Hispanic (59)	161	0.09
Alaska Athabascan (Ala. Nat.) (1)	1	<0.01
Aleut (Alaska Native) (5)	10	0.01
Apache (8)	23	0.01
Arapaho (1)	3	<0.01
Blackfeet (1)	37	0.02
Canadian/French Am. Ind. (2)	13	0.01
Central American Ind. (4)	4	<0.01
Cherokee (71)	256	0.14
Cheyenne (1)	2	<0.01
Chickasaw (2)	4	<0.01
Chippewa (224)	420	0.23
Choctaw (7)	11	0.01
Colville (2)	6	<0.01

Race*	Population	%
Comanche (1)	2	<0.01
Cree (1)	4	<0.01
Creek (3)	6	<0.01
Crow (0)	6	<0.01
Delaware (1)	3	<0.01
Hopi (1)	5	<0.01
Houma (0)	0	<0.01
Inupiat (Alaska Native) (1)	4	<0.01
Iroquois (30)	69	0.04
Kiowa (0)	0	<0.01
Lumbee (22)	33	0.02
Menominee (1)	2	<0.01
Mexican American Ind. (11)	18	0.01
Navajo (8)	13	0.01
Osage (1)	3	<0.01
Ottawa (30)	54	0.03
Paiute (1)	1	<0.01
Pima (0)	0	<0.01
Potawatomi (7)	14	0.01
Pueblo (0)	3	<0.01
Puget Sound Salish (0)	0	<0.01
Seminole (0)	0	<0.01
Shoshone (0)	1	<0.01
Sioux (17)	33	0.02
South American Ind. (0)	0	<0.01
Spanish American Ind. (0)	0	<0.01
Tlingit-Haida (Alaska Native) (2)	2	<0.01
Tohono O'Odham (0)	0	<0.01
Tsimshian (Alaska Native) (0)	0	<0.01
Ute (1)	5	<0.01
Yakama (0)	0	<0.01
Yaqui (0)	0	<0.01
Yuman (0)	0	<0.01
Yup'ik (Alaska Native) (4)	5	<0.01
Asian (1,424)	2,112	1.17
Not Hispanic (1,412)	2,055	1.14
Hispanic (12)	57	0.03
Bangladeshi (3)	3	<0.01
Bhutanese (0)	0	<0.01
Burmese (4)	5	<0.01
Cambodian (2)	6	<0.01
Chinese, ex. Taiwanese (321)	429	0.24
Filipino (223)	390	0.22
Hmong (42)	43	0.02
Indian (199)	269	0.15
Indonesian (0)	15	0.01
Japanese (125)	262	0.14
Korean (216)	314	0.17
Laotian (16)	26	0.01
Malaysian (10)	11	0.01
Nepalese (0)	2	<0.01
Pakistani (26)	35	0.02
Sri Lankan (3)	3	<0.01
Taiwanese (26)	35	0.02
Thai (22)	31	0.02
Vietnamese (137)	173	0.10
Hawaii Native/Pacific Islander (76)	198	0.11
Not Hispanic (73)	184	0.10
Hispanic (3)	14	0.01
Fijian (0)	0	<0.01
Guamanian/Chamorro (8)	12	0.01
Marshallese (1)	1	<0.01
Native Hawaiian (23)	85	0.05
Samoan (4)	8	<0.01
Tongan (1)	1	<0.01
White (175,015)	177,196	97.92
Not Hispanic (172,513)	174,424	96.38
Hispanic (2,502)	2,772	1.53

Macomb County

Population: 840,978

Ancestry	Population	%
Afghan (41)	41	<0.01
African, Sub-Saharan (3,949)	4,553	0.54
African (3,215)	3,728	0.45
Cape Verdean (11)	58	0.01
Ethiopian (0)	0	<0.01
Ghanaian (119)	119	0.01
Kenyan (40)	40	<0.01
Liberian (19)	19	<0.01
Nigerian (164)	164	0.02
Senegalese (20)	20	<0.01
Sierra Leonean (0)	0	<0.01
Somalian (75)	75	0.01
South African (49)	93	0.01
Sudanese (0)	0	<0.01
Ugandan (0)	0	<0.01
Zimbabwean (18)	18	<0.01
Other Sub-Saharan African (219)	219	0.03
Albanian (9,485)	10,147	1.21
Alsatian (0)	20	<0.01
American (34,352)	34,352	4.10
Arab (14,047)	21,199	2.53
Arab (2,959)	3,844	0.46
Egyptian (650)	742	0.09
Iraqi (5,071)	6,222	0.74
Jordanian (410)	559	0.07
Lebanese (3,522)	7,414	0.89
Moroccan (57)	115	0.01
Palestinian (147)	214	0.03
Syrian (523)	1,247	0.15
Other Arab (708)	842	0.10
Armenian (1,109)	1,892	0.23
Assyrian/Chaldean/Syriac (10,615)	12,680	1.51
Australian (202)	323	0.04
Austrian (514)	2,319	0.28
Basque (0)	10	<0.01
Belgian (4,569)	17,487	2.09
Brazilian (108)	137	0.02
British (841)	2,175	0.26
Bulgarian (154)	475	0.06
Cajun (0)	0	<0.01
Canadian (2,293)	5,339	0.64
Carpatho Rusyn (0)	23	<0.01
Celtic (83)	106	0.01
Croatian (987)	2,716	0.32
Cypriot (0)	0	<0.01
Czech (610)	3,697	0.44
Czechoslovakian (655)	1,838	0.22
Danish (356)	1,707	0.20
Dutch (2,159)	10,880	1.30
Eastern European (155)	240	0.03
English (15,215)	66,018	7.88
Estonian (0)	13	<0.01
European (4,216)	4,682	0.56
Finnish (1,287)	5,774	0.69
French, ex. Basque (5,387)	46,666	5.57
French Canadian (5,808)	17,709	2.11
German (50,777)	193,380	23.09
German Russian (0)	28	<0.01
Greek (3,262)	6,905	0.82
Guyanese (32)	46	0.01
Hungarian (1,898)	8,951	1.07
Icelander (10)	78	0.01
Iranian (387)	441	0.05
Irish (20,017)	99,693	11.90
Israeli (33)	44	0.01
Italian (46,142)	109,426	13.07
Latvian (18)	92	0.01
Lithuanian (808)	2,885	0.34
Luxemburger (8)	22	<0.01
Macedonian (3,758)	4,339	0.52
Maltese (648)	1,748	0.21
New Zealander (8)	24	<0.01
Northern European (265)	313	0.04
Norwegian (1,010)	4,475	0.53
Pennsylvania German (53)	267	0.03

Ancestry	Population	%
Polish (63,831)	156,887	18.73
Portuguese (153)	558	0.07
Romanian (4,108)	6,202	0.74
Russian (1,666)	6,770	0.81
Scandinavian (138)	385	0.05
Scotch-Irish (4,101)	12,603	1.50
Scottish (4,747)	19,742	2.36
Serbian (1,172)	2,144	0.26
Slavic (290)	847	0.10
Slovak (1,641)	4,934	0.59
Slovene (162)	449	0.05
Soviet Union (0)	0	<0.01
Swedish (1,605)	6,858	0.82
Swiss (179)	1,106	0.13
Turkish (108)	140	0.02
Ukrainian (3,454)	7,597	0.91
Welsh (441)	3,714	0.44
West Indian, ex. Hispanic (221)	350	0.04
Bahamian (13)	22	<0.01
Barbadian (0)	0	<0.01
Belizean (14)	14	<0.01
Bermudan (0)	0	<0.01
British West Indian (0)	0	<0.01
Dutch West Indian (0)	0	<0.01
Haitian (111)	145	0.02
Jamaican (47)	92	0.01
Trinidadian/Tobagonian (0)	0	<0.01
U.S. Virgin Islander (0)	0	<0.01
West Indian (36)	77	0.01
Other West Indian (0)	0	<0.01
Yugoslavian (4,681)	6,360	0.76

Hispanic Origin	Population	%
Hispanic or Latino (of any race)	19,095	2.27
Central American, ex. Mexican	573	0.07
Costa Rican	52	0.01
Guatemalan	223	0.03
Honduran	61	0.01
Nicaraguan	25	<0.01
Panamanian	100	0.01
Salvadoran	108	0.01
Other Central American	4	<0.01
Cuban	525	0.06
Dominican Republic	174	0.02
Mexican	12,719	1.51
Puerto Rican	1,952	0.23
South American	1,027	0.12
Argentinean	197	0.02
Bolivian	17	<0.01
Chilean	73	0.01
Colombian	272	0.03
Ecuadorian	140	0.02
Paraguayan	3	<0.01
Peruvian	135	0.02
Uruguayan	33	<0.01
Venezuelan	145	0.02
Other South American	12	<0.01
Other Hispanic or Latino	2,125	0.25

Race*	Population	%
African-American/Black (72,723)	80,122	9.53
Not Hispanic (72,053)	78,910	9.38
Hispanic (670)	1,212	0.14
American Indian/Alaska Native (2,646)	7,944	0.94
Not Hispanic (2,351)	7,152	0.85
Hispanic (295)	792	0.09
Alaska Athabascan (Ala. Nat.) (2)	5	<0.01
Aleut (Alaska Native) (2)	4	<0.01
Apache (22)	100	0.01
Arapaho (3)	8	<0.01
Blackfeet (38)	323	0.04
Canadian/French Am. Ind. (51)	126	0.02
Central American Ind. (2)	3	<0.01
Cherokee (286)	1,739	0.21
Cheyenne (2)	10	<0.01
Chickasaw (0)	7	<0.01
Chippewa (528)	1,076	0.13
Choctaw (21)	110	0.01
Colville (0)	0	<0.01

	Population	%
Comanche (11)	22	<0.01
Cree (10)	37	<0.01
Creek (7)	24	<0.01
Crow (2)	8	<0.01
Delaware (12)	20	<0.01
Hopi (1)	11	<0.01
Houma (0)	0	<0.01
Inupiat (Alaska Native) (4)	8	<0.01
Iroquois (180)	330	0.04
Kiowa (1)	2	<0.01
Lumbee (182)	301	0.04
Menominee (2)	5	<0.01
Mexican American Ind. (62)	91	0.01
Navajo (14)	52	0.01
Osage (2)	16	<0.01
Ottawa (81)	150	0.02
Paiute (0)	6	<0.01
Pima (2)	3	<0.01
Potawatomi (23)	78	0.01
Pueblo (9)	13	<0.01
Puget Sound Salish (3)	3	<0.01
Seminole (11)	32	<0.01
Shoshone (2)	7	<0.01
Sioux (26)	129	0.02
South American Ind. (7)	12	<0.01
Spanish American Ind. (1)	2	<0.01
Tlingit-Haida (Alaska Native) (2)	3	<0.01
Tohono O'Odham (1)	2	<0.01
Tsimshian (Alaska Native) (1)	2	<0.01
Ute (0)	1	<0.01
Yakama (0)	1	<0.01
Yaqui (2)	3	<0.01
Yuman (0)	0	<0.01
Yup'ik (Alaska Native) (3)	9	<0.01
Asian (25,063)	30,511	3.63
Not Hispanic (24,908)	30,110	3.58
Hispanic (155)	401	0.05
Bangladeshi (1,290)	1,418	0.17
Bhutanese (0)	0	<0.01
Burmese (15)	25	<0.01
Cambodian (144)	216	0.03
Chinese, ex. Taiwanese (2,550)	3,091	0.37
Filipino (5,015)	6,347	0.75
Hmong (1,885)	1,964	0.23
Indian (7,143)	7,878	0.94
Indonesian (37)	76	0.01
Japanese (418)	893	0.11
Korean (1,516)	2,099	0.25
Laotian (257)	335	0.04
Malaysian (15)	22	<0.01
Nepalese (22)	26	<0.01
Pakistani (1,127)	1,283	0.15
Sri Lankan (24)	27	<0.01
Taiwanese (73)	85	0.01
Thai (169)	269	0.03
Vietnamese (2,278)	2,554	0.30
Hawaii Native/Pacific Islander (179)	967	0.11
Not Hispanic (168)	904	0.11
Hispanic (11)	63	0.01
Fijian (4)	6	<0.01
Guamanian/Chamorro (32)	88	0.01
Marshallese (0)	0	<0.01
Native Hawaiian (38)	172	0.02
Samoan (22)	53	0.01
Tongan (0)	0	<0.01
White (717,973)	733,845	87.26
Not Hispanic (705,693)	720,129	85.63
Hispanic (12,280)	13,716	1.63

*Notes: † The Census 2010 population figure is used to calculate the percentages in the Hispanic Origin and Race categories. Ancestry percentages are based on the 2006-2010 American Community Survey population (not shown); ‡ Numbers in parentheses indicate the number of people reporting a single ancestry; * Numbers in parentheses indicate the number of persons reporting this race alone, not in combination with any other race; Please refer to the User Guide for more information.*

Marquette County

Population: 67,077

Ancestry	Population	%
Afghan (0)	0	<0.01
African, Sub-Saharan (9)	21	0.03
African (9)	13	0.02
Cape Verdean (0)	0	<0.01
Ethiopian (0)	0	<0.01
Ghanaian (0)	0	<0.01
Kenyan (0)	0	<0.01
Liberian (0)	0	<0.01
Nigerian (0)	0	<0.01
Senegalese (0)	0	<0.01
Sierra Leonean (0)	0	<0.01
Somalian (0)	8	0.01
South African (0)	0	<0.01
Sudanese (0)	0	<0.01
Ugandan (0)	0	<0.01
Zimbabwean (0)	0	<0.01
Other Sub-Saharan African (0)	0	<0.01
Albanian (0)	0	<0.01
Alsatian (0)	0	<0.01
American (1,723)	1,723	2.59
Arab (124)	146	0.22
Arab (45)	45	0.07
Egyptian (0)	0	<0.01
Iraqi (0)	0	<0.01
Jordanian (0)	0	<0.01
Lebanese (12)	34	0.05
Moroccan (10)	10	0.02
Palestinian (30)	30	0.05
Syrian (27)	27	0.04
Other Arab (0)	0	<0.01
Armenian (0)	18	0.03
Assyrian/Chaldean/Syriac (29)	29	0.04
Australian (7)	7	0.01
Austrian (19)	253	0.38
Basque (0)	1	<0.01
Belgian (188)	559	0.84
Brazilian (0)	0	<0.01
British (73)	152	0.23
Bulgarian (0)	13	0.02
Cajun (0)	0	<0.01
Canadian (126)	226	0.34
Carpatho Rusyn (0)	0	<0.01
Celtic (0)	0	<0.01
Croatian (88)	436	0.66
Cypriot (0)	0	<0.01
Czech (46)	381	0.57
Czechoslovakian (20)	43	0.06
Danish (88)	454	0.68
Dutch (290)	1,494	2.25
Eastern European (36)	56	0.08
English (1,695)	9,830	14.78
Estonian (12)	28	0.04
European (704)	758	1.14
Finnish (6,073)	14,162	21.29
French, ex. Basque (1,230)	8,535	12.83
French Canadian (811)	2,516	3.78
German (2,556)	13,184	19.82
German Russian (0)	0	<0.01
Greek (180)	380	0.57
Guyanese (0)	0	<0.01
Hungarian (63)	345	0.52
Icelander (0)	0	<0.01
Iranian (0)	0	<0.01
Irish (897)	7,494	11.27
Israeli (0)	0	<0.01
Italian (1,557)	6,395	9.61
Latvian (0)	19	0.03
Lithuanian (6)	168	0.25
Luxemburger (12)	12	0.02
Macedonian (2)	4	0.01
Maltese (7)	21	0.03
New Zealander (0)	0	<0.01
Northern European (7)	7	0.01
Norwegian (440)	1,919	2.89
Pennsylvania German (7)	20	0.03

Ancestry	Population	%
Polish (915)	3,501	5.26
Portuguese (34)	145	0.22
Romanian (0)	39	0.06
Russian (66)	332	0.50
Scandinavian (323)	459	0.69
Scotch-Irish (257)	1,046	1.57
Scottish (142)	1,431	2.15
Serbian (3)	24	0.04
Slavic (0)	11	0.02
Slovak (10)	50	0.08
Slovene (14)	58	0.09
Soviet Union (0)	0	<0.01
Swedish (1,268)	6,752	10.15
Swiss (0)	91	0.14
Turkish (32)	35	0.05
Ukrainian (91)	166	0.25
Welsh (62)	389	0.58
West Indian, ex. Hispanic (0)	97	0.15
Bahamian (0)	0	<0.01
Barbadian (0)	0	<0.01
Belizean (0)	0	<0.01
Bermudan (0)	0	<0.01
British West Indian (0)	0	<0.01
Dutch West Indian (0)	0	<0.01
Haitian (0)	0	<0.01
Jamaican (0)	97	0.15
Trinidadian/Tobagonian (0)	0	<0.01
U.S. Virgin Islander (0)	0	<0.01
West Indian (0)	0	<0.01
Other West Indian (0)	0	<0.01
Yugoslavian (37)	61	0.09

Hispanic Origin	Population	%
Hispanic or Latino (of any race)	767	1.14
Central American, ex. Mexican	43	0.06
Costa Rican	1	<0.01
Guatemalan	28	0.04
Honduran	4	0.01
Nicaraguan	1	<0.01
Panamanian	7	0.01
Salvadoran	2	<0.01
Other Central American	0	<0.01
Cuban	34	0.05
Dominican Republic	3	<0.01
Mexican	468	0.70
Puerto Rican	89	0.13
South American	29	0.04
Argentinean	7	0.01
Bolivian	0	<0.01
Chilean	6	0.01
Colombian	2	<0.01
Ecuadorian	2	<0.01
Paraguayan	0	<0.01
Peruvian	9	0.01
Uruguayan	1	<0.01
Venezuelan	2	<0.01
Other South American	0	<0.01
Other Hispanic or Latino	101	0.15

Race*	Population	%
African-American/Black (1,141)	1,432	2.13
Not Hispanic (1,126)	1,384	2.06
Hispanic (15)	48	0.07
American Indian/Alaska Native (1,161)	1,990	2.97
Not Hispanic (1,139)	1,931	2.88
Hispanic (22)	59	0.09
Alaska Athabascan (Ala. Nat.) (1)	6	0.01
Aleut (Alaska Native) (0)	0	<0.01
Apache (7)	10	0.01
Arapaho (0)	0	<0.01
Blackfeet (0)	5	0.01
Canadian/French Am. Ind. (3)	16	0.02
Central American Ind. (0)	3	<0.01
Cherokee (14)	82	0.12
Cheyenne (0)	1	<0.01
Chickasaw (3)	6	0.01
Chippewa (769)	1,182	1.76
Choctaw (0)	3	<0.01
Colville (0)	0	<0.01

	Population	%
Comanche (0)	1	<0.01
Cree (0)	0	<0.01
Creek (0)	0	<0.01
Crow (0)	1	<0.01
Delaware (0)	0	<0.01
Hopi (0)	0	<0.01
Houma (0)	0	<0.01
Inupiat (Alaska Native) (0)	3	<0.01
Iroquois (7)	15	0.02
Kiowa (0)	1	<0.01
Lumbee (0)	0	<0.01
Menominee (2)	6	0.01
Mexican American Ind. (2)	4	0.01
Navajo (1)	2	<0.01
Osage (0)	0	<0.01
Ottawa (33)	50	0.07
Paiute (0)	0	<0.01
Pima (1)	1	<0.01
Potawatomi (12)	26	0.04
Pueblo (1)	3	<0.01
Puget Sound Salish (0)	1	<0.01
Seminole (0)	1	<0.01
Shoshone (0)	0	<0.01
Sioux (6)	36	0.05
South American Ind. (0)	0	<0.01
Spanish American Ind. (0)	0	<0.01
Tlingit-Haida (Alaska Native) (0)	0	<0.01
Tohono O'Odham (0)	0	<0.01
Tsimshian (Alaska Native) (0)	0	<0.01
Ute (0)	1	<0.01
Yakama (0)	0	<0.01
Yaqui (0)	0	<0.01
Yuman (0)	0	<0.01
Yup'ik (Alaska Native) (0)	0	<0.01
Asian (385)	602	0.90
Not Hispanic (384)	582	0.87
Hispanic (1)	20	0.03
Bangladeshi (0)	3	<0.01
Bhutanese (0)	0	<0.01
Burmese (0)	0	<0.01
Cambodian (2)	8	0.01
Chinese, ex. Taiwanese (64)	104	0.16
Filipino (61)	116	0.17
Hmong (0)	1	<0.01
Indian (64)	93	0.14
Indonesian (0)	1	<0.01
Japanese (30)	66	0.10
Korean (68)	105	0.16
Laotian (0)	0	<0.01
Malaysian (0)	2	<0.01
Nepalese (1)	1	<0.01
Pakistani (23)	26	0.04
Sri Lankan (0)	0	<0.01
Taiwanese (4)	7	0.01
Thai (21)	30	0.04
Vietnamese (16)	23	0.03
Hawaii Native/Pacific Islander (13)	48	0.07
Not Hispanic (11)	37	0.06
Hispanic (2)	11	0.02
Fijian (0)	0	<0.01
Guamanian/Chamorro (5)	17	0.03
Marshallese (0)	2	<0.01
Native Hawaiian (6)	18	0.03
Samoan (0)	4	0.01
Tongan (0)	0	<0.01
White (62,911)	64,206	95.72
Not Hispanic (62,412)	63,589	94.80
Hispanic (499)	617	0.92

*Notes: † The Census 2010 population figure is used to calculate the percentages in the Hispanic Origin and Race categories. Ancestry percentages are based on the 2006-2010 American Community Survey population (not shown); ‡ Numbers in parentheses indicate the number of people reporting a single ancestry; * Numbers in parentheses indicate the number of persons reporting this race alone, not in combination with any other race; Please refer to the User Guide for more information.*

Midland County

Population: 83,629

Ancestry	Population	%
Afghan (0)	0	<0.01
African, Sub-Saharan (35)	46	0.06
African (22)	33	0.04
Cape Verdean (0)	0	<0.01
Ethiopian (0)	0	<0.01
Ghanaian (0)	0	<0.01
Kenyan (0)	0	<0.01
Liberian (0)	0	<0.01
Nigerian (0)	0	<0.01
Senegalese (0)	0	<0.01
Sierra Leonean (0)	0	<0.01
Somalian (0)	0	<0.01
South African (11)	11	0.01
Sudanese (0)	0	<0.01
Ugandan (0)	0	<0.01
Zimbabwean (0)	0	<0.01
Other Sub-Saharan African (2)	2	<0.01
Albanian (12)	12	0.01
Alsatian (0)	0	<0.01
American (5,451)	5,451	6.52
Arab (254)	354	0.42
Arab (83)	83	0.10
Egyptian (34)	34	0.04
Iraqi (0)	0	<0.01
Jordanian (130)	130	0.16
Lebanese (4)	41	0.05
Moroccan (0)	0	<0.01
Palestinian (0)	0	<0.01
Syrian (3)	66	0.08
Other Arab (0)	0	<0.01
Armenian (15)	52	0.06
Assyrian/Chaldean/Syriac (4)	4	<0.01
Australian (6)	13	0.02
Austrian (33)	182	0.22
Basque (0)	0	<0.01
Belgian (114)	223	0.27
Brazilian (12)	48	0.06
British (266)	580	0.69
Bulgarian (0)	0	<0.01
Cajun (0)	0	<0.01
Canadian (261)	608	0.73
Carpatho Rusyn (0)	0	<0.01
Celtic (36)	36	0.04
Croatian (17)	29	0.03
Cypriot (0)	0	<0.01
Czech (251)	877	1.05
Czechoslovakian (74)	176	0.21
Danish (68)	379	0.45
Dutch (632)	2,558	3.06
Eastern European (49)	131	0.16
English (3,293)	11,335	13.55
Estonian (2)	2	<0.01
European (791)	823	0.98
Finnish (137)	638	0.76
French, ex. Basque (975)	6,289	7.52
French Canadian (917)	2,148	2.57
German (9,743)	27,017	32.31
German Russian (0)	0	<0.01
Greek (55)	269	0.32
Guyanese (6)	6	0.01
Hungarian (162)	640	0.77
Icelander (0)	0	<0.01
Iranian (7)	7	0.01
Irish (2,445)	11,644	13.92
Israeli (29)	29	0.03
Italian (673)	2,391	2.86
Latvian (12)	12	0.01
Lithuanian (4)	63	0.08
Luxemburger (15)	15	0.02
Macedonian (0)	0	<0.01
Maltese (0)	26	0.03
New Zealander (0)	0	<0.01
Northern European (84)	122	0.15
Norwegian (421)	1,462	1.75
Pennsylvania German (14)	47	0.06

Ancestry (cont.)	Population	%
Polish (2,095)	7,209	8.62
Portuguese (6)	60	0.07
Romanian (4)	23	0.03
Russian (142)	529	0.63
Scandinavian (52)	208	0.25
Scotch-Irish (551)	1,613	1.93
Scottish (516)	2,423	2.90
Serbian (9)	23	0.03
Slavic (11)	61	0.07
Slovak (100)	223	0.27
Slovene (22)	102	0.12
Soviet Union (0)	0	<0.01
Swedish (600)	1,977	2.36
Swiss (39)	249	0.30
Turkish (0)	20	0.02
Ukrainian (71)	293	0.35
Welsh (94)	454	0.54
West Indian, ex. Hispanic (0)	22	0.03
Bahamian (0)	0	<0.01
Barbadian (0)	0	<0.01
Belizean (0)	0	<0.01
Bermudan (0)	0	<0.01
British West Indian (0)	0	<0.01
Dutch West Indian (0)	22	0.03
Haitian (0)	0	<0.01
Jamaican (0)	0	<0.01
Trinidadian/Tobagonian (0)	0	<0.01
U.S. Virgin Islander (0)	0	<0.01
West Indian (0)	0	<0.01
Other West Indian (0)	0	<0.01
Yugoslavian (15)	28	0.03

Hispanic Origin	Population	%
Hispanic or Latino (of any race)	1,704	2.04
Central American, ex. Mexican	55	0.07
Costa Rican	8	0.01
Guatemalan	16	0.02
Honduran	9	0.01
Nicaraguan	12	0.01
Panamanian	10	0.01
Salvadoran	0	<0.01
Other Central American	0	<0.01
Cuban	54	0.06
Dominican Republic	7	0.01
Mexican	1,139	1.36
Puerto Rican	124	0.15
South American	160	0.19
Argentinean	53	0.06
Bolivian	5	0.01
Chilean	11	0.01
Colombian	49	0.06
Ecuadorian	11	0.01
Paraguayan	0	<0.01
Peruvian	9	0.01
Uruguayan	3	<0.01
Venezuelan	15	0.02
Other South American	4	<0.01
Other Hispanic or Latino	165	0.20

Race*	Population	%
African-American/Black (1,013)	1,435	1.72
Not Hispanic (983)	1,383	1.65
Hispanic (30)	52	0.06
American Indian/Alaska Native (369)	824	0.99
Not Hispanic (336)	756	0.90
Hispanic (33)	68	0.08
Alaska Athabascan (Ala. Nat.) (2)	2	<0.01
Aleut (Alaska Native) (1)	1	<0.01
Apache (6)	9	0.01
Arapaho (0)	0	<0.01
Blackfeet (2)	21	0.03
Canadian/French Am. Ind. (4)	7	0.01
Central American Ind. (0)	0	<0.01
Cherokee (12)	69	0.08
Cheyenne (0)	1	<0.01
Chickasaw (1)	2	<0.01
Chippewa (155)	268	0.32
Choctaw (2)	9	0.01
Colville (0)	0	<0.01

Race* (cont.)	Population	%
Comanche (0)	2	<0.01
Cree (2)	5	0.01
Creek (1)	3	<0.01
Crow (0)	1	<0.01
Delaware (0)	1	<0.01
Hopi (0)	0	<0.01
Houma (0)	0	<0.01
Inupiat (Alaska Native) (2)	2	<0.01
Iroquois (5)	11	0.01
Kiowa (0)	0	<0.01
Lumbee (0)	0	<0.01
Menominee (0)	0	<0.01
Mexican American Ind. (7)	9	0.01
Navajo (0)	1	<0.01
Osage (0)	1	<0.01
Ottawa (18)	36	0.04
Paiute (0)	0	<0.01
Pima (0)	0	<0.01
Potawatomi (13)	19	0.02
Pueblo (0)	0	<0.01
Puget Sound Salish (0)	1	<0.01
Seminole (0)	1	<0.01
Shoshone (0)	0	<0.01
Sioux (5)	24	0.03
South American Ind. (1)	1	<0.01
Spanish American Ind. (0)	0	<0.01
Tlingit-Haida (Alaska Native) (0)	0	<0.01
Tohono O'Odham (0)	0	<0.01
Tsimshian (Alaska Native) (0)	0	<0.01
Ute (0)	0	<0.01
Yakama (0)	0	<0.01
Yaqui (0)	0	<0.01
Yuman (0)	0	<0.01
Yup'ik (Alaska Native) (0)	0	<0.01
Asian (1,556)	1,860	2.22
Not Hispanic (1,555)	1,853	2.22
Hispanic (1)	7	0.01
Bangladeshi (6)	6	0.01
Bhutanese (0)	0	<0.01
Burmese (0)	0	<0.01
Cambodian (3)	6	0.01
Chinese, ex. Taiwanese (505)	551	0.66
Filipino (99)	143	0.17
Hmong (5)	5	0.01
Indian (478)	513	0.61
Indonesian (3)	4	<0.01
Japanese (93)	159	0.19
Korean (175)	221	0.26
Laotian (2)	4	<0.01
Malaysian (4)	5	0.01
Nepalese (0)	0	<0.01
Pakistani (49)	61	0.07
Sri Lankan (2)	4	<0.01
Taiwanese (24)	25	0.03
Thai (17)	29	0.03
Vietnamese (61)	70	0.08
Hawaii Native/Pacific Islander (46)	84	0.10
Not Hispanic (46)	84	0.10
Hispanic (0)	0	<0.01
Fijian (0)	0	<0.01
Guamanian/Chamorro (4)	10	0.01
Marshallese (0)	0	<0.01
Native Hawaiian (17)	28	0.03
Samoan (2)	7	0.01
Tongan (2)	4	<0.01
White (79,063)	80,250	95.96
Not Hispanic (77,846)	78,880	94.32
Hispanic (1,217)	1,370	1.64

Notes: † The Census 2010 population figure is used to calculate the percentages in the Hispanic Origin and Race categories. Ancestry percentages are based on the 2006-2010 American Community Survey population (not shown); ‡ Numbers in parentheses indicate the number of people reporting a single ancestry; * Numbers in parentheses indicate the number of persons reporting this race alone, not in combination with any other race; Please refer to the User Guide for more information.

Monroe County

Population: 152,021

Ancestry	Population	%
Afghan (0)	0	<0.01
African, Sub-Saharan (69)	150	0.10
African (69)	150	0.10
Cape Verdean (0)	0	<0.01
Ethiopian (0)	0	<0.01
Ghanaian (0)	0	<0.01
Kenyan (0)	0	<0.01
Liberian (0)	0	<0.01
Nigerian (0)	0	<0.01
Senegalese (0)	0	<0.01
Sierra Leonean (0)	0	<0.01
Somalian (0)	0	<0.01
South African (0)	0	<0.01
Sudanese (0)	0	<0.01
Ugandan (0)	0	<0.01
Zimbabwean (0)	0	<0.01
Other Sub-Saharan African (0)	0	<0.01
Albanian (86)	86	0.06
Alsatian (0)	12	0.01
American (7,307)	7,307	4.78
Arab (589)	959	0.63
Arab (159)	252	0.16
Egyptian (0)	25	0.02
Iraqi (101)	101	0.07
Jordanian (13)	13	0.01
Lebanese (234)	377	0.25
Moroccan (0)	0	<0.01
Palestinian (0)	0	<0.01
Syrian (36)	145	0.09
Other Arab (46)	46	0.03
Armenian (68)	263	0.17
Assyrian/Chaldean/Syriac (4)	4	<0.01
Australian (73)	123	0.08
Austrian (35)	259	0.17
Basque (0)	0	<0.01
Belgian (408)	1,767	1.16
Brazilian (0)	17	0.01
British (192)	530	0.35
Bulgarian (41)	107	0.07
Cajun (7)	7	<0.01
Canadian (154)	563	0.37
Carpatho Rusyn (0)	0	<0.01
Celtic (6)	15	0.01
Croatian (78)	126	0.08
Cypriot (18)	18	0.01
Czech (212)	804	0.53
Czechoslovakian (91)	281	0.18
Danish (60)	148	0.10
Dutch (804)	3,665	2.40
Eastern European (55)	55	0.04
English (3,740)	14,854	9.72
Estonian (0)	15	0.01
European (1,064)	1,121	0.73
Finnish (112)	487	0.32
French, ex. Basque (2,987)	17,933	11.74
French Canadian (1,279)	3,307	2.16
German (16,498)	52,973	34.67
German Russian (0)	0	<0.01
Greek (364)	1,013	0.66
Guyanese (0)	0	<0.01
Hungarian (1,191)	4,057	2.66
Icelander (0)	0	<0.01
Iranian (0)	0	<0.01
Irish (4,401)	23,261	15.22
Israeli (49)	49	0.03
Italian (3,129)	8,704	5.70
Latvian (0)	0	<0.01
Lithuanian (71)	250	0.16
Luxemburger (0)	0	<0.01
Macedonian (17)	38	0.02
Maltese (51)	158	0.10
New Zealander (0)	0	<0.01
Northern European (0)	0	<0.01
Norwegian (268)	813	0.53
Pennsylvania German (61)	89	0.06

	Population	%
Polish (5,161)	15,376	10.06
Portuguese (0)	37	0.02
Romanian (112)	330	0.22
Russian (191)	851	0.56
Scandinavian (34)	75	0.05
Scotch-Irish (692)	2,370	1.55
Scottish (980)	4,124	2.70
Serbian (210)	398	0.26
Slavic (20)	41	0.03
Slovak (63)	356	0.23
Slovene (25)	55	0.04
Soviet Union (0)	0	<0.01
Swedish (207)	1,574	1.03
Swiss (74)	546	0.36
Turkish (0)	29	0.02
Ukrainian (158)	408	0.27
Welsh (71)	719	0.47
West Indian, ex. Hispanic (39)	114	0.07
Bahamian (0)	0	<0.01
Barbadian (0)	0	<0.01
Belizean (0)	0	<0.01
Bermudan (0)	0	<0.01
British West Indian (0)	0	<0.01
Dutch West Indian (0)	10	0.01
Haitian (0)	28	0.02
Jamaican (39)	76	0.05
Trinidadian/Tobagonian (0)	0	<0.01
U.S. Virgin Islander (0)	0	<0.01
West Indian (0)	0	<0.01
Other West Indian (0)	0	<0.01
Yugoslavian (49)	233	0.15

Hispanic Origin	Population	%
Hispanic or Latino (of any race)	4,667	3.07
Central American, ex. Mexican	75	0.05
Costa Rican	7	<0.01
Guatemalan	38	0.02
Honduran	4	<0.01
Nicaraguan	8	0.01
Panamanian	11	0.01
Salvadoran	6	<0.01
Other Central American	1	<0.01
Cuban	65	0.04
Dominican Republic	7	<0.01
Mexican	3,590	2.36
Puerto Rican	414	0.27
South American	88	0.06
Argentinean	12	0.01
Bolivian	6	<0.01
Chilean	5	<0.01
Colombian	11	0.01
Ecuadorian	10	0.01
Paraguayan	6	<0.01
Peruvian	17	0.01
Uruguayan	5	<0.01
Venezuelan	14	0.01
Other South American	2	<0.01
Other Hispanic or Latino	428	0.28

Race*	Population	%
African-American/Black (3,237)	4,372	2.88
Not Hispanic (3,144)	4,182	2.75
Hispanic (93)	190	0.12
American Indian/Alaska Native (467)	1,548	1.02
Not Hispanic (397)	1,368	0.90
Hispanic (70)	180	0.12
Alaska Athabascan (Ala. Nat.) (2)	2	<0.01
Aleut (Alaska Native) (0)	0	<0.01
Apache (9)	25	0.02
Arapaho (1)	2	<0.01
Blackfeet (12)	58	0.04
Canadian/French Am. Ind. (6)	12	0.01
Central American Ind. (0)	0	<0.01
Cherokee (74)	380	0.25
Cheyenne (1)	5	<0.01
Chickasaw (2)	4	<0.01
Chippewa (80)	170	0.11
Choctaw (2)	9	0.01
Colville (0)	0	<0.01

	Population	%
Comanche (4)	7	<0.01
Cree (1)	7	<0.01
Creek (3)	9	0.01
Crow (0)	2	<0.01
Delaware (1)	7	<0.01
Hopi (0)	0	<0.01
Houma (0)	0	<0.01
Inupiat (Alaska Native) (0)	0	<0.01
Iroquois (16)	35	0.02
Kiowa (3)	8	0.01
Lumbee (5)	14	0.01
Menominee (4)	10	0.01
Mexican American Ind. (10)	27	0.02
Navajo (2)	6	<0.01
Osage (0)	0	<0.01
Ottawa (25)	55	0.04
Paiute (0)	0	<0.01
Pima (0)	0	<0.01
Potawatomi (6)	15	0.01
Pueblo (1)	6	<0.01
Puget Sound Salish (0)	0	<0.01
Seminole (2)	6	<0.01
Shoshone (0)	1	<0.01
Sioux (11)	29	0.02
South American Ind. (5)	7	<0.01
Spanish American Ind. (0)	1	<0.01
Tlingit-Haida (Alaska Native) (2)	2	<0.01
Tohono O'Odham (0)	0	<0.01
Tsimshian (Alaska Native) (0)	0	<0.01
Ute (0)	0	<0.01
Yakama (0)	0	<0.01
Yaqui (1)	1	<0.01
Yuman (0)	0	<0.01
Yup'ik (Alaska Native) (0)	0	<0.01
Asian (842)	1,187	0.78
Not Hispanic (837)	1,166	0.77
Hispanic (5)	21	0.01
Bangladeshi (2)	3	<0.01
Bhutanese (0)	0	<0.01
Burmese (0)	0	<0.01
Cambodian (2)	2	<0.01
Chinese, ex. Taiwanese (123)	148	0.10
Filipino (119)	210	0.14
Hmong (0)	0	<0.01
Indian (233)	271	0.18
Indonesian (5)	7	<0.01
Japanese (53)	113	0.07
Korean (134)	180	0.12
Laotian (1)	2	<0.01
Malaysian (6)	6	<0.01
Nepalese (0)	0	<0.01
Pakistani (26)	31	0.02
Sri Lankan (1)	1	<0.01
Taiwanese (10)	10	0.01
Thai (17)	30	0.02
Vietnamese (55)	71	0.05
Hawaii Native/Pacific Islander (26)	82	0.05
Not Hispanic (24)	72	0.05
Hispanic (2)	10	0.01
Fijian (0)	0	<0.01
Guamanian/Chamorro (4)	9	0.01
Marshallese (0)	0	<0.01
Native Hawaiian (7)	18	0.01
Samoan (6)	22	0.01
Tongan (0)	0	<0.01
White (143,476)	146,036	96.06
Not Hispanic (140,609)	142,780	93.92
Hispanic (2,867)	3,256	2.14

*Notes: † The Census 2010 population figure is used to calculate the percentages in the Hispanic Origin and Race categories. Ancestry percentages are based on the 2006-2010 American Community Survey population (not shown); ‡ Numbers in parentheses indicate the number of people reporting a single ancestry; * Numbers in parentheses indicate the number of persons reporting this race alone, not in combination with any other race; Please refer to the User Guide for more information.*

Montcalm County

Population: 63,342

Ancestry	Population	%
Afghan (0)	0	<0.01
African, Sub-Saharan (20)	40	0.06
African (20)	40	0.06
Cape Verdean (0)	0	<0.01
Ethiopian (0)	0	<0.01
Ghanaian (0)	0	<0.01
Kenyan (0)	0	<0.01
Liberian (0)	0	<0.01
Nigerian (0)	0	<0.01
Senegalese (0)	0	<0.01
Sierra Leonean (0)	0	<0.01
Somalian (0)	0	<0.01
South African (0)	0	<0.01
Sudanese (0)	0	<0.01
Ugandan (0)	0	<0.01
Zimbabwean (0)	0	<0.01
Other Sub-Saharan African (0)	0	<0.01
Albanian (0)	0	<0.01
Alsatian (0)	0	<0.01
American (4,571)	4,571	7.19
Arab (64)	106	0.17
Arab (15)	37	0.06
Egyptian (0)	0	<0.01
Iraqi (0)	0	<0.01
Jordanian (0)	0	<0.01
Lebanese (14)	25	0.04
Moroccan (9)	9	0.01
Palestinian (12)	12	0.02
Syrian (14)	23	0.04
Other Arab (0)	0	<0.01
Armenian (0)	0	<0.01
Assyrian/Chaldean/Syriac (18)	55	0.09
Australian (0)	0	<0.01
Austrian (7)	59	0.09
Basque (0)	0	<0.01
Belgian (15)	116	0.18
Brazilian (2)	2	<0.01
British (30)	92	0.14
Bulgarian (0)	0	<0.01
Cajun (0)	0	<0.01
Canadian (104)	276	0.43
Carpatho Rusyn (0)	0	<0.01
Celtic (0)	0	<0.01
Croatian (7)	28	0.04
Cypriot (0)	0	<0.01
Czech (58)	151	0.24
Czechoslovakian (20)	51	0.08
Danish (1,165)	2,971	4.67
Dutch (1,850)	5,909	9.30
Eastern European (0)	0	<0.01
English (2,884)	8,693	13.68
Estonian (0)	0	<0.01
European (295)	379	0.60
Finnish (153)	294	0.46
French, ex. Basque (420)	2,545	4.00
French Canadian (329)	1,086	1.71
German (6,170)	18,547	29.18
German Russian (0)	0	<0.01
Greek (62)	126	0.20
Guyanese (0)	0	<0.01
Hungarian (53)	204	0.32
Icelander (12)	12	0.02
Iranian (0)	5	0.01
Irish (1,789)	8,713	13.71
Israeli (0)	0	<0.01
Italian (336)	1,034	1.63
Latvian (5)	15	0.02
Lithuanian (69)	139	0.22
Luxemburger (0)	0	<0.01
Macedonian (0)	0	<0.01
Maltese (0)	0	<0.01
New Zealander (0)	0	<0.01
Northern European (34)	34	0.05
Norwegian (58)	322	0.51
Pennsylvania German (198)	249	0.39

Ancestry (cont.)	Population	%
Polish (842)	2,543	4.00
Portuguese (15)	23	0.04
Romanian (53)	67	0.11
Russian (56)	170	0.27
Scandinavian (48)	90	0.14
Scotch-Irish (165)	630	0.99
Scottish (323)	1,156	1.82
Serbian (37)	37	0.06
Slavic (0)	3	<0.01
Slovak (17)	128	0.20
Slovene (0)	0	<0.01
Soviet Union (0)	0	<0.01
Swedish (259)	1,429	2.25
Swiss (17)	258	0.41
Turkish (0)	0	<0.01
Ukrainian (15)	48	0.08
Welsh (179)	352	0.55
West Indian, ex. Hispanic (4)	4	0.01
Bahamian (0)	0	<0.01
Barbadian (0)	0	<0.01
Belizean (0)	0	<0.01
Bermudan (0)	0	<0.01
British West Indian (0)	0	<0.01
Dutch West Indian (0)	0	<0.01
Haitian (4)	4	0.01
Jamaican (0)	0	<0.01
Trinidadian/Tobagonian (0)	0	<0.01
U.S. Virgin Islander (0)	0	<0.01
West Indian (0)	0	<0.01
Other West Indian (0)	0	<0.01
Yugoslavian (6)	16	0.03

Hispanic Origin	Population	%
Hispanic or Latino (of any race)	1,932	3.05
Central American, ex. Mexican	41	0.06
Costa Rican	4	0.01
Guatemalan	21	0.03
Honduran	10	0.02
Nicaraguan	1	<0.01
Panamanian	1	<0.01
Salvadoran	4	0.01
Other Central American	0	<0.01
Cuban	22	0.03
Dominican Republic	6	0.01
Mexican	1,530	2.42
Puerto Rican	120	0.19
South American	21	0.03
Argentinean	0	<0.01
Bolivian	1	<0.01
Chilean	6	0.01
Colombian	3	<0.01
Ecuadorian	1	<0.01
Paraguayan	0	<0.01
Peruvian	6	0.01
Uruguayan	0	<0.01
Venezuelan	4	0.01
Other South American	0	<0.01
Other Hispanic or Latino	192	0.30

Race*	Population	%
African-American/Black (1,483)	1,748	2.76
Not Hispanic (1,476)	1,714	2.71
Hispanic (7)	34	0.05
American Indian/Alaska Native (298)	785	1.24
Not Hispanic (269)	708	1.12
Hispanic (29)	77	0.12
Alaska Athabascan (Ala. Nat.) (1)	2	<0.01
Aleut (Alaska Native) (1)	1	<0.01
Apache (3)	6	0.01
Arapaho (1)	1	<0.01
Blackfeet (5)	17	0.03
Canadian/French Am. Ind. (1)	7	0.01
Central American Ind. (0)	0	<0.01
Cherokee (17)	84	0.13
Cheyenne (0)	2	<0.01
Chickasaw (0)	0	<0.01
Chippewa (53)	164	0.26
Choctaw (1)	2	<0.01
Colville (2)	2	<0.01

Race* (cont.)	Population	%
Comanche (0)	0	<0.01
Cree (0)	2	<0.01
Creek (2)	7	0.01
Crow (1)	1	<0.01
Delaware (0)	1	<0.01
Hopi (0)	0	<0.01
Houma (0)	0	<0.01
Inupiat (Alaska Native) (0)	1	<0.01
Iroquois (2)	6	0.01
Kiowa (0)	1	<0.01
Lumbee (5)	8	0.01
Menominee (1)	2	<0.01
Mexican American Ind. (7)	10	0.02
Navajo (0)	4	0.01
Osage (0)	0	<0.01
Ottawa (46)	81	0.13
Paiute (0)	0	<0.01
Pima (0)	0	<0.01
Potawatomi (12)	25	0.04
Pueblo (0)	0	<0.01
Puget Sound Salish (0)	0	<0.01
Seminole (0)	0	<0.01
Shoshone (0)	0	<0.01
Sioux (4)	16	0.03
South American Ind. (1)	2	<0.01
Spanish American Ind. (0)	0	<0.01
Tlingit-Haida (Alaska Native) (0)	0	<0.01
Tohono O'Odham (0)	0	<0.01
Tsimshian (Alaska Native) (0)	0	<0.01
Ute (0)	0	<0.01
Yakama (0)	0	<0.01
Yaqui (0)	0	<0.01
Yuman (0)	0	<0.01
Yup'ik (Alaska Native) (0)	0	<0.01
Asian (224)	349	0.55
Not Hispanic (220)	333	0.53
Hispanic (4)	16	0.03
Bangladeshi (0)	0	<0.01
Bhutanese (0)	0	<0.01
Burmese (2)	2	<0.01
Cambodian (0)	0	<0.01
Chinese, ex. Taiwanese (22)	27	0.04
Filipino (42)	84	0.13
Hmong (1)	1	<0.01
Indian (58)	65	0.10
Indonesian (2)	7	0.01
Japanese (16)	44	0.07
Korean (45)	83	0.13
Laotian (0)	0	<0.01
Malaysian (0)	1	<0.01
Nepalese (0)	0	<0.01
Pakistani (3)	3	<0.01
Sri Lankan (0)	0	<0.01
Taiwanese (0)	0	<0.01
Thai (5)	7	0.01
Vietnamese (12)	19	0.03
Hawaii Native/Pacific Islander (19)	56	0.09
Not Hispanic (15)	45	0.07
Hispanic (4)	11	0.02
Fijian (0)	0	<0.01
Guamanian/Chamorro (4)	7	0.01
Marshallese (0)	0	<0.01
Native Hawaiian (10)	33	0.05
Samoan (0)	8	0.01
Tongan (0)	0	<0.01
White (59,752)	60,700	95.83
Not Hispanic (58,635)	59,392	93.76
Hispanic (1,117)	1,308	2.06

Notes: † The Census 2010 population figure is used to calculate the percentages in the Hispanic Origin and Race categories. Ancestry percentages are based on the 2006-2010 American Community Survey population (not shown); ‡ Numbers in parentheses indicate the number of people reporting a single ancestry; * Numbers in parentheses indicate the number of persons reporting this race alone, not in combination with any other race; Please refer to the User Guide for more information.

Muskegon County

Population: 172,188

Ancestry	Population	%
Afghan (0)	0	<0.01
African, Sub-Saharan (199)	379	0.22
African (199)	374	0.22
Cape Verdean (0)	0	<0.01
Ethiopian (0)	0	<0.01
Ghanaian (0)	0	<0.01
Kenyan (0)	0	<0.01
Liberian (0)	0	<0.01
Nigerian (0)	5	<0.01
Senegalese (0)	0	<0.01
Sierra Leonean (0)	0	<0.01
Somalian (0)	0	<0.01
South African (0)	0	<0.01
Sudanese (0)	0	<0.01
Ugandan (0)	0	<0.01
Zimbabwean (0)	0	<0.01
Other Sub-Saharan African (0)	0	<0.01
Albanian (0)	4	<0.01
Alsatian (0)	0	<0.01
American (7,305)	7,305	4.22
Arab (358)	476	0.27
Arab (13)	54	0.03
Egyptian (0)	0	<0.01
Iraqi (251)	251	0.14
Jordanian (0)	0	<0.01
Lebanese (39)	116	0.07
Moroccan (46)	46	0.03
Palestinian (0)	0	<0.01
Syrian (0)	0	<0.01
Other Arab (9)	9	0.01
Armenian (4)	33	0.02
Assyrian/Chaldean/Syriac (9)	9	0.01
Australian (20)	56	0.03
Austrian (78)	310	0.18
Basque (0)	0	<0.01
Belgian (202)	633	0.37
Brazilian (0)	7	<0.01
British (126)	300	0.17
Bulgarian (15)	26	0.02
Cajun (0)	0	<0.01
Canadian (156)	337	0.19
Carpatho Rusyn (0)	0	<0.01
Celtic (11)	11	0.01
Croatian (65)	177	0.10
Cypriot (0)	0	<0.01
Czech (258)	1,068	0.62
Czechoslovakian (100)	282	0.16
Danish (258)	1,199	0.69
Dutch (6,214)	18,354	10.60
Eastern European (30)	30	0.02
English (3,878)	16,485	9.52
Estonian (37)	37	0.02
European (1,022)	1,133	0.65
Finnish (565)	1,092	0.63
French, ex. Basque (1,239)	9,513	5.49
French Canadian (1,006)	2,992	1.73
German (10,234)	38,055	21.97
German Russian (32)	40	0.02
Greek (190)	464	0.27
Guyanese (0)	0	<0.01
Hungarian (395)	1,455	0.84
Icelander (0)	0	<0.01
Iranian (0)	0	<0.01
Irish (3,559)	18,681	10.78
Israeli (0)	0	<0.01
Italian (1,154)	4,839	2.79
Latvian (3)	10	0.01
Lithuanian (190)	651	0.38
Luxemburger (0)	18	0.01
Macedonian (0)	0	<0.01
Maltese (9)	30	0.02
New Zealander (0)	0	<0.01
Northern European (99)	99	0.06
Norwegian (759)	2,529	1.46
Pennsylvania German (150)	224	0.13

Ancestry (cont.)	Population	%
Polish (3,524)	11,622	6.71
Portuguese (10)	81	0.05
Romanian (36)	127	0.07
Russian (129)	574	0.33
Scandinavian (197)	425	0.25
Scotch-Irish (713)	2,345	1.35
Scottish (487)	2,599	1.50
Serbian (45)	56	0.03
Slavic (28)	52	0.03
Slovak (268)	770	0.44
Slovene (70)	144	0.08
Soviet Union (0)	0	<0.01
Swedish (1,506)	7,043	4.07
Swiss (35)	350	0.20
Turkish (8)	21	0.01
Ukrainian (169)	359	0.21
Welsh (56)	529	0.31
West Indian, ex. Hispanic (106)	190	0.11
Bahamian (0)	0	<0.01
Barbadian (0)	0	<0.01
Belizean (0)	0	<0.01
Bermudan (0)	0	<0.01
British West Indian (0)	0	<0.01
Dutch West Indian (0)	0	<0.01
Haitian (31)	40	0.02
Jamaican (75)	141	0.08
Trinidadian/Tobagonian (0)	0	<0.01
U.S. Virgin Islander (0)	0	<0.01
West Indian (0)	9	0.01
Other West Indian (0)	0	<0.01
Yugoslavian (108)	235	0.14

Hispanic Origin	Population	%
Hispanic or Latino (of any race)	8,261	4.80
Central American, ex. Mexican	139	0.08
Costa Rican	22	0.01
Guatemalan	50	0.03
Honduran	20	0.01
Nicaraguan	5	<0.01
Panamanian	27	0.02
Salvadoran	15	0.01
Other Central American	0	<0.01
Cuban	67	0.04
Dominican Republic	17	0.01
Mexican	6,814	3.96
Puerto Rican	542	0.31
South American	95	0.06
Argentinean	7	<0.01
Bolivian	4	<0.01
Chilean	16	0.01
Colombian	30	0.02
Ecuadorian	6	<0.01
Paraguayan	1	<0.01
Peruvian	25	0.01
Uruguayan	0	<0.01
Venezuelan	5	<0.01
Other South American	1	<0.01
Other Hispanic or Latino	587	0.34

Race*	Population	%
African-American/Black (24,882)	27,322	15.87
Not Hispanic (24,599)	26,792	15.56
Hispanic (283)	530	0.31
American Indian/Alaska Native (1,407)	3,213	1.87
Not Hispanic (1,240)	2,786	1.62
Hispanic (167)	427	0.25
Alaska Athabascan (Ala. Nat.) (3)	4	<0.01
Aleut (Alaska Native) (0)	1	<0.01
Apache (9)	21	0.01
Arapaho (0)	0	<0.01
Blackfeet (16)	86	0.05
Canadian/French Am. Ind. (8)	21	0.01
Central American Ind. (2)	2	<0.01
Cherokee (49)	235	0.14
Cheyenne (0)	0	<0.01
Chickasaw (1)	4	<0.01
Chippewa (229)	436	0.25
Choctaw (6)	28	0.02
Colville (0)	0	<0.01

Race* (cont.)	Population	%
Comanche (0)	0	<0.01
Cree (2)	7	<0.01
Creek (3)	7	<0.01
Crow (0)	5	<0.01
Delaware (1)	1	<0.01
Hopi (0)	0	<0.01
Houma (0)	0	<0.01
Inupiat (Alaska Native) (4)	4	<0.01
Iroquois (8)	19	0.01
Kiowa (1)	1	<0.01
Lumbee (6)	13	0.01
Menominee (3)	3	<0.01
Mexican American Ind. (9)	29	0.02
Navajo (7)	13	0.01
Osage (1)	2	<0.01
Ottawa (463)	821	0.48
Paiute (1)	1	<0.01
Pima (1)	4	<0.01
Potawatomi (101)	145	0.08
Pueblo (1)	1	<0.01
Puget Sound Salish (0)	0	<0.01
Seminole (0)	3	<0.01
Shoshone (0)	0	<0.01
Sioux (9)	29	0.02
South American Ind. (4)	6	<0.01
Spanish American Ind. (0)	2	<0.01
Tlingit-Haida (Alaska Native) (1)	2	<0.01
Tohono O'Odham (0)	0	<0.01
Tsimshian (Alaska Native) (1)	2	<0.01
Ute (0)	0	<0.01
Yakama (0)	0	<0.01
Yaqui (0)	0	<0.01
Yuman (0)	3	<0.01
Yup'ik (Alaska Native) (0)	0	<0.01
Asian (941)	1,478	0.86
Not Hispanic (919)	1,423	0.83
Hispanic (22)	55	0.03
Bangladeshi (0)	0	<0.01
Bhutanese (0)	0	<0.01
Burmese (2)	4	<0.01
Cambodian (7)	12	0.01
Chinese, ex. Taiwanese (208)	276	0.16
Filipino (114)	248	0.14
Hmong (0)	0	<0.01
Indian (204)	249	0.14
Indonesian (6)	9	0.01
Japanese (49)	124	0.07
Korean (190)	304	0.18
Laotian (11)	18	0.01
Malaysian (1)	1	<0.01
Nepalese (0)	0	<0.01
Pakistani (11)	14	0.01
Sri Lankan (0)	1	<0.01
Taiwanese (2)	3	<0.01
Thai (13)	46	0.03
Vietnamese (68)	106	0.06
Hawaii Native/Pacific Islander (28)	119	0.07
Not Hispanic (18)	89	0.05
Hispanic (10)	30	0.02
Fijian (0)	2	<0.01
Guamanian/Chamorro (6)	25	0.01
Marshallese (0)	1	<0.01
Native Hawaiian (8)	44	0.03
Samoan (3)	12	0.01
Tongan (0)	2	<0.01
White (137,679)	142,208	82.59
Not Hispanic (133,132)	136,772	79.43
Hispanic (4,547)	5,436	3.16

Oakland County

Population: 1,202,362

Ancestry	Population	%
Afghan (0)	0	<0.01
African, Sub-Saharan (5,000)	6,666	0.55
African (3,241)	4,386	0.37
Cape Verdean (0)	0	<0.01
Ethiopian (330)	352	0.03
Ghanaian (93)	107	0.01
Kenyan (108)	108	0.01
Liberian (62)	62	0.01
Nigerian (693)	931	0.08
Senegalese (76)	76	0.01
Sierra Leonean (0)	0	<0.01
Somalian (0)	0	<0.01
South African (53)	170	0.01
Sudanese (0)	0	<0.01
Ugandan (0)	0	<0.01
Zimbabwean (65)	65	0.01
Other Sub-Saharan African (279)	409	0.03
Albanian (6,006)	6,374	0.53
Alsatian (9)	19	<0.01
American (47,656)	47,656	3.97
Arab (18,390)	25,644	2.14
Arab (4,896)	5,787	0.48
Egyptian (920)	1,101	0.09
Iraqi (5,645)	7,367	0.61
Jordanian (293)	477	0.04
Lebanese (3,459)	6,628	0.55
Moroccan (71)	130	0.01
Palestinian (395)	468	0.04
Syrian (1,015)	1,568	0.13
Other Arab (1,696)	2,118	0.18
Armenian (4,033)	6,463	0.54
Assyrian/Chaldean/Syriac (13,637)	16,412	1.37
Australian (176)	462	0.04
Austrian (1,029)	4,415	0.37
Basque (10)	105	0.01
Belgian (1,369)	6,374	0.53
Brazilian (378)	593	0.05
British (2,878)	5,886	0.49
Bulgarian (650)	781	0.07
Cajun (12)	44	<0.01
Canadian (4,490)	10,241	0.85
Carpatho Rusyn (16)	56	<0.01
Celtic (55)	219	0.02
Croatian (892)	3,120	0.26
Cypriot (10)	10	<0.01
Czech (1,298)	6,422	0.53
Czechoslovakian (809)	1,882	0.16
Danish (1,033)	4,686	0.39
Dutch (4,686)	22,526	1.88
Eastern European (3,434)	3,644	0.30
English (32,417)	127,848	10.64
Estonian (82)	121	0.01
European (13,537)	15,363	1.28
Finnish (3,611)	12,641	1.05
French, ex. Basque (7,154)	53,803	4.48
French Canadian (7,390)	22,501	1.87
German (61,007)	237,928	19.81
German Russian (22)	22	<0.01
Greek (4,489)	10,012	0.83
Guyanese (32)	32	<0.01
Hungarian (4,690)	14,395	1.20
Icelander (45)	227	0.02
Iranian (1,353)	1,750	0.15
Irish (36,543)	155,400	12.94
Israeli (483)	670	0.06
Italian (24,685)	74,897	6.24
Latvian (234)	608	0.05
Lithuanian (1,858)	4,969	0.41
Luxemburger (16)	81	0.01
Macedonian (797)	1,468	0.12
Maltese (809)	2,076	0.17
New Zealander (43)	66	0.01
Northern European (690)	747	0.06
Norwegian (2,771)	10,476	0.87
Pennsylvania German (75)	443	0.04

Ancestry	Population	%
Polish (42,549)	122,157	10.17
Portuguese (431)	1,023	0.09
Romanian (4,411)	7,814	0.65
Russian (12,571)	26,861	2.24
Scandinavian (546)	1,836	0.15
Scotch-Irish (7,387)	21,568	1.80
Scottish (10,116)	37,266	3.10
Serbian (981)	2,062	0.17
Slavic (300)	1,121	0.09
Slovak (1,648)	4,346	0.36
Slovene (258)	1,066	0.09
Soviet Union (0)	0	<0.01
Swedish (4,423)	18,565	1.55
Swiss (455)	3,049	0.25
Turkish (458)	585	0.05
Ukrainian (3,939)	9,395	0.78
Welsh (1,318)	8,973	0.75
West Indian, ex. Hispanic (1,343)	3,047	0.25
Bahamian (11)	20	<0.01
Barbadian (22)	86	0.01
Belizean (18)	24	<0.01
Bermudan (50)	89	0.01
British West Indian (20)	87	0.01
Dutch West Indian (0)	20	<0.01
Haitian (146)	735	0.06
Jamaican (985)	1,474	0.12
Trinidadian/Tobagonian (19)	146	0.01
U.S. Virgin Islander (8)	52	<0.01
West Indian (64)	314	0.03
Other West Indian (0)	0	<0.01
Yugoslavian (1,343)	2,649	0.22

Hispanic Origin	Population	%
Hispanic or Latino (of any race)	41,920	3.49
Central American, ex. Mexican	2,180	0.18
Costa Rican	133	0.01
Guatemalan	583	0.05
Honduran	344	0.03
Nicaraguan	102	0.01
Panamanian	185	0.02
Salvadoran	820	0.07
Other Central American	13	<0.01
Cuban	881	0.07
Dominican Republic	262	0.02
Mexican	26,756	2.23
Puerto Rican	5,621	0.47
South American	2,644	0.22
Argentinean	611	0.05
Bolivian	60	<0.01
Chilean	230	0.02
Colombian	736	0.06
Ecuadorian	240	0.02
Paraguayan	79	0.01
Peruvian	370	0.03
Uruguayan	27	<0.01
Venezuelan	251	0.02
Other South American	40	<0.01
Other Hispanic or Latino	3,576	0.30

Race*	Population	%
African-American/Black (164,078)	175,395	14.59
Not Hispanic (162,303)	172,360	14.34
Hispanic (1,775)	3,035	0.25
American Indian/Alaska Native (3,376)	10,491	0.87
Not Hispanic (2,872)	9,212	0.77
Hispanic (504)	1,279	0.11
Alaska Athabascan (Ala. Nat.) (2)	3	<0.01
Aleut (Alaska Native) (7)	11	<0.01
Apache (25)	110	0.01
Arapaho (0)	2	<0.01
Blackfeet (36)	333	0.03
Canadian/French Am. Ind. (61)	125	0.01
Central American Ind. (12)	22	<0.01
Cherokee (303)	2,038	0.17
Cheyenne (3)	18	<0.01
Chickasaw (7)	29	<0.01
Chippewa (847)	1,578	0.13
Choctaw (33)	160	0.01
Colville (0)	1	<0.01

	Population	%
Comanche (14)	21	<0.01
Cree (5)	44	<0.01
Creek (16)	65	0.01
Crow (1)	12	<0.01
Delaware (10)	26	<0.01
Hopi (2)	8	<0.01
Houma (1)	2	<0.01
Inupiat (Alaska Native) (3)	9	<0.01
Iroquois (145)	336	0.03
Kiowa (4)	4	<0.01
Lumbee (74)	132	0.01
Menominee (3)	9	<0.01
Mexican American Ind. (120)	199	0.02
Navajo (21)	54	<0.01
Osage (11)	11	<0.01
Ottawa (95)	216	0.02
Paiute (0)	6	<0.01
Pima (0)	0	<0.01
Potawatomi (68)	149	0.01
Pueblo (1)	3	<0.01
Puget Sound Salish (0)	0	<0.01
Seminole (7)	52	<0.01
Shoshone (4)	7	<0.01
Sioux (47)	142	0.01
South American Ind. (11)	34	<0.01
Spanish American Ind. (8)	12	<0.01
Tlingit-Haida (Alaska Native) (8)	18	<0.01
Tohono O'Odham (1)	3	<0.01
Tsimshian (Alaska Native) (1)	1	<0.01
Ute (1)	7	<0.01
Yakama (0)	1	<0.01
Yaqui (6)	16	<0.01
Yuman (1)	1	<0.01
Yup'ik (Alaska Native) (1)	2	<0.01
Asian (67,828)	77,076	6.41
Not Hispanic (67,577)	76,375	6.35
Hispanic (251)	701	0.06
Bangladeshi (555)	612	0.05
Bhutanese (0)	0	<0.01
Burmese (27)	31	<0.01
Cambodian (109)	160	0.01
Chinese, ex. Taiwanese (11,651)	12,922	1.07
Filipino (5,220)	7,244	0.60
Hmong (1,387)	1,453	0.12
Indian (29,582)	31,122	2.59
Indonesian (78)	141	0.01
Japanese (4,970)	6,243	0.52
Korean (6,210)	7,127	0.59
Laotian (149)	198	0.02
Malaysian (49)	99	0.01
Nepalese (265)	285	0.02
Pakistani (2,837)	3,119	0.26
Sri Lankan (283)	310	0.03
Taiwanese (893)	984	0.08
Thai (394)	536	0.04
Vietnamese (1,765)	2,090	0.17
Hawaii Native/Pacific Islander (254)	1,201	0.10
Not Hispanic (212)	1,059	0.09
Hispanic (42)	142	0.01
Fijian (3)	4	<0.01
Guamanian/Chamorro (58)	106	0.01
Marshallese (3)	3	<0.01
Native Hawaiian (76)	297	0.02
Samoan (25)	64	0.01
Tongan (2)	4	<0.01
White (928,912)	951,546	79.14
Not Hispanic (903,398)	922,942	76.76
Hispanic (25,514)	28,604	2.38

Notes: † The Census 2010 population figure is used to calculate the percentages in the Hispanic Origin and Race categories. Ancestry percentages are based on the 2006-2010 American Community Survey population (not shown); ‡ Numbers in parentheses indicate the number of people reporting a single ancestry; * Numbers in parentheses indicate the number of persons reporting this race alone, not in combination with any other race; Please refer to the User Guide for more information.

Ottawa County
Population: 263,801

Ancestry	Population	%
Afghan (0)	0	<0.01
African, Sub-Saharan (61)	163	0.06
African (28)	118	0.05
Cape Verdean (0)	0	<0.01
Ethiopian (18)	30	0.01
Ghanaian (0)	0	<0.01
Kenyan (0)	0	<0.01
Liberian (0)	0	<0.01
Nigerian (0)	0	<0.01
Senegalese (15)	15	0.01
Sierra Leonean (0)	0	<0.01
Somalian (0)	0	<0.01
South African (0)	0	<0.01
Sudanese (0)	0	<0.01
Ugandan (0)	0	<0.01
Zimbabwean (0)	0	<0.01
Other Sub-Saharan African (0)	0	<0.01
Albanian (64)	89	0.03
Alsatian (0)	0	<0.01
American (10,031)	10,031	3.84
Arab (273)	690	0.26
Arab (0)	21	0.01
Egyptian (0)	0	<0.01
Iraqi (0)	0	<0.01
Jordanian (0)	0	<0.01
Lebanese (153)	418	0.16
Moroccan (0)	0	<0.01
Palestinian (55)	70	0.03
Syrian (0)	93	0.04
Other Arab (65)	88	0.03
Armenian (0)	99	0.04
Assyrian/Chaldean/Syriac (0)	14	0.01
Australian (0)	34	0.01
Austrian (71)	493	0.19
Basque (0)	0	<0.01
Belgian (147)	586	0.22
Brazilian (71)	104	0.04
British (690)	997	0.38
Bulgarian (0)	0	<0.01
Cajun (0)	0	<0.01
Canadian (313)	929	0.36
Carpatho Rusyn (0)	0	<0.01
Celtic (0)	0	<0.01
Croatian (59)	336	0.13
Cypriot (0)	0	<0.01
Czech (226)	1,099	0.42
Czechoslovakian (120)	317	0.12
Danish (218)	1,302	0.50
Dutch (55,006)	88,087	33.70
Eastern European (60)	87	0.03
English (5,671)	23,567	9.02
Estonian (0)	0	<0.01
European (2,277)	2,820	1.08
Finnish (388)	1,942	0.74
French, ex. Basque (1,350)	9,491	3.63
French Canadian (775)	2,570	0.98
German (13,695)	58,514	22.39
German Russian (0)	0	<0.01
Greek (212)	664	0.25
Guyanese (0)	0	<0.01
Hungarian (529)	1,559	0.60
Icelander (0)	15	0.01
Iranian (105)	119	0.05
Irish (4,562)	25,452	9.74
Israeli (0)	0	<0.01
Italian (1,858)	7,337	2.81
Latvian (72)	186	0.07
Lithuanian (238)	1,120	0.43
Luxemburger (0)	11	<0.01
Macedonian (0)	73	0.03
Maltese (21)	58	0.02
New Zealander (0)	0	<0.01
Northern European (172)	172	0.07
Norwegian (513)	3,029	1.16
Pennsylvania German (126)	231	0.09

Ancestry (cont.)	Population	%
Polish (4,264)	14,801	5.66
Portuguese (51)	109	0.04
Romanian (84)	176	0.07
Russian (283)	1,012	0.39
Scandinavian (67)	383	0.15
Scotch-Irish (912)	2,990	1.14
Scottish (940)	4,895	1.87
Serbian (19)	87	0.03
Slavic (78)	219	0.08
Slovak (196)	485	0.19
Slovene (37)	127	0.05
Soviet Union (0)	0	<0.01
Swedish (1,536)	6,706	2.57
Swiss (157)	561	0.21
Turkish (66)	90	0.03
Ukrainian (262)	470	0.18
Welsh (159)	1,175	0.45
West Indian, ex. Hispanic (127)	262	0.10
Bahamian (0)	0	<0.01
Barbadian (0)	0	<0.01
Belizean (14)	43	0.02
Bermudan (0)	18	0.01
British West Indian (0)	0	<0.01
Dutch West Indian (0)	39	0.01
Haitian (34)	34	0.01
Jamaican (79)	114	0.04
Trinidadian/Tobagonian (0)	0	<0.01
U.S. Virgin Islander (0)	0	<0.01
West Indian (0)	14	0.01
Other West Indian (0)	0	<0.01
Yugoslavian (179)	265	0.10

Hispanic Origin	Population	%
Hispanic or Latino (of any race)	22,761	8.63
Central American, ex. Mexican	593	0.22
Costa Rican	25	0.01
Guatemalan	217	0.08
Honduran	122	0.05
Nicaraguan	59	0.02
Panamanian	42	0.02
Salvadoran	128	0.05
Other Central American	0	<0.01
Cuban	462	0.18
Dominican Republic	87	0.03
Mexican	18,314	6.94
Puerto Rican	1,169	0.44
South American	436	0.17
Argentinean	31	0.01
Bolivian	20	0.01
Chilean	102	0.04
Colombian	90	0.03
Ecuadorian	36	0.01
Paraguayan	4	<0.01
Peruvian	89	0.03
Uruguayan	9	<0.01
Venezuelan	51	0.02
Other South American	4	<0.01
Other Hispanic or Latino	1,700	0.64

Race*	Population	%
African-American/Black (3,874)	5,635	2.14
Not Hispanic (3,551)	5,010	1.90
Hispanic (323)	625	0.24
American Indian/Alaska Native (1,141)	2,456	0.93
Not Hispanic (806)	1,904	0.72
Hispanic (335)	552	0.21
Alaska Athabascan (Ala. Nat.) (1)	2	<0.01
Aleut (Alaska Native) (1)	4	<0.01
Apache (22)	38	0.01
Arapaho (0)	1	<0.01
Blackfeet (1)	41	0.02
Canadian/French Am. Ind. (17)	27	0.01
Central American Ind. (3)	4	<0.01
Cherokee (55)	241	0.09
Cheyenne (0)	1	<0.01
Chickasaw (2)	4	<0.01
Chippewa (206)	410	0.16
Choctaw (17)	35	0.01
Colville (1)	1	<0.01

Race* (cont.)	Population	%
Comanche (1)	4	<0.01
Cree (1)	1	<0.01
Creek (1)	2	<0.01
Crow (1)	1	<0.01
Delaware (1)	1	<0.01
Hopi (0)	0	<0.01
Houma (0)	0	<0.01
Inupiat (Alaska Native) (1)	5	<0.01
Iroquois (11)	28	0.01
Kiowa (0)	0	<0.01
Lumbee (8)	9	<0.01
Menominee (0)	0	<0.01
Mexican American Ind. (85)	121	0.05
Navajo (18)	33	0.01
Osage (0)	0	<0.01
Ottawa (125)	263	0.10
Paiute (0)	0	<0.01
Pima (0)	0	<0.01
Potawatomi (121)	225	0.09
Pueblo (2)	4	<0.01
Puget Sound Salish (0)	0	<0.01
Seminole (0)	9	<0.01
Shoshone (1)	2	<0.01
Sioux (13)	42	0.02
South American Ind. (4)	5	<0.01
Spanish American Ind. (4)	8	<0.01
Tlingit-Haida (Alaska Native) (1)	3	<0.01
Tohono O'Odham (0)	0	<0.01
Tsimshian (Alaska Native) (1)	1	<0.01
Ute (1)	1	<0.01
Yakama (0)	0	<0.01
Yaqui (1)	1	<0.01
Yuman (0)	0	<0.01
Yup'ik (Alaska Native) (0)	1	<0.01
Asian (6,738)	8,194	3.11
Not Hispanic (6,576)	7,859	2.98
Hispanic (162)	335	0.13
Bangladeshi (15)	16	0.01
Bhutanese (24)	33	0.01
Burmese (17)	20	0.01
Cambodian (994)	1,243	0.47
Chinese, ex. Taiwanese (716)	967	0.37
Filipino (329)	585	0.22
Hmong (23)	30	0.01
Indian (700)	820	0.31
Indonesian (12)	60	0.02
Japanese (86)	212	0.08
Korean (699)	977	0.37
Laotian (1,489)	1,788	0.68
Malaysian (6)	6	<0.01
Nepalese (4)	13	<0.01
Pakistani (25)	29	0.01
Sri Lankan (6)	10	<0.01
Taiwanese (20)	29	0.01
Thai (81)	165	0.06
Vietnamese (943)	1,146	0.43
Hawaii Native/Pacific Islander (74)	243	0.09
Not Hispanic (64)	205	0.08
Hispanic (10)	38	0.01
Fijian (0)	0	<0.01
Guamanian/Chamorro (8)	13	<0.01
Marshallese (1)	1	<0.01
Native Hawaiian (18)	67	0.03
Samoan (10)	19	0.01
Tongan (1)	2	<0.01
White (237,638)	242,506	91.93
Not Hispanic (226,156)	229,641	87.05
Hispanic (11,482)	12,865	4.88

Notes: † The Census 2010 population figure is used to calculate the percentages in the Hispanic Origin and Race categories. Ancestry percentages are based on the 2006-2010 American Community Survey population (not shown); ‡ Numbers in parentheses indicate the number of people reporting a single ancestry; * Numbers in parentheses indicate the number of persons reporting this race alone, not in combination with any other race; Please refer to the User Guide for more information.

Saginaw County

Population: 200,169

Ancestry	Population	%
Afghan (0)	0	<0.01
African, Sub-Saharan (532)	732	0.36
African (423)	590	0.29
Cape Verdean (0)	0	<0.01
Ethiopian (0)	6	<0.01
Ghanaian (55)	55	0.03
Kenyan (0)	0	<0.01
Liberian (13)	13	0.01
Nigerian (0)	0	<0.01
Senegalese (14)	14	0.01
Sierra Leonean (0)	0	<0.01
Somalian (0)	0	<0.01
South African (16)	43	0.02
Sudanese (0)	0	<0.01
Ugandan (0)	0	<0.01
Zimbabwean (11)	11	0.01
Other Sub-Saharan African (0)	0	<0.01
Albanian (0)	0	<0.01
Alsatian (0)	0	<0.01
American (7,788)	7,788	3.85
Arab (492)	711	0.35
Arab (65)	65	0.03
Egyptian (0)	0	<0.01
Iraqi (0)	22	0.01
Jordanian (51)	51	0.03
Lebanese (175)	279	0.14
Moroccan (43)	43	0.02
Palestinian (73)	73	0.04
Syrian (0)	10	<0.01
Other Arab (85)	168	0.08
Armenian (14)	51	0.03
Assyrian/Chaldean/Syriac (81)	103	0.05
Australian (0)	4	<0.01
Austrian (86)	533	0.26
Basque (0)	0	<0.01
Belgian (145)	508	0.25
Brazilian (0)	0	<0.01
British (186)	435	0.21
Bulgarian (0)	22	0.01
Cajun (0)	7	<0.01
Canadian (216)	468	0.23
Carpatho Rusyn (0)	0	<0.01
Celtic (0)	5	<0.01
Croatian (12)	91	0.04
Cypriot (0)	0	<0.01
Czech (438)	1,597	0.79
Czechoslovakian (197)	753	0.37
Danish (97)	620	0.31
Dutch (459)	3,692	1.82
Eastern European (22)	22	0.01
English (4,270)	16,828	8.32
Estonian (16)	19	0.01
European (1,003)	1,133	0.56
Finnish (237)	688	0.34
French, ex. Basque (1,774)	13,299	6.57
French Canadian (1,414)	4,162	2.06
German (25,681)	64,884	32.07
German Russian (0)	0	<0.01
Greek (302)	528	0.26
Guyanese (0)	0	<0.01
Hungarian (516)	2,163	1.07
Icelander (0)	11	0.01
Iranian (66)	66	0.03
Irish (4,263)	20,553	10.16
Israeli (0)	11	0.01
Italian (1,832)	5,592	2.76
Latvian (117)	137	0.07
Lithuanian (209)	750	0.37
Luxemburger (0)	0	<0.01
Macedonian (0)	16	0.01
Maltese (20)	38	0.02
New Zealander (0)	0	<0.01
Northern European (7)	7	<0.01
Norwegian (242)	1,167	0.58
Pennsylvania German (55)	148	0.07

Ancestry	Population	%
Polish (5,641)	18,282	9.04
Portuguese (118)	128	0.06
Romanian (38)	186	0.09
Russian (238)	1,285	0.64
Scandinavian (55)	138	0.07
Scotch-Irish (802)	2,839	1.40
Scottish (951)	4,552	2.25
Serbian (11)	126	0.06
Slavic (6)	116	0.06
Slovak (201)	681	0.34
Slovene (0)	11	0.01
Soviet Union (0)	0	<0.01
Swedish (356)	1,687	0.83
Swiss (74)	440	0.22
Turkish (23)	29	0.01
Ukrainian (126)	506	0.25
Welsh (113)	696	0.34
West Indian, ex. Hispanic (169)	258	0.13
Bahamian (0)	0	<0.01
Barbadian (31)	31	0.02
Belizean (0)	0	<0.01
Bermudan (0)	0	<0.01
British West Indian (16)	16	0.01
Dutch West Indian (0)	0	<0.01
Haitian (14)	14	0.01
Jamaican (2)	57	0.03
Trinidadian/Tobagonian (96)	130	0.06
U.S. Virgin Islander (0)	0	<0.01
West Indian (10)	10	<0.01
Other West Indian (0)	0	<0.01
Yugoslavian (104)	185	0.09

Hispanic Origin	Population	%
Hispanic or Latino (of any race)	15,573	7.78
Central American, ex. Mexican	162	0.08
Costa Rican	6	<0.01
Guatemalan	60	0.03
Honduran	26	0.01
Nicaraguan	11	0.01
Panamanian	24	0.01
Salvadoran	34	0.02
Other Central American	1	<0.01
Cuban	65	0.03
Dominican Republic	10	<0.01
Mexican	13,666	6.83
Puerto Rican	379	0.19
South American	113	0.06
Argentinean	12	0.01
Bolivian	12	0.01
Chilean	10	<0.01
Colombian	35	0.02
Ecuadorian	4	<0.01
Paraguayan	3	<0.01
Peruvian	18	0.01
Uruguayan	7	<0.01
Venezuelan	11	0.01
Other South American	1	<0.01
Other Hispanic or Latino	1,178	0.59

Race*	Population	%
African-American/Black (38,114)	40,895	20.43
Not Hispanic (37,222)	39,332	19.65
Hispanic (892)	1,563	0.78
American Indian/Alaska Native (877)	2,022	1.01
Not Hispanic (660)	1,607	0.80
Hispanic (217)	415	0.21
Alaska Athabascan (Ala. Nat.) (0)	0	<0.01
Aleut (Alaska Native) (0)	0	<0.01
Apache (7)	20	0.01
Arapaho (0)	0	<0.01
Blackfeet (9)	40	0.02
Canadian/French Am. Ind. (5)	20	0.01
Central American Ind. (1)	1	<0.01
Cherokee (39)	210	0.10
Cheyenne (2)	2	<0.01
Chickasaw (0)	1	<0.01
Chippewa (296)	560	0.28
Choctaw (3)	17	0.01
Colville (0)	0	<0.01

Race*	Population	%
Comanche (3)	4	<0.01
Cree (0)	4	<0.01
Creek (2)	4	<0.01
Crow (2)	3	<0.01
Delaware (0)	1	<0.01
Hopi (0)	0	<0.01
Houma (0)	0	<0.01
Inupiat (Alaska Native) (0)	2	<0.01
Iroquois (9)	26	0.01
Kiowa (0)	0	<0.01
Lumbee (8)	11	0.01
Menominee (0)	0	<0.01
Mexican American Ind. (45)	61	0.03
Navajo (5)	11	0.01
Osage (0)	0	<0.01
Ottawa (12)	37	0.02
Paiute (1)	1	<0.01
Pima (2)	6	<0.01
Potawatomi (25)	32	0.02
Pueblo (1)	3	<0.01
Puget Sound Salish (0)	0	<0.01
Seminole (1)	7	<0.01
Shoshone (0)	1	<0.01
Sioux (6)	18	0.01
South American Ind. (0)	5	<0.01
Spanish American Ind. (2)	5	<0.01
Tlingit-Haida (Alaska Native) (1)	1	<0.01
Tohono O'Odham (0)	0	<0.01
Tsimshian (Alaska Native) (0)	0	<0.01
Ute (2)	2	<0.01
Yakama (0)	0	<0.01
Yaqui (3)	5	<0.01
Yuman (1)	5	<0.01
Yup'ik (Alaska Native) (0)	0	<0.01
Asian (2,108)	2,634	1.32
Not Hispanic (2,067)	2,516	1.26
Hispanic (41)	118	0.06
Bangladeshi (19)	21	0.01
Bhutanese (0)	0	<0.01
Burmese (0)	0	<0.01
Cambodian (1)	1	<0.01
Chinese, ex. Taiwanese (390)	470	0.23
Filipino (269)	390	0.19
Hmong (58)	62	0.03
Indian (726)	789	0.39
Indonesian (5)	6	<0.01
Japanese (43)	91	0.05
Korean (226)	318	0.16
Laotian (4)	13	0.01
Malaysian (0)	5	<0.01
Nepalese (5)	6	<0.01
Pakistani (164)	172	0.09
Sri Lankan (7)	10	<0.01
Taiwanese (20)	24	0.01
Thai (23)	37	0.02
Vietnamese (87)	103	0.05
Hawaii Native/Pacific Islander (65)	180	0.09
Not Hispanic (55)	139	0.07
Hispanic (10)	41	0.02
Fijian (4)	4	<0.01
Guamanian/Chamorro (19)	46	0.02
Marshallese (1)	2	<0.01
Native Hawaiian (16)	38	0.02
Samoan (2)	4	<0.01
Tongan (1)	2	<0.01
White (149,272)	153,553	76.71
Not Hispanic (141,187)	144,101	71.99
Hispanic (8,085)	9,452	4.72

Notes: † The Census 2010 population figure is used to calculate the percentages in the Hispanic Origin and Race categories. Ancestry percentages are based on the 2006-2010 American Community Survey population (not shown); ‡ Numbers in parentheses indicate the number of people reporting a single ancestry; * Numbers in parentheses indicate the number of persons reporting this race alone, not in combination with any other race; Please refer to the User Guide for more information.

Shiawassee County

Population: 70,648

Ancestry	Population	%
Afghan (0)	0	<0.01
African, Sub-Saharan (17)	24	0.03
African (11)	11	0.02
Cape Verdean (0)	0	<0.01
Ethiopian (0)	0	<0.01
Ghanaian (0)	0	<0.01
Kenyan (0)	0	<0.01
Liberian (0)	0	<0.01
Nigerian (0)	0	<0.01
Senegalese (0)	0	<0.01
Sierra Leonean (0)	0	<0.01
Somalian (0)	0	<0.01
South African (6)	13	0.02
Sudanese (0)	0	<0.01
Ugandan (0)	0	<0.01
Zimbabwean (0)	0	<0.01
Other Sub-Saharan African (0)	0	<0.01
Albanian (0)	0	<0.01
Alsatian (0)	0	<0.01
American (5,483)	5,483	7.66
Arab (49)	105	0.15
Arab (1)	1	<0.01
Egyptian (0)	0	<0.01
Iraqi (17)	17	0.02
Jordanian (0)	0	<0.01
Lebanese (31)	71	0.10
Moroccan (0)	0	<0.01
Palestinian (0)	0	<0.01
Syrian (0)	16	0.02
Other Arab (0)	0	<0.01
Armenian (5)	5	0.01
Assyrian/Chaldean/Syriac (87)	87	0.12
Australian (17)	17	0.02
Austrian (17)	103	0.14
Basque (0)	0	<0.01
Belgian (64)	241	0.34
Brazilian (6)	8	0.01
British (37)	231	0.32
Bulgarian (0)	0	<0.01
Cajun (0)	0	<0.01
Canadian (278)	569	0.79
Carpatho Rusyn (0)	0	<0.01
Celtic (0)	0	<0.01
Croatian (31)	154	0.22
Cypriot (0)	0	<0.01
Czech (863)	2,280	3.18
Czechoslovakian (299)	553	0.77
Danish (133)	295	0.41
Dutch (382)	2,320	3.24
Eastern European (14)	24	0.03
English (3,545)	11,831	16.52
Estonian (0)	0	<0.01
European (555)	622	0.87
Finnish (132)	336	0.47
French, ex. Basque (546)	4,004	5.59
French Canadian (462)	1,359	1.90
German (5,991)	20,683	28.88
German Russian (0)	0	<0.01
Greek (22)	232	0.32
Guyanese (0)	0	<0.01
Hungarian (357)	885	1.24
Icelander (0)	0	<0.01
Iranian (10)	10	0.01
Irish (2,366)	10,967	15.31
Israeli (0)	0	<0.01
Italian (488)	1,821	2.54
Latvian (12)	12	0.02
Lithuanian (19)	70	0.10
Luxemburger (3)	3	<0.01
Macedonian (25)	39	0.05
Maltese (11)	14	0.02
New Zealander (0)	0	<0.01
Northern European (25)	64	0.09
Norwegian (182)	436	0.61
Pennsylvania German (36)	47	0.07

Ancestry	Population	%
Polish (1,301)	4,112	5.74
Portuguese (5)	28	0.04
Romanian (42)	87	0.12
Russian (148)	328	0.46
Scandinavian (16)	39	0.05
Scotch-Irish (388)	1,348	1.88
Scottish (566)	1,876	2.62
Serbian (8)	24	0.03
Slavic (5)	90	0.13
Slovak (175)	533	0.74
Slovene (0)	0	<0.01
Soviet Union (0)	0	<0.01
Swedish (139)	879	1.23
Swiss (47)	110	0.15
Turkish (0)	0	<0.01
Ukrainian (28)	108	0.15
Welsh (91)	344	0.48
West Indian, ex. Hispanic (0)	8	0.01
Bahamian (0)	8	0.01
Barbadian (0)	0	<0.01
Belizean (0)	0	<0.01
Bermudan (0)	0	<0.01
British West Indian (0)	0	<0.01
Dutch West Indian (0)	0	<0.01
Haitian (0)	0	<0.01
Jamaican (0)	0	<0.01
Trinidadian/Tobagonian (0)	0	<0.01
U.S. Virgin Islander (0)	0	<0.01
West Indian (0)	0	<0.01
Other West Indian (0)	0	<0.01
Yugoslavian (27)	99	0.14

Hispanic Origin	Population	%
Hispanic or Latino (of any race)	1,695	2.40
Central American, ex. Mexican	28	0.04
Costa Rican	0	<0.01
Guatemalan	6	0.01
Honduran	3	<0.01
Nicaraguan	2	<0.01
Panamanian	10	0.01
Salvadoran	7	0.01
Other Central American	0	<0.01
Cuban	33	0.05
Dominican Republic	3	<0.01
Mexican	1,320	1.87
Puerto Rican	85	0.12
South American	51	0.07
Argentinean	6	0.01
Bolivian	5	0.01
Chilean	0	<0.01
Colombian	29	0.04
Ecuadorian	2	<0.01
Paraguayan	0	<0.01
Peruvian	4	0.01
Uruguayan	5	0.01
Venezuelan	0	<0.01
Other South American	0	<0.01
Other Hispanic or Latino	175	0.25

Race*	Population	%
African-American/Black (325)	613	0.87
Not Hispanic (305)	576	0.82
Hispanic (20)	37	0.05
American Indian/Alaska Native (350)	797	1.13
Not Hispanic (303)	693	0.98
Hispanic (47)	104	0.15
Alaska Athabascan (Ala. Nat.) (3)	3	<0.01
Aleut (Alaska Native) (0)	0	<0.01
Apache (2)	18	0.03
Arapaho (0)	0	<0.01
Blackfeet (5)	28	0.04
Canadian/French Am. Ind. (7)	12	0.02
Central American Ind. (0)	0	<0.01
Cherokee (24)	112	0.16
Cheyenne (0)	0	<0.01
Chickasaw (2)	2	<0.01
Chippewa (111)	200	0.28
Choctaw (4)	7	0.01
Colville (0)	0	<0.01

	Population	%
Comanche (0)	0	<0.01
Cree (0)	1	<0.01
Creek (3)	3	<0.01
Crow (0)	2	<0.01
Delaware (0)	0	<0.01
Hopi (0)	0	<0.01
Houma (0)	0	<0.01
Inupiat (Alaska Native) (1)	1	<0.01
Iroquois (12)	25	0.04
Kiowa (0)	0	<0.01
Lumbee (1)	3	<0.01
Menominee (0)	0	<0.01
Mexican American Ind. (8)	12	0.02
Navajo (4)	8	0.01
Osage (0)	0	<0.01
Ottawa (29)	63	0.09
Paiute (0)	0	<0.01
Pima (0)	0	<0.01
Potawatomi (9)	10	0.01
Pueblo (6)	6	0.01
Puget Sound Salish (0)	0	<0.01
Seminole (0)	0	<0.01
Shoshone (0)	0	<0.01
Sioux (4)	11	0.02
South American Ind. (0)	3	<0.01
Spanish American Ind. (2)	2	<0.01
Tlingit-Haida (Alaska Native) (0)	0	<0.01
Tohono O'Odham (1)	1	<0.01
Tsimshian (Alaska Native) (0)	0	<0.01
Ute (1)	1	<0.01
Yakama (0)	0	<0.01
Yaqui (0)	0	<0.01
Yuman (0)	0	<0.01
Yup'ik (Alaska Native) (0)	0	<0.01
Asian (256)	411	0.58
Not Hispanic (247)	384	0.54
Hispanic (9)	27	0.04
Bangladeshi (4)	4	0.01
Bhutanese (0)	0	<0.01
Burmese (0)	0	<0.01
Cambodian (0)	0	<0.01
Chinese, ex. Taiwanese (59)	70	0.10
Filipino (52)	88	0.12
Hmong (23)	24	0.03
Indian (45)	56	0.08
Indonesian (0)	0	<0.01
Japanese (11)	42	0.06
Korean (24)	45	0.06
Laotian (0)	2	<0.01
Malaysian (0)	0	<0.01
Nepalese (0)	0	<0.01
Pakistani (6)	14	0.02
Sri Lankan (0)	0	<0.01
Taiwanese (1)	2	<0.01
Thai (9)	16	0.02
Vietnamese (8)	21	0.03
Hawaii Native/Pacific Islander (27)	59	0.08
Not Hispanic (22)	44	0.06
Hispanic (5)	15	0.02
Fijian (0)	0	<0.01
Guamanian/Chamorro (1)	2	<0.01
Marshallese (0)	0	<0.01
Native Hawaiian (10)	18	0.03
Samoan (5)	5	0.01
Tongan (1)	1	<0.01
White (68,315)	69,318	98.12
Not Hispanic (67,240)	68,028	96.29
Hispanic (1,075)	1,290	1.83

Notes: † The Census 2010 population figure is used to calculate the percentages in the Hispanic Origin and Race categories. Ancestry percentages are based on the 2006-2010 American Community Survey population (not shown); ‡ Numbers in parentheses indicate the number of people reporting a single ancestry; * Numbers in parentheses indicate the number of persons reporting this race alone, not in combination with any other race; Please refer to the User Guide for more information.

St. Clair County

Population: 163,040

Ancestry	Population	%
Afghan (0)	0	<0.01
African, Sub-Saharan (92)	113	0.07
African (92)	113	0.07
Cape Verdean (0)	0	<0.01
Ethiopian (0)	0	<0.01
Ghanaian (0)	0	<0.01
Kenyan (0)	0	<0.01
Liberian (0)	0	<0.01
Nigerian (0)	0	<0.01
Senegalese (0)	0	<0.01
Sierra Leonean (0)	0	<0.01
Somalian (0)	0	<0.01
South African (0)	0	<0.01
Sudanese (0)	0	<0.01
Ugandan (0)	0	<0.01
Zimbabwean (0)	0	<0.01
Other Sub-Saharan African (0)	0	<0.01
Albanian (55)	55	0.03
Alsatian (0)	0	<0.01
American (8,299)	8,299	5.01
Arab (452)	1,052	0.63
Arab (20)	107	0.06
Egyptian (33)	51	0.03
Iraqi (3)	3	<0.01
Jordanian (0)	0	<0.01
Lebanese (320)	703	0.42
Moroccan (0)	0	<0.01
Palestinian (0)	0	<0.01
Syrian (63)	175	0.11
Other Arab (13)	13	0.01
Armenian (65)	109	0.07
Assyrian/Chaldean/Syriac (106)	106	0.06
Australian (0)	28	0.02
Austrian (83)	580	0.35
Basque (0)	0	<0.01
Belgian (712)	3,358	2.03
Brazilian (7)	19	0.01
British (233)	585	0.35
Bulgarian (103)	172	0.10
Cajun (0)	0	<0.01
Canadian (665)	1,917	1.16
Carpatho Rusyn (0)	0	<0.01
Celtic (55)	55	0.03
Croatian (70)	321	0.19
Cypriot (0)	0	<0.01
Czech (157)	529	0.32
Czechoslovakian (139)	370	0.22
Danish (60)	361	0.22
Dutch (606)	3,302	1.99
Eastern European (57)	87	0.05
English (4,832)	19,361	11.68
Estonian (0)	0	<0.01
European (1,071)	1,173	0.71
Finnish (290)	1,281	0.77
French, ex. Basque (1,922)	13,320	8.04
French Canadian (1,446)	4,745	2.86
German (16,592)	55,022	33.20
German Russian (0)	6	<0.01
Greek (306)	884	0.53
Guyanese (0)	0	<0.01
Hungarian (528)	1,722	1.04
Icelander (0)	0	<0.01
Iranian (39)	39	0.02
Irish (5,637)	24,711	14.91
Israeli (11)	15	0.01
Italian (2,594)	9,780	5.90
Latvian (13)	50	0.03
Lithuanian (125)	441	0.27
Luxemburger (0)	0	<0.01
Macedonian (19)	50	0.03
Maltese (63)	152	0.09
New Zealander (0)	0	<0.01
Northern European (78)	92	0.06
Norwegian (285)	1,254	0.76
Pennsylvania German (39)	72	0.04

Ancestry (cont.)	Population	%
Polish (7,178)	21,303	12.85
Portuguese (36)	134	0.08
Romanian (120)	490	0.30
Russian (275)	1,540	0.93
Scandinavian (103)	164	0.10
Scotch-Irish (1,256)	3,614	2.18
Scottish (1,678)	6,845	4.13
Serbian (104)	178	0.11
Slavic (10)	42	0.03
Slovak (203)	435	0.26
Slovene (11)	25	0.02
Soviet Union (0)	0	<0.01
Swedish (359)	2,088	1.26
Swiss (48)	290	0.17
Turkish (24)	24	0.01
Ukrainian (290)	895	0.54
Welsh (135)	770	0.46
West Indian, ex. Hispanic (36)	98	0.06
Bahamian (0)	24	0.01
Barbadian (0)	0	<0.01
Belizean (0)	0	<0.01
Bermudan (0)	0	<0.01
British West Indian (0)	0	<0.01
Dutch West Indian (0)	10	0.01
Haitian (0)	0	<0.01
Jamaican (36)	64	0.04
Trinidadian/Tobagonian (0)	0	<0.01
U.S. Virgin Islander (0)	0	<0.01
West Indian (0)	0	<0.01
Other West Indian (0)	0	<0.01
Yugoslavian (99)	209	0.13

Hispanic Origin	Population	%
Hispanic or Latino (of any race)	4,708	2.89
Central American, ex. Mexican	108	0.07
Costa Rican	0	<0.01
Guatemalan	34	0.02
Honduran	25	0.02
Nicaraguan	18	0.01
Panamanian	25	0.02
Salvadoran	4	<0.01
Other Central American	2	<0.01
Cuban	69	0.04
Dominican Republic	7	<0.01
Mexican	3,667	2.25
Puerto Rican	284	0.17
South American	92	0.06
Argentinean	8	<0.01
Bolivian	2	<0.01
Chilean	2	<0.01
Colombian	38	0.02
Ecuadorian	14	0.01
Paraguayan	1	<0.01
Peruvian	15	0.01
Uruguayan	5	<0.01
Venezuelan	2	<0.01
Other South American	5	<0.01
Other Hispanic or Latino	481	0.30

Race*	Population	%
African-American/Black (3,976)	5,432	3.33
Not Hispanic (3,860)	5,155	3.16
Hispanic (116)	277	0.17
American Indian/Alaska Native (729)	2,032	1.25
Not Hispanic (647)	1,814	1.11
Hispanic (82)	218	0.13
Alaska Athabascan (Ala. Nat.) (0)	4	<0.01
Aleut (Alaska Native) (0)	0	<0.01
Apache (5)	17	0.01
Arapaho (0)	1	<0.01
Blackfeet (19)	70	0.04
Canadian/French Am. Ind. (44)	69	0.04
Central American Ind. (0)	0	<0.01
Cherokee (55)	313	0.19
Cheyenne (0)	7	<0.01
Chickasaw (0)	19	0.01
Chippewa (205)	387	0.24
Choctaw (2)	18	0.01
Colville (0)	0	<0.01

Race* (cont.)	Population	%
Comanche (4)	6	<0.01
Cree (1)	9	0.01
Creek (3)	5	<0.01
Crow (0)	5	<0.01
Delaware (10)	19	0.01
Hopi (2)	3	<0.01
Houma (0)	0	<0.01
Inupiat (Alaska Native) (0)	2	<0.01
Iroquois (43)	77	0.05
Kiowa (0)	0	<0.01
Lumbee (4)	14	0.01
Menominee (1)	3	<0.01
Mexican American Ind. (19)	31	0.02
Navajo (2)	2	<0.01
Osage (0)	1	<0.01
Ottawa (17)	48	0.03
Paiute (0)	0	<0.01
Pima (0)	3	<0.01
Potawatomi (12)	32	0.02
Pueblo (1)	2	<0.01
Puget Sound Salish (0)	0	<0.01
Seminole (0)	5	<0.01
Shoshone (0)	1	<0.01
Sioux (14)	40	0.02
South American Ind. (0)	0	<0.01
Spanish American Ind. (2)	2	<0.01
Tlingit-Haida (Alaska Native) (0)	0	<0.01
Tohono O'Odham (0)	0	<0.01
Tsimshian (Alaska Native) (0)	0	<0.01
Ute (0)	0	<0.01
Yakama (0)	0	<0.01
Yaqui (0)	1	<0.01
Yuman (1)	1	<0.01
Yup'ik (Alaska Native) (0)	0	<0.01
Asian (777)	1,202	0.74
Not Hispanic (763)	1,142	0.70
Hispanic (14)	60	0.04
Bangladeshi (11)	11	0.01
Bhutanese (0)	0	<0.01
Burmese (0)	0	<0.01
Cambodian (5)	6	<0.01
Chinese, ex. Taiwanese (118)	152	0.09
Filipino (166)	295	0.18
Hmong (74)	90	0.06
Indian (141)	186	0.11
Indonesian (8)	9	0.01
Japanese (33)	78	0.05
Korean (105)	164	0.10
Laotian (8)	9	0.01
Malaysian (0)	2	<0.01
Nepalese (0)	0	<0.01
Pakistani (24)	28	0.02
Sri Lankan (0)	2	<0.01
Taiwanese (3)	3	<0.01
Thai (29)	45	0.03
Vietnamese (28)	49	0.03
Hawaii Native/Pacific Islander (29)	94	0.06
Not Hispanic (27)	72	0.04
Hispanic (2)	22	0.01
Fijian (0)	0	<0.01
Guamanian/Chamorro (6)	8	<0.01
Marshallese (0)	0	<0.01
Native Hawaiian (12)	38	0.02
Samoan (3)	12	0.01
Tongan (0)	0	<0.01
White (153,052)	156,201	95.81
Not Hispanic (150,213)	152,841	93.74
Hispanic (2,839)	3,360	2.06

*Notes: † The Census 2010 population figure is used to calculate the percentages in the Hispanic Origin and Race categories. Ancestry percentages are based on the 2006-2010 American Community Survey population (not shown); ‡ Numbers in parentheses indicate the number of people reporting a single ancestry; * Numbers in parentheses indicate the number of persons reporting this race alone, not in combination with any other race; Please refer to the User Guide for more information.*

St. Joseph County

Population: 61,295

Ancestry	Population	%
Afghan (0)	0	<0.01
African, Sub-Saharan (55)	70	0.11
African (55)	67	0.11
Cape Verdean (0)	3	<0.01
Ethiopian (0)	0	<0.01
Ghanaian (0)	0	<0.01
Kenyan (0)	0	<0.01
Liberian (0)	0	<0.01
Nigerian (0)	0	<0.01
Senegalese (0)	0	<0.01
Sierra Leonean (0)	0	<0.01
Somalian (0)	0	<0.01
South African (0)	0	<0.01
Sudanese (0)	0	<0.01
Ugandan (0)	0	<0.01
Zimbabwean (0)	0	<0.01
Other Sub-Saharan African (0)	0	<0.01
Albanian (0)	0	<0.01
Alsatian (0)	0	<0.01
American (10,001)	10,001	16.17
Arab (52)	61	0.10
Arab (4)	4	0.01
Egyptian (0)	0	<0.01
Iraqi (6)	6	0.01
Jordanian (0)	0	<0.01
Lebanese (16)	16	0.03
Moroccan (0)	0	<0.01
Palestinian (0)	0	<0.01
Syrian (7)	16	0.03
Other Arab (19)	19	0.03
Armenian (0)	0	<0.01
Assyrian/Chaldean/Syriac (0)	25	0.04
Australian (0)	4	0.01
Austrian (14)	45	0.07
Basque (0)	0	<0.01
Belgian (4)	80	0.13
Brazilian (0)	0	<0.01
British (38)	57	0.09
Bulgarian (0)	0	<0.01
Cajun (14)	14	0.02
Canadian (40)	200	0.32
Carpatho Rusyn (0)	0	<0.01
Celtic (0)	3	<0.01
Croatian (17)	29	0.05
Cypriot (0)	0	<0.01
Czech (90)	246	0.40
Czechoslovakian (28)	48	0.08
Danish (70)	203	0.33
Dutch (885)	3,394	5.49
Eastern European (0)	0	<0.01
English (2,928)	7,403	11.97
Estonian (0)	0	<0.01
European (477)	520	0.84
Finnish (60)	130	0.21
French, ex. Basque (366)	1,899	3.07
French Canadian (89)	359	0.58
German (10,518)	20,289	32.80
German Russian (0)	0	<0.01
Greek (43)	153	0.25
Guyanese (2)	2	<0.01
Hungarian (92)	410	0.66
Icelander (0)	0	<0.01
Iranian (0)	0	<0.01
Irish (1,574)	6,159	9.96
Israeli (0)	0	<0.01
Italian (388)	957	1.55
Latvian (153)	153	0.25
Lithuanian (12)	95	0.15
Luxemburger (0)	0	<0.01
Macedonian (0)	0	<0.01
Maltese (0)	0	<0.01
New Zealander (0)	0	<0.01
Northern European (15)	15	0.02
Norwegian (130)	460	0.74
Pennsylvania German (401)	493	0.80

Ancestry (cont.)	Population	%
Polish (725)	2,266	3.66
Portuguese (10)	16	0.03
Romanian (63)	89	0.14
Russian (25)	175	0.28
Scandinavian (13)	38	0.06
Scotch-Irish (220)	717	1.16
Scottish (284)	1,287	2.08
Serbian (10)	35	0.06
Slavic (4)	7	0.01
Slovak (12)	28	0.05
Slovene (0)	0	<0.01
Soviet Union (0)	0	<0.01
Swedish (211)	746	1.21
Swiss (319)	703	1.14
Turkish (0)	0	<0.01
Ukrainian (24)	139	0.22
Welsh (115)	288	0.47
West Indian, ex. Hispanic (3)	3	<0.01
Bahamian (0)	0	<0.01
Barbadian (0)	0	<0.01
Belizean (0)	0	<0.01
Bermudan (0)	0	<0.01
British West Indian (0)	0	<0.01
Dutch West Indian (0)	0	<0.01
Haitian (3)	3	<0.01
Jamaican (0)	0	<0.01
Trinidadian/Tobagonian (0)	0	<0.01
U.S. Virgin Islander (0)	0	<0.01
West Indian (0)	0	<0.01
Other West Indian (0)	0	<0.01
Yugoslavian (0)	16	0.03

Hispanic Origin	Population	%
Hispanic or Latino (of any race)	4,034	6.58
Central American, ex. Mexican	63	0.10
Costa Rican	4	0.01
Guatemalan	10	0.02
Honduran	17	0.03
Nicaraguan	1	<0.01
Panamanian	9	0.01
Salvadoran	22	0.04
Other Central American	0	<0.01
Cuban	32	0.05
Dominican Republic	5	0.01
Mexican	3,587	5.85
Puerto Rican	197	0.32
South American	27	0.04
Argentinean	4	0.01
Bolivian	1	<0.01
Chilean	0	<0.01
Colombian	7	0.01
Ecuadorian	1	<0.01
Paraguayan	2	<0.01
Peruvian	2	<0.01
Uruguayan	0	<0.01
Venezuelan	10	0.02
Other South American	0	<0.01
Other Hispanic or Latino	123	0.20

Race*	Population	%
African-American/Black (1,600)	2,196	3.58
Not Hispanic (1,555)	2,115	3.45
Hispanic (45)	81	0.13
American Indian/Alaska Native (280)	706	1.15
Not Hispanic (234)	625	1.02
Hispanic (46)	81	0.13
Alaska Athabascan (Ala. Nat.) (0)	0	<0.01
Aleut (Alaska Native) (0)	0	<0.01
Apache (7)	24	0.04
Arapaho (0)	1	<0.01
Blackfeet (2)	31	0.05
Canadian/French Am. Ind. (2)	3	<0.01
Central American Ind. (0)	0	<0.01
Cherokee (41)	155	0.25
Cheyenne (0)	1	<0.01
Chickasaw (0)	2	<0.01
Chippewa (51)	79	0.13
Choctaw (4)	10	0.02
Colville (0)	0	<0.01

Race (cont.)	Population	%
Comanche (1)	1	<0.01
Cree (0)	1	<0.01
Creek (1)	2	<0.01
Crow (0)	0	<0.01
Delaware (0)	1	<0.01
Hopi (0)	0	<0.01
Houma (0)	0	<0.01
Inupiat (Alaska Native) (0)	0	<0.01
Iroquois (6)	8	0.01
Kiowa (0)	0	<0.01
Lumbee (5)	11	0.02
Menominee (0)	1	<0.01
Mexican American Ind. (7)	8	0.01
Navajo (5)	6	0.01
Osage (0)	0	<0.01
Ottawa (6)	11	0.02
Paiute (0)	2	<0.01
Pima (0)	0	<0.01
Potawatomi (21)	41	0.07
Pueblo (0)	0	<0.01
Puget Sound Salish (0)	0	<0.01
Seminole (0)	1	<0.01
Shoshone (0)	1	<0.01
Sioux (5)	22	0.04
South American Ind. (2)	4	<0.01
Spanish American Ind. (0)	0	<0.01
Tlingit-Haida (Alaska Native) (0)	0	<0.01
Tohono O'Odham (0)	0	<0.01
Tsimshian (Alaska Native) (0)	0	<0.01
Ute (0)	0	<0.01
Yakama (0)	0	<0.01
Yaqui (0)	0	<0.01
Yuman (0)	0	<0.01
Yup'ik (Alaska Native) (0)	1	<0.01
Asian (418)	595	0.97
Not Hispanic (416)	574	0.94
Hispanic (2)	21	0.03
Bangladeshi (6)	6	0.01
Bhutanese (0)	0	<0.01
Burmese (2)	2	<0.01
Cambodian (40)	49	0.08
Chinese, ex. Taiwanese (41)	45	0.07
Filipino (75)	110	0.18
Hmong (0)	2	<0.01
Indian (120)	149	0.24
Indonesian (1)	1	<0.01
Japanese (18)	42	0.07
Korean (57)	95	0.15
Laotian (7)	11	0.02
Malaysian (0)	0	<0.01
Nepalese (0)	0	<0.01
Pakistani (2)	4	0.01
Sri Lankan (0)	0	<0.01
Taiwanese (1)	3	<0.01
Thai (9)	15	0.02
Vietnamese (27)	39	0.06
Hawaii Native/Pacific Islander (2)	27	0.04
Not Hispanic (2)	23	0.04
Hispanic (0)	4	0.01
Fijian (0)	0	<0.01
Guamanian/Chamorro (0)	1	<0.01
Marshallese (0)	0	<0.01
Native Hawaiian (1)	13	0.02
Samoan (0)	0	<0.01
Tongan (1)	5	0.01
White (55,519)	56,792	92.65
Not Hispanic (53,930)	54,965	89.67
Hispanic (1,589)	1,827	2.98

*Notes: † The Census 2010 population figure is used to calculate the percentages in the Hispanic Origin and Race categories. Ancestry percentages are based on the 2006-2010 American Community Survey population (not shown); ‡ Numbers in parentheses indicate the number of people reporting a single ancestry; * Numbers in parentheses indicate the number of persons reporting this race alone, not in combination with any other race; Please refer to the User Guide for more information.*

Tuscola County

Population: 55,729

Ancestry	Population	%
Afghan (0)	0	<0.01
African, Sub-Saharan (15)	24	0.04
African (15)	24	0.04
Cape Verdean (0)	0	<0.01
Ethiopian (0)	0	<0.01
Ghanaian (0)	0	<0.01
Kenyan (0)	0	<0.01
Liberian (0)	0	<0.01
Nigerian (0)	0	<0.01
Senegalese (0)	0	<0.01
Sierra Leonean (0)	0	<0.01
Somalian (0)	0	<0.01
South African (0)	0	<0.01
Sudanese (0)	0	<0.01
Ugandan (0)	0	<0.01
Zimbabwean (0)	0	<0.01
Other Sub-Saharan African (0)	0	<0.01
Albanian (2)	2	<0.01
Alsatian (0)	0	<0.01
American (3,923)	3,923	6.94
Arab (193)	219	0.39
Arab (8)	8	0.01
Egyptian (0)	0	<0.01
Iraqi (1)	3	0.01
Jordanian (5)	5	0.01
Lebanese (153)	175	0.31
Moroccan (26)	26	0.05
Palestinian (0)	0	<0.01
Syrian (0)	2	<0.01
Other Arab (0)	0	<0.01
Armenian (10)	17	0.03
Assyrian/Chaldean/Syriac (0)	10	0.02
Australian (38)	49	0.09
Austrian (30)	141	0.25
Basque (0)	0	<0.01
Belgian (171)	424	0.75
Brazilian (0)	0	<0.01
British (19)	88	0.16
Bulgarian (0)	9	0.02
Cajun (0)	0	<0.01
Canadian (91)	280	0.50
Carpatho Rusyn (0)	0	<0.01
Celtic (0)	0	<0.01
Croatian (8)	29	0.05
Cypriot (0)	0	<0.01
Czech (21)	151	0.27
Czechoslovakian (61)	82	0.15
Danish (49)	178	0.31
Dutch (362)	1,516	2.68
Eastern European (3)	3	0.01
English (2,157)	7,037	12.45
Estonian (0)	3	0.01
European (148)	197	0.35
Finnish (57)	232	0.41
French, ex. Basque (486)	3,922	6.94
French Canadian (546)	1,553	2.75
German (8,084)	19,785	34.99
German Russian (0)	0	<0.01
Greek (31)	107	0.19
Guyanese (0)	0	<0.01
Hungarian (359)	1,285	2.27
Icelander (0)	0	<0.01
Iranian (0)	0	<0.01
Irish (1,617)	7,030	12.43
Israeli (0)	0	<0.01
Italian (419)	1,315	2.33
Latvian (0)	0	<0.01
Lithuanian (10)	83	0.15
Luxemburger (0)	0	<0.01
Macedonian (3)	8	0.01
Maltese (6)	9	0.02
New Zealander (0)	0	<0.01
Northern European (44)	44	0.08
Norwegian (94)	255	0.45
Pennsylvania German (35)	58	0.10

Polish (1,790)	5,666	10.02
Portuguese (0)	30	0.05
Romanian (15)	136	0.24
Russian (125)	408	0.72
Scandinavian (51)	69	0.12
Scotch-Irish (391)	1,057	1.87
Scottish (449)	1,726	3.05
Serbian (13)	13	0.02
Slavic (4)	13	0.02
Slovak (25)	89	0.16
Slovene (0)	4	0.01
Soviet Union (0)	0	<0.01
Swedish (78)	541	0.96
Swiss (9)	92	0.16
Turkish (0)	0	<0.01
Ukrainian (98)	186	0.33
Welsh (43)	277	0.49
West Indian, ex. Hispanic (0)	0	<0.01
Bahamian (0)	0	<0.01
Barbadian (0)	0	<0.01
Belizean (0)	0	<0.01
Bermudan (0)	0	<0.01
British West Indian (0)	0	<0.01
Dutch West Indian (0)	0	<0.01
Haitian (0)	0	<0.01
Jamaican (0)	0	<0.01
Trinidadian/Tobagonian (0)	0	<0.01
U.S. Virgin Islander (0)	0	<0.01
West Indian (0)	0	<0.01
Other West Indian (0)	0	<0.01
Yugoslavian (40)	86	0.15

Hispanic Origin	Population	%
Hispanic or Latino (of any race)	1,571	2.82
Central American, ex. Mexican	13	0.02
Costa Rican	0	<0.01
Guatemalan	9	0.02
Honduran	0	<0.01
Nicaraguan	0	<0.01
Panamanian	1	<0.01
Salvadoran	3	0.01
Other Central American	0	<0.01
Cuban	12	0.02
Dominican Republic	0	<0.01
Mexican	1,309	2.35
Puerto Rican	71	0.13
South American	3	0.01
Argentinean	0	<0.01
Bolivian	0	<0.01
Chilean	0	<0.01
Colombian	1	<0.01
Ecuadorian	0	<0.01
Paraguayan	0	<0.01
Peruvian	1	<0.01
Uruguayan	0	<0.01
Venezuelan	1	<0.01
Other South American	0	<0.01
Other Hispanic or Latino	163	0.29

Race*	Population	%
African-American/Black (634)	772	1.39
Not Hispanic (621)	740	1.33
Hispanic (13)	32	0.06
American Indian/Alaska Native (268)	659	1.18
Not Hispanic (233)	579	1.04
Hispanic (35)	80	0.14
Alaska Athabascan (Ala. Nat.) (1)	1	<0.01
Aleut (Alaska Native) (0)	0	<0.01
Apache (4)	11	0.02
Arapaho (0)	0	<0.01
Blackfeet (1)	24	0.04
Canadian/French Am. Ind. (2)	2	<0.01
Central American Ind. (0)	0	<0.01
Cherokee (26)	106	0.19
Cheyenne (1)	2	<0.01
Chickasaw (0)	0	<0.01
Chippewa (102)	187	0.34
Choctaw (0)	2	<0.01
Colville (0)	0	<0.01

Comanche (0)	0	<0.01
Cree (0)	0	<0.01
Creek (3)	3	0.01
Crow (0)	2	<0.01
Delaware (0)	0	<0.01
Hopi (0)	0	<0.01
Houma (0)	0	<0.01
Inupiat (Alaska Native) (2)	2	<0.01
Iroquois (5)	8	0.01
Kiowa (0)	0	<0.01
Lumbee (1)	6	0.01
Menominee (0)	0	<0.01
Mexican American Ind. (6)	9	0.02
Navajo (0)	0	<0.01
Osage (0)	0	<0.01
Ottawa (14)	17	0.03
Paiute (0)	0	<0.01
Pima (0)	0	<0.01
Potawatomi (2)	3	0.01
Pueblo (0)	1	<0.01
Puget Sound Salish (0)	0	<0.01
Seminole (0)	0	<0.01
Shoshone (3)	3	0.01
Sioux (0)	7	0.01
South American Ind. (0)	0	<0.01
Spanish American Ind. (0)	1	<0.01
Tlingit-Haida (Alaska Native) (0)	0	<0.01
Tohono O'Odham (0)	0	<0.01
Tsimshian (Alaska Native) (1)	3	0.01
Ute (0)	0	<0.01
Yakama (0)	0	<0.01
Yaqui (0)	0	<0.01
Yuman (0)	0	<0.01
Yup'ik (Alaska Native) (0)	0	<0.01
Asian (160)	253	0.45
Not Hispanic (155)	246	0.44
Hispanic (5)	7	0.01
Bangladeshi (0)	0	<0.01
Bhutanese (0)	0	<0.01
Burmese (0)	0	<0.01
Cambodian (1)	1	<0.01
Chinese, ex. Taiwanese (21)	28	0.05
Filipino (34)	56	0.10
Hmong (23)	23	0.04
Indian (20)	32	0.06
Indonesian (0)	0	<0.01
Japanese (11)	14	0.03
Korean (27)	50	0.09
Laotian (0)	5	<0.01
Malaysian (0)	0	<0.01
Nepalese (0)	0	<0.01
Pakistani (1)	6	0.01
Sri Lankan (0)	0	<0.01
Taiwanese (0)	0	<0.01
Thai (4)	8	0.01
Vietnamese (6)	12	0.02
Hawaii Native/Pacific Islander (17)	38	0.07
Not Hispanic (15)	33	0.06
Hispanic (2)	5	0.01
Fijian (0)	0	<0.01
Guamanian/Chamorro (0)	0	<0.01
Marshallese (1)	1	<0.01
Native Hawaiian (8)	19	0.03
Samoan (6)	6	0.01
Tongan (0)	0	<0.01
White (53,578)	54,244	97.34
Not Hispanic (52,547)	53,084	95.25
Hispanic (1,031)	1,160	2.08

Notes: † The Census 2010 population figure is used to calculate the percentages in the Hispanic Origin and Race categories. Ancestry percentages are based on the 2006-2010 American Community Survey population (not shown); ‡ Numbers in parentheses indicate the number of people reporting a single ancestry; * Numbers in parentheses indicate the number of persons reporting this race alone, not in combination with any other race; Please refer to the User Guide for more information.

Van Buren County

Population: 76,258

Ancestry	Population	%
Afghan (0)	0	<0.01
African, Sub-Saharan (85)	187	0.24
African (85)	173	0.23
Cape Verdean (0)	0	<0.01
Ethiopian (0)	0	<0.01
Ghanaian (0)	0	<0.01
Kenyan (0)	0	<0.01
Liberian (0)	14	0.02
Nigerian (0)	0	<0.01
Senegalese (0)	0	<0.01
Sierra Leonean (0)	0	<0.01
Somalian (0)	0	<0.01
South African (0)	0	<0.01
Sudanese (0)	0	<0.01
Ugandan (0)	0	<0.01
Zimbabwean (0)	0	<0.01
Other Sub-Saharan African (0)	0	<0.01
Albanian (10)	10	0.01
Alsatian (0)	0	<0.01
American (6,990)	6,990	9.13
Arab (56)	110	0.14
Arab (20)	62	0.08
Egyptian (0)	0	<0.01
Iraqi (0)	0	<0.01
Jordanian (0)	0	<0.01
Lebanese (33)	41	0.05
Moroccan (0)	0	<0.01
Palestinian (0)	0	<0.01
Syrian (0)	4	0.01
Other Arab (3)	3	<0.01
Armenian (4)	10	0.01
Assyrian/Chaldean/Syriac (0)	0	<0.01
Australian (14)	14	0.02
Austrian (67)	222	0.29
Basque (0)	0	<0.01
Belgian (18)	103	0.13
Brazilian (0)	0	<0.01
British (81)	167	0.22
Bulgarian (0)	0	<0.01
Cajun (0)	0	<0.01
Canadian (71)	152	0.20
Carpatho Rusyn (13)	13	0.02
Celtic (145)	163	0.21
Croatian (100)	240	0.31
Cypriot (0)	0	<0.01
Czech (255)	677	0.88
Czechoslovakian (14)	64	0.08
Danish (62)	401	0.52
Dutch (1,973)	6,819	8.90
Eastern European (2)	2	<0.01
English (2,435)	9,364	12.23
Estonian (0)	0	<0.01
European (539)	552	0.72
Finnish (50)	245	0.32
French, ex. Basque (329)	2,971	3.88
French Canadian (234)	788	1.03
German (6,495)	20,470	26.73
German Russian (0)	8	0.01
Greek (78)	214	0.28
Guyanese (0)	0	<0.01
Hungarian (146)	493	0.64
Icelander (0)	0	<0.01
Iranian (0)	0	<0.01
Irish (2,429)	11,161	14.57
Israeli (0)	0	<0.01
Italian (812)	2,451	3.20
Latvian (45)	45	0.06
Lithuanian (86)	395	0.52
Luxemburger (0)	0	<0.01
Macedonian (24)	42	0.05
Maltese (0)	0	<0.01
New Zealander (0)	0	<0.01
Northern European (20)	20	0.03
Norwegian (309)	983	1.28
Pennsylvania German (73)	217	0.28

	Population	%
Polish (1,508)	4,374	5.71
Portuguese (6)	6	0.01
Romanian (0)	0	<0.01
Russian (137)	354	0.46
Scandinavian (39)	192	0.25
Scotch-Irish (416)	1,065	1.39
Scottish (382)	1,741	2.27
Serbian (4)	4	0.01
Slavic (4)	16	0.02
Slovak (39)	147	0.19
Slovene (3)	3	<0.01
Soviet Union (0)	0	<0.01
Swedish (369)	1,697	2.22
Swiss (45)	130	0.17
Turkish (0)	7	0.01
Ukrainian (55)	211	0.28
Welsh (86)	355	0.46
West Indian, ex. Hispanic (27)	30	0.04
Bahamian (0)	0	<0.01
Barbadian (0)	0	<0.01
Belizean (0)	0	<0.01
Bermudan (0)	0	<0.01
British West Indian (0)	0	<0.01
Dutch West Indian (0)	0	<0.01
Haitian (23)	26	0.03
Jamaican (4)	4	0.01
Trinidadian/Tobagonian (0)	0	<0.01
U.S. Virgin Islander (0)	0	<0.01
West Indian (0)	0	<0.01
Other West Indian (0)	0	<0.01
Yugoslavian (6)	46	0.06

Hispanic Origin	Population	%
Hispanic or Latino (of any race)	7,758	10.17
Central American, ex. Mexican	78	0.10
Costa Rican	2	<0.01
Guatemalan	42	0.06
Honduran	12	0.02
Nicaraguan	1	<0.01
Panamanian	11	0.01
Salvadoran	10	0.01
Other Central American	0	<0.01
Cuban	42	0.06
Dominican Republic	10	0.01
Mexican	6,896	9.04
Puerto Rican	181	0.24
South American	50	0.07
Argentinean	7	0.01
Bolivian	1	<0.01
Chilean	2	<0.01
Colombian	19	0.02
Ecuadorian	4	0.01
Paraguayan	0	<0.01
Peruvian	13	0.02
Uruguayan	0	<0.01
Venezuelan	4	0.01
Other South American	0	<0.01
Other Hispanic or Latino	501	0.66

Race*	Population	%
African-American/Black (3,100)	3,946	5.17
Not Hispanic (3,007)	3,783	4.96
Hispanic (93)	163	0.21
American Indian/Alaska Native (669)	1,470	1.93
Not Hispanic (530)	1,255	1.65
Hispanic (139)	215	0.28
Alaska Athabascan (Ala. Nat.) (0)	2	<0.01
Aleut (Alaska Native) (0)	0	<0.01
Apache (2)	12	0.02
Arapaho (1)	1	<0.01
Blackfeet (0)	24	0.03
Canadian/French Am. Ind. (12)	20	0.03
Central American Ind. (0)	0	<0.01
Cherokee (48)	219	0.29
Cheyenne (0)	0	<0.01
Chickasaw (0)	1	<0.01
Chippewa (73)	166	0.22
Choctaw (4)	13	0.02
Colville (0)	0	<0.01

	Population	%
Comanche (0)	3	<0.01
Cree (0)	0	<0.01
Creek (5)	22	0.03
Crow (1)	5	0.01
Delaware (1)	11	0.01
Hopi (0)	0	<0.01
Houma (0)	0	<0.01
Inupiat (Alaska Native) (0)	0	<0.01
Iroquois (3)	13	0.02
Kiowa (0)	0	<0.01
Lumbee (0)	0	<0.01
Menominee (0)	0	<0.01
Mexican American Ind. (33)	40	0.05
Navajo (1)	1	<0.01
Osage (0)	0	<0.01
Ottawa (31)	70	0.09
Paiute (0)	0	<0.01
Pima (0)	0	<0.01
Potawatomi (191)	289	0.38
Pueblo (2)	2	<0.01
Puget Sound Salish (0)	0	<0.01
Seminole (0)	4	0.01
Shoshone (0)	0	<0.01
Sioux (7)	16	0.02
South American Ind. (0)	0	<0.01
Spanish American Ind. (3)	3	<0.01
Tlingit-Haida (Alaska Native) (1)	1	<0.01
Tohono O'Odham (0)	0	<0.01
Tsimshian (Alaska Native) (0)	0	<0.01
Ute (0)	0	<0.01
Yakama (0)	0	<0.01
Yaqui (1)	1	<0.01
Yuman (0)	0	<0.01
Yup'ik (Alaska Native) (0)	0	<0.01
Asian (313)	554	0.73
Not Hispanic (300)	510	0.67
Hispanic (13)	44	0.06
Bangladeshi (2)	2	<0.01
Bhutanese (0)	0	<0.01
Burmese (0)	0	<0.01
Cambodian (0)	1	<0.01
Chinese, ex. Taiwanese (41)	67	0.09
Filipino (34)	96	0.13
Hmong (1)	1	<0.01
Indian (102)	123	0.16
Indonesian (7)	8	0.01
Japanese (24)	65	0.09
Korean (52)	91	0.12
Laotian (3)	4	0.01
Malaysian (2)	2	<0.01
Nepalese (0)	0	<0.01
Pakistani (7)	18	0.02
Sri Lankan (0)	0	<0.01
Taiwanese (2)	2	<0.01
Thai (3)	17	0.02
Vietnamese (15)	30	0.04
Hawaii Native/Pacific Islander (17)	59	0.08
Not Hispanic (15)	48	0.06
Hispanic (2)	11	0.01
Fijian (0)	0	<0.01
Guamanian/Chamorro (5)	9	0.01
Marshallese (0)	0	<0.01
Native Hawaiian (7)	25	0.03
Samoan (3)	9	0.01
Tongan (0)	0	<0.01
White (66,129)	68,011	89.19
Not Hispanic (63,028)	64,490	84.57
Hispanic (3,101)	3,521	4.62

*Notes: † The Census 2010 population figure is used to calculate the percentages in the Hispanic Origin and Race categories. Ancestry percentages are based on the 2006-2010 American Community Survey population (not shown); ‡ Numbers in parentheses indicate the number of people reporting a single ancestry; * Numbers in parentheses indicate the number of persons reporting this race alone, not in combination with any other race; Please refer to the User Guide for more information.*

Washtenaw County

Population: 344,791

Ancestry	Population	%
Afghan (25)	59	0.02
African, Sub-Saharan (3,156)	3,690	1.07
African (1,698)	2,073	0.60
Cape Verdean (12)	12	<0.01
Ethiopian (78)	140	0.04
Ghanaian (119)	119	0.03
Kenyan (0)	0	<0.01
Liberian (0)	0	<0.01
Nigerian (693)	736	0.21
Senegalese (22)	22	0.01
Sierra Leonean (0)	0	<0.01
Somalian (261)	274	0.08
South African (114)	123	0.04
Sudanese (0)	0	<0.01
Ugandan (13)	13	<0.01
Zimbabwean (0)	9	<0.01
Other Sub-Saharan African (146)	169	0.05
Albanian (216)	282	0.08
Alsatian (0)	18	0.01
American (15,151)	15,151	4.41
Arab (4,070)	5,315	1.55
Arab (1,231)	1,303	0.38
Egyptian (234)	257	0.07
Iraqi (137)	182	0.05
Jordanian (291)	291	0.08
Lebanese (397)	975	0.28
Moroccan (8)	46	0.01
Palestinian (850)	935	0.27
Syrian (25)	291	0.08
Other Arab (897)	1,035	0.30
Armenian (359)	741	0.22
Assyrian/Chaldean/Syriac (85)	115	0.03
Australian (57)	158	0.05
Austrian (279)	1,048	0.30
Basque (0)	20	0.01
Belgian (309)	1,508	0.44
Brazilian (165)	285	0.08
British (1,329)	2,445	0.71
Bulgarian (81)	87	0.03
Cajun (32)	38	0.01
Canadian (1,043)	2,078	0.60
Carpatho Rusyn (0)	0	<0.01
Celtic (15)	44	0.01
Croatian (203)	565	0.16
Cypriot (0)	0	<0.01
Czech (375)	2,086	0.61
Czechoslovakian (160)	433	0.13
Danish (347)	1,794	0.52
Dutch (2,019)	8,431	2.45
Eastern European (993)	1,216	0.35
English (11,163)	42,349	12.31
Estonian (36)	36	0.01
European (5,874)	6,463	1.88
Finnish (975)	3,207	0.93
French, ex. Basque (1,984)	12,780	3.72
French Canadian (1,543)	5,091	1.48
German (22,483)	76,537	22.25
German Russian (0)	37	0.01
Greek (1,362)	2,746	0.80
Guyanese (9)	64	0.02
Hungarian (1,215)	4,397	1.28
Icelander (34)	142	0.04
Iranian (526)	632	0.18
Irish (8,776)	41,122	11.96
Israeli (163)	246	0.07
Italian (4,683)	15,089	4.39
Latvian (235)	408	0.12
Lithuanian (375)	1,167	0.34
Luxemburger (11)	37	0.01
Macedonian (56)	89	0.03
Maltese (120)	418	0.12
New Zealander (24)	24	0.01
Northern European (396)	458	0.13
Norwegian (834)	3,342	0.97
Pennsylvania German (68)	118	0.03

Ancestry	Population	%
Polish (7,335)	25,182	7.32
Portuguese (56)	333	0.10
Romanian (1,121)	1,719	0.50
Russian (1,957)	5,796	1.69
Scandinavian (234)	573	0.17
Scotch-Irish (1,989)	6,834	1.99
Scottish (2,397)	11,101	3.23
Serbian (219)	403	0.12
Slavic (59)	271	0.08
Slovak (275)	891	0.26
Slovene (25)	131	0.04
Soviet Union (0)	0	<0.01
Swedish (1,214)	5,787	1.68
Swiss (194)	1,377	0.40
Turkish (353)	499	0.15
Ukrainian (601)	1,607	0.47
Welsh (418)	3,194	0.93
West Indian, ex. Hispanic (561)	991	0.29
Bahamian (108)	108	0.03
Barbadian (0)	26	0.01
Belizean (0)	0	<0.01
Bermudan (0)	0	<0.01
British West Indian (31)	55	0.02
Dutch West Indian (0)	13	<0.01
Haitian (95)	176	0.05
Jamaican (201)	361	0.10
Trinidadian/Tobagonian (31)	126	0.04
U.S. Virgin Islander (0)	0	<0.01
West Indian (95)	126	0.04
Other West Indian (0)	0	<0.01
Yugoslavian (96)	447	0.13

Hispanic Origin	Population	%
Hispanic or Latino (of any race)	13,860	4.02
Central American, ex. Mexican	1,609	0.47
Costa Rican	191	0.06
Guatemalan	434	0.13
Honduran	383	0.11
Nicaraguan	97	0.03
Panamanian	137	0.04
Salvadoran	353	0.10
Other Central American	14	<0.01
Cuban	490	0.14
Dominican Republic	155	0.04
Mexican	7,107	2.06
Puerto Rican	1,329	0.39
South American	1,758	0.51
Argentinean	255	0.07
Bolivian	90	0.03
Chilean	146	0.04
Colombian	557	0.16
Ecuadorian	162	0.05
Paraguayan	7	<0.01
Peruvian	258	0.07
Uruguayan	39	0.01
Venezuelan	240	0.07
Other South American	4	<0.01
Other Hispanic or Latino	1,412	0.41

Race*	Population	%
African-American/Black (43,767)	49,305	14.30
Not Hispanic (43,152)	48,202	13.98
Hispanic (615)	1,103	0.32
American Indian/Alaska Native (1,174)	3,939	1.14
Not Hispanic (976)	3,384	0.98
Hispanic (198)	555	0.16
Alaska Athabascan (Ala. Nat.) (6)	7	<0.01
Aleut (Alaska Native) (3)	4	<0.01
Apache (5)	30	0.01
Arapaho (0)	3	<0.01
Blackfeet (22)	152	0.04
Canadian/French Am. Ind. (18)	45	0.01
Central American Ind. (4)	5	<0.01
Cherokee (87)	663	0.19
Cheyenne (0)	1	<0.01
Chickasaw (4)	16	<0.01
Chippewa (201)	466	0.14
Choctaw (20)	61	0.02
Colville (1)	1	<0.01

Race*	Population	%
Comanche (3)	10	<0.01
Cree (4)	25	0.01
Creek (20)	58	0.02
Crow (0)	9	<0.01
Delaware (4)	14	<0.01
Hopi (0)	1	<0.01
Houma (0)	1	<0.01
Inupiat (Alaska Native) (0)	5	<0.01
Iroquois (38)	102	0.03
Kiowa (0)	0	<0.01
Lumbee (12)	34	0.01
Menominee (12)	18	0.01
Mexican American Ind. (62)	107	0.03
Navajo (13)	28	0.01
Osage (4)	6	<0.01
Ottawa (26)	72	0.02
Paiute (1)	2	<0.01
Pima (0)	0	<0.01
Potawatomi (23)	56	0.02
Pueblo (3)	5	<0.01
Puget Sound Salish (4)	4	<0.01
Seminole (4)	19	0.01
Shoshone (4)	7	<0.01
Sioux (37)	85	0.02
South American Ind. (16)	50	0.01
Spanish American Ind. (0)	2	<0.01
Tlingit-Haida (Alaska Native) (9)	14	<0.01
Tohono O'Odham (3)	3	<0.01
Tsimshian (Alaska Native) (0)	2	<0.01
Ute (1)	7	<0.01
Yakama (2)	2	<0.01
Yaqui (0)	3	<0.01
Yuman (0)	1	<0.01
Yup'ik (Alaska Native) (1)	5	<0.01
Asian (27,109)	31,250	9.06
Not Hispanic (27,005)	30,935	8.97
Hispanic (104)	315	0.09
Bangladeshi (139)	156	0.05
Bhutanese (0)	0	<0.01
Burmese (16)	26	0.01
Cambodian (49)	63	0.02
Chinese, ex. Taiwanese (8,884)	9,977	2.89
Filipino (1,017)	1,633	0.47
Hmong (39)	41	0.01
Indian (6,894)	7,652	2.22
Indonesian (91)	129	0.04
Japanese (1,674)	2,362	0.69
Korean (4,330)	4,853	1.41
Laotian (86)	120	0.03
Malaysian (89)	115	0.03
Nepalese (54)	62	0.02
Pakistani (787)	861	0.25
Sri Lankan (137)	165	0.05
Taiwanese (1,057)	1,186	0.34
Thai (254)	369	0.11
Vietnamese (744)	946	0.27
Hawaii Native/Pacific Islander (128)	469	0.14
Not Hispanic (118)	432	0.13
Hispanic (10)	37	0.01
Fijian (3)	7	<0.01
Guamanian/Chamorro (19)	47	0.01
Marshallese (2)	10	<0.01
Native Hawaiian (30)	122	0.04
Samoan (26)	59	0.02
Tongan (12)	17	<0.01
White (256,880)	267,055	77.45
Not Hispanic (248,675)	257,659	74.73
Hispanic (8,205)	9,396	2.73

*Notes: † The Census 2010 population figure is used to calculate the percentages in the Hispanic Origin and Race categories. Ancestry percentages are based on the 2006-2010 American Community Survey population (not shown); ‡ Numbers in parentheses indicate the number of people reporting a single ancestry; * Numbers in parentheses indicate the number of persons reporting this race alone, not in combination with any other race; Please refer to the User Guide for more information.*

Wayne County

Population: 1,820,584

Ancestry	Population	%
Afghan (42)	42	<0.01
African, Sub-Saharan (14,503)	18,110	0.97
African (10,730)	13,869	0.74
Cape Verdean (25)	25	<0.01
Ethiopian (178)	260	0.01
Ghanaian (56)	84	<0.01
Kenyan (297)	297	0.02
Liberian (323)	323	0.02
Nigerian (1,955)	2,101	0.11
Senegalese (92)	152	0.01
Sierra Leonean (0)	0	<0.01
Somalian (128)	138	0.01
South African (126)	126	0.01
Sudanese (150)	184	0.01
Ugandan (18)	35	<0.01
Zimbabwean (0)	0	<0.01
Other Sub-Saharan African (425)	516	0.03
Albanian (4,613)	4,777	0.26
Alsatian (0)	27	<0.01
American (49,458)	49,458	2.64
Arab (67,117)	75,541	4.04
Arab (18,049)	19,667	1.05
Egyptian (485)	661	0.04
Iraqi (4,571)	5,009	0.27
Jordanian (1,848)	2,004	0.11
Lebanese (27,553)	32,000	1.71
Moroccan (425)	571	0.03
Palestinian (1,748)	2,043	0.11
Syrian (1,380)	2,057	0.11
Other Arab (11,058)	11,529	0.62
Armenian (2,172)	4,262	0.23
Assyrian/Chaldean/Syriac (1,063)	1,264	0.07
Australian (98)	312	0.02
Austrian (563)	2,884	0.15
Basque (24)	32	<0.01
Belgian (1,269)	4,981	0.27
Brazilian (319)	534	0.03
British (1,989)	4,198	0.22
Bulgarian (182)	427	0.02
Cajun (46)	84	<0.01
Canadian (3,171)	7,366	0.39
Carpatho Rusyn (0)	24	<0.01
Celtic (72)	114	0.01
Croatian (776)	3,091	0.17
Cypriot (16)	45	<0.01
Czech (1,058)	5,056	0.27
Czechoslovakian (748)	1,960	0.10
Danish (519)	3,201	0.17
Dutch (4,215)	19,136	1.02
Eastern European (706)	863	0.05
English (26,822)	104,287	5.58
Estonian (15)	41	<0.01
European (8,517)	10,004	0.53
Finnish (3,153)	9,681	0.52
French, ex. Basque (7,999)	61,318	3.28
French Canadian (7,888)	24,187	1.29
German (51,231)	219,518	11.74
German Russian (83)	178	0.01
Greek (4,022)	8,815	0.47
Guyanese (53)	106	0.01
Hungarian (8,257)	26,623	1.42
Icelander (0)	135	0.01
Iranian (318)	394	0.02
Irish (34,693)	156,009	8.34
Israeli (82)	162	0.01
Italian (29,781)	80,023	4.28
Latvian (262)	384	0.02
Lithuanian (2,051)	5,373	0.29
Luxemburger (0)	51	<0.01
Macedonian (1,372)	1,825	0.10
Maltese (2,450)	5,353	0.29
New Zealander (35)	35	<0.01
Northern European (472)	498	0.03
Norwegian (1,684)	7,266	0.39
Pennsylvania German (198)	528	0.03

Ancestry	Population	%
Polish (63,552)	154,979	8.29
Portuguese (204)	738	0.04
Romanian (4,587)	7,244	0.39
Russian (2,153)	8,155	0.44
Scandinavian (353)	831	0.04
Scotch-Irish (8,143)	22,644	1.21
Scottish (7,564)	31,442	1.68
Serbian (702)	1,691	0.09
Slavic (276)	986	0.05
Slovak (1,531)	4,867	0.26
Slovene (171)	653	0.03
Soviet Union (0)	0	<0.01
Swedish (2,017)	12,374	0.66
Swiss (286)	1,867	0.10
Turkish (361)	530	0.03
Ukrainian (3,291)	8,110	0.43
Welsh (833)	6,345	0.34
West Indian, ex. Hispanic (2,807)	4,167	0.22
Bahamian (66)	95	0.01
Barbadian (41)	52	<0.01
Belizean (61)	61	<0.01
Bermudan (0)	10	<0.01
British West Indian (13)	13	<0.01
Dutch West Indian (0)	5	<0.01
Haitian (198)	362	0.02
Jamaican (2,047)	2,832	0.15
Trinidadian/Tobagonian (145)	298	0.02
U.S. Virgin Islander (24)	24	<0.01
West Indian (212)	415	0.02
Other West Indian (0)	0	<0.01
Yugoslavian (2,299)	3,710	0.20

Hispanic Origin	Population	%
Hispanic or Latino (of any race)	95,260	5.23
Central American, ex. Mexican	2,977	0.16
Costa Rican	105	0.01
Guatemalan	877	0.05
Honduran	761	0.04
Nicaraguan	193	0.01
Panamanian	286	0.02
Salvadoran	722	0.04
Other Central American	33	<0.01
Cuban	1,784	0.10
Dominican Republic	1,016	0.06
Mexican	70,090	3.85
Puerto Rican	10,629	0.58
South American	2,011	0.11
Argentinean	371	0.02
Bolivian	67	<0.01
Chilean	151	0.01
Colombian	600	0.03
Ecuadorian	224	0.01
Paraguayan	31	<0.01
Peruvian	277	0.02
Uruguayan	25	<0.01
Venezuelan	228	0.01
Other South American	37	<0.01
Other Hispanic or Latino	6,753	0.37

Race*	Population	%
African-American/Black (737,943)	760,835	41.79
Not Hispanic (732,801)	753,330	41.38
Hispanic (5,142)	7,505	0.41
American Indian/Alaska Native (6,991)	20,245	1.11
Not Hispanic (5,635)	17,275	0.95
Hispanic (1,356)	2,970	0.16
Alaska Athabascan (Ala. Nat.) (3)	5	<0.01
Aleut (Alaska Native) (2)	5	<0.01
Apache (50)	156	0.01
Arapaho (3)	8	<0.01
Blackfeet (105)	863	0.05
Canadian/French Am. Ind. (122)	229	0.01
Central American Ind. (11)	34	<0.01
Cherokee (603)	3,602	0.20
Cheyenne (2)	24	<0.01
Chickasaw (13)	43	<0.01
Chippewa (1,027)	1,885	0.10
Choctaw (67)	337	0.02
Colville (0)	1	<0.01

	Population	%
Comanche (15)	33	<0.01
Cree (4)	53	<0.01
Creek (74)	185	0.01
Crow (2)	26	<0.01
Delaware (49)	110	0.01
Hopi (3)	13	<0.01
Houma (0)	1	<0.01
Inupiat (Alaska Native) (3)	23	<0.01
Iroquois (369)	739	0.04
Kiowa (1)	4	<0.01
Lumbee (164)	311	0.02
Menominee (26)	53	<0.01
Mexican American Ind. (297)	434	0.02
Navajo (54)	115	0.01
Osage (11)	28	<0.01
Ottawa (159)	278	0.02
Paiute (3)	8	<0.01
Pima (1)	5	<0.01
Potawatomi (78)	169	0.01
Pueblo (24)	37	<0.01
Puget Sound Salish (4)	7	<0.01
Seminole (13)	89	<0.01
Shoshone (3)	12	<0.01
Sioux (61)	215	0.01
South American Ind. (19)	78	<0.01
Spanish American Ind. (17)	20	<0.01
Tlingit-Haida (Alaska Native) (3)	15	<0.01
Tohono O'Odham (0)	2	<0.01
Tsimshian (Alaska Native) (0)	1	<0.01
Ute (7)	8	<0.01
Yakama (2)	7	<0.01
Yaqui (10)	17	<0.01
Yuman (0)	4	<0.01
Yup'ik (Alaska Native) (3)	6	<0.01
Asian (45,915)	57,829	3.18
Not Hispanic (45,590)	56,889	3.12
Hispanic (325)	940	0.05
Bangladeshi (5,647)	6,172	0.34
Bhutanese (0)	0	<0.01
Burmese (11)	14	<0.01
Cambodian (102)	145	0.01
Chinese, ex. Taiwanese (5,468)	6,495	0.36
Filipino (4,631)	6,439	0.35
Hmong (581)	627	0.03
Indian (17,986)	20,103	1.10
Indonesian (79)	131	0.01
Japanese (1,216)	2,240	0.12
Korean (1,987)	2,704	0.15
Laotian (122)	182	0.01
Malaysian (38)	63	<0.01
Nepalese (69)	72	<0.01
Pakistani (3,520)	3,849	0.21
Sri Lankan (114)	125	0.01
Taiwanese (237)	281	0.02
Thai (231)	390	0.02
Vietnamese (1,802)	2,121	0.12
Hawaii Native/Pacific Islander (404)	1,748	0.10
Not Hispanic (304)	1,424	0.08
Hispanic (100)	324	0.02
Fijian (2)	6	<0.01
Guamanian/Chamorro (93)	209	0.01
Marshallese (2)	2	<0.01
Native Hawaiian (116)	431	0.02
Samoan (69)	161	0.01
Tongan (3)	11	<0.01
White (951,936)	987,104	54.22
Not Hispanic (902,180)	931,383	51.16
Hispanic (49,756)	55,721	3.06

Notes: † The Census 2010 population figure is used to calculate the percentages in the Hispanic Origin and Race categories. Ancestry percentages are based on the 2006-2010 American Community Survey population (not shown); ‡ Numbers in parentheses indicate the number of people reporting a single ancestry; * Numbers in parentheses indicate the number of persons reporting this race alone, not in combination with any other race; Please refer to the User Guide for more information.

Place Profiles

Ann Arbor

Place Type: City
County: Washtenaw
Population: 113,934

Ancestry	Population	%
Afghan (13)	23	0.02
African, Sub-Saharan (1,060)	1,399	1.21
African (535)	809	0.70
Cape Verdean (0)	0	<0.01
Ethiopian (12)	59	0.05
Ghanaian (48)	48	0.04
Kenyan (0)	0	<0.01
Liberian (0)	0	<0.01
Nigerian (338)	338	0.29
Senegalese (0)	0	<0.01
Sierra Leonean (0)	0	<0.01
Somalian (2)	2	<0.01
South African (114)	123	0.11
Sudanese (0)	0	<0.01
Ugandan (0)	0	<0.01
Zimbabwean (0)	9	0.01
Other Sub-Saharan African (11)	11	0.01
Albanian (132)	162	0.14
Alsatian (0)	13	0.01
American (3,530)	3,530	3.06
Arab (1,620)	2,158	1.87
Arab (300)	327	0.28
Egyptian (166)	189	0.16
Iraqi (42)	67	0.06
Jordanian (104)	104	0.09
Lebanese (195)	367	0.32
Moroccan (0)	0	<0.01
Palestinian (353)	410	0.36
Syrian (10)	172	0.15
Other Arab (450)	522	0.45
Armenian (137)	274	0.24
Assyrian/Chaldean/Syriac (60)	60	0.05
Australian (33)	95	0.08
Austrian (154)	484	0.42
Basque (0)	12	0.01
Belgian (105)	605	0.53
Brazilian (120)	174	0.15
British (642)	1,287	1.12
Bulgarian (26)	32	0.03
Cajun (32)	32	0.03
Canadian (326)	638	0.55
Carpatho Rusyn (0)	0	<0.01
Celtic (5)	24	0.02
Croatian (102)	216	0.19
Cypriot (0)	0	<0.01
Czech (194)	842	0.73
Czechoslovakian (9)	58	0.05
Danish (158)	721	0.63
Dutch (624)	2,277	1.98
Eastern European (649)	719	0.62
English (3,270)	13,447	11.67
Estonian (36)	36	0.03
European (2,470)	2,664	2.31
Finnish (173)	786	0.68
French, ex. Basque (597)	3,984	3.46
French Canadian (247)	1,281	1.11
German (6,586)	22,916	19.89
German Russian (0)	37	0.03
Greek (661)	1,161	1.01
Guyanese (9)	9	0.01
Hungarian (287)	1,847	1.60
Icelander (11)	78	0.07
Iranian (274)	336	0.29
Irish (3,015)	12,142	10.54
Israeli (73)	147	0.13
Italian (1,591)	5,212	4.52
Latvian (48)	136	0.12
Lithuanian (133)	450	0.39
Luxemburger (11)	26	0.02
Macedonian (24)	40	0.03

Ancestry	Population	%
Maltese (39)	92	0.08
New Zealander (24)	24	0.02
Northern European (188)	203	0.18
Norwegian (308)	1,312	1.14
Pennsylvania German (44)	62	0.05
Polish (2,298)	7,858	6.82
Portuguese (22)	88	0.08
Romanian (364)	650	0.56
Russian (1,168)	3,214	2.79
Scandinavian (92)	229	0.20
Scotch-Irish (549)	2,326	2.02
Scottish (652)	3,574	3.10
Serbian (106)	166	0.14
Slavic (7)	64	0.06
Slovak (136)	270	0.23
Slovene (19)	67	0.06
Soviet Union (0)	0	<0.01
Swedish (523)	2,065	1.79
Swiss (62)	537	0.47
Turkish (278)	373	0.32
Ukrainian (223)	607	0.53
Welsh (112)	1,064	0.92
West Indian, ex. Hispanic (228)	380	0.33
Bahamian (12)	12	0.01
Barbadian (0)	16	0.01
Belizean (0)	0	<0.01
Bermudan (0)	0	<0.01
British West Indian (11)	35	0.03
Dutch West Indian (0)	0	<0.01
Haitian (4)	14	0.01
Jamaican (121)	181	0.16
Trinidadian/Tobagonian (25)	58	0.05
U.S. Virgin Islander (0)	0	<0.01
West Indian (55)	64	0.06
Other West Indian (0)	0	<0.01
Yugoslavian (60)	112	0.10

Hispanic Origin	Population	%
Hispanic or Latino (of any race)	4,666	4.10
Central American, ex. Mexican	394	0.35
Costa Rican	43	0.04
Guatemalan	130	0.11
Honduran	54	0.05
Nicaraguan	41	0.04
Panamanian	52	0.05
Salvadoran	74	0.06
Other Central American	0	<0.01
Cuban	226	0.20
Dominican Republic	78	0.07
Mexican	2,056	1.80
Puerto Rican	466	0.41
South American	963	0.85
Argentinean	169	0.15
Bolivian	46	0.04
Chilean	87	0.08
Colombian	292	0.26
Ecuadorian	73	0.06
Paraguayan	4	<0.01
Peruvian	162	0.14
Uruguayan	19	0.02
Venezuelan	108	0.09
Other South American	3	<0.01
Other Hispanic or Latino	483	0.42

Race*	Population	%
African-American/Black (8,804)	10,363	9.10
Not Hispanic (8,658)	10,057	8.83
Hispanic (146)	306	0.27
American Indian/Alaska Native (301)	1,110	0.97
Not Hispanic (224)	885	0.78
Hispanic (77)	225	0.20
Alaska Athabascan (Ala. Nat.) (3)	4	<0.01
Aleut (Alaska Native) (0)	0	<0.01
Apache (3)	12	0.01
Arapaho (0)	2	<0.01
Blackfeet (8)	36	0.03

Race*	Population	%
Canadian/French Am. Ind. (6)	16	0.01
Central American Ind. (0)	1	<0.01
Cherokee (9)	161	0.14
Cheyenne (0)	0	<0.01
Chickasaw (1)	6	0.01
Chippewa (46)	125	0.11
Choctaw (8)	12	0.01
Colville (0)	0	<0.01
Comanche (1)	4	<0.01
Cree (2)	14	0.01
Creek (7)	21	0.02
Crow (0)	3	<0.01
Delaware (1)	3	<0.01
Hopi (0)	1	<0.01
Houma (0)	0	<0.01
Inupiat (Alaska Native) (0)	3	<0.01
Iroquois (10)	23	0.02
Kiowa (0)	0	<0.01
Lumbee (4)	14	0.01
Menominee (3)	4	<0.01
Mexican American Ind. (26)	48	0.04
Navajo (6)	8	0.01
Osage (0)	0	<0.01
Ottawa (8)	18	0.02
Paiute (1)	1	<0.01
Pima (0)	0	<0.01
Potawatomi (11)	17	0.01
Pueblo (1)	1	<0.01
Puget Sound Salish (4)	4	<0.01
Seminole (3)	3	<0.01
Shoshone (4)	4	<0.01
Sioux (6)	19	0.02
South American Ind. (6)	22	0.02
Spanish American Ind. (0)	0	<0.01
Tlingit-Haida (Alaska Native) (0)	1	<0.01
Tohono O'Odham (1)	1	<0.01
Tsimshian (Alaska Native) (0)	0	<0.01
Ute (0)	0	<0.01
Yakama (0)	0	<0.01
Yaqui (0)	1	<0.01
Yuman (0)	0	<0.01
Yup'ik (Alaska Native) (0)	1	<0.01
Asian (16,353)	18,345	16.10
Not Hispanic (16,293)	18,205	15.98
Hispanic (60)	140	0.12
Bangladeshi (90)	102	0.09
Bhutanese (0)	0	<0.01
Burmese (9)	16	0.01
Cambodian (19)	29	0.03
Chinese, ex. Taiwanese (5,938)	6,555	5.75
Filipino (341)	580	0.51
Hmong (17)	17	0.01
Indian (3,826)	4,216	3.70
Indonesian (57)	83	0.07
Japanese (1,048)	1,428	1.25
Korean (2,924)	3,159	2.77
Laotian (7)	12	0.01
Malaysian (65)	81	0.07
Nepalese (25)	29	0.03
Pakistani (283)	324	0.28
Sri Lankan (66)	77	0.07
Taiwanese (788)	858	0.75
Thai (124)	168	0.15
Vietnamese (320)	395	0.35
Hawaii Native/Pacific Islander (38)	144	0.13
Not Hispanic (34)	126	0.11
Hispanic (4)	18	0.02
Fijian (1)	2	<0.01
Guamanian/Chamorro (10)	21	0.02
Marshallese (2)	8	0.01
Native Hawaiian (8)	36	0.03
Samoan (6)	9	0.01
Tongan (5)	6	0.01
White (83,171)	86,809	76.19
Not Hispanic (80,158)	83,380	73.18
Hispanic (3,013)	3,429	3.01

Notes: † The Census 2010 population figure is used to calculate the percentages in the Hispanic Origin and Race categories. Ancestry percentages are based on the 2006-2010 American Community Survey population (not shown); ‡ Numbers in parentheses indicate the number of people reporting a single ancestry; * Numbers in parentheses indicate the number of persons reporting this race alone, not in combination with any other race; Please refer to the User Guide for more information.

Battle Creek

Place Type: City
County: Calhoun
Population: 52,347

Ancestry	Population	%
Afghan (0)	0	<0.01
African, Sub-Saharan (76)	138	0.26
African (35)	97	0.18
Cape Verdean (0)	0	<0.01
Ethiopian (0)	0	<0.01
Ghanaian (0)	0	<0.01
Kenyan (9)	9	0.02
Liberian (0)	0	<0.01
Nigerian (0)	0	<0.01
Senegalese (0)	0	<0.01
Sierra Leonean (0)	0	<0.01
Somalian (0)	0	<0.01
South African (0)	0	<0.01
Sudanese (0)	0	<0.01
Ugandan (9)	9	0.02
Zimbabwean (23)	23	0.04
Other Sub-Saharan African (0)	0	<0.01
Albanian (9)	9	0.02
Alsatian (0)	0	<0.01
American (3,106)	3,106	5.89
Arab (50)	50	0.09
Arab (41)	41	0.08
Egyptian (0)	0	<0.01
Iraqi (0)	0	<0.01
Jordanian (0)	0	<0.01
Lebanese (0)	0	<0.01
Moroccan (9)	9	0.02
Palestinian (0)	0	<0.01
Syrian (0)	0	<0.01
Other Arab (0)	0	<0.01
Armenian (0)	0	<0.01
Assyrian/Chaldean/Syriac (0)	0	<0.01
Australian (0)	13	0.02
Austrian (0)	18	0.03
Basque (10)	10	0.02
Belgian (9)	19	0.04
Brazilian (24)	24	0.05
British (84)	179	0.34
Bulgarian (43)	43	0.08
Cajun (0)	0	<0.01
Canadian (83)	182	0.34
Carpatho Rusyn (0)	0	<0.01
Celtic (6)	6	0.01
Croatian (29)	44	0.08
Cypriot (0)	0	<0.01
Czech (23)	112	0.21
Czechoslovakian (0)	18	0.03
Danish (10)	122	0.23
Dutch (532)	1,828	3.46
Eastern European (0)	0	<0.01
English (2,259)	6,221	11.79
Estonian (0)	0	<0.01
European (276)	319	0.60
Finnish (79)	178	0.34
French, ex. Basque (255)	1,741	3.30
French Canadian (261)	513	0.97
German (4,195)	10,192	19.32
German Russian (0)	0	<0.01
Greek (69)	130	0.25
Guyanese (0)	0	<0.01
Hungarian (101)	265	0.50
Icelander (0)	0	<0.01
Iranian (6)	6	0.01
Irish (1,611)	5,662	10.73
Israeli (0)	0	<0.01
Italian (381)	942	1.79
Latvian (11)	34	0.06
Lithuanian (0)	92	0.17
Luxemburger (0)	0	<0.01
Macedonian (100)	194	0.37
Maltese (0)	37	0.07
New Zealander (0)	0	<0.01
Northern European (0)	0	<0.01
Norwegian (167)	311	0.59
Pennsylvania German (13)	81	0.15
Polish (452)	1,512	2.87
Portuguese (93)	101	0.19
Romanian (0)	0	<0.01
Russian (56)	171	0.32
Scandinavian (50)	106	0.20
Scotch-Irish (280)	661	1.25
Scottish (186)	754	1.43
Serbian (0)	28	0.05
Slavic (0)	9	0.02
Slovak (0)	165	0.31
Slovene (0)	0	<0.01
Soviet Union (0)	0	<0.01
Swedish (136)	455	0.86
Swiss (58)	73	0.14
Turkish (12)	12	0.02
Ukrainian (34)	47	0.09
Welsh (22)	207	0.39
West Indian, ex. Hispanic (101)	109	0.21
Bahamian (0)	0	<0.01
Barbadian (51)	51	0.10
Belizean (0)	0	<0.01
Bermudan (0)	0	<0.01
British West Indian (0)	0	<0.01
Dutch West Indian (0)	0	<0.01
Haitian (0)	0	<0.01
Jamaican (0)	8	0.02
Trinidadian/Tobagonian (50)	50	0.09
U.S. Virgin Islander (0)	0	<0.01
West Indian (0)	0	<0.01
Other West Indian (0)	0	<0.01
Yugoslavian (56)	70	0.13

Hispanic Origin	Population	%
Hispanic or Latino (of any race)	3,517	6.72
Central American, ex. Mexican	37	0.07
Costa Rican	8	0.02
Guatemalan	12	0.02
Honduran	3	0.01
Nicaraguan	0	<0.01
Panamanian	12	0.02
Salvadoran	2	<0.01
Other Central American	0	<0.01
Cuban	52	0.10
Dominican Republic	26	0.05
Mexican	2,713	5.18
Puerto Rican	245	0.47
South American	68	0.13
Argentinean	1	<0.01
Bolivian	0	<0.01
Chilean	1	<0.01
Colombian	34	0.06
Ecuadorian	4	0.01
Paraguayan	0	<0.01
Peruvian	24	0.05
Uruguayan	0	<0.01
Venezuelan	4	0.01
Other South American	0	<0.01
Other Hispanic or Latino	376	0.72

Race*	Population	%
African-American/Black (9,502)	11,026	21.06
Not Hispanic (9,347)	10,733	20.50
Hispanic (155)	293	0.56
American Indian/Alaska Native (377)	941	1.80
Not Hispanic (292)	796	1.52
Hispanic (85)	145	0.28
Alaska Athabascan (Ala. Nat.) (5)	6	0.01
Aleut (Alaska Native) (0)	2	<0.01
Apache (6)	19	0.04
Arapaho (0)	0	<0.01
Blackfeet (5)	55	0.11
Canadian/French Am. Ind. (1)	3	0.01
Central American Ind. (0)	0	<0.01
Cherokee (26)	165	0.32
Cheyenne (0)	2	<0.01
Chickasaw (0)	0	<0.01
Chippewa (46)	77	0.15
Choctaw (0)	4	0.01
Colville (0)	0	<0.01
Comanche (0)	1	<0.01
Cree (0)	4	0.01
Creek (0)	3	0.01
Crow (0)	6	0.01
Delaware (0)	0	<0.01
Hopi (1)	2	<0.01
Houma (1)	1	<0.01
Inupiat (Alaska Native) (0)	0	<0.01
Iroquois (3)	9	0.02
Kiowa (0)	0	<0.01
Lumbee (1)	2	<0.01
Menominee (0)	0	<0.01
Mexican American Ind. (9)	15	0.03
Navajo (4)	7	0.01
Osage (0)	0	<0.01
Ottawa (32)	42	0.08
Paiute (0)	0	<0.01
Pima (0)	0	<0.01
Potawatomi (43)	81	0.15
Pueblo (0)	1	<0.01
Puget Sound Salish (3)	3	0.01
Seminole (0)	1	<0.01
Shoshone (0)	0	<0.01
Sioux (6)	18	0.03
South American Ind. (2)	3	0.01
Spanish American Ind. (0)	0	<0.01
Tlingit-Haida (Alaska Native) (0)	1	<0.01
Tohono O'Odham (0)	0	<0.01
Tsimshian (Alaska Native) (0)	0	<0.01
Ute (1)	1	<0.01
Yakama (0)	0	<0.01
Yaqui (5)	5	0.01
Yuman (0)	0	<0.01
Yup'ik (Alaska Native) (0)	0	<0.01
Asian (1,271)	1,518	2.90
Not Hispanic (1,254)	1,482	2.83
Hispanic (17)	36	0.07
Bangladeshi (5)	5	<0.01
Bhutanese (0)	0	<0.01
Burmese (285)	301	0.58
Cambodian (1)	1	<0.01
Chinese, ex. Taiwanese (120)	143	0.27
Filipino (112)	159	0.30
Hmong (0)	0	<0.01
Indian (279)	325	0.62
Indonesian (8)	21	0.04
Japanese (254)	313	0.60
Korean (82)	120	0.23
Laotian (1)	2	<0.01
Malaysian (0)	0	<0.01
Nepalese (0)	0	<0.01
Pakistani (2)	2	<0.01
Sri Lankan (0)	0	<0.01
Taiwanese (2)	2	<0.01
Thai (10)	21	0.04
Vietnamese (49)	57	0.11
Hawaii Native/Pacific Islander (16)	83	0.16
Not Hispanic (15)	68	0.13
Hispanic (1)	15	0.03
Fijian (0)	0	<0.01
Guamanian/Chamorro (6)	14	0.03
Marshallese (0)	0	<0.01
Native Hawaiian (2)	19	0.04
Samoan (3)	15	0.03
Tongan (0)	0	<0.01
White (37,522)	39,558	75.57
Not Hispanic (35,911)	37,693	72.01
Hispanic (1,611)	1,865	3.56

*Notes: † The Census 2010 population figure is used to calculate the percentages in the Hispanic Origin and Race categories. Ancestry percentages are based on the 2006-2010 American Community Survey population (not shown); ‡ Numbers in parentheses indicate the number of people reporting a single ancestry; * Numbers in parentheses indicate the number of persons reporting this race alone, not in combination with any other race; Please refer to the User Guide for more information.*

Canton

Place Type: Charter Township
County: Wayne
Population: 90,173

Ancestry	Population	%
Afghan (0)	0	<0.01
African, Sub-Saharan (500)	664	0.75
African (170)	279	0.32
Cape Verdean (0)	0	<0.01
Ethiopian (135)	135	0.15
Ghanaian (0)	0	<0.01
Kenyan (0)	0	<0.01
Liberian (0)	0	<0.01
Nigerian (195)	233	0.26
Senegalese (0)	0	<0.01
Sierra Leonean (0)	0	<0.01
Somalian (0)	0	<0.01
South African (0)	0	<0.01
Sudanese (0)	0	<0.01
Ugandan (0)	17	0.02
Zimbabwean (0)	0	<0.01
Other Sub-Saharan African (0)	0	<0.01
Albanian (213)	213	0.24
Alsatian (0)	0	<0.01
American (4,185)	4,185	4.76
Arab (1,878)	2,465	2.80
Arab (664)	709	0.81
Egyptian (19)	27	0.03
Iraqi (57)	126	0.14
Jordanian (23)	23	0.03
Lebanese (694)	969	1.10
Moroccan (0)	0	<0.01
Palestinian (236)	255	0.29
Syrian (57)	173	0.20
Other Arab (128)	183	0.21
Armenian (174)	376	0.43
Assyrian/Chaldean/Syriac (113)	113	0.13
Australian (0)	9	0.01
Austrian (0)	165	0.19
Basque (0)	8	0.01
Belgian (63)	329	0.37
Brazilian (9)	30	0.03
British (320)	468	0.53
Bulgarian (27)	27	0.03
Cajun (0)	0	<0.01
Canadian (266)	572	0.65
Carpatho Rusyn (0)	0	<0.01
Celtic (0)	0	<0.01
Croatian (43)	200	0.23
Cypriot (0)	0	<0.01
Czech (40)	457	0.52
Czechoslovakian (34)	93	0.11
Danish (37)	144	0.16
Dutch (356)	1,514	1.72
Eastern European (29)	49	0.06
English (2,244)	8,145	9.26
Estonian (0)	0	<0.01
European (988)	1,228	1.40
Finnish (86)	547	0.62
French, ex. Basque (522)	4,267	4.85
French Canadian (347)	1,371	1.56
German (4,399)	17,180	19.53
German Russian (0)	0	<0.01
Greek (259)	537	0.61
Guyanese (0)	16	0.02
Hungarian (326)	927	1.05
Icelander (0)	0	<0.01
Iranian (61)	72	0.08
Irish (2,118)	9,745	11.08
Israeli (0)	0	<0.01
Italian (1,808)	5,771	6.56
Latvian (0)	0	<0.01
Lithuanian (109)	364	0.41
Luxemburger (0)	0	<0.01
Macedonian (103)	113	0.13
Maltese (151)	366	0.42
New Zealander (0)	0	<0.01
Northern European (8)	8	0.01

Ancestry	Population	%
Norwegian (178)	675	0.77
Pennsylvania German (7)	32	0.04
Polish (4,503)	11,542	13.12
Portuguese (10)	33	0.04
Romanian (506)	699	0.79
Russian (222)	728	0.83
Scandinavian (20)	119	0.14
Scotch-Irish (546)	1,393	1.58
Scottish (672)	2,402	2.73
Serbian (72)	161	0.18
Slavic (65)	154	0.18
Slovak (118)	323	0.37
Slovene (19)	44	0.05
Soviet Union (0)	0	<0.01
Swedish (189)	1,022	1.16
Swiss (82)	254	0.29
Turkish (133)	142	0.16
Ukrainian (190)	582	0.66
Welsh (127)	444	0.50
West Indian, ex. Hispanic (117)	211	0.24
Bahamian (0)	0	<0.01
Barbadian (0)	0	<0.01
Belizean (0)	0	<0.01
Bermudan (0)	0	<0.01
British West Indian (0)	0	<0.01
Dutch West Indian (0)	0	<0.01
Haitian (10)	31	0.04
Jamaican (107)	180	0.20
Trinidadian/Tobagonian (0)	0	<0.01
U.S. Virgin Islander (0)	0	<0.01
West Indian (0)	0	<0.01
Other West Indian (0)	0	<0.01
Yugoslavian (46)	182	0.21

Hispanic Origin	Population	%
Hispanic or Latino (of any race)	2,822	3.13
Central American, ex. Mexican	120	0.13
Costa Rican	13	0.01
Guatemalan	39	0.04
Honduran	28	0.03
Nicaraguan	5	0.01
Panamanian	23	0.03
Salvadoran	10	0.01
Other Central American	2	<0.01
Cuban	98	0.11
Dominican Republic	27	0.03
Mexican	1,837	2.04
Puerto Rican	266	0.29
South American	196	0.22
Argentinean	35	0.04
Bolivian	7	0.01
Chilean	5	0.01
Colombian	79	0.09
Ecuadorian	27	0.03
Paraguayan	6	0.01
Peruvian	14	0.02
Uruguayan	1	<0.01
Venezuelan	21	0.02
Other South American	1	<0.01
Other Hispanic or Latino	278	0.31

Race*	Population	%
African-American/Black (9,176)	9,984	11.07
Not Hispanic (9,070)	9,812	10.88
Hispanic (106)	172	0.19
American Indian/Alaska Native (224)	702	0.78
Not Hispanic (206)	649	0.72
Hispanic (18)	53	0.06
Alaska Athabascan (Ala. Nat.) (0)	0	<0.01
Aleut (Alaska Native) (0)	0	<0.01
Apache (2)	3	<0.01
Arapaho (2)	2	<0.01
Blackfeet (2)	31	0.03
Canadian/French Am. Ind. (4)	9	0.01
Central American Ind. (0)	0	<0.01
Cherokee (22)	124	0.14
Cheyenne (0)	0	<0.01
Chickasaw (0)	2	<0.01
Chippewa (46)	98	0.11

Race*	Population	%
Choctaw (1)	14	0.02
Colville (0)	0	<0.01
Comanche (0)	1	<0.01
Cree (0)	1	<0.01
Creek (4)	7	0.01
Crow (0)	0	<0.01
Delaware (4)	5	0.01
Hopi (0)	0	<0.01
Houma (0)	0	<0.01
Inupiat (Alaska Native) (0)	3	<0.01
Iroquois (11)	22	0.02
Kiowa (0)	0	<0.01
Lumbee (4)	12	0.01
Menominee (0)	0	<0.01
Mexican American Ind. (3)	5	0.01
Navajo (4)	4	<0.01
Osage (0)	2	<0.01
Ottawa (13)	22	0.02
Paiute (0)	0	<0.01
Pima (0)	0	<0.01
Potawatomi (1)	3	<0.01
Pueblo (1)	1	<0.01
Puget Sound Salish (0)	1	<0.01
Seminole (0)	0	<0.01
Shoshone (0)	0	<0.01
Sioux (0)	3	<0.01
South American Ind. (1)	10	0.01
Spanish American Ind. (0)	0	<0.01
Tlingit-Haida (Alaska Native) (0)	0	<0.01
Tohono O'Odham (0)	0	<0.01
Tsimshian (Alaska Native) (0)	0	<0.01
Ute (0)	0	<0.01
Yakama (0)	0	<0.01
Yaqui (0)	0	<0.01
Yuman (0)	0	<0.01
Yup'ik (Alaska Native) (0)	0	<0.01
Asian (12,739)	13,875	15.39
Not Hispanic (12,720)	13,816	15.32
Hispanic (19)	59	0.07
Bangladeshi (122)	125	0.14
Bhutanese (0)	0	<0.01
Burmese (0)	1	<0.01
Cambodian (7)	10	0.01
Chinese, ex. Taiwanese (1,849)	2,022	2.24
Filipino (646)	849	0.94
Hmong (6)	6	0.01
Indian (7,174)	7,546	8.37
Indonesian (24)	34	0.04
Japanese (307)	435	0.48
Korean (404)	481	0.53
Laotian (8)	16	0.02
Malaysian (2)	11	0.01
Nepalese (28)	30	0.03
Pakistani (1,396)	1,479	1.64
Sri Lankan (31)	31	0.03
Taiwanese (95)	100	0.11
Thai (39)	45	0.05
Vietnamese (288)	347	0.38
Hawaii Native/Pacific Islander (27)	83	0.09
Not Hispanic (21)	73	0.08
Hispanic (6)	10	0.01
Fijian (0)	0	<0.01
Guamanian/Chamorro (8)	15	0.02
Marshallese (2)	2	<0.01
Native Hawaiian (4)	17	0.02
Samoan (1)	4	<0.01
Tongan (0)	0	<0.01
White (65,140)	66,962	74.26
Not Hispanic (63,165)	64,802	71.86
Hispanic (1,975)	2,160	2.40

Notes: † The Census 2010 population figure is used to calculate the percentages in the Hispanic Origin and Race categories. Ancestry percentages are based on the 2006-2010 American Community Survey population (not shown); ‡ Numbers in parentheses indicate the number of people reporting a single ancestry; * Numbers in parentheses indicate the number of persons reporting this race alone, not in combination with any other race; Please refer to the User Guide for more information.

Clinton

Place Type: Charter Township
County: Macomb
Population: 96,796

Ancestry	Population	%
Afghan (0)	0	<0.01
African, Sub-Saharan (614)	614	0.63
African (414)	414	0.43
Cape Verdean (0)	0	<0.01
Ethiopian (0)	0	<0.01
Ghanaian (110)	110	0.11
Kenyan (0)	0	<0.01
Liberian (0)	0	<0.01
Nigerian (90)	90	0.09
Senegalese (0)	0	<0.01
Sierra Leonean (0)	0	<0.01
Somalian (0)	0	<0.01
South African (0)	0	<0.01
Sudanese (0)	0	<0.01
Ugandan (0)	0	<0.01
Zimbabwean (0)	0	<0.01
Other Sub-Saharan African (0)	0	<0.01
Albanian (746)	757	0.78
Alsatian (0)	10	0.01
American (4,195)	4,195	4.31
Arab (862)	1,873	1.93
Arab (192)	312	0.32
Egyptian (0)	0	<0.01
Iraqi (92)	95	0.10
Jordanian (44)	44	0.05
Lebanese (450)	1,184	1.22
Moroccan (0)	41	0.04
Palestinian (0)	0	<0.01
Syrian (41)	154	0.16
Other Arab (43)	43	0.04
Armenian (39)	132	0.14
Assyrian/Chaldean/Syriac (0)	0	<0.01
Australian (0)	0	<0.01
Austrian (64)	259	0.27
Basque (0)	0	<0.01
Belgian (457)	1,840	1.89
Brazilian (6)	13	0.01
British (153)	353	0.36
Bulgarian (0)	10	0.01
Cajun (0)	0	<0.01
Canadian (278)	612	0.63
Carpatho Rusyn (0)	0	<0.01
Celtic (0)	0	<0.01
Croatian (73)	334	0.34
Cypriot (0)	0	<0.01
Czech (56)	637	0.65
Czechoslovakian (45)	218	0.22
Danish (32)	176	0.18
Dutch (228)	1,146	1.18
Eastern European (0)	0	<0.01
English (1,558)	6,730	6.92
Estonian (0)	0	<0.01
European (331)	403	0.41
Finnish (131)	585	0.60
French, ex. Basque (535)	4,802	4.94
French Canadian (518)	1,822	1.87
German (5,962)	21,482	22.08
German Russian (0)	0	<0.01
Greek (276)	705	0.72
Guyanese (15)	15	0.02
Hungarian (233)	958	0.98
Icelander (0)	14	0.01
Iranian (22)	22	0.02
Irish (1,963)	10,861	11.16
Israeli (0)	11	0.01
Italian (6,881)	14,389	14.79
Latvian (0)	0	<0.01
Lithuanian (108)	331	0.34
Luxemburger (8)	8	0.01
Macedonian (214)	242	0.25
Maltese (37)	183	0.19
New Zealander (0)	0	<0.01
Northern European (19)	53	0.05

Ancestry (cont.)	Population	%
Norwegian (56)	371	0.38
Pennsylvania German (0)	10	0.01
Polish (7,011)	17,913	18.41
Portuguese (0)	16	0.02
Romanian (527)	810	0.83
Russian (74)	654	0.67
Scandinavian (7)	68	0.07
Scotch-Irish (312)	1,119	1.15
Scottish (367)	2,496	2.57
Serbian (136)	246	0.25
Slavic (8)	60	0.06
Slovak (140)	493	0.51
Slovene (35)	45	0.05
Soviet Union (0)	0	<0.01
Swedish (213)	762	0.78
Swiss (9)	87	0.09
Turkish (14)	14	0.01
Ukrainian (164)	598	0.61
Welsh (52)	484	0.50
West Indian, ex. Hispanic (13)	25	0.03
Bahamian (13)	13	0.01
Barbadian (0)	0	<0.01
Belizean (0)	0	<0.01
Bermudan (0)	0	<0.01
British West Indian (0)	0	<0.01
Dutch West Indian (0)	0	<0.01
Haitian (0)	0	<0.01
Jamaican (0)	12	0.01
Trinidadian/Tobagonian (0)	0	<0.01
U.S. Virgin Islander (0)	0	<0.01
West Indian (0)	0	<0.01
Other West Indian (0)	0	<0.01
Yugoslavian (825)	850	0.87

Hispanic Origin	Population	%
Hispanic or Latino (of any race)	2,290	2.37
Central American, ex. Mexican	75	0.08
Costa Rican	6	0.01
Guatemalan	24	0.02
Honduran	5	0.01
Nicaraguan	5	0.01
Panamanian	9	0.01
Salvadoran	26	0.03
Other Central American	0	<0.01
Cuban	72	0.07
Dominican Republic	14	0.01
Mexican	1,534	1.58
Puerto Rican	210	0.22
South American	128	0.13
Argentinean	17	0.02
Bolivian	3	<0.01
Chilean	2	<0.01
Colombian	36	0.04
Ecuadorian	29	0.03
Paraguayan	0	<0.01
Peruvian	7	0.01
Uruguayan	13	0.01
Venezuelan	21	0.02
Other South American	0	<0.01
Other Hispanic or Latino	257	0.27

Race*	Population	%
African-American/Black (12,623)	13,832	14.29
Not Hispanic (12,509)	13,614	14.06
Hispanic (114)	218	0.23
American Indian/Alaska Native (267)	893	0.92
Not Hispanic (230)	798	0.82
Hispanic (37)	95	0.10
Alaska Athabascan (Ala. Nat.) (0)	0	<0.01
Aleut (Alaska Native) (0)	0	<0.01
Apache (3)	11	0.01
Arapaho (0)	0	<0.01
Blackfeet (5)	45	0.05
Canadian/French Am. Ind. (3)	12	0.01
Central American Ind. (1)	2	<0.01
Cherokee (33)	209	0.22
Cheyenne (0)	0	<0.01
Chickasaw (0)	0	<0.01
Chippewa (47)	111	0.11

Race* (cont.)	Population	%
Choctaw (3)	11	0.01
Colville (0)	0	<0.01
Comanche (1)	4	<0.01
Cree (0)	0	<0.01
Creek (0)	1	<0.01
Crow (0)	0	<0.01
Delaware (0)	0	<0.01
Hopi (0)	0	<0.01
Houma (0)	0	<0.01
Inupiat (Alaska Native) (2)	5	0.01
Iroquois (8)	32	0.03
Kiowa (0)	0	<0.01
Lumbee (12)	18	0.02
Menominee (0)	0	<0.01
Mexican American Ind. (5)	11	0.01
Navajo (1)	1	<0.01
Osage (0)	1	<0.01
Ottawa (5)	16	0.02
Paiute (0)	0	<0.01
Pima (0)	0	<0.01
Potawatomi (1)	10	0.01
Pueblo (0)	2	<0.01
Puget Sound Salish (0)	0	<0.01
Seminole (3)	7	0.01
Shoshone (0)	0	<0.01
Sioux (2)	13	0.01
South American Ind. (0)	0	<0.01
Spanish American Ind. (0)	0	<0.01
Tlingit-Haida (Alaska Native) (0)	0	<0.01
Tohono O'Odham (0)	0	<0.01
Tsimshian (Alaska Native) (0)	0	<0.01
Ute (0)	0	<0.01
Yakama (0)	0	<0.01
Yaqui (0)	0	<0.01
Yuman (0)	0	<0.01
Yup'ik (Alaska Native) (0)	0	<0.01
Asian (1,737)	2,266	2.34
Not Hispanic (1,723)	2,220	2.29
Hispanic (14)	46	0.05
Bangladeshi (8)	10	0.01
Bhutanese (0)	0	<0.01
Burmese (0)	3	<0.01
Cambodian (20)	25	0.03
Chinese, ex. Taiwanese (246)	336	0.35
Filipino (383)	531	0.55
Hmong (100)	101	0.10
Indian (409)	501	0.52
Indonesian (1)	4	<0.01
Japanese (55)	115	0.12
Korean (152)	224	0.23
Laotian (17)	17	0.02
Malaysian (1)	2	<0.01
Nepalese (4)	4	<0.01
Pakistani (85)	108	0.11
Sri Lankan (1)	3	<0.01
Taiwanese (1)	1	<0.01
Thai (13)	20	0.02
Vietnamese (143)	164	0.17
Hawaii Native/Pacific Islander (31)	74	0.08
Not Hispanic (29)	66	0.07
Hispanic (2)	8	0.01
Fijian (0)	0	<0.01
Guamanian/Chamorro (0)	2	<0.01
Marshallese (0)	0	<0.01
Native Hawaiian (5)	21	0.02
Samoan (5)	5	0.01
Tongan (0)	0	<0.01
White (79,447)	81,257	83.95
Not Hispanic (78,062)	79,688	82.33
Hispanic (1,385)	1,569	1.62

Notes: † The Census 2010 population figure is used to calculate the percentages in the Hispanic Origin and Race categories. Ancestry percentages are based on the 2006-2010 American Community Survey population (not shown); ‡ Numbers in parentheses indicate the number of people reporting a single ancestry; * Numbers in parentheses indicate the number of persons reporting this race alone, not in combination with any other race; Please refer to the User Guide for more information.

Dearborn

Place Type: City
County: Wayne
Population: 98,153

Ancestry	Population	%
Afghan (42)	42	0.04
African, Sub-Saharan (141)	351	0.36
African (46)	183	0.19
Cape Verdean (0)	0	<0.01
Ethiopian (0)	0	<0.01
Ghanaian (0)	0	<0.01
Kenyan (0)	0	<0.01
Liberian (0)	0	<0.01
Nigerian (3)	3	<0.01
Senegalese (0)	0	<0.01
Sierra Leonean (0)	0	<0.01
Somalian (41)	41	0.04
South African (0)	0	<0.01
Sudanese (0)	0	<0.01
Ugandan (0)	0	<0.01
Zimbabwean (0)	0	<0.01
Other Sub-Saharan African (51)	124	0.13
Albanian (591)	666	0.68
Alsatian (0)	11	0.01
American (1,835)	1,835	1.86
Arab (35,960)	38,503	39.13
Arab (7,455)	8,134	8.27
Egyptian (328)	356	0.36
Iraqi (2,618)	2,820	2.87
Jordanian (785)	805	0.82
Lebanese (17,582)	18,812	19.12
Moroccan (60)	121	0.12
Palestinian (680)	792	0.80
Syrian (249)	309	0.31
Other Arab (6,203)	6,354	6.46
Armenian (345)	542	0.55
Assyrian/Chaldean/Syriac (13)	33	0.03
Australian (12)	26	0.03
Austrian (63)	218	0.22
Basque (11)	11	0.01
Belgian (41)	339	0.34
Brazilian (60)	77	0.08
British (122)	276	0.28
Bulgarian (23)	55	0.06
Cajun (0)	0	<0.01
Canadian (173)	417	0.42
Carpatho Rusyn (0)	0	<0.01
Celtic (16)	22	0.02
Croatian (45)	147	0.15
Cypriot (0)	0	<0.01
Czech (128)	398	0.40
Czechoslovakian (16)	91	0.09
Danish (29)	162	0.16
Dutch (167)	911	0.93
Eastern European (120)	176	0.18
English (1,336)	5,649	5.74
Estonian (0)	0	<0.01
European (638)	688	0.70
Finnish (190)	458	0.47
French, ex. Basque (238)	2,748	2.79
French Canadian (520)	1,773	1.80
German (2,855)	12,189	12.39
German Russian (0)	0	<0.01
Greek (226)	399	0.41
Guyanese (0)	0	<0.01
Hungarian (593)	1,569	1.59
Icelander (0)	0	<0.01
Iranian (33)	43	0.04
Irish (1,894)	9,225	9.38
Israeli (32)	32	0.03
Italian (2,319)	4,907	4.99
Latvian (25)	25	0.03
Lithuanian (137)	528	0.54
Luxemburger (0)	11	0.01
Macedonian (138)	165	0.17
Maltese (326)	662	0.67
New Zealander (0)	0	<0.01
Northern European (92)	92	0.09
Norwegian (35)	413	0.42
Pennsylvania German (9)	9	0.01
Polish (4,194)	10,629	10.80
Portuguese (32)	32	0.03
Romanian (779)	916	0.93
Russian (143)	534	0.54
Scandinavian (9)	9	0.01
Scotch-Irish (464)	1,388	1.41
Scottish (482)	1,516	1.54
Serbian (36)	93	0.09
Slavic (15)	68	0.07
Slovak (78)	236	0.24
Slovene (8)	48	0.05
Soviet Union (0)	0	<0.01
Swedish (154)	954	0.97
Swiss (5)	75	0.08
Turkish (12)	35	0.04
Ukrainian (424)	988	1.00
Welsh (82)	353	0.36
West Indian, ex. Hispanic (45)	180	0.18
Bahamian (0)	0	<0.01
Barbadian (0)	0	<0.01
Belizean (0)	0	<0.01
Bermudan (0)	0	<0.01
British West Indian (0)	0	<0.01
Dutch West Indian (0)	0	<0.01
Haitian (0)	25	0.03
Jamaican (0)	0	<0.01
Trinidadian/Tobagonian (45)	155	0.16
U.S. Virgin Islander (0)	0	<0.01
West Indian (0)	0	<0.01
Other West Indian (0)	0	<0.01
Yugoslavian (29)	233	0.24

Hispanic Origin	Population	%
Hispanic or Latino (of any race)	3,386	3.45
Central American, ex. Mexican	97	0.10
Costa Rican	0	<0.01
Guatemalan	38	0.04
Honduran	9	0.01
Nicaraguan	10	0.01
Panamanian	11	0.01
Salvadoran	29	0.03
Other Central American	0	<0.01
Cuban	72	0.07
Dominican Republic	33	0.03
Mexican	2,320	2.36
Puerto Rican	383	0.39
South American	141	0.14
Argentinean	21	0.02
Bolivian	1	<0.01
Chilean	13	0.01
Colombian	42	0.04
Ecuadorian	9	0.01
Paraguayan	3	<0.01
Peruvian	7	0.01
Uruguayan	0	<0.01
Venezuelan	43	0.04
Other South American	2	<0.01
Other Hispanic or Latino	340	0.35

Race*	Population	%
African-American/Black (3,965)	4,413	4.50
Not Hispanic (3,895)	4,296	4.38
Hispanic (70)	117	0.12
American Indian/Alaska Native (220)	555	0.57
Not Hispanic (166)	450	0.46
Hispanic (54)	105	0.11
Alaska Athabascan (Ala. Nat.) (0)	0	<0.01
Aleut (Alaska Native) (0)	0	<0.01
Apache (0)	2	<0.01
Arapaho (0)	0	<0.01
Blackfeet (2)	9	0.01
Canadian/French Am. Ind. (4)	5	0.01
Central American Ind. (0)	1	<0.01
Cherokee (17)	92	0.09
Cheyenne (0)	1	<0.01
Chickasaw (0)	0	<0.01
Chippewa (42)	69	0.07
Choctaw (2)	17	0.02
Colville (0)	0	<0.01
Comanche (0)	2	<0.01
Cree (0)	2	<0.01
Creek (1)	4	<0.01
Crow (0)	0	<0.01
Delaware (1)	1	<0.01
Hopi (0)	0	<0.01
Houma (0)	0	<0.01
Inupiat (Alaska Native) (0)	6	0.01
Iroquois (30)	39	0.04
Kiowa (0)	0	<0.01
Lumbee (3)	6	0.01
Menominee (0)	1	<0.01
Mexican American Ind. (9)	15	0.02
Navajo (2)	3	<0.01
Osage (0)	1	<0.01
Ottawa (3)	3	<0.01
Paiute (0)	0	<0.01
Pima (0)	0	<0.01
Potawatomi (2)	9	0.01
Pueblo (0)	0	<0.01
Puget Sound Salish (0)	0	<0.01
Seminole (0)	0	<0.01
Shoshone (1)	1	<0.01
Sioux (1)	5	0.01
South American Ind. (5)	12	0.01
Spanish American Ind. (0)	0	<0.01
Tlingit-Haida (Alaska Native) (1)	1	<0.01
Tohono O'Odham (0)	0	<0.01
Tsimshian (Alaska Native) (0)	0	<0.01
Ute (0)	0	<0.01
Yakama (0)	0	<0.01
Yaqui (5)	9	0.01
Yuman (0)	0	<0.01
Yup'ik (Alaska Native) (0)	0	<0.01
Asian (1,706)	4,603	4.69
Not Hispanic (1,696)	4,522	4.61
Hispanic (10)	81	0.08
Bangladeshi (7)	7	0.01
Bhutanese (0)	0	<0.01
Burmese (0)	0	<0.01
Cambodian (8)	13	0.01
Chinese, ex. Taiwanese (176)	236	0.24
Filipino (172)	269	0.27
Hmong (1)	1	<0.01
Indian (547)	695	0.71
Indonesian (6)	8	0.01
Japanese (17)	64	0.07
Korean (74)	104	0.11
Laotian (2)	2	<0.01
Malaysian (4)	7	0.01
Nepalese (6)	7	0.01
Pakistani (346)	379	0.39
Sri Lankan (0)	1	<0.01
Taiwanese (16)	17	0.02
Thai (8)	13	0.01
Vietnamese (131)	157	0.16
Hawaii Native/Pacific Islander (32)	208	0.21
Not Hispanic (31)	201	0.20
Hispanic (1)	7	0.01
Fijian (0)	0	<0.01
Guamanian/Chamorro (0)	2	<0.01
Marshallese (0)	0	<0.01
Native Hawaiian (4)	16	0.02
Samoan (16)	18	0.02
Tongan (1)	5	0.01
White (87,454)	91,285	93.00
Not Hispanic (85,116)	88,708	90.38
Hispanic (2,338)	2,577	2.63

Notes: † The Census 2010 population figure is used to calculate the percentages in the Hispanic Origin and Race categories. Ancestry percentages are based on the 2006-2010 American Community Survey population (not shown); ‡ Numbers in parentheses indicate the number of people reporting a single ancestry; * Numbers in parentheses indicate the number of persons reporting this race alone, not in combination with any other race; Please refer to the User Guide for more information.

Dearborn Heights

Place Type: City
County: Wayne
Population: 57,774

Ancestry	Population	%
Afghan (0)	0	<0.01
African, Sub-Saharan (98)	119	0.20
African (92)	113	0.19
Cape Verdean (0)	0	<0.01
Ethiopian (0)	0	<0.01
Ghanaian (0)	0	<0.01
Kenyan (0)	0	<0.01
Liberian (0)	0	<0.01
Nigerian (0)	0	<0.01
Senegalese (0)	0	<0.01
Sierra Leonean (0)	0	<0.01
Somalian (0)	0	<0.01
South African (0)	0	<0.01
Sudanese (0)	0	<0.01
Ugandan (0)	0	<0.01
Zimbabwean (0)	0	<0.01
Other Sub-Saharan African (6)	6	0.01
Albanian (50)	61	0.11
Alsatian (0)	0	<0.01
American (1,967)	1,967	3.39
Arab (9,307)	10,397	17.91
Arab (858)	1,002	1.73
Egyptian (27)	27	0.05
Iraqi (524)	578	1.00
Jordanian (226)	265	0.46
Lebanese (6,743)	7,446	12.82
Moroccan (0)	0	<0.01
Palestinian (166)	196	0.34
Syrian (430)	512	0.88
Other Arab (333)	371	0.64
Armenian (115)	303	0.52
Assyrian/Chaldean/Syriac (48)	48	0.08
Australian (0)	0	<0.01
Austrian (45)	198	0.34
Basque (0)	0	<0.01
Belgian (61)	97	0.17
Brazilian (11)	23	0.04
British (61)	102	0.18
Bulgarian (0)	28	0.05
Cajun (0)	0	<0.01
Canadian (95)	250	0.43
Carpatho Rusyn (0)	0	<0.01
Celtic (0)	0	<0.01
Croatian (11)	60	0.10
Cypriot (0)	0	<0.01
Czech (41)	231	0.40
Czechoslovakian (112)	181	0.31
Danish (25)	121	0.21
Dutch (205)	762	1.31
Eastern European (63)	63	0.11
English (1,445)	5,091	8.77
Estonian (0)	0	<0.01
European (387)	409	0.70
Finnish (190)	417	0.72
French, ex. Basque (166)	2,147	3.70
French Canadian (388)	1,102	1.90
German (1,883)	8,682	14.95
German Russian (0)	0	<0.01
Greek (164)	408	0.70
Guyanese (0)	5	0.01
Hungarian (263)	952	1.64
Icelander (0)	0	<0.01
Iranian (0)	0	<0.01
Irish (1,282)	6,820	11.75
Israeli (0)	9	0.02
Italian (1,793)	4,117	7.09
Latvian (0)	0	<0.01
Lithuanian (160)	272	0.47
Luxemburger (0)	0	<0.01
Macedonian (298)	393	0.68
Maltese (236)	286	0.49
New Zealander (0)	0	<0.01
Northern European (21)	39	0.07

Ancestry	Population	%
Norwegian (35)	204	0.35
Pennsylvania German (0)	0	<0.01
Polish (4,862)	9,260	15.95
Portuguese (5)	13	0.02
Romanian (456)	560	0.96
Russian (33)	343	0.59
Scandinavian (20)	33	0.06
Scotch-Irish (323)	931	1.60
Scottish (225)	1,474	2.54
Serbian (54)	54	0.09
Slavic (16)	16	0.03
Slovak (44)	175	0.30
Slovene (13)	13	0.02
Soviet Union (0)	0	<0.01
Swedish (138)	569	0.98
Swiss (0)	113	0.19
Turkish (24)	39	0.07
Ukrainian (162)	456	0.79
Welsh (20)	194	0.33
West Indian, ex. Hispanic (61)	75	0.13
Bahamian (0)	0	<0.01
Barbadian (0)	0	<0.01
Belizean (0)	0	<0.01
Bermudan (0)	0	<0.01
British West Indian (0)	0	<0.01
Dutch West Indian (0)	0	<0.01
Haitian (0)	0	<0.01
Jamaican (61)	75	0.13
Trinidadian/Tobagonian (0)	0	<0.01
U.S. Virgin Islander (0)	0	<0.01
West Indian (0)	0	<0.01
Other West Indian (0)	0	<0.01
Yugoslavian (199)	279	0.48

Hispanic Origin	Population	%
Hispanic or Latino (of any race)	2,712	4.69
Central American, ex. Mexican	87	0.15
Costa Rican	11	0.02
Guatemalan	14	0.02
Honduran	10	0.02
Nicaraguan	16	0.03
Panamanian	8	0.01
Salvadoran	28	0.05
Other Central American	0	<0.01
Cuban	60	0.10
Dominican Republic	18	0.03
Mexican	1,861	3.22
Puerto Rican	352	0.61
South American	100	0.17
Argentinean	23	0.04
Bolivian	0	<0.01
Chilean	1	<0.01
Colombian	33	0.06
Ecuadorian	11	0.02
Paraguayan	2	<0.01
Peruvian	3	0.01
Uruguayan	0	<0.01
Venezuelan	24	0.04
Other South American	3	0.01
Other Hispanic or Latino	234	0.41

Race*	Population	%
African-American/Black (4,546)	5,011	8.67
Not Hispanic (4,490)	4,892	8.47
Hispanic (56)	119	0.21
American Indian/Alaska Native (237)	561	0.97
Not Hispanic (196)	472	0.82
Hispanic (41)	89	0.15
Alaska Athabascan (Ala. Nat.) (1)	1	<0.01
Aleut (Alaska Native) (0)	0	<0.01
Apache (0)	5	0.01
Arapaho (0)	0	<0.01
Blackfeet (0)	15	0.03
Canadian/French Am. Ind. (7)	9	0.02
Central American Ind. (0)	0	<0.01
Cherokee (25)	101	0.17
Cheyenne (0)	0	<0.01
Chickasaw (3)	3	0.01
Chippewa (49)	78	0.14

Race*	Population	%
Choctaw (3)	4	0.01
Colville (0)	0	<0.01
Comanche (2)	3	0.01
Cree (1)	1	<0.01
Creek (0)	1	<0.01
Crow (0)	0	<0.01
Delaware (1)	1	<0.01
Hopi (0)	1	<0.01
Houma (0)	0	<0.01
Inupiat (Alaska Native) (0)	0	<0.01
Iroquois (37)	61	0.11
Kiowa (0)	1	<0.01
Lumbee (7)	8	0.01
Menominee (2)	2	<0.01
Mexican American Ind. (0)	6	0.01
Navajo (3)	4	0.01
Osage (0)	0	<0.01
Ottawa (3)	15	0.03
Paiute (2)	2	<0.01
Pima (0)	0	<0.01
Potawatomi (0)	3	0.01
Pueblo (0)	0	<0.01
Puget Sound Salish (0)	0	<0.01
Seminole (0)	3	0.01
Shoshone (0)	0	<0.01
Sioux (0)	7	0.01
South American Ind. (1)	1	<0.01
Spanish American Ind. (0)	0	<0.01
Tlingit-Haida (Alaska Native) (0)	0	<0.01
Tohono O'Odham (0)	0	<0.01
Tsimshian (Alaska Native) (0)	0	<0.01
Ute (0)	0	<0.01
Yakama (0)	0	<0.01
Yaqui (0)	0	<0.01
Yuman (0)	0	<0.01
Yup'ik (Alaska Native) (0)	0	<0.01
Asian (999)	1,696	2.94
Not Hispanic (995)	1,673	2.90
Hispanic (4)	23	0.04
Bangladeshi (0)	1	<0.01
Bhutanese (0)	0	<0.01
Burmese (0)	0	<0.01
Cambodian (4)	9	0.02
Chinese, ex. Taiwanese (137)	157	0.27
Filipino (132)	199	0.34
Hmong (0)	0	<0.01
Indian (288)	317	0.55
Indonesian (3)	3	0.01
Japanese (16)	45	0.08
Korean (37)	59	0.10
Laotian (0)	0	<0.01
Malaysian (0)	0	<0.01
Nepalese (0)	0	<0.01
Pakistani (89)	99	0.17
Sri Lankan (2)	2	<0.01
Taiwanese (3)	3	0.01
Thai (9)	22	0.04
Vietnamese (214)	219	0.38
Hawaii Native/Pacific Islander (12)	73	0.13
Not Hispanic (9)	69	0.12
Hispanic (3)	4	0.01
Fijian (0)	0	<0.01
Guamanian/Chamorro (1)	7	0.01
Marshallese (0)	0	<0.01
Native Hawaiian (3)	10	0.02
Samoan (7)	8	0.01
Tongan (0)	0	<0.01
White (49,772)	51,263	88.73
Not Hispanic (47,943)	49,214	85.18
Hispanic (1,829)	2,049	3.55

Notes: † The Census 2010 population figure is used to calculate the percentages in the Hispanic Origin and Race categories. Ancestry percentages are based on the 2006-2010 American Community Survey population (not shown); ‡ Numbers in parentheses indicate the number of people reporting a single ancestry; * Numbers in parentheses indicate the number of persons reporting this race alone, not in combination with any other race; Please refer to the User Guide for more information.

Detroit

Place Type: City
County: Wayne
Population: 713,777

Ancestry	Population	%
Afghan (0)	0	<0.01
African, Sub-Saharan (9,758)	12,021	1.58
African (7,657)	9,726	1.28
Cape Verdean (16)	16	<0.01
Ethiopian (43)	106	0.01
Ghanaian (0)	28	<0.01
Kenyan (286)	286	0.04
Liberian (81)	81	0.01
Nigerian (1,207)	1,282	0.17
Senegalese (28)	28	<0.01
Sierra Leonean (0)	0	<0.01
Somalian (87)	97	0.01
South African (75)	75	0.01
Sudanese (37)	37	<0.01
Ugandan (0)	0	<0.01
Zimbabwean (0)	0	<0.01
Other Sub-Saharan African (241)	259	0.03
Albanian (214)	233	0.03
Alsatian (0)	0	<0.01
American (7,086)	7,086	0.93
Arab (8,077)	8,642	1.14
Arab (4,276)	4,349	0.57
Egyptian (20)	92	0.01
Iraqi (1,072)	1,125	0.15
Jordanian (106)	117	0.02
Lebanese (362)	566	0.07
Moroccan (313)	398	0.05
Palestinian (121)	132	0.02
Syrian (9)	26	<0.01
Other Arab (1,798)	1,837	0.24
Armenian (139)	234	0.03
Assyrian/Chaldean/Syriac (630)	656	0.09
Australian (50)	129	0.02
Austrian (19)	157	0.02
Basque (13)	13	<0.01
Belgian (80)	422	0.06
Brazilian (0)	0	<0.01
British (323)	405	0.05
Bulgarian (44)	53	0.01
Cajun (41)	62	0.01
Canadian (371)	743	0.10
Carpatho Rusyn (0)	0	<0.01
Celtic (0)	9	<0.01
Croatian (64)	216	0.03
Cypriot (0)	0	<0.01
Czech (60)	326	0.04
Czechoslovakian (14)	52	0.01
Danish (80)	230	0.03
Dutch (327)	1,226	0.16
Eastern European (49)	61	0.01
English (2,251)	5,767	0.76
Estonian (7)	7	<0.01
European (349)	736	0.10
Finnish (238)	624	0.08
French, ex. Basque (691)	3,837	0.51
French Canadian (243)	906	0.12
German (2,715)	11,126	1.47
German Russian (83)	119	0.02
Greek (171)	451	0.06
Guyanese (0)	0	<0.01
Hungarian (340)	1,137	0.15
Icelander (0)	0	<0.01
Iranian (10)	10	<0.01
Irish (2,594)	10,866	1.43
Israeli (0)	0	<0.01
Italian (1,909)	4,785	0.63
Latvian (8)	8	<0.01
Lithuanian (149)	261	0.03
Luxemburger (0)	9	<0.01
Macedonian (17)	17	<0.01
Maltese (118)	266	0.04
New Zealander (0)	0	<0.01
Northern European (25)	25	<0.01
Norwegian (106)	292	0.04
Pennsylvania German (17)	78	0.01
Polish (5,452)	10,573	1.39
Portuguese (9)	42	0.01
Romanian (515)	608	0.08
Russian (211)	635	0.08
Scandinavian (84)	94	0.01
Scotch-Irish (486)	1,253	0.17
Scottish (377)	1,309	0.17
Serbian (40)	111	0.01
Slavic (53)	89	0.01
Slovak (96)	378	0.05
Slovene (0)	9	<0.01
Soviet Union (0)	0	<0.01
Swedish (115)	717	0.09
Swiss (25)	149	0.02
Turkish (31)	40	0.01
Ukrainian (272)	647	0.09
Welsh (64)	317	0.04
West Indian, ex. Hispanic (1,859)	2,609	0.34
Bahamian (59)	59	0.01
Barbadian (18)	29	<0.01
Belizean (11)	11	<0.01
Bermudan (0)	10	<0.01
British West Indian (0)	0	<0.01
Dutch West Indian (0)	0	<0.01
Haitian (149)	199	0.03
Jamaican (1,412)	1,946	0.26
Trinidadian/Tobagonian (100)	119	0.02
U.S. Virgin Islander (15)	15	<0.01
West Indian (95)	221	0.03
Other West Indian (0)	0	<0.01
Yugoslavian (31)	45	0.01

Hispanic Origin	Population	%
Hispanic or Latino (of any race)	48,679	6.82
Central American, ex. Mexican	1,813	0.25
Costa Rican	33	<0.01
Guatemalan	542	0.08
Honduran	566	0.08
Nicaraguan	69	0.01
Panamanian	124	0.02
Salvadoran	451	0.06
Other Central American	28	<0.01
Cuban	773	0.11
Dominican Republic	688	0.10
Mexican	36,452	5.11
Puerto Rican	5,783	0.81
South American	337	0.05
Argentinean	41	0.01
Bolivian	3	<0.01
Chilean	24	<0.01
Colombian	101	0.01
Ecuadorian	38	0.01
Paraguayan	0	<0.01
Peruvian	77	0.01
Uruguayan	7	<0.01
Venezuelan	38	0.01
Other South American	8	<0.01
Other Hispanic or Latino	2,833	0.40

Race*	Population	%
African-American/Black (590,226)	601,988	84.34
Not Hispanic (586,573)	596,963	83.63
Hispanic (3,653)	5,025	0.70
American Indian/Alaska Native (2,636)	8,448	1.18
Not Hispanic (1,927)	6,965	0.98
Hispanic (709)	1,483	0.21
Alaska Athabascan (Ala. Nat.) (0)	1	<0.01
Aleut (Alaska Native) (0)	1	<0.01
Apache (15)	59	0.01
Arapaho (1)	4	<0.01
Blackfeet (43)	441	0.06
Canadian/French Am. Ind. (23)	45	0.01
Central American Ind. (7)	15	<0.01
Cherokee (158)	1,321	0.19
Cheyenne (0)	6	<0.01
Chickasaw (3)	19	<0.01
Chippewa (126)	285	0.04
Choctaw (32)	193	0.03
Colville (0)	0	<0.01
Comanche (7)	16	<0.01
Cree (1)	32	<0.01
Creek (14)	71	0.01
Crow (2)	17	<0.01
Delaware (6)	28	<0.01
Hopi (1)	8	<0.01
Houma (0)	0	<0.01
Inupiat (Alaska Native) (0)	3	<0.01
Iroquois (65)	140	0.02
Kiowa (0)	1	<0.01
Lumbee (15)	48	0.01
Menominee (3)	15	<0.01
Mexican American Ind. (170)	238	0.03
Navajo (15)	46	0.01
Osage (0)	1	<0.01
Ottawa (34)	59	0.01
Paiute (0)	1	<0.01
Pima (0)	0	<0.01
Potawatomi (22)	61	0.01
Pueblo (5)	5	<0.01
Puget Sound Salish (4)	5	<0.01
Seminole (12)	63	0.01
Shoshone (0)	4	<0.01
Sioux (27)	68	0.01
South American Ind. (7)	29	<0.01
Spanish American Ind. (10)	10	<0.01
Tlingit-Haida (Alaska Native) (1)	3	<0.01
Tohono O'Odham (0)	2	<0.01
Tsimshian (Alaska Native) (0)	0	<0.01
Ute (7)	7	<0.01
Yakama (2)	3	<0.01
Yaqui (1)	2	<0.01
Yuman (0)	2	<0.01
Yup'ik (Alaska Native) (2)	2	<0.01
Asian (7,559)	9,925	1.39
Not Hispanic (7,436)	9,598	1.34
Hispanic (123)	327	0.05
Bangladeshi (2,597)	2,825	0.40
Bhutanese (0)	0	<0.01
Burmese (0)	3	<0.01
Cambodian (9)	13	<0.01
Chinese, ex. Taiwanese (597)	852	0.12
Filipino (538)	875	0.12
Hmong (545)	578	0.08
Indian (1,959)	2,588	0.36
Indonesian (5)	12	<0.01
Japanese (107)	307	0.04
Korean (203)	341	0.05
Laotian (82)	112	0.02
Malaysian (5)	8	<0.01
Nepalese (17)	17	<0.01
Pakistani (86)	124	0.02
Sri Lankan (39)	46	0.01
Taiwanese (30)	38	0.01
Thai (41)	96	0.01
Vietnamese (127)	182	0.03
Hawaii Native/Pacific Islander (129)	673	0.09
Not Hispanic (82)	503	0.07
Hispanic (47)	170	0.02
Fijian (2)	2	<0.01
Guamanian/Chamorro (49)	117	0.02
Marshallese (0)	0	<0.01
Native Hawaiian (30)	130	0.02
Samoan (18)	71	0.01
Tongan (4)	4	<0.01
White (75,758)	86,039	12.05
Not Hispanic (55,604)	63,384	8.88
Hispanic (20,154)	22,655	3.17

Farmington Hills

Place Type: City
County: Oakland
Population: 79,740

Ancestry	Population	%
Afghan (0)	0	<0.01
African, Sub-Saharan (639)	871	1.09
African (255)	395	0.49
Cape Verdean (0)	0	<0.01
Ethiopian (26)	26	0.03
Ghanaian (22)	22	0.03
Kenyan (15)	15	0.02
Liberian (0)	0	<0.01
Nigerian (236)	269	0.34
Senegalese (0)	0	<0.01
Sierra Leonean (0)	0	<0.01
Somalian (0)	0	<0.01
South African (43)	69	0.09
Sudanese (0)	0	<0.01
Ugandan (0)	0	<0.01
Zimbabwean (16)	16	0.02
Other Sub-Saharan African (26)	59	0.07
Albanian (856)	866	1.08
Alsatian (0)	0	<0.01
American (3,057)	3,057	3.81
Arab (2,121)	2,505	3.12
Arab (553)	587	0.73
Egyptian (12)	12	0.01
Iraqi (657)	777	0.97
Jordanian (0)	0	<0.01
Lebanese (221)	451	0.56
Moroccan (0)	0	<0.01
Palestinian (92)	92	0.11
Syrian (174)	174	0.22
Other Arab (412)	412	0.51
Armenian (476)	564	0.70
Assyrian/Chaldean/Syriac (1,094)	1,226	1.53
Australian (0)	78	0.10
Austrian (93)	268	0.33
Basque (0)	0	<0.01
Belgian (44)	225	0.28
Brazilian (94)	106	0.13
British (207)	340	0.42
Bulgarian (18)	18	0.02
Cajun (0)	32	0.04
Canadian (166)	435	0.54
Carpatho Rusyn (0)	0	<0.01
Celtic (11)	11	0.01
Croatian (38)	190	0.24
Cypriot (0)	0	<0.01
Czech (72)	328	0.41
Czechoslovakian (72)	178	0.22
Danish (115)	386	0.48
Dutch (231)	938	1.17
Eastern European (481)	501	0.62
English (1,625)	6,565	8.19
Estonian (9)	9	0.01
European (602)	794	0.99
Finnish (215)	779	0.97
French, ex. Basque (459)	2,726	3.40
French Canadian (296)	1,026	1.28
German (3,204)	12,353	15.40
German Russian (0)	0	<0.01
Greek (242)	466	0.58
Guyanese (0)	0	<0.01
Hungarian (659)	1,546	1.93
Icelander (11)	11	0.01
Iranian (76)	101	0.13
Irish (1,871)	7,439	9.28
Israeli (75)	78	0.10
Italian (1,526)	3,683	4.59
Latvian (11)	62	0.08
Lithuanian (308)	584	0.73
Luxemburger (0)	0	<0.01
Macedonian (0)	11	0.01
Maltese (115)	220	0.27
New Zealander (0)	17	0.02
Northern European (48)	48	0.06

Ancestry	Population	%
Norwegian (136)	503	0.63
Pennsylvania German (0)	0	<0.01
Polish (3,391)	8,787	10.96
Portuguese (17)	81	0.10
Romanian (505)	794	0.99
Russian (2,025)	3,395	4.23
Scandinavian (41)	181	0.23
Scotch-Irish (363)	1,146	1.43
Scottish (324)	1,821	2.27
Serbian (179)	195	0.24
Slavic (28)	37	0.05
Slovak (124)	298	0.37
Slovene (40)	185	0.23
Soviet Union (0)	0	<0.01
Swedish (156)	656	0.82
Swiss (0)	233	0.29
Turkish (51)	61	0.08
Ukrainian (633)	1,053	1.31
Welsh (73)	372	0.46
West Indian, ex. Hispanic (165)	254	0.32
Bahamian (0)	0	<0.01
Barbadian (22)	22	0.03
Belizean (0)	0	<0.01
Bermudan (0)	0	<0.01
British West Indian (20)	47	0.06
Dutch West Indian (0)	0	<0.01
Haitian (38)	46	0.06
Jamaican (85)	100	0.12
Trinidadian/Tobagonian (0)	29	0.04
U.S. Virgin Islander (0)	0	<0.01
West Indian (0)	10	0.01
Other West Indian (0)	0	<0.01
Yugoslavian (288)	374	0.47

Hispanic Origin	Population	%
Hispanic or Latino (of any race)	1,544	1.94
Central American, ex. Mexican	93	0.12
Costa Rican	5	0.01
Guatemalan	35	0.04
Honduran	11	0.01
Nicaraguan	12	0.02
Panamanian	11	0.01
Salvadoran	18	0.02
Other Central American	1	<0.01
Cuban	60	0.08
Dominican Republic	22	0.03
Mexican	796	1.00
Puerto Rican	148	0.19
South American	204	0.26
Argentinean	60	0.08
Bolivian	10	0.01
Chilean	10	0.01
Colombian	60	0.08
Ecuadorian	14	0.02
Paraguayan	15	0.02
Peruvian	15	0.02
Uruguayan	7	0.01
Venezuelan	13	0.02
Other South American	0	<0.01
Other Hispanic or Latino	221	0.28

Race*	Population	%
African-American/Black (13,848)	14,574	18.28
Not Hispanic (13,768)	14,436	18.10
Hispanic (80)	138	0.17
American Indian/Alaska Native (157)	567	0.71
Not Hispanic (139)	498	0.62
Hispanic (18)	69	0.09
Alaska Athabascan (Ala. Nat.) (0)	0	<0.01
Aleut (Alaska Native) (0)	0	<0.01
Apache (1)	7	0.01
Arapaho (0)	0	<0.01
Blackfeet (0)	19	0.02
Canadian/French Am. Ind. (3)	4	0.01
Central American Ind. (0)	2	<0.01
Cherokee (14)	126	0.16
Cheyenne (0)	0	<0.01
Chickasaw (3)	8	0.01
Chippewa (29)	60	0.08

Race*	Population	%
Choctaw (1)	20	0.03
Colville (0)	0	<0.01
Comanche (0)	0	<0.01
Cree (0)	3	<0.01
Creek (0)	4	0.01
Crow (0)	0	<0.01
Delaware (0)	3	<0.01
Hopi (0)	0	<0.01
Houma (1)	2	<0.01
Inupiat (Alaska Native) (0)	0	<0.01
Iroquois (2)	10	0.01
Kiowa (0)	0	<0.01
Lumbee (3)	3	<0.01
Menominee (0)	1	<0.01
Mexican American Ind. (9)	9	0.01
Navajo (0)	0	<0.01
Osage (0)	0	<0.01
Ottawa (2)	4	0.01
Paiute (0)	0	<0.01
Pima (0)	0	<0.01
Potawatomi (0)	4	0.01
Pueblo (0)	0	<0.01
Puget Sound Salish (0)	0	<0.01
Seminole (0)	2	<0.01
Shoshone (0)	0	<0.01
Sioux (0)	3	<0.01
South American Ind. (0)	3	<0.01
Spanish American Ind. (0)	0	<0.01
Tlingit-Haida (Alaska Native) (1)	2	<0.01
Tohono O'Odham (0)	0	<0.01
Tsimshian (Alaska Native) (0)	0	<0.01
Ute (0)	0	<0.01
Yakama (0)	0	<0.01
Yaqui (0)	0	<0.01
Yuman (1)	1	<0.01
Yup'ik (Alaska Native) (0)	0	<0.01
Asian (8,072)	8,910	11.17
Not Hispanic (8,063)	8,868	11.12
Hispanic (9)	42	0.05
Bangladeshi (16)	17	0.02
Bhutanese (0)	0	<0.01
Burmese (1)	1	<0.01
Cambodian (2)	8	0.01
Chinese, ex. Taiwanese (776)	864	1.08
Filipino (357)	468	0.59
Hmong (7)	10	0.01
Indian (5,037)	5,216	6.54
Indonesian (6)	9	0.01
Japanese (542)	643	0.81
Korean (533)	580	0.73
Laotian (5)	10	0.01
Malaysian (5)	7	0.01
Nepalese (17)	19	0.02
Pakistani (447)	500	0.63
Sri Lankan (41)	51	0.06
Taiwanese (37)	51	0.06
Thai (18)	24	0.03
Vietnamese (100)	131	0.16
Hawaii Native/Pacific Islander (13)	85	0.11
Not Hispanic (12)	77	0.10
Hispanic (1)	8	0.01
Fijian (0)	0	<0.01
Guamanian/Chamorro (1)	6	0.01
Marshallese (1)	1	<0.01
Native Hawaiian (2)	19	0.02
Samoan (1)	5	0.01
Tongan (0)	0	<0.01
White (55,539)	56,938	71.40
Not Hispanic (54,466)	55,749	69.91
Hispanic (1,073)	1,189	1.49

*Notes: † The Census 2010 population figure is used to calculate the percentages in the Hispanic Origin and Race categories. Ancestry percentages are based on the 2006-2010 American Community Survey population (not shown); ‡ Numbers in parentheses indicate the number of people reporting a single ancestry; * Numbers in parentheses indicate the number of persons reporting this race alone, not in combination with any other race; Please refer to the User Guide for more information.*

Flint

Place Type: City
County: Genesee
Population: 102,434

Ancestry	Population	%
Afghan (0)	0	<0.01
African, Sub-Saharan (1,391)	1,740	1.61
African (1,189)	1,515	1.41
Cape Verdean (0)	0	<0.01
Ethiopian (38)	38	0.04
Ghanaian (0)	0	<0.01
Kenyan (0)	0	<0.01
Liberian (0)	0	<0.01
Nigerian (115)	138	0.13
Senegalese (0)	0	<0.01
Sierra Leonean (0)	0	<0.01
Somalian (0)	0	<0.01
South African (0)	0	<0.01
Sudanese (0)	0	<0.01
Ugandan (0)	0	<0.01
Zimbabwean (0)	0	<0.01
Other Sub-Saharan African (49)	49	0.05
Albanian (0)	0	<0.01
Alsatian (0)	0	<0.01
American (3,644)	3,644	3.38
Arab (358)	492	0.46
Arab (76)	89	0.08
Egyptian (15)	15	0.01
Iraqi (20)	39	0.04
Jordanian (0)	0	<0.01
Lebanese (145)	236	0.22
Moroccan (49)	49	0.05
Palestinian (11)	11	0.01
Syrian (42)	53	0.05
Other Arab (0)	0	<0.01
Armenian (9)	9	0.01
Assyrian/Chaldean/Syriac (258)	277	0.26
Australian (0)	0	<0.01
Austrian (0)	0	<0.01
Basque (0)	0	<0.01
Belgian (0)	111	0.10
Brazilian (0)	0	<0.01
British (38)	92	0.09
Bulgarian (0)	0	<0.01
Cajun (0)	0	<0.01
Canadian (149)	378	0.35
Carpatho Rusyn (0)	0	<0.01
Celtic (0)	0	<0.01
Croatian (0)	0	<0.01
Cypriot (0)	0	<0.01
Czech (59)	147	0.14
Czechoslovakian (46)	70	0.06
Danish (34)	83	0.08
Dutch (251)	1,046	0.97
Eastern European (0)	0	<0.01
English (2,165)	5,391	5.00
Estonian (0)	0	<0.01
European (372)	496	0.46
Finnish (75)	249	0.23
French, ex. Basque (315)	2,105	1.95
French Canadian (557)	1,300	1.21
German (2,242)	7,597	7.05
German Russian (0)	6	0.01
Greek (33)	126	0.12
Guyanese (0)	58	0.05
Hungarian (165)	310	0.29
Icelander (0)	0	<0.01
Iranian (0)	0	<0.01
Irish (1,309)	5,535	5.13
Israeli (0)	0	<0.01
Italian (395)	1,379	1.28
Latvian (0)	14	0.01
Lithuanian (19)	44	0.04
Luxemburger (0)	0	<0.01
Macedonian (27)	41	0.04
Maltese (12)	12	0.01
New Zealander (0)	0	<0.01
Northern European (0)	0	<0.01

Ancestry	Population	%
Norwegian (173)	411	0.38
Pennsylvania German (23)	23	0.02
Polish (628)	1,732	1.61
Portuguese (40)	55	0.05
Romanian (18)	29	0.03
Russian (82)	201	0.19
Scandinavian (11)	101	0.09
Scotch-Irish (288)	601	0.56
Scottish (262)	1,116	1.04
Serbian (36)	36	0.03
Slavic (0)	0	<0.01
Slovak (39)	62	0.06
Slovene (0)	0	<0.01
Soviet Union (0)	0	<0.01
Swedish (105)	487	0.45
Swiss (25)	50	0.05
Turkish (11)	11	0.01
Ukrainian (69)	118	0.11
Welsh (26)	258	0.24
West Indian, ex. Hispanic (105)	219	0.20
Bahamian (7)	7	0.01
Barbadian (0)	0	<0.01
Belizean (0)	0	<0.01
Bermudan (0)	0	<0.01
British West Indian (0)	0	<0.01
Dutch West Indian (0)	23	0.02
Haitian (0)	0	<0.01
Jamaican (32)	89	0.08
Trinidadian/Tobagonian (55)	76	0.07
U.S. Virgin Islander (0)	0	<0.01
West Indian (11)	24	0.02
Other West Indian (0)	0	<0.01
Yugoslavian (0)	14	0.01

Hispanic Origin	Population	%
Hispanic or Latino (of any race)	3,976	3.88
Central American, ex. Mexican	65	0.06
Costa Rican	4	<0.01
Guatemalan	11	0.01
Honduran	14	0.01
Nicaraguan	4	<0.01
Panamanian	18	0.02
Salvadoran	14	0.01
Other Central American	0	<0.01
Cuban	59	0.06
Dominican Republic	13	0.01
Mexican	3,087	3.01
Puerto Rican	324	0.32
South American	50	0.05
Argentinean	3	<0.01
Bolivian	0	<0.01
Chilean	2	<0.01
Colombian	29	0.03
Ecuadorian	3	<0.01
Paraguayan	0	<0.01
Peruvian	10	0.01
Uruguayan	3	<0.01
Venezuelan	0	<0.01
Other South American	0	<0.01
Other Hispanic or Latino	378	0.37

Race*	Population	%
African-American/Black (57,939)	60,928	59.48
Not Hispanic (57,451)	60,166	58.74
Hispanic (488)	762	0.74
American Indian/Alaska Native (550)	1,950	1.90
Not Hispanic (455)	1,724	1.68
Hispanic (95)	226	0.22
Alaska Athabascan (Ala. Nat.) (1)	1	<0.01
Aleut (Alaska Native) (0)	0	<0.01
Apache (11)	36	0.04
Arapaho (0)	3	<0.01
Blackfeet (17)	141	0.14
Canadian/French Am. Ind. (3)	11	0.01
Central American Ind. (0)	1	<0.01
Cherokee (51)	423	0.41
Cheyenne (3)	12	0.01
Chickasaw (4)	14	0.01
Chippewa (123)	231	0.23

Race*	Population	%
Choctaw (8)	51	0.05
Colville (0)	0	<0.01
Comanche (0)	2	<0.01
Cree (1)	3	<0.01
Creek (6)	16	0.02
Crow (1)	3	<0.01
Delaware (0)	2	<0.01
Hopi (0)	0	<0.01
Houma (0)	0	<0.01
Inupiat (Alaska Native) (0)	4	<0.01
Iroquois (5)	25	0.02
Kiowa (0)	0	<0.01
Lumbee (0)	0	<0.01
Menominee (1)	1	<0.01
Mexican American Ind. (17)	40	0.04
Navajo (2)	11	0.01
Osage (1)	2	<0.01
Ottawa (20)	41	0.04
Paiute (0)	0	<0.01
Pima (1)	1	<0.01
Potawatomi (4)	16	0.02
Pueblo (1)	1	<0.01
Puget Sound Salish (1)	2	<0.01
Seminole (4)	4	<0.01
Shoshone (1)	1	<0.01
Sioux (9)	26	0.03
South American Ind. (0)	2	<0.01
Spanish American Ind. (0)	0	<0.01
Tlingit-Haida (Alaska Native) (0)	0	<0.01
Tohono O'Odham (0)	1	<0.01
Tsimshian (Alaska Native) (0)	0	<0.01
Ute (0)	0	<0.01
Yakama (0)	0	<0.01
Yaqui (0)	0	<0.01
Yuman (0)	0	<0.01
Yup'ik (Alaska Native) (0)	0	<0.01
Asian (464)	746	0.73
Not Hispanic (450)	700	0.68
Hispanic (14)	46	0.04
Bangladeshi (0)	0	<0.01
Bhutanese (0)	0	<0.01
Burmese (0)	0	<0.01
Cambodian (11)	16	0.02
Chinese, ex. Taiwanese (117)	153	0.15
Filipino (75)	148	0.14
Hmong (15)	18	0.02
Indian (91)	145	0.14
Indonesian (1)	2	<0.01
Japanese (20)	56	0.05
Korean (51)	84	0.08
Laotian (6)	11	0.01
Malaysian (0)	0	<0.01
Nepalese (9)	9	0.01
Pakistani (6)	9	0.01
Sri Lankan (0)	0	<0.01
Taiwanese (2)	9	0.01
Thai (9)	13	0.01
Vietnamese (15)	27	0.03
Hawaii Native/Pacific Islander (16)	72	0.07
Not Hispanic (14)	63	0.06
Hispanic (2)	9	0.01
Fijian (1)	1	<0.01
Guamanian/Chamorro (2)	12	0.01
Marshallese (0)	0	<0.01
Native Hawaiian (6)	25	0.02
Samoan (2)	7	0.01
Tongan (0)	0	<0.01
White (38,328)	41,527	40.54
Not Hispanic (36,537)	39,292	38.36
Hispanic (1,791)	2,235	2.18

*Notes: † The Census 2010 population figure is used to calculate the percentages in the Hispanic Origin and Race categories. Ancestry percentages are based on the 2006-2010 American Community Survey population (not shown); ‡ Numbers in parentheses indicate the number of people reporting a single ancestry; * Numbers in parentheses indicate the number of persons reporting this race alone, not in combination with any other race; Please refer to the User Guide for more information.*

Grand Rapids

Place Type: City
County: Kent
Population: 188,040

Ancestry	Population	%
Afghan (0)	0	<0.01
African, Sub-Saharan (2,279)	2,553	1.34
African (1,099)	1,313	0.69
Cape Verdean (72)	72	0.04
Ethiopian (306)	335	0.18
Ghanaian (0)	0	<0.01
Kenyan (17)	34	0.02
Liberian (309)	309	0.16
Nigerian (18)	18	0.01
Senegalese (0)	0	<0.01
Sierra Leonean (0)	0	<0.01
Somalian (68)	68	0.04
South African (53)	67	0.04
Sudanese (285)	285	0.15
Ugandan (0)	0	<0.01
Zimbabwean (0)	0	<0.01
Other Sub-Saharan African (52)	52	0.03
Albanian (28)	65	0.03
Alsatian (0)	0	<0.01
American (3,510)	3,510	1.84
Arab (465)	894	0.47
Arab (137)	242	0.13
Egyptian (0)	0	<0.01
Iraqi (0)	0	<0.01
Jordanian (0)	12	0.01
Lebanese (207)	379	0.20
Moroccan (0)	0	<0.01
Palestinian (43)	43	0.02
Syrian (17)	89	0.05
Other Arab (61)	129	0.07
Armenian (37)	37	0.02
Assyrian/Chaldean/Syriac (0)	0	<0.01
Australian (33)	86	0.05
Austrian (56)	357	0.19
Basque (0)	0	<0.01
Belgian (153)	335	0.18
Brazilian (42)	96	0.05
British (208)	667	0.35
Bulgarian (9)	9	<0.01
Cajun (0)	0	<0.01
Canadian (315)	649	0.34
Carpatho Rusyn (0)	0	<0.01
Celtic (0)	14	0.01
Croatian (96)	296	0.16
Cypriot (0)	0	<0.01
Czech (150)	666	0.35
Czechoslovakian (90)	217	0.11
Danish (200)	1,324	0.70
Dutch (16,182)	29,229	15.35
Eastern European (78)	108	0.06
English (3,152)	14,001	7.35
Estonian (10)	10	0.01
European (1,621)	2,054	1.08
Finnish (116)	703	0.37
French, ex. Basque (643)	5,485	2.88
French Canadian (566)	1,455	0.76
German (6,681)	30,522	16.03
German Russian (0)	0	<0.01
Greek (82)	378	0.20
Guyanese (0)	0	<0.01
Hungarian (128)	603	0.32
Icelander (0)	0	<0.01
Iranian (70)	116	0.06
Irish (3,359)	18,575	9.75
Israeli (13)	13	0.01
Italian (1,636)	5,060	2.66
Latvian (110)	204	0.11
Lithuanian (383)	1,236	0.65
Luxemburger (16)	49	0.03
Macedonian (11)	46	0.02
Maltese (19)	35	0.02
New Zealander (0)	0	<0.01
Northern European (87)	87	0.05

Ancestry (cont.)	Population	%
Norwegian (206)	1,190	0.62
Pennsylvania German (14)	76	0.04
Polish (6,048)	15,189	7.98
Portuguese (43)	89	0.05
Romanian (302)	399	0.21
Russian (386)	989	0.52
Scandinavian (30)	138	0.07
Scotch-Irish (633)	2,161	1.13
Scottish (544)	2,430	1.28
Serbian (0)	11	0.01
Slavic (26)	91	0.05
Slovak (30)	169	0.09
Slovene (0)	27	0.01
Soviet Union (0)	0	<0.01
Swedish (857)	3,385	1.78
Swiss (47)	639	0.34
Turkish (0)	11	0.01
Ukrainian (96)	351	0.18
Welsh (119)	743	0.39
West Indian, ex. Hispanic (169)	352	0.18
Bahamian (0)	0	<0.01
Barbadian (14)	14	0.01
Belizean (0)	0	<0.01
Bermudan (0)	12	0.01
British West Indian (0)	0	<0.01
Dutch West Indian (14)	14	0.01
Haitian (42)	42	0.02
Jamaican (68)	160	0.08
Trinidadian/Tobagonian (0)	0	<0.01
U.S. Virgin Islander (0)	11	0.01
West Indian (22)	90	0.05
Other West Indian (9)	9	<0.01
Yugoslavian (394)	492	0.26

Hispanic Origin	Population	%
Hispanic or Latino (of any race)	29,261	15.56
Central American, ex. Mexican	4,051	2.15
Costa Rican	20	0.01
Guatemalan	3,372	1.79
Honduran	197	0.10
Nicaraguan	45	0.02
Panamanian	35	0.02
Salvadoran	348	0.19
Other Central American	34	0.02
Cuban	417	0.22
Dominican Republic	1,342	0.71
Mexican	18,698	9.94
Puerto Rican	2,712	1.44
South American	337	0.18
Argentinean	41	0.02
Bolivian	21	0.01
Chilean	25	0.01
Colombian	99	0.05
Ecuadorian	41	0.02
Paraguayan	6	<0.01
Peruvian	65	0.03
Uruguayan	2	<0.01
Venezuelan	35	0.02
Other South American	2	<0.01
Other Hispanic or Latino	1,704	0.91

Race*	Population	%
African-American/Black (39,251)	44,032	23.42
Not Hispanic (37,890)	41,741	22.20
Hispanic (1,361)	2,291	1.22
American Indian/Alaska Native (1,390)	3,327	1.77
Not Hispanic (788)	2,337	1.24
Hispanic (602)	990	0.53
Alaska Athabascan *(Ala. Nat.)* (2)	3	<0.01
Aleut *(Alaska Native)* (0)	0	<0.01
Apache (6)	30	0.02
Arapaho (1)	1	<0.01
Blackfeet (8)	104	0.06
Canadian/French Am. Ind. (14)	17	0.01
Central American Ind. (73)	77	0.04
Cherokee (31)	269	0.14
Cheyenne (1)	5	<0.01
Chickasaw (3)	4	<0.01
Chippewa (229)	436	0.23

Race* (cont.)	Population	%
Choctaw (0)	15	0.01
Colville (0)	1	<0.01
Comanche (2)	9	<0.01
Cree (1)	4	<0.01
Creek (5)	12	0.01
Crow (0)	3	<0.01
Delaware (0)	0	<0.01
Hopi (0)	0	<0.01
Houma (0)	0	<0.01
Inupiat *(Alaska Native)* (1)	4	<0.01
Iroquois (2)	20	0.01
Kiowa (0)	0	<0.01
Lumbee (7)	15	0.01
Menominee (0)	0	<0.01
Mexican American Ind. (131)	166	0.09
Navajo (10)	26	0.01
Osage (0)	1	<0.01
Ottawa (148)	286	0.15
Paiute (0)	0	<0.01
Pima (0)	0	<0.01
Potawatomi (84)	166	0.09
Pueblo (0)	2	<0.01
Puget Sound Salish (0)	1	<0.01
Seminole (0)	16	0.01
Shoshone (0)	0	<0.01
Sioux (10)	43	0.02
South American Ind. (14)	25	0.01
Spanish American Ind. (12)	16	0.01
Tlingit-Haida *(Alaska Native)* (3)	4	<0.01
Tohono O'Odham (1)	1	<0.01
Tsimshian *(Alaska Native)* (0)	0	<0.01
Ute (0)	1	<0.01
Yakama (0)	0	<0.01
Yaqui (2)	3	<0.01
Yuman (1)	1	<0.01
Yup'ik *(Alaska Native)* (0)	0	<0.01
Asian (3,495)	4,532	2.41
Not Hispanic (3,445)	4,365	2.32
Hispanic (50)	167	0.09
Bangladeshi (42)	45	0.02
Bhutanese (86)	98	0.05
Burmese (398)	424	0.23
Cambodian (17)	26	0.01
Chinese, ex. Taiwanese (356)	511	0.27
Filipino (244)	451	0.24
Hmong (16)	19	0.01
Indian (344)	474	0.25
Indonesian (30)	59	0.03
Japanese (60)	173	0.09
Korean (641)	821	0.44
Laotian (24)	33	0.02
Malaysian (5)	5	<0.01
Nepalese (29)	41	0.02
Pakistani (21)	27	0.01
Sri Lankan (15)	23	0.01
Taiwanese (21)	27	0.01
Thai (24)	59	0.03
Vietnamese (967)	1,090	0.58
Hawaii Native/Pacific Islander (116)	314	0.17
Not Hispanic (58)	208	0.11
Hispanic (58)	106	0.06
Fijian (3)	9	<0.01
Guamanian/Chamorro (53)	73	0.04
Marshallese (1)	4	<0.01
Native Hawaiian (30)	81	0.04
Samoan (5)	10	0.01
Tongan (0)	0	<0.01
White (121,411)	128,050	68.10
Not Hispanic (110,890)	115,639	61.50
Hispanic (10,521)	12,411	6.60

*Notes: † The Census 2010 population figure is used to calculate the percentages in the Hispanic Origin and Race categories. Ancestry percentages are based on the 2006-2010 American Community Survey population (not shown); ‡ Numbers in parentheses indicate the number of people reporting a single ancestry; * Numbers in parentheses indicate the number of persons reporting this race alone, not in combination with any other race; Please refer to the User Guide for more information.*

Kalamazoo

Place Type: City
County: Kalamazoo
Population: 74,262

Ancestry	Population	%
Afghan (0)	0	<0.01
African, Sub-Saharan (389)	447	0.60
African (222)	280	0.38
Cape Verdean (0)	0	<0.01
Ethiopian (0)	0	<0.01
Ghanaian (0)	0	<0.01
Kenyan (23)	23	0.03
Liberian (0)	0	<0.01
Nigerian (0)	0	<0.01
Senegalese (0)	0	<0.01
Sierra Leonean (0)	0	<0.01
Somalian (0)	0	<0.01
South African (37)	37	0.05
Sudanese (0)	0	<0.01
Ugandan (61)	61	0.08
Zimbabwean (46)	46	0.06
Other Sub-Saharan African (0)	0	<0.01
Albanian (17)	17	0.02
Alsatian (0)	0	<0.01
American (1,987)	1,987	2.67
Arab (475)	503	0.68
Arab (210)	217	0.29
Egyptian (0)	0	<0.01
Iraqi (59)	59	0.08
Jordanian (0)	0	<0.01
Lebanese (74)	95	0.13
Moroccan (0)	0	<0.01
Palestinian (0)	0	<0.01
Syrian (0)	0	<0.01
Other Arab (132)	132	0.18
Armenian (37)	114	0.15
Assyrian/Chaldean/Syriac (26)	40	0.05
Australian (0)	35	0.05
Austrian (86)	315	0.42
Basque (0)	0	<0.01
Belgian (13)	193	0.26
Brazilian (0)	0	<0.01
British (180)	308	0.41
Bulgarian (0)	55	0.07
Cajun (0)	9	0.01
Canadian (69)	228	0.31
Carpatho Rusyn (0)	0	<0.01
Celtic (47)	47	0.06
Croatian (59)	85	0.11
Cypriot (0)	0	<0.01
Czech (128)	400	0.54
Czechoslovakian (68)	123	0.17
Danish (46)	223	0.30
Dutch (2,297)	6,165	8.30
Eastern European (172)	180	0.24
English (2,037)	7,733	10.41
Estonian (0)	0	<0.01
European (629)	758	1.02
Finnish (55)	307	0.41
French, ex. Basque (287)	2,458	3.31
French Canadian (185)	938	1.26
German (4,772)	15,282	20.56
German Russian (0)	0	<0.01
Greek (95)	193	0.26
Guyanese (0)	0	<0.01
Hungarian (128)	506	0.68
Icelander (25)	65	0.09
Iranian (33)	44	0.06
Irish (1,856)	8,753	11.78
Israeli (14)	14	0.02
Italian (787)	2,422	3.26
Latvian (76)	146	0.20
Lithuanian (32)	226	0.30
Luxemburger (0)	24	0.03
Macedonian (40)	40	0.05
Maltese (0)	0	<0.01
New Zealander (0)	0	<0.01
Northern European (0)	5	0.01

Ancestry	Population	%
Norwegian (240)	843	1.13
Pennsylvania German (13)	51	0.07
Polish (1,130)	4,217	5.67
Portuguese (0)	37	0.05
Romanian (49)	91	0.12
Russian (44)	327	0.44
Scandinavian (82)	135	0.18
Scotch-Irish (385)	1,279	1.72
Scottish (528)	1,932	2.60
Serbian (2)	19	0.03
Slavic (21)	21	0.03
Slovak (46)	138	0.19
Slovene (0)	29	0.04
Soviet Union (0)	0	<0.01
Swedish (260)	1,224	1.65
Swiss (23)	122	0.16
Turkish (0)	0	<0.01
Ukrainian (49)	173	0.23
Welsh (134)	534	0.72
West Indian, ex. Hispanic (0)	26	0.03
Bahamian (0)	0	<0.01
Barbadian (0)	0	<0.01
Belizean (0)	0	<0.01
Bermudan (0)	0	<0.01
British West Indian (0)	0	<0.01
Dutch West Indian (0)	0	<0.01
Haitian (0)	0	<0.01
Jamaican (0)	26	0.03
Trinidadian/Tobagonian (0)	0	<0.01
U.S. Virgin Islander (0)	0	<0.01
West Indian (0)	0	<0.01
Other West Indian (0)	0	<0.01
Yugoslavian (30)	91	0.12

Hispanic Origin	Population	%
Hispanic or Latino (of any race)	4,736	6.38
Central American, ex. Mexican	160	0.22
Costa Rican	5	0.01
Guatemalan	73	0.10
Honduran	18	0.02
Nicaraguan	5	0.01
Panamanian	27	0.04
Salvadoran	32	0.04
Other Central American	0	<0.01
Cuban	108	0.15
Dominican Republic	189	0.25
Mexican	3,430	4.62
Puerto Rican	340	0.46
South American	138	0.19
Argentinean	42	0.06
Bolivian	7	0.01
Chilean	7	0.01
Colombian	27	0.04
Ecuadorian	19	0.03
Paraguayan	1	<0.01
Peruvian	11	0.01
Uruguayan	1	<0.01
Venezuelan	22	0.03
Other South American	1	<0.01
Other Hispanic or Latino	371	0.50

Race*	Population	%
African-American/Black (16,460)	18,823	25.35
Not Hispanic (16,117)	18,255	24.58
Hispanic (343)	568	0.76
American Indian/Alaska Native (384)	1,341	1.81
Not Hispanic (312)	1,134	1.53
Hispanic (72)	207	0.28
Alaska Athabascan (Ala. Nat.) (1)	2	<0.01
Aleut (Alaska Native) (1)	1	<0.01
Apache (3)	14	0.02
Arapaho (0)	0	<0.01
Blackfeet (8)	40	0.05
Canadian/French Am. Ind. (2)	5	0.01
Central American Ind. (1)	1	<0.01
Cherokee (30)	202	0.27
Cheyenne (0)	2	<0.01
Chickasaw (0)	1	<0.01
Chippewa (63)	116	0.16

Race*	Population	%
Choctaw (4)	23	0.03
Colville (0)	0	<0.01
Comanche (2)	4	0.01
Cree (1)	2	<0.01
Creek (2)	11	0.01
Crow (2)	2	<0.01
Delaware (0)	2	<0.01
Hopi (0)	0	<0.01
Houma (0)	0	<0.01
Inupiat (Alaska Native) (0)	0	<0.01
Iroquois (6)	17	0.02
Kiowa (0)	0	<0.01
Lumbee (1)	1	<0.01
Menominee (0)	0	<0.01
Mexican American Ind. (13)	25	0.03
Navajo (7)	9	0.01
Osage (0)	0	<0.01
Ottawa (20)	23	0.03
Paiute (0)	0	<0.01
Pima (0)	0	<0.01
Potawatomi (34)	81	0.11
Pueblo (4)	4	0.01
Puget Sound Salish (0)	0	<0.01
Seminole (2)	2	<0.01
Shoshone (1)	1	<0.01
Sioux (7)	17	0.02
South American Ind. (1)	2	<0.01
Spanish American Ind. (0)	1	<0.01
Tlingit-Haida (Alaska Native) (0)	2	<0.01
Tohono O'Odham (0)	0	<0.01
Tsimshian (Alaska Native) (0)	0	<0.01
Ute (0)	0	<0.01
Yakama (0)	0	<0.01
Yaqui (6)	10	0.01
Yuman (0)	0	<0.01
Yup'ik (Alaska Native) (0)	0	<0.01
Asian (1,279)	1,766	2.38
Not Hispanic (1,266)	1,708	2.30
Hispanic (13)	58	0.08
Bangladeshi (12)	12	0.02
Bhutanese (0)	0	<0.01
Burmese (0)	1	<0.01
Cambodian (10)	22	0.03
Chinese, ex. Taiwanese (270)	325	0.44
Filipino (80)	178	0.24
Hmong (6)	6	0.01
Indian (396)	466	0.63
Indonesian (10)	20	0.03
Japanese (76)	125	0.17
Korean (161)	222	0.30
Laotian (6)	13	0.02
Malaysian (36)	43	0.06
Nepalese (10)	11	0.01
Pakistani (44)	51	0.07
Sri Lankan (2)	3	<0.01
Taiwanese (21)	22	0.03
Thai (21)	60	0.08
Vietnamese (72)	94	0.13
Hawaii Native/Pacific Islander (27)	123	0.17
Not Hispanic (20)	91	0.12
Hispanic (7)	32	0.04
Fijian (1)	1	<0.01
Guamanian/Chamorro (5)	6	0.01
Marshallese (0)	0	<0.01
Native Hawaiian (8)	28	0.04
Samoan (4)	15	0.02
Tongan (0)	1	<0.01
White (50,604)	53,580	72.15
Not Hispanic (48,752)	51,354	69.15
Hispanic (1,852)	2,226	3.00

Notes: † The Census 2010 population figure is used to calculate the percentages in the Hispanic Origin and Race categories. Ancestry percentages are based on the 2006-2010 American Community Survey population (not shown); ‡ Numbers in parentheses indicate the number of people reporting a single ancestry; * Numbers in parentheses indicate the number of persons reporting this race alone, not in combination with any other race; Please refer to the User Guide for more information.

Lansing

Place Type: City
County: Ingham
Population: 114,297

Ancestry	Population	%
Afghan (0)	0	<0.01
African, Sub-Saharan (1,615)	1,905	1.65
African (634)	906	0.78
Cape Verdean (0)	0	<0.01
Ethiopian (107)	107	0.09
Ghanaian (0)	0	<0.01
Kenyan (0)	0	<0.01
Liberian (0)	0	<0.01
Nigerian (41)	41	0.04
Senegalese (0)	0	<0.01
Sierra Leonean (0)	0	<0.01
Somalian (305)	316	0.27
South African (0)	7	0.01
Sudanese (239)	239	0.21
Ugandan (0)	0	<0.01
Zimbabwean (0)	0	<0.01
Other Sub-Saharan African (289)	289	0.25
Albanian (0)	0	<0.01
Alsatian (0)	0	<0.01
American (6,973)	6,973	6.03
Arab (751)	1,000	0.86
Arab (77)	110	0.10
Egyptian (28)	28	0.02
Iraqi (246)	246	0.21
Jordanian (0)	0	<0.01
Lebanese (382)	579	0.50
Moroccan (0)	0	<0.01
Palestinian (0)	0	<0.01
Syrian (10)	10	0.01
Other Arab (8)	27	0.02
Armenian (15)	54	0.05
Assyrian/Chaldean/Syriac (0)	0	<0.01
Australian (13)	13	0.01
Austrian (13)	179	0.15
Basque (0)	0	<0.01
Belgian (48)	326	0.28
Brazilian (10)	19	0.02
British (200)	451	0.39
Bulgarian (31)	77	0.07
Cajun (0)	0	<0.01
Canadian (76)	276	0.24
Carpatho Rusyn (0)	0	<0.01
Celtic (15)	24	0.02
Croatian (106)	255	0.22
Cypriot (9)	9	0.01
Czech (47)	431	0.37
Czechoslovakian (63)	140	0.12
Danish (10)	223	0.19
Dutch (908)	3,759	3.25
Eastern European (45)	65	0.06
English (2,707)	10,696	9.25
Estonian (0)	11	0.01
European (955)	1,260	1.09
Finnish (115)	462	0.40
French, ex. Basque (311)	3,355	2.90
French Canadian (246)	1,314	1.14
German (5,318)	21,220	18.35
German Russian (6)	6	0.01
Greek (237)	465	0.40
Guyanese (0)	0	<0.01
Hungarian (178)	805	0.70
Icelander (0)	0	<0.01
Iranian (7)	26	0.02
Irish (2,924)	12,586	10.88
Israeli (0)	0	<0.01
Italian (1,066)	3,473	3.00
Latvian (31)	41	0.04
Lithuanian (120)	241	0.21
Luxemburger (0)	0	<0.01
Macedonian (11)	33	0.03
Maltese (0)	9	0.01
New Zealander (0)	9	0.01
Northern European (77)	106	0.09

Ancestry	Population	%
Norwegian (156)	774	0.67
Pennsylvania German (41)	83	0.07
Polish (1,141)	4,385	3.79
Portuguese (23)	41	0.04
Romanian (11)	115	0.10
Russian (101)	626	0.54
Scandinavian (57)	128	0.11
Scotch-Irish (542)	1,369	1.18
Scottish (415)	2,375	2.05
Serbian (46)	73	0.06
Slavic (9)	35	0.03
Slovak (101)	164	0.14
Slovene (21)	31	0.03
Soviet Union (0)	0	<0.01
Swedish (277)	1,420	1.23
Swiss (17)	187	0.16
Turkish (22)	22	0.02
Ukrainian (126)	369	0.32
Welsh (83)	606	0.52
West Indian, ex. Hispanic (468)	601	0.52
Bahamian (0)	0	<0.01
Barbadian (0)	37	0.03
Belizean (0)	0	<0.01
Bermudan (0)	0	<0.01
British West Indian (0)	0	<0.01
Dutch West Indian (0)	0	<0.01
Haitian (312)	336	0.29
Jamaican (138)	194	0.17
Trinidadian/Tobagonian (18)	18	0.02
U.S. Virgin Islander (0)	0	<0.01
West Indian (0)	0	<0.01
Other West Indian (0)	16	0.01
Yugoslavian (94)	145	0.13

Hispanic Origin	Population	%
Hispanic or Latino (of any race)	14,292	12.50
Central American, ex. Mexican	211	0.18
Costa Rican	19	0.02
Guatemalan	86	0.08
Honduran	39	0.03
Nicaraguan	10	0.01
Panamanian	26	0.02
Salvadoran	27	0.02
Other Central American	4	<0.01
Cuban	1,193	1.04
Dominican Republic	56	0.05
Mexican	10,870	9.51
Puerto Rican	701	0.61
South American	251	0.22
Argentinean	37	0.03
Bolivian	12	0.01
Chilean	17	0.01
Colombian	78	0.07
Ecuadorian	39	0.03
Paraguayan	8	0.01
Peruvian	29	0.03
Uruguayan	6	0.01
Venezuelan	25	0.02
Other South American	0	<0.01
Other Hispanic or Latino	1,010	0.88

Race*	Population	%
African-American/Black (27,138)	31,830	27.85
Not Hispanic (26,194)	30,058	26.30
Hispanic (944)	1,772	1.55
American Indian/Alaska Native (882)	2,601	2.28
Not Hispanic (681)	2,048	1.79
Hispanic (201)	553	0.48
Alaska Athabascan (Ala. Nat.) (0)	1	<0.01
Aleut (Alaska Native) (0)	2	<0.01
Apache (14)	40	0.03
Arapaho (0)	1	<0.01
Blackfeet (18)	147	0.13
Canadian/French Am. Ind. (20)	29	0.03
Central American Ind. (2)	2	<0.01
Cherokee (39)	241	0.21
Cheyenne (1)	3	<0.01
Chickasaw (1)	3	<0.01
Chippewa (179)	381	0.33

Race*	Population	%
Choctaw (7)	36	0.03
Colville (0)	0	<0.01
Comanche (1)	3	<0.01
Cree (0)	6	0.01
Creek (0)	6	0.01
Crow (0)	0	<0.01
Delaware (2)	2	<0.01
Hopi (1)	1	<0.01
Houma (1)	1	<0.01
Inupiat (Alaska Native) (2)	3	<0.01
Iroquois (19)	49	0.04
Kiowa (0)	0	<0.01
Lumbee (0)	3	<0.01
Menominee (2)	4	<0.01
Mexican American Ind. (46)	91	0.08
Navajo (5)	8	0.01
Osage (0)	1	<0.01
Ottawa (110)	191	0.17
Paiute (1)	2	<0.01
Pima (0)	0	<0.01
Potawatomi (26)	51	0.04
Pueblo (2)	2	<0.01
Puget Sound Salish (0)	0	<0.01
Seminole (1)	13	0.01
Shoshone (0)	1	<0.01
Sioux (8)	43	0.04
South American Ind. (4)	8	0.01
Spanish American Ind. (1)	1	<0.01
Tlingit-Haida (Alaska Native) (4)	5	<0.01
Tohono O'Odham (1)	2	<0.01
Tsimshian (Alaska Native) (0)	0	<0.01
Ute (0)	1	<0.01
Yakama (0)	0	<0.01
Yaqui (1)	4	<0.01
Yuman (0)	0	<0.01
Yup'ik (Alaska Native) (3)	3	<0.01
Asian (4,256)	5,060	4.43
Not Hispanic (4,202)	4,924	4.31
Hispanic (54)	136	0.12
Bangladeshi (6)	6	0.01
Bhutanese (219)	281	0.25
Burmese (353)	383	0.34
Cambodian (11)	17	0.01
Chinese, ex. Taiwanese (565)	689	0.60
Filipino (149)	272	0.24
Hmong (604)	643	0.56
Indian (576)	674	0.59
Indonesian (19)	25	0.02
Japanese (56)	157	0.14
Korean (321)	404	0.35
Laotian (45)	60	0.05
Malaysian (18)	20	0.02
Nepalese (70)	113	0.10
Pakistani (39)	57	0.05
Sri Lankan (18)	21	0.02
Taiwanese (18)	21	0.02
Thai (43)	60	0.05
Vietnamese (928)	993	0.87
Hawaii Native/Pacific Islander (54)	194	0.17
Not Hispanic (38)	148	0.13
Hispanic (16)	46	0.04
Fijian (0)	0	<0.01
Guamanian/Chamorro (13)	22	0.02
Marshallese (2)	2	<0.01
Native Hawaiian (15)	77	0.07
Samoan (10)	34	0.03
Tongan (1)	1	<0.01
White (69,983)	76,134	66.61
Not Hispanic (63,381)	68,146	59.62
Hispanic (6,602)	7,988	6.99

Notes: † The Census 2010 population figure is used to calculate the percentages in the Hispanic Origin and Race categories. Ancestry percentages are based on the 2006-2010 American Community Survey population (not shown); ‡ Numbers in parentheses indicate the number of people reporting a single ancestry; * Numbers in parentheses indicate the number of persons reporting this race alone, not in combination with any other race; Please refer to the User Guide for more information.

Livonia

Place Type: City
County: Wayne
Population: 96,942

Ancestry	Population	%
Afghan (0)	0	<0.01
African, Sub-Saharan (232)	255	0.26
African (54)	77	0.08
Cape Verdean (0)	0	<0.01
Ethiopian (0)	0	<0.01
Ghanaian (0)	0	<0.01
Kenyan (0)	0	<0.01
Liberian (0)	0	<0.01
Nigerian (37)	37	0.04
Senegalese (0)	0	<0.01
Sierra Leonean (0)	0	<0.01
Somalian (0)	0	<0.01
South African (27)	27	0.03
Sudanese (0)	0	<0.01
Ugandan (0)	0	<0.01
Zimbabwean (0)	0	<0.01
Other Sub-Saharan African (114)	114	0.12
Albanian (381)	420	0.43
Alsatian (0)	0	<0.01
American (5,356)	5,356	5.47
Arab (1,779)	2,374	2.42
Arab (904)	1,013	1.03
Egyptian (0)	15	0.02
Iraqi (50)	50	0.05
Jordanian (152)	216	0.22
Lebanese (268)	668	0.68
Moroccan (0)	0	<0.01
Palestinian (220)	220	0.22
Syrian (92)	99	0.10
Other Arab (93)	93	0.09
Armenian (358)	580	0.59
Assyrian/Chaldean/Syriac (65)	95	0.10
Australian (0)	10	0.01
Austrian (54)	432	0.44
Basque (0)	0	<0.01
Belgian (55)	314	0.32
Brazilian (0)	0	<0.01
British (345)	652	0.67
Bulgarian (49)	60	0.06
Cajun (0)	0	<0.01
Canadian (359)	885	0.90
Carpatho Rusyn (0)	0	<0.01
Celtic (44)	51	0.05
Croatian (101)	301	0.31
Cypriot (0)	0	<0.01
Czech (100)	428	0.44
Czechoslovakian (51)	174	0.18
Danish (142)	494	0.50
Dutch (255)	1,539	1.57
Eastern European (98)	133	0.14
English (2,521)	11,053	11.29
Estonian (8)	8	0.01
European (747)	832	0.85
Finnish (749)	2,019	2.06
French, ex. Basque (644)	5,107	5.22
French Canadian (925)	2,931	2.99
German (5,336)	22,261	22.74
German Russian (0)	0	<0.01
Greek (695)	1,272	1.30
Guyanese (0)	0	<0.01
Hungarian (596)	1,923	1.96
Icelander (0)	11	0.01
Iranian (76)	76	0.08
Irish (3,587)	16,361	16.71
Israeli (0)	0	<0.01
Italian (3,212)	8,822	9.01
Latvian (45)	65	0.07
Lithuanian (348)	637	0.65
Luxemburger (0)	0	<0.01
Macedonian (225)	293	0.30
Maltese (305)	845	0.86
New Zealander (10)	10	0.01
Northern European (126)	126	0.13
Norwegian (173)	789	0.81
Pennsylvania German (0)	47	0.05
Polish (7,033)	17,428	17.80
Portuguese (21)	71	0.07
Romanian (322)	524	0.54
Russian (340)	1,101	1.12
Scandinavian (51)	104	0.11
Scotch-Irish (783)	2,368	2.42
Scottish (1,086)	4,098	4.19
Serbian (172)	253	0.26
Slavic (8)	95	0.10
Slovak (199)	667	0.68
Slovene (25)	72	0.07
Soviet Union (0)	0	<0.01
Swedish (158)	1,449	1.48
Swiss (11)	174	0.18
Turkish (26)	49	0.05
Ukrainian (374)	1,041	1.06
Welsh (39)	873	0.89
West Indian, ex. Hispanic (27)	32	0.03
Bahamian (0)	0	<0.01
Barbadian (12)	12	0.01
Belizean (0)	0	<0.01
Bermudan (0)	0	<0.01
British West Indian (0)	0	<0.01
Dutch West Indian (0)	0	<0.01
Haitian (0)	0	<0.01
Jamaican (15)	15	0.02
Trinidadian/Tobagonian (0)	5	0.01
U.S. Virgin Islander (0)	0	<0.01
West Indian (0)	0	<0.01
Other West Indian (0)	0	<0.01
Yugoslavian (83)	343	0.35

Hispanic Origin	Population	%
Hispanic or Latino (of any race)	2,399	2.47
Central American, ex. Mexican	104	0.11
Costa Rican	1	<0.01
Guatemalan	49	0.05
Honduran	11	0.01
Nicaraguan	4	<0.01
Panamanian	12	0.01
Salvadoran	26	0.03
Other Central American	1	<0.01
Cuban	90	0.09
Dominican Republic	21	0.02
Mexican	1,542	1.59
Puerto Rican	203	0.21
South American	179	0.18
Argentinean	51	0.05
Bolivian	9	0.01
Chilean	11	0.01
Colombian	40	0.04
Ecuadorian	17	0.02
Paraguayan	12	0.01
Peruvian	31	0.03
Uruguayan	3	<0.01
Venezuelan	3	<0.01
Other South American	2	<0.01
Other Hispanic or Latino	260	0.27

Race*	Population	%
African-American/Black (3,309)	3,691	3.81
Not Hispanic (3,264)	3,609	3.72
Hispanic (45)	82	0.08
American Indian/Alaska Native (237)	632	0.65
Not Hispanic (204)	561	0.58
Hispanic (33)	71	0.07
Alaska Athabascan (Ala. Nat.) (0)	0	<0.01
Aleut (Alaska Native) (0)	0	<0.01
Apache (0)	1	<0.01
Arapaho (0)	0	<0.01
Blackfeet (5)	13	0.01
Canadian/French Am. Ind. (2)	11	0.01
Central American Ind. (2)	2	<0.01
Cherokee (10)	84	0.09
Cheyenne (0)	0	<0.01
Chickasaw (0)	0	<0.01
Chippewa (50)	116	0.12

	Population	%
Choctaw (3)	10	0.01
Colville (0)	1	<0.01
Comanche (0)	0	<0.01
Cree (0)	3	<0.01
Creek (4)	7	0.01
Crow (0)	2	<0.01
Delaware (3)	4	<0.01
Hopi (0)	0	<0.01
Houma (0)	0	<0.01
Inupiat (Alaska Native) (0)	1	<0.01
Iroquois (27)	48	0.05
Kiowa (0)	0	<0.01
Lumbee (13)	20	0.02
Menominee (3)	7	0.01
Mexican American Ind. (20)	28	0.03
Navajo (3)	3	<0.01
Osage (0)	1	<0.01
Ottawa (8)	18	0.02
Paiute (1)	3	<0.01
Pima (0)	0	<0.01
Potawatomi (4)	4	<0.01
Pueblo (3)	6	0.01
Puget Sound Salish (0)	1	<0.01
Seminole (0)	0	<0.01
Shoshone (0)	0	<0.01
Sioux (2)	14	0.01
South American Ind. (0)	0	<0.01
Spanish American Ind. (0)	0	<0.01
Tlingit-Haida (Alaska Native) (0)	0	<0.01
Tohono O'Odham (0)	0	<0.01
Tsimshian (Alaska Native) (0)	0	<0.01
Ute (0)	0	<0.01
Yakama (0)	0	<0.01
Yaqui (0)	0	<0.01
Yuman (0)	0	<0.01
Yup'ik (Alaska Native) (0)	0	<0.01
Asian (2,459)	3,022	3.12
Not Hispanic (2,441)	2,980	3.07
Hispanic (18)	42	0.04
Bangladeshi (11)	11	0.01
Bhutanese (0)	0	<0.01
Burmese (0)	0	<0.01
Cambodian (11)	11	0.01
Chinese, ex. Taiwanese (509)	597	0.62
Filipino (433)	566	0.58
Hmong (1)	3	<0.01
Indian (882)	930	0.96
Indonesian (4)	10	0.01
Japanese (95)	175	0.18
Korean (166)	227	0.23
Laotian (3)	5	0.01
Malaysian (3)	5	0.01
Nepalese (2)	2	<0.01
Pakistani (70)	81	0.08
Sri Lankan (6)	8	0.01
Taiwanese (11)	19	0.02
Thai (15)	27	0.03
Vietnamese (193)	208	0.21
Hawaii Native/Pacific Islander (12)	60	0.06
Not Hispanic (11)	55	0.06
Hispanic (1)	5	0.01
Fijian (0)	0	<0.01
Guamanian/Chamorro (1)	5	0.01
Marshallese (0)	0	<0.01
Native Hawaiian (2)	21	0.02
Samoan (2)	3	<0.01
Tongan (0)	0	<0.01
White (89,159)	90,446	93.30
Not Hispanic (87,332)	88,468	91.26
Hispanic (1,827)	1,978	2.04

Notes: † The Census 2010 population figure is used to calculate the percentages in the Hispanic Origin and Race categories. Ancestry percentages are based on the 2006-2010 American Community Survey population (not shown); ‡ Numbers in parentheses indicate the number of people reporting a single ancestry; * Numbers in parentheses indicate the number of persons reporting this race alone, not in combination with any other race; Please refer to the User Guide for more information.

Macomb

Place Type: Township
County: Macomb
Population: 79,580

Ancestry	Population	%
Afghan (0)	0	<0.01
African, Sub-Saharan (527)	527	0.70
African (454)	454	0.61
Cape Verdean (0)	0	<0.01
Ethiopian (0)	0	<0.01
Ghanaian (0)	0	<0.01
Kenyan (0)	0	<0.01
Liberian (19)	19	0.03
Nigerian (28)	28	0.04
Senegalese (0)	0	<0.01
Sierra Leonean (0)	0	<0.01
Somalian (0)	0	<0.01
South African (26)	26	0.03
Sudanese (0)	0	<0.01
Ugandan (0)	0	<0.01
Zimbabwean (0)	0	<0.01
Other Sub-Saharan African (0)	0	<0.01
Albanian (1,820)	2,016	2.69
Alsatian (0)	0	<0.01
American (3,167)	3,167	4.23
Arab (874)	1,625	2.17
Arab (203)	260	0.35
Egyptian (0)	7	0.01
Iraqi (86)	124	0.17
Jordanian (48)	95	0.13
Lebanese (348)	808	1.08
Moroccan (0)	0	<0.01
Palestinian (19)	35	0.05
Syrian (54)	169	0.23
Other Arab (116)	127	0.17
Armenian (97)	262	0.35
Assyrian/Chaldean/Syriac (346)	430	0.57
Australian (0)	0	<0.01
Austrian (27)	99	0.13
Basque (0)	0	<0.01
Belgian (514)	1,860	2.48
Brazilian (0)	0	<0.01
British (52)	90	0.12
Bulgarian (0)	53	0.07
Cajun (0)	0	<0.01
Canadian (203)	571	0.76
Carpatho Rusyn (0)	12	0.02
Celtic (36)	36	0.05
Croatian (139)	220	0.29
Cypriot (0)	0	<0.01
Czech (79)	412	0.55
Czechoslovakian (29)	119	0.16
Danish (35)	69	0.09
Dutch (290)	1,243	1.66
Eastern European (47)	55	0.07
English (886)	4,987	6.66
Estonian (0)	0	<0.01
European (303)	315	0.42
Finnish (60)	458	0.61
French, ex. Basque (499)	4,292	5.73
French Canadian (482)	1,401	1.87
German (4,199)	17,908	23.92
German Russian (0)	28	0.04
Greek (240)	664	0.89
Guyanese (0)	0	<0.01
Hungarian (119)	884	1.18
Icelander (0)	16	0.02
Iranian (0)	0	<0.01
Irish (1,605)	7,998	10.68
Israeli (0)	0	<0.01
Italian (5,997)	13,499	18.03
Latvian (0)	0	<0.01
Lithuanian (20)	186	0.25
Luxemburger (0)	0	<0.01
Macedonian (964)	1,123	1.50
Maltese (108)	192	0.26
New Zealander (0)	0	<0.01
Northern European (0)	0	<0.01

Ancestry (cont.)	Population	%
Norwegian (46)	336	0.45
Pennsylvania German (0)	14	0.02
Polish (5,644)	15,670	20.93
Portuguese (7)	40	0.05
Romanian (378)	621	0.83
Russian (94)	533	0.71
Scandinavian (0)	11	0.01
Scotch-Irish (299)	861	1.15
Scottish (227)	1,376	1.84
Serbian (83)	268	0.36
Slavic (126)	204	0.27
Slovak (70)	190	0.25
Slovene (0)	58	0.08
Soviet Union (0)	0	<0.01
Swedish (291)	841	1.12
Swiss (31)	217	0.29
Turkish (36)	48	0.06
Ukrainian (147)	528	0.71
Welsh (18)	342	0.46
West Indian, ex. Hispanic (7)	7	0.01
Bahamian (0)	0	<0.01
Barbadian (0)	0	<0.01
Belizean (0)	0	<0.01
Bermudan (0)	0	<0.01
British West Indian (0)	0	<0.01
Dutch West Indian (0)	0	<0.01
Haitian (0)	0	<0.01
Jamaican (0)	0	<0.01
Trinidadian/Tobagonian (0)	0	<0.01
U.S. Virgin Islander (0)	0	<0.01
West Indian (7)	7	0.01
Other West Indian (0)	0	<0.01
Yugoslavian (782)	1,041	1.39

Hispanic Origin	Population	%
Hispanic or Latino (of any race)	1,803	2.27
Central American, ex. Mexican	74	0.09
Costa Rican	5	0.01
Guatemalan	43	0.05
Honduran	1	<0.01
Nicaraguan	0	<0.01
Panamanian	17	0.02
Salvadoran	8	0.01
Other Central American	0	<0.01
Cuban	51	0.06
Dominican Republic	14	0.02
Mexican	1,182	1.49
Puerto Rican	122	0.15
South American	113	0.14
Argentinean	21	0.03
Bolivian	0	<0.01
Chilean	6	0.01
Colombian	32	0.04
Ecuadorian	16	0.02
Paraguayan	0	<0.01
Peruvian	16	0.02
Uruguayan	4	0.01
Venezuelan	18	0.02
Other South American	0	<0.01
Other Hispanic or Latino	247	0.31

Race*	Population	%
African-American/Black (3,131)	3,522	4.43
Not Hispanic (3,096)	3,450	4.34
Hispanic (35)	72	0.09
American Indian/Alaska Native (161)	465	0.58
Not Hispanic (136)	409	0.51
Hispanic (25)	56	0.07
Alaska Athabascan (Ala. Nat.) (0)	0	<0.01
Aleut (Alaska Native) (0)	0	<0.01
Apache (1)	6	0.01
Arapaho (0)	0	<0.01
Blackfeet (1)	13	0.02
Canadian/French Am. Ind. (3)	8	0.01
Central American Ind. (0)	0	<0.01
Cherokee (15)	91	0.11
Cheyenne (0)	0	<0.01
Chickasaw (0)	1	<0.01
Chippewa (53)	78	0.10

Race* (cont.)	Population	%
Choctaw (3)	10	0.01
Colville (0)	0	<0.01
Comanche (0)	1	<0.01
Cree (0)	0	<0.01
Creek (0)	0	<0.01
Crow (0)	0	<0.01
Delaware (0)	2	<0.01
Hopi (0)	0	<0.01
Houma (0)	0	<0.01
Inupiat (Alaska Native) (0)	0	<0.01
Iroquois (20)	29	0.04
Kiowa (0)	0	<0.01
Lumbee (5)	18	0.02
Menominee (0)	0	<0.01
Mexican American Ind. (8)	10	0.01
Navajo (0)	3	<0.01
Osage (2)	6	0.01
Ottawa (8)	15	0.02
Paiute (0)	0	<0.01
Pima (0)	0	<0.01
Potawatomi (0)	1	<0.01
Pueblo (1)	1	<0.01
Puget Sound Salish (0)	0	<0.01
Seminole (1)	1	<0.01
Shoshone (0)	0	<0.01
Sioux (0)	2	<0.01
South American Ind. (0)	0	<0.01
Spanish American Ind. (0)	0	<0.01
Tlingit-Haida (Alaska Native) (0)	0	<0.01
Tohono O'Odham (0)	0	<0.01
Tsimshian (Alaska Native) (0)	0	<0.01
Ute (0)	0	<0.01
Yakama (0)	0	<0.01
Yaqui (0)	0	<0.01
Yuman (0)	0	<0.01
Yup'ik (Alaska Native) (1)	4	0.01
Asian (2,462)	2,957	3.72
Not Hispanic (2,446)	2,929	3.68
Hispanic (16)	28	0.04
Bangladeshi (17)	17	0.02
Bhutanese (0)	0	<0.01
Burmese (0)	2	<0.01
Cambodian (12)	18	0.02
Chinese, ex. Taiwanese (361)	421	0.53
Filipino (602)	774	0.97
Hmong (84)	86	0.11
Indian (657)	714	0.90
Indonesian (7)	7	0.01
Japanese (36)	82	0.10
Korean (192)	268	0.34
Laotian (18)	18	0.02
Malaysian (2)	2	<0.01
Nepalese (8)	8	0.01
Pakistani (114)	134	0.17
Sri Lankan (4)	4	0.01
Taiwanese (8)	11	0.01
Thai (7)	14	0.02
Vietnamese (238)	273	0.34
Hawaii Native/Pacific Islander (17)	68	0.09
Not Hispanic (15)	64	0.08
Hispanic (2)	4	0.01
Fijian (0)	0	<0.01
Guamanian/Chamorro (5)	13	0.02
Marshallese (0)	0	<0.01
Native Hawaiian (2)	11	0.01
Samoan (1)	4	0.01
Tongan (0)	0	<0.01
White (72,050)	73,177	91.95
Not Hispanic (70,906)	71,917	90.37
Hispanic (1,144)	1,260	1.58

Novi

Place Type: City
County: Oakland
Population: 55,224

Ancestry	Population	%
Afghan (0)	0	<0.01
African, Sub-Saharan (89)	171	0.32
African (89)	102	0.19
Cape Verdean (0)	0	<0.01
Ethiopian (0)	0	<0.01
Ghanaian (0)	0	<0.01
Kenyan (0)	0	<0.01
Liberian (0)	0	<0.01
Nigerian (0)	32	0.06
Senegalese (0)	0	<0.01
Sierra Leonean (0)	0	<0.01
Somalian (0)	0	<0.01
South African (0)	0	<0.01
Sudanese (0)	0	<0.01
Ugandan (0)	0	<0.01
Zimbabwean (0)	0	<0.01
Other Sub-Saharan African (0)	37	0.07
Albanian (240)	240	0.45
Alsatian (0)	0	<0.01
American (1,895)	1,895	3.52
Arab (973)	1,215	2.26
Arab (392)	392	0.73
Egyptian (0)	0	<0.01
Iraqi (110)	208	0.39
Jordanian (38)	48	0.09
Lebanese (265)	374	0.69
Moroccan (0)	0	<0.01
Palestinian (38)	38	0.07
Syrian (104)	104	0.19
Other Arab (26)	51	0.09
Armenian (202)	432	0.80
Assyrian/Chaldean/Syriac (373)	450	0.84
Australian (55)	72	0.13
Austrian (14)	91	0.17
Basque (0)	0	<0.01
Belgian (63)	295	0.55
Brazilian (27)	35	0.07
British (177)	390	0.72
Bulgarian (64)	84	0.16
Cajun (0)	0	<0.01
Canadian (149)	466	0.87
Carpatho Rusyn (0)	0	<0.01
Celtic (0)	0	<0.01
Croatian (9)	95	0.18
Cypriot (0)	0	<0.01
Czech (46)	242	0.45
Czechoslovakian (34)	50	0.09
Danish (28)	129	0.24
Dutch (180)	662	1.23
Eastern European (24)	36	0.07
English (1,271)	5,566	10.34
Estonian (0)	0	<0.01
European (640)	725	1.35
Finnish (100)	894	1.66
French, ex. Basque (173)	2,240	4.16
French Canadian (399)	1,132	2.10
German (2,366)	10,119	18.80
German Russian (0)	0	<0.01
Greek (277)	677	1.26
Guyanese (12)	12	0.02
Hungarian (150)	692	1.29
Icelander (0)	69	0.13
Iranian (52)	120	0.22
Irish (1,697)	6,629	12.32
Israeli (33)	70	0.13
Italian (1,496)	4,511	8.38
Latvian (0)	10	0.02
Lithuanian (21)	128	0.24
Luxemburger (0)	0	<0.01
Macedonian (46)	57	0.11
Maltese (79)	120	0.22
New Zealander (0)	0	<0.01
Northern European (67)	77	0.14

Ancestry	Population	%
Norwegian (263)	598	1.11
Pennsylvania German (0)	35	0.07
Polish (2,207)	5,841	10.85
Portuguese (17)	17	0.03
Romanian (136)	227	0.42
Russian (236)	770	1.43
Scandinavian (17)	140	0.26
Scotch-Irish (504)	1,175	2.18
Scottish (583)	2,051	3.81
Serbian (75)	142	0.26
Slavic (0)	16	0.03
Slovak (19)	196	0.36
Slovene (10)	31	0.06
Soviet Union (0)	0	<0.01
Swedish (138)	1,111	2.06
Swiss (17)	96	0.18
Turkish (0)	0	<0.01
Ukrainian (101)	398	0.74
Welsh (101)	490	0.91
West Indian, ex. Hispanic (17)	17	0.03
Bahamian (0)	0	<0.01
Barbadian (0)	0	<0.01
Belizean (0)	0	<0.01
Bermudan (0)	0	<0.01
British West Indian (0)	0	<0.01
Dutch West Indian (0)	0	<0.01
Haitian (17)	17	0.03
Jamaican (0)	0	<0.01
Trinidadian/Tobagonian (0)	0	<0.01
U.S. Virgin Islander (0)	0	<0.01
West Indian (0)	0	<0.01
Other West Indian (0)	0	<0.01
Yugoslavian (0)	47	0.09

Hispanic Origin	Population	%
Hispanic or Latino (of any race)	1,634	2.96
Central American, ex. Mexican	141	0.26
Costa Rican	3	0.01
Guatemalan	92	0.17
Honduran	13	0.02
Nicaraguan	5	0.01
Panamanian	5	0.01
Salvadoran	17	0.03
Other Central American	6	0.01
Cuban	53	0.10
Dominican Republic	22	0.04
Mexican	1,003	1.82
Puerto Rican	113	0.20
South American	131	0.24
Argentinean	14	0.03
Bolivian	3	0.01
Chilean	9	0.02
Colombian	40	0.07
Ecuadorian	2	<0.01
Paraguayan	3	0.01
Peruvian	30	0.05
Uruguayan	0	<0.01
Venezuelan	30	0.05
Other South American	0	<0.01
Other Hispanic or Latino	171	0.31

Race*	Population	%
African-American/Black (4,482)	4,848	8.78
Not Hispanic (4,451)	4,785	8.66
Hispanic (31)	63	0.11
American Indian/Alaska Native (111)	338	0.61
Not Hispanic (96)	299	0.54
Hispanic (15)	39	0.07
Alaska Athabascan (Ala. Nat.) (0)	0	<0.01
Aleut (Alaska Native) (0)	0	<0.01
Apache (1)	4	0.01
Arapaho (0)	0	<0.01
Blackfeet (1)	5	0.01
Canadian/French Am. Ind. (2)	6	0.01
Central American Ind. (0)	2	<0.01
Cherokee (12)	64	0.12
Cheyenne (1)	1	<0.01
Chickasaw (0)	1	<0.01
Chippewa (22)	41	0.07

Race*	Population	%
Choctaw (1)	4	0.01
Colville (0)	0	<0.01
Comanche (5)	5	0.01
Cree (0)	2	<0.01
Creek (1)	4	0.01
Crow (0)	0	<0.01
Delaware (0)	0	<0.01
Hopi (0)	0	<0.01
Houma (0)	0	<0.01
Inupiat (Alaska Native) (0)	4	0.01
Iroquois (3)	7	0.01
Kiowa (0)	0	<0.01
Lumbee (2)	4	0.01
Menominee (0)	0	<0.01
Mexican American Ind. (2)	2	<0.01
Navajo (1)	4	0.01
Osage (0)	0	<0.01
Ottawa (9)	10	0.02
Paiute (0)	1	<0.01
Pima (0)	0	<0.01
Potawatomi (0)	4	0.01
Pueblo (0)	0	<0.01
Puget Sound Salish (0)	0	<0.01
Seminole (0)	0	<0.01
Shoshone (1)	1	<0.01
Sioux (1)	2	<0.01
South American Ind. (1)	2	<0.01
Spanish American Ind. (0)	0	<0.01
Tlingit-Haida (Alaska Native) (0)	5	0.01
Tohono O'Odham (0)	0	<0.01
Tsimshian (Alaska Native) (0)	0	<0.01
Ute (0)	0	<0.01
Yakama (0)	0	<0.01
Yaqui (0)	0	<0.01
Yuman (0)	0	<0.01
Yup'ik (Alaska Native) (0)	0	<0.01
Asian (8,767)	9,354	16.94
Not Hispanic (8,756)	9,318	16.87
Hispanic (11)	36	0.07
Bangladeshi (20)	23	0.04
Bhutanese (0)	0	<0.01
Burmese (0)	0	<0.01
Cambodian (1)	1	<0.01
Chinese, ex. Taiwanese (1,637)	1,745	3.16
Filipino (225)	324	0.59
Hmong (7)	7	0.01
Indian (3,542)	3,657	6.62
Indonesian (11)	18	0.03
Japanese (1,984)	2,120	3.84
Korean (829)	893	1.62
Laotian (3)	4	0.01
Malaysian (6)	10	0.02
Nepalese (11)	11	0.02
Pakistani (89)	100	0.18
Sri Lankan (15)	15	0.03
Taiwanese (114)	131	0.24
Thai (14)	16	0.03
Vietnamese (146)	161	0.29
Hawaii Native/Pacific Islander (5)	51	0.09
Not Hispanic (2)	46	0.08
Hispanic (3)	5	0.01
Fijian (0)	0	<0.01
Guamanian/Chamorro (2)	9	0.02
Marshallese (0)	0	<0.01
Native Hawaiian (2)	15	0.03
Samoan (0)	3	0.01
Tongan (0)	0	<0.01
White (40,313)	41,290	74.77
Not Hispanic (39,228)	40,098	72.61
Hispanic (1,085)	1,192	2.16

*Notes: † The Census 2010 population figure is used to calculate the percentages in the Hispanic Origin and Race categories. Ancestry percentages are based on the 2006-2010 American Community Survey population (not shown); ‡ Numbers in parentheses indicate the number of people reporting a single ancestry; * Numbers in parentheses indicate the number of persons reporting this race alone, not in combination with any other race; Please refer to the User Guide for more information.*

Pontiac

Place Type: City
County: Oakland
Population: 59,515

Ancestry	Population	%
Afghan (0)	0	<0.01
African, Sub-Saharan (569)	776	1.27
African (389)	580	0.95
Cape Verdean (0)	0	<0.01
Ethiopian (39)	39	0.06
Ghanaian (0)	0	<0.01
Kenyan (0)	0	<0.01
Liberian (62)	62	0.10
Nigerian (15)	31	0.05
Senegalese (50)	50	0.08
Sierra Leonean (0)	0	<0.01
Somalian (0)	0	<0.01
South African (0)	0	<0.01
Sudanese (0)	0	<0.01
Ugandan (0)	0	<0.01
Zimbabwean (0)	0	<0.01
Other Sub-Saharan African (14)	14	0.02
Albanian (20)	20	0.03
Alsatian (0)	0	<0.01
American (1,737)	1,737	2.85
Arab (50)	135	0.22
Arab (17)	17	0.03
Egyptian (0)	0	<0.01
Iraqi (0)	0	<0.01
Jordanian (0)	0	<0.01
Lebanese (9)	72	0.12
Moroccan (9)	9	0.01
Palestinian (0)	0	<0.01
Syrian (0)	0	<0.01
Other Arab (15)	37	0.06
Armenian (43)	52	0.09
Assyrian/Chaldean/Syriac (0)	9	0.01
Australian (0)	0	<0.01
Austrian (0)	57	0.09
Basque (0)	0	<0.01
Belgian (0)	20	0.03
Brazilian (0)	9	0.01
British (60)	118	0.19
Bulgarian (0)	0	<0.01
Cajun (0)	0	<0.01
Canadian (28)	148	0.24
Carpatho Rusyn (0)	0	<0.01
Celtic (0)	0	<0.01
Croatian (27)	81	0.13
Cypriot (0)	0	<0.01
Czech (9)	86	0.14
Czechoslovakian (16)	24	0.04
Danish (0)	7	0.01
Dutch (66)	620	1.02
Eastern European (0)	0	<0.01
English (691)	2,250	3.69
Estonian (0)	0	<0.01
European (84)	115	0.19
Finnish (40)	143	0.23
French, ex. Basque (37)	906	1.49
French Canadian (218)	687	1.13
German (890)	3,983	6.53
German Russian (0)	0	<0.01
Greek (46)	286	0.47
Guyanese (0)	0	<0.01
Hungarian (78)	321	0.53
Icelander (0)	0	<0.01
Iranian (0)	0	<0.01
Irish (851)	2,896	4.75
Israeli (0)	0	<0.01
Italian (263)	1,003	1.64
Latvian (0)	0	<0.01
Lithuanian (0)	0	<0.01
Luxemburger (0)	0	<0.01
Macedonian (7)	35	0.06
Maltese (13)	13	0.02
New Zealander (0)	0	<0.01
Northern European (0)	0	<0.01

Ancestry	Population	%
Norwegian (77)	115	0.19
Pennsylvania German (4)	4	0.01
Polish (739)	1,458	2.39
Portuguese (0)	92	0.15
Romanian (47)	56	0.09
Russian (26)	192	0.31
Scandinavian (0)	0	<0.01
Scotch-Irish (219)	499	0.82
Scottish (150)	531	0.87
Serbian (0)	0	<0.01
Slavic (6)	6	0.01
Slovak (12)	42	0.07
Slovene (0)	0	<0.01
Soviet Union (0)	0	<0.01
Swedish (53)	174	0.29
Swiss (0)	0	<0.01
Turkish (0)	28	0.05
Ukrainian (0)	41	0.07
Welsh (28)	191	0.31
West Indian, ex. Hispanic (129)	814	1.33
Bahamian (0)	0	<0.01
Barbadian (0)	0	<0.01
Belizean (0)	0	<0.01
Bermudan (50)	89	0.15
British West Indian (0)	0	<0.01
Dutch West Indian (0)	0	<0.01
Haitian (10)	502	0.82
Jamaican (63)	120	0.20
Trinidadian/Tobagonian (0)	77	0.13
U.S. Virgin Islander (0)	20	0.03
West Indian (6)	6	0.01
Other West Indian (0)	0	<0.01
Yugoslavian (16)	16	0.03

Hispanic Origin	Population	%
Hispanic or Latino (of any race)	9,835	16.53
Central American, ex. Mexican	457	0.77
Costa Rican	2	<0.01
Guatemalan	20	0.03
Honduran	147	0.25
Nicaraguan	2	<0.01
Panamanian	20	0.03
Salvadoran	266	0.45
Other Central American	0	<0.01
Cuban	50	0.08
Dominican Republic	25	0.04
Mexican	6,605	11.10
Puerto Rican	2,309	3.88
South American	41	0.07
Argentinean	2	<0.01
Bolivian	3	0.01
Chilean	1	<0.01
Colombian	8	0.01
Ecuadorian	12	0.02
Paraguayan	0	<0.01
Peruvian	3	0.01
Uruguayan	0	<0.01
Venezuelan	10	0.02
Other South American	2	<0.01
Other Hispanic or Latino	348	0.58

Race*	Population	%
African-American/Black (30,988)	32,910	55.30
Not Hispanic (30,384)	31,897	53.59
Hispanic (604)	1,013	1.70
American Indian/Alaska Native (350)	990	1.66
Not Hispanic (242)	775	1.30
Hispanic (108)	215	0.36
Alaska Athabascan (Ala. Nat.) (1)	1	<0.01
Aleut (Alaska Native) (0)	0	<0.01
Apache (2)	13	0.02
Arapaho (0)	1	<0.01
Blackfeet (3)	44	0.07
Canadian/French Am. Ind. (3)	4	0.01
Central American Ind. (1)	1	<0.01
Cherokee (40)	186	0.31
Cheyenne (0)	0	<0.01
Chickasaw (0)	1	<0.01
Chippewa (65)	102	0.17

Race*	Population	%
Choctaw (2)	10	0.02
Colville (0)	0	<0.01
Comanche (0)	0	<0.01
Cree (0)	1	<0.01
Creek (1)	3	0.01
Crow (0)	7	0.01
Delaware (0)	0	<0.01
Hopi (0)	0	<0.01
Houma (0)	0	<0.01
Inupiat (Alaska Native) (0)	0	<0.01
Iroquois (5)	8	0.01
Kiowa (0)	1	<0.01
Lumbee (7)	10	0.02
Menominee (0)	0	<0.01
Mexican American Ind. (26)	36	0.06
Navajo (2)	4	0.01
Osage (0)	0	<0.01
Ottawa (12)	16	0.03
Paiute (0)	0	<0.01
Pima (0)	0	<0.01
Potawatomi (6)	15	0.03
Pueblo (0)	0	<0.01
Puget Sound Salish (0)	0	<0.01
Seminole (0)	6	0.01
Shoshone (0)	0	<0.01
Sioux (4)	14	0.02
South American Ind. (0)	0	<0.01
Spanish American Ind. (3)	3	0.01
Tlingit-Haida (Alaska Native) (0)	0	<0.01
Tohono O'Odham (0)	0	<0.01
Tsimshian (Alaska Native) (0)	0	<0.01
Ute (0)	0	<0.01
Yakama (0)	0	<0.01
Yaqui (3)	6	0.01
Yuman (0)	0	<0.01
Yup'ik (Alaska Native) (0)	0	<0.01
Asian (1,372)	1,615	2.71
Not Hispanic (1,359)	1,564	2.63
Hispanic (13)	51	0.09
Bangladeshi (1)	2	<0.01
Bhutanese (0)	0	<0.01
Burmese (0)	0	<0.01
Cambodian (34)	44	0.07
Chinese, ex. Taiwanese (186)	205	0.34
Filipino (93)	164	0.28
Hmong (675)	695	1.17
Indian (138)	171	0.29
Indonesian (2)	4	0.01
Japanese (9)	35	0.06
Korean (22)	44	0.07
Laotian (39)	47	0.08
Malaysian (1)	1	<0.01
Nepalese (0)	0	<0.01
Pakistani (7)	9	0.02
Sri Lankan (0)	0	<0.01
Taiwanese (4)	4	0.01
Thai (27)	31	0.05
Vietnamese (49)	67	0.11
Hawaii Native/Pacific Islander (12)	86	0.14
Not Hispanic (2)	46	0.08
Hispanic (10)	40	0.07
Fijian (0)	0	<0.01
Guamanian/Chamorro (5)	8	0.01
Marshallese (0)	0	<0.01
Native Hawaiian (7)	27	0.05
Samoan (0)	1	<0.01
Tongan (0)	1	<0.01
White (20,466)	22,597	37.97
Not Hispanic (15,815)	17,293	29.06
Hispanic (4,651)	5,304	8.91

Notes: † The Census 2010 population figure is used to calculate the percentages in the Hispanic Origin and Race categories. Ancestry percentages are based on the 2006-2010 American Community Survey population (not shown); ‡ Numbers in parentheses indicate the number of people reporting a single ancestry; * Numbers in parentheses indicate the number of persons reporting this race alone, not in combination with any other race; Please refer to the User Guide for more information.

Rochester Hills

Place Type: City
County: Oakland
Population: 70,995

Ancestry	Population	%
Afghan (0)	0	<0.01
African, Sub-Saharan (146)	219	0.31
African (40)	68	0.10
Cape Verdean (0)	0	<0.01
Ethiopian (0)	0	<0.01
Ghanaian (0)	0	<0.01
Kenyan (0)	0	<0.01
Liberian (0)	0	<0.01
Nigerian (12)	12	0.02
Senegalese (0)	0	<0.01
Sierra Leonean (0)	0	<0.01
Somalian (0)	0	<0.01
South African (0)	45	0.06
Sudanese (0)	0	<0.01
Ugandan (0)	0	<0.01
Zimbabwean (20)	20	0.03
Other Sub-Saharan African (74)	74	0.10
Albanian (821)	831	1.18
Alsatian (9)	9	0.01
American (2,436)	2,436	3.45
Arab (1,294)	1,483	2.10
Arab (248)	248	0.35
Egyptian (204)	213	0.30
Iraqi (280)	331	0.47
Jordanian (8)	8	0.01
Lebanese (259)	351	0.50
Moroccan (0)	0	<0.01
Palestinian (0)	0	<0.01
Syrian (134)	171	0.24
Other Arab (161)	161	0.23
Armenian (50)	86	0.12
Assyrian/Chaldean/Syriac (357)	500	0.71
Australian (9)	9	0.01
Austrian (89)	268	0.38
Basque (0)	0	<0.01
Belgian (131)	586	0.83
Brazilian (64)	75	0.11
British (213)	398	0.56
Bulgarian (12)	12	0.02
Cajun (0)	0	<0.01
Canadian (362)	733	1.04
Carpatho Rusyn (0)	0	<0.01
Celtic (11)	11	0.02
Croatian (18)	141	0.20
Cypriot (0)	0	<0.01
Czech (182)	497	0.70
Czechoslovakian (38)	107	0.15
Danish (100)	353	0.50
Dutch (294)	1,469	2.08
Eastern European (70)	83	0.12
English (1,857)	7,261	10.28
Estonian (0)	0	<0.01
European (747)	806	1.14
Finnish (145)	550	0.78
French, ex. Basque (757)	3,842	5.44
French Canadian (420)	1,183	1.68
German (4,207)	15,757	22.32
German Russian (0)	0	<0.01
Greek (356)	722	1.02
Guyanese (0)	0	<0.01
Hungarian (180)	738	1.05
Icelander (0)	0	<0.01
Iranian (189)	206	0.29
Irish (1,714)	9,197	13.03
Israeli (0)	0	<0.01
Italian (1,939)	5,615	7.95
Latvian (0)	21	0.03
Lithuanian (131)	350	0.50
Luxemburger (0)	0	<0.01
Macedonian (136)	217	0.31
Maltese (52)	221	0.31
New Zealander (0)	0	<0.01
Northern European (51)	51	0.07

Ancestry (cont.)	Population	%
Norwegian (153)	647	0.92
Pennsylvania German (0)	7	0.01
Polish (2,749)	7,882	11.16
Portuguese (87)	128	0.18
Romanian (496)	642	0.91
Russian (212)	647	0.92
Scandinavian (39)	57	0.08
Scotch-Irish (475)	1,248	1.77
Scottish (699)	2,398	3.40
Serbian (240)	382	0.54
Slavic (0)	45	0.06
Slovak (168)	480	0.68
Slovene (11)	46	0.07
Soviet Union (0)	0	<0.01
Swedish (237)	1,031	1.46
Swiss (59)	213	0.30
Turkish (0)	8	0.01
Ukrainian (459)	1,108	1.57
Welsh (114)	671	0.95
West Indian, ex. Hispanic (81)	173	0.25
Bahamian (0)	0	<0.01
Barbadian (0)	0	<0.01
Belizean (8)	8	0.01
Bermudan (0)	0	<0.01
British West Indian (0)	0	<0.01
Dutch West Indian (0)	0	<0.01
Haitian (21)	60	0.08
Jamaican (44)	44	0.06
Trinidadian/Tobagonian (0)	0	<0.01
U.S. Virgin Islander (8)	8	0.01
West Indian (0)	53	0.08
Other West Indian (0)	0	<0.01
Yugoslavian (22)	119	0.17

Hispanic Origin	Population	%
Hispanic or Latino (of any race)	2,183	3.07
Central American, ex. Mexican	92	0.13
Costa Rican	11	0.02
Guatemalan	36	0.05
Honduran	15	0.02
Nicaraguan	9	0.01
Panamanian	10	0.01
Salvadoran	11	0.02
Other Central American	0	<0.01
Cuban	49	0.07
Dominican Republic	2	<0.01
Mexican	1,331	1.87
Puerto Rican	229	0.32
South American	319	0.45
Argentinean	132	0.19
Bolivian	4	0.01
Chilean	31	0.04
Colombian	60	0.08
Ecuadorian	9	0.01
Paraguayan	3	<0.01
Peruvian	25	0.04
Uruguayan	4	0.01
Venezuelan	46	0.06
Other South American	5	0.01
Other Hispanic or Latino	161	0.23

Race*	Population	%
African-American/Black (3,228)	3,606	5.08
Not Hispanic (3,177)	3,516	4.95
Hispanic (51)	90	0.13
American Indian/Alaska Native (132)	425	0.60
Not Hispanic (108)	371	0.52
Hispanic (24)	54	0.08
Alaska Athabascan (Ala. Nat.) (0)	0	<0.01
Aleut (Alaska Native) (0)	0	<0.01
Apache (0)	4	0.01
Arapaho (0)	0	<0.01
Blackfeet (0)	7	0.01
Canadian/French Am. Ind. (1)	6	0.01
Central American Ind. (1)	1	<0.01
Cherokee (18)	103	0.15
Cheyenne (0)	0	<0.01
Chickasaw (2)	5	0.01
Chippewa (30)	67	0.09

Race* (cont.)	Population	%
Choctaw (0)	4	0.01
Colville (0)	0	<0.01
Comanche (1)	1	<0.01
Cree (0)	4	0.01
Creek (0)	3	<0.01
Crow (0)	0	<0.01
Delaware (0)	0	<0.01
Hopi (0)	0	<0.01
Houma (0)	0	<0.01
Inupiat (Alaska Native) (2)	2	<0.01
Iroquois (3)	16	0.02
Kiowa (0)	0	<0.01
Lumbee (4)	7	0.01
Menominee (0)	0	<0.01
Mexican American Ind. (9)	10	0.01
Navajo (0)	2	<0.01
Osage (1)	1	<0.01
Ottawa (1)	4	0.01
Paiute (0)	0	<0.01
Pima (0)	0	<0.01
Potawatomi (3)	10	0.01
Pueblo (0)	0	<0.01
Puget Sound Salish (0)	0	<0.01
Seminole (1)	5	0.01
Shoshone (0)	0	<0.01
Sioux (0)	6	0.01
South American Ind. (1)	1	<0.01
Spanish American Ind. (0)	0	<0.01
Tlingit-Haida (Alaska Native) (0)	0	<0.01
Tohono O'Odham (0)	0	<0.01
Tsimshian (Alaska Native) (1)	1	<0.01
Ute (0)	0	<0.01
Yakama (0)	0	<0.01
Yaqui (0)	0	<0.01
Yuman (0)	0	<0.01
Yup'ik (Alaska Native) (0)	0	<0.01
Asian (7,458)	8,144	11.47
Not Hispanic (7,447)	8,104	11.41
Hispanic (11)	40	0.06
Bangladeshi (74)	80	0.11
Bhutanese (0)	0	<0.01
Burmese (4)	4	0.01
Cambodian (7)	12	0.02
Chinese, ex. Taiwanese (1,367)	1,487	2.09
Filipino (504)	655	0.92
Hmong (67)	70	0.10
Indian (3,337)	3,470	4.89
Indonesian (14)	17	0.02
Japanese (211)	299	0.42
Korean (847)	891	1.26
Laotian (6)	10	0.01
Malaysian (9)	18	0.03
Nepalese (15)	15	0.02
Pakistani (498)	522	0.74
Sri Lankan (36)	36	0.05
Taiwanese (124)	133	0.19
Thai (40)	50	0.07
Vietnamese (169)	208	0.29
Hawaii Native/Pacific Islander (9)	31	0.04
Not Hispanic (6)	27	0.04
Hispanic (3)	4	0.01
Fijian (0)	0	<0.01
Guamanian/Chamorro (1)	1	<0.01
Marshallese (0)	0	<0.01
Native Hawaiian (8)	15	0.02
Samoan (0)	1	<0.01
Tongan (0)	0	<0.01
White (58,309)	59,497	83.80
Not Hispanic (56,818)	57,852	81.49
Hispanic (1,491)	1,645	2.32

*Notes: † The Census 2010 population figure is used to calculate the percentages in the Hispanic Origin and Race categories. Ancestry percentages are based on the 2006-2010 American Community Survey population (not shown); ‡ Numbers in parentheses indicate the number of people reporting a single ancestry; * Numbers in parentheses indicate the number of persons reporting this race alone, not in combination with any other race; Please refer to the User Guide for more information.*

Royal Oak

Place Type: City
County: Oakland
Population: 57,236

Ancestry	Population	%
Afghan (0)	0	<0.01
African, Sub-Saharan (33)	58	0.10
African (20)	45	0.08
Cape Verdean (0)	0	<0.01
Ethiopian (13)	13	0.02
Ghanaian (0)	0	<0.01
Kenyan (0)	0	<0.01
Liberian (0)	0	<0.01
Nigerian (0)	0	<0.01
Senegalese (0)	0	<0.01
Sierra Leonean (0)	0	<0.01
Somalian (0)	0	<0.01
South African (0)	0	<0.01
Sudanese (0)	0	<0.01
Ugandan (0)	0	<0.01
Zimbabwean (0)	0	<0.01
Other Sub-Saharan African (0)	0	<0.01
Albanian (238)	238	0.41
Alsatian (0)	0	<0.01
American (2,007)	2,007	3.48
Arab (477)	910	1.58
Arab (42)	94	0.16
Egyptian (0)	17	0.03
Iraqi (124)	181	0.31
Jordanian (16)	16	0.03
Lebanese (162)	411	0.71
Moroccan (0)	0	<0.01
Palestinian (0)	0	<0.01
Syrian (10)	68	0.12
Other Arab (123)	123	0.21
Armenian (139)	351	0.61
Assyrian/Chaldean/Syriac (59)	116	0.20
Australian (0)	19	0.03
Austrian (98)	466	0.81
Basque (0)	0	<0.01
Belgian (122)	424	0.73
Brazilian (12)	26	0.05
British (206)	445	0.77
Bulgarian (0)	22	0.04
Cajun (0)	0	<0.01
Canadian (269)	559	0.97
Carpatho Rusyn (7)	39	0.07
Celtic (0)	13	0.02
Croatian (66)	154	0.27
Cypriot (10)	10	0.02
Czech (92)	449	0.78
Czechoslovakian (54)	103	0.18
Danish (60)	247	0.43
Dutch (260)	1,581	2.74
Eastern European (160)	181	0.31
English (2,238)	8,727	15.11
Estonian (0)	0	<0.01
European (802)	865	1.50
Finnish (277)	747	1.29
French, ex. Basque (277)	2,993	5.18
French Canadian (411)	1,318	2.28
German (3,817)	14,457	25.04
German Russian (0)	0	<0.01
Greek (341)	654	1.13
Guyanese (20)	20	0.03
Hungarian (223)	882	1.53
Icelander (0)	0	<0.01
Iranian (18)	18	0.03
Irish (2,282)	9,767	16.92
Israeli (0)	0	<0.01
Italian (1,353)	4,293	7.43
Latvian (34)	51	0.09
Lithuanian (84)	353	0.61
Luxemburger (0)	16	0.03
Macedonian (0)	43	0.07
Maltese (59)	88	0.15
New Zealander (43)	43	0.07
Northern European (123)	123	0.21
Norwegian (129)	596	1.03
Pennsylvania German (0)	10	0.02
Polish (2,827)	7,841	13.58
Portuguese (46)	46	0.08
Romanian (44)	310	0.54
Russian (414)	1,263	2.19
Scandinavian (28)	80	0.14
Scotch-Irish (468)	1,472	2.55
Scottish (735)	2,460	4.26
Serbian (98)	264	0.46
Slavic (13)	59	0.10
Slovak (79)	191	0.33
Slovene (57)	110	0.19
Soviet Union (0)	0	<0.01
Swedish (231)	1,302	2.25
Swiss (38)	228	0.39
Turkish (41)	41	0.07
Ukrainian (95)	603	1.04
Welsh (124)	492	0.85
West Indian, ex. Hispanic (11)	88	0.15
Bahamian (11)	11	0.02
Barbadian (0)	64	0.11
Belizean (0)	0	<0.01
Bermudan (0)	0	<0.01
British West Indian (0)	0	<0.01
Dutch West Indian (0)	0	<0.01
Haitian (0)	0	<0.01
Jamaican (0)	7	0.01
Trinidadian/Tobagonian (0)	6	0.01
U.S. Virgin Islander (0)	0	<0.01
West Indian (0)	0	<0.01
Other West Indian (0)	0	<0.01
Yugoslavian (21)	44	0.08

Hispanic Origin	Population	%
Hispanic or Latino (of any race)	1,340	2.34
Central American, ex. Mexican	66	0.12
Costa Rican	4	0.01
Guatemalan	17	0.03
Honduran	12	0.02
Nicaraguan	9	0.02
Panamanian	8	0.01
Salvadoran	15	0.03
Other Central American	1	<0.01
Cuban	68	0.12
Dominican Republic	11	0.02
Mexican	741	1.29
Puerto Rican	111	0.19
South American	168	0.29
Argentinean	33	0.06
Bolivian	3	0.01
Chilean	14	0.02
Colombian	49	0.09
Ecuadorian	21	0.04
Paraguayan	1	<0.01
Peruvian	20	0.03
Uruguayan	3	0.01
Venezuelan	24	0.04
Other South American	0	<0.01
Other Hispanic or Latino	175	0.31

Race*	Population	%
African-American/Black (2,435)	2,866	5.01
Not Hispanic (2,399)	2,795	4.88
Hispanic (36)	71	0.12
American Indian/Alaska Native (153)	453	0.79
Not Hispanic (127)	403	0.70
Hispanic (26)	50	0.09
Alaska Athabascan (Ala. Nat.) (0)	0	<0.01
Aleut (Alaska Native) (0)	0	<0.01
Apache (4)	11	0.02
Arapaho (0)	0	<0.01
Blackfeet (6)	24	0.04
Canadian/French Am. Ind. (2)	10	0.02
Central American Ind. (1)	1	<0.01
Cherokee (21)	75	0.13
Cheyenne (0)	1	<0.01
Chickasaw (0)	1	<0.01
Chippewa (41)	84	0.15

Choctaw (2)	8	0.01
Colville (0)	0	<0.01
Comanche (0)	0	<0.01
Cree (0)	0	<0.01
Creek (2)	4	0.01
Crow (0)	0	<0.01
Delaware (0)	1	<0.01
Hopi (1)	1	<0.01
Houma (0)	0	<0.01
Inupiat (Alaska Native) (0)	0	<0.01
Iroquois (15)	20	0.03
Kiowa (0)	0	<0.01
Lumbee (5)	11	0.02
Menominee (0)	0	<0.01
Mexican American Ind. (2)	6	0.01
Navajo (1)	1	<0.01
Osage (0)	2	<0.01
Ottawa (4)	23	0.04
Paiute (0)	0	<0.01
Pima (0)	0	<0.01
Potawatomi (2)	5	0.01
Pueblo (1)	1	<0.01
Puget Sound Salish (0)	0	<0.01
Seminole (0)	3	0.01
Shoshone (0)	0	<0.01
Sioux (3)	8	0.01
South American Ind. (0)	0	<0.01
Spanish American Ind. (1)	1	<0.01
Tlingit-Haida (Alaska Native) (1)	1	<0.01
Tohono O'Odham (0)	0	<0.01
Tsimshian (Alaska Native) (0)	0	<0.01
Ute (0)	0	<0.01
Yakama (0)	0	<0.01
Yaqui (0)	0	<0.01
Yuman (0)	0	<0.01
Yup'ik (Alaska Native) (0)	0	<0.01
Asian (1,359)	1,759	3.07
Not Hispanic (1,339)	1,719	3.00
Hispanic (20)	40	0.07
Bangladeshi (7)	7	0.01
Bhutanese (0)	0	<0.01
Burmese (2)	2	<0.01
Cambodian (10)	17	0.03
Chinese, ex. Taiwanese (286)	354	0.62
Filipino (258)	378	0.66
Hmong (4)	6	0.01
Indian (382)	442	0.77
Indonesian (3)	10	0.02
Japanese (60)	128	0.22
Korean (161)	219	0.38
Laotian (3)	8	0.01
Malaysian (2)	5	0.01
Nepalese (11)	11	0.02
Pakistani (28)	36	0.06
Sri Lankan (5)	5	0.01
Taiwanese (8)	12	0.02
Thai (17)	23	0.04
Vietnamese (57)	77	0.13
Hawaii Native/Pacific Islander (23)	62	0.11
Not Hispanic (22)	56	0.10
Hispanic (1)	6	0.01
Fijian (0)	0	<0.01
Guamanian/Chamorro (11)	12	0.02
Marshallese (0)	0	<0.01
Native Hawaiian (1)	19	0.03
Samoan (3)	10	0.02
Tongan (0)	0	<0.01
White (51,941)	52,915	92.45
Not Hispanic (50,975)	51,861	90.61
Hispanic (966)	1,054	1.84

Notes: † The Census 2010 population figure is used to calculate the percentages in the Hispanic Origin and Race categories. Ancestry percentages are based on the 2006-2010 American Community Survey population (not shown); ‡ Numbers in parentheses indicate the number of people reporting a single ancestry; * Numbers in parentheses indicate the number of persons reporting this race alone, not in combination with any other race; Please refer to the User Guide for more information.

Saginaw

Place Type: City
County: Saginaw
Population: 51,508

Ancestry	Population	%
Afghan (0)	0	<0.01
African, Sub-Saharan (164)	164	0.31
African (151)	151	0.28
Cape Verdean (0)	0	<0.01
Ethiopian (0)	0	<0.01
Ghanaian (0)	0	<0.01
Kenyan (0)	0	<0.01
Liberian (13)	13	0.02
Nigerian (0)	0	<0.01
Senegalese (0)	0	<0.01
Sierra Leonean (0)	0	<0.01
Somalian (0)	0	<0.01
South African (0)	0	<0.01
Sudanese (0)	0	<0.01
Ugandan (0)	0	<0.01
Zimbabwean (0)	0	<0.01
Other Sub-Saharan African (0)	0	<0.01
Albanian (0)	0	<0.01
Alsatian (0)	0	<0.01
American (1,372)	1,372	2.57
Arab (46)	109	0.20
Arab (0)	0	<0.01
Egyptian (0)	0	<0.01
Iraqi (0)	0	<0.01
Jordanian (0)	0	<0.01
Lebanese (0)	0	<0.01
Moroccan (12)	12	0.02
Palestinian (0)	0	<0.01
Syrian (0)	0	<0.01
Other Arab (34)	97	0.18
Armenian (0)	22	0.04
Assyrian/Chaldean/Syriac (21)	21	0.04
Australian (0)	0	<0.01
Austrian (24)	106	0.20
Basque (0)	0	<0.01
Belgian (16)	64	0.12
Brazilian (0)	0	<0.01
British (31)	124	0.23
Bulgarian (0)	0	<0.01
Cajun (0)	7	0.01
Canadian (52)	114	0.21
Carpatho Rusyn (0)	0	<0.01
Celtic (0)	0	<0.01
Croatian (0)	0	<0.01
Cypriot (0)	0	<0.01
Czech (9)	139	0.26
Czechoslovakian (7)	98	0.18
Danish (11)	51	0.10
Dutch (43)	483	0.90
Eastern European (9)	9	0.02
English (713)	2,717	5.08
Estonian (0)	0	<0.01
European (215)	290	0.54
Finnish (25)	51	0.10
French, ex. Basque (233)	2,179	4.08
French Canadian (320)	945	1.77
German (3,172)	8,373	15.66
German Russian (0)	0	<0.01
Greek (41)	51	0.10
Guyanese (0)	0	<0.01
Hungarian (34)	297	0.56
Icelander (0)	0	<0.01
Iranian (0)	0	<0.01
Irish (648)	3,068	5.74
Israeli (0)	0	<0.01
Italian (473)	926	1.73
Latvian (19)	35	0.07
Lithuanian (33)	90	0.17
Luxemburger (0)	0	<0.01
Macedonian (0)	0	<0.01
Maltese (0)	0	<0.01
New Zealander (0)	0	<0.01
Northern European (0)	0	<0.01
Norwegian (13)	242	0.45
Pennsylvania German (2)	2	<0.01
Polish (860)	2,887	5.40
Portuguese (0)	0	<0.01
Romanian (0)	40	0.07
Russian (72)	327	0.61
Scandinavian (0)	0	<0.01
Scotch-Irish (56)	446	0.83
Scottish (188)	711	1.33
Serbian (0)	0	<0.01
Slavic (0)	0	<0.01
Slovak (0)	87	0.16
Slovene (0)	7	0.01
Soviet Union (0)	0	<0.01
Swedish (21)	125	0.23
Swiss (0)	69	0.13
Turkish (0)	6	0.01
Ukrainian (0)	44	0.08
Welsh (9)	102	0.19
West Indian, ex. Hispanic (71)	117	0.22
Bahamian (0)	0	<0.01
Barbadian (0)	0	<0.01
Belizean (0)	0	<0.01
Bermudan (0)	0	<0.01
British West Indian (16)	16	0.03
Dutch West Indian (0)	0	<0.01
Haitian (4)	4	0.01
Jamaican (2)	48	0.09
Trinidadian/Tobagonian (39)	39	0.07
U.S. Virgin Islander (0)	0	<0.01
West Indian (10)	10	0.02
Other West Indian (0)	0	<0.01
Yugoslavian (16)	16	0.03

Hispanic Origin	Population	%
Hispanic or Latino (of any race)	7,344	14.26
Central American, ex. Mexican	47	0.09
Costa Rican	1	<0.01
Guatemalan	17	0.03
Honduran	9	0.02
Nicaraguan	2	<0.01
Panamanian	10	0.02
Salvadoran	8	0.02
Other Central American	0	<0.01
Cuban	35	0.07
Dominican Republic	3	0.01
Mexican	6,487	12.59
Puerto Rican	162	0.31
South American	29	0.06
Argentinean	7	0.01
Bolivian	3	0.01
Chilean	4	0.01
Colombian	11	0.02
Ecuadorian	0	<0.01
Paraguayan	0	<0.01
Peruvian	1	<0.01
Uruguayan	2	<0.01
Venezuelan	1	<0.01
Other South American	0	<0.01
Other Hispanic or Latino	581	1.13

Race*	Population	%
African-American/Black (23,721)	25,266	49.05
Not Hispanic (23,127)	24,231	47.04
Hispanic (594)	1,035	2.01
American Indian/Alaska Native (268)	657	1.28
Not Hispanic (180)	490	0.95
Hispanic (88)	167	0.32
Alaska Athabascan (Ala. Nat.) (0)	0	<0.01
Aleut (Alaska Native) (0)	0	<0.01
Apache (3)	4	0.01
Arapaho (0)	0	<0.01
Blackfeet (5)	21	0.04
Canadian/French Am. Ind. (2)	5	0.01
Central American Ind. (0)	0	<0.01
Cherokee (6)	73	0.14
Cheyenne (1)	1	<0.01
Chickasaw (0)	0	<0.01
Chippewa (46)	102	0.20
Choctaw (1)	5	0.01
Colville (0)	0	<0.01
Comanche (3)	3	0.01
Cree (0)	3	0.01
Creek (0)	0	<0.01
Crow (0)	0	<0.01
Delaware (0)	0	<0.01
Hopi (0)	0	<0.01
Houma (0)	0	<0.01
Inupiat (Alaska Native) (0)	0	<0.01
Iroquois (2)	11	0.02
Kiowa (0)	0	<0.01
Lumbee (4)	4	0.01
Menominee (0)	0	<0.01
Mexican American Ind. (11)	14	0.03
Navajo (0)	0	<0.01
Osage (0)	0	<0.01
Ottawa (2)	6	0.01
Paiute (0)	0	<0.01
Pima (0)	0	<0.01
Potawatomi (8)	12	0.02
Pueblo (0)	0	<0.01
Puget Sound Salish (0)	0	<0.01
Seminole (1)	5	0.01
Shoshone (0)	0	<0.01
Sioux (2)	5	0.01
South American Ind. (0)	0	<0.01
Spanish American Ind. (1)	3	0.01
Tlingit-Haida (Alaska Native) (0)	0	<0.01
Tohono O'Odham (0)	0	<0.01
Tsimshian (Alaska Native) (0)	0	<0.01
Ute (2)	2	<0.01
Yakama (0)	0	<0.01
Yaqui (0)	0	<0.01
Yuman (1)	3	0.01
Yup'ik (Alaska Native) (0)	0	<0.01
Asian (165)	298	0.58
Not Hispanic (145)	244	0.47
Hispanic (20)	54	0.10
Bangladeshi (0)	0	<0.01
Bhutanese (0)	0	<0.01
Burmese (0)	0	<0.01
Cambodian (0)	0	<0.01
Chinese, ex. Taiwanese (28)	48	0.09
Filipino (29)	72	0.14
Hmong (31)	35	0.07
Indian (21)	36	0.07
Indonesian (0)	0	<0.01
Japanese (14)	27	0.05
Korean (30)	42	0.08
Laotian (1)	5	0.01
Malaysian (0)	1	<0.01
Nepalese (0)	0	<0.01
Pakistani (2)	3	0.01
Sri Lankan (0)	0	<0.01
Taiwanese (3)	3	0.01
Thai (1)	2	<0.01
Vietnamese (3)	7	0.01
Hawaii Native/Pacific Islander (15)	56	0.11
Not Hispanic (10)	31	0.06
Hispanic (5)	25	0.05
Fijian (3)	3	0.01
Guamanian/Chamorro (8)	17	0.03
Marshallese (0)	1	<0.01
Native Hawaiian (2)	10	0.02
Samoan (0)	1	<0.01
Tongan (0)	0	<0.01
White (22,401)	24,229	47.04
Not Hispanic (19,310)	20,468	39.74
Hispanic (3,091)	3,761	7.30

Notes: † The Census 2010 population figure is used to calculate the percentages in the Hispanic Origin and Race categories. Ancestry percentages are based on the 2006-2010 American Community Survey population (not shown); ‡ Numbers in parentheses indicate the number of people reporting a single ancestry; * Numbers in parentheses indicate the number of persons reporting this race alone, not in combination with any other race; Please refer to the User Guide for more information.

Shelby

Place Type: Charter Township
County: Macomb
Population: 73,804

Ancestry	Population	%
Afghan (0)	0	<0.01
African, Sub-Saharan (408)	438	0.60
African (390)	390	0.54
Cape Verdean (0)	0	<0.01
Ethiopian (0)	0	<0.01
Ghanaian (0)	0	<0.01
Kenyan (0)	0	<0.01
Liberian (0)	0	<0.01
Nigerian (0)	0	<0.01
Senegalese (0)	0	<0.01
Sierra Leonean (0)	0	<0.01
Somalian (0)	0	<0.01
South African (0)	30	0.04
Sudanese (0)	0	<0.01
Ugandan (0)	0	<0.01
Zimbabwean (18)	18	0.02
Other Sub-Saharan African (0)	0	<0.01
Albanian (1,484)	1,549	2.13
Alsatian (0)	0	<0.01
American (3,530)	3,530	4.85
Arab (1,351)	2,092	2.87
Arab (244)	397	0.55
Egyptian (134)	134	0.18
Iraqi (522)	639	0.88
Jordanian (29)	40	0.05
Lebanese (342)	686	0.94
Moroccan (0)	0	<0.01
Palestinian (0)	0	<0.01
Syrian (60)	176	0.24
Other Arab (20)	20	0.03
Armenian (97)	276	0.38
Assyrian/Chaldean/Syriac (1,179)	1,454	2.00
Australian (0)	0	<0.01
Austrian (69)	231	0.32
Basque (0)	10	0.01
Belgian (307)	1,336	1.84
Brazilian (0)	0	<0.01
British (134)	325	0.45
Bulgarian (60)	174	0.24
Cajun (0)	0	<0.01
Canadian (197)	597	0.82
Carpatho Rusyn (0)	0	<0.01
Celtic (0)	0	<0.01
Croatian (82)	197	0.27
Cypriot (0)	0	<0.01
Czech (69)	458	0.63
Czechoslovakian (66)	158	0.22
Danish (59)	266	0.37
Dutch (208)	1,077	1.48
Eastern European (0)	0	<0.01
English (1,941)	7,589	10.43
Estonian (0)	0	<0.01
European (520)	544	0.75
Finnish (83)	685	0.94
French, ex. Basque (346)	3,667	5.04
French Canadian (411)	1,199	1.65
German (4,734)	17,369	23.87
German Russian (0)	0	<0.01
Greek (504)	996	1.37
Guyanese (17)	17	0.02
Hungarian (223)	781	1.07
Icelander (0)	0	<0.01
Iranian (0)	13	0.02
Irish (1,519)	8,159	11.21
Israeli (0)	0	<0.01
Italian (5,130)	10,823	14.87
Latvian (0)	0	<0.01
Lithuanian (90)	257	0.35
Luxemburger (0)	0	<0.01
Macedonian (537)	639	0.88
Maltese (25)	65	0.09
New Zealander (0)	0	<0.01
Northern European (47)	47	0.06

Ancestry (cont.)	Population	%
Norwegian (119)	493	0.68
Pennsylvania German (8)	44	0.06
Polish (4,995)	12,829	17.63
Portuguese (32)	49	0.07
Romanian (478)	728	1.00
Russian (109)	549	0.75
Scandinavian (22)	57	0.08
Scotch-Irish (290)	1,108	1.52
Scottish (525)	1,845	2.54
Serbian (168)	265	0.36
Slavic (10)	64	0.09
Slovak (194)	669	0.92
Slovene (15)	34	0.05
Soviet Union (0)	0	<0.01
Swedish (78)	743	1.02
Swiss (14)	169	0.23
Turkish (0)	0	<0.01
Ukrainian (233)	517	0.71
Welsh (76)	419	0.58
West Indian, ex. Hispanic (29)	37	0.05
Bahamian (0)	0	<0.01
Barbadian (0)	0	<0.01
Belizean (0)	0	<0.01
Bermudan (0)	0	<0.01
British West Indian (0)	0	<0.01
Dutch West Indian (0)	0	<0.01
Haitian (0)	0	<0.01
Jamaican (0)	8	0.01
Trinidadian/Tobagonian (0)	0	<0.01
U.S. Virgin Islander (0)	0	<0.01
West Indian (29)	29	0.04
Other West Indian (0)	0	<0.01
Yugoslavian (402)	638	0.88

Hispanic Origin	Population	%
Hispanic or Latino (of any race)	1,777	2.41
Central American, ex. Mexican	54	0.07
Costa Rican	5	0.01
Guatemalan	22	0.03
Honduran	4	0.01
Nicaraguan	7	0.01
Panamanian	8	0.01
Salvadoran	7	0.01
Other Central American	1	<0.01
Cuban	54	0.07
Dominican Republic	13	0.02
Mexican	1,186	1.61
Puerto Rican	131	0.18
South American	163	0.22
Argentinean	37	0.05
Bolivian	2	<0.01
Chilean	14	0.02
Colombian	40	0.05
Ecuadorian	25	0.03
Paraguayan	2	<0.01
Peruvian	22	0.03
Uruguayan	0	<0.01
Venezuelan	21	0.03
Other South American	0	<0.01
Other Hispanic or Latino	176	0.24

Race*	Population	%
African-American/Black (2,331)	2,706	3.67
Not Hispanic (2,287)	2,634	3.57
Hispanic (44)	72	0.10
American Indian/Alaska Native (194)	536	0.73
Not Hispanic (171)	488	0.66
Hispanic (23)	48	0.07
Alaska Athabascan (Ala. Nat.) (0)	0	<0.01
Aleut (Alaska Native) (0)	0	<0.01
Apache (2)	3	<0.01
Arapaho (2)	2	<0.01
Blackfeet (3)	12	0.02
Canadian/French Am. Ind. (1)	3	<0.01
Central American Ind. (0)	0	<0.01
Cherokee (22)	117	0.16
Cheyenne (0)	0	<0.01
Chickasaw (0)	0	<0.01
Chippewa (42)	79	0.11

Race* (cont.)	Population	%
Choctaw (2)	6	0.01
Colville (0)	0	<0.01
Comanche (0)	1	<0.01
Cree (2)	7	0.01
Creek (0)	2	<0.01
Crow (0)	0	<0.01
Delaware (0)	0	<0.01
Hopi (0)	0	<0.01
Houma (0)	0	<0.01
Inupiat (Alaska Native) (0)	0	<0.01
Iroquois (30)	35	0.05
Kiowa (0)	0	<0.01
Lumbee (11)	25	0.03
Menominee (0)	1	<0.01
Mexican American Ind. (10)	10	0.01
Navajo (0)	9	0.01
Osage (0)	0	<0.01
Ottawa (6)	9	0.01
Paiute (0)	0	<0.01
Pima (0)	0	<0.01
Potawatomi (2)	6	0.01
Pueblo (3)	3	<0.01
Puget Sound Salish (0)	0	<0.01
Seminole (7)	16	0.02
Shoshone (0)	0	<0.01
Sioux (2)	12	0.02
South American Ind. (0)	0	<0.01
Spanish American Ind. (0)	0	<0.01
Tlingit-Haida (Alaska Native) (0)	0	<0.01
Tohono O'Odham (0)	0	<0.01
Tsimshian (Alaska Native) (0)	0	<0.01
Ute (0)	0	<0.01
Yakama (0)	0	<0.01
Yaqui (0)	1	<0.01
Yuman (0)	0	<0.01
Yup'ik (Alaska Native) (0)	0	<0.01
Asian (2,411)	2,909	3.94
Not Hispanic (2,403)	2,889	3.91
Hispanic (8)	20	0.03
Bangladeshi (48)	48	0.07
Bhutanese (0)	0	<0.01
Burmese (4)	7	0.01
Cambodian (3)	8	0.01
Chinese, ex. Taiwanese (237)	269	0.36
Filipino (337)	444	0.60
Hmong (37)	48	0.07
Indian (1,009)	1,064	1.44
Indonesian (0)	5	0.01
Japanese (40)	76	0.10
Korean (292)	359	0.49
Laotian (6)	14	0.02
Malaysian (0)	0	<0.01
Nepalese (2)	2	<0.01
Pakistani (155)	163	0.22
Sri Lankan (0)	0	<0.01
Taiwanese (11)	13	0.02
Thai (14)	27	0.04
Vietnamese (151)	161	0.22
Hawaii Native/Pacific Islander (14)	75	0.10
Not Hispanic (14)	75	0.10
Hispanic (0)	0	<0.01
Fijian (3)	4	0.01
Guamanian/Chamorro (2)	4	0.01
Marshallese (0)	0	<0.01
Native Hawaiian (0)	6	0.01
Samoan (1)	11	0.01
Tongan (0)	0	<0.01
White (67,121)	68,257	92.48
Not Hispanic (65,966)	67,019	90.81
Hispanic (1,155)	1,238	1.68

Notes: † The Census 2010 population figure is used to calculate the percentages in the Hispanic Origin and Race categories. Ancestry percentages are based on the 2006-2010 American Community Survey population (not shown); ‡ Numbers in parentheses indicate the number of people reporting a single ancestry; * Numbers in parentheses indicate the number of persons reporting this race alone, not in combination with any other race; Please refer to the User Guide for more information.

Southfield

Place Type: City
County: Oakland
Population: 71,739

Ancestry	Population	%
Afghan (0)	0	<0.01
African, Sub-Saharan (1,677)	2,102	2.88
African (1,243)	1,632	2.24
Cape Verdean (0)	0	<0.01
Ethiopian (99)	121	0.17
Ghanaian (0)	14	0.02
Kenyan (10)	10	0.01
Liberian (0)	0	<0.01
Nigerian (248)	248	0.34
Senegalese (19)	19	0.03
Sierra Leonean (0)	0	<0.01
Somalian (0)	0	<0.01
South African (0)	0	<0.01
Sudanese (0)	0	<0.01
Ugandan (0)	0	<0.01
Zimbabwean (12)	12	0.02
Other Sub-Saharan African (46)	46	0.06
Albanian (88)	88	0.12
Alsatian (0)	0	<0.01
American (1,357)	1,357	1.86
Arab (1,441)	1,650	2.26
Arab (299)	299	0.41
Egyptian (0)	13	0.02
Iraqi (983)	1,164	1.60
Jordanian (10)	10	0.01
Lebanese (18)	18	0.02
Moroccan (27)	42	0.06
Palestinian (11)	11	0.02
Syrian (18)	18	0.02
Other Arab (75)	75	0.10
Armenian (230)	241	0.33
Assyrian/Chaldean/Syriac (662)	863	1.18
Australian (0)	0	<0.01
Austrian (88)	203	0.28
Basque (0)	0	<0.01
Belgian (0)	27	0.04
Brazilian (6)	14	0.02
British (49)	145	0.20
Bulgarian (0)	0	<0.01
Cajun (12)	12	0.02
Canadian (152)	332	0.46
Carpatho Rusyn (0)	0	<0.01
Celtic (0)	0	<0.01
Croatian (17)	68	0.09
Cypriot (0)	0	<0.01
Czech (36)	288	0.39
Czechoslovakian (18)	39	0.05
Danish (0)	64	0.09
Dutch (76)	371	0.51
Eastern European (173)	173	0.24
English (485)	1,861	2.55
Estonian (0)	0	<0.01
European (431)	478	0.66
Finnish (61)	173	0.24
French, ex. Basque (137)	831	1.14
French Canadian (93)	326	0.45
German (728)	3,332	4.57
German Russian (0)	0	<0.01
Greek (108)	170	0.23
Guyanese (0)	0	<0.01
Hungarian (341)	594	0.81
Icelander (0)	0	<0.01
Iranian (17)	51	0.07
Irish (461)	2,274	3.12
Israeli (51)	60	0.08
Italian (334)	794	1.09
Latvian (0)	0	<0.01
Lithuanian (186)	269	0.37
Luxemburger (0)	0	<0.01
Macedonian (0)	6	0.01
Maltese (33)	33	0.05
New Zealander (0)	0	<0.01
Northern European (0)	0	<0.01

Ancestry	Population	%
Norwegian (33)	168	0.23
Pennsylvania German (0)	0	<0.01
Polish (972)	2,791	3.83
Portuguese (0)	14	0.02
Romanian (123)	262	0.36
Russian (1,274)	1,961	2.69
Scandinavian (7)	17	0.02
Scotch-Irish (162)	494	0.68
Scottish (200)	734	1.01
Serbian (0)	0	<0.01
Slavic (11)	11	0.02
Slovak (52)	87	0.12
Slovene (17)	25	0.03
Soviet Union (0)	0	<0.01
Swedish (67)	266	0.36
Swiss (0)	64	0.09
Turkish (26)	26	0.04
Ukrainian (211)	287	0.39
Welsh (23)	250	0.34
West Indian, ex. Hispanic (464)	726	1.00
Bahamian (0)	9	0.01
Barbadian (0)	0	<0.01
Belizean (10)	10	0.01
Bermudan (0)	0	<0.01
British West Indian (0)	0	<0.01
Dutch West Indian (0)	20	0.03
Haitian (23)	55	0.08
Jamaican (362)	461	0.63
Trinidadian/Tobagonian (11)	26	0.04
U.S. Virgin Islander (0)	24	0.03
West Indian (58)	121	0.17
Other West Indian (0)	0	<0.01
Yugoslavian (0)	0	<0.01

Hispanic Origin	Population	%
Hispanic or Latino (of any race)	957	1.33
Central American, ex. Mexican	53	0.07
Costa Rican	2	<0.01
Guatemalan	5	0.01
Honduran	7	0.01
Nicaraguan	5	0.01
Panamanian	20	0.03
Salvadoran	14	0.02
Other Central American	0	<0.01
Cuban	54	0.08
Dominican Republic	21	0.03
Mexican	443	0.62
Puerto Rican	168	0.23
South American	82	0.11
Argentinean	17	0.02
Bolivian	1	<0.01
Chilean	5	0.01
Colombian	27	0.04
Ecuadorian	6	0.01
Paraguayan	0	<0.01
Peruvian	15	0.02
Uruguayan	0	<0.01
Venezuelan	7	0.01
Other South American	4	0.01
Other Hispanic or Latino	136	0.19

Race*	Population	%
African-American/Black (50,432)	51,817	72.23
Not Hispanic (50,181)	51,445	71.71
Hispanic (251)	372	0.52
American Indian/Alaska Native (143)	689	0.96
Not Hispanic (135)	645	0.90
Hispanic (8)	44	0.06
Alaska Athabascan (Ala. Nat.) (0)	0	<0.01
Aleut (Alaska Native) (0)	0	<0.01
Apache (0)	9	0.01
Arapaho (0)	0	<0.01
Blackfeet (0)	28	0.04
Canadian/French Am. Ind. (5)	10	0.01
Central American Ind. (0)	0	<0.01
Cherokee (11)	119	0.17
Cheyenne (0)	2	<0.01
Chickasaw (0)	2	<0.01
Chippewa (13)	26	0.04

Race*	Population	%
Choctaw (2)	14	0.02
Colville (0)	0	<0.01
Comanche (0)	1	<0.01
Cree (0)	6	0.01
Creek (0)	9	0.01
Crow (0)	1	<0.01
Delaware (2)	6	0.01
Hopi (0)	1	<0.01
Houma (0)	0	<0.01
Inupiat (Alaska Native) (0)	0	<0.01
Iroquois (2)	5	0.01
Kiowa (0)	1	<0.01
Lumbee (1)	1	<0.01
Menominee (0)	0	<0.01
Mexican American Ind. (1)	1	<0.01
Navajo (0)	0	<0.01
Osage (0)	0	<0.01
Ottawa (2)	4	0.01
Paiute (0)	0	<0.01
Pima (0)	0	<0.01
Potawatomi (2)	7	0.01
Pueblo (0)	0	<0.01
Puget Sound Salish (0)	0	<0.01
Seminole (0)	6	0.01
Shoshone (0)	1	<0.01
Sioux (1)	3	<0.01
South American Ind. (0)	1	<0.01
Spanish American Ind. (0)	1	<0.01
Tlingit-Haida (Alaska Native) (0)	0	<0.01
Tohono O'Odham (0)	0	<0.01
Tsimshian (Alaska Native) (0)	0	<0.01
Ute (0)	0	<0.01
Yakama (0)	0	<0.01
Yaqui (0)	0	<0.01
Yuman (0)	0	<0.01
Yup'ik (Alaska Native) (0)	0	<0.01
Asian (1,233)	1,602	2.23
Not Hispanic (1,217)	1,554	2.17
Hispanic (16)	48	0.07
Bangladeshi (4)	8	0.01
Bhutanese (0)	0	<0.01
Burmese (2)	2	<0.01
Cambodian (4)	7	0.01
Chinese, ex. Taiwanese (179)	225	0.31
Filipino (263)	365	0.51
Hmong (22)	24	0.03
Indian (406)	461	0.64
Indonesian (2)	5	0.01
Japanese (29)	56	0.08
Korean (75)	88	0.12
Laotian (8)	10	0.01
Malaysian (2)	3	<0.01
Nepalese (3)	3	<0.01
Pakistani (56)	72	0.10
Sri Lankan (25)	28	0.04
Taiwanese (5)	5	0.01
Thai (23)	28	0.04
Vietnamese (71)	88	0.12
Hawaii Native/Pacific Islander (17)	74	0.10
Not Hispanic (16)	69	0.10
Hispanic (1)	5	0.01
Fijian (0)	0	<0.01
Guamanian/Chamorro (0)	3	<0.01
Marshallese (0)	0	<0.01
Native Hawaiian (4)	15	0.02
Samoan (2)	4	0.01
Tongan (1)	1	<0.01
White (17,876)	19,077	26.59
Not Hispanic (17,537)	18,613	25.95
Hispanic (339)	464	0.65

Notes: † The Census 2010 population figure is used to calculate the percentages in the Hispanic Origin and Race categories. Ancestry percentages are based on the 2006-2010 American Community Survey population (not shown); ‡ Numbers in parentheses indicate the number of people reporting a single ancestry; * Numbers in parentheses indicate the number of persons reporting this race alone, not in combination with any other race; Please refer to the User Guide for more information.

St. Clair Shores

Place Type: City
County: Macomb
Population: 59,715

Ancestry	Population	%
Afghan (0)	0	<0.01
African, Sub-Saharan (127)	161	0.26
African (116)	126	0.21
Cape Verdean (11)	35	0.06
Ethiopian (0)	0	<0.01
Ghanaian (0)	0	<0.01
Kenyan (0)	0	<0.01
Liberian (0)	0	<0.01
Nigerian (0)	0	<0.01
Senegalese (0)	0	<0.01
Sierra Leonean (0)	0	<0.01
Somalian (0)	0	<0.01
South African (0)	0	<0.01
Sudanese (0)	0	<0.01
Ugandan (0)	0	<0.01
Zimbabwean (0)	0	<0.01
Other Sub-Saharan African (0)	0	<0.01
Albanian (351)	351	0.58
Alsatian (0)	0	<0.01
American (2,044)	2,044	3.36
Arab (625)	992	1.63
Arab (152)	222	0.37
Egyptian (90)	90	0.15
Iraqi (12)	12	0.02
Jordanian (0)	0	<0.01
Lebanese (284)	558	0.92
Moroccan (0)	0	<0.01
Palestinian (9)	9	0.01
Syrian (78)	101	0.17
Other Arab (0)	0	<0.01
Armenian (49)	79	0.13
Assyrian/Chaldean/Syriac (0)	50	0.08
Australian (0)	0	<0.01
Austrian (30)	311	0.51
Basque (0)	0	<0.01
Belgian (716)	2,178	3.58
Brazilian (15)	15	0.02
British (49)	109	0.18
Bulgarian (0)	0	<0.01
Cajun (0)	0	<0.01
Canadian (471)	716	1.18
Carpatho Rusyn (0)	0	<0.01
Celtic (0)	0	<0.01
Croatian (157)	334	0.55
Cypriot (0)	0	<0.01
Czech (41)	290	0.48
Czechoslovakian (37)	102	0.17
Danish (0)	60	0.10
Dutch (123)	917	1.51
Eastern European (30)	30	0.05
English (1,276)	5,786	9.52
Estonian (0)	0	<0.01
European (333)	398	0.65
Finnish (80)	312	0.51
French, ex. Basque (426)	4,772	7.85
French Canadian (523)	1,601	2.63
German (3,950)	16,348	26.90
German Russian (0)	0	<0.01
Greek (343)	617	1.02
Guyanese (0)	0	<0.01
Hungarian (201)	586	0.96
Icelander (0)	0	<0.01
Iranian (0)	0	<0.01
Irish (1,817)	9,621	15.83
Israeli (0)	0	<0.01
Italian (3,208)	8,779	14.44
Latvian (0)	0	<0.01
Lithuanian (119)	324	0.53
Luxemburger (0)	0	<0.01
Macedonian (28)	84	0.14
Maltese (106)	191	0.31
New Zealander (0)	0	<0.01
Northern European (19)	19	0.03
Norwegian (147)	473	0.78
Pennsylvania German (0)	14	0.02
Polish (4,818)	12,345	20.31
Portuguese (10)	80	0.13
Romanian (147)	223	0.37
Russian (80)	460	0.76
Scandinavian (10)	25	0.04
Scotch-Irish (628)	1,611	2.65
Scottish (734)	2,269	3.73
Serbian (20)	86	0.14
Slavic (8)	44	0.07
Slovak (127)	475	0.78
Slovene (7)	7	0.01
Soviet Union (0)	0	<0.01
Swedish (152)	576	0.95
Swiss (25)	96	0.16
Turkish (0)	0	<0.01
Ukrainian (220)	599	0.99
Welsh (37)	192	0.32
West Indian, ex. Hispanic (0)	0	<0.01
Bahamian (0)	0	<0.01
Barbadian (0)	0	<0.01
Belizean (0)	0	<0.01
Bermudan (0)	0	<0.01
British West Indian (0)	0	<0.01
Dutch West Indian (0)	0	<0.01
Haitian (0)	0	<0.01
Jamaican (0)	0	<0.01
Trinidadian/Tobagonian (0)	0	<0.01
U.S. Virgin Islander (0)	0	<0.01
West Indian (0)	0	<0.01
Other West Indian (0)	0	<0.01
Yugoslavian (4)	91	0.15

Hispanic Origin	Population	%
Hispanic or Latino (of any race)	1,040	1.74
Central American, ex. Mexican	40	0.07
Costa Rican	6	0.01
Guatemalan	13	0.02
Honduran	7	0.01
Nicaraguan	1	<0.01
Panamanian	8	0.01
Salvadoran	5	0.01
Other Central American	0	<0.01
Cuban	35	0.06
Dominican Republic	15	0.03
Mexican	672	1.13
Puerto Rican	84	0.14
South American	61	0.10
Argentinean	19	0.03
Bolivian	0	<0.01
Chilean	1	<0.01
Colombian	17	0.03
Ecuadorian	9	0.02
Paraguayan	0	<0.01
Peruvian	9	0.02
Uruguayan	1	<0.01
Venezuelan	4	0.01
Other South American	1	<0.01
Other Hispanic or Latino	133	0.22

Race*	Population	%
African-American/Black (2,350)	2,719	4.55
Not Hispanic (2,333)	2,678	4.48
Hispanic (17)	41	0.07
American Indian/Alaska Native (188)	601	1.01
Not Hispanic (169)	536	0.90
Hispanic (19)	65	0.11
Alaska Athabascan (Ala. Nat.) (0)	0	<0.01
Aleut (Alaska Native) (0)	0	<0.01
Apache (2)	9	0.02
Arapaho (0)	0	<0.01
Blackfeet (5)	26	0.04
Canadian/French Am. Ind. (1)	9	0.02
Central American Ind. (1)	1	<0.01
Cherokee (16)	139	0.23
Cheyenne (0)	0	<0.01
Chickasaw (0)	1	<0.01
Chippewa (43)	86	0.14

	Population	%
Choctaw (0)	7	0.01
Colville (0)	0	<0.01
Comanche (0)	2	<0.01
Cree (1)	1	<0.01
Creek (0)	0	<0.01
Crow (0)	0	<0.01
Delaware (1)	4	0.01
Hopi (0)	4	0.01
Houma (0)	0	<0.01
Inupiat (Alaska Native) (0)	0	<0.01
Iroquois (11)	24	0.04
Kiowa (0)	0	<0.01
Lumbee (20)	28	0.05
Menominee (0)	0	<0.01
Mexican American Ind. (2)	2	<0.01
Navajo (1)	7	0.01
Osage (0)	7	0.01
Ottawa (6)	10	0.02
Paiute (0)	2	<0.01
Pima (0)	0	<0.01
Potawatomi (2)	2	<0.01
Pueblo (0)	1	<0.01
Puget Sound Salish (0)	0	<0.01
Seminole (0)	1	<0.01
Shoshone (0)	1	<0.01
Sioux (1)	13	0.02
South American Ind. (0)	0	<0.01
Spanish American Ind. (0)	0	<0.01
Tlingit-Haida (Alaska Native) (0)	0	<0.01
Tohono O'Odham (0)	0	<0.01
Tsimshian (Alaska Native) (0)	0	<0.01
Ute (0)	0	<0.01
Yakama (0)	0	<0.01
Yaqui (0)	0	<0.01
Yuman (0)	0	<0.01
Yup'ik (Alaska Native) (0)	0	<0.01
Asian (614)	913	1.53
Not Hispanic (611)	888	1.49
Hispanic (3)	25	0.04
Bangladeshi (0)	2	<0.01
Bhutanese (0)	0	<0.01
Burmese (0)	0	<0.01
Cambodian (1)	4	0.01
Chinese, ex. Taiwanese (107)	144	0.24
Filipino (227)	332	0.56
Hmong (14)	16	0.03
Indian (87)	105	0.18
Indonesian (0)	1	<0.01
Japanese (27)	71	0.12
Korean (66)	130	0.22
Laotian (2)	6	0.01
Malaysian (0)	0	<0.01
Nepalese (0)	0	<0.01
Pakistani (9)	12	0.02
Sri Lankan (0)	0	<0.01
Taiwanese (1)	4	0.01
Thai (15)	20	0.03
Vietnamese (38)	51	0.09
Hawaii Native/Pacific Islander (9)	31	0.05
Not Hispanic (9)	31	0.05
Hispanic (0)	0	<0.01
Fijian (0)	1	<0.01
Guamanian/Chamorro (4)	9	0.02
Marshallese (0)	0	<0.01
Native Hawaiian (2)	10	0.02
Samoan (0)	0	<0.01
Tongan (0)	0	<0.01
White (55,373)	56,353	94.37
Not Hispanic (54,575)	55,454	92.86
Hispanic (798)	899	1.51

Notes: † The Census 2010 population figure is used to calculate the percentages in the Hispanic Origin and Race categories. Ancestry percentages are based on the 2006-2010 American Community Survey population (not shown); ‡ Numbers in parentheses indicate the number of people reporting a single ancestry; * Numbers in parentheses indicate the number of persons reporting this race alone, not in combination with any other race; Please refer to the User Guide for more information.

Sterling Heights

Place Type: City
County: Macomb
Population: 129,699

Ancestry	Population	%
Afghan (41)	41	0.03
African, Sub-Saharan (932)	966	0.74
African (782)	802	0.62
Cape Verdean (0)	14	0.01
Ethiopian (0)	0	<0.01
Ghanaian (0)	0	<0.01
Kenyan (0)	0	<0.01
Liberian (0)	0	<0.01
Nigerian (33)	33	0.03
Senegalese (0)	0	<0.01
Sierra Leonean (0)	0	<0.01
Somalian (75)	75	0.06
South African (0)	0	<0.01
Sudanese (0)	0	<0.01
Ugandan (0)	0	<0.01
Zimbabwean (0)	0	<0.01
Other Sub-Saharan African (42)	42	0.03
Albanian (3,206)	3,414	2.63
Alsatian (0)	0	<0.01
American (4,311)	4,311	3.32
Arab (7,011)	8,488	6.54
Arab (1,807)	1,888	1.46
Egyptian (252)	283	0.22
Iraqi (3,473)	4,199	3.24
Jordanian (113)	161	0.12
Lebanese (994)	1,441	1.11
Moroccan (0)	0	<0.01
Palestinian (0)	29	0.02
Syrian (119)	187	0.14
Other Arab (253)	300	0.23
Armenian (282)	288	0.22
Assyrian/Chaldean/Syriac (6,987)	8,026	6.19
Australian (9)	18	0.01
Austrian (90)	526	0.41
Basque (0)	0	<0.01
Belgian (450)	1,835	1.41
Brazilian (57)	57	0.04
British (59)	163	0.13
Bulgarian (12)	24	0.02
Cajun (0)	0	<0.01
Canadian (265)	604	0.47
Carpatho Rusyn (0)	0	<0.01
Celtic (20)	20	0.02
Croatian (151)	347	0.27
Cypriot (0)	0	<0.01
Czech (106)	463	0.36
Czechoslovakian (185)	456	0.35
Danish (35)	261	0.20
Dutch (209)	1,216	0.94
Eastern European (40)	53	0.04
English (2,422)	8,908	6.87
Estonian (0)	0	<0.01
European (481)	516	0.40
Finnish (133)	854	0.66
French, ex. Basque (669)	6,116	4.72
French Canadian (669)	1,986	1.53
German (6,203)	23,659	18.24
German Russian (0)	0	<0.01
Greek (728)	1,148	0.89
Guyanese (0)	9	0.01
Hungarian (206)	1,195	0.92
Icelander (0)	10	0.01
Iranian (135)	163	0.13
Irish (2,457)	11,759	9.07
Israeli (17)	17	0.01
Italian (6,769)	15,325	11.82
Latvian (10)	39	0.03
Lithuanian (120)	310	0.24
Luxemburger (0)	0	<0.01
Macedonian (1,264)	1,382	1.07
Maltese (103)	235	0.18
New Zealander (0)	0	<0.01
Northern European (115)	115	0.09

Ancestry	Population	%
Norwegian (159)	712	0.55
Pennsylvania German (0)	0	<0.01
Polish (11,674)	23,071	17.79
Portuguese (35)	94	0.07
Romanian (1,447)	1,620	1.25
Russian (418)	1,070	0.83
Scandinavian (0)	12	0.01
Scotch-Irish (596)	1,593	1.23
Scottish (535)	2,501	1.93
Serbian (301)	369	0.28
Slavic (24)	69	0.05
Slovak (297)	1,027	0.79
Slovene (0)	32	0.02
Soviet Union (0)	0	<0.01
Swedish (207)	899	0.69
Swiss (11)	93	0.07
Turkish (14)	14	0.01
Ukrainian (791)	1,410	1.09
Welsh (46)	398	0.31
West Indian, ex. Hispanic (11)	20	0.02
Bahamian (0)	9	0.01
Barbadian (0)	0	<0.01
Belizean (0)	0	<0.01
Bermudan (0)	0	<0.01
British West Indian (0)	0	<0.01
Dutch West Indian (0)	0	<0.01
Haitian (0)	0	<0.01
Jamaican (11)	11	0.01
Trinidadian/Tobagonian (0)	0	<0.01
U.S. Virgin Islander (0)	0	<0.01
West Indian (0)	0	<0.01
Other West Indian (0)	0	<0.01
Yugoslavian (1,357)	1,665	1.28

Hispanic Origin	Population	%
Hispanic or Latino (of any race)	2,523	1.95
Central American, ex. Mexican	55	0.04
Costa Rican	13	0.01
Guatemalan	12	0.01
Honduran	9	0.01
Nicaraguan	1	<0.01
Panamanian	11	0.01
Salvadoran	9	0.01
Other Central American	0	<0.01
Cuban	69	0.05
Dominican Republic	33	0.03
Mexican	1,537	1.19
Puerto Rican	301	0.23
South American	192	0.15
Argentinean	36	0.03
Bolivian	9	0.01
Chilean	16	0.01
Colombian	59	0.05
Ecuadorian	16	0.01
Paraguayan	0	<0.01
Peruvian	22	0.02
Uruguayan	0	<0.01
Venezuelan	31	0.02
Other South American	3	<0.01
Other Hispanic or Latino	336	0.26

Race*	Population	%
African-American/Black (6,697)	7,313	5.64
Not Hispanic (6,638)	7,213	5.56
Hispanic (59)	100	0.08
American Indian/Alaska Native (281)	832	0.64
Not Hispanic (246)	735	0.57
Hispanic (35)	97	0.07
Alaska Athabascan (Ala. Nat.) (0)	0	<0.01
Aleut (Alaska Native) (0)	0	<0.01
Apache (2)	10	0.01
Arapaho (0)	1	<0.01
Blackfeet (6)	30	0.02
Canadian/French Am. Ind. (2)	5	<0.01
Central American Ind. (0)	0	<0.01
Cherokee (27)	164	0.13
Cheyenne (0)	0	<0.01
Chickasaw (0)	2	<0.01
Chippewa (59)	104	0.08

Race*	Population	%
Choctaw (1)	15	0.01
Colville (0)	0	<0.01
Comanche (0)	0	<0.01
Cree (6)	6	<0.01
Creek (0)	2	<0.01
Crow (0)	0	<0.01
Delaware (4)	7	0.01
Hopi (0)	0	<0.01
Houma (0)	0	<0.01
Inupiat (Alaska Native) (0)	0	<0.01
Iroquois (8)	23	0.02
Kiowa (0)	0	<0.01
Lumbee (12)	20	0.02
Menominee (0)	1	<0.01
Mexican American Ind. (4)	11	0.01
Navajo (5)	9	0.01
Osage (0)	0	<0.01
Ottawa (10)	19	0.01
Paiute (0)	0	<0.01
Pima (0)	0	<0.01
Potawatomi (5)	7	0.01
Pueblo (0)	0	<0.01
Puget Sound Salish (0)	0	<0.01
Seminole (1)	2	<0.01
Shoshone (1)	1	<0.01
Sioux (6)	13	0.01
South American Ind. (1)	3	<0.01
Spanish American Ind. (0)	0	<0.01
Tlingit-Haida (Alaska Native) (0)	0	<0.01
Tohono O'Odham (0)	0	<0.01
Tsimshian (Alaska Native) (0)	0	<0.01
Ute (0)	0	<0.01
Yakama (0)	0	<0.01
Yaqui (0)	0	<0.01
Yuman (0)	0	<0.01
Yup'ik (Alaska Native) (0)	0	<0.01
Asian (8,742)	10,282	7.93
Not Hispanic (8,713)	10,193	7.86
Hispanic (29)	89	0.07
Bangladeshi (205)	223	0.17
Bhutanese (0)	0	<0.01
Burmese (5)	5	<0.01
Cambodian (20)	25	0.02
Chinese, ex. Taiwanese (929)	1,023	0.79
Filipino (1,733)	1,981	1.53
Hmong (171)	175	0.13
Indian (3,340)	3,551	2.74
Indonesian (8)	14	0.01
Japanese (98)	170	0.13
Korean (406)	489	0.38
Laotian (31)	47	0.04
Malaysian (11)	15	0.01
Nepalese (5)	7	0.01
Pakistani (454)	501	0.39
Sri Lankan (11)	11	0.01
Taiwanese (34)	36	0.03
Thai (37)	46	0.04
Vietnamese (961)	1,027	0.79
Hawaii Native/Pacific Islander (19)	320	0.25
Not Hispanic (16)	306	0.24
Hispanic (3)	14	0.01
Fijian (0)	0	<0.01
Guamanian/Chamorro (7)	12	0.01
Marshallese (0)	0	<0.01
Native Hawaiian (7)	17	0.01
Samoan (3)	10	0.01
Tongan (0)	0	<0.01
White (110,426)	112,990	87.12
Not Hispanic (108,750)	111,121	85.68
Hispanic (1,676)	1,869	1.44

Notes: † The Census 2010 population figure is used to calculate the percentages in the Hispanic Origin and Race categories. Ancestry percentages are based on the 2006-2010 American Community Survey population (not shown); ‡ Numbers in parentheses indicate the number of people reporting a single ancestry; * Numbers in parentheses indicate the number of persons reporting this race alone, not in combination with any other race; Please refer to the User Guide for more information.

Taylor

Place Type: City
County: Wayne
Population: 63,131

Ancestry	Population	%
Afghan (0)	0	<0.01
African, Sub-Saharan (274)	305	0.48
African (218)	249	0.39
Cape Verdean (0)	0	<0.01
Ethiopian (0)	0	<0.01
Ghanaian (56)	56	0.09
Kenyan (0)	0	<0.01
Liberian (0)	0	<0.01
Nigerian (0)	0	<0.01
Senegalese (0)	0	<0.01
Sierra Leonean (0)	0	<0.01
Somalian (0)	0	<0.01
South African (0)	0	<0.01
Sudanese (0)	0	<0.01
Ugandan (0)	0	<0.01
Zimbabwean (0)	0	<0.01
Other Sub-Saharan African (0)	0	<0.01
Albanian (385)	385	0.60
Alsatian (0)	0	<0.01
American (2,291)	2,291	3.59
Arab (172)	356	0.56
Arab (51)	111	0.17
Egyptian (0)	0	<0.01
Iraqi (0)	0	<0.01
Jordanian (0)	0	<0.01
Lebanese (51)	145	0.23
Moroccan (0)	0	<0.01
Palestinian (7)	7	0.01
Syrian (63)	93	0.15
Other Arab (0)	0	<0.01
Armenian (70)	155	0.24
Assyrian/Chaldean/Syriac (11)	11	0.02
Australian (0)	23	0.04
Austrian (35)	94	0.15
Basque (0)	0	<0.01
Belgian (44)	101	0.16
Brazilian (86)	101	0.16
British (10)	47	0.07
Bulgarian (8)	8	0.01
Cajun (0)	0	<0.01
Canadian (39)	353	0.55
Carpatho Rusyn (0)	10	0.02
Celtic (0)	0	<0.01
Croatian (13)	115	0.18
Cypriot (0)	0	<0.01
Czech (79)	295	0.46
Czechoslovakian (103)	222	0.35
Danish (10)	168	0.26
Dutch (136)	923	1.45
Eastern European (10)	10	0.02
English (1,275)	5,231	8.19
Estonian (0)	0	<0.01
European (494)	613	0.96
Finnish (35)	291	0.46
French, ex. Basque (762)	4,438	6.95
French Canadian (708)	1,822	2.85
German (2,786)	10,727	16.80
German Russian (0)	0	<0.01
Greek (78)	350	0.55
Guyanese (10)	32	0.05
Hungarian (663)	2,139	3.35
Icelander (0)	0	<0.01
Iranian (0)	0	<0.01
Irish (2,185)	10,032	15.72
Israeli (0)	0	<0.01
Italian (1,048)	3,179	4.98
Latvian (10)	42	0.07
Lithuanian (126)	381	0.60
Luxemburger (0)	0	<0.01
Macedonian (7)	7	0.01
Maltese (163)	342	0.54
New Zealander (0)	0	<0.01
Northern European (0)	0	<0.01
Norwegian (26)	275	0.43
Pennsylvania German (74)	118	0.18
Polish (2,805)	6,619	10.37
Portuguese (20)	154	0.24
Romanian (138)	162	0.25
Russian (88)	305	0.48
Scandinavian (44)	98	0.15
Scotch-Irish (560)	1,226	1.92
Scottish (380)	1,341	2.10
Serbian (0)	11	0.02
Slavic (0)	20	0.03
Slovak (25)	243	0.38
Slovene (0)	8	0.01
Soviet Union (0)	0	<0.01
Swedish (135)	438	0.69
Swiss (0)	15	0.02
Turkish (0)	0	<0.01
Ukrainian (75)	101	0.16
Welsh (38)	314	0.49
West Indian, ex. Hispanic (74)	74	0.12
Bahamian (0)	0	<0.01
Barbadian (0)	0	<0.01
Belizean (0)	0	<0.01
Bermudan (0)	0	<0.01
British West Indian (0)	0	<0.01
Dutch West Indian (0)	0	<0.01
Haitian (0)	0	<0.01
Jamaican (18)	18	0.03
Trinidadian/Tobagonian (0)	0	<0.01
U.S. Virgin Islander (0)	0	<0.01
West Indian (56)	56	0.09
Other West Indian (0)	0	<0.01
Yugoslavian (0)	16	0.03

Hispanic Origin	Population	%
Hispanic or Latino (of any race)	3,209	5.08
Central American, ex. Mexican	77	0.12
Costa Rican	4	0.01
Guatemalan	16	0.03
Honduran	15	0.02
Nicaraguan	17	0.03
Panamanian	11	0.02
Salvadoran	14	0.02
Other Central American	0	<0.01
Cuban	55	0.09
Dominican Republic	7	0.01
Mexican	2,344	3.71
Puerto Rican	446	0.71
South American	56	0.09
Argentinean	23	0.04
Bolivian	2	<0.01
Chilean	6	0.01
Colombian	4	0.01
Ecuadorian	7	0.01
Paraguayan	0	<0.01
Peruvian	10	0.02
Uruguayan	2	<0.01
Venezuelan	2	<0.01
Other South American	0	<0.01
Other Hispanic or Latino	224	0.35

Race*	Population	%
African-American/Black (10,004)	10,865	17.21
Not Hispanic (9,896)	10,671	16.90
Hispanic (108)	194	0.31
American Indian/Alaska Native (336)	920	1.46
Not Hispanic (285)	808	1.28
Hispanic (51)	112	0.18
Alaska Athabascan (Ala. Nat.) (0)	0	<0.01
Aleut (Alaska Native) (0)	0	<0.01
Apache (4)	10	0.02
Arapaho (0)	0	<0.01
Blackfeet (12)	39	0.06
Canadian/French Am. Ind. (10)	13	0.02
Central American Ind. (0)	3	<0.01
Cherokee (41)	217	0.34
Cheyenne (0)	2	<0.01
Chickasaw (1)	5	0.01
Chippewa (59)	114	0.18
Choctaw (1)	8	0.01
Colville (0)	0	<0.01
Comanche (3)	3	<0.01
Cree (1)	2	<0.01
Creek (3)	4	0.01
Crow (0)	2	<0.01
Delaware (6)	18	0.03
Hopi (0)	2	<0.01
Houma (0)	0	<0.01
Inupiat (Alaska Native) (0)	0	<0.01
Iroquois (13)	43	0.07
Kiowa (0)	0	<0.01
Lumbee (27)	43	0.07
Menominee (0)	1	<0.01
Mexican American Ind. (4)	7	0.01
Navajo (1)	5	0.01
Osage (2)	4	0.01
Ottawa (9)	16	0.03
Paiute (0)	0	<0.01
Pima (0)	1	<0.01
Potawatomi (1)	3	<0.01
Pueblo (0)	1	<0.01
Puget Sound Salish (0)	0	<0.01
Seminole (0)	4	0.01
Shoshone (0)	0	<0.01
Sioux (0)	13	0.02
South American Ind. (0)	5	0.01
Spanish American Ind. (1)	1	<0.01
Tlingit-Haida (Alaska Native) (1)	4	0.01
Tohono O'Odham (0)	0	<0.01
Tsimshian (Alaska Native) (0)	0	<0.01
Ute (0)	0	<0.01
Yakama (0)	0	<0.01
Yaqui (4)	4	0.01
Yuman (0)	1	<0.01
Yup'ik (Alaska Native) (0)	0	<0.01
Asian (1,121)	1,324	2.10
Not Hispanic (1,111)	1,294	2.05
Hispanic (10)	30	0.05
Bangladeshi (0)	0	<0.01
Bhutanese (0)	0	<0.01
Burmese (0)	0	<0.01
Cambodian (15)	17	0.03
Chinese, ex. Taiwanese (98)	123	0.19
Filipino (234)	308	0.49
Hmong (5)	8	0.01
Indian (289)	312	0.49
Indonesian (4)	5	0.01
Japanese (31)	81	0.13
Korean (49)	69	0.11
Laotian (1)	5	0.01
Malaysian (2)	2	<0.01
Nepalese (0)	0	<0.01
Pakistani (243)	252	0.40
Sri Lankan (0)	0	<0.01
Taiwanese (0)	0	<0.01
Thai (14)	20	0.03
Vietnamese (86)	90	0.14
Hawaii Native/Pacific Islander (20)	63	0.10
Not Hispanic (16)	49	0.08
Hispanic (4)	14	0.02
Fijian (0)	0	<0.01
Guamanian/Chamorro (3)	3	<0.01
Marshallese (0)	0	<0.01
Native Hawaiian (7)	19	0.03
Samoan (1)	2	<0.01
Tongan (0)	0	<0.01
White (49,229)	50,686	80.29
Not Hispanic (47,177)	48,415	76.69
Hispanic (2,052)	2,271	3.60

Notes: † The Census 2010 population figure is used to calculate the percentages in the Hispanic Origin and Race categories. Ancestry percentages are based on the 2006-2010 American Community Survey population (not shown); ‡ Numbers in parentheses indicate the number of people reporting a single ancestry; * Numbers in parentheses indicate the number of persons reporting this race alone, not in combination with any other race; Please refer to the User Guide for more information.

Troy

Place Type: City
County: Oakland
Population: 80,980

Ancestry	Population	%
Afghan (0)	0	<0.01
African, Sub-Saharan (191)	191	0.24
African (69)	69	0.09
Cape Verdean (0)	0	<0.01
Ethiopian (0)	0	<0.01
Ghanaian (37)	37	0.05
Kenyan (0)	0	<0.01
Liberian (0)	0	<0.01
Nigerian (63)	63	0.08
Senegalese (0)	0	<0.01
Sierra Leonean (0)	0	<0.01
Somalian (0)	0	<0.01
South African (0)	0	<0.01
Sudanese (0)	0	<0.01
Ugandan (0)	0	<0.01
Zimbabwean (0)	0	<0.01
Other Sub-Saharan African (22)	22	0.03
Albanian (612)	612	0.76
Alsatian (0)	0	<0.01
American (2,507)	2,507	3.10
Arab (2,511)	3,081	3.80
Arab (750)	929	1.15
Egyptian (286)	286	0.35
Iraqi (594)	722	0.89
Jordanian (60)	66	0.08
Lebanese (621)	752	0.93
Moroccan (0)	0	<0.01
Palestinian (29)	29	0.04
Syrian (87)	145	0.18
Other Arab (84)	152	0.19
Armenian (133)	338	0.42
Assyrian/Chaldean/Syriac (1,350)	1,643	2.03
Australian (54)	54	0.07
Austrian (62)	269	0.33
Basque (0)	0	<0.01
Belgian (162)	722	0.89
Brazilian (38)	38	0.05
British (109)	275	0.34
Bulgarian (44)	44	0.05
Cajun (0)	0	<0.01
Canadian (124)	446	0.55
Carpatho Rusyn (0)	0	<0.01
Celtic (0)	60	0.07
Croatian (89)	274	0.34
Cypriot (0)	0	<0.01
Czech (23)	280	0.35
Czechoslovakian (111)	258	0.32
Danish (113)	376	0.46
Dutch (266)	1,546	1.91
Eastern European (137)	163	0.20
English (1,902)	8,083	9.98
Estonian (13)	13	0.02
European (760)	913	1.13
Finnish (235)	674	0.83
French, ex. Basque (350)	3,424	4.23
French Canadian (474)	1,265	1.56
German (3,915)	15,482	19.12
German Russian (22)	22	0.03
Greek (608)	1,057	1.31
Guyanese (0)	0	<0.01
Hungarian (190)	685	0.85
Icelander (0)	0	<0.01
Iranian (202)	218	0.27
Irish (2,069)	9,427	11.64
Israeli (0)	0	<0.01
Italian (2,327)	6,643	8.20
Latvian (32)	32	0.04
Lithuanian (62)	444	0.55
Luxemburger (0)	9	0.01
Macedonian (186)	223	0.28
Maltese (28)	90	0.11
New Zealander (0)	0	<0.01
Northern European (91)	91	0.11

Ancestry (cont.)	Population	%
Norwegian (144)	594	0.73
Pennsylvania German (8)	20	0.02
Polish (3,348)	9,135	11.28
Portuguese (45)	98	0.12
Romanian (915)	1,184	1.46
Russian (419)	931	1.15
Scandinavian (66)	86	0.11
Scotch-Irish (426)	1,480	1.83
Scottish (615)	2,454	3.03
Serbian (148)	333	0.41
Slavic (24)	139	0.17
Slovak (140)	277	0.34
Slovene (0)	44	0.05
Soviet Union (0)	0	<0.01
Swedish (433)	1,278	1.58
Swiss (19)	246	0.30
Turkish (61)	70	0.09
Ukrainian (423)	845	1.04
Welsh (40)	609	0.75
West Indian, ex. Hispanic (119)	198	0.24
Bahamian (0)	0	<0.01
Barbadian (0)	0	<0.01
Belizean (0)	0	<0.01
Bermudan (0)	0	<0.01
British West Indian (0)	0	<0.01
Dutch West Indian (0)	0	<0.01
Haitian (10)	28	0.03
Jamaican (109)	156	0.19
Trinidadian/Tobagonian (0)	0	<0.01
U.S. Virgin Islander (0)	0	<0.01
West Indian (0)	14	0.02
Other West Indian (0)	0	<0.01
Yugoslavian (279)	338	0.42

Hispanic Origin	Population	%
Hispanic or Latino (of any race)	1,710	2.11
Central American, ex. Mexican	210	0.26
Costa Rican	7	0.01
Guatemalan	25	0.03
Honduran	15	0.02
Nicaraguan	5	0.01
Panamanian	2	<0.01
Salvadoran	156	0.19
Other Central American	0	<0.01
Cuban	47	0.06
Dominican Republic	8	0.01
Mexican	825	1.02
Puerto Rican	130	0.16
South American	262	0.32
Argentinean	42	0.05
Bolivian	5	0.01
Chilean	13	0.02
Colombian	77	0.10
Ecuadorian	26	0.03
Paraguayan	4	<0.01
Peruvian	62	0.08
Uruguayan	1	<0.01
Venezuelan	27	0.03
Other South American	5	0.01
Other Hispanic or Latino	228	0.28

Race*	Population	%
African-American/Black (3,240)	3,655	4.51
Not Hispanic (3,210)	3,595	4.44
Hispanic (30)	60	0.07
American Indian/Alaska Native (151)	445	0.55
Not Hispanic (124)	384	0.47
Hispanic (27)	61	0.08
Alaska Athabascan (Ala. Nat.) (0)	0	<0.01
Aleut (Alaska Native) (0)	0	<0.01
Apache (1)	7	0.01
Arapaho (0)	0	<0.01
Blackfeet (0)	4	<0.01
Canadian/French Am. Ind. (3)	5	0.01
Central American Ind. (1)	3	<0.01
Cherokee (4)	80	0.10
Cheyenne (0)	0	<0.01
Chickasaw (0)	4	<0.01
Chippewa (17)	52	0.06

Race* (cont.)	Population	%
Choctaw (2)	8	0.01
Colville (0)	0	<0.01
Comanche (0)	0	<0.01
Cree (0)	0	<0.01
Creek (0)	1	<0.01
Crow (0)	0	<0.01
Delaware (0)	0	<0.01
Hopi (0)	3	<0.01
Houma (0)	0	<0.01
Inupiat (Alaska Native) (0)	0	<0.01
Iroquois (13)	22	0.03
Kiowa (0)	0	<0.01
Lumbee (1)	5	0.01
Menominee (0)	1	<0.01
Mexican American Ind. (5)	9	0.01
Navajo (1)	1	<0.01
Osage (0)	1	<0.01
Ottawa (7)	14	0.02
Paiute (0)	0	<0.01
Pima (0)	0	<0.01
Potawatomi (3)	9	0.01
Pueblo (0)	0	<0.01
Puget Sound Salish (0)	0	<0.01
Seminole (0)	4	<0.01
Shoshone (0)	0	<0.01
Sioux (2)	4	<0.01
South American Ind. (2)	3	<0.01
Spanish American Ind. (1)	1	<0.01
Tlingit-Haida (Alaska Native) (0)	0	<0.01
Tohono O'Odham (0)	0	<0.01
Tsimshian (Alaska Native) (0)	0	<0.01
Ute (0)	0	<0.01
Yakama (0)	0	<0.01
Yaqui (0)	4	<0.01
Yuman (0)	0	<0.01
Yup'ik (Alaska Native) (0)	0	<0.01
Asian (15,462)	16,417	20.27
Not Hispanic (15,439)	16,356	20.20
Hispanic (23)	61	0.08
Bangladeshi (213)	232	0.29
Bhutanese (0)	0	<0.01
Burmese (1)	4	<0.01
Cambodian (8)	14	0.02
Chinese, ex. Taiwanese (3,653)	3,809	4.70
Filipino (953)	1,121	1.38
Hmong (36)	36	0.04
Indian (7,331)	7,564	9.34
Indonesian (6)	10	0.01
Japanese (301)	386	0.48
Korean (1,373)	1,465	1.81
Laotian (20)	20	0.02
Malaysian (10)	11	0.01
Nepalese (31)	36	0.04
Pakistani (607)	663	0.82
Sri Lankan (34)	36	0.04
Taiwanese (393)	415	0.51
Thai (42)	50	0.06
Vietnamese (241)	257	0.32
Hawaii Native/Pacific Islander (1)	90	0.11
Not Hispanic (1)	84	0.10
Hispanic (0)	6	0.01
Fijian (0)	0	<0.01
Guamanian/Chamorro (0)	4	<0.01
Marshallese (0)	0	<0.01
Native Hawaiian (0)	12	0.01
Samoan (0)	2	<0.01
Tongan (0)	0	<0.01
White (59,998)	61,356	75.77
Not Hispanic (58,869)	60,096	74.21
Hispanic (1,129)	1,260	1.56

Warren

Place Type: City
County: Macomb
Population: 134,056

Ancestry	Population	%
Afghan (0)	0	<0.01
African, Sub-Saharan (539)	591	0.44
African (438)	490	0.36
Cape Verdean (0)	0	<0.01
Ethiopian (0)	0	<0.01
Ghanaian (0)	0	<0.01
Kenyan (40)	40	0.03
Liberian (0)	0	<0.01
Nigerian (0)	0	<0.01
Senegalese (20)	20	0.01
Sierra Leonean (0)	0	<0.01
Somalian (0)	0	<0.01
South African (0)	0	<0.01
Sudanese (0)	0	<0.01
Ugandan (0)	0	<0.01
Zimbabwean (0)	0	<0.01
Other Sub-Saharan African (41)	41	0.03
Albanian (524)	534	0.39
Alsatian (0)	0	<0.01
American (4,766)	4,766	3.51
Arab (1,921)	2,804	2.06
Arab (190)	309	0.23
Egyptian (8)	62	0.05
Iraqi (707)	932	0.69
Jordanian (164)	174	0.13
Lebanese (528)	891	0.66
Moroccan (0)	0	<0.01
Palestinian (13)	19	0.01
Syrian (92)	160	0.12
Other Arab (219)	257	0.19
Armenian (460)	528	0.39
Assyrian/Chaldean/Syriac (2,077)	2,627	1.93
Australian (0)	26	0.02
Austrian (115)	351	0.26
Basque (0)	0	<0.01
Belgian (465)	1,678	1.24
Brazilian (0)	0	<0.01
British (207)	441	0.32
Bulgarian (7)	44	0.03
Cajun (0)	0	<0.01
Canadian (219)	635	0.47
Carpatho Rusyn (0)	0	<0.01
Celtic (0)	23	0.02
Croatian (99)	406	0.30
Cypriot (0)	0	<0.01
Czech (69)	386	0.28
Czechoslovakian (87)	276	0.20
Danish (70)	225	0.17
Dutch (328)	1,603	1.18
Eastern European (8)	8	0.01
English (2,046)	9,746	7.18
Estonian (0)	0	<0.01
European (549)	600	0.44
Finnish (281)	969	0.71
French, ex. Basque (1,042)	7,214	5.31
French Canadian (1,135)	2,892	2.13
German (7,035)	26,458	19.48
German Russian (0)	0	<0.01
Greek (331)	894	0.66
Guyanese (0)	0	<0.01
Hungarian (235)	1,275	0.94
Icelander (0)	0	<0.01
Iranian (213)	226	0.17
Irish (3,645)	16,937	12.47
Israeli (0)	0	<0.01
Italian (5,164)	13,557	9.98
Latvian (8)	29	0.02
Lithuanian (157)	597	0.44
Luxemburger (0)	0	<0.01
Macedonian (104)	114	0.08
Maltese (133)	320	0.24
New Zealander (0)	0	<0.01
Northern European (27)	27	0.02

Ancestry (cont.)	Population	%
Norwegian (182)	765	0.56
Pennsylvania German (10)	30	0.02
Polish (12,605)	26,655	19.63
Portuguese (17)	82	0.06
Romanian (599)	955	0.70
Russian (331)	1,211	0.89
Scandinavian (5)	34	0.03
Scotch-Irish (626)	1,965	1.45
Scottish (704)	2,448	1.80
Serbian (161)	237	0.17
Slavic (9)	102	0.08
Slovak (429)	821	0.60
Slovene (57)	108	0.08
Soviet Union (0)	0	<0.01
Swedish (174)	1,004	0.74
Swiss (23)	130	0.10
Turkish (9)	18	0.01
Ukrainian (1,353)	1,999	1.47
Welsh (61)	557	0.41
West Indian, ex. Hispanic (96)	109	0.08
Bahamian (0)	0	<0.01
Barbadian (0)	0	<0.01
Belizean (14)	14	0.01
Bermudan (0)	0	<0.01
British West Indian (0)	0	<0.01
Dutch West Indian (0)	0	<0.01
Haitian (60)	73	0.05
Jamaican (22)	22	0.02
Trinidadian/Tobagonian (0)	0	<0.01
U.S. Virgin Islander (0)	0	<0.01
West Indian (0)	0	<0.01
Other West Indian (0)	0	<0.01
Yugoslavian (710)	990	0.73

Hispanic Origin	Population	%
Hispanic or Latino (of any race)	2,758	2.06
Central American, ex. Mexican	87	0.06
Costa Rican	1	<0.01
Guatemalan	35	0.03
Honduran	11	0.01
Nicaraguan	6	<0.01
Panamanian	8	0.01
Salvadoran	23	0.02
Other Central American	3	<0.01
Cuban	76	0.06
Dominican Republic	42	0.03
Mexican	1,650	1.23
Puerto Rican	405	0.30
South American	135	0.10
Argentinean	35	0.03
Bolivian	2	<0.01
Chilean	25	0.02
Colombian	20	0.01
Ecuadorian	19	0.01
Paraguayan	1	<0.01
Peruvian	13	0.01
Uruguayan	1	<0.01
Venezuelan	18	0.01
Other South American	1	<0.01
Other Hispanic or Latino	363	0.27

Race*	Population	%
African-American/Black (18,123)	19,712	14.70
Not Hispanic (17,978)	19,443	14.50
Hispanic (145)	269	0.20
American Indian/Alaska Native (562)	1,588	1.18
Not Hispanic (524)	1,461	1.09
Hispanic (38)	127	0.09
Alaska Athabascan (Ala. Nat.) (2)	3	<0.01
Aleut (Alaska Native) (0)	2	<0.01
Apache (5)	22	0.02
Arapaho (0)	0	<0.01
Blackfeet (2)	45	0.03
Canadian/French Am. Ind. (16)	38	0.03
Central American Ind. (0)	0	<0.01
Cherokee (72)	320	0.24
Cheyenne (1)	2	<0.01
Chickasaw (0)	2	<0.01
Chippewa (87)	171	0.13

Race* (cont.)	Population	%
Choctaw (3)	17	0.01
Colville (0)	0	<0.01
Comanche (0)	2	<0.01
Cree (1)	5	<0.01
Creek (0)	3	<0.01
Crow (0)	1	<0.01
Delaware (2)	2	<0.01
Hopi (0)	6	<0.01
Houma (0)	0	<0.01
Inupiat (Alaska Native) (0)	0	<0.01
Iroquois (21)	55	0.04
Kiowa (0)	0	<0.01
Lumbee (55)	77	0.06
Menominee (1)	1	<0.01
Mexican American Ind. (4)	8	0.01
Navajo (2)	8	0.01
Osage (0)	0	<0.01
Ottawa (23)	34	0.03
Paiute (0)	0	<0.01
Pima (1)	1	<0.01
Potawatomi (4)	14	0.01
Pueblo (0)	0	<0.01
Puget Sound Salish (3)	3	<0.01
Seminole (2)	2	<0.01
Shoshone (1)	2	<0.01
Sioux (8)	29	0.02
South American Ind. (0)	1	<0.01
Spanish American Ind. (0)	1	<0.01
Tlingit-Haida (Alaska Native) (1)	1	<0.01
Tohono O'Odham (0)	0	<0.01
Tsimshian (Alaska Native) (0)	0	<0.01
Ute (0)	0	<0.01
Yakama (0)	0	<0.01
Yaqui (2)	2	<0.01
Yuman (0)	0	<0.01
Yup'ik (Alaska Native) (0)	0	<0.01
Asian (6,212)	7,263	5.42
Not Hispanic (6,170)	7,175	5.35
Hispanic (42)	88	0.07
Bangladeshi (956)	1,061	0.79
Bhutanese (0)	0	<0.01
Burmese (0)	2	<0.01
Cambodian (30)	55	0.04
Chinese, ex. Taiwanese (297)	381	0.28
Filipino (1,183)	1,432	1.07
Hmong (1,170)	1,218	0.91
Indian (1,051)	1,254	0.94
Indonesian (5)	9	0.01
Japanese (65)	137	0.10
Korean (140)	202	0.15
Laotian (141)	178	0.13
Malaysian (0)	0	<0.01
Nepalese (3)	5	<0.01
Pakistani (192)	203	0.15
Sri Lankan (7)	7	0.01
Taiwanese (9)	11	0.01
Thai (33)	58	0.04
Vietnamese (544)	608	0.45
Hawaii Native/Pacific Islander (20)	153	0.11
Not Hispanic (18)	136	0.10
Hispanic (2)	17	0.01
Fijian (0)	0	<0.01
Guamanian/Chamorro (2)	3	<0.01
Marshallese (0)	0	<0.01
Native Hawaiian (5)	36	0.03
Samoan (3)	7	0.01
Tongan (0)	0	<0.01
White (105,088)	108,186	80.70
Not Hispanic (103,308)	106,146	79.18
Hispanic (1,780)	2,040	1.52

Notes: † The Census 2010 population figure is used to calculate the percentages in the Hispanic Origin and Race categories. Ancestry percentages are based on the 2006-2010 American Community Survey population (not shown); ‡ Numbers in parentheses indicate the number of people reporting a single ancestry; * Numbers in parentheses indicate the number of persons reporting this race alone, not in combination with any other race; Please refer to the User Guide for more information.

Waterford

Place Type: Charter Township
County: Oakland
Population: 71,707

Ancestry	Population	%
Afghan (0)	0	<0.01
African, Sub-Saharan (111)	133	0.19
African (63)	85	0.12
Cape Verdean (0)	0	<0.01
Ethiopian (0)	0	<0.01
Ghanaian (34)	34	0.05
Kenyan (0)	0	<0.01
Liberian (0)	0	<0.01
Nigerian (14)	14	0.02
Senegalese (0)	0	<0.01
Sierra Leonean (0)	0	<0.01
Somalian (0)	0	<0.01
South African (0)	0	<0.01
Sudanese (0)	0	<0.01
Ugandan (0)	0	<0.01
Zimbabwean (0)	0	<0.01
Other Sub-Saharan African (0)	0	<0.01
Albanian (82)	153	0.21
Alsatian (0)	0	<0.01
American (3,571)	3,571	4.97
Arab (361)	666	0.93
Arab (72)	110	0.15
Egyptian (19)	47	0.07
Iraqi (123)	135	0.19
Jordanian (0)	0	<0.01
Lebanese (95)	253	0.35
Moroccan (0)	29	0.04
Palestinian (0)	0	<0.01
Syrian (0)	0	<0.01
Other Arab (52)	92	0.13
Armenian (213)	435	0.61
Assyrian/Chaldean/Syriac (463)	527	0.73
Australian (0)	38	0.05
Austrian (46)	163	0.23
Basque (0)	0	<0.01
Belgian (21)	120	0.17
Brazilian (0)	0	<0.01
British (108)	271	0.38
Bulgarian (108)	108	0.15
Cajun (0)	0	<0.01
Canadian (219)	625	0.87
Carpatho Rusyn (0)	0	<0.01
Celtic (11)	56	0.08
Croatian (81)	174	0.24
Cypriot (0)	0	<0.01
Czech (157)	364	0.51
Czechoslovakian (25)	168	0.23
Danish (81)	326	0.45
Dutch (310)	1,900	2.65
Eastern European (42)	42	0.06
English (2,859)	10,085	14.05
Estonian (0)	0	<0.01
European (511)	647	0.90
Finnish (228)	690	0.96
French, ex. Basque (477)	4,372	6.09
French Canadian (555)	1,465	2.04
German (5,185)	18,164	25.30
German Russian (0)	0	<0.01
Greek (209)	571	0.80
Guyanese (0)	0	<0.01
Hungarian (294)	813	1.13
Icelander (0)	0	<0.01
Iranian (0)	0	<0.01
Irish (3,416)	12,416	17.29
Israeli (13)	26	0.04
Italian (1,316)	4,000	5.57
Latvian (7)	7	0.01
Lithuanian (35)	142	0.20
Luxemburger (0)	0	<0.01
Macedonian (17)	28	0.04
Maltese (30)	125	0.17
New Zealander (0)	0	<0.01
Northern European (11)	11	0.02
Norwegian (263)	786	1.09
Pennsylvania German (17)	56	0.08
Polish (2,070)	6,336	8.82
Portuguese (27)	34	0.05
Romanian (213)	352	0.49
Russian (309)	825	1.15
Scandinavian (61)	103	0.14
Scotch-Irish (739)	1,716	2.39
Scottish (789)	2,800	3.90
Serbian (0)	62	0.09
Slavic (39)	69	0.10
Slovak (95)	186	0.26
Slovene (24)	83	0.12
Soviet Union (0)	0	<0.01
Swedish (303)	1,259	1.75
Swiss (44)	84	0.12
Turkish (0)	0	<0.01
Ukrainian (150)	324	0.45
Welsh (41)	725	1.01
West Indian, ex. Hispanic (33)	46	0.06
Bahamian (0)	0	<0.01
Barbadian (0)	0	<0.01
Belizean (0)	0	<0.01
Bermudan (0)	0	<0.01
British West Indian (0)	0	<0.01
Dutch West Indian (0)	0	<0.01
Haitian (12)	12	0.02
Jamaican (21)	34	0.05
Trinidadian/Tobagonian (0)	0	<0.01
U.S. Virgin Islander (0)	0	<0.01
West Indian (0)	0	<0.01
Other West Indian (0)	0	<0.01
Yugoslavian (41)	136	0.19

Hispanic Origin	Population	%
Hispanic or Latino (of any race)	4,557	6.36
Central American, ex. Mexican	124	0.17
Costa Rican	16	0.02
Guatemalan	30	0.04
Honduran	26	0.04
Nicaraguan	10	0.01
Panamanian	3	<0.01
Salvadoran	38	0.05
Other Central American	1	<0.01
Cuban	39	0.05
Dominican Republic	14	0.02
Mexican	3,316	4.62
Puerto Rican	639	0.89
South American	103	0.14
Argentinean	11	0.02
Bolivian	0	<0.01
Chilean	18	0.03
Colombian	29	0.04
Ecuadorian	11	0.02
Paraguayan	3	<0.01
Peruvian	22	0.03
Uruguayan	0	<0.01
Venezuelan	9	0.01
Other South American	0	<0.01
Other Hispanic or Latino	322	0.45

Race*	Population	%
African-American/Black (3,374)	4,071	5.68
Not Hispanic (3,266)	3,871	5.40
Hispanic (108)	200	0.28
American Indian/Alaska Native (306)	807	1.13
Not Hispanic (254)	694	0.97
Hispanic (52)	113	0.16
Alaska Athabascan (Ala. Nat.) (0)	0	<0.01
Aleut (Alaska Native) (0)	0	<0.01
Apache (2)	11	0.02
Arapaho (0)	0	<0.01
Blackfeet (2)	28	0.04
Canadian/French Am. Ind. (2)	5	0.01
Central American Ind. (3)	4	0.01
Cherokee (21)	157	0.22
Cheyenne (2)	2	<0.01
Chickasaw (0)	0	<0.01
Chippewa (103)	167	0.23

Choctaw (2)	2	<0.01
Colville (0)	0	<0.01
Comanche (1)	2	<0.01
Cree (0)	1	<0.01
Creek (1)	1	<0.01
Crow (0)	0	<0.01
Delaware (4)	4	0.01
Hopi (1)	1	<0.01
Houma (0)	0	<0.01
Inupiat (Alaska Native) (1)	1	<0.01
Iroquois (8)	30	0.04
Kiowa (0)	1	<0.01
Lumbee (3)	9	0.01
Menominee (0)	0	<0.01
Mexican American Ind. (8)	17	0.02
Navajo (2)	8	0.01
Osage (0)	0	<0.01
Ottawa (6)	22	0.03
Paiute (0)	1	<0.01
Pima (0)	0	<0.01
Potawatomi (10)	14	0.02
Pueblo (0)	0	<0.01
Puget Sound Salish (0)	0	<0.01
Seminole (0)	1	<0.01
Shoshone (0)	0	<0.01
Sioux (6)	12	0.02
South American Ind. (1)	1	<0.01
Spanish American Ind. (1)	1	<0.01
Tlingit-Haida (Alaska Native) (1)	3	<0.01
Tohono O'Odham (0)	0	<0.01
Tsimshian (Alaska Native) (0)	0	<0.01
Ute (0)	0	<0.01
Yakama (0)	0	<0.01
Yaqui (0)	0	<0.01
Yuman (0)	0	<0.01
Yup'ik (Alaska Native) (0)	0	<0.01
Asian (1,143)	1,527	2.13
Not Hispanic (1,131)	1,488	2.08
Hispanic (12)	39	0.05
Bangladeshi (11)	11	0.02
Bhutanese (0)	0	<0.01
Burmese (0)	0	<0.01
Cambodian (4)	6	0.01
Chinese, ex. Taiwanese (137)	186	0.26
Filipino (236)	361	0.50
Hmong (213)	217	0.30
Indian (145)	178	0.25
Indonesian (2)	7	0.01
Japanese (51)	113	0.16
Korean (109)	166	0.23
Laotian (13)	15	0.02
Malaysian (0)	1	<0.01
Nepalese (57)	62	0.09
Pakistani (18)	22	0.03
Sri Lankan (0)	1	<0.01
Taiwanese (9)	11	0.02
Thai (18)	26	0.04
Vietnamese (75)	95	0.13
Hawaii Native/Pacific Islander (12)	58	0.08
Not Hispanic (10)	49	0.07
Hispanic (2)	9	0.01
Fijian (1)	1	<0.01
Guamanian/Chamorro (4)	5	0.01
Marshallese (0)	0	<0.01
Native Hawaiian (3)	16	0.02
Samoan (0)	1	<0.01
Tongan (0)	0	<0.01
White (63,937)	65,528	91.38
Not Hispanic (61,103)	62,353	86.96
Hispanic (2,834)	3,175	4.43

West Bloomfield

Place Type: Charter Township
County: Oakland
Population: 64,690

Ancestry	Population	%
Afghan (0)	0	<0.01
African, Sub-Saharan (238)	395	0.61
African (96)	96	0.15
Cape Verdean (0)	0	<0.01
Ethiopian (25)	25	0.04
Ghanaian (0)	0	<0.01
Kenyan (0)	0	<0.01
Liberian (0)	0	<0.01
Nigerian (93)	250	0.39
Senegalese (7)	7	0.01
Sierra Leonean (0)	0	<0.01
Somalian (0)	0	<0.01
South African (0)	0	<0.01
Sudanese (0)	0	<0.01
Ugandan (0)	0	<0.01
Zimbabwean (17)	17	0.03
Other Sub-Saharan African (0)	0	<0.01
Albanian (281)	315	0.49
Alsatian (0)	0	<0.01
American (2,747)	2,747	4.25
Arab (3,524)	4,594	7.10
Arab (1,263)	1,506	2.33
Egyptian (74)	83	0.13
Iraqi (1,385)	1,775	2.74
Jordanian (32)	32	0.05
Lebanese (257)	453	0.70
Moroccan (0)	0	<0.01
Palestinian (53)	53	0.08
Syrian (93)	125	0.19
Other Arab (367)	567	0.88
Armenian (691)	814	1.26
Assyrian/Chaldean/Syriac (4,689)	5,475	8.46
Australian (0)	0	<0.01
Austrian (92)	398	0.62
Basque (0)	0	<0.01
Belgian (33)	276	0.43
Brazilian (18)	78	0.12
British (121)	157	0.24
Bulgarian (0)	0	<0.01
Cajun (0)	0	<0.01
Canadian (468)	611	0.94
Carpatho Rusyn (0)	0	<0.01
Celtic (8)	8	0.01
Croatian (28)	61	0.09
Cypriot (0)	0	<0.01
Czech (40)	253	0.39
Czechoslovakian (19)	101	0.16
Danish (12)	152	0.23
Dutch (89)	541	0.84
Eastern European (831)	842	1.30
English (1,105)	3,993	6.17
Estonian (0)	0	<0.01
European (1,037)	1,081	1.67
Finnish (234)	429	0.66
French, ex. Basque (371)	1,658	2.56
French Canadian (170)	823	1.27
German (1,845)	7,192	11.11
German Russian (0)	0	<0.01
Greek (227)	347	0.54
Guyanese (0)	0	<0.01
Hungarian (506)	1,200	1.85
Icelander (0)	0	<0.01
Iranian (583)	640	0.99
Irish (1,144)	4,166	6.44
Israeli (208)	268	0.41
Italian (896)	2,337	3.61
Latvian (41)	76	0.12
Lithuanian (129)	293	0.45
Luxemburger (10)	10	0.02
Macedonian (14)	36	0.06
Maltese (19)	44	0.07
New Zealander (0)	0	<0.01
Northern European (12)	12	0.02

Ancestry (cont.)	Population	%
Norwegian (82)	281	0.43
Pennsylvania German (0)	0	<0.01
Polish (2,677)	6,341	9.80
Portuguese (8)	8	0.01
Romanian (222)	469	0.72
Russian (2,578)	4,873	7.53
Scandinavian (71)	101	0.16
Scotch-Irish (207)	594	0.92
Scottish (278)	924	1.43
Serbian (21)	84	0.13
Slavic (0)	35	0.05
Slovak (142)	224	0.35
Slovene (0)	31	0.05
Soviet Union (0)	0	<0.01
Swedish (239)	647	1.00
Swiss (29)	81	0.13
Turkish (85)	85	0.13
Ukrainian (335)	433	0.67
Welsh (58)	221	0.34
West Indian, ex. Hispanic (9)	20	0.03
Bahamian (0)	0	<0.01
Barbadian (0)	0	<0.01
Belizean (0)	0	<0.01
Bermudan (0)	0	<0.01
British West Indian (0)	0	<0.01
Dutch West Indian (0)	0	<0.01
Haitian (0)	0	<0.01
Jamaican (9)	20	0.03
Trinidadian/Tobagonian (0)	0	<0.01
U.S. Virgin Islander (0)	0	<0.01
West Indian (0)	0	<0.01
Other West Indian (0)	0	<0.01
Yugoslavian (61)	118	0.18

Hispanic Origin	Population	%
Hispanic or Latino (of any race)	1,042	1.61
Central American, ex. Mexican	64	0.10
Costa Rican	5	0.01
Guatemalan	22	0.03
Honduran	9	0.01
Nicaraguan	6	0.01
Panamanian	12	0.02
Salvadoran	10	0.02
Other Central American	0	<0.01
Cuban	42	0.06
Dominican Republic	12	0.02
Mexican	514	0.79
Puerto Rican	93	0.14
South American	162	0.25
Argentinean	34	0.05
Bolivian	3	<0.01
Chilean	23	0.04
Colombian	51	0.08
Ecuadorian	8	0.01
Paraguayan	9	0.01
Peruvian	21	0.03
Uruguayan	4	0.01
Venezuelan	7	0.01
Other South American	2	<0.01
Other Hispanic or Latino	155	0.24

Race*	Population	%
African-American/Black (7,396)	7,750	11.98
Not Hispanic (7,338)	7,662	11.84
Hispanic (58)	88	0.14
American Indian/Alaska Native (72)	285	0.44
Not Hispanic (61)	261	0.40
Hispanic (11)	24	0.04
Alaska Athabascan (Ala. Nat.) (0)	0	<0.01
Aleut (Alaska Native) (0)	0	<0.01
Apache (1)	3	<0.01
Arapaho (0)	0	<0.01
Blackfeet (1)	6	0.01
Canadian/French Am. Ind. (0)	0	<0.01
Central American Ind. (1)	2	<0.01
Cherokee (6)	44	0.07
Cheyenne (0)	0	<0.01
Chickasaw (0)	0	<0.01
Chippewa (9)	16	0.02

Race* (cont.)	Population	%
Choctaw (0)	2	<0.01
Colville (0)	0	<0.01
Comanche (0)	0	<0.01
Cree (2)	2	<0.01
Creek (0)	1	<0.01
Crow (0)	0	<0.01
Delaware (0)	0	<0.01
Hopi (0)	0	<0.01
Houma (0)	0	<0.01
Inupiat (Alaska Native) (0)	0	<0.01
Iroquois (3)	10	0.02
Kiowa (0)	0	<0.01
Lumbee (1)	6	0.01
Menominee (0)	0	<0.01
Mexican American Ind. (3)	3	<0.01
Navajo (2)	4	0.01
Osage (0)	0	<0.01
Ottawa (2)	3	<0.01
Paiute (0)	0	<0.01
Pima (0)	0	<0.01
Potawatomi (3)	9	0.01
Pueblo (0)	0	<0.01
Puget Sound Salish (0)	0	<0.01
Seminole (0)	4	0.01
Shoshone (0)	0	<0.01
Sioux (1)	6	0.01
South American Ind. (0)	5	0.01
Spanish American Ind. (0)	0	<0.01
Tlingit-Haida (Alaska Native) (2)	2	<0.01
Tohono O'Odham (0)	0	<0.01
Tsimshian (Alaska Native) (0)	0	<0.01
Ute (0)	0	<0.01
Yakama (0)	0	<0.01
Yaqui (0)	0	<0.01
Yuman (0)	0	<0.01
Yup'ik (Alaska Native) (0)	0	<0.01
Asian (5,421)	6,156	9.52
Not Hispanic (5,412)	6,123	9.47
Hispanic (9)	33	0.05
Bangladeshi (33)	36	0.06
Bhutanese (0)	0	<0.01
Burmese (4)	4	0.01
Cambodian (0)	0	<0.01
Chinese, ex. Taiwanese (730)	800	1.24
Filipino (256)	327	0.51
Hmong (0)	0	<0.01
Indian (2,225)	2,336	3.61
Indonesian (8)	8	0.01
Japanese (872)	946	1.46
Korean (464)	518	0.80
Laotian (1)	3	<0.01
Malaysian (4)	5	0.01
Nepalese (7)	7	0.01
Pakistani (565)	600	0.93
Sri Lankan (8)	10	0.02
Taiwanese (72)	78	0.12
Thai (14)	23	0.04
Vietnamese (63)	72	0.11
Hawaii Native/Pacific Islander (6)	129	0.20
Not Hispanic (6)	127	0.20
Hispanic (0)	2	<0.01
Fijian (0)	0	<0.01
Guamanian/Chamorro (0)	4	0.01
Marshallese (0)	0	<0.01
Native Hawaiian (2)	11	0.02
Samoan (1)	3	<0.01
Tongan (0)	0	<0.01
White (50,227)	51,374	79.42
Not Hispanic (49,474)	50,541	78.13
Hispanic (753)	833	1.29

*Notes: † The Census 2010 population figure is used to calculate the percentages in the Hispanic Origin and Race categories. Ancestry percentages are based on the 2006-2010 American Community Survey population (not shown); ‡ Numbers in parentheses indicate the number of people reporting a single ancestry; * Numbers in parentheses indicate the number of persons reporting this race alone, not in combination with any other race; Please refer to the User Guide for more information.*

Westland

Place Type: City
County: Wayne
Population: 84,094

Ancestry	Population	%
Afghan (0)	0	<0.01
African, Sub-Saharan (339)	529	0.62
African (219)	321	0.38
Cape Verdean (0)	0	<0.01
Ethiopian (0)	19	0.02
Ghanaian (0)	0	<0.01
Kenyan (0)	0	<0.01
Liberian (0)	0	<0.01
Nigerian (106)	115	0.14
Senegalese (14)	74	0.09
Sierra Leonean (0)	0	<0.01
Somalian (0)	0	<0.01
South African (0)	0	<0.01
Sudanese (0)	0	<0.01
Ugandan (0)	0	<0.01
Zimbabwean (0)	0	<0.01
Other Sub-Saharan African (0)	0	<0.01
Albanian (829)	829	0.98
Alsatian (0)	0	<0.01
American (4,473)	4,473	5.27
Arab (833)	1,262	1.49
Arab (357)	536	0.63
Egyptian (11)	21	0.02
Iraqi (0)	0	<0.01
Jordanian (180)	180	0.21
Lebanese (100)	245	0.29
Moroccan (0)	0	<0.01
Palestinian (119)	119	0.14
Syrian (27)	109	0.13
Other Arab (39)	52	0.06
Armenian (59)	94	0.11
Assyrian/Chaldean/Syriac (0)	0	<0.01
Australian (0)	24	0.03
Austrian (82)	200	0.24
Basque (0)	0	<0.01
Belgian (60)	187	0.22
Brazilian (7)	7	0.01
British (115)	254	0.30
Bulgarian (20)	93	0.11
Cajun (0)	0	<0.01
Canadian (298)	768	0.91
Carpatho Rusyn (0)	0	<0.01
Celtic (0)	0	<0.01
Croatian (91)	227	0.27
Cypriot (0)	0	<0.01
Czech (46)	469	0.55
Czechoslovakian (40)	55	0.06
Danish (25)	285	0.34
Dutch (288)	1,255	1.48
Eastern European (24)	24	0.03
English (1,934)	6,916	8.15
Estonian (0)	0	<0.01
European (669)	760	0.90
Finnish (228)	835	0.98
French, ex. Basque (571)	3,679	4.34
French Canadian (687)	1,562	1.84
German (3,675)	15,599	18.39
German Russian (0)	0	<0.01
Greek (206)	554	0.65
Guyanese (0)	0	<0.01
Hungarian (284)	989	1.17
Icelander (0)	0	<0.01
Iranian (0)	0	<0.01
Irish (2,566)	11,189	13.19
Israeli (24)	24	0.03
Italian (1,938)	4,529	5.34
Latvian (11)	11	0.01
Lithuanian (81)	323	0.38
Luxemburger (0)	0	<0.01
Macedonian (61)	61	0.07
Maltese (120)	287	0.34
New Zealander (0)	0	<0.01
Northern European (34)	34	0.04

Ancestry	Population	%
Norwegian (202)	497	0.59
Pennsylvania German (8)	52	0.06
Polish (4,073)	9,616	11.34
Portuguese (5)	39	0.05
Romanian (446)	623	0.73
Russian (110)	564	0.66
Scandinavian (0)	17	0.02
Scotch-Irish (620)	1,528	1.80
Scottish (416)	2,029	2.39
Serbian (20)	171	0.20
Slavic (11)	77	0.09
Slovak (162)	248	0.29
Slovene (31)	31	0.04
Soviet Union (0)	0	<0.01
Swedish (69)	863	1.02
Swiss (19)	72	0.08
Turkish (10)	30	0.04
Ukrainian (105)	515	0.61
Welsh (51)	376	0.44
West Indian, ex. Hispanic (153)	211	0.25
Bahamian (0)	0	<0.01
Barbadian (0)	0	<0.01
Belizean (0)	0	<0.01
Bermudan (0)	0	<0.01
British West Indian (0)	0	<0.01
Dutch West Indian (0)	0	<0.01
Haitian (0)	0	<0.01
Jamaican (131)	131	0.15
Trinidadian/Tobagonian (0)	0	<0.01
U.S. Virgin Islander (0)	0	<0.01
West Indian (22)	80	0.09
Other West Indian (0)	0	<0.01
Yugoslavian (265)	292	0.34

Hispanic Origin	Population	%
Hispanic or Latino (of any race)	3,165	3.76
Central American, ex. Mexican	59	0.07
Costa Rican	4	<0.01
Guatemalan	14	0.02
Honduran	9	0.01
Nicaraguan	14	0.02
Panamanian	7	0.01
Salvadoran	11	0.01
Other Central American	0	<0.01
Cuban	94	0.11
Dominican Republic	16	0.02
Mexican	2,287	2.72
Puerto Rican	273	0.32
South American	118	0.14
Argentinean	15	0.02
Bolivian	8	0.01
Chilean	4	<0.01
Colombian	30	0.04
Ecuadorian	15	0.02
Paraguayan	0	<0.01
Peruvian	34	0.04
Uruguayan	4	<0.01
Venezuelan	8	0.01
Other South American	0	<0.01
Other Hispanic or Latino	318	0.38

Race*	Population	%
African-American/Black (14,489)	15,552	18.49
Not Hispanic (14,347)	15,336	18.24
Hispanic (142)	216	0.26
American Indian/Alaska Native (391)	1,034	1.23
Not Hispanic (353)	896	1.07
Hispanic (38)	138	0.16
Alaska Athabascan (Ala. Nat.) (0)	0	<0.01
Aleut (Alaska Native) (1)	1	<0.01
Apache (0)	1	<0.01
Arapaho (0)	0	<0.01
Blackfeet (2)	28	0.03
Canadian/French Am. Ind. (8)	11	0.01
Central American Ind. (0)	0	<0.01
Cherokee (21)	160	0.19
Cheyenne (0)	2	<0.01
Chickasaw (1)	3	<0.01
Chippewa (118)	179	0.21

Race*	Population	%
Choctaw (0)	4	<0.01
Colville (0)	0	<0.01
Comanche (1)	4	<0.01
Cree (0)	3	<0.01
Creek (15)	25	0.03
Crow (0)	0	<0.01
Delaware (9)	15	0.02
Hopi (0)	0	<0.01
Houma (0)	1	<0.01
Inupiat (Alaska Native) (0)	0	<0.01
Iroquois (18)	40	0.05
Kiowa (0)	0	<0.01
Lumbee (11)	20	0.02
Menominee (0)	1	<0.01
Mexican American Ind. (8)	16	0.02
Navajo (3)	3	<0.01
Osage (1)	1	<0.01
Ottawa (9)	14	0.02
Paiute (0)	0	<0.01
Pima (0)	0	<0.01
Potawatomi (2)	4	<0.01
Pueblo (0)	0	<0.01
Puget Sound Salish (0)	0	<0.01
Seminole (1)	1	<0.01
Shoshone (0)	0	<0.01
Sioux (4)	8	0.01
South American Ind. (0)	0	<0.01
Spanish American Ind. (1)	2	<0.01
Tlingit-Haida (Alaska Native) (0)	0	<0.01
Tohono O'Odham (0)	0	<0.01
Tsimshian (Alaska Native) (0)	1	<0.01
Ute (0)	0	<0.01
Yakama (0)	0	<0.01
Yaqui (0)	0	<0.01
Yuman (0)	0	<0.01
Yup'ik (Alaska Native) (0)	1	<0.01
Asian (2,548)	2,986	3.55
Not Hispanic (2,526)	2,934	3.49
Hispanic (22)	52	0.06
Bangladeshi (25)	25	0.03
Bhutanese (0)	0	<0.01
Burmese (2)	2	<0.01
Cambodian (5)	16	0.02
Chinese, ex. Taiwanese (329)	367	0.44
Filipino (485)	602	0.72
Hmong (4)	4	<0.01
Indian (1,130)	1,188	1.41
Indonesian (0)	8	0.01
Japanese (51)	135	0.16
Korean (95)	132	0.16
Laotian (7)	10	0.01
Malaysian (11)	13	0.02
Nepalese (0)	0	<0.01
Pakistani (113)	126	0.15
Sri Lankan (7)	7	0.01
Taiwanese (4)	8	0.01
Thai (11)	22	0.03
Vietnamese (211)	241	0.29
Hawaii Native/Pacific Islander (13)	70	0.08
Not Hispanic (13)	63	0.07
Hispanic (0)	7	0.01
Fijian (0)	0	<0.01
Guamanian/Chamorro (6)	12	0.01
Marshallese (0)	0	<0.01
Native Hawaiian (1)	15	0.02
Samoan (5)	13	0.02
Tongan (0)	0	<0.01
White (63,737)	65,538	77.93
Not Hispanic (61,826)	63,362	75.35
Hispanic (1,911)	2,176	2.59

Wyoming

Place Type: City
County: Kent
Population: 72,125

Ancestry	Population	%
Afghan (0)	0	<0.01
African, Sub-Saharan (157)	186	0.26
African (106)	135	0.19
Cape Verdean (0)	0	<0.01
Ethiopian (0)	0	<0.01
Ghanaian (0)	0	<0.01
Kenyan (14)	14	0.02
Liberian (4)	4	0.01
Nigerian (0)	0	<0.01
Senegalese (0)	0	<0.01
Sierra Leonean (0)	0	<0.01
Somalian (0)	0	<0.01
South African (0)	0	<0.01
Sudanese (33)	33	0.05
Ugandan (0)	0	<0.01
Zimbabwean (0)	0	<0.01
Other Sub-Saharan African (0)	0	<0.01
Albanian (0)	0	<0.01
Alsatian (0)	0	<0.01
American (2,297)	2,297	3.20
Arab (26)	257	0.36
Arab (11)	59	0.08
Egyptian (0)	0	<0.01
Iraqi (0)	0	<0.01
Jordanian (0)	0	<0.01
Lebanese (0)	48	0.07
Moroccan (0)	0	<0.01
Palestinian (0)	10	0.01
Syrian (15)	140	0.19
Other Arab (0)	0	<0.01
Armenian (59)	98	0.14
Assyrian/Chaldean/Syriac (0)	0	<0.01
Australian (7)	7	0.01
Austrian (0)	22	0.03
Basque (0)	0	<0.01
Belgian (39)	70	0.10
Brazilian (12)	12	0.02
British (24)	169	0.24
Bulgarian (13)	25	0.03
Cajun (0)	0	<0.01
Canadian (82)	134	0.19
Carpatho Rusyn (0)	0	<0.01
Celtic (0)	29	0.04
Croatian (23)	38	0.05
Cypriot (0)	0	<0.01
Czech (54)	182	0.25
Czechoslovakian (22)	82	0.11
Danish (95)	259	0.36
Dutch (7,514)	16,185	22.54
Eastern European (12)	12	0.02
English (1,370)	6,612	9.21
Estonian (0)	0	<0.01
European (497)	566	0.79
Finnish (147)	458	0.64
French, ex. Basque (334)	2,725	3.79
French Canadian (88)	478	0.67
German (3,215)	13,797	19.21
German Russian (0)	0	<0.01
Greek (32)	52	0.07
Guyanese (0)	0	<0.01
Hungarian (86)	305	0.42
Icelander (0)	0	<0.01
Iranian (13)	13	0.02
Irish (1,516)	8,298	11.55
Israeli (0)	0	<0.01
Italian (608)	2,131	2.97
Latvian (19)	31	0.04
Lithuanian (38)	155	0.22
Luxemburger (0)	0	<0.01
Macedonian (22)	182	0.25
Maltese (0)	0	<0.01
New Zealander (0)	0	<0.01
Northern European (8)	19	0.03

Ancestry	Population	%
Norwegian (88)	402	0.56
Pennsylvania German (15)	35	0.05
Polish (1,276)	4,679	6.52
Portuguese (14)	70	0.10
Romanian (0)	0	<0.01
Russian (63)	342	0.48
Scandinavian (74)	175	0.24
Scotch-Irish (233)	849	1.18
Scottish (216)	1,319	1.84
Serbian (0)	0	<0.01
Slavic (0)	0	<0.01
Slovak (29)	57	0.08
Slovene (0)	29	0.04
Soviet Union (0)	0	<0.01
Swedish (234)	1,403	1.95
Swiss (43)	217	0.30
Turkish (0)	0	<0.01
Ukrainian (53)	112	0.16
Welsh (23)	300	0.42
West Indian, ex. Hispanic (33)	125	0.17
Bahamian (0)	0	<0.01
Barbadian (0)	0	<0.01
Belizean (0)	0	<0.01
Bermudan (0)	0	<0.01
British West Indian (13)	13	0.02
Dutch West Indian (0)	0	<0.01
Haitian (11)	21	0.03
Jamaican (9)	91	0.13
Trinidadian/Tobagonian (0)	0	<0.01
U.S. Virgin Islander (0)	0	<0.01
West Indian (0)	0	<0.01
Other West Indian (0)	0	<0.01
Yugoslavian (299)	299	0.42

Hispanic Origin	Population	%
Hispanic or Latino (of any race)	14,010	19.42
Central American, ex. Mexican	1,109	1.54
Costa Rican	6	0.01
Guatemalan	698	0.97
Honduran	138	0.19
Nicaraguan	26	0.04
Panamanian	6	0.01
Salvadoran	235	0.33
Other Central American	0	<0.01
Cuban	747	1.04
Dominican Republic	543	0.75
Mexican	9,419	13.06
Puerto Rican	1,460	2.02
South American	148	0.21
Argentinean	15	0.02
Bolivian	3	<0.01
Chilean	6	0.01
Colombian	42	0.06
Ecuadorian	15	0.02
Paraguayan	2	<0.01
Peruvian	37	0.05
Uruguayan	4	0.01
Venezuelan	24	0.03
Other South American	0	<0.01
Other Hispanic or Latino	584	0.81

Race*	Population	%
African-American/Black (5,215)	6,610	9.16
Not Hispanic (4,756)	5,843	8.10
Hispanic (459)	767	1.06
American Indian/Alaska Native (450)	1,109	1.54
Not Hispanic (292)	814	1.13
Hispanic (158)	295	0.41
Alaska Athabascan (Ala. Nat.) (2)	2	<0.01
Aleut (Alaska Native) (0)	0	<0.01
Apache (4)	7	0.01
Arapaho (0)	0	<0.01
Blackfeet (2)	27	0.04
Canadian/French Am. Ind. (0)	1	<0.01
Central American Ind. (1)	1	<0.01
Cherokee (17)	75	0.10
Cheyenne (0)	0	<0.01
Chickasaw (0)	0	<0.01
Chippewa (78)	152	0.21

Race*	Population	%
Choctaw (5)	9	0.01
Colville (0)	0	<0.01
Comanche (0)	2	<0.01
Cree (0)	0	<0.01
Creek (0)	7	0.01
Crow (0)	0	<0.01
Delaware (0)	0	<0.01
Hopi (0)	0	<0.01
Houma (0)	0	<0.01
Inupiat (Alaska Native) (0)	0	<0.01
Iroquois (5)	24	0.03
Kiowa (0)	0	<0.01
Lumbee (1)	1	<0.01
Menominee (0)	1	<0.01
Mexican American Ind. (15)	19	0.03
Navajo (4)	6	0.01
Osage (0)	2	<0.01
Ottawa (57)	122	0.17
Paiute (0)	0	<0.01
Pima (1)	1	<0.01
Potawatomi (48)	86	0.12
Pueblo (0)	0	<0.01
Puget Sound Salish (0)	1	<0.01
Seminole (0)	0	<0.01
Shoshone (0)	0	<0.01
Sioux (3)	9	0.01
South American Ind. (3)	4	0.01
Spanish American Ind. (7)	9	0.01
Tlingit-Haida (Alaska Native) (0)	0	<0.01
Tohono O'Odham (0)	0	<0.01
Tsimshian (Alaska Native) (0)	0	<0.01
Ute (0)	0	<0.01
Yakama (0)	0	<0.01
Yaqui (0)	0	<0.01
Yuman (0)	2	<0.01
Yup'ik (Alaska Native) (0)	0	<0.01
Asian (2,022)	2,386	3.31
Not Hispanic (1,992)	2,306	3.20
Hispanic (30)	80	0.11
Bangladeshi (5)	5	0.01
Bhutanese (0)	0	<0.01
Burmese (13)	17	0.02
Cambodian (2)	9	0.01
Chinese, ex. Taiwanese (176)	244	0.34
Filipino (91)	168	0.23
Hmong (0)	0	<0.01
Indian (150)	185	0.26
Indonesian (5)	10	0.01
Japanese (21)	60	0.08
Korean (161)	234	0.32
Laotian (11)	17	0.02
Malaysian (1)	1	<0.01
Nepalese (0)	0	<0.01
Pakistani (8)	10	0.01
Sri Lankan (0)	0	<0.01
Taiwanese (4)	4	0.01
Thai (13)	34	0.05
Vietnamese (1,309)	1,389	1.93
Hawaii Native/Pacific Islander (35)	111	0.15
Not Hispanic (26)	65	0.09
Hispanic (9)	46	0.06
Fijian (0)	0	<0.01
Guamanian/Chamorro (3)	10	0.01
Marshallese (0)	0	<0.01
Native Hawaiian (14)	28	0.04
Samoan (3)	4	0.01
Tongan (0)	0	<0.01
White (54,696)	57,143	79.23
Not Hispanic (49,208)	50,833	70.48
Hispanic (5,488)	6,310	8.75

Notes: † The Census 2010 population figure is used to calculate the percentages in the Hispanic Origin and Race categories. Ancestry percentages are based on the 2006-2010 American Community Survey population (not shown); ‡ Numbers in parentheses indicate the number of people reporting a single ancestry; * Numbers in parentheses indicate the number of persons reporting this race alone, not in combination with any other race; Please refer to the User Guide for more information.

Ypsilanti

Place Type: Charter Township
County: Washtenaw
Population: 53,362

Ancestry	Population	%
Afghan (0)	0	<0.01
African, Sub-Saharan (1,121)	1,227	2.31
African (594)	634	1.20
Cape Verdean (0)	0	<0.01
Ethiopian (19)	34	0.06
Ghanaian (71)	71	0.13
Kenyan (0)	0	<0.01
Liberian (0)	0	<0.01
Nigerian (201)	216	0.41
Senegalese (22)	22	0.04
Sierra Leonean (0)	0	<0.01
Somalian (114)	127	0.24
South African (0)	0	<0.01
Sudanese (0)	0	<0.01
Ugandan (0)	0	<0.01
Zimbabwean (0)	0	<0.01
Other Sub-Saharan African (100)	123	0.23
Albanian (0)	0	<0.01
Alsatian (0)	0	<0.01
American (3,184)	3,184	6.01
Arab (388)	551	1.04
Arab (117)	142	0.27
Egyptian (26)	26	0.05
Iraqi (0)	0	<0.01
Jordanian (0)	0	<0.01
Lebanese (13)	113	0.21
Moroccan (8)	46	0.09
Palestinian (17)	17	0.03
Syrian (0)	0	<0.01
Other Arab (207)	207	0.39
Armenian (10)	30	0.06
Assyrian/Chaldean/Syriac (0)	0	<0.01
Australian (0)	0	<0.01
Austrian (30)	72	0.14
Basque (0)	0	<0.01
Belgian (10)	53	0.10
Brazilian (0)	0	<0.01
British (92)	208	0.39
Bulgarian (0)	0	<0.01
Cajun (0)	0	<0.01
Canadian (82)	319	0.60
Carpatho Rusyn (0)	0	<0.01
Celtic (10)	10	0.02
Croatian (0)	5	0.01
Cypriot (0)	0	<0.01
Czech (33)	200	0.38
Czechoslovakian (0)	16	0.03
Danish (46)	157	0.30
Dutch (192)	1,162	2.19
Eastern European (0)	0	<0.01
English (1,035)	4,649	8.77
Estonian (0)	0	<0.01
European (597)	693	1.31
Finnish (147)	503	0.95
French, ex. Basque (262)	1,539	2.90
French Canadian (409)	714	1.35
German (2,548)	8,668	16.35
German Russian (0)	0	<0.01
Greek (37)	311	0.59
Guyanese (0)	32	0.06
Hungarian (178)	275	0.52
Icelander (0)	0	<0.01
Iranian (0)	0	<0.01
Irish (1,007)	5,123	9.66
Israeli (0)	0	<0.01
Italian (346)	1,553	2.93
Latvian (0)	19	0.04
Lithuanian (0)	53	0.10
Luxemburger (0)	0	<0.01
Macedonian (8)	8	0.02
Maltese (12)	63	0.12
New Zealander (0)	0	<0.01
Northern European (0)	0	<0.01

Ancestry	Population	%
Norwegian (50)	192	0.36
Pennsylvania German (0)	20	0.04
Polish (624)	2,371	4.47
Portuguese (26)	80	0.15
Romanian (102)	260	0.49
Russian (19)	327	0.62
Scandinavian (0)	12	0.02
Scotch-Irish (235)	831	1.57
Scottish (304)	1,497	2.82
Serbian (8)	24	0.05
Slavic (0)	33	0.06
Slovak (0)	139	0.26
Slovene (0)	19	0.04
Soviet Union (0)	0	<0.01
Swedish (121)	453	0.85
Swiss (0)	140	0.26
Turkish (6)	30	0.06
Ukrainian (101)	226	0.43
Welsh (54)	415	0.78
West Indian, ex. Hispanic (134)	269	0.51
Bahamian (0)	0	<0.01
Barbadian (0)	0	<0.01
Belizean (0)	0	<0.01
Bermudan (0)	0	<0.01
British West Indian (0)	0	<0.01
Dutch West Indian (0)	0	<0.01
Haitian (58)	107	0.20
Jamaican (41)	97	0.18
Trinidadian/Tobagonian (6)	14	0.03
U.S. Virgin Islander (0)	0	<0.01
West Indian (29)	51	0.10
Other West Indian (0)	0	<0.01
Yugoslavian (0)	57	0.11

Hispanic Origin	Population	%
Hispanic or Latino (of any race)	2,476	4.64
Central American, ex. Mexican	473	0.89
Costa Rican	65	0.12
Guatemalan	104	0.19
Honduran	110	0.21
Nicaraguan	15	0.03
Panamanian	33	0.06
Salvadoran	139	0.26
Other Central American	7	0.01
Cuban	65	0.12
Dominican Republic	16	0.03
Mexican	1,329	2.49
Puerto Rican	247	0.46
South American	105	0.20
Argentinean	5	0.01
Bolivian	1	<0.01
Chilean	7	0.01
Colombian	27	0.05
Ecuadorian	18	0.03
Paraguayan	0	<0.01
Peruvian	24	0.04
Uruguayan	6	0.01
Venezuelan	17	0.03
Other South American	0	<0.01
Other Hispanic or Latino	241	0.45

Race*	Population	%
African-American/Black (17,528)	19,204	35.99
Not Hispanic (17,321)	18,884	35.39
Hispanic (207)	320	0.60
American Indian/Alaska Native (227)	842	1.58
Not Hispanic (200)	743	1.39
Hispanic (27)	99	0.19
Alaska Athabascan (Ala. Nat.) (0)	0	<0.01
Aleut (Alaska Native) (1)	2	<0.01
Apache (0)	2	<0.01
Arapaho (0)	1	<0.01
Blackfeet (8)	48	0.09
Canadian/French Am. Ind. (1)	3	0.01
Central American Ind. (0)	0	<0.01
Cherokee (22)	166	0.31
Cheyenne (0)	0	<0.01
Chickasaw (1)	1	<0.01
Chippewa (39)	79	0.15

Race* (cont.)	Population	%
Choctaw (4)	27	0.05
Colville (0)	0	<0.01
Comanche (1)	1	<0.01
Cree (0)	2	<0.01
Creek (6)	11	0.02
Crow (0)	0	<0.01
Delaware (2)	5	0.01
Hopi (0)	0	<0.01
Houma (0)	0	<0.01
Inupiat (Alaska Native) (0)	0	<0.01
Iroquois (9)	20	0.04
Kiowa (0)	0	<0.01
Lumbee (4)	5	0.01
Menominee (0)	0	<0.01
Mexican American Ind. (3)	6	0.01
Navajo (3)	7	0.01
Osage (0)	0	<0.01
Ottawa (5)	7	0.01
Paiute (0)	1	<0.01
Pima (0)	0	<0.01
Potawatomi (0)	12	0.02
Pueblo (0)	2	<0.01
Puget Sound Salish (0)	0	<0.01
Seminole (1)	2	<0.01
Shoshone (0)	0	<0.01
Sioux (13)	24	0.04
South American Ind. (2)	7	0.01
Spanish American Ind. (0)	0	<0.01
Tlingit-Haida (Alaska Native) (6)	9	0.02
Tohono O'Odham (0)	0	<0.01
Tsimshian (Alaska Native) (0)	0	<0.01
Ute (0)	1	<0.01
Yakama (1)	1	<0.01
Yaqui (0)	0	<0.01
Yuman (0)	1	<0.01
Yup'ik (Alaska Native) (0)	0	<0.01
Asian (1,101)	1,552	2.91
Not Hispanic (1,092)	1,502	2.81
Hispanic (9)	50	0.09
Bangladeshi (0)	1	<0.01
Bhutanese (0)	0	<0.01
Burmese (1)	1	<0.01
Cambodian (3)	5	0.01
Chinese, ex. Taiwanese (175)	246	0.46
Filipino (176)	272	0.51
Hmong (2)	2	<0.01
Indian (247)	306	0.57
Indonesian (9)	17	0.03
Japanese (41)	94	0.18
Korean (120)	204	0.38
Laotian (31)	40	0.07
Malaysian (6)	14	0.03
Nepalese (1)	1	<0.01
Pakistani (70)	77	0.14
Sri Lankan (10)	17	0.03
Taiwanese (11)	14	0.03
Thai (30)	47	0.09
Vietnamese (107)	154	0.29
Hawaii Native/Pacific Islander (28)	89	0.17
Not Hispanic (26)	84	0.16
Hispanic (2)	5	0.01
Fijian (1)	1	<0.01
Guamanian/Chamorro (1)	9	0.02
Marshallese (0)	0	<0.01
Native Hawaiian (4)	21	0.04
Samoan (15)	30	0.06
Tongan (1)	3	0.01
White (31,171)	33,245	62.30
Not Hispanic (29,956)	31,781	59.56
Hispanic (1,215)	1,464	2.74

Notes: † The Census 2010 population figure is used to calculate the percentages in the Hispanic Origin and Race categories. Ancestry percentages are based on the 2006-2010 American Community Survey population (not shown); ‡ Numbers in parentheses indicate the number of people reporting a single ancestry; * Numbers in parentheses indicate the number of persons reporting this race alone, not in combination with any other race; Please refer to the User Guide for more information.

Ancestry Group Rankings

Afghan

Top 10 Places Sorted by Population
Based on all places, regardless of total population

Place	Population	%
Dearborn (city) Wayne County	42	0.04
Sterling Heights (city) Macomb County	41	0.03
Lima (township) Washtenaw County	36	1.13
Oshtemo (charter twp) Kalamazoo County	32	0.15
Ann Arbor (city) Washtenaw County	23	0.02
Acme (township) Grand Traverse County	0	0.00
Ada (township) Kent County	0	0.00
Adams (township) Arenac County	0	0.00
Adams (township) Hillsdale County	0	0.00
Adams (township) Houghton County	0	0.00

Top 10 Places Sorted by Percent of Total Population
Based on all places, regardless of total population

Place	Population	%
Lima (township) Washtenaw County	36	1.13
Oshtemo (charter twp) Kalamazoo County	32	0.15
Dearborn (city) Wayne County	42	0.04
Sterling Heights (city) Macomb County	41	0.03
Ann Arbor (city) Washtenaw County	23	0.02
Acme (township) Grand Traverse County	0	0.00
Ada (township) Kent County	0	0.00
Adams (township) Arenac County	0	0.00
Adams (township) Hillsdale County	0	0.00
Adams (township) Houghton County	0	0.00

Top 10 Places Sorted by Percent of Total Population
Based on places with total population of 50,000 or more

Place	Population	%
Dearborn (city) Wayne County	42	0.04
Sterling Heights (city) Macomb County	41	0.03
Ann Arbor (city) Washtenaw County	23	0.02
Battle Creek (city) Calhoun County	0	0.00
Canton (charter twp) Wayne County	0	0.00
Clinton (charter twp) Macomb County	0	0.00
Dearborn Heights (city) Wayne County	0	0.00
Detroit (city) Wayne County	0	0.00
Farmington Hills (city) Oakland County	0	0.00
Flint (city) Genesee County	0	0.00

African, Sub-Saharan

Top 10 Places Sorted by Population
Based on all places, regardless of total population

Place	Population	%
Detroit (city) Wayne County	12,021	1.58
Grand Rapids (city) Kent County	2,553	1.34
Southfield (city) Oakland County	2,102	2.88
Lansing (city) Ingham County	1,905	1.65
Flint (city) Genesee County	1,740	1.61
Jackson (city) Jackson County	1,671	4.86
Ann Arbor (city) Washtenaw County	1,399	1.21
Ypsilanti (charter twp) Washtenaw County	1,227	2.31
East Lansing (city) Ingham County	1,223	2.54
Sterling Heights (city) Macomb County	966	0.74

Top 10 Places Sorted by Percent of Total Population
Based on all places, regardless of total population

Place	Population	%
Manistee (township) Manistee County	489	12.06
Grayling (charter twp) Crawford County	327	5.43
Fife Lake (township) Grand Traverse County	138	5.27
Oronoko (charter twp) Berrien County	459	4.97
Berrien Springs (village) Berrien County	121	4.90
Jackson (city) Jackson County	1,671	4.86
Maple Forest (township) Crawford County	18	4.81
Buena Vista (cdp) Saginaw County	311	4.75
Kinross (charter twp) Chippewa County	319	3.97
Lathrup Village (city) Oakland County	146	3.56

Top 10 Places Sorted by Percent of Total Population
Based on places with total population of 50,000 or more

Place	Population	%
Southfield (city) Oakland County	2,102	2.88
Ypsilanti (charter twp) Washtenaw County	1,227	2.31
Lansing (city) Ingham County	1,905	1.65
Flint (city) Genesee County	1,740	1.61
Detroit (city) Wayne County	12,021	1.58
Grand Rapids (city) Kent County	2,553	1.34
Pontiac (city) Oakland County	776	1.27
Ann Arbor (city) Washtenaw County	1,399	1.21
Farmington Hills (city) Oakland County	871	1.09
Canton (charter twp) Wayne County	664	0.75

African, Sub-Saharan: African

Top 10 Places Sorted by Population
Based on all places, regardless of total population

Place	Population	%
Detroit (city) Wayne County	9,726	1.28
Jackson (city) Jackson County	1,634	4.76
Southfield (city) Oakland County	1,632	2.24
Flint (city) Genesee County	1,515	1.41
Grand Rapids (city) Kent County	1,313	0.69
Lansing (city) Ingham County	906	0.78
Ann Arbor (city) Washtenaw County	809	0.70
Sterling Heights (city) Macomb County	802	0.62
East Lansing (city) Ingham County	782	1.62
Oak Park (city) Oakland County	653	2.18

Top 10 Places Sorted by Percent of Total Population
Based on all places, regardless of total population

Place	Population	%
Manistee (township) Manistee County	489	12.06
Grayling (charter twp) Crawford County	327	5.43
Fife Lake (township) Grand Traverse County	138	5.27
Berrien Springs (village) Berrien County	121	4.90
Maple Forest (township) Crawford County	18	4.81
Jackson (city) Jackson County	1,634	4.76
Oronoko (charter twp) Berrien County	414	4.49
Buena Vista (cdp) Saginaw County	242	3.69
Kinross (charter twp) Chippewa County	269	3.34
Woodland Beach (cdp) Monroe County	60	3.17

Top 10 Places Sorted by Percent of Total Population
Based on places with total population of 50,000 or more

Place	Population	%
Southfield (city) Oakland County	1,632	2.24
Flint (city) Genesee County	1,515	1.41
Detroit (city) Wayne County	9,726	1.28
Ypsilanti (charter twp) Washtenaw County	634	1.20
Pontiac (city) Oakland County	580	0.95
Lansing (city) Ingham County	906	0.78
Ann Arbor (city) Washtenaw County	809	0.70
Grand Rapids (city) Kent County	1,313	0.69
Sterling Heights (city) Macomb County	802	0.62
Macomb (township) Macomb County	454	0.61

African, Sub-Saharan: Cape Verdean

Top 10 Places Sorted by Population
Based on all places, regardless of total population

Place	Population	%
Grand Rapids (city) Kent County	72	0.04
St. Clair Shores (city) Macomb County	35	0.06
Detroit (city) Wayne County	16	<0.01
Sterling Heights (city) Macomb County	14	0.01
York (charter twp) Washtenaw County	12	0.14
Mount Clemens (city) Macomb County	9	0.05
Trenton (city) Wayne County	9	0.05
Albion (township) Calhoun County	4	0.32
North Plains (township) Ionia County	3	0.23
Sturgis (township) St. Joseph County	3	0.15

Top 10 Places Sorted by Percent of Total Population
Based on all places, regardless of total population

Place	Population	%
Albion (township) Calhoun County	4	0.32
North Plains (township) Ionia County	3	0.23
Sturgis (township) St. Joseph County	3	0.15
York (charter twp) Washtenaw County	12	0.14
St. Clair Shores (city) Macomb County	35	0.06
Mount Clemens (city) Macomb County	9	0.05
Trenton (city) Wayne County	9	0.05
Grand Rapids (city) Kent County	72	0.04
Sterling Heights (city) Macomb County	14	0.01
Detroit (city) Wayne County	16	<0.01

Top 10 Places Sorted by Percent of Total Population
Based on places with total population of 50,000 or more

Place	Population	%
St. Clair Shores (city) Macomb County	35	0.06
Grand Rapids (city) Kent County	72	0.04
Sterling Heights (city) Macomb County	14	0.01
Detroit (city) Wayne County	16	<0.01
Ann Arbor (city) Washtenaw County	0	0.00
Battle Creek (city) Calhoun County	0	0.00
Canton (charter twp) Wayne County	0	0.00
Clinton (charter twp) Macomb County	0	0.00
Dearborn (city) Wayne County	0	0.00
Dearborn Heights (city) Wayne County	0	0.00

African, Sub-Saharan: Ethiopian

Top 10 Places Sorted by Population
Based on all places, regardless of total population

Place	Population	%
Grand Rapids (city) Kent County	335	0.18
Canton (charter twp) Wayne County	135	0.15
Southfield (city) Oakland County	121	0.17
Lansing (city) Ingham County	107	0.09
Detroit (city) Wayne County	106	0.01
Kentwood (city) Kent County	104	0.22
Oak Park (city) Oakland County	88	0.29
Waverly (cdp) Eaton County	59	0.24
Delta (charter twp) Eaton County	59	0.18
Ann Arbor (city) Washtenaw County	59	0.05

Top 10 Places Sorted by Percent of Total Population
Based on all places, regardless of total population

Place	Population	%
Norwich (township) Newaygo County	6	1.02
Cheshire (township) Allegan County	13	0.56
Parma (village) Jackson County	3	0.37
Pentland (township) Luce County	9	0.35
Williamston (city) Ingham County	12	0.32
James (township) Saginaw County	6	0.31
Oak Park (city) Oakland County	88	0.29
Mount Morris (township) Genesee County	57	0.26
Waverly (cdp) Eaton County	59	0.24
Kentwood (city) Kent County	104	0.22

Top 10 Places Sorted by Percent of Total Population
Based on places with total population of 50,000 or more

Place	Population	%
Grand Rapids (city) Kent County	335	0.18
Southfield (city) Oakland County	121	0.17
Canton (charter twp) Wayne County	135	0.15
Lansing (city) Ingham County	107	0.09
Pontiac (city) Oakland County	39	0.06
Ypsilanti (charter twp) Washtenaw County	34	0.06
Ann Arbor (city) Washtenaw County	59	0.05
Flint (city) Genesee County	38	0.04
West Bloomfield (charter twp) Oakland County	25	0.04
Farmington Hills (city) Oakland County	26	0.03

African, Sub-Saharan: Ghanaian

Top 10 Places Sorted by Population
Based on all places, regardless of total population

Place	Population	%
Clinton (charter twp) Macomb County	110	0.11
Ypsilanti (charter twp) Washtenaw County	71	0.13
Taylor (city) Wayne County	56	0.09
Buena Vista (cdp) Saginaw County	55	0.84
Buena Vista (charter twp) Saginaw County	55	0.61
Ann Arbor (city) Washtenaw County	48	0.04
Troy (city) Oakland County	37	0.05
Waterford (charter twp) Oakland County	34	0.05
Detroit (city) Wayne County	28	<0.01
Farmington Hills (city) Oakland County	22	0.03

Top 10 Places Sorted by Percent of Total Population
Based on all places, regardless of total population

Place	Population	%
Buena Vista (cdp) Saginaw County	55	0.84
Buena Vista (charter twp) Saginaw County	55	0.61
Westwood (cdp) Kalamazoo County	15	0.17
Ypsilanti (charter twp) Washtenaw County	71	0.13
Clinton (charter twp) Macomb County	110	0.11
Taylor (city) Wayne County	56	0.09
Niles (city) Berrien County	11	0.09
Holt (cdp) Ingham County	18	0.08
Delhi (charter twp) Ingham County	18	0.07
Kalamazoo (charter twp) Kalamazoo County	15	0.07

Top 10 Places Sorted by Percent of Total Population
Based on places with total population of 50,000 or more

Place	Population	%
Ypsilanti (charter twp) Washtenaw County	71	0.13
Clinton (charter twp) Macomb County	110	0.11
Taylor (city) Wayne County	56	0.09
Troy (city) Oakland County	37	0.05
Waterford (charter twp) Oakland County	34	0.05
Ann Arbor (city) Washtenaw County	48	0.04
Farmington Hills (city) Oakland County	22	0.03
Southfield (city) Oakland County	14	0.02
Detroit (city) Wayne County	28	<0.01
Battle Creek (city) Calhoun County	0	0.00

African, Sub-Saharan: Kenyan

Top 10 Places Sorted by Population
Based on all places, regardless of total population

Place	Population	%
Detroit (city) Wayne County	286	0.04
Adrian (city) Lenawee County	87	0.40
Grandville (city) Kent County	70	0.45
Huntington Woods (city) Oakland County	66	1.06
Haslett (cdp) Ingham County	53	0.27
Meridian (charter twp) Ingham County	53	0.13
Bay City (city) Bay County	52	0.15
East Lansing (city) Ingham County	44	0.09
Warren (city) Macomb County	40	0.03
Grand Rapids (city) Kent County	34	0.02

Top 10 Places Sorted by Percent of Total Population
Based on all places, regardless of total population

Place	Population	%
Huntington Woods (city) Oakland County	66	1.06
Leslie (city) Ingham County	14	0.73
Grandville (city) Kent County	70	0.45
Calvin (township) Cass County	9	0.42
Adrian (city) Lenawee County	87	0.40
Berrien (township) Berrien County	15	0.30
Haslett (cdp) Ingham County	53	0.27
Vevay (township) Ingham County	7	0.20
Bay City (city) Bay County	52	0.15
Meridian (charter twp) Ingham County	53	0.13

Top 10 Places Sorted by Percent of Total Population
Based on places with total population of 50,000 or more

Place	Population	%
Detroit (city) Wayne County	286	0.04
Warren (city) Macomb County	40	0.03
Kalamazoo (city) Kalamazoo County	23	0.03
Grand Rapids (city) Kent County	34	0.02

Place	Population	%
Farmington Hills (city) Oakland County	15	0.02
Wyoming (city) Kent County	14	0.02
Battle Creek (city) Calhoun County	9	0.02
Southfield (city) Oakland County	10	0.01
Ann Arbor (city) Washtenaw County	0	0.00
Canton (charter twp) Wayne County	0	0.00

African, Sub-Saharan: Liberian

Top 10 Places Sorted by Population
Based on all places, regardless of total population

Place	Population	%
Grand Rapids (city) Kent County	309	0.16
Hamtramck (city) Wayne County	97	0.43
Detroit (city) Wayne County	81	0.01
Pontiac (city) Oakland County	62	0.10
Inkster (city) Wayne County	61	0.23
Romulus (city) Wayne County	47	0.20
Kentwood (city) Kent County	38	0.08
Wayne (city) Wayne County	37	0.21
Grand Rapids (charter twp) Kent County	23	0.14
Macomb (township) Macomb County	19	0.03

Top 10 Places Sorted by Percent of Total Population
Based on all places, regardless of total population

Place	Population	%
Bethany (township) Gratiot County	11	0.81
Hamtramck (city) Wayne County	97	0.43
South Haven (charter twp) Van Buren County	14	0.35
Inkster (city) Wayne County	61	0.23
Ontwa (township) Cass County	14	0.22
Wayne (city) Wayne County	37	0.21
Romulus (city) Wayne County	47	0.20
Grand Rapids (city) Kent County	309	0.16
Grand Rapids (charter twp) Kent County	23	0.14
Pontiac (city) Oakland County	62	0.10

Top 10 Places Sorted by Percent of Total Population
Based on places with total population of 50,000 or more

Place	Population	%
Grand Rapids (city) Kent County	309	0.16
Pontiac (city) Oakland County	62	0.10
Macomb (township) Macomb County	19	0.03
Saginaw (city) Saginaw County	13	0.02
Detroit (city) Wayne County	81	0.01
Wyoming (city) Kent County	4	0.01
Ann Arbor (city) Washtenaw County	0	0.00
Battle Creek (city) Calhoun County	0	0.00
Canton (charter twp) Wayne County	0	0.00
Clinton (charter twp) Macomb County	0	0.00

African, Sub-Saharan: Nigerian

Top 10 Places Sorted by Population
Based on all places, regardless of total population

Place	Population	%
Detroit (city) Wayne County	1,282	0.17
Ann Arbor (city) Washtenaw County	338	0.29
Farmington Hills (city) Oakland County	269	0.34
West Bloomfield (charter twp) Oakland County	250	0.39
Southfield (city) Oakland County	248	0.34
Canton (charter twp) Wayne County	233	0.26
Inkster (city) Wayne County	232	0.88
Ypsilanti (charter twp) Washtenaw County	216	0.41
Pittsfield (charter twp) Washtenaw County	155	0.45
East Lansing (city) Ingham County	143	0.30

Top 10 Places Sorted by Percent of Total Population
Based on all places, regardless of total population

Place	Population	%
Penn (township) Cass County	17	0.96
Inkster (city) Wayne County	232	0.88
Kinde (village) Huron County	3	0.66
Pittsfield (charter twp) Washtenaw County	155	0.45
Ypsilanti (charter twp) Washtenaw County	216	0.41
West Bloomfield (charter twp) Oakland County	250	0.39
Lincoln (township) Huron County	3	0.35
Farmington Hills (city) Oakland County	269	0.34
Southfield (city) Oakland County	248	0.34
East Lansing (city) Ingham County	143	0.30

Top 10 Places Sorted by Percent of Total Population
Based on places with total population of 50,000 or more

Place	Population	%
Ypsilanti (charter twp) Washtenaw County	216	0.41
West Bloomfield (charter twp) Oakland County	250	0.39
Farmington Hills (city) Oakland County	269	0.34
Southfield (city) Oakland County	248	0.34
Ann Arbor (city) Washtenaw County	338	0.29
Canton (charter twp) Wayne County	233	0.26
Detroit (city) Wayne County	1,282	0.17
Westland (city) Wayne County	115	0.14
Flint (city) Genesee County	138	0.13
Clinton (charter twp) Macomb County	90	0.09

African, Sub-Saharan: Senegalese

Top 10 Places Sorted by Population
Based on all places, regardless of total population

Place	Population	%
Haslett (cdp) Ingham County	84	0.43
Meridian (charter twp) Ingham County	84	0.21
Westland (city) Wayne County	74	0.09
Romulus (city) Wayne County	50	0.21
Pontiac (city) Oakland County	50	0.08
Detroit (city) Wayne County	28	<0.01
Ypsilanti (charter twp) Washtenaw County	22	0.04
Warren (city) Macomb County	20	0.01
Southfield (city) Oakland County	19	0.03
Holland (charter twp) Ottawa County	15	0.04

Top 10 Places Sorted by Percent of Total Population
Based on all places, regardless of total population

Place	Population	%
Haslett (cdp) Ingham County	84	0.43
Meridian (charter twp) Ingham County	84	0.21
Romulus (city) Wayne County	50	0.21
Buena Vista (cdp) Saginaw County	14	0.21
Buena Vista (charter twp) Saginaw County	14	0.16
Westland (city) Wayne County	74	0.09
Pontiac (city) Oakland County	50	0.08
Ypsilanti (charter twp) Washtenaw County	22	0.04
Holland (charter twp) Ottawa County	15	0.04
Jackson (city) Jackson County	13	0.04

Top 10 Places Sorted by Percent of Total Population
Based on places with total population of 50,000 or more

Place	Population	%
Westland (city) Wayne County	74	0.09
Pontiac (city) Oakland County	50	0.08
Ypsilanti (charter twp) Washtenaw County	22	0.04
Southfield (city) Oakland County	19	0.03
Warren (city) Macomb County	20	0.01
West Bloomfield (charter twp) Oakland County	7	0.01
Detroit (city) Wayne County	28	<0.01
Ann Arbor (city) Washtenaw County	0	0.00
Battle Creek (city) Calhoun County	0	0.00
Canton (charter twp) Wayne County	0	0.00

African, Sub-Saharan: Sierra Leonean

Top 10 Places Sorted by Population
Based on all places, regardless of total population

Place	Population	%
Flushing (city) Genesee County	13	0.15
Grass Lake (charter twp) Jackson County	10	0.18
Acme (township) Grand Traverse County	0	0.00
Ada (township) Kent County	0	0.00
Adams (township) Arenac County	0	0.00
Adams (township) Hillsdale County	0	0.00
Adams (township) Houghton County	0	0.00
Addison (village) Lenawee County	0	0.00
Addison (township) Oakland County	0	0.00
Adrian (city) Lenawee County	0	0.00

Top 10 Places Sorted by Percent of Total Population
Based on all places, regardless of total population

Place	Population	%
Grass Lake (charter twp) Jackson County	10	0.18
Flushing (city) Genesee County	13	0.15
Acme (township) Grand Traverse County	0	0.00

Ada (township) Kent County	0	0.00
Adams (township) Arenac County	0	0.00
Adams (township) Hillsdale County	0	0.00
Adams (township) Houghton County	0	0.00
Addison (village) Lenawee County	0	0.00
Addison (township) Oakland County	0	0.00
Adrian (city) Lenawee County	0	0.00

Top 10 Places Sorted by Percent of Total Population
Based on places with total population of 50,000 or more

Place	Population	%
Ann Arbor (city) Washtenaw County	0	0.00
Battle Creek (city) Calhoun County	0	0.00
Canton (charter twp) Wayne County	0	0.00
Clinton (charter twp) Macomb County	0	0.00
Dearborn (city) Wayne County	0	0.00
Dearborn Heights (city) Wayne County	0	0.00
Detroit (city) Wayne County	0	0.00
Farmington Hills (city) Oakland County	0	0.00
Flint (city) Genesee County	0	0.00
Grand Rapids (city) Kent County	0	0.00

African, Sub-Saharan: Somalian

Top 10 Places Sorted by Population
Based on all places, regardless of total population

Place	Population	%
Lansing (city) Ingham County	316	0.27
Ypsilanti (charter twp) Washtenaw County	127	0.24
Detroit (city) Wayne County	97	0.01
Sterling Heights (city) Macomb County	75	0.06
Pittsfield (charter twp) Washtenaw County	73	0.21
Ypsilanti (city) Washtenaw County	72	0.36
Grand Rapids (city) Kent County	68	0.04
Dearborn (city) Wayne County	41	0.04
White Cloud (city) Newaygo County	36	2.05
East Lansing (city) Ingham County	32	0.07

Top 10 Places Sorted by Percent of Total Population
Based on all places, regardless of total population

Place	Population	%
White Cloud (city) Newaygo County	36	2.05
Ypsilanti (city) Washtenaw County	72	0.36
Lansing (city) Ingham County	316	0.27
Negaunee (township) Marquette County	8	0.27
Ypsilanti (charter twp) Washtenaw County	127	0.24
Pittsfield (charter twp) Washtenaw County	73	0.21
Walton (township) Eaton County	3	0.14
East Lansing (city) Ingham County	32	0.07
Sterling Heights (city) Macomb County	75	0.06
Okemos (cdp) Ingham County	13	0.06

Top 10 Places Sorted by Percent of Total Population
Based on places with total population of 50,000 or more

Place	Population	%
Lansing (city) Ingham County	316	0.27
Ypsilanti (charter twp) Washtenaw County	127	0.24
Sterling Heights (city) Macomb County	75	0.06
Grand Rapids (city) Kent County	68	0.04
Dearborn (city) Wayne County	41	0.04
Detroit (city) Wayne County	97	0.01
Ann Arbor (city) Washtenaw County	2	<0.01
Battle Creek (city) Calhoun County	0	0.00
Canton (charter twp) Wayne County	0	0.00
Clinton (charter twp) Macomb County	0	0.00

African, Sub-Saharan: South African

Top 10 Places Sorted by Population
Based on all places, regardless of total population

Place	Population	%
Ann Arbor (city) Washtenaw County	123	0.11
Detroit (city) Wayne County	75	0.01
Farmington Hills (city) Oakland County	69	0.09
Grand Rapids (city) Kent County	67	0.04
East Lansing (city) Ingham County	64	0.13
Hartland (township) Livingston County	56	0.39
Flint (charter twp) Genesee County	52	0.16
Rochester Hills (city) Oakland County	45	0.06
Kalamazoo (city) Kalamazoo County	37	0.05
Lyon (township) Roscommon County	36	2.39

Top 10 Places Sorted by Percent of Total Population
Based on all places, regardless of total population

Place	Population	%
Lyon (township) Roscommon County	36	2.39
Fremont (township) Saginaw County	27	1.37
Perry (city) Shiawassee County	13	0.60
Hartland (township) Livingston County	56	0.39
Royalton (township) Berrien County	16	0.35
Pennfield (charter twp) Calhoun County	31	0.34
Milton (township) Antrim County	7	0.34
Kingsford (city) Dickinson County	14	0.27
Westwood (cdp) Kalamazoo County	16	0.18
East Bay (township) Grand Traverse County	18	0.17

Top 10 Places Sorted by Percent of Total Population
Based on places with total population of 50,000 or more

Place	Population	%
Ann Arbor (city) Washtenaw County	123	0.11
Farmington Hills (city) Oakland County	69	0.09
Rochester Hills (city) Oakland County	45	0.06
Kalamazoo (city) Kalamazoo County	37	0.05
Grand Rapids (city) Kent County	67	0.04
Shelby (charter twp) Macomb County	30	0.04
Livonia (city) Wayne County	27	0.03
Macomb (township) Macomb County	26	0.03
Detroit (city) Wayne County	75	0.01
Lansing (city) Ingham County	7	0.01

African, Sub-Saharan: Sudanese

Top 10 Places Sorted by Population
Based on all places, regardless of total population

Place	Population	%
Grand Rapids (city) Kent County	285	0.15
Lansing (city) Ingham County	239	0.21
Lincoln Park (city) Wayne County	64	0.17
Inkster (city) Wayne County	59	0.22
East Lansing (city) Ingham County	58	0.12
Detroit (city) Wayne County	37	<0.01
Wyoming (city) Kent County	33	0.05
Flint (charter twp) Genesee County	31	0.09
Reed City (city) Osceola County	14	0.52
Romulus (city) Wayne County	13	0.05

Top 10 Places Sorted by Percent of Total Population
Based on all places, regardless of total population

Place	Population	%
Reed City (city) Osceola County	14	0.52
Inkster (city) Wayne County	59	0.22
Lansing (city) Ingham County	239	0.21
Lincoln Park (city) Wayne County	64	0.17
Grand Rapids (city) Kent County	285	0.15
East Lansing (city) Ingham County	58	0.12
Flint (charter twp) Genesee County	31	0.09
Wyoming (city) Kent County	33	0.05
Romulus (city) Wayne County	13	0.05
Plymouth (charter twp) Wayne County	11	0.04

Top 10 Places Sorted by Percent of Total Population
Based on places with total population of 50,000 or more

Place	Population	%
Lansing (city) Ingham County	239	0.21
Grand Rapids (city) Kent County	285	0.15
Wyoming (city) Kent County	33	0.05
Detroit (city) Wayne County	37	<0.01
Ann Arbor (city) Washtenaw County	0	0.00
Battle Creek (city) Calhoun County	0	0.00
Canton (charter twp) Wayne County	0	0.00
Clinton (charter twp) Macomb County	0	0.00
Dearborn (city) Wayne County	0	0.00
Dearborn Heights (city) Wayne County	0	0.00

African, Sub-Saharan: Ugandan

Top 10 Places Sorted by Population
Based on all places, regardless of total population

Place	Population	%
Kalamazoo (city) Kalamazoo County	61	0.08
Canton (charter twp) Wayne County	17	0.02
Superior (charter twp) Washtenaw County	13	0.10

Woodhaven (city) Wayne County	11	0.09
Northview (cdp) Kent County	11	0.08
Plainfield (charter twp) Kent County	11	0.04
Battle Creek (city) Calhoun County	9	0.02
Southgate (city) Wayne County	7	0.02
Acme (township) Grand Traverse County	0	0.00
Ada (township) Kent County	0	0.00

Top 10 Places Sorted by Percent of Total Population
Based on all places, regardless of total population

Place	Population	%
Superior (charter twp) Washtenaw County	13	0.10
Woodhaven (city) Wayne County	11	0.09
Kalamazoo (city) Kalamazoo County	61	0.08
Northview (cdp) Kent County	11	0.08
Plainfield (charter twp) Kent County	11	0.04
Canton (charter twp) Wayne County	17	0.02
Battle Creek (city) Calhoun County	9	0.02
Southgate (city) Wayne County	7	0.02
Acme (township) Grand Traverse County	0	0.00
Ada (township) Kent County	0	0.00

Top 10 Places Sorted by Percent of Total Population
Based on places with total population of 50,000 or more

Place	Population	%
Kalamazoo (city) Kalamazoo County	61	0.08
Canton (charter twp) Wayne County	17	0.02
Battle Creek (city) Calhoun County	9	0.02
Ann Arbor (city) Washtenaw County	0	0.00
Clinton (charter twp) Macomb County	0	0.00
Dearborn (city) Wayne County	0	0.00
Dearborn Heights (city) Wayne County	0	0.00
Detroit (city) Wayne County	0	0.00
Farmington Hills (city) Oakland County	0	0.00
Flint (city) Genesee County	0	0.00

African, Sub-Saharan: Zimbabwean

Top 10 Places Sorted by Population
Based on all places, regardless of total population

Place	Population	%
Comstock Northwest (cdp) Kalamazoo County	175	2.74
Comstock (charter twp) Kalamazoo County	175	1.20
Okemos (cdp) Ingham County	48	0.23
Meridian (charter twp) Ingham County	48	0.12
Kalamazoo (city) Kalamazoo County	46	0.06
Battle Creek (city) Calhoun County	23	0.04
East Lansing (city) Ingham County	20	0.04
Rochester Hills (city) Oakland County	20	0.03
Shelby (charter twp) Macomb County	18	0.02
West Bloomfield (charter twp) Oakland County	17	0.03

Top 10 Places Sorted by Percent of Total Population
Based on all places, regardless of total population

Place	Population	%
Comstock Northwest (cdp) Kalamazoo County	175	2.74
Comstock (charter twp) Kalamazoo County	175	1.20
Okemos (cdp) Ingham County	48	0.23
Oregon (township) Lapeer County	11	0.18
Meridian (charter twp) Ingham County	48	0.12
Fair Plain (cdp) Berrien County	8	0.11
Kalamazoo (city) Kalamazoo County	46	0.06
Gaines (township) Kent County	12	0.05
Benton (charter twp) Berrien County	8	0.05
Battle Creek (city) Calhoun County	23	0.04

Top 10 Places Sorted by Percent of Total Population
Based on places with total population of 50,000 or more

Place	Population	%
Kalamazoo (city) Kalamazoo County	46	0.06
Battle Creek (city) Calhoun County	23	0.04
Rochester Hills (city) Oakland County	20	0.03
West Bloomfield (charter twp) Oakland County	17	0.03
Shelby (charter twp) Macomb County	18	0.02
Farmington Hills (city) Oakland County	16	0.02
Southfield (city) Oakland County	12	0.02
Ann Arbor (city) Washtenaw County	9	0.01
Canton (charter twp) Wayne County	0	0.00
Clinton (charter twp) Macomb County	0	0.00

African, Sub-Saharan: Other

Top 10 Places Sorted by Population
Based on all places, regardless of total population

Place	Population	%
Lansing (city) Ingham County	289	0.25
Detroit (city) Wayne County	259	0.03
Fraser (city) Macomb County	136	0.92
Dearborn (city) Wayne County	124	0.13
Ypsilanti (charter twp) Washtenaw County	123	0.23
Lathrup Village (city) Oakland County	116	2.83
Livonia (city) Wayne County	114	0.12
Kentwood (city) Kent County	100	0.21
Rochester Hills (city) Oakland County	74	0.10
Farmington Hills (city) Oakland County	59	0.07

Top 10 Places Sorted by Percent of Total Population
Based on all places, regardless of total population

Place	Population	%
Lathrup Village (city) Oakland County	116	2.83
Fraser (city) Macomb County	136	0.92
Kinross (charter twp) Chippewa County	50	0.62
Hillman (village) Montmorency County	4	0.58
Royalton (township) Berrien County	24	0.52
Lansing (city) Ingham County	289	0.25
Orchard Lake Village (city) Oakland County	5	0.24
Ypsilanti (charter twp) Washtenaw County	123	0.23
Oronoko (charter twp) Berrien County	21	0.23
Kentwood (city) Kent County	100	0.21

Top 10 Places Sorted by Percent of Total Population
Based on places with total population of 50,000 or more

Place	Population	%
Lansing (city) Ingham County	289	0.25
Ypsilanti (charter twp) Washtenaw County	123	0.23
Dearborn (city) Wayne County	124	0.13
Livonia (city) Wayne County	114	0.12
Rochester Hills (city) Oakland County	74	0.10
Farmington Hills (city) Oakland County	59	0.07
Novi (city) Oakland County	37	0.07
Southfield (city) Oakland County	46	0.06
Flint (city) Genesee County	49	0.05
Detroit (city) Wayne County	259	0.03

Albanian

Top 10 Places Sorted by Population
Based on all places, regardless of total population

Place	Population	%
Sterling Heights (city) Macomb County	3,414	2.63
Macomb (township) Macomb County	2,016	2.69
Shelby (charter twp) Macomb County	1,549	2.13
Farmington Hills (city) Oakland County	866	1.08
Rochester Hills (city) Oakland County	831	1.18
Westland (city) Wayne County	829	0.98
Clinton (charter twp) Macomb County	757	0.78
Dearborn (city) Wayne County	666	0.68
Troy (city) Oakland County	612	0.76
Warren (city) Macomb County	534	0.39

Top 10 Places Sorted by Percent of Total Population
Based on all places, regardless of total population

Place	Population	%
Utica (city) Macomb County	225	4.73
Grosse Pointe Park (city) Wayne County	472	4.02
Bruce (township) Macomb County	281	3.24
Oakland (charter twp) Oakland County	467	2.90
Macomb (township) Macomb County	2,016	2.69
Sterling Heights (city) Macomb County	3,414	2.63
Holly (village) Oakland County	134	2.19
Shelby (charter twp) Macomb County	1,549	2.13
Wixom (city) Oakland County	235	1.75
Madison Heights (city) Oakland County	514	1.72

Top 10 Places Sorted by Percent of Total Population
Based on places with total population of 50,000 or more

Place	Population	%
Macomb (township) Macomb County	2,016	2.69
Sterling Heights (city) Macomb County	3,414	2.63
Shelby (charter twp) Macomb County	1,549	2.13
Rochester Hills (city) Oakland County	831	1.18
Farmington Hills (city) Oakland County	866	1.08
Westland (city) Wayne County	829	0.98
Clinton (charter twp) Macomb County	757	0.78
Troy (city) Oakland County	612	0.76
Dearborn (city) Wayne County	666	0.68
Taylor (city) Wayne County	385	0.60

Alsatian

Top 10 Places Sorted by Population
Based on all places, regardless of total population

Place	Population	%
Grosse Pointe Park (city) Wayne County	16	0.14
Ann Arbor (city) Washtenaw County	13	0.01
Lambertville (cdp) Monroe County	12	0.12
Bedford (township) Monroe County	12	0.04
Dearborn (city) Wayne County	11	0.01
Ogden (township) Lenawee County	10	0.96
Iron Mountain (city) Dickinson County	10	0.13
Birmingham (city) Oakland County	10	0.05
Washington (township) Macomb County	10	0.04
Clinton (charter twp) Macomb County	10	0.01

Top 10 Places Sorted by Percent of Total Population
Based on all places, regardless of total population

Place	Population	%
Ogden (township) Lenawee County	10	0.96
Liberty (township) Wexford County	8	0.90
Bay (township) Charlevoix County	4	0.27
Sylvan (township) Washtenaw County	5	0.18
Grosse Pointe Park (city) Wayne County	16	0.14
Iron Mountain (city) Dickinson County	10	0.13
Lambertville (cdp) Monroe County	12	0.12
Alma (city) Gratiot County	7	0.07
Birmingham (city) Oakland County	10	0.05
Bedford (township) Monroe County	12	0.04

Top 10 Places Sorted by Percent of Total Population
Based on places with total population of 50,000 or more

Place	Population	%
Ann Arbor (city) Washtenaw County	13	0.01
Dearborn (city) Wayne County	11	0.01
Clinton (charter twp) Macomb County	10	0.01
Rochester Hills (city) Oakland County	9	0.01
Battle Creek (city) Calhoun County	0	0.00
Canton (charter twp) Wayne County	0	0.00
Dearborn Heights (city) Wayne County	0	0.00
Detroit (city) Wayne County	0	0.00
Farmington Hills (city) Oakland County	0	0.00
Flint (city) Genesee County	0	0.00

American

Top 10 Places Sorted by Population
Based on all places, regardless of total population

Place	Population	%
Detroit (city) Wayne County	7,086	0.93
Lansing (city) Ingham County	6,973	6.03
Livonia (city) Wayne County	5,356	5.47
Warren (city) Macomb County	4,766	3.51
Westland (city) Wayne County	4,473	5.27
Sterling Heights (city) Macomb County	4,311	3.32
Clinton (charter twp) Macomb County	4,195	4.31
Canton (charter twp) Wayne County	4,185	4.76
Flint (city) Genesee County	3,644	3.38
Waterford (charter twp) Oakland County	3,571	4.97

Top 10 Places Sorted by Percent of Total Population
Based on all places, regardless of total population

Place	Population	%
Napoleon (cdp) Jackson County	661	53.48
Nessen City (cdp) Benzie County	24	33.33
Matchwood (township) Ontonagon County	37	31.36
Marenisco (township) Gogebic County	483	31.00
Marenisco (cdp) Gogebic County	80	30.30
Burr Oak (village) St. Joseph County	201	29.96
Delton (cdp) Barry County	296	29.90
Westphalia (village) Clinton County	246	28.91
Ovid (village) Clinton County	492	27.39
Nashville (village) Barry County	461	27.13

Top 10 Places Sorted by Percent of Total Population
Based on places with total population of 50,000 or more

Place	Population	%
Lansing (city) Ingham County	6,973	6.03
Ypsilanti (charter twp) Washtenaw County	3,184	6.01
Battle Creek (city) Calhoun County	3,106	5.89
Livonia (city) Wayne County	5,356	5.47
Westland (city) Wayne County	4,473	5.27
Waterford (charter twp) Oakland County	3,571	4.97
Shelby (charter twp) Macomb County	3,530	4.85
Canton (charter twp) Wayne County	4,185	4.76
Clinton (charter twp) Macomb County	4,195	4.31
West Bloomfield (charter twp) Oakland County	2,747	4.25

Arab: Total

Top 10 Places Sorted by Population
Based on all places, regardless of total population

Place	Population	%
Dearborn (city) Wayne County	38,503	39.13
Dearborn Heights (city) Wayne County	10,397	17.91
Detroit (city) Wayne County	8,642	1.14
Sterling Heights (city) Macomb County	8,488	6.54
West Bloomfield (charter twp) Oakland County	4,594	7.10
Hamtramck (city) Wayne County	4,285	18.97
Troy (city) Oakland County	3,081	3.80
Warren (city) Macomb County	2,804	2.06
Farmington Hills (city) Oakland County	2,505	3.12
Canton (charter twp) Wayne County	2,465	2.80

Top 10 Places Sorted by Percent of Total Population
Based on all places, regardless of total population

Place	Population	%
Dearborn (city) Wayne County	38,503	39.13
Hamtramck (city) Wayne County	4,285	18.97
Dearborn Heights (city) Wayne County	10,397	17.91
St. James (cdp) Charlevoix County	27	14.36
Harrietta (village) Wexford County	16	14.16
St. James (township) Charlevoix County	27	10.47
West Bloomfield (charter twp) Oakland County	4,594	7.10
Coldwater (city) Branch County	775	7.06
Sterling Heights (city) Macomb County	8,488	6.54
Village of Grosse Pointe Shores (city) Wayne Co.	193	6.49

Top 10 Places Sorted by Percent of Total Population
Based on places with total population of 50,000 or more

Place	Population	%
Dearborn (city) Wayne County	38,503	39.13
Dearborn Heights (city) Wayne County	10,397	17.91
West Bloomfield (charter twp) Oakland County	4,594	7.10
Sterling Heights (city) Macomb County	8,488	6.54
Troy (city) Oakland County	3,081	3.80
Farmington Hills (city) Oakland County	2,505	3.12
Shelby (charter twp) Macomb County	2,092	2.87
Canton (charter twp) Wayne County	2,465	2.80
Livonia (city) Wayne County	2,374	2.42
Southfield (city) Oakland County	1,650	2.26

Arab: Arab

Top 10 Places Sorted by Population
Based on all places, regardless of total population

Place	Population	%
Dearborn (city) Wayne County	8,134	8.27
Detroit (city) Wayne County	4,349	0.57
Hamtramck (city) Wayne County	2,280	10.09
Sterling Heights (city) Macomb County	1,888	1.46
West Bloomfield (charter twp) Oakland County	1,506	2.33
Livonia (city) Wayne County	1,013	1.03
Dearborn Heights (city) Wayne County	1,002	1.73
Troy (city) Oakland County	929	1.15
Canton (charter twp) Wayne County	709	0.81
Farmington Hills (city) Oakland County	587	0.73

Top 10 Places Sorted by Percent of Total Population
Based on all places, regardless of total population

Place	Population	%
St. James (cdp) Charlevoix County	27	14.36
St. James (township) Charlevoix County	27	10.47
Hamtramck (city) Wayne County	2,280	10.09

Place	Population	%
Dearborn (city) Wayne County	8,134	8.27
Hulbert (township) Chippewa County	14	6.14
Dollar Bay (cdp) Houghton County	26	3.17
Melvindale (city) Wayne County	329	3.06
Whitefish (township) Chippewa County	16	2.84
Excelsior (township) Kalkaska County	21	2.35
West Bloomfield (charter twp) Oakland County	1,506	2.33

Top 10 Places Sorted by Percent of Total Population
Based on places with total population of 50,000 or more

Place	Population	%
Dearborn (city) Wayne County	8,134	8.27
West Bloomfield (charter twp) Oakland County	1,506	2.33
Dearborn Heights (city) Wayne County	1,002	1.73
Sterling Heights (city) Macomb County	1,888	1.46
Troy (city) Oakland County	929	1.15
Livonia (city) Wayne County	1,013	1.03
Canton (charter twp) Wayne County	709	0.81
Farmington Hills (city) Oakland County	587	0.73
Novi (city) Oakland County	392	0.73
Westland (city) Wayne County	536	0.63

Arab: Egyptian

Top 10 Places Sorted by Population
Based on all places, regardless of total population

Place	Population	%
Dearborn (city) Wayne County	356	0.36
Troy (city) Oakland County	286	0.35
Sterling Heights (city) Macomb County	283	0.22
Rochester Hills (city) Oakland County	213	0.30
Ann Arbor (city) Washtenaw County	189	0.16
Madison Heights (city) Oakland County	172	0.57
Shelby (charter twp) Macomb County	134	0.18
Detroit (city) Wayne County	92	0.01
St. Clair Shores (city) Macomb County	90	0.15
West Bloomfield (charter twp) Oakland County	83	0.13

Top 10 Places Sorted by Percent of Total Population
Based on all places, regardless of total population

Place	Population	%
Barton (township) Newaygo County	6	0.94
Center Line (city) Macomb County	76	0.91
Hatton (township) Clare County	7	0.82
Exeter (township) Monroe County	25	0.63
Madison Heights (city) Oakland County	172	0.57
Grosse Pointe (city) Wayne County	25	0.46
Pleasant Ridge (city) Oakland County	11	0.43
Richmond (township) Osceola County	8	0.43
Union (charter twp) Isabella County	49	0.41
Oakland (charter twp) Oakland County	62	0.38

Top 10 Places Sorted by Percent of Total Population
Based on places with total population of 50,000 or more

Place	Population	%
Dearborn (city) Wayne County	356	0.36
Troy (city) Oakland County	286	0.35
Rochester Hills (city) Oakland County	213	0.30
Sterling Heights (city) Macomb County	283	0.22
Shelby (charter twp) Macomb County	134	0.18
Ann Arbor (city) Washtenaw County	189	0.16
St. Clair Shores (city) Macomb County	90	0.15
West Bloomfield (charter twp) Oakland County	83	0.13
Waterford (charter twp) Oakland County	47	0.07
Warren (city) Macomb County	62	0.05

Arab: Iraqi

Top 10 Places Sorted by Population
Based on all places, regardless of total population

Place	Population	%
Sterling Heights (city) Macomb County	4,199	3.24
Dearborn (city) Wayne County	2,820	2.87
West Bloomfield (charter twp) Oakland County	1,775	2.74
Southfield (city) Oakland County	1,164	1.60
Detroit (city) Wayne County	1,125	0.15
Warren (city) Macomb County	932	0.69
Farmington Hills (city) Oakland County	777	0.97
Troy (city) Oakland County	722	0.89
Shelby (charter twp) Macomb County	639	0.88
Dearborn Heights (city) Wayne County	578	1.00

Top 10 Places Sorted by Percent of Total Population
Based on all places, regardless of total population

Place	Population	%
Orchard Lake Village (city) Oakland County	107	5.03
Sterling Heights (city) Macomb County	4,199	3.24
Dearborn (city) Wayne County	2,820	2.87
West Bloomfield (charter twp) Oakland County	1,775	2.74
Lennon (village) Shiawassee County	17	2.63
Hazel Park (city) Oakland County	277	1.64
Manlius (township) Allegan County	49	1.64
Southfield (city) Oakland County	1,164	1.60
Madison Heights (city) Oakland County	424	1.42
Walled Lake (city) Oakland County	95	1.37

Top 10 Places Sorted by Percent of Total Population
Based on places with total population of 50,000 or more

Place	Population	%
Sterling Heights (city) Macomb County	4,199	3.24
Dearborn (city) Wayne County	2,820	2.87
West Bloomfield (charter twp) Oakland County	1,775	2.74
Southfield (city) Oakland County	1,164	1.60
Dearborn Heights (city) Wayne County	578	1.00
Farmington Hills (city) Oakland County	777	0.97
Troy (city) Oakland County	722	0.89
Shelby (charter twp) Macomb County	639	0.88
Warren (city) Macomb County	932	0.69
Rochester Hills (city) Oakland County	331	0.47

Arab: Jordanian

Top 10 Places Sorted by Population
Based on all places, regardless of total population

Place	Population	%
Dearborn (city) Wayne County	805	0.82
Dearborn Heights (city) Wayne County	265	0.46
Livonia (city) Wayne County	216	0.22
Westland (city) Wayne County	180	0.21
Brownstown (charter twp) Wayne County	179	0.61
Warren (city) Macomb County	174	0.13
Sterling Heights (city) Macomb County	161	0.12
Plymouth (charter twp) Wayne County	147	0.53
Lee (township) Midland County	130	3.00
Detroit (city) Wayne County	117	0.02

Top 10 Places Sorted by Percent of Total Population
Based on all places, regardless of total population

Place	Population	%
Lee (township) Midland County	130	3.00
Bowne (township) Kent County	89	2.94
James (township) Saginaw County	37	1.90
Addison (township) Oakland County	84	1.32
Dexter (township) Washtenaw County	78	1.31
Dearborn (city) Wayne County	805	0.82
Brownstown (charter twp) Wayne County	179	0.61
Plymouth (charter twp) Wayne County	147	0.53
Auburn Hills (city) Oakland County	110	0.52
Dearborn Heights (city) Wayne County	265	0.46

Top 10 Places Sorted by Percent of Total Population
Based on places with total population of 50,000 or more

Place	Population	%
Dearborn (city) Wayne County	805	0.82
Dearborn Heights (city) Wayne County	265	0.46
Livonia (city) Wayne County	216	0.22
Westland (city) Wayne County	180	0.21
Warren (city) Macomb County	174	0.13
Macomb (township) Macomb County	95	0.13
Sterling Heights (city) Macomb County	161	0.12
Ann Arbor (city) Washtenaw County	104	0.09
Novi (city) Oakland County	48	0.09
Troy (city) Oakland County	66	0.08

Arab: Lebanese

Top 10 Places Sorted by Population
Based on all places, regardless of total population

Place	Population	%
Dearborn (city) Wayne County	18,812	19.12
Dearborn Heights (city) Wayne County	7,446	12.82
Sterling Heights (city) Macomb County	1,441	1.11

Place	Population	%
Clinton (charter twp) Macomb County	1,184	1.22
Canton (charter twp) Wayne County	969	1.10
Warren (city) Macomb County	891	0.66
Macomb (township) Macomb County	808	1.08
Troy (city) Oakland County	752	0.93
Shelby (charter twp) Macomb County	686	0.94
Livonia (city) Wayne County	668	0.68

Top 10 Places Sorted by Percent of Total Population
Based on all places, regardless of total population

Place	Population	%
Dearborn (city) Wayne County	18,812	19.12
Dearborn Heights (city) Wayne County	7,446	12.82
Village of Grosse Pointe Shores (city) Wayne Co.	175	5.88
Mulliken (village) Eaton County	27	5.33
Oden (cdp) Emmet County	26	5.16
Logan (township) Mason County	11	4.51
Pearl Beach (cdp) St. Clair County	122	3.88
Au Sable (cdp) Iosco County	41	3.72
Summerfield (township) Monroe County	113	3.38
Cedarville (township) Menominee County	10	3.08

Top 10 Places Sorted by Percent of Total Population
Based on places with total population of 50,000 or more

Place	Population	%
Dearborn (city) Wayne County	18,812	19.12
Dearborn Heights (city) Wayne County	7,446	12.82
Clinton (charter twp) Macomb County	1,184	1.22
Sterling Heights (city) Macomb County	1,441	1.11
Canton (charter twp) Wayne County	969	1.10
Macomb (township) Macomb County	808	1.08
Shelby (charter twp) Macomb County	686	0.94
Troy (city) Oakland County	752	0.93
St. Clair Shores (city) Macomb County	558	0.92
Royal Oak (city) Oakland County	411	0.71

Arab: Moroccan

Top 10 Places Sorted by Population
Based on all places, regardless of total population

Place	Population	%
Detroit (city) Wayne County	398	0.05
Kinross (charter twp) Chippewa County	152	1.89
Dearborn (city) Wayne County	121	0.12
Ionia (city) Ionia County	72	0.60
Blackman (charter twp) Jackson County	72	0.92
Coldwater (township) Branch County	59	0.92
Flint (city) Genesee County	49	0.05
Muskegon (city) Muskegon County	46	0.12
Ypsilanti (charter twp) Washtenaw County	46	0.09
Southfield (city) Oakland County	42	0.06

Top 10 Places Sorted by Percent of Total Population
Based on all places, regardless of total population

Place	Population	%
McMillan (township) Ontonagon County	10	2.02
Kinross (charter twp) Chippewa County	152	1.89
Pentland (township) Luce County	27	1.06
Coldwater (township) Branch County	59	0.92
Ionia (city) Ionia County	72	0.60
St. Louis (city) Gratiot County	39	0.53
Freeland (cdp) Saginaw County	31	0.44
Indianfields (township) Tuscola County	26	0.42
Manistique (township) Schoolcraft County	4	0.40
Fife Lake (township) Grand Traverse County	10	0.38

Top 10 Places Sorted by Percent of Total Population
Based on places with total population of 50,000 or more

Place	Population	%
Dearborn (city) Wayne County	121	0.12
Ypsilanti (charter twp) Washtenaw County	46	0.09
Southfield (city) Oakland County	42	0.06
Detroit (city) Wayne County	398	0.05
Flint (city) Genesee County	49	0.05
Clinton (charter twp) Macomb County	41	0.04
Waterford (charter twp) Oakland County	29	0.04
Saginaw (city) Saginaw County	12	0.02
Battle Creek (city) Calhoun County	9	0.02
Pontiac (city) Oakland County	9	0.01

Please refer to the Explanation of Data in the front of the book for more detailed information.

Arab: Palestinian

Top 10 Places Sorted by Population
Based on all places, regardless of total population

Place	Population	%
Dearborn (city) Wayne County	792	0.80
Ann Arbor (city) Washtenaw County	410	0.36
Pittsfield (charter twp) Washtenaw County	336	0.99
Canton (charter twp) Wayne County	255	0.29
Livonia (city) Wayne County	220	0.22
Dearborn Heights (city) Wayne County	196	0.34
Garden City (city) Wayne County	138	0.49
Grand Blanc (charter twp) Genesee County	134	0.37
Detroit (city) Wayne County	132	0.02
Westland (city) Wayne County	119	0.14

Top 10 Places Sorted by Percent of Total Population
Based on all places, regardless of total population

Place	Population	%
Ann Arbor (charter twp) Washtenaw County	65	1.48
Lapeer (township) Lapeer County	63	1.22
Pittsfield (charter twp) Washtenaw County	336	0.99
Boyne City (city) Charlevoix County	33	0.88
Dearborn (city) Wayne County	792	0.80
Sylvan (township) Washtenaw County	22	0.78
Tyrone (township) Livingston County	71	0.71
Atlas (township) Genesee County	56	0.70
Hayes (township) Charlevoix County	12	0.63
Bingham (township) Leelanau County	16	0.62

Top 10 Places Sorted by Percent of Total Population
Based on places with total population of 50,000 or more

Place	Population	%
Dearborn (city) Wayne County	792	0.80
Ann Arbor (city) Washtenaw County	410	0.36
Dearborn Heights (city) Wayne County	196	0.34
Canton (charter twp) Wayne County	255	0.29
Livonia (city) Wayne County	220	0.22
Westland (city) Wayne County	119	0.14
Farmington Hills (city) Oakland County	92	0.11
West Bloomfield (charter twp) Oakland County	53	0.08
Novi (city) Oakland County	38	0.07
Macomb (township) Macomb County	35	0.05

Arab: Syrian

Top 10 Places Sorted by Population
Based on all places, regardless of total population

Place	Population	%
Dearborn Heights (city) Wayne County	512	0.88
Dearborn (city) Wayne County	309	0.31
Flint (charter twp) Genesee County	267	0.82
Allen Park (city) Wayne County	219	0.77
Bloomfield (charter twp) Oakland County	191	0.46
Sterling Heights (city) Macomb County	187	0.14
Shelby (charter twp) Macomb County	176	0.24
Farmington Hills (city) Oakland County	174	0.22
Canton (charter twp) Wayne County	173	0.20
Ann Arbor (city) Washtenaw County	172	0.15

Top 10 Places Sorted by Percent of Total Population
Based on all places, regardless of total population

Place	Population	%
Brevort (township) Mackinac County	17	2.66
Sanford (village) Midland County	27	2.47
Pearl Beach (cdp) St. Clair County	61	1.94
Armada (village) Macomb County	34	1.89
New Era (village) Oceana County	11	1.78
Burleigh (township) Iosco County	10	1.29
Bingham (township) Leelanau County	32	1.24
Farmington (city) Oakland County	114	1.10
Saugatuck (township) Allegan County	31	1.08
Freedom (township) Washtenaw County	14	1.05

Top 10 Places Sorted by Percent of Total Population
Based on places with total population of 50,000 or more

Place	Population	%
Dearborn Heights (city) Wayne County	512	0.88
Dearborn (city) Wayne County	309	0.31
Shelby (charter twp) Macomb County	176	0.24
Rochester Hills (city) Oakland County	171	0.24

Place	Population	%
Macomb (township) Macomb County	169	0.23
Farmington Hills (city) Oakland County	174	0.22
Canton (charter twp) Wayne County	173	0.20
Wyoming (city) Kent County	140	0.19
West Bloomfield (charter twp) Oakland County	125	0.19
Novi (city) Oakland County	104	0.19

Arab: Other

Top 10 Places Sorted by Population
Based on all places, regardless of total population

Place	Population	%
Dearborn (city) Wayne County	6,354	6.46
Hamtramck (city) Wayne County	1,973	8.73
Detroit (city) Wayne County	1,837	0.24
West Bloomfield (charter twp) Oakland County	567	0.88
Coldwater (city) Branch County	557	5.07
Ann Arbor (city) Washtenaw County	522	0.45
Farmington Hills (city) Oakland County	412	0.51
Dearborn Heights (city) Wayne County	371	0.64
Sterling Heights (city) Macomb County	300	0.23
Melvindale (city) Wayne County	292	2.71

Top 10 Places Sorted by Percent of Total Population
Based on all places, regardless of total population

Place	Population	%
Harrietta (village) Wexford County	16	14.16
Hamtramck (city) Wayne County	1,973	8.73
Dearborn (city) Wayne County	6,354	6.46
Coldwater (city) Branch County	557	5.07
Boon (township) Wexford County	16	2.80
Melvindale (city) Wayne County	292	2.71
East Jordan (city) Charlevoix County	39	2.02
Grass Lake (charter twp) Jackson County	92	1.66
Bloomfield Hills (city) Oakland County	62	1.60
Churchill (township) Ogemaw County	25	1.23

Top 10 Places Sorted by Percent of Total Population
Based on places with total population of 50,000 or more

Place	Population	%
Dearborn (city) Wayne County	6,354	6.46
West Bloomfield (charter twp) Oakland County	567	0.88
Dearborn Heights (city) Wayne County	371	0.64
Farmington Hills (city) Oakland County	412	0.51
Ann Arbor (city) Washtenaw County	522	0.45
Ypsilanti (charter twp) Washtenaw County	207	0.39
Detroit (city) Wayne County	1,837	0.24
Sterling Heights (city) Macomb County	300	0.23
Rochester Hills (city) Oakland County	161	0.23
Canton (charter twp) Wayne County	183	0.21

Armenian

Top 10 Places Sorted by Population
Based on all places, regardless of total population

Place	Population	%
West Bloomfield (charter twp) Oakland County	814	1.26
Bloomfield (charter twp) Oakland County	583	1.41
Livonia (city) Wayne County	580	0.59
Farmington Hills (city) Oakland County	564	0.70
Dearborn (city) Wayne County	542	0.55
Warren (city) Macomb County	528	0.39
Waterford (charter twp) Oakland County	435	0.61
Novi (city) Oakland County	432	0.80
Canton (charter twp) Wayne County	376	0.43
Southfield (township) Oakland County	356	2.45

Top 10 Places Sorted by Percent of Total Population
Based on all places, regardless of total population

Place	Population	%
Lake Angelus (city) Oakland County	17	5.78
Indian River (cdp) Cheboygan County	77	4.44
Burlington (township) Calhoun County	85	4.24
Orchard Lake Village (city) Oakland County	77	3.62
Beverly Hills (village) Oakland County	307	2.99
Port Hope (village) Huron County	6	2.76
Novi (township) Oakland County	3	2.50
Tuscarora (township) Cheboygan County	77	2.49
Southfield (township) Oakland County	356	2.45
Royalton (township) Berrien County	88	1.92

Top 10 Places Sorted by Percent of Total Population
Based on places with total population of 50,000 or more

Place	Population	%
West Bloomfield (charter twp) Oakland County	814	1.26
Novi (city) Oakland County	432	0.80
Farmington Hills (city) Oakland County	564	0.70
Waterford (charter twp) Oakland County	435	0.61
Royal Oak (city) Oakland County	351	0.61
Livonia (city) Wayne County	580	0.59
Dearborn (city) Wayne County	542	0.55
Dearborn Heights (city) Wayne County	303	0.52
Canton (charter twp) Wayne County	376	0.43
Troy (city) Oakland County	338	0.42

Assyrian/Chaldean/Syriac

Top 10 Places Sorted by Population
Based on all places, regardless of total population

Place	Population	%
Sterling Heights (city) Macomb County	8,026	6.19
West Bloomfield (charter twp) Oakland County	5,475	8.46
Warren (city) Macomb County	2,627	1.93
Troy (city) Oakland County	1,643	2.03
Shelby (charter twp) Macomb County	1,454	2.00
Madison Heights (city) Oakland County	1,310	4.37
Farmington Hills (city) Oakland County	1,226	1.53
Commerce (charter twp) Oakland County	1,119	2.85
Southfield (city) Oakland County	863	1.18
Oak Park (city) Oakland County	706	2.36

Top 10 Places Sorted by Percent of Total Population
Based on all places, regardless of total population

Place	Population	%
Hamlin (township) Eaton County	410	12.42
Keego Harbor (city) Oakland County	329	11.23
West Bloomfield (charter twp) Oakland County	5,475	8.46
Sterling Heights (city) Macomb County	8,026	6.19
Orchard Lake Village (city) Oakland County	114	5.36
Madison Heights (city) Oakland County	1,310	4.37
Hazel Park (city) Oakland County	561	3.32
Otisco (township) Ionia County	80	3.13
Commerce (charter twp) Oakland County	1,119	2.85
Rock River (township) Alger County	35	2.49

Top 10 Places Sorted by Percent of Total Population
Based on places with total population of 50,000 or more

Place	Population	%
West Bloomfield (charter twp) Oakland County	5,475	8.46
Sterling Heights (city) Macomb County	8,026	6.19
Troy (city) Oakland County	1,643	2.03
Shelby (charter twp) Macomb County	1,454	2.00
Warren (city) Macomb County	2,627	1.93
Farmington Hills (city) Oakland County	1,226	1.53
Southfield (city) Oakland County	863	1.18
Novi (city) Oakland County	450	0.84
Waterford (charter twp) Oakland County	527	0.73
Rochester Hills (city) Oakland County	500	0.71

Australian

Top 10 Places Sorted by Population
Based on all places, regardless of total population

Place	Population	%
Chesterfield (township) Macomb County	218	0.51
St. Joseph (city) Berrien County	138	1.64
Detroit (city) Wayne County	129	0.02
Ann Arbor (city) Washtenaw County	95	0.08
Grand Rapids (city) Kent County	86	0.05
Farmington Hills (city) Oakland County	78	0.10
Holt (cdp) Ingham County	77	0.33
Delhi (charter twp) Ingham County	77	0.30
Novi (city) Oakland County	72	0.13
Monroe (city) Monroe County	70	0.33

Top 10 Places Sorted by Percent of Total Population
Based on all places, regardless of total population

Place	Population	%
Lake Ann (village) Benzie County	8	2.61
Clifford (village) Lapeer County	7	2.01
Bath (cdp) Clinton County	45	1.98

Place	Population	%
St. Joseph (city) Berrien County	138	1.64
Fruitport (village) Muskegon County	16	1.50
Montague (township) Muskegon County	20	1.15
Convis (township) Calhoun County	19	1.13
Caro (village) Tuscola County	49	1.07
Coldsprings (township) Kalkaska County	12	0.87
Hay (township) Gladwin County	11	0.84

Top 10 Places Sorted by Percent of Total Population
Based on places with total population of 50,000 or more

Place	Population	%
Novi (city) Oakland County	72	0.13
Farmington Hills (city) Oakland County	78	0.10
Ann Arbor (city) Washtenaw County	95	0.08
Troy (city) Oakland County	54	0.07
Grand Rapids (city) Kent County	86	0.05
Waterford (charter twp) Oakland County	38	0.05
Kalamazoo (city) Kalamazoo County	35	0.05
Taylor (city) Wayne County	23	0.04
Dearborn (city) Wayne County	26	0.03
Westland (city) Wayne County	24	0.03

Austrian

Top 10 Places Sorted by Population
Based on all places, regardless of total population

Place	Population	%
Sterling Heights (city) Macomb County	526	0.41
Ann Arbor (city) Washtenaw County	484	0.42
Royal Oak (city) Oakland County	466	0.81
Livonia (city) Wayne County	432	0.44
West Bloomfield (charter twp) Oakland County	398	0.62
Grand Rapids (city) Kent County	357	0.19
Warren (city) Macomb County	351	0.26
Kalamazoo (city) Kalamazoo County	315	0.42
St. Clair Shores (city) Macomb County	311	0.51
Troy (city) Oakland County	269	0.33

Top 10 Places Sorted by Percent of Total Population
Based on all places, regardless of total population

Place	Population	%
Carp Lake (cdp) Emmet County	18	4.57
Greilickville (cdp) Leelanau County	59	3.50
Manistique (city) Schoolcraft County	99	3.03
Eagle River (cdp) Keweenaw County	2	3.03
Cedarville (township) Menominee County	9	2.77
Port Hope (village) Huron County	6	2.76
De Tour Village (village) Chippewa County	7	2.75
Hart (township) Oceana County	54	2.64
Beal City (cdp) Isabella County	9	2.60
Norway (township) Dickinson County	41	2.47

Top 10 Places Sorted by Percent of Total Population
Based on places with total population of 50,000 or more

Place	Population	%
Royal Oak (city) Oakland County	466	0.81
West Bloomfield (charter twp) Oakland County	398	0.62
St. Clair Shores (city) Macomb County	311	0.51
Livonia (city) Wayne County	432	0.44
Ann Arbor (city) Washtenaw County	484	0.42
Kalamazoo (city) Kalamazoo County	315	0.42
Sterling Heights (city) Macomb County	526	0.41
Rochester Hills (city) Oakland County	268	0.38
Dearborn Heights (city) Wayne County	198	0.34
Troy (city) Oakland County	269	0.33

Basque

Top 10 Places Sorted by Population
Based on all places, regardless of total population

Place	Population	%
Traverse City (city) Grand Traverse County	74	0.50
Bloomfield (charter twp) Oakland County	59	0.14
Oakland (charter twp) Oakland County	32	0.20
Hillsdale (city) Hillsdale County	14	0.17
Independence (charter twp) Oakland County	14	0.04
Lansing (charter twp) Ingham County	13	0.16
Detroit (city) Wayne County	13	<0.01
Ann Arbor (city) Washtenaw County	12	0.01
Flint (charter twp) Genesee County	11	0.03
Dearborn (city) Wayne County	11	0.01

Top 10 Places Sorted by Percent of Total Population
Based on all places, regardless of total population

Place	Population	%
Onota (township) Alger County	9	3.10
Traverse City (city) Grand Traverse County	74	0.50
Oakland (charter twp) Oakland County	32	0.20
Hillsdale (city) Hillsdale County	14	0.17
Lansing (charter twp) Ingham County	13	0.16
Bloomfield (charter twp) Oakland County	59	0.14
Lodi (township) Washtenaw County	8	0.13
Berlin (township) Ionia County	2	0.10
West Branch (township) Marquette County	1	0.06
Independence (charter twp) Oakland County	14	0.04

Top 10 Places Sorted by Percent of Total Population
Based on places with total population of 50,000 or more

Place	Population	%
Battle Creek (city) Calhoun County	10	0.02
Ann Arbor (city) Washtenaw County	12	0.01
Dearborn (city) Wayne County	11	0.01
Shelby (charter twp) Macomb County	10	0.01
Canton (charter twp) Wayne County	8	0.01
Detroit (city) Wayne County	13	<0.01
Clinton (charter twp) Macomb County	0	0.00
Dearborn Heights (city) Wayne County	0	0.00
Farmington Hills (city) Oakland County	0	0.00
Flint (city) Genesee County	0	0.00

Belgian

Top 10 Places Sorted by Population
Based on all places, regardless of total population

Place	Population	%
St. Clair Shores (city) Macomb County	2,178	3.58
Macomb (township) Macomb County	1,860	2.48
Clinton (charter twp) Macomb County	1,840	1.89
Sterling Heights (city) Macomb County	1,835	1.41
Warren (city) Macomb County	1,678	1.24
Shelby (charter twp) Macomb County	1,336	1.84
Chesterfield (township) Macomb County	1,276	2.99
Roseville (city) Macomb County	978	2.04
Grosse Pointe Woods (city) Wayne County	776	4.74
Troy (city) Oakland County	722	0.89

Top 10 Places Sorted by Percent of Total Population
Based on all places, regardless of total population

Place	Population	%
West Branch (township) Dickinson County	11	28.95
Gourley (township) Menominee County	46	13.81
Stephenson (township) Menominee County	75	10.64
Ira (township) St. Clair County	528	9.45
Emmett (village) St. Clair County	30	9.12
Escanaba (township) Delta County	303	8.68
Brampton (township) Delta County	79	7.00
Berlin (township) St. Clair County	229	6.94
Norway (city) Dickinson County	183	6.32
Ford River (township) Delta County	127	6.23

Top 10 Places Sorted by Percent of Total Population
Based on places with total population of 50,000 or more

Place	Population	%
St. Clair Shores (city) Macomb County	2,178	3.58
Macomb (township) Macomb County	1,860	2.48
Clinton (charter twp) Macomb County	1,840	1.89
Shelby (charter twp) Macomb County	1,336	1.84
Sterling Heights (city) Macomb County	1,835	1.41
Warren (city) Macomb County	1,678	1.24
Troy (city) Oakland County	722	0.89
Rochester Hills (city) Oakland County	586	0.83
Royal Oak (city) Oakland County	424	0.73
Novi (city) Oakland County	295	0.55

Brazilian

Top 10 Places Sorted by Population
Based on all places, regardless of total population

Place	Population	%
Ann Arbor (city) Washtenaw County	174	0.15
Oronoko (charter twp) Berrien County	107	1.16
Farmington Hills (city) Oakland County	106	0.13

Place	Population	%
Taylor (city) Wayne County	101	0.16
Grand Rapids (city) Kent County	96	0.05
West Bloomfield (charter twp) Oakland County	78	0.12
Ypsilanti (city) Washtenaw County	77	0.38
Brownstown (charter twp) Wayne County	77	0.26
Dearborn (city) Wayne County	77	0.08
Romulus (city) Wayne County	75	0.31

Top 10 Places Sorted by Percent of Total Population
Based on all places, regardless of total population

Place	Population	%
Alba (cdp) Antrim County	12	4.20
Chestonia (township) Antrim County	12	3.49
Eau Claire (village) Berrien County	7	1.30
Oronoko (charter twp) Berrien County	107	1.16
Bruce (township) Chippewa County	23	1.12
Romeo (village) Macomb County	34	0.99
Calumet (village) Houghton County	7	0.97
Shoreham (village) Berrien County	8	0.92
Matteson (township) Branch County	11	0.85
Rollin (township) Lenawee County	26	0.79

Top 10 Places Sorted by Percent of Total Population
Based on places with total population of 50,000 or more

Place	Population	%
Taylor (city) Wayne County	101	0.16
Ann Arbor (city) Washtenaw County	174	0.15
Farmington Hills (city) Oakland County	106	0.13
West Bloomfield (charter twp) Oakland County	78	0.12
Rochester Hills (city) Oakland County	75	0.11
Dearborn (city) Wayne County	77	0.08
Novi (city) Oakland County	35	0.07
Grand Rapids (city) Kent County	96	0.05
Troy (city) Oakland County	38	0.05
Royal Oak (city) Oakland County	26	0.05

British

Top 10 Places Sorted by Population
Based on all places, regardless of total population

Place	Population	%
Ann Arbor (city) Washtenaw County	1,287	1.12
Grand Rapids (city) Kent County	667	0.35
Livonia (city) Wayne County	652	0.67
Canton (charter twp) Wayne County	468	0.53
East Lansing (city) Ingham County	454	0.94
Lansing (city) Ingham County	451	0.39
Independence (charter twp) Oakland County	450	1.31
Royal Oak (city) Oakland County	445	0.77
Warren (city) Macomb County	441	0.32
Midland (city) Midland County	415	0.99

Top 10 Places Sorted by Percent of Total Population
Based on all places, regardless of total population

Place	Population	%
Pilgrim (cdp) Benzie County	3	15.79
Bay View (cdp) Emmet County	10	10.10
Bohemia (township) Ontonagon County	4	9.76
Eastport (cdp) Antrim County	10	5.05
Crystal Downs Country Club (cdp) Benzie County	4	4.60
Ironton (cdp) Charlevoix County	8	4.57
Barnes Lake-Millers Lake (cdp) Lapeer County	43	3.98
Stronach (cdp) Manistee County	6	3.87
Empire (village) Leelanau County	9	3.46
Paradise (township) Grand Traverse County	151	3.24

Top 10 Places Sorted by Percent of Total Population
Based on places with total population of 50,000 or more

Place	Population	%
Ann Arbor (city) Washtenaw County	1,287	1.12
Royal Oak (city) Oakland County	445	0.77
Novi (city) Oakland County	390	0.72
Livonia (city) Wayne County	652	0.67
Rochester Hills (city) Oakland County	398	0.56
Canton (charter twp) Wayne County	468	0.53
Shelby (charter twp) Macomb County	325	0.45
Farmington Hills (city) Oakland County	340	0.42
Kalamazoo (city) Kalamazoo County	308	0.41
Lansing (city) Ingham County	451	0.39

Bulgarian

Top 10 Places Sorted by Population
Based on all places, regardless of total population

Place	Population	%
Shelby (charter twp) Macomb County	174	0.24
Wixom (city) Oakland County	162	1.20
Waterford (charter twp) Oakland County	108	0.15
Westland (city) Wayne County	93	0.11
Berlin (township) St. Clair County	86	2.61
Novi (city) Oakland County	84	0.16
Port Huron (city) St. Clair County	80	0.26
Lansing (city) Ingham County	77	0.07
Rochester (city) Oakland County	71	0.58
Ontwa (township) Cass County	68	1.05

Top 10 Places Sorted by Percent of Total Population
Based on all places, regardless of total population

Place	Population	%
Leland (cdp) Leelanau County	14	4.39
Berlin (township) St. Clair County	86	2.61
Iron River (city) Iron County	54	1.75
Johnstown (township) Barry County	46	1.51
Wixom (city) Oakland County	162	1.20
Sugar Island (township) Chippewa County	9	1.15
Reading (township) Hillsdale County	23	1.13
Hesperia (village) Oceana County	11	1.06
Ontwa (township) Cass County	68	1.05
Riverside (township) Missaukee County	11	0.92

Top 10 Places Sorted by Percent of Total Population
Based on places with total population of 50,000 or more

Place	Population	%
Shelby (charter twp) Macomb County	174	0.24
Novi (city) Oakland County	84	0.16
Waterford (charter twp) Oakland County	108	0.15
Westland (city) Wayne County	93	0.11
Battle Creek (city) Calhoun County	43	0.08
Lansing (city) Ingham County	77	0.07
Kalamazoo (city) Kalamazoo County	55	0.07
Macomb (township) Macomb County	53	0.07
Livonia (city) Wayne County	60	0.06
Dearborn (city) Wayne County	55	0.06

Cajun

Top 10 Places Sorted by Population
Based on all places, regardless of total population

Place	Population	%
Detroit (city) Wayne County	62	0.01
Tecumseh (city) Lenawee County	52	0.60
Kinross (charter twp) Chippewa County	45	0.56
Oakfield (township) Kent County	42	0.74
Eastwood (cdp) Kalamazoo County	41	0.66
Kalamazoo (charter twp) Kalamazoo County	41	0.19
Flint (charter twp) Genesee County	38	0.12
Farmington Hills (city) Oakland County	32	0.04
Ann Arbor (city) Washtenaw County	32	0.03
Colfax (township) Wexford County	15	1.67

Top 10 Places Sorted by Percent of Total Population
Based on all places, regardless of total population

Place	Population	%
Colfax (township) Wexford County	15	1.67
Oakfield (township) Kent County	42	0.74
Eastwood (cdp) Kalamazoo County	41	0.66
Tecumseh (city) Lenawee County	52	0.60
Waucedah (township) Dickinson County	4	0.60
Kinross (charter twp) Chippewa County	45	0.56
West Branch (city) Ogemaw County	12	0.54
Park (township) St. Joseph County	14	0.53
Hersey (township) Osceola County	10	0.50
Riverton (township) Mason County	5	0.46

Top 10 Places Sorted by Percent of Total Population
Based on places with total population of 50,000 or more

Place	Population	%
Farmington Hills (city) Oakland County	32	0.04
Ann Arbor (city) Washtenaw County	32	0.03
Southfield (city) Oakland County	12	0.02
Detroit (city) Wayne County	62	0.01

Place	Population	%
Kalamazoo (city) Kalamazoo County	9	0.01
Saginaw (city) Saginaw County	7	0.01
Battle Creek (city) Calhoun County	0	0.00
Canton (charter twp) Wayne County	0	0.00
Clinton (charter twp) Macomb County	0	0.00
Dearborn (city) Wayne County	0	0.00

Canadian

Top 10 Places Sorted by Population
Based on all places, regardless of total population

Place	Population	%
Livonia (city) Wayne County	885	0.90
Westland (city) Wayne County	768	0.91
Detroit (city) Wayne County	743	0.10
Rochester Hills (city) Oakland County	733	1.04
St. Clair Shores (city) Macomb County	716	1.18
Grand Rapids (city) Kent County	649	0.34
Ann Arbor (city) Washtenaw County	638	0.55
Warren (city) Macomb County	635	0.47
Waterford (charter twp) Oakland County	625	0.87
Clinton (charter twp) Macomb County	612	0.63

Top 10 Places Sorted by Percent of Total Population
Based on all places, regardless of total population

Place	Population	%
Prescott (village) Ogemaw County	37	17.62
Maple Grove (cdp) Benzie County	8	7.69
Wedgewood (cdp) Wexford County	14	6.45
Manistique (city) Schoolcraft County	190	5.82
Wheatland (township) Sanilac County	24	5.47
Michiana (village) Berrien County	8	5.30
Columbus (township) Luce County	10	4.83
Manton (city) Wexford County	69	4.74
Baldwin (township) Delta County	34	4.59
Woodland Beach (cdp) Monroe County	77	4.07

Top 10 Places Sorted by Percent of Total Population
Based on places with total population of 50,000 or more

Place	Population	%
St. Clair Shores (city) Macomb County	716	1.18
Rochester Hills (city) Oakland County	733	1.04
Royal Oak (city) Oakland County	559	0.97
West Bloomfield (charter twp) Oakland County	611	0.94
Westland (city) Wayne County	768	0.91
Livonia (city) Wayne County	885	0.90
Waterford (charter twp) Oakland County	625	0.87
Novi (city) Oakland County	466	0.87
Shelby (charter twp) Macomb County	597	0.82
Macomb (township) Macomb County	571	0.76

Carpatho Rusyn

Top 10 Places Sorted by Population
Based on all places, regardless of total population

Place	Population	%
Flushing (city) Genesee County	57	0.67
Royal Oak (city) Oakland County	39	0.07
Fenton (charter twp) Genesee County	36	0.24
Watertown (charter twp) Clinton County	27	0.57
Sylvan Lake (city) Oakland County	17	0.94
Okemos (cdp) Ingham County	15	0.07
Meridian (charter twp) Ingham County	15	0.04
Plymouth (city) Wayne County	14	0.15
Almena (township) Van Buren County	13	0.27
Elba (township) Lapeer County	12	0.22

Top 10 Places Sorted by Percent of Total Population
Based on all places, regardless of total population

Place	Population	%
Sylvan Lake (city) Oakland County	17	0.94
Flushing (city) Genesee County	57	0.67
Watertown (charter twp) Clinton County	27	0.57
Almena (township) Van Buren County	13	0.27
Fenton (charter twp) Genesee County	36	0.24
Mecosta (township) Mecosta County	6	0.23
Elba (township) Lapeer County	12	0.22
Plymouth (city) Wayne County	14	0.15
Royal Oak (city) Oakland County	39	0.07
Okemos (cdp) Ingham County	15	0.07

Top 10 Places Sorted by Percent of Total Population
Based on places with total population of 50,000 or more

Place	Population	%
Royal Oak (city) Oakland County	39	0.07
Macomb (township) Macomb County	12	0.02
Taylor (city) Wayne County	10	0.02
Ann Arbor (city) Washtenaw County	0	0.00
Battle Creek (city) Calhoun County	0	0.00
Canton (charter twp) Wayne County	0	0.00
Clinton (charter twp) Macomb County	0	0.00
Dearborn (city) Wayne County	0	0.00
Dearborn Heights (city) Wayne County	0	0.00
Detroit (city) Wayne County	0	0.00

Celtic

Top 10 Places Sorted by Population
Based on all places, regardless of total population

Place	Population	%
Paw Paw (township) Van Buren County	145	2.05
Flint (charter twp) Genesee County	109	0.33
Troy (city) Oakland County	60	0.07
Waterford (charter twp) Oakland County	56	0.08
Livonia (city) Wayne County	51	0.05
Athens (township) Calhoun County	48	1.86
Kalamazoo (city) Kalamazoo County	47	0.06
Ironwood (city) Gogebic County	46	0.84
St. Clair (city) St. Clair County	46	0.82
Macomb (township) Macomb County	36	0.05

Top 10 Places Sorted by Percent of Total Population
Based on all places, regardless of total population

Place	Population	%
Omena (cdp) Leelanau County	35	12.54
Paw Paw (township) Van Buren County	145	2.05
Leelanau (township) Leelanau County	35	1.90
Athens (township) Calhoun County	48	1.86
Home (township) Newaygo County	3	1.32
Pipestone (township) Berrien County	28	1.28
Mansfield (township) Iron County	2	1.07
Ironwood (city) Gogebic County	46	0.84
Center (township) Emmet County	5	0.84
St. Clair (city) St. Clair County	46	0.82

Top 10 Places Sorted by Percent of Total Population
Based on places with total population of 50,000 or more

Place	Population	%
Waterford (charter twp) Oakland County	56	0.08
Troy (city) Oakland County	60	0.07
Kalamazoo (city) Kalamazoo County	47	0.06
Livonia (city) Wayne County	51	0.05
Macomb (township) Macomb County	36	0.05
Wyoming (city) Kent County	29	0.04
Ann Arbor (city) Washtenaw County	24	0.02
Lansing (city) Ingham County	24	0.02
Warren (city) Macomb County	23	0.02
Dearborn (city) Wayne County	22	0.02

Croatian

Top 10 Places Sorted by Population
Based on all places, regardless of total population

Place	Population	%
Warren (city) Macomb County	406	0.30
Sterling Heights (city) Macomb County	347	0.27
St. Clair Shores (city) Macomb County	334	0.55
Clinton (charter twp) Macomb County	334	0.34
Livonia (city) Wayne County	301	0.31
Grand Rapids (city) Kent County	296	0.16
Troy (city) Oakland County	274	0.34
Lansing (city) Ingham County	255	0.22
Escanaba (city) Delta County	244	1.92
Orion (charter twp) Oakland County	234	0.67

Top 10 Places Sorted by Percent of Total Population
Based on all places, regardless of total population

Place	Population	%
Ahmeek (village) Keweenaw County	21	11.60
Ensign (township) Delta County	86	9.90
Mansfield (township) Iron County	15	8.02

Stanton (township) Houghton County	86	6.96
Garfield (township) Mackinac County	86	6.95
Allouez (township) Keweenaw County	103	6.60
Lake Linden (village) Houghton County	63	6.47
Adams (township) Houghton County	153	5.93
White Pine (cdp) Ontonagon County	23	5.58
Laurium (village) Houghton County	111	5.16

Top 10 Places Sorted by Percent of Total Population
Based on places with total population of 50,000 or more

Place	Population	%
St. Clair Shores (city) Macomb County	334	0.55
Clinton (charter twp) Macomb County	334	0.34
Troy (city) Oakland County	274	0.34
Livonia (city) Wayne County	301	0.31
Warren (city) Macomb County	406	0.30
Macomb (township) Macomb County	220	0.29
Sterling Heights (city) Macomb County	347	0.27
Westland (city) Wayne County	227	0.27
Shelby (charter twp) Macomb County	197	0.27
Royal Oak (city) Oakland County	154	0.27

Cypriot

Top 10 Places Sorted by Population
Based on all places, regardless of total population

Place	Population	%
Grosse Pointe Woods (city) Wayne County	27	0.17
Wayne (city) Wayne County	18	0.10
Monroe (city) Monroe County	18	0.08
Royal Oak (city) Oakland County	10	0.02
Lansing (city) Ingham County	9	0.01
Acme (township) Grand Traverse County	0	0.00
Ada (township) Kent County	0	0.00
Adams (township) Arenac County	0	0.00
Adams (township) Hillsdale County	0	0.00
Adams (township) Houghton County	0	0.00

Top 10 Places Sorted by Percent of Total Population
Based on all places, regardless of total population

Place	Population	%
Grosse Pointe Woods (city) Wayne County	27	0.17
Wayne (city) Wayne County	18	0.10
Monroe (city) Monroe County	18	0.08
Royal Oak (city) Oakland County	10	0.02
Lansing (city) Ingham County	9	0.01
Acme (township) Grand Traverse County	0	0.00
Ada (township) Kent County	0	0.00
Adams (township) Arenac County	0	0.00
Adams (township) Hillsdale County	0	0.00
Adams (township) Houghton County	0	0.00

Top 10 Places Sorted by Percent of Total Population
Based on places with total population of 50,000 or more

Place	Population	%
Royal Oak (city) Oakland County	10	0.02
Lansing (city) Ingham County	9	0.01
Ann Arbor (city) Washtenaw County	0	0.00
Battle Creek (city) Calhoun County	0	0.00
Canton (charter twp) Wayne County	0	0.00
Clinton (charter twp) Macomb County	0	0.00
Dearborn (city) Wayne County	0	0.00
Dearborn Heights (city) Wayne County	0	0.00
Detroit (city) Wayne County	0	0.00
Farmington Hills (city) Oakland County	0	0.00

Czech

Top 10 Places Sorted by Population
Based on all places, regardless of total population

Place	Population	%
Ann Arbor (city) Washtenaw County	842	0.73
Owosso (city) Shiawassee County	816	5.28
Grand Rapids (city) Kent County	666	0.35
Clinton (charter twp) Macomb County	637	0.65
Midland (city) Midland County	571	1.36
Rochester Hills (city) Oakland County	497	0.70
Westland (city) Wayne County	469	0.55
Sterling Heights (city) Macomb County	463	0.36
Shelby (charter twp) Macomb County	458	0.63
Canton (charter twp) Wayne County	457	0.52

Top 10 Places Sorted by Percent of Total Population
Based on all places, regardless of total population

Place	Population	%
New Haven (township) Shiawassee County	149	11.42
Alpha (village) Iron County	14	10.85
Eagle Harbor (cdp) Keweenaw County	6	9.23
Britton (village) Lenawee County	71	9.15
Fairfield (township) Shiawassee County	60	8.55
Elk (township) Lake County	69	7.91
Omena (cdp) Leelanau County	21	7.53
Gourley (township) Menominee County	25	7.51
Hazelton (township) Shiawassee County	145	6.43
Lake Michigan Beach (cdp) Berrien County	64	5.83

Top 10 Places Sorted by Percent of Total Population
Based on places with total population of 50,000 or more

Place	Population	%
Royal Oak (city) Oakland County	449	0.78
Ann Arbor (city) Washtenaw County	842	0.73
Rochester Hills (city) Oakland County	497	0.70
Clinton (charter twp) Macomb County	637	0.65
Shelby (charter twp) Macomb County	458	0.63
Westland (city) Wayne County	469	0.55
Macomb (township) Macomb County	412	0.55
Kalamazoo (city) Kalamazoo County	400	0.54
Canton (charter twp) Wayne County	457	0.52
Waterford (charter twp) Oakland County	364	0.51

Czechoslovakian

Top 10 Places Sorted by Population
Based on all places, regardless of total population

Place	Population	%
Sterling Heights (city) Macomb County	456	0.35
Lincoln Park (city) Wayne County	280	0.73
Warren (city) Macomb County	276	0.20
Troy (city) Oakland County	258	0.32
Saginaw (charter twp) Saginaw County	237	0.58
Washington (township) Macomb County	236	0.97
Taylor (city) Wayne County	222	0.35
Flint (charter twp) Genesee County	220	0.67
Clinton (charter twp) Macomb County	218	0.22
Grand Rapids (city) Kent County	217	0.11

Top 10 Places Sorted by Percent of Total Population
Based on all places, regardless of total population

Place	Population	%
Twining (village) Arenac County	11	5.85
Faithorn (township) Menominee County	12	5.11
Brady (township) Saginaw County	95	4.10
Henderson (township) Wexford County	6	3.57
Laird (township) Houghton County	13	3.16
Hazelton (township) Shiawassee County	71	3.15
Venice (township) Shiawassee County	72	2.77
Indian River (cdp) Cheboygan County	43	2.48
Ossineke (cdp) Alpena County	26	2.43
Ashley (village) Gratiot County	15	2.43

Top 10 Places Sorted by Percent of Total Population
Based on places with total population of 50,000 or more

Place	Population	%
Sterling Heights (city) Macomb County	456	0.35
Taylor (city) Wayne County	222	0.35
Troy (city) Oakland County	258	0.32
Dearborn Heights (city) Wayne County	181	0.31
Waterford (charter twp) Oakland County	168	0.23
Clinton (charter twp) Macomb County	218	0.22
Farmington Hills (city) Oakland County	178	0.22
Shelby (charter twp) Macomb County	158	0.22
Warren (city) Macomb County	276	0.20
Livonia (city) Wayne County	174	0.18

Danish

Top 10 Places Sorted by Population
Based on all places, regardless of total population

Place	Population	%
Grand Rapids (city) Kent County	1,324	0.70
Ann Arbor (city) Washtenaw County	721	0.63
Livonia (city) Wayne County	494	0.50

Ludington (city) Mason County	431	5.28
Greenville (city) Montcalm County	419	4.95
Plainfield (charter twp) Kent County	405	1.31
Eureka (township) Montcalm County	389	10.05
Grand Rapids (charter twp) Kent County	388	2.39
Farmington Hills (city) Oakland County	386	0.48
Troy (city) Oakland County	376	0.46

Top 10 Places Sorted by Percent of Total Population
Based on all places, regardless of total population

Place	Population	%
Stronach (cdp) Manistee County	20	12.90
Crystal Downs Country Club (cdp) Benzie County	9	10.34
Eureka (township) Montcalm County	389	10.05
Stanton (city) Montcalm County	146	9.43
Maple Valley (township) Montcalm County	182	8.27
Lake City (city) Missaukee County	65	7.64
Matchwood (township) Ontonagon County	9	7.63
Pine (township) Montcalm County	153	7.51
Montcalm (township) Montcalm County	235	7.00
Belvidere (township) Montcalm County	160	6.61

Top 10 Places Sorted by Percent of Total Population
Based on places with total population of 50,000 or more

Place	Population	%
Grand Rapids (city) Kent County	1,324	0.70
Ann Arbor (city) Washtenaw County	721	0.63
Livonia (city) Wayne County	494	0.50
Rochester Hills (city) Oakland County	353	0.50
Farmington Hills (city) Oakland County	386	0.48
Troy (city) Oakland County	376	0.46
Waterford (charter twp) Oakland County	326	0.45
Royal Oak (city) Oakland County	247	0.43
Shelby (charter twp) Macomb County	266	0.37
Wyoming (city) Kent County	259	0.36

Dutch

Top 10 Places Sorted by Population
Based on all places, regardless of total population

Place	Population	%
Grand Rapids (city) Kent County	29,229	15.35
Georgetown (charter twp) Ottawa County	19,742	42.55
Wyoming (city) Kent County	16,185	22.54
Holland (charter twp) Ottawa County	9,456	27.26
Holland (city) Ottawa County	9,167	27.20
Kentwood (city) Kent County	8,913	18.48
Byron (township) Kent County	7,207	36.27
Jenison (cdp) Ottawa County	7,138	41.41
Gaines (charter twp) Kent County	6,541	26.89
Plainfield (charter twp) Kent County	6,200	20.05

Top 10 Places Sorted by Percent of Total Population
Based on all places, regardless of total population

Place	Population	%
Overisel (township) Allegan County	1,733	60.13
Jamestown (charter twp) Ottawa County	4,013	59.63
Blendon (township) Ottawa County	3,432	59.09
Zeeland (charter twp) Ottawa County	5,488	56.97
Zeeland (city) Ottawa County	3,110	55.44
Hudsonville (city) Ottawa County	3,637	50.65
Olive (township) Ottawa County	2,124	44.38
Laketown (township) Allegan County	2,459	44.12
Fillmore (township) Allegan County	1,186	43.55
Richland (township) Missaukee County	629	43.02

Top 10 Places Sorted by Percent of Total Population
Based on places with total population of 50,000 or more

Place	Population	%
Wyoming (city) Kent County	16,185	22.54
Grand Rapids (city) Kent County	29,229	15.35
Kalamazoo (city) Kalamazoo County	6,165	8.30
Battle Creek (city) Calhoun County	1,828	3.46
Lansing (city) Ingham County	3,759	3.25
Royal Oak (city) Oakland County	1,581	2.74
Waterford (charter twp) Oakland County	1,900	2.65
Ypsilanti (charter twp) Washtenaw County	1,162	2.19
Rochester Hills (city) Oakland County	1,469	2.08
Ann Arbor (city) Washtenaw County	2,277	1.98

Eastern European

Top 10 Places Sorted by Population
Based on all places, regardless of total population

Place	Population	%
West Bloomfield (charter twp) Oakland County	842	1.30
Ann Arbor (city) Washtenaw County	719	0.62
Farmington Hills (city) Oakland County	501	0.62
Bloomfield (charter twp) Oakland County	313	0.76
Huntington Woods (city) Oakland County	309	4.98
Southfield (township) Oakland County	222	1.53
Oak Park (city) Oakland County	199	0.67
Royal Oak (city) Oakland County	181	0.31
Kalamazoo (city) Kalamazoo County	180	0.24
Dearborn (city) Wayne County	176	0.18

Top 10 Places Sorted by Percent of Total Population
Based on all places, regardless of total population

Place	Population	%
Huntington Woods (city) Oakland County	309	4.98
Franklin (village) Oakland County	151	4.81
Barton Hills (village) Washtenaw County	12	4.27
Orchard Lake Village (city) Oakland County	43	2.02
Southfield (township) Oakland County	222	1.53
Coleman (city) Midland County	17	1.41
Delton (cdp) Barry County	13	1.31
West Bloomfield (charter twp) Oakland County	842	1.30
Milan (city) Washtenaw County	71	1.25
Lake (township) Missaukee County	31	1.12

Top 10 Places Sorted by Percent of Total Population
Based on places with total population of 50,000 or more

Place	Population	%
West Bloomfield (charter twp) Oakland County	842	1.30
Ann Arbor (city) Washtenaw County	719	0.62
Farmington Hills (city) Oakland County	501	0.62
Royal Oak (city) Oakland County	181	0.31
Kalamazoo (city) Kalamazoo County	180	0.24
Southfield (city) Oakland County	173	0.24
Troy (city) Oakland County	163	0.20
Dearborn (city) Wayne County	176	0.18
Livonia (city) Wayne County	133	0.14
Rochester Hills (city) Oakland County	83	0.12

English

Top 10 Places Sorted by Population
Based on all places, regardless of total population

Place	Population	%
Grand Rapids (city) Kent County	14,001	7.35
Ann Arbor (city) Washtenaw County	13,447	11.67
Livonia (city) Wayne County	11,053	11.29
Lansing (city) Ingham County	10,696	9.25
Waterford (charter twp) Oakland County	10,085	14.05
Warren (city) Macomb County	9,746	7.18
Sterling Heights (city) Macomb County	8,908	6.87
Royal Oak (city) Oakland County	8,727	15.11
Canton (charter twp) Wayne County	8,145	9.26
Troy (city) Oakland County	8,083	9.98

Top 10 Places Sorted by Percent of Total Population
Based on all places, regardless of total population

Place	Population	%
Crystal Downs Country Club (cdp) Benzie County	39	44.83
Eagle Harbor (cdp) Keweenaw County	27	41.54
Brutus (cdp) Emmet County	91	39.06
Bay View (cdp) Emmet County	38	38.38
Crystal Mountain (cdp) Benzie County	12	37.50
Alden (cdp) Antrim County	47	35.34
Canada Creek Ranch (cdp) Montmorency County	97	32.88
Eagle Harbor (township) Keweenaw County	85	32.57
Sherwood (village) Branch County	95	31.67
Empire (village) Leelanau County	81	31.15

Top 10 Places Sorted by Percent of Total Population
Based on places with total population of 50,000 or more

Place	Population	%
Royal Oak (city) Oakland County	8,727	15.11
Waterford (charter twp) Oakland County	10,085	14.05
Battle Creek (city) Calhoun County	6,221	11.79
Ann Arbor (city) Washtenaw County	13,447	11.67

Place	Population	%
Livonia (city) Wayne County	11,053	11.29
Shelby (charter twp) Macomb County	7,589	10.43
Kalamazoo (city) Kalamazoo County	7,733	10.41
Novi (city) Oakland County	5,566	10.34
Rochester Hills (city) Oakland County	7,261	10.28
Troy (city) Oakland County	8,083	9.98

Estonian

Top 10 Places Sorted by Population
Based on all places, regardless of total population

Place	Population	%
Ann Arbor (city) Washtenaw County	36	0.03
Cambridge (township) Lenawee County	30	0.52
Inkster (city) Wayne County	26	0.10
Niles (township) Berrien County	25	0.18
Oakland (charter twp) Oakland County	24	0.15
Lowell (charter twp) Kent County	20	0.34
Norton Shores (city) Muskegon County	19	0.08
Sands (township) Marquette County	16	0.65
Lathrup Village (city) Oakland County	16	0.39
Rochester (city) Oakland County	16	0.13

Top 10 Places Sorted by Percent of Total Population
Based on all places, regardless of total population

Place	Population	%
Lincoln (village) Alcona County	9	2.54
Gustin (township) Alcona County	9	1.12
Sands (township) Marquette County	16	0.65
Cambridge (township) Lenawee County	30	0.52
Lathrup Village (city) Oakland County	16	0.39
Lowell (charter twp) Kent County	20	0.34
Sullivan (township) Muskegon County	8	0.33
Maple Ridge (township) Delta County	3	0.31
Gilford (township) Tuscola County	3	0.29
Armada (township) Macomb County	13	0.24

Top 10 Places Sorted by Percent of Total Population
Based on places with total population of 50,000 or more

Place	Population	%
Ann Arbor (city) Washtenaw County	36	0.03
Troy (city) Oakland County	13	0.02
Lansing (city) Ingham County	11	0.01
Grand Rapids (city) Kent County	10	0.01
Farmington Hills (city) Oakland County	9	0.01
Livonia (city) Wayne County	8	0.01
Detroit (city) Wayne County	7	<0.01
Battle Creek (city) Calhoun County	0	0.00
Canton (charter twp) Wayne County	0	0.00
Clinton (charter twp) Macomb County	0	0.00

European

Top 10 Places Sorted by Population
Based on all places, regardless of total population

Place	Population	%
Ann Arbor (city) Washtenaw County	2,664	2.31
Grand Rapids (city) Kent County	2,054	1.08
Lansing (city) Ingham County	1,260	1.09
Canton (charter twp) Wayne County	1,228	1.40
West Bloomfield (charter twp) Oakland County	1,081	1.67
Meridian (charter twp) Ingham County	953	2.40
Oak Park (city) Oakland County	935	3.13
Troy (city) Oakland County	913	1.13
Royal Oak (city) Oakland County	865	1.50
Livonia (city) Wayne County	832	0.85

Top 10 Places Sorted by Percent of Total Population
Based on all places, regardless of total population

Place	Population	%
Lewiston (cdp) Montmorency County	249	17.52
Caberfae (cdp) Wexford County	19	14.96
Bridgehampton (township) Sanilac County	109	11.71
Albert (township) Montmorency County	249	9.70
South Branch (township) Wexford County	27	8.91
West Branch (township) Missaukee County	25	7.18
Byron (village) Shiawassee County	39	6.38
Bingham Farms (village) Oakland County	69	6.32
Williamston (city) Ingham County	229	6.05
Haynes (township) Alcona County	39	6.05

Top 10 Places Sorted by Percent of Total Population
Based on places with total population of 50,000 or more

Place	Population	%
Ann Arbor (city) Washtenaw County	2,664	2.31
West Bloomfield (charter twp) Oakland County	1,081	1.67
Royal Oak (city) Oakland County	865	1.50
Canton (charter twp) Wayne County	1,228	1.40
Novi (city) Oakland County	725	1.35
Ypsilanti (charter twp) Washtenaw County	693	1.31
Rochester Hills (city) Oakland County	806	1.14
Troy (city) Oakland County	913	1.13
Lansing (city) Ingham County	1,260	1.09
Grand Rapids (city) Kent County	2,054	1.08

Finnish

Top 10 Places Sorted by Population
Based on all places, regardless of total population

Place	Population	%
Calumet (charter twp) Houghton County	2,757	42.38
Marquette (city) Marquette County	2,593	12.20
Ishpeming (city) Marquette County	2,142	32.95
Livonia (city) Wayne County	2,019	2.06
Hancock (city) Houghton County	1,552	33.98
Adams (township) Houghton County	1,526	59.17
Negaunee (city) Marquette County	1,313	28.77
Ishpeming (township) Marquette County	1,243	35.40
Negaunee (township) Marquette County	1,200	39.95
Ironwood (city) Gogebic County	1,164	21.20

Top 10 Places Sorted by Percent of Total Population
Based on all places, regardless of total population

Place	Population	%
Bohemia (township) Ontonagon County	34	82.93
Stanton (township) Houghton County	874	70.77
Hancock (township) Houghton County	341	59.82
Adams (township) Houghton County	1,526	59.17
South Range (village) Houghton County	225	55.28
Covington (township) Baraga County	333	54.95
Humboldt (township) Marquette County	245	54.44
Quincy (township) Houghton County	182	52.00
Allouez (township) Keweenaw County	801	51.35
Chassell (township) Houghton County	886	50.69

Top 10 Places Sorted by Percent of Total Population
Based on places with total population of 50,000 or more

Place	Population	%
Livonia (city) Wayne County	2,019	2.06
Novi (city) Oakland County	894	1.66
Royal Oak (city) Oakland County	747	1.29
Westland (city) Wayne County	835	0.98
Farmington Hills (city) Oakland County	779	0.97
Waterford (charter twp) Oakland County	690	0.96
Ypsilanti (charter twp) Washtenaw County	503	0.95
Shelby (charter twp) Macomb County	685	0.94
Troy (city) Oakland County	674	0.83
Rochester Hills (city) Oakland County	550	0.78

French, except Basque

Top 10 Places Sorted by Population
Based on all places, regardless of total population

Place	Population	%
Warren (city) Macomb County	7,214	5.31
Sterling Heights (city) Macomb County	6,116	4.72
Grand Rapids (city) Kent County	5,485	2.88
Livonia (city) Wayne County	5,107	5.22
Clinton (charter twp) Macomb County	4,802	4.94
St. Clair Shores (city) Macomb County	4,772	7.85
Taylor (city) Wayne County	4,438	6.95
Waterford (charter twp) Oakland County	4,372	6.09
Macomb (township) Macomb County	4,292	5.73
Canton (charter twp) Wayne County	4,267	4.85

Top 10 Places Sorted by Percent of Total Population
Based on all places, regardless of total population

Place	Population	%
Crystal Mountain (cdp) Benzie County	18	56.25
Maple Grove (cdp) Benzie County	43	41.35
Nessen City (cdp) Benzie County	25	34.72

Garden (village) Delta County	66	32.67
Spalding (township) Menominee County	476	29.01
Hubbell (cdp) Houghton County	361	28.76
Wells (township) Delta County	1,400	28.36
Arvon (township) Baraga County	86	28.29
Eastport (cdp) Antrim County	55	27.78
Fairbanks (township) Delta County	89	24.59

Top 10 Places Sorted by Percent of Total Population
Based on places with total population of 50,000 or more

Place	Population	%
St. Clair Shores (city) Macomb County	4,772	7.85
Taylor (city) Wayne County	4,438	6.95
Waterford (charter twp) Oakland County	4,372	6.09
Macomb (township) Macomb County	4,292	5.73
Rochester Hills (city) Oakland County	3,842	5.44
Warren (city) Macomb County	7,214	5.31
Livonia (city) Wayne County	5,107	5.22
Royal Oak (city) Oakland County	2,993	5.18
Shelby (charter twp) Macomb County	3,667	5.04
Clinton (charter twp) Macomb County	4,802	4.94

French Canadian

Top 10 Places Sorted by Population
Based on all places, regardless of total population

Place	Population	%
Livonia (city) Wayne County	2,931	2.99
Warren (city) Macomb County	2,892	2.13
Sterling Heights (city) Macomb County	1,986	1.53
Taylor (city) Wayne County	1,822	2.85
Clinton (charter twp) Macomb County	1,822	1.87
Dearborn (city) Wayne County	1,773	1.80
St. Clair Shores (city) Macomb County	1,601	2.63
Westland (city) Wayne County	1,562	1.84
Waterford (charter twp) Oakland County	1,465	2.04
Grand Rapids (city) Kent County	1,455	0.76

Top 10 Places Sorted by Percent of Total Population
Based on all places, regardless of total population

Place	Population	%
Au Sable (township) Roscommon County	61	18.77
Faithorn (township) Menominee County	39	16.60
Webberville (village) Ingham County	220	14.93
Lake Linden (village) Houghton County	128	13.16
Akron (village) Tuscola County	38	12.58
Jennings (cdp) Missaukee County	35	12.41
Wells (township) Delta County	582	11.79
Backus (township) Roscommon County	29	11.69
Weidman (cdp) Isabella County	93	11.34
Escanaba (township) Delta County	378	10.83

Top 10 Places Sorted by Percent of Total Population
Based on places with total population of 50,000 or more

Place	Population	%
Livonia (city) Wayne County	2,931	2.99
Taylor (city) Wayne County	1,822	2.85
St. Clair Shores (city) Macomb County	1,601	2.63
Royal Oak (city) Oakland County	1,318	2.28
Warren (city) Macomb County	2,892	2.13
Novi (city) Oakland County	1,132	2.10
Waterford (charter twp) Oakland County	1,465	2.04
Dearborn Heights (city) Wayne County	1,102	1.90
Clinton (charter twp) Macomb County	1,822	1.87
Macomb (township) Macomb County	1,401	1.87

German

Top 10 Places Sorted by Population
Based on all places, regardless of total population

Place	Population	%
Grand Rapids (city) Kent County	30,522	16.03
Warren (city) Macomb County	26,458	19.48
Sterling Heights (city) Macomb County	23,659	18.24
Ann Arbor (city) Washtenaw County	22,916	19.89
Livonia (city) Wayne County	22,261	22.74
Clinton (charter twp) Macomb County	21,482	22.08
Lansing (city) Ingham County	21,220	18.35
Waterford (charter twp) Oakland County	18,164	25.30
Macomb (township) Macomb County	17,908	23.92
Shelby (charter twp) Macomb County	17,369	23.87

Top 10 Places Sorted by Percent of Total Population
Based on all places, regardless of total population

Place	Population	%
Beal City (cdp) Isabella County	268	77.46
Moltke (township) Presque Isle County	191	67.49
Westphalia (township) Clinton County	1,713	67.05
Dallas (township) Clinton County	1,653	65.21
Belknap (township) Presque Isle County	496	65.01
Pewamo (village) Ionia County	368	64.90
Bloomfield (township) Huron County	318	63.10
Fowler (village) Clinton County	781	62.73
Blumfield (township) Saginaw County	1,192	60.82
Westphalia (village) Clinton County	514	60.40

Top 10 Places Sorted by Percent of Total Population
Based on places with total population of 50,000 or more

Place	Population	%
St. Clair Shores (city) Macomb County	16,348	26.90
Waterford (charter twp) Oakland County	18,164	25.30
Royal Oak (city) Oakland County	14,457	25.04
Macomb (township) Macomb County	17,908	23.92
Shelby (charter twp) Macomb County	17,369	23.87
Livonia (city) Wayne County	22,261	22.74
Rochester Hills (city) Oakland County	15,757	22.32
Clinton (charter twp) Macomb County	21,482	22.08
Kalamazoo (city) Kalamazoo County	15,282	20.56
Ann Arbor (city) Washtenaw County	22,916	19.89

German Russian

Top 10 Places Sorted by Population
Based on all places, regardless of total population

Place	Population	%
Detroit (city) Wayne County	119	0.02
Southgate (city) Wayne County	49	0.16
Ann Arbor (city) Washtenaw County	37	0.03
Macomb (township) Macomb County	28	0.04
Holton (township) Muskegon County	24	0.94
Manistee (city) Manistee County	24	0.38
Troy (city) Oakland County	22	0.03
Otsego (township) Allegan County	19	0.34
Bay City (city) Bay County	11	0.03
Portage (city) Kalamazoo County	11	0.02

Top 10 Places Sorted by Percent of Total Population
Based on all places, regardless of total population

Place	Population	%
Holton (township) Muskegon County	24	0.94
Bangor (township) Van Buren County	8	0.41
Manistee (city) Manistee County	24	0.38
Otsego (township) Allegan County	19	0.34
Capac (village) St. Clair County	6	0.30
Newberry (village) Luce County	3	0.19
Southgate (city) Wayne County	49	0.16
Mussey (township) St. Clair County	6	0.14
Grant (township) Newaygo County	4	0.12
Cassopolis (village) Cass County	2	0.12

Top 10 Places Sorted by Percent of Total Population
Based on places with total population of 50,000 or more

Place	Population	%
Macomb (township) Macomb County	28	0.04
Ann Arbor (city) Washtenaw County	37	0.03
Troy (city) Oakland County	22	0.03
Detroit (city) Wayne County	119	0.02
Flint (city) Genesee County	6	0.01
Lansing (city) Ingham County	6	0.01
Battle Creek (city) Calhoun County	0	0.00
Canton (charter twp) Wayne County	0	0.00
Clinton (charter twp) Macomb County	0	0.00
Dearborn (city) Wayne County	0	0.00

Greek

Top 10 Places Sorted by Population
Based on all places, regardless of total population

Place	Population	%
Livonia (city) Wayne County	1,272	1.30
Ann Arbor (city) Washtenaw County	1,161	1.01
Sterling Heights (city) Macomb County	1,148	0.89

Troy (city) Oakland County	1,057	1.31
Shelby (charter twp) Macomb County	996	1.37
Warren (city) Macomb County	894	0.66
Rochester Hills (city) Oakland County	722	1.02
Clinton (charter twp) Macomb County	705	0.72
Novi (city) Oakland County	677	1.26
Macomb (township) Macomb County	664	0.89

Top 10 Places Sorted by Percent of Total Population
Based on all places, regardless of total population

Place	Population	%
Walloon Lake (cdp) Charlevoix County	32	14.16
Saline (township) Washtenaw County	96	4.70
Petersburg (city) Monroe County	49	4.06
Fowlerville (village) Livingston County	116	3.89
Village of Grosse Pointe Shores (city) Wayne Co.	114	3.83
Meade (township) Huron County	29	3.83
Duncan (township) Houghton County	8	3.48
Crystal Downs Country Club (cdp) Benzie County	3	3.45
Leslie (city) Ingham County	66	3.42
Erie (township) Monroe County	155	3.40

Top 10 Places Sorted by Percent of Total Population
Based on places with total population of 50,000 or more

Place	Population	%
Shelby (charter twp) Macomb County	996	1.37
Troy (city) Oakland County	1,057	1.31
Livonia (city) Wayne County	1,272	1.30
Novi (city) Oakland County	677	1.26
Royal Oak (city) Oakland County	654	1.13
Rochester Hills (city) Oakland County	722	1.02
St. Clair Shores (city) Macomb County	617	1.02
Ann Arbor (city) Washtenaw County	1,161	1.01
Sterling Heights (city) Macomb County	1,148	0.89
Macomb (township) Macomb County	664	0.89

Guyanese

Top 10 Places Sorted by Population
Based on all places, regardless of total population

Place	Population	%
Flint (city) Genesee County	58	0.05
Redford (charter twp) Wayne County	35	0.07
Ypsilanti (charter twp) Washtenaw County	32	0.06
Taylor (city) Wayne County	32	0.05
Scio (township) Washtenaw County	23	0.12
Royal Oak (city) Oakland County	20	0.03
Wayne (city) Wayne County	18	0.10
Shelby (charter twp) Macomb County	17	0.02
Canton (charter twp) Wayne County	16	0.02
Clinton (charter twp) Macomb County	15	0.02

Top 10 Places Sorted by Percent of Total Population
Based on all places, regardless of total population

Place	Population	%
Eau Claire (village) Berrien County	5	0.93
Arcada (township) Gratiot County	8	0.47
Sherwood (township) Branch County	6	0.32
St. Ignace (city) Mackinac County	7	0.27
Leonidas (township) St. Joseph County	2	0.18
Scio (township) Washtenaw County	23	0.12
Oronoko (charter twp) Berrien County	11	0.12
Wayne (city) Wayne County	18	0.10
Berrien (township) Berrien County	5	0.10
Redford (charter twp) Wayne County	35	0.07

Top 10 Places Sorted by Percent of Total Population
Based on places with total population of 50,000 or more

Place	Population	%
Ypsilanti (charter twp) Washtenaw County	32	0.06
Flint (city) Genesee County	58	0.05
Taylor (city) Wayne County	32	0.05
Royal Oak (city) Oakland County	20	0.03
Shelby (charter twp) Macomb County	17	0.02
Canton (charter twp) Wayne County	16	0.02
Clinton (charter twp) Macomb County	15	0.02
Novi (city) Oakland County	12	0.02
Ann Arbor (city) Washtenaw County	9	0.01
Sterling Heights (city) Macomb County	9	0.01

Hungarian

Top 10 Places Sorted by Population
Based on all places, regardless of total population

Place	Population	%
Lincoln Park (city) Wayne County	2,225	5.76
Taylor (city) Wayne County	2,139	3.35
Livonia (city) Wayne County	1,923	1.96
Ann Arbor (city) Washtenaw County	1,847	1.60
Southgate (city) Wayne County	1,630	5.40
Dearborn (city) Wayne County	1,569	1.59
Farmington Hills (city) Oakland County	1,546	1.93
Brownstown (charter twp) Wayne County	1,529	5.21
Allen Park (city) Wayne County	1,456	5.10
Warren (city) Macomb County	1,275	0.94

Top 10 Places Sorted by Percent of Total Population
Based on all places, regardless of total population

Place	Population	%
Grand Island (township) Alger County	27	48.21
Zilwaukee (township) Saginaw County	20	31.75
Conway (cdp) Emmet County	21	14.19
Fostoria (cdp) Tuscola County	79	10.79
Backus (township) Roscommon County	24	9.68
Holmes (township) Menominee County	25	8.53
Columbus (township) Luce County	17	8.21
Brethren (cdp) Manistee County	29	7.21
Milton (township) Cass County	252	6.85
Trenton (city) Wayne County	1,187	6.23

Top 10 Places Sorted by Percent of Total Population
Based on places with total population of 50,000 or more

Place	Population	%
Taylor (city) Wayne County	2,139	3.35
Livonia (city) Wayne County	1,923	1.96
Farmington Hills (city) Oakland County	1,546	1.93
West Bloomfield (charter twp) Oakland County	1,200	1.85
Dearborn Heights (city) Wayne County	952	1.64
Ann Arbor (city) Washtenaw County	1,847	1.60
Dearborn (city) Wayne County	1,569	1.59
Royal Oak (city) Oakland County	882	1.53
Novi (city) Oakland County	692	1.29
Macomb (township) Macomb County	884	1.18

Icelander

Top 10 Places Sorted by Population
Based on all places, regardless of total population

Place	Population	%
Ann Arbor (city) Washtenaw County	78	0.07
Novi (city) Oakland County	69	0.13
Kalamazoo (city) Kalamazoo County	65	0.09
Grosse Pointe Farms (city) Wayne County	55	0.58
Union (charter twp) Isabella County	43	0.36
Ypsilanti (city) Washtenaw County	38	0.19
Berkley (city) Oakland County	32	0.21
Cadillac (city) Wexford County	31	0.30
Fenton (charter twp) Genesee County	29	0.19
Redford (charter twp) Wayne County	29	0.06

Top 10 Places Sorted by Percent of Total Population
Based on all places, regardless of total population

Place	Population	%
Lewiston (cdp) Montmorency County	24	1.69
Montrose (city) Genesee County	18	1.07
Albert (township) Montmorency County	24	0.94
McKinley (township) Huron County	3	0.77
Onekama (village) Manistee County	3	0.74
Orchard Lake Village (city) Oakland County	15	0.71
Mentor (township) Oscoda County	9	0.69
Grosse Pointe Farms (city) Wayne County	55	0.58
Munro (township) Cheboygan County	3	0.55
Portland (city) Ionia County	19	0.49

Top 10 Places Sorted by Percent of Total Population
Based on places with total population of 50,000 or more

Place	Population	%
Novi (city) Oakland County	69	0.13
Kalamazoo (city) Kalamazoo County	65	0.09
Ann Arbor (city) Washtenaw County	78	0.07
Macomb (township) Macomb County	16	0.02

Place	Population	%
Clinton (charter twp) Macomb County	14	0.01
Farmington Hills (city) Oakland County	11	0.01
Livonia (city) Wayne County	11	0.01
Sterling Heights (city) Macomb County	10	0.01
Battle Creek (city) Calhoun County	0	0.00
Canton (charter twp) Wayne County	0	0.00

Iranian

Top 10 Places Sorted by Population
Based on all places, regardless of total population

Place	Population	%
West Bloomfield (charter twp) Oakland County	640	0.99
Ann Arbor (city) Washtenaw County	336	0.29
Warren (city) Macomb County	226	0.17
Troy (city) Oakland County	218	0.27
Rochester Hills (city) Oakland County	206	0.29
Sterling Heights (city) Macomb County	163	0.13
Pittsfield (charter twp) Washtenaw County	145	0.43
Novi (city) Oakland County	120	0.22
Grand Rapids (city) Kent County	116	0.06
Bloomfield Hills (city) Oakland County	112	2.89

Top 10 Places Sorted by Percent of Total Population
Based on all places, regardless of total population

Place	Population	%
Bloomfield Hills (city) Oakland County	112	2.89
Franklin (village) Oakland County	45	1.43
Carp Lake (cdp) Emmet County	5	1.27
Lake Fenton (cdp) Genesee County	59	1.11
Lodi (township) Washtenaw County	66	1.09
Canada Creek Ranch (cdp) Montmorency County	3	1.02
Ann Arbor (charter twp) Washtenaw County	44	1.00
West Bloomfield (charter twp) Oakland County	640	0.99
Ferrysburg (city) Ottawa County	28	0.96
New Buffalo (city) Berrien County	17	0.83

Top 10 Places Sorted by Percent of Total Population
Based on places with total population of 50,000 or more

Place	Population	%
West Bloomfield (charter twp) Oakland County	640	0.99
Ann Arbor (city) Washtenaw County	336	0.29
Rochester Hills (city) Oakland County	206	0.29
Troy (city) Oakland County	218	0.27
Novi (city) Oakland County	120	0.22
Warren (city) Macomb County	226	0.17
Sterling Heights (city) Macomb County	163	0.13
Farmington Hills (city) Oakland County	101	0.13
Livonia (city) Wayne County	76	0.08
Canton (charter twp) Wayne County	72	0.08

Irish

Top 10 Places Sorted by Population
Based on all places, regardless of total population

Place	Population	%
Grand Rapids (city) Kent County	18,575	9.75
Warren (city) Macomb County	16,937	12.47
Livonia (city) Wayne County	16,361	16.71
Lansing (city) Ingham County	12,586	10.88
Waterford (charter twp) Oakland County	12,416	17.29
Ann Arbor (city) Washtenaw County	12,142	10.54
Sterling Heights (city) Macomb County	11,759	9.07
Westland (city) Wayne County	11,189	13.19
Detroit (city) Wayne County	10,866	1.43
Clinton (charter twp) Macomb County	10,861	11.16

Top 10 Places Sorted by Percent of Total Population
Based on all places, regardless of total population

Place	Population	%
Ponshewaing (cdp) Emmet County	26	49.06
Filer City (cdp) Manistee County	73	48.99
Eagle (village) Clinton County	82	41.00
Grand Beach (village) Berrien County	108	36.24
Emmett (village) St. Clair County	116	35.26
Breedsville (village) Van Buren County	35	33.33
St. James (cdp) Charlevoix County	62	32.98
Attica (cdp) Lapeer County	322	31.23
St. James (township) Charlevoix County	78	30.23
Clare (city) Clare County	947	29.63

Top 10 Places Sorted by Percent of Total Population
Based on places with total population of 50,000 or more

Place	Population	%
Waterford (charter twp) Oakland County	12,416	17.29
Royal Oak (city) Oakland County	9,767	16.92
Livonia (city) Wayne County	16,361	16.71
St. Clair Shores (city) Macomb County	9,621	15.83
Taylor (city) Wayne County	10,032	15.72
Westland (city) Wayne County	11,189	13.19
Rochester Hills (city) Oakland County	9,197	13.03
Warren (city) Macomb County	16,937	12.47
Novi (city) Oakland County	6,629	12.32
Kalamazoo (city) Kalamazoo County	8,753	11.78

Israeli

Top 10 Places Sorted by Population
Based on all places, regardless of total population

Place	Population	%
West Bloomfield (charter twp) Oakland County	268	0.41
Flint (charter twp) Genesee County	192	0.59
Ann Arbor (city) Washtenaw County	147	0.13
Grand Blanc (charter twp) Genesee County	145	0.40
Kalamazoo (charter twp) Kalamazoo County	111	0.51
Farmington Hills (city) Oakland County	78	0.10
Novi (city) Oakland County	70	0.13
Bloomfield (charter twp) Oakland County	63	0.15
Southfield (city) Oakland County	60	0.08
Jackson (city) Jackson County	59	0.17

Top 10 Places Sorted by Percent of Total Population
Based on all places, regardless of total population

Place	Population	%
Orange (township) Kalkaska County	14	1.19
Lee (township) Midland County	29	0.67
Birch Run (village) Saginaw County	11	0.65
Marenisco (township) Gogebic County	10	0.64
Flint (charter twp) Genesee County	192	0.59
Pickford (township) Chippewa County	7	0.52
Kalamazoo (charter twp) Kalamazoo County	111	0.51
Saline (township) Washtenaw County	9	0.44
West Bloomfield (charter twp) Oakland County	268	0.41
Grand Blanc (charter twp) Genesee County	145	0.40

Top 10 Places Sorted by Percent of Total Population
Based on places with total population of 50,000 or more

Place	Population	%
West Bloomfield (charter twp) Oakland County	268	0.41
Ann Arbor (city) Washtenaw County	147	0.13
Novi (city) Oakland County	70	0.13
Farmington Hills (city) Oakland County	78	0.10
Southfield (city) Oakland County	60	0.08
Waterford (charter twp) Oakland County	26	0.04
Dearborn (city) Wayne County	32	0.03
Westland (city) Wayne County	24	0.03
Kalamazoo (city) Kalamazoo County	14	0.02
Dearborn Heights (city) Wayne County	9	0.02

Italian

Top 10 Places Sorted by Population
Based on all places, regardless of total population

Place	Population	%
Sterling Heights (city) Macomb County	15,325	11.82
Clinton (charter twp) Macomb County	14,389	14.79
Warren (city) Macomb County	13,557	9.98
Macomb (township) Macomb County	13,499	18.03
Shelby (charter twp) Macomb County	10,823	14.87
Livonia (city) Wayne County	8,822	9.01
St. Clair Shores (city) Macomb County	8,779	14.44
Troy (city) Oakland County	6,643	8.20
Roseville (city) Macomb County	6,401	13.38
Chesterfield (township) Macomb County	6,132	14.39

Top 10 Places Sorted by Percent of Total Population
Based on all places, regardless of total population

Place	Population	%
Faithorn (township) Menominee County	84	35.74
Quinnesec (cdp) Dickinson County	296	29.34
Pilgrim (cdp) Benzie County	5	26.32

Place	Population	%
Norway (township) Dickinson County	381	22.95
Cedar (cdp) Leelanau County	21	22.34
Gaastra (city) Iron County	56	21.13
Caspian (city) Iron County	151	20.97
Crystal Falls (city) Iron County	307	20.73
Chatham (village) Alger County	49	20.50
Tustin (village) Osceola County	19	20.21

Top 10 Places Sorted by Percent of Total Population
Based on places with total population of 50,000 or more

Place	Population	%
Macomb (township) Macomb County	13,499	18.03
Shelby (charter twp) Macomb County	10,823	14.87
Clinton (charter twp) Macomb County	14,389	14.79
St. Clair Shores (city) Macomb County	8,779	14.44
Sterling Heights (city) Macomb County	15,325	11.82
Warren (city) Macomb County	13,557	9.98
Livonia (city) Wayne County	8,822	9.01
Novi (city) Oakland County	4,511	8.38
Troy (city) Oakland County	6,643	8.20
Rochester Hills (city) Oakland County	5,615	7.95

Latvian

Top 10 Places Sorted by Population
Based on all places, regardless of total population

Place	Population	%
Grand Rapids (city) Kent County	204	0.11
Fabius (township) St. Joseph County	153	4.66
Kalamazoo (city) Kalamazoo County	146	0.20
Ann Arbor (city) Washtenaw County	136	0.12
Portage (city) Kalamazoo County	115	0.25
Kalamazoo (charter twp) Kalamazoo County	101	0.46
Saginaw (charter twp) Saginaw County	92	0.23
Scio (township) Washtenaw County	87	0.45
Bloomfield (charter twp) Oakland County	84	0.20
West Bloomfield (charter twp) Oakland County	76	0.12

Top 10 Places Sorted by Percent of Total Population
Based on all places, regardless of total population

Place	Population	%
Weidman (cdp) Isabella County	39	4.76
Fabius (township) St. Joseph County	153	4.66
Village of Grosse Pointe Shores (city) Wayne Co.	71	2.39
Lake (township) Menominee County	15	2.28
Michiana (village) Berrien County	3	1.99
Haring (cdp) Wexford County	5	1.43
Potterville (city) Eaton County	36	1.41
Dexter (village) Washtenaw County	53	1.37
Sherman (township) Isabella County	39	1.33
Sylvan (township) Washtenaw County	35	1.23

Top 10 Places Sorted by Percent of Total Population
Based on places with total population of 50,000 or more

Place	Population	%
Kalamazoo (city) Kalamazoo County	146	0.20
Ann Arbor (city) Washtenaw County	136	0.12
West Bloomfield (charter twp) Oakland County	76	0.12
Grand Rapids (city) Kent County	204	0.11
Royal Oak (city) Oakland County	51	0.09
Farmington Hills (city) Oakland County	62	0.08
Livonia (city) Wayne County	65	0.07
Taylor (city) Wayne County	42	0.07
Saginaw (city) Saginaw County	35	0.07
Battle Creek (city) Calhoun County	34	0.06

Lithuanian

Top 10 Places Sorted by Population
Based on all places, regardless of total population

Place	Population	%
Grand Rapids (city) Kent County	1,236	0.65
Livonia (city) Wayne County	637	0.65
Warren (city) Macomb County	597	0.44
Farmington Hills (city) Oakland County	584	0.73
Dearborn (city) Wayne County	528	0.54
Ann Arbor (city) Washtenaw County	450	0.39
Troy (city) Oakland County	444	0.55
Walker (city) Kent County	395	1.70
Taylor (city) Wayne County	381	0.60
Canton (charter twp) Wayne County	364	0.41

Top 10 Places Sorted by Percent of Total Population
Based on all places, regardless of total population

Place	Population	%
Michiana (village) Berrien County	12	7.95
Elk (township) Lake County	59	6.77
Fountain (village) Mason County	9	5.49
New Buffalo (township) Berrien County	94	4.78
Sauble (township) Lake County	18	4.76
Weidman (cdp) Isabella County	37	4.51
Walkerville (village) Oceana County	7	4.46
Arcadia (township) Manistee County	24	4.43
Chikaming (township) Berrien County	131	4.10
Custer (township) Mason County	44	3.86

Top 10 Places Sorted by Percent of Total Population
Based on places with total population of 50,000 or more

Place	Population	%
Farmington Hills (city) Oakland County	584	0.73
Grand Rapids (city) Kent County	1,236	0.65
Livonia (city) Wayne County	637	0.65
Royal Oak (city) Oakland County	353	0.61
Taylor (city) Wayne County	381	0.60
Troy (city) Oakland County	444	0.55
Dearborn (city) Wayne County	528	0.54
St. Clair Shores (city) Macomb County	324	0.53
Rochester Hills (city) Oakland County	350	0.50
Dearborn Heights (city) Wayne County	272	0.47

Luxemburger

Top 10 Places Sorted by Population
Based on all places, regardless of total population

Place	Population	%
Grand Rapids (city) Kent County	49	0.03
Greenwood (township) Oscoda County	39	2.95
Flushing (city) Genesee County	35	0.41
Commerce (charter twp) Oakland County	32	0.08
Escanaba (city) Delta County	31	0.24
East Grand Rapids (city) Kent County	30	0.28
Pavilion (township) Kalamazoo County	26	0.42
Ann Arbor (city) Washtenaw County	26	0.02
Kalamazoo (city) Kalamazoo County	24	0.03
Kingsford (city) Dickinson County	18	0.34

Top 10 Places Sorted by Percent of Total Population
Based on all places, regardless of total population

Place	Population	%
Greenwood (township) Oscoda County	39	2.95
Bessemer (township) Gogebic County	17	1.40
Henderson (cdp) Shiawassee County	3	0.79
Greenbush (township) Clinton County	16	0.78
North Allis (township) Presque Isle County	3	0.75
Ford River (township) Delta County	14	0.69
Bearinger (township) Presque Isle County	2	0.67
Franklin (township) Houghton County	9	0.65
Ellis (township) Cheboygan County	4	0.61
Pavilion (township) Kalamazoo County	26	0.42

Top 10 Places Sorted by Percent of Total Population
Based on places with total population of 50,000 or more

Place	Population	%
Grand Rapids (city) Kent County	49	0.03
Kalamazoo (city) Kalamazoo County	24	0.03
Royal Oak (city) Oakland County	16	0.03
Ann Arbor (city) Washtenaw County	26	0.02
West Bloomfield (charter twp) Oakland County	10	0.02
Dearborn (city) Wayne County	11	0.01
Troy (city) Oakland County	9	0.01
Clinton (charter twp) Macomb County	8	0.01
Detroit (city) Wayne County	9	<0.01
Battle Creek (city) Calhoun County	0	0.00

Macedonian

Top 10 Places Sorted by Population
Based on all places, regardless of total population

Place	Population	%
Sterling Heights (city) Macomb County	1,382	1.07
Macomb (township) Macomb County	1,123	1.50
Shelby (charter twp) Macomb County	639	0.88

Place	Population	%
Dearborn Heights (city) Wayne County	393	0.68
Washington (township) Macomb County	342	1.41
Livonia (city) Wayne County	293	0.30
Clinton (charter twp) Macomb County	242	0.25
Troy (city) Oakland County	223	0.28
Rochester Hills (city) Oakland County	217	0.31
Battle Creek (city) Calhoun County	194	0.37

Top 10 Places Sorted by Percent of Total Population
Based on all places, regardless of total population

Place	Population	%
Onota (township) Alger County	7	2.41
Village of Grosse Pointe Shores (city) Wayne Co.	54	1.81
Reeder (township) Missaukee County	19	1.69
Novi (township) Oakland County	2	1.67
Macomb (township) Macomb County	1,123	1.50
Tyrone (township) Livingston County	147	1.47
Au Gres (township) Arenac County	14	1.46
Washington (township) Macomb County	342	1.41
East Jordan (city) Charlevoix County	26	1.35
Lake Fenton (cdp) Genesee County	60	1.13

Top 10 Places Sorted by Percent of Total Population
Based on places with total population of 50,000 or more

Place	Population	%
Macomb (township) Macomb County	1,123	1.50
Sterling Heights (city) Macomb County	1,382	1.07
Shelby (charter twp) Macomb County	639	0.88
Dearborn Heights (city) Wayne County	393	0.68
Battle Creek (city) Calhoun County	194	0.37
Rochester Hills (city) Oakland County	217	0.31
Livonia (city) Wayne County	293	0.30
Troy (city) Oakland County	223	0.28
Clinton (charter twp) Macomb County	242	0.25
Wyoming (city) Kent County	182	0.25

Maltese

Top 10 Places Sorted by Population
Based on all places, regardless of total population

Place	Population	%
Livonia (city) Wayne County	845	0.86
Dearborn (city) Wayne County	662	0.67
Redford (charter twp) Wayne County	432	0.88
Canton (charter twp) Wayne County	366	0.42
Taylor (city) Wayne County	342	0.54
Warren (city) Macomb County	320	0.24
Westland (city) Wayne County	287	0.34
Dearborn Heights (city) Wayne County	286	0.49
Detroit (city) Wayne County	266	0.04
Sterling Heights (city) Macomb County	235	0.18

Top 10 Places Sorted by Percent of Total Population
Based on all places, regardless of total population

Place	Population	%
Wells (township) Marquette County	21	8.86
Millen (township) Alcona County	15	5.40
Wedgewood (cdp) Wexford County	7	3.23
Caseville (village) Huron County	22	3.16
Springdale (township) Manistee County	25	2.74
Wilson (township) Charlevoix County	45	2.35
Trout Lake (township) Chippewa County	9	2.17
Iosco (township) Livingston County	70	1.86
Whitefish (township) Chippewa County	10	1.78
Grant (township) Grand Traverse County	17	1.64

Top 10 Places Sorted by Percent of Total Population
Based on places with total population of 50,000 or more

Place	Population	%
Livonia (city) Wayne County	845	0.86
Dearborn (city) Wayne County	662	0.67
Taylor (city) Wayne County	342	0.54
Dearborn Heights (city) Wayne County	286	0.49
Canton (charter twp) Wayne County	366	0.42
Westland (city) Wayne County	287	0.34
Rochester Hills (city) Oakland County	221	0.31
St. Clair Shores (city) Macomb County	191	0.31
Farmington Hills (city) Oakland County	220	0.27
Macomb (township) Macomb County	192	0.26

Please refer to the Explanation of Data in the front of the book for more detailed information.

New Zealander

Top 10 Places Sorted by Population
Based on all places, regardless of total population

Place	Population	%
Ionia (township) Ionia County	71	1.87
Royal Oak (city) Oakland County	43	0.07
Northville (city) Oakland County	25	0.41
Ann Arbor (city) Washtenaw County	24	0.02
Lake Fenton (cdp) Genesee County	17	0.32
Fenton (charter twp) Genesee County	17	0.11
Farmington Hills (city) Oakland County	17	0.02
Harrison (charter twp) Macomb County	16	0.06
Aurelius (township) Ingham County	10	0.29
Livonia (city) Wayne County	10	0.01

Top 10 Places Sorted by Percent of Total Population
Based on all places, regardless of total population

Place	Population	%
Ionia (township) Ionia County	71	1.87
Northville (city) Oakland County	25	0.41
Lake Fenton (cdp) Genesee County	17	0.32
Aurelius (township) Ingham County	10	0.29
Galesburg (city) Kalamazoo County	4	0.22
Lake Orion (village) Oakland County	6	0.20
Hayes (township) Charlevoix County	3	0.16
Richmond (city) Macomb County	8	0.14
Rockford (city) Kent County	8	0.14
Fenton (charter twp) Genesee County	17	0.11

Top 10 Places Sorted by Percent of Total Population
Based on places with total population of 50,000 or more

Place	Population	%
Royal Oak (city) Oakland County	43	0.07
Ann Arbor (city) Washtenaw County	24	0.02
Farmington Hills (city) Oakland County	17	0.02
Livonia (city) Wayne County	10	0.01
Lansing (city) Ingham County	9	0.01
Battle Creek (city) Calhoun County	0	0.00
Canton (charter twp) Wayne County	0	0.00
Clinton (charter twp) Macomb County	0	0.00
Dearborn (city) Wayne County	0	0.00
Dearborn Heights (city) Wayne County	0	0.00

Northern European

Top 10 Places Sorted by Population
Based on all places, regardless of total population

Place	Population	%
Ann Arbor (city) Washtenaw County	203	0.18
Traverse City (city) Grand Traverse County	128	0.87
Livonia (city) Wayne County	126	0.13
Royal Oak (city) Oakland County	123	0.21
Sterling Heights (city) Macomb County	115	0.09
Midland (city) Midland County	108	0.26
Lansing (city) Ingham County	106	0.09
Dearborn (city) Wayne County	92	0.09
Troy (city) Oakland County	91	0.11
Grand Rapids (city) Kent County	87	0.05

Top 10 Places Sorted by Percent of Total Population
Based on all places, regardless of total population

Place	Population	%
Hazelton (township) Shiawassee County	57	2.53
Barnes Lake-Millers Lake (cdp) Lapeer County	27	2.50
Barton Hills (village) Washtenaw County	7	2.49
Baldwin (township) Delta County	16	2.16
Selma (township) Wexford County	41	1.87
Ann Arbor (charter twp) Washtenaw County	79	1.80
Brampton (township) Delta County	16	1.42
Williamstown (township) Ingham County	67	1.35
Almer (township) Tuscola County	39	1.26
China (township) St. Clair County	44	1.23

Top 10 Places Sorted by Percent of Total Population
Based on places with total population of 50,000 or more

Place	Population	%
Royal Oak (city) Oakland County	123	0.21
Ann Arbor (city) Washtenaw County	203	0.18
Novi (city) Oakland County	77	0.14
Livonia (city) Wayne County	126	0.13

Troy (city) Oakland County	91	0.11
Sterling Heights (city) Macomb County	115	0.09
Lansing (city) Ingham County	106	0.09
Dearborn (city) Wayne County	92	0.09
Rochester Hills (city) Oakland County	51	0.07
Dearborn Heights (city) Wayne County	39	0.07

Norwegian

Top 10 Places Sorted by Population
Based on all places, regardless of total population

Place	Population	%
Ann Arbor (city) Washtenaw County	1,312	1.14
Grand Rapids (city) Kent County	1,190	0.62
Midland (city) Midland County	1,021	2.43
Kalamazoo (city) Kalamazoo County	843	1.13
Portage (city) Kalamazoo County	835	1.82
Livonia (city) Wayne County	789	0.81
Waterford (charter twp) Oakland County	786	1.09
Lansing (city) Ingham County	774	0.67
Warren (city) Macomb County	765	0.56
Sterling Heights (city) Macomb County	712	0.55

Top 10 Places Sorted by Percent of Total Population
Based on all places, regardless of total population

Place	Population	%
Bay View (cdp) Emmet County	19	19.19
Pilgrim (cdp) Benzie County	3	15.79
Crystal Downs Country Club (cdp) Benzie County	10	11.49
Glen Arbor (cdp) Leelanau County	22	11.28
Mueller (township) Schoolcraft County	25	9.69
Northport (village) Leelanau County	39	9.49
Cedarville (township) Menominee County	30	9.23
Eagle Harbor (cdp) Keweenaw County	6	9.23
Suttons Bay (village) Leelanau County	55	9.06
Bear Lake (village) Manistee County	30	8.98

Top 10 Places Sorted by Percent of Total Population
Based on places with total population of 50,000 or more

Place	Population	%
Ann Arbor (city) Washtenaw County	1,312	1.14
Kalamazoo (city) Kalamazoo County	843	1.13
Novi (city) Oakland County	598	1.11
Waterford (charter twp) Oakland County	786	1.09
Royal Oak (city) Oakland County	596	1.03
Rochester Hills (city) Oakland County	647	0.92
Livonia (city) Wayne County	789	0.81
St. Clair Shores (city) Macomb County	473	0.78
Canton (charter twp) Wayne County	675	0.77
Troy (city) Oakland County	594	0.73

Pennsylvania German

Top 10 Places Sorted by Population
Based on all places, regardless of total population

Place	Population	%
Homer (township) Calhoun County	309	10.27
Algansee (township) Branch County	262	12.71
Nottawa (township) St. Joseph County	140	3.58
Richland (township) Montcalm County	131	4.65
Flynn (township) Sanilac County	126	12.84
Taylor (city) Wayne County	118	0.18
Ransom (township) Hillsdale County	98	9.35
Holland (charter twp) Ottawa County	84	0.24
Brandon (charter twp) Oakland County	83	0.55
Lansing (city) Ingham County	83	0.07

Top 10 Places Sorted by Percent of Total Population
Based on all places, regardless of total population

Place	Population	%
Flynn (township) Sanilac County	126	12.84
Algansee (township) Branch County	262	12.71
Homer (township) Calhoun County	309	10.27
Ransom (township) Hillsdale County	98	9.35
Orient (township) Osceola County	69	8.32
Wilcox (township) Newaygo County	68	6.75
Hartwick (township) Osceola County	34	6.05
Holland (township) Missaukee County	9	5.73
Sylvan (township) Osceola County	59	5.57
Gladwin (township) Gladwin County	74	5.35

Top 10 Places Sorted by Percent of Total Population
Based on places with total population of 50,000 or more

Place	Population	%
Taylor (city) Wayne County	118	0.18
Battle Creek (city) Calhoun County	81	0.15
Waterford (charter twp) Oakland County	56	0.08
Lansing (city) Ingham County	83	0.07
Kalamazoo (city) Kalamazoo County	51	0.07
Novi (city) Oakland County	35	0.07
Westland (city) Wayne County	52	0.06
Shelby (charter twp) Macomb County	44	0.06
Ann Arbor (city) Washtenaw County	62	0.05
Livonia (city) Wayne County	47	0.05

Polish

Top 10 Places Sorted by Population
Based on all places, regardless of total population

Place	Population	%
Warren (city) Macomb County	26,655	19.63
Sterling Heights (city) Macomb County	23,071	17.79
Clinton (charter twp) Macomb County	17,913	18.41
Livonia (city) Wayne County	17,428	17.80
Macomb (township) Macomb County	15,670	20.93
Grand Rapids (city) Kent County	15,189	7.98
Shelby (charter twp) Macomb County	12,829	17.63
St. Clair Shores (city) Macomb County	12,345	20.31
Canton (charter twp) Wayne County	11,542	13.12
Dearborn (city) Wayne County	10,629	10.80

Top 10 Places Sorted by Percent of Total Population
Based on all places, regardless of total population

Place	Population	%
Posen (village) Presque Isle County	201	78.82
Posen (township) Presque Isle County	689	77.16
Pulawski (township) Presque Isle County	231	68.55
Metz (township) Presque Isle County	157	58.15
Paris (township) Huron County	179	45.78
Cedar (cdp) Leelanau County	41	43.62
Parkdale (cdp) Manistee County	221	43.50
Bingham (township) Huron County	744	42.01
Krakow (township) Presque Isle County	287	41.12
Dwight (township) Huron County	350	40.94

Top 10 Places Sorted by Percent of Total Population
Based on places with total population of 50,000 or more

Place	Population	%
Macomb (township) Macomb County	15,670	20.93
St. Clair Shores (city) Macomb County	12,345	20.31
Warren (city) Macomb County	26,655	19.63
Clinton (charter twp) Macomb County	17,913	18.41
Livonia (city) Wayne County	17,428	17.80
Sterling Heights (city) Macomb County	23,071	17.79
Shelby (charter twp) Macomb County	12,829	17.63
Dearborn Heights (city) Wayne County	9,260	15.95
Royal Oak (city) Oakland County	7,841	13.58
Canton (charter twp) Wayne County	11,542	13.12

Portuguese

Top 10 Places Sorted by Population
Based on all places, regardless of total population

Place	Population	%
Taylor (city) Wayne County	154	0.24
Rochester Hills (city) Oakland County	128	0.18
Taymouth (township) Saginaw County	108	2.38
Jackson (city) Jackson County	102	0.30
Battle Creek (city) Calhoun County	101	0.19
Troy (city) Oakland County	98	0.12
Sterling Heights (city) Macomb County	94	0.07
Pontiac (city) Oakland County	92	0.15
Genoa (township) Livingston County	89	0.45
Grand Rapids (city) Kent County	89	0.05

Top 10 Places Sorted by Percent of Total Population
Based on all places, regardless of total population

Place	Population	%
Eagle Harbor (cdp) Keweenaw County	4	6.15
Newton (township) Mackinac County	23	5.07
Republic (cdp) Marquette County	20	3.55

Place	Population	%
Elsie (village) Clinton County	31	3.51
Taymouth (township) Saginaw County	108	2.38
Mancelona (village) Antrim County	35	2.37
West Ishpeming (cdp) Marquette County	66	2.30
Duplain (township) Clinton County	48	2.16
Republic (township) Marquette County	20	2.09
Roscommon (township) Roscommon County	87	1.96

Top 10 Places Sorted by Percent of Total Population
Based on places with total population of 50,000 or more

Place	Population	%
Taylor (city) Wayne County	154	0.24
Battle Creek (city) Calhoun County	101	0.19
Rochester Hills (city) Oakland County	128	0.18
Pontiac (city) Oakland County	92	0.15
Ypsilanti (charter twp) Washtenaw County	80	0.15
St. Clair Shores (city) Macomb County	80	0.13
Troy (city) Oakland County	98	0.12
Farmington Hills (city) Oakland County	81	0.10
Wyoming (city) Kent County	70	0.10
Ann Arbor (city) Washtenaw County	88	0.08

Romanian

Top 10 Places Sorted by Population
Based on all places, regardless of total population

Place	Population	%
Sterling Heights (city) Macomb County	1,620	1.25
Troy (city) Oakland County	1,184	1.46
Warren (city) Macomb County	955	0.70
Dearborn (city) Wayne County	916	0.93
Clinton (charter twp) Macomb County	810	0.83
Farmington Hills (city) Oakland County	794	0.99
Shelby (charter twp) Macomb County	728	1.00
Canton (charter twp) Wayne County	699	0.79
Ann Arbor (city) Washtenaw County	650	0.56
Rochester Hills (city) Oakland County	642	0.91

Top 10 Places Sorted by Percent of Total Population
Based on all places, regardless of total population

Place	Population	%
Vineyard Lake (cdp) Jackson County	31	4.16
York (charter twp) Washtenaw County	311	3.63
Pioneer (township) Missaukee County	12	3.20
Boyne Falls (village) Charlevoix County	8	2.68
Michiana (village) Berrien County	4	2.65
Stockbridge (village) Ingham County	29	2.64
Arenac (township) Arenac County	22	2.57
Novi (township) Oakland County	3	2.50
Calumet (charter twp) Houghton County	158	2.43
Saline (township) Washtenaw County	47	2.30

Top 10 Places Sorted by Percent of Total Population
Based on places with total population of 50,000 or more

Place	Population	%
Troy (city) Oakland County	1,184	1.46
Sterling Heights (city) Macomb County	1,620	1.25
Shelby (charter twp) Macomb County	728	1.00
Farmington Hills (city) Oakland County	794	0.99
Dearborn Heights (city) Wayne County	560	0.96
Dearborn (city) Wayne County	916	0.93
Rochester Hills (city) Oakland County	642	0.91
Clinton (charter twp) Macomb County	810	0.83
Macomb (township) Macomb County	621	0.83
Canton (charter twp) Wayne County	699	0.79

Russian

Top 10 Places Sorted by Population
Based on all places, regardless of total population

Place	Population	%
West Bloomfield (charter twp) Oakland County	4,873	7.53
Farmington Hills (city) Oakland County	3,395	4.23
Ann Arbor (city) Washtenaw County	3,214	2.79
Bloomfield (charter twp) Oakland County	2,201	5.31
Southfield (city) Oakland County	1,961	2.69
Oak Park (city) Oakland County	1,391	4.65
Royal Oak (city) Oakland County	1,263	2.19
Warren (city) Macomb County	1,211	0.89
Livonia (city) Wayne County	1,101	1.12
Sterling Heights (city) Macomb County	1,070	0.83

Top 10 Places Sorted by Percent of Total Population
Based on all places, regardless of total population

Place	Population	%
Conway (cdp) Emmet County	16	10.81
Huntington Woods (city) Oakland County	650	10.47
Franklin (village) Oakland County	254	8.09
Orchard Lake Village (city) Oakland County	162	7.62
Bingham Farms (village) Oakland County	83	7.60
West Bloomfield (charter twp) Oakland County	4,873	7.53
Lexington (township) Sanilac County	263	7.07
Beaver (township) Newaygo County	43	6.79
Port Hope (village) Huron County	13	5.99
Walled Lake (city) Oakland County	386	5.56

Top 10 Places Sorted by Percent of Total Population
Based on places with total population of 50,000 or more

Place	Population	%
West Bloomfield (charter twp) Oakland County	4,873	7.53
Farmington Hills (city) Oakland County	3,395	4.23
Ann Arbor (city) Washtenaw County	3,214	2.79
Southfield (city) Oakland County	1,961	2.69
Royal Oak (city) Oakland County	1,263	2.19
Novi (city) Oakland County	770	1.43
Troy (city) Oakland County	931	1.15
Waterford (charter twp) Oakland County	825	1.15
Livonia (city) Wayne County	1,101	1.12
Rochester Hills (city) Oakland County	647	0.92

Scandinavian

Top 10 Places Sorted by Population
Based on all places, regardless of total population

Place	Population	%
Ann Arbor (city) Washtenaw County	229	0.20
Grand Blanc (charter twp) Genesee County	204	0.56
Porter (township) Cass County	187	4.88
Walker (city) Kent County	187	0.80
Farmington Hills (city) Oakland County	181	0.23
Wyoming (city) Kent County	175	0.24
Meridian (charter twp) Ingham County	162	0.41
Norton Shores (city) Muskegon County	155	0.65
Novi (city) Oakland County	140	0.26
Grand Rapids (city) Kent County	138	0.07

Top 10 Places Sorted by Percent of Total Population
Based on all places, regardless of total population

Place	Population	%
Omena (cdp) Leelanau County	39	13.98
Lake Leelanau (cdp) Leelanau County	14	6.06
Star (township) Antrim County	46	5.46
Porter (township) Cass County	187	4.88
Laird (township) Houghton County	19	4.62
Breen (township) Dickinson County	19	4.58
Burt (township) Alger County	15	4.03
Laurium (village) Houghton County	86	4.00
Breedsville (village) Van Buren County	4	3.81
Lakes of the North (cdp) Antrim County	46	3.72

Top 10 Places Sorted by Percent of Total Population
Based on places with total population of 50,000 or more

Place	Population	%
Novi (city) Oakland County	140	0.26
Wyoming (city) Kent County	175	0.24
Farmington Hills (city) Oakland County	181	0.23
Ann Arbor (city) Washtenaw County	229	0.20
Battle Creek (city) Calhoun County	106	0.20
Kalamazoo (city) Kalamazoo County	135	0.18
West Bloomfield (charter twp) Oakland County	101	0.16
Taylor (city) Wayne County	98	0.15
Canton (charter twp) Wayne County	119	0.14
Waterford (charter twp) Oakland County	103	0.14

Scotch-Irish

Top 10 Places Sorted by Population
Based on all places, regardless of total population

Place	Population	%
Livonia (city) Wayne County	2,368	2.42
Ann Arbor (city) Washtenaw County	2,326	2.02
Grand Rapids (city) Kent County	2,161	1.13
Warren (city) Macomb County	1,965	1.45
Waterford (charter twp) Oakland County	1,716	2.39
St. Clair Shores (city) Macomb County	1,611	2.65
Sterling Heights (city) Macomb County	1,593	1.23
Westland (city) Wayne County	1,528	1.80
Troy (city) Oakland County	1,480	1.83
Royal Oak (city) Oakland County	1,472	2.55

Top 10 Places Sorted by Percent of Total Population
Based on all places, regardless of total population

Place	Population	%
Conway (cdp) Emmet County	20	13.51
Gagetown (village) Tuscola County	42	12.61
Gaines (village) Genesee County	44	11.83
Leland (cdp) Leelanau County	36	11.29
Horton Bay (cdp) Charlevoix County	75	10.20
Pickford (township) Chippewa County	121	8.94
Watersmeet (cdp) Gogebic County	49	8.15
Harrisville (city) Alcona County	40	7.65
Eastlake (village) Manistee County	35	7.10
Emmett (village) St. Clair County	23	6.99

Top 10 Places Sorted by Percent of Total Population
Based on places with total population of 50,000 or more

Place	Population	%
St. Clair Shores (city) Macomb County	1,611	2.65
Royal Oak (city) Oakland County	1,472	2.55
Livonia (city) Wayne County	2,368	2.42
Waterford (charter twp) Oakland County	1,716	2.39
Novi (city) Oakland County	1,175	2.18
Ann Arbor (city) Washtenaw County	2,326	2.02
Taylor (city) Wayne County	1,226	1.92
Troy (city) Oakland County	1,480	1.83
Westland (city) Wayne County	1,528	1.80
Rochester Hills (city) Oakland County	1,248	1.77

Scottish

Top 10 Places Sorted by Population
Based on all places, regardless of total population

Place	Population	%
Livonia (city) Wayne County	4,098	4.19
Ann Arbor (city) Washtenaw County	3,574	3.10
Waterford (charter twp) Oakland County	2,800	3.90
Sterling Heights (city) Macomb County	2,501	1.93
Clinton (charter twp) Macomb County	2,496	2.57
Royal Oak (city) Oakland County	2,460	4.26
Troy (city) Oakland County	2,454	3.03
Warren (city) Macomb County	2,448	1.80
Grand Rapids (city) Kent County	2,430	1.28
Canton (charter twp) Wayne County	2,402	2.73

Top 10 Places Sorted by Percent of Total Population
Based on all places, regardless of total population

Place	Population	%
Bendon (cdp) Benzie County	28	16.00
South Gull Lake (cdp) Kalamazoo County	175	14.01
Houghton (township) Keweenaw County	12	13.33
Wedgewood (cdp) Wexford County	28	12.90
Canada Creek Ranch (cdp) Montmorency County	37	12.54
Bois Blanc (township) Mackinac County	9	12.50
Oscoda (cdp) Iosco County	106	12.46
Sunfield (village) Eaton County	90	12.08
Ashley (village) Gratiot County	70	11.35
Glen Arbor (township) Leelanau County	82	10.62

Top 10 Places Sorted by Percent of Total Population
Based on places with total population of 50,000 or more

Place	Population	%
Royal Oak (city) Oakland County	2,460	4.26
Livonia (city) Wayne County	4,098	4.19
Waterford (charter twp) Oakland County	2,800	3.90
Novi (city) Oakland County	2,051	3.81
St. Clair Shores (city) Macomb County	2,269	3.73
Rochester Hills (city) Oakland County	2,398	3.40
Ann Arbor (city) Washtenaw County	3,574	3.10
Troy (city) Oakland County	2,454	3.03
Ypsilanti (charter twp) Washtenaw County	1,497	2.82
Canton (charter twp) Wayne County	2,402	2.73

Serbian

Top 10 Places Sorted by Population
Based on all places, regardless of total population

Place	Population	%
Rochester Hills (city) Oakland County	382	0.54
Sterling Heights (city) Macomb County	369	0.28
Troy (city) Oakland County	333	0.41
Macomb (township) Macomb County	268	0.36
Shelby (charter twp) Macomb County	265	0.36
Royal Oak (city) Oakland County	264	0.46
Livonia (city) Wayne County	253	0.26
Clinton (charter twp) Macomb County	246	0.25
Warren (city) Macomb County	237	0.17
Farmington Hills (city) Oakland County	195	0.24

Top 10 Places Sorted by Percent of Total Population
Based on all places, regardless of total population

Place	Population	%
Hendricks (township) Mackinac County	20	15.63
Middle Branch (township) Osceola County	33	4.17
Memphis (city) Macomb County	47	4.15
Metamora (village) Lapeer County	23	4.13
Onota (township) Alger County	7	2.41
Mitchell (township) Alcona County	7	2.35
Detroit Beach (cdp) Monroe County	38	2.15
Lake Angelus (city) Oakland County	6	2.04
Wakefield (city) Gogebic County	35	1.79
Mio (cdp) Oscoda County	39	1.77

Top 10 Places Sorted by Percent of Total Population
Based on places with total population of 50,000 or more

Place	Population	%
Rochester Hills (city) Oakland County	382	0.54
Royal Oak (city) Oakland County	264	0.46
Troy (city) Oakland County	333	0.41
Macomb (township) Macomb County	268	0.36
Shelby (charter twp) Macomb County	265	0.36
Sterling Heights (city) Macomb County	369	0.28
Livonia (city) Wayne County	253	0.26
Novi (city) Oakland County	142	0.26
Clinton (charter twp) Macomb County	246	0.25
Farmington Hills (city) Oakland County	195	0.24

Slavic

Top 10 Places Sorted by Population
Based on all places, regardless of total population

Place	Population	%
Macomb (township) Macomb County	204	0.27
Independence (charter twp) Oakland County	174	0.51
Canton (charter twp) Wayne County	154	0.18
Delta (charter twp) Eaton County	143	0.44
Troy (city) Oakland County	139	0.17
Waverly (cdp) Eaton County	128	0.52
Lyon (charter twp) Oakland County	123	0.88
Warren (city) Macomb County	102	0.08
Livonia (city) Wayne County	95	0.10
Grand Rapids (city) Kent County	91	0.05

Top 10 Places Sorted by Percent of Total Population
Based on all places, regardless of total population

Place	Population	%
Calumet (village) Houghton County	19	2.62
Au Train (township) Alger County	24	2.08
Amber (township) Mason County	45	1.83
Wakefield (township) Gogebic County	5	1.65
Ironwood (city) Gogebic County	76	1.38
Stanwood (village) Mecosta County	2	1.37
Acme (township) Grand Traverse County	56	1.27
Lupton (cdp) Ogemaw County	4	1.18
Spring Lake (village) Ottawa County	27	1.12
Bennington (township) Shiawassee County	35	1.10

Top 10 Places Sorted by Percent of Total Population
Based on places with total population of 50,000 or more

Place	Population	%
Macomb (township) Macomb County	204	0.27
Canton (charter twp) Wayne County	154	0.18
Troy (city) Oakland County	139	0.17
Livonia (city) Wayne County	95	0.10
Waterford (charter twp) Oakland County	69	0.10
Royal Oak (city) Oakland County	59	0.10
Westland (city) Wayne County	77	0.09
Shelby (charter twp) Macomb County	64	0.09
Warren (city) Macomb County	102	0.08
Dearborn (city) Wayne County	68	0.07

Slovak

Top 10 Places Sorted by Population
Based on all places, regardless of total population

Place	Population	%
Sterling Heights (city) Macomb County	1,027	0.79
Warren (city) Macomb County	821	0.60
Shelby (charter twp) Macomb County	669	0.92
Livonia (city) Wayne County	667	0.68
Clinton (charter twp) Macomb County	493	0.51
Rochester Hills (city) Oakland County	480	0.68
St. Clair Shores (city) Macomb County	475	0.78
Detroit (city) Wayne County	378	0.05
Chesterfield (township) Macomb County	366	0.86
Canton (charter twp) Wayne County	323	0.37

Top 10 Places Sorted by Percent of Total Population
Based on all places, regardless of total population

Place	Population	%
Bancroft (village) Shiawassee County	39	6.25
Oakley (village) Saginaw County	13	5.14
Hanover (village) Jackson County	14	4.20
Whitefish (township) Chippewa County	20	3.55
Hazelton (township) Shiawassee County	74	3.28
Elk Rapids (village) Antrim County	61	3.27
Mansfield (township) Iron County	6	3.21
Fairfield (township) Shiawassee County	22	3.13
Williamstown (township) Ingham County	145	2.91
Mueller (township) Schoolcraft County	7	2.71

Top 10 Places Sorted by Percent of Total Population
Based on places with total population of 50,000 or more

Place	Population	%
Shelby (charter twp) Macomb County	669	0.92
Sterling Heights (city) Macomb County	1,027	0.79
St. Clair Shores (city) Macomb County	475	0.78
Livonia (city) Wayne County	667	0.68
Rochester Hills (city) Oakland County	480	0.68
Warren (city) Macomb County	821	0.60
Clinton (charter twp) Macomb County	493	0.51
Taylor (city) Wayne County	243	0.38
Canton (charter twp) Wayne County	323	0.37
Farmington Hills (city) Oakland County	298	0.37

Slovene

Top 10 Places Sorted by Population
Based on all places, regardless of total population

Place	Population	%
Farmington Hills (city) Oakland County	185	0.23
Royal Oak (city) Oakland County	110	0.19
Warren (city) Macomb County	108	0.08
Midland (city) Midland County	91	0.22
Norton Shores (city) Muskegon County	90	0.38
Waterford (charter twp) Oakland County	83	0.12
East Lansing (city) Ingham County	78	0.16
Redford (township) Wayne County	74	0.15
Calumet (charter twp) Houghton County	73	1.12
Livonia (city) Wayne County	72	0.07

Top 10 Places Sorted by Percent of Total Population
Based on all places, regardless of total population

Place	Population	%
Harrietta (village) Wexford County	7	6.19
Boon (cdp) Wexford County	8	4.71
Limestone (township) Alger County	16	4.34
Mathias (township) Alger County	19	4.12
Grant (township) Keweenaw County	5	4.10
Metamora (village) Lapeer County	20	3.59
Sherman (township) Keweenaw County	3	3.37
Boon (township) Wexford County	18	3.15
Elberta (village) Benzie County	7	2.47
Gaastra (city) Iron County	5	1.89

Top 10 Places Sorted by Percent of Total Population
Based on places with total population of 50,000 or more

Place	Population	%
Farmington Hills (city) Oakland County	185	0.23
Royal Oak (city) Oakland County	110	0.19
Waterford (charter twp) Oakland County	83	0.12
Warren (city) Macomb County	108	0.08
Macomb (township) Macomb County	58	0.08
Livonia (city) Wayne County	72	0.07
Rochester Hills (city) Oakland County	46	0.07
Ann Arbor (city) Washtenaw County	67	0.06
Novi (city) Oakland County	31	0.06
Dearborn (city) Wayne County	48	0.05

Soviet Union

Top 10 Places Sorted by Population
Based on all places, regardless of total population

Place	Population	%
Long Lake (township) Grand Traverse County	52	0.61
Acme (township) Grand Traverse County	0	0.00
Ada (township) Kent County	0	0.00
Adams (township) Arenac County	0	0.00
Adams (township) Hillsdale County	0	0.00
Adams (township) Houghton County	0	0.00
Addison (village) Lenawee County	0	0.00
Addison (township) Oakland County	0	0.00
Adrian (city) Lenawee County	0	0.00
Adrian (township) Lenawee County	0	0.00

Top 10 Places Sorted by Percent of Total Population
Based on all places, regardless of total population

Place	Population	%
Long Lake (township) Grand Traverse County	52	0.61
Acme (township) Grand Traverse County	0	0.00
Ada (township) Kent County	0	0.00
Adams (township) Arenac County	0	0.00
Adams (township) Hillsdale County	0	0.00
Adams (township) Houghton County	0	0.00
Addison (village) Lenawee County	0	0.00
Addison (township) Oakland County	0	0.00
Adrian (city) Lenawee County	0	0.00
Adrian (township) Lenawee County	0	0.00

Top 10 Places Sorted by Percent of Total Population
Based on places with total population of 50,000 or more

Place	Population	%
Ann Arbor (city) Washtenaw County	0	0.00
Battle Creek (city) Calhoun County	0	0.00
Canton (charter twp) Wayne County	0	0.00
Clinton (charter twp) Macomb County	0	0.00
Dearborn (city) Wayne County	0	0.00
Dearborn Heights (city) Wayne County	0	0.00
Detroit (city) Wayne County	0	0.00
Farmington Hills (city) Oakland County	0	0.00
Flint (city) Genesee County	0	0.00
Grand Rapids (city) Kent County	0	0.00

Swedish

Top 10 Places Sorted by Population
Based on all places, regardless of total population

Place	Population	%
Grand Rapids (city) Kent County	3,385	1.78
Ann Arbor (city) Washtenaw County	2,065	1.79
Marquette (city) Marquette County	1,868	8.79
Norton Shores (city) Muskegon County	1,521	6.36
Livonia (city) Wayne County	1,449	1.48
Lansing (city) Ingham County	1,420	1.23
Wyoming (city) Kent County	1,403	1.95
Escanaba (city) Delta County	1,359	10.67
Royal Oak (city) Oakland County	1,302	2.25
Troy (city) Oakland County	1,278	1.58

Top 10 Places Sorted by Percent of Total Population
Based on all places, regardless of total population

Place	Population	%
West Branch (township) Dickinson County	14	36.84
Felch (township) Dickinson County	277	36.02
Quinnesec (cdp) Dickinson County	333	33.00

Bay de Noc (township) Delta County	122	32.28
Breen (township) Dickinson County	117	28.19
Palmer (cdp) Marquette County	133	24.09
Tustin (village) Osceola County	21	22.34
Ensign (township) Delta County	192	22.09
Arvon (township) Baraga County	67	22.04
Shorewood-Tower Hills-Harbert (cdp) Berrien County	315	
21.60		

Top 10 Places Sorted by Percent of Total Population
Based on places with total population of 50,000 or more

Place	Population	%
Royal Oak (city) Oakland County	1,302	2.25
Novi (city) Oakland County	1,111	2.06
Wyoming (city) Kent County	1,403	1.95
Ann Arbor (city) Washtenaw County	2,065	1.79
Grand Rapids (city) Kent County	3,385	1.78
Waterford (charter twp) Oakland County	1,259	1.75
Kalamazoo (city) Kalamazoo County	1,224	1.65
Troy (city) Oakland County	1,278	1.58
Livonia (city) Wayne County	1,449	1.48
Rochester Hills (city) Oakland County	1,031	1.46

Swiss

Top 10 Places Sorted by Population
Based on all places, regardless of total population

Place	Population	%
Grand Rapids (city) Kent County	639	0.34
Ann Arbor (city) Washtenaw County	537	0.47
Bloomfield (charter twp) Oakland County	300	0.72
Canton (charter twp) Wayne County	254	0.29
Troy (city) Oakland County	246	0.30
Farmington Hills (city) Oakland County	233	0.29
Royal Oak (city) Oakland County	228	0.39
Portage (city) Kalamazoo County	220	0.48
Wyoming (city) Kent County	217	0.30
Macomb (township) Macomb County	217	0.29

Top 10 Places Sorted by Percent of Total Population
Based on all places, regardless of total population

Place	Population	%
Hickory Corners (cdp) Barry County	26	9.56
Eden (township) Mason County	58	9.35
Elmer (township) Oscoda County	86	6.67
Highland (township) Osceola County	92	6.61
Sylvan (township) Osceola County	63	5.94
Garfield (township) Newaygo County	148	5.85
Sanborn (township) Alpena County	120	5.59
Pine (township) Montcalm County	106	5.20
Nottawa (township) St. Joseph County	196	5.01
Moore (township) Sanilac County	66	4.97

Top 10 Places Sorted by Percent of Total Population
Based on places with total population of 50,000 or more

Place	Population	%
Ann Arbor (city) Washtenaw County	537	0.47
Royal Oak (city) Oakland County	228	0.39
Grand Rapids (city) Kent County	639	0.34
Troy (city) Oakland County	246	0.30
Wyoming (city) Kent County	217	0.30
Rochester Hills (city) Oakland County	213	0.30
Canton (charter twp) Wayne County	254	0.29
Farmington Hills (city) Oakland County	233	0.29
Macomb (township) Macomb County	217	0.29
Ypsilanti (charter twp) Washtenaw County	140	0.26

Turkish

Top 10 Places Sorted by Population
Based on all places, regardless of total population

Place	Population	%
Ann Arbor (city) Washtenaw County	373	0.32
Canton (charter twp) Wayne County	142	0.16
Meridian (charter twp) Ingham County	138	0.35
West Bloomfield (charter twp) Oakland County	85	0.13
Okemos (cdp) Ingham County	82	0.39
White Lake (charter twp) Oakland County	72	0.24
Troy (city) Oakland County	70	0.09
Farmington Hills (city) Oakland County	61	0.08
Haslett (cdp) Ingham County	56	0.28

Cambridge (township) Lenawee County	55	0.96

Top 10 Places Sorted by Percent of Total Population
Based on all places, regardless of total population

Place	Population	%
Carp Lake (cdp) Emmet County	4	1.02
Cambridge (township) Lenawee County	55	0.96
Frankfort (city) Benzie County	10	0.70
Franklin (village) Oakland County	21	0.67
Carp Lake (township) Emmet County	4	0.52
Briley (township) Montmorency County	9	0.49
Markey (township) Roscommon County	11	0.46
New Buffalo (city) Berrien County	9	0.44
Grosse Pointe Park (city) Wayne County	50	0.43
Robinson (township) Ottawa County	24	0.40

Top 10 Places Sorted by Percent of Total Population
Based on places with total population of 50,000 or more

Place	Population	%
Ann Arbor (city) Washtenaw County	373	0.32
Canton (charter twp) Wayne County	142	0.16
West Bloomfield (charter twp) Oakland County	85	0.13
Troy (city) Oakland County	70	0.09
Farmington Hills (city) Oakland County	61	0.08
Royal Oak (city) Oakland County	41	0.07
Dearborn Heights (city) Wayne County	39	0.07
Macomb (township) Macomb County	48	0.06
Ypsilanti (charter twp) Washtenaw County	30	0.06
Livonia (city) Wayne County	49	0.05

Ukrainian

Top 10 Places Sorted by Population
Based on all places, regardless of total population

Place	Population	%
Warren (city) Macomb County	1,999	1.47
Sterling Heights (city) Macomb County	1,410	1.09
Rochester Hills (city) Oakland County	1,108	1.57
Farmington Hills (city) Oakland County	1,053	1.31
Livonia (city) Wayne County	1,041	1.06
Dearborn (city) Wayne County	988	1.00
Troy (city) Oakland County	845	1.04
Detroit (city) Wayne County	647	0.09
Ann Arbor (city) Washtenaw County	607	0.53
Royal Oak (city) Oakland County	603	1.04

Top 10 Places Sorted by Percent of Total Population
Based on all places, regardless of total population

Place	Population	%
Cross Village (cdp) Emmet County	11	15.49
Prescott (village) Ogemaw County	13	6.19
Cross Village (township) Emmet County	11	5.45
Carsonville (village) Sanilac County	21	5.26
Warner (township) Antrim County	18	4.66
Bay (township) Charlevoix County	63	4.21
Cedarville (township) Menominee County	13	4.00
Selma (township) Wexford County	86	3.92
Mentor (township) Oscoda County	51	3.90
Otisville (village) Genesee County	36	3.81

Top 10 Places Sorted by Percent of Total Population
Based on places with total population of 50,000 or more

Place	Population	%
Rochester Hills (city) Oakland County	1,108	1.57
Warren (city) Macomb County	1,999	1.47
Farmington Hills (city) Oakland County	1,053	1.31
Sterling Heights (city) Macomb County	1,410	1.09
Livonia (city) Wayne County	1,041	1.06
Troy (city) Oakland County	845	1.04
Royal Oak (city) Oakland County	603	1.04
Dearborn (city) Wayne County	988	1.00
St. Clair Shores (city) Macomb County	599	0.99
Dearborn Heights (city) Wayne County	456	0.79

Welsh

Top 10 Places Sorted by Population
Based on all places, regardless of total population

Place	Population	%
Ann Arbor (city) Washtenaw County	1,064	0.92

Livonia (city) Wayne County	873	0.89
Grand Rapids (city) Kent County	743	0.39
Waterford (charter twp) Oakland County	725	1.01
Rochester Hills (city) Oakland County	671	0.95
Troy (city) Oakland County	609	0.75
Lansing (city) Ingham County	606	0.52
Warren (city) Macomb County	557	0.41
Kalamazoo (city) Kalamazoo County	534	0.72
Royal Oak (city) Oakland County	492	0.85

Top 10 Places Sorted by Percent of Total Population
Based on all places, regardless of total population

Place	Population	%
Maple Grove (cdp) Benzie County	43	41.35
Pilgrim (cdp) Benzie County	5	26.32
Pointe Aux Barques (township) Huron County	2	18.18
Bois Blanc (township) Mackinac County	8	11.11
Vineyard Lake (cdp) Jackson County	67	8.99
Mathias (township) Alger County	34	7.38
Eagle (village) Clinton County	13	6.50
St. James (cdp) Charlevoix County	12	6.38
Vanderbilt (village) Otsego County	35	5.38
Maybee (village) Monroe County	33	5.13

Top 10 Places Sorted by Percent of Total Population
Based on places with total population of 50,000 or more

Place	Population	%
Waterford (charter twp) Oakland County	725	1.01
Rochester Hills (city) Oakland County	671	0.95
Ann Arbor (city) Washtenaw County	1,064	0.92
Novi (city) Oakland County	490	0.91
Livonia (city) Wayne County	873	0.89
Royal Oak (city) Oakland County	492	0.85
Ypsilanti (charter twp) Washtenaw County	415	0.78
Troy (city) Oakland County	609	0.75
Kalamazoo (city) Kalamazoo County	534	0.72
Shelby (charter twp) Macomb County	419	0.58

West Indian, excluding Hispanic

Top 10 Places Sorted by Population
Based on all places, regardless of total population

Place	Population	%
Detroit (city) Wayne County	2,609	0.34
Pontiac (city) Oakland County	814	1.33
Southfield (city) Oakland County	726	1.00
Oronoko (charter twp) Berrien County	678	7.35
Lansing (city) Ingham County	601	0.52
Ann Arbor (city) Washtenaw County	380	0.33
Grand Rapids (city) Kent County	352	0.18
Ypsilanti (charter twp) Washtenaw County	269	0.51
Farmington Hills (city) Oakland County	254	0.32
Flint (city) Genesee County	219	0.20

Top 10 Places Sorted by Percent of Total Population
Based on all places, regardless of total population

Place	Population	%
Portage (township) Mackinac County	155	18.07
Oronoko (charter twp) Berrien County	678	7.35
Harvey (cdp) Marquette County	83	5.58
Berrien Springs (village) Berrien County	134	5.43
Dimondale (village) Eaton County	63	5.07
Alden (cdp) Antrim County	5	3.76
Penn (township) Cass County	63	3.57
Mackinac Island (city) Mackinac County	12	3.02
Wheeler (township) Gratiot County	74	2.64
North Branch (village) Lapeer County	24	2.60

Top 10 Places Sorted by Percent of Total Population
Based on places with total population of 50,000 or more

Place	Population	%
Pontiac (city) Oakland County	814	1.33
Southfield (city) Oakland County	726	1.00
Lansing (city) Ingham County	601	0.52
Ypsilanti (charter twp) Washtenaw County	269	0.51
Detroit (city) Wayne County	2,609	0.34
Ann Arbor (city) Washtenaw County	380	0.33
Farmington Hills (city) Oakland County	254	0.32
Westland (city) Wayne County	211	0.25
Rochester Hills (city) Oakland County	173	0.25
Canton (charter twp) Wayne County	211	0.24

West Indian: Bahamian, excluding Hispanic

Top 10 Places Sorted by Population
Based on all places, regardless of total population

Place	Population	%
Pittsfield (charter twp) Washtenaw County	96	0.28
Detroit (city) Wayne County	59	0.01
Brownstown (charter twp) Wayne County	29	0.10
Emmett (township) St. Clair County	24	0.90
Oronoko (charter twp) Berrien County	13	0.14
Kentwood (city) Kent County	13	0.03
Clinton (charter twp) Macomb County	13	0.01
Ann Arbor (city) Washtenaw County	12	0.01
Whitewater (township) Grand Traverse County	11	0.43
Royal Oak (city) Oakland County	11	0.02

Top 10 Places Sorted by Percent of Total Population
Based on all places, regardless of total population

Place	Population	%
Emmett (township) St. Clair County	24	0.90
Whitewater (township) Grand Traverse County	11	0.43
Pittsfield (charter twp) Washtenaw County	96	0.28
Oronoko (charter twp) Berrien County	13	0.14
Harris (township) Menominee County	2	0.11
Brownstown (charter twp) Wayne County	29	0.10
Owosso (city) Shiawassee County	8	0.05
Dowagiac (city) Cass County	3	0.05
Kentwood (city) Kent County	13	0.03
Romulus (city) Wayne County	7	0.03

Top 10 Places Sorted by Percent of Total Population
Based on places with total population of 50,000 or more

Place	Population	%
Royal Oak (city) Oakland County	11	0.02
Detroit (city) Wayne County	59	0.01
Clinton (charter twp) Macomb County	13	0.01
Ann Arbor (city) Washtenaw County	12	0.01
Southfield (city) Oakland County	9	0.01
Sterling Heights (city) Macomb County	9	0.01
Flint (city) Genesee County	7	0.01
Battle Creek (city) Calhoun County	0	0.00
Canton (charter twp) Wayne County	0	0.00
Dearborn (city) Wayne County	0	0.00

West Indian: Barbadian, excluding Hispanic

Top 10 Places Sorted by Population
Based on all places, regardless of total population

Place	Population	%
Royal Oak (city) Oakland County	64	0.11
Battle Creek (city) Calhoun County	51	0.10
Lansing (city) Ingham County	37	0.03
Saginaw (charter twp) Saginaw County	31	0.08
Detroit (city) Wayne County	29	<0.01
Farmington Hills (city) Oakland County	22	0.03
Ann Arbor (city) Washtenaw County	16	0.01
Lapeer (city) Lapeer County	14	0.15
Jackson (city) Jackson County	14	0.04
Grand Rapids (city) Kent County	14	0.01

Top 10 Places Sorted by Percent of Total Population
Based on all places, regardless of total population

Place	Population	%
Lake Odessa (village) Ionia County	12	0.53
Odessa (township) Ionia County	12	0.31
Lapeer (city) Lapeer County	14	0.15
Oronoko (charter twp) Berrien County	11	0.12
Berrien Springs (village) Berrien County	3	0.12
Royal Oak (city) Oakland County	64	0.11
Battle Creek (city) Calhoun County	51	0.10
Saginaw (charter twp) Saginaw County	31	0.08
Albion (city) Calhoun County	6	0.07
Ypsilanti (city) Washtenaw County	10	0.05

Top 10 Places Sorted by Percent of Total Population
Based on places with total population of 50,000 or more

Place	Population	%
Royal Oak (city) Oakland County	64	0.11

Place	Population	%
Battle Creek (city) Calhoun County	51	0.10
Lansing (city) Ingham County	37	0.03
Farmington Hills (city) Oakland County	22	0.03
Ann Arbor (city) Washtenaw County	16	0.01
Grand Rapids (city) Kent County	14	0.01
Livonia (city) Wayne County	12	0.01
Detroit (city) Wayne County	29	<0.01
Canton (charter twp) Wayne County	0	0.00
Clinton (charter twp) Macomb County	0	0.00

West Indian: Belizean, excluding Hispanic

Top 10 Places Sorted by Population
Based on all places, regardless of total population

Place	Population	%
Inkster (city) Wayne County	50	0.19
Zeeland (charter twp) Ottawa County	43	0.45
Oronoko (charter twp) Berrien County	15	0.16
Warren (city) Macomb County	14	0.01
Holt (cdp) Ingham County	11	0.05
Delhi (charter twp) Ingham County	11	0.04
Detroit (city) Wayne County	11	<0.01
Okemos (cdp) Ingham County	10	0.05
Meridian (charter twp) Ingham County	10	0.03
Southfield (city) Oakland County	10	0.01

Top 10 Places Sorted by Percent of Total Population
Based on all places, regardless of total population

Place	Population	%
Zeeland (charter twp) Ottawa County	43	0.45
Inkster (city) Wayne County	50	0.19
Oronoko (charter twp) Berrien County	15	0.16
Holt (cdp) Ingham County	11	0.05
Okemos (cdp) Ingham County	10	0.05
Comstock (charter twp) Kalamazoo County	7	0.05
Delhi (charter twp) Ingham County	11	0.04
Meridian (charter twp) Ingham County	10	0.03
Oxford (charter twp) Oakland County	6	0.03
Niles (city) Berrien County	3	0.03

Top 10 Places Sorted by Percent of Total Population
Based on places with total population of 50,000 or more

Place	Population	%
Warren (city) Macomb County	14	0.01
Southfield (city) Oakland County	10	0.01
Rochester Hills (city) Oakland County	8	0.01
Detroit (city) Wayne County	11	<0.01
Ann Arbor (city) Washtenaw County	0	0.00
Battle Creek (city) Calhoun County	0	0.00
Canton (charter twp) Wayne County	0	0.00
Clinton (charter twp) Macomb County	0	0.00
Dearborn (city) Wayne County	0	0.00
Dearborn Heights (city) Wayne County	0	0.00

West Indian: Bermudan, excluding Hispanic

Top 10 Places Sorted by Population
Based on all places, regardless of total population

Place	Population	%
Pontiac (city) Oakland County	89	0.15
North Branch (village) Lapeer County	24	2.60
North Branch (township) Lapeer County	24	0.65
Jenison (cdp) Ottawa County	18	0.10
Georgetown (charter twp) Ottawa County	18	0.04
Grand Rapids (city) Kent County	12	0.01
Detroit (city) Wayne County	10	<0.01
Acme (township) Grand Traverse County	0	0.00
Ada (township) Kent County	0	0.00
Adams (township) Arenac County	0	0.00

Top 10 Places Sorted by Percent of Total Population
Based on all places, regardless of total population

Place	Population	%
North Branch (village) Lapeer County	24	2.60
North Branch (township) Lapeer County	24	0.65
Pontiac (city) Oakland County	89	0.15
Jenison (cdp) Ottawa County	18	0.10
Georgetown (charter twp) Ottawa County	18	0.04
Grand Rapids (city) Kent County	12	0.01
Detroit (city) Wayne County	10	<0.01

Place	Population	%
Acme (township) Grand Traverse County	0	0.00
Ada (township) Kent County	0	0.00
Adams (township) Arenac County	0	0.00

Top 10 Places Sorted by Percent of Total Population
Based on places with total population of 50,000 or more

Place	Population	%
Pontiac (city) Oakland County	89	0.15
Grand Rapids (city) Kent County	12	0.01
Detroit (city) Wayne County	10	<0.01
Ann Arbor (city) Washtenaw County	0	0.00
Battle Creek (city) Calhoun County	0	0.00
Canton (charter twp) Wayne County	0	0.00
Clinton (charter twp) Macomb County	0	0.00
Dearborn (city) Wayne County	0	0.00
Dearborn Heights (city) Wayne County	0	0.00
Farmington Hills (city) Oakland County	0	0.00

West Indian: British West Indian, excluding Hispanic

Top 10 Places Sorted by Population
Based on all places, regardless of total population

Place	Population	%
Oronoko (charter twp) Berrien County	62	0.67
Farmington Hills (city) Oakland County	47	0.06
Ann Arbor (city) Washtenaw County	35	0.03
Farmington (city) Oakland County	33	0.32
Pittsfield (charter twp) Washtenaw County	20	0.06
Saginaw (city) Saginaw County	16	0.03
Kingsford (city) Dickinson County	14	0.27
Lansing (charter twp) Ingham County	13	0.16
Melvindale (city) Wayne County	13	0.12
Wyoming (city) Kent County	13	0.02

Top 10 Places Sorted by Percent of Total Population
Based on all places, regardless of total population

Place	Population	%
Oronoko (charter twp) Berrien County	62	0.67
Farmington (city) Oakland County	33	0.32
Grout (township) Gladwin County	6	0.28
Kingsford (city) Dickinson County	14	0.27
Lansing (charter twp) Ingham County	13	0.16
Kinross (charter twp) Chippewa County	12	0.15
Melvindale (city) Wayne County	13	0.12
Westwood (cdp) Kalamazoo County	10	0.11
Farmington Hills (city) Oakland County	47	0.06
Pittsfield (charter twp) Washtenaw County	20	0.06

Top 10 Places Sorted by Percent of Total Population
Based on places with total population of 50,000 or more

Place	Population	%
Farmington Hills (city) Oakland County	47	0.06
Ann Arbor (city) Washtenaw County	35	0.03
Saginaw (city) Saginaw County	16	0.03
Wyoming (city) Kent County	13	0.02
Battle Creek (city) Calhoun County	0	0.00
Canton (charter twp) Wayne County	0	0.00
Clinton (charter twp) Macomb County	0	0.00
Dearborn (city) Wayne County	0	0.00
Dearborn Heights (city) Wayne County	0	0.00
Detroit (city) Wayne County	0	0.00

West Indian: Dutch West Indian, excluding Hispanic

Top 10 Places Sorted by Population
Based on all places, regardless of total population

Place	Population	%
Morenci (city) Lenawee County	40	1.66
Zeeland (city) Ottawa County	39	0.70
Kalamo (township) Eaton County	27	1.34
Flint (city) Genesee County	23	0.02
Lee (township) Midland County	22	0.51
Southfield (city) Oakland County	20	0.03
Penn (township) Cass County	17	0.96
Grand Rapids (city) Kent County	14	0.01
Lodi (township) Washtenaw County	13	0.22
Byron Center (cdp) Kent County	12	0.24

Top 10 Places Sorted by Percent of Total Population
Based on all places, regardless of total population

Place	Population	%
Morenci (city) Lenawee County	40	1.66
Kalamo (township) Eaton County	27	1.34
Penn (township) Cass County	17	0.96
Zeeland (city) Ottawa County	39	0.70
Elba (township) Gratiot County	8	0.57
Lee (township) Midland County	22	0.51
Marlette (township) Sanilac County	6	0.33
Byron Center (cdp) Kent County	12	0.24
Benona (township) Oceana County	3	0.23
Lincoln (township) Newaygo County	3	0.23

Top 10 Places Sorted by Percent of Total Population
Based on places with total population of 50,000 or more

Place	Population	%
Southfield (city) Oakland County	20	0.03
Flint (city) Genesee County	23	0.02
Grand Rapids (city) Kent County	14	0.01
Ann Arbor (city) Washtenaw County	0	0.00
Battle Creek (city) Calhoun County	0	0.00
Canton (charter twp) Wayne County	0	0.00
Clinton (charter twp) Macomb County	0	0.00
Dearborn (city) Wayne County	0	0.00
Dearborn Heights (city) Wayne County	0	0.00
Detroit (city) Wayne County	0	0.00

West Indian: Haitian, excluding Hispanic

Top 10 Places Sorted by Population
Based on all places, regardless of total population

Place	Population	%
Pontiac (city) Oakland County	502	0.82
Lansing (city) Ingham County	336	0.29
Oronoko (charter twp) Berrien County	213	2.31
Detroit (city) Wayne County	199	0.03
Ypsilanti (charter twp) Washtenaw County	107	0.20
Warren (city) Macomb County	73	0.05
River Rouge (city) Wayne County	68	0.82
Rochester Hills (city) Oakland County	60	0.08
Southfield (city) Oakland County	55	0.08
Farmington Hills (city) Oakland County	46	0.06

Top 10 Places Sorted by Percent of Total Population
Based on all places, regardless of total population

Place	Population	%
Dimondale (village) Eaton County	45	3.62
Oronoko (charter twp) Berrien County	213	2.31
Carsonville (village) Sanilac County	5	1.25
Pontiac (city) Oakland County	502	0.82
River Rouge (city) Wayne County	68	0.82
Baraga (village) Baraga County	18	0.76
Windsor (charter twp) Eaton County	45	0.65
Utica (city) Macomb County	31	0.65
Berrien Springs (village) Berrien County	13	0.53
South Haven (city) Van Buren County	23	0.51

Top 10 Places Sorted by Percent of Total Population
Based on places with total population of 50,000 or more

Place	Population	%
Pontiac (city) Oakland County	502	0.82
Lansing (city) Ingham County	336	0.29
Ypsilanti (charter twp) Washtenaw County	107	0.20
Rochester Hills (city) Oakland County	60	0.08
Southfield (city) Oakland County	55	0.08
Farmington Hills (city) Oakland County	46	0.06
Warren (city) Macomb County	73	0.05
Canton (charter twp) Wayne County	31	0.04
Detroit (city) Wayne County	199	0.03
Troy (city) Oakland County	28	0.03

West Indian: Jamaican, excluding Hispanic

Top 10 Places Sorted by Population
Based on all places, regardless of total population

Place	Population	%
Detroit (city) Wayne County	1,946	0.26
Southfield (city) Oakland County	461	0.63
Oronoko (charter twp) Berrien County	253	2.74
Lansing (city) Ingham County	194	0.17
Ann Arbor (city) Washtenaw County	181	0.16
Canton (charter twp) Wayne County	180	0.20
Grand Rapids (city) Kent County	160	0.08
Troy (city) Oakland County	156	0.19
Portage (township) Mackinac County	155	18.07
Oak Park (city) Oakland County	142	0.48

Top 10 Places Sorted by Percent of Total Population
Based on all places, regardless of total population

Place	Population	%
Portage (township) Mackinac County	155	18.07
Harvey (cdp) Marquette County	83	5.58
Berrien Springs (village) Berrien County	113	4.58
Alden (cdp) Antrim County	5	3.76
Mackinac Island (city) Mackinac County	12	3.02
Oronoko (charter twp) Berrien County	253	2.74
Wheeler (township) Gratiot County	74	2.64
Penn (township) Cass County	46	2.61
Ford River (township) Delta County	49	2.40
White Cloud (city) Newaygo County	36	2.05

Top 10 Places Sorted by Percent of Total Population
Based on places with total population of 50,000 or more

Place	Population	%
Southfield (city) Oakland County	461	0.63
Detroit (city) Wayne County	1,946	0.26
Canton (charter twp) Wayne County	180	0.20
Pontiac (city) Oakland County	120	0.20
Troy (city) Oakland County	156	0.19
Ypsilanti (charter twp) Washtenaw County	97	0.18
Lansing (city) Ingham County	194	0.17
Ann Arbor (city) Washtenaw County	181	0.16
Westland (city) Wayne County	131	0.15
Wyoming (city) Kent County	91	0.13

West Indian: Trinidadian and Tobagonian, excluding Hispanic

Top 10 Places Sorted by Population
Based on all places, regardless of total population

Place	Population	%
Dearborn (city) Wayne County	155	0.16
Detroit (city) Wayne County	119	0.02
Pontiac (city) Oakland County	77	0.13
Flint (city) Genesee County	76	0.07
Carrollton (township) Saginaw County	67	1.08
Ann Arbor (city) Washtenaw County	58	0.05
Oronoko (charter twp) Berrien County	57	0.62
Battle Creek (city) Calhoun County	50	0.09
Saginaw (city) Saginaw County	39	0.07
East Lansing (city) Ingham County	29	0.06

Top 10 Places Sorted by Percent of Total Population
Based on all places, regardless of total population

Place	Population	%
Carrollton (township) Saginaw County	67	1.08
Oronoko (charter twp) Berrien County	57	0.62
River Rouge (city) Wayne County	19	0.23
Dearborn (city) Wayne County	155	0.16
Houghton (city) Houghton County	12	0.16
Westwood (cdp) Kalamazoo County	14	0.15
Pontiac (city) Oakland County	77	0.13
Hillsdale (city) Hillsdale County	10	0.12
Battle Creek (city) Calhoun County	50	0.09
Ypsilanti (city) Washtenaw County	19	0.09

Top 10 Places Sorted by Percent of Total Population
Based on places with total population of 50,000 or more

Place	Population	%
Dearborn (city) Wayne County	155	0.16
Pontiac (city) Oakland County	77	0.13
Battle Creek (city) Calhoun County	50	0.09
Flint (city) Genesee County	76	0.07
Saginaw (city) Saginaw County	39	0.07
Ann Arbor (city) Washtenaw County	58	0.05
Farmington Hills (city) Oakland County	29	0.04
Southfield (city) Oakland County	26	0.04
Ypsilanti (charter twp) Washtenaw County	14	0.03
Detroit (city) Wayne County	119	0.02

West Indian: U.S. Virgin Islander, excluding Hispanic

Top 10 Places Sorted by Population
Based on all places, regardless of total population

Place	Population	%
Southfield (city) Oakland County	24	0.03
Pontiac (city) Oakland County	20	0.03
Detroit (city) Wayne County	15	<0.01
Spring Arbor (cdp) Jackson County	13	0.59
Spring Arbor (township) Jackson County	13	0.16
Grand Rapids (city) Kent County	11	0.01
Garden City (city) Wayne County	9	0.03
Rochester Hills (city) Oakland County	8	0.01
Niles (township) Berrien County	5	0.04
Custer (township) Antrim County	3	0.27

Top 10 Places Sorted by Percent of Total Population
Based on all places, regardless of total population

Place	Population	%
Spring Arbor (cdp) Jackson County	13	0.59
Custer (township) Antrim County	3	0.27
Spring Arbor (township) Jackson County	13	0.16
Niles (township) Berrien County	5	0.04
Southfield (city) Oakland County	24	0.03
Pontiac (city) Oakland County	20	0.03
Garden City (city) Wayne County	9	0.03
Grand Rapids (city) Kent County	11	0.01
Rochester Hills (city) Oakland County	8	0.01
Detroit (city) Wayne County	15	<0.01

Top 10 Places Sorted by Percent of Total Population
Based on places with total population of 50,000 or more

Place	Population	%
Southfield (city) Oakland County	24	0.03
Pontiac (city) Oakland County	20	0.03
Grand Rapids (city) Kent County	11	0.01
Rochester Hills (city) Oakland County	8	0.01
Detroit (city) Wayne County	15	<0.01
Ann Arbor (city) Washtenaw County	0	0.00
Battle Creek (city) Calhoun County	0	0.00
Canton (charter twp) Wayne County	0	0.00
Clinton (charter twp) Macomb County	0	0.00
Dearborn (city) Wayne County	0	0.00

West Indian: West Indian, excluding Hispanic

Top 10 Places Sorted by Population
Based on all places, regardless of total population

Place	Population	%
Detroit (city) Wayne County	221	0.03
Southfield (city) Oakland County	121	0.17
Grand Rapids (city) Kent County	90	0.05
Westland (city) Wayne County	80	0.09
Ann Arbor (city) Washtenaw County	64	0.06
East Lansing (city) Ingham County	62	0.13
Lansing (charter twp) Ingham County	61	0.74
Taylor (city) Wayne County	56	0.09
Rochester Hills (city) Oakland County	53	0.08
Ypsilanti (charter twp) Washtenaw County	51	0.10

Top 10 Places Sorted by Percent of Total Population
Based on all places, regardless of total population

Place	Population	%
Dimondale (village) Eaton County	18	1.45
Leroy (township) Calhoun County	40	1.10
Lansing (charter twp) Ingham County	61	0.74
Kalamo (township) Eaton County	14	0.70
Oronoko (charter twp) Berrien County	45	0.49
St. Ignace (city) Mackinac County	12	0.46
Milford (village) Oakland County	27	0.44
Beverly Hills (village) Oakland County	31	0.30
Windsor (charter twp) Eaton County	18	0.26
Mount Clemens (city) Macomb County	41	0.25

Top 10 Places Sorted by Percent of Total Population
Based on places with total population of 50,000 or more

Place	Population	%
Southfield (city) Oakland County	121	0.17

Please refer to the Explanation of Data in the front of the book for more detailed information.

Place	Population	%
Ypsilanti (charter twp) Washtenaw County	51	0.10
Westland (city) Wayne County	80	0.09
Taylor (city) Wayne County	56	0.09
Rochester Hills (city) Oakland County	53	0.08
Ann Arbor (city) Washtenaw County	64	0.06
Grand Rapids (city) Kent County	90	0.05
Shelby (charter twp) Macomb County	29	0.04
Detroit (city) Wayne County	221	0.03
Flint (city) Genesee County	24	0.02

West Indian: Other, excluding Hispanic

Top 10 Places Sorted by Population
Based on all places, regardless of total population

Place	Population	%
Lansing (city) Ingham County	16	0.01
Oronoko (charter twp) Berrien County	9	0.10
Grand Rapids (city) Kent County	9	<0.01
Evart (township) Osceola County	5	0.34
Niles (township) Berrien County	3	0.02
Acme (township) Grand Traverse County	0	0.00
Ada (township) Kent County	0	0.00
Adams (township) Arenac County	0	0.00
Adams (township) Hillsdale County	0	0.00
Adams (township) Houghton County	0	0.00

Top 10 Places Sorted by Percent of Total Population
Based on all places, regardless of total population

Place	Population	%
Evart (township) Osceola County	5	0.34
Oronoko (charter twp) Berrien County	9	0.10
Niles (township) Berrien County	3	0.02
Lansing (city) Ingham County	16	0.01
Grand Rapids (city) Kent County	9	<0.01
Acme (township) Grand Traverse County	0	0.00
Ada (township) Kent County	0	0.00
Adams (township) Arenac County	0	0.00
Adams (township) Hillsdale County	0	0.00
Adams (township) Houghton County	0	0.00

Top 10 Places Sorted by Percent of Total Population
Based on places with total population of 50,000 or more

Place	Population	%
Lansing (city) Ingham County	16	0.01
Grand Rapids (city) Kent County	9	<0.01
Ann Arbor (city) Washtenaw County	0	0.00
Battle Creek (city) Calhoun County	0	0.00
Canton (charter twp) Wayne County	0	0.00
Clinton (charter twp) Macomb County	0	0.00
Dearborn (city) Wayne County	0	0.00
Dearborn Heights (city) Wayne County	0	0.00
Detroit (city) Wayne County	0	0.00
Farmington Hills (city) Oakland County	0	0.00

Yugoslavian

Top 10 Places Sorted by Population
Based on all places, regardless of total population

Place	Population	%
Sterling Heights (city) Macomb County	1,665	1.28
Kentwood (city) Kent County	1,378	2.86
Hamtramck (city) Wayne County	1,162	5.14
Macomb (township) Macomb County	1,041	1.39
Warren (city) Macomb County	990	0.73
Clinton (charter twp) Macomb County	850	0.87
Shelby (charter twp) Macomb County	638	0.88
Grand Rapids (city) Kent County	492	0.26
Farmington Hills (city) Oakland County	374	0.47
Harrison (charter twp) Macomb County	373	1.51

Top 10 Places Sorted by Percent of Total Population
Based on all places, regardless of total population

Place	Population	%
Waverly (township) Cheboygan County	23	5.28
Hamtramck (city) Wayne County	1,162	5.14
Sherman (township) Keweenaw County	4	4.49
Vicksburg (village) Kalamazoo County	93	3.22
Stony Point (cdp) Monroe County	56	3.13
Kentwood (city) Kent County	1,378	2.86
Addison (township) Oakland County	148	2.33
Meade (township) Mason County	2	2.11

Place	Population	%
Lodi (township) Washtenaw County	122	2.02
Little Traverse (township) Emmet County	44	1.87

Top 10 Places Sorted by Percent of Total Population
Based on places with total population of 50,000 or more

Place	Population	%
Macomb (township) Macomb County	1,041	1.39
Sterling Heights (city) Macomb County	1,665	1.28
Shelby (charter twp) Macomb County	638	0.88
Clinton (charter twp) Macomb County	850	0.87
Warren (city) Macomb County	990	0.73
Dearborn Heights (city) Wayne County	279	0.48
Farmington Hills (city) Oakland County	374	0.47
Troy (city) Oakland County	338	0.42
Wyoming (city) Kent County	299	0.42
Livonia (city) Wayne County	343	0.35

Hispanic Origin Rankings

Hispanic or Latino (of any race)

Top 10 Places Sorted by Population
Based on all places, regardless of total population

Place	Population	%
Detroit (city) Wayne County	48,679	6.82
Grand Rapids (city) Kent County	29,261	15.56
Lansing (city) Ingham County	14,292	12.50
Wyoming (city) Kent County	14,010	19.42
Pontiac (city) Oakland County	9,835	16.53
Holland (charter twp) Ottawa County	8,347	23.42
Holland (city) Ottawa County	7,512	22.73
Saginaw (city) Saginaw County	7,344	14.26
Lincoln Park (city) Wayne County	5,676	14.88
Kalamazoo (city) Kalamazoo County	4,736	6.38

Top 10 Places Sorted by Percent of Total Population
Based on all places, regardless of total population

Place	Population	%
Shelby (village) Oceana County	942	45.62
Fennville (city) Allegan County	547	39.13
Clyde (township) Allegan County	718	34.45
Covert (township) Van Buren County	881	30.51
Hartford (city) Van Buren County	793	29.50
Imlay City (city) Lapeer County	1,042	28.97
Shelby (township) Oceana County	1,150	28.26
Breedsville (village) Van Buren County	56	28.14
Lee (township) Allegan County	1,121	27.92
Lawrence (village) Van Buren County	271	27.21

Top 10 Places Sorted by Percent of Total Population
Based on places with total population of 50,000 or more

Place	Population	%
Wyoming (city) Kent County	14,010	19.42
Pontiac (city) Oakland County	9,835	16.53
Grand Rapids (city) Kent County	29,261	15.56
Saginaw (city) Saginaw County	7,344	14.26
Lansing (city) Ingham County	14,292	12.50
Detroit (city) Wayne County	48,679	6.82
Battle Creek (city) Calhoun County	3,517	6.72
Kalamazoo (city) Kalamazoo County	4,736	6.38
Waterford (charter twp) Oakland County	4,557	6.36
Taylor (city) Wayne County	3,209	5.08

Central American, excluding Mexican

Top 10 Places Sorted by Population
Based on all places, regardless of total population

Place	Population	%
Grand Rapids (city) Kent County	4,051	2.15
Detroit (city) Wayne County	1,813	0.25
Wyoming (city) Kent County	1,109	1.54
Ypsilanti (charter twp) Washtenaw County	473	0.89
Pontiac (city) Oakland County	457	0.77
Ann Arbor (city) Washtenaw County	394	0.35
Pittsfield (charter twp) Washtenaw County	345	1.00
Kentwood (city) Kent County	273	0.56
Lansing (city) Ingham County	211	0.18
Troy (city) Oakland County	210	0.26

Top 10 Places Sorted by Percent of Total Population
Based on all places, regardless of total population

Place	Population	%
Chandler (township) Charlevoix County	7	2.82
Grand Rapids (city) Kent County	4,051	2.15
Daggett (village) Menominee County	4	1.55
Wyoming (city) Kent County	1,109	1.54
Shelby (village) Oceana County	29	1.40
Oronoko (charter twp) Berrien County	109	1.19
Spurr (township) Baraga County	3	1.09
Berrien Springs (village) Berrien County	19	1.06
Banks (township) Antrim County	17	1.06
Pittsfield (charter twp) Washtenaw County	345	1.00

Top 10 Places Sorted by Percent of Total Population
Based on places with total population of 50,000 or more

Place	Population	%
Grand Rapids (city) Kent County	4,051	2.15
Wyoming (city) Kent County	1,109	1.54
Ypsilanti (charter twp) Washtenaw County	473	0.89
Pontiac (city) Oakland County	457	0.77
Ann Arbor (city) Washtenaw County	394	0.35
Troy (city) Oakland County	210	0.26
Novi (city) Oakland County	141	0.26
Detroit (city) Wayne County	1,813	0.25
Kalamazoo (city) Kalamazoo County	160	0.22
Lansing (city) Ingham County	211	0.18

Central American: Costa Rican

Top 10 Places Sorted by Population
Based on all places, regardless of total population

Place	Population	%
Ypsilanti (charter twp) Washtenaw County	65	0.12
Pittsfield (charter twp) Washtenaw County	50	0.14
Ann Arbor (city) Washtenaw County	43	0.04
Detroit (city) Wayne County	33	<0.01
Grand Rapids (city) Kent County	20	0.01
Lansing (city) Ingham County	19	0.02
Oronoko (charter twp) Berrien County	16	0.17
Waterford (charter twp) Oakland County	16	0.02
Canton (charter twp) Wayne County	13	0.01
Sterling Heights (city) Macomb County	13	0.01

Top 10 Places Sorted by Percent of Total Population
Based on all places, regardless of total population

Place	Population	%
Spurr (township) Baraga County	3	1.09
Woodbridge (township) Hillsdale County	4	0.30
Buckley (village) Wexford County	2	0.29
Brooklyn (village) Jackson County	3	0.25
Coleman (city) Midland County	3	0.24
Limestone (township) Alger County	1	0.23
Vicksburg (village) Kalamazoo County	6	0.21
Chums Corner (cdp) Grand Traverse County	2	0.21
Mackinac Island (city) Mackinac County	1	0.20
Oronoko (charter twp) Berrien County	16	0.17

Top 10 Places Sorted by Percent of Total Population
Based on places with total population of 50,000 or more

Place	Population	%
Ypsilanti (charter twp) Washtenaw County	65	0.12
Ann Arbor (city) Washtenaw County	43	0.04
Lansing (city) Ingham County	19	0.02
Waterford (charter twp) Oakland County	16	0.02
Dearborn Heights (city) Wayne County	11	0.02
Rochester Hills (city) Oakland County	11	0.02
Battle Creek (city) Calhoun County	8	0.02
Grand Rapids (city) Kent County	20	0.01
Canton (charter twp) Wayne County	13	0.01
Sterling Heights (city) Macomb County	13	0.01

Central American: Guatemalan

Top 10 Places Sorted by Population
Based on all places, regardless of total population

Place	Population	%
Grand Rapids (city) Kent County	3,372	1.79
Wyoming (city) Kent County	698	0.97
Detroit (city) Wayne County	542	0.08
Ann Arbor (city) Washtenaw County	130	0.11
Ypsilanti (charter twp) Washtenaw County	104	0.19
Kentwood (city) Kent County	102	0.21
Novi (city) Oakland County	92	0.17
Lansing (city) Ingham County	86	0.08
Kalamazoo (city) Kalamazoo County	73	0.10
Pittsfield (charter twp) Washtenaw County	68	0.20

Top 10 Places Sorted by Percent of Total Population
Based on all places, regardless of total population

Place	Population	%
Grand Rapids (city) Kent County	3,372	1.79
Daggett (village) Menominee County	4	1.55
Shelby (village) Oceana County	26	1.26
Banks (township) Antrim County	17	1.06
Wyoming (city) Kent County	698	0.97
Eagle (village) Clinton County	1	0.81
Torch Lake (township) Antrim County	9	0.75
Clam Union (township) Missaukee County	6	0.68
Shelby (township) Oceana County	27	0.66
Parchment (city) Kalamazoo County	11	0.61

Top 10 Places Sorted by Percent of Total Population
Based on places with total population of 50,000 or more

Place	Population	%
Grand Rapids (city) Kent County	3,372	1.79
Wyoming (city) Kent County	698	0.97
Ypsilanti (charter twp) Washtenaw County	104	0.19
Novi (city) Oakland County	92	0.17
Ann Arbor (city) Washtenaw County	130	0.11
Kalamazoo (city) Kalamazoo County	73	0.10
Detroit (city) Wayne County	542	0.08
Lansing (city) Ingham County	86	0.08
Livonia (city) Wayne County	49	0.05
Macomb (township) Macomb County	43	0.05

Central American: Honduran

Top 10 Places Sorted by Population
Based on all places, regardless of total population

Place	Population	%
Detroit (city) Wayne County	566	0.08
Grand Rapids (city) Kent County	197	0.10
Pontiac (city) Oakland County	147	0.25
Wyoming (city) Kent County	138	0.19
Pittsfield (charter twp) Washtenaw County	123	0.35
Ypsilanti (charter twp) Washtenaw County	110	0.21
Kentwood (city) Kent County	58	0.12
Ann Arbor (city) Washtenaw County	54	0.05
Holland (city) Ottawa County	46	0.14
Lansing (city) Ingham County	39	0.03

Top 10 Places Sorted by Percent of Total Population
Based on all places, regardless of total population

Place	Population	%
Chandler (township) Charlevoix County	7	2.82
Springdale (township) Manistee County	4	0.51
Fruitport (village) Muskegon County	5	0.46
Geneva (township) Midland County	4	0.38
Northport (village) Leelanau County	2	0.38
Pittsfield (charter twp) Washtenaw County	123	0.35
New Lothrop (village) Shiawassee County	2	0.34
Burdell (township) Osceola County	4	0.30
Bangor (township) Van Buren County	6	0.28
Berrien Springs (village) Berrien County	5	0.28

Top 10 Places Sorted by Percent of Total Population
Based on places with total population of 50,000 or more

Place	Population	%
Pontiac (city) Oakland County	147	0.25
Ypsilanti (charter twp) Washtenaw County	110	0.21
Wyoming (city) Kent County	138	0.19
Grand Rapids (city) Kent County	197	0.10
Detroit (city) Wayne County	566	0.08
Ann Arbor (city) Washtenaw County	54	0.05
Waterford (charter twp) Oakland County	26	0.04
Lansing (city) Ingham County	39	0.03
Canton (charter twp) Wayne County	28	0.03
Kalamazoo (city) Kalamazoo County	18	0.02

Central American: Nicaraguan

Top 10 Places Sorted by Population
Based on all places, regardless of total population

Place	Population	%
Detroit (city) Wayne County	69	0.01
Grand Rapids (city) Kent County	45	0.02
Ann Arbor (city) Washtenaw County	41	0.04
Holland (charter twp) Ottawa County	33	0.09
Wyoming (city) Kent County	26	0.04
Oronoko (charter twp) Berrien County	23	0.25
Holland (city) Ottawa County	18	0.05
Pittsfield (charter twp) Washtenaw County	17	0.05
Taylor (city) Wayne County	17	0.03
Dearborn Heights (city) Wayne County	16	0.03

Top 10 Places Sorted by Percent of Total Population
Based on all places, regardless of total population

Place	Population	%
Alden (cdp) Antrim County	1	0.80
Meade (township) Mason County	1	0.55
Baroda (village) Berrien County	3	0.34
Wawatam (township) Emmet County	2	0.30
Albion (township) Calhoun County	3	0.27
Oronoko (charter twp) Berrien County	23	0.25
Mackinaw City (village) Emmet County	2	0.25
Perrinton (village) Gratiot County	1	0.25
Bertrand (township) Berrien County	6	0.23
Bates (township) Iron County	2	0.22

Top 10 Places Sorted by Percent of Total Population
Based on places with total population of 50,000 or more

Place	Population	%
Ann Arbor (city) Washtenaw County	41	0.04
Wyoming (city) Kent County	26	0.04
Taylor (city) Wayne County	17	0.03
Dearborn Heights (city) Wayne County	16	0.03
Ypsilanti (charter twp) Washtenaw County	15	0.03
Grand Rapids (city) Kent County	45	0.02
Westland (city) Wayne County	14	0.02
Farmington Hills (city) Oakland County	12	0.02
Royal Oak (city) Oakland County	9	0.02
Detroit (city) Wayne County	69	0.01

Central American: Panamanian

Top 10 Places Sorted by Population
Based on all places, regardless of total population

Place	Population	%
Detroit (city) Wayne County	124	0.02
Ann Arbor (city) Washtenaw County	52	0.05
Grand Rapids (city) Kent County	35	0.02
Ypsilanti (charter twp) Washtenaw County	33	0.06
Kalamazoo (city) Kalamazoo County	27	0.04
Lansing (city) Ingham County	26	0.02
Canton (charter twp) Wayne County	23	0.03
Oronoko (charter twp) Berrien County	22	0.24
Pontiac (city) Oakland County	20	0.03
Southfield (city) Oakland County	20	0.03

Top 10 Places Sorted by Percent of Total Population
Based on all places, regardless of total population

Place	Population	%
Deckerville (village) Sanilac County	3	0.36
Sanford (village) Midland County	3	0.35
Vermontville (township) Eaton County	6	0.29
Middlebury (township) Shiawassee County	4	0.26
Yates (township) Lake County	2	0.26
Oronoko (charter twp) Berrien County	22	0.24
Lamotte (township) Sanilac County	2	0.22
Wolverine Lake (village) Oakland County	8	0.19
Whitewater (township) Grand Traverse County	5	0.19
Jonesville (village) Hillsdale County	4	0.18

Top 10 Places Sorted by Percent of Total Population
Based on places with total population of 50,000 or more

Place	Population	%
Ypsilanti (charter twp) Washtenaw County	33	0.06
Ann Arbor (city) Washtenaw County	52	0.05
Kalamazoo (city) Kalamazoo County	27	0.04
Canton (charter twp) Wayne County	23	0.03

Pontiac (city) Oakland County	20	0.03
Southfield (city) Oakland County	20	0.03
Detroit (city) Wayne County	124	0.02
Grand Rapids (city) Kent County	35	0.02
Lansing (city) Ingham County	26	0.02
Flint (city) Genesee County	18	0.02

Central American: Salvadoran

Top 10 Places Sorted by Population
Based on all places, regardless of total population

Place	Population	%
Detroit (city) Wayne County	451	0.06
Grand Rapids (city) Kent County	348	0.19
Pontiac (city) Oakland County	266	0.45
Wyoming (city) Kent County	235	0.33
Troy (city) Oakland County	156	0.19
Ypsilanti (charter twp) Washtenaw County	139	0.26
Kentwood (city) Kent County	88	0.18
Ann Arbor (city) Washtenaw County	74	0.06
Pittsfield (charter twp) Washtenaw County	64	0.18
Holland (charter twp) Ottawa County	58	0.16

Top 10 Places Sorted by Percent of Total Population
Based on all places, regardless of total population

Place	Population	%
Pontiac (city) Oakland County	266	0.45
Wixom (city) Oakland County	54	0.40
Lake Linden (village) Houghton County	4	0.40
Wilcox (township) Newaygo County	4	0.36
Port Sheldon (township) Ottawa County	15	0.35
Wyoming (city) Kent County	235	0.33
Superior (charter twp) Washtenaw County	43	0.33
Clawson (city) Oakland County	37	0.31
Ypsilanti (charter twp) Washtenaw County	139	0.26
Oronoko (charter twp) Berrien County	23	0.25

Top 10 Places Sorted by Percent of Total Population
Based on places with total population of 50,000 or more

Place	Population	%
Pontiac (city) Oakland County	266	0.45
Wyoming (city) Kent County	235	0.33
Ypsilanti (charter twp) Washtenaw County	139	0.26
Grand Rapids (city) Kent County	348	0.19
Troy (city) Oakland County	156	0.19
Detroit (city) Wayne County	451	0.06
Ann Arbor (city) Washtenaw County	74	0.06
Waterford (charter twp) Oakland County	38	0.05
Dearborn Heights (city) Wayne County	28	0.05
Kalamazoo (city) Kalamazoo County	32	0.04

Central American: Other Central American

Top 10 Places Sorted by Population
Based on all places, regardless of total population

Place	Population	%
Grand Rapids (city) Kent County	34	0.02
Detroit (city) Wayne County	28	<0.01
Ypsilanti (charter twp) Washtenaw County	7	0.01
Pittsfield (charter twp) Washtenaw County	6	0.02
Novi (city) Oakland County	6	0.01
Walled Lake (city) Oakland County	4	0.06
Brighton (city) Livingston County	4	0.05
Lansing (city) Ingham County	4	<0.01
Delhi (charter twp) Ingham County	3	0.01
Holt (cdp) Ingham County	3	0.01

Top 10 Places Sorted by Percent of Total Population
Based on all places, regardless of total population

Place	Population	%
Leland (cdp) Leelanau County	1	0.27
Northport (village) Leelanau County	1	0.19
Newberry (village) Luce County	1	0.07
Walled Lake (city) Oakland County	4	0.06
Brighton (city) Livingston County	4	0.05
Leelanau (township) Leelanau County	1	0.05
Leland (township) Leelanau County	1	0.05
McMillan (township) Luce County	1	0.04
Pipestone (township) Berrien County	1	0.04
Bear Creek (township) Emmet County	2	0.03

Top 10 Places Sorted by Percent of Total Population
Based on places with total population of 50,000 or more

Place	Population	%
Grand Rapids (city) Kent County	34	0.02
Ypsilanti (charter twp) Washtenaw County	7	0.01
Novi (city) Oakland County	6	0.01
Detroit (city) Wayne County	28	<0.01
Lansing (city) Ingham County	4	<0.01
Warren (city) Macomb County	3	<0.01
Canton (charter twp) Wayne County	2	<0.01
Farmington Hills (city) Oakland County	1	<0.01
Livonia (city) Wayne County	1	<0.01
Royal Oak (city) Oakland County	1	<0.01

Cuban

Top 10 Places Sorted by Population
Based on all places, regardless of total population

Place	Population	%
Lansing (city) Ingham County	1,193	1.04
Detroit (city) Wayne County	773	0.11
Wyoming (city) Kent County	747	1.04
Grand Rapids (city) Kent County	417	0.22
Ann Arbor (city) Washtenaw County	226	0.20
Delta (charter twp) Eaton County	167	0.52
Kentwood (city) Kent County	151	0.31
Waverly (cdp) Eaton County	143	0.60
Holland (charter twp) Ottawa County	123	0.35
Kalamazoo (city) Kalamazoo County	108	0.15

Top 10 Places Sorted by Percent of Total Population
Based on all places, regardless of total population

Place	Population	%
Maple Grove (cdp) Benzie County	3	2.27
Michiana (village) Berrien County	3	1.65
Lansing (charter twp) Ingham County	97	1.19
Lansing (city) Ingham County	1,193	1.04
Wyoming (city) Kent County	747	1.04
Edgemont Park (cdp) Ingham County	23	0.98
Kaleva (village) Manistee County	4	0.85
Beechwood (cdp) Ottawa County	24	0.80
Ravenna (village) Muskegon County	8	0.66
Grandville (city) Kent County	99	0.64

Top 10 Places Sorted by Percent of Total Population
Based on places with total population of 50,000 or more

Place	Population	%
Lansing (city) Ingham County	1,193	1.04
Wyoming (city) Kent County	747	1.04
Grand Rapids (city) Kent County	417	0.22
Ann Arbor (city) Washtenaw County	226	0.20
Kalamazoo (city) Kalamazoo County	108	0.15
Royal Oak (city) Oakland County	68	0.12
Ypsilanti (charter twp) Washtenaw County	65	0.12
Detroit (city) Wayne County	773	0.11
Canton (charter twp) Wayne County	98	0.11
Westland (city) Wayne County	94	0.11

Dominican Republic

Top 10 Places Sorted by Population
Based on all places, regardless of total population

Place	Population	%
Grand Rapids (city) Kent County	1,342	0.71
Detroit (city) Wayne County	688	0.10
Wyoming (city) Kent County	543	0.75
Kentwood (city) Kent County	308	0.63
Kalamazoo (city) Kalamazoo County	189	0.25
Oronoko (charter twp) Berrien County	97	1.06
Ann Arbor (city) Washtenaw County	78	0.07
Lincoln Park (city) Wayne County	65	0.17
Lansing (city) Ingham County	56	0.05
Melvindale (city) Wayne County	42	0.39

Top 10 Places Sorted by Percent of Total Population
Based on all places, regardless of total population

Place	Population	%
Oronoko (charter twp) Berrien County	97	1.06
Berrien Springs (village) Berrien County	15	0.83
Wyoming (city) Kent County	543	0.75

Grand Rapids (city) Kent County	1,342	0.71
Kentwood (city) Kent County	308	0.63
Clarksville (village) Ionia County	2	0.51
Centerville (township) Leelanau County	6	0.47
Melvindale (city) Wayne County	42	0.39
Berrien (township) Berrien County	16	0.31
Hillman (township) Montmorency County	6	0.28

Top 10 Places Sorted by Percent of Total Population
Based on places with total population of 50,000 or more

Place	Population	%
Wyoming (city) Kent County	543	0.75
Grand Rapids (city) Kent County	1,342	0.71
Kalamazoo (city) Kalamazoo County	189	0.25
Detroit (city) Wayne County	688	0.10
Ann Arbor (city) Washtenaw County	78	0.07
Lansing (city) Ingham County	56	0.05
Battle Creek (city) Calhoun County	26	0.05
Pontiac (city) Oakland County	25	0.04
Novi (city) Oakland County	22	0.04
Warren (city) Macomb County	42	0.03

Mexican

Top 10 Places Sorted by Population
Based on all places, regardless of total population

Place	Population	%
Detroit (city) Wayne County	36,452	5.11
Grand Rapids (city) Kent County	18,698	9.94
Lansing (city) Ingham County	10,870	9.51
Wyoming (city) Kent County	9,419	13.06
Holland (charter twp) Ottawa County	6,950	19.50
Pontiac (city) Oakland County	6,605	11.10
Saginaw (city) Saginaw County	6,487	12.59
Holland (city) Ottawa County	6,241	18.88
Lincoln Park (city) Wayne County	4,696	12.31
Kalamazoo (city) Kalamazoo County	3,430	4.62

Top 10 Places Sorted by Percent of Total Population
Based on all places, regardless of total population

Place	Population	%
Shelby (village) Oceana County	849	41.11
Fennville (city) Allegan County	516	36.91
Clyde (township) Allegan County	673	32.29
Breedsville (village) Van Buren County	56	28.14
Covert (township) Van Buren County	808	27.98
Hartford (city) Van Buren County	720	26.79
Imlay City (city) Lapeer County	943	26.22
Lawrence (village) Van Buren County	254	25.50
Shelby (township) Oceana County	1,034	25.41
Lee (township) Allegan County	1,005	25.03

Top 10 Places Sorted by Percent of Total Population
Based on places with total population of 50,000 or more

Place	Population	%
Wyoming (city) Kent County	9,419	13.06
Saginaw (city) Saginaw County	6,487	12.59
Pontiac (city) Oakland County	6,605	11.10
Grand Rapids (city) Kent County	18,698	9.94
Lansing (city) Ingham County	10,870	9.51
Battle Creek (city) Calhoun County	2,713	5.18
Detroit (city) Wayne County	36,452	5.11
Kalamazoo (city) Kalamazoo County	3,430	4.62
Waterford (charter twp) Oakland County	3,316	4.62
Taylor (city) Wayne County	2,344	3.71

Puerto Rican

Top 10 Places Sorted by Population
Based on all places, regardless of total population

Place	Population	%
Detroit (city) Wayne County	5,783	0.81
Grand Rapids (city) Kent County	2,712	1.44
Pontiac (city) Oakland County	2,309	3.88
Wyoming (city) Kent County	1,460	2.02
Lansing (city) Ingham County	701	0.61
Waterford (charter twp) Oakland County	639	0.89
Kentwood (city) Kent County	532	1.09
Lincoln Park (city) Wayne County	514	1.35
Ann Arbor (city) Washtenaw County	466	0.41
Holland (city) Ottawa County	450	1.36

Top 10 Places Sorted by Percent of Total Population
Based on all places, regardless of total population

Place	Population	%
Pontiac (city) Oakland County	2,309	3.88
Morley (village) Mecosta County	12	2.43
Melvindale (city) Wayne County	243	2.27
Wyoming (city) Kent County	1,460	2.02
Novi (township) Oakland County	3	2.00
Eau Claire (village) Berrien County	12	1.92
Berrien Springs (village) Berrien County	33	1.83
Oronoko (charter twp) Berrien County	152	1.65
Attica (cdp) Lapeer County	16	1.61
Copemish (village) Manistee County	3	1.55

Top 10 Places Sorted by Percent of Total Population
Based on places with total population of 50,000 or more

Place	Population	%
Pontiac (city) Oakland County	2,309	3.88
Wyoming (city) Kent County	1,460	2.02
Grand Rapids (city) Kent County	2,712	1.44
Waterford (charter twp) Oakland County	639	0.89
Detroit (city) Wayne County	5,783	0.81
Taylor (city) Wayne County	446	0.71
Lansing (city) Ingham County	701	0.61
Dearborn Heights (city) Wayne County	352	0.61
Battle Creek (city) Calhoun County	245	0.47
Kalamazoo (city) Kalamazoo County	340	0.46

South American

Top 10 Places Sorted by Population
Based on all places, regardless of total population

Place	Population	%
Ann Arbor (city) Washtenaw County	963	0.85
Grand Rapids (city) Kent County	337	0.18
Detroit (city) Wayne County	337	0.05
Rochester Hills (city) Oakland County	319	0.45
Troy (city) Oakland County	262	0.32
Lansing (city) Ingham County	251	0.22
Pittsfield (charter twp) Washtenaw County	216	0.62
Oronoko (charter twp) Berrien County	205	2.23
Farmington Hills (city) Oakland County	204	0.26
Canton (charter twp) Wayne County	196	0.22

Top 10 Places Sorted by Percent of Total Population
Based on all places, regardless of total population

Place	Population	%
Barton Hills (village) Washtenaw County	10	3.40
Berrien Springs (village) Berrien County	42	2.33
Oronoko (charter twp) Berrien County	205	2.23
Sherman (township) Keweenaw County	1	1.49
Shoreham (village) Berrien County	11	1.28
Oscoda (cdp) Iosco County	10	1.11
Sand Lake (village) Kent County	5	1.00
Berrien (township) Berrien County	48	0.94
Dexter (village) Washtenaw County	38	0.93
Honor (village) Benzie County	3	0.91

Top 10 Places Sorted by Percent of Total Population
Based on places with total population of 50,000 or more

Place	Population	%
Ann Arbor (city) Washtenaw County	963	0.85
Rochester Hills (city) Oakland County	319	0.45
Troy (city) Oakland County	262	0.32
Royal Oak (city) Oakland County	168	0.29
Farmington Hills (city) Oakland County	204	0.26
West Bloomfield (charter twp) Oakland County	162	0.25
Novi (city) Oakland County	131	0.24
Lansing (city) Ingham County	251	0.22
Canton (charter twp) Wayne County	196	0.22
Shelby (charter twp) Macomb County	163	0.22

South American: Argentinean

Top 10 Places Sorted by Population
Based on all places, regardless of total population

Place	Population	%
Ann Arbor (city) Washtenaw County	169	0.15
Rochester Hills (city) Oakland County	132	0.19
Farmington Hills (city) Oakland County	60	0.08

Livonia (city) Wayne County	51	0.05
Midland (city) Midland County	46	0.11
Kalamazoo (city) Kalamazoo County	42	0.06
Troy (city) Oakland County	42	0.05
Grand Rapids (city) Kent County	41	0.02
Detroit (city) Wayne County	41	0.01
Bloomfield (charter twp) Oakland County	39	0.09

Top 10 Places Sorted by Percent of Total Population
Based on all places, regardless of total population

Place	Population	%
Quincy (township) Houghton County	2	0.74
Michiana (village) Berrien County	1	0.55
Chandler (township) Huron County	2	0.42
Barton Hills (village) Washtenaw County	1	0.34
Berrien Springs (village) Berrien County	6	0.33
Cleveland (township) Leelanau County	3	0.29
Oronoko (charter twp) Berrien County	24	0.26
Trowbridge Park (cdp) Marquette County	5	0.23
Hardwood Acres (cdp) Benzie County	1	0.23
Milan (city) Washtenaw County	12	0.21

Top 10 Places Sorted by Percent of Total Population
Based on places with total population of 50,000 or more

Place	Population	%
Rochester Hills (city) Oakland County	132	0.19
Ann Arbor (city) Washtenaw County	169	0.15
Farmington Hills (city) Oakland County	60	0.08
Kalamazoo (city) Kalamazoo County	42	0.06
Royal Oak (city) Oakland County	33	0.06
Livonia (city) Wayne County	51	0.05
Troy (city) Oakland County	42	0.05
Shelby (charter twp) Macomb County	37	0.05
West Bloomfield (charter twp) Oakland County	34	0.05
Canton (charter twp) Wayne County	35	0.04

South American: Bolivian

Top 10 Places Sorted by Population
Based on all places, regardless of total population

Place	Population	%
Ann Arbor (city) Washtenaw County	46	0.04
Grand Rapids (city) Kent County	21	0.01
Kentwood (city) Kent County	19	0.04
Northville (township) Wayne County	13	0.05
Lansing (city) Ingham County	12	0.01
Delta (charter twp) Eaton County	11	0.03
Scio (township) Washtenaw County	10	0.05
Plainfield (charter twp) Kent County	10	0.03
Farmington Hills (city) Oakland County	10	0.01
Saginaw (charter twp) Saginaw County	9	0.02

Top 10 Places Sorted by Percent of Total Population
Based on all places, regardless of total population

Place	Population	%
Sand Lake (village) Kent County	3	0.60
Pleasant Plains (township) Lake County	3	0.19
Elmira (township) Otsego County	3	0.18
Baldwin (village) Lake County	2	0.17
Berrien (township) Berrien County	8	0.16
Ann Arbor (charter twp) Washtenaw County	6	0.14
Krakow (township) Presque Isle County	1	0.14
Burr Oak (village) St. Joseph County	1	0.12
Nelson (township) Kent County	5	0.10
Burlington (township) Calhoun County	2	0.10

Top 10 Places Sorted by Percent of Total Population
Based on places with total population of 50,000 or more

Place	Population	%
Ann Arbor (city) Washtenaw County	46	0.04
Grand Rapids (city) Kent County	21	0.01
Lansing (city) Ingham County	12	0.01
Farmington Hills (city) Oakland County	10	0.01
Livonia (city) Wayne County	9	0.01
Sterling Heights (city) Macomb County	9	0.01
Westland (city) Wayne County	8	0.01
Canton (charter twp) Wayne County	7	0.01
Kalamazoo (city) Kalamazoo County	7	0.01
Troy (city) Oakland County	5	0.01

South American: Chilean

Top 10 Places Sorted by Population
Based on all places, regardless of total population

Place	Population	%
Ann Arbor (city) Washtenaw County	87	0.08
Holland (charter twp) Ottawa County	43	0.12
Holland (city) Ottawa County	36	0.11
Oronoko (charter twp) Berrien County	31	0.34
Rochester Hills (city) Oakland County	31	0.04
Warren (city) Macomb County	25	0.02
Grand Rapids (city) Kent County	25	0.01
Detroit (city) Wayne County	24	<0.01
West Bloomfield (charter twp) Oakland County	23	0.04
Grosse Pointe Park (city) Wayne County	19	0.16

Top 10 Places Sorted by Percent of Total Population
Based on all places, regardless of total population

Place	Population	%
Shoreham (village) Berrien County	4	0.46
Cleveland (township) Leelanau County	4	0.39
Wexford (township) Wexford County	4	0.37
Oronoko (charter twp) Berrien County	31	0.34
Boyne Valley (township) Charlevoix County	4	0.33
Berrien (township) Berrien County	14	0.28
Penn (township) Cass County	4	0.23
Berrien Springs (village) Berrien County	4	0.22
Onsted (village) Lenawee County	2	0.22
Caledonia (village) Kent County	3	0.20

Top 10 Places Sorted by Percent of Total Population
Based on places with total population of 50,000 or more

Place	Population	%
Ann Arbor (city) Washtenaw County	87	0.08
Rochester Hills (city) Oakland County	31	0.04
West Bloomfield (charter twp) Oakland County	23	0.04
Waterford (charter twp) Oakland County	18	0.03
Warren (city) Macomb County	25	0.02
Royal Oak (city) Oakland County	14	0.02
Shelby (charter twp) Macomb County	14	0.02
Troy (city) Oakland County	13	0.02
Novi (city) Oakland County	9	0.02
Grand Rapids (city) Kent County	25	0.01

South American: Colombian

Top 10 Places Sorted by Population
Based on all places, regardless of total population

Place	Population	%
Ann Arbor (city) Washtenaw County	292	0.26
Detroit (city) Wayne County	101	0.01
Grand Rapids (city) Kent County	99	0.05
Canton (charter twp) Wayne County	79	0.09
Lansing (city) Ingham County	78	0.07
Troy (city) Oakland County	77	0.10
Pittsfield (charter twp) Washtenaw County	72	0.21
East Lansing (city) Ingham County	70	0.14
Scio (township) Washtenaw County	62	0.31
Farmington Hills (city) Oakland County	60	0.08

Top 10 Places Sorted by Percent of Total Population
Based on all places, regardless of total population

Place	Population	%
Berrien Springs (village) Berrien County	21	1.17
Honor (village) Benzie County	3	0.91
Parma (village) Jackson County	5	0.65
Oronoko (charter twp) Berrien County	55	0.60
Fairfield (township) Shiawassee County	4	0.53
Orange (township) Kalkaska County	6	0.49
Dexter (village) Washtenaw County	19	0.47
Custer (township) Antrim County	5	0.44
Mecosta (township) Mecosta County	9	0.34
Edgemont Park (cdp) Ingham County	8	0.34

Top 10 Places Sorted by Percent of Total Population
Based on places with total population of 50,000 or more

Place	Population	%
Ann Arbor (city) Washtenaw County	292	0.26
Troy (city) Oakland County	77	0.10
Canton (charter twp) Wayne County	79	0.09
Royal Oak (city) Oakland County	49	0.09

Place	Population	%
Farmington Hills (city) Oakland County	60	0.08
Rochester Hills (city) Oakland County	60	0.08
West Bloomfield (charter twp) Oakland County	51	0.08
Lansing (city) Ingham County	78	0.07
Novi (city) Oakland County	40	0.07
Wyoming (city) Kent County	42	0.06

South American: Ecuadorian

Top 10 Places Sorted by Population
Based on all places, regardless of total population

Place	Population	%
Ann Arbor (city) Washtenaw County	73	0.06
Grand Rapids (city) Kent County	41	0.02
Lansing (city) Ingham County	39	0.03
Detroit (city) Wayne County	38	0.01
Clinton (charter twp) Macomb County	29	0.03
Canton (charter twp) Wayne County	27	0.03
Troy (city) Oakland County	26	0.03
Shelby (charter twp) Macomb County	25	0.03
East Lansing (city) Ingham County	23	0.05
Oronoko (charter twp) Berrien County	21	0.23

Top 10 Places Sorted by Percent of Total Population
Based on all places, regardless of total population

Place	Population	%
Sherman (township) Keweenaw County	1	1.49
Barton Hills (village) Washtenaw County	3	1.02
Clement (township) Gladwin County	4	0.44
Elsie (village) Clinton County	4	0.41
Maple Ridge (township) Delta County	3	0.39
Lake Michigan Beach (cdp) Berrien County	3	0.25
Oronoko (charter twp) Berrien County	21	0.23
Duplain (township) Clinton County	4	0.17
Reed City (city) Osceola County	4	0.16
Bear Lake (township) Kalkaska County	1	0.15

Top 10 Places Sorted by Percent of Total Population
Based on places with total population of 50,000 or more

Place	Population	%
Ann Arbor (city) Washtenaw County	73	0.06
Royal Oak (city) Oakland County	21	0.04
Lansing (city) Ingham County	39	0.03
Clinton (charter twp) Macomb County	29	0.03
Canton (charter twp) Wayne County	27	0.03
Troy (city) Oakland County	26	0.03
Shelby (charter twp) Macomb County	25	0.03
Kalamazoo (city) Kalamazoo County	19	0.03
Ypsilanti (charter twp) Washtenaw County	18	0.03
Grand Rapids (city) Kent County	41	0.02

South American: Paraguayan

Top 10 Places Sorted by Population
Based on all places, regardless of total population

Place	Population	%
Farmington Hills (city) Oakland County	15	0.02
Livonia (city) Wayne County	12	0.01
West Bloomfield (charter twp) Oakland County	9	0.01
Lansing (city) Ingham County	8	0.01
Adrian (city) Lenawee County	7	0.03
Bloomfield (charter twp) Oakland County	6	0.01
Canton (charter twp) Wayne County	6	0.01
Kentwood (city) Kent County	6	0.01
Grand Rapids (city) Kent County	6	<0.01
Northville (city) Oakland County	5	0.08

Top 10 Places Sorted by Percent of Total Population
Based on all places, regardless of total population

Place	Population	%
Onaway (city) Presque Isle County	3	0.34
Shoreham (village) Berrien County	2	0.23
Grawn (cdp) Grand Traverse County	1	0.13
Milan (township) Monroe County	2	0.12
Northville (city) Oakland County	5	0.08
Breckenridge (village) Gratiot County	1	0.08
Sylvan (township) Washtenaw County	2	0.07
Village of Grosse Pointe Shores (city) Wayne Co.	2	0.07
Standish (city) Arenac County	1	0.07
Blissfield (village) Lenawee County	2	0.06

Top 10 Places Sorted by Percent of Total Population
Based on places with total population of 50,000 or more

Place	Population	%
Farmington Hills (city) Oakland County	15	0.02
Livonia (city) Wayne County	12	0.01
West Bloomfield (charter twp) Oakland County	9	0.01
Lansing (city) Ingham County	8	0.01
Canton (charter twp) Wayne County	6	0.01
Novi (city) Oakland County	3	0.01
Grand Rapids (city) Kent County	6	<0.01
Ann Arbor (city) Washtenaw County	4	<0.01
Troy (city) Oakland County	4	<0.01
Dearborn (city) Wayne County	3	<0.01

South American: Peruvian

Top 10 Places Sorted by Population
Based on all places, regardless of total population

Place	Population	%
Ann Arbor (city) Washtenaw County	162	0.14
Detroit (city) Wayne County	77	0.01
Grand Rapids (city) Kent County	65	0.03
Troy (city) Oakland County	62	0.08
Kentwood (city) Kent County	60	0.12
Wyoming (city) Kent County	37	0.05
Oronoko (charter twp) Berrien County	34	0.37
Westland (city) Wayne County	34	0.04
East Lansing (city) Ingham County	33	0.07
Livonia (city) Wayne County	31	0.03

Top 10 Places Sorted by Percent of Total Population
Based on all places, regardless of total population

Place	Population	%
Oscoda (cdp) Iosco County	9	1.00
Shoreham (village) Berrien County	5	0.58
Oronoko (charter twp) Berrien County	34	0.37
Greenwood (township) Wexford County	2	0.34
Barton Hills (village) Washtenaw County	1	0.34
Wakefield (township) Gogebic County	1	0.33
Brampton (township) Delta County	3	0.29
Berrien (township) Berrien County	14	0.28
Berrien Springs (village) Berrien County	5	0.28
Bismarck (township) Presque Isle County	1	0.26

Top 10 Places Sorted by Percent of Total Population
Based on places with total population of 50,000 or more

Place	Population	%
Ann Arbor (city) Washtenaw County	162	0.14
Troy (city) Oakland County	62	0.08
Wyoming (city) Kent County	37	0.05
Novi (city) Oakland County	30	0.05
Battle Creek (city) Calhoun County	24	0.05
Westland (city) Wayne County	34	0.04
Rochester Hills (city) Oakland County	25	0.04
Ypsilanti (charter twp) Washtenaw County	24	0.04
Grand Rapids (city) Kent County	65	0.03
Livonia (city) Wayne County	31	0.03

South American: Uruguayan

Top 10 Places Sorted by Population
Based on all places, regardless of total population

Place	Population	%
Ann Arbor (city) Washtenaw County	19	0.02
Clinton (charter twp) Macomb County	13	0.01
Chesterfield (township) Macomb County	7	0.02
Farmington Hills (city) Oakland County	7	0.01
Detroit (city) Wayne County	7	<0.01
Oronoko (charter twp) Berrien County	6	0.07
Lansing (city) Ingham County	6	0.01
Ypsilanti (charter twp) Washtenaw County	6	0.01
Raisinville (township) Monroe County	5	0.09
Owosso (city) Shiawassee County	5	0.03

Top 10 Places Sorted by Percent of Total Population
Based on all places, regardless of total population

Place	Population	%
Novi (township) Oakland County	1	0.67
Lyndon (township) Washtenaw County	4	0.15
Butman (township) Gladwin County	2	0.10

Place	Population	%
Manitou Beach-Devils Lake (cdp) Lenawee County	2	0.10
Raisinville (township) Monroe County	5	0.09
Spring Lake (village) Ottawa County	2	0.09
Springvale (township) Emmet County	2	0.09
Springfield (city) Calhoun County	4	0.08
Oronoko (charter twp) Berrien County	6	0.07
Casco (township) Allegan County	2	0.07

Top 10 Places Sorted by Percent of Total Population
Based on places with total population of 50,000 or more

Place	Population	%
Ann Arbor (city) Washtenaw County	19	0.02
Clinton (charter twp) Macomb County	13	0.01
Farmington Hills (city) Oakland County	7	0.01
Lansing (city) Ingham County	6	0.01
Ypsilanti (charter twp) Washtenaw County	6	0.01
Macomb (township) Macomb County	4	0.01
Rochester Hills (city) Oakland County	4	0.01
West Bloomfield (charter twp) Oakland County	4	0.01
Wyoming (city) Kent County	4	0.01
Royal Oak (city) Oakland County	3	0.01

South American: Venezuelan

Top 10 Places Sorted by Population
Based on all places, regardless of total population

Place	Population	%
Ann Arbor (city) Washtenaw County	108	0.09
Rochester Hills (city) Oakland County	46	0.06
Dearborn (city) Wayne County	43	0.04
Pittsfield (charter twp) Washtenaw County	38	0.11
Detroit (city) Wayne County	38	0.01
Grand Rapids (city) Kent County	35	0.02
Portage (city) Kalamazoo County	31	0.07
Sterling Heights (city) Macomb County	31	0.02
Novi (city) Oakland County	30	0.05
Scio (township) Washtenaw County	28	0.14

Top 10 Places Sorted by Percent of Total Population
Based on all places, regardless of total population

Place	Population	%
Barton Hills (village) Washtenaw County	4	1.36
Benzonia (village) Benzie County	3	0.60
Powers (village) Menominee County	2	0.47
Cassopolis (village) Cass County	5	0.28
Dexter (village) Washtenaw County	10	0.25
Oronoko (charter twp) Berrien County	22	0.24
Bunker Hill (township) Ingham County	5	0.24
Berrien Springs (village) Berrien County	4	0.22
Milan (city) Washtenaw County	12	0.21
Ann Arbor (charter twp) Washtenaw County	9	0.21

Top 10 Places Sorted by Percent of Total Population
Based on places with total population of 50,000 or more

Place	Population	%
Ann Arbor (city) Washtenaw County	108	0.09
Rochester Hills (city) Oakland County	46	0.06
Novi (city) Oakland County	30	0.05
Dearborn (city) Wayne County	43	0.04
Dearborn Heights (city) Wayne County	24	0.04
Royal Oak (city) Oakland County	24	0.04
Troy (city) Oakland County	27	0.03
Wyoming (city) Kent County	24	0.03
Kalamazoo (city) Kalamazoo County	22	0.03
Shelby (charter twp) Macomb County	21	0.03

South American: Other South American

Top 10 Places Sorted by Population
Based on all places, regardless of total population

Place	Population	%
Detroit (city) Wayne County	8	<0.01
Blackman (charter twp) Jackson County	6	0.02
Independence (charter twp) Oakland County	6	0.02
Northville (township) Wayne County	6	0.02
Oak Park (city) Oakland County	6	0.02
Lansing (charter twp) Ingham County	5	0.06
Port Huron (city) St. Clair County	5	0.02
Rochester Hills (city) Oakland County	5	0.01
Troy (city) Oakland County	5	0.01
Handy (township) Livingston County	4	0.05

Top 10 Places Sorted by Percent of Total Population
Based on all places, regardless of total population

Place	Population	%
Bismarck (township) Presque Isle County	1	0.26
Clio (city) Genesee County	2	0.08
Au Sable (cdp) Iosco County	1	0.07
Lansing (charter twp) Ingham County	5	0.06
Berrien Springs (village) Berrien County	1	0.06
Handy (township) Livingston County	4	0.05
Sparta (village) Kent County	2	0.05
Au Sable (charter twp) Iosco County	1	0.05
Hayes (township) Charlevoix County	1	0.05
Walled Lake (city) Oakland County	3	0.04

Top 10 Places Sorted by Percent of Total Population
Based on places with total population of 50,000 or more

Place	Population	%
Rochester Hills (city) Oakland County	5	0.01
Troy (city) Oakland County	5	0.01
Southfield (city) Oakland County	4	0.01
Dearborn Heights (city) Wayne County	3	0.01
Detroit (city) Wayne County	8	<0.01
Ann Arbor (city) Washtenaw County	3	<0.01
Sterling Heights (city) Macomb County	3	<0.01
Dearborn (city) Wayne County	2	<0.01
Grand Rapids (city) Kent County	2	<0.01
Livonia (city) Wayne County	2	<0.01

Other Hispanic or Latino

Top 10 Places Sorted by Population
Based on all places, regardless of total population

Place	Population	%
Detroit (city) Wayne County	2,833	0.40
Grand Rapids (city) Kent County	1,704	0.91
Lansing (city) Ingham County	1,010	0.88
Holland (charter twp) Ottawa County	613	1.72
Wyoming (city) Kent County	584	0.81
Saginaw (city) Saginaw County	581	1.13
Holland (city) Ottawa County	509	1.54
Ann Arbor (city) Washtenaw County	483	0.42
Flint (city) Genesee County	378	0.37
Battle Creek (city) Calhoun County	376	0.72

Top 10 Places Sorted by Percent of Total Population
Based on all places, regardless of total population

Place	Population	%
Alba (cdp) Antrim County	13	4.41
Eagle Harbor (cdp) Keweenaw County	3	3.95
Shelby (village) Oceana County	61	2.95
Huron (township) Huron County	12	2.75
Hart (city) Oceana County	53	2.49
Bohemia (township) Ontonagon County	2	2.44
Hartford (city) Van Buren County	61	2.27
Shelby (township) Oceana County	82	2.02
Applegate (village) Sanilac County	5	2.02
Lee (township) Allegan County	77	1.92

Top 10 Places Sorted by Percent of Total Population
Based on places with total population of 50,000 or more

Place	Population	%
Saginaw (city) Saginaw County	581	1.13
Grand Rapids (city) Kent County	1,704	0.91
Lansing (city) Ingham County	1,010	0.88
Wyoming (city) Kent County	584	0.81
Battle Creek (city) Calhoun County	376	0.72
Pontiac (city) Oakland County	348	0.58
Kalamazoo (city) Kalamazoo County	371	0.50
Waterford (charter twp) Oakland County	322	0.45
Ypsilanti (charter twp) Washtenaw County	241	0.45
Ann Arbor (city) Washtenaw County	483	0.42

Racial Group Rankings

African-American/Black

Top 10 Places Sorted by Population
Based on all places, regardless of total population

Place	Population	%
Detroit (city) Wayne County	601,988	84.34
Flint (city) Genesee County	60,928	59.48
Southfield (city) Oakland County	51,817	72.23
Grand Rapids (city) Kent County	44,032	23.42
Pontiac (city) Oakland County	32,910	55.30
Lansing (city) Ingham County	31,830	27.85
Saginaw (city) Saginaw County	25,266	49.05
Warren (city) Macomb County	19,712	14.70
Inkster (city) Wayne County	19,324	76.17
Ypsilanti (charter twp) Washtenaw County	19,204	35.99

Top 10 Places Sorted by Percent of Total Population
Based on all places, regardless of total population

Place	Population	%
Royal Oak (charter twp) Oakland County	2,372	98.06
Highland Park (city) Wayne County	11,258	95.60
Benton Harbor (city) Berrien County	9,170	91.35
Detroit (city) Wayne County	601,988	84.34
Muskegon Heights (city) Muskegon County	8,828	81.32
Buena Vista (cdp) Saginaw County	5,227	76.69
Inkster (city) Wayne County	19,324	76.17
Southfield (city) Oakland County	51,817	72.23
Beecher (cdp) Genesee County	7,346	71.79
Benton Heights (cdp) Berrien County	2,628	64.35

Top 10 Places Sorted by Percent of Total Population
Based on places with total population of 50,000 or more

Place	Population	%
Detroit (city) Wayne County	601,988	84.34
Southfield (city) Oakland County	51,817	72.23
Flint (city) Genesee County	60,928	59.48
Pontiac (city) Oakland County	32,910	55.30
Saginaw (city) Saginaw County	25,266	49.05
Ypsilanti (charter twp) Washtenaw County	19,204	35.99
Lansing (city) Ingham County	31,830	27.85
Kalamazoo (city) Kalamazoo County	18,823	25.35
Grand Rapids (city) Kent County	44,032	23.42
Battle Creek (city) Calhoun County	11,026	21.06

African-American/Black: Not Hispanic

Top 10 Places Sorted by Population
Based on all places, regardless of total population

Place	Population	%
Detroit (city) Wayne County	596,963	83.63
Flint (city) Genesee County	60,166	58.74
Southfield (city) Oakland County	51,445	71.71
Grand Rapids (city) Kent County	41,741	22.20
Pontiac (city) Oakland County	31,897	53.59
Lansing (city) Ingham County	30,058	26.30
Saginaw (city) Saginaw County	24,231	47.04
Warren (city) Macomb County	19,443	14.50
Inkster (city) Wayne County	19,106	75.31
Ypsilanti (charter twp) Washtenaw County	18,884	35.39

Top 10 Places Sorted by Percent of Total Population
Based on all places, regardless of total population

Place	Population	%
Royal Oak (charter twp) Oakland County	2,346	96.98
Highland Park (city) Wayne County	11,172	94.87
Benton Harbor (city) Berrien County	9,101	90.67
Detroit (city) Wayne County	596,963	83.63
Muskegon Heights (city) Muskegon County	8,731	80.43
Inkster (city) Wayne County	19,106	75.31
Buena Vista (cdp) Saginaw County	5,095	74.75
Southfield (city) Oakland County	51,445	71.71
Beecher (cdp) Genesee County	7,264	70.99
Lathrup Village (city) Oakland County	2,591	63.58

Top 10 Places Sorted by Percent of Total Population
Based on places with total population of 50,000 or more

Place	Population	%
Detroit (city) Wayne County	596,963	83.63
Southfield (city) Oakland County	51,445	71.71
Flint (city) Genesee County	60,166	58.74
Pontiac (city) Oakland County	31,897	53.59
Saginaw (city) Saginaw County	24,231	47.04
Ypsilanti (charter twp) Washtenaw County	18,884	35.39
Lansing (city) Ingham County	30,058	26.30
Kalamazoo (city) Kalamazoo County	18,255	24.58
Grand Rapids (city) Kent County	41,741	22.20
Battle Creek (city) Calhoun County	10,733	20.50

African-American/Black: Hispanic

Top 10 Places Sorted by Population
Based on all places, regardless of total population

Place	Population	%
Detroit (city) Wayne County	5,025	0.70
Grand Rapids (city) Kent County	2,291	1.22
Lansing (city) Ingham County	1,772	1.55
Saginaw (city) Saginaw County	1,035	2.01
Pontiac (city) Oakland County	1,013	1.70
Wyoming (city) Kent County	767	1.06
Flint (city) Genesee County	762	0.74
Kalamazoo (city) Kalamazoo County	568	0.76
Kentwood (city) Kent County	409	0.84
Southfield (city) Oakland County	372	0.52

Top 10 Places Sorted by Percent of Total Population
Based on all places, regardless of total population

Place	Population	%
Saginaw (city) Saginaw County	1,035	2.01
Buena Vista (cdp) Saginaw County	132	1.94
Rockland (township) Ontonagon County	4	1.75
Pontiac (city) Oakland County	1,013	1.70
Buena Vista (charter twp) Saginaw County	139	1.60
Lansing (city) Ingham County	1,772	1.55
Baldwin (village) Lake County	18	1.49
Zilwaukee (township) Saginaw County	1	1.49
Millersburg (village) Presque Isle County	3	1.46
Morley (village) Mecosta County	7	1.42

Top 10 Places Sorted by Percent of Total Population
Based on places with total population of 50,000 or more

Place	Population	%
Saginaw (city) Saginaw County	1,035	2.01
Pontiac (city) Oakland County	1,013	1.70
Lansing (city) Ingham County	1,772	1.55
Grand Rapids (city) Kent County	2,291	1.22
Wyoming (city) Kent County	767	1.06
Kalamazoo (city) Kalamazoo County	568	0.76
Flint (city) Genesee County	762	0.74
Detroit (city) Wayne County	5,025	0.70
Ypsilanti (charter twp) Washtenaw County	320	0.60
Battle Creek (city) Calhoun County	293	0.56

American Indian/Alaska Native

Top 10 Places Sorted by Population
Based on all places, regardless of total population

Place	Population	%
Detroit (city) Wayne County	8,448	1.18
Grand Rapids (city) Kent County	3,327	1.77
Sault Ste. Marie (city) Chippewa County	3,167	22.39
Lansing (city) Ingham County	2,601	2.28
Flint (city) Genesee County	1,950	1.90
Warren (city) Macomb County	1,588	1.18
Kalamazoo (city) Kalamazoo County	1,341	1.81
Ann Arbor (city) Washtenaw County	1,110	0.97
Wyoming (city) Kent County	1,109	1.54
Kinross (charter twp) Chippewa County	1,077	14.24

Top 10 Places Sorted by Percent of Total Population
Based on all places, regardless of total population

Place	Population	%
Bay Mills (township) Chippewa County	836	56.60
Zeba (cdp) Baraga County	260	54.17
St. Ignace (township) Mackinac County	350	37.27
St. Ignace (city) Mackinac County	847	34.54
Hudson (township) Mackinac County	61	33.70
Watersmeet (cdp) Gogebic County	138	32.24
Sugar Island (township) Chippewa County	208	31.90
Superior (township) Chippewa County	366	27.37
Moran (township) Mackinac County	269	27.06
Harris (township) Menominee County	518	26.32

Top 10 Places Sorted by Percent of Total Population
Based on places with total population of 50,000 or more

Place	Population	%
Lansing (city) Ingham County	2,601	2.28
Flint (city) Genesee County	1,950	1.90
Kalamazoo (city) Kalamazoo County	1,341	1.81
Battle Creek (city) Calhoun County	941	1.80
Grand Rapids (city) Kent County	3,327	1.77
Pontiac (city) Oakland County	990	1.66
Ypsilanti (charter twp) Washtenaw County	842	1.58
Wyoming (city) Kent County	1,109	1.54
Taylor (city) Wayne County	920	1.46
Saginaw (city) Saginaw County	657	1.28

American Indian/Alaska Native: Not Hispanic

Top 10 Places Sorted by Population
Based on all places, regardless of total population

Place	Population	%
Detroit (city) Wayne County	6,965	0.98
Sault Ste. Marie (city) Chippewa County	3,137	22.18
Grand Rapids (city) Kent County	2,337	1.24
Lansing (city) Ingham County	2,048	1.79
Flint (city) Genesee County	1,724	1.68
Warren (city) Macomb County	1,461	1.09
Kalamazoo (city) Kalamazoo County	1,134	1.53
Kinross (charter twp) Chippewa County	1,044	13.81
Chippewa (township) Isabella County	923	19.83
Westland (city) Wayne County	896	1.07

Top 10 Places Sorted by Percent of Total Population
Based on all places, regardless of total population

Place	Population	%
Bay Mills (township) Chippewa County	833	56.40
Zeba (cdp) Baraga County	256	53.33
St. Ignace (township) Mackinac County	346	36.85
St. Ignace (city) Mackinac County	831	33.89
Hudson (township) Mackinac County	61	33.70
Watersmeet (cdp) Gogebic County	138	32.24
Sugar Island (township) Chippewa County	203	31.13
Superior (township) Chippewa County	365	27.30
Moran (township) Mackinac County	266	26.76
Harris (township) Menominee County	502	25.51

Top 10 Places Sorted by Percent of Total Population
Based on places with total population of 50,000 or more

Place	Population	%
Lansing (city) Ingham County	2,048	1.79
Flint (city) Genesee County	1,724	1.68
Kalamazoo (city) Kalamazoo County	1,134	1.53
Battle Creek (city) Calhoun County	796	1.52
Ypsilanti (charter twp) Washtenaw County	743	1.39
Pontiac (city) Oakland County	775	1.30
Taylor (city) Wayne County	808	1.28
Grand Rapids (city) Kent County	2,337	1.24
Wyoming (city) Kent County	814	1.13
Warren (city) Macomb County	1,461	1.09

American Indian/Alaska Native: Hispanic

Top 10 Places Sorted by Population
Based on all places, regardless of total population

Place	Population	%
Detroit (city) Wayne County	1,483	0.21
Grand Rapids (city) Kent County	990	0.53
Lansing (city) Ingham County	553	0.48
Wyoming (city) Kent County	295	0.41
Flint (city) Genesee County	226	0.22
Ann Arbor (city) Washtenaw County	225	0.20
Pontiac (city) Oakland County	215	0.36
Kalamazoo (city) Kalamazoo County	207	0.28
Holland (city) Ottawa County	172	0.52
Saginaw (city) Saginaw County	167	0.32

Top 10 Places Sorted by Percent of Total Population
Based on all places, regardless of total population

Place	Population	%
Lake Leelanau (cdp) Leelanau County	13	5.14
Suttons Bay (township) Leelanau County	93	3.12
Chippewa (township) Isabella County	120	2.58
Rothbury (village) Oceana County	11	2.55
Millersburg (village) Presque Isle County	5	2.43
Rockland (township) Ontonagon County	4	1.75
Lake City (city) Missaukee County	14	1.67
Sherman (township) Keweenaw County	1	1.49
Wawatam (township) Emmet County	9	1.36
Deckerville (village) Sanilac County	11	1.33

Top 10 Places Sorted by Percent of Total Population
Based on places with total population of 50,000 or more

Place	Population	%
Grand Rapids (city) Kent County	990	0.53
Lansing (city) Ingham County	553	0.48
Wyoming (city) Kent County	295	0.41
Pontiac (city) Oakland County	215	0.36
Saginaw (city) Saginaw County	167	0.32
Kalamazoo (city) Kalamazoo County	207	0.28
Battle Creek (city) Calhoun County	145	0.28
Flint (city) Genesee County	226	0.22
Detroit (city) Wayne County	1,483	0.21
Ann Arbor (city) Washtenaw County	225	0.20

Alaska Native: Alaska Athabascan

Top 10 Places Sorted by Population
Based on all places, regardless of total population

Place	Population	%
Battle Creek (city) Calhoun County	6	0.01
Pennfield (charter twp) Calhoun County	5	0.06
Drummond (township) Chippewa County	4	0.38
Greenwood (township) St. Clair County	4	0.26
Ann Arbor (city) Washtenaw County	4	<0.01
Gwinn (cdp) Marquette County	3	0.16
Newaygo (city) Newaygo County	3	0.15
Manchester (township) Washtenaw County	3	0.07
Calumet (charter twp) Houghton County	3	0.05
Forsyth (township) Marquette County	3	0.05

Top 10 Places Sorted by Percent of Total Population
Based on all places, regardless of total population

Place	Population	%
Alden (cdp) Antrim County	1	0.80
Drummond (township) Chippewa County	4	0.38
Maybee (village) Monroe County	2	0.36
Greenwood (township) St. Clair County	4	0.26
Vernon (village) Shiawassee County	2	0.26
Whittemore (city) Iosco County	1	0.26
Augusta (village) Kalamazoo County	2	0.23
Helena (township) Antrim County	2	0.20
Bancroft (village) Shiawassee County	1	0.18
Gwinn (cdp) Marquette County	3	0.16

Top 10 Places Sorted by Percent of Total Population
Based on places with total population of 50,000 or more

Place	Population	%
Battle Creek (city) Calhoun County	6	0.01
Ann Arbor (city) Washtenaw County	4	<0.01
Grand Rapids (city) Kent County	3	<0.01
Warren (city) Macomb County	3	<0.01

Place	Population	%
Kalamazoo (city) Kalamazoo County	2	<0.01
Wyoming (city) Kent County	2	<0.01
Dearborn Heights (city) Wayne County	1	<0.01
Detroit (city) Wayne County	1	<0.01
Flint (city) Genesee County	1	<0.01
Lansing (city) Ingham County	1	<0.01

Alaska Native: Aleut

Top 10 Places Sorted by Population
Based on all places, regardless of total population

Place	Population	%
Shelby (village) Oceana County	9	0.44
Shelby (township) Oceana County	9	0.22
Bad Axe (city) Huron County	8	0.26
Highland (charter twp) Oakland County	5	0.03
Conway (township) Livingston County	4	0.11
Rockford (city) Kent County	4	0.07
Bay City (city) Bay County	4	0.01
White Lake (charter twp) Oakland County	4	0.01
Buchanan (city) Berrien County	3	0.07
Adrian (township) Lenawee County	3	0.05

Top 10 Places Sorted by Percent of Total Population
Based on all places, regardless of total population

Place	Population	%
Shelby (village) Oceana County	9	0.44
Bad Axe (city) Huron County	8	0.26
Shelby (township) Oceana County	9	0.22
Mulliken (village) Eaton County	1	0.18
Lake (township) Benzie County	1	0.13
Conway (township) Livingston County	4	0.11
Beaverton (township) Gladwin County	2	0.10
Rockford (city) Kent County	4	0.07
Buchanan (city) Berrien County	3	0.07
Croton (township) Newaygo County	2	0.06

Top 10 Places Sorted by Percent of Total Population
Based on places with total population of 50,000 or more

Place	Population	%
Battle Creek (city) Calhoun County	2	<0.01
Lansing (city) Ingham County	2	<0.01
Warren (city) Macomb County	2	<0.01
Ypsilanti (charter twp) Washtenaw County	2	<0.01
Detroit (city) Wayne County	1	<0.01
Kalamazoo (city) Kalamazoo County	1	<0.01
Westland (city) Wayne County	1	<0.01
Ann Arbor (city) Washtenaw County	0	0.00
Canton (charter twp) Wayne County	0	0.00
Clinton (charter twp) Macomb County	0	0.00

American Indian: Apache

Top 10 Places Sorted by Population
Based on all places, regardless of total population

Place	Population	%
Detroit (city) Wayne County	59	0.01
Lansing (city) Ingham County	40	0.03
Flint (city) Genesee County	36	0.04
Grand Rapids (city) Kent County	30	0.02
Warren (city) Macomb County	22	0.02
Battle Creek (city) Calhoun County	19	0.04
Muskegon (city) Muskegon County	16	0.04
Flint (charter twp) Genesee County	14	0.04
Holland (city) Ottawa County	14	0.04
Kalamazoo (city) Kalamazoo County	14	0.02

Top 10 Places Sorted by Percent of Total Population
Based on all places, regardless of total population

Place	Population	%
Lake City (city) Missaukee County	10	1.20
Luther (village) Lake County	3	0.94
Hopkins (village) Allegan County	5	0.82
Greenwood (township) Wexford County	3	0.51
Newkirk (township) Lake County	3	0.47
Raber (township) Chippewa County	3	0.46
Rothbury (village) Oceana County	2	0.46
Leonidas (township) St. Joseph County	5	0.42
Nester (township) Roscommon County	1	0.34
Convis (township) Calhoun County	5	0.31

Top 10 Places Sorted by Percent of Total Population
Based on places with total population of 50,000 or more

Place	Population	%
Flint (city) Genesee County	36	0.04
Battle Creek (city) Calhoun County	19	0.04
Lansing (city) Ingham County	40	0.03
Grand Rapids (city) Kent County	30	0.02
Warren (city) Macomb County	22	0.02
Kalamazoo (city) Kalamazoo County	14	0.02
Pontiac (city) Oakland County	13	0.02
Royal Oak (city) Oakland County	11	0.02
Waterford (charter twp) Oakland County	11	0.02
Taylor (city) Wayne County	10	0.02

American Indian: Arapaho

Top 10 Places Sorted by Population
Based on all places, regardless of total population

Place	Population	%
Harbor Springs (city) Emmet County	8	0.67
Garfield (charter twp) Grand Traverse County	4	0.02
Detroit (city) Wayne County	4	<0.01
Westwood (cdp) Kalamazoo County	3	0.03
Kalamazoo (charter twp) Kalamazoo County	3	0.01
Roseville (city) Macomb County	3	0.01
Flint (city) Genesee County	3	<0.01
Custer (township) Mason County	2	0.16
Luna Pier (city) Monroe County	2	0.14
Ann Arbor (city) Washtenaw County	2	<0.01

Top 10 Places Sorted by Percent of Total Population
Based on all places, regardless of total population

Place	Population	%
Harbor Springs (city) Emmet County	8	0.67
Custer (township) Mason County	2	0.16
Luna Pier (city) Monroe County	2	0.14
Pellston (village) Emmet County	1	0.12
Lakeview (village) Montcalm County	1	0.10
Newark (township) Gratiot County	1	0.09
Sagola (township) Dickinson County	1	0.09
Curtis (township) Alcona County	1	0.08
McKinley (township) Emmet County	1	0.08
Bronson (city) Branch County	1	0.04

Top 10 Places Sorted by Percent of Total Population
Based on places with total population of 50,000 or more

Place	Population	%
Detroit (city) Wayne County	4	<0.01
Flint (city) Genesee County	3	<0.01
Ann Arbor (city) Washtenaw County	2	<0.01
Canton (charter twp) Wayne County	2	<0.01
Shelby (charter twp) Macomb County	2	<0.01
Grand Rapids (city) Kent County	1	<0.01
Lansing (city) Ingham County	1	<0.01
Pontiac (city) Oakland County	1	<0.01
Sterling Heights (city) Macomb County	1	<0.01
Ypsilanti (charter twp) Washtenaw County	1	<0.01

American Indian: Blackfeet

Top 10 Places Sorted by Population
Based on all places, regardless of total population

Place	Population	%
Detroit (city) Wayne County	441	0.06
Lansing (city) Ingham County	147	0.13
Flint (city) Genesee County	141	0.14
Grand Rapids (city) Kent County	104	0.06
Battle Creek (city) Calhoun County	55	0.11
Ypsilanti (charter twp) Washtenaw County	48	0.09
Clinton (charter twp) Macomb County	45	0.05
Warren (city) Macomb County	45	0.03
Pontiac (city) Oakland County	44	0.07
Kalamazoo (city) Kalamazoo County	40	0.05

Top 10 Places Sorted by Percent of Total Population
Based on all places, regardless of total population

Place	Population	%
Backus (township) Roscommon County	6	1.82
Allen (village) Hillsdale County	2	1.05
Clarendon (township) Calhoun County	9	0.79

Place	Population	%
Ossineke (cdp) Alpena County	7	0.75
Deckerville (village) Sanilac County	6	0.72
Spurr (township) Baraga County	2	0.72
Vanderbilt (village) Otsego County	4	0.71
Parchment (city) Kalamazoo County	12	0.67
Gilford (township) Tuscola County	5	0.67
Canada Creek Ranch (cdp) Montmorency County	2	0.66

Top 10 Places Sorted by Percent of Total Population
Based on places with total population of 50,000 or more

Place	Population	%
Flint (city) Genesee County	141	0.14
Lansing (city) Ingham County	147	0.13
Battle Creek (city) Calhoun County	55	0.11
Ypsilanti (charter twp) Washtenaw County	48	0.09
Pontiac (city) Oakland County	44	0.07
Detroit (city) Wayne County	441	0.06
Grand Rapids (city) Kent County	104	0.06
Taylor (city) Wayne County	39	0.06
Clinton (charter twp) Macomb County	45	0.05
Kalamazoo (city) Kalamazoo County	40	0.05

American Indian: Canadian/French American Indian

Top 10 Places Sorted by Population
Based on all places, regardless of total population

Place	Population	%
Detroit (city) Wayne County	45	0.01
Sault Ste. Marie (city) Chippewa County	40	0.28
Warren (city) Macomb County	38	0.03
Lansing (city) Ingham County	29	0.03
Port Huron (city) St. Clair County	23	0.08
Lincoln Park (city) Wayne County	18	0.05
Grand Rapids (city) Kent County	17	0.01
Redford (charter twp) Wayne County	16	0.03
Ann Arbor (city) Washtenaw County	16	0.01
Bay Mills (township) Chippewa County	13	0.88

Top 10 Places Sorted by Percent of Total Population
Based on all places, regardless of total population

Place	Population	%
Bay Mills (township) Chippewa County	13	0.88
Hendricks (township) Mackinac County	1	0.65
Zeba (cdp) Baraga County	3	0.63
Hudson (township) Mackinac County	1	0.55
Rapid River (township) Kalkaska County	6	0.52
Eastport (cdp) Antrim County	1	0.46
Winterfield (township) Clare County	2	0.44
Parma (village) Jackson County	3	0.39
Skandia (township) Marquette County	3	0.36
Au Train (township) Alger County	4	0.35

Top 10 Places Sorted by Percent of Total Population
Based on places with total population of 50,000 or more

Place	Population	%
Warren (city) Macomb County	38	0.03
Lansing (city) Ingham County	29	0.03
Taylor (city) Wayne County	13	0.02
Royal Oak (city) Oakland County	10	0.02
Dearborn Heights (city) Wayne County	9	0.02
St. Clair Shores (city) Macomb County	9	0.02
Detroit (city) Wayne County	45	0.01
Grand Rapids (city) Kent County	17	0.01
Ann Arbor (city) Washtenaw County	16	0.01
Clinton (charter twp) Macomb County	12	0.01

American Indian: Central American Indian

Top 10 Places Sorted by Population
Based on all places, regardless of total population

Place	Population	%
Grand Rapids (city) Kent County	77	0.04
Detroit (city) Wayne County	15	<0.01
Trenton (city) Wayne County	6	0.03
Kalamazoo (charter twp) Kalamazoo County	5	0.02
Pittsfield (charter twp) Washtenaw County	4	0.01
Waterford (charter twp) Oakland County	4	0.01
Burton (city) Genesee County	3	0.01
Hamtramck (city) Wayne County	3	0.01
Marquette (city) Marquette County	3	0.01

Place	Population	%
Taylor (city) Wayne County	3	<0.01

Top 10 Places Sorted by Percent of Total Population
Based on all places, regardless of total population

Place	Population	%
Levering (cdp) Emmet County	1	0.47
Casnovia (village) Kent County	1	0.31
Eau Claire (village) Berrien County	1	0.16
Dimondale (village) Eaton County	1	0.08
McKinley (township) Emmet County	1	0.08
Brooks (township) Newaygo County	2	0.06
Churchill (township) Ogemaw County	1	0.06
James (township) Saginaw County	1	0.05
Leslie (city) Ingham County	1	0.05
Grand Rapids (city) Kent County	77	0.04

Top 10 Places Sorted by Percent of Total Population
Based on places with total population of 50,000 or more

Place	Population	%
Grand Rapids (city) Kent County	77	0.04
Waterford (charter twp) Oakland County	4	0.01
Detroit (city) Wayne County	15	<0.01
Taylor (city) Wayne County	3	<0.01
Troy (city) Oakland County	3	<0.01
Clinton (charter twp) Macomb County	2	<0.01
Farmington Hills (city) Oakland County	2	<0.01
Lansing (city) Ingham County	2	<0.01
Livonia (city) Wayne County	2	<0.01
Novi (city) Oakland County	2	<0.01

American Indian: Cherokee

Top 10 Places Sorted by Population
Based on all places, regardless of total population

Place	Population	%
Detroit (city) Wayne County	1,321	0.19
Flint (city) Genesee County	423	0.41
Warren (city) Macomb County	320	0.24
Grand Rapids (city) Kent County	269	0.14
Lansing (city) Ingham County	241	0.21
Taylor (city) Wayne County	217	0.34
Clinton (charter twp) Macomb County	209	0.22
Kalamazoo (city) Kalamazoo County	202	0.27
Pontiac (city) Oakland County	186	0.31
Ypsilanti (charter twp) Washtenaw County	166	0.31

Top 10 Places Sorted by Percent of Total Population
Based on all places, regardless of total population

Place	Population	%
Watersmeet (cdp) Gogebic County	10	2.34
Copper Harbor (cdp) Keweenaw County	2	1.85
Meade (township) Mason County	3	1.66
Bear Lake (cdp) Kalkaska County	5	1.53
Forestville (village) Sanilac County	2	1.47
Boon (cdp) Wexford County	2	1.20
Gourley (township) Menominee County	5	1.19
Interior (township) Ontonagon County	4	1.19
Clarendon (township) Calhoun County	13	1.14
Rust (township) Montmorency County	6	1.07

Top 10 Places Sorted by Percent of Total Population
Based on places with total population of 50,000 or more

Place	Population	%
Flint (city) Genesee County	423	0.41
Taylor (city) Wayne County	217	0.34
Battle Creek (city) Calhoun County	165	0.32
Pontiac (city) Oakland County	186	0.31
Ypsilanti (charter twp) Washtenaw County	166	0.31
Kalamazoo (city) Kalamazoo County	202	0.27
Warren (city) Macomb County	320	0.24
St. Clair Shores (city) Macomb County	139	0.23
Clinton (charter twp) Macomb County	209	0.22
Waterford (charter twp) Oakland County	157	0.22

American Indian: Cheyenne

Top 10 Places Sorted by Population
Based on all places, regardless of total population

Place	Population	%
Flint (city) Genesee County	12	0.01

Place	Population	%
Kimball (township) St. Clair County	6	0.06
Rochester (city) Oakland County	6	0.05
Detroit (city) Wayne County	6	<0.01
Otter Lake (village) Lapeer County	5	1.29
Marathon (township) Lapeer County	5	0.11
Escanaba (city) Delta County	5	0.04
Roseville (city) Macomb County	5	0.01
Grand Rapids (city) Kent County	5	<0.01
Augusta (village) Kalamazoo County	4	0.45

Top 10 Places Sorted by Percent of Total Population
Based on all places, regardless of total population

Place	Population	%
Crystal Mountain (cdp) Benzie County	1	1.85
Otter Lake (village) Lapeer County	5	1.29
Augusta (village) Kalamazoo County	4	0.45
Sheridan (township) Mason County	4	0.37
Luna Pier (city) Monroe County	4	0.28
Beaver (township) Newaygo County	1	0.20
Deerfield (township) Lenawee County	3	0.19
Dansville (village) Ingham County	1	0.18
Weldon (township) Benzie County	1	0.18
Au Sable (cdp) Iosco County	2	0.14

Top 10 Places Sorted by Percent of Total Population
Based on places with total population of 50,000 or more

Place	Population	%
Flint (city) Genesee County	12	0.01
Detroit (city) Wayne County	6	<0.01
Grand Rapids (city) Kent County	5	<0.01
Lansing (city) Ingham County	3	<0.01
Battle Creek (city) Calhoun County	2	<0.01
Kalamazoo (city) Kalamazoo County	2	<0.01
Southfield (city) Oakland County	2	<0.01
Taylor (city) Wayne County	2	<0.01
Warren (city) Macomb County	2	<0.01
Waterford (charter twp) Oakland County	2	<0.01

American Indian: Chickasaw

Top 10 Places Sorted by Population
Based on all places, regardless of total population

Place	Population	%
Detroit (city) Wayne County	19	<0.01
Flint (city) Genesee County	14	0.01
Clay (township) St. Clair County	13	0.14
Farmington Hills (city) Oakland County	8	0.01
Ann Arbor (city) Washtenaw County	6	0.01
Kentwood (city) Kent County	6	0.01
Port Huron (city) St. Clair County	5	0.02
Portage (city) Kalamazoo County	5	0.01
Rochester Hills (city) Oakland County	5	0.01
Taylor (city) Wayne County	5	0.01

Top 10 Places Sorted by Percent of Total Population
Based on all places, regardless of total population

Place	Population	%
Presque Isle Harbor (cdp) Presque Isle County	3	0.50
Albion (township) Calhoun County	3	0.27
Roscommon (village) Roscommon County	2	0.19
Presque Isle (township) Presque Isle County	3	0.18
Weare (township) Oceana County	2	0.17
Florence (township) St. Joseph County	2	0.16
Newkirk (township) Lake County	1	0.16
Merrill (township) Newaygo County	1	0.15
Clay (township) St. Clair County	13	0.14
Pickford (township) Chippewa County	2	0.13

Top 10 Places Sorted by Percent of Total Population
Based on places with total population of 50,000 or more

Place	Population	%
Flint (city) Genesee County	14	0.01
Farmington Hills (city) Oakland County	8	0.01
Ann Arbor (city) Washtenaw County	6	0.01
Rochester Hills (city) Oakland County	5	0.01
Taylor (city) Wayne County	5	0.01
Dearborn Heights (city) Wayne County	3	0.01
Detroit (city) Wayne County	19	<0.01
Grand Rapids (city) Kent County	4	<0.01
Troy (city) Oakland County	4	<0.01
Lansing (city) Ingham County	3	<0.01

American Indian: Chippewa

Top 10 Places Sorted by Population
Based on all places, regardless of total population

Place	Population	%
Sault Ste. Marie (city) Chippewa County	2,558	18.09
Kinross (charter twp) Chippewa County	826	10.92
Chippewa (township) Isabella County	782	16.80
Bay Mills (township) Chippewa County	749	50.71
Baraga (township) Baraga County	685	17.96
St. Ignace (city) Mackinac County	681	27.77
Soo (township) Chippewa County	645	20.53
Suttons Bay (township) Leelanau County	453	15.19
L'Anse (township) Baraga County	448	11.66
Baraga (village) Baraga County	446	21.72

Top 10 Places Sorted by Percent of Total Population
Based on all places, regardless of total population

Place	Population	%
Bay Mills (township) Chippewa County	749	50.71
Zeba (cdp) Baraga County	185	38.54
Hudson (township) Mackinac County	53	29.28
St. Ignace (township) Mackinac County	274	29.18
St. Ignace (city) Mackinac County	681	27.77
Sugar Island (township) Chippewa County	171	26.23
Superior (township) Chippewa County	303	22.66
Moran (township) Mackinac County	219	22.03
Watersmeet (cdp) Gogebic County	93	21.73
Baraga (village) Baraga County	446	21.72

Top 10 Places Sorted by Percent of Total Population
Based on places with total population of 50,000 or more

Place	Population	%
Lansing (city) Ingham County	381	0.33
Grand Rapids (city) Kent County	436	0.23
Flint (city) Genesee County	231	0.23
Waterford (charter twp) Oakland County	167	0.23
Westland (city) Wayne County	179	0.21
Wyoming (city) Kent County	152	0.21
Saginaw (city) Saginaw County	102	0.20
Taylor (city) Wayne County	114	0.18
Pontiac (city) Oakland County	102	0.17
Kalamazoo (city) Kalamazoo County	116	0.16

American Indian: Choctaw

Top 10 Places Sorted by Population
Based on all places, regardless of total population

Place	Population	%
Detroit (city) Wayne County	193	0.03
Flint (city) Genesee County	51	0.05
Lansing (city) Ingham County	36	0.03
Ypsilanti (charter twp) Washtenaw County	27	0.05
Kalamazoo (city) Kalamazoo County	23	0.03
Farmington Hills (city) Oakland County	20	0.03
Dearborn (city) Wayne County	17	0.02
Warren (city) Macomb County	17	0.01
Grand Rapids (city) Kent County	15	0.01
Sterling Heights (city) Macomb County	15	0.01

Top 10 Places Sorted by Percent of Total Population
Based on all places, regardless of total population

Place	Population	%
Sherwood (village) Branch County	5	1.62
Logan (township) Mason County	2	0.64
White Pine (cdp) Ontonagon County	3	0.63
New Troy (cdp) Berrien County	3	0.60
South Branch (township) Wexford County	2	0.52
Pellston (village) Emmet County	4	0.49
Parchment (city) Kalamazoo County	8	0.44
Carp Lake (township) Ontonagon County	3	0.42
Owendale (village) Huron County	1	0.41
Wheatland (township) Mecosta County	5	0.36

Top 10 Places Sorted by Percent of Total Population
Based on places with total population of 50,000 or more

Place	Population	%
Flint (city) Genesee County	51	0.05
Ypsilanti (charter twp) Washtenaw County	27	0.05
Detroit (city) Wayne County	193	0.03
Lansing (city) Ingham County	36	0.03

Kalamazoo (city) Kalamazoo County	23	0.03
Farmington Hills (city) Oakland County	20	0.03
Dearborn (city) Wayne County	17	0.02
Canton (charter twp) Wayne County	14	0.02
Southfield (city) Oakland County	14	0.02
Pontiac (city) Oakland County	10	0.02

American Indian: Colville

Top 10 Places Sorted by Population
Based on all places, regardless of total population

Place	Population	%
Hartland (township) Livingston County	5	0.03
Belvidere (township) Montcalm County	2	0.09
Kentwood (city) Kent County	2	<0.01
Allendale (cdp) Ottawa County	1	0.01
Howell (city) Livingston County	1	0.01
York (charter twp) Washtenaw County	1	0.01
Allendale (charter twp) Ottawa County	1	0.01
Grand Rapids (city) Kent County	1	<0.01
Livonia (city) Wayne County	1	<0.01
White Lake (charter twp) Oakland County	1	<0.01

Top 10 Places Sorted by Percent of Total Population
Based on all places, regardless of total population

Place	Population	%
Belvidere (township) Montcalm County	2	0.09
Hartland (township) Livingston County	5	0.03
Allendale (cdp) Ottawa County	1	0.01
Howell (city) Livingston County	1	0.01
York (charter twp) Washtenaw County	1	0.01
Kentwood (city) Kent County	2	<0.01
Allendale (charter twp) Ottawa County	1	0.01
Grand Rapids (city) Kent County	1	<0.01
Livonia (city) Wayne County	1	<0.01
White Lake (charter twp) Oakland County	1	<0.01

Top 10 Places Sorted by Percent of Total Population
Based on places with total population of 50,000 or more

Place	Population	%
Grand Rapids (city) Kent County	1	<0.01
Livonia (city) Wayne County	1	<0.01
Ann Arbor (city) Washtenaw County	0	0.00
Battle Creek (city) Calhoun County	0	0.00
Canton (charter twp) Wayne County	0	0.00
Clinton (charter twp) Macomb County	0	0.00
Dearborn (city) Wayne County	0	0.00
Dearborn Heights (city) Wayne County	0	0.00
Detroit (city) Wayne County	0	0.00
Farmington Hills (city) Oakland County	0	0.00

American Indian: Comanche

Top 10 Places Sorted by Population
Based on all places, regardless of total population

Place	Population	%
Detroit (city) Wayne County	16	<0.01
Grand Rapids (city) Kent County	9	<0.01
Lee (township) Calhoun County	6	0.49
Suttons Bay (township) Leelanau County	6	0.20
Niles (city) Berrien County	5	0.04
Novi (city) Oakland County	5	0.01
Alpena (city) Alpena County	4	0.04
Monroe (city) Monroe County	4	0.02
Holland (charter twp) Ottawa County	4	0.01
Kalamazoo (city) Kalamazoo County	4	0.01

Top 10 Places Sorted by Percent of Total Population
Based on all places, regardless of total population

Place	Population	%
Lee (township) Calhoun County	6	0.49
Wolverine (village) Cheboygan County	1	0.41
Mitchell (township) Alcona County	1	0.28
Otisville (village) Genesee County	2	0.23
Au Sable (cdp) Iosco County	3	0.21
Suttons Bay (township) Leelanau County	6	0.20
Au Sable (charter twp) Iosco County	3	0.15
Brockway (township) St. Clair County	2	0.10
Attica (cdp) Lapeer County	1	0.10
Nunda (township) Cheboygan County	1	0.10

Top 10 Places Sorted by Percent of Total Population
Based on places with total population of 50,000 or more

Place	Population	%
Novi (city) Oakland County	5	0.01
Kalamazoo (city) Kalamazoo County	4	0.01
Dearborn Heights (city) Wayne County	3	0.01
Saginaw (city) Saginaw County	3	0.01
Detroit (city) Wayne County	16	<0.01
Grand Rapids (city) Kent County	9	<0.01
Ann Arbor (city) Washtenaw County	4	<0.01
Clinton (charter twp) Macomb County	4	<0.01
Westland (city) Wayne County	4	<0.01
Lansing (city) Ingham County	3	<0.01

American Indian: Cree

Top 10 Places Sorted by Population
Based on all places, regardless of total population

Place	Population	%
Detroit (city) Wayne County	32	<0.01
Ann Arbor (city) Washtenaw County	14	0.01
Auburn Hills (city) Oakland County	10	0.05
Flint (charter twp) Genesee County	8	0.03
Shelby (charter twp) Macomb County	7	0.01
Grand Ledge (city) Eaton County	6	0.08
Lansing (city) Ingham County	6	0.01
Roseville (city) Macomb County	6	0.01
Southfield (city) Oakland County	6	0.01
Sterling Heights (city) Macomb County	6	<0.01

Top 10 Places Sorted by Percent of Total Population
Based on all places, regardless of total population

Place	Population	%
Greenleaf (township) Sanilac County	4	0.51
Minden City (village) Sanilac County	1	0.51
Marenisco (cdp) Gogebic County	1	0.39
Clinton (township) Oscoda County	1	0.23
Melrose (township) Charlevoix County	3	0.21
Ortonville (village) Oakland County	3	0.21
Eveline (township) Charlevoix County	3	0.20
Manistique (township) Schoolcraft County	2	0.18
Minden (township) Sanilac County	1	0.18
Vanderbilt (village) Otsego County	1	0.18

Top 10 Places Sorted by Percent of Total Population
Based on places with total population of 50,000 or more

Place	Population	%
Ann Arbor (city) Washtenaw County	14	0.01
Shelby (charter twp) Macomb County	7	0.01
Lansing (city) Ingham County	6	0.01
Southfield (city) Oakland County	6	0.01
Battle Creek (city) Calhoun County	4	0.01
Rochester Hills (city) Oakland County	4	0.01
Saginaw (city) Saginaw County	3	0.01
Detroit (city) Wayne County	32	<0.01
Sterling Heights (city) Macomb County	6	<0.01
Warren (city) Macomb County	5	<0.01

American Indian: Creek

Top 10 Places Sorted by Population
Based on all places, regardless of total population

Place	Population	%
Detroit (city) Wayne County	71	0.01
Westland (city) Wayne County	25	0.03
Ann Arbor (city) Washtenaw County	21	0.02
Flint (city) Genesee County	16	0.02
Grand Rapids (city) Kent County	12	0.01
Ypsilanti (charter twp) Washtenaw County	11	0.02
Kalamazoo (city) Kalamazoo County	11	0.01
Huron (charter twp) Wayne County	10	0.06
Southfield (city) Oakland County	9	0.01
Pittsfield (charter twp) Washtenaw County	8	0.02

Top 10 Places Sorted by Percent of Total Population
Based on all places, regardless of total population

Place	Population	%
Breedsville (village) Van Buren County	6	3.02
Fairgrove (village) Tuscola County	3	0.53
Hanover (village) Jackson County	2	0.45

Place	Population	%
Wheatland (township) Sanilac County	2	0.41
Goodwell (township) Newaygo County	2	0.37
Bliss (township) Emmet County	2	0.32
Arcada (township) Gratiot County	5	0.30
Harrisville (township) Alcona County	4	0.30
Columbia (township) Van Buren County	7	0.27
Gilmore (township) Benzie County	2	0.24

Top 10 Places Sorted by Percent of Total Population
Based on places with total population of 50,000 or more

Place	Population	%
Westland (city) Wayne County	25	0.03
Ann Arbor (city) Washtenaw County	21	0.02
Flint (city) Genesee County	16	0.02
Ypsilanti (charter twp) Washtenaw County	11	0.02
Detroit (city) Wayne County	71	0.01
Grand Rapids (city) Kent County	12	0.01
Kalamazoo (city) Kalamazoo County	11	0.01
Southfield (city) Oakland County	9	0.01
Canton (charter twp) Wayne County	7	0.01
Livonia (city) Wayne County	7	0.01

American Indian: Crow

Top 10 Places Sorted by Population
Based on all places, regardless of total population

Place	Population	%
Detroit (city) Wayne County	17	<0.01
Pontiac (city) Oakland County	7	0.01
Mecosta (village) Mecosta County	6	1.31
Morton (township) Mecosta County	6	0.14
Flint (charter twp) Genesee County	6	0.02
Battle Creek (city) Calhoun County	6	0.01
Tyrone (township) Livingston County	4	0.04
Burton (city) Genesee County	4	0.01
Hartford (township) Van Buren County	3	0.09
Kinross (charter twp) Chippewa County	3	0.04

Top 10 Places Sorted by Percent of Total Population
Based on all places, regardless of total population

Place	Population	%
Mecosta (village) Mecosta County	6	1.31
Aetna (township) Missaukee County	1	0.24
Montmorency (township) Montmorency County	2	0.18
Port Sanilac (village) Sanilac County	1	0.16
Morton (township) Mecosta County	6	0.14
Wisner (township) Tuscola County	1	0.14
Vermontville (village) Eaton County	1	0.13
Antioch (township) Wexford County	1	0.12
Portage (township) Mackinac County	1	0.10
Hartford (township) Van Buren County	3	0.09

Top 10 Places Sorted by Percent of Total Population
Based on places with total population of 50,000 or more

Place	Population	%
Pontiac (city) Oakland County	7	0.01
Battle Creek (city) Calhoun County	6	0.01
Detroit (city) Wayne County	17	<0.01
Ann Arbor (city) Washtenaw County	3	<0.01
Flint (city) Genesee County	3	<0.01
Grand Rapids (city) Kent County	3	<0.01
Kalamazoo (city) Kalamazoo County	2	<0.01
Livonia (city) Wayne County	2	<0.01
Taylor (city) Wayne County	2	<0.01
Southfield (city) Oakland County	1	<0.01

American Indian: Delaware

Top 10 Places Sorted by Population
Based on all places, regardless of total population

Place	Population	%
Detroit (city) Wayne County	28	<0.01
Taylor (city) Wayne County	18	0.03
Westland (city) Wayne County	15	0.02
South Haven (charter twp) Van Buren County	7	0.18
Lyon (charter twp) Oakland County	7	0.05
Sterling Heights (city) Macomb County	7	0.01
Garden City (city) Wayne County	6	0.02
Southgate (city) Wayne County	6	0.02
Southfield (city) Oakland County	6	0.01
Canton (charter twp) Wayne County	5	0.01

Top 10 Places Sorted by Percent of Total Population
Based on all places, regardless of total population

Place	Population	%
Rockland (township) Ontonagon County	1	0.44
Omena (cdp) Leelanau County	1	0.37
Case (township) Presque Isle County	2	0.22
Camden (village) Hillsdale County	1	0.20
Noble (township) Branch County	1	0.19
South Haven (charter twp) Van Buren County	7	0.18
Port Sanilac (village) Sanilac County	1	0.16
Alanson (village) Emmet County	1	0.14
Skidway Lake (cdp) Ogemaw County	4	0.12
St. Ignace (city) Mackinac County	3	0.12

Top 10 Places Sorted by Percent of Total Population
Based on places with total population of 50,000 or more

Place	Population	%
Taylor (city) Wayne County	18	0.03
Westland (city) Wayne County	15	0.02
Sterling Heights (city) Macomb County	7	0.01
Southfield (city) Oakland County	6	0.01
Canton (charter twp) Wayne County	5	0.01
Ypsilanti (charter twp) Washtenaw County	5	0.01
St. Clair Shores (city) Macomb County	4	0.01
Waterford (charter twp) Oakland County	4	0.01
Detroit (city) Wayne County	28	<0.01
Livonia (city) Wayne County	4	<0.01

American Indian: Hopi

Top 10 Places Sorted by Population
Based on all places, regardless of total population

Place	Population	%
Detroit (city) Wayne County	8	<0.01
Warren (city) Macomb County	6	<0.01
Green Oak (township) Livingston County	5	0.03
St. Clair Shores (city) Macomb County	4	0.01
Crystal Falls (city) Iron County	3	0.20
Bangor (charter twp) Bay County	3	0.02
Bay City (city) Bay County	3	0.01
Troy (city) Oakland County	3	<0.01
East China (township) St. Clair County	2	0.05
Williams (charter twp) Bay County	2	0.04

Top 10 Places Sorted by Percent of Total Population
Based on all places, regardless of total population

Place	Population	%
Crystal Falls (city) Iron County	3	0.20
Ortonville (village) Oakland County	1	0.07
Lake Isabella (village) Isabella County	1	0.06
East China (township) St. Clair County	2	0.05
Woodland (township) Barry County	1	0.05
Williams (charter twp) Bay County	2	0.04
Green Oak (township) Livingston County	5	0.03
Ithaca (city) Gratiot County	1	0.03
Sherman (township) Isabella County	1	0.03
Bangor (charter twp) Bay County	3	0.02

Top 10 Places Sorted by Percent of Total Population
Based on places with total population of 50,000 or more

Place	Population	%
St. Clair Shores (city) Macomb County	4	0.01
Detroit (city) Wayne County	8	<0.01
Warren (city) Macomb County	6	<0.01
Troy (city) Oakland County	3	<0.01
Battle Creek (city) Calhoun County	2	<0.01
Taylor (city) Wayne County	2	<0.01
Ann Arbor (city) Washtenaw County	1	<0.01
Dearborn Heights (city) Wayne County	1	<0.01
Lansing (city) Ingham County	1	<0.01
Royal Oak (city) Oakland County	1	<0.01

American Indian: Houma

Top 10 Places Sorted by Population
Based on all places, regardless of total population

Place	Population	%
Farmington Hills (city) Oakland County	2	<0.01
Wheatland (township) Mecosta County	1	0.07
Blissfield (village) Lenawee County	1	0.03

Place	Population	%
Blissfield (township) Lenawee County	1	0.03
LaGrange (township) Cass County	1	0.03
Benton (charter twp) Berrien County	1	0.01
Fenton (city) Genesee County	1	0.01
Mundy (township) Genesee County	1	0.01
Raisin (township) Lenawee County	1	0.01
St. Joseph (city) Berrien County	1	0.01

Top 10 Places Sorted by Percent of Total Population
Based on all places, regardless of total population

Place	Population	%
Wheatland (township) Mecosta County	1	0.07
Blissfield (village) Lenawee County	1	0.03
Blissfield (township) Lenawee County	1	0.03
LaGrange (township) Cass County	1	0.03
Benton (charter twp) Berrien County	1	0.01
Fenton (city) Genesee County	1	0.01
Mundy (township) Genesee County	1	0.01
Raisin (township) Lenawee County	1	0.01
St. Joseph (city) Berrien County	1	0.01
Farmington Hills (city) Oakland County	2	<0.01

Top 10 Places Sorted by Percent of Total Population
Based on places with total population of 50,000 or more

Place	Population	%
Farmington Hills (city) Oakland County	2	<0.01
Battle Creek (city) Calhoun County	1	<0.01
Lansing (city) Ingham County	1	<0.01
Westland (city) Wayne County	1	<0.01
Ann Arbor (city) Washtenaw County	0	0.00
Canton (charter twp) Wayne County	0	0.00
Clinton (charter twp) Macomb County	0	0.00
Dearborn (city) Wayne County	0	0.00
Dearborn Heights (city) Wayne County	0	0.00
Detroit (city) Wayne County	0	0.00

Alaska Native: Inupiat (Eskimo)

Top 10 Places Sorted by Population
Based on all places, regardless of total population

Place	Population	%
Calumet (charter twp) Houghton County	6	0.09
Dearborn (city) Wayne County	6	0.01
Clinton (charter twp) Macomb County	5	0.01
Mason (township) Cass County	4	0.14
Rockford (city) Kent County	4	0.07
Alpena (township) Alpena County	4	0.04
Wyandotte (city) Wayne County	4	0.02
Novi (city) Oakland County	4	0.01
Flint (city) Genesee County	4	<0.01
Grand Rapids (city) Kent County	4	<0.01

Top 10 Places Sorted by Percent of Total Population
Based on all places, regardless of total population

Place	Population	%
North Adams (village) Hillsdale County	3	0.63
Sheridan (township) Mason County	3	0.28
Forest (township) Cheboygan County	2	0.19
Turner (township) Arenac County	1	0.18
Elmwood (township) Tuscola County	2	0.17
Lake (township) Roscommon County	2	0.16
Mason (township) Cass County	4	0.14
Lake (township) Benzie County	1	0.13
Adams (township) Hillsdale County	3	0.12
Hatton (township) Clare County	1	0.11

Top 10 Places Sorted by Percent of Total Population
Based on places with total population of 50,000 or more

Place	Population	%
Dearborn (city) Wayne County	6	0.01
Clinton (charter twp) Macomb County	5	0.01
Novi (city) Oakland County	4	0.01
Flint (city) Genesee County	4	<0.01
Grand Rapids (city) Kent County	4	<0.01
Ann Arbor (city) Washtenaw County	3	<0.01
Canton (charter twp) Wayne County	3	<0.01
Detroit (city) Wayne County	3	<0.01
Lansing (city) Ingham County	3	<0.01
Rochester Hills (city) Oakland County	2	<0.01

American Indian: Iroquois

Top 10 Places Sorted by Population
Based on all places, regardless of total population

Place	Population	%
Detroit (city) Wayne County	140	0.02
Dearborn Heights (city) Wayne County	61	0.11
Warren (city) Macomb County	55	0.04
Lansing (city) Ingham County	49	0.04
Livonia (city) Wayne County	48	0.05
Redford (charter twp) Wayne County	45	0.09
Taylor (city) Wayne County	43	0.07
Westland (city) Wayne County	40	0.05
Chesterfield (township) Macomb County	39	0.09
Dearborn (city) Wayne County	39	0.04

Top 10 Places Sorted by Percent of Total Population
Based on all places, regardless of total population

Place	Population	%
Harrisville (city) Alcona County	6	1.22
Lennon (village) Shiawassee County	5	0.98
Haight (township) Ontonagon County	2	0.94
Wolverine (village) Cheboygan County	2	0.82
Pinora (township) Lake County	5	0.70
Sugar Island (township) Chippewa County	4	0.61
Caspian (city) Iron County	5	0.55
South Branch (township) Wexford County	2	0.52
Mentor (township) Cheboygan County	4	0.49
Elmer (township) Oscoda County	5	0.44

Top 10 Places Sorted by Percent of Total Population
Based on places with total population of 50,000 or more

Place	Population	%
Dearborn Heights (city) Wayne County	61	0.11
Taylor (city) Wayne County	43	0.07
Livonia (city) Wayne County	48	0.05
Westland (city) Wayne County	40	0.05
Shelby (charter twp) Macomb County	35	0.05
Warren (city) Macomb County	55	0.04
Lansing (city) Ingham County	49	0.04
Dearborn (city) Wayne County	39	0.04
Waterford (charter twp) Oakland County	30	0.04
Macomb (township) Macomb County	29	0.04

American Indian: Kiowa

Top 10 Places Sorted by Population
Based on all places, regardless of total population

Place	Population	%
Greenwood (township) Oscoda County	4	0.36
St. Johns (city) Clinton County	4	0.05
Bangor (charter twp) Bay County	4	0.03
Temperance (cdp) Monroe County	3	0.04
Bedford (township) Monroe County	3	0.01
Grand Blanc (charter twp) Genesee County	3	0.01
Monroe (city) Monroe County	3	0.01
Washington (township) Macomb County	2	0.01
Joyfield (township) Benzie County	1	0.13
Lake (township) Lake County	1	0.12

Top 10 Places Sorted by Percent of Total Population
Based on all places, regardless of total population

Place	Population	%
Greenwood (township) Oscoda County	4	0.36
Joyfield (township) Benzie County	1	0.13
Lake (township) Lake County	1	0.12
Bear Lake (township) Manistee County	1	0.06
Rich (township) Lapeer County	1	0.06
St. Johns (city) Clinton County	4	0.05
Temperance (cdp) Monroe County	3	0.04
Bangor (charter twp) Bay County	4	0.03
Pierson (township) Montcalm County	1	0.03
Summerfield (township) Monroe County	1	0.03

Top 10 Places Sorted by Percent of Total Population
Based on places with total population of 50,000 or more

Place	Population	%
Dearborn Heights (city) Wayne County	1	<0.01
Detroit (city) Wayne County	1	<0.01
Pontiac (city) Oakland County	1	<0.01
Southfield (city) Oakland County	1	<0.01
Waterford (charter twp) Oakland County	1	<0.01
Ann Arbor (city) Washtenaw County	0	0.00
Battle Creek (city) Calhoun County	0	0.00
Canton (charter twp) Wayne County	0	0.00
Clinton (charter twp) Macomb County	0	0.00
Dearborn (city) Wayne County	0	0.00

American Indian: Lumbee

Top 10 Places Sorted by Population
Based on all places, regardless of total population

Place	Population	%
Warren (city) Macomb County	77	0.06
Detroit (city) Wayne County	48	0.01
Taylor (city) Wayne County	43	0.07
Lincoln Park (city) Wayne County	32	0.08
St. Clair Shores (city) Macomb County	28	0.05
Shelby (charter twp) Macomb County	25	0.03
Hazel Park (city) Oakland County	23	0.14
Roseville (city) Macomb County	20	0.04
Livonia (city) Wayne County	20	0.02
Sterling Heights (city) Macomb County	20	0.02

Top 10 Places Sorted by Percent of Total Population
Based on all places, regardless of total population

Place	Population	%
Kinde (village) Huron County	8	1.79
Lincoln (township) Huron County	8	0.99
Bear Lake (village) Manistee County	2	0.70
Wellston (cdp) Manistee County	2	0.64
Grass Lake (village) Jackson County	7	0.60
Metamora (village) Lapeer County	3	0.53
Mesick (village) Wexford County	2	0.51
Argyle (township) Sanilac County	3	0.40
Lakewood Club (village) Muskegon County	5	0.39
Sheridan (township) Mecosta County	5	0.36

Top 10 Places Sorted by Percent of Total Population
Based on places with total population of 50,000 or more

Place	Population	%
Taylor (city) Wayne County	43	0.07
Warren (city) Macomb County	77	0.06
St. Clair Shores (city) Macomb County	28	0.05
Shelby (charter twp) Macomb County	25	0.03
Livonia (city) Wayne County	20	0.02
Sterling Heights (city) Macomb County	20	0.02
Westland (city) Wayne County	20	0.02
Clinton (charter twp) Macomb County	18	0.02
Macomb (township) Macomb County	18	0.02
Royal Oak (city) Oakland County	11	0.02

American Indian: Menominee

Top 10 Places Sorted by Population
Based on all places, regardless of total population

Place	Population	%
Detroit (city) Wayne County	15	<0.01
Trenton (city) Wayne County	9	0.05
Whitmore Lake (cdp) Washtenaw County	7	0.11
Menominee (city) Menominee County	7	0.08
Northfield (township) Washtenaw County	7	0.08
Frenchtown (township) Monroe County	7	0.03
Delta (charter twp) Eaton County	7	0.02
Southgate (city) Wayne County	7	0.02
Livonia (city) Wayne County	7	0.01
Norway (city) Dickinson County	6	0.21

Top 10 Places Sorted by Percent of Total Population
Based on all places, regardless of total population

Place	Population	%
Posen (village) Presque Isle County	2	0.85
Bliss (township) Emmet County	3	0.48
Posen (township) Presque Isle County	2	0.24
Norway (city) Dickinson County	6	0.21
Bergland (township) Ontonagon County	1	0.21
Zeba (cdp) Baraga County	1	0.21
Breen (township) Dickinson County	1	0.20
Superior (township) Chippewa County	2	0.15
Whitmore Lake (cdp) Washtenaw County	7	0.11
McMillan (township) Luce County	3	0.11

Top 10 Places Sorted by Percent of Total Population
Based on places with total population of 50,000 or more

Place	Population	%
Livonia (city) Wayne County	7	0.01
Detroit (city) Wayne County	15	<0.01
Ann Arbor (city) Washtenaw County	4	<0.01
Lansing (city) Ingham County	4	<0.01
Dearborn Heights (city) Wayne County	2	<0.01
Dearborn (city) Wayne County	1	<0.01
Farmington Hills (city) Oakland County	1	<0.01
Flint (city) Genesee County	1	<0.01
Shelby (charter twp) Macomb County	1	<0.01
Sterling Heights (city) Macomb County	1	<0.01

American Indian: Mexican American Indian

Top 10 Places Sorted by Population
Based on all places, regardless of total population

Place	Population	%
Detroit (city) Wayne County	238	0.03
Grand Rapids (city) Kent County	166	0.09
Lansing (city) Ingham County	91	0.08
Ann Arbor (city) Washtenaw County	48	0.04
Holland (charter twp) Ottawa County	41	0.12
Flint (city) Genesee County	40	0.04
Pontiac (city) Oakland County	36	0.06
Holland (city) Ottawa County	30	0.09
Livonia (city) Wayne County	28	0.03
Kalamazoo (city) Kalamazoo County	25	0.03

Top 10 Places Sorted by Percent of Total Population
Based on all places, regardless of total population

Place	Population	%
Meade (township) Mason County	1	0.55
Claybanks (township) Oceana County	4	0.51
Burdell (township) Osceola County	6	0.45
Columbia (township) Van Buren County	11	0.43
White Pine (cdp) Ontonagon County	2	0.42
Harrisville (city) Alcona County	2	0.41
Center (township) Emmet County	2	0.35
Golden (township) Oceana County	6	0.34
Bear Lake (cdp) Kalkaska County	1	0.31
Moran (township) Mackinac County	3	0.30

Top 10 Places Sorted by Percent of Total Population
Based on places with total population of 50,000 or more

Place	Population	%
Grand Rapids (city) Kent County	166	0.09
Lansing (city) Ingham County	91	0.08
Pontiac (city) Oakland County	36	0.06
Ann Arbor (city) Washtenaw County	48	0.04
Flint (city) Genesee County	40	0.04
Detroit (city) Wayne County	238	0.03
Livonia (city) Wayne County	28	0.03
Kalamazoo (city) Kalamazoo County	25	0.03
Wyoming (city) Kent County	19	0.03
Battle Creek (city) Calhoun County	15	0.03

American Indian: Navajo

Top 10 Places Sorted by Population
Based on all places, regardless of total population

Place	Population	%
Detroit (city) Wayne County	46	0.01
Grand Rapids (city) Kent County	26	0.01
Flint (city) Genesee County	11	0.01
Garden City (city) Wayne County	9	0.03
Kalamazoo (city) Kalamazoo County	9	0.01
Shelby (charter twp) Macomb County	9	0.01
Sterling Heights (city) Macomb County	9	0.01
Zeeland (charter twp) Ottawa County	8	0.08
Wayne (city) Wayne County	8	0.05
Ann Arbor (city) Washtenaw County	8	0.01

Top 10 Places Sorted by Percent of Total Population
Based on all places, regardless of total population

Place	Population	%
Sherwood (village) Branch County	3	0.97
Richland (township) Missaukee County	5	0.34

Place	Population	%
Grass Lake (village) Jackson County	4	0.34
Omer (city) Arenac County	1	0.32
Hesperia (village) Oceana County	3	0.31
Hickory Corners (cdp) Barry County	1	0.31
Hancock (township) Houghton County	1	0.22
Weidman (cdp) Isabella County	2	0.21
Standish (township) Arenac County	3	0.16
Grant (township) Mecosta County	1	0.15

Top 10 Places Sorted by Percent of Total Population
Based on places with total population of 50,000 or more

Place	Population	%
Detroit (city) Wayne County	46	0.01
Grand Rapids (city) Kent County	26	0.01
Flint (city) Genesee County	11	0.01
Kalamazoo (city) Kalamazoo County	9	0.01
Shelby (charter twp) Macomb County	9	0.01
Sterling Heights (city) Macomb County	9	0.01
Ann Arbor (city) Washtenaw County	8	0.01
Lansing (city) Ingham County	8	0.01
Warren (city) Macomb County	8	0.01
Waterford (charter twp) Oakland County	8	0.01

American Indian: Osage

Top 10 Places Sorted by Population
Based on all places, regardless of total population

Place	Population	%
Garden City (city) Wayne County	7	0.03
St. Clair Shores (city) Macomb County	7	0.01
Lincoln Park (city) Wayne County	6	0.02
Macomb (township) Macomb County	6	0.01
Salem (township) Allegan County	4	0.09
Trenton (city) Wayne County	4	0.02
Taylor (city) Wayne County	4	0.01
Saline (city) Washtenaw County	3	0.03
Mundy (township) Genesee County	3	0.02
Springfield (charter twp) Oakland County	3	0.02

Top 10 Places Sorted by Percent of Total Population
Based on all places, regardless of total population

Place	Population	%
Lakes of the North (cdp) Antrim County	1	0.11
Onsted (village) Lenawee County	1	0.11
Salem (township) Allegan County	4	0.09
Ferry (township) Oceana County	1	0.08
Pittsford (township) Hillsdale County	1	0.06
Richmond (township) Osceola County	1	0.06
Oneida (charter twp) Eaton County	2	0.05
Briley (township) Montmorency County	1	0.05
Colfax (township) Huron County	1	0.05
Hayes (township) Clare County	2	0.04

Top 10 Places Sorted by Percent of Total Population
Based on places with total population of 50,000 or more

Place	Population	%
St. Clair Shores (city) Macomb County	7	0.01
Macomb (township) Macomb County	6	0.01
Taylor (city) Wayne County	4	0.01
Canton (charter twp) Wayne County	2	<0.01
Flint (city) Genesee County	2	<0.01
Royal Oak (city) Oakland County	2	<0.01
Wyoming (city) Kent County	2	<0.01
Clinton (charter twp) Macomb County	1	<0.01
Dearborn (city) Wayne County	1	<0.01
Detroit (city) Wayne County	1	<0.01

American Indian: Ottawa

Top 10 Places Sorted by Population
Based on all places, regardless of total population

Place	Population	%
Grand Rapids (city) Kent County	286	0.15
Lansing (city) Ingham County	191	0.17
Muskegon (city) Muskegon County	181	0.47
Petoskey (city) Emmet County	178	3.14
Manistee (city) Manistee County	154	2.47
Bear Creek (township) Emmet County	140	2.26
Muskegon (charter twp) Muskegon County	137	0.77
Wyoming (city) Kent County	122	0.17
Norton Shores (city) Muskegon County	101	0.42
Manistee (township) Manistee County	85	2.08

Top 10 Places Sorted by Percent of Total Population
Based on all places, regardless of total population

Place	Population	%
Cross Village (township) Emmet County	30	10.68
Cross Village (cdp) Emmet County	6	6.45
Pellston (village) Emmet County	45	5.47
Conway (cdp) Emmet County	9	4.41
Center (township) Emmet County	22	3.87
Meade (township) Mason County	7	3.87
Bay Shore (cdp) Charlevoix County	29	3.85
Eastlake (village) Manistee County	19	3.71
McKinley (township) Emmet County	48	3.70
Harbor Springs (city) Emmet County	42	3.52

Top 10 Places Sorted by Percent of Total Population
Based on places with total population of 50,000 or more

Place	Population	%
Lansing (city) Ingham County	191	0.17
Wyoming (city) Kent County	122	0.17
Grand Rapids (city) Kent County	286	0.15
Battle Creek (city) Calhoun County	42	0.08
Flint (city) Genesee County	41	0.04
Royal Oak (city) Oakland County	23	0.04
Warren (city) Macomb County	34	0.03
Kalamazoo (city) Kalamazoo County	23	0.03
Waterford (charter twp) Oakland County	22	0.03
Pontiac (city) Oakland County	16	0.03

American Indian: Paiute

Top 10 Places Sorted by Population
Based on all places, regardless of total population

Place	Population	%
Speaker (township) Sanilac County	4	0.27
Milford (village) Oakland County	4	0.06
Milford (charter twp) Oakland County	4	0.03
Detour (township) Chippewa County	3	0.37
Livonia (city) Wayne County	3	<0.01
Sturgis (city) St. Joseph County	2	0.02
Davison (township) Genesee County	2	0.01
Eastpointe (city) Macomb County	2	0.01
Chesterfield (township) Macomb County	2	<0.01
Dearborn Heights (city) Wayne County	2	<0.01

Top 10 Places Sorted by Percent of Total Population
Based on all places, regardless of total population

Place	Population	%
Detour (township) Chippewa County	3	0.37
Speaker (township) Sanilac County	4	0.27
Wilmot (township) Cheboygan County	1	0.11
Milford (village) Oakland County	4	0.06
Milford (charter twp) Oakland County	4	0.03
Belleville (city) Wayne County	1	0.03
Cedar Creek (township) Muskegon County	1	0.03
Onondaga (township) Ingham County	1	0.03
Sturgis (city) St. Joseph County	2	0.02
Davison (township) Genesee County	2	0.01

Top 10 Places Sorted by Percent of Total Population
Based on places with total population of 50,000 or more

Place	Population	%
Livonia (city) Wayne County	3	<0.01
Dearborn Heights (city) Wayne County	2	<0.01
Lansing (city) Ingham County	2	<0.01
St. Clair Shores (city) Macomb County	2	<0.01
Ann Arbor (city) Washtenaw County	1	<0.01
Detroit (city) Wayne County	1	<0.01
Novi (city) Oakland County	1	<0.01
Waterford (charter twp) Oakland County	1	<0.01
Ypsilanti (charter twp) Washtenaw County	1	<0.01
Battle Creek (city) Calhoun County	0	0.00

American Indian: Pima

Top 10 Places Sorted by Population
Based on all places, regardless of total population

Place	Population	%
Fremont (township) Saginaw County	6	0.29

Place	Population	%
Redford (charter twp) Wayne County	4	0.01
Cheshire (township) Allegan County	3	0.14
North Muskegon (city) Muskegon County	3	0.08
Vevay (township) Ingham County	3	0.08
Port Huron (charter twp) St. Clair County	2	0.02
Garfield (charter twp) Grand Traverse County	2	0.01
Watersmeet (cdp) Gogebic County	1	0.23
Bay Mills (township) Chippewa County	1	0.07
Watersmeet (township) Gogebic County	1	0.07

Top 10 Places Sorted by Percent of Total Population
Based on all places, regardless of total population

Place	Population	%
Fremont (township) Saginaw County	6	0.29
Watersmeet (cdp) Gogebic County	1	0.23
Cheshire (township) Allegan County	3	0.14
North Muskegon (city) Muskegon County	3	0.08
Vevay (township) Ingham County	3	0.08
Bay Mills (township) Chippewa County	1	0.07
Watersmeet (township) Gogebic County	1	0.07
Trowbridge Park (cdp) Marquette County	1	0.05
Marquette (charter twp) Marquette County	1	0.03
Port Huron (charter twp) St. Clair County	2	0.02

Top 10 Places Sorted by Percent of Total Population
Based on places with total population of 50,000 or more

Place	Population	%
Flint (city) Genesee County	1	<0.01
Taylor (city) Wayne County	1	<0.01
Warren (city) Macomb County	1	<0.01
Wyoming (city) Kent County	1	<0.01
Ann Arbor (city) Washtenaw County	0	0.00
Battle Creek (city) Calhoun County	0	0.00
Canton (charter twp) Wayne County	0	0.00
Clinton (charter twp) Macomb County	0	0.00
Dearborn (city) Wayne County	0	0.00
Dearborn Heights (city) Wayne County	0	0.00

American Indian: Potawatomi

Top 10 Places Sorted by Population
Based on all places, regardless of total population

Place	Population	%
Harris (township) Menominee County	335	17.02
Grand Rapids (city) Kent County	166	0.09
Dowagiac (city) Cass County	140	2.38
Wyoming (city) Kent County	86	0.12
Escanaba (city) Delta County	84	0.67
Battle Creek (city) Calhoun County	81	0.15
Kalamazoo (city) Kalamazoo County	81	0.11
LaGrange (township) Cass County	75	2.14
Detroit (city) Wayne County	61	0.01
Niles (township) Berrien County	58	0.41

Top 10 Places Sorted by Percent of Total Population
Based on all places, regardless of total population

Place	Population	%
Harris (township) Menominee County	335	17.02
Zeba (cdp) Baraga County	12	2.50
Dowagiac (city) Cass County	140	2.38
LaGrange (township) Cass County	75	2.14
Gourley (township) Menominee County	8	1.90
Hartford (city) Van Buren County	50	1.86
Athens (township) Calhoun County	38	1.49
Breen (township) Dickinson County	7	1.40
Levering (cdp) Emmet County	3	1.40
Wayne (township) Cass County	35	1.32

Top 10 Places Sorted by Percent of Total Population
Based on places with total population of 50,000 or more

Place	Population	%
Battle Creek (city) Calhoun County	81	0.15
Wyoming (city) Kent County	86	0.12
Kalamazoo (city) Kalamazoo County	81	0.11
Grand Rapids (city) Kent County	166	0.09
Lansing (city) Ingham County	51	0.04
Pontiac (city) Oakland County	15	0.03
Flint (city) Genesee County	16	0.02
Waterford (charter twp) Oakland County	14	0.02
Saginaw (city) Saginaw County	12	0.02
Ypsilanti (charter twp) Washtenaw County	12	0.02

American Indian: Pueblo

Top 10 Places Sorted by Population
Based on all places, regardless of total population

Place	Population	%
Wyandotte (city) Wayne County	6	0.02
Livonia (city) Wayne County	6	0.01
Huron (charter twp) Wayne County	5	0.03
Bay City (city) Bay County	5	0.01
Kentwood (city) Kent County	5	0.01
Roseville (city) Macomb County	5	0.01
Detroit (city) Wayne County	5	<0.01
Union (charter twp) Isabella County	4	0.03
Genesee (charter twp) Genesee County	4	0.02
Summit (township) Jackson County	4	0.02

Top 10 Places Sorted by Percent of Total Population
Based on all places, regardless of total population

Place	Population	%
Merrill (village) Saginaw County	3	0.39
Humboldt (township) Marquette County	1	0.22
Jonesfield (township) Saginaw County	3	0.18
Petersburg (city) Monroe County	2	0.17
Vicksburg (village) Kalamazoo County	3	0.10
Orange (township) Ionia County	1	0.10
Bennington (township) Shiawassee County	3	0.09
Marcellus (village) Cass County	1	0.08
Scottville (city) Mason County	1	0.08
London (township) Monroe County	2	0.07

Top 10 Places Sorted by Percent of Total Population
Based on places with total population of 50,000 or more

Place	Population	%
Livonia (city) Wayne County	6	0.01
Kalamazoo (city) Kalamazoo County	4	0.01
Detroit (city) Wayne County	5	<0.01
Shelby (charter twp) Macomb County	3	<0.01
Clinton (charter twp) Macomb County	2	<0.01
Grand Rapids (city) Kent County	2	<0.01
Lansing (city) Ingham County	2	<0.01
Ypsilanti (charter twp) Washtenaw County	2	<0.01
Ann Arbor (city) Washtenaw County	1	<0.01
Battle Creek (city) Calhoun County	1	<0.01

American Indian: Puget Sound Salish

Top 10 Places Sorted by Population
Based on all places, regardless of total population

Place	Population	%
Flint (charter twp) Genesee County	6	0.02
Grant (township) Clare County	5	0.15
Detroit (city) Wayne County	5	<0.01
Niles (township) Berrien County	4	0.03
Ann Arbor (city) Washtenaw County	4	<0.01
Battle Creek (city) Calhoun County	3	0.01
Warren (city) Macomb County	3	<0.01
Flint (city) Genesee County	2	<0.01
Meyer (township) Menominee County	1	0.10
Wayne (township) Cass County	1	0.04

Top 10 Places Sorted by Percent of Total Population
Based on all places, regardless of total population

Place	Population	%
Grant (township) Clare County	5	0.15
Meyer (township) Menominee County	1	0.10
Wayne (township) Cass County	1	0.04
Niles (township) Berrien County	4	0.03
Portage (charter twp) Houghton County	1	0.03
Flint (charter twp) Genesee County	6	0.02
Calumet (charter twp) Houghton County	1	0.02
Battle Creek (city) Calhoun County	3	0.01
Alpena (township) Alpena County	1	0.01
Argentine (township) Genesee County	1	0.01

Top 10 Places Sorted by Percent of Total Population
Based on places with total population of 50,000 or more

Place	Population	%
Battle Creek (city) Calhoun County	3	0.01
Detroit (city) Wayne County	5	<0.01
Ann Arbor (city) Washtenaw County	4	<0.01
Warren (city) Macomb County	3	<0.01

Flint (city) Genesee County	2	<0.01
Canton (charter twp) Wayne County	1	<0.01
Grand Rapids (city) Kent County	1	<0.01
Livonia (city) Wayne County	1	<0.01
Wyoming (city) Kent County	1	<0.01
Clinton (charter twp) Macomb County	0	0.00

American Indian: Seminole

Top 10 Places Sorted by Population
Based on all places, regardless of total population

Place	Population	%
Detroit (city) Wayne County	63	0.01
Shelby (charter twp) Macomb County	16	0.02
Grand Rapids (city) Kent County	16	0.01
Lansing (city) Ingham County	13	0.01
Flint (charter twp) Genesee County	8	0.03
Clinton (charter twp) Macomb County	7	0.01
Crockery (township) Ottawa County	6	0.15
Oak Park (city) Oakland County	6	0.02
Pontiac (city) Oakland County	6	0.01
Southfield (city) Oakland County	6	0.01

Top 10 Places Sorted by Percent of Total Population
Based on all places, regardless of total population

Place	Population	%
Watersmeet (cdp) Gogebic County	3	0.70
Vandalia (village) Cass County	1	0.33
Barryton (village) Mecosta County	1	0.28
Watersmeet (township) Gogebic County	3	0.21
Mathias (township) Alger County	1	0.18
Crockery (township) Ottawa County	6	0.15
Yates (township) Lake County	1	0.13
Maple Ridge (township) Alpena County	2	0.12
Decatur (village) Van Buren County	2	0.11
Indian River (cdp) Cheboygan County	2	0.10

Top 10 Places Sorted by Percent of Total Population
Based on places with total population of 50,000 or more

Place	Population	%
Shelby (charter twp) Macomb County	16	0.02
Detroit (city) Wayne County	63	0.01
Grand Rapids (city) Kent County	16	0.01
Lansing (city) Ingham County	13	0.01
Clinton (charter twp) Macomb County	7	0.01
Pontiac (city) Oakland County	6	0.01
Southfield (city) Oakland County	6	0.01
Rochester Hills (city) Oakland County	5	0.01
Saginaw (city) Saginaw County	5	0.01
Taylor (city) Wayne County	4	0.01

American Indian: Shoshone

Top 10 Places Sorted by Population
Based on all places, regardless of total population

Place	Population	%
Ashland (township) Newaygo County	4	0.14
East Lansing (city) Ingham County	4	0.01
Ann Arbor (city) Washtenaw County	4	<0.01
Detroit (city) Wayne County	4	<0.01
Petoskey (city) Emmet County	3	0.05
Wayne (city) Wayne County	3	0.02
Millington (township) Tuscola County	2	0.05
Pavilion (township) Kalamazoo County	2	0.03
New Baltimore (city) Macomb County	2	0.02
Berkley (city) Oakland County	2	0.01

Top 10 Places Sorted by Percent of Total Population
Based on all places, regardless of total population

Place	Population	%
Ashland (township) Newaygo County	4	0.14
Petoskey (city) Emmet County	3	0.05
Millington (township) Tuscola County	2	0.05
Calvin (township) Cass County	1	0.05
Dayton (township) Tuscola County	1	0.05
Indian River (cdp) Cheboygan County	1	0.05
Marlette (city) Sanilac County	1	0.05
Pinckney (village) Livingston County	1	0.04
Sylvan (township) Washtenaw County	1	0.04
Pavilion (township) Kalamazoo County	2	0.03

American Indian: Sioux

Top 10 Places Sorted by Percent of Total Population
Based on places with total population of 50,000 or more

Place	Population	%
Ann Arbor (city) Washtenaw County	4	<0.01
Detroit (city) Wayne County	4	<0.01
Warren (city) Macomb County	2	<0.01
Dearborn (city) Wayne County	1	<0.01
Flint (city) Genesee County	1	<0.01
Kalamazoo (city) Kalamazoo County	1	<0.01
Lansing (city) Ingham County	1	<0.01
Novi (city) Oakland County	1	<0.01
Southfield (city) Oakland County	1	<0.01
St. Clair Shores (city) Macomb County	1	<0.01

American Indian: Sioux

Top 10 Places Sorted by Population
Based on all places, regardless of total population

Place	Population	%
Detroit (city) Wayne County	68	0.01
Lansing (city) Ingham County	43	0.04
Grand Rapids (city) Kent County	43	0.02
Warren (city) Macomb County	29	0.02
Flint (city) Genesee County	26	0.03
Ypsilanti (charter twp) Washtenaw County	24	0.04
Escanaba (city) Delta County	21	0.17
Ann Arbor (city) Washtenaw County	19	0.02
Kentwood (city) Kent County	18	0.04
Battle Creek (city) Calhoun County	18	0.03

Top 10 Places Sorted by Percent of Total Population
Based on all places, regardless of total population

Place	Population	%
Meade (township) Mason County	4	2.21
Brutus (cdp) Emmet County	2	0.92
Whittemore (city) Iosco County	3	0.78
Hendricks (township) Mackinac County	1	0.65
White Pine (cdp) Ontonagon County	3	0.63
Wilmot (township) Cheboygan County	5	0.57
Baldwin (township) Delta County	4	0.53
Marquette (township) Mackinac County	3	0.50
Medina (township) Lenawee County	5	0.46
Wilcox (township) Newaygo County	5	0.46

Top 10 Places Sorted by Percent of Total Population
Based on places with total population of 50,000 or more

Place	Population	%
Lansing (city) Ingham County	43	0.04
Ypsilanti (charter twp) Washtenaw County	24	0.04
Flint (city) Genesee County	26	0.03
Battle Creek (city) Calhoun County	18	0.03
Grand Rapids (city) Kent County	43	0.02
Warren (city) Macomb County	29	0.02
Ann Arbor (city) Washtenaw County	19	0.02
Kalamazoo (city) Kalamazoo County	17	0.02
Pontiac (city) Oakland County	14	0.02
St. Clair Shores (city) Macomb County	13	0.02

American Indian: South American Indian

Top 10 Places Sorted by Population
Based on all places, regardless of total population

Place	Population	%
Detroit (city) Wayne County	29	<0.01
Grand Rapids (city) Kent County	25	0.01
Ann Arbor (city) Washtenaw County	22	0.02
Dearborn (city) Wayne County	12	0.01
Scio (township) Washtenaw County	10	0.05
Canton (charter twp) Wayne County	10	0.01
Lansing (city) Ingham County	8	0.01
Ypsilanti (charter twp) Washtenaw County	7	0.01
Ludington (city) Mason County	6	0.07
Jackson (city) Jackson County	6	0.02

Top 10 Places Sorted by Percent of Total Population
Based on all places, regardless of total population

Place	Population	%
Chippewa (township) Chippewa County	1	0.47
Birch Run (village) Saginaw County	5	0.32
Brampton (township) Delta County	3	0.29

Place	Population	%
Lamotte (township) Sanilac County	2	0.22
Mecosta (village) Mecosta County	1	0.22
Garden (township) Delta County	1	0.13
Rich (township) Lapeer County	2	0.12
Benton Heights (cdp) Berrien County	4	0.10
Bath (cdp) Clinton County	2	0.10
Custer (township) Antrim County	1	0.09

Top 10 Places Sorted by Percent of Total Population
Based on places with total population of 50,000 or more

Place	Population	%
Ann Arbor (city) Washtenaw County	22	0.02
Grand Rapids (city) Kent County	25	0.01
Dearborn (city) Wayne County	12	0.01
Canton (charter twp) Wayne County	10	0.01
Lansing (city) Ingham County	8	0.01
Ypsilanti (charter twp) Washtenaw County	7	0.01
Taylor (city) Wayne County	5	0.01
West Bloomfield (charter twp) Oakland County	5	0.01
Wyoming (city) Kent County	4	0.01
Battle Creek (city) Calhoun County	3	0.01

American Indian: Spanish American Indian

Top 10 Places Sorted by Population
Based on all places, regardless of total population

Place	Population	%
Grand Rapids (city) Kent County	16	0.01
Detroit (city) Wayne County	10	<0.01
Wyoming (city) Kent County	9	0.01
Marshall (city) Calhoun County	5	0.07
Zeeland (charter twp) Ottawa County	5	0.05
Union (charter twp) Isabella County	5	0.04
Solon (township) Kent County	4	0.07
Meridian (charter twp) Ingham County	4	0.01
Breckenridge (village) Gratiot County	3	0.23
Wheeler (township) Gratiot County	3	0.11

Top 10 Places Sorted by Percent of Total Population
Based on all places, regardless of total population

Place	Population	%
Hillman (village) Montmorency County	2	0.29
Breckenridge (village) Gratiot County	3	0.23
Wheeler (township) Gratiot County	3	0.11
Washington (township) Gratiot County	1	0.11
Hillman (township) Montmorency County	2	0.09
Lake Michigan Beach (cdp) Berrien County	1	0.08
Marshall (city) Calhoun County	5	0.07
Solon (township) Kent County	4	0.07
Sandusky (city) Sanilac County	2	0.07
Edwards (township) Ogemaw County	1	0.07

Top 10 Places Sorted by Percent of Total Population
Based on places with total population of 50,000 or more

Place	Population	%
Grand Rapids (city) Kent County	16	0.01
Wyoming (city) Kent County	9	0.01
Pontiac (city) Oakland County	3	0.01
Saginaw (city) Saginaw County	3	0.01
Detroit (city) Wayne County	10	<0.01
Westland (city) Wayne County	2	<0.01
Kalamazoo (city) Kalamazoo County	1	<0.01
Lansing (city) Ingham County	1	<0.01
Royal Oak (city) Oakland County	1	<0.01
Southfield (city) Oakland County	1	<0.01

Alaska Native: Tlingit-Haida

Top 10 Places Sorted by Population
Based on all places, regardless of total population

Place	Population	%
Ypsilanti (charter twp) Washtenaw County	9	0.02
Novi (city) Oakland County	5	0.01
Lansing (city) Ingham County	5	<0.01
Walker (city) Kent County	4	0.02
Ypsilanti (city) Washtenaw County	4	0.02
Taylor (city) Wayne County	4	0.01
Grand Rapids (city) Kent County	4	<0.01
Indian River (cdp) Cheboygan County	3	0.15
Inverness (township) Cheboygan County	3	0.13

Place	Population	%
Tuscarora (township) Cheboygan County	3	0.10

Top 10 Places Sorted by Percent of Total Population
Based on all places, regardless of total population

Place	Population	%
Eden (township) Mason County	2	0.34
South Boardman (cdp) Kalkaska County	1	0.19
Readmond (township) Emmet County	1	0.17
Lake (township) Roscommon County	2	0.16
Indian River (cdp) Cheboygan County	3	0.15
Inverness (township) Cheboygan County	3	0.13
Greenleaf (township) Sanilac County	1	0.13
Posen (township) Presque Isle County	1	0.12
Tuscarora (township) Cheboygan County	3	0.10
Bath (cdp) Clinton County	2	0.10

Top 10 Places Sorted by Percent of Total Population
Based on places with total population of 50,000 or more

Place	Population	%
Ypsilanti (charter twp) Washtenaw County	9	0.02
Novi (city) Oakland County	5	0.01
Taylor (city) Wayne County	4	0.01
Lansing (city) Ingham County	5	<0.01
Grand Rapids (city) Kent County	4	<0.01
Detroit (city) Wayne County	3	<0.01
Waterford (charter twp) Oakland County	3	<0.01
Farmington Hills (city) Oakland County	2	<0.01
Kalamazoo (city) Kalamazoo County	2	<0.01
West Bloomfield (charter twp) Oakland County	2	<0.01

American Indian: Tohono O'Odham

Top 10 Places Sorted by Population
Based on all places, regardless of total population

Place	Population	%
Pickford (township) Chippewa County	3	0.19
Huntington Woods (city) Oakland County	3	0.05
York (charter twp) Washtenaw County	2	0.02
Harrison (charter twp) Macomb County	2	0.01
Detroit (city) Wayne County	2	<0.01
Lansing (city) Ingham County	2	<0.01
Boyne Falls (village) Charlevoix County	1	0.34
Boyne Valley (township) Charlevoix County	1	0.08
Leslie (city) Ingham County	1	0.05
Vernon (township) Shiawassee County	1	0.02

Top 10 Places Sorted by Percent of Total Population
Based on all places, regardless of total population

Place	Population	%
Boyne Falls (village) Charlevoix County	1	0.34
Pickford (township) Chippewa County	3	0.19
Boyne Valley (township) Charlevoix County	1	0.08
Huntington Woods (city) Oakland County	3	0.05
Leslie (city) Ingham County	1	0.05
York (charter twp) Washtenaw County	2	0.02
Vernon (township) Shiawassee County	1	0.02
Harrison (charter twp) Macomb County	2	0.01
Schoolcraft (township) Kalamazoo County	1	0.01
Detroit (city) Wayne County	2	<0.01

Top 10 Places Sorted by Percent of Total Population
Based on places with total population of 50,000 or more

Place	Population	%
Detroit (city) Wayne County	2	<0.01
Lansing (city) Ingham County	2	<0.01
Ann Arbor (city) Washtenaw County	1	<0.01
Flint (city) Genesee County	1	<0.01
Grand Rapids (city) Kent County	1	<0.01
Battle Creek (city) Calhoun County	0	0.00
Canton (charter twp) Wayne County	0	0.00
Clinton (charter twp) Macomb County	0	0.00
Dearborn (city) Wayne County	0	0.00
Dearborn Heights (city) Wayne County	0	0.00

Alaska Native: Tsimshian

Top 10 Places Sorted by Population
Based on all places, regardless of total population

Place	Population	%
Oakfield (township) Kent County	5	0.09

Place	Population	%
Elkland (township) Tuscola County	3	0.09
Dexter (village) Washtenaw County	2	0.05
Wayland (city) Allegan County	2	0.05
Kawkawlin (township) Bay County	2	0.04
Fraser (city) Macomb County	2	0.01
Norton Shores (city) Muskegon County	2	0.01
Scio (township) Washtenaw County	2	0.01
Eaton Rapids (city) Eaton County	1	0.02
Robinson (township) Ottawa County	1	0.02

Top 10 Places Sorted by Percent of Total Population
Based on all places, regardless of total population

Place	Population	%
Oakfield (township) Kent County	5	0.09
Elkland (township) Tuscola County	3	0.09
Dexter (village) Washtenaw County	2	0.05
Wayland (city) Allegan County	2	0.05
Kawkawlin (township) Bay County	2	0.04
Eaton Rapids (city) Eaton County	1	0.02
Robinson (township) Ottawa County	1	0.02
Fraser (city) Macomb County	2	0.01
Norton Shores (city) Muskegon County	2	0.01
Scio (township) Washtenaw County	2	0.01

Top 10 Places Sorted by Percent of Total Population
Based on places with total population of 50,000 or more

Place	Population	%
Rochester Hills (city) Oakland County	1	<0.01
Westland (city) Wayne County	1	<0.01
Ann Arbor (city) Washtenaw County	0	0.00
Battle Creek (city) Calhoun County	0	0.00
Canton (charter twp) Wayne County	0	0.00
Clinton (charter twp) Macomb County	0	0.00
Dearborn (city) Wayne County	0	0.00
Dearborn Heights (city) Wayne County	0	0.00
Detroit (city) Wayne County	0	0.00
Farmington Hills (city) Oakland County	0	0.00

American Indian: Ute

Top 10 Places Sorted by Population
Based on all places, regardless of total population

Place	Population	%
Detroit (city) Wayne County	7	<0.01
Saline (city) Washtenaw County	5	0.06
Putnam (township) Livingston County	4	0.05
Pinckney (village) Livingston County	3	0.12
Birmingham (city) Oakland County	3	0.01
Commerce (charter twp) Oakland County	3	0.01
Saginaw (city) Saginaw County	2	<0.01
Bay Mills (township) Chippewa County	1	0.07
Shiawassee (township) Shiawassee County	1	0.04
Ishpeming (city) Marquette County	1	0.02

Top 10 Places Sorted by Percent of Total Population
Based on all places, regardless of total population

Place	Population	%
Pinckney (village) Livingston County	3	0.12
Bay Mills (township) Chippewa County	1	0.07
Saline (city) Washtenaw County	5	0.06
Putnam (township) Livingston County	4	0.05
Shiawassee (township) Shiawassee County	1	0.04
Ishpeming (city) Marquette County	1	0.02
Peninsula (township) Grand Traverse County	1	0.02
Birmingham (city) Oakland County	3	0.01
Commerce (charter twp) Oakland County	3	0.01
Alma (city) Gratiot County	1	0.01

Top 10 Places Sorted by Percent of Total Population
Based on places with total population of 50,000 or more

Place	Population	%
Detroit (city) Wayne County	7	<0.01
Saginaw (city) Saginaw County	2	<0.01
Battle Creek (city) Calhoun County	1	<0.01
Grand Rapids (city) Kent County	1	<0.01
Lansing (city) Ingham County	1	<0.01
Ypsilanti (charter twp) Washtenaw County	1	<0.01
Ann Arbor (city) Washtenaw County	0	0.00
Canton (charter twp) Wayne County	0	0.00
Clinton (charter twp) Macomb County	0	0.00
Dearborn (city) Wayne County	0	0.00

American Indian: Yakama

Top 10 Places Sorted by Population
Based on all places, regardless of total population

Place	Population	%
Van Buren (charter twp) Wayne County	4	0.01
Detroit (city) Wayne County	3	<0.01
Kingsford (city) Dickinson County	2	0.04
Ronald (township) Ionia County	1	0.05
Fenton (charter twp) Genesee County	1	0.01
Hillsdale (city) Hillsdale County	1	0.01
York (charter twp) Washtenaw County	1	0.01
Eastpointe (city) Macomb County	1	<0.01
Mount Morris (township) Genesee County	1	<0.01
Oxford (charter twp) Oakland County	1	<0.01

Top 10 Places Sorted by Percent of Total Population
Based on all places, regardless of total population

Place	Population	%
Ronald (township) Ionia County	1	0.05
Kingsford (city) Dickinson County	2	0.04
Van Buren (charter twp) Wayne County	4	0.01
Fenton (charter twp) Genesee County	1	0.01
Hillsdale (city) Hillsdale County	1	0.01
York (charter twp) Washtenaw County	1	0.01
Detroit (city) Wayne County	3	<0.01
Eastpointe (city) Macomb County	1	<0.01
Mount Morris (township) Genesee County	1	<0.01
Oxford (charter twp) Oakland County	1	<0.01

Top 10 Places Sorted by Percent of Total Population
Based on places with total population of 50,000 or more

Place	Population	%
Detroit (city) Wayne County	3	<0.01
Ypsilanti (charter twp) Washtenaw County	1	<0.01
Ann Arbor (city) Washtenaw County	0	0.00
Battle Creek (city) Calhoun County	0	0.00
Canton (charter twp) Wayne County	0	0.00
Clinton (charter twp) Macomb County	0	0.00
Dearborn (city) Wayne County	0	0.00
Dearborn Heights (city) Wayne County	0	0.00
Farmington Hills (city) Oakland County	0	0.00
Flint (city) Genesee County	0	0.00

American Indian: Yaqui

Top 10 Places Sorted by Population
Based on all places, regardless of total population

Place	Population	%
Kalamazoo (city) Kalamazoo County	10	0.01
Dearborn (city) Wayne County	9	0.01
Pontiac (city) Oakland County	6	0.01
Battle Creek (city) Calhoun County	5	0.01
Riley (township) Clinton County	4	0.20
Buena Vista (cdp) Saginaw County	4	0.06
Buena Vista (charter twp) Saginaw County	4	0.05
Richfield (township) Genesee County	4	0.05
Taylor (city) Wayne County	4	0.01
Lansing (city) Ingham County	4	<0.01

Top 10 Places Sorted by Percent of Total Population
Based on all places, regardless of total population

Place	Population	%
Centerville (township) Leelanau County	3	0.24
Riley (township) Clinton County	4	0.20
Coloma (city) Berrien County	3	0.20
Frederic (township) Crawford County	2	0.15
Evart (city) Osceola County	2	0.11
North Branch (village) Lapeer County	1	0.10
Blissfield (village) Lenawee County	3	0.09
Sagola (township) Dickinson County	1	0.09
Blissfield (township) Lenawee County	3	0.08
Dimondale (village) Eaton County	1	0.08

Top 10 Places Sorted by Percent of Total Population
Based on places with total population of 50,000 or more

Place	Population	%
Kalamazoo (city) Kalamazoo County	10	0.01
Dearborn (city) Wayne County	9	0.01
Pontiac (city) Oakland County	6	0.01
Battle Creek (city) Calhoun County	5	0.01

Taylor (city) Wayne County	4	0.01
Lansing (city) Ingham County	4	<0.01
Troy (city) Oakland County	4	<0.01
Grand Rapids (city) Kent County	3	<0.01
Detroit (city) Wayne County	2	<0.01
Warren (city) Macomb County	2	<0.01

American Indian: Yuman

Top 10 Places Sorted by Population
Based on all places, regardless of total population

Place	Population	%
North Muskegon (city) Muskegon County	3	0.08
Saginaw (city) Saginaw County	3	0.01
Ithaca (city) Gratiot County	2	0.07
Carrollton (township) Saginaw County	2	0.03
Detroit (city) Wayne County	2	<0.01
Wyoming (city) Kent County	2	<0.01
Frankenlust (township) Bay County	1	0.03
Marysville (city) St. Clair County	1	0.01
Farmington Hills (city) Oakland County	1	<0.01
Garden City (city) Wayne County	1	<0.01

Top 10 Places Sorted by Percent of Total Population
Based on all places, regardless of total population

Place	Population	%
North Muskegon (city) Muskegon County	3	0.08
Ithaca (city) Gratiot County	2	0.07
Carrollton (township) Saginaw County	2	0.03
Frankenlust (township) Bay County	1	0.03
Saginaw (city) Saginaw County	3	0.01
Marysville (city) St. Clair County	1	0.01
Detroit (city) Wayne County	2	<0.01
Wyoming (city) Kent County	2	<0.01
Farmington Hills (city) Oakland County	1	<0.01
Garden City (city) Wayne County	1	<0.01

Top 10 Places Sorted by Percent of Total Population
Based on places with total population of 50,000 or more

Place	Population	%
Saginaw (city) Saginaw County	3	0.01
Detroit (city) Wayne County	2	<0.01
Wyoming (city) Kent County	2	<0.01
Farmington Hills (city) Oakland County	1	<0.01
Grand Rapids (city) Kent County	1	<0.01
Taylor (city) Wayne County	1	<0.01
Ypsilanti (charter twp) Washtenaw County	1	<0.01
Ann Arbor (city) Washtenaw County	0	0.00
Battle Creek (city) Calhoun County	0	0.00
Canton (charter twp) Wayne County	0	0.00

Alaska Native: Yup'ik

Top 10 Places Sorted by Population
Based on all places, regardless of total population

Place	Population	%
Ashland (township) Newaygo County	6	0.22
Sault Ste. Marie (city) Chippewa County	6	0.04
Bruce (township) Macomb County	5	0.06
Macomb (township) Macomb County	4	0.01
Solon (township) Leelanau County	3	0.20
Flushing (city) Genesee County	3	0.04
Pittsfield (charter twp) Washtenaw County	3	<0.01
Lansing (city) Ingham County	3	<0.01
Addison (township) Oakland County	2	0.03
Whitmore Lake (cdp) Washtenaw County	2	0.03

Top 10 Places Sorted by Percent of Total Population
Based on all places, regardless of total population

Place	Population	%
Ashland (township) Newaygo County	6	0.22
Solon (township) Leelanau County	3	0.20
Claybanks (township) Oceana County	1	0.13
Riverton (township) Mason County	1	0.09
Harrisville (township) Alcona County	1	0.07
Bruce (township) Macomb County	5	0.06
Tecumseh (township) Lenawee County	1	0.05
Sault Ste. Marie (city) Chippewa County	6	0.04
Flushing (city) Genesee County	3	0.04
Big Prairie (township) Newaygo County	1	0.04

(Top 10 Places Sorted by Percent of Total Population)
Based on places with total population of 50,000 or more

Place	Population	%
Macomb (township) Macomb County	4	0.01
Lansing (city) Ingham County	3	<0.01
Detroit (city) Wayne County	2	<0.01
Ann Arbor (city) Washtenaw County	1	<0.01
Westland (city) Wayne County	1	<0.01
Battle Creek (city) Calhoun County	0	0.00
Canton (charter twp) Wayne County	0	0.00
Clinton (charter twp) Macomb County	0	0.00
Dearborn (city) Wayne County	0	0.00
Dearborn Heights (city) Wayne County	0	0.00

Asian

Top 10 Places Sorted by Population
Based on all places, regardless of total population

Place	Population	%
Ann Arbor (city) Washtenaw County	18,345	16.10
Troy (city) Oakland County	16,417	20.27
Canton (charter twp) Wayne County	13,875	15.39
Sterling Heights (city) Macomb County	10,282	7.93
Detroit (city) Wayne County	9,925	1.39
Novi (city) Oakland County	9,354	16.94
Farmington Hills (city) Oakland County	8,910	11.17
Rochester Hills (city) Oakland County	8,144	11.47
Warren (city) Macomb County	7,263	5.42
West Bloomfield (charter twp) Oakland County	6,156	9.52

Top 10 Places Sorted by Percent of Total Population
Based on all places, regardless of total population

Place	Population	%
Hamtramck (city) Wayne County	5,539	24.70
Troy (city) Oakland County	16,417	20.27
Ann Arbor (charter twp) Washtenaw County	825	18.92
Novi (city) Oakland County	9,354	16.94
Ann Arbor (city) Washtenaw County	18,345	16.10
Okemos (cdp) Ingham County	3,358	15.71
Canton (charter twp) Wayne County	13,875	15.39
Pittsfield (charter twp) Washtenaw County	5,273	15.21
Farmington (city) Oakland County	1,549	14.93
Northville (township) Wayne County	3,520	12.35

Top 10 Places Sorted by Percent of Total Population
Based on places with total population of 50,000 or more

Place	Population	%
Troy (city) Oakland County	16,417	20.27
Novi (city) Oakland County	9,354	16.94
Ann Arbor (city) Washtenaw County	18,345	16.10
Canton (charter twp) Wayne County	13,875	15.39
Rochester Hills (city) Oakland County	8,144	11.47
Farmington Hills (city) Oakland County	8,910	11.17
West Bloomfield (charter twp) Oakland County	6,156	9.52
Sterling Heights (city) Macomb County	10,282	7.93
Warren (city) Macomb County	7,263	5.42
Dearborn (city) Wayne County	4,603	4.69

Asian: Not Hispanic

Top 10 Places Sorted by Population
Based on all places, regardless of total population

Place	Population	%
Ann Arbor (city) Washtenaw County	18,205	15.98
Troy (city) Oakland County	16,356	20.20
Canton (charter twp) Wayne County	13,816	15.32
Sterling Heights (city) Macomb County	10,193	7.86
Detroit (city) Wayne County	9,598	1.34
Novi (city) Oakland County	9,318	16.87
Farmington Hills (city) Oakland County	8,868	11.12
Rochester Hills (city) Oakland County	8,104	11.41
Warren (city) Macomb County	7,175	5.35
West Bloomfield (charter twp) Oakland County	6,123	9.47

Top 10 Places Sorted by Percent of Total Population
Based on all places, regardless of total population

Place	Population	%
Hamtramck (city) Wayne County	5,495	24.51
Troy (city) Oakland County	16,356	20.20
Ann Arbor (charter twp) Washtenaw County	824	18.89

Novi (city) Oakland County	9,318	16.87
Ann Arbor (city) Washtenaw County	18,205	15.98
Okemos (cdp) Ingham County	3,340	15.63
Canton (charter twp) Wayne County	13,816	15.32
Pittsfield (charter twp) Washtenaw County	5,233	15.10
Farmington (city) Oakland County	1,542	14.87
Northville (township) Wayne County	3,501	12.29

Top 10 Places Sorted by Percent of Total Population
Based on places with total population of 50,000 or more

Place	Population	%
Troy (city) Oakland County	16,356	20.20
Novi (city) Oakland County	9,318	16.87
Ann Arbor (city) Washtenaw County	18,205	15.98
Canton (charter twp) Wayne County	13,816	15.32
Rochester Hills (city) Oakland County	8,104	11.41
Farmington Hills (city) Oakland County	8,868	11.12
West Bloomfield (charter twp) Oakland County	6,123	9.47
Sterling Heights (city) Macomb County	10,193	7.86
Warren (city) Macomb County	7,175	5.35
Dearborn (city) Wayne County	4,522	4.61

Asian: Hispanic

Top 10 Places Sorted by Population
Based on all places, regardless of total population

Place	Population	%
Detroit (city) Wayne County	327	0.05
Grand Rapids (city) Kent County	167	0.09
Holland (charter twp) Ottawa County	143	0.40
Ann Arbor (city) Washtenaw County	140	0.12
Lansing (city) Ingham County	136	0.12
Holland (city) Ottawa County	95	0.29
Sterling Heights (city) Macomb County	89	0.07
Warren (city) Macomb County	88	0.07
Dearborn (city) Wayne County	81	0.08
Wyoming (city) Kent County	80	0.11

Top 10 Places Sorted by Percent of Total Population
Based on all places, regardless of total population

Place	Population	%
Applegate (village) Sanilac County	5	2.02
North Allis (township) Presque Isle County	7	1.34
Eagle Harbor (cdp) Keweenaw County	1	1.32
Wolverine (village) Cheboygan County	3	1.23
Walloon Lake (cdp) Charlevoix County	3	1.03
Argyle (township) Sanilac County	6	0.79
Grawn (cdp) Grand Traverse County	6	0.78
Washington (township) Sanilac County	11	0.66
Richland (township) Ogemaw County	6	0.66
Berrien Springs (village) Berrien County	11	0.61

Top 10 Places Sorted by Percent of Total Population
Based on places with total population of 50,000 or more

Place	Population	%
Ann Arbor (city) Washtenaw County	140	0.12
Lansing (city) Ingham County	136	0.12
Wyoming (city) Kent County	80	0.11
Saginaw (city) Saginaw County	54	0.10
Grand Rapids (city) Kent County	167	0.09
Pontiac (city) Oakland County	51	0.09
Ypsilanti (charter twp) Washtenaw County	50	0.09
Dearborn (city) Wayne County	81	0.08
Troy (city) Oakland County	61	0.08
Kalamazoo (city) Kalamazoo County	58	0.08

Asian: Bangladeshi

Top 10 Places Sorted by Population
Based on all places, regardless of total population

Place	Population	%
Hamtramck (city) Wayne County	3,083	13.75
Detroit (city) Wayne County	2,825	0.40
Warren (city) Macomb County	1,061	0.79
Troy (city) Oakland County	232	0.29
Sterling Heights (city) Macomb County	223	0.17
Canton (charter twp) Wayne County	125	0.14
Ann Arbor (city) Washtenaw County	102	0.09
Madison Heights (city) Oakland County	95	0.32
Rochester Hills (city) Oakland County	80	0.11
Shelby (charter twp) Macomb County	48	0.07

Top 10 Places Sorted by Percent of Total Population
Based on all places, regardless of total population

Place	Population	%
Hamtramck (city) Wayne County	3,083	13.75
Barton Hills (village) Washtenaw County	5	1.70
Warren (city) Macomb County	1,061	0.79
Center Line (city) Macomb County	42	0.51
Detroit (city) Wayne County	2,825	0.40
Madison Heights (city) Oakland County	95	0.32
Troy (city) Oakland County	232	0.29
Oronoko (charter twp) Berrien County	25	0.27
Cassopolis (village) Cass County	4	0.23
Bad Axe (city) Huron County	6	0.19

Top 10 Places Sorted by Percent of Total Population
Based on places with total population of 50,000 or more

Place	Population	%
Warren (city) Macomb County	1,061	0.79
Detroit (city) Wayne County	2,825	0.40
Troy (city) Oakland County	232	0.29
Sterling Heights (city) Macomb County	223	0.17
Canton (charter twp) Wayne County	125	0.14
Rochester Hills (city) Oakland County	80	0.11
Ann Arbor (city) Washtenaw County	102	0.09
Shelby (charter twp) Macomb County	48	0.07
West Bloomfield (charter twp) Oakland County	36	0.06
Novi (city) Oakland County	23	0.04

Asian: Bhutanese

Top 10 Places Sorted by Population
Based on all places, regardless of total population

Place	Population	%
Lansing (city) Ingham County	281	0.25
Grand Rapids (city) Kent County	98	0.05
Grand Haven (city) Ottawa County	18	0.17
Kentwood (city) Kent County	12	0.02
Georgetown (charter twp) Ottawa County	9	0.02
Lansing (charter twp) Ingham County	7	0.09
Grandville (city) Kent County	7	0.05
Fremont (city) Newaygo County	5	0.12
Spring Lake (township) Ottawa County	5	0.03
Robinson (township) Ottawa County	1	0.02

Top 10 Places Sorted by Percent of Total Population
Based on all places, regardless of total population

Place	Population	%
Lansing (city) Ingham County	281	0.25
Grand Haven (city) Ottawa County	18	0.17
Fremont (city) Newaygo County	5	0.12
Lansing (charter twp) Ingham County	7	0.09
Grand Rapids (city) Kent County	98	0.05
Grandville (city) Kent County	7	0.05
Spring Lake (township) Ottawa County	5	0.03
Kentwood (city) Kent County	12	0.02
Georgetown (charter twp) Ottawa County	9	0.02
Robinson (township) Ottawa County	1	0.02

Top 10 Places Sorted by Percent of Total Population
Based on places with total population of 50,000 or more

Place	Population	%
Lansing (city) Ingham County	281	0.25
Grand Rapids (city) Kent County	98	0.05
Ann Arbor (city) Washtenaw County	0	0.00
Battle Creek (city) Calhoun County	0	0.00
Canton (charter twp) Wayne County	0	0.00
Clinton (charter twp) Macomb County	0	0.00
Dearborn (city) Wayne County	0	0.00
Dearborn Heights (city) Wayne County	0	0.00
Detroit (city) Wayne County	0	0.00
Farmington Hills (city) Oakland County	0	0.00

Asian: Burmese

Top 10 Places Sorted by Population
Based on all places, regardless of total population

Place	Population	%
Grand Rapids (city) Kent County	424	0.23
Lansing (city) Ingham County	383	0.34
Springfield (city) Calhoun County	349	6.63

Battle Creek (city) Calhoun County	301	0.58
Kentwood (city) Kent County	36	0.07
Sault Ste. Marie (city) Chippewa County	34	0.24
Meridian (charter twp) Ingham County	17	0.04
Wyoming (city) Kent County	17	0.02
Ann Arbor (city) Washtenaw County	16	0.01
Portage (city) Kalamazoo County	12	0.03

Top 10 Places Sorted by Percent of Total Population
Based on all places, regardless of total population

Place	Population	%
Springfield (city) Calhoun County	349	6.63
Muir (village) Ionia County	9	1.49
Battle Creek (city) Calhoun County	301	0.58
Eckford (township) Calhoun County	7	0.54
Lansing (city) Ingham County	383	0.34
Berrien Springs (village) Berrien County	5	0.28
Lyons (township) Ionia County	9	0.26
Sault Ste. Marie (city) Chippewa County	34	0.24
Dimondale (village) Eaton County	3	0.24
Grand Rapids (city) Kent County	424	0.23

Top 10 Places Sorted by Percent of Total Population
Based on places with total population of 50,000 or more

Place	Population	%
Battle Creek (city) Calhoun County	301	0.58
Lansing (city) Ingham County	383	0.34
Grand Rapids (city) Kent County	424	0.23
Wyoming (city) Kent County	17	0.02
Ann Arbor (city) Washtenaw County	16	0.01
Shelby (charter twp) Macomb County	7	0.01
Rochester Hills (city) Oakland County	4	0.01
West Bloomfield (charter twp) Oakland County	4	0.01
Sterling Heights (city) Macomb County	5	<0.01
Troy (city) Oakland County	4	<0.01

Asian: Cambodian

Top 10 Places Sorted by Population
Based on all places, regardless of total population

Place	Population	%
Holland (charter twp) Ottawa County	749	2.10
Holland (city) Ottawa County	295	0.89
Park (township) Ottawa County	77	0.43
Zeeland (charter twp) Ottawa County	74	0.74
Warren (city) Macomb County	55	0.04
Beechwood (cdp) Ottawa County	52	1.72
Pontiac (city) Oakland County	44	0.07
Eastpointe (city) Macomb County	31	0.10
Ann Arbor (city) Washtenaw County	29	0.03
Roseville (city) Macomb County	27	0.06

Top 10 Places Sorted by Percent of Total Population
Based on all places, regardless of total population

Place	Population	%
Holland (charter twp) Ottawa County	749	2.10
Beechwood (cdp) Ottawa County	52	1.72
Holland (city) Ottawa County	295	0.89
Zeeland (charter twp) Ottawa County	74	0.74
White Pigeon (village) St. Joseph County	8	0.53
Fillmore (township) Allegan County	14	0.52
Palmer (cdp) Marquette County	2	0.48
Park (township) Ottawa County	77	0.43
Nottawa (township) St. Joseph County	13	0.34
Flowerfield (township) St. Joseph County	5	0.32

Top 10 Places Sorted by Percent of Total Population
Based on places with total population of 50,000 or more

Place	Population	%
Pontiac (city) Oakland County	44	0.07
Warren (city) Macomb County	55	0.04
Ann Arbor (city) Washtenaw County	29	0.03
Clinton (charter twp) Macomb County	25	0.03
Kalamazoo (city) Kalamazoo County	22	0.03
Royal Oak (city) Oakland County	17	0.03
Taylor (city) Wayne County	17	0.03
Sterling Heights (city) Macomb County	25	0.02
Macomb (township) Macomb County	18	0.02
Flint (city) Genesee County	16	0.02

Asian: Chinese, except Taiwanese

Top 10 Places Sorted by Population
Based on all places, regardless of total population

Place	Population	%
Ann Arbor (city) Washtenaw County	6,555	5.75
Troy (city) Oakland County	3,809	4.70
East Lansing (city) Ingham County	2,124	4.37
Canton (charter twp) Wayne County	2,022	2.24
Novi (city) Oakland County	1,745	3.16
Rochester Hills (city) Oakland County	1,487	2.09
Pittsfield (charter twp) Washtenaw County	1,441	4.16
Meridian (charter twp) Ingham County	1,138	2.87
Sterling Heights (city) Macomb County	1,023	0.79
Farmington Hills (city) Oakland County	864	1.08

Top 10 Places Sorted by Percent of Total Population
Based on all places, regardless of total population

Place	Population	%
Ann Arbor (charter twp) Washtenaw County	325	7.45
Houghton (city) Houghton County	510	6.62
Ann Arbor (city) Washtenaw County	6,555	5.75
Troy (city) Oakland County	3,809	4.70
East Lansing (city) Ingham County	2,124	4.37
Pittsfield (charter twp) Washtenaw County	1,441	4.16
Okemos (cdp) Ingham County	841	3.94
Scio (township) Washtenaw County	745	3.71
Novi (city) Oakland County	1,745	3.16
Meridian (charter twp) Ingham County	1,138	2.87

Top 10 Places Sorted by Percent of Total Population
Based on places with total population of 50,000 or more

Place	Population	%
Ann Arbor (city) Washtenaw County	6,555	5.75
Troy (city) Oakland County	3,809	4.70
Novi (city) Oakland County	1,745	3.16
Canton (charter twp) Wayne County	2,022	2.24
Rochester Hills (city) Oakland County	1,487	2.09
West Bloomfield (charter twp) Oakland County	800	1.24
Farmington Hills (city) Oakland County	864	1.08
Sterling Heights (city) Macomb County	1,023	0.79
Livonia (city) Wayne County	597	0.62
Royal Oak (city) Oakland County	354	0.62

Asian: Filipino

Top 10 Places Sorted by Population
Based on all places, regardless of total population

Place	Population	%
Sterling Heights (city) Macomb County	1,981	1.53
Warren (city) Macomb County	1,432	1.07
Troy (city) Oakland County	1,121	1.38
Detroit (city) Wayne County	875	0.12
Canton (charter twp) Wayne County	849	0.94
Macomb (township) Macomb County	774	0.97
Rochester Hills (city) Oakland County	655	0.92
Westland (city) Wayne County	602	0.72
Ann Arbor (city) Washtenaw County	580	0.51
Livonia (city) Wayne County	566	0.58

Top 10 Places Sorted by Percent of Total Population
Based on all places, regardless of total population

Place	Population	%
Wolverine (village) Cheboygan County	6	2.46
Daggett (village) Menominee County	5	1.94
Port Austin (village) Huron County	12	1.81
Sterling Heights (city) Macomb County	1,981	1.53
Minden City (village) Sanilac County	3	1.52
Ponshewaing (cdp) Emmet County	1	1.45
Levering (cdp) Emmet County	3	1.40
Oronoko (charter twp) Berrien County	128	1.39
Troy (city) Oakland County	1,121	1.38
Walloon Lake (cdp) Charlevoix County	4	1.38

Top 10 Places Sorted by Percent of Total Population
Based on places with total population of 50,000 or more

Place	Population	%
Sterling Heights (city) Macomb County	1,981	1.53
Troy (city) Oakland County	1,121	1.38
Warren (city) Macomb County	1,432	1.07
Macomb (township) Macomb County	774	0.97

Canton (charter twp) Wayne County	849	0.94
Rochester Hills (city) Oakland County	655	0.92
Westland (city) Wayne County	602	0.72
Royal Oak (city) Oakland County	378	0.66
Shelby (charter twp) Macomb County	444	0.60
Farmington Hills (city) Oakland County	468	0.59

Asian: Hmong

Top 10 Places Sorted by Population
Based on all places, regardless of total population

Place	Population	%
Warren (city) Macomb County	1,218	0.91
Pontiac (city) Oakland County	695	1.17
Lansing (city) Ingham County	643	0.56
Detroit (city) Wayne County	578	0.08
Waterford (charter twp) Oakland County	217	0.30
Sterling Heights (city) Macomb County	175	0.13
Roseville (city) Macomb County	108	0.23
Eastpointe (city) Macomb County	106	0.33
Clinton (charter twp) Macomb County	101	0.10
Macomb (township) Macomb County	86	0.11

Top 10 Places Sorted by Percent of Total Population
Based on all places, regardless of total population

Place	Population	%
Clarksville (village) Ionia County	7	1.78
Pontiac (city) Oakland County	695	1.17
Ortonville (village) Oakland County	15	1.04
Elmer (township) Sanilac County	8	0.99
Warren (city) Macomb County	1,218	0.91
Resort (township) Emmet County	21	0.78
Ridgeway (township) Lenawee County	12	0.78
Denmark (township) Tuscola County	22	0.72
Riley (township) St. Clair County	22	0.66
Olive (township) Clinton County	16	0.65

Top 10 Places Sorted by Percent of Total Population
Based on places with total population of 50,000 or more

Place	Population	%
Pontiac (city) Oakland County	695	1.17
Warren (city) Macomb County	1,218	0.91
Lansing (city) Ingham County	643	0.56
Waterford (charter twp) Oakland County	217	0.30
Sterling Heights (city) Macomb County	175	0.13
Macomb (township) Macomb County	86	0.11
Clinton (charter twp) Macomb County	101	0.10
Rochester Hills (city) Oakland County	70	0.10
Detroit (city) Wayne County	578	0.08
Shelby (charter twp) Macomb County	48	0.07

Asian: Indian

Top 10 Places Sorted by Population
Based on all places, regardless of total population

Place	Population	%
Troy (city) Oakland County	7,564	9.34
Canton (charter twp) Wayne County	7,546	8.37
Farmington Hills (city) Oakland County	5,216	6.54
Ann Arbor (city) Washtenaw County	4,216	3.70
Novi (city) Oakland County	3,657	6.62
Sterling Heights (city) Macomb County	3,551	2.74
Rochester Hills (city) Oakland County	3,470	4.89
Detroit (city) Wayne County	2,588	0.36
West Bloomfield (charter twp) Oakland County	2,336	3.61
Hamtramck (city) Wayne County	1,751	7.81

Top 10 Places Sorted by Percent of Total Population
Based on all places, regardless of total population

Place	Population	%
Farmington (city) Oakland County	1,240	11.96
Troy (city) Oakland County	7,564	9.34
Canton (charter twp) Wayne County	7,546	8.37
Hamtramck (city) Wayne County	1,751	7.81
Novi (city) Oakland County	3,657	6.62
Farmington Hills (city) Oakland County	5,216	6.54
Auburn Hills (city) Oakland County	1,275	5.95
Northville (township) Wayne County	1,660	5.83
Okemos (cdp) Ingham County	1,217	5.70
Rochester Hills (city) Oakland County	3,470	4.89

Top 10 Places Sorted by Percent of Total Population
Based on places with total population of 50,000 or more

Place	Population	%
Troy (city) Oakland County	7,564	9.34
Canton (charter twp) Wayne County	7,546	8.37
Novi (city) Oakland County	3,657	6.62
Farmington Hills (city) Oakland County	5,216	6.54
Rochester Hills (city) Oakland County	3,470	4.89
Ann Arbor (city) Washtenaw County	4,216	3.70
West Bloomfield (charter twp) Oakland County	2,336	3.61
Sterling Heights (city) Macomb County	3,551	2.74
Shelby (charter twp) Macomb County	1,064	1.44
Westland (city) Wayne County	1,188	1.41

Asian: Indonesian

Top 10 Places Sorted by Population
Based on all places, regardless of total population

Place	Population	%
Ann Arbor (city) Washtenaw County	83	0.07
Oronoko (charter twp) Berrien County	62	0.67
Grand Rapids (city) Kent County	59	0.03
East Lansing (city) Ingham County	47	0.10
Canton (charter twp) Wayne County	34	0.04
Lansing (city) Ingham County	25	0.02
Meridian (charter twp) Ingham County	22	0.06
Battle Creek (city) Calhoun County	21	0.04
Kalamazoo (city) Kalamazoo County	20	0.03
Georgetown (charter twp) Ottawa County	18	0.04

Top 10 Places Sorted by Percent of Total Population
Based on all places, regardless of total population

Place	Population	%
Bay View (cdp) Emmet County	1	0.75
Berrien Springs (village) Berrien County	13	0.72
Oronoko (charter twp) Berrien County	62	0.67
Lake (charter twp) Berrien County	17	0.57
Elberta (village) Benzie County	1	0.27
Hartford (city) Van Buren County	6	0.22
Bay Port (cdp) Huron County	1	0.21
Burlington (township) Lapeer County	3	0.20
New Troy (cdp) Berrien County	1	0.20
Sylvan Lake (city) Oakland County	3	0.17

Top 10 Places Sorted by Percent of Total Population
Based on places with total population of 50,000 or more

Place	Population	%
Ann Arbor (city) Washtenaw County	83	0.07
Canton (charter twp) Wayne County	34	0.04
Battle Creek (city) Calhoun County	21	0.04
Grand Rapids (city) Kent County	59	0.03
Kalamazoo (city) Kalamazoo County	20	0.03
Novi (city) Oakland County	18	0.03
Ypsilanti (charter twp) Washtenaw County	17	0.03
Lansing (city) Ingham County	25	0.02
Rochester Hills (city) Oakland County	17	0.02
Royal Oak (city) Oakland County	10	0.02

Asian: Japanese

Top 10 Places Sorted by Population
Based on all places, regardless of total population

Place	Population	%
Novi (city) Oakland County	2,120	3.84
Ann Arbor (city) Washtenaw County	1,428	1.25
West Bloomfield (charter twp) Oakland County	946	1.46
Farmington Hills (city) Oakland County	643	0.81
Canton (charter twp) Wayne County	435	0.48
Troy (city) Oakland County	386	0.48
Battle Creek (city) Calhoun County	313	0.60
Detroit (city) Wayne County	307	0.04
Rochester Hills (city) Oakland County	299	0.42
Northville (township) Wayne County	293	1.03

Top 10 Places Sorted by Percent of Total Population
Based on all places, regardless of total population

Place	Population	%
Novi (city) Oakland County	2,120	3.84
Ann Arbor (charter twp) Washtenaw County	101	2.32
Filer City (cdp) Manistee County	2	1.72

Place	Population	%
West Bloomfield (charter twp) Oakland County	946	1.46
Pulawski (township) Presque Isle County	5	1.46
Ann Arbor (city) Washtenaw County	1,428	1.25
Carney (village) Menominee County	2	1.04
Northville (township) Wayne County	293	1.03
New Troy (cdp) Berrien County	5	1.01
Scio (township) Washtenaw County	194	0.97

Top 10 Places Sorted by Percent of Total Population
Based on places with total population of 50,000 or more

Place	Population	%
Novi (city) Oakland County	2,120	3.84
West Bloomfield (charter twp) Oakland County	946	1.46
Ann Arbor (city) Washtenaw County	1,428	1.25
Farmington Hills (city) Oakland County	643	0.81
Battle Creek (city) Calhoun County	313	0.60
Canton (charter twp) Wayne County	435	0.48
Troy (city) Oakland County	386	0.48
Rochester Hills (city) Oakland County	299	0.42
Royal Oak (city) Oakland County	128	0.22
Livonia (city) Wayne County	175	0.18

Asian: Korean

Top 10 Places Sorted by Population
Based on all places, regardless of total population

Place	Population	%
Ann Arbor (city) Washtenaw County	3,159	2.77
Troy (city) Oakland County	1,465	1.81
East Lansing (city) Ingham County	1,007	2.07
Meridian (charter twp) Ingham County	996	2.51
Novi (city) Oakland County	893	1.62
Rochester Hills (city) Oakland County	891	1.26
Grand Rapids (city) Kent County	821	0.44
Pittsfield (charter twp) Washtenaw County	661	1.91
Okemos (cdp) Ingham County	655	3.07
Farmington Hills (city) Oakland County	580	0.73

Top 10 Places Sorted by Percent of Total Population
Based on all places, regardless of total population

Place	Population	%
Oronoko (charter twp) Berrien County	380	4.13
Okemos (cdp) Ingham County	655	3.07
Ann Arbor (city) Washtenaw County	3,159	2.77
Meridian (charter twp) Ingham County	996	2.51
East Lansing (city) Ingham County	1,007	2.07
Pittsfield (charter twp) Washtenaw County	661	1.91
Berrien Springs (village) Berrien County	34	1.89
Troy (city) Oakland County	1,465	1.81
Haslett (cdp) Ingham County	345	1.80
Ann Arbor (charter twp) Washtenaw County	78	1.79

Top 10 Places Sorted by Percent of Total Population
Based on places with total population of 50,000 or more

Place	Population	%
Ann Arbor (city) Washtenaw County	3,159	2.77
Troy (city) Oakland County	1,465	1.81
Novi (city) Oakland County	893	1.62
Rochester Hills (city) Oakland County	891	1.26
West Bloomfield (charter twp) Oakland County	518	0.80
Farmington Hills (city) Oakland County	580	0.73
Canton (charter twp) Wayne County	481	0.53
Shelby (charter twp) Macomb County	359	0.49
Grand Rapids (city) Kent County	821	0.44
Sterling Heights (city) Macomb County	489	0.38

Asian: Laotian

Top 10 Places Sorted by Population
Based on all places, regardless of total population

Place	Population	%
Holland (charter twp) Ottawa County	1,250	3.51
Warren (city) Macomb County	178	0.13
Holland (city) Ottawa County	156	0.47
Zeeland (charter twp) Ottawa County	153	1.53
Park (township) Ottawa County	150	0.84
Detroit (city) Wayne County	112	0.02
Lansing (city) Ingham County	60	0.05
Pontiac (city) Oakland County	47	0.08
Sterling Heights (city) Macomb County	47	0.04
Ypsilanti (charter twp) Washtenaw County	40	0.07

Top 10 Places Sorted by Percent of Total Population
Based on all places, regardless of total population

Place	Population	%
Vandalia (village) Cass County	18	5.98
Holland (charter twp) Ottawa County	1,250	3.51
Cassopolis (village) Cass County	32	1.80
Penn (township) Cass County	28	1.58
Zeeland (charter twp) Ottawa County	153	1.53
LaGrange (township) Cass County	32	0.91
Tustin (village) Osceola County	2	0.87
Park (township) Ottawa County	150	0.84
Beechwood (cdp) Ottawa County	25	0.83
Fillmore (township) Allegan County	18	0.67

Top 10 Places Sorted by Percent of Total Population
Based on places with total population of 50,000 or more

Place	Population	%
Warren (city) Macomb County	178	0.13
Pontiac (city) Oakland County	47	0.08
Ypsilanti (charter twp) Washtenaw County	40	0.07
Lansing (city) Ingham County	60	0.05
Sterling Heights (city) Macomb County	47	0.04
Detroit (city) Wayne County	112	0.02
Grand Rapids (city) Kent County	33	0.02
Troy (city) Oakland County	20	0.02
Macomb (township) Macomb County	18	0.02
Clinton (charter twp) Macomb County	17	0.02

Asian: Malaysian

Top 10 Places Sorted by Population
Based on all places, regardless of total population

Place	Population	%
Ann Arbor (city) Washtenaw County	81	0.07
East Lansing (city) Ingham County	65	0.13
Kalamazoo (city) Kalamazoo County	43	0.06
Oronoko (charter twp) Berrien County	21	0.23
Lansing (city) Ingham County	20	0.02
Oshtemo (charter twp) Kalamazoo County	19	0.09
Rochester Hills (city) Oakland County	18	0.03
Sterling Heights (city) Macomb County	15	0.01
Meridian (charter twp) Ingham County	14	0.04
Ypsilanti (charter twp) Washtenaw County	14	0.03

Top 10 Places Sorted by Percent of Total Population
Based on all places, regardless of total population

Place	Population	%
Oronoko (charter twp) Berrien County	21	0.23
Berrien (township) Berrien County	9	0.18
Galien (village) Berrien County	1	0.18
Brown City (city) Sanilac County	2	0.15
Hudson (township) Charlevoix County	1	0.14
East Lansing (city) Ingham County	65	0.13
Felch (township) Dickinson County	1	0.13
Alaiedon (township) Ingham County	3	0.10
Bath (cdp) Clinton County	2	0.10
Oshtemo (charter twp) Kalamazoo County	19	0.09

Top 10 Places Sorted by Percent of Total Population
Based on places with total population of 50,000 or more

Place	Population	%
Ann Arbor (city) Washtenaw County	81	0.07
Kalamazoo (city) Kalamazoo County	43	0.06
Rochester Hills (city) Oakland County	18	0.03
Ypsilanti (charter twp) Washtenaw County	14	0.03
Lansing (city) Ingham County	20	0.02
Westland (city) Wayne County	13	0.02
Novi (city) Oakland County	10	0.02
Sterling Heights (city) Macomb County	15	0.01
Canton (charter twp) Wayne County	11	0.01
Troy (city) Oakland County	11	0.01

Asian: Nepalese

Top 10 Places Sorted by Population
Based on all places, regardless of total population

Place	Population	%
Lansing (city) Ingham County	113	0.10
Waterford (charter twp) Oakland County	62	0.09
Wixom (city) Oakland County	54	0.40

Place	Population	%
Grand Rapids (city) Kent County	41	0.02
Troy (city) Oakland County	36	0.04
East Lansing (city) Ingham County	35	0.07
Canton (charter twp) Wayne County	30	0.03
Ann Arbor (city) Washtenaw County	29	0.03
Madison Heights (city) Oakland County	27	0.09
Portage (city) Kalamazoo County	20	0.04

Top 10 Places Sorted by Percent of Total Population
Based on all places, regardless of total population

Place	Population	%
Wixom (city) Oakland County	54	0.40
Orange (township) Kalkaska County	3	0.24
Frankenlust (township) Bay County	8	0.22
Kalkaska (village) Kalkaska County	3	0.15
Walled Lake (city) Oakland County	9	0.13
Big Rapids (charter twp) Mecosta County	5	0.12
Farmington (city) Oakland County	11	0.11
Kalkaska (township) Kalkaska County	5	0.11
Lansing (city) Ingham County	113	0.10
Waterford (charter twp) Oakland County	62	0.09

Top 10 Places Sorted by Percent of Total Population
Based on places with total population of 50,000 or more

Place	Population	%
Lansing (city) Ingham County	113	0.10
Waterford (charter twp) Oakland County	62	0.09
Troy (city) Oakland County	36	0.04
Canton (charter twp) Wayne County	30	0.03
Ann Arbor (city) Washtenaw County	29	0.03
Grand Rapids (city) Kent County	41	0.02
Farmington Hills (city) Oakland County	19	0.02
Rochester Hills (city) Oakland County	15	0.02
Novi (city) Oakland County	11	0.02
Royal Oak (city) Oakland County	11	0.02

Asian: Pakistani

Top 10 Places Sorted by Population
Based on all places, regardless of total population

Place	Population	%
Canton (charter twp) Wayne County	1,479	1.64
Troy (city) Oakland County	663	0.82
West Bloomfield (charter twp) Oakland County	600	0.93
Brownstown (charter twp) Wayne County	579	1.89
Rochester Hills (city) Oakland County	522	0.74
Sterling Heights (city) Macomb County	501	0.39
Farmington Hills (city) Oakland County	500	0.63
Dearborn (city) Wayne County	379	0.39
Ann Arbor (city) Washtenaw County	324	0.28
Pittsfield (charter twp) Washtenaw County	308	0.89

Top 10 Places Sorted by Percent of Total Population
Based on all places, regardless of total population

Place	Population	%
Brownstown (charter twp) Wayne County	579	1.89
Canton (charter twp) Wayne County	1,479	1.64
West Bloomfield (charter twp) Oakland County	600	0.93
Pittsfield (charter twp) Washtenaw County	308	0.89
Troy (city) Oakland County	663	0.82
Rochester Hills (city) Oakland County	522	0.74
Hamtramck (city) Wayne County	160	0.71
Farmington Hills (city) Oakland County	500	0.63
Bloomfield (charter twp) Oakland County	247	0.60
Orchard Lake Village (city) Oakland County	11	0.46

Top 10 Places Sorted by Percent of Total Population
Based on places with total population of 50,000 or more

Place	Population	%
Canton (charter twp) Wayne County	1,479	1.64
West Bloomfield (charter twp) Oakland County	600	0.93
Troy (city) Oakland County	663	0.82
Rochester Hills (city) Oakland County	522	0.74
Farmington Hills (city) Oakland County	500	0.63
Taylor (city) Wayne County	252	0.40
Sterling Heights (city) Macomb County	501	0.39
Dearborn (city) Wayne County	379	0.39
Ann Arbor (city) Washtenaw County	324	0.28
Shelby (charter twp) Macomb County	163	0.22

Asian: Sri Lankan

Top 10 Places Sorted by Population
Based on all places, regardless of total population

Place	Population	%
Ann Arbor (city) Washtenaw County	77	0.07
Farmington Hills (city) Oakland County	51	0.06
Detroit (city) Wayne County	46	0.01
Meridian (charter twp) Ingham County	37	0.09
Rochester Hills (city) Oakland County	36	0.05
Troy (city) Oakland County	36	0.04
Pittsfield (charter twp) Washtenaw County	34	0.10
Bloomfield (charter twp) Oakland County	33	0.08
Canton (charter twp) Wayne County	31	0.03
Okemos (cdp) Ingham County	28	0.13

Top 10 Places Sorted by Percent of Total Population
Based on all places, regardless of total population

Place	Population	%
Ann Arbor (charter twp) Washtenaw County	8	0.18
Bloomfield Hills (city) Oakland County	7	0.18
Okemos (cdp) Ingham County	28	0.13
Milton (township) Cass County	5	0.13
Berrien Springs (village) Berrien County	2	0.11
Pittsfield (charter twp) Washtenaw County	34	0.10
Meridian (charter twp) Ingham County	37	0.09
Farmington (city) Oakland County	9	0.09
Bloomfield (charter twp) Oakland County	33	0.08
Oak Park (city) Oakland County	22	0.08

Top 10 Places Sorted by Percent of Total Population
Based on places with total population of 50,000 or more

Place	Population	%
Ann Arbor (city) Washtenaw County	77	0.07
Farmington Hills (city) Oakland County	51	0.06
Rochester Hills (city) Oakland County	36	0.05
Troy (city) Oakland County	36	0.04
Southfield (city) Oakland County	28	0.04
Canton (charter twp) Wayne County	31	0.03
Ypsilanti (charter twp) Washtenaw County	17	0.03
Novi (city) Oakland County	15	0.03
Lansing (city) Ingham County	21	0.02
West Bloomfield (charter twp) Oakland County	10	0.02

Asian: Taiwanese

Top 10 Places Sorted by Population
Based on all places, regardless of total population

Place	Population	%
Ann Arbor (city) Washtenaw County	858	0.75
Troy (city) Oakland County	415	0.51
East Lansing (city) Ingham County	192	0.40
Rochester Hills (city) Oakland County	133	0.19
Novi (city) Oakland County	131	0.24
Pittsfield (charter twp) Washtenaw County	123	0.35
Meridian (charter twp) Ingham County	119	0.30
Canton (charter twp) Wayne County	100	0.11
Okemos (cdp) Ingham County	86	0.40
West Bloomfield (charter twp) Oakland County	78	0.12

Top 10 Places Sorted by Percent of Total Population
Based on all places, regardless of total population

Place	Population	%
Ann Arbor (charter twp) Washtenaw County	66	1.51
Ann Arbor (city) Washtenaw County	858	0.75
Troy (city) Oakland County	415	0.51
East Lansing (city) Ingham County	192	0.40
Okemos (cdp) Ingham County	86	0.40
Pittsfield (charter twp) Washtenaw County	123	0.35
Onsted (village) Lenawee County	3	0.33
Meridian (charter twp) Ingham County	119	0.30
South Branch (township) Wexford County	1	0.26
Lodi (township) Washtenaw County	15	0.25

Top 10 Places Sorted by Percent of Total Population
Based on places with total population of 50,000 or more

Place	Population	%
Ann Arbor (city) Washtenaw County	858	0.75
Troy (city) Oakland County	415	0.51
Novi (city) Oakland County	131	0.24
Rochester Hills (city) Oakland County	133	0.19

West Bloomfield (charter twp) Oakland County	78	0.12
Canton (charter twp) Wayne County	100	0.11
Farmington Hills (city) Oakland County	51	0.06
Sterling Heights (city) Macomb County	36	0.03
Kalamazoo (city) Kalamazoo County	22	0.03
Ypsilanti (charter twp) Washtenaw County	14	0.03

Asian: Thai

Top 10 Places Sorted by Population
Based on all places, regardless of total population

Place	Population	%
Ann Arbor (city) Washtenaw County	168	0.15
Detroit (city) Wayne County	96	0.01
Holland (charter twp) Ottawa County	85	0.24
East Lansing (city) Ingham County	85	0.17
Kalamazoo (city) Kalamazoo County	60	0.08
Lansing (city) Ingham County	60	0.05
Grand Rapids (city) Kent County	59	0.03
Warren (city) Macomb County	58	0.04
Pittsfield (charter twp) Washtenaw County	55	0.16
Rochester Hills (city) Oakland County	50	0.07

Top 10 Places Sorted by Percent of Total Population
Based on all places, regardless of total population

Place	Population	%
Meade (township) Mason County	5	2.76
Fountain (village) Mason County	5	2.59
Stephenson (township) Menominee County	5	0.75
Hudson (township) Charlevoix County	5	0.72
Grawn (cdp) Grand Traverse County	5	0.65
Honor (village) Benzie County	2	0.61
Bingham Farms (village) Oakland County	6	0.54
Parma (village) Jackson County	4	0.52
McKinley (township) Huron County	2	0.45
Sherman (township) Mason County	5	0.42

Top 10 Places Sorted by Percent of Total Population
Based on places with total population of 50,000 or more

Place	Population	%
Ann Arbor (city) Washtenaw County	168	0.15
Ypsilanti (charter twp) Washtenaw County	47	0.09
Kalamazoo (city) Kalamazoo County	60	0.08
Rochester Hills (city) Oakland County	50	0.07
Troy (city) Oakland County	50	0.06
Lansing (city) Ingham County	60	0.05
Canton (charter twp) Wayne County	45	0.05
Wyoming (city) Kent County	34	0.05
Pontiac (city) Oakland County	31	0.05
Warren (city) Macomb County	58	0.04

Asian: Vietnamese

Top 10 Places Sorted by Population
Based on all places, regardless of total population

Place	Population	%
Kentwood (city) Kent County	1,786	3.67
Wyoming (city) Kent County	1,389	1.93
Grand Rapids (city) Kent County	1,090	0.58
Sterling Heights (city) Macomb County	1,027	0.79
Lansing (city) Ingham County	993	0.87
Gaines (charter twp) Kent County	773	3.07
Holland (charter twp) Ottawa County	633	1.78
Warren (city) Macomb County	608	0.45
Ann Arbor (city) Washtenaw County	395	0.35
Canton (charter twp) Wayne County	347	0.38

Top 10 Places Sorted by Percent of Total Population
Based on all places, regardless of total population

Place	Population	%
Kentwood (city) Kent County	1,786	3.67
Gaines (charter twp) Kent County	773	3.07
Cutlerville (cdp) Kent County	332	2.31
Wyoming (city) Kent County	1,389	1.93
Holland (charter twp) Ottawa County	633	1.78
Holt (cdp) Ingham County	288	1.20
Delhi (charter twp) Ingham County	296	1.14
Waverly (cdp) Eaton County	247	1.03
Byron (township) Kent County	193	0.95
Delta (charter twp) Eaton County	302	0.93

Top 10 Places Sorted by Percent of Total Population
Based on places with total population of 50,000 or more

Place	Population	%
Wyoming (city) Kent County	1,389	1.93
Lansing (city) Ingham County	993	0.87
Sterling Heights (city) Macomb County	1,027	0.79
Grand Rapids (city) Kent County	1,090	0.58
Warren (city) Macomb County	608	0.45
Canton (charter twp) Wayne County	347	0.38
Dearborn Heights (city) Wayne County	219	0.38
Ann Arbor (city) Washtenaw County	395	0.35
Macomb (township) Macomb County	273	0.34
Troy (city) Oakland County	257	0.32

Hawaii Native/Pacific Islander

Top 10 Places Sorted by Population
Based on all places, regardless of total population

Place	Population	%
Detroit (city) Wayne County	673	0.09
Sterling Heights (city) Macomb County	320	0.25
Grand Rapids (city) Kent County	314	0.17
Dearborn (city) Wayne County	208	0.21
Lansing (city) Ingham County	194	0.17
Warren (city) Macomb County	153	0.11
Ann Arbor (city) Washtenaw County	144	0.13
West Bloomfield (charter twp) Oakland County	129	0.20
Kalamazoo (city) Kalamazoo County	123	0.17
Wyoming (city) Kent County	111	0.15

Top 10 Places Sorted by Percent of Total Population
Based on all places, regardless of total population

Place	Population	%
Posen (village) Presque Isle County	4	1.71
Lake Ann (village) Benzie County	4	1.49
Fairbanks (township) Delta County	4	1.42
Bear Lake (village) Manistee County	4	1.40
Oronoko (charter twp) Berrien County	101	1.10
Walloon Lake (cdp) Charlevoix County	3	1.03
South Range (village) Houghton County	7	0.92
Haring (cdp) Wexford County	3	0.91
Buckley (village) Wexford County	6	0.86
Parkdale (cdp) Manistee County	6	0.85

Top 10 Places Sorted by Percent of Total Population
Based on places with total population of 50,000 or more

Place	Population	%
Sterling Heights (city) Macomb County	320	0.25
Dearborn (city) Wayne County	208	0.21
West Bloomfield (charter twp) Oakland County	129	0.20
Grand Rapids (city) Kent County	314	0.17
Lansing (city) Ingham County	194	0.17
Kalamazoo (city) Kalamazoo County	123	0.17
Ypsilanti (charter twp) Washtenaw County	89	0.17
Battle Creek (city) Calhoun County	83	0.16
Wyoming (city) Kent County	111	0.15
Pontiac (city) Oakland County	86	0.14

Hawaii Native/Pacific Islander: Not Hispanic

Top 10 Places Sorted by Population
Based on all places, regardless of total population

Place	Population	%
Detroit (city) Wayne County	503	0.07
Sterling Heights (city) Macomb County	306	0.24
Grand Rapids (city) Kent County	208	0.11
Dearborn (city) Wayne County	201	0.20
Lansing (city) Ingham County	148	0.13
Warren (city) Macomb County	136	0.10
West Bloomfield (charter twp) Oakland County	127	0.20
Ann Arbor (city) Washtenaw County	126	0.11
Oronoko (charter twp) Berrien County	95	1.03
Kalamazoo (city) Kalamazoo County	91	0.12

Top 10 Places Sorted by Percent of Total Population
Based on all places, regardless of total population

Place	Population	%
Posen (village) Presque Isle County	4	1.71
Lake Ann (village) Benzie County	4	1.49

Place	Population	%
Fairbanks (township) Delta County	4	1.42
Bear Lake (village) Manistee County	4	1.40
Oronoko (charter twp) Berrien County	95	1.03
South Range (village) Houghton County	7	0.92
Buckley (village) Wexford County	6	0.86
Parkdale (cdp) Manistee County	6	0.85
Oscoda (cdp) Iosco County	7	0.78
Burt (township) Alger County	4	0.77

Top 10 Places Sorted by Percent of Total Population
Based on places with total population of 50,000 or more

Place	Population	%
Sterling Heights (city) Macomb County	306	0.24
Dearborn (city) Wayne County	201	0.20
West Bloomfield (charter twp) Oakland County	127	0.20
Ypsilanti (charter twp) Washtenaw County	84	0.16
Lansing (city) Ingham County	148	0.13
Battle Creek (city) Calhoun County	68	0.13
Kalamazoo (city) Kalamazoo County	91	0.12
Dearborn Heights (city) Wayne County	69	0.12
Grand Rapids (city) Kent County	208	0.11
Ann Arbor (city) Washtenaw County	126	0.11

Hawaii Native/Pacific Islander: Hispanic

Top 10 Places Sorted by Population
Based on all places, regardless of total population

Place	Population	%
Detroit (city) Wayne County	170	0.02
Grand Rapids (city) Kent County	106	0.06
Wyoming (city) Kent County	46	0.06
Lansing (city) Ingham County	46	0.04
Pontiac (city) Oakland County	40	0.07
Kalamazoo (city) Kalamazoo County	32	0.04
Saginaw (city) Saginaw County	25	0.05
River Rouge (city) Wayne County	21	0.27
Holland (city) Ottawa County	19	0.06
Lincoln Park (city) Wayne County	19	0.05

Top 10 Places Sorted by Percent of Total Population
Based on all places, regardless of total population

Place	Population	%
Walloon Lake (cdp) Charlevoix County	2	0.69
Haring (cdp) Wexford County	2	0.61
Robin Glen-Indiantown (cdp) Saginaw County	4	0.55
Lake Victoria (cdp) Clinton County	4	0.43
Capac (village) St. Clair County	7	0.37
Burr Oak (village) St. Joseph County	3	0.36
Oliver (township) Kalkaska County	1	0.36
Sunfield (village) Eaton County	2	0.35
Locke (township) Ingham County	6	0.34
North Star (township) Gratiot County	3	0.34

Top 10 Places Sorted by Percent of Total Population
Based on places with total population of 50,000 or more

Place	Population	%
Pontiac (city) Oakland County	40	0.07
Grand Rapids (city) Kent County	106	0.06
Wyoming (city) Kent County	46	0.06
Saginaw (city) Saginaw County	25	0.05
Lansing (city) Ingham County	46	0.04
Kalamazoo (city) Kalamazoo County	32	0.04
Battle Creek (city) Calhoun County	15	0.03
Detroit (city) Wayne County	170	0.02
Ann Arbor (city) Washtenaw County	18	0.02
Taylor (city) Wayne County	14	0.02

Hawaii Native/Pacific Islander: Fijian

Top 10 Places Sorted by Population
Based on all places, regardless of total population

Place	Population	%
Grand Rapids (city) Kent County	9	<0.01
Oronoko (charter twp) Berrien County	6	0.07
Burton (city) Genesee County	6	0.02
Mayfield (township) Grand Traverse County	4	0.26
Fife Lake (township) Grand Traverse County	4	0.14
Clayton (charter twp) Genesee County	4	0.05
Shelby (charter twp) Macomb County	4	0.01
Berrien Springs (village) Berrien County	3	0.17
Pittsfield (charter twp) Washtenaw County	3	0.01

Place	Population	%
Saginaw (city) Saginaw County	3	0.01

Top 10 Places Sorted by Percent of Total Population
Based on all places, regardless of total population

Place	Population	%
Mayfield (township) Grand Traverse County	4	0.26
Berrien Springs (village) Berrien County	3	0.17
Fife Lake (township) Grand Traverse County	4	0.14
Lakefield (township) Saginaw County	1	0.10
Oronoko (charter twp) Berrien County	6	0.07
Clayton (charter twp) Genesee County	4	0.05
Burton (city) Genesee County	6	0.02
Blair (township) Grand Traverse County	2	0.02
Lathrup Village (city) Oakland County	1	0.02
Shelby (charter twp) Macomb County	4	0.01

Top 10 Places Sorted by Percent of Total Population
Based on places with total population of 50,000 or more

Place	Population	%
Shelby (charter twp) Macomb County	4	0.01
Saginaw (city) Saginaw County	3	0.01
Grand Rapids (city) Kent County	9	<0.01
Ann Arbor (city) Washtenaw County	2	<0.01
Detroit (city) Wayne County	2	<0.01
Flint (city) Genesee County	1	<0.01
Kalamazoo (city) Kalamazoo County	1	<0.01
St. Clair Shores (city) Macomb County	1	<0.01
Waterford (charter twp) Oakland County	1	<0.01
Ypsilanti (charter twp) Washtenaw County	1	<0.01

Hawaii Native/Pacific Islander: Guamanian or Chamorro

Top 10 Places Sorted by Population
Based on all places, regardless of total population

Place	Population	%
Detroit (city) Wayne County	117	0.02
Grand Rapids (city) Kent County	73	0.04
Lansing (city) Ingham County	22	0.02
Ann Arbor (city) Washtenaw County	21	0.02
Saginaw (city) Saginaw County	17	0.03
Canton (charter twp) Wayne County	15	0.02
Eastpointe (city) Macomb County	14	0.04
Battle Creek (city) Calhoun County	14	0.03
Macomb (township) Macomb County	13	0.02
Inkster (city) Wayne County	12	0.05

Top 10 Places Sorted by Percent of Total Population
Based on all places, regardless of total population

Place	Population	%
Waverly (township) Cheboygan County	2	0.44
Harbor Springs (city) Emmet County	5	0.42
Edwardsburg (village) Cass County	4	0.32
Drummond (township) Chippewa County	3	0.28
Dowling (cdp) Barry County	1	0.27
James (township) Saginaw County	5	0.25
Torch Lake (township) Antrim County	3	0.25
Antioch (township) Wexford County	2	0.25
Grant (township) Cheboygan County	2	0.24
Koehler (township) Cheboygan County	3	0.23

Top 10 Places Sorted by Percent of Total Population
Based on places with total population of 50,000 or more

Place	Population	%
Grand Rapids (city) Kent County	73	0.04
Saginaw (city) Saginaw County	17	0.03
Battle Creek (city) Calhoun County	14	0.03
Detroit (city) Wayne County	117	0.02
Lansing (city) Ingham County	22	0.02
Ann Arbor (city) Washtenaw County	21	0.02
Canton (charter twp) Wayne County	15	0.02
Macomb (township) Macomb County	13	0.02
Royal Oak (city) Oakland County	12	0.02
Novi (city) Oakland County	9	0.02

Hawaii Native/Pacific Islander: Marshallese

Top 10 Places Sorted by Population
Based on all places, regardless of total population

Place	Population	%
Ann Arbor (city) Washtenaw County	8	0.01
Portage (city) Kalamazoo County	4	<0.01
Grand Rapids (city) Kent County	4	<0.01
Big Rapids (charter twp) Mecosta County	2	0.05
Leighton (township) Allegan County	2	0.04
Lowell (charter twp) Kent County	2	0.03
Lyon (charter twp) Oakland County	2	0.01
Marquette (city) Marquette County	2	0.01
Ypsilanti (city) Washtenaw County	2	0.01
Canton (charter twp) Wayne County	2	<0.01

Top 10 Places Sorted by Percent of Total Population
Based on all places, regardless of total population

Place	Population	%
North Branch (village) Lapeer County	1	0.10
Richmond (township) Osceola County	1	0.06
Big Rapids (charter twp) Mecosta County	2	0.05
Newaygo (city) Newaygo County	1	0.05
Leighton (township) Allegan County	2	0.04
Reed City (city) Osceola County	1	0.04
Lowell (charter twp) Kent County	2	0.03
North Branch (township) Lapeer County	1	0.03
Acme (township) Grand Traverse County	1	0.02
Caro (village) Tuscola County	1	0.02

Top 10 Places Sorted by Percent of Total Population
Based on places with total population of 50,000 or more

Place	Population	%
Ann Arbor (city) Washtenaw County	8	0.01
Grand Rapids (city) Kent County	4	<0.01
Canton (charter twp) Wayne County	2	<0.01
Lansing (city) Ingham County	2	<0.01
Farmington Hills (city) Oakland County	1	<0.01
Saginaw (city) Saginaw County	1	<0.01
Battle Creek (city) Calhoun County	0	0.00
Clinton (charter twp) Macomb County	0	0.00
Dearborn (city) Wayne County	0	0.00
Dearborn Heights (city) Wayne County	0	0.00

Hawaii Native/Pacific Islander: Native Hawaiian

Top 10 Places Sorted by Population
Based on all places, regardless of total population

Place	Population	%
Detroit (city) Wayne County	130	0.02
Grand Rapids (city) Kent County	81	0.04
Lansing (city) Ingham County	77	0.07
Ann Arbor (city) Washtenaw County	36	0.03
Warren (city) Macomb County	36	0.03
Kalamazoo (city) Kalamazoo County	28	0.04
Wyoming (city) Kent County	28	0.04
Pontiac (city) Oakland County	27	0.05
Lincoln Park (city) Wayne County	25	0.07
Flint (city) Genesee County	25	0.02

Top 10 Places Sorted by Percent of Total Population
Based on all places, regardless of total population

Place	Population	%
Posen (village) Presque Isle County	4	1.71
Lake Ann (village) Benzie County	4	1.49
Fairbanks (township) Delta County	4	1.42
Bear Lake (village) Manistee County	4	1.40
Walloon Lake (cdp) Charlevoix County	3	1.03
South Range (village) Houghton County	7	0.92
Parkdale (cdp) Manistee County	6	0.85
Burt (township) Alger County	4	0.77
Adams (township) Arenac County	4	0.71
Zeba (cdp) Baraga County	3	0.63

Top 10 Places Sorted by Percent of Total Population
Based on places with total population of 50,000 or more

Place	Population	%
Lansing (city) Ingham County	77	0.07

Place	Population	%
Pontiac (city) Oakland County	27	0.05
Grand Rapids (city) Kent County	81	0.04
Kalamazoo (city) Kalamazoo County	28	0.04
Wyoming (city) Kent County	28	0.04
Ypsilanti (charter twp) Washtenaw County	21	0.04
Battle Creek (city) Calhoun County	19	0.04
Ann Arbor (city) Washtenaw County	36	0.03
Warren (city) Macomb County	36	0.03
Royal Oak (city) Oakland County	19	0.03

Hawaii Native/Pacific Islander: Samoan

Top 10 Places Sorted by Population
Based on all places, regardless of total population

Place	Population	%
Detroit (city) Wayne County	71	0.01
Oronoko (charter twp) Berrien County	68	0.74
Lansing (city) Ingham County	34	0.03
Ypsilanti (charter twp) Washtenaw County	30	0.06
Dearborn (city) Wayne County	18	0.02
Battle Creek (city) Calhoun County	15	0.03
Kalamazoo (city) Kalamazoo County	15	0.02
Westland (city) Wayne County	13	0.02
Mount Pleasant (city) Isabella County	12	0.05
Shelby (charter twp) Macomb County	11	0.01

Top 10 Places Sorted by Percent of Total Population
Based on all places, regardless of total population

Place	Population	%
Oronoko (charter twp) Berrien County	68	0.74
Adams (township) Arenac County	4	0.71
Redding (township) Clare County	3	0.57
McBride (village) Montcalm County	1	0.49
Warner (township) Antrim County	2	0.48
Newton (township) Mackinac County	2	0.47
Maple Valley (township) Montcalm County	7	0.36
Brevort (township) Mackinac County	2	0.34
Churchill (township) Ogemaw County	5	0.29
Berrien Springs (village) Berrien County	5	0.28

Top 10 Places Sorted by Percent of Total Population
Based on places with total population of 50,000 or more

Place	Population	%
Ypsilanti (charter twp) Washtenaw County	30	0.06
Lansing (city) Ingham County	34	0.03
Battle Creek (city) Calhoun County	15	0.03
Dearborn (city) Wayne County	18	0.02
Kalamazoo (city) Kalamazoo County	15	0.02
Westland (city) Wayne County	13	0.02
Royal Oak (city) Oakland County	10	0.02
Detroit (city) Wayne County	71	0.01
Shelby (charter twp) Macomb County	11	0.01
Grand Rapids (city) Kent County	10	0.01

Hawaii Native/Pacific Islander: Tongan

Top 10 Places Sorted by Population
Based on all places, regardless of total population

Place	Population	%
Oronoko (charter twp) Berrien County	10	0.11
Springfield (city) Calhoun County	6	0.11
Windsor (charter twp) Eaton County	6	0.09
Summit (township) Jackson County	6	0.03
Ann Arbor (city) Washtenaw County	6	0.01
Sturgis (city) St. Joseph County	5	0.05
Dearborn (city) Wayne County	5	0.01
Macon (township) Lenawee County	4	0.27
Benton Harbor (city) Berrien County	4	0.04
Lincoln (charter twp) Berrien County	4	0.03

Top 10 Places Sorted by Percent of Total Population
Based on all places, regardless of total population

Place	Population	%
Macon (township) Lenawee County	4	0.27
Central Lake (village) Antrim County	2	0.21
Oronoko (charter twp) Berrien County	10	0.11
Springfield (city) Calhoun County	6	0.11
Lake (charter twp) Berrien County	3	0.10
Windsor (charter twp) Eaton County	6	0.09
Central Lake (township) Antrim County	2	0.09
Sturgis (city) St. Joseph County	5	0.05

Place	Population	%
Lodi (township) Washtenaw County	3	0.05
Benton Harbor (city) Berrien County	4	0.04

Top 10 Places Sorted by Percent of Total Population
Based on places with total population of 50,000 or more

Place	Population	%
Ann Arbor (city) Washtenaw County	6	0.01
Dearborn (city) Wayne County	5	0.01
Ypsilanti (charter twp) Washtenaw County	3	0.01
Detroit (city) Wayne County	4	<0.01
Kalamazoo (city) Kalamazoo County	1	<0.01
Lansing (city) Ingham County	1	<0.01
Pontiac (city) Oakland County	1	<0.01
Southfield (city) Oakland County	1	<0.01
Battle Creek (city) Calhoun County	0	0.00
Canton (charter twp) Wayne County	0	0.00

White

Top 10 Places Sorted by Population
Based on all places, regardless of total population

Place	Population	%
Grand Rapids (city) Kent County	128,050	68.10
Sterling Heights (city) Macomb County	112,990	87.12
Warren (city) Macomb County	108,186	80.70
Dearborn (city) Wayne County	91,285	93.00
Livonia (city) Wayne County	90,446	93.30
Ann Arbor (city) Washtenaw County	86,809	76.19
Detroit (city) Wayne County	86,039	12.05
Clinton (charter twp) Macomb County	81,257	83.95
Lansing (city) Ingham County	76,134	66.61
Macomb (township) Macomb County	73,177	91.95

Top 10 Places Sorted by Percent of Total Population
Based on all places, regardless of total population

Place	Population	%
Lincoln (village) Alcona County	337	100.00
Wakefield (township) Gogebic County	305	100.00
Loud (township) Montmorency County	293	100.00
Grand Beach (village) Berrien County	272	100.00
Burlington (village) Calhoun County	261	100.00
Mansfield (township) Iron County	241	100.00
Wells (township) Marquette County	231	100.00
Copper City (village) Houghton County	190	100.00
Henderson (township) Wexford County	163	100.00
Stronach (cdp) Manistee County	162	100.00

Top 10 Places Sorted by Percent of Total Population
Based on places with total population of 50,000 or more

Place	Population	%
St. Clair Shores (city) Macomb County	56,353	94.37
Livonia (city) Wayne County	90,446	93.30
Dearborn (city) Wayne County	91,285	93.00
Shelby (charter twp) Macomb County	68,257	92.48
Royal Oak (city) Oakland County	52,915	92.45
Macomb (township) Macomb County	73,177	91.95
Waterford (charter twp) Oakland County	65,528	91.38
Dearborn Heights (city) Wayne County	51,263	88.73
Sterling Heights (city) Macomb County	112,990	87.12
Clinton (charter twp) Macomb County	81,257	83.95

White: Not Hispanic

Top 10 Places Sorted by Population
Based on all places, regardless of total population

Place	Population	%
Grand Rapids (city) Kent County	115,639	61.50
Sterling Heights (city) Macomb County	111,121	85.68
Warren (city) Macomb County	106,146	79.18
Dearborn (city) Wayne County	88,708	90.38
Livonia (city) Wayne County	88,468	91.26
Ann Arbor (city) Washtenaw County	83,380	73.18
Clinton (charter twp) Macomb County	79,688	82.33
Macomb (township) Macomb County	71,917	90.37
Lansing (city) Ingham County	68,146	59.62
Shelby (charter twp) Macomb County	67,019	90.81

Top 10 Places Sorted by Percent of Total Population
Based on all places, regardless of total population

Place	Population	%
Loud (township) Montmorency County	293	100.00
Burlington (village) Calhoun County	261	100.00
Wells (township) Marquette County	231	100.00
Henderson (township) Wexford County	163	100.00
Alpha (village) Iron County	145	100.00
Copper Harbor (cdp) Keweenaw County	108	100.00
Houghton (township) Keweenaw County	82	100.00
Eagle River (cdp) Keweenaw County	71	100.00
Caberfae (cdp) Wexford County	64	100.00
Crystal Mountain (cdp) Benzie County	54	100.00

Top 10 Places Sorted by Percent of Total Population
Based on places with total population of 50,000 or more

Place	Population	%
St. Clair Shores (city) Macomb County	55,454	92.86
Livonia (city) Wayne County	88,468	91.26
Shelby (charter twp) Macomb County	67,019	90.81
Royal Oak (city) Oakland County	51,861	90.61
Dearborn (city) Wayne County	88,708	90.38
Macomb (township) Macomb County	71,917	90.37
Waterford (charter twp) Oakland County	62,353	86.96
Sterling Heights (city) Macomb County	111,121	85.68
Dearborn Heights (city) Wayne County	49,214	85.18
Clinton (charter twp) Macomb County	79,688	82.33

White: Hispanic

Top 10 Places Sorted by Population
Based on all places, regardless of total population

Place	Population	%
Detroit (city) Wayne County	22,655	3.17
Grand Rapids (city) Kent County	12,411	6.60
Lansing (city) Ingham County	7,988	6.99
Wyoming (city) Kent County	6,310	8.75
Pontiac (city) Oakland County	5,304	8.91
Holland (charter twp) Ottawa County	4,218	11.84
Holland (city) Ottawa County	4,124	12.48
Saginaw (city) Saginaw County	3,761	7.30
Lincoln Park (city) Wayne County	3,451	9.05
Ann Arbor (city) Washtenaw County	3,429	3.01

Top 10 Places Sorted by Percent of Total Population
Based on all places, regardless of total population

Place	Population	%
Shelby (village) Oceana County	395	19.13
Fennville (city) Allegan County	246	17.60
Imlay City (city) Lapeer County	595	16.54
Crystal (township) Oceana County	109	13.01
Hart (city) Oceana County	273	12.84
Beechwood (cdp) Ottawa County	381	12.64
Holland (city) Ottawa County	4,124	12.48
Shelby (township) Oceana County	502	12.34
Clyde (township) Allegan County	256	12.28
Adrian (city) Lenawee County	2,535	12.00

Top 10 Places Sorted by Percent of Total Population
Based on places with total population of 50,000 or more

Place	Population	%
Pontiac (city) Oakland County	5,304	8.91
Wyoming (city) Kent County	6,310	8.75
Saginaw (city) Saginaw County	3,761	7.30
Lansing (city) Ingham County	7,988	6.99
Grand Rapids (city) Kent County	12,411	6.60
Waterford (charter twp) Oakland County	3,175	4.43
Taylor (city) Wayne County	2,271	3.60
Battle Creek (city) Calhoun County	1,865	3.56
Dearborn Heights (city) Wayne County	2,049	3.55
Detroit (city) Wayne County	22,655	3.17

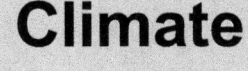

Climate

Michigan Physical Features and Climate Narrative

PHYSICAL FEATURES. Michigan is located in the heart of the Great Lakes region and is composed of two large peninsulas. Many smaller peninsulas jut from these two peninsulas into the world's largest bodies of fresh water to give most of Michigan a quasi-marine type climate in spite of its midcontinent location.

The Upper Peninsula is long and narrow, lying primarily between 45° and 47° N. latitude. It averages only 75 miles in width and extends from Northern Wisconsin eastward over 300 miles into Northern Lake Huron. Lake Superior lies to the north while the northern portion of Lake Michigan forms the boundary to the southeast. Isle Royale, separated from the mainland, is located in Lake Superior about 50 miles northwest of the tip of the Keweenaw Peninsula. The Lower Peninsula, shaped like a mitten and occupying about 70 percent of Michigan's total land area, extends northward nearly 300 miles from the Indiana and Ohio border or about 42° N. latitude to the eastern end of the Upper Peninsula. Lake Michigan extends the entire length of the Lower Peninsula on the west while Lakes Huron, St. Clair and Erie form the eastern boundary. The total coastline for the state exceeds 3,100 miles. In addition, Michigan has over 11,000 smaller lakes with a total surface area of over 1,000 square miles. These lakes are scattered throughout 81 of the 83 counties while more than 36,000 miles of streams wind their way across the state.

While latitude, by determining the amount of solar insolation, is the major climatic control, the Great Lakes and variations in elevation play an important role in the amelioration of Michigan's climate. Because of its mid-latitude location, prevailing winds are from a westerly direction. During the summer months winds are predominantly from the southwest when the semi-permanent Bermuda High Pressure Center is located over the southeastern United States. During the winter months the prevailing winds are west to northwest, but change quite frequently for short periods as migrating cyclones and anticyclones move through the area.

The eastern half of the Upper Peninsula varies from level to gently rolling hills with elevation generally between 600 and 1,000 feet above sea level. The western tablelands rise to elevations generally between 1,400 and 1,600 feet with Porcupine Mountain, the State's highest point, 2,023 feet, located in Ontonagan County overlooking Lake Superior. The rugged hills extend northeastward from Ontonagan County through the center of the Keweenaw Peninsula and play an important role in the larger precipitation amounts received in this area.

The Lower Peninsula features range from quite level terrain in the southeast to gently rolling hills in the southwest with elevations generally between 800 and 1,000 feet. A series of sand dunes along the Lake Michigan shoreline rise to heights of nearly 400 feet above the lake level. These are the result of the prevailing westerly winds which blow across the lake. Tablelands cover the northern part of the Lower Peninsula and reach a maximum elevation of 1,700 feet in Osecola County near Cadillac. In the northwestern section of the Lower Peninsula a number of finger-like peninsulas extend into Grand Traverse Bay and Lake Michigan.

GENERAL CLIMATE. The lake effect imparts many interesting departures to Michigan's climate which one would not ordinarily expect to find at a midcontinental location. Because of the lake waters' slow response to temperature changes and the dominating westerly winds, the arrival of both summer and winter are retarded. In the spring, the cooler temperatures slow the development of vegetation until the danger of frost is past. In the fall, the warmer lake waters temper the first outbreaks of cold air allowing additional time for crops to mature. With the first cold air outbreaks in the fall, Michigan experiences a considerable increase in cloudiness. When cold air passes over the warmer lake water, a shal-

low layer of unstable, moisture-laden air develops in the lower levels of the atmosphere. This air, when forced to rise, produces the increased cloudiness and frequent snow flurry activity observed in the fall and early winter months.

On warm, summer days when prevailing winds are generally light, the lake's shore area frequently develops a localized wind pattern which may extend inland for only a few miles. This is frequently referred to as the "lake breeze." It develops when the much warmer air over the land masses begins to rise, allowing the cooler air over the lakes to move inland. At night this pattern may be reversed creating what is known as a "land breeze". A wind of this type may also be observed, but on a much smaller scale, along the shores of the larger inland lakes.

The length of Michigan's growing season or freeze-free period does not decrease in the normal manner from south to north. Instead, isolines for the length of the growing season follow closely the contours of the lake shores. The shortest average growing season, about 60 days, occurs in the interior section of the Western Upper Peninsula. The growing season increases to between 140 and 160 days, as one goes towards the lake shores. A similar pattern exists in the Lower Peninsula where the growing season in the northern tablelands averages only 70 days, but increases rapidly to 140 days near the lakes. Michigan's maximum average growing season, 170 days, is found in the southwest and southeastern corners of the state.

PRECIPITATION. Michigan averages about 31 inches of precipitation per year. About 55-60 percent of the annual total is recorded during the normal growing season. Summer precipitation falls primarily in the form of showers or thunderstorms, while a more steady type of precipitation of lighter intensity dominates the winter months. The annual number of thunderstorms observed decreases from about 40 in the south to around 25 in the Upper Peninsula area with nearly 50 percent of these recorded during the summer months, June through August.

The frequency of floods is quite low in Michigan with the greatest likelihood occurring in late winter or early spring when sudden warming and rain may be combined with snowmelt. Mild meteorological drought conditions are not uncommon in Michigan, but meteorological droughts reaching severe conditions are infrequent and generally of short duration. The normally even distribution of precipitation and higher humidities observed in Michigan are helpful in reducing the high demands for moisture.

SNOWFALL. Michigan receives some of the heaviest snowfall totals east of the Rockies except for isolated points in the New England States. The maximum average annual snowfall amounts of over 170 inches are located along the escarpment which rises abruptly to an elevation of over 1,400 feet above Lake Superior, at the western end of the Upper Peninsula. Another area with amounts exceeding 120 inches is centered in the western section of the tableland region of the Lower Peninsula. The prevailing westerlies, passing over the Great Lakes, become moisture laden in the lower levels and when forced upward by the land masses, drop much of their excessive moisture in the form of snow squalls in these areas.

STORMS. Damaging or dangerous storms do not occur as frequently in Michigan as in the states to the south and west. Recorded tornado occurrences have averaged four per year. About 90 percent of these tornadoes occurred in the southern one-half of the Lower Peninsula. Damaging wind storms and blizzards are not as frequent but do cause considerable damage from time to time. Hail is most frequently observed in the spring months. A higher frequency of hail is noted in the fall months over the northwestern section of the Lower Peninsula. This is attributed mainly to the strong lake influence in this region.

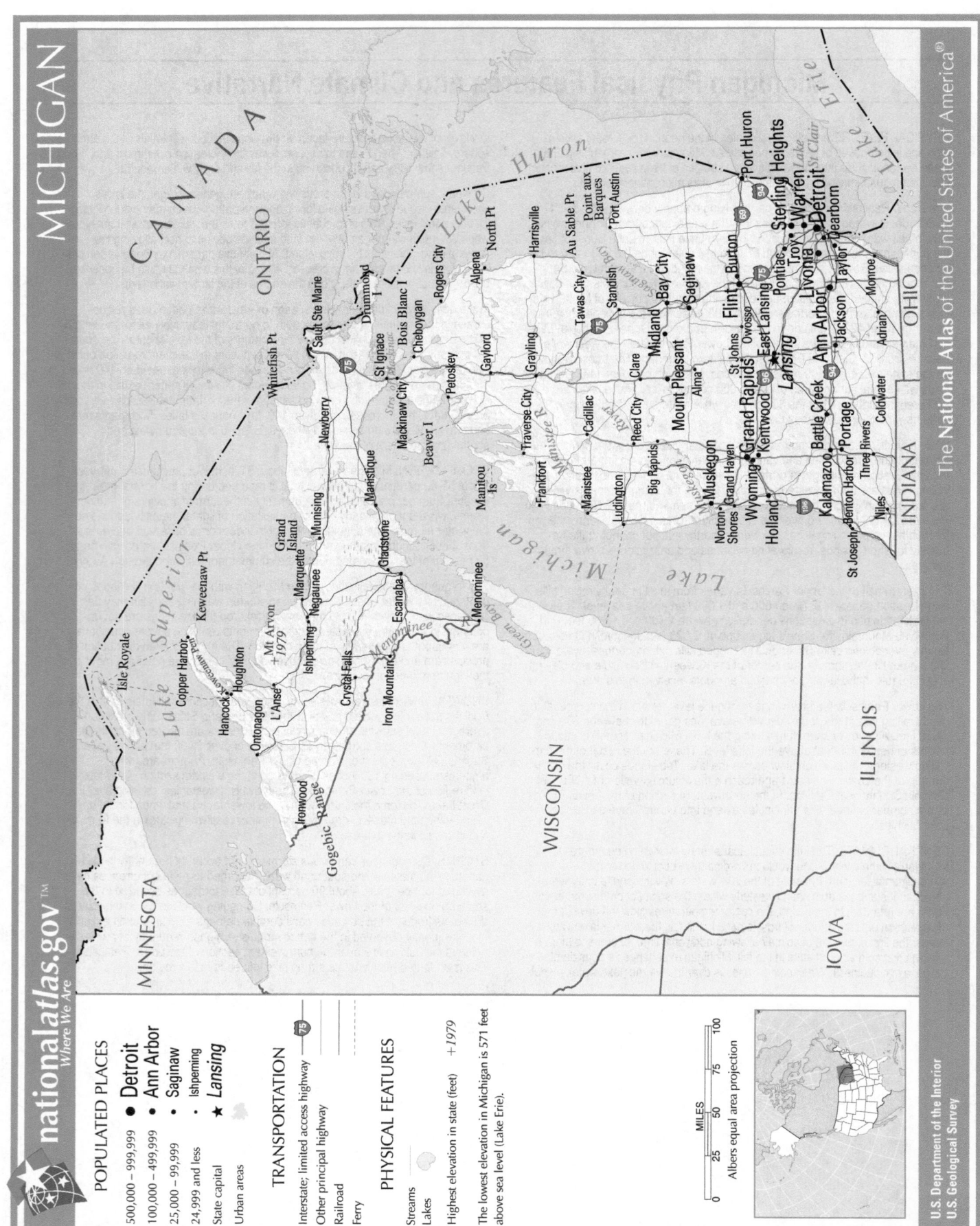

MICHIGAN

nationalatlas.gov ™
Where We Are

POPULATED PLACES
● **Detroit**   500,000 – 999,999
● Ann Arbor   100,000 – 499,999
● Saginaw   25,000 – 99,999
● Ishpeming   24,999 and less
★ *Lansing*   State capital
     Urban areas

TRANSPORTATION
〔75〕 Interstate; limited access highway
       Other principal highway
       Railroad
       Ferry

PHYSICAL FEATURES
       Streams
       Lakes
+1979 Highest elevation in state (feet)

The lowest elevation in Michigan is 571 feet above sea level (Lake Erie).

MILES
0   25   50   75   100
Albers equal area projection

U.S. Department of the Interior
U.S. Geological Survey

The **National Atlas** of the United States of America ®

CANADA

ONTARIO

Lake Superior

Lake Huron

Lake Michigan

Lake Erie

Lake St Clair

Green Bay

Saginaw Bay

MINNESOTA

WISCONSIN

ILLINOIS

IOWA

INDIANA

OHIO

Isle Royale

Copper Harbor
Keweenaw Pt
Hancock
Houghton
Ontonagon
L'Anse
+Mt Arvon
1979
Ironwood
Gogebic Range
Crystal Falls
Iron Mountain
Ishpeming
Negaunee
Marquette
Grand Island
Munising
Escanaba
Gladstone
Menominee
Manistique

Whitefish Pt
Sault Ste Marie
Newberry
Drummond I
Bois Blanc I
St Ignace
Mackinaw City
Cheboygan
Beaver I
Petoskey
Rogers City
Alpena
Gaylord
North Pt
Harrisville
Au Sable Pt
Point aux Barques
Port Austin

Manitou Is
Frankfort
Traverse City
Grayling
Manistee
Cadillac
Reed City
Ludington
Big Rapids
Tawas City
Standish
Midland
Bay City
Saginaw
Mount Pleasant
Clare
Alma
St Johns
Owosso
East Lansing
Lansing
Grand Rapids
Kentwood
Wyoming
Norton Shores
Muskegon
Grand Haven
Holland
Battle Creek
Portage
Kalamazoo
Benton Harbor
Three Rivers
St Joseph
Niles
Coldwater

Port Huron
Sterling Heights
Warren
Troy
Pontiac
Flint
Burton
Livonia
Detroit
Dearborn
Taylor
Ann Arbor
Jackson
Adrian
Monroe

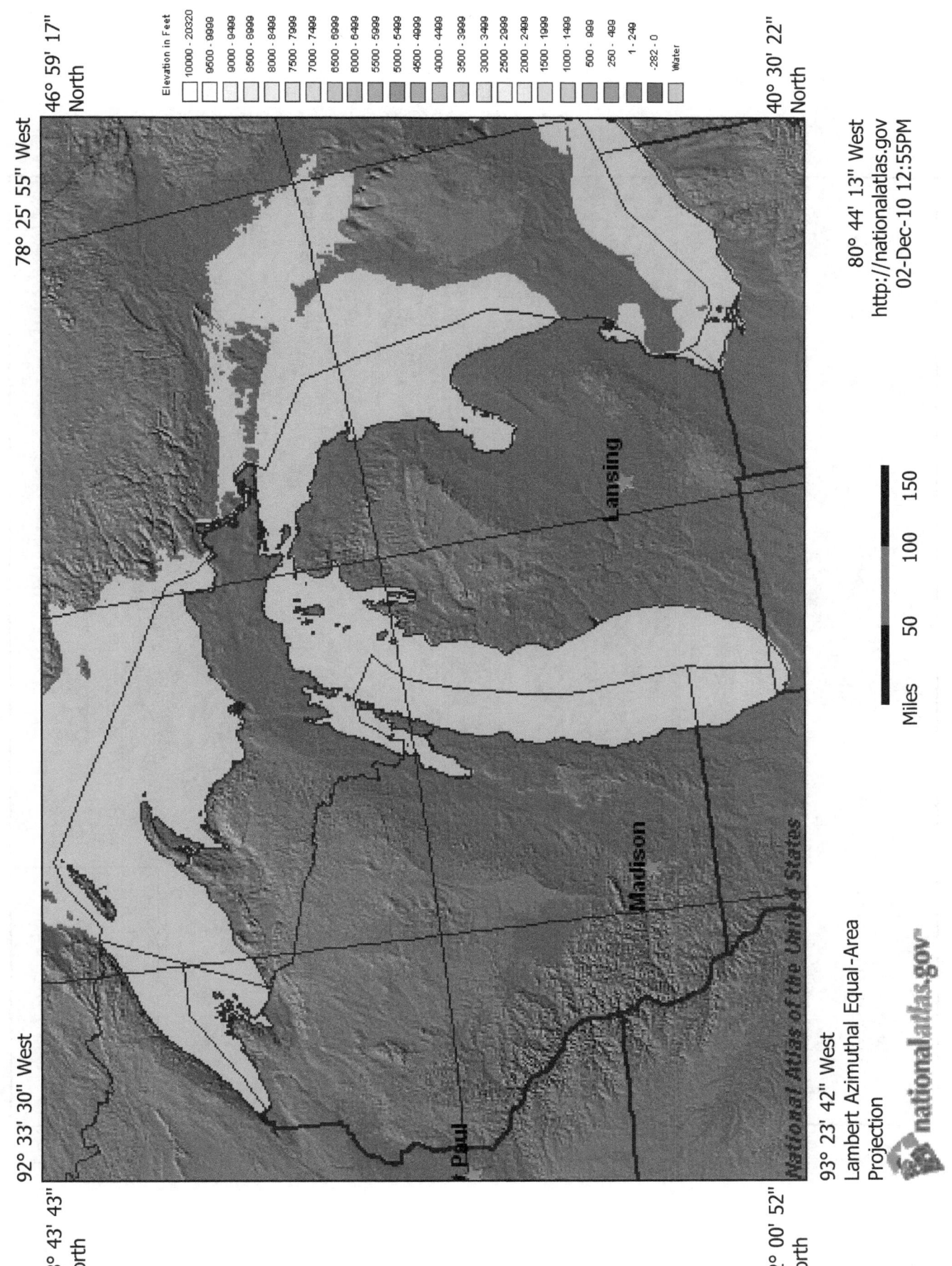

46° 59' 17" West
North

78° 25' 55" West

Elevation in Feet

10000 - 20320
9500 - 9999
9000 - 9499
8500 - 8999
8000 - 8499
7500 - 7999
7000 - 7499
6500 - 6999
6000 - 6499
5500 - 5999
5000 - 5499
4500 - 4999
4000 - 4499
3500 - 3999
3000 - 3499
2500 - 2999
2000 - 2499
1500 - 1999
1000 - 1499
500 - 999
250 - 499
1 - 249
-282 - 0
Water

40° 30' 22"
North

80° 44' 13" West
http://nationalatlas.gov
02-Dec-10 12:55PM

Lansing

Madison

St Paul

92° 33' 30" West

48° 43' 43"
North

Miles   50   100   150

93° 23' 42" West
Lambert Azimuthal Equal-Area
Projection

National Atlas of the United States

nationalatlas.gov™

42° 00' 52"
North

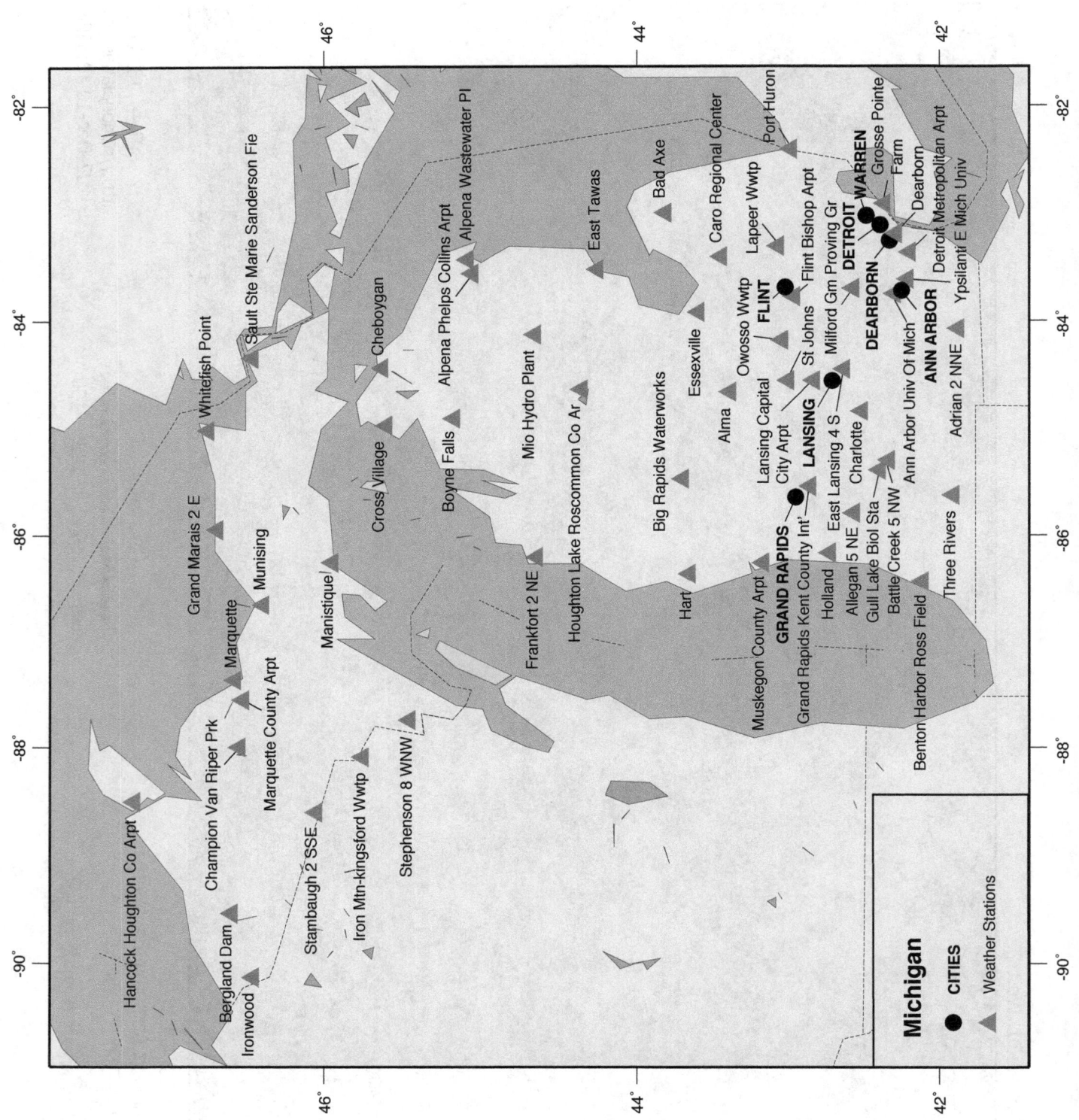

Michigan

● CITIES

◤ Weather Stations

Michigan Weather Stations by County

County	Station Name
Alger	Grand Marais 2 E
	Munising
Allegan	Allegan 5 NE
Alpena	Alpena Phelps Collins Arpt
	Alpena Wastewater Pl
Bay	Essexville
Benzie	Frankfort 2 NE
Berrien	Benton Harbor Ross Field
Calhoun	Battle Creek 5 NW
Charlevoix	Boyne Falls
Cheboygan	Cheboygan
Chippewa	Sault Ste Marie Sanderson Field
	Whitefish Point
Clinton	Lansing Capital City Arpt
	St Johns
Dickinson	Iron Mtn-Kingsford WWTP
Eaton	Charlotte
Emmet	Cross Village
Genesee	Flint Bishop Arpt
Gogebic	Ironwood
Gratiot	Alma
Houghton	Hancock Houghton Co Arpt
Huron	Bad Axe
Ingham	East Lansing 4 S
Iosco	East Tawas
Iron	Stambaugh 2 SSE
Kalamazoo	Gull Lake Biol Sta
Kent	Grand Rapids Kent County Intl
Lapeer	Lapeer WWTP
Lenawee	Adrian 2 NNE
Livingston	Milford Gm Proving Ground
Marquette	Champion Van Riper Prk
	Marquette
	Marquette County Arpt
Mecosta	Big Rapids Waterworks

County	Station Name
Menominee	Stephenson 8 WNW
Muskegon	Muskegon County Arpt
Oceana	Hart
Ontonagon	Bergland Dam
Oscoda	Mio Hydro Plant
Ottawa	Holland
Roscommon	Houghton Lake Roscommon Co Arpt
Schoolcraft	Manistique
Shiawassee	Owosso Wwtp
St. Clair	Port Huron
St. Joseph	Three Rivers
Tuscola	Caro Regional Center
Washtenaw	Ann Arbor Univ of Mich
	Ypsilanti E Mich Univ
Wayne	Dearborn
	Detroit Metropolitan Arpt
	Grosse Pointe Farms

See User Guide for station inclusion criteria.

Michigan Weather Stations by City

City	Station Name	Miles
Ann Arbor	Ann Arbor Univ of Mich	1.9
	Detroit Metropolitan Arpt	20.0
	Milford Gm Proving Ground	21.4
	Ypsilanti E Mich Univ	6.6
Battle Creek	Battle Creek 5 NW	5.3
	Charlotte	24.9
	Gull Lake Biol Sta	11.4
Canton	Ann Arbor Univ of Mich	12.5
	Dearborn	12.2
	Detroit Metropolitan Arpt	9.3
	Milford Gm Proving Ground	21.8
	Ypsilanti E Mich Univ	9.3
Clinton	Dearborn	24.3
	Grosse Pointe Farms	13.8
Dearborn	Dearborn	1.0
	Detroit Metropolitan Arpt	9.9
	Grosse Pointe Farms	16.6
	Ypsilanti E Mich Univ	21.4
Detroit	Dearborn	8.2
	Detroit Metropolitan Arpt	17.2
	Grosse Pointe Farms	10.6
Farmington Hills	Ann Arbor Univ of Mich	21.5
	Dearborn	13.8
	Detroit Metropolitan Arpt	18.6
	Milford Gm Proving Ground	17.8
	Ypsilanti E Mich Univ	21.2
Flint	Flint Bishop Arpt	5.2
	Lapeer WWTP	20.1
	Owosso Wwtp	24.7
Grand Rapids	Grand Rapids Kent County Intl	8.7
Kalamazoo	Allegan 5 NE	23.2
	Battle Creek 5 NW	17.8
	Gull Lake Biol Sta	13.6
	Three Rivers	23.9
Lansing	Charlotte	17.9
	East Lansing 4 S	4.9
	Lansing Capital City Arpt	5.1
	St Johns	21.1
Livonia	Ann Arbor Univ of Mich	18.9
	Dearborn	8.9
	Detroit Metropolitan Arpt	12.4
	Grosse Pointe Farms	24.0
	Milford Gm Proving Ground	21.2
	Ypsilanti E Mich Univ	16.9
Macomb Twp	Grosse Pointe Farms	18.9
Novi	Ann Arbor Univ of Mich	17.1
	Dearborn	16.6
	Detroit Metropolitan Arpt	19.0
	Milford Gm Proving Ground	13.6
	Ypsilanti E Mich Univ	18.1

City	Station Name	Miles
Pontiac	Dearborn	23.2
	Milford Gm Proving Ground	21.3
Rochester Hills	Dearborn	24.5
	Grosse Pointe Farms	23.6
Royal Oak	Dearborn	13.8
	Detroit Metropolitan Arpt	22.5
	Grosse Pointe Farms	15.4
Saginaw	Essexville	14.3
Shelby	Grosse Pointe Farms	20.6
Southfield	Dearborn	11.4
	Detroit Metropolitan Arpt	19.0
	Grosse Pointe Farms	19.2
	Milford Gm Proving Ground	23.9
St. Clair Shores	Dearborn	21.0
	Grosse Pointe Farms	7.5
Sterling Heights	Dearborn	20.9
	Grosse Pointe Farms	15.1
Taylor	Ann Arbor Univ of Mich	23.5
	Dearborn	6.2
	Detroit Metropolitan Arpt	4.3
	Grosse Pointe Farms	21.5
	Ypsilanti E Mich Univ	17.9
Troy	Dearborn	18.9
	Grosse Pointe Farms	18.5
Warren	Dearborn	16.1
	Grosse Pointe Farms	10.0
Waterford	Dearborn	24.8
	Milford Gm Proving Ground	17.0
West Bloomfield Twp	Ann Arbor Univ of Mich	24.9
	Dearborn	18.8
	Detroit Metropolitan Arpt	24.1
	Milford Gm Proving Ground	16.1
Westland	Ann Arbor Univ of Mich	17.2
	Dearborn	7.5
	Detroit Metropolitan Arpt	7.3
	Grosse Pointe Farms	24.9
	Milford Gm Proving Ground	24.5
	Ypsilanti E Mich Univ	13.4
Wyoming	Allegan 5 NE	22.2
	Grand Rapids Kent County Intl	9.5
	Holland	22.5
Ypsilanti Twp	Ann Arbor Univ of Mich	8.5
	Dearborn	20.0
	Detroit Metropolitan Arpt	12.7
	Ypsilanti E Mich Univ	1.7

Note: Miles is the distance between the geographic center of the city and the weather station.

Michigan Weather Stations by Elevation

Feet	Station Name
1,564	Champion Van Riper Prk
1,560	Stambaugh 2 SSE
1,430	Ironwood
1,415	Marquette County Arpt
1,299	Bergland Dam
1,149	Houghton Lake Roscommon Co Arpt
1,074	Hancock Houghton Co Arpt
1,060	Iron Mtn-Kingsford WWTP
990	Milford Gm Proving Ground
959	Mio Hydro Plant
930	Battle Creek 5 NW
930	Big Rapids Waterworks
910	Gull Lake Biol Sta
901	Charlotte
899	Ann Arbor Univ of Mich
879	East Lansing 4 S
865	Frankfort 2 NE
840	Lansing Capital City Arpt
819	Lapeer WWTP
810	Three Rivers
784	Grand Rapids Kent County Intl
779	Ypsilanti E Mich Univ
766	Flint Bishop Arpt
759	Adrian 2 NNE
759	Alma
750	Allegan 5 NE
743	Cross Village
743	St Johns
734	Boyne Falls
729	Owosso Wwtp
717	Sault Ste Marie Sanderson Field
714	Bad Axe
709	Stephenson 8 WNW
700	Hart
688	Alpena Phelps Collins Arpt
680	Munising
669	Caro Regional Center
665	Marquette
632	Detroit Metropolitan Arpt
627	Benton Harbor Ross Field
625	Muskegon County Arpt
624	Grand Marais 2 E
620	Manistique
612	Grosse Pointe Farms
609	Holland
604	Dearborn
604	Whitefish Point
589	Alpena Wastewater Pl
589	Cheboygan
589	Port Huron
587	Essexville
585	East Tawas

See User Guide for station inclusion criteria.

Alpena Phelps Collins Airport

The city of Alpena lies on the northwest shore of Thunder Bay, eight miles from the open waters of Lake Huron. Lake Huron and Thunder Bay lie at an elevation of 580 feet above sea level. Generally, the land slopes up westward from the lakeshore to 689 feet at the airport. Farther to the west and southwest the land becomes higher and more rolling. A range of hills with tops 1,000 to 1,350 feet lies northwest to southeast about 25 miles southwest of the station.

Summer showers moving from the southwest weaken and sometimes dissipate as they approach Alpena. Winter storms often bring winds with an easterly component. Precipitation from these is increased by moisture and instability picked up from Lake Huron and by forced upslope flow.

The normal wintertime storm track is south of the city, and most passing storms bring snow. Rain, freezing rain, and sleet are uncommon, but not unknown, in winter. In summer, most storms pass to the north, often bringing brief showers to the area, but occasionally, heavy thunderstorms with damaging winds occur. The Great Lakes modify most climatic extremes. Precipitation amounts are distributed evenly throughout the year. The lake effect is most pronounced in early winter, before ice forms. Minimum temperatures during this season are higher than would be expected at this latitude.

Summers in Alpena are warm and sunny. Brief showers usually occur every few days, often falling on only part of the area. Hailstorms average less than one a year. During prolonged heat waves the highest temperatures in Michigan often occur in the forest area southwest of Alpena. Winter months are cloudy and marked by frequent snow flurries. Storms bring heavier snowfall. Snow cover is sufficiently deep and persistent to provide good protection for grasses and winter grains.

The climate along the immediate Lake Huron shore is semi-maritime and lacks the temperature extremes experienced just a few miles inland. Maximum temperatures near the lake shore average 1.6 degrees lower than those at the airport, minimum temperatures average five degrees higher. Afternoon lake breezes which are strongest in the late spring and early summer cause lake shore maximum temperatures to average 3.6 degrees lower during the month of May.

Freezing temperatures have occurred as late as late June and as early as late August. Principal crops in the area are hay, potatoes, berries, and apples.

Prevailing winds are from the northwest except during May and June when southeast winds predominate. Southeast winds are common in the afternoon during all the summer months.

Alpena Phelps Collins Airport *Alpena County*   Elevation: 688 ft.   Latitude: 45° 04' N   Longitude: 83° 35' W

	JAN	FEB	MAR	APR	MAY	JUN	JUL	AUG	SEP	OCT	NOV	DEC	YEAR
Mean Maximum Temp. (°F)	27.3	29.6	38.3	52.5	64.9	74.9	79.8	77.4	69.4	56.2	43.4	32.1	53.8
Mean Temp. (°F)	19.4	20.4	28.7	41.7	52.6	62.2	67.5	65.6	57.9	46.3	35.8	25.1	43.6
Mean Minimum Temp. (°F)	11.3	11.2	19.0	30.9	40.3	49.5	55.3	53.7	46.5	36.4	28.3	18.1	33.4
Extreme Maximum Temp. (°F)	52	65	80	90	93	103	102	102	94	90	75	65	103
Extreme Minimum Temp. (°F)	-28	-25	-17	-7	21	29	37	30	25	16	-6	-18	-28
Days Maximum Temp. ≥ 90°F	0	0	0	0	0	2	3	1	0	0	0	0	6
Days Maximum Temp. ≤ 32°F	21	18	9	1	0	0	0	0	0	0	4	15	68
Days Minimum Temp. ≤ 32°F	30	27	28	18	5	0	0	0	1	11	21	29	170
Days Minimum Temp. ≤ 0°F	7	6	3	0	0	0	0	0	0	0	0	2	18
Heating Degree Days (base 65°F)	1,409	1,254	1,120	694	389	137	40	65	230	574	868	1,229	8,009
Cooling Degree Days (base 65°F)	0	0	0	2	13	61	125	91	25	3	0	0	320
Mean Precipitation (in.)	1.65	1.30	1.87	2.46	2.63	2.55	2.95	3.25	2.86	2.58	2.10	1.76	27.96
Maximum Precipitation (in.)*	3.3	3.2	4.4	4.1	8.3	8.4	7.2	6.3	7.1	6.5	7.4	4.4	35.2
Minimum Precipitation (in.)*	0.2	0.1	0.3	1.2	1.0	0.2	0.2	0.9	0.3	0.6	0.6	0.4	21.4
Extreme Maximum Daily Precip. (in.)	1.41	1.51	1.85	1.22	2.11	1.55	2.59	2.01	1.54	3.44	1.58	1.28	3.44
Days With ≥ 0.1" Precipitation	5	4	5	6	6	6	6	6	6	6	6	5	67
Days With ≥ 0.5" Precipitation	0	1	1	2	2	2	2	2	2	1	1	1	17
Days With ≥ 1.0" Precipitation	0	0	0	0	0	0	1	1	1	0	0	0	3
Mean Snowfall (in.)	*21.4*	*18.0*	*11.0*	na	na	na	na	na	*trace*	*0.4*	*8.0*	*19.3*	na
Maximum Snowfall (in.)*	44	33	36	13	4	0	0	0	trace	4	35	46	146
Maximum 24-hr. Snowfall (in.)*	16	11	17	11	4	0	0	0	trace	2	15	16	17
Maximum Snow Depth (in.)	*28*	*37*	*28*	na	na	na	na	na	*trace*	*1*	*12*	*26*	na
Days With ≥ 1.0" Snow Depth	*29*	*27*	*21*	na	na	na	na	na	*0*	*0*	*7*	*20*	na
Thunderstorm Days*	< 1	< 1	1	2	4	5	7	6	4	1	< 1	< 1	30
Foggy Days*	10	9	13	12	13	14	14	17	16	14	14	12	158
Predominant Sky Cover*	OVR	OVR	OVR	OVR	OVR	OVR	OVR	OVR	OVR	OVR	OVR	OVR	OVR
Mean Relative Humidity 7am (%)*	81	80	82	80	78	81	85	90	91	86	84	83	83
Mean Relative Humidity 4pm (%)*	67	62	59	53	51	53	54	59	61	62	68	72	60
Mean Dewpoint (°F)*	13	12	20	29	40	51	57	56	50	39	29	19	35
Prevailing Wind Direction*	WNW	WNW	WNW	WNW	ESE	SE	WNW	SW	W	WSW	WNW	SW	WNW
Prevailing Wind Speed (mph)*	10	9	10	10	9	8	8	7	7	8	9	8	9
Maximum Wind Gust (mph)*	53	54	54	60	53	58	53	60	45	47	56	54	60

Note: (*) Period of record is 1959-1995

Detroit Metropolitan Airport

Detroit and the immediate suburbs, including nearby urban areas in Canada, occupy an area approximately 25 miles in radius. The waterway, consisting of the Detroit and St. Clair Rivers, Lake St. Clair, and the west end of Lake Erie, lies at an elevation of 568 to 580 feet above sea level. Nearly flat land slopes up gently from the waters edge northwestward for about 10 miles and then gives way to increasingly rolling terrain. The Irish Hills, parallel to and about 40 miles northwest of the water-way, have tops 1,000 to 1,250 feet above sea level. On the Canadian side of the waterway the land is relatively level.

Northwest winds in winter bring snow flurry accumulations to all of Michigan except in the Detroit Metropolitan area while summer showers moving from the northwest weaken and sometimes dissipate as they approach Detroit. On the other hand, much of the heaviest precipitation in winter comes from southeast winds, especially to the northwest suburbs of the city.

The climate of Detroit is influenced by its location with respect to major storm tracks and the influence of the Great Lakes. The normal wintertime storm track is south of the city, which brings on the average, about three inch snowfalls. Winter storms can bring combinations of rain, snow, freezing rain, and sleet with heavy snowfall accumulations possible at times. In summer, most storms pass to the north allowing for intervals of warm, humid, sunny skies with occasional thunderstorms followed by days of mild, dry, and fair weather. Temperatures of 90 degrees or higher are reached during each summer.

Local climatic variations are due largely to the immediate effect of Lake St. Clair and the urban heat island. On warm days in late spring or early summer, lake breezes often lower temperatures by 10 to 15 degrees in the eastern part of the city and the northeastern suburbs. The urban heat island effect shows up mainly at night where minimum temperatures at the Metropolitan Airport average four degrees lower than downtown Detroit. On humid summer nights or on very cold winter nights, this difference can exceed 10 degrees.

The growing season averages 180 days and has ranged from 145 days to 205 days. On average, the last freezing temperature occurs in late April while the average first freezing temperature occurs in late October. A freeze has occurred as late as mid-May and as early as late September.

Detroit Metropolitan Airport *Wayne County*   Elevation: 632 ft.   Latitude: 42° 13' N   Longitude: 83° 21' W

	JAN	FEB	MAR	APR	MAY	JUN	JUL	AUG	SEP	OCT	NOV	DEC	YEAR
Mean Maximum Temp. (°F)	32.1	35.1	45.4	58.7	69.9	79.2	83.3	81.3	74.1	61.2	48.6	36.3	58.7
Mean Temp. (°F)	25.3	27.7	36.6	48.7	59.4	69.0	73.3	71.8	64.2	51.9	41.1	29.9	49.9
Mean Minimum Temp. (°F)	18.4	20.3	27.8	38.7	48.8	58.7	63.3	62.2	54.2	42.5	33.6	23.5	41.0
Extreme Maximum Temp. (°F)	64	70	81	87	93	104	102	100	94	90	75	69	104
Extreme Minimum Temp. (°F)	-21	-15	-4	10	29	38	44	38	33	20	12	-10	-21
Days Maximum Temp. ≥ 90°F	0	0	0	0	0	3	5	3	1	0	0	0	12
Days Maximum Temp. ≤ 32°F	16	12	4	0	0	0	0	0	0	0	1	10	43
Days Minimum Temp. ≤ 32°F	28	25	22	7	0	0	0	0	0	3	14	25	124
Days Minimum Temp. ≤ 0°F	2	1	0	0	0	0	0	0	0	0	0	1	4
Heating Degree Days (base 65°F)	1,224	1,048	874	488	210	36	3	8	102	408	709	1,081	6,191
Cooling Degree Days (base 65°F)	0	0	0	7	41	162	267	225	83	8	0	0	793
Mean Precipitation (in.)	1.95	1.98	2.37	2.96	3.31	3.55	3.31	3.18	3.25	2.53	2.70	2.49	33.58
Maximum Precipitation (in.)*	3.9	5.0	4.5	5.4	6.2	7.0	6.0	7.8	7.5	4.9	5.7	6.0	42.6
Minimum Precipitation (in.)*	0.3	0.1	0.8	0.9	0.9	1.0	0.6	0.7	0.4	0.3	0.8	0.5	21.0
Extreme Maximum Daily Precip. (in.)	1.59	2.28	1.69	3.58	1.78	2.59	4.34	2.51	3.71	2.02	2.30	1.45	4.34
Days With ≥ 0.1" Precipitation	6	5	6	7	7	6	7	6	6	5	6	6	73
Days With ≥ 0.5" Precipitation	1	1	1	2	2	2	2	2	2	2	2	1	20
Days With ≥ 1.0" Precipitation	0	0	0	0	1	1	1	1	1	0	0	0	5
Mean Snowfall (in.)	12.3	10.1	7.3	1.8	trace	trace	0.0	0.0	trace	0.3	1.5	9.8	43.1
Maximum Snowfall (in.)*	30	21	16	9	trace	0	0	0	0	3	12	35	75
Maximum 24-hr. Snowfall (in.)*	11	8	8	5	trace	0	0	0	0	3	6	18	18
Maximum Snow Depth (in.)	24	18	9	6	trace	trace	0	0	trace	1	3	12	24
Days With ≥ 1.0" Snow Depth	17	12	6	1	0	0	0	0	0	0	1	8	45
Thunderstorm Days*	< 1	< 1	2	3	4	6	6	5	4	1	1	< 1	32
Foggy Days*	12	11	13	11	12	12	13	17	15	15	14	14	159
Predominant Sky Cover*	OVR	OVR	OVR	OVR	OVR	OVR	SCT	OVR	OVR	OVR	OVR	OVR	OVR
Mean Relative Humidity 7am (%)*	80	79	79	78	78	79	82	86	87	84	82	81	81
Mean Relative Humidity 4pm (%)*	67	63	58	53	51	52	52	54	54	55	64	69	58
Mean Dewpoint (°F)*	17	18	26	35	46	56	61	60	53	42	32	22	39
Prevailing Wind Direction*	WSW	SW	WNW	WSW	WSW	SW	SW	SW	SW	SW	SW	SW	SW
Prevailing Wind Speed (mph)*	14	14	14	14	13	10	9	9	10	12	13	13	12
Maximum Wind Gust (mph)*	66	64	64	66	61	94	71	69	54	52	58	61	94

Note: (*) Period of record is 1958-1995

Flint Bishop Airport

Flint, Michigan, is located in the Flint River Valley, in the center of Genesee County. Lake Huron lies approximately 65 miles to the east, while Saginaw Bay is about 40 miles to the north. The surrounding terrain is generally level with a slight rising tendency to a range of hills 15 to 20 miles southeast of the city.

Flint is generally under the climatic influence of the Great Lakes. Temperatures of 100 degrees or higher are rare and cold waves are less severe then expected. During the winter months, snow showers occur with strong northwesterly winds, and Lake Michigan, lying 120 miles to the west, causes a tempering effect upon cold waves coming from the northwest. The lake effect also results in delaying the coming of spring and prolonging warmer weather in late autumn. This results in conditions favorable for orchards and small fruit.

Precipitation is usually ample for growth and development of vegetation. The wettest periods normally occur in the late spring, early summer, and early fall. The driest period is normally during the winter, and although there is an occasional heavy snowfall, most of the snow occurs in the form of frequent light flurries.

Winter months are marked by considerable cloudiness and rather high relative humidity, while during the summer relative humidity is usually not excessive and sunshine is plentiful.

Violent windstorms associated with thunderstorms and squall lines occasionally hit this area. Tornadoes are infrequent but have caused extensive property damage and loss of life.

Weather changes are frequent throughout the year, since a majority of atmospheric disturbances moving eastward across the country pass near enough to affect the weather in Flint.

Flint Bishop Airport *Genesee County*   Elevation: 766 ft.   Latitude: 42° 58' N   Longitude: 83° 45' W

	JAN	FEB	MAR	APR	MAY	JUN	JUL	AUG	SEP	OCT	NOV	DEC	YEAR
Mean Maximum Temp. (°F)	30.2	33.2	43.5	57.3	68.9	78.2	82.2	79.9	72.7	59.7	46.9	34.5	57.3
Mean Temp. (°F)	23.0	25.2	34.4	46.7	57.3	66.9	71.0	69.2	61.6	49.7	39.2	27.9	47.7
Mean Minimum Temp. (°F)	15.8	17.3	25.1	36.0	45.8	55.4	59.7	58.5	50.4	39.8	31.5	21.2	38.0
Extreme Maximum Temp. (°F)	61	68	80	87	93	101	101	98	94	89	75	70	101
Extreme Minimum Temp. (°F)	-21	-19	-11	6	23	33	40	37	26	20	9	-13	-21
Days Maximum Temp. ≥ 90°F	0	0	0	0	0	2	4	2	1	0	0	0	9
Days Maximum Temp. ≤ 32°F	18	14	5	0	0	0	0	0	0	0	2	12	51
Days Minimum Temp. ≤ 32°F	29	25	24	11	1	0	0	0	0	7	17	27	141
Days Minimum Temp. ≤ 0°F	4	3	1	0	0	0	0	0	0	0	0	2	10
Heating Degree Days (base 65°F)	1,294	1,117	944	549	264	59	12	25	151	472	766	1,142	6,795
Cooling Degree Days (base 65°F)	0	0	1	6	33	121	203	162	55	6	0	0	587
Mean Precipitation (in.)	1.64	1.46	1.96	2.94	3.01	3.04	3.42	3.28	3.78	2.46	2.63	1.96	31.58
Maximum Precipitation (in.)*	3.2	5.3	4.2	5.6	6.8	6.5	7.9	11.0	10.9	4.2	4.9	4.7	45.4
Minimum Precipitation (in.)*	0.3	0.2	0.3	1.0	0.3	0.6	0.7	0.4	0.3	0.4	0.7	0.4	18.1
Extreme Maximum Daily Precip. (in.)	1.17	1.49	1.37	2.25	2.23	3.46	2.72	3.89	3.62	1.90	1.87	0.96	3.89
Days With ≥ 0.1" Precipitation	5	4	5	7	6	6	6	6	6	6	6	6	69
Days With ≥ 0.5" Precipitation	1	1	1	1	2	2	3	2	2	2	1	1	19
Days With ≥ 1.0" Precipitation	0	0	0	0	1	1	1	1	1	0	0	0	5
Mean Snowfall (in.)	13.0	10.3	6.8	2.6	trace	trace	trace	trace	0.0	0.4	2.5	11.8	47.4
Maximum Snowfall (in.)*	29	21	19	17	1	0	0	0	trace	4	16	25	84
Maximum 24-hr. Snowfall (in.)*	15	10	13	12	1	0	0	0	trace	4	11	9	15
Maximum Snow Depth (in.)	18	12	10	7	trace	trace	trace	trace	0	2	6	20	20
Days With ≥ 1.0" Snow Depth	21	17	8	1	0	0	0	0	0	0	2	13	62
Thunderstorm Days*	< 1	< 1	1	3	4	6	6	6	4	1	1	< 1	32
Foggy Days*	11	10	12	11	10	10	12	16	14	14	13	13	146
Predominant Sky Cover*	OVR	OVR	OVR	OVR	OVR	OVR	OVR	OVR	OVR	OVR	OVR	OVR	OVR
Mean Relative Humidity 6am (%)*	81	81	81	80	81	85	88	91	90	86	83	83	84
Mean Relative Humidity 3pm (%)*	70	67	60	53	51	53	52	55	56	57	65	72	59
Mean Dewpoint (°F)*	17	18	25	34	45	55	60	59	52	42	31	22	38
Prevailing Wind Direction*	SW	WSW	WNW	WSW	WSW	WSW	SW	SW	S	S	SW	SW	SW
Prevailing Wind Speed (mph)*	12	12	14	13	12	10	9	8	9	10	13	12	12
Maximum Wind Gust (mph)*	61	54	69	68	56	76	73	71	63	49	63	69	76

Note: (*) Period of record is 1949-1995

Grand Rapids Int'l Airport

Grand Rapids, Michigan, is located in the west-central part of Kent County, in the picturesque Grand River valley about 30 air miles east of Lake Michigan. The Grand River, the longest stream in Michigan, flows through the city and bisects it into east and west sections. High hills rise on either side of the valley. Elevations range from 602 feet on the valley floor to 1,020 feet in the extreme southern part of Kent County, southwest of the airport.

Grand Rapids is under the natural climatic influence of Lake Michigan. In spring the cooling effect of Lake Michigan helps retard the growth of vegetation until the danger of frost has passed. The warming effect in the fall retards frost until most of the crops have matured. Fall is a colorful time of year in western Michigan, compensating for the late spring. During the winter, excessive cloudiness and numerous snow flurries occur with strong westerly winds. The tempering effect of Lake Michigan on cold waves coming in from the west and northwest is quite evident.

The tempering effect of the lake promotes the growth of a great variety of fruit trees and berries, especially apples, peaches, cherries, and blueberries. The intense cold of winter is modified, thus reducing winter kill of fruit trees. Summer days are pleasantly warm and most summer nights are quite comfortable, although there are about three weeks of hot, humid weather during most summers. Prolonged severe cold waves with below-zero temperatures are infrequent. The temperature usually rises to above zero during the daytime hours regardless of early morning readings.

July is the sunniest month and December is the month with the least sunshine. November through January is usually a period of excessive cloudiness and minimal sunshine.

Precipitation is usually ample for the growth and development of all vegetation. About one-half of the annual precipitation falls during the growing season, May through September. Droughts occur occasionally, but are seldom of protracted length. The snowfall season extends from mid-November to mid-March. Some winters have had continuous snow cover throughout this period, although there is usually a mid-winter thaw. The Grand River flows through the city and reaches critical heights a couple of times each year. Overflow is generally limited to the lowlands of the flood plain.

November is one of the windiest months and although violent windstorms are infrequent, gusts have on occasion exceeded 65 mph. Summer thunderstorms occasionally produce gusty winds over 60 mph.

Grand Rapids Int'l Airport *Kent County*   Elevation: 784 ft.   Latitude: 42° 53' N   Longitude: 85° 31' W

	JAN	FEB	MAR	APR	MAY	JUN	JUL	AUG	SEP	OCT	NOV	DEC	YEAR
Mean Maximum Temp. (°F)	30.4	33.2	43.6	57.5	69.2	78.5	82.4	80.1	72.6	59.6	46.6	34.4	57.3
Mean Temp. (°F)	23.8	26.0	34.7	47.1	58.0	67.6	71.8	70.1	62.2	50.1	39.3	28.4	48.3
Mean Minimum Temp. (°F)	17.1	18.7	25.8	36.6	46.8	56.6	61.1	60.0	51.7	40.6	32.0	22.4	39.1
Extreme Maximum Temp. (°F)	63	69	78	86	91	98	100	98	92	88	74	69	100
Extreme Minimum Temp. (°F)	-22	-17	-7	3	26	35	41	41	27	18	9	-18	-22
Days Maximum Temp. ≥ 90°F	0	0	0	0	0	3	4	2	0	0	0	0	9
Days Maximum Temp. ≤ 32°F	18	14	5	0	0	0	0	0	0	0	2	13	52
Days Minimum Temp. ≤ 32°F	28	26	23	10	1	0	0	0	0	5	17	27	137
Days Minimum Temp. ≤ 0°F	3	2	0	0	0	0	0	0	0	0	0	1	6
Heating Degree Days (base 65°F)	1,272	1,096	933	537	246	50	8	18	140	460	763	1,127	6,650
Cooling Degree Days (base 65°F)	0	0	1	7	36	134	225	182	61	6	0	0	652
Mean Precipitation (in.)	2.11	1.77	2.39	3.33	3.92	3.63	3.81	3.63	4.33	3.23	3.44	2.53	38.12
Maximum Precipitation (in.)*	4.4	3.3	5.8	6.1	8.3	8.2	8.8	8.5	11.8	8.3	7.8	6.6	47.5
Minimum Precipitation (in.)*	0.3	0.3	0.7	1.8	0.9	0.3	0.6	0.1	trace	trace	0.6	0.7	22.8
Extreme Maximum Daily Precip. (in.)	2.15	2.96	1.36	2.35	4.15	3.17	3.56	3.61	3.21	2.83	2.94	1.51	4.15
Days With ≥ 0.1" Precipitation	6	5	6	7	7	6	6	6	7	7	7	7	77
Days With ≥ 0.5" Precipitation	1	1	1	2	2	3	3	3	3	2	2	1	24
Days With ≥ 1.0" Precipitation	0	0	0	1	1	1	1	1	1	1	1	0	8
Mean Snowfall (in.)	20.8	14.2	8.3	2.0	trace	trace	trace	trace	trace	0.6	6.8	21.9	74.6
Maximum Snowfall (in.)*	46	30	36	16	2	0	0	0	trace	trace	8	27	51	118
Maximum 24-hr. Snowfall (in.)*	16	9	10	12	1	0	0	0	trace	8	10	10	16
Maximum Snow Depth (in.)	20	21	14	7	trace	trace	trace	trace	trace	1	11	17	21
Days With ≥ 1.0" Snow Depth	23	17	8	1	0	0	0	0	0	0	3	16	68
Thunderstorm Days*	< 1	< 1	2	4	4	6	6	5	4	2	1	< 1	34
Foggy Days*	11	11	12	11	10	10	12	15	13	13	12	13	143
Predominant Sky Cover*	OVR	OVR	OVR	OVR	OVR	OVR	OVR	OVR	OVR	OVR	OVR	OVR	OVR
Mean Relative Humidity 7am (%)*	82	81	81	79	79	81	84	89	89	85	83	83	83
Mean Relative Humidity 4pm (%)*	72	66	61	54	50	51	53	56	58	59	68	74	60
Mean Dewpoint (°F)*	17	17	25	34	45	55	60	60	53	41	31	22	39
Prevailing Wind Direction*	WSW	WSW	ENE	WSW	WSW	WSW	WSW	WSW	S	S	WSW	WSW	WSW
Prevailing Wind Speed (mph)*	14	13	12	13	12	10	10	10	8	9	13	13	12
Maximum Wind Gust (mph)*	62	62	71	68	68	63	61	61	61	48	78	62	78

Note: (*) Period of record is 1948-1995

Houghton Lake Airport

Houghton Lake is located in north-central lower Michigan. The present station is on the northeast shore of Houghton Lake, the largest inland lake in Michigan, with a circumference of about 32 miles. The Muskegon River source is Higgins Lake, eight miles to the north. It flows through Houghton Lake, then southwestward to Lake Michigan. The station lies within an elongated bowl shaped 1,000-foot plateau, which extends roughly 50 miles north, 75 miles southwest, and about 20 miles south-east of Houghton Lake. In the immediate area, the land is level to rolling, but there are hills and ridges from 100 to 300 feet higher in elevation surrounding the station. Soils are generally sand, or sandy loam supporting little agricultural production, but the area is rich in natural resources of forests, lakes, and streams.

The interior location diminishes the influence of the larger Great Lakes, which lie 70 to 80 miles east and west of Houghton Lake. Hence, the daily temperature range is larger, especially in summer, and temperature extremes are greater than are found nearer the shores of either Lake Michigan or Lake Huron. Temperatures reach the 100 degree mark about one summer out of ten, and at the other extreme, fall below zero an average of 22 times during the winter season.

Precipitation is normally a little heavier during the summer season. About 60 percent of the annual total falls in the six-month period from April through September. The heaviest precipitation occurs with summertime thunderstorms.

Snowfall averages above 80 inches per year at Houghton Lake, with considerable variation from year to year. Much heavier snows, averaging over 100 inches a sea-son, fall within a 30- to 60-mile radius to the north and west of Houghton Lake. Seasonal totals have ranged from 24 inches to over 124 inches. Measurable amounts of snow have occurred in nine of the 12 months, and the average number of months with measurable snowfall is six.

Cloudiness is greatest in the late fall and early winter, while sunshine percentage is highest in the spring and summer. Cloudiness is increased in the late fall due to the moisture and warmth picked up by the westerly and northwesterly winds while crossing Lake Michigan.

The growing season is normally quite short, averaging about 90 days between spring and fall freezes.

Houghton Lake Airport *Roscommon County*   Elevation: 1,149 ft.   Latitude: 44° 22' N   Longitude: 84° 41' W

	JAN	FEB	MAR	APR	MAY	JUN	JUL	AUG	SEP	OCT	NOV	DEC	YEAR
Mean Maximum Temp. (°F)	26.5	29.6	39.5	54.0	66.5	75.7	79.9	77.3	69.2	55.7	42.5	30.8	54.0
Mean Temp. (°F)	18.7	20.5	29.5	43.0	54.5	63.4	67.7	65.6	57.9	46.4	35.5	24.5	43.9
Mean Minimum Temp. (°F)	10.9	11.4	19.4	31.9	42.4	51.1	55.4	53.8	46.6	37.0	28.5	18.1	33.9
Extreme Maximum Temp. (°F)	54	59	76	86	90	103	98	96	92	85	70	64	103
Extreme Minimum Temp. (°F)	-26	-31	-20	2	22	29	34	29	21	18	-5	-18	-31
Days Maximum Temp. ≥ 90°F	0	0	0	0	0	1	2	1	0	0	0	0	4
Days Maximum Temp. ≤ 32°F	23	18	8	1	0	0	0	0	0	0	4	17	71
Days Minimum Temp. ≤ 32°F	30	27	28	16	4	0	0	0	2	10	22	29	168
Days Minimum Temp. ≤ 0°F	7	6	3	0	0	0	0	0	0	0	0	2	18
Heating Degree Days (base 65°F)	1,428	1,252	1,095	656	336	111	40	68	231	573	878	1,249	7,917
Cooling Degree Days (base 65°F)	0	0	0	3	18	70	129	93	26	2	0	0	341
Mean Precipitation (in.)	1.55	1.22	1.85	2.51	2.79	3.05	2.63	3.41	3.13	2.57	2.32	1.67	28.70
Maximum Precipitation (in.)*	3.1	3.4	5.7	4.7	6.0	6.7	5.3	7.2	9.5	8.1	5.1	4.5	37.7
Minimum Precipitation (in.)*	0.6	0.3	0.6	1.0	0.4	0.8	0.5	0.8	trace	0.5	0.4	0.5	20.2
Extreme Maximum Daily Precip. (in.)	0.93	1.45	1.55	1.81	1.85	2.84	3.55	3.12	2.30	3.47	1.65	1.20	3.55
Days With ≥ 0.1" Precipitation	5	4	5	6	6	6	5	7	6	6	6	5	67
Days With ≥ 0.5" Precipitation	1	0	1	1	2	2	2	2	2	1	1	1	16
Days With ≥ 1.0" Precipitation	0	0	0	0	0	1	1	1	1	0	0	0	4
Mean Snowfall (in.)	*18.0*	*12.0*	*8.7*	na	na	na	na	*trace*	*trace*	0.7	9.2	16.4	na
Maximum Snowfall (in.)*	38	24	29	12	2	0	0	0	trace	4	42	30	117
Maximum 24-hr. Snowfall (in.)*	15	7	12	6	2	0	0	0	trace	4	14	13	15
Maximum Snow Depth (in.)	*21*	*20*	*18*	na	na	na	na	*trace*	*trace*	1	17	22	na
Days With ≥ 1.0" Snow Depth	*29*	*27*	*18*	na	na	na	na	0	0	0	7	22	na
Thunderstorm Days*	< 1	< 1	1	2	4	5	6	6	4	1	1	< 1	30
Foggy Days*	11	10	12	10	11	12	12	17	16	14	14	13	152
Predominant Sky Cover*	OVR	OVR	OVR	OVR	OVR	OVR	OVR	OVR	OVR	OVR	OVR	OVR	OVR
Mean Relative Humidity 7am (%)*	83	82	84	80	78	81	85	91	91	88	87	85	85
Mean Relative Humidity 4pm (%)*	72	66	61	53	47	51	52	58	61	62	72	76	61
Mean Dewpoint (°F)*	13	13	21	30	41	52	58	57	50	39	29	19	35
Prevailing Wind Direction*	W	W	W	NW	W	W	SW	WSW	SW	SW	W	W	W
Prevailing Wind Speed (mph)*	12	9	9	12	9	9	8	8	9	10	13	12	10
Maximum Wind Gust (mph)*	62	48	61	61	60	58	58	59	48	54	61	43	62

Note: (*) Period of record is 1964-1995

Lansing Capital City Airport

The climate at Lansing alternates between continental and semi-marine, depending on meteorological conditions. The marine type is due to the influence of the Great Lakes and is governed by the force and direction of the wind. When there is little or no wind, the weather becomes continental in character, which means pronounced fluctuation in temperature, hot weather in summer and severe cold in winter. On the other hand, a strong wind from the Lakes may immediately transform the weather into a semi-marine type.

Since large bodies of water are less responsive to temperature changes, the Great Lakes hold the winter cold longer in the spring and the summer heat longer in the fall than do the land areas. This fact is illustrated by looking at some monthly mean temperatures at Lansing as compared to similar latitudes west of the Lakes. Such a comparison shows cooler summers and milder winters in Lansing because of the lake effect.

Based on the 1951-1980 period, the average first occurrence of 32 degrees Fahrenheit in the fall is September 30 and the average last occurrence in the spring is May 13.

Precipitation is fairly well distributed through the year, and no conspicuous annual variation is noted, although there is about one inch less per month in winter than in summer. The heavier amounts in summer occur in thunderstorms. The wettest months are May and June. Snowfall for Lansing is moderate, averaging about 52 inches per year.

There are almost twice as many cloudy days as clear days throughout the year. Much cloudiness prevails during the winter season, but sunshine is abundant during the summer months. Similarly, relative humidity remains rather high during the winter, but is only moderate in summer.

Tornadoes sometimes occur in this area, but their frequency is less than in states farther to the south and west. Destructive thunder and wind storms are not uncommon. Flooding of streams and rivers in the upper grand Basin occurs in about one year out of three, with floods causing considerable damage in about one year out of ten.

Lansing Capital City Airport *Clinton County*   Elevation: 840 ft.   Latitude: 42° 47' N   Longitude: 84° 35' W

	JAN	FEB	MAR	APR	MAY	JUN	JUL	AUG	SEP	OCT	NOV	DEC	YEAR
Mean Maximum Temp. (°F)	30.1	33.1	43.7	57.5	68.9	78.3	82.3	80.0	72.7	59.6	46.6	34.3	57.3
Mean Temp. (°F)	22.8	25.0	34.1	46.5	57.0	66.7	70.8	69.1	61.3	49.4	38.8	27.6	47.4
Mean Minimum Temp. (°F)	15.3	16.8	24.4	35.4	45.2	55.1	59.2	58.0	49.8	39.2	30.9	20.8	37.5
Extreme Maximum Temp. (°F)	62	69	79	86	91	99	100	100	93	87	74	69	100
Extreme Minimum Temp. (°F)	-29	-25	-13	-2	23	33	38	36	22	19	8	-18	-29
Days Maximum Temp. ≥ 90°F	0	0	0	0	0	2	4	2	1	0	0	0	9
Days Maximum Temp. ≤ 32°F	18	14	6	1	0	0	0	0	0	0	2	13	54
Days Minimum Temp. ≤ 32°F	29	26	25	12	2	0	0	0	1	8	18	27	148
Days Minimum Temp. ≤ 0°F	5	3	1	0	0	0	0	0	0	0	0	2	11
Heating Degree Days (base 65°F)	1,303	1,124	952	555	272	62	14	29	160	483	780	1,153	6,887
Cooling Degree Days (base 65°F)	0	0	0	6	32	120	200	162	55	6	0	0	582
Mean Precipitation (in.)	1.64	1.46	2.11	3.02	3.28	3.45	2.89	3.37	3.44	2.50	2.73	1.92	31.81
Maximum Precipitation (in.)*	3.6	4.2	4.4	5.2	6.6	10.2	6.4	9.8	8.3	5.6	5.4	4.7	39.6
Minimum Precipitation (in.)*	0.4	0.2	0.9	1.1	0.6	0.2	0.5	0.2	trace	0.3	0.5	0.4	21.2
Extreme Maximum Daily Precip. (in.)	1.59	2.14	1.24	2.10	3.22	4.95	2.12	2.70	3.43	1.43	2.16	1.02	4.95
Days With ≥ 0.1" Precipitation	4	4	5	8	7	6	6	6	6	6	6	6	70
Days With ≥ 0.5" Precipitation	1	1	1	2	2	2	2	2	2	2	2	1	20
Days With ≥ 1.0" Precipitation	0	0	0	0	1	1	1	1	1	0	1	0	6
Mean Snowfall (in.)	13.7	11.0	*7.3*	*2.1*	*trace*	*trace*	*trace*	*0.0*	*trace*	*0.4*	*3.5*	*13.2*	*51.2*
Maximum Snowfall (in.)*	34	24	20	17	trace	0	0	0	trace	8	17	28	80
Maximum 24-hr. Snowfall (in.)*	15	8	14	10	trace	0	0	0	trace	8	8	9	15
Maximum Snow Depth (in.)	23	17	13	*6*	*trace*	*trace*	*trace*	*0*	*trace*	*1*	*7*	*16*	*23*
Days With ≥ 1.0" Snow Depth	23	17	8	*1*	*0*	*0*	*0*	*0*	*0*	*0*	*2*	*15*	*66*
Thunderstorm Days*	< 1	< 1	1	3	4	6	6	6	4	1	1	< 1	32
Foggy Days*	13	12	13	12	11	11	12	16	14	14	14	14	156
Predominant Sky Cover*	OVR	OVR	OVR	OVR	OVR	OVR	SCT	OVR	OVR	OVR	OVR	OVR	OVR
Mean Relative Humidity 7am (%)*	83	82	83	80	79	81	85	90	90	87	85	84	84
Mean Relative Humidity 4pm (%)*	72	67	62	55	52	53	53	56	58	59	68	74	61
Mean Dewpoint (°F)*	17	17	25	35	45	56	60	60	53	41	32	22	39
Prevailing Wind Direction*	W	W	W	W	W	W	W	W	SSW	SW	SSW	SW	W
Prevailing Wind Speed (mph)*	14	14	14	14	12	10	10	9	10	12	12	13	12
Maximum Wind Gust (mph)*	60	52	64	70	62	69	64	54	48	55	60	62	70

Note: (*) Period of record is 1948-1995

Marquette County Airport

The Marquette County Airport lies about 7.5 miles southwest of the nearest shoreline of Lake Superior and about eight miles west of the city of Marquette. Lake Superior is the largest body of fresh water in the world and the deepest and coldest of the Great Lakes. An irregular northwest-southeast ridge line lies just to the east of the airport. There are several water storage basins in the vicinity of the station. One basin, about 20 miles long, is three miles northwest and another, about eight miles in diameter, is three miles west.

The climate is influenced considerably by the proximity of Lake Superior. As a consequence of the cool expanse of water in the summer, there is rarely a long period of sweltering hot weather. Periods of drought are extremely rare. In the winter, cold outbreaks are tempered considerably by the waters of Lake Superior if the lake is unfrozen. However, winds blowing across these relatively warmer waters pick up moisture and cause cloudy weather throughout the winter, as well as frequent periods of light snow. Lake-formed snow showers and snow squalls are intensified near the station by upslope winds, especially from the northwest through northeast. With a northeast through east wind, especially in autumn, the upslope condition will cause light snow at the airport, while along the lakeshore, only drizzle or no precipitation may occur.

The growing season averages 117 days. Precipitation is rather evenly distributed throughout the year, with an average precipitation of four inches or more in June and September and less than two inch averages only in January and February. One hundred inches or more of snow occur in nine of ten winter seasons.

Marquette County Airport *Marquette County*   Elevation: 1,415 ft.   Latitude: 46° 32' N   Longitude: 87° 33' W

	JAN	FEB	MAR	APR	MAY	JUN	JUL	AUG	SEP	OCT	NOV	DEC	YEAR
Mean Maximum Temp. (°F)	22.2	25.9	34.6	48.0	62.2	71.9	76.4	74.2	65.8	51.8	37.5	26.0	49.7
Mean Temp. (°F)	14.1	16.3	24.5	38.0	50.8	60.4	65.2	63.5	55.7	43.1	30.6	18.9	40.1
Mean Minimum Temp. (°F)	6.0	6.6	14.3	27.9	39.3	48.8	54.0	52.8	45.5	34.4	23.6	11.8	30.4
Extreme Maximum Temp. (°F)	49	61	71	92	93	96	99	96	93	87	73	59	99
Extreme Minimum Temp. (°F)	-27	-32	-30	-9	17	28	36	34	24	14	-8	-28	-32
Days Maximum Temp. ≥ 90°F	0	0	0	0	0	1	2	1	0	0	0	0	4
Days Maximum Temp. ≤ 32°F	26	21	13	3	0	0	0	0	0	0	10	23	96
Days Minimum Temp. ≤ 32°F	31	28	29	22	8	0	0	0	2	15	26	30	191
Days Minimum Temp. ≤ 0°F	10	10	5	0	0	0	0	0	0	0	0	7	32
Heating Degree Days (base 65°F)	1,571	1,373	1,250	806	447	182	80	106	295	673	1,026	1,424	9,233
Cooling Degree Days (base 65°F)	0	0	0	2	12	51	95	68	22	2	0	0	252
Mean Precipitation (in.)	2.43	2.07	3.00	3.09	3.06	2.71	2.77	3.10	3.72	3.85	3.18	2.53	35.51
Maximum Precipitation (in.)*	4.5	3.6	6.1	6.6	7.9	12.3	5.6	8.6	7.6	7.6	8.3	6.9	51.6
Minimum Precipitation (in.)*	0.6	0.5	0.3	0.9	0.1	0.6	0.6	0.6	1.2	0.9	1.0	0.4	22.7
Extreme Maximum Daily Precip. (in.)	2.21	1.53	2.42	3.09	3.15	1.87	2.46	2.30	4.29	2.89	2.18	2.30	4.29
Days With ≥ 0.1" Precipitation	7	5	7	7	6	7	7	6	8	8	7	7	82
Days With ≥ 0.5" Precipitation	1	1	1	2	2	2	2	2	2	2	2	1	20
Days With ≥ 1.0" Precipitation	0	0	1	1	1	0	0	1	1	1	1	0	7
Mean Snowfall (in.)	43.4	35.8	34.8	14.5	1.3	trace	trace	trace	0.1	6.4	24.5	42.2	203.0
Maximum Snowfall (in.)*	69	64	61	29	23	trace	0	0	2	19	49	83	269
Maximum 24-hr. Snowfall (in.)*	23	18	21	16	14	trace	0	0	2	11	18	24	24
Maximum Snow Depth (in.)	45	44	63	41	17	trace	trace	trace	trace	10	24	47	63
Days With ≥ 1.0" Snow Depth	31	28	30	14	1	0	0	0	0	3	16	29	152
Thunderstorm Days*	< 1	< 1	1	1	3	6	6	5	4	2	< 1	< 1	28
Foggy Days*	7	7	9	9	10	11	10	13	14	12	11	9	122
Predominant Sky Cover*	na	na	na	na	na	na	na	na	na	na	na	na	na
Mean Relative Humidity 7am (%)*	na	na	na	na	na	na	na	na	na	na	na	na	na
Mean Relative Humidity 4pm (%)*	na	na	na	na	na	na	na	na	na	na	na	na	na
Mean Dewpoint (°F)*	na	na	na	na	na	na	na	na	na	na	na	na	na
Prevailing Wind Direction*	na	na	na	na	na	na	na	na	na	na	na	na	na
Prevailing Wind Speed (mph)*	na	na	na	na	na	na	na	na	na	na	na	na	na
Maximum Wind Gust (mph)*	na	na	na	na	na	na	na	na	na	na	na	na	na

Note: (*) Period of record is 1963-1995

Muskegon County Airport

Muskegon is located on the eastern shore of Lake Michigan approximately 100 miles north of the southern tip of the lake. The terrain is generally level with several sand dunes along the shoreline. Much of the soil is sandy and vegetation grows well, as evidenced by the trees and grass which grow on the dunes. Many crops grow in the area. Asparagus and celery are the principal truck- garden vegetables. A variety of fruits is raised and blueberries lead as a principal product. The main industry in this area is manufacturing with emphasis on foundry and machined products. The area is also a resort center due to features such as extensive sandy beaches, both on Lake Michigan and inland lakes.

Lake Michigan has a very decided effect upon the weather and climate of this area. The prevailing westerly winds tend to moderate the temperatures, resulting in warmer winters than further inland. In the summer the effect is just the opposite. The air temperature usually remains below the uncomfortable readings of the high 90s. Spring arrives about three to four weeks later than normal for this latitude. Autumn is also delayed, as is the cold of early winter.

Precipitation is fairly moderate, but snowfall is moderate to heavy. The heaviest snows occur during late December, January, and February. Precipitation is also influenced by the lake, especially during the winter. Instability in snow showers along the lakeshore vary enormously in intensity, resulting in traces of snow to more than a foot in 24 hours. The heavier snow squalls tend to concentrate over small sections of the shoreline, depending on their intensity and the direction of the wind. With strong winds most snowshowers will fall further inland, sometimes as much as 30 to 40 miles. Snowfall is likely to occur every day for weeks at a time. The daily accumulation of lake effect snow varies greatly. However, due to low water content of most of the storms, the snow settles rapidly.

Summertime thunderstorms have a tendency, as they move inland, to follow the Muskegon and Grand River Valleys. Thus, these areas are more often frequented by severe electrical storms which will pass without a drop of rain two to three miles from the immediate river valleys. Thunderstorms near the shoreline are most frequent at night. The afternoon convection-type storms seldom occur within five miles of the lake. Lake Michigan-spawned thunderstorms give shoreline areas a surprising number of occurrences.

Based on the 1951-1980 period, the average first occurrence of 32 degrees Fahrenheit in the fall is October 11 and the average last occurrence in the spring is May 8.

Muskegon County Airport *Muskegon County*   Elevation: 625 ft.   Latitude: 43° 10' N   Longitude: 86° 14' W

	JAN	FEB	MAR	APR	MAY	JUN	JUL	AUG	SEP	OCT	NOV	DEC	YEAR
Mean Maximum Temp. (°F)	30.7	33.0	42.6	55.5	66.8	75.8	80.3	78.6	71.3	58.5	46.2	35.0	56.2
Mean Temp. (°F)	24.9	26.5	34.2	45.9	56.3	65.6	70.5	69.3	61.5	49.9	39.6	29.6	47.8
Mean Minimum Temp. (°F)	18.9	19.9	25.8	36.2	45.7	55.4	60.7	59.8	51.7	41.3	32.9	24.1	39.4
Extreme Maximum Temp. (°F)	61	67	80	84	89	98	96	95	91	83	72	64	98
Extreme Minimum Temp. (°F)	-11	-19	-6	1	25	32	39	38	27	21	10	-8	-19
Days Maximum Temp. ≥ 90°F	0	0	0	0	0	1	1	1	0	0	0	0	3
Days Maximum Temp. ≤ 32°F	17	14	6	0	0	0	0	0	0	0	2	11	50
Days Minimum Temp. ≤ 32°F	28	26	24	10	1	0	0	0	0	5	15	26	135
Days Minimum Temp. ≤ 0°F	2	1	0	0	0	0	0	0	0	0	0	0	3
Heating Degree Days (base 65°F)	1,237	1,082	947	570	286	72	13	22	149	465	756	1,090	6,689
Cooling Degree Days (base 65°F)	0	0	0	0	23	97	191	161	51	4	0	0	531
Mean Precipitation (in.)	2.05	1.78	2.37	2.98	3.21	2.55	2.37	3.52	3.82	3.11	3.37	2.59	33.72
Maximum Precipitation (in.)*	4.5	2.8	6.6	6.1	6.5	5.5	6.6	9.9	13.5	7.3	6.6	5.4	42.3
Minimum Precipitation (in.)*	0.4	0.4	0.5	0.7	0.3	0.2	0.5	0.1	0.2	0.5	0.6	0.9	23.1
Extreme Maximum Daily Precip. (in.)	1.18	1.65	4.00	2.66	2.30	2.52	1.57	3.45	4.33	2.58	2.12	2.58	4.33
Days With ≥ 0.1" Precipitation	6	5	6	7	6	5	5	6	7	7	7	7	74
Days With ≥ 0.5" Precipitation	1	1	1	2	2	2	2	2	3	2	2	1	21
Days With ≥ 1.0" Precipitation	0	0	0	0	1	1	0	1	1	1	1	0	6
Mean Snowfall (in.)	29.2	18.8	9.2	2.5	*trace*	*trace*	*trace*	*trace*	*trace*	*0.2*	6.3	28.9	**95.1**
Maximum Snowfall (in.)*	102	46	36	20	trace	0	0	0	trace	5	26	83	182
Maximum 24-hr. Snowfall (in.)*	22	14	9	12	trace	0	0	0	trace	5	9	15	22
Maximum Snow Depth (in.)	30	30	15	13	trace	*trace*	*trace*	*trace*	*trace*	*1*	11	24	**30**
Days With ≥ 1.0" Snow Depth	24	20	9	1	0	*0*	*0*	*0*	*0*	*0*	3	17	**74**
Thunderstorm Days*	< 1	< 1	2	3	4	6	6	6	5	2	1	< 1	35
Foggy Days*	11	10	12	11	11	11	11	14	12	13	12	12	140
Predominant Sky Cover*	OVR	OVR	OVR	OVR	OVR	OVR	CLR	OVR	OVR	OVR	OVR	OVR	OVR
Mean Relative Humidity 7am (%)*	81	81	80	78	76	80	84	88	88	84	80	81	82
Mean Relative Humidity 4pm (%)*	75	70	63	55	52	55	56	59	61	62	70	75	63
Mean Dewpoint (°F)*	18	18	25	33	43	54	60	60	53	42	32	23	38
Prevailing Wind Direction*	WNW	WNW	E	WNW	SW	SW	SW	SW	SSW	SSW	WNW	WNW	WNW
Prevailing Wind Speed (mph)*	14	13	12	13	13	12	12	12	13	15	15	14	13
Maximum Wind Gust (mph)*	62	67	59	63	54	55	58	63	54	55	59	56	67

Note: (*) Period of record is 1948-1995

Sault Ste Marie Sanderson Field

Sault Ste. Marie is located at the extreme eastern tip of the Upper Peninsula of Michigan at the intersection of Lake Superior, Michigan, and Huron. Consequently, the regional climate is essentially maritime during ice-free periods of the year. Lake ice development usually begins in December and progresses to maximum coverage in February. As ice cover develops, the character of the regional climate gradually changes to continental polar by the time of maximum lake ice development. Lake Superior, to the northwest, is the largest, deepest, and coldest of the Great Lakes and is the dominant climatic control for the area. Water in the northern Great Lakes remains relatively cool during the summer and seldom freezes over during the winter. Therefore, temperatures are moderated throughout most of the year, whereas cloudiness and precipitation are increased.

Terrain on the Michigan side of the international border is nearly flat and lies 700 to 800 feet above sea level. Very little climatological influence is related to Michigan terrain. However, terrain on the Canadian side of the border rises rather abruptly to about 1,500 feet above sea level and this definite topographic influence increases the rain and snow shower activity over the Canadian hills.

Heavy fog occurrences reach a maximum in August, September, and October and form in response to the passage of relatively cold air masses over the warmer waters of the northern Great Lakes. Destructive tornadoes and thunderstorms have occurred on rare occasions.

Most summers pass without a temperature reaching 90 degrees. Winters are cold and snowy with total seasonal snowfall ranging from about 30 inches to more than 175 inches. November 21 is the average date for the appearance of the permanent winter snow cover which normally lasts until April 7.

Annual percent of possible sunshine is low but is especially low during late fall and early winter because of cloud cover produced by lake moisture evaporated into the cold air. Sunshine amounts increase as ice development increases in the winter season. Daylight during most of June and July lasts almost 16 hours, whereas winter daylight reaches a minimum of less than 9 hours a day in late December.

Based on the 1951-1980 period, the average first occurrence of 32 degrees Fahrenheit in the fall is September 27 and the average last occurrence in the spring is May 26.

Sault Ste Marie Sanderson Field *Chippewa County*   Elevation: 717 ft.   Latitude: 46° 28' N   Longitude: 84° 21' W

	JAN	FEB	MAR	APR	MAY	JUN	JUL	AUG	SEP	OCT	NOV	DEC	YEAR
Mean Maximum Temp. (°F)	22.7	25.4	33.8	48.7	62.5	71.0	75.8	74.4	66.2	52.7	39.7	28.2	50.1
Mean Temp. (°F)	14.6	16.8	25.1	39.3	51.1	59.2	64.5	63.9	56.4	44.7	33.4	21.4	40.9
Mean Minimum Temp. (°F)	6.5	8.1	16.3	29.9	39.7	47.5	53.1	53.4	46.6	36.5	27.0	14.6	31.6
Extreme Maximum Temp. (°F)	44	49	63	85	89	93	97	94	90	81	68	62	97
Extreme Minimum Temp. (°F)	-36	-28	-21	-2	24	26	36	29	25	16	-4	-31	-36
Days Maximum Temp. ≥ 90°F	0	0	0	0	0	0	1	0	0	0	0	0	1
Days Maximum Temp. ≤ 32°F	25	21	13	2	0	0	0	0	0	0	6	19	86
Days Minimum Temp. ≤ 32°F	31	28	29	19	6	1	0	0	1	10	22	29	176
Days Minimum Temp. ≤ 0°F	10	9	4	0	0	0	0	0	0	0	0	5	28
Heating Degree Days (base 65°F)	1,558	1,358	1,230	764	428	193	78	85	268	624	942	1,345	8,873
Cooling Degree Days (base 65°F)	0	0	0	0	5	27	70	58	17	1	0	0	178
Mean Precipitation (in.)	2.26	1.35	1.92	2.47	2.56	2.65	2.88	3.10	3.64	3.79	3.34	2.87	32.83
Maximum Precipitation (in.)*	4.5	3.7	5.0	5.2	5.3	7.3	6.0	9.5	7.8	6.5	7.7	6.2	45.8
Minimum Precipitation (in.)*	0.5	0.2	0.3	0.6	0.8	0.5	0.6	0.5	1.0	0.2	0.9	0.6	25.5
Extreme Maximum Daily Precip. (in.)	1.21	0.90	1.08	1.63	1.63	1.91	1.75	3.15	2.20	1.65	2.33	1.46	3.15
Days With ≥ 0.1" Precipitation	7	4	5	6	6	6	6	7	8	10	9	9	83
Days With ≥ 0.5" Precipitation	1	0	1	1	2	2	2	2	2	2	2	1	18
Days With ≥ 1.0" Precipitation	0	0	0	0	0	0	0	1	1	1	0	0	3
Mean Snowfall (in.)	*32.5*	*18.2*	*13.2*	na	na	na	na	*trace*	*trace*	2.1	16.5	37.8	na
Maximum Snowfall (in.)*	71	40	35	26	5	0	0	0	3	12	47	99	209
Maximum 24-hr. Snowfall (in.)*	15	12	12	9	3	0	0	0	3	7	11	27	27
Maximum Snow Depth (in.)	*38*	*36*	*37*	na	na	na	na	*trace*	*trace*	4	*14*	*49*	na
Days With ≥ 1.0" Snow Depth	*29*	*28*	*29*	na	na	na	na	*0*	*0*	1	*10*	*27*	na
Thunderstorm Days*	< 1	< 1	1	1	3	6	6	5	4	2	< 1	< 1	28
Foggy Days*	8	7	11	10	10	14	15	18	18	15	12	11	149
Predominant Sky Cover*	OVR	OVR	OVR	OVR	OVR	OVR	OVR	OVR	OVR	OVR	OVR	OVR	OVR
Mean Relative Humidity 7am (%)*	80	80	82	80	80	85	89	92	92	89	86	84	85
Mean Relative Humidity 4pm (%)*	74	70	67	59	53	59	60	62	67	68	76	78	66
Mean Dewpoint (°F)*	8	9	17	28	39	50	56	56	49	39	27	16	33
Prevailing Wind Direction*	E	NW	NW	NW	WNW	WNW	WNW	NW	NW	ESE	ESE	E	NW
Prevailing Wind Speed (mph)*	8	13	13	13	12	10	9	10	12	9	9	8	10
Maximum Wind Gust (mph)*	61	56	59	58	55	52	54	56	55	61	71	60	71

Note: (*) Period of record is 1947-1995

Adrian 2 NNE *Lenawee County* Elevation: 759 ft.   Latitude: 41° 55' N   Longitude: 84° 01' W

	JAN	FEB	MAR	APR	MAY	JUN	JUL	AUG	SEP	OCT	NOV	DEC	YEAR
Mean Maximum Temp. (°F)	32.5	35.3	46.2	59.5	70.6	80.0	83.6	81.5	74.5	61.6	48.6	36.1	59.2
Mean Temp. (°F)	24.4	26.6	36.0	47.8	58.1	67.7	71.5	69.7	62.2	50.2	39.6	28.6	48.5
Mean Minimum Temp. (°F)	16.2	17.9	25.7	36.1	45.6	55.3	59.4	57.8	49.8	38.8	30.5	21.0	37.8
Extreme Maximum Temp. (°F)	62	70	80	88	94	104	100	100	94	88	76	69	104
Extreme Minimum Temp. (°F)	-22	-16	-6	8	25	35	41	32	27	15	7	-14	-22
Days Maximum Temp. ≥ 90°F	0	0	0	0	1	3	5	3	1	0	0	0	13
Days Maximum Temp. ≤ 32°F	15	11	3	0	0	0	0	0	0	0	1	11	41
Days Minimum Temp. ≤ 32°F	29	26	24	11	1	0	0	0	1	7	19	28	146
Days Minimum Temp. ≤ 0°F	4	2	0	0	0	0	0	0	0	0	0	2	8
Heating Degree Days (base 65°F)	1,252	1,080	894	515	238	47	8	21	135	457	757	1,122	6,526
Cooling Degree Days (base 65°F)	0	0	0	6	30	133	218	173	57	5	0	0	622
Mean Precipitation (in.)	2.05	1.95	2.48	3.22	3.68	3.93	3.19	3.92	3.63	2.77	2.91	2.58	36.31
Extreme Maximum Daily Precip. (in.)	2.25	2.35	1.61	2.06	3.00	3.25	2.90	4.20	4.74	1.88	2.00	1.79	4.74
Days With ≥ 0.1" Precipitation	6	5	7	7	8	7	6	6	7	6	7	7	79
Days With ≥ 0.5" Precipitation	1	1	1	2	2	3	2	2	2	2	2	2	22
Days With ≥ 1.0" Precipitation	0	0	0	1	1	1	1	1	1	1	1	0	8
Mean Snowfall (in.)	8.9	6.8	4.5	0.7	0.0	0.0	0.0	0.0	0.0	0.1	1.6	7.0	29.6
Maximum Snow Depth (in.)	21	16	11	8	0	0	0	0	0	3	7	10	21
Days With ≥ 1.0" Snow Depth	18	15	6	0	0	0	0	0	0	0	2	10	51

Allegan 5 NE *Allegan County* Elevation: 750 ft.   Latitude: 42° 35' N   Longitude: 85° 47' W

	JAN	FEB	MAR	APR	MAY	JUN	JUL	AUG	SEP	OCT	NOV	DEC	YEAR
Mean Maximum Temp. (°F)	30.9	33.9	43.8	*57.9*	69.2	*78.2*	*82.5*	*80.3*	73.1	60.3	47.8	34.8	*57.7*
Mean Temp. (°F)	23.3	25.5	33.8	*46.4*	57.2	*66.2*	70.5	68.7	*61.3*	49.5	39.4	28.1	*47.5*
Mean Minimum Temp. (°F)	15.7	17.1	23.8	*34.9*	45.0	*54.2*	58.5	57.2	*49.6*	38.7	30.9	21.3	*37.2*
Extreme Maximum Temp. (°F)	60	70	79	*88*	91	*97*	*100*	*97*	93	84	75	70	*100*
Extreme Minimum Temp. (°F)	-21	-25	-10	*0*	23	*32*	*39*	*36*	26	18	6	-18	*-25*
Days Maximum Temp. ≥ 90°F	0	0	0	*0*	0	*2*	*4*	*2*	1	0	0	0	*9*
Days Maximum Temp. ≤ 32°F	17	13	5	*0*	0	*0*	*0*	*0*	0	0	2	11	*48*
Days Minimum Temp. ≤ 32°F	29	25	25	*13*	3	*0*	*0*	*0*	1	8	19	26	*149*
Days Minimum Temp. ≤ 0°F	4	2	1	*0*	0	*0*	*0*	*0*	0	0	0	1	*8*
Heating Degree Days (base 65°F)	1,285	1,110	960	*559*	268	*68*	*17*	*28*	*157*	478	762	1,137	*6,829*
Cooling Degree Days (base 65°F)	0	0	1	*7*	32	*110*	*194*	*150*	*53*	5	0	0	*552*
Mean Precipitation (in.)	2.98	2.14	2.48	*3.41*	4.55	*3.55*	*3.86*	*3.85*	3.95	3.25	*3.79*	3.17	*40.98*
Extreme Maximum Daily Precip. (in.)	1.90	1.36	1.75	*2.12*	3.73	*5.80*	*4.79*	*3.52*	3.40	2.52	*3.28*	2.23	*5.80*
Days With ≥ 0.1" Precipitation	8	7	6	*7*	8	*6*	*6*	*7*	7	7	7	9	*85*
Days With ≥ 0.5" Precipitation	2	1	1	*2*	3	*2*	*3*	*3*	3	2	2	1	*25*
Days With ≥ 1.0" Precipitation	0	0	0	*1*	1	*1*	*1*	*1*	1	0	1	0	*7*
Mean Snowfall (in.)	25.6	17.3	8.5	*2.6*	trace	*0.0*	*0.0*	*0.0*	0.0	0.4	7.4	24.8	*86.6*
Maximum Snow Depth (in.)	27	25	23	*10*	trace	*0*	*0*	*0*	0	*5*	20	22	*27*
Days With ≥ 1.0" Snow Depth	25	21	10	*1*	0	*0*	*0*	*0*	0	*0*	4	17	*78*

Alma *Gratiot County* Elevation: 759 ft.   Latitude: 43° 23' N   Longitude: 84° 40' W

	JAN	FEB	MAR	APR	MAY	JUN	JUL	AUG	SEP	OCT	NOV	DEC	YEAR
Mean Maximum Temp. (°F)	29.8	32.8	42.8	56.7	69.0	78.6	82.9	80.7	72.9	59.6	46.1	34.0	57.2
Mean Temp. (°F)	21.9	24.0	32.8	45.4	56.8	66.5	70.7	68.7	60.7	48.6	37.6	26.9	46.7
Mean Minimum Temp. (°F)	14.0	15.2	22.7	34.0	44.6	54.3	58.4	56.8	48.5	37.6	29.0	19.7	36.2
Extreme Maximum Temp. (°F)	59	67	79	88	94	100	103	101	93	90	76	68	103
Extreme Minimum Temp. (°F)	-22	-15	-8	5	24	34	41	36	27	20	6	-8	-22
Days Maximum Temp. ≥ 90°F	0	0	0	0	0	3	5	3	1	0	0	0	12
Days Maximum Temp. ≤ 32°F	19	14	5	0	0	0	0	0	0	0	2	13	53
Days Minimum Temp. ≤ 32°F	30	27	27	14	2	0	0	0	1	9	22	29	161
Days Minimum Temp. ≤ 0°F	5	3	1	0	0	0	0	0	0	0	0	1	10
Heating Degree Days (base 65°F)	1,329	1,152	993	587	275	66	14	28	167	506	816	1,176	7,109
Cooling Degree Days (base 65°F)	0	0	0	5	29	117	198	151	46	4	0	0	550
Mean Precipitation (in.)	1.90	1.63	2.11	3.05	3.46	3.33	2.78	3.42	3.52	2.96	2.84	2.13	33.13
Extreme Maximum Daily Precip. (in.)	1.28	1.86	1.39	3.40	3.22	3.22	2.38	2.51	9.33	4.04	3.00	1.80	9.33
Days With ≥ 0.1" Precipitation	5	4	5	7	7	6	5	6	6	6	6	6	69
Days With ≥ 0.5" Precipitation	1	1	1	2	2	2	2	2	2	2	2	1	20
Days With ≥ 1.0" Precipitation	0	0	0	0	1	1	1	1	1	0	1	0	6
Mean Snowfall (in.)	11.0	8.3	6.0	1.8	trace	0.0	0.0	0.0	0.0	0.3	2.8	9.8	40.0
Maximum Snow Depth (in.)	17	22	15	5	trace	0	0	0	0	2	8	16	22
Days With ≥ 1.0" Snow Depth	23	21	11	1	0	0	0	0	0	0	2	15	73

Alpena Wastewater Pl *Alpena County* Elevation: 589 ft.   Latitude: 45° 04' N   Longitude: 83° 26' W

	JAN	FEB	MAR	APR	MAY	JUN	JUL	AUG	SEP	OCT	NOV	DEC	YEAR
Mean Maximum Temp. (°F)	27.7	29.5	37.2	50.2	61.4	71.6	77.2	76.1	68.6	55.7	43.2	33.2	52.6
Mean Temp. (°F)	20.6	21.7	29.5	41.8	52.5	62.6	68.2	67.2	59.8	47.7	36.7	26.9	44.6
Mean Minimum Temp. (°F)	13.3	13.8	21.7	33.4	43.6	53.6	59.2	58.2	50.9	39.7	30.2	20.6	36.5
Extreme Maximum Temp. (°F)	55	62	75	88	92	100	100	100	92	87	75	65	100
Extreme Minimum Temp. (°F)	-21	-18	-12	6	21	36	39	36	29	22	4	-12	-21
Days Maximum Temp. ≥ 90°F	0	0	0	0	0	1	2	1	0	0	0	0	4
Days Maximum Temp. ≤ 32°F	21	17	9	1	0	0	0	0	0	0	3	13	64
Days Minimum Temp. ≤ 32°F	30	27	26	13	2	0	0	0	0	5	18	28	149
Days Minimum Temp. ≤ 0°F	4	4	1	0	0	0	0	0	0	0	0	1	10
Heating Degree Days (base 65°F)	1,371	1,219	1,095	690	391	125	31	40	183	531	842	1,174	7,692
Cooling Degree Days (base 65°F)	0	0	0	0	10	61	138	116	32	3	0	0	362
Mean Precipitation (in.)	1.83	1.52	1.73	2.46	2.94	2.62	3.14	3.48	3.27	2.72	2.15	1.93	29.79
Extreme Maximum Daily Precip. (in.)	1.60	1.58	*1.61*	1.86	2.04	2.05	2.97	2.22	2.50	2.31	1.52	1.06	*2.97*
Days With ≥ 0.1" Precipitation	5	4	4	6	7	6	6	7	7	7	6	6	71
Days With ≥ 0.5" Precipitation	1	1	1	2	2	2	2	2	2	2	1	1	19
Days With ≥ 1.0" Precipitation	0	0	0	0	1	0	1	1	1	0	0	0	4
Mean Snowfall (in.)	*15.3*	*11.8*	*6.3*	2.4	trace	0.0	0.0	0.0	0.0	0.3	3.2	13.1	*52.4*
Maximum Snow Depth (in.)	34	50	53	17	trace	0	0	0	0	4	10	34	53
Days With ≥ 1.0" Snow Depth	26	25	18	2	0	0	0	0	0	0	3	15	89

The period of record for all cooperative weather station data is 1980 – 2009. See User Guide for detailed explanation of data.

Ann Arbor Univ of Mich *Washtenaw County*   Elevation: 899 ft.   Latitude: 42° 18' N   Longitude: 83° 43' W

	JAN	FEB	MAR	APR	MAY	JUN	JUL	AUG	SEP	OCT	NOV	DEC	YEAR
Mean Maximum Temp. (°F)	31.5	35.1	45.8	59.6	70.9	79.8	83.3	81.3	74.5	61.5	48.0	35.2	58.9
Mean Temp. (°F)	24.8	27.4	36.4	48.8	59.5	68.8	72.7	71.2	64.0	51.9	40.5	29.1	49.6
Mean Minimum Temp. (°F)	17.9	19.7	26.9	37.9	48.1	57.7	62.1	61.0	53.4	42.2	33.0	22.9	40.2
Extreme Maximum Temp. (°F)	62	67	80	87	92	101	100	98	94	89	75	67	101
Extreme Minimum Temp. (°F)	-22	-13	-8	7	27	36	43	39	30	21	10	-12	-22
Days Maximum Temp. ≥ 90°F	0	0	0	0	0	3	5	2	1	0	0	0	11
Days Maximum Temp. ≤ 32°F	17	12	4	0	0	0	0	0	0	0	2	12	47
Days Minimum Temp. ≤ 32°F	28	25	23	9	1	0	0	0	0	4	15	27	132
Days Minimum Temp. ≤ 0°F	2	1	0	0	0	0	0	0	0	0	0	1	4
Heating Degree Days (base 65°F)	1,241	1,056	881	489	206	37	5	12	106	408	728	1,106	6,275
Cooling Degree Days (base 65°F)	0	0	1	8	44	156	251	211	82	8	0	0	761
Mean Precipitation (in.)	2.58	2.36	2.75	3.31	3.31	3.56	3.51	3.84	3.50	2.86	3.00	2.94	37.52
Extreme Maximum Daily Precip. (in.)	1.57	1.88	1.65	2.09	2.19	3.17	2.58	4.54	2.66	2.23	1.90	1.46	4.54
Days With ≥ 0.1" Precipitation	7	6	6	8	7	7	7	7	6	6	7	7	81
Days With ≥ 0.5" Precipitation	1	1	2	2	2	3	2	3	3	2	2	2	25
Days With ≥ 1.0" Precipitation	0	0	0	0	1	1	1	1	1	1	0	0	6
Mean Snowfall (in.)	16.2	12.1	9.0	2.7	trace	0.0	0.0	0.0	trace	0.3	3.2	13.5	57.0
Maximum Snow Depth (in.)	18	19	22	6	trace	0	trace	0	trace	1	4	16	22
Days With ≥ 1.0" Snow Depth	21	17	7	1	0	0	0	0	0	0	1	13	60

Bad Axe *Huron County*   Elevation: 714 ft.   Latitude: 43° 49' N   Longitude: 83° 00' W

	JAN	FEB	MAR	APR	MAY	JUN	JUL	AUG	SEP	OCT	NOV	DEC	YEAR
Mean Maximum Temp. (°F)	28.4	30.8	39.7	53.3	65.7	75.8	80.3	78.3	71.0	58.3	45.2	32.7	55.0
Mean Temp. (°F)	21.5	23.1	31.2	43.4	54.6	64.6	69.2	67.6	60.4	49.1	38.1	26.8	45.8
Mean Minimum Temp. (°F)	14.7	15.4	22.6	33.4	43.5	53.3	58.1	56.9	49.8	39.9	31.0	20.9	36.6
Extreme Maximum Temp. (°F)	61	66	80	88	92	97	101	98	92	89	74	68	101
Extreme Minimum Temp. (°F)	-20	-18	-9	14	25	32	42	34	27	23	6	-6	-20
Days Maximum Temp. ≥ 90°F	0	0	0	0	0	2	3	1	0	0	0	0	6
Days Maximum Temp. ≤ 32°F	20	16	9	1	0	0	0	0	0	0	2	14	62
Days Minimum Temp. ≤ 32°F	30	27	27	15	2	0	0	0	0	6	19	28	154
Days Minimum Temp. ≤ 0°F	4	3	1	0	0	0	0	0	0	0	0	1	9
Heating Degree Days (base 65°F)	1,341	1,178	1,043	646	335	97	25	41	173	491	801	1,176	7,347
Cooling Degree Days (base 65°F)	0	0	0	4	20	92	163	129	43	6	0	0	457
Mean Precipitation (in.)	1.81	1.81	1.97	2.91	3.16	2.92	3.20	3.64	3.95	2.66	2.80	2.10	32.93
Extreme Maximum Daily Precip. (in.)	1.68	2.02	1.99	1.62	2.87	2.01	2.85	2.63	6.46	1.56	2.25	0.96	6.46
Days With ≥ 0.1" Precipitation	5	5	5	7	7	6	6	6	7	7	6	6	73
Days With ≥ 0.5" Precipitation	1	1	1	2	2	2	2	2	2	2	2	1	20
Days With ≥ 1.0" Precipitation	0	0	0	1	1	1	1	1	1	0	0	0	6
Mean Snowfall (in.)	12.3	9.7	7.2	2.2	0.1	0.0	0.0	0.0	0.0	0.4	3.4	10.8	46.1
Maximum Snow Depth (in.)	24	31	10	7	trace	0	0	0	0	1	6	21	31
Days With ≥ 1.0" Snow Depth	23	22	11	1	0	0	0	0	0	0	3	15	75

Battle Creek 5 NW *Calhoun County*   Elevation: 930 ft.   Latitude: 42° 22' N   Longitude: 85° 16' W

	JAN	FEB	MAR	APR	MAY	JUN	JUL	AUG	SEP	OCT	NOV	DEC	YEAR
Mean Maximum Temp. (°F)	31.9	35.5	46.4	59.8	70.9	79.3	82.7	*80.9*	*73.3*	60.8	*47.2*	35.6	*58.7*
Mean Temp. (°F)	24.2	26.8	36.1	48.2	58.8	67.7	71.3	*69.7*	*61.8*	50.5	*39.1*	28.5	*48.6*
Mean Minimum Temp. (°F)	16.5	18.0	25.7	36.6	46.7	55.9	59.9	*58.4*	*50.5*	40.1	*30.8*	21.2	*38.4*
Extreme Maximum Temp. (°F)	62	72	79	87	94	97	100	99	95	87	75	69	100
Extreme Minimum Temp. (°F)	-20	-19	-6	5	22	30	40	37	25	16	7	-18	-20
Days Maximum Temp. ≥ 90°F	0	0	0	0	0	2	4	2	0	0	0	0	8
Days Maximum Temp. ≤ 32°F	17	12	3	0	0	0	0	0	0	0	2	12	46
Days Minimum Temp. ≤ 32°F	29	26	24	11	2	0	0	0	1	7	18	27	145
Days Minimum Temp. ≤ 0°F	3	2	0	0	0	0	0	0	0	0	0	1	6
Heating Degree Days (base 65°F)	1,257	1,075	892	506	225	50	12	*23*	*150*	447	*772*	1,125	*6,534*
Cooling Degree Days (base 65°F)	0	0	1	8	39	136	214	*175*	*61*	5	*0*	0	*639*
Mean Precipitation (in.)	1.74	1.49	2.06	2.93	3.76	3.17	3.51	3.75	3.93	3.38	2.80	2.15	34.67
Extreme Maximum Daily Precip. (in.)	1.54	2.24	1.88	1.96	2.43	2.65	3.35	2.75	*3.83*	2.80	2.46	1.25	*3.83*
Days With ≥ 0.1" Precipitation	5	4	5	7	8	6	6	7	7	7	5	6	73
Days With ≥ 0.5" Precipitation	1	1	1	2	3	2	2	3	2	2	2	1	22
Days With ≥ 1.0" Precipitation	0	0	0	0	1	1	1	1	1	1	1	0	7
Mean Snowfall (in.)	16.3	11.7	6.3	2.1	trace	0.0	0.0	0.0	trace	0.6	5.2	17.0	59.2
Maximum Snow Depth (in.)	18	24	21	5	trace	0	0	0	0	3	*11*	20	*24*
Days With ≥ 1.0" Snow Depth	22	17	7	0	0	0	0	0	0	0	*3*	15	*64*

Benton Harbor Ross Field *Berrien County*   Elevation: 627 ft.   Latitude: 42° 08' N   Longitude: 86° 26' W

	JAN	FEB	MAR	APR	MAY	JUN	JUL	AUG	SEP	OCT	NOV	DEC	YEAR
Mean Maximum Temp. (°F)	33.1	36.3	46.4	58.8	69.6	79.0	83.4	81.5	75.2	63.1	49.5	36.9	59.4
Mean Temp. (°F)	26.2	28.4	36.8	47.9	57.9	67.6	72.2	70.4	63.5	52.4	41.3	30.1	49.6
Mean Minimum Temp. (°F)	19.0	20.5	27.1	36.9	46.3	56.2	60.9	59.3	51.7	41.7	33.1	23.2	39.7
Extreme Maximum Temp. (°F)	66	70	84	89	97	100	104	101	98	92	76	69	104
Extreme Minimum Temp. (°F)	-17	-12	-3	9	24	31	37	37	23	15	8	-15	-17
Days Maximum Temp. ≥ 90°F	0	0	0	0	1	4	6	4	1	0	0	0	16
Days Maximum Temp. ≤ 32°F	15	10	3	0	0	0	0	0	0	0	2	10	40
Days Minimum Temp. ≤ 32°F	28	25	23	10	2	0	0	0	1	5	15	26	135
Days Minimum Temp. ≤ 0°F	2	1	0	0	0	0	0	0	0	0	0	1	4
Heating Degree Days (base 65°F)	1,197	1,028	870	517	256	63	13	22	121	397	705	1,076	6,265
Cooling Degree Days (base 65°F)	0	0	2	11	45	148	241	197	82	12	0	0	738
Mean Precipitation (in.)	1.97	1.60	2.08	3.27	3.52	3.24	3.22	4.05	4.07	3.51	3.32	2.28	36.13
Extreme Maximum Daily Precip. (in.)	1.80	2.37	2.20	1.88	1.87	2.10	3.14	3.25	2.42	2.81	2.78	2.37	3.25
Days With ≥ 0.1" Precipitation	5	4	6	8	7	6	6	6	7	8	7	7	77
Days With ≥ 0.5" Precipitation	1	1	1	2	3	2	2	3	3	2	2	1	23
Days With ≥ 1.0" Precipitation	0	0	0	1	1	1	1	1	1	1	1	0	8
Mean Snowfall (in.)	29.6	20.0	7.6	0.8	trace	0.0	0.0	0.0	trace	0.4	3.5	23.8	85.7
Maximum Snow Depth (in.)	61	80	12	4	trace	0	0	0	trace	4	12	72	80
Days With ≥ 1.0" Snow Depth	15	10	4	0	0	0	0	0	0	0	2	10	41

The period of record for all cooperative weather station data is 1980 – 2009. See User Guide for detailed explanation of data.

Bergland Dam *Ontonagon County* Elevation: 1,299 ft. Latitude: 46° 35' N Longitude: 89° 33' W

	JAN	FEB	MAR	APR	MAY	JUN	JUL	AUG	SEP	OCT	NOV	DEC	YEAR
Mean Maximum Temp. (°F)	21.3	25.8	35.7	50.3	64.5	73.3	77.5	76.0	67.1	53.1	37.9	25.2	50.6
Mean Temp. (°F)	11.7	13.9	23.0	38.0	51.0	60.5	64.8	63.3	55.3	42.7	30.0	16.8	39.2
Mean Minimum Temp. (°F)	1.9	1.9	10.3	25.7	37.4	47.6	52.0	50.6	43.4	32.2	22.1	8.3	27.8
Extreme Maximum Temp. (°F)	53	58	70	89	93	96	97	96	91	86	73	59	97
Extreme Minimum Temp. (°F)	-38	-39	-31	-11	15	27	35	32	21	13	-10	-30	-39
Days Maximum Temp. ≥ 90°F	0	0	0	0	0	0	1	1	0	0	0	0	2
Days Maximum Temp. ≤ 32°F	26	20	11	2	0	0	0	0	0	1	10	23	93
Days Minimum Temp. ≤ 32°F	31	28	29	25	10	1	0	0	3	18	26	31	202
Days Minimum Temp. ≤ 0°F	14	13	8	0	0	0	0	0	0	0	1	9	45
Heating Degree Days (base 65°F)	1,650	1,440	1,295	804	438	174	80	103	304	685	1,043	1,489	9,505
Cooling Degree Days (base 65°F)	0	0	0	1	10	44	81	57	18	1	0	0	212
Mean Precipitation (in.)	2.99	1.91	2.46	2.74	3.38	3.71	3.97	3.58	3.90	4.05	3.22	3.44	39.35
Extreme Maximum Daily Precip. (in.)	1.36	1.41	2.43	2.24	2.12	4.52	2.26	3.07	2.04	2.06	1.88	1.75	4.52
Days With ≥ 0.1" Precipitation	9	6	6	7	7	8	8	7	9	10	9	10	96
Days With ≥ 0.5" Precipitation	1	1	1	1	2	2	3	3	3	3	1	1	22
Days With ≥ 1.0" Precipitation	0	0	0	0	1	1	1	1	1	1	0	0	6
Mean Snowfall (in.)	41.9	25.8	26.0	9.7	1.2	0.0	0.0	0.0	0.2	5.2	25.1	42.7	177.8
Maximum Snow Depth (in.)	49	43	49	33	16	0	0	0	3	14	41	42	49
Days With ≥ 1.0" Snow Depth	31	28	29	14	1	0	0	0	0	3	16	29	151

Big Rapids Waterworks *Mecosta County* Elevation: 930 ft. Latitude: 43° 42' N Longitude: 85° 29' W

	JAN	FEB	MAR	APR	MAY	JUN	JUL	AUG	SEP	OCT	NOV	DEC	YEAR
Mean Maximum Temp. (°F)	29.4	33.0	42.6	56.4	68.6	78.0	82.0	79.5	71.7	58.2	44.9	33.2	56.4
Mean Temp. (°F)	20.9	23.4	31.5	44.3	55.7	65.3	69.5	67.3	59.3	47.2	36.3	25.7	45.5
Mean Minimum Temp. (°F)	12.4	13.7	20.4	32.3	42.9	52.5	56.9	55.1	46.8	36.2	27.8	18.2	34.6
Extreme Maximum Temp. (°F)	58	64	76	89	93	98	100	101	92	87	75	66	101
Extreme Minimum Temp. (°F)	-25	-29	-15	1	19	30	37	32	24	16	3	-15	-29
Days Maximum Temp. ≥ 90°F	0	0	0	0	0	2	4	2	0	0	0	0	8
Days Maximum Temp. ≤ 32°F	19	14	6	1	0	0	0	0	0	0	3	14	57
Days Minimum Temp. ≤ 32°F	30	27	28	16	4	0	0	0	1	11	22	29	168
Days Minimum Temp. ≤ 0°F	6	4	2	0	0	0	0	0	0	0	0	2	14
Heating Degree Days (base 65°F)	1,359	1,170	1,031	617	303	80	23	42	197	547	853	1,212	7,434
Cooling Degree Days (base 65°F)	0	0	0	2	22	95	168	121	33	3	0	0	444
Mean Precipitation (in.)	2.16	1.71	2.43	3.26	3.42	3.31	3.20	4.02	4.02	3.30	3.17	2.41	36.41
Extreme Maximum Daily Precip. (in.)	1.80	1.66	2.22	1.70	1.93	3.24	3.94	3.53	7.64	2.73	1.90	2.13	7.64
Days With ≥ 0.1" Precipitation	6	5	6	7	7	6	6	7	8	7	7	7	79
Days With ≥ 0.5" Precipitation	1	1	2	2	2	2	2	3	2	2	2	1	22
Days With ≥ 1.0" Precipitation	0	0	0	1	1	1	1	1	1	1	1	0	8
Mean Snowfall (in.)	18.1	12.6	8.1	2.0	trace	0.0	0.0	0.0	trace	0.3	5.0	16.4	62.5
Maximum Snow Depth (in.)	18	26	14	8	trace	0	0	0	trace	4	12	16	26
Days With ≥ 1.0" Snow Depth	27	23	11	1	0	0	0	0	0	0	4	20	86

Boyne Falls *Charlevoix County* Elevation: 734 ft. Latitude: 45° 10' N Longitude: 84° 55' W

	JAN	FEB	MAR	APR	MAY	JUN	JUL	AUG	SEP	OCT	NOV	DEC	YEAR
Mean Maximum Temp. (°F)	28.3	31.8	41.8	56.9	69.7	78.6	82.7	80.6	72.6	58.9	44.6	32.7	56.6
Mean Temp. (°F)	20.7	22.4	30.8	44.3	55.7	65.1	69.5	68.0	60.8	48.8	37.2	26.3	45.8
Mean Minimum Temp. (°F)	13.1	12.8	19.7	31.7	41.7	51.6	56.3	55.4	49.0	38.6	29.8	19.8	35.0
Extreme Maximum Temp. (°F)	56	65	82	89	94	97	101	100	95	91	76	66	101
Extreme Minimum Temp. (°F)	-32	-32	-23	-6	20	28	33	30	24	19	-3	-17	-32
Days Maximum Temp. ≥ 90°F	0	0	0	0	0	3	5	2	1	0	0	0	11
Days Maximum Temp. ≤ 32°F	21	16	6	0	0	0	0	0	0	0	3	15	61
Days Minimum Temp. ≤ 32°F	30	27	27	17	7	1	0	0	1	9	20	29	168
Days Minimum Temp. ≤ 0°F	6	6	3	0	0	0	0	0	0	0	0	2	17
Heating Degree Days (base 65°F)	1,366	1,200	1,053	619	308	93	26	39	174	504	826	1,194	7,402
Cooling Degree Days (base 65°F)	0	0	0	5	27	102	172	140	56	8	0	0	510
Mean Precipitation (in.)	2.39	1.57	1.84	2.49	2.89	2.84	2.64	3.58	3.76	3.89	3.04	2.69	33.62
Extreme Maximum Daily Precip. (in.)	1.76	0.83	2.03	1.69	1.86	2.20	2.11	3.15	2.55	1.95	1.81	1.24	3.15
Days With ≥ 0.1" Precipitation	8	5	6	6	7	6	6	7	8	9	9	9	86
Days With ≥ 0.5" Precipitation	1	1	1	2	2	2	2	2	2	2	1	1	19
Days With ≥ 1.0" Precipitation	0	0	0	0	1	1	1	1	1	1	0	0	6
Mean Snowfall (in.)	31.1	21.3	11.0	4.5	0.3	0.0	0.0	0.0	trace	0.8	12.7	32.4	114.1
Maximum Snow Depth (in.)	29	33	25	13	trace	0	0	0	trace	4	16	26	33
Days With ≥ 1.0" Snow Depth	29	27	20	2	0	0	0	0	0	0	7	23	108

Caro Regional Center *Tuscola County*, Elevation: 669 ft. Latitude: 43° 27' N Longitude: 83° 24' W

	JAN	FEB	MAR	APR	MAY	JUN	JUL	AUG	SEP	OCT	NOV	DEC	YEAR
Mean Maximum Temp. (°F)	30.1	32.7	43.3	57.8	69.7	*79.1*	*83.2*	80.8	*73.2*	60.4	46.7	33.9	*57.6*
Mean Temp. (°F)	22.6	24.1	33.7	46.2	56.9	*66.3*	70.9	68.9	*61.4*	49.9	38.9	27.3	*47.3*
Mean Minimum Temp. (°F)	15.0	15.5	23.9	34.5	44.0	*53.5*	58.6	56.9	*49.5*	39.4	31.0	20.7	*36.9*
Extreme Maximum Temp. (°F)	61	65	80	88	94	*100*	101	*101*	92	89	76	69	*101*
Extreme Minimum Temp. (°F)	-24	-24	-15	9	23	*31*	38	32	25	16	1	-18	*-24*
Days Maximum Temp. ≥ 90°F	0	0	0	0	1	*3*	5	*3*	1	0	0	0	*13*
Days Maximum Temp. ≤ 32°F	18	14	6	1	0	*0*	0	*0*	0	0	2	13	*54*
Days Minimum Temp. ≤ 32°F	29	26	25	14	3	*0*	0	*0*	1	8	18	27	*151*
Days Minimum Temp. ≤ 0°F	5	4	1	0	0	*0*	0	*0*	0	0	0	2	*12*
Heating Degree Days (base 65°F)	1,308	1,150	965	564	278	*69*	*14*	*30*	*155*	467	778	1,162	*6,940*
Cooling Degree Days (base 65°F)	0	0	0	1	33	*115*	*205*	*157*	*52*	6	0	0	*575*
Mean Precipitation (in.)	1.86	1.38	2.00	3.15	3.01	*3.52*	*3.13*	*3.07*	4.33	3.01	2.79	2.07	*33.32*
Extreme Maximum Daily Precip. (in.)	1.22	1.98	1.53	2.40	1.71	*4.02*	*2.61*	*2.55*	7.28	1.75	2.34	2.60	*7.28*
Days With ≥ 0.1" Precipitation	6	4	6	8	7	*7*	6	*6*	7	7	6	6	*76*
Days With ≥ 0.5" Precipitation	1	1	1	2	2	*2*	2	*2*	3	2	2	1	*21*
Days With ≥ 1.0" Precipitation	0	0	0	0	1	*1*	1	*1*	1	0	0	0	*5*
Mean Snowfall (in.)	11.6	7.3	5.2	1.0	trace	*0.0*	*0.0*	*0.0*	0.0	0.1	2.0	9.6	*36.8*
Maximum Snow Depth (in.)	16	18	12	4	trace	*0*	*0*	*0*	0	0	1	*16*	*18*
Days With ≥ 1.0" Snow Depth	21	18	7	1	0	*0*	*0*	*0*	0	0	2	14	*63*

The period of record for all cooperative weather station data is 1980 – 2009. See User Guide for detailed explanation of data.

Champion Van Riper Prk *Marquette County*   Elevation: 1,564 ft.   Latitude: 46° 31' N   Longitude: 87° 59' W

	JAN	FEB	MAR	APR	MAY	JUN	JUL	AUG	SEP	OCT	NOV	DEC	YEAR
Mean Maximum Temp. (°F)	22.9	27.4	37.8	51.9	65.6	74.3	78.8	76.4	67.4	54.3	37.8	25.6	51.7
Mean Temp. (°F)	12.3	14.7	24.2	38.0	50.2	59.4	64.4	62.6	54.7	42.9	29.3	16.6	39.1
Mean Minimum Temp. (°F)	1.5	2.0	10.5	24.0	34.7	44.5	49.9	48.8	41.9	31.5	20.8	7.6	26.5
Extreme Maximum Temp. (°F)	50	61	69	92	91	95	98	96	94	85	72	60	98
Extreme Minimum Temp. (°F)	-38	-40	-33	-16	12	17	26	27	15	10	-11	-38	-40
Days Maximum Temp. ≥ 90°F	0	0	0	0	0	1	1	0	0	0	0	0	2
Days Maximum Temp. ≤ 32°F	24	18	9	1	0	0	0	0	0	0	9	22	83
Days Minimum Temp. ≤ 32°F	30	26	29	24	14	3	0	1	5	18	26	29	205
Days Minimum Temp. ≤ 0°F	14	12	8	1	0	0	0	0	0	0	1	9	45
Heating Degree Days (base 65°F)	1,630	1,417	1,258	805	462	195	89	119	315	679	1,064	1,494	9,527
Cooling Degree Days (base 65°F)	0	0	0	1	7	35	76	53	15	1	0	0	188
Mean Precipitation (in.)	1.81	1.23	2.07	2.40	3.01	3.34	3.75	3.29	3.54	3.54	2.23	1.85	32.06
Extreme Maximum Daily Precip. (in.)	*1.52*	*1.27*	2.13	*2.49*	2.40	*2.96*	*3.61*	2.55	2.30	*1.92*	1.49	1.15	*3.61*
Days With ≥ 0.1" Precipitation	5	3	5	5	5	6	7	6	8	7	6	5	68
Days With ≥ 0.5" Precipitation	1	0	1	1	2	2	2	2	2	2	1	1	17
Days With ≥ 1.0" Precipitation	0	0	0	0	0	1	1	1	1	1	0	0	5
Mean Snowfall (in.)	25.9	16.1	19.3	6.8	0.5	0.0	0.0	0.0	0.1	4.2	*15.6*	26.1	*114.6*
Maximum Snow Depth (in.)	54	60	53	44	19	0	0	0	trace	7	24	31	60
Days With ≥ 1.0" Snow Depth	27	25	26	12	1	0	0	0	0	2	14	24	131

Charlotte *Eaton County*   Elevation: 901 ft.   Latitude: 42° 33' N   Longitude: 84° 50' W

	JAN	FEB	MAR	APR	MAY	JUN	JUL	AUG	SEP	OCT	NOV	DEC	YEAR
Mean Maximum Temp. (°F)	30.1	33.2	43.1	56.7	68.1	77.8	81.2	79.4	72.2	59.5	46.5	34.1	56.8
Mean Temp. (°F)	22.4	24.6	33.4	45.8	56.8	66.5	70.0	68.4	60.7	49.0	38.3	27.2	46.9
Mean Minimum Temp. (°F)	14.7	16.0	23.7	34.8	45.4	55.1	58.7	57.3	49.1	38.5	30.0	20.2	37.0
Extreme Maximum Temp. (°F)	60	70	79	88	91	99	100	101	93	87	73	69	101
Extreme Minimum Temp. (°F)	-21	-17	-8	3	25	31	41	36	27	18	6	-15	-21
Days Maximum Temp. ≥ 90°F	0	0	0	0	0	2	3	2	0	0	0	0	7
Days Maximum Temp. ≤ 32°F	18	14	6	0	0	0	0	0	0	0	3	13	54
Days Minimum Temp. ≤ 32°F	29	27	25	13	2	0	0	0	0	9	20	28	153
Days Minimum Temp. ≤ 0°F	4	3	1	0	0	0	0	0	0	0	0	2	10
Heating Degree Days (base 65°F)	1,313	1,135	972	575	278	65	18	32	170	493	794	1,165	7,010
Cooling Degree Days (base 65°F)	0	0	1	5	30	115	178	143	47	4	0	0	523
Mean Precipitation (in.)	1.78	1.46	2.13	3.14	3.65	3.30	3.04	3.59	3.68	3.18	2.88	2.18	34.01
Extreme Maximum Daily Precip. (in.)	1.80	1.55	1.60	2.42	2.45	3.15	2.46	3.18	3.60	2.31	2.26	1.37	3.60
Days With ≥ 0.1" Precipitation	5	4	5	7	7	6	7	7	6	7	7	6	74
Days With ≥ 0.5" Precipitation	1	1	1	2	2	2	2	2	3	2	2	1	21
Days With ≥ 1.0" Precipitation	0	0	0	0	1	1	1	1	1	1	0	0	6
Mean Snowfall (in.)	13.3	8.7	6.4	1.2	0.0	0.0	0.0	0.0	0.0	0.5	1.9	10.9	42.9
Maximum Snow Depth (in.)	27	18	16	8	0	0	0	0	0	5	6	28	28
Days With ≥ 1.0" Snow Depth	22	17	8	1	0	0	0	0	0	0	2	14	64

Cheboygan *Cheboygan County*   Elevation: 589 ft.   Latitude: 45° 39' N   Longitude: 84° 28' W

	JAN	FEB	MAR	APR	MAY	JUN	JUL	AUG	SEP	OCT	NOV	DEC	YEAR
Mean Maximum Temp. (°F)	27.1	29.2	37.3	49.9	62.2	72.0	77.5	76.2	68.8	55.7	43.4	32.3	52.6
Mean Temp. (°F)	18.7	19.5	27.5	40.4	51.6	61.7	67.5	66.4	59.0	46.9	36.3	25.3	43.4
Mean Minimum Temp. (°F)	10.2	9.7	17.5	30.8	40.9	51.3	57.5	56.6	49.1	38.0	29.2	18.3	34.1
Extreme Maximum Temp. (°F)	55	62	74	86	90	96	98	98	92	88	72	64	98
Extreme Minimum Temp. (°F)	-27	-28	-18	-2	17	32	41	36	26	19	8	-15	-28
Days Maximum Temp. ≥ 90°F	0	0	0	0	0	1	1	1	0	0	0	0	3
Days Maximum Temp. ≤ 32°F	22	18	9	1	0	0	0	0	0	0	3	15	68
Days Minimum Temp. ≤ 32°F	30	28	29	18	3	0	0	0	0	7	20	29	164
Days Minimum Temp. ≤ 0°F	7	7	3	0	0	0	0	0	0	0	0	2	19
Heating Degree Days (base 65°F)	1,429	1,281	1,155	733	412	143	39	50	206	558	854	1,223	8,083
Cooling Degree Days (base 65°F)	0	0	0	1	4	49	124	101	32	3	0	0	314
Mean Precipitation (in.)	1.72	1.32	1.76	2.58	2.75	2.62	3.05	3.40	3.35	3.45	2.48	2.04	30.52
Extreme Maximum Daily Precip. (in.)	2.20	1.13	1.64	2.88	2.14	2.51	3.21	4.48	2.70	2.09	1.51	1.67	4.48
Days With ≥ 0.1" Precipitation	5	4	5	6	6	5	5	6	7	8	7	6	70
Days With ≥ 0.5" Precipitation	1	1	1	1	2	2	2	2	2	2	1	1	18
Days With ≥ 1.0" Precipitation	0	0	0	0	0	1	1	1	1	1	0	0	5
Mean Snowfall (in.)	25.4	19.3	12.1	4.0	0.1	0.0	0.0	0.0	0.0	0.6	7.0	24.3	92.8
Maximum Snow Depth (in.)	32	41	30	18	2	0	0	0	0	11	11	30	41
Days With ≥ 1.0" Snow Depth	28	27	21	3	0	0	0	0	0	0	7	21	107

Cross Village *Emmet County*   Elevation: 743 ft.   Latitude: 45° 38' N   Longitude: 85° 02' W

	JAN	FEB	MAR	APR	MAY	JUN	JUL	AUG	SEP	OCT	NOV	DEC	YEAR
Mean Maximum Temp. (°F)	27.3	29.6	38.3	51.8	63.6	71.5	76.0	74.9	68.2	55.4	43.4	32.3	52.7
Mean Temp. (°F)	20.2	21.0	28.7	41.4	52.4	61.2	66.5	65.9	59.6	47.8	37.3	26.7	44.1
Mean Minimum Temp. (°F)	13.1	12.3	19.0	31.1	41.2	50.9	57.0	56.9	50.9	40.2	31.2	21.1	35.4
Extreme Maximum Temp. (°F)	55	61	76	89	90	90	95	93	90	82	73	65	95
Extreme Minimum Temp. (°F)	-27	-23	-19	-4	22	31	36	38	25	18	6	-12	-27
Days Maximum Temp. ≥ 90°F	0	0	0	0	0	0	0	0	0	0	0	0	0
Days Maximum Temp. ≤ 32°F	22	18	9	1	0	0	0	0	0	0	3	15	68
Days Minimum Temp. ≤ 32°F	30	27	28	18	5	0	0	0	0	5	17	28	158
Days Minimum Temp. ≤ 0°F	5	5	2	0	0	0	0	0	0	0	0	1	13
Heating Degree Days (base 65°F)	1,382	1,239	1,120	702	392	150	48	53	188	528	823	1,179	7,804
Cooling Degree Days (base 65°F)	0	0	0	2	8	43	102	88	31	3	0	0	277
Mean Precipitation (in.)	1.78	1.19	1.77	2.61	2.71	2.55	2.09	3.20	3.38	3.56	2.62	2.12	29.58
Extreme Maximum Daily Precip. (in.)	1.10	1.24	1.55	2.17	1.94	1.98	1.56	2.72	2.08	2.01	1.66	1.50	2.72
Days With ≥ 0.1" Precipitation	5	4	5	6	6	6	5	6	7	8	7	7	72
Days With ≥ 0.5" Precipitation	1	0	1	2	2	1	1	2	2	2	1	1	16
Days With ≥ 1.0" Precipitation	0	0	0	0	0	0	0	1	1	1	0	0	3
Mean Snowfall (in.)	21.4	16.3	10.5	4.9	0.1	0.0	0.0	0.0	trace	0.3	5.8	20.5	79.8
Maximum Snow Depth (in.)	35	30	27	19	trace	0	0	0	trace	4	14	26	35
Days With ≥ 1.0" Snow Depth	28	28	22	5	0	0	0	0	0	0	6	21	110

The period of record for all cooperative weather station data is 1980 – 2009. See User Guide for detailed explanation of data.

Dearborn *Wayne County*   Elevation: 604 ft.   Latitude: 42° 19' N   Longitude: 83° 14' W

	JAN	FEB	MAR	APR	MAY	JUN	JUL	AUG	SEP	OCT	NOV	DEC	YEAR
Mean Maximum Temp. (°F)	32.9	36.1	45.8	59.1	70.7	80.3	84.5	82.9	76.0	62.4	49.4	37.1	59.8
Mean Temp. (°F)	25.1	27.5	36.2	48.2	58.9	68.5	73.1	71.6	64.2	51.6	40.9	29.5	49.6
Mean Minimum Temp. (°F)	17.3	18.9	26.4	37.2	47.0	56.7	61.6	60.2	52.4	40.8	32.3	22.2	39.4
Extreme Maximum Temp. (°F)	65	71	83	90	95	104	102	102	100	91	76	69	104
Extreme Minimum Temp. (°F)	-20	-12	-9	10	25	36	41	40	29	19	11	-9	-20
Days Maximum Temp. ≥ 90°F	0	0	0	0	0	4	6	4	1	0	0	0	15
Days Maximum Temp. ≤ 32°F	15	10	3	0	0	0	0	0	0	0	1	10	39
Days Minimum Temp. ≤ 32°F	28	25	23	9	1	0	0	0	0	5	16	26	133
Days Minimum Temp. ≤ 0°F	3	1	0	0	0	0	0	0	0	0	0	1	5
Heating Degree Days (base 65°F)	1,229	1,052	888	504	223	43	5	12	105	415	716	1,092	6,284
Cooling Degree Days (base 65°F)	0	0	1	7	41	156	261	222	88	8	0	0	784
Mean Precipitation (in.)	2.04	2.04	2.41	2.98	3.06	3.34	3.31	2.80	3.39	2.95	2.76	2.53	33.61
Extreme Maximum Daily Precip. (in.)	1.85	1.85	1.79	2.05	2.39	2.95	2.22	2.32	3.93	2.64	1.95	1.19	3.93
Days With ≥ 0.1" Precipitation	5	5	6	7	6	7	6	6	6	6	7	7	74
Days With ≥ 0.5" Precipitation	1	1	2	2	2	2	2	2	2	2	2	2	22
Days With ≥ 1.0" Precipitation	0	0	0	0	1	1	1	1	1	1	0	0	6
Mean Snowfall (in.)	10.6	8.0	5.3	0.7	0.0	0.0	0.0	0.0	0.0	0.1	1.0	7.1	32.8
Maximum Snow Depth (in.)	24	24	16	5	0	0	0	0	0	1	5	14	24
Days With ≥ 1.0" Snow Depth	19	16	7	0	0	0	0	0	0	0	1	9	52

East Lansing 4 S *Ingham County*   Elevation: 879 ft.   Latitude: 42° 40' N   Longitude: 84° 29' W

	JAN	FEB	MAR	APR	MAY	JUN	JUL	AUG	SEP	OCT	NOV	DEC	YEAR
Mean Maximum Temp. (°F)	30.4	33.3	43.4	57.0	68.7	78.3	82.2	80.7	*73.6*	60.0	47.2	34.5	*57.4*
Mean Temp. (°F)	22.7	24.7	33.9	46.3	57.2	66.7	70.5	69.2	*61.5*	49.2	38.9	27.4	*47.3*
Mean Minimum Temp. (°F)	14.9	16.1	24.4	35.5	45.7	55.2	58.9	57.6	*49.3*	38.4	30.6	20.2	*37.2*
Extreme Maximum Temp. (°F)	62	63	80	87	92	98	101	100	94	88	75	67	101
Extreme Minimum Temp. (°F)	-20	-19	-8	3	25	34	39	33	26	19	9	-12	-20
Days Maximum Temp. ≥ 90°F	0	0	0	0	0	2	3	3	1	0	0	0	9
Days Maximum Temp. ≤ 32°F	18	13	6	1	0	0	0	0	0	0	2	13	53
Days Minimum Temp. ≤ 32°F	29	26	25	12	2	0	0	0	0	8	19	28	149
Days Minimum Temp. ≤ 0°F	4	3	1	0	0	0	0	0	0	0	0	2	10
Heating Degree Days (base 65°F)	1,306	1,133	957	560	268	64	16	29	*156*	488	776	1,160	*6,913*
Cooling Degree Days (base 65°F)	0	0	1	5	33	123	195	166	*57*	5	0	0	*585*
Mean Precipitation (in.)	1.61	1.42	1.70	2.83	3.26	3.37	3.12	3.31	3.59	2.64	2.58	1.64	31.07
Extreme Maximum Daily Precip. (in.)	1.63	1.42	1.60	2.20	3.10	2.87	2.11	3.56	*4.50*	2.82	2.17	1.17	*4.50*
Days With ≥ 0.1" Precipitation	5	4	5	7	7	6	6	6	6	6	5	5	68
Days With ≥ 0.5" Precipitation	1	1	1	2	2	2	2	2	3	2	2	1	21
Days With ≥ 1.0" Precipitation	0	0	0	0	1	1	1	1	1	0	0	0	5
Mean Snowfall (in.)	12.0	8.7	4.9	1.0	0.0	0.0	0.0	0.0	0.0	0.3	1.7	9.7	38.3
Maximum Snow Depth (in.)	14	24	17	6	0	0	0	0	0	4	5	13	24
Days With ≥ 1.0" Snow Depth	20	17	8	1	0	0	0	0	0	0	2	13	61

East Tawas *Iosco County*   Elevation: 585 ft.   Latitude: 44° 17' N   Longitude: 83° 30' W

	JAN	FEB	MAR	APR	MAY	JUN	JUL	AUG	SEP	OCT	NOV	DEC	YEAR
Mean Maximum Temp. (°F)	29.8	32.2	40.6	53.0	65.1	75.1	80.1	78.4	71.1	58.1	45.5	34.3	55.3
Mean Temp. (°F)	21.5	22.9	31.0	43.1	54.2	63.9	68.9	67.5	60.2	48.2	37.7	27.1	45.5
Mean Minimum Temp. (°F)	13.2	13.5	21.4	33.1	43.3	52.7	57.6	56.5	49.2	38.3	29.8	20.0	35.7
Extreme Maximum Temp. (°F)	58	59	78	91	92	101	102	100	95	93	76	65	102
Extreme Minimum Temp. (°F)	-18	-21	-18	6	26	32	39	31	26	19	1	-19	-21
Days Maximum Temp. ≥ 90°F	0	0	0	0	0	1	2	1	0	0	0	0	4
Days Maximum Temp. ≤ 32°F	18	14	6	1	0	0	0	0	0	0	1	12	52
Days Minimum Temp. ≤ 32°F	30	27	27	14	3	0	0	0	1	8	19	28	157
Days Minimum Temp. ≤ 0°F	6	5	1	0	0	0	0	0	0	0	0	1	13
Heating Degree Days (base 65°F)	1,341	1,183	1,047	652	341	102	25	40	172	517	813	1,167	7,400
Cooling Degree Days (base 65°F)	0	0	0	1	15	77	151	123	35	3	0	0	405
Mean Precipitation (in.)	2.04	1.69	2.10	2.83	3.00	3.03	2.69	3.37	3.45	2.75	2.62	2.06	31.63
Extreme Maximum Daily Precip. (in.)	1.41	1.51	1.54	3.52	1.94	2.40	3.07	2.20	2.62	3.06	1.56	1.77	3.52
Days With ≥ 0.1" Precipitation	5	5	5	6	7	6	6	6	6	6	6	6	70
Days With ≥ 0.5" Precipitation	1	1	1	2	2	2	2	2	3	2	2	1	21
Days With ≥ 1.0" Precipitation	0	0	0	1	1	1	0	1	1	0	0	0	5
Mean Snowfall (in.)	16.8	12.7	8.1	1.9	0.1	0.0	0.0	0.0	trace	0.1	2.7	11.2	53.6
Maximum Snow Depth (in.)	24	23	21	9	2	0	0	0	trace	2	14	16	24
Days With ≥ 1.0" Snow Depth	25	25	17	2	0	0	0	0	0	0	3	15	87

Essexville *Bay County*   Elevation: 587 ft.   Latitude: 43° 37' N   Longitude: 83° 52' W

	JAN	FEB	MAR	APR	MAY	JUN	JUL	AUG	SEP	OCT	NOV	DEC	YEAR
Mean Maximum Temp. (°F)	29.3	31.7	41.0	54.8	66.9	77.0	81.5	79.3	72.1	58.9	46.0	33.9	56.0
Mean Temp. (°F)	22.5	24.4	33.0	45.7	57.4	67.3	71.7	69.9	62.3	50.1	39.1	27.9	47.6
Mean Minimum Temp. (°F)	15.6	17.0	24.9	36.7	47.9	57.4	61.8	60.3	52.4	41.3	32.1	21.8	39.1
Extreme Maximum Temp. (°F)	60	68	81	90	95	101	99	100	92	90	75	68	101
Extreme Minimum Temp. (°F)	-18	-13	-7	14	28	37	42	39	32	23	7	-5	-18
Days Maximum Temp. ≥ 90°F	0	0	0	0	0	3	4	2	1	0	0	0	10
Days Maximum Temp. ≤ 32°F	19	15	7	1	0	0	0	0	0	0	2	13	57
Days Minimum Temp. ≤ 32°F	29	27	25	10	0	0	0	0	0	4	16	28	139
Days Minimum Temp. ≤ 0°F	3	2	0	0	0	0	0	0	0	0	0	1	6
Heating Degree Days (base 65°F)	1,312	1,142	987	578	263	57	10	21	134	462	772	1,144	6,882
Cooling Degree Days (base 65°F)	0	0	0	6	35	131	224	177	59	7	0	0	639
Mean Precipitation (in.)	1.67	1.46	1.80	3.09	3.33	3.19	2.60	3.40	4.18	2.90	2.66	1.83	32.11
Extreme Maximum Daily Precip. (in.)	1.21	1.68	1.40	1.81	2.48	2.50	2.81	2.47	7.72	2.05	1.85	1.42	7.72
Days With ≥ 0.1" Precipitation	5	4	5	7	7	6	6	6	6	6	6	6	70
Days With ≥ 0.5" Precipitation	1	1	1	2	2	2	2	2	3	2	2	1	21
Days With ≥ 1.0" Precipitation	0	0	0	1	1	1	1	0	1	1	1	0	7
Mean Snowfall (in.)	12.6	8.4	5.3	0.9	0.0	0.0	0.0	0.0	0.0	trace	1.4	9.9	38.5
Maximum Snow Depth (in.)	*16*	*21*	9	3	0	0	0	0	0	0	0	5	*32*
Days With ≥ 1.0" Snow Depth	*14*	*12*	5	0	0	0	0	0	0	0	1	7	*39*

The period of record for all cooperative weather station data is 1980 – 2009. See User Guide for detailed explanation of data.

Frankfort 2 NE *Benzie County*   Elevation: 865 ft.   Latitude: 44° 39' N   Longitude: 86° 12' W

	JAN	FEB	MAR	APR	MAY	JUN	JUL	AUG	SEP	OCT	NOV	DEC	YEAR
Mean Maximum Temp. (°F)	29.1	31.1	39.3	52.7	64.0	73.2	77.7	76.1	69.0	56.6	44.3	33.1	53.9
Mean Temp. (°F)	23.8	25.1	32.0	43.8	54.1	63.3	68.5	67.9	61.0	49.3	38.5	28.1	46.3
Mean Minimum Temp. (°F)	18.5	19.0	24.7	35.0	44.1	53.3	59.3	59.6	52.9	41.9	32.5	23.0	38.6
Extreme Maximum Temp. (°F)	56	63	73	85	88	91	93	95	91	84	79	62	95
Extreme Minimum Temp. (°F)	-15	-11	-10	11	25	34	39	40	31	24	10	-3	-15
Days Maximum Temp. ≥ 90°F	0	0	0	0	0	0	1	0	0	0	0	0	1
Days Maximum Temp. ≤ 32°F	19	16	8	1	0	0	0	0	0	0	2	13	59
Days Minimum Temp. ≤ 32°F	29	26	25	12	2	0	0	0	0	3	16	27	140
Days Minimum Temp. ≤ 0°F	1	1	0	0	0	0	0	0	0	0	0	0	2
Heating Degree Days (base 65°F)	1,270	1,122	1,015	629	342	112	23	27	158	484	790	1,138	7,110
Cooling Degree Days (base 65°F)	0	0	0	2	11	68	138	123	43	4	0	0	389
Mean Precipitation (in.)	2.49	1.83	1.98	2.72	3.04	3.09	2.97	3.34	4.02	3.51	3.04	2.67	34.70
Extreme Maximum Daily Precip. (in.)	1.34	1.15	2.45	1.74	2.08	2.81	2.40	4.08	3.20	2.20	2.02	1.56	4.08
Days With ≥ 0.1" Precipitation	8	6	6	6	6	6	5	6	7	8	8	9	81
Days With ≥ 0.5" Precipitation	1	1	1	2	2	2	2	2	2	2	2	1	20
Days With ≥ 1.0" Precipitation	0	0	0	0	1	1	1	1	1	1	0	0	6
Mean Snowfall (in.)	30.6	20.3	13.9	4.0	0.1	0.0	0.0	0.0	trace	0.3	8.0	27.7	104.9
Maximum Snow Depth (in.)	42	48	27	9	trace	0	0	0	trace	2	10	35	48
Days With ≥ 1.0" Snow Depth	27	26	21	2	0	0	0	0	0	0	7	21	104

Grand Marais 2 E *Alger County*   Elevation: 624 ft.   Latitude: 46° 40' N   Longitude: 85° 57' W

	JAN	FEB	MAR	APR	MAY	JUN	JUL	AUG	SEP	OCT	NOV	DEC	YEAR
Mean Maximum Temp. (°F)	26.3	29.4	37.6	49.9	62.4	71.4	76.4	76.3	68.6	55.2	41.3	30.8	52.1
Mean Temp. (°F)	18.8	20.6	27.4	39.0	49.7	58.3	63.8	64.4	57.6	45.4	34.1	23.9	41.9
Mean Minimum Temp. (°F)	11.2	11.7	17.2	28.0	37.0	45.3	51.1	52.5	46.6	35.6	26.8	16.9	31.7
Extreme Maximum Temp. (°F)	48	56	73	87	92	97	99	97	94	84	71	57	99
Extreme Minimum Temp. (°F)	-25	-31	-23	4	17	26	30	31	24	16	-4	-17	-31
Days Maximum Temp. ≥ 90°F	0	0	0	0	0	1	2	1	0	0	0	0	4
Days Maximum Temp. ≤ 32°F	23	18	9	0	0	0	0	0	0	0	5	17	72
Days Minimum Temp. ≤ 32°F	31	28	29	23	10	2	0	0	1	11	24	30	189
Days Minimum Temp. ≤ 0°F	5	5	2	0	0	0	0	0	0	0	0	2	14
Heating Degree Days (base 65°F)	1,427	1,250	1,158	774	475	231	106	82	240	601	921	1,266	8,531
Cooling Degree Days (base 65°F)	0	0	0	1	8	38	76	71	26	1	0	0	221
Mean Precipitation (in.)	2.23	1.18	1.31	1.21	2.41	2.60	2.97	2.61	3.58	3.42	2.22	2.05	27.79
Extreme Maximum Daily Precip. (in.)	0.97	0.98	1.43	1.36	1.71	2.00	3.00	2.88	2.32	1.90	*1.03*	*0.97*	*3.00*
Days With ≥ 0.1" Precipitation	8	4	4	3	6	6	6	5	8	9	7	8	74
Days With ≥ 0.5" Precipitation	1	0	1	0	1	2	2	2	2	2	1	0	14
Days With ≥ 1.0" Precipitation	0	0	0	0	0	0	1	1	0	0	0	0	3
Mean Snowfall (in.)	40.9	24.6	15.1	4.1	0.3	0.0	0.0	0.0	trace	0.6	11.6	*35.7*	*132.9*
Maximum Snow Depth (in.)	36	42	40	26	8	0	0	0	trace	*5*	12	33	*42*
Days With ≥ 1.0" Snow Depth	30	27	28	10	0	0	0	0	0	*0*	10	26	*131*

Grosse Pointe Farms *Wayne County*   Elevation: 612 ft.   Latitude: 42° 23' N   Longitude: 82° 54' W

	JAN	FEB	MAR	APR	MAY	JUN	JUL	AUG	SEP	OCT	NOV	DEC	YEAR
Mean Maximum Temp. (°F)	32.7	35.2	44.4	57.6	68.9	78.5	83.0	80.9	73.8	61.1	48.8	36.5	58.5
Mean Temp. (°F)	26.0	27.9	36.0	48.0	58.9	68.5	73.3	72.0	64.6	52.6	41.6	30.4	50.0
Mean Minimum Temp. (°F)	19.3	20.6	27.6	38.3	48.8	58.3	63.6	63.1	55.4	44.0	34.4	24.2	41.5
Extreme Maximum Temp. (°F)	60	69	81	90	93	105	102	101	92	88	75	69	105
Extreme Minimum Temp. (°F)	-17	-7	-6	12	29	38	43	40	33	19	14	-7	-17
Days Maximum Temp. ≥ 90°F	0	0	0	0	0	3	6	3	0	0	0	0	12
Days Maximum Temp. ≤ 32°F	15	11	4	0	0	0	0	0	0	0	1	10	41
Days Minimum Temp. ≤ 32°F	28	25	22	7	0	0	0	0	0	2	13	24	121
Days Minimum Temp. ≤ 0°F	1	1	0	0	0	0	0	0	0	0	0	1	3
Heating Degree Days (base 65°F)	1,202	1,041	892	511	223	42	5	9	93	385	694	1,068	6,165
Cooling Degree Days (base 65°F)	0	0	1	6	40	153	269	233	88	8	0	0	798
Mean Precipitation (in.)	1.94	1.96	2.37	3.09	3.26	3.64	3.51	3.47	3.47	2.90	2.81	2.57	34.99
Extreme Maximum Daily Precip. (in.)	1.42	1.95	2.08	1.72	2.16	3.31	2.91	2.21	3.48	4.30	1.91	1.98	4.30
Days With ≥ 0.1" Precipitation	6	5	6	8	7	7	6	6	7	6	7	6	77
Days With ≥ 0.5" Precipitation	1	1	1	2	2	2	2	2	2	2	2	2	21
Days With ≥ 1.0" Precipitation	0	0	0	0	1	1	1	1	1	1	0	0	5
Mean Snowfall (in.)	8.7	6.9	3.6	0.6	0.0	0.0	0.0	0.0	0.0	trace	0.6	6.5	26.9
Maximum Snow Depth (in.)	23	18	12	5	0	0	0	0	0	0	4	13	23
Days With ≥ 1.0" Snow Depth	18	15	7	0	0	0	0	0	0	0	1	8	49

Gull Lake Biol Sta *Kalamazoo County*   Elevation: 910 ft.   Latitude: 42° 24' N   Longitude: 85° 23' W

	JAN	FEB	MAR	APR	MAY	JUN	JUL	AUG	SEP	OCT	NOV	DEC	YEAR
Mean Maximum Temp. (°F)	32.4	36.3	47.4	60.8	72.6	81.6	85.0	82.7	75.5	62.8	48.9	36.4	60.2
Mean Temp. (°F)	24.9	27.6	37.0	49.1	60.2	69.3	73.1	71.5	64.0	52.3	41.0	29.4	50.0
Mean Minimum Temp. (°F)	17.4	18.8	26.6	37.3	47.8	57.0	61.3	60.2	52.5	41.7	33.0	22.4	39.7
Extreme Maximum Temp. (°F)	61	70	79	88	94	98	101	98	*95*	*88*	74	69	*101*
Extreme Minimum Temp. (°F)	-20	-19	-7	4	25	34	40	39	*29*	*22*	10	-13	*-20*
Days Maximum Temp. ≥ 90°F	0	0	0	0	1	5	6	3	1	0	0	0	16
Days Maximum Temp. ≤ 32°F	16	10	3	0	0	0	0	0	0	0	1	10	40
Days Minimum Temp. ≤ 32°F	28	25	22	10	1	0	0	0	0	5	15	27	133
Days Minimum Temp. ≤ 0°F	3	2	0	0	0	0	0	0	0	0	0	1	6
Heating Degree Days (base 65°F)	1,236	1,052	861	480	193	34	4	13	109	395	714	1,096	6,187
Cooling Degree Days (base 65°F)	0	0	1	9	51	170	263	221	85	7	0	0	807
Mean Precipitation (in.)	2.17	1.88	2.61	3.57	3.89	3.67	3.70	4.17	4.69	3.44	3.28	2.77	39.84
Extreme Maximum Daily Precip. (in.)	1.63	2.10	1.77	2.70	3.20	3.23	4.18	2.31	*6.05*	2.05	*2.35*	1.32	*6.05*
Days With ≥ 0.1" Precipitation	6	5	6	8	8	7	6	7	7	7	7	7	81
Days With ≥ 0.5" Precipitation	1	1	2	2	3	3	3	3	3	2	2	1	26
Days With ≥ 1.0" Precipitation	0	0	0	1	1	1	1	1	1	1	1	0	8
Mean Snowfall (in.)	17.1	10.9	5.5	0.9	trace	0.0	0.0	0.0	0.0	*0.4*	3.9	16.9	*55.6*
Maximum Snow Depth (in.)	20	25	17	7	0	0	0	0	0	*0*	17	24	*25*
Days With ≥ 1.0" Snow Depth	22	19	7	1	0	0	0	0	0	*0*	2	15	*66*

The period of record for all cooperative weather station data is 1980 – 2009. See User Guide for detailed explanation of data.

Hancock Houghton Co Arpt *Houghton County*   Elevation: 1,074 ft.   Latitude: 47° 10' N   Longitude: 88° 30' W

	JAN	FEB	MAR	APR	MAY	JUN	JUL	AUG	SEP	OCT	NOV	DEC	YEAR
Mean Maximum Temp. (°F)	22.4	24.6	32.8	46.9	61.1	70.4	75.4	73.8	64.5	50.9	37.3	26.2	48.9
Mean Temp. (°F)	16.4	17.5	25.2	38.6	51.0	60.1	65.5	64.6	56.1	43.9	31.9	20.8	41.0
Mean Minimum Temp. (°F)	10.4	10.3	17.6	30.2	40.8	49.8	55.6	55.3	47.7	36.7	26.4	15.4	33.0
Extreme Maximum Temp. (°F)	50	56	65	88	90	96	102	95	90	83	71	53	102
Extreme Minimum Temp. (°F)	-26	-23	-23	-4	22	32	37	35	24	17	-6	-13	-26
Days Maximum Temp. ≥ 90°F	0	0	0	0	0	1	1	0	0	0	0	0	2
Days Maximum Temp. ≤ 32°F	26	21	15	3	0	0	0	0	0	0	10	22	97
Days Minimum Temp. ≤ 32°F	30	27	29	19	4	0	0	0	1	9	24	30	173
Days Minimum Temp. ≤ 0°F	6	6	3	0	0	0	0	0	0	0	0	3	18
Heating Degree Days (base 65°F)	1,499	1,338	1,226	787	439	180	69	80	279	649	986	1,364	8,896
Cooling Degree Days (base 65°F)	0	0	0	1	10	40	93	73	19	1	0	0	237
Mean Precipitation (in.)	2.82	1.54	1.78	1.88	2.48	2.64	2.77	2.37	3.32	3.07	2.29	2.59	29.55
Extreme Maximum Daily Precip. (in.)	1.82	1.79	2.49	1.49	1.80	2.07	2.99	3.23	3.58	2.03	1.36	1.53	3.58
Days With ≥ 0.1" Precipitation	9	5	5	5	6	6	6	5	7	8	6	8	76
Days With ≥ 0.5" Precipitation	1	1	1	1	1	2	2	1	2	2	1	1	16
Days With ≥ 1.0" Precipitation	0	0	0	0	0	0	1	1	1	0	0	0	3
Mean Snowfall (in.)	na	na	na	na	na	na	na	na	na	na	na	na	na
Maximum Snow Depth (in.)	na	na	na	na	na	na	na	na	na	na	na	na	na
Days With ≥ 1.0" Snow Depth	na	na	na	na	na	na	na	na	na	na	na	na	na

Hart *Oceana County*   Elevation: 700 ft.   Latitude: 43° 41' N   Longitude: 86° 21' W

	JAN	FEB	MAR	APR	MAY	JUN	JUL	AUG	SEP	OCT	NOV	DEC	YEAR
Mean Maximum Temp. (°F)	29.6	32.3	40.9	54.6	66.2	75.2	79.8	77.8	70.5	57.5	45.6	34.1	55.3
Mean Temp. (°F)	23.0	24.9	32.1	44.6	55.0	64.3	69.1	67.7	60.2	48.4	38.3	28.1	46.3
Mean Minimum Temp. (°F)	16.4	17.4	23.3	34.5	43.8	53.5	58.3	57.6	49.8	39.2	31.0	22.1	37.2
Extreme Maximum Temp. (°F)	59	65	77	84	88	98	97	94	89	87	71	68	98
Extreme Minimum Temp. (°F)	-14	-19	-6	1	24	33	39	37	26	22	7	-7	-19
Days Maximum Temp. ≥ 90°F	0	0	0	0	0	1	1	1	0	0	0	0	3
Days Maximum Temp. ≤ 32°F	19	14	7	1	0	0	0	0	0	0	2	12	55
Days Minimum Temp. ≤ 32°F	29	26	25	13	3	0	0	0	1	8	19	27	151
Days Minimum Temp. ≤ 0°F	2	2	1	0	0	0	0	0	0	0	0	1	6
Heating Degree Days (base 65°F)	1,294	1,128	1,012	610	322	95	26	35	180	511	793	1,137	7,143
Cooling Degree Days (base 65°F)	0	0	0	3	19	82	160	127	42	3	0	0	436
Mean Precipitation (in.)	2.59	1.89	2.13	2.95	3.71	3.22	3.01	3.81	3.88	3.57	3.33	2.68	36.77
Extreme Maximum Daily Precip. (in.)	1.70	1.51	1.28	1.80	4.65	3.75	4.60	4.83	5.43	2.50	3.45	1.90	5.43
Days With ≥ 0.1" Precipitation	8	5	5	6	6	6	6	6	7	8	7	8	78
Days With ≥ 0.5" Precipitation	1	1	1	2	3	2	2	3	3	3	2	1	24
Days With ≥ 1.0" Precipitation	0	0	0	1	1	1	1	1	1	1	1	0	8
Mean Snowfall (in.)	25.7	17.3	6.7	1.8	trace	0.0	0.0	0.0	0.0	trace	3.9	22.7	78.1
Maximum Snow Depth (in.)	39	35	15	8	trace	0	0	0	0	1	10	31	39
Days With ≥ 1.0" Snow Depth	20	18	8	1	0	0	0	0	0	0	2	13	62

Holland *Ottawa County*   Elevation: 609 ft.   Latitude: 42° 47' N   Longitude: 86° 07' W

	JAN	FEB	MAR	APR	MAY	JUN	JUL	AUG	SEP	OCT	NOV	DEC	YEAR
Mean Maximum Temp. (°F)	33.0	35.9	45.3	58.3	69.7	79.2	83.3	81.8	74.4	61.3	48.6	36.8	59.0
Mean Temp. (°F)	26.0	28.1	36.0	47.7	58.2	67.6	72.2	70.9	63.2	51.4	40.9	30.2	49.4
Mean Minimum Temp. (°F)	18.8	20.4	26.4	37.0	46.8	56.1	61.0	59.9	52.1	41.5	33.1	23.5	39.7
Extreme Maximum Temp. (°F)	65	72	80	91	93	101	100	97	93	86	75	70	101
Extreme Minimum Temp. (°F)	-11	-11	-4	5	25	33	41	40	27	22	11	-9	-11
Days Maximum Temp. ≥ 90°F	0	0	0	0	0	3	5	2	0	0	0	0	10
Days Maximum Temp. ≤ 32°F	14	10	3	0	0	0	0	0	0	0	1	9	37
Days Minimum Temp. ≤ 32°F	28	26	23	10	1	0	0	0	0	4	14	26	132
Days Minimum Temp. ≤ 0°F	1	1	0	0	0	0	0	0	0	0	0	0	2
Heating Degree Days (base 65°F)	1,203	1,038	894	521	245	54	9	14	117	422	716	1,074	6,307
Cooling Degree Days (base 65°F)	0	0	0	9	40	139	238	203	71	8	0	0	708
Mean Precipitation (in.)	na	1.32	1.71	3.00	3.85	3.53	3.40	3.53	3.83	3.71	3.31	2.60	na
Extreme Maximum Daily Precip. (in.)	2.00	2.00	1.50	2.37	4.10	6.87	7.99	3.00	2.97	3.20	2.50	2.50	7.99
Days With ≥ 0.1" Precipitation	4	4	4	6	7	6	5	5	7	7	6	5	66
Days With ≥ 0.5" Precipitation	1	1	1	2	3	2	2	2	3	2	2	1	22
Days With ≥ 1.0" Precipitation	0	0	0	1	1	1	1	1	1	1	1	0	8
Mean Snowfall (in.)	20.8	13.7	5.2	1.1	trace	0.0	0.0	0.0	0.0	0.2	3.3	20.4	64.7
Maximum Snow Depth (in.)	36	23	14	12	trace	0	0	0	0	2	7	22	36
Days With ≥ 1.0" Snow Depth	15	12	5	1	0	0	0	0	0	0	2	10	45

Iron Mtn-Kingsford WWTP *Dickinson County*   Elevation: 1,060 ft.   Latitude: 45° 47' N   Longitude: 88° 05' W

	JAN	FEB	MAR	APR	MAY	JUN	JUL	AUG	SEP	OCT	NOV	DEC	YEAR
Mean Maximum Temp. (°F)	24.5	29.1	38.9	53.7	66.8	76.2	80.4	78.1	69.6	55.6	40.7	28.2	53.5
Mean Temp. (°F)	13.7	17.6	27.7	41.7	53.9	63.6	68.1	66.3	57.8	44.9	32.2	19.4	42.2
Mean Minimum Temp. (°F)	2.9	6.1	16.5	29.7	40.9	51.0	55.7	54.5	46.0	34.1	23.7	10.6	31.0
Extreme Maximum Temp. (°F)	53	60	77	94	95	100	100	98	98	88	75	64	100
Extreme Minimum Temp. (°F)	-33	-39	-24	0	16	29	37	35	22	13	-8	-23	-39
Days Maximum Temp. ≥ 90°F	0	0	0	0	0	2	3	1	0	0	0	0	6
Days Maximum Temp. ≤ 32°F	24	18	9	1	0	0	0	0	0	0	6	20	78
Days Minimum Temp. ≤ 32°F	31	28	29	19	5	0	0	0	2	15	26	30	185
Days Minimum Temp. ≤ 0°F	14	10	4	0	0	0	0	0	0	0	0	8	36
Heating Degree Days (base 65°F)	1,585	1,334	1,149	693	354	112	37	56	236	618	978	1,407	8,559
Cooling Degree Days (base 65°F)	0	0	0	0	17	77	139	103	26	1	0	0	364
Mean Precipitation (in.)	1.29	1.00	1.59	2.30	3.04	3.30	3.37	3.52	3.45	3.07	1.89	1.53	29.35
Extreme Maximum Daily Precip. (in.)	1.55	1.17	2.38	1.61	2.00	2.82	4.05	2.68	1.91	2.72	1.84	1.02	4.05
Days With ≥ 0.1" Precipitation	4	3	5	6	7	8	7	7	7	6	5	5	70
Days With ≥ 0.5" Precipitation	0	0	1	2	2	2	2	3	2	2	1	1	18
Days With ≥ 1.0" Precipitation	0	0	0	0	1	1	0	1	1	1	0	0	5
Mean Snowfall (in.)	14.2	9.4	10.6	4.6	0.6	0.0	0.0	0.0	trace	0.7	5.8	13.8	59.7
Maximum Snow Depth (in.)	34	34	31	18	8	0	0	0	trace	8	10	27	34
Days With ≥ 1.0" Snow Depth	30	28	23	3	0	0	0	0	0	0	6	24	114

The period of record for all cooperative weather station data is 1980 – 2009. See User Guide for detailed explanation of data.

Ironwood *Gogebic County*　Elevation: 1,430 ft.　Latitude: 46° 28' N　Longitude: 90° 11' W

	JAN	FEB	MAR	APR	MAY	JUN	JUL	AUG	SEP	OCT	NOV	DEC	YEAR
Mean Maximum Temp. (°F)	20.6	25.5	35.3	49.9	63.2	72.3	76.5	74.7	66.2	52.3	37.5	24.5	49.9
Mean Temp. (°F)	11.5	15.0	24.6	39.2	51.9	61.3	65.8	64.0	55.8	43.1	30.0	16.6	39.9
Mean Minimum Temp. (°F)	2.3	4.4	13.9	28.4	40.4	50.2	55.0	53.3	45.4	33.9	22.3	8.6	29.8
Extreme Maximum Temp. (°F)	55	60	72	84	92	94	97	96	90	86	72	59	97
Extreme Minimum Temp. (°F)	-41	-37	-34	-12	16	26	35	32	22	5	-10	-36	-41
Days Maximum Temp. ≥ 90°F	0	0	0	0	0	0	1	1	0	0	0	0	2
Days Maximum Temp. ≤ 32°F	26	20	13	2	0	0	0	0	0	1	10	24	96
Days Minimum Temp. ≤ 32°F	31	28	29	21	7	1	0	0	2	15	26	31	191
Days Minimum Temp. ≤ 0°F	13	11	5	0	0	0	0	0	0	0	1	9	39
Heating Degree Days (base 65°F)	1,656	1,409	1,246	770	414	159	70	93	292	673	1,042	1,495	9,319
Cooling Degree Days (base 65°F)	0	0	0	2	14	56	102	70	22	1	0	0	267
Mean Precipitation (in.)	1.96	1.25	1.98	2.63	3.08	3.51	4.14	3.42	4.02	3.92	2.65	2.11	34.67
Extreme Maximum Daily Precip. (in.)	1.46	1.12	1.64	2.26	4.09	2.25	2.82	2.06	2.54	2.10	2.26	1.13	4.09
Days With ≥ 0.1" Precipitation	6	4	5	7	7	8	7	7	8	8	7	7	81
Days With ≥ 0.5" Precipitation	1	0	1	2	2	2	3	2	3	2	1	1	20
Days With ≥ 1.0" Precipitation	0	0	0	0	1	1	1	1	1	1	0	0	6
Mean Snowfall (in.)	45.2	26.7	24.6	11.4	1.8	0.0	0.0	0.0	0.3	6.8	24.9	45.5	187.2
Maximum Snow Depth (in.)	47	44	42	27	13	0	0	0	0	6	15	27	32	47
Days With ≥ 1.0" Snow Depth	31	28	27	9	1	0	0	0	0	0	3	16	30	145

Lapeer WWTP *Lapeer County*　Elevation: 819 ft.　Latitude: 43° 04' N　Longitude: 83° 18' W

	JAN	FEB	MAR	APR	MAY	JUN	JUL	AUG	SEP	OCT	NOV	DEC	YEAR
Mean Maximum Temp. (°F)	30.2	33.1	43.3	57.2	68.9	77.9	82.1	79.9	73.1	60.0	47.1	34.3	57.3
Mean Temp. (°F)	22.7	24.5	33.6	46.1	57.0	66.1	70.7	68.7	61.5	49.7	39.0	27.5	47.3
Mean Minimum Temp. (°F)	15.1	15.9	23.8	35.1	45.1	54.4	59.2	57.5	49.8	39.3	30.9	20.7	37.2
Extreme Maximum Temp. (°F)	61	68	81	87	92	100	100	99	94	*86*	75	69	*100*
Extreme Minimum Temp. (°F)	-26	-24	-16	7	24	32	36	32	26	*17*	8	-10	*-26*
Days Maximum Temp. ≥ 90°F	0	0	0	0	0	2	4	2	0	0	0	0	8
Days Maximum Temp. ≤ 32°F	18	14	6	1	0	0	0	0	0	0	2	13	54
Days Minimum Temp. ≤ 32°F	29	27	26	13	2	0	0	0	1	7	18	28	151
Days Minimum Temp. ≤ 0°F	5	4	1	0	0	0	0	0	0	0	0	2	12
Heating Degree Days (base 65°F)	1,304	1,140	968	565	274	69	15	29	154	472	774	1,155	6,919
Cooling Degree Days (base 65°F)	0	0	1	6	34	110	198	151	54	4	0	0	558
Mean Precipitation (in.)	1.59	1.50	1.75	2.73	3.12	3.02	3.74	3.34	3.85	2.86	2.64	1.76	31.90
Extreme Maximum Daily Precip. (in.)	1.22	1.18	1.36	2.14	1.95	2.32	3.60	2.39	3.72	*3.53*	1.70	1.34	*3.72*
Days With ≥ 0.1" Precipitation	5	4	5	6	6	6	6	7	6	6	6	5	68
Days With ≥ 0.5" Precipitation	1	1	1	2	2	2	3	2	3	2	2	1	22
Days With ≥ 1.0" Precipitation	0	0	0	0	1	1	1	1	1	0	0	0	5
Mean Snowfall (in.)	*10.0*	7.8	4.7	1.3	0.0	0.0	0.0	0.0	0.0	*0.1*	1.4	8.1	*33.4*
Maximum Snow Depth (in.)	*19*	*14*	12	6	0	0	0	0	0	*1*	5	*17*	*19*
Days With ≥ 1.0" Snow Depth	*18*	*17*	7	1	0	0	0	0	0	*0*	1	12	*56*

Manistique *Schoolcraft County*　Elevation: 620 ft.　Latitude: 45° 57' N　Longitude: 86° 15' W

	JAN	FEB	MAR	APR	MAY	JUN	JUL	AUG	SEP	OCT	NOV	DEC	YEAR
Mean Maximum Temp. (°F)	25.6	27.5	34.9	46.9	57.8	67.7	73.3	73.6	65.7	52.9	41.1	30.3	49.8
Mean Temp. (°F)	17.6	19.1	26.7	38.9	49.4	59.1	64.8	64.8	57.2	45.4	34.5	23.4	41.7
Mean Minimum Temp. (°F)	9.6	10.7	18.3	30.8	40.8	50.5	56.2	56.0	48.6	37.7	27.8	16.3	33.6
Extreme Maximum Temp. (°F)	46	47	69	84	87	96	93	94	87	74	65	59	96
Extreme Minimum Temp. (°F)	-25	-25	-19	3	25	34	39	38	19	20	3	-15	-25
Days Maximum Temp. ≥ 90°F	0	0	0	0	0	0	0	0	0	0	0	0	0
Days Maximum Temp. ≤ 32°F	23	19	11	1	0	0	0	0	0	0	5	17	76
Days Minimum Temp. ≤ 32°F	31	28	28	17	3	0	0	0	1	9	22	29	168
Days Minimum Temp. ≤ 0°F	8	6	2	0	0	0	0	0	0	0	0	4	20
Heating Degree Days (base 65°F)	1,461	1,289	1,182	776	479	188	64	63	241	602	909	1,284	8,538
Cooling Degree Days (base 65°F)	0	0	0	1	1	18	64	64	13	0	0	0	161
Mean Precipitation (in.)	na	*0.66*	1.33	2.35	2.58	2.90	2.93	2.94	3.36	3.30	2.38	*1.45*	na
Extreme Maximum Daily Precip. (in.)	*0.84*	*0.58*	*1.30*	*3.86*	*2.46*	*1.61*	*3.70*	*2.41*	*3.85*	*2.71*	*1.43*	*1.50*	*3.86*
Days With ≥ 0.1" Precipitation	2	2	3	5	6	6	6	6	7	7	5	3	58
Days With ≥ 0.5" Precipitation	0	0	1	1	2	2	1	2	2	2	2	1	16
Days With ≥ 1.0" Precipitation	0	0	0	0	0	1	0	1	1	1	0	0	4
Mean Snowfall (in.)	*21.6*	14.3	11.0	2.7	trace	0.0	0.0	0.0	0.0	0.2	4.7	19.6	*74.1*
Maximum Snow Depth (in.)	55	61	48	19	1	0	0	0	0	*1*	13	42	*61*
Days With ≥ 1.0" Snow Depth	26	27	23	3	0	0	0	0	0	0	4	18	101

Marquette *Marquette County*　Elevation: 665 ft.　Latitude: 46° 33' N　Longitude: 87° 23' W

	JAN	FEB	MAR	APR	MAY	JUN	JUL	AUG	SEP	OCT	NOV	DEC	YEAR
Mean Maximum Temp. (°F)	26.1	29.1	36.9	48.2	60.3	69.2	75.1	74.9	67.4	54.4	41.0	30.0	51.0
Mean Temp. (°F)	19.3	21.5	29.2	40.1	50.8	59.8	66.1	66.4	59.1	47.0	35.1	23.9	43.2
Mean Minimum Temp. (°F)	12.5	13.8	21.5	32.0	41.2	50.3	57.1	57.9	50.7	39.5	29.2	17.8	35.3
Extreme Maximum Temp. (°F)	52	59	77	91	91	99	102	99	97	85	74	60	102
Extreme Minimum Temp. (°F)	-22	-24	-11	4	23	31	41	42	30	19	1	-17	-24
Days Maximum Temp. ≥ 90°F	0	0	0	0	0	1	1	1	0	0	0	0	3
Days Maximum Temp. ≤ 32°F	23	18	10	1	0	0	0	0	0	0	5	18	75
Days Minimum Temp. ≤ 32°F	31	27	27	16	3	0	0	0	0	5	20	29	158
Days Minimum Temp. ≤ 0°F	5	4	1	0	0	0	0	0	0	0	0	2	12
Heating Degree Days (base 65°F)	1,409	1,223	1,103	742	444	193	62	52	204	553	889	1,267	8,141
Cooling Degree Days (base 65°F)	0	0	0	0	2	9	43	104	103	33	2	0	0	296
Mean Precipitation (in.)	1.86	1.30	2.01	2.38	2.57	2.54	2.57	2.64	3.33	3.16	2.64	1.93	28.93
Extreme Maximum Daily Precip. (in.)	1.28	1.28	1.12	1.88	5.12	2.13	2.48	2.76	2.53	2.25	1.95	1.11	5.12
Days With ≥ 0.1" Precipitation	6	4	5	6	6	6	6	6	7	8	7	6	73
Days With ≥ 0.5" Precipitation	0	0	1	1	1	2	2	2	2	2	1	1	15
Days With ≥ 1.0" Precipitation	0	0	0	0	1	0	0	0	0	1	0	0	1
Mean Snowfall (in.)	28.3	21.2	20.7	7.6	0.6	0.0	0.0	0.0	0.0	1.0	10.8	25.1	115.3
Maximum Snow Depth (in.)	37	33	41	23	9	0	0	0	trace	4	15	26	41
Days With ≥ 1.0" Snow Depth	30	28	28	8	1	0	0	0	0	1	9	26	130

The period of record for all cooperative weather station data is 1980 – 2009. See User Guide for detailed explanation of data.

Milford Gm Proving Ground *Livingston County* Elevation: 990 ft. Latitude: 42° 35' N Longitude: 83° 42' W

	JAN	FEB	MAR	APR	MAY	JUN	JUL	AUG	SEP	OCT	NOV	DEC	YEAR
Mean Maximum Temp. (°F)	30.2	32.8	43.0	56.3	67.9	76.8	80.9	78.9	71.3	58.7	46.4	33.6	56.4
Mean Temp. (°F)	22.6	24.6	33.5	45.9	56.9	66.2	70.3	68.9	61.2	49.2	38.5	26.7	47.0
Mean Minimum Temp. (°F)	15.2	16.1	23.9	35.4	46.0	55.5	59.6	58.7	51.1	39.7	30.5	19.9	37.6
Extreme Maximum Temp. (°F)	61	67	79	86	92	94	97	97	93	84	75	64	97
Extreme Minimum Temp. (°F)	-23	-16	-8	12	24	35	41	39	26	20	8	-18	-23
Days Maximum Temp. ≥ 90°F	0	0	0	0	0	1	2	1	0	0	0	0	4
Days Maximum Temp. ≤ 32°F	18	14	6	1	0	0	0	0	0	0	3	14	56
Days Minimum Temp. ≤ 32°F	28	26	25	12	2	0	0	0	0	7	18	27	145
Days Minimum Temp. ≤ 0°F	4	3	1	0	0	0	0	0	0	0	0	2	10
Heating Degree Days (base 65°F)	1,307	1,138	970	572	275	65	14	27	156	485	789	1,180	6,978
Cooling Degree Days (base 65°F)	0	0	0	4	30	108	185	154	50	4	0	0	535
Mean Precipitation (in.)	1.59	1.91	1.78	2.46	3.17	3.29	2.82	3.03	2.99	2.43	2.45	1.98	29.90
Extreme Maximum Daily Precip. (in.)	1.75	2.67	1.53	2.36	na	na	2.52	2.56	5.08	2.00	1.70	1.34	na
Days With ≥ 0.1" Precipitation	4	4	5	6	6	6	5	6	6	5	5	5	63
Days With ≥ 0.5" Precipitation	1	1	1	1	2	2	2	2	2	1	2	1	18
Days With ≥ 1.0" Precipitation	0	0	0	0	1	1	1	1	1	0	0	0	5
Mean Snowfall (in.)	11.0	7.6	3.5	1.2	trace	0.0	0.0	0.0	0.0	0.1	1.6	8.4	33.4
Maximum Snow Depth (in.)	18	12	13	5	trace	0	0	0	0	trace	4	14	18
Days With ≥ 1.0" Snow Depth	18	16	5	0	0	0	0	0	0	0	1	11	51

Mio Hydro Plant *Oscoda County* Elevation: 959 ft. Latitude: 44° 40' N Longitude: 84° 08' W

	JAN	FEB	MAR	APR	MAY	JUN	JUL	AUG	SEP	OCT	NOV	DEC	YEAR
Mean Maximum Temp. (°F)	28.3	31.9	41.0	54.6	67.2	76.9	81.9	79.3	71.0	57.5	44.2	33.0	55.6
Mean Temp. (°F)	19.2	21.1	29.6	42.7	54.1	63.8	68.9	66.6	58.6	46.6	36.0	25.1	44.3
Mean Minimum Temp. (°F)	10.0	10.3	18.1	30.8	41.0	50.7	55.8	53.7	46.0	35.6	27.7	17.1	33.1
Extreme Maximum Temp. (°F)	55	61	78	88	95	103	101	101	94	85	74	66	103
Extreme Minimum Temp. (°F)	-29	-31	-22	-1	22	30	37	24	25	17	-8	-21	-31
Days Maximum Temp. ≥ 90°F	0	0	0	0	0	2	4	2	0	0	0	0	8
Days Maximum Temp. ≤ 32°F	21	15	7	1	0	0	0	0	0	0	3	14	61
Days Minimum Temp. ≤ 32°F	30	27	28	18	6	0	0	0	2	12	22	29	174
Days Minimum Temp. ≤ 0°F	8	7	3	0	0	0	0	0	0	0	0	4	22
Heating Degree Days (base 65°F)	1,412	1,235	1,091	664	351	108	28	53	217	566	864	1,231	7,820
Cooling Degree Days (base 65°F)	0	0	0	3	20	79	156	108	29	2	0	0	397
Mean Precipitation (in.)	1.42	1.10	1.46	2.22	2.62	2.73	2.83	3.26	2.83	2.56	2.14	1.42	26.59
Extreme Maximum Daily Precip. (in.)	1.00	1.05	2.12	1.30	1.58	2.39	3.75	3.13	2.31	2.10	1.62	1.06	3.75
Days With ≥ 0.1" Precipitation	5	4	4	6	7	6	6	7	7	6	6	4	68
Days With ≥ 0.5" Precipitation	1	1	1	1	2	2	2	2	2	2	1	1	18
Days With ≥ 1.0" Precipitation	0	0	0	0	0	0	1	0	1	0	0	0	2
Mean Snowfall (in.)	na	4.7	na	1.4	trace	0.0	0.0	0.0	0.0	0.1	2.0	na	na
Maximum Snow Depth (in.)	29	32	27	7	4	0	0	0	0	3	14	14	32
Days With ≥ 1.0" Snow Depth	25	23	16	3	0	0	0	0	0	0	6	18	91

Munising *Alger County* Elevation: 680 ft. Latitude: 46° 25' N Longitude: 86° 40' W

	JAN	FEB	MAR	APR	MAY	JUN	JUL	AUG	SEP	OCT	NOV	DEC	YEAR
Mean Maximum Temp. (°F)	24.9	27.1	35.2	47.5	60.9	69.6	74.7	74.0	66.1	53.4	40.6	29.4	50.3
Mean Temp. (°F)	18.0	19.2	27.6	38.8	50.2	59.0	64.9	64.7	57.5	45.8	34.4	23.2	42.0
Mean Minimum Temp. (°F)	11.0	11.3	19.8	30.1	39.5	48.4	55.0	55.4	48.9	38.0	28.2	17.0	33.6
Extreme Maximum Temp. (°F)	47	57	71	89	92	93	101	98	90	83	70	57	101
Extreme Minimum Temp. (°F)	-27	-21	-18	3	20	29	35	33	28	13	5	-21	-27
Days Maximum Temp. ≥ 90°F	0	0	0	0	0	0	1	1	0	0	0	0	2
Days Maximum Temp. ≤ 32°F	24	20	12	2	0	0	0	0	0	0	5	19	82
Days Minimum Temp. ≤ 32°F	31	28	28	19	6	1	0	0	0	7	21	30	171
Days Minimum Temp. ≤ 0°F	6	5	1	0	0	0	0	0	0	0	0	3	15
Heating Degree Days (base 65°F)	1,451	1,288	1,151	780	458	210	81	76	240	591	910	1,289	8,525
Cooling Degree Days (base 65°F)	0	0	0	1	7	37	85	75	22	1	0	0	228
Mean Precipitation (in.)	3.30	2.11	2.21	2.18	2.83	2.77	3.24	3.04	3.92	4.22	3.08	3.61	36.51
Extreme Maximum Daily Precip. (in.)	1.40	1.16	1.86	1.22	1.76	1.64	3.12	3.16	2.13	2.00	2.14	1.41	3.16
Days With ≥ 0.1" Precipitation	12	7	7	7	7	7	7	6	9	10	9	12	100
Days With ≥ 0.5" Precipitation	1	1	1	1	2	2	2	2	3	3	2	1	21
Days With ≥ 1.0" Precipitation	0	0	0	0	0	1	1	1	1	1	0	0	5
Mean Snowfall (in.)	42.4	28.2	19.3	7.2	0.4	0.0	0.0	0.0	trace	1.8	12.9	39.5	151.7
Maximum Snow Depth (in.)	na	na	na	na	1	0	0	0	trace	4	19	na	na
Days With ≥ 1.0" Snow Depth	na	na	na	11	0	0	0	0	0	1	9	23	na

Owosso Wwtp *Shiawassee County* Elevation: 729 ft. Latitude: 43° 01' N Longitude: 84° 11' W

	JAN	FEB	MAR	APR	MAY	JUN	JUL	AUG	SEP	OCT	NOV	DEC	YEAR
Mean Maximum Temp. (°F)	29.7	32.5	43.1	56.9	68.5	78.0	81.9	79.8	72.8	59.8	47.4	34.8	57.1
Mean Temp. (°F)	22.1	24.3	33.4	45.8	56.8	66.3	70.3	68.8	61.6	49.7	39.3	28.0	47.2
Mean Minimum Temp. (°F)	14.4	16.0	23.7	34.7	45.0	54.6	58.7	57.7	50.4	39.5	31.3	21.2	37.3
Extreme Maximum Temp. (°F)	62	67	80	88	91	99	101	97	92	89	76	69	101
Extreme Minimum Temp. (°F)	-20	-17	-8	3	25	33	40	37	26	21	9	-10	-20
Days Maximum Temp. ≥ 90°F	0	0	0	0	0	2	3	2	0	0	0	0	7
Days Maximum Temp. ≤ 32°F	19	14	6	1	0	0	0	0	0	0	2	12	54
Days Minimum Temp. ≤ 32°F	29	26	25	14	2	0	0	0	0	8	18	28	150
Days Minimum Temp. ≤ 0°F	5	3	1	0	0	0	0	0	0	0	0	1	10
Heating Degree Days (base 65°F)	1,324	1,144	973	573	277	66	17	30	151	474	763	1,138	6,930
Cooling Degree Days (base 65°F)	0	0	0	1	30	113	189	154	57	6	0	0	554
Mean Precipitation (in.)	1.59	1.48	1.77	3.02	3.46	3.16	3.05	3.26	3.66	2.86	2.58	2.06	31.95
Extreme Maximum Daily Precip. (in.)	1.56	1.63	1.60	1.88	2.54	2.44	1.95	3.62	3.00	4.67	1.68	1.81	4.67
Days With ≥ 0.1" Precipitation	5	4	5	7	6	6	6	6	6	7	6	6	70
Days With ≥ 0.5" Precipitation	1	1	1	2	2	2	2	2	3	2	2	1	21
Days With ≥ 1.0" Precipitation	0	0	0	0	1	1	1	1	1	0	0	0	5
Mean Snowfall (in.)	10.3	7.7	4.3	0.9	trace	0.0	0.0	0.0	0.0	0.2	1.6	10.6	35.6
Maximum Snow Depth (in.)	19	22	10	5	trace	0	0	0	0	0	3	16	22
Days With ≥ 1.0" Snow Depth	18	13	6	0	0	0	0	0	0	0	1	12	50

The period of record for all cooperative weather station data is 1980 – 2009. See User Guide for detailed explanation of data.

Port Huron *St. Clair County*   Elevation: 589 ft.   Latitude: 42° 59' N   Longitude: 82° 25' W

	JAN	FEB	MAR	APR	MAY	JUN	JUL	AUG	SEP	OCT	NOV	DEC	YEAR
Mean Maximum Temp. (°F)	31.4	33.6	42.4	55.2	67.0	77.1	81.9	80.5	73.4	60.4	47.6	35.3	57.2
Mean Temp. (°F)	24.4	26.0	34.1	45.7	56.7	66.8	72.2	71.1	63.8	51.4	40.4	28.8	48.5
Mean Minimum Temp. (°F)	17.3	18.4	25.7	36.1	46.4	56.3	62.5	61.7	54.2	42.4	33.1	22.2	39.7
Extreme Maximum Temp. (°F)	60	69	80	87	96	102	101	102	95	90	75	66	102
Extreme Minimum Temp. (°F)	-19	-8	-7	13	28	35	43	41	32	20	12	-7	-19
Days Maximum Temp. ≥ 90°F	0	0	0	0	1	3	4	2	1	0	0	0	11
Days Maximum Temp. ≤ 32°F	17	13	6	0	0	0	0	0	0	0	1	11	48
Days Minimum Temp. ≤ 32°F	29	26	25	9	0	0	0	0	0	2	15	26	132
Days Minimum Temp. ≤ 0°F	2	1	0	0	0	0	0	0	0	0	0	1	4
Heating Degree Days (base 65°F)	1,252	1,096	950	577	278	63	6	12	106	421	732	1,115	6,608
Cooling Degree Days (base 65°F)	0	0	0	3	29	122	237	209	78	7	0	0	685
Mean Precipitation (in.)	1.94	1.93	2.13	2.90	3.07	3.42	3.22	3.27	3.76	2.75	3.03	2.21	33.63
Extreme Maximum Daily Precip. (in.)	1.45	1.80	1.65	1.95	2.98	2.61	3.72	2.74	3.97	2.87	2.06	1.52	3.97
Days With ≥ 0.1" Precipitation	5	5	6	8	7	7	7	6	7	6	7	6	77
Days With ≥ 0.5" Precipitation	1	1	1	1	2	2	2	2	2	2	2	1	19
Days With ≥ 1.0" Precipitation	0	0	0	0	1	1	1	1	1	0	1	0	6
Mean Snowfall (in.)	10.9	9.0	4.7	0.7	0.0	0.0	0.0	0.0	0.0	0.0	1.3	8.3	34.9
Maximum Snow Depth (in.)	16	18	11	8	0	0	0	0	0	0	12	19	19
Days With ≥ 1.0" Snow Depth	17	16	6	0	0	0	0	0	0	0	1	11	51

St Johns *Clinton County*   Elevation: 743 ft.   Latitude: 43° 01' N   Longitude: 84° 33' W

	JAN	FEB	MAR	APR	MAY	JUN	JUL	AUG	SEP	OCT	NOV	DEC	YEAR
Mean Maximum Temp. (°F)	30.2	33.2	43.8	57.5	69.5	78.9	82.9	80.7	73.8	60.5	47.0	34.6	57.7
Mean Temp. (°F)	22.7	25.0	34.1	46.4	57.7	67.2	71.3	69.4	62.1	50.1	38.8	27.7	47.7
Mean Minimum Temp. (°F)	15.0	16.7	24.4	35.2	45.8	55.6	59.6	58.1	50.3	39.7	30.6	20.8	37.6
Extreme Maximum Temp. (°F)	61	69	79	89	93	98	100	100	92	88	75	69	100
Extreme Minimum Temp. (°F)	-19	-12	-10	7	25	34	41	38	27	20	0	-13	-19
Days Maximum Temp. ≥ 90°F	0	0	0	0	0	3	5	2	1	0	0	0	11
Days Maximum Temp. ≤ 32°F	18	14	5	1	0	0	0	0	0	0	2	12	52
Days Minimum Temp. ≤ 32°F	29	26	25	13	2	0	0	0	0	7	19	28	149
Days Minimum Temp. ≤ 0°F	4	3	0	0	0	0	0	0	0	0	0	1	8
Heating Degree Days (base 65°F)	1,306	1,126	952	558	254	55	12	24	142	461	781	1,149	6,820
Cooling Degree Days (base 65°F)	0	0	1	6	35	130	212	167	61	6	0	0	618
Mean Precipitation (in.)	1.79	1.50	2.10	3.26	3.58	3.23	3.23	3.35	3.73	2.97	2.67	1.73	33.14
Extreme Maximum Daily Precip. (in.)	1.50	2.40	1.80	4.50	4.86	3.45	3.36	2.80	3.82	6.50	2.18	1.18	6.50
Days With ≥ 0.1" Precipitation	5	4	5	8	7	6	6	6	6	7	6	5	71
Days With ≥ 0.5" Precipitation	1	1	1	2	2	2	2	2	3	2	2	1	21
Days With ≥ 1.0" Precipitation	0	0	0	0	1	1	1	1	1	0	1	0	6
Mean Snowfall (in.)	13.5	9.5	5.8	1.3	trace	0.0	0.0	0.0	0.0	0.3	2.1	9.7	42.2
Maximum Snow Depth (in.)	24	27	10	6	trace	0	0	0	0	3	5	14	27
Days With ≥ 1.0" Snow Depth	18	15	6	1	0	0	0	0	0	0	1	10	51

Stambaugh 2 SSE *Iron County*   Elevation: 1,560 ft.   Latitude: 46° 03' N   Longitude: 88° 37' W

	JAN	FEB	MAR	APR	MAY	JUN	JUL	AUG	SEP	OCT	NOV	DEC	YEAR
Mean Maximum Temp. (°F)	22.0	26.5	36.5	51.5	64.6	73.4	77.2	75.3	66.5	53.1	37.9	25.5	50.8
Mean Temp. (°F)	10.9	13.7	23.7	38.7	50.8	59.9	63.8	61.9	53.5	41.7	29.2	16.2	38.7
Mean Minimum Temp. (°F)	-0.3	0.8	10.8	25.8	37.0	46.3	50.3	48.6	40.6	30.4	20.4	6.9	26.5
Extreme Maximum Temp. (°F)	55	60	73	92	90	97	96	96	94	84	72	59	97
Extreme Minimum Temp. (°F)	-40	-45	-31	-11	16	25	32	29	20	10	-11	-41	-45
Days Maximum Temp. ≥ 90°F	0	0	0	0	0	0	1	0	0	0	0	0	1
Days Maximum Temp. ≤ 32°F	26	20	11	2	0	0	0	0	0	0	10	23	92
Days Minimum Temp. ≤ 32°F	31	28	30	24	11	2	0	1	6	20	27	31	211
Days Minimum Temp. ≤ 0°F	16	14	8	0	0	0	0	0	0	0	1	10	49
Heating Degree Days (base 65°F)	1,675	1,447	1,275	784	439	184	97	133	348	715	1,069	1,507	9,673
Cooling Degree Days (base 65°F)	0	0	0	1	8	37	67	45	11	1	0	0	170
Mean Precipitation (in.)	1.03	0.84	1.35	2.24	3.03	3.61	4.08	3.13	3.54	3.07	1.91	1.29	29.12
Extreme Maximum Daily Precip. (in.)	0.96	0.87	1.21	1.78	1.74	3.70	5.20	1.96	2.94	2.94	1.84	0.88	5.20
Days With ≥ 0.1" Precipitation	4	3	4	6	7	8	8	7	8	7	5	4	71
Days With ≥ 0.5" Precipitation	0	0	1	1	2	2	3	2	2	2	1	0	16
Days With ≥ 1.0" Precipitation	0	0	0	0	1	1	1	1	1	1	0	0	6
Mean Snowfall (in.)	14.9	10.6	11.5	5.8	0.4	0.0	0.0	trace	trace	2.0	8.7	15.2	69.1
Maximum Snow Depth (in.)	39	32	34	34	7	0	0	trace	trace	6	11	39	39
Days With ≥ 1.0" Snow Depth	31	28	27	6	0	0	0	0	0	1	10	27	130

Stephenson 8 WNW *Menominee County*   Elevation: 709 ft.   Latitude: 45° 27' N   Longitude: 87° 45' W

	JAN	FEB	MAR	APR	MAY	JUN	JUL	AUG	SEP	OCT	NOV	DEC	YEAR
Mean Maximum Temp. (°F)	26.3	29.6	40.2	54.2	67.0	76.3	80.2	78.2	69.6	57.0	42.0	30.1	54.2
Mean Temp. (°F)	15.5	17.6	28.6	41.9	53.4	62.9	67.0	65.5	57.1	45.4	32.9	21.0	42.4
Mean Minimum Temp. (°F)	4.6	5.5	16.9	29.6	39.8	49.4	53.8	52.8	44.6	33.6	23.7	11.7	30.5
Extreme Maximum Temp. (°F)	56	58	78	91	93	96	99	99	93	88	76	62	99
Extreme Minimum Temp. (°F)	-39	-45	-21	0	19	28	35	30	21	13	-12	-24	-45
Days Maximum Temp. ≥ 90°F	0	0	0	0	0	2	3	1	0	0	0	0	6
Days Maximum Temp. ≤ 32°F	23	17	7	1	0	0	0	0	0	0	5	17	70
Days Minimum Temp. ≤ 32°F	31	27	28	20	7	1	0	0	3	15	25	30	187
Days Minimum Temp. ≤ 0°F	12	11	4	0	0	0	0	0	0	0	0	7	34
Heating Degree Days (base 65°F)	1,530	1,335	1,122	686	366	124	46	63	250	604	955	1,359	8,440
Cooling Degree Days (base 65°F)	0	0	0	2	14	67	116	87	21	2	0	0	309
Mean Precipitation (in.)	1.14	0.75	1.55	2.38	3.01	3.36	3.44	3.42	3.47	2.92	2.30	1.42	29.16
Extreme Maximum Daily Precip. (in.)	1.69	1.08	1.70	2.05	2.18	2.83	3.35	2.95	2.40	2.13	2.35	1.00	3.35
Days With ≥ 0.1" Precipitation	4	2	4	6	7	7	6	6	7	6	5	4	64
Days With ≥ 0.5" Precipitation	0	0	1	1	2	2	2	2	3	2	1	1	17
Days With ≥ 1.0" Precipitation	0	0	0	0	1	1	1	1	1	1	0	0	6
Mean Snowfall (in.)	15.0	8.2	9.5	3.8	0.4	0.0	0.0	0.0	trace	0.6	4.3	12.1	53.9
Maximum Snow Depth (in.)	36	37	24	12	7	0	0	0	0	2	10	28	37
Days With ≥ 1.0" Snow Depth	26	26	20	3	0	0	0	0	0	0	4	18	97

The period of record for all cooperative weather station data is 1980 – 2009. See User Guide for detailed explanation of data.

Three Rivers *St. Joseph County*   Elevation: 810 ft.   Latitude: 41° 56' N   Longitude: 85° 38' W

	JAN	FEB	MAR	APR	MAY	JUN	JUL	AUG	SEP	OCT	NOV	DEC	YEAR
Mean Maximum Temp. (°F)	32.5	36.2	46.6	59.8	71.1	80.5	83.9	82.0	75.2	62.5	49.2	36.4	59.7
Mean Temp. (°F)	24.4	27.0	36.1	48.1	58.8	68.4	72.0	70.3	62.8	50.9	40.2	28.8	49.0
Mean Minimum Temp. (°F)	16.2	17.9	25.5	36.4	46.5	56.3	60.0	58.5	50.3	39.3	31.1	21.2	38.3
Extreme Maximum Temp. (°F)	66	72	80	88	93	103	102	100	96	88	79	72	103
Extreme Minimum Temp. (°F)	-23	-14	-4	7	25	35	41	38	28	18	9	-15	-23
Days Maximum Temp. ≥ 90°F	0	0	0	0	1	4	6	3	1	0	0	0	15
Days Maximum Temp. ≤ 32°F	16	10	4	0	0	0	0	0	0	0	1	11	42
Days Minimum Temp. ≤ 32°F	29	26	24	11	1	0	0	0	0	8	18	27	144
Days Minimum Temp. ≤ 0°F	4	2	0	0	0	0	0	0	0	0	0	1	7
Heating Degree Days (base 65°F)	1,252	1,067	891	506	227	44	8	17	128	436	737	1,114	6,427
Cooling Degree Days (base 65°F)	0	0	1	8	42	153	231	187	69	6	0	0	697
Mean Precipitation (in.)	2.27	1.79	2.37	3.18	4.13	3.52	4.31	4.23	3.88	3.40	3.18	2.59	38.85
Extreme Maximum Daily Precip. (in.)	2.33	1.37	1.66	2.31	2.31	4.35	4.08	3.30	5.05	3.19	3.17	1.46	5.05
Days With ≥ 0.1" Precipitation	6	5	6	7	8	6	7	7	6	7	7	7	79
Days With ≥ 0.5" Precipitation	1	1	1	2	3	2	3	3	2	2	2	1	23
Days With ≥ 1.0" Precipitation	0	0	0	1	1	1	1	1	1	1	1	0	8
Mean Snowfall (in.)	9.6	6.4	4.8	0.9	trace	0.0	0.0	0.0	0.0	0.4	2.5	9.5	34.1
Maximum Snow Depth (in.)	18	18	16	4	trace	0	0	0	0	3	5	19	19
Days With ≥ 1.0" Snow Depth	19	16	7	1	0	0	0	0	0	0	2	14	59

Whitefish Point *Chippewa County*   Elevation: 604 ft.   Latitude: 46° 45' N   Longitude: 84° 59' W

	JAN	FEB	MAR	APR	MAY	JUN	JUL	AUG	SEP	OCT	NOV	DEC	YEAR
Mean Maximum Temp. (°F)	24.8	26.8	34.4	45.6	57.7	66.8	72.4	73.4	66.3	52.9	40.4	29.8	49.3
Mean Temp. (°F)	18.4	18.9	25.6	37.3	47.7	56.3	62.2	64.1	57.8	46.0	34.9	24.3	41.1
Mean Minimum Temp. (°F)	12.0	10.9	16.8	28.9	37.6	45.7	52.1	54.9	49.3	39.1	29.4	18.8	32.9
Extreme Maximum Temp. (°F)	43	50	61	78	85	89	96	94	90	74	68	57	96
Extreme Minimum Temp. (°F)	-23	-26	-22	0	23	29	33	33	26	19	6	-14	-26
Days Maximum Temp. ≥ 90°F	0	0	0	0	0	0	0	0	0	0	0	0	0
Days Maximum Temp. ≤ 32°F	25	20	11	1	0	0	0	0	0	0	5	18	80
Days Minimum Temp. ≤ 32°F	30	28	29	20	7	1	0	0	0	6	20	29	170
Days Minimum Temp. ≤ 0°F	5	6	3	0	0	0	0	0	0	0	0	1	15
Heating Degree Days (base 65°F)	1,438	1,298	1,214	825	531	265	121	76	226	582	895	1,254	8,725
Cooling Degree Days (base 65°F)	0	0	0	0	1	11	43	56	17	0	0	0	128
Mean Precipitation (in.)	2.27	1.49	1.84	2.17	2.48	2.72	3.19	3.05	3.51	3.72	2.82	2.78	32.04
Extreme Maximum Daily Precip. (in.)	0.79	0.87	1.60	1.20	1.83	1.76	3.00	2.20	2.12	2.30	1.45	2.20	3.00
Days With ≥ 0.1" Precipitation	9	5	5	6	6	6	7	6	8	10	8	10	86
Days With ≥ 0.5" Precipitation	0	0	1	1	2	2	2	2	2	2	1	1	16
Days With ≥ 1.0" Precipitation	0	0	0	0	0	0	1	1	0	0	0	0	2
Mean Snowfall (in.)	36.0	21.7	12.7	4.7	0.1	0.0	0.0	0.0	trace	1.1	11.6	34.7	122.6
Maximum Snow Depth (in.)	34	38	39	36	7	0	0	0	trace	3	12	28	39
Days With ≥ 1.0" Snow Depth	31	28	30	16	0	0	0	0	0	1	8	25	139

Ypsilanti E Mich Univ *Washtenaw County*   Elevation: 779 ft.   Latitude: 42° 14' N   Longitude: 83° 37' W

	JAN	FEB	MAR	APR	MAY	JUN	JUL	AUG	SEP	OCT	NOV	DEC	YEAR
Mean Maximum Temp. (°F)	32.6	36.4	46.7	60.8	71.9	81.1	*84.8*	82.4	75.3	62.8	48.8	36.6	*60.0*
Mean Temp. (°F)	25.7	28.6	37.4	50.0	60.7	69.9	*74.0*	72.1	64.6	52.9	41.1	*30.2*	*50.6*
Mean Minimum Temp. (°F)	19.0	20.8	28.1	39.1	49.4	58.7	*63.1*	61.7	53.9	43.0	33.4	24.0	41.2
Extreme Maximum Temp. (°F)	64	69	82	87	96	102	100	99	95	90	74	68	102
Extreme Minimum Temp. (°F)	-20	-11	-6	10	29	38	38	38	33	22	9	-10	-20
Days Maximum Temp. ≥ 90°F	0	0	0	0	1	4	7	4	1	0	0	0	17
Days Maximum Temp. ≤ 32°F	15	10	3	0	0	0	0	0	0	0	1	10	39
Days Minimum Temp. ≤ 32°F	27	24	21	7	0	0	0	0	0	3	15	25	122
Days Minimum Temp. ≤ 0°F	2	1	0	0	0	0	0	0	0	0	0	0	4
Heating Degree Days (base 65°F)	1,211	1,021	849	452	181	29	*2*	8	97	377	709	*1,072*	*6,008*
Cooling Degree Days (base 65°F)	0	0	1	8	53	185	*288*	234	92	10	0	*0*	871
Mean Precipitation (in.)	1.93	1.76	2.30	3.00	3.60	3.19	3.27	3.46	3.50	2.73	2.86	2.34	33.94
Extreme Maximum Daily Precip. (in.)	1.57	2.10	1.51	1.87	3.34	2.17	*2.06*	4.07	2.17	2.43	1.96	*1.47*	*4.07*
Days With ≥ 0.1" Precipitation	5	4	6	7	7	6	6	6	6	5	6	5	69
Days With ≥ 0.5" Precipitation	1	1	1	2	2	2	2	2	3	2	2	1	21
Days With ≥ 1.0" Precipitation	0	0	0	0	1	1	1	1	1	1	0	0	6
Mean Snowfall (in.)	10.8	6.8	5.1	1.0	trace	0.0	0.0	0.0	0.0	0.1	1.3	*8.3*	*33.4*
Maximum Snow Depth (in.)	23	24	10	5	trace	0	0	0	0	1	6	20	24
Days With ≥ 1.0" Snow Depth	18	14	7	1	0	0	0	0	0	0	1	10	51

Michigan Weather Station Rankings

Annual Extreme Maximum Temperature

	Highest			Lowest	
Rank	Station Name	°F	Rank	Station Name	°F
1	Grosse Pointe Farms	105	1	Cross Village	95
2	Adrian 2 NNE	104	1	Frankfort 2 NE	95
2	Benton Harbor Ross Field	104	3	Manistique	96
2	Dearborn	104	3	Whitefish Point	96
2	Detroit Metropolitan Arpt	104	5	Bergland Dam	97
6	Alma	103	5	Ironwood	97
6	Alpena Phelps Collins Arpt	103	5	Milford Gm Proving Ground	97
6	Houghton Lake Roscommon Co Arpt	103	5	Sault Ste Marie Sanderson Field	97
6	Mio Hydro Plant	103	5	Stambaugh 2 SSE	97
6	Three Rivers	103	10	Champion Van Riper Prk	98
11	East Tawas	102	10	Cheboygan	98
11	Hancock Houghton Co Arpt	102	10	Hart	98
11	Marquette	102	10	Muskegon County Arpt	98
11	Port Huron	102	14	Grand Marais 2 E	99
11	Ypsilanti E Mich Univ	102	14	Marquette County Arpt	99
16	Ann Arbor Univ of Mich	101	14	Stephenson 8 WNW	99
16	Bad Axe	101	17	Allegan 5 NE	100
16	Big Rapids Waterworks	101	17	Alpena Wastewater Pl	100
16	Boyne Falls	101	17	Battle Creek 5 NW	100
16	Caro Regional Center	101	17	Grand Rapids Kent County Intl	100
16	Charlotte	101	17	Iron Mtn-Kingsford WWTP	100
16	East Lansing 4 S	101	17	Lansing Capital City Arpt	100
16	Essexville	101	17	Lapeer WWTP	100
16	Flint Bishop Arpt	101	17	St Johns	100
16	Gull Lake Biol Sta	101	25	Ann Arbor Univ of Mich	101

Annual Mean Maximum Temperature

	Highest			Lowest	
Rank	Station Name	°F	Rank	Station Name	°F
1	Gull Lake Biol Sta	60.2	1	Hancock Houghton Co Arpt	48.9
2	Ypsilanti E Mich Univ	60.0	2	Whitefish Point	49.3
3	Dearborn	59.8	3	Marquette County Arpt	49.7
4	Three Rivers	59.7	4	Manistique	49.8
5	Benton Harbor Ross Field	59.4	5	Ironwood	49.9
6	Adrian 2 NNE	59.2	6	Sault Ste Marie Sanderson Field	50.1
7	Holland	59.0	7	Munising	50.3
8	Ann Arbor Univ of Mich	58.9	8	Bergland Dam	50.6
9	Detroit Metropolitan Arpt	58.8	9	Stambaugh 2 SSE	50.8
10	Battle Creek 5 NW	58.7	10	Marquette	51.1
11	Grosse Pointe Farms	58.5	11	Champion Van Riper Prk	51.7
12	Allegan 5 NE	57.7	12	Grand Marais 2 E	52.1
12	St Johns	57.7	13	Alpena Wastewater Pl	52.6
14	Caro Regional Center	57.6	13	Cheboygan	52.6
15	East Lansing 4 S	57.4	15	Cross Village	52.7
15	Grand Rapids Kent County Intl	57.4	16	Iron Mtn-Kingsford WWTP	53.5
17	Flint Bishop Arpt	57.3	17	Alpena Phelps Collins Arpt	53.8
17	Lansing Capital City Arpt	57.3	18	Frankfort 2 NE	53.9
17	Lapeer WWTP	57.3	19	Houghton Lake Roscommon Co Arpt	54.0
20	Alma	57.2	20	Stephenson 8 WNW	54.2
20	Port Huron	57.2	21	Bad Axe	55.0
22	Owosso Wwtp	57.1	22	East Tawas	55.3
23	Charlotte	56.8	23	Hart	55.4
24	Boyne Falls	56.6	24	Mio Hydro Plant	55.6
25	Big Rapids Waterworks	56.5	25	Essexville	56.0

Rankings include 25 highest/lowest stations. If state has less than 25 stations, all stations are included. The period of record is 1980–2009. See User Guide for detailed explanation of data.

Annual Mean Temperature

	Highest			Lowest	
Rank	**Station Name**	**°F**	**Rank**	**Station Name**	**°F**
1	Ypsilanti E Mich Univ	**50.6**	1	Stambaugh 2 SSE	38.7
2	Grosse Pointe Farms	50.0	2	Champion Van Riper Prk	39.1
2	Gull Lake Biol Sta	50.0	3	Bergland Dam	39.2
4	Detroit Metropolitan Arpt	49.9	4	Ironwood	39.9
5	Ann Arbor Univ of Mich	49.6	5	Marquette County Arpt	40.1
5	Benton Harbor Ross Field	49.6	6	Sault Ste Marie Sanderson Field	40.9
5	Dearborn	49.6	7	Hancock Houghton Co Arpt	41.0
8	Holland	49.4	8	Whitefish Point	41.1
9	Three Rivers	49.0	9	Manistique	41.7
10	Battle Creek 5 NW	**48.6**	10	Grand Marais 2 E	41.9
11	Adrian 2 NNE	48.5	11	Munising	**42.0**
11	Port Huron	48.5	12	Iron Mtn-Kingsford WWTP	42.3
13	Grand Rapids Kent County Intl	48.3	13	Stephenson 8 WNW	**42.4**
14	Muskegon County Arpt	47.8	14	Marquette	43.2
15	Flint Bishop Arpt	47.7	15	Cheboygan	43.4
15	St Johns	47.7	16	Alpena Phelps Collins Arpt	43.6
17	Essexville	47.6	17	Houghton Lake Roscommon Co Arpt	43.9
18	Allegan 5 NE	**47.5**	18	Cross Village	44.1
19	East Lansing 4 S	**47.4**	19	Mio Hydro Plant	**44.4**
19	Lansing Capital City Arpt	47.4	20	Alpena Wastewater Pl	44.6
21	Caro Regional Center	**47.3**	21	Big Rapids Waterworks	45.5
21	Lapeer WWTP	47.3	21	East Tawas	45.5
23	Owosso Wwtp	47.2	23	Bad Axe	45.8
24	Milford Gm Proving Ground	**47.0**	23	Boyne Falls	45.8
25	Charlotte	46.9	25	Frankfort 2 NE	46.3

Annual Mean Minimum Temperature

	Highest			Lowest	
Rank	**Station Name**	**°F**	**Rank**	**Station Name**	**°F**
1	Grosse Pointe Farms	41.5	1	Champion Van Riper Prk	26.5
2	Ypsilanti E Mich Univ	**41.2**	1	Stambaugh 2 SSE	26.5
3	Detroit Metropolitan Arpt	41.0	3	Bergland Dam	27.8
4	Ann Arbor Univ of Mich	40.2	4	Ironwood	29.8
5	Benton Harbor Ross Field	39.7	5	Marquette County Arpt	30.4
5	Gull Lake Biol Sta	39.7	6	Stephenson 8 WNW	**30.5**
5	Holland	39.7	7	Iron Mtn-Kingsford WWTP	31.0
5	Port Huron	39.7	8	Sault Ste Marie Sanderson Field	31.6
9	Dearborn	39.4	9	Grand Marais 2 E	31.7
9	Muskegon County Arpt	39.4	10	Hancock Houghton Co Arpt	33.0
11	Essexville	39.1	10	Whitefish Point	33.0
11	Grand Rapids Kent County Intl	39.1	12	Mio Hydro Plant	**33.1**
13	Frankfort 2 NE	38.6	13	Alpena Phelps Collins Arpt	33.4
14	Battle Creek 5 NW	**38.4**	14	Manistique	33.6
15	Three Rivers	38.3	14	Munising	**33.6**
16	Flint Bishop Arpt	38.0	16	Houghton Lake Roscommon Co Arpt	33.9
17	Adrian 2 NNE	37.8	17	Cheboygan	34.1
18	Milford Gm Proving Ground	**37.6**	18	Big Rapids Waterworks	34.6
18	St Johns	37.6	19	Boyne Falls	35.0
20	Lansing Capital City Arpt	37.5	20	Marquette	35.3
21	Owosso Wwtp	37.3	21	Cross Village	35.4
22	Allegan 5 NE	**37.2**	22	East Tawas	35.7
22	East Lansing 4 S	**37.2**	23	Alma	36.2
22	Hart	**37.2**	24	Alpena Wastewater Pl	36.5
22	Lapeer WWTP	37.2	25	Bad Axe	36.6

Rankings include 25 highest/lowest stations. If state has less than 25 stations, all stations are included. The period of record is 1980–2009. See User Guide for detailed explanation of data.

Annual Extreme Minimum Temperature

	Highest			Lowest	
Rank	Station Name	°F	Rank	Station Name	°F
1	Holland	-11	1	Stambaugh 2 SSE	-45
2	Frankfort 2 NE	-15	1	Stephenson 8 WNW	*-45*
3	Benton Harbor Ross Field	-17	3	Ironwood	-41
3	Grosse Pointe Farms	-17	4	Champion Van Riper Prk	-40
5	Essexville	-18	5	Bergland Dam	-39
6	Hart	*-19*	5	Iron Mtn-Kingsford WWTP	-39
6	Muskegon County Arpt	-19	7	Sault Ste Marie Sanderson Field	-36
6	Port Huron	-19	8	Boyne Falls	-32
6	St Johns	-19	8	Marquette County Arpt	-32
10	Bad Axe	-20	10	Grand Marais 2 E	-31
10	Battle Creek 5 NW	-20	10	Houghton Lake Roscommon Co Arpt	-31
10	Dearborn	-20	10	Mio Hydro Plant	*-31*
10	East Lansing 4 S	-20	13	Big Rapids Waterworks	-29
10	Gull Lake Biol Sta	*-20*	13	Lansing Capital City Arpt	-29
10	Owosso Wwtp	*-20*	15	Alpena Phelps Collins Arpt	-28
10	Ypsilanti E Mich Univ	-20	15	Cheboygan	-28
17	Alpena Wastewater Pl	-21	17	Cross Village	-27
17	Charlotte	-21	17	Munising	*-27*
17	Detroit Metropolitan Arpt	-21	19	Hancock Houghton Co Arpt	-26
17	East Tawas	-21	19	Lapeer WWTP	*-26*
17	Flint Bishop Arpt	-21	19	Whitefish Point	-26
22	Adrian 2 NNE	-22	22	Allegan 5 NE	*-25*
22	Alma	-22	22	Manistique	-25
22	Ann Arbor Univ of Mich	-22	24	Caro Regional Center	*-24*
22	Grand Rapids Kent County Intl	-22	24	Marquette	-24

July Mean Maximum Temperature

	Highest			Lowest	
Rank	Station Name	°F	Rank	Station Name	°F
1	Gull Lake Biol Sta	85.0	1	Whitefish Point	72.4
2	Ypsilanti E Mich Univ	*84.8*	2	Manistique	73.3
3	Dearborn	84.5	3	Munising	74.7
4	Three Rivers	83.9	4	Marquette	75.1
5	Adrian 2 NNE	83.6	5	Hancock Houghton Co Arpt	75.4
6	Benton Harbor Ross Field	83.4	6	Sault Ste Marie Sanderson Field	75.8
7	Ann Arbor Univ of Mich	83.3	7	Cross Village	76.0
7	Detroit Metropolitan Arpt	83.3	8	Grand Marais 2 E	76.4
7	Holland	83.3	8	Marquette County Arpt	76.4
10	Caro Regional Center	*83.2*	10	Ironwood	76.5
11	Grosse Pointe Farms	83.0	11	Alpena Wastewater Pl	77.2
12	Alma	82.9	11	Stambaugh 2 SSE	77.2
12	St Johns	82.9	13	Bergland Dam	77.5
14	Battle Creek 5 NW	82.7	13	Cheboygan	77.5
14	Boyne Falls	82.7	15	Frankfort 2 NE	77.7
16	Allegan 5 NE	*82.5*	16	Champion Van Riper Prk	78.8
17	Grand Rapids Kent County Intl	82.4	17	Alpena Phelps Collins Arpt	79.8
18	Lansing Capital City Arpt	82.3	18	Hart	*79.9*
19	East Lansing 4 S	82.2	18	Houghton Lake Roscommon Co Arpt	79.9
19	Flint Bishop Arpt	82.2	20	East Tawas	80.1
21	Lapeer WWTP	82.1	21	Stephenson 8 WNW	*80.2*
22	Big Rapids Waterworks	82.0	22	Bad Axe	80.3
23	Mio Hydro Plant	81.9	22	Muskegon County Arpt	80.3
23	Owosso Wwtp	81.9	24	Iron Mtn-Kingsford WWTP	80.4
23	Port Huron	81.9	25	Milford Gm Proving Ground	80.9

Rankings include 25 highest/lowest stations. If state has less than 25 stations, all stations are included. The period of record is 1980–2009. See User Guide for detailed explanation of data.

January Mean Minimum Temperature

Highest			Lowest		
Rank	Station Name	°F	Rank	Station Name	°F
1	Grosse Pointe Farms	19.3	1	Stambaugh 2 SSE	-0.3
2	Benton Harbor Ross Field	19.0	2	Champion Van Riper Prk	1.5
2	Ypsilanti E Mich Univ	19.0	3	Bergland Dam	1.9
4	Muskegon County Arpt	18.9	4	Ironwood	2.3
5	Holland	18.8	5	Iron Mtn-Kingsford WWTP	2.9
6	Frankfort 2 NE	18.5	6	Stephenson 8 WNW	4.6
7	Detroit Metropolitan Arpt	18.4	7	Marquette County Arpt	6.0
8	Ann Arbor Univ of Mich	17.9	8	Sault Ste Marie Sanderson Field	6.5
9	Gull Lake Biol Sta	17.4	9	Manistique	9.6
10	Dearborn	17.3	10	Mio Hydro Plant	10.0
10	Port Huron	17.3	11	Cheboygan	10.2
12	Grand Rapids Kent County Intl	17.1	12	Hancock Houghton Co Arpt	10.4
13	Battle Creek 5 NW	16.5	13	Houghton Lake Roscommon Co Arpt	10.9
14	Hart	16.4	14	Munising	11.0
15	Adrian 2 NNE	16.2	15	Grand Marais 2 E	11.2
15	Three Rivers	16.2	16	Alpena Phelps Collins Arpt	11.3
17	Flint Bishop Arpt	15.8	17	Whitefish Point	12.0
18	Allegan 5 NE	15.7	18	Big Rapids Waterworks	12.5
19	Essexville	15.6	18	Marquette	12.5
20	Lansing Capital City Arpt	15.3	20	Boyne Falls	13.1
21	Lapeer WWTP	15.2	20	Cross Village	13.1
21	Milford Gm Proving Ground	15.2	22	East Tawas	13.2
23	Caro Regional Center	15.0	23	Alpena Wastewater Pl	13.4
23	St Johns	15.0	24	Alma	14.0
25	East Lansing 4 S	14.9	25	Owosso Wwtp	14.4

Number of Days Annually Maximum Temperature ≥ 90°F

Highest			Lowest		
Rank	Station Name	Days	Rank	Station Name	Days
1	Ypsilanti E Mich Univ	17	1	Cross Village	0
2	Benton Harbor Ross Field	16	1	Manistique	0
2	Gull Lake Biol Sta	16	1	Whitefish Point	0
4	Dearborn	15	4	Frankfort 2 NE	1
4	Three Rivers	15	4	Sault Ste Marie Sanderson Field	1
6	Adrian 2 NNE	13	4	Stambaugh 2 SSE	1
6	Caro Regional Center	13	7	Bergland Dam	2
8	Alma	12	7	Champion Van Riper Prk	2
8	Detroit Metropolitan Arpt	12	7	Hancock Houghton Co Arpt	2
8	Grosse Pointe Farms	12	7	Ironwood	2
11	Ann Arbor Univ of Mich	11	7	Munising	2
11	Boyne Falls	11	12	Cheboygan	3
11	Port Huron	11	12	Hart	3
11	St Johns	11	12	Marquette	3
15	Essexville	10	12	Muskegon County Arpt	3
15	Holland	10	16	Alpena Wastewater Pl	4
17	Allegan 5 NE	9	16	East Tawas	4
17	East Lansing 4 S	9	16	Grand Marais 2 E	4
17	Flint Bishop Arpt	9	16	Houghton Lake Roscommon Co Arpt	4
17	Grand Rapids Kent County Intl	9	16	Marquette County Arpt	4
17	Lansing Capital City Arpt	9	16	Milford Gm Proving Ground	4
22	Battle Creek 5 NW	8	22	Alpena Phelps Collins Arpt	6
22	Big Rapids Waterworks	8	22	Bad Axe	6
22	Lapeer WWTP	8	22	Iron Mtn-Kingsford WWTP	6
22	Mio Hydro Plant	8	22	Stephenson 8 WNW	6

Number of Days Annually Maximum Temperature ≤ 32°F

	Highest			Lowest	
Rank	Station Name	Days	Rank	Station Name	Days
1	Hancock Houghton Co Arpt	97	1	Holland	37
2	Ironwood	96	2	Dearborn	39
2	Marquette County Arpt	96	2	Ypsilanti E Mich Univ	39
4	Bergland Dam	93	4	Benton Harbor Ross Field	40
5	Stambaugh 2 SSE	92	4	Gull Lake Biol Sta	40
6	Sault Ste Marie Sanderson Field	86	6	Adrian 2 NNE	41
7	Champion Van Riper Prk	83	6	Grosse Pointe Farms	41
8	Munising	82	8	Three Rivers	42
9	Whitefish Point	80	9	Detroit Metropolitan Arpt	43
10	Iron Mtn-Kingsford WWTP	78	10	Battle Creek 5 NW	46
11	Manistique	76	11	Ann Arbor Univ of Mich	47
12	Marquette	75	12	Allegan 5 NE	*48*
13	Grand Marais 2 E	72	12	Port Huron	48
14	Houghton Lake Roscommon Co Arpt	71	14	Muskegon County Arpt	50
15	Stephenson 8 WNW	70	15	Flint Bishop Arpt	51
16	Alpena Phelps Collins Arpt	68	16	East Tawas	52
16	Cheboygan	68	16	Grand Rapids Kent County Intl	52
16	Cross Village	68	16	St Johns	52
19	Alpena Wastewater Pl	64	19	Alma	53
20	Bad Axe	62	19	East Lansing 4 S	53
21	Boyne Falls	61	21	Caro Regional Center	*54*
21	Mio Hydro Plant	*61*	21	Charlotte	54
23	Frankfort 2 NE	59	21	Lansing Capital City Arpt	54
24	Big Rapids Waterworks	57	21	Lapeer WWTP	54
24	Essexville	57	21	Owosso Wwtp	54

Number of Days Annually Minimum Temperature ≤ 32°F

	Highest			Lowest	
Rank	Station Name	Days	Rank	Station Name	Days
1	Stambaugh 2 SSE	211	1	Grosse Pointe Farms	121
2	Champion Van Riper Prk	205	2	Ypsilanti E Mich Univ	122
3	Bergland Dam	202	3	Detroit Metropolitan Arpt	124
4	Ironwood	191	4	Ann Arbor Univ of Mich	132
4	Marquette County Arpt	191	4	Holland	132
6	Grand Marais 2 E	189	4	Port Huron	132
7	Stephenson 8 WNW	187	7	Dearborn	133
8	Iron Mtn-Kingsford WWTP	185	7	Gull Lake Biol Sta	133
9	Sault Ste Marie Sanderson Field	176	9	Benton Harbor Ross Field	135
10	Mio Hydro Plant	*174*	9	Muskegon County Arpt	135
11	Hancock Houghton Co Arpt	173	11	Grand Rapids Kent County Intl	137
12	Munising	171	12	Essexville	139
13	Alpena Phelps Collins Arpt	170	13	Frankfort 2 NE	140
13	Whitefish Point	170	14	Flint Bishop Arpt	141
15	Big Rapids Waterworks	168	15	Three Rivers	144
15	Boyne Falls	168	16	Battle Creek 5 NW	145
15	Houghton Lake Roscommon Co Arpt	168	16	Milford Gm Proving Ground	145
15	Manistique	168	18	Adrian 2 NNE	146
19	Cheboygan	164	19	Lansing Capital City Arpt	148
20	Alma	161	20	Allegan 5 NE	*149*
21	Cross Village	158	20	Alpena Wastewater Pl	149
21	Marquette	158	20	East Lansing 4 S	149
23	East Tawas	157	20	St Johns	149
24	Bad Axe	154	24	Owosso Wwtp	150
25	Charlotte	153	25	Caro Regional Center	*151*

Rankings include 25 highest/lowest stations. If state has less than 25 stations, all stations are included. The period of record is 1980–2009. See User Guide for detailed explanation of data.

Number of Days Annually Minimum Temperature ≤ 0°F

	Highest			Lowest	
Rank	Station Name	Days	Rank	Station Name	Days
1	Stambaugh 2 SSE	49	1	Frankfort 2 NE	2
2	Bergland Dam	45	1	Holland	2
2	Champion Van Riper Prk	45	3	Grosse Pointe Farms	3
4	Ironwood	39	3	Muskegon County Arpt	3
5	Iron Mtn-Kingsford WWTP	36	5	Ann Arbor Univ of Mich	4
6	Stephenson 8 WNW	34	5	Benton Harbor Ross Field	4
7	Marquette County Arpt	32	5	Detroit Metropolitan Arpt	4
8	Sault Ste Marie Sanderson Field	28	5	Port Huron	4
9	Mio Hydro Plant	*22*	5	Ypsilanti E Mich Univ	4
10	Manistique	20	10	Dearborn	5
11	Cheboygan	19	11	Battle Creek 5 NW	6
12	Alpena Phelps Collins Arpt	18	11	Essexville	6
12	Hancock Houghton Co Arpt	18	11	Grand Rapids Kent County Intl	6
12	Houghton Lake Roscommon Co Arpt	18	11	Gull Lake Biol Sta	6
15	Boyne Falls	17	11	Hart	*6*
16	Munising	15	16	Three Rivers	7
16	Whitefish Point	15	17	Adrian 2 NNE	8
18	Big Rapids Waterworks	14	17	Allegan 5 NE	*8*
18	Grand Marais 2 E	14	17	St Johns	8
20	Cross Village	13	20	Bad Axe	9
20	East Tawas	13	21	Alma	10
22	Caro Regional Center	*12*	21	Alpena Wastewater Pl	10
22	Lapeer WWTP	12	21	Charlotte	10
22	Marquette	12	21	East Lansing 4 S	10
25	Lansing Capital City Arpt	11	21	Flint Bishop Arpt	10

Number of Annual Heating Degree Days

	Highest			Lowest	
Rank	Station Name	Num.	Rank	Station Name	Num.
1	Stambaugh 2 SSE	9,673	1	Ypsilanti E Mich Univ	*6,008*
2	Champion Van Riper Prk	9,527	2	Grosse Pointe Farms	6,165
3	Bergland Dam	9,505	3	Gull Lake Biol Sta	6,187
4	Ironwood	9,319	4	Detroit Metropolitan Arpt	6,191
5	Marquette County Arpt	9,233	5	Benton Harbor Ross Field	6,265
6	Hancock Houghton Co Arpt	8,896	6	Ann Arbor Univ of Mich	6,275
7	Sault Ste Marie Sanderson Field	8,873	7	Dearborn	6,284
8	Whitefish Point	8,725	8	Holland	6,307
9	Iron Mtn-Kingsford WWTP	8,559	9	Three Rivers	6,427
10	Manistique	8,538	10	Adrian 2 NNE	6,526
11	Grand Marais 2 E	8,531	11	Battle Creek 5 NW	*6,534*
12	Munising	*8,525*	12	Port Huron	6,608
13	Stephenson 8 WNW	*8,440*	13	Grand Rapids Kent County Intl	6,650
14	Marquette	8,141	14	Muskegon County Arpt	6,689
15	Cheboygan	8,083	15	Flint Bishop Arpt	6,795
16	Alpena Phelps Collins Arpt	8,009	16	St Johns	6,820
17	Houghton Lake Roscommon Co Arpt	7,917	17	Allegan 5 NE	*6,829*
18	Mio Hydro Plant	*7,820*	18	Essexville	6,882
19	Cross Village	7,804	19	Lansing Capital City Arpt	6,887
20	Alpena Wastewater Pl	7,692	20	East Lansing 4 S	*6,913*
21	Big Rapids Waterworks	7,434	21	Lapeer WWTP	6,919
22	Boyne Falls	7,402	22	Owosso Wwtp	6,930
23	East Tawas	7,400	23	Caro Regional Center	*6,940*
24	Bad Axe	7,347	24	Milford Gm Proving Ground	*6,978*
25	Hart	*7,143*	25	Charlotte	7,010

Rankings include 25 highest/lowest stations. If state has less than 25 stations, all stations are included. The period of record is 1980–2009. See User Guide for detailed explanation of data.

Number of Annual Cooling Degree Days

	Highest			Lowest	
Rank	Station Name	Num.	Rank	Station Name	Num.
1	Ypsilanti E Mich Univ	**871**	1	Whitefish Point	128
2	Gull Lake Biol Sta	807	2	Manistique	161
3	Grosse Pointe Farms	798	3	Stambaugh 2 SSE	170
4	Detroit Metropolitan Arpt	793	4	Sault Ste Marie Sanderson Field	178
5	Dearborn	784	5	Champion Van Riper Prk	188
6	Ann Arbor Univ of Mich	761	6	Bergland Dam	212
7	Benton Harbor Ross Field	738	7	Grand Marais 2 E	221
8	Holland	708	8	Munising	**228**
9	Three Rivers	697	9	Hancock Houghton Co Arpt	237
10	Port Huron	685	10	Marquette County Arpt	252
11	Grand Rapids Kent County Intl	652	11	Ironwood	267
12	Battle Creek 5 NW	**639**	12	Cross Village	277
12	Essexville	639	13	Marquette	296
14	Adrian 2 NNE	622	14	Stephenson 8 WNW	**309**
15	St Johns	618	15	Cheboygan	314
16	Flint Bishop Arpt	587	16	Alpena Phelps Collins Arpt	320
17	East Lansing 4 S	**585**	17	Houghton Lake Roscommon Co Arpt	341
18	Lansing Capital City Arpt	582	18	Alpena Wastewater Pl	362
19	Caro Regional Center	**575**	19	Iron Mtn-Kingsford WWTP	364
20	Lapeer WWTP	558	20	Frankfort 2 NE	389
21	Owosso Wwtp	554	21	Mio Hydro Plant	**397**
22	Allegan 5 NE	**552**	22	East Tawas	405
23	Alma	550	23	Hart	**436**
24	Milford Gm Proving Ground	**535**	24	Big Rapids Waterworks	444
25	Muskegon County Arpt	531	25	Bad Axe	457

Annual Precipitation

	Highest			Lowest	
Rank	Station Name	Inches	Rank	Station Name	Inches
1	Allegan 5 NE	**40.98**	1	Mio Hydro Plant	**26.59**
2	Gull Lake Biol Sta	39.84	2	Grand Marais 2 E	27.79
3	Bergland Dam	39.35	3	Alpena Phelps Collins Arpt	27.96
4	Three Rivers	38.85	4	Houghton Lake Roscommon Co Arpt	28.70
5	Grand Rapids Kent County Intl	38.12	5	Marquette	28.93
6	Ann Arbor Univ of Mich	37.52	6	Stambaugh 2 SSE	29.12
7	Hart	**36.77**	7	Stephenson 8 WNW	29.16
8	Munising	**36.51**	8	Iron Mtn-Kingsford WWTP	29.35
9	Big Rapids Waterworks	36.41	9	Hancock Houghton Co Arpt	29.55
10	Adrian 2 NNE	36.31	10	Cross Village	29.58
11	Benton Harbor Ross Field	36.13	11	Alpena Wastewater Pl	29.79
12	Marquette County Arpt	35.51	12	Milford Gm Proving Ground	**29.90**
13	Grosse Pointe Farms	34.99	13	Cheboygan	30.52
14	Frankfort 2 NE	34.70	14	East Lansing 4 S	31.07
15	Battle Creek 5 NW	34.67	15	Flint Bishop Arpt	31.58
15	Ironwood	34.67	16	East Tawas	31.63
17	Charlotte	34.01	17	Lansing Capital City Arpt	31.81
18	Ypsilanti E Mich Univ	33.94	18	Lapeer WWTP	31.90
19	Muskegon County Arpt	33.72	19	Owosso Wwtp	31.95
20	Port Huron	33.63	20	Whitefish Point	32.04
21	Boyne Falls	33.62	21	Champion Van Riper Prk	32.06
22	Dearborn	33.61	22	Essexville	32.11
23	Detroit Metropolitan Arpt	33.58	23	Sault Ste Marie Sanderson Field	32.83
24	Caro Regional Center	**33.32**	24	Bad Axe	32.93
25	St Johns	33.14	25	Alma	33.13

Rankings include 25 highest/lowest stations. If state has less than 25 stations, all stations are included. The period of record is 1980–2009. See User Guide for detailed explanation of data.

Annual Extreme Maximum Daily Precipitation

	Highest			Lowest	
Rank	Station Name	Inches	Rank	Station Name	Inches
1	Alma	9.33	1	Cross Village	2.72
2	Holland	*7.99*	2	Alpena Wastewater Pl	*2.97*
3	Essexville	7.72	3	Grand Marais 2 E	*3.00*
4	Big Rapids Waterworks	7.64	3	Whitefish Point	3.00
5	Caro Regional Center	*7.28*	5	Boyne Falls	3.15
6	St Johns	6.50	5	Sault Ste Marie Sanderson Field	3.15
7	Bad Axe	6.46	7	Munising	*3.16*
8	Gull Lake Biol Sta	*6.05*	8	Benton Harbor Ross Field	3.25
9	Allegan 5 NE	*5.80*	9	Stephenson 8 WNW	*3.35*
10	Hart	*5.43*	10	Alpena Phelps Collins Arpt	3.44
11	Stambaugh 2 SSE	5.20	11	East Tawas	3.52
12	Marquette	5.12	12	Houghton Lake Roscommon Co Arpt	3.55
13	Three Rivers	5.05	13	Hancock Houghton Co Arpt	3.58
14	Lansing Capital City Arpt	4.95	14	Charlotte	3.60
15	Adrian 2 NNE	4.74	15	Champion Van Riper Prk	*3.61*
16	Owosso Wwtp	*4.67*	16	Lapeer WWTP	*3.72*
17	Ann Arbor Univ of Mich	4.54	17	Mio Hydro Plant	*3.75*
18	Bergland Dam	4.52	18	Battle Creek 5 NW	*3.83*
19	East Lansing 4 S	*4.50*	19	Manistique	*3.86*
20	Cheboygan	4.48	20	Flint Bishop Arpt	3.89
21	Detroit Metropolitan Arpt	4.34	21	Dearborn	3.93
22	Muskegon County Arpt	4.33	22	Port Huron	3.97
23	Grosse Pointe Farms	4.30	23	Iron Mtn-Kingsford WWTP	4.05
24	Marquette County Arpt	4.29	24	Ypsilanti E Mich Univ	*4.07*
25	Grand Rapids Kent County Intl	4.15	25	Frankfort 2 NE	4.08

Number of Days Annually With ≥ 0.1 Inches of Precipitation

	Highest			Lowest	
Rank	Station Name	Days	Rank	Station Name	Days
1	Munising	*100*	1	Manistique	58
2	Bergland Dam	96	2	Milford Gm Proving Ground	*63*
3	Boyne Falls	86	3	Stephenson 8 WNW	64
3	Whitefish Point	86	4	Holland	66
5	Allegan 5 NE	*85*	5	Alpena Phelps Collins Arpt	67
6	Sault Ste Marie Sanderson Field	83	5	Houghton Lake Roscommon Co Arpt	67
7	Marquette County Arpt	82	7	Champion Van Riper Prk	68
8	Ann Arbor Univ of Mich	81	7	East Lansing 4 S	68
8	Frankfort 2 NE	81	7	Lapeer WWTP	68
8	Gull Lake Biol Sta	81	7	Mio Hydro Plant	*68*
8	Ironwood	81	11	Alma	69
12	Adrian 2 NNE	79	11	Flint Bishop Arpt	69
12	Big Rapids Waterworks	79	11	Ypsilanti E Mich Univ	69
12	Three Rivers	79	14	Cheboygan	70
15	Hart	*78*	14	East Tawas	70
16	Benton Harbor Ross Field	77	14	Essexville	70
16	Grand Rapids Kent County Intl	77	14	Iron Mtn-Kingsford WWTP	70
16	Grosse Pointe Farms	77	14	Lansing Capital City Arpt	70
16	Port Huron	77	14	Owosso Wwtp	70
20	Caro Regional Center	*76*	20	Alpena Wastewater Pl	71
20	Hancock Houghton Co Arpt	76	20	St Johns	71
22	Charlotte	74	20	Stambaugh 2 SSE	71
22	Dearborn	74	23	Cross Village	72
22	Grand Marais 2 E	74	24	Bad Axe	73
22	Muskegon County Arpt	74	24	Battle Creek 5 NW	73

Rankings include 25 highest/lowest stations. If state has less than 25 stations, all stations are included. The period of record is 1980–2009. See User Guide for detailed explanation of data.

Number of Days Annually With ≥ 0.5 Inches of Precipitation

	Highest			Lowest	
Rank	Station Name	Days	Rank	Station Name	Days
1	Gull Lake Biol Sta	26	1	Grand Marais 2 E	14
2	Allegan 5 NE	25	2	Marquette	15
2	Ann Arbor Univ of Mich	25	3	Cross Village	16
4	Grand Rapids Kent County Intl	24	3	Hancock Houghton Co Arpt	16
4	Hart	24	3	Houghton Lake Roscommon Co Arpt	16
6	Benton Harbor Ross Field	23	3	Manistique	16
6	Three Rivers	23	3	Stambaugh 2 SSE	16
8	Adrian 2 NNE	22	3	Whitefish Point	16
8	Battle Creek 5 NW	22	9	Alpena Phelps Collins Arpt	17
8	Bergland Dam	22	9	Champion Van Riper Prk	17
8	Big Rapids Waterworks	22	9	Stephenson 8 WNW	17
8	Dearborn	22	12	Cheboygan	18
8	Holland	22	12	Iron Mtn-Kingsford WWTP	18
8	Lapeer WWTP	22	12	Milford Gm Proving Ground	18
15	Caro Regional Center	21	12	Mio Hydro Plant	18
15	Charlotte	21	12	Sault Ste Marie Sanderson Field	18
15	East Lansing 4 S	21	17	Alpena Wastewater Pl	19
15	East Tawas	21	17	Boyne Falls	19
15	Essexville	21	17	Flint Bishop Arpt	19
15	Grosse Pointe Farms	21	17	Port Huron	19
15	Munising	21	21	Alma	20
15	Muskegon County Arpt	21	21	Bad Axe	20
15	Owosso Wwtp	21	21	Detroit Metropolitan Arpt	20
15	St Johns	21	21	Frankfort 2 NE	20
15	Ypsilanti E Mich Univ	21	21	Ironwood	20

Number of Days Annually With ≥ 1.0 Inches of Precipitation

	Highest			Lowest	
Rank	Station Name	Days	Rank	Station Name	Days
1	Adrian 2 NNE	8	1	Marquette	1
1	Benton Harbor Ross Field	8	2	Mio Hydro Plant	2
1	Big Rapids Waterworks	8	2	Whitefish Point	2
1	Grand Rapids Kent County Intl	8	4	Alpena Phelps Collins Arpt	3
1	Gull Lake Biol Sta	8	4	Cross Village	3
1	Hart	8	4	Grand Marais 2 E	3
1	Holland	8	4	Hancock Houghton Co Arpt	3
1	Three Rivers	8	4	Sault Ste Marie Sanderson Field	3
9	Allegan 5 NE	7	9	Alpena Wastewater Pl	4
9	Battle Creek 5 NW	7	9	Houghton Lake Roscommon Co Arpt	4
9	Essexville	7	9	Manistique	4
9	Marquette County Arpt	7	12	Caro Regional Center	5
13	Alma	6	12	Champion Van Riper Prk	5
13	Ann Arbor Univ of Mich	6	12	Cheboygan	5
13	Bad Axe	6	12	Detroit Metropolitan Arpt	5
13	Bergland Dam	6	12	East Lansing 4 S	5
13	Boyne Falls	6	12	East Tawas	5
13	Charlotte	6	12	Flint Bishop Arpt	5
13	Dearborn	6	12	Grosse Pointe Farms	5
13	Frankfort 2 NE	6	12	Iron Mtn-Kingsford WWTP	5
13	Ironwood	6	12	Lapeer WWTP	5
13	Lansing Capital City Arpt	6	12	Milford Gm Proving Ground	5
13	Muskegon County Arpt	6	12	Munising	5
13	Port Huron	6	12	Owosso Wwtp	5
13	St Johns	6	25	Alma	6

Annual Snowfall

	Highest			Lowest	
Rank	Station Name	Inches	Rank	Station Name	Inches
1	Marquette County Arpt	203.0	1	Grosse Pointe Farms	26.9
2	Ironwood	187.2	2	Adrian 2 NNE	29.6
3	Bergland Dam	177.8	3	Dearborn	32.8
4	Munising	*151.7*	4	Lapeer WWTP	*33.4*
5	Grand Marais 2 E	*132.9*	4	Milford Gm Proving Ground	*33.4*
6	Whitefish Point	122.6	4	Ypsilanti E Mich Univ	*33.4*
7	Marquette	115.3	7	Three Rivers	34.1
8	Champion Van Riper Prk	*114.6*	8	Port Huron	34.9
9	Boyne Falls	114.1	9	Owosso Wwtp	*35.6*
10	Frankfort 2 NE	104.9	10	Caro Regional Center	*36.8*
11	Muskegon County Arpt	*95.1*	11	East Lansing 4 S	38.3
12	Cheboygan	92.8	12	Essexville	38.5
13	Allegan 5 NE	*86.6*	13	Alma	40.0
14	Benton Harbor Ross Field	85.7	14	St Johns	42.2
15	Cross Village	79.8	15	Charlotte	42.9
16	Hart	*78.1*	16	Detroit Metropolitan Arpt	43.1
17	Grand Rapids Kent County Intl	74.6	17	Bad Axe	46.1
18	Manistique	*74.1*	18	Flint Bishop Arpt	47.4
19	Stambaugh 2 SSE	69.1	19	Lansing Capital City Arpt	*51.2*
20	Holland	64.7	20	Alpena Wastewater Pl	*52.4*
21	Big Rapids Waterworks	62.5	21	East Tawas	53.6
22	Iron Mtn-Kingsford WWTP	59.7	22	Stephenson 8 WNW	53.9
23	Battle Creek 5 NW	59.2	23	Gull Lake Biol Sta	*55.6*
24	Ann Arbor Univ of Mich	57.0	24	Ann Arbor Univ of Mich	57.0
25	Gull Lake Biol Sta	*55.6*	25	Battle Creek 5 NW	59.2

Annual Maximum Snow Depth

	Highest			Lowest	
Rank	Station Name	Inches	Rank	Station Name	Inches
1	Benton Harbor Ross Field	80	1	Caro Regional Center	*18*
2	Marquette County Arpt	63	1	Milford Gm Proving Ground	*18*
3	Manistique	*61*	3	Lapeer WWTP	*19*
4	Champion Van Riper Prk	60	3	Port Huron	19
5	Alpena Wastewater Pl	53	3	Three Rivers	19
6	Bergland Dam	49	6	Flint Bishop Arpt	20
7	Frankfort 2 NE	48	7	Adrian 2 NNE	21
8	Ironwood	47	7	Grand Rapids Kent County Intl	21
9	Grand Marais 2 E	*42*	9	Alma	22
10	Cheboygan	41	9	Ann Arbor Univ of Mich	22
10	Marquette	41	9	Owosso Wwtp	*22*
12	Hart	*39*	12	Grosse Pointe Farms	23
12	Stambaugh 2 SSE	39	12	Lansing Capital City Arpt	*23*
12	Whitefish Point	39	14	Battle Creek 5 NW	*24*
15	Stephenson 8 WNW	*37*	14	Dearborn	24
16	Holland	36	14	Detroit Metropolitan Arpt	24
17	Cross Village	35	14	East Lansing 4 S	24
18	Iron Mtn-Kingsford WWTP	34	14	East Tawas	24
19	Boyne Falls	33	14	Ypsilanti E Mich Univ	24
20	Essexville	*32*	20	Gull Lake Biol Sta	*25*
20	Mio Hydro Plant	*32*	21	Big Rapids Waterworks	26
22	Bad Axe	31	22	Allegan 5 NE	*27*
23	Muskegon County Arpt	*30*	22	St Johns	27
24	Charlotte	28	24	Charlotte	28
25	Allegan 5 NE	*27*	25	Muskegon County Arpt	*30*

Rankings include 25 highest/lowest stations. If state has less than 25 stations, all stations are included. The period of record is 1980–2009. See User Guide for detailed explanation of data.

Number of Days Annually With ≥ 1.0 Inch Snow Depth

	Highest			Lowest	
Rank	Station Name	Days	Rank	Station Name	Days
1	Marquette County Arpt	152	1	Essexville	39
2	Bergland Dam	151	2	Benton Harbor Ross Field	41
3	Ironwood	145	3	Detroit Metropolitan Arpt	45
4	Whitefish Point	139	3	Holland	45
5	Champion Van Riper Prk	131	5	Grosse Pointe Farms	49
5	Grand Marais 2 E	131	6	Owosso Wwtp	50
7	Marquette	130	7	Adrian 2 NNE	51
7	Stambaugh 2 SSE	130	7	Milford Gm Proving Ground	51
9	Iron Mtn-Kingsford WWTP	114	7	Port Huron	51
10	Cross Village	110	7	St Johns	51
11	Boyne Falls	108	7	Ypsilanti E Mich Univ	51
12	Cheboygan	107	12	Dearborn	52
13	Frankfort 2 NE	104	13	Lapeer WWTP	56
14	Manistique	101	14	Three Rivers	59
15	Stephenson 8 WNW	97	15	Ann Arbor Univ of Mich	60
16	Mio Hydro Plant	91	16	East Lansing 4 S	61
17	Alpena Wastewater Pl	89	17	Flint Bishop Arpt	62
18	East Tawas	87	17	Hart	62
19	Big Rapids Waterworks	86	19	Caro Regional Center	63
20	Allegan 5 NE	78	20	Battle Creek 5 NW	64
21	Bad Axe	75	20	Charlotte	64
22	Muskegon County Arpt	74	22	Gull Lake Biol Sta	66
23	Alma	73	22	Lansing Capital City Arpt	66
24	Grand Rapids Kent County Intl	68	24	Grand Rapids Kent County Intl	68
25	Gull Lake Biol Sta	66	25	Alma	73

Significant Storm Events in Michigan: 2000 – 2009

Location or County	Date	Type	Mag.	Deaths	Injuries	Property Damage ($mil.)	Crop Damage ($mil.)
Wayne	09/11/00	Flood	na	0	0	20.0	0.0
Southeast Lower Michigan	08/06/01	Excessive Heat	na	1	200	0.0	0.0
Eaton	09/09/01	Tornado	F1	0	1	10.0	0.1
Northwest Upper Michigan	04/12/02	Flood	na	0	0	18.5	0.0
Dickinson	09/30/02	Tornado	F1	0	0	7.0	0.0
Southeast Lower Michigan	04/03/03	Ice Storm	na	1	2	161.1	0.0
Marquette County	05/15/03	Flood	na	0	0	14.0	0.0
Southeast Michigan	11/12/03	High Wind	87 mph	0	0	21.0	0.0
Southwestern and South Central Lower Michigan	05/21/04	Flood	na	0	0	25.0	4.6
Southeast Michigan	05/23/04	Flood	na	0	0	100.0	0.0
Southeast Lower Michigan	11/15/05	Strong Wind	55 mph	0	0	7.2	0.0
Marquette	06/20/07	Hail	1.75 in.	0	0	20.0	0.0
Marquette	06/20/07	Hail	1.50 in.	0	0	18.0	0.0
Eaton	08/24/07	Tornado	F3	0	5	40.0	0.0
Genesee	08/24/07	Tornado	F2	0	1	13.0	0.0
Livingston	08/24/07	Tornado	F2	0	0	7.0	0.0
Ingham	10/18/07	Tornado	F2	2	0	15.0	0.0
Kalamazoo	09/13/08	Flood	na	0	0	11.0	0.0
Ottawa	06/19/09	Flash Flood	na	0	0	34.0	0.0

Note: Deaths, injuries, and damages are date and location specific.

2015 Title List
Visit www.GreyHouse.com for Product Information, Table of Contents, and Sample Pages.

General Reference
An African Biographical Dictionary
America's College Museums
American Environmental Leaders: From Colonial Times to the Present
Encyclopedia of African-American Writing
Encyclopedia of Constitutional Amendments
Encyclopedia of Gun Control & Gun Rights
An Encyclopedia of Human Rights in the United States
Encyclopedia of Invasions & Conquests
Encyclopedia of Prisoners of War & Internment
Encyclopedia of Religion & Law in America
Encyclopedia of Rural America
Encyclopedia of the Continental Congress
Encyclopedia of the United States Cabinet, 1789-2010
Encyclopedia of War Journalism
Encyclopedia of Warrior Peoples & Fighting Groups
The Environmental Debate: A Documentary History
The Evolution Wars: A Guide to the Debates
From Suffrage to the Senate: America's Political Women
Global Terror & Political Risk Assessment
Media & Communications 1900-2020
Nations of the World
Political Corruption in America
Privacy Rights in the Digital Era
The Religious Right: A Reference Handbook
Speakers of the House of Representatives, 1789-2009
This is Who We Were: 1880-1900
This is Who We Were: A Companion to the 1940 Census
This is Who We Were: In the 1910s
This is Who We Were: In the 1920s
This is Who We Were: In the 1940s
This is Who We Were: In the 1950s
This is Who We Were: In the 1960s
This is Who We Were: In the 1970s
U.S. Land & Natural Resource Policy
The Value of a Dollar 1600-1865: Colonial Era to the Civil War
The Value of a Dollar: 1860-2014
Working Americans 1770-1869 Vol. IX: Revolutionary War to the Civil War
Working Americans 1880-1999 Vol. I: The Working Class
Working Americans 1880-1999 Vol. II: The Middle Class
Working Americans 1880-1999 Vol. III: The Upper Class
Working Americans 1880-1999 Vol. IV: Their Children
Working Americans 1880-2015 Vol. V: Americans At War
Working Americans 1880-2005 Vol. VI: Women at Work
Working Americans 1880-2006 Vol. VII: Social Movements
Working Americans 1880-2007 Vol. VIII: Immigrants
Working Americans 1880-2009 Vol. X: Sports & Recreation
Working Americans 1880-2010 Vol. XI: Inventors & Entrepreneurs
Working Americans 1880-2011 Vol. XII: Our History through Music
Working Americans 1880-2012 Vol. XIII: Education & Educators
World Cultural Leaders of the 20th & 21st Centuries

Education Information
Charter School Movement
Comparative Guide to American Elementary & Secondary Schools
Complete Learning Disabilities Directory
Educators Resource Directory
Special Education: A Reference Book for Policy and Curriculum Development

Health Information
Comparative Guide to American Hospitals
Complete Directory for Pediatric Disorders
Complete Directory for People with Chronic Illness
Complete Directory for People with Disabilities
Complete Mental Health Directory
Diabetes in America: Analysis of an Epidemic
Directory of Drug & Alcohol Residential Rehab Facilities
Directory of Health Care Group Purchasing Organizations
Directory of Hospital Personnel
HMO/PPO Directory
Medical Device Register
Older Americans Information Directory

Business Information
Complete Television, Radio & Cable Industry Directory
Directory of Business Information Resources
Directory of Mail Order Catalogs
Directory of Venture Capital & Private Equity Firms
Environmental Resource Handbook
Food & Beverage Market Place
Grey House Homeland Security Directory
Grey House Performing Arts Directory
Grey House Safety & Security Directory
Grey House Transportation Security Directory
Hudson's Washington News Media Contacts Directory
New York State Directory
Rauch Market Research Guides
Sports Market Place Directory

Statistics & Demographics
American Tally
America's Top-Rated Cities
America's Top-Rated Smaller Cities
America's Top-Rated Small Towns & Cities
Ancestry & Ethnicity in America
The Asian Databook
Comparative Guide to American Suburbs
The Hispanic Databook
Profiles of America
"Profiles of" Series – State Handbooks
Weather America

Financial Ratings Series
TheStreet Ratings' Guide to Bond & Money Market Mutual Funds
TheStreet Ratings' Guide to Common Stocks
TheStreet Ratings' Guide to Exchange-Traded Funds
TheStreet Ratings' Guide to Stock Mutual Funds
TheStreet Ratings' Ultimate Guided Tour of Stock Investing
Weiss Ratings' Consumer Guides
Weiss Ratings' Guide to Banks
Weiss Ratings' Guide to Credit Unions
Weiss Ratings' Guide to Health Insurers
Weiss Ratings' Guide to Life & Annuity Insurers
Weiss Ratings' Guide to Property & Casualty Insurers

Bowker's Books In Print® Titles
American Book Publishing Record® Annual
American Book Publishing Record® Monthly
Books In Print®
Books In Print® Supplement
Books Out Loud™
Bowker's Complete Video Directory™
Children's Books In Print®
El-Hi Textbooks & Serials In Print®
Forthcoming Books®
Large Print Books & Serials™
Law Books & Serials In Print™
Medical & Health Care Books In Print™
Publishers, Distributors & Wholesalers of the US™
Subject Guide to Books In Print®
Subject Guide to Children's Books In Print®

Canadian General Reference
Associations Canada
Canadian Almanac & Directory
Canadian Environmental Resource Guide
Canadian Parliamentary Guide
Canadian Venture Capital & Private Equity Firms
Financial Services Canada
Governments Canada
Health Guide Canada
The History of Canada
Libraries Canada
Major Canadian Cities

2015 Title List

Visit **www.SalemPress.com** for Product Information, Table of Contents, and Sample Pages.

Science, Careers & Mathematics

Ancient Creatures: Unearthed
Applied Science
Applied Science: Engineering & Mathematics
Applied Science: Science & Medicine
Applied Science: Technology
Biomes and Ecosystems
Careers in Business
Careers in Chemistry
Careers in Communications & Media
Careers in Environment & Conservation
Careers in Healthcare
Careers in Hospitality & Tourism
Careers in Human Services
Careers in Law, Criminal Justice & Emergency Services
Careers in Physics
Careers in Technology Services & Repair
Computer Technology Innovators
Contemporary Biographies in Business
Contemporary Biographies in Chemistry
Contemporary Biographies in Communications & Media
Contemporary Biographies in Environment & Conservation
Contemporary Biographies in Healthcare
Contemporary Biographies in Hospitality & Tourism
Contemporary Biographies in Law & Criminal Justice
Contemporary Biographies in Physics
Earth Science
Earth Science: Earth Materials & Resources
Earth Science: Earth's Surface and History
Earth Science: Physics & Chemistry of the Earth
Earth Science: Weather, Water & Atmosphere
Encyclopedia of Energy
Encyclopedia of Environmental Issues
Encyclopedia of Environmental Issues: Atmosphere and Air Pollution
Encyclopedia of Environmental Issues: Ecology and Ecosystems
Encyclopedia of Environmental Issues: Energy and Energy Use
Encyclopedia of Environmental Issues: Policy and Activism
Encyclopedia of Environmental Issues: Preservation/Wilderness Issues
Encyclopedia of Environmental Issues: Water and Water Pollution
Encyclopedia of Global Resources
Encyclopedia of Global Warming
Encyclopedia of Mathematics & Society
Encyclopedia of Mathematics & Society: Engineering, Tech, Medicine
Encyclopedia of Mathematics & Society: Great Mathematicians
Encyclopedia of Mathematics & Society: Math & Social Sciences
Encyclopedia of Mathematics & Society: Math Development/Concepts
Encyclopedia of Mathematics & Society: Math in Culture & Society
Encyclopedia of Mathematics & Society: Space, Science, Environment
Encyclopedia of the Ancient World
Forensic Science
Geography Basics
Internet Innovators
Inventions and Inventors
Magill's Encyclopedia of Science: Animal Life
Magill's Encyclopedia of Science: Plant life
Notable Natural Disasters
Principles of Chemistry
Science and Scientists
Solar System
Solar System: Great Astronomers
Solar System: Study of the Universe
Solar System: The Inner Planets
Solar System: The Moon and Other Small Bodies
Solar System: The Outer Planets
Solar System: The Sun and Other Stars
World Geography

Literature

American Ethnic Writers
Classics of Science Fiction & Fantasy Literature
Critical Insights: Authors
Critical Insights: New Literary Collection Bundles
Critical Insights: Themes
Critical Insights: Works
Critical Survey of Drama
Critical Survey of Graphic Novels: Heroes & Super Heroes
Critical Survey of Graphic Novels: History, Theme & Technique
Critical Survey of Graphic Novels: Independents/Underground Classics
Critical Survey of Graphic Novels: Manga
Critical Survey of Long Fiction
Critical Survey of Mystery & Detective Fiction
Critical Survey of Mythology and Folklore: Heroes and Heroines
Critical Survey of Mythology and Folklore: Love, Sexuality & Desire
Critical Survey of Mythology and Folklore: World Mythology
Critical Survey of Poetry
Critical Survey of Poetry: American Poets
Critical Survey of Poetry: British, Irish & Commonwealth Poets
Critical Survey of Poetry: Cumulative Index
Critical Survey of Poetry: European Poets
Critical Survey of Poetry: Topical Essays
Critical Survey of Poetry: World Poets
Critical Survey of Shakespeare's Sonnets
Critical Survey of Short Fiction
Critical Survey of Short Fiction: American Writers
Critical Survey of Short Fiction: British, Irish, Commonwealth Writers
Critical Survey of Short Fiction: Cumulative Index
Critical Survey of Short Fiction: European Writers
Critical Survey of Short Fiction: Topical Essays
Critical Survey of Short Fiction: World Writers
Cyclopedia of Literary Characters
Holocaust Literature
Introduction to Literary Context: American Poetry of the 20th Century
Introduction to Literary Context: American Post-Modernist Novels
Introduction to Literary Context: American Short Fiction
Introduction to Literary Context: English Literature
Introduction to Literary Context: Plays
Introduction to Literary Context: World Literature
Magill's Literary Annual 2015
Magill's Survey of American Literature
Magill's Survey of World Literature
Masterplots
Masterplots II: African American Literature
Masterplots II: American Fiction Series
Masterplots II: British & Commonwealth Fiction Series
Masterplots II: Christian Literature
Masterplots II: Drama Series
Masterplots II: Juvenile & Young Adult Literature, Supplement
Masterplots II: Nonfiction Series
Masterplots II: Poetry Series
Masterplots II: Short Story Series
Masterplots II: Women's Literature Series
Notable African American Writers
Notable American Novelists
Notable Playwrights
Notable Poets
Recommended Reading: 500 Classics Reviewed
Short Story Writers

Grey House Publishing | Salem Press | **H.W. Wilson** | 4919 Route, 22 PO Box 56, Amenia NY 12501-0056

2015 Title List

Visit **www.SalemPress.com** for Product Information, Table of Contents, and Sample Pages.

History and Social Science

The 2000s in America
50 States
African American History
Agriculture in History
American First Ladies
American Heroes
American Indian Culture
American Indian History
American Indian Tribes
American Presidents
American Villains
America's Historic Sites
Ancient Greece
The Bill of Rights
The Civil Rights Movement
The Cold War
Countries, Peoples & Cultures
Countries, Peoples & Cultures: Central & South America
Countries, Peoples & Cultures: Central, South & Southeast Asia
Countries, Peoples & Cultures: East & South Africa
Countries, Peoples & Cultures: East Asia & the Pacific
Countries, Peoples & Cultures: Eastern Europe
Countries, Peoples & Cultures: Middle East & North Africa
Countries, Peoples & Cultures: North America & the Caribbean
Countries, Peoples & Cultures: West & Central Africa
Countries, Peoples & Cultures: Western Europe
Defining Documents: American Revolution (1754-1805)
Defining Documents: Civil War (1860-1865)
Defining Documents: Emergence of Modern America (1868-1918)
Defining Documents: Exploration & Colonial America (1492-1755)
Defining Documents: Manifest Destiny (1803-1860)
Defining Documents: Post-War 1940s (1945-1949)
Defining Documents: Reconstruction (1865-1880)
Defining Documents: The 1920s
Defining Documents: The 1930s
Defining Documents: The American West (1836-1900)
Defining Documents: The Ancient World (2700 B.C.E.-50 C.E.)
Defining Documents: The Middle Ages (524-1431)
Defining Documents: World War I
Defining Documents: World War II (1939-1946)
The Eighties in America
Encyclopedia of American Immigration
Encyclopedia of Flight
Encyclopedia of the Ancient World
The Fifties in America
The Forties in America
Great Athletes
Great Athletes: Baseball
Great Athletes: Basketball
Great Athletes: Boxing & Soccer
Great Athletes: Cumulative Index
Great Athletes: Football
Great Athletes: Golf & Tennis
Great Athletes: Olympics
Great Athletes: Racing & Individual Sports
Great Events from History: 17th Century
Great Events from History: 18th Century
Great Events from History: 19th Century
Great Events from History: 20th Century (1901-1940)
Great Events from History: 20th Century (1941-1970)
Great Events from History: 20th Century (1971-2000)
Great Events from History: Ancient World
Great Events from History: Cumulative Indexes
Great Events from History: Gay, Lesbian, Bisexual, Transgender Events
Great Events from History: Middle Ages
Great Events from History: Modern Scandals
Great Events from History: Renaissance & Early Modern Era

Great Lives from History: 17th Century
Great Lives from History: 18th Century
Great Lives from History: 19th Century
Great Lives from History: 20th Century
Great Lives from History: African Americans
Great Lives from History: Ancient World
Great Lives from History: Asian & Pacific Islander Americans
Great Lives from History: Cumulative Indexes
Great Lives from History: Incredibly Wealthy
Great Lives from History: Inventors & Inventions
Great Lives from History: Jewish Americans
Great Lives from History: Latinos
Great Lives from History: Middle Ages
Great Lives from History: Notorious Lives
Great Lives from History: Renaissance & Early Modern Era
Great Lives from History: Scientists & Science
Historical Encyclopedia of American Business
Immigration in U.S. History
Magill's Guide to Military History
Milestone Documents in African American History
Milestone Documents in American History
Milestone Documents in World History
Milestone Documents of American Leaders
Milestone Documents of World Religions
Musicians & Composers 20th Century
The Nineties in America
The Seventies in America
The Sixties in America
Survey of American Industry and Careers
The Thirties in America
The Twenties in America
United States at War
U.S.A. in Space
U.S. Court Cases
U.S. Government Leaders
U.S. Laws, Acts, and Treaties
U.S. Legal System
U.S. Supreme Court
Weapons and Warfare
World Conflicts: Asia and the Middle East

Health

Addictions & Substance Abuse
Adolescent Health
Cancer
Complementary & Alternative Medicine
Genetics & Inherited Conditions
Health Issues
Infectious Diseases & Conditions
Magill's Medical Guide
Psychology & Behavioral Health
Psychology Basics

2015 Title List

Visit www.HWWilsonInPrint.com for Product Information, Table of Contents and Sample Pages

Current Biography
Current Biography Cumulative Index 1946-2013
Current Biography Monthly Magazine
Current Biography Yearbook: 2003
Current Biography Yearbook: 2004
Current Biography Yearbook: 2005
Current Biography Yearbook: 2006
Current Biography Yearbook: 2007
Current Biography Yearbook: 2008
Current Biography Yearbook: 2009
Current Biography Yearbook: 2010
Current Biography Yearbook: 2011
Current Biography Yearbook: 2012
Current Biography Yearbook: 2013
Current Biography Yearbook: 2014
Current Biography Yearbook: 2015

Core Collections
Children's Core Collection
Fiction Core Collection
Middle & Junior High School Core
Public Library Core Collection: Nonfiction
Senior High Core Collection

The Reference Shelf
Aging in America
American Military Presence Overseas
The Arab Spring
The Brain
The Business of Food
Conspiracy Theories
The Digital Age
Dinosaurs
Embracing New Paradigms in Education
Faith & Science
Families: Traditional and New Structures
The Future of U.S. Economic Relations: Mexico, Cuba, and Venezuela
Global Climate Change
Graphic Novels and Comic Books
Immigration in the U.S.
Internet Safety
Marijuana Reform
The News and its Future
The Paranormal
Politics of the Ocean
Reality Television
Representative American Speeches: 2008-2009
Representative American Speeches: 2009-2010
Representative American Speeches: 2010-2011
Representative American Speeches: 2011-2012
Representative American Speeches: 2012-2013
Representative American Speeches: 2013-2014
Representative American Speeches: 2014-2015
Revisiting Gender
Robotics
Russia
Social Networking
Social Services for the Poor
Space Exploration & Development
Sports in America
The Supreme Court
The Transformation of American Cities
U.S. Infrastructure
U.S. National Debate Topic: Surveillance
U.S. National Debate Topic: The Ocean
U.S. National Debate Topic: Transportation Infrastructure
Whistleblowers

Readers' Guide
Abridged Readers' Guide to Periodical Literature
Readers' Guide to Periodical Literature

Indexes
Index to Legal Periodicals & Books
Short Story Index
Book Review Digest

Sears List
Sears List of Subject Headings
Sears: Lista de Encabezamientos de Materia

Facts About Series
Facts About American Immigration
Facts About China
Facts About the 20th Century
Facts About the Presidents
Facts About the World's Languages

Nobel Prize Winners
Nobel Prize Winners: 1901-1986
Nobel Prize Winners: 1987-1991
Nobel Prize Winners: 1992-1996
Nobel Prize Winners: 1997-2001

World Authors
World Authors: 1995-2000
World Authors: 2000-2005

Famous First Facts
Famous First Facts
Famous First Facts About American Politics
Famous First Facts About Sports
Famous First Facts About the Environment
Famous First Facts: International Edition

American Book of Days
The American Book of Days
The International Book of Days

Junior Authors & Illustrators
Tenth Book of Junior Authors & Illustrations

Monographs
The Barnhart Dictionary of Etymology
Celebrate the World
Guide to the Ancient World
Indexing from A to Z
The Poetry Break
Radical Change: Books for Youth in a Digital Age

Wilson Chronology
Wilson Chronology of Asia and the Pacific
Wilson Chronology of Human Rights
Wilson Chronology of Ideas
Wilson Chronology of the Arts
Wilson Chronology of the World's Religions
Wilson Chronology of Women's Achievements

Grey House Publishing | Salem Press | H.W. Wilson | 4919 Route, 22 PO Box 56, Amenia NY 12501-0056